DICTIONARY
of the
CHRISTIAN CHURCH

DICTIONARY
of the
CHRISTIAN CHURCH

Edited by F. L. Cross & E. A. Livingstone

 HENDRICKSON PUBLISHERS

Dictionary of the Christian Church
Hendrickson Publishers, Inc.
P. O. Box 3473
Peabody, Massachusetts 01961-3473

ISBN 978-1-59856-250-7

© 1997 Oxford University Press

Originally published as *The Oxford Dictionary of the Christian Church.*
First published 1957
Second edition 1974
Reprinted (with revisions) 1983
Third edition 1997

Hendrickson Publishers' edition published by arrangement with
Oxford University Press.

Printed in the United States of America

First Hendrickson Publishers' Printing—October 2007

PREFACE

THE first edition of the *Dictionary* was an immediate success, unforeseen by anyone except perhaps the Editor, who had visions of a copy in every parsonage house in the country. In the decade that followed its publication in 1957, the outward practices of the Church underwent changes unparalleled in any similar time-span in modern history, many of them popularly associated with Second Vatican Council (1962–5), though their origins can often be traced earlier. The liturgical changes in the RC Church and its more liberal attitude both to Biblical scholarship and towards other communions were reflected in the second edition, published in 1974. In the last twenty years or so the shifts in attitude that marked the earlier period have increased in strength; changes in practice may have been less dramatic but perhaps more fundamental. The challenges to accepted orthodoxy encapsulated in Feminist Theology, Liberation Theology, and a more positive evaluation of other religions have made significant changes in the life and thought of the Church. Feminist Theology, for instance, has promoted a new perspective on the position of women in the Church and (indirectly) the divisions stemming from the ordination of women to the priesthood (and episcopate) in some parts of the Church which claim Catholic continuity. The new insights which have arisen out of these approaches have also led to changes in the understanding of some of the most basic doctrines. Doctrinal articles which could remain unaltered in the second edition have often had to be revised to take account of this thinking. There has also been a parallel resistance to change and a yearning for certainty, reflected in the strength of Evangelicals in England and of Fundamentalists in parts of the USA, and in the attraction of Orthodoxy for the Western World. The majority of Christians are now in Africa, Asia, and South America, not Europe and North America. This edition endeavours to record these changes, including new articles on a number of countries not separately treated in the past and increasing the coverage of Evangelical figures. It also includes more recent bibliographical material. Some may feel there is too much of this, but St Gregory the Great commented that the Scriptures provide water in which lambs may walk and elephants swim,[1] and a dictionary of this kind has to provide for a similar range of readers. What one person finds useless is just what another needs, and with interlibrary loans most books are eventually obtainable if sufficient detail is provided.

The first edition was largely the personal work of the Revd Dr F. L. Cross, assisted by a small group of helpers who, with a few exceptions, were junior when the work began, even if they held senior posts by the time it was published. For the second edition, he commissioned the Rt. Revd Dr K. T. Ware to fill gaps in the coverage of Eastern Orthodoxy. After Dr Cross's death, a wonderfully generous group of his friends and colleagues, led by Dr R. W. Hunt, the Revd Prof. H. F. D. Sparks, and Dr J. F. Mason, rallied round and pressed into service their colleagues and pupils; the Rt. Revd Mgr. J. D. Crichton and the Rt. Revd Mgr. L. L. McReavy looked after changes in RC liturgy and canon law. Much of their work has stood the test of time and survives in this edition, to which some of them have contributed new material.

The third edition is more of a corporate effort, with a larger number of scholars contributing their expertise. To all of them I am immensely grateful, and it is to them that the *Dictionary* owes whatever merit it may have. I am especially indebted to the Revd Prof. M. F. Wiles, who

---

[1] *Moralia sive Expositio in Iob*, Dedication, 4.

encouraged me in the beginning and has provided wise guidance whenever I ran into problems that seemed insuperable; to Dr Andrew Louth, who has written many articles and for fourteen years has generously put at my disposal his immense learning; to Dr Paul Joyce, the Revd Prof. J. Barton, the Revd G. M. Styler, and the Revd R. C. Morgan, who revised articles on Biblical subjects; to Prof. Peter Brunt, who wrote on subjects touching Roman history; to Dr S. P. Brock, who looked after much to do with the Middle East; to the Revd H. E. J. Cowdrey, who told me about medieval Popes and other Churchmen; to the Very Revd Dr Simon Tugwell, OP, who wrote articles and fielded queries about matters of spirituality and Dominican history; to the Revd Dr A. E. McGrath, the Revd Dr Diarmaid MacCulloch, and Dr Richard Rex, who taught me about the Reformation; to the Revd Robert Ombres, OP, and the Revd Dr S. J. Pix who looked after the entries on canon law in the RC and Anglican Churches respectively; and to Prof. A. Hastings and Dr D. L. Hilliard who guided me on things African and Asiatic. The Revd Dr G. F. Nuttall, from whom I sought guidance over Nonconformity, went beyond even the second mile and read the second edition from cover to cover, pointing out what needed attention at every turn. On American matters Prof. J. Pelikan agreed to answer questions and never failed to respond with a helpful suggestion, and the Revd Dr R. W. Pfaff went through the book showing me opportunities to drop or abbreviate what was no longer important and suggesting gaps to be filled. Besides the contributors listed on pp. xiii–xxii, and the multitude too numerous to mention by name who have answered individual questions, I am indebted for advice on various points to Revd E. W. F. Agar, Prof. J. W. Allan, Revd Pio G. Alves de Sousa, Mr H. Anderson, Revd J. Andriessen, SJ, Rt. Revd Dr G. W. Ashby, the late Canon J. G. B. Ashworth, Miss Karen Aveyard, Dr W. Baier, Miss I. D. Baird, Prof. J. W. Baldwin, Prof. B. W. Ball, the late Dr C. P. Bammel, Miss Melanie Barber, Dr Alexandra Barratt, Rt. Revd T. Bavin, Prof. P. Bayley, Mr A. S. Bell, Revd Dom Aidan Bellenger, OSB, Dr B. S. Benedikz, Rt. Revd J. M. Bickersteth, KCVO, Dr E. G. W. Bill, OBE, Mrs Joan Bloodworth, M. F. Boespflug, Mr John A. Bollier, Sr. M. Borgia, OSU, M. M.-L. Bossuat, Revd W. Boulton, Revd Dr Leonard E. Boyle, OP, Mrs Ann Bradshaw, Revd Dr T. Bradshaw, Revd J. Brady, Revd I. F. M. Brayley, SJ, Miss G. M. Briggs, the late Canon H. M. Brown, Dr Michelle P. Brown, Rt. Revd Mgr. R. Brown, Revd Thomas Brown, SSM, Canon W. R. F. Browning, Mr David Brunton, Dr C. E. Bryant, Miss A. Buchan, Dr Charles Burnett, the late Rt. Revd Dr B. C. Butler, OSB, Mrs C. Butler, Mr P. A. Byrnes, Revd G. M. Cagni, Barnabite, Revd D. A. Cameron, Revd F. D. G. Campbell, SSJE, Dr G. N. Cantor, Revd Dr Elizabeth D. H. Carmichael, Revd Danilo Castello, CM, Revd G. R. Chapman, Revd Graeme Chatfield, Revd Huw Chiplin, Canon T. R. Christie, Mr Colin T. Clarkson, Revd K. E. Claus, Mr A. W. F. Coghill, the late Mr L. S. Colchester, Miss G. E. Coldham, Revd Dr Richard Conrad, OP, Mr M. Conway, Most Revd Dr Maurice Couve de Murville, the late Dr R. W. Cowley, Mrs Barbara Crossland, Revd Dr Eugene Csocsán de Várallja, Dr J. R. Curran, Dr Mark Curthoys, the late Canon M. E. Dahl, Revd W. Davage, the late Canon E. T. Davies, Dr G. I. Davies, the late Revd Dr R. E. Davies, Revd Thomas Davitt, CM, Prof. A. C. de la Mare, OBE, FBA, Mrs Lyle Dennen, Dr G. E. M. de Ste Croix, Dom Adalbert de Vogüé, OSB, Revd G. R. Dimock, OP, Dr Alexis Doval, FSC, Revd J. M. V. Drummond, Rt. Revd Michael Hare Duke, Revd Prof. G. R. Dunstan, CBE, Revd Dr H. D. Dupree, Revd G. D'Urso, OP, Révd. Père A. Duval, OP, Mrs E. R. Ehrhardt, Revd J. T. Ellis, Revd Prof. J. A. Emerton, FBA, the late Revd Dr H. Escott, Prof. J. M. Estes, Revd Ambrogio Eszer, OP, Dr P. Évieux, Dr P. J. Fedwick, Canon J. C. Fenton, Revd Dr Paul S. Fiddes, Dr John Fines, Dr R. A. Fletcher, DSC, OBE, Revd Dr T. S. Flynn, OP, Mrs M. J. Fox, Revd Fr. Gamelin, OSB, Prof. D. Ganz, Revd J. Garrow, Revd A. Gilmore, Revd R. J. Ginn, Mr J. P. Godwin, Rt. Revd Ronald Gordon, Mr R. J. Goulden, Dr M. D. Goulder, Dr R. Goulet, Mr B. J. Grant, Revd Benedict Green, CR, Metropolitan P. Gregorios, Mr Stephen Gregory, Mª Cristina

Guillén, Prof. H. F. Guite, Mr R. E. Gurney, Revd Dom Rhaban Haacke, OSB, Mr I. T. Hall, Revd Prof. S. G. Hall, Revd Serge Hallette, Revd Dr R. J. Halliburton, Prof. M. Harl, Dr Andreas Haug, Rt. Revd Mgr. G. A. Hay, Dr Felicity Heal, the late Very Revd Dr E. W. Heaton, the late Miss W. A. G. Herrington, Prof. Y.-M. Hilaire, Rt. Revd Dom Giles Hill, OSB, Mr D. B. Hindmarsh, the late Revd Prof. W. A. Hinnebusch, OP, Dr Mary Hobbs, Prof. P. M. Holt, FBA, Prof. A. M. Honoré, FBA, Mr David J. Hooson, Miss B. Horley, Mr J. E. Horsch, Revd Austin Horsley, SM, Revd Ulrich Horst, OP, Dr James Howard-Johnston, Rt. Revd Dr J. W. A. Howe, Dr David Howlett, Very Revd E. Hubner, SJ, the late Revd Dr Gordon Huelin, Revd Alvaro Huerga, OP, Mr R. Ironman, Revd Robin Isherwood, Revd Miguel Itza, OP, Mrs Ritva Jacobbson, Dr N. W. James, Mr R. C. Johnson, Canon Brian H. Kelly, Sir Anthony Kenny, FBA, Dr E. J. King, Mrs Sophie Kisling, Revd J. M. Knight, Miss A. S. Kroese, Revd Prof. M. Lacko, SJ, Mr J. B. Lasek, Dr J. Latham, SJ, Prof. C. H. Lawrence, Mrs J. G. McK. Laws, the late Revd Dr J. S. Lawton, Revd Dr A. Lenox-Conyngham, Very Revd Bertie Lewis, Prof. W. Liebeschuetz, Revd Dr J. T. Lienhard, SJ, Dr S. N. L. Lieu, Most Revd F. G. Linale, Mr G. M. Longley, Mr M. H. Lowes, Revd Dr T. M. McCoog, SJ, Revd Catherine T. R. Mac-Donald, Revd Dr J. A. McGuckin, Prof. Dr Maria Leonar Machado de Sousa, Rt. Revd Mgr. T. G. McKenna, Dr C. M. MacRobert, Dr John Maddicott, FBA, Mr L. Maddison, Archimandrite J. H. Maitland Moir, Revd Dr G. A. Maloney, SJ, Dr W. S. Maltby, Revd George Marcil, OFM, Miss Jackie Marsh, Mr J. K. Martin, Prof. H. C. G. Matthew, FBA, Dr D. L. Mealand, Revd Renzo Meneghini, IMC, Revd Dr B. M. Metzger, M. Hubert Meyer, Revd Dr Dennis Minns, OP, Very Revd P. R. Mitchell, the late Prof. E. Molland, the late Révd. Père C. Mondésert, SJ, Mr Michael Montgomery, Dr Densil Morgan, Revd B. Mountford, Canon M. A. Moxon, Mr David Murphy, Revd A. Nadson, Mr S. R. Nairn, the late Very Revd Michael Napier, Cong. Orat., the late Revd F. J. Nash, Canon C. B. Naylor, Rt. Revd Dr Michael Nazir-Ali, Mr J. D. R. Newhouse, Mr J. S. Nicoll, Mrs M. Nixon, Dr J. O. W. Norris, Dr Ragnar Norrman, Revd Dr D. W. Norwood, Revd M. K. O'Halloran, SJ, Very Revd Dom Alexander Olivar, OSB, Revd Dr E. Panella, OP, Miss K. F. Pantzer, Mrs J. H. Parker, Dr Philip Pattenden, the late Canon B. C. Pawley, Revd Dr A. R. Peacocke, MBE, Revd Isacio Pérez Fernández, OP, Mr D. C. Peterson, M. Pierre Petitmengin, Prof. M. Philonenko, Mr Neil Plummer, Dr Colin Podmore, Dr Alex Popescu, Dr Karen Pratt, Dr R. D. F. Pring-Mill, FBA, Canon D. Probets, Dr Huw Pryce, Revd S. Rajamancickam, SJ, Dr Nigel L. Ramsay, Dr G. Redworth, Revd Dom D. D. Rees, OSB, Revd M. Rees, Prof. T. B. W. Reid, Mr D. H. Rice, Mr C. R. Riches, Revd G. M. Roberts, Mr R. Robinson, Dr Frank E. Robson, OBE, Revd H. Rooke, Canon James M. Rosenthal, Revd G. W. Rusling, Prof. P. Russell, Very Revd Patrick Ryall, OSM, Very Revd José Maria Salaverri, SM, Revd A. T. J. Salter, Revd Andrew Saville, Rt. Revd Dr Christoph Schönborn, OP, Revd Dom Jeremias Schröder, OSB, Revd Dom Gregory Scott, OSB, Mr R. D. Scott, Revd M. Searle, OFM, Revd Prof. A. P. F. Sell, Revd E. Simmons, CR, Miss Kate Skrebutenas, the late Miss Beryl Smalley, the late Dr Elsie Smith, Mrs J. J. M. Smith, Révd. Père L. Soltner, OSB, Revd Dr B. D. Spinks, Prof. H. F. Stander, Very Revd H. E. C. Stapleton, Revd Dr J. N. Steenson, Dr Elizabeth B. Stuart, Prof. Dr R. Stupperich, Dr Henry Summerson, Miss B. M. Swinson, Revd G. A. Tancred, Revd Michael Tavinor, Revd Dr Michael Tavuzzi, OP, the late Canon C. V. Taylor, Revd Dr J. J. Taylor, SM, Mr N. C. Thomas, Revd T. C. G. Thornton, Revd B. G. Thorogood, OBE, Very Revd J. H. Tidy, the late Ven. G. B. Timms, Miss R. B. Tingley, Revd A. Trabucchi, MCCJ, Miss M. S. Travis, the late Dr K. Treu, Dr J. Vennebusch, Dr G. Vermes, FBA, Canon R. D. Vicary, Dr P. A. Wakely, Revd Dom Henry Wansbrough, OSB, the late Canon M. A. C. Warren, Mr D. S. Watson, the late Revd Prof. J. A. Weisheipl, OP, Ven. F. V. Weston, Sr. M. Immolata Wetter, IBMV, Revd Dr L. R. Wickham, Miss Audrey Wild, Miss Elizabeth Wilford, Miss Alice Wilkinson, Prof. G. H.

Preface

Williams, Miss Joan Williams, the Rt. Revd Dr R. D. Williams, FBA, Mr N. G. Wilson, FBA, the late Prof E. Wind, Prof. Dr Wolgast, Revd Dr J. L. Womer, Mr Richard Wood, Rt. Revd Dr K. J. Woollcombe, and Mr D. G. Wright. Thanks for bibliographical and other assistance are also due to the staffs of the Biblioteca Nacional, Madrid; the Bibliothèque Nationale, Paris; the British Library; Lambeth Palace Library; the Vatican Library; the Libraries of the Universities of Birmingham, Cambridge, Leeds, Manchester, Princeton, and Yale, and the University of Wales, Bangor; of Princeton Theological Seminary, the Courtauld Institute, Queen Mary and Westfield College, London, the Union Seminary, New York, and Yale Divinity School; the Victoria and Albert Museum; the Indian and Bangladeshi High Commissions in London; and above all to the staff of the Bodleian Library and other libraries in Oxford, and therein especially to Mr P. G. Allmond, Dr B. Barker-Benfield, Mr R. D. Bell, Ms C. Blundell, Miss J. Dean, Dr G. A. Evison, Mrs A. L. Flavell, Dr M. R. Kauffmann, Mr R. A. Lindo, Mr R. A. McNeil, Mr J. P. Mialon, Mrs S. J. Miles, Mrs W. L. F. Minty, Ms A. M. Northover, Miss A. J. Peters, Miss M. Sheldon-Williams, Mrs P. J. Skinner, and Mr P. Warren, who have all gone far beyond the call of duty. All these, and those whose names occur in the List of Contributors, gave unstintingly, but of course what remains amiss is my responsibility.

Production of the book has been a long and complicated process. Modern typographical conventions, such as the use of arabic rather than roman numerals, have been introduced in the hope that this will prove easier for a new generation of readers. The reordering of articles has been designed with the same end in view. Short titles have normally been used for English statutes rather than the older system of citation by regnal years. Thus the Roman Catholic Relief Act 1926 replaces 16 & 17 Geo. V, c. 55. Where the date incorporated in the official short title differs from the more familiar one when the legislation was passed, both dates are indicated. For example, 'The Toleration Act 1688, passed in 1689 . . .'. The terms man, mankind, etc., are normally used in an inclusive sense; to spell out men and women every time seemed an unnecessary use of space and the distinction is normally made only when there is a particular point at issue, as in discussion of the early chapters of Genesis. In the absence of agreement about the superiority of one modern translation of the Bible over another, quotations are usually from the Authorized Version, though other translations are used in exceptional cases.

For invaluable help in dealing with the various stages in the production process I am grateful to the Very Revd Ephrem Lash, who read the structured proofs and told me much about Orthodox practice; the Revd Dr Simon Francis Gaine, OP, who read all the galley proofs against the original copy, not only picking up printer's errors but also alerting me to recent shifts in RC practice and teaching; and the Rt. Revd Michael Manktelow, who achieved the herculean task of reading both galley and page proofs to a strict (and often inconvenient) timetable, and pointing me to improvements at every stage. To all these my debt is incalculable. I have also been assisted in checking and settling queries by Mrs Skinner, Dr Mark Vessey, Dr R. A. Cross, the Revd Dr J. R. Garrard, Dr Peter Cramer, Dr Gaine, Miss Paula Gooder, Miss Christine Joynes, Miss Ruth Owen, and Dr Maria Sherwood-Smith. Without their help, the *Dictionary* would not have been published before the millennium.

15 St. Giles   E. A. LIVINGSTONE
Oxford
October 1996

PREFACE TO THE FIRST EDITION

THE Christian Church has been so closely interwoven with the course of Western civilization that her history, life, and institutions are matters of deep concern not only to those who through Holy Baptism have been admitted to membership in the Body of Christ, but to all who take an intelligent interest in contemporary culture. The present *Dictionary* has been compiled in order to bring together, in a concise and handy form, as large a body of information as possible directly bearing on the Christian Church. It is addressed to the needs not merely of those whose primary vocation lies in the Christian ministry or in the professional study of theology or church history, nor even only to the general body of professing Christians who seek information about their faith and its growth, but to the educated public as a whole. For this and other reasons technicalities have been avoided, and it is hoped that throughout the entries are so written as to be immediately intelligible to the layman. If the *Dictionary* has any apologetic purpose, it seeks to achieve it solely through the objective presentation of fact.

The scope of the *Dictionary* need not be outlined here, as it will be discovered most readily from a rapid perusal of its pages. If a historical treatment predominates, the employment of this method will need no defence in the case of a faith which is so evidently rooted in history as is Christianity. The attempt has been made to give due and proportionate attention to the several parts and aspects of a vast field, covering over nineteen centuries. But history, as modern studies in its structure by Wilhelm Dilthey, Ernst Troeltsch, and a host of others have made abundantly clear, is by its nature selective, and a discipline in which the employment of objective canons, for example on a statistical basis, is an intrinsically unattainable ideal. If in the present work fuller attention has been paid to Western Christendom than to later Eastern Orthodoxy, to Christianity in Britain than to that of the Continent, to the events of the nineteenth century than to those of the tenth, this disproportion is only relative. In any case it may be presumed that the reader will welcome fuller information on matters at closer range. If, on the other hand, to some readers outside Europe it seems that insufficient attention has been given to the non-European lands where Christianity is now firmly planted, it must be recalled that the Church's connexion with Mediterranean and European countries is of far longer standing, and this fact is necessarily reflected in the subject-matter of a work in which the treatment is historical.

Perhaps some readers will look for a rather fuller treatment of Biblical matters in a *Dictionary of the Christian Church* than will be found here; and reasonably. The importance of the Bible throughout the history of the Church—and especially whenever she has been fully alive to her theological vocation—has always been fundamental. But it would have been impossible to give any adequate treatment of Biblical subjects in the present work without making disproportionate demands on space. There seemed the less need for doing so in view of the abundance of Biblical aids in the form of dictionaries (lexical, factual, and theological), concordances, and compendious commentaries of varying dimensions. These works are readily accessible in libraries. But as they are seldom privately possessed except by the clergy and others with a direct interest in theological studies, it was felt that some information of an elementary kind would be welcomed by a considerable body of lay people whose needs the *Dictionary* might be expected to serve. It is primarily for such readers that the entries on Biblical subjects are included.

Preface to the First Edition

A notable constituent of the *Dictionary* is the bibliographies in small type at the end of the articles. To enable the reader to use these to the best advantage it may be of service to add a few details about their construction and purpose. They were mostly compiled independently of the articles, and their form, it must be confessed, was devised as the *Dictionary* developed, so that complete consistency has not been achieved. They do not set out to record (as is not infrequently the case in dictionary works) the sources which the compiler happens to have found specially useful. Their purpose, rather, is to record the principal items of primary and permanent interest bearing on the subject of the entry. The reader is asked, therefore, not to be too hasty in his strictures when he finds a work listed which the best critics assure him is 'superseded'. Still less must he suppose that the inclusion of a book implies an editorial *nihil obstat*. It is sufficiently familiar that a bad book has sometimes had great intrinsic importance in relation to a particular subject; and since the historical student may need to discover details of such a book, they have been included. Careful attention has also been given to recording the original date of publication of all items, partly to enable the bibliographies to be used by those interested in the authors as well as the contents of the books. Unless the contrary is expressly stated, the date given is always to be taken as that of the first edition. For those who want further readily accessible material, either by way of bibliography or on the subject itself, a liberal citation of articles in the larger standard dictionaries and encyclopaedic works has been made on a selective basis. Our own experience of dictionary works is that *PRE*[1] is to be especially commended for its thoroughness and accuracy, *DTC* for its amplitude, and *EC* for its modernity. We have found no reason to contest what appears to be the general verdict about the limitations of *DACL*. But that dictionary, despite its inaccuracies, is so often the only pointer to further material on archaeological and liturgical matters that we have frequently cited it. With use, the reader will perhaps accustom himself to finding guidance from the bibliography also by its omissions. Thus, where in the case of a person no biography is recorded, it can ordinarily be assumed that none is known to the Editor.

We hope, finally, that the inclusion of this relatively extensive bibliography needs no apology. Those who pursue theological and historical studies rarely possess a large private library in these days, and are more than hitherto dependent on public libraries, often at some distance. It is believed that the *Dictionary* will put the student of church history in possession of a larger body of bibliographical material than any other work of similar compass. If a good deal of this information will be rarely, if ever, wanted by many users of the *Dictionary*, this is a common phenomenon in a reference book. The same is true of *Bradshaw* or *Whitaker* or *Crockford*.

In the construction of the *Dictionary* constant use has naturally been made of the standard sets of texts, historical collections, and histories, as well as the larger dictionaries, encyclopaedias, chronological tables, gazetteers, atlases, and other works of reference. Where any question of accuracy arose, the attempt was always made to verify details from first-hand sources. The extent to which this process could be carried had obvious limits. Where there are many hundreds of opportunities for error on every page, doubtless many inaccuracies survive. But it may be worth pointing out that in some instances considerable labour has been involved in the establishment of a single reference or date; and hence where such, as given in this *Dictionary*, differs from that currently found elsewhere, while it might be prudent to treat it with reserve, it would be mistaken to conclude that it was necessarily wrong.

---

[1] The full titles corresponding to these and the many other abbreviations used will be found in the 'List of Abbreviations', pp. xxiii–xxxii.

It is unnecessary to recount in detail the stages by which the *Dictionary* has assumed its present shape. It owes its inception to Mr G. F. J. Cumberlege of the Oxford University Press, who invited the Editor to undertake the work as long ago as 1939. Reference to the list of Contributors on pp. [x–xii][1] will show that it is the work of many hands, among them several scholars of high distinction. Roughly half the entries, including most of those of major importance, were drafted by these Contributors working independently. The rest, together with the bibliographies, were compiled by the Editor and his immediate associates. In some cases the reader who is versed in contemporary theological literature will have little difficulty in identifying the authorship of certain articles. But in order to secure the maximum uniformity it was agreed at the outset that all contributions should be subject to such editorial modification and reconstruction as seemed desirable, and that anonymity should be preserved. In the event many of the articles in the *Dictionary* are the work of several hands.

A consequence of this method of composition is that revision has been continuous. The material as put at the Editor's disposal needed welding, as far as possible, into a unity. By the close interrelation of the articles much economy of space has been achieved. In this connexion the Publisher generously allowed a great deal of recasting in the proof stage. The Editor is conscious that with the expenditure of further time and labour this process could with profit have been carried further, especially, he believes, in the earlier sections of the work. But a year or so ago it seemed to the Press and the Editor alike that the time had come to eschew further revision and to start the book on its way. In a dictionary (and particularly in one on a new pattern) perfection is an unattainable ideal. If in its future editions this work is to be less imperfect, the Editor must look to the goodwill of his readers to inform him of points needing correction.

There remains the happy task of expressing my own thanks, and also, I doubt not, those of future users of the *Dictionary*, to the very large company of those who in innumerable ways have contributed to its making. It is possible to mention by name only a few of them.

There are, first, my immediate associates. In the earliest stages of the work I had as a collaborator in the Editorship my then colleague the Revd T. M. Parker, *cuius eruditionis fontes plurimi gustavimus exhausit nemo.*[2] Though he had a decisive formative influence on the *Dictionary*, he was, alas, soon compelled to withdraw by pressure of other work. At this period valuable assistance was also given by the Revd H. J. Sutters who, among other labours, compiled the original list of entries. During several of the War years, when progress was necessarily slow, Miss Hilda C. Graef, now known as the biographer of Therese Neumann and Edith Stein, drafted or revised a great number of the early entries; and it was to her, more than to anyone else, that the possession of a continuous first draft was due. In the herculean task of finally producing from a vast assemblage of material a work which had form, unity, and completeness, my principal debt is to Miss Elizabeth A. Livingstone. For over five years the *Dictionary* has engaged her devoted and untiring energies. No problem that arose could be allowed to rest until it had been pursued to its limits, whether by research, correspondence, or personal interviews, and in some cases by all three means; and in this connexion abundant thanks are also due to the large body of those who have generously responded to Miss Livingstone's inquiries. The drafting of the bibliographies is almost wholly due to the same collaborator. There are relatively few of the books or articles cited which Miss Livingstone has not handled, or, where this proved impossible, pursued to an unimpeachable source; and, it need hardly be said, there are a vast number of others which, though examined, have been passed by unrecorded, either through the exigencies of space or through

[1] These pages relate to the first edition.
[2] Words originally applied to F. E. Brightman, an earlier Librarian of Pusey House, by C. H. Turner.

their want of permanent interest. This task has involved the consultation of what must be almost, if not quite, a record number of books in public libraries; and it would be impossible not to mention our indebtedness to the staffs of the Bodleian Library and of the Reading Room of the British Museum, on whom the compilation of the *Dictionary* has imposed (in the literal sense as well as in others) many very heavy burdens. At the Bodleian Library, particular thanks are due to Mr R. G. Chapman, MA, Mr R. J. Key, MA, and Miss Angela M. Jackson.

At a comparatively early stage in the work, the Press invited Professor F. M. Powicke and the Revd Professor S. L. Greenslade to report on and, as far as opportunity allowed, to read the proofs. Professor Powicke's valuable comments on the earlier drafts of the medieval articles preserved us from many pitfalls, while Professor Greenslade, who scrutinized the whole work, made innumerable suggestions which were of untold service. It must be insisted, however, that so many modifications have been made in the text since these two scholars concluded their task several years ago, that they must not be held in any way responsible for errors. In the later stages of the work much assistance was received with the medieval articles from Dr R. W. Hunt, the Keeper of Western Manuscripts at the Bodleian Library, and, in the matter of the medieval bibliographies, from Dr Daniel Callus, OP. The Editor hopes that in consequence of this abundant assistance even specialists in medieval studies will find the work a useful reference book. In Semitic matters, where the Editor's own incompetence has made him much in need of guidance, he has also to thank Professors G. R. Driver, C. A. Simpson, and H. F. D. Sparks, and Mr O. H. M. Lehmann for help on specific points.

A word of special thanks is due for help of another kind. With a generosity which would be unbelievable to those who do not know him, Mr Samuel Gurney went through the whole of the galley proofs, almost line by line, assiduously checking references against standard works and producing lively comments and suggestions from his wide store of learning about all things ecclesiastical and unecclesiastical.

It need hardly be said that the production of the *Dictionary* has involved a great deal of typing and other secretarial work. Usually each article needed to be drafted many times before it was in the right form for the printer. In this connexion thanks are due to some of those already mentioned as well as to Miss G. I. Johns, to Mrs M. Bridge, and to Mrs J. Barnicoat, among others.

Finally, a word of thanks must be said to the Oxford University Press and their printers. The Editor had the good fortune to have a publisher with unique experience in Dictionaries. To learn that the construction of a dictionary is not the wholly humdrum task of Dr Johnson's lexicographer, the reader need but turn to the fascinating Preface to the new *Liddell and Scott*. If the finished work is not quite the companionable and attractive book that I believe Mr Cumberlege originally envisaged, this is because it became clear, as the work proceeded, that it was not within the present Editor's capacity to produce it. But I am grateful to him for his generous and continuous interest in the work until he retired from the Press last September, and also to all other members of the staff of Amen House who have been concerned with the *Dictionary* since its inception. The printers, Messrs. R. & R. Clark of Edinburgh, have earned the gratitude of the Press, the readers of the *Dictionary*, and myself by their patience and accuracy at every stage of the long and complicated process of production, and through them the Scottish, as well as the English, tradition of academic printing and publishing has contributed to this book.

Christ Church   F. L. CROSS
Oxford
May 1957

LIST OF CONTRIBUTORS

†N. J. ABERCROMBIE, MA, D.Phil., sometime Editor of the *Dublin Review*

†The Revd A. W. ADAMS, DD, sometime Dean of Divinity, Magdalen College, Oxford

P. S. ALEXANDER, MA, D.Phil., Nathan Laski Professor of Postbiblical Jewish Literature, University of Manchester

†D. J. ALLAN, MA, FBA, sometime Professor of Greek, University of Glasgow

The Revd G. W. ANDERSON, MA, Hon.DD, Hon.Theol.D., FRSE, FBA, Professor Emeritus of Hebrew and Old Testament Studies, University of Edinburgh

A. ELIZABETH ARMSTRONG, MA, D.Phil., Emeritus Fellow of Somerville College, Oxford

A. H. ARMSTRONG, MA, FBA, Emeritus Professor of Greek, University of Liverpool, and Emeritus Professor of Classics, Dalhousie University, Halifax, Nova Scotia

The Ven. D. J. ATKINSON, MA, Ph.D., M.Litt., Archdeacon of Lewisham

The Revd J. BACKHOUSE, BA, sometime priest-in-charge of Bitteswell, Leics

IRENA BACKUS, D.Phil., Dr.theol.hab., titular professor, Institut d'histoire de la Réformation, University of Geneva

†The Revd D. S. BAILEY, D.Litt., sometime Canon Residentiary and Precentor of Wells

The Revd AELRED BAKER, OSB, MA, Prinknash Abbey

†The Revd M. B. BANISTER, MA, sometime Vicar of King's Sutton, Banbury, Oxon

The Revd ANSELM BANKS, OSB, MA, Buckfast Abbey

The Revd MICHAEL BANNER, MA, D.Phil., Ph.D., F. D. Maurice Professor of Moral and Social Theology, King's College London

GILES BARBER, MA, B.Litt., sometime Librarian, The Taylorian Institution, Oxford

MALCOLM BARBER, BA, Ph.D., Reader in Medieval History, University of Reading

W. H. BARBER, MA, D.Phil., Emeritus Professor of French, Birkbeck College, London

RUTH BARBOUR, MA, sometime Assistant in the Department of Western Manuscripts, Bodleian Library, Oxford

FRANK BARLOW, CBE, MA, D.Phil., Hon.D.Litt., FBA, Emeritus Professor of History, University of Exeter

The Revd L. W. BARNARD, MA, Ph.D., sometime Senior Lecturer in Theology, University of Leeds

T. C. BARNARD, MA, D.Phil., Fellow of Hertford College, Oxford

ANNIE BARNES, MA, D.Phil., Honorary Fellow of St Anne's College, Oxford

S. J. B. BARNISH, MA, D.Phil., Lecturer in Late Antique and Early Medieval European History, Royal Holloway, University of London

†The Revd J. W. B. BARNS, MA, D.Phil., sometime Professor of Egyptology, University of Oxford

The Revd JAMES BARR, DD, FBA, Professor of Hebrew Bible, Vanderbilt University, and Regius Professor of Hebrew Emeritus, University of Oxford

The Revd C. K. BARRETT, DD, FBA, Emeritus Professor of Divinity, Durham University

The Revd P. L. S. BARRETT, MA, BD, LL M, Rector of Compton and Otterbourne

†The Revd J. V. BARTLET, MA, Hon.DD, sometime Professor of Church History, Mansfield College, Oxford

The Revd J. BARTON, MA, D.Phil., D.Litt., Oriel and Laing Professor of the Interpretation of Holy Scripture, University of Oxford

†The Rt. Revd Mgr. J. M. T. BARTON, DD, sometime Consultor, Pontifical Biblical Commission, and Canon of Westminster Cathedral

R. J. BAUCKHAM, MA, Ph.D., Professor of New Testament Studies, University of St Andrews

RICHARD BEADLE, Ph.D., Lecturer in English, University of Cambridge, and Fellow of St John's College

JAMES A. BECKFORD, D.Litt., Professor in the Department of Sociology, University of Warwick

R. A. P. J. BEDDARD, MA, D.Phil., Fellow and Tutor in Modern History, Oriel College, Oxford

The Very Revd T. R. BEESON, OBE, MA, sometime Dean of Winchester

†A. F. L. BEESTON, MA, D.Phil., FBA, sometime Laudian Professor of Arabic, University of Oxford

S. BERTELLI, Professor of Modern History, University of Florence

The Revd THOMAS F. BEST, Ph.D., Executive Secretary in the Secretariat of the Faith and Order Commission, World Council of Churches, Geneva

MARTIN BIDDLE, MA, FBA, Fellow of Hertford College, Oxford

†L. BIELER, D.Phil., sometime Professor of Palaeography and Late Latin, University College, Dublin

T. J. BINYON, MA, D.Phil., Fellow of Wadham College, Oxford

†The Revd HUGH BISHOP, CR, MA, sometime Superior of the Community of the Resurrection, Mirfield

E. BLACKBURN, Wakefield

†The Revd ANDREW BLAIR, CR, MA, sometime of the Community of the Resurrection, Mirfield

W. J. BLAIR, MA, D.Phil., FSA, Fellow and Praelector in Modern History, The Queen's College, Oxford

†T. S. R. BOASE, MA, Hon.DCL, sometime President of Magdalen College, Oxford

REINHARD BODENMANN, D.Th., Research Fellow, University of Geneva

GERALD BONNER, MA, Reader-Emeritus, University of Durham, and sometime Distinguished Professor of

List of Contributors

Early Christian Studies, Catholic University of America

The Revd M. A. BOURDEAUX, MA, BD, DD (Lambeth), Director, Keston Institute, Oxford, and Hon. Canon of Rochester

The Revd JOHN BOWDEN, MA, Hon.DD, Editor and Managing Director, SCM Press Ltd., London

FIONA BOWIE, BA, D.Phil., Lecturer in Theology and Religious Studies, University of Wales, Lampeter

The Revd J. W. BOWKER, MA, Adjunct Professor, University of Pennsylvania

†The Revd H. S. BOX, BD, Ph.D., sometime Vicar of St Barnabas, Bexhill

†The Revd H. R. T. BRANDRETH, OGS, sometime Vicar of St Saviour's, Highbury, and St Dunstan's, Fleet Street, London

D. BRASS, BA, Ph.D., sometime Senior Lecturer in Spanish and Portuguese, University of Bristol

MARTIN BRETT, D.Phil., Fellow and Tutor, Robinson College, Cambridge

LORD BRIGGS, MA, Hon.D.Litt., FBA, sometime Provost of Worcester College, Oxford

S. P. BROCK, MA, D.Phil., FBA, Reader in Syriac Studies, and Fellow of Wolfson College, Oxford

C. N. L. BROOKE, CBE, Litt.D., FBA, Dixie Professor Emeritus of Ecclesiastical History, University of Cambridge, and Life Fellow of Gonville and Caius College

G. J. BROOKE, MA, Ph.D., Senior Lecturer in Intertestamental Literature, Department of Religions and Theology, University of Manchester

PETER NEWMAN BROOKS, MA, D.Phil., Fellow of Robinson College and Lecturer in Divinity, University of Cambridge

The Revd D. W. BROWN, MA, Ph.D., Van Mildert Professor of Divinity in the University of Durham and Canon of Durham Cathedral

P. R. L. BROWN, MA, Hon.D.Theol., Hon.DHL, Hon.D.Litt., FBA, Rollins Professor of History, Princeton University

The Revd RAYMOND BROWN, BD, M.Th., Ph.D., sometime Principal of Spurgeon's College, London

†J. H. BRUMFITT, MA, D.Phil., sometime Professor of French, University of St Andrews

P. A. BRUNT, MA, FBA, Camden Professor Emeritus of Ancient History, University of Oxford, and Emeritus Fellow of Brasenose College

The Rt. Revd C. O. BUCHANAN, MA, DD (Lambeth), Bishop Suffragan of Woolwich

D. A. BULLOUGH, MA, FSA, Emeritus Professor of Mediaeval History, University of St Andrews

J. A. BURROW, MA, FBA, Winterstoke Professor of English, University of Bristol

J. A. CALDWELL, B.Mus., MA, D.Phil., University Reader in Music, University of Oxford

†The Revd DANIEL CALLUS, OP, MA, D.Phil., sometime of Blackfriars, Oxford

E. K. CAMERON, MA, D.Phil., Reader in Reformation History, University of Newcastle upon Tyne

†The Revd J. T. CAMPION, MA, sometime Chaplain of the Blue Nile Province

†The Revd A. C. CANNER, MA, sometime Vicar of Tintagel, Cornwall

†The Revd R. E. CANT, MA, sometime Canon Residentiary and Chancellor of York

The Very Revd E. F. CARPENTER, KCVO, MA, BD, Ph.D., Hon.DD, sometime Dean of Westminster

†The Rt. Revd H. J. CARPENTER, MA, Hon.DD, sometime Bishop of Oxford

J. I. CATTO, MA, D.Phil., Fellow of Oriel College, Oxford

The Revd HENRY CHADWICK, KBE, DD, FBA, sometime Master of Peterhouse, Cambridge

ALLAN CHAPMAN, MA, D.Phil., FRAS, Faculty of Modern History, University of Oxford

†C. R. CHENEY, CBE, D.Litt., FBA, sometime Professor of Medieval History and Fellow of Corpus Christi College, Cambridge

The Revd A. C. CHEYNE, Professor Emeritus of Ecclesiastical History, New College, University of Edinburgh

The Revd J. P. H. CLARK, MA, BD, DD (Lambeth), Vicar of Longframlington, Northumberland

STUART CLARK, Ph.D., Lecturer in History, University of Wales, Swansea

W. H. CLENNELL, MA, sometime Senior Assistant Librarian, Bodleian Library, Oxford

R. A. COLES, MA, D.Phil., Papyrology Rooms, Ashmolean Museum, Oxford

The Revd EDMUND COLLEDGE, OSA, MA, Emeritus Professor, Pontifical Institute of Mediaeval Studies, Toronto

BARRY COLLETT, MA, D.Phil., Senior Lecturer in the Department of History, University of Melbourne

The Revd D. COOK, MA, Chaplain, Cranbrook School

JOYCE COOMBS, sometime member of the Mothers' Union Central Council, London

M. P. COSTELOE, BA, Ph.D., Professor of Hispanic and Latin American Studies, University of Bristol

JOHN COTTINGHAM, MA, D.Phil., Professor of Philosophy, University of Reading

WILLIAM J. COURTENAY, Ph.D., C. H. Haskins Professor of History, University of Wisconsin, Madison

†The Revd F. COURTNEY, SJ, DD, sometime Librarian and Lecturer, Heythrop College, University of London

The Revd H. E. J. COWDREY, MA, FBA, Emeritus Fellow, St Edmund Hall, Oxford

†The Revd C. STUART CRAIG, BA, sometime General Secretary of the Congregational Council for World Mission

P. J. CRAMER, MA, Ph.D., Winchester College

†The Revd W. J. CRATCHLEY, Ph.D., DD, sometime Vicar of St Mark's, Swindon, and Honorary Canon of Bristol

The Very Revd Mgr. J. D. CRICHTON, Hon.DSL, sometime Parish Priest of Pershore and editor of *Life and Worship*

The Revd G. CROFT, SJ, MA, Ph.D., Lecturer in Psychology, The Seminary, Harare

†A. C. CROMBIE, MA, B.Sc., Ph.D., FBA, sometime Fellow of Trinity College, Oxford

†The Revd F. L. CROSS, DD, FBA, sometime Lady Margaret Professor of Divinity and Canon of Christ Church, Oxford

R. A. CROSS, MA, D.Phil., Fellow of Oriel College, Oxford

†The Revd J. Crozier, sometime Parish Priest at Abingdon and Hon. Canon of Portsmouth diocese

†The Revd G. J. Cuming, DD, sometime Canon Theologian of Leicester Cathedral

The Revd Colin Davey, Ph.D., Co-ordinating Secretary for Church Life, Council of Churches for Britain and Ireland, London

The Revd Brian Davies, OP, MA, D.Phil., M.Th., Professor of Philosophy, Fordham University, New York

The Revd G. Henton Davies, M.Litt., MA, Hon.DD, Principal Emeritus of Regent's Park College, Oxford

Oliver Davies, MA, D.Phil., Lecturer in Theology, University of Wales, Lampeter

R. T. Davies, MA, sometime Reader in English Literature, University of Liverpool

†N. Davis, MBE, MA, FBA, sometime Merton Professor of English Language and Literature, University of Oxford

†R. H. C. Davis, MA, FBA, sometime Professor of Medieval History, University of Birmingham

N. R. M. de Lange, MA, D.Phil., Lecturer in Rabbinics, University of Cambridge

†The Revd V. A. Demant, MA, D.Litt., Hon.DD, sometime Regius Professor of Moral and Pastoral Theology and Canon of Christ Church, Oxford

†The Revd D. R. Dendy, MA, BD, sometime Vicar of Bledington, Oxford

The Revd R. A. Denniston, MA, M.Sc., sometime Academic and General Publisher, Oxford University Press

†Sirapie Der Nersessian, Litt.D., sometime Professor of Byzantine Art and Archaeology, Dumbarton Oaks, Washington

A. M. Devine, MA, Ph.D., sometime Fellow of Wolfson College, Oxford

A. G. Dickens, CMG, MA, D.Litt., FBA, FSA, Emeritus Professor of History, University of London

†The Revd J. C. Dickinson, MA, B.Litt., sometime Senior Lecturer in Theology, University of Birmingham

J. P. B. Dobbs, BA, M.Ed., M.Phil., D.Phil., Dip.Ed., Dip.Theol., FRSA, FRAS, sometime Director of Music Studies and Deputy Principal of Dartington College of Arts

†Sir Godfrey R. Driver, MA, Hon.DD, FBA, sometime Professor of Semitic Philology, University of Oxford

The Very Revd J. H. Drury, MA, Dean of Christ Church, Oxford

E. T. Dubois, D.Phil., D.-ès-Lettres, sometime Reader in French, University of Newcastle upon Tyne

Jean Dunbabin, MA, D.Phil., Fellow and Tutor in History, St Anne's College, Oxford

The Revd A. Ian Dunlop, TD, MA, BD, Edinburgh

The Revd A. O. Dyson, MA, BD, D.Phil., Professor of Social and Pastoral Theology, University of Manchester

T. F. Earle, MA, D.Phil., University Lecturer in Portuguese, University of Oxford

Robert Easting, MA, D.Phil., Reader in English Language and Literature, Victoria University of Wellington, New Zealand

Revd Canon Peter Eaton, BA, Rector of St James Episcopal Church, Lancaster, Penn.

Brother Elias, O.Carm., BA, M.Phil., Aylesford

†A. B. Emden, MA, Hon.D.Litt., FBA, FSA, sometime Principal of St Edmund Hall, Oxford

The Revd Philip Endean, SJ, MA, BD, D.Phil., Lecturer in Systematic Theology, Heythrop College, University of London

The Revd G. H. Ettlinger, SJ, MA, D.Phil., Professor of Patristics, St John's University, Jamaica, New York

R. J. W. Evans, MA, D.Phil., FBA, Professor of European History, University of Oxford

The Revd M. Everitt, MA, Chaplain and Fellow of Merton College, Oxford

†The Revd H. H. Farmer, MA, Hon.DD, sometime Norris-Hulse Professor of Divinity and Fellow of Peterhouse, Cambridge

Margot Fassler, MA, Ph.D., Director, Yale Institute of Sacred Music; Professor of Religion and Music, Yale Divinity School; and Professor of Musicology, Yale School of Music

E. Ferguson, Ph.D., Professor Emeritus of Church History, Abilene Christian University, Abilene, Texas

The Revd Ronald Ferguson, MA, BD, Th.M., Minister of St Magnus Cathedral, Kirkwall, Orkney

The Rt. Revd Mgr. B. E. Ferme, D.Phil., DCL, Professor of Canon Law, Università Pontificia Gregoriana, Rome

K. C. Fincham, MA, Ph.D., Senior Lecturer in History, University of Kent

The Revd C. B. Firth, MA, sometime Asia Secretary of the Conference of Missionary Societies of Great Britain and Ireland, London

Ian Fisher, MA, Royal Commission on the Ancient and Historical Monuments of Scotland, Edinburgh

†The Revd J. D. C. Fisher, MA, BD, sometime Honorary Canon of Chichester

†The Revd B. FitzGibbon, SJ, MA, sometime Lecturer in History, Campion Hall, Oxford

The Revd Joseph A. Fitzmyer, SJ, Professor Emeritus, Biblical Studies, Catholic University of America

A. J. Flavell, MA, Assistant Librarian, Bodleian Library, Oxford

†J. D. Fleeman, MA, D.Phil., sometime Fellow of Pembroke College, Oxford

R. A. Fletcher, MA, Reader, University of York

Derek W. Flitter, MA, D.Phil., Lecturer in Modern Spanish Language and Literature, University of Birmingham

†Sir Idris Foster, MA, FBA, sometime Jesus Professor of Celtic, University of Oxford

†Ruth Fraenkel, Ph.D., Oxford

The Revd J. E. Francis, BD, sometime Principal of Overdale College, Birmingham

†The Revd R. S. Franks, MA, D.Litt., sometime Principal of Western College, Bristol

The Revd R. H. Fuller, MA, Professor Emeritus, Virginia Theological Seminary

The Revd Simon Francis Gaine, OP, MA, D.Phil., Blackfriars, Oxford

List of Contributors

The Revd C. GALLAGHER, SJ, MA, DCL, sometime Rector of the Pontifical Oriental Institute, Rome

†Dame HELEN L. GARDNER, MA, D.Litt., FBA, FRSL, sometime Merton Professor of English Literature, University of Oxford

The Revd J. R. GARRARD, D.Phil., Assistant Curate, Team Parish of Elland

D. J. GAZELEY, Director of Watts and Co., London

†Sir FREDERICK GIBBERD, RA, FRIBA, London

†M. T. GIBSON, MA, D.Phil., sometime Senior Research Fellow, St Peter's College, Oxford

R. N. GILDEA, MA, D.Phil., University Reader in Modern History and Fellow of Merton College, Oxford

†The Revd J. GILL, SJ, BA, Ph.D., sometime Rector of the Pontifical Oriental Institute, Rome

MARK GOLDIE, MA, Ph.D., Fellow and Lecturer in History, Churchill College, Cambridge

B. J. GOLDING, MA, D.Phil., Senior Lecturer, Department of History, University of Southampton

†The Revd N. GOODALL, MA, D.Phil., sometime Assistant General Secretary of the World Council of Churches

P. R. GOODER, MA, Lecturer, Ripon College Cuddesdon, Oxford

M. D. GOODMAN, MA, D.Phil., FBA, Professor of Jewish Studies and Fellow of Wolfson College, Oxford

†The Revd E. L. H. GORDON, MA, sometime Rector of Great Chart, Ashford, Kent

PAMELA O. E. GRADON, MA, Ph.D., Emeritus Fellow of St Hugh's College, Oxford

†HILDA C. GRAEF, sometime Senior Assistant on the *Patristic Greek Lexicon*

The Revd J. W. GRANT, MA, D.Phil., Hon.DD, Hon. LL D, sometime Professor of Church History, Victoria University, Toronto

The Revd K. GRAYSTON, MA, D.Litt., Emeritus Professor of Theology, University of Bristol

The Revd V. H. H. GREEN, DD, Honorary Fellow and sometime Rector of Lincoln College, Oxford

†The Revd S. L. GREENSLADE, DD, FBA, sometime Regius Professor of Ecclesiastical History and Canon of Christ Church, Oxford

DIANA GREENWAY, Ph.D., Reader in Medieval History, Institute of Historical Research, University of London

The Revd JACQUES GRES-GAYER, D.Theol., D.Hist., Associate Professor of Church History, Catholic University of America

MARTIN GRIFFITHS, MA, Dip.Law., of the Inner Temple, Barrister

R. M. GRIFFITHS, MA, Ph.D., Professor of French, King's College London

†E. M. GRINLING, MA, sometime Principal Lecturer in Religious Education, Darlington College of Education

W. J. GRISBROOKE, MA, BD, sometime Lecturer at the Queen's College, Birmingham, and at St Mary's College, Oscott

ERIK GUNNES, dr.philos., Emeritus Professor of Medieval History, University of Oslo

†SAMUEL GURNEY, MA, Trinity College, Oxford

The Revd J. R. GUY, BA, Ph.D., Vicar of Betws Cedewain and Tregynon and Llanwyddelan, Powys, and Editor of the *Journal of Welsh Religious History*

The Revd BENEDICT HACKETT, OSA, Ph.D., St Mary's Priory, Birmingham, formerly Assistant General of the Order

The Revd JACQUES HAERS, SJ, D.Phil., Lecturer in Theology, Catholic University of Leuven

C. A. HAIGH, MA, Ph.D., Tutor in Modern History and Student of Christ Church, Oxford

A. HAMILTON, MA, Ph.D., Professor of the History of the Radical Reformation, University of Amsterdam

B. HAMILTON, Ph.D., Professor of Crusading History, University of Nottingham

†The Revd R. J. HAMMER, MA, BD, Ph.D., sometime Lecturer at the Queen's College, Birmingham, and Recognized Lecturer in the Faculty of Theology, University of Birmingham

ROBERT T. HANDY, M.Div., Ph.D., Hon.LHD, Hon.DD, Henry Sloane Coffin Professor Emeritus of Church History, Union Theological Seminary, New York

†The Rt. Revd R. P. C. HANSON, DD, FBA, MRIA, sometime Professor of Theology, University of Manchester

C. G. HARDIE, MA, Emeritus Fellow of Magdalen College, Oxford

G. L. HARRISS, MA, D.Phil., FBA, Emeritus Fellow, Magdalen College, Oxford

The Revd H. St. J. HART, BD, Life Fellow and Hebrew Lecturer at Queens' College, Cambridge, and Emeritus Reader in Hebrew and Intertestamental Studies in the University

†The Very Revd F. P. HARTON, BD, sometime Dean of Wells

The Revd A. E. HARVEY, MA, DD, Canon Residentiary and Sub-Dean of Westminster

M. M. HARVEY, MA, D.Phil., Lecturer in History, University of Durham

The Revd A. HASTINGS, MA, D.Theol., Hon.DD, Emeritus Professor of Theology, University of Leeds

P. J. HEATHER, MA, D.Phil., Lecturer in Early Medieval History, University College London

The Revd B. L. HEBBLETHWAITE, MA, BD, Lecturer in Divinity, University of Cambridge, Life Fellow of Queens' College, and Canon Theologian of Leicester Cathedral

†The Revd M. M. HENNELL, MA, sometime Canon of Manchester

J. R. L. HIGHFIELD, MA, D.Phil., FSA, Emeritus Fellow of Merton College, Oxford

CHRISTOPHER HILL, MA, FBA, sometime Fellow and Tutor in Modern History and then Master, Balliol College, Oxford

The Revd D. I. HILL, MA, Hon.DD, sometime Canon Residentiary of Canterbury Cathedral

DAVID HILLIARD, MA, Ph.D., Reader in History, The Flinders University of South Australia

†The Revd P. B. HINCHLIFF, DD, sometime Regius Professor of Ecclesiastical History and Canon of Christ Church, Oxford

The Revd P. D. HOCKEN, Ph.D., Mother of God Community, Gaithersburg, Maryland

†The Revd J. P. HODGES, MA, sometime Rector of Streatham

The Revd MARCUS HODGES, OP, STL, M.Theol., Blackfriars, Cambridge

C. HOLDSWORTH, MA, Ph.D., Professor of Medieval History, University of Exeter

The Revd Dom P. D. HOLDSWORTH, OSB, MA, STL, sometime Master of St Benet's Hall, Oxford

GEORGE HOLMES, MA, Ph.D., FBA, Chichele Professor Emeritus of Medieval History, University of Oxford

The Very Revd R. T. HOLTBY, MA, BD, FSA, sometime Dean of Chichester

†The Revd A. F. HOOD, CBE, MA, sometime Canon and Chancellor of St Paul's Cathedral, London

IRVIN B. HORST, MA, D.Theol., Emeritus Professor in Church History, University of Amsterdam

I. H. HOSKINS, MA, member of the General Council of the Theosophical Society (Adyar)

R. J. HOWELLS, BA, Ph.D., Reader in French, Birkbeck College, London

ANNE HUDSON, MA, D.Phil., FBA, Professor of Medieval English, University of Oxford

†The Revd Dom ANSELM HUGHES, OSB, MA, sometime monk of Nashdom Abbey, Bucks

JEREMY HUGHES, MA, D.Phil., Pusey and Ellerton Fellow, University of Oxford

E. D. HUNT, MA, D.Phil., Lecturer in Classics and Ancient History, University of Durham

†G. N. S. HUNT, MA, Wadham College, Oxford

†R. W. HUNT, MA, D.Phil., FBA, sometime Keeper of Western Manuscripts, Bodleian Library, and Fellow of Balliol College, Oxford

R. L. HUNTER, B.Sc., TD, Edinburgh

S. S. HUSSEY, MA, Ph.D., Professor Emeritus of English, University of Lancaster

†M. B. HUTCHINSON, MA, Balliol College, Oxford

The Revd S. ICKERT, Ph.D., sometime Lutheran Fellow, Mansfield College, Oxford

†The Revd E. O. JAMES, D.Litt., FSA, sometime Professor of the History and Philosophy of Religion, University of London

H. T. JENKINS, MA, B.Litt., sometime Assistant Editor, *Victoria County History of Oxfordshire*

K. JENSEN, Ph.D., Assistant Librarian, Bodleian Library, Oxford

The Revd E. R. G. JOB, MA, ARCM, sometime Vice-Dean and Precentor of Winchester Cathedral

The Revd S. A. C. B. JOHN, MA, sometime Vicar of Barlow, Derbyshire

J. JOHNS, MA, D.Phil., University Lecturer in Islamic Archaeology and Fellow of Wolfson College, Oxford

The Revd P. F. JOHNSON, MA, Canon Residentiary of Bristol Cathedral

P. M. JOYCE, MA, D.Phil., University Lecturer in Old Testament Studies and Fellow of St Peter's College, Oxford

ELAINE KAYE, MA, BD, Ph.D., College Historian, Mansfield College, Oxford

†The Revd J. N. D. KELLY, DD, FBA, sometime Principal of St Edmund Hall, Oxford

The Rt. Revd E. W. KEMP, DD, Bishop of Chichester

M. S. KEMPSHALL, MA, D.Phil., Murray Fellow in History, Faculty of Modern History, University of Oxford

†Sir FREDERIC KENYON, MA, D.Litt., FBA, sometime Director and Principal Librarian, British Museum, London

†Dame KATHLEEN M. KENYON, MA, D.Litt., FBA, FSA, sometime Principal of St Hugh's College, Oxford

The Revd D. A. KERR, SS, MA, D.Phil., Professor of Ecclesiastical History, Maynooth

The Very Revd F. KERR, OP, MA, STM, Blackfriars, Edinburgh

S. D. KEYNES, MA, Ph.D., Litt.D., Reader in Anglo-Saxon History, University of Cambridge, and Fellow of Trinity College

†The Revd G. D. KILPATRICK, DD, sometime Dean Ireland's Professor of Exegesis of Holy Scripture, University of Oxford

†The Revd H. P. KINGDON, MA, sometime Vicar of Chewton Mendip

W. J. TORRANCE KIRBY, MA, D.Phil., Tutor, St John's College, Santa Fe, New Mexico

R. KLIBANSKY, MA, Ph.D., D.Habil., FRSC, Emeritus Frothingham Professor of Logic and Metaphysics, McGill University, and Emeritus Professor of the University of Heidelberg

GEORGE KNIGHT, OBE, MA, RN, Retired Naval Officer

†The Revd H. KNIGHT, BD, D.Phil., sometime Assistant Master, Gordonstoun School

†The Revd M. D. KNOWLES, MA, Litt.D., FBA, FSA, sometime Regius Professor of Modern History and Fellow of Peterhouse, Cambridge

The Revd R. BUICK KNOX, DD, sometime Professor of Church History, Westminster College, Cambridge

H. G. KOENIGSBERGER, MA, Ph.D., FBA, Professor of History Emeritus, King's College London

A. J. KRAILSHEIMER, MA, Ph.D., Emeritus Student of Christ Church, Oxford

W. G. LAMBERT, MA, FBA, Professor Emeritus of Assyriology, University of Birmingham

†The Revd G. W. H. LAMPE, DD, sometime Regius Professor of Divinity and Fellow of Gonville and Caius College, Cambridge

E. LAMPERT, Lic.ès-Lettres, D.Phil., FRSL, Emeritus Professor of Russian Studies, University of Keele

JOHN LANKFORD, MS, Ph.D., Special Assistant to the Provost and Adjunct Professor of History, Kansas State University

FRANCES LANNON, MA, D.Phil., Fellow of Lady Margaret Hall, Oxford

MICHAEL LAPIDGE, Litt.D., FBA, Elrington-Bosworth Professor of Anglo-Saxon, University of Cambridge

The Very Revd E. C. LASH, MA, STB, sometime Lecturer in Biblical and Patristic Studies, University of Newcastle upon Tyne

†The Revd A. C. LAWSON, DD, sometime Vicar of St Michael's, Shrewsbury

†KATHLEEN M. LEA, MA, sometime Fellow of Lady Margaret Hall, Oxford

The Revd JÉSUS M. LECEA, Sch.P., Procurator General of the Piarist Fathers

†The Revd Dom JEAN LECLERCQ, OSB, STD, sometime monk of Clervaux Abbey, Luxembourg

O. H. M. LEHMAN, MA, B.Litt., D.Phil., Hebrew Union College, Cincinnati, and Miami University, Oxford, Ohio

GILLIAN LEWIS, MA, D.Phil., Fellow and Tutor in Modern History, St Anne's College, Oxford

P. S. LEWIS, MA, Fellow of All Souls College, Oxford

†The Revd P. OSMUND LEWRY, OP, STL, D.Phil., sometime of Blackfriars, Oxford, and Fellow of the Pontifical Institute of Mediaeval Studies, Toronto

†K. J. LEYSER, MA, FBA, sometime Chichele Professor of Medieval History, University of Oxford

The Revd F. LINYARD, BA, BD, sometime Chairman of the Provincial Board of the Moravian Church in Great Britain and Ireland

ELIZABETH A. LIVINGSTONE, MBE, MA, DD (Lambeth), St Anne's College, Oxford

Sir CHRISTOPHER LLOYD, MA, B.Litt., Surveyor of The Queen's Pictures

The Revd G. LLOYD JONES, BD, MA, STM, Ph.D., Hon.DD, Senior Lecturer, School of Theology and Religious Studies, University of Wales, Bangor, and Canon Chancellor of Bangor Cathedral

ANN LOADES, MA, Ph.D., Professor of Theology, University of Durham

A. LOUTH, DD, Reader in Patristics, University of Durham

D. E. LUSCOMBE, Litt.D., FBA, Leverhulme Personal Research Professor of Medieval History, University of Sheffield

The Revd D. McL. LYNCH, CBE, MA, sometime Chief Secretary of the Church Army and Prebendary of St Paul's Cathedral

The Revd JAMES McCONICA, CSB, MA, D.Phil., Hon.D.Litt., FRSC, Fellow of All Souls College, Oxford, and President of the Pontifical Institute of Mediaeval Studies, Toronto

The Revd DIARMAID MacCULLOCH, MA, Ph.D., FSA, University Lecturer in Church History and Fellow of St Cross College, Oxford

D. McDIARMID, MA, Ph.D., Fundraising Director, Royal Melbourne Institute of Technology, Melbourne

The Revd JOHN MACDONALD, MA, B.Litt., sometime Lecturer in Theology, University College, Lampeter

The Revd B. J. MACDONALD-MILNE, MA, Rector of Radwinter with Hempstead, and Rural Dean of Saffron Walden, Essex

The Revd A. E. McGRATH, BD, MA, D.Phil., Principal of Wycliffe Hall, Research Lecturer in Theology, University of Oxford, and Professor of Systematic Theology, Regent College, Vancouver

†ANGUS MACINTYRE, MA, D.Phil., sometime Fellow and Tutor in Modern History, Magdalen College, and Principal-elect, Hertford College, Oxford

The Revd DONALD K. McKIM, BA, M.Div., Ph.D., Minister, Presbyterian Church (USA), Berwyn, Pennsylvania

†D. M. MacKINNON, MA, FBA, FRSA, sometime Norris-Hulse Professor of Divinity and Fellow of Corpus Christi College, Cambridge

†MAY McKISACK, MA, sometime Professor of History, Westfield College, London

R. D. McKITTERICK, MA, Ph.D., Litt.D., Professor of Early Medieval European History, University of Cambridge, and Fellow of Newnham College

I. W. F. MACLEAN, MA, D.Phil., Professor of French and Fellow of The Queen's College, Oxford

N. B. McLYNN, MA, D.Phil., Lecturer, Faculty of Law, Keio University, Yokohama, Japan

The Revd J. McMANNERS, D.Litt., FBA, Fellow of All Souls College and Emeritus Regius Professor of Ecclesiastical History, University of Oxford

ALAN MACQUARRIE, MA, Ph.D., Research Centre in Scottish History, University of Strathclyde

The Revd J. MACQUARRIE, D.Litt., DD, FBA, Lady Margaret Professor Emeritus of Divinity, University of Oxford

†The Rt. Revd Mgr. L. L. McREAVY, JCD, MA, sometime member of the Pontifical Commission for the Revision of the Code of Canon Law

The Rt. Revd MICHAEL MANKTELOW, MA, sometime Bishop Suffragan of Basingstoke

†The Revd W. W. S. MARCH, MA, BD, sometime Canon Residentiary of Chichester

ELIZABETH MARCHANT, Taizé

R. A. MARKUS, MA, Ph.D., FBA, Professor Emeritus, University of Nottingham

†The Revd J. MARSH, MA, D.Phil., sometime Principal of Mansfield College, Oxford

†The Revd P. M. MARTIN, MA, sometime Canon Residentiary and Chancellor of Wells

†The Revd E. L. MASCALL, DD, FBA, sometime Professor of Historical Theology, University of London

J. F. A. MASON, MA, D.Phil., Emeritus Student of Christ Church, Oxford

†The Revd A. GERVASE MATHEW, OP, MA, sometime of Blackfriars, Oxford

R. A. MAY, MA, sometime Leonard Stein Lecturer in Medieval Hebrew, University of Oxford

The Revd A. MEREDITH, SJ, MA, D.Phil., Farm Street, London

C. MEWS, D.Phil., Lecturer in History, Monash University, Australia

The Very Revd R. L. P. MILBURN, MA, FSA, Honorary Fellow of Worcester College, Oxford; sometime Dean of Worcester

BELLA MILLETT, MA, B.Phil., D.Phil., Reader in English, University of Southampton

E. H. MILLIGAN, BA, sometime Librarian of the Religious Society of Friends, London

The Revd J. O. MILLS, OP, MA, sometime Counsellor on Communication Development to the Master of the Order of Preachers, Rome

The Revd L. MINHINNICK, MA, sometime Vicar of St John's, Lytham

A. G. MOLLAND, MA, Ph.D., Honorary Senior Lecturer in History, University of Aberdeen

INGUN MONTGOMERY, Professor of Church History, University of Oslo

†The Revd E. GARTH MOORE, MA, DCL, barrister, sometime Fellow of Corpus Christi College, Cambridge, and Chancellor of Southwark, Durham, and Gloucester dioceses

P. R. S. MOOREY, MA, D.Phil., FBA, FSA, Keeper of Antiquities, Ashmolean Museum, Oxford

†The Rt. Revd J. R. H. MOORMAN, DD, FSA, sometime Bishop of Ripon

The Revd R. MORGAN, MA, Priest-in-charge of Sandford-on-Thames, and University Lecturer in Theology, University of Oxford

†The Revd Dom AUGUSTINE MORRIS, OSB, sometime Abbot of Nashdom Abbey, Bucks

The Revd COLIN MORRIS, MA, Emeritus Professor of Medieval History, University of Southampton, and Emeritus Fellow of Pembroke College, Oxford

†The Rt. Revd R. C. MORTIMER, DD, sometime Bishop of Exeter

†The Revd C. B. MOSS, DD, sometime Vice-Principal, St Boniface College, Warminster

The Revd J. MUDDIMAN, MA, D.Phil., University Lecturer in Theology and Fellow and Tutor, Mansfield College, Oxford

The Revd J. A. MUNITIZ, SJ, MA, D.ès Lettres, Master of Campion Hall, Oxford

ALEXANDER MURRAY, MA, B.Phil., FBA, Fellow and Praelector in Modern History, University College, Oxford

†P. MURRAY, Ph.D., FSA, sometime Professor of the History of Art, Birkbeck College, University of London

†The Rt. Revd S. C. NEILL, MA, Hon.DD, FBA, sometime Professor of Philosophy and Religious Studies, University of Nairobi

The Revd S. A. NELSON, BA, M.Div., Ph.D., Professor of Theology, Golden Gate Baptist Seminary, Strawberry Point, California

B. C. NEVEU, MA, D.ès L., D.en D., President of the École pratique des Hautes Études (Sorbonne), Paris

The Revd G. M. NEWLANDS, MA, BD, Ph.D., Professor of Divinity, University of Glasgow

D. H. NEWSOME, MA, D.Litt., FRSL, sometime Lecturer in Ecclesiastical History, University of Cambridge

†The Revd R. W. NICHOLLS, BA, AKC, sometime Vicar of Barnham, Bognor Regis

The Revd A. NICHOLS, OP, MA, Ph.D., STL, Blackfriars, Cambridge

The Revd D. NICHOLSON, MA, Dipl.Th., sometime Vice-Principal of Edinburgh Theological College, Life-President of the Society of Retreat Conductors, and Hon. Canon of Edinburgh and Aberdeen

The Revd E. W. NICHOLSON, DD, FBA, Provost of Oriel College, Oxford

OLIVER NICHOLSON, MA, D.Phil., Associate Professor, Department of Classical and Near Eastern Studies, University of Minnesota

J. B. W. NIGHTINGALE, MA, Fellow of Magdalen College, Oxford

The Revd D. E. NINEHAM, DD, Emeritus Professor of Theology, University of Bristol, and Honorary Canon of Bristol Cathedral and sometime Warden of Keble College, Oxford

The Revd K. W. NOAKES, MA, D.Phil., sometime Librarian of Pusey House, Oxford

PETER R. NOCKLES, MA, D.Phil., Assistant Librarian, John Rylands University Library of Manchester

The Revd E. R. NORMAN, DD, Canon Residentiary and Treasurer of York Minster

J. L. NORTH, MA, Ph.D., Barmby Lecturer in New Testament Studies, University of Hull

Sir DIMITRI OBOLENSKY, MA, Ph.D., D.Litt., FBA, FSA, Emeritus Professor of Russian and Balkan History, University of Oxford

†The Revd J. B. O'CONNELL, MA, BD, sometime Honorary Canon of the Diocese of Menevia, Wales

DONNCHADH Ó CORRÁIN, MA, D.Litt., MRIA, Professor of History, University College, Cork

The Revd O. M. T. O'DONOVAN, MA, D.Phil., Regius Professor of Moral and Pastoral Theology and Canon of Christ Church, Oxford

†H. S. OFFLER, MA, FBA, sometime Professor of Medieval History, University of Durham

The Revd J. O'MALLEY, SJ, MA, Ph.D., Professor of Church History, Weston School of Theology, Cambridge, Mass.

The Revd ROBERT OMBRES, OP, STL, JCL, LL B, LL M, Barrister, Blackfriars, Oxford

D. M. OWEN, MA, Litt.D., FSA, sometime Keeper of the Archives, University of Cambridge

NIGEL F. PALMER, MA, D.Phil., Professor of German Medieval and Linguistic Studies, University of Oxford

RICHARD PARISH, MA, D.Phil., Professor of French and Fellow of St Catherine's College, Oxford

†The Revd T. M. PARKER, DD, sometime Fellow of University College, Oxford

R. A. PATERSON, MA, LL B, Solicitor of the Church, Church of Scotland

THOMAS S. PATTIE, MA, Curator of Manuscripts, British Library, London

†The Revd E. A. PAYNE, CH, MA, B.Litt., Hon.DD, Hon.LL D, sometime General Secretary and later President, Baptist Union of Great Britain and Ireland

†The Revd A. F. SCOTT PEARSON, D.Litt., sometime Professor of Ecclesiastical History and Symbolics, Presbyterian College, Belfast

R. PETERS, Oxford

†SIMONE PÉTREMENT, Docteur ès lettres, sometime Conservateur honoraire à la Bibliothèque Nationale, Paris

The Revd R. W. PFAFF, MA, D.Phil., DD, Professor of History, University of North Carolina

†The Very Revd R. PILKINGTON, DCL, sometime Honorary Canon of the Chapter of Westminster Cathedral

M. LOUISE PIROUET, BA, Ph.D., sometime Lecturer in Religious Studies, Makerere University, Kampala; Nairobi University; and Homerton College, Cambridge

†The Revd W. N. PITTENGER, STD, sometime Senior Resident, King's College, Cambridge

The Revd S. J. PIX, MA, Dip.Th., Hon.D.Litt., Vicar of St Michael at the North Gate with St Martin and All Saints, Oxford

The Revd J. E. PLATT, MA, M.Th., D.Phil., Fellow and Chaplain of Pembroke College, Oxford

V. POHLE, Liverpool

D. S. PORTER, MA, sometime Senior Assistant Librarian, Bodleian Library, Oxford

D. C. POTTS, MA, D.Phil., Emeritus Fellow of Keble College, Oxford

†Sir MAURICE POWICKE, MA, D.Litt., FBA, sometime Regius Professor of Modern History, University of Oxford

†The Revd G. L. PRESTIGE, DD, sometime Canon and Treasurer of St Paul's Cathedral, London

The Revd D. T. W. PRICE, MA, Senior Lecturer in History and Theology, University of Wales, Lampeter, and Canon of St David's Cathedral

W. W. PRICE, BA, BD, Th.M., D.Theol., Mansfield College, Oxford

ANTONY QUINTON (Lord Quinton), MA, FBA, sometime President of Trinity College, Oxford, and Chairman of the British Library Board

ALBERT J. RABOTEAU, MA, Ph.D., Henry W. Putman Professor of Religion, Princeton University

The Revd A. RACE, B.Tech., MA, Rector of St Andrew's, Aylestone, Leicester

The Revd HENRY D. RACK, MA, Ph.D., Honorary Fellow, formerly Bishop Fraser Senior Lecturer in Ecclesiastical History, University of Manchester

†The Revd A. A. H. RADICE, MA, sometime Rector of Hepworth, Norfolk

The Revd P. RAEDTS, SJ, D.Phil., Professor of Medieval History, University of Nijmegen, and Lecturer in Church History, University of Leiden

The Revd OLIVER P. RAFFERTY, SJ, BA, M.Th., Christ Church and Campion Hall, Oxford

RENÉ RANCOEUR, Conservateur en chef honoraire à la Bibliothèque Nationale, Paris

†The Revd E. C. RATCLIFF, MA, sometime Regius Professor of Divinity, Cambridge

The Revd BERNARD M. G. REARDON, MA, sometime Head of the Department of Religious Studies, University of Newcastle upon Tyne

S. R. REBENICH, Dr.phil., Privatdozent, Seminar of Ancient History, Mannheim University

R. REECE, B.Sc., D.Phil., Institute of Archaeology, University College London

M. E. REEVES, CBE, MA, D.Phil., D.Litt., FBA, Honorary Fellow of St Anne's and St Hugh's Colleges, Oxford

RICHARD REX, MA, Ph.D., Lecturer in Church History, University of Cambridge

J. S. C. RILEY-SMITH, MA, Ph.D., Dixie Professor of Ecclesiastical History, University of Cambridge

R. H. ROBBINS, MA, D.Phil., Fellow and Tutor in English, Wadham College, Oxford

A. D. S. ROBERTS, MA, M.Litt., Keeper of Oriental Books, Bodleian Library, Oxford

†The Revd B. J. ROBERTS, DD, sometime Professor of Hebrew and Semitics, University College of North Wales, Bangor

†C. H. ROBERTS, CBE, MA, FBA, sometime Fellow of St John's College, Oxford

The Revd J. ROBINSON, M.Th., BD, FKC, Master of the Temple, London, and Canon Emeritus of Canterbury Cathedral

†The Revd C. F. ROGERS, MA, sometime Professor of Pastoral Theology, King's College, London

†D. M. ROGERS, MA, D.Phil., sometime Head of Special Collections, Bodleian Library, Oxford

M. I. ROGERS, London

N. J. ROGERS, MA, M.Litt., Archivist, Sidney Sussex College, Cambridge

Sr. M. JOHN RONAYNE, OP, BA, Monjas Dominicanas, Lisbon

The Revd ANDREW C. ROSS, MA, BD, STM, Ph.D., sometime Principal of New College, Edinburgh; Senior Lecturer in the History of Missions, University of Edinburgh

R. H. ROUSE, MA, Ph.D., Professor of History, University of California, Los Angeles

PHILIP ROUSSEAU, MA, D.Phil., Associate Professor of History, University of Auckland, New Zealand

The Rt. Revd D. G. ROWELL, MA, D.Phil., Bishop Suffragan of Basingstoke and Emeritus Fellow of Keble College, Oxford

The Revd C. C. ROWLAND, MA, Ph.D., Dean Ireland's Professor of Exegesis of Holy Scripture and Fellow of The Queen's College, Oxford

†The Revd E. G. RUPP, DD, FBA, sometime Dixie Professor of Ecclesiastical History, University of Cambridge

The Revd JOY RUSSELL-SMITH, MA, BD, sometime Lecturer in English, Birkbeck College, London

†Sr. FRIDESWIDE SANDEMAN, OSB, BA, Stanbrook Abbey, Worcs

The Very Revd W. ROY SANDERSON, MA, Hon.D.D., sometime Moderator of the General Assembly of the Church of Scotland

The Rt. Revd J. R. SATTERTHWAITE, CMG, BA, sometime Bishop of Gibraltar in Europe

†The Revd H. P. SAUNDERS, MA, BD, sometime Principal of Ely Theological College and Canon of Ely

J. E. SAYERS, MA, Ph.D., Litt.D., Professor of Archive Studies, University College London

The Revd R. J. SCHIEFEN, CSB, MA, STB, M.Ed., Ph.D., Professor in History, University of St Thomas, Houston

The Rt. Revd J. L. SCHUSTER, MA, sometime Bishop of St John's

A. B. SCOTT, D.Phil., Emeritus Professor of Late Latin, Queen's University, Belfast

R. D. SCOTT, MA, Reader in Classics, University of Melbourne

TOM SCOTT, MA, Ph.D., FRSA, Reader in History, University of Liverpool

The Revd M. A. SCREECH, D.Litt., FBA, FRSL, Extraordinary Fellow of Wolfson College and Emeritus Fellow of All Souls College, Oxford; sometime Fielden Professor of French Language and Literature, University College London

†The Revd W. B. SELBIE, DD, sometime Principal of Mansfield College, Oxford

†The Revd E. N. C. Sergeant, MA, sometime Chaplain of Millfield School, Street, Somerset

J. R. Sharp, MA, Worcester College, Oxford

R. Sharpe, MA, Ph.D., FSA, Reader in Diplomatic, University of Oxford

The Very Revd M. W. Sheehan, OFM Cap., MA, D.Phil., sometime Warden, Greyfriars, Oxford

†I. P. Sheldon Williams, D.Litt., sometime Visiting Lecturer, University College, Dublin

†G. T. Shepherd, MA, sometime Professor of Mediaeval English Language and Literature, University of Birmingham

†A. N. Sherwin-White, MA, FBA, sometime Reader in Ancient History and Fellow of St John's College, Oxford

The Revd Aylward Shorter, WF, President of the Missionary Institute, London

J. S. G. Simmons, OBE, MA, Hon.D.Litt., FLA, FSA, Emeritus Fellow of All Souls College, Oxford

†The Very Revd C. A. Simpson, DD, sometime Dean of Christ Church, Oxford

The Revd C. D. Smith, MA, sometime Vicar of St Mary Magdalene, Oxford

Lesley Smith, M.Sc., D.Phil., Senior Research Fellow, Linacre College, Oxford

The Rt. Revd A. Smithson, MA, Bishop Suffragan of Jarrow

R. J. Song, MA, D.Phil., Lecturer in Theology, St John's College, Durham

Sir Richard Southern, MA, Hon.D.Litt., FBA, sometime President of St John's College, Oxford

†The Revd H. F. D. Sparks, DD, FBA, sometime Oriel Professor of the Interpretation of Holy Scripture, University of Oxford

†G. D. Squibb, QC, BCL, MA, sometime Bencher of the Inner Temple

†The Revd Dom Aelred Squire, OSB Cam., B.Litt., sometime of New Camaldoli Hermitage, Big Sur, California

The Revd Dom A. J. Stacpoole, OSB, MC, MA, D.Phil., sometime Senior Tutor, St Benet's Hall, Oxford

Clare E. Stancliffe, MA, D.Phil., Honorary Lecturer in the Department of Theology, University of Durham

The Revd G. C. Stead, Litt.D., FBA, sometime Ely Professor of Divinity, University of Cambridge

Stephen J. Stein, MA, Ph.D., Professor of Religious Studies, Indiana University, Bloomington

†S. M. Stern, MA, D.Phil., sometime Fellow of All Souls College, Oxford

†C. E. Stevens, B.Litt., MA, sometime Fellow of Magdalen College, Oxford

†The Revd Dom Anselm Stoelin, O.Carth., Parkminster

†The Revd D. Stone, DD, sometime Principal of Pusey House and Honorary Canon of Christ Church, Oxford

†The Revd John Sturdy, MA, sometime Dean of Gonville and Caius College, Cambridge

The Revd G. M. Styler, MA, Fellow of Corpus Christi College, Cambridge

The Revd H. J. Sutters, MA, St John's College, Oxford

N. T. J. A. Swarbrick, MA, Assistant Teacher, Grandpont Nursery School, Oxford

†The Very Revd. N. Sykes, MA, D.Litt., Hon.DD, FBA, sometime Dean of Winchester

The Rt. Revd S. W. Sykes, MA, Bishop of Ely

†The Revd H. Edward Symonds, CR, DD, sometime of the Community of the Resurrection, Mirfield

The Revd N. Tanner, SJ, MA, D.Phil., Tutor in Medieval History, Campion Hall, Oxford

Robert Brian Tate, MA, Ph.D., FBA, Emeritus Professor, University of Nottingham

The Revd David W. A. Taylor, BA, BD, Th.M., Hon.DD, sometime General Secretary, Consultation on Church Union

The Revd Colin P. Thompson, MA, D.Phil., Fellow of St Catherine's College, Oxford

David M. Thompson, MA, Ph.D., BD, University Lecturer in Modern Church History and Fellow of Fitzwilliam College, Cambridge

†The Revd G. I. F. Thomson, MA, sometime Chaplain of All Souls College, Oxford

Robert W. Thomson, MA, Ph.D., FBA, Calouste Gulbenkian Professor of Armenian Studies, University of Oxford

†The Revd J. P. Thornton-Duesbery, MA, sometime Master of St Peter's Hall, Oxford

†Jocelyn M. C. Toynbee, MA, D.Phil., FSA, FBA, sometime Laurence Professor of Classical Archaeology, Cambridge

†The Revd G. C. Triffitt, BA, SSJE, sometime Superior General of the Society of St John the Evangelist, Oxford

The Revd A. W. Trotman, Th.B., BD, AKC, minister of Wesleyan Holiness Church, Leytonstone, London

R. W. Truman, MA, D.Phil., Student of Christ Church, Oxford

†C. A. Trypanis, MA, D.Litt., FRSL, sometime Bywater and Sotheby Professor of Byzantine and Modern Greek Language and Literature, University of Oxford, Professor of Classics, Chicago University, and President of the Academy of Athens

The Revd Geraint Tudur, BD, D.Phil., Lecturer in Church History, University of Wales, Bangor

The Very Revd Simon Tugwell, OP, STM, DD, STD, President of the Dominican Historical Institute, Rome, and Consultor to the Congregation for Causes of Saints

†The Revd H. E. W. Turner, DD, sometime Van Mildert Professor of Divinity, University of Durham, and Canon of Durham Cathedral

K. C. Turpin, B.Litt., MA, sometime Provost of Oriel College, Oxford

†W. G. Urry, MA, Ph.D., sometime Reader in Palaeography, University of Oxford

Werner Ustorf, D.Th., Professor of Mission, Selly Oak Colleges, Birmingham, and University of Birmingham

M. G. A. Vale, MA, D.Phil., Fellow of St John's College, Oxford

J. van den Berg, D.Theol., Emeritus Professor of Church History, State University of Leiden

Mark Vessey, MA, D.Phil., Lecturer in English, University of British Columbia

J. A. Vickers, BA, BD, Ph.D., sometime Head of Religious and Social Studies, Bognor Regis College of Education

List of Contributors

†The Revd A. R. VIDLER, DD, sometime Fellow and Dean of King's College, Cambridge

The Revd F. E. VOKES, MA, BD, sometime Professor of Divinity, Trinity College, Dublin

The Revd G. S. WAKEFIELD, MA, M.Litt., DD (Lambeth), sometime Principal of Queen's College, Birmingham

The Rt. Revd P. K. WALKER, MA, sometime Bishop of Ely

†J. M. WALLACE-HADRILL, CBE, MA, D.Litt., FBA, sometime Chichele Professor of Medieval History, University of Oxford

A. F. WALLS, OBE, MA, B.Litt., DD, FSA Scot., Director of the Centre for the Study of Christianity in the Non-Western World and Hon. Professor, University of Edinburgh

J. J. WALTERS, MA, Hertford College, Oxford

P. A. WARD JONES, MA, FRCO, Music Librarian, Bodleian Library, Oxford

BRYAN WARD-PERKINS, MA, D.Phil., Fellow and Tutor in History, Trinity College, Oxford

The Rt. Revd KALLISTOS T. WARE, MA, D.Phil., Bishop of Diokleia, Spalding Lecturer in Eastern Orthodox Studies, and Fellow of Pembroke College, Oxford

†S. WATSON, OBE, MA, D.Mus., sometime Organist of Christ Church, Oxford, and Choragus to the University

D. E. R. WATT, MA, D.Phil., FRSE, Emeritus Professor of Scottish Church History, University of St Andrews

The Revd P. A. WELSBY, MA, Ph.D., sometime Canon Residentiary of Rochester

†The Revd H. K. WHITE, MA, sometime Vicar of St Mary Aldermary, London

The Revd W. A. WHITEHOUSE, B.Litt., MA, Hon.DD, Emeritus Professor of Theology, University of Kent at Canterbury

†The Revd D. E. H. WHITELEY, MA, sometime Fellow and Chaplain of Jesus College, Oxford

†The Revd W. T. WHITLEY, MA, LL D, sometime Principal of Melbourne Baptist College, Victoria, Australia

The Revd R. E. WHYTE, BA, Vicar of St Paul's Church, Rusthall, Tunbridge Wells

The Revd L. R. WICKHAM, MA, Ph.D., Lecturer in the Faculty of Divinity, University of Cambridge

†The Revd B. J. WIGAN, MA, sometime Honorary Canon of Rochester

The Revd M. F. WILES, DD, FBA, Regius Professor Emeritus of Divinity, University of Oxford

M. J. WILKS, MA, Ph.D., Professor Emeritus of Medieval History, Birkbeck College, London

The Revd TREVOR WILLIAMS, MA, Chaplain, Fellow, and Lecturer in Theology, Trinity College, Oxford

†The Revd G. G. WILLIS, DD, sometime Editor of the *Chronicle of the Convocation of Canterbury*

B. R. WILSON, MA, D.Litt., Emeritus Fellow of All Souls College, Oxford

The Revd R. McL. WILSON, DD, FBA, Emeritus Professor of Biblical Criticism, University of St Andrews

†The Ven. C. WITTON-DAVIES, MA, sometime Archdeacon of Oxford

DIANA WOOD, BA, Ph.D., Lecturer in History, University of East Anglia, Norwich

†H. G. WOOD, DD, sometime Professor of Theology, University of Birmingham

The Revd G. W. WOOLFENDEN, Ph.B., STB, M.Phil., Lecturer in Liturgy and Worship, Ripon College Cuddesdon, Oxford

A. D. WRIGHT, MA, D.Phil., Senior Lecturer in Modern History, University of Leeds

J. R. C. WRIGHT, MA, D.Phil., Student of Christ Church, Oxford

†The Very Revd RONALD SELBY WRIGHT, CVO, DD, FRSE, sometime Minister of the Canongate, Edinburgh, and Moderator of the General Assembly of the Church of Scotland

The Revd P. H. WYLD, MC, MA, sometime General Editor, USPG, London

The Revd E. J. YARNOLD, SJ, DD, University Research Lecturer, Campion Hall, Oxford

The Revd Dom RICHARD YEO, OSB, MA, JCD, Downside Abbey, Bath

RONALD JOHN ZAWILLA, MSL, Ph.D., Director, Gallery Genesis, Chicago

C. J. ZEALLEY, MA, Wolfson College, Oxford

GROVER A. ZINN, BA, BD, Ph.D., Danforth Professor of Religion, Oberlin College, Oberlin, Ohio

ABBREVIATIONS

Abbreviations

[The editions mentioned are those cited in the *Dictionary*]

AAS	**Acta Apostolicae Sedis* (Rome, 1909 ff.).
AASS	*Acta Sanctorum (Antwerp, 1643–1770; Brussels, 1780–86, 1845–83, and 1894 ff.; Tongerloo, 1794; and Paris, 1875–87).
Abh. (Bayr.)	*Abhandlungen der philosophisch-philologischen (und historischen) Classe der (königlich) bayerischen Akademie der Wissenschaften* (Munich, 1835 ff.).
Abh. (Berl.)	*Abhandlungen der (königlichen) preussischen [from 1947 deutschen] Akademie der Wissenschaften* (Berlin, 1815–1907; philosoph.-hist. Kl., ibid., 1908–49).
Abh. (Gött.)	*Abhandlungen der (königlichen) Gesellschaft (Academie) der Wissenschaften zu Göttingen.* Philolog.-hist. Kl., NF (Berlin, 1897–1939).
Abh. (Gött.), Dritte Folge	*Abhandlungen der Gesellschaft (Akademie) der Wissenschaften zu Göttingen.* Philolog.-hist. Kl., Dritte Folge (Berlin, 1932–9; Göttingen, 1937 ff.).
Abh. (Heid.)	*Abhandlungen der Heidelberger Akademie der Wissenschaften.* Philosoph.-hist. Kl. (Heidelberg, 1913 ff.).
Abh. (Sächs.)	*Abhandlungen der philologisch-historischen Classe der (königlich) sächsischen Gesellschaft (Akademie) der Wissenschaften* (Leipzig, 1850–1943; Berlin, 1950 ff.).
ACO	*Acta Conciliorum Oecumenicorum* [Series I], ed. E. *Schwartz and J. Straub (Strasbourg, 1914; Berlin, 1922–84); Series II, ed. sub auspiciis Academiae Scientiarum Bavaricae (Berlin, 1984 ff.).
ACW	Ancient Christian Writers, ed. J. Quasten and others (Westminster, Md., and London, 1946–67; Westminster, Md., 1970 ff.).
AFH	*Archivum Franciscanum Historicum* (Quaracchi, 1908 ff.).
AHDLMA	*Archives d'histoire doctrinale et littéraire du moyen âge* (Paris, 1926 ff.).
AHMA	Analecta Hymnica Medii Aevi, ed. G. M. Dreves, SJ, and C. Blume, SJ (55 vols., Leipzig, 1886–1922); Register, ed. M. Lütolf (3 vols., Bern and Munich, 1978).
Altaner and Stuiber (1966)	B. *Altaner, *Patrologie: Leben, Schriften und Lehre der Kirchenväter* (6th edn. revised by A. Stuiber, 1966).
Altaner and Stuiber (1978)	B. *Altaner, *Patrologie: Leben, Schriften und Lehre der Kirchenväter* (8th edn. revised by A. Stuiber, 1978).
AM	**Hymns Ancient and Modern* (London, Standard Edition, 1916).
Anal. Boll.	*Analecta Bollandiana* (Paris and Brussels, 1882 ff.).
ANCL	Ante-Nicene Christian Library (25 vols., Edinburgh, 1864–97).
ASS	*Acta Sanctae Sedis* (41 vols., Rome, 1865–1908).
Bardenhewer, 1	O. *Bardenhewer, *Geschichte der altkirchlichen Literatur*, 1 (2nd edn., 1913).
Bardenhewer, 2	O. *Bardenhewer, *Geschichte der altkirchlichen Literatur*, 2 (2nd edn., 1914).
Bardenhewer, 3	O. *Bardenhewer, *Geschichte der altkirchlichen Literatur*, 3 (1912).
Bardenhewer, 4	O. *Bardenhewer, *Geschichte der altkirchlichen Literatur*, 4 (1924).
Bardenhewer, 5	O. *Bardenhewer, *Geschichte der altkirchlichen Literatur*, 5 (1932).
Beck	H.-G. Beck, *Kirche und theologische Literatur im byzantinischen Reich* (Byzantinisches Handbuch, 2.2; Munich, 1959).
Ber. (Sächs.)	*Berichte (from 1962 Sitzungsberichte) über die Verhandlungen der (königlich) sächsischen Gesellschaft (Akademie) der Wissenschaften zu Leipzig.* Philologisch-historische Classe (Leipzig, 1849–1947; Berlin, 1950 ff.).
Bettenson	H. Bettenson (ed.), *Documents of the Christian Church* (World's Classics, London, 1943). [Also pub., with different pagination, in Galaxy Edition, New York, 1947.]
Bettenson (2nd edn., 1963)	H. Bettenson (ed.), *Documents of the Christian Church* (2nd edn., 1963).

BGPM	Beiträge zur Geschichte der Philosophie des Mittelalters. Texte und Untersuchungen, begründet von C. Baeumker (Münster i.W., 1891 ff.; from 1930 *Beiträge zur Geschichte der Philosophie und Theologie des Mittelalters*; NF, 1970 ff.; Supplementbände, 1913 ff.).
BHG (3rd edn., 1957)	*Bibliotheca Hagiographica Graeca*, 3rd edn. by F. Halkin, SJ (3 vols., Brussels, 1957).
BHL	*Bibliotheca Hagiographica Latina Antiquae et Mediae Aetatis*, ediderunt Socii Bollandiani (Subsidia Hagiographica, 6; 2 vols., Brussels, 1898–1901; Novum Supplementum, ed. H. Fros, ibid. 70; 1986).
BHO	*Bibliotheca Hagiographica Orientalis*, ediderunt Socii Bollandiani (Subsidia Hagiographica, 10; Brussels, 1910).
Black's N.T. Comm.	Black's New Testament Commentaries, ed. H. Chadwick (London, 1957 ff.).
Braun, *AG*	J. Braun, SJ, *Das christliche Altargerät* (1932).
Braun, *CA*	J. Braun, SJ, *Der christliche Altar* (2 vols., 1924).
Braun, *LG*	J. Braun, SJ, *Die liturgische Gewandung im Occident und Orient nach Ursprung und Entwicklung, Verwendung und Symbolik* (1907).
Braun, *LP*	J. Braun, SJ, *Die liturgischen Paramente in Gegenwart und Vergangenheit* (2nd edn., 1924).
Bremond	H. *Bremond, *Histoire littéraire du sentiment religieux en France depuis la fin des guerres de religion jusqu'à nos jours* (11 vols., 1916–33, + index, 1936).
Brightman, *LEW*	F. E. *Brightman, *Liturgies Eastern and Western*, vol. 1: Eastern (1896; all pub.).
BRUC	A. B. Emden, *A Biographical Register of the University of Cambridge to 1500* (Cambridge, 1963).
BRUO	A. B. Emden, *A Biographical Register of the University of Oxford to A.D. 1500* (3 vols., Oxford, 1957–9).
BRUO, 1501–1540	A. B. Emden, *A Biographical Register of the University of Oxford A.D. 1501 to 1540* (Oxford, 1974).
BZ	*Byzantinische Zeitschrift* (Leipzig, 1892–1943; Munich, 1943–89; Stuttgart, 1990 ff.).
Camb. Bib.	The Cambridge Bible for Schools (1878–1936; RV, 1903–30).
C. Anc. H.	*The Cambridge Ancient History*, ed. J. B. Bury and others (12 vols., 1923–39).
C. Anc. H. (rev. edn.)	*The Cambridge Ancient History* (revised edition of vols. 1–2; originally issued in fascicles, 1961–71).
C. Anc. H. (2nd edn.)	*The Cambridge Ancient History*, 2nd edn. by J. Boardman and others (1982 ff.).
C. Anc. H. (3rd edn.)	*The Cambridge Ancient History*, 3rd edn. by I. E. S. Edwards and others (1970 ff.).
CBEL	*The Cambridge Bibliography of English Literature*, ed. F. W. Bateson (4 vols., Cambridge, 1940, + supplement, 1957).
CC	Corpus Christianorum (Turnhout, 1954 ff.).
CCCM	Corpus Christianorum, Continuatio Mediaevalis (Turnhout, 1967 ff.).
CCSA	Corpus Christianorum, Series Apocrypha (Turnhout, 1983 ff.).
CCSG	Corpus Christianorum, Series Graeca (Turnhout, 1977 ff.).
CCSL	Corpus Christianorum, Series Latina (Turnhout, 1954 ff.).
CE	*Catholic Encyclopedia* (15 vols. + index, New York, 1907–14).
Cent. Bib.	The Century Bible, ed. W. F. Adeney (34 vols., Edinburgh, 1901–22).
CGT	The Cambridge Greek Testament for Schools (and Colleges) [ed. J. J. S. Perowne and others] (20 vols., Cambridge, 1881–1933).
CHS	*Church Historical Society.
Clar. Bib.	The Clarendon Bible (Oxford, 1922 ff.).

Abbreviations

C. Med. H.	*Cambridge Medieval History*, planned by J. B. Bury, ed. H. M. Gwatkin, J. P. Whitney and others (8 vols., 1911–36, and vol. of maps, 1936; vol. 4 revised under the editorship of J. M. Hussey, 2 parts, 1966–7).
CMH	*Cambridge Modern History*, planned by Lord *Acton, ed. A. W. Ward, G. W. Prothero, and S. Leathes (12 vols., 1902–10, + index, 1911, and atlas, 1912).
CPG	*Clavis Patrum Graecorum*, ed. M. Geerard and F. Glorie (5 vols., Turnhout, 1974–87).
CPL (3rd edn., 1995)	*Clavis Patrum Latinorum*, ed. E. Dekkers [OSB] and A. Gaar (3rd edn., CCSL; Turnhout and Steenbrugge, 1995).
CQR	*Church Quarterly Review* (169 vols., London, 1875–1968).
CRS	*Catholic Record Society (London, 1905 ff.).
CSCO	Corpus Scriptorum Christianorum Orientalium:
	Scriptores Aethiopici (Paris etc., 1903–12; Louvain, 1953 ff.).
	Scriptores Arabici (Paris etc., 1903–12; Rome, 1922; Louvain, 1926 ff.).
	Scriptores Armeniaci (Louvain, 1953 ff.).
	Scriptores Coptici (Paris etc., 1906–49; Louvain, 1949 ff.).
	Scriptores Iberici (Louvain, 1950 ff.).
	Scriptores Syri (Paris etc., 1907–19; Louvain, 1919 ff.).
	Subsidia (Louvain, 1950 ff.).
CSEL	Corpus Scriptorum Ecclesiasticorum Latinorum (Vienna, 1866 ff.).
CSH Byz.	Corpus Scriptorum Historiae Byzantinae (49 vols., Bonn, 1828–78).
DAC	*Dictionary of the Apostolic Church*, ed. J. *Hastings (2 vols., 1915–18).
DACL	*Dictionnaire d'Archéologie Chrétienne et de Liturgie*, ed. F. *Cabrol, OSB, and H. *Leclercq, OSB (15 vols., 1907–53).
Darlow and Moule	T. H. Darlow and H. F. Moule, *Historical Catalogue of the Printed Editions of Holy Scripture in the Library of the British and Foreign Bible Society* (2 vols. bound in 4, 1903–11).
Darlow and Moule, ed. A. S. Herbert, 1 (1968)	A. S. Herbert, *Historical Catalogue of Printed Editions of the English Bible 1525–1961. Revised and Expanded from the Edition of T. H. Darlow and H. F. Moule*, 1903 (1968).
DCA	*Dictionary of Christian Antiquities*, ed. W. Smith and S. Cheetham (2 vols., 1875–80).
DCB	*Dictionary of Christian Biography*, ed. W. Smith and H. Wace (4 vols., 1877–87).
DCG	*Dictionary of Christ and the Gospels*, ed. J. *Hastings (2 vols., 1906–8).
DDC	*Dictionnaire de Droit Canonique*, ed. R. Naz (7 vols., 1935–65).
DECH	*Dictionary of English Church History*, ed. S. L. Ollard and G. Crosse (1912).
DECH (3rd edn., 1948)	*Dictionary of English Church History*, 3rd edn. by S. L. Ollard, G. Crosse, and M. F. Bond (1948).
Denz. and Bann.	H. Denzinger, *Enchiridion Symbolorum Definitionum et Declarationum de Rebus Fidei et Morum*, 28th edn. after that of C. Bannwart, SJ, and I. B. Umberg, SJ, by C. *Rahner, SJ (Freiburg i.B., 1952).
Denz. and Schön. (36th edn., 1976)	H. Denzinger, *Enchiridion Symbolorum Definitionum et Declarationum de Rebus Fidei et Morum*, 36th edn. by A. Schönmetzer, SJ (Freiburg i.B., 1976).
Denzinger and Hünermann (37th edn., 1991)	H. Denzinger, *Enchiridion Symbolorum Definitionum et Declarationum de Rebus Fidei et Morum*, 37th edn., with Ger. tr., by P. Hünermann (Freiburg i.B., 1991).
DHGE	*Dictionnaire d'Histoire et de Géographie Ecclésiastiques*, ed. A. Baudrillart and others (1912 ff.).

Dict. Amer. Biog.	*Dictionary of American Biography*, published under the Auspices of the American Council of Learned Societies, ed. A. Johnson and others (20 vols., 1928–36, + index, 1937, and 7 Supplements, 1944–81).
Dict. Bibl.	*Dictionnaire de la Bible*, ed. F. Vigouroux, PSS (5 vols., 1895–1912).
Dict. Bibl., Suppl.	*Dictionnaire de la Bible*, Supplément, ed. L. Pirot (1928 ff.).
Dict. Sp.	*Dictionnaire de Spiritualité*, ed. M. Viller, SJ, and others (16 vols. + index, 1937–95).
DIP	*Dizionario Italiano di Perfezione*, ed. G. Pelliccia and G. Rocca (1974 ff.).
DNB	*Dictionary of National Biography*, founded by G. Smith, ed. L. Stephen and S. Lee (63 vols., 1885–1900). [Also repr., with some corrections, in 21 vols., 1908–9.]
DNB, Suppl.	*Dictionary of National Biography*, Supplement, ed. S. Lee (3 vols., 1901). [Also repr. in 1 vol., 1909.]
DNB, 1901–1911	*Dictionary of National Biography, Supplement January 1901–December 1911*, ed. S. Lee (3 vols., 1912).
DNB, 1912–1921	*Dictionary of National Biography, 1912–1921*, ed. H. W. C. Davis and J. R. H. Weaver (1927).
DNB, 1922–1930	*Dictionary of National Biography, 1922–1930*, ed. J. R. H. Weaver (1937).
DNB, 1931–1940	*Dictionary of National Biography, 1931–1940*, ed. L. G. Wickham Legg (1949).
DNB, 1941–1950	*Dictionary of National Biography, 1941–1950*, ed. L. G. Wickham Legg and E. T. Williams (1959).
DNB, 1951–1960	*Dictionary of National Biography, 1951–1960*, ed. E. T. Williams and H. M. Palmer (1971).
DNB, 1961–1970	*Dictionary of National Biography, 1961–1970*, ed. E. T. Williams and C. S. Nicholls (1981).
DNB, 1971–1980	*Dictionary of National Biography, 1971–1980*, ed. R. Blake and C. S. Nicholls (1986).
DNB, 1981–1985	*Dictionary of National Biography, 1981–1985*, ed. R. Blake and C. S. Nicholls (1990).
DNB, 1986–1990	*Dictionary of National Biography, 1986–1990*, ed. C. S. Nicholls (1996).
DPAC	*Dizionario Patristico e di Antichità Cristiane*, ed. A. Di Berardino (3 vols., Casale Monferrato, 1983–88).
DTC	*Dictionnaire de Théologie Catholique*, ed. A. Vacant, E. Mangenot, and É. Amann (15 vols., 1903–50); Tables Générales by B. Loth and A. Michel (3 vols., 1951–72).
Duchesne	[see *LP*].
EB (11th edn.)	*Encyclopaedia Britannica*, 11th edn. (28 vols. and index, 1910–11).
EB (14th edn.)	*Encyclopaedia Britannica*, 14th edn. (23 vols. and index, 1929).
EB (1968 edn.)	*Encyclopaedia Britannica* (23 vols. and index; Chicago, 1968).
EB (1974 edn.)	*The New Encyclopaedia Britannica* (30 vols., Chicago, 1974).
EB (1977 edn.)	*The New Encyclopaedia Britannica* (30 vols., Chicago, 1977).
EB (1985 edn.)	*The New Encyclopaedia Britannica* (30 vols. + index in 2 vols., Chicago, 1985).
E.Bi.	*Encyclopaedia Biblica*, ed. T. K. *Cheyne and J. S. Black (4 vols., 1899–1903).
EC	*Enciclopedia Cattolica*, ed. P. Paschini and others (12 vols., 1949–54).
EETS	Early English Text Society (London, 1864–1980; Oxford, 1976 ff.).
EH	Exegetisches Handbuch zum Alten Testament, ed. J. Nickel and others (Münster i.W., 1911 ff.).
EH	**English Hymnal* (London, 1906).
EHR	*English Historical Review* (London, 1886 ff.).
Eissfeldt	O. Eissfeldt, *The Old Testament* (Eng. tr. by P. R. Ackroyd, Oxford, 1966).
EJ	*Encyclopaedia Judaica*, ed. J. Klatzkin and others (10 vols., Berlin, 1928–1934).

Abbreviations

EKL	*Evangelisches Kirchenlexikon*, ed. H. Brunotte and O. Weber (4 vols., incl. Registerband, 1956–62).
EKL (3rd edn.)	*Evangelisches Kirchenlexikon*, 3rd edn. by E. Falbusch and others (4 vols, 1986–96).
EL	*Ephemerides Liturgicae* (Rome, 1887 ff.).
Enc. *Jud.*	*Encyclopaedia Judaica*, ed. C. Roth and others (16 vols., Jerusalem, 1971–2, + Yearbooks).
ÉO	*Échos d'Orient* (39 vols., Paris, 1897–1942).
EOMIA	*Ecclesiae Occidentalis Monumenta Iuris Antiquissima*, ed. C. H. *Turner (Oxford, 1899 ff.).
Fliche and Martin	A. Fliche and V. Martin (eds.), *Histoire de l'Église depuis les origines jusqu'à nos jours* (Paris, 1935 ff.).
GCS	Die griechischen christlichen Schriftsteller der ersten drei Jahrhunderte (Leipzig, 1897–1941; Berlin and Leipzig, 1953; Berlin, 1954 ff.).
Gee and Hardy	H. Gee and W. J. Hardy (eds.), *Documents Illustrative of English Church History* (1896).
Gel. Anz. (Gött.)	*Göttingische gelehrte Anzeigen unter der Aufsicht der (königl.) Gesellschaft (Academie) der Wissenschaften* (Göttingen, 1884 ff.).
Hardouin	J. *Hardouin [Harduinus], *Acta Conciliorum et Epistolae Decretales, ac Constitutiones Summorum Pontificum* (12 vols., Paris, '1714–15').
Hardy	T. D. Hardy, *Descriptive Catalogue of Materials Relating to the History of Great Britain and Ireland to the End of the Reign of Henry VII* (3 vols. bound in 4, Rolls Series, 1862–71).
HAT	Handbuch zum Alten Testament, ed. O. Eissfeldt and others (Tübingen, 1934 ff.).
Hb. NT	Handbuch zum Neuen Testament, begründet von H. *Lietzmann (1906 ff.).
HBS	*Henry Bradshaw Society (1891 ff.).
HDB	J. *Hastings (ed.), *Dictionary of the Bible* (4 vols., 1898–1902, with extra vol., 1904).
HE	*Historia Ecclesiastica.*
Hefele and Leclercq	C. J. *Hefele (tr. into Fr. by H. *Leclercq, OSB), *Histoire des conciles d'après les documents originaux* (11 vols., 1907–52).
Heimbucher	M. Heimbucher, *Die Orden und Kongregationen der katholischen Kirche*, 1 (3rd edn., 1933), 2 (1934).
HERE	J. *Hastings (ed.), *Encyclopaedia of Religion and Ethics* (12 vols. + index, 1908–26).
Hist. Eccl.	*Historia Ecclesiastica.*
Hist. *J.*	*Historisches Jahrbuch* (Münster i.W., 1880–82; Munich, 1883–1930; Cologne, 1931–50; Munich and Freiburg i.B., 1950 ff.).
HKAT	Handkommentar zum Alten Testament, ed. W. Nowack (18 vols., Göttingen, 1892–1933).
HTR	*Harvard Theological Review* (New York, 1908 f.; Cambridge, Mass., 1910 ff.).
HTS	Harvard Theological Studies (Cambridge, Mass., 1916 ff.).
HUL	Home University Library (London, 1911 ff.).
HZ	*Historische Zeitschrift* (Munich etc., 1859 ff.).
ICC	International Critical Commentary (Edinburgh, 1895 ff.).
ILS	*Inscriptiones Latinae Selectae*, ed. H. Dessau (3 vols. in 5, Berlin, 1892–1916).

Jaffé	P. Jaffé, *Regesta Pontificum Romanorum ab Condita Ecclesia ad Annum post Christum Natum MCXCVIII*, 2nd edn. by G. Wattenbach (2 vols., Leipzig, 1885–8).
JE	*Jewish Encyclopedia*, ed. I. Singer and others (12 vols., New York and London, 1901–6).
JEH	*Journal of Ecclesiastical History* (London, 1950 ff.).
JLW	*Jahrbuch für Liturgiewissenschaft* (Münster i.W., 1921–41).
Joannou	P.-P. Joannou, *Discipline Générale Antique* (Pontificia Commissione per la Redazione del Codice di Diritto Canonico Orientale, Fonti, 9; 2 vols. in 3 parts, Rome, 1962–3).
JQR	*Jewish Quarterly Review* (London, 1888–1908; Philadelphia, 1910 ff.).
JTS	*Journal of Theological Studies* (London, 1900–5; Oxford, 1906–49; NS, ibid., 1950 ff.).
Jungmann (1952)	J. A. Jungmann, SJ, *Missarum Sollemnia: Eine genetische Erklärung der römischen Messe* (3rd edn., 2 vols., 1952).
Jungmann (1958 edn.)	J. A. Jungmann, SJ, *Missarum Sollemnia: Eine genetische Erklärung der römischen Messe* (4th edn., 2 vols., 1958).
Jungmann (Eng. tr.)	J. A. Jungmann, SJ, *The Mass of the Roman Rite* (Eng. tr. of 1948 edn. of *Missarum Sollemnia*; 2 vols., New York, 1951–5).
Kaeppeli	T. Kaeppeli, OP, and E. Panella, OP, *Scriptores Ordinis Praedicatorum Medii Aevi* (4 vols., Rome, 1970–93).
KAT	Kommentar zum Alten Testament, ed. E. Sellin and others (Leipzig, 1913–39; Gütersloh, 1962 ff.).
KEH	Kurzgefasstes exegetisches Handbuch zum Alten Testament (Leipzig, 1838 ff.).
KEK	Kritisch-exegetischer Kommentar über das Neue Testament, ed. H. A. W. *Meyer (16 vols., Göttingen, 1832–52; Eng. tr., 20 vols., 1873–95; also subsequent edns.).
KHAT	Kurzer Hand-Commentar zum Alten Testament, ed. K. Marti (21 vols., Freiburg i.B., 1897–1906).
Kidd	B. J. Kidd (ed.), *Documents Illustrative of the Continental Reformation* (1911).
Krumbacher	K. Krumbacher, *Geschichte der byzantinischen Literatur von Justinian bis zum Ende des oströmischen Reiches, 527–1453* (2nd edn., 1897).
Kümmel	W. G. Kümmel, *Introduction to the New Testament* (Eng. tr. by H. C. Kee, 1975).
LACT	Library of *Anglo-Catholic Theology (97 vols., Oxford, 1841–63).
Latourette	K. S. Latourette, *History of the Expansion of Christianity* (7 vols., New York and London, 1938–45).
Lauchert	F. Lauchert, *Die Kanones der wichtigsten altkirchlichen Concilien* (1896).
LF	*Library of the Fathers (43 vols., Oxford, 1838–74).
LLE	Library of Liturgiology and Ecclesiology for English Readers, ed. V. Staley (9 vols., 1902–11).
Loeb	Loeb Classical Library (London and Cambridge, Mass., 1912 ff.).
LP (Duchesne)	Le *Liber Pontificalis*, ed. L. *Duchesne (Bibliothèque des Écoles Françaises d'Athènes et de Rome, 2 vols., 1886–92).
L.Th.K.	*Lexikon für Theologie und Kirche*, ed. M. Buchberger (10 vols., 1930–8).
L.Th.K. (2nd edn.)	*Lexikon für Theologie und Kirche*, 2nd edn. by J. Höfer and K. *Rahner (10 vols. and index, 1957–67, + 3 supplementary vols., *Das zweite vatikanische Konzil*, 1967–8).
L.Th.K. (3rd edn.)	*Lexikon für Theologie und Kirche*, 3rd edn. by W. Kasper and others (1993 ff.).

Abbreviations

LW	L. Brinkhoff, OFM, and others (eds.), *Liturgisch Woordenboek* (2 vols., 1958–68).
McNeile	A. H. McNeile, *An Introduction to the Study of the New Testament* (2nd edn. by C. S. C. Williams, 1953).
Mai, *NPB*	A. *Mai (ed.), *Nova Patrum Bibliotheca* (8 vols., Rome, 1844–71).
Mai, *SR*	A. *Mai (ed.), *Spicilegium Romanum* (10 vols., Rome, 1839–44).
Mai, *SVNC*	A. *Mai (ed.), *Scriptorum Veterum Nova Collectio e Vaticanis Codicibus edita* (10 vols., Rome, 1825–38).
Manitius	M. Manitius, *Geschichte der lateinischen Literatur des Mittelalters* (Handbuch der klassischen Altertumswissenschaft, ed. I. von Müller, 9, Abt. 2; 3 vols., 1911–31).
Mann	H. K. Mann, *The Lives of the Popes in the (Early) Middle Ages* (18 vols., bound in 19, 1902–32).
Mansi	J. D. *Mansi, *Sacrorum Conciliorum Nova et Amplissima Collectio* (31 vols., Florence, 1759–98).
MGH	*Monumenta Germaniae Historica.*
Mirbt	C. Mirbt, *Quellen zur Geschichte des Papsttums und des römischen Katholizismus* (4th edn., 1924).
Mirbt and Aland (1967)	C. Mirbt, *Quellen zur Geschichte des Papsttums und des römischen Katholizismus*, 6th edn., ed. K. Aland, Band 1: *Von den Anfängen bis zum Tridentium* (1967).
Moff. Comm.	The *Moffatt Commentaries.
Mordek	H. Mordek, *Kirchenrecht und Reform im Frankenreich* (Beiträge zur Geschichte und Quellenkunde des Mittelalters, 1; 1975).
NA	*Neues Archiv der Gesellschaft für ältere deutsche Geschichtskunde zur Beförderung einer Gesammtausgabe der Quellenschriften deutscher Geschichte des Mittelalters* (Hanover, 1876–1922; Berlin, 1922–35).
Nachr. (Gött.)	*Nachrichten von der (königlichen) Gesellschaft (Academie) der Wissenschaften zu Göttingen.* Philolog.-hist. Kl. (Göttingen, 1894 ff.).
Nachr. (Gött. Gesch. Mitt.)	*Nachrichten von der (königlichen) Gesellschaft (Academie) der Wissenschaften zu Göttingen.* Geschaftliche Mitteilungen (Göttingen, 1894–1939; *Jahrbuch der Akademie der Wissenschaften zu Göttingen,* 1940 ff.).
NCBEL	*The New Cambridge Bibliography of English Literature*, ed. G. Watson and others (5 vols., Cambridge, 1969–77).
NCE	*New Catholic Encyclopedia* (14 vols. + index, New York, etc., 1967, + 3 supplementary vols., 16–18; 1974–89).
New Cent. Bib.	The Century Bible, New Edition (1966 ff.; entitled The New Century Bible, 1967 ff.).
New Clar. Bib.	New Clarendon Bible (Oxford, 1963 ff.).
NF	Neue Folge.
Novum Auctarium	*Novum Auctarium Bibliothecae Hagiographicae Graecae*, by F. Halkin, SJ (Subsidia Hagiographica, 65; Brussels, 1984).
NPB	[see Mai].
NPNCF	Nicene and Post-Nicene Christian Fathers (New York, 1887–92; Oxford, 1890–1900).
NS	New Series.
OC	*Oriens Christianus* (Leipzig, 1901 ff. For details see s.v.).
OCD (2nd edn.)	*The Oxford Classical Dictionary*, 2nd edn., ed. N. G. L. Hammond and H. H. Scullard (1970).

OCD (3rd edn.)	*The Oxford Classical Dictionary*, 3rd edn., ed. S. Hornblower and A. Spawforth (1996).
OCP	*Orientalia Christiana Periodica* (Rome, 1935 ff.).
OCT	Oxford Classical Texts (1894 ff.).
OED	*A New [Oxford] English Dictionary on Historical Principles* founded mainly on the Materials collected by the Philological Society, ed. J. A. H. Murray, H. Bradley, W. A. Craigie, and C. T. Onions (10 vols. + supplement, 1884–1933).
OED (2nd edn.)	*The Oxford English Dictionary*, 2nd edn., ed. J. A. Simpson and E. S. C. Weiner (20 vols., 1989).
OHS	Oxford Historical Society (Oxford, 1885 ff.).
Pastor	L. *Pastor, *The History of the Popes from the Close of the Middle Ages*, Eng. tr. (40 vols., 1891–1954).
PBD (1912)	*Prayer Book Dictionary*, ed. G. Harford, M. Stevenson, and J. W. Tyrer (1912).
PBD (1925)	*Prayer Book Dictionary*, ed. G. Harford, M. Stevenson, and J. W. Tyrer (1925 edn.).
PG	*Patrologia Graeca*, ed. J. P. *Migne (162 vols., Paris, 1857–66).
PL	*Patrologia Latina*, ed. J. P. *Migne (221 vols., Paris, 1844–64).
PO	*Patrologia Orientalis*, ed. R. Graffin and F. Nau (Paris, 1907 ff.).
Polgár	L. Polgár, SJ, *Bibliographie sur l'Histoire de la Compagnie de Jésus 1901–1980*, 3: *Les Personnes* (3 vols., Rome, 1990).
Pourrat	P. Pourrat, PSS, *La Spiritualité chrétienne* (4 vols., 1918–28).
PRE (3rd edn.)	*Realencyklopädie für protestantische Theologie und Kirche*, begründet von J. J. *Herzog, 3rd edn. by A. *Hauck (21 vols., 1898–1908, + Register, 1909, and Ergänzungen und Nachträge, 2 vols., 1913).
PW	A. Pauly, *Real-Encyclopädie der classischen Altertumswissenschaft*, ed. G. Wissowa and others (1893 ff.).
Quasten (cont.), *Patrology*, 4 (1986)	A. Di Berardino (ed.), *Patrology*, 4 (Eng. tr. of *Patrologia*, 3; Turin, 1978) (Westminster, Md., 1986), designed as a continuation of J. Quasten, *Patrology* 1–3 (1950–60).
Quétif and Échard	J. Quétif, OP, and J. Échard, OP, *Scriptores Ordinis Praedicatorum Recensiti* (2 vols., Paris, 1719–21).
Raby	F. J. E. Raby, *A History of Christian Latin Poetry from the Beginnings to the Close of the Middle Ages* (1927).
Raby (1953)	F. J. E. Raby, *A History of Christian Latin Poetry from the Beginnings to the Close of the Middle Ages* (2nd edn., 1953).
RAC	*Reallexikon für Antike und Christentum*, ed. T. Klauser, E. Dassmann, and others (Stuttgart, 1950 ff.).
R. Bén.	*Revue Bénédictine* (vols. 1–5 pub. under the title *Le Messager des Fidèles*; Lille and Bruges, 1884; Maredsous, 1885 ff.).
R. Bibl.	*Revue Biblique* (Paris, 1892 ff.).
Rech. S.R.	*Recherches de Science Religieuse* (Paris, 1910 ff.).
Rev. S.R.	*Revue des Sciences Religieuses* (Paris, 1921 f.; Strasbourg and Paris, 1923 f.; Strasbourg, 1925 ff.).
RGG (2nd edn.)	*Die Religion in Geschichte und Gegenwart*, 2nd edn. by H. *Gunkel and L. Zscharnack (5 vols., 1927–31).
RGG (3rd edn.)	*Die Religion in Geschichte und Gegenwart*, 3rd edn. by K. Galling (6 vols. + Register, 1957–65).
RH	*Revue Historique* (Paris, 1876 ff.).

RHE	*Revue d'Histoire Ecclésiastique* (Louvain, 1900 ff.).
RHPR	*Revue d'Histoire et de Philosophie religieuses* (Strasbourg, 1921–4; Strasbourg and Paris, 1925–49; Paris, 1950 ff.).
Riv. A.C.	*Rivista di Archeologia Cristiana* (Rome, 1924 ff.).
Rohault	C. Rohault de Fleury, *La Messe: Études archéologiques sur ses monuments* (8 vols., 1883–9).
RQ	*Römische Quartalschrift für die christliche Alterthumskunde und für Kirchengeschichte* (Rome, 1887 ff., + 28 Supplementhefte, 1893–1931).
RQH	*Revue des Questions Historiques* (Paris, 1866–1933; Blois, 1933; Paris, 1934; Blois, 1935 f.; Bourges, 1937–9).
RS	Rolls Series (1858 ff.).
RSPT	*Revue des Sciences Philosophiques et Théologiques* (Kain and Paris, 1907–12; Paris, 1913 ff.).
RTAM	*Recherches de Théologie Ancienne et Médiévale* (Louvain, 1929 ff.).
Sb. (Bayr.)	*Sitzungsberichte der (königlich) bayerischen Akademie der Wissenschaften (zu München)* (Munich, 1860–71; philosoph.-philolog. und hist. Cl., 1871–1930; philosoph.-hist. Abt., 1930 ff.).
Sb. (Berl.)	*Sitzungsberichte der (königlichen) preussischen [from 1948 deutschen] Akademie der Wissenschaften zu Berlin* (Berlin, 1882–1921; philosoph.-hist. Kl., 1922–49).
Sb. (Heid.)	*Sitzungsberichte der Heidelberger Akademie der Wissenschaften. Philosoph.-hist. Kl.* (Heidelberg, 1910 ff.).
Sb. (Wien)	*Sitzungsberichte der (kaiserlichen) [from 1947 Österreichischen] Akademie der Wissenschaften (in Wien). Hist.-philolog. or Philolog.-hist. Kl.* (Vienna, 1848 ff.).
SC	Sources Chrétiennes (Paris, 1942 ff.).
Schneemelcher	E. Hennecke, *Neutestamentliche Apokryphen in deutscher Übersetzung*, 3rd edn. by W. Schneemelcher (2 vols., 1959–64; Eng. tr., 1963–5).
Schneemelcher (5th edn.)	E. Hennecke, *Neutestamentliche Apokryphen in deutscher Übersetzung*, 5th edn. by W. Schneemelcher (2 vols., 1987–9; Eng. tr., 1991–2).
Schottenloher	K. Schottenloher, *Bibliographie zur deutschen Geschichte im Zeitalter der Glaubensspaltung, 1517–1585* (7 vols., 1933–66).
Soggin	J. A. Soggin, *Introduction to the Old Testament* (3rd edn., 1989; Eng. tr. of *Introduzione all'Antico Testamento*, 4th edn., Brescia, 1987).
Sommervogel	Augustin de Backer, SJ, Aloys de Backer, SJ, and A. Carayon, SJ, *Bibliothèque de la Compagnie de Jésus*, ed. C. Sommervogel, SJ (12 vols., 1890–1932; repr., Louvain, 1960).
SPCK	*Society for Promoting Christian Knowledge. (See p. 1527 f.)
SPG	*Society for the Propagation of the Gospel. (See p. 1529.)
SR	[see Mai].
SSL	Spicilegium Sacrum Lovaniense (Louvain, 1922 ff.).
ST	Studi e Testi (Rome, 1900 ff.).
ST	*Summa Theologica or Summa Theologiae.
Stammler	W. Stammler and others (eds.), *Die Deutsche Literatur des Mittelalters: Verfasserlexikon* (5 vols., 1933–55).
Summa Theol.	*Summa Theologica or Summa Theologiae.*
SVNC	[see Mai].
Tanner, *Decrees*	N. P. Tanner, SJ (ed.), *Decrees of the Ecumenical Councils* (2 vols., 1990).
Teub.	*Bibliotheca Scriptorum Graecorum et Romanorum Teubneriana* (Leipzig, 1849 ff.).
Th.Q.	*Theologische Quartalschrift* (Tübingen, 1831–1928; various places, 1929 ff.).
TLS	*The Times Literary Supplement* (London, 1902 ff.).
TLZ	*Theologische Literaturzeitung* (Leipzig, 1876 ff., + Bibliographisches Beiblatt, ibid., 1922 ff.).

TRE	*Theologische Realenzyklopädie*, ed. G. Krause, G. Müller, and others (Berlin etc., 1977 ff.).
TU	*Texte und Untersuchungen zur Geschichte der altchristlichen Literatur, begründet von O. von Gebhardt und A. *Harnack (Leipzig, 1882–1943; Berlin, 1951 ff.).
Turner	[see *EOMIA*].
TWNT	*Theologisches Wörterbuch zum Neuen Testament*, ed. G. *Kittel and G. Friedrich (1933–73 + Register and Supplement, 1978–9; Eng. tr., 10 vols., Nashville, 1964–76).
Überweg, 1	F. Überweg, *Grundriss der Geschichte der Philosophie*, 1 (12th edn. by K. Praechter, 1926).
Überweg, 2	F. Überweg, *Grundriss der Geschichte der Philosophie*, 2 (11th edn. by B. Geyer, 1928).
Überweg, 3	F. Überweg, *Grundriss der Geschichte der Philosophie*, 3 (12th edn. by M. Frischeisen-Köhler and W. Moog, 1924).
Überweg, 4	F. Überweg, *Grundriss der Geschichte der Philosophie*, 4 (12th edn. by T. K. Oesterreich, 1923).
Überweg, 5	F. Überweg, *Grundriss der Geschichte der Philosophie*, 5 (12th edn. by T. K. Oesterreich, 1928).
VC	*Vigiliae Christianae* (Amsterdam, 1947 ff.).
VCH	*Victoria County History* (London, 1900–75; Oxford, 1976 ff.).
Verfasserlexikon (2nd edn.)	*Die Deutsche Literatur des Mittelalters: Verfasserlexikon*, begun by J. Stammler and others, 2nd edn., ed. K. Ruh and others (1978 ff.).
Vogel, *Sources*	C. Vogel, *Medieval Liturgy: An Introduction to the Sources* (rev. Eng. tr. by W. Storey and N. Rasmussen, OP, of Vogel's *Introduction aux sources de l'histoire du culte chrétien aux moyen âge* (Biblioteca degli 'Studi Medievali', 1 [1966]); Washington, DC [1986]).
West. Comm.	Westminster Commentaries [until 1903, 'Oxford Commentaries'], ed. W. Lock and others (London, 1899 ff.).
ZATW	*Zeitschrift für die alttestamentliche Wissenschaft (und die Kunde des nachbiblischen Judentums)* (Giessen, 1881–1932; Berlin, 1933 ff.; + Beihefte, Giessen, 1896–1934; Berlin, 1936 ff.).
ZKG	*Zeitschrift für Kirchengeschichte* (Gotha, 1877–1930; Stuttgart, 1931 ff.).
ZKT	*Zeitschrift für katholische Theologie* (Innsbruck, 1877–1940; Vienna, 1947 ff.).
ZNTW	*Zeitschrift für die neutestamentliche Wissenschaft und die Kunde des Urchristentums (und der älteren Kirche)* (Giessen, 1900–32; Berlin, 1933 ff.; + Beihefte, Giessen, 1923–34; Berlin, 1936 ff.).

(C) BIBLICAL BOOKS

OT: Gen., Exod., Lev., Num., Deut., Jos., Jgs., Ruth, 1, 2 Sam. (= 1, 2 Reg., Vulg.), 1, 2 Kgs. (= 3, 4 Reg., Vulg.), 1, 2 Chron. (= 1, 2 Paralip., Vulg.), Ez. (= 1 Esd., Vulg.), Neh. (= 2 Esd., Vulg.), Est., Job, Pss., Prov., Eccles., Song of Songs (= Cant., Vulg.), Is. (= Es., Vulg.), Jer., Lam., Ezek., Dan., Hos., Joel, Am., Obad., Jon., Mic., Nah., Hab., Zeph., Hag., Zech., Mal.

Apocrypha: 1, 2 Esd. (= 3, 4 Esd., Vulg.), Tob., Judith, Rest of Est., Wisd. Sol., Ecclus. (= Sirach, Vulg.), Bar., S. of III Ch., Sus., Bel (or Dragon), Pr. Man., 1, 2 Macc.

NT: Mt., Mk., Lk., Jn., Acts, Rom., 1, 2 Cor., Gal., Eph., Phil., Col., 1, 2 Thess., 1, 2 Tim., Tit., Philem., Heb., Jas., 1, 2 Pet., 1, 2, 3 Jn., Jude, Rev. (= Apoc., Vulg.).

FRANK LESLIE CROSS
1900–1968

To a younger generation of English-speaking theologians the name of F. L. Cross has become almost synonymous with the *Oxford Dictionary of the Christian Church*. On the Continent of Europe it is revered in connexion with international conferences on academic aspects of theology which somehow broke through denominational barriers at a time when ecumenical dialogue between Catholics and Protestants was virtually prohibited. However his achievements are estimated, it may well be that those who did not know him personally will ask what manner of man Cross was. The answer that would be almost universally given is that he was a shy and retiring scholar, and a man of God.

Frank Leslie Cross was born exactly a year before Queen Victoria died. He was the eldest child of parents who were not young; his father retired from business when Leslie was eleven and the family then moved from Honiton to Bournemouth. As a day-boy he attended the local grammar school, which at that time specialized in science. While he was still at school he passed the London Intermediate B.Sc. examination and won the Domus Scholarship for Natural Science at Balliol College, Oxford.

After one term at Oxford Cross was involved in military service during the last months of the First World War. The letters which he sent home suggest that he was less unhappy than might be expected and looking back on his time in the Army he described the exercises as futile rather than positively frustrating. The Armistice was signed before he was sent to the Front, and in due course he returned to Balliol. He took Honours in Chemistry and Crystallography at Oxford in 1920 and in the same year completed the London B.Sc. He devoted the rest of his life to the study of theology, though the scientific habit of taking nothing verifiable on trust never left him. Since Balliol had no theologians among their Fellows, Cross was sent to Keble for tuition by D. C. Simpson and K. E. Kirk. Despite the handicap of having to learn Greek at a late stage, Cross took First Class Honours in Theology in 1922. He also collected a number of University prizes and scholarships, which in those days were sought for their financial as well as for their honorific value. He went to Germany for a year to work at Marburg and Freiburg on the material for his doctoral dissertation on Husserl, eventually taking his D.Phil. at Oxford in 1930. In 1923 he became an ordinand at Ripon Hall, of which H. D. A. Major was then Principal. He co-operated with Major in editing the papers left unpublished on Hastings Rashdall's death in 1924; these formed three volumes published in 1927–30. Cross certainly came under Major's influence, but it may well be doubted if he ever accepted the more extreme tenets of the so-called Modernism. In 1925 he was ordained to the title of Tutor and Chaplain of Ripon Hall.

In 1927, rather surprisingly, Cross received from the Governors an invitation to become one of the priest-librarians of Pusey House, a house of study founded in memory of E. B. Pusey, with 'the pursuit of personal holiness' as one of its avowed aims. He seems to have met with some suspicion in his early years on account of his continued association with the Modernist movement, but gradually, particularly under the influence of Darwell Stone, he made it clear that his theological position was basically Anglo-Catholic. His little book, *Religion and the Realm of Science*, published in 1930, reflects the influence upon his mind at this time of the scientific method, the moralism of Rashdall and Major, and the intense aesthetic attraction of Catholic ceremonial and sacramental religion. The centenary of the Oxford Movement in 1933 provided the occasion for a number of small works on the subject and probably led him to embark on a study of Newman, published in 1935. This contains letters of Newman which were previously unknown.

Also in 1933 Cross became an Examining Chaplain to the Bishop of Bradford, a post which he conscientiously filled for ten years. His correspondence makes it clear that he found the work arduous and inclined to interfere with his other interests, but it was a task which he valued for the contact it gave him with the parochial ministry. It is also worth recording that despite all his diffidence he was exercising a strong pastoral influence over the many undergraduates who sought his counsel at Pusey House, and that the strength of his spirituality impressed others who came in contact with him at this time. He was during the 1930s an ardent pacifist, and he persuaded many to share his views. In 1934 he became Custodian of the Library of Pusey House. He did much to expand as well as to catalogue the library and made known its uses among non-theologians in the University.

In 1934 he was appointed University Lecturer in the Philosophy of Religion and from 1935 to 1938 he was also Wilde Lecturer in Natural and Comparative Religion, choosing as his subject the history of the relations between religion and scientific theory. It would seem, however, that his interests were turning in other directions. In 1935 he published a collection of extracts from 17th-century Anglican divines which he edited with P. E. More under the title *Anglicanism*; from its continued sales it appears that this has become a standard work. The following year he produced his adaptation of Huck's *Synopsis of the First Three Gospels*, also widely used. But he was already drawn to the early Fathers. On a walking tour in Majorca in December 1935 to January 1936 he records that he spent a good many evenings translating Bardenhewer. He had already lectured for a number of years on Leo and Athanasius, and in 1939 he published a students' edition of the *De Incarnatione*. Both from his Inaugural Lecture on Athanasius when he became Lady Margaret Professor of Divinity (1944) and from the papers he left unfinished, it seems clear that he meant to produce a critical edition of the text; but his energies were diverted to other channels. On Stone's death in 1941 Cross succeeded him as Editor of the *Lexicon of Patristic Greek* (as it was then called). On this project he toiled much, working in the Bodleian Library on the intractable slips, persuading others to give freely of their time, and raising funds by appeal and by his own work. When he undertook to look after parishes during the University vacation he would ask for his fees to be paid to the *LPG*. In 1941 he was also concerned with the foundation of the Theological Literature Association, of which he was one of the two secretaries throughout its useful life. In addition, he set to work, as a labour of piety, on a life of Darwell Stone, which he completed in record time. The book was published in 1943. Even if it fails to give a vivid portrait of its subject, the material it contains remains one of the sources for the history of the Church of England during the period of the Modernist crisis and the controversy over the revision of the Book of Common Prayer.

On Maundy Thursday 1939 Cross and his fellow-librarian, the Revd Dr T. M. Parker, were invited by the Oxford University Press to produce a semi-popular volume to be called *The Oxford Companion to the Christian Religion*; it was to be analogous to *The Oxford Companion to Music*. After a year it became clear that it would not be quickly completed, and Dr Parker resigned. Cross continued to work at the first draft in spasms, but with the intervention of the Second World War and other troubles the completion of the book, and its metamorphosis into the first edition of this *Dictionary*, had to wait until he had become Lady Margaret Professor of Divinity. On the death of Dr N. P. Williams in April 1943 this chair became vacant. At that time it was filled by an election in which all holders of Oxford degrees in Divinity were entitled to vote. When it was first suggested to Cross that he should stand he refused, but after an overnight journey he changed his mind and allowed his name to go forward. Partly because of war-time conditions, the election was not held until January 1944, when Cross was elected by a respectable majority.

The Lady Margaret Chair carries with it a canonry of Christ Church and a large mansion of over thirty rooms in the heart of the college. To this abode Cross took his books in suitcases and devoted his afternoons to taming the garden. At first he had a housekeeper and tried to turn his lodgings into an almost monastic house of study. Later, after his mother's death, his father and sisters came to live in his house, but he still offered accommodation to many generations of undergraduates, in many cases without charge. In the Cathedral his influence was quickly felt, partly because of his regular attendance at every office and partly because he soon introduced an additional weekday celebration of the Holy Communion at an early hour which at times drew a sizeable congregation; at first he was himself the normal celebrant, but as others wished to join in he gladly took his turn in the rota.

The principal achievements of his Professorship were the publication in 1957 of the *Oxford Dictionary of the Christian Church*, as it was eventually called, and the organization of international conferences. The *Dictionary* was very largely his own work. Other scholars supplied him with information, and assistants helped with compiling bibliographies and first drafts, but he himself welded the material into a unity and his hand is clearly visible throughout. The book has become a standard work of reference, and at the time of his death he was working on the second edition.

The international conferences grew out of his desire for peace and co-operation among scholars and Christians. Almost immediately after the end of the Second World War he took part in a mission to Germany to try to restore relations with German Christians, and when Patrick McLaughlin suggested to him that a gathering of scholars interested in the study of the Fathers of the Church would further relations between Christians of different denominations, he readily agreed to convene such a meeting. The First International Conference on Patristic Studies took place in 1951. In those days the academic nature of the assembly had to be stressed, and even then all members of one of the principal Roman Catholic orders were forbidden at the last moment to attend, on the ground that the gathering was 'crypto-ecumenical'. This was a severe blow. But about 200 people came, from every continent. The value of the Conference for exchange of views was so obvious that a small delegation asked Cross to arrange another; and since at a late stage he had suddenly begun to call the 1951 meeting 'The *First* International Conference on Patristic Studies' it was not difficult to see that a series was envisaged. The Second took place in 1955, and from then until long after his death the Proceedings were published by the Berlin Academy in *Texte und Untersuchungen*. The Conferences, at four-yearly intervals, grew, until that of 1967, opened by Cardinal Pellegrino, was more than double the size of the first, and everyone took part without denominational distinction. In 1957, at the first of the parallel New Testament Congresses, which developed from earlier congresses intended to foster the exchange of ideas between the Anglican clergy and academics, Dr [later Cardinal] Heenan, then Archbishop of Liverpool, took the chair for Dr Ramsey, then Archbishop of York. These conferences owed their being to Cross's powers of organization and their success to his attention to every detail and to his powers of control and persuasion; he somehow contrived to keep Continental professors content with their ration of 18 minutes, while he was able to encourage the diffident and young. It is likely that the conferences on Patristic studies played some part in bringing about the enormous increase in popularity of the Fathers as a field of research which is reflected in the output of the University Presses over the next twenty years; it is also likely that they played some part—though it is impossible to assess precisely what—in bringing together Christians of different allegiances and making for an atmosphere in which ecumenism became fashionable. This search for unity certainly figured largely in his plans for his conferences and in his prayers.

Partly at least because of these labours Cross did not produce a large output of original work.

He took enormous care over the supervision of his pupils and the encouragement of other scholars. He contributed to the *Journal of Theological Studies* a number of important articles, including those on the pre-Leonine elements in the Roman Mass in 1949, the African Canons in 1961, and the development of Western liturgical manuscripts in 1965. At the time of his death he was working on the Stowe Missal; he felt confident that he had discovered the purpose for which the original manuscript was written and he was concerned to see just how it fitted into the development of the Roman Mass. He published an interesting reconstruction of 1 Peter as a Paschal Homily in 1954, a view which he later doubted. Other insights on particular points he buried in unlikely places: he propounded his interpretation of Melito's *Peri Pascha* in a lecture which he never published and he printed his findings first in a review of someone else's edition and then in his own handbook, *Early Christian Fathers* (1960).

His lectures were badly attended, largely because his delivery was painful. It was equally difficult to follow his sermons, which were frequently first-rate pieces of work and read well. It is something of a surprise to find that he was chosen as Select Preacher at Cambridge on more than one occasion and that he also preached in St Paul's Cathedral in 1939.

He was personally shy and by nature retiring. Throughout his life he disliked parties and found social contacts difficult. He was completely lacking in small-talk and on a superficial level a bad judge of character, and he frequently overestimated people's ability. On the other hand few were able to refuse his requests and he was deeply respected by the college servants who said that he was almost unique in his appreciation of what they did. When he was in charge of college and university livings he invariably visited the parishes in which an incumbent was to be appointed, and he got on well with the country people. He enjoyed walking and, up to 1960, bicycling both in Britain and on the Continent. He spent much time with religious communities, making it his habit during vacations to act as chaplain to communities of nuns whose own priests were on holiday or during an interregnum. These visits provided him with a peace of mind which he seldom seemed to find elsewhere.

Towards the end of his life honours came to him from many quarters. He had obtained his own Oxford DD in 1950; in 1959 and 1960 he received honorary degrees from Aberdeen and Bonn and was later offered others in America; in 1967 he was elected a Fellow of the British Academy. He retired from his chair in September 1968 and died on 29 December of the same year.

A

Aaron. In Hebrew tradition *Moses' brother. He is first mentioned in the narrative of Moses' vision on Mt. Horeb (Exod. 4: 14), when Yahweh assigns him to Moses as his assistant. Yahweh afterwards appointed him and his descendants to be priests (Exod. 28 and 29; Num. 8 and 18), an office he kept despite his share in setting up the *golden calf (Exod. 32: 1–6). The power of his priestly intercession is emphasized in the story of his staying a plague (Num. 16: 43–8), and his authority is miraculously confirmed by the budding rod (Num. 17: 1–8). Aaron's priesthood, whose chief function was the offering of acceptable sacrifice to God, gave him a unique position. He was the head of his sons and the Levites; he alone offered incense in the Holy of Holies and mediated between God and the people; and, like a king, he was anointed and crowned with diadem and tiara (Exod. 28).

In Christian theology he is a type of Christ. This conception of Aaron as at once foreshadowing and being replaced by Him is worked out in the Ep. to the Hebrews, where the superiority of the perfect sacrifice of Calvary to the animal sacrifices of the Aaronic priesthood is established.

H. Valentin, *Aaron: Eine Studie zur vor-priesterschriftlichen Aaron-Überlieferung* (Orbis Biblicus et Orientalis, 18; 1978). E. Rivkin in *The Interpreter's Dictionary of the Bible*, suppl. vol. (Nashville, 1976), pp. 1–3, s.v. 'Aaron, Aaronides', with bibl. See also works on Priesthood in the OT cited s.v. PRIEST.

Abailard. See ABELARD.

Abba. The Aramaic word for 'Father'. It occurs three times in the NT, Mk. 14: 36, Rom. 8: 15, and Gal. 4: 6, in each case with its Greek equivalent ('Αββᾶ, ὁ Πατήρ, 'Abba, Father'). It is used as a title for individual Desert Fathers, e.g. in the *Apophthegmata Patrum*.

S. V. McCasland, ' "Abba, Father" ', *Journal of Biblical Literature*, 72 (1953), pp. 79–91. J. C. G. Greig, 'Abba and Amen: Their Relevance to Christology', in F. L. Cross (ed.), *Studia Evangelica*, 5 (TU 103; 1968), pp. 3–13, esp. pp. 3–10, with refs. J. Barr, ' "Abbā" isn't "Daddy" ', *JTS* NS 39 (1988), pp. 28–47. G. Kittel in *TWNT* 1 (1933), pp. 4–6 (Eng. tr., 1964, pp. 5 f.), s.v. ἀββᾶ. See also comm. to Mk. etc.

abbé. A French term, originally restricted to the *abbot of a monastery, but in modern times applied to every person wearing secular ecclesiastical dress. The extension of meaning took place in the 16th cent., when the Concordat of 1516 authorized Francis I to nominate secular priests abbots *in commendam*. As the number of nominations far exceeded the abbacies available, many 'abbés', who often were not even in *major orders, devoted themselves to other work, e.g. educational and literary pursuits, whence the term was transferred to secular clerics in general. Today such clerics are correctly addressed as 'M. l'Abbé'.

abbess. The superior of certain *sui generis* (i.e. autonomous) houses of nuns. The title is used among the *Benedictines, *Cistercians, *Trappists, *Poor Clares, and some *canonesses. Its earliest known use (Lat. *abbatissa*) is in a sepulchral inscription (514) on the site of an ancient convent near the basilica of St Agnes extra muros at *Rome. The power of an abbess is determined by the fact that her house is *sui iuris*: because of this, she is a major superior (*CIC* (1983), can. 613, s. 2), and, depending on the Constitutions of her house or Order, she may hold office for a term of years, for an indefinite period, until a certain retiring age, and sometimes even for life (cf. *CIC*, can. 624, s. 1). A newly elected abbess normally receives a liturgical blessing, at which she may be invested with a *ring. In the Middle Ages wide powers were claimed by certain abbesses, e.g. the Abbess of Conversano on election, vested in a mitre, received the homage of the local clergy, while *Innocent III had to forbid the Abbesses of Burgos and Palencia from hearing the confessions of their nuns. In England abbesses attended councils on several occasions, e.g. St *Hilda was present at *Whitby in 664. The Council of *Trent put an end to most special prerogatives.

A. Tamburinius, OSB, *De Jure Abbatissarum et Monialium* (Rome, 1638). T. J. Bowe, *Religious Superioresses: A Historical Synopsis and a Commentary* (Catholic University of America Canon Law Studies, 228; 1946). E. Power, *Medieval English Nunneries, c.1275 to 1535* (1922), pp. 42–95. J. de Puniet in *Dict. Sp.* 1 (1937), cols. 57–61, s.v. 'Abbesse'; A. Pantone in *DIP* 1 (1974), cols. 14–22, s.v. 'Abbadessa'.

Abbo, St (*c*.945–1004), otherwise 'Abbon', Abbot of *Fleury. He was born nr. Orleans, entered the Benedictine abbey of Fleury, and studied at *Paris, *Reims, and Fleury. From 985 to 987 he was in charge of studies at the monastery school of Ramsey, at the same time helping *Oswald, Abp. of *York, in the restoration of monasticism in England. While at Ramsey he composed his *Passio S. Eadmundi*; and shortly after returning to Fleury he addressed his *Quaestiones Grammaticales* to the Ramsey monks. He was elected Abbot of Fleury in 988. He supported the *Cluniac Reform and was an ardent defender of Papal authority and of the freedom of the monasteries from both episcopal and secular interference. He was killed in a revolt occasioned by the reform of the priory of La Réole in Gascony. His correspondence is a valuable source for the relations between France and the Papacy during the reign of Robert the Pious. He also issued writings on logic, mathematics, and astronomy and an Epitome of the Lives of the Popes. Feast day, 13 Nov.

Works and Letters in J. P. Migne, *PL* 139. 417–578 (incomplete). *Opera inedita* ed. A. Van de Vyver, posthumously pub. with introd. by R. Raes (Rijksuniversiteit te Gent. Werken uitgegeven door de Faculteit van de Letteren en Wijsbegeerte, 140, etc.; Bruges, 1966 ff.). *Passio S. Eadmundi* also ed. M. Winterbottom, *Three Lives of English Saints* (Toronto Medieval Latin Texts, 1972), pp. 67–87. *Quaestiones Grammaticales*, ed., with Fr. tr., by A. Guerreau-Jalabert (Paris, 1982). The principal authority is the Vita by a monk Aimonus repr. from the *Acta Sanctorum

Ordinis Sancti Benedicti in J. P. Migne, loc. cit., 375–414. P. Cousin, OSB, *Abbon de Fleury-sur-Loire* (Paris, 1954). A. Van de Vyver, 'Les Œuvres inédites d'Abbon de Fleury', *R. Bén.* 47 (1935), pp. 125–69. A Fliche, *La Réforme grégorienne*, 1 (SSL 6; 1924), pp. 47–60. U. Berlière, OSB, in *DHGE* 1 (1912), cols. 49–51, s.v. 'Abbon de Fleury', with details of his works and edns. of them. A. Amanieu in *DDC* 1 (1935), cols. 71–6, s.v. 'Abbon de Fleury'.

abbot (from Aram. and Syr. *abba*, i.e. father; Gk. ἀββᾶς, Lat. *abbas*). In the W. Church it is the official title of the superior of certain monasteries of monks or monastic *Congregations belonging to the *Benedictine, *Cistercian, or *Trappist families, or of some houses of certain orders of *Canons Regular (e.g. the *Augustinian Canons Regular of the Lateran and the *Premonstratensians). Acc. to the Rule of St *Benedict, the abbot is to be regarded as the father of his monastic family, and as such has far-reaching powers in the government of his house, the rules of which he may regulate in accordance with the needs of climate, customs of the times, etc. Nowadays abbots are always elected and hold office in accordance with the Constitutions of their Order or Congregation: sometimes for life, sometimes for an indefinite term, sometimes until reaching a certain retiring age, sometimes for a term of years (cf. *CIC* (1983), can. 624, s. 1). An abbot is a major superior (*CIC* (1983), can. 613, s. 2), and, since all the Orders and Congregations which have abbots are recognized by canon law as clerical institutes (cf. *CIC* (1983), can. 588, s. 2), an abbot must be a priest, he exercises ecclesiastical power (*CIC* (1983), can. 596, s. 2), and is recognized as an *Ordinary (*CIC* (1983), can. 134, s. 1). Unlike other major superiors, an abbot receives a liturgical blessing, at which he may be invested with a *ring, *mitre, and *crosier. The abbot of a territorial abbey (formerly known as an 'abbot nullius [*sc.* dioecesis]') also has quasi-episcopal jurisdiction over the territory of his abbey (*CIC* (1983), can. 370). The older practice of occasionally conferring the title of abbot on a monk as a mark of honour, without jurisdiction, is now falling into disuse. In the Middle Ages, certain abbots gradually acquired the right to certain insignia and privileges normally reserved to bishops, and also the right to assist at Church Councils (since the 8th Council of *Toledo in 653). The ancient distinction between mitred abbots (in pre-Reformation England, peers of Parliament) and others does not now exist. The superiors of certain prominent monasteries have the name of 'Archabbot', and, in addition, the presiding abbot of a *Congregation (q.v.) is often known as the 'Abbot President' or 'Abbot General'. Since 1893 the Benedictine Confederation has had an 'Abbot Primate' who presides over the whole order. The corresponding rank in the E. Church is *hegumenos or *archimandrite (q.v.).

Chs. 2, 3, 46, and 64 of the 'Rule of St Benedict' are esp. concerned with the abbot; *RB 1980: The Rule of St Benedict in Latin and English with Notes*, ed. T. Fry, OSB (Collegeville, Minn. [1982]), pp. 322–78 (app. 2, 'The Abbot', by C. Peifer, OSB); see also other comm. to rule cited under BENEDICT, RULE OF ST. A. Tamburinius, OSB, *De Iure Abbatum* (3 vols., Lyons 1640). B. Hegglin, OSB, *Der Benediktinische Abt in rechtsgeschichtlicher Entwicklung und geltendem Kirchenrecht* (Kirchengeschichtliche Quellen und Studien, 5; 1961). A. de Vogüé, OSB, *La Communauté et l'Abbé dans la Règle de Saint Benoît* (Textes et études théologiques [Bruges], 1961; Eng. tr., Cistercian Studies

Series, 5; 2 vols., Kalamazoo, Mich., 1979–88). P. Salmon, OSB, *L'Abbé dans la Tradition monastique: Contribution à l'histoire du caractère perpétuel des supérieurs religieux en Occident* (Histoire et sociologie de l'Église, 2; Sirey, 1962; Eng. tr., Cistercian Studies Series, 14; Washington, DC, 1972). A. Veilleux, OSB, 'The Abbatial Office in Cenobitic Life', *Monastic Studies*, 6 (1968), pp. 3–45; A. de Vogüé and A. Veilleux, 'Apropos of the Abbatial Office', ibid. 7 (1969), pp. 160–4. U. Berlière, OSB, *Les Élections Abbatiales au Moyen Age* (Académie Royale de Belgique. Classe des Lettres et des Sciences Morales et Politiques, Mémoires. Collection in-8°, deuxième série, 20, fasc. 3; 1927). J. Baucher, OSB, in *DDC* 1 (1935), cols. 29–62, s.v. 'Abbés'; J. de Puniet, OSB, in *Dict. Sp.* 1 (1937), cols. 49–57, s.v. 'Abbé'; A. Nocent in *DIP* 1 (1974), cols. 3–14, s.v. 'Abate'. See also works cited s.v. MONASTICISM.

Abbot of Misrule. See MISRULE, LORD OF.

Abbot, Ezra (1819–84), biblical scholar. A native of Maine, USA, and a *Unitarian by belief, in 1856 he became assistant librarian at Harvard university and in 1872 professor of NT at the Harvard divinity school. In 1871 he was appointed one of the original members of the American NT Revision Company in charge of the RV, where his judgement exercised great influence. Several of his textual researches were incorporated into C. R. Gregory's *Prolegomena* (1890) to the 8th (last) edition of C. *Tischendorf's Greek NT. Though extreme care for detail much restricted the extent of his own publications, his work bore fruit in the writings of many others, who sought his assistance. His other writings included 'The Authorship of the Fourth Gospel: External Evidences', an able defence of the Johannine authorship, in the *Unitarian Review* (1880), and a very thorough discussion of the punctuation of Rom. 9: 5 in the *Journal of the Society of Biblical Literature and Exegesis* for 1883. These items, as well as several other of his papers, were reprinted after his death in *Critical Essays* (1888).

Ezra Abbot (Cambridge, Mass., 1884), with pref. by S. J. Barrows, addresses by J. H. Thayer (pp. 28–60) and others, memorial tributes, short biog. note (p. 7), and list of Abbot's publications (pp. 69–73). B. W. Bacon in *Dict. Amer. Biog.* 1 (1928), pp. 10 f.

Abbot, George (1562–1633), Abp. of *Canterbury. A native of Guildford, he was educated and later taught at Balliol College, Oxford. In 1597 he became master of University College, Oxford, and in 1600, 1603, and 1605 he was vice-chancellor. In 1600 he also became Dean of *Winchester. He displayed from an early date strong *Puritan sympathies which brought him increasingly into conflict with the rising party of *High Churchmen in the university, esp. W. *Laud. He won *James I's favour by his mission to Scotland (1608) in which he persuaded the Presbyterians of the lawfulness of episcopacy. Preferments followed rapidly. In 1609 he was made Bp. of *Lichfield and Coventry; early in the following year he was translated to London; and in 1611 he became Abp. of Canterbury. As his long archiepiscopate was marked by the decline of Puritanism among the influential classes, Abbot found himself forced to fight a losing battle. He was severe on RCs and correspondingly partial to *Calvinists both at home and abroad. Thus he encouraged the King's endeavours to secure the dismissal of C. *Vorstius as an *Arminian from his chair at *Leiden; he arranged for the settlement of M. A. *de Dominis, the apostate Abp. of

Spalato, in English benefices; and he ensured that England was represented at the Synod of *Dort. The strong line he took in the Essex nullity suit (1613), however, in which he upheld justice against the King and others in high position, won him deserved respect and a temporary popularity among Anglicans of all schools. His unhappiness culminated in the curious consequences of an accident while hunting at Bramshill, Hants, in 1621. Having accidentally shot a gamekeeper, Abbot was considered by some of his fellow-bishops to have become irregular as a man of blood. When the case was tried by a commission of six bishops and four laymen, and opinion was equally divided as to the irregularity, James gave his decision in Abbot's favour. On 24 Dec. James signed on his behalf a formal dispensation and Abbot resumed his duties. In 1625 he crowned *Charles I, but, owing to various differences with the monarch, esp. on the subject of the *Divine Right of Kings, he exercised little influence during his reign, and for a time he was sequestered from his jurisdiction in 1627. His writings include a widely circulated *Geography, or a Brief Description of the Whole World* (1599), and an *Exposition on the Prophet Jonah* (1600).

His elder brother, **Robert Abbot** (1560–1618), was Bp. of *Salisbury from 1615 till his death.

Standard modern Life by P. A. Welsby (London, 1962). K. Fincham, 'Prelacy and Politics: Archbishop Abbot's Defence of Protestant Orthodoxy', *Bulletin of the Institute of Historical Research*, 61 (1988), pp. 36–64. R. A. Christophers, *George Abbot, Archbishop of Canterbury 1562–1633: A Bibliography* (Charlottesville, Va., 1966). S. L. Lee in *DNB* 1 (1885), pp. 5–20, s.v.

abbreviator. An official of the Roman chancery, whose principal duty was the preparation of letters and writs for the collation of Church dignities. He was so named from the extensive abbreviations employed in Papal documents. *Pius II erected the abbreviators into a college of prelates divided into three ranks (1463). In 1814 Pius VII abolished the junior ranks, and in 1908, when *Pius X reorganized the chancery, the college as a whole was suppressed and its functions transferred to a group of *protonotaries (*protonotarii apostolici participantes*).

J. Ciampinus, *De Abbreviatorum de Parco maiori, sive assistentium S.R.E. vicecancellario in literarum apostolicarum expeditionibus antiquo statu, illorumve in Collegium erectione, munere, dignitate, praerogativis, ac privilegiis dissertatio historica* (Rome, 1691). E. Fournier in *DDC* 1 (1935), cols. 98–106, s.v. 'Abbréviateurs'.

Abdisho'. See EBEDJESUS.

à Becket, St Thomas. See BECKET, ST THOMAS.

Abel. Acc. to Gen. 4: 2, the second son of *Adam and *Eve, who became a shepherd, whilst his brother Cain cultivated the land. He was slain by Cain, jealous that Abel's sacrifice of the firstlings of his flock had been accepted by Yahweh, whereas his own was rejected (Gen. 4: 3 ff.). Gen. 4 contains the only mention of him in the OT. In the NT the Lord places him at the beginning of the line of prophets who were killed ('from the blood of righteous Abel', Mt. 23: 35), and the author of Heb., who attributes the acceptance of his sacrifice to his faith (11: 4), opposes his blood to that of Christ 'that speaketh better things than that of Abel' (12: 24; cf. also 1 Jn. 3: 12). The

Fathers, who frequently commented on his story, regarded him as a type of Christ, the principal points of comparison being his innocent life as a shepherd, his accepted sacrifice, and his violent death. As the first of martyrs he also sometimes stands for the persecuted Christians, belonging to the city which is in heaven (St *Augustine, *De Civ. Dei*, 15. 1). In the Liturgy, his name is mentioned with those of *Abraham and *Melchizedek in the *Canon of the Roman Mass (and is also mentioned in the Liturgy of St *Basil), and in the prayers for the dying he was until recently invoked to assist the soul. See also ABELITES.

V. Aptowitzer, *Kain und Abel in der Agada, den Apokryphen, der hellenistischen, christlichen und muhammedanischen Literatur* (1922). J. Hennig, 'Abel's Place in the Liturgy', *Woodstock Studies*, 7 (1946), pp. 126–41; Y. *Congar, 'Ecclesia ab Abel' in *Abhandlungen über Theologie und Kirche: Festgabe für Karl Adam*, ed. M. Reding (Düsseldorf, 1952), pp. 79–108. J. Lewinsohn, I. Chanoch, and B. Heller in *Encyclopaedia Judaica*, 1 (Berlin, 1928), cols. 207–14, s.v., with bibl. See also comm. on Gen.

Abelard, Peter (1079–1142/3), philosopher and theologian. (Abailard, used by some scholars, is prob. nearer the original form of his name and its pronunciation than the conventional spelling.) He was born at Le Pallet, near Nantes, the son of a Breton knight. The pupil successively of *Roscelin, *William of Champeaux, and of *Anselm of Laon, he early showed evidence of a lively, restless, and independent mind which brought him into frequent conflict with his masters. His brilliant refutation of the *Realism of William of Champeaux at once established his renown as a teacher. He went on to lecture at *Paris to large audiences of enthusiastic students, first in dialectics and later in theology, until the tragic issue of his love-affair with Héloïse, the niece of Fulbert, Canon of *Notre-Dame, caused him to retire to the monastery of *St-Denis in 1117/18. Roscelin and others then attacked the orthodoxy of his teaching on the Trinity; he was condemned unheard at the Council of *Soissons (1121) and made to burn his book on the subject (the 'Theologia Summi Boni'). He returned to St-Denis, but, having already provoked the monks' hostility, he was forced to flee when he criticized the legend of St *Dionysius, the patron of the abbey. He established a small oratory called the Paraclete, near Troyes, where he was soon joined by a band of pupils; it was here that Héloïse was later to become Abbess of a house of nuns. In 1127 Abelard became Abbot of St-Gildas, but by 1136 he was back in Paris, where he had among his students *John of Salisbury and *Arnold of Brescia. In June 1140, after St *Bernard of Clairvaux had denounced his teaching to Rome, a list of propositions ascribed to him was condemned at the Council of *Sens. The sentence was confirmed by Pope Innocent II, but, as a result of the intervention of *Peter the Venerable, Abelard was reconciled to Bernard, restored to communion, and received by Peter at Cluny. He died at the Cluniac priory of St-Marcel, near Chalon-sur-Saône.

Abelard's versatility is reflected in his writings. His philosophical works include 'Scito te ipsum' (also called 'Ethics'), a 'Dialectica', and some 'Glossulae' on *Porphyry. His 'Sic et Non', a collection of apparently contradictory excerpts from the Bible and the Fathers on a large number of questions, was intended to help the reader to reconcile the contradictions by making him aware of the difference between authority itself and the many forms in which it is expressed. In his 'Theologia Summi Boni' (*c.*1119–20), he did not apply reason directly to the doctrine of the Trinity, but rather sought to show how this doctrine might be understood by way of 'analogies provided by human reason'. He continued to refine and defend this method in a series of new versions of the 'Theologia'. In his 'Dialogus' (*c.*1125–6), he displayed a sympathy in debate (with a Jew and a philosopher) at variance with his earlier more combative style. He was also the author of a collection of hymns, written at the request of Héloïse for the nuns of the Paraclete. These include the well-known 'O quanta qualia' ('O what the joy and the glory must be'), to be sung at Vespers on Saturday, which, with its characteristic combination of devotional feeling and dialectical play, hymns the joys of an endless Sabbath in heaven.

Abelard's philosophical and theological doctrines were to a great extent determined by his early interest in the problem of *universals. Inspired no doubt by his lessons with the *Nominalist Roscelin, he maintained that only individuals could be described as things ('res'), and that language represented an abstraction from these things. The 'vox' or 'nomen' of language could not be considered a thing, but only a concept, because the qualities shared by individuals are not in themselves things, but the results of a mental act. Later he came to give more importance to the question of meaning in language. The understanding of the thing, which is required for words to have meaning, is at least in part (he said) a true understanding of the thing as it was conceived in the mind of God. With this thinking he moved from his earlier scepticism back to a position nearer to the Realism he had begun by attacking. In his 'Ethics', he argued that sin, 'properly speaking', consisted not in any action but in contempt for the wishes of God; while thus emphasizing the importance of intention in moral action, he held that it must nevertheless be informed by a knowledge of right and wrong which depended ultimately on revealed truth. Similarly, his stress on the suffering and death of Christ as our supreme example (his exemplarist theory of the *Atonement) involved no denial of the place of Christ's death in effecting salvation through the sacraments.

It was never Abelard's purpose simply to set reason against faith. His writings are best seen as a sustained attempt to question the content of faith, and so to gain a fuller, more lucid perception of it. The 'Historia Calamitatum', the account which he gave of his life to *c.*1132, records some of the difficulties, private and public, caused by such an approach. As well as the pleasure he took in his own powers of argument, it tells of the disappointments which he suffered when he felt that his ideas had been misunderstood. Despite his frequent immersion in controversy, after his separation from Héloïse he held increasingly to an ideal (derived partly from St *Jerome) of the monk as one engaged in a solitary, intellectual search for God. His influence is evident in the many authors who took up his method and, in a sense, in the history of scholasticism itself.

There is not yet a complete edn. of Abelard's works, which have only slowly come to light in modern times. Early edn. by A. Du Chesne (Paris, 1616), repr., with additions, in J. P. Migne, *PL* 178; modern collections of *Ouvrages inédits* (Paris, 1836), and

Opera hactenus seorsim edita (2 vols., ibid., 1849–59), both by V. Cousin. *Opera theologica*, ed. E. M. Buytaert, OFM, and C. J. Mews (CCCM 11, 12, 13, etc., 1969 ff.; vol. 13, 1987, incl. recent bibl.). Crit. edn. of hymns by G. M. Dreves, SJ (Paris, 1891; also *AHMA* 48 (1905), pp. 141–232); and by J. Szövérffy (Medieval Classics, Texts and Studies, 2–3; Albany, NY, 1975). I '*Planctus*' ed., with musical transcription, by G. Vecchi (Modena, 1951). Short early glosses on logical texts ed. M. Dal Pra (Rome and Milan, 1954); further writings on logic ed. B. Geyer (BGPM 21, Hefte 1–4; 1919–33; 2nd edn. of Heft 4, 1973). *Glossae super librum Porphyrii secundum vocales*, attributed to Abelard, ed. C. Ottaviano, *Testi medioevali inediti* (Fontes Ambrosiani, 3; Florence, 1933), pp. 95–207. *Super Periermenias*, 12–14, and *Sententie secundum M. Petrum*, prob. by Abelard, ed. L. Minio-Paluello, *Twelfth Century Logic: Texts and Studies*, 2 (Rome, 1958). *Dialectica*, ed. L. M. De Rijk (Assen, 1956). *Sic et Non*, ed. B. Boyer and R. McKeon (6 fasc., Chicago and London, 1976–7). Crit. edn. of *Historia Calamitatum*, with Fr. tr., by J. Monfrin (Bibliothèque des Textes Philosophiques, 1959; 3rd edn., 1967); *Ethics*, ed., with Eng. tr., D. E. Luscombe (Oxford, 1971); *Dialogus inter Philosophum, Iudaeum et Christianum*, ed. R. Thomas (Stuttgart and Bad Cannstatt [1970]); Eng. tr. by P. J. Payer (Mediaeval Sources in Translation, 20; Toronto, 1979); *Soliloquium*, ed., with Eng. tr., by C. Burnett in *Studi Medievali*, 3rd ser. 25 (1984), pp. 857–94. Various letters between Abelard and Héloïse, ed. J. T. Muckle, CSB, *Mediaeval Studies*, 15 (1953), pp. 47–94; 17 (1955), pp. 240–81, and by T. P. McLaughlin, CSB, ibid. 18 (1956), pp. 241–92 [the letters are here described as 1–7; they were subsequently renumbered, the *Historia Calamitatum* being counted as letter 1]. Letters 9–14 (of the new enumeration), ed. E. R. Smits (Groningen, 1983). Eng. tr. of the *Historia Calamitatum* and some letters by B. Radice (Harmondsworth, 1974). C. Waddell, OCSO, has identified elements in the late 13th-cent. *Ordinal of the Paraclete prob. by Abelard: *The Old French Paraclete Ordinary and the Paraclete Breviary* (Cistercian Liturgy Series, 3–7; Gethsemani Abbey, Ky., 1983–5). Principal modern studies by J. G. Sikes (Cambridge, 1932); E. *Gilson, *Héloïse et Abélard* (1938; 3rd edn., 1964; Eng. tr., 1953); R. Oursel, *La Dispute et la Grâce: Essai sur la Rédemption d'Abélard* (Publications de l'Université de Dijon, 19; 1959); J. Jolivet, *Arts du langage et théologie chez Abélard* (Etudes de Philosophie Médiévale, 57; 1969; 2nd edn., 1982); D. E. Luscombe, *The School of Peter Abelard: The Influence of Abelard's Thought in the Early Scholastic Period* (Cambridge, 1969); R. Weingart, *The Logic of Divine Love: A Critical Analysis of the Soteriology of Peter Abailard* (Oxford, 1970). *Peter Abelard: Proceedings of the International Conference, Louvain, May 10–12, 1971*, ed. E. M. Buytaert (Mediaevalia Lovaniensia, Series 1, Studia, 2; 1974); *Pierre Abélard—Pierre le Vénérable: Les courants philosophiques, littéraires et artistiques en Occident au milieu du XIIe siècle, Abbaye de Cluny, 2 au 9 juillet 1972*, ed. R. Louis, J. Jolivet, and J. Châtillon (Colloques internationaux du centre national de la recherche scientifique, 546; 1975); *Abélard en son temps: Actes du colloque international organisé à l'occasion du 9e centenaire de la naissance de Pierre Abélard (14–19 mai 1979)*, ed. J. Jolivet (1981); *Petrus Abaelardus (1079–1142): Person, Werk und Wirkung*, ed. R. Thomas (Trierer Theologische Studien, 38; 1980). D. E. Luscombe, 'From Paris to the Paraclete: The Correspondence of Abelard and Heloise', *Proceedings of the British Academy*, 74 (1988), pp. 247–83. Raby, pp. 319–26. E. Portalié in *DTC* 1 (1903), cols. 36–55; R. Peppermüller in *TRE* 1 (1977), pp. 7–17.

Abelites (also **Abelians** and **Abelonians**). A small African sect which originated in the diocese of Hippo and is known only from St *Augustine (*De Haer.* 87). Admitting marriage and, indeed, holding it to be obligatory, its members lived in complete continence after the alleged example of *Abel. They perpetuated their existence by each husband and wife adopting a boy and a girl. By St Augustine's time it had ceased to exist as a sect, the few surviving Abelite families having been received back into the Church.

Abercius, Inscription of.

The Greek epitaph of Abercius Marcellus, Bp. of Hieropolis (not Hierapolis), in Phrygia Salutaris (d. *c.*200) Discovered by W. M. *Ramsay in 1883, it had been composed and apparently set up by Abercius over his future tomb. It mentions his travels to Rome and Nisibis and, making allusive use of early Christian symbolism, gives Abercius' testimony to the currency everywhere of the Eucharist. The inscription, which was presented by the Sultan Abdul Hamid to *Leo XIII, is now in the *Vatican Museum. The attempts of certain scholars (e.g. G. Ficker, A. Dieterich) to maintain that Abercius was a pagan priest, not a Christian bishop, have now been abandoned.

The 'Life of Abercius', which exists in three recensions, is of much later date. It attributes to Abercius a 'Book of Teaching' (βίβλος διδασκαλίας) as well as a letter to the Emp. *Marcus Aurelius, and also incorporates the text of the Inscription. The original form of this 'Life' was apparently written at Hieropolis towards the end of the 4th cent. Despite J. B. *Pitra's defence, the *Vita* appears to be of no independent historical value. Abercius is commemorated in both E. and W. as a saint. Feast day, 22 Oct.

The Greek text with Eng. tr. is in J. B. *Lightfoot, *The Apostolic Fathers* (1889), 2. 1, pp. 492–501; also, with introd. and Lat. tr., in J. Quasten, *Monumenta Eucharistica et Liturgica Vetustissima* (Bonn, 1935), 1, pp. 21–4. The three texts of the Life are in *S. Abercii Vita*, ed. T. Nissen (Teub., 1912). W. Lüdtke and T. Nissen, *Die Grabschrift des Aberkios: Ihre Überlieferung und ihr Text* (ibid., 1910). A. Abel, 'Étude sur l'Inscription d'Abercius', *Byzantion*, 3 ('1926' [1928]), pp. 321–411, with full bibl. W. Wischmeyer, 'Der Aberkiosinschrift als Grabepigramm', *Jahrbuch für Antike und Christentum*, 23 (1980), pp. 22–47, incl. text. H. *Leclercq, OSB, in *DACL* 1 (pt. 1; 1907), cols. 66–87, s.v.

Abgar, Legend of.

An old tradition ascribes to Abgar V (reigned 4 BC–AD 7 and 13–50), one of the kings of *Edessa, an exchange of letters with the Lord. The King, being ill, wrote to Christ asking Him to visit and heal him; He, though declining to come Himself, promised that, after His Ascension, He would send a disciple to cure the King and preach the Gospel to the people. In one version of the story is added a special blessing for Edessa. The legend is reported in variant forms by *Eusebius (*HE* 1. 13) and in the 'Doctrine of *Addai'. In the account of Eusebius the letter is followed by a recital of the mission of *Thaddaeus, one of the Seventy, who is sent by St *Thomas 'who is also called Jude', heals the King and converts many inhabitants of the city. Acc. to the 'Pilgrimage of *Egeria', the letter of Christ, written in Syriac on parchment, was preserved at Edessa; there existed many copies of it to which were ascribed miraculous powers of healing and protection. In the 'Doctrine of Addai' Abgar's emissary brings back a portrait of Christ, as well as his reply to Abgar's letter; it is disputed whether Eusebius has suppressed this detail, or whether it represents a later development. Acc. to some scholars the legend as a whole is a retrojection into the 1st cent. of the conversion (itself uncertain) of Abgar VIII (177–212); acc. to others it was an invention of the late 3rd or early 4th cent. (possibly designed to counter *Manichaean propaganda). The letter

was placed among the apocryphal books in the *Decretum Gelasianum*, but long remained popular in both E. and W.

R. A. *Lipsius, *Die edessenische Abgarsage kritisch untersucht* (1880); L. J. Tixeront, *Les Origines de l'Église d'Édesse et la légende d'Abgar* (1888); E. von Dobschütz, 'Der Briefwechsel zwischen Abgar und Jesus', *Zeitschrift für wissenschaftliche Theologie*, 43 (1900), pp. 422–86. H. C. Youtie, 'A Gothenburg Papyrus and the Letter to Abgar', *HTR* 23 (1930), pp. 299–302; id., 'Gothenburg Papyrus 21 and the Coptic Version of the Letter to Abgar', ibid. 24 (1931), pp. 61–5, with further refs. S. Giversen, 'Ad Abgarum: The Sahidic Version of the Letter to Abgar on a Wooden Tablet', *Acta Orientalia*, 24 (1959), pp. 71–82, with refs. R. Peppermüller, 'Griechische Papyrusfragmente der Doctrina Addai', *VC* 25 (1971), pp. 289–301. A. Cameron, *The Sceptic and the Shroud* (Inaugural Lecture, London, 1980; repr. in id., *Continuity and Change in Sixth-Century Byzantium*, 1981, no. 5). H. J. W. Drijvers in Schneemelcher (5th edn., 1987), 1 pp. 389–95; Eng. tr., 1 (1991), pp. 492–500. E. Kirsten in *RAC* 4 (1959), cols. 588–93, s.v. 'Edessa'.

abjuration.

The act of renouncing any idea, person, or thing to which one has previously adhered. It was in the past defined in RC canon law as an external retractation, made before witnesses, of errors contrary to Catholic faith and unity, such as apostasy, heresy, and schism. There are examples of it in the reconciliation of penitents during the first centuries, in the ecclesiastical legislation of the Middle Ages, and in the practice of the *Inquisition, which imposed abjuration on formal heretics as well as suspects. In modern times the term has usually been restricted to the public retractation imposed on Catholics who, having knowingly and publicly defected from the faith or communion of the Catholic Church, sought to be reconciled to her. From 1857 to 1967 some form of abjuration was imposed on those who were received into the RC Church from other (esp. Protestant) bodies. Abjuration is not mentioned in the 1983 *Codex Iuris Canonici*.

The Greek Church has also set forms of abjuration, esp. for *Manichaeans, *Jews, and Muslims, containing short descriptions of the errors renounced. There also exist numerous formulae for RCs seeking admission to the Greek Church, renouncing esp. the *Filioque and the Council of *Florence (1439), to which has been added more recently a special anathema against Papal *infallibility. During the last three centuries there have been many conversions from Protestantism to Orthodoxy, for which are required abjurations of the *Double Procession, and also of the denials of the *Real Presence, the Priesthood, the cult of the saints and images, and various Protestant tenets.

Abjuration, Oath of.

An oath for renouncing the Stuart dynasty, to be sworn by everyone who took office, civil, military, or spiritual, was first proposed in 1690, but not made compulsory until 1702 by the Abjuration Act 1701. It was reimposed by the Security of the Sovereign Act 1714 and the Treason Act 1766. In 1778 it was imposed on RCs in England as a condition of the removal of various disabilities. Among the matters to be abjured were the claims of the Pretender, the temporal power of the Pope and his right to depose, and the tenets that heretics may lawfully be put to death and that faith need not be kept with them. Its imposition was finally abolished in 1858 and its place taken by a new form of the Oath of *Allegiance.

ablutions. (1) The washing of fingers and chalice by the celebrant after the Communion in the Mass. The ceremony became part of the Eucharistic rite in the 10th or 11th cent. Its performance varied; the chalice usually received only one ablution with wine, and the fingers were rinsed either with wine or with water or, later, with both. In the RC Church the rite was regulated in the *Missal of *Pius V, which prescribed a twofold ablution of the chalice first with wine, then with wine and water, the ablution of the fingers with wine and water being connected with the latter. Since 1969 it has been permissible to use one ablution, of water only, and the ablution now may be postponed until after the end of the Mass. In the *Mozarabic and Greek rites the ablutions are performed privately after the Mass; in the other E. rites, however, immediately after the Communion and before the concluding prayers. The development of the ceremony is a consequence of the belief in the Eucharistic Presence and an expression of reverence due to Christ present under the Sacred Species.

(2) In the RC Church the rinsing of the mouth after the reception of the Bl Sacrament with wine by the new priests in the Ordination Mass, which was customary until 1968, and a similar rinsing with water formerly common at the Communion of the Sick. The W. custom was probably connected with the medieval practice of giving the communicants a draught of unconsecrated wine immediately after Communion to cleanse the mouth. A similar custom exists in the E., where in many places the communicants receive unconsecrated wine after Communion at the Liturgy.

On (1), W. Lockton, *The Treatment of the Remains at the Eucharist* (1920).

On (2), P. Browe, SJ, 'Mittelalterliche Kommunionriten', *JLW* 15 (1941), pp. 23–66; '5, Die Ablution', pp. 48–57. Jungmann (1958 edn.), 2, pp. 510–20; Eng. tr., 2, pp. 411–19.

F. *Cabrol, OSB, and S. Pétridès in *DACL* 1 (pt. 1; 1907), cols. 103–11, s.v.

abortion. See CONTRACEPTION, PROCREATION, AND ABORTION, ETHICS OF.

Abraham (or **Abram**, Gen. 11: 26–17: 5), OT *Patriarch. His story is told in Gen. 11: 26–25: 18. Having journeyed from Ur of the Chaldeans, he settled in Haran, whence he set out for the land of Canaan, in response to a Divine command (Gen. 12: 1). Famine then drove him into Egypt. On his return, he delivered his nephew Lot from the captivity of Chedorlaomer, king of Elam, and was blessed by *Melchizedek, king of Salem (Gen. 14). Yahweh promised him a son by his wife Sarai (Sarah) and an innumerable posterity, confirming His promises by a covenant. After the birth of his son *Isaac, Abraham's faith was put to a severe test by a command to sacrifice his son (Gen. 22). When Abraham had shown his readiness even for this act of obedience, a ram was substituted before the sacrifice was actually offered, and Abraham was rewarded by the formal renewal of God's promises.

Scholarly opinion is divided about both the historicity and the date of the Abraham traditions. The older view, still held by some critics, is that Abraham lived c.1800 BC; others (e.g. T. L. Thompson) see the Abraham material as having its origins in the period of Israel's settlement in Palestine (c.1200 BC), whilst J. Van Seters argues that the tradition is essentially a literary creation of the age of the Exile (c.550 BC).

The Christian Church has always recognized in Abraham her spiritual ancestor on account of his faith, a conception worked out by St *Paul (Rom. 4: 11; Gal. 3: 7), St James (2: 21–3), and the author of Hebrews (11: 8–10). The Fathers, e.g. St *Clement of Rome, St *Ambrose, and St *Augustine, exalted his obedience in leaving his homeland. His willingness to sacrifice his son furnished the Fathers with a model of perfect obedience to the will of God, even in the severest trials. It came to prefigure the death of Christ, and many writers, e.g. *Tertullian, *Origen, St *Cyril of Alexandria, elaborated on the similarities. In the *Canon of the Mass and in the sequence '*Lauda Sion' the immolation of Isaac prefigures the Sacrifice of the Mass. There is a parallel Jewish Rabbinic tradition of lively speculation upon the so-called 'Binding' of Isaac. The story of Abraham has continued to be a rich source of theological reflection, figuring, e.g., in the work of S. *Kierkegaard.

The term 'Abraham's bosom' is of Rabbinic origin and is used by Christ in the parable of Dives and Lazarus (Lk. 16: 22). Since the time of St Augustine it has been understood to signify the place of repose where Abraham is.

Abraham has a major place in histories of Israel and in works on the Patriarchs (q.v.). A. Parrot, *Abraham et son temps* (Cahiers d'Archéologie Biblique, 14; 1962); T. L. Thompson, *The Historicity of the Patriarchal Narratives: The Quest for the Historical Abraham* (Beihefte zur *ZATW*, 133; 1974); J. Van Seters, *Abraham in History and Tradition* (1975). A. Alt, *Der Gott der Väter* (Beiträge zur Wissenschaft von Alten und Neuen Testament, Dritte Folge, 12; 1929); Eng. tr. in Alt's *Essays on Old Testament History and Religion* (Oxford, 1966), pp. 1–77. R. E. Clements, *Abraham and David: Genesis XV and its Meaning for Israelite Tradition* (Studies in Biblical Theology, 2nd ser. 5; 1967). *Abraham, Père des Croyants* (Cahiers Sioniens, 5. 2; June 1951, with contributions by E. Tisserant, J. *Daniélou, SJ, and others); R. Martin-Achard, *Actualité d'Abraham* (Bibliothèque Théologique; Neuchâtel, 1969). See also comm. on Gen. cited s.v.

Abraham, Apocalypse of. An apocryphal writing, dating from perhaps as early as the 1st cent. AD. The opening chapters (1–8) recount *Abraham's conversion from idolatry. The rest of the book (9–32) describes a series of visions seen by Abraham in the heavens, showing the nature of sin and the Fall and its issue in God's destruction of the *Temple. The book ends (32) with a promise that God will deliver His chosen. The work in all probability goes back to a lost Greek or even Hebrew or Aramaic original, but the text survives only in a late Slavonic version. The earliest MS ('Codex Sylvester') dates from the 14th cent. In its present form the book shows clear traces of Christian influence, particularly in the later chapters, although the opening 'legendary' part of the book is based on Jewish tradition.

The Slavonic text has been pub. twice—by two Russian scholars, N. Tikhonravov and J. Sreznevsky (both at St Petersburg, 1863). A facsimile ed. was issued ibid., 1891. Ger. tr., with app. crit., by G. N. Bonwetsch (Leipzig, 1897). Eng. trs., with introd., by G. H. Box (London, 1918); R. Rubinkiewicz and H. G. Lunt in J. H. Charlesworth (ed.), *The Old Testament Pseudepigrapha*, 1 (1983), pp. 681–705; and by A. Pennington in H. F. D. Sparks (ed.), *The Apocryphal Old Testament* (Oxford, 1984), pp. 363–91.

Abraham, Testament of. An apocryphal writing, describing how *Abraham, unwilling to face death, is taken to heaven by the Archangel *Michael and has a vision of the two roads leading to hell and paradise and learns how most men choose the former. After praying for the forgiveness of sinners, he is brought back to earth and finally borne by the Angel of Death to paradise. The Testament exists in two Greek recensions (apparently its original language), as well as in Romanian, Arabic, Ethiopic, and Coptic versions. In the last three of these versions it is supplemented by 'Testaments' of Isaac and of Jacob. It was very popular in the E. Church from the 5th cent. onwards. It may have been written as early as the 2nd cent., but opinions have differed both as to its date and as to whether the author was a Jew or a Christian.

Gk. text ed. M. R. James, with extracts from the Arabic version ed. W. E. Barnes (Texts and Studies, 2, no. 2; Cambridge, 1892). Gk. text also ed., with Fr. tr. and introd., by F. Schmidt (Texte und Studien zum Antiken Judentum, 11; Tübingen, 1986). Eng. tr. of the Gk. text by G. H. Box, with tr. of the Coptic version of the Testaments of Isaac and Jacob by S. Gaselee (London, 1927). Further Eng. tr. of the Gk. text by N. Turner in H. F. D. Sparks (ed.), *The Apocryphal Old Testament* (Oxford, 1984), pp. 393–421, with bibl. Fr. tr. of Gk. text and Oriental versions, with full introd. and bibl., by M. Delcor (Studia in Veteris Testamenti Pseudepigrapha, 2; Leiden, 1973). G. E. W. Nickelsburg, Jun. (ed.), *Studies on the Testament of Abraham* (Society of Biblical Literature, Septuagint and Cognate Studies, 6 [1976]).

Abraham Ecchellensis (1600–64), *Maronite scholar. A native of Hekel or Ecchel on Mt. Lebanon, he studied at the Maronite College in Rome and taught Syriac and Arabic in Rome and Paris. In 1660 he became a scriptor in the *Vatican library. He published several important works on oriental languages, among them an edition of 84 spurious Arabic *Nicene Canons (1645) and Syriac and Arabic versions of 3 Macc. and of Ruth for the Paris *Polyglot.

J. Lamy in *DTC* 1 (1903), cols. 116–18; L. Petit in *DHGE* 1 (1912), cols. 169–71, both s.v.

Abrahams, Israel (1858–1925), Rabbinic scholar. Educated at University College, London, he was appointed reader in Talmudic and Rabbinic literature at Cambridge in 1902. He became prominent as a leader of 'Liberal Judaism'. In his later years he applied himself esp. to the study of Christian origins in their relation to their Rabbinic background, setting out his conclusions in two series of *Studies in Pharisaism and the Gospels* (1917, 1924). From 1889 to 1907 he edited (with C. J. Goldsmid *Montefiore) the *Jewish Quarterly Review*.

G. A. Kohut (ed.), *Jewish Studies in Memory of Israel Abrahams* (New York, 1927), with select bibl. of Abrahams' works, pp. xix–xlvii; suppl. bibl. by S. Levy in *Jewish Historical Society of England*, Miscellanies, 3 (1937), pp. 41–6. H. Loewe, *Israel Abrahams* (1944).

Absolute Idealism. 'Idealism' is the name sometimes given to philosophical theories according to which reality is mental or spiritual (ideal from 'idea') rather than material or independent of mind. Absolute Idealism is a kind of Idealism chiefly associated with G. W. F. *Hegel, but it can also be found in varying degrees in writers such as J. G. *Fichte, F. W. J. von *Schelling, T. *Carlyle, S. T.

*Coleridge, F. H. *Bradley, and B. *Bosanquet. It is called 'Absolute' in order to distinguish it from 'Subjective Idealism'. Subjective Idealism is typically understood as holding that the only reality is ideas in the human mind. Absolute Idealism, by contrast, says that there is significant reality outside the human mind. It came to exercise a strong influence on British speculative thought, including philosophical theology, in the decades immediately preceding World War I.

For its influence on British theology see C. C. J *Webb, *A Study of Religious Thought in England from 1850* (1933).

absolution. The formal act of a bishop or priest pronouncing the forgiveness of sins by Christ to penitent sinners, in virtue of Christ's gift of the Holy Spirit to the Apostles empowering them to forgive or to retain sins (Jn. 20: 23). A formula of absolution is included in many liturgical acts of worship, but, acc. to the traditional Catholic belief, *mortal sins (in modern formularies 'grave sins') are normally absolved only in the Sacrament of *Penance. The medieval development of private confession, and in particular the devotional practice of frequent confession, led to a widespread tendency to seek formal absolution even for venial sins, though this was never officially required. The need for a formal absolution by an ordained minister is commonly denied among Protestants, who also generally do not ascribe any sacramental force to such an absolution.

Two methods of absolution have been, and still are, in use—the indicative and the precatory. By *indicative* is meant the use by the absolver of such formulae as 'I absolve thee', whereas in *precatory* methods of absolution the priest prays formally that God will absolve an individual or a congregation. In the E., the precatory form is always used, though in the Russian Church, and possibly elsewhere, the indicative is added. The RC Church uses the indicative (preceded by the precatory, but holding this insufficient if used alone) within the Sacrament of Penance, and the precatory for other liturgical purposes. The Anglican BCP provides the indicative form of absolution for individuals in the Office for the *Visitation of the Sick and the precatory form for use in e.g. the Communion Office. The American BCP (1979), however, provides for the use of either the indicative or the precatory form in its rite for the Reconciliation of a Penitent. The form of absolution in Morning and Evening Prayer in the BCP is usually held to be only *declaratory*, i.e. the pronouncement that God forgives those who repent.

A. Villien in *DDC* 1 (1935), cols. 120–3. See also bibl. under PENANCE.

absolution prayer, a prayer until recently found in the Divine Office after the Psalms and before the lessons of each *nocturn. The name has been derived from *absolutio* in the sense of completion, on the ground that the prayer ended a section of the office; but the prayer did not appear in its final form until the 13th cent., when *absolutio* was already a technical term, and further, one of the prayers was of a penitential character.

Absolutions of the Dead. The title given to the service in the RC Church formerly said after the *Requiem Mass in the presence of the body before it was taken from the church. It could also be said even though the body was not present. The title is derived from the occurrence of the word 'absolve' in two of the prayers. The service consisted of prayers for the departed soul, and the censing and aspersing of the body during the saying of the *Lord's Prayer. One of the concluding prayers is found in the earliest Gregorian MSS, but the service as a whole was medieval. An account of a funeral by St *Theodore of Tarsus, Abp. of Canterbury (d. 690), definitely excludes it.

In 1969 it was replaced by a final commendation. After a short address and silence, the body is sprinkled with water and censed. After responses a collect is said and a chant sung as the body is carried to the church door.

abstinence. A penitential practice, consisting in abstaining from the use of certain kinds of food. It is thus commonly distinguished from *fasting (q.v.), which means the refusal of all, or all but a strictly limited quantity of, food, irrespective of its kind. It is practised among most peoples in different forms and for various reasons, e.g. among Egyptians, Indians, Greeks, Arabs. The Jewish Law contained elaborate food prohibitions (Lev. 11), which, however, were abrogated by the New Dispensation, the only apparent exceptions being blood and things strangled (Acts 15). From early Christian times, however, other kinds of abstinence were practised, esp. among the hermits. Thus St *Antony and his followers abstained from all food save bread, salt, and water, and *Pachomius and the Egyptian monks followed a similar diet. It was carried to excess in several early heretical sects who taught dualistic doctrines, e.g. the *Manichees and various other *Gnostic bodies. In the W. more or less severe abstinence throughout the year is practised by most contemplative orders, such as the *Carthusians, *Carmelites, and some *Benedictine congregations. Both in E. and W. the Friday abstinence of all Christians in commemoration of the Passion was in use from early times. It is mentioned by *Clement of Alexandria and *Tertullian as an established custom, and was extended to Saturday in the W. at about the same time. The practice was attacked by *Jovinian in the 4th cent., and later by the *Reformers, who considered it to be contrary to the Gospel.

Among RCs abstinence from flesh-meat has traditionally been observed on all Fridays in the year (except such as coincided with *Feasts of Obligation), Wednesdays in Lent, and certain other occasions such as *Vigils and *Rogation Days. By the Apostolic Constitution *Paenitemini* of 17 Feb. 1966, the penitential days were reduced to Fridays (except when Feasts of Obligation), *Ash Wednesday or the first day of Lent, and *Good Friday, and Episcopal Conferences were permitted to vary these days and to substitute for abstinence other forms of penance, particularly works of charity or piety; advantage of this concession was taken in many countries. The *CIC* (1983), cans. 1250 f. enjoins 'abstinence from meat, or from some other food as determined by the Episcopal Conference', on the same days, while still allowing Episcopal conferences to substitute other forms of penance (can. 1253). The law of abstinence is binding from the age of 14 (can. 1252). In the Greek and other E. Churches the practice of abstinence (ξηροφαγία, 'dry food') is far more rigid. It extends to all Wednesdays and Fridays of the year, all days of the Major (Lent) Fast including Sundays, and

several other periods, bringing up the number of days of abstinence to about 150; and not only meat, but fish, eggs, milk, cheese, oil, and wine are also generally forbidden (fish is allowed on *Palm Sunday and 25 Mar., and oil and wine on Saturdays and Sundays in Lent, except *Holy Saturday, when no oil is permitted). In the C of E, though there is nothing formally enjoined in the matter of abstinence as distinct from fasting, the Friday abstinence has never been completely abandoned. Its wider observance in modern times has been due esp. to the *Oxford Movement. See also FASTS AND FASTING.

Arts. s.v. in *DTC* 1 (1903), cols. 261–77 (several authors). See also bibl. to FASTS AND FASTING.

Abuna (Eth. and Arab. *abu-na*, 'our father'). The Patriarch of the *Ethiopian Church.

Abyssinian Church. See ETHIOPIAN CHURCH.

Acacian schism. In the *Monophysite controversy, a temporary schism (482–519) between *Rome and the E. which arose out of the Emp. *Zeno's *Henoticon (q.v.). It began during the Patriarchate of Acacius (471–89) at *Constantinople. Despite the attempts of Flavitas (490) and Euphemius (490–6), Acacius' successors, to heal it, it continued till the accession of Justin (518).

On Acacius, see M. Jugie, AA, in *DHGE* 1 (1912), cols. 244–8, s.v. E. *Schwartz, *Publizistische Sammlungen zum Acacianischen Schisma* (Abh. (Bayr.), 1934, Heft 10). W. H. C. Frend, *The Rise of the Monophysite Movement* (Cambridge, 1972), pp. 143–254, *passim*.

Acacius of Caesarea (d. 365), *Arian theologian. A disciple of *Eusebius Pamphili and his successor in the see of *Caesarea (in Palestine) in 341, he was a representative of strict Arianism. Under the Emp. Constantius he was pronounced deposed by the Council of *Sardica (343) and became one of the principal representatives of the *Homoeans. He proposed a Homoean Creed at the Council of *Seleucia in 359 and drew up the acts (now lost) of the Homoean Synod of Constantinople in 360. Under *Jovian he signed the Creed of *Nicaea at Antioch in 363, but returned to Arianism under Valens. He was deposed in 365 by the *Semiarian Synod of Lampsacus. Among his works were 17 vols. on Eccles. and other treatises, which now exist only in fragments. His followers ('Acacians') were for a short time (357–61) a distinct and important theological party.

The main sources are *Jerome, *De Vir. Ill.* 98, and *Socrates, *HE* 2. 4, together with St Jerome's letters. Part of a polemical treatise against *Marcellus of Ancyra is preserved by *Epiphanius, *Haer.* 72. 6–10. Fragments on the Ep. to the *Romans ed. by K. Staab, *Pauluskommentare aus der griechischen Kirche* (1933), pp. 53–6; further fragments ed. R. Devreesse, *Les anciens commentateurs grecs de l'Octateuque et des Rois* (ST 201; 1959), pp. 105–22. J.-M. Leroux, 'Acace, évêque de Césarée de Palestine, (341–365)', in F. L. Cross (ed.), *Studia Patristica*, 8 (1966), pp. 82–5.

Acarie, Mme (1566–1618), 'Mary of the Incarnation', one of the founders of the Reformed *Carmelites in France. Barbe Jeanne Avrillot was educated by the *Poor Clares at Longchamps, outside Paris; she wanted to enter the community, but, in obedience to her parents, in 1584 she married Pierre Acarie, who was a distant relation. They had six children and Mme Acarie was a devoted wife and mother. Their house (the *hôtel Acarie*) became a centre of charitable works and intense spirituality. In her life of prayer she experienced visions and *ecstasies, but her spiritual directors, *Benet of Canfield and the *Carthusian Richard Beaucousin, advised her to hold them at bay as inimical to a truly contemplative life. Reading F. de Ribera's 1601 translation of the Life of St *Teresa of Ávila, she felt called to introduce the Reformed Carmelites into France; she was helped by Mlle de Longueville and P. de *Bérulle (a relation of her husband), and the first house was founded in 1604. She also assisted Mme de Sainte-Beuve in bringing the *Ursulines to Paris and supported Bérulle in the foundation of the *Oratory in 1611. After her husband's death in 1613 she entered the Carmelite house in Amiens as a lay sister, taking the name 'Marie de l'Incarnation'. In 1616 she transferred to Pontoise. She died there in 1618, having spent some thirty years as a married woman and some four as a Carmelite. She was beatified in 1791. She was frequently called upon to give spiritual guidance, but only *Les Vrays Exercises de la Bienheureuse Sœur Marie de l'Incarnation ... Très propres à toutes Ames qui désirent ensuyvre sa bonne vie* (1622) was posthumously published from her papers.

A. Duval, *La Vie admirable de Sœur Marie de l'Incarnation* (1621; repr. 1893). J.-B.-A. Boucher, *Vie de la Bienheureuse Sœur Marie de l'Incarnation* (1800); Bruno de J[ésus] M[arie], OCD, *La Belle Acarie* [1942], incl. text of her *Exercises*, pp. 727–50, and bibl. Other Lives by E. de Broglie ('Les Saints', 1903) and L. C. Sheppard (London, 1953). E. Dubois, 'The hôtel Acarie: a meeting place for European currents of spirituality in early seventeenth-century France', *Durham University Journal*, 71 (1979), pp. 187–96. Bremond, 2 (1916), pp. 193–262; Eng. tr., 2 (1930), pp. 145–94.

Acathistus (Gk. ἀκάθιστος, 'not sitting', because it was sung standing), a famous liturgical hymn in honour of the BVM, sung in the Orthodox Church on the Saturday of the fifth week of *Lent. It consists of 24 stanzas, alternately long and short, each beginning with one of the letters of the Greek alphabet. The first part of the text is based on the events of Christ's life, from the *Annunciation to His *Presentation in the Temple; the second praises the mystery of the Incarnation. Dating prob. from the early 6th cent., it may be the work of St *Romanos 'Melodus', although this attribution is disputed. It is possible that Patr. *Sergius of Constantinople appointed it to be sung in thanksgiving for the deliverance of his city from the Avars and Slavs in 626, and that Patr. *Germanus established a special feast, at which it was recited, in memory of the defeat of the Arabs before the capital in 717–18; but neither of these is likely to be the author. The attributions to George Pisides (early 6th cent.), George of Nicomedia (late 9th cent.), and Patr. *Photius are impossible.

E. Wellesz, *The Akathistos Hymn* (Monumenta Musicae Byzantinae Transcripta, 9; Copenhagen, 1957); G. G. Meersseman, OP, *Der Hymnos Akathistos im Abendland* (Spicilegium Friburgense, 2–3; 1958–60); C. A. Trypanis, *Fourteen Early Byzantine Cantica* (Wiener Byzantinische Studien, 5; 1968), pp. 17–39, incl. text. D. Attwater, *The Akathistos Hymn: Translated from the original Greek. With historical and liturgical notes* (1934). R. A. Fletcher, 'Three Early Byzantine Hymns and their Place in the Liturgy of the Church of Constantinople', *BZ* 51 (1958), pp. 53–65, esp. pp. 63–5.

accentus. The name given since the 16th cent. to *plainsong of the simple recitation type as sung by the officiant (celebrant, deacon, etc.). The more elaborate kind of chant, as found in antiphons or hymns, whether sung by choir or congregation, is termed *concentus*.

Acceptants. Those who 'accepted' the bull '*Unigenitus' (1713) in the *Jansenist controversy, as contrasted with the *Appellants who appealed against it.

Accession Service. The form of prayer for use on the anniversary of the accession of the reigning sovereign, printed at the end of the BCP. Such forms have been in use in England and Wales since 1576. The Order is put out by the Sovereign in Council. Strictly it has no other authority and is not part of the BCP, though can. 2 of the 1640 canons recognized the service. No service was issued for *Charles II's reign, as 30 Jan., the date of his *de jure* accession, was provided for by the commemoration of King *Charles the Martyr. Various revisions have been made from time to time. The last and most comprehensive, that of 1901, is the model of the service still in use. Here provision is made (1) for special forms of Morning and Evening Prayer (with proper Psalms, Lessons, etc.); (2) for a proper Collect, Epistle, and Gospel at the Eucharist; and (3) for a separate service, opening with the *Te Deum. A fresh Order in Council is issued at the beginning of every reign, and when modifications are required through other changes in the Royal Family. Since 1936, the first revision after the disestablishment of the Church in *Wales, the use of the service has been ordered only for churches in the provinces of *Canterbury and *York, and even there its use is now rare.

For the forms put out in 1576 and 1578, see W. K. Clay (ed.), *Liturgies and Occasional Forms of Prayer set forth in the Reign of Queen Elizabeth* (*Parker Soc., 1847), pp. 548–61. D. Maclean in *PBD* (1912), p. 2.

accident. In medieval philosophy, following *Aristotle, an entity whose essential nature it is to inhere in another entity as a subject (*ens in alio*). It is thus to be contrasted with a substance (*ens per se*).

The term has played an important part in Eucharistic doctrine since the *Schoolmen evolved the theory of the *accidentia sine subjecto* ('accidents without a subject') to elucidate the mystery of the Presence. The concept was used to explain how, after the changing of the substances of the bread and wine into those of the Body and Blood of Christ, the accidents of the former, e.g. quantity, colour, taste, etc., continued to exist and be perceptible by the senses. St *Thomas Aquinas, e.g., taught (*Summa Theol.* 3. q. 77) that after the consecration through miraculous Divine intervention the accident of quantity continued to exist without inhering in a substance and that in this accident the other accidents inhered in a natural manner. By the end of the 14th cent. the explanation in terms of accidents had come to be widely accepted, but J. *Wycliffe and J. *Huss, as well as M. *Luther and the *Reformers generally, rejected it. The Council of *Trent taught the continuance of the *species* of bread and wine after consecration, but without mention of accidents. The doctrine of the *accidentia sine subjecto*, though very generally accepted among RC theologians, has in fact never been formally defined. See also TRANSUBSTANTIATION.

P. Mielle in *DTC* 1 (1903), cols. 302–4; C. Fabro in *EC* 1 (1949), cols. 191 f., with bibl. Full discussion of accidents in Eucharistic theology by F. Jansen, SJ, in *DTC* 5 (1913), cols. 1368–452, s.v. 'Eucharistiques (Accidents)', with bibl.

accidie (Gk. ἀκηδία, 'negligence', 'indifference'). In its general sense the word is used several times in the *Septuagint (e.g. Ps. 119: 28, Is. 61: 3), but later its meaning was modified to convey sadness, spiritual torpor, and sloth, as in *Hermas (*Vis.* 3. 11. 3). The conception was first fully analysed by *Evagrius Ponticus, and from then on the word became a technical term of Christian asceticism. It figures as one of the deadly sins in the lists of the spiritual writers of antiquity and the Middle Ages. The classical description of it, given by *Cassian (*Instit.* 10. 2), depicts it as a state of restlessness and inability either to work or pray. It is treated at length by St *Thomas Aquinas (*Summa Theol.* 2^a 2^{ae}, q. 35) and mentioned in the '*Ancren Riwle' and the writings of Richard *Rolle of Hampole. Accidie is generally regarded as affecting particularly monks and hermits, who are more liable to it than other persons owing to the outward monotony of their life. The term received a new lease of life in England through the influence of F. *Paget, who, in his 'Introductory Essay Concerning Accidie' in *The Spirit of Discipline* (1891), studied it in a number of ancient and modern authors as well as in its modern manifestations.

S. Wenzel, *The Sin of Sloth: Acedia in Medieval Thought and Literature* (Chapel Hill, NC [1967]). G. Bardy in *Dict. Sp.* 1 (1937), cols. 166–9, s.v. 'Acedia', with extensive patristic refs.

accommodation. In theology, the adaptation of a text or teaching to altered circumstances.

(1) It is sometimes used to connote the giving to a text in Scripture a meaning not intended by the writer, e.g. St *Matthew's application of 'Out of Egypt have I called my son' (Hos. 11: 1; cf. Mt. 2: 15) to Christ where 'son' meant originally the nation of Israel, or the reference formerly in the Roman Mass of Pharaoh's words 'Ite ad Joseph' ('Go to Joseph', Gen. 41: 55) to the Lord's foster-father. This usage of the word is mainly found in RC writers.

(2) 'Accommodation' (Ger. *Herablassung*, lit. 'condescension'; also *Akkommodation*) was also used by liberal German theologians of the 18th cent. to expound the mode of Divine communication through the Bible. J. S. *Semler and other exegetes maintained that beside the timeless and unchangeable element in Scripture, there were passages in which the Divine revelation was accommodated to the human understanding by being clothed in transitory forms. Such accommodation was met with esp. in the teaching of Christ. His explicit words and implicit assumptions about, e.g., the authorship of particular parts of the OT, the Messianic character of certain prophecies, or the objective reality of demon-possession, were explained, not as the necessary limitations of His human knowledge consequent on the reality of the Incarnation, but as the deliberate adjustment of His words and actions to the ideas and beliefs of contemporary Judaism. Under the influence of the rationalistic tendencies of the

*Enlightenment this form of exegesis often reduced the core of eternal truth to small proportions; e.g. the NT teaching on the *Atonement was explained as merely 'accommodation' to Jewish thought-forms and therefore without validity for later ages.

(3) The word is also used in a more general sense of the teaching by Christians of part only of the truth for the sake of prudence, or of the modification of the form of Christian teaching to secure its more ready acceptance. A notable instance of accommodation in this sense was the practice of the *Jesuit missionaries in China to use the word 't'ien' for God and to allow converts to continue in practices akin to ancestor-worship. Such accommodation was forbidden in 1715 by Clement XI and again in 1742 by *Benedict XIV. The method of 'reserve' advocated by I. *Williams in No. 80 of *Tracts for the Times*, entitled *On Reserve in Communicating Religious Knowledge*, has certain affinities with this form of 'accommodation'; but here the chief motive for adjustment was the need for reverence in speaking of sacred subjects.

Aceldama (RV, **Akeldama**). 'The field of blood', a piece of land in the neighbourhood of *Jerusalem, so named (1) acc. to Mt. 27: 8, because it was bought with the price of the Lord's blood; but (2) acc. to Acts 1: 18 f., because it was the scene of *Judas Iscariot's tragic end.

Acoemetae (Gk. ἀκοίμηται, 'sleepless ones'). A celebrated body of Orthodox monks. They were founded *c.*400 by Abbot Alexander (*c.*350–*c.*430), who, after having established a monastery on the Euphrates, went to *Constantinople, where he established a religious house whose monks were to observe absolute poverty, do no manual work, exercise a vigorous apostolate by means of missions, and keep up perpetual psalmody in alternating choirs. These ideas, which were complete novelties in Byzantine monasticism, attracted a great number of monks from other convents. They provoked, however, such hostility from the Patr. *Nestorius and others that Alexander was driven from Constantinople and, after many difficulties, founded a monastery on these lines at Gomon in Bithynia. Under his successor it was transferred to the modern Tchiboukli, on the middle Bosphorus, where the monks were first given by the populace their name of 'Acoemetae', which they henceforth kept. The Acoemetae, many of whom were taken for other foundations, e.g. *Studios, became ardent defenders of orthodoxy against the *Monophysites, their most famous member being their abbot St Marcellus, who signed the condemnation of *Eutyches at Constantinople in 448. In their struggle against Eutychianism, however, the monks later fell into the Nestorian heresy, for which they were excommunicated by Pope John II in 534. There are few mentions of them after this period. At an uncertain date they transferred their monastery to Constantinople, where they are mentioned in the 12th cent. As early as the time of Marcellus they had modified the exaggerated poverty enjoined by Alexander, and later possessed one of the most famous monastic libraries in the East.

Greek Life of St Alexander, ed., with Lat. tr. and introd., by E. de Stoop in *PO* 6 (1911), pp. 641–705. [E.] Marin, *Les Moines de Constantinople depuis la fondation de la ville jusqu'à la mort de Photius, 330–898* (1897), *passim*. J. Pargoire, AA, 'Un Mot sur les Acémètes' in *ÉO* 2 (1898), pp. 304–8 and 365–72. I. M. Phoundoules, Ἡ Εἰκοσιτετράωρος Ἀκοίμητος Δοξολογία (1963). E. Marin in *DTC* 1 (1903), cols. 304–8; J. Pargoire, AA, in *DACL* 1 (1907), cols. 307–21; S. Vailhé, AA, in *DHGE* 1 (1912), cols. 272–82, all s.v. 'Acémètes', with bibl.

acolyte. The first in rank of the two Lesser Ministries in the RC Church. Until 1972 acolytes formed one of the four *Minor Orders. They were specially delegated to the service of the altar, assisting priest and deacon, and administering the Eucharist both inside and outside Mass. The earliest mention of acolytes in Rome dates from 251, and about this time they were subjected to the regional deacons, prob. six to each region. In the early *Ordines Romani* they have a multitude of duties, incl. that of carrying the Eucharist. Gradually the *subdeacons and acolytes absorbed most of the functions of the other Minor Orders at Mass and Baptism. Some acolytes also became officers or secretaries to the Pope. The office of acolyte is also found in Africa in the time of St *Cyprian but seldom elsewhere in the W. in the early centuries.

Since 1972 the ministry of acolyte may be conferred on lay men, who thereby acquire no clerical status. Where the needs of the Church require, and no ministers are available, lay people may carry out most of their liturgical functions. The regulations are laid down in *CIC* (1983), can. 230.

J. *Morin, *Commentarius de Sacris Ecclesiae Ordinationibus*, 2 (Paris, 1655), pp. 197 f., 236–9, and *passim*. F. Wieland, *Die genetische Entwicklung der sog. Ordines Minores in den drei ersten Jahrhunderten* (RQ, Suppl. Heft 7; 1897), pp. 48–54 and 154–61. H. *Leclercq, OSB, in *DACL* 1 (pt. 1; 1907), cols. 348–56; F. [Philip] Oppenheim, OSB, in *EC* 1 (1949), cols. 198 f.

acosmism (Gk. ἀ, privative, and κόσμος, the 'ordered universe'). An extreme form of *pantheism (q.v.) which asserts that the totality of individual things is nothing but a manifestation of the Absolute and has no real being. It may be contrasted with those forms of pantheism which conceive of the Absolute as in some sense ingredient into individual things. The term was used by G. W. F. *Hegel, who apparently coined the word (*Encyclopädie*, § 50) to describe B. *Spinoza's system.

Acquaviva, Claudius. See AQUAVIVA, CLAUDIO.

act, human. In moral theology the term denotes the free and voluntary actions of a human being done with knowledge and attention. To such acts alone can moral praise or blame be accorded, since those which fall below this level are not full expressions of the will of man, as a being endowed with free will. An act can be made less than human by: (1) ignorance, insofar as this is not the fault of the person acting (see INVINCIBLE IGNORANCE), (2) force or constraint applied by an outside agent, (3) passion, insofar as its influence is independent of the will, (4) fear, if sufficient seriously to cloud the mind, or (5) habit, insofar as it destroys advertence to what one is doing.

Acta Apostolicae Sedis. The official gazette of the *Vatican, founded by *Pius X in the decree, 'Promulgandi Pontificias Constitutiones' (29 Sept. 1908). Publication began in Jan. 1909. About 12 issues appear each year.

Acta Sanctorum. The celebrated series of lives of the saints, arranged in the order of their feasts in the ecclesiastical year, which was begun by the *Bollandists, a small body of *Jesuit scholars, in the 17th cent. The plan was conceived by H. Rosweyde (d. 1629), who did not, however, see any of it completed. The first two vols. (Jan.) were published at Antwerp in 1643. By the date of the suppression of the order (1773), 50 vols. (to 7 Oct.) had been brought out. Three further vols. were edited by former Jesuits, *Premonstratensians, and others shortly afterwards, and in 1837 the work was resumed by the Society. In 1925 it reached 10 Nov., and in 1940 the introduction (or Propylaeum) to December was published.

New edn. of section Jan., vol. 1, to Oct., vol. 6, by J. Carnandet (Paris, 1863–8). M. D. Knowles, 'Great Historical Enterprises, 1. The Bollandists', *Transactions of the Royal Historical Society*, 5th ser. 5 (1958), pp. 147–66; repr. in his *Great Historical Enterprises* (1963), pp. 1–32. See also other works cited under BOLLANDISTS.

Acta Sanctorum Ordinis Sancti Benedicti. The history of the saints of the *Benedictine Order, of which J. *Mabillon published the first volume in 1668. It was completed in 1701.

Vols. 1–3 (pt. 1) repr. by the Benedictines of *Solesmes (Mâcon, 1935–9).

action (Lat. *actio*). A name once applied to the whole Mass either as a single sacrificial action or possibly as a contraction of the phrase *gratiarum actio*, i.e. 'thanksgiving', 'Eucharist'. Later it was applied in a more restricted sense to the *Canon of the Mass as the sacrificial action *par excellence*. The phrase survives in the Roman Missal in the heading of the *Communicantes prayer, 'Infra actionem'.

Action Française, French political movement. At the height of the Dreyfus affair in 1898, the teacher Henri Vaugeois and writer Maurice Pujo formed a Comité d'Action Française; it was made known to the public in a lecture by Vaugeois on 20 June and on 10 July 1899 appeared the first issue of *L'Action Française*, originally a fortnightly review. The Provençal intellectual, Charles Maurras, soon the leading figure, converted the movement to monarchism. Maurras blamed the internal and international weakness of France on the democracy of the Third Republic and argued that only a restoration of the monarchy could promote French glory abroad and ensure the right combination of authority and the autonomy of families, corporations, and regions at home. He was clerical rather than Catholic, and valued the Church as a principle of order and hierarchy rather than as a spiritual force. The movement flourished as the threat from Germany became greater. The Ligue de l'Action Française was set up in 1905. *L'Action Française* became a daily newspaper in 1908, edited by Léon Daudet, and was distributed by young hawkers, the Camelots du Roy, who also served as fighting squads. Support was always middle-class and strongest among the right-wing students of the Latin Quarter, who resented the *anticlericalism and pacificism of their professors and of certain republican politicians. During the 1914–18 war the Action Française was fiercely annexionist and after the war took a hard line against reconciliation with Germany. The movement was supported by integralist RCs but opposed by RCs of Le Sillon, the Association Catholique de la Jeunesse Française, and liberal bishops. In 1926 these opponents of the Action Française obtained its condemnation by Pope *Pius XI on the grounds of extreme nationalism and a cynical misappropriation of Catholic doctrine. Relations with the official royalist movement were equally strained, and in 1937 the royal Pretender, Henri, Comte de Paris, announced that only the House of France was qualified to define what the monarchy of the future would be. The Action Française responded late but vehemently to the threat of international Communism, and refused after 1936 to countenance a war with Nazi Germany that would lead to a triumph of Communism. In the period 1940–44 Maurras was isolated at Lyons between the government of Vichy and the collaborationists of Paris, but was tried for collaboration in 1945 and condemned to life imprisonment and national degradation. The last number of L'Action Française had appeared on 24 Aug. 1944. In 1951 Maurras was released; he died the following year, by which time the movement had disintegrated.

E. [J.] Weber, Action Française: Royalism and Reaction in Twentieth Century France (Stanford, Calif., 1962); E. R. Tannenbaum, The Action Française: Diehard Reactionaries in Twentieth-Century France (New York and London, 1962); L. Thomas, L'Action française devant l'Église (de Pie X à Pie XII) [1965]. E. Nolte, Der Faschismus in seiner Epoche (Munich, 1963), pp. 61–190; Eng. tr. (1965), pp. 29–141. S. M. Osgood, French Royalism since 1870 (2nd. edn., The Hague, 1970). C. Capitan Peter, Charles Maurras et l'idéologie d'Action française (1972); M. Sutton, Nationalism, Positivism and Catholicism: The Politics of Charles Maurras and the French Catholics 1890–1914 (Cambridge, 1982), passim; P. Boutang, Maurras: La destinée et l'œuvre [1984]. A. Dansette in NCE 1 (1967), pp. 97 f., s.v.

action sermon. Among Scottish *Presbyterians, the sermon preached before the administration of the Lord's Supper. J. *Calvin used the expression action de grâces for the thanksgiving which followed Communion, and from this use J. *Knox probably took it as a name for the whole service. The sermon has now become less important than the prayers preceding Communion, and is frequently omitted.

active life. As distinguished from the '*contemplative life', the 'active life' means (1) the cultivation of the Christian virtues and (2) a life devoted to Christian works, esp. works of fraternal charity, sometimes subdivided into *corporal works of mercy and such spiritual works as preaching. In sense (1) the active life is necessary for all Christians and is normally regarded as an essential preliminary to the contemplative life. Spiritual writers have disagreed about whether the active life in sense (2) is incumbent on all Christians in this world, at least sometimes, though most assert that some Christians are obliged to it by their state of life and vocation.

For bibl. see CONTEMPLATION.

Acton, John. See AYTON, JOHN.

Acton, John Emerich Edward Dalberg, first Baron Acton (1834–1902), historian. Born at Naples of émigré RC parents, he was educated at *Paris, Oscott (under N. *Wiseman), and Munich, where he formed a lifelong friendship with J. J. I. von *Döllinger. He was debarred from Cambridge by the unrepealed religious tests. From his early years an ardent liberal in politics, he became Whig MP for Carlow in 1859, and was thus brought into relations with W. E. *Gladstone, whom he much admired. He also became actively interested in the cause of religious liberty, taking over from J. H. *Newman in 1859 the editorship of the RC *Rambler (from 1862, Home and Foreign Review) in defence of liberal views. His own contributions reflected his immense range of knowledge, but the threat of a Papal veto owing to its anti-*Ultramontane tendencies led him to suspend it in 1864. Henceforward he endeavoured to resist the movement towards Ultramontanism in the RC Church. He strongly opposed the *Syllabus Errorum (1864), and in 1869 went to Rome to organize resistance to the definition of Papal Infallibility at the *Vatican Council, working in close conjunction with Döllinger when publishing in the Allgemeine Zeitung the famous series of letters under the signature '*Quirinus'. But he never formally broke with the RC Church, and in 1874 in some letters to The Times publicly explained his position on the basis of Gladstone's pamphlet on The Vatican Decrees. In his later years Acton's main energies were devoted to encouraging the study of modern history. He helped to found (1886), and often contributed to, the English Historical Review. In 1895 Lord Rosebery appointed him Regius Professor of Modern History at Cambridge in succession to Sir John *Seeley, where he delivered his famous inaugural lecture on the study of history (reprinted in Lectures on Modern History, ed. by J. N. *Figgis and R. V. Laurence, 1906). His last great work was to plan the Cambridge Modern History (12 vols., and index, 1901–11), for which he wrote the introductory chapter, though most of the work was not published till after his death. His posthumously published writings include Historical Essays and Studies (1907), The History of Freedom (1907), and Lectures on the French Revolution (1910), books partly based on studies which grew out of a long-projected, but never executed, 'History of Liberty'. A further collection of his writings was published under the title Essays on Church and State (1952).

Letters of Lord Acton to Mary, Daughter of the Right Hon. W. E. Gladstone, ed. with introd. memoir (pp. xi–lxxvii) by H. Paul (1904); F. A. *Gasquet, OSB, Lord Acton and his Circle [1906]; J. N. Figgis and R. V. Laurence (eds.), Selections from the Correspondence of the First Lord Acton (1917); Ignaz von Döllinger and Lord Acton, Briefwechsel 1850–1890, ed. V. Conzemius (3 vols., Munich, 1963–71); The Correspondence of Lord Acton and Richard Simpson, ed. J. L. Altholz, D. McElrath, and J. C. Holland (3 vols., Cambridge, 1971–5). Acton's Journal, 22 Nov. 1869–24 Jan. 1870, ed. E. Campion (Sydney, 1975). D. McElrath, Lord Acton: The Decisive Decade 1864–1874. Essays and Documents (Bibliothèque de la RHE 51; 1970). D. Mathew, Acton (1946); id., Lord Acton and his Times (1968); G. Himmelfarb, Lord Acton: A Study in Conscience and Politics (1952). Studies by U. Noack (Frankfurt, 1935, 1936, and 1947). G. E. Fasnacht, Acton's Political Philosophy (1952); L. Kochan, Acton on History (1954); H. A. MacDougall, OMI, The Acton–Newman Relations (New York, 1962). [W.] O. Chadwick, 'Lord Acton at the First Vatican Council', JTS NS 28 (1977), pp. 465–97. H. Tulloch, Acton (Historians on Historians; 1988). Bibl. in W. A. Shaw, A Bibliography of the Historical Works of Dr Creighton, etc. (Royal Historical Society, 1903), pp. 3–63.

Acts of the Apostles. The fifth Book of the NT, written by St *Luke the author of the Third Gospel. It outlines the mission of the Church from Christ's Ascension and the gift of the Holy Spirit to St *Paul's visit to Rome *c.* AD 62. The identity of authorship between the Third Gospel and Acts is now virtually undisputed, and there are some grounds for holding that both are the work of Luke, the companion of Paul mentioned in Col. 4: 14, Philem. 24, and 2 Tim. 4: 11. This is definitely stated by Christian writers from the latter part of the 2nd cent. onwards, e.g. the *Muratorian Canon, St *Irenaeus, *Clement of Alexandria, and *Tertullian. The chief objections to Lucan authorship are the inconsistencies between Acts and the Pauline Epistles, but these can be explained in part by their different aims. The accuracy of the author's information probably varies in different parts of the Book. There are errors (e.g. concerning *Theudas), but it would be unreasonable to expect modern attitudes to historical precision, and at some points where Acts coincides with profane history Luke has been supported by modern archaeological finds (e.g. by Sir William *Ramsay). In general the narrative is condensed and impressionistic, not exact in its details.

Scholars are far from unanimous on the question of date. Two different views were already held in antiquity. Acc. to the so-called *Anti-Marcionite 'Prologue of Luke' (at one time dated *c.*160–80), Acts was written in Achaia some time after the death of Paul. The more common early opinion dated the Book at the end of or shortly after the Apostle's first Roman captivity. *Eusebius based this view chiefly on 2 Tim. 4: 16 ff. It was followed by A. *Harnack, who considered it unlikely that Acts would have omitted any mention of Paul's martyrdom if it had already taken place. At the other extreme a few have put forward a 2nd-cent. date. Some have thought that parallels with *Josephus imply that the author had read his 'Antiquities' (93), but the majority would probably settle for the 80s. This is late enough to account for an idealized picture of the nascent Church, but prior to systematic *persecution by the Roman authorities.

The author will have used oral and perhaps written traditions; the apparent existence of doublets in the earlier chapters has been thought to support the latter hypothesis, and scholars such as Harnack once claimed success in separating these sources. Acc. to C. C. Torrey, Acts 1: 2–15: 35 is Luke's translation of a single Aramaic document emanating from *Jerusalem which was concerned to show the universal mission of Christianity. The so-called 'We-sections' (Acts 16: 10–17; 20: 5–15; 21: 1–18; 27: 1–28: 16, to which *Codex Bezae adds 11: 28) are still often believed to come from the author's own travel diary, thus revealing him as an eyewitness of many of the events he related, but many critics ascribe the use of the first person to one of the author's sources, or his own desire to achieve vividness in his narrative. In any case there are extensive sequences that supply detailed information, as well as others which give a more generalized account.

The text of Acts, which has come down to us in two recensions, presents a difficult critical problem. The shorter text is represented by most of the great uncial MSS, e.g. the *Codices Sinaiticus, Vaticanus, and Alexandrinus; the other, longer, text by the so-called '*Western text', esp. Codex Bezae. Several theories have been put forward to account for this divergence. Acc. to one view, represented e.g. by F. *Blass and T. *Zahn, Luke himself issued his work in two versions; acc. to another, which is much more widely held, the original text was expanded and smoothed over by some writer versed in tradition early in the 2nd cent.

The Book of Acts may be conveniently divided into six parts, tracing the progress of Christianity from Jerusalem to Rome. 1: 1–6: 7 describes the Jerusalem Church and the preaching of St *Peter; 6: 8–9: 31 the extension of the Church throughout Palestine and the preaching of St *Stephen; 9: 32–12: 24 the extension of the Church to *Antioch and the conversion of Cornelius; 12: 25–16: 5 Paul's first missionary journey and the Council of Jerusalem; 16: 6–19: 20 the conversion of Macedonia, Greece, and Asia; and 19: 21–28: 31 ends with Paul's journey to Rome as a prisoner and his witness to the Gospel there.

The Book emphasizes the Divine origin of Christianity, which is attested by the Apostles and their miracles and martyrdoms. In their discourses with the Jews they affirm that Jesus is the Messiah (2: 36; 4: 27; 9: 22, etc.), proclaimed as such by His Resurrection, of which they are the authorized witnesses (e.g. 1: 22; 3: 15), and foretold in the OT (2: 25–36; 13: 16–38). Salvation is offered through Him, but it is not so clearly associated with His death as it is by Paul. The most striking proofs of the Divine origin of the infant Church are the miraculous intervention of the Holy Spirit in her foundation (2: 1–4), the fervent charity of the first Christians (2: 44–7), the rapid propagation of Christianity, and the Divine help given to the Apostles, esp. to Peter and Paul (chs. 12 and 16). Belief in the Divine status of Christ is reflected, notably in the title 'Lord'. Sins are forgiven through *Baptism (2: 38), mention is made of the imposition of *hands (8: 15–17; 19: 6), which some have seen as foreshadowing *Confirmation, and all the faithful remain in fellowship in 'the breaking of bread' (ἡ κλάσις τοῦ ἄρτου, 2: 42; cf. 2: 46; 20: 7), the term used in Acts for the Eucharistic rite. Thus, acc. to Acts, the Church has her special rites from the beginning, by which Christianity is distinguished from Judaism. This distinction becomes noticeable esp. with the conversion of pagans (ch. 11) and through the decision of the Council of Jerusalem (ch. 15) to abrogate certain of the Mosaic observances. The infant Church seems to have been governed first only by the Apostles (2: 42; 4: 33), to whom the 'Seven' were added later (6: 1–6), as well as elders (πρεσβύτεροι, 14: 23; 15: 2, etc.) and bishops (ἐπίσκοποι, 20: 28), the latter two evidently not yet being distinguished.

The author may have had a number of aims: to defend Christianity against the charge of political subversion; to demonstrate the essential unity of the Church in its worldwide mission (and here he seems at least to have played down the dissensions which the Epp. show to have been serious), and perhaps to vindicate the part played by Paul. But his main aim can best be seen as to give a picture of what Christianity is, and how the Gospel spread from Jerusalem to Rome. This he does with the help of sermons and speeches, an emphasis on the main stages, and a selection of illuminating incidents. He has undoubtedly given a dramatic picture; a majority of scholars accept it as at least substantially reliable, however partial.

Modern comm. by A. *Loisy (Paris, 1920); E. Jacquier (Études Bibliques, 2nd edn., 1926); F. J. Foakes Jackson (Moff. Comm., 1931); F. F. Bruce (London, 1951; 3rd edn., Grand Rapids, Mich., and Leicester, 1990); E. Haenchen (KEK, 10th edn., 1956; 14th edn., 1965; Eng. tr., 1971); C. S. C. Williams (Black's NT Comm., 1957); H. Conzelmann (Hb. NT 1963; 2nd edn., 1972; Eng. tr., Philadelphia, Pa. [1987]); R. P. C. Hanson (New Clarendon Bible, 1967); J. Munck, ed. W. F. Albright and C. S. Mann (Anchor Bible, 1967), and C. K. Barrett (ICC, 1994 ff.). M.-É. Boismard and A. Lamouille, *Le Texte Occidental des Actes des Apôtres: Reconstitution et Réhabilitation* (2 vols., 1984). A. Harnack, *Die Apostelgeschichte* (1908; Eng. tr., 1909), and other works; C. C. Torrey, *The Composition and Date of Acts* (Harvard Theological Studies, no. 1, 1916); F. J. Foakes Jackson and K. *Lake (eds.), *The Beginnings of Christianity* (5 vols., 1920–33); W. L. Knox, *St Paul and the Church of Jerusalem* (1925); H. J. *Cadbury, *The Making of Luke–Acts* (1927); A. C. Clark, *The Acts of the Apostles* (1933; on the text); W. L. Knox, *The Acts of the Apostles* (1948); M. *Dibelius, *Aufsätze zur Apostelgeschichte* (1951; Eng. tr., 1956); H. J. Cadbury, *The Book of Acts in History* (1955); E. Trocmé, *Le 'Livre des Actes' et l'Histoire* (1957); J. Dupont, OSB, *Les Sources du Livre des Actes* (1960; Eng. tr., 1964); id., *Études sur les Actes des Apôtres* (1967); J. C. O'Neill, *The Theology of Acts in its Historical Setting* (1961); C. K. Barrett, *Luke the Historian in Recent Study* (A. S. Peake Memorial Lecture, 1961); M. Wilcox, *The Semitisms of Acts* (Oxford, 1965); L. E. Keck and J. L. Martyn (eds.), *Studies in Luke–Acts* (1968); A. [A. T.] Ehrhardt, *The Acts of the Apostles* (Manchester, 1969); M. Hengel, *Zur urchristlichen Geschichtsschreibung* (1979; Eng. tr., *Acts and the History of Earliest Christianity*, 1979); P. F. Esler, *Community and Gospel in Luke–Acts: The Social and Political Motivations of Lucan Theology* (Society for New Testament Studies, Monograph Series, 57; Cambridge, 1987); G. Lüdemann, *Das frühe Christentum nach den Traditionen der Apostelgeschichte* (1987; Eng. tr., *Early Christianity according to the Traditions in Acts*, 1989); R. C. Tannehill, *The Narrative Unity of Luke–Acts: A Literary Interpretation*, 2 (Minneapolis [1990]). [W.] W. Gasque, *A History of Criticism of the Acts of the Apostles* (Beiträge zur Geschichte der biblischen Exegese, 17; 1975; repr. with addendum, Peabody, Mass. [1989]). See also works cited under LUKE, GOSPEL OF ST, and historical works on PAUL, ST, cited s.v., esp. those of J. Knox, G. Bornkamm, and R. Jewett.

Acts of the Martyrs. Of the numerous separate accounts of early Christian martyrdoms of varying authenticity, the most reliable are those that follow the official shorthand reports of the trials. Very few of these, however, have survived, perhaps the most perfect specimen of this type being the 'Acta Proconsularia' of St *Cyprian. A second category, the so-called 'Passiones', are the stories of martyrdoms written by Christian authors and based on eyewitness accounts. To this type belong the 'Martyrdoms' of St *Ignatius, of St *Polycarp, of the Martyrs of Lyons, the famous 'Passion of St *Perpetua and St Felicitas', the 'Passion of St *Irenaeus', and others. In all these the miraculous element is much restricted, a feature which did not appeal to the popular taste. In their later versions the sober account of the original was frequently embellished with miraculous and other apocryphal or legendary material, e.g. in the cases of St Perpetua, the *Scillitan Martyrs, and other authentic Acts. A third category belongs completely to the realm of legend, with probably no historical kernel whatever. Such are the Acts of St *Catherine of Alexandria and those of St *George.

*Eusebius of Caesarea was probably the first Christian author to produce a collection of Acts of Martyrs; his great work, the Συναγωγὴ τῶν Ἀρχαίων Μαρτυρίων, is unfortunately lost, but a smaller one on the Palestinian martyrs survives in Greek fragments and in a complete Syriac version. In the W. Church the Acts of the Martyrs were carefully collected and used in the Liturgy from early times, as is testified by St *Augustine.

The most comprehensive collection is contained in the *Bollandist *Acta Sanctorum*. Another well-known set is that of T. *Ruinart, *Acta Primorum Martyrum Sincera et Selecta* (1689). Convenient edn., with Eng. tr., by H. Musurillo, SJ (Oxford Early Christian Texts, 1972). G. Lanata, *Gli Atti dei Martiri come Documenti Processuali* (Studi e Testi per un Corpus Iudiciorum, 1; Milan, 1973). J. den Boeft and J. Bremmer, 'Notiunculae Martyrologicae', *VC* 35 (1981), pp. 43–56; 36 (1982), pp. 383–402; 39 (1985), pp. 110–30. Critical studies appear in the *Analecta Bollandiana* and in the many writings of H. *Delehaye.

Acts of Sts Paul and Thecla. See PAUL AND THECLA, ACTS OF STS.

Acts of St Peter, of Pilate, of Thomas, etc. See PETER, ACTS OF; PILATE, ACTS OF; THOMAS, ACTS OF, etc.

Actual Grace. See GRACE.

Actual Sin. A sin, whether of commission or omission, which is the outcome of a free personal act of the individual will. In Christian theology it is contrasted with *Original Sin (q.v.). See also SIN.

Actus Purus (Lat., 'Pure Actuality'). The Scholastic term used (e.g. by St *Thomas Aquinas) as a way of characterizing the nature of God and distinguishing Him from His creatures. It derives from the *Aristotelian distinction between 'potentiality' and 'actuality', though it employs the distinction in a way that Aristotle does not. To call God *Actus Purus* is to say two things: that God is in no way changeable (that He has no 'potentiality' for change), and that the existence of God is not and could not be caused by anything (that God has no 'potential' non-existence). It is thus to say that God is eternally all that He could be, and that He is eternally uncreated. The distinction between potentiality and actuality is employed by Aquinas in the *Quinque Viae* and elsewhere.

Adalbert of Bremen (c.1000–72), German Archbishop. He was the descendant of a noble Saxon family. In 1032 he became canon at Bremen, later provost of Halberstadt Cathedral, and in 1043 Abp. of Bremen-Hamburg. He was an energetic promoter of missionary activities, esp. in the Nordic countries, Scandinavia, Iceland, Greenland, and the Orkneys, and planned to become Patriarch of the North. In 1053 *Leo IX nominated him Papal Vicar and Legate of the Nordic nations. During the minority of *Henry IV he gradually gained considerable influence over the young King, who loaded him with rich counties and abbeys. In 1066 Henry was compelled to dismiss him from his court by the jealousy of enemies, who also invaded his archbishopric and robbed him of his possessions. In 1069 he was recalled by Henry and part of his property restored. His last years were darkened by the invasion of the pagan Wends, who destroyed Hamburg in 1071–2.

O. H. May, *Regesten der Erzbischöfe von Bremen*, 1, fasc. 1 (Veröffentlichungen der Historischen Kommission für Hannover, Oldenburg, Braunschweig, Schaumburg-Lippe und Bremen, 11; 1928), pp. 53–79. Contemporary account by Adam of Bremen (d. c. 1085) in his *Gesta Hammaburgensis Ecclesiae Pontificum*, 3 (ed. B. Schmeidler, *MGH*, Scriptores Rerum Germanicarum in usum scholarum, 1917, pp. 142–226; Eng. tr. by F. J. Tschan, Records of Civilization, Sources and Studies, 53; 1959, pp. 114–85). G. Meyer von Knonau, *Jahrbücher des deutschen Reiches unter Heinrich IV und Heinrich V*, 2 (1894), pp. 121–47. C. Grünhagen, *Adalbert, Erzbischof von Hamburg und die Idee eines nordischen Patriarchats* (1854). E. N. Johnson, 'Adalbert of Hamburg-Bremen: A Politician of the Eleventh Century', *Speculum*, 9 (1934), pp. 147–79, with refs. to date. G. Misch, 'Studien zur Geschichte der Autobiographie III: Das Bild des Erzbischofs Adalbert in der Hamburgischen Kirchengeschichte des Domscholasters Adam von Bremen', *Nachr.* (Gött.), 1956, pp. 203–80. F. Knöpp, 'Adalbert, Erzbischof von Hamburg-Bremen 1043–1072', in id. (ed.), *Die Reichsabtei Lorsch*, 1 (Darmstadt, 1973), pp. 335–46. W. Seegrün in *TRE* 1 (1977), pp. 407–410.

Adam. Acc. to the biblical story, the first human being. 'Adam' is in fact a transliteration of one of the words for 'man' in Hebrew (אָדָם). In Genesis there are two accounts of the creation of humankind—1: 26–31, attributed to a priestly editor (*P), and 2: 5–7, attributed to the Yahwist (*J); the stories of the *Fall and subsequent history (Gen. 2: 15–4: 1 and 25) are, on a documentary hypothesis, all J material. Acc. to the P account, humans were created on the sixth day, after the animals (1: 26); were made in the image and likeness of God (1: 26 f.); commanded to multiply; and given dominion over the earth (1: 28–30). The J account, more anthropomorphic, assigns man's creation to the time when the earth was still void. It describes God's breathing into Adam's nostrils the breath of life (2: 7), the creation of *Eve from his rib (2: 21 f.; cf. 3: 20), and his work in the garden of Eden, with its Tree of Knowledge and forbidden fruit (2: 17). Ch. 3 narrates the Fall (q.v.), the curse laid on humanity, and the expulsion from Paradise. There is, however, now less general agreement among scholars over the analysis of the Pentateuch into documentary sources than there was in earlier decades (see PENTATEUCH). Various traditions about the story of Adam and Eve from the time of their expulsion from Paradise until their deaths are recorded in such apocryphal works as the Greek 'Apocalypse of Moses' and the Latin 'Life of Adam and Eve'.

Traditional theology has utilized the scriptural statements in its doctrine of man and his relation to God. As the father of the human race Adam has been held to have been endowed with great intellectual gifts, enabling him, e.g., to give names to all the animals (2: 19 f.). He was also held to possess infused knowledge (Ecclus. 17. 6 f.). The Councils of *Orange (529, can. 19) and of *Trent (sess. 5, cans. 1 and 2) defined that he was created in the state of sanctifying grace in conformity with the belief that Christ, the *Second Adam (Rom. 5: 14 and 1 Cor. 15: 45), restored mankind to the state of righteousness which had been lost by the first Adam. This state of grace has been held to consist with certain preternatural privileges, such as the absence of concupiscence and the possession of immortality and impassibility, which were bestowed on Adam in his original condition. It was through the Fall that these prerogatives were lost.

Acc. to Christian tradition, Christ delivered Adam from *limbo. The notion of *Tatian and the *Encratites that Adam had been damned was rejected by St *Irenaeus, who taught that Christ's victory over the old Serpent would not have been complete had He not delivered Adam from his power. Acc. to a Jewish tradition, taken up by St

*Jerome and long accepted in the W., he was buried at Hebron. This supposition gradually gave way to another, first found in *Origen and widespread esp. in the E., which places his tomb on *Calvary, so that at the Crucifixion the Blood of the Second Adam was poured out over the head of the First. St *Augustine (*In Ps.* 95 [96], no. 15) found in the four letters of Adam's name allusion to the four points of the compass (*Anatole, Dysis, Arctos, Mesembria*) and hence a sign of his identity with fallen humanity scattered over the whole world.

The biblical account is discussed in comm. on Gen., cited s.v. Convenient Eng. tr. of the 'Life of Adam and Eve', with introd. and refs. to original text, in H. F. D. Sparks (ed.), *The Apocryphal Old Testament* (Oxford, 1984), pp. 141–67. A. Vitti, SJ, 'Christus-Adam: De Paulino hoc concepto interpretando eiusque ab extraneis fontibus independentia vindicanda', *Biblica*, 7 (1926), pp. 121–45, 270–85, 384–401. J. *Daniélou, SJ, *Sacramentum Futuri: Études sur les Origines de la Typologie Biblique* (1950), pp. 3–52; Eng. tr. (1960), pp. 11–65. C. K. Barrett, *From First Adam to Last: A Study in Pauline Theology* (1962), pp. 1–21; R. Scroggs, *The Last Adam: A Study in Pauline Anthropology* (Oxford, 1966). J. Jeremias in *TWNT* 1 (1933; Eng. tr. 1964), pp. 141–3; G. W. H. Lampe (ed.), *A Patristic Greek Lexicon* (Oxford, 1968), pp. 26–9, s.v. Ἀδάμ. O. Betz and others in *TRE* 1 (1977), pp. 414–37, s.v. See also H. *Leclercq, OSB, in *DACL* 1 (pt. 1; 1907), cols. 509–19, s.v. 'Adam et Eve'. See also works cited s.v. ORIGINAL SIN.

Adam of Marsh (Adama de Marisco) (d. *c*.1258), English *Franciscan theologian. He was probably a native of Somerset, educated at *Oxford, and after being ordained priest received the living of *Wearmouth from his uncle, Richard, Bp. of *Durham. In 1232 or 1233 he entered the Franciscan Order at *Worcester and later was sent to Oxford. In 1245 he accompanied Robert *Grosseteste, his lifelong friend, to the Council of *Lyons. Despite the plans of the French to give him a chair at the university of *Paris, he returned to Oxford, where, from *c*.1247, he was regent of the Franciscan house of studies. Apart from his work as a scholar he exercised great influence in English political and social life. Together with Grosseteste and Simon de Montfort he defended the national liberties, and his advice was frequently sought by the most influential men of the country, among them Henry III and *Boniface, Abp. of *Canterbury. In 1256 both Henry and Boniface endeavoured to have him appointed to the see of *Ely, but the monks of Ely objected and obtained a Papal decision in their favour. Besides letters, he probably also wrote commentaries on Cant. and Heb., and he is perhaps the author of a treatise on the tides usually ascribed to Grosseteste. His learning, highly esteemed, e.g. by Roger *Bacon, gained him the title of 'Doctor Illustris'.

Letters ed. J. S. Brewer, *Monumenta Franciscana*, 1 (RS, 1858), pp. 77–489, with introd., pp. lxxvi–ci. The other principal source is the mid-13th-cent. *Tractatus de Adventu Fratrum Minorum in Angliam* of Thomas of Eccleston, OFM, esp. Collationes 3, 11, and 13 f., ed. A. C. Little (2nd edn., Manchester, 1951), pp. 17 f., 50, 71, and 84. Cuthbert [Hess], OSFC, *The Romanticism of St Francis and other Studies* (new edn., 1924), pp. 190–235. D. Douie, 'Adam "de Marisco", an English Franciscan', *Durham University Journal*, 32 (1940), pp. 81–97. G. Cantini, OFM, 'Adam de Marisco O.F.M. auctor spiritualis', *Antonianum*, 23 (1948), pp. 441–74. A. G. Little, 'The Franciscan School at Oxford in the Thirteenth Century', *AFH* 19 (1926), pp. 803–74, esp. pp. 831–7. R. C. Dales, 'Adam Marsh, Robert Grosseteste, and the Treatise on the

Tides', *Speculum*, 52 (1977), pp. 900 f. C. H. Lawrence, 'The Letters of Adam Marsh and the Franciscan School at Oxford', *JEH* 42 (1991), pp. 218–38. M. *Creighton in *DNB* 1 (1855), p. 79, s.v.; *BRUO* 2 (1958), pp. 1225–6, s.v. 'Marsh, Adam'.

Adam of St-Victor (12th cent.), *sequence-writer and composer. The *Augustinian canon of the abbey of St-Victor in Paris (see VICTORINES) to whom some of the finest sequences have been attributed, was long thought to have been a Breton ('Brito'), who entered the abbey *c.*1130 and died between 1177 and 1192. He has recently been identified with the Adam who was *Precentor of the cathedral of *Notre-Dame by 1107 (hence called Adam Precentor), donated his prebend to the abbey of St-Victor in 1133, entered the abbey some time later, and died in 1146. While it is not possible to say with certainty which of the some 60 sequences surviving from 12th-cent. Paris are Adam's work, he prob. wrote a core of early texts including 'Zima vetus', 'Ecce dies celebris', and 'Mundi renovatio' (all for *Easter), 'Lux iocunda, lux insignis' (for *Whitsunday), 'Heri mundus' (for the feast of St *Stephen), and 'Prunus datum' (for that of St *Laurence), and some of their melodies as well; the famous 'Laudes crucis' (for the *Invention and *Exaltation of the Cross) may also be by him. It is likely that his influence permeated the whole corpus of Victorine sequences, which for the first time made extensive use of OT typology and developed a melodic tradition closely integrated with the text.

Collections of the sequences attributed to Adam ed. by L. Gautier (2 vols., Paris, 1858–9; 3rd edn., Paris, 1894; Eng. tr. of 1st edn. by D. S. Wrangham, 3 vols., 1881); by E. Misset and P. Aubry (Paris, 1900, incl. music); and by C. Blume, SJ, and H. M. Bannister (eds.), *Liturgische Prosen des Übergangsstiles und der zweiten Epoche insbesondere die dem Adam von Sanct Victor zugeschriebenen* (AHMA 54; 1915). E. Hegener, *Studien zur "zweiten Sprache" in der religiösen Lyrik des zwölften Jahrhunderts: Adam von St Victor, Walter von Châtillon* (Beihefte zum Mittellateinischen Jahrbuch, 6; Ratingen [1971]). esp. pp. 4–132. M. E. Fassler, 'Who was Adam of St. Victor? The Evidence of the Sequence Manuscripts', *Journal of the American Musicological Society*, 37 (1984), pp. 233–69. Id., *Gothic Song: Victorine Sequences and Augustinian Reform in Twelfth-Century Paris* (Cambridge, 1993). J. Szövérffy, *Die Annalen der lateinischen Hymnendichtung*, 2 (1965), pp. 106–20, with further refs. Raby, pp. 348–55, with further bibl. p. 482.

Adam, Karl (1876–1966), Catholic theologian. A native of Bavaria, Karl Adam was ordained to the priesthood in 1900. He spent several years in pastoral work and taught at the University of Munich before he was appointed professor first at Strasbourg in 1918 and then in 1919 at Tübingen, where he remained until 1949. At many points he anticipated the aims of the *Ecumenical Movement, combining a liberal and modern outlook with full Catholic orthodoxy, and he exercised great influence, esp. over a lay public, by his writings, of which the best known was *Das Wesen des Katholizismus* (1924; Eng. tr., 1929). His other books include *Christus unser Bruder* (1926; Eng. tr., 1931), *Jesus Christus* (1933; Eng. tr., 1934), *Una Sancta in katholischer Sicht* (1948; Eng. tr., 1954), and *Der Christus des Glaubens* (1954; Eng. tr., 1957).

Abhandlungen über Theologie und Kirche: Festgabe für Karl Adam, ed. M. Reding (Düsseldorf, 1952), with list of his works,

pp. 319 f.; *Vitae et Veritati: Festgabe für Karl Adam* (ibid., 1956). H. Kreidler, *Eine Theologie des Lebens: Grundzüge im theologischen Denken Karl Adams* (Tübinger theologische Studien, 29; Mainz [1988]); R. A. Krieg, *Karl Adam: Catholicism in German Culture* (Notre Dame, Ind., 1992).

Adamantius. The name of the orthodox protagonist in the dialogue 'De recta in Deum fide', which dates from the early 4th cent. and is prob. a product of Asia Minor or Syria. It is commonly supposed that he was the author of the dialogue, but nothing further is known of him. If the note at the end of the *Philocalia, ch. 24, is genuine (the authenticity of the chapter has been seriously questioned), St *Basil the Great and St *Gregory Nazianzus wrongly identified him with *Origen. The dialogue, in five books, is a disputation first with two disciples of *Marcion, and then with followers of *Bardesanes and *Valentinus. At the end, Eutropius, a pagan arbitrator, gives the palm of victory to Adamantius. The work was translated into Latin by *Rufinus.

Ed. princeps by J. R. Wetstein (Basle, 1674), repr. in edns. of Origen (e.g. *PG* 11. 1711–1884). Rufinus' Lat. text, which survives only in a 12th-cent. MS at Schlettstadt, formerly at Hirschau, was first pub. by C. P. *Caspari, *Kirchenhistorische Anecdota* (Christiania, 1883), 1, pp. 1–129. Crit. edn., with Rufinus' Lat., by W. H. van de Sande Bakhuyzen (GCS, 1901). F. J. A. *Hort in *DCB* 1 (1877), pp. 39–41, s.v.

Adamites. A small Christian sect, first mentioned by St *Epiphanius (*Haer.* 52) and St *Augustine (*Haer.* 31), who aimed at returning to man's primitive innocence in Paradise by the practice of nudity. They are perhaps to be identified with a group of *Carpocratians, referred to by *Clement of Alexandria (*Strom.* 3. 2), who advocated community of wives and sexual promiscuity. In more recent times, small groups among the *Waldenses, Dutch *Anabaptists, and others, also calling themselves 'Adamites', have advocated similar doctrines and practices.

G. Bareille in *DTC* 1 (1903), cols. 391 f., s.v.

Adamnan, St. The older form of the name of Adomnán, St (q.v.).

Adamson, Patrick (1537–92), also 'Coustance' or 'Constance', Abp. of St Andrews. Educated at Perth Grammar School and St Andrews university, he was minister at Ceres from 1563 to 1566. He then went abroad for some years, living in France and for a time also at *Geneva, where he studied *Calvinist theology under T. *Beza. He was imprisoned in Paris for six months for describing the infant son of *Mary Queen of Scots as 'serenissimus princeps' of Scotland, England, France, and Ireland. After his return he published a catechism of his own compilation as well as a Latin version of the '*Scottish Confession' (1572). Appointed in 1576 Abp. of St Andrews in succession to John Douglas (1571–4), he now became involved in a long controversy with the *Presbyterian party. In 1583 some sermons preached before *James VI (I) led to his winning the royal favour and becoming Ambassador at *Elizabeth I's court later in the same year. During his stay in London he used his great powers of oratory to bring discredit on the Presbyterian party. Strongly supported by the King, he returned to Scotland in May 1584, but his disfavour with the *General Assembly continued to increase, and his *Declaration of the King's Majesty's Intention and Meaning towards the late Acts of Parliament* (1585) provoked much hostility. At the synod of Fife (April 1586), James Melville, the nephew of Andrew *Melville and professor of theology at St Andrews, made a fierce attack on his character and opinions and, though Adamson brought the matter before the King, the synod excommunicated him. Further charges were made on his character at the meeting of the General Assembly in 1587, and in the following year Adamson lost the King's favour. Adamson now sought the support of A. Melville and is credited with a *Recantation* of his earlier *Declaration*, though there are grounds for believing the recantation (pub. at Middelburg, 1598) to be spurious. His writings include Latin renderings of the Lamentations of Jeremiah and of the Book of Revelation (both 1590).

The most reliable authority is D. *Calderwood, *History of the Kirk of Scotland* (1678; crit. edn. from unpub. MSS by T. Thomson, Wodrow Society, esp. vols. 1–5, 1842–4). There is also a Life by T. Wilson appended to his edn. of Adamson's *De Sacro Pastoris Munere* (1619; sep. pagination). G. Donaldson, 'The Attitude of Whitgift and Bancroft to the Scottish Church', *Transactions of the Royal Historical Society*, 4th ser. 24 (1942), pp. 95–115, repr. in id., *Scottish Church History* (Edinburgh, 1985), pp. 164–77. D. G. Mullan, *Episcopacy in Scotland: The History of an Idea, 1560–1638* (ibid. [1986]), pp. 54–73.

Addai. The traditional founder of the Church at *Edessa. In Syriac tradition he was one of the 72 (*al.* 70) disciples of Lk. 10: 1, and acc. to the 'Doctrine of Addai' (q.v.) he was sent by St *Thomas the Apostle to heal King *Abgar. In the account of the conversion of Edessa given by *Eusebius (*HE* 1. 12. 3) he is identified with *Thaddaeus.
See bibl. to foll. entry.

Addai, Doctrine of. A Syriac writing which describes how King *Abgar (q.v.) was brought into contact with Christ and *Addai was sent to *Edessa to convert him. It is preserved *in toto* only in a single St Petersburg MS and in an early Armenian version. In its present form it dates from the early 5th cent. and incorporates the more recent legend of the *Invention of the Cross by Protonice, described as the wife of the future Emp. Claudius (d. AD 54), and the older legend of Abgar's correspondence with Christ, already known to *Eusebius (*HE* 1. 13. 6–8). Though older scholars accepted the historicity of the narrative, more recent opinion supposes that it is either an entire fabrication, perhaps modelled on the conversion of King Izates of Adiabene (*c.*36–60) to Judaism (*Josephus, *Ant.* 20. 2. 3–4), or a reflection on the conversion of Abgar VIII (177–212).

The complete Syriac text, with Eng. tr., was pub. by G. Phillips, *The Doctrine of Addai, the Apostle* (1876); it was repr., with a new Eng. tr. by G. Howard (Chico, Calif., 1981). Bardenhewer, 1, pp. 591–6, and 4, p. 326. See also bibl. to ABGAR, LEGEND OF, and EDESSA.

Addai and Mari, Liturgy of. The Syriac Liturgy which is still the normal rite of the *Church of the East and the *Chaldeans. The rite prob. originated in *Edessa, perhaps going back to the 3rd cent. It is thus of great importance for the early history of the Liturgy. The earliest MS of the *Anaphora belongs to the 10th or 11th cent.; from it are absent certain additions found in all later witnesses.

The most notable feature of the Anaphora, in its original form, is the address to Christ (not to God the Father). Furthermore, the Institution Narrative is absent from most MSS; it is disputed whether this is an original feature of the Anaphora or whether, e.g., it was cut out by Isho'yahb III in the 7th cent. The attribution to *Addai and Mari, the traditional founders of Christianity in Mesopotamia, appears not to be attested before the 11th cent.; earlier sources speak of the 'Anaphora of the Apostles'. It is closely related to the *Maronite Anaphora known (from the opening word) as the 'Sharrar', attributed variously to St *Peter or to the Twelve Apostles.

The *editio princeps* of the Syriac text is in *Liturgia Sanctorum Apostolorum Adaei et Maris* (Urmi, 1890–2). Modern edn., with Eng. tr. and comm., by A. Gelston (Oxford, 1992). Earlier Eng. tr. in Brightman, *LEW*, pp. 245–305. E. C. Ratcliff, 'The Original Form of the Anaphora of Addai and Mari: A Suggestion', *JTS* 30 (1929), pp. 23–32; G. *Dix, OSB, *The Shape of the Liturgy* (1945), esp. pp. 177–87; B. Botte, OSB, 'L'Anaphore Chaldéenne des Apôtres', *OCP* 15 (1949), pp. 259–76; W. F. Macomber, SJ, 'The Oldest Known Text of the Anaphora of the Apostles Addai and Mari', ibid. 32 (1966), pp. 335–71; id., 'The Maronite and Chaldean Versions of the Anaphora of the Apostles', ibid. 37 (1971), pp. 55–84; id., 'The Ancient Form of the *Anaphora of the Apostles*', in N. G. Garsoïan, T. F. Mathews, and R. W. Thomson (eds.), *East of Byzantium: Syria and Armenia in the Formative Period* (Washington, DC, 1982), pp. 73–88.

Adelard of Bath (early 12th cent.), English Scholastic philosopher. Few facts about his life survive, but he is known to have studied at Tours, prob. taught at Laon, and visited Salerno and Sicily and perhaps Asia Minor. He translated the 'Elements' of Euclid, and in his 'Quaestiones Naturales' defended Democritus' theory of atoms as well as the Aristotelian proof of God's existence from motion. In his principal work, 'De Eodem et Diverso' (between 1105 and 1116), written in epistolary form, Adelard developed a theory of the Liberal Arts and also attempted to reconcile the *Platonic and *Aristotelian doctrines of *universals, holding that in reality the universal and the particular were identical, and distinct only in our mode of apprehending them.

Adelard's 'De Eodem et Diverso', ed. H. Willner (BGPM 4, Heft 1; 1903); 'Quaestiones Naturales', ed. M. Müller (ibid. 31, Heft 2; 1934); tr. of Euclid's 'Elements', 1–8 and 10. 36–15. 2, ed. H. L. L. Busard (Pontifical Institute of Mediaeval Studies, Studies and Texts, 64; Toronto [1983]). F. J. P. Bliemetzrieder, *Adelhard von Bath* (Munich, 1935). C. H. Haskins, *Studies in the History of Mediaeval Science* (Cambridge, Mass., 1924), pp. 20–42. C. Burnett (ed.), *Adelard of Bath: An English Scientist and Arabist of the Early Twelfth Century* (Warburg Institute Surveys and Texts, 14: 1987). M. Clagett in *Dictionary of Scientific Biography*, ed. C. G. Gillispie and others, 1 (New York, 1970), pp. 61–4, with details of works, pub. and unpub.

Adeste Fideles. Anonymous Christmas hymn, probably written in the 17th or 18th cent., of French or German authorship. J. F. Wade (*c.*1711–86) has been suggested as the composer of its most popular tune, but was prob. only the copyist. It has been frequently translated, the best-known version being based on that by F. *Oakeley, 'O come, all ye faithful, joyful and triumphant'.

J. Stéphan, OSB, *The 'Adeste Fideles': A Study on its Origin and Development* (Buckfast Abbey, 1947; enlarged Fr. edn., 1949).

Adhemar de Monteil (d. 1098), Bp. of Le Puy. Of noble family and at one time a knight, he became Bp. of Le Puy some time between 1080 and 1087. In 1095 *Urban II summoned the Council of *Clermont from Le Puy and made Adhemar his representative on the First *Crusade (*hujus itineris ac laboris ducem, vice nostra*), during which Adhemar was closely associated with Raymond of Toulouse. He died on 1 August 1098, soon after the capture of Antioch; his death is usually regarded as a severe blow to any hopes of maintaining the unity of the Crusading leaders, and certainly decreased any likelihood of Papal control of the Franks in the E.

His career is discussed in J. H. and L. L. Hill, 'Contemporary accounts and later reputation of Adhemar, bishop of Puy', *Medievalia et Humanistica*, 9 (1955), pp. 30–38; J. A. Brundage, 'Adhemar of Puy: The Bishop and his Critics', *Speculum*, 34 (1959), pp. 201–12; and H. E. Mayer, 'Zur Beurteilung Adhémars von Le Puy', *Deutsches Archiv*, 16 (1960), pp. 547–52. See also works cited under CRUSADES.

Adherents. In the Church of *Scotland, baptized persons who, although non-communicants, are intimately connected with a congregation. If parishioners and seat-holders over 21 years of age, they have the right to be placed on the electoral register. This right is controlled by the *kirk session, to whose jurisdiction they are subject.

Adiaphorists (from Gk. ἀδιάφορα, 'things indifferent'). A party in German Protestantism which held that certain rites and actions were matters of indifference. The first controversy on the subject broke out in connection with the Leipzig Interim (1548). In this compromise between the theologians of *Wittenberg, esp. P. *Melanchthon, and the ecclesiastical and civil authorities of Saxony, the Wittenberg group declared certain Catholic practices such as *Confirmation and Extreme *Unction, the *Mass without *transubstantiation, and the veneration of *saints 'adiaphora', i.e. matters on which concessions might be made in the interest of peace without prejudice to Protestant doctrine. This policy was fiercely opposed by M. *Flacius Illyricus, who, in his *De Veris et Falsis Adiaphoris* (1549), stressed the dangers to integral *Lutheranism of these concessions. The controversy continued till after the Peace of *Augsburg (1555) and was brought to an end only by Article 10 of the Formula of *Concord (1577), which ruled that in times of persecution concessions were not to be made, but otherwise ceremonies not commanded or forbidden by Scripture might be altered acc. to the decisions of individual Churches. Similar problems were discussed by theologians in England in the 16th cent.

Another controversy on 'adiaphora' broke out in the latter half of the 17th cent. between the Pietistical followers of P. J. *Spener and A. H. *Francke, who declared all worldly pleasures such as theatres and dances to be sinful in themselves, and the orthodox Lutherans who held them to be indifferent and therefore permitted. A harmonizing of the two points of view was later given by F. D. E. *Schleiermacher, who, though denying the conception of matters of indifference, considered ordinary pleasures part of the whole of human life and therefore not only permissible but even demanded by duty.

F. H. R. Frank, *Die Theologie der Concordienformel historisch-diplomatisch entwickelt und beleuchtet*, 4 (1865), pp. 1–120. A.

*Ritschl, *Geschichte des Pietismus*, 2 (1884), pp. 174–83. J. Gottschick in *PRE* (3rd edn.), 1 (1896), pp. 168–79, s.v. 'Adiaphora'; E. T. Horn in *HERE* 1 (1908), pp. 91–3, s.v. 'Adiaphorism'. See also bibl. to GNESIO–LUTHERANS.

ad Limina Apostolorum, i.e., lit., 'to the thresholds of the Apostles'. Pilgrimages *ad Limina Apostolorum, sc.* to the tombs of St *Peter and St *Paul in *Rome, usually undertaken in fulfilment of a vow, were very popular in the Middle Ages. In modern times the term is ordinarily used in a technical sense, denoting the visits which RC bishops are required to pay to Rome to venerate the tombs of the Apostles and to report on the state of their dioceses to the Pope. This custom originated in the decree of a Roman synod (743) which enjoined such visits on all bishops who had been ordained at Rome (can. 4). *Gregory VII extended this obligation to all metropolitans of the W., and from the 13th cent. it was imposed on all bishops consecrated by the Pope himself or by his special representative. *Sixtus V, by the bull 'Romanus Pontifex' of 20 Dec. 1584, required the visit from all bishops every three to ten years, acc. to the distance of their dioceses. Since then the regulations have changed from time to time. The 1983 *Codex Iuris Canonici* (can. 400) requires that a diocesan bishop should normally go to Rome in person every five years to venerate the tombs of the Apostles Peter and Paul and to present himself to the Pope. If legitimate hindrances prevent the visit, a representative is to be appointed.

F. M. Cappello, *De Visitatione Liminum* (2 vols., Rome, 1912–13). J. J. Carroll, *The Bishop's Quinquennial Report: A Historical Synopsis and a Commentary* (Catholic University of America Canon Law Studies, 259; 1956), with bibl. J. Cottier, 'Éléments nouveaux des normes de la visite "Ad limina" et leur valeur juridique respective, des décrétales au Concile de Trente', *Ephemerides Iuris Canonici*, 8 (1952), pp. 174–206.

Admission to Candidacy for Ordination of Deacons and Priests. In the RC Church, a rite introduced in 1972 when the two remaining *minor orders of *acolyte and *lector ceased to be a stage on the way to the priesthood. It takes place either during Mass or in the course of some other service involving 'the proclamation of God's word'. After the homily, the candidates, who have previously made their petition in writing to the diocesan bishop, are called and presented to the bishop. He examines them and prays for them. After further prayers of intercession the service concludes with two collects and the episcopal blessing.

Admission to Holy Communion Measure 1972. The BCP provided that no-one should be admitted to Holy Communion until confirmed or 'ready and desirous to be confirmed'. The 1972 Measure allows the General Synod of the C of E to provide for the admission of other baptized persons. These now include communicant members of other Churches which subscribe to the doctrine of the Holy Trinity, and who are in good standing in their own Church (Canon B 15A).

Admonition to Parliament, An (1572). A manifesto against all ecclesiastical dignitaries, demanding a non-episcopal constitution for the English Church. It attacked *inter alia* the use of wafer-bread at the Communion, then still current, reception of Communion kneeling, and the admission of Papists to Communion; it demanded a radical restructuring of the ecclesiastical courts to produce more effective discipline. Cast in the form of an open letter to Parliament, it was accompanied by a 'View of Popish Abuses yet remaining in the English Church'. Though issued anonymously from unknown presses, authorship of the two parts was correctly attributed to two London *Puritan clergymen, Thomas Wilcox and John *Field, who were both committed to Newgate on 7 July 1572. When the bishops commissioned replies to the *Admonition*, it was defended in a *Second Admonition* (?by Christopher Goodman, Nov. 1572), and more cogently in a *Reply to an Answer made of Mr. Dr. Whitgift* by T. *Cartwright (April 1573). Both the *Admonition* and the defences of it were suppressed by a royal proclamation on 11 June 1573, and Cartwright, on the issue of a warrant for his arrest, was compelled to leave the country. J. *Whitgift again answered Cartwright, who retaliated from exile abroad with two parts of a *Second Reply* in 1575 and 1577.

Text in *Puritan Manifestoes*, ed. W. H. *Frere and C. E. Douglas (CHS 72; 1907), pp. 5–19; *Second Admonition*, ibid., pp. 79–133. D. J. McGinn, *Admonition Controversy* (Rutgers University Studies in English, 5; New Brunswick, NJ 1949). P. Lake, *Anglicans and Puritans? Presbyterianism and English Conformist Thought from Whitgift to Hooker* (1988), esp. pp. 13–70.

Ado, Martyrology of. The *martyrology compiled between 853 and 860 by St Ado (*c*.800–75), then a *Benedictine monk, later Abp. of Vienne. Acc. to Ado his basis was an ancient Roman martyrology ('Martyrologium Romanum Parvum') which he had discovered at *Ravenna, but this work, which is full of blunders, was certainly spurious and may even have been fabricated by Ado himself. The highly convenient plan and arrangement of the compilation were the pattern for later martyrologies. It directly influenced the Martyrology of *Usuard and mediately the '*Roman Martyrology', and was thus the source of most of the merits and defects of its successors.

The Martyrology of Ado was edited by H. Rosweyde, SJ, at Antwerp in 1613 (repr. in J. P. Migne, *PL* 123. 139–436), and by D. Giorgi (Rome, 1745). Modern edn., with comm., by J. Dubois, OSB, and G. Renaud (Paris, 1984). H. *Quentin, *Les Martyrologes historiques* (1908), pp. 465–681.

Adomnán, St (*c*.624–704), also 'Adamnan', Abbot of *Iona. Of the same Irish royal lineage as St *Columba, he became a novice at the monastery of Iona, where he was elected abbot in 679. Visits to *Wearmouth in 686 and 688 led him to accept the Roman dating of *Easter, but according to *Bede he was unable to persuade the monks of Iona and its dependencies to adopt it. In 692 he went to Ireland, where he was more successful in furthering the Roman observance. He also proposed a law to protect non-combatants in war, first accepted at the Synod of Birr (697) and thereafter periodically enforced as the 'Law of Adomnán'. His 'Life of St Columba' (written 688–92, or perhaps later, *c*.700) is of great historical value for its information on monastic life. He also wrote 'De Locis Sanctis', an account of a visit to the Holy Land by Arculf, a bishop from Gaul; and there are some Latin canons in his name. He was venerated in Scotland and Ireland, where the modern form of his name is St Eunan. Feast day, 23 Sept.

Modern edns. of his 'Life of St Columba' by W. Reeves (Irish Archaeological and Celtic Society; Dublin, 1857) and, with Eng. tr., by A. O. and M. O. Anderson (London, 1961), and of his 'De Locis Sanctis' by L. Bieler (CCSL 175, 1965, pp. 175–234) and, with Eng. tr., by D. Meehan (Scriptores Latini Hiberniae, 3; Dublin, 1958). The so-called 'Canones Adomnani' are ed., with Eng. tr., by L. Bieler, *The Irish Penitentials* (ibid. 5; 1963), pp. 176–81. The 'Law of Adomnán' is ed., with Eng. tr., by K. Meyer (Anecdota Oxoniensia, 4th ser., pt. 12; Oxford, 1905). The chief authority for his life is Bede, *HE* 5. 15–7 and 21; comm. by J. M. Wallace-Hadrill (Oxford, 1988), pp. 187–9. Irish Life (prob. 10th cent.) ed., with Eng. tr., by M. Herbert and P. Ó Riain (Irish Texts Society, 54; London, 1988); on this Life also M. Herbert, *Iona, Kells, and Derry* (Oxford, 1988), pp. 151–79. G. Brüning, 'Adamnans Vita Columbae und ihre Ableitungen', *Zeitschrift für celtische Philologie*, 11 (1917), pp. 213–304; D. A. Bullough, 'Columba, Adomnan and the Achievement of Iona', *Scottish Historical Review*, 43 (1964), pp. 111–30, and 44 (1965), pp. 17–33; J. M. Picard, 'The Purpose of Adomnán's *Vita Columbae*', *Peritia*, 1 (1982), pp. 160–77; M. Ní Dhonnchadha, 'The Guarantor List of *Cáin Adomnáin*, 697', ibid., pp. 178–215; A. P. Smyth, *Warlords and Holy Men: Scotland AD 80–1000* (The New History of Scotland, 1; 1984), pp. 116–40.

Adonai (Heb. אֲדֹנָי, plur. of אָדוֹן, 'master', 'Lord'; the use of the plural prob. implies a 'sense of majesty'). Divine name, frequently used in the OT. The Jews also read it for the unutterable name of Yahweh, which, in the text of the Hebrew Bible, is usually pointed with the vowel signs proper to Adonai. The *Gnostics employed it as a name for one of their aeons.

In the Christian Liturgy the term is applied esp. to the Second Person of the Trinity in the great antiphon to the Magnificat for 18 Dec., 'O Adonai' (see O-ANTIPHONS).

G. H. *Dalman, *Studien zur biblischen Theologie: Der Gottesname Adonaj und seine Geschichte* (1889).

Adoptianism. (1) The heresy, originating in Spain in the 8th cent., acc. to which Christ, in His humanity, is not the true, but only the adoptive, Son of God. Its chief representatives were *Elipandus, Abp. of *Toledo, and *Felix, Bp. of Urgel. The heresy probably arose out of Elipandus' fight against the error of *Migetius, who seems to have held the bizarre doctrine that the Trinity consisted of three historical figures, David, Jesus, and St Paul, and who made no distinction between Christ's position as son of David and as Son of God. Elipandus drew a sharp distinction between the humanity of Christ ('of the seed of David') and His Divine Sonship, and maintained that the human Jesus was only the adoptive Son of God. Elipandus was supported by Felix of Urgel, who recanted, however, at a synod held at Ratisbon in 792. Having repeated his abjuration before the Pope, Felix returned to his diocese, but again fell into error and was obliged to flee. The Spanish bishops sided with Elipandus and tried to prove their views from Scripture and the Fathers. After they had communicated to the Pope a letter they had sent to *Charlemagne, the latter called the Council of *Frankfurt (794), where the bishops attacked the Spanish arguments in two documents. These, together with a third drawn up by *Hadrian I, were sent to Spain. A reply from Felix in favour of the heresy provoked *Alcuin's famous seven books 'Contra Felicem', and in 798 *Leo III called a synod at *Rome which anathematized Felix. In the same year, after a long dispute, he once more recanted. Elipandus, however, remained firm, and Alcuin wrote another treatise against him. The archbishop died soon afterwards and the heresy disappeared.

It was revived, however, in the 12th cent. in a modified form by *Abelard, *Gilbert de la Porrée, and others, who, through identifying the rational nature with the Person, arrived also at Adoptianist views. In later times several attempts were made, e.g. by *Duns Scotus, *Durandus, F. *Suárez, and others, to interpret in an orthodox sense the statement that Jesus as Man is the adopted Son of God, but these theories were all rejected as subversive of a sound Christology.

(2) Through the influence of A. *Harnack's *Dogmengeschichte* the term (usually spelt 'Adoptionism') has also been frequently applied to the heretical stream in early Greek theology which regarded Christ as a man gifted with Divine powers. This view, first represented by the *Ebionites, was later developed by the *Monarchians, e.g. *Theodotus and *Paul of Samosata. *Theodore of Mopsuestia, *Nestorius, and the *Antiochene School in general also tend to what may be called, in a rather loose sense, an Adoptionist Christology.

On (1), see C. W. F. Walch, *Historia Adoptianorum* (Göttingen, 1755); Hefele and Leclercq, 3. 2 (1910), pp. 1001–60. É. Amann, 'L'Adoptianisme espagnol du VIIIᵉ siècle', *Rev. S.R.* 16 (1936), pp. 281–317; R. de Abadal y de Vinyals, *La Batalla del Adopcionismo en la Desintegración de la Iglesia Visigoda* (Barcelona, 1949); W. Heil, 'Der Adoptianismus, Alkuin und Spanien', in *Karl der Grosse: Lebenswerk und Nachleben*, 2, ed. B. Bischoff (1965), pp. 95–155; id., *Alkuinstudien*, 1: *Zur Chronologie und Bedeutung des Adoptianismusstreites* (Düsseldorf, 1970); K. Schäferdiek, 'Der adoptianische Streit im Rahmen der spanischen Kirchengeschichte', *ZKG* 80 (1969), pp. 291–311; 81 (1970), pp. 1–16. Useful summary [in Eng.] by G. B. Blumenshine in his edn. of Alcuin's *Liber Contra Haeresim Felicis* (ST 285; 1980), pp. 9–24 ('The Adoptionist Heresy of the Eighth Century'). J. F. Rivera Recio, *El adopcionismo en España (s. VIII)* (Toledo, 1980). J. C. Cavadini, *The Last Christology of the West: Adoptionism in Spain and Gaul, 785–820* (Philadelphia [1993]).

adoration. In strict terminology the expression, from the Lat. *adoratio*, is equivalent to the Greek theological term λατρεία, designating an act of worship due to God alone. If used more loosely, however, it also covers the Greek προσκύνησις which, in early times, was used for adoration of God as well as for veneration such as is paid to persons or objects of sacred character. In this second sense it was frequently used among E. peoples and also in the Bible, e.g. in the narrative of Joseph and his brethren (Gen. 43: 26), whereas in the first sense it is used, e.g., in the Second Commandment. The Lord inculcates that adoration (προσκύνησις) is due to God alone (Mt. 4: 10). He Himself is frequently adored (e.g. Jn. 9: 38), whereas, on the other hand, St *Peter refuses the adoration of Cornelius (Acts 10: 25 f.). The Divine prerogative of adoration was emphasized esp. by the early Christian martyrs, who refused to 'adore' the statues of the Emperor. It was claimed for the Son and the Holy Spirit, e.g. by *Origen and other early Fathers, a fact which suggests the equality of the Three Divine Persons, whereas it is denied to all creatures, not excepting the BVM. Until the 5th cent. Christians seem not to have distinguished between λατρεία and προσκύνησις. But the increasing veneration of images and the ensuing *Iconoclastic Controversy necessitated a

stricter terminology. The Second Council of *Nicaea (787) reserved the term λατρεία to the worship of God alone (including God incarnate), whereas προσκύνησις might be applied also to the cult of creatures. After some controversy this distinction was accepted also in the W., and from the age of Scholasticism W. theologians term adoration of God '*latria', but veneration of creatures '*dulia' (Gk. δουλεία).

God is to be worshipped 'in spirit and in truth' (Jn. 4: 24) but this injunction is not normally understood to exclude bodily gestures of adoration, such as prostrations or the utterance of spoken prayers. In RC theology the Eucharistic sacrifice is often regarded as the principal act of adoration. The adoration paid to the Bl Sacrament depends on the doctrine of the Real Presence, among its most striking manifestations being the practices of the *Forty Hours and of Perpetual Adoration, cultivated by many religious congregations. Among Anglicans a service of Eucharistic devotion, sometimes resembling the RC *Benediction service, is also frequently termed 'Adoration'.

A. Molien in *Dict. Sp.* 1 (1937), cols. 210–22, s.v., with bibl.

Adoro Te devote, or, more correctly, 'Adoro devote'. Eucharistic hymn, attributed by the MSS to St *Thomas Aquinas, though his authorship has been contested. It is a simple, but very personal and deeply felt, prayer to the Lord hidden under the sacramental species. Unlike St Thomas's other Eucharistic hymns, it was not written for the Office of *Corpus Christi. Until recently it was printed in the Roman *Missal and *Breviary among the 'Orationes pro Opportunitate Sacerdotis Dicendae'. There are many English translations, the most famous of which, found in several slightly varying forms, is that by J. R. Woodford (1850), Bp. of *Ely, 'Thee we adore, O hidden Saviour'. That of G. M. *Hopkins, 'Godhead here in hiding, whom I do adore', is also widely used.

Crit. edn. of traditional text by C. M. Dreves (ed.), *Lateinische Hymnendichter des Mittelalters*, 2 (AHMA 50; 1907), pp. 589–91. A. *Wilmart, OSB, 'La Tradition littéraire et textuelle de l' "Adoro te devote" ', *RTAM* 1 (1929), pp. 21–40 and 149–76, with rev. text, pp. 159–61; repr. in Wilmart's *Auteurs spirituels et textes dévots* (1932), pp. 361–414 (ch. 12), with rev. text, pp. 393–5. This is now printed in the section of the *Rituale Romanum, De Sacra Communione et de Cultu Mysterii Eucharistici extra Missam* (1973), pp. 61 f. F. J. E. Raby, 'The Date and Authorship of the Poem *Adoro Te Devote*', *Speculum*, 20 (1945), pp. 236–8; P.-M. Gy [OP], 'L'Office du Corpus Christi et la théologie des accidents eucharistiques', *RSPT* 66 (1982), pp. 81–6.

Adrian I, IV, VI. See HADRIAN I, IV, VI.

Advent (Lat. *Adventus*, 'coming', i.e. of Christ). The ecclesiastical season immediately before *Christmas. In W. Christendom Advent Sunday, i.e. the first day of Advent, is the Sunday nearest to St Andrew's Day (30 Nov.). Four Sundays in Advent thus always precede Christmas Day. In the E. Advent is a much longer season, beginning in the middle of Nov. Advent Sunday is traditionally the day on which the ecclesiastical year begins. The first clear references to the season in the W. come from the latter half of the 6th cent. In the *Gelasian Sacramentary Advent Collects, Epistles, and Gospels are provided for the five

Sundays preceding Christmas and for the corresponding Wednesdays and Fridays. The Wednesday and Friday *propers of the Mass remained in England until the BCP of 1549.

Advent was formerly kept as *Lent, but with less strictness. In the W. fasting is no longer formally ordered, though festivites are discouraged and the solemn character of the season is marked by the liturgical use of purple (except on the Third Sunday, '*Gaudete', q.v., when rose-coloured vestments may be used) and, in the Roman Missal, by the omission of *Gloria in Excelsis at the Sunday Masses. The season is observed as a time of preparation not only for Christmas but also for the Second Coming of Christ as Judge at the Last Day. See also O—ANTIPHONS.

M. Jugie, AA, ' La Première Fête mariale en orient et occident, l'Avent primitif', ÉO 26 (1923), pp. 130–52; B. Botte, OSB, Les Origines de la Noël et de l'Épiphanie (Louvain, 1932), pp. 263–84; J. A. Jungmann, SJ, Gewordene Liturgie (1941), pp. 232–94 ('Advent und Voradvent'); A. Chavasse, 'L'Avent romain, du VIᵉ au VIIIᵉ Siècle', EL 67 (1953), pp. 297–308; W. Croce, SJ, 'Die Adventsliturgie im Licht ihrer geschichtlichen Entwicklung', ZKT 76 (1954), pp. 257–96, 440–72. F. *Cabrol, OSB, in DACL 1 (1907), cols. 3223–30, s.v. 'Avent'; A. *Baumstark in RAC 1 (1950), cols. 112–25, s.v.; J. H. Crehan, SJ, in Catholic Dictionary of Theology, 1 (1962), pp. 41–3, s.v., with bibl.

Adventists. Various Christian groups which hold in common that the Second Coming of Christ is to be expected immediately. As a denomination the Adventists date from 1831, when William Miller (1782–1849) first began to proclaim at Dresden, NY, the imminence of the Second Coming. On the basis of study of dates in the OT he came to fix the Second Coming in 1843–4. He made converts from many Christian bodies; pre-millennium conferences were held; and a paper called The Midnight Cry started. After the year had passed uneventfully, various later dates were suggested. Miller himself always maintained that the Coming was imminent, though in his later years he became less ready to pronounce dates. Differences of opinion as to the date of the Second Advent and also on the question of the immortality of the soul produced schisms. The 'Evangelical Adventists', who were the original body and retained a Catholic belief in the after-life, have died out. The chief bodies now are the 'Second Advent Christians' and the 'Seventh-day Adventists' (q.v.).

D. T. Taylor, The Reign of Christ on Earth (Boston, 1855; ed. H. L. Hastings, London, 1882). H. C. Sheldon, Studies in Recent Adventism (New York, 1915). E. S. Gaustad (ed.), The Rise of Adventism: Religion and Society in mid-nineteenth-century America (New York and London, 1974), with bibl. essay, pp. 207–317. See also bibl. to SEVENTH-DAY ADVENTISTS.

Advertisements, book of. The book entitled Advertisements, partly for due Order in the public Administration of Common Prayers and using the Holy Sacraments, and partly for the Apparel of all Persons Ecclesiastical by virtue of the Queen's Majesty's Letters commanding the same, issued in Mar. 1556 by Abp. M. *Parker. Of 39 items in all, it ordered inter alia the use of the surplice (in place of the traditional Mass vestments) in the Eucharist and kneeling at the reception of Communion. It has long been disputed whether this book of Advertisements is to be understood as

the 'other order' in the paragraph in the Act of *Uniformity of 1559 providing that the Ornaments (see *ORNAMENTS RUBRIC) in use in the second year of *Edward VI should be retained 'until other order shall therein be taken by the authority of the Queen's Majesty'. Though the 19th-cent. courts upheld that the Advertisements were covered by the Act of 1559, there are good grounds for questioning this opinion, one of the most cogent being the survival of the rubric in the BCP of 1662. See also VESTIARIAN CONTROVERSY.

Text in Gee and Hardy, no. 81 (pp. 467–75).

advocatus diaboli (Lat., 'devil's advocate'). A popular term for the '*promotor fidei' (q.v.).

advowson. The right of appointing a clergyman to a parish or other ecclesiastical benefice. Advowsons are of two kinds: (1) 'Collative', when they are held by the *Ordinary under whose jurisdiction the benefice is, normally the bishop of the diocese; and (2) 'Presentative', when they are held by some other person ('patron'), who presents the nominee for institution. In the latter case the patron, who may be clerical or lay, an individual or a corporation, does not possess the right of putting his candidate in spiritual or even legal possession of the office. He presents him to the bishop or other ecclesiastical superior for *institution and *induction (qq.v.), and the latter may for due cause reject the nominee. The right of advowson is historically the survival of an originally much more extensive control exercised by the feudal lord over churches on his estates.

In most RC countries advowson has died out, though it survives in a few places. In the C of E, where it still exists, its exercise is governed by English civil law, which since the time of the Constitutions of *Clarendon (1164) has succeeded in maintaining control of this valuable right. Thus a bishop who without legal cause refuses to accept a patron's nominee can be compelled to do so by an action of *Quare impedit in the civil courts. In the 14th cent. the Papal method of overriding these rights of private patronage by means of Provisions was fought by the State in the Statute of *Provisors (1351).

In English law an advowson is a property right which can pass by gift, by inheritance or (formerly) by sale. It was common for part only of the right to be sold, e.g. the right to the next presentation only, or the right to take turns at presenting. It was valuable mainly because it was a gift of income and position, but it also allowed the patron to influence the character of the ministry. A Measure of 1923 ended the sale but not the transfer of advowsons. It also ended the practice of patrons presenting themselves or their husbands to benefices.

Before 1986, an advowson could be exercised by any person, whether or not a Christian, except aliens, outlaws, lunatics (for whom the Lord Chancellor acted) and RCs (whose rights were exercised by the Universities of Oxford and Cambridge, dividing the country between them for this purpose). The Patronage (Benefices) Measure 1986 introduced a new regime, replacing most of the old law. All rights of patronage must now be registered before they can be exercised, and no person can exercise a right of patronage unless he declares in writing that he is an 'actual communicant member' of the C of E or a Church in communion with it. Those who cannot make the declaration must appoint a qualified representative to act for them. Nominations must be made in consultation with the Bishop and representatives of the *Parochial Church Council, and must have their approval. If approval is refused, it can be reviewed by the Archbishop.

In the Church of *Scotland the rights of private patronage were resisted by a large party in the Kirk and were the chief cause of the secessions which eventually produced the *Free Church of Scotland (1843).

P. Thomas, *Le Droit de Propriété des Laïques sur les Églises et le Patronage laïque au moyen âge* (Bibliothèque de l'École des Hautes Études, Sciences religieuses, 19; 1906). J. W. Gray, 'The Ius Praesentandi in England from the Constitutions of Clarendon to Bracton', *EHR* 67 (1952), pp. 481–509. P. Landau, *Jus Patronatus: Studien zur Entwicklung des Patronats im Dekretalenrecht und der Kanonistik des 12. und 13. Jahrhunderts* (Forschungen zur kirchlichen Rechtsgeschichte und zum Kirchenrecht, 12; 1975).

Aegidius, St. See GILES, ST.

Aegidius Romanus. See GILES OF ROME.

AEGM. See ANGLICAN EVANGELICAL GROUP MOVEMENT.

Aelfheah, St. See ALPHEGE, ST.

Aelfric (*c*.955–*c*.1020), 'the Grammarian', Abbot of Eynsham. His early training was at the *Benedictine abbey at *Winchester under *Ethelwold, who implanted in him the ideals of the monastic reform movement. In 987 he was transferred to the newly founded abbey at Cerne Abbas in Dorset and here issued two sets of homilies in English, dealing with the events of the liturgical year and with doctrinal and historical subjects. These homilies gained a revived notoriety at the time of the Reformation, as Aelfric not only used language which excluded the doctrine of the *Immaculate Conception of the BVM but was also held to have maintained a view of the Eucharist incompatible with *transubstantiation. In his Eucharistic theology he was probably influenced by *Ratramnus, though his unorthodoxy was apparently much exaggerated. The use of alliterative prose in some of these homilies was developed in a third series on the 'Lives of the Saints', where the arrangement is commonly printed as verse. In 1005 he was appointed the first Abbot of Eynsham in Oxfordshire. His writings of this period include an abridgement of the *Regularis Concordia* (addressed to his monks at Eynsham), a Latin Life of Ethelwold, and an English rendering of *Bede's *De Temporibus*. He was a dedicated pedagogue, and composed the earliest Latin grammar in any vernacular language; he also composed a *Colloquy* to serve as an introduction to Latin conversation for monastic *oblates. His greatest claim to fame was his provision of books with real literary merit for the rural clergy in their native language.

W. Skeat (ed.), *Ælfric's Lives of the Saints* (EETS, orig. ser. 76, 82, 94, and 114 bound in 2 vols.; 1881–1900); B. Thorpe (ed.), *The Homilies of the Anglo-Saxon Church, containing the Homilies of Ælfric* (2 vols., 1844–6, with Eng. tr.); M. Godden (ed.), *Ælfric's Catholic Homilies: The Second Series Text* (EETS, suppl. ser. 5; 1979); J. C. Pope (ed.), *Homilies of Ælfric: A Supplementary Collection* (ibid., orig. ser. 259–60; 1967–8). Facsimile of his 1st ser. of Catholic Homilies, in British Library MS Royal 7 C. XII, ed. by N. Eliason and P. [A. M.] Clemoes (Early English Manuscripts in Facsimile, 13; Copenhagen, 1966). Grammar and Glossary, ed. J. Zupitza (Sammlung englischer Denkmäler, 1; 1880; repr., with introd. by H. Gneuss, 1966); *Exameron Anglice*, ed. S. J. Crawford (Bibliothek der angelsächsischen Prosa, 10; 1921); *Colloquy*, ed. G. N. Garmonsway (London, 1939); *De Temporibus*, ed. H. Henel (EETS, orig. ser. 213; 1942); Life of Ethelwold, ed. M. Lapidge and M. Winterbottom as an appendix to their edn. of Wulfstan of Winchester's Life of Ethelwold (Oxford Medieval Texts, 1991), pp. 70–80, with useful discussion pp. cxlvi–clv; and abridgement of the *Regularis Concordia*, ed. H. Nocent, OSB, and others in *Consuetudinum Saeculi X/XI/XII Monumenta non-Cluniacensia* (Corpus Consuetudinum Monasticarum, 7, pt. 3; Siegburg, 1984), pp. 149–85.
C. L. White, *Ælfric: A new Study of his Life and Writings* (Yale Studies in English, 2; 1898); M. M. Dubois, *Ælfric, sermonnaire, docteur et grammairien* (Paris, 1942), with full bibl. P. A. M. Clemoes, 'The Chronology of Ælfric's Works', in id. (ed.), *The Anglo-Saxons: Studies in some Aspects of their History and Culture presented to Bruce Dickins* (1959), pp. 212–47, with refs. J. Hurt, *Ælfric* (New York, [1972]). M. McC. Gatch, *Preaching and Theology in Anglo-Saxon England: Ælfric and Wulfstan* (Toronto, 1977). L. Grundy, *Books and Grace: Ælfric's Theology* (King's College London Medieval Studies, 6; 1991). L. M. Reinsma, *Ælfric: An Annotated Bibliography* (New York and London, 1987).

Aelia Capitolina. The new city which Hadrian built in *c*.130 on the site of *Jerusalem (destroyed AD 70). It was so named after the Emperor himself (Publius Aelius Hadrianus) and Jupiter Capitolinus. Statues to both Hadrian and Jupiter were erected in the area of the Temple. Its exact limits are unknown, but it probably extended as far as the present N. wall of Jerusalem and included the northern part of the western hill.

[L.] H. Vincent, OP and F. M. Abel, OP, *Jérusalem*, 2 (1914–1926), pp. 1–39, with map as pl. 1.

Aelred, St. See AILRED, ST.

Aeneas of Gaza (d. 518), Christian philosopher. He studied under Hierocles, the *Neoplatonist, at *Alexandria, and became a strong supporter of *Platonist and Neoplatonist doctrines. In his dialogue 'Theophrastus' he defended the immortality of the soul and the resurrection of the body, though he rejected such tenets of Platonism as conflicted with orthodox Christian doctrine, e.g. the pre-existence of the soul and the eternity of the world. Twenty-five of his letters have also survived. With *Procopius of Gaza and *Zacharias Scholasticus, he made up the 'Gaza Triad'.

Gk. text of the 'Theophrastus' in A. *Gallandi, *Bibliotheca Veterum Patrum*, 10 (1774), pp. 629–64, repr. J. P. Migne, *PG* 85. 865–1004; crit. edn. by M. E. Colonna (Naples, 1958). Letters ed. R. Hercher, *Epistolographi Graeci* (Paris, 1873), pp. 24–32; crit. edn. by L. M. Positano (Naples, 1950; 2nd edn., 1962). M. Wacht, *Aeneas von Gaza als Apologet* (Theophania, 21; Bonn, 1969), with bibl.

Aeneas Silvius Piccolomini. See PIUS II.

Aengus, St. See OENGUS, ST.

aequiprobabilism. See EQUIPROBABILISM.

aer (Gk. ἀήρ). A large veil, used in the E. Church to cover the chalice and paten during the Liturgy.

Aerius (4th cent.), presbyter of Pontus. He was at first an associate of *Eustathius (who in 355 became Bp. of Sebaste), with whose ascetic movement he was closely identified and by whom he was ordained; but later (*c*.360) the two quarrelled. Acc. to St *Epiphanius (*Haer.* 75), from whom our knowledge of him is mainly derived, he maintained that there was no distinction between the function and rank of bishops and priests; that the observance of *Easter was a Jewish superstition (1 Cor. 5: 7); that prescribed fasts were wrong; and that it was useless to pray and give alms for the dead. Hence his followers refused to fast even in *Holy Week, though they observed a purely voluntary fast on *Sundays. Aerius was also charged by Epiphanius with being an *Arian. His followers (Aerians) are mentioned by St *Philaster (*Haer.* 72) and by St *Augustine (*De Haeresibus*, 53), but appear to have died out soon after his death. Aerius has prob. received from modern controversialists (*Bellarmine; some 17th-cent. Anglicans) more attention than his importance merits.

V. Ermoni in *DHGE* 1 (1912), col. 663, and H. C. Brennecke in *L.Th.K* (3rd edn.), 1 (1993), cols. 185 f., s.v.

Aeterni Patris. The encyclical of *Leo XIII (4 Aug. 1879), commending to the Church the study of philosophy, and esp. of the works of St *Thomas Aquinas. It gave the impetus to the revival of Scholastic philosophy.

Text in *Acta Leonis XIII* (1887), pp. 88–108. Comm. by F. *Ehrle, SJ, orig. pub. in *Stimmen aus Maria-Laach*, 18 (1880), pp. 13–28, 292–317, 388–407, and 485–98, together with the text of the Encyclical, ed. F. Pelster, SJ (Sussidi Eruditi, 6; Rome, 1954). *Atti del'VIII Congresso Tomistico Internazionale: L'Enciclica Aeterni Patris* (Studi Tomistici, 10–12; Vatican City, 1981). V. B. Brezik, CSB (ed.), *One Hundred Years of Thomism: Aeterni Patris and Afterwards, A Symposium* (Houston, Tex., 1981), esp. pp. 7–27, with Eng. tr. of the Encyclical, pp. 173–97.

Aethelbert, Aethelburga, etc. See ETHELBERT, ETHELBURGA, etc.

Aetius (d. *c*.366). A Christian sophist who carried the principles of *Arianism to their farthest limits. His enemies, by a play on his name, surnamed him ἄθεος, 'the godless one'. Originally a craftsman of *Antioch, he travelled to *Alexandria, where he became a subtle dialectician and skilled in the philosophy of *Aristotle. Under the Emp. *Julian (361–3) he was ordained a bishop by the Arians without fixed see. He and his followers, also known as *Anomoeans, asserted that the Son, being begotten, was in essence unlike the Father, the Ingenerate. A short writing of his (Συνταγμάτιον περὶ ἀγεννήτου θεοῦ καὶ γεννητοῦ) is preserved by *Epiphanius (*Haer.* 76. 11) and in a few fragments elsewhere.

G. Bardy, 'L'Héritage littéraire d'Aétius', *RHE* 24 (1928), pp. 809–27; V. Grumel, 'Les Textes monothélites d'Aétius', *ÉO* 18 (1929), pp. 159–66; L. R. Wickham, 'The *Syntagmation* of Aetius the Anomean', *JTS* NS 19 (1968), pp. 532–69, incl. text and Eng. tr. E. Venables in *DCB* 1 (1877), pp. 51–3, s.v.

affective prayer. A kind of prayer in which the emphasis is on making aspirations of love towards God, rather than on formulating precise petitions or engaging in discursive reflection. It was taught particularly in the 16th and 17th cents., though its roots are much older.

affinity. In moral theology, relationship created by marriage. It arises from a valid marriage, whether consummated or not, and is held to form an impediment to subsequent marriage between the one party and certain blood relations of the other. The impediment is not extinguished by death. In the C of E the sphere of affinity is regulated by the 'Table of *Kindred and Affinity' (q.v.), originally drawn up in 1563 and in 1969 substantially revised (Canon B 31), which superseded the complicated rules of the medieval canonists. Marriages within the *prohibited degrees were voidable in civil law until 1835, when Lord *Lyndhurst's Marriage Act rendered them *ipso facto* void. In the 20th cent. a stream of legislation beginning with the *Deceased Wife's Sister's Marriage Act 1907 has legalized marriage within many of the formerly prohibited degrees, including notably union with a father- or mother-in-law, but a clergyman is not obliged to solemnise such a marriage if he chooses not to. Most of these provisions refer to marriages terminated by death, and not by divorce. The RC rulings on affinity, affecting marriage and other matters, will be found in *CIC* (1983), cans. 109, 492 § 3, 1092, 1298, and 1448 § 1. RC canon law no longer recognizes spiritual affinity, which arises between the *godparent and the baptized.

P. Dib in *DDC* 1 (1935), cols. 264–85, s.v. 'Affinité'; C. Henry in *NCE* 1 (1967), pp. 167–71, s.v.

affirmation. In English civil law, a solemn declaration in place of an oath made by those who have conscientious objection to being sworn, either because of their religious convictions or because they have no religious belief. In the 17th cent. *Quakers suffered severe persecution for refusing to be sworn. The *Toleration Act 1688 began the process of relief by allowing 'certain persons, dissenters from the Church of England', to make an affirmation instead of an Oath of *Allegiance, and in 1691 a similar concession was made in respect of the Oath of Supremacy in *Ireland. The position was regularized for the 'people called Quakers' by an Act of 1696 which expressly granted them the general right of making an affirmation in place of an oath. This permission was limited, however, to official oaths, and criminal proceedings were exempted. This last restriction was removed by two Acts of 1833, the Quakers and Moravians Act and the 'Separatists' Affirmations Act, and in 1838 the exemption was extended to include former adherents of those sects. In 1854 the Common Law Procedure Act allowed the right of affirmation to all who conscientiously objected to being sworn. This was not construed to include atheists, who were uniquely prevented from giving evidence altogether, because it was thought that without fear of divine sanction evidence could not be relied upon. The Evidence Further Amendment Act 1869 and the Evidence Act 1870 allowed atheists to give oral evidence on affirmation, and the Oaths Act 1888 provided for depositions by atheists.

In practice the right to affirm was little used except by Quakers, because the 1888 Act required unbelievers to make public profession of their atheism. Since its replacement by the Oaths Act 1978, this is no longer necessary, and affirmation, although not usual, is now more frequently heard. It is also permitted when an oath would be inconvenient, e.g. because the appropriate religious book is not available.

affusion (or, occasionally, **infusion**). The method of
*Baptism now ordinarily practised in the W. Church
whereby water is poured over the head of the candidate.
It did not become general until the later Middle Ages,
*immersion and *submersion being the usual methods in
earlier times. The change was doubtless due to the wish
to avoid possible dangers to the candidate's health. It was
perhaps adopted from the first in cases where immersion
was not easily possible, e.g. on the Day of *Pentecost (Acts
2: 41) or in the gaoler's house at Philippi (Acts 16: 33). In
the BCP, modern Anglican liturgies, and the RC rite of
1969 it is a recognized alternative to immersion. See also
ASPERSION.

Afraates. See APHRAHAT.

Africa, Christianity in. Apart from Egypt and the
Mediterranean coast (Roman 'Africa', on which see the
following entry), Christianity had by the 4th cent. penetrated to *Nubia, where it died out in the 16th cent., and
to *Ethiopia, but it did not spread further south until the
era of Portuguese expansion from the late 15th cent. In
the 16th and 17th cents. Christianity penetrated most
deeply into the *Congo kingdom. Its presence in Warri on
the *Nigerian coast and Monomotapa (see ZIMBABWE) was
more superficial. Otherwise it took root within the
Portuguese colonies of *Angola and, to a lesser extent,
*Mozambique. Angola retains the largest degree of con-
tinuity with a pre-19th-cent. Church. At the close of the
18th cent. Christianity remained restricted to a few coastal
pockets.

A new Christian era began with the settlements of
*Black Christians from Nova Scotia at Freetown in
*Sierra Leone in 1787 and with a missionary advance
inland from the Dutch and then British colony of Cape
Town effectively beginning with the arrival there of J. T.
*van der Kemp in 1799. New missionary societies (the
*London Missionary Society, the *Church Missionary
Society, the *Holy Ghost Fathers, the *White Fathers,
etc.) began work in many parts of the continent as the
19th cent. advanced, while new missionary strategies were
developed by planners such as H. *Venn the younger,
Card. C.-M. A.-*Lavigerie, and Bl D. *Comboni. Early
missionaries varied greatly. They included explorers and
publicists such as D. *Livingstone, translators such as R.
*Moffat, political activists such as J. *Philip, and African
converts such as S. A. *Crowther. Apart from the extreme
south and the Horn of Africa, the interior was hardly
touched before the final quarter of the 19th cent. The missions founded in 1875 on Lake *Malawi (see LAWS, R.) and
in 1877 by the CMS in Buganda (see UGANDA) mark a new
beginning. In the following thirty years, coinciding with
the political 'Scramble for Africa', missions were established almost everywhere and a vast process of Church
growth got under way. The principal factors in conversion
were the bush school, the *catechist, and the vernacular
printed texts of Scripture, hymns, and the like. In many
African languages almost nothing else has even now been
printed.

In general missionary activity benefited from the new
conditions created by colonial rule; nevertheless at times
some missionaries voiced strong criticism of colonial
abuses (see ZAIRE, ANGOLA, COLENSO, J., and PHILIP, J.).

After 1920 there was an increasing alliance in the fields of
education and medicine between the missions and more
benevolent colonial governments. In the late colonial
period, however, esp. in southern Africa, relations were
more often strained (e.g. in Zimbabwe, Mozambique,
*South Africa). Since political independence, Church–
State relations have varied. While mostly co-operative,
there have been considerable conflicts as in Uganda under
I. Amin, in Zaire under President Mobutu, and in the
*Sudan.

From the 1890s African Christians began in some countries, notably Nigeria and South Africa, to reject missionary control and some aspects of missionary teaching and
to form independent Churches of their own. This movement at times took the form of a schism within, esp.
*Methodist, *Baptist, *Congregational, and *Low Church
Anglican missions, resulting in a Church not greatly different from that which had been left. At other times the
new Church was a consequence of the preaching and healing activity of a 'prophet' such as W. W. *Harris or S.
*Kimbangu. New Churches and movements went on
being born and subdividing through every decade of the
20th cent., esp. in South Africa, Zimbabwe, *Kenya, Nigeria, Zaire, and *Ghana. While the character of these
Churches (in all several thousand, of which many are
exceedingly small) greatly varied, most were much concerned with *spiritual healing, including the acceptance of
a traditional African interpretation of sickness in terms of
spirit possession and *witchcraft.

Everywhere the mainline, formerly mission, Churches
remain numerically far larger as a group than the 'independent' Churches. They mostly moved from white missionary to black indigenous leadership about the time of
the political independence of the country concerned.
Joseph Kiwanuka, consecrated RC Bp. of Masaka,
Uganda, in 1939, was the first African diocesan bishop of
the Latin rite in any mission Church in the 20th cent. It
was another twenty years before such appointments
became commonplace. In the latter part of the 20th cent.
(roughly since the coming of independence to most of
black Africa c.1960), the growth of all the Churches has
been prodigious, with a membership of some 25 million in
1950 increasing to well over 150 million in 1990. By this
time there were over 350 RC African bishops, and there
were over 150 Anglican African bishops at the *Lambeth
Conference of 1988. In many countries RCs are the largest
Church; in some, incl. Zaire, they include a total majority
of Christians. In Namibia *Lutherans form a majority. In
other countries, notably South Africa, there are a large
number of Churches and no one predominates. A recognizable African theology has developed since the 1960s
concerned esp. with the relationship between Christianity
and traditional religion and culture, but in southern Africa
it has focused more on issues of politics and race. In the
1990s the African Churches remain the fastest growing but
also structurally the least stable part of world Christianity.

C. P. Groves, *The Planting of Christianity in Africa* (4 vols.,
1948–58); A. Hastings, *The Church in Africa, 1450–1950* (Oxford
History of the Christian Church, 1994) with bibl.; id., *A History
of African Christianity 1950–1975* (Cambridge, 1979). Four symposia are also wide-ranging: C. G. Baëta (ed.), *Christianity in
Tropical Africa: Studies presented . . . at the Seventh International
African Seminar, University of Ghana, April 1965* (1968); T. O.

Ranger and J. Weller (eds.), *Themes in the Christian History of Central Africa* (1975); E. Fasholé-Luke and others (eds.), *Christianity in Independent Africa* (Ibadan and London, 1978); and G. Ruggieri (ed.), *Église et Histoire de l'Église en Afrique* (1990). For 19th-cent. mission history see also R. [A.] Oliver, *The Missionary Factor in East Africa* (1952; 2nd edn., 1965); R. M. Slade, *English-Speaking Missions in the Congo Independent State (1878–1908)* (Académie royale des Sciences coloniales, Classe des Sciences morales et politiques, Mémoires in-8°, NS 16, fasc. 2; Brussels, 1959); and J. F. A. Ajayi, *Christian Missions in Nigeria 1841–1891* (1965). Other local studies include J. V. Taylor, *The Growth of the Church in Buganda* (1958); B. A. Pauw, *Christianity and Xhosa Tradition: Belief and Ritual among Xhosa-speaking Christians* (1975); and B. [G. M.] Sundkler, *Bara Bukoba: Kyrka och miljo i Tanzania* (Stockholm, 1974; Eng. tr., *Bara Bukoba: Church and Community in Tanzania*, 1980). Aspects of Christian life are treated by id., *The Christian Ministry in Africa* (1960); A. Shorter, WF, and E. Kataza, *Missionaries to Yourselves: African Catechists Today* (1972); and A. Hastings, *Christian Marriage in Africa: Being a Report Commissioned by the Archbishops of Cape Town, Central Africa . . .* (1973).

On independent Churches and prophet movements, B. G. M. Sundkler, *Bantu Prophets in South Africa* (1948; 2nd edn., 1961); G. Shepperson and T. Price, *Independent African: John Chilembwe and the Origins, Setting and Significance of the Nyasaland Native Rising of 1915* (Edinburgh, 1958); D. B. Barrett, *Schism and Renewal in Africa: An Analysis of the Six Thousand Contemporary Religious Movements* (Nairobi, etc., 1968); B. [G. M.] Sundkler, *Zulu Zion and some Swazi Zionists* (1976); H. W. Turner, *Religious Innovation in Africa: Collected Essays on New Religious Movements* (Boston, 1979); R. I. J. Hackett (ed.), *New Religious Movements in Nigeria* (Lewiston, NY [1987]); and H. W. Turner, *Bibliography of New Religious Movements in Primal Societies, 1: Black Africa* (Boston, 1977).

On African theology, J. S. Pobee, *Toward an African Theology* (Nashville, Tenn. [1979]); K. A. Dickson, *Theology in Africa* (1984); J. S. Mbiti, *Bible and Theology in African Christianity* (Nairobi, 1986); P. [W. E.] Frostin, *Liberation Theology in Tanzania and South Africa: A First World Interpretation* (Studia Theologica Lundiensia, 42; 1988); and A. Hastings, *African Catholicism* (1989).

Africa, the Church in Roman. How Christianity spread to Roman 'Africa' (i.e. roughly Tripoli, Tunisia, Algeria, and Morocco) is unknown. The earliest evidence is that of the '*Acts' of the *Scillitan martyrs (180); and the 'Passion' of St *Perpetua (203) and the works of *Tertullian (*c.*197–*c.*220) reveal a Church widespread and organized. While Roman Christians were still speaking Greek, the African Church was already using a Latin Bible and liturgy. By *Cyprian's time (*c.*250) there were fully 100 bishops under the primacy of Carthage. The Romanized towns and the coastal regions were the chief, but not the only, areas of evangelization; and, though sees were more frequent in Africa Proconsularis and Numidia, parts of Mauretania had been touched. *Persecution by the Emp. *Decius (250) weakened the Church, leading to controversy over the readmission of lapsed members and to the *Novatianist schism, which in turn produced controversy with Rome over rebaptism. But, led by Cyprian, the faithful recovered strength and withstood fresh persecution under the Emp. Valerian (258). At the end of the century Africa added *Arnobius and *Lactantius to the as yet short roll of Latin theologians.

The 4th cent. saw the partly theological, partly social struggle against *Donatism, arising out of *Diocletian's persecution; the writings of *Tyconius and *Optatus; and

the rise of St *Augustine. Notable features of this period were the war against paganism, the growth of monasticism, African resistance to Papal claims, and the series of African Councils, the canons of which were incorporated into both Greek and Latin *canon law.

Such achievements were ended by the Vandal invaders (429), whose *Arian kings normally repressed Catholic Christianity, with intermittent toleration, as when Hilderic allowed an important council to assemble in 525. The chief writers of this later period were the historian *Victor Vitensis, the poet Dracontius, *Vigilius of Thapsus, and *Fulgentius of Ruspe. The reconquest (534) by *Justinian's general, Belisarius, restored orthodoxy, and some African theologians, notably *Facundus, were prominent in defence of the *Three Chapters; while monasticism became strong and canonists again active. Later still, *Gregory I (590–604) corresponded with African bishops, the Berber tribes were gradually converted, and, *c.*640, Africa strongly challenged *Monothelitism. But at the end of the 7th cent. the Arab conquest (Carthage fell in 698) reduced to a shadow the Church which had bred so many martyrs and thinkers. Its ruined shrines are now being uncovered.

C. Diehl, *L'Afrique Byzantine: Histoire de la Domination Byzantine en Afrique (533–709)* (1896); H. *Leclercq, OSB, *L'Afrique chrétienne* (2 vols., 1904); P. Monceaux, *Histoire littéraire de l'Afrique Chrétienne* (7 vols., 1901–23). E. Buonaiuti, *Il cristianesimo nell'Africa romana* (Bari, 1928). W. H. C. Frend, *The Donatist Church: A Movement of Protest in Roman North Africa* (Oxford, 1952; reissued, with extended bibl., 1985). C. Courtois, *Les Vandales et l'Afrique* (1955). J. P. Brisson, *Autonomisme et Christianisme dans l'Afrique romaine de Septime Sévère à l'Invasion vandale* (1958). F. Decret, *L'Afrique Manichéenne (IVᵉ–Vᵉ siècles)* (2 vols., Études Augustiniennes, 1978). C. Lepelley, *Les Cités de l'Afrique romaine au Bas-Empire* (2 vols., ibid., 1979–81). N. Duval, *Les Églises africaines à deux Absides* (Bibliothèque des Écoles françaises d'Athènes et Rome, 218; 2 vols., 1971–3), and other works of this author. Y. Duval, *Loca Sanctorum Africae: Le Culte des Martyrs en Afrique du IVᵉ au VIIᵉ siècle* (Collection de l'École française de Rome, 58; 2 vols., 1982). J. Christern, *Das frühchristliche Pilgerheiligtum von Tebessa* (Wiesbaden, 1976). J. Cuoq, *L'Église d'Afrique du Nord du deuxième au douzième siècle* [1984]. J. B. Ward Perkins and R. G. Goodchild, 'The Christian Antiquities of Tripolitania', *Archaeologia*, 95 (1953), pp. 1–82. H. Leclercq, OSB, in *DACL* 1 (1907), cols. 575–775, s.v. 'Afrique'; A. Schindler in *TRE* 1 (1977), cols. 640–700, s.v. 'Afrika, I', with copious bibl.; V. Saxer and P.-A. Février in *DPAC* 1 (1983), cols. 61–74, s.v.; Eng. tr., *Encyclopedia of the Early Church*, 1 (1992), pp. 13–16.

African Missions, Society of (Societas Missionum ad Afros, SMA), RC society of priests and lay brothers, dedicated to the evangelization of Africa and people of African origin. The founder, Melchior de Marion Brésillac (1813–79), a French aristocrat from Languedoc, served first in *India as a priest of the Paris Foreign Missions Society. He was made Bp. of Coimbatore in 1846 but in 1855 resigned his see over missionary policy concerning the caste system and reluctance to train indigenous clergy. He founded the Society of African Missions at Lyons, in 1856, and went with the first missionaries to *Sierra Leone, where he died of fever in 1859. Leadership of the society until 1901 passed to Augustine Planque (1826–1907), whom *Pius IX confirmed as first Superior General. In the 1860s foundations were made in *Nigeria and Benin and missions were eventually established along the entire W. African coast from Liberia to the Niger River. In 1875 Planque founded the sisters' Congregation of Our Lady of the Apostles. The Society of African Missions spread throughout Europe and N. America, and, in addition to its W. African foundations, began missionary work in Egypt. In the *United States members of the Society work among Black and Hispanic Americans. New foundations have recently been made in Latin America, Asia, and *Poland.

J. M. Todd, *African Mission: A historical study of the Society of African Missions* . . . [1962]. F. Gantly and E. Thorp, *For this cause: The life of Melchior de Marion Brésillac, founder of the Society of African Missions* (Rome, 1970). M. J. Bane, SMA, *Catholic Pioneers in West Africa* (1956), esp. pp. 127–93; E. M. Hogan, *Catholic Missionaries and Liberia: A Study of Christian Enterprise in West Africa, 1842–1950* (Cork, 1981), *passim.* N. Douai, SMA, in *DIP* 6 (1988), cols. 1652–4, s.v. 'Società delle Missioni Africane'.

Africanus, Sextus Julius. See JULIUS AFRICANUS, SEXTUS.

Agabus, St, prophet. He is mentioned in Acts as foretelling the famine (AD 44–8) under Claudius (11: 28) and St Paul's imprisonment (21: 10). In the E. Church he is held to be one of the seventy disciples (Lk. 10: 1) and dignified as an Apostle. Feast day, in the E., 8 April; in the W., 13 Feb.

agape (ἀγάπη, 'love'). (1) For reasons unknown, the *Septuagint generally uses ἀγάπη and related words instead of the more normal Greek word ἔρως to cover 'love' in all its senses. In the NT the word acquires a special connotation because of the kind of love revealed in Christ, taken as an indication of an essential quality in God and as a model for human imitation. This made it possible for a contrast to be made in Christian usage between ἀγάπη, seen as a spiritual and unselfish love, and ἔρως, seen as a carnal passion; but *Origen (prologue to *Comm. Cant.*) and *Dionysius the Pseudo-Areopagite (*Divine Names*, 4. 12) protested against this distinction on philological and theological grounds. In modern times a further distinction has been suggested, esp. by A. Nygren: the Christian doctrine of ἀγάπη is based on the selfless love which originates in God, whereas the pagan ἔρως, when used in a religious context, means the hunger of the creature reaching out in desire towards God. But the late Neoplatonist *Proclus explicitly has a doctrine of providential ἔρως on God's part, and some scholars, notably J. M. Rist and G. Quispel, have argued that this is not foreign to the earlier Platonist tradition. 'Αγάπη was normally translated into Latin by *caritas*; hence the original meaning of 'charity' in English. For the noun 'charity' is used in the AV, but most modern versions of the Bible prefer 'love', which has always been used for the cognate verbal form. See also LOVE.

(2) The term is applied also to the religious meal which seems to have been in use in the early Church in close relation to the Eucharist. The classic NT ref. is 1 Cor. 11: 17–34, where abuses which accompanied the common meals that preceded the Eucharist are condemned. The most important early documents held to attest the practice are St *Ignatius' reference to the Christian love-feasts in his letter to the Smyrnaeans (8) and esp. *Pliny's letter to

Trajan (10. 96). The latter contains a description of two separate Christian meetings, the one an early morning assembly for prayer, traditionally regarded as a Eucharistic celebration, the other an ordinary meal, believed to be the Agape. St *Hippolytus in the *Apostolic Tradition* (26) gives instructions about a liturgical meal which is differentiated from the Eucharist; this is often taken to be an Agape, though the word does not occur in the text. *Tertullian also seems to refer to the Agape in his *Apology* (39), though what he describes is not entirely clear. The connection of the Agape with the Eucharist had virtually ceased by the time of St *Cyprian; the Eucharist was then celebrated fasting in the morning, the Agape in the evening. It seems to have been more and more a charity supper and is described as such by St *Augustine (*contra Faustum*, 20. 20). It is still mentioned at the *Trullan Synod (692), but it soon fell into disuse generally, though there are signs of its longer persistence in the *Ethiopian Church. There has been some interest in reviving it in modern times, and the C of E Services and Prayers for *Lent, Holy Week, Easter* (1986) allows for an Agape within the Eucharist. Some scholars link the Agape with the custom of distributing the 'antidoron' or *'pain bénit' (q.v.).

(3) In the 18th cent. the Agape was introduced among various *Pietist communities, including the *Moravians (in 1727); it was brought to London by John *Wesley in 1738. 'Love feasts', as they were called, became an established feature of *Methodism until the mid-19th cent. In the C of E the Agape was revived in the parish of Hilgay in Norfolk in 1949 in an attempt to bring together separated Churches, esp. Anglicans and Methodists. The experiment was repeated overseas, beginning at Makerere College in *Uganda, as a means of reconciling diverse Christian traditions in a simple liturgical rite thought to stem from the early Church, but not confused with the Eucharist.

(1) A. Nygren, *Den Kristna Kärlekstanken genom tiderna: Eros och Agape* (2 vols., 1930–6; Eng. tr. (*Agape and Eros*), in 3 vols., 1932–9, pt. 1 by A. G. Hebert, SSM, and pt. 2, 2 vols., by P. S. Watson; new tr. by P. S. Watson, 1953); J. M. Rist, *Eros and Psyche: Studies in Plato, Plotinus, and Origen* (Phoenix, Suppl. Vol. 6; Toronto, 1964); G. Quispel, 'God is Eros', in W. R. Schoedel and R. L. Wilken (eds.), *Early Christian Literature and the Classical Intellectual Tradition* (Théologie Historique, 53 [1979]), pp. 189–205. See also bibl. to LOVE.

(2) Apart from 1 Cor. 11, the chief NT texts are Acts 2: 42, 46; Acts 6; Acts 20: 7, 11; 2 Pet. 2: 13; Jude 12. Cf. also *Did.* 9 and 10 (acc. to F. *Kattenbusch, T. *Zahn, G. *Dix, ref. here to Agape; acc. to P. *Batiffol, H. *Lietzmann, K. Völker ref. to Eucharist); Ignatius, *Smyrn.* 6. 8, 8. 2, and 12. 2, *Trall.* 2. 3, *Magn.* 1. 1, etc.; *Epist. Apost.*, 15; *Clement Alex., *Paedag.* 2. 1. J. F. Keating, *The Agape and the Eucharist in the Early Church* (1901); P. Batiffol in *DTC* 1 (1901), cols. 551–6, s.v.; id., *Études d'histoire et de théologie positive*, 1 (3rd edn., 1904), pp. 283–325; H. Lietzmann, *Messe und Herrenmahl* (1926), pp. 197–210 and 230–8; Eng. tr. (Leiden, 1979), pp. 161–71 and 188–94; cf. pp. 271 f.; K. Völker, *Mysterium und Agape: Die gemeinsamen Mahlzeiten in der alten Kirche* (1926); J. M. Hanssens, SJ, 'L'Agape et l'Eucharistie', *EL* 41 (1927), pp. 525–48; 42 (1928), pp. 545–74; 43 (1929), pp. 177–98 and 520–9; A. Arnold, *Der Ursprung des christlichen Abendmahls im Lichte der neuesten liturgiegeschichtlichen Forschung* (1937); G. Dix, OSB, *The Shape of the Liturgy* (1944), pp. 82–102. B. Reicke, *Diakonie, Festfreunde und Zelos in Verbindung mit der Altchristlichen Agapenfeier* (Acta Universitatis Upsaliensis, 1951, pt. 5; 1951). A. Hamman, *Vie liturgique et Vie Sociale* (Bibliothèque de Théologie [1968]), pp. 151–227 ('L'Agape et les repas de charité'). [B.] T. Lloyd, *Celebrating the Agape Today*

(Grove Worship Booklets, 97; 1986). See also H. *Leclercq, OSB, in *DACL* 1 (pt. 1; 1907), cols. 775–848 (holds that the Agape was a funeral meal). C. Bernas in *NCE* 1 (1967), pp. 193 f., s.v.; K. Richter in *L.Th.K.* (3rd edn.), 1 (1993), cols. 222 f., s.v.

(3) [G.] I. [F.] Thomson, *An Experiment in Worship: The Revival of the Agape* (1951). F. Baker, *Methodism and the Love-Feast* (1957).

Agapemone, Church of the. A small 19th-cent. English sect. It was founded by Henry James Prince (1811–99), who in 1840 was ordained as curate of Charlynch, nr. Bridgwater in Somerset. Together with his rector, Samuel Starky, he started a revivalist movement which soon resulted in illusions of the grossest kind. Both left the C of E and began a ministry of their own, asserting that they were the Holy Spirit personified, the Two Witnesses of Rev. 11, or *Elijah. In 1849 they opened the 'Agapemone' or 'Abode of Love' in the village of Spaxton (in Somerset), being amply supported by their followers, who believed Prince to be a Divine being. The morals of the sect caused great scandal and a trial in 1860 revealed the licentiousness of Prince and his followers. In the early 1890s the sect conducted a campaign in Clapton in NE London, calling themselves the 'Children of the Resurrection'. J. H. Smyth-Pigott, Prince's successor in the leadership, proclaimed himself to be Christ. The sect disappeared early in the 20th cent.

Material on the Agapemonites is to be found in Prince's own writings, e.g. *A Hook in the Nose of Leviathan* (1877) and *The Man Christ Jesus* (1886), as well as in those of his opponents, among which are J. G. Dick, *A Word of Warning* (1845), and O. Piers, *The Door not Shut* (1846).

agapetae (Gk. ἀγαπηταί, 'beloved'). Another name for *subintroductae.

Agapetus, St (d. 536), Pope from 535. He was a strong defender of orthodoxy. In 536 he visited *Constantinople where, in spite of Imperial opposition from *Justinian and Theodora, he deposed Anthimus the *Monophysite Patr. of Constantinople, and consecrated *Menas as his successor. He died soon afterwards, after a reign of ten months. Feast day, in the E., 17 April (day of death); in the W., 20 Sept.

Letters and other items in J. P. Migne, *PL* 66. 35–80. Jaffé, 1, pp. 113–15. *LP* (Duchesne), 1, pp. 287–9. H. I. Marrou, 'Autour de la bibliothèque du Pape Agapit', *Mélanges d'Archéologie et d'Histoire*, 48 (1931), pp. 124–69. W. Ennslin, 'Papst Agapet I. und Kaiser Justinian I.', *Hist. J.* 77 (1958), pp. 459–66. J. P. Kirsch in *DHGE* 1 (1912), cols. 887–90, s.v.; J. Chapin in *NCE* 1 (1967), pp. 194 f., s.v.

Agatha, St. A virgin martyred at Catania in Sicily. In the 5th and succeeding cents. she was held in great veneration. Her name occurs in the *Canon of the Roman Mass and in the ancient *martyrologies; and two early churches were dedicated to her in Rome. The date of her death is quite uncertain, and the *acts of her martyrdom, which derive from the beginning of the 6th cent., are legendary. Besides being the patron saint of the city of Catania and of bell-founders, she is invoked against fire. Feast day, 5 Feb.

'Acta' in *AASS*, Feb. 1 (1658), pp. 598–602. S. Romeo, *S. Agata, V. e M., e il suo culto* (Catania, 1922). V. L. Kennedy, CSB, *The Saints of the Canon of the Mass* (Studi di Antichità

Cristiana, 14; Rome, 1938), pp. 169–73; F. di Capua, 'La concezione agonistica del martirio nei primi secoli del cristianesimo e l'introito della messa di S. Agata', *EL* 61 (1947), pp. 229–40. 'Studi su S. Agata e il suo Culto nella Ricorrenza del xvii Centenario del Martirio', *Archivio Storico per la Sicilia Orientale*, 4. 5 (1953 [for 1952]). On the early Roman church (mentioned by St *Gregory the Great, *Dialog.* 3. 30) dedicated to her, see C. Huelsenn, C. Cecchelli, and others, *S. Agata dei Goti* (Monografie sulle chiese di Roma, 1; 1924), G. N. Verrando, 'Note di Topografia Martiriale della Via Aurelia', *Riv. A.C.* 57 (1981), pp. 255–82, esp. pp. 275–82. J. P. Kirsch in *CE* 1 (1907), pp. 203 f., s.v.; P. Allard in *DACL* 1 (pt. 1; 1907), cols. 848–50, s.v., with further bibl.; H. Dörrie in *RAC* 1 (1950), cols. 179–84, s.v.

Agathangelos. The reputed author of a 'History of the Armenians' which gives an account of the life of St *Gregory the Illuminator (q.v.) and the conversion of *Armenia. Perhaps 'Agathangelos' is only a pseudonym of an Armenian Christian, proclaiming to his countrymen the 'good tidings' of their conversion. The writer asserts that he was a contemporary of St Gregory and wrote his life at the command of King Tiridates (298–?330). A. von Gutschmid argued that the Armenian text dates from *c*.450, and that it made use of earlier sources. The Greek text is secondary to the Armenian.

Armenian text of the 'History of the Armenians' pub. at Constantinople, 1709; modern edn. at Tiflis, 1909; Eng. tr. of the part known as *The Teaching of St Gregory* [paragraphs 259–715 of the 'History'] by R. W. Thomson (Cambridge, Mass., 1970) and of the remainder of the 'History' by id. (Albany, NY, 1976). Greek text in *AASS*, Sept. 8 (1762), pp. 320–402; modern edn. by G. Lafontaine (Publications de l'Institut Orientaliste de Louvain, 7; 1973). A. von Gutschmid, 'Agathangelos', *Zeitschrift der deutschen morgenländischen Gesellschaft*, 31 (1877), pp. 1–60. G. Garitte, *Documents pour l'Étude du Livre d'Agathange* (ST 127; 1946), with additional texts. G. Winkler, 'Our present knowledge of the *History* of Agat 'angełos and its oriental versions', *Revue des Études Arméniennes*, NS 14 (1980), pp. 125–41.

Agathias (*c*.532–*c*.582), poet and historian. He practised as an advocate at *Constantinople. His Περὶ τῆς Ἰουστινιανοῦ Βασιλείας is our principal authority for the history of the years 552–8 of the reign of *Justinian. He also made a collection of contemporary epigrams (including several of his own) and wrote erotic myths in nine books of Δαφνιακά. It is doubtful if he was a Christian.

'History' first edited with notes and Lat. tr. by B. Vulcanius (Leiden, 1594), with 'Epigrammata Graeca' appended. Crit. edns. by B. G. Niebuhr (CSH Byz., 1828; repr. J. P. Migne, *PG* 88. 1269–1596) and R. Keydell (Corpus Fontium Historiae Byzantinae, 2; Berlin, 1967), with introd. and bibl. Eng. tr. of Keydell's text by J. D. Frendo (ibid. 2a; 1975). A. [M.] Cameron, *Agathias* (Oxford, 1970).

Agatho (*c*.577–681), Pope from 678. He was a Sicilian by birth. In 680 he held a council at Rome against the *Monothelites, the doctrinal formula set forth at which was adopted at the Sixth Oecumenical Council of *Constantinople. He also took up the cause of St *Wilfrid of York in his dispute with *Theodore, Abp. of *Canterbury, and the King of Northumbria, and furthered the spread of the Roman Liturgy in England. Feast day, 10 Jan.

Jaffé, 1, pp. 238–40. *LP* (Duchesne), 1, pp. cclvii and 350–8. L. Magi, *La Sede Romana nella corrispondenza degli imperatori e patriarchi bizantini (VI–VII sec.)* (Bibliothèque de la *RHE* 57; 1972), pp. 235–53. A. Vacant and H. Quentin, OSB, in *DTC* 1

(1903), cols. 559–63, s.v.; J. P. Kirsch in *DHGE* 1 (1912), cols. 916–18, s.v.; J. N. D. Kelly, *The Oxford Dictionary of Popes* (1986), pp. 77 f.

Agde, Council of (*Concilium Agathense*). A council held in 506 at Agde in the S. of France under the presidency of St *Caesarius of Arles. Its 47 genuine canons deal with such subjects as clerical celibacy, the canonical age for ordination, the relations of a bishop and his diocesan synod, church property, public peace, and the religious obligations of the faithful.

Hardouin, 2, cols. 995–1006; Hefele and Leclercq, 2 (pt. 2; 1908), pp. 973–1002. K. Schäferdiek, *Die Kirche in den Reichen der Westgoten und Suewen bis zur Errichtung der westgotischen katholischen Staatskirche* (Arbeiten zur Kirchengeschichte, 39; 1967), pp. 55–67 and 243–5. C. Munier, *Concilia Galliae A. 314–A. 506* (CCSL 148; 1963), pp. 189–228. Id. in *DPAC* 1 (1983), col. 78 f.; Eng. tr. in *Encyclopaedia of the Early Church*, 1 (1992), p. 17.

age, canonical. The age, fixed by *canon law, at which a person becomes capable of undertaking special duties, of enjoying special privileges, or of entering specified new states of life. The term is esp. used in connection with *ordination, for which in the C of E the canonical age for a deacon is 'twenty-three . . . unless he have a *faculty'; for a priest 'twenty-four . . . unless being over twenty-three he have a faculty'; and for a bishop at least thirty.

'Age of Reason'. (1) The traditional term for the age at which a child may be supposed to be capable of discerning right from wrong and therefore being responsible for his conduct. In RC moral theology this age is held to be reached at about 7 years, and current canon law (*CIC* (1983), can. 97 § 2) expressly states that on the completion of his 7th year a child is presumed to have the use of reason. The assumption of moral responsibility is commonly marked by the First Communion.

(2) A name sometimes applied to the 18th cent., when the prevailing tendency in philosophy and religion was rationalistic and opposed to all belief in the supernatural. W. *Cave described it as the *saeculum rationalisticum*.

Agenda (Lat., 'things to be performed'). (1) A term occasionally found in English 17th-cent. divines for matters of religious practice as opposed to those of belief (*credenda*).

(2) In certain primitive (particularly African) liturgies it is used of the central part of the *Mass, elsewhere called the *Canon, *Anaphora, etc. In the Council of *Carthage of 390 (can. 9), it is used of the Eucharist as a whole.

(3) Among German-speaking Protestants on the Continent, the term is in regular use for the prescribed forms of service.

aggiornamento (Ital., 'renewal'). A term closely connected with the pontificate of *John XXIII denoting a fresh presentation of the faith, together with a recognition of the wide natural rights of man and support of freedom of worship and the welfare state. In his opening speech at the Second *Vatican Council the Pope made it clear that, while a renewal of the method of the presentation of truth was required, a clear distinction had to be drawn between the unchangeable *depositum fidei* and the form of its enunciation.

Agios o Theos (Gk. ἅγιος ὁ θεός, 'Holy God'). An anthem, so named from its first words, which occurs in the E. liturgies. It has survived, in the original Greek, in the Roman *Good Friday Liturgy, where it has traditionally been sung during the *Veneration of the Cross. See also TRISAGION.

Agnellus of Pisa, Bl (*c*.1194–1236), founder of the English *Franciscan Province. According to tradition, he was received into the Order at Pisa, his native city, by St *Francis, who later sent him to *Paris to erect a convent. After his return to Italy, he was sent to England in 1224, and on 10 Sept. arrived at Dover with eight other friars, four of them English. Shortly afterwards he established friaries at *Canterbury, London, and *Oxford. He engaged R. *Grosseteste to teach at the Oxford friary, which rapidly became a centre of learning. He exercised considerable political influence in the conflict between Henry III and the Earl Marshal. He was a deacon until late in life when he received priest's orders at the wish of his province. He died in March 1236 at Oxford, where his remains were venerated until the Reformation. His cultus was confirmed by *Leo XIII in 1892. His feast used to be observed in some dioceses on 13 March; as this date invariably fell in Lent, the English Franciscans now celebrate his memory on 10 Sept., the date of the arrival of the first friars in England.

The principal authority is Thomas of Eccleston, *Tractatus de Adventu Fratrum Minorum in Angliam*, ed. A. G. Little (Collection d'Études et Documents, 7, Paris, 1909; 2nd edn., Manchester, 1951; in the 1909 edn. the relevant passages from the Chronicle of Lanercost and Bartholomew of Pisa's *Liber Conformitatum* are pr. in appendices). Eng. trs. of the *Tractatus* by Father Cuthbert, OSFC (London, 1903), E. G. Salter, *The Coming of the Friars Minor to England & Germany* (1926), pp. 3–126, and by L. Sherley-Price (London, 1964). Father Gilbert, OSFC, *B. Agnellus and the English Grey Friars* (1937). Antoine de Sérent, OFM, in *DHGE* 1 (1912), cols. 907 f., s.v., with further refs.; *BRUO* 3 (1959), p. 1484, s.v. 'Pisa, Agnellus de'.

Agnellus, Andreas (*c*.800–*c*.845), historian of *Ravenna. He had the title of Abbot, but appears to have remained a secular priest. His principal writing, 'Liber Pontificalis Ecclesiae Ravennatis', is an elaborate account of the see, modelled on the '*Liber Pontificalis' of Rome, which traces the history from St *Apollinaris to his own age. It is full of historical errors, but also embodies valuable information about the buildings and customs of Ravenna, esp. in Agnellus' own time. The work was written largely to support the claims of Ravenna against *Rome. He has often been confused with St Agnellus, Abp. of Ravenna (*c*.556–*c*.566).

Editio princeps of the *Liber Pontificalis Ecclesiae Ravennatis* was pub. in 2 vols., Leipzig, 1708; crit. edn. by O. Holder-Egger in *MGH*, Scriptores Rerum Langobardicarum et Italicarum Saec. VI–IX (1878), pp. 265–391; also ed. A. Testi Rasponi in *Rerum Italicarum Scriptores* founded by L. A. *Muratori, 2nd edn. cont. by C. Carducci and V. Fiorini, 2. 3 (1924; only to ch. 104 (AD 606); no more pub.). G. Fasoli, 'Rileggendo il "Liber Pontificalis" di Agnello Ravennate', *Settimane di Studio del Centro Italiano di Studi sull'Alto Medioevo*, 17 (1970), pp. 457–95. P. Lamma in *Dizionario Biografico degli Italiani*, 1 (1960), pp. 429 f., s.v. 'Agnello'.

Agnes, St. She has been venerated as a virgin in Rome since the 4th cent., but the early legends of her martyrdom vary considerably, and nothing certain can be deduced as to the date or manner of her death. A *basilica was built in *c*.350 on the Via Nomentana on the site of her remains. Her name occurs in the Roman *Canon of the Mass and in all *martyrologies both in E. and W., though on different days. In art she is represented with a lamb, no doubt on account of the similarity of 'agnus' with 'Agnes', and the archiepiscopal *pallium is made from the wool of two lambs, blessed each year in her basilica on her feast (21 Jan.). In the Roman Calendar a second feast used to be kept on the octave day, 28 Jan.

Lat. text of her Acta, ascribed to St *Ambrose, in *AASS*, Jan. 2 (1643), pp. 351–4; F. de' Cavalieri, *S. Agnese nella tradizione e nella leggenda* (*RQ*, suppl. 10; 1899), with Gk. texts, pp. 71–92; repr. in *Scritti Agiografici*, 1 (ST 221; 1962), pp. 293–354; with other arts. on St Agnes repr. ibid. 2 (ST 222; 1962), pp. 337–64. F. Jubaru, SJ, *Sainte Agnès vierge et martyre de la voie Nomentane d'après de nouvelles recherches* (1907), on which see F. de' Cavalieri, *Hagiographica* (ST 19; 1908), pp. 141–64. V. L. Kennedy, CSB, *The Saints of the Canon of the Mass* (Studi di Antichità Cristiana, 14; 1938), pp. 173–7. A. J. Denomy, CSB (ed.), *The Old French Lives of Saint Agnes and Other Vernacular Versions of the Middle Ages* (Harvard Studies in Romance Languages, 13; 1938), with full introd., pp. 4–38, and hagiographical bibl., pp. 263–5. A. P. Frutaz, *Il Complesso Monumentale di Sant'Agnese e di Santa Costanzia* (1960), pp. 5–71, with Eng. summary, pp. 99–101. P. Allard and H. *Leclercq, OSB, in *DACL* 1 (1907), cols. 915–65; A. P. Frutaz in *EC* 1 (1948), cols. 467–74, s.v. 'Agnese'; E. Josi and R. Aprili in *Bibliotheca Sanctorum*, 1 (Rome, 1961), cols. 382–411, s.v. 'Agnese'; all with bibl.

Agnoetae (Gk. ἀγνοέω 'to be ignorant of'). A *Monophysite sect founded by Themistius, a deacon of *Alexandria (6th cent.; hence also 'Themistians'). On the basis of Mk. 13: 32, Jn. 11: 34, etc., they attributed ignorance to the human soul of Christ. Most Monophysites rejected their teaching. It was also attacked by Eulogius, Patr. of Alexandria, in 598–9, and declared heretical by Pope *Gregory I.

A. Grillmeier, SJ, *Jesus der Christus im Glauben der Kirche*, 2/2 (1989), pp. 379–402; Eng. tr. (1995), pp. 362–84. P. *Schaff in *DCB* 1 (1877), pp. 62 f., s.v.; A. Vacant in *DTC* 1 (1903), cols. 586–96, s.v. 'Agnoètes', with patristic refs.

agnosticism. As most commonly understood, the view that we cannot really know whether there is a God or not. The invention of the word is generally ascribed to T. H. *Huxley, who is said to have coined it in 1869 on the basis of Acts 17: 23. Agnosticism is sometimes associated with those who stress the importance of faith (rather than philosophical speculation) in religion. More frequently, however, it is identified with religious scepticism, esp. of the kind influenced by such writers as D. *Hume and I. *Kant. In the later 19th cent. agnosticism was favoured by people of sceptical inclinations who wished to avoid professing dogmatic *atheism. In popular usage the term has come to be applied to all forms of scepticism.

H. *Spencer, *First Principles* (1862); L. Stephen, *An Agnostic's Apology and other Essays* (1893); J. Ward, *Naturalism and Agnosticism* (*Gifford Lectures for 1896–8; 2 vols., 1899; 2nd edn., 1903); R. Flint, *Agnosticism* (1903); R. A. Armstrong, *Agnosticism and Theism in the Nineteenth Century* (1905); J. [A.] Passmore, *A Hundred Years of Philosophy* (1957; 2nd edn., 1966), chs. 1–2;

B. Lightman, *The Origins of Agnosticism: Victorian Unbelief and the Limits of Knowledge* [1987].

Agnus Dei. (1) The formula beginning with the words 'O Lamb of God' said or sung in the Latin liturgy shortly before the Communion. The scriptural basis is Jn. 1: 29 (itself derived from Is. 53: 7), but the repetition is first found in the *Gloria in excelsis*, introduced at Rome for episcopal Masses by Pope *Symmachus (498–514). Its independent use is ascribed by the *Liber Pontificalis* to *Sergius I (687–701), a Syrian, who ordered it to be sung at the time of the Fraction. Its origin may have been a practical protest by Sergius against can. 82 of the *Trullan Council (692) forbidding the representation of the Lord under the form of a lamb. Originally recited once only, by the beginning of the 11th cent. it was said three times, though the third 'have mercy upon us' was changed to 'grant us peace', perhaps as a preparation for the *Kiss of Peace, which then came immediately after it, or possibly, as *Innocent III says, because of the calamities afflicting the Church. By the regulations of the *Ordo Missae* of 1969 it again accompanies the Fraction and may be repeated any number of times. In the Middle Ages the Agnus, like the *Kyrie, was extensively interpolated. In *Requiems 'grant them rest' used to be substituted for the second part. It is now quite widely used in the C of E, where its legality was upheld by the *Lincoln Judgement; it is included in both Holy Communion rites in the ASB.

(2) A wax medallion bearing the figure of a lamb, blessed by the Pope in the first year of his pontificate and every 7th year afterwards. These objects of devotion are first heard of early in the 9th cent. at Rome, where the Archdeacon manufactured them on Holy Saturday from the remnants of the previous year's *paschal candle. They may represent a Christian substitute for a pagan charm. Agnus Dei's are also made of a mixture of wax and dust believed to be that of the bones of martyrs.

On (1), *LP* (Duchesne) 1, p. 376. F. *Cabrol, OSB, in *DACL* 1 (1907), cols. 965–9, s.v., and Jungmann (1958 edn.), 2, pp. 413–22; Eng. tr., 2, pp. 332–40.
On (2), E. Mangenot in *DTC* 1 (1903), cols. 605–13, s.v., with bibl.; W. Henry in *DACL* 1 (1907), cols. 969–71, s.v.

Agobard (*c*.769–840), Abp. of Lyons. Appointed coadjutor to Leidrad of Lyons in 813, he succeeded to his see in 816. His support of Lothair in the latter's revolt against his father, the Emp. *Louis I, led to his deposition at the Council of Thionville (835), but he was reinstated four years later. He was a versatile scholar whose works were marked by much originality. He attacked the excessive veneration of images, trial by ordeal, belief in witchcraft, and the 'absurd opinion of the vulgar concerning hail and thunder' (that it was due to magic). His theological writings include a treatise against the *Adoptionist views of *Felix of Urgel. He may also have attacked the liturgical speculations of *Amalarius of Metz. However, the authenticity of the work in question is contested, as is that of various other treatises in which some scholars claim to detect the hand of *Florus of Lyons.

Works first pub. by P. Masson (Paris, 1605) and re-ed. by S. *Baluzius (2 vols. bound in 1, Paris, 1666), repr. in J. P. Migne, *PL* 104. 159–352. Crit. edn. by L. Van Acker (CCCM 52; 1981). [A.] Bressolles, *Saint Agobard: Évêque de Lyon* (L'Église et l'État au moyen-âge, 9, 1949); [J.] A. Cabaniss, *Agobard of Lyons* (Syracuse, NY, 1953); E. Boshof, *Erzbischof Agobard von Lyon* (Kölner historische Abhandlungen, 17; 1969). Id. in *TRE* 2 (1978), pp. 101–3, s.v.

Agonizants (from Med. Lat. *agonizo*, 'to be at the point of death'), the fraternity, also known as 'Camillians', which was founded by St *Camillus de Lellis (q.v.) at Rome in 1586. In 1591 the Order was given a rule by Gregory XIV, and soon grew rapidly in riches and popularity. Its work has always been to minister to the sick and dying.

P. Sannazzaro, MI, in *DIP* 2 (1975), cols. 912–24, s.v. 'Chierici Regolari Ministri degli Infermi'.

Agrapha (i.e. 'unwritten [sayings]'). A name given esp. to the sayings of Christ not contained in the four canonical Gospels. Some occur in various NT MSS (e.g. Lk. 6: 4 in the *Codex Bezae); one in Acts (20: 35); others are found in apocryphal Gospels, e.g. the 'Gospel acc. to the *Hebrews' and esp. the 'Gospel of *Thomas', and the writings of the Fathers.

A. Resch, *Agrapha: Aussercanonische Evangelienfragmente* (TU 5, Heft 4; 1889); id., *Agrapha: Aussercanonische Schriftfragmente* (ibid. 30, Hefte 3–4; 1906). J. H. *Ropes, *Die Sprüche Jesu die in den kanonischen Evangelien nicht überliefert sind* (ibid. 14, Heft 2; 1896). B. Jackson, *Twenty-five Agrapha* (1900; incl. Eng. tr.). J. Jeremias, *Unbekannte Jesusworte* (Abhandlungen zur Theologie des Alten und Neuen Testaments, 16; 1948; 3rd edn., 1963; Eng. tr., 1957, and 2nd edn., 1964). R. Dunkerley, *Beyond the Gospels* (Pelican Books, 1957). O. Hofius in Schneemelcher, 1 (5th edn., 1987), pp. 76–9; Eng. tr., 1 (1991), pp. 88–91. J. K. Elliott, *The Apocryphal New Testament* (Oxford, 1993), pp. 26–30. J. H. Ropes in *HDB*, extra vol. (1904), pp. 343–52, s.v.; L. Vaganay in *Dict. Bibl. Suppl.* 1 (1928), cols. 158–98, s.v.; O. Hofius in *TRE* 2 (1978), pp. 103–10, s.v.

Agreed Statement. See ANGLICAN–ROMAN CATHOLIC INTERNATIONAL COMMISSION.

Agricola, Johann (*c.*1494–1566), German Protestant reformer. A native of Eisleben, he studied theology under M. *Luther at *Wittenberg and in 1519 accompanied him to the *Leipzig Disputation. In 1523 he began to teach theology at Wittenberg. He moved to Eisleben in 1525. In 1527 his *antinomian views brought him into conflict with P. *Melanchthon. In 1536 he returned to Wittenberg for discussions over the *Schmalkaldic Articles which he in due course signed. However, his antinomian views involved him in another conflict in 1536, this time with Luther. He did not wish to separate himself from the Lutheran Church and was called in 1539 to the newly-founded Wittenberg Consistory. In 1540 he moved to Berlin and published a recantation which put an end to the controversy, at least officially. John II, Elector of Brandenburg, appointed him to the offices of *General Superintendent and court preacher which he filled until his death. He was associated in the preparation of the *Augsburg Interim of 1548 and supported the traditional Lutherans against the *Adiaphorists. The author of numerous treatises and exegetical works, he also published collections of German proverbs (1528, 1529, 1548).

Life by G. Kawerau (Berlin, 1881). J. Rogge, *Johann Agricolas Lutherverständnis* (Theologische Arbeiten, 14 [1960]). L. W. Spitz, *The Religious Renaissance of the German Humanists* (Cambridge,

Mass., 1963), pp. 20–40. B. Kordes, *M. Johann Agricola's aus Eisleben Schriften möglichst vollständig verzeichnet* (Altona, 1817; repr., Leipzig, 1973). J. Rogge in *TRE* 2 (1978), pp. 110–18, s.v. with bibl.

Agrippa von Nettesheim, Heinrich Cornelius (1486–1535), scholar and adventurer. After studying in *Cologne and *Paris, in 1508 he fought in Spain, probably in the service of *Ferdinand V of Aragon. In 1509 he was at Dôle, lecturing on J. *Reuchlin's *De Verbo Mirificio*, and was attacked for teaching heresy. Around this time he wrote his *De Nobilitate et Praecellentia Foeminei Sexus*, a striking example of the Renaissance re-evaluation of the status of women. In 1510 he was in London, apparently on some secret mission, and while there studied St *Paul's Epistles with J. *Colet. From 1511 to 1517 he was in N. Italy. He attended the Council of Pisa and subsequently lectured on the *Hermetica at Pavia and Turin. About 1518 he was appointed advocate and orator of Metz. He took an interest in contemporary theological controversies, but his fierce criticism of abuses was qualified by protestations of loyalty to the Catholic Church. After spending the early 1520s in Germany and Switzerland, in 1524 he moved to France to become physician to Louis of Savoy. He soon fell into disgrace, and in 1529 went to the Low Countries to become historiographer to the Emp. *Charles V. His most important works were *De Incertitudine et Vanitate Scientiarum et Artium* (1530) and *De Occulta Philosophia* (1531). The *De Occulta* (composed *c.*1510) was an attempt to recover what he believed to have been an ancient tradition of secret magical wisdom which encompassed all branches of knowledge and was in harmony with, and ultimately derived from, Divine revelation. The *De Incertitudine* was a work of profound scepticism, or rather *fideism, which not only repudiated the esoteric tradition but strongly attacked *scholasticism, denied the power of reason to attain truth, and made revelation the only source of knowledge. The publication of these works, which were condemned by the universities of Paris, Louvain, and Cologne, cost him the Emperor's favour. But the dedication of *De Occulta* to *Hermann of Wied, the reforming Abp. of Cologne, earned him a place in his entourage from 1532. He probably stayed with Hermann until 1535, when he seems to have returned to France and died there.

Works (2 vols., Lyons, no date; repr. Lyons, 1600; repr., with introd. [in Eng.] by R. H. Popkin, Hildesheim and New York, 1970). Crit. edn. of *De Nobilitate et Praecellentia Foeminei Sexus* by R. Antonioli and others (Travaux d'Humanisme et Renaissance, 243; 1990), with good bibl. Fr. tr. of *De Occulta* by J. Servier (3 vols., Paris, 1981–2). H. Morley, *The Life of Henry Cornelius Agrippa von Nettesheim* (2 vols., 1856); J. Orsier, *Henri Cornélis Agrippa* (1911); C. G. Nauert, Jun., *Agrippa and the Crisis of Renaissance Thought* (Illinois Studies in the Social Sciences, 55; 1965), with extensive bibl.

Ahikar legend. A story which occurs in various forms but in essence tells of a Grand Vizier of Sennacherib, Ahikar the Wise, against whom his adopted son, Nadan, plotted and received appropriate retribution. The legend was widely spread in the East. It is met with in the *Elephantine papyri and in Romanian, Slavonic, Armenian, Arabic, and Syriac literature. Since G. Hoffmann (1880) pointed out the identity of 'Achiacharus', *Tobit's nephew (Tob. 1: 21), with 'Ahikar', its influence on the Book of Tobit has been universally admitted.

F. C. *Conybeare, J. R. Harris, and A. S. Lewis, *The Story of Ahikar from the Syriac, Arabic, Armenian, Ethiopic, Greek and Slavonic Versions* (1898); R. H. *Charles, *The Apocrypha and Pseudepigrapha of the Old Testament*, 2 (Oxford, 1913), pp. 715–84; F. Nau, *Histoire et sagesse d'Ahikar l'Assyrien* (1909). J. M. Lindenberger, *The Aramaic Proverbs of Ahiqar* (Baltimore and London, 1983). Id. in J. H. Charlesworth (ed.), *The Old Testament Pseudepigrapha*, 2 (1985), pp. 479–507. R. Degen in *Enzyklopädie des Märchens*, ed. K. Ranke, 1 (1977), cols. 53–9, s.v. 'Achikar', with bibl.

Aidan, St

Aidan, St (d. 651), Irish monk of *Iona and Bp. of *Lindisfarne. At the request of St *Oswald, King of Northumbria, he was sent from Iona to revive the missionary work of *Paulinus. Consecrated bishop in 635, he established his headquarters on the island of Lindisfarne, whence he made long journeys on the mainland, strengthening the Christian communities and founding new missionary outposts. The Christian practices taught by Aidan were those of the *Celtic Church. He carefully educated a group of twelve English boys to be future ecclesiastical leaders of their people, among them St *Chad. His asceticism and gentleness won rapid success for his mission, and his personal relations with Oswald (d. 642) and Oswald's successor, St *Oswine (d. 651), were close and intimate. Feast day, 31 Aug.

The principal authority is *Bede, *HE* 3. 3, 5 f., 14–17, 25; comm. by J. M. Wallace-Hadrill (Oxford, 1988), pp. 90 f., 95 f., and 108–11 *passim*, with further refs. A. C. Fryer, *Aidan, the Apostle of the North* [1884]. J. B. *Lightfoot, *Leaders in the Northern Church* (Sermons, 1890), pp. 39–54. W. *Bright, *Chapters of Early English Church History* (1878), pp. 134–46 and 163 f.

Ailly, Pierre d'

Ailly, Pierre d'. See D'AILLY, PIERRE.

Ailred, St

Ailred, St (1109–67), also 'Aelred', the 'Bernard of the North', Abbot of *Rievaulx. The son of a Saxon priest of *Hexham, he was for some years at the court of King David of Scotland, son of St *Margaret. He entered the *Cistercian house at Rievaulx *c.*1133, became Abbot of Revesby in 1143, and Abbot of Rievaulx in 1147. In 1142–3 Ailred, at the invitation of St *Bernard of Clairvaux, wrote his first important work, the 'Speculum Caritatis'. His extensive spiritual writings show marked similarity of interest and attitude with those of St Bernard and *William of St-Thierry. He shared the latter's concern with psychology, and his analysis of the nature of the 'affections' and of love is in many ways parallel to that of the continental Cistercians. His devotion was marked by a strong attachment to the suffering humanity of Christ; and his 'De Spirituali Amicitia', a rewriting of Cicero's 'De Amicitia', is the fullest medieval discussion of the theme of friendship. He also wrote a life of *Edward the Confessor. In recent times, ninety-five sermons in an anonymous collection of homilies in the Bibliothèque Nationale in Paris (nouv. acq. Lat. 294) and eighteen in a similar MS in the Municipal Library at Troyes (MS 868) have been attributed to Ailred. His biography was written by his pupil, Walter Daniel. Feast day, 12 Jan., also 3 Mar.

Collections of Ailred's 'Opera Ascetica' in B. Tissier, *Bibliotheca Patrum Cisterciensium*, 5 (Bono-Fonte, 1662), pp. 162–388; *Opera Historica* in R. Twysden, *Historiae Anglicanae Scriptores Decem* (London, 1652), cols. 337–422; both repr. in J. P. Migne,

PL 195. 209–796. Modern edn. of the *Opera Ascetica* by A. Hoste, OSB, and C. H. Talbot (CCCM 1; 1971); *Sermones inediti B. Aelredi Abbatis Rievallensis* ed. C. H. Talbot (Series Scriptorum S. Ordinis Cisterciensis, 1; Rome, 1952). The sermons recently attributed to Ailred ed. G. Raciti, OCSO (CCCM 2A ff.; 1989 ff.). There are separate edns. of *De Spirituali Amicitia*, with Fr. tr. and notes, by J. Dubois (Bibliothèque de Spiritualité Médiévale, 1948); of *Cum factus esset Jesus annorum duodecim* by A. Hoste, OSB, with Fr. tr. by J. Dubois (SC 60; 1958); of *De Institutione Inclusarum* and *Oratio Pastoralis*, with Fr. tr. by C. Dumont, OCSO (ibid. 66; 1961); and of selected prayers, with introd. by A. Hoste, OSB, with Eng. tr. by Sr Rose of Lima (Steenbrugge, 1965). There are Eng. trs. of Ailred's *Treatises* [*Cum factus esset Jesus annorum duodecim* and *De Institutione Inclusarum*] and his *Oratio Pastoralis* (Cistercian Fathers Series, 2; 1971), *De Spirituali Amicitia* (ibid. 5; 1977), and *De Anima* (ibid. 22; 1981). F. M. Powicke (ed.), *The Life of Ailred of Rievaulx by Walter Daniel* (tr. and notes; 1950). A. Hallier, O.Cist.SO, *Un Éducateur Monastique: Aelred de Rievaulx* (1959; Eng. tr., Cistercian Studies Series, 2; 1969). A. Squire, OP, *Aelred of Rievaulx: A Study* (1969; rev. edn., Cistercian Studies Series, 50; Kalamazoo, Mich., 1981; also London, 1981). B. P. McGuire, *Brother and Lover: Aelred of Rievaulx* (New York, 1994) A. Hoste, OSB, *Bibliotheca Aelrediana: A Survey of the Manuscripts, Old Catalogues, Editions and Studies concerning St Aelred of Rievaulx* (Instrumenta Patristica, 2; Steenbrugge, 1962). *Collectanea Cisterciensia*, 29 (1967), pp. 3–99 [special issue to mark the 8th centenary of Ailred's death].

'Ain Karim

'Ain Karim. A village about 5 miles W. of *Jerusalem, in the hill country, traditionally regarded as the home of *Zacharias and *Elizabeth, the birthplace of St *John Baptist, and the scene of the *Visitation.

aisle

aisle (Fr. *aile*, 'wing'). Commonly any extension of the nave of a church made by the piercing of its side walls with a series of arches and the building on of an extension with a separate and lower roof, for the purpose of increased accommodation. Less frequently a similar extension of the chancel or transept. It is often, but quite wrongly, used of a gangway up the centre of the nave or elsewhere; and the corresponding expression 'centre aisle' is a contradiction in terms.

Akathistos

Akathistos. See ACATHISTUS.

Akhmîm fragment

Akhmîm fragment. See PETER, APOCALYPSE OF ST, and PETER, GOSPEL OF ST.

Akiba

Akiba or **Aqiba** (*c.*50–132), Jewish Rabbi. Akiba ben Joseph was the most influential rabbi of his generation. As teacher of the renowned Rabbi Meir he prob. much influenced the *Mishnah. He actively supported the revolt of *Bar-Cochba, recognizing his claims as *Messiah. He was taken prisoner by the Romans and burnt alive. *Aquila's version of the OT was probably a product of the School of Akiba.

L. Finkelstein, *Akiba: Saint and Martyr* (New York, 1936). P. Benoit, OP, 'Rabbi Aqiba ben Joseph, sage et héros du Judaïsme', *R. Bibl.* 54 (1947), pp. 54–89, repr. in id., *Exégèse et Théologie*, 2 (1961), pp. 340–79. P. Lenhardt and P. von der Osten-Sacken, *Rabbi Akiva: Texte und Interpretationen zum rabbinischen Judentum und Neuen Testament* (Arbeiten zur neutestamentlichen Theologie und Zeitgeschichte, 1; 1987). H. Freedman and others in *Encyclopaedia Judaica*, 2 (Jerusalem, 1971), cols. 488–92, s.v. 'Akiva'.

Akoimetae

Akoimetae. See ACOEMETAE.

Aksum. See AXUM.

Alacoque, St Margaret Mary. See MARGARET MARY ALACOQUE, ST.

Alan (or Alain) of Lille (d. 1203), poet, theologian, and preacher. He prob. studied and taught at Paris *c*.1150–*c*.1185. Later he moved to the S. of France, prob. to Montpellier, where he was engaged in combating the *Catharist heresy. Towards the end of his life he entered the abbey of *Cîteaux where he died.

He had a thorough training in the liberal arts before turning his attention to theology, and it is prob. that the *De planctu naturae*, a mixture of prose and verse, in which Nature personified plays the chief role, is an early work. His earliest theological work seems to be the incomplete *Summa Quoniam homines* and a number of unpublished *quaestiones*. Not much later are the *Regulae caelestis iuris*, in which an attempt is made to state theological truths in a series of rules or axioms, and the allegorical poem *Anticlaudianus* (1182–3). His subsequent works include a set of *Distinctiones*, a dictionary of biblical terms with literal and moral and allegorical interpretations, an *Ars praedicandi*, to which was attached a set of 27 model sermons, and a *Liber poenitentialis*, the earliest of the medieval manuals for confessors. Alan is reckoned among the 'Porretani' or disciples of *Gilbert de la Porrée, but his work has a highly personal character, which is also reflected in his style; the width of his interests is celebrated in his epitaph: 'Qui duo [i.e. the Old and New Testaments], qui septem [the liberal arts], qui totum scibile scivit'. The 'Ars Fidei Catholicae', an attempt to confute non-Christians on rational grounds alone, which until recently was attributed to him, has been shown to be the work of Nicholas of Amiens.

Collections of his works by C. de Visch (Antwerp, 1654) and, with additions, in the *Bibliotheca Scriptorum Ordinis Cisterciensis* (ibid., 1654) and J. P. Migne, *PL* 210; but these are not all satisfactory, since some still remain unpub.; see M. T. d'Alverny, *Alain de Lille: Textes inédits avec une introduction sur sa vie et ses œuvres* (Études de Philosophie médiévale, 52; 1965), with bibl. *De planctu naturae*, ed. N. M. Häring in *Studi Medievali*, 3rd ser. 19 (1978), pp. 797–879; Eng. tr. by J. J. Sheridan (Toronto, 1980). *Summa Quoniam homines*, ed. P. Glorieux in *AHDLMA* 20 (1954), pp. 113–364. *De Virtutibus et Vitiis*, ed. O. Lottin, OSB, *Psychologie et Morale aux XIIe et XIIIe Siècles*, 6 (Gembloux, 1960), pp. 27–92. *Anticlaudianus*, ed. R. Bossuat (Textes Philosophiques du Moyen Age, 1; 1955; Eng. tr. by J. J. Sheridan, Toronto, 1973). *Liber poenitentialis*: middle and short versions [this last is the work of a follower of Alan] ed. J. Longère in *AHDLMA* 32 (1965), pp. 169–242; long version ed. id. (Analecta Mediaevalia Namurcensia, 17–18; Louvain, 1965). For edns. of sermons and shorter poems, see M. T. d'Alverny, op. cit. M. Baumgartner, *Die Philosophie des Alanus de Insulis* (BGPM 2, Heft 4; 1896); G. Raynaud de Lage, *Alain de Lille: Poète du XIIe Siècle* (Université de Montréal Publications de l'Institut d'Études Médiévales, 1951). H. Roussel and F. Suard (eds.), *Alain de Lille, Gautier de Châtillon, Jakemart Giélée et leurs temps (Actes du Colloque de Lille, octobre 1978)* (Lille, 1980), pp. 27–169, incl. art. on attributions by M. T. d'Alverny; G. R. Evans, *Alan of Lille: The Frontiers of Theology in the later Twelfth Century* (1983). J. Ziolkowski, *Alan of Lille's Grammar of Sex: The Meaning of Grammar to a Twelfth-Century Intellectual* (Speculum Anniversary Monographs, 10; Cambridge, Mass., 1985). M. *Grabmann, *Die Geschichte der scholastischen Methode*, 2 (1911), pp. 452–76; Überweg, 2, pp. 245–7, with bibl. p. 706. J. M. Canivez in *Dict. Sp.* 1 (1927), cols. 270–2, s.v. 'Alain de

Lille'; G. Silagi in *TRE* 2 (1978), pp. 155–60, s.v. 'Alanus ab Insulis'.

Alane, Alexander. See ALESIUS, ALEXANDER.

alapa. According to W. usage, the light blow formerly delivered by the bishop on the cheek (*leviter in maxilla caedit*) of those being confirmed. It was perhaps an imitation of the blow with the sword by which a young Teutonic warrior was dubbed a knight and, if so, symbolized the spiritual warfare lying ahead of the candidate. More prob. it is to be associated with the *Kiss of Peace.

Alaric (*c*.370?–410), Visigothic leader. Belonging to a noble family, until 395 he combined a prominent position in the Gothic world with high office in the military hierarchy of the E. Empire; he was a commander of Gothic Federate troops under the Emp. *Theodosius I. On the latter's death he sought a more important and regular position within the Empire, and, on being frustrated, turned to violence. From 395 to 410 he enjoyed intermittent periods when he was recognized as a *Magister Militum* of the Empire; these periods were interspersed with military action, in the course of which he increased the strength of his following. In 408 he turned the attention of his forces definitively to the W. and mounted his second invasion of Italy. Once again, however, no lasting settlement was reached and Alaric besieged Rome in 408 and 409 before sacking it on the third occasion in 410. He entered the city on 24 August 410. This event caused consternation throughout the Empire and prompted St *Augustine's *City of God*. Even the sack of Rome led to no settlement, and when Alaric died later in the same year his group had not found a permanent position in the Empire. Like all those Goths who had been influenced by *Ulphilas, Alaric was *homoean in belief and was thus denounced by Augustine as an *Arian.

The major sources for his career are Olympiodorus, *Zosimus (based on Olympiodorus), Claudian, *Orosius, and Jordanes. Good secondary accounts by T. *Mommsen, 'Stilicho und Alarich', *Hermes*, 38 (1903), pp. 101–15; J. [F.] Matthews, *Western Aristocracies and Imperial Court*, A.D. 364–425 (Oxford, 1975), pp. 270–306; P. J. Heather, *Goths and Romans 332–489* (Oxford Historical Monographs, 1991), pp. 193–224.

à Lasco, John. See LASKI, JOHN.

alb. A white linen garment, reaching from the neck to the ankles with tight-fitting sleeves and held in at the waist by a girdle, worn by the ministers at Mass. It is derived from the under-tunic common in the Roman and Greek world. It has been used in Christian worship from an early date, but it was not regarded as a specifically liturgical garment until long after the other Eucharistic vestments. Sometimes it is ornamented, near the hem, with strips of embroidery or other coloured material, known as 'apparels'. The alb was taken to symbolize purity, and it was customary for the celebrant to say 'Make me white . . .' when putting it on. Albs of silk and in colours have also sometimes been used.

Braun, *LG* pp. 57–92 (ch. 3). C. Calleweart, 'De Alba Liturgica', *Collationes Brugenses*, 25 (1925), pp. 370–4, repr. in his *Sacris Erudiri* (Steenbrugge, 1940), no. 20, pp. 211–14.

Alban, St, the first British martyr (*Protomartyr Anglorum*). His martyrdom has traditionally been connected with the *Diocletianic persecution (c.305), but most modern scholars have accepted the reading preserved in a Turin MS (D.V. 3), according to which he suffered under Septimius Severus (c.209). According to all sources he was a pagan of Verulamium (now *St Albans in Herts) who was converted and baptized by a fugitive priest whom he sheltered. When the Emperor sent soldiers to search the house, Alban disguised himself in the priest's cloak, was arrested, and condemned to death. The priest, traditionally named Amphibalus from some confusion with the cloak (*amphibalus*), is said to have been stoned to death a few days later at Redbourn. St Alban is commemorated by *Venantius Fortunatus (c.580) in the line *Albanum egregium fecunda Britannia profert*. His shrine still stands in St Albans Abbey. He is not to be identified with the St Alban venerated at Cologne. Feast day, 22 June (dropped from the RC Calendar of 1969; now observed locally on 20 June); 17 June in the BCP (prob. by a misreading of xxii as xvii).

AASS, Jun. 4 (1707), pp. 146–70; W. Meyer, 'Die Legende des h. Albanus des Protomartyr Angliae in Texten vor Beda', *Abh.* (Gött.), NS 8, No. 1 (1904). Life in verse by John Lydgate (d. c.1450), ed. J. E. van der Westhuizen (Leiden, 1974). For various forms of the legend see Hardy, 1, pp. 3–30. W. Levison, 'St Alban and St Albans', *Antiquity*, 15 (1941), pp. 337–59. J. Morris, 'The Date of Saint Alban', *Hertfordshire Archaeology*, 1 (1968), pp. 1–8.

Alban, St, and St Sergius, Fellowship of. An organization, founded in 1928, which aims at promoting better understanding between Christians, and particularly between the Anglican and Orthodox Churches, by means of prayer, meetings, conferences, and the publication of the periodical *Sobornost* (from 1979 incorporating *Eastern Churches Review*). It maintains a permanent centre (now in Oxford) and has branches in various parts of England.

Journal of the Fellowship of S. Alban and S. Sergius. Quarterly (London, 1928–33, typewritten; 1934, printed); *Sobornost* (ibid., 1935 ff.). N. Zernov in R. Rouse and S. C. Neill (eds.), *A History of the Ecumenical Movement, 1517–1948* (1954), pp. 662–4. N. and M. Zernov, *The Fellowship of St Alban & St Sergius: A Historical Memoir* (Oxford, 1979).

Albania, Christianity in. Christianity probably reached what is now Albania at an early date through traders from Epirus and Macedonia, but with the fall of the W. Empire in the 5th and 6th cents. its influence was largely destroyed. In the Dark Ages, the native Illyrians, who later became known as Albanians, were partly conquered by Slav invaders from the N. In the 9th cent. some of the Albanians were incorporated into the Bulgarian realm (thus adhering to Eastern *Orthodox Christianity), and in the 11th cent. fell under *Serbian sway. At the religious schism between E. and W. a section of Albanians transferred their religious allegiance from *Constantinople to Rome. In 1389 the medieval Serbian Empire, into which the Albanians were later incorporated, fell to the Turks, who overran the country. Nevertheless, for ninety years resistance was effectively made to the Turkish power, esp. under G. K. Skanderbeg (1403–68), a national leader who maintained an independent kingdom in Upper Albania from 1443 till his death. He also encouraged his followers to abandon Orthodoxy for Rome. Many remained faithful to Orthodoxy, however, and under centuries of Turkish rule the proportion of Orthodox to Latins increased. Although the Turks, who finally subjugated Albania in 1521, treated the Albanians as allies rather than subjects, imperial favour was dependent upon the profession of *Islam, and there was much apostasy. Local Turkish lords indulged for centuries in every kind of persecution. In 1913 Albania became independent and the Orthodox Albanian Church became autocephalous in 1922. Under Communist rule after the Second World War, all places of worship were closed. When the outward practice of religion was again allowed in 1991, there were no Orthodox bishops surviving and only a few priests. The *Oecumenical Patriarch appointed Anastasios Yannoulatos acting Exarch in 1991. The following year he became Abp. of Tirana and full Exarch. Other bishops have since been appointed.

W. Peacock, *Albania: The Foundling State of Europe* (1914). D. Attwater, *The Christian Churches of the East*, 2 (1961), pp. 119–21. P. R. Prifti, *Socialist Albania since 1944* [1978], pp. 150–66 ('The Abolition of Religion'); P. Walters (ed.), *World Christianity: Eastern Europe* (Keston Book, 29; Eastbourne, 1988), pp. 237–46. M. Lacko in NCE 1 (1967), pp. 246 f., s.v.; G. Stadtmüller and B. Spuler in TRE 2 (1978), pp. 160–7, s.v. 'Albanien', with bibl.

Albert of Brandenburg (1490–1545), Cardinal Abp. and Elector of Mainz. He was successively a prebendary of Mainz (1509), Abp. of Magdeburg (1513), and Abp. of Mainz (1514). In 1518 he was created cardinal. Entrusted by *Leo X in 1517 with the publication in Saxony and Brandenburg of the Indulgence for *St Peter's in Rome, he secured the services of the notorious *Dominican, J. *Tetzel, to preach it. He was himself a man of liberal ideas and a friend of the humanists, notably of Ulrich von *Hutten, but he was never a supporter of M. *Luther's ideas. Having temporized somewhat during the *Peasants' War (1525), he threw in his lot with the German Catholic princes at the Dessau Meeting (1525). He was a resolute defender of the Papacy, though he tried to discourage extreme measures against the Protestants. In 1538 he took part in the Nuremberg Meeting which opposed the League of *Schmalkalden. In 1542 he became, through the influence of the *Jesuit Peter Faber, who resided in his diocese for a year, a warm admirer of the new Order, and in his last years worked strenuously on its behalf.

Crit. text of 9 primary documents by P. Fabisch and E. Iserloh, *Dokumente zur Causa Lutheri (1517–1521)*, 1 (Corpus Catholicorum, 41; 1988), pp. 202–309. J. May, *Der Kurfürst, Cardinal und Erzbischof Albrecht II von Mainz und Magdeburg* (2 vols., 1865–75). F. Jürgensmeier (ed.), *Erzbischof Albrecht von Brandenberg (1490–1545): Ein Kirchen- und Reichsfürst der Frühen Neuzeit* (Beiträge zur Mainzer Kirchengeschichte, 3; Frankfurt am Main, 1991). F. Winkler, *Das Gebetbuch des Kardinal Albrecht von Brandenburg* (1962). F. Schrader, 'Kardinal Albrecht von Brandenburg, Erzbischof von Magdeburg, im Spannungsfeld zwischen alter und neuer Kirche', in R. Bäumer (ed.), *Von Konstanz nach Trient . . .: Festgabe für August Franzen* (Paderborn, etc., 1972), pp. 419–45. G. A. Benrath in TRE 2 (1978), pp. 184–7, s.v. 'Albrecht von Mainz'.

Albert of Prussia (1490–1568). The last Grand Master of the *Teutonic Order and first Hohenzollern Duke of Prussia. Albert von Brandenburg-Ansbach was drawn towards *Lutheranism by A. *Osiander at the Diet of Nuremberg in 1522, and, with M. *Luther's support, determined to make Prussia a hereditary Duchy. In 1525 he achieved this end, but was obliged to recognize the Polish King as suzerain. In the same year he married Dorothea of Denmark. He encouraged education, established schools in his duchy, and founded the university of Königsberg in 1544, where he appointed Osiander professor in 1549. After the quarrel between the latter and P. *Melanchthon over *justification by faith, a strict form of Lutheranism was established in his dominions.

E. M. Wermter (ed.), *Kardinal Stanislaus Hosius Bischof von Ermland und Herzog Albrecht von Preussen: Ihr Briefwechsel über das Konzil von Trient (1560–62)* (Reformationsgeschichtliche Studien und Texte, 82; 1957). P. G. Thielen, *Die Kultur am Hofe Herzog Albrechts von Preussen (1525–1568)* (1953); W. Hubatsch, *Albrecht von Brandenburg-Ansbach* (Heidelberg, 1960); H. Freiwald, *Markgraf Albrecht von Ansbach-Kulmbach und seine Landständische Politik als Deutschordens-Hochmeister und Herzog in Preussen während der Entscheidungsjahre 1521–1528* (1961); J. R. Fligge, *Herzog Albrecht von Preussen und der Osiandrismus, 1522–1568* (Bonn diss., 1972). W. Hubatsch in *TRE* 2 (1978), pp. 188–93, s.v. 'Albrecht von Preussen', with extensive bibl.

Albert the Great, St. See ALBERTUS MAGNUS, ST.

Albertus Magnus, St (d. 1280, over 80 years old), theologian, philosopher, and scientist. Born of knightly stock at Lauingen on the Danube, near Ulm, he studied at Padua, where he entered the *Dominican Order, prob. in 1229. He returned almost immediately to *Cologne to study theology, and then became lecturer in the Dominican houses of Hildesheim, Freiberg (in Saxony), Ratisbon, and Strasbourg. From his earliest years he was keenly interested in natural science and went out of his way to observe curious natural phenomena. During his early years as a teacher he wrote his first theological work, the *De Natura Boni*. Between 1240 and 1244 he was sent to the university of *Paris and from 1245 to 1248 he held one of the Dominican chairs in theology; from 1246 he had St *Thomas Aquinas among his pupils. In 1248 he was sent back to Cologne to take charge of the new international Dominican house of studies. He composed a *Summa de Creaturis* (completed by 1246), a commentary on the Sentences of *Peter Lombard (completed in 1249), and a set of lectures on all the writings of *Dionysius the Pseudo-Areopagite (completed in 1250). In Cologne he lectured on the new, complete translation of *Aristotle's *Ethics* and embarked, at the request of his students, on the huge project of making the complete Aristotelian corpus 'intelligible to the Latins', a work which occupied much of the rest of his life. In addition to his teaching and writing, he was often employed as arbitrator in ecclesiastical disputes. From 1254 to 1257 he was Provincial of Germany. In 1256 he visited the Papal court, prob. because Alexander IV wanted to consult him about an apparent growth of heterodox Aristotelianism in Paris; he conducted a disputation there against the doctrine of the non-individual nature of the intellect attributed to *Averroes, and was also incidentally present at the condemnation of William of St Amour (d. 1272), the leading Parisian enemy of the *mendicants. In 1260, at the Pope's insistence, he became Bp. of Ratisbon, where he quickly managed to set the spiritual and material affairs of the diocese in better order. In 1261

he went to the papal court to tender his resignation, which was accepted by Urban IV in 1262, though Albert remained in the Papal entourage until 1263, when he was sent back to Germany as Papal emissary to preach the crusade and perform a variety of other tasks. Between 1264 and 1267 he prob. lived in the Dominican house in Würzburg. In 1268 he was teaching in Strasbourg, and in 1269 or 1270 he returned to Cologne, where he was still teaching in 1277. In 1274 he assisted at the Second Council of *Lyons, and in 1277 he intervened to prevent the condemnation of Thomas Aquinas in Paris, though it is not certain that he went to Paris in person.

Albert taught at a time when many theologians were reacting against the various influences coming from the E., including Greek negative (or *apophatic) theology and the new Aristotelianism mediated by Arab and Jewish commentators, and in particular against some of the philosophical tenets learned from Aristotle. Albert insisted that philosophical problems must be faced honestly and dealt with philosophically, and he defended unpopular theses on the incomprehensibility of God and the nature of human self-knowledge, for instance. He commented on almost the whole Aristotelian corpus, including the *Liber de Causis*, which he believed to be the crown of *peripatetic philosophy, though he did not accept its ascription to Aristotle. His own observations of natural phenomena allowed him to expand Aristotle's *naturalia* considerably. He also wrote on mathematics. His philosophical works won him considerable acclaim. He also wrote several biblical commentaries and, towards the end of his life, embarked on a *Summa Theologiae*.

Apart from his very profound influence on Thomas Aquinas, he initiated a more *Neoplatonist kind of speculation, which flourished among the German Dominicans, such as Ulrich of Strasbourg (d. 1277), Dietrich of Freiberg (d. after 1310), and Berthold of Moosburg (d. after 1361). In the 15th cent. an 'Albertist' school was recognized, esp. in Cologne, as distinct from the 'Thomists', and he remained influential, particularly among philosophers. His more popular fame, though, rested to some extent on works falsely ascribed to him, such as the *De adhaerendo Deo* (prob. the work of John of Kastl, d. after 1418) and a variety of works on magic and alchemy. There has been a revival of interest in his genuine writings in the 20th cent.

Albert was beatified in 1622 and canonized and declared a *Doctor of the Church by *Pius XI in 1931. In 1941 *Pius XII proclaimed him patron of natural scientists. Feast day, 15 Nov.

Works, ed. P. Jammy (21 vols., Lyons, 1651), A. Borgnet (38 vols., Paris, 1890–9), and by B. Geyer and others (Münster i. W., 1951 ff.). *De Animalibus*, ed. H. Stadler (BGPM 15–16; 1916–21); some of the sermons ed. J. B. Schneyer in *RTAM* 36 (1969), pp. 100–47, and by B. Geyer, *Die Universitätspredigten des Albertus Magnus* (*Sb.* (Bayr.), 1966, Heft 3); *Quaestio Disputata de Prophetia*, ed. J. P. Torrell, *RSTP* 65 (1981), pp. 5–53 and 197–232; part of the comm. on Euclid, ed. P. M. J. E. Tummers (Leiden Diss., 2 vols., Nijmegen, 1984). Eng. tr. of his comm. on Dionysius' *Mystical Theology* by S. [C. ff.] Tugwell, OP, *Albert & Thomas: Selected Writings* (Classics of Western Spirituality, 1988), pp. 131–98, with important introd., pp. 1–129. P. de Loë, OP, 'De Vita et Scriptis B. Alberti Magni', *Anal. Boll.* 19 (1900), pp. 257–84; 20 (1901), pp. 273–316; and 21 (1902), pp. 361–71. F. Pelster, SJ, *Kritische Studien zum Leben* *und zu den Schriften des Alberts des Grossen* (Freiburg i. B., 1920); H. C. Scheeben, *Albert der Grosse: Zur Chronologie seines Lebens* (Quellen und Forschungen zur Geschichte des Dominikanerordens in Deutschland, 27; Vechta, 1931). G. Meersseman, OP, *Introductio in Opera Omnia B. Alberti Magni* (Bruges, 1931). E. *Gilson, 'L'Âme raisonnable chez Albert le Grand', *AHDLMA* 14 (1943), pp. 5–72. H. Ostlender (ed.), *Studia Albertina: Festschrift für Bernhard Geyer zum 70. Geburtstage* (BGPM Suppl. 4; 1952). A. Fries, CSSR, *Die unter dem Namen des Albertus Magnus überlieferten Mariologischen Schriften* (BGPM 17, Heft 4; 1954); id., *Die Gedanken des heiligen Albertus Magnus über die Gottesmutter* (Thomistische Studien, 7; 1958). F. Ruello, *Les 'Noms Divins' et les 'Raisons' selon Saint Albert le Grand* (Bibliothèque Thomiste, 25; 1963). P. Michaud-Quantin, *La Psychologie de l'Activité chez Albert le Grand* (ibid. 36; 1966). J. Schneider, *Das Gute und die Liebe nach der Lehre Alberts des Grossen* (Veröffentlichungen des Grabmann-Institutes, NS 3; 1967). F.-J. Nocke, *Sakrament und personaler Vollzug bei Albertus Magnus* (BGPM 41, Heft 4; 1967). L. Hödl, 'Albert der Grosse und die Wende der lateinischen Philosophie im 13. Jahrundert', in *Virtus Politica: Festgabe zum 75. Geburtstag von Alfons Hugnagel* (Stuttgart, 1974), pp. 251–75. *Archives de Philosophie*, 43 (1980), pp. 529–711 (special issue for the 7th centenary of Albert's death); F. J. Kovack and R. W. Shahan (eds.), *Albert the Great: Commemorative Essays* (Norman, Okla. [1980]); G. Meyer, OP, and A. Zimmermann (eds.), *Albertus Magnus, Doctor Universalis, 1280/1980* (Walberger Studien, Philosophische Reihe, 6; Mainz, 1980); J. A. Weisheipl, OP (ed.), *Albertus Magnus and the Sciences* (Studies and Texts, 49; Toronto, 1980); *RSTP* 65 (1981), pp. 55–99 (special issue for the 7th centenary of Albert's death). P. Hossfeld, *Albertus Magnus als Naturphilosoph und Naturwissenschaftler* (Bonn, 1983). A. Fries, *Der Doppeltraktat über die Eucharistie unter dem Namen des Albertus Magnus* (BGPM NS 25; 1984). A. de Libera, *Introduction à la Mystique Rhénane d'Albert le Grand à Maître Eckhart* [1984], esp. pp. 37–56. B. Thomassen, *Metaphysik als Lebensform: Untersuchungen zur Grundlegung der Metaphysik im Metaphysikkommentar Alberts des Grossen* (BGPM NS, 27; 1985). E. Gilson, *History of Christian Philosophy in the Middle Ages* (1955), pp. 277–94 and 666–73. F. Van Steenberghen, *La Philosophie au XIIIᵉ siècle* (2nd edn., Philosophes Médiévaux, 28; 1991), pp. 245–75. J. A. Weisheipl, OP, in *NCE* 1 (1967), pp. 254–8, s.v.

Albigenses. A medieval term for the inhabitants of parts of S. France, and hence applied to the heretics who were strong there in the late 12th and early 13th cents. These were a branch of the *Cathari (q.v.). The Albigenses were condemned by successive Councils, at Lombers in 1165 and at *Verona in 1184. *Innocent III promoted a series of preaching missions, but after the assassination of the Papal legate Peter of Castelnau in 1208, he authorized a *Crusade against them. The expedition led to a long period of warfare in S. France, in which the N. French forces, led by Simon de Montfort, were opposed, not only by those who sympathized with heresy, but by a great part of S. French society. The Treaty of Paris in 1229 prepared the way for the incorporation of Languedoc into the domain of the French monarchy and marked the victory of the Catholic forces. In 1233 a new procedure, the *Inquisition, began effective action against the heretics. By 1300, these survived only in a few remote outposts.

For their beliefs, see CATHARI.

The main sources are the records of the prosecutions. C. Douais (ed.), *Les Sources de l'histoire de l'Inquisition dans le midi de la France* (1881); id., *Documents pour servir à l'histoire de l'Inquisition dans le Languedoc* (2 vols., 'Société de l'Histoire de France', 1900); J. Duvernoy (ed.), *Le Régistre d'Inquisition de Jacques Fournier, évêque de Pamiers (1318–1325)* (Bibliothèque Méridion-

ale, 2nd ser. 41; 3 vols., Toulouse, 1965). C. Thouzellier, *Catharisme et Valdéisme en Languedoc à la Fin du XIIᵉ et au Début du XIIIᵉ Siècle* (Publications de la Faculté des Lettres et Sciences Humaines de Paris, Série 'Recherches', 27; 1966; 2nd edn., 1969). É Griffe, *Les débuts de l'aventure cathare en Languedoc (1140–1190)* (1969); id., *Le Languedoc cathare de 1190 à 1210* (1971); id., *Le Languedoc cathare au temps de la Croisade (1209–1229)* (1973), id., *Le Languedoc cathare et l'Inquisition (1229–1329)* (1980). There has been much modern work on the Albigensian Crusades, and the results are presented in J. R. Strayer, *The Albigensian Crusades* (New York, 1971); W. L. Wakefield, *Heresy, Crusade and Inquisition in Southern France 1100–1250* (1974); and J. [P. C.] Sumption, *The Albigensian Crusade* (1978). Account of life in a village where the Albigenses had strong support, based on the register of Jacques Fournier [later *Benedict XII], by E. Le Roy Ladurie, *Les Paysans de Languedoc* (1966; shorter version, 1969; Eng. tr., 1976; revised edn., *Montaillou, village occitan de 1294 à 1324*, 1975, revised edn., 1982; abbrev. Eng. tr., 1978). R. Manselli and Y. Dossat in *Lexikon des Mittelalters*, 1 (1980), cols. 302–7, s.v. 'Albigenser'. There is much valuable material in the annual *Cahiers de Fanjeaux* (Toulouse, 1966 ff.). See also works cited under CATHARI and INQUISITION.

Albright Brethren. See EVANGELICAL CHURCH.

Alcoran. See KORAN.

Alcuin (*c.*740–804), a major contributor to the *Carolingian Renaissance. A native of Northumberland, he was educated at the cathedral school of *York. Under Aelberht, Bishop (767–73) and Archbishop (773–78) of York, he visited Rome and the Frankish court and helped create a library at the cathedral, the contents of which are evoked in his poem 'On the Bishops, Kings, and Saints of York'. Following a meeting with *Charlemagne at Parma in 781 he was invited to join his court and the scholars already there. He was in England in 786 and again in 790–93, but, whether reluctantly or not, France was his normal country of residence until his death in 804. From 796 he was Abbot of St Martin's at Tours. A competent and versatile scholar, he appears to have had a particular talent for instruction, and both at the court and at Tours he played an important role in developing the resources of contemporary ecclesiastical culture. His extant literary production includes a quantity of biblical exegesis; a major work on the Trinity; three treatises directed against the *Adoptianism of Felix of Urgel, whom he opposed in person at the Council of Aachen in 799 or 800; moral and philosophical writings; 'Lives' of the saints *Willibrord, *Vedast, Richarius, and *Martin (the last of these in verse); manuals of grammar, rhetoric, dialectic, orthography, and mathematics; an abundant correspondence (mainly from the period after 793); and poems on a wide variety of subjects. As Abbot of St Martin's, Alcuin supervised the production of several pandects (or complete editions) of the Bible written in a fully developed 'Caroline minuscule'; his preference for the *Vulgate text probably contributed to its final acceptance in the W. At different times in his career he also revised the Roman *Lectionary and adapted the *Gregorian Sacramentary for use in Gaul by incorporating certain *Gelasian elements and adding a series of *votive and festal Masses of his own composition. (The supplement to the Sacramentary sent by Pope *Hadrian I to Charlemagne, known as the *'Hucusque', which was long attributed to Alcuin, is now thought to be the work of *Benedict of Aniane.) In the American BCP (1979), feast day, 20 May.

Works ed. by A. Quercetanus (Paris, 1617) and Frobenius Forster (2 vols., Ratisbon, 1777), repr. in J. P. Migne, *PL* 100 and 101. Critical edns. of poems by E. Dümmler in *MGH*, Poetae Latini Medii Aevi, 1, pt. 1 (1880), of letters by id. in *MGH*, Epistolae, 4 (1895), pp. 1–493, of *Liber contra haeresim Felicis* by G. B. Blumenshine (ST 285, 1980), and of 'The Bishops, Kings, and Saints of York' by P. Godman (Oxford Medieval Texts, 1982), with Eng. tr. and valuable introd. Alcuin's votive Masses ed. by J. Deshusses, OSB, in *Archiv für Liturgiewissenschaft*, 14 (1972), pp. 7–41. Text of a book of private prayers, attributable to Alcuin or to a member of his circle, ed. A. *Wilmart, OSB, *Precum Libelli Quattuor Aevi Karolini*, 1 (Rome, 1940), pp. 9–30. Selections from his letters in Eng. tr. by S. Allot (York, 1974). There is an early Life of Alcuin written between 823 and 829, pr. among his works (J. P. Migne, *PL* 100, cols. 89–106) and critically ed. by W. Arndt in *MGH*, Scriptores, 15, pt. 1 (1887), pp. 182–97. E. Dümmler, 'Zur Lebensgeschichte Alchvins', *NA* 18 (1893), pp. 53–70. Modern biographies by C. J. B. Gaskoin (London, 1904), A. Kleinclausz (Annales de l'Université de Lyon, 3rd ser., fasc. 15; Paris, 1948), and E. S. Duckett (New York, 1951). M. Roger, *L'Enseignement des lettres classiques d'Ausone à Alcuin* (1905), pp. 313–402, 440–8. A. Wilmart, OSB, 'Le lectionnaire d'Alcuin', *EL* 51 (1937), pp. 136–97. W. Levison, *England and the Continent in the Eighth Century* (Oxford, 1946), esp. pp. 148–73. B. Fischer, OSB, *Die Alkuin Bibel* (Aus der Geschichte der lateinischen Bibel, 1; Freiburg i. Br., 1957). G. Ellard, SJ, *Master Alcuin, Liturgist* (Chicago, 1956). L. Wallach, *Alcuin and Charlemagne: Studies in Carolingian History and Literature* (Cornell Studies in Classical Philology, 32; Ithaca, NY, 1959). B. Bischoff (ed.), *Karl der Grosse: Lebenswerk und Nachleben*, 2: *Das geistige Leben* (Düsseldorf, 1965). W. Heil, *Alkuinstudien*, 1: *Zur Chronologie und Bedeutung des Adoptianismusstreites* (Düsseldorf, 1970). J. Deshusses, OSB, 'Les anciens sacramentaires de Tours', *R. Bén.* 89 (1979), pp. 281–302, with refs. to other arts. by this scholar. J. Marenbon, *From the Circle of Alcuin to the School of Auxerre: Logic, Theology and Philosophy in the Early Middle Ages* (Cambridge, 1981), pp. 30–66. D. A. Bullough, 'Alcuin and the Kingdom of Heaven', in U.-R. Blumenthal (ed.), *Carolingian Essays* (Washington, DC [1983]), pp. 1–69; repr. in Bullough, *Carolingian Renewal: Sources and Heritage* (Manchester and New York, 1991), pp. 161–240. D. Schaller in *Verfasserlexikon* (2nd edn.), 1 (1978), cols. 241–53; W. Heil in *TRE* 2 (1978), pp. 266–76, both s.v. 'Alkuin', with bibl.

Alcuin Club. An Anglican society founded in 1897 'to encourage and assist in the practical study of ceremonial, and the arrangement of churches, their furniture and ornaments, in accordance with the rubrics of the BCP, strict obedience to which is the guiding principle of the Club'. In recent years its widening sympathies have been recognized by a modification of its expressed aims, which are now said to be the promotion of 'the study of Christian liturgy in general, and in particular the liturgies of the Anglican Communion'. It has issued several series of publications.

P. J. Jagger, *The Alcuin Club and its Publications 1897–1987: An Annotated Bibliography* (2nd edn. [1986]).

Aldhelm, St (d. 709), first Bp. of *Sherborne. The details of his life are uncertain as they derive from the two late (12th-cent.) writers Faricius of Abingdon and *William of Malmesbury. He was a near relation of Ine, King of Wessex. About 675 he became Abbot of *Malmesbury and in 705 Bp. of the new diocese of Sherborne, when the old see of Wessex was divided. He took a prom-

inent part in the reforming movement initiated by Abp. *Theodore and the monk Hadrian, and founded some monasteries as well as several churches. According to William of Malmesbury, he built the small church at Bradford-on-Avon dedicated to St Lawrence; some work of Aldhelm's date may survive. Much of his Latin writing, composed in a flamboyant style studded with apparently learned words and drawing on an impressively wide range of authorities, survives to attest his learning. He was held in high repute as a poet, but none of his English poems has been preserved. Feast day, 25 May.

Works, with Vita by Faricius, ed. J. A. Giles (Oxford, 1844), repr. J. P. Migne, *PL* 89. 63–314. Modern edn. of Works by R. Ehwald in *MGH*, Auctores Antiquissimi, 15 (1913–19). Facsimile of *De Laudibus Virginitatis* with Latin and Old English Glosses. MS 1650 of the Royal Library in Brussels, with introd. by G. van Langenhove (Rijksuniversiteit te Gent. Werken uitgegeven door de Faculteit van de Wijsbegeerte en Letteren. Extra Series: Facsimiles, 2; Brussels, 1941). Eng. tr. of his *Prose Works* by M. Lapidge and M. Herren (Ipswich and Cambridge, 1979), with introd.; and of his *Poetic Works* by M. Lapidge and J. L. Rosier (ibid., 1985), with introd. Life by William of Malmesbury, ed. N. E. S. A. Hamilton, *Gesta Pontificum Anglorum*, bk. 5 (RS, 1870), pp. 330–443. G. F. Browne, *St Aldhelm* (1903); W. B. Wildman, *Life of St Ealdhelm* (1905). M. Winterbottom, 'Aldhelm's Prose Style and its Origins', *Anglo-Saxon England*, 6 (1977), pp. 39–76; M. Lapidge, 'Aldhelm's Latin Poetry and Old English Verse', *Comparative Literature*, 31 (1979), pp. 209–31. See also A. S. Cook, *Sources for the Biography of Aldhelm* (Transactions of the Connecticut Academy of Arts and Sciences, 28; 1927).

Aldrich, Henry (1647–1710), Dean of *Christ Church. Educated at Westminster and at Christ Church, Oxford, he became Canon of Christ Church in 1682, and in 1689, as an opponent of the High Church party and as a supporter of the Revolution, was appointed to succeed the RC Dean, J. Massey. He was remarkable for his versatility. His *Artis Logicae Compendium* (1691; revised by H. L. *Mansel, 1849) remained a standard textbook until the end of the 19th cent. He was a skilful architect, and Peckwater Quadrangle and other buildings in Oxford are ascribed to him. He also composed several anthems largely based on Italian models.

W. G. Hiscock, *Henry Aldrich of Christ Church 1648–1710* (privately pr., Oxford, 1960).

Aleander, Girolamo (1480–1542), humanist scholar. Educated at Venice and Padua, at the suggestion of *Erasmus in 1508 he went to seek his fortune in Paris, where he gave lectures on Greek. There he also graduated and in 1513 was chosen Rector of the University. The important part that he took in the history of the Reformation began with his appointment by *Leo X as one of the two Papal envoys commissioned to present M. *Luther with the bull '*Exsurge Domine', and to negotiate with the Emperor for support against him. In his Ash Wednesday sermon (13 Feb. 1521) at the Diet of *Worms, he vigorously denounced Luther and demanded his condemnation without trial. Unlike many at Rome, Aleander was never in doubt either as to the fact of Luther's popularity in Germany or as to the pressing need for disciplinary reform in the Church. In 1524 he was appointed Abp. of Brindisi and in 1538 a cardinal.

H. Omont, 'Journal Autobiographique du Cardinal Jérôme Aléandre (1480—1530): Notices des Manuscrits de Paris et Udine', *Notices et Extraits des Manuscrits de la Bibliothèque Nationale*, 35 (1896), pp. 1–116, incl. text. T. Brieger, *Aleander und Luther, 1521* (Gotha, 1884). W. Friedensburg (ed.), *Legation Aleanders 1538-1539* (Nuntiaturberichte aus Deutschland, Abt. 1: 1533–1559, 3-4; 1893); G. Müller (ed.), *Legation Lorenzo Campeggios* [1530–32] *und Nuntiatur Girolamo Aleandros* [1531–2] (ibid., Ergänzbände 1–2; 1963–9); J. Hoyoux (ed.), *Le Carnet de Voyage de Jérôme Aléandre en France et à Liège (1510–1516)* (Bibliothèque de l'Institut Historique Belge de Rome, 18; 1969). J. Paquier, *Jérôme Aléandre de sa naissance à la fin de son séjour à Brindes, 1480-1529* (1900). P. Kalkoff, *Aleander gegen Luther* (1908); id., 'Zur Charakteristik Aleanders', *ZKG* 43 (1924), pp. 209–19. F. Gaeta, *Un Nunzio Pontificio a Venezia nel Cinquecento* (Civiltà Veneziana, Saggi, 9; 1960). G. Alberigo in *Dizionario Biografico degli Italiani*, 2 (1960), pp. 128–35; G. Müller in *TRE* 2 (1978), pp. 227–31, both s.v. 'Aleandro'. Further bibl. in Schottenloher, 1 (1933), pp. 11–13.

Alembert, J. le R. D'. See D'ALEMBERT, J. LE R'.

aleph (א). The first letter of the Hebrew alphabet, numerically equivalent to one. Textual critics of the NT use it to denote the *Codex Sinaiticus.

Alesius, Alexander (1500–65), alternatively 'Aless' or 'Alane', Scottish *Lutheran divine. A native of Edinburgh, he studied at St Andrews, where he became a canon. Selected in 1527 to confute Patrick *Hamilton, who had become an adherent of Lutheran doctrines, he was himself won over by Hamilton's arguments and steadfastness at the stake (1528), and shortly after delivered a Latin sermon at St Andrews attacking the morals of the clergy for which he was imprisoned. In 1532 he escaped to Germany, where in 1533 he made the acquaintance of M. *Luther and P. *Melanchthon at *Wittenberg and signed the *Augsburg Confession. In the same year he wrote against a Scottish decree forbidding the laity to read the Bible and in 1534 he was excommunicated at Holyrood. In 1535 he brought a letter to England from Melanchthon to *Henry VIII. On his arrival he was warmly welcomed, esp. by T. *Cranmer, and T. *Cromwell, the new chancellor, made him a divinity lecturer at Cambridge. The opposition to his Protestantism, however, soon caused him to leave Cambridge and for a time he practised in London, as a physician, where at Cromwell's request he disputed with J. Stokesley, Bp. of London, on the number of the Sacraments. After the passing of the Act of *Six Articles (1539) he left again for Germany and in 1540 became professor of theology at Frankfurt-on-Oder. After various other academic offices and missions in the cause of the Reformation, he may have revisited England under *Edward VI, when he was employed by Cranmer to translate parts of the First BCP of 1549 into Latin (pub. Leipzig, 1551) for the information of M. *Bucer and *Peter Martyr. He was the author of many exegetical and controversial writings.

J. Thomasius, *Orationes* (Leipzig, 1683), Oratio 14, delivered at Leipzig on 20 Apr. 1661, pp. 300–22. G. Wiedermann, 'Alexander Alesius' Lectures on the Psalms at Cambridge, 1536', *JEH* 37 (1986), pp. 15–41. J. E. McGoldrick, *Luther's Scottish Connection* (Cranbury, NJ, etc. [1989]), pp. 58–60. A. W. Ward in *DNB* 1 (1885), pp. 254–9, s.v., with further refs.

Alexander, St (d. 328), Bp. of *Alexandria from 312. He was actively concerned in putting down the *Melitian and *Arian schisms. At a council of his clergy at Alexandria *c*.321 he excommunicated *Arius, one of his presbyters, who shortly before had begun to propagate his doctrines. He then got into touch with the leading theologian of the W., Bp. *Hosius of Córdoba, and, with the energetic support of his deacon *Athanasius (who was shortly afterwards to succeed him in his see), took a leading part at the Council of *Nicaea. Two of his Epistles survive (*Theodoret, *HE* 1. 4; *Socrates, *HE* 1. 6). Also ascribed to him is a 'Sermo de Anima et Corpore deque Passione Domini', which survives in Syriac, Coptic, and Georgian, as well as in two Gk. fragments. Feast day, in the W., 26 Feb.; in the Greek Church, 29 May; in the *Coptic Church, 22 April.

Collected edn. of his writings in J. P. Migne, *PG* 18. 523–608. Crit. edn. of Epp. in H. G. Opitz (ed.), *Athanasius Werke*, 3, Lief. 1–2 (1934–5), pp. 6–11, 19–31. G. Bardy, 'Saint Alexandre d'Alexandrie a-t-il connu la Thalie d'Arius?' in *Rev. SR* 6 (1926), pp. 527–32. W. Schneemelcher, 'Der Sermo "De Anima et corpore". Ein Werk Alexanders von Alexandrien?', in id. (ed.), *Festschrift für Günther Dehn* (Neukirchen, 1957), pp. 119–43. Bardenhewer, 3, pp. 34–41; Altaner and Stuiber (1978), pp. 269 and 602; *CPG* 2 (1974), pp. 1–4 (nos. 2000–21). C. Kannengiesser, SJ, in *DPAC* 1 (1983), cols. 132 f., s.v. 'Alessandro di Alesandria'; Eng. tr. in *Encyclopedia of the Early Church*, 1 (1992), p. 20.

Alexander II (d. 1073), Bp. Anselm I of Lucca (1056–73) and Pope from 1061. A native of Baggio, nr. Milan, he supported the *Patarenes. In order to dispose of him the Abp. of Milan sent him on a mission to the Emp. Henry III (1039–56). In 1056 he became Bp. of Lucca. Elected Pope in 1061 with the support of Hildebrand (later *Gregory VII), he was enthroned without the support of *Henry IV (1056–1106), who had an antipope (Honorius II) elected. Although the schism was not entirely ended until Honorius' death (1072), Alexander was generally recognized, except in Parma, after the Synod of Mantua of 1064. As Pope he tried to realize the ideals of the reforming party. He dispatched legates to Lombardy, France, Spain, and England and held four synods at Rome. He renewed the decrees against simony and enforcing clerical celibacy, adding a prohibition against attendance at the Mass of an incontinent priest, laid down regulations for the freedom of episcopal elections, and legislated on marriage. He took strong action to enforce these measures, summoning to Rome the Abps. of Mainz and Cologne and the Bp. of Bamberg, and deposing the Abp. of Milan for simony. He strengthened the influence of the Papacy by insisting on personal attendance at Rome before he would confer the *pallium, and he persuaded Philip I of France to accord the same significance to Papal decrees as to canons. His blessing was asked and given to William of Normandy's invasion of England (1066). The last important act of his pontificate was his excommunication of the advisers of Henry IV. His considerable stature as a Pope and as a moderate and diplomatic reformer has become more widely appreciated in modern times. He is not to be confounded with (St) *Anselm of Lucca (*c*.1035–1088, q.v.).

146 genuine and six doubtful letters or bulls printed in J. P. Migne, *PL* 146, 1279–1430. O. Delarc, *Saint Grégoire VII et la*

réforme de l'Église au XIe siècle, 2 (1889), pp. 161–526. T. Schmidt, *Alexander II. (1061–1073) und die römische Reformgruppe seiner Zeit* (Päpste und Papsttum, 11; 1977). A. Fliche, *La Réforme grégorienne*, 1 (SSL, fasc. 6; 1924), pp. 341–84; Mann, 6 (1925), pp. 261–369; A. Fliche in Fliche and Martin, 8 (1944), pp. 31–54. C. Violante in *Dizionario Biografico degli Italiani*, 2 (1960), pp. 176–83, s.v. 'Alessandro II', with bibl.

Alexander III (d. 1181), Pope. Orlando ('Roland') Bandinelli first rose to prominence as a teacher, prob. at *Bologna. Papal chancellor under *Eugenius III, he exercised a strong influence on *Hadrian IV, whom he succeeded in 1159. An *antipope, Victor IV, was immediately set up and supported by the Emp. *Frederick I (Barbarossa). The schism lasted for 17 years and was ended only by the acceptance of Alexander by the Emperor at Venice in 1177. During the schism, Alexander lived mostly in France, where he was brought into close contact with Henry II of England in the affair of *Becket. The Pope as a subtle diplomatist was embarrassed by the impetuous Archbishop, but showed himself very firm in imposing penance upon Henry for Becket's murder. In 1179 he assembled and presided over the Third *Lateran Council, one of the most important measures of which was to vest the exclusive right of electing a Pope in a two-thirds majority of the cardinals. He strongly encouraged the scholastic revival of the 12th cent. It is, however, unlikely that he was the author of the commentary on the 'Decretum' of *Gratian or the 'Sententiae Rolandi' which were long attributed to him; they appear to be the work of a different Magister Rolandus. The city of Alessandria, founded in the plain of Lombardy at this time, was named after Alexander in gratitude for his support of the liberties of the Lombard Communes against Barbarossa.

Much of his Correspondence in J. P. Migne, *PL* 200; further letters and information on his part in the Becket controversy in J. C. Robertson and J. B. Sheppard (eds.), *Materials for the History of Thomas Becket*, 5–7 (RS 1881–5); see also Jaffé, 2, pp. 145–418. W. Holtzmann, 'Die Register Papst Alexander III. in den Händen der Kanonisten', *Quellen und Forschungen aus italienischen Archiven und Bibliotheken*, 30 (1940), pp. 13–87. The chief authority up to 1178 is the account by Card. Boso, his favourite Cardinal, in *LP* (Duchesne), 2, pp. 397–446; Eng. tr. by G. M. Ellis (Oxford, 1973), with introd. by P. Munz. H. Reuter, *Geschichte Alexanders des Dritten und der Kirche seiner Zeit* (3 vols., 1845; 2nd edn., Leipzig, 1860). M. Pacaut, *Alexandre III: Étude sur la Conception du Pouvoir Pontifical dans sa Pensée et dans son Œuvre* (1956). M. W. Baldwin, *Alexander III and the Twelfth Century* (Glen Rock, NJ, 1968). R. Somerville, *Pope Alexander III and the Council of Tours (1163)* [1977]. J. T. Noonan, 'Who was Rolandus?', in K. Pennington and R. Somerville (eds.), *Law, Church, and Society: Essays in Honor of Stephan Kuttner* (Philadelphia, 1977), pp. 21–48; R. Weigand, 'Magister Rolandus und Papst Alexander III.', *Archiv für katholisches Kirchenrecht*, 149 (1980), pp. 3–44; F. Liotta (ed.), *Miscellanea Rolando Bandinelli, Papa Alessandro III* (Siena, 1986). Mann, 10 (1925), pp. 1–238, with full refs. P. Brezzi in *Dizionario Biografico degli Italiani*, 2 (1960), pp. 183–9, s.v. 'Alessandro III'; J. Ehlers in *TRE* 2 (1978), pp. 237–41, s.v.

Alexander V (c.1339–1410), Pope. Peter of Candia (Crete), also 'Peter Philarges', having become a *Franciscan, studied at Oxford and later was a Master of Theology at Paris (1381), where he lectured on the *Sentences. His academic career was brought to an end by preferment. He became Bp. successively of Piacenza (1386), Vicenza (1388), Novara (1389), Abp. of Milan

(1402); and in 1409 at the Council of *Pisa he was unanimously elected to fill the Papal chair, presumed vacant, despite the two existing claimants. His strong character and extensive learning aroused great hopes; but he died after ten months. RC theologians still dispute whether he can claim a place in the true Papal succession. His importance in medieval thought has recently been increasingly recognized. His surviving 'Commentary on the Sentences' shows marked *nominalistic leanings.

M. Renières, Ἱστορικαὶ μελέται. Ὁ Ἕλλην πάπας Ἀλέξανδρος ἐ (Athens, 1881). F. *Ehrle, SJ, *Der Sentenzenkommentar Peters von Candia des Pisaner Papstes Alexanders V* (Franziskanische Studien, Beiheft 9; 1925). Pastor, 1 (1891), pp. 190 f. L. Salembier in *DTC* 1 (1903), cols. 772–4; A. Clerval in *DHGE* 2 (1914), cols. 216–18; *BRUO* 1 (1957), pp. 345 f., s.v. 'Candia, Peter de'; A. Petrucci in *Dizionario Biografico degli Italiani*, 2 (1960), pp. 193–6, s.v. 'Alessandro V, antipapa'.

Alexander VI (1431–1503), Pope from 1492. Rodrigo Borgia, a Spaniard by birth and nephew of Pope *Callistus III (1455–8), who created him a Cardinal in 1456, after studying at *Bologna, was appointed Chancellor of the Roman Church in 1457. He exercised considerable influence under Paul II (1464–71), and was largely responsible for the election of *Sixtus IV (1471). His own election having been secured largely through bribery, the course of his pontificate was determined almost solely by political and family considerations, esp. his favouritism of his son, Caesar. Among the most notable acts of his pontificate were the series dividing the New World between *Spain and *Portugal (1493–4), his prosecution and execution of G. *Savonarola in 1498, the *Jubilee which he organized in 1500, and the Crusade against the Moors (1499–1500). A man of immoral life, he was an astute politician and generous patron of artists, esp. D. Bramante, G. and A. Sangallo, and 'Pinturicchio'. Under him the Leonine city was largely replanned and the castle of Sant' Angelo rebuilt.

P. de Roo (ed.), *Materials for a History of Pope Alexander VI, his Relatives and his Times* (5 vols., Brussels, 1924). Eng. tr. of the account of his reign from the diary of his Master of Ceremonies, John Burchard (based on edn. of Diary by E. Celani, Città di Castello, 1906), by G. Parker, *At the Court of the Borgia* (Folio Society, 1963). V. Nemec, *Papst Alexander VI* (1879); A. Leonetti, *Papa Alessandro VI* (3 vols., with documents, 1880); J. Schnitzer, *Der Tod Alexanders VI: Eine quellenkristische Untersuchung* (1929); O. Ferrara, *El Papa Borgia* (1943; Eng. tr., New York, 1940, London, 1942). G. Soranzo, *Studi Intorno a Papa Alessandro VI (Borgia)* (Pubblicazioni dell'Università Cattolica del Sacro Cuore, NS 34; Milan [1950]). L. Weckman, *Las Bulas Alejandrinas de 1493 y la Teoria Politica del Papado Medieval* (Mexico, 1949); M. Batllori, SJ, *Alejandro VI y la Casa Real de Aragón 1492–1495* (Madrid, 1958). Pastor, 5 (1898), pp. 375–523, and 6 (1898), pp. 3–181. J. Paquier in *DTC* 1 (1903), cols. 724–7; P. Richard in *DHGE* 2 (1914), cols. 218–29, both s.v.; G. B. Picotti in *Dizionario Biografico degli Italiani*, 2 (1960), pp. 196–205, s.v. 'Alessandro VI', with bibl.; M. Batllori in *NCE* 1 (1967), pp. 290–2, s.v.

Alexander VII (1599–1667), Pope from 1655. Fabio Chigi was a native of Siena, where he studied philosophy, law, and theology. In 1626 he entered upon an ecclesiastical career at Rome. After being *Inquisitor of Malta, he became Papal *Nuncio at *Cologne in 1639. As such he followed the negotiations of the Peace of *Westphalia and protested against several of its clauses. After his return to

Rome (1651), he was created Cardinal in 1652 and became Papal secretary of state. During the first year of his pontificate he showed himself an enemy of nepotism, but in 1656 he gave way to the pressure of his advisers, who feared a weakening of the Papal position through the absence of his family, and called his brother and nephews to Rome. As a theologian he was of strongly anti-*Jansenist views, and, to make Jansenist subterfuges impossible, condemned in 1656 the five propositions drawn from *Augustinus in the sense in which C. O. *Jansen had meant them. In this attitude he was supported by Louis XIV, though political troubles arose between the Pope and the King, owing to a dispute between the Papal *entourage* and the French ambassador. Louis thereupon seized *Avignon and Venaissin, and threatened to invade the States of the Church, and Alexander had to sign the humiliating peace of Pisa in 1664. Following the controversy on *Probabilism, he condemned, in 1665 and 1666, forty-five *Laxist propositions, though not the Probabilist system. He was a friend of the *Jesuits, esp. of Cardinal Sforza Pallavicini, the historian of the Council of *Trent, and he procured the readmission of the order to the republic of *Venice. He also did much for the embellishment and modernization of Rome.

His official correspondence as Apostolic Delegate in Malta, 1634–9, ed. V. Borg (ST 249; 1967); Correspondence on Jansenism while he was Papal Nuncio at Cologne, 1639–51, ed. A. Legrand and L. Ceyssens, OFM (Bibliothèque de l'Institut Historique Belge de Rome, 8; 1957); Letters and Diaries while he was Nuncio at the Congress of Westphalia (1640–51), ed. V. Kybal and G. Incisa della Rocchetta (Miscellanea della R. Deputazione Romana di Storia Patria, 14, 16, etc.; 1943 ff.). S. Pallavicini, SJ, *Della vita di Alessandro VII* (only to 1659; 2 vols., 1839–40). M. Albert, *Nuntius Fabio Chigi und die Anfänge des Jansenismus 1639–1651* (RQ Suppl. 44; 1988). Pastor, 31 (1940), pp. 1–313. H. Hemmer and E. Deshayes in DTC 1 (1903), cols. 727–47, s.v.; P. Richard in DHGE 2 (1914), cols. 229–44, s.v.; M. Rosa in *Dizionario Biografico degli Italiani*, 2 (1960), pp. 205–15, s.v. 'Alessandro VII'; each with bibl.

Alexander VIII (1610–91), Pope from 1689. Pietro Ottoboni, the descendant of a noble Venetian family, studied at Padua, where he became a doctor of canon and civil law in 1627. Having been an auditor of the *Rota for 14 years, he was created Cardinal by *Innocent X in 1652, and subsequently became Bp. of Brescia. After his election to the Papacy in 1689, he effected a reconciliation with Louis XIV, who in 1690 gave back *Avignon and Venaissin, which he had taken from *Alexander VII. His most important doctrinal decisions were the condemnations of the Four *Gallican Propositions of 1682 and of 31 propositions of C. O. *Jansen, both in 1690. In the same year he also condemned the doctrine of *Philosophic Sin. Despite the condemnation of Gallicanism his relations with France remained satisfactory. During his short pontificate he helped his native city of *Venice against the Turks, and brought about several social improvements in the States of the Church by a diminution of taxes and an increase of cheap food imports. He also enriched the *Vatican Library by the purchase of the valuable MSS ('Reginenses') of Queen *Christina of Sweden.

S. Freiherr von Bischoffshausen, *Papst Alexander VIII und der Wiener Hof, 1689–1691* (1900); C. Gérin, 'Le Pape Alexandre VIII et Louis XIV d'après des documents inédits', RQH, 22 (1877),

pp. 135–210; E. Michaud, *La Politique de compromis avec Rome en 1689: Le Pape Alexandre VIII et le Duc de Chaulnes d'après les correspondances diplomatiques inédites du Ministère des Affaires étrangères de France* (1888); M. Dubruel, 'Le Pape Alexandre VIII et les affaires de France', RHE 15 (1914), pp. 282–302 and 495–514. Pastor, 32 (1940), pp. 525–60. H. Hemmer and X. Le Bachelet in DTC 1 (1905), cols. 747–63, s.v., P. Richard in DHGE 2 (1914), cols. 244–51, s.v.; A. Petrucci in *Dizionario Biografico degli Italiani*, 2 (1960), pp. 215–18, s.v. 'Alessandro VIII'; each with bibl.

Alexander of Hales (c.1186–1245), the 'Doctor Irrefragabilis'. Born at Halesowen, West Midlands, he studied arts and theology at *Paris, and became a doctor c.1220–1. It was he who took the fateful step of using the Sentences of *Peter Lombard, instead of the Bible, as the basic text for his lectures on theology. His glosses on the Sentences have survived in more than one redaction, as well as collections of *quaestiones*. After the dispersion of Paris University in 1229 he was one of its representatives to Pope *Gregory IX. In 1231–2 he was in England and was made Archdeacon of *Coventry, but he soon returned to his chair in Paris. In 1236 he joined the *Franciscan Order; he was able to keep his chair, which was henceforth filled by a Franciscan. He is regarded as the founder of the Franciscan school of theology, but the 'Summa theologica' which goes under his name was only begun by him and was continued by William of Melitona and others. He also had some part in the composition of an 'Expositio in Regulam S. Francisci' (1242), popularly known as 'The Four Masters'.

Glossa in quatuor libros Sententiarum ed. by the Franciscans of Quaracchi (Bibliotheca Francescana Scholastica Medii Aevi, 12–15; 1951–7), with prolegomena in vol. 1, pp. 5*–130*. *Quaestiones Disputatae 'Antequam Esset Frater'*, ed. idd. (ibid. 19–21; 1960). The *Summa Theologica*, which was first pub. at Venice in 1475 under the name of Thomas of Hales, also ed. idd. (4 vols., Quaracchi, 1924–48), with prolegomena by V. Doucet, OFM, in vol. 4, pp. xiii–cclxx. E. Gössmann, *Metaphysik und Heilsgeschichte: Eine theologische Untersuchung der Summa Halensis* (Mitteilungen des Grabmann-Instituts der Universität München, Sonderband, 1964). V. Marcolino, *Das Alte Testament in der Heilsgeschichte: Untersuchungen zum dogmatischen Verständnis des Alten Testaments als heilsgeschichtliche Periode nach Alexander von Hales* (BGPM NS 2; 1970). E. Bettoni, *Il Problema della Conoscibilità di Dio nella Scuola Francescana* (Il Pensiero medioevale, 1st ser. 1; Padua, 1950), pp. 1–106. B. Smalley, 'The Gospels in the Paris Schools in the late 12th and early 13th centuries. Peter the Chanter, Hugh of St. Cher, Alexander of Hales, John of La Rochelle', *Franciscan Studies*, 39 (1979), pp. 230–54; 40 (1980), pp. 298–369, esp. pp. 317–44. I. Herscher, OFM, 'A Bibliography of Alexander of Hales', ibid. 26 (1945), pp. 435–54. A. Emmen in NCE 1 (1967), pp. 296 f., s.v.

Alexander of Lycopolis (3rd cent.), writer against *Manichaeism. He was probably a pagan who became a Manichaean and later a Christian, though some modern scholars, notably L. S. Le N. *Tillemont and, more recently, A. Brinkmann, contend that he never embraced Christianity. Acc. to *Photius (*Contra Manichaeos* 1. 11) he became a bishop. His fame rests on his treatise against the Manichaeans, Πρὸς τὰς Μανιχαίου δόξας, in which he praises the simplicity and efficacy of the Christian philosophy and contrasts it with the illogical and contradictory doctrines of the Manichaeans. Though his style and thought are often obscure, the work is a primary source for the study of Manichaeism.

The treatise, first pub. by F. *Combefis in 1672, is repr. in J. P. Migne, *PG* 18. 411–48. Crit. edn. by A. Brinkmann (Teub., 1895). Eng. tr. by P. W. van der Horst and J. Mansfeld (Leiden, 1974). Fr. tr., with full comm. and introd., by A. Villey (Sources Gnostiques et Manichéennes, 2; 1985). M. *Dibelius in *RAC* 1 (1950), cols. 270 f., s.v.

Alexander, Michael Solomon (1799–1845), first Anglican Bp. in *Jerusalem. Born in Schönlanke in Posen, he was trained in strictly orthodox *Judaism. He came to England in 1820 and here was brought into personal contact with Christianity, was suspended from his duties as rabbi, and baptized in 1825. Upon his ordination in 1827 he joined the London Society for Promoting Christianity among the Jews and served as a missionary in Danzig from 1827 to 1830. From 1830 to 1841 he had a mission in London, and from 1832 was also professor of Hebrew at *King's College. Here he took an active part in revising the Hebrew NT and also translated the BCP into Hebrew. On the establishment of the Anglican bishopric at Jerusalem, he was consecrated as first bishop of the see (1841), where his short term of service was successful alike among Arabs and Jews. See also JERUSALEM, ANGLICAN BISHOPRIC IN.

Autobiogr. account of his conversion appended to J. Hatchard, *The Predictions and Promises of God Respecting Israel* (sermon, 1825), pp. 37–40. J. F. A. De la Roi, *Michael Solomon Alexander, der erste evangelische Bischof in Jerusalem* (1897).

Alexandre, Noël (1639–1724), Church historian. He entered the *Dominican Order at Rouen in 1654; in 1655 he moved to Paris, where he spent most of the rest of his life and became one of the leading theologians. He wrote a number of theological works, including *Theologia dogmatica et moralis* (10 vols., 1694), but the most important of his writings is his *Selecta Historiae Ecclesiasticae Capita* (26 vols., 1676–86), a treatise of great erudition. The earlier volumes were praised by *Innocent XI in 1681 and 1682, but the *Gallican sympathies noticeable in his treatment of the conflict between the Empire and the Papacy led to the whole work being put on the *Index in 1684. Alexandre tried to make it unobjectionable in a revision published under the title *Historia Ecclesiastica* (1699), but this did not satisfy the authorities in Rome. Only two posthumous editions, annotated by C. Roncaglia (1734) and G. D. *Mansi (1749), were published with ecclesiastical approval. His initial opposition to '*Unigenitus' and support of the *Appellants in 1717 earned him a reputation of being a *Jansenist sympathizer, apparently unjustly, as he explicitly criticized Jansenism.

A. Hänggi, *Der Kirchenhistoriker Natalis Alexander (1639–1724)* (Studia Friburgensia, NS 11; 1955), with bibl. R. Coulon, OP, 'Jacobin, Gallican et "appelan". Le P. Noël Alexandre', *RSPT* 6 (1912), pp. 49–80, 279–331; A. Mercati, 'Intorno alla "Romanità" di Natale Alexandre Ord. Praed.', *Archivum Fratrum Praedicatorum*, 16 (1946), pp. 5–82. R. Coulon, OP, and A. Papillon, *Scriptores Ordinis Praedicatorum* (Paris, 1934), pp. 380–98. R. Coulon in *DHGE* 2 (1914), cols. 280–7, s.v.

Alexandria. In size and importance, Alexandria in Egypt was the second city of the Roman Empire. It was a centre not only of Hellenism but also of Semitism, with the largest community of Jews in any single city of the ancient world (see PHILO, SEPTUAGINT); and it has therefore sometimes been found surprising that St *Paul never preached there. The foundation of the Church in Alexandria is traditionally ascribed to St *Mark, but we have no reliable knowledge of its early history. Gnostic teachers, such as *Basilides and *Heracleon, were active in the city in the mid-2nd cent., but its fame as a centre of Christian thought dates from the end of that century with the work of *Clement and *Origen. Its importance increased during the 4th and 5th cents., especially under its bishops *Athanasius and *Cyril. The Council of *Nicaea (325) assigned to Alexandria a place of honour second only to Rome, and superior to *Antioch, but its importance was diminished by the rise of *Constantinople, which was granted precedence over Alexandria by the Councils of *Constantinople (381) and *Chalcedon (451). The great majority of Christians in Egypt supported the *Monophysite schisms, and by the time Egypt passed under the Persians (616) and then under the Arabs (642), the Greek Orthodox Patriarchate of Alexandria had lost most of its influence. At the division between E. and W. Alexandria remained on the side of Constantinople. Besides the Greek Orthodox Patriarch, the head of the *Coptic Church also has the title 'Patriarch of Alexandria'; and since the 13th cent. there has been a Latin Patriarch of Alexandria, but he is purely titular.

See also following two entries and CODEX ALEXANDRINUS.

M. *Le Quien, *Oriens Christianus*, 2 (Paris, 1740), cols. 329–640. J. M. *Neale, *A History of the Holy Eastern Church: The Patriarchate of Alexandria* (2 vols., 1847). C. A. Papadopoulos, Ἱστορία τῆς Ἐκκλησίας Ἀλεξανδρείας (62–1934) (Alexandria, 1935). T. Orlandi, *Storia della Chiesa di Alessandria* (Coptic texts with Italian tr. and comm.; Milan, 1968 ff.). J. Faivre in *DHGE* 2 (1914), cols. 289–369, s.v. 'Alexandrie'. W. Schubart and A. Calderini in *RAC* 1 (1950), cols. 271–83, s.v.

Alexandrian text. An early form of the Greek text of the NT, known also as the Egyptian, which B. F. *Westcott and F. J. A. *Hort treated as a later scholarly recension and distinguished from their preferred *Neutral text—a distinction which is rarely now maintained. It is represented by *Codex Vaticanus (B), and in part by other uncials, e.g. ℵ, A, C, W, and by the citations of the early Alexandrian Fathers, *Origen and *Clement. The same type of text is displayed in 20th-cent. *papyrus discoveries from Egypt, esp. the *Bodmer papyri P75 and P66 and the *Chester Beatty papyrus P46, and their early date calls into question the theory of a later recension. The Alexandrian text has largely resisted stylistic improvement, harmonization and expansion (in contrast to the *Western and *Caesarean texts) and seems to be the result of careful transmission. This does not necessarily mean, however, that it is the earliest form of NT text; the scarcity of evidence other than from the preserving sands of Egypt may disguise a wider variation in the NT text of the 2nd cent.

C. M. Martini, SJ, *Il Problema della Recensionalità del Codice B alla luce del papiro Bodmer XIV* (Analecta Biblica, 26; 1966); id., 'Is there a late Alexandrian text of the Gospels?', *New Testament Studies*, 24 (1978), pp. 285–96; E. J. Epp, 'The Twentieth Century Interlude in New Testament Textual Criticism', *Journal of Biblical Literature*, 93 (1974), pp. 386–414; id., 'The Significance of the Papyri for Determining the Nature of the New Testament Text in the Second Century: A Dynamic View of Textual Transmission', in W. L. Petersen (ed.), *Gospel Traditions in the Second Century: Origins, Recensions, Text, and Transmission* (Notre Dame, Ind., and London [1989]), pp. 71–103; G. D. Fee, 'P75, P66 and Origen: The Myth of Early Textual Recension in Alexandria', in R. N. Longenecker and M. C. Tenney (eds.), *New Dimensions in New Testament Study* (Grand Rapids [1974]), pp. 19–45; the last three arts. are repr. in E. J. Epp and G. D. Fee, *Studies in the Theory and Method of New Testament Textual Criticism* (Grand Rapids, 1993), chs. 5, 13 and 14.

Alexandrian theology. This is a modern designation for a style of theology associated with the Church at *Alexandria and markedly influenced by the Platonic tradition. Its characteristic emphases on the reality of the spiritual world and the *allegorical exegesis of Scripture are clearly evidenced in the work of *Origen. The term is particularly used (in contrast to *Antiochene theology) to refer to forms and expressions of belief which laid special stress on the Divine nature of Christ and the unity of His person. Its primary exemplar is to be seen in St *Cyril and his opposition to *Nestorianism. A result of this stress was that even the orthodox among the Alexandrians (e.g. St Cyril) did not hesitate to say of the Incarnate Christ that 'God suffered', while the less orthodox, beginning with *Apollinarius (who, though not in fact an Alexandrian, can be seen as belonging to the same theological tradition), undermined the completeness of Christ's humanity, holding that His highest human faculties were simply replaced by the Divine Nature, so that He could neither be tempted nor suffer. *Monophysitism must be considered an extreme form of the Alexandrian school of thought, which, by verbal adherence to Cyril's language, taught that there was only one nature in Christ, a view which practically nullified His humanity; while *Monothelitism, in the 7th cent., carried on the same tradition in different terms by asserting the unity of Christ's Divine and Human Will.

See also CATECHETICAL SCHOOL OF ALEXANDRIA.

C. *Bigg, *The Christian Platonists of Alexandria* (*Bampton Lectures, 1886; ed. F. E. *Brightman, 1913); R. B. Tollinton, *Alexandrine Teaching on the Universe* (1932); E. Molland, *The Conception of the Gospel in the Alexandrian Theology* (Oslo, 1938); R. V. Sellers, *Two Ancient Christologies* (1940). P. Brezzi, *La Gnosi cristiana di Alessandria et le antiche scuole cristiane* [1950]. G. Bardy, 'Aux Origines de l'École d'Alexandrie' *Rech. S.R.* 27 (1937), pp. 65–90; id., 'Pour l'Histoire de l'École d'Alexandrie', *Vivre et Penser* [wartime title of *R. Bibl.*], 2 (1942), pp. 80–109. F. M. Young, 'A Reconsideration of Alexandrian Christology', *JEH* 22 (1971), pp. 103–14. J. Quasten, *Patrology*, 2 (Utrecht, 1953), pp. 1–118, esp. pp. 2–4, with bibl. W. R. *Inge in HERE 1 (1908), pp. 308–19, s.v. See also bibl. to ANTIOCHENE THEOLOGY and CATECHETICAL SCHOOL OF ALEXANDRIA.

Alford, Henry (1810–71), Dean of *Canterbury. He entered Trinity College, Cambridge, in 1829, and was elected fellow in 1834. In 1835 he became Vicar of Wymeswold, Leicestershire. From 1853 to 1857 he ministered to a large congregation at Quebec Chapel, Marylebone, and then became Dean of Canterbury, where he remained till his death. His most important work was an edition of the Greek NT (1849–61), in which he united freshness of treatment with wide learning. He also translated the *Odyssey*, wrote several well-known hymns (among them, 'Come, ye thankful people, come' and 'Ten thousand times ten thousand'), edited the writings of

J. *Donne (1839), published some original verse, and was the first editor of the *Contemporary Review*.

Poetical Works, 2 vols., 1845. Life, Journal and Letters, ed. by F. Alford, his widow (1873). W. H. Fremantle in *DNB* 1 (1885), pp. 282–4, s.v.

Alfred the Great (849–99), King of Wessex from 871. He was born at Wantage. Apart from his defeat of the Danes, which contributed materially to the maintenance of Christianity in England, Alfred is chiefly memorable in Church history for the care with which he promoted ecclesiastical reform and the revival of learning. Himself a man of deep piety and considerable education, he gathered round him a band of scholars from England, Wales, and the Continent, and with their help translated a number of the most popular Latin works of the time. He himself was largely responsible for translating the 'Pastoral Care' of *Gregory the Great, the 'Consolation of Philosophy' of *Boethius, the 'Soliloquies' of St *Augustine, and the first 50 psalms of the Psalter; at his instigation Werferth, Bp. of *Worcester, translated the 'Dialogues' of Gregory the Great, and an anonymous translator produced an English version of the 'History' of *Orosius. He promoted the interests of the Church, founding monastic communities at Shaftesbury and Athelney; he also apparently made plans for one at *Winchester. He has been remembered for a thousand years as one who did his utmost for the education of his clergy and nobles, and, in his own life, as the pattern of a Christian king. Feast day, 26 Oct.

Crit. edns. of Alfred's versions of Gregory's *Pastoral Care* by H. Sweet (EETS 45 and 50; 1871–2), of Boethius' *De Consolatione Philosophiae* by W. J. Sedgefield (Oxford, 1899), of the 'Soliloquies' of St Augustine by W. Endter (Bibliothek der angelsächsischen Prosa, 11; Hamburg, 1922) and by T. A. Carnicelli (Cambridge, Mass., 1969), and of the first 50 Psalms by J. W. Bright and R. L. Ramsay, *Liber Psalmorum: The West-Saxon Psalms* (Boston and London, 1907). Werferth's tr. of Gregory's 'Dialogues' is ed. H. Hecht (Bibliothek der angelsächsischen Prosa, 5; 2 parts, Leipzig and Hamburg, 1900–7), and the anonymous tr. of the 'History' of Orosius by J. Bately (EETS suppl. ser. 6; 1980). The primary sources for Alfred's life are the contemporary biography by Asser (crit. edn. by W. H. Stevenson, Oxford, 1904; new impression, with art. on recent work by D. Whitelock, 1959) and the 'Anglo-Saxon Chronicle' for the years of his reign; Eng. tr. of these, with full comm. (and selected passages from Alfred's writings) by S. Keynes and M. Lapidge, *Alfred the Great* (Penguin Classics, 1983). C. Plummer, *The Life and Times of Alfred the Great* (Ford Lectures for 1901; Oxford, 1902); A. J. Frantzen, *King Alfred* (Boston [1986]); A. P. Smyth, *King Alfred the Great* (Oxford, 1995; cf. S. Keynes in *JEH* 47 (1996), pp. 529–51). On his reign, R. H. Hodgkin, *A History of the Anglo-Saxons*, 2 (Oxford, 1935), pp. 537–688; 3rd edn. (1952), pp. 537–695; F. M. Stenton, *Anglo-Saxon England* (ibid., 1943), pp. 246–73; 3rd edn. (1971), pp. 248–76.

aliturgical days. Days on which the Eucharist may not be celebrated. In the Roman rite there are now only two such days, namely *Good Friday and *Holy Saturday; in the E. Church there are many more.

All Saints' Day. The feast, kept in the W. on 1 Nov., to celebrate all the Christian saints, known and unknown. Reference to such a feast occurs in St *Ephrem Syrus (d. 373), while in St *Chrysostom (d. 407) it is assigned to a definite day, namely the first Sunday after *Pentecost, that still observed in the E. This same day was apparently associated with the saints also at *Rome in the 6th cent.; but in the W. the feast did not become firmly established until the consecration of the Pantheon at Rome (*dedicatio S. Mariae ad martyres*) to Christian usage by Boniface IV on 13 May 609 or 610. From then on an annual commemoration of 'All Saints' was made on 13 May. Its observance on 1 Nov. appears to date from the time of Gregory III (d. 741), who dedicated on that day a chapel in the basilica of St Peter to 'All the Saints'. Gregory IV (d. 844) ordered its universal observance and *Sixtus IV (d. 1484) added the Octave (suppressed 1955). In the calendar in the ASB, the Octave Day (8 Nov.) is assigned to the 'Saints and Martyrs of England'.

Serm. of Chrysostom, *Laudatio Sanctorum Omnium* (J. P. Migne, *PG* 1. 705–12). L. Eisenhofer, *Handbuch der katholischen Liturgik*, 1 (1932), pp. 606 f. G. Löw in *EC* 9 (1952), cols. 86–90, s.v. 'Ognissanti'; B. Luykx, O Praem., in *LW* 1 (1962), cols. 99–102, s.v. 'Allerheiligen', with further bibl.

All Souls' Day. The commemoration of the souls of the faithful departed on 2 Nov., the day following *All Saints' Day. (Until 1970, when 2 Nov. was a Sunday, All Souls' Day was 3 Nov.) Its observance became universal through the influence of *Odilo of Cluny, who in 998 commanded its annual celebration in the *Benedictine houses of his congregation. In 1915 *Benedict XV gave permission for priests to celebrate three Masses on All Souls' Day (a privilege confined to this day and *Christmas). The Mass contains the famous sequence, '*Dies Irae' (since 1969 no longer obligatory). In the C of E, the observance of All Souls' Day was dropped at the Reformation, but provision is made for it in the ASB and many other modern Anglican liturgies.

The 'Statutum Odilonis pro Defunctis' is printed in J. P. Migne, *PL* 142. 1037 f. The commemoration is first met with at Rome in the 14th cent. (*Ordo Romanus* XIV (Mabillon), no. 101). For the Apostolic Constitution (10 Aug. 1915), permitting the three Masses on the day, see *AAS* 7 (1915), pp. 401–4. C. A. Kneller, SJ, 'Geschichte über die drei Messen am Allerseelentag', *ZKT* 42 (1918), pp. 74–113.

Allah. An Arabic word used as the name of God by all Muslims (and in some circumstances also by Arabic-speaking Christians). It has often been thought to be a combination of '*al* (the definite article) and *ilah* ('god'). The Muslim use of the word may be interpreted to mean 'The Only God'. In Muslim belief, God has 99 further names, each of which is represented by a bead on their rosary, the hundredth and largest of them representing the name Allah itself.

Allamano, Bl Giuseppe (1851–1926), founder of the *Consolata Missionaries. Born at Castelnuova, at school he came under the guidance of St John *Bosco. After ordination in 1873 he joined the staff of the Turin seminary, where he had himself been trained, and in 1880 he was appointed guardian of the Sanctuario della Consolata, a Marian shrine in Turin. From 1882 he was involved in the spiritual direction of the diocesan clergy. On recovering from a severe illness in 1891, he vowed to found a missionary society for priests and laymen. He fulfilled this vow in 1901 and founded a missionary congregation

for women in 1910. He directed both congregations until his death, sending missionaries to *Kenya, *Ethiopia, Tanzania, and *Mozambique. He was beatified in 1990.

L. Sales, IMC, *Il Canonico Giuseppe Allamano, fondatore dei Missionari e delle Missionarie della Consolata* (Turin, 1936); id., *La Dottrina Spirituale de Servo di Dio Can. Giuseppe Allamo* (2 vols., ibid., 1949; 2nd edn., 1 vol., 1963; Eng. tr., Rome [1982]). The Eng. tr. includes an introd. by C. Bona, IMC, which was reissued, with other material, as C. Bona, *Fr. Joseph Allamano* (London and Dublin [1986]). Popular Life by D. Agasso (Cinisello Balsamo, 1990; Eng. tr., Slough, 1991).

Allatius, Leo (1587 or 1588–1669), Greek RC theologian and historian. He was a native of Chios. In 1622 he supervised the transference of the valuable collection of Palatinate MSS from Heidelberg to the Vatican Library, of which he became custodian in 1661. A zealous advocate of reunion between the Orthodox and RC Churches, he wrote several works seeking to establish the unity in essential doctrine between them, the chief being his *De ecclesiae occidentalis atque orientalis perpetua consensione libri III* (Cologne, 1648). He also wrote extensively on *patristics.

MS *Vita* by S. Gradi, partly pr. in A. *Mai, *NPB* 6 (pt. 2; 1853), pp. v–xxviii. P. P. Argenti, *The Religious Minorities of Chios* (Cambridge, 1970), pp. 233–69. C. Jacono, *Bibliografia di Leone Allacci (1588–1669)* (Quaderni dell'Istituto di Filologia Greca della Università di Palermo, 2; 1962). G. Podskalsky, *Griechische Theologie in der Zeit der Türkenherrschaft (1453–1821)* (Munich, 1988), pp. 213–19. L. Bréhier in *DHGE* 2 (1914), cols. 479–84, s.v.

Allegiance, Oath of. An ancient oath of fidelity and true allegiance to the Sovereign now prescribed by the Promissory Oaths Act 1868 s. 2. All holders of clerical office in England are required to take it, by Canon C 13 and the *Clerical Subscription Act 1865. The accompanying Oath of Supremacy, which acknowledged the Sovereign as Supreme Governor in matters spiritual or temporal, was abolished in 1868, but the principle of Royal Supremacy continues to be acknowledged by the C of E as a whole in Canon A 7.

allegory. In Christian exegesis, one of the traditional ways of interpreting Scripture in distinction to the literal or historical sense. The Greek word, ἀλληγορία, belongs to ancient literary theory and is defined as 'speaking one thing and signifying something other than what is said' (Heraclitus, *Quaestiones Homericae*); it was applied by the *Stoics and others to the interpretation of Homer. A form of allegorical interpretion of Scripture was practised in the Palestinian Rabbinic schools. From the earliest days Christians applied allegory to the OT in order to make it yield a Christian meaning. It can be seen as an extension of the argument from *prophecy. As certain specific prophecies in the OT were fulfilled in Christ, so the literal, historical events recorded in the OT were regarded as *types, having a deeper spiritual significance for Christians (e.g. the crossing of the Red Sea was fulfilled in Christian *Baptism). St *Paul used the term in Gal. 4: 24, 'which things contain an allegory' (ἅτινά ἐστιν ἀλληγορούμενα), to point to the relationship between the old Israel and the Church which is its fulfilment, but 2 Cor. 3, with its contrast between the letter and the Spirit, prob. had greater influence on the development of Christian allegory. In the later development of Christian exegesis pagan ideas about allegory played their part (as had already been the case with *Philo). *Origen is regarded as the great exponent of allegory, distinguishing a threefold literal, moral, and spiritual sense, corresponding to the human body, soul, and spirit, though in practice he usually worked with a twofold distinction between letter and spirit, history and deeper allegorical meaning, as is characteristic of the Fathers generally. Most of the Fathers were anxious to safeguard the literal, historic meaning of the biblical text; this concern was esp. characteristic of the school of *Antioch. Origen is often regarded as having failed in this respect. In the W. more systematic accounts of the senses of Scripture emerged, the most fundamental being the distinction of four senses, the literal, the allegorical (its doctrinal significance), the tropological or moral (its application to the individual Christian life), and the anagogical (lifting the mind to the goal of the Christian life). The Middle Ages witnessed both an elaboration of these interpretations which lost sight of the literal sense and a growing attempt to recover the literal, historical, original meaning (which involved recourse to the text in the original language).

The Renaissance and the Reformation brought a renewed mistrust of allegory. Although *Erasmus had a deep appreciation of its place in the patristic exegesis of Scripture, allegorical interpretation was, in theory at least, rejected by the Reformers as enabling human tradition to pervert the plain meaning of the Bible (they none the less used it in their sermons). With the *Enlightenment and the Romantics allegory in any context was rejected as artificial and arbitrary, in contrast to symbol. J. *Keble's *Tract 89* contains a defence of patristic allegory, but it had little influence. In modern times there has been renewed appreciation of patristic allegory, often called typology (though that term is not ancient), by several scholars, notably J. *Daniélou and H. de *Lubac.

See also EXEGESIS.

J. Daniélou, SJ, *Sacramentum Futuri: Études sur les origines de la typologie biblique* (1950; Eng. tr., 1960); H. de Lubac, SJ, *Histoire et Esprit: L'Intelligence de l'Écriture d'après Origène* (Théologie, 16; 1950); id., *Exégèse médiévale: Les quatre sens de l'écriture* (ibid. 41; 2 vols. in 4 parts, 1959–64); B. Smalley, *The Study of the Bible in the Middle Ages* (Oxford, 1952; 3rd edn., 1983); R. M. Grant, *The Letter and the Spirit* (1957); J. Pépin, *Mythe et allégorie: Les origines grecques et les contestations judéo-chrétiennes* (1958; 2nd edn., Études Augustiniennes, 1976); R. P. C. Hanson, *Allegory and Event: A Study of the Sources and Significance of Origen's Interpretation of Scripture* (1959), pp. 9–129 ('The Sources of Christian Allegory'); D. E. Nineham (ed.), *The Church's Use of the Bible, Past and Present* (1963), esp. chs. by H. Chadwick, J. N. D. Kelly, and B. Smalley; R. P. C. Hanson, 'Biblical Exegesis in the Early Church', in *Cambridge History of the Bible*, 1, ed. P. R. Ackroyd and C. P. Evans (1970), pp. 412–53; M. F. Wiles, 'Origen as Biblical Scholar', ibid., pp. 454–89; G. W. H. Lampe, J. Leclercq, OSB, B. Smalley, and E. I. J. Rosenthal, 'The Exposition and Exegesis of Scripture', ibid. 2, ed. G. W. H. Lampe (1969), pp. 155–220 and 252–79; A. Louth, *Discerning the Mystery* (Oxford, 1983), pp. 96–131; id., 'The Oxford Movement, the Fathers and the Bible', *Sobornost/Eastern Churches Review*, 6, no. 1 (1984), pp. 30–45.

Alleluia (Heb. הַלְלוּיָהּ, 'Praise ye Yah'), liturgical expression of praise. It occurs in a number of Psalms, esp. in Pss. 111–17, where its position indicated that it was chanted as a kind of *antiphon by the choir of the

*Levites. It is found elsewhere in the Bible only in Tobit (13: 18) and the Book of Rev. (19: 1, 3, 4, 6), in both places as the chant of the saints in heaven. It was taken over into the liturgy of the Church at an early date. In the W. it became the characteristic expression of joy and was therefore sung esp. in *Paschaltide, as is witnessed by St *Augustine (*Serm*. 252, De diebus paschalibus, 23. 9), but whether, as *Sozomen (*Hist. Eccl.* 7. 19) affirms, it was restricted at *Rome to *Easter Day or not, remains doubtful. The Roman usage was regulated by St *Gregory the Great, who ordered the Alleluia to be said at Mass and the Office throughout the year except in the penitential time between *Septuagesima and Easter. It was later omitted also in funeral offices. In the Greek Church, on the other hand, it remained a part of all offices, and its omission at certain times was made one of the grievances of the E. Church against the W. in the struggle which led to the schism of the 11th cent.

Acc. to the Roman rite the Alleluia is now sung at all Masses except in Lent; formerly it was omitted on some other penitential occasions as well. It is chanted before the Gospel and normally consists of a twofold Alleluia, a verse from Scripture, and another Alleluia. In Paschaltide Alleluias are inserted in many places both in the Mass and in the Divine Office. The name 'Alleluia Saturday' is sometimes applied to *Holy Saturday because, to mark the return of the Alleluia after its absence since the beginning of Lent, the celebrant solemnly intones it three times, each time at a higher pitch. In the E. Alleluias are also sung before the Gospel, and in many other places in the liturgical office; in contrast to the W., however, they are not regarded as festal, and occur with especial frequency during the Lenten services. In the *Ambrosian rite the form 'Hallelujah' was used until 1976.

On the orig. use of the word, cf. F. H. Woods in *HDB* 2 (1899), p. 287. T. Nöldeke, 'Hallelyua', *Beihefte zur ZATW*, 33 (1918), pp. 375–80. Jungmann, *MS* (1958 edn.), 1, pp. 540–57; Eng. tr. 1 [1950], pp. 422–36, with refs. A. G. Martimort, 'Origine et signification de l'Alleluia de la Messe Romaine', in R. Granfield and J. A. Jungmann (eds.), *Kyriakon: Festschrift Johannes Quasten*, 2 (1970), pp. 811–34; E. Jammers, *Das Alleluia in der Gregorianischen Messe* (Liturgiewissenschaftliche Quellen und Forschungen, 55; 1973); A. Rose, 'L'usage et la signification de l'Alleluia en Orient et en Occident', in *Gestes et Paroles dans les diverses familles liturgiques: Conférence Saint-Serge XXIV* semaine d'études liturgiques* (Bibliotheca Ephemerides Liturgicae, Subsidia, 14; 1978), pp. 205–33. T. Bailey, *The Ambrosian Alleluias* (Egham, Surrey, 1983). E. Wellesz, *Eastern Elements in Western Chant: Studies in the Early History of Ecclesiastical Music* (Monumenta Musicae Byzantinae, Subsidia, 2; Boston, 1947), esp. pp. 175–85; id., 'Gregory the Great's Letter on the *Alleluia*', *Annales Musicologiques*, 2 (1954), pp. 7–26. W. Apel, *Gregorian Chant* [1958], pp. 375–92. C. Thodberg, *Der byzantinische Alleluiarionzyklus* (Monumenta Musicae Byzantinae, Subsidia, 8; Copenhagen, 1966). K. Schlager and C. Thodberg in *The New Grove Dictionary of Music and Musicians*, 1 (1980), pp. 269–76, s.v.

Alleluyatic Sequence. A name popularly given to the hymn 'Cantemus cuncti melodum' ('The strain upraise of joy and praise, Alleluia', *EH*, no. 494), on account of its frequent repetition of 'Alleluia'. It was written in the early 10th cent., and used before or at *Septuagesima for the 'farewell to Alleluia' since, acc. to traditional liturgical practice, the word Alleluia, as an expression of joy, was not used between Septuagesima and *Easter. The words are based on Ps. 147.

Crit. edn. of text by C. Blume, SJ, and H. Bannister (eds.), *Thesauri Hymnologici Prosarium* (AHMA 53; 1911), pp. 60–2. W. A. Shoults and J. Julian in J. Julian (ed.), *Dictionary of Hymnology* (2nd edn., 1907), pp. 203 f., s.v. 'Cantemus Cuncti Melodum Nunc'.

Allen, Roland (1868–1947), missionary and missionary theorist. The son of a clergyman, he was educated at St John's College, Oxford, and Leeds Clergy School. He was ordained priest in 1893 and joined the North China Mission of the *SPG in 1895. He left Peking in 1903 when his health broke. In 1904 he became Rector of Chalfont St Peter in Buckinghamshire, but resigned in 1907 because he would not baptize where there was no evidence of Christian commitment. For the rest of his life he wrote and canvassed industriously and combatively, being provided by the Survey Application Trust with a vehicle for his ideas. These centred on the local and indigenous character of the NT Church, reflecting apostolic trust in the Holy Spirit to provide new believers with everything needed for the Church's life and leadership, and expansion by 'the unexhorted and unorganized activity of individual members of the Church explaining to others the Gospel which they had found for themselves'. By contrast, he felt that modern missions imposed foreign direction, kept financial control, and established an alienated professional ministry. Allen's views gained attention from *Evangelicals, and more widely after his death. His best known works are *Missionary Methods: St Paul's or ours?* (1912, 2nd edn., 1927) and *The Spontaneous Expansion of the Church and the Causes which Hinder it* (1927).

Selected Writings ed. D. M. Paton as *The Ministry of the Spirit* (1960), with memoir by A. McLeish, pp. ix–xvi. D. M. Paton (ed.), *Reform of the Ministry: A Study in the Work of Roland Allen* (1968).

Allen, William (1532–94), Cardinal. He was a fellow of Oriel College, Oxford. In 1561 he left England for Louvain, returned in the next year, and was finally forced to leave the country in 1565. From that time he concentrated on the work of training RC mission priests for the conversion of England, believing that the majority of English people were still Catholic at heart, and that Protestantism was only a temporary phase of opinion. He founded colleges for this work at *Douai (1568) and Rome (1575–9), and encouraged the foundation at Valladolid (1589). From the press at Douai there issued a stream of RC propaganda, and the *Douai version of the Bible was produced under his inspiration. By supporting *Philip II's invasion of England in 1588, however, he incurred the serious hostility of many English RCs. Towards the end of his life, he was created a cardinal in 1587 and nominated Abp. of Malines in 1589. He ended his days at the *English College at Rome.

Modern repr. of his *Brief History of the Glorious Martyrdom of Twelve Reverend Priests, Father Edmund Campion and his Companions*, by J. H. Pollen, SJ (1908). *The Letters and Memorials of William Cardinal Allen (1532–94)*, ed. with hist. introd. by T. F. Knox, Cong. Orat. (Records of the English Catholics under the Penal Laws, 2; 1882). 'Some Correspondence of Cardinal Allen, 1579–85, from the Jesuit Archives' contributed by P. Ryan, SJ,

to the CRS, *Miscellanea*, 7 (CRS 9; 1911), pp. 12–105. *Letters of William Allen and Richard Barret 1572–1598*, ed. P. Renold (ibid. 58; 1967). Life by Bede Camm, OSB (1908). T. H. Clancy, *Papist Pamphleteers: The Allen–Persons Party and the Political Thought of the Counter Reformation in England 1572–1615* (Chicago, 1964). A. Pritchard, *Catholic Loyalism in Elizabethan England* (1979), pp. 11–36 ('Allen and Parsons: The Political Theory of Militant Catholicism'). A. F. Allison and D. M. Rogers, 'A Catalogue of Catholic Books in English . . .', *Biographical Studies*, 3 (1956), pp. 133 f. (nos. 5–13); idd., *The Contemporary Printed Literature of the English Counter-Reformation*, 1 (Aldershot, 1989), pp. 3–5 (nos. 6–18). T. Cooper in *DNB* 1 (1885) pp. 314–22, s.v.

Allestree, Richard (1619–81), Anglican divine. He was educated at *Christ Church, Oxford, where Richard Busby (afterwards Headmaster of Westminster) was his tutor. For a time he served in the royalist forces and throughout his life remained loyal in support of the Stuart cause. During the Commonwealth he assisted J. *Fell in continuing the C of E service in a private dwelling-house in Oxford. From 1663 to 1679 he was Regius Professor of Divinity at Oxford and in 1665 he also became Provost of Eton. He is best remembered as the probable author of 'The *Whole Duty of Man'.

Collected edn. of *The Works of the Learned and Pious Author of The Whole Duty of Man* (2 parts, Oxford, 1684). Anon. Life by [J. Fell] prefixed to *Forty Sermons* (1684; no pagination); repr. separately, 1848. See also bibl. to WHOLE DUTY OF MAN.

Allies, Thomas William (1813–1903), theologian. From 1833 to 1841 he was a Fellow of Wadham College, Oxford. In 1842 he became Vicar of Launton, near Bicester. He became closely associated with the leaders of the *Oxford Movement, esp. E. B. *Pusey; but having begun to doubt the Anglican position during travels abroad in 1845 and 1847 (described in his *Journal in France* [1848]), he joined the RC Church after the *Gorham Judgement. He was a man of wide learning, and in his later life a prominent apologist for Roman Catholicism both by lectures and writings. The latter include *The See of St Peter* (1850) and 8 vols. under the general title *The Formation of Christendom* (1865–96). From 1853 to 1890 he was secretary of the Catholic Poor Schools Committee, the RC equivalent of the *National Society and the British and Foreign Schools Society.

M. H. Allies (daughter), *Thomas William Allies* (1907; repr., with additional appendices, 1924). W. B. Owen in *DNB, 1901–1911*, 1, pp. 37 f.

Almachius, St. See TELEMACHUS, ST.

almery. An obsolete form of the word '*aumbry' (q.v.).

almoner. An officer who has the duty of dispensing alms. Very frequently he is in holy orders. The Lord High Almoner of the King of England, who has the disposing of the Sovereign's alms and on *Maundy Thursday, in the absence of the Sovereign, normally distributes the royal 'maundy', is usually a bishop. In France *aumonier* is used in a more general sense of 'chaplain'.

almuce, alternatively **amice** or **amess**. An item of ecclesiastical costume, usually a cape lined with fur, worn in certain religious orders. Its use can be traced back to the

12th cent. In more recent times it has been worn esp. by canons in *France, who carry their almuce as a mark of dignity over the left arm. The word 'amice' (Lat. *almutia*) in this sense is independent in derivation from that of the *amice (q.v.) worn at the Eucharist, though the two have often been confused.

Alogi. A group of heretics in Asia Minor (*c.* AD 170). They seem to have been strongly opposed to *Montanism and to have ascribed the Fourth Gospel and Revelation to *Cerinthus, but their exact doctrines are not easy to ascertain. Acc. to *Epiphanius (*Haer.* 51), they denied the divinity of the Holy Spirit and of the Logos. The word '*Alogi*' (ἄλογοι) was coined for them by their opponents, who used it in the double sense of 'unreasonable' and 'disbelievers in the Logos'.

V. Rose, OP, 'Question johannine. Les Aloges asiatiques et les aloges romains', *R. Bibl.* 6 (1897), pp. 516–34. A. Bludau, *Die ersten Gegner der Johannes-Schriften* (Biblische Studien, 22, Hefte 1 and 2; 1925). S. G. Hall in *TRE* 2 (1978), pp. 290–95, s.v. 'Aloger', with further refs.

Aloysius Gonzaga, St (1568–91), patron of RC youth. Of noble descent, he was destined for a military career, and from 1577 to 1579 was at Florence as a page at the court of Francesco de' Medici, where he first began to feel a vocation to religion. After joining the suite of Mary of Austria in 1581, he followed her to Spain, but in 1584 he returned to Italy, where, in the face of great opposition, he entered the novitiate of the *Jesuits in 1585. He made his vows in 1587, and died, at the age of 23, a victim to his labours among the plague-stricken of Rome. He was canonized in 1726. Feast day, 21 June.

Opera Omnia, partim Italice, partim Latine (incomplete), ed. A. Heuser (Bibliotheca Mystica et Ascetica, 3; Cologne, etc., 1850). Works listed in Sommervogel, 3 (1892), cols. 1575–81, and 9 (1900), col. 420. Life by his contemporary and associate, V. Cepari, SJ (Rome, 1606; Lat. tr., Cologne, 1608; Eng. tr., Paris, 1627, repr. London, 1974); ed., with additional matter, by A. Schroeber, SJ (Einsiedeln, 1891; Eng. tr., 1891). The account in *AASS*, Jun. 4 (1707), pp. 847–1167, utilizes the process of beatification. C. C. Martindale, SJ, *The Vocation of Aloysius Gonzaga* (1927), with bibl. Polgár, 2 (1990), pp. 39–54. W. V. Bangert, SJ, in *NCE* 1 (1967), pp. 332 f., s.v.

alpha and omega (*A* and *Ω*). The first and last letters of the Greek alphabet, used in the Christian Church to denote God's eternity and infinitude. In the NT they are found in Rev. 1: 8, 21: 6, and also in 22: 13 (of Christ). Their adoption is probably derived from the Heb. use of the word 'truth', אמת, the first and last letters of which are the first and last letters of the Heb. alphabet.

G. Kittel in *TWNT* 1 (1933; Eng. tr., 1964), pp. 1–3, s.v., with refs. F. *Cabrol, OSB, in *DACL* 1 (pt. 1; 1907), cols. 1–25, s.v.

Alphege, St (954–1012), also **Aelfheah**, Abp. of *Canterbury. A monk of Deerhurst, or possibly of *Glastonbury, and then Abbot of Bath, he succeeded St *Ethelwold as Bp. of *Winchester in 984. In 1006 he was translated to Canterbury. He was murdered by the Danes during a drunken feast because he would not ransom himself at the expense of his poor tenants, and was therefore regarded as a martyr. Feast day, 19 Apr.

Life by Osbern, monk of Canterbury (d. *c.*1090), in [H. Wharton] *Anglia Sacra*, 2 (1691), pp. 122–42, with Osbern's account of translation of Alphege's relics from London to Canterbury (1023), pp. 143–7. E. A. Freeman, *The History of the Norman Conquest*, 1 (1867), pp. 387–9, with note on sources in 3rd edn. (1877), pp. 673–8; N. Brooks, *The Early History of the Church of Canterbury* (Leicester, 1984), esp. pp. 278–81 and 283–5.

Alphonsus Liguori, St (1696–1787), founder of the *Redemptorists and moral theologian. The son of a Neapolitan noble, Giuseppe dei Liguori, Alfonso Maria dei Liguori was born at Marianella near Naples. After taking the degree of Doctor of Laws at the age of 16, he practised with marked success at the bar for eight years; but in 1723 the loss, by an oversight, of an important suit in which a Neapolitan noble was suing the Grand Duke of Tuscany for £100,000 convinced him of the transitoriness of worldly glory and he withdrew from his profession. He received the tonsure, joined an association of mission preachers, was ordained priest in 1726, and became a successful evangelist in the country around Naples. In 1729 he took up residence in a missionary college in Naples where he made the close friendship of Tommaso Falcoia (1663–1743), of the congregation of the *Pii Operarii*, who had taken part in the foundation (1719) of a convent of nuns at Scala, near Amalfi, and was to exercise great influence on him. When in 1730 Falcoia became Bp. of Castellammare, the diocese in which Scala was situated, Alphonsus moved to Scala, in 1731 reorganized the nuns (the first house of 'Redemptoristines'), and then in 1732 founded the 'Congregation of the Most Holy Redeemer' or 'Redemptorists' (q.v.) for men in a neighbouring hospice. Originally there were seven postulants under Alphonsus' guidance, who devoted themselves to pastoral work among the poor in the country districts. Falcoia was technically their director until his death (1743), when Alphonsus was formally elected Superior-General; but, owing to internal dissensions, growth was slow. In 1745 Alphonsus wrote the first of his many devotional and spiritual works. In 1749 *Benedict XIV approved the rule and institute for men and in 1750 the corresponding ones for women. In 1762 Alphonsus accepted with much reluctance the see of Sant'Agata dei Goti, in the province of Beneventum (he had declined the archbishopric of Palermo in 1747). Here, continuing to live an austere life, he was largely engaged in literary and missionary labours. In 1775 he resigned his see on the plea of ill-health and retired to Nocera. But he lived another twelve years, and became involved in much controversy arising from the affairs of his Order. His last years were clouded by severe spiritual trials and darkness.

Alphonsus sought to commend the Gospel to a sceptical age by gentle and direct methods. Spurning the florid oratory of his contemporaries, he preached simply and to the heart and believed that the rigorism of the contemporary confessional (largely under *Jansenist influences) repelled rather than won back the sinful. He set out these ideals in a system of *moral theology, first outlined in his *Annotations* to Hermann Busembaum (a much esteemed Jesuit casuist, 1600–68), published at Naples in 1748. This teaching he recast in his celebrated *Theologia Moralis* (2 vols., 1753 and 1755), of which seven further editions appeared before his death, as well as a number of compendiums, e.g. the *Homo Apostolicus* (1759). In the debate on how far it is allowable to follow any 'probable' opinion in matters of conduct, Alphonsus, in contradistinction to the Jesuits, developed the system known as *Equiprobabilism (q.v.).

His innumerable devotional writings include (Eng. titles) *Visits to the Blessed Sacrament and the Blessed Virgin* (1745), *The Glories of Mary* (1750), *Novena of Christmas* (1758), *Novena of the Heart of Jesus* (1758), *The Great Means of Prayer* (1759), *The True Spouse of Jesus Christ* (1760), and *The Way of Salvation* (1767). They became very popular and remained in general use down to the later 19th cent. There is no doubt that they fostered devotion; but their exuberance became a frequent target of criticism, esp. by Protestant writers.

Alphonsus was beatified in 1816, canonized in 1839, and declared a *doctor ecclesiae* by *Pius IX in 1871. Feast day, 1 (formerly 2) Aug.

Opere Ascetiche (Rome, 1933 ff., with Introduzione Generale by O. Gregorio, G. Cacciatore, and D. Capione, 1960, incl. recent bibl.). His Letters ed. P. Kuntz, CSSR (3 vols., Rome, 1887). There are many eds. of his *Theologia Moralis* and his popular devotional works. The primary source is A. M. Tannoia, CSSR, *Della vita ed istituto del venerabile Alfonso Maria Liguori* (3 vols., 1798–1802; Eng. tr., 5 vols., 1848–9). This should be corrected in its details by the scholarly Life [in Germ.] by K. Dilgskron, CSSR (Regensburg and New York, 1887). R. Telleria, CSSR, *San Alfonso Maria de Ligorio* (2 vols., Madrid 1950–1); T. Rey-Mermet, CSSR, *Le Saint du Siècle des Lumières: Alfonso de Liguori* (1982; 2nd edn., 1987), and other works of this author; F. M. Jones, CSSR, *Alphonsus de Liguori: The Saint of Bourbon Naples 1696–1787* [1992]. Writings associated with the bicentenary of Alphonsus' death include two special numbers of *Studia Moralia*, vol. 25 (Rome, 1987); J. Delumeau (ed.), *Alphonse de Liguori, Pasteur et Docteur* (Théologie Historique, 77 [1987]); and the acts of an international conference held 15–19 May 1988, P. Giannantonio (ed.), *Alphonso M. de Liguori e la Società Civile del suo Tempo* (Biblioteca dell' 'Archivium Romanicum', 1st ser., vol. 243; 2 vols., Florence, 1990). On Alphonsus' spiritual teaching, see Pourrat, 4, pp. 449–91. A. Palmieri in *DHGE* 2 (1914), cols. 715–35, s.v., with extensive bibl. to date; G. Cacciatore in *Dizionario Biografico degli Italiani*, 2 (1960), pp. 342–50, s.v., also with bibl.

Altaner, Berthold (1885–1964), patristic scholar. A native of Silesia, he was ordained in 1910 and began to teach Church history at Breslau in 1919. Ten years later he was appointed professor of patrology, ancient Church history, and Christian archaeology at Breslau. He was the first theologian to be deprived of his university position by the Nazis in 1933. He held a post at Breslau cathedral until expelled in 1945, when he fled to Bavaria. Until he retired in 1950 he was professor of patrology and the history of liturgy at Würzburg.

His early works deal with the history of the *Dominican Order: *Venturino von Bergamo O. Pr.* (1911), *Der hl. Dominikus* (1922), *Die Dominikanermission des 13. Jahrhunderts* (1924), and *Die Briefe Jordans von Sachsen* (1925). He is best known for his one-volume *Patrologie: Leben, Schriften und Lehre der Kirchenväter* (1938; Eng. tr. based on 5th German edn. of 1958 by H. C. Graef, 1960), which has become a standard textbook and work of reference. A rev. edn. by A. Stuiber was issued in 1966.

His *Kleine patristische Schriften*, ed. G. Glockmann (TU 83; 1967). B. Altaner, *Verzeichnis meiner Veröffentlichungen 1907–1953* (Würzburg, 1953). List of his works to date in *Hist. J.* 77 (1958), pp. 576–600.

altar (Gk. θυσιαστήριον; Lat. *altare, ara*). The word was used of the Eucharistic table (if not already in Heb. 13: 10) in *Ignatius, *Tertullian, and *Cyprian, and this usage has been general in Catholic Christianity ever since. At the *Reformation, however, it gave rise to much controversy owing to the disputes concerning the doctrine of the *sacrifice of the Mass, of which the (stone) altar was taken as a natural symbol.

The earliest altars were doubtless of wood, being the tables in private houses normally used for domestic purposes, and *Optatus, *Augustine, and others mention wooden altars in the 4th and 5th cents. No doubt the custom of celebrating the Eucharist on the tombs of martyrs first caused stone altars to come into use. After the persecutions, bodies of martyrs were placed under altars; later, as the available relics grew smaller, they were enclosed in the altar and their presence was required for the consecration of all altars in RC Churches. The 1977 *Ordo Dedicationis Ecclesiae et Altaris*, however, lays down that relics are to be used in the dedication of altars only if they are of a size to suggest a complete human body, or at least the major part of it; they are then to be placed under the altar. For centuries there was only one altar in each Christian church, but the practice of celebrating private *Masses caused others to be added, the original altar being then known as the 'High Altar', and it became customary for each of these additional altars to be dedicated to some saint other than that to which the church itself was dedicated. In the E. Church, where private Masses are unknown, churches commonly have only one altar, though the E. regulation that the Eucharist must always be offered on a 'fasting altar' explains the occasional occurrence of two altars in the same church, to allow for two Masses on a single day. The Roman rite permits the celebration of Mass only on an altar blessed or consecrated by a bishop, except where a temporary altar is set up in a place where Mass is not customarily celebrated. In early times the altar seems to have been normally free-standing in the church, and the celebrant seems to have stood on the far side of the altar facing the congregation. Recently altars have been restored to this position in many places and the celebrant of the Eucharist has adopted a *westward position.

It was customary for altars to be covered with three cloths (which first appear in the 9th cent.) but since 1969 one is sufficient. Before the 10th cent. the cross and candlesticks were not placed on the altar, but the cross surmounted the *ciborium magnum which covered the altar, and the candles were held round during the Eucharist or suspended in candelabra from the ciborium (see foll. entry).

In the C of E, a deliberate change was made at the Reformation, from altars made of stone, fixed and immovable, to free-standing tables of wood, in order to emphasize the imagery of the Lord's Supper against the doctrine of the sacrifice of the Mass. The BCP uses the expression 'Holy Table' throughout, although versions before the Prayer Book of 1552 had retained the word 'altar'. Immovable stone altars survived, e.g. in *Westminster Abbey and Eton College, but they were exceptions to a rule which was recognized in a series of 19th-cent. cases as enforceable by law. The Holy Table Measure 1964 reversed these cases by permitting the Holy Table to be 'either movable or immovable' and 'of wood, stone or any other material suitable'; and in recent times the use of stone altars has become fairly common. In a case concerning St Stephen's, Walbrook (1987) an attempt was made to revive the old law by arguing that the proposed altar (a cylindrical piece of marble carved by Henry Moore, eight feet in diameter and weighing 10 tons) was not a 'table' as required by the 1969 *Canons (can. F 2). The *Court of Ecclesiastical Cases Reserved rejected this approach, defining a table as a 'horizontal surface raised above the ground' and, incidentally, authorizing a limited doctrine of Eucharistic sacrifice.

Comprehensive collection of material in J. Braun's two works (*CA* and *AG*). Rohault, 1, pp. 93–240, with pls. xxiii–lxxxix. E. *Bishop, *Liturgica Historica* (1918), no. 2, 'On the History of the Christian Altar', pp. 20–38. W. H. St J. Hope (ed.), *English Altars from Illuminated Manuscripts* (*Alcuin Club Collections, 1; 1899); P. *Dearmer, *Fifty Pictures of Gothic Altars* (ibid. 10; 1910). G. [F.] Webb, *The Liturgical Altar* (1933; 2nd edn., 1939); J. N. Comper, *On the Christian Altar and the Buildings which contain it* (1950); J. [B.] O'Connell, *Church Building and Furnishing: The Church's Way. A Study in Liturgical Law* (1955), pp. 127 214. Historical, doctrinal, and legal aspects in the C of E are authoritatively discussed in 'Re St Stephen's, Walbrook', *Law Reports* (1987) Family Division, pp. 146–98. H. *Leclercq, OSB, in *DACL* 1 (1907), cols. 3155–89, s.v. 'Autel', with bibl.; J. P. Kirsch and T. Klauser in *RAC* 1 (1950), cols. 334–54, s.v. 'Altar. III (christlich)'.

altar lights. The use of candles on the Christian altar seems to derive from the lighted candles which were carried in early times before the Pope as a mark of honour and at first placed on the floor behind the altar. The custom of placing them upon the altar is not definitely attested before *c.*1175, when two candles flanking an altar cross are mentioned as 'the present custom' of the Papal chapel. Subsequently mention is made of seven or more candles, acc. to the dignity of the feast, though one candle alone, to light the Missal, was also frequent. Since 1969 it has been permissible to put candles on the altar or on the floor around the altar, and the number is no longer specified in the RC Church. *Cranmer's Visitation Articles (1547) implied the permissibility of two altar lights. *Edward VI's 2nd *Injunction (1549) prohibited them, but they have now been widely restored in England. The *Lincoln Judgement (1890) recognized the legality in the C of E of two altar candles, provided they were not used ceremonially, and in 1951 the use of six candles was permitted by the Court of *Arches, although two 'must be regarded as the recognised and traditional use in the Church of England.'

D. R. Dendy, *The Use of Lights in Christian Worship* (1959). Braun, *AG*, 'Die Altarleuchter', pp. 492–530; E. *Bishop, *Liturgica Historica* (1918), pp. 301–13 ('Of Six Candles on the Altar: An Enquiry').

altar rails. Rails to protect the altar from profanation were widely introduced into English churches in the early years of *Elizabeth I, when the rood-screens and their protecting doors were removed. The *Puritans disliked them as implying that the altar was specially sacred, and in many cases they were taken out again. In his Archiepiscopal Visitation (1634), W. *Laud ordered altars which had been removed into the body of the church to be restored to the E. wall and required their protection by altar rails, at

which the communicants were to receive the Sacrament; and many fine examples of altar rails date from this period. Their removal, however, was again ordered by Parliament in 1641, and they finally came back at the Restoration in 1660. In the RC Church altar rails prob. came into use in Italy in the 16th cent. Since 1970 they have not been legally required.

F. Bond, *The Chancel of English Churches* (1916), pp. 131–9.

Alternative Services. The Prayer Book (Alternative and Other Services) Measure 1965 provided that the Act of *Uniformity 1662, as amended, should temporarily cease to govern the worship of the C of E, and that other services could be sanctioned, initially by the *Church Assembly and subsequently by the General *Synod, for an experimental period. This was replaced by the Church of England (*Worship and Doctrine) Measure 1974, which repealed almost the whole of the Act of Uniformity. The new Measure came into force on 1 Sept. 1975 and allows the use of alternative services on a permanent basis to be authorized by the General Synod by Canon (see cans. B 1–5). These powers must be exercised so as to ensure that the forms of service contained in the BCP 'continue to be available for use in the Church of England'. Of the rites so authorized, Series I in general legalized the use of the Deposited Book of 1928. Series II gave effect to the work of the Liturgical Commission appointed by the Abps. of *Canterbury and *York in 1955, and Series III introduced modern English.

The Alternative Service Book (1980) was authorized by the General Synod in 1979 as a supplement to the BCP, for a period of ten years; this was later extended to the year 2000. It reflects modern study of liturgical origins, esp. in the Eucharist, and the revisions made by other religious bodies, notably the RC Church. The *Calendar includes many new names, moves some saints' days, and makes minor changes in the arrangement of the Seasons (see YEAR, LITURGICAL). Morning and Evening Prayer follow the pattern of the BCP, with a wide choice of *Canticles; provision is made for a shortened form of service. In the Eucharist two rites are given, both more traditional in structure than the BCP. Rite A has four alternative *Eucharistic Prayers, and throughout there are many options. The Initiation Services include a form of 'Thanksgiving for the Birth of a Child' (see CHURCHING OF WOMEN). *Baptism and *Confirmation may be administered in one service or separately. In Baptism the *sign of the cross, which may be made with blessed oil, is placed after the *renunciation, and a triple administration of the water is recommended. Confirmation is administered with the formula 'Confirm, O Lord, your servant N. with your Holy Spirit', and the candidate may be anointed. In the Marriage Service the traditional pattern is retained, though the changed status of women is recognized. In the Funeral Services prayer may be offered for the dead. In the *Ordinal, stress is laid on the distinction of *orders and the priest's power to consecrate and absolve; the assent of the people is required, and the formula of ordination is precatory, not imperative. Supplementary material issued after 1980 includes *Lent, Holy Week, Easter: Services and Prayers* (1986) and *The Promise of His Glory: Services and Prayers for the Season from All Saints to Candlemas* (1991).

See also BAPTISM, BURIAL SERVICES, CONFIRMATION, EVEN-SONG, LECTIONARY, MATTINS, and PSALTER, and for parallel developments in other Provinces, COMMON PRAYER, BOOK OF.

The Alternative Service Book 1980: A Commentary by the Liturgical Commission (1980).

Alumbrados (also *Illuminati*, i.e. 'enlightened'). The name given to loosely knit groups of spiritual persons in *Spain in the 16th cent. They led a retired life given to prayer and contemplation, and their practices were propagated esp. by the reformed *Franciscans, St *John of Ávila, and some members of the *Jesuit Order. Whether or not several of them were doctrinally unorthodox is uncertain; recent research has shown some of the accusations against them to have been ill founded. Some *alumbrados*, however, were spiritually unbalanced and exercised an unhealthy influence on those whom they excited by their pretended visions and revelations. They were severely treated by the *Inquisition, though many of their adherents were saintly people and some were later even canonized. In 1527 St *Ignatius Loyola, while a student at Salamanca, was charged with showing them sympathy.

A. Huerga, *Historia de los Alumbrados* (5 vols., 1978–94). A. Márquez, *Los Alumbrados: Orígenes y filosofía (1525–1559)* (1972; 2nd edn., 1980). M. Bataillon, *Érasme et l'Espagne* (Bibliothèque de l'École des Hautes Études Hispaniques, 21; 1937; rev. edn. by D. Devoto and C. Amiel, Travaux d'Humanisme et Renaissance, 250; 3 vols., Geneva, 1991), *passim*. A. Selke, *El Santo Oficio de la Inquisición: Proceso de Fr. Francisco Ortiz (1529–1532)* (1968); M. Ortega Costa, *Proceso de la Inquisición contra María de Cazalla* (1978); A. [A. H.] Hamilton, *Proceso de Rodrigo de Bivar (1539)* (1979); id., *Heresy and Mysticism in Sixteenth-Century Spain: The Alumbrados* (Cambridge, 1992). J. E. Longhurst, *Luther's Ghost in Spain (1517–1546)* (Lawrence, Kan., 1969).

Amalarius of Metz (*c.*780–850 [or 851]), liturgical scholar. A pupil and admirer of *Alcuin, he was a prominent figure in the *Carolingian Renaissance. It seems likely that he was Bp. of Trier from *c.*809 to 813, when he was sent on a mission to Constantinople. He then retired to Hornbach and devoted himself to writing. In 835 he was appointed to administer the see of Lyons after the deposition of its archbishop, *Agobard. His principal treatise, the 'De ecclesiasticis officiis' (in four books), which was partly an attempt to further the fusion of Roman and *Gallican ceremonial practices, exercised great influence in the Middle Ages and remains a fundamental source for the history of liturgy. Its explanations of ritual are sometimes very fanciful and artificial, and at the Synod of Quiercy in 838 some of its contents were pronounced heretical and he was removed from Lyons. Among his other surviving writings are a small treatise on the ceremonies of *Baptism and the 'Eclogae de officio missae', a description of the Roman Pontifical Mass. He compiled an *antiphonary which has not survived but can be partly reconstructed on the basis of references in another of his works. (The contention of J. *Sirmond and some older scholars that the Bp. of Trier was a different person of the same name seems to have been generally abandoned.)

His 'Regula Canonicorum et Sanctimonialium', 'Eclogae de Officio Missae', and 'Epistolae' in J. P. Migne, *PL* 105. 815–1340; crit. edns. of his 'Epistolae' by E. Duemmler in *MGH*, Epistolae, 5 (1899), pp. 240–724, of his 'Opera Liturgica Omnia' by J. M.

Hanssens, SJ (ST 138–140; 1948–50), with introd. and bibl. J. Sirmond, SJ, 'De Duobus Amalariis' in *Opera Varia*, 4 (Paris, 1696), cols. 641–7. R. Mönchemeier, *Amalar von Metz* (Kirchengeschichtliche Studien, 1, Hefte 3–4; 1893); [J.] A. Cabaniss, *Amalarius of Metz* (Amsterdam, 1954). O. B. Hardison, Jun., *Christian rite and Christian drama in the Middle Ages* (Baltimore, 1965), pp. 35–79. R.-J. Hesbert, OSB, 'L'Antiphonaire d'Amalaire', *EL* 94 (1980), pp. 176–94. J. M. Wallace-Hadrill, *The Frankish Church* (Oxford, 1983), pp. 326–9.

Amalric (d. *c.*1207), scholastic philosopher. He was a native of Bène, near *Chartres, and taught at *Paris. In a series of *pantheistic treatises, which had many points of contact with those of *Erigena, he maintained (*inter alia*) that God was the one essence underlying all created beings (*deum esse essentiam omnium creaturarum et esse omnium*) and that those who remain in the love of God cannot sin. He founded a sect, the 'Amalricians', who further developed his teachings. His leading theses were expressly condemned by a synod at Paris in 1210 and again at the *Lateran Council of 1215. See also DAVID OF DINANT.

The principal sources are *Caesarius of Heisterbach, *Dialogus Miraculorum* (ed. J. Strange, Cologne, 1851, pp. 304–7) and Martin Oppaviensis, *Chronicon Pontificum et Imperatorum* (ed. L. Weiland in *MGH*, Scriptores, 22, 1872, p. 438). Eng. tr. of the former, and other primary material, in W. L. Wakefield and A. P. Evans, *Heresies of the High Middle Ages* (Records of Civilization, Sources and Studies, 81; 1969), pp. 258–63. C. Baeumker (ed.), 'Contra Amaurianos. Ein anonymer wahrscheinlich dem Garnerius von Rochefort zugehöriger Traktat gegen die Amalrikaner aus dem Anfang des XIII. Jahrhunderts' in *BGPM* 24 (1926), Hefte 5–6. G. C. Capelle, *Autour du décret de 1210*, 3: *Amaury de Bène: Étude sur son panthéisme formel* (Bibliothèque Thomiste, 16; 1932). M. dal Pra, *Amalrico di Bène* (Storia universale della filosofia, 8; Milan, 1951). M. T. d'Alverny, 'Un Fragment du Procès des Amauriciens', *AHDLMA* 18 (1951), pp. 325–36. N. Cohn, *Pursuit of the Millennium* (rev. edn., 1970), pp. 152–6. G. Dickson, 'The Burning of the Amalricians', *JEH* 40 (1989), pp. 347–69.

Amana Society. A Christian sect, otherwise known as the Community of True Inspiration. It originated in Germany in 1714, under the influence of the writings of E. L. Grüber and J. F. Rock, who were deeply imbued with *Pietist views, but centred all their teaching in the doctrine of present-day inspiration. A large part of the body sailed for America in 1842. In 1855 they finally settled at Amana, Iowa, and were granted a formal constitution under the laws of the state in 1859. Their settlements were organized on a strictly communal basis, with minimum contact with the outside world, until economic difficulties during the Great Depression led to the conversion of the Amana Society into a modified joint stock corporation in 1932. As a co-operative, the Society runs farms, a woollen mill, and other industries. The Amana Church Society, which became a separate legal entity in 1932, had 535 adult members in 1994.

W. R. Perkins and B. L. Wick, *History of the Amana Society, or Community of True Inspiration* (State University of Iowa Publications. Historical Monograph, 1, 1891; repr., Westport, Conn., 1976); B. M. H. Shambaugh, *Amana: The Community of True Inspiration* (Iowa, 1908); id., *Amana That Was and Amana That Is* (Iowa, 1932). Id. in *HERE* 1 (1908), pp. 358–69, s.v.

Amandus, St (d. *c.*675), Merovingian Apostle of Flanders. Born near Nantes, in early manhood he made his way to Tours, and then to Bourges, where he lived an ascetic life under the direction of St Austregisilus, the Bishop. In 628, having been consecrated Bishop at the behest of Chlotar II without any fixed see, he began active missionary work in Flanders and Carinthia, and in 633 founded two monasteries at Ghent under the patronage of St *Peter (one of them taking the name of St Bavon, the benefactor). Later he founded a large monastery at Elnon, near Tournai, of which he was in his last years Abbot; afterwards it was known as St-Amand. He is said, but on very doubtful authority, to have been Bp. of Maastricht from 649 to 652. His 'Testamentum' survives, but otherwise the evidence for his life is not very trustworthy. Feast day, 6 Feb.

Testamentum ed. by B. Krusch in *MGH*, Scriptores Rerum Merovingicarum, 5 (1910), pp. 483–5. One recension of the Vita Amandi, attributed to Amandus' disciple, Baudemundus, pr. in *AASS*, Feb. 1 (1658), pp. 848–72; another by B. Krusch, op. cit., pp. 428–49; the ascription to Baudemundus is denied by Krusch, who considers the life to be late 8th cent. (ibid., pp. 395–428). Further life by Milo, a monk of St Amand (*c*.845–55), ed. L. Traube, *MGH*, Poetae, 3 (1896), pp. 567–610; prose suppl. ed. B. Krusch, op. cit., pp. 450–85. L. Van der Essen, *Étude critique et littéraire sur les Vitae des saints mérovingiens de l'ancienne Belgique* (1907), pp. 336–49. E. de Moreau, SJ, *Saint Amand* (Museum Lessianum, Section Missiologique, 7; 1927), with bibl.; id., *Saint Amand, le principal évangélisateur de la Belgique* (Collection nationale, Brussels, 1942 [more popular]). Id., 'La Vita Amandi Prima et les Fondations monastiques de S. Amand', *Anal. Boll.* 67 (1949), pp. 447–64. A. Verhulst and G. Declercq, 'L'action et le souvenir de saint Amand en Europe centrale. À propos de la découverte d'une *Vita Amandi antiqua*', in M. Van Uytfanghe and R. Demeulenaere (eds.), *Aevum inter Utrumque: Mélanges offerts à Gabriel Sanders* (Instrumenta Patristica, 23; 1991), pp. 503–26.

Amarna Tablets. See TELL EL-AMARNA TABLETS.

Amaury. See AMALRIC.

ambo. A raised platform in a Christian *basilica, from which the Scriptures could be read to the people and litanies and other public parts of the liturgy conducted. Originally there was only one, but later two were built, one for the Epistle and one for the Gospel, on the S. and N. sides respectively. Several early examples survive, notably in Italy, but after the 14th cent. they were superseded by the *lectern and *pulpit. Recently there has been a tendency in some places to reintroduce them, and a Vatican Instruction of 1964 suggests the use of an ambo for reading the lessons and for preaching unless the pulpit is near the sanctuary.

Rohault, 3 (1883), pp. 1–72. D. Hickley, 'The Ambo in Early Liturgical Planning—a study with special reference to the Syrian *Bema*', *Heythrop Journal*, 7 (1966), pp. 407–27. H. *Leclercq, OSB, in *DACL* 1 (1907), cols. 1330–47, s.v. 'Ambon', with refs.

Ambrose, St (*c*.339–97), Bp. of Milan. He was born at Trier, the son of the Praetorian Prefect of Gaul. He followed a traditional administrative career, practising in the law-courts and in due course being appointed governor of Aemilia-Liguria, with his seat at Milan. On the death in 373 or 374 of *Auxentius, the Arian Bp. of Milan, the Milanese laity demanded that Ambrose should succeed him. Though brought up in a Christian family, he was not yet baptized, i.e. he was still a *catechumen. After initial resistance, he accepted the see, was baptized and ordained,

and devoted himself to the study of theology, perhaps under the guidance of *Simplicianus. As a bishop he was famous as a preacher, and a zealous upholder of orthodoxy against *Arianism. To him was partly due the conversion of St *Augustine (386), who greatly revered him. Events brought him into close touch with successive W. Emperors, and in his dealings with them he asserted a remarkable degree of authority: he persuaded Gratian to refuse a hearing to those who objected to the removal of the Altar of Victory from the Senate House at Rome and threatened ecclesiastical sanctions against Valentinian II if he restored it; he insisted that *Theodosius should abandon any plan to restore the synagogue burnt down by Christians at Callinicum in 388 and excommunicated him for a massacre at *Thessalonica in 390. Equally, he maintained the independence of the Church against the civil power, refusing to cede a basilica to Valentinian II's Arian protégés in 386 and protesting against the action of the Gallic bishops in involving Maximus in the execution of *Priscillian as a heretic in the same year. Apart from the *De Sacramentis* (q.v.), of which the Ambrosian authorship is now generally recognized, his most notable work is 'De Officiis Ministrorum', a treatise on Christian ethics, based on Cicero, with special reference to the clergy. The rest consist largely of the substance of sermons or instruction given to candidates for Baptism, on the faith and Sacraments. Knowledge of Greek enabled him to introduce much E. theology into the W. He also wrote on ascetical subjects, and did much to encourage monasticism and the cult of the martyrs (e.g. Sts *Gervasius and Protasius) in N. Italy. His Letters are of great historical value. He was the author of Latin *hymns (q.v.), and it was through his influence that hymns became an integral part of the liturgy of the W. Church. At the beginning of the 20th century some scholars (H. Brewer and A. E. Burn) attributed to him the so-called *Athanasian Creed.

With St *Jerome, St Augustine, and St *Gregory the Great, St Ambrose is one of the four traditional *Doctors of the Latin Church. Feast day, 7 Dec.; in the BCP calendar, 4 Apr.

Editio princeps of his Works, Venice, 1485. Benedictine edn. [F. du Frische and N. Le Nourry], 2 vols., Paris, 1686–90; repr. in J. P. Migne, *PL* 14–17. Crit. edns. by C. Schenkl, M. Petschenig, and others (CSEL, 1897 ff.) and M. Adriaen and others (CCSL, 1957 ff.); also of *De Virginibus* by E. Cazzaniga (Corpus Scriptorum Latinorum Paravianum; Turin, 1948), of *De Virginitate* by id. (ibid., 1952), and, with Fr. tr., of his hymns, by J. Fontaine and others (Patrimoines Christianisme, 1992). For edns. of the Life by *Paulinus, see s.v. F. H. Dudden, *The Life and Times of St Ambrose* (2 vols., Oxford, 1935). H. F. v. Campenhausen, *Ambrosius von Mailand als Kirchenpolitiker* (1929); J. R. Palanque, *Saint Ambroise et l'empire romain* (1933). *Ambrosiana: Scritti di storia, archeologia ed arte pubblicati nel XVI centenario della nascita di Sant'Ambrogio, CCCXL–MCMXL* (1942). P. Courcelle, *Recherches sur les Confessions de Saint Augustin* (1950), pp. 93–174, 211–21. R. H. *Connolly, *The Explanatio Symboli ad Initiandos, A Work of Saint Ambrose* (Texts and Studies, 10; 1952). A. Paredi, *S. Ambrogio e la sua età* (2nd edn., Milan [1960]). J. Pépin, *Théologie cosmique et théologie chrétienne (Ambrose, Exam. 1. 1. 1–4)* (Bibliothèque de Philosophie Contemporaine, 1964). E. Dassmann, *Die Frömmigkeit des Kirchenvaters Ambrosius von Mailand* (Münsterische Beiträge zur Theologie, 29; 1965). P. Courcelle, *Recherches sur saint Ambroise: 'Vies' anciennes, culture, iconographie* (Études Augustiniennes, 1973); G. Madec, *Saint Ambroise et la Philosophie* (ibid., 1974); Y.-M. Duval (ed.),

Ambroise de Milan (ibid., 1974); G. Lazzati (ed.), *Ambrosius Episcopus: Atti del Congresso internazionale di studi ambrosiani nel xvi centenario della elevazione di sant'Ambrogio alla cattedra episcopale, Milano 2–7 decembre 1974* (Studia Patristica Mediolanensia, 6–7; 1976); N. B. McLynn, *Ambrose of Milan: Church and Court in a Christian Capital* (Berkeley, Calif., and London, 1994); D. H. Williams, *Ambrose and the End of the Arian–Nicene Conflicts* (Oxford Early Christian Studies, 1995); C. Markschies, *Ambrosius von Mailand und die Trinitätstheologie* (Beiträge zur historischen Theologie, 90; 1995). *Cento anni di bibliografia ambrosiana (1874–1974)*, ed. P. F. Beatrice and others (Studia Patristica Mediolanensia, 11; 1981). Bardenhewer, 3, pp. 498–547; Altaner and Stuiber (1978), pp. 378–89 and 629–32. See also bibl. to DE SACRAMENTIS and ATHANASIAN CREED.

Ambrose, St, of Camaldoli. See TRAVERSARI, AMBROGIO.

Ambrose, Isaac (1604–64), *Puritan divine. The son of a Lancashire clergyman, he was educated at Brasenose College, Oxford, and ordained priest before 1627. After serving cures in Derbyshire and N. Yorkshire, he became one of the King's four Preachers in Lancashire (from 1634) and resided at Garstang, near Preston. About 1640 he became Vicar of Preston. He adopted *Presbyterianism in 1641 and subsequently took a prominent part in the seventh Lancashire Classis, several times acting as Moderator. He was twice taken prisoner by the royal army. In 1650 he was still minister in Preston, but in 1654 he moved to Garstang. He served on the committee for the ejection of 'scandalous, ignorant and insufficient ministers and schoolmasters' in Lancashire. He was himself ejected in 1662.

He was a man of peaceful disposition, who spent a month each year in solitary meditation, prayer, and study. After an illness he determined to write a devotional description of what the Lord had done for his soul. Written in 1653, it was published in 1658 under the title, *Looking unto Jesus, or the Soul's Eyeing of Jesus as Carrying on the Great Work of Man's Salvation*. The work is marked by deep piety, combined with vividness and freshness of imagination. His other publications include *Prima, Media, and Ultima, the First, Middle, and Last Things: in Three Treatises* (1650); *Redeeming the Time* (1658); and *War with Devils—Ministration of Angels* (1661).

Complete Works ed., 3 parts, London, 1674–89; new edn., 2 vols., Manchester, 1799–1802. A. *Wood, *Athenae Oxonienses* (ed. P. Bliss), 3 (1817), cols. 659–61.

Ambrosian chant. The chant of Milan survives only in MSS of the 12th cent. and later, although its roots are clearly older. The earliest MS of importance, British Library Add. 34209, contains the Office and Mass, in a continuous sequence, of the *pars hiemalis* only; the rest of the year is supplied by other MSS, from which the modern editions of the *Antiphonale Missarum* and the *Liber Vesperalis* are for the most part derived.

The chant is characterized by its tendency to prolixity and modal freedom when compared with the *Gregorian. It is classified under four, rather than eight, modes (ignoring the distinction between authentic and plagal modes), and the psalm-tones, which lack the mediation, are grouped in four corresponding series with variable reciting-notes or tenors.

The chief primary sources are British Library Add. MS 34209, ed. by the Benedictines of *Solesmes (Paléographie Musicale, 5–7; 1896–1900), *Antiphonale Missarum iuxta ritum S. E. Mediolanensis* (Rome, 1935), and *Liber Vesperalis iuxta ritum S. E. Mediolanensis* (ibid., 1939). [H.] Huglo and others, *Fonti e Paleografia del Canto Ambrosiano* (Archivio Ambrosiano, 7; 1956). T. Bailey, *The Ambrosian Alleluias* (Egham, Surrey, 1983). R. Jesson in W. Apel, *Gregorian Chant* (1958), pp. 465 83.

Ambrosian rite. The rite used in the old archiepiscopal province of Milan and one of the very few non-Roman rites which survive in the RC Church in the W. Its name is derived from St *Ambrose, Bp. of Milan, but there is no definite evidence of connection with him. Although since his time the rite has contained the Roman *Canon of the Mass it differs widely from the Roman rite. Thus, for example, the *Offertory takes place before and not after the Creed (as in the Roman rite) and has always been accompanied by a procession (see VECCHIONI). In 1976 the Missal was revised in accordance with the principles of the Second *Vatican Council and the traditions of the rite. It was followed by a revised Breviary in 1983.

Three main theories of the origin of the rite have been put forward: (1) It is merely a development of the traditional Roman rite; (2) it is an older W. rite which has survived only at Milan; (3) it is an Oriental rite introduced at Milan by the Greek and Arian Bishop *Auxentius (or one of the other six Greek bishops who appear among the ten predecessors of St Ambrose) which, purged of heresy (it is suggested) by St Ambrose, became the parent of the whole family of *Gallican rites. This last theory (originated by L. *Duchesne) was widely held in the earlier years of the 20th cent., but the rite is now commonly regarded as of purely W. ancestry, though it has some E. features and importations from N. of the Alps.

The Ambrosian Missal was first ed. at Milan in 1475. That in use before 1976 appeared in 1902; crit. edn. by A. Ratti (*Pius XI) and M. Magistretti (Milan, 1913). Eng. tr. by E. G. C. F. Atchley (London, 1909). *Corpus Ambrosiano-Liturgicum*, ed. O. Heiming and J. Frei (Liturgiewissenschaftliche Quellen und Forschungen, 49 (1 and 2), 51, 56; 1969–83). M. Magistretti (ed.), *Beroldus, sive Ecclesiae Ambrosianae Mediolanensis Kalendarium et Ordines Saec. XII* (Milan, 1894); id., *Monumenta Veteris Liturgiae Ambrosianae* (3 vols., ibid., 1897–1905) and other works. W. C. Bishop, *The Mozarabic and Ambrosian Rites* (*Alcuin Club Tracts, 15; 1924), pp. 98–134. A. Paredi, *I prefazi ambrosiani* (Pubbl. Univ. Catt. del Sacro Cuore, 4th ser. 25; Milan, 1937). P. Borelli, *Il Rito Ambrosiano* (Brescia, 1964), with bibl. L. Duchesne, *Origines du culte chrétien* (1889), ch. 3, pp. 81–99; Eng. tr. (1903), pp. 86–105. A. A. King, *Liturgies of the Primatial Sees* (1957), pp. 286–456. P. Lejay in *DACL* 1 (1907), cols. 1373–1442, s.v. 'Ambrosien (Rit)'; J. D. Crichton in *Catholic Dictionary of Theology*, 1 (1962), pp. 67–9, s.v.; A. M. Triacca, SDB, in *Nuovo Dizionario di Liturgia*, ed. D. Sartore, CJS, and A. M. Triacca, SDB (1984), pp. 16–52, s.v., incl. extensive bibl.

Ambrosiana. The Ambrosian Library at Milan, founded *c.*1605 by Federico Borromeo (1564–1631), was one of the first large libraries to be open to the public without distinction. The books were originally protected from theft by the severest ecclesiastical penalties, the removal of a book being a sin from which only the Pope could absolve. Borromeo sent agents all over the world to collect MSS, and *c.*1803 it received many ancient MSS from the library at *Bobbio. *Pius XI (Achille Ratti) was Librarian from 1888 to 1912 (Prefect from 1907).

A. Martini and D. Bassi, *Catalogus Codicum Graecorum Biblio-thecae Ambrosianae* (2 vols., Milan, 1906); A. Rivolta, *Catalogo dei Codici pinelliani dell'Ambrosiana* (1932). Mai, *SR* 5 (1841), pp. 24–50, 'De Nonnullis Codicibus Bibliothecae Ambrosianae'; E. Griffini, 'Lista dei manoscritti arabi nuovi fondo della Biblioteca Ambrosiana di Milan', *Rivista degli Studi Orientali*, 3 (1910), pp. 253–78. A. Saba, 'La biblioteca Ambrosiana', *Aevum*, 6 (1932), pp. 531–620.

Ambrosiaster. The name given (apparently first by the Benedictine editors of St *Ambrose) to the author of a set of Latin commentaries on the 13 Epp. of St Paul, ascribed in all the MSS but one, and by most medieval writers, to Ambrose. St *Augustine and certain Irish authorities quote that on Romans as by 'Sanctus Hilarius'. Their ascription to Ambrose, which was first questioned in modern times by F. *Torres in 1522, is now universally denied, and various persons have been suggested as their author, e.g. Isaac, an ex-Jew, who relapsed into Judaism, and opposed *Damasus in 374; 'Hilary the Deacon'; Hilary, a layman and Proconsul of Africa; and *Evagrius of Antioch. The commentaries are on the *Old Latin text of the Epistles and thus an important witness to the pre-Vulgate text. The writer avoids allegory, is practical, and has a good sense of history. Ambrosiaster is almost certainly also the author of 'Quaestiones Veteris et Novi Testamenti', wrongly ascribed to Augustine, and possibly of the 'Mosaicarum et Romanarum Legum Collectio'.

Comm. in J. P. Migne, *PL* 17. 45–508. Crit. edn. by H. I. Vogels (CSEL 81, 3 parts; 1966–9). 'Quaestiones', ed. A. *Souter (ibid. 50; 1908). A. Souter, *A Study of Ambrosiaster* (Texts and Studies, 7. 4; Cambridge, 1905); id., *The Earliest Latin Comment-aries on the Epistles of St Paul* (1927). C. Martini, OFM, *Ambrosiaster: De Auctore, Operibus, Theologia* (Spicilegium Ponti-ficii Athenaei Antoniani, 4; Rome, 1944). A. Pollastri, *Ambrosiaster: Commento alla Lettera ai Romani. Aspetti Cristologici* (L'Aquila, 1977). Further arts. by id. in *Studi Storico Religiosi*, 2 (1978), pp. 93–127 (Eng. summary, p. 238), and 4 (1980), pp. 313–72 (Eng. summary, p. 404). R. Hoven, 'Notes sur Érasme et les auteurs anciens', *L'Antiquité Classique*, 38 (1969), pp. 169–74, esp. pp. 172–4. *CPL* (ed. 3, 1995), pp. 58 f. (nos. 184–8). M. G. Mara in Quasten (cont.), *Patrology*, 4 (1986), pp. 180–90, with bibl. G. Bardy in *Dict. Bibl.*, Suppl. 1 (1928), cols. 225–41, s.v.; A. Stuiber in *TRE* 2 (1978), pp. 356–62, s.v.

ambulatory. The 'walking-space' which arises when an apsidal sanctuary in certain churches of the Norman period is surrounded by continuous *aisles. The ambulat-ory is bounded on one side by the arches of the sanctuary, and on the other may give access to a series of chapels of a later date.

AMDG ('*Ad Maiorem Dei Gloriam*', 'To the greater glory of God'). The motto of the *Jesuits, but it also frequently appears elsewhere in Christian use.

Amen (Heb. אָמֵן; Gk. ἀμήν). A Hebrew word meaning 'verily'. It is used to express assent by Jews (Deut. 27: 15 ff.) and Christians (1 Cor. 14: 16) at the end of religious formulae, prayers, hymns, and creeds. Cf. the *Catechism of the BCP: 'and therefore I say, Amen, so be it'.

P. I. Cecchetti, 'L'"Amen" nella Bibbia e nella Liturgia', *Bol-lettino Ceceliano*, 37 (1942), pp. 87–93 and 109–15; repr. in id.,

Scritti (Lateranum, NS 33; 1967), pp. 171–86. H. Schlier in *TWNT*, 1 (1933), pp. 339–42 (Eng. tr., 1964, pp. 335–8), with further bibl., 10/2 (1979), pp. 973 f.; W. Bauer, *Griechisch-deutsches Wörterbuch zu den Schriften des Neuen Testaments* (6th edn. by K. and B. Aland, 1988), col. 89; Eng. tr. of 5th edn. (1979), pp. 45 f., both s.v. ἀμήν. F. *Cabrol in *DACL* 1 (1907), cols. 1554–73, s.v.

Americanism. A movement propagated esp. among American RCs in the last decade of the 19th cent. with a view to adapting as far as possible the external life of the Church to supposed modern cultural ideals; it also had repercussions in France. After the publication of the life of I. T. *Hecker in 1891, Americanism was associated with his teaching. Stress was laid on the value of the 'active' virtues (e.g. humanitarianism, eugenic reform, demo-cracy), and the 'passive' attitudes such as humility and subjection to authority were depreciated. It was also urged that the Church should relax as far as possible the rigour of her requirements on converts, emphasize what was held in common by RCs and other Christians, and minimize points of difference. In an Apostolic Letter, 'Testem Benevolentiae' (22 Jan. 1899), addressed to Cardinal J. Gibbons, Abp. of Baltimore, *Leo XIII condemned it in moderate but quite definite terms; and in consequence it quickly disappeared.

'Testem Benevolentiae' in *Acta Leonis XIII*, 7 (1906), pp. 223–33). A. Houtin, *L'Américanisme* (Namur, 1904); T. T. McAvoy, CSC, *The Great Crisis in American Catholic History 1895–1900* (Chicago, 1957), incl. Eng. tr. of 'Testem Benevolentiae', pp. 379–91, and bibl. J. T. Ellis, *The Life of James Cardinal Gibbons*, 2 (Milwaukee, 1952), pp. 1–80. M. M. Reher, 'Pope Leo XIII and "Americanism"', *Theological Studies*, 34 (1973), pp. 679–89. G. P. Fogarty, SJ, *The Vatican and the Americanist Crisis: Denis J. O'Connell, American Agent in Rome, 1885–1903* (Miscellanea Historiae Pontificae, 36; Rome, 1974). T. T. McAvoy, CSC, in *NCE* 1 (1967), pp. 443 f., s.v. See also bibl. under HECKER.

Ames, William (1576–1633), *Calvinist moral theolo-gian and controversialist. Educated at Christ's College, Cambridge, where his tutor was W. *Perkins, he became an extreme *Puritan, refusing to wear the surplice in his college chapel and in 1609 attacking card-playing in a sermon. Leaving Cambridge c.1610, he settled for a time at Colchester and then moved to Holland. Here he took a prominent part in the *Remonstrant controversies and became recognized by the Calvinists as one of their best theologians. In 1622 he became Professor of Theology at Franeker, where he attracted hearers from all parts of Protestant Europe. A few months before his death he gave up his professorship for reasons of health and took charge of the English congregation at Rotterdam. His most important work, *De Conscientia, eius Jure et Casibus* (1632), is one of the first Protestant treatises on *casuistry and was long held in high repute for its incisive decisions. Of his theological works, the principal was *Medulla Theologiae* (1st edn., 1627), a systematic exposition of Calvinist prin-ciples. Among his controversial writings were *Bellarminus Enervatus* (4 vols., 1628) and *Animadversiones in Synodalia* (1629).

His *Latin Works* were ed., with a Life, by M. Nethenus (5 vols., Amsterdam, 1658). K. Reuter, *Wilhelm Amesius der führende Theologe der erwachenden reformierten Pietismus* (Beiträge zur Ge-schichte und Lehre der Reformierten Kirche, 4; Neukirchen [1940]). Eng. tr. by D. Horton of Nethenus' Life, a Dutch Life by H. Visscher (Haarlem, 1894), and Reuter (Cambridge, Mass. [1965]). K. L. Sprunger, *The Learned Doctor William Ames* [1972]. E. Rose, *Cases of Conscience: Alternatives open to Recusants and Puritans under Elizabeth I and James I* (Cambridge, 1975), pp. 194–200. R. T. Kendall, *Calvin and English Calvinism to 1649* (Oxford Theological Monographs, 1979), pp. 151–64.

Amiatinus, Codex. See CODEX AMIATINUS.

amice (Lat. *amictus*). A linen cloth, square or oblong in shape, with strings attached. In the W. Church it may be worn round the neck by the priest when celebrating the Eucharist, and by other ministers who wear the *alb. Its original significance is obscure. Since the bishop conveyed the amice to the *subdeacon at his ordination with the admonition that it signified the *castigatio vocis*, it is natural to suppose that it was originally a sort of scarf to protect the throat. But in the prayers which until 1969 were said before Mass when the amice is being put on, it is referred to as *galea salutis* ('helmet of salvation'), from which it would be natural to deduce that it was originally a head-covering. This view is supported by the fact that certain religious orders still wear the amice in the form of a head-covering when approaching the altar for Mass, and during parts of the service. In some orders (e.g. the *Benedictine) the amice has the shape of a hood and is worn in such a way as to a form an outer covering for the hood of the religious habit. In the E. the amice as such is not used, but it is customary for some priests to use an ordinary handkerchief in the same way, as a practical method of preventing the vestments becoming stained by perspiration. See also ALMUCE.

Braun, *LG*, pp. 21–52. V. Ermoni in *DACL* 1 (1907), cols. 1597–9, s.v. 'Amict'.

Amidah. See EIGHTEEN BENEDICTIONS.

Amish (or **Amish Mennonites**), a conservative group in the USA and Canada which originated in a division among the *Swiss Brethren under the leadership of Jakob Ammann (*c*.1656–before 1730), an elder of Erlenbach (in the Canton of Berne), later of Markirch (Sainte-Marie-aux-Mines) in Alsace. Ammann and his group differed from other Swiss Brethren in their more frequent observance of the Lord's Supper, in their practices of washing each other's feet during the service and at all times shunning (*Meidung*) those who had been excommunicated, and in wearing 'plain' dress. They gained adherents in S. Germany and esp. in Alsace, as well as in Switzerland. Most of them migrated to N. America during the 18th and 19th cents.; the small numbers remaining in Europe returned to the parent body. In America they have undergone various divisions but most are members of the Old Order Amish Mennonite Church. In doctrine and Church order they differ little from the *Mennonites but they worship in each other's houses and retain the use of 'Pennsylvania Dutch' (German) in their services. Though they avoid publicity, they have attracted attention because of their traditional dress, their educational methods, their farming without modern machinery, and their high-quality craft work, esp. quilts made by the women. They practise forms of mutual aid based on personal and community sharing rather than on commercial insurance; their

application for exemption from the taxes and benefits of state social security has been allowed in some states. They have communities in Pennsylvania, Ohio, Indiana, and Iowa, as well as elsewhere in the USA and in Ontario in Canada. In 1984 the number of their baptized members was estimated at 35,000.

J. A. Hostetler, *Amish Society* (Baltimore, 1963; 3rd edn., ibid. and London, 1980), with extensive bibl. Good entry in *EB* (15th edn.; 1974), Micropaedia, 1, p. 316, s.v. 'Amish Mennonites'.

Ammon, St (d. *c*.350), also **Amun**, Egyptian hermit. One of the most celebrated ascetics of the *Nitrian desert, he is mentioned by St *Athanasius in his *Vita Antonii*. On St *Antony's advice he sought to bring his monks together under his immediate supervision. Feast day, 4 Oct.

Other sources include *Palladius, *Lausiac history*, ch. 8, and the *Historia Monachorum*, ch. 29. Introd. by C. Byeus, SJ, to extract from Palladius in *AASS*, Oct. 2 (1768), pp. 413–21. I. G. Smith in *DCB* 1 (1877), p. 102, s.v.

Ammonas, St (d. before 396), Egyptian hermit. After 14 years living as a monk at *Scete, he became a disciple of St *Antony of Egypt and succeeded him as leader of the monastery of Pispir after his death. Several of his sayings are preserved in the *Apophthegmata Patrum* (acc. to which he was consecrated bishop by St *Athanasius, but this assertion is prob. based on confusion with another Ammonas); the collection of 14 letters ascribed to him is also very prob. authentic. Feast day, 16 Jan.

Syr. tr. of his letters ed., with Lat. tr., by M. Kmosko, *PO* 10 (1915), pp. 555–616; Eng. tr. of this by D. J. Chitty and S. [P.] Brock (Fairacres Publications, 72; Oxford, 1979). Less authentic Gk. text and Syr. tr., with modern Fr. tr. and introd., ed. F. Nau, *PO* 11 (1915), pp. 391–504. For the complicated tradition of the versions of his works, see *CPG* 2 (1974), pp. 68–71 (nos. 2380–93). F. Klejna, SJ, 'Antonius und Ammonas. Eine Untersuchung über Herkunft und Eigenart der ältesten Mönchsbriefe', *ZKT* 62 (1938), pp. 309–48.

Ammonian Sections. See EUSEBIAN CANONS AND SECTIONS.

Ammonius Saccas (*c*. AD 175–242). The reputed founder of *Neoplatonism. An Alexandrian by birth, he was held in high repute as a teacher, and appears to have considerably influenced *Plotinus, who, on hearing a discourse of Ammonius, remarked, 'This is the man I was looking for' (τοῦτον ἐζήτουν). Acc. to *Porphyry (in *Eusebius, *HE* 6. 19), who also states (prob. wrongly) that Ammonius was a lapsed Christian, he had *Origen (but perhaps not the Christian Origen) among his pupils. He is said to have committed none of his teachings to writing. See also EUSEBIAN CANONS AND SECTIONS.

H. von Arnim, 'Quelle der Ueberlieferung über Ammonius Sakkas', *Rheinisches Museum für Philologie*, NS 42 (1887), pp. 276–85; E. Zeller, 'Ammonius Sakkas und Plotinus', *Archiv für Geschichte der Philosophie*, 7 (1894), pp. 295–312. W. Theiler, *Forschungen zum Neuplatonismus* (Quellen und Studien zur Geschichte der Philosophie, 10; 1966), pp. 1–45 ('Ammonios der Lehrer des Origenes'). E. R. Dodds, 'Numenius and Ammonius', in *Les Sources de Plotin* (Fondation Hardt pour l'étude de l'antiquité classique, Entretiens, 5; Vandœuvres and Geneva, 21–9 Aug. 1957 [1960]), pp. 3–61 (incl. discussion). A. H. Armstrong in id. (ed.), *The Cambridge History of Later Greek and Early Medi-*

eval Philosophy (1967), pp. 196–8. H.-R. Schwyzer, *Ammonios Sakkas, der Lehrer Plotins* (Rheinisch-Westfälische Akademie der Wissenschaften, Vorträge G 260; Opladen, 1983). Überweg, 1, pp. 593–5, with further bibl. p. 188*. H. Dörrie in *TRE* 2 (1978), pp. 463–71, s.v. 'Ammonios Sakkos', with bibl.

Amos, Book of. Amos was the earliest of the canonical prophets of the OT. He is said (1: 1) to have prophesied 'in the days of Uzziah king of Judah, and in the days of Jeroboam the son of Joash king of Israel', i.e. between 760 and 750 BC. Acc. to 7: 14 f. he differentiated himself from the *nebi'm* or official prophets and claimed that his prophetic inspiration derived from a direct call from Yahweh received while he was exercising a secular calling as a shepherd (or, possibly, a sheep-farmer). The two principal themes of his message were that increasing affluence among the leaders of Israelite society had produced an unjust social order in which the poor were being exploited, and that in consequence Yahweh, the God of Israel, was about to put an end to Israel's special status by causing the nation's downfall. This national calamity would come about through a combination of natural disasters and of military defeat, perhaps at the hands of the rising Assyrian Empire. Amos shares with his hearers the expectation of a 'day of Yahweh' but reverses the popular expectation that this will be a day of triumph for the Israelites; instead, he says, it will be a day of darkness and despair. Amos thus stands at the beginning of the 'eschatological' tradition in OT prophecy, looking for a decisive and irreversible Divine intervention in human history. His oracles are also notable for their mature literary style, perhaps indebted to the '*Wisdom' tradition, and for their assumption that Yahweh is the God not only of Israel but of all nations, who avenges injustice and oppression wherever they are to be found and who has no favourites. Later prophets mitigated Amos's belief that the election of Israel had been annulled by Yahweh and restored faith in the covenant promises, but Amos's uncompromising commitment to ethical monotheism became the hallmark of prophetic teaching. The Book seems to have undergone a series of editings, and in the last of these (perhaps in the 6th or 5th cent. BC) an oracle of promise (9: 13–15) was added to give the Book an incongruous 'happy ending'.

Modern comm. by W. R. Harper (on Amos and Hosea, ICC, 1905, pp. 1–200), E. Hammershaimb (Copenhagen, 1946; 3rd edn., 1967; Eng. tr., Oxford, 1970); J. L. Mays (London, 1969); H. W. Wolff (on Joel and Amos, *Dodekapropheton*, 2; Biblischer Kommentar, Altes Testament, 14/2, Neukirchen, 1969, pp. 105–410; Eng. tr., Philadelphia [1977], pp. 87–355); W. Rudolph (on Joel, Amos, Obad., and Jon., KAT 13/2, 1971, pp. 93–292); and J. A. Soggin (Brescia, 1982; Eng. tr., 1987). A. S. Kapelrud, *Central Ideas in Amos* (Oslo, 1956; repr., 1961). H. Reventlow, *Das Amt des Propheten bei Amos* (Forschungen zur Religion und Literatur des Alten und Neuen Testaments, 80; 1962); H. W. Wolff, *Amos' geistige Heimat* (Wissenschaftliche Monographien zum Alten und Neuen Testament, 18; Neukirchen, 1964; Eng. tr., Philadephia [1973]). R. Martin-Achard, *Amos: L'homme, le message, l'influence* (Publications de la Faculté de Théologie de l'Université de Genève, 7 [1984]). E. Würthwein, 'Amos-Studien', *ZATW* 62 (1950), pp. 10–52; R. Smend, 'Das Nein des Amos', *Evangelische Theologie*, 23 (1963), pp. 404–23. J. Blenkinsopp, *A History of Prophecy in Israel* (1984), pp. 86–96.

amphibalum (or -us). (1) A *Gallican name for the *chasuble; (2) the *birrus*, a garment put on first and covering the head, and perhaps to be identified with the *amictus* or *amice. Acc. to tradition, St Amphibalus was the name of a martyr closely associated with St *Alban.

Amphilochius, St (c.340–95), Bp. of Iconium from 373. A cousin of *Gregory Nazianzus, he stood in close personal relations with all the *Cappadocian Fathers. He was present at a council of Iconium in 376 in which the full Divinity of the Holy Spirit was zealously defended, and was head of the Council of Side in 390 which excommunicated the *Messalians. Most of his surviving writings are in a fragmentary condition; but a few are complete, including some sermons and the *Iambics for Seleucus*, which contains a list of books of the Bible, of some importance for the history of the *Canon. Feast day, 23 Nov.

Writings and Life in J. P. Migne, *PG* 39. 9–130 (incomplete). Crit. edn. of his *Iambi ad Seleucum* (previously pr. among the works of Gregory of Nazianzus in *PG* 37. 1577–1600) by E. Oberg (Patristische Texte und Studien, 9; 1969). *Opera* ed. C. Datema (CCSG 3; 1978), with introd. and bibl. K. *Holl, *Amphilochius von Ikonium in seinem Verhältnis zu den grossen Kappadoziern* (Tübingen, 1904); G. Ficker, *Amphilochiana*, 1 (Leipzig, 1906, all pub.). *CPG* 2 (1974), pp. 230–42 (nos. 3230–54). J. Quasten, *Patrology*, 3 (Utrecht and Westminster, Md., 1960), pp. 296–300; Altaner and Stuiber (1978), pp. 308 f. and 612 f., both with bibl.

Ampleforth Abbey, N. Yorks. In 1802 the community of English *Benedictine monks of St Lawrence's Priory (1608–1793), Dieulouard, Lorraine, settled at Ampleforth Lodge; this community claims continuity with the Benedictines of *Westminster Abbey, at least as these were restored under *Mary. Though the monastery was in exile for two centuries, many of the monks served on pastoral missions in England; these developed into parishes in the late 18th and 19th cents. Ampleforth College, the school founded in 1803, grew in size and academic quality, esp. after the foundation in 1897 of St Benet's Hall, Oxford, as a house of a study for the monks. The monastery became an abbey in 1899. In 1955 it founded a priory in the USA, at St Louis. During the abbacy of Basil *Hume (1963–76) it opened a retreat centre which has continued to flourish. Earlier members of the community include Gabriel Gifford (1554–1629), Abp. of *Reims and Primate of France, Augustine *Baker (1575–1641), and Alban Roe (1583–1642), one of the *Forty Martyrs of England and Wales canonized in 1970.

J. C. Almond, OSB, *The History of Ampleforth Abbey from the foundation of St Lawrence's at Dieulouard to the present time* (1903). J. McCann, OSB, and C. Cary-Elwes, OSB (eds.), *Ampleforth and its Origins* (1952).

ampulla. Lat., a globular vessel for holding liquid. The term is used of three classes of objects.

(1) Of certain bottle-shaped vessels, usually of glass, found at tombs in the *catacombs. Such have often been known as *ampullae sanguinis* from an identification, going back to the 17th cent., of the dark-red sediment frequently found in them with the blood of a martyr. But their date (4th cent. onwards), the proportion found in the graves of small children, the discovery of similar ampullae at Jewish catacombs, e.g. on the *Via Labicana*, together with the scientific analysis of their contents, have discredited this view. It would appear rather that they were used to pre-

serve drops of the perfume poured on the bodies of the dead.

(2) Of certain coarsely made vases of baked clay often bearing the image or symbol of the saint, which were used to preserve oil from the lights burnt in *martyria*. A number sent by Pope *Gregory I from the tombs of Roman martyrs are preserved at the Cathedral at Monza. Those brought by pilgrims from the tomb of St *Menas in Egypt are esp. common.

(3) Of vessels to preserve the sacramental oils. They are referred to e.g. in St *Optatus of Milevis (*Contra Donatistas* 2. 19) and the *Gregorian Sacramentary. The most famous of such ampullae is the 'Sainte Ampoule' which, acc. to a legend in Flodoard (10th cent.), already mentioned by *Hincmar (d. 882), was brought by a dove at the prayers of St *Remigius for the Baptism of *Clovis. In the developed form of the legend, current from the 12th cent., the 'Sainte Ampoule' preserved at *Reims was miraculously replenished with *chrism for each coronation. It is known to have have been used for the coronation of French kings from 1131 (Louis VII) until the Revolution. Although it was broken in 1793, a fragment was preserved and used at the coronation of Charles X (1824). It appears to have been made of a metal similar to tin and engraved with a representation of the Adoration of the Magi and Shepherds. Similar legends of the miraculous origin of ampullae are found elsewhere in Europe. That among the English coronation regalia is in the unusual form of an eagle with outstretched wings. It dates from 1660 and was prob. copied from an earlier one, which, acc. to legend, was entrusted by the BVM to St Thomas *Becket.

The memorandum prepared by G. B. *De Rossi and circulated privately in 1862 was ed., with other docs., by A. Ferrua, SJ, *Sulla Questione del Vaso de Sangue* (Studi di Antichità Cristiana, 18; 1944). O. M. Dalton, *Catalogue of Christian Antiquities of the British Museum* (1901), pp. 154–9; C. M. Kaufmann, *Zur Ikonographie der Menas-Ampullen* (1910); C. Cecchelli, 'Note iconografiche su alcune ampolle bobbiesi', *Riv. A.C.* 4 (1927), pp. 115–39. H. *Leclercq, OSB, in *DACL* 1 (pt. 2; 1907), cols. 1722–78, s.v. 'Ampoules', and E. Josi in *EC* 1 (1949), cols. 1113–15, s.v. 'Ampolla'. On (3), Sir Francis Oppenheimer, *The Legend of the Ste. Ampoule* (1953); P. E. Schramm, *Der König von Frankreich*, 1 (1939; 2nd edn., 1960), pp. 145–50.

Amsdorf, Nikolaus von (1483–1565), *Lutheran theologian. A native of Torgau, he studied at Leipzig and Wittenberg, where he became lecturer in philosophy and theology in 1508. In 1517 he joined M. *Luther, whom he accompanied to the Disputation at *Leipzig in 1519 and to the Diet of *Worms in 1521. In 1524 he went to Magdeburg to lead the Protestant opposition against the Catholic clergy and to reform the services on Wittenberg lines. In 1528 and 1531 he did the same for Goslar. In 1534 he was responsible for Luther's renewed dispute with *Erasmus. He later quarrelled with P. *Melanchthon and M. *Bucer and alienated the Emperor during the Colloquy of *Ratisbon in 1541. In the same year he was appointed Bp. of Naumburg by the Elector of Saxony against the candidate of the Cathedral chapter and the wishes of the Emperor, but had to give up the appointment after the war of *Schmalkalden (1547) and went to Eisenach. He was a violent opponent of the Leipzig Interim, and, with *Flacius Illyricus, became a leader of the *Gnesio-

Lutheran party opposed to the *Adiaphorists (q.v.). During the *Synergist controversy he maintained against G. *Major, J. Pfeffinger, and others not only the uselessness but the actual harmfulness of good works, but did not subscribe to the teaching of Flacius Illyricus on sin as the substance of natural man. His one-sided interpretation of Luther caused a split within the Lutheran party, and his teaching on the harmfulness of good works was criticized in the Formula of *Concord. He was the author of numerous theological treatises.

Ausgewählte Schriften, ed. O. Lerche (Gütersloh, 1938). Short Life by T. Pressel (Elberfeld, 1862). P. Brunner, *Nikolaus von Amsdorf als Bischof von Naumburg* (Schriften des Vereins für Reformationsgeschichte, 179; 1961). O. H. Nebe, *Reine Lehre: Zur Theologie des Niklas von Amsdorff* (1935). R. Kolb, *Nikolaus von Amsdorf (1483–1565): Popular Polemics in the Preservation of Luther's Legacy* (Bibliotheca Humanistica & Reformatorica, 24; Nieuwkoop, 1978). J. Rogge in *TRE* 2 (1978), pp. 487–97, s.v. 'Amsdorff, Nikolaus von'.

Amsterdam Assembly (1948). The Assembly in the Concertgebouw, Amsterdam, from 22 Aug. to 4 Sept. which formally constituted the '*World Council of Churches' (q.v.). The Church leaders present included Marc Boegner, Pastor of Passy and President of the Protestant Federation of France; Erling Eidem, *Lutheran Abp. of Uppsala; Geoffrey *Fisher, Abp. of Canterbury; Germanos Strenopoulos, Abp. of Thyateira, under the *Oecumenical Patriarch; and J. R. *Mott (q.v.). The theme of the discussions was 'Man's Disorder and God's Design', under the four separate heads 'The Universal Church in God's Design' (by G. *Aulén, K. *Barth, G. *Florovsky, R. *Niebuhr, E. Schlink, O. Tomkins, W. A. Visser 't Hooft, etc.); 'The Church's Witness to God's Design' (by E. *Brunner, W. M. Horton, H. Kraemer, S. C. Neill, P. *Tillich, etc.); 'The Church and the Disorder of Society' (by Kathleen Bliss, E. Brunner, R. Niebuhr, J. H. *Oldham, etc.); and 'The Church and International Disorder' (by E. Brunner, J. F. Dulles, J. L. Hromadka, etc.).

The Official Report, with the 4 vols. under the separate titles named above, was issued in 1948–9. H. G. G. Herklots, *Amsterdam, 1948* (1948; popular).

Amyraut, Moïse (1596–1644). French Protestant theologian. Born in Bourgueil, he first studied Law at the University of Poitiers, then (from *c*.1618) Theology at the Protestant Academy of Saumur, where he came under the influence of John *Cameron. In July 1626 he became a minister at Saumur and began lecturing in Theology at the Academy, a post he was to retain until his death while becoming Principal in 1641. In 1631 he was Saumur delegate to the Charenton Synod where he successfully pleaded that the French Protestants (*Huguenots) be granted certain rights, including the right to address the King without kneeling. In 1634 he published the *Brief Traitté de la prédestination* which initiated the controversy over universal grace. Without espousing *Arminianism and while explicitly identifying his own teaching with that of J. *Calvin, Amyraut taught that the Son had been sent into the world to redeem all men provided they had faith. This doctrine was strongly criticized by Calvinist theologians in France (notably P. *du Moulin), Switzerland, and the Netherlands (notably Frederick Spanheim, 1600–49). In 1637 Amyraut was tried for heresy at the Protestant Synod of Alençon, but surprisingly escaped condemnation. As well as numerous treatises on grace, and sermons and biblical paraphrases in French, he wrote *La Morale chrestienne* (1652), the first important work of Calvinist ethics. Ecumenically minded, he also remained royalist during the rebellions of French nobility against the King ('La Fronde') in 1648–52.

There are no modern edns. of his works and most of his personal papers have not survived. A primary source is the account of the proceedings of the Charenton and Alençon synods issued first in Eng. tr. by J. Quick, *Synodicon in Gallia reformata*, 2 (London, 1692), pp. 255–422, and then in French by J. Aymon, *Tous les synodes nationaux des églises réformées de France*, 2 (The Hague, 1710), pp. 447–619. F. Laplanche, *Orthodoxie et Prédiction: L'Œuvre d'Amyraut et la querelle de la grâce universelle* (1965); B. G. Armstrong, *Calvinism and the Amyraut Heresy: Protestant Scholasticism and Humanism in Seventeenth-Century France* (Madison, Wis., and London, 1969). R. Nicole, *Moyse Amyraut: A Bibliography with special reference to the controversy on Universal Grace* (New York and London, 1981). J. Dedieu in *DHGE* 2 (1914), cols. 1380 f., s.v.

Anabaptists ('re-baptizers', from Gk. ἀνά and βαπτίζω). The comprehensive designation of various closely related groups on the Continent who in the 16th cent. refused to allow their children to be baptized and reinstituted the baptism of believers. Their denial that infant baptism was true baptism led to the nickname. The main groups to be distinguished are: (1) Thomas *Müntzer (*c.*1489–1525) and the *Zwickau Prophets who appeared in *Wittenberg in 1521. Müntzer sympathized with the *Peasants' War (1525) and taught a doctrine of the *Inner Light similar to that later adopted by the *Quakers. (2) The *Swiss Brethren, who reintroduced believers' baptism as the basis of Church fellowship near Zurich in 1525; unlike Müntzer, they believed in non-resistance and rejected Christian participation in the magistracy. Their views quickly spread in the Swiss valleys, and into the Rhineland and SW Germany. To this group belonged Balthasar *Hubmaier (*c.*1485–1528) and, for a time, Hans Denck (1495?–1527). (3) Communities which found asylum in Moravia and, under the leadership of Jacob Hutter (d. 1536), established settlements based on the common ownership of property. After many sufferings and wanderings certain of their descendants, now known as Hutterites or Hutterian Brethren, are now to be found in Canada and the USA. (4) The South German Anabaptists, who shared the eschatological and spiritual interests of Hans Hut (d. 1527), but, esp. under the leadership of Pilgram Marpeck (d. 1556), moderated their views in line with those of the Swiss Brethren. Marpeck was an able writer and in many books entered into debate with the *Lutherans and C. *Schwenckfeld. (5) Melchiorites or Hoffmanites, that is, Anabaptists influenced by Melchior *Hoffmann (*c.*1500–*c.*1543), mainly in NW Germany and the Low Countries. Hoffmann taught an unorthodox Christology of a *docetic kind and held *apocalyptic views. (6) A group of Anabaptist refugees in Münster who in 1533–5 attempted to establish a Kingdom of the Saints under the leadership first of Jan Mattys (d. 1534) and then of Jan Bockelson (John of *Leiden, 1510–36). During the siege of the city a form of polygamy was introduced, and the grave excesses and

fanaticism brought the whole of the left-wing movement into a disrepute which long continued. (7) The *Mennonites, shepherded and reorganized in the Netherlands and NW Germany by Menno Simons after the Münster episode. Their views were similar to those of the Swiss Brethren, with pacifism and non-resistance strongly emphasized. They later became in the Netherlands an influential community of rather liberal theological views and also spread to other Continental lands and to America.

Miguel *Servetus is sometimes classed among the Anabaptists, but he was not the organizer of Churches as were those listed above. Faustus *Socinus also rejected infant baptism, and Socinian influences are to be traced on some of the later Mennonites.

The Anabaptists were vigorously denounced by M. *Luther, H. *Zwingli, and J. *Calvin and severely persecuted by both Roman Catholics and Protestants. Those put to death probably ran into tens of thousands. Down to modern times they have suffered from hostile criticism; and Anabaptist hymnology and martyrology are only now receiving sympathetic and scholarly study.

There were Anabaptists in England as early as 1534, but throughout the 16th cent. Anabaptist views seem to have been mainly confined to refugees from the Low Countries. The early *Separatists and *Brownists, however, were probably influenced by them, and John *Smyth was certainly in close touch with the Mennonites. In the 17th and 18th cents. Baptists were often described as Anabaptists, but the name had then become one of abuse with evil associations and was largely repudiated.

Quellen zur Geschichte der Wiedertäufer [later *Täufer*] (Quellen und Forschungen zur Reformationsgeschichte, vols. 13, 16, 20, 22–4, 26–7, 29–31, 34, 41, 50, 53–4 etc.; 1930 ff., incl. H. J. Hillerbrand, *Bibliographie des Täufertums, 1520–1630* as vol. 10, 1962; also pub. in Eng., Elkhart, Ind., 1962). Id., *A Bibliography of Anabaptism, 1520–1630: A Sequel—1962–1974* (Sixteenth Century Bibliography, 1; St Louis, 1975). *Documenta Anabaptistica Neederlandica* (Kerkhistorische Bijdragen, 6, parts 1 and 2, 10, 15 etc.; 1975 ff.). H. Fast (ed.), *Der linke Flügel der Reformation: Glaubenszeugnisse der Täufer, Spiritualisten, Schwärmer und Antitrinitarier* (Klassiker der Protestantismus, 4; Bremen, 1962). Eng. tr. of useful collection of extracts ed. G. H. Williams, *Spiritual and Anabaptist Writers* (Library of Christian Classics, 25; 1957); Eng. tr. of further docs. ed. W. R. Estep, *Anabaptist Beginnings (1523–1533): A Source Book* (Bibliotheca Humanistica & Reformatorica, 16; Nieuwkoop, 1976). *The Writings of Pilgram Marpeck*, ed., with Eng. tr., by W. Klassen and W. Klaassen (Classics of the Radical Reformation Series, 2; Scottdale, Pa., 1978). *The Chronicle of the Hutterian Brethren*, tr. and ed. by the Hutterian Brethren (2 vols., Rifton, NY, etc., 1987 ff.).

The standard work is G. H. Williams, *The Radical Reformation* (Philadelphia, 1957; London, 1962; 3rd edn., Sixteenth Century Essays & Studies, 15; Kirksville, Mo., 1992). There is another modern account by U. Gastaldi, *Storia dell'Anabattismo* (2 vols., Turin, 1972–81). W. R. Estep, *The Anabaptist Story* (Nashville, 1963; repr., with rev. bibl., Grand Rapids, 1975). F. H. Littell, *The Anabaptist View of the Church* ([American] Studies in Church History, 8; 1952; rev. as *The Origins of Sectarian Protestantism*, New York and London, 1964); R. Friedmann, *Hutterite Studies*, ed. H. S. Bender (Goshen, Ind., 1961); id., *The Theology of Anabaptism: An Interpretation* (posthumously pub.; Studies in Anabaptist and Mennonite History, 15; Scottdale, Pa., 1973); J. M. Stayer, *Anabaptists and the Sword* (Lawrence, Kan., 1972; 2nd edn., 1976). K. R. Davis, *Anabaptism and Asceticism: A Study in Intellectual Origins* (Scottdale, Pa., 1974). H.-J. Goertz, *Die*

Täufer: Geschichte und Deutung (Munich, 1980; 2nd edn., 1988; Eng. tr., 1996). V. Peters, *All Things Common: The Hutterian Way of Life* (Minneapolis, 1965); J. W. Bennett, *Hutterian Brethren: The agricultural economy and social organization of a communal people* (Stanford, Calif., 1967); C.-P. Clasen, *Anabaptism: A Social History, 1525–1618. Switzerland, Austria, Moravia, South and Central Germany* (Ithaca, NY, and London, 1972), and other works of this author. J. S. Oyer, *Lutheran Reformers against Anabaptists: Luther, Melanchthon and Menius and the Anabaptists of Central Germany* (The Hague, 1964). H. J. Hillerbrand, *Die politische Ethik des Oberdeutschen Täufertums* (Beihefte der Zeitschrift für Religions- und Geistesgeschichte, 7; 1962). R. Friedmann, *Die Schriften der Huterischen Täufergemeinschaften: Gesamtkatalog ihrer Manuskriptbücher, ihrer Schreiber und ihrer Literatur 1529–1667* (Österreichische Akademie der Wissenschaften, Philosophisch-historische Klasse, Denkschriften, 86; 1965). W. O. Packull, *Mysticism and the Early South German–Austrian Anabaptist Movements 1525–1531* (Studies in Anabaptist and Mennonite History, 19; Scottdale, Pa., 1977). C. Krahn, *Dutch Anabaptism: Origin, Spread, Life and Thought (1450–1600)* (The Hague, 1968). I. B. Horst, *The Radical Brethren: Anabaptism and the English Reformation to 1558* (Bibliotheca Humanistica & Reformatorica, 2; Nieuwkoop, 1972). E. A. Payne in *The New Cambridge Modern History*, 2, ed. G. R. Elton (1958), pp. 119–33. See also works cited under MENNONITES.

Anacletus, St (1st cent.), also 'Anencletus', Gk. ἀνέγκλητος i.e. 'blameless', early Bp. of *Rome. He is probably to be identified with 'Cletus' (so *Irenaeus, *Eusebius, *Optatus, *Augustine), though the *Liberian Catalogue and the *Liber Pontificalis distinguish them. He followed St *Linus (the successor to St *Peter) and preceded St *Clement of Rome (d. c.96). Nothing further is known of him, though tradition attributes the division of Rome into 25 parishes to him. The feast of St Cletus (with St Marcellinus, d. c.304) used to be kept on 26 Apr. (suppressed 1969).

Jaffé, 1, p. 1 f. *LP* (Duchesne), 1, pp. lxix f. and 125. J. P. Kirsch in *DHGE* 2 (1914), cols. 1407 f., s.v. 'Anaclet'; P. Goggi in *EC* 1 (1948), col. 1126, s.v. 'Anacleto'; J. N. D. Kelly, *The Oxford Dictionary of Popes* (1986), p. 7.

anakephalaiosis. See RECAPITULATION.

Analecta Bollandiana. A quarterly review which has been issued since 1882 by the *Bollandists. It is devoted to hagiographical studies and research and from time to time prints hitherto unpublished documents.

analogy (Gk. ἀναλογία, orig. a mathematical term denoting proportion, but already used in a more general sense by *Plato and *Aristotle). In common modern usage the word signifies a resemblance or similarity between objects of discourse. More technically, however, analogy is a linguistic and semantic phenomenon which occurs when one word bears different but related meanings so that its use on different occasions involves neither equivocation nor univocity. In cricket and zoology, 'bat' can mean something entirely different and its use is therefore equivocal. In 'Fido is a dog' and 'Rover is a dog', the word 'dog' means exactly the same thing and its use is univocal. When, however, we speak, for example, of a healthy diet and a healthy complexion, 'healthy' has a different but related meaning. Its use here may therefore be regarded as analogical. For this reason analogy has sometimes been confused with metaphor, though most writers on analogy have resisted the identification on the ground that an analogical statement is literally true while a metaphorical one is not.

In theological circles the general intelligibility of analogy has been cited as a help to understanding how one can significantly refer to God by means of words more usually used of creatures. The general idea here is that one can, for instance, truly and meaningfully say 'God is wise' and 'Solomon is wise' even though the wisdom of God is fundamentally incomprehensible. The advantage of this theory is held to be twofold. First, the use of analogy in talking about God allows us to employ arguments concerning Him which abide by common rules of logic and which proceed by means of terms for which there is already some (non-theological) meaning. Second, the recognition that our discourse about God can be analogical is a necessary corrective to *anthropomorphism or any tendency to imply that God is the same kind of thing as any nameable or describable creature.

The role of analogy in theology was much discussed by medieval writers, esp. St *Thomas Aquinas; his treatment of the subject, together with that of Thomas de Vio *Cajetan, proved very influential. In modern times the concept has again come into prominence: the RC philosopher Erich Przywara (1899–1972) made the analogy of being (*analogia entis*) central to his thought, whereas K. *Barth rejected the notion as an attempt to subjugate the Divine to human categories and propounded as an alternative the notion of *analogia fidei* (analogy of faith).

Crit. edn. of Cajetan, *De Nominum Analogia* (completed 1498, first pub. Venice, 1506) by P. N. Zammit, OP (Rome, 1934; rev. by P. H. Hering, OP, ibid., 1952; Eng. tr., Duquesne Studies, Philosophical Series, 4; Pittsburgh, 1953). T. L. Penido, OP, *Le Rôle de l'analogie en théologie dogmatique* (1931); E. L. Mascall, *Existence and Analogy* (1949); H. Lyttkens, *The Analogy between God and the World: An Investigation of its Background and Interpretation of its Use by Thomas of Aquino* (Acta Universitatis Upsaliensis, 1953, 5; 1953); G. P. Klubertanz, SJ, *St Thomas Aquinas on Analogy* (Jesuit Studies; Chicago, 1960); R. M. McInerny, *The Logic of Analogy: An Interpretation of St Thomas* (The Hague, 1961); B. Montagnes, OP, *La Doctrine de l'Analogie de l'Être d'après Saint Thomas d'Aquin* (Philosophes Médiévaux, 6; 1963); B. Mondin, SX, *The Principle of Analogy in Protestant and Catholic Theology* (The Hague, 1963). H. G. Pöhlmann, *Analogia entis oder Analogia fidei? Die Frage der Analogie bei Karl Barth* (Forschungen zur systematischen und ökumenischen Theologie, 16; 1965). J. F. Ross, *Portraying Analogy* (Cambridge Studies in Philosophy, 1981).

Analogy of Religion, The (1736). A famous work of *apologetics by J. *Butler, the full title of which is *The Analogy of Religion, Natural and Revealed, to the Constitution and Course of Nature*. Written as an answer to certain forms of *Deism, it seeks to show both that Christianity is not unreasonable and that both Natural and Revealed Religion are positively reasonable. A characteristic strategy of the book is to argue that various objections to particular religious beliefs are not decisive since similar objections can be raised with respect to non-religious beliefs concerning nature. Butler also holds that truths about nature are an indication of the truth of religious beliefs, for which they serve to prepare us. To a large extent his case is pragmatic and relies on the notion that 'to us, probability is the very guide of life' (Introduction). We are right, he thinks, to act in accordance with the balance of probability; and this points to the truth of Natural and Revealed Religion whose propositions are of great practical importance and not just matters of theory to which we can afford to be indifferent.

The best modern edition is that of W. E. *Gladstone, *The Works of Joseph Butler*, 1 (Oxford, 1896), pp. 1–411. For other works, see bibl. to BUTLER, JOSEPH.

Anamnesis (Gk. ἀνάμνησις, 'memorial'). The word, which is used in the narrative of the Eucharist in the NT (1 Cor. 11: 24 f., Lk. 22: 19), is employed by liturgists for the commemoration of the Passion, Resurrection, and Ascension of Christ, which in most liturgies is included in the *Eucharistic Prayer after the Words of Institution.

O. Casel, OSB, 'Das Mysteriengedächtnis der Messliturgie im Lichte der Tradition', *JLW* 6 (1926), pp. 113–204. N. A. Dahl, 'Anamnesis. Mémoire et commémoration dans le christianisme primitif', *Studia Theologica* (Lund), 1 (1948), pp. 69–95. B. Botte, OSB, 'Problèmes de l'Anamnèse', *JEH* 5 (1954), pp. 16–24. D. Gregg, *Anamnesis in the Eucharist* (Grove Liturgical Study, 5; Bramcote, 1976 [from a Protestant perspective]). R. Cabié in A. G. Martimort, *L'Église en Prière*, new edn., 2 [1983], pp. 113–18 and 223–7; Eng. tr. (1986), pp. 96–100 and 207–11. F. *Cabrol, OSB, in *DACL* 1 (pt. 2; 1907), cols. 1880–96.

Ananias and Sapphira. The man and his wife who, acc. to Acts 5: 1–11, held back part of their property when the Apostolic Church was experimenting with community of goods and, on being challenged in turn by St *Peter, suddenly fell dead.

Anaphora (Gk. ἀναφορά, lit. 'offering'). The central prayer in the Eucharistic liturgy. The traditional order of its parts is *Sursum Corda (usually introduced by some form of benediction), *Preface, *Sanctus, Memorial of the Incarnation, Words of *Institution, *Anamnesis, *Epiclesis, Intercession (missing in some cases), and *Doxology. Among the oldest known Anaphoras are those of the '*Apostolic Tradition' of *Hippolytus, the Liturgy of *Addai and Mari, and the Egyptian form of the Liturgy of St *Basil.

The word is also used in a wider sense to cover the whole liturgy from the *Great Entrance to the end (including the *Communion).

Anastasia, St (c.304), martyr. A curious liturgical interest attaches to this saint as, though originally unconnected with *Rome, she is mentioned in the Roman *Canon of the Mass and used to be commemorated in the Second Mass for *Christmas Day. She was apparently martyred at Sirmium in Pannonia, whence her relics were translated to *Constantinople by St *Gennadius (458–71) and interred in the church of the *Anastasis, founded by St *Gregory Nazianzen. Hence the cultus spread, probably through the agency of Byzantine officials, to the ancient church in Rome near the Circus Maximus known as the *titulus Anastasiae* (perhaps from the name of its founder) and the only church near the Imperial palace; the dedication was now understood of the Sirmian saint; and the Pope celebrated here the stational Mass of Dawn on Christmas Day. Acc. to later and quite untrustworthy legends, Anastasia was a Roman lady of noble birth, the wife of a pagan Publius and spiritual disciple of St *Chry-

sogonus, and was martyred on the island of Palmaria. Feast day in W. until 1969, 25 Dec.; in E. 22 Dec.

'Acta' discussed in H. *Delehaye, SJ, *Étude sur le légendier romain* (Subsidia Hagiographica, 23; 1936), pp. 151–71. V. L. Kennedy, CSB, *The Saints of the Canon of the Mass* (Studi di Antichità Cristiana, 14; 1938), pp. 183–5. L. *Duchesne, 'Notes sur la topographie de Rome au moyen âge', no. 3, 'Sainte-Anastasie', *Mélanges d'archéologie et d'histoire*, 7 (1887), pp. 387–413; H. Grisar, SJ, 'S. Anastasia di Roma', *Analecta Romana*, 1 (1899), pp. 595–610; P. B. Whitehead, 'The Church of S. Anastasia in Rome', *American Journal of Archaeology*, 31 (1927), pp. 405–20; P. Devos, 'Sainte Anastasie la vierge et la source de sa passion', *Anal. Boll.* 80 (1962), pp. 33–47. C. Pietri, *Roma Christiana: Recherches sur l'Église de Rome . . . (311–440)* (Bibliothèque des Écoles françaises d'Athènes et de Rome, 224; 1976), pp. 461–4.

Anastasis (Gk. ἀνάστασις, 'resurrection'). From the first the word was used of the resurrection both of Christ Himself and of mankind in general. There were early churches dedicated to the Anastasis (of Christ) at *Jerusalem and *Constantinople; and it is possible (but see previous entry) that the present church of 'St Anastasia' at *Rome, at the foot of the Palatine Hill, originally had that dedication.

Anastasius I (d. 598), Patr. of *Antioch 559–70 and 593–598. Though a key figure in the dogmatic discussions of the second half of the 6th cent., he has not yet clearly emerged from the shadows cast by inadequate identification and publication of his works. A critic of *Justinian I's *aphthartodocetism, he was deposed by Justinian II and spent twenty-three years in exile, composing dogmatic treatises—against a tritheist, on the Trinity and the Incarnation, on the providence of God, and (incidentally) numerous problems of biblical interpretation. He prob. wrote as a neo-Chalcedonian (staunchly defending the orthodox creed of *Chalcedon, but attempting to close the gap with the *Monophysites). His works greatly influenced later authors, e.g. *Maximus the Confessor and *John of Damascus.

Collection of works attributed to him in J. P. Migne, *PG* 89. 1289–408. Crit. edns. by K.-H. Uthemann of his 'Dialogue with a Tritheist', *Traditio*, 37 (1981), pp. 73–108, and of his 'Philosophical Chapters', *OCP* 46 (1980), pp. 306–66. The edn. of his works by S. N. Sakkos (Thessalonica, 1976) needs to be used with caution; cf. *CPG* 3 (1979), pp. 313–19 (nos. 6944–69). G. Weiss, *Studia Anastasiana I: Studien zum Leben, zu den Schriften und zur Theologie des Patriarchen Anastasius I. von Antiochien (559–598)* (Miscellanea Byzantina Monacensia, 4; Munich, 1965). Krumbacher, pp. 59 f.; Beck (1959), pp. 380 f.

Anastasius, St (d. c.700) (Anastasius Sinaita), Abbot of the monastery of St Catherine on Mount *Sinai. A strong supporter of orthodoxy against all forms of heresy, he is believed to have attacked *Monophysitism at *Alexandria as early as 640, and it was against the same heresy that his most important treatise, the 'Hodegos' (Gk. Ὁδηγός, i.e. 'Guide'), was primarily directed. The 154 'Questions and Answers' included in editions of his writings are not in their present form his work, and the textual tradition of the popular 'Narrationes' attributed to him requires clarification. Feast in E., 21 April.

The fullest collection of his works is in J. P. Migne, *PG* 89. 35–1288; further works under the title 'Anastasiana' in J. B. *Pitra, *Iuris Ecclesiastici Graecorum Historia et Monumenta*, 2

(1868), pp. 238–94. 'Synopsis de haeresibus et synodis', also ed. K.-H. Uthemann, in *Annuarium Historiae Conciliorum*, 14 (1982), pp. 58–94. Crit. edn. of 'Hodegos' (entitled *Viae Dux*) by id. (CCSG 8; 1981) and of Homilies and *Opuscula adversus Monotheletas* by id. (ibid. 12; 1985); that of the genuine 'Questions and Answers' by M. Richard and J. A. Munitiz in preparation. J. B. Kumpfmüller, *De Anastasio Sinaita* (Würzburg, 1865). S. N. Sakkos, Περὶ Ἀναστασίων Σιναϊτῶν (Thessalonica, 1964; conclusions not generally accepted, but valuable for list of MSS). T. Spacil, SJ, 'La teologia di S. Anastasio Sinaita', *Bessarione*, 26 (1922), pp. 157–78, and 27 (1923), pp. 14–44. M. Richard, 'Anastase le Sinaïte, l'Hodegos et le Monothélisme', *Revue des Études Byzantines*, 16 (1958), pp. 29–42. CPG 3 (1979), nos. 7745–58 (pp. 453–62). Altaner and Stuiber (1978), pp. 524 f. and 661.

Anastasius Bibliothecarius (9th cent.), scholar. Apparently a native of Rome, he was educated by Greek monks with whom he retained close associations. In Aug. 855 he allowed the Imperial party to proclaim him antipope against Benedict III, but soon proved himself too rash and undisciplined for the office and was disowned by his supporters a month later. He was the best Greek scholar of his age in the W. *Nicholas I gave him the Abbacy of S. Maria in Trastevere, while later Popes made him their Librarian (hence 'Bibliothecarius') and rewarded him with important posts in the Chancery, where he tried to stem the threatening schism in the E. He attended the final session of the Eighth *Oecumenical Council (869) and later (871) translated its Acts into Latin. In 873 he translated the Acts of the Seventh Council (787). Among his other writings are a *Chronographia Tripartita*, based on earlier Byzantine historians, and several works on dogmatic theology.

'Epistolae sive Praefationes', ed. E. Perels and G. Laehr in *MGH, Epistolae*, 7 (1928), pp. 395–442. A. Lapôtre, *De Anastasio Bibliothecario sedis apostolicae* (Paris, 1885). E. Perels, *Papst Nikolaus I und Anastasius Bibliothecarius* (1920), esp. pp. 181–241. U. Westerbergh, *Anastasius Bibliothecarius, Sermo Theodori Studitae de Sancto Bartholomeo apostolo: A Study* (Acta Universitatis Stockholmiensis. Studia Latina Stockholmiensia, 9; 1963). P. Devos, SJ, 'Anastase le Bibliothécaire. Sa contribution à la correspondance pontificale. La date de sa mort', *Byzantion*, 32 (1962), pp. 97–115; id., 'Une Passion grecque inédite de S. Pierre d'Alexandrie et sa traduction par Anastase le Bibliothécaire', *Anal. Boll.* 83 (1965), pp. 157–87. C. Leonardi, 'Anastasio Bibliotecario e l'Ottavo Concilio Ecumenico' in *Studi Medievali*, 3rd ser. 8 (1967), pp. 59–192. *LP* (Duchesne), 1, p. xxxv (on his reputed authorship of the *Liber Pontificalis*). P. Devos, SJ, in *NCE* 1 (1967), pp. 480 f., s.v. 'Anastasius the Librarian'.

anathema (Gk. ἀνάθεμα, lit. 'suspended', 'set up above'). It is the equivalent of the Heb. word חֵרֶם, the root meaning of which is 'to cut off', 'curse', 'separate'. In the OT the term is used of votive offerings, e.g. Lev. 21: 5; but more often of things 'devoted to God', and hence 'under a ban' (e.g. in Deut. 7: 26), i.e. not for common use (cf. Lev. 27: 28 f.). Thus people, animals, cities, nations, and things could all become 'anathema', which frequently involved complete extermination (cf. Joshua 6, Deut. 7: 1 f., 1 Sam. 15). The practice was later alleviated, and after the Exile was normally confined to exclusion from the community and loss of goods. In this form it survived until the time of the Lord (e.g. Mt. 18: 17, Jn. 9: 22, though the term itself is not used in these and similar Gospel passages). St *Paul uses the word to denote separation

from the Christian community inflicted for sins such as preaching a gospel other than his (Gal. 1: 8 f.) or for not loving the Lord (1 Cor. 16: 22).

In the post-Apostolic Church the earliest recorded instance of anathematizing offenders is at the Council of *Elvira (c.306). It soon became the regular procedure against heretics. In 431, St *Cyril of Alexandria issued his famous twelve anathematisms against *Nestorius. By the 5th cent., anathematization appears clearly distinguished from *excommunication. *Gratian tends to play down the distinction, but in C. 11 q. 3 c. 24 he identifies the latter as involving only exclusion from the sacraments and from worship, whereas the former means complete separation from the body of the faithful. This corresponds to the distinction made later by *Gregory IX between minor and major excommunication (*Decretals*, 5. 39. 59), and classical canonists thereafter identified anathema with major excommunication, though the former was sometimes reserved to the solemn ritual in which the bishop pronounced excommunication, surrounded by twelve priests carrying lighted candles, which were thrown to the ground when sentence had been uttered (*Decretum*, C. 11 q. 3 c. 106). *Pius IX's apostolic constitution, *Apostolicae Sedis* (12 Oct. 1869), suppressed the category of minor excommunication, and in the 1917 *Codex Iuris Canonici* the only difference between excommunication and anathema was that the latter involved the solemn ritual which was still theoretically available in the *Pontifical. The 1983 *Codex* abolished even this distinction, so that the term 'anathema' no longer has any official application in the penal code.

W. C. van Unnik, 'Jesus: Anathema or Kyrios (I Cor. 12: 3)', in B. Lindars, SSF, and S. S. Smalley (eds.), *Christ and Spirit in the New Testament: In honour of Charles Francis Digby Moule* (Cambridge, 1973), pp. 113–26. J. Behm in *TWNT* 1 (1933), pp. 356 f.; Eng. tr., 1 (1964), pp. 354 f. L. Brun, *Segen und Fluch im Urchristentum* (Oslo, 1931). A. Vacant in *DTC* 1 (1903), cols. 1168–71; A. Amanieu in *DDC* 1 (1935), cols. 512–16; K. Hofmann in *RAC* 1 (1950), cols. 427–30, s.v.

Anatolius, St (d. *c.*282), Bp. of Laodicea. He was a native of *Alexandria, where he established a school of *Aristotelian philosophy and obtained a seat in the senate. During the siege of the Alexandrian suburb Brychion, in the revolt under the Prefect Aemilian (262), Anatolius devised a successful stratagem to relieve his fellow-Christians. Soon afterwards he was consecrated, apparently as coadjutor-bishop, by Theotecnus, Bp. of *Caesarea in Palestine, and in 268, on his way to the Synod at *Antioch to deal with *Paul of Samosata, made Bp. of Laodicea. Though a man of great learning and held in high repute by *Eusebius (*HE* 7. 32. 6–12) and St *Jerome (*De Viris Ill.* 73), his writings were few. They included a treatise on the date of Easter (Περὶ τοῦ Πάσχα), based on the 19-year cycle still used, from which Eusebius (loc. cit.) quotes a passage, and a work in 10 Books on the Elements of Arithmetic (Ἀριθμητικαὶ εἰσαγωγαί), though what were thought to be fragments of this work (J. P. *Migne, *PG* 10. 232–6) are prob. not genuine. It seems that the attribution to Anatolius of the 'Liber Anatoli de Ratione Paschali' (acc. to B. Krusch, compiled in England in the 6th cent.; acc. to C. H. *Turner, at *Iona between 580 and 600) is also mistaken. Feast day, 3 July.

The 'Liber Anatoli de Ratione Paschali' was first pub. by A. Bucher, SJ, *De Doctrina Temporum Commentarius* (Antwerp, 1634;

repr. in J. P. Migne, *PL* 10. 209–32). A new edn. was issued by B. Krusch, *Studien zur christlichmittelalterlichen Chronologie: Der 84-jährige Osterzyklus und seine Quellen* (1880). C. H. Turner, 'The Paschal Canon of "Anatolius of Laodicea" ', *EHR* 10 (1895), pp. 699–710. V. Grumel, 'La date de l'équinoxe vernal dans le canon pascal d'Anatole de Laodicée', in *Mélanges Eugène Tisserant*, 2 (ST 232; 1964), pp. 217–40. *CPG* 1 (1983), pp. 199 f. (nos. 1620–4). See also works cited under PASCHAL CONTROVERSIES.

Anatolius (*c*.400–58), Patr. of *Constantinople. A native of *Alexandria, he was sent to Constantinople by St *Cyril. When *Flavian was deposed in 449, Anatolius was elected Bp. of Constantinople and consecrated by *Dioscorus. Pope *Leo I demanded that he should explicitly condemn *Eutyches and *Nestorius and endorse the *Tome of Leo; on the accession of the Emp. *Marcian and *Pulcheria (450), Anatolius agreed. He seems to have encouraged Marcian to summon the Council of *Chalcedon and took his place after the Papal legates. By agreeing to the condemnation of Dioscorus for uncanonical behaviour at the *Latrocinium, and not on account of his doctrine, he helped to convince the Illyrian and Egyptian bishops of the orthodoxy of the Tome of Leo, and he had some part in formulating the Definition of Chalcedon. Canon 28 of the Council, which confirmed the prerogatives of the see of Constantinople and ranked it second only to that of Rome, led to acrimony, while Leo also complained that Anatolius had exceeded his jurisdiction in consecrating Maximus Bp. of *Antioch. In general, however, they cooperated in pursuing an anti-*Monophysite policy. His coronation of the Emp. Leo I in 457 set the pattern of future Byzantine coronations.

V. Grumel, AA (ed.), *Les Regestes des Actes du Patriarcat de Constantinople*, 1, fasc. 1 (2nd edn., 1972), pp. 85–101 (nos. 111–42). The other main sources are the letters of Leo and the Acts of the Council of Chalcedon (cited s.vv.). The Life printed in *AASS*, Jul. 1 (1719), pp. 659–66, is of little historical value. M. Jugie, AA, in *DHGE* 2 (1914), cols. 1497–500, s.v. 'Anatole (9)'; T. Camelot, OP, in *NCE* 1 (1967), pp. 482 f., s.v.

anchorite (*m.*), **anchoress** (*f.*) (Gk. ἀναχωρέω, 'to withdraw'). A person who withdraws from the world to live a solitary life of silence, prayer, and mortification. Technically the term covers *coenobites as well as *hermits, but it is commonly restricted to the latter, i.e. persons who live entirely alone. The word, in distinction from 'hermit', is now used esp. of one who lives in strictly confined quarters (his 'cell'). In the early Church this way of life was at the will of the anchorite, who was free to leave his retirement if necessary, but later it was recognized and ordered acc. to rules by the Church, the bishop himself enclosing the anchorite, who was thenceforward confined within the walls of his cell. In the later Middle Ages an anchorite's cell was sometimes attached to parish churches.

R. M. Clay, *The Hermits and Anchorites of England* (1914), pp. 73–198 and 203–63; id., 'Further Studies on Medieval Recluses', *Journal of the British Archaeological Association*, 3rd ser. 16 (1953), pp. 74–86. F. D. S. Darwin, *The English Mediaeval Recluse* [1944].

Ancient of Days. A designation of Yahweh found in Dan. 7: 9, 13, and 22. The expression in the original Aramaic יוֹם הַכִּפֻּרִים means literally 'one aged in days' and

apparently described the Deity under the figure of an old man.

Ancren(e) Riwle (or *Ancrene Wisse*), an early 13th-cent. 'Rule' or 'Guide for Anchoresses', written in a west Midlands dialect of English. It was originally composed for three well-born sisters, and later revised by the author for a larger group of recluses; the revised version refers to visits by *Dominican and *Franciscan friars, and so cannot have been written before the second quarter of the 13th cent. It is connected by style, preoccupations, and MS tradition with a number of other west Midlands prose works for women religious, the 'Katherine Group' and the 'Wooing Group'. The identity of the author is uncertain, but his work shows close links with the tradition of monastic legislation running from the *Augustinian canons to the Dominicans. The eight parts of the 'Rule' deal with: (1) the recluses' devotional routine; (2) the custody of the senses, and (3) of the thoughts; (4) temptation, (5) confession, and (6) penance; (7) the love of God; and (8) external regulations. The author emphasizes that the 'outer rule' of the first and final parts is no more than a handmaid to the 'lady' or 'inner rule'—the Divine commands governing the heart and conscience—to which he devotes the main body of his work; but he is less concerned with mystical experience than with general spiritual advice on the ascetic life and its problems. Most of his material is taken over from Latin sources, esp. the works of St *Augustine, St *Gregory I, and St *Bernard of Clairvaux; a significant minor source is *Ailred of Rievaulx's treatise *De vita eremetica ad sororem*. His style is clear, lively, and rhetorically accomplished, drawing on both Latin and native English prose traditions. During the later Middle Ages the 'Rule' was frequently copied, translated into Latin and French, and adapted for other communities both of men and of women; it retained its place in English devotional literature until the early 16th cent.

The EETS has pub. diplomatic texts of almost all the MSS, incl. the French and Latin versions. The text now usually accepted as standard is the author's rev. version, which survives only in Corpus Christi College, Cambridge, MS 402; this is ed. by J. R. R. Tolkien (EETS orig. ser. 249; 1962), and tr. into modern Eng. by M. B. Salu, with introd. by G. Sitwell, OSB (Orchard Books, 1955; repr., Exeter, 1990) and by A. Savage and N. Watson, *Anchoritic Spirituality* (Classics of Western Spirituality, New York [1991]), pp. 41–207. There are good general introds. and notes in the crit. edns. by G. Shepherd, *Ancrene Wisse: Parts Six and Seven* (1959) (based on the Corpus MS) and R. W. Ackerman and R. Dahood, *Ancrene Riwle: Introduction and Part I* (Medieval and Renaissance Texts and Studies, 31; Binghamton, NY, 1984) (based on British Library MS Cleopatra C. VI, an early MS with corrections possibly by the author). Full discussion of date and authorship by E. J. Dobson, *The Origins of Ancrene Wisse* (Oxford, 1976). B. Millett, 'The Origins of Ancrene Wisse: New Answers, New Questions', *Medium Ævum*, 61 (1992), pp. 206–28. Detailed bibl. survey by R. Dahood, 'Ancrene Wisse, the Katherine Group and the Wohunge Group', in A. S. G. Edwards (ed.), *Middle English Prose: A Critical Guide to Major Authors and Genres* (New Brunswick, NJ, 1984), pp. 1–33.

Ancyra (also **Angora**, now **Ankara**). Among the important early Church synods held here were:

(1) 314. A council of from twelve to eighteen bishops from Asia Minor and Syria. It dealt with the question of the '*lapsi'. In its first nine canons ecclesiastical penalties

were allotted acc. to the gravity and scandal of the lapse, but eventual reconciliation was granted to all. The remaining canons (10–25), which were concerned with various other offences, are of importance in the development of the *penitential system. Canon 13 has caused some controversy since it seems to favour ordination by presbyters.

(2) 358. A council of the *Semiarians under the presidency of *Basil of Ancyra, which rejected both extreme Arian teaching and also the Nicene *Homoousios ('of one substance'), and asserted that the Son was 'like in substance' to the Father.

On (1), Hardouin, 1 (1715), cols. 269–82; Mansi, 2 (1759), cols. 513–40. Canons, with Fr. tr. and introd., also pr. in Joannou, 1, pt. 2 (1962), pp. 54–73. Crit. edn. of Lat. texts in C. H. *Turner, *EOMIA* 2. 1 (1907). Hefele and Leclercq, 1 (pt. 1; 1907), pp. 298–326. R. B. Rackham, 'The Text of the Canons of Ancyra', *Studia Biblica et Ecclesiastica*, 3 (Oxford, 1891), pp. 139–216. C. H. Turner, 'Canon xiii of Ancyra', in C. *Gore, *The Church and the Ministry* (new edn., 1919), pp. 327–30. *CPG* 4 (1980), pp. 2 f. (nos. 8501 f.)

On (2), Hardouin, 1 (1715), cols. 707–10; Mansi, 3 (1759), cols. 265–90. Hefele and Leclercq, 1 (pt. 2; 1907), pp. 903–8. *CPG* 4 (1980), pp. 20 f. (no. 8579).

Andreae, Jakob (1528–90), *Lutheran theologian. Of humble origins, he owed most of his education to the patronage of Duke Ulrich of Württemberg. The next Duke appointed him Superintendent of the churches in the area of Göppingen in 1553, and in 1561 Professor of Theology and Chancellor of the University of *Tübingen. He worked to establish Lutheran forms of Church life and discipline both in Württemberg and elsewhere; he took part in various negotiations between the Lutherans and RCs in Germany and attended the Colloquy of *Poissy (1561) in France; above all he strove to secure harmony among the Lutheran Churches. He was one of the authors of the Formula of *Concord (q.v.) and travelled extensively in his efforts to secure its acceptance. He was bitterly attacked by the *Calvinists and his meeting with T. *Beza and others at Montbéliard in 1586 failed to produce any agreement.

His autobiography, written in Latin in 1562, ed., with Ger. tr., by H. Ehmer (Quellen und Forschungen zur württembergischen Kirchengeschichte, 10 [1991]). Short Life by M. Fittbogen (Leipzig, 1881). H. Gürsching, 'Jakob Andreae und seine Zeit', *Blätter für württembergische Kirchengeschichte*, 54 (1954), pp. 123–56; R. Müller-Streisand, 'Theologie und Kirchenpolitik bei Jakob Andreä bis zum Jahr 1568', ibid. 60–1 (1960–1), pp. 224–395, with bibl. R. Kolb, 'Jakob Andreae', in J. Raitt (ed.), *Shapers of Religious Traditions in Germany, Switzerland, and Poland, 1560–1600* (1981), pp. 53–68. M. Brecht in *TRE* 2 (1978), pp. 672–80.

Andrew, St, *Apostle. He was the brother of St *Peter, with whom he appears in the Gospels (Mk. 1: 16–20, 29, etc.). Though not a member of the inner band of three (Peter, *James, and *John), several incidents concerning him are recorded (Jn. 1: 35–42, Mt. 4: 18–20, Jn. 6: 8 f., Mk. 13: 3 f., etc.). *Eusebius (*HE* 3. 1. 1) states that he later went to Scythia. The *Muratorian Fragment connects him with the writing of St John's Gospel. Acc. to a late and unreliable tradition he was crucified at Patras, in Achaia, in 60. The earliest evidence for the form of his cross taking the shape of an X (as it appears in the Union

Jack) dates from the 10th cent. Feast day, 30 Nov. In the Anglican Communion, St Andrewstide is widely observed by intercessions for foreign missions. Since *c.*750 he has been regarded as the patron saint of Scotland. He is also the patron saint of Greece and Russia. See also following entry.

P. M. Peterson, *Andrew, Brother of Simon Peter: His History and his Legends* (Supplements to *Novum Testamentum*, 1; 1958); F. Dvornik, *The Idea of Apostolicity and the Legend of the Apostle Andrew* (Cambridge, Mass., 1958), pp. 138–299. M. R. James in *HDB* 1 (1898), pp. 92 f., s.v. On St Andrew's connection with Scotland, W. F. Skene, *Celtic Scotland*, 1 (1876), pp. 296–99, with refs. to orig. sources. On iconography, R. Pillinger, *Der Apostel Andreas: Ein Heilger von Ost und West im Bild der frühen Kirche* (*Sb.* (Wien), 612; 1994). Cf. also foll. bibl.

Andrew, Acts of St. An apocryphal book dating probably from the late 2nd cent., and held in favour among the *Encratites. In its original form it no longer survives, but fragments are contained in various Greek MSS, parts survive in Coptic and Armenian translations, and *Gregory of Tours gives a long epitome of it. It depicts the apostle as imprisoned at Patras, and prosecuted for his advocacy of ascetic practices. The 'Martyrdom' of St Andrew, a variant text of part of the work, describes the Apostle's death by crucifixion, but without mention of the 'St Andrew's cross' (see previous entry).

Texts in R. A. Lipsius and M. Bonnet, *Acta Apocrypha*, 2. 1 (Leipzig, 1898), pp. 1–127. Crit. edn., with additional material, by J.-M. Prieur (CC, Series Apocryphorum, 5–6; 1989). Eng. tr. in J. K. Elliott, *The Apocryphal New Testament* (Oxford, 1993), pp. 244–83, with introd. pp. 231–9. J. Flamion, *Les Actes Apocryphes de l'Apôtre André* (1911). Ger. tr., with introd. by J.-M. Prieur, in Schneemelcher, 2 (5th edn., 1989), pp. 93–137; Eng. tr., 2 [1992], pp. 101–51. See also works cited in previous entry.

Andrew of Crete, St (*c.*660–740), theologian and hymnwriter. A native of Damascus, he became Abp. of Gortyna in Crete *c.*692. In 712 he acquiesced in a brief imposition of *Monothelitism. During the early stages of the *Iconoclastic controversy, he defended the veneration of icons. He wrote many hymns, notably a series of '*canons', of which form of composition he is said to have been the inventor. His most famous piece, the 'Great Canon' (ὁ μέγας κανών), contains no less than 250 strophes. A considerable number of his homilies have also survived. Feast day, in E., 4 July. (He is not to be confounded with St Andrew of Crete, 'the Colybite', d. 766; feast day, 20 Oct.)

Opera, with Lat. tr., ed. by F. Combefis, OP, Paris, 1644; repr. from A. *Gallandi in J. P. Migne, *PG* 97. 805–1444. Eng. trs. of the 'Great Canon' by D. J. Chitty (London, 1957) and by Sister Katherine and Sister Thekla (Newport Pagnell, 1974). S. Vailhé, AA, 'St André de Crète', *ÉO* 5 (1902), pp. 378–87. A. Heisenberg, 'Ein jambisches Gedicht des Andreas von Kreta', *BZ* 10 (1901), pp. 505–14. T. Nissen, 'Diatribe und Consolatio in einer christlichen Predigt des achten Jahrhunderts', *Philologus*, 92 (1937), pp. 177–98, with further note, pp. 382–5. P. Sanz, 'Ein Fragment eines neuen Kanon des Andreas von Kreta', *Jahrbuch der Österreichischen Byzantinischen Gesellschaft*, 4 (1955), pp. 1–11, incl. text. *CPG* 3 (1979), pp. 541–53 (nos. 8164–228), with further bibl.

Andrew of St-Victor (d. 1175), biblical exegete. Canon of St-Victor at Paris (see VICTORINES), he was first (*c.*1147)

Abbot of the Victorine abbey at Wigmore in Hereford-shire. Difficulties arose with the monks and he went back to St-Victor after a few years, but between 1161 and 1163 he returned to Wigmore, where he died. He wrote commentaries on the *Octateuch, the Prophets, Proverbs, and Ecclesiastes. Basing himself on the work of *Hugh of St-Victor and using Jewish sources, he concentrated on the literal sense of Scripture to an extent not found elsewhere in the Middle Ages.

Comm. on Ecclesiastes, ed. G. Calandra (Palermo, 1948); on Jonah, ed. A. Penna, *Biblica*, 36 (1955), pp. 305–31; on the *Heptateuch, ed. C. Lohr and R. Berndt (CCCM 53; 1986); on Prov. and Eccles., ed. R. Berndt (ibid. 53B; 1991); on Ez., ed. M. Signer (ibid. 53E; 1991); on Dan., ed. M. Zier (ibid. 53F; 1990); and on Sam. and Kgs., ed. F. A. van Liere (Groningen Diss., 1995). R. Berndt, *André de Saint-Victor († 1175), exégète et théologien* (Bibliotheca Victorina, 2; 1991). B. Smalley, *The Study of the Bible in the Middle Ages* (3rd edn., Oxford, 1983), pp. xii and 112–95. W. McKane, *Selected Christian Hebraists* (Cambridge, 1989), pp. 42–75, with notes pp. 215–25 and bibl. pp. 248 f.

Andrewes, Lancelot (1555–1626), Bp. of *Winchester. Born in the parish of All Hallows, Barking, he was educated at Merchant Taylors' School and Pembroke Hall, Cambridge, where he was elected Fellow in 1576 and Catechist in 1580. He was a devoted scholar, hard-working and accurate, who became the master of 15 languages. In 1589 he became Vicar of St Giles, Cripplegate, and in the same year, in succession to W. *Fulke, Master of Pembroke Hall. His incumbency at Cripplegate was attached to a prebend at *St Paul's, where his remarkable preaching abilities first attracted notice. *Elizabeth I offered him two bishoprics (*Salisbury, *Ely); but he declined both owing to conditions which involved the alienation of some of the revenues. In 1601 he became Dean of *Westminster. Under *James I (1603), who held Andrewes in high esteem, he rapidly rose. He became Bp. of *Chichester in 1605, of Ely in 1609, and of Winchester in 1619. In 1604 he attended the *Hampton Court Conference, which appointed him one of the translators of the *Authorized Version of the Bible; he was largely responsible for the Pentateuch and the historical Books. In the next years he became involved in the controversy over the Oath of Allegiance, imposed after the *Gunpowder Plot (1605). When St Robert *Bellarmine, under the pseudonym of 'Matthaeus Tortus' (his almoner), had attacked King James's *Apology for the Oath* (1608), Andrewes wrote a vigorous and able reply under the title *Tortura Torti* (1609). After a further attack on the King by Bellarmine, who now wrote in his own name, Andrewes issued a second work, *Responsio ad Apologiam Cardinalis Bellarmini* (1610). In 1613 he sat on the commission which investigated the Essex nullity suit where he was one of the seven members who voted for the divorce. In 1617 he accompanied James I to Scotland in an attempt to persuade the Scots to accept episcopacy. Later he was put on the commission on the irregularity of G. *Abbot, Abp. of *Canterbury, who had accidentally shot a gamekeeper while hunting (Oct. 1621). He died at Winchester House, *Southwark, prob. on 25 Sept. 1626, and was buried in the parish church which is now Southwark Cathedral. In different parts of the Anglican Communion a feast day is observed on 25 or 26 September, the divergence reflecting the uncertainty over the date of his death.

Theologically, Andrewes was one of the principal influences in the formation of a distinctive Anglican theology, which, in reaction from the rigidity of Puritanism, should be reasonable in outlook and Catholic in tone. Convinced that true theology must be built on sound learning, he cultivated the friendship of such divines as R. *Hooker and G. *Herbert, as well as of liberal scholars from abroad, e.g. I. *Casaubon and P. *du Moulin, and he opposed the *Lambeth Articles (1595), though at the time he was chaplain to Abp. J. *Whitgift. Probably his known aversion to Calvinism explains his absence from the Anglican delegation to the Synod of *Dort (1618). He held a high doctrine of the Eucharist, emphasizing that in the sacrament we receive the true body and blood of Christ and constantly using sacrificial language of the rite. He wanted the C of E to express its worship in an ordered ceremonial and in his own chapel used the mixed chalice, incense, and altar-lights.

But in his lifetime Andrewes's fame rested esp. on his preaching. He regularly preached at court on the greater Church feasts; and his 'Ninety-Six Sermons', first pub. in a collected edition by W. *Laud and J. Buckeridge in 1629, remain a classic of Anglican homiletic works. They are characterized by verbal conceits, a minute and (to modern feeling) overworked analysis of the text, and constant Greek and Latin quotations. His famous *Preces Privatae* is a collection of devotions, mainly in Greek, compiled for his personal use. Though there were various partial English translations from 1630 onwards, the first comprehensive edition was that issued (with Lat. tr. apparently based on Andrewes's own material) by J. Lamphire in 1675; this was the basis of the classic (and enlarged) English translation by F. E. *Brightman (1903). Andrewes's *Patterne of Catechisticall Doctrine* (1630; also posthumous) was based on lectures delivered at Pembroke Hall, Cambridge.

Works ed. J. P. Wilson and J. Bliss in *LACT* (11 vols., 1841–54). Modern selection of his sermons ed. G. M. Story (Oxford, 1967), with biog. introd. Brief Life by Henry Isaacson (1581–1654), Andrewes's pupil, amanuensis, and intimate friend (London, 1650 [1651]; new edn. by S. Isaacson, London, 1829; also incl. in works). Other Lives and studies by A. T. Russell (Cambridge, 1860), R. L. Ottley (London, 1894), M. F. Reidy, SJ (Chicago, 1955), P. A. Welsby (London, 1958), and N. Lossky (Paris, 1986; Eng. tr., Oxford, 1991). R. W. *Church, 'Lancelot Andrewes', in A. Barry (ed.), *Masters of English Theology* (1877), pp. 61–112. T. S. *Eliot, *For Lancelot Andrewes: Essays on Style and Order* (1928), ch. 1, pp. 13–32. J. H. Overton in *DNB* 1 (1885), pp. 401–5, s.v.

Anencletus, St. See ANACLETUS, ST.

angel (from Gk. ἄγγελος, 'messenger'). The belief in angels is amply attested in the Bible, both in the OT and in the NT. They are represented as an innumerable multitude (e.g. Gen. 32: 1 f., Dan. 7: 10) of beings intermediate between God and man. In the older books interest is chiefly confined to their mission (cf. Gen. 16: 7 ff.; Jgs. 6: 11 ff.), whereas in the later ones their nature is more clearly defined. In Isaiah's vision (Is. 6) and in Job they form the heavenly court and sing the praises of God, whose commands they obediently perform for nations (Dan. 10: 13 and 21, 12: 1) as well as for individuals, and even three proper names, *Michael (Dan. 10: 13),

*Gabriel (Dan. 8: 16), and *Raphael (Tob. 3: 17), are recorded. In *Philo and the Jewish apocryphal writings, esp. *Enoch, angelology is highly developed, and angels, being the constant intermediators between God and man, were also regarded as the promulgators of the Law, a view accepted by the NT writers (Acts 7: 53, Gal. 3: 19, Heb. 2: 2). The Lord Himself sanctioned the popular belief. Acc. to His teaching the angels are spiritual beings (Mt. 22: 30) who enjoy always the vision of God in heaven (Mt. 18: 10) and will accompany Him at His Second Coming (Mt. 16: 27). The NT authors represent Christ as surrounded by angels at the most important periods of His life. They announce His Incarnation (Mt. 1: 20, 24) and His Birth (Lk. 2: 9–15); they minister to Him in the desert (Mt. 4: 11), strengthen Him in His agony (Lk. 22: 43), would be ready to defend Him when He is captured (Mt. 26: 53), and are the first witnesses of His Resurrection (Mt. 28: 2–7; Jn. 20: 12 f.). In Rev. the role of angels is paramount; their worship in heaven is the prototype of the worship of the Church, and their ministry at the end of the world is the visionary development of the Lord's teaching. On the other hand, the dangers of an exaggerated cult paid to them by some heretical sects in the early days of Christianity are reflected in Col. (2: 18) and perhaps also in Heb., which lays special emphasis on the superiority of Christ to the angels (1: 4 ff.).

In the first cents., while the great Trinitarian and Christological doctrines were being worked out, interest in angels was largely confined to Jewish–Christian circles, where Christ was sometimes seen as a kind of angel. Otherwise, their existence was accepted by the Fathers as a truth of faith; their immaterial and spiritual nature, however, was not fully recognized until *Dionysius the Ps.-Areopagite and St *Gregory the Great. *Origen attributed to them an ethereal body, an opinion which seems to have been shared by St *Augustine. There was similar uncertainty on the subject of their present state. St *Ignatius of Antioch had affirmed that they must believe in the Blood of Christ in order to be saved (Smyrn. 6. 1), and Origen held the good angels to be no less capable of falling than the demons were of being saved. This teaching was rejected by most of the orthodox Fathers, though traces of it are to be found in *Didymus, *Cyril of Jerusalem, and others. Perhaps the greatest interest was taken in the question of the angelic orders, raised by the two enumerations in Eph. 1: 21 and Col 1: 16 respectively. By amalgamating both passages five different ranks were arrived at, to which were sometimes added 'Angels' (here understood as a separate species of beings) and '*Archangels' (so *Irenaeus), and also the *Seraphim of Is. 6: 2 and the *Cherubim of Ez. 1: 5; but their number and order were only fixed by Dionysius in his 'Celestial Hierarchies', where they are arranged in three hierarchies containing three choirs each, in the order of Seraphim, Cherubim, and Thrones; Dominations, Virtues, and Powers; Principalities, Archangels, and Angels. Of these only the last two choirs have an immediate mission to men.

In the Middle Ages Dionysius' speculative doctrine was taken over and developed by the *Schoolmen, and a treatise on angels became a part of the Commentaries on the 'Sentences' of *Peter Lombard from the 13th cent. onwards. The doctrines of St *Thomas Aquinas and *Duns Scotus were foreshadowed by St *Albert the Great

and St *Bonaventure respectively. St Thomas and all the Schoolmen after him are at one on the point that angels are intelligences not destined to be united to a body, and thereby differ from the human soul. Acc. to St Thomas they are not composed of 'form' and 'matter', but are subsistent forms, each differing from the other and forming a species in himself. From their immateriality follows that they are by nature immortal and incorruptible; having neither extension nor dimensions they cannot be in a place, but can move and act on material beings by applying their power to the place in which they want to be. Duns Scotus, on the other hand, regards angels as composite beings consisting of form and matter, though the latter is not corporeal. There may be several angels in the same species, and several angels may occupy the same place. The angelic mode of knowledge had already been discussed by St Augustine (Civ. Dei, 11. 29), from whom St Thomas took over the distinction between scientia matutina and scientia vespertina, the former being supernatural knowledge which sees its objects in the Divine Word, and the latter natural, which knows individual things not, indeed, as man, through the senses, but through the intelligible species infused into the angelic intelligence at its creation. St Thomas held that its proper object was the immaterial, and its mode not discursive reasoning, but the intuitive perception of conclusions in their principles, a view contested by Duns Scotus, and later by F. *Suárez, who held that angels can reason. On the question of the Fall, St Thomas taught that the angelic will is such that one good or bad act fixes him irrevocably in good or evil, whereas Duns Scotus regarded a succession of acts as necessary. On several other points both schools of thought were in agreement. Thus most Scholastics taught that the angels were created at the same time as the material universe, that they were elevated to a state of grace in order to undergo a test followed either by supernatural beatitude or eternal damnation, and that the chief Divine mysteries, esp. the Incarnation, were then revealed to them. In the question of the hierarchy they all followed Dionysius more or less closely.

The teaching of post-medieval theologians runs on the lines of a Thomist–Scotist synthesis as developed by Suárez. The RC Church has made few pronouncements on the subject. While Catholic Christianity in general teaches the existence of angels, their perfect spirituality, and their creation before man, and enjoins a cult similar to that given to the saints, Protestants have tended to shrink from definition and speculation in the matter. See also GUARDIAN ANGELS.

F. Suárez, SJ, Summa Theologiae de Deo Rerum Omnium Creatore, pars secunda, 'De Angelis' (Lyons, 1620). J. Turmel, 'Histoire de l'angélologie des temps apostoliques à la fin du V' siècle', Revue d'histoire et de littérature religieuses, 3 (1898), pp. 289–308, 407–34, 533–52; id., 'L'Angélologie depuis le faux Denys l'Aréopagite', ibid. 4 (1899), pp. 217–38, 289–309, 414–34, 537–62; J. *Daniélou, SJ, Les Anges et leur mission d'après les Pères de l'Église (Collection Irénikon, NS 5; 1952). M.-T. d'Alverny, 'Les Anges et les jours', Cahiers Archéologiques, 9 (1957), pp. 271–300. E. Peterson, Das Buch von den Engeln: Stellung und Bedeutung der heiligen Engel im Kultus (Leipzig, 1935; Eng. tr. 1964). J. Barbel, CSSR, Christos Angelos: Die Anschauung von Christus als Bote und Engel in der gelehrten und volkstümlichen Literatur des christlichen Altertums (Theophaneia, 3; Bonn, 1941). [A.] W. Carr, Angels and Principalities: The Background, meaning and development of the

Pauline phrase hai archai kai hai exousiai (Society for New Testament Studies, Monograph Series, 42; 1981). C. A. Patrides, *Premises and Motifs in Renaissance Thought and Literature* (Princeton, NJ [1982]), pp. 3–30 ('The Orders of the Angels'). G. Davidson, *A Dictionary of Angels* (New York and London [1967]). A. Vacant, G. Bareille, L. Petit, J. Parisot, J. Miskgian in *DTC* 1 (1903), cols. 1189–1272, s.v. 'Anges'; H. L. Pass in *HERE* 4 (1911), pp. 578–83, s.v. 'Demons and Spirits (Christian)'; J. Duhr in *Dict. Sp.* 1 (1937), cols. 580–625, s.v. 'Anges'; J. Michl in *RAC* 5 (1962), cols. 109–200, s.v. 'Engel IV (christlich)', with bibl. cols. 256–8. For representation in art, also H. *Leclercq, OSB, in *DACL* 1 (1907), cols. 2080–2161, s.v. 'Anges', with bibl.; J. Villette, *L'Ange dans l'art d'Occident du XIIe au XVIe siècle* (1940), with bibl.; T. Klauser in *RAC* 5 (1962), cols. 258–322, s.v. 'Engel X (in der Kunst)'. Popular account (good on iconography) by P. L. Wilson, *Angels* [1980].

Angela of Foligno, Bl (c.1248–1309), Umbrian mystic.

She came of a wealthy family and spent almost her whole life at Foligno. After the death of her husband she was converted to a life of austerity and prayer and later became a *Franciscan tertiary. She was the recipient of frequent visions, esp. relating to the Lord's Passion. The accounts of them, taken down from dictation by her confessor, Brother Arnold, and later circulated as 'Liber Visionum et Instructionum', reflect early Franciscan piety at its highest. Angela was beatified by Innocent XII in 1693. Feast day, 4 Jan.

Her 'Liber Visionum', pub. at Alcalá, 1502, ed. L. P. Rosello (Venice, c.1510); also Paris, 1598, and Cologne, 1601. Crit. edns. after the MS Assisi 342 by P. Doncœur, SJ, and M. Faloci Pulignani (Bibliothèque d'Ascétique et de Mystique, 2; Paris, 1925), with Fr. tr., ed. M. J. Ferré and L. Baudry (Paris, 1927), and by L. Thier, OFM, and A. Calufetti, OFM (Grottaferrata, 1985). Eng. tr. by M. G. Steegman, with preface by A. Thorold ('1909' [1908]). L. Leclève, *Sainte Angèle de Foligno* (1936). P. Lachance, OFM, *The Spiritual Journey of the Blessed Angela of Foligno according to the Memorial of the Frater A.* (Studia Antoniana, 29; Rome, 1984). C. Schmitt, OFM (ed.), *Vita e Spiritualità della Beata Angela da Foligno: Atti del Convegno di Studi per il VII Centenario della Conversione della Beata Angela da Foligno (1285–1985), Foligno 11–14 dicembre 1985* (Perugia, 1987). H. Graef in *NCE* 1 (1967), pp. 501 f., s.v.

Angela Merici, St (1470/75–1540), foundress of the

*Ursulines. She lived most of her mature life at Brescia. In her early years she was a Franciscan *tertiary. After devoting some years to the education of young girls and the care of sick women, she made a pilgrimage to Palestine in 1524–5 during which she was smitten with blindness for a time. As the result of visions she founded at Brescia in 1535 a religious community for women which she named after her patron, St Ursula. In 1537 she herself was elected superior. She was canonized in 1807. Feast day, 27 Jan.

The earliest biography, compiled by G. B. Nazari in 1568, is partially pr. as an appendix to G. Bertoletti, *Storia di S. Angela Merici, 1474–1540* (Brescia, 1923). Later lives by O. Gondi, SJ (ibid., 1600) and C. Doneda (ibid., 1768). *Ste Angèle Merici et l'ordre des Ursulines*, par une religieuse du même ordre (2 vols., 1922); Sister M[ary] Monica, OSU, *Angela Merici and her Teaching Idea, 1474–1540* (New York, 1927), with bibl.; T. Ledóchowska, OSU, *Angèle Merici et la Compagnie de Sainte-Ursule* (2 vols., Rome [1968]; Eng. tr., ibid. [1970]). More popular Life by P. Caraman (London, 1963).

Angelic Doctor, the. A title applied from medieval times

to St *Thomas Aquinas in reference to 'the almost angelic quality of his intellect' (Motu Proprio, *Doctoris Angelici*, 29 June 1914). See also DOCTORS, SCHOLASTIC.

Angelic Hymn (Lat. hymnus angelicus). Another name

for the *Gloria in excelsis* (q.v.), the opening words of which were the hymn of the angelic host at *Bethlehem (Lk. 2: 14).

Angelico, Bl Fra (1395/1400–1455), Giovanni da Fie-

sole, painter. On the basis of the Life by Giorgio Vasari (1511–71), it was long held that he was born in 1387 and entered the *Dominican Order in 1407. It now seems that he was active in Florence as a painter in 1417, but still at that time a layman; he is first recorded as a friar at the Convent of San Domenico at Fiesole in 1423, and he remained there for some time after 1435, when some members of the community moved to Florence to found a new convent. During the 1430s he was also active in Cortona, where some of his greatest pictures still are. The first evidence of his presence at San Marco in Florence dates from 1441. His work here included the high altarpiece in the church and the frescoed decoration of the cells, cloisters, and corridors of the convent. Probably in 1445 he was summoned to Rome and is said to have been offered the archbishopric of Florence. Between 1446 and 1449 he painted four fresco cycles in chapels at the *Vatican. He became Prior of San Domenico, Fiesole, in 1450. He was beatified in 1982. Feast day in the Dominican Order, 18 February.

His great artistic contribution lay in his narrative power and use of brilliant colour; many of the most memorable images in Christian art were conceived by Fra Angelico. In the 19th cent. he was widely regarded as the supreme example of a mystical or spiritual artist. Modern critics tend to stress the innovative nature of his work and his place in the development of Renaissance art.

G. Vasari, *Le vite de piu eccellenti architetti, pittori, et scultori Italiani* (2 vols., Florence, 1550), 1, pp. 367–72; convenient Eng. tr. by G. Bull (Penguin Classics, 1965), pp. 199–207. Modern studies by F. Schottmüller (Klassiker der Kunst, 18; Stuttgart, 1911), J. Pope-Hennessy (London, 1952; 2nd edn., 1974), S. Orlandi, OP (Florence, 1964), C. Lloyd (Oxford and New York, 1979), and T. S. Centi, OP (Siena, 1984; argues in favour of traditional chronology). *Beato Angelico: Miscellanea di Studi* a cura della Postulazione Generale dei Domenicani (1984). L. Castelfranchi Vegas, *L'Angelico e l'Umanismo* (Milan, 1989); W. Hood, *Fra Angelico at San Marco* (New Haven, Conn., 1993).

Angels of the Churches. The seven angels of the

Churches of *Ephesus, *Smyrna, *Pergamum, *Thyatira, *Sardis, *Philadelphia, and *Laodicea mentioned in Rev. 1–3. To whom or what is the reference is much disputed. If the angels are men they may be bishops occupying their sees; if heavenly beings, they are perhaps the spiritual protectors of the respective Churches.

W. M. *Ramsay, *The Letters to the Seven Churches of Asia* (1904), pp. 69–72; C. J. Hemer, *The Letters to the Seven Churches of Asia in their Local Setting* (Journal for the Study of the New Testament, Supplement Series, 11; Sheffield [1986]), pp. 32–34. See also comm. to Rev. cited s.v.

Angelus. In the W. Church, the devotion consisting in the repetition thrice daily (early morning, noon, and evening) of three *Ave Marias with *versicles and a *collect as a memorial of the Incarnation. A bell is rung three times for each Ave and nine times for the collect. The name comes from the first word of the opening versicle in the Latin. During *Paschaltide its place is taken by a devotion beginning with the verse, 'Regina coeli laetare, alleluia'. Its history is obscure. The use of a similar devotion, recited at night to a bell, was adopted in Germany in the 13th cent. The morning Angelus first appears in the 14th cent., while the earliest evidence for the midday Angelus is from the 15th cent. The devotion did not come into general use until the 17th cent. The evening Angelus bell is commonly known in Italy as the 'Ave Maria'.

H. Thurston, SJ, 'Our Popular Devotions', Sect. 5: 'The Angelus', *Month*, 98 (1901), pp. 483–99, 607–16; 99 (1902), pp. 61–73, 518–32; also 100 (1902), pp. 89 f. T. Esser, OP, 'Geschichte des englischen Grusses', *Hist. J.* 5 (1884), pp. 88–116; id., 'Das Ave-Maria-Läuten und der "Engel des Herrn" in ihrer geschichtlichen Entwickelung', ibid. 23 (1902), pp. 22–51, 247–69, 775–825. Hefele and Leclercq, 5 (pt. 2; 1913), Appendix IV, 'Sur la salutation angélique prescrite par le canon 7 du Concile de Béziers en 1246', pp. 1734–59. U. Berlière in *DTC* 1 (pt. 1; 1903), cols. 1273–7, s.v. 'Angélique (Salutation)'; H. Thurston, SJ, in *Dict. Sp.* 1 (1937), cols. 1164 f., s.v. 'Ave Maria', both with bibl.

Angelus Silesius (1624–77) (**Johannes Scheffler**), mystical poet and controversialist. The son of a Lutheran Polish noble, he became (*c*.1649) court physician to the Duke of Oels, in Silesia. In 1653 he became a RC, and thenceforward devoted his time and energies to writing. In 1661 he was ordained priest. His chief fame lies in his mystical poems, published under the titles of *Heilige Seelenlust* (1657) and *Cherubinischer Wandersmann* (1675; 1st edn. with different title, 1657). The former interprets the spiritual life with the imagery of the Song of Solomon; the latter was written under the influence of a tradition of German mysticism that owes much to *Eckhart. He also began in 1663 a series of 55 controversial tracts in which he attacked various Christian sects. Some of these were collected in his *Ecclesiologia* (1677).

Edns. of his works by H. L. Held (3 vols., Munich, 1921; 2nd edn., 1924) and G. Ellinger (2 vols., Berlin [1924]). *Cherubinischer Wandersmann*, ed., with Fr. tr. and introd., by E. Susini (Publications de la Faculté des Lettres et Sciences Humaines de Paris, Série 'Textes et Documents', 4–5; 1964). Selected passages tr. into Eng. by J. E. C. Flitch (London, 1932). G. Ellinger, *Angelus Silesius: Ein Lebensbild* (Breslau, 1927). J. Baruzi, *Création religieuse et pensée contemplative* (1951), pp. 99–239. E. O. Reichert, *Johannes Scheffler als Streittheologe: Dargestellt an den konfessionspolemischen Traktaten der 'Ecclesiologia'* (Studien zu Religion, Geschichte und Geisteswissenschaft, 4; 1969).

Anglican and Eastern Churches Association. A body founded in 1864, partly on the initiative of J. M. *Neale, to pray and work for the reunion of the Orthodox Church and the Anglican Communion. It was originally known as the 'Eastern Church Association', and in its present form it also embodies another organization, founded in 1906, the 'Anglican and Eastern Orthodox Churches Union'. During 1920–39 and 1950–4 it issued *The Christian East*, since 1955 *The Eastern Churches News-Letter*.

Anglican chant. The music of the Psalms, as widely used in the Anglican Communion. It consists of a tune in barred music, harmonized, in which the first part of each half-verse is sung on a reciting note, and the concluding words fitted to a tune in metrical rhythm. It developed out of the plainchant psalm-tones about the end of the 17th cent., harmony and more rigid time being introduced; and it became widely popular about the middle of the 19th, when parish churches began to copy the choral services of cathedrals. In the 20th cent. a movement began to adapt the Anglican chant to a less rigid time, in order to avoid distortion of the words, and various methods, such as rearrangements of verses, the use of speech-rhythm, etc., have been employed to this end. The Anglican chant is still very widely used, but there has been, since the middle of the 19th cent., a parallel revival of *plainsong.

C. H. Phillips, *The Singing Church* (1945), pp. 112 f. and 201–10. K. R. Long, *The Music of the English Church* (1972), esp. pp. 235 f. N. Timperley, *The Music of the English Parish Church* (2 vols., Cambridge, 1979), esp. 1, pp. 167–76. R. [S.] *Bridges in *PBD* (1912), pp. 171–81, s.vv. 'Chant, Anglican' and 'Chanting'; P. A. Scholes and C. Moore in D. Arnold (ed.), *The New Oxford Companion to Music* (1983), pp. 77–80, s.v.

Anglican Communion. The Church in communion with, and recognizing the leadership of, the see of *Canterbury, whether in Britain or abroad. It consists of the *Church of England (the only part still retaining state *establishment), the Church of *Ireland, the Church in *Wales, the *Scottish Episcopal Church, the *Episcopal Church in the USA, the Anglican Churches of *Australia, *Canada, Papua New Guinea, and the Southern Cone of America; the Anglican Church in Aotearoa, New Zealand and Polynesia; the Provinces of *Southern Africa, the *West Indies, *West Africa, Central Africa, *Uganda, *Kenya, Myanmar (*Burma), Tanzania, the Indian Ocean, Melanesia, *Sudan, *Nigeria, Burundi, Rwanda, *Zaire, *Korea, *Mexico, and South East Asia; the Nippon Sei Ko Kai (*Japan), the Church of Ceylon (*Sri Lanka), the Episcopal Church of *Brazil, the Episcopal Church in *Jerusalem and the Middle East, the *Philippine Episcopal Church, and various 'extra-provincial' dioceses under the jurisdiction of the Abp. of Canterbury or another Anglican Primate (or his see). The Lusitanian Church (*Portuguese Episcopal Church) and the Spanish Reformed Episcopal Church are also members of the Anglican Communion. The United Churches of *South India, *North India, *Pakistan, and Bangladesh are members of the Anglican Consultative Council, the *Lambeth Conference, and the Primates' Meeting. The Anglican Communion is in communion with them and with the Philippine Independent Church; the *Old Catholic Churches and the Mar Thoma Syrian Church of *Malabar are in communion with most Anglican Churches.

For the first 250 years after the *Reformation, the Anglican Communion, except for the Episcopal Church in Scotland (disestablished from the days of William III) consisted solely of the one (state) Church of England, Ireland, and Wales. Efforts to found sees in the colonies (dating from the time of W. *Laud) were hindered by supposed legal objections and real political ambiguities, and priests working there, who were for the most part state chaplains rather than missionaries, were placed under the jurisdiction of the Bp. of London. In 1784 the Scottish bishops accepted an invitation to consecrate S. *Seabury as the first bishop of the Church in the United States. After the Consecration of Bishops Abroad Act 1786 had made possible the consecration in England of bishops for sees in other parts of the world, two further American bishops were consecrated by the English Archbishops in 1787 and a fourth in 1790. With the episcopal succession secured, the Episcopal Church in the United States formed itself into an autonomous body in full communion with the see of Canterbury by the action of its first General Convention in 1789, when it also produced its own revision of the BCP.

Meanwhile in 1787 the first colonial bishop (C. Inglis, Bp. of Nova Scotia) was consecrated, with jurisdiction over British N. America, and new sees were shortly afterwards set up in this area. In 1814 T. F. *Middleton was consecrated first Bp. of Calcutta, a diocese which at its height extended over *India, Sri Lanka, the E. Indies, and New South Wales, but which was soon divided by the creation of the sees of Madras (1835) and of Bombay (1837), and by the appointment of W. G. Broughton as first Bp. of Australia in 1836. The diocese of New Zealand was set up in 1841, with G. A. *Selwyn as its first bishop. In the same year the Colonial Bishoprics' Council was formed, through the efforts of C. J. *Blomfield, Bp. of London, and a great increase in the number of overseas bishoprics followed. Provincial organization began in 1835, when the Bp. of Calcutta became Metropolitan of India. It was extended to Australia in 1847, to South Africa in 1853, to New Zealand in 1858, to Canada in 1860, and to the West Indies in 1883. During the same period diocesan councils and provincial synods developed, and towards the end of the 19th cent. the title of Abp. was assumed by some of the Metropolitans. In 1855 for the first time an Anglican (non US) bishop was consecrated outside the British Isles when F. T. McDougall was made Bp. of Labuan and Sarawak (Borneo) by D. *Wilson, Bp. of Calcutta. Gradually complete independence was secured by those dioceses with provincial organization, which in the second half of the 20th cent. was extended almost everywhere. Dioceses outside provincial organization, though free from state control, depend directly on the Abp. of Canterbury or another Primate (or his see), but few of these remain. In Britain the Church of Ireland was disestablished in 1869 and that of Wales in 1920. Overseas Churches within the British Empire have been similarly disestablished (e.g. most of those in the West Indies in the latter part of the 19th cent. and the Church of India in 1928). Outside the British Empire a few Anglican sees were founded, e.g. in *China and Japan (where English, Canadian, and American missionaries worked together), in Jerusalem, Iran, and Egypt, and in scattered places elsewhere, e.g. Madagascar. The British Anglican chaplaincies in the whole of Europe were under the care of the Bp. of London until 1842, when responsibility for the areas bordering the Mediterranean was vested in the newly-created diocese of Gibraltar. In 1980 the chaplaincies in northern and central Europe were joined with the diocese of Gibraltar to form the diocese of *Europe.

In addition to the office of the Abp. of Canterbury, the Anglican Communion has a network of support and communication in the Lambeth Conferences, the regular Primates' Meetings, and the Anglican Consultative Council. Anglican bishops meet periodically as a body at the Lambeth Conference, which was first called by Abp. C. T. *Longley in 1867. The Conference has no legislative power and does not make decisions which are binding on member Churches, but its reports and resolutions carry weight and indicate the opinions of the contemporary Anglican episcopate. In 1969 the Anglican Consultative Council, which includes clerical and lay as well as episcopal representatives from each Province or Church of the Anglican Communion, was established as an advisory body. The Primates have met regularly for consultation since 1979.

H. Lowther Clarke, *Constitutional Church Government in the Dominions Beyond the Seas and in other Parts of the Anglican Communion* (1924). J. W. C. Wand (ed.), *The Anglican Communion: A Survey* (1948). H. G. G. Herklots, *Frontiers of the Church: The Making of the Anglican Communion* (1961). J. Howe, *Highways and Hedges: Anglicanism and the Universal Church* (1985; 2nd edn., *Anglicanism and the Universal Church: Highways and Hedges*, Toronto, 1990). The Eucharistic rites of the various branches of the Anglican Communion are collected in B. [J.] Wigan (ed.), *The Liturgy in English* (1962); C. O. Buchanan (ed.), *Modern Anglican Liturgies 1958–1968* (1968); id. (ed.), *Further Anglican Liturgies 1968–1975* (1975); id. (ed.), *Latest Anglican Liturgies 1976–1984* (1985). *The Anglican Communion: A Guide issued by the Anglican Communion Office* (1991). See also works cited under ANGLICANISM, CHURCH OF ENGLAND, and LAMBETH CONFERENCES. Current information is contained in the *Official Yearbook of the Church of England* and the official publications of individual Provinces and Churches.

Anglicanism. The word was coined in the 19th cent. from the much older 'Anglican', perhaps under the influence of the contemporary French term, *Gallicanisme*. It properly denotes the system of doctrine and practice of those Christians who are in communion with the see of *Canterbury but it has come to be used esp. in a more restricted sense of that system in so far as it claims to possess a religious and theological outlook distinguishable from that of other Christian communions, whether Catholic, Orthodox, or Protestant. The original formulation of Anglican principles is to be sought in the reign of *Elizabeth I rather than that of *Henry VIII or *Edward VI, for it was under her that a *via media between the opposing factions of Rome and Geneva (later called the 'Elizabethan Settlement') became a political necessity and Anglicanism as a doctrinal system took shape. Its formularies, including the Book of *Common Prayer, the *Ordinal, the *Thirty-Nine Articles, and the two Books of *Homilies became from Elizabeth's reign the basis of Anglican self-understanding, preaching, and doctrine. The Elizabethan BCP was the focus of controversies in the 17th cent., but, although the Book underwent subsequent revision, these alterations were of little theological significance.

After a period in which *Calvinist influences were dominant, the 17th cent. is often seen as the Golden Age of Anglicanism. In the lives and writings of L. *Andrewes, W. *Laud, H. *Thorndike, J. *Taylor, J. *Cosin, T. *Ken, and many others, often collectively known as the '*Caroline Divines', the C of E at once confirmed her rejection of the claims of Rome and refused to adopt the theological and ecclesiastical systems of the Continental reformers. Classical Anglicanism avoided the tendency to confessional systems and refused to recognize any form of *authority as absolute. The historic episcopate was preserved, even though many (e.g. R. *Hooker) did not regard it as of divine institution. The Church's right to adapt its ministry and even the form of its doctrine to changing circumstances was not denied, but the extent of legitimate change was held to be limited by appeal to Scripture as containing all things necessary to salvation. Truth was therefore to be sought from the joint testimony of Scripture and ecclesiastical authority, which in its turn was to be based on the tradition of the first four cents. The role of reason has always been affirmed in the Anglican tradition; it is reason itself that recognizes the authority of Scripture. As Jeremy Taylor put it, 'Scripture, tradition, councils, and fathers, are the evidence in question, but reason is the judge'.

At the Restoration of 1660 the dominant party belonged to the school of W. Laud (d. 1645) and other *High Churchmen who emphasized the continuity of the C of E with its Catholic roots. This influence was weakened by the secession of the *Nonjurors in 1690, but as writers they continued to play an important part in the defence of the Church against the secular learning of the European *Enlightenment. An initial reaction to such secular learning had come from the *Cambridge Platonists (1633–88) who sought to bypass both the doctrinal rigidities of *predestinarian Calvinism and what they felt to be a secular reaction to such over-confident and morally repugnant theology. Their emphasis on devotional religion and a conservative respect for the wisdom of the past that they feared was being undermined by mechanistic notions of nature and human society foreshadowed much that was to be characteristic of later Anglicanism. They found intellectual successors in W. *Law, J. *Butler, and D. *Waterland who answered the attacks of the *Deists and rationalists in the 18th cent., but their immediate heritage was a *latitudinarianism that gained strength in the early part of the 18th cent., with its emphasis on practical Christian living, morality, and a distrust of every kind of enthusiasm. The emergence of *Evangelicalism among Anglicans both in Britain and the USA in the later 18th cent. may be seen as in part a reaction against this trend. It did much for the spiritual life of the Church, but its appeal to the emotions and its emphasis on the primacy of Scripture and the importance of preaching sometimes went beyond the traditional ethos of Anglicanism, and the followers of J. *Wesley broke away from the C of E. Those who remained within it included such powerful laymen as W. *Wilberforce and those who were influenced by the preaching of C. *Simeon. Evangelicals still form a sizeable group within Anglicanism; their tendency is to emphasize its Reformation heritage rather than its Catholic elements.

The continuity of the High Church tradition within the C of E in the 18th cent. has recently been recognized; it is seen in the activities of J. *Potter, E. *Gibson, and S. *Johnson, as well as those, such as the *Hutchinsonians, who took part in the theological and philosophical controversies of the Enlightenment. Nevertheless, the beginning of the *Oxford Movement is traditionally dated in 1833. The Catholic Revival, as it is sometimes called, sought to restore to Anglicanism a proper sense of its roots and sacramental life as a part of the Catholic Church. It began as a scholarly movement among a group in Oxford centred round J. *Keble, E. B. *Pusey, and J. H. *Newman, who issued a series of *Tracts for the Times* (see TRACTARIANISM). By the end of the 19th cent., partly under the influence of *Ultramontanism, it had developed a strong, and often controversial, emphasis on Catholic ritual and outward symbols. However, by the mid-20th cent. many of the practices advocated by its leaders had been generally accepted, even though the influence of the *Anglo-Catholics began to wane thereafter.

Another influence on the theological framework of Anglicanism developed during the 19th cent. The latitudinarianism of the 17th cent. laid the foundations for the development of the *Broad Church or '*Liberal' theological movement of the mid-1800s, and the publication of *Essays and Reviews* (1860), though it incurred public condemnation at the time, assured within the bounds of Anglicanism a place for the new biblical and doctrinal criticism from Germany. Scholarship has traditionally held a high place in the Anglican tradition which is reflected in the appointment of scholarly bishops such as J. B. *Lightfoot and B. F. *Westcott. Anglican scholars have been in the forefront of historical and patristic studies. They have been free in every field to adopt radical or conservative traditions.

The principle of *lex orandi lex credendi* has traditionally been a distinctive feature of Anglicanism, and until 1948 *Lambeth Conferences held the BCP to be a bond in the Anglican Communion. In one language or another the Prayer Book (with comparatively minor revisions authorized in the second quarter of the 20th cent.) was used throughout the world. The second half of the 20th cent. has witnessed a period of liturgical experimentation in Anglican Churches and almost every Province has produced a different Prayer Book, so that there is now considerable diversity where there was general uniformity. A greater spirit of independence among Provinces in the Anglican Communion, together with the increasing proportion of Anglicans in non-English-speaking countries and cultures, contributes to the challenge of maintaining a unity of ethos in contemporary Anglicanism. The ordination of *women to the priesthood and episcopate in some Provinces and not in others has strained the bounds of comprehensiveness of Anglicanism and highlighted disputed questions of authority within that tradition. It has also called into question the central position of Anglicanism as a bridge in ecumenical discussions with other Churches, most notably the Orthodox. On the other hand, the traditional view that Anglicanism has no doctrines of its own but only those of the universal Church, has been challenged by S. W. Sykes and others; they argue that Anglican ecclesiology, with its vision of freedom and diversity within the limits imposed by Scripture, reason, and tradition, has a positive contribution to make to the ecumenical debate.

P. E. More and F. L. Cross, *Anglicanism: The Thought and Practice of the Church of England illustrated from the Religious Literature of the Seventeenth Century* (1935); G. R. Evans and J. R. Wright (eds.), *The Anglican Tradition: A Handbook of Sources* (1991). S. [C.] Neill, *Anglicanism* (Harmondsworth, 1958; 3rd edn., 1965); S. F. Bayne, *An Anglican Turning Point: Documents and Interpretations* (Austin, Tex., 1964); H. R. McAdoo, *The Spirit of Anglicanism: A Survey of Anglican Theological Method in the Seventeenth Century* (Hale Lectures, 1965); id., *The Unity of*

Anglicanism (Wilton, Conn., 1983); W. J. Wolf (ed.), *The Spirit of Anglicanism* (ibid., 1979; London, 1982); S. W. Sykes, *The Integrity of Anglicanism* (1979); id. and J. Booty (eds.), *The Study of Anglicanism* (1988); S. W. Sykes (ed.), *Authority in the Anglican Communion* (1988); P. Avis, *Anglicanism and the Christian Church* (Edinburgh, 1989); W. L. Sachs, *The Transformation of Anglicanism from State Church to Global Communion* (Cambridge, 1993). The ethos and spirit of recent Anglicanism can be studied in the writings and biographies of modern Church leaders, e.g. of A. C. *Tait, E. W. *Benson, M. *Creighton, R. T. *Davidson, C. *Gore, C. G. *Lang, W. *Temple, H. H. *Henson, G. K. A. *Bell, G. F. *Fisher, and A. M. *Ramsey. See also works cited under ANGLICAN COMMUNION and CHURCH OF ENGLAND.

Anglican Evangelical Group Movement. An association of the Anglican clergy and laity who held *Liberal Evangelical views. The movement originated in 1906 as a private body with the title of the 'Group Brotherhood', led by J. C. Wright (then Canon of Manchester), F. S. Guy Warman (then Vicar of Birkenhead, later Bp. of Manchester), and J. E. Watts-Ditchfield (then Vicar of St. James-the-less, Bethnal Green, later Bp. of Chelmsford), and arose from the desire of some of the younger Evangelicals to free Evangelicalism from what they regarded as an unduly conservative interpretation of Christianity, to welcome the help of science and criticism in the search for truth, and to infuse more dignity and beauty into worship. The 1923 annual conference at Coleshill, nr. Birmingham, decided to establish a public body under the title of 'Anglican Evangelical Group Movement' and to issue a public statement of its aims. Its members were pledged to study the social and economic implications of the Gospel, and to work for effective unity among all Christian people. Its activities included group study and the holding of retreats and conventions, esp. an annual conference which for many years from 1928 met at Cromer, for the deepening of spiritual life. Under the leadership of V. F. Storr (d. 1940) the movement saw the heyday of its influence from 1923 to 1939. Attempts to revive the movement after the end of the Second World War were not entirely successful and in 1967 it formally terminated its existence.

T. G. Rogers (ed.), *Liberal Evangelicalism. By Members of the Church of England* (1923). L. Hickin, 'Liberal Evangelicals in the Church of England', *CQR* 169 (1968), pp. 43–54.

Anglican–Methodist Conversations. In a Cambridge University sermon on 3 Sept. 1946, G. F. *Fisher, Abp. of Canterbury, suggested that a fresh start in the search for unity between the C of E and the Free Churches might be made if the latter would consider accepting episcopacy and coming into communion with the C of E. A conference of delegates appointed by the Archbishop and representatives of the Free Churches met and in 1950 issued a Report, *Church Relations in England*, which outlined a possible course of action but emphasized that it must be left to individual Churches to decide whether to pursue the matter. Of the Free Churches only the *Methodists decided to do so. In 1955 the Methodist Conference and the *Convocations of Canterbury and York decided to enter into conversations on the basis of the *Church Relations in England* Report and representatives on both sides were appointed. In 1958 an *Interim Report* was issued, mainly because those taking part in the Conversations felt that Dr Fisher's original proposal would be acceptable

only if it were viewed as the first stage of a scheme to bring about constitutional reunion, and it was thought necessary to seek approval for this new aim. This was given by the Methodist Conference and the *Lambeth Conference in the summer of 1958 and by the Convocations in Jan. 1959. The *Final Report* was issued in 1963. This outlined a plan in two stages. Stage I was to be inaugurated by a Service of Reconciliation, which included a pledge to seek organic union and a rite of unification of the existing ministries of the two Churches. The service was to be followed by the consecration of the first Methodist bishops, in which Anglican bishops would take part, and thereafter all ordinations in the Methodist Church would be performed by bishops. In other matters the authority of the Methodist Conference was to remain unimpaired during Stage I, and no timetable was set for the achievement of Stage II. In 1965 outline proposals were approved by the Convocations and the Methodist Conference, and a new Anglican–Methodist Unity Commission was set up. In 1967 it issued an interim statement, *Towards Reconciliation*, and in 1968 the final report was published in two parts: Part I, *The Ordinal*, and Part II, *The Scheme*. The Ordinal contained a Preface on the doctrine of ministry, which had been drawn up in consultation with RC and Orthodox theologians, and represented a wide area of ecumenical agreement. More opposition was aroused by the Scheme, esp. the proposals for unifying the existing ministries in the Service of Reconciliation. It was agreed that the Convocations and the Methodist Conference should vote on the Scheme simultaneously on 8 July 1969 and that a 75 per cent majority should be required before it could be implemented. The Methodist Conference produced a 77 per cent vote in favour, the Convocations only a 69 per cent majority. The Standing Committee of the General *Synod (which came into being in 1970) set up a working party and the Synod gave provisional approval to the Scheme in July 1971, but when it came before the Synod for a final decision on 3 May 1972 it received just under 66 per cent approval and so lapsed. New talks were initiated in 1995.

Alternative proposals to the 1968 Scheme were put forward by C. O. Buchanan and others, *Growing into Union: Proposals for a united Church in England* (1970). J. M. Turner, *Conflict and Reconciliation: Studies in Methodism and Ecumenism in England 1740–1982* (1985), pp. 194–214.

Anglican Ordinations. Until the subject was removed from the sphere of public discussion in the RC Church by *Leo XIII's bull '*Apostolicae Curae' (1896), there was diversity of opinion in that Communion on the *validity of the Orders of *bishop, *priest, and *deacon conferred by the Reformation *Ordinals of the C of E. The grounds on which their validity has been and is attacked fall into two classes: (1) Attacks on the actual historical continuity by the laying-on of hands. These usually assert either that Abp. M. *Parker was not himself consecrated or that his principal consecrator, W. *Barlow, had not been consecrated. Only rarely is either of these theses nowadays maintained by scholars; and even if the succession had been lost with Parker, it would have been restored with W. *Laud, from whom the present English episcopate derives, and who was consecrated by bishops, some of whom were in the undisputed Irish and Italian successions. (2) Attacks on the sufficiency of the Ordinal introduced under *Edward VI. These have been of two kinds:

(a) Assertions that the omission of the *porrectio instrumentorum* (see INSTRUMENTS, TRADITION OF THE) and other ceremonies renders the rite invalid. The recognition that such ceremonies were not in use in the early Church has led this objection to be abandoned. (b) The arguments of Leo XIII that the *intention of the Anglican Church as expressed in the rite is defective because there are no acts or words explicitly conferring the power for priests to offer sacrifice, and that the acts and words formerly used for this purpose were omitted by the Reformers. To this charge the Abps. of *Canterbury and *York replied in an Encyclical Letter, dated 29 Mar. 1897, in which they argued that the Anglican Church makes it clear that she intends to confer the Office instituted by Christ and all that it contains; they contended that the C of E teaches the doctrine of the *Eucharistic Sacrifice in terms at least as explicit as those of the *Canon of the Mass; and finally they pointed out that the words and acts required by the Pope are not found in the earliest Roman Ordinals, so that if their omission renders an Ordination invalid, the Orders of the Church of Rome are on no surer footing than those of the C of E. It has also been made a ground of complaint against the Edwardine Ordinal that the *formulae* for the Ordination of bishop and priest are the same, 'Accipe Spiritum Sanctum'; but to this objection it is replied that the intention to distinguish between the two is sufficiently expressed in the existence of two separate services, the contents of the services themselves, and the Preface to the Ordinal. In recent times the refusal of the RC Church to recognize the validity of Anglican Orders has been seen as a serious impediment in ecumenical relations; individual acts by modern Popes have sometimes been taken to indicate a softening of attitude, but there has been no change in the official position. See also the following entry.

The validity of Anglican Orders has been recognized by the *Old Catholics, and many parts of the Orthodox Church hold that they are as valid as those of the RC Church.

Besides the official documents mentioned, there were several important pamphlets issued by the Church Historical Society (SPCK) pub. *c.*1896. E. Denny and T. A. *Lacey, *De Hierarchia Anglicana Dissertatio Apologetica* (1895); T. A. Lacey, *A Roman Diary and other Documents* (1910); Viscount *Halifax, *Leo XIII and Anglican Orders* (1912); G. *Dix, *The Question of Anglican Orders* (1944); F. Clark, SJ, *Anglican Orders and Defect of Intention* (1956); id., *Eucharistic Sacrifice and the Reformation* (1960; 2nd edn., Oxford, 1967); J. J. Hughes, *Absolutely Null and Utterly Void: The Papal Condemnation of Anglican Orders 1896* (1968); id., *Stewards of the Lord* (1970). R. W. Franklin (ed.), *Anglican Orders: Essays on the Centenary of* Apostolicae Curae, *1896–1996* (1996), incl. Eng. tr. of texts. C. Androutsos, *The Validity of English Ordinations from an Orthodox Catholic Point of View* (1909); C. Papadopoulos, *The Validity of Anglican Ordinations* (Eng. tr., 1931); E. R. Hardy (ed.), *Orthodox Statements on Anglican Orders* (New York, 1946). L. Marchal in *DTC* 11. 2 (1932), cols. 1154–1193, s.v. 'Ordinations anglicanes', with bibl.

Anglican–Roman Catholic International Commission (ARCIC).

A joint commission of the RC Church and the whole Anglican Communion. In 1966, when M. *Ramsey, Abp. of Canterbury, met Pope *Paul VI in Rome, in a Common Declaration they inaugurated a dialogue which, it was hoped, would lead to 'that unity in truth and faith for which Christ prayed'; such unity they explained as 'complete communion of faith and sacra-

mental life'. A Joint Preparatory Commission was established, which after three meetings completed a Report at Malta in 1968, setting out the agenda for the full Commission.

The International Commission, which consisted of nine members from each side, held a series of residential meetings (known as 'Conversations') lasting about nine days, generally once a year, in different places, beginning in 1970. As a result of these meetings a series of 'Agreed Statements' was issued: on 'Eucharistic Doctrine' (Windsor, 1971); 'Ministry and Ordination' (Canterbury, 1973); and 'Authority in the Church' (Venice, 1976). 'Elucidations' (Salisbury, 1979) attempted to answer questions which had been raised concerning the first two documents. The Commission's 'Final Report' (Windsor, 1981; pub. 1982) included these four documents, adding an introduction on the Church, a second Agreed Statement on Authority, and a further 'Elucidation'. It was submitted to the two Churches for evaluation. The 1988 *Lambeth Conference resolved that the statements on the Eucharist and Ministry were 'consonant in substance with the faith of Anglicans', but, while welcoming the statement on Authority, called for further study of questions connected with Papal primacy. A preliminary and somewhat critical RC assessment was contained in the 'Observations' made by the Congregation for the *Doctrine of the Faith in 1982. The formal Response was made in 1991; while points of convergence and agreement were acknowledged, 'differences or ambiguities' were judged to remain.

Before this a new Commission (ARCIC II) was set up by Pope *John Paul II and Abp. R. Runcie after a meeting in Canterbury in 1982. This Commission, consisting at first of twenty-four members (the number was reduced later), issued Agreed Statements on 'Salvation and the Church' (Llandaff, 1986; pub. 1987) and 'The Church as Communion' (Dublin, 1990). The former document formulated an agreement over the doctrine of *justification by faith, which had been a central issue at the Reformation and is of particular concern to *Evangelicals in the Anglican Communion. The Congregation for the Doctrine of the Faith made 'Observations' on it in 1988.

In its approach to the questions which divided the Anglican and RC Churches, the first Commission sought to avoid the conventional method of comparing parallel accounts of their views, which would necessarily emphasize the differences, and sought rather to formulate statements expressing 'substantial agreement' on the points under consideration. This was explained as agreement on essential matters, such that remaining points of difference could be resolved on the basis of the fundamentals held in common. The same policy was adopted by the second Commission. While this positive attitude has yielded a measure of accord which has surprised many in both Churches, some problems remain to be resolved. The study of the mutual recognition of ministries, made necessary by the RC condemnation of *Anglican Orders in 1896, was placed on the agenda of the second Commission by Pope John Paul II and Abp. Runcie, but has been complicated by the ordination of women as priests and bishops in some Provinces of the Anglican Communion. The two primates, meeting in Rome in 1989, acknowledged this new obstacle to reunion, but reaffirmed their respective

Churches' commitment to the 'restoration of visible unity and full ecclesial communion'.

C. Hill and E. [J.] Yarnold, SJ (eds.), *Anglicans and Roman Catholics: The Search for Unity* (1994), incl. text of ARCIC I Final Report and official responses.

Anglo-Catholicism. The term 'Anglo-Catholic' has sometimes been applied to the C of E as a whole, signifying its claim to be part of the Catholic Church without being *Roman* Catholic, but it is more commonly used to distinguish that section or party within the Anglican Communion which stems from the *Tractarian Movement of the 1830s; indeed the term in its English form appears to date from 1838 (the Lat. *Anglo-Catholicus* is found in the 17th cent.). Anglo-Catholics hold a high doctrine of the Church and Sacraments; they attach great importance to the '*apostolic succession', that is, to an episcopal order derived from the apostles; to the historical continuity of the existing C of E with the Church of the earliest centuries; and to the Church's ultimate independence of the State.

The original Tractarians were concerned with basic doctrines of the Church. They revived *religious communities and various practices of personal discipline (such as the use of auricular *confession and *fasting), largely based on current RC models. They were not much concerned with ritual and ceremonial. But as the movement developed and moved into the parishes, Anglo-Catholics came to be regarded as preoccupied with the externals of worship and so were known as 'ritualists'. Disturbances occurred and legal actions were taken against them in both the ecclesiastical and civil courts. Nevertheless, despite the initial opposition of nearly all the bishops, and the attempts of Parliament to control *Public Worship, many of the practices originally regarded as Anglo-Catholic (such as the use of *candles or the wearing of *stoles) gradually spread throughout the C of E. The increased frequency of celebrations of the Eucharist owed much to their influence.

In its early days Anglo-Catholicism was conservative both theologically and politically, but in the latter part of the 19th cent. a division arose between those who sought to liberalize its theology by accepting the results of biblical criticism and those who resisted all concessions to modernity: Charles *Gore and the authors of *Lux Mundi* (1889) were pioneers in this respect; they were opposed by E. B. *Pusey, H. P. *Liddon, and G. A. *Denison. At the same time Anglo-Catholics who had been influenced by F. D. *Maurice became active in promoting more or less radical and socialist organizations, such as the Guild of St Matthew and the Christian Social Union.

These divisions continued into the 20th cent. and were compounded by differences concerning the revision of the Book of *Common Prayer. The movement seemed to reach its apogee after the First World War when five spectacular Anglo-Catholic Congresses were held in London and elsewhere between 1920 and 1933. Hopes were entertained of converting the whole Anglican Communion which had already been influenced in many (often unacknowledged) ways by the diffusion of Anglo-Catholic ideals. Anglo-Catholicism had already changed the face, though not the character, of Anglicanism. Meanwhile, in *Essays Catholic and Critical* (1926) a group of Anglo-

Catholic scholars had made a notable attempt to reconcile the findings of modern scholarship with traditional doctrine. Since the 1930s Anglo-Catholics have been less conspicuous as an organized and identifiable party, though the movement has continued to have its adherents and periodically shows signs of revival (notably the Catholic Renewal Conferences at Loughborough in 1978 and 1983). In recent years groups of Anglo-Catholics, prob. by themselves a minority, but sometimes acting in conjunction with *Evangelicals, have opposed schemes for union with the *Free Churches; they have also opposed projects for the ordination of women. In face of this apparently negative attitude, 'Affirming Catholicism' (technically an educational charity) was founded in 1990, to provide a forum for the discussion of issues raised by the tension between scholarship and free enquiry on the one hand, and the Catholic tradition within Anglicanism on the other. In some countries where women have been ordained to the priesthood (and episcopate) small numbers of Anglo-Catholics have formed secession Churches (e.g. the 'Anglican Catholic Church' in the USA).

See also OXFORD MOVEMENT.

W. J. Sparrow Simpson, *The History of the Anglo-Catholic Revival from 1845* (1932); N. P. *Williams and C. Harris (eds.), *Northern Catholicism* (1933); W. L. Knox and A. R. Vidler, *The Development of Modern Catholicism* (1933); [D.] G. Rowell, *The Vision Glorious: Themes and Personalities of the Catholic Revival in Anglicanism* (Oxford, 1983); W. S. F. Pickering, *Anglo-Catholicism: A study in religious ambiguity* (1989).

Anglo-Saxon Church. By this title is meant the Church in England from the end of the 6th cent. to the Norman Conquest (1066). During the 6th and 7th cents. England was being evangelized from two sides. In 597 the Roman mission of St *Augustine landed at Thanet in the south and sees were quickly set up at *Canterbury, London, *Rochester, and *York. In the north, the Irishman St *Aidan established himself at *Lindisfarne c.635. For a time the work of the missions was hindered by disputes over differences in such customs as the date of observing *Easter and the cutting of the *tonsure. But in 664 union between north and south was set in train after the Synod of *Whitby, and in 669 *Theodore of Tarsus arrived as Abp. of Canterbury and began his great work of reform and organization. Further important synods of the English bishops were held at *Hertford in 672 or 673 and at *Hatfield in 679, and many new dioceses were formed. In 787, at a synod presided over by two papal legates, *Lichfield was made an archbishopric, but the arrangement lasted for less than 16 years. The Danish invasions were a great blow to the Church, although the victory of *Alfred secured the nominal acceptance of Christianity by the invaders. In the 10th cent., reforms were initiated by St *Dunstan and St *Ethelwold and a closer connection with the Continent was established. At the Norman Conquest, most of the surviving Anglo-Saxon bishops were removed, but the most outstanding of them, St *Wulfstan, continued at *Worcester till his death in 1095.

Monasticism was very strong in the Anglo-Saxon Church, most of the work of evangelization being done by monks, and it is to this period that we may trace the origin of the English custom of having cathedrals with monastic chapters. Double monasteries of men and women, often under the rule of an abbess, were not uncommon during the period, but most of these did not survive the Viking incursions of the 9th cent. The connection between Church and State was particularly close. The conversion of a district usually began in the royal palace; bishoprics were conterminous with tribal areas; and it is very often difficult to decide whether a particular assembly was primarily ecclesiastical or secular. In some of these respects, however, the Anglo-Saxon Church did not differ from many Continental Churches of the time. Despite a popular belief to the contrary, relations between the Anglo-Saxon Church and the rest of W. Christendom seem to have been constant and good.

Eng. tr. of much primary material in D. Whitelock, M. Brett, and C. N. L. Brooke (eds.), *Councils & Synods and other Documents Relating to the English Church*, 1: A.D. 871–1204, pt. 1: 871–1066 (Oxford, 1981). W. *Bright, *Chapters of Early English Church History* (1873; 3rd edn., 1897); F. M. Stenton, *Anglo-Saxon England* (1943; 3rd edn., 1971). M. Deanesly, *The Pre-Conquest Church in England* (1961); id., *Sidelights on the Anglo-Saxon Church* (1962); J. Godfrey, *The Church in Anglo-Saxon England* (1962); F. Barlow, *The English Church 1000–1066: A Constitutional History* (1963; 2nd edn., 1979); H. [M. R. E.] Mayr-Harting, *The Coming of Christianity to Anglo-Saxon England* (1972). C. Cubitt, *Anglo-Saxon Church Councils c.650–c.850* [1995].

Angola, Christianity in. The *Portuguese colony of Angola, developing from the port of Luanda, dates from 1576. From 1596 it was placed within the newly established (RC) diocese of San Salvador, comprising the *Congo and Angola. The bishop's residence was soon moved from San Salvador, within the independent kingdom of the Congo, to Luanda in the Portuguese colony, but the official translation was delayed until 1716. The *Jesuits staffed a college in Luanda, but elsewhere missionary work was carried out mainly by Italian *Capuchins.

Conditions were unfavourable to the growth of the Church. The main reason for Luanda's existence was as a slave port for Brazil. The slave trade devastated African society here more than elsewhere in Africa and demoralized the Portuguese. Nevertheless the Church survived, with some local clergy, despite long periods when there was no bishop and despite Portuguese anticlerical laws from the late 18th cent. and the suppression of religious orders. Areas within Angola are the only part of sub-Saharan Africa in which there has been a continuous local Church since the 16th cent., though by the mid-19th cent. there were few priests.

In 1865 French *Holy Ghost Fathers accepted responsibility for the mission and the Church began to revive. In 1881 Antonio Barroso, an outstanding Portuguese missionary and later Bp. of Oporto, began work around San Salvador. Protestant activity began when the British *Baptist Missionary Society came to include the north of the country within its field (see ZAIRE). In the centre and south the American Board of Commissioners for Foreign Missions began work in 1880 and the *Methodist Episcopal Church in 1884.

The anticlericalism which had characterized Portuguese governments for many years ended with that of A. de Salazar, whose Colonial Act of 1930 re-established a privileged position for RC missions. This was reinforced by the Con-

cordat and Missionary Agreement between Portugal and the Vatican in 1940. Government policy was to regard Angola as a province of Portugal and the Protestant missions, staffed by British and American missionaries, were often attacked as an anti-Portuguese influence. The nationalist movements drew their leadership largely from the Protestant community. An African rising in the north of Angola in 1961 was countered by widespread Portuguese attacks on African suspects, esp. Protestants. The Independence of Angola in 1975 has been followed by almost continuous civil war in which Baptists and Methodists have often been linked with forces opposed to the government, while RCs have been more sympathetic to the Marxist government. About half the population belongs to the RC Church and under a quarter to Protestant denominations.

For the pre-18th-cent. Church the basic documents are pr. in A. Brásio, C.S.Sp. (ed.), *Monumenta Missionária Africana: África Occidental* (20 vols., Lisbon, 1952–88). Id., *História et Missiologia: Inéditos e esparsos* (Luanda, 1973). L. Jadin, 'Le Clergé séculier et les Capucins du Congo et d'Angola aux XVIᵉ et XVIIᵉ siècles. Conflits de juridiction, 1700–1726', *Bulletin de l'Institut historique Belge de Rome*, 36 (1964), pp. 185–483. D. Birmingham, *Trade and Conflict in Angola: The Mbundu and their Neighbours under the Influence of the Portuguese 1483–1730* (Oxford, 1966). A. Hastings, *The Church in Africa 1450–1950* (Oxford History of the Christian Church, 1994), *passim* (see index). For the 19th-cent. RC revival the primary docs. include those relating to the mission of the Holy Ghost Fathers, ed. A Brásio, C.S.Sp., *Angola* (Spiritana Monumenta Historica, Series Africa, 1; 5 vols., Pittsburgh and Louvain, 1966–71), and a collection relating to the work of Barroso, also ed. A. Brásio, C.S.Sp., *D. António Barroso, Missionário, Cientista, Missiólogo* (1961). The background is described by J. Duffy, *Portuguese Africa* (1959), pp. 49–78 and *passim*. L. Addicott, *Cry Angola!* (Living Church Books, 1962). A. Hastings, op. cit.; id., *A History of African Christianity 1950–1975* (Cambridge, 1979), *passim*.

Anima Christi (Lat., 'Soul of Christ'), the well-known prayer, beginning

Soul of Christ, sanctify me,
Body of Christ, save me,

used esp. as a private Eucharistic devotion. From its use at the outset of the **Spiritual Exercises* it has been traditionally ascribed to St *Ignatius Loyola ('Aspirationes S. Ignatii ad Sanctissimum Redemptorem'), but is really very much older. It appears to date from the early 14th cent. (not 12th cent., as L. Eisenhofer). *John XXII (d. 1334; probably not its author, despite G. M. Dreves) enriched it with indulgences. Early occurrences of it are in the British Library MS Harl. 1260, fol. 158 (AD 1370); a prayer-book of Card. Peter of Luxembourg (d. 1387), preserved at *Avignon; and on an inscription of Moorish workmanship on the gates of the Alcazar at Seville (c.1364).

H. Thurston, SJ, 'The Anima Christi', *Month*, 125 (1915), pp. 493–505; repr. in his *Familiar Prayers*, ed. P. Grosjean, SJ (1953), ch. 3, pp. 38–53. D. Prideaux, OSB, 'A Note on the Prayer "Anima Christi"', *Laudate*, 1 (1923), pp. 9–21. H. L. Pass, *Anima Christi: A Little Treatise on the Spiritual Life* (1934), esp. pp. 293–302. P. Schepens, 'Pour l'histoire de la prière *Anima Christi*', *Nouvelle Revue théologique*, 62 (1935), pp. 699–710. P. Leturia, SJ, 'Libros de Horas, Anima Christi y Ejercicios Espirituales de S. Ignacio', *Archivum Historicum Societatis Iesu*, 17 (for 1948; 1949), pp. 3–50, esp. pp. 35–50. B. Fischer, 'Das Trierer *Anima Christi*. Der bisher unveröffentlichte älteste nichtlateinische Text des *Anima Christi* aus einer Hs. des frühen XIV. Jhts. in der Trierer Stadtbibliothek', *Trierer Theologische Zeitschrift*, 60 (1951), pp.

189–96. H. Thurston, SJ, in *Dict. Sp.* 1 (1937), cols. 670–2, s.v., with further bibl.

animism. The belief, widespread among primitive peoples, that certain material objects, e.g. trees and stones, are possessed by spirits which are the cause of their movements and characteristic qualities. Echoes of animism are found in the OT, e.g. *Jacob's treatment of the stone at Bethel as if it were Divine (Gen. 28: 22). Anti-Christian writers have sometimes held all worship of a personal god, particularly if connected with special holy places, to be a survival of primitive animism; while the Christian need not deny that in early times animistic ideas assisted, e.g., the growth of such beliefs as that in *immortality.

E. B. Tylor, *Primitive Culture* (2 vols., 1871), chs. 11–17. E. O. James, *Prehistoric Religion: A Study in Primitive Archaeology* (1957). E. E. Evans-Pritchard in *Catholic Dictionary of Theology*, 1 (1962), pp. 98 f., s.v.; K. W. Bolle in M. Eliade (ed.), *The Encyclopedia of Religion*, 1 (1987), pp. 296–302, s.v. 'Animism and Animatism'. See also bibl. to ANTHROPOLOGY.

Anna Comnena (b. 1083; d. after 1148). The daughter of the Emp. Alexius I, Comnenus, and Irene, she was one of the earliest women historians and among the most outstanding writers of the Byzantine age. Having conspired unsuccessfully after her father's death to depose her brother, John, in the interests of her husband, Nicephorus Bryennius, she retired to a convent where she wrote a history of her father's reign, the 'Alexiad' (*'Αλεξιάς*). This work, finished after 1148, is less a history than an apology or panegyric, being full of extravagant adulation and almost devoid of critical judgement. It is, however, of great interest as a representation of the Orthodox hostility to the W. Church and to the *Crusades as a menace to the E. Empire. She praises Alexius' persecution of the *Bogomil heretics which culminated in the execution of Basilius, their leader.

The best edns. of the Alexiad are those of A. Reifferscheid (2 vols., Teub., 1884) and (with Fr. tr.) B. Leib (3 vols., Paris, 1937–45, index by P. Gautier, 1976). Eng. trs. of the Alexiad by E. A. S. Dawes (London, 1928) and E. R. A. Sewter (Penguin Classics, 1969). G. Buckler, *Anna Comnena* (1929).

Annas. The Jewish *High Priest from AD 6 (or 7) to 15. In the latter year he was deposed by the procurator, Valerius Gratus, and succeeded by his son-in-law, *Caiaphas, though, as appears from Lk. 3: 2, Jn. 18: 13, and Acts 4: 6, he continued to have at least a share in his former office, and could even be referred to as High Priest—perhaps (because) strict Jews held him to be so. Acc. to Jn. 18: 13, Jesus, after His arrest, was first brought to Annas and had a preliminary trial in his palace before being sent on to Caiaphas. In Acts 4: 6 he takes a leading part in the trial of the Apostles at Jerusalem.

annates (Lat. *annata*, from *annus*, 'year'). The first year's revenue of an ecclesiastical benefice, paid to the Papal curia. These payments, later known as 'first-fruits', became general through the increase of direct Papal nomination to livings in the 13th cent. The actual term *annata* was at first applied to the tax paid upon minor benefices only, but in the 15th cent. it came to be used also of the *servitia* paid on bishoprics and the headships of monaster-

ies. In 1532 the payment of ani ates from English archbishoprics and bishoprics to the Holy See was restrained, but the Act was passed condition illy, so that the King could use it as a threat against the Pope to gain his wishes over the royal 'divorce'. This failed, although it did result in the Pope's issuing the necessary instruments for the consecration of T. *Cranmer as Abp. of Canterbury; and *Henry VIII brought the Act into force by letters patent dated 9 July 1533. The Appointment of Bishops Act 1533 in 1534 confirmed the 1532 Act, and annates and tithes were annexed to the Crown in 1535 by the First Fruits and Tenths Act 1534. In 1704 they were assigned by the Crown to the Governors of *Queen Anne's Bounty for the augmentation of poor livings, and were abolished in 1926.

W. E. Lunt, *Papal Revenues in the Middle Ages* (New York, 2 vols., 1934), esp. 1. 93–9, and 2. 315–72, with full refs.; id., *Financial Relations of the Papacy with England 1327–1534* (Cambridge, Mass., 1962), pp. 307–445, with bibl. refs. The Reformation legislation is pr. in J. R. Tanner, *Constitutional Documents 1485–1603* (Cambridge, 2nd edn., 1930), pp. 25–39. J. P. Kirsch in *CE* 1 (1907), pp. 537 f.

Anne, St, Mother of the BVM. Her name (not found in the Bible) and the legend of her life occur already in the *Protevangelium of James (2nd cent.). A church was erected at *Constantinople in her honour by the Emp. *Justinian I (d. 565) and relics and pictures at *Rome (S. Maria Antiqua) date from the 8th cent. In the 10th cent. her feast was observed at Naples and it was widely current in the W. by 1350. Urban VI expressly ordered it for all England, to popularize the marriage of Richard II to Anne of Bohemia (Jan. 1382). By the end of the Middle Ages the cult had become extremely popular and was an object of special attack by M. *Luther and other Reformers. In 1584 it was ordered for the Universal Church, and Gregory XV even made it a *Feast of Obligation. The feast is now observed with esp. devotion in *Canada and also in Brittany (of which country she is Patroness). Feast day in the W., 26 July (with St *Joachim from 1969); in the E., 25 July.

The primary source is the *Protevangelium Jacobi*, 1–8. B. Kleinschmidt, OFM, *Die heilige Anna, ihre Verehrung in Geschichte, Kunst und Volkstum* (Forschungen zur Volkskunde, 1930). P. V. Charland, *La Bonne Sainte, ou l'Histoire de la Dévotion à sainte Anne* (Quebec, 1904), and other works of this author. M. V. Ronan, *S. Anne: Her Cult and her Shrines* (1927). K. Ashley and P. Sheingorn (eds.), *Interpreting Cultural Symbols: Saint Anne in late Medieval Society* (Athens, Ga., and London [1990]). A. *Wilmart, OSB, 'Sur les Fêtes de la Conception et de Ste Anne. Chants en l'honneur de Ste Anne dans un manuscrit français du XIᵉ Siècle', *EL* 42 (1928), pp. 258–68; repr. in id., *Auteurs spirituels et textes dévots du Moyen Age Latin* (1932), pp. 46–55.

Anne (1665–1714), Queen of Great Britain and Ireland. The second daughter of *James II, she continued to be brought up as an Anglican even after her father had been received into the RC Church. In 1702 she succeeded her brother-in-law, William III, her brother, James, being excluded from the succession as a RC. Her political views varied during her reign, but in religious matters she remained consistently true to the *High Church tradition of her grandfather, *Charles I. Early in her reign (1704) she created '*Queen Anne's Bounty' for the clergy. By exercising her right to nominate bishops, she introduced a

High Church and Tory element on the Bench, which at her accession was composed almost entirely of Whigs and *Latitudinarians out of sympathy with the predominantly High Church inferior clergy. She strongly supported the *Occasional Conformity Bill, first introduced into Parliament in 1702, to end the scandal of Dissenters' qualifying for public office by occasional communion in their parish churches; but the bill was not passed till the end of her reign, when there was a decided Tory majority in the Commons. In 1710 she was present at the trial of H. *Sacheverell, which achieved the discomfiture of the Whigs at the ensuing elections, and she was thought by the general public to be a strong supporter of the accused. The Tory ascendancy of 1711–14 was used for political measures against Dissent (such as the *Schism Act 1713), instead of constructive enactments, and it did not long survive the Queen's death. Though the power of the Latitudinarian party in the Church, dominant at her accession, was somewhat checked during her reign and the Caroline High Church tradition revived, the success of her policy was weakened by the effects of the secession of the *Nonjurors, as well as by the political incompetence of the Tory party, who alone gave it active support. In the next reign it was almost destroyed by the association of High Churchmanship with Jacobitism.

B. C. Brown (ed.), *The Letters and Diplomatic Instructions of Queen Anne* (1935). Anon., *The Life of Her Late Majesty Queen Anne* (2 vols., 1721). A. Boyer, *The History of the Reign of Queen Anne* (11 vols., 1703–13). The best modern study is that of E. Gregg, *Queen Anne* (1980). There is also much information in G. V. Bennett, *The Tory Crisis in Church and State 1688–1730: The Career of Francis Atterbury, Bishop of Rochester* (Oxford, 1975), pp. 3–182 *passim*.

Anne Boleyn (?1501–36), second Queen of *Henry VIII. A daughter of Sir Thomas Boleyn, she spent her youth at the Netherlands and French Courts, and came to the English Court in 1521. Her charm, intelligence, and strong personality won her many admirers; from 1526 these included Henry, who was tiring of Catherine of Aragon and beginning to think of divorce. Probably in 1527 they were informally betrothed, and by Aug. Henry opened negotiations with the Pope for a marriage annulment. These moved slowly, but Anne began living openly with Henry during 1531; when in 1532 the King determined to secure an end to his marriage with Catherine unilaterally, Anne was created Marchioness of Pembroke in her own right, and became pregnant towards the end of 1532. A secret marriage took place on 24 or 25 Jan. 1533, and, after Abp. T. *Cranmer had pronounced Henry's marriage to Catherine null in May, Anne was crowned Queen, despite widespread distaste. Though her first child was not the son Henry desired but the future *Elizabeth I (Sept. 1533), her position did not become dangerous until after a stillbirth in Jan. 1536. By then, Henry, increasingly intimidated by her forceful personality, had found a new love in Jane Seymour and began to listen to Anne's conservative enemies, who were joined by T. *Cromwell; during April Anne was accused of treacherous adultery, Cranmer declared her marriage to Henry null (the reasons given are not known), and on 19 May 1536 she was executed. Apart from her importance in precipitating the 'divorce' crisis, she played a major role during her brief reign in promoting

reform and advancing reformers to positions of power in the Church.

Anne Boleyn figures in the primary sources for the reign of Henry VIII and the Reformation. The history in her defence by George Wyatt (d. 1624) is ed. by D. M. Loades, *The Papers of George Wyatt* (Camden 4th ser. 5; 1968), pp. 19–30; M. Dowling (ed.), 'William Latymer's Cronickille of Anne Bulleyne', *Camden Miscellany*, 30 (ibid. 39; 1990), pp. 23–65. Id., 'Anne Boleyn and Reform', *JEH* 35 (1984), pp. 30–46. E. W. Ives, *Anne Boleyn* (Oxford, 1986). See also bibl. to HENRY VIII.

Anne's Bounty, Queen. See QUEEN ANNE'S BOUNTY.

Annexed Book, the. A name given to the actual BCP annexed to the Act of *Uniformity of 1662, which prescribed the use throughout the realm of 'true and perfect copies' of it. The MS original was a fair copy made from the 'Convocation Book' (i.e. the text finally approved by Convocation in 1661), which was signed by the members of Convocation, and then presented to Parliament.

A *Facsimile of the BCP signed by Convocation, Dec. 20th, 1661, and attached to the Act of Uniformity, 1662*, was pub. in 1891.

annihilationism. See CONDITIONAL IMMORTALITY.

Anno Domini (Lat., 'in the year of the Lord'). The current system of dating by 'AD', based on the traditional year of the birth of Christ, was devised by *Dionysius Exiguus (6th cent.). It is now commonly held that the actual birth was several years earlier, between 7 and 4 BC, since it is established that Herod the Great died (cf. Mt. 2: 19) in the latter year. Some authorities, however, have preferred the date AD 6, the date usually given to the great census under Quirinius (Lk. 2: 1 f.). See also CHRONOLOGY, BIBLICAL.

Annunciation of the BVM. The feast, observed on 25 Mar. ('Lady Day'), commemorates the announcement of the Incarnation by the angel *Gabriel to the Virgin and the conception of Christ in her womb (Lk. 1: 26–38). The date is usually taken to depend on that of Christ's nativity (25 Dec.), though a different tradition held that the dependence was the other way round, and associated the date of the Lord's conception with that of His crucifixion (see CHRISTMAS). In the E. there is evidence for the observance of the feast of the Annunciation in a sermon by Abraham of Ephesus preached prob. between 530 and 553 in either Constantinople or Ephesus, and in one of the hymns of *Romanos Melodus. In the W. the first authentic reference is in the *Gelasian Sacramentary. In the Acts of the Council *in Trullo (692) it is exempted from the ban on feasts in *Lent, while in Spain the observance was long kept on 18 Dec. to prevent its occurrence in Lent. By the 8th cent. its observance in the W. had become universal. In the BCP it is a '*red letter' day and in the Table of Proper Lessons is described as the 'Annunciation of Our Lady', the only place where the Book uses this title of the BVM. In the RC Church it is now called the 'Annunciation of the Lord', and in some modern Anglican rites (incl. the ASB) it is designated the 'Annunciation of Our Lord to the Blessed Virgin Mary'.

St *Bernard's famous Homilies 'Super *Missus Est*' are repr. in J. P. Migne, *PL* 183. 55–88. The sermon by Abraham of Ephesus was ed. by M. Jugie, AA, 'Abraham d'Éphèse et ses écrits', *BZ* 22 (1913–4), pp. 37–59. S. Vailhé, AA, 'Origines de la fête de l'Annonciation', *ÉO* 9 (1906), pp. 138–45; M. Jugie, AA, 'La Première Fête mariale en Orient et en Occident: l'avent primitif', ibid. 26 (1923), pp. 130–52. I. Cecchetti, 'L'Annunciazione. Il racconto biblico e la festa liturgica', *Bollettino Ceciliano*, 38 (1943), pp. 46–8 and 98–114. R. A. Fletcher, 'Three Early Byzantine Hymns and their Place in the Liturgy of the Church of Constantinople', *BZ* 51 (1958), pp. 53–65. For works on the biblical narrative, see comm. to Lk.

anointing. A ceremonial action performed on persons and things to separate them from profane use and obtain on their behalf the infusion of Divine grace. The ceremonial use of oil is common to many religions, e.g. Hinduism, the worship of ancient Greece and Rome, and many primitive peoples. In the OT priests and kings are anointed to symbolize their sanctity and endowment with the Spirit of God; hence the future deliverer of Israel was designated the 'Messiah' or 'Anointed One', and this title was taken over by the Apostles and appears in the NT in its Greek form 'Christ' (Χριστός). In the NT anointing is used as a charismatic means of healing (e.g. Mk. 6: 13) and combined with prayer in Jas. 5: 14 (see UNCTION). The Church from early times made sacramental use of it in the rites of *Baptism, *Confirmation, and *Ordination (qq.v.), as well as in the consecration of churches, altars, bells, etc. The anointing of kings, which is first met with (in Visigothic Spain) in the 7th cent., was influenced immediately by the OT (see CORONATION RITE IN ENGLAND). See also CHRISM.

See bibl. to BAPTISM, CHRISM, CONFIRMATION, ORDERS AND ORDINATION, and UNCTION.

Anomoeans (from ἀνόμοιος, 'unlike' or 'dissimilar'). The 4th cent. exponents of a doctrine akin to *Arianism and in modern times frequently called 'Neo-Arians'. They held that the Son, being begotten, was in essence unlike (ἀνόμοιος) the Father, the Ingenerate or Unbegotten. Their leaders were *Aetius and *Eunomius; they were also known as 'Aetians' and '*Exoucontians'.

See bibl. to AETIUS and ARIANISM.

Anschar, St. See ANSKAR, ST.

Anselm, St (c.1033–1109), Abp. of *Canterbury. He was the son of a Lombard landowner and a native of Aosta. After several years of undisciplined life he crossed the Alps into *France in 1056 and in 1059 entered the monastic school at *Bec in Normandy, then directed by *Lanfranc of Pavia, his fellow-countryman. Here he was persuaded by Lanfranc and Maurilius, Abp. of Rouen, to take monastic vows (1060) and in 1063 he succeeded Lanfranc as prior. His devotion and remarkable intellectual abilities gained him a high reputation as a teacher and spiritual director. His earliest writings were prayers to various saints and letters mainly addressed to the Norman monks who followed Lanfranc to Canterbury in 1070. Then followed the *Monologion* and the *Proslogion* (1078–9) and a series of philosophical and theological works, *De Veritate*, *De Libero Arbitrio* and *De Casu Diaboli*, as well as an introduction to dialectic entitled *De Grammatico*. Meanwhile Abbot Herluin of Bec had died in 1078, and Anselm succeeded to the Abbacy of Bec. From now on he paid several visits to England, where he renewed his personal contact with Lanfranc and the former monks of Bec at Canterbury, and won the respect of *William I and many of the barons.

On Lanfranc's death (1089) the archbishopric of Canterbury was vacant until 1093, but in March of this year King William II, then gravely ill, was persuaded to appoint an archbishop. He nominated Anselm, who reluctantly consented, and he was consecrated in December 1093. Disputes had already broken out between him and the King over the lands and tenants of the archbishopric, and these disputes continued with increasing violence until 1097. They were further complicated by disputes over the recognition of Pope *Urban II, over the right of the Archbishop to hold a council, and finally over Anselm's wish to go to Rome for Papal advice. In the end, after a series of violent disputes which are fully described by Anselm's biographer, *Eadmer, the King allowed him to go and he reached Rome in April 1098.

During the previous five years of conflict Anselm had not been unproductive theologically. In 1095 he had completed his *De Incarnatione Verbi* which he had begun before he left Bec; and in 1098 in Italy he completed the greatest of his theological works, *Cur Deus Homo*. In October 1098 he attended the Council of Bari and defended the *Double Procession against the Greeks with arguments later embodied in his *De Processione Sancti Spiritus*. At the Vatican Council of April 1099 he first learned of the Papal decrees against lay *investiture, and when the new King Henry I recalled him to England on William II's death (2 Aug. 1100) he insisted on observing these decrees without compromise. Consequently he refused to renew the homage he had paid to William II or to consecrate bishops whom Henry had invested. After more than two years of argument, in 1103 Anselm agreed to go to Rome again to try to get a Papal relaxation of the decrees on Henry's behalf. When this attempt failed he resigned himself to a further period of exile which lasted until 1107, when the Pope and King agreed to a compromise behind Anselm's back. In the last two years of his life Anselm held a council which enforced clerical *celibacy and he became increasingly engaged in the long-standing conflict with York over the primacy of Canterbury. He died on 21 April 1109.

Both as a philosopher and a theologian, Anselm has a foremost place among medieval thinkers. His was the most luminous and penetrating intellect between St *Augustine and St *Thomas Aquinas. He differed from most of his predecessors in preferring to defend the faith by intellectual reasoning instead of employing scriptural and patristic authorities. The object of his *Monologion* was to establish the being of God solely on rational grounds, though he claimed that everything in it was derived from, and could be supported by, the words of St Augustine. In the *Proslogion* this reasoning was given the more systematic form of the *ontological argument (q.v.). Anselm here maintained that if we mean by God (as he held that we do) 'that than which nothing greater can be thought' (*id quo nihil maius cogitari possit*), then we cannot think of this entity except as existing; for, if it did not exist, it would not be 'that than which nothing greater can be thought'. This argument, which seems to imply that the power to think of such a Being implies the existence of a Being consistent with the terms of the definition, was at once challenged by Gaunilo, a monk of Marmoutier, who retorted with an argument similar to that later used by I. *Kant. Anselm, however, held the argument relating to degrees of being was valid in this single case.

Like St Augustine, Anselm saw in faith the precondition of the right use of reason ('credo ut intelligam'); but it yet remains our duty, so far as we can, to exercise our minds in apprehending revealed truth. The whole of his theology is a working out of this programme. His *Cur Deus Homo* was the most considerable contribution to the theology of the *Atonement in the Middle Ages. It interpreted the doctrine in terms of the satisfaction which is needed to restore the universal harmony of the Creation dislocated by sin. He strongly repudiated the notion, current since *Origen and St *Gregory of Nyssa, that the devil had rights over fallen man which it was a leading purpose of the Cross to satisfy. He was also the author of many letters. Of these, the earlier ones (before 1093) are important for Anselm's spiritual and monastic teaching, and those written while he was Archbishop give the fullest surviving account of the ecclesiastical disputes of his pontificate.

Feast day, 21 April. It seems unlikely that he was ever formally canonized, despite several attempts from 1163 onwards, but his cult became firmly established in the later Middle Ages; in 1720 *Clement XI declared him a '*Doctor of the Church'.

The unsatisfactory edn. of Anselm's Works by the *Maurist, G. Gerberon, OSB (Paris, 1675) is repr. in J. P. Migne, *PL* 158 and 159. Crit. edn. by F. S. Schmitt, OSB (begun Seckau, 1938; repr. and cont., 6 vols., Edinburgh, 1946–61). Eng. tr. of vols. 1–2 by J. Hopkins and H. Richardson (4 vols.: 1, London, Toronto, and New York, 1974; 2–4, Toronto and New York, 1976), with extensive bibl. Unfinished fragments and reports of Anselm's teaching pr. in *Memorials of St Anselm*, ed. R. W. Southern and F. S. Schmitt (Auctores Britannici Medii Aevi, 1; 1969). The principal sources for his life are the 'Historia Novorum' and the 'Vita Anselmi' by his chaplain, Eadmer, ed. M. Rule (Rolls Series, 81; 1884); 'Vita Anselmi' also ed., with Eng. tr., by R. W. Southern (London [1962]); Eng. tr. of 'Historia Novorum' by G. Bosanquet (ibid., 1964). Modern studies by R. W. *Church (London, 1870) and R. W. Southern, *Saint Anselm and his Biographer: A study of monastic life and thought 1059–c.1130* (Birkbeck Lectures, 1959; Cambridge 1963); id., *Saint Anselm: A Portrait in a Landscape* (ibid., 1990); for a different view, see S. N. Vaughn, *Anselm of Bec and Robert of Meulan* (Los Angeles and London, 1987). M. J. Charlesworth, *St Anselm's Proslogion* (Oxford 1965), incl. text, Eng. tr., and an account of recent interpretations of Anselm's argument for the existence of God; there is an older and highly original interpretation by K. *Barth, *Fides Quaerens Intellectum* (Munich, 1931; 2nd edn., Zollikon, 1958; Eng. tr., 1960); on this question also R. [J.] Campbell, *From Belief to Understanding: A Study of Anselm's Proslogion Argument on the Existence of God* (Canberra, 1976). D. P. Henry, *The De Grammatico of St Anselm* (University of Notre Dame Publications in Medieval Studies, 18; Notre Dame, Ind., 1964), includes text and Eng. tr.; id., *The Logic of Saint Anselm* (Oxford, 1967); id., *Commentary on De Grammatico: The Historical-Logical Dimensions of a Dialogue of St Anselm's* (Synthese Historical Library, 8; Dordrecht and Boston [1974]). J. McIntyre, *St Anselm and his Critics: A Re-interpretation of the Cur Deus Homo* (Edinburgh, 1954). J. Hopkins, *A Companion to the Study of St Anselm* (Minneapolis, 1972). G. R. Evans, *Anselm and Talking about God* (Oxford, 1978); id., *Anselm* (1989). P. Gilbert, SJ, *Dire l'Ineffable: Lecture du 'Monologion' de S. Anselme* (1984). F. S. Schmitt in *NCE* 1 (1967), pp. 581–3, s.v. See also bibl. to CUR DEUS HOMO.

Anselm (Ansellus) of Laon (d. 1117), 'Laudunensis',

theologian. It is not known where he studied. The statement usually made that he was educated at *Bec under St *Anselm lacks foundation. Towards the end of the 11th cent. he was teaching at the cathedral school at Laon, where he was joined by his brother Ralph (d. 1133). Anselm seems to have combined the chancellorship with being dean of the cathedral (1106–14) and archdeacon (1115–17). He was famous as a teacher of the liberal arts as well as of theology. His theological teaching was given in lectures on the Books of the Bible, in the course of which points of interest were discussed as they arose in elementary *quaestio* form with reference to the authority of the Fathers. After his death these were reworked and enlarged into systematic 'Summae', of which the two most important are the 'Sententiae divinae paginae' and the 'Sententiae Anselmi'. Anselm was traditionalist in his views and stuck close to the Fathers, but his methods were new. In his lectures on the Bible he discussed the substance of the text and so opened the way for systematic enquiry. He was an influential teacher, and among those who came to his school were *William of Champeaux, *Gilbert de la Porrée, and Peter *Abelard.

The corpus of Anselm's work is not yet settled, but it is certain that he arranged commentaries (*Glossae*) on the Psalter, the Pauline Epistles ('Pro altercatione'), and on the Gospel of St John, which were the foundation of the *Glossa ordinaria*.

The edn. of works ascribed to him in J. P. Migne (*PL* 162. 1187–586) is unsatisfactory. The text of the two comm. is given in the edns. of *Nicholas of Lyra. The *Enarrationes in Evangelium S. Matthaei* is a work of the middle of the 12th cent., possibly by Geoffrey Babion (see D. van den Eynde, OFM, in *RTAM* 26 (1959), pp. 50–84). For his life see G. Lefèvre, *De Anselmo Laudunensi Scholastico* (Paris thesis; Évreux, 1895), and A. *Wilmart, OSB, 'Un commentaire des Psaumes restitué à Anselme de Laon', *RTAM* 8 (1936), pp. 325–44 [but this comm. is not his work]. For his work, O. Lottin, OSB, *Psychologie et Morale aux XIIe et XIIIe Siècles*, 5 (Gembloux, 1959), esp. pp. 9–183. F. P. Bliemetzrieder, *Anselms von Laon Systematische Sentenzen* (BGPM 18, Hefte 2–3; 1919); H. Weisweiler, SJ, *Das Schrifttum der Schule Anselms von Laon und Wilhelms von Champeaux in deutschen Bibliotheken* (ibid. 33, Hefte 1–2; 1936). B. Smalley, *The Study of the Bible in the Middle Ages* (3rd edn., Oxford, 1983), pp. ix f. and 49–51. M. *Grabmann, *Die Geschichte der scholastischen Methode*, 2 (1911), pp. 136–68; A. M. Landgraf, *Einführung in die Geschichte der theologischen Literatur der Frühscholastik unter dem Gesichtspunkte der Schulenbildung* (Regensburg, 1948), pp. 55–60; rev. Fr. tr. (Montreal and Paris, 1973), pp. 67–74.

Anselm of Lucca, Pope (d. 1073). See ALEXANDER II.

Anselm of Lucca, St (*c*.1035–86). He is not to be confused with his uncle, Pope *Alexander II (q.v.; he was also Bp. Anselm I of Lucca, 1056–73), by whom he was nominated to the see of Lucca in 1073. After hesitation he accepted investiture from *Henry IV, but resigned his bishopric and retired to a monastery, prob. St-Gilles on the Rhône. In 1075, at the insistence of *Gregory VII, he resumed his see; he lived an austere life and sought to impose strict discipline on an unwilling chapter. Prob. late in 1080 partisans of Henry IV expelled him from Lucca. From that time he was Gregory's standing legate in Lombardy. He made a collection of canons (*c*.1083) and wrote a polemical treatise in support of Gregory against the antipope ('Contra Guibertum et Sequaces eius', 1085/6). Feast day, 18 Mar.

His *Liber contra Guibertum*, the capitula of his *Collectio Canonum*, and extracts from his *Collectanea* are repr. in J. P. Migne, *PL* 149. 445–536; crit. edn. of his *Liber contra Guibertum* by E. Bernheim in *MGH*, Libelli de lite, 1 (1891), pp. 517–28; the unfinished edn. of the *Collectio Canonum* by F. Thaner (Innsbruck, 2 fascs , 1906–15; repr , Aalen, 1965) is unsatisfactory; it prints only bks. 1–10 and 11, caps. 1–15; bk. 13, ed. by E. Pásztor in *Sant'Anselmo, Mantova e la Lotta per le Investiture: Atti del Convegno Internazionale di Studi (Mantova, 23–24–25 maggio 1986)*, ed. P. Golinelli (Bologna, 1987), pp. 405–21. The principal authority for his life is the Vita formerly attributed to Bardo, ed. R. Wilmans in *MGH*, Scriptores, 12 (1856), pp. 1–35. There is also a metrical Life by Rangerius, Bp. of Lucca, of 1096/9, ed. E. Sackur, G. Schwartz, and B. Schmeidler, ibid. 30 (pt. 2; 1934), pp. 1152–307. P. Fournier, 'Observations sur diverses Recensions de la Collection canonique d'Anselme de Lucques', *Annales de l'Université de Grenoble*, 13 (1901), pp. 427–58; id. and G. Le Bras, *Histoire des Collections Canoniques en Occident*, 2 (1932), pp. 25–37 and 192–203. A. Stickler, 'Il Potere Coattivo Materiale della Chiesa nella Riforma Gregoriana secondo Anselmo di Lucca', in G. B. Borino (ed.), *Studi Gregoriani*, 2 (1947), pp. 235–85; G. B. Borino, 'Il Monacato e l'Investitura di Anselmo Vescovo di Lucca', ibid. 5 (1956), pp. 361–74. E. Pásztor, 'Una fonte per la storia dell'età gregoriana: la "Vita Anselmi episcopi Lucensis" ', *Bulletino dell'Istituto Storico Italiano*, 72 (1960), pp. 1–33; id., 'Motivi dell'ecclesiologia di Anselmo di Lucca. In margine a un sermone inedito', ibid. 77 (1965), pp. 45–104, incl. text. H. Fuhrmann, *Einfluss und Verbreitung der pseudoisidorischen Fälschungen*, 2 (Schriften der *MGH*, 24/2; 1973), pp. 509–522. P. Landau, 'Erweiterte Fassungen der Kanonessammlung des Anselm von Lucca aus dem 12. Jahrhundert', in *Sant'Anselmo*, op. cit., pp. 323–38. C. Violante in *Dizionario Biografico degli Italiani*, 3 (1961), pp. 399–407, s.v. 'Anselmo da Baggio'; T. Kölzer in *Lexikon des Mittelalters*, 1 (1980), cols. 679 f., s.v. 'Anselm, 3'.

Anskar, St (801–65), or **Ansgar**, the 'Apostle of the North'. A native of Picardy, he became a monk at *Corbie. Thence he went to Corvey in Westphalia, and later to *Denmark, whose king had been recently converted. He established a school in Schleswig, but was soon expelled by the local heathen. He then went to *Sweden, where he built the first Christian church. About 832 he was appointed by Gregory IV Bp. of Hamburg and c.848 first Abp. of Bremen. In 854 he was in Denmark again, converted Erik, King of Jutland, and did much to mitigate the horrors of the slave trade. After his death the Scandinavian countries relapsed completely into paganism. In Germany he is also known as 'St Scharies'. Feast day, 3 Feb.

The principal authority is the Life attributed to Rimbert, his successor in the see of Bremen (crit. edn. by G. Waitz in Scriptores Rerum Germanicarum, 1884; rev., with Ger. tr. and introd., by W. Trillmich in id. and R. Buchner (eds.), *Quellen des 9. und 11. Jahrhunderts zur Geschichte der Hamburgischen Kirchen und des Reiches* (1961), pp. 3–133; Eng. tr., with introd., notes and bibl., by C. H. Robinson, 1921). W. Levison, 'Die echte und die verfälschte Gestalt von Rimberts Vita Anskarii', *Zeitschrift des Vereins für Hamburgische Geschichte*, 23 (1919), pp. 89–146; repr. in Levison's *Aus Rheinischer und Frankischer Frühzeit* (Düsseldorf, 1948), pp. 567–609, with further art. repr. pp. 610–30. G. H. Kippel, *Historische Forschungen und Darstellungen*, 2: *Lebensbeschreibung des Erzbischofs Ansgar* (1845), with text of St Anskar's 'Pigmenta', pp. 230–50, and other important docs. in appendices. E. de Moreau, SJ, *Saint Anschaire* (Museum Lessianum, Section Missiologique, 12; 1930); P. Oppenheim, OSB, *Der heilige Ansgar und die Anfänge des Christentums in den nordischen Ländern* (1931). C. J. A. Opper-

mann, *The English Missionaries in Sweden and Finland* (1937), pp. 38–45, 162–4.

Anson By-law. The law allowing a child to be withdrawn from a primary school during any time allotted to religious observance or instruction if the parent so desires and if arrangement has been made for him to attend religious observance or instruction elsewhere. It was so named after Sir William Reynell Anson (1843–1914), who was Parliamentary Secretary to the Board of Education when the Education Act of 1902 was passed. The Education Act of 1936 made the principles of this by-law everywhere applicable, and a similar provision was retained in the Education Reform Act 1988 (sect. 9).

ante-chapel. The W. end of certain medieval college chapels, which usually projects N. and S. of the choir, from which it is separated by a screen. It is structurally a truncated nave, added to give technical completeness to the building and thus avoid the architectural anomaly of a chancel *in vacuo*.

Ante-Communion. In the C of E the earlier portion of the service of Holy Communion down to and including the Prayer for the Church Militant, esp. when recited without the remainder of the service. The essential parts of the full rite (offering and consecration of the Bread and Wine and the Communion) being omitted, it is in no sense a real Eucharist. Analogies have been found for it elsewhere in the Mass of the *Presanctified and the '*Dry Mass', but liturgically the only real parallel is the 'Mass of the Catechumens' in the early Church.

Antelapsarianism. See SUPRALAPSARIANISM.

antependium. A vesture or *frontal, varying in colour acc. to the ecclesiastical season, which hangs in front of the altar.

anthem. The Anglicized form of the word *antiphon. It was used originally in connection with Psalmody, but in current English usage it is commonly applied to sacred vocal music usually set to scriptural words. In the BCP it has the meanings antiphon (as in the preface 'Concerning the Service of the Church'), *canticle (so applied to the Easter 'Anthems', e.g., and by implication to Ps. 95), and its usual modern sense. A rubric introduced into the BCP in 1662 provides for an anthem after the third collect at Morning and Evening Prayer 'in Quires and Places where they sing'. In many modern Anglican liturgies, 'a canticle, psalm, hymn or anthem' may be sung before the Gospel or at various other points in the Eucharist.

From the late 16th to the 19th cent. anthems were divided into 'full anthems' in which the whole choir sang throughout, and 'verse anthems' in which sections ('verses') for one or more solo voices were contrasted with those for the full choir.

E. A. Wienandt and R. H. Young, *The Anthem in England and America* (1970). E. H. Fellowes, *English Cathedral Music from Edward VI to Edward VII* (1941; rev. by J. A. Westrup, 1969); N. Temperley, *The Music of the English Parish Church* (2 vols., Cambridge, 1979), esp. 1, pp. 162–7. P. Le Huray and R. T. Daniel in S. Sadie (ed.), *The New Grove Dictionary of Music and Musicians*, 1 (1980), pp. 454–63.

Anthony, St. See ANTONY, ST.

anthropology. In its more exact sense as used by theologians the study of man as contrasted, e.g., with that of God, or of angels, and more particularly the study 'of his creation, elevation to supernatural status, and his fall' (A. *Tanquerey). It enables the Christian apologist to exhibit the true nature and end of man, and his superior status to the animal creation, as against views which represent him as a purely biological species, or an economic unit, or a mass of psychological reflexes. This, the traditional meaning of the word, has been revived in theological discussion in the present century.

Esp. since the middle of the 19th cent., the word has been widely used for the science which studies the life and environment of primitive man, and in more recent times for the study of man in society. Social anthropology, as it is generally called, has profoundly affected modern man's understanding of himself, and theology has not escaped this influence.

(1) A collection of Patristic texts, in Eng. tr., is ed., with introd., by J. Patout Burns, *Theological Anthropology* (Sources of Early Christian Thought; Philadelphia [1981]). W. *Pannenberg, *Anthropologie in theologische Perspektive* (1983; Eng. tr., 1985). The subject is also treated in all manuals of dogmatic theology, incl. J. Feiner and others in *Mysterium Salutis*, ed. J. Feiner and M. Löhrer, 2 (Einsiedeln [1967]), pp. 559–706.

(2) Modern introds., which discuss the development of the subject, incl. L. [P.] Mair, *An Introduction to Social Anthropology* (Oxford, 1965; 2nd edn., 1972), and E. [R.] Leach, *Social Anthropology* (New York and Oxford, 1982). An earlier view is represented by R. Munro in *HERE* 1 (1908), pp. 561–73, s.v.

anthropomorphism (Gk. ἄνθρωπος, 'man', and μορφή, 'form'). In theology the term signifies the attribution to God of human characteristics, feelings, and situations. Jews and Christians have regularly insisted that God is strictly incomparable and incomprehensible; so there has always been much criticism of anthropomorphism within the Judaeo-Christian tradition. Yet that tradition has also wanted to stress that God is somehow personal; so anthropomorphism may also be regarded an an integral part of Judaeo-Christianity. These facts have led to much discussion concerning the interpretation and propriety of various anthropomorphic statements about God. In this connection, discussion has often centred around the notion of *analogy.

anthroposophy. A system evolved by R. *Steiner (q.v.), based on the premiss that the human soul can, of its own power, contact the spiritual world. The concepts of reincarnation and karma are central to it. It acknowledges Christ as a cosmic being, but its understanding of Him is very different from that of orthodox Christianity; He is regarded as a 'Sun Being' ('Sonnenwesen') who became incarnate at the turning-point of man's spiritual evolution, bringing the impulses of the highest Divine love to earth. Anthroposophy has found adherents esp. among those in search of religious experience outside the normal channels of Church life. It was condemned by the RC Church in 1919.

G. Kaufmann, *Fruits of Anthroposophy* (1922); [L.] F. Edmunds, *Anthroposophy: A Way of Life* (Hartfield, E. Sussex, 1982); G. Ahern, *Sun at Midnight: The Rudolf Steiner Movement*

and the Western Esoteric Tradition (Wellingborough, Northants, 1984). See also bibl. to STEINER, R.

Antiburgher. A member of the group in the Secession Church in Scotland which separated in 1747 from the '*Burgher' group because it refused to admit that an adherent of that Church could take the civil 'Burgess Oath'.

Antichrist. The prince of Christ's enemies. In the NT he is referred to by name only in 1 Jn. 2: 18, 22, 4: 3, and 2 Jn. 7 (where he is identified with those who deny the Incarnation). Many see him, however, in the strange beasts of Rev., sometimes thought to represent Rome, and in 'the man of sin' of 2 Thess. 2: 3–10, who will appear after a great apostasy before 'the day of the Lord' and sit in God's sanctuary, claiming to be God, but will be finally slain by Christ. Some have maintained that there was a Jewish Antichrist legend which was adopted and expanded by Christians; others have connected Antichrist not with a person but with an evil principle; yet others have seen in Antichrist a reference to some historical person—Caligula, *Simon Magus, or *Nero. The attempt of Caligula to set up his statue in the Temple at Jerusalem, the deification of the Emperor, and Emperor-worship, suggested strongly that Antichrist would come from imperial Rome; and the effect of the Neronian persecutions, particularly in view of Rev. 17: 8, 13: 3, and the uncertainty concerning Nero's grave, led men to expect Nero to return from the tomb. Acc. to *Jerome and *Augustine, many believed that St John the Divine was not dead but sleeping, waiting to testify against *Nero redivivus* as Antichrist. In the 4th cent. Antichrist was sometimes identified with the *Arian heresy, whilst *Cyril of Jerusalem states that he will be a magician who will take control of the Roman Empire, claim to be Christ, deceive the Jews by pretending to be the Son of David and rebuilding the Temple, and who, after persecuting the Christians, will be slain at the Second Advent by the Son of God (*Cat. Lect.* 15. 11–15). Since the Reformation, the identification of the Pope with Antichrist has often been made, esp. in the less-educated circles of Protestantism.

W. *Bousset, *Der Antichrist* (1895; Eng. tr., 1896). B. Rigaux, *L'Antéchrist et l'Opposition au royaume messianique dans l'Ancien et le Nouveau Testament* (Louvain, diss., Gembloux and Paris, 1932). G. C. Jenks, *The Origins and Early Development of the Antichrist Myth* (Beihefte zur *ZNTW*, 59; Berlin, 1991). R. K. Emmerson, *Antichrist in the Middle Ages: A Study of Medieval Apocalypticism, Art, and Literature* (Manchester, 1981). [J. E.] C. Hill, *Antichrist in Seventeenth-Century England* (Riddell Memorial Lectures, 1969; 1971). E. Lohmeyer in *RAC* 1 (1950), cols. 450–7, s.v., with bibl.

Anticlericalism. A liberal movement in politics and religion which affected many parts of Europe and Latin America in the 19th and 20th cents. It was directed against the RC Church as a State religion, claiming a monopoly of religious truth and wide political powers. The French Revolution, which established religious toleration for all religions and subjected the RC Church to the civil power, was a breakthrough for anticlericalism. The dechristianization movement of 1793–4 attacked the Catholic religion as such, but to be anticlerical and a Catholic believer was not as a rule a contradiction. After 1815 the RC Church in France and in Europe generally regained many (but not all) of its powers and privileges from governments, to serve as a bastion against revolution, and its identification with reactionary regimes and conservative social élites drove many liberals and democrats to anticlericalism. It was clear to them that to gain and retain power it would be necessary to curtail the political power of the Church, and in particular its control of education. Anticlericalism came in waves, notably after the revolutions of 1830 in *France and *Belgium, the triumphs of Liberals in *Portugal (1834) and *Spain (1836), in the Paris Commune of 1871, and the Spanish Republic of 1873. Subsequent outbursts followed the coming to power of French Republicans (1879) and Radicals (1902), of Belgian (1879) and Spanish (1885) Liberals, and the Portuguese Revolution of 1910. Anticlericalism was rife in *Mexico after the Revolution of 1910, but the formation of the independent Mexican State in 1821 had already (1833 and 1857) given rise to attacks on the RC Church, which in Latin America was regarded as an arm of Spanish colonialism. The movement towards national unification was thus a second force behind anticlericalism. The loyalty of Catholic clergy and laity to Rome was seen by state-builders as a challenge to the sovereign state. Italy, in particular, could not be fully unified until the temporal power of the Pope had been eliminated (1870). The Pope ordered the faithful to boycott the political life of the new state, confirming the anticlericalism of the Liberal parties which held power until 1921. Catholic populations incorporated into the periphery of the new German Empire were considered to be insufficiently loyal and were subjected to the anticlerical persecution of the *Kulturkampf in 1872–87. Limits to anticlericalism were often set by tactical considerations. To antagonize the religious feelings of electorates sometimes only increased the political threat to liberal regimes. Liberal and democratic movements tried to neutralize revolutionary socialists by harnessing them to an anticlerical front, but the menace of class war induced anticlericals and Catholic conservatives to rally in defence of private property. This was the case in Belgium in the 1880s and France and Spain in the 1890s. Faced by the emergence of Communism, the Papacy came to terms with the Italian Fascist state in 1929, the Third Reich in 1933, Vichy France in 1940, and General Franco's Spain in 1953. This accommodation did not, however, prevent the persecution of the Catholic Church in Germany by Hitler. The return of the liberal and democratic regimes in W. Europe after 1944 was marked by a certain resurgence of anticlericalism.

See also ASSOCIATIONS, LAW OF; CONCORDAT OF 1801; and articles on the countries concerned.

E. Faguet L'anticléricalisme (1906). P. A. Dykema and H. A. Oberman (eds.), Anticlericalism in Late Medieval and Early Modern Europe (Studies in Medieval and Reformation Thought, 51; Leiden etc., 1993). A. Mellor, Histoire de l'anticléricalisme français ([Tours] 1966); R. Rémond, L'Anticléricalisme en France de 1815 à nos jours (1976); P. Pierrard, L'Église et les ouvriers en France, 1840–1940 (1984); E. Lecanuet, L'Église de France sous la Troisième République (2 vols., 1907–10; rev. edn., 4 vols., 1930–1), passim; E. M. Acomb, The French Laic Laws 1879–1889: The First Anticlerical Campaign of the Third Republic (New York, 1941); M. O. Partin, Waldeck-Rousseau, Combes and the Church: The Politics of Anticlericalism 1899–1905 (Durham, NC, 1969). P. Vercauteren, 'La Place de Paul Janson dans la vie politique belge de 1877 à 1884', Res Publica, 11 (1969), pp. 383–404. A. C. Jemelo, Chiesa e Stato in Italia dal Risorgimento ad oggi (1955;

Eng. tr., Church and State in Italy 1850–1950, Oxford, 1960). J. C. Ullman, The Tragic Week: A Study of Anticlericalism in Spain, 1875–1912 (Cambridge, Mass., 1968); J. M. Sánchez, Reform and Reaction: The politico-religious background of the Spanish Civil War (Chapel Hill, NC [1964]); J. Andrés Gallego, La Política religiosa en España 1889–1913 (1975). D. L. Wheeler, Republican Portugal: A Political History 1910–1926 (Madison, Wis., 1978), esp. pp. 67–72. J. L. Mecham, Church and State in Latin America (Chapel Hill, NC, rev. edn., 1966). J. S. Conway, The Nazi Persecution of the Churches, 1933–45 (1968).

Antididagma. The reply issued in 1544 by the cathedral chapter of *Cologne to the plan set out by Abp. *Hermann of Wied in his Consultatio to reform Catholic practice. It was a moderate restatement of traditional principles and apparently mainly the work of J. *Gropper. Its language exercised a certain influence on the BCP of 1549.

The work orig. appeared in Ger. early in 1544 with the title Christliche und katholische Gegenberichtung eines ehrwürdigen Domcapitals zu Köln wider das Buch der genannten Reformation. The Lat. version, which followed soon afterwards, has a long title beginning Antididagma, seu Christianae et Catholicae Religionis per . . . Canonicos Metropolitanae Ecclesiae Colonien: Propugnatio (Cologne, 1544; repr. Paris, 1549). F. E. *Brightman, The English Rite, 1 (1915), pp. xlviii f.

antidoron. See PAIN BÉNIT.

antilegomena (Gk. τὰ ἀντιλεγόμενα). The word is used by *Eusebius of Caesarea (HE 3. 25. 3 f.) of those scriptural books of which the claim to be considered a part of the NT canon was disputed. He subdivided them into: (1) those 'generally recognized' (γνώριμοι), viz. Jas., Jude, 2 Pet., 2 and 3 Jn.; and (2) the 'spurious' (νόθοι), viz. the 'Acts of St *Paul', the 'Shepherd of *Hermas' the 'Apoc. of St *Peter', the 'Ep. of *Barnabas', the '*Didache', and (perhaps) Rev.

Anti-Marcionite Prologues. The short introductory prologues, prefixed to the Gospels of Mk., Lk., and Jn. (that of Mt., if it ever existed, has been lost), which are contained in some 40 MSS of the Vulgate. They were written in Greek, but only that to Luke has survived in its original language. D. de Bruyne and A. *Harnack held that they were the earliest of the extant Gospel Prologues, dating from the latter half of the 2nd cent., and thus threw important light on the origins of the Gospels. They are now held to have been neither directed against *Marcion, nor written so early, nor even to be of the same date.

Text in A. *Huck, H. *Lietzmann, and F. L. Cross, A Synopsis of the First Three Gospels (Tübingen, 1936), p. viii; also ed., with full discussion, by J. Regul (Vetus Latina. Ergänzende Schriftenreihe aus der Geschichte der Lateinischen Bibel, 6; 1969), with bibl. In Eng. there is a good summary of the points at issue, with refs. to de Bruyne and Harnack and subsequent discussions, in E. Haenchen, The Acts of the Apostles (Eng. tr., Oxford, 1971), pp. 10–12.

antiminsion, also **antimension** (Gk. ἀντιμήνσιον, 'instead of a table'). In the E. Church, the portable altar, consisting of a cloth of silk or linen, decorated with representations of the Passion, and usually of the entombment of Christ, and containing relics. It was originally intended for use when there was no properly consecrated altar, but is now always used, even on consecrated altars, in the manner of the W. *corporal, with another corporal, the *eileton, underneath it. It is first met with at about the beginning of the 9th cent.

antinomianism. A general name for the view that Christians are by grace set free from the need of observing any moral law. It was attributed to St *Paul by his opponents (Rom. 3: 8) because of his disparagement of the Mosaic Law in favour of the Law of the New Covenant 'written in the heart'—an internal impulse towards good—and strenuously repudiated by him. The charge of antinomianism was plausibly made against many of the *Gnostic sects, e.g. the *Carpocratians, who held that, as matter was so sharply opposed to spirit, bodily actions were indifferent and therefore licentiousness was wholly admissible. At the Reformation, antinomian teaching was revived, e.g. by the *Anabaptists and J. *Agricola, as following from the *Lutheran doctrine of *justification by faith. In England some antinomian sects developed under the Commonwealth.

antinomy. In philosophy, one of a pair of mutually conflicting laws or sequences of thought ('thesis' and 'antithesis'), each of which possesses, or appears to possess, equal validity. In the *Critique of Pure Reason* (1781), I. *Kant elaborated four antinomies, the purpose of which was to show the inconsistencies to which the understanding is driven when it applies itself to philosophical speculation and thus to demonstrate the impossibility of theoretical metaphysics. Their subjects are: (1) the spatial and temporal limitations of the physical world; (2) the divisibility of substances; (3) causality and freedom; and (4) the relation of the First Cause to the world.

Antioch. In size and importance, Antioch in Syria was the third city of the Roman Empire. As appears from Acts, a Christian community existed there from almost the earliest days, and it was here that the disciples of Christ were first called 'Christians' (Acts 11: 26). Acc. to tradition, the first bishop of the city was St *Peter, and by the beginning of the 2nd cent. the Church had an organization, with the celebrated St *Ignatius as its bishop. By the 4th cent. the see ranked after Rome and Alexandria as the third patriarchal see of Christendom, reaching its greatest extent of jurisdiction at the end of that cent. Gradually, however, the rise in power of the see of *Constantinople, and to a less extent the erection of *Jerusalem into a patriarchate, reduced the importance of Antioch, and its influence also suffered later from the *Nestorian and *Monophysite schisms (the latter supported by the civil power of the Saracens). At the Schism of 1054, the patriarchate supported Constantinople, but in 1100 the Orthodox Patriarch of Antioch withdrew to Constantinople, and the Crusaders appointed a Latin Patriarch. From the 14th cent. the Latin patriarchate has been only titular. The Orthodox Patriarch now resides at Damascus, the most important city in Syria. Other patriarchs, *Uniat and Monophysite, take the title of Antioch, though these also do not reside there. A small Turkish township now exists on the site, where excavations were carried out by a Franco-American expedition in 1931–9. See also ANTIOCHENE THEOLOGY.

M. Lequien, *Oriens Christianus*, 2 (Paris, 1740), cols. 669–1076, and 3 (ibid., 1740), cols. 1153–240. J. M. *Neale, *A History*

of the Holy Eastern Church*, 5, 'The Patriarchate of Antioch' (1873). E. S. Bouchier, *A Short History of Antioch, 300 B.C.–A.D. 1268* (Oxford, 1921). R. Devreesse, *Le Patriarcat d'Antioche depuis la paix de l'Église jusqu'à la conquête arabe* (1945). C. A. Papadopoulos, Ἱστορία τῆς Ἐκκλησίας Ἀντιοχείας (Alexandria, 1951). A. J. Festugière, OP, *Antioche païenne et chrétienne* (Bibliothèque des Écoles françaises d'Athènes et de Rome, 194; 1959). V. Corwin, *St Ignatius and Christianity in Antioch* (Yale Publications in Religion, 1; 1960). G. Downey, *A History of Antioch in Syria from Seleucus to the Arab Conquest* (Princeton, NJ, 1961). J. H. W. G. Liebeschuetz, *Antioch: City and Imperial Administration in the later Roman Empire* (Oxford, 1972). D. S. Wallace-Hadrill, *Christian Antioch: A Study of Early Christian Thought in the East* (1982). C. Cahen, *La Syrie du nord à l'époque des croisades et la principauté d'Antioche* (1940). G. W. Elderkin, R. Stillwell, and others, *Antioch-on-the-Orontes* (Publications of the Committee for the Excavation of Antioch and its Vicinity; vols. 1–3 (Princeton, NJ, etc., 1934–41, on excavations of 1934–9); subsequent vols. on specific classes of find, 1948 ff.). D. Levi, *Antioch Mosaic Pavements* (2 vols., 1947). C. Karalevskij in *DHGE* 3 (1924), cols. 563–703, s.v. 'Antioche', with detailed bibl.; G. Downey and G. A. Maloney in *NCE* 1 (1967), pp. 623–7, s.v.

Antioch, Council of (341). The 'Dedication Council' (*concilium in encaeniis*), held on the occasion of the consecration of *Constantine's 'Golden Church' at *Antioch, was the first of the many 4th-cent. councils in which efforts were made to abandon strict *Nicene theology. It was attended by 97 bishops besides the Emp. Constantius himself. No less than four creeds were put forward, all of them defective from the standpoint of orthodoxy since they were intended not to supplement, but to replace, that of *Nicaea.

The 25 (mainly disciplinary) 'Canons of Antioch' preserved in many of the ancient collections, both Greek and Latin, were long thought to have been the work of this Council but are now generally held to belong to a Council held at Antioch in 330.

Hardouin, 1, cols. 589–610; Mansi, 2 (1759), cols. 1305–50. Canons, with Fr. tr. and introd., pr. in Joannou, 1, pt. 2 (1962), pp. 100–26; crit. edn. of Lat. texts in C. H. *Turner, *EOMIA* 2.2 (1913), pp. 215–320. Hefele and Leclercq, 1 (pt. 2; 1907), pp. 702–33. E. *Schwartz, 'Zur Geschichte des Athanasius, IX', *Nachr.* (Gött.), 1911, pp. 469–522, repr. in his *Gesammelte Schriften*, 3 (1959), pp. 265–334. W. Schneemelcher, 'Die Kirchweihsynode von Antiochien 341', in A. Lippold and N. Himmelmann (eds.), *Bonner Festgabe Johannes Straub zum 65. Geburtstag* (Beiheft der Bonner Jahrbücher, 39; 1977), pp. 319–46. H. [H.] Hess, *The Canons of the Council of Sardica AD 343* (Oxford, 1958), pp. 145–50 (Appendix II; 'The Origin of the Canons of Antioch'). For the Creeds connected with the Council, see J. N. D. Kelly, *Early Christian Creeds* (1950; 3rd edn., 1972), pp. 263–74; also G. Bardy, *Recherches sur S. Lucien d'Antioche et son école* (1936), pp. 85–132. *CPG* 4 (1980), pp. 15 f. (nos. 8556–9); cf. p. 11 (nos. 8535 f.).

Antiochene theology. This is a modern designation for a style of theology associated with the Church at *Antioch, contrasted with *Alexandrian theology. In scriptural exegesis it placed more emphasis on the literal and historical sense, though still stressing the importance of insight (θεωρία) into the deeper, spiritual meaning of the biblical text. Some earlier figures, such as *Paul of Samosata and *Lucian of Antioch, are loosely associated with this style of approach, but it is primarily exemplified by a tradition of theological teaching, developed largely in reaction to

*Arianism in the 4th and 5th cents. Its most famous exponents are *Diodore of Tarsus, John *Chrysostom, *Theodore of Mopsuestia, *Nestorius, and *Theodoret of Cyrrhus. In its Christological teaching, stress was laid on the humanity of Christ and the reality of His moral choices. To achieve this, and to preserve the impassibility of His Divine nature, the unity of His person was described in a looser way than in Alexandrian theology. It was primarily this difference, and the mutual suspicion to which it gave rise, that was the theological nub of the Nestorian controversy. The tradition was discredited after the Council of *Ephesus (431), and did not altogether recover its prestige when the opposing tendency, which produced *Apollinarianism and *Eutychianism, fell into disrepute.

D. S. Wallace-Hadrill, *Christian Antioch: A Study of Early Christian Thought in the East* (1982). F. Loofs, *Paulus von Samosata* (TU 44, Heft 5; 1924); R. V. Sellers, *Two Ancient Christologies* (1940), pp. 107–257. E. Boularand, 'Aux sources de la doctrine d'Arius. [II.] La théologie antiochienne', *Bulletin de Littérature Ecclésiastique*, 68 (1967), pp. 241–72. A. Vaccari, SJ, 'La "teoria" esegetica antiochena', *Biblica*, 15 (1934), pp. 94–101; J. Guillet, SJ, 'Les Exégèses d'Alexandrie et d'Antioche, conflit ou malentendu?', *Rech. S.R.* 34 (1947), pp. 257–302; R. M. Grant, *A Short History of the Interpretation of the Bible* (2nd edn., 1965), pp. 69–79; C. Schäublin, *Untersuchungen zu Methode und Herkunft der Antiochenischen Exege* (Theophaneia, 23; Cologne and Bonn, 1974); B. de Margerie, SJ, *Introduction à l'histoire de l'exégèse*, 1 (1980), pp. 188–213. A. van Roey in *NCE* 1 (1967), pp. 627 f., s.v. 'Antioch, School of'.

Antiochus Epiphanes (d. 164 BC), King of Syria from 175 BC. (The epithet 'Epiphanes' means 'illustrious'.) His policy of attaining political unity by propagating Greek culture eventually met with violent resistance from the Jews. At first he succeeded in using as his pawns the high priests Jason and Menelaus, who had in turn bought the *high priesthood from him. In 169 BC he attacked *Jerusalem and despoiled the *Temple, and in 167 BC made a renewed and fiercer onslaught in a determination to exterminate Judaism. Jewish customs were forbidden under penalty of death, the Temple defiled and pagan cults instituted. This led to the *Maccabean revolt, after which Antiochus retired to Persia, where he died. His policy and actions are described in the Books of the Maccabees.

The chief biblical refs. are Dan. 11: 11–45; 1 Macc. 1: 10–64, 2 and 3, and 6: 1–16; and 2 Macc. 4: 7–9: 29. The other authorities include Livy (41. 20), Polybius (26. 1; 28. 18–20; 29. 24–7; 31. 9; etc.), and Diodorus Siculus (29. 32, 31. 16, and 34. 1), as well as *Josephus. H. L. Jansen, *Die Politik Antiochos' des IV* (Skrifter utgitt av det Norske Videnskaps-Akademi, 1; Oslo, 1942. Historisk-Filosofisk Klasse no. 3; 1943). O. Mørkholm, *Antiochus IV of Syria* (Classica et Mediaevalia, Dissertationes '8' [7]; Copenhagen, 1966). E. *Schürer, *The History of the Jewish People in the Age of Jesus Christ*, rev. Eng. tr. by G. Vermes and others, 1 (Edinburgh, 1973), pp. 128 f., 146–8, and 150–5.

Antipas, Herod. See HEROD FAMILY.

antiphon (Gk. ἀντίφωνον, orig. 'something sung alternately by two choirs'). In the W. Church, sentences, usually from Scripture, recited before and after the *Psalms and *Canticles in the Divine Office. They vary with the season or feast, and are often intended to indicate the spirit in which the (invariable) Psalms and Canticles are sung. They are now recited completely before and after the Psalms or Canticles. The name is also applied to the Four Anthems of Our Lady, sung, according to the season, at the close of *Compline. In the E. Church the word is used in a different sense, and applied to the three anthems sung antiphonally in the early part of the Eucharistic Liturgy, and varying acc. to the feast or season. There are also antiphons at *Vespers and *Mattins, consisting of Psalms sung antiphonally, and at other offices and functions. Such antiphonal singing may be divided either between two choirs or else between a soloist and the choir, and may consist either of verses sung thus in alternation, or of a Psalm broken at intervals by a refrain. See also ANTHEM.

Antiphonal (also **Antiphonary**). Orig. the liturgical book in the W. Church containing all parts both of the Choir *Office and of the *Mass which were sung by the choir antiphonally. It therefore included the *Graduale. In later times the Office (*Antiphonarium officii*) and Mass (*Antiphonarium missae*) portions were separated, and in current usage the word is restricted to the former book. The official 'Vatican edition' of 1907 is now being revised. The second volume of the *Antiphonale Romanum, Liber Hymnarius* (Solesmes, 1983) contains the *invitatory antiphons, the Psalter, and some fifty *responsories.

antipope. A person set up as Bp. of Rome in opposition to the person already holding the see or held to be lawfully elected to it. There have been about thirty-five antipopes in the history of the Church.

A. *Mercati (Eng. tr.), 'The New List of the Popes', *Mediaeval Studies*, 9 (1947), pp. 71–80, incl. list of Popes and antipopes. A. Amanieu in *DDC* 1 (1935), cols. 598–622, s.v. 'Antipape'.

Antitrinitarianism. A term used to denote various professedly Christian systems which agree only in rejecting the Catholic doctrine of the *Trinity. Such were those of the *Ebionite Jewish Christians of the 1st cent., who thought that to recognize Christ as God would involve the abandonment of *Monotheism; the *Gnostic sects of the 2nd, who subordinated Christ to God as being merely a manifestation of the Father, instead of a coequal Person (see SUBORDINATIONISM); and the Monarchian *Modalists who refused to admit distinct Persons within the Trinity, regarding the Son and Holy Spirit as aspects of the Father's Being. The *Arian view of Christ's Person, which in all its forms fell short of conceding Him full divinity, is also antitrinitarian. In the Middle Ages several obscure pseudo-mystical and pantheistic sects held antitrinitarian views. For the better-known post-Reformation forms of Antitrinitarianism, see under SOCINUS and UNITARIANISM. Unitarianism is the most radical form in which it exists today.

Antonelli, Giacomo (1806–76), Cardinal Secretary of State. He never proceeded beyond the diaconate, to which he was ordained in 1840. After holding various offices under *Gregory XVI, he was created a *cardinal by *Pius IX on his accession (1847). In 1848 he arranged the flight of the Pope to Gaeta, where he was appointed Secretary of State. Returning to Rome in 1850, he influenced the Pope in favour of a reactionary and ultramontane policy, and virtually became the temporal ruler of Rome down to 1870, being nicknamed the 'Red Pope'. He opposed the convening of the First *Vatican Council, and while it was sitting advised the Pope to drop the *Infallibility question. After 1870 he was chiefly concerned with maintaining the claims of the Papacy in its struggle with the *Risorgimento*. A statesman rather than a prelate, he was loaded with praise by his friends, but regarded as unscrupulous by his enemies.

Il Carteggio Antonelli-Sacconi (1858–1860), ed. M. Gabriele (Istituto per la Storia del Risorgimento Italiano, Biblioteca Scientifica, 2nd ser. 41–2; 1962); *Il Carteggio Antonelli-Barili 1859–1861*, ed. C. Menegussi Rostagni (ibid. 65; 1973); *Il Carteggio Antonelli-De Luca 1859–1861*, ed. id. (ibid. 72; 1983). C. Falconi, *Il Cardinale Antonelli: Vita e carriera del Richelieu italiano nella Chiesa di Pio IX* (Milan, 1983). F. J. Coppa, *Cardinal Giacomo Antonelli and Papal Politics in European Affairs* (Albany, NY [1990]). P. Pirri, 'Il Cardinale Antonelli tra il mito e la storia', *Rivista di Storia della Chiesa in Italia*, 12 (1958), pp. 81–120. R. Aubert in *Dizionario Biografico degli Italiani*, 3 (1961), pp. 484–93, s.v.

Antonians. Several communities claiming the patronage of, or descent from, St *Antony of Egypt.

(1) The original disciples of St Antony in the desert, with whom the present Antonians of the *Maronites [(3) below] in the Near East claim (but on insufficient historical evidence) continuity.

(2) A congregation founded by Gaston de Dauphiné in 1095, which spread through France, Spain, and Italy, and survived till the French Revolution. They were known as the 'Hospital Brothers of Saint Antony'.

(3) An order in the *Armenian Church, founded in the 17th cent. to maintain the connection with the RC Church. There are also Antonians among the Chaldean and Maronite *Uniats, and the monastery of Mount *Sinai among the Orthodox claims to follow the rule of St Antony.

(4) A congregation founded in Flanders in 1615.

The name was also taken by an antinomian sect founded in Switzerland in 1802 by a certain Anton Unternäher (1759–1824; hence the name) who pretended to be the redeemer of mankind.

On (1) and (3), Heimbucher, 1, pp. 67–76. E. El-Hayek in *NCE* 1 (1967), pp. 644–6; J. Gribomont, OSB, and others in *DIP* 1 (1974), cols. 687–98, both s.v.
On (2), V. Advielle, *Histoire de l'Ordre Hospitalier de Saint Antoine le Viennois et ses Commanderies et Prieurés*, 1 (1883); L. Maillet-Guy, *La Commanderie de Saint-Antoine de Vienne en Dauphiné* (Vienne [1925]), and other works of this author. Heimbucher, 1, pp. 423 f. I. Ruffino in *DIP* 2 (1975), cols. 134–41, s.v. 'Canonici Regolari di Sant'Agostino di Sant'Antonio', with bibl.

Antoninus, St (1389–1459), Abp. of Florence. He joined the *Dominican Order in 1404/5, under the influence of Bl John Dominic (c.1355–1419), and was one of the first members of his new foundation at Fiesole, which was intended to embody the Dominican reform, with its desire to return to the primitive observances and austerities of the Order. Antoninus quickly rose to prominence and was Prior successively in Cortona, Fiesole, Naples, Rome, and Florence. In 1432 he was appointed Vicar General for the Dominican reform in Tuscany. In 1436 he became the first Dominican Prior of the former *Sylvestrine monastery of San Marco, Florence, which had just been given to the Dominicans and which was to be splendidly restored and

enlarged by the munificence of Cosimo de' Medici. In 1446 he was made Abp. of Florence by *Eugenius IV. The appointment is said to have been due to the advice of Fra *Angelico, but this is not certain. By his integrity Antoninus became the counsellor of popes and statesmen, and by his care for the sick and needy in times of plague and famine endeared himself to the people. As a writer he was distinguished for his 'Summa theologica moralis', several treatises on the Christian life, and a general history of the world. As an economist, he was among the first to adapt Catholic traditions to modern conditions, maintaining that money invested in business was true capital and that it was not therefore necessarily wrong to receive interest on it. Feast day, 10 May.

His works are listed in Kaeppeli, 1 (1970), pp. 80–100, with bibl. *Summa Theologica* (first pub. Venice, 1477–9), ed. P. *Ballerini (Verona, 1740). R. Morçay (ed.), *Chroniques de Saint Antonin: Fragments originaux du titre xxii, 1378–1459* (1913). Life by Francesco di Castiglione, a member of Antoninus' household, pr. in *AASS*, Mai. 1 (1680), pp. 313–25, with almost contemporary additions by Leonard de Suburti, OP, pp. 326–34, and account, with extracts, of the Process of Canonization, pp. 335–51. R. Morçay, *Saint Antonin archevêque de Florence, 1389–1459* (1914). J. B. Walker [OP], *The 'Chronicles' of Saint Antoninus* (Catholic University of America Studies in Medieval History, 6; 1933); W. T. Gaughan, *Social Theories of Saint Antoninus from his Summa Theologica* (Catholic University of America Studies in Sociology, 35; '1950' [1951]). S. Orlandi, OP, 'S. Antonino: La sua famiglia. Gli anni giovanili', *Memorie Domenicane*, 76 (1959), pp. 81–118; id., 'I primi cinque anni di episcopato', ibid., pp. 119–72; id., 'Il Convento di S. Domenico in Fiesole', ibid. 77 (1960), pp. 3–36 and 93–140; id., 'Gli ultimi otto anni di episcopato', ibid., pp. 169–248; also issued as *S. Antonino* (2 vols., Florence, 1959–60). U. Horst, OP, 'Papst, Bischöfe und Konzil nach Antonin von Florenz', *RTAM* 32 (1965), pp. 76–116. R. [A.] de Roover, *San Bernardino of Siena and Sant'Antonino of Florence: Two Great Economic Thinkers of the Middle Ages* (Kress Library of Business and Economics, 19; Boston, 1967). S. Orlandi, OP, *Bibliografia Antoniniana: Descrizione dei manoscritti, della Vita e delle Opere di S. Antonino* (Vatican City, 1961). J. B. Walker, OP, in *NCE* 1 (1967), pp. 646 f., s.v.

Antony, St, of Egypt (251?–356), hermit. About 269 Antony gave away his possessions, and devoted himself to a life of asceticism, and c.285 retired completely into the desert, to the 'Outer Mountain' at Pispir, where he is said to have fought with demons under the guise of wild beasts. The holiness and ordered discipline of his life, esp. compared with the more eccentric austerities of other solitaries, attracted a number of disciples; and c.305 he came out of his solitude to organize them into a community of hermits who lived under rule (an innovation) but with little common life comparable to that of the later religious orders. About 310 Antony retired again into solitude to his 'Inner Mountain' (still called Dêr Mar Antonios, near the Red Sea), but he later exercised his influence in support of the Nicene party in the *Arian controversy, in which he was closely associated with St *Athanasius. Towards the end of his life the numbers of those who turned to the solitary life of the desert increased and his authority grew correspondingly. The evidence for his life is the 'Vita Antonii', traditionally regarded as by Athanasius, though many scholars attribute it to an Athanasian milieu rather than to Athanasius himself. Feast day, 17 Jan.

The seven Epp. of Antony, mentioned by *Jerome (De vir. ill. 88) and surviving in toto only in a Lat. tr. pr. in J. P. Migne, *PG*

40. 977–1000, are prob. genuine; Georgian version with Coptic fragments, ed. G. Garitte (CSCO 148; 1955, with Lat. tr., ibid. 149; 1955); Eng. tr. by D. J. Chitty (Fairacres Publications, 50; Oxford, 1975); Fr. tr., with introd. by A. Louf, OCR (Spiritualité Orientale, 19; Bellefontaine, 1976). The collection of twenty *Epp.* printed *PG* 40. 999–1066, a working over of the earlier set through the Arabic, appears to contain nothing further authentic. A letter to Abbot Theodore and his monks 'On proper Repentance' (*PG* 40. 1065) seems to be genuine; but the twenty Sermons (40. 961–78) and the so-called 'Rule of St Antony' (40. 1065–79) are spurious. Crit. ed. of the 'Vita Antonii' (*PG* 26. 835–978) by G. J. M. Bartelink (SC 400; 1994). It survives also in a number of early versions; Lat. text ed. G. Garitte (Études de Philologie, d'Archéologie et d'Histoire anciennes publiées par l'Institut Historique Belge de Rome, 3; 1939); it is also ed. H. Hoppenbrouwers, OSB (Latinitas Christianorum Primaeva, 14; Nijmegen, 1960), and by G. J. M. Bartelink, with introd. by C. Mohrmann, and Ital. tr. (Vite dei Santi, 1 [Milan] 1974); Syriac text ed. R. Draguet (CSCO 417, with discussion and Fr. tr., 418; 1980). Modern Eng. trs. by R. T. Meyer (ACW 10; 1950) and R. C. Gregg (Classics of Western Spirituality, 1980). L. Bouyer, Cong. Orat., *La Vie de Saint Antoine* (1950); B. Steidel, OSB (ed.), *Antonius Magnus Eremita 356–1956: Studia ad Antiquum Monachismum Spectantia* (Studia Anselmiana, 38; 1956). H. Dörries, 'Die Vita Antonii als Geschichtsquelle', *Nachr.* (Gött.), 1949, pp. 357–410, repr., with additional material, in Dörries, *Wort und Stunde*, 1 (Göttingen, 1966), pp. 145–224. S. Rubenson, *The Letters of St Antony: Origenist Theology, Monastic Tradition and Making of a Saint* (Bibliotheca Historico-Ecclesiastica Lundensis, 24; 1990). J. Quasten, *Patrology*, 3 (Utrecht and Westminster, Md., 1960), pp. 39–45, 148–53; Altaner and Stuiber (1978), pp. 261 f., 276, 604, with further bibl. *CPG*, 2 (1974), pp. 60–3 (nos. 2330–50), and pp. 16 f. (no. 2101). G. Bardy in *Dict. Sp.* 1 (1937), cols. 702–8, s.v.

Antony, St, of Padua (1188/95–1231), *Franciscan friar. Born in Lisbon, perhaps of noble family, he was educated at the cathedral school and when he was 15 joined the *Augustinian canons nearby. Two years later he was transferred to Coimbra. He was disappointed by the religious spirit of the house and deeply moved when the relics of some Franciscan missionaries killed in Morocco were brought to Coimbra in 1220. He obtained his release and received the Franciscan habit in the chapel of San Antonio at Olivares, near Coimbra, changing his name from Ferdinand to Antony. Late in 1220 he sailed to Morocco, but he was forced by illness to return to Europe. He attended the General Chapter at *Assisi in 1221, and was sent to the hermitage of San Paolo near Forlì. When he was called upon to preach at an ordination, his unexpected eloquence and learning were discovered. With the approval of St *Francis, he was appointed lector in theology to the Order, being the first to hold the post. He taught at *Bologna (1223–4), and then at Montpellier and Toulouse. He became Custodian at Limoges, prob. in 1226, and provincial of Bologna in 1227, but was released from office in 1230 to devote himself more fully to preaching. He was one of seven friars sent to the Pope by the General Chapter of 1230 to seek a clarification of the Franciscan Rule. He spent the rest of his life near Padua, where his relics have always been venerated. He was canonized in 1232 and declared a *Doctor of the Church in 1946. Feast day, 13 June.

St Antony's preaching gained a considerable reputation during his life; it was largely directed against the vices of usury and avarice; it also met with notable success among the heretics of France and N. Italy. Possibly during his life, and certainly after his death, he was widely regarded as a worker of miracles. His cultus, always popular, further developed in the late 19th cent., and he is now one of the most popular Christian saints. He is chiefly invoked for the return of lost property, possibly because of the incident related in the *Chronica XXIV Generalium* (no. 21) of the novice who ran away with a Psalter which St Antony was using and was forced by an alarming apparition to return it. He is also the patron of the poor, alms given to obtain his intercession being known since *c.*1870 as 'St Antony's Bread'; and he is believed to protect the pregnant and travellers. In early art he is usually depicted with a book or lily, symbolizing his knowledge of Scripture, or occasionally with an ass, which is supposed to have knelt before the Bl Sacrament upheld by St Antony; today he is usually represented holding the Holy Child.

Collections of his sermons were pub. at Paris in 1520 and 1521; collected edn. of his works by J. de la Haye (ed.), *Sancti Francisci Assisiatis . . . nec non Sancti Antonii Paduani Opera Omnia* (Paris, 1641), pp. 97–792; additional sermons ed. A. Pagus, OFM (Avignon, 1684). Crit. edn. of his *Sermones Dominicales et Festivi* by B. Costa, L. Frasson, J. Luisetto, and P. Marangon (3 vols., Padua, 1979), with introd. 'De Vita et Operibus', 1, pp. xiii–xlv, with refs. Eng. tr. of his *Moral Concordances* by J. M. *Neale (London, 1856). The most important source for his life is the *Legenda Prima* written shortly after his death; crit. edn., with later appendix, by L. de Kerval in *Collection d'Études et de Documents*, 5 (1904), pp. 1–157, with notes on other sources, pp. 237–71; also ed. G. Abate, OFM Conv., in *Il Santo*, 8 (1968), pp. 127–226, and V. Gamboso (Fonti Agiografiche Antoniniane, 1; Padua, 1981). L. de Kerval, *L'Évolution et le développement du merveilleux dans les légendes de S. Antoine de Padua* (Opuscules de Critique Historique, 13–14; 1906). E. Gilliat-Smith, *Saint Anthony of Padua according to his Contemporaries* (1926); R. M. Huber, OFM, *St Anthony of Padua, Doctor of the Church Universal* (Milwaukee, 1948); S. Clasen, OFM, *Antonius, Diener des Evangeliums und der Kirche* (1959; Eng. tr., Chicago, 1961); *S. Antonio di Padova fra storia e pietà: Colloquio interdisciplinare su 'il fenomeno antoniano'* (Centro Studi Antoniani, 1; Padua, 1977); A. Poppi (ed.), *Le Fonti et la Teologia dei Sermoni Antoniani: Atti del Congresso Internazionale di Studio sui 'Sermones' di S. Antonio di Padova (Padova, 5–10 ottobre 1981)* (Il Santo, 22, fasc. 1–3; Padua, 1982). There are many excellent articles on St Antony in other volumes of *Il Santo: Rivista Antoniana di Storia, Dottrina, Arte* (1961 ff.). J. Toussaert, *Antonius von Padua: Versuch einer kritischen Biographie* (Cologne, 1967). S. Clasen, OFM, in *NCE* 1 (1967), pp. 595 f., with bibl.

apatheia (Gk. ἀπάθεια, 'impassibility' or 'passionlessness'), a term used in ascetical theology in the E. Church, often translated 'dispassion'. When applied to God, it is used in its literal sense, but from *Clement of Alexandria onwards it is also used as a technical term for human perfection, denoting mastery of the passions or serenity. *Apatheia* has *Stoic roots and is handled in the Greek tradition in a variety of ways. For *Evagrius, who popularized the word, it means the quelling of passions that disturb the soul, leading to a serenity that makes spiritual love possible; other writers are more positive, and *Diadochus of Photike even speaks of the 'fire of *apatheia*' (πῦρ ἀπαθείας: *Cent.* 17). Evagrius was attacked by St *Jerome, who, thinking that *apatheia* meant insensibility, rejected it (*Ep.* 133. 3). *Cassian used the phrase *puritas cordis* to represent the Evagrian *apatheia*, and the term never established itself in the W.

T. Rüther, *Die sittliche Forderung der Apatheia in den beiden ersten christlichen Jahrhunderten und bei Klemens von Alexandrien* (Freiburger Theologische Studien, 63; 1949). A. and C. Guillaumont in the introd. to their edn. of Evagrius, *Practicos*, 1 (SC 170; 1971), pp. 98–112. G. Bardy in *Dict. Sp.* 1 (1937), cols. 727–46, s.v.

Apelles (2nd cent.), founder of a *Gnostic sect. Our slight knowledge of him comes mainly from fragments of his antagonist, Rhodo (in *Eusebius, *HE* 5. 13), and refs. in *Tertullian's *De Praescriptione* (30; 34). Originally a disciple of *Marcion at *Rome, he taught at *Alexandria and later returned to Rome, where he came under the influence of a visionary, Philumene, whose oracles he collected. He embodied his system in an extended work, Συλλογισμοί. He modified Marcion's dualism in an endeavour to defend a less *Docetic doctrine of the Person of Christ. Christ came down from the good God, who was not himself the creator of the world, however, and really lived and really suffered in a body miraculously formed out of the elements. Those who believed in Christ would gain salvation not by knowledge alone or by faith alone, but by good works. Tertullian wrote a book against him, now lost.

For sources see A. *Harnack, *Marcion* (TU, 45; 1921), pp. 213–30, and Appendix 7 (pp. 323*–39*). Useful discussion by J.-P. Mahé in his introd. to Tertullian, *La Chair du Christ*, 1 (SC 216; 1975), pp. 59–61 and 94–110. E. Junod, 'Les attitudes d'Apelles, disciple de Marcion, à l'égard de l'Ancien Testament', *Augustinianum*, 22 (1982), pp. 113–33. J. Quasten, *Patrology*, 1 (Utrecht, 1950), pp. 272–4.

Aphrahat (early 4th cent.), the first of the *Syriac Church Fathers. He was an ascetic, evidently holding some important ecclesiastical office, and lived through the persecution of the Sasanid king, Shapur II (310–79). Our knowledge of him comes from 23 'Demonstrations' (inaccurately known as his 'Homilies'), the first 10 of which were completed in 337, the next 12 in 344, and the final one in 345. The first 22 are arranged on an acrostic plan, each beginning with a different letter of the alphabet, and give a survey of the Christian faith. The 23rd, in the nature of an appendix, is a short treatise 'On the berry' (Is. 65: 8). His writings show that he attached importance to asceticism, esp. celibacy, and that, at least in intention, he was orthodox in his theology. His works throw valuable light on early Christianity in Persia and on the text of the NT. He was known as 'the Persian Sage' and at an early date was confused with *Jacob of Nisibis, to whom the early Armenian translation of his works is attributed.

Syr. text of Homilies ed. by W. Wright (London, 1869) and, with Lat. tr., by J. Parisot, OSB (Patrologia Syriaca, Pars I, vols. 1–2; 1894–1907). Fr. tr., with introd. and notes, by M.-J. Pierre (SC 349 and 359; 1988–89); Eng. tr. of eight Homm. by J. Gwynn in *NPNCF*, 2nd ser., 13 (1898), pp. 345–412, and of nine (mainly different) Homm. and some fragments by J. Neusner, *Aphrahat and Judaism* (Studia Post-Biblica, 19; Leiden, 1971), pp. 19–119. I. Ortiz de Urbina, SJ, *Die Gottheit Christi bei Afrahat* (Orientalia Christiana, 31, fasc. 1 (no. 87); 1933). E. J. Duncan, *Baptism in the Demonstrations of Aphraates the Persian Sage* (Catholic University of America Studies in Christian Antiquity, 8; 1945). T. Baarda, *The Gospel Quotations of Aphrahat the Persian Sage*, 1: *Aphrahat's Text of the Fourth Gospel* (Amsterdam diss., 2 vols.; 1975). P. Bruns, *Das Christusbild Aphrahats des persischen Weisen* (Hereditas, 4; Bonn, 1990). Bardenhewer, 4, pp. 327–40; I. Ortiz de Urbina, SJ, *Patrologia Syriaca* (2nd edn., Rome, 1965), pp.

46–51, with full bibl. I. Hausherr in *Dict. Sp.* 1 (1937), cols. 746–52, s.v.; A. Vööbus, 'Nachträge zum Reallexikon für Antike und Christentum. Aphrahat', *Jahrbuch für Antike und Christentum*, 3 (1960), pp. 152–5, with bibl.

Aphthartodocetae. An extreme *Monophysite group, led by *Julian, Bp. of Halicarnassus, and hence known also as 'Julianists'. They taught that from the first moment of the incarnation the earthly body of Christ was in its nature incorruptible (ἄφθαρτος), impassible, and immortal, though this fact did not preclude Him from accepting suffering and death by a free act of His will. The doctrine was attacked (on grounds acceptable also to Catholic orthodoxy) by *Severus, the *Syrian Orthodox Patr. of Antioch, as incompatible with belief in the true humanity of Christ.

R. Draguet, *Julien d'Halicarnasse et sa controverse avec Sévère* (1924). M. Jugie, AA, 'Julien d'Halicarnasse et Sévère d'Antioche', *ÉO* 24 (1925), pp. 129–62 and 257–85; id., 'L'empereur Justinien a-t-il été aphthartodocète?', ibid. 31 (1932), pp. 399–402; id., *Theologia Dogmatica Christianorum Orientalium ab Ecclesia Catholica Dissentium*, 5 (Paris, 1935), pp. 432–7. A. Grillmeier, SJ, *Jesus der Christus im Glauben der Kirche*, 2/2 (1989), pp. 83–116; Eng. tr. (1995), pp. 79–111.

Apiarius. A priest of the diocese of Sicca in proconsular Africa, who was deposed by his bishop for misconduct. The incident is important in connection with the growth of Papal jurisdiction. Apiarius appealed to Pope *Zosimus (417–18), who thereupon ordered him to be reinstated. In consequence a council held at *Carthage in May 419 forbade appeals beyond the sea. The Pope protested at this decree, and the case dragged on for some years. About 423 Apiarius was again excommunicated, and again appealed to Rome with the same result. The incident also led to a fresh examination of the authority attaching to the *Sardican Canons and thus indirectly had a decisive influence on the beginnings of the codification of *canon law.

C. Munier (ed.), *Concilia Africae A. 345–A. 525* (CCSL 149; 1974), pp. 79–149. Hefele and Leclercq, 2, pp. 196–215 *passim*, with bibl. note p. 196. C. Pietri, *Roma Christiana* (Bibliothèque des Écoles Françaises d'Athènes et de Rome, 224; 1976), 2, pp. 1250–75 *passim*. A. Audollent in *DHGE* 3 (1924), cols. 951–4, s.v., with bibl.

Apocalypses. See ABRAHAM, APOCALYPSE OF; BARUCH, II; PETER, APOCALYPSE OF; REVELATION, BOOK OF.

Apocalyptic literature. The word 'apocalypse' (ἀποκάλυψις) means a 'revelation' or 'unveiling', so that an apocalyptic book claims to reveal things which are normally hidden and to unveil the future. The Jewish Apocalyptic books belong approximately to the period from 200 BC to AD 100 and deal with the end of the present world order and with the next world. Whereas the Israelite Prophets were primarily preachers, concerned with current problems of their own generation and nation, the Apocalyptists were pre-eminently writers, directing their attention towards the end of things and to the destiny of the world in general. The origins and growth of this literature reflect the history of Israel's conflicts with other nations and the conviction that trust in military power was useless. As the nation continued to be subjected to foreign domination, it despaired of ever attaining political supremacy, and the conclusion was drawn that God would eventually intervene, destroy Israel's enemies, and set up His Kingdom on earth. Some scholars have argued that the Apocalyptic literature, at least in part, represents the protest of visionaries excluded from power by the priestly group which controlled the *Temple after the *Exile.

Apocalyptic literature proper begins with the Book of *Daniel, probably written during the persecution of *Antiochus Epiphanes (175–164 BC) to comfort the Jews in their distress and to assure them of the approaching Divine intervention. However, the beginnings of Apocalyptic tendencies can be seen in the prophetic writings (e.g. Joel 2, Is. 65, Amos 5: 16–20, 9: 11–15, Is. 24–7, Zech. 9–14, Ezek. 38, 39), where there are frequent references to the approaching 'day of the Lord'. The Apocalyptic writings appear to be indebted also to certain elements of the '*Wisdom literature', and even to foreign influences, esp. those of Persian religion. They are almost always pseudonymous and written in the names of Israel's past heroes, a circumstance which is perhaps to be ascribed to the fact that, owing to the supremacy of the Law (which was regarded as containing the complete and final revelation of the Divine will), the only way to secure a hearing after the formation of the earliest form of the OT *Canon in about the 3rd cent. BC was to attribute these writings to some famous person of remote times.

Important Jewish Apocalyptic writings outside the OT are the First and Second Books of *Enoch, the Apocalypse of *Baruch, the Fourth Book of Ezra (2 *Esdras), the Assumption of *Moses, the Book of *Jubilees, the Ascension of *Isaiah, and the *Testament of the Twelve Patriarchs.

In the NT, the element of Apocalyptic appears in various places. The two most important Christian Apocalypses are Rev. and the (non-canonical) 'Apocalypse of *Peter'. Whatever interpretation the Lord Himself wished His disciples to put upon His apocalyptic utterances, it is clear that, at least in the earlier part of the Apostolic age, a speedy Second Coming of Christ was expected (see e.g. Mt. 24 and 25, Mk. 13, Lk. 21, 1 Thess. 4, 1 Cor. 15 for typical Apocalyptic passages). 2 Pet. and Rev. probably belong to a slightly later period, when severe persecution was troubling the Church.

Eng. trs. of most of the Jewish Apocalyptic writings not in the OT will be found in R. H. *Charles, *The Apocrypha and Pseudepigrapha of the Old Testament* (2 vols., Oxford, 1913); J. H. Charlesworth (ed.), *The Old Testament Pseudepigrapha* (2 vols., 1983–5); and H. F. D. Sparks (ed.), *The Apocryphal Old Testament* (Oxford, 1984). H. H. Rowley, *The Relevance of Apocalyptic: A Study of Jewish and Christian Apocalypses from Daniel to Revelation* (1944); D. S. Russell, *The Method and Message of Jewish Apocalyptic* (1964); P. D. Hanson, *The Dawn of Apocalyptic* (Philadelphia [1975]); C. Rowland, *The Open Heaven: A Study of Apocalyptic in Judaism and Early Christianity* (1982). G. Lanczkowski and others in *TRE* 3 (1978), pp. 189–257, s.v. 'Apokalypten/Apocalypsen, I–IV', with extensive bibl.

Apocatastasis. The Greek name (ἀποκατάστασις) for the doctrine that ultimately all free moral creatures—angels, men, and devils—will share in the grace of salvation. It is to be found in *Clement of Alexandria, in *Origen and St *Gregory of Nyssa. It was strongly attacked by St *Augustine of Hippo and formally con-

demned in the first anathema against *Origenism, probably put out by the Council of Constantinople in AD 543. In more modern times the doctrine has been defended by certain *Anabaptists, *Moravians, *Christadelphians (modified in some of these by a form of *conditional immortality), and also by certain individual theologians, of whom perhaps the most important is F. D. E. *Schleiermacher. Such teaching is also known as *Universalism.

apocrisarius (from Gk. ἀποκρίνομαι 'to answer, make response'). An ecclesiastical deputy or other official of high rank.

(1) The envoys used by the Patriarchates as their diplomatic representatives in other Patriarchal cities or at Imperial courts. *Apocrisarii* were at first, from the 5th cent., sent on specific missions, but by the 9th cent. at any rate they had acquired the character of permanent legates. In recent years the *Oecumenical Patriarch has appointed an 'apocrisarius' to the Abp. of *Canterbury, and the Anglican chaplains in Athens, Belgrade, Bucharest, Istanbul, Moscow, and Sofia are 'apocrisarii' to their respective Archbishop or Patriarchs.

(2) The title was also used of the senior court chaplains of the Frankish courts, also known as 'archicapellani'.

Apocrypha, the (Gk. τὰ ἀπόκρυφα (plur.), 'the hidden [things]'). The biblical Books received by the early Church as part of the Gk. version of the OT, but not included in the Heb. Bible, being excluded by the non-Hellenistic Jews from their *canon. Their position in Christian usage has been somewhat ambiguous. In the *Vulgate and versions derived from it they are mostly part of the OT; but in the AV, RV, NEB, and other non-Roman modern versions, they either form a separate section between the OT and NT, or are omitted altogether. They comprise (in the order of the AV): 1 and 2 Esdras, Tobit, Judith, the Rest of Esther, the Wisdom of Solomon, Ecclesiasticus, Baruch with the Epistle of Jeremy, the Song of the three Holy Children, the History of Susanna, Bel and the Dragon, the Prayer of Manasses, and 1 and 2 Maccabees (qq.v.).

The Church received these writings from Hellenistic Judaism, esp. that of *Alexandria. In the *Septuagint (LXX), which incorporated all except 2 Esd., they were in no way differentiated from the other Books of the OT. The narrative Books (1 Esd., Tobit, Judith, 1 and 2 Macc.) are grouped in the principal MSS with the later historical Books 1 Chron.–Esth., the Wisdom Books (Wisd., Ecclus.) with Prov., etc., and Pr. of Man. is appended to the Psalter. The three items, Song of III Ch., Susanna, and Bel and Dragon (collectively known as 'the Additions to Daniel'), are here integral parts of the Book of Dan., being the parts of the Gk. text to which nothing corresponds in the Heb. Similarly the disjointed chapters (by no means a complete Book) appearing in the Eng. versions of the Apocrypha as 'the Rest of Esther' are here simply the portions of the Gk. text of Esth. not found in the Heb. Baruch and Ep. of Jer. are appended in LXX MSS to Jer., though not derived from the Heb. Book. Under the name of 'Esdras' (the Gk. form of Heb. 'Ezra') the LXX contains two Books: one (Ἔσδρας αʹ, i.e. '1 Ezra') corresponds to portions of (the Heb.) 2 Chron., Ezr., and Neh., but contains also a passage (1 Esd. 3: 1–5: 6.) not found there; the other (Ἔσδρας βʹ, i.e. '2 Ezra') is a faithful rendering of

Ezr. and Neh. The latter therefore is regarded as the LXX version of these OT Books, while the former, which diverges from the Heb., appears among the Apocrypha as '1 Esdras'. The '2 Esdras' of the Apocrypha is a different work altogether. It is not extant in Gk. and found only in Lat. MSS; but it was doubtless translated from the Gk., and is, like the rest, of Jewish origin. This last is also known as the 'Ezra Apocalypse'.

In date of writing, the Books of the Apocrypha derive from the period 300 BC–AD 100 approx., and mostly from 200 BC–AD 70, i.e. before the definite separation of the Church from Judaism. In this period, though the *Canon of the Jewish Scriptures was closed as far as the 'Law' and the 'Prophets' were concerned, it was still possible for works which came to be known technically as 'Writings' to attain for the first time the status of Scripture, and some of the Canonical Books of the OT (e.g. Dan.) date from this period. Some of the Apocrypha, e.g. Ecclus. (cf. the Prologue to the Book), being written originally in Heb., might have gained canonical status, but did not; others (e.g. 2 Macc.), being written in Gk., were never current among Aramaic-speaking Jews. When the Heb. Canon of Scripture was settled (perhaps around AD 100), the Heb. text of the excluded Books ceased to be copied. Hence, with the exception of fragments recovered in modern times (e.g. considerable portions of Ecclus. discovered in an ancient *geniza), this has hence been lost. On the other hand, the Gk. survived because of its use by Christians, who at first received all the Books of the Septuagint equally as Scripture. Though no Book of the Apocrypha is quoted in the NT, *Clement of Rome and other early Fathers, notably *Clement of Alexandria and *Origen, cite them frequently. The considerable use made of them by Christians for apologetic purposes, e.g. of texts held to refer to such Christian doctrines as the Incarnation and the Eternal Generation of the *Wisdom (equated with the Word (*Logos), i.e. Son) of God (Wis. 7: 26), may have contributed to the Jewish rejection of the Books. In the later Gk. version of the Scriptures made by the Jew *Aquila (q.v.), the Heb. Canon was followed exactly.

Down to the 4th cent. the Church generally accepted all the Books of the Septuagint as canonical. Gk. and Lat. Fathers alike (e.g. *Irenaeus, *Tertullian, *Cyprian) cite both classes of Books without distinction. In the 4th cent., however, many Gk. Fathers (e.g. *Eusebius, *Athanasius, *Cyril of Jerusalem, *Epiphanius, *Gregory of Nazianzus) came to recognize a distinction between those canonical in Heb. and the rest, though the latter were still customarily cited as Scripture. St *Jerome, through his E. contacts and his Heb. studies, accepted this distinction, and introduced the term 'apocrypha' for the latter class, which he also described as the 'libri ecclesiastici' as distinguished from the 'libri canonici'. But with a few exceptions (e.g. *Hilary, *Rufinus), W. writers (esp. *Augustine) continued to consider all as equally canonical. In the E. Church opinion varied, and for some centuries the Books continued to be widely accepted; but at the Synod of *Jerusalem in 1672 it was decided that Tobit, Judith, Ecclus., and Wisd. (together with the full LXX text of Jer., Dan., and Est.) alone were to be regarded as canonical. Opinion in the W. also was not unanimous, some authorities considering certain books uncanonical; but,

despite Jerome's distinction, all, including '2 Esdras' (see above), were commonly included in the Vulgate and cited as Scripture. (In the Vulgate, 'I, II Esdras' = Ezr. and Neh. (from the Heb.); 'III Esdras' = '1 Esdras' (i.e. Ἔσδρας α΄ of the LXX); and 'IV Esdras' = '2 Esdras' (the Ezra Apocalypse).)

At the Reformation, Protestant leaders, ignoring the traditional acceptance of all the Books of the LXX in the early Church and desiring to return to biblical authority purged of medieval tradition, refused the status of inspired Scripture to those Books of the Vulg. not to be found in the Heb. Canon. M. *Luther, however, included the Apocrypha (except 1 and 2 Esd.) as an appendix to his translation of the Bible (1534), and in his preface allowed them to be 'useful and good to be read'. The Geneva translators (see BIBLE, ENGLISH VERSIONS) translated them, with a preface recognizing their value for 'knowledge of history and instruction of godly manners', and the C of E, in the *Thirty-Nine Articles (1562) (Art. VI), stated that 'the Church doth read [them] for example of life and instruction of manners; but yet doth it not apply them to establish any doctrine'. At the Council of *Trent (Sess. IV, 8 April 1548), the full canonicity of the Books was confirmed, with the exception of 1 and 2 (i.e. III and IV) Esdras and Pr. of Man., which were placed thenceforth in an appendix to the Vulgate, after the NT. This decision was confirmed for the RC Church by the First *Vatican Council (1870). In the C of E, in accordance with Art. VI, the Apocrypha, as a separate section between the OT and NT, were included as an integral part of the *Authorized Version of 1611. Under Puritan ascendancy, however, it was declared in the *Westminster Confession (1646–7) that the Apocrypha were not 'to be otherwise approved or made use of than other human writings'. The common attitude to them in Great Britain, maintained officially by the Church of *Scotland and favoured by Nonconformists, was of rejection or at least suspicion, and this, perhaps combined with Anglican apathy, and reinforced by the decision of the *British and Foreign Bible Society not to distribute Bibles containing them, led to their general omission from the editions commonly sold. In the BCP of 1662, portions of some of them were included in the Lectionary, and this was continued in the Lectionary of 1871 as far as Wisd., Ecclus., and Baruch were concerned. In the Revised Lectionary of 1922 portions of Pr. of Man., 1 and 2 Macc., and Tobit were also included. The ASB includes (optional) readings from Tobit, Wisd., Ecclus., Baruch, Song of III Ch., Susanna, and 1 and 2 Macc.

With the growth of a historical perspective in biblical studies in the 19th cent., and increased knowledge and interest in the Hellenistic and non-biblical background of the NT, the great value of the Apocrypha as historical sources came to be generally recognized, and there came also a new recognition of their religious value. Historically they are invaluable for the light which they throw on the period between the end of the OT historical narrative in Ezra-Neh. (c.400 BC) and the opening of the NT. They witness to the rise of the belief in eternal life and in the resurrection of the body, championed by the Pharisees in the NT period (cf. Mk. 12: 18–27, Acts 23: 6–9), and bear upon questions that were very much alive in the Apostolic Age (e.g. the Jewish Law, good works, sin and its origin in the *Fall, eschatology). Having been read as Scripture by the pre-Nicene Church and many post-Nicene Fathers, they have gained increasing respect in modern times even from those who do not hold them to be equally canonical with the rest of the OT.

Revision of AV Eng. tr., with crit. comm. ed. H. *Wace (Speaker's Commentary, 2 vols., 1888), with valuable 'General Introduction' by G. *Salmon, 1, pp. ix–xlvi; Eng. tr., with full introd., bibl., and notes, also in R. H. *Charles, *The Apocrypha and Pseudepigrapha of the Old Testament*, 1 (Oxford, 1913). RSV Apocrypha with comm. ed. by B. M. Metzger (New York, 1965). W. O. E. Oesterley, *The Books of the Apocrypha: Their Origin, Teaching and Contents* (1914); id., *An Introduction to the Books of the Apocrypha* (1935). E. J. Goodspeed, *The Story of the Apocrypha* (Chicago, 1939). B. M. Metzger, *An Introduction to the Apocrypha* (New York, 1957). L. H. Brockington, *A Critical Introduction to the Apocrypha* (1961). C. C. Torrey, *The Apocryphal Literature: A Brief Introduction* (New Haven, Conn., 1945; London, 1963). Eissfeldt, pp. 571–603, with bibl. R. T. Herford, *Talmud and Apocrypha: A Comparative Study of the Jewish Ethical Teaching in the Rabbinical and non-Rabbinical Sources in the Early Centuries* (1933). R. [T.] Beckwith, *The Old Testament Canon of the New Testament Church* (1985), pp. 338–433. R. H. Pfeiffer, *History of New Testament Times with an Introduction to the Apocrypha* (New York, 1949; London, 1954), pp. 233–522. E. *Schürer, *The History of the Jewish People in the Age of Jesus Christ*, rev. Eng. tr. by G. Vermes and others, 3 (pt. 1; Edinburgh, 1986), pp. 180–5, 198–212, 216–32, 568–79; 3 (pt. 2; ibid., 1987), pp. 705–45. H.-P. Rüger in *TRE* 3 (1978), pp. 289–316, s.v. 'Apokryphen des Alten Testaments'. See also works cited under CANON OF SCRIPTURE and under individual books.

Apocryphal New Testament. A modern title for various early Christian books outside the *Canon of the NT which are similar in form or content to the corresponding canonical Scriptures. The epithet 'apocryphal' does not of itself convey the modern sense of fictitious invention.

GOSPELS. Many of these exist. It is possible that some may embody trustworthy traditions, but this applies only to the earliest, not much later than the Gospels recognized as canonical (e.g. the *Egerton Papyrus or perhaps the Coptic *Gospel of *Thomas*). A second group was clearly and unmistakably intended to support heretical, and esp. *Gnostic, views (e.g. the *Gospel of the *Ebionites*, the *Gospel of *Philip*; see also below). A third group set out to satisfy popular curiosity with tales about the childhood of Christ (the *Infancy Gospel of *Thomas*), His Passion (the *Gospel of *Peter*, the *Gospel of Nicodemus* [see PILATE, ACTS OF]), or His meetings with His disciples in the period between the Resurrection and the Ascension (the *Dialogue of the Redeemer*, *Apocryphon of *John*, and the (orthodox) *Testament of Our Lord in Galilee*). 'Revelation Gospels' of this last type were popular among the Gnostics, who extended the period from 40 days to 18 months. Another feature is that subordinate figures in the canonical narratives sometimes become the central characters, as with the BVM in the *Protevangelium* or *Book of *James*, or Joseph in the *History of Joseph the Carpenter*. Most of these works lie between the 1st and 3rd cent., but some of their content was incorporated into works of later centuries.

ACTS. Of the Apocryphal Acts, the most important are those of *Peter, *Paul, *John, *Andrew, and *Thomas, all probably late 2nd cent. They are sometimes known collectively as the 'Leucian Acts', because all were ascribed

by *Photius to one Leucius Charinus; but wide differences of style, matter, and doctrinal standpoint forbid the assumption of common authorship. Their subject-matter is partly made up of stories parallel to and perhaps inspired by the canonical Acts of the Apostles, partly credible oral traditions, partly evident romance. The *Acts of Paul* (from which the *Acts of Paul and Thecla*, which was current as a separate work, was later extracted) is not markedly heretical; but nearly all the others in varying degrees reflect current heretical influences.

EPISTLES AND OTHER WRITINGS. Of the non-canonical epistles the best known are those of *Clement ('ep. 1') and Barnabas (qq.v.; *c.* AD 100), though these hardly rank as NT apocrypha in the normal sense. Among others are the spurious Epp. of St. Paul *To the Corinthians* and *To the Laodiceans*. There are also various apocryphal apocalypses besides the Revelation of St John, which itself long remained on the borders of the NT canon.

M. R. James, *The Apocryphal New Testament* (Oxford, 1924); J. K. Elliott, *The Apocryphal New Testament* (ibid., 1993); both give the principal texts in Eng. tr. C. *Tischendorf (ed.), *Evangelia Apocrypha* (Leipzig, 1853; 2nd edn., 1876). A. de Santos Otero (ed.), *Los Evangelios Apócrifos* (1956; 6th edn., 1988; convenient edn. of Gk. and Lat. texts, with Sp. tr.). R. A. *Lipsius and M. Bonnet, *Acta Apostolorum Apocrypha* (2 vols., Leipzig, 1891–1903). Ger. tr. by E. Hennecke, *Neutestamentliche Apokryphen* (1904; 5th edn. by W. Schneemelcher, 2 vols., 1987–9; Eng. tr., with tr. of texts from their original languages, 1991–2). M. R. James, *Anecdota Apocrypha* (Cambridge 'Texts and Studies'; 1893 and 1897). J. Hervieux, *Ce que l'Évangile ne dit pas* ([1958]; Eng. tr. as *What are Apocryphal Gospels?*, 1960). See also lit. under separate items.

Apodeipnon (Gk. ἀπόδειπνον, 'after supper'). In the E. Church, the late evening liturgical service which is the counterpart of *Compline in the W. There are two forms: the normal one, called 'small', and a much longer one, called 'great', which is used on weekdays in *Lent and as part of the all-night *Vigil on certain important feast days.

Apollinaris, St (date unknown), first Bp. of *Ravenna. The earliest mention of him is in a sermon of St Peter *Chrysologus (d. *c.*450), who styles him a martyr; but the principal authority is some (historically worthless) 7th-cent. *acta* which put him in the 1st cent. and make him a disciple of St *Peter at Antioch. His body was venerated in early times at Classe, near Ravenna, the supposed scene of his sufferings, later in the cathedral of Ravenna itself. His name still occurs in the canon of the *Ambrosian rite. Feast day, 23 July.

AASS, Jul. 5 (1727), pp. 328–85, incl. medieval accounts of the translation of his relics. F. Lanzoni, *Le origini delle diocesi antiche d'Italia: Studio critico* (ST 35; 1923), pp. 452–75 (on Ravenna, with bibl. refs.). E. Will, *Saint Apollinaire de Ravenne* (1936); G. Lucchesi, *Note agiografiche sui primi vescovi di Ravenna* (Faenza, 1941). H. *Delehaye, SJ, 'L'Hagiographie ancienne de Ravenne', *Anal. Boll.* 47 (1929), pp. 5–30.

Apollinaris, Sidonius. See SIDONIUS APOLLINARIS.

Apollinarius, Claudius (2nd cent.), Bp. of Hierapolis, early Christian *Apologist. His writings included a 'Defence of the Faith', presented to *Marcus Aurelius (prob. in 172), treatises 'Against the Pagans' (Πρòς

Ἕλληνας), on 'Truth' (Περὶ Ἀληθείας), and on *Easter (Περὶ τοῦ Πάσχα), and a work against the *Montanists. Apart from a few fragments, all his writings are lost. Feast day, 8 Jan.

The chief authority is *Eusebius, *HE*, 4. 27, and 5. 19. The fragments are collected in M. J. *Routh, *Reliquiae Sacrae*, 1 (2nd edn., Oxford, 1846), pp. 155–74, and in J. C. T. Otto, *Corpus Apologetarum Christianorum*, 9 (1872), pp. 479–95.

Apollinarius and Apollinarianism.

Apollinarius (or Apollinaris) ('the Younger', *c*.310–*c*.390) was the son of a grammarian of Beirut, also named Apollinarius ('the Elder'), in conjunction with whom he rewrote much of the Bible in classical forms when the Emp. *Julian (361–3) forbade Christians to use the pagan classics. A vigorous advocate of orthodoxy against the *Arians, he became Bp. of Laodicea *c*.360 and was a close friend of St *Athanasius (whom he had received on his return from exile in 346). His characteristic Christological teaching described below does not appear to have been the object of special criticism until towards the end of his career, but it was explicitly condemned by synods at Rome in 374–80 and by the Council of *Constantinople of 381. Apollinarius himself seceded from the Church *c*.375, and from 381 the State forbade Apollinarian public worship.

Of Apollinarius' extensive writings, most have been lost. Among his dogmatic works which survive under the false names of orthodox writers are: (1) a 'Detailed Confession of Faith' (ἡ κατὰ μέρος πίστις), attributed to St *Gregory Thaumaturgus; (2) three writings attributed to St Athanasius: a Profession of Faith addressed to the Emp. *Jovian, 'Quod unus sit Christus', and 'De Incarnatione Dei Verbi' (though in the case of the last two the ascription to Apollinarius rather than to a follower of his cannot be regarded as certain); and (3) three writings under the name of Pope *Julius (337–52). Another dogmatic work ('Απόδειξις) can be partially reconstructed from St *Gregory of Nyssa's attack on it in his 'Antirrheticus'. Fragments of his many Commentaries on the OT and NT, as well as of his apologetic works against *Porphyry (in 30 books) and the Emp. Julian, have also been preserved, largely in *catenae*. A Paraphrase of the Pss. in hexameters attributed to Apollinarius is spurious; it dates from the 5th–6th cent.

The fragmentary nature of the surviving sources makes the interpretation of Apollinarius' teaching a difficult task. He shared with St Athanasius the conviction that only the unchangeable Divine *Logos could be the saviour of man with his inherently changeable and fallible mind or soul. This led him to deny explicitly (in a way that St Athanasius did not) the presence of a human mind or soul in Christ. While this enabled him to stress the unity of Godhead and flesh in the person of Christ and to repudiate any conception of moral development in Christ's life, it carried the implication that Christ's manhood was not complete. It is that fact which is distinctive of Apollinarianism. The fundamental objection raised from the outset by Catholic orthodoxy is that if there is no complete manhood in Christ, He is not a perfect example for us, nor did He redeem the whole of human nature, but only its physical elements.

Texts in H. *Lietzmann, *Apollinaris von Laodicea und seine Schule: Texte und Untersuchungen*, 1 (Tübingen, 1904; all pub.); this supersedes the collection of texts in J. Dräseke, *Apollinaris*

von Laodicea (TU 7, Hefte 3 and 4; 1892; conclusions generally rejected). Additional texts: K. Staab, *Pauluskommentare aus der griechischen Kirche* (1933), pp. 57–82; H. de Riedmatten, OP, 'Les Fragments d'Apollinaire à l'"Éranistes" ' in *Das Konzil von Chalkedon: Geschichte und Gegenwart*, ed. A. Grillmeier, SJ, and H. Bacht, SJ, 1 (1951), pp. 203–12; id., 'La Correspondance entre Basile de Césarée et Apollinaire de Laodicée', *JTS* NS 7 (1956), pp. 199–210; 8 (1957), pp. 53–70; J. Reuss (ed.), *Matthäus-Kommentare aus der griechischen Kirche* (TU 61; 1957), pp. 1–54; id. (ed.), *Johannes-Kommentare aus der griechischen Kirche* (ibid. 89; 1966), pp. 3–64; R. Devreesse (ed.), *Les Anciens Commentaires grecs de l'Octateuque et des Rois* (ST 201; 1959), pp. 128–54; E. Mühlenberg, *Psalmenkommentare aus der Katenenüberlieferung*, 1 (Patristische Texte und Studien, 15; 1975), pp. 1–118. G. Voisin, *L'Apollinarisme* (1901); C. E. Raven, *Apollinarianism* (1923); G. L. Prestige, *Fathers and Heretics* (Bampton Lectures for 1940; 1940), Lect. 5, pp. 193–246; id., *St Basil the Great and Apollinaris of Laodicea*, ed. H. Chadwick (1956). H. de Riedmatten, OP, 'Some Neglected Aspects of Apollinarist Christology', *Dominican Studies*, 1 (1948), pp. 239–60; id., 'La Christologie d'Apollinaire de Laodicée', in K. Aland and F. L. Cross (eds.), *Studia Patristica*, 2 (TU 64; 1957), pp. 208–34. E. Mühlenberg, *Apollinaris von Laodicea* (Forschungen zur Kirchen- und Dogmengeschichte, 23; 1969). T. F. Torrance, *Theology in Reconciliation* (1975), pp. 139–214 ('The Mind of Christ in Worship. The Problem of Apollinarianism in the Liturgy'). R. M. Hübner, *Die Schrift des Apollinarius von Laodicea gegen Photin (Pseudo-Athanasius, Contra Sabellianos) und Basilius von Caesarea* (Patristische Texte und Studien, 30; 1989). *CPG* 2 (1974), pp. 301–17 (nos. 3645–700). R. Aigrian in *DHGE* 3 (1924), cols. 962–82, s.v. On the Psalm Metaphrasis (ed. A. Ludwich, Teub., 1912) see J. Golega, *Der Homerische Psalter: Studien über die dem Apolinarios von Laodikeia zugeschriebene Psalmenparaphrase* (Studia Patristica et Byzantina, 6; 1960).

Apollonius of Tyana

(d. *c*.98), Neopythagorean philosopher. His virtuous life and reforming religious tendencies were constantly exaggerated after his death, so that it became possible for anti-Christian writers to compose biographies of him consciously parallel with the Gospel life of Christ. The Life of him by Flavius Philostratus (*c*.220), though perhaps not inspired by this motive, furnished by its exaggeration and pretensions matter for anti-Christians in later times, and in particular for Hierocles, Governor of Bithynia *c*.303, who wrote a Life of Apollonius which called forth a refutation from *Eusebius of Caesarea. In modern times opponents of Christianity have occasionally used Philostratus to disparage the uniqueness of the Christian Gospel, but the alleged parallels are generally admitted to be unconvincing. A collection of letters, of doubtful authenticity, is ascribed to Apollonius.

There is a convenient edn. of Philostratus' *Vita Apollonii* in the Loeb Classical Library (2 vols., 1912, ed. F. C. Conybeare). Also Eng. tr., with valuable introd., by J. S. Phillimore (2 vols., 1912). Further Eng. tr. by C. P. Jones, ed. and abridged, with introd., by G. M. Bowersock (Penguin Classics, 1970). Crit. edn. of letters, with Eng. tr., by R. J. Penella (Mnemosyne, suppl. 56; Leiden, 1979). G. Petzke, *Die Traditionen über Apollonius von Tyana und das Neue Testament* (Leiden, 1969); E. Koskenniemi, *Apollonios von Tyana in der neutestamentlichen Exegese* (Tübingen [1994]). M. Dzielska, *Apollonius of Tyana in Legend and History*, Eng. tr. by P. Pieńkowski (Problemi e Ricerche di Storia Antica, 10; Rome, 1986). G. Anderson, *Philostratus: Biography and Belles Lettres in the Third Century A.D.* [1986], pp. 121–239. K. Gross in *RAC* 1 (1950), cols. 529–33, s.v., with bibl.

Apollos.

A 'learned' Jew of Alexandria, 'mighty in the scriptures', and apparently already a Christian, though 'knowing only the baptism of John [the Baptist]' (Acts 18: 24–5). His Christian education was completed *c.*54 at *Ephesus by *Priscilla and Aquila. He then preached at Corinth, where some Christians wished to set him up as a rival to St Paul (Acts 18: 24, 1 Cor. 3: 4, etc.). Many, from M. *Luther onwards, have argued that he was the author of the Epistle to the Hebrews.

apologetics. The defence of Christian belief and of the Christian way against alternatives and against criticism. St *Paul in Athens 'argued in the synagogue with the Jews and the devout persons, and in the market place every day with those who chanced to be there' (Acts 17: 17 RSV; Acts goes on to provide an example of such argument in its account of Paul's words on the *Areopagus to the *Epicurean and *Stoic philosophers). The works of the 2nd-cent. *Apologists, whether against the Jews or pleading the case of Christianity before the Roman authorities, continue this tradition, as does St *Augustine's *City of God*, written to defend a faith accused by pagans of leading to the fall of Rome. St *Thomas Aquinas, too, in the *Summa Contra Gentiles*, sets himself the task 'of making known, as far as my limited power will allow, the truth that the Catholic faith professes, and of setting aside the errors that are opposed to it' (1. 2. 9). F. D. E. *Schleiermacher, in his *Brief Outline on the Study of Theology* (Eng. tr. of *Kurze Darstellung des theologischen Studiums*, 1811), distinguishes apologetics, 'which seeks to ward off hostility towards the [Christian] community' (§ 39), from polemics, which defends Christianity's essence against internal deviations.

Powerful objections to apologetics were raised by K. *Barth, who insisted that the Gospel's basis in revelation alone yielded no common ground for a defence of Christianity by natural reason. This view has been widely disputed by theologians, both Protestant (e.g. P. *Tillich and W. *Pannenberg) and RC (e.g. K. *Rahner and H. *Küng), for whom man's reason cannot be thought of as wholly corrupt and for whom the natural world, and especially human nature, themselves provide rationally defensible intimations of transcendence. For such theologians, Christianity, too, especially in its central Christological and eschatological emphases, itself yields a rationally defensible view and way of life.

A. Richardson, *Christian Apologetics* (1947); B. Ramm, *Types of Apologetic Systems* (Wheaton, Ill., 1953; rev. as *Varieties of Christian Apologetics*, Grand Rapids, Mich., 1961). B. Lindars, SSF, *New Testament Apologetic: The Doctrinal Significance of the Old Testament Quotations* (1961). W. Pannenberg, *Basic Questions in Theology* [Eng. tr. of articles pub. in various places], 3 (1973), pp. 99–115 (ch. 3, 'Speaking about God in the Face of Atheist Criticism', orig. Ger. pub. in 1969). B. [G.] Mitchell, *The Justification of Religious Belief* (1973). H. Küng, *Christ sein* (1974; Eng. tr., *On being a Christian*, 1977); id., *Existiert Gott?* (1978; Eng. tr., *Does God Exist?*, 1980). E. [F.] Osborn, *The Beginning of Christian Philosophy* (1981). T. W. Crafer in *HERE* 1 (1908), pp. 611–23; E. Kamlah, C. Andresen, H.-H. Schrey, and others in *RGG* (3rd edn.), 1 (1957), cols. 477–95; J.-B. Metz in *Sacramentum Mundi*, 1 (1968), pp. 66–70; L. W. Barnard, K. G. Steck, and H.-R. Müller-Schwefe in *TRE* 3 (1978), pp. 371–429, all s.v.

Apologia pro vita sua (1864). J. H. *Newman's 'history of [his] religious opinions' down to his reception into the RC Church, 9 Oct. 1845. It is a primary historical source for the *Oxford Movement, not least because of the letters and other historical documents which it contains. This moving and tragic work, one of the greatest autobiographies in the language, was provoked by a gibe of C. *Kingsley in *Macmillan's Magazine* for January 1864 (cited s.v. KINGSLEY). Early in Feb. 1864 Newman published in a pamphlet some correspondence with Kingsley and the publisher over the passage with the title *Mr Kingsley and Dr Newman*. Kingsley promptly issued a reply ('*What, then does Dr Newman mean?*'). The *Apologia*, Newman's answer, was orig. issued in weekly parts.

Many repr., e.g. in *Everyman's Library* (1912). Crit. edn., with introd. by Wilfrid Ward, London, 1913; reissued 1931; more elaborate crit. edn. by M. J. Svaglic (Oxford, 1967). C. H. Collette, *Dr. Newman and his Religious Opinions* (1866; anti-Roman critique). W. E. Houghton, *The Art of Newman's Apologia* (New Haven, Conn., 1945). V. F. Blehl, SJ, and F. X. Connolly (eds.), *Newman's* Apologia: *A Classic Reconsidered* (New York [1964]).

Apologists. The name esp. given to the Christian writers who (*c.*120–220) first addressed themselves to the task of making a reasoned defence and recommendation of their faith to outsiders. They include *Aristides, *Justin Martyr, *Tatian, *Athenagoras, *Theophilus, *Minucius Felix, and *Tertullian. They belonged to the period when Christianity was first making converts among the educated classes, and was also in conflict with the State over its very right to exist. Their object was to gain a fair hearing for Christianity, to dispel popular slanders and misunderstandings, and sometimes to show that Christians were loyal subjects, and to provide for this purpose some account of Christian belief and practice. They had to meet: (1) pagan philosophy and the general outlook which it influenced, and (2) the specifically Jewish objections. They devoted much attention to the application of OT prophecy to Christianity, and to the position of the divinity of Christ in relation to Monotheism, and esp. in connection with the latter doctrine elaborated the teaching on the *Logos and won for it a permanent place in Christian theology. Except for Tertullian, they were not primarily theologians. Their method was to exhibit Christianity to emperors and to the public as politically harmless and morally and culturally superior to paganism.

Collected crit. edn. of texts by J. C. T. Otto, *Corpus Apologetarum* (9 vols., Jena, 1847–72; 3rd edn. of vols. 1–5 [Justin], 1876–81); more recent text (except Theophilus) in E. J. Goodspeed, *Die ältesten Apologeten* (1914). E. J. Goodspeed, *Index Apologeticus* (Leipzig, 1912; vocabulary). J. Geffcken, *Zwei griechische Apologeten* (1907; Aristides and Athenagoras); A. Puech, *Les Apologistes grecs du deuxième siècle de notre ère* (1912); M. Pellegrino, *Studi su l'antica apologetica* (1947). N. Zeegers-Vander Vorst, *Les Citations des Poètes Grecs chez les Apologistes Chrétiens du II*e* Siècle* (Université de Louvain, Recueil de Travaux d'Histoire et de Philologie, 4th ser. 47; 1972). H. B. Timothy, *The Early Christian Apologists and Greek philosophy exemplified by Irenaeus, Tertullian and Clement of Alexandria* (Assen, 1973). R. M. Grant, *Greek Apologists of the Second Century* (Philadelphia, 1988). V. A. Spence Little, *The Christology of the Apologists* (1934). A. L. Williams, *Adversus Judaeos: A Bird's-Eye View of Christian* Apologiae *until the Renaissance* (Cambridge, 1935), esp. book 1. See also standard Patrologies and bibls. under separate Apologists.

Apolysis (Gk. ἀπόλυσις, 'dismissal'). The concluding blessing in the E. rites, said by the priest at the end of the Liturgy and of the offices.

apolytikion (Gk. ἀπολυτίκιον). In the E. rites, the principal *troparion of the day, celebrating the particular feast or saint commemorated in the calendar. It is sung at the end of Vespers (hence its name, 'dismissal hymn'), and is repeated in *Orthros, the Liturgy and almost all the other offices.

apophatic theology (Gk. ἀποφατικὴ θεολογία), or negative theology, a way of approaching God by denying that any of our concepts can properly be affirmed of Him. The term is first used by *Dionysius the Pseudo-Areopagite in contrast with cataphatic or affirmative theology and symbolic theology (*Myst.* 3). In apophatic theology the soul rejects all ideas or images of God and enters the 'darkness that is beyond understanding', where it is 'wholly united with the Ineffable' (ibid.). The roots of apophatic theology can be traced back a long way, to the ban on *images in parts of the OT, and to a similar rejection of *anthropomorphism by the Greek philosopher Xenophanes, developed by Parmenides and *Plato into a tradition which characterizes the Divine in largely negative terms. This tradition was taken up by the *Gnostics, philosophers such as *Philo and Numenius, by *Plotinus and other *Neoplatonists, and by the Christian Fathers, esp. St *Gregory of Nyssa. Apophatic theology can be seen as an assertion of the inadequacy of human understanding in matters Divine, and therefore a corrective within theology, forming part of the way of *analogy (q.v.), an approach perhaps more characteristic of the W. Church. In the E., on the other hand, apophatic theology is regarded as fundamental. Here it is seen as an affirmation that God cannot be an object of knowledge at all; this doctrine is given classic expression in the teaching of St *Gregory Palamas that God's essence is unknowable, while He makes Himself known to us through His energies.

See also GOD.

E. Norden, *Agnostos Theos: Untersuchungen zur Formengeschichte religiöser Rede* (1913); A.-J. Festugière, OP, *La Révélation d'Hermès Trismégiste*, 4: *Le Dieu inconnu et la Gnose* (1954). J. Hochstaffl, *Negative Theologie: Ein Versuch zur Vermittlung des patristischen Begriffs* (Munich, 1976), with bibl. D. Turner, *The Darkness of God: Negativity in Christian Mysticism* (Cambridge, 1995). V. *Lossky, *Essai sur la Théologie mystique de l'Église d'Orient* (1944; Eng. tr., 1957); P. Evdokimov, *La Connaissance de Dieu selon la tradition orientale* (Lyons, 1967). J. Pieper, *Philosophia negativa: Zwei Versuche über Thomas von Aquin* (Munich, 1953; Eng. tr., with other material, *The Silence of St Thomas*, 1957).

Apophthegm. A designation used by R. *Bultmann and other *Form Critics for those items in the Gospels which M. *Dibelius describes as '*Paradigms'. The term had been used previously for stories of a similar type in secular Greek literature.

Apophthegmata Patrum (Gk. ἀποφθέγματα, terse, pointed sayings). Collections of sayings of, or brief stories about, Egyptian monks, commonly known in English as 'Sayings of the Desert Fathers'. They are mainly arranged either alphabetically acc. to the speakers or subjects of the stories, or systematically by subject-matter. The material dates from the 4th–5th cents., a large proportion being ascribed to one Poemen, who lived well into the 5th cent. The surviving collections in their present form date from the late 5th to early 6th cent. In addition to the Greek, there are collections in Latin, Syriac, Armenian, Coptic, Georgian, and Ethiopic. Direct and unsophisticated, they vividly convey the spirit of the early desert spirituality.

The most widely diffused collection is the alphabetically arranged one first pr. by J. B. *Cotelier, *Ecclesiae Graecae Monumenta*, 1 (1677), pp. 338–712, repr. J. P. Migne, *PG* 65. 71–440; Eng. tr. by B. Ward, SLG, *The Sayings of the Desert Fathers* (1975); reliable Fr. tr. by L. Regnault, OSB, *Les Sentences des Pères du Désert* (Solesmes [1981]). Other collections and a Lat. version pub. by H. Rosweyde, SJ, as bk. 7 of his *Vitae Patrum* (1617; this and other texts repr. in *PL* 73 and 74). Coptic version in Sahidic dialect ed., with Fr. tr., by M. Chaîne (Cairo, 1960). Ethiopic version ed., with Lat. tr., by V. Arras (CSCO 238–9, Scriptores Aethiopici, 45–46; 1963). Eng. tr. of Syriac version by E. A. W. Budge, *Wit and Wisdom of the Christian Fathers of Egypt* (1934). W. *Bousset, *Apophthegmata: Studien zur Geschichte des ältesten Mönchtums* (ed. T. Hermann and G. Krüger, 1923). J.-C. Guy, SJ, *Recherches sur la Tradition grecque des* Apophthegmata Patrum (Subsidia Hagiographica, 36; 1962). L. Regnault, OSB, 'Aux Origines des Collections d'Apophthegmes', in E. A. Livingstone (ed.), *Studia Patristica*, 18.2 (Kalamazoo, Mich., and Louvain, 1989), pp. 61–74. G. [E.] Gould, *The Desert Fathers on Monastic Community* (Oxford Early Christian Studies, 1993). *CPG* 3 (1979), pp. 84–95 (nos. 5558–95).

apostasy. In the discipline of the early Church the term was used of the abandonment of Christianity, which was, with murder and fornication, one of the three sins at first accounted unpardonable, if committed by a baptized person, and later pardonable only after public penance. Until recently the word was used in the RC Church in three senses: (1) total defection from the Christian faith; (2) public defection from the RC Church; (3) desertion by a professed religious who had taken perpetual vows. The 1983 *Codex Iuris Canonici* (can. 751), however, defines apostasy as the total renunciation of the Christian faith.

On apostasy in the early Church, see bibl. s.v. LAPSI. On modern RC legislation, J. A. Coriden in id. and others (eds.), *The Code of Canon Law: A Text and Commentary* (1985), pp. 547 f.

aposticha (Gk. ἀπόστιχα). In the E. Church, brief liturgical hymns or *stichera attached to verses from the Psalter. They occur at the end of *Vespers, and (except on feast days) of *Orthros.

apostil. See POSTIL.

Apostle (Gk. ἀπόστολος). (1) A title given in the early Church to some of its leaders (1 Cor. 12: 28), esp. missionaries, and at Heb. 3: 1 to Christ Himself. The origin and precise significance of the term is disputed, but some reference to being sent (Gk. ἀποστέλλω, 'I send') is certain. St *Paul claimed the title for himself (Rom. 1: 1, Gal. 1: 1, etc.) on the basis of a commission from the Risen Christ, and used it of others (e.g. Rom. 16: 7), incl. St *James the Lord's Brother (Gal. 1: 19). It is used, most frequently by St *Luke, of the twelve disciples whose names are recorded in Mk. 3: 14–19, Mt. 10: 2–4, Lk. 6: 13–16, the slight variations perhaps indicating uncertainty rather than fluctuating membership of the group or different names for the same person. The later restriction of the title to the twelve (cf. Rev. 21: 14) was apparently unknown to Paul (cf. 1 Cor. 15: 5 with 15: 7), or at least resisted by him. It was popularized by Luke, who sees the election of St *Matthias (Acts 1: 15–26) as the reconstitution of an apostolic twelve after the defection and death of *Judas Iscariot. In modern usage the term is sometimes applied to the leader of the first Christian mission to a country, e.g. to St *Patrick, the 'Apostle of Ireland', Sts. *Cyril and Methodius, the 'Apostles of the Slavs', and many others. Where the traditional beliefs of the operation of grace and authority in the Church are maintained, it is through the twelve apostles that this grace and authority are held to descend from Christ, and from them to their lawfully appointed successors (see APOSTOLIC SUCCESSION, EPISCOPACY). Acc. to later tradition, all twelve apostles, except St *John, were also martyrs.

(2) A name given to the Epistle read in the E. Liturgy. It is always a portion of an epistle of one of the apostles or is taken from the Acts, and never, as in W. rites on occasion, an extract from the OT. The word is also used for the book which contains these readings set out as appointed.

(3) An official in the *Catholic Apostolic Church.

On (1) J. B. *Lightfoot, *St Paul's Epistle to the Galatians* (1865), pp. 89–97 ('On the Name and Office of Apostle'). K. *Lake in *The Beginnings of Christianity*, pt. 1, ed. F. J. Foakes Jackson and K. Lake, 5 (1933), pp. 37–59: note 6 ('The Twelve and the Apostles'). K. H. Rengstorf in *TWNT*, 1 (1933), pp. 406–48 (Eng. tr., 1 (1964), pp. 407–47), s.v. ἀπόστολος. G. Saas, *Apostelamt und Kirche: Eine theologisch-exegetische Untersuchung des paulinischen Apostelbegriffs* (1939); K. E. *Kirk (ed.), *The Apostolic Ministry: Essays on the History and the Doctrine of Episcopacy* (1946); A. Fridrichsen, *The Apostle and his Message* (Uppsala, 1947); H. von Campenhausen, 'Der urchristliche Apostelbegriff', *Studia Theologica* (Lund), 1 (1948), pp. 96–130; W. Schmithals, *Das kirchliche Apostelamt: Eine historische Untersuchung* (Göttingen, 1961; Eng. tr., Nashville, 1969; London, 1971); G. Klein, *Die zwölf Apostel: Ursprung und Gehalt einer Idee* (Forschungen zur Religion und Literatur des Alten und Neuen Testaments, 77; Göttingen, 1961); E. Klostermann, *Das Christliche Apostolat* (Innsbruck, etc., 1962); C. Burchard, *Der dreizehnte Zeuge* (Forschungen zur Religion und Literatur des Alten und Neuen Testaments, 103; Göttingen, 1970). J. A. Kirk, 'Apostleship since Rengstorf: Towards a synthesis', *New Testament Studies*, 21 (1975), pp. 249–64. W. A. Bienert, 'Das Apostelbild in der altchristlichen Überlieferung' in Schneemelcher, 2 (5th edn., 1989), pp. 6–28 (Eng. tr., 2 [1992], pp. 5–27), with recent bibl.

Apostle of England. St *Augustine of *Canterbury (q.v.).

Apostle of the Gentiles. St *Paul. The title does not occur in the NT; but cf. Gal. 2: 7.

Apostle of Rome. Title of St *Philip Neri (q.v.).

Apostles' Creed. A statement of faith used only in the W. Church. Like other ancient *Creeds, it falls into three sections, concerned with God, Jesus Christ, and the Holy Spirit, corresponding to the three Baptismal questions of the primitive Church. Terse in expression, it is less overtly theological than E. Creeds, but it includes such distinctive articles as the *Descent into Hell and the *Communion of Saints. Though its affirmations can be supported by NT evidence, the formula itself is not of apostolic origin. Its title is first found c.390 (*Ep.* 42. 5 of St *Ambrose), by which time the legend of its joint composition by the twelve Apostles was already current. Its present form, first quoted by St *Pirminius (early 8th cent.), is an elaboration

of the shorter *Old Roman Creed (q.v.), which had itself evolved from earlier, simpler texts based on the Lord's threefold baptismal command (Mt. 28: 19). This developed form seems to have had a Hispano-Gallic origin, was given a monopoly in his dominions by *Charlemagne, and was eventually accepted at Rome, where the Old Roman Creed or similar forms had survived for centuries. By the early Middle Ages it was everywhere employed at Baptism in the W., and between the 7th and 9th cents. secured a place in the daily offices. The BCP prescribes its use at Baptism (in an interrogative form) and daily at *Mattins and *Evensong, except on the thirteen days in the year on which the *Athanasian Creed is to be said in its place at Mattins. Its use at Mattins and Evensong is retained in most modern Anglican liturgies. In the 20th cent. it has been increasingly treated in discussions about Church union as a binding formulary of faith.

J. *Pearson, *An Exposition of the Creed* (1659). J. N. D. Kelly, *Early Christian Creeds* (1950; 3rd edn., 1972), esp. pp. 368–434. H. B. *Swete, *The Apostles' Creed: Its relation to primitive Christianity* (1894). F. *Kattenbusch, *Das apostolische Symbol* (2 vols., 1894–1900). T. *Zahn, *Das apostolische Symbolum* (1893; Eng. tr., 1899); A. *Harnack, 'Apostolisches Symbolum', *PRE* (3rd edn.), 1 (1897), pp. 741–55 (Eng. tr. as sep. work, *The Apostles' Creed*, 1901); E. Vacandard, 'Les Origines du symbole des apôtres', *RQH* 67 (1899), pp. 329–77; H. *Lietzmann, 'Die Anfänge des Glaubensbekenntnisses', in *Festgabe . . . A. Harnack* (1921), pp. 226–42. P. Feine, *Die Gestalt des apostolischen Glaubensbekenntnisses in der Zeit des Neuen Testaments* (1925). K. *Barth, *Credo: Die Hauptprobleme der Dogmatik dargestellt im Anschluss an das Apostolische Glaubensbekenntnis* (1935; Eng. tr., 1936). E. *Brunner, *Ich glaube an den lebendigen Gott* (1945; Eng. tr., 1961). O. S. Barr, *From the Apostles' Faith to the Apostles' Creed* (New York, 1964). H. de *Lubac, SJ, *La Foi chrétienne: Essai sur la structure du Symbole des Apôtres* (1969). J. de Ghellinck, SJ, *Patristique et moyen-âge*, 1: *Les Recherches sur les origines du symbole des apôtres* (1946; 2nd edn., 1949), fundamental with full summary of modern literature. See also bibl. to OLD ROMAN CREED.

Apostles, The Doctrine of the Twelve. See DIDACHE.

Apostles, The Epistle of the. See TESTAMENT OF OUR LORD IN GALILEE.

Apostleship of Prayer. A RC pious association under the guidance of the *Jesuit Order, with special devotion to the *Sacred Heart of Jesus. There are three degrees of membership, acc. to the rule of devotion undertaken. It was founded at Vals, France, in 1844 by F. X. Gautrelet, and in 1879 received from the Pope formal statutes, which were revised in 1896.

Apostolic Age. A modern title in use esp. among biblical scholars for the first period in the history of the Christian Church, approximately falling within the lifetime of the *Apostles (q.v.). Great importance is attached, esp. by Protestants, to the practices and beliefs of the Church during this period.

Apostolic Canons. A series of eighty-five canons attributed to the Apostles. They form the concluding chapter (8. 47) of the '*Apostolic Constitutions', the author of which (c.350–80) probably compiled them himself. Most of them deal with the ordination, the official responsibilities, and the moral conduct of the clergy, though a few are concerned with the duties of Christians in general. The last canon gives a list of scriptural Books which includes the Apostolic Constitutions itself. Twenty of the set are based on canons of *Antioch (?341). The first 50 were translated into Latin in the 6th cent. by *Dionysius Exiguus, and thus became part of the early canon law of the W. Church, while the *Trullan Council (692), though it condemned the 'Apostolic Constitutions' as a whole, secured their formal recognition in the E.

F. X. Funk, *Didascalia et Constitutiones Apostolorum* (1905), i, pp. 564–93; also, with Fr. tr., in Joannou, i, pt. 2 (1962), pp. 1–53. Eng. tr. in ANCL 17 (1870), pt. 2, pp. 257–69. *CPG* i (1983), pp. 231–3 (no. 1740).

Apostolic Church Order. An early Christian document, containing regulations on ecclesiastical practice and moral discipline. It is so named because its contents are ascribed to the various apostles, who speak at a reputed council at which Mary and Martha are present. It is thought to have been composed in Egypt *c*. AD 300. The document was evidently the work of an eccentric compiler, as it treats 'Peter' and 'Cephas' as different persons and deals with *readers as though they ranked between *presbyters and *deacons. It contains a text of the Two Ways parallel to, or based on, that in the '*Didache'. It was originally written in Greek, but it survives also in Latin (in a *Verona codex, lv [53]) and in Syriac, Coptic, Arabic, and Ethiopic versions (in the *Sinodos).

The Gk. text was first ed. by J. W. Bickell, *Geschichte des Kirchenrechts* (1843), pp. 107–32; also in T. Schermann (ed.), *Die allgemeine Kirchenordnung: Frühchristliche Liturgien und kirchliche Überlieferung*, i (Paderborn, 1914), pp. 12–34. Fragments of Lat. tr. ed. E. Tidner, *Didascaliae Apostolorum Canonum Ecclesiasticorum Traditionis Apostolicae Versiones Latinae* (TU 75; 1963), pp. 107–13. Arabic and Ethiopic texts ed., with Eng. tr., together with Eng. tr. of Coptic text by G. Horner, *The Statutes of the Apostles or Canones Ecclesiastici* (1904). A. *Harnack, *Die Quellen der sogenannten Apostolischen Kirchenordnung* (TU 2, Heft 5; 1886; Eng. tr., 1895 [despite misleading title]). E. Hennecke, 'Zur Apostolischen Kirchenordnung' in ZNTW 20 (1921), pp. 241–8; cf. H. *Lietzmann, ibid., pp. 254–6. *CPG* i (1983), pp. 229–31 (no. 1739). J. Quasten, *Patrology*, 2 (Utrecht, 1953), pp. 119 f.

Apostolic Constitutions. A collection of ecclesiastical law dating from *c*.350–80, and almost certainly of Syrian provenance. The full title is 'Ordinances of the Holy Apostles through Clement'. The *Trullan Synod (692) believed that the *Arian tendency of the work was due to the influence of interpolators, but C. H. *Turner demonstrated the Arian intention of the original text. Of its eight books 1 to 6 are based on the '*Didascalia'; 7. 1–32 on the '*Didache'; 7. 33–49 is liturgical material apparently derived from Jewish blessings; 8. 1–2 may be connected with the work 'Concerning Spiritual Gifts' listed on the base of the statue associated with St *Hippolytus; 8. 3–46 is loosely based on Hippolytus' '*Apostolic Tradition' and contains an elaborate version of the Antiochene Liturgy; while 8. 47 is the '*Apostolic Canons'. Various attempts have been made to identify the compiler. J. *Ussher (1644) believed the same hand was responsible for the Long Recension of the Letters of St *Ignatius of Antioch; D. Hagedorn argued that the author of both works was *Julian, an Arian author of a commentary on Job. Despite the wealth of liturgical material contained in the work

(there are three accounts of Baptism and one of the Eucharist), it cannot be uncritically accepted as evidence for the usage of the later 4th cent.

Ed. princeps by F. *Torres, Venice, 1563, repr. by J. B. *Cotelier in *Patres Apostolici*, i (1672), with new Lat. tr.; a later edn. of Cotelier's text was repr. in J. P. Migne, *PG* 1. 555–1156. Crit. edns. by F. X. Funk (Paderborn, 1905) and M. Metzger (SC 320, 329, and 336; 1985–7), with full introd. and bibl. Liturgy in bk. 8 also pr. in Brightman, *LEW*, pp. 3–30, with introd. pp. xvii–xlvii. Eng. tr. by J. Donaldson in ANCL 17 (1870), pt. 2. Eng. tr. of liturgical portions, with notes, by W. J. Grisbrooke (Grove Liturgical Study, 61; 1990). F. X. Funk, *Die apostolischen Konstitutionen* (1891), and later works. C. H. Turner, 'Notes on the Apostolic Constitutions', *JTS* 16 (1915), pp. 54–61 and 523–38; and 31 (1930), pp. 128–41; D. Hagedorn, *Die Hiobkommentar des Arianers Julian* (Patristische Texte und Studien, 14; 1973). D. A. Fiensy, *Prayers Alleged to be Jewish: An Examination of the Constitutiones Apostolorum* (Brown Judaic Studies, 65; Chico, Calif. [1985]). *CPG* i (1983), pp. 220 f. (no. 1730).

Apostolic Delegate. A person appointed by the Pope to keep the *Vatican informed of ecclesiastical matters in the territory which the *Holy See has assigned to him. He is not a diplomatic official, his status being purely ecclesiastical. The Vatican appointed an Apostolic Delegate to Great Britain for the first time in 1938 in the person of Mgr. William Godfrey (1889–1963).

Apostolic Fathers. The title given since the later 17th cent. to those Fathers of the age immediately succeeding the NT period whose works in whole or in part have survived. They are *Clement of Rome, *Ignatius, *Hermas, *Polycarp, and *Papias, and the authors of the 'Ep. of *Barnabas', of the 'Ep. to *Diognetus', of '2 Clement', and of the '*Didache'. In modern printed editions the 'Martyrdoms' of Clement, Ignatius, and Polycarp are sometimes included with them. Some of these writings hovered for a time on the edge of the NT canon, Herm. and Barn., e.g., being found in the *Codex Sinaiticus and 1 Clem. in the *Codex Alexandrinus.

J. B. *Cotelier, *SS. Patrum qui Temporibus Apostolicis floruerunt ... Opera* (Paris, 1672). J. P. Migne, *PG* 1–2. Collected modern edns. by O. Gebhardt, A. *Harnack, and T. *Zahn (3 vols., Leipzig, 1875–7; ed. minor, ibid., 1877); by J. B. *Lightfoot (5 vols., 1885–90, fine edn. of Clement, Ignatius, and Polycarp only, with full comm. and notes; edn. of texts, with Eng. tr., in one vol., 1891); by F. X. Funk (2 vols., Tübingen, 1878–81); by K. *Lake (Loeb, 2 vols., 1917–19, with Eng. tr.); rev. of Funk's edn. by K. Bihlmeyer (vol. 1 only (incl. all except Hermas), Tübingen, 1924; 2nd edn., by W. Schneemelcher, 1956, 3rd edn., 1970). Eng. trs. also by J. A. Kleist (ACW 6; 1948), E. J. Goodspeed (New York, 1950) and M. Staniforth (Harmondsworth, 1968; 2nd edn. by A. Louth, 1987), and, with comm., ed. R. M. Grant (6 vols.: 1–3, New York and London, 4–6, Camden, NJ, and London; 1964–8). For edns. and trs. of individual Fathers, see the sep. entries. For vocabulary, H. Kraft, *Clavis Patrum Apostolorum: Catalogus Vocum in Libris Patrum qui dicuntur Apostolici non raro occurrentium* (Munich, 1963). *The New Testament in the Apostolic Fathers* (ed. Oxford Society of Hist. Theology, 1905). T. F. Torrance, *The Doctrine of Grace in the Apostolic Fathers* (1948). J. Lawson, *A Theological and Historical Introduction to the Apostolic Fathers* (1961). L. W. Barnard, *Studies in the Apostolic Fathers and their Background* (Oxford [1966]). A. P. O'Hagan, *Material Re-Creation in the Apostolic Fathers* (TU 100; 1968); J. Liebaert, *Les Enseignements moraux des Pères Apostoliques* [1970]; T. H. C. van Eijk, *La résurrection des morts chez les Pères Apostoliques* (Théologie historique, 25 [1974]). S. [C. ff.] Tugwell, OP, *The*

Apostolic Fathers (Outstanding Christian Thinkers, 1989). *CPG* 1 (1983), pp. 1–3 (no. 1000) for further bibl.

Apostolic King. A title traditionally borne by the King of Hungary. It is supposed to have been conferred on the first King, *Stephen I (d. 1038), by Pope *Sylvester II on account of his apostolic zeal. He was also known as 'His Apostolic Majesty'.

Apostolic See. The see of Rome, so called from its traditional association with the two apostles, St *Peter and St *Paul.

apostolic succession. The method whereby the ministry of the Christian Church is held to be derived from the apostles by a continuous succession. It has usually been associated with an assertion that the succession has been maintained by a series of bishops. These bishops have been regarded as succeeding the apostles because: (1) they perform the functions of the apostles; (2) their commission goes back to the apostles; (3) they succeed one another in the same sees, the derivation of which may be traced back to the communion of the apostles; and (4) by some writers because through their consecration to the episcopal office they inherit from the apostles the transmission of the Holy Spirit which empowers them for the performance of their work. The fact of the succession of the ministry from the apostles, and of the apostles from Christ, was strongly emphasized by *Clement of Rome before the end of the 1st cent.; and the necessity for it has been very widely taught within the historic Church. The fact of continuity in the succession has occasionally been disputed; and the necessity has been denied by most Protestant writers, and asserted only with qualifications by some other theologians.

Doubts about the continuity of the apostolic succession were among the reasons which led to the condemnation of *Anglican Orders (q.v.) by the see of Rome in 1896; in more recent years the maintenance of the 'historic episcopate' has been among the major issues in schemes for *reunion involving Anglican and other bodies. The 1982 statement on '*Baptism, Eucharist and Ministry', issued by the *Faith and Order Commission of the *World Council of Churches, was disposed to accept 'episcopal succession as a sign of the apostolicity of the life of the whole Church'. See also ANGLICAN–METHODIST CONVERSATIONS, and SOUTH INDIA, CHURCH OF.

A. W. Haddan, *Apostolical Succession in the Church of England* (1869); C. *Gore, *The Ministry of the Christian Church* (1889; ed. C. H. Turner, 1919); A. C. *Headlam in *The Prayer Book Dictionary* (1912 and 1925); C. H. Turner in *Essays on the Early History of the Church and the Ministry*, ed. H. B. *Swete (1918; 2nd edn., 1921); K. E. *Kirk (ed.), *The Apostolic Ministry* (1946); A. Ehrhardt, *The Apostolic Succession in the First Two Centuries of the Church* (1953). E. Benz, *Bischofsamt und apostolische Sukzession im deutschen Protestantismus* (1953). W. Telfer, *The Office of a Bishop* (1962), pp. 107–20.

Apostolic Tradition, The (Gk. ἡ ἀποστολικὴ παράδοσις). The document formerly known as the '*Egyptian Church Order', now generally held to be the work of St *Hippolytus. The treatise is apparently referred to in the words ἀποστολικὴ παράδοσις which occur in the list of writings attributed to Hippolytus on the statue preserved in the *Vatican Library. It contains a detailed description of rites and practices which are alleged to be traditional, though it cannot be assumed that they correspond in every particular with the Roman usage of the early 3rd cent. The document includes rites of *Ordination and *Baptism, and a *Eucharistic Prayer; this last was used as the basis of the second Eucharistic prayer in the 1970 Roman Missal. Apart from fragments, the original Greek text is lost. The most important translation is the Latin, preserved in part in a palimpsest at *Verona (lv [53]), in which it is combined with versions of the '*Didascalia Apostolorum' and the '*Apostolic Church Order'. There are also oriental versions (*Coptic, Arabic made from the Coptic, and *Ethiopic made from the Arabic) incorporated into the '*Sinodus Alexandrina'. Use was made of it in a number of other works (such as the '*Apostolic Constitutions', bk. 8, the *Testamentum Domini*, and the 'Canons of *Hippolytus') which have survived in a variety of E. languages. The Verona text was first published by E. Hauler in 1900, but the credit for establishing its Hippolytean authorship belongs to R. H. *Connolly, and, in a less degree, to E. *Schwartz.

There are critical reconstructions of the text by G. *Dix, OSB (London, 1937, incl. Eng. tr.; repr. with preface by H. Chadwick, 1968) and, most authoritatively, by B. Botte, OSB (Liturgiewissenschaftliche Quellen und Forschungen, 39; 1963). Simplified text by B. Botte, OSB (SC 11 bis, 1968; repr. with some revisions, 1984). Other Eng. trs. by B. S. Eaton (Cambridge, 1934) and G. J. Cuming (Grove Liturgical Study, 8; 1976). Lat. text ed. E. Hauler, *Didascaliae Apostolorum Fragmenta Veronensia Latina* (Leipzig, 1900), pp. 101–21, and E. Tidner, *Didascaliae Apostolorum, Canonum Ecclesiasticorum, Traditionis Apostolicae Versiones Latinae* (TU 75; 1963), pp. 117–50; Coptic ed., with Ger. tr., by W. Till and J. Leipoldt (TU 58; 1954); Arabic edn., with Fr. tr., by J. and A. Périer, 'Les "127 canons des Apôtres"', *PO* 8 (1912), pp. 590–622; Ethiopic (the first version to be pub. when an incomplete Lat. tr., was pr. by J. Ludolf, *Ad suam Historiam Aethiopicam . . . Commentarius* (Frankfurt a. Main, 1691), pp. 328–8), ed. G. Horner, *The Statutes of the Apostles* (1904), pp. 10–48, with Eng. tr., pp. 138–86; also, with Ger. tr., by H. Duensing (*Abh.* (Gött.), Dritte Folge, 32; 1946). E. Schwartz, *Über die Pseudoapostolischen Kirchenordnungen* (Strasbourg, 1910); R. H. Connolly, *The So-called Egyptian Church Order and Derived Documents* (Texts and Studies, 8.4; Cambridge, 1916). J. M. Hanssens, SJ, *La Liturgie d'Hippolyte: Ses documents, son titulaire, ses origines et son caractère* (Orientalia Christiana Analecta, 155; 1959); id., *La liturgie d'Hippolyte: Documents et Etudes* (Rome 1970). J. Magne, *Tradition Apostolique sur les Charismes et Diatexeis des saints Apôtres* (Origines Chrétiennes, 1; 1975 [argues against Hippolytean authorship]). G. J. Cuming (ed.), *Essays on Hippolytus* (Grove Liturgical Study, 15; 1978). E. Mazza, 'Omelie pasquali e Birkat ha-mazon: Fonti dell'Anafora di Ippolito?', *EL* 97 (1983), pp. 409–81. A. Faivre, *Naissance d'une hiérarchie: Les premières étapes du cursus clérical* (Théologie historique, 40 [1977]), esp. pp. 47–67; id., 'La documentation canonico-liturgique de l'église ancienne', *Rev. S.R.* 54 (1980), pp. 204–19 and 273–97, esp. pp. 279–86. *CPG* 1 (1983), pp. 226–8 (no. 1737).

Apostolicae Curae. Pope *Leo XIII's Bull, issued on 13 Sept. 1896, in which Anglican Orders were condemned as invalid through defect of both form and intention. A 'Responsio' was issued in 1897 by the Abps. of Canterbury and York. For the history of the question see ANGLICAN ORDINATIONS.

The text is in *Leonis Papae XIII Allocutiones, Epistolae, Constitutiones*, 6 (1900), pp. 198–210. Bettenson (2nd edn.), pp. 385–6. See also works cited under ANGLICAN ORDINATIONS.

Apostolici (Lat.), 'Apostolics'. Among the several sects and religious bodies to whom this title has been applied, either by themselves or by others are:

(1) Some *Gnostic communities of the 2nd–4th cents. They are described by *Epiphanius (*Haer.* 61).

(2) An ascetic body which flourished in the 12th cent. around Cologne and at Périgueux in France. They rejected marriage, oaths, and the use of flesh-meat, and attacked many Catholic doctrines. St *Bernard of Clairvaux preached against them.

(3) A sect begun at Parma in 1260 by one Gerard Segarelli. It drew its inspiration from the *Franciscan teaching on poverty. It was condemned at Rome in 1286 and again in 1291, and in 1300 Segarelli was burnt to death at Parma. Shortly afterwards the sect was revived under Fra Dolcino, who expounded apocalyptic doctrines derived from *Joachim of Fiore. In 1307 he too was burnt at the stake.

(4) The name has also been assumed by certain Protestant groups, e.g. some *Anabaptist sects.

Apostolicity. One of the four marks of the Church set forth in the *Nicene Creed ([*Credo*] *in unam sanctam catholicam et apostolicam ecclesiam*). On a Catholic view, the word means identifiable with the Church of the Apostles by succession (see APOSTOLIC SUCCESSION) and continuity of doctrine, to which RCs would add by communion with the 'see of Peter'. By Protestants it is generally understood to mean 'primitive', in contrast with real or supposed corruptions of post-apostolic times. (See also NOTES OF THE CHURCH.)

Apostolicum. A name given, esp. on the Continent, to the *Apostles' Creed.

apotheosis (Gk. ἀποθέωσις from θεός, 'god'), the assimilation of a man to a god. Greeks and Romans made no firm distinction between gods and men, and at latest from the reign of Alexander (356–323 BC) cults were rendered to rulers both before and after their death, as if to gods, though it does not appear that they were normally credited with supernatural powers; A. D. Nock held that the cults indicated homage rather than worship. The subjects of Rome commonly honoured the reigning emperor in this way, though no emperor was officially recognized as a god at Rome before death. The Christians' refusal to take part in the cult has sometimes been seen as a reason for their persecution by the government, but implausibly, since participation was not legally obligatory on any subject. Deified emperors were termed 'divi'; the same title was used by Christian emperors down to *Theodosius I, who claimed only to rule by the grace of God. The use of the same term to denote saints has sometimes been thought to support the theory that the pagan practice of apotheosis can be connected with the origins of Christian *canonization, but the saints were certainly not reckoned to be more than human. Rarely in Gnosticism, and once in *Gregory Thaumaturgus, the word ἀποθέωσις is used in the sense of 'union with God'; but this idea of 'divinization' through religious union, though common in E.

Christian mysticism and theology, is much more generally described as θέωσις or θεοποίησις. See also DEIFICATION.

M. P. Nilsson, *Geschichte der Griechischen Religion*, 2 (Handbuch der Altertumswissenschaft, 5/2; 1950), pp. 125–75 and 366–76 (3rd edn., 1974, pp. 132–85 and 384–95); K. Latte, *Römische Religionsgeschichte* (ibid. 5/4; 1960), ch. 12. L. Cerfaux and J. Tondriau, *Un concurrent du Christianisme: Le Culte des Souverains dans la Civilisation Gréco-Romaine* (Bibliothèque de Théologie, 3rd ser. 5; 1957). F. Taeger, *Charisma: Studien zur Geschichte des antiken Herrscherkultes* (2 vols., Stuttgart, 1957–60). A. D. Nock in *C. Anc. H.* 10 (1934), ch. 15, esp. pp, 481–503; id., 'Deification and Julian', *Journal of Roman Studies*, 47 (1957), pp. 115–23, repr. in his *Essays on Religion and the Ancient World*, ed. Z. Stewart (2 vols., Oxford, 1972), no. 49; cf. also nos. 6, 11, 40, and 45. J. H. W. G. Liebeschuetz, *Continuity and Change in Roman Religion* (Oxford, 1979), pp. 64–90, 235–43, and 289.

Apparitions of the BVM, the. The eighteen manifestations of the BVM to St *Bernadette (q.v.) in the grotto near *Lourdes between 11 Feb. and 16 July 1858. They are commemorated in the RC Church on 11 Feb. by a feast which was of universal observance from 1907 to 1969.

apparitor. An officer appointed by an ecclesiastical judge to execute the orders and decrees of his court, and to summon persons to appear before it (hence the name). They were also anciently called 'summoners' or 'sumners'. Their number and privileges were restricted by a *Canon (138) of 1604. They continue to be appointed, and usually carry the mace before the *chancellor.

R. *Phillimore, *The Ecclesiastical Law of the Church of England*, 2 (2nd edn. by W. G. F. Phillimore, 1895), pp. 951–4.

appeals. Applications from a lower to a higher judicial authority, a term commonly used in connection with the ecclesiastical courts. Appeals by clergy and laity to authorities higher than their diocesans were based upon Roman civil law and regulated by several councils from *Nicaea (325) to *Trent (1545–63). During the Middle Ages appeal to the Papal *Curia from the English ecclesiastical courts occasioned intermittent friction between Church and State. From the time of Henry II, the Kings of England attempted to limit appeals to Rome, until in 1534 *Henry VIII abolished them, substituting the Court of *Delegates as final arbiter in ecclesiastical causes. Appeals are now governed by the *Ecclesiastical Jurisdiction Measure 1963 (q.v.).

appearance. A word once popular in philosophy through the use made of it by F. H. *Bradley in his *Appearance and Reality* (1893). Acc. to Bradley, the only reality is an absolute all-inclusive experience ('the richer for every discord'), and everything other than this, including morality and religion, is convicted on analysis of contradiction and hence assigned to the realm of 'appearance'. In a somewhat different sense, the word is also used of those elements in our knowledge which we obtain through our senses. It is this meaning which is found in the *Platonist emphasis on the need for 'saving the appearances' (σώζειν τὰ φαινόμενα, *Proclus, *Hyp.* 5. 10), i.e. for securing that the facts of sense-observation have their due place in any rationalized theory or system about the world.

Appellants. (1) The 31 RC secular priests, headed by William Bishop (c.1553–1624), titular Bp. of *Chalcedon from 1623, who appealed to Rome in 1598–9 for the cancellation of G. *Blackwell's appointment as *archpriest and superior of the mission on the ground that his pro-*Jesuit policy was damaging the RC cause in England. Since Card. W. *Allen's death (1594), the English RCs had become divided into an extreme party, mostly Jesuits, under R. *Parsons, who wished to destroy *Elizabeth I's government, and the remainder who were politically loyal; and Blackwell's appointment in 1598 had brought matters to a head. The original Appeal was a failure. But, as Blackwell persevered in his policy, the seculars made further Appeals in 1601 and 1602, the third time with the support of the French ambassador. Blackwell was reprimanded, his connection with the Jesuits severed, and several Appellant priests put on the controlling council. On his return, Bishop drew up a 'Protestation of Allegiance' to Elizabeth (31 Jan. 1603) in which he and 12 other priests formally repudiated the use of political means for the conversion of England. The immediate controversy came to an end when in 1608 Blackwell himself took the Oath of Allegiance to *James I, but tensions between regulars and seculars continued.

(2) The name given to those of *Jansenist and *Gallican sentiments who rejected the condemnation by '*Unigenitus' (1713) of 101 propositions extracted from P. *Quesnel's *Reflexions morales*. In March 1717 four bishops solemnly appealed against the Papal Bull to the next General Council; in the following months they were joined by eight other bishops, incl. Card. L. A. *de Noailles, Abp. of Paris, by the *Sorbonne and other universities, and by a significant number of clergy. In Sept. 1718 *Clement XI in his brief 'Pastoralis Officii' formally condemned and excommunicated them and from 1720 the French court concurred in attacking them. With the support of the *Parlements* they were able to keep up some resistance and played a part in the expulsion of the *Jesuits from France.

On (1) T. G. Law (ed.), *The Archpriest Controversy: Documents relating to the Dissensions of the Roman Catholic Clergy, 1597–1602* (Camden Society, NS 66 and 68; 1896–8); narrative by John Bennett (written in 1621) and other 17th-cent. papers in *Miscellanea*, 12 (CRS 22; 1921), pp. 132–86. A. Pritchard, *Catholic Loyalism in Elizabethan England* (1979), pp. 120–201.
On (2) J. Carreyre, *Le Jansénisme durant la régence* (Bibliothèque de la RHE, 2–4; 1929–33). D. [K.] Van Kley, *The Jansenists and the Expulsion of the Jesuits from France 1757–1765* (New Haven, Conn., and London, 1975). See also works on JANSENISM, cited s.v.

Appian Way (Lat. *Via Appia*). The famous road constructed by the censor Appius Claudius Caecus in 312 BC from *Rome to the S. of Italy. It was orig. carried as far as Capua, but later taken through to Brindisi. After disembarking at Puteoli, St *Paul travelled on the Appian Way on his first journey to Rome, being met (Acts 28: 15) by groups of Christian disciples at 'Appii Forum' (43 miles) and Three Taverns (33 miles from Rome).

Owing to the construction of the Via Appia Nuova, for the first few miles out of Rome the old road remains much as it was in ancient times. It is still flanked by many monuments, mostly tombs. The Christian sanctuaries and remains along it include the '*Domine quo vadis?' chapel (q.v.); the *catacombs of St *Callistus (the burying-place

of most of the Popes in the 3rd cent.) and of Praetextatus; and the basilica of St *Sebastian (near the reputed resting-place of the remains of St *Peter and St Paul during the persecution of Valerian, 258).

appropriation. The practice common in the Middle Ages of permanently annexing to a monastery, Dean and Chapter, college or other spiritual body the *tithes and profits of a parish. It was then usually necessary to endow and appoint a *vicar or substitute to perform the parochial duties, and this was made law by the Appropriation of Benefices Acts in 1391 and 1402 (15 Ric. II c. 6, 4 Hen. IV c. 12). However, monasteries with benefices for their table (*ad mensam monachorum*) or with a dispensation because the house was poor or the church was close, were permitted instead to license a curate, often one of their number, who had no endowment and could be recalled at any time. See also IMPROPRIATION.

R. Burn, *Ecclesiastical Law*, 1 (9th edn. rev. by R. *Phillimore, 1842), pp. 65–92, s.v.; and 2, pp. 55–55c, s.v. 'Curate'

apron. The 'apron' which is part of the traditional distinctive dress of Anglican bishops, deans, and archdeacons is really a shortened form of the *cassock, extending to the knees; it is now seldom worn. Formerly this dress was widely worn on the Continent, but in the 19th cent. its use was very much restricted by *Pius IX.

apse. A semicircular or polygonal E. end to a chancel. This was a universal feature of the primitive *basilican type of church architecture, adapted from the model of Roman public buildings. The altar stood on the chord of the apse, with the seats of the bishop and presbyters in the curved space behind. It was introduced into England by St *Augustine's mission, but the Celtic square-ended chancel continued to prevail. The Norman builders again favoured the apse, but in later building there was a general reversion to the indigenous square end, only a few examples of apsidal sanctuaries still remaining, e.g. at *Norwich Cathedral. See also BASILICA.

APUC ('Association for the Promotion of the Unity of Christendom'). A society formed in 1857 in F. G. *Lee's rooms to further the cause of reunion, esp. between the C of E and Rome. Its members were required to say daily the prayer for the unity of the Church in the Latin Missal. It owed its foundation chiefly to A. L. M. Phillipps *de Lisle, a leading RC layman, who had earlier (c.1838) established a 'Society for Prayers for the Conversion of England'; and it included Anglicans (among them A. P. *Forbes) and also some Orthodox. After 1864, when it was condemned by the *Holy Office RCs were compelled to withdraw from it. It was finally disbanded in 1921.

Members of the Association used two organs, *The Union Newspaper* (1857–62) and *The Union Review* (1862–75). B. [C.] and M. Pawley, *Rome and Canterbury through Four Centuries* (1974), pp. 187–97 (rev. edn. 1981, pp. 170–79). E. B. Stuart, 'Unjustly Condemned?: Roman Catholic Involvement in the APUC 1857–64', *JEH* 41 (1990), pp. 44–63. H. R. T. Brandreth, *Dr. Lee of Lambeth: A Chapter in Parenthesis in the History of the Oxford Movement* (1951), pp. 76–117.

Aquarians (Lat. *Aquarii*, from *aqua*, 'water'). A name given by *Philaster (*Haer.* 77) and *Augustine (*Haer.* 64) to a sect or sects which, for ascetic or other reasons, used water instead of wine in the Eucharist. They were sometimes known as 'Hydroparastatae' (Gk. Ὑδροπαραστάται, 'those who offer water').

P. Lebeau, SJ, *Le Vin nouveau du Royaume* (1966), pp. 142–84 ('La contestation aquarienne'). P. *Batiffol in *DACL* 1 (1907), cols. 2648–54, s.v. See also other works cited under WINE.

Aquaviva, Claudio (1543–1615), fifth General of the *Jesuits. The youngest son of the Duke of Atri, he studied law at Perugia and entered the Jesuit novitiate in 1567. Ordained in 1574, he became Provincial of Naples in 1576 and of Rome in 1579 and was elected General in 1581. His qualities of leadership helped to bring about the Society's consolidation, both in respect of its internal structures and its characteristic approaches to ministry. Under his rule its membership increased from *c.*5,000 to *c.*13,000. The famous '*Ratio Studiorum', outlining Jesuit teaching procedures, was completed, as well as a set of authoritative guidelines (or 'Directory') for the use of the *Spiritual Exercises. Important norms regarding the spiritual life and training of Jesuits became established in the Society's law, and Aquaviva wrote two seminal letters addressed to all Jesuits on prayer (1599 and 1612). He also overcame a number of attempts to amend the Society's form of government. These were instigated by Spanish Jesuits, with the support on different occasions of *Philip II, the *Inquisition, and Popes *Sixtus V and *Clement VIII. The settlement which he achieved was decisive for the subsequent history of the Jesuits.

As General, Aquaviva had to govern and support various individuals and groups of Jesuits who encountered severe difficulties, including temporary exile from *France and *Venice and persecutions in England and *Japan. Jesuits were also involved in fierce theological controversies, notably Luis de *Molina on grace and free will and St Robert *Bellarmine over the temporal power of the Pope.

Works listed in Sommervogel, 1 (1890), cols. 480–91; 8 (1898), cols. 1669 f.; Polgár, 1 (1990), pp. 129 f. A. Astráin, SJ, *Historia de la Compañia de Jesús en la asistencia de España*, vols. 3 (1910), pt. 2, and 4 (1913). W. V. Bangert, SJ, *A History of the Society of Jesus* (St Louis, 1972; 2nd edn., 1986), esp. pp. 97–107 and 110–13. J. de Guibert, SJ, *La Spiritualité de la Compagnie de Jésus* (posthumous; Bibliotheca Instituti Historici S.I., 4; Rome, 1953), pp. 219–37; Eng. tr. (Chicago, 1964), pp. 230–47. B. Schneider, SJ, 'Der Konflikt zwischen Claudius Aquaviva und Paul Hoffaeus', *Archivum Historicum Societatis Iesu*, 26 (1957), pp. 3–56; 27 (1958), pp. 279–306. M. Rosa in *Dizionario Biografico degli Italiani*, 1 (1960), pp. 168–78; B. Schneider, SJ, in *NCE* 1 (1967), pp. 89 f., both s.v. 'Acquaviva'; I. Iparraguirre, SJ, and M. de Certeau, SJ, in *Dict. Sp.* 8 (1974), cols. 979–94, s.v. 'Jésuites'.

Aquila, St. See PRISCILLA, ST.

Aquila, Version of. Greek version of the OT. It was the work of Aquila, a native of Sinope in Pontus, who lived under Hadrian (117–38). Acc. to St *Epiphanius (*Mens. et Pond.* 14), he was a relative of the Emperor and was converted to Christianity during a stay in *Jerusalem, but, having refused to give up his astrological studies, he was excommunicated and became a proselyte to Judaism. Having become a disciple of the *Rabbis, from whom he learned Hebrew and the rabbinical method of exegesis, he used this knowledge to make a revision of the *Septuagint, bringing it into line with the official Hebrew text. It was soon adopted by Greek-speaking Jews in preference to the LXX, which was used by the Christians. His translation, which was finished probably *c.*140, was extremely literal, attempting to reproduce individual Hebrew words and phrases exactly. This procedure frequently obscured the sense; but the fidelity of Aquila's version to the Hebrew original was admitted by the Fathers most competent to judge, such as *Origen and *Jerome.

Surviving fragments of Aquila's version ed. F. *Field in *Origenis Hexaplorum quae supersunt* (2 vols., Oxford, 1871–5); more recently discovered passages ed. G. *Mercati, *Un palimpsesto ambrosiano de salmi esapli* (Turin, 1896), and F. C. *Burkitt, *Fragments of the Book of Kings according to the Translation of Aquila* (1897, with pref. by C. Taylor; texts from the Cairo Geniza). D. Barthélemy, OP, *Les Devanciers d'Aquila: Première publication intégrale du Texte des Fragments du Dodécaprophéton trouvés dans le désert de Juda* (Supplements to *Vetus Testamentum*, 10; Leiden, 1963), with introd. M. Abrahams, *Aquila's Greek Versions of the Hebrew Bible* (1919); A. E. Silverstone, *Aquila and Onkelos* (Publications of the University of Manchester. Semitic Languages Series, no. 1, 1931; claims to identify Aquila with Onkelos). L. L. Grabbe, 'Aquila's Translation and Rabbinic Exegesis', *Journal of Jewish Studies*, 33 (1982), pp. 527–36. J. Reider, *An Index to Aquila: Greek–Hebrew, Hebrew–Greek, Latin–Hebrew with the Syriac and Armenian Evidence*, completed and rev. by N. Turner (Supplements to *Vetus Testamentum*, 12; 1966). H. B. *Swete, *An Introduction to the Old Testament in Greek* (1900), pp. 31–42; S. Jellicoe, *The Septuagint and Modern Study* (Oxford, 1968), pp. 76–83. E. *Schürer, *A History of the Jewish People in the Age of Jesus Christ*, rev. Eng. tr. by G. Vermes and others, 3 (pt. 1; Edinburgh, 1986), pp. 493–9. See also bibl. to HEXAPLA.

Aquileia, a village on the Adriatic coast which was an important city during the later Roman Empire, and long the seat of a W. Patriarchate. Acc. to a 5th-cent. legend it was evangelized by St *Mark, but in fact the beginnings of the Church cannot be traced beyond the 3rd cent. In 381 its bishop, Valerian, appears as Metropolitan of the Churches in the area, holding a synod of bishops directed against *Arianism, over which St *Ambrose presided. Under Valerian and his successor, *Chromatius, it was a centre of learning, and *Jerome (*Chron.* s.a. 374), who spent some years there, refers to the 'clerici' of Aquileia as a 'choir of the blessed' (*chorus beatorum*). In 452 the city was sacked by *Attila, but not destroyed. In the 6th cent. the bishops assumed the title of patriarch. During the dispute over the *Three Chapters (553) the patriarch withstood *Justinian and the Pope and was declared schismatic. Owing to the attacks of the Lombards in 568 the patriarch took refuge in Grado, which is now joined to the mainland by a causeway but was then an island in the lagoon; from the early 7th cent. there were two rival patriarchs, one at Grado ('new' Aquileia) which was eventually transferred to Venice in 1451, and one ('old' Aquileia) at Cormons (later Cividale). The territory of the latter was greatly enlarged N. of the Alps in the reign of *Charlemagne under the Patriarch *Paulinus. It survived with diminished territory, and came in 1420 under Venetian and in 1509 under Austrian domination. It was suppressed in 1751. The present basilica was reconstructed by the Patriarch Poppo (1019–42) on the site of one of the early 4th cent. Its floor, which was revealed by excavation in 1909, is covered with early 4th-cent. mosaics which are among the most remarkable survivals of early Christian art. There has been much speculation by scholars about the rite of Aquileia, but owing to the loss of early material nothing certain is known. The surviving books show only certain local uses.

J. B. M. de Rubeis, *Monumenta Ecclesiae Aquileiensis commentario historico-chronologico-critico illustrata* ('Argentinae' [either Venice or Verona], 1740). P. F. Kehr, *Italia Pontificia*, 7 (pt. 1; Berlin, 1923), pp. 8–71; (pt. 2; 1925), pp. 27–72. P. Paschini, *Storia del Friuli* (3 vols., 1934–6; 2nd edn., 2 vols., 1953–4). *La basilica di Aquileia* (ed. Comitato per le cerimonie celebrative del IX° centenario della basilica; Bologna, 1933). G. Brusin, *Aquileia e Grado: Guida storico-artistica* (25th edn., Padua, 1964). *Mostra di Codici Liturgici Aquileiesi* (Udine, 1968). G. Cuscito, *Cristianesimo antico ad Aquileia e in Istria* (Fonti e Studi per la Storia della Venezia Giulia, 2nd ser. 3; 1977). Recent discoveries and theories are recorded in the journal *Aquileia Nostra: Bolletino dell'Associazione Nazionale per Aquileia* (Milan, 1930 ff.) and in the occasional pubs. Antichità Altoadriatiche (Udine, 1972 ff.), of which vol. 11 is S. Piussi, *Bibliografia Aquileiese* (1978), with index to other vols. in the series. P. L. Zovatto in *Reallexikon zur Byzantinischen Kunst*, ed. K. Wessel, 1 (1966), pp. 293–306; H. Schmidinger in *Lexikon des Mittelalters*, 1 (1980), cols. 827 f., both s.v.

Aquinas, St Thomas. See THOMAS AQUINAS, ST.

Arabic Versions of the Bible. There are conflicting traditions about the earliest attempts to translate substantial portions of the Bible into Arabic, but it is clear that it was only after the *Koran had made Arabic into a literary language and the conquests of *Islam had turned large parts of Christian Syria and Egypt into Arabic-speaking areas that the need for translations of Scripture into Arabic was felt. By the 9th cent. there were a number of Arabic versions of the NT, in some cases made directly from the Greek, in others through the *Syriac and *Coptic (*Bohairic) versions; the oldest surviving MS (Vaticanus arabicus 13, dated 8th or possibly early 9th cent.) is a translation from the Syriac *Peshitta. This MS originally also contained the Psalter. Fragments of an Arabic translation of the Psalter (in Greek letters, hence obviously intended for *Melchites) are dated in the 8th cent. Subsequent translations of Books of the OT were made from Greek, Syriac, and Hebrew (notably the version of Saadia ben Joseph ha-Gaon, d. 942). The Arabic OT text printed in the Paris *Polyglot reflects this variety; Saadia's version is used for the Pentateuch, but in other Books the Arabic was translated from Greek or Syriac. In the 13th cent. two revisions of the Arabic NT were sponsored by the Patriarchate of *Alexandria; the latter of these, the so-called 'Alexandrian Vulgate', is that followed in modern printed editions.

The earliest text to be pr. was Psalms, incl. in the Polyglot Psalter pub. at Genoa in 1516. The NT was ed. by T. Erpenius at Leiden in 1616. Crit. edn. of the Gospels by P. A. de *Lagarde (Leipzig, 1864), with valuable introd. B. Violet, 'Ein zweisprächiges Psalmenfragment aus Damascus', *Orientalistische Literatur-Zeitung*, 4 (1901), cols. 384–403, 425–41, 475–88. This fragment and selected other texts, with glossary, ed. P. [E.] Kahle, *Die arabischen Bibelübersetzungen* (Leipzig, 1904). I. Guidi, 'Le traduzioni degli evangelii in arabo e in etiopico', *Atti della R. Accademia dei Lincei*, 4th ser., Classe di Scienze Morali, Storiche et Filologiche, 4. 1 (1888), pp. 5–37. B. M. Metzger, *The Early Versions of the New Testament* (Oxford, 1977), pp. 257–68. S. H.

Griffith, 'The Gospel in Arabic: An Inquiry into its Appearance in the First Abbasid Century', *OC* 69 (1985), pp. 126–67. G. Graf, *Geschichte der christlichen arabischen Literatur*, 1 (ST 118; 1944), pp. 85–185. G. Mink and S. P. Brock in *TRE* 6 (1980), pp. 207–11, s.v. 'Bibelübersetzungen'. For literature on the Arabic version of the Diatessaron, see DIATESSARON.

Aramaic. The Semitic language which was the vernacular in Palestine in the time of Christ, and which He Himself almost certainly used. It had long been spoken by the Aramaeans in N. Syria and in Mesopotamia, and came to be used increasingly throughout the Levant for commercial and diplomatic transactions (cf. 2 Kgs. 18: 26). In later OT times it more and more ousted Hebrew as the language of Palestine. A few sections of the OT itself (Ezra 4: 8–6: 18, 7: 12–26; Dan. 2: 4–7: 28; Jer. 10: 11) are written in Aramaic and by NT times Hebrew was cultivated mainly by the learned. To satisfy the needs of the people, the Hebrew Scriptures were issued in the form of Aramaic paraphrases, known as the *Targums. *Syriac (q.v.) and Mandaic are both dialects of Aramaic, each with its own script. In the NT there are many places where the Greek reflects the Aramaic modes of thought or background of the writers, and occasionally Aramaic words are preserved, e.g. Mk. 5: 41, 7: 34, 15: 34. It is very unlikely, however, that any parts of the NT are direct translations from Aramaic (as scholars such as C. F. *Burney and C. C. Torrey claimed). See also CHALDEE.

C. Brockelmann, *Grundriss der vergleichenden Grammatik der semitischen Sprachen* (2 vols., 1908–13); F. Rosenthal, *Die aramaistische Forschung seit Theodor Nöldekes Veröffentlichungen* (1939); id., *A Grammar of Biblical Aramaic* (Porta Linguarum Orientalium, NS 5; 1961); id. (ed.), *An Aramaic Handbook* (2 parts in 4; ibid. 10; 1967). H. Bauer and P. Leander, *Grammatik des Biblisch-Aramäischen* (1927). M. Black, *An Aramaic Approach to the Gospels and Acts* (Oxford, 1946; 3rd edn., 1967). W. B. Stevenson, *Grammar of Palestinian Jewish Aramaic* (1924; 2nd edn., 1962); G. *Dalman, *Grammatik des jüdisch-palästinischen Aramäisch* (1894; 2nd edn., rev., 1905); id., *Die Worte Jesu* (1898; 2nd edn., 1930). F. Schulthess and E. Littmann, *Grammatik des christlich-palästinischen Aramäisch* (1924). E. Y. Kutscher, *Hebrew and Aramaic Studies* (Jerusalem, 1977), pp. 90–155; J. C. Greenfield, 'Aramaic and its Dialects', in H. H. Paper (ed.), *Jewish Languages ...: Proceedings of Regional Conferences of the Association for Jewish Studies held at the University of Michigan and New York University in March–April 1975* (Cambridge, Mass., 1978), pp. 29–43; id., 'The Language of Palestine, 200 B.C.E.–200 C.E.', ibid., pp. 143–54. J. A. Fitzmyer, SJ, *A Wandering Aramean* (Society of Biblical Literature, Monograph Series, 25; 1979). A. Dupont-Sommer, *Les Araméens* (1949). For full bibl. H. J. W. Drijvers in J. H. Hospers (ed.), *A Basic Bibliography for the Study of the Semitic Languages*, 1 (Leiden, 1973), pp. 283–335. R. Degen and H. P. Rüger in *TRE* 3 (1978), pp. 599–610, s.v. 'Aramäisch, I–II'.

Arator (6th cent.), Christian Latin poet. Born (perhaps *c.*490) in Liguria, he received his early education in Milan, where he was befriended by *Ennodius, and subsequently studied the classics in *Ravenna. He went as imperial ambassador to Dalmatia in 526 and was ultimately *comes privatarum* under the Emp. Athalaric. He left the imperial service to become a subdeacon in Rome, where he enjoyed a close association with Pope *Vigilius (537–55). At Rome he completed his major work, the *De actibus apostolorum*, a hexametrical version of the Book of Acts, which was read publicly in the church of San Pietro in Vincoli at *Rome in 544. The poem is not simply a metrical paraphrase, in the manner of *Juvencus, but an exegetical elaboration of the symbolic meaning in the biblical narrative. Although the poem is difficult, it was widely studied in the early Middle Ages, being eclipsed as a curriculum text only in the 12th cent. The date of his death is unknown.

Works (repr. from 1769 edn.) in J. P. Migne, *PL* 68. 63–252; crit. edn. by A. P. McKinlay (CSEL 72; 1951). Id., *Arator: The Codices* (Mediaeval Academy of America, publication 43; Cambridge, Mass., 1942); G. R. Wieland, *The Latin Glosses on Arator and Prudentius in Cambridge University Library MS Gg. 5. 35* (Pontifical Institute of Mediaeval Studies, Studies and Texts, 61; Toronto, 1983). R. Hillier, *Arator on the Acts of the Apostles* (Oxford Early Christian Studies, 1993). Manitius, 1, pp. 162–7. K. Thraede, 'Arator', *Jahrbuch für Antike und Christentum*, 4 (1961), pp. 187–96.

Arbuthnott, Missal of. A Scottish MS missal dated 1491, now in the Paisley Museum. It survives complete, on 244 leaves. It corresponds closely with the typical edition of 1498 of the *Sarum Missal, with differences chiefly in the *Propers for Saints. It also contains some *Sequences not found in the English pre-Reformation uses. As the only surviving specimen of the medieval Scottish use, the MS is of considerable interest.

Ed. G. H. *Forbes, *Liber Ecclesie Beati Terrenani de Arbuthnott* (Burntisland, 1864).

archaeology, Christian. In ancient Greek writers the word ἀρχαιολογία (lit. 'discourse on things ancient') meant antiquarian lore, as distinct from the narrative history of persons and events. Its Latin equivalent, *antiquitates*, yielded the English word 'antiquities' which long served to define a branch of historical inquiry that concerned itself with materials and records of all kinds, in so far as they could be used to illustrate the condition of earlier societies. The classic English example of this type of research, in the field of ecclesiastical history, is J. *Bingham's *Antiquities of the Christian Church* (1708–22), 'being an essay upon the ancient usages and customs of the primitive Church' based mainly on literary evidence. The specialized use of the word 'archaeologia' or its vernacular equivalent to mean a science of the monuments (as opposed to the documents) of antiquity does not appear to have gained currency until the early 19th cent. The expression 'Christian archaeology' was popularized by G. B. *de Rossi's *Bullettino di Archeologia Cristiana*, first published in 1863. As traditionally defined, Christian archaeology is a historical science of the monuments of early Christianity, the function of which is 'to make known as fully as possible the thought and religious life of Christian antiquity' (G. P. Kirsch). In this context, 'Christian antiquity' is usually taken to mean the first six cents. of the Christian era.

Although evidence of an interest in early Christian monuments (esp. those of *Rome and the Holy Land) can be found in all periods from the 4th cent. onwards, the beginnings of Christian archaeology may be associated with the first exploration of the Roman *catacombs in the late 16th and early 17th cent., the results of which appear most clearly in A. *Bosio's *Roma sotterranea* (1632). Much of this early work is characterized by a spirit of *Counter-Reformation apologetic, it then being widely believed that archaeological evidence could demonstrate the primitive origins of Catholic observances (e.g. the cult of *relics). Rome, and the catacombs in particular, continued to provide the main focus of Christian archaeology throughout the following two and a half cents., a state of affairs that is reflected in the foundation of the Pontificia Commissione di Archeologia Sacra under Pope *Pius IX in 1852 (to be followed by the foundation of the Pontificio Istituto di Archeologia Cristiana in 1925) and in the magisterial works of G. B. de Rossi. The latter, whose *Roma sotterranea cristiana* began to appear in 1864, is generally credited with establishing Christian archaeology as a modern scientific discipline. His work was carried on by J. Wilpert (1857–1944), who assembled major *corpora* of Roman frescoes, mosaics, and early Christian *sarcophagi. See also ROME, CHURCHES OF, and ST PETER'S, ROME.

The history of Christian archaeology since the beginning of the 20th cent. has been marked by three major developments, each of which may be seen as freeing the science from earlier constraints. (1) The attention of researchers has been drawn increasingly to areas of early Christian civilization outside Rome; nowadays the sphere of Christian archaeology encompasses the whole of the ancient Mediterranean world, as well as a number of adjacent regions that were either touched by early Christianity or whose native traditions help account for particular features of Christian material culture. (2) The erosion of long-standing prejudices against the intellectual and artistic achievements of the period now known as 'late antiquity' (2nd–7th cent. AD) has led to a new interest, shared by secular and ecclesiastical historians alike, in the relationship between early Christianity and classical culture. (3) Partly as a result of the two preceding developments, the traditional link between Christian archaeology and historical theology has been considerably weakened, to the extent that some scholars now question the viability of a specifically 'Christian' archaeology, while others favour the concept of a combined 'late antique, early Christian and early medieval archaeology' (P. Testini). A further trend, particularly noticeable in Britain in recent years, has been towards the excavation and scientific study of Christian sites of the medieval period.

The techniques of Christian archaeology (survey, excavation, recording, dating, interpretation, and reconstruction) are essentially the same as those employed in other fields of archaeological science. The main classes of early Christian monuments are *cemeteries, buildings (chiefly churches, *baptisteries, and *monasteries but also, on occasion, private houses; see DURA EUROPOS), sculpture, paintings, mosaic, textiles, liturgical apparatus, together with such objects as glass, *lamps, medals, and *rings. Epigraphy, the study of inscriptions, is a special branch of Christian archaeology. Where buildings and artefacts are studied for their aesthetic qualities, they form the subject-matter of a history of Christian architecture and art, an important part of which is concerned with the pedigree of representational themes (*iconography).

While the correct interpretation of the material finds made by Christian archaeologists regularly depends on a thorough understanding of the relevant literary evidence (including that of papyri; see PAPYROLOGY), archaeological research also provides much information on the early history of the Church that could never be obtained from the literary record alone. This is particularly so with regard to the lives of members of the lower orders of Christian society and the ordinary routine of Christian observance. In view of the improbability of any major future increase in our literary documentation, it is indeed likely that 'for the year-to-year growth of his subject the Church historian will continue to look to the archaeologist' (W. H. C. Frend).

G. P. Kirsch, 'L'Archeologia cristiana, suo carattere proprio e suo metodo scientifico. Prolusione per l'inaugurazione del Pont. Istituto di Archeologia Cristiana', *Rivista di Archeologia Cristiana,* 4 (1927), pp. 49–57; G. Ferretto, *Note Storico-Bibliografiche di Archeologia Cristiana* (Vatican City, 1942); P. Testini, *Archeologia Cristiana: Nozioni generali dalle origini alla fine del sec. VI* [1958]; R. Krautheimer, *Early Christian and Byzantine Architecture* (Pelican History of Art, 1965); A. Grabar, *Le premier art chrétien (200–395)* ([1966]; Eng. tr. 1967); C. Andresen, *Einführung in die Christliche Archäologie* (Die Kirche in ihrer Geschichte, I.B. 1; Göttingen, 1971); K. Weitzmann (ed.), *Age of Spirituality: Late Antique and Early Christian Art, Third to Seventh Century. Catalogue of the exhibition at the Metropolitan Museum of Art, November 19, 1977, through February 12, 1978* (New York [1979]); W. Rodwell, *The Archaeology of the English Church* (1981); [A.] C. Thomas, *Christianity in Roman Britain to AD 500* (1981); P. Testini, 'L'"Archaeologia Cristiana". Quale disciplina oggi?', in *Atti del V Congresso Nazionale di Archeologia Cristiana . . . 22–29 settembre 1979,* 1 (1982), pp. 17–35; F. W. Deichmann, *Einführung in die Christliche Archäologie* (Darmstadt, 1983); W. Wischmeyer, 'Perspektiven frühchristlicher Kunst für die Geschichte der Kirche', *RQ* 79 (1984), pp. 145–62; H. R. Seeliger, 'Christliche Archäologie oder spätantike Kunstgeschichte? Aktuelle Grundlagenfragen aus der Sicht der Kirchengeschichte', *Rivista di Archeologia Cristiana,* 61 (1985), pp. 167–87; W. H. C. Frend, 'Archaeology and patristic studies', in E. A. Livingstone (ed.), *Studia Patristica,* 18, pt. 1 (Kalamazoo, Mich., 1985), pp. 9–21; id., *The Archaeology of Early Christianity: A History* (1996). W. Smith and S. Cheetham, *Dictionary of Christian Antiquities* (2 vols., 1875–80); F. *Cabrol, OSB, and H. *Leclercq, OSB, *Dictionnaire d'archéologie chrétienne et de liturgie* (15 vols., 1907–53); A. Baudrillart and others (eds.), *Dictionnaire d'histoire et de géographie ecclésiastiques* (1912 ff.); T. Klauser and others (eds.), *Reallexikon für Antike und Christentum* (1950 ff.). The progress of Christian archaeology may be followed in periodicals such as *Römische Quartalschrift* (1887 ff.), *Revista di Archeologia Cristiana* (1924 ff.), *Jahrbuch für Antike und Christentum* (1958 ff.) and in the pub. proceedings of the Congresso Internazionale di Archeologia Cristiana (since the 3rd Congress, of 1932, pub. in the series Studi di Antichità Cristiana, 1934 ff.). J. Quasten in *NCE* 1 (1967), pp. 761–8.

archangel (Gk. ἀρχάγγελος, 'chief angel'). In the NT the word occurs only twice, at Jude v. 9, where *Michael is referred to as 'the archangel', and at 1 Thess. 4; 16 ('the voice of the archangel'). In Christian tradition *Gabriel and *Raphael are also commonly reckoned with Michael among the archangels. Acc. to traditional angelology, as expounded by *Dionysius the Pseudo-Areopagite, the archangels belong to the third and lowest hierarchy of the angelic beings. See also ANGEL.

archbishop (Gk. ἀρχιεπίσκοπος). In the 4th and 5th cents. the title was applied to the *patriarchs and holders of other outstanding sees. Later its use was extended to *metropolitans (or *primates) having jurisdiction over an ecclesiastical province. In the Latin Church it has now almost become a title of honour for a bishop of a distinguished see.

A. S. Popek, *The Rights and Obligations of Metropolitans* (Catholic University of America Canon Law Studies, 260; 1947). See also bibl. to BISHOP.

archdeacon. A cleric having a defined administrative authority delegated to him by the bishop in the whole or part of the diocese. The territory assigned to him is known as an archdeaconry and gives him a territorial title, e.g. 'Archdeacon of Lindsey'. In the C of E and other Churches of the Anglican Communion an archdeacon is styled 'Venerable'. The duties of archdeacons vary widely but they usually include a general disciplinary supervision of the clergy of their archdeaconry and a more particular care over the temporal administration of its ecclesiastical property. Thus they usually *induct parish priests to new benefices and admit *churchwardens to their offices. The Anglican *Ordinal presupposes that among their functions is the examination and presentation of candidates for *Ordination. By the 1969 *Canons (can. C 22) they are required to hold annual visitations within their archdeaconry. Originally, as the name implies, an archdeacon was merely the chief of the *deacons who assisted diocesan bishops in their work. They were in deacon's orders and gradually acquired what was almost a right of succession to the episcopal throne. The transition from this to the present position of archdeacons was accomplished by the 9th cent. but the steps by which it came about are not clear. In England since 1662 an archdeacon must be in priest's orders, and since 1840 must have been so for six years.

J. *Bingham, *Origines Ecclesiasticae,* Bk. 2, ch. 21 (1708), pp. 287–301. A. Gréa, 'Essai historique sur les archidiacres', *Bibliothèque de l'École des Chartes,* 12 (1851), pp. 39–67 and 215–47; F. X. Glasschröder, 'Zur Geschichte des Archidiakonates', in S. Ehses (ed.), *Festschrift zum elfhundertjährigen Jubiläum des Deutschen Campo in Rom* (1897), pp 139–49. A. H. Thompson, 'Diocesan Organization in the Middle Ages. Archdeacons and Rural Deans', *Proceedings of the British Academy,* 29 (1943), pp. 153–94, esp. pp. 153–84. R. *Phillimore, *The Ecclesiastical Law of the Church of England,* 1 (2nd edn. by W. G. F. Phillimore, 1895), esp. pp. 194–207 (see also index); *Halsbury's Laws of England* (4th edn.), 14 (1975), pp. 240–4 (paras. 496–502). R. Peters, *Oculus Episcopi: Administration in the Archdeaconry of St Albans 1580–1625* (Manchester, 1963). J. Addy, *The Archdeacon and Ecclesiastical Discipline in Yorkshire 1598–1714: The Clergy and the Churchwardens* (St Anthony's Hall Publications, 24; York, 1963). J. P. Kirsch in *CE* 1 (1907), pp. 693 f., s.v. E. W. Watson in *DECH,* pp. 18–21, s.v. A. Amanieu in *DDC* 1 (1935), cols. 948–1004, s.v. 'Archidiacre', with extensive bibl.; P. Palazzini in *EC* 4 (1950), cols. 1538–44, s.v. 'Diacono e Arcidiacono', pt. 4.

archdiocese. A diocese of which the holder is *ex officio* *archbishop, e.g. *Canterbury. The word is used esp. of RC archdioceses, e.g. *Westminister.

Arches Court of Canterbury. The Court of the province of *Canterbury which formerly met in *Bow Church ('S. Maria de Arcubus'). Originally it was presided over by the Archbishop's *Official Principal, but the office is now combined with that of the 'Dean of the Arches' (the judge of the Archbishop's 'Court of Peculiars' which sat in the same church). Since the reorganization of ecclesiastical courts by the *Ecclesiastical Jurisdiction Measure 1963, it now has no original jurisdiction, but hears appeals from the diocesan *Consistory Courts within the province of

Canterbury in cases not involving doctrine, ritual, or ceremonial. Formerly an appeal from this Court lay only to the Pope; in 1534, by the Act for the Submission of the Clergy and the Restraint of Appeals, this was transferred to the King in Chancery. There is now no appeal except in causes of *faculty, which are heard by the *Judicial Committee of the Privy Council.

Very few medieval records of the Court are known; those from the *Restoration to 1914, with a few exceptions, are catalogued in M. D. Slatter, *Lists of the Records of the Court of Arches deposited for Temporary Safe Keeping in the Bodleian Library in 1941* (1951; not pub. but widely circulated). For the later records, see also J. Houston, *Index of Cases in the Records of the Court of Arches at Lambeth Palace Library, 1660–1913* (Index Library, 85; 1972). I. J. Churchill, *Canterbury Administration* (2 vols., 1933), 1, pp. 424–69, and 2, App. 1, pp. 186–210. M. D. Slatter, 'The Records of the Court of Arches', *JEH* 4 (1953), pp. 139–53; M. Barber, 'Records of the Court of Arches in Lambeth Palace Library', *Ecclesiastical Law Journal*, 3 (1995) pp. 10–19. See also bibl. to DEAN OF THE ARCHES.

archimandrite (Gk. ἀρχιμανδρίτης, 'the ruler of a *mandra* or fold'). This title, which has been in use in the E. Church from the 4th cent., was used originally in two senses: (1) a monastic superior, equivalent to the Greek term '*hegumenos' and to the W. term '*abbot'; (2) the superior of a group of several monasteries. Thus in 6th-cent. Palestine there were two archimandrites of this type, one charged with the supervision of all the *coenobitic houses, and the other with that of the hermits. In the Orthodox Church today it is used most frequently as a title of honour for an unmarried priest, who need not necessarily be the head of a community.

J. Pargoire in *DACL* 1 (1907), cols. 2739–61, s.v.

archpriest. An ecclesiastic in priest's orders who occupies a position of pre-eminence among other priests. From the early 5th cent. the title was applied to the senior presbyter of a city, either by years or appointment, who performed many of the bishop's liturgical and governmental functions in his absence or during a vacancy. In later times, while the *archdeacon had become responsible for the governmental work of the bishop, the archpriest continued to perform the bishop's sacerdotal duties in his absence. Though there is some doubt as to which was originally superior, by the 13th cent. the archdeacon had vindicated his position. Gradually, except at *Rome, most of the work of both these officials during a vacancy was taken over by the *Vicar General. In some Continental cathedrals the archpriest survives as a capitular dignitary.

As Christianity spread in the 4th cent. from the cities to the countryside, the title was also given, esp. in Gaul, to the cleric who presided over the groups of parishes which united for the principal Sunday Mass and other functions previously performed by the bishop. In this sense the word is first found in the Second Council of Tours (576). With the formation of separate parishes the importance of the archpriest declined, and most of his duties were taken over by the *rural dean. Acc. to the 1983 *Codex Iuris Canonici* (can. 553) the modern *dean (or vicar forane) is now sometimes called an archpriest. The title was also given to the superior appointed by the Pope to govern the secular priests sent to England from foreign seminaries between 1598 and 1621 (see following entry).

In the Orthodox Church the title is still one of honour, which may or may not carry any specific function; it is borne by senior married priests and is the highest rank they can attain.

A. Amanieu in *DDC* 1 (1935), cols. 1004–26, s.v. 'Archiprêtre', with extensive bibl.

Archpriest Controversy. The dispute between the pro-*Jesuit and anti-Jesuit RC clergy in England which followed the death of Card. W. *Allen in 1594. For details, see APPELLANTS (1) and BLACKWELL, G.

arcosolium. An arched burial niche of the Roman period, built or excavated either above or below ground. The word is used esp. of those dug from *c.* AD 250 in the walls of galleries and *cubicula* in the *catacombs. Bodies were placed in one or more *loculi* cut into the niche, or, esp. in Sicily, in a receding series of floor graves. They were also sometimes placed on or under a stone slab (*mensa*) which divided the niche horizontally. In some cases a stone *sarcophagus (*solium*) was used; and, in the more elaborate *arcosolia*, esp. those of popes and *martyrs, the *mensae* sometimes served as altars. *Arcosolia* often have rich decorations and interesting painting, although many have been damaged by later burials.

G. B. *de Rossi, *La Roma sotterranea cristiana*, esp. 3 (1877), pp. 418–20 and 490–3. J. M. C. Toynbee *Death and Burial in the Roman World* [1971], pp. 134 f., 138, 188–90, 200, 209–12, 237, and 242–4. J. Stevenson, *The Catacombs* [1978], pp. 18 f., 27, 66, 80, 131 f., and 140 f. H. *Leclercq, OSB, in *DACL* 1 (pt. 2; 1907), cols. 2774–87, s.v., with full refs.

area bishop. In the C of E, a common, but unofficial, designation of a *suffragan bishop to whom certain powers have been legally delegated by the diocesan bishop when a diocese has been divided into areas under the Dioceses Measure 1978.

Areopagite, the. The mystical writer, *Dionysius (6) (? 5th cent.), so named from a wrong identification with the Dionysius who was converted by St *Paul's speech on the *Areopagus (Acts 17: 34).

Areopagus (Gk., Ἄρειος πάγος, 'Mars' Hill'), a spur jutting out and separated by a short saddle from the western end of the Acropolis, Athens, prob. so called from a myth that Mars had here cleared himself of the murder of Halirrhothius, the son of Neptune. The name Areopagus was also applied to an oligarchical council which, from very early times, met on the hill. Its functions appear to have been mainly judicial (esp. trials for homicide), though at times it endeavoured to exert political influence. Under the Roman Empire it seems to have been increasingly concerned with religious matters. It is not entirely clear whether, when St *Paul was brought to the Areopagus to explain his 'new teaching' (Acts 17: 19), it was before the official court or whether the place was merely chosen as convenient for a meeting. The language of Acts suggests the latter view, though a marginal note in some MSS indicates the other alternative, which was that adopted by St *Chrysostom. Traces of ancient stone seats on the Areopagus are still visible.

B. Keil, *Beitrage zur Geschichte des Areopags* (*Ber.* (Sächs.), 71. 8; 1920). W. S. Ferguson, 'Researches in Athenian and Delian Documents III', *Klio*, 9 (1909), pp. 304–40, remarks on the Council, pp. 325–30. W. M. *Ramsay, *St Paul the Traveller and Roman Citizen* (1895), pp. 243–9, with note p. 260; B. Gärtner, *The Areopagus Speech and Natural Revelation* (Acta Seminarii Neotestamentici Upsaliensis, 21; 1955), with extensive bibl.; T. D. Barnes, 'An Apostle on Trial', *JTS* NS 20 (1969), pp. 407–19; C. J. Hemer, 'Paul at Athens: a topographical note', *New Testament Studies*, 20 (1973–4), pp. 341–50. H. *Leclercq, OSB, in *DACL* 1 (pt. 2; 1907), cols. 3040–6, s.v. 'Athènes' (§ 2). See also comm. to Acts, cited s.v.

Argentina, Christianity in. Argentina, originally a Spanish colony, obtained its complete independence in 1816 after the revolution of 1810. The first missionaries, who arrived in 1539, were *Franciscans, followed by the *Jesuits some 40 years later. The RC Church claims a membership of 25 million—over 90 per cent of the population—organized in 54 dioceses and 12 provinces. The State religion has always been RC (until 1994 the president of the republic had to be of that faith), but there is complete religious toleration. Mass attendance is unusually small for Latin America and there is a grave shortage of priests. There is a large body of strongly *anticlerical feeling in the country. The Protestant Churches, who began missionary work in the 19th cent., constitute just under 3 per cent of the population. Of these the *Pentecostals form the largest group, though they are less numerous than elsewhere in Latin America. The *Lutheran Church has 100,000 members, mainly immigrants from Germany and Scandinavia, while the *Baptist Churches have strong connections with the Southern Baptist Convention of the USA. The *Presbyterian and *Methodist Churches are small. There are two Anglican dioceses, with about 15,000 members, in the Province of the Southern Cone of America (created in 1983).

There is much relevant material (up to 1852) in V. F. López, *Historia de la República Argentina* (10 vols., Buenos Aires, 1883–93; new edn., 1911), and P. Denis, *La République Argentine* (1920; Eng. tr., 1922), *passim*. R. Levene, *Lecciones de historia argentina* (11th edn., 2 vols., Buenos Aires, 1928), esp. ch. 14 (Eng. tr., The Inter-American Historical Series, 1; Chapel Hill, NC, 1937, pp. 148–56). J. C. Zuretti, *Historia eclesiástica argentina* (Buenos Aires, 1945); id., *Nueva historia eclesiástica argentina, del Concilio de Trento al Vaticano II* (ibid., 1972). E. Amato, *La Iglesia en Argentina* (Estudios Socio-Religiosos Latino-Americanos, 5(2); Brussels, Bogatá, and Buenos Aires, 1965). J. L. Mecham, *Church and State in Latin America: A History of Politico-Ecclesiastical Relations* (Chapel Hill, NC, 1934), pp. 275–303; 2nd edn. (1966), pp. 225–51. E. F. Every, *The Anglican Church in South America* (1915), pp. 17–40. T. [R.] Beeson and J. Pearce, *A Vision of Hope: The Churches and Change in Latin America* (1984), pp. 100–22, esp. pp. 117–22. G. Furlong in *NCE* 1 (1967), pp. 779–85, s.v.

Arianism. The principal heresy which denied the full Divinity of Jesus Christ, so called after its author, *Arius (q.v.).

Arius appears to have held that the Son of God was not eternal but created before the ages by the Father from nothing as an instrument for the creation of the world; He was therefore not God by nature, but a creature, and so susceptible of change, even though different from all other creatures in being the one direct creation of God; His dignity as Son of God was bestowed on Him by the Father on account of his foreseen abiding righteousness. The Arian movement included many who were sympathetic to the approach of Arius, without themselves agreeing with every aspect of his teaching. Earlier scholars tended to see this teaching as an adulteration of Christian faith by essentially pagan philosophical concerns. More recent writers have argued that a major objective of the Arians was to distinguish the Divinity of the Father from that of the Son in order to express the *Incarnation of Christ in a way which did not ascribe the limitations of the Incarnate Son to the full Divinity which they attributed uniquely to the Father.

The teaching of Arius, though condemned by his bishop *Alexander at a synod at *Alexandria (*c.*320), continued to spread and to agitate the masses, until the Emp. *Constantine, anxious for the peace of the newly unified Empire, called a General Council at *Nicaea, which met in 325. There the opponents of Arianism, largely under the spiritual leadership of St *Athanasius, then a deacon at Alexandria, defined the Catholic faith in the coeternity and coequality of the Father and the Son, using the famous term '*homoousios' to express their consubstantiality, while Arius and some bishops who supported him, among them *Eusebius of Nicomedia, were banished. Constantine, at first an ardent promoter of the Nicene settlement, soon began to waver. In 328 the influential Eusebius of Nicomedia and the other exiled bishops were permitted to return and at once began to intrigue against the Nicene party. *Eustathius of Antioch was deposed and banished in 330, and Athanasius, since 328 Bp. of Alexandria, had to go into exile to Trier in 336. Arius himself was to be recognized as orthodox and to be received back into the Church in the same year, when his sudden death prevented his reinstatement.

After the death of Constantine (337), Athanasius and some other Nicene bishops returned to their dioceses. But the new Emperor of the E., Constantius, soon openly embraced Arianism, the extent of his support being restrained only by his fear of his brother Constans, the ruler of the W., who protected the Catholics. In 339 Athanasius was again deprived of his see and fled to Rome, where his orthodoxy was recognized by a Council held in 341. In the same year a Council was held at *Antioch by the bishops of the E. Four different statements of faith are associated with this Council. Their general tenor is to repudiate the teaching of Arius, while also avoiding any use of the term 'homoousios'. To restore peace to the Empire another Council was convoked by both Emperors at *Sardica in 343, which, however, the Eusebian bishops left for fear of being defeated. At Sardica Athanasius was again recognized as the rightful Bp. of Alexandria and several Arian bishops were deposed.

A short period of peace followed after Athanasius had returned to Alexandria in 346, but with the death of Constans in 350, which left Constantius sole ruler, new persecutions began for the Catholics. Not only was Athanasius exiled once more, but so also were many W. bishops, including Pope *Liberius and St *Hilary of Poitiers. In the course of the ensuing debates, three major groups emerged. The extreme party, usually called '*Anomoeans' (from ἀνόμοιος, 'dissimilar') and known in modern times also as 'Neo-Arians', pressed the differences between the Father and Son; the middle party, called '*Homoeans' (from ὅμοιος, 'similar'), aimed at avoiding dogmatic precision as far as possible by affirming that the Son is similar to the Father 'acc. to the Scriptures'; while a third group, the '*Semi-Arians' (q.v.), favoured the term 'homoiousios' as expressing both the similarity and the distinction between the first Two Persons of the Trinity. These different views were laid down in further formulas of faith. Among them a Homoean formula, drawn up at a Council of *Sirmium (357), was accepted by a double Council of E. and W. bishops who met at Seleucia and *Ariminum respectively in 359. It was of this year that St *Jerome wrote his well-known comment; 'The whole world groaned and marvelled to find itself Arian' (*Dial. adv. Lucif.* 19; *PL* 23. 172C).

This crowning victory of Arianism was the turning-point of its history, since it frightened the Semi-Arians into the ranks of orthodoxy. With the death of Constantius (361) it lost its chief supporter; Athanasius returned to Alexandria and, in 362, held a Council at which a more conciliatory approach helped to reunite a wide spectrum of the opponents of Arianism. In the W. Arius had little direct influence. But a more straightforwardly biblical form of *subordinationism was a powerful force there (esp. in Illyria) until the time of the Emp. Valentian. In the E. the triumph of orthodoxy was retarded by the Emp. Valens. Athanasius had died in 373; but the brilliant theological expositions of the Nicene faith by the three Cappadocians, St *Basil, St *Gregory of Nazianzus, and St *Gregory of Nyssa, prepared the way for the final victory of orthodoxy under the Emp. *Theodosius at the Council of *Constantinople in 381. After being driven from the Empire, Arianism retained a foothold among the Teutonic tribes, esp. through *Ulphilas' *Gothic Bible and liturgy, which prevented their rapid assimilation with their Catholic subjects when they occupied the greater part of the W. Empire and caused persecution of Catholics in N. Africa and Spain. The conversion of the Franks to Catholicism (496) was the prelude to the gradual disappearance of Arianism from the religious creed of the Teutonic tribes.

The subject of necessity fills a central place in all the Church histories of the 4th cent. H. M. Gwatkin, *Studies of Arianism* (1882; 2nd edn., 1900); id., *The Arian Controversy* (1889). M. Simonetti, *Studi sull'Arianesimo* (Verba Seniorum, NS 5 [1965]); M. Meslin, *Les Ariens d'Occident, 335–430* (Patristica Sorbonensia, 8; 1967). É Boularand, *L'Hérésie d'Arius et la 'Foi' de Nicée* (1972 ff.). T. A. Kopecek, *A History of Neo-Arianism* (Patristic Monograph Series, 8; 2 vols., Philadelphia, 1979). R. Lorenz, *Arius judaizans? Untersuchungen zur dogmengeschichtlichen Einordnung des Arius* (Forschungen zur Kirchen- und Dogmengeschichte, 31 [1979]). R. C. Gregg and D. E. Groh, *Early Arianism: A View of Salvation* (1981). R. C. Gregg (ed.), *Arianism: Historical and Theological Reassessments* (Patristic Monograph Series, 11; 1985). R. [D.] Williams, *Arius: Heresy and Tradition* (1987). R. P. C. Hanson, *The Search for the Christian Doctrine of God: The Arian Controversy 318–381* (Edinburgh, 1988). H. C. Brennecke, *Studien zur Geschichte der Homöer: Der Osten bis zum Ende der homöischen Reichskirche* (Beiträge zur historischen Theologie, 73 [1988]). M. R. Barnes and D. H. Williams (eds.), *Arianism after Arius* (Edinburgh, 1993). M. F. Wiles, *Archetypal Heresy: Arianism through the Centuries* (Oxford, 1996). G. Bardy, *Recherches sur S. Lucien d'Antioche et son école* (1936). J. Gummerus, *Die homöusianische Partei bis zum Tode des Konstantius* (1900). A. Grillmeier, SJ, 'Die theologische und sprachliche Vorbereitung der christologischen Formel von Chalkedon', in id. and H. Bacht, SJ (eds.), *Das Konzil von Chalkedon*, 1 (Würzburg, 1951), pp. 5–202; rev. Eng. tr. as *Christ in Christian Tradition: From the Apostolic Age to Chalcedon* (1965; 2nd edn., 1975). M. Wiles, 'In defence of Arius', *JTS* NS 13 (1962), pp. 339–47; G. C. Stead, 'The Platonism of Arius', ibid. 15 (1964), pp. 16–31. A. M. Ritter in *TRE* 3 (1978), pp. 692–719, s.v., with bibl.; M. Simonetti in *DPAC*, 1 (1983), cols. 337–45, s.v. 'Ario-Arianesimo'; Eng. tr. in *Encyclopedia of the Early Church*, 1 (1992), pp. 76–8. See also works cited under ATHANASIUS, ST, and HOMOOUSION.

aridity or dryness. The term is used to refer either generally to a lack of conscious fervour and delight in the Christian life as a whole, or more specifically to a lack of fervour and delight in prayer and other spiritual exercises. Such a condition may be due either to a deliberate turning away from God or to factors outside a person's control. In the latter case, all spiritual writers agree that it provides an occasion to recall humbly one's own weakness and to appreciate that the service of God does not depend on felt consolations. Regular Christian practices should not be abandoned just because of a feeling of aridity. Different authorities assess the significance of aridity diversely: those who regard conscious joy in the Lord as a normal and desirable feature of the Christian life recommend various active ways of trying to escape from aridity, whereas others regard the lack of sensible devotion as a sign of God's purification of the soul and the readiness to do without consolations as a sign of spiritual maturity; other authorities treat the presence or absence of conscious fervour as a matter of complete indifference, with no effect on the practice of the Christian life.

The subject is treated in books on the spiritual life; see bibl. to PRAYER. R. Daeschler, SJ, in *Dict. Sp.* 1 (1937), cols. 845–55, s.v. 'Aridité'.

Ariel. A name used of *Jerusalem in Is. 29: 1. The most probable interpretation appears to be 'altar-hearth' (cf. Ezek. 43: 15 f.).

S. Feigin, 'The Meaning of Ariel', *Journal of Biblical Literature*, 39 (1920), pp. 131–7; W. F. Albright, 'The Babylonian Temple-Tower and the Altar of Burnt Offering', ibid., pp. 137–42; H. G. May, '*Ephod* and *Ariel*', *American Journal of Semitic Languages and Literatures*, 56 (1939), pp. 44–69, esp. pp. 52–69. See also comm. on ISAIAH and EZEKIEL.

Ariminum and Seleucia, Synods of. Two synods to which the Emp. Constantius summoned the bishops of the W. and E. respectively in 359 in an attempt to settle the *Arian dispute. That at Ariminum (Rimini) was much the larger of the two assemblies, and the great majority of its adherents were orthodox. The Arian minority, however, included a group of skilled diplomats, among them *Valens and *Ursacius, who succeeded in undoing the effect of the anti-Arian decision of the Council when it reached the Emperor. In consequence, under imperial pressure, the orthodox bishops at Ariminum, who had not dispersed, were induced later in the year, and in the interest of peace to subscribe an Arianizing Creed, drawn up at Nice in Thrace.

At Seleucia, under the leadership of the *Anomoeans, Acacius and Eudoxius, the Creed of Nice was also accepted.

It was these and similar events that led St *Jerome to remark of the year 359 that 'the whole world groaned and marvelled to find itself Arian' ('ingemuit totus orbis et se

Arianum esse miratus est', *Dial. adv. Lucif.* 19, *PL* 23. 172C).

Hardouin, 1 (1715), cols. 711–26; Mansi, 3 (1759), cols. 293–310 and 315–26. Hefele and Leclercq, 1 (2; 1907), pp. 929–55. Y.-M. Duval, 'La "manœuvre frauduleuse" de Rimini. A la recherche du *Liber aduersus Vrsacium et Valentem*', in *Hilaire et son temps: Acts du Colloque de Poitiers 29 septembre—3 octobre 1968* (Études Augustiniennes, 1969), pp. 51–103. G. Bardy in Fliche and Martin, 3 (1936), pp. 161–9. *CPG* 4 (1980), pp. 21–4 (nos. 8582–90).

Aristeas, Letter of. A Jewish pseudepigraphic letter written in Greek which claims to have been written by one Aristeas, an official at the court of Ptolemy Philadelphus (285–247 BC). It contains a legend describing how the *Septuagint came to be miraculously written. Its composition has been variously dated between 200 BC and AD 33.

Crit. edns. of Gk. text by P. Wendland (Teub., Leipzig, 1900), H. St J. Thackeray in H. B. *Swete, *An Introduction to the Old Testament in Greek* (1900), pp. 499–574, and, with Fr. tr., by A. Pelletier, SJ (SC 89; 1962). Eng. trs. by H. St J. Thackeray (London, 1917) and M. Hadas (New York, 1951). H. G. Meecham, *The Letter of Aristeas: A Linguistic Study with special reference to the Greek Bible* (Manchester, 1935; with repr. of Thackeray's text). S. Jellicoe, *The Septuagint and Modern Study* (Oxford, 1968), pp. 29–58; E. *Schürer, *The History of the Jewish People in the Age of Jesus Christ*, rev. Eng. tr. by G. Vermes and others, 3 (pt. 1; Edinburgh, 1986), pp. 677–87, with bibl. K. Müller in *TRE* 3 (1978), pp. 719–25, s.v. 'Aristeasbrief', with bibl.

Aristides (2nd cent.) of Athens, Christian philosopher and Apologist. Until recent times our only knowledge of him came from brief references in *Eusebius and St *Jerome. In 1878, however, part of his 'Apology' in an *Armenian translation was published at *Venice by the *Mechitarists; and, in spite of the incredulity of E. *Renan and others, its authenticity was established. In 1891 a Syriac translation of the whole work, discovered in 1889 on Mt *Sinai, was edited by J. R. *Harris; and, in an appendix, J. A. *Robinson gave reasons for believing that the original Greek, somewhat modified and expanded, was to be found in the apology for Christianity in the 'Lives of *Barlaam and Josaphat'. Acc. to Eusebius, Aristides delivered his Apology to the Emp. Hadrian at the same time as another Apologist, *Quadratus, that is, in 124. J. R. Harris, however, argued that these Apologies were in fact both addressed to Antoninus Pius (d. 161) early in his reign.

Aristides sought to defend the existence and eternity of God, and to show that Christians had a fuller understanding of His nature than either the barbarians, the Greeks, or the Jews, and that they alone live acc. to His precepts. Like *Justin and *Tatian, he retained the status and garb of a philosopher after his conversion. A sermon on Lk. 23: 43 has been ascribed to him, prob. wrongly.

Eusebius, *HE* 4. 3. 3, and *Chron.* ad a. 2140; Jerome, *De vir. illustr.* 20. Crit. edn. of Gk. text by J. Geffcken, *Zwei griechische Apologeten* (1907), pp. 1–96; other attempts at reconstruction of Gk. text by R. Seeberg (Erlangen, 1893); Syr. text ed. J. R. Harris, 'The Apology of Aristides on Behalf of the Christians', with appendix with Gk. text ed. J. A. Robinson, in Camb. *Texts and Studies*, 1 (1) (1891); Arm. frag. in G. B. *Pitra, *Analecta Sacra*, 4 (1883), pp. 6–10 and 282–6. A papyrus frag. of the Gk. text has also been pub. with Eng. tr. by H. J. M. Milne in *JTS* 25 (1924), pp. 73–7. Eng. tr. by D. M. Kay in *ANCL*. Additional vol. (1897),

pp. 259–79. Ital. tr. of the Syriac, with full introd., by C. Vona (Lateranum, NS 16; 1950). W. C. van Unnik, 'Die Gotteslehre bei Aristides und in gnostischen Schriften', *Theologische Zeitschrift*, 17 (1961), pp. 166–74. Bardenhewer, 1, pp. 187–202; Altaner and Stuiber (1978), pp. 64 f.; J. Quasten, *Patrology*, 1 (Utrecht, 1950), pp. 191–5. *CPG* 1 (1983), pp. 26–8 (nos. 1062–7), with bibl.

Aristion (1st cent.). Acc to *Papias, as reported by *Eusebius (*HE* 3. 39. 4), he was a primary authority, with the Presbyter *John, for the traditions about the Lord. He is certainly to be distinguished from *Aristo of Pella, whom Eusebius (4. 6. 3) cites as an authority for the *Bar Cochba revolt, though the two are identified by St *Maximus Confessor. In an *Armenian MS dated 986, [Mk.] 16: 9–20 (the concluding twelve verses of the Gospel in most texts) is attributed to 'the Presbyter Ariston'. But F. C. *Conybeare's theory that the MS preserves a genuine tradition which recognized Papias' Aristion as their real author has received little following.

F. C. Conybeare, 'Aristion the Author of the Last Twelve Verses of Mark', *The Expositor*, 4th ser. 8 (1893), pp. 241–54, id., 'On the Last Twelve Verses of St Mark's Gospel', ibid. 5th ser. 2 (1895), pp. 401–21; J. *Chapman, OSB, 'Aristion, author of the Ep. to the Hebrews', *R. Bén.* 22 (1905), pp. 50–64. Bardenhewer, 1, pp. 448 f. B. W. Bacon in *DCG* 1 (1906), pp. 114–18, and E. Peterson in *EC* 1 (1949), cols. 1908 f.

Aristo of Pella (*c*.140), early Christian *Apologist. His work has perished, but *Origen, in *Contra Celsum* (4. 52) mentions, without giving the author's name, a 'Disputation between Jason and Papiscus concerning Christ'; this work is attributed to Aristo by John of Scythopolis (in his Paraphrase on *Dionysius the Pseudo-Areopagite, ascribed to St Maximus the Confessor: *PG* 4. 421B). Jason, a baptized Jew, converts his fellow-Jew, Papiscus, by proving the fulfilment of the Messianic prophecies in Christ. Origen defends its allegorical interpretation of the OT against the mockeries of Celsus. Acc. to *Eusebius (*HE* 4. 6. 3), Aristo wrote an account of the destruction of *Jerusalem under Hadrian (135).

Fragments of the 'Disputation' quoted in the works of St *Jerome and Origen were pr. by H. J. *Routh, *Reliquiae Sacrae*, 1 (2nd edn., Oxford, 1846), pp. 91–109; repr. (from 1st edn.) in J. P. Migne, *PG* 5. 1277–86; also ed. J. C. T. Otto, *Corpus Apologetarum*, 9 (Jena, 1872), pp. 349–63. *CPG* 1 (1983), p. 43 (no. 1101). Bardenhewer, 1 (2nd edn., 1913), pp. 202–6; Altaner and Stuiber (1978), pp. 62 and 554. E. Peterson in *EC* 1 (1949), cols. 1911 f., s.v.

Aristobulus, St. In Rom. 16: 10 St *Paul sent greeting to the 'household of Aristobulus' (τοὺς ἐκ τῶν 'Αριστοβούλου). Nothing further is known of this Aristobulus, unless he be the grandson of *Herod the Great and friend of the Emp. Claudius of this name. It is possible that he came to be considered a Christian merely because of his mention in the NT. Acc. to a Spanish tradition, he made his way to Britain in the second year of the reign of *Nero and finally became Bp. of Britonia (modern Mondoñedo) in Spain. Feast day, 30 or 31 Oct.

He has sometimes been identified with an Aristobulus who, acc. to the Gk. menologies, was one of the 70 disciples (Lk. 10: 1) and brother of St *Barnabas and whose daughter married St *Peter. This Aristobulus was believed to have been consecrated bishop by St Paul and to have organized a Church in Britain; but the story is without credible authority. He was apparently the Aristobulus, 'the disciple of the Apostles', named in the Roman *Martyrology. Feast day, 15 or 16 March.

Extr. on Aristobulus from Gk. Menology in *AASS*, Mart. 1 (1668), p. 869; cf. also ibid. 2 (1668), pp. 374–6, R. Aigrain in *DHGE* 4 (1930), col. 194, s.v.

Aristobulus of Paneas (3rd–2nd cent, BC), Jewish philosopher of *Alexandria who most prob. taught some time between 180 and 145 BC. His Commentary on the Law, fragments of which are preserved by *Eusebius (*Praep. Ev.* 8. 10 and 13. 12 and *HE* 7. 32. 17), seeks to prove that the OT was the source of much Greek philosophy and by an elaborate system of allegorical interpretation to reconcile philosophical conceptions with the Jewish creed. His citation of a *Peripatetic source (in Eus., *Praep. Ev.* 13. 12. 10) led *Clement of Alexandria and Eusebius to assign him to that school, but it is clear that he was also influenced by *Plato and the Pythagoreans. The eclectic character of the work has suggested doubts about its authorship, but the ascription to Aristobulus is now generally accepted. By the early Christian Fathers Aristobulus was regarded as the founder of Jewish philosophy in Alexandria.

N. Walter, *Der Thoraausleger Aristobulos: Untersuchungen zu seinen Fragmenten und zu pseudepigraphischen Resten der jüdisch-hellenistischen Literatur* (TU 86; 1964). E. Schürer, *The History of the Jewish People in the Age of Jesus Christ*, rev. Eng. tr. by G. Vermes and others, 3 (pt. 1; Edinburgh, 1986), pp. 579–87, with bibl.

Aristotle (384–322 BC), Greek philosopher. He was the son of Nicomachus, the court physician to Amyntas II of Macedonia, and born at Stagirus (later Stagira) on the peninsula of Chalcidice. In 367 he went to Athens, where he became a member of the scientific group gathered round *Plato. After Plato's death (347), when Speusippus became head of the Academy, Aristotle left for Asia Minor, where he spent three years with his friend and former fellow-student Hermeias, who had risen to be tyrant of the cities of Assos and Atarneus in the Troad. Here he married Pythias, Hermeias' niece, and c.344 removed with his wife to Mitylene in Lesbos. After Hermeias' assassination by the Persians (343), Aristotle joined the Macedonian court, and became tutor to the crown prince, afterwards Alexander the Great, then a boy of 13; of his relations with Alexander there is very little contemporary evidence. When Alexander became king (336), Aristotle returned to Athens, where the headship of Plato's Academy happened to be vacant on Speusippus' death. Aristotle, however, was not elected, the choice falling on Xenocrates of Chalcedon. Though he never wholly severed his connection with the Academy, he opened a rival school at the Lyceum (335), to which he attracted some of the Academy's most distinguished members. Here he devoted himself for the next 12 years to lecturing, organizing the school, fostering scientific research and collecting a large library, the model for those of *Alexandria and *Pergamum. In contrast to the Academy, where the emphasis was on mathematics, Aristotle presented a wide-ranging programme of studies, including the natural sciences. From the circumstance that the instruction was given in a covered portico ('peripatos'), his school obtained the name of 'Peripatetic'. On the death of Alexander (323), the strong anti-Macedonian agitation forced Aristotle to leave Athens, whence he withdrew with his disciples to Chalcis, where he died in the following year.

Aristotle, like Plato, appears to have made regular use of the dialogue in his earliest years; but lacking Plato's imaginative gifts he probably never found the form congenial. Apart from fragments in later writers, his dialogues have been wholly lost. The works on which his reputation rests are apparently texts based on his lecture notes and memoranda which he had prepared for his pupils. Among the chief are the two famous editions of the *Ethics*—the *Nicomachean Ethics*, issued by his son Nicomachus, and the *Eudemian Ethics*, possibly a recasting by his pupil Eudemus, a mathematician; the *Physics*, of which the earlier books deal with the science of nature in general, the later ones with motion; the *Metaphysics* on the science of Being (the title, given to it because it followed the *Physics* in the Aristotelian *corpus*, first appears in Nicolaus of Damascus); the celebrated writings on logic (the *Categories*, *De Interpretatione*, the *Prior* and *Posterior Analytics*, the *Topics*, *De Sophisticis Elenchis*) collectively known as the *Organon*; and a large number of writings on natural science (among others *De Caelo*, *De Generatione et Corruptione*, *De Anima*, *De Partibus Animalium*); the *Politics*; the *Rhetoric*; and the *Poetics*. In 1890 a lost treatise on the *Constitution of Athens* (not before 329–328) was found among the Egyptian papyri (1st cent. AD); it was published in 1891 by F. G. Kenyon and is preserved in the British Library.

Though a disciple of *Plato, his philosophical position was very different. Whereas Plato deduced a world of 'ideas', entities which he conceived as arranged in a hierarchy, at the head of which was the 'Idea of the Good', and as alone having reality, Aristotle asserted that an idea exists only as expressed in the individual object. Thus he maintained that, far from there being an idea 'tree' possessing existence in its own right, it is the union of the 'form' tree with 'matter' which makes the real individual tree. This view required a theory of causation to account for the conjunction of form and matter, and Aristotle was thus led to postulate a 'First Cause', though he did not hold this supreme cause to be personal in the Christian sense. In explaining his doctrine he analysed the four senses in which the word 'cause' may be used. A cause, he affirmed, might be 'formal', 'material', 'final', or 'efficient'. The 'material cause' is the matter upon which the form (or in the case of change, the new form) is imposed; the 'formal cause' is the form which in conjunction with matter makes the new object a distinct entity; the 'final cause' is the end which, in processes of growth or change, determines the course of the development; and the 'efficient cause' is the motive agent which produces the event. God is the world's prime mover (πρῶτον κινοῦν), eternally inspiring it to imitate his perfection (κινεῖ ὡς ἐρώμενον).

The science of 'Logic' was Aristotle's creation, and for many centuries his treatment of it was accepted as definitive, to the neglect of important developments made by the Stoics; but since the latter part of the 19th cent., esp. under the influence of G. Frege and Bertrand Russell, the scope of logic has been greatly widened. Aristotle treats of concepts, judgements and propositions, the syllogism, demonstration, the problematic syllogism, and fallacies.

His works on Physics have formed the basis of all subsequent study of the subject. His 'Ethics' has also had an enormous influence. His moral ideal was happiness in accordance with virtue, virtue being the highest value, though natural advantages could also contribute to happiness. In practical terms he saw virtue as a mean between two extremes—courage, e.g., being a mean between cowardice and foolhardiness.

In the early centuries of the Christian Church, Aristotle's philosophy was regarded with suspicion, largely because his teachings were thought to lead to a materialistic view of the world. This attitude was further encouraged by the high repute in which Plato, conceived as the diametrically opposed philosopher to Aristotle, was held by the Christian Fathers. *Boethius (6th cent.), however, vigorously expounded Aristotelian doctrines. In the W., knowledge of Aristotle began in the 9th cent. with the slow recovery of his logical writings (completed only c.1130), progressed during the 12th cent. to the translation of his scientific writings, and culminated in the reception of the Ethics c.1200 and of the Politics in the mid-13th cent. A number of scientific texts were transmitted indirectly via Arabic translations, with Arabic commentaries. Hence they were theologically suspect. Even when such great Christian philosophers as St *Albertus Magnus and St *Thomas Aquinas built up their systems on an avowedly Aristotelian basis, that suspicion was never entirely dissipated. The thinkers of the Renaissance (and their eminent precursor, *Nicholas of Cusa) gave Platonism a new lease of life. In 1879 the encyclical *Aeterni Patris of *Leo XIII commended Thomistic Aristotelianism in terms that made it for the first time the highroad of philosophical orthodoxy in the modern RC Church.

TEXT: Editio princeps, by Aldine Press, 5 vols. fol., Venice, 1495–8. The best collected edn. (from which citations are normally given) is that of the Prussian Academy, ed. I. Bekker (5 vols., Berlin, 1831–70; fragments ed. V. Rose, scholia ed. C. A. Brandis, index ed. H. Bonitz). Many items also in OCT. Gk. texts of single works ed. with modern comm. incl.: Ethics, ed. J. Burnet (London, 1900); also (comm. only) by H. H. Joachim, ed. D. A. Rees (Oxford, 1951). Politics, ed. W. L. Newman (4 vols., Oxford, 1887–1902). Poetics, ed. S. H. Butcher (London, 1895; 4th edn., 1907, frequently repr.); also by D. W. Lucas, with comm. (Oxford, 1968). And all by [W.] D. Ross, pub. Oxford: Prior and Posterior Analytics (1949); Physics (1936); De Anima (1961); Metaphysics (2 vols., 1924; corrected repr., 1953). The ancient Gk. comms., of various dates between the 1st cent. and the 12th cent. AD were pub. by the Berlin Academy under the editorship of H. Diels, M. Hayduck, and others (23 vols., 1882–1909); 'Supplementum Aristotelicum' ed. S. P. Lambros and others (3 vols., Berlin, 1885–1903). On the medieval versions of Aristotle, see G. Lacombe and L. Minio-Paluello, Aristoteles Latinus, in 'Corpus Philosophorum Medii Aevi Academiarum Consociatarum Auspiciis et Consilio Editum' (Codicum descriptio, pars prior, Rome, 1939; pars posterior, Cambridge, 1955; with supplement by L. Minio-Paluello, Bruges and Paris, 1961). The comms. themselves are also being pub. under the title Aristoteles Latinus in the same series originally under the general editorship of L. Minio-Paluello (Rome, 1951, and Bruges and Paris, 1953 ff.). A. Jourdain, Recherches sur l'âge et l'origine des traductions d'Aristote (1819). M. *Grabmann, Forschungen über die lateinischen Aristoteles-Übersetzungen des XIII. Jahrhunderts (BGPM 17, Hefte 5–6; 1916). Collected arts. by L. Minio-Paluello repr. as Opuscula: The Latin Aristotle (Amsterdam, 1972). B. G. Dod and G. H. Lohr, 'Aristotle in the Middle Ages', in N. Kretzmann and others (eds.),

The Cambridge History of Later Medieval Philosophy (1982), pp. 43–98.

TRANSLATIONS: Complete works, ed. J. A. Smith and W. D. Ross (12 vols., Oxford, 1908–52; revised ed. by J. Barnes, 2 vols., Princeton, NJ, 1984). Selections: R. McKeon (ed.), The Basic Works of Aristotle (New York, 1941); J. R. Bambrough, The Philosophy of Aristotle (New York, 1963). Loeb series includes Ethics (both versions), Politics, Poetics, On the Heavens, Metaphysics, var. dates. The Clarendon Aristotle ser. of selected works with valuable comm. includes Categories and De Interpretatione, by J. L. Ackrill (1963); Physics 1 and 2, by W. Charlton (1970); 3 and 4, by E. Hussey (1983); De Generatione et Corruptione, by C. F. J. Williams (1982); De Anima 1 in part, 2 and 3, by D. W. Hamlyn (1968); Metaphysics Books Γ, Δ, and E, by C. Kirwan (1971; 2nd edn., 1993); Books M and N, by J. Annas (1976); and Z and H by D. Bostock (1994). Other trs. of Nicomachean Ethics by [W.] D. Ross (repr. from vol. 9 of the Works, World Classics, 1954; rev. edn., 1980) and by J. A. K. Thomson (London, 1953; Penguin Classics, 1955; rev. edn., 1976), of Politics by E. Barker (Oxford, 1946; shorter edn. 1948).

STUDIES: Good introductions include W. D. Ross, Aristotle (London, 1923; 5th edn., 1949); D. J. Allan, The Philosophy of Aristotle (1952; 2nd edn., 1970); M. Grene, A Portrait of Aristotle (1963); G. E. R. Lloyd, Aristotle: The Growth and Structure of his Thought (Cambridge, 1968); J. L. Ackrill, Aristotle the Philosopher (Oxford, 1981). Authoritative full-scale surveys: I. Düring, Aristoteles: Darstellung und Interpretation seines Denkens (Heidelberg, 1966); W. K. C. Guthrie, A History of Greek Philosophy, 6 (Cambridge, 1981); F. Ueberweg, Die Philosophie der Antike, 3, ed. H. Flashar (Basle, 1983), pp. 177–457. See also J. Barnes and others, Aristotle: A Bibliography (Study Aids, 7; Oxford, 1977). On Aristotle's development the basic work is W. Jaeger, Aristoteles: Grundlegung einer Geschichte seiner Entwicklung (1923; Eng. tr., 1934, rev. 1948). For criticism, see W. D. Ross, 'The Development of Aristotle's Thought', Proceedings of the British Academy, 43 (1957), pp. 63–78, and G. E. L. Owen, 'The Platonism of Aristotle', ibid. 50 (1965), pp. 125–50.

Ethics: P. Aubenque, La Prudence chez Aristote (1963; 2nd edn., 1976); W. R. F. Hardie, Aristotle's Ethical Theory (1968; 2nd edn., 1980); A. Kenny, The Aristotelian Ethics: A Study of the Relationship between the Eudemian and Nicomachean Ethics of Aristotle (Oxford, 1978).

Politics: E. Barker, The Political Thought of Plato and Aristotle (1906; repr., New York, 1959), pp. 208–524; R. G. Mulgan, Aristotle's Political Theory (Oxford, 1977).

Logic: E. Kapp, Greek Foundations of Traditional Logic (New York, 1942); J. Łukasiewicz, Aristotle's Syllogistic from the Standpoint of Modern Formal Logic (Oxford, 1951; 2nd edn., 1957); W. [C.] and M. Kneale, The Development of Logic (ibid., 1962) pp. 23–112.

Philosophy of Mind: O. Hamelin, La théorie de l'intellect d'après Aristote et ses commentateurs (Bibliothèque d'histoire de philosophie, 1953); G. E. R. Lloyd and G. E. L. Owen, Aristotle on Mind and the Senses (Cambridge, 1978).

Natural Philosophy: A. Mansion, Introduction à la Physique Aristotélicienne (Louvain, 1913; 2nd edn., 1946); F. [R. H.] Solmsen, Aristotle's System of the Physical World (Cornell Studies in Classical Philology, 33; New York, 1960); S. [J.] Waterlow, Nature, Change and Agency in Aristotle's Physics (Oxford, 1982).

Metaphysics: P. Aubenque, Le problème de l'être chez Aristote (Bibliothèque de philosophie contemporaine, 1962; 3rd edn., 1972); J. Owens, CSSR, The Doctrine of Being in the Aristotelian 'Metaphysics' (Toronto, 1951; 3rd edn., 1978); J. Barnes and others, Articles on Aristotle, 3 (1979); M. L. Gill, Aristotle on Substance: The Paradox of Unity (Princeton, NJ, 1989).

Theology: H. von Arnim, Die Entstehung der Gotteslehre des Aristoteles (Sb. (Wien), 212, Abh. 5; 1931); W. K. C. Guthrie, 'The Development of Aristotle's Theology', Classical Quarterly, 27

(1933), pp. 162–71; F.-P. Hager (ed.), *Metaphysik und Theologie des Aristoteles* (Darmstadt, 1969); G. Patzig, 'Theology and Ontology in Aristotle's *Metaphysics*' [Eng. tr. of a lecture pub. in *Kant-Studien*, 52 (1960/1), pp. 185–205], in J. Barnes, op. cit., pp. 33–49.

Later Influence: J. L. Stocks, *Aristotelianism* (1925; introductory); F. Wehrli in F. Ueberweg, op. cit., pp. 461–597 (detailed). R. Sorabji (ed.), *Aristotle Transformed: The Ancient Commentators and their Influence* (1990).

J. Barnes (ed.), *The Cambridge Companion to Aristotle* (1995). G. B. Kerferd in P. Edwards (ed.), *The Encyclopedia of Philosophy*, 1 (New York and London, 1967), pp. 151–62, with bibl.; O. Gigon, H. Dörrie, and others in *TRE* 3 (1978), pp. 726–96, s.v. 'Aristoteles/Aristotelismus'; M. Nussbaum in *OCD* (3rd edn., 1996), pp. 165–9, s.v.

Arius (d. 336), heresiarch. There is much divergence between the authorities for his life. He was prob. born in Libya, between *c*.260 and 280, and was a pupil of *Lucian of Antioch; if *Sozomen (*HE* 1. 15) can be trusted, he was ordained deacon by St *Peter, Bp. of *Alexandria (d. 311), who later excommunicated him as a member of the *Melitian sect. Under Achillas (312–13), Peter's successor, he was ordained priest and put in charge of Baucalis, one of the principal churches at Alexandria. Here he seems to have met with marked success as a preacher and been revered for his asceticism. Under the next bishop, St *Alexander, he came forward prob. *c*.319 (not 323, as E. *Schwartz) as a champion of subordinationist teaching about the Person of Christ. The controversy quickly spread, Arius seeking support among other disciples of Lucian, notably *Eusebius of Nicomedia, while a synod at Alexandria under Alexander proceeded to excommunicate him. Shortly after his arrival in the E. (Sept. 324), the Emp. *Constantine sent *Hosius to Alexandria to attempt a settlement; but the mission failed. Accordingly an *Oecumenical Council was convened (orig. to Ancyra), met at *Nicaea in the early summer of 325, and, largely through the influence of St *Athanasius, condemned Arius. Arius spent the next few years in banishment in Illyria, but, owing to the Court influence of Eusebius of Nicomedia, he was recalled from exile prob. *c*.334. He returned to Alexandria, where Athanasius was ordered to receive him back into communion, but refused. He died suddenly in the streets of Constantinople in 336.

Arius seems to have written little. He embodied his doctrine in a verse composition, known as the Thalia (Θάλεια, 'Banquet'), of which fragments survive, and in popular songs, now lost. There also exist a letter seeking support from Eusebius of Nicomedia (ap. *Theodoret, *HE* 1. 5 [*PG* 82. 909–12]) and a statement of belief in a letter to Alexander (Athanasius, *De Synodis*, 16). See also ARIANISM.

The chief sources for his life are the writings of Athanasius, supplemented by *Epiphanius (*Haer.* 69) and the Church historians, *Rufinus, *Socrates, *Sozomen, *Philostorgius. See also bibl. to ARIANISM.

Ark. (1) The Ark of *Noah, which the Patriarch was bidden to build of gopher wood to preserve life during the *Flood, is described in Gen. 6. It was borne on the waters and finally rested on the 'Mountains of Ararat' (Gen. 8: 4), and was the means by which Noah and his family ('eight persons' acc. to 1 Pet. 3: 20) and representatives of all living creatures were saved from the catastrophe.

Critics are widely agreed that the Hebrew narrative has been influenced by Babylonian versions of the flood story which describe the building of a comparable vessel. The Babylonian historian Berossus (*c*.300 BC) claimed that remains of the ark were extant in his day and used for making amulets and bracelets. See also GILGAMESH, EPICS OF.

(2) The Ark of the Covenant, the most sacred religious symbol of the Hebrew people and believed to represent the Presence of God. It was in form a rectangular box or chest made of acacia or shittim wood, overlaid with gold inside and out. Its length was two and a half cubits, and its height and breadth one and a half cubits (i.e. *c*.45 × 27 × 27 inches). On top of the Ark was a gold plate or *mercy-seat (q.v.). It was surmounted, acc. to the account in Ex. 25: 18–21, by two *cherubim, and was carried on gold poles which passed through gold rings on the sides.

Acc. to the traditional accounts the Ark was carried by the Israelites from the time of the *Exodus (prob. 13th cent. BC) into the land of Canaan, and, until the *Temple was built, was kept in the holy tent or *tabernacle. For a brief period it was in the hands of Israel's enemy, the Philistines (1 Sam. 4–6). It was considered to be of such sanctity that for an unauthorized person to touch it, even accidentally, was sacrilege, punishable by death (cf. e.g. 2 Sam. 6: 6). When it was permanently lodged within the Temple of *Solomon its home was the 'Holy of Holies', which the High Priest alone entered once a year. The Ark seems at one time to have contained only the Tables of the Law (1 Kgs. 8: 9), but several traditions exist (e.g. Heb. 9: 4) of other things which were kept inside it. The Ark was apparently captured when *Jerusalem fell to the Babylonians *c*.586 BC, and nothing is certainly known of its later history. See also SYNAGOGUE.

Both the Ark of Noah and the Ark of the Covenant have been symbolically interpreted by the Christian Fathers and theologians. Acc. to *Tertullian, St *Jerome, and others, the Ark of Noah typifies the Church, which, like it, is the only means of salvation, containing saints and sinners symbolized by the pure and impure animals, and being tossed about by tempests but never submerged. The Ark of the Covenant, on the other hand, is a symbol of the Lord. Acc. to St *Thomas Aquinas the gold with which it is overlaid signifies His wisdom and charity; the golden vase it contains represents His soul, Aaron's rod His priestly dignity, and the Tables of the Law His office as law-giver. St *Bonaventure saw in it a figure of the Eucharist; acc. to a sermon attributed to St *Ambrose it symbolizes the BVM, in whom was enclosed the heir of the Law as the Law itself was contained in the Ark of the Covenant. In this sense the symbolism is applied in the Litany of *Loreto, where the BVM is called 'Foederis Arca'. This imagery is very common in E. hymnography.

(1) A. Parrot, *Déluge et Arche de Noé* (Cahiers d'Archéologie Biblique, 1 [1953], esp. pp. 39–51; Eng. tr. (1955), pp. 54–67. E. Ullendorff, 'The Construction of Noah's Ark', *Vetus Testamentum*, 4 (1954), pp. 95 f. See also comm. on Gen.

(2) M. *Dibelius, *Die Lade Jahwes* (1906). W. R. Arnold, *Ephod and Ark* (Harvard Theological Studies, 3; 1917). H. Gressmann, *Die Lade Jahwes und das Allerheiligste des salomonischen Tempels* (Beiträge zur Wissenschaft vom Alten Testament, 26; 1920). K. *Budde, 'Ephod und Lade', *ZATW* 39 (1921), pp. 1–42. O. Eissfeldt, 'Lade und Stierbild', ibid. 58 (1940–1), pp. 190–215. J. Morgenstern, 'The Ark, the Ephod, and the "Tent of

Meeting" ', pt. 1, *Hebrew Union College Annual*, 17 (1942–3), pp. 153–266, esp. pp. 153–7, 229–66, with refs. to earlier works of this author. E. Nielsen, 'Some Reflections on the History of the Ark', *Supplements to Vetus Testamentum*, 7 (1960), pp. 61–74, with refs. P. D. Miller and J. J. M. Roberts, *The Hand of the Lord: A Reassessment of the 'Ark Narrative' of 1 Samuel* (Johns Hopkins Near Eastern Studies [1977]). R. de Vaux, OP, *Les Institutions de l'Ancien Testament*, 2 (1960), pp. 127–33, with bibl. pp. 439 f.; Eng. tr. (2nd edn., 1965), pp. 297–302, with bibl. p. 540. H. Lesêtre in *Dict. Bibl.* 1 (1895), cols. 912–23, s.v. 'Arche d'alliance'.

H. Hurter, SJ, 'De Arca Noe, Ecclesiae Typo, Patrum Sententiae' in *Opuscula Patrum Selecta*, 3 (Innsbruck, 1868), pp. 217–33. H. *Leclercq, OSB, in *DACL* 1 (pt. 2; 1907), cols. 2709–32, s.v. 'Arche [de Noé]', with refs. H. Lesêtre, op. cit., col. 923. See also bibl. to FLOOD and NOAH.

Arles (Lat. *Arelate*), **Synods of.** At least 15 Councils were held at Arles between 314 and 1275. Among the more important were:

(1) 314. Summoned by *Constantine to deal with the *Donatist schism. It passed 22 canons dealing with abuses resulting from the persecutions.

(2) 353. An *Arianizing Council.

[(2a). The 25 canons of the so-called 'Second Council of Arles' of the 5th cent. appear to be a private collection of canons based on those of earlier councils held elsewhere and not to have ever received conciliar authority.]

(3) 813. Canons passed concerning preaching and the education of the clergy.

(4) 1234. Canons passed against the *Albigensians.

(5) 1263 (earlier authorities, 1260). Condemned the doctrines of *Joachim of Fiore.

(1) Hardouin, 1 (1715), cols. 259–70; Mansi, 2 (1759), cols. 463–512. Crit. edns. of Canons in Turner, *EOMIA* 1. 2. 2 (1939), pp. 372–416, and C. Munier (ed.), *Concilia Galliae A. 314–A. 506* (CCSL 148; 1963), pp. 3–24, with Fr. tr. and introd. by J. Gaudemet, *Conciles Gaulois du IVᵉ Siècle* (SC 241; 1977), pp. 35–63. Hefele and Leclercq, 1 (1; 1907), pp. 275–98. F. X. Funk, 'Die Zeit der ersten Synode von Arles', *Th. Q.* 72 (1890), pp. 296–304, repr. in id., *Kirchengeschichtliche Abhandlungen und Untersuchungen*, 1 (1897), pp. 352–8; L. *Duchesne, 'La Date du concile d'Arles', *Mélanges d'Archéologie et d'Histoire*, 10 (1890), pp. 640–4. H. Schrörs, 'Drei Aktenstücke in Betreff des Konzils von Arles', *Zeitschrift der Savigny-Stiftung für Rechtsgeschichte*, 42, Kan. Abt., 11 (1921), pp. 429–39.

(2) Hardouin, 1 (1715), cols. 697 f.; Mansi, 3 (1759), cols. 231 f.; C. Munier, op. cit., p. 30; J. Gaudemet, op. cit., pp. 81–83. Hefele and Leclercq, 1 (2; 1907), pp. 869–72.

(3) Hardouin, 4 (1714), cols. 1001–6; Mansi, 14 (1769), cols. 55–64. Hefele and Leclercq, 3 (2; 1910), pp. 1135 f.

(4) Hardouin, 7 (1714), cols. 235–40; Mansi, 23 (1779), cols. 335–42. Hefele and Leclercq, 5 (2; 1913), pp. 1560 f.

(5) Hardouin, 7 (1714), cols. 509–16; Mansi, 23 (1779), cols. 1001–12. Hefele and Leclercq, 6 (1; 1914), pp. 113–17.

Armada, Spanish. This great fleet was intended by *Philip II of Spain for the invasion of England in the interests of Roman Catholicism and to avenge English attacks upon Spanish trade. Its defeat after a week's fighting in the English Channel (20–7 July 1588) was hailed as a 'great deliverance' by countless Anglican preachers.

Armagh (Ard Macha, 'Height of Macha', a legendary queen). Archiepiscopal see in the North of *Ireland. Acc. to tradition it was founded by St *Patrick, and from the

7th cent. it was the most powerful Church in Ireland. The succession of *coarbs of St Patrick, who controlled the Church and its resources, is known from the Annals of Ulster. Reforms were carried through in the face of much opposition under St Cellach (or Celsus, 1105–29) and St *Malachy (1134–6). The English conquest of Ireland, with government centred on *Dublin, diminished Armagh's independence, though most of the archbishops continued to be Irish. Abp. Richard *FitzRalph (1347–60) was a scholar of international reputation. Under *Henry VIII, Abp. George Cromer (1522–43) refused to recognize the royal supremacy and opposed the reforming measures. His successor, George Dowdall (d. 1558), took the Oath of Supremacy and hence was not recognized by Paul III, but he too was a zealous supporter of the old faith. Under *Edward VI he left the country, and in 1552 the first Protestant bishop, Hugh Goodacre (d. 1553), was appointed. Henceforward there was both a Protestant and a RC succession, though for many generations bishops of the latter lived in exile or destitution, St Oliver *Plunkett (1669–81) suffering martyrdom. Among the Protestant archbishops were J. *Ussher, the famous scholar (1624–56), and Richard Robinson, first Baron Rokeby (1765–94), to whose munificence Armagh owes the archbishop's palace, a library, and other public institutions. Towards the end of the 18th cent. the Catholic archbishops resumed their normal way of life. A new RC cathedral, dedicated to St Patrick, was built (1840–1904), and many religious Orders and Congregations were established in the diocese. The present Anglican cathedral of St Patrick is on a fortified hill, acc. to tradition given to Patrick by King Daire. It was mainly rebuilt in the 18th cent., but followed in general plan the original 13th-cent. structure.

From the Middle Ages the archbishops of Armagh's claim to the primacy was contested by the archbishops of Dublin, both Catholic and Protestant. The long literary feud, which followed the conflict between Oliver Plunkett and Peter Talbot, Abp. of Dublin, in 1670, culminated in the learned work of Hugh MacMahon, *Jus Primatiale Armacanum* (1728). See also following entry.

J. Stuart, *Historical Memoirs of the City of Armagh* (Newry, 1819; ed. A. Coleman, OP, Dublin, 1900). R. King, *A Memoir Introductory to the Early History of the Primacy of Armagh* (2nd edn., Armagh, 1854). J. B. Leslie, *Armagh Clergy and Parishes* (Dundalk, 1911; suppl. to 1947, ibid., 1948). A. Gwynn, SJ, *The Medieval Province of Armagh 1470–1545* (ibid., 1946). A. Coleman, OP, in *CE* 1 (1907), pp. 729–33, with bibl. See also works cited in bibl. to IRELAND, CHRISTIANITY IN.

Armagh, Book of (Lat. *Liber Ardmachanus*). A celebrated 9th cent. vellum codex containing a miscellaneous collection of documents, partly in Latin, partly in Irish. These include a complete non-*Vulgate text of the Latin NT, in the order Gospels, Pauline Epp. (with prefaces by *Pelagius and the Ep. to the *Laodiceans), Catholic Epp., Rev., and Acts. It is preceded by a collection of documents relating to St *Patrick, of the first importance for the history of the Irish Church. After the NT is a copy of the Life of St *Martin of Tours by *Sulpicius Severus.

The MS was written in 807–8, by the master-scribe Ferdomnach and one or two assistants, at the request of Torbach (d. 808), *coarb of St Patrick. The MS was regarded as part of the coarb's insignia and was treated as a relic of St Patrick, and was used for the swearing of oaths until after the Middle Ages. In the 17th cent. it passed from its hereditary keepers into private hands and is now in the library of Trinity College, Dublin (MS 52). It is referred to by biblical scholars as the 'Codex Dubliniensis'.

Complete text ed. with introd. and appendices by J. Gwynn (Dublin, 1913). Collotype facsimile of the Patrician documents, with introd. by E. Gwynn (ibid., 1937). The Patrician texts also ed., with introd. and Eng. tr., by L. Bieler (Scriptores Latini Hiberniae, 10; 1979). R. Sharpe, 'Palaeographical considerations in the study of the Patrician documents in the Book of Armagh', *Scriptorium*, 36 (1982), pp. 3–28.

Armenia, Christianity in. The Armenians were the first nation to embrace Christianity officially. They were converted by *Gregory the Illuminator, who was consecrated bishop by the Metropolitan of Caesarea in Cappadocia in 314, and who baptized their king Tiridates III (or IV) (reigned 298–?330). Gregory established the patriarchal see at Ashitishat in Taron, and for a time the office of *Catholicos (or Primate) was hereditary in his family. About 390 Armenia became divided between the Byzantine and Persian empires. At that time Etchmiadzin, near Mount Ararat, became the patriarchal see. The monarchy in the W. (Byzantine) part of Armenia soon disappeared, and that in the E. part under Persian suzerainty was suppressed in 428. Since then the Armenians have been subject to Persians, Arabs, Turks, and Russians, and their unity has consisted in the bond of race, language, culture, literature, and religion.

In 374 (after the death of St *Nerses) the Armenians repudiated their dependence on the Church of Caesarea. In the early part of the 5th cent. St *Isaac the Great (Catholicos c.389–c.438) and St *Mesrob greatly strengthened the Church by the invention of a national script, and the Bible and Liturgy were translated into Armenian. Owing to the wars in which they were involved, the Armenians were not represented at the Council of *Chalcedon, but in 555 the Armenian Church definitively repudiated that Council and has since been reputed *Monophysite. The decision seems to have been partly motivated by fear of domination by Constantinople, and the Armenians never entered into full communion with the other *Oriental Orthodox Churches.

The next 700 years was a period of persecution from Persians and Arabs, though there was an independent kingdom of the Bagratids in Armenia from the end of the 9th to the middle of the 11th cent., and the medieval kingdom of Cilicia, or Little Armenia, was an independent entity from the end of the 12th cent. to 1375. The Armenians of Little Armenia accepted union with Rome at the Council of Sis in 1307 and this was confirmed at the Council of *Florence (1438–9). The Armenians of Greater Armenia, however, did not accept papal authority, and, though they were represented at the Council of Florence, which issued the famous instruction 'Pro Armenis' on the Sacraments, the union there achieved had little practical result and in protest they re-established a line of independent patriarchs at Etchmiadzin in 1441.

In modern times the Armenians have suffered serious persecution, esp. at the hands of the Turks in 1915, and the Russians often endeavoured to suppress Armenian traditions. There are thought to be some 5 million Armenians

(mainly in the Republic of Armenia, countries of the former Soviet Union, and N. America); the majority profess allegiance to the Armenian Church, and something over 100,000 are in communion with Rome. The non-Roman Armenians are sometimes distinguished as 'Gregorian Armenians'. Their church is organized as two Catholicates, with individual congregations choosing their allegiance on the basis of authority and jurisdiction, and not on any difference of faith or ritual. The Catholicos of Etchmiadzin has wide acceptance throughout the Armenian world; the Catholicos of Sis, who is resident in Antelias (a suburb of Beirut) gained support from Armenians opposed to the communist regime in Armenia. Under them there are two classes of priests—the 'vardapets' or doctors, who are unmarried, and the parish priests, who, unless monks, must be married before ordination to the diaconate. The monks are not a distinct class and bishops are usually chosen from among the vardapets.

Their dogmas are similar to those of the Orthodox Church, and their Liturgy is substantially that of St *Basil, in classical Armenian. The chief vestment is the chasuble (*shurjar*), shaped like a cope. For the Eucharist, they use unleavened bread in the form of a large Latin host, and do not mix water with the wine (see MIXED CHALICE). They give Communion in both kinds by intinction. They follow the Julian Calendar. They are unique among non-Protestant Christians in not observing *Christmas as a separate feast. Instead, they celebrate the Nativity of the Lord as part of the *Epiphany, from 5 to 13 January. They make the sign of the Cross after the manner of the Latins.

S. Weber, *Die katholische Kirche in Armenien: Ihre Begründung und Entwicklung vor der Trennung* (1903); M. Ormanian, *L'Église arménienne: Son histoire, sa doctrine, son régime, sa discipline, sa liturgie, son présent* (1910; Eng. tr., 1912; rev. edn., 1954; Eng. tr., 1955). L. Arpee, *A History of Armenian Christianity from the Beginning to Our Own Time* (New York, 1946). Crit. edn. of the *Narratio de Rebus Armeniae*, a fundamental doc. for the early history of the Armenian Church, with comm., by G. Garitte (CSCO 132, Subsidia, 4; 1952). J. Mécérian, SJ, *Histoire et Institutions de l'Église Arménienne* (Recherches publiées sous la direction des l'Institut de Lettres Orientales de Beyrouth, 30 [1965]). K. Sarkissian, *The Council of Chalcedon and the Armenian Church* (1965). F. Tournebize, *Histoire politique et religieuse de l'Arménie.* 1: *Depuis les origines des Arméniens jusqu'à la mort de leur dernier roi (l'an 1393)* (1910; all pub.). H. F. B. Lynch, *Armenia: Travels and Studies* (2 vols., 1901). F. Heyer (ed.), *Die Kirche Armeniens: Eine Volkskirche zwischen Ost und West* (Die Kirchen der Welt, 18; Stuttgart, 1978). F. C. *Conybeare and A. J. Maclean (eds. and trs.), *Rituale Armenorum* (1905); A. A. King, *The Rites of Eastern Christendom* (Rome, 1948), ch. 10, pp. 521–646. G. Winkler, *Das armenische Initiationsrituale: Entwicklungsgeschichtliche und liturgievergleichende Untersuchung der Quellen des 3. bis 10. Jahrunderts* (Orientalia Christiana Analecta, 217; 1982). J. Muyldermans, 'Le Costume liturgique arménien: Étude historique', *Le Muséon*, 39 (1925), pp. 253–324. A. *Fortescue, *The Lesser Eastern Churches* (1913), pp. 383–445; D. Attwater, *The Dissident Eastern Churches* (Milwaukee, Wis. [1937]), pp. 293–308, rev. as *The Christian Churches of the East*, 1 ([Leominster] 1961; London, 1963), pp. 173–87. K. Sarkissian, *A Brief Introduction to Armenian Christian Literature* (1960); S. Der Nersessian, *L'Art Arménien* ([1977]; Eng. tr. 1978), esp. pp. 21–80 (of both French and English), on Christian churches and artefacts. G. Amadouni in *DIP* 1 (1974), cols. 879–99, s.v. 'Armeno, monachesimo'; W. Hage and B. Spuler in *TRE* 4 (1979), pp. 40–63, s.v. 'Armenien'.

Armenian Version of NT. The Gospels, Acts, and Pauline Epp. were translated into Armenian in the early 5th cent., probably from an *Old Syriac version. Traditionally this translation has been ascribed to Sts *Mesrob and *Isaac the Great. After the Council of *Ephesus (431), two Armenians returned from *Constantinople with 'correct' copies of the Greek Bible (i.e. with MSS of the *Lucianic text) and proceeded to bring the then existing Armenian text into conformity. In one Armenian MS the concluding 12 verses of Mk. (16: 9–20) are attributed to 'the presbyter Ariston' (see ARISTION).

Editio princeps of whole Armenian Bible, Amsterdam, 1666; first crit. edn. by J. Zohrab, Venice, 1805, photographically repr., Delmar, NY, 1984, with introd. (in Eng.) by C. [E.] Cox, pp. x–xxvi. NT pub. separately Amsterdam, 1668; ed. J. Zohrab, Venice, 1789. Book of Rev. ed. F. C. *Conybeare (Text and Translation Society, 3, 1907, pp. 1–163). F. Macler, *Le Texte arménien de l'Évangile d'après Matthieu et Marc* (Annales du Musée Guimet. Bibliothèque d'Études, 28; 1919). S. Lyonnet, SJ, *Les Origines de la Version arménienne et le Diatessaron* (Biblica et Orientalia, 13; 1950). B. M. Metzger, *The Early Versions of the New Testament* (Oxford, 1977), pp. 153–81. F. C. Conybeare in *HDB* 1 (1900), pp. 153 f.

armill. One of the *Coronation regalia. Although the word means 'bracelet', it was applied to a garment resembling a *stole, both in the '*Liber Regalis' and in the English Coronation rite from 1661 to 1937. It was held to signify the quasi-priestly character of the anointed king. In former times it was crossed over the breast, and was so found on the body of Edward I, when his tomb was opened in 1774. The *Lambeth MS of *Charles I's Coronation ordered the words 'Receive the Bracelets of Sincerity and Wisdom' to be said by the prelate who placed the armill on the king. Later it was placed on the king's shoulders by the Dean of *Westminster, as one of the 'garments of salvation'. It is perhaps identical with the Greek λῶρος, a long jewelled scarf worn by the Byzantine emperors. At the Coronation of Queen Elizabeth II (1953) the use of armills in the form of bracelets was restored, the stole royal being given immediately afterwards.

P. E. Schramm, *Herrschaftszeichen und Staatssymbolik* (Schriften der Monumenta Germaniae Historica, 13), 2 (1955), pp. 538–53 ('Baugen-armillae: Zur Geschichte der königlichen Armspangen'), with further refs. in 3 (1956), p. 1102, and Nachträge (1978), pp. 31–3. E. C. Ratcliff, *The Coronation Service of Her Majesty Queen Elizabeth II* (1953), pp. 31 f.

Arminianism. Jacobus Arminius (Jakob Hermansz or Harmensz), the celebrated Dutch Reformed theologian (1560–1609), was the son of Hermand Jacobszoon, a cutler of Oudewater in S. Holland. He was schooled at Utrecht and later studied for a time at Marburg. On hearing that most of his relatives had been massacred by the Spaniards, he returned to the Netherlands and took refuge at Rotterdam. Here his evident theological abilities won him influential friends and support. He continued his theological studies at *Leiden (1576–81), at Geneva under T. *Beza, and (for a short time) at Basle, as well as at Padua and Rome. On his return to the Netherlands in 1587 he received a call to minister at Amsterdam and was ordained there in the following year. Studies in the Ep. to the Romans having led him to doubt the Calvinistic doctrine of predestination, he was accused of *Pelagianism and disloyalty to the Confessions of his Church. After an unsuccessful attempt of J. Uitenbogaert to mediate, his opposition to Calvinistic doctrines became more pronounced. An extensive correspondence with Francis Junius, professor at Leiden, and an attempted refutation (not published till after Arminius' death) of W. *Perkins's treatise on predestination led him to work out his doctrines with greater precision. He also found himself increasingly drawn into the political struggle in the Netherlands, as his views on the absolute authority of the State brought him the support of J. van Oldenbarnevelt against the military ideals of Prince Maurice of Orange. Appointed professor at Leiden in 1603, he was at once drawn into a conflict with the zealous Calvinist F. *Gomar, who had taught at Leiden since 1594, but after a disputation at The Hague in the presence of Oldenbarnevelt on 6 May 1603, Arminius successfully cleared himself of the charges of Pelagianism and *Socinianism, and obtained possession of his chair. He now found himself at one of the chief centres of learning in Europe, with J. J. *Scaliger as his colleague, and provided with wide opportunities for furthering his beliefs. For the rest of his life, though his temper remained conciliatory and he was steadily supported by the curators of the university, he was engaged in controversy. He made it one of his chief ends to obtain the revision of the two chief Calvinistic documents of the Dutch Church, the *Belgic Confession and the *Heidelberg Catechism. But though negotiations for a National Synod for this purpose were unsuccessful he commanded widespread respect, and from 1608 H. *Grotius threw in his lot with him. The disputes continued down to the time of his death.

As a system of faith, Arminian doctrines, formally set forth in the *Remonstrance (q.v.) of 1610, were a theological reaction against the deterministic logic of Calvinism. The Arminians insisted that the Divine sovereignty was compatible with a real human free will; that Jesus Christ died for all and not only for the elect; and that both the *Supralapsarian and *Sublapsarian views of *predestination were unbiblical. At first the opposition to Arminianism was led by F. Gomar. The struggle was long and bitter. Suspected of favouring the pro-Spanish party in politics, the Arminians were attacked by Prince Maurice of Orange. After their condemnation at the Synod of *Dort (1618–19), many were banished and others persecuted. By 1630 a less rigid policy had been adopted, but it was not until 1795 that the Remonstrants were admitted to full toleration.

As representatives of a more liberal school of theology than the strict Calvinists, the Arminians exercised considerable influence on the formation of modern Dutch and European Protestant theology. In England the anti-Calvinistic trend in 17th-cent. theology, and esp. in the Laudian revival, was widely termed 'Arminian' by its opponents, though it is doubtful if here the direct influence of Arminius' teaching was at all considerable. In the *Methodist movement J. *Wesley held an Arminian position, as contrasted with G. *Whitefield's Calvinist teaching, thus giving rise to the division in theological outlook between *Wesleyan and *Calvinistic Methodists which has persisted down to modern times. On the Continent the reputation of Arminianism sank very low in the 18th cent., owing to the association which grew up between it and Socinianism. More recently the tension between the Arminian and Calvinist trends in theology had been less acute, until the theological revival of Calvinism under the influence of K. *Barth.

J. Arminius' Theological Works, ed. Leiden, 1629 (repr. Frankfurt, 1631, 1635). Eng. tr. by J. and W. Nichols (3 vols., London, 1825–75; repr., with introd. by C. Bangs, Grand Rapids, 1986). Lives by C. Brandt (Amsterdam, 1724; Eng. tr., 1854) and J. H. Maronier (ibid., 1905). A. W. Harrison, *The Beginnings of Arminianism to the Synod of Dort* (1926); id., *Arminianism* (1937). R. L. Colie, *Light and Englightenment: A Study of the Cambridge Platonists and the Dutch Arminians* (Cambridge, 1957), esp. pp. 1–21. C. Bangs, *Arminius: A Study in the Dutch Reformation* (New York, 1971). E. More, 'John Goodwin and the Origins of the New Arminianism', *Journal of British Studies*, 22, pt. 1 (1982), pp. 50–70. J. M. Atkins, 'Calvinist Bishops, Church Unity, and the Rise of Arminianism', *Albion*, 18 (1986), pp. 411–27. N. Tyacke, *Anti-Calvinists: The Rise of English Arminianism c.1590–1640* (Oxford Historical Monographs, 1987); H. [R.] Trevor-Roper, *Catholics, Anglicans and Puritans* (1987), pp. 40–119 ('Laudianism and Political Power'); P. White, *Predestination, Policy and Polemic: Conflict and Consensus in the English Church from the Reformation to the Civil War* (Cambridge, 1992).

Arnauld, Antoine (1612–94), 'the Great Arnauld', French theologian and philosopher. He was the twentieth son of a bourgeois family, born in Paris, who, after the death of his father in 1619, came increasingly under the influence of his mother and of his sister, Angélique (see foll. entry). In 1633 he entered the *Sorbonne, where the subject of his bachelor's thesis was the doctrine of *grace. For some years he was a prominent figure in the intellectual society of Paris, but, after receiving the subdiaconate in 1638, he began to enter into association with *Port-Royal and *Saint-Cyran. He was priested in 1641 and the following day retired to Port-Royal. In 1643 he published *De la fréquente communion*, which with its stress on the need for thorough preparation for Communion and its emphasis on the right interior dispositions did much to propagate *Jansenist principles among a wide public. The book provoked a storm from the *Jesuits which necessitated Arnauld's withdrawal from public life. In the next year he published (anon.) his *Apologie de M. Jansenius*, a semi-official manifesto of the Jansenist theological position and Arnauld now became the acknowledged leader of the Jansenists, writing extensively on their behalf. The publication of two outspoken *Lettres . . . à un duc et pair*, directed against the Jesuit method in the confessional, provoked an attack from the Sorbonne. The support of the *Dominicans and also of B. *Pascal, who sought to justify Arnauld in the first of his *Lettres provinciales*, failed to save him, and he was censured by the Sorbonne in Jan. 1656 and in Feb. 1656 solemnly degraded; and until the 'Peace of the Church' of 1668 he remained in retirement. In 1669 he was received by Louis XIV, restored to his position as a Doctor of the Sorbonne and treated as a popular hero. With P. *Nicole (q.v.) he then began a major treatise against the *Calvinists, *La Perpétuité de la foi catholique touchant l'Eucharistie* (1669–74). When the Jansenist controversy began to revive in 1679, Arnauld left France for the Netherlands, where he was joined by P. *Quesnel; and here he continued to write untiringly, until his death, against N. *Malebranche, on *Gallicanism, and on various biblical subjects. If he was less radical than Jansen in his teaching on the all-embracing power of grace, it was to him more than to anyone else that Jansenist principles owed their diffusion.

Arnauld was the author of over 320 works. Many of his letters are in MS in the Bibliothèque Nationale, Paris. *Œuvres de Messire Antoine Arnauld* (43 vols., Lausanne, 1775–83; with Life in vol. 43). Modern edn. by P. Clair and F. Girbal of *La Logique ou l'Art de Penser* by Arnauld and P. Nicole (Paris, 1965). Eng. tr. of the Leibniz–Arnauld Correspondence by H. T. Mason (Manchester, 1967). P. Quesnel, *Histoire abrégée de la vie et des ouvrages de M. Arnauld* (Cologne, 1695). É Jacques, *Les années d'exil de Antoine Arnauld (1679–1694)* (Bibliothèque de la *RHE*, 63; 1976). A. R. Ndiaye, *La Philosophie d'Antoine Arnauld* (Bibliothèque d'Histoire de la Philosophie, 1991). J. Carreyre, PSS, in *DHGE* 4 (1930), cols. 447–85, s.v. and with bibl.

Arnauld, Jacqueline Marie Angélique (1591–1661), 'Mère Angélique', Abbess of *Port-Royal. She was the sister of Antoine *Arnauld (see preceding entry), and christened Jacqueline, but at her confirmation took the name of Angélique by which she is commonly known. Born at Paris, she was procured succession at the age of 7 to the abbacy of Port-Royal, and after residence in the *Benedictine convents of St-Antoine, Paris, and at Maubuisson, she became Abbess of Port-Royal in 1602. At first she shared without protest in the very relaxed (but not immoral) discipline of the house, until in 1608 she was converted by a sermon from a visiting *Capuchin friar. She promptly introduced drastic reforms (community of goods, enclosure, regular office, uniformity of dress, abstinence, and silence) and also laid great emphasis on the inner discipline of the spirit. In 1618 she carried through similar reforms at Maubuisson. In 1619 she fell in with St *Francis de Sales and wished to join the *Visitation nuns, but, permission being refused, she returned to Port-Royal in 1623. The community now increased rapidly in numbers and came to include Angélique's four sisters and their mother, and in 1625 Angélique moved it to a larger house in the Faubourg Saint-Jacques in Paris. A proposal of Sébastien Zamet, Bp. of Langres (Bp. 1615–55), to amalgamate the community with the reformed Benedictine house of Tard, nr. Dijon, led to serious differences, and in 1630 Angélique was forced to resign as Abbess. After her sister Agnes succeeded to this office in 1636, Angélique again exercised (indirect) power. She came under the influence of *Saint-Cyran, under whom the community became an enthusiastic upholder of *Jansenist principles and practice, and Angélique herself for long periods abstained from Communion. From 1642 to 1654 she was again Abbess. She died shortly after the signing of the Formulary of 1661. See also PORT-ROYAL.

Her spiritual doctrines, based on papers written by herself or under her immediate inspiration, may be studied in *Mémoires pour servir à l'histoire de Port-Royal et à la vie de la Révérende Mère Marie-Angélique . . . Arnauld* (3 vols., Utrecht, 1742–4), *Entretiens ou conférences de la Révérende Mère Angélique Arnauld* (3 vols., ibid., 1757), and other collections. Modern edn. of her autobiography up to 1638 ed. L. Cognet, *Relation écrite par la Mère Angélique Arnauld sur Port-Royal* (1949). A. Gazier, *Jeanne de Chantal et Angélique Arnauld d'après leur correspondance, 1620–1641* (Paris, 1915). L. Cognet, *La Mère Angélique et Saint François de Sales 1618–1626* (1951), and other works of this author. P. Bugnion-Secrétan, *La Mère Angelique Arnauld 1591–1661 d'après ses écrits* (1991).

Arndt, Ernst Moritz (1769–1860), German patriot and poet. A native of Schoritz in the island of Rügen and of a strict Protestant family, he studied at Greifswald (1791) and Jena (1793), where he came under the influence of the *Aufklärung and of the Critical Philosophy (esp. J. G. *Fichte). Philosophical doubts led him to give up his intention of becoming a pastor in 1797. In 1800 he became lecturer in history at Greifswald university. His work, *Vom Geist der Zeit* (1806), directed against Napoleon, endangered his freedom and he fled to Sweden. During the wars from 1812 onwards he exercised a great influence by his patriotic publications. In 1818 he was appointed professor of history at the newly founded university of Bonn. In 1819 appeared a fourth part of *Vom Geist der Zeit*, in which he attacked the reactionary policy of the German princes. Suspension from his professorship followed in 1820, and for the next 20 years Arndt devoted himself to literary work. In 1840 he was reinstalled in his office by Frederick William IV.

Despite his change-over from theology to history Arndt always retained his religious interests. After a period of doubt, during which he tried to combine *Lutheranism with the contemporary German Idealistic philosophy, he began, in 1817, to occupy himself more with the Bible and the Reformation, and, under the influence of friends, esp. F. D. E. *Schleiermacher, he adopted a more definitely Christian attitude. To this period belong his hymns to Christ, among them his popular '*Ich weiss, an wen ich glaube*'. His hopes of a union between Protestants and Catholics in a German National Church were disappointed through the growing influence of *Ultramontanism, and in his later years he became one of the sturdiest representatives of German Protestantism, his most important work on the subject being *Über den gegenwärtigen Stand des Protestantismus* (1844).

Works ed. H. Rösch and others (14 vols., Leipzig and Magdeburg, 1892–1909). Lives by W. Baur (2nd edn., Hamburg, 1863), E. Langenberg (Bonn, 1865), E. Muesebeck (vol. 1, Gotha, 1914; all pub.), and P. Breitenkamp (Berlin, 1939). R. Wolfram, *Ernst Moritz Arndt und Schweden* (1933). A. G. Pundt, *Arndt and the National Awakening in Germany* (Columbia University thesis; New York, 1935). R. Fahrner, *Arndt: Geistiges und politisches Verhalten* (1937). U. E. W. Willers, *Ernst Moritz Arndt och hans Svenska Förbindelser: Studier i svensk-pommersk Historiografi och svensk Opinionsbildning* (1945), with portrait and bibl. G. Ott, *Ernst Moritz Arndt: Religion, Christentum und Kirche in der Entwicklung des deutschen Publizisten und Patrioten* (Düsseldorf, 1966). K. H. Schäfer, *Ernst Moritz Arndt als politischer Publizist* (Veröffentlichungen des Stadtarchivs Bonn, 13; 1974). Id. and J. Schawe, *Ernst Moritz Arndt: Ein bibliographes Handbuch 1769–1969* (ibid. 8; 1971).

Arndt, Johann (1555–1621), *Lutheran theologian and mystical writer. A devoted follower of P. *Melanchthon, he studied at Helmstedt (1576) and *Wittenberg (1577) and later at Strasbourg and Basle. In 1583 he was made pastor of Badeborn, but aroused *Calvinist hostility by his uncompromising Lutheranism. In 1590 he was compelled to move to Quedlinburg and in 1599 to Brunswick. He is chiefly remembered for his *Vier Bücher vom wahren Christentum* (1606), in which, in contrast to the prevalent forensic view of the Atonement, he dwelt on the work of Christ in the heart of man. Arndt was much venerated by the German *Pietists.

Works ed. by J. J. Rambach (8 vols., Leipzig, 1734–6). Eng. tr. of parts of *Vier Bücher vom wahren Christentum* as *True Christianity*

by P. Erb (Classics of Western Spirituality, 1979), with introd. W. Koepp, *Johann Arndt: Eine Untersuchung über die Mystik im Luthertum* (1912), with bibl. F. J. Winter, *Johann Arndt, der Verfasser des 'Wahren Christentums'* (Schriften des Vereins für Reformationsgeschichte, 101–2, 1911); E. Weber, *Johann Arndts Vier Bücher vom Wahren Christentum als Beitrag zur protestantischen Irenik des 17. Jahrhunderts* (Schriften des Instituts für Wissenschaftliche Irenik der Johann Wolfgang Goethe Universität, Frankfurt am Main, 2; Marburg, 1969). C. Braw, *Bücher im Staube: Die Theologie Johann Arndts in ihrem Verhältnis zur Mystik* (Studies in Medieval and Reformation Thought, 39; Leiden, 1985). M. Schmidt in *TRE* 4 (1979), pp. 121–9, s.v.

Arnobius (3rd–4th cent.). A Christian apologist who flourished in the time of *Diocletian (284–305). Acc. to *Jerome, he was a rhetorician at Sicca in proconsular Africa, converted to Christianity by a dream. In his 'Adversus Nationes', a treatise full of curious learning, he defended the consonance of the Christian religion with the best pagan philosophy. *Lactantius was his pupil.

Editio princeps of the *Adversus Nationes* by Faustus Sabaeus [Brixianus] at Rome, 1543. J. P. Migne, *PL* 5. 349–1372. Crit. edns. by A. Reifferscheid (CSEL 4; 1875), C. Marchesi (Turin, 1934; 2nd edn., 1953), and H. Le Bonniec (Collection des Universités de France, 1982 ff.). Eng. trs. by A. H. Bryce and H. Campbell (ANCL 19; 1871) and G. E. McCracken (ACW 7–8; 1949). F. Gabarrou, *Arnobe, son œuvre* (1921); id., *Le Latin d'Arnobe* (1921); E. Rapisarda, *Arnobio* (1946); P. Krafft, *Beiträge zur Wirkungsgeschichte des älteren Arnobius* (Klassisch-Philologische Studien, 32; 1966); M. B. Simmons, *Arnobius of Sicca* (Oxford Early Christian Studies, 1995). P. Monceaux, *Histoire littéraire de l'Afrique chrétienne*, 3 (1905), pp. 241–86. L. Berkowitz, *Index Arnobianus* (Hildesheim, 1967). J. Quasten, *Patrology*, 2 (Utrecht, 1953), pp. 383–92. P. Siniscalco in *DPAC* 1 (1983), cols. 377–9, s.v.; Eng. tr., *Encyclopedia of the Early Church*, 1 (1992), p. 82, with further bibl.

Arnobius Junior (5th cent.). He was a monk, possibly of African origin, who has left an account of a debate held *c*.450 between himself and an Egyptian *Monophysite ('Conflictus cum Serapione'). He also wrote allegorizing 'Commentaries' on the Pss., some notes on the Gospels, and a 'Liber ad Gregoriam', a letter to an aristocratic lady of Rome. G. *Morin ascribed to him the '*Praedestinatus' (q.v.), but this attribution is problematic.

Editio princeps of his Commentaries by *Erasmus (Basle, 1522), of his 'Expositiunculae in Evangelium' by G. Cognatus [i.e. Cousin] (Basle, 1543). Complete text of the latter pr. by G. Morin, OSB, in *Anecdota Maredsolana*, 3 (pt. 3; Maredsous and Oxford, 1903), pp. 129–51. Collected edn. in J. P. Migne, *PL* 53. 237–692, and suppl. 3 (1963), 213–56. Crit. edn. of his *Opera* by K.-D. Daur (CCLS, 25 and 25A; 1990–2). C. Pifarré, *Arnobio el Joven y la Cristología del 'Conflictus'* (Scripta et Documenta, 35; Montserrat, 1988). B. Studer in Quasten (cont.), *Patrology*, 4 (1986), pp. 567–9, with further bibl. P. de Labriolle in *DHGE* 4 (1930), cols. 547–9.

Arnold of Brescia (d. 1155), reformer. Almost certainly a native of Brescia, Arnold studied in France before returning to Italy and becoming a *canon regular. His preaching against the worldliness of the Church led him to take a leading part in the conflict between the bishop and reformers in Brescia. As a result, in *c*.1139, he was forced to return to France. He became a supporter of Peter *Abelard, and at the Council of *Sens (1140), St *Bernard of Clairvaux secured his condemnation along with

Abelard, on the grounds that he taught the same errors. Arnold later (1146/7) made his way to Rome. After a brief reconciliation with the Church, he gave his support to the Roman senate in its rejection of the temporal dominion of the popes; he was excommunicated by *Eugenius III on 15 July 1148. After the accession of the Emp. *Frederick Barbarossa, who made a treaty with the Pope on 16 Oct. 1152, the senate lost control of Rome. Arnold was captured by Barbarossa and condemned to death. He was handed over to the Prefect of the now subdued city and hanged; the ashes of his body were thrown into the Tiber. While *John of Salisbury showed respect for his austerity and quickness of mind, *Otto of Freising, less sympathetic, attributed to Arnold 'unsound' teaching on infant baptism and the Eucharist. It is probable that he discouraged his followers from receiving the sacraments from priests guilty of *simony; and told them to confess to one another rather than to such priests. It seems, however, that like other reformers at the time, he was mainly concerned to revive the ideal of apostolic poverty. He developed this into an assault (readily adopted by political rebels) on the possession of worldly goods and the exercise of secular authority by the Church.

The primary sources are the *Gesta Friderici* of Otto of Freising, the letters of Bernard of Clairvaux and the *Historia Pontificalis* of John of Salisbury; on the last, see text of R. L. Poole (Oxford, 1927), pp. lviii–lxx. W. v. Giesebrecht, 'Ueber Arnold von Brescia', *Sb.* (Bayr.), 3 (1873), pp. 122–54; K. Hampe, 'Zur Geschichte Arnolds von Brescia', *Historische Zeitschrift*, 130 (1924), pp. 58–69; G. W. Greenaway, *Arnold of Brescia* (1931), with discussion of sources, pp. 205–10, and of modern studies, pp. 211–17. A. Frugoni, *Arnaldo da Brescia nelle fonti del secolo XII* (Istituto storico Italiano per il medio evo. Studi storici, 8–9; 1954). H. Grundmann, *Bibliographie zur Ketzergeschichte des Mittelalters (1900–1966)* (Sussidi Eruditi, 20; Rome, 1967), pp. 22 f. (nos. 101–13). A. Frugoni in *Dizionario Biografico degli Italiani*, 4 (1962), pp. 247–50; R. Manselli in *TRE* 4 (1979), pp. 129–33, both s.v.

Arnold, Gottfried (1666–1714), German Protestant theologian and devotional writer. A native of Annaberg in Saxony, he studied theology at *Wittenberg from 1685 to 1689, when, following the advice of P. J. *Spener, he accepted a position as private tutor at Dresden. Under Spener's influence he experienced a conversion. In 1693 he went to Quedlinburg, where he wrote his first important work, *Die erste Liebe* (1696), an enthusiastic account of the life of the first Christians, founded on his *patristic studies and especially the work of W. *Cave. The book earned him a call to Giessen as professor of Church history in 1697, a post which he resigned in the following year because he found it too distracting. He returned to Quedlinburg, where he wrote his principal work, the *Unparteiische Kirchen- und Ketzer-Historie* (1699–1700). Though not as impartial as its title claims, it is important esp. as a history of Protestant mysticism and for its use of many out-of-the-way documents on the movement. The opposition of the official Lutheran Church led him to form close connections with representatives of a more personal spirituality such as J. G. *Gichtel. His *Geheimnis der göttlichen Sophia* (1700) abounds in strange speculations on the androgynous nature of the first man, lost by the Fall, and recovered through Christ. After his marriage in 1701 he devoted himself increasingly to pastoral work. In 1704

he became inspector and pastor at Werben, and in 1707 at Perleberg. His writings of this later period are devotional and less eccentric, among the most popular being his *Historia et Descriptio Theologiae Mysticae* (Frankfurt, 1702; Ger. tr., 1703), *Geistliche Gestalt eines evangelischen Lehrers* (1704), and *Wahre Abbildung des inwendigen Christentums* (1709). He is also well known as an author of hymns, and he published translations of M. *Molinos and Mme *Guyon, and edited the works of *Angelus Silesius.

Modern edn. of his *Geistliche Lieder* by R. C. Ehmann (Stuttgart, 1856; with Life, pp. 1–43). Selected writings reproduced in facsimile, with introd, in vol. 1 by W. Nigg (Stuttgart and Bad Cannstatt, 1963 ff.). F. Dibelius, *Gottfried Arnold: Sein Leben und seine Bedeutung für Kirche und Theologie* (1873); E. Seeberg, *Gottfried Arnold: Die Wissenschaft und die Mystik seiner Zeit* (1923); H. Dörries, *Geist und Geschichte bei Gottfried Arnold* (*Abh.* (Gött.), Dritte Folge, 51; 1963); T. Stählin, *Gottfried Arnolds geistliche Dichtung: Glaube und Mystik* (Veröffentlichungen der Evangelischen Gesellschaft für Liturgieforschung, 15; 1966). J. Büchsel, *Gottfried Arnold: Sein Verständnis von Kirche und Wiedergeburt* (Arbeiten zur Geschichte des Pietismus, 8; 1970). P. C. Erb, *Pietists, Protestants, and Mysticism: The Use of Late Medieval Spiritual Texts in the Work of Gottfried Arnold (1666–1714)* (Pietist and Wesleyan Studies, 2; Metuchen, NJ, and London, 1989). M. Schmidt in *TRE* 4 (1979), pp. 136–40, s.v.

Arnold, Matthew (1822–88), poet and literary critic. He was the eldest son of T. *Arnold (q.v.). Born at Laleham, Surrey, he was educated at *Winchester, Rugby, and Balliol College, *Oxford, where he won the Newdigate Prize with his poem *Cromwell* (1843). In 1845 he was elected a Fellow of Oriel College; from 1847 to 1851 he was private secretary to Lord Lansdowne; and from 1851 to 1883 a Government Inspector of Schools. From 1857 to 1867 he was also Professor of Poetry at Oxford. In 1853 he published his *Poems* (including 'Sohrab and Rustum' and 'The Scholar Gipsy'); in 1855 his *Poems* (Second Series). 'Thyrsis' and 'Rugby Chapel' both first appeared in *New Poems* (1867). His prose writings include *On Translating Homer* (1861), *Essays in Criticism* (1865; 2nd ser., 1888), and *Culture and Anarchy* (1869). For his religious views, *St Paul and Protestantism* (1870), *Literature and Dogma* (1873), *God and the Bible* (1875), and *Last Essays on Church and Religion* (1877) are of particular interest.

Matthew Arnold made it his mission to condemn the boorishness of the English, finding in 'culture' the cure for contemporary ills and a potent help towards the formation of human character. Religion, he held, was to be concerned with conduct and not with speculation about the nature of things. The power behind the universe is a moral one, and with it a moral tendency which resides in man is in sympathy. These truths Arnold held to be manifested in the OT belief that righteousness, which God approves, exalts a nation; but he deplored the superstitious *bibliolatry, alien from the scientific spirit of the age, which interpreted with literalness such poetic images as the hope of the *Messiah. The religion of Jesus had shown advance by laying stress on personal rather than national conduct, and had suffused morality with emotion and, therefore, with happiness.

Collected Works, 15 vols., London, 1903–4 (with bibl. by T. B. Smart). Prose Works also ed. R. H. Super (11 vols., Ann Arbor, Mich., 1960–77). Modern edns. of his Poems by C. B. Tinker and H. F. Lowry (London, 1950) and K. Allott (ibid.,

1965). *Letters, 1848–1888*, ed. G. W. E. Russell (2 vols., 1895); *Letters to Arthur Hugh Clough*, ed. H. F. Lowry (1932). *Note-Books*, ed. H. F. Lowry, K. Young, and W. H. Dunn (1952). Studies by G. Saintsbury ('Modern English Writers', 1899), H. W. Paul ('English Men of Letters', 1902), W. H. Dawson (New York and London, 1904), G. W. E. Russell ('Literary Lives', 1904), Hugh Kingsmill (pseud., 1928), L. Trilling (New York, 1939), E. K. Chambers (Oxford, 1947), D. G. James (ibid., 1961), H. C. Duffin (London, 1962), W. D. Anderson (Ann Arbor, Mich., 1965), A. D. Culler (New Haven, Conn., and London, 1966), G. R. Strange (Princeton, NJ, 1967), D. Bush (London, 1971), and ed. K. Allott (ibid., 1975). Life by P. Honan (London, 1981). C. B. Tinker and H. F. Lowry, *The Poetry of Matthew Arnold: A Commentary* (1940). W. Robbins, *The Ethical Idealism of Matthew Arnold: A Study of the Nature and Sources of his Moral and Religious Ideas* (1959). R. apRoberts, *Arnold and God* (Berkeley, Calif., and London, 1983); J. C. Livingston, *Matthew Arnold and Christianity* (Columbia, SC [1986]). R. Garnett in *DNB*, Suppl. 1 (1901), pp. 70–5, s.v.

Arnold, Thomas (1795–1842), Headmaster of Rugby. A widely-read classical scholar, he was a Fellow of Oriel College, Oxford, from 1815 to 1819, where he was a contemporary of John *Keble and R. D. *Hampden. In 1828 he was appointed Headmaster of Rugby. Here he aimed at fostering a system of education based on a carefully laid foundation of religious training. He made it his goal to educate the sons of middle-class parents, who began to flock into the public schools towards the close of his lifetime, into a high sense of duty, of public service, and of the importance of personal character. He believed in the essential unity of the secular and religious, of Church and State, and in the universal priesthood of the laity. His influence on the young men of his generation was considerable; he was one of the founders of the *Broad Church movement, and his liberalism, both theological and political, found sympathetic echoes in later Victorian thought. He objected to the *Tractarians on the ground of their ecclesiasticism, and vigorously attacked them in an article entitled 'Dr Hampden and the Oxford Malignants' in the *Edinburgh Review* of 1836. In 1841 he was appointed Regius Professor of Modern History at Oxford, but died while still in his prime in the following year. His ecclesiastical ideals were epitomized in his *Principles of Church Reform* (1833). He also issued works on classical subjects and some volumes of sermons.

Miscellaneous Works collected and ed. by A. P. *Stanley (London, 1845). Id., *The Life and Correspondence of Thomas Arnold* (2 vols., 1844). Other studies by E. J. Worboise (London, 1859), J. J. Findlay (ed.; Cambridge, 1897), R. J. Campbell (London, 1927), A. Whitridge (ibid., 1928), N. Wymer (ibid., 1953), T. W. Bamford (ibid., 1960), and E. L. Williamson, Jun. (University, Ala., 1964). M. McCrum, *Thomas Arnold, Headmaster: A Reassessment* (Oxford, 1989). T. Walrond in *DNB* 2 (1885), pp. 113–17, s.v.

Arnulf, St (*c*.580–*c*.640), also Arnoul, Bp. of Metz. A member of a noble Frankish family whose lands were concentrated around Metz and Verdun, he rapidly rose to high position in the court of Theodebert II, King of Austrasia (595–612). Renouncing his desire for a solitary life, he became *domesticus* to Theodebert and then took an active part in securing the accession of Clothar II in 613. He was consecrated Bp. of Metz *c*.614, and from 623 assisted Clothar's son, Dagobert, in the government of his kingdom in the Ardennes. He took part in the Councils of Clichy (*c*.626–7) and of *Reims (*c*.627), and was eventually allowed to resign his see. He joined his friend Romaric in retirement in a deserted place near Remiremont in the Vosges, where he spent the rest of his life in meditation and prayer. Before he was consecrated bishop he had been married to the daughter of the Count of Boulogne. One of his sons, Clodulf, was his third successor in the see of Metz; by the marriage of the other, Ansegisel, with Begga, daughter of Pepin II, Mayor of the Palace of Austrasia, he became an ancestor of the Carolingian kings of France. The liturgical cult of Arnulf was established by the late 8th cent. Feast day, 18 July or 16 Aug.

The principal authority is an anonymous contemporary Lat. Life pr. in *AASS*, Jul. 4 (1735), pp. 435–40; a further Life, mainly dependent on it, dating from the reign of Louis II (846–79) and attributed to Umno, ibid., pp. 440–5; crit. edn. of the former by B. Krusch in *MGH*, Scriptores Rerum Merovingicarum, 2 (1888), pp. 426–46. J. Depoin, 'Grandes Figures monacales des temps mérovingiens: Saint Arnoul de Metz. Études de critique historique', *Revue Mabillon*, 11 (1921), pp. 245–58; 12 (1922), pp. 13–25, 105–18. E. Hlawitschka, 'Die Vorfahren Karls des Grossen', in W. Braunfels (ed.), *Karl der Grosse*, 1 (Düsseldorf, 1965), pp. 50–82, esp. pp. 51–8 and 73; O. G. Oexle, 'Die Karolinger und die Stadt des heiligen Arnulf', *Frühmittelalterliche Studien*, 1 (1967), pp. 250–364, esp. pp. 270–9 and 345–61 (on the cult).

ars praedicandi (Lat., 'the art of preaching'). The medieval *artes praedicandi* provided instruction in the composition of sermons either as an adjunct to a collection of sermons or as a manual which circulated with other aids for the preacher. Although this literature reflects the teaching of earlier Church writers such as St *Augustine, St *Gregory, St *Isidore, or *Rabanus Maurus, and is influenced by the rhetorical principles of Cicero, Quintilian, and the *Rhetorica ad Herennium*, it did not assume its distinctive form until the 12th cent. Guibert of Nogent's (d. 1124) *Quo Ordine Sermo Fieri Debeat* is an early witness to a systematic study of sermon composition. The sermon collections of *Honorius 'of Autun', Maurice of Sully (d. 1196) and *Peter the Chanter also contain material of this kind, but the first major example is *Alan of Lille's *Ars Praedicandi*. Alan deals with preaching as public instruction in morals and faith, addressed to those who seek to be informed, drawing on reason and authority, and besides general advice supplies an anthology of source material.

Over 300 *artes praedicandi* have survived from the 13th to the 16th cent. Some are intended for mendicant missioners or priests with a care of souls; others are designed for preachers of the highly structured thematic sermon to learned congregations. *Humbert of Romans in his *De Eruditione Praedicatorum* displays a concern with the adaptation of preaching to different congregations. Robert of Basevorn, *Forma Praedicandi* (1322) and Thomas Waleys, OP, *De Modo Componendi Sermones* (*c*.1340), are representative of manuals for thematic preaching, with sections on the choice of theme and protheme, the technique of division and subdivision, the use of confirmatory authorities and development (*dilatatio*) of the divisions, as well as advice on delivery.

Description of the *artes*, with indications of the MSS, are given by T. M. Charland, OP, *Artes Praedicandi* (Publications de l'Institut d'Études Médiévales d'Ottawa, 7; 1936); and H. Caplan, *Mediaeval Artes Praedicandi: A Hand-List* (Cornell Studies in

Classical Philology, 24; 1934); id., *Mediaeval Artes Praedicandi: A Supplementary Hand-List* (ibid. 25; 1936). Pr. edns. are listed by H. Caplan and H. H. King, 'Latin Tractates on Preaching: A Book-List', *HTR* 42 (1949), pp. 185–206; S. Gallick, '*Artes praedicandi*: Early Printed Editions', *Mediaeval Studies*, 39 (1977), pp. 477–89. Edns. of texts mentioned: Guibert of Nogent, *Quo Ordine Sermo Fieri Debeat*, in J. P. Migne, *PL* 156. 21–32; Alan of Lille, *Ars Praedicandi*, ibid. 210. 109–98; Eng. tr. by G. R. Evans (Cistercian Fathers Series, 23; Kalamazoo, Mich., 1981); Humbert of Romans, *De Eruditione Praedicatorum*, lib. 1, in his *Opera de Vita Regulari*, ed. J. J. Berthier, OP, 2 (Rome, 1889; repr. Turin, 1956), pp. 373–484; Eng. tr., ed. W. M. Conlon (Westminster, Md., 1951); lib. 2, partial edn., *Bibliotheca Maxima Veterum Patrum*, 25 (Lyons, 1677), pp. 456–567; Robert of Basevorn, *Forma Praedicandi*, ed. Charland, op. cit., pp. 233–323; Eng. tr. by L. Krul, OSB, in J. J. Murphy (ed.), *Three Medieval Rhetorical Arts* (Berkeley and Los Angeles, 1971), pp. 109–215; Thomas Waleys, OP, *De Modo Componendi Sermones*, ed. Charland, op. cit., pp. 327–403. Study by J. Longère, *La prédication médiévale* (1983), pp. 195–202. M. G. Briscoe in J. R. Strayer (ed.), *Dictionary of the Middle Ages*, 1 (1982), pp. 555–58, s.v.

Artemon (also **Artemas**) (3rd cent.),*Adoptionist heretic. He is mentioned twice by *Eusebius, who says that *Paul of Samosata revived his heresy (*HE* 5. 28 and 7. 30. 16 f.). Eusebius asserts that the '*Little Labyrinth' was directed against Artemon's teaching, though the passages he quotes concern only the heresy of *Theodotus the Cobbler and his namesake; there is no other evidence about the teaching of Artemon. If the 'Little Labyrinth' was directed against Artemon, it would appear that he taught in Rome, perhaps before 235. However, the letter of the synod which condemned Paul of Samosata in 268, quoted by Eusebius, names 'Artemas' as the father of Paul's heresy, and implies that he was then still alive (ibid. 7. 30. 16 f.). Later writers who mention Artemon appear to derive their information from Eusebius.

*Epiphanius, *Haer.* 65. 1. 4; *Theodoret, *Haer. Fab.* 2. 4; and *Photius, *Biblioth.* 48. R. H. *Connolly, OSB, 'Eusebius *H.E.* v. 28', *JTS* 49 (1948), pp. 73–9. P. Salmon in *DCB* 1 (1877), p. 174, s.v.

Articles. See FORTY-TWO ARTICLES; IRISH ARTICLES; LAMBETH ARTICLES; ORGANIC ARTICLES; SIX ARTICLES; TEN ARTICLES; THIRTEEN ARTICLES; THIRTY-NINE ARTICLES; TWELVE ARTICLES.

artophorion (Gk. ἀρτοφόριον). In the E. Church, the *tabernacle on the altar in which the Blessed Sacrament is reserved; also the small portable ones used for taking Communion to the sick.

Arundel, Thomas (1353–1414), Abp. of *Canterbury. A prominent politician and twice Chancellor under Richard II (1386–9 and 1391–6), he was consecrated Bp. of *Ely in 1374, and translated to *York in 1388 and to Canterbury in 1396. In 1397 he was impeached in parliament and banished. At the request of Richard II, Pope Boniface IX deprived him of the see of Canterbury by translating him to St Andrews (which did not recognize the authority of Boniface). Restored to Canterbury in 1399, he was three times Chancellor under Henry IV, and remained in possession of his see until his death. He was a prominent opponent of the *Lollards, holding a provincial

council against them at *Oxford in 1408, seeking out Lollard writings, and showing himself active in the persecution carried out against them; his *Constitutions*, drafted in 1407 and issued in 1409, were intended to ensure orthodoxy in the English Church.

M. [E.] Aston, *Thomas Arundel: A Study of Church Life in the Reign of Richard II* (Oxford, 1967). K. B. McFarlane, *John Wycliffe and the Beginnings of English Nonconformity* [1953], pp. 150–5 and 161–5. R. G. Davies, 'Thomas Arundel as Archbishop of Canterbury, 1396–1414', *JEH* 24 (1973), pp. 9–21. J. Gairdner in *DNB* 2 (1885), pp. 137–41, s.v.; *BRUO* 1 (1957), pp. 51–3.

Asaph, St (late 6th cent.), Welsh saint. Jocelin of Furness (12th cent.) refers to a little book on the life of St Asaph in which he is said to have been a disciple of St *Kentigern, when the latter was in exile at Llanelwy (later called *St Asaph, q.v.) in Wales. When Kentigern returned to Scotland, Asaph succeeded him as head of the monastery of Llanelwy, and became the first Welsh bishop of the see. Nothing more is definitely known of him. Names from the OT were popular in early Wales; Asaph doubtless took his name from the Asaph to whom are attributed Pss. 50 and 73–83.

Jocelin's 'Life of Kentigern', chs. 25 and 31; conveniently pr. by A. P. *Forbes, *Lives of S. Ninian and S. Kentigern* (Historians of Scotland, 5; 1874), pp. 204–6 and 215–16, with Eng. tr., pp. 78–81 and 90–2. S. Baring-Gould and J. Fisher, *The Lives of the British Saints*, 1 (1907), pp. 177–85; A. W. Wade-Evans, *Welsh Christian Origins* (Oxford, 1934), pp. 191–4.

Asbury, Francis (1745–1816). One of the two first *Methodist bishops in America. Sent to America by J. *Wesley in 1771, he was very soon given supervision of all Methodist work in the country. When the American Methodists became a separate organization in 1784, he and Thomas *Coke became joint superintendents. His journal from 1771 has much valuable historical matter. He travelled widely throughout the newly independent American States and continued the work of organization and administration until his death.

Modern edn. of his Journal and Letters by E. T. Clark and others (3 vols., London and Nashville, 1958). Lives by J. Lewis (London, 1927), H. Asbury (New York, 1927), W. L. Duren (ibid., 1928), and La V. C. Rudolph (Nashville, 1966). F. Baker, *From Wesley to Asbury* (Durham, NC, 1976), esp. pp. 105–41.

Ascension of Christ. The statement in the Creeds that Christ 'ascended into heaven' is based mainly on Acts 1: 1–9 where, after 40 days of appearances, the Risen Lord speaks to the Apostles about the coming of the *Holy Spirit and the Church's mission, and is then taken up in a cloud. The reference to the Apostles' return to Jerusalem from the Mount of *Olives (Acts 1: 12) gave rise to the tradition that this is where it took place. Lk. 24: 50–3 by contrast seems to imply that this withdrawal of Christ into Heaven occurred at *Bethany on the evening of the day of the Resurrection. Behind St *Luke's narrative stands the universal conviction of the early Church that God had vindicated Jesus after His crucifixion, and the expression of this mystery in the biblical language of exaltation, heavenly session, and resurrection (see RESURRECTION OF CHRIST). The language of exaltation and ascension is developed most profoundly in the Fourth Gospel where it balances that of *Incarnation. Its roots may be found in early Judaism (e.g. Dan. 7: 13; cf. Jn. 6: 62) and legends of the Assumption of *Moses and the Ascension of *Elijah, *Enoch, *Isaiah, etc. The idea is present in other parts of the NT: Eph. 4: 8–10, Heb. 4: 14, 6: 20, 7: 26, 8: 1, 1 Pet. 3: 22, 1 Tim. 3: 16.

For Christians the Ascension marks the solemn close of the post-Resurrection appearances and signifies the rule of Christ in the present (cf. 1 Cor. 15: 25). It is associated through Ps. 110: 1 with the idea of heavenly session at God's right hand (cf. Mk. 12: 36 and parallels, 14: 62 and parallels, 16: 19; Acts 2: 33, Rom. 8: 34, Col. 3: 1, Eph. 1: 20, Heb. 1: 3 and 13, 8: 1, 10: 12 f., 12: 2). Doctrinally it implies Christ's humanity being taken into Heaven and its hold on the Christian imagination is evidenced by the importance of the motif in Christian *iconography.

Ascension Day is one of the chief feasts of the Christian year. It is kept on the sixth Thursday, i.e. the 40th day, after *Easter. There is widespread testimony (e.g. in *Chrysostom, *Egeria, and *Socrates) to its celebration from the later years of the 4th cent. In early times its observance was frequently, if not always, marked by a procession, apparently to commemorate Christ's journey to the Mount of Olives. Acc. to W. usage, the *Paschal Candle, lighted during more important services in Eastertide, was until 1970 extinguished after the Gospel at Mass on Ascension Day. In the BCP Proper Psalms (8, 15, 21; 24, 47, 108) are appointed for the day itself and a Proper Preface for use throughout the *octave. Modern Anglican liturgies make similar provision, in some cases following the 1970 *Missale Romanum* in directing that the Preface for the Ascension be used until the Saturday before *Whitsunday.

V. Larrañaga, SJ, *La Ascensión del Señor en el Nuevo Testamento* (2 vols., 1943; earlier Fr. tr., Rome, 1938). J. G. Davies, *He Ascended into Heaven: A Study in the History of Doctrine* (Bampton Lectures, 1958; 1958), with bibl. R. Cabié, *La Pentecôte: L'Évolution de la Cinquantaine pascale au cours des cinq premiers siècles* [1965], pp. 185–97. G. Lohfink, *Die Himmelfahrt Jesu: Untersuchungen zu den Himmelfahrts- und Erhöhungstexten bei Lukas* (Studien zum Alten und Neuen Testament, 26; 1971). N. Gkioles, Ἡ Ἀνάληψις τοῦ Χριστοῦ βάσει τῶν μνημειῶν τῆς α' χιλιετήριδος (Βιβλιοθήκη Σοφίας Ν. Σαριπόλου, 41; Athens, 1981). B. K. Donne, *Christ Ascended: A Study in the Significance of the Ascension of Jesus Christ in the New Testament* (Exeter, 1983).

Ascension of Isaiah. See ISAIAH, ASCENSION OF.

Ascent of Mount Carmel, The. The title of a famous treatise by St *John of the Cross (q.v.).

ascetical theology. See SPIRITUALITY and PURGATIVE, ILLUMINATIVE, AND UNITIVE WAYS.

asceticism. The term is derived from Gk. ἄσκησις ('exercise', 'training') already applied by the Greek philosophers to moral training, often with the connotation of voluntary abstention from certain pleasures; it denotes (1) practices employed to combat vices and develop virtues and (2) the renunciation of various facets of customary social life and comfort or the adoption of painful conditions for religious reasons. It is found in one form or another in many of the world's religions, esp. those of the Indian subcontinent. In the NT the word occurs only

once—as a verb, ἀσκεῖν, 'to strive'—at Acts 24: 16. In 1 Cor. 9: 25 the Christian life is compared to the games in which 'every man that striveth ... is temperate in all things'. But the idea, present already in the OT, esp. in the *Wisdom books, is prominent throughout the NT. It is summed up in the Lord's call to His disciples: 'If any man would come after Me, let him deny himself and take up his cross and follow Me' (Mk. 8: 34), with its emphasis on the two sides of Christian asceticism, the negative one of self-denial and the positive one of the following of Christ. This invitation to practice self-abnegation is frequently reiterated, mostly in very strong terms (Mt. 10: 38 f., Jn. 12: 25), being shown to involve constant watchfulness (Mt. 24: 42, 25: 13, etc.) and fasting (Mt. 6: 16–18; Mk. 2: 18–20) and, in many cases, renunciation of all earthly possessions (Mt. 19: 21, Mk. 10: 28, Lk. 9: 57–62) and perpetual chastity (Mt. 19: 12). St *Paul counsels the same ideal, repeatedly inculcating the necessity of keeping up the struggle against the inclinations of the 'old man' (e.g. Rom. 8: 13 and 1 Cor. 9: 26 f.).

In the early Christian centuries many ascetic practices seem to have become fairly widespread, the chief of them being renunciation of marriage, home, and property; some ascetics practised extreme forms of fasting and self-deprivation. In the popular mind there seems to have been an association between the abandonment of human comforts and the acquisition of miraculous powers. *Clement of Alexandria and *Origen appear to have been the first Fathers to study the theoretical foundations of asceticism. Taking over from the *Stoics the idea of ascetic action as a purification of the soul from its passions, they see in it a necessary means for loving God more perfectly and for attaining to contemplation. Origen also stresses its value as preparation for martyrdom. The Desert Fathers from the late 3rd cent. and the subsequent monastic tradition increasingly tended to favour a more temperate external asceticism and laid more stress on interior abnegation and the cultivation of the virtues. The monks came to be regarded as the leading representatives of asceticism and it is from them that the most influential ascetic treatises come, such as the 'Conferences' of *Cassian and of *Dorotheus.

With the growing devotion to the humanity of Christ, esp. to His Passion, in the Middle Ages asceticism underwent a certain modification in that it became increasingly inspired by the desire for conformation to the sufferings of the Redeemer. This desire, often coupled with a strongly penitential attitude and a rather pessimistic view of human life, led to the adoption of rather more violent forms of asceticism, such as flagellation and the wearing of hair shirts and chains. This devotional, penitential asceticism was popularized esp. by the *Mendicant orders, whose members produced many treatises on the ascetic life. Early in the 15th cent. the '*Imitation of Christ' developed a new doctrine of the inner life on the basis of an exacting asceticism.

At the close of the Middle Ages there appeared a twofold reaction against the late medieval ascetic ideal. On the one hand a variety of movements, some of them inspired by the humanism of the Renaissance, stressed the interior life and called into question the value of external ascetic practices; on the other hand the Protestant Reformers, with their insistence on *justification by faith, denied the propriety of many conventional works of penance, though they did allow a certain value to some works of self-discipline, such as fasting, provided these were not seen as in any way contributing to justification. Despite these challenges the ascetical ideal, upheld by the Council of *Trent, continued to find its champions in such austere saints as *Peter of Alcántara, *John of the Cross, and later in the *Curé d'Ars, as well as in new *congregations and reformed branches of old orders such as the *Passionists or the *Trappists. At the same time a more exclusively interior and hidden asceticism of complete renunciation of the will found expression in other modern Institutes, e.g. the *Jesuits and the *Visitation Nuns. Among the *Puritans asceticism, in the negative sense of abstinence from particular pleasures or recreations, was widely upheld and practised. In a more positive sense it also found an important place in *Methodism and esp. among the *Tractarian divines and their successors. It led to the wide revival of religious communities in England in the 19th cent. An exaggerated asceticism has been the mark of some sects, e.g. of the *Montanists, *Gnostics, and *Manichaeans of the patristic period, and of the medieval *Cathari and *Waldenses, where it was usually combined with dualistic tendencies in theology.

Acc. to its classical Christian exponents asceticism is a necessary means of fighting the concupiscence of the flesh, of the eyes, and the pride of life, mentioned in 1 Jn. 2: 16. It is also of great value as an imitation of the sacrificial life of Christ and as a means of expiation of one's own sins and those of others, in virtue of the doctrine of the Mystical Body. It springs from the love of God and aims at overcoming all the obstacles to this love in the soul. It is thus not an end in itself but essentially a preparation for the life of union with God, since, in its positive aspect, it seeks to foster the interior tendencies that serve to develop the life of charity.

M. J. Rouët de Journel, SJ, and J. Dutilleul, SJ (eds.), *Enchiridion Asceticum* (Freiburg i.B., 1930; mainly patristic); H. Koch, *Quellen zur Geschichte der Askese und des Mönchtums in der alten Kirche* (1933). O. Zöckler, *Kritische Geschichte der Askese* (1863; 2nd edn. as *Askese und Mönchtum*, 2 vols., 1897). H. Strathmann, *Geschichte der frühchristlichen Askese bis zur Entstehung des Mönchtums* (1914). M. Viller, SJ, and K. *Rahner, SJ, *Aszese und Mystik in der Väterzeit* (1939). P. Nagel, *Die Motivierung der Askese in der Alten Kirche und der Ursprung des Mönchtums* (TU 95; 1966). B. Lohse, *Askese und Mönchtum im der Antike und in den alten Kirche* (Religion und Kultur der alten Mittelmeerwelt in Parallelforschungen, 1; 1969). W. J. Sheils (ed.), *Monks, Hermits and the Ascetic Tradition* (Studies in Church History, 22; Oxford, 1985). S. Elm, '*Virgins of God': The Making of Asceticism in Late Antiquity* (Oxford Classical Monographs, 1994). V. L. Wimbush and R. Valantasis (eds.), *Asceticism* (New York and Oxford, 1995). A. Vööbus, *History of Asceticism in the Syrian Orient* (CSCO 184, 197, and 500; Subsidia, 14, 17, and 81; Louvain, 1958–88). M. Black, 'The Tradition of Hasidaean-Essene Asceticism: its origins and its influence', in *Aspects du Judéo-Christianisme: Colloque de Strasbourg 23–25 avril 1964* (Travaux du Centre d'Études supérieures spécialisé d'Histoire des Religions de Strasbourg, 1965), pp. 19–33; G. Quispel, 'L'Évangile selon Thomas et les origines de l'ascèse chrétienne', ibid., pp. 35–52. R. Murray, SJ, 'The Features of the Earliest Christian Asceticism', in P. Brooks (ed.), *Christian Spirituality: Essays in Honour of Gordon Rupp* (1975), pp. 66–77. L. Gougaud, OSB, *Dévotions et pratiques ascétiques du moyen âge* (Collection 'Pax', 21; 1925; Eng. tr., 1927). J. de Ghellinck, SJ, *Patristique et Moyen Age*, 3 (1948), pp. 185–244 (Étude 5: Un Programme de lectures spirituelles dans les écrits des pères). O. Zöckler in *HERE* 2 (1907), pp. 73–80, s.v. 'Asceticism (Christian)'; J. de Guibert, SJ, and others in *Dict. Sp.* 1 (1937), cols. 936–1010, s.v. 'Ascèse, Ascétisme'. See also works cited under SPIRITUALITY.

aseity (Lat. *aseitas*, from [*ens*] *a se*, 'being from itself'). The quality in virtue of which a being exists of and from itself alone. Acc. to Christian teaching, it is realized solely in God and distinguishes Him from all created beings, whose existence, as it issues ultimately from Him, is derivative from something outside itself (*ens ab alio*).

Ash Wednesday. The first day of *Lent, six and a half weeks before *Easter. Down to the 7th cent., Lent began with *Quadragesima Sunday, as it still does in the *Ambrosian Rite. The four extra days were added later to secure the exact number of 40 week-days for the fast. At one time public penitents at Rome were ceremonially admitted to begin their penance on this day; and when this discipline fell into disuse, between the 8th and 10th cents., the general penance of the whole congregation took its place. This was symbolized by the imposition of ashes, in token of mourning and penitence, upon the heads of clergy and people, a rite still ordered for Ash Wednesday in the Roman Missal. In the BCP of 1549 and in subsequent editions the *Commination Service is prescribed for this day. In the American Books of 1929 and 1979 Ash Wednesday is mentioned as a special fast-day (with *Good Friday), and in the Scottish Book of 1929 it is named (together with the six days before Easter) a 'Greater Fast'. In the RC Church Ash Wednesday and Good Friday are now the only days on which fasting is prescribed universally.

H. Thurston, SJ, *Lent and Holy Week* (1904), pp. 84–99. K. W. Stevenson, *Worship: Wonderful and Sacred Mystery* (Washington, DC [1992]), pp. 159–87 ('Origins and Development of Ash Wednesday'). F. *Cabrol, OSB, in *DACL* 2 (1910), cols. 3037–44, s.v. 'Cendres', with bibl.

Asherah. A Hebrew feminine proper name, used in the OT of a *Canaanite goddess (1 Kgs. 15: 13, 2 Kgs. 21: 7 [RV]) and of the sacred pole erected as her symbol (1 Kgs. 16: 33, 2 Kgs. 13: 6 [RV]). (The AV consistently renders the word 'grove'; cf. LXX ἄλσος, Vulg. *lucus*.) The poles were set up near the Canaanite altars, which in early times were often built under green trees. The Israelites adopted them, along with other appurtenances of the religion which they found in existence when they settled in Canaan, but their destruction was ordered in the Hebrew legislation (Deut. 7: 5, 12: 3).

J. Day, 'Asherah in the Hebrew Bible and Northwest Semitic Literature', *Journal of Biblical Literature*, 105 (1986), pp. 385–408. W. A. Maier, '*Ašerah: Extrabiblical Evidence* (Harvard Semitic Monographs, 37; Atlanta, 1986). S. M. Olyan, *Asherah and the Cult of Yahweh in Israel* (Society of Biblical Literature, Monograph Series, 34; Atlanta, 1988). T. S. Frymer in *Encyclopaedia Judaica*, 3 (Jerusalem, 1972), cols. 703–5, s.v., with bibl.

Aske, Robert (d. 1537), leader of the '*Pilgrimage of Grace' (q.v.). Descended from an old Yorkshire family, he became an attorney and Fellow of Gray's Inn. On 13 Oct. 1536 he put himself at the head of the 'Pilgrimage' when rebellion broke out in Yorkshire. After treating on equal terms with the royal leaders sent to suppress the rising and obtaining a safe-conduct to *Henry VIII, he returned northwards early in 1537 with a promise that the grievances would be redressed. A fresh outbreak provided a pretext for a change in the outwardly conciliatory attitude of the King, and by May 1537 Aske had been seized and found himself a prisoner in the Tower of London. He was charged and condemned at Westminster for high treason, taken back to the North, and in July 1537 hanged in chains at *York.

Aske's own account of his capture in Lincs, his examination, and other related documents preserved in the Public Record Office are ed. by M. Bateson in *EHR* 5 (1890), pp. 330–45 and 550–73. J. *Gairdner in *DNB* 2 (1885), pp. 189 f., s.v. See also bibl. to PILGRIMAGE OF GRACE.

Askew (or **Ayscough**), Anne (1521–46), Protestant martyr. Of Lincolnshire descent, she separated from Thomas Kyme, her husband, a religious conservative, and in 1545 was arrested on account of her Eucharistic beliefs. Both Bp. E. *Bonner and Bp. S. *Gardiner examined her in a vain effort to make her recant; in an equally fruitless attempt to obtain incriminating information on leading Protestants at Court, she was subsequently illegally tortured by two Privy Councillors, Sir Richard Rich and the Lord Chancellor, Thomas Lord Wriothesley, apparently in person. She was burnt at *Smithfield on 16 July 1546. For the facts, the chief authority is two tracts by J. *Bale.

The tracts are J. Bale, *The First Examination of the worthy Servant of God, Mistress Anne Askew* (Marburg, 1546); id., *The Latter Examination of Anne Askew* (ibid., 1547); cf. also *The Account of the Sufferings of Anne Askew ...* written by herself (London, 1849). Charles Wriothesley, *A Chronicle of England during the Reigns of the Tudors*, ed. by W. D. Hamilton, 1 (Camden Society, 2nd ser. 11; 1875), pp. 155, 167–9. J. *Foxe, *Acts and Monuments*, ed. G. Townsend, 5 (1846), pp. 537–50.

Asperges. In the W. Church the ceremony of sprinkling *holy water over the altar and people after the entrance rite at Mass on Sundays. During the ceremony a chant from Ps. 51, 'Asperges me, Domine, hyssopo' ('Cleanse me, Lord') etc., has traditionally been sung, except in *Eastertide, when it was replaced by '*Vidi aquam'. Since 1970 alternative anthems have been provided and other suitable chants may be used. The ceremony certainly goes back to the 9th cent., when it was referred to by *Hincmar of Reims in his 'Epistola synodica'; it may now be omitted. The sprinkler used for the purpose is known as the 'aspergillum', 'aspersorium', or 'goupillon'.

L. Eisenhofer, *Handbuch der katholischen Liturgik*, 1 (1932), pp. 476–80. C. Goeb, OSB, 'The Asperges', *Orate Fratres*, 2 (1927–8), pp. 338–42.

aspersion. The method of baptism whereby the candidate is merely sprinkled with the baptismal water. It is a variant of *affusion (in which the water is actually poured on the candidate), and is held to be permissible only in exceptional circumstances.

aspirant. One who aspires to a vocation to the *religious life.

Assemani (Syriac = 'Simon'). The family name of four famous *Maronite Orientalists of the 18th cent.

(1) **Joseph Simonius** (1687–1768). He was a native of Tripoli in Syria, who entered the Maronite College at Rome in 1703. After being ordained priest he obtained a post at the *Vatican Library and was sent to collect MSS in the E. by Clement XI in 1715, and again in 1735. In 1736 he attended the first National Maronite Council, where he used his influence to bring his countrymen into closer connection with Rome. Shortly afterwards he was nominated Abp. of Tyre and Prefect of the Vatican Library. His principal work, the *Bibliotheca Orientalis* (4 vols., 1719–28), is a collection of *Syriac documents, esp. on the history of the Churches of Syria, Chaldaea, and Egypt, by which Syriac literature was introduced into the W., and which, for great parts, has not been superseded. He also edited the works of St *Ephraem Syrus, *Opera Ephraemi* (6 vols., 1732–46), with Latin and Greek translations, and this is still the only complete edition. Among his other works are the unfinished *Kalendaria Ecclesiae Universae* (6 vols., 1755), designed as a collection of texts, inscriptions, etc., on all the saints of the world, *Italicae Historiae Scriptores* (4 vols., 1751–53), and the *Bibliotheca Juris Orientalis Canonici et Civilis* (5 vols., 1762–6).

(2) **Stephen Evodius** (1707–82), nephew of the former. He also studied at the Maronite College in Rome, was appointed missionary of the *Propaganda and travelled in Syria, Mesopotamia, and Egypt as well as in Europe, esp. in England. He assisted his uncle in cataloguing the MSS of the Vatican Library. At the suggestion of *Benedict XIV he edited *Bibliothecae Mediceae-Laurentianae et Palatinae Codicum MSS Orientalium Catalogus* (2 vols., 1742), *Acta Sanctorum Martyrum Orientalium et Occidentalium* (2 vols., 1748), and *Bibliothecae Apostolicae Vaticanae Codicum MSS Catalogus*.

(3) **Joseph Aloysius** (1710–82). His precise relationship to Joseph Simonius is not clear. He was professor of Syriac, later of Liturgy, at the Sapienza in Rome and edited *Codex Liturgicus Ecclesiae Universae* (13 vols., 1749–66), a valuable collection for the study of the E. liturgies; *Commentarius Criticus de Ecclesiis* (1766); and *Commentaria de Catholicis seu Patriarchis Chaldaeorum et Nestorianorum* (1775).

(4) **Simon** (1752–1821). He was a grand-nephew of Joseph Simonius. After studying at Rome, he went to Syria as a missionary. In 1785 he became professor of Oriental languages at the seminary of Padua, and in 1807 at Padua university. He published several works on Arabic subjects, among them an 'Essay on the Origin, Cult, Literature, and Customs of the Arabs before Mohammed' (1787) and the 'Catalogue of the Naniana Library' (2 vols., 1787–92), both in Italian, containing important MS extracts and essays on Arabic literature, coins, etc.

(1) J. Notain Daraunis (ed.), *Series Chronologica Patriarcharum Antiochiae per Josephum Simonium Assemanum ...* (1881), pp. 1–11. J. Debs, *Kitâb tarîkh Sûriya*, pt. 4, vol. 8 (Beirut, 1905), pp. 553–68. G. Levi Della Vida, *Ricerche sulla formazione del più antico fondo dei manoscritti orientali della Bibliotheca Vaticana* (ST 92; 1939), *passim*. P. Mahfoud, *Joseph Simon Assimani et la Célébration du Concile libanais maronite de 1736. Traduction française des mémoires d'un témoin avec introduction et notes* (Corona Lateranensis, 5; 1965). G. Levi Della Vida in *Dizionario Biographico degli Italiani*, 4 (1962), pp. 437–40, s.v.
(2) J. Debs, op. cit., pp. 568–70. G. Levi Della Vida, *Ricerche*, *passim*.
(3 and 4) J. Debs, op. cit., pp. 570 f.

L. Petit, AA, in *DACL* 1 (1907), cols. 2973–80, s.vv.; P. Stair in *EC* 1 (1949), cols. 159–61, s.vv., both with bibl.

Assemblies of God. The name taken by many autonomous but normally loosely-associated national groupings of individual *Pentecostal Churches virtually forming a denomination within the Pentecostal movement. It was first taken by the earliest national organization of white Pentecostal Churches in the USA formed from independent assemblies in 1914. The importance of the Assemblies of God in comparison with other Pentecostal Churches varies in different countries. Their structure is generally Presbyterian in character, combining the autonomy of the local assembly with district and national councils. They commonly insist on *glossolalia ('tongues') as initial evidence of '*baptism in the Holy Spirit'. Extensive missions, among Christians and non-Christians, have been undertaken, particularly by the American Assemblies of God.

See works cited in bibl. to PENTECOSTALISM.

Assemblies of the French Clergy (*Assemblées du Clergé de France*). The quinquennial meetings of deputies of the French clergy which were an established institution in France from the end of the 16th cent. to the French Revolution. They were composed of elected representatives (half bishops, half other beneficed clergy) from the 16 provinces. Their functions were primarily to apportion the heavy financial burden laid on the clergy by the king, but increasingly they came to discuss ecclesiastical matters. The 'extraordinary' Assembly of 1682 incurred the disapproval of *Innocent XI by approving and adopting, at the behest of Louis XIV, the *Gallican Articles. An elaborate and successful technique of procedure enabled the Assemblies to exercise considerable financial influence.

Collection des Procès-verbaux des Assemblées-générales du Clergé de France, depuis l'année 1560, jusqu'à présent (10 vols., 1767–80). L. Serbat, *Les Assemblées du Clergé de France: Origines, Organisation, Développement 1561–1615* (Bibliothèque de l'École des Hautes Études, 154; 1906). P. Blet, SJ, *Le Clergé de France et la Monarchie: Étude sur les Assemblées Générales du Clergé de 1615 à 1666* (Analecta Gregoriana, 106–7; 1959); id., *Les Assemblées du Clergé et Louis XIV de 1670 à 1693* (ibid., 189; 1972). N. Ravitch, *Sword and Mitre: Government and Episcopate in France and England in the Age of Aristocracy* (The Hague and Paris, 1966), pp. 154–94 *passim*; R. [E.] Mousnier, *Les Institutions de la France sous la Monarchie Absolue*, 1 (1974), pp. 282–99; Eng. tr. (Chicago and London, 1979), pp. 358–82. M. Peronnet, 'Naissance d'une institution: les assemblées du clergé', in A. Stegmann (ed.), *Pouvoir et institution en Europe au XVIème siècle: Vingt-septième Colloque International d'Études Humanistes, Tours* (De Pétrarque à Descartes, 51; 1987), pp. 249–61. M. Marion in *DHGE* 4 (1930), cols. 1103–14, s.v. 'Assemblées du Clergé'.

Assent, Declaration of. A formal declaration of assent to the *Thirty-Nine Articles, the Book of *Common Prayer, and the *Ordinal (described as 'the historic formularies' of the C of E) which is legally required of all bishops, clergy, deaconesses, readers, registrars, chancellors, and lay workers of the C of E as a condition of taking office. The current form of the Declaration is prescribed by canon C 15 (1975). It is worded as a declaration of 'belief in the faith which is revealed in the Holy Scriptures and set forth in the catholic creeds and to which the historic formularies of the C of E bear witness'. The 1969 canon (amended in 1975) replaces the form of 1865, which

was itself significantly looser than canon 36 of 1604 demanding 'that he acknowledgeth *all and every* the articles ... being in number nine and thirty'. The Declaration also contains an undertaking only to use authorized forms of service.

Asses, Feast of (Lat. *Festum asinorum*). A religious celebration formerly observed at *Christmas (or in some cases on 14 Jan.) in certain French towns (e.g. Rouen, Beauvais), at which the prophecy of Balaam's ass (Num. 22) or alternatively the Flight of the Holy Family into Egypt (Mt. 2: 13–15) was dramatically represented.

T. J. Crowley in *CE* 1 (1907), pp. 798 f., s.v., with refs.

Assisi. The city in the Umbrian Hills, famous as the birthplace of St *Francis. At one end of the town is the huge three-storeyed *basilica of San Francesco (1228–53, with the remains of the saint) and at the other, the much smaller one wherein is the body of St *Clare. A further basilica, Sta Maria degli Angeli, below in the plain, shelters the little chapel known as the *Portiuncula, where the Franciscan Order originated. Other famous shrines in the neighbourhood are 'San Damiano', the 11th-cent. chapel and the 13th-cent. convent in which St Clare lived, and the 'Eremo delle Carceri' in the rocks above the city.

Mrs R. [C.] Goff, *Assisi of St. Francis* (1908); A. Fortini, *Assisi nel Medio Evo: Leggende, Avventure, Battaglie* (1940); T. Desbonnets, OFM, *Assise: Sur les pas de saint François. Guide spirituel* [1971]; Società Internazionale di Studi Francescani, *Assisi al tempo di san Francesco: Atti del V Convegno Internazionale, Assisi 13–16 ottobre 1977* (Assisi, 1978); L. Temperini, TOR, *Assisi romana e medioevale: Profilo storico-archeologico* (1985).

Assizes of Jerusalem. The series of law-books which state the customary law of the Latin kingdom of Jerusalem and were compiled by various authors (notably John of Ibelin) at various dates from 1197 onwards. Their ultimate source was the feudal customs of W. Europe at the time of the First *Crusade; the *Livre au Roi* (compiled 1197–1205) best represents the customs of the 12th-cent. kingdom, in which the monarchy had been relatively strong, but the remaining texts describe the institutions of its 13th cent. successor, and reflect the interests of the nobility.

Standard edn. of the text pub. by le Comte Beugnot ('Recueil des historiens des croisades', 2 vols., Paris, 1841–3). F. Monnier, 'Godfrey de Bouillon et les assises de Jérusalem', *Séances et travaux de l'Académie des Sciences Morales et Politiques*, 100 (1873), pp. 73–105, 663–94, and 101, NS 1 (1874), pp. 444–93; M. Grandclaude, *Étude critique sur les livres des assises de Jérusalem* (1923). M. Greilsammer, 'Structure and Aims of the *Livre au Roi*', in B. Z. Kedar and others (eds.), *Outremer: Studies in the History of the Crusading Kingdom of Jerusalem, presented to Joshua Prawer* (Jerusalem, 1982), pp. 218–26.

Associations, Law of. The law promulgated by the French government on 1 July 1901 which enlarged trade-union rights but also required religious congregations which should have requested authorization under a decree of 1804, but had not done so, to regularize their position. (The term 'congrégations' was used by French civil lawyers to cover monastic orders as well as *congregations as defined in canon law.) A parliamentary commission insisted that the right to authorize congregations be given to the Chamber of Deputies and the Senate, instead of to the Council of State, as the government proposed. The Radical government which came to power after the elections of 1902 applied the law with particular severity. Congregations which had not requested authorization were closed forthwith. Male congregations which had requested authorization were grouped by the government into three categories of teaching, preaching, and commercial (only the *Cistercians), and three bills rejecting their requests were passed by the Assembly in March 1903. A bill rejecting the request of female congregations, except those engaged in charitable work, was passed in June 1903. A law of 7 July 1904 banned all congregations from teaching, including those which had been authorized, exempting only their overseas missions.

Text of law in *Journal officiel* for 2 July 1901, pp. 4025–7; of bills rejecting authorization in *Journal officiel, Débats parlementaires, Chambre*, of 13 Mar. 1903, p. 1117; 25 Mar. 1903, p. 1281; 27 Mar. 1903, p. 1337; 6 June 1903, p. 1849; of law of 7 July 1904 in *Journal officiel*, 8 July 1904, pp. 4129–30. Texts of the laws of 1 July 1901 and 7 July 1904 also in A. Debidour, *L'Église catholique et l'État sous la troisième République (1870–1906)*, 2 (1909), pp. 540–7. M. O. Partin, *Waldeck-Rousseau, Combes, and the Church: The politics of anti-clericalism, 1899–1905* (Durham, NC, 1969).

Assumption of the BVM. The belief that the BVM, having completed her earthly life, was in body and soul assumed into heavenly glory ('Immaculatam Deiparam semper Virginem Mariam, expleto terrestris vitae cursu, fuisse corpore et anima ad caelestem gloriam assumptam'; definition *Munificentissimus Deus* of 1950).

It is now generally agreed that the belief was unknown in the earliest ages of the Church. St *Ambrose (*Exposit. Evan. sec. Luc.* 2. 35; *PL* 15. 1574) and St *Epiphanius (*Haer.* 79. 11; *PG* 42. 716) were apparently still ignorant of it. It is first met with in certain NT apocrypha dating from the later 4th cent. onwards, some of them *Gnostic in sympathy. These texts, which bear such titles as 'The Passing Away of Mary' and 'The Obsequies of Mary', survive in Greek, Latin, Syriac, Coptic, Arabic, and Ethiopic and are assigned in the MSS to various authors, e.g. to St *John the Evangelist and St *Melito of Sardis. They record the death of the BVM at *Jerusalem amid varying miraculous circumstances, in some cases alleging that her body was assumed on the way to the burial, in others that it was raised after three days. The date of the Virgin's death is variously assigned, e.g. to three or fifty years after the *Ascension. It appears that one such work was condemned in the *Decretum Gelasianum*, though the condemnation may have been directed against its Gnostic teachings rather than specifically against its doctrine of the corporal assumption. A homily attributed in most MSS to Timothy of Jerusalem (prob. 4th–5th cent.) may imply the alternative belief that the BVM was assumed in body and soul during her natural life.

The doctrine of the corporal assumption was first formulated in orthodox circles in the W. by St *Gregory of Tours (d. 594), who accepted as historical the account attributed in MSS to Melito. In the E. a passage in *Dionysius the Ps.-Areopagite's *Concerning the Divine Names* (5th–6th cent.) was taken by *Andrew of Crete (d. 740) to mean that *Dionysius (the presumed disciple of St *Paul) had witnessed the assumption, while the writings of St *Germanus of Constantinople and other 7th-cent. authors testify to the acceptance of the doctrine by this period. In the next cent. St *John Damascene related that at the Council of *Chalcedon, *Juvenal, Bp. of Jerusalem, had told the Emp. Marcian and his wife *Pulcheria, who wished to possess the body of the BVM, that her death had been witnessed by all the Apostles, but that when her tomb was later opened, it was found empty. This account, which claimed the authority of Dionysius, presented the doctrine as ancient Catholic tradition; it was of particular influence in the W. because of its inclusion from the 16th cent. in the Roman Breviary among the lessons for the feast of the Octave of the Assumption.

Feasts celebrating the death of the BVM were observed in Palestine during the 5th cent., possibly at *Antioch in the 4th cent. The Greek Church was, however, divided as to the date between 18 Jan. (associating it with the *Epiphany) and 15 Aug. (prob. connecting it with the dedication of some church in her honour), until the Emp. Maurice (582–603) ordered that the latter date should be observed. In Rome, unless the Mass for the BVM given under 15 Aug. in the *Gelasian Sacramentary (which does not mention any corporal assumption) be original, it appears that one general feast in honour of Our Lady was observed until the last years of the 7th cent., that is, on 1 Jan. The Byzantine feasts of the BVM, incl. that of the Assumption, seem to have been introduced in the time of Pope *Sergius I (687–701). From Rome they spread to the countries of the Gallican rite, where a feast of Our Lady had previously been kept on 18 Jan. (the other E. date); and by the end of the 8th cent. the feast of the Assumption was universally observed in the W. on 15 Aug. In 847 Pope *Leo IV ordered that the octave be kept and in 863 *Nicholas I made the feast equal to those of *Easter, *Christmas, and *Whitsunday. In the C of E the feast disappeared from the BCP in 1549, and has not been officially restored. It has been retained, however, in the Oxford University Calendar, and is now observed in many places. In a number of Provinces of the Anglican Communion 15 August is kept as the principal feast of the BVM, though without reference to the Assumption.

The doctrine was prob. first upheld on grounds of deductive theology in an 8th- or 9th-cent. letter attributed to St *Augustine (*PL* 40. 1141–8) and was later defended by St *Albertus Magnus, St *Thomas Aquinas, and St *Bonaventure. *Benedict XIV declared it a probable opinion. In answer to repeated demands to the Popes from 1870 onwards, on 1 Nov. 1950 Pope *Pius XII in *Munificentissimus Deus* defined the doctrine and provided a new Mass for the Feast. The Mass was further changed in 1969. In the E. Church belief in the corporal assumption of the BVM is general, though prob. in terms less precise than those of the Roman definition. It is there known as the *Koimesis* (lit. 'falling asleep').

O. Faller, SJ, *De Priorum Saeculorum Silentio circa Assumptionem B. Mariae Virginis* (Analecta Gregoriana, 36, Sectio A, n. 5; 1946). J. K. Elliott, *The Apocryphal New Testament* (Oxford, 1993), pp. 691–723, incl. Eng. tr. of main texts with refs. to original edns. F. Cavallera, 'A propos d'une enquête patristique sur l'Assomption', *Bulletin de Littérature Ecclésiastique*, 27 (1926), pp. 97–116. Sermons by *Jacob of Sarug and James, Bp. of Birta, ed. A. *Baumstark, 'Zwei syrische Dichtungen auf das

Entschlafen der allerseligsten Jungfrau', *Oriens Christianus*, 5 (1905), pp. 82–125. B. *Capelle, OSB, 'La Fête de l'Assomption dans l'histoire liturgique', *Ephemerides Theologicae Lovanienses*, 3 (1926), pp. 33–45; id., 'La Fête de la Vierge à Jérusalem au Ve siècle', *Le Muséon*, 56 (1943), pp. 1–33; id., 'La Messe gallicane de l'Assomption, son rayonnement, ses sources', in *Miscellanea Liturgica in Honorem L. Cunibert Mohlberg*, 1 (1948), pp. 33–59; V. Grumel, 'Le Mois de Marie des Byzantins', *ÉO* 35 (1932), pp. 257–69; A. Raes, SJ, 'Λux origines de la fête de l'Assomption', *OCP* 12 (1946), pp. 262–74. *LP* (Duchesne), 1 (1886), p. 376. A. Wenger, AA, *L'Assomption de la T. S. Vierge dans la tradition byzantine du VIe au Xe siècle: Études et documents* (Archives de l'Orient Chrétien, 6; 1955), with extensive refs. C. Piana, OFM, *Assumptio Beatae Virginis Mariae apud Scriptores saec. XIII* (1942). M. Jugie, AA, *La Mort et l'assomption de la Sainte Vierge: Étude historico-doctrinale* (ST 114; 1944), with refs. G. Hentrich and R. G. de Moos (eds.), *Petitiones de Assumptione Corporea B.V. Mariae in Caelum Definienda ad Sanctam Sedem Delatae* (2 vols., Rome, 1942). V. Bennett and R. Winch, *The Assumption of Our Lady and Catholic Theology* (1950). F. *Heiler (ed.), *Das neue Mariendogma im Lichte der Geschichte und im Urteil der Oekumene* (Oekumenische Einheit, 1951, Heft 2; Munich, 1951). H. S. Box in E. L. Mascall and H. S. Box (eds.), *The Blessed Virgin Mary* (1963), pp. 89–102. S. C. Mimouni, *Dormition et Assomption de Marie: Histoire des Traditions Anciennes* (Théologie Historique, 98 [1995]. H. F. Davis in *Catholic Dictionary of Theology*, 1 (1962), pp. 170–9, s.v. See also bibl. to MUNIFICENTISSIMUS DEUS.

Assumption of Moses, The. See MOSES, THE ASSUMPTION OF.

Assumptionists (Augustinians of the Assumption). A religious congregation, founded at Nîmes in 1845 for the active religious life, and approved in 1864 by *Pius IX. Its members follow a modification of the *Augustinian rule. They have spread to many parts of the world, esp. since 1900, when their congregations in France were dispersed by State decree. Their work includes the care of asylums and schools, the dissemination of literature, and missionary work in many parts of the world. Several ancillary orders and confraternities have been formed to support their work. Their house at *Constantinople has esp. fostered the study of the theology and institutions of the E. Church, notably through its review, *Échos d'Orient* (1897 ff.), and a group of notable scholars (L. Petit, E. Bouvy, F. Cayré, M. Jugie, S. Salaville, and R. Janin).

J. Monval, *Les Assomptionnistes* (1939). Heimbucher, 2, pp. 384–6. M. Lombard in *DHGE* 1 (1930), cols. 1136–42, s.v.; R. Touveneraud, AA, in *DIP* 1 (1974), cols. 381–7, s.v. 'Agostiniani dell'Assunzione'.

Assyrian Christians. A name adopted in modern times by members of the *Church of the East (q.v.) who, in their search for an ethnic identity, claim descent from the ancient Assyrians. The Patriarch is now officially styled 'Catholicos Patriarch of the Assyrian Church of the East'. In the 19th cent. A. H. Layard, the excavator of Nineveh, first suggested that the local *Syriac Christian communities in the region were descended from the ancient Assyrians, and the idea was later popularized by W. A. Wigram, a member of the Abp. of *Canterbury's Mission to the Church of the East (1885–1915). More recently, as a result of large-scale emigration of Christians from the Middle East to the USA, Europe, and elsewhere, the term 'Assyrian' has also sometimes been adopted by members

of the *Syrian Orthodox Church abroad, thus often becoming a source of friction and confusion.

W. A. Wigram, *The Assyrians and their Neighbours* (1929); J.-M. Fiey, OP, ' "Assyriens" ou Araméens?', *L'Orient Syrien*, 10 (1965), pp. 141–60; J. Joseph, *The Nestorians and their Muslim Neighbours* (Princeton Oriental Studies, 20; 1961), pp. 11–18. G. Yonan, *Assyrer heute* (Reihe Pogrom, 59; Hamburg, 1978). See also works cited under CHURCH OF THE EAST.

asteriscus (Gk. ἀστερίσκος, from ἀστήρ, 'a star'). In the Byzantine rites, a utensil consisting of two metal strips crossed and bent and placed over the bread during the Liturgy to keep it from contact with the veil that covers it. It is removed at the *Sanctus.

Asterius (d. after 341), the 'Sophist', *Arian theologian. He was a pupil of *Lucian of Antioch and was present at the Council of *Antioch of 341. Fragments are preserved by St *Athanasius (from Asterius' 'Syntagmation') and by *Marcellus of Ancyra. Homilies on the Pss. ascribed to him have been recovered in modern times and edited by M. Richard and E. Skard, though some scholars think that these are the work of a different Asterius. If genuine, they throw important light on the early interests and methods of the Arian school.

His writings are listed by St *Jerome, *De Vir. Ill.* 94. Fragments ed., with Germ. tr. and comm., by M. Vinzent (Supplements to *VC*, 20; 1993). *Asterii Sophistae commentariorum in Psalmos quae supersunt: Accedunt aliquot homiliae anonymae*, ed. M. Richard (Symbolae Osloenses. Fasc. Supplet. 16; 1956; Index by E. Skard, ibid. 17; 1962). G. Bardy, 'Astérius le Sophiste', *RHE* 22 (1926), pp. 221–72; id., *Recherches sur S. Lucien d'Antioche et son école* (1936), pp. 316–57; E. Skard, 'Asterios von Amaseia und Asterios der Sophist', *Symbolae Osloenses*, 20 (1940), pp. 86–132; cf. ibid. 25 (1947), pp. 80–82, and ibid. 27 (1949), pp. 54–69. H. auf der Maur, *Die Osterhomilien des Asterios Sophistes als Quelle für die Geschichte der Osterfeier* (Trierer Theologische Studien, 19; Trier, 1967), with bibl. M. F. Wiles and R. C. Gregg, 'Asterius: A New Chapter in the History of Arianism?', in R. C. Gregg (ed.), *Arianism: Historical and Theological Reassessments* (Patristic Monograph Series, 11; Philadelphia, 1985), pp. 111–51. W. Kinzig, *In Search of Asterius* (Forschungen zur Kirchen- und Dogmengeschichte, 47; Göttingen, 1990; argues that the homilies are by an Asterius who lived in the late 4th or early 5th cent.). W. Speyer in *RAC*, Suppl.-Lief. 4 (1986), cols. 626–39, s.v.

astrology. The study of the supposed influence of the stars upon human fortunes. In modern usage the term is confined to 'judicial astrology', i.e. the 'science' which professes to forecast the fortunes of a man, e.g. from the positions of the stars at the moment of his birth. Astrology was much practised in the ancient world, but the influence of Christian teaching, as illustrated in St *Augustine, *De Civ. Dei*, 5. 1–8, suppressed it in the Empire, until in the 13th cent. it re-entered the W. through Jewish and Arabic scholars, who for centuries had studied it in the E. The 16th cent. was the period when its influence was most powerful in Europe, among Catholics and Protestants alike. The scepticism of the 18th cent., with the growth of scientific knowledge, greatly reduced its popularity; and in England its credit was much shaken by a satirical pamphlet by J. *Swift, called *Prediction for the Year 1708*. In the 20th century the growth of unbelief and superstition has encouraged the revival of astrology in certain quarters.

Astruc, Jean (1684–1766), physician and Pentateuchal critic. The son of a Protestant pastor, he was converted at an early age to Catholicism. In 1730 he became physician to Louis XV and in the following year professor at the Collège de France. From 1743 he was attached to the Faculty of Medicine at Paris. In 1753 he published anonymously his celebrated work *Conjectures sur les Mémoires originaux dont il paroît que Moyse s'est servi pour composer le Livre de la Genèse*, in which he maintained that in its present form the Book of Genesis was a piecing together of earlier documents. He based this view on the varying use of '*Elohim' and '*Yahweh' for the Divine name, and on the duplication of narratives. He did not dispute that it was *Moses who brought the documents together. Astruc also wrote a *Dissertation sur l'immortalité et sur l'immatérialité de l'âme* (1755).

A. Lods, *Jean Astruc et la critique biblique au XVIIIᵉ siècle* (1924). J. de Savignac, 'L'Œuvre et la personnalité de Jean Astruc', *Nouvelle Clio*, 5 (1953), pp. 138–47. E. Böhmer in *PRE* (3rd edn.), 2 (1897), pp. 162–70, s.v. Astruc's many medical publications do not call for mention here.

asylum, right of. See SANCTUARY.

Athanasian Creed. A profession of faith widely used in W. Christendom, and also known from its opening words as the 'Quicunque Vult'. It differs from the *Apostles' and *Nicene Creeds in form, as well as in embodying *anathemas, and is not a recognized standard of faith in the E., though it has appeared (without the *Filioque clause) in the Greek *Horologion since *c.*1780 and in Russian service books from the 17th cent. Of the Protestant bodies, some (notably the *Lutherans) retain it as a statement of faith; the old *Breviary ordered its recitation at *Prime on most Sundays; and in the Anglican BCP (where it is printed immediately before the Litany) it replaces the Apostles' Creed at Morning Prayer on thirteen holy days, chosen apparently as being at roughly equal intervals apart.

The attribution to St *Athanasius has been generally abandoned since the researches of G. J. *Voss (1642), chiefly on the ground that the Creed contains doctrinal expressions which arose only in later controversies. Not only is there no early authority for ascribing it to him, but it was evidently composed in Latin, not in Greek, and till modern times it has circulated solely in the W. Most recent scholars incline to the view that it originated in S. Gaul, prob. in the region of *Lérins, although earlier this century the thesis of H. Brewer, SJ, that it was the work of St *Ambrose, enjoyed considerable vogue. A Gallic origin is confirmed by the fact that the creed first appears in a sermon of St *Caesarius of Arles and by the remarkable correspondences between it and the *Excerpta* of St *Vincent of Lérins. The date of the Creed is equally disputed. It used to be held that the terminology employed pointed to a time when the controversy over *Apollinarianism was acute and before the outbreak of the *Nestorian and *Eutychian heresies; a date between 381 and 428 was generally accepted. More recently J. N. D. Kelly has argued that the Christological heresy attacked was not Apollinarianism but Nestorianism, and that therefore the Creed was composed after 428.

Its subject-matter falls into two halves, which expound respectively the doctrines of the Trinity and of the Incarnation. To the latter is added a list of the important events of the Lord's redeeming work in a form resembling that of the Apostles' Creed. The creed is prefaced and concluded with the assertion that belief in the truths it asserts is necessary to salvation.

Since 1867 many efforts have been made in the C of E to have it removed from the service, or truncated, especial objection being made to the 'damnatory clauses' (vv. 2 and 42), but conservative opinion has generally held that, even if it may be considered desirable in the abstract that certain expressions should be explained or retranslated, any alteration would give the impression that something of the traditional faith was being surrendered. The BCP version, however, is in places inaccurate and misleading, partly because of mistranslation, and partly because the Reformers based their rendering on an inaccurate text. In the Anglican Churches outside England its use in worship has for some time been considerably restricted or abandoned, and even in England it is now rarely used. It does not occur in the ASB.

A. E. Burn, *The Athanasian Creed and its Early Commentaries* (Texts and Studies, 4, no. 1; Cambridge, 1896). G. D. W. Ommanney, *A Critical Dissertation on the Athanasian Creed* (1897). The standard work now is J. N. D. Kelly, *The Athanasian Creed* (The Paddock Lectures for 1962–3; 1964). H. Brewer, SJ, *Das sogenannte Athanasianische Glaubensbekenntnis ein Werk des hl. Ambrosius* (1909). G. *Morin, OSB, 'A propos du Quicumque. Extraits d'homélies de S. Césaire d'Arles sous le nom de S. Athanase', *R. Bén.* 28 (1911), pp. 417–24. J. Stiglmayr, SJ, 'Das Quicunque und Fulgentius von Ruspe', *ZKT* 49 (1925), pp. 341–57 [Ath. Creed, work of Fulgentius]. A. E. Burn, 'The Authorship of the *Quicumque Vult*', *JTS* 27 (1925–6), pp. 19–28. G. Morin, OSB, 'L'Origine du symbole d'Athanase: témoignage inédit de S. Césaire d'Arles', *R. Bén.* 44 (1932), pp. 207–19. N. M. Haring, SAC, 'Commentaries on the Pseudo-Athanasian Creed', *Mediaeval Studies*, 34 (1972), pp. 208–52. F. *Loofs in *PRE* (3rd edn.), 2 (1897), pp. 177–94.

Athanasius, St (*c.*296–373), Bp. of *Alexandria. He seems to have been born and brought up in Alexandria. He received a good classical education before becoming deacon and secretary to the bishop of the diocese, *Alexander, whom he attended at the Council of *Nicaea (325) and succeeded in 328. By his refusal to compromise with *Arianism he incurred the enmity of the powerful Arianizing party in the reigns of *Constantine and Constantius. His use of violence and intimidation also contributed to the strength of the opposition to him and was the specific ground for his deposition at the Council of Tyre in 335 and his exile to Trier in 336; he returned on the death of Constantine in 337; but in 339 he was forced to flee to *Rome, where he established close contacts with the W. Church, which continued throughout his life to support him. He was restored in 346 by the influence of Constans, the W. Emperor, against the will of Constantius, who in 356 again drove him from the see. He remained in hiding near Alexandria till the accession of *Julian (361). He returned to the city in Feb. 362, but Julian exiled him again later in the year. On Julian's death (363) he was able to come back in 364, and, after yet another brief exile (365–6), helped for the rest of his life to build up the new Nicene party by whose support orthodoxy triumphed over Arianism at the Council of *Constantinople in 381. He died at Alexandria on 2–3 May 373.

His most famous work is the *De Incarnatione*, the second of two closely linked treatises. In it he expounds how God the Word (*Logos), by His union with manhood, restored to fallen man the image of God in which he had been created (Gen. 1: 27), and by His death and resurrection met and overcame death, the consequence of sin. Many scholars date the work before *c*.318, when Athanasius was still in his twenties, but others place it 15–20 years later. As bishop he was the greatest and most consistent theological opponent of Arianism. From 339 to 359 he wrote a series of works in defence of the faith proclaimed at Nicaea—that is, the true deity of God the Son. From about 361 onwards he especially sought the reconciliation of the large *Semiarian party to the Nicene term *homoousios ('of one substance'), which they were reluctant to accept. The Council of Alexandria (362), under his direction, greatly furthered this end, by clearing up misunderstandings of the terms ὑπόστασις (translated 'person') and οὐσία ('substance'). He also argued for the deity of the Holy Spirit in his *Epistles to Serapion*. As the friend of the monks *Serapion and *Pachomius, and closely linked with (perhaps the biographer of) *Antony, he aided the ascetic movement in Egypt and he was the first to introduce knowledge of monasticism to the W. His resolute character as well as his theology was the outstanding obstacle of the triumph of Arianism in the E. Feast day, 2 May. See also MELITIAN SCHISM (1).

Ed. princeps of Gk. text 'ex officina Commeliniana', 2 vols., Heidelberg, 1600–1. All earlier edns. superseded by the Maurist text, ed. B. *Montfaucon, 3 vols., Paris, 1698; repr., with additions, by N. A. Giustiniani, Bp. of Padua, 4 vols., Padua, 1777; with further additions in J. P. Migne, *PG* 25–28. Crit. text ed. H. G. Opitz, W. Schneemelcher, and M. Tetz for the Berlin Academy, in progress, Berlin, 1934 ff. Sep. edns. of *De Incarnatione* by A. *Robertson (London, 1882; 2nd edn., 1893), F. L. Cross (ibid., 1939), R. W. Thomson (with *Contra Gentes*, Oxford Early Christian Texts, 1971; incl. Eng. tr.), and C. Kannengiesser (SC 199, 1973; with Fr. tr.); *Contra Gentes* also ed. P. T. Camelot, OP (SC 18 bis, 1977); of *Orations against Arians* by W. *Bright (Oxford, 1873) and *Historical Writings* by id. (ibid., 1881); of the *Apologies* by J. M. Szymusiak, SJ (SC 56, 1958; with Fr. tr.; 2nd edn., 1987); and of Five Homilies, *Expositio fidei* and *Sermo Maior* by H. Nordberg (Societas Scientiarum Fennica. Commentationes Humanarum Litterarum, 30/2; Helsinki, 1962). New text of Comm. on Pss. ed. G. M. Vian (Studia Ephemerides 'Augustinianum', 14; Rome 1978). Syriac text of *Festal Epp.* ed. W. *Cureton (London, 1848); Coptic text ed. L. T. Lefort (CSCO 150, with Lat. tr. 151; 1955). Syriac texts of other works, with Eng. tr., ed. as *Athanasiana Syriaca* by R. W. Thomson (ibid. 257–8, 272–3, 324–5, and 386–7; 1965–77). On the text H. G. Opitz, *Untersuchungen zur Überlieferung der Schriften des Athanasius* (1935; indispensable); M. Tetz, 'Zur Edition der dogmatischen Schriften des Athanasius von Alexandrien', *ZKG* 67 (1955–6), pp. 1–28. *CPG* 2 (1974), pp. 12–60 (nos. 2090–309). Eng. trs. of 'Select Treatises [against] the Arians' by J. H. *Newman (LF, 2 vols., 1842–4; 2nd edn., much rev., 1881); A. Robertson in NPNCF (1892). Fr. tr. of *Epp. to Serapion*, with introd. and notes, by J. Lebon (SC 15, 1947); Eng. tr. by C. R. B. Shapland (London, 1951).

There is no contemporary Life. Important is the 'Vita Acephala' pub. 1738 by F. S. *Maffei (q.v.); modern edn., with Fr. tr. and full introd., by A. Martin (SC 317, 1985). Fundamental is series of papers by E. *Schwartz in *Nachr.* (Gött.) ('Zur Geschichte des Athanasius', various dates, 1904–11); collected and repr. in his *Gesammelte Schriften*, 3 (1959). H. M. Gwatkin, *Studies of Arianism* (1882; 2nd edn., 1900), *passim*. F. L. Cross, *The Study of St Athanasius* (1945; lecture). M. Richard, 'Saint Athanase et

la psychologie du Christ selon les Ariens', *Mélanges de Science Religieuse*, 4 (1947), pp. 5–54. E. P. Meijering, *Orthodoxy and Platonism in Athanasius: Synthesis or Antithesis?* (Leiden, 1968). J. Roldanus, *Le Christ et l'Homme dans la Théologie d'Athanase d'Alexandrie* (Studies in the History of Christian Thought, 4; ibid., 1968). P. Merendino, OSB, *Paschale Sacramentum: Eine Untersuchung über die Osterkatechese des hl. Athanasius von Alexandrien in ihrer Beziehung zu den frühchristlichen exegetisch-theologischen Überlieferungen* (Liturgiewissenschaftliche Quellen und Forschungen, 42; 1965). C. Kannengiesser, SJ (ed.), *Politique et théologie chez Athanase d'Alexandrie: Actes du Colloque de Chantilly 23–25 septembre 1973* (Théologie historique, 27 [1974]); id., *Athanase d'Alexandrie, évêque et écrivain: Une lecture des traités Contre les Ariens* (ibid. 70 [1983]). K. M. Girardet, *Kaisergericht und Bischofsgericht: Studien zu den Anfängen des Donatistenstreites (313–315) und zum Prozess des Athanasius von Alexandrien (328–346)* (Antiquitas, 1. Abhandlungen zur alten Geschichte, 21; 1975), esp. pp. 43–162. T. D. Barnes, *Athanasius and Constantius* (Cambridge, Mass., and London, 1993). G. Mueller, *Lexicon Athanasianum* (Berlin, 1952). F. M. Young, *From Nicaea to Chalcedon: A Guide to the Literature and its Background* (1983), pp. 65–83, with bibl. pp. 339–41 and 362–7. Altaner and Stuiber (1978), pp. 271–9 and 603 f. G. C. Stead in *DPAC* 1 (1983), cols. 423–32, s.v. 'Atanasio'; Eng. tr., *Encyclopedia of the Early Church*, 1 (1992), pp. 93–5, s.v. with further bibl. For material on his Life of St Antony, see s.v. ANTONY, ST.

Athanasius (the Athonite), St (*c*.920–1003). A native of Trebizond, he became a monk in Bithynia, but migrated thence to Mount *Athos, where he established (961) the first of its famous monasteries (the *Lavra). His foundation, though resisted by the eremites already settled on Athos, prospered through the support of the Emperors Nicephorus Phocas and John Tzimisces (969–76). He became Abbot-General (πρῶτος) of all the communities on the Mount, of which 58, including Iveron, Vatopedi, and Esphigmenou, were in being by his death. Feast day, 5 July. (He is not to be confused with the Athanasius mentioned in the Roman Martyrology for this date, a 5th cent. deacon of *Jerusalem.)

His Typicon and Testament are pr. in P. Meyer, *Die Haupturkunden für die Geschichte der Athosklöster* (1894), pp. 102–22 and 123–30 respectively. Early Gk. Life by a monk named Athanasius, ed. J. Pomialovsky (St Petersburg, 1895); further Gk. life, based on an earlier text, ed. L. Petit, AA, *Anal. Boll.* 25 (1906), pp. 5–89, with Fr. tr. by Hiéromoine Pierre in *Irénikon*, 8 (1931), pp. 457–99, 667–89; 9 (1932), pp. 71–95 and 240–64; also pub. separately, Chevetogne, 1963. Both lives ed. J. Noret (CCSG 9; 1982), with introd. and bibl. Id., 'La Vie la plus ancienne de saint Athanase l'Athonite confrontée aux écrits laissés par le saint', *Anal. Boll.* 100 (1982), pp. 545–66. J. Leroy, OSB, 'S. Athanase l'Athonite et la Règle de S. Benoît', *Revue d'Ascétique et de Mystique*, 29 (1953), pp. 108–22. See also bibl. to ATHOS, MT.

atheism (from Gk. ἄθεος, 'without God'). The word was originally used in Greece of all those who, whether they believed in God or not, disbelieved in the official gods of the State. Of such men Socrates was the classic instance. In the Roman Empire the term was applied in a similar sense by the pagans to Christians, but sometimes Christians, like St *Polycarp, would turn the term against their persecutors.

Until the expression '*agnosticism' came into general use in the 19th cent., the term 'atheist' was used, at least popularly, to describe also those who thought of the existence of God as an unprovable thesis. Of such there are three chief divisions: philosophical agnostics, materialists, and *pantheists. Any of these may be atheists in the strict sense of the word, but none need be. The philosophical agnostic normally says that the evidence is not sufficient to compel us either to assert or to deny the existence of God; but it is only if he adds further that the assertion of God's existence is meaningless, and not merely rash, that he is strictly to be called an atheist. The materialist, similarly, is strictly to be called an atheist only if he asserts that nothing can exist outside a closed system of matter; but often he will not say more than that for practical purposes it is necessary to treat the material world as a closed system. The pantheist view, also, has taken many forms; but it does not become truly atheistic until it makes its immanent divinity into such a limited being that he is no longer recognizable as God in any ordinary sense of the word.

Modern atheism is usually seen by its adherents as a way of safeguarding an affirmation of human freedom and creativity, and man's ability to control his own destiny; the dialectical materialism of Marxism is a case in point, but the same concerns can be detected in secular *existentialism which is usually atheistic and in the philosophy of M. *Heidegger. Under the influence of the Marxist philosopher E. Bloch, 'atheism' is sometimes paradoxically regarded by modern Christian theologians (e.g. J. *Moltmann) as a legitimate element of Christian theology; it is seen as a means of avoiding the danger of positing God as one entity among others, an infinite Being encroaching on finite beings (a concept termed 'ontotheology' by Heidegger).

F. A. Lange, *Geschichte des Materialismus und Kritik seiner Bedeutung in der Gegenwart* (1866; Eng. tr., 3 vols., 1877–81). A. B. Drachmann, *Atheism in Pagan Antiquity* (1922). H. de *Lubac, SJ, *Le Drame de l'Humanisme athée* (1945; Eng. tr., 1949). C. Fabro, *Introduzione all'ateismo moderno* (1964; Eng. tr., *God in Exile*, Westminster, Md., 1968). E. Bloch, *Atheismus im Christentum: Zur Religion des Exodus und des Reiches* (Frankfurt am Main, 1968). J. Moltmann, *Der gekreuzigte Gott* (1972; 2nd edn., 1973), pp. 205–14; Eng. tr., *The Crucified God* (1974), pp. 219–27. P. Masterson, *Atheism and Alienation: A Study of the Philosophical Sources of Contemporary Atheism* (Dublin, 1971; Harmondsworth, 1973). M. J. Buckley, SJ, *At the Origins of Modern Atheism* (New Haven, Conn., and London [1987]).

On the pagan attacks on the early Christians as 'atheists', see A. *Harnack, *Der Vorwurf des Atheismus in den drei ersten Jahrhunderten* (TU 13/1; 1905). For a modern philosophical defence of atheism, see J. L. Mackie, *The Miracle of Theism: Arguments for and against the Existence of God* (Oxford, 1982). C. B. Upton in *HERE* 2 (1909), pp. 173–83; J. Murray, SJ, in *Catholic Dictionary of Theology*, 1 (1962), pp. 182–9, s.v., with bibl.

Athelstan (c.894–939), King of England from 927. The eldest son of King Edward the Elder, he was recognized as king of the Mercians on his father's death in 924, and soon afterwards came to be recognized as king of the West Saxons as well; he extended his rule over the Northumbrians in 927, and thereby became the first king of all England. Renowned as a collector of *relics, and as a generous benefactor of the Church, he was also reputed to be a man of justice and learning. During his reign many contacts were established with rulers and ecclesiastics on the Continent; and both St *Dunstan and St *Ethelwold began their careers at his court. In many respects the ori-

gins of the 10th-cent. monastic reform movement in England can be traced back to this period.

An important source of information is *William of Malmesbury, *De gestis regum Anglorum*, ed. W. *Stubbs, 1 (RS; 1887), pp. 141–52; on William's account see M. Lapidge, 'Some Latin Poems as Evidence for the Reign of Athelstan', *Anglo-Saxon England*, 9 (1981), pp. 61–98. J. A. *Robinson, *The Times of Saint Dunstan* (Ford Lectures, 1922; Oxford, 1923), pp. 25–80, remains invaluable. M. Wood, 'The Making of King Aethelstan's Empire: an English Charlemagne?', in [C.] P. Wormald (ed.), *Ideal and Reality in Frankish and Anglo-Saxon Society: Studies Presented to J. M. Wallace-Hadrill* (Oxford, 1983), pp. 250–72; S. [D.] Keynes, 'King Athelstan's Books', in M. Lapidge and H. Gneuss (eds.), *Learning and Literature in Anglo-Saxon England: Studies Presented to Peter Clemoes on the Occasion of his Sixty-Fifth Birthday* (Cambridge, 1985), pp. 143–201.

Athenagoras (2nd cent.), Christian *Apologist. He is described in the earliest MS of his works as 'the Christian Philosopher of *Athens'. His 'Apology' or 'Supplication', addressed c.177 to *Marcus Aurelius and his son Commodus, sought to rebut current calumnies against the Christians: *atheism (chs. 4–30), Thyestian banquets, and Oedipean incest (chs. 31–6). A treatise 'On the Resurrection of the Dead' has traditionally been ascribed to him, but the attribution has been challenged. In this work the author endeavours to refute objections (chs. 1–10) and then to defend the doctrine positively. As a writer Athenagoras was one of the ablest of the Apologists, lucid in style and forceful in argument. He was the first to elaborate a philosophical defence of the Christian doctrine of God as Three in One. He upheld the indissolubility of marriage, even by death.

The Gk. text is preserved in the 'Arethas Codex' (Par. gr. 451), written in AD 914, on which all the other MSS depend. *Ed. princeps* by H. *Stephanus (Paris, 1557). Later edns. by P. *Maran (Paris, 1742; repr. in J. P. Migne, *PG* 6. 887–1024), E. *Schwartz in TU 4.2 (1891), P. Ubaldi and M. Pellegrino (Corona Patrum Salesiana, Serie Greca 14; Turin, 1947), M. Marcovich (Patristische Texte und Studien, 31; 1990), B. Pouderon (SC 379; 1992, with Fr. tr.) and, with Eng. tr., by W. R. Schoedel (Oxford Early Christian Texts, 1972). Earlier Eng. tr. by J. H. Crehan, SJ (ACW 23; 1956). H. A. Lucks, *The Philosophy of Athenagoras: Its Sources and Value* (Catholic University of America Philosophical Studies, 32; 1936). L. W. Barnard, *Athenagoras: A Study in Second Century Christian Apologetic* (Théologie historique, 18 [1972]). B. Pouderon, *Athénagore d'Athènes: Philosophe Chrétien* (ibid. 82 [1989]). *CPG* 1 (1983), pp. 28 f. (nos. 1070 f.). J. Quasten, *Patrology*, 1 (Utrecht, 1950), pp. 229–36, with good bibl. See also works cited under APOLOGISTS.

Athenagoras (1886–1972), Patr. of *Constantinople. Born at Vasilikon near Ioánnina in N. Greece, he studied at Constantinople in the Theological School at Halki (1903–10). In 1922 he became Metropolitan of Corfu and in 1930 Greek Abp. of N. and S. America, where he brought to an end a schism dividing the Greek Church in the USA and thoroughly reorganized the archdiocese. In 1948 he became *Oecumenical Patriarch. During his tenure of this office he did much to counteract attempts by the Patriarchate of Moscow to assume leadership in the Orthodox world. In his work as Patriarch he was inspired by two major aims: (1) closer co-operation between the *autocephalous Churches of the Orthodox communion: on his initiative the 'Panorthodox Conferences' met in Rhodes in 1961 and the years following; (2) better understanding between divided Christians: here his most striking achievements were his meeting with Pope *Paul VI at *Jerusalem in 1964, and the revocation of the *anathemas between Rome and Constantinople in 1965.

Studies by B. Ohse (Göttingen [1968]), ed. J. E. Anastasios (Ioánnina, 1975), and A. J. Delicostopoulos (Athens, 1988). *Towards the Healing of Schism: The Sees of Rome and Constantinople. Public statements and correspondence between the Holy See and the Ecumenical Patriarchate, 1958–1984*, ed. and tr. E. J. Stormon, SJ (Ecumenical Documents 3; New York [1987]), pp. 25–249 passim.

Athens. By the 1st cent. AD Athens had become a provincial city of the Roman Empire, important only for its schools of philosophy, to which upper-class Romans went as to a university. Its first known Christian connection was the visit (c. AD 50) of St *Paul on his second missionary journey (Acts 17: 15–18: 1). His sermon to the *Epicureans and *Stoics, as given in Acts 17: 22–31, took the form of an academic discourse and the preacher evidently did not meet with his usual success. Among his few converts was St *Dionysius the Areopagite (q.v.: 17: 34). Apart from this passage, the NT has no other references to Christianity at Athens, except the passing mention in 1 Thess. 3: 1.

The earliest evidence for a Christian community comes from the middle of the 2nd cent. Acc. to *Melito of Sardis (*Eusebius, *HE* 4. 26. 10), Antoninus Pius (138–61) endeavoured to check the unofficial, and possibly riotous, persecution of Christians in Athens and elsewhere. At or about this time Publius, Bp. of Athens, was martyred and the Church almost extinguished; but it was revived under his successor, Quadratus. Athens appears to have been one of the earliest centres of a philosophical interpretation of Christianity and was the home of the *Apologists, *Quadratus (perhaps to be distinguished from the Bishop just mentioned), *Aristides, and *Athenagoras.

In the next centuries the history of the city was uneventful. The philosophical schools continued and the city was twice visited by *Origen, who is said to have combated an outbreak of heresy there. St *Basil and St *Gregory of Nazianzus both studied at Athens. In 529 *Justinian closed its schools as exponents of surviving paganism, and shortly afterwards the Parthenon and other temples were converted into churches. In the Byzantine period many churches and monasteries were built. After the Latin Conquest in 1204 (Fourth *Crusade) the Parthenon became the cathedral of a W. bishop using the Latin rite, while a Greek bishop and the Greek rite were allowed to continue in the lower town for the native population. When the city fell to the Turks (1456), its conquerors turned the Parthenon into a mosque, expelling all W. influence but tolerating, as elsewhere, the Greek Church. They remained in possession of the Acropolis until 1833 when the Kingdom of Greece was set up and the Orthodox Church of Greece became *autocephalous with Athens as the metropolitical see.

M. *Le Quien, *Oriens Christianus*, 2 (Paris, 1740), cols. 169–178, 3 (1740), cols. 837–44. A. Mommsen, *Athenae Christianae* (Leipzig, 1868). F. *Gregorovius, *Geschichte der Stadt Athen im Mittelalter von der Zeit Justinians bis zur türkischen Eroberung* (2 vols., 1889). A. Frantz, 'From Paganism to Christianity in the

Temples of Athens', *Dumbarton Oaks Papers*, 19 (1965), pp. 185–205. K. M. Setton, 'Athens in the Later Twelfth Century', *Speculum*, 19 (1944), pp. 179–209, repr. in id., *Athens in the Middle Ages* (1975), no. 3. N. T. Philadelpheus, Ἱστορία τῶν Ἀθηνῶν ἐπὶ Τουρκοκρατίας ἀπὸ τοῦ 1400 μέχρι τοῦ 1800 (2 vols., Athens, 1902). I. T. Hill, *The Ancient City of Athens: Its Topography and Monuments* (1953). D. Sicilianos, *Old and New Athens* (rev. Eng. tr., 1960: orig. Greek in 3 vols., 1953–5). J. Travlos, *Pictorial Dictionary of Ancient Athens* (1971), and other works of this author. R. Janin, AA, *Les Églises et les Monastères des Grands Centres Byzantins* (1975), pp. 298–340. V. Laurent, AA, 'La Liste épiscopale de la métropole d'Athènes', in *Mémorial Louis Petit* (Bucarest, 1948), pp. 272–91. R. Janin, AA, in *DHGE* 5 (1931), cols. 15–42, s.v.

Athon, John. See AYTON, JOHN.

Athos, Mount, 'the Holy Mountain'. The peninsula which projects into the Aegean Sea from the coast of Macedonia and terminates in Mount Athos has long been entirely the property of monasteries of the E. Orthodox Church. The first monastic settlement of which there is reliable evidence is the foundation of the monastery of the '*Lavra' by St *Athanasius the Athonite in 961. There are now 20 virtually independent monasteries on the peninsula. Such matters as are of common concern to the whole mountain are legislated for by a council, made up of one representative from each monastery, and an executive committee of four members. The monasteries contain many valuable MSS and works of art. The peninsula, cut off from the mainland by forest, forms a natural monastic enclosure, from which women are excluded.

R. Curzon, *Visits to Monasteries in the Levant* (1849), pt. 4, pp. 327–449. A. Riley, *Athos, or the Mountain of the Monks* (1887); P. Meyer, *Die Haupturkunden für die Geschichte der Athosklöster* (1894). G. Smurnakes, Τὸ Ἅγιον Ὄρος (Athens, 1903); R. M. Dawkins, *The Monks of Athos* (1936). P. Sherrard, *Athos: The Mountain of Silence* (1960). *Le Millénaire du Mont Athos 963–1963: Études et mélanges* (2 vols., Chevetogne [1963–4]), with bibl. E. Amand de Mendieta, *Mount Athos: The Garden of the Panaghia* (Berliner Byzantinische Arbeiten, 46; 1972). P. Sherrard, *Athos: The Holy Mountain* (1982). R. F. Taft, SJ, 'Mount Athos: A Late Chapter in the History of the Byzantine Rite', *Dumbarton Oaks Papers*, 42 (1988), pp. 179–94, with other arts. pp. 157–78. G. Millet (ed.), *Monuments de l'Athos*, 1: *Les Peintures* (Monuments de l'art byzantin, 5; 1927). *Archives de l'Athos* (Paris, 1937 ff.). Catalogues of MSS include S. P. Lambros, *Catalogue of the Greek Manuscripts on Mount Athos* (2 vols., Cambridge, 1895–1900) and those of S. Eustratiades and Arcadios (MSS of the Monastery of Vatopedi; Harvard Theological Studies, Cambridge, Mass., 11; 1924) and Spyridon and S. Eustratiades (MSS of the Lavra; ibid. 12; 1925). G. A. Maloney in *NCE* 1 (1967), pp. 1008–10, s.v.

Atonement (i.e. 'at-one-ment'). In Christian theology, man's reconciliation with God through the sacrificial death of Christ.

The need for such reconciliation is implicit in the OT conception of God's absolute righteousness, to which nothing impure or sinful can approach. Its achievement is here represented as dependent on an act of God Himself, whether by the Divine appointment of the sacrificial system through which uncleanness, both ritual and moral, may be purged by the shedding of blood (cf. Heb. 9: 22), or, in a Prophetic view, by the future Divine gift of a new covenant to replace the old covenant which sinful Israel has broken (Jer. 31: 31), or, in certain passages of the Book of Is., by the action of a Divinely sent *Servant of the Lord who was 'wounded for our transgressions' and 'bare the sin of many' (Is. 53: 5, 12). But the Prophets also insisted that without repentance the offering of sacrifice for sins was futile (Is. 1: 10–17, Hos. 6: 6). In the post-exilic period, atoning value was attributed to the death of martyrs (2 Macc. 7: 38; 4 Macc. 6: 28, 17: 22).

As recorded in the NT, Christ, like *John the Baptist, began His ministry with a call to universal repentance for sin (Mk. 1: 4, 15). While He proclaimed the uselessness of blood-sacrifices considered as a substitute for repentance (Mt. 9: 13), He spoke also of giving His life 'a ransom for many' (Mk. 10: 45) and at the institution of the *Eucharist declared the shedding of His blood to constitute 'the new covenant' (Lk. 22: 20, 1 Cor. 11: 25) and to be 'unto remission of sins' (Mt. 26: 28). He also applied to Himself the words of Is. 53 relating to the Suffering Servant (Lk. 22: 37). In St *John's Gospel Christ is set forth as 'the Lamb of God which taketh away the sin of the world' (Jn. 1: 29) and His death shown in a sacrificial light by being placed in juxtaposition to the sacrifice of the *Paschal Lamb at the *Passover (Jn. 19: 14, 36). Hence in the earliest Christian preaching His death was already proclaimed to be 'for our sins' (1 Cor. 15: 3) and His work expounded on the basis of Is. 53 (Acts 8: 32–5).

For the elaboration of the doctrine, the Church owed a unique debt to St *Paul. Christ's death and resurrection were the means by which we are redeemed from the effects of Law and its transgression, namely sin, from God's condemnation, and from death. By Baptism the Christian mystically shares in Christ's death and His victory over it (that is the resurrection), and acquires, by God's free gift, a new status of sonship or justification; and peace was made between God and man 'through the blood of His cross' (Col. 1: 20). Hence the death of Christ was an expiation (ἱλαστήριον, Rom. 3: 25). Elsewhere in the NT, the believer is said to be redeemed 'with precious blood' (1 Pet. 1: 18 f.), and the author of Hebrews makes constant use of sacrificial language in the same connection (cf. esp. ch. 9).

The Fathers took up and developed the doctrine of the NT, but posed new questions. For *Origen the death of Christ was the ransom paid to Satan, who had acquired rights over man by the Fall, but was deceived into thinking he could hold the sinless Christ. This view was accepted with various modifications by many of the Latin Fathers, among them St *Hilary of Poitiers, St *Augustine, and St *Leo, and among the Greeks by St *Gregory of Nyssa (though it was rejected by St *Gregory of Nazianzus). But while maintaining that the devil had rights over sinful man, the exponents of this doctrine also commonly stressed that in trying to exercise them on the sinless Christ he abused them, and was thus himself conquered by the power of the resurrection. Another view is that God the Son, by taking our nature upon Him, has effected a change in human nature as such. It is typified in such a saying as St *Athanasius' 'He became man that we might be made divine' (De Inc. 54). The general patristic teaching is that Christ is our representative, not our substitute; and that the effect of His sufferings, His perfect obedience, and His resurrection extends to the whole of humanity and beyond.

In the 11th–12th cents. with St *Anselm's Cur Deus Homo the emphasis shifted. The role of Satan gave way to the idea of satisfaction. Sin, being an infinite offence against God, required a satisfaction equally infinite. As no finite being, man or angel, could offer such satisfaction, it was necessary that an infinite being, i.e. God Himself, should take the place of man and, by His death, make complete satisfaction to Divine Justice. Hence the death of Christ was not a ransom paid to the devil but a debt paid to the Father. P. *Abelard, on the other hand, sought the explanation in terms of love. Christ's atoning death was effective primarily as the final proof of a love for man which evoked a response of love in the sinner. This break with tradition, too radical to meet with much acceptance, was violently criticized by St *Bernard. The later Scholastic teaching set out from Anselm. *Thomas Aquinas, while accepting Anselm's satisfactional view as a correct account of what took place, denied that the method of satisfaction was imperative. However 'convenient' the method, it had no intrinsic necessity, because God might have redeemed us without exacting full satisfaction. In the circumstances, however, the satisfaction was not only adequate but superabundant, for whereas the offence against God, being perpetrated by a finite being, was only morally infinite, the satisfaction, being the work of a divine Person, was objectively, as well as morally, infinite. This teaching, which became the current opinion among Catholic theologians, was challenged by the *Scotists and *Nominalists, who held that the Atonement was adequate, not because of its own intrinsic value, but because of its 'extrinsic acceptance' by God.

The Reformers, though leaving the core of the traditional doctrine intact, developed it in a different direction. M. *Luther rejected the Scholastic satisfaction theory and taught that Christ, in bearing by voluntary substitution the punishment due to man, was reckoned by God a sinner in his place. J. *Calvin went even further in teaching that the Saviour 'bore in His soul the tortures of a condemned and ruined man'. In reaction against the exaggerations of this 'penal theory' arose the doctrine, first defended by the Socinians, which denied the objective efficacy of the Cross and looked upon the death of Christ as primarily an example to His followers. Notable modern exponents of this view in England were B. *Jowett and H. *Rashdall. More recently there has been a return to traditional views. G. *Aulén (Christus Victor, 1931) defended the traditional theme of Christ's victory as the 'classic idea' of redemption, but he has been criticized for not coming to grips with mythological language. *Demythologized interpretations draw on *existentialist and sociological concepts of alienation as descriptive of humanity's fallen state. Christ, by His resistance to demonic false absolutes, opens the way to liberation and right relationship with God. In contrast, *Barthian theology has renewed stress on the objectivity of the Atonement, with the Cross at the centre of the Christian Creed. It should be added finally that there has never been any official formulation in orthodox Christianity of the mystery of the Lord's redemptive work and that there is every likelihood that a variety of emphases and interpretations will continue.

For the history of the doctrine, see J. Rivière, Le Dogme de la Rédemption: Essai d'Étude Historique (1905; Eng. tr., 1909); id., Le

Dogme de la Rédemption: Études Critiques et Documents (1931); R. S. Franks, *The History of the Doctrine of the Work of Christ* (2 vols., 1918); H. Rashdall, *The Idea of Atonement in Christian Theology* (1919); L. W. Grensted, *A Short History of the Doctrine of the Atonement* (1920); H. E. W. Turner, *The Patristic Doctrine of Redemption: A Study of the Development of the Doctrine in the First Five Centuries* (1952); R. E. Weingart, *The Logic of Divine Love: A Critical Analysis of the Soteriology of Peter Abailard* (Oxford, 1970), pp. 120–84; Λ. C. Clifford, *Atonement and Justification: English Evangelical Theology 1640–1790. An Evaluation* (ibid., 1990).

For the NT teaching, see V. Taylor, *Jesus and His Sacrifice: A Study of the Passion-Sayings in the Gospels* (1937); id., *The Atonement in New Testament Teaching* (1940); id., *Forgiveness and Reconciliation: A Study in New Testament Teaching* (1941); id., *The Cross of Christ* (1956); L. Morris, *The Apostolic Preaching of the Cross* (1955); M. Hengel, *The Atonement: A Study of the Origins of the Doctrine in the New Testament* (1981; expanded Eng. tr. of an art. in the *Internationale katholische Zeitschrift*, 9 (1980), pp. 1–25 and 135–47).

For systematic presentations, see J. McLeod Campbell, *The Nature of the Atonement* (1856); R. W. *Dale, *The Atonement* (1885); R. C. *Moberly, *Atonement and Personality* (1901; worked out on the basis of Vicarious Penitence); P. T. Forsyth, *The Work of Christ* (1910); J. Rivière, *Le Dogme de la Rédemption: Étude théologique* (1914); J. *Denney, *The Christian Doctrine of Reconciliation* (1917; posthumous); *The Atonement: Papers from the Summer School of Catholic Studies held at Cambridge, July 31–Aug. 9, 1926* (1928); E. *Brunner, *Der Mittler* (1927; Eng. tr., *The Mediator*, 1934); id., *Das Gebot und die Ordnungen* (1932; Eng. tr., *The Divine Imperative*, 1937); L. S. Thornton, CR, *The Doctrine of the Atonement* (1937); L. Hodgson, *The Doctrine of the Atonement* (Hale Lectures, 1950; 1951). K. Barth, *Die kirchliche Dogmatik*, 4: *Die Lehre von der Versöhnung* (3 parts in 4 vols., 1953–9; Eng. tr., 1956–62), *passim*; S. Lyonnet, SJ, *De Peccato et Redemptione* (Theologia Biblica Novi Testamenti; Rome, 2 vols. pub. to date, 1957–60; Eng. tr., with other material, in id. and L. Sabourin, SJ, *Sin, Redemption, and Sacrifice: A Biblical and Patristic Study*, Analecta Biblica, 48; 1970); P. *Tillich, *Systematic Theology*, 2 (Chicago, 1957; repr. London, 1978), pp. 165–80 (London, 1957, pp. 191–208); R. S. Paul, *The Atonement and the Sacraments: The Relation of the Atonement to the Sacraments of Baptism and the Lord's Supper* (Nashville, 1960; London, 1961); W. *Pannenberg, *Grundzüge der Christologie* (1964), pp. 251–88 (Eng. tr., *Jesus— God and Man* (1968), pp. 245–80); F. W. Dillistone, *The Christian Understanding of Atonement* (1968); F. M. Young, *Sacrifice and the Death of Christ* (1975); C. E. Gunton, *The Actuality of Atonement: A Study of Metaphor, Rationality and the Christian Tradition* (Edinburgh, 1988); P. S. Fiddes, *Past Event and Present Salvation: The Christian Idea of Atonement* (1989); T. [S. M.] Williams, 'The Atonement', in R. [C.] Morgan (ed.), *The Religion of the Incarnation: Anglican Essays in Commemoration of Lux Mundi* (Bristol, 1989), pp. 99–118; R. [G.] Swinburne, *Responsibility and Atonement* (Oxford, 1989), esp. pp. 148–62.

Atonement, Day of. The annual Jewish fast day (יוֹם הַכִּפֻּרִים, ἡμέρα ἐξιλασμοῦ) which falls on the 10th day of the 7th month (Tishri), i.e. roughly in Oct. It is commonly called 'Yom Kippur'. Its observance is regulated by Lev. 16: 23, 27–32, and Num. 29: 7–11, all prob. dating from the period of the *Exile or later. Its purpose is the cleansing of sanctuary, priesthood, and people from sin and the re-establishment of good relations between God and His chosen ones. It is the only fast which the Mosaic Law provides. Much of the ritual ordered in the OT has necessarily lapsed, e.g. the entry of the priest into the Holy of Holies in the *Temple, the offering of incense before the *Mercy Seat and its sprinkling with blood, and

the scapegoat for *Azazel dispatched to the wilderness. The basis of present observance is to be found in the Tractate 'Yoma' of the *Mishnah, wholly devoted to the subject. The Day is still observed by strict abstinence from food, and many Jews who rarely attend public worship on other occasions attend the synagogue. The imagery of the Day of Atonement deeply influenced the NT author of the Ep. to the Heb., who saw in Christ the Great High Priest whose Atonement on the Cross abolished the need for the annual repetition of the observance.

Convenient collection of texts, in Eng. tr., S. Y. Agnon, *Days of Awe* (New York, 1948, repr. 1965), pp. 183–279. S. Landersdorfer, *Studien zum biblischen Versöhnungstag* (1924). I. Elbogen, *Der jüdische Gottesdienst in seiner geschichtlichen Entwicklung* (1913), pp. 149–54. J. Morgenstern, 'Two Prophecies from the Fourth Century B.C. and the Evolution of Yom Kippur', *Hebrew Union College Annual* 24 (1952–3), pp. 1–74. R. de Vaux, OP, *Les Institutions de l'Ancien Testament*, 2 (1960), pp. 415–20, with bibl. pp. 459 f.; Eng. tr. (2nd edn., 1965), pp. 507–10, with bibl. p. 552. M. D. Herr and J. Milgrom in *Encyclopaedia Judaica*, 5 (Jerusalem, 1972), cols. 1376–87, s.v. 'Day of Atonement'. See also comm. on Lev. and Num.

atrium. The main court of the Roman house. From an early date the word was used of the forecourt attached to Christian churches, which usually consisted of a colonnaded quadrangle with a fountain in the middle. It was connected with the interior of the church by a *narthex or portico, which ran the length of one side, and by which from *c*. the 6th cent. it was replaced as the main way of approach from without. An atrium with porticoes attached to the church erected by St *Paulinus at Tyre is described by *Eusebius (*Hist. Eccl.* 10. 4. 39).

Atterbury, Francis (1662–1732), Bp. of *Rochester. He was a Tory High Churchman. After some years of academic controversy at Christ Church, Oxford, he became Lecturer of St Bride's London, chaplain to William III and Mary, and preacher at Bridewell Hospital. In his (anonymous) *Letter of a Convocation Man* (1697) and his *Rights and Privileges of an English Convocation Stated and Vindicated* (1700), he became the champion of *Convocation against the Crown and of the inferior clergy against the bishops. In 1701 he became Archdeacon of Totnes, in 1704 Dean of Carlisle, in 1711 Dean of Christ Church, and in 1713 Bp. of Rochester and Dean of *Westminster. In 1723 he was deprived of all his offices and banished from the country for alleged complicity in a Jacobite plot, and he died in exile. He was regarded as the best preacher of his day.

His Memoirs and Correspondence were edited by F. Williams (2 vols., 1869). Studies by H. C. Beeching (London, 1909) and G. V. Bennett (Oxford, 1975), J. H. Overton in *DNB* 2 (1885), pp. 233–8.

Atticus (d. 425), Patr. of *Constantinople from 406. A native of Sebaste in *Armenia, he was brought up in the *Pneumatomachian heresy, but was converted to orthodoxy in Constantinople. Here he became the bitter opponent of St John *Chrysostom. As Patriarch, however, he realized that the quarrel with Rome about the condemnation of Chrysostom weakened the prestige of his see; he re-established communion with Rome, and, to the vexation of St *Cyril of Alexandria, he restored Chrysostom's name to the *diptychs. He asserted the right to consecrate bishops in provinces near Constantinople and won support from the Emp. *Theodosius II for his jurisdiction in Illyricum and Asia Minor. *Apiarius and *Pelagian refugees in Constantinople brought him into direct contact with the Churches of N. Africa. In 419 he sent to Carthage a copy of the *Nicene canons with a covering letter. At the request of *Aurelius, Bp. of Carthage, he repelled Pelagians, but pained St *Augustine by failing to write to him as well as to Aurelius and by expressing anxieties about the *Manichaean attitude to sex attributed by the Pelagians to Augustine. Augustine wrote to protest, c.420–1. A letter 'on Virginity' to the Empress *Pulcheria and her two sisters, known to *Gennadius of Marseilles, has not survived, but there are extant fragments of a letter on Christology to an otherwise unknown Eupsychius, appealed to by both sides in the controversy for and against the *Chalcedonian definition. In the E. Church Atticus is venerated as a saint; feast days, 8 Jan. and 11 Oct.

V. Grumel, AA, Les Regestes des Actes du Patriarcat de Constantinople, 1 (2nd edn., 1972), pp. 27–36 (nos. 34a–48a). Lat. text of his recension of the Nicene canons in Turner, EOMIA 1 (1939), pp. 104–42, with his covering letter, pp. 611–3; this letter also in C. Munier (ed.), Concilia Africae A. 345–A. 525 (CCSL 149; 1974), p. 163. Syriac text of the letter to Eupsychius, ed., with Fr. tr., by M. Brière, Revue de l'Orient Chrétien, 29 (1933–4), pp. 378–424; further Gk. and Syriac fragments ed. M. Geerard and A. Van Roey in Corona Gratiarum: Miscellanea Patristica, Historica et Liturgica Eligio Dekkers ... Oblata, 1 (Instrumenta Patristica, 10; 1975), pp. 69–81. Sermon on the BVM in Syriac, ed., with Lat. tr., by J. Lebon, Le Muséon, 46 (1933), pp. 167–202, and with Fr. tr., by M. Brière, Revue de l'Orient Chrétien, 29 (1933–4), pp. 160–86. Augustine's letter to Atticus, ep. 6, ed. J. Divjak (CSEL 88, 1981, pp. 32–38). The principal authorities for his Life are *Socrates, HE 7. 2, *Sozomen, HE 8. 27, and *Palladius, Dialogus de Vita S. Johannis Chrysostomi, 9–11. Life from various sources printed in AASS, Jan. 1 (1643), pp. 473–82; also ibid., Aug. 1 (1753), pp. 32 f. CPG 3 (1979), pp. 105–7 (nos. 5650–7).

Attila (d. 453), King of the Huns from c.433. Attila united all the Hun tribes, prob. for the first time in their history, completing the process with the murder of his brother Bleda (c.445), with whom he had previously shared power. The united Huns dominated the surrounding tribes, so that Attila was able to gather a still larger military force. Using as a pretext the charge that the Bp. of Margus on the Danube had been plundering the tombs of Hun princes, he launched a series of attacks on the Roman Empire in the 440s. After devastating the East, he invaded Gaul in 451, but was defeated on the Catalaunian Plains near Troyes. The story that he spared the town at the request of its bishop, *Lupus, is prob. unhistorical. In 452 he turned to Italy, ravaging its northern cities; unreliable sources say that he was persuaded to leave *Rome in peace by Pope *Leo I. He died after a drinking bout on his wedding night. Christian sources know him as the 'Scourge of God'—a minister of divine vengeance— while Teutonic legends represent him as hospitable and magnanimous.

The main sources are Jordanes, Getica, esp. sections 34–49 passim (ed. T. Mommsen, MGH, Auctores Antiqui, 5, pt. 1; 1882, pp. 104–25; Eng. tr. by C. C. Mierow, Princeton, NJ, and London, 1915, pp. 101–125); and fragments of Priscus (ed. and tr. by R. C. Blockley, The Fragmentary Classicising Historians of the Later Roman Empire, 2, ARCA Classical and Medieval Texts, Papers and Monographs 10, Liverpool, 1983, pp. 222–377, esp. pp. 234–69 and 274–321). E. A. Thompson, A History of Attila and the Huns (Oxford, 1948); J. O. Maenchen-Helfen, The World of the Huns, ed. M. Knight (Berkeley, Calif., and London, 1973), passim.

Atto (c.885–961), Bp. of Vercelli from 924. He was a canonist and theologian remarkable for his great erudition in an unlearned age. His writings included a long commentary on the Pauline Epistles (dependent on *Augustine, *Jerome, *Claudius of Turin, and others) and a collection of ecclesiastical canons. Some of his letters and sermons have also survived.

Works ed. C. Buronzo del Signore (2 vols., Vercelli, 1768), repr. J. P. Migne, PL 134. 9–916. Modern edn. of the 'Polypticum', an incisive critique of affairs in N. Italy in his day, attributed to Atto (though the authorship remains contested), with Ger. tr. by G. Goetz (Abh. (Sächs.), 37, Heft 2; 1922). S. F. Wemple, Atto of Vercelli: Church State and Christian Society in Tenth Century Italy (Temi e Testi, 27; Rome, 1979). C. Frova, 'Il "Polittico" attribuito ad Attone vescovo di Vercelli (924–960 ca.): tra storia e grammatica', Bullettino dell'Istituto Storico Italiano per il medio evo e Archivio Muratoriano, 90 (1982/3), pp. 1–75. A. Fliche, La Réforme grégorienne, 1 (SSL 6; 1924), pp. 61–74.

attrition. The sorrow for sin which proceeds from fear of punishment or a sense of the ugliness of sin. It is contrasted with *contrition (q.v.), which is held to proceed from the love of God. Its value was denied by M. *Luther and upheld by the Council of *Trent. Acc. to St *Thomas Aquinas and most medieval scholastics and moral theologians, attrition is a sufficient disposition for forgiveness within the sacrament of penance. Some theologians, such as *Peter Lombard, however, insisted on the need for perfect contrition. In 1667 *Alexander VII terminated this dispute by declaring that either opinion could be held without heresy.

J. Périnelle, OP, L'Attrition d'après le Concile de Trente et d'après Saint Thomas d'Aquin (Bibliothèque Thomiste, 10; 1927); H. Dondaine, OP, L'Attrition suffisante (ibid. 25; 1943). J. McDonald in Catholic Dictionary of Theology, 1 (1962), pp. 206–9, with further bibl.

Aubigné, J. H. M. d'. See MERLE D'AUBIGNÉ, J. H.

Auburn Declaration (1837). A statement issued in 1837 in which the principal doctrines of the American *Presbyterians of the 'New School' were set forth. It was compiled by the Revd Baxter Dickinson (d. 1876) in reply to the charges made by the 'Old School' against the 'New School' to the effect that they had departed from the traditional *Calvinist teaching as embodied in the *Westminster standards. The statement, which was accepted in Aug. 1837 at Auburn, New York State, was made the theological basis on which the 'New School' was organized as a separate body. In 1868 the Declaration was admitted by the General Assembly of the 'Old School' to contain 'all fundamentals of the Calvinistic Creed' and thus paved the way for the reunion of 1870. Its 16 propositions are concerned rather to rebut a number of imputed soteriological and anthropological errors than to frame a set of positive beliefs.

The text is in P. *Schaff, The Creeds of Christendom (1877), vol. 3, pp. 777–80.

Auctorem Fidei. The bull of *Pius VI, dated 28 Aug. 1794, which condemned 85 articles of the Synod of *Pistoia (1786).

Text in A. Barbèri and R. Segreti (eds.), *Bullarii Romani Continuatio*, 9 (Rome, 1845), pp. 395–418; the greater part, incl. the propositions condemned, is repr. Denzinger and Hünermann (37th edn., 1991), pp. 711–51 (nos. 2600–2700). See also bibl. to PISTOIA, SYNOD OF, and PIUS VI.

Audiani. A 4th-cent. rigorist sect founded in Syria by Audius, a layman or perhaps a deacon, which separated from the Church on the ground that the clergy were too secularized. They were also accused of holding an *anthropomorphic view of the Godhead. Banished by *Constantine to Scythia, they there carried on missionary activity among the Goths.

The principal authorities are *Epiphanius, *Haer.* 70, and *Theodoret, *HE* 4. 10. L. E. Islein, 'Audios und die Audianer', *Jahrbücher für protestantische Theologie*, 16 (1890), pp. 298–305. H. C. Puech in *RAC* 1 (1950), cols. 910–15, s.v. 'Audianer', with refs.

Audience, Court of. Formerly an ecclesiastical court of the province of *Canterbury. Originally the Archbishop exercised his legatine jurisdiction in person, but later was assisted by assessors ('Auditors'), who were gradually reduced to one. Later still, this remaining Auditor sat at *St Paul's as judge of the court. In 1536 an attempt was made to abolish the court; but it survived until the next century, when it was superseded by the Court of *Arches, which had the same jurisdiction.

M. *Parker, *De Antiquitate Britannicae Ecclesiae* (1605), pp. 30–3. W. S. Holdsworth, *A History of English Law*, 1 (1903), pp. 371 f. I. J. Churchill, *Canterbury Administration*, 1 (1933), pp. 470–99, with refs.

audiences, pontifical. Receptions given by the Pope to visitors to Rome and to officials having business with the Holy See. They are for the most part private, but the general public are received in large numbers three or four times a week.

audientes (Lat., 'hearers'). In the early Church, those belonging to the first state of the *catechumenate. When they definitely desired to commit themselves to immediate pre-baptismal instruction, they were admitted to the higher order of '*competentes'.

Audoin, St. See OUEN, ST.

Audry, St. See ETHELDREDA, ST.

Aufer a nobis. In the Roman Mass the collect for purity formerly said by the celebrant at the end of the *Preparation as he went up to the altar. The text is first found in the *Leonine Sacramentary as the collect in the fourth of a collection of Masses headed 'In Natale Episcoporum'. The use of the collect was dropped in the *Ordo Missae* of 1969.

Jungmann (1952), 1, esp. pp. 378 f. and 401 f.; Eng. tr., 1, pp. 291–3 and 308 f.

Aufklärung (Ger., 'Enlightenment'). The term is applied in a technical sense to a movement of thought which appeared in an esp. clear-cut form in 18th-cent. Germany and is connected with the names of H. S. *Reimarus, G. E. *Lessing, and J. G. *Herder. Set within the world-wide tendency to Rationalism, characteristic of the period, the 'Aufklärung' combines opposition to all supernatural religion and belief in the all-sufficiency of human reason with an ardent desire to promote the happiness of men in this life. One of its chief ideals was religious toleration, represented by Lessing's *Nathan der Weise* and the policy of Frederick the Great. Most of its representatives preserved the belief in God, freedom, and immortality as consonant with reason, but rejected the Christian dogma and were hostile to Catholicism as well as to Protestant orthodoxy, which they regarded as powers of spiritual darkness depriving humanity of the use of its rational faculties. Their fundamental belief in the goodness of human nature, which blinded them to the fact of sin, produced an easy optimism and absolute faith in the progress and perfectibility of human society once the principles of enlightened reason had been recognized. The spirit of the 'Aufklärung' penetrated deeply into German Protestantism, where it disintegrated faith in the authority of the Bible and encouraged biblical criticism on the one hand and an emotional '*Pietism' on the other. In German Catholicism it had its exponents among the educated laity and the higher clergy, being favoured by the policy of *Joseph II. It directed itself esp. against the religious orders, the celibacy of the clergy, devotion to the saints, and such popular expressions of piety as pilgrimages and the veneration of relics.

See also ENLIGHTENMENT.

Augsburg, Confession of (1530). The *Lutheran confession of faith, mainly the work of P. *Melanchthon, which, after receiving M. *Luther's approval, was presented at Augsburg to the Emp. *Charles V on 25 June 1530. To make the Lutheran position as inoffensive as possible to the Catholic party, its language was studiously moderate. In form it is divided (apart from an introductory preface) into two parts. The first epitomizes in 21 articles the essential Lutheran doctrines. Of these the 20th, which expounds the Lutheran doctrines on faith and good works, is the most elaborate. The second half reviews the abuses for which remedy is demanded, among them communion in one kind, clerical celibacy, private masses, monastic vows, and compulsory confession. After receiving it, the Emperor transmitted it to a body of RC theologians which included J. *Eck, J. *Faber, and J. *Cochlaeus and their reply, designated the 'Confutatio pontificia', was read on 3 Aug. Melanchthon answered this with an 'Apology for the Confession', which the Emperor refused to receive.

The Confession was, from the first, an authoritative Lutheran document, and in the spring of 1531 (with a few slight changes) the *editio princeps* was published. In the ensuing years it was issued in a number of forms which varied somewhat in doctrine. In 1580, when the 'Book of *Concord' was drawn up, an endeavour was made to revert to the text presented to the Diet in 1530, and this 1580 text, the so-called 'Invariata', though it differs in over 450 places (mostly of no significance) from that of the Diet, remains the chief standard of faith in the Lutheran Churches. The considerably revised text issued by Melanchthon in 1540 (the 'Variata') is accepted by the

Reformed (i.e. Calvinist) Churches in certain parts of Germany.

Crit. eds. of text (Ger. and Lat.) by H. Bornkamm in *Die Bekenntnisschriften der evangelisch-lutheranischen Kirche*, herausgegeben im Gedenkjahr der Augsburgischen Konfession 1930 (10th edn., Göttingen, 1986), pp. 31–137, with 'Apology', pp. 139–404. Lat. text also in Kidd, pp. 259–89 (no. 116); Eng. tr. in T. G. Tappert (ed.), *The Book of Concord* (Philadelphia [1959]), pp. 23–96, with 'Apology', pp. 97–285. Crit. edn. of the 'Confutatio', with introd. and bibl., by H. Immenkötter (Corpus Catholicorum, 33; Münster, 1979). W. Gussmann, *Quellen und Forschungen zur Geschichte des Augsburgischen Glaubensbekenntnisses* (2 vols., 1911). H. Bornkamm, *Der authentische Text der Confessio Augustana (1530)* (Sb. (Heid.), 1956, Abh. 2). W. Maurer, *Historischer Kommentar zur Confessio Augustana* (2 vols., 1976–8; Eng. tr., Philadelphia [1986]). V. Pfnür, *Einig in der Rechtfertigungslehre? Die Rechtfertigungslehre der Confessio Augustana (1530) und die Stellungnahme der katholischen Kontroverstheologie zwischen 1530 und 1535* (Veröffentlichungen des Instituts für Europäische Geschichte Mainz, 60; 1970). H. Fries and others, *Confessio Augustana: Hindernis oder Hilfe?* (Regensburg, 1979). E. Iserloh (ed.), *Confessio Augustana und Confutatio: Der Augsburger Reichstag 1530 und die Einheit der Kirche Internationales Symposion der Gesellschaft zur Herausgabe des Corpus Catholicorum in Augsburg vom 3.–7. September 1979* (Reformationsgeschichtliche Studien und Texte, 118; 1980). J. A. Burgess (ed.), *The Role of the Augsburg Confession: Catholic and Lutheran Views* (Philadelphia [1980]). B. Lohse, H. Immenkötter, and A. Sperl in *TRE* 4 (1979), pp. 616–39, s.v. 'Augsburger Bekenntnis, Confutatio und Apologie', with bibl.

Augsburg, Interim of. The doctrinal formula accepted as the provisional basis of religious settlement between Catholics and Protestants in 1548. After a joint commission of both groups, appointed by *Charles V in Feb. 1548, had failed to reach agreement, the Emperor had a formula prepared by J. *Pflug, Bp. of Naumburg, M. Helding, suffragan Bp. of Mainz, and J. *Agricola. This doctrinal compromise in 26 articles was designed as a provisional basis till the Council of *Trent made a final settlement. The chief points yielded to the Protestants were clerical marriage and communion in both kinds. After being secretly circulated, it was accepted at the Diet of Augsburg, 30 June 1548, and rigidly executed in parts of S. Germany. In the more Protestant parts of Germany, where the Augsburg Interim failed to obtain assent, a less Catholic edict, the so-called 'Leipzig Interim', put forth by the Elector Maurice in Dec. 1548, was adopted.

Ger. and Lat. text of the Augsburg Interim ed., with introd. and bibl., by J. Melhhausen (Texte zur Geschichte der evangelischen Theologie, 3; Neukirchen, 1970). Lat. text of ch. 26: 'De caeremoniis et usu Sacramentorum' also in Kidd, no. 148, pp. 359–62.

Augsburg, Peace of (1555). The settlement of religious affairs in the German Empire between Ferdinand I and the Electors at Augsburg on 25 Sept. 1555. It recognized the existence of both Catholicism and Lutheranism (but not Calvinism) in Germany, providing that in each land subjects should follow the religion of their ruler (*cuius regio eius religio*). Those not content with this settlement were permitted, after selling their property, to migrate to other lands. In the Imperial cities, both religions, if already established, were to continue. The official standard of Lutheran faith was the '*Augsburg Confession' of 1530 or any of its later recensions. Though Lutheranism then secured official recognition it was a victory for territorial-

ism, not toleration. All property in the hands of Protestants at the time of the Passau Treaty (1552) was to be confirmed to them. This 'Peace' remained the basis of the ecclesiastical settlement in the Empire until the Edict of Restitution (1629) and the Treaty of *Westphalia of 1648.

Crit. edn. of text in A. Druffel, *Beiträge zur Reichsgeschichte 1553–1555* (rev. edn. by K. Brandi; Briefe und Akten zur Geschichte des sechzehnten Jahrhunderts, 4; 1896). Eng. tr. of the main clauses is repr. in Kidd, pp. 363 f. (no. 149), and Bettenson (2nd edn.), 1963), pp. 301 f. C. W. Spieker, *Geschichte des Augsburger Religionsfriedens von 26 September 1555* (Schleiz, 1854). G. Wolf, *Der Augsburger Religionsfriede* (Stuttgart, 1890). Further bibl. in Schottenloher, 4 (1938), pp. 34 f. (nos. 34481–503). G. Pfeiffer in *TRE* 4 (1979), pp. 639–45, s.v. 'Augsburger Religionsfriede'.

Augusteum. The building erected at *Wittenberg in 1564–83 on the site of the *Augustinian monastery at which M. *Luther in his early life had taught. It at first served University purposes, but after many vicissitudes in the 18th cent. eventually became a Lutheran theological seminary.

Augustine, St, of Canterbury (d. between 604 and 609), missionary to Kent and first Abp. of *Canterbury. The prior of St Andrew's monastery at Rome, he was in 596 dispatched by St *Gregory the Great, then Pope, to refound the Church in England. He wished to turn back while in Gaul, but, encouraged by letters from Gregory, he finally landed in Kent in the spring of 597. He was favourably received and given every opportunity for his work, and after a few months Christianity was formally adopted by *Ethelbert, King of Kent, whose wife Bertha had been a Christian before marriage. Augustine's capacity for organization seems to have been limited, for he wrote to ask for Gregory's instruction on the smallest points. About 603, with Ethelbert's assistance, he tried to reach an agreement with representatives of the ancient *Celtic Church', which still survived in Britain and was at variance with Rome on questions of discipline and practice; but the attempt was a failure. In 604 he sent *Justus to preach west of the Medway, with the title of Bp. of *Rochester, and *Mellitus to work, as Bp. of London, among the East Saxons. His final (recorded) act was to consecrate Laurence to be his successor at Canterbury, some time between 604 and 609. Feast day, 26 May; in the RC Church since 1969, 27 May.

The principal authority is *Bede, *HE* 1. 23–2. 3; comm. by J. M. Wallace-Hadrill (Oxford, 1988), esp. pp. 31–48. Life by Goscelin in *AASS*, Mai. 6 (1688), pp. 375–95. Docs. of primary importance for his mission and episcopate in A. W. Haddan and W. *Stubbs (eds.), *Councils and Ecclesiastical Documents Relating to Great Britain and Ireland* (1871), pp. 3–60. A. J. Mason (ed.), *The Mission of St Augustine to England according to the Original Documents* (1897). M. Deanesly, *Augustine of Canterbury* (1964). N. Brooks, *The Early History of the Church of Canterbury* (Leicester, 1984), esp. pp. 3–14 and 87–93. On the controversy over the genuineness of the correspondence of Pope Gregory I with Augustine and others, preserved in Bede, *HE* 1. 23–32, see P. Meyvaert, 'Bede's text of the *Libellus Responsionum* of Gregory the Great to Augustine of Canterbury', in P. Clemoes and K. Hughes (eds.), *England Before the Conquest: Studies in primary sources presented to Dorothy Whitelock* (Cambridge, 1971), pp. 15–33, with refs. to earlier lit. F. M. Stenton, *Anglo-Saxon England*

(Oxford History of England, 2, 1943), pp. 103–12; 3rd edn. (1971), pp. 102–13. M. *Creighton in *DNB* 2 (1885), pp. 255–7.

Augustine, St, of Hippo (354–430), Bp. of Hippo Regius (modern Annaba, on the coast of Algeria) and '*Doctor of the Church'. Aurelius Augustinus was born at Thagaste (modern Souk-Ahras, in Algeria), to a pagan father Patricius, a member of the town council, and his Christian wife (St *Monica), through whom he was made a *catechumen in infancy. Augustine's home culture was Latin, and teachers at Thagaste, nearby Madauros, and Carthage gave him a mastery of Latin literature and rhetoric, with some knowledge of Greek. In adolescence he lost his faith, and at the age of 17 he took a concubine with whom he lived for 15 years; she bore him a son, Adeodatus (d. 389). In 373, when he was 18, Augustine read Cicero's (lost) *Hortensius*. This reawakened his religious aspirations, but disillusionment with the *Old Latin Bible's style and content led him away from his mother's faith to *Manichaeism. The Manichees retained his loose adherence for a decade, as he passed through successive teaching posts at Carthage, Rome, and Milan. Here, for reasons of secular ambition, he painfully abandoned the liaison with the mother of his son and was betrothed to a 12-year-old heiress found by Monica. This turmoil coincided with a religious crisis to which various factors contributed: loss of belief in Mani's mythology, the positive influence of St *Ambrose's sermons (which he attended initially for their rhetorical power but increasingly for their content), attachment to a group of enthusiastic students of *Plotinus and *Porphyry, and asthmatic attacks which forced him to retire from his Milan professorship when he was 32. In July 386 in a garden in Milan he came to a decision to abandon secular hopes, his career in rhetoric, and marriage. On Easter Eve 387 he was baptized by Ambrose. He moved to Rome and, having buried Monica at Ostia, returned to Africa in the late summer of 388. At Thagaste he and a group of friends established an ascetic lay community. In 391, when visiting Hippo Regius, Augustine was seized by the people and against his will ordained priest by the aged Bp. Valerius. Probably in the summer of 395 be became coadjutor bishop and was in sole charge after Valerius' death soon afterwards. He himself died on 28 Aug. 430, when the Vandals were besieging Hippo.

Augustine's consecration as bishop was controversial, not least on account of his Manichaean past. During his priesthood he produced tracts against the Manichees and in the three years after he became bishop he wrote the deeply anti-Manichaean *Confessions (q.v.). Against Mani he used *Neoplatonist arguments to counter belief in an ultimate power of darkness too strong for the good Light to eliminate; he defended the canonical OT (rejected by Mani), and he upheld the use of wine in both natural and sacramental contexts as well as the admission of married Christians to full Church membership by Baptism. Crucial to Augustine's rebuttal of Mani is the vindication of religious authority both in the biblical canon and in the worldwide Church: 'I would not have believed the gospel unless the universal Church had constrained me to do so' (*C. Ep. Fund.* 5. 6). Augustine nevertheless remained influenced by Mani's contention that unregenerate humanity lacks free will to perform any good action, and the proposition

that sexuality exercises a downward pull on the soul (common to Mani and the Platonists) was important to Augustine both in his ascetic ideals and in his articulation of the doctrine of '*original sin'.

Augustine's opposition to *Donatism helped him to win the confidence of the Catholic community. He wrote a popular, versified narrative of the schism's origin and invited Donatist bishops to public debate on the central issue of unity versus holiness. He persuaded the primate, *Aurelius, Bp. of Carthage, to call episcopal councils to achieve a common front, and he sought to induce his colleagues to recognize the sacraments conferred by Donatists, including *Orders. To this end he developed the distinction between *validity (q.v.) and efficacy: even though valid, Baptism or Ordination does not benefit the recipient until brought within the fold. This conciliatory sacramental theology was assisted by the doctrine of *predestination: 'Many who seem to be without are within, and many who seem to be within are without.' Augustine initially opposed the use of coercion against the Donatists, but from 405 Imperial government pressure was increasingly successful in reconciling Donatists to Catholicism, and by the time of the conference at Carthage in May 411, he accepted its legitimacy within certain limitations.

In *Confessions*, 10. 29 (40) Augustine prayed 'You have commanded continence. Grant what you command and command what you will'. In 405 this was quoted at Rome by a bishop condoning Christians of unregenerate sexual life; it caused outrage to *Pelagius, a respected spiritual director. He felt that Augustine's doctrine destroyed human responsibility; if God gives a moral command one cannot say that its keeping is inherently impossible, and while the assistance of grace is necessary, the agent of a moral action has a part to play. Against this, in a vast body of anti-Pelagian writings, Augustine argued that without grace there could be no faith, no act of good will; the catastrophic consequences of Adam's *fall have made humanity corrupt and selfish, locked into a sinful social tradition: therefore the grace needed is more than external instruction and example and has to be the love of God poured into the passive heart by which humanity is enabled to do right because it is then enjoyable. Nevertheless, though Baptism is the sacrament of remission of sins both actual and 'original' (i.e. corporately transmitted from Adam), no believer attains perfection, being tied down by the body's desires. The sexual instinct is never without some flaw of egotism, even if procreative marriage makes good use of it. Even the virtuous actions of good pagans are flawed. That salvation is wholly by grace is the logic of predestination: by an eternal decree antecedent to merit God has shown His mercy in choosing a substantial minority of souls who are granted the gift of perseverance. Augustine sometimes thought it possible that God's decree not only brought the elect to salvation but also consigned the reprobate to hell; more often in his later works he preferred to say that God allowed but did not decree the latter.

During the years of the Pelagian controversy, Augustine was also engaged in writing a massive vindication of Christianity against pagan critics who held that the abandonment of the old gods was responsible for the sack of Rome in 410. The 22 books of *The City of God* appeared in instalments (416–22). The old Republic had been sordid and its religion trivial, and its gods had not delivered the human happiness and order they promised. Augustine then discussed the State under a Christian emperor. He disapproved of torture and capital punishment, though conceding that judges had to punish criminals to protect society; slavery was a symptom of humanity's fallen estate, and in a violent world the Church was called to represent forgiveness and humanity. But the city of God is an otherworldly society towards which one can struggle now to restraining injustice, but which is realized beyond this life. The two 'cities', earthly and heavenly, are distinct.

Augustine's ethic is ascetic. The corruption of society is seen in lust for dehumanizing or degrading entertainments (gladiators killing in the amphitheatre, eroticism in the theatre); in inhuman torture and capital punishment; in war for aggression rather than for self-defence, which he thought 'just' provided also that its end was to achieve fraternal peace with the enemy; in the selfish quest for power, honour, wealth, and sex, though all four could also be used for positive social ends. The root cause of injustice and wrong is the treatment of means as ends and ends as means. We enjoy what we ought only to use and vice versa. The morality of an individual action depends on its intention in the situation, and the one moral absolute is the '*Golden Rule'. The purpose of the conjugal act is procreation, but its use for mutual delight is pardonable. The foundation of Christian marriage is consent, mutual fidelity, and recognition that in God's sight it is indissoluble. The problems of sexuality lie in its involuntary and irrational impulses, from which Adam and Eve in paradise were free.

Between 399 and 419 Augustine wrote *On the Trinity* in 15 books. The central theme is that there is nothing irrational in the notion of being one and three, since being, knowing, and willing are all constitutive of human personality. There are, however, difficulties in using this analogy to understand the relationship of Father, Son, and Holy Spirit, one God yet distinct in their mutual relations. An ascending series of triads culminates in the unity of thought, speech, and will, and in the interpenetration of knowing and loving. Perhaps the Holy Spirit is the bond of love between the Father and the Son. Jn. 20: 22 suggests that the coming forth of the Spirit is from the Father through the Son, and to join the Son with the Father averts an *Arianizing understanding of the Trinity as an unequal Triad. Augustine's speculation, later taken as formal theology, laid the foundation for the *Filioque.

The heart of Augustine's religion is seen in his Tractates on St John's Gospel, his Sermons, esp. on the Psalms, and his Rule for monks and nuns (see following entry). These express not only his spirituality, the yearning (*desiderium*) for God which for him is the hallmark of authentic faith, but also his profound sense of the ecclesial community, the body which with Christ as its head is the *totus Christus*. No scandal is bad enough to make anyone right to leave it. Exegesis of Scripture became increasingly important to Augustine. His treatise *De Doctrina Christiana* sought both to place biblical study in relation to secular culture and to articulate principles of interpretation so that one can discern what is literal and what allegorical. His *Harmony of the Evangelists* answers pagan criticism that the inconsistencies of the Gospels invalidate their authority. Other tracts include *De cura pro mortuis*, arguing that prayer for the faithful departed is right, but that whether they are buried in any particular place is a matter

of indifference; two treatises on lying, which is held to be wrong if intended to deceive and always dangerously likely to diminish respect for the truth; *De bono conjugali*, implicitly rebutting St *Jerome's negative evaluation of marriage and sex; and *Enchiridion*, a handbook of his theology. There are also numerous letters, recently increased by the discoveries of J. Divjak. Near the end of his life he composed a review of his writings (*Retractationes*), partly correcting and partly defending himself. This work, together with the catalogue of his library made by *Possidius, his biographer, gives the chronology and order of his writings, most of which have survived.

Augustine's influence on the course of subsequent theology has been immense. It moulded that of the W. Church in the early Middle Ages, and even the reaction against Augustinianism with the gradual rediscovery of *Aristotle by the 13th cent. was less complete than has often been supposed. The Reformers appealed to elements of Augustine's teaching in their attack on the *Schoolmen, and later the *Jansenists invoked his authority. It is still one of the most potent elements in W. religious thought. Feast day, 28 Aug.

See also CONFESSIONS OF ST AUGUSTINE, DONATISM, MANI AND MANICHAEISM, and PELAGIANISM.

ST AUGUSTINE'S WRITINGS: Earliest are his Dialogues (no doubt an idealization of the actual conversations in which he took part at Cassiciacum), which include *Contra Academicos*, *De Beata Vita*, *De Ordine*, *Soliloquia*, and *De Immortalitate Animae* (all AD 386–7; J. P. Migne, *PL* 32). Among his anti-Manichaean writings are *Acta contra Fortunatum Manichaeum* (392), *Contra Faustum Manichaeum* (33 Bks., 397–8), and *Contra Secundinum Manichaeum* (399), all in *PL* 42; among his works against the Donatists, *Psalmus contra Partem Donati* (394), *Contra Epistolam Parmeniani* (400), *De Baptismo contra Donatistas* (400–1), and *Breviculus Collationis cum Donatistis* (411–12), all in *PL* 43; among those against the Pelagians, *De Peccatorum Meritis et Remissione* (411–12), *De Spiritu et Littera* (412), *De Natura et Gratia* (413–15), *De Gestis Pelagii* (417), *Contra Julianum* (6 Bks., 421), all in *PL* 44; among those against the *Semipelagians, *De Gratia et Libero Arbitrio* (426–7), *De Correptione et Gratia* (426–7), *De Praedestinatione Sanctorum* (428–9), and *De Dono Perseverantiae* (428–9), in *PL* 44 and 45. He also wrote a short general treatise, *De Haeresibus* (428; *PL* 42. 21–50). Of his biblical writings the chief are *De Genesi ad Litteram* (12 Bks., 401–14; *PL* 34), *De Consensu Evangelistarum* (4 Bks., 400; *PL* 34), *Tractatus CXXIV in Joannis Evangelium* (414–416/17) and *Tractatus X in Ep. Joannis* (415–16, both perhaps begun 407–8; *PL* 35), and *Enarrationes in Psalmos* (392–420; *PL* 36–37). His chief dogmatic works include *De Diversis Quaestionibus ad Simplicianum* (396; *PL* 40), *De Trinitate* (15 Bks., 399–419; *PL* 42), *Enchiridion ad Laurentium* (421–3; *PL* 41. 229–90), and *De Civitate Dei* (22 Bks., 416–22; *PL* 41). The *Confessions* are in *PL* 32. 583–656. Augustine also wrote many important letters, nearly all on dogmatic subjects, of which some 250 survive. To his large collection of Sermons many additions have been made in recent times, esp. through the researches of G. *Morin, OSB, C. Lambot, OSB, and A. *Wilmart, OSB. At the end of his life Augustine reviewed his several works in his *Retractationes* (426; *PL* 32. 659–868). For the catalogue of his works by Possidius, see s.v.; also *CPL* (3rd edn., 1995), pp. 97–153 (nos. 250–386).

COLLECTED EDITIONS: First collected edn. of his Works by J. Amerbach (9 vols. Basle, 1506). Other imp. early edns. by *Erasmus (10 vols. Basle, 1528–9) and the 'Theologi Lovanienses' (11 vols., Antwerp, 1577). All previous edns. were superseded by that of the *Maurists (T. Blampin, P. *Constant, and others; 11 vols., Paris, 1679–1700, with valuable index in vol. 11); repr.

frequently, incl. J. P. Migne, *PL* 32–47 (unfortunately with varying pagination in the several Migne reprints); on the Maurist edn. see J. de Ghellinck, SJ, *Patristique et Moyen Age*, 3 (1948), pp. 339–484 (Étude 8: Une Édition patristique célèbre). Since 1887 crit. edn. of individual works in the CSEL (some items, however, not up to the usual standard of this series); also in CCSL 27–57, 1954 ff., and, with Fr. tr., under the auspices of the Augustinians of Paris, Bibliothèque Augustinienne, 1936 ff.

Eng. trs. in the *Library of the Fathers by M. Dods, by P. *Schaff in 'Nicene and Post Nicene Christian Fathers' (8 vols., 1887–92) and by various contributors in 'Fathers of the Church' (1948 ff.) and in 'Ancient Christian Writers' (1949 ff).

LIVES: Contemporary Life by his friend and disciple, Possidius, Bp. of Calama (q.v.). Classic Life in edn. Ben. (repr. *PL* 32. 65–578). Le N. *Tillemont, *Mémoires pour servir à l'Histoire Ecclés.*, 13 (2nd edn., 1710). Modern Lives by G. Bardy (Montpellier, 1940), G. [I.] Bonner (1963; repr., Norwich, 1986), P. [R. L.] Brown (London, 1967), A. Mandouze (Paris, 1968) and J. J. O'Donnell (Boston, Mass. [1985]).

STUDIES ON HIS EARLY CHRISTIAN PERIOD: P. Alfaric, *L'Évolution intellectuelle de S. Augustin*. 1: *Du manichéisme au néoplationisme* (all pub., 1918); C. Boyer, SJ, *Christianisme et néoplatonisme dans la formation de Saint Augustin* (1921); J. Nörregaard, *Augustins Bekehrung* (Tübingen, 1923); A. Pincherle, *La formazione teologica di Sant'Agostino* [1947]; P. Courcelle, *Recherches sur les 'Confessions' de S. Augustin* (1950; 2nd edn., 1968); M. Testard, *S. Augustin et Cicéron* (2 vols., 1958); R. Holte, *Béatitude et sagesse* (1962); O. du Roy, *L'Intelligence de la foi en la Trinité selon Saint Augustin* (1966); R. J. O'Connell, *Saint Augustine's Early Theory of Man* (Cambridge, Mass., 1968). E. Feldmann, *Der Einfluss des Hortensius und des Manichäismus auf das Denken des jungen Augustinus von 373* (Dissertation, 2 vols., Münster, 1975).

EDITIONS AND MONOGRAPHS ON INDIVIDUAL TREATISES: These include (1) *De Civitate Dei*: Ed. princeps, Subiaco, 1467. Ed. J. E. C. Welldon (2 vols., London, 1924). Eng. tr. by H. Bettenson (Harmondsworth, 1972). J. N. *Figgis, *The Political Aspects of St Augustine's 'City of God'* (1921); H. S. Burleigh, *The City of God: A study of St Augustine's Philosophy* (1949); R. H. Barrow, *Introduction to St Augustine 'The City of God'* (1950); H. I. Marrou, *L'Ambivalence du Temps de l'Histoire chez Saint Augustin* (1950); F. G. Maier, *Augustin und das antike Rom* (Tübinger Beiträge zur Altertumswissenschaft, 39; 1955); A. Wachtel, *Beiträge zur Geschichtstheologie des Aurelius Augustinus* (Bonner historische Forschungen, 17; 1960); J. C. Guy, SJ, *Unité et structure logique de la 'Cité de Dieu' de saint Augustin* (1961); P. R. L. Brown, 'Saint Augustine', in B. Smalley (ed.), *Trends in Medieval Political Thought* (Oxford, 1965), pp. 1–21; U. Duchrow, *Christenheit und Weltverantwortung* (Forschungen und Berichte der Evangelistischen Studiengemeinschaft, 25; Stuttgart, 1970; 2nd edn., 1983); G. Corcoran, *St Augustine on Slavery* (Studia Ephemeridis 'Augustinianum', 22; Rome, 1985); J. van Oort, *Jerusalem and Babylon* (Supplements to *VC*, 14; 1991).
(2) Sermons: C. Morin, OSB (ed.), *Sermones post Maurinos reperti* (Miscellanea Agostiniana, 1; Rome 1930); C. Lambot, OSB (ed.), *Sermones selecti* (Stromata patristica et mediaevalia, 1; Utrecht and Brussels, 1950); F. Dolbeau, 'Nouveaux sermons de saint Augustin pour la conversion des païens et des donatistes', *Revue des Études Augustiniennes*, 37 (1991), pp. 37–77 and 261–306. C. Mohrmann, *Die altchristliche Sondersprache in den Sermones des hl. Augustin* (Latinitas Christianorum primaeva, 3; 1932). M. Pontet, *L'Exégèse de S. Augustin prédicateur* (Théologie, 7; 1945); B. Blumenkranz, *Die Judenpredigt Augustins* (Basler Beiträge zur Geschichtswissenschaft, 25; 1946); A. M. La Bonnardière, *Recherches de chronologie augustinienne* (1965). P. P. Verbraken, OSB, *Études critiques sur les sermones authentiques de saint Augustin* (Instrumenta Patristica, 12; 1976).
(3) Epistles: Excellent edn. by A. Goldbacher in CSEL 34 (1), 1895; 34 (2), 1898; 44, 1904; 57, 1911. Further letters ed. J. Divjak (ibid. 88, 1981; rev. edn., with Fr. tr., as *Œuvres de Saint Augustin*,

46B; Bibliothèque Augustinienne, 1987); cf. H. Chadwick, 'New Letters of St Augustine', *JTS* NS 34 (1983), pp. 425–52. Eng. tr. of new letters by R. B. Eno, SS (Fathers of the Church, 81; 1989).

ON HIS PLACE IN THE HISTORY OF WESTERN CIVILIZATION: cf. E. *Troeltsch, *Augustin, die christliche Antike und das Mittelalter im Anschluss an die Schrift*, De Civitate Dei (1915); E. Przywara, SJ (ed.), *Augustinus: Die Gestalt als Gefüge* (Leipzig, 1934), introd. repr. separately as *Augustinisch: Ur-Haltung des Geistes* (Kriterien, 17; Einsiedeln [1970]); H. I. Marrou, *St Augustin et la fin de la culture antique* (1938); id., *Saint Augustin et l'Augustinisme* (1955; Eng. tr., 1957); H. Hagendahl, *Augustine and the Latin Classics* (Studia Graeca et Latina Gothoburgensia, 20; 2 vols., 1967).

ON HIS THEOLOGY AND OUTLOOK: O. Rottmanner, *Der Augustinismus* (1892); K. *Adam, *Die Eucharistielehre des hl. Augustin* (1908); J. Mausbach, *Die Ethik des hl. Augustinus* (2 vols., 1909); T. A. *Lacey, *Nature, Miracle and Sin: A Study of St Augustine's Conception of the Natural Order* (1916); P. *Batiffol, *Le Catholicisme de S. Augustin* (2 vols., 1920); E. *Gilson, *Introduction à l'étude de saint Augustin* (Études de philosophie médiévale, 11; 1929; 2nd edn., 1943; Eng. tr., New York, 1960; London, 1961); *A Monument to St Augustine* (by various authors, London, 1930); J. Burnaby, *Amor Dei: A Study of the Religion of St Augustine* (1938; repr., Norwich, 1991); F. van der Meer, *Augustinus de Zielzorger* (1947; Eng. tr., 1961); T. J. van Bavel, OESA, *Recherches sur la Christologie de saint Augustin* (Paradosis, 10; Fribourg, Switzerland, 1954); J. Ratzinger, *Volk und Haus Gottes in Augustins Lehre von der Kirche* (Münchener Theologische Studien, 2. Systematische Abteilung, 7; 1954); G. Nygren, *Das Prädestinationsproblem in der Theologie Augustins* (Forschungen zur Kirchen- und Dogmengeschichte, 5; 1956); H. A. Deane, *The Political and Social Ideas of St Augustine* (New York and London 1963); R. A. Markus, *Saeculum: History and Society in the Theology of St Augustine* (Cambridge, 1970); E. TeSelle, *Augustine the Theologian* (1970); J. Pépin, *Saint Augustin et la dialectique* (Saint Augustine Lecture, 1972; Villanova, Pa., 1976). W. Wieland, *Offenbarung bei Augustinus* (Tübinger theologische Studien, 12; 1978); O. [M. T.] O'Donovan, *The Problem of Self-Love in St Augustine* (New Haven, Conn., and London [1980]); K. Flasch, *Augustin: Einführung in sein Denken* (Stuttgart, 1980); G. O'Daly, *Augustine's Philosophy of Mind* (1987); C. Kirwan, *Augustine* (London and New York, 1989); G. Madec, AA, *La Patrie et la Voie: Le Christ dans la vie et la pensée de S. Augustin* (1989); J. M. Rist, *Augustine: Ancient thought baptised* (Cambridge, 1994). Introd. by H. Chadwick, *Augustine* (Past Masters; Oxford, 1986). C. Mayer (ed.), *Augustinus-Lexikon* (Basle and Stuttgart, 1086 ff.).

C. Andresen, *Bibliographia Augustiniana* (Darmstadt, 1962; 2nd edn., 1973); T. van Bavel, OESA, *Répertoire Bibliographique de Saint Augustin 1950–1960* (Instrumenta Patristica, 3; The Hague, 1963); T. L. Miethe, *Augustinian Bibliography, 1970–1980* (Westport, Conn., and London, 1982). Current literature is noted in *Revue des études augustiniennes* (1955 ff.).

Of the arts. in all dictionaries and encyclopaedic works, one of the fullest is that by E. Portalié, *DTC* 1 (1903), cols. 2268–472, with bibl.; separate Eng. tr. by R. J. Bastian, SJ, *A Guide to the Thought of St Augustine* (1960).

Augustine of Hippo, Rule of St.

Augustine of Hippo, Rule of St. A title applied to various monastic texts whose precise relationship has long been a matter of dispute. Despite various permutations in different MSS, there appear to be three main texts: (1) the *Ordo Monasterii* (Regulations for a Monastery, or System), (2) the *Praeceptum* (Precept), and (3) St *Augustine's *Epistula* 211, paragraphs 5–16, which is closely parallel to the *Praeceptum*, but addressed to women, whereas the *Praeceptum* is addressed to men. While Augustine's interest in monasticism is clear both from the *Confessions* and *Possidius' Life, the absence of any reference to a separate Rule in the *Retractationes* has cast doubts upon his authorship of some of the documents. *Erasmus suggested that the Rule was first written for women and adapted for men. In modern times Luc Verheijen has proposed an ingenious solution, that at Hippo Augustine founded two monasteries, one for priests for whom the *Praeceptum* was composed; the other for brothers who were to follow his *Ordo*; this idea has not won universal acceptance.

After monastic life in N. Africa died out, the Rule was little used until it was adopted at the end of the 11th cent. by the *Augustinian Canons. At a time when the Papacy was insisting that newly founded religious orders should take existing rules, the Rule of St Augustine, with its sanity and adaptability, was accepted by the *Dominicans, the *Augustinian Hermits or Friars, and the *Servites; it was later adopted by the *Ursuline and *Visitation nuns.

Crit. edn. of all the Latin texts, with full discussion, by L. Verheijen, OSA, *Le Règle de saint Augustin* (Études Augustiniennes, 2 vols., 1967). Lat. text of *Ordo Monasterii, Praeceptum*, and Augustine's *Ep.* 211 are repr., with Eng. tr., and full discussion, in G. [P.] Lawless, OSA, *Augustine of Hippo and his Monastic Rule* (Oxford, 1987). Further Eng. tr. of the *Praeceptum* by R. Canning, OSA, with comm. by T. J. van Bavel, OSA (London, 1984). A. Zumkeller, OSA, *Das Mönchtum des heiligen Augustinus* (Cassiciacum, 11; 1950; 2nd edn., 1968; Eng. tr., New York, 1986). Agatha Mary [Crabb], SPB, *The Rule of St Augustine: An Essay in Understanding* (Villanova, Pa., 1992).

Augustinian Canons. (They were also known as **Austin**, or **Black**, or **Regular Canons**). Though the ideal of the *Canons Regular had been foreshadowed by various attempts in the early Church to establish a full common life for houses of clerks (notably that by St *Augustine of Hippo), as a family of religious in the W. Church they date from the first years of the movement later known as the Gregorian Reform.

Their origin is to be found in certain communities of clerks in N. Italy and the S. of France, who in the middle decades of the 11th cent. sought to live the common life of poverty, celibacy, and obedience, in accordance with what they believed to be the example of the early Christians. Their way of life received official approval at *Lateran synods in 1059 and 1063 and in the following cent. was widely adopted in W. Europe. By the opening decades of the 12th cent., members of these communities had come to be known as 'regular canons' (*canonici regulares*) and had generally adopted the Rule of St Augustine (which half a cent. before was almost unknown to them; see previous entry). From now on a regular canon is almost synonymous with an Augustinian canon, i.e. one who follows the Rule of St Augustine. From the early 12th cent., a number of independent Augustinian congregations were established, of which some of the more influential, e.g. the *Victorines and the *Premonstratensians, were much influenced by *Cistercian customs. In subsequent times Augustinian canons suffered considerably from the disorders and changes of the later Middle Ages and the disturbances of the *Reformation, and many houses were suppressed and replaced by other orders, esp. the *clerks regular. But certain of the older congregations still survive in the RC Church, notably the 'Canons Regular of the Lateran' (CRL), whom Pope *Alexander II (1061–73) instituted in his cathedral church.

Of clerical origin, the Augustinian canons were liable to episcopal visitation and able to undertake parochial responsibilities, though this was a privilege of which they did not always make extensive use in the Middle Ages. The flexibility of their rule enabled regular canons to follow various vocations, active and contemplative. They had a notable connection with hospitals; in London St Bartholomew's and St Thomas's Hospitals were formerly both Augustinian houses.

E. Amort, *Vetus Disciplina Canonicorum Regularium et Secularium ex Documentis magna parte hucusque ineditis a Temporibus Apostolicis usque ad Saeculum xvii critice et moraliter expensa* (2 vols., Venice, 1747). *La vita comune del clero nei secoli XI e XII* (Miscellanea del Centro di Studi Medioevali, 3; Pubblicazioni dell'Università Cattolica del S. Cuore, 3rd ser. 2; 2 vols., Milan, 1962); C. D. Fonseca, *Medioevo Canonicale* (ibid. 12; 1970). H. E. Salter (ed.), *Chapters of the Augustinian Canons* (Canterbury and York Society, 29; 1922). J. C. Dickinson, *The Origins of the Austin Canons and their Introduction into England* (CHS, 1950). N. Widloecher, *La Congregazione dei Canonici Regolari Lateranensi: Periodo di Formazione (1402–1483)* (Gubbio, 1929). C. Dereine, SJ, 'Vie commune, règle de Saint Augustin et chanoines réguliers au XI⁴ siècle', *RHE* 41 (1946), pp. 365–406. C. W. Bynum, *Jesus as Mother: Studies in the Spirituality of the High Middle Ages* (Publications of the Center for Medieval and Renaissance Studies, UCLA, 16; Berkeley, Calif., etc. [1982]), pp. 22–58. J. C. Dickinson in *NCE* 3 (1967), pp. 62–4, s.v. 'Canons Regular of St Augustine'; C. Egger, CRL, in *DIP* 2 (1975), cols. 46–63, s.v. 'Canonici Regolari', with bibl.

Augustinian Hermits or Friars. A religious order living according to the Rule of St *Augustine of Hippo. In 1244 *Innocent IV directed the Tuscan hermits to accept this Rule, which had already been adopted by the Zanbonini in 1225 and the Brettini in 1228; in 1256 Pope Alexander IV united these three congregations (and certain others who seceded soon afterwards) to form the Friars Hermit from whom the present-day order descends. It was formerly thought that they then also received the Dominican 'Constitutions', but there is no evidence for this theory. The hermits had settled in remote places; while the friars did not abandon these settlements, they soon tended to concentrate their work in towns, and became widely established in W. Europe. The later Middle Ages saw the rise of certain local reformed congregations, such as that of Saxony (1419–1560), to which M. *Luther belonged. The friars suffered considerably from the effects of the *Reformation and the secularizations of later times, but they still survive, notably in Europe, N. and S. America, and in the *Philippines. They undertake extensive pastoral, educational, and missionary work. The 'Augustinian *Recollects' (q.v.) and the 'Discalced Augustinians', who were of Silician origin and founded in 1593, are reformed congregations.

L. Empoli, OESA (ed.), *Bullarium Ordinis Eremitarum S. Augustini, in quo plures Constitutiones Apostolicae . . . ab Innocentio Tertio usque ad Urbanum Octavum ad eundem spectantes collectae sunt* (Rome, 1628). B. [A. L.] van Luijk, OSA (ed.), *Bullarium Ordinis Eremitarum S. Augustini: Periodus formationis 1187–1256* (Cassiciacum, 18; Würzburg, 1964). I. Arambury Cendoya, OSA (ed.), *Las primitivas constituciones de los Agustinos (Ratisbonenses del año 1290)* (Valladolid, 1966). Henry of Friemar [c. 1243–1340], 'Treatise on the Origin and Development of the Order of the Hermit Friars and its true and real title', ed. R. Arbesmann, OSA, *Augustiniana*, 6 (1956), pp. 37–145. Jordan of Saxony [c.1299–c.1370 or 1380], *Liber Vitasfratrum*, ed. id. and W. Hümpfner, OSA (Cassiciacum, 1; New York, 1943). An official history of the Order is being pub.: D. Gutiérrez [Moran],

OSA, *Los Agustinos en la edad media 1256–1356* (Rome, 1980; Eng. tr., Villanova, Pa., 1984); id., *Los Agustinos en la edad media 1357–1517* (1977; Eng. tr., 1983); *Los Agustinos desde el protestantismo hasta la restauración católica 1518–1648* (1971; Eng. tr., 1979); J. J. Gavigan, *The Augustinians from the French Revolution to the Present* (1989). B. A. L. van Luijk, OSA, *L'Ordine Agostiniano e la riforma monastica dal Cinquecento alla vigilia della Rivoluzione Francese* (Heverlee and Louvain, 1973). M. Elm, 'Italienische Eremitengemeinschaften des 12. und 13. Jahrhunderts. Studien zur Vorgeschichte des Augustiner-Eremitenordens', *L'Eremitismo in Occidente nei Secoli XI e XII: Atti della seconda Settimana internazionale di studio Mendola, 30 agosto–6 settembre 1962* (Pubblicazioni dell'Università Cattolica del Sacro Cuore, Miscellanea del Centro di Studi Medioevali, 4; 1965), pp. 491–559. F. Roth, OSA, 'Cardinal Richard Annibaldi, first Protector of the Augustinian Order, 1243–1276', *Augustiniana*, 2 (1952), pp. 26–60, 108–49, 230–47; 3 (1953), pp. 21–34, 283–313; 4 (1954), pp. 5–24. Id., *The English Austin Friars 1249–1538* (Cassiciacum, 6–7; New York, 1961–6). A. Gwynn, SJ, *The English Austin Friars in the Time of Wyclif* (1940). D. A. Perini, OESA, *Bibliographia Augustiniana, cum notis biographicis: Scriptores Itali* (4 pts. [1929]–1937). E. Gindele and others, *Bibliographie zur Geschichte und Theologie des Augustiner-Eremitenordens bis zum Beginn der Reformation* (Spätmittelalter und Reformation. Texte und Untersuchungen, 1; 1977). M. T. Disdier, AA, in *DHGE* 5 (1930), cols. 499–595, s.v. 'Augustin (1er Ordre dit de Saint) (Érémites)', with full bibl.; B. Rano [Gundin], OSA, in *DIP* 1 (1974), cols. 278–381, s.v. 'Agostiniani'; separate Eng. tr., *The Order of Saint Augustine* (Rome, 1975). A. Zumkeller, OSA, in *TRE* 4 (1979), pp. 728–39, s.v. 'Augustiner-Eremiten', with bibl.

Augustinians of the Assumption. See ASSUMPTIONISTS.

Augustinus. The title of the treatise by C. O. *Jansen (d. 1638) on grace and human nature, as presented in the works of St *Augustine. Based upon his anti-*Pelagian writings, and embodying many of the conclusions of M. *Baius, it was directed against the neo-scholastic theologians. It was published in 1640 and became the accepted exposition of the dogmatic principles of *Jansenism.

After the 'privilège' necessary for publication had been granted on 13 Feb. 1640, the work appeared at Louvain in Aug. of the same year (repr., Paris, 1641, and Rouen, 1643). N. [J.] Abercrombie, *The Origins of Jansenism* (Oxford, 1936), esp. pp. 125–58. J. Carreyre in *DTC* 8 (pt. 1; 1924), cols. 330–448, s.v. 'Jansénisme', gives full analysis. See also other items cited s.v. JANSENISM, esp. arts. by L. Ceyssens, OFM.

Aulén, Gustaf (1879–1977), Bp. of Strängnäs. He was appointed professor of systematic theology of the University of *Lund in 1913. From 1933 to 1952 he was Bp. of Strängnäs. With A. Nygren (1890–1978), he was a leader of the *Motivsforschung* school, which sought to see the essential Christian truth behind a doctrine rather than to stress the actual form in which it is presented. The main works of his early period are *Den allmänneliga kristna tron* ('The Faith of the Christian Church', 1923; Eng. tr. 1948), *Den kristna gudsbilden* ('The Christian Idea of God', 1927), and his Olaus *Petri Lectures for 1930, published as *Den kristna försoningstanken* ('The Christian Idea of the Atonement'), of which an abridged version in English was produced by A. G. Hebert under the title of *Christus Victor* (1931). In these lectures Aulén defended a modified version of the 'ransom to the devil' theory of the *Atonement. After his retirement he continued to write on many topics. Though he did not change his theological position in its

essentials, his later writings laid more stress on the elements of coherence and continuity in doctrine, and on the historical trustworthiness of the Gospel record. These later writings include *Reformation och katolicitet* ('Reformation and Catholicity', 1959; Eng. tr. 1961), *Jesus i nutida historisk forskning* ('Jesus in Contemporary Research', 1973; Eng. tr. 1976), and his autobiography, *Från mina nittiosex år* (1975).

Scripta Minora Regiae Societatis Humaniorum Litterarum Lundensis, 1978–1979: In memoriam Gustavi Aulén (1979), incl. list of his works by K. Gierow and P. Ekström [separate pagination].

aumbry (also **ambry**). A small recess in the wall of a church or sacristy in which, in medieval times, sacred vessels, books, and sometimes, but not usually, the reserved Sacrament might be kept. Its use for the last-named purpose was formerly forbidden by the RC Church, but it has long been common in the Anglican Communion.

G. *Dix, *A Detection of Aumbries* (1942); E. Maffei, *La Réservation eucharistique jusqu'à la Renaissance* (1942); S. J. P. van Dijk, OFM, and J. H. Walker, *The Myth of the Aumbry* (1957; critique of G. Dix).

Aurelius, St (d. *c.*430), Bp. of *Carthage from *c.*391. He presided over a long series of ecclesiastical councils, mostly at Carthage. Some of the letters addressed to him by St *Augustine (Aug., *epp.* 22, 41, 60, 174), who held him in high honour, survive. Feast day, 20 July.

AASS, Oct. 11 (1864), pp. 852–60. A. Mandouze, *Prosopographie Chrétienne du Bas-Empire*, 1: *Prosopographie de l'Afrique Chrétienne (303–533)* (1982), pp. 105–27. A. Audollent in *DHGE* 5 (1930), cols. 726–38, s.v., with bibl.

aureole (Lat. *aureolus*, 'golden'). In sacred pictures, the background of gold, typifying glory, which often surrounds the figure, as distinct from the 'nimbus' (or halo), which covers only the head.

auricular confession. Confession 'to the ear' [Lat. *ad auriculam*, sc. of a priest], i.e. the confession of sins to God in the presence of a priest authorized to forgive them in His name. See also PENANCE.

Ausculta fili (Lat., 'Listen, my son'). The opening words (1) of the Rule of St *Benedict and (2) of *Boniface VIII's bull of 5 Dec. 1301 to Philip the Fair of France.

Ausonius (*c.*310–*c.*395), Roman poet. Decimus Magnus Ausonius was a native of Burdigala (Bordeaux), where he established a school of rhetoric. About 365 he became tutor to the future Emp. Gratian, who in 379 raised him to the consulship. To judge by a few of his poems, he made at least some profession of Christianity in his mature years, though the letters (in verse) which he addressed to his former pupil, *Paulinus of Nola, to dissuade him from his project of giving up his wealth to the poor and becoming a monk, reveal little of the Christian ascetic ideal. Of his 'Epigrams', three—the 'Versus paschales pro Augusto', the 'Oratio Matutina', and the 'Oratio versibus rhopalicis'—are ostensibly the work of an orthodox Christian. Of his many secular poems, perhaps the most successful was his 'Mosella', a poem describing the region of the Moselle and the city of Trier.

Ed. princeps, Venice, 1472. Crit. edns. by C. Schenkl (*MGH*, Auct. Ant. 5. 2; 1883), R. Peiper (Teub., 1886), S. Prete (ibid., 1978; cf. M. D. Reeve in *Gnomon*, 52 (1980), pp. 444–51), R. H. P. Green (Oxford, 1991, with introd., comm., and extensive bibl.), and, with Eng. tr., by H. G. E. White (Loeb, 2 vols., 1919–21). J. Fontaine, 'Unité et diversité du mélange des genres et des tons chez quelques écrivains latins de la fin du IVe siècle: Ausone, Ambroise, Ammien', in M. Fuhrmann (ed.), *Christianisme et Formes littéraires de l'Antiquité tardive en Occident* (Fondation Hardt Entretiens sur l'Antiquité classique, 23; 1977), pp. 425–82, repr. in id., *Études sur la poesie latine tardive d'Ausone à Prudence* (1980), pp. 25–82. N. K. Chadwick, *Poetry and Letters in Early Christian Gaul* (1955), pp. 47–62 (ch. 2: 'Ausonius and his circle'). J. [F.] Matthews, *Western Aristocracies and the Imperial Court A.D. 364–425* (Oxford, 1975), pp. 51–5, 69–87, and 150–3. Bardenhewer, 3, pp. 436–40; Altaner and Stuiber (1978), pp. 406 f. and 634 f.

Austin. An older English form of '*Augustine*'.

Australia, Christianity in. When the British Government founded a convict colony in New South Wales in 1788, the C of E was given land for schools and churches and in many ways enjoyed official status. In 1836 W. G. Broughton (1788–1853), Archdeacon of New South Wales since 1829, was consecrated the first Anglican bishop. However, almost from the beginning of the settlement, there were adherents of other denominations, and in the interests of maintaining social order and morality the colonial government generally encouraged their worship and from the 1820s paid their clergy. The large number of RC convicts were served, first by convict priests, then by official chaplains, and, after 1833, by missionary priests who included W. B. *Ullathorne and J. B. Polding (1794–1877), a scholarly monk from *Downside sent to Australia as the first RC bishop in 1835. The *London Missionary Society supported *Congregational preachers in and around Sydney from 1798. The first *Methodist minister, S. Leigh (1785–1852), arrived in 1815. The *Presbyterians, mostly Scottish free settlers, from 1823 were ministered to by the fiery preacher and politician, J. D. Lang (1799–1878), and during the 1830s *Baptists began work in Sydney. In 1836 South Australia was established as a separate colony to encourage the free settlement of dissenters, amongst whom were *Lutheran refugees from Prussia who helped to build up the region's wine industry. Denominational conflict was endemic as each group resisted the others' religious teaching and social advancement. The claims of the C of E to the status of an established Church exacerbated the Irish nationalism of many RCs and the opposition of Presbyterians. All denominations were suspicious of any real or imagined attempt by each other to gain special status.

Various denominational missions to the Aboriginal people were established, including that of Spanish *Benedictine monks in W. Australia in 1846, but few Aborigines were baptized. Their religion is unwritten, closely tied to the land and to tribal life, and not easily related to W. Christian notions of sin and salvation. However, as tribal life and traditional religion disintegrated, Aborigines were gradually drawn into Christianity.

During the 19th cent., esp. after the gold rushes of the 1850s, the spread of secular views led to the withdrawal of state aid to religion. During the 1870s state school systems were established to provide 'free, compulsory and secular' education, though the RC Church maintained its own schools and all the major Churches kept a small number of élite grammar schools and university colleges. After 1880 evangelical piety underwent a decline in both urban and rural areas, esp. in the Congregational Church, though attendant moralistic attitudes ('wowserism') survived as a social force. In the same period the social work of the *Salvation Army enabled it to establish a presence in areas of urban poverty. By the early 20th cent. most denominations had a majority of Australian-born clergy. They established theological colleges and attempted to tackle the problems presented by the vast inland distances: Anglican Bush Brothers, notably the Brotherhood of the Good Shepherd (1903–72), ministered to the outback by horse, car, and aeroplane, and in 1912 the Presbyterian Church founded the Australian Inland Mission, which later began a 'flying doctor' service. Many Australian denominations also undertook missionary work in the *South Pacific, *India, *Korea, and East Africa.

In the 1914–18 war the allied cause was supported by Church leaders in what was regarded as a war in defence of civilization and Christianity, though there was anti-British feeling amongst some Irish RCs, and Abp. D. Mannix (Abp. of Melbourne, 1917–63) strongly opposed conscription. After 1918 there was a gradual change of emphasis from denominational issues to the wider problems and social concerns of Australian society. Councils of Churches were established in the various states, where they pursued matters of public morality and social need—though rarely theological questions. The economic depression of the 1930s further stimulated the Churches to become more directly involved in social and political affairs. From 1940 the RC bishops issued an annual Social Justice Statement and a committee of the General Synod of the C of E set up the Christian Social Order Movement (1943–51).

After 1945, there were changes. Denominational traditions became more consciously Australian, and in 1981 the C of E became the Anglican Church in Australia. In 1977 the Methodist Church, most Congregationalists, and a majority of Presbyterians joined to form the Uniting Church in Australia. Migration brought large numbers of European RCs, esp. from Italy. There also now exist substantial Greek, Russian, and other national Orthodox communities which have maintained strong cultural identities with an Australian flavour and which have an active laity. Since the 1960s denominational conflict has lessened and been generally replaced by much practical co-operation. In 1977 an interdenominational *Australian Hymn Book* was published. This is widely used outside Australia under the title *With One Voice*.

The diminishing antagonism between the denominations has been balanced by an increase of conflict within them. During the 1950s RCs were divided over the active involvement of anti-communist religious groups in the affairs of trade unions and politics. Since the 1960s there have been strong debates within each denomination over questions of personal morality and social problems, esp. poverty, and the appropriate political role of Christians. Amongst Anglicans the question of the ordination of *women to the priesthood has been divisive, with the problem being compounded by the virtual autonomy of each diocese. The first women priests were ordained in 1992.

During the 1980s some Australian Christians campaigned for Aboriginal welfare and land rights. Aboriginal and white writers and artists have fostered an understanding of Aboriginal spirituality as another element in Australian Christianity.

At the 1991 census 27 per cent of Australians described themselves as RC, 24 per cent as Anglican, 8 per cent Uniting Church, 4 per cent (continuing) Presbyterian, and 3 per cent Orthodox. The *Pentecostal Churches and similar charismatic groups, many with strong American influence, are growing rapidly.

R. A. Giles, *The Constitutional History of the Australian Church* (1929); [J. T.] R. Border, *Church and State in Australia 1788–1872: A Constitutional Study of the Church of England in Australia* (1962). D. [L.] Hilliard, *Godliness and Good Order: A History of the Anglican Church in South Australia* (Netley, SA, 1986); R. A. F. Webb, *Brothers in the Sun: A History of the Bush Brotherhood Movement in the Outback of Australia* (Adelaide, 1978); S. Judd and K. [J.] Cable, *Sydney Anglicans: A History of the Diocese* (Sydney, 1987). P. F. Moran, *History of the Catholic Church in Australasia* (Sydney [1895]); P. [J.] O'Farrell, *The Catholic Church in Australia. A Short History: 1788–1967* (Melbourne, 1968; London, 1969; 3rd edn., entitled *The Catholic Church and Community*, Sydney, 1985); E. Campion, *Australian Catholics* (Ringwood, Victoria, 1978); R. Fogarty, FMS, *Catholic Education in Australia 1806–1950* (2 vols., Carlton, Victoria, 1959); T. [C.] Truman, *Catholic Action and Politics* (Melbourne, 1959; rev. edn., London, 1960). A. D. Hunt, *This Side of Heaven: A History of Methodism in South Australia* (Adelaide, 1985). M. Owen (ed.), *Witness of Faith: Historic Documents of the Uniting Church in Australia* (Melbourne, 1984). J. Barrett, *That Better Country: The Religious Aspect of Life in Eastern Australia, 1835–1850* (Carlton, Victoria, and London, 1966); H. R. Jackson, *Churches and People in Australia and New Zealand, 1860–1930* (Sydney, 1987); W. Phillips, *Defending 'A Christian Country': Churchmen and Society in New South Wales in the 1880s and After* (Brisbane, 1981); J. S. Gregory, *Church and State: Changing Government Policies towards Religion in Australia* (Melbourne, 1973); M. C. Hogan, *The Sectarian Strand: Religion in Australian History* (Ringwood, Victoria, 1987); T. W. Swain and D. B. Rose, (eds.), *Aboriginal Australians and Christian Missions: Ethnographic and Historical Studies* (Bedford Park, SA, 1988); H. Mol, *The Faith of Australians* (Studies in Society, 25; Sydney and London, 1985); I. Gillman (ed.), *Many Faiths, One Nation: A Guide to the Major Faiths and Denominations in Australia* (Sydney [1988]). Information on prominent religious figures is to be found in *Australian Dictionary of Biography* (Carlton, Victoria, and London, 1966 ff.).

authority. The power or right to persuade individuals or groups to obey precepts or recommendations. In the State, the coercive power of the government can ensure compliance, and in the period when the Church was identified with organized society, Church authority was enforced with temporal penalties. In the Christian community authority operates on the ground of an appeal to individual *conscience, with the understanding that deviation from what is acceptable to the community, in faith or morals, may entail exclusion or spiritual censure. An individual accepts authority without necessarily discerning the grounds of a ruling, because he acknowledges that private reason is seldom fully informed, may be led by unconscious egocentricity into defending an opinion for reasons other than its evident truth, and may be insensitive to the experience and wisdom of other believers. Obedience enters into the primary act of believing which submits to divine *grace and *revelation.

For Christians the ultimate authority is God, revealed in Jesus Christ and His redeeming work, experienced and interpreted by the community of His disciples. The NT writings presuppose the authority of Jesus and also of the Christian community's interpretation both of His teaching and of the OT as fulfilled in Him. For this community the Jesus of history is the Christ of faith, immanent in His Church by the Holy Spirit, but also the Church's judge and Lord. Error in the earliest traditions behind the Gospels becomes problematic for authority only if it is held that the Apostles completely misunderstood Him.

Within the Church an exclusive stress on authority in belief has sometimes failed to leave room for rational understanding of the faith. Apart from this central issue, there are four main polarities on the role of authority in Christian thought: (1) between the individual and the community, where the deeper the sense of human sin and blindness, the stronger the dependence on Church and Bible; (2) between charismatic, immediate prophetic inspiration and a mediated or transmitted authority, in which the pastor's commission to minister word and sacrament depends on the juridical *validity of the *Orders of the person who ordained him; (3) between Scripture and the interpreting consensus of the community if and when the natural sense of Scripture asks for correction in the life and tradition of the community—a tension which can lead to the divorce of biblical study from faith; (4) between the guiding hand of the clergy and the general consent of the laity—a polarity which becomes sharp if the clergy are regarded as a radically separate order independent of lay people whose role is to be receptive and passive, but no less sharp if the laity, in affirming the priestliness of the total body of believers, fails to acknowledge a special mandate in the pastorate entrusted with a commission to minister *absolution and *blessing and to safeguard the celebration of the sacraments. Related to this last issue is the historic W. tension between the collective or collegial voice of the episcopate as a whole and the primatial independence of the Roman see. For the RC Church this was decided in favour of the Pope, as independent of the collective mind of the bishops, at the first *Vatican Council (1870); at the second Vatican Council this was partially balanced by the decree 'Lumen Gentium' (1964), which enshrined the principle of *collegiality, recognizing the bishops' shared responsibility. As yet this conception does not seem to have greatly influenced RC practice or thinking. Whereas Orthodox and Anglicans think of major Councils as decision-making bodies, for RCs they are expressions of Christian opinion to advise the Pope who gives the authoritative ruling. Connected with this polarity is the question whether teaching authority needs to be linked with power in the form of centralized bureaucratic control or universal jurisdiction.

Church authority has been enforced in the past by temporal penalties, but it is now generally imposed, as in primitive times before the conversion of the Roman Empire, by spiritual censures alone, esp. that of *excommunication.

See also ANGLICAN–ROMAN CATHOLIC INTERNATIONAL COMMISSION, CONCILIAR MOVEMENT, INFALLIBILITY, and OECUMENICAL COUNCILS.

J. *Martineau, *The Seat of Authority in Religion* (1890); A. *Sabatier, *Les Religions d'autorité et la religion de l'esprit* (1903; Eng. tr., 1904); P. T. *Forsyth, *The Principle of Authority in Relation to Certainty, Sanctity and Society* ([1913]; 2nd edn., 1952); A. E. J. Rawlinson, *Authority and Freedom* (1924); T. A. *Lacey, *Authority in the Church: A Study of Principles* (1928); H. von Campenhausen, *Kirchliches Amt und geistliche Vollmacht in der ersten drei Jahrhunderten* (Beiträge zur historischen Theologie, 14; 1953, Eng. tr., 1969); J. M. Todd (ed.), *Problems of Authority* (1962); N. [L. A.] Lash, *Voices of Authority* (1976); G. Philips, *Primauté et Collégialité: Le dossier . . . sur la Nota Explicativa Praevia (Lumen Gentium, Chap. III)*, ed. J. Grootaers (Bibliotheca Ephemeridum Theologicarum Lovaniensium, 72; 1986); G. R. Evans, *Problems of Authority in the Reformation Debates* (Cambridge, 1992). See also bibl. to BIBLE (section on Authority and Inspiration); also CHURCH.

Authorized Version of the Bible. At the *Hampton Court Conference (1604) Dr John *Rainolds (or Reynolds, 1549–1607), the *Puritan President of Corpus Christi College, Oxford, suggested that there should be a new translation of the Bible. R. *Bancroft, Bp. of London, having reluctantly concurred, *James I ordered that the work should be begun, and a strong body of revisers was formed, including the professors of Hebrew and Greek at Oxford and Cambridge and other leading scholars, over fifty in all, who sat in six groups, two at Oxford, two at Cambridge, and two at Westminister. Their instructions were to take the *Bishops' Bible as their basis, to consult all earlier versions, esp. the *Reims NT (see DOUAI) and the *Geneva Bible, to retain the old ecclesiastical terms (such as 'Church' for 'Congregation' and 'Baptism' for 'Washing'), and to exclude all marginal notes, unless required to explain some Hebrew or Greek word. Each group worked separately at first, with a special portion of the Bible assigned to it. They then sent their work to all the others for criticism, and final settlement was made at a general meeting of the chief members of each group, learned men from outside being called in to discuss cases of special difficulty. William *Tyndale's influence through various versions down to the Bishops' Bible fixed the general tone of the translation, which is also indebted to the 'Wycliffe' versions. The work, begun in 1607, took two years and nine months to prepare for the press, and was paid for at 30s. each man per week, and by preferment. The final MS (now lost) was bought by Robert Barker (d. 1645), the King's Printer, for £3,500, which included the copyright. It was seen through the press by Dr Miles Smith (d. 1624) and Bp. T. Bilson (1547–1616), and first appeared in large folio volumes, including the *Apocrypha, printed in black letter, with headings and chapter-summaries in Roman type, at 25s. in sheets, 30s. bound, in 1611. The 'Preface of the translators', probably by Dr Miles Smith, explains that it is a revision, not a new translation, and that the revisers, who had the original Hebrew and Greek texts before them, steered a course between the Puritan and Roman versions. On the title-page are the words 'Appointed to be read in Churches', but it has never otherwise been officially 'authorized'. It immediately superseded the Bishops' Bible, and won favour by its intrinsic merits rather than by official backing. Modern editions often omit the Preface and the Apocrypha, and the current text differs considerably in orthography from the first edition of 1611. In the USA it is commonly known as the 'King James Version'.

F. H. [A.] *Scrivener, *The Cambridge Paragraph Bible* (1873), introd., pp. ix–cix; largely repr. with revisions, id., *The Authorized Edition of the English Bible, 1611: Its Subsequent Reprints and Modern Representatives* (1884). B. F. *Westcott, *A General View of the History of the English Bible* (3rd edn. by W. A. Wright, 1905), pp. 107–21 and 255–78; A. W. Pollard, *Records of the English Bible* (1911), pp. 37–76, with docs. pp. 331–77. J. Isaacs in H. Wheeler Robinson (ed.), *The Bible in its Ancient and English Versions* (1940), pp. 196–227. D. Norton, *A history of the Bible as literature*, 1 (Cambridge, 1993), esp. pp. 144–61, 174–6, and 211–15. R. C. *Trench, *On the Authorized Version of the New Testament in Connection with some Recent Proposals for Revision* (1858). Darlow and Moule, ed. A. S. Herbert, 1 (1968), pp. 130–3, with refs. See further bibl. s.v. BIBLE (ENGLISH VERSIONS).

auto de fe (Sp., 'the delivering of sentence in matters of faith'). The public ceremony of the Spanish *Inquisition at which, after a Procession, Mass, and Sermon, sentences were read and executed. Heretics were clad in the ceremonial *sanbenito (if unrepentant, grotesquely embroidered), with yellow mitre. Those sentenced to death were handed over to the secular power with a formal exhortation to mercy, though by *Innocent IV's bull 'Ad Extirpanda' (1252) execution had to follow within five days, and, until the last case at Seville in 1781, this was carried out by *burning at the stake.

auto sacramental (Sp. *auto*, 'ordinance'). A form of entertainment formerly common in Spain, analogous to the English *morality plays. These plays date from well into the medieval times, but the classical period was the 15th–16th cents., when the chief writers were J. de la Enzina, G. Vicente, and, best known of all, Pedro Calderón (1600–81). By this period the autos were always associated with the feast of *Corpus Christi, and in their later development took the form of allegorical treatments of the mystery of the Eucharist. They were preceded by a procession of the Host through the streets of the town to a space outside the house of some dignitary, where the performance was given. The procession and whole performance were at the public expense, and their magnificence was limited only by the resources of the city or town producing the play, which were strained to the utmost. Many of the plays are of considerable artistic merit, and they had a wide popularity. They were officially prohibited in 1765 by King Charles III, but for many years after this date they continued to be shown in the remoter districts.

E. González Pedroso (ed.), *Autos sacramentales desde su origen hasta fines del siglo XVII* (Biblioteca de Autores Españoles [58]; 1865), with introd. pp. vii–lxi. H. A. Rennert, *The Spanish Stage in the Time of Lope de Vega* (New York, 1909), esp. pp. 297–333. A. A. Parker, 'Notes on the Religious Drama in Medieval Spain and the Origins of the "Auto Sacramental"', *Modern Language Review*, 30 (1935), pp. 170–82. Id., *The Allegorical Drama of Calderón: An Introduction to the Autos Sacramentales* (1943), with refs. N. D. Shergold, *A History of the Spanish Stage from Medieval Times until the End of the Seventeenth Century* (Oxford, 1967), esp. pp. 85–112 and 415–504, with extensive bibl.

autocephalous (Gk. αὐτοκέφαλος, lit. 'himself the head'). A term used in the early Church to describe bishops who were under no superior authority and thus independent both of *Patriarch and *Metropolitan. Such were the bishops of *Cyprus, the bishops of *Armenia and Iberia down to the time of *Photius, and probably the

British bishops before 597. The bishops of *Ravenna may also have had such autonomy for a time. In another sense, the word was used of E. bishops who were directly dependent on the Patriarch, without intermediate reference to a Metropolitan, as well as of priests belonging to patriarchal dioceses. Its principal later and current use, however, is for the modern national Churches that make up the E. Orthodox Church which, though normally in communion with *Constantinople, are governed by their own national synods. In the same connection it is used of the independent monastery on Mount *Sinai.

Autpert, Ambrose (d. 784), abbot. A native of Provence, he went to Italy as a young man and became a monk of St Vincent, near Capua, c.740. He was elected abbot in 777, but left the monastery in 778 in circumstances which are unclear. He was summoned to Rome by *Hadrian I in 784, but died on the way there.

His main work is a commentary on Rev. which became a standard text in the Middle Ages. This made a clean break with eschatological speculation and refused to admit any references to actual times or places; rather it depicted a vision of the Church universal, transcending time and space. It is remarkable for its stress on preaching: the spread of preaching is a continuing miracle and proof of Christ's presence in the Church when other miracles ceased. Autpert is said to have written commentaries on Lev., the Song of Songs, and Psalms, but no trace of these has been found. His other genuine works include a book 'De Conflictu vitiorum et virtutum', a Life of the founders of his monastery, and sermons.

Editio princeps of his comm. on Rev. by G. Hittorp (Cologne, 1536). Crit. edn. of his works by R. Weber, OSB (CCCM 27, 27A and 27B; 1975–9). J. Winandy, OSB, *Ambroise Autpert, moine et théologien* [1953].

Auxentius (d. 373 or 374), Arian Bp. of Milan. A Cappadocian by birth, he was ordained c.343 by Gregory, the intruded Bp. of *Alexandria, and soon became the most prominent supporter of *Arianism in the W. Though apparently ignorant of Latin, he was appointed to the see of Milan by Constantius in 355. Despite condemnation for heresy, acc. to St *Athanasius at the Council of *Ariminum (359), and certainly at Paris (360), he continued to hold his bishopric. Neither the approaches of St *Hilary of Poitiers to the Emp. Valentinian on the subject in 364–365 nor Athanasius' attack on him in 369 nor his condemnation by a synod held at Rome in 372 dislodged him, and he continued in his see till his death; he was a beneficiary of Valentinian's policy of doctrinal neutrality. He was succeeded by the orthodox St *Ambrose. The theory that he was responsible for the introduction of oriental elements in the *Ambrosian rite is no longer accepted.

Our knowledge of Auxentius derives from scattered refs. in Athanasius, St *Basil, Hilary of Poitiers, and St *Eusebius of Vercelli. M. Meslin, *Les Ariens d'Occident 335–430* (Patristica Sorbonensia, 8; 1967), esp. pp. 41–4 and 291–4. C. Pietri, *Roma Christiana: Recherches sur l'Église de Rome ... (311–400)* (Bibliothèque des Écoles françaises d'Athènes et de Rome, 224; 1976), pp. 249–65 *passim* and 731–6.

Auxiliary Saints (Lat. *auxilium*, 'assistance'). A group of 14 saints, also known as the Fourteen Holy Helpers, vener-

ated for the supposed efficacy of their prayers on behalf of human necessities. They are: Sts *George (23 Apr.), *Blaise (3 Feb.), *Erasmus (2 June), *Pantaleon (27 July), *Vitus (15 June), *Christopher (25 July), *Denys (9 Oct.), Cyriacus (8 Aug.), Acacius (8 May), *Eustace (20 Sept.), *Giles (1 Sept.), *Margaret (20 July), *Barbara (4 Dec.), *Catherine of Alexandria (25 Nov.). These are the traditional dates of their festivals, many of which have now been suppressed in the W.

Avancini, Nikola (1611–86), *Jesuit ascetic writer and theologian. A native of Bretz, near *Trent, he entered the Society of Jesus in 1627 and held teaching appointments at Trieste (1634), Laibach (1635) and Vienna (1641). He became successively rector of the Colleges of Passau (1664), Vienna (1666), and Graz (1672). In 1675 he was appointed Visitor of Bohemia, in 1676 Provincial of the Austrian Province, and in 1682 Assistant for the German Provinces. He had just been nominated temporary Vicar-General of the Order at his death. He wrote extensively on philosophy and theology, esp. during the earlier years of his life. His *Vita et Doctrina Jesu Christi ex Quattuor Evangelistis Collecta* (Vienna, 1665), a collection of terse and pithy daily meditations, deservedly established itself as a classic. It has been translated into most modern European languages and is still widely used, esp. by the clergy. He was also a notable dramatist. His other published works include *Poesis Lyrica* (1659) and *Orationes* (3 vols., 1656–60).

There is a modern Eng. tr. (somewhat adapted) of Avancini's *Vita et Doctrina Jesu Christi* by K. D. Mackenzie (London, 1937). Works listed in Sommervogel, 1 (1890), cols. 668–80, and 8 (1898), cols. 1711 f.; Polgár, 1 (1990), pp. 182 f. E. Lamalle, SJ, in *DHGE* 5 (1931), cols. 991 f., s.v. with bibl.

Ave Maria. See HAIL MARY.

Ave Maris Stella. One of the most popular Marian hymns, dating at least from the 9th cent. It is contained in the 9th-cent. Codex Sangallensis 95 and has been attributed to various authors, one of the most probable assignations being that to *Paul the Deacon. The rhythmical hymn is a prayer of great simplicity and beauty for the maternal intercession of the BVM. In the Roman breviary it is one of the hymns for the Second Vespers of the Common of Feasts of the BVM. It has frequently been paraphrased and translated, perhaps the best-known version being that by E. *Caswall, 'Hail Thou Star of Ocean'.

Crit. text, with notes, in C. Blume, SJ (ed.), *Die Hymnen des Thesaurus Hymnologicus H. A. Daniels und andere Hymnen-Ausgaben* (AHMA 51, 1908), pp. 140–2. H. Lausberg, *Der Hymnus 'Ave maris stella'* (Abhandlungen der Rheinisch-Westfälischen Akademie der Wissenschaften, 61; 1976), with refs. A dal Zotto, 'Ricerche sull'auctore del l'"Ave Maris Stella"', *Aevum*, 25 (1951), pp. 494–503; S. de Ibero, OFM Cap., J. Garcia Garcia, E. R. Panyagua, CM, 'Estudio del "Ave Maris Stella"', *Helmantica*, 8 (1957), pp. 421–75. J. Szövérffy, *Die Annalen der Lateinischen Hymnendichtung*, 1 (1964), pp. 219 f., with further refs.

Ave Verum Corpus. Short anonymous Eucharistic hymn, probably dating from the 14th cent., beginning 'Ave verum corpus, natum Ex Maria Virgine' ('Hail true body, Born of the Virgin Mary'). It was sung, esp. in Italy, France, and Germany, after the *Preface or during the

*Consecration at Mass, and is still frequently chanted, e.g. at *Benediction (settings by W. A. Mozart, W. *Byrd, and others).

Crit. text in C. Blume, SJ, and H. M. Bannister (eds.), *Liturgische Prosen des Übergangstiles und der zweiten Epoche insbesondere die dem Adam von Sanct Victor zugeschriebenen* (AHMA 54; 1915), no. 167, pp. 257 f. J. Szövérffy, *Die Annalen der Lateinischen Hymnendichtung*, 2 (1965), pp. 298 f.

Avempace (d. 1139, at an early age), Muslim Andalusian philosopher. The name by which he is known in W. Christendom is a Latinized form of Abu Bakr Muhammad ibn Yahya ibn Bajjah. He taught that the 'ascent of the soul' was less a matter of moral and spiritual purification than a progressive stripping of all materiality until the soul achieves fusion with the 'active intellect' which is an emanation of the Godhead (see AVICENNA). The Arabic text of his most important work, *Tadbir al-mutawahhid* ('Rule of the Solitary'), survives complete only in a *Bodleian MS (Pococke 206); it was also known from Hebrew translations. He wrote other works on a variety of subjects.

The 'Rule of the Solitary', ed., with Eng. tr., by D. M. Dunlop, *Journal of the Royal Asiatic Society of Great Britain and Ireland* (1945), pp. 61–81; also ed., with Sp. tr. and full introd. by M. Asín Palacios (Madrid and Granada, 1946). D. M. Dunlop in *Encyclopaedia of Islam*, 2nd edn., 3 (1971), pp. 728 f., s.v. 'Ibn Bādjdja', with extensive bibl.

Averroism. Averroes (Ibn Rushd, 1126–98) was from an important Muslim family of Córdoba, where he studied the Muslim sciences of law and theology, as well as the non-Muslim sciences of medicine, mathematics, and philosophy. Having gained the favour of the ruler, Abū Ya'qūb Yūsuf (1163–84), he became quādī at Seville and Córdoba, and in 1182, chief physician to the caliph at Marrakesh. After 1195 he was in disgrace for a time, when the government adopted a policy of hostility to the non-Islamic sciences, but he was recalled to the court in Marrakesh shortly before his death. His chief claim to fame rests on his Commentaries on *Aristotle, for which he was known in the Middle Ages as 'The Commentator'. Though generally a faithful interpreter of the philosopher, whom he venerated as the greatest genius of all times, his Aristotelianism, like that of most Arabic philosophers, is tinged with *Neoplatonist ideas. Acc. to him God, the Prime Mover, is entirely separated from the world, in which He exercises no Providence, while the celestial spheres are intelligences, emanating from God in a descending series until they reach man. He taught, further, the eternity and potentiality of matter and the unity of the human intellect ('monopsychism'), i.e. the doctrine that only one intellect exists for the whole human race in which every individual participates, to the exclusion of personal immortality. He consequently interpreted the *Koran allegorically, though retaining the literal interpretation as the only one suitable for the common people.

The theories of Averroes became known in Catholic Europe c.1230. At first the danger to the Catholic faith was not recognized. Both Roger *Bacon and, in his earlier work, *Albert the Great misunderstood the doctrine of Averroes on the intellect. There is no certain evidence before 1256 that the bearing of the views of Averroes on the personal immortality of man was understood. In that year Pope Alexander IV commanded Albert the Great, then at the Papal court, to examine the question. Albert did this in his *De Unitate Intellectus contra Averroem*. A year earlier, in Paris the Faculty of Arts had prescribed the study of Aristotle's *Metaphysics* and of his works on natural science. As a result, within a decade, there were members of the Faculty who were teaching doctrines of Aristotle and his commentators which were destructive of the Christian faith. Their leader was *Siger of Brabant. A reaction to their teaching is clearly seen in the later works of St *Bonaventure, and also in the *De Unitate Intellectus contra Averroistas* which St *Thomas Aquinas, who had returned to Paris in 1269, directed chiefly against Siger. In the year of its publication (1270) Stephen Tempier, Bp. of Paris, condemned a series of 13 errors, dealing with the eternity of the world, the denial of the universal providence of God, the unity of the human intellect, and the denial of free will. In 1277 he issued a more comprehensive list of errors. In the preamble he accused Siger and his followers of saying that 'things are true according to philosophy but not according to the Catholic faith, as though there were two contradictory truths'. This is the doctrine known as that of the double truth. After 1277 Averroism could no longer be taught in the University of Paris, but it infiltrated again in the 14th cent., when it was proclaimed e.g. by John of Jandun. It survived in Italy, esp. at Padua, until the time of the Renaissance.

Lat. tr. of Averroes' comm. on Aristotle in the Works of Aristotle, 11 vols. Venice, 1550–52, repr. several times during the 16th cent. Modern edn. of comm. and other works surviving in Arabic, Hebrew, and Latin, under the aegis of the Mediaeval Academy of America (Pubs. 54, 59, 62, 65, 71, 78–80, and 96; Cambridge, Mass., 1949–86; cf. H. A. Wolfson, 'Revised Plan for the Publication of a *Corpus Commentariorum Averrois in Aristotelem*', *Speculum*, 38 (1963), pp. 88–104), and then of the International Union of Academies (*Averrois Opera*, Madrid, 1983 ff.). Eng. trs. of his treatises *Tahafut al-Tahafut* (The Incoherence of the Incoherence) by S. van den Bergh (2 vols., London, 1954); of 'On the Harmony of Religion and Philosophy' by G. F. Hournai (ibid., 1961); of his comm. on *Plato's *Republic* by R. Lerner (Ithaca, NY, and London, 1974); of his 'Epistle on the Possibility of Conjunction with the Active Intellect' by K. P. Bland (New York, 1982), and of his comm. on Aristotle's *Metaphysics*, Book Lām, by C. Genequand (Leiden, 1984).

E. *Renan, *Averroès et l'averroïsme* (1852). L. Gauthier, *La Théorie d'Ibn Rochd (Averroès) sur les Rapports de la Religion et de la Philosophie* (Paris, 1909); M. *Grabmann, *Der lateinische Averroismus des 13. Jahrhunderts und seine Stellung zur christlichen Weltanschauung* (Sb. (Bayr.), 1931, Heft 2). R. de Vaux, OP, 'La Première Entrée d'Averroès chez les Latins', *Revue des Sciences Philosophiques et Théologiques*, 22 (1933), pp. 193–245; D. Salmon, OP, 'Note sur la première influence d'Averroès', *Revue Néoscolastique de Philosophie*, 60 (1937), pp. 203–12. B. Nardi, *Saggi sull'aristotelismo padovano dal secolo XIV al XVI* (Florence, 1958), *passim*; F. van Steenberghen, 'Une Légende tenace: la théorie de la double vérité', *Académie royale de Belgique, Bulletin de la Classe des Lettres et des Sciences morales et politiques*, 5th ser. 56 (1970), pp. 179–96. *Multiple Averroès: Actes du Colloque International organisé à l'occasion du 850ᵉ anniversaire de la naissance d'Averroès, Paris, 20–23 septembre 1976*, ed. J. Jolivet (1978); *Convegno internazionale l'Averroismo in Italia (Roma, 18–20 Aprile 1977)* (Accademia nazionale dei Lincei, Atti dei Convegni Lincei, 40; 1979). B. S. Kogan, *Averroes and the Metaphysics of Causation* (Albany, NY [1985]). O. [N. H.] Leaman, *Averroes and his Philosophy* (Oxford, 1988). Further bibl. in W. Totok, *Handbuch der Geschichte der Philosophie*, 2 (Frankfurt am Main, 1973), pp. 277–83, 455–7, and 586 f. G. C. Anawati, *Bibliographie d'Averroès* (Algiers, 1978).

M.-M. Gorce, OP, in *DHGE* 5 (1931), cols. 1032–92, s.v.; R. Arnaldez in *Encyclopaedia of Islam* (2nd edn.), 3 (1971), pp. 909–20, s.v. 'Ihn Rushd'; id. and A. Z. Iskandar in *Dictionary of Scientific Biography*, 12 (1975), pp. 1–9, s.v. 'Rushd'; J. Hjärpe and others in *TRE* 5 (1980), pp. 51–61, s.v.

Avesta. The sacred books of the *Zoroastrians or Parsis, which set forth the theology and religious system of the ancient Iranians. The title used by earlier modern scholars, 'Zend-Avesta', rests on a misunderstanding. The work, which was based on much older matter, was put together under Shapur II (309–79), when it reached substantially its present outline. Considerable additions were made after the Arab Conquest of Iran (637–51) and a very great deal has been lost since. The main subjects dealt with are the ritual, hymns, liturgy, and law of the Parsis, and it is divided into five sections. The comparatively short portion known as the Gathas (versified sermons), written in a slightly different dialect, appears to be the oldest part of the work and perhaps goes back to Zoroaster himself. Knowledge of the work was first brought to the W. by a French scholar, Anquetil du Perron, who journeyed to India in 1754 with the express purpose of procuring the text, and after many difficulties returned with a copy for publication in 1771.

The standard edn. is that of K. F. Geldner (8 fascs., Stuttgart, 1885–96). Eng. tr. in *The Sacred Books of the East* (ed. F. *Max Müller), 4, 23, 31, by J. Darmesteter and L. H. Mills. J. Kellens in E. Yarshater (ed.), *Encyclopedia Iranica*, 3 (London and New York, 1989), pp. 35–44, s.v., with bibl. See also works cited under ZOROASTRIANISM.

Avicebron or **Avicebrol** (*c*.1020–*c*.1060), the Latin name of the Spanish Jewish philosopher Solomon Ibn Gabirol. Medieval Christian writers wrongly supposed him to have been an Arab Muslim. His system contained both *Aristotelian and *Neoplatonist elements; against his view that the distinction between matter and form applied in the non-material as well as in the material sphere, St *Thomas Aquinas directed his *Opusculum* 15, 'De substantiis separatis'. His principal work was the *Fons Vitae*, written in Arabic, of which the Latin translation became very popular in the Middle Ages. He also wrote poems and hymns.

The Arabic original of the *Fons Vitae* has been lost; extracts surviving in medieval Heb. tr. were rediscovered and ed., with Fr. tr. and important introd. on his life and works, by S. Munk, *Mélanges de philosophie juive et arabe* (1859); 12th-cent. Lat. tr. ed., with introd., by C. Baeumker (BGPM, 1, Hefte 2–4; 1892–5); abridged Eng. tr. of vol. 3 by H. E. Wedeck (New York, 1962; London, 1963). Arabic text of 'The Improvement of Moral Qualities', ed., with Eng. tr. and introd., by S. S. Wise (Columbia University Oriental Studies, New York, 1901). Modern edn. of his poems, written in Heb., by H. N. Bialik and J. H. Ravnitzki (3 vols., Berlin and Tel-Aviv, 1924–32). J. M. Millás Vallicrosa, *Selomó ibn Gabirol como poeta y filósofo* (Biblioteca Hebraicoespañola, 1; 1945); E. Bertola, *Salomon ibn Gabirol (Avicebron): Vita, opere e pensiero* (1953); F. Brunner, *Platonisme et aristotélisme: La Critique d'ibn Gabirol par Saint Thomas d'Aquin* (1965); J. Schlanger, *La Philosophie de Salomon ibn Gabirol* (Études sur le judaïsme médiéval, 3; Leiden, 1968). I. Husik, *A History of Mediaeval Jewish Philosophy* (New York, 1916), pp. 59–79. M.-M. Gorce, OP, in *DHGE* 5 (1931), cols. 1104–7, s.v., with bibl.

Avicenna (980–1037), Muslim philosopher, who also acted as the court physician to a number of Iranian princes. His full name was Abu 'Ali al Husain ibn 'Abdallah ibn Sina. His teaching exercised a great influence on the earlier *Schoolmen. His philosophy was in the main *Aristotelian, but it was also much influenced by *Neoplatonism. He held that there was a hierarchy of emanations from the Godhead which mediate between God and man. Of these the most important is the 'active intellect', which Avicenna conceived as an entity in a Platonic world of ideas. The 'passive intellect', which is his name for the individual mind, can acquire ideas only by contact with the active, and is thus secondary. He distinguished, in the usual Aristotelian fashion, between necessary and contingent being, holding that God was necessary and the universe contingent; but between the two he set the world of ideas, which he held to be necessary, not of itself, but because God has made it so. He was the author of *c*.100 treatises, including a *Canon of Medicine*, which long enjoyed a great reputation, and a vast philosophical Summa called *Al-Shifa* or 'Sanatio'.

His works, which were written mainly in Arabic, were known to the Middle Ages in Heb. and (esp.) Lat. trs. (the latter often made from the Heb.). Collections of his works were pub. in Lat. tr. at Venice, 1495, 1508, and 1546. Crit. edn. of medieval Lat. tr. by S. Van Riet and others, *Avicenna Latinus* (Louvain and Leiden, 1968 ff.), with introds. by G. Verbeke. Modern Fr. trs. from the Arabic of Bks. 1–5 of the section on Metaphysics in *Al-Shifa*, with introd. and notes, by G. C. Anawati (Études Musulmanes, 21; 1978) and of his *Instructions and Remarks* by A.-M. Goichon (Collection d'Œuvres Arabes de L'Unesco, 1951). Eng. tr. from the Persian of the section on Metaphysics in *Dānish Nāma-i 'alā'ī* (The Book of Scientific Knowledge) by P. Morewedge (Persian Heritage Series, 13; 1973). His autobiography was ed., with Eng. tr., by W. E. Gohlman (Studies in Islamic Philosophy and Science; Albany, NY, 1974).

S. M. Afnan, *Avicenna: His Life and Works* (1958). A.-M. Goichon, *La Distinction de l'essence et de l'existence d'après Ibn Sīnā (Avicenne)* (1937); id., *La Philosophie d'Avicenne et son Influence en Europe médiévale* (1944; 2nd edn., 1951); L. Gardet, *La Pensée religieuse d'Avicenne* (Études de Philosophie Médiévale, 41; 1951), with refs. to recent edns. of his religious works. E. *Gilson, 'Avicenne et le point de départ de Duns Scot', *AHDLMA* 2 (1927), pp. 89–149; id., 'Les Sources gréco-arabes de l'augustinisme avicennisant', ibid. 4 (1930), pp. 5–158. E. R. Harvey, *The Inward Wits: Psychological Theory in the Middle Ages and the Renaissance* (Warburg Institute Surveys, 6; 1975). H. Corbin, *Avicenne et le récit visionnaire* (Commission des monuments nationaux de l'Iran. Collection du millénaire d'Avicenne, 25; 2 vols, Teheran, 1952–5; Eng. tr., '1960' [1961]). J. R. Michot, *La Destinée de l'homme selon Avicenne* (Académie Royale de Belgique, Classe de lettres, Fonds René Draguet, 5; 1986). D. Gutas, *Avicenna and the Aristotelian Tradition* (Islamic Philosophy and Theology, Texts and Studies, 4; Leiden, etc., 1988). O. C. Gruner, *A Treatise on the Canon of Avicenna* (incorporating a translation of the first Book; 1930). E. Gilson, *History of Christian Philosophy in the Middle Ages* (1955), pp. 187–216; M. Fakhry, *A History of Islamic Philosophy* (New York and London, 1970), pp. 147–83; (2nd edn., 1983), pp. 128–62. Full bibl. in W. Totok, *Handbuch der Geschichte der Philosophie*, 2 (Frankfurt am Main, 1973), pp. 264–72. M.-M. Gorce, OP, in *DHGE* 5 (1931), cols. 1107–19, s.v.; A.-M. Goichon in *Encyclopaedia of Islam* (2nd edn.), 3 (1971), pp. 941–7, s.v. 'Ibn Sīnā'; G. C. Anawati and A. Z. Iskandar in *Dictionary of Scientific Biography*, 15 (supp. 1; 1978), pp. 494–501, s.v. 'Sīnā', all with extensive bibl.

Avignon. Acc. to tradition, its first bishop was St Rufus, a disciple of St *Paul. It was in the 12th cent. a centre of the *Albigenses, and for this reason its defences were dismantled by Louis VIII in 1226. From 1309 till 1377 it was the residence ('*Babylonian Captivity') of the Popes, though it did not become Papal property until 1348, when *Clement VI bought it from Joanna, the Queen of Naples. After the Papal court had returned to Rome, two *antipopes, Clement VII and Benedict XIII, lived in Avignon, the latter being finally expelled in 1408.

T. Okey, *The Story of Avignon* ('Medieval Towns Series', 1911). E. Duprat, *Les Origines de l'église d'Avignon: Des Origines à 879* (1909). J. Girard and P. Pansier, *La Cour temporelle d'Avignon aux XIVᵉ et XVIᵉ siècles* (Recherches Historiques et Documents sur Avignon, le Comtat-Venaissin et la Principauté d'Orange, 1; 1909). G. Mollat, *Les Papes d'Avignon, 1305–1378* (1912; Eng. tr. of 1949 edn., 1963; 10th edn. [1965]). Y. Renouard, *La Papauté à Avignon* (1954; Eng. tr., 1970). B. Guillemain, *La Cour Pontificale d'Avignon (1309–1327): Étude d'une société* (Bibliothèque des Écoles françaises d'Athènes et de Rome, 201; 1962). H. Labande, *Les Palais des papes et les monuments d'Avignon au XIVᵉ siècle* (2 vols., Marseilles, 1925). H. Hoberg (ed.), *Die Inventare des päpstlichen Schatzes in Avignon 1314–1376* (ST 111; 1944). J. Girard in *DHGE* 5 (1931), cols. 1121–53, s.v.; A.-M. Hayez and J. Verger in *Lexikon des Mittelalters*, 1 (1980), cols. 1301–4, s.v.

Avitus, St (d. *c*.518), Bp. of Vienne from *c*.490. Alcimus Ecdidius Avitus was born in Auvergne of a Roman senatorial family. Succeeding to the see of Vienne in Gaul on the death of his father, Hesychius (490), he exercised an enduring influence on the ecclesiastical life of Burgundy and won the *Arian King Sigismund to the acceptance of Catholic orthodoxy. He was also a strong advocate of the movement for the closer ecclesiastical union of Gaul with Rome. His reputation for learning greatly impressed King *Clovis, then still a pagan. Among his surviving works are a poem *De Spiritalis Historiae Gestis* (in five books, also called *De Mosaicae Historiae Gestis*), another *De Consolatoria Castitatis Laude* (or *De Virginitate*), a treatise *Contra Eutychianum*, three complete homilies (and fragments of many others), and some 90 letters. Feast day, 5 Feb.

Works ed. J. *Sirmond, SJ (Paris, 1643), repr. (*via* A. *Gallandi) in J. P. Migne, *PL* 59. 191–398. Rev. text by R. Peiper in *MGH*, Auctores Antiquissimi, 6 (pt. 2; 1883); sections not incl. in *PL* are repr. in A. Hamman, OFM (ed.), *PL*, Suppl. 3, cols. 798–830. Bks. 1–3 of *De Spiritalis Historiae Gestis* ed. D. J. Nodes (Toronto Medieval Latin Texts, 16 [1985]). H. Goelzer, *Le Latin de S. Avit* (1909); M. Burckhardt, *Die Briefsammlung des Bischofs Avitus von Vienne* (1938). M. Reydellet, *La Royauté dans la littérature latine de Sidoine à Isidore de Séville* (Bibliothèque des Écoles françaises d'Athènes et de Rome, 243; 1981), pp. 87–137. M. Simonetti, 'Letteratura antimonofisita d'Occidente', *Augustinianum*, 18 (1978), pp. 487–532, esp. pp. 522–31. S. Isetta, 'Rassegna di Studi Avitani (1857–1982)', *Bollettino di Studi Latini*, 13 (1983), pp. 59–73. J.-R. Palanque in *DHGE* 5 (1931), cols. 1205–8, s.v. 'Avit (15)'.

Avrillon, Jean Baptiste Élie (1652–1729), French theologian and spiritual writer. He made his profession as a *Minim in 1671. Among his writings were *Réflexions théologiques, morales et affectives sur les attributs de Dieu* (1705) and manuals for the observance of *Lent and *Advent. E. B. *Pusey published in 1844 adapted English versions of *A Guide for passing Advent holily*, and *A Guide for passing Lent holily*, and, in 1845, of *The Year of Affections*.

Pourrat, 4 (1928), pp. 333–6; J. de Guibert in *Dict. Sp.* 1 (1937), cols. 1185 f.

Axum (or Aksum) in N. *Ethiopia, capital of a kingdom flourishing from the 2nd to the 7th cent. Despite claims of a 4th-cent. evangelization by St *Frumentius, it was not until the beginning of the 6th cent. that it emerged as a major Christian power under King Caleb. After the disappearance of the kingdom, the Churches of Axum retained their prestige throughout Ethiopia until the 20th century.

J. T. Bent, *The Sacred City of the Ethiopians: Being a record of Travel and Research in Abyssinia in 1893* (1893, new edn., 1896), esp. pp. 152–97 and 238–85. *Deutsche Aksum-Expedition*, herausgegeben von der Generalverwaltung der königlichen Museen zu Berlin (by E. Littmann and others; 4 vols. 1913). Y. M. Kobishchanov, *Axum* (Eng. tr. of Russian, Moscow, 1966, by L. T. Kapitanov [1979]). H. Brakmann in *RAC*, Suppl. 1 ('1992'), cols. 718–810, s.v. 'Axomis (Aksum)'.

Ayliffe, John (1676–1732), English jurist. He was educated at Winchester and at New College, Oxford. His strong Whig sympathies brought him into conflict with the dominant Jacobitism of Oxford, and his *Ancient and Present State of the University of Oxford* (2 vols., 1714) led to expulsion from the university and loss of his degrees. In 1726 he published his *Parergon Iuris Canonici Anglicani* (2nd edn., 1734), arranged alphabetically, which remains a treatise of high authority. In 1734 his *New Pandect of the Civil Law* (vol. 1, on Roman law; all pub.) appeared posthumously.

S. Gibson, 'A Neglected Oxford Historian', in *Oxford Essays in Medieval History Presented to Herbert Edward Salter* (1934), no. 11, pp. 234–41. G. P. Macdonell in *DNB* 2 (1885), pp. 279–81, s.v.

Ayscough. See ASKEW, A.

Ayton, John (d. before 1350), English canonist. His name occurs in several forms, among them 'Acton' (so in *DNB*), 'Athone', 'Achedune'. He was a pupil of Abp. J. *Stratford and became a canon of *Lincoln. He wrote a commentary on the 'Constitutions' of the Papal legates Otto and Ottobon, which was printed in the 1496 and later editions of W. *Lyndwood's *Provinciale*.

Besides the prefaces to the various edns. of Lyndwood, see also F. W. *Maitland, *Roman Canon Law in the Church of England* (1898), pp. 6–14, 55, and 76. S. L. Lee in *DNB* 1 (1885), p. 67; *BRUO* 1 (1957), pp. 11–12; *BRUC*, p. 2, all s.v. 'Acton, John'.

Azazel (Heb., עֲזָאזֵל). The mysterious figure, dwelling in the desert, to whom the 'scapegoat' of the sin-offering was dispatched as part of the ritual of the Day of *Atonement (Lev. 16: 1–28). Originally perhaps a desert-demon or goat-deity was intended. In 1 Enoch 6, 8 and 10. 4–8 he is a leader of the fallen angels, a Prometheus-like instructor of mankind in crafts, and the author of all sin. In later Jewish, *Gnostic and *Islamic traditions, he is a leader of demons.

T. K. *Cheyne, 'The date and origin of the ritual of the "Scapegoat"', *ZATW* 15 (1895), pp. 153–6; G. R. *Driver, 'Three Technical Terms in the Pentateuch', *Journal of Semitic Studies*, 1 (1956), pp. 97–105, esp. pp. 97 f. M. H. Segal, 'The

Religion of Israel before Sinai', *JQR* 53 (1962–3), pp. 226–56, esp. pp. 248–51. J. G. Frazer, *The Golden Bough*, 6, 'The Scapegoat' (1913), p. 210, n. 4. S. Ahituv in *Encyclopaedia Judaica*, 3 (Jerusalem, 1971), cols. 1000–1002, s.v. with further refs. See also comm. on Lev.

Azymites (also Lat. *Infermentarii*). The name given to the W. Church by the E. at the time of the Schism of 1054, with reference to their use of unleavened bread (τὰ ἄζυμα) in the Liturgy, which, on the E. view, invalidated the rite. See also BREAD, LEAVENED AND UNLEAVENED.

B

Baal (Heb. בַּעַל, Gk. Βάαλ or Βαάλ). The word, which means literally 'lord' or 'owner', e.g. of a house (Ex. 22: 7, [EVV 22: 8], Jgs. 19: 22), was used esp. of the Semitic deities who were held to produce agricultural and animal fertility. The discoveries at *Ras Shamra (ancient Ugarit) in Syria from 1929 onwards furnished fresh evidence concerning Baal-worship in pre-Israelite Canaan. The older view that there was a supreme deity, Baal, to be identified with the sun god, rests on insufficient evidence. The debased rites which arose in connection with Baal-worship caused it to be vigorously attacked by the Hebrew prophets, who constantly found themselves compelled to resist attempts to fuse the worship of Yahweh with that of the local Baalim. The '*high places' at which the cultus was centred were finally destroyed through the efforts of such men as *Elijah and King Josiah. It was the abhorrence of Baal-worship that in later times led the Jews to read the word 'Bosheth' ('shame') as a substitute wherever Baal occurred in the sacred text; cf. the appearance of two forms of the same name, 'Eshbaal' (1 Chr. 9: 39) and 'Ishbosheth' (2 Sam. 2: 8). See also BEL.

Primary texts transliterated, with Eng. tr., in G. R. *Driver, *Canaanite Myths and Legends*, 2nd edn. by J. C. L. Gibson (Edinburgh, 1977), pp. 37–81, with introd. pp. 2–19. W. R. *Smith, *Lectures on the Religion of the Semites* (3rd edn. by S. A. *Cook, 1927), passim. A. S. Kapelrud, *Baal in the Ras Shamra Texts* (Copenhagen, 1952). J. Gray, *The Legacy of Canaan: The Ras Shamra Texts and their Relevance to the Old Testament* (Supplements to *Vetus Testamentum*, 5; 2nd edn., 1965), esp. 163–9. F. Nötscher, T. Klauser, H. Bacht, SJ, A. *Baumstark, and O. Eissfeldt in *RAC* 1 (1950), cols. 1063–113, s.v., with extensive refs.; J. Gray in *The Interpreter's Dictionary of the Bible*, 1 (1962), pp. 328 f., s.v.

Babel, Tower of. Acc. to Gen. 11: 1–9, the tower reaching to heaven, the presumptuous construction of which was frustrated by Yahweh through confusion of languages among its builders. The story was probably inspired by the famous Babylonian temple-tower ('ziggurat') of Etemenanki, which symbolized for the Israelites the pride of the nations destined by God to dissolution from within. The immediate purpose of the narrative, which plays upon the Hebrew words בָּבֶל (Babel, 'Babylon') and בָּלַל (balal, 'to confuse'), seems to have been to account for the division of languages.

H. Gressmann, *The Tower of Babel* (Hilda Stroock Lectures for 1927; posthumously ed. J. Obermann, New York, 1928). A. Parrot, *La Tour de Babel* (Cahiers d'Archéologie Biblique, 2; 1953; Eng. tr., 1955). See also comm. on Gen., cited s.v.

Babylas, St (d. c.250), Bp. of *Antioch. He succeeded Zebinus in the see of Antioch c.240. St John *Chrysostom relates that he once refused an emperor access to a church on the ground of an unrepented crime. (The emperor has sometimes been identified with *Philip the Arabian (q.v.), of whom *Eusebius tells a similar story.) He was imprisoned in the *Decian persecution and died in bonds.

In 351 his remains were translated to Daphne, a suburb of Antioch, to hallow a former temple of Apollo for Christian worship. In 362 *Julian the Apostate ordered their removal when unable to obtain a reply from the oracle of Apollo, and they were brought back to Antioch with Psalms ridiculing the heathen idols. Babylas became the object of a devoted cultus at Antioch, and Chrysostom preached two panegyrics (untrustworthy as historical sources) in his honour. Later his cultus extended to the W., and he was celebrated in both prose and verse by St *Aldhelm of Sherborne. Feast day, 24 Jan. in W., 4 Sept. in E.

Eusebius, *HE* 6. 29. 4 and 39. 4; *Sozomen, *HE* 5. 19; *Theodoret, *HE* 3. 6. Chrysostom's sermons on Babylas are in *PG* 1. 527–72; on their slight historical value see II. *Delehaye, SJ, *Les Passions des martyrs et les genres littéraires* (1921), pp. 209 and 232. Three series of Acta (all late) are pr. in *AASS*, Jan. 2 (1643), pp. 569–78; P. Peeters, SJ, 'La Passion de S. Basile d'Epiphanie', *Anal. Boll.* 48 (1930), pp. 302–23, incl. text and refs. to Georgian material on St Babylas. Aldhelm, *De Virginitate Prosa*, 33, ed. R. Ehwald in *MGH*, Auctores Antiquissimi, 15 (1919), pp. 274 f., and id., *De Virginitate Carmen*, lines 1035–70, ibid., pp. 397 f. 'Les Deux Saints Babylas', *Anal. Boll.* 19 (1900), pp. 5–8. J.-M. Sauget in *DPAC* 1 (1983), cols. 464 f., s.v. 'Babila di Antiochia'; Eng. tr. in *Encyclopedia of the Early Church*, 1 (1992), p. 106.

Babylonian captivity. The captivity in Babylon, whither under Nebuchadnezzar (604–562 BC) a significant proportion of the population of *Judah was deported in two batches c.597 and c.586 BC respectively (2 Kgs. 24: 14–16; 25: 11). Acc. to Ez. 1–2, they were permitted to return after the Persian ruler, Cyrus, had captured Babylon c.539 BC, though many of them did not return until at least 100 years later (Neh. 1 ff.).

The expression was used metaphorically by F. *Petrarch and subsequent writers of the exile of the Popes at *Avignon from 1309 to 1377. M. *Luther's treatise on the *Babylonish Captivity of the Church* (1520) was a sustained attack on the 'bondage' in which the Church had been held by the withdrawal of the chalice from the laity, the doctrine of *transubstantiation, and the *Sacrifice of the Mass.

Bach, Johann Sebastian (1685–1750), German composer. After being court organist and 'Konzertmeister' at Weimar (1708–17), and court 'Kapellmeister' at Cöthen (1717–23), he became *cantor at the Thomaskirche in Leipzig in 1723, a post he retained till his death. In his theological outlook Bach appears to have adhered to an orthodox *Lutheran position, although his choice of *cantata and *Passion texts sometimes suggests some sympathy with *Pietistic thought. Although the c.200 extant Church cantatas (many more are lost) cover most of his creative life, the majority date from the early Leipzig years, a period of astonishing fecundity, which also saw the two great settings of the Passion (acc. to St John, 1724;

acc. to St Matthew, 1727). Both intersperse the Gospel narrative with arias and chorales to produce large-scale *oratorio Passions. The Protestant chorale also lies at the heart of many of the cantatas, while in the chorale-based organ works Bach often achieved a uniquely expressive interpretation of both text and melody. His other major works include the 'Magnificat', the 'Christmas Oratorio' (a series of six cantatas for the Christmas season), and the Mass in B minor. This last gigantic creation was completed only in the final years of Bach's life, although some of the music originated up to 25 years earlier. Too monumental for liturgical use (though some individual movements were so performed in Bach's time), it is best regarded as a personal summing up of the possibilities of the genre. Bach's music had to wait until the 19th cent. and the advocacy of F. Mendelssohn and others before its true greatness was widely recognized. The combination of supreme technical skill with immense creative imagination resulted in music of such spiritual power that it has transcended all denominational boundaries.

Collected edn. of his works pub. for the Bach-Gesellschaft (61 vols., Leipzig, 1851–1926); new edn. (*Neue Bach-Ausgabe*) for the Johann-Sebastian Bach-Institut, Göttingen, and the Bach-Archiv, Leipzig (Kassel, 1954 ff.). Supplements to the latter include *Bach-Dokumente*, ed. W. Neumann and H.-J. Schulze (1963 ff.). Eng. tr. of many docs. in H. T. David and A. Mendel (eds.), *The Bach Reader* (New York, 1945; London, 1946; rev. edn. [1966]). Thematic catalogues ed. W. Schmieder (Leipzig, 1950) and H.-J. Schulze and C. Wolff, *Bach Compendium* (1985 ff.). Lives by J. N. Forkel (Leipzig, 1802; Eng. tr., 1820; modern Eng. tr., with notes and appendices by C. S. Terry, 1920), P. Spitta (2 vols., Leipzig, 1873–80; Eng. tr., 3 vols., 1884–5), A. *Schweitzer (in Fr., Leipzig, 1905; Eng. tr., 2 vols., 1911), C. S. Terry (London, 1928), and M. Boyd (ibid., 1983). J. A. Westrup, *Bach Cantatas* (BBC Music Guides, 1966). G. Stiller, *Johann Sebastian Bach und das Leipziger gottesdienstliche Leben seiner Zeit* (Kassel [1970]; Eng. tr., St Louis [1984]). M. Petzoldt (ed.), *Bach als Ausleger der Bibel* (Göttingen, 1985). G. Herz, *Essays on J. S. Bach* (Studies in Musicology, 73; Ann Arbor, Mich., 1985). J. [J.] Pelikan, *Bach among the Theologians* (Philadelphia [1986]). P. [F.] Williams, *The Organ Music of J. S. Bach* (3 vols., Cambridge, 1980–4). C. Wolff (ed.), *Bach-Bibliographie* (1985). W. Emery and others in S. Sadie (ed.), *The New Grove Dictionary of Music and Musicians*, 1 (1980), pp. 785–840, s.v.

Bacon, Francis (1561–1626), philosopher. He was the son of Sir Nicholas Bacon (1509–79), *Elizabeth I's Lord Keeper, and Ann Cooke, whose sister was married to Elizabeth's chief minister, Lord Burleigh. Born in London, from the age of 12 Bacon was for two and a half years at Trinity College, Cambridge, and then spent three years in Paris. Left ill-provided by his father's death, he trained and went to work as a barrister. The Queen was not well disposed towards him, despite his readiness to prosecute the Earl of Essex, her fallen favourite and his former friend. He represented various places in Parliament between 1584 until his elevation to the House of Lords as Lord Verulam in 1618. *James I made him successively Solicitor-General (1607), Attorney-General (1613), Lord Keeper (1617), and Lord Chancellor (1618). In 1621 he was raised to the rank of Viscount St Albans. In the same year he was accused of, and confessed to, bribery and corruption. The heavy fine and banishment from London were soon remitted, but they marked the end of his public career.

Bacon was the first English philosopher of importance since *William of Ockham (d. 1347). In his *Proficience and Advancement of Learning* (1605) he defended the pursuit of natural knowledge and attacked three unsatisfactory modes of enquiry (i.e. 'disputatious' learning or *Scholasticism, 'delicate' (i.e. dilettante) learning or humanism, which he regarded as preoccupied with style rather than substance, and 'fantastical' learning or occultism). He then provided an elaborate classification of the varieties of knowledge which has had lasting influence. His *De Augmentis Scientiarum* (1623) is an expanded Latin version of this work. His *Novum Organum* (written c.1608; pub. 1620) opens with his 'Great Instauration', a further classification of the sciences, and his famous account of the four kinds of 'idols' which mislead man in his pursuit of truth: the idols of the tribe which are mental weaknesses typical of the whole human species; idols of the cave which are individual peculiarities serving to distinguish one cast of mind from another; idols of the market which are forms of error connected with the influence of language; and idols of the theatre which are the received but erroneous systems of philosophy described in the *Advancement of Learning*. The main business of the book, however, is to describe a method of eliminative induction by which the inquiring student of nature can ascend by gradual steps from observed matters of particular fact to comprehensive natural laws. His most important philosophical contribution in these works was his emphasis on two characteristics of natural knowledge. He held the almost unprecedented view that knowledge was cumulative, that it is possible to enlarge it rather than simply to preserve the wisdom of the past. And he insisted that the sort of knowledge that should be pursued is for practical ends, as the indispensable means to 'the relief of man's estate'. *The New Atlantis* (1627, posthumous), describing the ideal state, embodies Bacon's conception of natural inquiry as an essentially co-operative undertaking. His *Essays*, consisting mainly of worldly moralizing, appeared with additions in each new edition (1597, 1612, and 1625); that on 'Atheism' first came out in 1612.

Bacon divided knowledge as a whole into natural knowledge (or 'philosophy') and divinity, by which he meant inspired revelation. The sole task of 'divine philosophy' (a small section of natural knowledge) was to establish the existence of God as presupposed by the existence and character of the natural world. Since it can tell us nothing more than that, we have to depend on revelation for knowledge of God's nature, action, and purposes. This apparently unquestioning dependence on scriptural authority is consistent with his *Puritan upbringing, though it is hard to reconcile with his critically inquiring outlook. In line with *Aristotle, as scholastically interpreted, Bacon took the rational soul to be implanted in the human body by God, thus securing its immortality. As superhuman it is beyond the competence of scientific investigation. Yet he insisted that 'human philosophy', i.e. the study of man and society, is to be carried out in the same inductive way as the study of non-human nature, and that every event has a cause. While Bacon has been acclaimed by freethinkers, it seems that he was at least a *deist; he wrote a number of prayers, a group of 'holy meditations', some defences of religious toleration, and he translated seven Psalms into pedestrian English.

Opera Omnia, pub. in 6 vols., Amsterdam 1661–84; standard edn. by J. Spedding, R. L. Ellis, and D. D. Heath (14 vols., London, 1857–74), of which the last 7 vols. comprise the *Letters and Life of Francis Bacon* (incl. his Occasional Works, ed. J. Spedding). *Philosophical Works*, partly repr. with introd, by J. M. Robertson (London, 1905). Modern edns. (with introd. and notes) of his *Essays* by E. A. Abbott ('London Series of English Classics', 2 vols., 1876); of his *Novum Organum* by T. Fowler (Oxford, 1878; 2nd edn., 1889); and of his *Advancement of Learning* and *The New Atlantis* by T. Case ('World's Classics', 1906). Lives by R. W. *Church ('English Men of Letters', 1884), J. Nichol (Edinburgh and London, 1888), and J. O. Fuller (London and The Hague [1981]). The many studies of his thought include: T. Fowler, *Francis Bacon* ('English Philosophers', 1881); F. H. Anderson, *The Philosophy of Francis Bacon* (Chicago, 1948); P. Rossi, *Francesco Bacone: dalla magia alla scienza* (Bari, 1957; Eng. tr., 1968); J. G. Crowther, *Francis Bacon: The First Statesman of Science* (1960); B. Vickers (ed.), *Essential Articles for the Study of Francis Bacon* (Hamden, Conn., 1968; London, 1972); and A. Quinton, *Francis Bacon* (Past Masters, Oxford, 1980). M. Purver, *The Royal Society: Concept and Creation* (1967), pp. 20–62. R. W. Gibson, *Francis Bacon: A Bibliography of his Works and of Baconiana to the Year 1750* (Oxford, 1950; supp., privately issued, 1959).

Bacon, Roger (b. *c.*1214 or perhaps more prob *c.*1220; d. 1292 or later), 'Doctor mirabilis', *Franciscan philosopher. Born, acc. to late evidence, at either Ilminister in Somerset or Bisley in Glos., he possibly studied at *Oxford, and certainly in *Paris. His earliest writings are a series of *quaestiones* on *Aristotle's 'Physics' and 'Metaphysics', on the Pseudo-Aristotelian 'De Plantis', and on the *'Liber de Causis'. They are among the earliest lectures on these books, and may be assigned to the years between 1240/1 and 1245/6. About 1247 he turned to the study of languages, mathematics, and natural sciences. The date at which he moved to Oxford is not known. It was probably here that, *c.*1257, he entered the Franciscan Order, in which he came under the influence of *Adam of Marsh and other disciples of Robert *Grosseteste, for whom he later expressed an unbounded admiration.

A new stage in Bacon's career was reached in the mid-1260s. Back in Paris at the Franciscan convent, he had a chance of expounding his ideas on the defects he saw in western education to a clerk in the household of Cardinal Guy le Gros de Foulques, who not long afterwards (Feb. 1265) became Pope Clement IV. The Pope bade him dispatch to Rome an account of his doctrines 'secretly and without delay'. Bacon set to work, and in late 1267 or early 1268 sent to the Pope an encyclopedic work in seven parts, known as the 'Opus maius', in which he outlined the causes which had hindered the progress of philosophy among the Latins and had weakened W. Christendom in its struggle against *Islam. The work also gave a fervent account of the importance of the study of languages for a proper understanding of the Bible, and of the value of mathematics, optics, the natural sciences, and moral philosophy in rebuilding and strengthening W. Christendom against its enemies. He also wrote two briefer works, the 'Opus minus' and 'Opus tertium', which were partly synopses and partly elaborations of sections of the 'Opus maius'; the first was sent to the Pope, the second probably not.

The death of Pope Clement IV in Nov. 1268 brought to an end any hope of a Papal commendation for his ideas. Bacon lived more than 20 years longer, and was able to

continue writing. The 'Communia Naturalium' and 'Communia Mathematica' are usually assigned to this period, though they may have been written earlier, but the 'Compendium Studii Philosophiae' is known to have been written *c.*1272, and the fragmentary 'Compendium Studii Theologiae' in 1292. In 1277 Bacon is said to have been condemned by the General of the Franciscan Order for 'suspect novelties' and 'dangerous doctrine' and imprisoned for a time. The background to this condemnation is not known. According to the Oxford chronicler, John Rous, he was buried in the Franciscan convent at Oxford.

Bacon's place in the history of thought is hard to assess. In philosophy and in science he had an exceptionally wide knowledge of works translated from Greek and Arabic, but he was never able to construct a unified system. His irascible nature and his intemperate criticism of those who disagreed with him worked against the acceptance of his proposals for the reform of theological studies. Nevertheless he was a man of wide vision. The history of his posthumous reputation remains to be written. Never entirely forgotten in the Middle Ages, his real achievement was submerged in that of a man of magical powers and imaginary mechanical inventions.

'Opus Maius', ed. J. H. Bridges (3 vols., Oxford, 1897–1900); 'Opus Minus', 'Opus Tertium', and 'Compendium Studii Philosophiae', ed. J. S. Brewer in *Rogeri Bacon Opera quaedam hactenus inedita*, 1 (all pub., London, 1859). 'Opus Tertium', ed. P. Duhem (Quaracchi, 1909). Bacon's 'Moralis Philosophia', ed. F. Delorme, OFM, and E. Massa (Zurich, 1953). 'Compendium Studii Theologiae', ed. H. *Rashdall (British Society for Franciscan Studies, Aberdeen, 1911; in an appendix in the vol., A. G. Little attempts the difficult task of listing Bacon's complete works, pp. 71–122). Many items ed. (not very satisfactorily) by R. Steele and others in *Opera hactenus inedita Rogeri Baconi* (London and Oxford, 1905 ff.; 16 vols. to 1940). His Gk. grammar and fragments of Heb. grammar ed. E. Nolan and S. A. Hirsch (Cambridge, 1902). Crit. edn., with Eng. tr., of his 'De multiplicatione specierum' and 'De speculis comburentibus' by D. C. Lindberg (Oxford, 1983). K. M. Fredborg and others, 'An unedited part of Roger Bacon's "Opus Maius": "De signis" ', *Traditio*, 34 (1978), pp. 75–136, incl. text. A. G. Little (ed.), *Roger Bacon* (Commemorative Essays, 1914). D. E. Sharp, *Franciscan Philosophy at Oxford in the Thirteenth Century* (British Society of Franciscan Studies, 16; 1930), pp. 115–71. T. Crowley, *Roger Bacon: The Problem of the Soul in his Philosophical Commentaries* (Louvain and Dublin, 1950). S. E. Easton, *Roger Bacon and his Search for a Universal Science* (1952). E. Massa, *Ruggero Bacone: Etica e poetica nella storia dell''Opus Maius'* (Uomini e Dottrine, 3; 1955). F. Alessio, *Mito e scienza in Ruggero Bacone* (Pubblicazioni della Facoltà di Filosofia e Lettere dell'Università di Pavia; Milan, 1957). Id., 'Un Secolo di Studi su Ruggero Bacone (1848–1957)', *Rivista Critica di Storia della Filosofia*, 14 (1959), pp. 81–102. J. M. G. Hackett, 'The Attitude of Roger Bacon to the *Scientia* of Albertus Magnus', in J. A. Weisheipl, OP (ed.), *Albertus Magnus and the Sciences: Commemorative Essays 1980* (Pontifical Institute of Mediaeval Studies, Studies and Texts, 49; 1980), pp. 53–72. A. C. Crombie and J. D. North in *Dictionary of Scientific Biography*, 1 (1970), pp. 377–85, s.v., with detailed bibl.

Baeda. See BEDE, ST.

Baeumer, Suitbert. See BÄUMER, SUITBERT.

Bagot, Richard (1782–1854), Bp. successively of *Oxford and of *Bath and Wells. He was educated at

Rugby and at *Christ Church, Oxford, and in 1804 elected a Fellow of All Souls. From 1829 to 1845 he was Bp. of Oxford. His relations with the *Tractarians are his chief interest to the historian. When in a charge of 1838 he reproved them for practices 'which hitherto had ended in superstition', E. B. *Pusey addressed to him an Open Letter. After the publication of *Tract 90* in 1841, Bagot induced J. H. *Newman to cease issuing the tracts altogether, but in a charge of 1842 he defended the Tractarians against current attacks, though he denounced the 'lamentable want of judgement' of the rank and file of the movement. In 1845 he was translated at his own desire to the see of Bath and Wells, where the closing months of his life were taken up by a controversy with G. A. *Denison, Vicar of East Brent, on Eucharistic doctrine.

S. Lee in *DNB* 2 (1885), pp. 339 f., s.v., with bibl.

Baillie, John (1886–1960), Scottish theologian. Born in the *Free Church of Scotland manse at Gairloch, Wester Ross, he went from Inverness Royal Academy to Edinburgh to study philosophy at the university and theology at New College (then a seminary of the *United Free Church for whose ministry he trained). After some years of teaching in Canada and the USA, from 1934 until his retirement in 1956 he was Professor of Divinity at Edinburgh, latterly serving also as Principal of New College. He attracted students from all over the world. He was Moderator of the General Assembly of the Church of Scotland in 1943, and Joint President of the *World Council of Churches from 1954. His numerous publications, which included *And the Life Everlasting* (1934), *Our Knowledge of God* (1939), *The Idea of Revelation in Recent Thought* (1956), and *The Sense of the Presence of God* (*Gifford Lectures for 1961–2; 1962), were marked by literary grace, loyalty to the substance of the Christian faith despite unease at some of its traditional formulations, and avoidance of philosophical and theological extremes. While giving a strictly limited welcome to the fashionable *Barthianism of his day, he made plain his deepest concerns in the eloquent apologetic of *Invitation to Pilgrimage* (1942) and the warm piety of *A Diary of Private Prayer* (1936).

His brother, **Donald Macpherson Baillie** (1887–1954) was an equally distinguished preacher, theologian, and ecumenical statesman. Teaching systematic theology at St Mary's College, St Andrews, from 1934 until his death, he won international acclaim for his *God was in Christ* (1948), with its imaginative use of the Pauline 'paradox of grace' to illuminate *Christology. Like John, Donald was deeply indebted to the *Calvinist faith and devotion of his Highland upbringing. He became a friend of the *Student Christian Movement and the *Iona Community, and a prominent figure in the Faith and Order conferences at *Edinburgh (1937) and *Lund (1952).

D. M. Baillie, *The Theology of the Sacraments and other papers* (1957), with a biographical essay by J. Baillie, pp. 11–36. D. [A. S.] Fergusson (ed.), *Christ, Church and Society: Essays on John Baillie and Donald Baillie* (Edinburgh, 1993).

Bainbridge, Christopher (*c.*1464–1514), Abp. of *York and cardinal. He was born at Hilton, near Appleby, in Cumbria, and educated at The Queen's College, Oxford, of which he was appointed provost in 1496. He held a number of benefices and was made Dean of *Windsor in 1505. In 1507 he was consecrated Bp. of *Durham, and translated to York in 1508. *Henry VIII sent him to Rome as ambassador in 1509 and *Julius II created him cardinal in 1511. As such, Julius II entrusted him with a military expedition against Ferrara. In the same year (1511), Henry chose him to inform the Pope of England's adhesion to the Holy League against France. Bainbridge died of poison administered by one of his chaplains, who accused Sylvester de Gigli, Bp. of *Worcester and resident English ambassador at Rome, of instigating him to the murder from motives of rivalry (though de Gigli was finally acquitted). A man of violent temper, Bainbridge proved himself a courageous defender of English interests at the Curia.

Liber Pontificalis Chr. Bainbridge Archiepiscopi Eboracensis, ed. W. G. Henderson (Surtees Society, 61; 1875). D. S. Chambers, *Cardinal Bainbridge in the Court of Rome 1509 to 1514* (Oxford, 1965). J. *Gairdner in *DNB* 2 (1885), pp. 433 f.; *BRUO* 1 (1957), pp. 91–3.

Baird Lectures. A series of at least six lectures established in 1871 on the benefaction of James Baird (1802–76), a wealthy ironmaster, for the defence of orthodox *Presbyterian teaching and delivered annually at Glasgow, and also if required at one other Scottish university. The lecturer must be a minister of the Church of Scotland.

Baius, Michel (1513–89), Flemish theologian. He was educated at Louvain, became principal of Standonck College in 1541, and held various appointments in the University of Louvain in the years following. Shortly after 1550 he joined John Hessels (1522–66) in asserting theological propositions on the subjects of grace and sin which were held to be unorthodox, and met with the displeasure of the Chancellor of the University and the Abp. of Malines. In 1560 eighteen of his propositions were censured by the *Sorbonne. Even so, Baius and Hessels were chosen to represent the University in 1563 at the Council of *Trent, and received the powerful protection of the King of Spain. Further publications by Baius resulted in the bull 'Ex omnibus afflictionibus' (1 Oct. 1567), in which a large number of propositions from his writings, or embodying his doctrine, were condemned, but which did not mention him by name. For the rest of his life he seems to have hesitated between loyalty to his principles and the desire to remain in the RC Church, and to have been seeking ways of verbal reconciliation between his teaching and official pronouncements. In 1579 the bull 'Provisionis Nostrae' reaffirmed that of 1567, and Baius made a formal recantation of his main views, but his subsequent writings appear to show that they still underlay his teachings.

His system, 'Baianism', is often considered an anticipation of *Jansenism. It is contained in a series of small works, in which Baius interprets in his own way the anti-*Pelagian teaching of St *Augustine. Its main principles were: (1) That in the primitive state, innocence was not a supernatural gift of God to man, but the necessary complement of human nature itself. (2) That *original sin is not merely a privation of grace, but habitual *concupiscence, transmitted by heredity, and so even in unconscious infants is a sin or moral evil of itself. (3) That the sole work of *redemption is to enable us to recover the gifts of original innocence and live moral lives; and that this end is achieved by the substitution of charity for concupiscence as the motive for each meritorious act. The grace conferred by redemption was thus not considered to be supernatural.

Opera, ed. G. Gerberon, OSB, Cologne, 1696. The 18 censured propositions, together with Baius' annotations, and a further explanation of his doctrine made to the Theology Faculty at Louvain, and part of a letter of 1569, were repr. by H. Lennerz, SJ (Pontificia Universitas Gregoriana, Textus et Documenta. Series Theologia, 24; 1938). J. B. Du Chesne, SJ, *Histoire du baïanisme ou l'hérésie de Michel Baïus* (Douai, 1731). F. X. Linsenmann, *Michael Baius und die Grundlegung des Jansenismus* (Tübingen, 1867). F.-X. Jansen, SJ, *Baius et la baianisme* (Museum Lessianum, Section Théologique, 18; Louvain, 1927). G. Fourure, *Les Châtiments divins: Étude historique et doctrinale* (Bibliothèque de Théologie, 2nd ser., Théologie Morale, 5 [1959]). G. Galeota, SJ, *Bellarmino contro Baio a Lovanio: Studio e testo di un inedito bellarminiano* (Aloisiana. Scritti Pubblicati sotto la Direzione della Pontificia Facoltà Teologica Napoletana 'S. Luigi', 5; Rome 1966), with extensive bibl.; V. Grossi, OSA, *Baio e Bellarmino interpreti di S. Agostino nelle questioni del Soprannaturale* (Studia Ephemeridis 'Augustinianum', 3; 1968). H. de *Lubac, SJ, 'Deux Augustiniens fourvoyés, Baïus et Jansénius; I. Baïus', *Rech. S.R.* 21 (1931), pp. 422–43; id., *Surnaturel: Études historiques* (Théologie, 8; 1946), esp. pp. 15–37; repr. and enlarged in id., *Augustinisme et théologie moderne* (ibid. 63; 1965), pp. 15–48; Eng. tr. (1969), pp. 1–33. É. [J. M.] van Eijl, OFM, 'L'Interprétation de la Bulle de Pie V portant condamnation de Baius', *RHE* 50 (1955), pp. 499–542. N. J. Abercrombie, *The Origins of Jansenism* (1936), pp. 87–93, 137–42, and *passim*. X. Le Bachelet, SJ, in *DTC* 2 (1905), cols. 38–111, s.v.; É. J. M. van Eijl, OFM, in *Nationaal Biografisch Woordenboek*, 1 (1964), cols. 113–29, s.v. 'Bay (Baius) Michaelde', with extensive bibl.; P. J. Donnelly in *NCE* 2 (1967), pp. 19–21, s.v. See also works cited under JANSENISM.

Baker, Augustine (baptismal name, David) (1575–1641), *Benedictine writer on ascetical theology and history. He became a RC, entered the Benedictine Order at Padua in 1605, and was ordained priest in 1613. He worked at Cambrai and *Douai, and as a chaplain in England. Of his ascetical writings the most famous survive in *Sancta Sophia, or Holy Wisdom* (2 vols., 1657), a collection made posthumously. It expounds the way of contemplation, under the headings 'Of an Internal Life in General', 'Of Mortification', and 'Of Prayer'. His important researches into the history of the origins of the Benedictine Order in England were published in *Apostolatus Benedictinorum in Anglia* (Douai, 1626). He also left in MS a Life of Dame Gertrude *More (q.v. for details).

Confessions, ed. J. McCann, OSB (1922). A short treatise, *The Substance of the Rule of St Bennet*, is ed. by the nuns of Stanbrook Abbey (Worcester, 1981). Lives by P. Salvin [OSB] and S. Cressy [OSB], ed. by J. McCann (1933); 'Memorials' incl. his autobiography and life by Fr. Leander Prichard in *Memorials of Father Augustine Baker and other Documents relating to the English Benedictines*, ed. J. McCann and [R.] H. *Connolly (Catholic Record Society, 33; 1933), pp. 1–154, with Descriptive Catalogue of Baker MSS, pp. 274–93. Modern study by A. Low (New York, 1970). J. Gaffney, *Augustine Baker's Inner Light* (Scranton, Pa. [1989]). [M.] D. *Knowles, *The English Mystical Tradition* (1961), pp. 151–87. V. M. Lagorio and R. Bradley, *The 14th-Century English Mystics: A Comprehensive Annotated Bibliography* (New York and London, 1981), pp. 166–170 (nos. 804–26). P. Spearitt, OSB, in G. S. Wakefield (ed.), *A Dictionary of Spirituality* (1983), p. 36, s.v.

Baker, Sir Henry Williams, Bart. (1821–77), hymn-writer. The son of Vice-Admiral Sir Henry Loraine Baker, he was educated at Trinity College, Cambridge. From 1851 until his death he was Vicar of Monkland, near Leominster. His many hymns, written under the influence of the *High Church Movement, of which he was a devoted supporter, were marked by simplicity of expression and smoothness of rhythm. Among those which have become well known are 'The King of Love my Shepherd is' (paraphrase of Ps. 23), 'Lord, Thy Word abideth', and 'O praise ye the Lord'. He translated a number of hymns from Latin, notably those of the 17th-cent. *Victorine hymn-writer, Jean-Baptiste de Santeuil. He was also the promoter and compiler of the original edition (1861) of *Hymns, Ancient and Modern* (q.v.) as well as the editor of other hymn-books and a devotional manual.

A. H. Grant in *DNB* 3 (1885), p. 11.

baldachino (from Ital. *Baldacco*, 'Baghdad', whence came the materials used in its construction). A canopy used to cover an altar, also called umbraculum or *ciborium. It may be made of wood, stone, or metal, in which case it is supported on pillars, or of silk or velvet when it is suspended from the ceiling or attached to the wall. It was originally surmounted by a cross, which was later placed on or behind the altar. The oldest existing example is of the 9th cent. at *Ravenna; the largest and most famous is G. L. Bernini's canopy on twisted pillars over the high altar of *St Peter's at Rome. The baldachino was required in the RC Church by the *Caeremoniale Episcoporum* of 1600 (1. 12. 13 and 1. 14. 1), but its use has ceased to be general in the 20th cent. and it is not mentioned in the 1984 revision. The Reformers objected to it on the ground that it tended to make the Lord's Table a fixture, and J. *Jewel, Bp. of *Salisbury, made it a subject of controversy with Thomas Harding (1516–72). The word is also used of the canopy over a bishop's throne, over statues, and of the movable canopy carried in processions, e.g. of the Blessed Sacrament.

Braun, *CA* 2, pp. 185–9 and 262–71. O. Treitinger in *RAC* 1 (1950), cols. 1150–3, s.v. with refs.

Baldwin (d. 1190), Abp. of *Canterbury. A native of *Exeter, he became a member of the household of Bp. Bartholomew (Bp. of Exeter, 1161–4), and was Archdeacon of Totnes, *c.*1161–1170. He was a distinguished scholar and friend of *John of Salisbury. At the height of the dispute between Henry II and Abp. Thomas *Becket, he became a *Cistercian monk at Forde in Devonshire, and by 1175 had been appointed Abbot. In 1180 he became Bp. of *Worcester. Like his predecessor, Bp. Roger, a notable Papal judge-delegate, Baldwin may have had a hand in compiling the important Worcester collection of *decretals. In 1184 he was translated to Canterbury, the suffragan bishops and the monks of Christ Church, who both claimed the right to elect, having chosen him separately. A dispute between Baldwin and the monks over property and patronage culminated in a struggle in the Papal court at Rome; in England the King had backed Baldwin, who planned to found a college of secular canons, first at Hackington, near Canterbury, and later at *Lambeth. His objective was, if not to set up an alternative cathedral, at least to provide income and status for his clerks and counsellors. In this enterprise he was unsuccessful, as was his successor, *Hubert Walter. In 1188 Baldwin held a metropolitan visitation of the Welsh dioceses, so affirming the jurisdiction of Canterbury in *Wales. In March 1190 he set out on the Third *Crusade, and died in Nov. at Acre. He was the author of sermons and several theological works, the best known being the treatise De Sacramento Altaris.

Opera repr. from B. Tissier, Bibliotheca Patrum Cisterciensium, 5 (1662), pp. 1–159, in J. P. Migne, PL 204. 401–774. De Sacramento Altaris, ed. J. Morson, OCSO, with Fr. tr. by E. de Solmes, OSB, and introd. by J. Leclercq, OSB (SC 93–4; 1963). Treatises also ed., with Fr. tr., by R. Thomas, OCSO (Pain de Cîteaux, 35–40 [1973–5]). P. Guébin, 'Deux sermons inédits de Baldwin, archevêque de Canterbury 1184–1190', JTS 13 (1912), pp. 571–4. His official letters as Abp. ed. C. R. Cheney and B. E. A. Jones, English Episcopal Acta, 2 (1986), pp. 203–75 (nos. 233–326). The correspondence over his dispute with his monks is ed. W. *Stubbs, Epistolae Cantuarienses (Chronicles and Memorials of the Reign of Richard I, 2; RS, 1865), pp. 4–329 passim, with admirable introd. On the circumstances of his translation to Canterbury, D. Whitelock, M. Brett, and C. N. L. Brooke (eds.), Councils & Synods . . . I: A.D. 871–1204, 2 (Oxford, 1981), pp. 1015–22. His journey into Wales was described by *Giraldus Cambrensis, Itinerarium Kambriae (Opera, ed. J. F. Dimock, 6, RS, 1868, pp. 3–152). On the Collectio Wigorniensis (analysed by H.-E. Lohmann in Zeitschrift der Savigny-Stiftung für Rechtsgeschichte, Kanonistische Abteilung, 22 (1933), pp. 36–187), C. Duggan, Twelfth-Century Decretal Collections (1963), pp. 110–15, and M. G. Cheney, Roger, Bishop of Worcester (Oxford, 1980), pp. 198–200.

Bale, John (1495–1563), Bp. of Ossory, 'Bilious Bale'. He entered the *Carmelite Priory at Norwich at the age of 11, and studied at Cambridge, Louvain, and Toulouse before being converted to Protestantism by Thomas Lord Wentworth c.1533; he renounced his celibacy and vigorously defended the Reformation, writing earthily Protestant plays which brought him favour from T. *Cromwell. On Cromwell's fall in 1540 he fled abroad, but returned in 1548 and in 1552 was nominated Bp. of Ossory. He and Abp. Hugh Goodacre of *Armagh provoked controversy by refusing to be consecrated by the traditional rite and insisting on the use of the Edwardine BCP; he made enemies by his energetic promotion of Protestantism. On *Mary's accession (1553), he tried to flee to Scotland, but after capture by pirates went to the Netherlands, Germany, and Switzerland. After his return to England on *Elizabeth I's accession in 1559, he retired to a prebend at *Canterbury, his literary savagery preserved to the last. His *millenarian views remained influential. Of 21 plays (mostly lost), King John (c.1536) anticipates later historical drama. Genuine if partisan historical scholarship is reflected in his Illustrium Maioris Britanniae Scriptorum, hoc est, Angliae, Cambriae, ac Scotiae Summarium (1548), an indispensable pioneering attempt at British bibliography.

Select Works, ed. H. Christmas (*Parker Society, 1849), with biogr. notice, pp. vii–xii; Complete Plays, ed. P. Happé (Tudor Interludes, 4–5; Cambridge, 1985–6). His 'Index Britanniae Scriptorum' has been ed. by R. L. Poole and M. Bateson (Anecdota Oxoniensia, Mediaeval and Modern Series, 9; 1902); his King John, ed., with modernized spelling, by W. A. Armstrong, Elizabethan History Plays (World's Classics, 1965), pp. 1–87. There is much autobiographical material in The Vocation

of John Bale to the Bishopric of Ossory in Ireland, his Persecutions in the same and final Deliverance (1553; repr. in the Harleian Miscellany, 6 [1745], pp. 402–28). Modern studies by J. W. Harris (Illinois Studies in Language and Literature, 25, pt. 4; 1940), H. McCusker (Bryn Mawr, Pa., 1942), K. Sperk (Anglistische Forschungen, 101; 1973), and L. P. Fairfield (West Lafayette, Ind., 1976). J. F. Mozley, 'John Bale', Notes and Queries, 189 (1945), pp. 276 f.; L. P. Fairfield, 'John Bale and the Development of Protestant Hagiography in England', JEH 24 (1973), pp. 145–60. W. T. Davies, 'A Bibliography of John Bale', Oxford Bibliographical Society Proceedings and Papers, 5 (1940), pp. 201–79.

Balfour, Arthur James (1848–1930), British philosopher and statesman, Prime Minister, 1902–5, and Foreign Secretary, 1916–19. In 1879 he published a work intended as an apology for religious faith with the somewhat misleading title A Defence of Philosophic Doubt. It endeavoured to show that all forms of human knowledge, including the natural sciences with their boasting claims, left certain basic residual problems which defied intellectual solution, and that the ultimate convictions of mankind rested on the non-rational ground of religious faith. This position Balfour developed in his Foundations of Belief (1895), which, in view of the eminence to which he had then risen as a statesman, attracted very wide attention. He worked out his position somewhat further in two sets of *Gifford Lectures, Theism and Humanism (1915), and Theism and Thought (1923). In public affairs, his Education Bill of 1902 provoked keen hostility from Nonconformists and in defence he published a Letter on the Criticisms of an Opponent [J. *Clifford] (subsequently included in his Essays and Addresses, 3rd edn., 1905). He was a communicant in both the C of E and the Church of Scotland.

His biography was written by B. E. C. Dugdale, his niece (2 vols. London, 1936). Further Lives by [C.] K. Young (ibid., 1963), S. [H.] Zebel (Cambridge, 1973), J. M. H. S. Wyndham, Baron Egremont (London, 1980), and R. F. Mackay (Oxford, 1985). D. Judd, Balfour and the British Empire (1968). A. Cecil in DNB 1922–1930, pp. 41–56, s.v.

Ball, John (d. 1381), priest, implicated in the insurrection of Wat Tyler. Little is known of his early life. Acc. to his own account he was first at *York and later at Colchester. In 1366, when living in Essex, he was summoned before the Abp. of *Canterbury for preaching *Wycliffite doctrines of property, and the faithful were forbidden to attend his sermons. In 1376 his arrest as an excommunicated person was ordered, but his popularity continued, esp. through his teaching of the equality of bondsmen and gentry. During Tyler's insurrection (1381) he was in custody in the Archbishop's prison at Maidstone, but was freed by the rebels and brought in triumph to Canterbury. At Blackheath he preached on the famous rhyme 'When Adam dalf and Eve span, Who was then a gentilman?' and incited the populace to kill the nobles and all others opposed to his ideal of social equality. He was present at the death of Abp. *Simon of Sudbury in the Tower, and also at the meeting of Wat Tyler and the King at *Smithfield. After Tyler's death he fled to the Midlands. He was captured at Coventry and brought before Richard II at *St Albans, where he was executed as a traitor.

The chief authorities for his life are Fasciculi Zizaniorum (ed. W. W. Shirley, Rolls Series, 1858), p. 273; Thomas Walsingham,

Historia Anglicana, 2 (ed. by H. T. Riley, RS, 1864), pp. 32–4; Henry Knighton, *Chronicon*, 2 (ed. by J. R. Lumby, RS, 1895), pp. 131 f. and 139 f. Eng. tr. of the sources, with comm. and introd., by R. B. Dobson, *The Peasants' Revolt of 1381* (2nd edn., 1983), pp. xxviii–xxx, 135–7, 369–78, and 380 f. J. *Gairdner in *DNB* 3 (1885), pp. 73 f.

Ballerini, Pietro (1698–1769), patristic scholar and canonist. He was the son of a surgeon, born at *Verona, and educated by the *Jesuits there. Ordained priest in 1722, he shortly afterwards became principal of a classical school in the same city. Attention was drawn to his work on moral theology when his extreme views on *usury were condemned by Pope *Benedict XIV in his bull *Vix pervenit* (1745). In 1748 he was sent by the republic of *Venice to defend its interests at Rome in a dispute over *Aquileia. He was then commissioned by the Pope to prepare a new edition of the works of St *Leo the Great to replace that of P. *Quesnel (1675), which had been written in the interest of *Gallicanism. This edition (3 vols., Venice, 1753–7), published in conjunction with his brother Girolamo Ballerini (1702–81), has remained the standard text of Leo; the last vol. contains a valuable collection of documents (not pub. elsewhere) and dissertations on the early history of *canon law. The joint work of the two brothers, which owed much of its success to their fruitful cooperation, also included *Henrici Norisii Veronensis . . . Opera* (4 vols., Verona, 1729–32), with valuable material on ecclesiastical history, *S. Zenonis, Episcopi Veronensis, Sermones*, with notes (ibid., 1739), *S. Antonini, Archiepiscopi Florentini, Summa Theologica*, with Life of the author (ibid., 4 pts., 1740–1) and *Ratherii, Episcopi Veronensis, Opera* (ibid., 1765). Pietro alone also pub., among other items, *Il Metodo di S. Agostino negli studi* (ibid., 1724), a history of *probabilism which seemed rather to defend the theory of *probabiliorism (ibid., 1736), an edition of the *S. Raymundi de Pennafort Summa* (ibid., 1744), a treatise on usury (Bologna, 1747) and, against *Febronianism, the *De Vi ac Ratione Primatus Romanorum Pontificum* (Verona, 1766) and the *De Potestate Ecclesiastica Summorum Pontificum et Conciliorum Generalium* (ibid., 1768).

Count Giammaria Mazzuchelli, *Gli scrittori d'Italia*, 2 (pt. 1; 1758), pp. 178–85, s.vv. T. Facchini, *Il Papato principio di unità e Pietro Ballerini di Verona* (Padua, 1950). C. da Remanzacco, 'Vita e Opere di Pietro Ballerini', *Studia Patavina*, 9 (1962), pp. 452–492. W. Telfer, 'Additional Note B. The Ballerini' appended to art. 'The Codex Verona LX (58)', *HTR* 36 (1943), pp. 231 f.; O. Capitani in *Dizionari Biografico degli Italiani*, 5 (1963), pp. 575–87, s.v.

Balsamon, Theodore (c.1140–after 1195), Greek canonist. He was born in *Constantinople and held several ecclesiastical appointments in the capital. Before 1191 he became Greek Patriarch of *Antioch, but he never exercised his official functions, as the see was held by a Latin Patriarch supported by the *Crusaders, and Balsamon continued to reside at Constantinople. His *Scholia*, his most important work, consists of: (1) a commentary on the 'Nomocanon' of *Photius, and (2) one of the principal collections of the *canon law of the E. In the latter he expounds how the civil legislation is to be treated when it conflicts with the ecclesiastical canon.

Extant works repr. from W. *Beveridge's Συνοδικόν (2 vols., Oxford, 1672) in J. P. Migne, *PG* 137 and 138. V. N. Bene-

shevich, *A Study of the Tradition of the Nomocanon of Photius and the Version of Balsamon* (in Russ.; 2 pts., St Petersburg, 1905). G. P. Stevens, *De Theodoro Balsamone: Analysis operum ac mentis juridicae* (Corona Lateranensis, 16; 1969). Krumbacher, pp. 607–9. E. Herman in *DDC* 2 (1937), cols. 76–83, with refs. to Russ. lit.

Balthasar, Hans Urs von (1905–88), Swiss theologian and writer. Born in Lucerne into a distinguished political and scholarly family, he studied German literature and philosophy at Vienna, Berlin, and Zurich. His doctoral thesis, *Die Apokalypse der deutschen Seele* (1937–9, vol. 1 repr. as *Prometheus*, 1947), is a massive study of German Idealism. In 1929 he became a *Jesuit. He continued his studies at Munich and Lyons, where his mentors were the philosopher Erich Przywara (1899–1972) and H. de *Lubac. The former's work on St *Augustine and *Ignatius Loyola and on the *analogia entis* influenced his theological development; the latter introduced him to the study of the Fathers, the fruits of which emerged in studies on *Origen (pub. in book form as *Parole et mystère chez Origène*, 1957), *Maximus the Confessor (*Kosmische Liturgie*, 1941; 2nd edn., 1961), and *Gregory of Nyssa (*Présence et Pensée*, 1942). From 1940 to 1948 he was university chaplain at Basle. Here he met K. *Barth, on whom he published an important study in 1951, and also Adrienne von Speyr, a Swiss medical doctor and mystic, who had a profound influence on his thought; he became the amanuensis of her visions, editor of her writings, and apologist of her mission. His first theological, as opposed to historical work, *Das Herz der Welt* (1945; Eng. tr., *Heart of the World*, 1979), shows her influence, as well as containing in outline the themes of his mature theology. In 1950 he left the Jesuits to set up a Secular *Institute, under von Speyr's inspiration, and also set up his own publishing house in Einsiedeln. He was nominated a cardinal in 1988 but died before he was admitted to the office.

Balthasar's literary output was enormous and very varied. It included translations into German of the Fathers and modern theologians (esp. de Lubac) but also of French Catholic literary figures such as P. L. C. *Claudel; studies of individual theologians, incl. M. *Buber (1958; Eng. tr., 1961), of the novelists Reinhold Schneider (1953) and Georges Bernanos (1954), and of the *Carmelite nuns St *Teresa of Lisieux (1950; Eng. tr., 1953) and Elizabeth of Dijon (1952; Eng. tr., 1956); a great work on prayer, *Das betrachtendes Gebet* (1955; Eng. tr., 1961); and a profound meditation of the trinitarian mystery of the *triduum sacrum, 'Mysterium Paschale' (in *Mysterium Salutis*, ed. J. Feiner and M. Löhrer, 3/2 (1969), pp. 133–326). His greatest achievement, however, lay in his theological trilogy: *Herrlichkeit: Eine theologische Ästhetik* (3 vols. in 7, 1961–9 [incomplete]; Eng. tr., *The Glory of the Lord*, 7 vols., 1982–91), to which *Glaubhaft is nur Liebe* (1963; Eng. tr., *Love Alone*, 1968) was an introduction; *Theodramatik* (1973–83); and *Theologik* (1985).

Balthasar's aim was to rescue theology from a narrowing of its concern which had resulted from a shrinking from seeing God's revelation of Himself under the transcendental category of the beautiful. God's glory was seen as the central concept of the biblical revelation, primarily beautiful, then also true and good. This conception both broadens the basis of theology—any production of the human spirit is relevant to theology—and saves theology from an arid scholasticism or ignorant piety, by uniting knowledge and love in contemplation: it is a theology of 'kneeling theologians'. The God thus discerned is God the Trinity and in the Incarnation of the Son the depths of man's godlessness are shared by the Son and drawn into the mystery of God's love by the Holy Spirit.

Balthasar's *Rechenschaft 1965* (Einsiedeln, 1965), incl. bibl. of works to date, pp. 37–79. H. de Lubac, SJ, *Paradoxe et Mystère de l'Église* [1967], pp. 180–212. J. [K.] Riches (ed.), *The Analogy of Beauty: The Theology of Hans Urs von Balthasar* (Edinburgh, 1986). L. Roberts, *The Theological Aesthetics of Hans Urs von Balthasar* (Washington, DC [1987]. K. Lehmann and W. Kasper (eds.), *Hans Urs von Balthasar: Gestalt und Werk* (Cologne, 1989). G. F. O'Hanlon, SJ, *The immutability of God in the theology of Hans Urs von Balthasar* (Cambridge, 1990). B. McGregor, OP, and T. Norris (eds.), *The Beauty of Christ: An Introduction to the Theology of Hans Urs von Balthasar* (Edinburgh, 1994). Bibl. ed. C. Capol (Freiburg [1990]).

Baltimore, Councils of. A series of ecclesiastical councils, three plenary (1852–84) and ten provincial (1829–69), by which many details of the administration and discipline of the RC Church in the USA were settled. Little was decreed on doctrinal matters; but the Second Plenary Council (1866) issued some warnings against the teachings which were later generally known as *Americanism and condemned by *Leo XIII in the letter 'Testem benevolentiae' (1899).

Acts and Decrees of the three Plenary Councils pub. at Baltimore in 1853, 1868, and 1886; Decrees and other documents of the Provincial Councils in *Acta et Decreta Sacrorum Conciliorum Recentium Collectio Lacensis*, 3 (Freiburg, 1875), cols. 9–122, 155–82, and 575–600 (also text of first two Plenary Councils, cols. 129–54 and 323–574). P. Guilday, *A History of the Councils of Baltimore: 1791–1884* (New York, 1932). W. H. W. Fanning in *CE* 2 (1907), pp. 235–41, s.v.; J. Hennesey in *NCE* 2 (1967), pp. 38–43, s.v., with further bibl.

Baluze, Étienne (1630–1718), 'Balusius', ecclesiastical historian and canonist. Born at Tulle, he was educated by the *Jesuits in Tulle and Toulouse. He became secretary to P. de *Marca, then Abp. of Toulouse, and went with him to Paris. After his death, Baluze presented a thesis on canon law at the *Sorbonne in 1665, and in 1667 became librarian to J. B. Colbert, through whose influence he was made professor of canon law at the Collège Royal in 1670 and its director in 1707. He greatly enlarged Colbert's library and incidentally built up his own (now part of the Bibliothèque Nationale). His *Histoire généalogique de la maison d'Auvergne* (1708), using documents later proved to be forgeries, sought to prove the ancient lineage of the family older than that of the King; it led to Baluze's banishment from Paris in 1710, though he was allowed to return in 1713. His writings include *Capitularia Regum Francorum* (1677), an edition of the Epistles of *Innocent III (1682; incomplete, since Baluze was denied access to the Vatican archives), *Conciliorum Nova Collectio* (1683), an edition of *Marius Mercator (1684), *Vitae Paparum Avenionensium* (1693; put on the Index for alleged *Gallicanism, 1698), and *Historia Tutelensis* (a history of Tulle, 1717).

New edn. of his *Vitae Paparum Avenionensium*, ed. G. Mollat (4 vols., Paris, 1914–28). R. Fage, *Les Œuvres de Baluze, cataloguées et décrites* (2 pts., Tulle, 1882–4). C. Godard, *De Stephano*

Baluzio Tutelensi, Libertatum Ecclesiae Gallicanae Propugnatore (Paris thesis, 1901). G. Mollat, *Étude critique sur les* Vitae Paparum Avenionensium *d'Étienne Baluze* (1917). J. Rambaud-Buhot, 'Baluze, bibliothécaire et canoniste', in *Études d'histoire du droit canonique dédiées à Gabriel Le Bras*, 1 (1965), pp. 325–42. H. *Quentin, OSB, *Jean-Dominique Mansi et les grandes collections conciliaires* (1900), pp. 32–8 and 204–69. L. Auvray and R. Poupardin, *Catalogue des Manuscrits de la Collection Baluze* (1921). G. Mollat in *DHGE* 6 (1932), cols. 439–52, s.v.; A. Martin in *Dictionnaire de Biographie Française*, 5 (1951), pp. 23–5, s.v.

Bampton Lectures. By the will of John Bampton, Canon of Salisbury (d. 1751), an endowment was created for eight annual lectures to be delivered in St Mary's, Oxford. Their subject is the exposition and defence of the Christian Faith as expressed in the Creeds, on the authority of Scripture and the Fathers. The first series was given in 1780. Since 1895 they have been delivered biennially. In modern times notable courses have been delivered by W. R. *Inge (1899), H. *Rashdall (1915), A. C. *Headlam (1920), N. P. *Williams (1924), K. E. *Kirk (1928), R. H. *Lightfoot (1934), A. M. Farrer (1948), D. E. Jenkins (1966), G. W. H. Lampe (1976), and others. Another series of lectures ('Sarum Lectures'), open to non-Anglican speakers, was established in 1952 from the Bampton fund; notable lecturers have included C. H. *Dodd (1954–5), J. *Daniélou, SJ (1956–7), B. *Capelle, OSB (1958–9), D. *Knowles, OSB (1964–5), C. Butler, OSB (1966–7), and P. Ricoeur (1978–9). In 1968 a 'Bampton Fellowship' was established for research into the subjects prescribed for the Bampton Lecturers.

Bancroft, Richard (1544–1610), Abp. of *Canterbury. He was educated at Christ's College, and later at Jesus College, Cambridge. He first became well known between 1580 and 1590 as a stern opponent and persecutor of the *Puritans. In 1586 he was made Treasurer of *St Paul's Cathedral, and in 1587 Canon of *Westminster. In a sermon preached on 1 Jn. 4: 1 in 1589 at St Paul's Cross in defence of the divine origin of episcopacy, he outspokenly condemned not only Puritanism but also *Presbyterianism. In 1597 he was appointed to the see of London, from which date, owing to J. *Whitgift's age and incapacity, he virtually possessed archiepiscopal powers. He played a leading role in the *Hampton Court Conference, at which he adopted an uncompromising position, and on Whitgift's death later in 1604 he was translated to Canterbury. The *canons passed by the Convocations of Canterbury and York in 1604 and 1606 respectively were largely his work. As archbishop, he imposed the royal policy against Puritans and endeavoured, but without success, to improve the income of the parochial clergy and to secure the complete independence of the ecclesiastical courts from secular control. He was more successful in protecting the Church's privileges against lay encroachments in Parliament. Shortly before his death, he assisted in the re-establishment of episcopacy in Scotland.

A. Peel (ed.), *Tracts ascribed to Richard Bancroft* (1953). R. G. Usher, *Reconstruction of the English Church* (2 vols., 1910). S. B. Babbage, *Puritanism and Richard Bancroft* (1962). W. D. J. C. Thompson, 'A Reconsideration of Richard Bancroft's Paul's Cross Sermon of 9 February 1588/9', *JEH* 20 (1969), pp. 253–66, with further refs. See also works cited under HAMPTON COURT CONFERENCE.

Báñez, Domingo (1528–1604), *Thomist theologian. In his youth he studied philosophy at Salamanca, and in 1547 made his profession in the *Dominican Order. For some years he studied under Domingo *Soto, and held professorships in the Spanish universities of Ávila, Valladolid, and elsewhere. In 1577 he returned to Salamanca, was elected to the chief chair in 1580, and acquired a great reputation as an exponent of the traditional Scholastic theology, in which he usually followed St Thomas down to the smallest details; and he took a prominent part in the Jesuit–Dominican controversy on *grace which led to the appointment of the 'Congregatio *de Auxiliis'. He became the director and confessor of St *Teresa of Ávila, who relied on his counsel in her own interior life, and in her reform of the *Carmelites.

Works listed in Quétif and Échard, 2 (1721), pp. 352 f. *Commentarios inéditos a la prima secundae de Santo Tomás*, ed. V. Beltrán de Heredia, OP (Consejo superior de investigaciones científicas, Institutos Francisco Suárez, 3 vols., 1942–8); *Commentarios inéditos a la tercera parte de Santo Tomás*, ed. id. (ibid., 2 vols. in 3 pts., 1951–3). *Domingo Báñez y las Controversias sobre la Gracia: Textos y Documentos*, ed. id. (ibid., 1968) M. Midali, SDB, *Corpus Christi Mysticum apud Dominicum Báñez eiusque fontes* (Analecta Gregoriana, 116; 1962). V. Beltrán de Heredia, OP, 'Actuación de Maestro Domingo Báñez en la universidad de Salamanca', *La Ciencia Tomista*, 25 (1922), pp. 64–73, 208–40; 26 (1922), pp. 63–73, 199–223; 27 (1923), pp. 40–51, 361–74; 28 (1923), pp. 36–47; id., 'El Maestro Fray Domingo Báñez y la inquisición española', ibid. 37 (1928), pp. 289–309; 38 (1928), pp. 35–58, 171–86; id., 'Valor doctrinal de las lecturas del P. Báñez', ibid. 39 (1929), pp. 60–81; id., 'Vindicando la memoria del Maestro Fray Domingo Báñez', ibid. 40 (1929), pp. 312–22; id., 'El Maestro Domingo Báñez', ibid. 47 (1933), pp. 26–39, 162–79. M. Lépée, *Báñez et Sainte Thérèse* (1947), esp. pp. 34–74, with bibl. pp. 7 f. P. Mandonnet, OP, in *DTC* 2 (1905), cols. 140–5, s.v.; F. Domínguez in *L.Th.K.* (3rd edn.), 1 (1993), cols. 1384–6, s.v. with list of works and edns.

Bangor. Of the many places of this name, the three best known are:

(1) 'Bangor Fawr' in Caernarfonshire and Merionethshire. The see was traditionally founded by the abbot-bishop, St *Deiniol (d. 584?), but scarcely anything is known of it till Norman times. The cathedral was rebuilt by Bp. Anian (1267–1305), who baptized Edward II, but it was burnt in 1402 by Owen Glendower, and lay in ruins until Bp. Henry Deane (d. 1503) began to rebuild the choir. The work was completed by Bp. Thomas Skevington (d. 1533), who had previously been Abbot of *Beaulieu. From 1716 to 1721 the see was filled by B. *Hoadly. See also BANGOR, USE OF.

(2) 'Bangor Iscoed' in Wrexham. The site of one of the greatest monasteries of Wales, which at one time held 2,000 monks. The early history of this Bangor is also uncertain; but its monks are known to have refused to cooperate with St *Augustine at the close of the 6th cent. In c.616 the Saxons under Ethelfrid of Northumbria put to death 1,200 of its monks. Little or nothing of the abbey exists today.

(3) Bangor in Co. Down, Ireland. St *Comgall founded an abbey in 555 or 559, from which many daughter monasteries arose, so that at his death (c.601) he ruled 3,000 monks. It was the original home of St *Columbanus and St *Gall. After it had been plundered by the Danes in 824 it remained derelict until rebuilt on a magnificent scale in the 12th cent. It soon decayed again, however. From 1469 *Franciscans were in possession, and a century later the *Augustinians. Very little of the abbey remains.

See also following entries.

On (1), B. Willis, *Survey of the Cathedral Church of Bangor* (1721). M. L. Clarke, *Bangor Cathedral* (Cardiff, 1969). A. I. Pryce, *The Diocese of Bangor in the XVIth Century, being a Digest of the Registers of the Bishops, 1512–1646* (Bangor, 1923); id., *The Diocese of Bangor during the Three Centuries, 1600–1899* (Cardiff, 1929). R. Graham in *DHGE* 6 (1932), cols. 494 f., s.v. See also works cited under WALES, CHRISTIANITY IN .

On (2), the chief authority is *Bede, *HE* 2. 2; notes in edn. by C. Plummer, 2 (1896), pp. 76–8.

On (3), A. Gwynn, SJ, 'The Irish Monastery of Bangor', *Irish Ecclesiastical Record*, 5th ser. 74 (1950), pp. 388–97. F. O'Briain, OFM, in *DHGE* 6 (1932), cols. 497–502, s.v.

Bangor, Antiphonary of. This *Antiphonary, written in the monastery at the Irish Bangor between 680 and 691, passed to *Bobbio, whence Federico Borromeo transferred it in 1609 to the *Ambrosiana at Milan (where it is now Cod. C. 5 inf.). It is the only surviving liturgical authority for the choir office in the early Irish Church. The familiar hymn 'Sancti venite, Christi Corpus sumite' (Eng. tr. by J. M. *Neale, 'Draw nigh and take the body of the Lord', *English Hymnal* 307) is taken from this source.

Crit. edn. by F. E. Warren (HBS 4 and 10; 1893–5). M. Curran, MSC, *The Antiphonary of Bangor and the Early Irish Monastic Liturgy* (Blackrock, Co. Dublin, 1984). F. *Cabrol, OSB, in *DACL* 2 (pt. 1; 1910), cols. 183–91.

Bangor, Use of. Of the pre-Reformation liturgical 'Use of [Welsh] Bangor' referred to by T. *Cranmer in the preface to the 1549 BCP (see CONCERNING THE SERVICE OF THE CHURCH) nothing definite can be discovered. It is likely that it preserved ancient Celtic elements and a calendar rich in Welsh saints. Earlier liturgists thought that it had survived in a MS Missal in use at Oswestry (then in the diocese of St Asaph) in 1554; but it now seems clear that this missal attests a predominantly '*Sarum Use'.

Bangorian Controversy. The dispute which followed the sermon preached by B. *Hoadly, Bp. of *Bangor, on 31 Mar. 1717 before George I on 'The Nature of the Kingdom or Church of Christ', endeavouring to prove from the text, 'My kingdom is not of this world' (Jn. 18: 36), that the Gospels afford no warrant for any visible Church authority. The subject is said to have been suggested by the King. The sermon, which was immediately published, provoked a large number of pamphlets attacking Hoadly. Among his more formidable antagonists were W. *Law, in his *Three Letters to the Bishop of Bangor* (1717–19), and T. *Sherlock. On 3 May 1717 the Lower House of *Convocation appointed a committee to consider the sermon, which reported on 10 May. When the Lower House resolved to send its findings to the Upper House, the King, to save Hoadly from synodical condemnation, which would have emphasized the opposition of the clergy to the government, prorogued Convocation, which did not meet again, except formally, until 1852.

The fullest bibliography is that by T. Herne, 'An Account of all the considerable pamphlets that have been published on either Side in the Present Controversy between the Bishop of Bangor, and Others to the End of the Year MDCCXIX', in *The Works of Benjamin Hoadly*, pub. by his son John Hoadly (1773), 2, pp. 381–

401, and 1, pp. 689–701. See also ibid. 2, pp. 379–990 and *passim*; J. O. Nash and C. *Gore, *William Law's Defence of Church Principles* (Westminster Library [1893]). H. D. Rack, ' "Christ's Kingdom not of this World": The Case of Benjamin Hoadly versus William Law Reconsidered', in D. Baker (ed.), *Church, Society and Politics* (Studies in Church History, 12; 1975), pp. 275–91. G. [E.] Rupp, *Religion in England 1688–1791* (Oxford History of the Christian Church, 1986), pp. 88–101.

banners, processional. A banner was originally the standard of a king or prince providing a rallying-point for his forces in battle. Christians of the 6th cent. had seen the symbolism of this, and were using crosses with red streamers (*vexilla*) attached for street processions in Rome. (Cf. the contemporary hymn **Vexilla Regis prodeunt*.) Medieval banners bore the armorial designs of knights and were not apparently used exclusively for Church functions.

banns of marriage. The custom of announcing a forthcoming marriage during Divine Service was probably taken over from pre-Christian practice, but it seems to have developed esp. after *Charlemagne's order for inquiry before marriage into possible *consanguinity between the parties. The word 'banns' is Middle English and means 'proclamation'. The practice was enjoined by the Synod of *Westminster of 1200 and the *Lateran Council of 1215. The BCP regards the publication of banns as the normal prelude to marriage, though the obtaining of a licence is a civil and canonical equivalent. Under the Marriage Act 1949 they must be published from an audible manner from a proper 'banns book' and not from loose papers, in the parish church or in some public chapel on three Sundays preceding the marriage, normally by a clergyman in the main morning service. If the persons to be married dwell in different parishes or chapelries, publication must take place in both, while if they are to be married in a parish on whose electoral roll at least one is entered, then publication must take place in that parish and in the parish or parishes of residence. The clergyman is entitled to seven days' notice of the first publication; and if the marriage is not solemnized within three months of the completion of publication, republication is necessary. In certain circumstances, banns may be published by a lay person, who will often be a *reader. See also MARRIAGE LICENCES.

J. B. Roberts, *Banns of Marriage: An historical Synopsis and commentary* (Catholic University of America Canon Law Studies, 64; 1931). P. M. Smith, ' "I publish the Banns of Marriage . . . " ', *Modern Churchman*, NS 12 (1969), pp. 299–308. R. D. H. Bursell, *Liturgy, Order and the Law* (Oxford, 1996), pp. 164–70.

Baptism. The *Sacramental rite which admits a candidate to the Christian Church. That it goes back to the earliest days is clear not only from the many references in Acts but also from the allusions in St *Paul's Epistles; he sometimes finds it necessary to remind his readers of its significance, but he takes for granted its existence and regular use. In Acts faith and repentance are the prerequisites (8: 13 and 2: 38), and acc. to St Paul it effects and represents the believer's union with Christ through which he participates in His death and resurrection (Rom. 6: 4), is cleansed from his sins (1 Cor. 6: 11), incorporated into the Body of Christ and 'made to drink of the Spirit' (1 Cor. 12: 13). In Acts it is associated with receiving the Spirit (2: 38), although the exact connection is not always the same (8: 15 f.; 10: 47; 19: 2–3). The chief precedents for it were the baptism of Jewish proselytes and baptism by *John the Baptist; Christians have often seen it foreshadowed in the *Flood, in *circumcision, and in other OT figures. Attempts to find its origin in paganism have won little acceptance, and the counterparts in mystery religions (apart from the question of their date) carry little weight.

It has been accepted in Christian tradition, on the basis of Matt. 28: 19 and the allusion to Baptism in Jn. 3: 5, that Christ Himself instituted the Sacrament. According to the Gospels as a whole, He saw Himself as sent by God for man's salvation, identified Himself with the human condition by accepting John's baptism (see BAPTISM OF CHRIST), and (Lk. 12: 50) spoke of His impending death as a baptism. The Church stems from His ministry, passion, and resurrection and preserved many of His parables and sayings, but how far He made His intentions explicit, and indeed how far He envisaged an organized Church as a continuing institution, is a matter of dispute among scholars.

Baptism has been in the name of the Father, Son, and Holy Spirit at least from the end of the 1st cent. Some passages in Acts (2: 38, 10: 48, and 19: 5) speak of Baptism 'in the name of (the Lord) Jesus (Christ)', but whether this formula was ever used has been questioned. Though *Infant Baptism is not mentioned in the NT, it is perhaps implied in such passages as Mt. 19: 14 and Acts 16: 33.

The rite of Baptism was developed in the early Church. In the 'Two Ways' of the *Didache* the principal duties of the candidate for Baptism and the method of administering it by triple *immersion or affusion on the head are outlined. The triple immersion is also attested by *Tertullian (*Adv. Prax.* 26), who in his *De Baptismo* and *De Corona* describes the other parts of the rite, such as the preparatory fast and vigil, the confession of sins, the renunciation of the devil and, after the immersion, the anointing, the imposition of the hand of the minister and the symbolic meal of milk and honey. A full description of what is virtually the same rite is found in the *Apostolic Tradition*. In the early Church the rite, normally presided over by the bishop, included the laying on of hands and anointing, and culminated in the Eucharist. (For the later division of these ceremonies in the W., see CONFIRMATION).

From the 2nd to the 4th cent. the proper seasons for Baptism were Easter and Pentecost, but other dates (e.g. *Epiphany and *Christmas) were added later. In cases of necessity, however, Baptism might be administered at any time and by any Christian, though, acc. to Tertullian, the *Apostolic Constitutions*, and the 'Fourth Council of *Carthage', not by women. A practice which was common in the first four or five cents. was to delay Baptism until maturity, or even until death was believed to be imminent, for fear of the responsibilities incurred by it. In the latter case Baptism was conferred without further ceremonies, but it was regarded as inferior to regular Baptism and constituted a canonical impediment debarring the persons thus baptized, who were called 'clinici' (Gk. κλίνη, 'bed'), from ordination to the priesthood. Clinical Baptism gradually fell into desuetude owing esp. to the increasing practice of Infant Baptism and the development of the penitential system.

The theology of Baptism was elucidated by the 3rd-cent. controversy on the *validity of heretical Baptism. The general practice in the W. came to be to admit persons baptized in heretical sects by mere imposition of hands. In the E., however, at least in Asia Minor, the Church refused to recognize Baptism conferred by heretics and generally rebaptized such people (on many occasions, both in antiquity and in modern times, this rule has been relaxed); this practice also prevailed in N. Africa, acc. to Tertullian, *De Baptismo*, 15. It was strongly supported by St *Cyprian and confirmed by two Councils at Carthage in 255 and 256. When the decisions of the latter were submitted to Pope *Stephen I he refused to sanction rebaptism and also threatened the African bishops with excommunication if they continued the practice. The controversy was stopped by the deaths of Stephen (257) and Cyprian (258) and a fresh outbreak of persecution, though each party continued to follow its own custom. The dispute was revived in the beginning of the 4th cent. by the *Donatists, who held Baptism to be invalid if conferred by a heretical or even an unworthy Catholic minister. The Council of *Arles in 314 opposed this view by declaring heretical Baptism valid if conferred in the name of the Trinity, and this teaching came to be generally accepted in the W. Church, esp. through the influence of St *Augustine. He established the dependence of the validity of the Sacrament on the correct form prescribed by Christ, regardless of the faith or worthiness of the minister ('*non cogitandum quis det, sed quid det*'). In defending the propriety of Infant Baptism against the *Pelagians, he also maintained that one of the chief effects of the Sacrament was the removal of the stain of *Original Sin on the soul which bars even the new-born child from the Kingdom of Heaven, thereby developing earlier teaching from NT times, acc. to which the remission of Actual Sins, the infusion of grace, and the incorporation into the Church had been generally recognized as results of Baptism. The doctrine of the Baptismal *character (Gk. σφραγίς) marking the baptized soul in a special way, which had been adumbrated by *Hermas and in the 'Acts of *Thomas' and developed in the 4th cent. by St *Cyril of Jerusalem, was taken even further by Augustine. He held that the Holy Spirit produced in Baptism an effect independent of sanctifying grace. This 'royal character' (*character regius, Contra Gaudentium*, 1. 12. 13), he held, marked the soul as God's. Elsewhere he compared it to the military mark, *nota militaris* (*De Baptismo*, 1. 4. 5), which could not be destroyed and was not to be repeated. The effects of Baptism were produced by Christ, who is the sole giver of sacramental grace, the minister being simply His instrument. Augustine allowed, however, the 'baptism of blood' by martyrdom and the 'baptism of desire' in certain cases as equivalents of the Sacrament.

The Augustinian doctrine was taken up and developed by the Schoolmen, esp. St *Thomas Aquinas, who distinguished between the 'remote matter' of water and the 'proximate matter' of immersion or affusion. Though remitting both Original and Actual Sin and their punishment, Baptism did not efface the consequences of Original Sin in the natural order such as ignorance, suffering, con-cupiscence, and death. It conferred habitual grace, the infused virtues and the gifts of the Holy Spirit. The Baptismal character formed the Christian in the image of Christ and bestowed on him a certain participation in His priesthood.

The 16th-cent. Reformers did not leave the medieval teaching on Baptism intact. The *Augsburg Confession contented itself with stating that Baptism was necessary to salvation, that by it the grace of God was offered, and that children were to be baptized and thus received into God's favour. M. *Luther sought to combine belief in the necessity of Baptism with his doctrine of justification by faith alone. Baptism was a promise of Divine grace after which a man's sins are no longer imputed to him. U. *Zwingli, on the other hand, denied the necessity of Baptism, seeing in it only a sign admitting man to the Christian community. J. *Calvin, though holding that Baptism gave man an assurance of pardon and of participation in the gifts of Christ, taught that it was efficacious only for the elect, since they alone have the faith without which the rite is worthless. The BCP preserved the traditional Catholic teaching. In the Orders for the Administration of Baptism it maintained the doctrine of Baptismal Regeneration, asserting that man is washed and sanctified with the Holy Spirit, delivered from the wrath of God, received into the ark of Christ's Church, accorded remission of sins, and made an heir of everlasting salvation. In the *Thirty-Nine Articles the teaching is less explicit, but they clearly exclude the Zwinglian view and regard Baptism as a 'sign of Regeneration' by which 'the promises of forgiveness of sin, and of our adoption to be the sons of God by the Holy Ghost, are visibly signed and sealed'. The doctrine of the RC Church was restated at the Council of *Trent, particular stress being laid on the fact that Baptism is not merely a sign of grace, but actually contains and confers it on those who put no obstacle (*obex*) in its way, and that, further, it is the instrument used by God for the justification of infidels. The modern RC legislation concerning Baptism is contained in the *CIC* (1983), cans. 849–78.

The rationalism of the 18th cent. contributed largely to the indifference towards Baptism in the Continental Protestant Churches as well as in the C of E. The revival of the Catholic doctrine of Baptismal Regeneration in the latter is due to the *Tractarian Movement, esp. E. B. *Pusey's three Tracts, nos. 67–9. The *Gorham Case (q.v.) in 1850 attracted the attention of the general public to the question, and, though the secular authorities decided against the Catholic view, the latter has become increasingly prevalent in the C of E. In recent times the need for some restatement of Baptismal theology has been widely felt. This has been esp. prompted by the custom of presenting for Baptism children from homes where there is little prospect of a Christian upbringing.

The forms of the rite used in the RC Church are still the most elaborate found in the W. The *Ordo Baptismi Parvulorum* of 1969 governs present practice. After an undertaking from the parents that the child shall be brought up in the Christian faith, the priest reads one or more passages from Scripture and delivers a homily. A prayer of *exorcism is followed by the anointing of the candidate's breast with the 'oil of catechumens', unless a local conference of bishops has authorized the omission of the latter rite. The priest then blesses the water, except in

*Paschaltide when the water blessed at the Easter Vigil is used. Both parents and *godparents renounce Satan and evil and make a declaration of faith. The priest baptizes the child, either by immersion or *affusion, using the traditional formula. He then anoints him with *chrism and the child is clothed with a white garment. The child's father lights a candle from the Paschal Candle in the baptistery and holds it. The rite of *Ephphatha may follow. The ceremony is concluded at the sanctuary with a recital of the *Lord's Prayer and a threefold blessing of the mother, father, and all present, which replaces the *Churching of Women. If Baptism is administered by a *catechist, the anointings are omitted; a form still further simplified is provided for use in danger of death. The *Ordo Initiationis Christianae Adultorum* (1972) provided a new Order for the Baptism of adults, which is not very different from that for the Baptism of children. The Sacrament is celebrated during the Easter Vigil or at least during Mass (after the homily); the rite consists of the *Litany of Saints, blessing of the water, the renunciation of evil and profession of faith (by the candidate answering for himself), the Baptism and other post-baptismal ceremonies, except for the chrismation. It is immediately followed by confirmation. Adult Baptism in the RC Church is the conclusion of the restored catechumenate (q.v.).

The rite of the C of E is much simpler. Acc. to the BCP, Baptism should be administered after the Second Lesson at Morning or Evening Prayer. After several prayers recited by the priest and a reading from the Gospel there follows the renunciation of the devil, the world, and the flesh, the confession of faith, the naming of the child by the godparents and the immersion in or affusion of water, accompanied by the Baptismal formula, followed by a signing with the cross and concluding prayers. The ASB provides, alternatively, for Baptism to be administered during the Eucharist, either at the beginning of the service or after the sermon. It also makes other modifications, including changes in the form of renunciation, a more elaborate formula for the signing with the cross, and the practice of giving a lighted candle to the parent or godparent of the child.

In conditional Baptism, which is given both in the RC Church and the C of E, when it is doubtful whether the candidate has already previously been validly baptized, most of the ceremonies are omitted and the Baptismal Formula is pronounced in a conditional form, beginning in the C of E 'If thou art not already baptized, I baptize thee'.

While the forms of the rite used in the W. have been simplified in modern times, that used by the Orthodox Church has remained unchanged. It falls into two parts: the rite for admission to the catechumenate, consisting of exorcisms, renunciation of Satan, and profession of faith, and the rite of Baptism proper, in which water and oil are blessed, the candidate is anointed with oil, immersed three times in water, and clothed with a white garment. Chrismation follows immediately, and the rite concludes with Epistle, Gospel, and final litany. Normally, though this is not always possible, Communion is given at the same time to the newly baptized.

See also BAPTISM OF CHRIST and INFANT BAPTISM.

The chief patristic authorities are *Didache*, 7; *Ep. *Barnabae*, 11; *Apostolic Tradition*, 20 f.; Tertullian, *De Baptismo*; Cyprian, *Epistulae*; Ps.-Cyprian, *De Rebaptismate*; Cyril of Jerusalem,

Catecheses, 19–21; *Ambrose, *De Mysteriis* and *De Sacramentis*; several treatises of *Gregory of Nyssa and St Augustine; John *Chrysostom, *Catecheses ad illuminandos* (Series 3), Hom. 2; *Theodore of Mopsuestia, *Homeliae catecheticae*, 12–14; *Maximus of Turin, *De Baptismo*; *Ildefonsus, *De Cognitione Baptismi*. The classical medieval treatment is in St Thomas Aquinas, *ST* 3. qq. 66–71; cf. also *Alexander of Hales, *ST* 4. qq. 1–8, and St *Bonaventure, *In quarto dist.* 1–6.

G. *Cassander, *De Baptismo Infantium* (Cologne, 1563); W. *Wall, *The History of Infant Baptism* (2 vols., 1705); J. W. F. Höfling, *Das Sacrament der Taufe* (2 vols., 1846–8; Lutheran); E. B. Pusey, *Scriptural Views of Holy Baptism* (Tracts for the Times, nos. 67–9; all 1835); J. B. *Mozley, *The Primitive Doctrine of Baptismal Regeneration* (1856); id., *A Review of the Baptismal Controversy* (1862).

J. Corblet, *Histoire dogmatique, liturgique et archéologique du sacrement de baptême* (2 vols., 1881–2); H. Windisch, *Taufe und Sünde im ältesten Christentum bis auf Origenes* (1908); W. Heitmüller, *Taufe und Abendmahl im Urchristentum* (1911); A. d'Alès, *Baptême et confirmation* (1928; Eng. tr., 1929); R. *Reitzenstein, *Die Vorgeschichte der christlichen Taufe* (1929); P. Lundberg, *La Typologie baptismale dans l'ancienne Église* (Acta Seminarii Neotestamentici Upsaliensis, 10; 1942). W. F. Flemington, *The New Testament Doctrine of Baptism* (1948); R. Schnackenburg, *Das Heilsgeschehen bei der Taufe nach dem Apostel Paulus* (Münchener Theologische Studien, 1. Historische Abteilung, 1; 1950; Eng. tr., 1964); G. W. H. Lampe, *The Seal of the Spirit* (1951); A. Benoît, *Le Baptême chrétien au second siècle: La théologie des pères* (1953). A. Stenzel, SJ, *Die Taufe: Eine genetische Erklärung der Taufliturgie* (Innsbruck, 1958). A. Gilmore (ed.), *Christian Baptism: A Fresh Attempt to Understand the Rite in terms of Scripture, History, and Theology* (1959). R. E. O. White, *The Biblical Doctrine of Initiation* (1960). E. C. Whitaker, *Documents of the Baptismal Liturgy* (1960; 2nd edn., 1970). G. R. Beasley-Murray, *Baptism in the New Testament* (1962). T. Maertens, *Histoire et pastorale du rituel du catéchuménat et du baptême* (Bruges, 1962). J. D. C. Fisher, *Christian Initiation: Baptism in the Medieval West: A Study in the Disintegration of the Primitive Rite of Initiation* (Alcuin Club Collections, 47; 1965); id., *Christian Initiation: The Reformation Period* (ibid. 51; 1970), pp. 3–156; P. J. Jagger, *Christian Initiation 1552–1969* (ibid. 52; 1970); L. L. Mitchell, *Baptismal Anointing* (ibid. 48; 1965). G. Wainwright, *Christian Initiation* (Ecumenical Studies in History, 10; 1969). E. [J.] Yarnold, SJ, *The Awe-Inspiring Rites of Initiation: Baptismal Homilies of the Fourth Century* [tr. into Eng., with full introd.] (Slough, 1972). R. F. G. Burnish, *The Meaning of Baptism: A Comparison of the Teaching and Practice of the Fourth Century with the Present Day* (Alcuin Club Collections, 67; 1985). P.-R. Tragan (ed.), *Alle Origini del Battesimo Cristiano: Atti del' VIII Convegno de Teologia Sacramentaria, Roma, 9–11 marzo 1989* (Studia Anselmiana, 106; 1991). P. [J.] Cramer, *Baptism and Change in the Early Middle Ages, c.200–c.1150* (Cambridge, 1993). J. D. Crichton, *Christian Celebration: The Sacraments* (1973), esp. pp. 29–87; A. Kavanagh, *The Shape of Baptism: The Rite of Christian Initiation* (Studies in the Reformed Rites of the Catholic Church, 1; New York, 1978); R. Cabié in A. G. Martimort, *L'Église en Prière* (1983–4 edn.), 3, pp. 23–114; Eng. tr. (1988), pp. 11–100. R. Schulte in *Mysterium Salutis*, ed. J. Feiner and M. Löhrer, 5 (Einsiedeln, 1976), pp. 136–221. Various authors in C. [P. M.] Jones, G. Wainwright and E. [J.] Yarnold, SJ (eds.), *The Study of Liturgy* (1978), pp. 79–146; 2nd edn. (1992), pp. 111–83. On Baptism in the E. Church, A. Schmemann, *Of Water and the Spirit* ([Tuckahoe, NY] 1974). B. Varghese, *Les onctions baptismales dans la tradition Syrienne* (CSCO 512, Subsidia, 82; Louvain, 1989).

Various authors in *HERE* 2 (1909), pp. 367–412 (on Christian and non-Christian Baptism), and in *DTC* 2 (1905), cols. 167–378; P. de Puniet, OSB, in *DACL* 2 (pt. 1, 1910), cols. 251–346; A. Oepke, βάπτω, βαπτίζω, βαπτισμός, βάπτισμα, βαπτιστής in *TWNT* 1 (1933), pp. 527–44 (Eng. tr., 1 (1964), pp. 529–46). J. Coppens in *Dict. Bibl.* suppl. 1 (1928), cols. 852–924, all with bibl. See also bibl. to CONFIRMATION and INFANT BAPTISM.

'Baptism, Eucharist and Ministry' (BEM). A major statement on these subjects was approved by the *Faith and Order Commission of the *World Council of Churches at Lima in Peru in 1982. It was the fruit of multilateral conversations going back to the *Lausanne Conference of 1927. Virtually all confessional traditions were represented. In the discussions past controversies were examined in the hope of setting divided Churches free to confront the future together, not in rivalry; the Churches were invited to consider the statement at the highest level and report their reactions. The text expressly affirms convergence, not consensus sufficient to remove all division; the restoration of unity is seen as a gradual process. Added commentaries identify unresolved differences (e.g. ordination of *women); questions of *authority (synods, primacy) remain unexamined, but a high estimate of Scripture is implicit throughout. Though the extent and depth of agreement has astonished the Churches, difficulties have been felt. Orthodox theologians believe that one Church already exists and is not something to be realized by the agreement of heterogeneous bodies on the theology of the sacraments. Non-episcopal bodies have been pained by the suggestion that they should consider the threefold ministry of bishops, priests, and deacons as a norm they would do well to recover. Baptists are asked to avoid rebaptism. RCs find the language about sacraments ambiguous and inadequate and ask for further study of the nature of the apostolic tradition and the issue of decisive authority in the Church. Reformed bodies desire explicit enthusiasm for the Reformation. Some Protestants would have preferred more symbolist and less realist accounts of the Eucharistic Presence and offering, and prefer to think of the pastor as representing Christ the Shepherd rather than as Priest. Nevertheless, *Baptism, Eucharist and Ministry* is one of the most important theological documents hitherto produced by the ecumenical movement, resolving many classical difficulties, and putting others into a new perspective.

The text, published by the World Council of Churches as Faith and Order Paper no. 111 (Geneva, 1982) is repr. in H. Meyer and L. Vischer (eds.), *Growth in Agreement* (Faith and Order Paper no. 108; New York and Geneva, 1984), pp. 465–503. The official reaction of the Churches, ed. M. Thurian, *Churches respond to BEM* (World Council of Churches, Faith and Order Papers, nos. 129, 132, 135, 137, 143, and 144; 1986). L. Vischer, *Die ordinierten Dienste in der Kirche* (Texte der Evangelischen Arbeitstelle Oekumene, 3; Bern, 1984). *Towards a Church of England Response to BEM and ARCIC* (General Synod Paper 661; 1985), pp. 1–61.

'baptism in the Holy Spirit'. A doctrine best known today in its *Pentecostal form. Pentecostals generally claim that the believer is empowered for Christian witness through a unique action of Christ (cf. Mark 1: 8), distinct from conversion or sacramental *Baptism ('water baptism'). They maintain that, as the Holy Spirit fell on the first Apostles, so those summoned to be likewise 'filled' (cf. Acts 2: 4) are 'baptized with the Holy Spirit' (cf. Acts 11: 15 f.), and that the normal outward sign of this 'baptism' is their breaking into tongues (*glossolalia) (cf. Acts 10: 44–7). This criterion is the specifically Pentecostal contribution to the doctrine, which had its origins in J. *Wesley's teaching on *perfection as it was developed in the 19th-cent. American *Holiness movement. Many NT

exegetes question the scriptural basis of the teaching, but it has been accepted in a modified form by many members of the *Charismatic Renewal Movement.

J. D. G. Dunn, *Baptism in the Holy Spirit: A Re-examination of the New Testament Teaching on the Gift of the Spirit in Relation to Pentecostalism Today* (Studies in Biblical Theology, 2nd. ser. 15; 1970); D. W. Dayton, *The Theological Roots of Pentecostalism* (Studies in Evangelicalism, 5; Metuchen, NJ, and London, 1987), pp. 87–113.

Baptism of Christ. This event is recorded by the first three Evangelists and implied by Jn. Even those critics who question the historical accuracy of many details in the Gospels accept that Jesus Christ came to hear St *John the Baptist and, like others, received baptism at his hands, thus endorsing John's mission. Mk. 1: 10–11 tells of a vision of the heavens opening and a Divine Voice declaring His Sonship. Later accounts, including *Ignatius, *Justin, the Gospels of the *Ebionites, *Nazarites, and *Hebrews, develop the tradition, reflecting some perplexity that the sinless Son of God should undergo a baptism of repentance, and at the hands of a subordinate figure.

Among patristic writers who regard the Lord's baptism as instituting Christian Baptism are *Ambrose, *In Luc.* 2. 83, and *Chrysostom, *Hom. in Mt.* 12. 3; cf. also St *Thomas Aquinas, *Summa Theolog.*, 3. 66. 2. G. R. Beasley-Murray, *Baptism in the New Testament* (1962), pp. 45–67. H. Anderson, *The Gospel of Mark* (New Cent. Bib., 1976), pp. 74–80. See also other comm. on MARK, GOSPEL OF ST, cited s.v.

baptistery. The building or part of the church in which *Baptism is administered. At least from the 3rd cent. onwards, esp. in Mediterranean lands, this was often a separate building west of the church and polygonal in plan. But the spread of infant Baptism (by *affusion) led to the increasingly common use of *fonts, quite often placed at the west end of the church. In modern churches, however, the fonts are sometimes placed below floor-level, to emphasize the Pauline doctrine of Baptism, and the RC *Ordo* of 1969 envisages that in some baptisteries there may be running water.

The earliest known baptistery is that at *Dura Europos (before AD 256). Another example is that at the *Lateran at Rome, which in its origins dates from the time of *Constantine I (much altered later). It is octagonal, with a low font (now lost), surrounded by eight columns and an ambulatory. The church of S. Costanza, orig. built as a tomb for the daughter of Constantine, is another round Roman edifice which was also formerly used as a baptistery. There are later examples at Pisa, *Ravenna, Florence, Nocera, Tebéssa, el-Kantara, Poitiers, and elsewhere.

J. Corbet, 'Des Lieux consacrés à l'administration du baptême', *Revue de l'Art Chrétien*, 23 (1877), pp. 276–81; 24 (1877), pp. 112–82, 300–10; 25 (1878), pp. 26–49, 275–316. C. F. Rogers, 'Baptism and Christian Archaeology', *Studia Biblica et Ecclesiastica*, 5 (Oxford, 1903), pp. 239–361, esp. pp. 321–59, *passim*. F. J. Dölger, *Antike und Christentum*, 4 (1934), pp. 153–87 ('Zur Symbolik des altchristlichen Taufhauses'). J. G. Davies, *The Architectural Setting of Baptism* (1962). A. Khatchatrian, *Les Baptistères Paléochrétiens: Plans, notices et bibliographie* (1962). P. [J.] Cramer, *Baptism and Change in the Early Middle Ages*, c.200–c.1150 (Cambridge, 1993), pp. 267–90. On the famous baptistery at the Lateran, see also G. Pelliccioni, *Le nuove scoperte sulle origini* del *Battistero Lateranense* (Atti della Pontificia Accademia Romana di Archeologia, 3rd ser. 3, Memorie, 12/1; 1973); on that at Ravenna, S. K. Kostof, *The Orthodox Baptistery at Ravenna* (Yale Publications in the History of Art, 18; 1965). R. [L. P.] Milburn, *Early Christian Art and Architecture* (1988), pp. 203–14. A. Nesbitt in *DCA* 1 (1875), pp. 173–8; H. *Leclercq, OSB, in *DACL* 2 (pt. 1; 1910), cols. 382–469; E. Josi and E. Lavagnino in *EC* 2 (1949), cols. 1050–6; F. W. Deichmann in *RAC* 1 (1950), cols. 1157–67, s.v. 'Baptisterium', with extensive refs.

Baptists. One of the largest Protestant and Free Church communions, to be found in every Continent. Its total membership in 1988 was over 35 million, with a much larger community strength. The origins of the Baptists in modern times have been traced to the action of John *Smyth, a *Separatist exile in Amsterdam who, in 1609, reinstituted the Baptism of committed believers as the basis of fellowship of a gathered Church. But Smyth was under *Mennonite influence, and Baptist beginnings have also been traced back to the *Anabaptist wing of the Continental *Reformation (esp. in Zurich), to the protests of medieval sects against prevailing baptismal theory and practice, and to the period of the early Church and the NT. Smyth and his associates were concerned to re-establish the Baptism of believers according to its NT meaning, in the interests of a true doctrine of the nature of the Church.

The first Baptist Church in England consisted of certain members of Smyth's Church who returned to London in 1612 under the leadership of Thomas *Helwys. From this a number of other Churches sprang in Stuart and Commonwealth times. *Arminian in theology with a connectional polity, they came to be known as 'General Baptists'. In 1633 the adoption of believers' Baptism by a group of *Calvinistic London Separatists, who were members of the Church which had Henry Jacob as pastor, led to the rise of 'Particular Baptist' Churches in many parts of the country. About the same time *immersion became their usual mode of Baptism, instead of *affusion or sprinkling, again in obedience to the NT. These Particular (Calvinistic) Baptist Churches were independent or congregational in polity but gave regular expression to their inter-Church relationships through Associations, which have continued to be a vital part of Baptist Church life.

Many Baptists were associated with the more radical spiritual and political movements of the 17th cent. They were pioneers in the quest for freedom of conscience and religious liberty. After the *Restoration they moved close to the *Presbyterians and *Independents and became recognized as one of the *Three Denominations of Protestant Dissenters. John *Bunyan was an outstanding figure among them and was important not only for his writings but because he encouraged a pattern of local Church membership which could include Baptists and Paedobaptists. From the mid-17th cent. there were Baptist Churches in the American colonies. The settlement of Roger *Williams at Providence, Rhode Island, and the Church formed there in 1639 on Baptist principles is generally regarded as the beginning of American Baptist history. A small 17th-cent. group who became known as Sabbatarian or Seventh Day Baptists, and whose descendants are still represented in both England and North America, regarded the Fourth *Commandment as requiring services on the seventh, not the first, day of the week.

In the 18th cent. many of the General Baptist Churches in England came under *Unitarian influences and ultimately ceased to maintain their witness to believers' Baptism. But Dan Taylor (1738–1816), under the stimulus of the *Evangelical Revival, in 1770 formed a 'New Connexion' among them, which maintained a vigorous life, and a century later united with the main stream of Baptist witness. The *Baptist Missionary Society, formed in 1792 by ministers of the Northamptonshire Association of Particular Baptists at the call of William *Carey, initiated the modern movement of missionary expansion among Protestant Churches. Northamptonshire Baptists had been stirred by reports of the *Great Awakening in New England. This revival quickened the Baptist Churches of America and led to the beginnings of the rapid and spectacular growth of Baptists in that continent. Baptist preachers were in the van as the frontier was carried westwards. As a result of their missionary zeal Baptists became the largest religious community in many of the southern States, and among the *Black Churches of the USA about two-thirds of the members are Baptists. By 1988 there were over 29 million Baptists in North America. They are organized in several Conventions, the Southern Baptist Convention being the largest and most conservative. American Baptists have been noted for their vigorous missionary work, Adoniram *Judson of Burma being its pioneer. Other notable American Baptists have included the historian K. S. Latourette (1884–1968), Martin Luther *King, and Billy *Graham. In South America there are over 850,000 Baptists with another 230,000 in Central America and the Caribbean.

The rigid Calvinism of the 18th cent. was gradually modified not only in America, but also in England, though not without some protests. There remained in England a number of 'Strict Baptist' Churches, strongly Calvinist in theology, where Communion was, and indeed still is, restricted to baptized believers. In the 19th cent. most other Baptist Churches welcomed all believers to Communion, many also adopting 'open communion' after the Bunyan pattern. The increase in their numbers more than kept pace with the growth in population, and from their ranks came outstanding preachers such as Robert *Hall, C. H. *Spurgeon, Alexander *Maclaren, and John *Clifford. The Baptist Union, formed in 1813, was gradually transformed into the Baptist Union of Great Britain and Ireland. Its modern development owed much to the leadership of J. H. *Shakespeare, who was secretary for over 25 years (1898–1924). In Britain there are some 216,000 Church members. Baptists in England and three Baptist Associations in Wales shared in the Free Church movement and are members of the *Free Church Federal Council, Churches Together in England, the *Council of Churches for Britain and Ireland (as they were of the *British Council of Churches), and of the *World Council of Churches. The Baptist Union of Wales is a member of CYTUN (Churches Together in Wales). The Baptists of *Scotland were much influenced by the life and teaching of Archibald McLean (1733–1812). He and his followers kept close to the NT in both doctrine and practice and were at one time known as 'Scotch Baptists' or '*Sandemanian Baptists'. Their work provided one of the sources of the *Disciples of Christ. Baptists have been numerous in *Wales since John Myles (or Miles,

1621–84) organized the first Church at Ilston (1649) and Vavasour Powell (1617–70) acted as the leader of a band of itinerant evangelists. Their most famous preacher was Christmas Evans (1766–1838). There has been a considerable emigration of Baptists from Wales to the USA. Baptists in *Ireland trace their roots back to Churches founded by Baptist officers and chaplains in Oliver *Cromwell's army and by settlers who remained there after the Restoration. These Churches, mainly of Particular Baptists with a leavening of General Baptists, survived through the 18th cent., later receiving support from English Particular Baptists.

In 1834 a Baptist Church was formed in Hamburg under the leadership of J. C. Oncken (1800–84) and from this came an extensive Baptist movement in Europe, spreading to Slavic-speaking people. Baptists were generally persecuted in Tsarist *Russia. They increased in numbers during the early years of the Soviet regime but later suffered from the general restrictions on religious freedom. In recent times their numbers have grown significantly (to some 548,000, according to the best estimates in 1988), and they form the largest Protestant community in the countries of the former USSR.

Baptist Churches were formed in *Australia and *New Zealand in the early 19th cent., and in the 20th cent. Baptist work has expanded throughout Asia, Africa, and South America. In 1905 the Baptist World Alliance was formed at a congress in London as a forum for international co-operation. It has several Commissions which deal with a variety of denominational concerns, including ecumenical relations. Its present headquarters is in McLean, Virginia.

In spite of their variety and individualism, most Baptists have remained strongly attached to the truths of evangelical Christianity. In their worship they follow in general the Reformed tradition. Their polity is a modified form of independency. Their ministers, or pastors, receive, in most countries, a careful training. Their oldest college in Britain (Bristol) traces its history back to the 1679 bequest of Edward Terrill. Regent's Park College, of which H. Wheeler *Robinson was principal from 1920 to 1942, is now a Permanent Private Hall of *Oxford University. Many colleges and universities in America and elsewhere are under Baptist auspices. In ecumenical relationships Baptists have been hesitant about schemes for organic union, partly because of their concern to preserve their witness to believers' Baptism and the autonomy of the local Church as the 'gathered community'; but they have been eager for partnership and co-operation with other Christians. Although only about 15 Baptist Conventions or Unions are members of the World Council of Churches, they comprise about 40 per cent of the world Baptist constituency.

T. Armitage, A History of the Baptists; Traced by their Vital Principles and Practices, from the Time of our Lord and Saviour Jesus Christ, to the Year 1886 (New York and London, 1888). H. L. McBeth, The Baptist Heritage (Nashville, 1987). T. Crosby, The History of the English Baptists, from the Reformation to the Beginning of the Reign of King George I (4 vols., 1738–40); J. Ivimey, A History of the English Baptists (4 vols., 1811–30). A. Taylor, The History of the English General Baptists (2 pts., privately pr., London, 1818). J. H. Wood, A Condensed History of the General Baptists of the New Connexion (1847). W. T. Whitley, A History of the British Baptists (1923); A. C. Underwood, A History of the English Baptists (1947). W. T. Whitley, The Baptists of London 1612–1928 [1928]. B. R. White, The English Baptists of the Seventeenth Century (A History of the English Baptists, 1 [1983]); R. Brown, The English Baptists of the Eighteenth Century (ibid. 2 [1986]); J. H. Y. Briggs, The English Baptists of the Nineteenth Century (ibid. 3 [1994]). E. A. Payne, The Baptist Union: A Short History (1959). T. M. Bassett, The Welsh Baptists (Swansea, 1977). D. W. Bebbington (ed.), The Baptists in Scotland: A History (Glasgow, 1988). G. K. Parker (ed.), Baptists in Europe: History & Confessions of Faith (Nashville [1982]). A. H. Newman, A History of the Baptist Churches in the United States (American Church History, 2; New York, 1894). O. K. and M. M. Armstrong, The Indomitable Baptists: A Narrative of their Role in Shaping American History (Garden City, NY, 1967). R. G. Torbet, Venture of Faith: The Story of the American Foreign Missionary Society ... 1814–1954 (Philadelphia [1955]). R. A. Baker, The Southern Baptist Convention and its People 1607–1972 (Nashville [1974]). L. Fitts, A History of Black Baptists (ibid. [1985]). E. R. Fitch, The Baptists of Canada (Toronto [1911]). B. S. Brown, Members One of Another: The Baptist Union of Victoria, 1862–1962 (Melbourne, 1962). W. L. Lumpkin, Baptist Confessions of Faith (Philadelphia [1959]). E. A. Payne, The Fellowship of Believers: Baptist Thought and Practice Yesterday and Today (1944; 2nd edn., 1952). A. Gilmore (ed.), Christian Baptism (1959). W. T. Whitley, A Baptist Bibliography (2 vols., 1916–22); E. C. Starr, A Baptist Bibliography (26 vols., Hamilton, NY, and later other places, 1947–76).

See also publications of the Baptist Historical Society, esp. The Baptist Quarterly (1908 ff.), and works cited under ANABAPTISTS.

Baptist Missionary Society.

It was founded at Kettering, Northants, on 2 Oct. 1792, with Andrew Fuller (1754–1815) as its first secretary. Its first missionary, W. *Carey, to whose earnest pleading the society owed its origin, went in 1793 to the Indian subcontinent, where the Society still has active links with Church bodies. Its other main fields have been: (1) Jamaica, where William Knibb (1803–45) and other missionaries gave vigorous support to the cause of slave emancipation, (2) *China, where Timothy Richard (1845–1919) was an outstanding pioneer, (3) *Zaire, where George Grenfell (1845–1906) and Holman Bentley (1855–1906) played notable parts in the opening up of the Congo River, and (4) *Brazil, which since 1953 has become an area of major involvement. The Society has about 200 missionaries working alongside Christian nationals engaged in pastoral, evangelistic, developmental, educational, and medical work.

Essays in J. B. Meyers (ed.), The Centenary Volume of the Baptist Missionary Society (1892); others in the BMS commemorative vol., Ter-Jubilee Celebrations, 1942–4 (1945); B. Stanley, The History of the Baptist Missionary Society 1792–1992 (Edinburgh, 1992). E. A. Payne, Freedom in Jamaica: Some Chapters in the Story of the Baptist Missionary Society [1933]; id., The First Generation: Early Leaders of the Baptist Missionary Society in England and India [1936]; id., The Great Succession: Leaders of the Baptist Missionary Society during the Nineteenth Century [1938].

Barabbas.

The 'robber' (λῃστής, Jn. 18: 40) whom (according to Mk. 15: 6–15 and parallels) *Pilate released from prison instead of Christ. It is possible (on the evidence of certain MSS), but unlikely, that his real name was 'Jesus Barabbas', Barabbas in that case being a patronymic.

H. A. Rigg, 'Barabbas', Journal of Biblical Literature, 64 (1945), pp. 417–56. See also comm. to MARK, ST, GOSPEL OF, cited s.v.

Barbara, St.

Acc. to tradition, the daughter of a pagan of Nicomedia, who on being converted to the Christian faith was handed over by her father to the prefect and martyred. A circumstantial account of her martyrdom is contained in the *Golden Legend*. She is one of the 14 *Auxiliary Saints. Her prayers are sought esp. as a protection against thunderstorms and fire; and, by an obvious extension of this idea, she is venerated as the patroness of artillerymen and firemen. Feast day, 4 Dec., suppressed in Roman Calendar of 1969.

The earliest accounts, apparently written in Gk., are now lost; various versions in Syr., Lat., and other languages survive. A late Gk. text is printed in J. P. Migne, *PG* 116. 301–16; another, prob. earlier, ed. A. Wirth, *Danae in christlichen Legenden* (Prague, etc., 1892), pp. 103–12. Syr. text ed. A. Smith Lewis, *Studia Sinaitica*, 9 (1900), pp. 101–10, with Eng. tr., 10 (1900), pp. 77–84; W. Weyh, *Der syrische Barbara-Legende* (1912). Lat. text in P. Paschini, *S. Barbara: Note agiografiche* ('Lateranum', 1927), pp. 38–52, with refs. B. de Gaiffier, SJ, 'La Légende latine de Sainte Barbe par Jean de Wackerzeele', *Anal. Boll.* 77 (1959), pp. 5–41. S. Peine, *St. Barbara, die Schutzheilige der Bergleute und der Artillerie, und ihre Darstellung in der Kunst* (1896). Comte de Lapparent, 'Sur quelques représentations de Sainte Barbe', *Bulletin Monumental*, 86 (1927), pp. 149–53.

Barbarossa. See FREDERICK I.

barbe (Fr. 'uncle', lit. 'the bearded'). A title of respect used by the *Waldenses of their preachers.

Barberini. A Roman family of Tuscan descent, several of whose members filled important offices in the Church in Italy in the 17th cent. In 1623 Maffeo Barberini was elected Pope as *Urban VIII. Francesco Barberini the elder (1597–1679), who built the fine Palazzo Barberini in Rome, founded in 1627 the 'Biblioteca Barberina', containing the famous collection of MSS which passed to the Vatican Library in 1902. Their reckless plundering of ancient monuments for their designs, e.g. Urban VIII's conversion of the bronze beams of the roof of the portico of the Pantheon into the *baldachino for the high altar at St Peter's and cannon for the Castel S. Angelo, gave rise to the *mot* 'Quod non fecerunt barbari, fecerunt Barberini'.

P. Pecchiai, *I Barberini* (Archivi d'Italia e Rassegna Internazionale degli Archivi, Quaderno doppio 5; 1959). T. H. Didier and F. Bonnard in *DHGE* 6 (1932), cols. 640–5, s.v.; G. Graglia in *EC* 2 (1949), cols. 825–7, s.v., with bibl.

Barclay, John (1734–98), founder of the '*Bereans' (q.v.) or 'Barclayites'. The son of a farmer at Muthill in Perthshire, he was educated at St Andrews University, where he came under the influence of Archibald Campbell (1691–1756), professor of Church history, whose teaching was attracting attention through its denial of natural theology. In 1759 Barclay was licensed by the presbytery of Auchterarder, and soon afterwards became assistant to James Jobson, the incumbent of Errol, a strong Evangelical. Differences of opinion with Jobson led him to move in 1763 to Fettercairn, Kincardine, where he was appointed assistant to A. Dow. In 1766 Barclay published *Rejoice Evermore, or Christ All in All*, in which he expounded a doctrine of immediate Divine revelation. Censure for heresy by the presbytery followed, and in consequence, despite a petition to the Crown from virtually all the parishioners, he was not appointed to succeed Dow on his death in 1772. Barclay then made his way to Edinburgh, where he gained only a small following. Unable to procure

ordination in Scotland, he went to Newcastle, and here he succeeded in being regularly ordained in 1773. Returning soon afterwards to Edinburgh, he constituted a new Church, known as the Berean Assembly, from its zeal for study of the Bible (cf. Acts 17: 10 f.). He laboured on behalf of the community in considerable poverty, but with great earnestness, and continued to publish writings. The chief was a collected work (1776) containing *inter alia* his earlier *The Psalms, paraphrased according to the New Testament Interpretation* (1766), illustrating Barclay's beliefs on Scripture. In 1776 Barclay went to London to propagate his doctrines; here he seems to have met with considerable success, and established Berean communities both in London and at Bristol. He returned to Scotland in 1778, continuing to work and travel for his cause, despite very straitened conditions, till his death.

The Works of John Barclay [i.e. his Essays], ed. J. Thomson and D. McMillan (Glasgow, 1852), with 'A Short Account of the Early Part of the Life of Mr. John Barclay', pp. 11–21. A. Miller in *HERE* 2 (1909), pp. 519–23, s.v. 'Bereans'.

Barclay, Robert (1648–90), Scottish *Quaker apologist. He was the son of David Barclay (1610–86), who served as a soldier under *Gustavus Adolphus, assisted in the defeat of Montrose before Inverness (1646) and was one of the 30 Scottish Members of Parliament under O. *Cromwell (1654 and 1656). Robert was born at Gordonstoun and educated at the (RC) Scots' Theological College at *Paris. His father having declared his adhesion to the Quakers in 1666, Robert followed his example in 1667. He soon acquired a wide learning which, combined with considerable intellectual powers, made him the most weighty of all Quaker theologians. In 1673 he published *A Catechism and Confession of Faith*. In 1676 there followed his principal work, his 'Apology', written to support 15 Quaker 'Theses Theologicae' which he had defended at Aberdeen and circulated in English, Latin, French, and Dutch. It was originally printed in Latin at Amsterdam as *Theologiae Verae Christianae Apologia* (1676); the English version, *Apology for the True Christian Religion, as the same is set forth and preached by the people called in Scorn 'Quakers'*, first appeared in 1678. Its impressive and eloquent defence of the doctrine of the '*Inner Light' against the sufficiency of external authorities, including the Bible, made it the classical exposition of Quaker principles. The work also included a strong attack on *Calvinism. During his travels in the Netherlands and Germany (1676) Barclay won the sympathy of Elizabeth, the Princess Palatine, for Quaker principles; and on his return he came into favour with the Duke of York (later *James II), a distant relative whom he believed to be a genuine advocate of toleration. He was thus able to be of service to W. *Penn in his foundation of Pennsylvania, which was given a constitution on Quaker principles, and in 1683 Barclay himself became (non-resident) governor of East New Jersey. In the course of his life Barclay often suffered imprisonment for his doctrines. His other writings include *The Anarchy of the Ranters* (1676).

His works were issued in 1692 in a collected folio vol., with the title *Truth Triumphant*. They were repub. in 3 vols. in 1717–18. The *Apology* has often been repr. M. C. Cadbury, *Robert Barclay: His Life and Work* (1912). L. Eeg-Olofsson, *The Conception of the Inner Light in Robert Barclay's Theology* (Lund, 1954). D. E.

Trueblood, *Robert Barclay* (New York and London [1968]). Introductory account, with extracts of his writings, by J. P. Wragge, *The Faith of Robert Barclay* (1948).

Barclay, William (1907–78), NT scholar. After taking degrees in classics and divinity at Glasgow, he studied for a year (1932–3) at *Marburg. From 1933 to 1946 he was minister of Trinity Church, Renfrew (a suburb of Glasgow); from 1947 until his retirement in 1977 he held teaching appointments at Glasgow University, being from 1963 Professor of Divinity and Biblical Criticism. His principal importance lay in his ability to distil the fruits of NT scholarship and to communicate the Gospel message in plain language to a very wide public, both through his writing and broadcasting.

There is much autobiographical material in his *Testament of Faith* (1975). J. R. McKay and J. F. Miller (eds.), *Biblical Studies: Essays in Honour of William Barclay* (1976). Life by C. L. Rawlins (Grand Rapids, Mich., and Exeter, 1984).

Bar Cochba (Aram. בר כוכבא, i.e. 'son of a star'; cf. Num. 24: 17). The leader of a Jewish rebellion in Palestine in AD 132. Its purpose was to resist the project of the Emp. Hadrian to rebuild *Jerusalem as a Graeco-Roman city, with a temple of Jupiter on the site of the former Jewish Temple. (See AELIA CAPITOLINA.) A guerrilla war was waged from 132 to 135 in which both sides suffered severe losses. He claimed to be, and was accepted as, the *Messiah, acc. to Christian sources, echoed in rabbinic literature. The name Bar Cochba is found only in some rabbinic and in Christian sources; most Jewish sources call him Bar Koziba ('son of a liar'). Recent finds of some of his letters in the Judaean desert show that his real name was Simeon bar Kosiba.

J. T. Milik in P. Benoit, OP, J. T. Milik, and R. de Vaux, OP, *Les Grottes de Murabba'at* (Discoveries in the Judaean Desert, 2; Oxford, 1961), pp. 159–61. J. A. Fitzmyer, SJ, 'The Bar Cochba Period', in J. L. McKenzie (ed.), *The Bible in Current Thought: Gruenthaner Memorial Volume* (New York, 1962), pp. 133–68, repr. in Fitzmyer's *Essays on the Semitic Background of the New Testament* (1971), pp. 305–54. E. *Schürer, *The History of the Jewish People in the Age of Jesus Christ* (Eng. tr. rev. by G. Vermes and others), 1 (Edinburgh, 1973), pp. 543–52, with bibl. pp. 534 f. P. Schäfer, *Der Bar Kokhba-Aufstand: Studien zum zweiten jüdischen Krieg gegen Rom* (Texte und Studien zum Antiken Judentum, 1; 1981). B. Isaac and A. Oppenheimer, 'The Revolt of Bar Kokhba: Ideology and Modern Scholarship', *Journal of Jewish Studies*, 36 (1985), pp. 33–60.

Bardenhewer, Otto (1851–1935), *patristic scholar. Born at München-Gladbach, he was educated at Bonn and Würzburg universities, lectured at Munich from 1879 to 1884, and was professor of OT Exegesis at Münster i.W. from 1884 to 1886 and of NT Exegesis at Munich from 1886 to 1924. His *Patrologie* in a single volume appeared in 1894 (Eng. tr., 1908). This was followed by his more ambitious *Geschichte der altkirchlichen Literatur* (1, 1902, 2nd edn., 1913; 2, 1903, 2nd edn., 1914; 3, 1912, with additions, 1923; 4, 1924; 5, 1932), which for its completeness, soundness of judgement and clarity of presentation was long unsurpassed; it remains a standard work of reference. His other works include *Des heiligen Hippolytus von Rom Commentar zum Buche Daniel* (1877), *Polychronius, Bruder Theodors von Mopsuestia und Bischof*

von Apamea (1879), and many contributions to *Biblische Studien.*

J. Sickenberger, *Erinnerungen an Otto Bardenhewer* (1937). E. Peterson in *EC* 2 (1949), cols. 839 f.

Bardesanes (154–222), correctly 'Bar-Daisan', regarded by later writers as a heretic. He was a speculative thinker associated with the court of Abgar VIII at *Edessa (where *Julius Africanus met him). The sources of any further biographical material are hostile and unreliable. Of his writings, a 'Dialogue of Destiny, or the Book of the Laws of the Lands' from which *Eusebius and other Christian Fathers preserve fragments (as from Περὶ εἱμαρμένης) has come down in the original Syriac. In this Bardesanes argues against the determinism of the 'Chaldaeans' (astrologers). The titles of several other works are preserved, and *Ephrem Syrus (*Hymni contra Haereses*, 55) quotes from his collection of 150 hymns. Bardesanes' cosmological teaching prob. influenced *Mani; his Christology was docetic and he denied the resurrection of the body. His disciples maintained a precarious existence for several centuries.

His 'Dialogue of Destiny', ed. W. *Cureton, *Spicilegium Syriacum* (London, 1855), pp. 1–21 (Syr.), with Eng. tr., pp. 1–34; later edns. by F. Nau in *Patrologia Syriaca*, 2 (1907), pp. 492–657, and, with Eng. tr., by H. J. W. Drijvers (Semitic Texts with Translations, 3; Assen, 1965). Early sources include Eusebius, *HE* 4. 30, *Epiphanius, *Haer.* 56, and *Moses of Chorene, *Hist.*, 2. 66. H. J. W. Drijvers, *Bardaisan of Edessa* (Studia Semitica Neerlandica, 6; Assen, 1966), with extensive bibl.; T. Jansma, *Natuur, Lot en Vrijheid: Bardesanes, de Filosoof der Arameeërs en zijn Images* (Cahiers bij het Nederlands Theologisch Tijdschrift, 6 [1969]). Bardenhewer, 1, pp. 364–8; Altaner and Stuiber (1978), pp. 101 f. and 563. J. Quasten, *Patrology*, 1 (Utrecht, 1950), pp. 263 f. F. *Hort in *DCB* 1 (1877), pp. 250–60, s.v.; H. J. W. Drijvers in *TRE* 5 (1980), cols. 206–12, s.v.

Bar Hebraeus (1226–86). The name by which Abû-l-Faraǧ, a *Jacobite Syrian bishop and polymath, is commonly known. He was the son of a physician of Jewish descent who was converted to the Christian faith. After studying medicine at Antioch and Tripoli, he was consecrated bishop in 1246, and in 1264 he became Primate of the East, with his residence at the monastery of Mar Mattai near Mosul. His works, which are mostly encyclopaedic in character, are mainly written in *Syriac (a few are in Arabic). They include 'The Candelabra of the Sanctuary', a vast theological compendium; 'The Storehouse of Mysteries' or scholia on the whole Bible; 'The Cream of Science', an encyclopaedia of *Aristotelian philosophy (most of it still unpublished); an important Chronicle; 'The Book of the Dove' on the monastic life; and two works on Church discipline and life, the *Nomocanon* and *Ethicon.*

The 'Candelabra' has mostly been pub., with Fr. tr., by J. Bakoš (*PO* 22, fasc. 4, and 24, fasc. 3; 1930–33), F. Graffin, SJ (ibid. 27, fasc. 4; 1957), M. Albert (ibid. 30, fasc. 2; 1961), A. Torbey (ibid. 30, fasc. 4; 1963), J. Khouri (ibid. 31, fasc. 1; 1965), É. Zigmund-Cerbü (ibid. 35, fasc. 2; 1969), and N. Séd (ibid. 40, fasc. 3, and 41, fasc. 3; 1981–3). Two 'bases' or parts were ed. separately by J. Bakoš, *Psychologie de Grégoire Aboulfaradj* (Leiden, 1948) and R. Kohlhaas, OSB, *Jakobitische Sakramententheologie im 13. Jahrhundert* (Liturgiewissenschaftliche Quellen und Forschungen, 36; 1959). The 'Chronicle' has been pub. in two parts: pt. 1, ed., with Eng. tr., by E. A. W. Budge, *The Chrono-*

graphy of Gregory Abû'l Faraj (2 vols., 1932); pt. 2, ed., with Lat. tr., by J. B. Abbeloos and T. J. Lamy, *Gregorii Barhebraei Chronicon Ecclesiasticum* (3 vols., Louvain, 1872–7). Autobiography also pub. by J. S. *Assemani, *Bibliotheca Orientalis*, 2 (Rome, 1721), pp. 248–63. J. Göttsberger, *Barhebräus und seine Scholia zur heiligen Schrift* (Biblische Studien, 5, Hefte 4–5; 1900). H. F. Janssens, *L'Entretien de la sagesse: Introduction aux œuvres philosophiques de Bar Hebraeus* (Bibliothèque de la Faculté de Philosophie et Lettres de l'Université de Liège, 75, 1937). Λ. *Baumstark, *Geschichte der syrischen Literatur* (1922), pp. 312–20.

Barlaam and Joasaph, Sts, two subjects of a popular medieval legend. It having been prophesied in the infancy of Joasaph (or *Josaphat), the son of a heathen Indian king, that he would be converted to Christianity, he was shut up in a palace so that he should know nothing of the facts or evils of life. Guided by a revelation, a monk Barlaam visits the prince in disguise and converts him to Christianity, using a series of 'Apologues' or fables. His father tries to win him back, by arranging a public disputation, but is himself eventually converted. For a time he ruled the kingdom with his father, but later retired to the wilderness with Barlaam.

The tale is an exhortation to renunciation of the world and is of Buddhist origin. The Greek text is traditionally ascribed to St *John of Damascus, but it is now widely accepted that it is an adapted translation from Georgian, perhaps made by St Euthymius of *Athos (d. 1028). The Georgian, which is the earliest Christianized form of the tale, goes back to an Arabic version, itself made from Middle Persian (lost). The Greek translator has incorporated many new elements, incl. the 'Apology' of *Aristides. The older of the two Latin translations was made before 1048. See also JOSAPHAT, ST.

The names of Barlaam and Josaphat were added to the *Roman Martyrology by C. *Baronius. Their feast is observed on 27 Nov. In W. calendars another St Barlaam, a martyr, is commemorated on 9 Nov.

Ed. princeps of Gk. text in J. F. Boissonade, *Anecdota Graeca*, 4 (1832), pp. 1–365; repr. in J. P. Migne, *PG* 96. 857–1250. Modern edn., with Eng. tr., by G. R. Woodward and H. Mattingly (Loeb, 1914; repr., 1967, with new introd. by D. M. Lang). Two recensions of the Georgian text ed. I. V. Abuladze (Tiflis, 1957); Eng. tr. by D. M. Lang of the short recension (London, 1957) and of the long recension (ibid., 1966). Ethiopic text ed. E. A. Wallis Budge (2 vols., Cambridge, 1923). R. L. Wolff, 'Barlaam and Joasaph', *HTR* 32 (1939), pp. 131–9. F. Dölger, *Der griechische Barlaam-Roman, ein Werk des H. Johannes von Damaskos* (Studia Patristica et Byzantina, 1; Ettal, 1953). H. Peri, *Der Religionsdisput der Barlaam–Legende, ein Motiv abendländischer Dichtung* (Acta Salmanticensia, Filosofía y Letras, 14, no. 3; 1959). D. Gimaret, *Le Livre de Bilawhar et Būḍāsf selon la Version Arabe Ismaélienne* (Centre de Recherches d'Histoire et de Philologie de la IVᵉ Section de l'École pratique des Hautes Études, 4: Hautes Études Islamiques et Orientales d'Histoire comparée, 3; 1971). Beck, pp. 35–41 (prefers attribution to John, a monk of St Sabas, who may be John of Damascus). A. Kazhdan, 'Where, when and by whom was the Greek Barlaam and Ioasaph not written?', in W. Will (ed.), *Zu Alexander d. Gr. Festschrift G. Wirth zum 60. Geburtstag am 9.12.86*, 2 (Amsterdam, 1988), pp. 1187–207. *CPG* 3 (1979), pp. 532–5 (no. 8120). H. Bacht, SJ, in *RAC* 1 (1950), cols. 1193–2000, with bibl. to date; B. Stuber in *Dict. Sp.* 8 (1974), cols. 464–6, s.v. 'Jean Damascène'.

Barlow, Thomas (1607–91), Bp. of *Lincoln. At *Oxford he became Librarian of the *Bodleian (1642),

Provost of Queen's (1657), and Lady Margaret Professor of Divinity (1660). Theologically he was a definite *Calvinist, but, by persistent trimming, he kept his offices through the many changes of the century. He became Bp. of Lincoln in 1675, but there is reason to doubt whether he ever visited his cathedral. His violent anti-Papalism found full scope in the *Popish Plot, but, on the accession of *James II, he professed his loyal affection. Undismayed, he took the oath to William III without demur. His published works include a treatise on natural theology entitled *Exercitationes aliquot metaphysicae de Deo* (1637), *Plain reasons why a Protestant of the Church of England should not turn Roman Catholic* (1688), and *Cases of Conscience* (1692).

The Genuine Remains of . . . Dr. Thomas Barlow (1936, ed. P. Pett). A. *Wood, *Athenae Oxonienses* (3rd edn. by P. Bliss), 4 (1820), cols. 333–41. S. Levy, 'Bishop Barlow on the "Case of the Jews" ', *Transactions of the Jewish Historical Society of England*, 3 (1899), pp. 151–6. E. Venables in *DNB* 3 (1885), pp. 224–9.

Barlow, William (d. 1568), Bp. of *Chichester. Born of an impoverished family of gentry, he became an *Augustinian canon, and was in royal diplomatic service possibly in the later 1520s and certainly in the 1530s. Gaining preferment through *Anne Boleyn's favour, he was chosen Bp. of *St Asaph in 1536, but was apparently transferred to *St David's before his consecration. He became Bp. of *Bath and Wells in 1548, resigned on *Mary's accession, and on *Elizabeth I's in 1559 he was appointed Bp. of Chichester. As the chief consecrator of Abp. M. *Parker in 1559, Barlow's position is at the centre of the controversy on *Anglican ordinations; there is no surviving record of his own consecration, but every indication that it took place regularly under the Catholic *Ordinal. He has been much confused with namesakes. He is not to be identified with the reformist Henrician pamphleteer Jerome Barlow, but certainly wrote the conservative *Dialogue describing the original ground of these Lutheran factions . . .* (1531). He also translated part of the *Apocrypha for the *Bishops' Bible. Five of his daughters were wives of bishops.

Facsimile repr. of his *Dialogue* (Amsterdam, 1974); also, with notes and full discussion by A. M. MacLean (Courtenay Library of Reformation Classics, 15; Sutton Courtenay [1981]). A. S. Barnes, *Bishop Barlow and Anglican Orders: A Study of the Original Documents* (1922). C. Jenkins, 'Bishop Barlow's Consecration and Archbishop Parker's Register: With some new documents', *JTS* 24 (1923–4), pp. 1–32; A. M. McLean, ' "Detestynge Thabomynacyon": William Barlow, Thomas More and the Anglican Episcopacy', *Moreana*, no. 49 (1976), pp. 67–77; id., ' "A noughtye and a false lyeng boke": William Barlow and the *Lutheran Factions*', *Renaissance Quarterly*, 31 (1978), pp. 173–85. [E.] G. Rupp, *Studies in the Making of the English Protestant Tradition* (Cambridge, 1947), pp. 62–72 ('The Early Career of Bishop Barlow'). J. Fines, *A Biographical Register of Early English Protestants*, 1 (Sutton Courtenay [1981]), s.v. [no pagination].

Barlow, William (c.1565–1613), Bp. of *Lincoln. Educated at St John's College, Cambridge, he was a Fellow of Trinity Hall from 1590 to 1596, when he was made chaplain to Abp. *Whitgift. He became Dean of *Chester in 1602, Bp. of *Rochester in 1605, and Bp. of Lincoln in 1608. He attended the *Hampton Court Conference in 1604 and is best known for his *Summe and Substance of the Conference . . . at Hampton Court* (1604), which, despite contemporary and later criticism, remains the most satisfactory account. He took part in the Cambridge dispute about *predestination in the late 1590s, and in his report to Whitgift criticized J. *Overall, then regius professor of theology, for indulging the *Calvinist faction; his own views seem to anticipate those of the Dutch *Arminians.

Barlow was an able preacher and an ardent supporter of *Divine Right. In 1606 he was employed by *James I to preach before A. *Melville in an attempt to urge the acceptance of episcopacy and the royal supremacy on the Church of Scotland. Two years later he replied to R. *Parson's attack on the Oath of Allegiance. As Bp. of Lincoln he was a determined opponent of Puritan nonconformity. He was one of the translators of the AV.

His *Summe and Substance* is repr. in E. *Cardwell, *A History of Conferences* (Oxford, 1840), pp. 167–212. K. Fincham, *Prelate as Pastor: The Episcopate of James I* (Oxford, 1990), pp. 242 f. and 279–82. E. Venables in *DNB* 3 (1885), pp. 231–3.

Barmen Declaration

Barmen Declaration (1934). The statement drawn up at the first Synod of the *Confessing Church at Barmen from 29 to 30 May 1934, to define the belief and mission of the Church in the face of the theologically liberal tendencies of the Nazi *German Christians. The foundation of the Church was held to be the Revelation of God in Jesus Christ and not any subordinate revelation in nature or history, and her primary mission was defined as to preach the Gospel of the free Grace of God. The Synod and its Declaration were deeply under the influence of K. *Barth.

Text, with full bibl., in K. D. Schmidt (ed.), *Die Bekenntnisse und grundsätzlichen Äusserungen zur Kirchenfrage*, 2 (1935), section 42, pp. 91–8. G. Niemöller, *Die erste Bekenntnissynode der Deutschen evangelischen Kirche zu Barmen* (Arbeiten zur Geschichte des Kirchenkampfes, 5–6; 1959). W.-D. Hauschild, G. Kretschmar and C. Nicolaisen (eds.), *Die lutherischen Kirchen und die Bekenntnissynode von Barmen: Referate des Internationalen Symposiums auf der Reisenburg 1984* (Göttingen, 1984). K. Scholder, *Die Kirchen und das Dritte Reich*, 2 [1987], esp. pp. 159–219; Eng. tr., 2 (1988), pp. 122–71.

Barnabas, St.

Barnabas, St. A Jewish *Levite of *Cyprus who became one of the earliest Christian disciples at *Jerusalem. Along with St *Paul, he is called an *Apostle (Acts 14: 14). His original name was Joseph, but he was 'surnamed Barnabas by the Apostles', the word 'Barnabas' being interpreted by St Luke as 'son of consolation' (υἱὸς παρακλήσεως, Acts 4: 36). It was he who introduced Paul, perhaps an acquaintance of long standing, to the Apostles after his conversion (Acts 9: 27), and was sent by them to inquire into the situation at *Antioch, where Christianity was being preached to Gentiles on a new scale (11: 22 ff.). Having approved, he fetched Paul from Tarsus to help him in the first 'missionary journey' which followed (Acts 13 and 14; see PAUL, ST), beginning with Cyprus. Indeed, in this he was originally the leader, though Paul very soon became the more prominent. At the so-called council at Jerusalem (Acts 15) he defended the claims of the Gentile Christians, and after it returned to Antioch with Paul (15: 30). Owing to a dispute with Paul over John *Mark, 'they parted asunder one from the other' (15: 39), and Barnabas sailed for Cyprus. He probably continued to travel widely, as later Paul mentions him as if he were known to the *Galatians (Gal. 2: 1, 2: 13), the *Corinthians (1 Cor. 9: 6), and possibly the *Colossians (Col. 4: 10). He is the traditional founder of the Cypriot Church, and legend asserts that he was martyred at Salamis in AD 61. Acc. to another tradition he was one the seventy of Lk. 10: 1, and to a third the founder of the Church of Milan and its first bishop. *Tertullian attributes to his authorship the Ep. to the *Hebrews. Feast day, 11 June. See also following entry.

AASS, Jun. 2 (1698), pp. 420–60. Crit. edn. of his Acta by M. Bonnet, *Acta Philippi et Acta Thomae accedunt Acta Barnabae* (Leipzig, 1903), pp. 292–302. O. Braunsberger, SJ, *Der Apostel Barnabas: Sein Leben und der ihm beigelegte Brief* (Mainz, 1876). L. *Duchesne, 'Saint Barnabé', in *Mélanges G. B. *de Rossi* (Suppl. aux Mélanges d'Archéologie et d'Histoire publiés par l'École française de Rome, 12; 1892), pp. 41–71. J. D. Burger, 'L'Énigme de Barnabas', *Museum Helveticum*, 3 (1946), pp. 180–93. S. [P.] Brock, 'Βαρναβᾶς: υἱὸς παρακλήσεως', *JTS* NS 25 (1974), pp. 93–8.

Barnabas, Epistle of.

Barnabas, Epistle of. An epistle of early Christian times ascribed by *Clement of Alexandria to the Apostle *Barnabas. Its Greek text was first discovered entire in the *Codex Sinaiticus. It contains a strong attack on Judaism, explaining animal sacrifices, the distinctive enactments of the Mosaic Law, and the material Temple as mistakes due to Jewish blindness and denying that they were ever God's will. The writer also maintains that the Hebrew Scriptures, so far from enjoining Judaic practices, had an esoteric sense, which he professes to reveal. In this way he succeeds in finding in the OT convincing testimonies for Christianity and against Judaism. It is very improbable that the author was really the Apostle Barnabas. He was a Christian, perhaps of *Alexandria, who wrote at some time between 70 and 150.

For edns. and trs. of text, see bibl. to APOSTOLIC FATHERS. Also ed. T. Klauser (Florilegium Patristicum, fasc. 1, new edn., 1940), R. A. Kraft, with Fr. tr., introd., and notes by P. Prigent (SC 172; 1971), and, with Ital. tr., by F. S. Barcellona (Corona Patrum; Turin, 1975). H. Windisch, *Der Barnabasbrief* (Hb NT, Ergänzungsband, 3; 1920); P. Prigent, *L' Épître de Barnabé I–XVI et ses sources* (Etudes Bibliques, 1961). K. Wengst, *Tradition und Theologie des Barnabasbriefes* (Arbeiten zur Kirchengeschichte, 42; 1971). P. Richardson and M. B. Schukster, 'Barnabas, Nerva, and the Yavnean Rabbis', *JTS* NS 34 (1983), pp. 31–55. J. Carleton Paget, *The Epistle of Barnabas: Outlook and Background* (Wissenschaftliche Untersuchungen zum Neuen Testament, 2. Reihe, 64; 1994). See also bibl. to APOSTOLIC FATHERS.

Barnabas, Gospel of.

Barnabas, Gospel of. A writing in Italian, apparently dating from the 14th cent., by a native of Italy who had renounced Christianity for Islam. An 'Evangelium secundum Barnabam' is also listed in the '*Decretum Gelasianum' among the *spuria*; but this is prob. an independent work, now wholly lost.

Ital. text ed. with Eng. tr. by L. and L. Ragg (Oxford, 1907). Ital. text reproduced photographically, with notes and Fr. tr. by L. Cirillo and M. Frémaux, and full introd. by L. Cirillo (Paris, 1977). R. Stichel, 'Bemerkungen zum Barnabas-Evangelium', *Byzantinoslavica*, 43 (1982), pp. 189–201.

Barnabites.

Barnabites. A small religious order founded at Milan in 1530 by St Antonio Maria Zaccaria (d. 1539). Officially known as the 'Clerks Regular of St Paul', its members obtained their popular name from their church of St Barnabas at Milan. Besides the usual monastic obligations, their rule provides for the study of St *Paul's Epistles and for education and mission work. In 1985 there were some 500 members of the order, in 85 houses: of these 40 were in Italy, and 15 in Brazil.

O. Premoli, Barnabite, *Storia dei Barnabiti nel cinquecento* (1913), *nel seicento* (1922), *dal 1700 al 1825* (1925). L. M. Levati and others, *Menologio dei Barnabiti* (12 vols., Genoa, 1932–8). G. Boffito, Barnabite, *Scrittori Barnabiti . . . (1533–1933)* (4 vols., Florence, 1933–7). Heimbucher, 2, pp. 106–10. V. M. Colciago in *EC* 4 (1950), cols. 298–301, s.v. 'Congregazione di S. Paolo'; A. M. Erba in *DIP* 2 (1973), cols. 945–74, s.v. 'Chierici Regolari di San Paolo', with bibl.

Barnett, Samuel Augustus (1844–1913), Anglican social reformer. After studying law and modern history at Wadham College, *Oxford, he was ordained deacon in 1867. In 1869 he founded the Charity Organization Society. From 1873 to 1894 he was Vicar of St Jude's Whitechapel, where his unorthodox methods (evening schools, entertainments, serving on the Board of Guardians) at first aroused much criticism, but soon led to his recognition as a loyal priest, devoted to the religious and cultural improvement of the East End of London. He encouraged tutors from Oxford to come to lecture to his parishioners, and from 1884 to 1896 was the first Warden of Toynbee Hall. In 1884 he helped to found the Education Reform League, and in 1885 he became a promoter of the Artisans' Dwellings Act. Throughout his life he was active in initiating projects directed to the reform of social conditions on Christian principles and urging Christians to study them. In 1893 Barnett became a canon of Bristol cathedral and in 1906 was made a canon of *Westminster. He was much assisted in his work by his wife (Henrietta Octavia, *née* Rowland), who before marriage had been a co-worker with Octavia Hill (1838–1912). 'Barnett House', for the study of social problems, was founded at Oxford in his memory. His writings include *Practicable Socialism: Essays on Social Reform* (1888), *The Service of God: Sermons, Essays, and Addresses* (1897), and *Religion and Politics* (1911).

His Life was written by his wife in 2 vols. (1918). J. Wells in *DNB, 1912–1921*, pp. 31 f.

Baro, Peter (1534–99), anti-*Calvinist divine. Born at Étampes, he studied for the law at Bourges, where he came under the influence of the recently introduced Protestant doctrines. Abandoning law for divinity, he made his way to *Geneva, where J. *Calvin admitted him to the ministry. After returning to France, he found himself compelled to flee to England. In 1574, mainly through the influence of Burghley, he was appointed Lady Margaret Professor of Divinity at Cambridge. Here, despite his earlier personal associations with Calvin, he became a critic of the more predestinarian of the Calvinist doctrines. The *Lambeth Articles seem to have been drafted partly to rebut his teaching, but Baro put an anti-Calvinist sense on them and thus justified his formal assent. He also challenged W. *Perkins's teaching on predestination, then in high repute at Cambridge. But though Burghley had interposed in his favour and J. *Overall and L. *Andrewes had given him their support, Baro found it expedient to flee from Cambridge in 1596. He lived for the rest of his life in London. He can be regarded as an early leader of the movement in Anglican theology later popularly termed '*Arminianism'.

His writings include *Praelectiones* on Jonah (1579), *De fide ejusque Ortu et Natura plana ac dilucida Explicatio* (1580), and *Summa Trium de Praedestinatione Sententiarum* (1613).

Abridged version of his autobiography from a Baker MS, vol. 39, p. 185, and other material pr. by R. Masters, *Memoirs of the Life and Writings of the late Rev. Thomas Baker* (1784), pp. 127–31. H. C. Porter, *Reformation and Reaction in Tudor Cambridge* (Cambridge, 1958), esp. pp. 376–97. P. [G.] Lake, *Moderate Puritans and the Elizabethan Church* (ibid., 1982), pp. 227–42.

barocco. See BAROQUE.

Baronius, Cesare (1538–1607), ecclesiastical historian. He became a member of the *Oratory under St *Philip Neri in 1557, and Superior in 1593. In 1596 he was made Cardinal and in 1597 Librarian of the *Vatican. His most important work, the *Annales Ecclesiastici* (12 folio volumes, 1588–1607), is a history of the Church in chapters each corresponding to a year, undertaken as a RC reply to the *Centuries of Magdeburg. At his death this work had only reached the year 1198, and various attempts, all worthless, were made to continue it, one by the Oratorians themselves. Baronius was at some pains to secure accuracy, as is clear from the long list of authorities he cites and compares. But on many matters, particularly where the E. Church is concerned, his information was scanty and in error, and throughout his critical powers failed to support his good intentions. In the eleventh volume, published in 1605, he included a note supporting Papal claims in Sicily against Spain, which was published as a separate treatise after his death (Paris, 1609; Leiden, 1619), and gave much offence to Philip III. At the time of the original publication it is said to have lost Baronius the Papacy, owing to Spanish opposition. He also published two new and corrected editions of the *Roman Martyrology (1586 and 1589).

The standard edn. of his *Annales Ecclesiastici*, with the various additions and an index to the whole, is that of J. D. *Mansi and D. Georgius (38 vols., Lucca, 1738–59). Early Life by H. Barnabeus, Cong. Orat. (Rome, 1651). G. Calenzio, *La vita e gli scritti del Cardinale Cesare Baronio* (1907); V. Simoncelli (ed.), *Per Cesare Baronio: Scritti vari nel terzo centenario della sua morte* (1911); A. Roncalli [*John XXIII], *Il Cardinale Cesare Baronio: Conferenza tenuta il 4 decembre 1907 nel Seminario di Bergamo ricorrendo il terzo centenario della morte* (1961); C. K. Pullapilly, *Caesar Baronius: Counter-Reformation Historian* (Notre Dame, Ind., and London, 1975). H. Jedin, *Kardinal Caesar Baronius: Der Anfang der katholischen Kirchengeschichtsschreibung im 16. Jahrhundert* (Katholisches Leben und Kirchenreform im Zeitalter der Glaubensspaltung, 38; 1978). *Baronio Storico e la Controriforma: Atti del convegno internazionale di studi, Sora, 6–10 ottobre 1979*, ed. R. De Maio and others (Fonti e Studi Baroniani, 1; Sora, 1982). A. Pincherle in *Dizionario Biografico degli Italiani*, 6 (1964), pp. 470–8, s.v.

baroque (Portug. *barroco*, a 'rough pearl'). The ornate style of art and architecture which flourished in Italy during the 17th and early 18th cents., and spread throughout mainland Europe, esp. in France and Spain. By means of complex spatial geometry, a harmonious richness of decoration and an unreserved appeal to the emotions, it sought to infuse new life and religious feeling into the cold rigidity of the later Renaissance. Its most notable Italian exponents were G. L. Bernini (1598–1680), C. Maderno (1556–1629), and F. Borromini (1599–1667). In Germany and Austria some of the most distinguished examples of the baroque style are in the buildings of Balthasar Neumann (1687–1753), J. B. Fischer von Erlach (1656–1723), and the Asam brothers, Cosmas Damian (1686–1739) and Aegid Quirin (1692–1750). Owing to the fantastic exuberance of some architects, the term 'baroque' came to signify anything florid or bizarre. See also ROCOCO.

H. Wölfflin, *Renaissance und Barock: Eine Untersuchung über Wesen und Entstehung des Barockstils in Italien* (1888; Eng. tr., with introd. by P. Murray, 1964); G. Bazin, *The Baroque: Principles, Styles, Modes, Themes*, tr. by P. Wardroper (1968); J. R. Martin, *Baroque* (1977). A. Pigler, *Barockthemen: Eine Auswahl von Verzeichnissen zur Ikonographie des 17. und 18. Jahrhunderts* (2 vols., Budapest, 1956; 2nd edn., 3 vols., 1974). R. Wittkower and I. B. Jaffe (eds.), *Baroque Art: The Jesuit Contribution* (New York, 1972). S. Sitwell, *Southern Baroque Art* (1924); id., *German Baroque Art* (1927); id., *Spanish Baroque Art* (1931). R. Wittkower, *Art and Architecture in Italy 1600 to 1750* (Pelican History of Art, 1958; 3rd edn., 1973); E. Hempel, *Baroque Art and Architecture in Central Europe*, tr. by E. Hempel and M. Kay (ibid., 1965). [C.] N. [P.] Powell, *From Baroque to Rococo: An Introduction to Austrian and German Architecture from 1580 to 1790* (1959). E. K. Waterhouse, *Italian Baroque Painting* (1962; 2nd edn., 1969). J. Hook, *The Baroque Age in England* [1976]. A. E. Brinckmann, *Barockskulptur* (Handbuch der Kunstwissenschaft [1919]). G. Briganti and others in *Encyclopedia of World Art*, 2 (1960), cols. 255–381, s.v. 'Baroque Art', with bibl.; H. Hatzfeld in *NCE* 2 (1967), pp. 106–13, s.v.; S. Galigani, ibid., pp. 113–22, s.v. 'Baroque Art'.

Barrier Act. The Act passed on 8 Jan. 1697 by the General Assembly of the Church of Scotland, which requires that proposals to make any important alteration in the constitution of the Church shall first be presented in the form of overtures to the Assembly, and if passed in this form shall then be sent down to presbyteries for their consideration and opinion, and thence remitted to a future Assembly. Its purpose was to prevent hasty legislation that might prejudice the doctrine, worship, or government of the Church. The Act is still in force.

J. T. Cox, *Practice and Procedure in the Church of Scotland* (6th edn. by D. F. M. MacDonald, 1976), pp. 15 f., 104, and 181, with text of the Act, p. 385.

Barrington, Shute (1734–1826), Bp. of *Durham. He was the youngest son of John Shute, first Viscount Barrington (1678–1734), a strong advocate of complete religious freedom for the Protestant dissenters. Educated at Eton and at Merton College, Oxford, he was ordained in 1756, and in 1761 became a canon of Christ Church. After other appointments he filled successively the sees of *Llandaff (1769), *Salisbury (1782), and Durham (1791), and was one of the most influential bishops of his age, highly regarded by his fellow-bishops and by politicians alike. He made generous distribution of his large episcopal revenues. In his attitude to the Nonconformists he was less liberal than his father, deprecating any relaxation of subscription on the ground that precise articles of faith were indispensable in an Established Church. Besides issuing an edition of his father's *Miscellanea Sacra* (3 vols., 1770) he published the *Life* of his brother, William Wildman, Viscount Barrington (1814), a collection of *Sermons* (1811), and some minor works.

Brief Memoir by G. Townsend in his edn. of *The Theological Works of the first Viscount Barrington*, 1 (1828), pp. xliv–lix. A. H. Grant in *DNB* 3 (1885), p. 294.

Barrow, Henry (*c.*1550–93), also Barrowe, *Congregationalist. Educated at Clare Hall, Cambridge, he was converted *c.*1580 from the profligate life of a courtier to a strict *Puritanism. In 1586, when visiting in prison J. *Greenwood, the *Separatist leader, with whom he had earlier come into association, he was detained by order of Abp. J. *Whitgift, and kept in confinement till his death. He wrote in defence of separatism and congregational independence, and also engaged in controversy with R. *Browne, although they differed little in their conviction that, according to Scripture, Church authority was vested primarily in the individual congregation. He was charged in 1590 with circulating seditious books, and three years later sentenced to be hanged. Most of his writings were printed in the Netherlands by his friends. They included *A True Description . . . of the Visible Congregation of the Saints, etc.* (1589) and *A Brief Discovery of the False Church* (1590 [?1591]). The suggestion that Barrow was the author of the *Marprelate Tracts is now generally rejected.

The Writings of Henry Barrow 1587–1590, ed. L. H. Carlson (Elizabethan Nonconformist Texts, 3; 1962); *The Writings of Henry Barrow, 1590–1591*, ed. id. (ibid. 5; 1966); *The Writings of John Greenwood 1587–1590, together with the joint writings of Henry Barrow and John Greenwood 1587–1590*, ed. id. (ibid. 4; 1962), pp. 95–273; *The Writings of John Greenwood and Henry Barrow 1591–1593*, ed. id. (ibid. 6; 1970), pp. 93–291. F. J. Powicke, *Henry Barrow, Separatist (1550?–1593), and the Exiled Church of Amsterdam* (1900); B. R. White, *The English Separatist Tradition from the Marian Martyrs to the Pilgrim Fathers* (Oxford Theological Monographs, 1971), esp. pp. 67–90; S. Brachlow, *The Communion of Saints: Radical Puritan and Separatist Ecclesiology 1570–1625* (ibid., 1988), *passim*.

Barrow, Isaac (1630–77), Anglican divine, classical scholar, and mathematician. He entered Trinity College, Cambridge, in 1643, and though a royalist and the son of a royalist, became a scholar in 1647, and a Fellow in 1649. From 1655 to 1659 he travelled in France, Italy, and the Near East, and on his return to England was ordained. He was appointed Professor of Greek at Cambridge in 1660, Professor of Geometry at Gresham College, London, shortly after, and the first Lucasian Professor of Mathematics at Cambridge in 1663. The last post he resigned in 1669, in favour of his pupil, I. *Newton, whose greater ability he recognized, while he himself had come to doubt whether his mathematical studies left him sufficient time for theology. Soon after this, *Charles II made him his chaplain, and in 1673 Master of Trinity. The precision of a mathematician's thought is reflected in his theology, and his *Treatise on the Pope's Supremacy* (1680, posthumous) remains a work of outstanding ability. He was also one of the most successful (and lengthy) preachers of his day.

Collected edn. of his Theological Works by J. *Tillotson (4 vols., London, 1683–7), incl. 'Some Account of the Life of Dr. Isaac Barrow' by A. H[ill]. Modern edn. by A. Napier (9 vols., Cambridge, 1859) incl. Life by A. Hill, vol. 1, pp. xxxvii–liv, and 'Barrow and his Academical Times as Illustrated in his Latin Works' by W. Whewell, vol. 9, pp. i–lv. Mathematical Works ed. W. Whewell (Cambridge, 1860). P. H. Osmond, *Isaac Barrow, His Life and Times* (1944); M. Feingold (ed.), *Before Newton: The Life and Times of Isaac Barrow* (Cambridge, 1990). J. H. Overton in *DNB* 3 (1885), pp. 299–305.

Barsanuphius, St (d. 540, at an advanced age), ascetical writer. Though born in Egypt, Barsanuphius spent most of his life as a hermit in the region S. of Gaza. He exerted much influence on E. spirituality (medieval and modern) through a collection of letters to and from John the Prophet or John of Gaza, a fellow-hermit of whom little is known. The correspondence is called *Questions and Answers*. Drawing on the tradition of desert spirituality best represented by the **Apophthegmata Patrum*, and violently opposed to the speculations of *Origen, the teaching of both men influenced *Dorotheus, *John Climacus, Paul *Evergetinos, *Simeon the New Theologian, and the *Hesychasts. Feast day in the E., 6 Feb.

The correspondence of Barsanuphius with John was ed. by *Nicodemus of the Holy Mountain (posthumously pub., Venice, 1816); this edn. was repr. by S. N. Schoinas (Volos, 1960). Crit. edn., with Eng. tr., of sections 1–124 by D. J. Chitty in *PO* 31 (1966), pp. 449–616. Correspondence also ed. by F. Neyt, OSB, and P. de Angelis-Noah (SC 426, 427, etc.; 1997 ff.). Fr. tr., based on MS, by L. Regnault, P. Lemaire, and B. Outtier (Solesmes [1972]). Fragment against the Origenists in *PG* 86. 892–901. S. Vailhé, 'Les Lettres spirituelles de Jean et de Barsanuphe', *ÉO* 7 (1904), pp. 268–76; id., 'Saint Barsanuphe', ibid. 8 (1905), pp. 14–25; id., 'Jean le Prophète et Séridos' ibid., pp. 154–60. P. de Angelis-Noah, 'La méditation de Barsanuphe sur la lettre '*HTA*', *Byzantion*, 53 (1983), pp. 494–506. Beck, pp. 395 f. *CPG* 3 (1979), p. 373 (no. 7350). I. Hausherr, SJ, in *Dict. Sp.*, 1 (1937), cols. 1255–62, s.v.

Barsumas (d. *c*.457), archimandrite and saint of the *Syrian Orthodox Church. He was invited by the Emp. *Theodosius II (d. 450) to defend *Eutyches at the Second Council of Ephesus (*Latrocinium, 449), and at the Council of *Chalcedon (451) he was among those who presented petitions in favour of *Dioscorus. The Syriac Life, written in the 6th–7th cent., is the source of the other oriental versions. Feast day, 3 Feb.

Text of Eth. Life, with Fr. tr., ed. S. Grébaut, 'Vie de Barsoma le Syrien', *Revue de l'Orient Chrétien*, 13 (1908), pp. 337–45, and 14 (1909), pp. 135–42, 264–75, and 401–14. Short extracts of the Syrian Life ed., with Fr. tr. by F. Nau, ibid. 18 (1913), pp. 272–6, 379–89, and 19 (1914), pp. 113–34, 278–89; an edn. of the full text by A. N. Palmer and J. Jarry in *PO* is announced. E. Honigmann, *Le Couvent de Barsaumā et le patriarcat jacobite d'Antioche et de Syrie* (CSCO 146, Subsidia, 7; 1954), esp. pp. 6–23. G. Bardy in *DHGE* 6 (1932), cols. 946 f.

Barsumas (d. before 496), Bp. of Nisibis in the *Church of the East. He studied at the Persian school in *Edessa and may have been the Barsauma whose banishment was demanded at the *Latrocinium (449). At an unknown date he became Metropolitan of Nisibis and a keen propagandist of the theology of *Theodore of Mopsuestia. Over several years he conducted a feud with the see of Seleucia-Ctesiphon, and at the Synod of Beth Lapat in 484 he secured the deposition of Babowai, the *Catholicos of Seleucia. He was instrumental in founding the influential theological school in Nisibis directed by *Narsai, who had fled from Edessa *c*.470. When the Persian school at Edessa was finally closed (489), Barsumas welcomed the exiles from there also. Six of his letters survive.

His letters are conveniently repr. by J. B. Chabot in his edn. of the *Synodicon Orientale* (Notices et Extraits des Manuscrits de la Bibliothèque Nationale, 37; 1902), pp. 525–39. Ger. tr. by O. Braun, *Das Buch der Synhados* (1900), pp. 75–83. J. Labourt, *Le Christianisme dans l'empire perse sous la dynastie sassanide (224–632)* (1904), pp. 131–52. S. Gero, *Barsauma of Nisibis and Persian*

Christianity in the Fifth Century (CSCO 426; Subsidia, 63; 1981). I. Ortiz de Urbina, SJ, *Patrologia Syriaca* (2nd edn., Rome, 1968), pp. 118–20. G. Bardy in *DHGE* 6 (1932), cols. 948–50, s.v.; J.-M. Sauget in *DPAC* 1 (1983), cols. 484–6, s.v.; Eng. tr. in *Encyclopedia of the Early Church*, 1 (1992), p. 112.

Barth, Karl (1886–1968), Protestant theologian. He was the son of Fritz Barth (1856–1912), Professor of NT Theology at Berne. After studying at Berne, Berlin, *Tübingen, and *Marburg, Karl Barth began as a minister at Geneva (1909–11) and was then for ten years (1911–21) pastor at Safenwil (Aargau). Here, under the shadow of the war of 1914–18 and in direct relation to his pastoral responsibility, he was led to a radical questioning of the prevailing liberal theology, and wrote his 'Commentary on Romans' (*Der Römerbrief*, '1919', pub. 1918). In this work he revived Pauline and *Reformation themes that had been muted or omitted in liberal theology—the sovereignty of God, the finitude and sinfulness of man, *eschatology, and God's judgement on human institutions and culture. The originality, critical power, and actuality of its message, particularly in the pessimism of the post-war situation, at once gave him a very wide hearing among German-speaking Protestant theologians. In 1921 he became extraordinary professor at Göttingen and later Professor at Münster i.W. (1925) and Bonn (1930).

On Hitler's accession to power and the outbreak of the 'Church Struggle' (1933), Barth at once threw in his lot with the *Confessing Church. As a Swiss subject he enjoyed a liberty of speech not open to a German and he had a strong backing. None the less his action demanded much courage. The formulation of Confessional theology in the *Barmen Declaration of 1934 was largely Barth's work. At the outset he held that National Socialism, being purely a matter of secular politics, was irrelevant to the Christian, provided the freedom of the Gospel was maintained. Later he came to the view that such neutrality was not possible, and vigorously attacked Nazism. On his refusal to take an oath of unconditional allegiance to the Führer, he was deprived of his chair. He left Germany and in 1935 became Professor of Theology at Basle, where he continued to teach until he retired in 1962.

Developing the positions already announced in *Romans*, Barth aimed to lead theology away from what he believed to be the fundamentally erroneous 19th-cent. synthesis between theology and culture. Theology was to be based on the Word of God communicated in the Bible, and to stand over against human philosophies. Among those who chiefly influenced his thought were the great Continental Reformers and such later thinkers as S. *Kierkegaard, F. M. *Dostoevsky, F. *Overbeck, and the *Blumhardts. Human reason, he held, has no power to attain to the knowledge of God which is given only in God's gracious revelation in Jesus Christ. This revelation comes from God to man and is contrasted with religion, which is described as man's sinful attempt to grasp God and which ends only in distortion and idolatry. Clearly this outlook rules out all *natural theology and makes any dialogue with non-Christian religions virtually impossible. It also led Barth to be very critical of such figures as F. D. E. *Schleiermacher, G. W. F. *Hegel, and A. *Ritschl, and to engage in sharp exchanges with A. *Harnack.

These doctrines Barth proclaimed with passionate fervour in a style at once graphic and forceful, and in language deeply influenced by the Bible. He made them the theme of innumerable sermons and addresses, as well as of more continuous writings. In 1927 he published the beginnings of a systematic exposition of his theology in *Die Christliche Dogmatik im Entwurf*, 1, 'Die Lehre vom Worte Gottes'; but he abandoned this work and a few years later began again on a vast scale. In 1932 there appeared the first volume of *Die kirchliche Dogmatik*, on which he was destined to be engaged for most of the rest of his life. After his retirement and a serious illness, it became impossible to complete the work according to the original plan and the final volume on 'The Doctrine of Redemption' was never written. Nevertheless, Barth's *Church Dogmatics* is by far the most detailed Protestant exposition of Christian doctrine to have appeared since the Reformation.

The vast work begins from 'The Doctrine of the Word of God' as the source of all revelation and the foundation of any genuinely Christian theology. But the doctrine of the Trinity is soon introduced and it becomes apparent that Barth's interpretation of the Word is made in the light of the classic theological tradition. This is clear also in his treatment of the *Incarnation. Although the adverse judgements on natural theology and religion remain, Barth introduces the idea of a 'humanity' of God, and while this leaves the initiative in grace and revelation decisively with God, it helps to narrow the gap between God and man, seemingly unbridgeable in the early writings.

In 1945 Münster University restored the doctorate of which it had deprived Barth in 1939. In politics he now declined to take up the same hostile attitude to Communism as he had hitherto done to Nazism on the ground that the Church, which must be essentially detached from politics, cannot decide in advance that Communism is necessarily evil. He continued to act as a potent astringent influence in Protestant theology, on secondary matters (e.g. *Infant Baptism) often taking up provocative and sometimes unexpected positions.

In English-speaking countries, the greatest impact of 'the Barthian Theology' was in the 1930s. By the 1950s, though Barth still had professed disciples, his theological influence had become widely diffused among many who did not share his particular views or comprise a specifically 'Barthian' movement. At the same time his personal prestige, based largely on his distinctive and forthright standpoint, gave him the position of the outstanding Protestant theologian, and perhaps the most notable Christian prophet, of his time.

Barth's other works include *Das Wort Gottes und die Theologie* (collected lectures, 1924; Eng. tr., 1928); *Die Theologie und die Kirche* (further lectures, 1928); *Credo* (an outline of dogmatics based on the *Apostles' Creed, 1935; Eng. tr., 1936); *The Knowledge of God and the Service of God* (*Gifford Lectures, 1937–8; pub. 1938; based on the *Scottish Confession of 1560); *Die kirchliche Lehre von der Taufe* (1943; Eng. tr., 1948); *Dogmatik in Grundriss* (Lectures delivered in Bonn, 1946; pub. 1947; Eng. tr., 1949); *Die protestantische Theologie im 19. Jahrhundert* (1947; Eng. tr. of part as *From Rousseau to Ritschl*, 1959; Eng. tr. of the whole, 1972); *Die christliche Lehre nach dem Heidelberger Katechismus* (1948; Eng. tr., 1964).

See also BRUNNER, E., and DIALECTICAL THEOLOGY.

A *Gesamtausgabe* has begun to appear (Zurich, 1971 ff.); it will include new edns. of his pub. works and much unpub. material in 6 sections: (1) Sermons, (2) Academic Works, (3) Lectures and Minor Works, (4) Talks, (5) Letters, and (6) Biographical Material. The Eng. tr. of Barth's *Römerbrief* by E. C. *Hoskyns (1933) did much to spread knowledge of his doctrines in Britain. Eng. tr. of his *Kirchliche Dogmatik* by G. T. Thomson, T. F. Torrance, G. W. Bromiley, and others (13 vols., 1936–69). Eng. tr. of his Göttingen lectures (from the *Gesamtausgabe*) by G. W. Bromiley as *Göttingen Dogmatics* (Grand Rapids, Mich., 1991 ff.). *Festschriften* were issued in honour of his 50th birthday, ed. E. Wolf (Munich, 1936); of his 60th birthday (Cahiers Théologiques de l'Actualité Protestante, Hors Série, 2; Neuchâtel and Paris, 1946) and ed. F. W. Camfield (London, 1947); of his 70th birthday, ed. E. Wolf and others (Zurich, 1956, with list of his works to date, pp. 945–60), ed. T. H. L. Parker (London, 1956) and a special issue of *Theologische Zeitschrift*, 12, Hefte 2–3 (1956); and for his 80th birthday, ed. E. Busch and others (Zurich, 1966, with list of his works from 1956 onwards, pp. 709–23) and ed. J. I. McCord and T. H. L. Parker (London, 1966). E. Busch, *Karl Barths Lebenslauf: nach seinen Briefen und autobiographischen Texten* (Munich, 1975; Eng. tr., 1976). A. Keller, *Der Weg der dialektischen Theologie durch die kirchliche Welt* (1931; Eng. tr. as *Karl Barth and Christian Unity* [1933]). C. van Til, *The New Modernism: An Appraisal of the Theology of Barth and Brunner* (1946). O. Weber, *Karl Barth's Kirchliche Dogmatik* (1950; Eng. tr., 1953). H. [U.] von *Balthasar, *Karl Barth: Darstellung und Deutung seiner Theologie* (1951; Eng. tr., 1972). J. Hamer, OP, *Karl Barth: L'Occasionalisme théologique de Karl Barth. Étude sur sa méthode dogmatique* (1949; Eng. tr., 1962). G. C. Berkouwer, *De Triomf der Genade in de Theologie van Karl Barth* (Kampen, 1955; Eng. tr., 1956). H. Bouillard, *Karl Barth* (Théologie, 38 and 39; 2 vols. in 3, 1957). H. *Küng, *Rechtfertigung: Die Lehre Karl Barths und eine katholische Besinnung* (Einsiedeln, 1957; Eng. tr., 1964). T. F. Torrance, *Karl Barth: An Introduction to his Early Theology, 1910–1931* (1962). F. Schmid, *Verkündigung und Dogmatik in der Theologie Karl Barths: Hermeneutik und Ontologie in einer Theologie des Wortes Gottes* (Forschungen zur Geschichte und Lehre des Protestantismus, Zehnte Reihe, 29; Munich, 1964). E. Jüngel, *Gottes Sein ist im Werden: Verantwortliche Rede vom Sein Gottes bei Karl Barth. Eine Paraphrase* (Tübingen, 1965; Eng. tr., *The Doctrine of the Trinity*, Monograph Supplements to the *Scottish Journal of Theology*, 4; 1976); id., various papers repr. in his *Barth-Studien* (Ökumenische Theologie, 9 [1982]). S. W. Sykes (ed.), *Karl Barth: Studies of his Theological Method* (Oxford, 1979). B. L. McCormack, *Karl Barth's Critically Realistic Dialectical Theology: Its Genesis and Development 1909–1936* (ibid., 1995). H. M. Wildi, *Bibliographie Karl Barth* (Zurich, 1984 ff.).

Bartholomew, St. One of the twelve Apostles. He is mentioned only in the Synoptic Gospels (Mk. 3: 18, Lk. 6: 14, Mt. 10: 3) and in Acts (1: 13). The name is a patronymic, meaning 'son of Tolmai', so that he may have had another (personal) name, and he has sometimes been identified with *Nathanael (Jn. 1: 45–51, 21: 2). Acc. to *Eusebius, when *Pantaenus of Alexandria visited *India between AD 150 and 200, he found there 'the Gospel according to Matthew' in Hebrew, left behind by 'Bartholomew, one of the Apostles' (*HE* 5. 10. 3). Bartholomew is traditionally said to have been flayed alive at Albanopolis in Armenia. Feast day in W., 24 Aug.; in E., 11 June.

A. Romeo in *EC* 2 (1949), cols. 916–18, s.v. 'Bartolomeo, Apostolo (I)', with bibl.

Bartholomew, Gospel of St. An apocryphal Gospel whose existence was known to *Jerome and *Bede (possibly only through Jerome). It has perhaps been incorporated into the 'Questions of Bartholomew' which survive in a number of Greek, Latin, and Slavonic MSS. These 'Questions' treat of the *descent of Christ into hell, the BVM's account of the Annunciation, a vision of the bottomless pit, the summons to the devil to judgement, questions about the deadly sins, and other subjects. They have a number of parallels with *Gnostic Gospels. There also exists in Coptic (apparently in three recensions) a 'Book of the Resurrection of Christ by Bartholomew the Apostle'.

A. *Wilmart, OSB, and E. Tisserant, 'Fragments grecs et latins de l'Évangile de Barthélemy', *R. Bibl.* NS 10 (1913), pp. 161–90, 321–68, incl. text of Lat. and Gk. and refs. to scattered edns. of other versions; U. Moricca, 'Un nuovo testo dell'"Evangelo di Bartolomeo" ', ibid. 30 (1921), pp. 481–516, and 31 (1922), pp. 20–30, incl. text. Gk. and Lat. texts. with Sp. tr., also in A. de Santos Otero (ed.), *Los Evangelios Apócrifos* (6th edn., 1988), pp. 530–66. Eng. tr. in J. K. Elliott, *The Apocryphal New Testament* (Oxford, 1993), pp. 652–68; also in Schneemelcher, cited below. Ger. tr., with useful introd. by F. Scheidweiler and W. Schnee-melcher and assessment of Coptic texts of the 'Book of the Resur-rection', in Schneemelcher, 1 (5th edn., 1987), pp. 424–40; Eng. tr., 1 (1991), pp. 537–57, incl. Eng. tr. of the 'Questions', pp. 539–53. F. Haase, 'Zur Rekonstruktion des Bartholomäusevange-liums', *ZNTW* 16 (1915), pp. 93–112. A. F. L. Beeston, 'The *Quaestiones Bartholomae*', *JTS* NS 25 (1974), pp. 124–7. The Coptic 'Book of the Resurrection', ed., with Eng. tr., by E. A. W. Budge, *Coptic Apocrypha in the Dialect of Upper Egypt* (1913), pp. 1–48, 179–230, Eng. summary in J. K. Elliott, op. cit., pp. 668–72.

Bartholomew of the Martyrs (1514–90), Portuguese theologian. Bartholomew Fernandez, who owes his sur-name 'A Martyribus' to the church in which he was bap-tized, entered the *Dominican monastery at Lisbon in 1528. After teaching philosophy and theology in various houses of his order, he was made Bp. of Braga in 1559. In 1561 he went to *Trent, where he took a prominent part in the last nine sessions, esp. in the drafting of the decrees on the reform of the clergy, which he did his best to put into practice after his return to his diocese. In 1582 he resigned his charge and retired to the Dominican convent at Viana. He was much esteemed for his personal holiness as well as for his energy in carrying out the Tridentine reforms. Among his works is the *Stimulus Pastorum* (1564) and a *Compendium Spiritualis Doctrinae* (1582), which was translated into many languages. In 1845 he was declared Venerable by *Gregory XVI.

Opera Omnia, ed. J. D. (in religion Dom Malachie) d'Inguim-bert (Rome, 2 pts. bound in 1, 1734–5). Modern edn. of *Theolog-ica Scripta*, by R. de Almeida Rolo, OP (6 vols., Braga, 1973–7). The primary source is the Life by *Luis of Granada (d. 1558; crit. edn. in *Opera*, ed. J. Cuervo, OP, vol. 14, Madrid, 1906, pp. 323–66); it was cont. by Luis of Cacegas, OP, and Luis of Sousa, OP, who pub. it under the names of Cacegas and himself (Viana, 1619); modern edn. under the name of Luis of Sousa, with preface and notes by A. R. Machado (Colecção de Clássicos Sá da Costa, 3 vols., Lisbon, 1946–8) and by G. Chaves de Melo and A. Pinto de Castro (Biblioteca de Autores Portugueses, ibid. [1984]). Sec-ondary Lives include that by the *Jansenists P. T. du Fossé and L. I. Le Maistre de Saci (pub. anonymously, Paris, 1663; Eng. tr., 1880). R. de Almeida Rolo, OP, *O Bispo e a sua missão pastoral segundo D. Frei Bartolomeu dos Mártires* (Porto, 1964; Fr. tr., Lisbon, 1965); id., *Formação e Vida Intelectual de D. Frei Bartolo-meu dos Mártires* (Porto, 1977). *IV Centenário da Morte de D. Frei Bartolomeu dos Mártires: Congresso Internacional. Actas* (Fatima, 1994).

Bartholomew of Pisa (c.1260–1347), *Dominican theo-logian. He is also sometimes called 'of San Concordio' after his native place. He entered the Dominican Order in 1277, and, after studying at *Bologna, Paris, and Pisa, he taught at several Dominican houses and was soon held in high reputation as a scholar. He is chiefly famous for his alphabetically arranged 'Summa de Casibus Conscientiae' (1338), also called 'Summa Pisana' or 'Summa Bartholo-mea'. It was much used during the 14th and 15th cents. and was later also frequently printed.

There is a description of him in 'Chronica Antiqua Conventus Sanctae Catherinae de Pisis', pr. in *Archivio Storico Italiano*, 6, par. 2, sez. 3 (1845), pp. 397–633, pp. 521–9. Kaeppeli, 1 (1970), pp. 157–68.

Bartholomew's Day, Massacre of St. The massacre that took place on the night of 23–24 Aug. 1572 and the two following days in which, chiefly, it appears, at the instigation of *Catherine de' Medici, between 5,000 and 10,000 *Huguenots, including G. de *Coligny, were put to death in Paris and other large French cities.

The massacre is discussed from different angles in all Lives of Catherine de' Medici and Gaspard de Coligny, cited s.vv. J. W. Thompson, *The Wars of Religion in France, 1559–1576* (1909), pp. 448–53. S. L. England, *The Massacre of Saint Bartholomew* (1938). P. Erlanger, *Le Massacre de la Saint-Barthélemy* (1960; Eng. tr., 1962). N. M. Sutherland, *The Massacre of St Bartholomew and the European Conflict 1559–1572* (1973), esp. pp. 312–50. A. Soman (ed.), *The Massacre of St Bartholomew: Reappraisals and Documents* (International Archives of the History of Ideas, 75; The Hague, 1974). R. M. Kingdon, *Myths about the St Bartholomew's Day Massacres, 1572–1576* (Cambridge, Mass., and London, 1988). H. Butterfield, *Man on his Past* (Cambridge, 1955), pp. 171–201.

Bartholomites. (1) *Armenian.* A community of *Armenian monks who fled from Armenia when the Sultan of Egypt invaded the country in 1296, and settled in 1307 at Genoa, where a church dedicated to St Barthol-omew was built for them, hence their name. Others from Armenia joined them, and they spread throughout Italy. At first they retained the Armenian Liturgy and the Rule of St *Basil, but later, with the approval of Innocent VI (1356), they adopted the Roman Liturgy and the Rule of St *Augustine, and wore a habit similar to that of the *Dominicans, whose privileges they were granted by Boni-face IX. In the 17th cent. they began to decline and were finally suppressed by *Innocent X in 1650.

(2) *German.* A congregation of secular priests, 'Institu-tum clericorum saecularium in communi viventium', known also as 'Bartholomaeans', 'United Brethren', and 'Communists'. They were founded in 1640 at Tittmoning by Bartholomew Holzhauser (1613–58), a German parish priest and ecclesiastical writer, in order to revive the morals and discipline of the clergy and laity, after the decline due to the *Thirty Years War (1618–48). They lived in community under obedience to a superior, but without vows, and were entrusted with many seminaries. After receiving formal approbation from Innocent XI in 1680, they spread into England, Poland, Italy, and other European countries. Their extinction was brought about by the secularization of the German ecclesiastical states under Napoleon in 1803; and recent attempts at restora-tion have been without effect.

(1) M. A. van den Oudenrijn, OP (ed.), *Les Constitutions des Frères Arméniens de Saint Basile en Italie* (Orientalia Christiana Analecta, 126; 1940). [P. Hélyot], *Histoire des ordres monastiques, religieux et militaires*, 1 (1714), pp. 243–8, Heimbucher, 1, pp. 104 f. J. M. Besse in *CE* 2 (1907), p. 317, s.v.; L.-A. Redigonda in *DIP* 1 (1973), cols. 1073–5, s.v. 'Bartolomiti Armeni', with bibl.

(2) J. P. L. Gaduel, *Vie du vénérable serviteur de Dieu Barthélemy Holzhauzer . . . fondateur de l'Institut des clercs séculiers vivant en communauté, avec une étude sur cet Institut* (Orléans, 1861). F. Busan, OSB, 'Das Leben und Institut des ehrwürdigen Bartholomäus Holzhauser', *Studien und Mitteilungen aus dem Benediktiner- und Cistercienser-Orden*, 23 (1902), pp. 403–31 and 634–55. M. Arneth, *Das Ringen um Geist und Form der Priesterbildung im Säkularklerus des siebzehnten Jahrhunderts* (Würzburg [1970]), pp. 179–279 and 380–434. Heimbucher, 2, pp. 595–7. M. Arneth in *Dict. Sp.* 7 (pt. 1; 1969), cols. 590–7, s.v. 'Holzhauser', with bibl.; J. Berdonces in *DIP* 1 (1973), cols. 1070–3, s.v. 'Bartolomiti', with bibl.

Bartimaeus. The blind beggar healed by Christ at or near *Jericho on His last journey to *Jerusalem. He is said to have afterwards 'followed Him in the way' (Mk. 10: 46–52).

Bartolommeo, Fra (1475–1517), Florentine painter. Bartolommeo (or Baccio) di Paolo del Fattorino, known as Baccio della Porta, was an admirer and follower of G. *Savonarola, whose portrait he painted. In 1500 he entered the *Dominican Order, and was based at San Marco, Florence; he gave up painting until 1504. His work exemplified the transition from the Early to the High Renaissance and for a time he was the most important painter in Florence after the departure of *Leonardo da Vinci and *Raphael from the city. He travelled to *Venice (1508), where he was impressed by Giovanni Bellini, and Rome (1514), but was mainly active in Florence, working in partnership with Mariotto Albertinelli. Among his most famous works are the 'Last Judgement', painted (1499–1500) for S. Maria Nuova (now in the Museo di San Marco) and the 'Lamentation' in the Pitti, both in Florence; he also painted numerous magnificent altar-pieces.

F. Knapp, *Fra Bartolommeo della Porta und die Schule von San Marco* (1903). H. von der Gabelentz, *Fra Bartolommeo und die Florentiner Renaissance* (2 vols., 1922). J. A. Crowe and G. B. Cavalcaselle, *A History of Painting in Italy*, 6 (1914), ch. 3, pp. 50–104; A. Venturi, *Storia dell'Arte Italiana*, 9, pt. 1 (Milan, 1925), pp. 223–347; S. J. Freedberg, *Painting in Italy 1500–1600* (Pelican History of Art, 1971), pp. 49–54, with bibl. p. 519 (rev. paperback edn., 1975, pp. 84–90, with bibl. p. 716).

Barton, Elizabeth (*c*.1506–34), the 'Maid of Kent'. She was a servant girl who, after an illness in 1525, had trances and claimed to utter prophecies. After inquiries and a public examination by the Prior of Christ Church, Canterbury (1526), she was admitted as a nun at St Sepulchre's Convent in the city. Her prophecies then took a political turn, consisting in personal attacks on *Henry VIII for his intention to divorce his queen. In 1533, under examination by Abp. T. *Cranmer, a confession, true or false, was extorted from her that her trances were feigned, and she was prosecuted by Bill of Attainder and executed in 1534.

The main sources for her life are the Act of Attainder by which she was condemned (Treason of Elizabeth Barton (Pretended Revelations) Act 1533), and J. *Gairdner (ed.), *Letters and Papers Foreign and Domestic of the Reign of Henry VIII*, 6 (1882) and 7 (1883), *passim*. Some material from the *Cottonian MSS is pr. by T. Wright, *Three Chapters of Letters Relating to the Suppression of the Monasteries* (Camden Society, 26; 1843), pp. 13–34. A. D. Cheney, 'The Holy Maid of Kent', *Transactions of the Royal Historical Society*, NS 18 (1904), pp. 107–29; E. J. Devereux, 'Elizabeth Barton and Tudor Censorship', *Bulletin of the John Rylands Library*, 49 (1966–7), pp. 91–106. A. Neame, *The Holy Maid of Kent* (1971).

Baruch, Book of. A Book of the *Apocrypha to which is attached the 'Epistle of *Jeremy' (q.v.), the two together, with *Lamentations, forming appendices to the Book of *Jeremiah. The book consists of (1) an introduction, which professes to have been written by Baruch, the disciple of Jeremiah, and read by him to the Jewish captives in Babylon in the 6th cent. BC (1: 1–14); (2) a liturgical confession (1: 15–3: 8); (3) a sermon (3: 9–4: 4); and (4) a set of canticles (4: 5–5: 9). On a critical view, the unmistakable dependence of the work upon *Daniel has led scholars to date it in post-Maccabaean times, and its liturgical use has suggested to some that it was either written or adapted for use in the cycle of sabbaths commemorating national disasters which began to be observed after the fall of *Jerusalem in AD 70. It is generally held that at any rate the earlier sections of the Book were originally written in Hebrew.

Gk. and Heb. text ed. and reconstructed, with Eng. tr., by E. Tov (Society of Biblical Literature, Texts and Translations, Pseudepigrapha Series, 6; Missoula, Mont. [1975]). Comm. by O. C. Whitehouse in R. H. *Charles, *The Apocrypha and Pseudepigrapha of the Old Testament*, 1 (Oxford, 1913), pp. 569–95, and C. A. Moore, *Daniel, Esther and Jeremiah: The Additions* (Anchor Bible, 44; 1977), pp. 256–316. R. R. Harwell, *The Principal Versions of Baruch* (Yale Diss., New Haven, Conn., 1915). D. G. Burke, *The Poetry of Baruch: A Reconstruction and Analysis of the original Hebrew Text of Baruch 3: 9–5: 5* (Society of Biblical Literature, Septuagint and Cognate Studies, 10; Chico, Calif. [1982]). E. *Schürer, *The History of the Jewish People in the Age of Jesus Christ*, rev. Eng. tr. by G. Vermes and others, 3 (pt. 2, Edinburgh, 1987), pp. 733–43, with bibl. J. Le Moyne, OSB, in *Dict. Bibl.*, Suppl. 8 (1972), cols. 729–36, s.v. 'Prophètes d'Israël'. See also bibl. to APOCRYPHA.

Baruch, II. The Syriac Apocalypse. A Jewish work which professes to have been written by Baruch, Jeremiah's secretary. Opinions about the date of its composition vary, but since it describes the capture of *Jerusalem by the Chaldeans *c*.586 BC, it has been inferred that it was written after the fall of Jerusalem in AD 70, to encourage the Jews after the destruction of the Temple. A reference to the 'twenty-fifth year' (in ch. 1) has led P. Bogaert to suggest that it dates from AD 95; other scholars have placed it variously between AD 70 and *c*.135. In language and ideas it has striking resemblances to IV Ezra (II *Esdras). The Apocalypse was originally composed in Greek, but the bulk of it is extant only in a single 6th-cent. Syriac MS in the *Ambrosiana at Milan. The theory that the book in its latest form was the work of a Christian has not been generally accepted.

Syr. text ed. by A. M. Ceriani in *Monumenta Sacra et Profana*, 5 (pt. 2; Milan, 1871), pp. 113–80; also by M. Kmosko in *Patrologia Syriaca* (ed. R. Graffin), 2 (1907), cols. 1056–207, and S. Dedering in *The Old Testament in Syriac according to the Peshitta Version*, pt. 4, fasc. 3 (Leiden, 1973), first item. Eng. trs. with introds., notes, and indices by R. H. *Charles (London, 1896); id., *The Apocrypha and Pseudepigrapha of the Old Testament*, 2 (1913), pp. 470–526; A. F. J. Klijn in J. H. Charlesworth (ed.), *The Old Testament Pseudepigrapha*, 1 (1983), pp. 615–52; and L. H. Brockington in H. F. D. Sparks (ed.), *The Apocryphal Old Testament* (Oxford, 1984), pp. 835–95. Fr. tr., with introd. and comm., by P. Bogaert, OSB (SC 144–5; 1969). Ger. tr. by B. Violet (GCS 32, 1924, pp. 205–336, with introd. pp. lvi–xcvi). A. M. Denis, *Introduction aux pseudépigraphes grecs d'Ancien Testament* (Studia in Veteris Testamenti Pseudepigrapha, 1; Leiden, 1970), pp. 182–6 ('Les fragments grecs de l'Apocryphe syriaque de Baruch'). J. B. Frey in *Dict. Bibl.*, Suppl. 1 (1928), cols. 418–23, s.v. 'Apocryphes de l'Ancien Testament. 9: L'Apocalypse syriaque de Baruch'.

Baruch, III and IV. 'The Greek Apocalypse of Baruch' (traditionally numbered III Baruch) is an apocryphal work, apparently of Jewish origin, but worked over by a Christian hand. It may date from the 2nd cent., and it was probably known to *Origen (*De princ.* 2. 3. 6). The Apocalypse described the visions of the seven heavens which were granted to Baruch, though the last two are wanting as the MS is defective. A Slavonic version also exists.

'The Paraleipomena of Jeremiah' or 'The Rest of the Words of Baruch' (traditionally called IV Baruch) also dates from the 2nd cent., and may be earlier than the above. It is prob. the work of a Jewish Christian and deals with the end of *Jeremiah's life. The Greek text appears to be the original, but there are also Ethiopic, Armenian, and Slavonic translations.

The numbering of III and IV Baruch is sometimes interchanged.

Gk. text of the 'Greek Apocalypse' ed. M. R. James, *Apocrypha Anecdota*, 2nd ser. (Texts and Studies, 5, no. 1; Cambridge, 1897), pp. 84–94; also ed. by J. C. Picard in *Pseudepigrapha Veteris Testamenti Graece*, 2 (Leiden, 1967), pp. 61–96. Eng. tr. of Slavonic text by W. R. Morfill in M. R. James, op. cit., pp. 95–102. Introd., ibid., pp. li–lxx. Eng. trs. of Gk. text, with introds. and notes, in R. H. *Charles, *The Apocrypha and Pseudepigrapha of the Old Testament*, 2 (1913), pp. 527–41, rev. by A. W. Argyle in H. F. D. Sparks (ed.), *The Apocryphal Old Testament* (Oxford, 1984), pp. 897–914, and of Gk. and Slavonic texts by H. E. Gaylord, Jun., in J. H. Charlesworth (ed.), *The Old Testament Pseudepigrapha*, 1 (1983), pp. 653–79.

Gk. text of the 'Rest of the Words of Baruch' first pub. by A. M. Ceriani, *Monumenta Sacra et Profana*, 5, pt. 1 (Milan, 1868), pp. 9–18; standard edn. with introd. by J. R. Harris (London, 1889). Eng. tr. by R. Thornhill in H. F. D. Sparks, op. cit., pp. 813–33; Ethiopic text ed. A. *Dillmann, *Chrestomathia Aethiopica* (Leipzig, 1866), pp. 1–15. G. Delling, *Jüdische Lehre und Frömmigkeit in den Paralipomena Jeremiae* (Beihefte zur *ZATW*, 100; 1967), with bibl.

Basel, Confessions and **Council of.** See BASLE, CONFESSIONS and COUNCIL OF.

Bashmuric. See FAYUMIC.

Basil, St, 'the Great' (*c.*330–79 [or possibly slightly earlier]). One of the three *Cappadocian Fathers. He was the brother of St *Gregory of Nyssa and St *Macrina. After being educated at Caesarea in Cappadocia, *Constantinople, and *Athens in the best pagan and Christian culture of his day, he forsook the world for the monastic life, and, after a brief period in Syria and Egypt, settled as a hermit by the river Iris near Neocaesarea (358).

Here his early friendship with St *Gregory of Nazianzus was renewed, and they preached missions together. It has been suggested that the Emp. *Julian (361–3) tried to bring him to court, but it is not clear that the letter (*ep.* 32, Bidez) was addressed to Basil the Great rather than another Basil. In any case, it was not until *c.*364 that he left his retirement at the behest of his bishop, Eusebius of Caesarea in Cappadocia, to defend orthodoxy against the Arian Emperor, Valens. In 370 he was appointed to succeed Eusebius in the see of Caesarea, and held this office for the rest of his life. It brought him into the thick of further controversies with the extreme *Arian party led by *Eunomius, as well as with the *Pneumatomachi, who denied the divinity of the Holy Spirit, and with the Bps. of Rome (*Damasus) and Alexandria (*Athanasius), who refused to recognize his revered supporter, St *Meletius, as Bp. of Antioch.

In character Basil, besides being eloquent, learned, and statesmanlike, was possessed of great personal holiness. His nature was at once sensitive and pugnacious. To these qualities he added an unusual talent for organization, and impressed on E. monasticism the structure and ethos which it has retained ever since. The vast series of buildings he established on the outskirts of Caesarea, which included, besides the church and episcopal residence, hospitals and hostels for the poor, who were cared for by a carefully planned system of relief, long remained a monument to his memory.

His more important writings include a large collection of letters, his treatise 'On the Holy Spirit', and his three 'Books against Eunomius'. In conjunction with Gregory of Nazianzus he compiled the *Philocalia, a selection of passages from the works of *Origen. In the field of doctrine he made a strong effort to reconcile the *Semiarians to the formula of *Nicaea, and to show that their word *Homoiousios* ('like in substance to the Father') had the same implications as the Nicene *Homoousios* ('of one substance'). The virtual termination of the Arian controversy at the Council of *Constantinople in 381/2 shortly after his death is a tribute to his success. In some quarters he was suspected of *Apollinarianism, because he corresponded with Apollinarius, but it is clear from other letters (236 and 261) that his Christology was not Apollinarian. Feast day in W., 2 Jan. (formerly 14 June, as now in parts of the Anglican Communion); in E., 1 Jan. See also the following entries.

Collected Works first ed. at Basle, 1532; best edn. that of J. *Garnier, OSB, and P. *Maran, OSB, Paris, 1721–30, repr., with additions, 'apud Gaume', 3 vols. in 6, Paris, 1839, and in J. P. Migne, *PG* 29–32. Crit. edns. of *De Spiritu Sancto*, by C. F. Johnston (Oxford, 1892) and B. Pruche, OP (SC 17 bis, 1968); of *Epp.* by R. Deferrari (Loeb, 4 vols., 1926–34) and Y. Courtonne (Collection des Universités de France, Paris, 3 vols., 1957–66); of *Hom.*, 22 ('Ad adolescentes'), by F. Boulenger (Paris, 1935; repr., with corrections, by N. G. Wilson, *Saint Basil on the Value of Greek Literature*, 1975); of *Hom. in Hexaëm.*, by S. Giet (SC 26; 1950); of *Hom.* on 'Observe-toi toi-même' by S. Y. Rudberg (Acta Universitatis Stockholmiensis, 2 [1962]); of *Comm. in Is.*, by P. Trevisan (2 vols., Turin, 1939); of *De Baptismo*, with Ital. tr., by U. Neri (Brescia, 1976), repr., with notes and Fr. tr. by J. Ducatillon (SC 357; 1989); and of *Contra Eunomium*, by B. de Sesboüé, SJ, G.-M. de Durand, OP, and L. Doutreleau, SJ (SC 299 and 305; 1982–3). The sermons *de creatione hominis*, ed. under the name of Basil by A. Smets, SJ, and M. Van Esbroeck, SJ (SC

160; 1970), may be the work of Gregory of Nyssa. Eng. tr. of selected works by B. Jackson (NPNCF, 1895).

P. Allard, *Saint Basile* (1903); W. K. L. Clarke, *St Basil the Great: A Study in Monasticism* (1913); Y. Courtonne, *Saint Basile et l'hellénisme* (1934); id., *Un témoin du IVe siècle oriental: Saint Basile et son temps d'après sa correspondance* (Collection d'Études anciennes, 1973). G. F. Reilly, *Imperium and Sacerdotium according to St Basil the Great* (Washington, DC, 1945); D. Amand, OSB, *L' Ascèse monastique de Saint Basile* (Maredsous, 1949). J. Gribomont, OSB, *Histoire du texte des Ascétiques de S. Basile* (Bibliothèque du Muséon, 32; 1953); S. Y. Rudberg, *Études sur la tradition manuscrite de Saint Basile* (Stockholm, 1953). H. Dörries, *De Spiritu Sancto: Der Beitrag des Basilius zum Abschluss des trinitarischen Dogmas* (Abh. (Gött.), Dritte Folge, 39; 1956). G. L. Prestige, *St Basil the Great and Apollinaris of Laodicea*, ed. H. Chadwick (1956). T. Špidlík, SJ, *La Sophiologie de S. Basile* (Orientalia Christiana Analecta, 162; 1961). H. Dehnhard, *Das Problem der Abhängigkeit des Basilius von Platon: Quellenuntersuchungen zu seinen Schriften De Spiritu Sancto* (Patristische Texte und Studien, 3; 1964). E. Amand de Mendieta and S. Y. Rudberg, *Basile de Césarée: La tradition manuscrite directe des neuf homélies sur l'Hexaémeron* (TU 123; 1980). P. J. Fedwick (ed.), *Basil of Caesarea, Christian Humanist, Ascetic: A Sixteen-Hundredth Anniversary Symposium* (Pontifical Institute of Mediaeval Studies, 2 vols., Toronto [1981]). J. Gribomont, OSB, *Saint Basile, Évangile et Église* (Spiritualité Orientale et Vie Monastique, 36–7; 1984 [collection of repr. papers]). P. Rousseau, *Basil of Caesarea* (Berkeley, Calif., 1994). *CPG* 2 (1974), pp. 140–78 (nos. 2835–3005). Bardenhewer, 3, pp. 130–62 and 670 f.; Altaner and Stuiber (1978), pp. 290–8 and 606–9. J. Gribomont, OSB, in *NCE* 2 (1967), pp. 143–6, with bibl.; id. in *DPAC* 1 (1983), cols. 491–7, s.v.; Eng. tr., *Encyclopedia of the Early Church*, 1 (1992), pp. 114 f.

See also works cited in the two following entries.

Basil, Liturgy of St. This liturgy is extant in two forms, the earlier and shorter of which is the ordinary liturgy of the *Coptic Church. An early MS of this form in a 7th-cent. Sahidic version (the original was Greek) contains an anaphora of Antiochene structure with some Egyptian features; it is comparable in brevity and simplicity to those of *Addai and Mari and the *Apostolic Tradition*. The expansion of this anaphora into the longer form may well be in part the work of St *Basil the Great. For some centuries this longer form was the chief liturgy of *Constantinople, but it was eventually superseded on most days of the ecclesiastical year by the 'Liturgy of St *Chrysostom', which it had prob. influenced. It is, however, still used in the Orthodox Church on the first five Sundays in *Lent, on *Maundy Thursday, on the eves of *Easter, of *Christmas, and of *Epiphany, and on the feast of St Basil (1 Jan.). The Egyptian form of the Liturgy of St Basil has served as a model for modern *Eucharistic Prayers, esp. those of the RC Church.

Text in Brightman, *LEW*, pp. 309–44, 400–11; also in J. P. Migne, *PG* 31. 1629–56. H. Engberding, OSB, *Das eucharistische Hochgebet der Basileiosliturgie* (1931). S. Euringer, *Die äthiopische Anaphora des hl. Basilius* (Rome, 1934; ed., with tr. and notes, from four MSS). J. Doresse and E. Lanne, *Un témoin archaïque de la liturgie copte de S. Basile*, with appendix by B. *Capelle, OSB, 'Les Liturgies "basiliennes" et saint Basile' (Bibliothèque du Muséon, 47; 1960). A. Raes, SJ, 'Un nouveau document de la Liturgie de S. Basile', *OCP* 26 (1960), pp. 401–11. W. E. Pitt, 'The Origin of the Anaphora of the Liturgy of St Basil', *JEH* 12 (1961), pp. 1–13. H. Engberding, OSB, 'Das anaphorische Fürbittgebet der Basiliusliturgie', *Oriens Christianus*, 47 (1963), pp. 16–52; 49 (1965), pp. 18–37. P. Scazzoso, *Introduzione alla*

ecclesiologia di san Basilio (Studia Patristica Mediolanensia, 4; 1975), pp. 144–70. *CPG* 2 (1974), pp. 163 f. (no. 2905). P. de Meester, OSB, in *DACL* 6 (pt. 2; 1925), cols. 1596–604 ('Authenticité des liturgies de Saint Basile et de Saint Jean Chrysostome'), s.v. 'Grecques (Liturgies)'.

Basil, Rule of St. The monastic Rule put forward by St *Basil the Great, which is the basis of the usual Rule still followed by religious in the E. Church. Basil's earliest attempt to provide rules for the monastic life is known as the 'moral rules' (*regulae morales*) or *Moralia*, composed at the beginning of his monastic life in 358/9; they form a collection of 80 rules, each supported by quotations from the NT. What is usually referred to as the 'Rule of St Basil' is his *Asceticon*, a collection of questions and answers on the monastic life, which originated in questions put to Basil on his travels by devout lay people. The earliest form of these (called the 'Short Asceticon') goes back to the early 360s and now exists only in a Latin translation made by *Rufinus in 397 and in fragments of a Syriac version. Some of the questions seem to betray a *Messalian influence. A later redaction of these questions and answers seems to have been made for the monastery Basil set up at Caesarea; to it is appended the *Epitimia*, rules for the punishment of monastic offenders. This form of the *Asceticon* was used by St *Theodore of Studios (d. 826) in his revision of the Rule. Basil prepared a further, more literary, redaction, which he sent, with the 'moral rules', to his disciples in Pontus. The most widespread form of the *Asceticon* (the so-called 'Vulgate') was, however, compiled in the 6th cent. This consists of the 'moral rules', the questions and answers, and the *Epitimia*, interspersed with 'prologues', most of which are authentically Basilian. In this form the questions and answers are divided into 55 'detailed rules' (*regulae fusius tractatae*), which provide a systematic presentation of the monastic life, and 313 'short rules' (*regulae brevius tractatae*), which discuss the detailed application of these principles to the cloistered life. This 'Great Asceticon' was further expanded in the Middle Ages by the addition of the *Constitutiones asceticae* and a treatise on Baptism.

While strict, the *Asceticon* avoided giving encouragement to the more extreme austerities of the hermits of the deserts. It conceived of asceticism as a means to the perfect service of God, to be achieved in community life under obedience. Hours of liturgical prayer were laid down, and manual and other work, in the form of set tasks, enjoined. Poverty and chastity similar to those later prescribed in the W. were also imposed. Children were to be trained in classes attached to the monasteries, and were to be given an opportunity of testing their vocation to the religious life. The monks were enjoined also to care for the poor.

The text of all three forms of *Regulae* (incl. the *moralia*), with the prologues and *Epitimia*, and the *Constitutiones asceticae*, is pr. in J. P. Migne, *PG* 31. 653–870, 881–1428. Crit. edn. of Rufinus' translation of the 'Short Asceticon' by K. Zelzer (CSEL 86; 1986). Eng. tr. by W. K. L. Clarke, *The Ascetic Works of Saint Basil* (1925).

E. F. Morison, *St Basil and his Rule: A Study in Early Monasticism* (1912). J. Gribomont, OSB, *Histoire du texte des Ascétiques de S. Basile* (Bibliothèque du Muséon, 32; 1953). K. Zelzer, 'L'histoire du text des Règles de saint Basile et de saint Benoît à la lumière de la tradition gallo-franque', *Regulae Benedicti Studia*, 13 (1986), pp. 75–89. J. Quasten, *Patrology*, 3 (Utrecht and

Westminster, Md., 1960), pp. 211–14. *CPG* 2 (1974), pp. 152–60 (nos. 2875–98).

Basil of Ancyra (4th cent.), *Arian Bp. He was a typical representative of the more moderate party of the Arians. Elected in 336 to succeed *Marcellus in the see of Ancyra, he was himself deposed by the Council of *Sardica in 343, but reinstated by Constantius *c*.348. He took part in the Arianizing synods of Sirmium (351), of Ancyra (358), and Seleucia (359). His constantly increasing criticisms of the more extreme Arian doctrines, however, led their exponents to remove him from his see in 360, and banish him to Illyria, where he died. A short dogmatic treatise which he composed in conjunction with *George of Laodicea has been preserved by *Epiphanius in his *Haer.* 73. 12–22. He was also perhaps the author of the treatise 'On Virginity' (so F. Cavallera) included among the works of St *Basil the Great.

For the writings mentioned, see J. P. Migne, *PG* 42. 425–44, and 30. 669–810. Old-Slav text of *De Virginitate* ed., with Fr. tr., by A. Vaillant (Textes publiés par l'Institut d'Études Slaves, 3; 1943). J. Gummerus, *Die homöusianische Partei bis zum Tode des Konstantius* (1900), pp. 121–34. F. Cavallera, 'Le "De Virginitae" de Basile d'Ancyre', *RHE* 6 (1905), pp. 5–14. J. J. Cuesta, 'Dieta y virginidad: Basilio de Ancira y san Gregorio de Nisa', *Miscelánea Comillas*, 14 (1950), pp. 187–97, esp. pp. 189–93. J. Quasten, *Patrology*, 3 (Utrecht and Westminster, Md., 1960), pp. 201–3.

Basil of Seleucia (d. after 468), Abp. of Seleucia by 448. He is remembered chiefly for his vacillating part in the events which preceded the Council of *Chalcedon in 451. Having condemned *Eutyches, the heresiarch, in 448, he acquiesced in his rehabilitation by the *Latrocinium in 449, but recanted shortly after and signed the *Tome of St *Leo I in 450. A series of 41 sermons of Basil on the Scriptures (two not genuine) have been preserved; and there are a few other writings, some of them spurious, that have come down under his name; these apparently include the 'De Vita et Miraculis Sanctae Theclae'.

Works in J. P. Migne, *PG* 85. 1–618; P. [T.] Camelot, OP, 'Une Homélie inédite de Basile de Séleucie', in *Mélanges offerts à A. M. Desrousseaux* (1937), pp. 35–48; Hesychius of Jerusalem, Basil of Seleucia, and others, *Homélies Pascales (cinq homélies inédites)*, ed. M. Aubineau (SC 187; 1972), pp. 167–277, with Fr. tr. and introd. B. Marx, 'Der homiletische Nachlass des Basileios von Seleukia', *OCP* 7 (1941), pp. 329–69. E. Honigmann, *Patristic Studies* (ST 173; 1953), pp. 180–3. M. Van Parys, 'L'évolution de la doctrine christologique de Basile de Séleucie', *Irénikon*, 44 (1971), pp. 493–514. *CPG* 3 (1979), pp. 278–83 (nos. 6655–75). See also bibl. to THECLA, ST.

basilica. An early form of the building used for Christian worship, especially common in W. Europe in the centuries which immediately followed the recognition of Christianity by *Constantine. It seems to have been modelled on the Roman building of the same name, which served as a law court and a commercial exchange; but some features were apparently derived from the Roman house and others from the chapels of the *catacombs, both of which had served as places of Christian worship before the conversion of the Empire. The building was often approached by an '*atrium', or outer courtyard, with its colonnaded cloister. The church itself consisted of a '*narthex', or narrow porch, leading by three or more doorways into the main building. This was built with a nave and two (or even four) narrower aisles with pillars supporting horizontal architraves at first, but in later times arches. Above these rose the clerestory pierced by windows. The building was usually orientated, with the E. end completed by an arch and semicircular apse, with mosaics in its vaulting. The altar, which stood out from the wall on the chord of the apse, was raised on a platform and surmounted by a canopy. Directly underneath the altar and partly below the level of the floor was the 'confessio' or chapel which sometimes contained the body of the patron Saint. While the basilica was being used for worship the bishop sat on a throne in the centre of the wall of the apse, with his clergy in a semicircle on either side. He moved to the altar for the celebration of the Eucharist. See also ORIENTATION.

Today the title of 'basilica' is given by the Pope to certain privileged churches. Such basilicas are 'major' or 'minor'. The four 'Major Basilicas' are the Roman churches of St John *Lateran (for the 'Patriarch of the West', the Pope), *St Peter's at the Vatican (for the Patriarch of *Constantinople), *St Paul's outside the Walls (for the Patriarch of *Alexandria), and *Santa Maria Maggiore (for the Patriarch of *Antioch). Each has a Papal altar, the use of which was until 1966 restricted to the Pope or his immediate delegate. There are a number of 'Minor Basilicas' in Rome and others throughout the world.

R. Krautheimer, *Corpus Basilicarum Christianarum Romae: The Early Christian Basilicas of Rome, IV–IX Cent.* (Monumenti di Antichità Pubblicati dal Pontificio Istituto di Archeologia Cristiana, 2nd ser. 2; 5 vols., 1937–77). L. Bréhier, 'Les Origines de la basilique chrétienne', *Bulletin Monumental*, 86 (1927), pp. 221–49. J. G. Davies, *The Origin and Development of Early Christian Church Architecture* (1952), pp. 12–50. J. B. Ward Perkins, 'Constantine and the Origins of the Christian Basilica', *Papers of the British School at Rome*, 22 (1954), pp. 69–90. R. Krautheimer, *Early Christian and Byzantine Architecture* (Pelican History of Art, 1965; 3rd edn., 1979). R [L. P.] Milburn, *Early Christian Art and Architecture* (1988), pp. 85–8 and 94–119. H. *Leclercq, OSB, in *DACL* 2 (pt. 1; 1910), cols. 525–602, s.v. 'Basilique'; E. Langlotz and F. W. Deichmann in *RAC* 1 (1950), cols. 1225–59, s.v. 'Basilika'.

Basilides. A theologian of *Gnostic tendencies who taught at *Alexandria in the second quarter of the 2nd cent. He wrote a biblical commentary, the *Exegetica*, in 24 books; perhaps also a work entitled 'the Gospel' (contents unknown); and some Odes. Besides biblical material he used secret traditions supposedly deriving from St *Peter and St *Matthias, some Gnostic doctrines, and elements of Platonic and Stoic philosophy. His system is difficult to reconstruct, since only fragments of his writings survive, and conflicting accounts are given by *Irenaeus, *Clement of Alexandria, and *Hippolytus. Acc. to Irenaeus, Basilides taught a form of *dualistic Gnosticism, reminiscent of *Valentinianism, but more elaborate, with 365 heavens; the ruler of the lowest is the creator God of the OT. Christ is a messenger of the supreme God, manifest in Jesus, who exchanged roles with *Simon of Cyrene before the Crucifixion. In complete contrast, Hippolytus' Basilides is perhaps the only seriously philosophical Gnostic; he taught a *monist system in which everything is derived from an ineffable 'non-existent' God. Jesus is an enlightened being who leads the elect back to God. Acc.

to Clement, Basilides was much more orthodox, though a dualist. His followers soon formed a separate sect, but his influence seems to have been largely confined to Egypt.

The chief authorities are Irenaeus, *Adv. Haer.* 1. 24; Clement of Alexandria, *Strom. passim*; Hippolytus, *Haer.* 7. 20–7. D. A. Hilgenfeld, *Die Ketzergeschichte des Urchristentums* (Leipzig, 1884), pp. 195–230. P. J. G. A. Hendrix, *De Alexandrijnsche Haeresiarch Basilides* (Amsterdam, 1926). W. Foerster, 'Das System des Basilides', *New Testament Studies*, 9 (1963), pp. 233–55; W. A. Löhr, *Basilides und seine Schule* (Wissenschaftliche Untersuchungen zum Neuen Testament, 83; 1996). A. Pourkier, *L'hérésiologie chez Épiphane de Salamine* (Christianisme Antique, 4 [1992]), pp. 205–56, with bibl. p. 505. F. J. A. *Hort in *DCB* 1 (1877), pp. 268–81; J. H. Waszink in *RAC* 1 (1950), cols. 1217–25, both s.v. See also works cited under GNOSTICISM.

Basilikon Doron (Gk. Βασιλικὸν Δῶρον, 'a royal gift'). The title of *James I's book addressed to his eldest son, Henry (d. 1612). Its professed purpose was to guide Henry in his duties when he succeeded to the throne, but its real object was to rebuke ministers of religion who meddled in State affairs. James had a private edition of seven copies printed in 1599, but published it openly in 1603 on the death of *Elizabeth I. It was immediately popular and within three years translations had been printed in French (two versions), Danish, Dutch, Latin, German, Welsh, and Swedish.

Crit. edn. by J. Craigie (Scottish Text Society, 3rd ser. 16 and 18; 1944–50). Text also in C. H. McIlwain (ed.), *The Political Works of James I* (Harvard Political Classics, 1; Cambridge, Mass., and London, 1918), pp. 3–52, with important introd. Facsimile of 1599 edn. (Menston, Yorks., 1969).

Basle, Confessions of.
The [first] 'Confession of Basle', which was compiled by O. *Myconius on the basis of a shorter formula put forward by J. *Oecolampadius in 1531, was made the basis of the reform introduced at Basle in 1534. Its theological standpoint represents a compromise between the positions of M. *Luther and H. *Zwingli. The 'First *Helvetic Confession' of 1536 is sometimes known also as the 'Second Confession of Basle'.

The text of the two Confessions is in H. A. Niemeyer, *Collectio Confessionum in ecclesiis reformatis publicataurm* (Leipzig, 1840), pp. 78–122; Eng. tr., with introd. and bibl., in A. C. Cochrane (ed.), *Reformed Confessions of the 16th Century* (1966), pp. 89–111.

Basle, Council of
(1431–49). The Council, which inherited both the tasks and the difficulties of the Council of *Constance (q.v.), was convoked by *Martin V and opened in 1431. It was presided over by Card. G. *Cesarini, who was confirmed in this office by the new Pope, *Eugenius IV. When the latter, acting on unfavourable reports, dissolved it by a bull of 18 Dec. 1431, the Council disregarded the Pope's action, which was opposed also by Cesarini, and reaffirmed the decrees of Constance on the superiority of a *General Council over a Pope. The assembly at that time consisted of only a few bishops and abbots, apart from the inferior clergy, but it grew rapidly and, in order to enhance its authority, it introduced new regulations for procedure which gave the lower grades a majority over the bishops. It was, moreover, widely supported by the princes and the great universities, one of its

best-known members being *Nicholas of Cusa, the humanist.

The Pope, pressed by the Council, the Emp. Sigismund, and even by Venice, and beset by political difficulties in Italy, in the bull 'Dudum sacrum' of 15 Dec. 1433 revoked his former decision and recognized the Council The Council continued, however, in its anti-Papal attitude, reasserted once again the decrees of Constance, imposed many restrictions on the Papal legates, and prescribed an oath to be taken by a Pope after his election. It also attempted to regulate the nominations of cardinals and other affairs of the *Curia. In 1436 Eugenius IV denounced the usurpations of the Council in a memorandum to all Catholic princes. In 1437 the *Hussite question was settled against the Papal views by the ratification of the 'Compactata', thereby conceding to the Bohemians Communion in both kinds and several other demands. In the same year occurred the final break of the Council with the Orthodox Church over the place of the proposed council for union. As the Pope, the Greek envoys, and the Papal minority of the Council preferred a place in Italy, Eugenius transferred the Council to Ferrara; while those who remained at Basle deposed the Pope as a heretic and elected Amadeus VIII of Savoy as antipope (Felix V) in 1439. The renewal of the schism cost the Council its prestige, and the nations submitted one by one to Eugenius. In 1448 the Council was driven from Basle and moved to Lausanne, where Felix V abdicated, and in 1449 it decreed its own closure.

The oecumenicity of the Council of Basle has been an object of much discussion, but most RC theologians now recognize the first 25 sessions, until the transfer of the Council to Ferrara and *Florence. See also CONCILIAR THEORY.

Texts in Hardouin, 8–9; Mansi, 29–31 (1788–98). Crit. texts in *Concilium Basiliense: Studien und Quellen zur Geschichte des Concils von Basel* (ed. J. Haller and others 1896 ff.; 8 vols. to 1936); other contemporary material in *Monumenta Conciliorum Generalium Seculi Decimi Quinti*, ed. by F. Palacky and others (3 vols., Vienna and Basle, 1857–1932; vol. 4, indices, Basle, 1935). Text of decrees, with Eng. tr. and introd., in Tanner, *Decrees* (1990), pp. 453–513. Eng. tr. of other primary docs. in C. M. D. Crowder, *Unity, Heresy and Reform, 1378–1460: The Conciliar Response to the Great Schism* (1977), pp. 146–65, 177–9, with introd., pp. 29–35. Hefele and Leclercq, 7 (pt. 2, 1916), pp. 663–1137, with extensive bibl. refs. J. Gill, SJ, *Constance et Bâle–Florence* (Histoire des Conciles Œcuméniques, 9; 1965), pp. 119–209 and 332–51. J. W. Stieber, *Pope Eugenius IV, the Council of Basel and the Secular and Ecclesiastical Authorities in the Empire* (Studies in the History of Christian Thought, 13; Leiden, 1978). G. Christianson, *Cesarini: The Conciliar Cardinal. The Basel Years, 1431–1438* (Kirchengeschichtliche Quellen und Studien, 10; 1979). A. [J.] Black, *Council and Commune: The conciliar movement and the fifteenth-century heritage* [in some issues subtitled *The Conciliar Movement and the Council of Basle*] (1979), esp. pp. 1–117 and 194–222. H. Müller, *Die Franzosen, Frankreich und das Basler Konzil (1431–1449)* (Konziliengeschichte, Reihe B; 2 vols., 1990). E. Delaruelle, E. R. Labande, and F. Ourliac in Fliche and Martin, 14 (1962), pp. 227–92, with extensive bibl. pp. 227 f. J. Gill, SJ, in *NCE* 2 (1967), pp. 141 f., s.v. 'Basel, Council of'; A. N. E. D. Schofield in *TRE* 5 (1980), pp. 284–9, s.v. 'Basel–Ferrara–Florenz, Konzil von. I. Das Konzil von Basel'.

Basnage, Jacques
(1653–1723), *Calvinist theologian and Church historian. Having become in 1676 a minister

at Rouen, his native town, he retired to the Netherlands in 1685 after the revocation of the Edict of *Nantes. He later took a prominent part in Dutch affairs of state. His two most important writings are his *Histoire de la religion des églises réformées* (2 vols., 1690) and his *Histoire de l'église* (2 vols., 1699), both pub. at Rotterdam. He also wrote against J. B. *Bossuet.

E.-A. Maihlet, *Jacques Basnage, théologien, controversiste, diplomate et historien: Sa vie et ses écrits* (Geneva, 1880; repr. 1978). G. Loirette in *DHGE* 6 (1932), cols. 1251–3, s.v.

Bassendyne Bible. The earliest edition of the Bible in English to be published in Scotland. In July 1575 Thomas Bassendyne (or Bassinden; d. 1577) was granted a licence by the Privy Council to print the Bible, with the stipulation that it should be ready in nine months, and in 1576 the NT appeared. The Bible was not completed, however, till 1579.

W. T. Dobson, *History of the Bassendyne Bible* (Edinburgh, 1887), esp. pp. 101–57. Darlow and Moule, 1, ed. A. S. Herbert (1968), no. 158, pp. 88 f.

Bath and Wells. A see of the Province of *Canterbury, roughly equal to the historical county of Somerset. It was founded c.909 by King Edward the Elder as the diocese of *Wells. Between 1088 and 1091 the see was moved from Wells to Bath by King William II and Bp. John de Villula (1088–1122), and John and his successors styled themselves Bishops of Bath until Bp. Savaric (1192–1205), having obtained the abbacy of *Glastonbury, changed the title to 'Bath and Glastonbury'. In 1219 *Honorius III dissolved the union of Glastonbury with Bath and authorized the title 'Bath and Wells', though Bp. Jocelin (1206–42) did not assume it. A protracted dispute between the canons of Wells and the monks of Bath over the right to elect the bishop was resolved by *Innocent IV in 1245. He confirmed the title of 'Bath and Wells ' (which was then taken by Bp. Roger, 1244–7, and all his successors), and ordered that elections should be made alternately in Wells and Bath by the two chapters jointly, and that enthronements should be at the place of election. This arrangement came to an end with the dissolution of Bath Abbey in 1540; since then, Wells has been the sole cathedral of the diocese, but the title of the see and the bishop has remained unchanged. Notable holders of the see have included R. *Fox (1492–4), T. *Wolsey (1518–23), W. *Barlow (1548–1553), T. *Ken (1685–90), and R. *Bagot (1845–54). The present abbey-church at Bath has served since the *dissolution of the monasteries as a parish church.

The following Episcopal Registers have been pub. by the Somerset Record Society: Walter Giffard, 1265–6 (13; 1899), John de Drokensford, 1309–29 (1; 1887), Ralph of Shrewsbury, 1329–1363 (9 and 10; 1896), Henry Bowett, 1401–7 (13; 1899), Nicholas Bubwith, 1407–24 (29 and 30; 1914), John Stafford, 1425–43 (31 and 32; 1915–16), Thomas Beckington, 1443–65 (49 and 50; 1934–5), Robert Stillington, 1466–91, and Richard Fox, 1492–4 (52; 1937), Oliver King, 1496–1503, and Hadrian de Castello, 1503–18 (54; 1939), Thomas Wolsey, 1518–23, John Clerke, 1523–41, William Knyght, 1541–7, and Gilbert Bourne, 1554–9 (55; 1940). A Survey of the Diocesan Archives, carried out by a committee appointed by the Pilgrim Trust in 1946, was circulated in typescript among the principal record libraries of England. H. *Wharton, *Anglia Sacra*, 1 (1691), pp. 551–77. S. H. Cassan, *Lives of the Bishops of Bath and Wells from the Earliest Times to the Pres-*

ent Period (1829). P. M. Hembry, *The Bishops of Bath and Wells, 1540–1640: Social and Economic Problems* (1967). T. S. Holmes in W. Page (ed.), *VCH*, Somerset, 2 (1911), pp. 1–67. On Bath Abbey, see W. *Dugdale, *Monasticon Anglicanum*, 2 (1819 edn.), pp. 256–73; T. S. Holmes in *VCH*, loc. cit., pp. 69–81. C. L. Marson in *DECH*, pp. 44–6, s.v. See also bibl. to WELLS.

Bath Qol (Heb. בַּת קוֹל, 'daughter of a voice'). The term in *Rabbinic theology for a voice from Heaven such as was believed to be a regular means of God's communication with men. Such a voice is referred to in the NT at Christ's *Baptism (Mk. 1: 11) and *Transfiguration (Mk. 9: 7) and before His Passion (Jn. 12: 28), and also in Acts (9: 4, cf. 10: 13).

Batiffol, Pierre (1861–1929), Church historian. A pupil of G. B. *de Rossi, from 1889 till his death he was at the École de Ste-Barbe at *Paris, except from 1898 to 1908 when he was rector of the Institut Catholique at Toulouse. In 1890 he produced a critical edition of the *Syntagma Doctrinae ad Monachos*, a work once attributed to St *Athanasius. His *Histoire du Bréviaire romain* (1893; much improved 1911; Eng. tr., 1912) exercised a considerable influence on the revival of liturgical studies. For some years he was closely associated with the group of scholars later condemned as *Modernists. His first series of *Études d'histoire et de théologie positive* (1902) was followed in 1903 by a second volume dealing with the Eucharist. This created such a storm that Batiffol was forced to resign from his rectorship at Toulouse, and in 1911 it was placed on the *Index. In 1913 he issued a much revised edition with the separate title *L'Eucharistie, la Présence réelle et la Transsubstantiation*. His later years were mainly taken up with a history of the Church and esp. of the growth of Papal power to the time of St *Leo, of which the successive volumes were *L'Église naissante et le catholicisme* (1909; Eng. tr., *Primitive Catholicism*, 1911), *La Paix constantinienne et le catholicisme* (1914), *Le Catholicisme de Saint Augustin* (1920), and *Le Siège apostolique, 359–451* (1924). In 1928 followed *Saint Grégoire le Grand* (Eng. tr., 1929). His writings, if not mostly of great originality, did much to encourage critical study in France and esp. to introduce to his country recent German work in patristics.

J. Rivière, *Monseigneur Batiffol* (1929). Id. in *DHGE* 6 (1932), cols. 1327–30, s.v.

Bauer, Bruno (1809–82), German theologian and historian. He was at first a conservative *Hegelian, but, after moving from Berlin to Bonn in 1839, he adopted a position even more extreme than that of D. F. *Strauss and attributed the Gospel story to the imagination, not, like Strauss, of the Christian community, but of a single mind. In 1842 he was deprived of his teaching post. The guiding principle of his many writings was a belief that the origins of Christianity were to be found in Graeco-Roman philosophy. He assigned the 'Original Gospel' to the reign of Hadrian (117–38) and the Epp. of St *Paul to that of *Marcus Aurelius (161–80). Besides his work on NT criticism, he wrote on the history of the 18th cent.

M. Kegel, *Bruno Bauer und seine Theorien über die Entstehung des Christentums* (Abhandlungen zur Philosophie und ihrer Geschichte, 6; 1908). E. Barnikol, *Bruno Bauer: Studien und Materialien aus dem Nachlass*, ed. P. Reimer and H.-M. Saas

(Assen, 1972). Z. Rosen, *Bruno Bauer and Karl Marx: The Influence of Bruno Bauer on Marx's Thought* (The Hague, 1977). A. *Schweitzer, *Geschichte der Leben-Jesu Forschung* (2nd edn., 1913), pp. 141–61; J. C. O'Neill, *The Bible's Authority* (Edinburgh, 1991), pp. 150–66. E. Barnikol in *RGG* (3rd edn.), 1 (1957), cols. 922–4, s.v.; J. Mehlhausen in *TRE* 5 (1980), pp. 314–17, s.v.

Bäumer, Suitbert (1845–94), liturgical scholar. After studying at Bonn and *Tübingen, he took the *Benedictine habit at *Beuron in 1865. From 1875 to 1890 he was in exile at *Maredsous, through the *Kulturkampf. He wrote extensively on liturgical subjects, esp. in *Der Katholik* of Mainz. His chief work, *Die Geschichte des Breviers* (Freiburg i. B., 1895; Fr. tr. by R. Biron, 2 vols., 1905), was the fruit of long and patient researches in the principal libraries of Europe. Among its theses were the liturgical importance of St *Gregory I and the widespread influence of *Gregory VII's rite in the Papal chapel through its subsequent adoption by the *Franciscans. In his later years he collaborated closely with E. *Bishop. His other works include a Life of J. *Mabillon (1892) and a treatise on the *Apostles' Creed (1893).

U. Berlière, OSB, 'Dom Suitbert Baeumer, OSB', *R. Bén.* 11 (1894), pp. 481–99 (incl. list of works; pp. 497–9). R. Biron, OSB, 'Notice biographique' prefixed to his tr. of Bäumer's *Geschichte des Breviers* ('Histoire du bréviaire'), 1 (1905), pp. xiii–xiv. R. Proost in *DACL* 2 (1910), cols. 623–6, s.v.; P. Séjourné, OSB, in *DHGE* 6 (1932), cols. 1474–81, s.v.

Baumstark, Anton (1872–1948), Semitic scholar and liturgist. A native of Constance, he studied classical and oriental philology at Heidelberg. From 1899 to 1905 he resided at the German Campo Santo at Rome. Later he was a schoolmaster at Sassbach in Baden (1905–21); then, simultaneously, Professor at Bonn (from 1921), Nijmegen (from 1923), and Utrecht (from 1926); and from 1930 to 1935 Professor Ordinarius in Oriental Studies at Münster i. W. In 1901 he began the periodical *Oriens Christianus* (3 series; to 1941) in which he published much of his best work. He was also a constant contributor to the *Maria Laach *Jahrbuch für Liturgiewissenschaft* (from 1921). His separate works include: *Die Messe im Morgenland* (1906), *Festbrevier und Kirchenjahr der syrischen Jakobiten* (1910), *Die christlichen Literaturen des Orients* (2 vols., Sammlung Göschen, 1911), *Geschichte der syrischen Literatur* (1922), *Die älteste erreichbare Gestalt des 'Liber sacramentorum anni circuli' der römischen Kirche* (with C. Mohlberg, 1927), *Liturgie comparée: Conférences faites au prieuré d'Amay* (1940; 3rd edn. by B. Botte, OSB, 1953; Eng. tr. by F. L. Cross, 1958), *Nocturna Laus: Typen frühchristlicher Vigilienfeier und ihr Fortleben vor allem im römischen und monastischen Ritus* (posthumously ed. by O. Heiming, 1957), and *Die Vorlage des althochdeutschen Tatians* (ed. J. Rathofer, 1964).

Short obituary by T. Klauser in *EL* 63 (1949), pp. 185–7, followed by full bibl. by H. E. Killy (1894–1948; 546 items), pp. 187–207.

Baur, Ferdinand Christian (1792–1860), German Protestant theologian, founder of the *Tübingen School (q.v.). A native of Schmiden in Württemberg, he was educated at Tübingen University. From 1817 to 1826 he taught classics at Blaubeuren and in 1824–5 he published

his work *Symbolik und Mythologie*. From 1826 until his death he taught New Testament and historical theology at Tübingen. A student of German Idealism, he was drawn to modern theology by F. D. E. *Schleiermacher's work *Die christliche Glaube* (1821–2), and from 1835 he was inspired by G. F. W. *Hegel's theory of historical development. This guided his theological interpretation of *Die christliche Gnosis* (1835), *Die christliche Lehre von der Versöhnung* (1838), and *Die christliche Lehre von der Dreieinigkeit und Menschwerdung Gottes in ihrer geschichtlichen Entwicklung* (3 vols., 1841–3), which set a new standard in the history of doctrine. In *Die Christuspartei in der korinthischen Gemeinde* (1831) he recognized the fact of conflict in early Christianity and later made this the key to his understanding of early Christianity. In *Die sogenannten Pastoralbriefe des Apostels Paulus* (1835) he denied the Pauline authorship of the *Pastoral Epistles, dating them in the 2nd cent. on account of the historical situation they presuppose. His view of the development is clearest in his monograph on St *Paul (*Paulus, der Apostel Jesu Christi*, 1845; Eng. tr., 1873–5). This denied the authenticity of all the Pauline Epistles except Gal., 1 and 2 Cor., and Rom., and assigned Acts to the later 2nd cent. In 1847 he concluded his researches into the NT canon with a work on the Gospels, *Kritische Untersuchungen über die kanonischen Evangelien*, in which he assigned the earliest date to Mt., as representing the Judaizing party, and the latest to Jn., as depicting the final reconciliation. This last Gospel reflected the *Gnostic and *Montanist controversies of the 2nd cent. and was devoid of historical value. In his later years he devoted himself chiefly to Church history, which he carried from the beginnings of Christianity to the 19th cent., the last vols. being published posthumously. The whole picture is summarized in *Das Christentum und die christliche Kirche der drei ersten Jahrhunderte* (1853; Eng. tr., *The Church History of the First Three Centuries*, 1878–1879). Among his other writings were *Lehrbuch der christlichen Dogmengeschichte* (1847), his *Vorlesungen über neutestamentliche Theologie* (ed. by his son, F. F. Baur, 1864), and *Vorlesungen über die christliche Dogmengeschichte* (ed. id., 3 vols., 1865–7).

Ausgewählte Werke in Einzelausgaben, ed. K. Scholder (5 vols., Stuttgart, 1963–75). Eng. tr. of some of his writings on Church History, with introd. by P. C. Hodgson (New York, 1968), and bibl. Life by G. Frädrich (Gotha, 1909). E. Zeller, *Vorträge und Abhandlungen*, 1 (2nd edn., 1875), pp. 390–479 (no. 11: F. C. Baur). W. Geiger, *Spekulation und Kritik: Die Geschichtstheologie Ferdinand Christian Baurs* (1964). P. C. Hodgson, *The Formation of Historical Theology: A Study of Ferdinand Christian Baur* (New York [1966]). J. Fitzer, *Möhler and Baur in Controversy, 1832–38: Romantic-Idealist Assessment of the Reformation and Counter-Reformation* (American Academy of Religion Studies in Religion, 7; Tallahassee, Fla., 1974), esp. pp. 1–20 and 45–116. H. Harris, *The Tübingen School* (Oxford, 1975), pp. 11–54. P. Friedrich, *Ferdinand Christian Baur als Symboliker* (Studien zur Theologie und Geistesgeschichte des Neunzehnten Jahrhunderts, 12; 1975). E. P. Meijering, *F. C. Baur als Patristiker: Die Bedeutung seiner Geschichtsphilosophie und Quellenforschung* (Amsterdam, 1986). R. [C.] Morgan in N. Smart and others (eds.), *Nineteenth Century Religious Thought in the West*, 1 (Cambridge, 1985), pp. 261–89, with bibl. H. Schmidt and J. Haussleiter in *PRE* (3rd edn.), 2 (1897), pp. 467–83, with full list of Baur's writings (pp. 467–9) and bibl. (pp. 469 f.); K. Scholder in *TRE* 5 (1980), pp. 352–9, s.v.

Bavon, St (d. *c*.653), also called **Allowin**. The patron saint of the cathedral and diocese of Ghent (feast days, 1 Oct. and 1 Aug.) and of the diocese of Haarlem (feast days, 9 Aug. and 10 May).

Three Lives are printed in *AASS*, Oct. 1 (1765), pp. 229–53; the first, and a short extract from the third, ed. by B. Krusch in *MGH*, Scriptores Rerum Merovingicarum, 4 (1902), pp. 527–46. R. Podevijn, OSB, *Bavo* (Bruges, 1945). M. Coens, SJ, 'S. Bavon était-il évêque?', *Anal. Boll.* 63 (1945), pp. 220–41, with refs.; id., 'Translations et miracles de Saint Bavon au XI⁰ siècle', ibid. 86 (1968), pp. 39–66. L. van der Essen in *DHGE* 7 (1934), cols. 14 f., s.v., incl. full bibl. M. Van Uytganghe in *Nationaal Biografisch Woordenboek*, 10 (1983), pp. 18–21, s.v. 'Bavo'.

Baxter, Richard (1615–91), *Puritan divine. Born at Rowton, Salop, he was largely self-educated. He studied first at the free school of Wroxeter, next under the nominal tutelage of Richard Wickstead, Chaplain at Ludlow Castle, and finally (1633) in London under the patronage of Sir Henry Herbert, Master of the Revels. In disgust at the frivolity of the Court he returned home to study divinity, in particular the Schoolmen. In 1634 he came into intimate contact with Joseph Symonds and Walter Cradock, two devout Nonconformist divines, who awakened his sympathies for the positive elements in dissent. In 1638 he was ordained by John Thornborough, Bp. of *Worcester, and in 1639 nominated assistant minister at Bridgnorth, where he remained for two years, increasing his knowledge of the issues between Nonconformity and the C of E. After the promulgation of the 'Et Cetera Oath' (1640) he rejected belief in episcopacy in its current English form. In 1641 he became curate of the incumbent of Kidderminster, where among a population of hand-loom workers he continued to minister with remarkable success until 1660. So far as possible he ignored the differences between Presbyterian, Episcopalian, and Independent, and secured cooperation among the local ministers in common pastoral work. In the early part of the Civil War he temporarily joined the Parliamentary Army, preaching at Alcester on the day of the Battle of Edgehill (23 Oct. 1642). A champion of moderation, he was opposed to the *Solemn League and Covenant (1643) and also disliked O. *Cromwell's religious views. After the Battle of Naseby (14 June 1645) he became Chaplain to Colonel Edward Whalley's regiment, seeking to counteract the sectaries and to curb republican tendencies. On leaving the army (1647) he retired for a time to Rous Lench, where he wrote his devotional classic, *The Saints' Everlasting Rest* (1650). In 1660 he played a prominent part in the recall of *Charles II; but his dissatisfaction with episcopacy led him to decline the bishopric of *Hereford. This refusal debarred him from ecclesiastical office and he was not permitted to return to Kidderminster or to hold any living. He took a prominent part at the *Savoy Conference (1661; q.v.), for which he had prepared a 'Reformed Liturgy'; here he presented the *Exceptions to the BCP. Between 1662 and the *Declaration of Indulgence of 1687 he endured persecution, suffering at the hands of the notorious Judge Jeffreys on the questionable charge of having 'libelled the Church' in his *Paraphrase on the New Testament* (1685). He was in sympathy with those responsible for the overthrow of *James II and readily complied with the *Toleration Act of William and Mary. He died on 8 Dec. 1691.

Baxter left nearly 200 writings. They breathe a spirit of deep unaffected piety and reflect his love of moderation. *Gildas Salvianus; The Reformed Pastor* (1656) illustrates the great care he took in his pastoral organization, and the *Reliquiae Baxterianae* (ed. Matthew Sylvester, 1696) is a long and careful autobiography. He also wrote several hymns, among them 'Ye holy angels bright' and 'He wants not friends that hath Thy love'.

The Practical Works of . . . Richard Baxter (London, 4 vols., 1707); new edn. with Life and examination of Baxter's writings by W. Orme (23 vols., 1830). *Calendar of the Correspondence of Richard Baxter* by N. H. Keeble and G. F. Nuttall (2 vols., Oxford, 1991). Many of his works were repr. in the 19th cent. Modern abridged edns. of *The Saints' Everlasting Rest*, by M. Monckton (Reunion edn. [1928]), *Gildas Salvianus; the Reformed Pastor*, by J. T. Wilkinson (1939) and of his autobiography, the *Reliquiae Baxterianae* by J. M. L. Thomas (1925; and in Everyman's Library, 1931). *Chapters from a Christian Directory*, selected by J. Tawney with a preface by C. *Gore (1925). F. J. Powicke (ed.), with introd. by G. Unwin, 'The Reverend Baxter's last Treatise', *Bulletin of the John Rylands Library*, 10 (1926), pp. 163–218; Various MSS in Dr Williams's Library pr. in R. Schlatter, *Richard Baxter & Puritan Politics* (New Brunswick, NJ [1957]). F. J. Powicke, *A Life of the Reverend Richard Baxter, 1615–1691* (1924); id., *The Reverend Richard Baxter Under the Cross, 1662–1691* (1927); I. Morgan, *The Nonconformity of Richard Baxter* (1926); G. F. Nuttall, *Richard Baxter* (1965); W. M. Lamont, *Richard Baxter and the Millennium: Protestant Imperialism and the English Revolution* (1979); N. H. Keeble, *Richard Baxter: Puritan Man of Letters* (Oxford, 1982). A. B. Grosart, *Annotated List of the Writings of Richard Baxter* (1868). N. H. Keeble, 'Richard Baxter's Preaching Ministry: its History and Texts', *JEH* 35 (1984), pp. 539–59, with checklist of his known sermons. J. T. Wilkinson, *Richard Baxter and Margaret Charlton: A Puritan Love Story. Being the Breviate of the Life of Margaret Baxter, by Richard Baxter 1681* (1928). H. Martin, *Puritanism and Richard Baxter* (1954), esp. pp. 122–92. A. H. Wood, *Church Unity without Uniformity: A Study of Seventeenth-Century English Church Movements and of Richard Baxter's Proposals for a Comprehensive Church* (1963). A. B. Grosart in *DNB* 3 (1885), pp. 429–37.

Bay Psalm Book. The metrical version of the Psalms produced at Cambridge, Massachusetts (popularly known in the USA as 'Bay State'), in 1640, and the first book to be printed in British America. It was the work of a body of *Congregationalists, among them Richard Mather (1596–1669).

Z. Haraszti, *The Enigma of the Bay Psalm Book* (Chicago [1956]), pub. together with facsimile repr. B. F. Swan, 'Some Thoughts on the Bay Psalm Book of 1640, with a Census of Copies', *Yale University Library Gazette*, 22 (1948), pp. 51–176.

Bayeux Tapestry. An embroidered band of linen, 231 ft. by 20 in., preserved at Bayeux in Normandy, which depicts the Norman invasion of England and the events preceding it. It was probably made for Bp. *Odo of Bayeux for use in his cathedral. In it appear Odo himself, Abp. *Stigand, and *Edward the Confessor's *Westminster Abbey, for the architecture of which it is a valuable authority. It is also an important witness to the ecclesiastical dress of the epoch.

Complete tapestry reproduced in colour, with introd. by D. M. Wilson (London, 1985). F. M. Stenton (ed.), *The Bayeux Tapestry* (1957; 2nd edn., 1965); D. J. Bernstein, *The Mystery of the Bayeux Tapestry* (1986).

Bayle, Pierre (1647–1706), sceptical writer. The son of a French Protestant minister, he became professor of philosophy and history at Rotterdam in 1681. In his *Pensées diverses sur le comète* (1683) he argued *inter alia* that, religion and morality being independent of one another, all the private and social virtues may be equally practised by atheists. By such views, and by his championship of universal toleration in his *Commentaire philosophique sur ces paroles de Jésus-Christ: 'Contrains-les d'entrer'* (1686–8; written in connection with the revocation of the Edict of *Nantes), he incurred the antagonism of influential French Protestants, and was deprived of his chair in 1693. His most famous work was his *Dictionnaire historique et critique* (1695–7; 2nd edition, enlarged, 1702). His accuracy, encyclopaedic knowledge, and sceptical temper made his work invaluable to the anti-Christian *Deists and *philosophes* of the 18th cent., both in France and in England, but his own religious position seems to have been one of *fideism within the French Reformed Church.

His *Œuvres diverses* (4 vols. in 5 parts, The Hague, 1725–31; 2nd edn., ibid., 1737) contains letters and all his works except the *Dictionnaire*. Further letters ed. E. Gigas (Copenhagen, 1890). Life by P. Des Maizeaux prefixed to *Dictionnaire historique et critique*, 1 (4th edn., 1730), pp. xvii–cviii, issued separately (2 vols., 1732). Studies by L. A. *Feuerbach (Ansbach, 1838; 2nd edn., Leipzig, 1844), J. Delvolé (Paris, 1906), C. Serrurier (Lausanne, 1912), H. Robinson (New York, 1931), ed. P. Dibon (Paris, 1959), É. Labrousse (2 vols., The Hague, 1963–4; also, more briefly in the series 'Past Masters', Oxford, 1983), and W. Rex (The Hague, 1965). H. T. Mason, *Pierre Bayle and Voltaire* (Oxford, 1963); P. Rétat, *Le Dictionnaire de Bayle et la lutte philosophique au XVIIIᵉ siècle* (1971); R. Whelan, *The Anatomy of superstition: A study of the historical theory and practice of Pierre Bayle* (Studies on Voltaire and the eighteenth century, 259; Oxford, 1989).

Bayly, Lewis (d. 1631), the author of *The Practice of Piety*. He was educated at Oxford, probably at Exeter College, and became chaplain to Henry, Prince of Wales. His *Puritan opinions gave offence at court; but he returned to favour and in 1616 became chaplain to *James I and later in the year Bp. of *Bangor. As a bishop, his opinions again made him unpopular; continual trouble with the Council led to his imprisonment in the Fleet (1621); and his laxity in ecclesiastical discipline was attacked constantly until his death. His *Practice of Piety* (3rd edn., 1613; the date of its original publication is not known) enjoyed remarkable popularity, esp. among the Puritans, and was translated into several languages; John *Bunyan regarded it as a great influence in his life.

Biog. Preface (inaccurate) by G. Webster to the 1842 edn. of Bayly's *Practice of Piety*. J. E. Bailey, 'Bishop Lewis Bayly and his "Practice of Piety"', *Manchester Quarterly*, 2 (1883), pp. 221–39, repr. separately, 1883. M. Schmidt, 'Eigenart und Bedeutung der Eschatologie im englischen Puritanismus', *Theologia Viatorum: Jahrbuch der Kirchlichen Hochschule, Berlin*, 4 (for 1952; 1953), pp. 205–66, esp. pp. 224–51. T. F. Tout in *DNB* 3 (1885), pp. 448 f.

BCMS (Bible Churchmen's Missionary Society). A society formed out of the *CMS when a group broke away from the parent body in 1922 in order to assert its fidelity to the traditional doctrines of the Evangelical party (in particular, to the belief in the complete inerrancy of the Scriptures), as opposed to any reinterpretation or alteration of emphasis adopted by *Liberal Evangelicals.

W. S. Hooton and J. Stafford Wright, *The First Twenty-Five Years of the Bible Churchmen's Missionary Society, 1922–47* (1947).

bead (Mid. Eng. 'bede'). Originally the word meant a prayer (cf. Ger. *beten*, 'to pray'), but later it was transferred to the small spherical bodies used for 'telling beads' (i.e. counting the beads of a *rosary), and hence also applied, e.g., to the parts of a necklace. 'To bid a bead' thus means 'to offer a prayer'. See also BIDDING PRAYER.

beadle. In the Church of Scotland an official appointed by the *session to care for the place of worship and to perform other similar functions. He is subject to the minister for direction in his duties, and hence used frequently to be known as 'the minister's man'. One of his most conspicuous tasks is to bear the books to the pulpit before divine service begins. In the newer branches of Presbyterianism he is generally called by the ambiguous title 'church officer'.

beard. See BEARDS, CLERICAL.

Beard, Charles (1827–88), *Unitarian divine. From 1867 he was in charge of Renshaw Street chapel, Liverpool, and from 1864 to 1879 was editor of the *Theological Review*. Besides some fine sermons and addresses, he published several historical works. Of these the best known is his series of Hibbert Lectures for 1883, *The Reformation in its relation to Modern Thought and Knowledge*, in which, in accordance with his own sympathies, he stressed the humanistic, as against the more definitely theological, aspects of the Reformers' work.

Study in H. McLachlan, *Records of a Family, 1800–1933* (Publications of the University of Manchester, no. 239; 1935), pp. 36–75. A. Gordon in *DNB*, Suppl. 1 (1901), pp. 154 f.

beards, clerical. The wearing of beards by clerics has remained the practice of the E. Church since apostolic times. From the 5th cent. onwards, however, largely under monastic influence, W. clerics adopted the practice of being clean-shaven, and at the time of *Photius, the beardlessness of the W. clergy became one of the points of controversy between E. and W. From the 12th cent. a long series of prohibitions were issued by W. Councils against clerics wearing beards, but in the 15th cent. they widely came in again under the influence of secular fashion, being worn, e.g., by 16th- and 17th-cent. Popes. They are still worn by *Capuchins.

The *Apologia de Barbis*, apparently by the *Cistercian Abbot Burchard of Bellevaux (d. 1163/5), was ed. by R. B. C. Huygens, *Apologiae Duae* (CCCM 62; 1985), pp. 130–224, with introd. on beards in the Middle Ages by G. Constable, pp. 47–130. H. *Leclercq, OSB, in *DACL* 2 (pt. 1; 1910), cols. 478–93, s.v. 'Barbe'; H. Thurston, SJ, in *CE* 2 (1907), p. 363, s.v.

Beatific Vision. The vision of the Divine Being in heaven which, acc. to Christian theology, is the final destiny of the redeemed. Its nature and conditions were a subject of much dispute in the later Middle Ages. *Benedict XII (1336) formally defined that the Divine Essence would be seen by direct intuition and face to face (*visione intuitiva et etiam faciali*), while against the Beghards and *Beguines the Council of *Vienne of 1311 laid down that it transcended man's natural capacities and hence was supernatural, and that it was through the Divine gift of the 'light of glory' (*lumen gloriae*) that it was made accessible to him. Whereas its primary object is the vision of the Divine Essence itself, it is held that the vision also extends in a secondary and complementary sense to cover all that the blessed may have a reasonable interest in knowing. Acc. to some theologians the vision is bestowed in exceptional circumstances for brief periods in this life, e.g. St *Thomas Aquinas held that it was granted to *Moses (Ex. 34: 28–35) and St *Paul (2 Cor. 12: 2–4).

C. Trottmann, *La Vision Béatifique: Des disputes scolastiques à sa définition par Benoît XII* (Bibliothèque des Écoles Françaises d'Athènes et de Rome, 289; 1995).

beatification. In the RC Church, the act by which the Pope permits the public veneration after his death of some faithful Catholic in parts of the Church. Before the 12th cent., and less generally from that date to the 17th cent., it was customary for local bishops to beatify people for their own dioceses. A person who has been beatified receives the title of 'Blessed'. Although the *CIC* (1983), can. 1187, distinguishes the Blessed from the Saints, there are indications that, at least in its present form, beatification may not survive. Normally one attested *miracle is required for beatification. In the Russian Church there is a similar process, though not bearing the same name, for authorizing the local cult of deceased Christians. See also CANONIZATION.

*Benedict XIV, *De Servorum Dei Beatificatione et de Beatorum Canonizatione* (Bonn, 4 vols. bound in 5, 1734–8), *passim*. On current procedures, A. Casieri, *Postulatorum Vademecum* (Studium Pro Causis Sanctorum Congregationis; 2nd edn., Rome, 1985). G. Löw, CSSR, in *EC* 2 (1949), cols. 1090–6, s.v. 'Beatificazione'. See also bibl. to CANONIZATION.

beating of the bounds. A ceremony common in medieval England, and associated with the *Rogationtide procession round the parish. When written maps, showing parish boundaries, were hardly known, this annual perambulation was a means of impressing these limits on the minds of the young. The bounds were solemnly beaten with willow rods, and on occasion boys of the parish were also beaten or bumped on the ground at the boundary. The custom is known to date back to the end of the 9th or beginning of the 10th cent., and lasted long after the religious part of the procession was abolished under *Elizabeth I. In modern times it has been revived in some parishes.

The *Injunctions of Elizabeth I (no. 18). J. H. MacMichael, 'Beating the Bounds: Its Origin', *Notes and Queries*, 10th ser. 2 (1904), pp. 113 f., with short bibl. Further bibl. by J. T. Page, ibid. 3 (1905), pp. 390 f., and by G. Potter, ibid. 4 (1905), p. 31.

Beatitudes, the. Christ's promises of coming blessings in the '*Sermon on the Mount' (Mt. 5: 3–11) and the 'Sermon on the Plain' (Lk. 6: 20–2). In Mt. there are eight (or nine) blessings, applicable to all, whereas in Lk. there are four blessings, spoken to the disciples, followed by four 'Woes'. The Beatitudes have formal analogies in the OT (e.g. Is. 32: 20, Ps. 1: 1) and elsewhere in the NT (e.g.

Lk. 12: 37, Mt. 13: 16). In Lk. their content refers to external conditions, in Mt. more to the moral and spiritual qualities of Christian discipleship. The sixth, on purity of heart, has had a particular influence on the mystical tradition.

J. Dupont, OSB, *Les Béatitudes: Le problème littéraire, le message doctrinal* (Louvain, 1954; 2nd edn. of chs. 1–2: *Les Béatitudes*, vol. 1: *Le problème littéraire: les deux versions du Sermon sur la montagne et des Béatitudes*, 1958; of ch. 3 as *Les Béatitudes*, vol. 2: *La bonne nouvelle*, 1969; of chs. 4–5 as *Les Béatitudes*, vol. 3: *Les Évangélistes*, 1973), with bibl. See also bibl. to SERMON ON THE MOUNT and comm. to MATTHEW and LUKE, GOSPELS OF, cited s.vv.

Beatitudes, Mount of the. The name traditionally given to the place where the *Sermon on the Mount is believed to have been delivered (cf. Mt. 5: 1). It has been identified since Crusading times with the mountain Karn Hattin, W. of the Sea of *Galilee.

Beaton (or Bethune), David (c.1494–1546), Cardinal Abp. of St Andrews. He became Abbot of Arbroath in 1523, and was sent by James V on various missions to France. In 1529 he became Keeper of the Privy Seal, Cardinal in 1538, and succeeded his uncle as Abp. of St Andrews in 1539. On the death of James (1542) he made a bid for the regency, and in spite of his failure to secure it, acquired considerable influence over his successful competitor, the Earl of Arran. It was largely through his influence that the English plans for the subjugation of Scotland were defeated; but after his death his countrymen preferred to remember and exaggerate his actions as a persecutor, and in particular his trial and condemnation of the propagandist G. *Wishart, whose zeal for the Reformation seems to have been involved with political plottings and designs on the Cardinal's life. He was assassinated by John Leslie at St Andrews on 29 May 1546.

R. K. Hannay (ed.), *Rentale Sancti Andree, being the Chamberlain and Granitar Accounts of the Archbishopric in the Time of Cardinal Betoun, 1538–1546* (Scottish History Society, 2nd ser. 4; 1913). The main sources for his life are J. *Knox's *History of the Reformation*, Bk. 1, *passim*, and J. *Spottiswoode, *History of the Church of Scotland* (1847–51 edn.), 1, pp. 134–65. M. H. B. Sanderson, *Cardinal of Scotland: David Beaton, c.1494–1546* (Edinburgh [1986]). M. MacArthur in *DNB* 4 (1885), pp. 17 f. See also works on the Scottish Reformation cited s.v. SCOTLAND, CHRISTIANITY IN.

Beauduin, Lambert (1873–1960), Belgian liturgist and founder of *Chevetogne. After ordination in 1897, he worked with a society of priests devoted to the care of working men and in 1906 entered the *Benedictine Abbey of Mont-César at Louvain. Here he took part in the organization of Liturgical Weeks in 1909, established the periodical *La Vie liturgique* (since 1911 *Les Questions liturgiques*), and wrote *La Piété de l'Église* (1914), which popularized the aims of the *Liturgical Movement. In 1921 he was sent to the Anselmo in Rome and became interested in E. liturgy. After Pope *Pius XI had urged that Benedictines should pray for Christian unity (*Equidem verba*, 21 March 1924), Dom Beauduin founded a monastery of Union at Amay-sur-Meuse (see CHEVETOGNE). He attended Cardinal *Mercier at the *Malines Conversations and in a report to him expressed the desire that the Anglican Church should be 'united to Rome, not absorbed' ('unie non absorbée'). When this phrase was published considerable criticism was directed against him. In 1928 he had to leave Amay and in 1930 he was condemned by a Roman tribunal. His preaching in 1942 was one of the factors leading to the establishment of the Centre de Pastorale Liturgique in Paris. In 1950 he was able to return to his community, now at Chevetogne. The validity of his approach to questions of reunion was recognized by Pope *John XXIII.

Beauduin's memorandum on 'L'Église Anglicane unie non absorbée' is pr. in *The Conversations at Malines 1912–1925: Original Documents*, ed. Lord Halifax (1930), pp. 241–61; Eng. tr. in G. K. A. *Bell (ed.), *Documents on Christian Unity*, 3rd ser. 1930–48 (1948), pp. 21–32 (no. 149). Lives by L. Bouyer, Cong. Orat. (Tournai, 1964) and S. A. Quitslund (New York, 1973). *Veilleur avant l'Aurore: Colloque Lambert Beauduin* [held at Chevetogne, 30 Aug.–3 Sept. 1976] (Chevetogne, 1978). M. Cappuyns, OSB, 'Dom Lambert Beauduin (1873–1960). Quelques Documents et Souvenirs', *RHE* 61 (1966), pp. 424–54 and 761–807. A. Haquin, 'L'Exile de dom Lambert Beauduin au monastère d'En-Calcat (1932–1934)', ibid. 80 (1985), pp. 51–99 and 415–40.

Beaufort, Henry (*c.* 1375–1447), Cardinal and Bp. of *Lincoln and *Winchester. He was born at Beaufort, Anjou, the son of John of Gaunt and Catherine Swynford. His parents having been married in 1396, he was declared legitimate in 1397. He was educated at Peterhouse, Cambridge, and at Queen's College, Oxford. After holding various benefices, incl. a prebend at Lincoln from 1389, he became Dean of *Wells in 1396 and in the following year Chancellor of the University of Oxford. In 1398 he was provided to the see of Lincoln. In 1403 he became Chancellor until he was translated to Winchester in 1404, succeeding *William of Wykeham. During most of the reign of Henry IV, however, he supported the party of the Prince of Wales in opposition to the King and Abp. *Arundel. In 1407 he was declared debarred from the succession. With the accession of Henry V in 1413 he was appointed Chancellor, but resigned in 1417, ostensibly to go on pilgrimage. On the way he attended the Council of *Constance. Here he was largely responsible for the election of Oddo Colonna as *Martin V, who issued a bull creating him Cardinal and *legatus a latere* and prob. granted him permission to hold the see of Winchester *in commendam* for life. Henry V, however, prevented him from accepting these favours. Appointed in 1421 as one of the guardians of Henry VI, he became Chancellor in 1424 and virtually ruled the realm for the next two years. After a serious quarrel with the Duke of Gloucester, he sought leave to go on pilgrimage again in 1426. In the same year he accepted a cardinalate, and led an unsuccessful expedition against the *Hussites; but his new office, which rendered his position ambiguous, made him very unpopular in England. In spite, however, of continued attacks by the Duke of Gloucester, esp. in 1439, he played a considerable part in foreign policy, being present at the Council of Arras in 1435 and the subsequent negotiations. He also took part in the trial of *Joan of Arc. After the fall of Gloucester (1441) his party was left supreme, but he personally seems to have taken little further part in politics. He died at Wolvesey Palace on Palm Sunday, 1447.

At Winchester Beaufort completed the transformation of the nave of the Cathedral, and greatly extended the Hospital of St Cross. But he stands out by his financial ability and shrewd statesmanship rather than as a Churchman. By lending money to the King at opportune moments and high rates of (disguised) interest, he amassed a fortune which made his support indispensable to the government. In general he upheld the ideals of constitutional government and strove for peace.

G. L. Harriss, *Cardinal Beaufort: A Study of Lancastrian Ascendancy and Decline* (Oxford, 1988), with full bibl. *BRUO* 1 (1957), pp. 139–42; *BRUC*, pp. 46–9, s.v.

Beaufort, Margaret. See MARGARET, LADY.

Beaulieu, Abbey of. This *Cistercian abbey in Hampshire was founded and endowed in 1204 by King *John for 30 monks from *Cîteaux, and dedicated in 1246 in the presence of Henry III and his queen, Eleanor. The abbey was from the first 'exempted' by *Innocent III, with right of sanctuary, which was sought by Ann Neville, wife of Warwick the King-Maker, Perkin Warbeck, and others. At the time of the suppression (1539) there were 32 sanctuary-men with their wives and families within the precincts. Among the portions still standing are the Early English refectory (now used as the parish church), the gatehouse (now a private residence), the guesthouse dormitory, and parts of the cloisters and chapter house. Beaulieu (*Bellus locus*) has preserved its original Norman-French pronunciation of 'Bewley'.

W. *Dugdale, *Monasticon Anglicanum*, 5 (1825 edn.), pp. 680–4. W. J. St John Hope and H. Brakespear, 'The Cistercian Abbey of Beaulieu', *Archaeological Journal*, 63 (1906), pp. 130–86. J. K. Fowler, *A History of Beaulieu Abbey A.D. 1204–1539* [1911]. J. C. Cox in *VCH*, Hampshire and the Isle of Wight, ed. H. A. Doubleday and W. Page, 2 (1903), pp. 140–6.

Bec, Abbey of. This celebrated Norman abbey, situated between *Rouen and *Lisieux, was founded by Bl Herluin (feast day, 26 Aug.) and consecrated by Mauger, Abp. of Rouen and uncle of William the Conqueror, in 1041. In 1060 it was rebuilt on a much larger scale. Its notable monks included Lanfranc (Prior, *c.*1045–63; later Abp. of *Canterbury), St *Anselm (Prior, 1063–78; Abbot, 1078–93; also later Abp. of Canterbury); Gundulf (Bp. of *Rochester, 1077–1108), Ernulf (also Bp. of Rochester, 1114–24), and Gilbert Crispin (Abbot of *Westminster, 1085–1117). It long enjoyed royal patronage and was visited by Henry I (1106) and Henry II (1152, 1159, 1178), kings of England. A fire in 1263 destroyed most of the abbey; the new church built soon afterwards lasted until the 19th cent. In 1467 the Tour St Nicholas, still extant, was constructed. After the concordat between Francis I and *Leo X in 1516, the government of the abbey passed into the hands of *commendatory abbots. In 1626 it was taken over and largely rebuilt by the *Maurists. It was suppressed in 1790 and partly demolished from 1810 onwards. In the latter part of the 19th cent. the buildings attracted the interest of historians and in 1948 the Benedictine life (*Olivetan Congregation) was re-established. The abbey at one time had considerable property in England (cf. Tooting Bec); and the modern community actively promotes religious relations between France and England.

M. P. Dickson, OSB (ed.), *Consuetudines Beccenses* (Corpus Consuetudinum Monasticarum, 4; Siegburg, 1967). Gilbert Crispin's 'Life of Herluin', ed. J. A. *Robinson, *Gilbert Crispin, Abbot of Westminster* (Cambridge, 1911), pp. 87–110. A. A. Porée, *Histoire de l'abbaye du Bec* (2 vols., Évreux, 1901). *Select Documents of the English Lands of the Abbey of Bec*, ed. M. Chibnall (Camden Society, 3rd ser. 73; 1951). M. [McC.] Morgan, *The English Lands of the Abbey of Bec* (Oxford Historical Series; Oxford, 1946). J. de La Varende, *L'Abbaye du Bec-Hellouin: vingt-quatre photographies* de J. M. Marcel (Paris, 1951). L. H. Cottineau, OSB, *Répertoire Topo-Bibliographique des Abbayes et Prieurés* (Mâcon, 1935), cols. 316–19. P. Cousin in *NCE* 2 (1967), pp. 209–11, s.v., with further bibl.

Becket, St Thomas (?1120–70), Abp. of *Canterbury. A son of Normans who had settled in London, Thomas was educated at Merton Priory (Surrey), at a school in London, and in *Paris, where *Robert of Melun may have been among his teachers; but he was never a great scholar. By 1146 he was a member of the household of *Theobald, Abp. of Canterbury, who sent him to study law at *Bologna and Auxerre and, after ordaining him deacon, appointed him Archdeacon of Canterbury in 1154. In 1155 Henry II made him his Chancellor, and his influence was enhanced by an intimate friendship with the King. He liked hunting and the display of pomp, and during a military expedition to France took a personal part in the fighting. His policy as Chancellor was generally in harmony with the wishes of the King, often against the interests of the Church; and when, in 1162, he was elected Abp. of Canterbury at the instigation of the King, he accepted the office with reluctance, knowing a break to be inevitable.

From now on Becket championed his own rights and those of his archbishopric and of the Church with surprising determination. He resigned the chancellorship, and disputes with the King, crucially over how criminous clerks should be tried and punished, led Henry in 1163 to require the bishops to sanction the 'ancient customs of the kingdom'. When a code of these customs, the 'Constitutions of *Clarendon', was promulgated in 1164, Becket was forced to submit, an act of which he soon repented. Henry, therefore, began to persecute him because of his 'ingratitude', required him to account for money he had received when Chancellor, and charged him with breaking his promise to observe the Constitutions. His trial and condemnation in the royal court at Northampton in October led him to flee to France and appeal for justice to *Alexander III, then at Sens. During the following negotiations between the Pope, Henry, and the Archbishop, Thomas stayed at first at the *Cistercian abbey of Pontigny in Burgundy, and when the King threatened to expel all Cistercians from his dominions (1166), he moved to the *Benedictine abbey of Ste-Colombe at Sens, which was under the special protection of the French King. After he had issued sentences of excommunication against some bishops and royal servants in 1166 and 1169, he made peace unexpectedly with Henry at Fréteval in July 1170. The King promised to make amends for the coronation of his son by the Abp. of *York (Roger of Pont-l'Évêque), a flagrant infringement of the prerogatives of Canterbury, while Thomas sent Papal letters of suspension to the bishops who had assisted at the ceremony.

Becket crossed to England on 30 Nov., where he was received with popular enthusiasm. He refused, however, to absolve the bishops, unless they would swear to accept penalties which the Pope would impose. Henry, naturally furious, uttered some words in a fit of rage which were enough to inspire four knights (Hugh de Morville, William de Tracy, Reginald Fitz-Urse, Richard le Breton) to make their way to Canterbury in revenge. Becket was assassinated in his cathedral in the late afternoon of 29 Dec. 1170.

The murder provoked great indignation throughout Europe. Miracles were soon recorded at Becket's tomb and a widespread cultus developed. On 21 Feb. 1173 he was canonized by Alexander III and on 12 July 1174 Henry did public penance at the shrine. Becket's remains were translated to their place in the choir (the 'Trinity Chapel') in 1220 and until the destruction of the shrine under Henry VIII (1538) it remained one of the principal pilgrimage centres of Christendom. Feast day, 29 Dec.; of his translation, 7 July.

J. C. Robertson and J. B. Sheppard, *Materials for the History of Thomas Becket* (RS, 7 vols., 1875–85); *The Life and Death of Thomas Becket . . . based on the account of William fitzStephen his clerk, with additions from other contemporary sources*, tr. and ed. G. Greenaway (Folio Society, 1961). A. Duggan, *Thomas Becket: A Textual History of his Letters* (Oxford, 1980); an edn. of the letters is in preparation.

F. Barlow, *Thomas Becket* [1986]. Earlier works include W. H. *Hutton, *Thomas Becket, Archbishop of Canterbury* (1910; rev. edn., 1926); E. Walberg, *La Tradition hagiographique de Saint Thomas Becket avant la fin du XIIe siècle: Études critiques* (1929); R. Foreville, *L'Église et la royauté en Angleterre sous Henri II Plantagenet, 1154–1189* (1943); id., *Le Jubilé de Saint Thomas Becket du XIIIe au XVe siècle (1220–1470): Étude et documents* (1958); [M.] D. *Knowles, *Thomas Becket* (1970), and other works of this author; B. Smalley, *The Becket Conflict and the Schools* (Oxford, 1973), esp. pp. 109–37. *Thomas Becket: Actes du Colloque International de Sédières, 19–24 Août 1973*, ed. R. Foreville (1975). Dramatic interpretation in T. S. *Eliot, *Murder in the Cathedral* (1935). M. D. Knowles in *NCE* 2 (1967), pp. 212–14, s.v.

Becon, Thomas (c.1511–67), Protestant Reformer. A native of Norfolk, he was educated at St John's College, Cambridge, where he came under the influence of *H. Latimer. He was ordained priest in 1538. He was arrested for preaching Protestant doctrines and forced to recant in 1541 and again in 1543, when he publicly destroyed his writings. At this time he lived as a layman in Kent, publishing under the pseudonym of Theodore Basil. Travelling around the country until the accession of *Edward VI (1547), he then became chaplain to Lord Protector *Somerset and to Abp. T. *Cranmer, who made him one of the *Six Preachers at *Canterbury. He was presented to the living of St Stephen Walbrook in London. Losing all preferment on *Mary's accession (1553), he was imprisoned for allegedly seditious preaching and on his release went to Strasbourg (1554) and Frankfurt (1555) and then seems to have taught at *Marburg University (1556–9). On his return to England under *Elizabeth I, he was installed as a canon of Canterbury Cathedral in 1559 and given other preferment.

Becon's prolific, lively and usually polemical writings enjoyed wide popularity. Until his exile, he remained more influenced by *Lutheranism than most English Reformers, but he was also an early opponent of images. He contributed the sermon 'Against Whoredom and Uncleanness' (usually known as the 'Homily against Adultery') to the 'Book of *Homilies' and may have assisted Cranmer in his controversial writings. His numerous other works include *The Jewel of Joy* (prob. written 1547–8; earliest extant copy perhaps 1550), and *The Sick Man's Salve* (composed before 1553; entered on the Stationers' Register, 1558–9). He revised and republished his works in a folio edition (3 vols., 1560–4), in which his *New Catechism* appeared for the first time.

Modern edn. of most of his works by J. Ayre (*Parker Society, 3 vols., 1843–4). D. S. Bailey, *Thomas Becon and the Reformation of the Church in England* (1952).

Beda, the ('Collegio Beda'). The college at Rome where English candidates for the RC priesthood who have discovered their vocation late in life, including converts from non-Roman ministries who wish to be ordained in the RC Church, are trained.

J. J. Curtin in *NCE* 2 (1967), pp. 215 f., s.v.

bede (prayer). See BEAD.

Bede, St (*c.*673–735), 'The Venerable', pedagogue, computist, biblical exegete, hagiographer, and historian, the foremost and most influential scholar from Anglo-Saxon England. The course of his uneventful life is known from the brief notice which he himself gave in the last chapter of his *Historia Ecclesiastica*: at the age of 7 he was given as an *oblate to the newly-founded monastery of *Wearmouth under the care of St *Benedict Biscop and subsequently, on the foundation of Jarrow in 682, was transferred to that abbey and to its abbot, Ceolfrith. Except for brief excursions to *Lindisfarne and *York, Bede spent the remainder of his life at Jarrow, devoting himself to reading, teaching, and the explication of Scripture. He was ordained deacon at the age of 19 and priested when he was 30; he died at Jarrow aged over 60.

Bede's pedagogical writings include treatises *De Orthographia*, an alphabetically arranged glossary of Latin words which are capable of confusion or misunderstanding by beginners; *De Arte Metrica*, a lucid account of the principles underlying quantitative verse, based on Late Latin grammatical treatises but including many quotations from Christian Latin poets; and *De Natura Rerum*, a cursory exposition of natural phenomena such as the motion of the planets, eclipses, tides, etc., based mainly on *Isidore and Pliny. Each of these pedagogical treatises survives in large numbers of manuscripts, indicating that they constituted an essential ingredient of the medieval curriculum. His computistical writings were equally influential. They include an early work, the *De Temporibus*, written to explain to his students the principles for the calculation of *Easter acc. to the Roman usage adopted by the Synod of *Whitby (664). This work was so highly compressed, however, that Bede later produced a longer and more discursive account of Paschal reckoning in his *De Temporum Ratione* (written in 725), and this work, which survives in some 250 manuscripts, proved to be the most widely studied computistical manual of the Middle Ages. Bede's pedagogical instincts were, however, best applied to the explication of Scripture. For his biblical exegesis he used both the *Vulgate and the *Old Latin texts as well as (for

Acts) the Greek text. His commentaries were largely based on the writings of St *Augustine, St *Jerome, St *Ambrose, and St *Gregory the Great, but they also embodied original comment: they were motivated above all by concern with clarity of exposition, and it was this concern which commended them to his contemporaries and successors. His commentaries include works on Gen. 1–20, Exod. 24: 12–30: 21, Sam., Kgs., Tobit, Song of Songs, Ez. and Neh., Mk., Lk., Acts, the *Catholic Epistles, and Rev. Bede's interest in hagiography is reflected in the extensive revision which he made of the *Hieronymian *Martyrologium* (his revision does not survive in its pristine form) as well as in the prose *Vita S. Felicis*, a recasting of various poems by *Paulinus of Nola on St Felix. But it was his two Lives of St *Cuthbert— one in verse and a later one in prose (*c.*721)—which secured Bede's reputation as a hagiographer and the establishment of the cult of St Cuthbert throughout Europe. Whereas during the Middle Ages Bede was widely known for all facets of his scholarly work, he is best known today as a historian; indeed he has been called the 'Father of English History'. His early interest in computus led him naturally to the study of chronology: to each of his major computistical treatises he appended a set of annals recording the history of the world from creation to his own day. The study of chronology culminated in the *Historia Ecclesiastica Gentis Anglorum* (completed in 731), one of the great works of medieval historiography and the single most important source for our understanding of early England.

To the end of his life Bede was occupied in teaching and expounding Scripture, as we learn from an eyewitness account of his last days by a devoted student (the *Epistula Cuthberti de obitu Bedae*). In a letter written towards the end of his life and addressed to *Egbert (Abp of *York, 732–66) he emphasized the importance of episcopal visitation, Confirmation, and frequent Communion as the remedy for the ills of the time. Less than a century after his death he was honoured with the title of Venerable, and in the 11th cent. his bones were translated to *Durham; a conspicuous tomb in the cathedral still commemorates him. In 1899 *Leo XIII declared him a '*Doctor of the Church'. Feast day, 25 (formerly 27) May.

Collected Works pub. in 3 vols., Paris, 1521–36, also ed., with Eng. tr., by J. A. Giles (12 vols., London, 1843–4); Lat. text repr. in J. P. Migne, *PL* 90–5. Crit. edn. in CCSL 118–23 (1955 ff. incl. his biblical comms. except that on Rev.). Other edns. of his *Opera Historica* by C. Plummer (with notes, Oxford, 1896) and of his *Historia Ecclesiastica*, with Eng. tr., by B. Colgrave and R. A. B. Mynors (Oxford Medieval Texts, 1969; historical comm. by J. M. Wallace-Hadrill, ibid., 1988); of his prose Life of St Cuthbert, with Eng. tr., by B. Colgrave, *Two Lives of St Cuthbert* (Cambridge, 1940; repr. 1985), pp. 142–307 and 341–59; of his metrical Life of St Cuthbert by W. Jaager (Palaestra, 198; 1935); of his *Expositio Actuum Apostolorum et Retractatio*, by M. L. W. Laistner (Mediaeval Academy of America, Publication 35; 1939; repr. in CCSL 121, pp. 1–178); and of his *Opera de Temporibus*, by C. W. Jones (Mediaeval Academy of America, Publication, 41; 1943; text repr., with glosses from a MS written in 873/4, in CCSL 123, pp. 263–460). M. L. W. Laistner and H. H. King, *A Hand-List of Bede Manuscripts* (New York, 1943), C. W. Jones, *Bedae Pseudepigrapha: Scientific Writings Falsely Attributed to Bede* (1939). A. H. Thompson (ed.), *Bede: His Life, Times and Writings. Essays in Commemoration of the Twelfth Centenary of his Death* (Oxford, 1935); three essays by B. *Capelle, OSB, M. Inguanez, OSB, and Beda Thum, OSB, *S. Beda Venerabilis* (Studia Anselmiana, 6; 1936); G. [I.] Bonner (ed.), *Famulus Christi: Essays in Commemoration of the Thirteenth Centenary of the Birth of the Venerable Bede* (1976). G. H. Brown, *Bede the Venerable* (1987). P. H. Blair, *The World of Bede* (1970). J. Campbell, *Essays in Anglo-Saxon History* (1986), pp. 1–48 and 85–119 [repr. four items orig. pub. between 1966 and 1979, with additional notes]. Various Jarrow lectures are devoted to Bede. *CPL* (3rd edn., 1995), pp. 444–58 (nos. 1343–84) and pp. 737 f. (nos. 2318–2323b). I. Cecchetti in *Bibliotheca Sanctorum*, 2 (Rome, 1962), cols. 1006–1072, s.v. 'Beda', with extensive refs.

Bedlam (= 'Bethlehem'). Originally the name given to the 'Hospital of St Mary of Bethlehem', in Bishopsgate, which the Sheriff of London founded in 1247 for the housing of the clergy of St Mary of Bethlehem when they visited Britain. It is uncertain when insane persons were first received here, but the house is mentioned as a hospital for the sick in 1330 and lunatics are definitely stated to have been there in 1402. On the *dissolution of the monasteries it passed to the London civic authorities, and in 1547 became a royal foundation for the reception of lunatics. Its place was taken in 1675 by a new hospital in Moorfields, and this again was transferred to the Lambeth Road in 1815. By an extension in meaning, the word 'Bedlam' has come to be applied to any lunatic asylum or any scene of disorder within doors.

R. M. Clay, *The Medieval Hospitals of England* ('The Antiquary's Books'; 1909), pp. 32–4, 210, and 238. E. G. O'Donoghue, *The Story of Bethlehem Hospital from its Foundation in 1247* (1914).

Beecher, Lyman (1775–1863), American Protestant minister. Born in New Haven, Connecticut, he went to Yale University, where he came under the influence of its first president, Timothy Dwight (1752–1817) and the spirit of *revivalism which led to the Second *Great Awakening. He became pastor of *Presbyterian churches in East Hampton, Long Island (1799) and Cincinnati, Ohio (1832) and of *Congregational churches in Litchfield, Connecticut (1810) and Boston, Massachusetts (1810). In Cincinnati he was also President of the newly founded Lane Theological Seminary (1832–50). A major figure in American evangelical Protestantism in the period before the Civil War, Beecher was a leader in revivals (at first he opposed C. G. *Finney and his 'new measures' but came to accept him), a committed advocate of social reform (the *temperance movement, women's suffrage, anti-*slavery), and a staunch opponent of *Unitarianism and RCism. At one time a defender of the *established Church (Congregational in Connecticut and Massachusetts), he came to recognize that disestablishment, fully realized in 1833, offered a great opportunity for the Churches. His *Plea for the West* (1835) was a recognition of the importance of the mid-west for the future of the nation, as well as an outspoken tract against imagined plots of the RC Church and European monarchies to control or influence the mid-western territories. In 1835 he was tried for heresy, but acquitted by his *presbytery and synod. His seven sons entered the ministry, and one of his daughters, Mrs Harriet Beecher Stowe, was the author of *Uncle Tom's Cabin* (1852). The Lyman Beecher Lectures on Preaching at Yale were established in 1871.

His *Autobiography*, with Correspondence, ed. by C. Beecher [son] (2 vols., New York, 1864–5), also ed. B. M. Cross (2 vols., Cambridge, Mass., 1961). M. Caskey, *Chariot of Fire: Religion and the Beecher Family* (New Haven, Conn., and London, 1978), pp. 3–67. J. W. Fraser, *Pedagogue for God's Kingdom: Lyman Beecher and the Second Great Awakening* (Lanham, Md., etc. [1985]).

Beelzebub. The name applied to 'the prince of devils' in the Gospels, where Christ's enemies accuse Him of 'casting out devils by Beelzebub' (Mk. 3: 22–6; cf. Mt. 12: 24–8, Lk. 11: 15–20), i.e. of acting by the power of, or of being an agent of, the evil one (cf. Mt. 10: 25), not of God. It is this direct and deliberate calling of good 'evil' which leads to the Lord's words on the sin that 'hath never forgiveness' (Mk. 3: 29, etc.).

In all the Gk. MSS of the Gospels the form is 'Beelzebul' (Βεελζεβούλ); the form 'Beelzebub' is due to the influence of the OT, where 'Baal-zebub' is the god of the Philistine city of Ekron mentioned in 2 Kgs. 1. Neither name is found elsewhere in the Bible or in contemporary sources, Jewish or pagan. 'Baal-zebub' appears to mean in Heb. 'lord of flies' and the word is so explained by ancient commentators; but the exact connection between this and the 'Beelzebul' evidently current in *Galilee in the time of Christ and regarded as practically equivalent to '*Satan' (Mk. 3: 23), is uncertain. 'Beelzebul' is variously regarded as (1) a mere corruption in pronunciation of 'Baal-zebub', possibly influenced by an *Aramaic word meaning 'enmity', which suggested the use of this OT name for the arch-fiend; (2) derived from a Heb. word meaning 'dung', i.e. 'lord of filth'; or (3) derived from an uncommon Hebrew word for house or mansion, i.e. 'lord of the underworld'. This last suggestion, though it would give added point to the references to 'a house divided' and 'the strong man's house' in the Gospel passages (cf. 'master of the house', Mt. 10: 25), seems etymologically very improbable. The *Mishnah contains one reference to Beelzebub, understood as 'fly-god'. From the general absence of other references from Jewish literature it would seem that the term was of only local or temporary currency.

A. *Loisy, 'Béelzeboul', *Revue d'Histoire et de Littérature Religieuses*, 9 (1904), pp. 434–66; W. E. M. Aitken, 'Beelzebul', *Journal of Biblical Literature*, 31 (1912), pp. 34–53. M. Limbeck, 'Beelzebul—eine ursprüngliche Bezeichnung für Jesus?', in H. Feld and J. Nolte (eds.), *Wort Gottes in der Zeit: Festschrift Karl Hermann Schelkle zum 65. Geburtstag dargebracht* (Düsseldorf, 1973), pp. 31–42. E. *Nestle in *DCG* 1 (1906), pp. 181 f., s.v.; W. Foerster in *TWNT* 1 (1933; Eng. tr., 1964), pp. 605 f.; further bibl. in 10/2 (1979), pp. 1014 f.; T. H. Gaster in *The Interpreter's Dictionary of the Bible*, 1 (1962), p. 374, s.v. 'Beelzebul'.

Beghards. See following entry.

Beguines, Beghards. The Beguines were women leading pious, but non-monastic lives, mainly in the late Middle Ages. Some lived alone, some in communities. They promised to remain celibate and obey a rule while living as Beguines, but retained the use of private property and were free to change their status and marry. They often wore a simple habit, but they were not a religious order with a common rule or structure. They usually engaged in communal prayer and in philanthropic work, but Beguines could be found in almost every profession open to women. Their male counterparts were the Beghards, who were usually weavers, dyers, or fullers, who had a common purse and held no private property; they were fewer in number.

The origin of the terms is obscure. *Beguina* (from which *beghardus* derived) appears to have been used first of the groups of women leading semi-religious lives in the towns of the Low Countries; one such group in the diocese of Liège was inspired by Lambert le Bègue (d. 1177), but it is not clear that the term derives from his name. While it was in the Low Countries that the movement was most complex and enduring, similar groups were numerous in Germany, France, and other countries of mainland Europe in the 13th and 14th cents. Beguine settlements (known as Beguinages) were established, often in the vicinity of *Dominican and *Franciscan friaries, with whom they often had close links. Beguines attracted criticism from the Church authorities on account of their lack of enclosure and regular status, often coupled with an enthusiastic piety which emphasized direct personal relationship with God. The Council of *Vienne (1311–14) condemned Beguines and Beghards as 'an abominable sect' (decree 28) on account of their association with the heresy attributed to the *Brethren of the Free Spirit, and tried to suppress Beguines living outside Beguinages (decree 16). In the 13th and 14th cents. some Beguines were executed (e.g. Margaret *Porette) and they suffered persecution and declined during the *Reformation and again in the French Revolution. The Beguinages of the Low Countries had a second period of growth in the 17th cent., but few Beguines now continue the tradition.

Beguines such as *Mechtild of Magdeburg and *Hadewijch were responsible for some of the earliest religious writing in the vernacular. Their writing, which is personal and poetic, is associated with 'bridal mysticism' (*Brautmystik*).

J. L. von *Mosheim, *De Beghardis et Beguinabus Commentarius* (Leipzig, 1790), with docs. Eng. tr. of works of three of the Beguines by [A.] O. Davies, ed., with introd. by F. Bowie, *Beguine Spirituality* (1989). L. J. M. Philippen, *De Begijnhoven* (Antwerp, 1918). H. Grundmann, *Religiöse Bewegungen im Mittelalter* (Historische Studien, 267; 1935), pp. 319–475; repr., Hildesheim, 1961, with additional material, pp. 524–38. E. W. McDonnell, *The Beguines and Beghards in Medieval Culture* (New Brunswick, 1954). B. M. Bolton, '*Vitae matrum*: A further aspect of the *Frauenfrage*', in D. Baker (ed.), *Medieval Women* (Studies in Church History, Subsidia, 1; Oxford, 1978), pp. 253–73; id., 'Some Thirteenth Century Women in the Low Countries. A Special Case?', *Nederlands Archief voor Kerkgeschiedenis*, 61 (1981), pp. 7–29. J. Asen, 'Die Beginen in Köln', *Annalen des Historischen Vereins für den Niederrhein*, 111 (1927), pp. 81–180; 112 (1928), pp. 71–148; and 113 (1928), pp. 13–96. D. Phillips, *Beguines in Medieval Strasburg: A Study of the Social Aspect of Beguine Life* (University of Columbia thesis; Stanford, Calif., 1941). A. Mens, OFM Cap., *Oorsprong en Betekenis van de Nederlandse Begijnen-en Begardenbeweging* (Verhandelingen van de Koninklijke Vlaamse Academie voor Wetenschappen, Letteren en Schone Kunsten van België. Klasse der Letteren, Jaargang 9, no. 7; Antwerp, 1947). R. Manselli, *Spirituali e Beghini in Provenza* (Istituto Storico Italiano per il Medio Evo. Studi Storici, 31–4; 1959). E. G. Neumann, *Rheinische Beginen- und Begardenwesen: Ein Mainzer Beitrag zur religiösen Bewegung am Rhein* (Mainzer Abhandlungen zur mittleren und neueren Geschichte, 4; Meisenheim am Glan, 1960). K. Ruh, 'Beginenmystik. Hadewijch, Mechthild von Magdeburg, Marguerite Porete', *Zeitschrift für deutsches Altertum und deutsche Literatur*, 106 (1977), pp. 265–77. U. Peters, *Religiöse Erfahrung als literarisches Faktum: Zur Vorgeschichte und Genese frauenmystischer Texte des 13. und 14. Jahrhunderts* (Tübingen, 1988), esp. pp. 41–100. R. W. Southern, *Western Society and the Church in the Middle Ages* (Pelican History of the Church, 2; 1970), pp. 318–

31. J. van Mierlo, SJ, in *DHGE* 7 (1934), cols. 426–41 and 457–73, s.vv. 'Bégardisme' and 'Béguinages'; R. E. Lerner in J. Strayer (ed.), *Dictionary of the Middle Ages*, 2 (1983), pp. 157–62, s.v.

Behemoth (Heb. בְּהֵמוֹת). This Heb. word, which occurs several times in the OT, is generally translated 'beast' except in Job 40: 15, where the AV, RV, and RSV all retain the form 'behemoth'. Here it means a particular beast, the greatest of all land animals (perhaps the hippopotamus), and the counterpart of the sea-beast, *Leviathan.

Bel. Another form of 'Baal' (q.v.). In Jer. 50: 2, 51: 44 and Is. 46: 1, he is the guardian deity of Babylon, the empire which held the Jews captive.

Bel and the Dragon (or **Bel and the Serpent** [or **Snake**]). Two stories attached to the Book of *Daniel in certain Gk. MSS (*Septuagint and *Theodotion) of the OT and hence included (as a single item) in the *Apocrypha of the English Bible. The former recounts (vv. 1–22; [Vulg.] Dan. 13: 65–14: 21) how Daniel convinced the Babylonian King that the offerings of food and drink which were daily set before the image of Bel were not really consumed by the god but removed secretly by the priests, leading to the execution of the priests and the destruction of the image. The latter story (vv. 23–42; [Vulg.] Dan. 14: 22–42), which appears to be based on an ancient Semitic myth, describes how Daniel, having obtained the King's consent to attack the dragon (or serpent), put him to death by feeding him cakes made of pitch, fat, and hair. The people in their rage insisted that Daniel should be cast into a den of seven lions, whence, with the aid of the prophet *Habakkuk, who was miraculously transported from Judaea to feed him, he was saved from death and liberated (cf. Dan. 6). In consequence the King became a worshipper of Yahweh.

The occurrence of these stories in the Septuagint led them to be accepted by *Irenaeus, *Tertullian, *Origen, and others, but they were already questioned by *Julius Africanus. *Jerome incorporated them into the *Vulgate, though he did not conceal his doubts about them. In the AV they are entitled 'The History of the Destruction of Bel and the Dragon, cut off from the End of Daniel'. In 1894 M. Gaster announced the discovery of a story of the Dragon in *Aramaic which appeared to underlie the Gk.; his arguments were widely challenged, but many now hold, on other grounds, that the narratives are based on a Semitic original.

Comm. by T. Witton Davies in R. H. *Charles, *The Apocrypha and Pseudepigrapha of the Old Testament*, 1 (Oxford, 1913), pp. 652–64, and C. A. Moore, *Daniel, Esther and Jeremiah: The Additions* (Anchor Bible, 44; 1977), pp. 23–38 and 117–49. M. Gaster, 'The Unknown Aramaic Original of Theodotion's Additions to the Book of Daniel', *Proceedings of the Society of Biblical Archeology*, 16 (1894), pp. 280–90 and 312–17. E. *Schürer, *The History of the Jewish People in the Age of Jesus Christ*, rev. Eng. tr. by G. Vermes and others, 3 (pt. 2; Edinburgh, 1987), pp. 723–30, with bibl. See also bibl. to APOCRYPHA.

Belgic Confession (1561). The 'Confession de Foi des Églises Réformées Wallonnes et Flamandes', originally drawn up in French by Guido de Brès (1522–67) on the basis of the *Gallican Confession (1559). In an attempt to conciliate the Netherlands' government it specifically repudiated *Anabaptist doctrines. Its adoption in synod at Antwerp in May 1566 marked the final acceptance of Calvinistic principles in the Netherlands. It was again adopted by the Synod of *Dort in 1619.

Both the original 1561 text and the amended form of 1619 are pr. in J. N. Bakhuisen van den Brink (ed.), *De Nederlandse Belijdenisgeschriften* (2nd edn., Amsterdam, 1976), pp. 59–146, with introd., pp. 1–27. Eng. tr. of the 1619 form, with introd., in A. C. Cochrane (ed.), *Reformed Confessions of the 16th Century* (1966), pp. 185–219.

Belgium, Christianity in. The history of Belgium as an independent country dates only from 1830, but Christianity can be traced back to the mid-4th cent., when Servatius, the first Bp. of Tongres and a strong opponent of *Arianism, attended the Councils of *Sardica and *Rimini. The area was more lastingly evangelized in the 7th cent. by St *Amandus and St *Eligius. A large number of monasteries were founded and important schools at Liège were fostered by Bp. *Notker. Throughout the Middle Ages there was considerable religious fervour, which found its expression in the religious movements of *Beguines and Beghards, and in the writings of the great mystics J. van *Ruysbroeck and *Hadewijch. In 1520 the University of Louvain, founded in 1425, condemned the first writings of M. *Luther. The *Reformation brought about the break-up of the Spanish Netherlands, sanctioned by the Peace of *Westphalia in 1648. Strong Spanish repression maintained the South, that was to become Belgium, within the Catholic sphere of influence. In the 17th cent. *Jansenism became influential and was the object of bitter controversy.

When Belgium became independent of the *Netherlands in 1830, the Church had suffered under the Austrian *Josephite, the French revolutionary and Napoleonic regimes, and then under the Dutch *Calvinist government of William I of Holland (reigned 1813–40), during which severe restrictions were imposed on RCs. The 'Sacred Union' between Catholics and Liberals that carried out the Revolution of 1830 and drew up a constitution in which the separation of Church and State is enshrined, lasted until *c.*1847, when tensions resulted in *Anticlericalism on the one hand and *Ultramontanism on the other. Interactions and tensions between the spheres of religion and politics have been reflected in recurrent problems over the financing of Catholic schools (1879–84 and 1952–8) and the so-called 'pillarization' (the development of separate Catholic, Socialist, and Liberal social networks covering every aspect of life), as well as in social and cultural-linguistic issues. Belgium is a predominantly RC country but, because of increasing secularization, the Church is losing more and more of its social significance. In recent times the Belgian Church has played an important international role: Belgian missionaries have worked throughout the world, most vigorously in *Zaire and *India; Card. D. J. *Mercier was instrumental in the development of neo-*Thomism and was largely responsible for the *Malines Conversations; Card. J. L. *Cardijn exercised great influence on the social thinking of the RC Church; and Card. L. J. Suenens played a leading role at the Second *Vatican Council. There are Protestant, Orthodox, Jewish, and growing Islamic minorities in Belgium.

É. de Moreau, SJ, *Histoire de l'Église en Belgique* [to 1633] (Museum Lessianum, Section historique, 1, 2, 3, 11, 12, and 15; 1940–52); id., *L'Église en Belgique: Des origines au début du XXᵉ siècle* (1944); R. Aubert, *150 ans de vie des églises* (1979). U. Berlière, OSB, and others, *Monasticon Belge* (Bruges and other places, 1890 ff. [Tome 7, vol. 4, 1984]); E. Michel, *Abbayes et monastères de Belgique: leur importance et leur rôle dans le développement du pays* (1923); H. Haag, *Les origines du catholicisme libéral en Belgique (1789–1839)* (Université de Louvain, Recueil de Travaux d'Histoire et de Philosophie, 3rd ser. 36; 1950). *Recherches Sociologiques*, 16 (1985), no. 3: special number devoted to 'La Belgique et ses dieux', with summaries in English. On the period 1914–58, A. Tihon in J.-M. Mayeur and others (eds.), *Histoire du Christianisme des origines à nos jours*, 12 (1990), pp. 538–54. There is also much information on the Church in H. Pirenne, *Histoire de Belgique* (7 vols., 1900–32; illustrated edn., 4 vols. [1948–52]), complemented by J. Bartier and others, *Histoire de la Belgique contemporaine, 1914–1970* [1975]. Useful introds. to Belgian history by P. Carson, *The Fair Face of Flanders* (Ghent, 1969) and G.-H. Dumont, *La Belgique* (Que Sais-Je? 319; 1991). There are many important monographs in the Cahiers/Bijdragen of the Centre Interuniversitaire d'Histoire Contemporaine (Louvain and Paris, 1957 ff.). The KA(tholiek) DO(cumentatie) C(entrum) at the University of Leuven has pub. yearbooks on aspects of Church life in Belgium since 1830. É. de Moreau, SJ, in *DHGE* 7 (1934), cols. 520–756, s.v. 'Belgique'; M. Dierickx in *NCE* 2 (1967), pp. 239–49, s.v.; É. Brouette in *TRE* 5 (1980), pp. 511–25, s.v. 'Belgien'.

Belial. A Heb. word (בְּלִיַּעַל) of uncertain etymology, probably meaning 'worthlessness', 'wickedness', or 'destruction'. It is usually found in combination with a noun, e.g. 'sons of Belial' (Deut. 13: 13; 1 Sam. 2: 12; 10: 27; 25: 17; 2 Chr. 13: 7, etc.). In 2 Cor. 6: 15, the only NT ref. (where the best MSS read Βελίαρ not Βελίαλ), St *Paul uses the word of Satan. In J. *Milton it is the name of the fallen angel who represents impurity (*Paradise Lost*, 1. 490–505, *Paradise Regained*, 2. 150).

Bell, George Kennedy Allen (1881–1958), Bp. of *Chichester. The son of a clergyman, Bell was educated at Westminster School and *Christ Church, Oxford. He was ordained deacon in 1907, priest in 1908. After a curacy at Leeds and a brief period as tutor and lecturer at Christ Church (1910–14), he became secretary to Abp. *Davidson. In 1920 he acted as assistant secretary to the *Lambeth Conference. During the period when he was Dean of *Canterbury (1924–9), various reforms were introduced, incl. the abolition of visitors' fees and the establishment of the *Friends of the Cathedral. In 1928 he arranged for the production of John Masefield's *The Coming of Christ*, the first dramatic performance in an English cathedral in modern times. As Bp. of Chichester from 1929 to 1958 he pursued a forward-looking policy, but it was in the field of ecumenical and international affairs that his chief contribution lay.

His interest in the *Ecumenical Movement dated from 1919, when he went as part of the British delegation to the meeting at Oud Wassenaar (near The Hague) of the World Alliance for International Friendship through the Churches. He became one of the leaders of the *Life and Work movement and played a prominent part at the first conference at *Stockholm in 1925. He was chairman of the Council from 1932 to 1934 and of the administrative committee from 1934 to 1938. He supported the *Confessing Church in its struggle against the Nazi government. His outspoken condemnation of indiscriminate Allied bombing of German towns during the Second World War was prob. a major factor in preventing his succession to William *Temple as Abp. of Canterbury in 1944. His contacts with German and other Churches after the war facilitated the first meeting of the *World Council of Churches in 1948. He was chairman of its central committee from 1948 to 1954 and then honorary president until his death. He was also a staunch supporter of the Church of *South India and acted as joint-chairman of the *Anglican–Methodist Conversations which began in 1956. He edited several volumes of *Documents on Christian Unity* (1924–58) and wrote other works on the subject. His Life of Randall Davidson (2 vols., 1935) is a notable contribution to contemporary English Church history. He resigned from the see of Chichester in Jan. 1958 and died later in the same year.

Correspondence with Alphons Koechlin, 1933–54 (in Ger. tr.), ed. A. Lindt (Zurich, 1969). R. C. D. Jasper, *George Bell, Bishop of Chichester* (1967). Further study by K. Slack (London, 1971). [E.] G. Rupp, *'I seek my brethren': Bishop Bell and the German Churches* (lecture, 1975). P. K. Walker, *The Anglican Church Today: Rediscovering the Middle Way* (1988), pp. 27–70. R. C. D. Jasper in *DNB*, *1951–1960* (1971), pp. 80–2.

Bellarmine, St Robert (1542–1621), theologian and controversialist. Roberto Francesco Romolo Bellarmino was born at Montepulciano in Tuscany. In 1560 he joined the *Jesuits and was ordained priest in 1570. As professor of theology at Louvain (1570), where he came into contact with non-Roman thought, he soon gained a reputation for learning and eloquence; but, partly owing to the cold climate of the N., he moved to Rome in 1576 where he became professor of controversial theology at the newly founded 'Collegium Romanum'. He was made a cardinal in 1599 and from 1602 to 1605 was Abp. of Capua. His later years were spent in the composition of works of spirituality.

His life was largely devoted to scholarship and controversy. He proved himself a vigorous and successful opponent of the Protestants, whom he sought to vanquish by reason and argument rather than by dogmatic assertion and abuse; and *James I of England engaged in controversy with him. His chief work was the *Disputationes de Controversiis Christianae Fidei adversus hujus temporis Haereticos* (3 vols., Ingolstadt, 1586–93), a systematic and clear apologia for the RC position. He also took a prominent part in the production of the revised edition of the *Vulgate, known as the Sixto-Clementine, in 1592. As regards the Papacy, he supported *Paul V in his struggle against *Venice and wrote a book against that of W. Barclay of Aberdeen (*c.*1547–1608) denying the temporal authority of the Pope; but Bellarmine held that the Pope had only an indirect, not a direct, power in temporal matters, a view which had previously brought him into disgrace with *Sixtus V. Finally his sympathetic interest in G. *Galileo reflects his reasonableness.

He became entitled to the appellation of 'Venerable' in 1627, but further recognition was long delayed, despite frequent attempts to secure it, owing to his minimizing view of Papal authority. He was eventually canonized in 1930 and declared to be a *Doctor of the Church in 1931. Feast day, 17 Sept. (formerly 13 May).

Collected edn. of his works pub. in 7 vols., Cologne, 1617–21, vol. 7 being ed. by S. Rychius; modern edns., 12 vols., Paris, 1870–4, and 8 vols., Naples, 1872; suppl. to his works ed. X. M. Le Bachelet, SJ, *Auctarium Bellarminianum* (Paris, 1913); *Opera Oratoria Postuma, adiunctis Documentis Variis ad Gubernium Animarum Spectantibus*, ed. S. Tromp, SJ (11 vols., Rome, 1942–1969). G. Galeota, SJ, *Bellarmino contro Baio a Lovanio: Studio e Testo di un inedito Bellarminiano* (Aloisiana. Scritti Pubblicati sotto la direzione della Pontificia Facoltà Teologica Napoletana 'S. Luigi', 5; Rome, 1966). Eng. tr. of some of his spiritual writings by J. P. Donnelly, SJ, and R. J. Teske, SJ (Classics of Western Spirituality, New York [1989]). His autobiography, written in 1613, was pr. at the time of his attempted beatification, Rome, 1676; repr. Louvain, 1753. The primary authorities for his life are the biographies of J. Fuligatti, SJ (Rome, 1624), D. Bartoli, SJ (ibid., 1678), and N. Frizon, SJ (Nancy, 1708). X. M. Le Bachelet, SJ, *Bellarmin avant son cardinalat, 1524–1598* (1911), with important docs.; id., *Bellarmin et la bible sixto-clémentine* (1911), also with docs. J. Brodrick, SJ, *The Life and Works of Blessed Robert Francis Cardinal Bellarmine* (2 vols., 1928); id., *Robert Bellarmine, Saint and Scholar* (1961). F. X. Arnold, *Die Staatslehre des Kardinals Bellarmin: Eine Beitrag zur Rechts- und Staatsphilosophie des konfessionellen Zeitalters* (Munich, 1934). E. A. Ryan, SJ, *The Historical Scholarship of Saint Bellarmine* (Université de Louvain. Recueil de Travaux publiés par les Membres des Conférences d'Histoire et de Philologie, 2nd ser. 35; 1936); A. Bernier, SJ, *Un Cardinal humaniste: Saint Robert Bellarmin ... et la musique liturgique* (Montreal and Paris, 1939). A. M. Artola, CP, *De la Revelación a la Inspiración: Los orígenes de la moderna teología católica sobre la Inspiración biblica* (Bilbao, 1983), pp. 30–6, 41–51, 62–5, and 79 f. Sommervogel, 1 (1890), cols. 1151–254; Polgár, 1 (1990), pp. 234–59. P. Dudon, SJ, in *DHGE* 7 (1934), cols. 798–824, s.v. 'Bellarmin'; G. Galeota, SJ, in *Dict. Sp.* 13 (1988), cols. 713–20, s.v. 'Robert (3) Bellarmin'.

Belloc, Joseph Hilaire Pierre (1870–1953), RC historical writer and critic. Half French, he was born at St-Cloud (nr. Versailles), educated at the *Oratory School in Birmingham under J. H. *Newman, served for a year with the French artillery, and then entered Balliol College, Oxford (1892). In 1906 he was elected Liberal MP for South Salford, but his fervent individualism and fear of State dominance made him critical of his party's alliance with the Socialists and he did not stand for the second election of 1910. He then joined G. K. *Chesterton and his brother, Cecil Chesterton, in a series of political broadsides popularly known as the 'Chesterbellocs'; and for the rest of his life he was a well-known figure in journalism, expounding Catholic economic liberalism and upholding the traditional values of European civilization as the true inheritance of the medieval system. On this general topic his chief work was *Europe and the Faith* (1912). He was the author of many historical writings which commanded attention by their brilliant and provocative style, though they were seldom contributions to serious knowledge. They include *The French Revolution* (1924), a *History of England* (1925–7), and Lives of *Joan of Arc (1929), *Richelieu (1930), *Wolsey (1930), Napoleon (1932), *Charles I (1933), *Cromwell (1934), and *Milton (1935). He also wrote the popular travel-book, *The Path to Rome* (1902), some volumes of light essays, and some successful light and satirical verse.

D. Woodruff (ed.), *For Hilaire Belloc: Essays in Honour of his 72nd Birthday* (1942), incl. an essay by D. Jerrold, 'On the Influence of Hilaire Belloc', pp. 9–17. R. Speaight, *The Life of Hilaire Belloc* (1957); A. N. Wilson, *Hilaire Belloc* (1984). Shorter study by E. and R. Jebb [daughter and son-in-law] (London, 1956).

bells. The legend that associates the introduction of the bell into Christian worship with *Paulinus of Nola in Campania (d. 431) lacks historical foundation; it was perhaps invented to account for the Latin words *campana* and *nola*, both meaning bell. The earliest reference to such usage occurs in a letter of *Ferrandus of Carthage (*c.*535), but St *Gregory of Tours is the first writer to mention it frequently. Handbells were much used in the British Isles and other areas under Celtic influence from the 5th to the 9th cent; a famous example is the Bell of St *Patrick's Will, now in the National Museum of Ireland, Dublin. Hanging bells had come into general use in the Church by the 8th cent. There was a peal of three bells in *St Peter's, Rome, in the time of Pope *Stephen II (752–7), and another at *Winchester is depicted in the Benedictional of St *Ethelwold (*c.*980). Both he and St *Dunstan cast bells for churches. From the 8th cent. bells were blessed by a bishop with *holy water and *chrism; since 1984 the ceremony (popularly called the 'baptism of bells') may be performed by a priest, and oil is no longer used. For centuries it has been customary to ring bells to summon the people to church and on other occasions, e.g. to announce the passing of a parishioner (the 'passing bell') or his death (still ordered in the 1604 Canons of the C of E, but not retained in those of 1969), or for the ringing of the '*Angelus' or the '*De profundis'. The 10th-cent. *Regularis Concordia* notes as an established English custom the frequent pealing of bells at feasts. From medieval times to the present it has been customary for bells to bear inscriptions, sometimes in the form of a hexameter line, such as *Stella Maria maris succurre piissima nobis*. In size they vary very widely from the quite small treble to the large tenor. Thus Great Paul in *St Paul's Cathedral (1882) weighs almost 16¾ tons, and the Petrusglocke in *Cologne Cathedral (1923) over 25 tons. Small bells are sometimes used at the altar and rung at the Eucharist at the *Elevation and the *Communion.

T. North, *English Bells and Bell Lore* (Leek, 1888); J. J. Raven, *The Bells of England* (The Antiquary's Books, 1906); H. B. Walters, *The Church Bells of England* (1912), with bibl., pp. ix–xx; E. Morris, *The History and Art of Change Ringing* (1931); id., *Towers and Bells of Britain* (1955); [F.] P. Price, *Bells and Man* (Oxford, 1983); E. V. Williams, *The Bells of Russia: History and Technology* (Princeton, NJ, 1985). H. *Leclercq, OSB, in *DACL* 3 (pt. 2; 1914), cols. 1954–77, s.v. 'Cloche, clochette'; P. Price in S. Sadie (ed.), *The New Grove Dictionary of Music and Musicians*, 2 (1980), pp. 424–37, s.v.

bell-tower. See CAMPANILE.

'beloved disciple'. The anonymous and idealized disciple in St. *John's Gospel, identified as the one 'whom Jesus loved' (13: 23, 19: 26, 20: 2, 21: 7, and 21: 20) and at 21: 24 (cf. 19: 35) as the eye witness source of this gospel's tradition. Some assume a reference to him also at 1: 37–9 and 18: 15. On account of his prominence and closeness to the Lord he has often been identified with St. *John, the Apostle, who is not named in the gospel but was later thought to be the Evangelist. Others have suggested *Lazarus or John Mark (see MARK, ST), or have seen here a purely fictitious character.

For bibl. see JOHN, ST, APOSTLE.

bema (Gk. βῆμα, 'platform'). Acc. to E. usage, the space, usually raised above the level of the *nave of a church, which is shut off by the *iconostasis and contains the *altar, i.e. the counterpart of the *sanctuary in the W. The word is also used, less correctly, for the altar itself.

Benedicamus Domino (Lat., 'Let us bless the Lord'). In the Roman rite a formula used from the 11th cent. until modern times to mark the end of the choir *office and in some circumstances also the end of Mass. It is now used only at the conclusion of the *Office of Readings and the midday office. The response is 'Deo gratias' ('Thanks be to God').

The formula is first found in Gallican sources. Jungmann (1958 edn.), 2, pp. 538–40; Eng. tr., 2, pp. 435–7.

Benedicite (Lat., 'Bless ye [the Lord]'). The *canticle or song of praise put into the mouths of Shadrach, Meshach, and Abednego, as they stood in the 'fiery furnace' before King Nebuchadnezzar. It forms part (vv. 35–66) of the *Song of the Three Children (q.v.). It has been used in Christian liturgical worship from early times. *Rufinus, writing *c.*406, says that it was sung by Christians throughout the world. It is found in certain orders for the *Paschal Vigil Service and it came to be widely used in the morning office of *Lauds in the W. and its E. equivalents. From the medieval Lauds, in which it was sung on all Sundays and festivals, it passed into the BCP as an alternative to the *Te Deum at *Mattins, used mainly in *Lent and *Advent. In modern revisions of the morning office, the ASB provides an abridged form of the Benedicite, and in the 1971 reordering of the RC Divine *Office it is preserved on festivals and at least two Sundays out of four. In the Byzantine *Orthros it is prescribed as the eighth daily canticle, but it is usually represented by a single chanting of the refrain.

F. *Cabrol, OSB, in *DACL* 2 (1910), cols. 660–4. See also works cited under CANTICLE and under SONG OF THE THREE CHILDREN.

Benedict, St (*c.*480–*c.*550), of Nursia, the 'Patriarch of Western monasticism'. Little is known of his life. Born at Nursia, he was educated at Rome, where the licentiousness of contemporary society led him to withdraw from the world and retire *c.*500 to a cave at *Subiaco. Here he lived as a hermit for some years. A community gradually grew up round him and he is said to have established a group of monasteries in the area. Local jealousy prompted him to leave Subiaco, and *c.*529, he moved with a small band of monks to *Monte Cassino, where he remained till his death. It was here that he elaborated his plans for the reform of monasticism and composed his Rule (see foll. entry). He does not appear to have been ordained or to have contemplated founding an order. He was buried at Monte Cassino in the same grave as his sister, St *Scholastica. Feast day, in W., 11 July (formerly 21 Mar.; within the *Benedictine Order, both feasts have long been and still are observed); in E., 14 Mar.

Practically the sole source for his life is St *Gregory I, *Dialogues*, Bk. 2 (ed. A. de Vogüé, OSB, with Fr. tr. by P. Antin, OSB, SC 260, 1979, pp. 120–249). Modern biographical studies by J. *Chapman, OSB (London, 1929), F. *Cabrol, OSB (Paris, 1933; Eng. tr., 1934), J. McCann, OSB (London, 1937; repr. 1979), I. Schuster, OSB (Milan, 1943; Eng. tr., St Louis, 1951; London, 1953). *Atti del 7° Congresso Internazionale di Studi* *sull'Alto Medioevo . . . 29 settembre–5 ottobre 1980* [devoted to 'San Benedetto nel suo Tempo'] (Centro Italiano di Studi sull'Alto Medioevo, 2 vols., Spoleto, 1982); *Monastica: Scritti Raccolti in Memoria del XV Centenario della Nascità di S. Benedetto (480–1980)* (Miscellanea Cassinese, 44, 46–8; Montecassino, 1981–4). *Il Sepolcro di San Benedetto* (ibid. 27 and 45; 1951–82). O. L. Kapsner, OSB, *A Benedictine Bibliography* (2nd edn., 2 vols.; Collegeville, Minn., 1962), esp. 2, pp. 15–30 (for works on Benedict himself), with suppl. (ibid., 1982), esp. pp. 439–47. A *Bulletin d'Histoire Bénédictine*, containing full bibl. information on the saint, his Rule and the history of the Benedictine order, has appeared at intervals in *R. Bén.* since 1895 and as separate suppl. since 1912.

Benedict, Rule of St. The monastic Rule drawn up by St *Benedict of Nursia *c.*540 for his monks, mostly laymen, of *Monte Cassino. Drawing freely from the earlier Rule of St Basil (see BASIL, RULE OF ST) in the version of *Rufinus, and from John *Cassian, as well as from the Fathers of the Desert, St *Augustine, and St *Caesarius of Arles, but probably predominantly from the *Regula Magistri*, Benedict created a taut, inclusive, and individual directory of the spiritual as well as of the administrative life of a monastery. The Rule is marked by prudence and humanity, and leads by observance and obedience to the perfect following of Christ. It is safeguarded and applied by a patriarchal *abbot, chosen by his monks, with full authority, who is directed to take counsel and to care for the individual. The chief task and central act of the community is the Divine Office (*opus Dei*) which with private prayer, spiritual reading, and work fills the day. All monks must renounce private ownership, though the monastery may own property; the regime is austere but not exacting.

There is an immense literature. Crit. edns. of the Rule include those by R. Hanslik (CSEL 75; 1960; 2nd edn., 1977), and, with Fr. tr. and comm. by J. Neufville, OSB, and A. de Vogüé, OSB, (SC 181–6; 1971–2; with additional vol. of doctrinal and spiritual comm. by A. de Vogüé, 1977; Eng. tr. of this vol., Cistercian Studies Series, 54; Kalamazoo, Mich., 1983). Text and Eng. tr. by J. McCann, OSB (London, 1952) and *RB 1980*, ed. T. Fry, OSB (Collegeville, Minn. [1981]), with good introd. and notes. Facsimile of text in Bodleian MS Hatton 48 (Early English Manuscripts in Facsimile, 15; Copenhagen, 1968), with introd. by D. H. Farmer, pp. 11–29. Comm. by P. Delatte, OSB (Paris, 1913; Eng. tr., 1921), G. Herwegen, OSB (Einsiedeln, 1944), and B. Steidle, OSB (Beuron, 1952). Id. (ed.), *Commentationes in Regulam S. Benedicti* (Studia Anselmiana, 42; Rome, 1957). P. Meyvaert, OSB, 'Problems concerning the "Autograph" manuscript of Saint Benedict's Rule', *R. Bén.* 69 (1959), pp. 3–21; repr. in id., *Benedict, Gregory, Bede and Others* (1977), no. 3. The modern history of the text of the Rule is documented by J. D. Broekaert, *Bibliographie de la Règle de Saint Benoît: Éditions latines et traductions imprimées de 1489 à 1929* (Studia Anselmiana, 77–8; Rome, 1980; 1213 items) and B. Jaspert, *Bibliographie der Regula Benedicti 1930–1980: Ausgaben und Übersetzungen* (Regula Benedicti Studia, suppl. 5; Hildesheim, 1983; 424 items). The annual *Regula Benedicti Studia* (ibid., 1972 ff.) provides a bibliography of secondary works on the Rule. See also works cited, s.v. BENEDICT, ST, BENEDICTINE ORDER, and REGULA MAGISTRI.

Benedict of Aniane, St (*c.*750–821), abbot. After serving under *Pepin and his son, *Charlemagne, he became a monk at St-Seine, near Dijon, prob. in 774. In 779 he founded on his own property at Aniane in Languedoc a monastery which became the centre of an extended reform of all the French monastic houses. His systematization of

the *Benedictine Rule received official approval at the Synods of Aachen of 816 and 817. His collection of early monastic Rules (known as the *Codex Regularum monasticarum et canonicarum*) is our most important single source of texts of this type. He was also responsible for a major dogmatic compilation (the *Munimenta fidei*) and, it is now widely thought, for the *Hucusque (q.v.). From *c.*795 he took a vigorous part in opposing the teaching of the *Adoptianist *Felix of Urgel. His personal life was one of severe asceticism. Feast day, 11 Feb.

His writings are in J. P. Migne, *PL* 103. 393–1440, with Life by his disciple and friend, Ardo, cols. 335–84; crit. ed. of the Life by G. Waitz in *MGH*, Scriptores, 15 (pt. 1; 1887), pp. 198–220; Eng. tr. by A. Cabaniss (Ilfracombe, Devon, 1979). Relevant decrees of the Synods of Aachen and related texts ed. J. Semmler in K. Hallinger, OSB (ed.), *Corpus Consuetudinum Monasticarum*, 1 (Siegburg, 1963), pp. 423–561; the 'Modus Penitentiarum' ascribed to Benedict, ibid., pp. 563–82. Contents of the *Munimenta fidei* described, with edn. of sections attributable to Benedict, by J. Leclercq, OSB, *Analecta Monastica*, 1st ser. (Studia Anselmiana, 20; 1948), pp. 21–74. Discussion of the contents of the *Codex Regularum* by A. de Vogüé, OSB, *Les Règles monastiques anciennes* (Typologie des Sources du Moyen Âge Occidental, 46; 1985), esp. pp. 42–5. J. Narberhaus, *Benedikt von Aniane* (Beiträge zur Geschichte des alten Mönchtums und des Benediktinerordens, 16; 1930); W. Williams, 'St Benedict of Aniane', *Downside Review*, 54 (1936), pp. 357–74; S. Dulcy, *La Règle de Saint Benoît d'Aniane et la réforme monastique à l'époque carolingienne* (Montpellier thesis; Nîmes, 1935); J. Winandy, OSB, 'L'Œuvre monastique de Saint Benoît d'Aniane', in *Mélanges bénédictins publiés à l'occasion du XIVᵉ Centenaire de la Mort de Saint Benoît par les Moines de l'Abbaye de Saint Jérôme de Rome* (Wandrille, 1947), pp. 235–58; P. Schmitz, OSB, 'L'Influence de Saint Benoît', in *Il monachesimo nell'alto medioevo e la formazione della civiltà occidentale* (Settimane di Studio del Centro Italiano di Studi sull'Alto Medioevo, 4; 1957), pp. 401–15. J. Semmler, 'Die Beschlüsse des Aachener Konzils im Jahre 816', *ZKG* 74 (1963), pp. 15–82. P. Schmitz, OSB, in *DHGE* 8 (1935), cols. 177–88, s.v. 'Benoît d'Aniane', with bibl. E. von Severus, OSB, in *TRE* 5 (1980), pp. 535–8; J. Semmler in *L.Th.K.* (3rd edn.), 2 (1994), cols. 200 f., both s.v. 'Benedikt von Aniane'.

Benedict Biscop, St (*c.*628–689 or 690), *Benedictine monk. Of noble Northumbrian birth, he spent his youth at the court of King Oswiu. After two journeys to *Rome (the first, 653, with St *Wilfrid), in 666 he became a monk of *Lérins. In 669 he accompanied Abp. *Theodore to *Canterbury, where he became Abbot of the monastery of St Peter and St Paul (later St *Augustine's). In 674 he founded the monastery of St Peter at *Wearmouth and in 682 that of St Paul at Jarrow. An enthusiast for learning and art, Benedict brought back from his journeys to Rome (five in all) many paintings, relics, and MSS. He also secured the services of John, the archcantor of St Peter's, Rome, to teach in England the Roman chant. He is further reputed to have introduced into England the use of glass windows and churches built in stone. He was an enthusiastic advocate of Roman liturgical practice. His Life was written by *Bede, who was entrusted to Benedict's care at the age of 7. Feast day, 12 Jan. He is the patron of the English Benedictines.

Bede, *HE* 4. 18 and 5. 19, and *Historia Abbatum*, 1; *William of Malmesbury, *Gesta Pontificum*, 4. 186, ed. by N. E. S. A. Hamilton (RS, 1870), pp. 327–9. P. Wormald, 'Bede and Benedict Biscop', in G. [I.] Bonner (ed.), *Famulus Christi: Essays in Commemoration of the Thirteenth Centenary of the Birth of the Venerable*

Bede (1976), pp. 141–69. K. Zelzer, 'Zur Frage der Observanz des Benedict Biscop', in E. A. Livingstone (ed.), *Studia Patristica*, 20 (Louvain, 1989), pp. 323–9.

Benedict Joseph Labre, St. See LABRE, ST BENEDICT JOSEPH.

Benedict XII (d. 1342), Pope from 1334. Jacques Fournier was the third of the *Avignon Popes. Of humble origin, he entered as a youth the *Cistercian abbey of Boulbonne and was later transferred to Fontfroide. Having studied at *Paris and become Master of Theology, he was installed Abbot of Fontfroide in 1311, appointed Bp. of Pamiers in 1317, and translated to Mirepoix in 1326. Created cardinal in 1327, he took part in the dogmatic controversies of the time, esp. on the questions of the poverty of Christ and on the *Beatific Vision. After being elected Pope in 1334, he at once inaugurated several ecclesiastical reforms. Himself entirely free from nepotism, he fought esp. the rapacity of the clergy, many of whom he sent back from Avignon to their dioceses without conferring benefices on them. He forbade the holding of benefices *in *commendam* except in the case of cardinals and was a zealous reformer of the religious orders, esp. the *Benedictines by his bull 'Summi magistri' (1336). He also ordered the establishment of houses of studies in every country and improved the training of novices, many of his measures being later adopted by the Council of *Trent. In the political field, where he tended to commit himself to the policy of Philip VI of France, he was less successful. French influence led his conciliatory attitude towards Louis of Bavaria to fail, and hence to the declaration of the Electors assembled at Rense to the effect that the Emperor holds his rights not through confirmation by the Pope but through the fact of his election. Louis, though allying himself with France in 1341, finally wrecked all hopes of better relations between Pope and Emperor by ignoring the Pope's remonstrations and giving his son, Louis of Brandenburg, in marriage to Margaret Maultasch, who had separated from her husband without ecclesiastical dispensation. Through the war between England and France Benedict's plan for a Crusade came to nothing, and his contemplated return to Rome was frustrated by the opposition of Philip VI and the unrest in Italy, though after 1339 *Verona, *Bologna, and Milan returned to the Papal allegiance. He also began the building of the famous palace of the Popes at Avignon. Benedict XII was a competent theologian, though most of his works have remained unpublished. His chief doctrinal pronouncement is the constitution 'Benedictus Deus' (1336) in which he defined the Catholic doctrine that the souls of the just who have no faults to expiate enjoy the Beatific Vision immediately after death, thereby resolving the conflict started by *John XXII in his private capacity.

His *Lettres closes, patentes et curiales se rapportant à la France*, ed. G. Daumet (Bibliothèque des Écoles Française d'Athènes et de Rome, 3rd ser. 2; 3 pts., 1899–1920); *Lettres communes*, ed. J.-M. Vidal (ibid. 2 bis; 3 vols., 1902–11); *Lettres closes et patentes intéressant les pays autres que la France*, ed. J.-M. Vidal and G. Mollat (ibid. 2 [ter], 5 pts., 2 vols., 1913–50); A. L. Tautu (ed.), *Acta . . . e regestis Vaticanis aliisque fontibus* (Pontificia Commissio ad Redigendum Codicem Iuris Canonici Orientalis. Fontes, 3rd ser., vol. 8, 1958). J. Duvernoy (ed.), *Le Registre d'Inquisition de Jacques Fournier, évêque de Pamiers (1318–1325)* (Bibliothèque Méridionale, 2nd ser. 41; 3 vols., Toulouse, 1965); see also E. Le

Roy Ladurie, *Montaillou, village occitan de 1294 à 1324* (1975; rev. edn., 1982; abbreviated Eng. tr., 1978). He also wrote a Comm. on Mt., part of which was pub. by G. Lazarus (Venice, 1603) under the name of 'Benedict XI'. S. *Baluse, *Vitae Paparum Avenionensium* (ed. G. Mollat, 1, 1914, pp. 195–240 and 576–80). C. Jacob, *Studien über Papst Benedikt XII* (1910). J. B. Mahn, *Le Pape Benoît XII et les Cisterciens* (Bibliothèque de l'École des Hautes Études, 295; 1950); B. Guillemain, *La Politique Bénéficiale du Pape Benoît XII* (ibid. 299; 1952); C. Schmitt, OSB, *Un Pape réformateur et un défenseur de l'unité de l'Église: Benoît XII et l'Ordre des Frères Mineurs* (Florence, 1959). J. M. Vidal, 'Notice sur les œuvres du Pape Benoît XII', *RHE* 6 (1905), pp. 557–65 and 785–810. H. Otto, 'Benedikt XII als Reformator des Kirchenstaates', *RQ* 36 (1928), pp. 59–110. G. Mollat, *Les Papes d'Avignon* (1912), esp. Bk. 1, ch. 4, and Bk. 2, ch. 1, pt. 4 (10th edn. [1965], pp. 72–88 and 200–212; Eng. tr. of an earlier edn., 1963, pp. 26–36 and 110–19). K. A. Fink in *Handbuch der Kirchengeschichte*, ed. H. Jedin, 3 (pt. 2; 1968), pp. 393–9; Eng. tr., vol. 4 (1980), pp. 315–24. X. Le Bachelet, SJ, in *DTC* 2 (1905), cols. 653–704, s.v. 'Benoît XII'; B. Guillemain in *Dizionario Biografico degli Italiani*, 8 (1966), pp. 378–84, s.v. 'Benedetto XII'.

Benedict XIII (d. 1423), *Antipope at *Avignon from 1394 to 1417. Pedro de Luna was a doctor of Canon Law of great learning and austerity of life. Created *cardinal in 1375 by *Gregory XI, he took part in the election of Gregory's successor, *Urban VI, but later became a partisan of his Antipope, Clement VII. After Clement's death (1394) he himself was elected Antipope, largely because he promised to put an end to the schism, even if it meant abdicating. After his enthronement, however, he refused to resign, and even sustained a long siege and subsequent imprisonment in the Papal castle of Avignon in defence of his dignity. Personal negotiations with the Roman Pope, Boniface IX, and his successors Innocent VII and Gregory XII were equally unsuccessful. The Council of *Pisa, against which he had called a synod at Perpignan, deposed him in 1409, and the Council of *Constance confirmed his deposition in 1417. After this even his last adherents (Scotland, Aragon, Castile, and Sicily) left him. He shut himself up in his castle at Peñiscola near Valencia, where he still claimed to be the rightful Pope until his death. As RC historians deny his rightful place in the Papal succession, the title of 'Benedict XIII' is attached to P. F. Orsini (d. 1730; see following entry).

Documents relatifs au Grand Schisme, 4–5: *Lettres de Benoît XIII (1394–1422)*, vol. 1, ed. J. Paye-Bourgeois (Analecta Vaticano-Belgica [première série], 31; 1983), vol. 2, ed. M.-J. Tits-Dieuaide (ibid. 19; 1960). F. McGurk (ed.), *Calendar of Papal Letters to Scotland of Benedict XIII of Avignon 1394–1419* (Scottish History Society, 4th ser. 13; 1976). H. Millett and E. Poulle, *Le vote de la soustraction d'obédience en 1398* (1988 ff.). L. Panzan, *Recordanzas en tiempo de Papa Luna (1407–1435)*, ed. G. de Andres (1987), pp. 76–103, 113–22, and 128–58. Martin de Alpartil, *Chronica Actitatorum Temporibus Domini Benedicti XIII*, ed. F. Ehrle, SJ (Quellen und Forschungen aus dem Gebiete der Geschichte, 12; 1906). S. Puig y Puig, *Episcopologio barcinonese: Pedro de Luna, último papa de Aviñon, 1387–1430* (Barcelona, 1920). A. Glasfurd, *The Antipope (Peter de Luna, 1342–1423): A Study in Obstinacy* (1965), with bibl. F. Ehrle, SJ, 'Aus den Akten des Afterkonzils von Perpignan 1408', *Archiv für Literatur- und Kirchengeschichte des Mittelalters*, 5 (1889), pp. 387–492, and 7 (1900), pp. 576–696; id., 'Neue Materialien zur Geschichte Peters von Luna (Benedikt XIII)', ibid. 6 (1892), pp. 138–308, and 7 (1900), pp. 1–306; id., 'Die kirchenrechtlichen Schriften Peters von Luna (Benedikt XIII)', ibid. 7 (1900), pp. 515–75. G. Mollat, 'Épisodes du siège du palais des papes au temps de Benoît XIII

(1398–1399)', *RHE* 23 (1927), pp. 489–501. W. Brandmüller, 'Die Gesandtschaft Benedikts XIII. an das Konzil von Pisa', in G. Schwaiger (ed.), *Konzil und Papst . . . Festgabe für Hermann Tüchle* (1975), pp. 169–205, repr. in Brandmüller, *Papst und Konzil im Grossen Schisma* (1990), pp. 42–70. N. Valois, *La France et le grand schisme d'occident* (4 vols., 1898–1902), *passim*. F. Baix and L. Jadin in *DHGE* 8 (1935), cols. 135–63, s.v. 'Benoît XIII', with bibl.

Benedict XIII (1649–1730), Pope from 1724. Pietro Francesco Orsini, who entered the *Dominican Order in 1667, became a cardinal in 1672 and Abp. of Benevento in 1686. As Pope, he presided at the provincial Lateran Council of 1725, which sought to reform clerical morals; but though well-intentioned and scholarly, he was of weak character, and his policy was determined by his unscrupulous favourite, Cardinal Coscia. In 1725 he confirmed the bull '*Unigenitus', though he suffered the Dominicans to preach a doctrine of *grace akin to that of the *Jansenists.

Quétif and Échard, 2 (1721), pp. 814–17. G. B. Pittoni, *Vita del sommo pontifice Benedetto Decimoterzo* (Venice, 1730); A. Borgia, *Benedicti XIII, Romani Pontificis Vita Commentario Excerpta* (Rome, 1741). G. B. Vignato, OP, *Storia di Benedetto XIII* (vol. 1–3 only pub. [dealing with his pre-papal period], [1952–6]) Pastor, 24 (1941), pp. 98–299. J. Carreyre in *DHGE* 7 (1935), cols. 163 f.; G. De Caro in *Dizionario Biografico degli Italiani*, 8 (1966), pp. 384–93, s.v. 'Benedetto XIII'.

Benedict XIV (1675–1758), Pope from 1740. A native of *Bologna, Prospero Lorenzo Lambertini was educated at Rome at the Collegium Clementinum. He became Consistorial Advocate in 1701, *Promotor Fidei in 1708, and assessor of the Congregation of *Rites in 1712. In 1718 he was appointed secretary of the Congregation of the Council, in 1727 Bp. of Ancona, in 1728 cardinal, and in 1731 Abp. of Bologna. On the death of Clement XII (6 Feb. 1740), after a conclave lasting six months he was elected to the Papacy on 17 Aug.

Of wide sympathies, a clear sense of order and proportion, and a real interest in science and learning, Benedict did much to commend his office to the *Aufklärung. He was an exemplary administrator, conciliatory in his dealings with the secular powers, and esp. concerned to strengthen the moral influence of the Papacy; and his prudence and ability were respected in the courts of Europe, Protestant as well as Catholic. His *De Servorum Dei Beatificatione et Beatorum Canonizatione* (1734–8; often repr.), which grew out of his practical experience as 'Promotor Fidei', has remained the classic treatise on the subject. Book 1 contains extensive material on the history of beatification and *canonization; Books 2 and 3 treat of the successive stages in the process, including the testimonies, virtuous life and special graces (*gratis datae*) to be sought in the candidate; and Book 4 deals with the requisite miracles (pt. 1) and with various liturgical questions (Office and Mass of the Saint, insertion in the *Roman Martyrology, and adoption as Patron; pt. 2). Benedict also compiled an extensive work of hardly less authority on Diocesan *Synods (*De Synodo Diœcesana*, Rome, 1748; often repr.). His official pronouncements, collected in *Bullarium Benedicti XIV* (1768), frequently embodied scientific disquisitions. His other writings included an elaborate treatise on the Sacrifice of the Mass (*De Sacrosancto Missae Sacrificio*, 1748) and further works on canon law; and in 1752 he issued a standard edition of the *Caeremoniale*

Episcoporum (q.v.). His pronouncements dealt, *inter alia*, with the suppression of pagan practices admitted into Christianity, notably by the *Jesuits in *China ('Ex quo singulari', 1742) and *Malabar ('Omnium sollicitudinum', 1744); *usury ('Vix pervenit', 1745); *mixed marriages ('Magnae nobis admirationis', 1748); and *Jansenism ('Ex omnibus christiani orbis', 1756). To encourage historical studies, Benedict also founded a number of academies at Rome. He was buried in St Peter's, Rome, where he is commemorated by a striking monument by Pietro Bracci.

Opera, ed. E. de Azevedo, SJ (12 vols., Rome, 1747–51), and, with *Bullarium*, ed. J. Silvester (17 vols., Prato, 1839–46); *Opera Omnia Inedita*, ed. F. Heiner (Freiburg i. B., 1904); *Correspondance*, ed. E. Heeckeren (2 vols., Paris, 1912). *Lettere . . . al Card. de Tencin*, ed. E. Morelli (Rome, 1955 ff.). Modern Eng. tr. of extracts of his *De Synodo Diœcesana* (London, 1926). Life by [L. A. de] Caraccioli (Paris, 1783). A. M. Beltanini, *Benedetto XIV e la repubblica di Venezia* (Milan, 1931). E. Morelli, *Tre Profili* (1955), pp. 1–45. R. Haynes, *Philosopher King: The Humanist Pope Benedict XIV* [1970]. M. Cecchelli (ed.), *Benedetto XIV (Prospero Lambertini): Convegno Internazionale di studi storici sotto il patrocinio dell'Archidiocesi di Bologna. Cento, 6–9 dicembre 1979* (3 vols., Cento, 1981–3). Pastor, 35 ('1949' [1950]) and 36 (1950), pp. 1–142, with bibl. to date. R. Naz in *DDC* 2 (1937), cols. 752–61, s.v. 'Benoît XIV'; J. Carreyre, PSS, in *DHGE* 8 (1935), cols. 164–7, s.v. 'Benoît XIV'; M. Rosa in *Dizionario Biografico degli Italiani*, 8 (1966), pp. 393–408, s.v. 'Benedetto XIV'.

Benedict XV (1854–1922), Pope from 1914. Giacomo P. G. B. della Chiesa was born at Pegli in the diocese of Genoa, and studied at Genoa and at the *Gregorian University, Rome. From 1883 to 1887 he was in Spain as secretary to Cardinal Rampolla, then Papal Nuncio at Madrid; and when the latter was recalled in 1887, della Chiesa returned to Rome with him, and remained there until appointed Abp. of *Bologna in 1907. On the death of *Pius X shortly after the outbreak of the war of 1914–1918 he was elected to succeed him. While endeavouring to preserve the neutrality of the Holy See, he protested against inhuman methods of warfare and made several strenuous efforts to bring about peace. After the war he continued to work for international reconciliation. In 1917 he promulgated the code of canon law (*Codex Iuris Canonici*), which was almost complete at the time of his election. He paved the way for a better understanding with the E. Churches by the establishment in the same year of the Congregation for the Oriental Church and the Pontifical Oriental Institute in Rome. In an apostolic letter of 30 Nov. 1919 ('Maximum illud') he urged missionary bishops to build up a native clergy as well as to seek the welfare of the people among whom they worked. During his pontificate a British representative was accredited to the Papal court for the first time since the 17th cent.

Official acts of his pontificate in *AAS*, vol. 6 (1914) p. 473–vol. 14 (1922), p. 92 (incl. the accounts of his election and funeral). W. Steglich (ed.), *Der Friedensappell Papst Benedikts XV. vom 1. August 1917 und die Mittelmächte: Diplomatische Aktenstücke des deutschen Auswärtigen Amtes . . . aus den Jahren 1915–1922* (Wiesbaden, 1970). The many Lives include those by F. Vistalli (Rome, 1928), G. Migliori (Milan, 1932), H. E. G. Rope (London, 1941), F. Hayward (Paris, 1955), and W. H. Peters (Milwaukee [1959]). [P. L. T.] G. Goyau, *Papauté et chrétienté sous Benoît XV* (1922); G. Rossini (ed.), *Benedetto XV, i cattolici e la prima guerra mondiale: Atti del Convegno di Studio tenuto a Spoleto nei giorni 7–8–9 settembre 1962* (1963). E. de Moreau, SJ, in *DHGE* 8

(1935), cols. 167–72, s.v. 'Benoît XV'; G. de Rosa in *Dizionario Biografico degli Italiani*, 8 (1966), pp. 408–17, s.v. 'Benedetto XV'; W. H. Peters in *NCE* 2 (1967), pp. 279 f., s.v.

Benedictine Order. St *Benedict of Nursia founded monasteries at *Subiaco and *Monte Cassino in central Italy, and he wrote a Rule (see BENEDICT, RULE OF ST), but he did not found an order. Although internal evidence suggests that he expected his Rule to be used in more than one monastery, it was only one among several rules which an individual monastery might adopt in determining its observance. In the 7th and 8th cents. it was increasingly widely followed in Gaul, in England (prob. largely through the influence of St *Wilfrid), and in Germany (through the missionary work of St *Boniface and other Anglo-Saxons), but there was no juridical link between the monasteries using it. Both *Charlemagne and *Louis the Pious wished to reform monasteries through promoting observance of the Rule of St Benedict, and Louis, assisted by St *Benedict of Aniane, in 816–17 issued legislation imposing on all monasteries within the Frankish domain a uniform observance based on the Rule (the 'capitulare monasticum') and instituting visitations to ensure that this was enforced. From this period there developed a consciousness among monks and nuns in the W. that they all belonged to the family, or Order, of St Benedict.

In the Middle Ages liturgical observance became more prolonged and more solemn, and manual work diminished in importance. Monasteries became large and wealthy institutions. Because individual monasteries were autonomous, i.e. with no superior above their own *abbot, one of the chief difficulties of medieval Benedictinism was reforming the abuses that inevitably crept into monastic observance. *Cluny (founded 909) was one of the main centres of reform; by the end of the 11th cent. well over a thousand monasteries had been either founded by, or affiliated to, Cluny, all of them obliged to follow the Cluniac observance. Several popes, esp. *Innocent III at the Fourth *Lateran Council (1215), attempted to promote reforms by establishing general chapters and visitations along the *Cistercian model. This method was relatively successful in England, but in many countries these efforts at reform were short-lived. Reform movements in N. Europe in the 15th cent. led to unions of independent monasteries, e.g. the Bursfeld Union in Germany (1446); in S. Europe there were some monastic *congregations founded in which the autonomy of the monasteries was virtually abolished, e.g. the Congregation of Santa Giustina in Italy (1419). In the 16th cent. the *Reformation put an end to monastic life in much of N. Europe and in England (see DISSOLUTION OF THE MONASTERIES), though English monasteries were later founded in Continental Europe and kept alive the English Benedictine tradition. The Council of *Trent in 1563 gave a renewed impetus to the institution of general chapters and visitations, and in the following years several new congregations were founded, notably the *Maurist Congregation in France (1621).

Reforms such as these from the 15th cent. onwards facilitated the growth of libraries and the development of biblical and patristic scholarship. The *Enlightenment, the French Revolution, and the *anticlerical legislation of the 19th cent. led to State interference in all Benedictine monasteries. The majority were suppressed; a few were able to survive. The mid-19th cent. witnessed a revival of Benedictine monasticism with the foundation of *Solesmes in France (1833), St Vincent, Pennsylvania, USA (1846), and *Beuron in Germany (1863), each of which became the centre of a new congregation. In 1893 *Leo XIII united all the Benedictine congregations of monks into the Benedictine Confederation, with an Abbot Primate resident at Rome; his intention was not to abolish the autonomy of monasteries but to promote co-operation. In recent years the smaller orders founded in the 11th–14th cents., which follow the Rule of St Benedict (*Vallombrosians, *Olivetans, *Camaldolese, *Sylvestrines), but not the *Cistercian Order, have joined the Benedictine Confederation.

Evidence of communities of nuns following the Rule of St Benedict goes back to at least the 7th cent. A number of Benedictine nuns, e.g. St *Hildegard of Bingen in the 12th cent. and St *Gertrude the Great and *Mechtild of Magdeburg in the 13th cent., illustrate the high degree of culture and spirituality that flourished among them. Many of the reform movements of the Middle Ages had counterparts among Benedictine nuns. In modern times most communities of nuns are autonomous, but subject to the supervision of the bishop; only since the mid-20th cent. have efforts been made to reduce the isolation of many communities. There are a few communities (esp. in England, Brazil, Belgium, and Germany) which are full members of a monastic congregation to which communities of monks also belong. The Council of Trent in 1563 imposed on all nuns a stricter enclosure (*clausura) than had previously been practised by many communities of Benedictine nuns. The 17th cent. saw the foundation of many new communities, esp. in France, including some communities of Englishwomen. Communities of Benedictine nuns, like those of monks, experienced decline and suppression, followed by revival, in the 18th and 19th cents.

There are also communities of Benedictine sisters, i.e. religious who are not nuns and have less strict rules of enclosure. Most are engaged in charitable work, e.g. education and care of the sick, and in missionary activity. The majority of these communities were founded in the 19th and 20th cents. They are most numerous in the USA, but there are increasing numbers in Africa and other parts of the Third World.

In the W. Church the Rule of St Benedict has been the norm of monastic piety, and it was Benedictines who preserved classical learning by their care and copying of MSS in the Dark Ages and by their teaching and civilizing influence (see MONASTICISM). In later generations Benedictines have been influential in fostering the ideals and practice of scholarship and have played an important part in the development of liturgical worship, esp. in the early days of the '*liturgical movement'.

In the 20th cent. Benedictine monasteries have been established in the Anglican Church (see RELIGIOUS ORDERS IN ANGLICANISM) and in the Lutheran Church of *Sweden.

There is an immense literature. The standard modern account is that of P. Schmitz, OSB, *Histoire de l'Ordre de Saint-Benoît* (7 vols., Maredsous, 1942–56). Useful introds. by [E.] C. Butler, OSB, *Benedictine Monachism* (1919; 2nd edn., 1924); H. van Zeller, OSB, *The Benedictine Idea* [1959]; and by T. Fry, OSB (ed.), *RB 1980: The Rule of St Benedict* (Collegeville, Minn. [1981]), pp. 113–51. More specialized works include Beiträge zur Geschichte des alten Mönchtums und des Benediktinerordens

(Hefte 1–22, ed. I. Herwegen, OSB; 1912–41; Hefte 23 ff., ed. S. Hilpisch, OSB, and E. v. Severus, OSB; 1959 ff.). S. Hilpisch, OSB, *Geschichte des Benediktinischen Mönchtums in ihren Grundzügen* (Freiburg, 1929); id., *Das Benediktinertum im Wandel der Zeiten* (St Ottilien, 1950). G. Penco, OSB, 'La Prima diffusione della Regola di S. Benedetto', in B. Steidle, OSB (ed.), *Commentationes in Regulam S. Benedicti* (Studia Anselmiana, 42; 1957), pp. 321–45; id., *Storia del Monachesimo in Italia dalle origini alla fine del Medio Evo* (Tempi e Figure, 2nd ser. 31 [1961]), *passim*. B. Collett, *Italian Benedictine Scholars and the Reformation: The Congregation of Santa Giustina of Padua* (Oxford Historical Monographs, 1985). The standard work on Benedictine nuns is by S. Hilpisch, OSB, *Geschichte der Benediktinerinnen* (St Ottilien, 1951; Eng. tr., Collegeville, Minn., 1958). On Benedictine life in England, W. *Dugdale, *Monasticon Anglicanum* (1655–73; new edn., 1817–30); [M.] D. *Knowles, OSB, *The Monastic Order in England: A History of its Development from the Times of St Dunstan to the Fourth Lateran Council, 943–1216* (Cambridge, 1940; 2nd edn., 1963, with bibl.); id., *The Religious Orders in England* (3 vols., ibid., 1948–59), *passim*; [M.] D. Knowles and R. N. Hadcock, *Medieval Religious Houses: England and Wales* (1953; rev. edn., 1971; catalogue, with maps). [M.] D. Knowles and J. K. S. St Joseph, *Monastic Sites from the Air* (Cambridge Air Surveys, no. 1, 1952). O. L. Kapsner, OSB, *A Benedictine Bibliography* (2nd edn., 2 vols., Collegeville, Minn., 1962, with suppl., 1982). A *Bulletin d'Histoire Bénédictine* has appeared in *R. Bén.* at intervals since 1895 and as a separate suppl. since 1912. Heimbucher, 1, pp. 154–314, and 2, pp. 650–5. P. Schmitz, OSB, in *DHGE* 7 (1934), cols. 1062–234; J. Leclercq, OSB, A. G. Biggs, and others in *NCE* 2 (1967), pp. 205–303; G. Lunardi, OSB, in *DIP* 1 (1974), cols. 1222–46, s.v. 'Benedettine, Monache', and cols. 1246–8, s.v. 'Benedettine, Suore'; P. Englebert, OSB, in *L.Th.K.* (3rd edn.), 2 (1994), cols. 211–18, s.v. 'Benediktiner'. See also works cited under BENEDICT, RULE OF ST, and MONASTICISM.

benedictio mensae. A liturgical form of grace developed in monastic circles from verses of the Psalms. Reference to it is found as early as *Cassian (*Inst. coenob.* 7. 12) and St *Benedict (*Regula* 43). Today the grace consists of a verse which varies acc. to the feasts, short prayers, and a blessing. After meals the prayers are preceded by a psalm and concluded by intercessions for benefactors and the dead, and the *Lord's Prayer.

benediction. See BLESSING.

Benediction of the Blessed Sacrament. A service in the W. Church culminating in the blessing of the people with the *Reserved Sacrament. A comparatively late form of worship, it developed from the fusion of the veneration of the Host exposed outside Mass, which dates from the 14th cent., with the custom of the confraternities and guilds singing the *Salve Regina* or other antiphons to the BVM on Saturday evenings. The *Exposition of the Blessed Sacrament concluded (as it normally still does) with the blessing of the people with the Host. The giving of such a blessing was in keeping with the medieval practice of ending popular devotions by blessing with a sacred object (e.g. a *crucifix or *relic) those who took part in them. The blessing or benediction with the Blessed Sacrament came to be regarded as the focal point of the service, and from about the 16th cent. it often followed a comparatively brief period of exposition, giving its name to the devotion which was the most common form of evening service in RC churches until the introduction of *Evening Masses after 1953. It is now forbidden to give such a blessing except at the end of a service including biblical readings and a reasonable period of exposition. For details of the service, see EXPOSITION OF THE BLESSED SACRAMENT. A comparable service came into use in parts of the Anglican Communion in the late 19th–early 20th cent., sometimes called 'Adoration' or 'Devotions'.

For current RC legislation on Benediction and Exposition, see bibl. to EXPOSITION. Series of arts. by H. Thurston, SJ, in *The Month*, 97 (1901), pp. 587–97; 98 (1901), pp. 58–69, 186–93, 264–76; and 106 (1905), pp. 394–404. Id., 'Benediction of the Blessed Sacrament', in *Report of the Nineteenth Eucharistic Congress, held at Westminster from 9th to 13th September 1908* (1909), pp. 452–64. N. Mitchell, OSB, *Cult and Controversy: The Worship of the Eucharist outside Mass* (Studies in the Reformed Rites of the Catholic Church, 4; New York, 1982), esp. pp. 181–5 and 322–31.

Benedictional. In the W. Church the liturgical book containing the formulae of the bishop's blessing formerly pronounced at Mass, esp. in Spain, France, and England, before the 'Pax Domini'. The oldest extant copy appears to date from the 7th cent.

Benedictus. The song of thanksgiving (Lk. 1: 68–79) uttered by *Zachariah at the birth of his son, St *John the Baptist. The hymn is addressed to God in thanksgiving for the fulfilment of the Messianic hopes, and to the child who is to be the Lord's forerunner. In the W. Church it is sung liturgically at *Lauds, whence it was taken over in the BCP, where it finds a place in Morning Prayer. In modern Anglican liturgies it often follows the First Lesson rather than the Second, as in the BCP. In the E. Church it is prescribed to be sung daily at the morning office (*Orthros), but in practice it is usually omitted, except in monasteries and in Lent.

P. Vielhauer, 'Das Benedictus des Zacharias', *Zeitschrift für Theologie und Kirche*, 49 (1952), pp. 253–72. See also comm. to LUKE, GOSPEL OF ST, cited s.v.

Benedictus qui venit. The Latin form of Mt. 21: 9: 'Blessed is he that cometh in the name of the Lord'. In most of the ancient liturgies, including the Roman *Mass, it is said or sung immediately after the *Sanctus, though in sung Masses at one time it followed the *Elevation in the Roman rite. It was included, in a slightly altered form, in the BCP of 1549, but dropped in the 1552 revision. It is allowed in the ASB and other modern Anglican rites.

It is first found in Gaul, viz. *Caesarius of Arles, *Serm.* 73. 4. Jungmann (1958 edn.), 2, pp. 170–3; Eng. tr., 2, pp. 136–8.

benefice. A term originally used for a grant of land for life as a reward (*beneficium*) for services. Under *canon law it came to imply an ecclesiastical office which prescribed certain duties or conditions ('spiritualities') for the due discharge of which it awarded certain revenues ('temporalities'). Parochial benefices in the C of E are of three kinds: rectories, vicarages, and (until 1968) perpetual curacies. In each case the duties of the incumbent include observance of the promises made at *Ordination, the showing of proper respect for his office, and due solicitude for the moral and spiritual welfare of his parishioners. The union of benefices is now governed by the Pastoral Measure 1983, and is effected by a pastoral scheme under that Measure. On a vacancy, the Patronage (Benefices) Measure 1986 regulates the way in which the registered patron is to consult with the bishop and two parish representatives before making a presentation. Once the *Institution or *Collation has taken place, the incumbent has a freehold of the benefice, subject to the fixed retirement age, and the possibility of removal under the *Ecclesiastical Jurisdiction Measure 1963 for misconduct or under the Incumbents (Vacation of Benefices) Measure 1977 for pastoral breakdown or mental or physical disability. See also ADVOWSON.

In the RC Church the Second *Vatican Council called for the abandonment or reform of the system of benefices. The 1983 *Codex Iuris Canonici (can. 1272) provides that where benefices in the strict sense still exist they are to be supervised by the local Conference of Bishops; gradually they are to be phased out in favour of other arrangements.

Benefit of Clergy. The exemption from trial by a secular court on being charged with a felony which was accorded to the clergy in the Middle Ages. It was granted to all who were tonsured as well as to nuns. In later times benefit of clergy was allowed on a first conviction for certain offences to all who could read, on the ground that ability to read was the accepted test of a cleric. The privilege was finally abolished in England by the Criminal Law Act 1827. It was last successfully claimed in South Carolina, USA, in *The State v. Bosse* [1855], 42 SC 276.

F. Pollock and F. W. *Maitland, *The History of English Law before the Time of Edward I*, 1 (Cambridge, 1895), pp. 424–40. L. C. Gabel, *Benefit of Clergy in England in the Later Middle Ages* (Smith College Studies in History, 14; Northampton, Mass., 1929). G. Crosse in *DECH* (3rd edn., 1948), p. 53, s.v.

Benet, St. An older English form of the name of St *Benedict.

Benet of Canfield (1562–1611), *Capuchin spiritual writer. William Fitch was born in Little Canfield, Essex, and educated at the Inns of Court. His reading of R. *Parsons, *The First Book of the Christian Exercise* (1582) prompted him to approach Robert Darbyshire, then in Newgate prison, who received him into the RC Church in August 1585. He left England the following year and entered the Capuchin Order in Paris in 1587. He was professed in 1588, completed his studies in Italy, and was ordained in 1591 or 1592. He returned to France and held various positions in Capuchin houses, becoming Definitor in Paris. He counselled his fellow Capuchins François de Tremblay ('Grey Eminence') and Ange de Joyeuse, acted as spiritual director to Mme *Acarie, and assisted in the reform of various religious houses (e.g. the *Benedictine nuns at Montmartre) and he helped Mme de Sainte-Beuve establish the *Ursulines in Paris. He returned to England in 1599 and was imprisoned in Wisbech Castle; he was released and went back to France in 1602 or 1603. During his captivity he wrote, in English, the first parts of *The Rule of Perfection*, as well as *Le Chevalier Chrétien* (pub., 1609). The first French version of the *Rule*, entitled *Exercise de la Volonté de Dieu*, began to circulate in MS from 1593. He revised the text at different times. The three parts of *La Règle de Perfection* (1610) cover the three forms of God's will: the exterior, the interior, and the essential. At first God's will is sought actively in the circumstances of life; then follow the manifestations of God's will through inspiration and illumination to the passive soul. In the third and difficult part the soul contemplates God's

will directly without the help of the intellect or images; this entails the annihilation of the self before God. The third part also contains several, perhaps intercalated, chapters on Christ's Passion. The *Rule* shows the influence of the *Cloud of Unknowing*, W. *Hilton's *Scala Perfectionis*, St *Bonaventura's *Itinerarium Mentis in Deum*, the Flemish spiritual writers, as well as *Dionysius, the Pseudo-Areopagite. H. *Bremond considered Benet 'the Master of Masters' in his spirituality.

The 1st and 2nd pts. of the *Rule* in Eng. were pub., Rouen, 1608; in Fr., Paris, '1609' [1608]. All 3 pts. of the Fr., ibid., 1610. It is unlikely that Benet himself produced an Eng. edn. of the 3rd pt. but a version of part of it by Augustine *Baker, OSB, underlines the adaptation by G. Randall, *A Bright Starre leading to and centering in Christ our perfection* (London, 1646). Crit. edn. of Eng. and Fr. texts by J. Orcibal (Bibliothèque de l'École des Hautes Études, Section des Sciences Religieuses, 83 [1982]). Life by J. Brousse, *La Vie du Révérend Père P. Ange de Joyeuse . . .* (Paris, 1621), pp. 429–668; Eng. tr. (Douai, 1623), ed. T. A. Birrell, *The Lives of Ange de Joyeuse and Benet of Canfield* (1959), pp. 87–175. Optat de Veghel, OFM Cap., *Benoît de Canfield (1562–1610): Sa vie, sa doctrine et son influence* (Bibliotheca Seraphico-Capuccina, Sectio Historica, 11; Rome, 1949). P. Renaudin, *Un Maître de la mystique française, Benoît de Canfield* [1956]. E. Gullick, 'The Life of Father Benet of Canfield', *Collectanea Franciscana*, 42 (1972), pp. 39–67, id., 'Benet of Canfield. The Rule of Perfection: the active and contemplative life', *Laurentianum*, 13 (1972), pp. 401–36. P. Mommaers, 'Benoît de Canfield et ses sources flamandes', *Revue d'Histoire de la Spiritualité*, 48 (1972), pp. 401–34; 49 (1973), pp. 37–66; K. Emery, ' "All and Nothing": Benet of Canfield's *Règle de perfection*', *Downside Review*, 92 (1974), pp. 46–61. Cuthbert [Hess], OSFC, *The Capuchins* (2 vols., 1928), esp. 2, pp. 421–4. Bremond, 2 (1916), pp. 135–68.

Bengel, Johannes Albrecht (1687–1752), *Lutheran NT scholar. He entered the Lutheran ministry in 1707, and in 1713 became professor at the seminary of Denkendorf. In 1741 he was made *General Superintendent at Herbrechtingen, and in 1749 at Alpirspach. He did some work on classical and patristic literature, but his chief importance is as a textual critic and expositor of the NT. His text and *critical apparatus (1734) mark the beginning of modern scientific work in that field. Hardly less celebrated was his penetrating and pithy exegesis of the NT, published in his *Gnomon Novi Testamenti* (1742; revised Eng. tr., 1857–8). It was much used and admired by J. *Wesley, and remains a classic.

Correspondence ed. J. C. F. Burk (great-grandson; Stuttgart, 1836). Life, also by Burk (ibid., 1831; Eng. tr., 1837). G. Mälzer, *Johann Albrecht Bengel: Leben und Werk* (Stuttgart [1970]), and other works of this author. Further studies by O. Wächter (ibid., 1865) and K. Hermann (ibid., 1937). M. Brecht in *TRE* 5 (1980), pp. 583–9, s.v.

Bennett, William James Early (1804–86), Anglican *High Churchman. An upholder of *Tractarian principles, he became in 1840 priest-in-charge of St Paul's, Knightsbridge, and in this capacity built St Barnabas's, Pimlico (opened 1850), where he introduced what was then regarded as very advanced ceremonial. This provoked fierce opposition and mob rioting; and C. J. *Blomfield, Bp. of London, despite a certain sympathy with Bennett, became alarmed, and induced him to resign. He was instituted, however, to the vicarage of Frome Selwood, in Somerset, in 1852. In 1867 a public letter to E. B. *Pusey

(*A Plea for Toleration in the Church of England*), in which he dealt with the *Real Presence in the *Eucharist, led to a series of legal actions which were significant as showing the inadequacy of the existing courts to deal with matters of doctrine. The legitimacy of his Eucharistic teaching, however, was allowed. *The Old Church Porch*, which he began at Frome in 1854 (pub. in London), is claimed as the first parish magazine. He published many controversial and other writings.

Life by F. Bennett (London, 1909). W. P. Courtney in *DNB*, suppl. 1 (1901), pp. 169–71.

ben Sira (i.e. 'the son of Sira'). Jesus ben Sira, the author of *Ecclesiasticus (q.v.). 'Sirach' is the Greek form, the termination 'ch' indicating that the word was indeclinable.

Benson, Edward White (1829–96), Abp. of *Canterbury. Educated at King Edward's School, Birmingham (where he made a lifelong friendship with his fellow-pupil, J. B. *Lightfoot), and Trinity College, Cambridge, he became at first an assistant master at Rugby (1852), and then Master of the newly-founded school at Wellington (1859). In 1872 Bp. C. *Wordsworth appointed him Chancellor of *Lincoln, where he was responsible for the foundation of the Theological College (1874). In 1877 he went as its first bishop to *Truro; his vigorous and forceful character was particularly well suited to the needs of the new diocese. In 1883 he succeeded Abp. A. C. *Tait at Canterbury, where he was intensely zealous and active in the Church's interests, but intolerant of opposition and criticism. A strong Tory, he vigorously upheld the Establishment; yet he remained a friend of W. E. *Gladstone, to whom he owed his appointment, and it was while on a visit to him that he died in Hawarden church. Convinced that the influence of the laity should be given institutional recognition, he encouraged the establishment of the House of Laymen, with consultative status, in 1886. In 1887 he reconstituted the Bishopric in *Jerusalem (q.v.). To deal with the ritual charges brought against E. *King, Bp. of *Lincoln, he revived the 'court of the Abp. of Canterbury', which based its decisions on the rubrics of the BCP and traditional practice in the C of E (see also LINCOLN JUDGEMENT). His great devotion to St *Cyprian bore fruit in *Cyprian, his Life, his Times, his Work* (1897), published a few months after his death.

Index to his Letters and Papers in Lambeth Palace Library, by M. Stewart and others (1980). His Life (2 vols., London, 1899–1900) by his son, A. C. Benson. Id., *The Trefoil: Wellington College, Lincoln, and Truro* (1923). D. Williams, *Genesis and Exodus: A Portrait of the Benson Family* (1979), esp. pp. 1–107. P. [B.] Hinchliff, *God and History: Aspects of British Theology 1875–1914* (Oxford, 1992), pp. 73–98. A. J. Mason in *DNB*, suppl. 1 (1901), pp. 171–9.

Benson, Richard Meux (1824–1915), founder of the *Society of St John the Evangelist (SSJE). Educated at *Christ Church, Oxford, of which he was a Student from 1846 to 1915, he was ordained in 1848 and in 1850 appointed Vicar of Cowley, then a village, some two miles from *Oxford, where he lived a studious, devoted life. In 1859 he was on the point of going to India on missionary work when Bp. S. *Wilberforce induced him to remain to take charge of the new suburb developing at the Oxford

end of his parish. A sermon preached by J. *Keble inspired him to found the SSJE in 1865. In 1890 he resigned his superiorship of the Society. His religious writings, mostly based on his sermons, reveal his penetrating originality and deeply spiritual mind.

'Letters' ed. G. Congreve, SSJE, and W. H. Longridge, SSJE (Oxford, 1916), 'Further Letters' ed. by idd. (1920). M. V. Woodgate, *Father Benson: Founder of the Cowley Fathers* (1953); M. L. Smith, SSJE (ed.), *Benson of Cowley* (Oxford, 1980). S. L. Ollard in *DNB, 1912–1921*, pp. 38 f.

Benson, Robert Hugh (1871–1914), RC apologist. The youngest son of E. W. *Benson, Abp. of Canterbury, he was educated at Eton and Trinity College, Cambridge. In 1894 Benson was ordained, then served in the Eton mission at Hackney Wick and elsewhere, and in 1898 went to the *Community of the Resurrection at Mirfield, where he was professed in 1901. In 1903 he was received into the RC Church. After (re-)ordination in 1904, he devoted most of the remainder of his life to preaching and literary work, residing, from 1908, at Buntingford. His novels, remarkable for their vivid characterization and fervent creed, include *The Light Invisible* (1903), *By What Authority?* (1904), *The Sentimentalists* (1906), *The Lord of the World* (1907), and *None other Gods* (1910). His published sermons include *Christ in the Church* (1911) and *The Friendship of Christ* (1912).

There is much autobiog. material in his *Confessions of a Convert* (1913). *Spiritual Letters*, with preface by A. C. Benson (brother; London, 1917). Life by C. C. Martindale, SJ (2 vols., ibid., 1916). Short Memoir by A. C. Benson (ibid., 1915). A. Wilkinson, *The Community of the Resurrection* (1992), pp. 82–7. C. C. Martindale, SJ, in *DNB, 1912–1921*, pp. 39–41.

Bentley, Richard (1662–1742), English classical scholar. He entered St John's College, Cambridge, at the early age of 14. After a year as headmaster of Spalding Grammar School, he became tutor to the son of E. *Stillingfleet. In his *Boyle Lectures (1692) on the *Evidences of Natural and Revealed Religion*, as in his attack (1713) on the freethinker A. *Collins, he appeared in the role of an able apologist for Christianity. But it was as a classical scholar that he made his real mark. Before his 24th year he had started a Hexapla dictionary and in 1691 he issued a Latin letter to John *Mills as an appendix to an edition of the 'Chronicle' of *John Malalas. His brilliant restoration in this appendix of many passages where the text was corrupt revealed his great powers as a critic to the few capable to judge. In 1699 his attack on Charles Boyle in his *Dissertation on the Epistles of Phalaris* was a still more remarkable performance. During the coming years an astonishing array of works, among them his notorious re-editing of J. *Milton's *Paradise Lost*, came from Bentley's pen. Nearly all the time, too, Bentley, who had been admitted Master of Trinity College, Cambridge, in 1700, was engaged in a bitter feud, largely provoked by his high-handed methods and reforms, with the Fellows of the College. They tried repeatedly, and almost successfully, to get their Master deposed from office, but he held it till his death.

Works, ed. A. Dyce (3 vols., 1836–8); J. H. Monk, *Life of Bentley* (2 vols., 1833); R. C. Jebb, *Life of Bentley* (1882); E. Hedicke, *Studia Bentleiana* (1902); R. J. White, *Dr. Bentley: A Study in Academic Scarlet* (1965). C. O. Brink, *English Classical Scholar-*

ship (Cambridge, 1986), pp. 21–83 and notes pp. 201–9. A. T. Bartholomew and J. W. Clark, *Bibliography of Richard Bentley* (1908).

Berakah (Heb. בְּרָכָה, 'blessing'). The characteristic Jewish prayer, which takes the form of a blessing or thanksgiving to God. Hence the name 'Berakoth' (the plural form of the word) is applied to the tractates of the *Talmud which contain directions about prayer, both public and private. The OT provides many examples of this type of prayer (e.g. Gen. 24: 27, Job 1: 21, Ps. 28: 6), which was carried over into Christian usage (2 Cor. 1: 3, 1 Pet. 1: 3), and there are parallelisms in ideas and phraseology between early Christian prayers and Jewish berakoth (cf. 1 Clem. 59 and the second of the *Eighteen Benedictions). It has been suggested that the use of 'Eucharist' (Gk. εὐχαριστία, one of the two translations of Heb. *berakah*), for the central Christian rite arose from the fact that the Eucharistic prayer was a Christian adaptation of the Jewish berakah which was recited over a cup of wine.

Berdyaev, Nicolas (1874–1948), Russian *existentialist religious philosopher. His works portray a philosophical evolution from Marxism to Idealism, and thence to Orthodox or would-be Orthodox mysticism; they are imbued with prophetic, apocalyptic presentiments and a keen sense of the transcendent meaning of history. From 1922 onwards Berdyaev lived as an émigré in Berlin and, mainly, in Paris. His seminal work, written before the Revolution in Russia, is *The Meaning of the Christian Act* (pub. in Russian in 1916; Eng. tr., 1955); it is an apologia of man as co-creator with God. His main post-revolutionary work begins with *Freedom and the Spirit* (Russian, 1927; Eng. tr., 1935), his most theological book, in which he sets out for the first time his version of religious existentialist or personalist philosophy. His next major work was *The Destiny of Man* (Russian, 1931; Eng. tr., 1937), which develops a theory of ethics, going, as he maintained, beyond the 'ethics of law' and the 'ethics of redemption'. Highly sensitive to the moods of his time, he believed that the 'contradictions of modern history' portend a new era of 'divine–human creation'. This belief is expressed in a number of smaller books, such as *The End of our Time* (Russian, 1924; Eng. tr., 1933), *The Bourgeois Mind and Other Essays* (Eng. tr. from various sources, 1934), *The Fate of Man in the Modern World* (Russian, 1934; Eng. tr., 1935), *Slavery and Freedom* (Russian, 1939; Eng. tr., 1943), and *The Origins of Russian Communism* (Eng. tr., 1937; Russian not pub. until 1955); in these works his critical, nonconformist allegiance to Orthodoxy is combined with moral and social radicalism and, in contrast to most of his fellow émigrés, an eventual acceptance of post-revolutionary Russia. His two outstanding late works are *The Beginning and the End* (Russian, 1947; Eng. tr., 1952), a restatement of specifically philosophical and metaphysical problems; and *Dream and Reality* (posthumously pub., Russian, 1949; Eng. tr., 1950), a largely non-factual, intellectual autobiography, a critical self-assessment, and a summing up of his outlook.

Studies by M. Spinka (Philadelphia [1950]), O. Fielding Clarke (London, 1950), E. Porret (Neuchâtel and Paris, 1951), M. A. Villon (London, 1961), J.-L. Segundo (Paris [1963]),

M.-M. Davy (Paris, 1964; Eng. tr., 1967), F. Nucho (London, 1967), D. B. Richardson (in Eng.; The Hague, 1968), and V. A. Kuvakin (Moscow, 1980). P. Klein, *Die 'kreative Freiheit' nach Nikolaj Berdjajew* (Studien zur Geschichte der katholischen Moraltheologie, 21; 1976); P. C. Murdoch, *Der Sakramentalphilosophische Aspekt im Denken Nikolaj Aleksandrovitsch Berdjaevs* (Oikonomia. Quellen und Studien zur orthodoxen Theologie, 14; Erlangen, 1981).

Bereans, also known as **Barclayans** or **Barclayites.** A religious sect founded at Edinburgh in 1773 by J. *Barclay (q.v.). The name was derived from the characteristics of the Bereans mentioned in Acts 17: 10 f. Barclay taught a modified form of *Calvinism, stressing at once its supernatural and mystical aspects. Natural theology he held to be impossible, since every attempt to prove the existence of God rests on a *petitio principii*. The sole fount of truth is Holy Scripture, which speaks throughout of Christ. The Christian, who is enabled to understand it by faith illuminated by the Holy Spirit, will find, e.g., that every single verse in the Psalms points forward to Christ or His Church. The act of faith implanted in the believer conveys assurance of salvation to him. It is thus the highest gift of God to man, and the 'blasphemy against the Holy Ghost' mentioned in the Gospels is unbelief. Any idea of a covenant-renewal at the Lord's Supper was repudiated as leading to the Romish doctrine of the Mass.

Barclay's doctrines won for a time an enthusiastic reception in a few widely scattered congregations in Scotland. Berean communities were also established in London and Bristol. After Barclay's death (1798), however, they soon melted away, and were for the most part merged in the *Congregationalists.

A. Miller in *HERE* 2 (1909), pp. 519–23, s.v.

Berengar of Tours (*c*.1010–88), pre-scholastic theologian. Berengar's family was associated with St Martin's, Tours, and by 1030 he was a canon there. After studying at *Chartres, *c*.1028, when *Fulbert was bishop, he took service with Geoffrey Martel, Count of Anjou (1040–60). By 1040 he was archdeacon and by 1047 treasurer of Angers cathedral. By 1053 he had ceased to be treasurer, but he remained archdeacon until 1060. The new Count (Geoffrey the Bearded) was hostile, and Berengar returned to St Martin's where he appears as 'master of the schools' from *c*.1070. Some time after 1080 he retired to the island hermitage of St Côme, three miles west of Tours, where he died.

Berengar was much criticized for his teaching on the *Eucharist. His case was discussed twice by *Leo IX in 1050, and again at a legatine synod at Tours in 1054; by Nicholas II in 1059; and at last definitively by *Gregory VII in 1078–9. Tractates were written against him in all parts of Europe, but esp. in Normandy. They include: John of Fécamp, *Confessio Fidei*, 4 (J. P. Migne, *PL* 101. 1085–91); *Durandus of Troarn, *De Corpore et Sanguine Christi* (ibid. 149. 1375–424); *Lanfranc of Bec, *De Corpore et Sanguine Domini* (ibid. 150. 407–42); and Guitmund of La Croix-St-Leufroy, *De Corporis et Sanguinis Domini Veritate* (ibid. 149. 1427–94). Berengar's surviving theological work consists almost entirely of his reply to Lanfranc, traditionally known as the *De Sacra Coena* and now (more correctly) as *Rescriptum contra Lanfrannum*. Here he maintains the fact of the Real Presence, but denies that any material change in the elements is needed to explain it.

Berengar's position was never diametrically opposed to that of his critics, and he was prob. never excommunicated. But the controversy that he aroused forced men to reconsider the Carolingian discussion of the Eucharist, as *Paschasius had left it, and to clarify the doctrine of *transubstantiation. Further, when both Berengar and his critics used the secular disciplines of logic and grammar to express a matter of Christian doctrine, the way was open to the *scholasticism of the 12th cent.

The text of Berengar's *Rescriptum* was discovered by G. E. *Lessing and ed. by A. F. and F. T. Vischer (Berlin, 1834). Crit. edn. by R. B. C. Huygens, with facsimile and paleographical introd. by W. Milde (CCSM 84 and 84A; 1988). Letters ed. C. Erdmann in id. and N. Fickermann (eds.), *Briefsammlung der Zeit Heinriches IV.* (*MGH*, Die deutschen Geschichtsquellen des Mittelalters 500–1500, 5; 1950), pp. 132–72. M. Matronola, OSB, (ed.), *Un testo inedito di Berengario di Tours e il Concilio Romano del 1079* (Orbis Romanus, 6; 1936). A. J. Macdonald, *Berengar and the Reform of Sacramental Doctrine* (1930). O. Capitani, *Studi su Berengario di Tours* (Lecce [1966]). J. de Montclos, *Lanfranc et Bérenger: La controverse eucharistique du XIᵉ siècle* (SSL, 37; 1971), esp. pp. 3–245. P. Ganz and others (eds.), *Auctoritas und Ratio: Studien zu Berengar von Tours* (Wolfenbüttler Mittelalter-Studien, 2; Wiesbaden, 1990). H. Chadwick, 'Ego Berengarius', *JTS* NS 40 (1989), pp. 414–45. D. *Stone, *A History of the Doctrine of the Eucharist*, 1 (1909), pp. 244–59; G. Macy, *The Theologies of the Eucharist in the Early Scholastic Period* (Oxford, 1984), esp. pp. 35–53. M. Cappuyns in *DHGE* 8 (1935), cols. 385–407, s.v., with detailed bibl.

Bereshith (Heb. בְּרֵאשִׁית, 'in the beginning'). The first word of the Hebrew text of *Genesis and hence the Hebrew name for the Book.

Berggrav, Eivind (1884–1959), Bp. of Oslo. Born at Stavanger, the son of a bishop and Minister for Church and Education in the Norwegian Government, he studied at Oslo, Oxford, Cambridge, Marburg, and Lund. In 1909 he was made editor of the monthly journal *Kirke og Kultur*, and began ten years' work as a teacher. In 1919 he became pastor at Hurdalen, in 1925 prison chaplain in Oslo, and in 1929 Bp. of Hålogaland in the extreme north of Norway. In 1937 he returned to Oslo as Primate of the Norwegian Church. In earlier years he had been influenced by N. *Söderblom, Abp. of Uppsala, and at Oslo he rapidly won leadership in the *Ecumenical Movement, being elected President of the World Alliance for Promoting International Friendship through the Churches in 1938 and calling a conference of Scandinavian Church leaders on the outbreak of war in 1939. After the occupation of Norway by the Nazis (9 Apr. 1940) Berggrav took an active part in organizing resistance to the Quisling Government. With six other Norwegian bishops he resigned (24 Feb. 1941) 'what the state has committed to my charge', at the same time declaring that 'the spiritual calling which has been ordained to me at the altar of God remains mine by God and by right'. Arrested on 9 Apr., he remained a solitary prisoner in a log cabin on the outskirts of Oslo until the defeat of Hitler (1945). After the war he took an active part in the foundation of the *World Council of Churches and its work. He retired from his see in 1950. His writings include *With God in the Darkness*

(1943), an account in English of the Norwegian Church Conflict.

Study by A. Johnson (Oslo, 1959; Eng. tr., Minneapolis, 1960).

Bergson, Henri (1859–1941), French philosopher. He was born at Paris, of Jewish descent, and studied at the École Normale Supérieure, where he fell under the spell of the activist doctrines of L. *Ollé-Laprune (1839–98) and É. Boutroux (1845–1921) and in 1889 submitted for his doctorate his celebrated *Essai* (see below). In 1900 he accepted a professorship at the Collège de France, remaining there until his retirement in 1924. His intellectual brilliance and daring gained him the hearing of large audiences in many countries. In 1914 he was honoured with election to the French Academy and in 1928 with the Nobel Prize.

Believing that the way to reality was by intuition, Bergson aimed at a radical criticism of all forms of intellectualism. He held that in real life the function of the intellect is subordinate; and that in man it is intuition which accomplishes those purposes which in the lower animals are carried out by instinct. All intellectualist conceptions of reality rest on spatial patterns akin to the diagrams and clock-time of the physicist, which distort the truth and must be abandoned for a new view of time (*durée*). Reality is evolutionary and progressive. Hence the traditional philosophic systems, which in the end can never escape a static and pantheistic determinism, must give way to a new philosophy of creativity and free will in which 'the gates of the future lie ever open'. At the root of moral action lies a 'life-force' (*élan vital*), which is an impulse found at its fullest development in heroes and prophets. Bergson's doctrines thus had close affinities with the thought of W. *James and the *Pragmatists generally.

Bergson's chief works were *Essai sur les données immédiates de la conscience* (1889; Eng. tr., *Time and Free Will*, 1910); *Matière et mémoire* (1896; Eng. tr., 1911); *L' Évolution créatrice* (1907; Eng. tr., 1911); *Les Deux Sources de la morale et de la religion* (1932; Eng. tr., 1935). His influence extended far beyond professed philosophers. His ideas, in whole or in part, were welcomed by many religious thinkers (notably the RC *Modernists) who were dissatisfied with the dominating position which traditional theology assigns to the human intellect.

Œuvres complètes d'Henri Bergson (7 vols., Geneva, 1945–6); his main *Œuvres* also ed. by A. Robinet (1959); *Écrits et Paroles*, ed. R.-M. Mossé Bastide (3 vols., 1957–9); and *Mélanges*, ed. A. Robinet and others (1972). Sympathetic interpretation by a disciple in H. W. Carr, *Henri Bergson: The Philosophy of Change* (1912) and id., *The Philosophy of Change* (1914). E. Le Roy, *Une Philosophie nouvelle: Henri Bergson* (1912; Eng. tr., 1913); J. *Maritain, *La Philosophie bergsonienne: Études critiques* (1914; Eng. tr., with additional material from *Ransoming the Time*, as *Bergsonian Philosophy and Thomism*, New York [1955]); A. Thibaudet, *Le Bergsonisme* (2 vols., 4th edn., 1923); J. Chevalier, *Bergson* (1926); R. Jolivet, *Essai sur le bergsonisme* (1931); A. Béguin and P. Thévenez (eds.), *Henri Bergson: Essais et témoignages* (Neuchâtel, 1943); L. Adolphe, *La Philosophie religieuse de Bergson* (1946); id., *La Dialectique des images chez Bergson* (1951); id., *L'Univers bergsonien* [1955]; J. Chevalier, *Entretiens avec Bergson* [1959]; V. Jankélévitch, *Henri Bergson* (Paris, 1959); T. Hanna (ed.), *The Bergsonian Heritage* (1962); M. Barthélemy-Madaule, *Bergson et Teilhard de Chardin* [1963]; id., *Bergson adversaire de Kant* (Bibliothèque de Philosophie Contemporaine, 1966); A. R. Lacey,

Bergson (The Arguments of the Philosophers, 1989); P. Soulez, *Bergson politique* [1989]; M. Cariou, *Lectures bergsoniennes* [1990], and other works of this author. Good introd. by L. Kolakowski, *Bergson* (Past Masters, Oxford, 1985). P. A. Y. Gunter, *Henri Bergson: A Bibliography* (Bowling Green, Oh. [1974]).

Berkeley, George (1685–1753), philosopher and divine. He was educated at Trinity College, Dublin, of which he became Fellow in 1707. After some time spent in travelling abroad, he was appointed Dean of Derry in 1724. From 1728 to 1732 he was in America, attempting to found a missionary college in Bermuda, but the refusal of the home government to support his plan led him to abandon it. In 1734 he was made Bp. of Cloyne, a position he held until his death in Oxford, where he spent the last five months of his life. His most important philosophical works, all of them the works of his youth, were *A New Theory of Vision* (1709), *Principles of Human Knowledge* (1710), and *Hylas and Philonous* (1713).

Berkeley is celebrated for his metaphysical doctrine, which was a form of Subjective Idealism. He held that, when we affirm material things to be real, we mean no more than that they are perceived (*esse est percipi*). Material objects, on Berkeley's view, continue to exist when not perceived by us solely because they are objects of the thought of God. The only things that exist in a primary sense are spirits, and material objects exist simply in the sense that they are perceived by spirits.

Berkeley was a philosopher rather than a theologian, but in a small work called *A Discourse on Passive Obedience* (1712) he upheld an ethical utilitarianism of a theological rather than a philosophical kind. He also wrote various short treatises on practical matters of the day.

Crit. edn. of his works by A. A. Luce and T. E. Jessop ('Bibliotheca Britannica Philosophica', 9 vols., 1948–57). Also useful is the edn. by A. C. *Fraser (4 vols., Oxford, 1871; rev. reissue, 1901). Life by A. A. Luce (London, 1949). Other studies by G. A. Johnston (London, 1923), J. M. Hone and M. M. Rossi (ibid., 1931), G. D. *Hicks (ibid., 1932), J. Wild (Cambridge, Mass., 1936), G. J. Warnock (Harmondsworth, 1953; reissued with additions, Oxford, 1982), I. C. Tipton (London, 1974), G. Pitcher (ibid., 1977), K. P. Winkler (Oxford, 1989), and D. Berman (ibid., 1994). A. A. Luce, *Berkeley and Malebranche* (1934); id., *Berkeley's Immaterialism* (1945); id., *The Dialectic of Immaterialism: An Account of the Making of Berkeley's* Principles (1963); E. A. Sillem, *George Berkeley and the Proofs for the Existence of God* (1957); A. D. Ritchie, *George Berkeley: A Reappraisal*, ed. G. E. Davie (Manchester, 1967). W. E. Steinkraus (ed.), *New Studies in Berkeley's Philosophy* (New York and London, 1966); J. Foster and H. Robinson (eds.), *Essays on George Berkeley: A Tercentennial Celebration* (Oxford, 1985). T. E. Jessop, *A Bibliography of George Berkeley* (1934; 2nd edn., The Hague, 1973).

Bernadette, St (1844–79), peasant girl of *Lourdes. She was the daughter of François Soubirous, a miller, and the eldest child of a family of six. She was baptized as 'Marie Bernarde', but became affectionately known to her family and neighbours as 'Bernadette'. After a childhood lived in a context of poverty, at the age of 14 she received 18 *apparitions of the BVM at the Massabielle Rock, near Lourdes. The first was on 11 Feb. 1858 and the last on 16 July of the same year. The Virgin, who manifested herself as the 'Immaculate Conception', revealed her presence by supernatural occurrences (esp. a miraculous spring of water) and commands (the building of a church). After a

period in which Bernadette suffered much from constant questionings and publicity, she joined the Sisters of Notre-Dame at Nevers, where she lived for the rest of her life. She was beatified by *Pius XI in 1925 and canonized in 1933. Feast day in France, 18 Feb. (not in the universal calendar). Her feast has also been observed on 16 Apr.

The principal collection of primary docs. is ed. by R. Laurentin, B. Billet, OSB, and P. Galland, *Lourdes: Documents authentiques* (7 vols. [1957–66]; to 1866); R. Laurentin and M.-T. Bourgeade, *Logia de Bernadette: Étude critique de ses paroles de 1866 à 1879* (3 vols., 1971). Smaller collection by L. [J. M.] Cros, SJ, and P. M. Olphe-Galliard, SJ, *Lourdes 1858* [1957]. *Les Écrits de Sainte Bernadette et sa voie spirituelle*, ed. A. Ravier, SJ (1961). H. Petitot, *Histoire exacte des apparitions de N.-D. de Lourdes à Bernadette* [1935]; id., *Histoire exacte de la vie intérieure et religieuse de Ste Bernadette* [1935]. The many popular Lives include those of E. Guynot (Paris [1937]), F. Trochu (ibid., 1954; Eng. tr., 1957), M. Trouncer (London, 1958), R. Laurentin (Paris, 1978; Eng. tr., 1979), and A. Ravier, SJ (Freiburg i. B., 1979; Eng. tr., 1979). See also bibl. TO LOURDES.

Bernard, St (1090–1153), Abbot of *Clairvaux. Born of noble parents at Fontaines near Dijon, in 1112 he entered the recently-founded monastery of *Cîteaux, together with 30 other young noblemen of Burgundy, including his own brothers. When three years later he was asked by the abbot, St *Stephen Harding, to choose a place for a new monastery, he established a house at Clairvaux, which soon became one of the chief centres of the *Cistercian Order. As Abbot of Clairvaux, Bernard came to exercise immense influence in ecclesiastical and political affairs. In 1129 he acted as secretary to the Synod of Troyes and there obtained recognition for the Rule of the new order of Knights *Templar, which he is said himself to have drawn up. In the disputed election which followed the death of Pope Honorius II in 1130, Bernard sided with Innocent II against the antipope, Anacletus, and was eventually successful in securing Innocent's victory. As a reward, the Pope showered privileges on the Cistercian Order. Bernard's relations with the Papacy became more intimate still with the election of a Cistercian monk and former pupil as Pope *Eugenius III in 1145. During the next few years Bernard attacked the heretical teaching of *Henry of Lausanne in Languedoc, and he preached the Second *Crusade. When the Crusade failed, Bernard blamed the crusaders for their lack of faith.

Bernard's best-known work is the unfinished series of sermons on the Song of Songs ('Sermones super Cantica Canticorum'). In it he ranges from the practical life of the monk to the mystical confrontation between the bridegroom and bride of the Canticle; by use of *allegory he interprets the bridegroom as Christ and the bride sometimes as the Church, sometimes as himself. The 'Sermones per annum' are sermons for liturgical feast days; some of these, as well as the sermons 'In laudibus virginis matris', convey his deep-felt devotion to the BVM, though its influence on the Marian cult has been exaggerated. His treatises single out particular themes of the ascetic life: humility in the 'De gradibus humilitatis et superbiae', love in the 'De diligendo Deo', in which he insists that God should be loved simply and purely because He is God. The longest treatise, 'De consideratione', is addressed to Pope Eugenius III; as well as a portrait of the ideal pope, it gives an elaborate account of the knowledge of God. The large body of his letters show his concern with political and moral matters, such as the abuse of feudal lordship. They also did much to prepare, and then secure, the condemnation of Peter *Abelard at the Council of *Sens (1140). In his denunciation of the luxury of the *Cluniac way of life and his attacks on Abelard and on *Gilbert de la Porrée in 1148, he gave less attention to his opponents' motives than to defending the ascetic ideal, as defined by tradition. He was above all else a monk. Nevertheless, for all his stubborn effort to limit the use of reason in theology, his language attains a formal beauty (itself an expression of the ritual order of the monastery) and a richness of imagery which associate him with the 12th-cent. rebirth of letters. In his opposition to the persecution of the Jews, he stood apart from most of his contemporaries. While the attribution to him of the poem '*Jesu, dulcis memoria' is almost certainly erroneous, the devotion it expresses is reflected in his genuine work. His writings were widely read in his own time and later, by monks and laymen alike, and after the Reformation by both Protestants and Catholics. He was canonized in 1174, and created a '*Doctor of the Church' in 1830. Feast day, 20 Aug.

Editio princeps of his works by A. Brocard (Paris, 1508). The classic edn. is 2nd edn. of that by J. *Mabillon, OSB (2 vols., Paris, 1690 [1st edn., 6 vols. in 9, 1667]), repr., with additions, in J. P. Migne, *PL* 182–5. Modern edn. by J. Leclercq, OSB, C. H. Talbot, and H. M. Rochais, OSB (8 vols., Rome, 1957–77). Eng. tr. of Mabillon's edn., with additional notes by S. J. Eales (Catholic Standard Library, 4 vols., 1889–96); Eng. tr. based on edn. of Leclercq, etc. (Cistercian Fathers Series, 1, 4, 7, 10, 13, 18, 19, 20, 25, 31, 37, 40, 53, etc.; 1970 ff.). Eng. tr. of his letters by B. S. James (London, 1953). J. Leclercq, OSB, *Études sur Saint Bernard et le texte de ses écrits* (Analecta Sacri Ordinis Cisterciensis, 9, fascs. 1–2; Rome, 1953); id., *Recueil d'études sur Saint Bernard et ses écrits* (Storia e Letteratura, 92, 104, 114, 167, and 182; Rome, 1962–92). The chief sources for the biog. of the saint are some contemporary Lives, pr. in J. Mabillon (also *PL* 185), esp. the 'Vita Prima' (ibid., cols. 225–454) and the 'Vita Secunda' (cols. 469–524). Eng. tr. of 'Vita Prima' by G. Webb and A. Walker (1960). A. H. Bredero, 'Études sur la "Vita Prima" de Saint Bernard', *Analecta Sacri Ordinis Cisterciensis*, 17 (1961), pp. 3–72, 215–60; 18 (1962), pp. 3–59. Classic modern Life by E. Vacandard (2 vols., Paris, 1895); also J. Leclercq, OSB, *Saint Bernard Mystique* [Bruges, 1948], and many other works of this author. E. *Gilson, *La Théologie mystique de Saint Bernard* (Études de philosophie médiévale, 20; 1934; Eng. tr., 1940). *Saint Bernard théologien: Actes du Congrès de Dijon 15–19 Septembre 1953* (Analecta Sacri Ordinis Cisterciensis, 9, fascs. 3–4; Rome, 1953). J. Leclercq, *Monks and Love in Twelfth-Century France: Psycho-Historical Essays* (Oxford, 1979), *passim*. G. R. Evans, *The Mind of St Bernard of Clairvaux* (Oxford, 1983). B. Jacqueline, *Papauté et Épiscopat selon Saint Bernard de Clairvaux* [1963]. A. H. Bredero, *Cluny et Cîteaux au douzième siècle: L'Histoire d'une controverse monastique* (Amsterdam and Maarssen, 1985). J. R. Sommerfeldt (ed.), *Bernardus Magister: Papers Presented at the Nonacentenary Celebration of the Birth of Saint Bernard of Clairvaux, Kalamazoo, Michigan . . . 10–13 May 1990* (Kalamazoo and Cîteaux, 1992). K. Elm (ed.), *Bernhard von Clairvaux: Rezeption und Wirkung im Mittelalter und in der Neuzeit* (Wolfenbütteler Mittelalter-Studien, 6; 1994). J. de la Croix Bouton, *Bibliographie Bernardine 1891–1957* (Commission d'histoire de l'Ordre de Cîteaux, 5 [1958]); E. Manning, *Bibliographie Bernardine 1957–1970* (Documentation Cistercienne, 6; Rochefort, 1972). E. Vacandard in *DTC* 2 (1905), cols. 746–85; J.-M. Canivez, O. Cist., in *DHGE* 8 (1935), cols. 610–44; J. Leclercq, OSB, in *TRE* 5 (1980), pp. 644–51, s.v. 'Bernhard von Clairvaux'.

Bernard of Chartres (*c*.1080–*c*.1130), grammarian. A canon of *Chartres, he was master in the cathedral school from *c*.1114 (prob. much earlier) and in 1124 Chancellor of the cathedral. A revered teacher of the 'artes', he was as concerned with his pupils' moral growth as with their intellectual development. He honoured the classical authors as giants, with whose support modern scholars could advance still further. He left only a few lines of verse, preserved by *John of Salisbury, whom he taught.

John of Salisbury, *Metalogicon*, 1. 5, 11, 24; 2. 17; 3. 2, 4; 4. 35, and *Polycraticus*, 2. 22; 7. 13. E. Jeauneau, 'Lectio Philosophorum': *Recherches sur l'école de Chartres* (Amsterdam, 1973), pp. 51–73, with refs. R. W. Southern, *Medieval Humanism and Other Studies* (Oxford, 1970), p. 68.

Bernard of Cluny (*c*.1100–*c*.1150), also called Bernard of Morlás (Dept. Hautes-Pyrénées) or Morval. He is not to be confused with the author of the 11th-cent. Cluniac *ordo* nor with any of the 12th-cent. priors of *Cluny. Bernard dedicated his major poem, *De contemptu mundi*, to *Peter the Venerable, and a prefatory letter (datable after 1125) implies that he himself is a Cluniac monk. Several famous hymns by J. M. *Neale derive from the *De contemptu mundi*, notably 'Jerusalem the Golden'. Bernard's *Mariale*, which includes 15 hymns to the BVM, was widely current. He wrote five further didactic poems, dedicating one to Pope *Eugenius III (1145–53), and the prose *Instructio sacerdotis*.

The *De contemptu mundi* is ed. by T. Wright, *The Anglo-Latin Satirical Poets and Epigrammatists of the Twelfth Century*, 2 (RS, 1872), pp. 3–102, by H. C. Hoskier (London, 1929), and, with Eng. tr., by R. E. Pepin (Medieval Texts and Studies, 8; East Lansing, Mich. [1991]). Eng. tr. of this and other works attributed to Bernard by H. Preble (Chicago, 1906). The *Mariale* is ed. by G. M. Dreves in *AHMA* 50 (1907), pp. 423–82. The poem *De vanitate mundi* (or 'Carmen ad Rainaldum') is pr. in J. P. Migne, *PL* 184. 1307–14, and the other four poems (identified by A. *Wilmart) are ed. by K. Halvarson (Acta Universitatis Stockholmiensis, Studia Latina Stockholmiensia, 9; 1963). The *Instructio sacerdotis* is pr. in J. P. Migne, *PL* 184. 771–92. A. Wilmart, OSB, 'Grands poèmes inédits de Bernard le Clunisien', *R. Bén.* 45 (1933), pp. 249–54; R. C. Petry, 'Mediaeval eschatology and social responsibility in Bernard of Morval's De contemptu mundi', *Speculum*, 24 (1949), pp. 207–17; G. J. Engelhardt, 'The "De contemptu mundi" of Bernardus Morvalensis', *Mediaeval Studies*, 22 (1960), pp. 108–35; 26 (1964), pp. 109–42; and 29 (1967), pp. 243–72. Raby, pp. 315–19. M.-T. Disdier, AA, in *DHGE* 8 (1935), cols. 699 f., s.v. 'Bernard de Morlaix'.

Bernard, John Henry (1860–1927), successively Abp. of *Dublin and Provost of *Trinity College, Dublin. He came of a Kerry family and was born in Bengal. He was educated at Trinity College, Dublin, where he was elected to a fellowship in 1884 and an important lectureship in Divinity in 1886. In his earlier years, when his interests were as much philosophical as theological, he collaborated with his colleague, J. P. Mahaffy (1839–1919), in his second edition of *Kant's Critical Philosophy for English Readers* (1889); and in 1892 he published the first English version of Kant's *Kritik der Urtheilskraft*. Theologically a *High Churchman, he came to fill a prominent place in the life of the Church of *Ireland. In 1911 he became Bp. of Ossory, and in 1915 Abp. of Dublin; and he played a notable part in the Convention on the self-government of Ireland, where he was one of the official representatives of the Protestant Church (1916–18). In 1919 he succeeded Mahaffy as Provost of Trinity College, successfully piloting the College through the revolution and its aftermath. His scholarly editions and commentaries include an English version of 'The Pilgrimage of Silvia' (see EGERIA) for the Palestine Pilgrims' Text Society (1891), the *Irish Liber Hymnorum* (with R. Atkinson, HBS, 13 and 14, 1898), and commentaries on the *Pastoral Epp. (Camb. Bible, 1899) and, his most considerable work, on St John's Gospel (posthumously ed. A. H. McNeile, 2 vols., ICC, 1928). His work was marked by accuracy and sound judgement rather than originality.

Life by R. H. Murray (London, 1931). On his family, see Bernard's own work, *The Bernards of Kerry* (Dublin, 1922). E. J. Gwynn in *DNB, 1922–1930* (1937), pp. 78–91.

Bernardines. The title popularly given to the 'Reformed Congregation of St *Bernard', i.e. the Italian branch of the *Feuillants (q.v.).

Bernardino of Siena, St (1380–1444), *Franciscan reformer, 'the Apostle of the Holy Name'. Born at Massa Marittima, a town of which his father was then governor, he became a Franciscan friar at the age of 22 and in 1438 was elected Vicar General of the Friars of the Strict *Observance in Italy. A preacher of great eloquence, to whom, said *Pius II, men listened as they might have listened to St *Paul, he made it his chief aim to regenerate the age in which he lived. He was responsible for moral reforms in many cities, and by the time of his death, although accused of heretical views on many occasions, he was perhaps the most influential religious force in Italy. He was a great promoter of devotion to the Holy *Name of Jesus. Feast day, 20 May.

Works ed. P. Rodulphius, 4 vols., Venice, 1591, and J. de la Haye, OFM, 4 vols., Paris, 1635; crit. edn. studio et cura PP. Collegii S. Bonaventurae (9 vols., Quaracchi, 1950–65). D. Pacetti, OFM, *De Sancti Bernardini Senensis Operibus: Ratio Criticae Editionis* (ibid., 1947), with details of edns. of vernacular works to date. *AASS*, Mai. 5 (1685), pp. 257*–318*. Life by Leonard Benvoglienti, dated 8 May 1446, ed. F. Van Ortroy, SJ, *Anal. Boll.* 21 (1902), pp. 53–80; 'Vie inédite de S. Bernardin de Sienne par un frère mineur, son contemporain', ed. id., ibid. 25 (1906), pp. 304–38. A. M. da Venezia, *Vita di S. Bernardino da Siena* (Venice, 1745; various later edns.). Modern Lives by P. Thureau-Dangin (Paris, 1896; Eng. tr., 1906), K. Hefele (Freiburg i.B., 1912), A. G. F. Howell (London, 1913), and V. Facchinetti, OFM (Milan, 1933). M. Sticco, *Il pensiero di S. Bernardino da Siena* [1924]. B. Stasiewski, *Der heilige Bernardin von Siena: Untersuchungen über die Quellen seiner Biographien* (Franziskanische Studien, Beiheft 13; 1931). M. Sticco and others, *S. Bernardino da Siena: Saggi e ricerche pubblicati nel quinto centenario della morte, 1444–1944* (Pubblicazioni dell'Università Cattolica del S. Cuore, NS 6; 1945). I. Origo, *The World of San Bernardino* (1963), with bibl. *Enciclopedia Bernardiniana: Opera edita per conto del Centro Promotore Generale delle Celebrazioni del VI Centenario della Nascita di S. Bernardino da Siena*, 1: *Bibliografia*, ed. E. d'Angelo [1980]. *Bullettino di Studi Bernardiniani* (10 vols., Siena, 1935–50). B. Korošak and R. Aprile in *Bibliotheca Sanctorum*, 2 (1962), cols. 1294–321; R. Manselli in *Dizionario Biografico degli Italiani*, 9 (1967), pp. 215–26; D. Pacetti in *NCE* 2 (1967), pp. 345–7.

Berne, Theses of. Ten theological propositions compiled by two Berne pastors, F. Kolb and B. *Haller, for the

Berne disputation of 6–26 Jan. 1528. The purpose of the disputation, convened on the decision of the City Council, was to establish the Reformation in Berne. The measure was a reaction not only to a religious crisis within Berne itself but also to the Baden disputation of 1526, which had attempted to consolidate Swiss opposition to the Reformation. The Theses express U. *Zwingli's teaching. They were directed against (1) the *Papacy, (2) *Tradition, (3) *Satisfaction, (4) the *Real Presence in the Eucharist, (5) the *Sacrifice of the Mass, (6) Mediation through the Saints, (7) *Purgatory, (8) *Images, (9) and (10) *Celibacy. After being debated by Protestants and RCs, they were embodied in a decree of 7 Feb. 1528 which enforced the Reformation in Berne, thus ending the confessionally isolated position of Zurich within Switzerland.

Text in R. Steck and G. Tobler (eds.), *Aktensammlung zur Geschichte der Berner Reformation 1521–1532* (Berne, 1923), pp. 518–21 (no. 1371). Lat. tr. (by Zwingli) in Kidd, pp. 459 f. (no. 217); Eng. tr. in P. *Schaff, *A History of the Creeds of Christendom*, 1 (1877), pp. 365 f., with introd. and bibl., pp. 364 f.; also, with introd., in A. C. Cochrane, *Reformed Confessions of the 16th Century* (1966), pp. 45–50. L. von Muralt, *Die Badener Disputation* (Quellen und Abhandlungen zur Schweizerischen Reformationsgeschichte, 3; 1926). K. Guggisberg, *Bernische Kirchengeschichte* (Berne, 1958), esp. pp. 101–20. I. Backus, *The Disputations of Baden, 1526, and Berne, 1528: Neutralizing the Early Church* (Studies in Reformed Theology and History, 1, no. 1; Princeton, NJ, 1993), esp. pp. 79–98.

Bérulle, Pierre de (1575–1629), cardinal, diplomat, theologian, and reformer. His family, members of the legal nobility, lived in Paris, where he was educated. He studied theology and was ordained priest in 1599. In the circle around his cousin, Mme *Acarie, he became acquainted with mystical experiences, and he then read the works of the Rheno-Flemish mystics. He went to Spain in 1604 and brought the reformed *Carmelites to Paris. In 1611 he founded the *Oratory on the pattern of that established by St *Philip Neri in 1564. At court, he reconciled Louis XIII with his mother in 1619 but he antagonized *Richelieu by his disapproval of his foreign policy. He negotiated the dispensation necessary for the marriage of *Henrietta Maria to *Charles I in 1625 and accompanied her to England. He was made a cardinal in 1627. In his main work, *Discours de l'État et des Grandeurs de Jésus* (1623) he expounded his Christocentric spirituality, his devotion to Christ as God-made-man; this led *Urban VIII to describe him as the 'Apostolus Verbi Incarnati'. He formulated a vow of spiritual servitude to Jesus and Mary which he tried to impose on those under his spiritual care, and he initiated a devotion to the Child Jesus. His spiritual teaching dominated the Oratory for the rest of the century.

Works ed. F. Bourgoing, Cong. Orat. (Paris, 1644); repr., with additions, by J. P. *Migne (ibid., 1856); also repr., 2 vols., Montsoult, 1960. *Correspondance*, ed. J. Dagens (Bibliothèque de la *RHE*, 17–19; 1937–9), with Essai biographique in vol. 1, pp. ix–xlv. G. Harbert, *La Vie du Cardinal de Bérulle* (1646). M. Houssaye, *M. de Bérulle et les Carmélites de France, 1575–1611* (1872); id., *Le Père de Bérulle et l'oratoire de Jésus, 1611–1625* (1874); id., *Le Cardinal de Bérulle et le Cardinal de Richelieu, 1625–1629* (1875). A. Molien, Cong. Orat., *Le Cardinal de Bérulle* (2 vols., 1947). J. Dagens, *Bérulle et les origines de la restauration catholique* [1952]. R. Bellemare, *Le Sens de la créature dans la doctrine de Bérulle* [1959]. P. Cochois, *Bérulle et l'École Française*

[1963]. M. Dupoy, *Bérulle: Une Spiritualité de l'adoration* [1964]; id., *Bérulle et le sacerdoce: Étude historique et doctrinale* (1969), incl. unpub. texts. J. Orcibal, *Le Cardinal de Bérulle: Évolution d'une spiritualité* (1965). F. Guillén Preckler, Sch.P., *Bérulle aujourd'hui, 1575–1975: Pour une spiritualité du Christ* [1978]. Bremond, 3, pp. 3–279; Pourrat, 3, pp. 491–515; L. Cognet, *La Spiritualité Moderne*, 1 (1966), pp. 210–410. A. Molien in *Dict. Sp.* 1 (1937), cols. 1539–81, s.v.

Bessarion (1403–72), cardinal, Greek scholar and statesman. He became a monk in 1423; and after studying under *Gemistos Plethon (1431–6) he was made Metropolitan of *Nicaea in 1437 by the Emp. John VIII Palaeologus. He accompanied the latter to the Council of Ferrara-*Florence, where in the course of the debates he was persuaded by the Latins' arguments and became an ardent advocate of the union of the Latin and Greek Churches. While he was still at sea on his way home, he was created a cardinal by Pope *Eugenius IV (1439). In *Constantinople the union was unpopular but, although many repudiated it, Bessarion remained in communion with Rome and shortly afterwards returned to Italy (1440). There he gained the patronage of Eugenius IV and his successors, fulfilled important ecclesiastical missions, and was nearly elected Pope. In 1463 *Pius II appointed him Patriarch of Constantinople (since 1453 in the hands of the Turks) and from Viterbo he addressed an Encyclical Letter to his flock to encourage them and explain his own position in respect of the union of the Churches.

Bessarion was an enthusiastic scholar and patron of scholars, and among his protégés were T. Gaza, D. Chalcondyles, and J. and C. Lascaris, all of whom played a prominent part in the revival of Greek studies in the Italian Renaissance. He himself translated into Latin *Aristotle's 'Metaphysics' and Xenophon's 'Memorabilia', and among other works he wrote a treatise 'In Calumniatorem Platonis', directed against the Aristotelian views of George of Trebizond, and a treatise on the Eucharist. Bessarion bequeathed his library, notable for its large collection of Greek and Latin MSS, to the Senate of Venice, where it became the foundation of the *Marciana.

Works in J. P. Migne, *PG* 160 and 161.137–746. L. Mohler, *Kardinal Bessarion als Theologe, Humanist und Staatsmann* (Quellen und Forschungen aus dem Gebiete der Geschichte, 20, 22, and 24; 1923–42), incl. Gk. text, with a Lat. tr., of his 'In Calumniatorem Platonis libri IV' and 'De Sacramento Eucharistiae'. His 'Oratio Dogmatica de Unione' ed., with introd., by E. Candal, SJ (Concilium Florentinum, Documenta et Scriptores, Series B, 7, fasc. 1; Rome, 1958); and his 'De Spiritus Sancti Processione ad Alexium Lascarin Philanthropinum' ed. id. (ibid. 7, fasc. 2; 1961). H. Vast, *Le Cardinal Bessarion (1403-1473): Étude sur la chrétienté et la renaissance vers le milieu du XVᵉ siècle* (1878). H. D. Saffrey [OP], 'Notes Autographes du Cardinal Bessarion dans un Manuscrit de Munich' *Byzantion*, 35 (1965), pp. 536–63. L. Labowsky, *Bessarion's Library and the Biblioteca Marciana: Six Early Inventories* (Sussidi Eruditi, 31; 1979). *Miscellanea Marciana di Studi Bessarionei (a coronamento del V Centenario della donazione nicena)* (Medioevo e Umanesimo, 24; Padua, 1976). J. Gill, SJ, 'Was Bessarion a conciliarist or a unionist before the Council of Florence?', in *Collectanea Byzantina* (Orientalia Christiana Analecta, 204; Rome, 1977), pp. 201–16. N. G. Wilson, *From Byzantium to Italy* (1992), esp. pp. 57–67. L. Bréhier in *DHGE* 8 (1935), cols. 1181–99; L. Labowsky in *Dizionario Biografico degli Italiani*, 9 (1967), pp. 686–96, with extensive bibl.; J. Gill, SJ, in *TRE* 5 (1980), pp. 725–30, s.v.

beth (Heb. בַּיִת, a 'house'). A word often occurring in biblical place-names. See following entries.

Bethabara. Acc. to Jn. 1: 28 (AV), the place 'beyond *Jordan' where St *John the Baptist baptized, and thus presumably the scene of Christ's *Baptism. It is possibly the modern ford 'Abarah', N. of Beisan; but (1) 'abarah' means only 'crossing', and (2) many important MSS, followed by the RV, read '*Bethany beyond Jordan', and this is almost certainly the correct text.

For readings of the different MSS, see comm. on Jn. F. M. Abel, OP, *Géographie de la Palestine*, 2 (1938), pp. 264 f. C. Kopp, *Die heiligen Stätten der Evangelien* (Regensburg, 1959), pp. 153–66; Eng. tr. as *The Holy Places of the Gospels* (1963), pp. 113–29. A. Barrois, OP, in *Dict. Bibl.* suppl. 1 (1928), cols. 968–70, s.v. 'Béthanie'.

Bethany. The village of Sts *Martha and *Mary and *Lazarus (Jn. 11: 1), about two miles (Jn. 11: 18) from *Jerusalem, on the SE slopes of the Mount of *Olives (Mk. 11: 1). There Christ supped with Simon (Mk. 14: 3), and lodged during the week before His Passion (Mt. 21: 17). Its modern name is 'Azaryah, i.e. 'the place of Lazarus'. 'Bethany beyond Jordan' (Jn. 1: 28 RV) is another village.

F. M. Abel, OP, *Géographie de la Palestine*, 2 (1938), pp. 266 f., with refs. P. Benoit, OP, and M. E. Boismard, OP, 'Un Ancien Sanctuaire chrétien à Béthanie', *R. Bibl.* 58 (1951), pp. 200–51. S. J. Saller, OFM, *Excavations at Bethany (1949–1953)* (Publications of the Studium Biblicum Franciscanum, 12; Jerusalem, 1957). J. Murphy-O'Connor, OP, *The Holy Land* (2nd edn., Oxford, 1986), pp. 115–18 [popular guidebook].

Bethel (lit., Heb. 'House of God'). (1) A major sanctuary to the north of *Jerusalem. Acc. to Gen. 28: 10–22, God appeared here in a dream to *Jacob, who thereupon erected the stone on which his head had rested as a sacred pillar. On the division of the Hebrew Kingdom after the death of *Solomon (c.930 BC), Jeroboam I, the first ruler of the independent northern kingdom (*Israel), set up a 'golden calf' here (1 Kgs. 12: 28 f.), the worship continuing (cf. Am. 7: 10–13) until King Josiah abolished sacrificial worship at all sanctuaries except Jerusalem in 621.

(2) The small town near Bielefeld in Westphalia which gives the popular name to the *Bodelschwinghsche Stiftungen*. These consist of homes for epileptics, training centres for deaconesses and male nurses, and a college for Protestant theological students. The aim of their founder, the *Lutheran pastor Friedrich Bodelschwingh (1831–1910), was to relieve the lot of the mentally defective by giving them a share in the work of the community acc. to their capacity and by providing for their spiritual needs. At the same time Bethel furnished a staff of men and women willing and able to help in the social activities of the Lutheran Church. See also INNERE MISSION.

(3) A name used, esp. by certain *Methodists and *Baptists, for a place of religious worship.

On (1) F. M. Abel, OP, *Géographie de la Palestine*, 2 (1938), pp. 270 f., with refs. to earlier lit. J. L. Kelso, *The Excavation of Bethel (1934–1960)*, with chs. by W. F. Albright and others (Annual of the American Schools of Oriental Research, 39; Cambridge, Mass., 1968), incl. ch. on 'The History of Bethel', pp. 45–53. J. L. Kelso in E. Stern and others (eds.), *The New Encyclopedia of Archaeological Excavations in the Holy Land*, 1 (Jerusalem and New York [1993]), pp. 192–4, s.v.

Bethesda. A pool at *Jerusalem (Jn. 5: 2; but some important MSS read 'Bethzatha' or similar variant) believed to possess miraculous properties connected with a periodical disturbance of the water. It has been variously identified, e.g. with the 'Virgin's Pool' SE of the *Temple, where a spring still bubbles intermittently.

J. Jeremias, *Die Wiederentdeckung von Bethesda, Johannes, 5, 2* (Forschungen zur Religion und Literatur des Alten und Neuen Testaments, NS 41; 1949; rev. Eng. tr., New Testament Archaeology Monograph, 1; Louisville, Ky., 1966). D. J. Wieand, 'John v. 2 and the Pool of Bethesda', *New Testament Studies*, 12 (1966), pp. 392–404; W. D. Davies, *The Gospel and the Land* (1974), pp. 302–13. B. Lindars, SSF, *The Gospel of John* (New Cent. Bib. [1972]), pp. 212 f. See also other comm. to Jn.

Bethlehem. The small town five miles S. of *Jerusalem which was the native city of King *David and the birthplace of Christ. About half of the inhabitants are now Christian. It contains one of the oldest churches in Christendom, the 'Church of the Holy Nativity', built by *Constantine in 330 upon the supposed site of the Holy Birth. In spite of rebuilding by *Justinian in the 6th cent., much of the original church survives, including a mosaic pavement unearthed in 1934. Both the Orthodox and Latin Churches have rights within it. For the Council of Bethlehem (1672), see JERUSALEM, SYNOD OF.

L. H. Vincent, OP, and F. M. Abel, OP, *Bethléem: Le Sanctuaire de la Nativité* (1914). L. H. Vincent, OP, 'Bethléem. Le Sanctuaire de la Nativité d'après les fouilles récentes', *R. Bibl.* 45 (1936), pp. 544–74, and 46 (1937), pp. 93–121. B. Bagatti, OFM, *Gli antichi Edifici Sacri di Betlemme* (Pubblicazioni dello Studium Biblicum Franciscanum, 9; Jerusalem 1952). R. W. Hamilton, *The Church of the Nativity, Bethlehem: A Guide* (Jerusalem, 1947). C. Kopp, *Die heiligen Stätten der Evangelien* (Regensburg, 1959), pp. 11–85; abridged Eng. tr., *The Holy Places of the Gospels* (1963), pp. 1–47. J. [D.] Wilkinson, *Jerusalem Pilgrims before the Crusades* (Warminster [1977]), pp. 151 f. M. Stekelis and others in E. Stern and others (eds.), *The New Encyclopedia of Archaeological Excavations in the Holy Land*, 1 (Jerusalem and New York [1993]), pp. 203–10, s.v.

Bethlehemites. The name of several orders of religious. *Matthew Paris attests the existence at Cambridge of a military order dedicated to Our Lady of Bethlehem in 1257. Two centuries later *Pius II founded a military order, dedicated to the 'Blessed Virgin Mary of Bethlehem', for the defence of the Aegean against the Turks after the fall of *Constantinople in 1453. Another order of Bethlehemites, or 'Belemites', was established *c.* 1655 in Guatemala for the purposes of tending the sick and education. None of these survives. In 1976 an order of monks and nuns of Bethlehem was founded in France and has spread to other countries. They are *Carthusian in inspiration, but have a special interest in religious art. See also BEDLAM.

J. M. Besse, OSB, in *CE* 2 (1907), pp. 534–6; D. [M.] *Knowles, A. Martínez Cuesta, and J. Berdonces in *DIP* 1 (1974), cols. 1420–5, s.v. 'Betlemiti'.

Bethphage. A village on the Mount of *Olives near *Bethany, with which it is usually associated in the NT

(Mk. 11: 1; Lk. 19: 29). Its site is uncertain, but it is traditionally located on the road linking Bethany and el Tur.

F. M. Abel, OP, *Géographie de la Palestine*, 2 (1938), p. 279, with refs. S. J. Saller, OFM, and E. Testa, OFM, *The Archaeological Setting of the Shrine of Bethphage* (Publications of the Studium Biblicum Franciscanum, Smaller Series, 1; Jerusalem, 1961). C. Kopp, *Die heiligen Stätten der Evangelien* (Regensburg, 1959), pp. 323–32; abridged Eng. tr., *The Holy Places of the Gospels* (1963), pp. 267–77; J. [D.] Wilkinson, *Jerusalem Pilgrims before the Crusades* (Warminster [1977]), pp. 152 f.

Bethsaida (lit. 'House of Fishing'). A town on the E. bank of the *Jordan where it enters the Sea of Galilee; its site has not been precisely identified. It was a predominantly Gentile city, and rebuilt by Herod Philip the tetrarch (d. AD 33 or 34), who renamed it 'Julias' in honour of the Roman Imperial house. Christ visited it in the course of His ministry (Mk. 8: 22, Lk. 9: 10). It has been suggested that 'Bethsaida of Galilee' (Jn. 12: 21), the home of the disciples *Philip, *Peter, and *Andrew (Jn. 1: 44), was a different place, and that, if so, this would be the city referred to at Mk. 6: 45.

F. M. Abel, OP, *Géographie de la Palestine*, 2 (1938), pp. 279 f., with refs. C. Kopp (Eng. tr. by J. Watt), 'Christian Sites around the Sea of Galilee. II. Bethsaida and El-Minyeh', *Dominican Studies*, 3 (1950), pp. 10–40. J. [D.] Wilkinson, *Jerusalem Pilgrims before the Crusades* (Warminster [1977]), p. 153.

Bethune, David. See BEATON, DAVID.

betrothal. A free promise of future marriage between two persons. In origin the Christian betrothal ceremonies date back, both in their Jewish and Roman counterparts, to the custom of 'wife purchase'. The giving of a ring is an earnest of the man's good faith. In many countries formal betrothal before witnesses is still the custom, but in England the Church has ceased to exercise any authority in the matter. See also MATRIMONY.

betting and gambling. A gamble is a contract whereby the loss or gain of something of value is made wholly dependent on an uncertain event. If either of the contracting parties is in a state of certainty about the event, the gamble is invalid and fraudulent. The common forms of a gamble are bets, games of chance, and lotteries. The morality of gambling, considered as a species of recreation, is debated. Some hold it to be always illicit, but the majority of Christians regard it as permissible, though highly open to abuse. Among the latter there is agreement that for a gamble to be allowable it must conform to certain conditions. It must not be about an unlawful matter, e.g. one may not bet someone that he will not get drunk; the stake must not be excessive; and it must be for some end other than mere avarice, e.g. recreation. There is now no explicit RC law proscribing it, though habitual gambling was long forbidden to the clergy. The Council of *Elvira (can. 79) condemns dice, perhaps because of their pagan associations. St *Alphonsus Liguori considers every bet at least a venial sin; but this is not the view of most RC theologians. The peculiar nature of the gambling contract and its doubtful morality are recognized by most civil codes of law, which do not allow the winner to sue at law for his gains. On the other hand they recognize it to the extent that they do not allow the loser, once he has paid, to sue for the recovery of his losses.

R. C. Mortimer, *Gambling* (1933). *Gambling: An Ethical Discussion. A Report of the Social and Industrial Commission of the Church Assembly* (1950).

Beuno, St (d. *c*.640), Abbot of Clynnog. He is the subject of many legends and superstitions, from which it seems impossible to disentangle any certain history. He is said to have founded monasteries in Herefordshire, but his chief mission work is believed to have been in N. Wales, where his tomb was long venerated at Clynnog Fawr (Caernarfonshire and Merionethshire). He is supposed to have restored to life St *Winifred, his niece. He is the titular saint of the modern Jesuit College at St Asaph, Denbighshire. Feast day, 21 Apr.

There is a Welsh Life of St Beuno (Buchedd Beuno), of which the earliest MS dates from 1346; text ed. J. Morris Jones and J. Rhŷs, *The Elucidarium and other tracts in Welsh from Llyvyr Agkyr Llandewivrevi* (Anecdota Oxoniensia, Oxford, 1894), pp. 105–18, and by A. W. Wade-Evans, *Vitae Sanctorum Britanniae et Genealogiae* (Board of Celtic Studies, University of Wales, History and Law Series, 9; Cardiff, 1944), pp. 16–22. Eng. tr. with notes by id., 'Beuno Sant', *Archaeologia Cambrensis*, 85 (1930), pp. 315–41. J. H. Pollen, SJ, 'Traces of a Great Welsh Saint', *The Month*, 80 (1894), pp. 235–47.

Beuron, Abbey of. The mother abbey of the 'Beuron Congregation' of *Benedictine monks in Hohenzollern, on the upper Danube. The present abbey was constituted in 1863, and the monastic *congregation established in 1873, though there were *Augustinian canons at Beuron as far back as the 11th cent. It has become famous through its work for *liturgical reform, in which it has been esp. assisted by its daughter abbey of *Maria Laach, and the creation of a school of religious art. Until 1920 the now separated Belgian abbeys of *Maredsous and Mont-César (at Louvain) belonged to the Beuron Congregation.

K. T. Zingeler, *Geschichte des Klosters Beuron im Donauthale* (1890; on the Augustinian foundation). The present Benedictine Monastery is described in O. Wolff, OSB, *Beuron: Bilder und Erinnerungen aus dem Mönchsleben der Jetztzeit* (1889; 6th edn., 1923). 'Regula S. Patris Benedicti, Abbatis et Monachorum Patriarchae, cum constitutionibus congregationis Beuronensis', *Archiv für katholisches Kirchenrecht*, 54 (1885), pp. 78–114. J. Kreitmaier, *Beuroner Kunst: Eine Ausdrucksform der christlichen Mystik* (3rd edn., 1921). S. Mayer, OSB, *Benediktinisches Ordensrecht in der Beuroner Kongregation* (4 vols., Beuron, 1929–30). Id., *Beuroner Bibliographie: Schriftsteller und Künstler während der ersten hundert Jahre des Benediktinerklosters Beuron 1863–1963* (ibid., 1963). *Festschrift zum hundertjährigen Bestehen der Erzabtei St Martin, Beuron* (ibid., 1963). V. E. Fiala, OSB, 'Die besondere Ausprägung des Benediktinischen Mönchtums in der Beuroner Kongregation', *R. Bén.* 83 (1973), pp. 181–228. The periodical *Benediktinische Monatsschrift zur Pflege religiösen und geistigen Lebens* is pub. from Beuron (1919 ff.). V. E. Fiala, OSB, in *DIP* 1 (1974), cols. 1427–36, s.v.

Beveridge, William (1637–1708), Bp. of *St Asaph. Educated at St John's College, Cambridge, he was ordained both deacon and priest in Jan. 1661 and immediately became Vicar of Ealing. In 1672 he published his Συνοδικόν, a collection of Greek canons, which contained an abundance of (in places misguided) erudition. In the same year he became Vicar of St Peter's Cornhill, where

he had a daily service and a Eucharist every Sunday. In 1681 he became Archdeacon of Colchester and in 1684 Prebendary of *Canterbury. When T. *Ken was deprived in 1691, Beveridge was offered (but through his *nonjuring sympathies declined) the vacated see of *Bath and Wells; and was not again offered a bishopric until 1704, when he became Bp. of St Asaph. As bishop he was sympathetic towards the Welsh language, and he was a strong supporter of the *SPCK, the translation of whose publications into Welsh he encouraged. His *Private Thoughts upon Religion* (posthumous, 1709) places him among the spiritual writers of the century, while the translation of several of his works into Welsh after his death witnesses to his continued influence.

Collected edns. of his Works [by T. Gregory] (2 vols., fol., London, 1720), T. H. Horne (9 vols., ibid., 1824), and J. Bliss (LACT, 12 vols., 1843–8); all incomplete. A. B. Grosart in *DNB* 4 (1885), pp. 447 f., s.v.

Beverley Minster. The minster, which stands on the site of a Saxon church founded by St *John of Beverley (d. 721) and is held to be one of the finest examples of early Gothic architecture in Britain, is now a parish church. In the 10th cent. a college of secular canons was established here. The existing building was constructed after the destruction of the earlier church by fire in 1188. At the *Reformation the minster survived until the Dissolution of Colleges Act 1547, as it was in the hands of secular canons. In 1713 a restoration prevented it from falling into ruin.

W. *Dugdale, *Monasticon Anglicanum*, 2 (1819 edn.), pp. 128–30, and 6 (pt. 2; 1830), pp. 1306–12. G. Poulson, *Beverlac; or, The Antiquities and History of the Town of Beverley*, 2 (1829), pp. 513–720; G. Oliver, *The History and Antiquities of the Town and Minster of Beverley* (1829). C. Hiatt, *Beverley Minster* (1898). A. Hamilton Thompson, in *VCH*, Yorkshire, 2 (1913), pp. 353–9; K. [R.] Miller and others, *Beverley* (Royal Commission on Historical Monuments, England, suppl. ser. 4; 1982), pp. 7–15, with refs.

Beyschlag, Willibald (1823–1900), German Evangelical theologian. In 1856 he became Court Preacher at Karlsruhe and in 1860 Professor of Pastoral Theology at Halle. One of the leading exponents of the '*Vermittlungstheologie', he rejected the *Chalcedonian Christology, but strongly attacked the rationalistic doctrines of E. *Renan and D. F. *Strauss. In his later years he took a prominent part in ecclesiastical politics. After 1870 he helped to draw up the new constitution of the Prussian Church, and he supported the Prussian Government in the *Kulturkampf, partly by lending his aid to the cause of the '*Old Catholics'. He was also one of the chief agents in founding the *Evangelischer Bund. His writings include *Karl Immanuel Nitzsch* (1871), *Der Altkatholizismus* (3rd edn., 1883), *Leben Jesu* (2 vols., 1885–6), *Neutestamentliche Theologie* (2 vols., 1891; Eng. tr., 2 vols., 1895) and *Aus meinem Leben: Erinnerungen und Erfahrungen der jüngeren Jahre* (2 vols., Halle, 1896–9).

K. H. Pahncke, *Willibald Beyschlag: Ein Gedenkblatt zur 5jähr. Wiederkehr seines Todestages (am 25.xi.1900). Auf Grund von Tagenbüchern, Briefen und eigenen Erinnerungen* (Tübingen, 1905). Id. in *PRE* (3rd edn.), 23 (1913), pp. 192–203.

Beza, Theodore (1519–1605), *Calvinist theologian. De Bèze (the original form of his name) came from an old

Catholic family of Vézelay in Burgundy. He was educated by his tutor M. Wolmar, first at Orléans, later at Bourges, where Wolmar became a Protestant and made his house a centre of the new religion, J. *Calvin being one of its most frequent guests. In 1534 Wolmar returned to Germany, and from 1535 to 1539 Beza studied law at Orléans with a view to embracing an ecclesiastical career. Having soon abandoned this plan he went to *Paris, where he wrote the *Poemata Juvenilia* (1548), later editions of which he partly expurgated. In 1548 he officially renounced the Catholic religion and went to *Geneva, where he formally married Claudine Denosses, with whom he had concluded a clandestine marriage in 1544. In 1549 he became professor of Greek at Lausanne. In 1554 he defended the burning of M. *Servetus at Geneva in his treatise *De Haereticis a civili Magistratu Puniendis*. In 1558 Calvin offered him a professorship at the newly founded academy at Geneva, a post which Beza held until 1595. In 1559 he published his *Confession de la foi chrétienne*, an exposition of Calvinist beliefs which was translated into Latin in 1560 and into several vernacular languages shortly afterwards. In 1561 he completed the edition of the Psalms begun by C. *Marot and in the same year he took a prominent part in the colloquy between Catholics and *Huguenots at *Poissy, urging the Huguenots not to accept a compromise solution. In 1562 when civil war broke out in France between the two religious groups, Beza tried to procure men and arms from the Protestant German princes. He returned to Geneva in 1563 and on the death of Calvin in 1564 succeeded him as head of the Genevan Church and leader of the Calvinist movement in Europe. He was involved in numerous theological controversies. In the 1550s and 1560s he disputed with S. *Castellio about free-will, and he defended the orthodox doctrine of the Trinity against L. *Socinus, G. Biandrata, and others. In defence of the view that the Holy Spirit makes Christ's Divine (but not His human) nature present to the faithful in the *Eucharist, between 1559 and 1593 Beza produced a series of writings against the Lutheran *Ubiquitarians, notably J. *Brenz, J. Westphal, and J. *Andreae. In 1571 he presided over the National Synod of La Rochelle which marked the consolidation of the French Huguenot Church. In his *Du Droit des magistrats*, published anonymously in 1574, Beza went against most political thinkers of his time in asserting that lower-placed government officials had the right to overthrow a tyrannical ruler. He is usually considered to have hardened Calvin's doctrine of *predestination by arguing (in his 'Tabula Praedestinationis' of 1555 and elsewhere) that even the *Fall was part of God's eternal plan; it followed the election of some to salvation and others to damnation, the atoning death of Christ being offered only for the former.

Beza's NT went through five editions during his lifetime. In 1556 he published an annotated Latin translation of the NT, adding the Greek text in 1565. The work was intended to replace *Erasmus' Greek text, Latin translation, and annotations which Beza considered doctrinally and textually unsound. In fact, his own Greek text, although based on R. *Stephanus' edition of 1550, on variants collected by H. Stephanus and on a number of hitherto unknown MSS, incl. (from 1582) the *Codex Bezae and the *Peshitta, differed little from Erasmus'. The principal differences lay in his Latin translation and in his detailed textual and theological annotations. The work remained influential all over Europe in the 17th cent., providing one of the chief sources for the translators of the AV.

See also CODEX BEZAE.

Some of his treatises and letters were collected by Beza and pub. as *Tractationes Theologicae* (3 vols., Geneva, 1570–82). Crit. edn. of his *Correspondance* collected by H. Aubert and pub. by F. Aubert and others (Geneva, 1960 ff., in the series Travaux d'Humanisme et Renaissance). Modern edns. of the *Histoire ecclésiastique des Églises réformées au Royaume de France* (compiled by Beza from memoirs sent to him from all over France, 1580) by G. Baum and E. Cunitz (3 vols., Paris, 1883–9), of Beza's *Chrestiennes Méditations* by M. Richter (Textes Littéraires Français, 113; 1964), of *Abraham Sacrifiant* by K. Cameron, K. M. Hall, and F. Higman (ibid. 135; 1967), of *Du droit des magistrats* by R. M. Kingdon (Classiques de la Pensée Politique, 7; '1970' [1971]), and of a student's notes on his lectures on Rom. and Heb., 1564–66, by P. Fraenkel and L. Perrotet (Travaux d'Humanisme et Renaissance, 226; 1988). Lives by F. C. Schlosser (Heidelberg, 1809), J. W. Baum ([only to 1563], 2 vols., Berlin, 1843–51), H. Heppe (Elberfeld, 1861), and P.-F. Geisendorf (Geneva, 1949). W. Kickel, *Vernunft und Offenbarung bei Theodor Beza: Zum Problem des Verhältnisses von Theologie, Philosophie und Staat* (Beiträge zur Geschichte und Lehre der Reformierten Kirche, 25; 1967). J. Raitt, *The Eucharistic Theology of Theodore Beza: Development of the Reformed Doctrine* (American Academy of Religion, Studies in Religion, 4; Chambersburg, Pa., 1972). J. S. Bray, *Theodore Beza's Doctrine of Predestination* (Bibliotheca Humanistica & Reformatorica, 12; Nieuwkoop, 1975). T. Maruyama, *The Ecclesiology of Theodore Beza: The Reform of the True Church* (Travaux d'Humanisme et Renaissance, 166; Geneva, 1978). I. D. Backus, *The Reformed Roots of the English New Testament: The Influence of Theodore Beza on the English New Testament* (Pittsburgh Theological Monograph Series, 28; Pittsburgh, 1980). F. Gardy, *Bibliographie des œuvres théologiques, littéraires, historiques et juridiques de Théodore de Bèze* (Travaux d'Humanisme et Renaissance, 41; 1960). E. Choisy, *L'État chrétien à Genève au temps de Théodore de Bèze* (1903). J. Raitt in *TRE* 5 (1980), pp. 765–74, s.v.

BFBS. See BRITISH AND FOREIGN BIBLE SOCIETY.

Biasca Sacramentary. The oldest surviving MS (10th cent.), of the *Ambrosian rite. It is preserved at Milan in the *Ambrosiana (A. 24 *bis* inf.).

Crit. edn. by O. Heiming (Liturgiewissenschaftliche Quellen und Forschungen, 51, etc.; 1969 ff.), with bibl.

Bible. (1) *Word*. The word 'Bible' is derived through the Fr. and Lat. from the Gk. βιβλία, 'books', used in the *Septuagint in such expressions as 'the Books of the Law' (1 Macc. 1: 56) and 'the holy Books' (1 Macc. 12: 9). The usual Gk. word (NT, *Philo, *Josephus) for the Jewish sacred writings, however, was not βιβλία but γραφαί ('scriptures'). But whereas γραφαί was translated into Lat. (*scripturae*), βιβλία was transliterated; and 'Biblia' thus became a new and distinctive term for the Holy Scriptures, denoting, as its plural form shows, a collection of books. As the biblical books were increasingly considered a unity, the word (orig. neut. pl.) came to be understood as a fem. sing., whence the Eng. 'Bible', Fr. *la Bible*, etc.

(2) *The Jewish Scriptures*. The Jews classified their Scriptures in three groups: (*a*) the Law (*Torah), (*b*) the Prophets, and (*c*) other Books, known collectively as the

'Writings'. The Law comprised the *Pentateuch or 'Five Books of Moses' (Gen., Exod., Lev., Num., Deut.), regarded as on a higher level than all the rest. The 'Prophets' fell into two groups, the 'Former Prophets' (Josh., Jgs., 1 and 2 Sam., and 1 and 2 Kgs.) and the 'Latter Prophets' (Is., Jer., Ezek., and the Twelve *Minor Prophets). The inclusion of the 'Former Prophets', properly historical Books, among the Prophets accords with the modern view which sees in them history written from an essentially prophetic point of view. The 'Writings' comprised all the remaining Books of the English OT (Ruth, 1 and 2 Chron., Ez., Neh., Est., Job, Pss., Prov., Eccles., Song of Songs, and Dan.) as well as some others, e.g. Ecclus., Tob., Macc., which the Jews later rejected. By the time of Christ, Jews everywhere recognized the Law and the Prophets as holy Scripture, but the exact compass of the 'Writings' was still undefined. While some, e.g. the Pss., were universally received, others, e.g. Est., which were later officially accepted, were still disputed, and others again, e.g. Ecclus., which were later rejected, were not yet definitely excluded. The *canon of the Jewish Scriptures was perhaps settled at about the end of the first century AD, though some scholars favour a rather later date.

(3) *The Greek Old Testament*. Before the Christian era the Hebrew Scriptures, including some which were later rejected from the canon, had been translated into Greek for the use of Greek-speaking Jews. This Greek Bible was extended by the inclusion of other Jewish writings of a similar kind, e.g. Wisd. Sol., which were not translations but original Greek compositions. The version of this Greek Bible in most general use was the Septuagint (q.v.). As soon as Christianity won its footing in the Hellenistic world, this was the version in which Christians received the Jewish Scriptures; hence it was the first Christian Bible. The early separation of Christianity from Judaism caused the Christian canon before long to differ from that of the Jews. The Jewish rejection of certain books *c*. AD 100 was unheeded by the Church, which continued to reckon all books in the Septuagint as Scripture. It was only at a later date that the Church became generally conscious of its divergence here from Judaism. Then the Church designated those Books (or parts of Books) which were not in the Hebrew canon as 'Deuterocanonical' or (as in the AV and RV) as *Apocrypha. They include some, e.g. Ecclus., Tob., Judith, 1 Macc., which it is fairly or quite certain were translations from the Heb. and others, e.g. Wisd. Sol. and 2 Macc., which are more probably original compositions by Jewish authors in Greek. Besides the Septuagint, other versions (*Symmachus, *Aquila, *Theodotion) also circulated to some extent among the Greek-speaking Jews and in the early Christian Church.

(4) *The New Testament*. During the 2nd cent. the Christian Church came to regard certain of her own writings, esp. if of Apostolic origin, as of equal authority and inspiration to those she had inherited from Judaism (cf. the collocation of St *Paul's Epp. with 'the other scriptures' in 2 Pet. 3: 16). The canon (q.v.) of the NT, based on the four Gospels and the Epp. of St Paul, came into existence largely without definition. It was prob. formally fixed at *Rome in 382, when the Christian OT canon (based on the Septuagint) was also defined. At *Alexandria

the present canon is already found in St *Athanasius' *Festal Ep.* for 367.

(5) *The Latin Bible, the Apocrypha, and other Versions*. Many early Latin versions of parts of the Bible ('*Old Latin') came into use in the Christian Church, esp. in Africa and Italy. The OT Books were translated, not from the Hebrew but from the Greek. To remedy the confusion created by a variety of translations, St *Jerome, encouraged by Pope *Damasus, revised the Gospels and subsequently made a fresh translation of the OT, wherever possible from the Hebrew original. St Jerome's version (the '*Vulgate', q.v.), which was given formal recognition at the Council of *Trent (sess. 4), became the authoritative Latin translation of the Bible in the RC Church.

Jerome's task necessarily drew his attention to the Deuterocanonical Books not found in the Heb. Bible. He himself sought to exclude them from the Christian canon ('libri canonici') as 'libri ecclesiastici' or Apocrypha. But though frequent doubts as to their status continued to be raised, the Latin Church retained them and finally settled their authority at Trent (scss. 4). At the Reformation, the Protestants in their vernacular versions either omitted the Apocrypha altogether or placed them in a separate section between the OT and the NT. At the Synod of *Jerusalem in 1672 the E. Church, which had hitherto continued to use the Septuagint canon, but with some doubts about certain of the Deuterocanonical Books, rejected all but four (Tob., Judith, Ecclus., and Wisd.), though retaining the full LXX text of Jer., Dan., and Est.

For the ancient versions other than the Septuagint and Vulgate, see SYRIAC, COPTIC, ETHIOPIC; for the principal English versions, see foll. entry and refs. there given; for translations into other modern languages, see under the names of the translators (M. *Luther, T. *Beza, etc.).

(6) *Authority and Interpretation*. The respect shown by Christ and the Apostolic Church to the Scriptures of Judaism forms the basis of the Christian attitude to the Bible. The OT Scriptures, regarded as inspired by the Holy Spirit (Lk. 24: 44, 2 Tim. 3: 15 f.) were seen as a revelation of God and a preparation for the coming of Christ, which in various ways they foretold (Heb. 1: 1 f.). Many OT ordinances were superseded, but the OT as a whole remained authoritative. Its message was completed by the NT, so that the two together formed a single and final revelation.

In patristic times the most serious challenge to this view of the Bible was that of *Marcion (q.v.), who repudiated the OT and accepted only part of what later came to constitute the NT. After the failure of Marcion's challenge the authority of the Bible was everywhere accepted. The other great heretics (e.g. *Arius) took a common stand with the orthodox and appealed to both OT and NT in support of their doctrines. In the matter of interpretation, *allegorical methods were much in use in the patristic, medieval, and Reformation periods, but the literal sense generally exercised control in matters of doctrine. The Reformers benefited from Renaissance humanist scholarship as they insisted more strongly on the priority of the literal and 'historical' (i.e. Christological) sense and appealed to Scripture against ecclesiastical tradition. But Luther's flexible Christocentric interpretation soon became petrified into theories of verbal inerrancy, and both Catholics and Protestants shared a common view of inspiration that insisted on the truth of the biblical statements, not only in matters of history, doctrine, and ethics, but also cosmology and natural science. Thus the heliocentric teaching of *Galileo was condemned as heretical.

Modern science and philosophy, esp. *Cartesianism, challenged this position from without, and in the 18th cent. modern linguistic, *text-critical, and historical study undermined it from within biblical scholarship itself. The critical radicalism of the English *Deists was combined in 19th-cent. German Protestantism with a sense of historical development and newer methods for reconstructing history (*source criticism). In 19th-cent. England it was geology and evolutionary theories that did most to shake biblical authority. Hostility to any notion of a supernatural revelation on the part of some critics of orthodoxy evoked a series of robust responses from those who maintained more traditional theologies, and the resulting polarization has been characteristic of the development of biblical criticism to the present day. By the end of the 19th cent., however, archaeology was making its mark and *higher criticism was widely accepted in the Protestant Churches of Europe and North America. Two important reactions against biblical criticism were the suppression of RC *Modernism by *Pius X and the emergence of *Fundamentalism in the United States of America. But following the encyclical '*Divino Afflante Spiritu' (1943) of *Pius XII RC biblical scholarship progressed more openly and since the Second *Vatican Council has played a major role. Evangelical scholarship has also developed and, despite continuing opposition to rational enquiry in Fundamentalist circles, the old hostilities have largely subsided. Newer literary approaches have directed attention away from the more contentious questions of historicity, and in recent years an interpretative pluralism has emerged.

See also BIBLICAL COMMISSION, BIBLICAL THEOLOGY, CANON OF SCRIPTURE, FORM CRITICISM, HISTORICAL JESUS, QUEST OF THE, MANUSCRIPTS OF THE BIBLE, TEXTUAL CRITICISM, and articles on individual biblical Books and persons, and on biblical scholars.

TEXTS. Edns. of the Hebrew OT by K. Elliger and W. Rudolph, *Biblia Hebraica Stuttgartensia* (1977; 2nd edn., 1983); Greek NT by B. F. *Westcott and F. J. A. *Hort (1881); E. B. *Nestle (1898, 27th edn. by B. and K. Aland, 1993); A. *Souter (1910; 2nd edn., 1947; text that underlying RV, apparatus only due to Souter); K. Aland and others (1966; 4th edn. by B. Aland and others, 1993). For edns. of the Septuagint and Vulgate, see s.vv. For Eng. versions see foll. entry.

DICTIONARIES. J. *Hastings (ed.), *A Dictionary of the Bible* (4 vols., Edinburgh, 1898–1902, and extra vol., 1904; still useful); T. K. *Cheyne and J. S. Black (eds.), *Encyclopaedia Biblica* (4 vols., 1899–1903; with some excellent and original articles but often erratic); F. Vigouroux (ed.), *Dictionnaire de la Bible* (5 vols., 1891–1912) and Supplément (ed. L. Pirot and others, 1928 ff.); G. A. Buttrick (ed.), *The Interpreter's Dictionary of the Bible* (4 vols., Nashville and New York [1962], and suppl. vol., ed. K. Crim [1976]); D. N. Freedman and others (eds.), *The Anchor Bible Dictionary* (6 vols. [1992]); B. M. Metzger and M. D. Coogan (eds.), *The Oxford Companion to the Bible* (New York and Oxford, 1993).

COMMENTARIES. Complete comm. ed. by A. S. *Peake (q.v.), 1919; the 1962 edn. is a completely new book ed. M. Black and H. H. Rowley); *The New Jerome Biblical Commentary*, ed. R. E.

Brown, SS, J. A. Fitzmyer, SJ, and R. E. Murphy, O.Carm. (1989); and *The Catholic Study Bible: The New American Bible*, ed. D. Senior (New York [1990]). Comm. on separate books in 'International Critical Commentary' (Edinburgh, 1895 ff.), 'New Clarendon Bible' (Oxford, 1963 ff.), 'New Century Bible' (London, 1966 ff.), 'Anchor Bible' (Garden City, NY, 1964–88; New York, 1989 ff.), 'Hermeneia' (Philadelphia, 1971–87; Minneapolis, 1989 ff.), 'Word Biblical Commentary' (Waco, Tex., 1982–8; Dallas, 1988 ff.); 'New International Commentary on the OT' (Grand Rapids, 1964 ff.), 'New International Commentary on the NT' (ibid., 1950 ff.; early vols. pub. in Britain as 'New London Commentary on the NT'); 'Black's NT Commentaries' (London, 1957 ff.), and 'Sacra Pagina' (Collegeville, Minn., 1991 ff.); also important comm. in German, many of them continuously revised: 'Kritisch-exegetischer Kommentar über das Neue Testament', founded by H. A. W. *Meyer (Göttingen, 1832 ff.); the 'Handbuch zum Neuen Testament' (Tübingen, 1906 ff.); the 'Handbuch zum Alten Testament' (ibid., 1934 ff.); 'Das Neue Testament Deutsch' (Göttingen, 1932 ff.); 'Das Alte Testament Deutsch' (ibid., 1951 ff.; the 'Old Testament Library', 1960 ff., is based on this series); 'Herders theologischer Kommentar zum Neuen Testament' (Freiburg i. B., 1953 ff.); 'Biblischer Kommentar: Altes Testament' (Neukirchen, 1955 ff.); and the 'Evangelisch-katholischer Kommentar zum Neuen Testament' (Neukirchen, 1969 ff.).

GENERAL WORKS. O. Eissfeldt, *Einleitung in das Alte Testament unter Einschluss der Apokryphen und Pseudepigraphen* (1934; 3rd edn., 1964; Eng. tr., Oxford, 1965); R. H. Pfeiffer, *Introduction to the Old Testament* (New York, 1948; London, 1952); J. A. Soggin, *Introduzione all'Antico Testamento* (2 vols., Brescia [1968–9]; 4th edn., 1987; Eng. tr., 1989); W. G. Kümmel, *Einleitung in das Neue Testament*, 17th edn. by P. Feine and J. Behm ([1973]; Eng. tr., 1975); J. L. Crenshaw, *Story and Faith: A Guide to the Old Testament* (New York, 1986). *The Cambridge History of the Bible*, ed. S. L. Greenslade and others (3 vols., Cambridge, 1963–70). H. von Campenhausen, *Die Entstehung der Christlichen Bibel* (Beiträge zur historischen Theologie, 39; 1968; Eng. tr., *The Formation of the Christian Bible*, 1972); *Bible de tous les temps*, ed. C. Kannengiesser, SJ (8 vols., 1984–9).

AUTHORITY AND INTERPRETATION. K. Scholder, *Ursprünge und Probleme der Bibelkritik im 17. Jahrhundert* (Forschungen zur Geschichte und Lehre des Protestantismus, Zehnte Reihe, 33; 1966; Eng. tr., *The Birth of Modern Critical Theology*, 1990); J. Barr, *The Bible in the Modern World* (1973), and other works of this author; H. W. Frei, *The Eclipse of Biblical Narrative: A Study in Eighteenth and Nineteenth Century Hermeneutics* (New Haven, Conn., and London, 1974); D. H. Kelsey, *The Uses of Scripture in Recent Theology* (1975); D. [E.] Nineham, *The Use and Abuse of the Bible: A Study of the Bible in an Age of Rapid Cultural Change* (1976); H. Reventlow, *Bibelautorität und Geist der Moderne* (Forschungen zur Kirchen- und Dogmengeschichte, 30; 1980; Eng. tr., with additional material, *The Authority of the Bible and the Rise of the Modern World*, 1984); J. Barton, *People of the Book? The Authority of the Bible in Christianity* (Bampton Lectures for 1988; 1988); R. [C.] Morgan and J. Barton, *Biblical Interpretation* (Oxford Bible Series, 1988). See also bibl. to HERMENEUTICS.

Bible (English versions).

I. PRE-REFORMATION VERSIONS. No complete Anglo-Saxon Bible, or even NT, exists. Translations of this period comprise (a) interlinear glosses (forming a crude word-by-word translation) of the Gospels and Pss., and (b) versions, sometimes abridged, of separate portions of the Bible, e.g. parts of Exod. 20–3 in the introductory section of King *Alfred's Laws, a prose version of Pss. 1–50 (possibly by Alfred himself), and the four Gospels in W. Saxon (perhaps 10th cent.). Free renderings of OT narrative passages occur in the homilies of *Aelfric (c.992), who also translated Gen. 1–35 (36–50 having been done by another hand previously) and (with considerable omissions) Exod. 1–Josh. 11. There are also numerous detached quotations and free renderings of other parts of the Bible in homilies.

In Middle English, from c.1250 onwards, metrical versions of certain Books (esp. Gen. and Exod.), of biblical history generally, and of the Psalter, were made. There followed in Midland and in Northern dialect prose versions of the Psalter, the latter by Richard *Rolle of Hampole.

In the 14th cent. several anonymous translations of NT Books in various dialects were produced, apparently in connection with *Lollardy and under the influence of J. *Wycliffe. But the popular view that Wycliffe himself was the first English translator of the complete Bible seems to be without foundation. There are two 'Wycliffite' versions:

(a) Early Version. The most important MS is Bodley 959, which covers the greater part of the OT (i.e. as far as Bar. 3: 20, in Vulgate order). This early version, which was made by the 1390s, has been associated with *Nicholas Hereford. It was very literal, and was soon revised.

(b) Later Version. This was produced on the basis of an intermediate version; later critics suggested it was connected with John *Purvey. In the prologue the translator explains his method of working 'with divers fellows and helpers' and with 'many good fellows and cunning at the correcting of the translation'. It is much more idiomatic than the early version.

Both these versions, esp. the former, follow the Vulgate (then the only text available), often so closely as to be detrimental to the clarity of the English. At the Council of Oxford in 1407 the making of any fresh translations of the whole or any portion of the Bible and the use of any translation made 'in the times of John Wycliffe or since' without diocesan or synodical sanction were forbidden. Nevertheless many MSS of the Wycliffite versions (esp. the later text) continued to be made and used until the appearance of W. *Tyndale's and M. *Coverdale's work.

2. THE REFORMATION PERIOD. The Wycliffite versions, being under ecclesiastical censure, were not printed. New facilities for textual study and translation of the Bible were opened up by the printing of the Vulgate (first in 1456), the Hebrew text (1488), *Erasmus' Greek Testament (1516, with four revisions by 1535), the *Complutensian Polyglot (1522), and S. *Pagninus' literal Latin rendering of the Hebrew OT (1528). The plan of a translation of the NT from the Greek is due to W. Tyndale and dates from c.1523. He failed to obtain the patronage of C. *Tunstall, Bp. of London, but for a short while was supported by Humphrey Monmouth, a London merchant. In 1524 he fled to Germany, where he probably met at *Wittenberg M. *Luther, whose German NT had appeared in 1522. The printing of Tyndale's NT (in 4to) was begun at *Cologne in 1525; but before it was complete Tyndale was forced to flee to Worms, where it was restarted and finished (in 8vo) in 1526. Subsequent editions were printed in the Netherlands, and copies soon reached England. Tyndale then translated the *Pentateuch, which was printed at Antwerp in 1529–30. His translation of Jonah appeared in 1531 and a revision of Gen. and of the NT in 1534, and of the NT again in 1535. He also translated, but never published, Josh.–2 Chron. inclusive. His NT and Pentateuch contained marginal notes, described by *Henry VIII as 'pestilent glosses', expressing his strongly Protestant views. In his prefaces, prologues, marginal references, etc., Tyndale is greatly dependent on Luther, but his translation is an independent and pioneer work, using Erasmus' Latin version of the NT, the Vulgate, and Luther's German, as well as his own interpretation of the original. His final version of the NT contains much which passed unchanged into the Authorized Version.

In 1534 Canterbury *Convocation petitioned Henry VIII that the whole Bible might be translated into English. Though no royal command to this effect was issued, Miles *Coverdale published in 1535 a complete Bible, dedicated to the King. He based his rendering on Tyndale's where available; the other OT books he translated from the German of Luther and the Zurich version of U. *Zwingli and Leo Juda, with guidance from Pagninus and the Vulgate. He does not appear to have known Hebrew. His Psalter has remained in constant use until modern times in the BCP version of the Psalms. In 1537 a revised English Bible known as '*Matthew's Bible' appeared. It was the first to bear the King's authorization and was printed in Antwerp for the London printers, R. *Grafton and E. *Whitchurch. The ascription to 'Thomas Matthew' was nominal (the suggested identification with one Thomas Matthew of Colchester is improbable), its real editor being John *Rogers. The text consisted of Tyndale's Pentateuch, a version of Josh.–2 Chron. made from the Hebrew and hitherto unpublished (prob. also Tyndale's, cf. above), Tyndale's NT of 1535, and the remainder in Coverdale's version. Rogers's work was confined to careful editing and adaptation. For the Prayer of Manasses, omitted by Coverdale, he translated the French version of *Olivetan, from whom also he took some editorial matter. At about the same time Coverdale's Bible, previously printed abroad, was for the first time printed in England.

Further revisions of the whole Bible followed. The '*Great Bible' of 1539, printed in Paris, was issued under T. *Cromwell's patronage. In 1540 it was revised and reissued with a preface by T. *Cranmer and a notice identifying it with the 'Bible in the largest volume in English' which the *Injunction of 1538 ordered to be set up in churches. Both these revisions, which claimed on the title-page of 1539 to have been made from the Hebrew and Greek 'by the diligent study of divers excellent learned men', were by Coverdale, though they did not bear his name. Among the 'learned men' whom Coverdale had consulted was S. *Münster, who in 1534–5 had issued a literal German translation of the Hebrew. All notes and controversial matter were deliberately excluded. In 1539 R. *Taverner also published a revision of 'Matthew's Bible' based on careful attention to the Greek and to the Vulgate OT. In 1542 S. *Gardiner, Bp. of *Winchester, headed a reaction in favour of the Vulgate, and in 1546 the use of Tyndale's or Coverdale's NT was forbidden by royal decree. Under *Edward VI this policy was reversed by the Protestant movement and the English versions were again reprinted.

In the reign of *Mary, W. *Whittingham issued at Geneva in 1557 a new English NT for the Protestant exiles (for the first time divided into verses and printed in roman type). Then followed in 1559 the Psalms, and in 1560 a complete Bible, dedicated to Queen *Elizabeth I. This version (the '*Geneva Bible' (q.v.), also popularly the '*Breeches Bible') was based on Tyndale and the Great Bible, but influenced by J. *Calvin and T. *Beza, as well as by the French Bibles of Lefèvre and Olivetan. It had marginal notes written from an extreme Protestant viewpoint. Many of its renderings, not found in previous English versions, were later adopted into the AV.

In the reign of Elizabeth I the Geneva Bible obtained great popularity in England, although it lacked the royal and ecclesiastical authorization still possessed by the Great Bible. In 1566 Abp. M. *Parker undertook a revision of the latter in co-operation with other bishops. This new translation (the '*Bishops' Bible') was published in 1568 and revised in 1572. It copied the Geneva Bible in the adoption of verse-divisions, but the rendering was explicitly based on the Great Bible, with attention to the Greek and to the Hebrew, for which Pagninus and Münster were taken as authorities. Phrases which savoured of 'lightness or obscenity' were altered and passages considered unedifying were marked for omission in public reading. All comment, in the form of marginal notes, was eschewed. As the several revisers worked without much co-ordination, this translation varies in quality from Book to Book.

Though not yet acknowledging the right of the laity to read the Bible in the vernacular without special ecclesiastical sanction, the RC Church also felt the need for an acceptable English version. The NT was translated by members of the English College at Reims, largely at the instigation of W. (later Cardinal) *Allen. The chief translators were Gregory *Martin and Richard Bristow, and it was issued in 1582. The OT followed from Douai in 1609–1610 (see DOUAI-REIMS BIBLE). Both NT and OT were translated from the Vulgate, in acc. with the Council of Trent's endorsement of this version; but in the NT at least the original language was consulted. Many words and turns of phrase show the close adherence (also deliberate) of the translators to their standard, e.g. 'Pasch' (Passover), 'Azymes' (Unleavened Bread), 'supersubstantial bread' (Mt. 6: 11), 'legates of Christ' (ambassadors). But in many places the English is vivid and direct. The Reims NT was among the versions consulted by the makers of the AV.

3. THE AUTHORIZED VERSION (1611) AND ITS SUCCESSORS. At the *Hampton Court Conference a new version of the Bible was suggested to *James I, who in the same year appointed for the task 54 divines, among them the Puritan J. *Rainolds, J. Bois of Cambridge, H. *Savile, J. *Overall, L. *Andrewes, and W. *Barlow. The 'Bishops' Bible' was used as a basis, but earlier English versions were taken into consideration, and the new Bible was designedly a revision rather than a completely original work. Careful marginal notes on matters of text and translation (not theology) were provided and the best resources of contemporary scholarship were utilized. The result, published in 1611, was a version of great felicity, which within a generation displaced all previous versions, and became the only familiar, and in most cases the only known, form of the Bible to generations of English-speaking people. Beyond the royal authority under which it was made, and the statement on the title-page 'Appointed to be read in churches', no formal authorization was given to it. In the BCP of 1662 it was adopted as the text for the Epistles and Gospels, though the Psalter remained in Coverdale's version. It was

carried from England to the American Colonies, and it continues in use in the USA, where it is known as the 'King James Version', and in other English-speaking countries. See also AUTHORIZED VERSION.

The Authorized Version was not accepted entirely without criticism, but projects for further revision, e.g. that of the Long Parliament of 1653, came to nothing. Modifications in spelling, punctuation, use of capitals, etc., were unobtrusively made by editors, esp. T. Paris at Cambridge (1762) and B. Blayney at Oxford (1769), and the headlines of pages and the marginal references altered in different editions. The only new translations or revisions from this period were private ones. J. *Wesley's *Explanatory Notes on the New Testament* (1755) embodied a conservative revision of the AV. Other 18th-cent. translators (e.g. D. *Mace, 1729) went further in the introduction of colloquialisms or in free paraphrase into the style of contemporary elegance, esp. E. Hardwood's *A Liberal Translation of the NT* (1768). Among scholarly translations of individual books was R. *Lowth's *Isaiah* (1778). The Reims-Douai version was revised by Bp. R. *Challoner (1749–50); and versions of the Pentateuch were issued by the Jewish scholars I. Delgado (1785) and D. Levi (1787).

4. THE REVISED VERSION (1881–5) and AMERICAN STANDARD VERSION (1901). The growth of biblical scholarship and the availability of new versions for comparison, as well as changes in English usage since 1611, led to occasional expressions of dissatisfaction with the AV from the early 19th cent., and from the middle of the century proposals for the revision of the AV were both advocated and opposed. In 1870 the Convocation of Canterbury took up the matter and a committee of revisers, to which non-Anglican scholars were co-opted, was appointed. They were instructed to 'introduce as few alterations as possible into the text of the AV, consistently with faithfulness' and 'to limit, as far as possible, the expression of such alterations to the language of the Authorized and earlier English versions'. No change in the text was to be finally approved except by a two-thirds majority; changes supported by only a simple majority were to be noted in the margin. The NT was published in 1881, the OT in 1885. The *Apocrypha was undertaken after the main work, and issued in 1895. As far as practicable, the revisers used the same English word or phrase for the same Hebrew or Greek, thus facilitating the study of the original through the medium of the English. The Psalms and other poetical OT books were printed in lines according to their original structure, the rest of the text in paragraphs instead of in separate verses. The *American Standard Version* (pub. 1901) incorporated into the text of the RV those renderings preferred by the American scholars who had co-operated (by correspondence).

5. MODERN TRANSLATIONS. Since the publication of the RV and its American counterpart there have been numerous translations of single books produced as parts of learned commentaries and separately. There have also been a number of private translations of the complete NT or the whole Bible, aiming increasingly at making the Bible intelligible to the common man. These have included, on the Protestant side, the NT of R. F. Weymouth (1903); the NT (1913) and OT (1924) of J. *Moffatt (whole Bible, revised, 1935); *The Bible: An American Translation* by E. J.

Goodspeed (NT, 1923, and Apocrypha, 1938) and J. M. Powis Smith (OT, 1935); *The New Testament in Modern English* (1958; revised 1973) by J. B. Phillips (1906–82, a parish priest of the C of E who retired in 1955 to devote himself to writing), originally pub. as *Letters to Young Churches* (1947), *The Gospels* (1952), and *The Young Church in Action* (Acts, 1955); two versions in completely non-ecclesiastical English: *The Good News Bible: Today's English Version* pub. by the American and other Bible Societies (NT, New York, 1966; in Britain, slightly adapted, 1968; whole Bible in both editions, 1976), and *The Living Bible* paraphrased by K. N. Taylor (Wheaton, Ill., NT, 1967; adapted British version, 1969; complete Bible in both editions, 1971); and the much more traditional NT version by W. *Barclay (2 vols., 1968–9). There have also been two RC translations: the *Westminster Version of the Holy Scriptures*, ed. by C. Lattey and J. Keating (NT, 1935; OT incomplete), translated from the original languages, with attention to the Vulgate, and the version of R. A. *Knox (NT, 1945; OT, 1948–9; whole Bible, 1955), made from the (Clementine) Vulgate with due attention to the Greek and Hebrew. The latter, which was commissioned by the English RC hierarchy, after some hesitation received ecclesiastical sanction and gained some approbation from non-RCs for its literary merit. It has now been largely superseded by the *Jerusalem Bible* (see below).

The most important 20th-cent. biblical translations, as in the past, have been corporate ventures. A version in Basic English (i.e. using a restricted vocabulary advocated for teaching English to foreigners) of the NT (1941) and of the complete Bible (1949) was made by a committee under the chairmanship of S. H. Hooke. Of far greater significance was the *Revised Standard Version* (NT, 1946; OT, 1952; Apocrypha, 1957). This was a revision of the *American Standard Version*, intended to stand 'in the Tyndale–King James tradition', undertaken by a committee representing the major Protestant Churches of N. America; the revisers took account of current scholarship and changes in language to produce a rendering more accurate than the *American Standard Version* and free from archaisms thought to be misleading, unintelligible, or unnecessary, but preserving a dignity suitable for public worship. The RSV came to be widely used not only in America but also in Britain (where it is printed in editions with British spellings) and other English-speaking countries. Its faithfulness to the original, and relative caution in modernization, have given it a wide appeal among all traditions, including conservative evangelicals (see FUNDAMENTALISM). In 1965 the NT, and in 1966 the whole Bible (in Vulgate order) appeared in a 'Catholic edition' bearing the *imprimatur; it had slight textual changes and some adaptations in the notes for RC readers. In what became known as the 'Common Bible' (1973), designed to appeal to RCs, Protestants, and Orthodox alike, the RSV text was rearranged so that those parts of the Apocrypha which were included in the OT in the Vulgate (e.g. Esther) were printed between the NT and OT and the material regarded by neither RCs or Protestants as canonical, but included as an appendix in the Vulgate (e.g. the Prayer of Manasseh), was printed as an appendix. A revision of the RSV, the *New Revised Standard Version* appeared in 1989.

While avoiding archaisms and almost always using inclusive language, this translation is in direct descent from the AV and retains much of its solemnity.

The *New English Bible* (NT 1961; whole Bible, with slightly revised NT, 1970) is in a different mould. It was designed as a new translation of the Bible into contemporary English, to be made from the original languages and drawing on the best scholarship and literary judgement. It was made under the direction of a Joint Committee of the non-RC Churches of the British Isles, established in 1947 on the initiative of the Church of Scotland, with the co-operation of the *British and Foreign Bible Society and the National Bible Society of Scotland. The panels of translators worked under the chairmanship of C. H. *Dodd from 1950 to 1965, and from 1965 under that of Dodd and Sir Godfrey *Driver jointly. The NEB won limited acceptance, partly because of its academic flavour, and in 1974 a revision was undertaken by a panel, including RCs, under the chairmanship of W. D. McHardy. The *Revised English Bible* (1989) is a radical revision of the NEB. While generally more conservative in its treatment of the original text, it avoids the eccentricities of individual views that are reflected in the NEB and is generally more satisfactory for public reading. Inclusive language is used where it is thought not to endanger the original sense, and 'thou' is no longer retained in passages where God is addressed.

The *Jerusalem Bible* (1966) is an English parallel, made by a group of English-speaking RCs under the chairmanship of Alexander Jones, of *La Bible de Jérusalem*. This was a French rendering of the original Hebrew, Greek, and Aramaic texts, with extensive notes, made by members of the *Dominican École Biblique in Jerusalem and published in France (1948–54; first one-volume edition, 1956). The English text generally follows the interpretation of the French but was made with reference to the original languages and is accompanied by revised notes. It follows the Vulgate order but has the traditional (AV/RV) English forms of biblical names rather than those of the Douai version (e.g. Hosea, not Osee); it uses 'Yahweh' not 'the Lord' to represent the *tetragrammaton in the OT and 'you' rather than 'thee' and 'thou' in passages addressing God. Its revision, *The New Jerusalem Bible* (1985), produced under the chairmanship of Dom Henry Wansbrough, OSB, makes use of the new edition of *La Bible de Jérusalem* (1973), whose interpretation it normally follows in the notes and introduction, though incorporating the results of biblical scholarship since 1973. The translation, again made from the original languages, uses the same word for key terms throughout. It was the first complete English version to make serious efforts at inclusive language. Both the JB and the NJB have been accepted by many outside the RC Church.

Other modern translations include the *New American Bible* (1970), made by members of the Catholic Biblical Association of America under the patronage of the Bishops' Committee of the Confraternity of Christian Doctrine and widely used by RCs in the USA; the *New International Version* (1978 in the USA; 1979 in Britain), the work of scholars from different parts of the English-speaking world, representing a broad range of *evangelical denominations, directed by the New York Bible Society; and the *New King James Version* (NT, 1979; whole Bible,

1982; text adapted to British usage as the *Revised Authorized Version*, 1982); the primary aim of this translation is to recast the AV in modern English without sacrificing its 'majestic and reverent style'.

In the C of E, the liturgical reading of the AV is assumed in the BCP, but the legality of reading the RV was established in 1899. In 1965 the Prayer Book (Versions of the Bible) Measure authorized the optional use, for any scriptural passage, of the RSV or NEB. Since then a wide variety of translations has been authorized, and the ASB includes passages from the RSV, NEB, JB, and Today's English Version (*The Good News Bible*) among the readings for the Eucharist. In the RC Church national hierarchies each authorize translations for liturgical use; those sanctioned in England and Wales include the Knox version, the RSV, NRSV, JB, and NJB; the *New American Bible* is favoured in the USA.

The principal edns. of the pre-Reformation versions are: W. W. Skeat (ed.), *The Gospel according to Saint Mark in Anglo-Saxon and Northumbrian Versions* (Cambridge, 1871); id. (ed.), *The Gospel according to Saint Luke* ... (ibid., 1874); id. (ed.), *The Gospel according to Saint John* ... (ibid., 1878); id. (ed.), *The Gospel according to Saint Matthew in Anglo-Saxon, Northumbrian, and Old Mercian Versions* (ibid., 1887); J. W. Bright (ed.), *The Gospel of Saint Luke in Anglo-Saxon* (Oxford, 1893); these will be superseded by R. M. Liuzza (ed.), *The Old English Version of the Gospels* (EETS 304, etc.; 1994 ff.); H. Sweet (ed.), *The Oldest English Texts* (ibid. 83; 1885), pp. 183–420 [Vespasian Psalter]); G. P. Krapp (ed.), *The Paris Psalter* (New York, 1932); K. D. Bülbring (ed.), *The Earliest Complete English Prose Psalter*, pt. 1 (EETS 97; 1891); H. R. Bramley (ed.), *The Psalter or Psalms of David and Certain Canticles with a Translation and Exposition in English by Richard Rolle of Hampole* (Oxford, 1884); A. C. Paues (ed.), *A Fourteenth Century English Biblical Version* (Cambridge, 1904); J. Forshall and F. Madden (eds.), *The Holy Bible ... in the Earliest English Versions made from the Latin Vulgate by John Wycliffe and his Followers* (5 vols., Oxford, 1850); C. Lindberg (ed.), *MS. Bodley 959* (Acta Universitatis Stockholmiensis, Stockholm Studies in English, 6, 8, 10, 13, 20; 1959–69); the remaining part of the early version of the OT ed. from MS Christ Church 145, by id. (ibid. 29; 1973).

M. Deanesly, *The Lollard Bible and other Medieval Biblical Versions* (1920). S. L. Fristedt, *The Wycliffite Bible*, pt. 1 (Stockholm Studies in English, 4; 1953); id., 'New Light on John Wycliffe and the First Full English Bible' in *Studier i modern Språkvetenskap*, NS 3 (1968), pp. 61–86. *The English Hexapla of the NT Scriptures* [Wycliffe, Tyndale, Cranmer, Genevan, Anglo-Rhemish, Authorized] (1841). B. F. Westcott, *A General View of the History of the English Bible* (1868; 3rd edn., rev. W. A. Wright, 1905); A. W. Pollard, *Records of the English Bible* (1911); H. W. *Robinson (ed.), *The Bible in its Ancient and English Versions* (1940); C. C. Butterworth, *The Literary Lineage of the King James Bible 1340–1611* (Philadelphia, 1941); H. Pope, OP, *English Versions of the Bible* (St Louis, 1952); F. F. Bruce, *The English Bible: A History of Translations* (1961; 3rd edn., 1979); F. C. Grant, *Translating the Bible* (1961). S. L. Greenslade (ed.), *The Cambridge History of the Bible: The West from the Reformation to the Present Day* (1963), esp. pp. 141–70 and 361–82; G. Hammond, *The Making of the English Bible* (Manchester, 1982); E. H. Robertson, *Makers of the English Bible* (Cambridge, 1990); D. Norton, *A History of the Bible as Literature* (2 vols., ibid., 1993). G. [N. S.] Hunt, *About the New English Bible* (1970); R. Coleman, *New Light and Truth: The Making of the Revised English Bible* (Oxford and Cambridge, 1989); B. M. Metzger and others, *The Making of the New Revised Standard Version of the Bible* (Grand Rapids, Mich., 1991). For printed edns., see list in Darlow and Moule, ed. A. S. Herbert, 1 (1968). M. T. Hills (ed.), *The English Bible in America: A Bibliography of Editions of the Bible & New Testament Published in America 1777–1957* (New York, 1961).

Bible Christians (or **Bryanites**). One of the bodies which went to form the *United Methodist Church in 1907. It traces its origin to William O'Bryan (1778–1868), a local preacher of the *Wesleyan Methodist Church. Finding many of the villages of Devon and Cornwall in almost complete ignorance of the Gospel, he extended his very successful evangelism beyond the limits of his own circuit. In the conflict with the local Wesleyan authorities which ensued, O'Bryan, not without hesitation and regret, separated himself, and in 1815 he founded the first society of a new community at Shebbear, in N. Devon. Although faced by much opposition and persecution the new movement spread rapidly. At the end of the first year there were 567 members, and after only five years of work in the west, missionaries were sent to Kent and London. In 1831 missions were founded in Canada and Prince Edward Island; in 1846, in the USA; in 1850, in Australia. Membership reached its maximum at 32,317 in 1906.

For several years O'Bryan, as the founder of the movement, was accepted as the natural head of the Society and president of its annual Conference. His assumption of autocratic control of the property and affairs of his Churches gradually led to disputes, which were temporarily settled in 1827 by the Conference being the recognized organ of government with O'Bryan continuing as president. O'Bryan, however, was dissatisfied and in 1829 left his Society; in 1831 he went to America. Later he was reconciled to the Conference, though he never rejoined it.

The Bible Christians held the doctrines common to all the branches of Methodism. When the Conference was officially constituted in 1831 provision was made for the inclusion of lay representatives. Women were admitted to the ministry equally with men, esp. in the earliest period. As it grew the movement did notable missionary work, e.g. that of Samuel Pollard in SW China.

In 1907 the Bible Christians united with the *Methodist New Connexion and the *United Methodist Free Churches to form the *United Methodist Church.

T. Shaw, *The Bible Christians 1815–1907* (1965). J. T. Wilkinson in R. [E.] Davies, A. R. George, and [E.] G. Rupp (eds.), *A History of the Methodist Church in Great Britain*, 2 (1978), pp. 294–303; 3 (1983), pp. 169–72, with bibl.

Bible Churchmen's Missionary Society. See BCMS.

Bible divisions and references. The division of major sections of the OT (such as the *Pentateuch) into Books was associated with the amount of material that would fit on to a single scroll. When the Hebrew was translated into Greek, which takes more space than Hebrew (partly because Greek is written with a full set of vowels), some Books (Sam., Kgs., Chron.) were divided into two. In other parts of the OT and in the NT single items which were collected in the Bible constituted Books. The Hebrew Bible was further divided into sections for liturgical reading in Jewish services; these divisions were marked in the margin in much the same way as was done in the Church (see LECTIONARY) and continue to appear in printed Hebrew Bibles. Paragraph and verse divisions existed in Hebrew MSS from a very early date; paragraphs are found in the *Dead Sea Scrolls and verses are referred to in the *Mishnah (Megillah, 4. 4). A reference system which used paragraphs denoted by letters of the alphabet was introduced in NT MSS from the middle of the 13th cent. Chapter divisions originated in Christian Bibles. Introduced for ease of reference, they followed a number of schemes, e.g. that of the *Eusebian Canons; the oldest known system of capitation of the Bible is that preserved in the margins of *Codex Vaticanus (4th cent.). The system in current use is attributed to S. *Langton (d. 1228). It was adapted to the Hebrew Bible in Rabbi Isaac Nathan's concordance produced in the middle of the 15th cent., though chapters in the Hebrew Bible do not always correspond exactly with those of the OT in Christian Bibles. The first printed Hebrew Bible to contain chapter divisions was that produced by D. Bomberg in 1517. Verse numbers were first used by Rabbi Nathan; they were taken over in the Latin translation of S. *Paginus and in the French (1553) and Latin (1555) Bibles of Robert Estienne I (*Stephanus). For the NT Estienne did not follow the cumbersome divisions of Paginus but in 1551 introduced numbered verses in his edition of the Gk. and Lat. NT. These have remained in use ever since. The first Bibles to have numbered verses throughout were those of Estienne just mentioned. The *Geneva Bible (1560) was the first such English Bible.

C. D. Ginsburg, *Introduction to the Massoretico-Critical Edition of the Hebrew Bible* (1897), pp. 1–108. J. M. Oesch, *Petucha und Setuma: Untersuchungen zu einer überlieferten Gliederung im hebräischen Text des Alten Testaments* (Orbis Biblicus et Orientalis, 27; 1979). G. F. Moore, 'The Vulgate Chapters and Numbered Verses in the Hebrew Bible', *Journal of Biblical Literature*, 13 (1893), pp. 73–8. J. H. Harris, 'Some Notes on the Verse-Division of the New Testament', ibid. 19 (1900), pp. 114–23. B. Smalley, *The Study of the Bible in the Middle Ages* (2nd edn., Oxford, 1952; 3rd edn., 1983), pp. 222–4, with refs. F. Kenyon, *Our Bible and the Ancient Manuscripts* (5th edn. by A. W. Adams, 1958), pp. 261 and 299. B. M. Metzger, *The Text of the New Testament* (Oxford, 1964; 3rd edn., 1992), pp. 22–5; id., *Manuscripts of the Greek Bible* (New York and Oxford, 1981), pp. 40–43. Darlow and Moule, pt. 2 (1911), p. 388 (no. 3719); pt. 3 (1911), pp. 588–90 (no. 4623), pp. 924 f. (no. 6108), and pp. 938 f. (nos. 6135 f.).

Bible Society, British and Foreign. See BRITISH AND FOREIGN BIBLE SOCIETY.

Biblia Pauperum (Lat., 'the Bible of Poor Men'). Though also employed from the early Middle Ages to describe various other short biblical summaries for elementary instruction, the title *Biblia Pauperum* is used to denote specifically a picture-book in which on each page a set group of figures illustrates a NT antitype flanked by two corresponding OT *types, with short explanatory texts from the Bible and mnemonic verses. More than 80 MS examples are known from the 14th cent.; they can be grouped into separately recognizable traditions from Austria and S. Germany. Soon after the invention of printing in the mid-15th cent., the *Biblia Pauperum* enjoyed a short vogue in the Netherlands and Germany in the form of various blockbook (xylographic) editions, each double page of pictures and text being printed from a single woodcut, or made up of a mixture of woodcut pictures and hand-written text. The text may be in Latin or German. A number of these blockbook editions have been reproduced in facsimile.

Description and discussion of MSS in [J.] H. Cornell, *Biblia Pauperum* (Stockholm, 1925). G. Schmidt, *Die Armenbibeln des XIV. Jahrhunderts* (Veröffentlichungen des Instituts für Österreichische Geschichtsforschung, 19; 1959). A. Henry, *Biblia Pauperum* (Aldershot, 1987) [facsimile of a blockbook of c.1460, with Eng. tr.], incl. general introd. pp. 3–46. R. L. P. Milburn in G. W. H. Lampe (ed.), *The Cambridge History of the Bible*, 2 (1969), pp. 280–308. K.-A. Wirth in *Verfasserlexikon* (2nd edn.), 1 (1978), cols. 843–52, s.v.

Bibliander (= Buchmann), Theodor (c.1504–64), Orientalist and Protestant theologian. He succeeded to U. *Zwingli's chair at Zurich University on the Reformer's death in 1531. He maintained that the heathen possessed by the law of nature a knowledge of God, and attacked the *Calvinistic doctrine of *predestination. Among his chief works were a Hebrew grammar (1535), editions of the *Koran (1543) and of the *Protevangelium Jacobi (1552), and some studies in chronology (1551; 1558).

E. Egli, *Analecta Reformatoria*, 2 (1901), pp. 1–144. R. Pfister, 'Das Türkenbüchlein Theodor Biblianders', *Theologische Zeitschrift*, 9 (1953), pp. 438–54. E. Egli in *PRE* (3rd edn.), 3 (1897), pp. 185–7, s.v.

Biblical Commission. Originally a committee of five *cardinals, assisted by 39 consultors, created as an organ for the study of the Bible in the RC Church. It was instituted by *Leo XIII in the apostolic letter 'Vigilantiae' (30 Oct. 1902) to further biblical studies in conformity with the requirements of modern scholarship and to safeguard the authority of Scripture against the attacks of exaggerated criticism. In 1904 it was empowered to confer ecclesiastical academic degrees. One of its chief tasks was to answer questions on biblical matters. Among its notable *responsa* were those on the Mosaic authorship of the *Pentateuch (1906), the authenticity and historicity of Jn. (1907), the authenticity and character of Is. (1908), the historicity of Gen. 1–3 (1909), and the *Synoptic Problem (1912). The *responsa* were never understood to have been issued infallibly. In his motu proprio 'Praestantia sacrae Scripturae' (1907) *Pius X considered them 'useful for the proper progress and guidance of biblical scholarship along safe lines'. He did, however, require the same submission by RCs to those *responsa* as to similar papally approved decrees of other *Roman Congregations, and consequently a dark cloud of fear and reactionary conservatism settled over RC biblical scholarship in the first half of the 20th cent. A more liberal attitude to biblical criticism was reflected in *Pius XII's encyclical 'Divino afflante Spiritu' (30 Sept. 1943). The *responsa* gave way to 'letters' and 'instructions' in which, though concern was at times expressed about excessive tendencies, the Commission gradually assumed a more positive stance. In 1954 a second edition of the *Enchiridion Biblicum* was issued. The Commission's secretary, A. Miller, and its subsecretary, A. Kleinhans, reviewed it in texts which were almost identical save for the language (German and Latin). They declared that *responsa* touching on faith and morals were still valid, whereas those that dealt with literary questions were to be regarded as conditioned by their time and corresponding to a historical context that no longer existed; in such cases the RC interpreter could proceed 'with full freedom' (*in aller Freiheit, plena libertate*). The Commission's instruction 'De historica evangeliorum veritate' (1964) explicitly reckoned with *form criticism and distinguished three stages in the development of the Gospel tradition. Its essential content was briefly summarized in 'Dei Verbum' (§ 19) of the Second *Vatican Council. In 1971 *Paul VI reorganized the Biblical Commission, making it the counterpart of the International Theological Commission, a part of the Congregation for the *Doctrine of the Faith. It is now composed of 20 RC biblical scholars who meet once a year and advise the Congregation and the Pope on biblical aspects of current theological issues. Since that reorganization the Commission has published various statements.

The names of the members of the Commission are given in *Annuario Pontificio*. The *responsa* are pr. in *Enchiridion Biblicum: Documenta Ecclesiastica Sacram Scripturam Spectantia auctoritate Pontificiae Commissionis de Re Biblica edita* (4th edn., Rome and Naples, 1961), nos. 160 f., 181–4, 187–9, 276–80, 324–39, 383–416, 513–21, 534–7, and 621; two letters, ibid., nos. 522–33 and 577–81; most are also pr. in Denzinger and Hünermann (37th edn., 1991), nos. 3372 f., 3394–400, 3505–9, 3512–28, 3561–78, 3581–93, 3628–30, 3750 f., 3792–6, and 3862–4. The instruction 'De historica evangeliorum veritate' is pr. in *AAS* 56 (1964), pp. 712–18; Eng. tr. and comm. by J. A. Fitzmyer, SJ, *A Christological Catechism* (New York, etc. [1982]), pp. 97–140. Reviews of *Enchiridion Biblicum* (2nd edn.) by A. Miller, OSB, in *Benediktinische Monatschrift*, 31 (1955), pp. 49 f., and by A. Kleinhans, OFM, in *Antonianum*, 30 (1955), pp. 63–5; cf. E. F. Siegman, CPPS, 'The Decrees of the Pontifical Biblical Commission. A recent clarification', *Catholic Biblical Quarterly*, 18 (1956), pp. 23–9. More recent statements of the Commission include 'Can Women be Priests?', *Origins*, 6 (1976–7), pp. 92–6; *Fede e cultura alla luce della Bibbia* (Turin, 1981); *Bible et Christologie* (Paris, 1984); *Unité et diversité dans l'église* (Vatican City, 1989); and *L'Interprétation de la Bible dans l'église* (ibid., 1993; also conveniently pr. in *Biblica*, 84 (1993), pp. 451–528).

Biblical Theology. In 1787 J. P. Gabler drew a distinction between biblical theology and dogmatic theology, the former being the non-dogmatic description of the religious doctrines contained in the Bible and the latter the traditional dogmatic interpretation of them. The term is now more often used with reference to a movement among biblical scholars in the mid-20th cent. which was derived from the thought of K. *Barth and others of similar outlook. Though by no means homogeneous, it usually exhibited the following characteristics: (1) Biblical concepts were held to be *sui generis*, and in particular a sharp contrast was drawn between Hebrew and Greek thought, to the advantage of the former. (2) Biblical concepts were held to be still adequate for all essential purposes. (3) God's action in history was taken to be the primary medium of revelation, and a distinctive stream of 'salvation history' was often isolated. Christian faith was held to be based on events as opposed to ideas. (4) Emphasis was placed on the inner coherence of the biblical material, often represented as centred upon certain key concepts, e.g. '*covenant' or '*kerygma'. (5) A fairly conservative attitude was taken with regard to the historical trustworthiness of the biblical records.

In Britain and America the movement was less conceptually based than it was in Germany, where it underlay G. *Kittel's influential *Wörterbuch* of the NT. It provided a route by which scientific study of the Bible could make its way in the RC Church and has had considerable influence on the choice and arrangement of the biblical material in the modern liturgies of the RC and other Churches. In 1961 it was seriously challenged by J. Barr on the ground that it failed to do justice to the complex interrelations of biblical and non-biblical cultures. Others have argued that it exaggerated the historical trustworthiness of the Bible. Considerable diversity is now found within the biblical material, and further study of cultural relativism has raised doubts whether biblical ways of thinking can be applied to the contemporary situation in the way the proponents of biblical theology presupposed. These included O. *Cullmann, C. H. *Dodd, G. von *Rad, and A. Richardson (1905–75).

G. E. Wright, *God Who Acts: Biblical Theology as Recital* (Studies in Biblical Theology, 8; 1952). J. Barr, *The Semantics of Biblical Language* (Oxford, 1961), esp. pp. 263–87, and other works of this author; B. S. Childs, *Biblical Theology in Crisis* (Philadelphia [1970]); H.-J. Kraus, *Die Biblische Theologie* (Neukirchen, 1970); W. J. Harrington, OP, *The Path of Biblical Theology* (Dublin, 1973); D. [E.] Nineham, *The Use and Abuse of the Bible* (1976), esp. pp. 73–93; J. D. G. Dunn, *Unity and Diversity in the New Testament* (1977; 2nd edn., 1990); J. D. Smart, *The Past, Present, and Future of Biblical Theology* (Philadelphia [1979]); H. Reventlow, *Hauptprobleme der Biblischen Theologie im 20. Jahrhundert* (Darmstadt, 1983; Eng. tr., 1986).

bibliolatry. Excessive veneration for the letter of Scripture, as found in certain *Protestants in *Reformation times and since. Cf. the cry that 'The Bible, and the Bible only, is the religion of Protestants' (based on a misunderstanding of W. *Chillingworth).

Bickell, Gustav (1838–1906), Orientalist and patristic scholar. A convert to the RC Church (1865), he was ordained priest in 1867 and was elected to professorships at Innsbruck (1874) and Vienna (1892). His patristic writings include editions of St *Ephraem's *Carmina Nisibena* (1866) and the works of Isaac of Antioch (2 vols., 1873–77). He also wrote on the origins of the Christian Eucharistic rite (*Messe und Pascha*, 1872) and on metre in biblical Hebrew.

Biog. sketch by D. M. Müller in *Almanach der kaiserlichen Akademie der Wissenschaften*, 56 (Vienna, 1906), pp. 347–51.

Bickersteth, Edward (1786–1850), leader of the Anglican *Evangelicals from the death of Charles *Simeon in 1836 until his own. The son of a surgeon, he left school at the age of 14, worked in the Post Office, became an articled clerk in a solicitor's office in London, and then entered into partnership with his brother-in-law, a solicitor in *Norwich. From his late teens he took religious duties very seriously, and in Norwich he founded a *CMS Association. He also wrote *A Help to the Study of the Scriptures* (1815), called in its later editions *A Scripture Help*. In 1815 he gave up the practice of law and was ordained deacon and priest in the same year, before going to Africa on behalf of the CMS to settle disputes among the missionaries. He was secretary of the CMS from 1824 to 1830, when he became Rector of Watton, Herts, though he continued to travel extensively on its behalf. Opposed both to Roman Catholicism and *Tractarianism, he was one of the founders of the *Parker Society. He was also active in the foundation of the *Evangelical Alliance. His books were designed to foster piety, but display considerable learning. They include *A Treatise on Prayer* (1818), *A Treatise on the Lord's Supper* (1822), and *A Treatise on Baptism* (1840). His *Christian Psalmody* (1833) long remained the most popular hymn book among Evangelicals. A friend of Lord *Shaftesbury, he campaigned on behalf of children working in factories. His son, **Edward Henry Bickersteth** (1825–1906), was Bp. of *Exeter, 1855–1906; his grandson, **Edward Bickersteth** (1850–97), Bp. of South Tokyo, 1886–97; his nephew **Robert Bickersteth** (1816–84), Bp. of *Ripon, 1857–84; and his great-great-grandson **John Monier Bickersteth** (b. 1921), Bp. of *Bath and Wells, 1975–87.

T. R. Birks (son-in-law), *Memoir of the Rev. Edward Bickersteth* (2 vols., 1851). M. [M.] Hennell, *Sons of the Prophets* (1979), pp. 29–49. W. Hunt in *DNB* 5 (1886), pp. 3 f.

Bidding Prayer. The form of prayer interceding for the Universal Church, the State, Clergy, Nobility, and Commons, and commemorating the departed, which the Anglican Canon 55 (1604) ordered to be used by preachers before the sermon. In origin it derives from the group of intercessions, usually in Litany form, which in ancient liturgies occurred after the Sermon or the Gospel. These survived in the Roman Solemn Prayers ('the Collects') of the *Good Friday Liturgy and in the isolated 'Oremus' in the ordinary Latin Mass (at the beginning of the 'Mass of the Faithful').

By the 9th cent. the priest prayed for all conditions of men and made commemoration of the departed after the sermon at Mass on Sundays and festivals. In England during the Middle Ages this was called 'Bidding the *Bedes'. These Biddings formed part of the vernacular devotions, instructions, and notices attached to the sermon, and together were known in France (where they survive in certain places) as the *Prône* (a word of uncertain origin). At first they were left to the discretion of the priest but gradually tended to assume fixed forms. The Bidding Prayer is now seldom used except in the universities, at Assize sermons, and on state occasions.

In the Liturgical Constitution of the Second *Vatican Council (4 Dec. 1963), provision was made for the restoration of the 'Community Prayer' or 'Prayer of the Faithful' in the Roman Mass, esp. on days on which there is a homily. 'By this prayer, in which the people are to take part, intercession will be made for Holy Church, for the civil authorities, for those oppressed by various needs, for all mankind and for the salvation of the entire world' (sect. 53). In the C of E a similar prayer, in the form of a series of biddings, has been incorporated in the Eucharist in the ASB.

F. E. *Brightman, *The English Rite*, 2 (1915), Appendix 1, pp. 1020–45. P. de Clerck, *La 'Prière Universelle' dans les liturgies latines anciennes* (Liturgiewissenschaftliche Quellen und Forschungen, 62; 1977).

Biddle, John (1615–62), English *Unitarian. Graduating in 1638 at Magdalen Hall, Oxford, he became shortly afterwards master of the free school at *Gloucester, where he wrote his 'XII Arguments' against the deity of the Holy Spirit. In 1645 the MS was seized and Biddle was imprisoned for a time. In 1647, however, the 'XII Arguments' were published, and on 6 Sept. they were ordered to be burned by the hangman. Notwithstanding the ordinance of 1648, visiting with death all who denied the Trinity, he published two anti-Trinitarian tracts, but he was saved by his friends among the *Independent Parliamentarians and retired to Staffordshire, where he preached and helped to edit an edition of the *Septuagint. On the passing of the Act of Oblivion of 1652, his adherents ('Biddellians', '*Socinians', or 'Unitarians') began regular Sunday worship. Biddle now published two catechisms, for which he was summoned before Parliament (1654) and again imprisoned. On release he was again put on trial, but banished by Cromwell to the Scilly Isles (1655). Returning to London on his release (1662), he was arrested, fined, and sent to prison, where he died.

Vita, said to be by J. Farrington (anon., London, 1682). J. Toulmin, *A Review of the Life, Character and Writings of the Rev. John Biddle, MA* (1791). H. J. McLachlan, *Socinianism in Seventeenth-Century England* (Oxford, 1951), esp. pp. 163–217. A. B. Grosart in *DNB* 5 (1886), pp. 13–16.

Biel, Gabriel (*c*.1420–95), scholastic philosopher. Educated at Heidelberg, Erfurt, and Cologne, he later joined the *Brethren of the Common Life at Marienthal and became first provost of the house at Butzbach, and in 1479 was appointed provost of the house at Urach. With Count Eberhard of Württemberg, he was responsible for founding the University of *Tübingen, where he held the professorial chair of theology. One of the last great medieval scholastic thinkers, he was a follower of the *nominalist thought of *William of Ockham, though he showed himself tolerant of opposite systems. His views on the relationship between the economy of commercial life and theology reflect the transitional nature of his age. Thus he held that the 'just price' was determined by supply and demand rather than by theological maxims, and that the merchant is a useful and necessary member of society. His works included a 'Commentary on the Sentences of *Peter Lombard', an exposition of the *Canon of the Mass, and a treatise 'De potestate et utilitate monetarum'.

Most of his works exist only in edns. of 15th and 16th cents.; list in Überweg, 2, p. 604. Mod. edn. of his 'Quaestiones de Justificatione', by C. Feckes (*Opuscula et Textus*, Series Scholastica, 4; Münster i.W., 1929), of his *Canonis Misse Expositio* by H. A. Oberman and W. J. Courtenay (Veröffentlichungen des Instituts für europäische Geschichte Mainz, 31–4; 1963–7; with index and *Disquisitio et consensus materiae* ed. W. Werbeck, ibid. 79; 1976), of his *Defensorium Obedientiae Apostolicae*, with Eng. tr., by H. A. Oberman, D. E. Zerfoss, and W. J. Courtenay (Cambridge, Mass., 1968), and of his *Collectorium circa quattuor libros Sententiarum* by W. Werbeck and U. Hofmann (4 vols. in 5 pts., Tübingen, 1973–84). Eng. tr. of his *Treatise on the Power and Utility of Moneys*, by R. B. Burke (Philadelphia and Oxford, 1930). M. *Luther, *Randbemerkungen zu Gabriel Biels* Collectorium in Quattuor Libros Sententiarum *und zu dessen* Sacri Canonis Missae Expositio (Lyons, 1514; repr. 1933). H. A. Oberman, *The Harvest of Medieval Theology: Gabriel Biel and Late Medieval Nominalism* (Cambridge, Mass., 1963), with bibl. L. Grane, *Contra Gabrielem: Luthers Auseinandersetzung mit Gabriel Biel in der Disputatio Contra Scholasticam Theologiam 1517* (Acta theologica Danica, 4; Copenhagen, 1962). W. Ernst, *Gott und Mensch am Vorabend der Reformation: Eine Untersuchung zur Moralphilosophie und -Theologie bei Gabriel Biel* (Erfurter theologische Studien, 28; Leipzig, 1972). F. J. Burkard, *Philosophische Lehrgehalte in Gabriel Biels*

*Sentenzenkommentar unter besonderer Berücksichtigung seiner Er-
kenntnislehre* (Monographien zur philosophischen Forschung, 122;
Meisenbeim am Glan, 1974). J. L. Farthing, *Thomas Aquinas and
Gabriel Biel: Interpretations of St Thomas Aquinas in German
Nominalism on the Eve of the Reformation* (Duke Monographs in
Medieval and Renaissance Studies, 9; Durham, NC, 1988). M.
Cappuyns, OSB, in *DHGE* 8 (1935), cols. 1429–35; V. Heynck
in *NCE* 2 (1967), p. 552; W. Dettloff in *TRE* 6 (1980), pp. 488–
91, all s.v.

bigamy. (1) A 'second marriage' contracted by a person
whose 'first' husband or wife is still alive, when the 'first'
marriage has not been declared null. The traditional view
of the W. Church is that such a union is no marriage.
English civil law takes the same view if a divorce has not
been obtained, and, moreover, regards bigamy in such circumstances as a criminal offence. See also DIVORCE.

(2) Acc. to older usage, the term relates to a second
marriage after the death of one of the partners to the first
marriage. In this sense it is also known as 'digamy' (q.v.).

J. Vergier-Boimond in *DDC* 2 (1937), cols. 853–88, s.v. 'Bigamie (l'Irrégularité de)', with extensive bibl.; R. Naz, ibid., cols.
888 f., s.v. 'Bigamie (le Délit de)'.

Bigg, Charles (1840–1908), Church historian. Educated
at Corpus Christi College, Oxford, he was in his early life
a college tutor and schoolmaster. In 1886 he delivered and
published his *Bampton Lectures on *The Christian Platonists of Alexandria*, one of the finest works of English theology in the 19th cent. From 1887 to 1901 he was Rector
of Fenny Compton, and in 1901 succeeded W. *Bright as
Regius Professor of Ecclesiastical History at Oxford.

A. Clark in *DNB, 1901–1911*, 1 (1912), pp. 162 f., s.v.

Bilney, Thomas (*c*.1495–1531), Protestant martyr. A
member of Trinity Hall, Cambridge, he is said to have
converted H. *Latimer to the doctrines of the
Reformation, as well as to have had some influence on M.
*Parker, the future archbishop. In 1527 he was arrested for
heresy, but escaped death by recanting. Four years later he
was again on trial for *Lollardy; and after recanting and
relapsing he was burnt at *Norwich on 19 Aug. 1531. The
grounds of his condemnation are obscure. He seems to
have been perfectly orthodox on such things as
*transubstantiation and the *sacrifice of the Mass, but to
have aroused hostility by preaching violent sermons
against *relics, *pilgrimages, and the cult of the saints.

The principal authority is J. *Foxe, *Acts and Monuments* (ed.
G. Townsend, 4, 1846, pp. 619–56 and 755–63). J. Y. Batley, *On
a Reformer's Latin Bible: Being an Essay on the* Adversaria *in the
Vulgate of Thomas Bilney* (Cambridge, 1940), with biographical
sketch, pp. 1–12. J. F. Davis, 'The trials of Thomas Bylney and
the English Reformation', *Historical Journal*, 24 (1981), pp. 775–
90; G. Walker, 'Saint or Schemer? The 1527 Heresy Trial of
Thomas Bilney Reconsidered', *JEH* 40 (1989), pp. 219–38.

bilocation. The presence of a person in more than one
place at the same moment. Certain saints, e.g. *Alphonsus
Liguori, *Antony of Padua, and *Philip Neri, are supposed to have been granted this gift on occasion.

bination. The celebration of two Masses on the same day
by the same priest. In the RC Church no priest may normally celebrate (or concelebrate) Mass more than once a day,
except on the few occasions, such as *Christmas and

*Maundy Thursday, when more than one Mass is pro-
vided. The local *ordinary may, however, allow priests to
celebrate twice in a day, or even three times on Sundays
and *Feasts of Obligation when pastoral necessity requires
it (*CIC* (1983), can. 905). In the Middle Ages the custom
gave rise to scandals through priests who multiplied their
Masses to obtain additional Mass stipends.

K. Holböck, *Die Bination: Rechtsgeschichtliche Untersuchung*
(Rome, 1941). É. Jombart in *DDC* 2 (1937), cols. 889–98, s.v.
'Binage'.

binding and loosing. The power which Mt. 16: 19
reports was given by Christ to St *Peter and later to all the
Apostles (Mt. 18: 18). It seems to be a general authority to
exercise discipline over the Church, and, while some have
identified it with the power of forgiving or retaining sins
(Jn. 20: 23), others hold it to be a wider and more inclusive
authority.

H. Vorgrimler, 'Das "Binden und Lösen" in der Exegese nach
dem Tridentinum bis zu Beginn des 20. Jahrhunderts', *ZKT* 85
(1963), pp. 460–77, with refs. F. Büschel in *TWNT* 2 (1935), pp.
59 f. (Eng. tr., 1964, pp. 60 f.), s.v. δέω; J. Jeremias, ibid. 3 (1938;
Eng. tr., 1965), pp. 749–53, s.v. 'κλείς. B. Die Schüsselgewalt';
O. Michel in *RAC* 2 (1954), cols. 374–80, s.v. 'Binden und
Lösen', with extensive bibl. See also comm. to JOHN, GOSPEL OF
ST, and MATTHEW, GOSPEL OF ST.

Bingham, Joseph (1668–1723), author of *The Antiquities
of the Christian Church*. He was educated at Wakefield
Grammar School and University College, Oxford, where
he became a Fellow in 1689. He was delated to the Vice-
Chancellor for a sermon preached in St Mary's, Oxford,
on 28 Oct. 1695 and on being condemned (with scant
justice) for teaching the tritheistic doctrines of W. *Sherlock, resigned his Fellowship. In the same year he became
Rector of Headbourne Worthy, near *Winchester, and in
1712 also Rector of Havant, holding the livings in plurality
until his death. In 1706 he argued in *The French Church's
Apology for the Church of England* that the real affinities of
the *Huguenots were with the C of E and not with the
English Dissenters. He also took an active part in the controversy on lay-baptism, of which he was a strong advocate. His most famous work, the *Origines Ecclesiasticae; or
the Antiquities of the Christian Church* (10 vols., 1708–22),
with its wealth of systematically arranged information, on
the hierarchy, organization, rites, discipline, and calendar
of the early Church, was the fruit of some 20 years' labours
and has not been superseded. In the preface to a projected
2nd edition he advocated the reunion of the Churches on
the basis of primitive episcopacy. A Latin version was
published at Halle in 1724–8 by the *Lutheran, J. H.
Grischow, and a RC abridgement at Augsburg in 1788–96.

Works in 2 vols., fol., London, 1726; best edn., 10 vols., Oxford,
1855, with Life by his great-grandson, R. Bingham (repr. from
edn. in 9 vols., 1821–9) in vol. 1, pp. xvii–xxxi. L. W. Barnard,
'The Use of the Patristic Tradition in the Late Seventeenth and
Early Eighteenth Centuries', in R. [J.] Bauckham and B. Drewery
(eds.), *Scripture, Tradition and Reason: . . . Essays in Honour of
Richard P. C. Hanson* (Edinburgh, 1988), pp. 174–203. J. H.
Overton in *DNB* 5 (1886), pp. 48–50; F. E. *Brightman in *DECH*
(1912), pp. 55 f.; N. Sykes in *DHGE* 8 (1935), cols. 1506–8, s.v.

Binitarianism. The belief that there are only two Persons in the Godhead instead of the three of the *Trinity,

thus involving the denial of the deity of the Holy Spirit. It has been held that a few early Christian theologians, e.g. *Tertullian before he became a *Montanist, had an imperfect apprehension of the Trinity and thought in binitarian terms. The word appears to have been coined by F. *Loofs in 1898.

W. Macholz, *Spuren binitarischer Denkweisen seit Tertullian* (1902). K. E. *Kirk, 'The Evolution of the Doctrine of the Trinity', in A. E. J. Rawlinson (ed.), *Essays on the Trinity and Incarnation* (1928), pp. 157–237.

bioethics. The term 'bioethics' was coined in 1971 to describe ethical reflection on issues arising within the sphere of the biological and medical sciences; it is preferable to 'medical ethics' which is often used to refer to the limited rules of conduct and etiquette contained in professional codes. The problems of bioethics have increased with recent technological developments and include contraception, *in vitro* fertilization, artifical insemination, genetic engineering, abortion, eugenics, experimentation, transplantation, the rationing of resources, the treatment of mental illness, and euthanasia. In Christian thinking bioethics is a part of *moral theology and is governed by its principles, variously derived from Scripture or the natural law. Chief among these principles have been the sacredness of human life, love of neighbour, and respect for the sovereignty and providence of God. For other writers it is a branch of ethics in which principles of autonomy, beneficence, confidentiality, and justice are to be applied. For discussion of some branches of bioethics see CONTRACEPTION, PROCREATION, AND ABORTION, ETHICS OF, and DYING, CARE OF THE.

W. T. Reich (ed.), *The Encyclopaedia of Bioethics* (4 vols. [1978]).

Bird, William. See BYRD, WILLIAM.

biretta. The hard square cap sometimes worn by clergy in the W. Church. In origin it was apparently a soft hat, the use of which was originally confined to the higher graduates of universities; but in the 16th cent. its use was allowed to all the clergy. Its colour is black for *priests, purple for *bishops, red for *cardinals, and white for *Premonstratensian canons and Cistercian abbots. In recent times the biretta has tended to go out of use.

Braun, *LG*, pp. 510–14. H. Thurston, SJ, in *CE* 2 (1907), pp. 577 f., with refs.

Birgitta, St, of Sweden. See BRIDGET, ST, OF SWEDEN.

Birinus, St (d. 649 or 650), first Bp. of *Dorchester, near Oxford, and Apostle to the West Saxons. He was consecrated bishop by Asterius at Genoa and landed in Wessex in 634. In the following year he converted and baptized the King, Cynegils, who gave him Dorchester as his episcopal see. It had been intended that he should evangelize the more remote parts of Britain, but he remained in Wessex. Feast day, 3 Dec. (in some places, 5 Dec.).

The principal authority is *Bede, *HE* 3. 7; comm. by J. M. Wallace-Hadrill (Oxford, 1988), pp. 97 f. and 231. Modern studies by J. E. Field (London, 1902) and T. Varley (Winchester, 1934). R. Graham in *DHGE* 8 (1935), cols. 1530 f., s.v.

Bischop, Simon. See EPISCOPIUS.

bishop (Gk. ἐπίσκοπος, lit. 'overseer'). The highest order of ministers in the Christian Church. The word is an Anglo-Saxon corruption of *episcopus*.

In Catholic Christendom (incl. the Anglican Communion) bishops are the chief pastors of the Church, who individually form a centre of unity in their dioceses, and together, by their sharing in the episcopal college, embody the unity of the Church, and by their consecration and power to confer *Orders, witness to the succession of the Church throughout the ages. They normally receive consecration at the hands of a *Metropolitan and two other bishops, and are consecrated to rule a particular diocese or part of the Church within that Metropolitan's *province. In addition to consecration two further things are necessary: election and mission. Election is the choosing of a particular person. The candidate must be of mature age (30 years in the C of E), have spent a certain period in priest's orders, and be of good character and sound doctrine. In the RC Church election is performed by the Pope; nowadays the clergy of the diocese may nominate candidates, but in every case the final choice is his. Elsewhere the usual method is for a bishop to be chosen by the dean and chapter of the cathedral of the diocese or some other ecclesiastical body existing specially for this purpose. Throughout the history of the Church secular rulers have from time to time secured the right to nominate candidates to vacant sees, but theoretically this has always been subject to ecclesiastical approval. In the C of E at the present day the *Crown Appointments Commission submits two names to the Prime Minister, who recommends one to the Sovereign; the Sovereign then gives leave to the *dean and *chapter to proceed to an election (the document containing this permission is known as the *congé d'élire) and nominates the person to be elected. After the election the royal assent is given to it. Should the chapter elect a person other than the one nominated, the royal assent would, presumably, be refused and the electors become subject to certain pains and penalties. When there is no recognized chapter in the diocese the Crown appoints a person directly by letters patent. Mission is the conveying of the powers of a bishop. In the C of E the Metropolitan of the province confirms the election and at the direction of the Crown proceeds to the consecration. If the candidate is nominated directly by the Crown there is no confirmation. After consecration the new bishop is enthroned in his cathedral and takes possession of his see. Acc. to Anglican theory this is the result of his acceptance into their company by the other bishops. In the RC Church every diocesan bishop is required either in person or by an approved deputy to visit Rome every five years and report on the state of his diocese. (See AD LIMINA APOSTOLORUM.)

The chief duties of a modern bishop in the W. Church consist in the general oversight of his diocese, in the leadership of his clergy and laity in the proclamation of the Gospel, and in administering those Sacraments which he alone is competent to confer (*Confirmation and Ordination). The diocesan bishop may be assisted by other bishops who are subordinate to him and known as *suffragans (q.v.), auxiliaries, coadjutors, or assistants. In the E. Church the position and spiritual powers of the bishop are similar to those in the W., with the exception of the additional requirement that bishops, unlike other priests, are required to be unmarried (or widowed). This practice virtually necessitates their recruitment from the monastic order.

In the C of E the diocesan bishop exercises jurisdiction either through his *Consistory Court, over which he himself presides in theory (though he usually delegates the presidency nowadays to his *chancellor), or through commissaries appointed under the Church Discipline Act 1840. From medieval times the English bishops have had seats in the House of Lords; but under the Bishoprics Act 1878 only 26 English bishops (that is the two archbishops and the bishops of London, *Durham, and *Winchester *ex officio*, and 21 others senior by nomination to an English see) enjoy this privilege. The bishop's connection with his cathedral church, which is governed by the statutes of the various cathedrals, varies considerably from diocese to diocese.

Among the *insignia* traditional to the bishop (most of them now widely in use in the Anglican Communion) are the throne in his cathedral (usually on the Gospel side of the sanctuary; at *Norwich behind the high altar; see CATHEDRA), *mitre, *pastoral staff, *pectoral cross, and *ring. In England he is addressed as 'Right Reverend'; if an archbishop, as 'Most Reverend'. In the RC Church he is styled 'Reverendissimus et Illustrissimus'. Here, and often elsewhere, he is mentioned throughout his diocese by name in the Eucharistic prayer.

The beginnings of the episcopate in early times have long been debated, partly because of the inconclusiveness of the NT evidence by itself, partly on account of its relevance to the many contemporary forms of Church government. It seems that at first the terms 'episcopos' and 'presbyter' were used interchangeably (cf. e.g. Acts 20: 17 and 20: 28). But for St *Ignatius (early 2nd cent.), bishops, presbyters, and deacons are already quite distinct. On the other hand, elsewhere, notably in Egypt, the threefold ministry does not seem to have established itself until considerably later. By the middle of the 2nd cent. all the leading centres of Christianity would appear to have had their bishops, and from then until the Reformation, Christianity was everywhere organized on an episcopal basis.

The title of bishop was retained after the Reformation in certain *Lutheran Churches, notably those of *Denmark, *Norway, *Finland, *Sweden, and Transylvania. It was temporarily restored in Prussia in 1701 and was customary in certain other German provinces such as Schleswig-Holstein; it was generally adopted for the *'Superintendents' of the German Lutheran Church in 1927. In the case of Lutheran bishops, however, with the exception of Sweden, and Finland until 1884, the title implied no claim to apostolic succession or any of the peculiar powers deriving therefrom, such as are normally connected with the Catholic use of the word. The title is also in use among certain other Protestant bodies such as the *Moravians and the *Methodist Episcopal Churches of America and Africa: the former claiming apostolic succession although it is Presbyterian in government; the latter derives its succession from the appointments made by J. *Wesley.

See also APOSTOLIC SUCCESSION, CHOREPISCOPUS, ORDERS AND ORDINATION, SUFFRAGAN BISHOP.

A. Barbosa, *Pastoralis Solicitudinis, siue de Officio, et Potestate Episcopi Tripartita Descriptio* (2 vols., Lyons, 1628); C. Ziegler, *De Episcopis, eorumque Juribus, Privilegiis et Vivendi Ratione* (Nuremberg, 1686). D. Bouix, *Tractatus de Episcopo, ubi et de Synodo Diocesana* (2 vols., Paris, 1859). R. *Phillimore, *The Ecclesiastical Law of the Church of England*, 1 (2nd edn., by W. G. F. Phillimore, 1895), esp. pp. 18–86; H. W. Cripps, *A Practical Treatise on the Law Relating to the Church and Clergy* (8th edn., by K. M. Macmorran, 1937), pp. 70–86; G. [E.] Moore, *Introduction to English Canon Law*, 3rd edn. by T. Briden and B. Hanson (1992), esp. pp. 16–20. G. Coulton in *DECH*, pp. 58–63, s.v. The main duties and rights of modern RC bishops are laid down in *CIC* (1983), cans. 375–430. T. J. Green in J. A. Coriden, T. J. Green, and D. E. Heintschel, *The Code of Canon Law: A Text and Commentary* (1985), pp. 319–49, with bibl. E. Valton in *DTC* 5 (1913), cols. 1701–25, s.v. 'Évêques. Questions théologiques et canoniques', with refs. F. Claeys-Bouuaert in *DDC* 5 (1953), cols. 569–89, s.v. 'Évêques', with bibl.

For the chief original texts on the early growth of episcopacy, D. *Stone, *Episcopacy and Valid Orders in the Primitive Church* (1910). J. *Bingham, *Origines Ecclesiasticae*, bk. 2, chs. 1–18 (1708), pp. 49–257. J. Réville, *Les Origines de l'épiscopat* (1894); R. L. Fox, *Pagans and Christians* (1986), pp. 493–545. A. J. Mason, *The Church of England and Episcopacy* (1914). C. Jenkins and K. D. Mackenzie (eds.), *Episcopacy, Ancient and Modern* (1930); N. Sykes, *The Church of England and Non-Episcopal Churches in the Sixteenth and Seventeenth Centuries* (1948); E. R. Fairweather and R. F. Hettlinger, *Episcopacy and Reunion* (Toronto, 1952; London, 1953); F. Benz, *Bischofsamt und apostolische Sukzession im deutschen Protestantismus* (1953); K. M. Carey (ed.), *The Historic Episcopate in the Fullness of the Church* (1954; 2nd edn., 1960); N. Sykes, *Old Priest and New Presbyter: Episcopacy and Presbyterianism since the Reformation with especial relation to the Churches of England and Scotland* (Cambridge, 1956); W. H. G. Simon (ed.), *Bishops* (1961); W. Telfer, *The Office of a Bishop* (1962); A. G. Hebert, SSM, *Apostle and Bishop* (1963); J. Colson, *L'Épiscopat catholique: Collégialité et primauté dans les trois premiers siècles de l'Église* (Unam Sanctam, 43; 1963), and other works of this author. [R.] J. Halliburton, *The Authority of a Bishop* (1987). J. A. *Robinson in *E.Bi.*, 1 (1899), cols. 578–84, s.v.; D. Stone in *HERE* 5 (1912), pp. 332–7, s.v. 'Episcopacy'; F. Prat, SJ, in *DTC* 5 (1913), cols. 1656–701, s.v. 'Évêques (origines de l'épiscopat)' See also works cited under ORDERS AND ORDINATION.

Bishop, Edmund (1846–1917), liturgist and historian. A native of Totnes, Devon, he had his schooling at *Exeter and in *Belgium. After a short time as secretary to T. *Carlyle, he held a government post from 1864 to 1885 in the Education Office, when he spent most of his leisure in research in the British Museum. In 1867 he was received into the Church of Rome. After leaving the Education Office he hoped to become a monk at *Downside Abbey; but his intention was frustrated by weak health. He continued, however, to maintain close connections with Downside, where he made the friendship of F. A. *Gasquet, who shared his liturgical interests. In 1890, in conjunction with Gasquet, he published *Edward VI and the Book of Common Prayer*; in 1908 a study of the early English calendars in the *Bosworth Psalter*, and in 1909 studies in various liturgical subjects in an appendix to R. H. *Connolly's *Liturgical Homilies of Narsai*. He also made notable contributions to the early history of the Roman liturgy, esp. the text of the *canon missae* and the history of the *Gregorian Sacramentary. Perhaps his most widely known writing was his paper on 'The Genius of the Roman Rite', originally delivered to the Historical Research Society on 8 May 1899, in which he maintained that the two chief characteristics of the Roman rite (when divested of *Gallican accretions) were 'soberness' and 'sense'. This and many of his other papers were collected in *Liturgica Historica* (1918; posthumous).

Life by N. [J.] Abercrombie (London, 1959). A. R. Vidler, *A Variety of Catholic Modernists* (Sarum Lectures, 1968–9; Cambridge, 1970), pp. 134–52.

Bishops' Bible. A new English translation of the Bible, compiled at the direction of Abp. M. *Parker, and first published in 1568. It was a revision of the *Great Bible version. All *churchwardens were ordered by *Convocation to obtain a copy for their churches in 1571, and in the following year it was republished with some corrections. A novel feature of this edition was the placing of each translator's initials at the end of his part. It remained the official English version till the publication of the *Authorized Version in 1611, but despite numerous editions by the Queen's Printers it won less popularity than the unauthorized *Calvinist translation known as the *Geneva Bible.

Darlow and Moule, ed. A. S. Herbert, 1 (1968), pp. 70 f. (no. 125).

Bishops' Book (1537). Under the title 'The Institution of a Christen Man', this book was an exposition of the *Creed, the *Seven Sacraments, the *Decalogue, the *Lord's Prayer, and the *Ave Maria, compiled by a committee of English bishops and divines in 1537. It also dealt with certain other vexed questions, among them the doctrines of *justification and *purgatory and the relation of the C of E to the Roman see. The book never received the authority of the King, who used it rather to test the temper of the people. In 1543 a revised edition was published by *Henry VIII which came to be known as the *King's Book.

The book was repr. in *Formularies of Faith set forth by Authority during the Reign of Henry VIII* (ed. C. *Lloyd, 1825), pp. 21–212. F. E. *Brightman, *The English Rite* (2 vols., 1915), Introd. (see index, p. 1064).

Bishops' Wars. The two brief campaigns in Scotland in 1639 and 1640. After the attempt of *Charles I to enforce the use of the Prayer Book in Scotland, the Scots had broken out into rebellion, and their avowed aim was to abolish episcopacy. The military importance of these campaigns was inconsiderable, but the need for money to conduct them obliged the King to summon the English Parliament, which had not met since 1629, and so gave his enemies in England a chance to gather their forces.

Black Canons. See BLACK MONKS.

Black Churches. Apart from the ancient Churches of *Nubia and *Ethiopia, Black Churches originated in the 18th cent. among the descendants of African slaves in the *United States of America. Beginning in the 1740s, evangelical *revivals attracted increasing numbers of Blacks to Christianity, perhaps largely because they were permitted to assume active roles as preachers and leaders. The *Baptist and *Methodist Churches that resulted from the revivals licensed Black men to preach. By the 1770s Black Baptists were acting as pastors of separate Black congrega-

tions of slave and free members. In the South, Black Churches were restricted and sometimes suppressed because Whites suspected they might foment slave rebellion. In the 19th cent. slaves became familiar with at least the rudiments of Christianity. Some attended church with Whites or met separately under White supervision, but the majority had no access to formal church services. Slaves regularly held their own religious meetings, with or without their owners' consent. In sermon and song they recounted biblical stories and identified themselves as a chosen people whom God would free as He had done Israel of old. The slaves generated a distinct religious culture, best expressed in the *spirituals (q.v.).

In the North, the abolition of slavery after the Revolution (1776–83) enabled Blacks to exercise religious freedom. Alienated by White discrimination, Blacks in Philadelphia founded two influential churches, Bethel African Methodist and St Thomas African Episcopal, both in 1794. Over the next decade, separate Black Churches of various denominations sprang up across the North. In 1816 the first major Black denomination, the African Methodist Episcopal Church was formed and Richard Allen (1760–1831), a former slave, elected as its bishop. As the one institution under Black control, the Church served to organize the socio-political, as well as the religious, life of free Black communities. It became the primary forum for promoting the causes of education, self-help, and anti-slavery. When, for example, delegates to the first National Negro Convention gathered in 1830 to try to improve conditions for Blacks, they met in Bethel African Methodist Episcopal church in Philadelphia, with Bp. Allen presiding. Black leaders in abolition, temperance, and moral reform movements were mainly ministers.

Most Black Churches were Protestant, because Blacks had little contact with RCism except in Maryland and Louisiana. Black RC communities in Baltimore and New Orleans organized two religious orders of Black women, the Oblate Sisters of Providence in 1829 and the Holy Family Sisters in 1842. The first African American priest, James Augustine Healy (1830–1900), was ordained in 1854. Black RCs did not, however, attain anything like the institutional independence of the Black Protestant Churches until the 20th cent.

Black Church membership was predominantly female, but, as in other Churches, the clergy were exclusively male, since women were barred from ordination until the 20th cent. With the rare exception of travelling evangelists such as Jarena Lee (b. 1783) and Amanda Berry Smith (1837–1915), women were not permitted to preach in church. They did, however, lead home prayer meetings, offer spiritual counsel, and wield considerable influence through auxiliary, missionary, and Sunday school boards.

Blacks began the first American foreign missions in the 1780s when George Liele (*c.*1750–1820) established Baptist Churches in Jamaica and David George (*c.*1742–1810) did the same in Nova Scotia and *Sierra Leone. In 1820 an African Methodist Episcopal Church missionary, Daniel Coker (born Isaac Wright, 1780–1846), sailed to Sierra Leone and a Black Baptist, Lott Carey (1780?–1828) arrived in Liberia in 1821.

After Emancipation in 1865, northern missionaries went South to organize Churches among the former slaves. The influx of southern members enlarged the rolls of northern

Black denominations and made them national in scope. Ex-slaves withdrew from White Churches in large numbers to found their own. When Reconstruction (1865–77) allowed Blacks to hold political office, ministers took active roles in government, until disfranchisement once again restricted Black leadership primarily to the Church.

After the demise of Reconstruction, worsening race relations prompted some Black Americans to consider emigrating to Africa, a position advocated most forcefully by the African Methodist Episcopal Church Bp. Henry McNeal Turner (1834–1915). Few emigrated, but many agreed with the Black Episcopalian, Alexander Crummell (1819–98), a former missionary to Liberia, that it was the divinely appointed destiny of African Americans to Christianize Africa. Although Black Churches were too poor to finance missions on a large scale, scores of Black American men and women served in Africa with the support of Black or White mission boards.

At the end of the 19th cent., Black Church membership reached 2.7 million out of a population of 8.3 million Blacks. In 1895 Black Baptists united to form the National Baptist Convention, soon the largest Black denomination. Blacks joined new *Holiness and *Pentecostal Churches that emphasized sanctification and speaking in tongues. A Black preacher, William J. Seymour (1870–1922), led the 1906 Azusa Street revival in Los Angeles that inspired Pentecostal Churches across America. At the beginning of the 20th cent. rural Blacks moved in increasing numbers to the cities of the South and North. Some of the larger Churches developed social agencies to assist in their relocation. Migrants increased the ranks of urban Churches and formed new congregations, usually in homes or rented shopfronts. In the cities new religious options emerged. RCism attracted significant numbers of Black converts, primarily by means of the parochial schools. Esoteric forms of Judaism and Islam, and charismatic religious leaders gained followers at the expense of mainstream Churches. In this setting of religious ferment, the emphasis of Holiness and Pentecostal Churches on charismatic experience exerted a wide appeal.

Twentieth cent. urbanization and modernization also brought criticism of the Church for alleged conservatism and other-worldliness. Secular alternatives competed with the Church and new professionals rivalled the minister's authority. The Church, none the less, remained the central institution for Black social, cultural, and political life. The struggle for civil rights depended heavily upon the support of Black Churches and Black clergy. The career of the Black Baptist minister Martin Luther *King epitomized for his followers the religious nature of the political struggle for racial equality. King drew upon the Black Church tradition to mobilize demonstrations against racism, poverty, and war.

In the late 1960s and 1970s militant critics accused the Church of retarding Black liberation. In response, some Black clergy developed a Black theology that emphasized the theme of liberation (see LIBERATION THEOLOGY). More recently Black women, as well as White, have articulated theological critiques of sexism in Church and society. Today the Black Church is no longer the only institution which Black Americans control. It remains, however, a central institution for Black communities throughout the country.

Historically Black Churches arose in the racially divided society of America, but they now also have a substantial presence in the urban areas of Britain. After the end of the Second World War (1945), a large number of Black people from the Caribbean were recruited to fill job vacancies in England. Many of those who came first belonged to mainstream Churches (esp. Anglican and Baptist), but, feeling unwelcome in the English congregations of these communions, a significant proportion of them came to disregard their denominational loyalties. Increasingly, later Caribbean immigrants came from Holiness and Pentecostal backgrounds. They suffered from liturgical and doctrinal incompatibilities, and, given the more evangelical emphasis of their Churches in the Caribbean, felt alienated by what they regarded as nominal Christianity. The regrouping of individuals around denominational loyalties within the Holiness–Pentecostal stream provided not only a common bond in worship but also some social and cultural cohesion for Afro-Caribbean Christians of various denominations, and they were joined by those who had become disaffected in other Churches. The majority of Black Churches in Britain fall within the Pentecostal–Holiness tradition, but there is a strong presence among the *Seventh-day Adventists and the emerging African Christian groups. Since the mid-1970s, concentration on social action has given rise to such groups as the Afro-West Indian United Council of Churches (established in 1976), and in more recent times they have become involved in wider ecumenical endeavours, such as the establishment of *Churches Together in England and Wales (1991). The term 'Black-led', formerly widely used, is disliked by these Churches.

Collections of primary material by M. C. Sernett (ed.), *Afro-American Religious History: A Documentary Witness* (Durham, NC, 1985) and G. S. Wilmore and J. H. Cone (eds.), *Black Theology: A Documentary History, 1966–1979* (Maryknoll, NY [1979]). C. G. Woodson, *The History of the Negro Church* (Washington, DC [1921]; 2nd edn. [1945]). G. S. Wilmore, *Black Religion and Black Radicalism: An Interpretation of the Religious History of Afro-American People* (Garden City, NY, 1972; 2nd edn., Maryknoll, NY [1983]). C. V. R. George, *Segregated Sabbaths: Richard Allen and the Emergence of Independent Black Churches 1760–1840* (New York, 1973). A. J. Raboteau, *Slave Religion: The 'Invisible Institution' of the Antebellum South* (ibid., 1978). R. K. Burkett and R. Newman (eds.), *Black Apostles: Afro-American Clergy Confront the Twentieth Century* (Boston [1978]); D. W. Wills and R. Newman (eds.), *Black Apostles at Home and Abroad: Afro-Americans and the Christian Mission from the Revolution to Reconstruction* (ibid. [1982]). J. M. Washington, *Frustrated Fellowship: The Black Baptist Quest for Social Power* (Macon, Ga. [1986]). E. Lincoln and L. H. Mamiya, *The Black Church in the African American Experience* (Durham, NC, and London, 1990).

Black Friars. Friars of the Order of Preachers or *Dominicans. They are so called from the black mantles worn over their white habits and *scapulars. The name is first attested in the 14th cent.

W. Gumbley, OP, 'On the Name Blackfriars', *Blackfriars*, 1 (1920–1), pp. 54 f.

Black Letter Days. The lesser (mainly non-scriptural) Saints' Days (printed in black), as distinct from the major festivals, which formerly appeared in red letters in the BCP calendar. They were omitted in 1549, but four appeared in the 1552 Book and the remainder in 1561 save for St *Evurtius (added, 1604), St *Alban, and the Ven. *Bede (added, 1662). In 1662 their purpose was defined by the revising bishops as the commemoration of Saints and the provision of useful calendrical notes for business purposes. The practice of distinguishing important feasts by the use of red letters goes back to the pre-Reformation service books. The Black Letter days were excluded from the Irish (1878) and American (1786) Prayer Books. Much more extensive lists are found in modern Anglican Prayer Books.

[W. *Sanday], *Minor Holy Days in the Church of England: Primary Authorities for the Early Names* [1901]. V. Staley, *The Liturgical Year: An Explanation of the Origin, History and Significance of the Festival Days and Fasting Days of the English Church* (1907), ch. 12, pp. 129–58.

Black Mass. The expression is used as a popular name for: (1) a *Requiem, or Mass for the Dead, so called from the custom of using black vestments; and (2) a parody of the Mass celebrated with blasphemous intention, in honour of the devil.

Black Monks. A name given in medieval England to the *Benedictine monks, as they were distinguished by wearing black habits. The analogous term 'Black Canons' is also found as a designation of *Augustinian canons.

Black Rubric. The name now commonly given to the 'Declaration on Kneeling' printed at the end of the Holy Communion service in the BCP. It is first found in the Book of 1552, when it was inserted at the last moment without Parliamentary authority. The Elizabethan edition of 1559 removed it; but a shortened version was replaced in the Book of 1662, with the significant change that the words 'real and essential' were altered to 'corporal' presence, thereby indicating that its purpose was rather to guard against *transubstantiation and popular medieval ideas of Eucharistic doctrine than to deny altogether Christ's presence in the Sacrament. The expression 'Black Rubric' dates only from the 19th cent. when the practice of printing the BCP with the rubrics in red was introduced and the fact that the 'Declaration' was really not a rubric at all was marked by printing it in black. In modern two-colour reprints of the BCP it will be found, however, printed in red.

J. G. Simpson in *PBD*, pp. 105 f., s.v. See also F. E. *Brightman, *The English Rite* (2 vols., 1915), index (p. 1062), s.v. 'Declaration on Kneeling'.

Blackwell, George (1547–1612), RC *archpriest. He was educated at Trinity College, Oxford, where he was elected to a fellowship in 1566, which he subsequently gave up through his RC sympathies. In 1574 he entered the English College at *Douai and was ordained priest in 1575. He returned to England on the RC mission in 1576. After the confusion in RC discipline that followed Card. W. *Allen's death (1594) through the absence of a supreme authority in England, Blackwell was put in control of the secular clergy by *Clement VIII, with the title of archpriest and with 12 assistants to help him. Though not himself a *Jesuit, Blackwell pursued a strongly pro-Jesuit policy hostile to the interests of the secular clergy,

who aimed at political *rapprochement* with the Crown. A group of 31 *Appellants (q.v.), headed by W. Bishop, sought redress from Rome, but on 6 Apr. 1599 a reply was issued in Blackwell's favour. On the strength of it Blackwell continued his previous policy, but after two further appeals he was reproved by Clement in a letter of 5 Oct. 1602. After imprisonment for a time in 1607, he took the Oath of Allegiance to *James I, which had been formally condemned by *Paul V in 1606 and 1607, and in 1608 the Pope appointed George Birket or Birkhead in his place.

Refs. to Blackwell will be found in the docs. of the Archpriest Controversy listed s.v. APPELLANTS. T. Cooper in *DNB* 5 (1886), pp. 144–6.

Blaise, St. See BLASIUS, ST.

Blake, William (1757–1827), poet, artist, and visionary. Apprenticed to an engraver from 1771 to 1778, he became, through frequent work in *Westminster Abbey, imbued with the spirit of Gothic art which remained his guiding ideal throughout his life. In 1789 he finished his *Songs of Innocence*, a collection of poems of childlike simplicity which included 'The Divine Image', where God and His image, man, are hymned as 'Mercy, Pity, Peace, and Love'. The book was engraved by hand and illustrated by coloured drawings, a technique adopted in most of his subsequent works. It was followed by *The Book of Thel* (1789) and *The Marriage of Heaven and Hell* (1793), allegorical poems full of obscure though often beautiful imagery, which Blake used to express his religious convictions. The *Songs of Experience* (1794) are a kind of complement to the *Songs of Innocence*, though on a sterner note and penetrated by a deep sense of the darker side of life, e.g. in the famous 'Tyger'. His later poetical works, written in something like free verse, are increasingly given over to theosophical speculations and unintelligible allegories. At the same time his compositions gained in artistic maturity. About 1795 he produced a series of large colour prints of much imaginative power, including the magnificent 'The Elohim creating Adam', and in 1797 his illustrations of Edward Young's *Night Thoughts*. In 1804 he published his poem *Milton*, the proem of which consists of the famous lines 'Jerusalem', much used (with the music of Hubert Parry) as a national hymn. In the following years he produced engravings for Robert Blair's *Grave* of high visionary qualities, but, like most of his drawings, not without flaws in technique. From 1808 to 1818 he was occupied with writing and illustrating his great allegorical poem *Jerusalem*, in which St *Teresa and Mme *Guyon figure among 'the gentle souls who guide the great wine-press of Love'. His unconventional religious beliefs found fresh expression in an unfinished poem, *The Everlasting Gospel*, which rejects the traditional picture of a meek and humble Christ. His greatest work, the *Illustrations to the Book of Job*, completed in the last years of his life (1821–1825, pub. 1826), consists of 21 engravings showing the dealings of God with Job from the peaceful contentment of the opening scene, through the despair of the tormented Job accusing his Creator, to the rapturous bliss of his final restoration. The figures, often of elemental strength and beauty, move in the atmosphere of crude black and white contrasts which invests Blake's works with their characteristic impression of haunting unreality.

Blake's art, which spurns reason as well as nature and lives solely in the realm of imagination, was inseparable from his religion, which was itself a religion of art. Opposed to both dogma and asceticism, it flowed from a boundless sympathy with all living things which Blake identified with the forgiveness of sins proclaimed by the Gospel. Though he was little understood by his contemporaries, his visionary genius, both as a poet and an artist, has been increasingly admired since its discovery by A. C. Swinburne and interpretation by W. B. Yeats. His insistence on the supremacy of the spiritual world, though unbalanced by reason and a sound sense of reality, has acted as a powerful antidote to 19th cent. materialism.

The best edns. of his writings are those by G. [L.] Keynes (3 vols., London, 1925, repr., with additional material, 1966) and G. E. Bentley, Jun. (2 vols., Oxford, 1978). Id., *Blake Records* (ibid., 1969). M. Butlin, *The Paintings and Drawings of William Blake* (2 vols., New Haven, Conn., and London, 1981). Life by A. Gilchrist (2 vols., London, 1863), repr. in Everyman's Library (1942). Modern studies by M. Wilson (London, 1927; 3rd edn. by G. [L.] Keynes, 1971), T. Wright (2 vols., Olney, Bucks, 1929), K. [J.] Raine (London, 1970), J. King (ibid., 1991), and P. Ackroyd (ibid., 1995).

G. [L.] Keynes, *Blake Studies* (1949; 2nd edn., Oxford, 1971); G. W. Digby, *Symbol and Image in William Blake* (ibid., 1957); G. M. Harper, *The Neoplatonism of William Blake* (Chapel Hill, NC, and London, 1961); M. D. Paley and M. Phillips (eds.), *William Blake: Essays in Honour of Sir Geoffrey Keynes* (Oxford, 1973). P. Berger, *William Blake: Mysticisme et poésie* (1906; Eng. tr., 1914); J. G. Davies, *The Theology of William Blake* (1948). D. Bindman, *Blake as an Artist* (Oxford, 1977). R. N. Essick, *William Blake Printmaker* (Princeton, NJ, 1980); id., *The Separate Plates of William Blake: A Catalogue* (ibid., 1983). M. Eaves, *William Blake's Theory of Art* (ibid., 1982). S. F. Damon, *A Blake Dictionary* (Providence, RI, 1965). G. [L.] Keynes, *A Bibliography of William Blake* (New York, 1921); G. E. Bentley, Jun., and M. K. Nurmi, *A Blake Bibliography* (Minneapolis, 1964; rev. as *Blake Books*, Oxford, 1977). *Blake Newsletter*, 1–10 (Berkeley, Calif., 1967–77); *Blake: An Illustrated Quarterly*, 11 ff. (ibid., 1977 ff.).

Blandina, St. A virgin slave girl martyred in 177 at Lyons, together with *Pothinus, the bishop of the city. Feast day in the W., 2 June; in E., 26 July.

Her heroic courage is described in the 'Letter of the Churches of Lyons and Vienne', preserved in *Eusebius, *HE* 5. 1. 3–63.

Blasius, St. Acc. to a late and historically worthless but widely distributed legend, St Blasius (Blaise) was Bp. of Sebaste in Armenia and martyred under *Licinius in the early 4th cent. He is said to have miraculously saved the life of a young child who was nearly choked by a fish-bone, and hence his intercessions have been sought by the sick, and esp. those with throat trouble. He is also invoked for the cure of diseases of cattle and is the patron saint of woolcombers. He is one of the 14 *Auxiliary Saints, and his cult used to be very popular in Germany. His feast is observed in the W. on 3 Feb. (formerly 15 Feb.); in the E. on 11 Feb.

AASS, Feb. 1 (1658), pp. 331–53. His Gk. Legend is pr. in J. P. Migne, *PG* 116. 817–30. G. Garitte, 'La Passion de S. Irénarque de Sébastée et la Passion de S. Blaise', *Anal. Boll.* 73 (1955), pp. 18–54. J. P. Kirsch in *CE* 2 (1907), p. 592; G. D. Gordini

and others in *Bibliotheca Sanctorum*, 3 (1963), cols. 157–70, s.v. 'Biagio, vescovo di Sebaste', both with bibl.

blasphemy (Gk. βλασφημία, from βλάπτω, 'to damage', and φήμη, 'reputation'). Speech, thought, or action manifesting contempt for God. In moral theology it is commonly regarded as a sin against the virtue of religion, though St *Thomas Aquinas defined it as a sin against faith. It may be directed either immediately against God or mediately against the Church or the saints, and is by its nature a mortal sin. Blasphemy was punished by stoning in the OT (Lev. 24: 16, 1 Kgs. 21: 10), and the Code of *Justinian, as well as the medieval canon law, also prescribed severe punishments. Thus the Council of Aachen of 818 re-established the death penalty. In post-Reformation England, blasphemy laws were passed in 1558 and reinforced in 1698. From the time of the *Enlightenment the secular authorities in most countries have regarded blasphemy no longer as a crime against God but as an offence against society and punished it as such. In recent times repeated attempts have been made in many countries to abolish the laws against blasphemy altogether. Thus in Great Britain only scurrilous attacks on Christianity can be sustained under the blasphemy laws, as calculated to offend believers or even to cause a breach of the peace.

Blass, Friedrich Wilhelm (1843–1907), German classical scholar, who also contributed much to the philology and *textual criticism of the NT. Besides editions of Matthew (1901), Luke (1897), John (1902), and Acts (1895), he published a *Grammatik des neutestamentlichen Griechisch* (1896; 16th edn. by A. Debrunner and F. Rehkopf, 1976; Eng. tr. by H. St J. Thackeray, 1898; Eng. tr. of 9–10th edns., incorporating notes by A. Debrunner, by R. W. Funk, Cambridge, 1961) and a *Philology of the Gospels* (London, 1898). He maintained that the *Western and non-Western texts of Lk. and Acts were different recensions both deriving from the same author (St Luke), a view, however, which has found little favour among most textual critics.

W. Crönert, 'Friedrich Blass', *Biographisches Jahrbuch für die Altertumswissenschaft*, 32 (1909), pp. 1–32 (with list of Blass's works, pp. 30–2). For his theory of Luke-Acts, see L. J. M. Bebb in *HDB* 3 (1900), pp. 164 f. A. Romeo in *EC* 2 (1949), cols. 1716 f.

Blastares, Matthew (fl. 1335). A monk of Thessalonica who composed an alphabetical handbook of *canon law (Σύνταγμα κατὰ στοιχεῖον) as well as treatises against 'the Latins' (i.e. W. Catholics) and the Jews. He seems also to be the author of a collection of hymns.

His *Syntagma* is repr. in J. P. Migne, *PG* 144. 960–1400. His hymns were ed. by P. B. Paschos (Athens, 1980); id., Ὁ Ματθαῖος Βλάσταρης καὶ τὸ ὑμνογραφικὸν ἔργον του (Thessalonica, 1978), with summary in Fr. Beck (1959), pp. 786 f., with refs. J. Herman in *DDC* 2 (1937), cols. 920–5, s.v.

Blemmydes, Nicephorus (1197–?1269). A Greek theologian who took an active part in the attempts to reunite the E. and W. Churches in the 13th cent. From 1214 to 1221 he studied medicine with his father; in 1223/4 he was ordained deacon, and priest in 1234. He wrote on a variety of subjects, including theology, physics, and logic, and also produced some poems and a monastic rule.

His theological writings are in J. P. Migne, *PG* 142. 527–1622. *Curriculum Vitae et Carmina* ed. A. Heisenberg (Teub., 1896); the edn. of the *Curriculum Vitae* is now superseded by that, accompanied by the *Epistula Universalior*, ed. J. A. Munitiz (CCSG 13; 1984); Eng. tr. of the *Curriculum Vitae (A Partial Account)*, with comm., by id. (SSL 48; 1988). P. Canart, 'Nicéphore Blemmyde et le Mémoire adressé aux envoyés de Grégoire IX (Nicée, 1234)', *OCP* 25 (1959), pp. 310–25, incl. text. Beck (1959), pp. 671–3, with lit. to date.

Blessed (as title). See BEATIFICATION.

Blessed Sacrament. A term used of the Sacrament of the Eucharist, and applied both to the service itself and more esp. to the consecrated elements.

Blessed Virgin, the. See MARY, THE BLESSED VIRGIN.

blessing. The authoritative pronouncement of God's favour. Instances in the OT are the blessing of Isaac (Gen. 27) and the prayer of Balaam (Num. 23 f.), both of which presuppose the automatic action of a blessing, independently of moral considerations. Later we see liturgical blessings of persons (Num. 6: 22 ff.) and of things, such as food (1 Sam. 9: 13, cf. Mt. 14: 19). In Christian practice blessing finds a frequent place in the liturgy, esp. in the blessing of the elements in consecration (so Mt. 26: 26). The blessing of the people at the end of the Mass did not become general until the later Middle Ages. Blessings are frequently given to individuals, e.g. the deacon who is to sing the Gospel, the penitent about to make a confession, and less formally outside liturgical services, by bishops and priests (and in the RC Church now also by deacons), and by parents to their children. In many places a custom has arisen of concluding all services with a blessing, often given at the altar. The right hand is raised to bless, and usually the *sign of the cross is made, though occasionally this is omitted. The section of the *Rituale Romanum, *De benedictionibus* (1984) provides forms of blessings of people in various circumstances of their life and for animals, buildings, fields, and food as well as other inanimate objects. These blessings are real services, incl. biblical readings and intercessions. Provision is also made for *grace at meals. See also BERAKAH.

A. Franz, *Die kirchlichen Benediktionen im Mittelalter* (1909). T. G. Simons, *Blessings: A reappraisal of their nature, purpose and celebration* (Saratoga, Calif., 1981); M. Collins and D. Power (eds.), *Blessing and Power* (Concilium, 178; 1985).

Blomfield, Charles James (1786–1857), Bp. of London. He was the son of a schoolmaster at Bury St Edmunds, and, after a distinguished career at Trinity College, Cambridge, was ordained in 1810. In the next 14 years he was appointed to a succession of benefices culminating in his nomination in 1824 to the see of *Chester. Here he set himself to raise the standard of clerical life and to root out abuses, esp. those of non-residence, though he himself retained his former living of St Botolph's, Aldgate, in *commendam. In 1828 he became Bp. of London. During his episcopate some 200 new churches were built and consecrated in his diocese, chiefly through his zeal and interest. In politics his position wavered.

Though nominally a Whig, he resisted Catholic Emancipation (1829), and absented himself in the early stages of the Reform Bill, but he finally voted in its favour. His Churchmanship also seemed inconsistent. While he drove W. J. E. *Bennett from St Paul's, Knightsbridge, and supported the *Jerusalem Bishopric scheme of 1841, he signed the protest against R. D. *Hampden's appointment to the see of *Hereford, and dissented from the judgement of the Privy Council in the *Gorham case. He was an active member of the *Ecclesiastical Commission. In 1856 he was forced by paralysis to resign his see. He was held in repute as a classical scholar and issued editions of *Prometheus Vinctus* (1810), Callimachus (1815), Euripides (1821) and other texts.

Memoir by his son, A. Blomfield (2 vols., 1893). P. J. Welch, 'Bishop Blomfield and Church Extension in London', *JEH* 4 (1953), pp. 203–15; id., 'Blomfield and Peel: A Study in Co-operation between Church and State, 1841–1846', ibid. 12 (1961), pp. 71–84. G. F. A. Best, *Temporal Pillars: Queen Anne's Bounty, the Ecclesiastical Commissioners, and the Church of England* (Cambridge, 1964), *passim*.

Blondel, David (1590–1655), French Protestant ecclesiastical historian. A native of Châlons-sur-Marne, he was educated at Sedan and at the *Genevan Academy. For most of his life he was a pastor at Roucy; in 1631 he was offered a chair of theology at Saumur, but the opposition of his patron led the synod of Charenton to revoke the invitation. In 1645 he was created an 'Honorary Professor' of Saumur, with a generous annual financial grant, and in 1650 finally left Roucy to succeed G. J. *Voss at the École Illustre at Amsterdam, where he came into prominence through his liberal sympathies. He was at once a learned historian and effective controversialist. His *Pseudo-Isidorus et Turrianus Vapulantes* (1928), perhaps his most important work, finally discredited the historicity of the '*False Decretals'. His *De la primauté en l'Église* (1641) was a defence of the Reformed ecclesiastical polity and his *Apologia pro Sententia Hieronymi de Episcopis et Presbyteris* (1646) an attack on episcopacy. He also wrote an erudite and successful criticism of the myth of Pope *Joan (in two writings, 1647 and 1657) which aroused hostility among many of his fellow Protestants.

All his works were on the *Index. E. and E. Haag, *La France Protestante* (2nd edn.), 2 (1879), pp. 623–31. A. Lambert in *DDC* 2 (1937), cols. 926 f.

Blondel, Maurice (1861–1949), French philosopher. He was a native of Dijon, where he was educated at the École Normale, and later held professorships of philosophy at Montauban, Lille, and Aix-Marseille. The work that first placed him in the front rank of contemporary thinkers was *L'Action* (1893; Eng. tr., 1984), with the significant sub-title, 'Essai d'une critique de la vie et d'une science de la pratique'. In it Blondel attempted to construct a 'philosophy of action', conceiving 'action' in its widest sense and all its ramifications, and to develop also a philosophy of the idea, as well as to expound the relations between science and belief and between philosophy and religion. His analysis of action led him to conclude that the human will which produces action cannot satisfy itself, because its fundamental desire is never fulfilled by any finite good. From this point of departure he developed an argument for the being of God resting on volition, in the light of which he modified the old Scholastic proofs. God imposes Himself on the will as the first principle and the last term; we must, therefore, 'opt' either for or against Him.

The teaching of *L'Action* was amplified in several later works, e.g. *Histoire et dogme* (1904; Eng. tr., 1964), *Le Procès de l'intelligence* (1922), and esp. *Le Problème de la philosophie catholique* (1932) and *La Pensée* (2 vols., 1934). The last-named work states his final position with regard to the intellectual aspects of experience. He here accords a greater place to abstract conceptions than in *L'Action* and affirms the legitimacy of methodical argumentation, e.g. in the rational proofs of the existence of God. Yet his position is not that of *Aristotle and St *Thomas Aquinas, but follows rather the *Platonic tradition as continued in St *Augustine, R. *Descartes, and G. W. *Leibniz. For Blondel it is not that knowledge of creatures precedes knowledge of God, but rather it is the existence of an obscure yet positive affirmation of God that is the very condition which makes the Aristotelian and Thomist proofs possible. The problem of the supernatural also played a large part in the thought of Blondel, who was a devout Catholic. He held that the whole mental life of man was directed to the possession of God in the Beatific Vision, and consequently he attributed to unaided human reason the capacity of demonstrating its positive possibility.

Blondel's thought has been of considerable influence in modern philosophy. For several years he was closely associated with the leading figures in the *Modernist Movement, which welcomed the pragmatist aspects of his teaching; and many contemporary thinkers, incl. R. Eucken (1846–1926), G. *Gentile, and F. *von Hügel, were indebted to him.

P. Archambault, *L'Œuvre philosophique de Maurice Blondel: Vers un réalisme intégral* (Cahiers de La Nouvelle Journée, 12; 1928); B. Romeyer, SJ, *La Philosophie religieuse de Maurice Blondel* (1943); H. Duméry, *La Philosophie de l'action: Essai sur l'intellectualisme blondélien* ('Philosophie de l'Esprit', 1948), with preface by Blondel; H. Bouillard, *Blondel et le christianisme* [1961]; C. Tresmontant, *Introduction à la métaphysique de Maurice Blondel* [1963]; R. Saint-Jean, SJ, *Genèse de l'Action: Blondel 1882–1893* (Museum Lessianum, section philosophique, 52; 1965); id., *L'Apologétique philosophique: Blondel 1893–1913* (Théologie, 67; 1966); J. J. McNeill, SJ, *The Blondelian Synthesis: A Study of the Influence of German Philosophical Sources on the Formation of Blondel's Method and Thought* (Studies in the History of Christian Thought, 1; Leiden, 1966); M. Jouhaud, *Le Problème de l'être de l'expérience morale chez Maurice Blondel* (1970); U. Hommes, *Tranzendenz und Personalität: Zum Begriff der Action bei Maurice Blondel* (Philosophische Abhandlungen, 41; Frankfurt am Main [1972]); R. Virgoulay, *Blondel et le Modernisme* (1980). D. Folscheid (ed.), *Maurice Blondel: Une Dramatique de la modernité. Actes du colloque . . . organisé par le séminaire Saint Luc, Aix-en-Provence, mars 1989* (1990). G. Baum, *Man Becoming: God in Secular Experience* (New York, 1970), esp. ch. 1. R. Virgoulay and C. Troisfontaines, *Maurice Blondel: Bibliographie analytique et critique* (Centre d'Archives Maurice Blondel, 2–3; Louvain [1975–6]). See also bibl. to LABERTHONNIÈRE, L.

Blount, Charles (1654–93), English *Deist. He is best known by his *Anima Mundi* (1679), a sceptical discussion of the subject of immortality, and *The Two First Books of Philostratus concerning the Life of Apollonius Tyaneus* (1680). The notes of the latter gave offence by their attacks

on priestcraft and sympathy with the free thought of T. *Hobbes.

The Miscellaneous Works of Charles Blount . . . to which is prefixed the life of the author [signed Lindamour, a pseudonym of Charles Gildon] (5 pts., 1685). Modern studies by U. Bonanate (Florence, 1972) and K.-J. Walber (Aspekte der englischen Geistes- und Kulturgeschichte, 15; Frankfurt [1988]).

Blow, John (1649–1708), composer and organist. He became one of the Children of the *Chapel Royal at the Restoration, and at an early age distinguished himself as a composer of *anthems. Already in 1668 he was appointed organist of *Westminster Abbey, an office which he gave up in 1679 in favour of his greater pupil, H. *Purcell, resuming it on Purcell's death in 1695. The most important of his other offices was that of Master of the Children of the Chapel Royal (1674). Of his works over 100 anthems and 10 services survive, besides secular compositions.

W. Shaw in S. Sadie (ed.), *The New Grove Dictionary of Music and Musicians*, 2 (1980), pp. 805–12, s.v., with detailed list of his works.

Bloxam, John Rouse (1807–91), Anglican ceremonialist and historian. Educated at Rugby School and at Worcester and Magdalen Colleges, *Oxford, he was ordained priest in 1833 and elected a Fellow of Magdalen in 1836. He held a succession of offices at Magdalen until appointed Vicar of Upper Beeding, W. Sussex (1862), where he remained till his death. He associated himself closely with the *Tractarian Movement and from 1837 to 1840 was J. H. *Newman's curate at Littlemore. A careful and learned ecclesiologist, Bloxam was the real originator of the ceremonial revival in the English Church. He introduced various ornaments into Littlemore church (gilded candlesticks, wooden alms-dish, black silk stole, credence table, litany desk, etc.), which were soon afterwards copied by F. *Oakeley at the Margaret Chapel in London and thence spread and came into general use. Through his correspondence with A. L. M. P. *de Lisle about reunion, he became one of the first Tractarians to establish relations with RCs, though these seem to have been abruptly terminated by the secession of R. W. Sibthorp in Oct. 1841. Deeply devoted to his college, he published a Magdalen College *Register* (7 vols., 1853–81) and also compiled a valuable (unpublished) collection of college papers.

R. D. Middleton, *Magdalen Studies* (1936), pp. 31–79; id., *Newman and Bloxam: An Oxford Friendship* (1947). W. P. Courtney in *DNB*, Suppl. 1 (1901), pp. 224 f.

Blumhardt, Johann Christoph (1805–80), Protestant evangelist. The nephew of Christian Gottlieb Blumhardt (1779–1838), who founded the Protestant 'Basel Mission', he was born at Stuttgart, studied at *Tübingen, taught at Basle from 1830, and in 1838 became pastor at Möttlingen in Württemberg, where his evangelical work attracted much attention, largely through the physical cures by which it was sometimes accompanied. As his motto he took the words 'Jesus is Conqueror' (*Jesus ist Sieger*). From 1852 until his death he worked at Bad Boll, near Göppingen, which became a centre of influential international missionary work. Blumhardt's theology was developed under the influence of Swabian *Pietism (J. A. *Bengel, P. M. Hahn), but its eschatological emphasis also anticipated some elements in *Dialectical Theology. His collected works were published in 3 vols., 1886–8.

His son, **Christoph Friedrich Blumhardt** (1842–1919), who took over the direction of Bad Boll after his father's death, was also a zealous missioner and a considerable theologian. Active sympathy with the needs of the working classes led him to become from 1900 to 1906 a Social Democrat member of the Württemberg Diet.

Modern edn. of J. C. Blumhardt's Collected Works, by J. Scharfenberg and others (Göttingen, 1968 ff.). F. Zuendel, *Pfarrer J. C. Blumhardt: Ein Lebensbild* (Zurich, 1880). L. Ragaz, *Der Kampf um das Reich Gottes in Blumhardt, Vater und Sohn* (ibid., 1922). E. Jäckh, *Blumhardt, Vater und Sohn und ihre Botschaft* (1924). G. Sauter, *Die Theologie des Reiches Gottes beim älteren und jüngeren Blumhardt* (Zurich and Stuttgart, 1962). E. *Thurneysen, *Christoph Blumhardt* (1926). E. Kerlen, *Zu den Füssen Gottes: Untersuchungen zur Predigt Christoph Blumhardts* (Munich, 1981). K. *Barth, *Die protestantische Theologie im 19. Jahrhundert* (Zurich, 1947), pp. 588–97; Eng. tr. (1972), pp. 643–53. J. Scharfenberg in *TRE* 6 (1980), pp. 721–7, s.v. 'Blumhardt, Johann Christoph'; E. Kerlen, ibid., pp. 719–21, s.v. 'Blumhardt, Christoph'.

Boanerges. The surname given by Christ (Mk. 3: 17) to *James and *John, the sons of Zebedee. The word is there stated to mean 'sons of thunder', but the derivation is quite uncertain.

Bobbio. A small town in the Apennines, some 40 miles NE of Genoa, once the seat of an important abbey founded in 612 by St *Columbanus (who died there in 615). Its celebrated collection of early MSS (many of them dating from the 10th cent.) has mostly passed to the *Vatican Library, the *Ambrosiana at Milan, and Turin (several of these were destroyed in the fire of 1904). The 'Bobbio Missal', now in the Bibliothèque Nationale at Paris (BN Lat. 13246) is an important collection of liturgical texts dating from the 8th cent. There are signs of Irish influence, but opinion is divided as to whether it was written in S. France or N. Italy.

L. H. Cottineau, OSB, *Répertoire topo-bibliographique des abbayes et prieurés* (Mâcon, 1935), cols. 400–2, s.v. A. Ratti (*Pius XI), *Le ultime vicende della Biblioteca e dell'Archivio di S. Colombano di Bobbio* (1901). C. Cipolla, *Codici bobbiesi della Biblioteca Nazionale Universitaria di Torino* (Collezione paleografica bobbiese, 1; 2 vols., 1907); id. and G. Buzzi, *Codice diplomatico del Monastero di San Colombano di Bobbio fino all'anno MCCVIII* (3 vols., 1918); P. Collura, *La Precarolina e la Carolina a Bobbio* (1943), with refs. These works are mainly superseded by G. *Mercati's 'Prolegomenon de Fatis Bibliothecae Monasterii S. Columbani Bobiensis' to his edn. of *M. Tulli Ciceronis De Re Publica Libri e Codice Rescripto Vaticano Latino 5757 Phototypice Expressi* (Codices e Vaticanis Selecti, 23; Vatican, 1934), pp. 1–174. E. A. Lowe, *Codices Latini Antiquiores*, 4 (Oxford, 1947), esp. pp. xx–xxviii. P. Engelbert, 'Zur Frühgeschichte des Bobbieser Skriptoriums', *R. Bén.* 78 (1968), pp. 220–60. P. Verrua, *Bibliografia bobbiese* (Piacenza, 1936). M. Passalacqua (ed.), *Tre testi grammaticali Bobbiesi* (Sussidi Eruditi, 38; Rome, 1984). The 'Bobbio Missal' ed., with facsimile reproduction, by E. A. Lowe (HBS 53, 58; 1917–20), with notes and studies by A. *Wilmart, OSB, E. A. Lowe, and H. A. Wilson (ibid. 61; 1924). K. Gamber, *Sakramentartypen* (Texte und Arbeiten, Abt. 1, Hefte 49/50; Beuron, 1958), pp. 39–43. A. Wilmart in *DACL* 2 (pt. 1; 1910), cols. 935–9, s.v. 'Bobbio (Manuscrits de)'; id., ibid., cols. 939–62, s.v. 'Bobbio (Missel de)'.

Bochart, Samuel (1599–1667), biblical scholar. A native of Rouen, he studied philosophy at Sedan and theology at Saumur and in 1628 became pastor at Caen. In 1652 he accompanied P. D. *Huet to the court of *Christina of Sweden. After his return he became a member of Caen Academy. His chief works are his *Geographia Sacra* (2 pts., 1646, 1651) and the *Hierozoicon, sive Historia Animalium S. Scripturae* (2 vols., 1663; 3rd edn., with notes by E. F. C. Rosenmüller, 3 vols. 1793–6); the latter esp. was drawn on by later biblical commentators. He was a very learned oriental linguist, though his long preoccupation with Phoenician and other Semitic languages sometimes led him to fantastic etymological conclusions.

Works pub. in 2 vols., Leiden, 1675; also ed. by J. Leusden and P. de Villemandy, with Life by E. Morin (3 vols., ibid., 1692). E. H. Smith, *Samuel Bochart: Recherches sur la vie et les ouvrages de cet auteur illustre* (Caen, 1833).

Bodleian Library. The library of the University of *Oxford. The oldest portion (15th cent.), over the Divinity School, is known as 'Duke Humfrey's Library'; but the 600 MSS presented by Humphrey, Duke of Gloucester (d. 1447), son of Henry IV, were dispersed in the 16th cent. The library was restocked and endowed early in the 17th cent. by Sir Thomas Bodley (d. 1613), a retired diplomat, who added the E. wing. Between 1635 and 1640 W. *Laud presented about 1,300 MSS, including the 'Codex Laudianus' of Acts. Its other benefactors have included J. *Selden; Richard Rawlinson (a *non-juring bp.; d. 1755), who bequeathed nearly 5,000 MSS, besides printed books and pictures; and Francis Douce (d. 1834), who left to the Bodleian his collection of illuminated service-books and other rarities. The library possesses a good collection of patristic MSS, oriental as well as Greek and Latin. It is one of the six libraries which under the Copyright Acts can claim a presentation copy of every new work published in Great Britain and Ireland.

F. Madan and H. H. E. Craster (eds.), *Summary Catalogue of the Western Manuscripts in the Bodleian Library, Oxford* (7 vols. bound in 13, 1895–1953; Supp. covering the post-medieval accessions 1916–75 by M. Clapinson and T. D. Rogers, 3 vols., 1991). Thomas James's orig. pr. catalogue (1605) was repr. in facsimile in 1986, with useful introd. W. D. Macray, *Annals of the Bodleian Library, Oxford: with a notice of the Earlier Library of the University* (1868, 2nd edn. enlarged, 1890, repr. 1984); [H. H.] E. Craster, *History of the Bodleian Library 1845–1945* (1952; repr. 1981). S. [G.] Gillam, *The Divinity School and Duke Humfrey's Library at Oxford* (1988); I. [G.] Philip, *The Bodleian Library in the Seventeenth and Eighteenth Centuries* (1983); D. [M.] Rogers, *The Bodleian Library and its Treasures 1320–1700* (Henley-on-Thames [1991]). G. W. Wheeler (ed.), *Letters of Sir Thomas Bodley to Thomas James, First Keeper of the Bodleian Library* (1926; repr. 1985).

Bodley, George Frederick (1827–1907), ecclesiastical architect and designer. Born at Hull, he was articled to Sir G. G. *Scott. His earliest churches, such as Selsley, Glos (1858–62) and St Martin's, Scarborough (1861–3), were built in a continental Gothic style, influenced by J. *Ruskin, and are notable for their decoration and stained glass by W. *Morris, D. G. *Rossetti, and E. Burne-Jones. All Saints', Jesus Lane, Cambridge (1863–70) marks his adoption of a more purely English late Decorated style. In 1869 he formed a partnership with Thomas Garner (1839–

1906) which lasted until 1898. Together they developed the 19th-cent. English Gothic tradition with great refinement in a number of outstanding church buildings, including St Augustine's, Pendlebury (1870–74), Holy Angels', Hoar Cross, Staffs (1872–6), and St Mary's, Clumber Park, Notts (1886–9). Bodley was an extremely influential architect; his particular style spread throughout the Anglican Communion. He designed St David's Cathedral, Hobart, Tasmania (1868–94), the high altar and reredos of *St Paul's Cathedral, London (1887, destroyed 1944), and, with Henry Vaughan, the Episcopal Cathedral in *Washington, DC. As an ecclesiastical designer he was responsible for the arrangements at ritualistic centres, such as St Paul's, Knightsbridge, (1882; reredos, rood screen, and stained glass). With Garner and G. C. Scott, Jun., in 1874 he founded the firm of Watts and Co. to produce furnishings to his designs. His pupils include Sir Ninian Comper (1864–1960).

D. Verey, 'George Frederick Bodley: climax of the Gothic Revival', in J. Fawcett (ed.), *Seven Victorian Architects* [1976], pp. 84–101, 145 f., and 153–6. P. Waterhouse in *DNB, 1901–1911*, 1 (1912), pp. 187–90.

Bodmer Papyri. A collection of unusually important MSS, most on papyrus (see PAPYROLOGY), some on parchment, all with one exception codices and all with a few exceptions containing works of Christian literature, acquired by purchase for his library in Geneva by M. Martin Bodmer, mostly in 1956. The earlier MSS are in Greek, the later in Coptic (mainly Sahidic). Their provenance is alleged to have been *Nag Hammadi, but may well have been Panopolis (Akhmîm); there are grounds for thinking that they and the *Chester Beatty Papyri come from the same site; in either case they may represent the remains of an ancient church or early monastic library, surviving in a *geniza when no longer required for use. This would explain both the widely varying dates of the MSS (ranging from *c.*AD 200 to the 7th cent.) as well as the relatively good state of preservation. If the texts of *Iliad* 1 and the Menander Codex belong to the same find, these are among the pagan authors whom Christians might be expected to read.

The most important Christian MSS are those of the fourth Gospel (P. 66) of *c.*AD 200 which survives nearly complete and another of a codex containing both the third and the fourth Gospels (P. 75), written in the 3rd cent., of which more than four-fifths remain, a nearly contemporary MS of the original Greek of the Acts of *Phileas, and a copy of *Melito, 'On the Pasch'.

Edn. of the texts by V. Martin, M. Testuz, and R. Kasser pub. by the Bibliotheca Bodmeriana (Coligny, Geneva, 1954 ff. [20 vols. to 1969]). Bodmer Papyrus II (containing Jn.) was reissued, with a Supp., under the editorship of V. Martin and J. W. B. Barnes, ibid., 1962. Bodmer Papyrus III (Coptic text of Jn. and Gen. 1–4: 2) ed. R. Kasser (CSCO, Scriptores Copti, 25, with Fr. tr., ibid. 26; 1958); Bodmer Papyrus VI (Coptic text of Proverbs), ed. id. (ibid. 27, with Fr. tr., ibid. 28; 1960). On the provenance of the collection and its relation with the Chester Beatty Papyri, see E. G. Turner, *Greek Papyri* (enlarged repr., Oxford, 1980), pp. 52 f., 163 f., 201.

Body of Christ. (1) The natural or human Body which the Lord took of Mary, and which, acc. to orthodox Chris-

tian theology, was changed but not abandoned at the Resurrection and remains for ever His in heaven.

(2) The *Church (q.v.), as the community whose members are incorporated into His life in Baptism (see 1 Cor., Eph., Col., etc.), and which since *Pentecost has formed the vehicle of His redemptive activity on earth.

(3) The consecrated Bread in the *Eucharist (q.v.).

(4) The Latin form, '*Corpus Christi' (q.v.), has been used as the title of a feast which since the 13th cent. has been kept in the W. Church on the Thursday after Trinity Sunday in honour of the *Blessed Sacrament; and as a designation of churches and colleges dedicated in honour of the Eucharist.

Boehme, Jakob (1575–1624), German *Lutheran theosophical author, known as 'philosophus Teutonicus'. He was the son of a farmer. At first a shepherd, he was later apprenticed to a shoemaker, and from 1599, when he was married, till 1613 followed that trade at Görlitz in Silesia. The recipient of mystical experiences, he claimed that in his writings he described only what he had learnt personally from Divine illumination. In 1612 he published his first work, *Morgenröte im Aufgang oder Aurora*, which aroused the opposition of the Lutheran pastor, Gregorius Richter, who forced the municipal authorities to intervene; and Boehme was ordered to cease writing. In 1618, however, he began a series of devotional treatises which were published under the title *Der Weg zu Christo* in 1623. As Richter continued his opposition, Boehme left Görlitz in 1624 and went to Dresden and later to the houses of several friends in Silesia, where he was much appreciated. He died soon after his return to Görlitz in the same year. His writings, most of them published posthumously, include *Die drei Prinzipien göttlichen Wesens*, an inquiry into the Divine essence; *Signatura Rerum*, containing his cosmological theories; *Mysterium Magnum*, an allegorical explanation of the Book of Genesis; and *Von Christi Testamenten*, a treatise on Baptism and the Eucharist.

Boehme is a very obscure and difficult writer who made abundant use of abstruse terminology, borrowed largely from *Paracelsus, the mystics, alchemy, and astrology; and his critics are still divided as to whether the foundation of his thought is pantheistic or dualist. Having lived from childhood in a state of religious exaltation, he believed himself called to penetrate the deepest mysteries concerning God, man, and nature. Acc. to him God, the Father, is the 'Ungrund', the indefinable matter of the universe, neither good nor evil, but containing the germs of either, unconscious and impenetrable. This 'abyss' tends to know itself in the Son, who is light and wisdom, and to expand and express itself in the Holy Spirit. The Godhead has two wills, one good and one evil, 'love' and 'wrath', which drive Him to create nature, which unfolds itself in the seven nature spirits or 'Quellgeister', the last of which is man. The unfolding of creation is revelation, or the birth of God. Man accepts this revelation through faith in Christ, and experiences the birth of God in his soul. He will then be a conqueror on earth and will ultimately replace Lucifer, the fallen angel, in the heavenly city.

Boehme has exercised a far-reaching influence, esp. in Germany and the English-speaking countries. The thinkers of German Romanticism, such as G. W. F.

*Hegel, F. W. J. von *Schelling and F. X. von Baader, acknowledge their debt to him; and in England he was a source of inspiration to P. *Sterry, the Cambridge Platonist, to the 17th–18th-cent. '*Philadelphian Society', and to W. *Law. I. *Newton also wrestled with his writings for three months. His teaching was propagated by circles of disciples called 'Behmenists'.

A modern Ger. edn. of his Works is that by K. W. Schiebler (1831–47, repr. 1922); repr. of J. W. Ueberfeld's 1730 edn. by A. Faust and W. E. Peuckert (11 vols., Stuttgart, 1955–60). Original MSS of *Morgenröte* and various other works ed. by W. Buddecke as *Die Urschriften* (2 vols., ibid., 1963–66). A complete Eng. tr. of his works was made by J. Ellistone and J. Sparrow (1644–62; re-ed. 1762–84). More recent Eng. tr. of *Der Weg zu Christ (The Way to Christ)* by P. [C.] Erb (Classics of Western Spirituality, New York, etc. [1978]). A. [A.] Koyré, *La Philosophie de Jacob Boehme* (1929); H. R. Brinton, *The Mystic Way, based on a Study of the Philosophy of Jacob Boehme* (1931); H. Grunsky, *Jacob Boehme* (Stuttgart, 1956); J. J. Stoudt, *Sunrise to Eternity: A Study in Jacob Boehme's Life and Thought* (Philadelphia [1957]); E. Benz, *Der Prophet Jakob Boehme: Eine Studie über den Typus nachreformatorischen Prophetentums* (Akademie der Wissenschaften und der Literatur [in Mainz]. Abhandlungen der Geistes- und Sozialwissenschaftlichen Klasse, Jahrgang 1959, Heft 3); H. Tesch, *Vom dreifachen Leben: Ein geistiges Porträt des Mystikers Jakob Böhme* (Remagen [1971]); G. Wehr and P. Deghaye, *Jacob Böhme* (1977), with bibl., pp. 227–36; P. Deghaye, *La Naissance de Dieu ou la doctrine de Jacob Boehme* (1985). *Jacob Boehme, ou L'obscure lumière de la connaissance mystique*, pub. under the auspices of the Centre de Recherche sur l'histoire des idées de l'Université de Picardie (1979). S. Hutin, *Les Disciples anglais de Jacob Boehme aux XVII⁴ et XVIII⁴ siècles* [1960]. N. Smith, *Perfection Proclaimed: Language and Literature in English Radical Religion 1640–1660* (Oxford, 1989), pp. 185–225. G. W. Allen in *HERE* 2 (1909), pp. 778–84; E. H. Pältz in *TRE* 6 (1980), pp. 748–54.

Boethius, Anicius Manlius Torquatus Severinus (*c*.480–*c*.524), philosopher and statesman. Of an old senatorial family (the Anicii), Boethius was himself consul in 510 and his sons together in 522. The consulship was ceremonial. Only in middle life did Boethius take an active part in politics: indirectly *c*.517–22 by writing the *Opuscula Sacra* (see below), directly in 522 by becoming 'Master of the Offices' at the Ostrogothic court in *Ravenna. In the latter capacity he was charged with treason, imprisoned in Pavia, and judicially murdered.

Boethius made Latin adaptations of Greek works on the *quadrivium, prob. including Euclid's *Geometry*, but his abiding interest was in logic, broadly understood. He made translations of, and commentaries on, *Aristotle's Περὶ ἑρμηνείας and 'Categories', and a commentary on Marius *Victorinus' translation of *Porphyry's *Isagoge*, all of them a main source of Aristotelian knowledge in the early Middle Ages. He also wrote on 'Topics' and on 'Hypothetical Syllogisms' (a major source for ancient propositional logic). Logic dominates the *Opuscula Sacra*, 1–3 and 5, Boethius' brief contributions to the debate with and within the Greek Church on the Trinity and the Person of Christ. Since the court in Ravenna was *Arian, such definitions had a political as well as a religious dimension. But Boethius' most famous work, the *De consolatione philosophiae*, was written in the face of death. In alternating verse and prose, he offers a Platonic vindication of providence, despite the ethical problem of evil and the logical hurdle of free will. Boethius' mind was formed by contem-

porary *Neoplatonists, esp. *Proclus and *Ammonius. His definition of 'person' as 'the individual substance of a rational nature' became classical; so also that of eternity as 'the simultaneous and perfect possession of limitless life'. Like Porphyry, he bequeathed to medieval philosophers an indecisiveness whether *universals are real apart from the concrete existents in which they are embodied; the distinction between Being and Existence; and the reconciliation of providence with freedom by the doctrine that what is contingent to us is not so to God, who is timeless.

Boethius was a major educator of the medieval west, initially as a logician and always as the author of *De consolatione philosophiae*. Despite the absence of specifically Christian teaching the moral of the *Consolation* was clear to the medieval commentator: through philosophy the soul attains to knowledge of the vision of God. An Anglo-Saxon translation is attributed to King *Alfred, and translations and commentaries continued in most W. languages until the Renaissance. Boethius was canonized as 'St Severinus', and his tomb is honoured at the church of San Pietro in Ciel d'Oro in Pavia; feast day, 23 Oct.

Works first ed. Venice, 1492. Later edns. and reprs. include J. P. Migne, *PL* 63–4. Modern edns. of the *Consolatio* by R. Pieper (Teub., 1871) and L. Bieler (CCSL 94; 1957; 2nd edn., 1984); the Pieper edn. is repr., with Eng. tr. by S. J. Tester, in *Theological Tractates*, ed. H. F. Stewart, E. K. Rand, and S. J. Tester (Loeb, 1973), pp. 130–435. *In Isagogen Porphyrii Commenta*, ed. S. Brandt (CSEL 48; 1906); comm. on Aristotle's Περὶ ἑρμηνείας ed. C. Meiser (Teub., 2 pts., 1877–80); *De Institutione Arithmetica* and *De Institutione Musica*, ed. G. Friedlein (ibid., 1867; repr. Frankfurt, 1966); his tr. of Porphyry's *Isagoge*, ed. L. Minio-Paluello, *Aristoteles Latinus*, 1. 6–7 (1966); his trs. of works of Aristotle are included in the relevant vols. of *Aristoteles Latinus*. *Theological Tractates* ('Opuscula Sacra'), ed., with Eng. tr., by H. F. Stewart and E. K. Rand (Loeb, 1918; rev. edn. by S. J. Tester, 1973). *Cassiodorus' testimony is pr. in the introd. to the edn. of his *Variae* by Å. J. Fridh (CCSL 96; 1973), pp. v f. L. Cooper, *A Concordance of Boethius: The five theological tractates and the Consolation of Philosophy* (Mediaeval Academy of America, Publication 1; 1928). M. Bernhard, *Wortkonkordanz zu Anicius Manlius Severinus Boethius De Institutione Musica* (Bayerische Akademie der Wissenschaften, Veröffentlichung der Musikhistorischen Kommission, 4; 1979). J. Shiel, 'Boethius' Commentaries on Aristotle', *Mediaeval and Renaissance Studies*, 4 (1958), pp. 217–44. H. Potiron, *Boèce, théoricien de la musique grecque* (Travaux de l'Institut Catholique de Paris, 9 [1961]). G. Schrimpf, *Die Axiomenschrift des Boethius (De Hebdomadibus) als philosophisches Lehrbuch des Mittelalters* (Studien zur Problemgeschichte der antiken und mittelalterlichen Philosophie 2; Leiden, 1966). P. Courcelle, *La Consolation de Philosophie dans la tradition littéraire: Antécédents et postérité de Boèce* (1967). L. Obertello, *Severino Boezio* (2 vols., Genoa, 1974). J. Gruber, *Kommentar zu Boethius De Consolatione Philosophiae* (1978). M. [T.] Gibson (ed.), *Boethius: His Life, Thought and Influence* (Oxford, 1981), incl. list of works on logic, with details of best edns., pp. 85 f. H. Chadwick, *Boethius: The Consolation of Music, Logic, Theology, and Philosophy* (ibid., 1981). *Congresso internazionale di Studi Boeziani (Pavia, 5–8 ottobre 1980): Atti*, ed. L. Obertello (1981). G. [J. P.] O'Daly, *The Poetry of Boethius* (1991). E. K. Rand, *Founders of the Middle Ages* (Cambridge, Mass., 1928), pp. 135–80. M. Cappuyns in *DHGE* 9 (1937), cols. 348–80, s.v. 'Boèce'.

Bogomils. A medieval Balkan sect of *Manichaean origin. In the 8th cent. the Byzantine emperors settled a number of *Paulicians in Thrace, and under their influence the heresy known as Bogomilism after its founder,

Bogomil (the Bulgarian for Theophilus, 'beloved of God'), was introduced into the Balkans. The earliest description of the heresy is found in a reply to the Bulgar Tsar Peter by the Patriarch Theophylact (c.950), who described it as 'Manichaeism mixed with Paulicianism'. The Bogomils were denounced c.972 by the Bulgarian priest Cosmas in his *Sermon against the Heretics*, which mentioned their refusal to obey authority, civil or ecclesiastical.

The Bogomils, whose doctrines are known principally through the writings of *Euthymius Zigabenus, taught that the world and the human body were the work of Satan, only the soul being created by God. The true Christian conquered matter by abstaining from marriage, meat, and wine, and by the renunciation of all possessions. Such an ideal was in practice possible only for the 'Perfect'; the ordinary faithful might sin but were under obligation to obey the Perfect and would receive 'spiritual baptism' on their death-beds. Like other dualist sects, they accepted only the NT and the Psalms, holding the rest of the OT to be the work of the devil. They held the *Docetic view that Christ did not have a human body but only the appearance of one. They rejected the Sacraments, churches, and relics, but retained a hierarchy of their own.

Bogomilism spread rapidly in the Balkans and Asia Minor in the 11th cent., and from the mid-12th cent. onwards exerted a formative influence on the sect of the *Cathari in France and Italy. The leader of a Bogomil organization in Constantinople was burnt at the stake c.1110, and strong measures were taken against the Bogomils in Serbia c.1180 and in Bulgaria in 1211. In the 13th cent. its votaries secured a notable success in Dalmatia, and esp. in Bosnia, where under the name of *Patarenes they later became the dominant religious group. Catholicism was nominally restored in 1450, but many Patarenes fled to Herzegovina, and when the Turks conquered Bosnia in 1463 and Herzegovina in 1482, large numbers of the people adopted *Islam. No traces of the heresy remain in the Balkans except perhaps tombstones with symbolic decorations which may go back to Manichaeism.

D. Obolensky, *The Bogomils: A Study in Balkan Neo-Manichaeism* (1948), with full bibl. H. C. Puech and A. Vaillant, *Le Traité contre les Bogomiles de Cosmas le Prêtre: Traduction et Étude* (1945). S. Runciman, *The Medieval Manichee: A Study of the Christian Dualist Heresy* (Cambridge, 1947), esp. pp. 63–115. E. Werner, 'Die Bogomilen in Bulgarien. Forschungen und Fortschritte', *Studi Medievali*, 3rd ser. 3 (1962), pp. 249–78. On the Bogomils in Bulgaria there is a magisterial work in Bulgarian by D. S. Angelov (Sofia, 1969). Id., 'Der Bogomilismus in Bulgarien', *Bulgarian Historical Review*, 3, no. 2 (ibid., 1975), pp. 34–54, repr. in id., *Les Balkans au Moyen Age: la Bulgarie des Bogomils aux Turcs* (1978), no. 1; see also nos. 2–6. M. D. Lambert, *Medieval Heresy: Popular Movements from Bogomil to Hus* (1977), esp. pp. 12–23. A. V. Soloviev in *NCE* 2 (1967), pp. 633 f., s.v.; A. de Santos Otero in *TRE* 7 (1981), pp. 28–42, s.v. 'Bogomilen', with extensive bibl.

Bohairic. One of the principal dialects of *Coptic; the name, from the Arabic 'Bohaïrah', indicates an origin in the northern part of the Nile Delta. The former popular designation of this dialect, 'Memphitic' (from Memphis, the great Egyptian city at the southern apex of the Delta) was misleading, since it referred to a stage in its history when its use had spread far south of its place of origin. Such literature as may have been written in it while it was merely a local dialect is almost wholly lost; but texts in Bohairic become very plentiful from about the 9th cent. when its use became general throughout Egypt, supplanting other dialects, particularly *Sahidic. As knowledge of Greek was widespread in Lower Egypt, the translation of the Scriptures was a less pressing need than further south; the Bohairic version which we have is much later than the Sahidic, dating probably from the 6th–7th cents., and has long been, and still is, the official version of the *Coptic Church. Although the vast majority of Bohairic MSS date from the 9th cent. and later, a small number from the 4th cent. are now known; the place of these early Bohairic texts within the development of the Coptic biblical text is not clear. See also SAHIDIC.

There is a critical edn. of the Bohairic NT by G. Horner (4 vols., Oxford, 1898–1905). R. Kasser (ed.), *Papyrus Bodmer III: Évangile de Jean et Genèse I–IV, 2 en bohairique* (CSCO, Scriptores, 25–6; 1958, incl. Fr. tr.). The best-known grammar of the Bohairic dialect of Coptic is A. Mallon, *Grammaire copte* (Beirut, 1904; 4th edn., rev. by M. Malinine, ibid., 1956). See also works cited under COPTIC.

Bohemian Brethren, later known as '*Moravian Brethren' and 'Unitas Fratrum'. They were a group of *Utraquists (q.v.) who, having for some years led an existence apart within that religious body, separated formally under the leadership of 'Brother Gregory' in 1467, in order to follow more closely the teaching of Peter Chelčický (d. c.1460). They rejected oaths and military service, deprecated town life and private property, stressed Christian discipline, and stood for a simple, pure, and unworldly Christianity. The Brethren were organized as a Church by Lukáš of Prague, who broke with the tradition of uncompromising asceticism of the earlier Brethren, exalted faith without works, and in 1494 had the writings of Chelčický and Gregory condemned by the Synod of Rychnov. Under Lukáš's leadership the sect spread rapidly, though persecuted by the Utraquists. Their efforts to associate with the *Lutherans, frustrated at first by refusal to give up the celibacy of the priesthood, the Seven Sacraments, and a strict Church discipline, were successful only in 1542, after the death of Lukáš (1528), when they accepted justification by faith alone and the *Real Presence, but retained their discipline of public and private confession of sins. After the victory of Mühlberg (1547) the Emp. Ferdinand took repressive measures against them and many emigrated. Some eventually settled in *Poland, where they allied themselves with the *Calvinists at the Synod of Koźminek (1555). Those who remained in Bohemia likewise became more Calvinist in doctrine; they obtained the freedom to practise their cult from Maximilian II in 1575, but fixed their principal seat in Moravia, hence the other name under which they are known. They became the leading sector in Bohemian Protestantism, though outnumbered by the quasi-Lutheran Utraquists. In 1609 Rudolf II handed over to both groups the university of Prague and gave them many other rights, but after the Battle of the White Mountain (1620) all Protestants were exiled, together with the last bishop of the Brethren, the famous educationist, J. A. *Comenius. The remains of the sect survived for a hundred years, and in 1721 accepted an offer of N. L. von *Zinzendorf to join the *Herrnhuter, with whom they amalgamated. Their doctrine rested on the authority of Scripture, the interpretation of which was entrusted to the community. Each member was to realize the ideal of the Sermon on the Mount by a life of poverty and renunciation under the supervision of the elders, though later this austerity was relaxed, and in the 16th cent. numerous noblemen joined the Brethren. The sect rejected the veneration of the saints and held that the efficacy of the Sacraments depended on the dignity of the minister and the faith of the recipients. They laid special emphasis on Church services, organization, and education. Their schools were famous and their contribution to Czech literature considerable (esp. through their complete translation of the Bible, 6 vols., 1579–93), though the remnant which later moved to Herrnhut were German-speaking. They greatly influenced *Methodism in its earlier stages.

For their later history, see under HERRNHUT and MORAVIAN BRETHREN.

For the bulk of the lit. see bibl. to MORAVIANS. J. Goll (ed.), *Quellen und Untersuchungen zur Geschichte der Böhmischen Brüder* (2 vols., Prague, 1878–82). J. T. Müller, *Geschichte der Böhmischen Brüder* (3 vols., Herrnhut, 1922–31). R. Říčan, *Die Böhmischen Brüder: Ihr Ursprung und ihre Geschichte*, tr. into Ger. by B. Polelár (1961); E. Peschke, *Die Böhmischen Brüder im Urteil ihrer Zeit* (Arbeiten zur Theologie, 1st ser. 17; 1964). P. Brock, *The Political and Social Doctrines of the Unity of Czech Brethren in the Fifteenth and Early Sixteenth Centuries* (Slavistic Printings and Reprintings, 11; The Hague, 1957); J. K. Zeman, *The Anabaptists and the Czech Brethren in Moravia, 1526–1618: A Study of Origins and Contacts* (The Hague, 1969). W. Eberhard, *Konfessionsbildung und Stände in Böhmen 1478–1530* (Veröffentlichungen des Collegium Carolinum, 38; Munich, 1981); id., *Monarchie und Widerstand: Zur ständischen Oppositionsbildung im Herrschaftssystem Ferdinands I. in Böhmen* (ibid. 54; 1985). M. L. Wagner, *Petr Chelčický: A Radical Separatist in Hussite Bohemia* (Studies in Anabaptist and Mennonite History, 25; Scottdale, Pa., 1983).

Bohemond I (*c*.1052–1111), Prince of Antioch. He was the eldest son of Duke Robert Guiscard, the Norman conqueror of Apulia, on whose death (1085) he was passed over in favour of his half-brother. As leader of the S. Italian contingent Bohemond played an important part in the success of the First *Crusade. In return for his undertaking to secure the surrender of Antioch, the other leaders promised Bohemond possession of that city, which should, however, as a recent Byzantine possession, have been returned to the Emp. Alexius I (June 1098). Bohemond remained in Antioch during the march on Jerusalem, received investiture from the new Latin Patriarch of Jerusalem, and was enlarging his new principality when he was captured by the Turks (August 1100–May 1103). After losses of territory to Alexius he left Antioch to raise an expedition in the W. against the Emperor, but his enterprise, which received Papal backing, ended in defeat (Treaty of Devol, 1108) and he died at Canosa in 1111. Bohemond's expulsion of the Greek Patriarch from Antioch and his appointment of a Latin successor (1100), together with his hostility towards Byzantium, contributed much to the hardening of the schism between Rome and the E. Churches.

The most important primary authority for Bohemond's career in 1097–9 is the *Gesta Francorum et aliorum Hierosolimitanorum*, written by an unknown knight in his army, separately ed. by H. Hagenmeyer (2 pts., Heidelberg, 1889–90), L. Bréhier (Paris, 1924), B. A. Lees (Oxford, 1924), and, with Eng. tr., R. Hill (London, 1962); it must be compared with other W. chronicles of the First Crusade written from different viewpoints. *Anna Comnena (q.v.), who as the 14-year-old daughter of Alexius I was clearly fascinated by Bohemond in 1097, gives a hostile Byzantine view in her *Alexiad*. Ralf of Caen, 'Gesta Tancredi in expeditione Hierosolymitana', in *Recueil des historiens des Croisades*, Historiens occidentaux, 3 (Paris, 1856), pp. 587–716, is an apologia for Bohemond's nephew and lieutenant Tancred. The standard modern Life is R. B. Yewdale, *Bohemond I, Prince of Antioch* (Princeton, NJ, 1924). A. R. Gadolin, 'Prince Bohemund's death and apotheosis in the church of San Sabino, Canosa di Puglia', *Byzantion*, 52 (1982), pp. 124–53. L. Bréhier in *DHGE* 9 (1937), cols. 484–98, s.v.; D. Girgensohn in *Dizionario Biografico degli Italiani*, 11 (1969), pp. 117–24, s.v. 'Boemondo I', with bibl.

Bollandists. The *Jesuit editors of the '*Acta Sanctorum', so called after John van Bolland (1596–1665), the founder and first editor of the work. The plan for a critical edition of the lives of the Saints, based on authentic sources, had been conceived by Heribert Rosweyde (1569–1629), who, however, did not live to see any of it published. Under Bolland and his successors nearly all the archives and libraries of religious houses were systematically combed for material, for which a special museum was founded at Antwerp. Work by the Bollandists was suspended when the Jesuits were suppressed in Belgium in 1773, but resumed in 1837. Among the most outstanding of modern Bollandists is H. *Delehaye. Since 1882 the '*Analecta Bollandiana' (q.v.) have been published as supplements.

H. Delehaye, SJ, *A travers trois siècles: L'œuvre des Bollandistes, 1615–1915* (1920; Eng. tr., 1922; revised edn. with additional bibl., 1959); P. Peeters, SJ, *L'Œuvre des Bollandistes* (Académie Royale de Belgique. Classe des Lettres. Mémoires. 2nd ser. (8vo), 39, fasc. 4; 1942; 2nd edn., 54, fasc. 5; 1961). Id., *Figures bollandiennes contemporaines* (Collection Durandal, no. 73; 1948). [M.] D. *Knowles, *Great Historical Enterprises* (Cambridge, 1963), pp. 1–32. R. Aigrain, *L'Hagiographie* (1953), pp. 329–50. C. De Smedt, SJ, in *CE* 2 (1907), pp. 630–9, s.v.; M. Scaduto, SJ, in *EC* 2 (1949), cols. 1782–90, s.v.

Bologna. The ancient Bononia, in N. Italy. In the Middle Ages its university (founded in the 12th cent.) was the chief centre in Europe for the study of canon and civil law. The city has retained since the 5th cent. its devotion to St *Petronius (d. *c*.450), an early bishop. The first general chapter of the *Dominican Order was held in the town in 1220, and in the church of S. Domenico lies the body of St *Dominic (d. 1221).

H. *Rashdall (ed. by F. M. Powicke and A. B. Emden), *The Universities of Europe in the Middle Ages*, 1 (1936), ch. 4, pp. 87–268, with bibl. A. Sorbelli and L. Simeoni, *Storia della università di Bologna* (2 vols., 1940). *Storia di Bologna*: vol. 1: *I Tempi Antichi*, by P. Ducati (Bologna, 1928); vol. 2: *Dalle Origini del Cristianesimo agli Albori del Comune*, by A. Sorbelli (ibid., 1938). R. Grandi, *I Monumenti dei Dottori e la Scultura a Bologna (1267–1348)* (ibid. [1982]). G. Zanelli, *Bibliografia per la Storia dell'Università di Bologna (Origini–1945)* (ibid., 1976). F. Bonnard in *DHGE* 9 (1937), cols. 645–60, incl. further bibl.

Bologna, Concordat of (1516). The agreement between Pope *Leo X and Francis I of France which ended the *Pragmatic Sanction of Bourges. The French king was to nominate ecclesiastics to metropolitan and cathedral churches, to abbeys, and to conventual priories, and, if certain rules were complied with, Papal confirmation was not to be refused. After two invalid nominations, however, the appointment was to lapse to the Pope.

Orig. indult, 'Primitiva illa Ecclesia', in Hardouin, 9 (1714), cols. 1810–25; Leo X's supplementary bull, 'Pastor Aeternus' (19 Dec. 1516), which finally abrogated the Pragmatic Sanction of Bourges, ibid., cols. 1826–31; extracts in Mirbt and Aland (1967), p. 498 (no. 785). L. Madelin, 'Les Premières Applications du concordat de 1516 d'après les dossiers du château Saint-Ange', Mélanges d'Archéologie et d'Histoire de l'École Française de Rome, 17 (1897), pp. 323–85. See also works cited s.v. FRANCE, CHRISTIANITY IN.

Bolsec, Hieronymus Hermes (d. 1584), physician and religious controversialist. Originally a *Carmelite friar in Paris, he adopted Protestantism c.1545 and settled first on the estates of the Duchess of Ferrara and subsequently (1547) in the Chablais (then under Bernese jurisdiction), working as a physician. Frequenting theological gatherings in Geneva, Bolsec came into conflict with J. *Calvin by arguing that *predestination to salvation or reprobation amounted to no more than man's own faith or lack of faith in God. Arrested in Oct. 1551, Bolsec was tried and banished from Genevan territory. This relatively light sentence was due to the intervention of the Bernese and other Swiss Protestant Churches who did not share Calvin's extreme view of predestination. Bolsec then travelled in France and Switzerland, continuing his attacks on Calvin. His doctrines were condemned by the Synod of Lyons in 1563. In his last years he returned to the RC Church, settled in France, and published very hostile Lives of Calvin (1577) and T. *Beza (1582).

Documents of his trial are printed in Calvin's Opera, ed. G. Baum and others, 8 (Corpus Reformatorum, 36; Brunswick, 1870), cols. 145–248; ed. H. Fazy in Mémoires de l'Institut national genevois, 10 (1865), pp. 3–74; and in Registres de la Compagnie des Pasteurs de Genève au temps de Calvin, ed. R.-M. Kingdon and J.-F. Bergier, 1: 1546–1553, ed. J.-F. Bergier (Travaux d'Humanisme et Renaissance, 55; 1964), pp. 80–131. F. Pfeilschifter, Das Calvinbild bei Bolsec und sein Fortwirken im französischen Katholizismus bis ins 20 Jhdt. (Augsburg, 1983), with details of edns. of Bolsec's Life of Calvin. E. and E. Hagg, La France protestante, 2 (2nd edn., 1879), cols. 745–76; J. Dedieu in DHGE 9 (1937), cols. 676–9, both s.v.

Bolsena, the Miracle of. The traditional story, familiar through *Raphael's fresco in the *Vatican stanze, has it that when a German priest on pilgrimage to Rome was once celebrating Mass in the church of St Cristina in the little Umbrian town of Bolsena, he was disturbed by doubts about the transubstantiation of the bread and wine, which were suddenly resolved when he saw blood issue from the elements and bathe the corporal. It is also narrated that when Pope Urban IV (1261–4) had been shown the corporal, which had been conveyed to Orvieto where he was staying, he at once determined to institute the feast of *Corpus Christi and also enjoined work to begin on the cathedral of Orvieto to enshrine such a precious relic. There is no contemporary evidence for the miracle, and there is no trace of it in Urban's bull instituting the feast.

Scenes from the legend are depicted on a *reliquary made in 1338 and in a fresco cycle begun in 1357, both in the cathedral at Orvieto. Mentioned in the 15th cent. by St *Antoninus of Florence (Chronica, 3, tit. 19, c. 13), it is found in a fuller form in

*Benedict XIV, Commentarii duo de D. N. Jesu Christi Matrisque Eius Festis, 1 (Lat. tr., 1745), p. 212.

Bombastus von Hohenheim, Theophrastus. See PARACELSUS.

Bonaventure, St (c.1217–74). *Franciscan theologian, 'Doctor seraphicus'. An Italian by birth, Giovanni di Fidanza studied in the Faculty of Arts in the University of *Paris. Probably in 1243 he entered the Franciscan Order and then studied theology under *Alexander of Hales. In 1248 he began to teach publicly; in 1253–4 he became doctor in theology; he continued teaching until 1257, with a short interruption due to the quarrel between the secular masters and the mendicant orders. On 2 Feb. 1257 he was elected Minister General of his order, and in this capacity he took a prominent part in settling the internal dissensions by which the order was then rent. He first codified its statutes in the 'Constitutions of Narbonne' in 1260. His Life of St *Francis was approved by his order in 1263 as the official biography of their founder, and in 1266 a general chapter at Paris decreed the destruction of all other 'legends' of the saint. In 1271 he was mainly responsible for securing the election of *Gregory X to the Papacy. In 1273 he was created Cardinal Bp. of Albano. He took a prominent part in the events of the Second Council of *Lyons in 1274 and died while it was still sitting. Feast day, 15 (until 1969, 14) July.

As a theologian he remained faithful to the tradition which derived from St *Augustine and was reasserted by St *Anselm, and had only limited sympathy with the new *Aristotelian doctrines, though he acknowledged that Aristotle's description of the facts was often correct. As against St *Thomas Aquinas, who gave a far more ready hearing to the new doctrines, St Bonaventure held that the creation of the world in time could be demonstrated by the light of reason. He emphasized that all human wisdom was folly when compared with the mystical illumination which God sheds on the faithful Christian; and this essentially mystical theory of knowledge he set forth in his 'Itinerarium Mentis in Deum'. His most extensive and systematic work is his 'Commentary on the *Sentences' of *Peter Lombard. He denied the doctrine of the *Immaculate Conception of the BVM. As a spiritual writer he had a great and lasting influence.

Crit. edn. of his Works by the Franciscans of Quaracchi (10 vols.; sep. index to vols. 1–6, Quaracchi, 1882–1902). Opera Theologica Selecta, ed. idd., Editio Minor (5 vols., ibid., 1934–64) [vols. 1–4 contain his comm. on the Sentences, vol. 5 various smaller works]. A different recension of the Collationes in Hexaëmeron from that in the complete works was ed. by F. Delorme, OFM (Bibliotheca Franciscana Scholastica Medii Aevi, 8; ibid., 1934). Modern Eng. tr of his works by J. de Vinck (5 vols., Patterson, NJ, 1960–70); also of his 'Itinerarium Mentis in Deum', 'Lignum Vitae' and Life of St Francis by E. Cousins (Classics of Western Spirituality [1978]). B. Distelbrink, Bonaventurae Scripta Authentica, Dubia vel Spuria critice Recensia (Subsidia Scientifica Franciscalia, 5; Rome 1975). E. *Gilson, La Philosophie de Saint Bonaventure (Études de Philosophie Médiévale, 4; 1924; 2nd edn., 1943, repr., 1978; Eng. tr., 1938). J. Ratzinger, Die Geschichtstheologie des heiligen Bonaventura (1959; Eng. tr., Chicago [1971]). J. G. Bougerol, OFM, Introduction à l'Étude de Saint Bonaventure (Bibliothèque de Théologie, 1st ser., Théologie dogmatique, 2 [1961]). J. F. Quinn, The Historical Constitution of St Bonaventure's Philosophy (Pontifical Institute of Mediaeval Studies, Studies and Texts, 23;

Toronto, 1973). *S. Bonaventura 1274–1974: Volumen commemorativum anni septies centenarii a morte S. Bonaventurae ... cura et studio Commissionis Internationalis Bonaventurianae* (5 vols., Rome [1974]); A. Pompei (ed.), *San Bonaventura Maestro di Vita Francescana et di Sapienza Cristiana: Atti del Congresso Internazionale per il VII centenario di san Bonaventura da Bagnoregio, Roma, 19–26 settembre 1974* (3 vols., ibid., 1979). Z. Hayes, OFM, *The Hidden Centre: Spirituality and Speculative Christology in St Bonaventure* (New York [1981]). F. Van Steenberghen, *La Philosophie au XIII᷎ siècle* (2nd edn., Philosophes Médiévaux, 28; 1991), pp. 177–244. J. Hamesse, *Thesaurus Bonaventurianus* (Travaux publiés par le Centre de Traitement Electronique des Documents de l'Université Catholique de Louvain, 3; 1972 ff.). E. Longpré, OFM, in *Dict. Sp.* 1 (1937), cols. 1768–843, s.v.; I. C. Brady, OFM, in *NCE* 2 (1967), pp. 658–64, s.v.; R. Sbardella, OFM, in *DIP* 1 (1974), cols. 1504–12, s.v.; A. Gerken, OFM, in *Lexikon des Mittelalters*, 2 (1983), cols. 402–7, s.v.

Bonhoeffer, Dietrich (1906–45), Lutheran pastor. The son of a professor of psychiatry at Berlin, Bonhoeffer studied at *Tübingen and Berlin, but was deeply influenced by K. *Barth. After his ordination, he worked in Barcelona and at the *Union Theological Seminary in New York (1928–9), and then returned to a university lectureship and pastoral work in Berlin in 1931, a year in which he also began his enduring connection with the *ecumenical movement. Opposed to the Nazi movement from the first, he sided with the *Confessing Church against the *German Christians, and signed the *Barmen Declaration in 1934. After serving as Chaplain to the Lutheran congregation in London, he returned to Germany in 1935 to become head of a seminary for the Confessing Church at Finkenwalde in Pomerania; here he put into practice ideas learnt in England at Kelham and *Mirfield. He was forbidden by the Nazis to teach, banned from Berlin and dismissed from his lectureship there in 1936; in 1937 the seminary at Finkenwalde was closed by the government. On the outbreak of the Second World War Bonhoeffer was in America on a lecture-tour, but he felt it his duty to return to Germany. In 1942 he tried to mediate between the Germans opposed to Hitler and the British government through his friendship with G. K. A. *Bell. He was arrested in 1943 and after imprisonment in Buchenwald he was hanged by the Gestapo at Flossenbürg in 1945.

His best-known work, *Widerstand und Ergebung* (ed. E. Bethge, 1951; Eng. tr. as *Letters and Papers from Prison*, 1953; enlarged edn., 1970; Eng. tr., 1971), needs to be read in the context of his surroundings and other writings. His first work, *Sanctorum Communio* (1930; Eng. tr., 1963), on the structure of the Church, is much modified by his second, *Akt und Sein* (1931; Eng. tr., *Act and Being*, 1962). This centres on the concept of revelation, which to him demanded a continuity to be found in Christ preached in the Church; the individual thus experiences revelation only in relation to the community. In *Widerstand und Ergebung* he is concerned with the growing secularization of modern man and the necessity of speaking in a secular way about God. Though writers of the 'Death of God' school have taken up his idea of religionless Christianity, his teaching represents a search for the beyond in the midst, and a demand for a radical reform of the Church, which in its existing form he thought to have no message for the present day. In its place he sought a form of Christianity

capable of dispensing with traditional religion as a prerequisite of biblical faith. His other works include *Die Nachfolge* (1937; Eng. tr., *The Cost of Discipleship*, 1948) and *Ethik* (ed. E. Bethge, 1949; Eng. tr., 1955).

Gesammelte Schriften, ed. E. Bethge (6 vols., Munich, 1958–74); new edn. of his *Werke* by E. Bethge and others (ibid., 1986 ff.). Eng. tr. of selections of Letters, Lectures, and Notes, from the Collected Works, by E. H. Robertson and J. Bowden, under the titles *No Rusty Swords* (1965), *The Way to Freedom* (1966), and *True Patriotism* (1973). Collection of extracts in Eng. tr. by J. de Gruchy, *Dietrich Bonhoeffer, Witness to Jesus Christ* (1988). E. Bethge, *Dietrich Bonhoeffer: Theologe, Christ, Zeitgenosse* (Munich, 1967; Eng. tr., 1970). Other studies by J. D. Godsey (Philadelphia and London, 1960), R. Marlé (Paris, 1967; Eng. tr., 1968), W. Kuhns (Dayton, Oh., 1967; London, 1968), M. Bosanquet (London, 1968), A. Dumas (Geneva, 1968; Eng. tr., 1972), and H. R. Pelikan (Vienna, etc. [1982]). H. Müller, *Von der Kirche zur Welt: Ein Beitrag zu der Beziehung des Wortes Gottes auf die Societas in Dietrich Bonhoeffers theologischer Entwicklung* (Hamburg, 1966); J. A. Phillips, *The Form of Christ in the World: A Study of Bonhoeffer's Christology* (1967). R. Mayer, *Christuswirklichkeit: Grundlagen, Entwicklung und Konsequenzen der Theologie Dietrich Bonhoeffers* (1969); G. T. Müller, *Bonhoeffers Theologie der Sakramente* (Frankfurter Theologische Studien, 28; 1979); id., *Für Andere da: Christus-Kirche-Gott in Bonhoeffers Sicht der mündig gewordenen Welt* (Konfessionskundliche und Kontroverstheologische Studien, 44 [1980]). E. G. Wendel, *Studien zur Homiletik Dietrich Bonhoeffers* (Hermeneutische Untersuchungen zur Theologie, 21; Tübingen, 1985). C. Marsh, *Reclaiming Dietrich Bonhoeffer: The Promise of his Theology* (New York and Oxford, 1994). E. Bethge and others, *Die Mündige Welt: Dem Andenken Dietrich Bonhoeffers* (5 vols., Munich, 1955–69). Useful collection of essays on Bonhoeffer in Eng. in R. G. Smith (ed.), *World Come of Age* (1967). G. Krause in *TRE* 7 (1981), pp. 55–66, s.v., with bibl.

Boniface, St (*c.*675–754), the 'Apostle of Germany'. Wynfrith, as he was originally called, was born in Wessex (at *Crediton, according to later tradition), educated at *Exeter, and entered the monastery of Nursling, near Southampton. He was a man of learning; besides a collection of hexametrical *enigmata*, he wrote a Latin grammar and possibly a treatise on metrics. In 716 he made a first, unsuccessful, missionary journey to Frisia. Undaunted, two years later he went to Rome, where in 719 *Gregory II commissioned him to preach to the heathen; at the same time he seems to have given him the name Boniface. After helping St *Willibrord in Frisia, Boniface turned south and converted many of the Hessians. He was summoned to Rome in 722 and ordained bishop, without being given a see. On his return to Germany, his courage in felling the Oak of Thor at Geismar, near Fritzlar, won him many converts in Hesse. He also worked in Thuringia and founded a number of monasteries, including Fritzlar, Taubersbischofsheim, Ohrdruf, Ochsenfurt, and Kitzingen. Prob. in 732 Gregory III sent him a *pallium and in the following years he laid the foundations of a settled ecclesiastical organization E. of the Rhine. After the death of *Charles Martel (741), he convened a series of Councils to reform the Frankish Church, and *c.*746 he became Abp. of Mainz. After a few years he resigned his see to return to his mission in Frisia, where he met with martyrdom from brigands at Dokkum in 754. His body was taken to *Fulda, which he had played some part in founding in 744. His devotion to the Papacy, coupled with the success of his work, may have assisted the spread of Papal influence N. of the Alps. Feast day, 5 June.

Opera Omnia, ed. J. A. Giles (2 vols., London, 1844); J. P. Migne, PL 89. 597–892. Crit. edn. of his Letters by M. Tangl (MGH, Epistolae Selectae, 1; 1916); Eng. tr. by E. Emerton (Records of Civilization, Sources and Studies, 31; New York, 1940). Hexametrical enigmata also ed. E. Duemmler in MGH, Poetae Latini Aevi Carolini, 1 (1881), pp. 1–23. Ars Grammatica and Ars Metrica, ed. G. J. Gebauer and B. Löfstedt (CCSL 133B; 1980). Of the early Lives (ed. W. Levison in MGH, Scriptores Rerum Germanicarum in Usum Scholarum, 1905), the most trustworthy is that by Willibald. The Letters, some other docs., and the Life by Willibald are also ed., with Ger. tr., by R. Rau (Ausgewählte Quellen zur deutschen Geschichte des Mittelalters, 4b; 1968). Eng. tr. of Life by Willibald and a selection of Boniface's letters in C. H. Talbot, The Anglo-Saxon Missionaries in Germany (1954), pp. 23–149. The standard modern work is T. Schieffer, Winfrid-Bonifatius und die christliche Grundelung Europas (Freiburg, 1954; repr. with new bibl., Darmstadt, 1972). Other studies include those of G. Kurth ('Les Saints', Paris, 1902), G. F. Browne (London, 1910), W. Lampen (Amsterdam, 1949), G. W. Greenaway (London, 1955), and J. C. Sladden (Exeter, 1980). Sankt Bonifatius: Gedenkgabe zum zwölfhundertsten Todestag (Fulda, 1954). T. Reuter (ed.), The Greatest Englishman: Essays on St Boniface and the Church at Crediton (Exeter, 1980). M. B. Parkes, 'The Handwriting of St Boniface: A Reassessment of the Problems', Beiträge zur Geschichte der deutschen Sprache und Literatur, 98 (1976), pp. 161–79. D. Parsons, 'Sites and Monuments of the Anglo-Saxon Mission in Central Germany', Archaeological Journal, 140 (1983), pp. 280–321. W. Levison, England and the Continent in the Eighth Century (Ford Lectures, 1943; Oxford, 1946), esp. pp. 70–93. J. M. Wallace-Hadrill, The Frankish Church (Oxford History of the Christian Church, 1983), pp. 150–61.

Boniface I, St (d. 422), Pope from 418. Before his election to the Papacy, he had been a presbyter at Rome. Immediately on the death of *Zosimus on 26 Dec. 418, both Boniface and the archdeacon Eulalius, a rival candidate, were elected and both were consecrated on the same day (29 Dec. 418). In consequence of the dispute, Boniface did not obtain possession of the see till 10 Apr. 419, after the Emp. Honorius had decided in his favour a week earlier at *Ravenna. After the caution shown by his predecessor, he took a decisive stand at the Imperial Court against *Pelagianism. He restored the rights of the metropolitans in the South of Gaul. He also secured the prefecture of Illyricum for his own jurisdiction when the E. Emp. *Theodosius II was endeavouring to transfer it to the obedience of the Patr. of *Constantinople. Feast day, 4 Sept.

Letters and decrees repr. in J. P. Migne, PL 20. 745–92. LP (Duchesne), 1 (1886), pp. 227–9. G. Bardy in DHGE 9 (1937), cols. 895–7, s.v.; J. Chapin in NCE 2 (1967), pp. 668 f., s.v.

Boniface VIII (c.1234–1303), Pope from 1294. Benedict Gaetani was a native of Anagni. After studying at Todi and Spoleto he became a canon at *Paris, Rome, and elsewhere, and in 1276 entered upon his career at the Curia, being appointed consistorial advocate and *notary apostolic. Having been created cardinal-deacon in 1281 and cardinal-priest in 1291, he was employed on important missions to France and Italy and took a decisive part in the abdication of St *Celestine V. Elected Pope at Naples in 1294, he immediately went to Rome, and from the first strove to realize his double aim of the pacification of Europe and the liberation of the Holy Land from the

Turks. His exertions, however, were destined to failure. After trying without success to reconcile Genoa and *Venice (1295), and to prevent the election of Frederick of Aragon as King of Sicily (1296), he became involved in his great struggle with Philip the Fair of France, which was to last until his death. In a professed attempt to stop the war between England and France by depriving the belligerents of their main financial resources, he issued the bull '*Clericis laicos' (q.v.; 25 Feb. 1296), forbidding the King to demand or receive extraordinary taxes from the clergy without Papal assent. When Philip replied by stopping all transports of gold and valuables to Rome, the Pope had to modify his claims and to concede to Philip the right to decide for himself cases of necessity in which he might levy taxes without consulting him, in the letter 'Ineffabilis Amoris' (20 Sept. 1296). At the same time the Papal position was aggravated by his difficulties with the powerful family of Colonna, with whom sided the *Fraticelli, whose exaggerated teachings Boniface had proscribed. The Papal armies, however, razed the Colonna fortresses to the ground, many members of the family finding refuge in France. In 1300 the Pope was able to celebrate the *Holy Year with great pomp, despite the absence of nearly all European princes. But in 1301 the struggle between Boniface and Philip broke out again when the King brought to trial the Papal legate, Bp. Bernard de Saisset, demanding his degradation and delivery to the secular power. The Pope replied by the bull '*Ausculta fili' (5 Dec. 1301), in which he enunciated the doctrine of Papal supremacy over princes and kingdoms, attacked Philip's government, and summoned the King or his representative to a synod in Rome. It was followed by the famous bull '*Unam Sanctam' (q.v.; 18 Nov. 1302), in which Boniface defended, with numerous patristic quotations, the jurisdiction of the Pope over every human creature. The struggle with Philip came to a head in 1303, when Philip refused to restore communications with Rome and endeavoured to bring the Pope to trial. Boniface replied by preparing a bull of excommunication, but Philip forestalled him, and William de Nogaret, at the head of a band of mercenaries, took the Pope prisoner at Anagni. Though Italian troops released him after three days, he was now broken in health and died at Rome a month later.

One of the great upholders of the absolute power of the Papacy, Boniface was the true successor of *Gregory VII and *Innocent III, but failed to understand the growth of national feeling which had taken place in the latter part of the 13th cent., and which increasingly diminished the political influence of the Popes. Among his many achievements is the compilation of the *Sext (q.v.), the embellishment of the Roman churches, and the foundation of the Roman university, the 'Sapienza' (1303).

G. Digard, M. Faucon, A. Thomas, and R. Fawtier (eds.), Les Registres de Boniface VIII (Bibliothèque des Écoles Françaises d'Athènes et de Rome, 2nd ser. 4; 4 vols., 1904–39). T. S. R. Boase, Boniface VIII (1933). F. M. Powicke, 'Pope Boniface VIII', History, NS 18 (1934), pp. 307–29. M. Seidlmayer, 'Papst Bonifaz VIII und der Kirchenstaat', Hist. J. 60 (1940), pp. 78–87. J. Rivière, Le Problème de l'Église et de l'État au temps de Philippe le Bel (SSL 8, 1926), passim, G. Digard, Philippe le Bel et le Saint-Siège de 1285 à 1304, ed. F. Lehoux (2 vols., 1936). T. Schmidt, Der Bonifaz-Prozess: Verfahren der Papstanklage in der Zeit Bonifaz' VIII. und Clemens' V. (Forschungen zur kirchlichen Rechtsgeschichte und zum Kirchenrecht, 19; 1989). H. Wolter, SJ, in

Handbuch der Kirchengeschichte, ed. H. Jedin, 3 (pt. 2; 1968), pp. 344–56, with bibl. pp. 340–2; Eng. tr., vol. 4 (1980), pp. 269–81, with bibl. pp. 708 f. B. Tierney in *NCE* 2 (1967), pp. 671–3; E. Dupré Theseider in *Dizionario Biografico degli Italiani*, 12 (1970), pp. 146–70, s.v. 'Bonifacio VIII', with extensive bibl.

Boniface of Savoy (d. 1270), Abp. of *Canterbury. He was the son of Thomas I, Count of Savoy, and through his sister's marriage became nearly related to Henry III. Having entered the *Carthusian Order while still a boy, in 1234 he was elected Bp. of Belley in Burgundy. In 1241 he was elected to succeed St *Edmund of Abingdon as Abp. of Canterbury, but Papal confirmation was delayed and he did not reach England until 1244, when he promptly carried through several important financial reforms. In the same year he left to attend the First Council of *Lyons (1245), where he was consecrated by *Innocent IV. He did not return until 1249, when he was enthroned at Canterbury on All Saints' Day. He instituted a metropolitical visitation of his province which met with strong resistance from the clergy generally, and he retired to Rome until 1252. In his later years he was frequently abroad, returning to England for the last time in 1265. In 1269 he set out with Edward I on a crusade, but died on the way at St Helena, Savoy. He became the subject of a cultus in Savoy (confirmed in 1830), where his feast is kept on 13 Mar.

G. Strickland, 'Ricerche storiche sopra il B. Bonifacio di Savoia, arcivescovo di Cantorbery 1207–70', *Miscellanea di Storia Italiana*, 3rd ser. 1 (no. 32 della Raccolta, 1895), pp. 349–432. R. Foreville, 'L'élection de Boniface de Savoie au Siège Primatial de Canterbury (1241–1243)', *Bulletin Philologique et Historique . . . du Comité des Travaux Historiques et Scientifiques*, 1 (1960), pp. 435–50. L. F. Wilshire, 'Boniface of Savoy, Carthusian and Archbishop of Canterbury 1207–1270', *Analecta Cartusiana*, 31 (Salzburg, 1977), pp. 1–89. M. *Creighton in *DNB* 5 (1886), pp. 350–2, s.v.

Bonifatiusverein (Ger., 'Boniface Society'). A society founded in 1849 under the patronage of St *Boniface for the support of Catholics living in those parts of Germany where the population is mainly Protestant. Its work is centred at Paderborn in Westphalia.

G. Walf in *L.Th.K.* (3rd edn.), 2 (1994), cols. 582 f., s.v. 'Bonifatiuswerk der deutschen Katholiken e. V.'.

Bonn Reunion Conferences. Two international conferences held at Bonn in 1874 and 1875 under the presidency of J. J. I. von *Döllinger to foster reunion between Churches which had retained the faith and order of historic Christianity. Their direction was in the hands of the newly separated *Old Catholics (though Döllinger himself never formally joined them). Others present included German Evangelicals, members of the E. Churches, and many theologians from Great Britain (including E. H. *Browne [Bp. of Winchester], H. P. *Liddon, and E. S. *Talbot) and America.

The Reports were pub. in English (London, 1875, 1876).

Bonner, Edmund (*c.*1500–69), Bp. of London. Trained at Oxford in *canon and civil law, he was employed by *Henry VIII on diplomatic missions from 1527, notably to Pope *Clement VII in 1532–3, to King Francis I of France in 1538–40, and to the Emp. *Charles V in 1542–3. He was appointed Bp. of *Hereford in 1538, and in 1539 translated to London, where he was responsible for enforcing the Act of the *Six Articles. Under *Edward VI he opposed the Royal *Injunctions of 1547 and evaded the provisions of the 1549 Book of *Common Prayer; he was deprived and imprisoned in 1549 for disobeying a Privy Council instruction. Restored by *Mary in 1553, he was energetic in the reconstruction of Catholic belief and worship and in the conviction of heretics. His reputation for cruelty may be exaggerated; he was pressed into action by Mary, and tried to obtain recantations. Under *Elizabeth I he refused to take the oath under the Act of *Supremacy and was deprived in 1559; he spent his last years imprisoned in the Marshalsea.

G. Alexander, 'Bonner and the Marian Persecutions', *History*, 60 (1975), pp. 374–91 (repr. in C. Haigh (ed.), *The English Reformation Revised* (Cambridge, 1987), pp. 157–75); id., 'Bishop Bonner and the Parliament of 1559', *Bulletin of the Institute of Historical Research*, 56 (1983), pp. 164–79. J. *Gairdner in *DNB* 5 (1886), pp. 356–60; *BRUO, 1501–1540*, pp. 57–9, both s.v., with bibl.

Bonosus (d. *c.*400). A Bp. of Naïssus (as *Innocent I implies, *epp.* 16 and 17) or *Sardica (acc. to *Marius Mercator), who denied the perpetual virginity of the BVM. His teaching was examined at a council at Capua in 391 and subsequently condemned; but Bonosus refused to submit and founded a sect (the 'Bonosians') which survived down to the 7th cent.

The earliest authority is Pope *Siricius, *ep.* 9 (ad Anysium, epis. Thessalonicensem); by an error, this letter is also ascribed to *Ambrose ('*ep.* 79'). Other sources include the Council of *Orange (538), can. 31, and *Vigilius, *ep.* 15. J. R. Palanque, *Saint Ambroise et l'empire romain* (1933), pp. 259–63. E. Venables in *DCB* 1 (1877), pp. 330 f.; F. *Loofs in *PRE* (3rd edn.), 3 (1897), pp. 314–17, with further refs. to sources; X. Le Bachelet, SJ, in *DTC* 2 (1905), cols. 1027–31.

Book Annexed, the. See ANNEXED BOOK, THE.

Book of Advertisements. See ADVERTISEMENTS, BOOK OF.

Book of Armagh. See ARMAGH, BOOK OF.

Book of Common Order [Common Prayer]. See COMMON ORDER [COMMON PRAYER], BOOK OF.

Book of Concord. See CONCORD, FORMULA AND BOOK OF.

Book of Jubilees. See JUBILEES, BOOK OF.

Book of Kells. See KELLS, BOOK OF.

book of life. The phrase occurs in six passages in the NT: Phil. 4: 3; Rev. 3: 5; 13: 8; 17: 8; 20: 12, 15; and 21: 27. (In AV, also at 22: 19, but here all the best MS evidence is for 'tree of life'.) The conception of a heavenly register of the elect is based on ideas found in the OT (e.g. Exod. 32: 32; Ps. 69: 28; Dan. 7: 10; 12: 1) and in 1 *Enoch (47. 3).

Book of Sports. See SPORTS, BOOK OF.

Books of Discipline. See DISCIPLINE, BOOKS OF.

Booth, William (1829–1912), founder and first General of the *Salvation Army (q.v.). A native of Nottingham and of partly Jewish origin, he was apprenticed to a pawn-broker in 1842. He became a *Methodist soon after, and in 1844 he had an experience of conversion. Two years later he became a revivalist preacher. In 1849 he went to London, and in 1855 married Catherine Mumford (1829–90), who shared his aspirations and became herself a famous preacher. In 1861 he left the Methodists, with whom he had come into conflict on account of his aggress-ive preaching, and established a revivalist movement of his own, called the Christian Mission, in Whitechapel, which undertook evangelistic, social, and rescue work. From 1880, when the Salvation Army spread to the USA, Aus-tralia, the Continent, and elsewhere, he spent much of his life travelling and organizing and addressing meetings. In 1890 he published *In Darkest England and the Way Out* in collaboration with W. T. Stead, in which he suggested a number of remedies for the social evils of the times, including farm colonies and rescue homes. His work was encouraged by Edward VII as well as by several foreign authorities.

Booth's chief characteristic was his love for the poor, whose souls he sought to save by his preaching while at the same time ministering to their bodily needs. Though he was ignorant of theology and of a rather narrow out-look, the strength of his emotions and sympathies, combined with a shrewd commercial sense, made his movement one of the most successful religious revivals of modern times.

In 1912 he was succeeded by his son, **William Bramwell Booth** (1856–1929), as General.

The Life of General Booth, by various authors (1912); H. Begbie, *Life of William Booth* (2 vols., 1920); St John Ervine, *God's Soldier* (2 vols., 1934); R. Collier, *The General next to God* (1965). H. Begbie in *DNB, 1912–1921*, pp. 50–2.
Life of Catherine Booth by her son-in-law, F. de L. Booth-Tucker (2 vols., London [1892]); modern Life by her grand-daughter, C. Bramwell Booth (ibid., 1970). Life of William Bramwell Booth by id. (ibid., 1933).

Booths, Feast of. See TABERNACLES, FEAST OF.

Borborians. A sect of libertine *Gnostics which flour-ished from the 2nd to the 5th cents. Their doctrines and practices are described by *Epiphanius (*Haer.* 26).

Bordeaux Pilgrim. The earliest known Christian pil-grim from W. Europe to the *Holy Land. He made his pilgrimage in AD 333–4, visiting *Constantinople and fin-ishing his journey at Milan. His account ('Itinerarium Burdigalense') is for the most part only a list of the stages in his route, but there is a brief description of some of the sites of Palestine.

Itinerarium first pub. by P. *Pithou (n.p., 1589); crit. edns. by P. Geyer, CSEL 39 (1889), pp. 1–33, with introd. pp. iv–viii, and O. Cuntz, *Itineraria Romana*, 1 (Leipzig, 1929), pp. 86–102. Edn. based on those of Geyer and Cuntz, CCSL 175 (1965), pp. 1–26. Eng. tr. by A. Stewart, with notes by C. W. Wilson (Palestine Pilgrims' Text Society, 1887). B. Kötting, *Peregrinatio Religiosa* (Forschungen zur Volkskunde, 33–5; 1950), pp. 89–110 and 343–

54, *passim*. R. Gelsomino, 'L'*Itinerarium Burdigalense* et la Puglia', *Vetera Christianorum*, 3 (1966), pp. 161–208.

Borgia, Cesare (1475–1507), Italian prince. An illegitim-ate son of Pope *Alexander VI, he was appointed to the archbishopric of Valencia and the cardinalate before he was 20 years of age. A few years later (1499) he was dispensed from the obligations of his orders so that he might marry Charlotte d'Albret, the sister of the King of Navarre. Soon after, King Louis XII created him Duke of Valentinois and his father made him 'Captain General of the Church'. A picturesque and able soldier, Cesare proved himself unscrupulous and merciless in securing his ends, though he ruled his subjects, once they were conquered, with just-ice and firmness, and on his activities N. Machiavelli is said to have based his portrait of *The Prince*. Cesare recov-ered many of the Papal provinces which had broken away from the Holy See, and was himself proclaimed Duke of Romagna. On his father's death, an illness precluded his taking part in the elections of his successors, Pius III (who lived only a few weeks) and *Julius II. The new Pope was a resolute enemy of the Borgia family and Cesare fled to Naples, where he was arrested and taken to Spain by order of *Ferdinand of Aragon. He escaped to Navarre, where he was employed on military service by his brother-in-law and killed while besieging the rebel castle of Viana.

E. Alvisi, *Cesare Borgia, Duca di Romagna: Notizie e documenti* (1878). Studies by C. Yriarte (2 vols., Paris, 1889; Eng. version (shortened), 1947), W. H. Woodward, (London, 1913), C. Beuf (Toronto and New York, 1942), and G. Sacerdote (Milan, 1950). M. Mallett, *The Borgias* (1969), *passim*. F. Gilbert in *Dizionario Biografico degli Italiani*, 12 (1970), pp. 696–708.

Borgia, St Francis (1510–72), *Jesuit. A Spanish court-ier and great-grandson of Pope *Alexander VI, he became Viceroy of Catalonia in 1539 until he succeeded to the dukedom of Gandía on the death of his father in 1534. In 1546 his wife died, and shortly afterwards he made a vow to join the Jesuits. He made his solemn profession in 1548, but in secret and with a dispensation regarding poverty for up to three years so that he could discharge all his family and administrative responsibilities. In the autumn of 1550 he travelled to Rome and from there let his membership of the Society of Jesus become public. Returning to Spain in 1551, he was ordained priest in the Basque country. From 1554 until 1560 he was in overall charge of the Jesuit provinces of Spain and Portugal. In 1561 he returned to Rome and became assistant to D. *Laínez, succeeding him as *General of the Society in 1565 and holding this office until his own death in 1572.

The membership of so significant a figure greatly increased the prestige of the new Society, and Borgia's eremitical inclinations may have had a decisive influence on the development of the Jesuit spiritual tradition. Through him the *Spiritual Exercises* of St *Ignatius Loyola were officially approved by Pope *Paul III in 1548, and both his money and influence were crucial in the establishment of the 'Roman College' (later *Gregorianum). Also important were his close, if not always easy, contacts with the Spanish and Portuguese courts: in particular, he was spiritual director to Princess Juana (regent of Spain during *Philip II's absence in England), who was admitted to secret membership of the

Society in 1555. Borgia nevertheless encountered difficulties with the *Inquisition in 1559–61, which were
resolved only by his return to Rome. As General, Borgia
developed the Society's legislation considerably and presided over continuing growth, inaugurating the Jesuit missions in the Spanish American colonies. He was canonized
in 1671. Feast day, 10 Oct.

Opera Omnia, pub. at Brussels, 1675. Letters and other material
in the Monumenta Historica Societatis Jesu (5 vols., Madrid, 1894–
1911). Further texts in edn. of M. Ruiz Jurado, SJ, in Archivum
Historicum Societatis Iesu, 41 (1972), pp. 176–206. Modern edn.
of his Tratados espirituales, with introd., by C. de Dalmases, SJ
(Espirituales Españoles, Serie A, Textos, 15; Barcelona, 1964).
Contemporary Lives by P. de Ribadeneira, SJ (Madrid, 1592;
modern edn. by E. Rey, SJ, under the title Historias de la Contrarreforma (1945), pp. 601–852) and D. Vásquez, SJ (unpub.).
Modern biographies by P. Suau (Paris, 1910), O. Karrer, SJ
(Freiburg i. B., 1921), and C. de Dalmases (Madrid, 1983; Eng.
tr., St Louis, 1991). M. Yeo, The Greatest of the Borgias (1936).
C. de Dalmases, SJ, and J. F. Gilmong, SJ, 'Las obras de San
Francisco de Borgia', Archivum Historicum Societatis Iesu, 30
(1961), pp. 125–79; C. de Dalmases, SJ, 'San Francisco de Borja
y la Inquisición española 1559–1561', ibid. 41 (1972), pp. 48–135;
M. Scaduto, SJ, 'Il governo di S. Francesco Borgia 1565–1572',
ibid., pp. 136–75. Polgár, 1 (1990), pp. 316–25. C. de Dalmases,
SJ, in Dict. Sp. 5 (1964), cols. 1019–32, s.v. 'François (5) de
Borgia'; id. in NCE 2 (1967), pp. 709 f., s.v.

Borromeo, St Charles. See CHARLES BORROMEO, ST.

Borrow, George Henry (1803–81), philologist and traveller. After education at Norwich Grammar School, he was
articled to a firm of solicitors. His ambition was to be a
writer, and soon he left the law to seek his fortune in
London. He went on tramp as a tinker for several years;
and from the wide experience thus gained he later wrote
the descriptions of gypsy life in Lavengro (1851) and The
Romany Rye (2 vols., 1857). As an agent of the *British
and Foreign Bible Society he travelled widely, distributing
copies of the Bible. His The Bible in Spain (3 vols., 1843)
became widely popular through its picturesque and viva-
cious narrative. He was also a considerable linguist, who
made several translations of portions of the Scriptures into
little-known tongues.

Collected edn. of his works by C. [K.] Shorter (16 vols.,
London, 1923–4). W. I. Knapp, The Life, Writings and Correspondence of George Borrow (1899). Studies by H. Jenkins (London,
1912), C. K. Shorter (ibid., 1913, incl. unpub. letters; also ibid.
[1920]), R. Fréchet (Paris, 1956), D. Williams (Oxford, 1982), and
M. Collie (Cambridge, 1982). M. Collie and A. Fraser, George
Borrow: A Bibliographical Study (Winchester, 1984).

Bosanquet, Bernard (1848–1923), idealist philosopher.
Educated at Balliol College, Oxford, where he came under
the influence of T. H. *Green and R. L. Nettleship, he
was elected a Fellow of University College in 1870 and
remained there until 1881. For most of the rest of his life
he lived privately in London, except from 1903 to 1908
when he was Professor of Moral Philosophy at St Andrews. With F. H. *Bradley he was the leading exponent
of *Absolute Idealism in England, though his interests
were wider and his outlook more conciliatory. In logic, the
judgement and not the concept was the fundamental form.
In his political theory he ascribed to the State, as the
'general' or 'rational will', almost limitless powers. His

understanding of religion was essentially *pantheistic. He
conceived of it as only a stage towards metaphysics, and
correspondingly of the God of religion as not more than
the highest of the appearances of the Absolute; and the
Incarnation at a moment in history he found meaningless.
Among his many writings the chief are: Logic, or the Morphology of Knowledge (2 vols., 1888), A History of Aesthetic
(1892), A Companion to *Plato's Republic (1895), The
Philosophical Theory of the State (1899), The Principle of
Individuality and Value (1912), The Value and Destiny of
the Individual (1913), What Religion Is (1920), and The
Meeting of Extremes in Contemporary Philosophy (1921).

His Life was written by his wife, H. Bosanquet (1924). J. H.
Muirhead, B. Bosanquet and his Friends: Letters (1935). C. Le Che-
valier, Éthique et idéalisme: Le Courant néo-hégélien en Angleterre,
Bernard Bosanquet et ses amis (Bibliothèque d'Histoire de la Philo-
sophie, 1963). C. C. J. *Webb, 'Bernard Bosanquet's Philosophy
of Religion', Hibbert Journal, 22 (1923–4), pp. 75–96. A. M.
McBriar, An Edwardian Mixed Doubles: The Bosanquets versus the
Webbs. A Study in British Social Policy 1890–1929 (Oxford, 1987).
A. D. Lindsay in DNB, 1922–1930, pp. 91–3.

Bosco, St John (1815–88). The founder of the *Salesian
Order (q.v.). The son of Piedmontese peasants, he was
brought up in and around Turin, where he spent most of
his life. A vision received at the age of 9 (the first of many
more throughout his life) aroused in him a keen interest
in winning lads to the Christian faith, and in 1859 he
founded the 'Pious Society of St *Francis de Sales', commonly known as the 'Salesians'. His influence over his
boys was achieved by using a minimum of restraint and
discipline, combined with a careful watch over his pupils'
development and the use of personal and religious encouragement. Don Bosco also actively promoted industrial
schools and evening classes where young men could be
apprenticed for secular vocations in a religious background. In the latter part of his life he did much to foster
missionary work. He was beatified in 1929 and canonized
in 1934. Feast day, 31 Jan.

Epistolario, ed. E. Ceria (4 vols., Turin, 1955–9). Memorie
dell'Oratorio di S. Francesco di Sales dal 1815 al 1855 [Bosco's
autobiography] ed. id. (ibid., 1946; Eng. tr., New Rochelle, NY,
1989). G. B. Lemoyne and E. Ceria, Memorie biografiche di don
Giovanni Bosco (19 vols., ibid., 1898–1939; Eng. tr., New Rochelle, NY, 1965 ff.). C. d'Espiney, Don Bosco (Nice, 1881; 10th
edn. with additional material, 1888). P. Stella, Don Bosco nella
storia della religiosità Cattolica (2 vols., Zurich, 1968–9). Other
Lives by A. Auffray, SDBL (Paris, 1929; Eng. tr., 1930), and
L. C. Sheppard (London, 1957). F. Desramaut, SDB, in Dict.
Sp. 8 (1974), cols. 291–303, s.v. 'Jean (35) Bosco'; id. in DIP 4
(1977), cols. 1246–53, s.v. 'Giovanni Bosco'.

Bosio, Antonio (c.1575–1629), Italian archaeologist,
dubbed by G. B. *de Rossi the 'Columbus of the
*Catacombs'. A native of Malta, he was sent to school at
Rome. After preliminary studies in philosophy and law, he
gave himself up at the age of 18 to archaeology, to which
he devoted the rest of his life. He was among the first to
recognize the significance of an accidental discovery on 31
May 1578 of a subterranean burial-place on the Via Salaria. Bosio's first descent was on 10 Dec. 1593 at the
Catacomb of *Domitilla (though Bosio could not yet name
it) on the Via Ardeatina, when, through inexperience, he
lost himself and only just succeeded in finding his way

out. His very extensive discoveries were described in his *Roma sotterranea* (finished 1620; not published until '1632', actually 1634 owing to delays with printing), which remained the standard work until G. B. de Rossi's researches. It was a remarkable achievement, methodical and deeply learned, the least satisfactory part of it being the engravings, which Bosio had entrusted to colleagues.

A. Valeri, *Cenni biografici di Antonio Bossio con documenti inediti* (1900); G. Ferretto, *Note storico-bibliografiche di archeologia cristiana* (1942), pp. 132–62. J. Stevenson, *The Catacombs* (1978), pp. 50–3. N. Parise in *Dizionario Biografico degli Italiani*, 13 (1971), pp. 257–9.

Bossey, Switzerland. An Ecumenical Institute of the *World Council of Churches was opened at the Château de Bossey, 12 miles from Geneva, in Sept. 1946. It owed its existence largely to the generosity of John D. Rockefeller, Jun. The Institute runs courses and conferences which aim at fostering characteristics of Christian leadership, as well as bringing together members of different Churches. By arrangement with the University of Geneva, it constitutes a Graduate School of Ecumenical Studies.

Bossuet, Jacques-Bénigne (1627–1704), French preacher and Bp. of Meaux. The fifth son of a judge in the Parlement of Dijon, he was educated first at the *Jesuit school at Dijon, later at Metz (whither his father had removed), and at the age of 13 appointed to a canonry in Metz cathedral. In 1642 he went to *Paris, where he entered the Collège de Navarre to train for the priesthood. His oratorical gifts attracted notice through a sermon with which as a boy of 16 he entertained a *salon* at the Hôtel de Rambouillet. In 1649 he was ordained deacon and, after preparation under St *Vincent de Paul, priest at Metz in 1652. After seven years at Metz, spent in study, controversy with the Protestants, and preaching, in 1659 he moved to Paris. Here his fame rapidly grew and he was a frequent preacher before the court. He was mainly responsible for the conversion of Marshal Turenne from Protestantism in 1668. In 1669 he was appointed Bp. of Condom in Gascony and in the same year delivered the first of his great 'Funeral Orations' (on *Henrietta Maria), which revealed to the full his powers as a pulpit orator. For the next 11 years he was tutor to the Dauphin (1670–1681). During this period he published his *Exposition de la doctrine catholique sur les matières de controverse* (1671), and also wrote (in the first place for his pupil's instruction) his *Traité de la connaissance de Dieu et de soi-même* (pub. 1722) and his *Discours sur l'histoire universelle* (1681). The latter was a compelling presentation of the Christian view of Divine overruling in history. On the completion of his duties as preceptor he was translated to the see of Meaux (1681), and now came to take an increasingly prominent part in French ecclesiastical affairs. At the *Assemblée générale du Clergé of 1682 he was mainly instrumental in securing the support of the French clergy for the moderate *Gallicanism of the Four *Gallican Articles (q.v.), which he himself drew up. In his zeal for the Catholic faith he approved of the Revocation of the Edict of *Nantes (1685) and also directed many publications against the Protestants, among which his *Histoire des variations des Églises protestantes* (2 vols., 1688) was the most notable. At the same time Bossuet hoped that Christian reunion might be fur-

thered by peaceful methods, and to this end conducted a long correspondence (1683–1700) with G. W. *Leibniz. His *Méditations sur l'Évangile* (pub. 1731) and his *Élévations sur les mystères* (pub. 1727), written in the concluding decade of his life, rank as classics of French devotional literature. In his last years the case of Mme *Guyon led him into a bitter controversy on mysticism with F. *Fénelon, and Bossuet was mainly responsible for his condemnation in 1699. His views were embodied in his *Relation sur le quiétisme* (1698). He was also a vigorous opponent of R. *Simon's theories of the Bible, notably in his *Défense de la tradition et des saints pères* (pub. 1763).

By common consent Bossuet is among the greatest preachers of all time. Not only did he possess the outward gifts which belong to the successful orator (an impressive presence, a pleasing voice, ease of manner, fitness of phrase); he also combined with them precision of thought, complete grasp of the subject and, above all, a strong hold on dogmatic truth; and to the dry light of argument he added the fire of passion. The fact that he was at his best on a large canvas made the funeral oration a form specially suited to his talents. The three on Henrietta Maria (1669), Henriette Anne d'Angleterre (1670), and the Prince de Condé (1687) will remain classics. But his real greatness as a preacher rests on the distinction he showed on less formal occasions.

Complete Works, ed. F. Lachat (31 vols., Paris, 1862–6). *Œuvres oratoires*, ed. J. Lebarq, rev. by C. Urbain and E. Levesque (7 vols., Paris, 1914–26). Correspondence, ed. C. Urbain and E. Levesque (15 vols., Paris, 1909–12). Modern Eng. tr. of Bossuet's *Politique tirée des propres paroles de l'Écriture Sainte* (1709), with introd. by P. Riley (Cambridge Texts in the History of Political Thought, 1990). Lives by A. Rébelliau ('Les Grands Écrivains français', 1900), W. J. Sparrow Simpson (London, 1937), and J. Calvet (Paris, 1941). R. Schmittlein, *L'Aspect politique du différend Bossuet–Fénelon* (Bade, 1954); L. Cognet, *Crépuscule des mystiques: Bossuet. Fénelon* (Tournai [1958]); J. Truchet, *La Prédication de Bossuet* (2 vols., 1960); id., *Bossuet panégyriste* (1962); id., *Politique de Bossuet* (1966); T. Goyet, *L'Humanisme de Bossuet* (2 vols. in 1 [1965]); J. Lebrun, *Bossuet* ('Les écrivains devant Dieu' [1970]); id., *La spiritualité de Bossuet* [1972]. F. *Cabrol, OSB, 'Bossuet, ses relations avec l'Angleterre', *RHE* 27 (1931), pp. 525–71. A. Largent in *DTC* 2 (1905), cols. 1049–89; E. Levesque in *DHGE* 9 (1937), cols. 1339–91.

Bötticher, Paul Anton. See LAGARDE, PAUL ANTON DE.

Botulph, St (mid-7th cent.), also Botolph, Botwulf. Acc. to the Anglo-Saxon Chronicle the founder and first abbot of a monastery at Icanhoe (or Ox-island) in 654; it is uncertain whether this was Iken in Suffolk, where the church is dedicated to St Botulph, or (less probably) Boston (i.e. Botulph's town) in Lincs. During the Middle Ages the cult of the saint was very popular, esp. in East Anglia and the north, and some 70 English churches have been dedicated to him. Feast day, 17 June.

Historia Abbatum Auctore Anonymo, cap. 4; pr. by C. Plummer in his edn. of the historical works of *Bede (2 vols., Oxford, 1896), 1, p. 389, with notes, 2, p. 372. Life by Folcard pr. in *AASS*, Jun. 3 (1701), pp. 402 f. For MSS, edns. and value of Folcard and other Lives, Hardy, 1, pp. 373–6. F. S. Stevenson, 'St Botolph (Botwulf) and Iken', *Proceedings of the Suffolk Institute of Archaeology and Natural History*, 18 (1922), pp. 29–52.

bounds, beating of the. See BEATING OF THE BOUNDS.

Bourchier, Thomas (c.1410–86), Abp. of *Canterbury. Educated at Oxford, of which University he later became Chancellor, he was appointed to the see of *Worcester in 1433, of *Ely in 1443, of Canterbury in 1454, and created cardinal in 1467. He became much involved in the political affairs of the time, maintaining an even balance between the conflicting interests of Lancaster and York, and retaining the favour of Edward IV. In 1457 he took a leading part in the trial of R. *Pecock, Bp. of *Chichester, for heresy. He lived to crown Henry VII king.

Registrum Thome Bourgchier Cantuariensis Archiepiscopi A.D. 1454–1486, ed. F. R. H. du Boulay (Canterbury and York Society, 54; 1957). W. F. *Hook, Lives of the Archbishops of Canterbury, 5 (1867), pp. 268–386. J. *Gairdner in DNB 5 (1886), pp. 15–18, s.v.; BRUO 1 (1957), pp. 230–2, s.v. 'Bourgchier, Thomas'; both with refs. For his part in Pecock's condemnation see also V. H. H. Green, Bishop Reginald Pecock (1945), pp. 49–60.

Bourdaloue, Louis (1632–1704), French preacher. He joined the *Jesuits in 1648, and was employed in teaching humanities and morals in various provincial houses. His preaching career began in 1666. His courses of sermons, twelve in all, delivered before Louis XIV and his court during Advent and Lent in and after 1670, earned him an outstanding reputation as a preacher. The published sermons exhibit qualities of clarity and logical construction; and notes taken at the time of their delivery tend to confirm the impression of rhetorical power which he made upon his contemporaries. For the most part he was concerned with the moral applications of Christianity, combining an inflexible austerity of principle with a remarkable psychological tact and insight, perfected in the practice of spiritual direction.

Sermons et autres œuvres, ed. by F. Bretonneau, SJ (16 vols., Lyons, etc., 1707–34). Œuvres complètes (18 vols., Toulouse, 1818); also ed. by E. Griselle (vols. 1 and 2 only, Paris, 1919–22). Selected sermons ed. by G. Truc (Paris, 1921); R. Daeschler (ibid., 1929); and L. Dimier (ibid., 1936). M. Lauras, SJ, Bourdaloue, sa vie et ses œuvres (2 vols., 1881). Other Lives by [A. A.] L. Pauthe (Paris, 1900), F. Castets (2 vols., ibid., 1901–4), and E. Byrne (ibid., 1929). E. Griselle, Bourdaloue: Histoire critique de sa prédication d'après les notes de ses auditeurs et les témoignages contemporains (3 vols., 1901–6); F. Brunetière, Études critiques, 8 (1907), pp. 121–82 ('L'éloquence de Bourdaloue'); G. Truc, 'L'actualité psychologique dans les sermons de Bourdaloue', Revue d'histoire littéraire de la France, 21 (1914), pp. 41–61; J. C. Reville, SJ, Herald of Christ: Louis Bourdaloue S.J., king of preachers and preacher of kings (New York [1922]); M. F. Hitz, Die Redekunst in Bourdaloues Predigt (Diss., Munich, 1936). Polgár, 1 (1990), pp. 360–7.

Bourignon, Antoinette (1616–80), Flemish enthusiast and mystical writer. She tried to found a new ascetic order, and to run an orphanage at Liège as an *Augustinian house, both unsuccessfully. After 1662 she was estranged from mainstream Christianity, and came to conceive herself to be the 'woman clothed with the sun' of Rev. 12. She influenced P. *Poiret, who published her works. John *Wesley included an edited version of her writings in his *Christian Library. Bourignonist ideas were particularly influential in Scotland in the early part of the 18th cent.; between 1711 and 1889 ministers of the Church of Scotland had to make an explicit denial of Bourignonism before ordination.

Collected works pub. in 19 vols., Amsterdam, 1669–86. A. v. d. Linde, Antoinette Bourignon: Das Licht der Welt (Leiden, 1895); A. R. Macewen, Antoinette Bourignon, Quietist (1910). G. D. Henderson, Mystics of the North-East (Third Spalding Club, Aberdeen, 1934), passim (see index). R. A. *Knox, Enthusiasm: Chapters in the History of Religion (Oxford, 1950), pp. 352–5.

Bousset, Wilhelm (1865–1920), NT scholar. In 1916 he became professor of NT theology at Giessen. He made extensive investigations into the connections of later *Judaism and early Christianity with the contemporary Hellenistic religions, and the growth of the so-called '*Religionsgeschichtliche Schule' owed much to his researches. Among his chief writings were Der Antichrist (1895), Die Religion des Judentums im neutestamentlichen Zeitalter (1903; 3rd edn. by H. Gressmann, 1926), Die Hauptprobleme der Gnosis (1907), Kyrios Christos (1913; Eng. tr., Nashville, 1970), and Apophthegmata: Studien zur Geschichte des ältesten Mönchtums (1923; posthumous).

Bousset edited, with W. Heitmüller, the Theologische Rundschau, 1897–1917, and with H. *Gunkel the Forschungen zur Religion und Geschichte des AT und NT, 1903 ff. A collection of his Religionsgeschichtliche Studien was ed. A. F. Verheule (Supplements to Novum Testamentum, 50; 1979), with introd., pp. 1–27. Id., Wilhelm Bousset: Leben und Werk (Utrecht thesis; Amsterdam, 1973). J. M. Schmidt in TRE 7 (1981), pp. 97–101, s.v.

Bow Church. The church of St Mary-le-Bow ('S. Maria de Arcubus') in Cheapside, so named from the stone arches of the original 11th-cent. church on the site. The present church, which was badly damaged in an air raid in 1940, was built by C. *Wren after the Great Fire of 1666. It gave its name to the '*Arches Court of Canterbury' which formerly met in the crypt of the church. The confirmation of those elected bishops in the province of *Canterbury still takes place here.

See bibl. to ARCHES, COURT OF CANTERBURY.

Bowden, John William (1798–1844), *Tractarian. A close friend and contemporary at Trinity College, Oxford, of J. H. *Newman, with whom he collaborated on a poem on 'St Bartholomew's Eve' (1821), he became a warm supporter of the *Oxford Movement. He wrote some of the *Tracts for the Times (nos. 5, 29, 30, 56, and perhaps 58), many articles for the *British Critic and a Life of *Gregory VII (1840). He also contributed six hymns to 'Lyra Apostolica' (1836).

His son, **John Edward Bowden** (1829–74), who became a RC in 1848, was a member of the London *Oratory and the biographer of F. W. *Faber.

C. Kent in DNB 6 (1886), p. 41, s.v.

bowing. From very early times Christians have bowed 'at the name of Jesus', on the authority of Phil. 2: 10. How far back the custom of bowing at other times, particularly to the altar, can be traced, is disputed. In the C of E, despite *Puritan objections, bowing at the Holy *Name was enjoined in Canon 18 (1604), and the practice of making their reverence and obeisance on entering and leaving the church was recommended to the people in Canon 7 (1640). The statutes of *Winchester Cathedral require that the clergy on entering and leaving the church shall 'severally bow themselves towards the altar, devoutly worshipping the Divine Majesty'.

boy bishop. In medieval times it was a widespread custom, in many English monasteries, schools, and country parishes, to elect on St *Nicholas's Day (6 Dec.) a boy who should execute till *Holy Innocents' Day (28 Dec.) various functions in church ordinarily performed by a bishop. The practice was abolished by *Henry VIII, revived by *Mary, and finally abolished by *Elizabeth I. On the Continent it was never so common, though analogous celebrations sometimes took place, esp. in Germany, on the Feast of St Gregory the Great (then 12 Mar.). The intention was to express in dramatic form the reverence for childhood shown in the Gospels.

E. K. Chambers, *The Mediaeval Stage* (2 vols., Oxford, 1903), 1, pp. 336–71, and 2, pp. 282–9; K. Young, *The Drama of the Medieval Church*, 1 (ibid., 1933), pp. 106–11 and 552.

Boyle, Robert (1627–91), scientist, 'the father of chemistry and son of the Earl of Cork'. From 1654 to 1668 he lived in Oxford, exercising great influence, but, partly because he did not wish to take the oaths which would be incumbent on taking office, he accepted no official position at any time. His experimental research on atmospheric pressure and chemical affinity by atomic or 'corpuscular' interaction was of fundamental importance. He saw his scientific work as demonstrating the Divine design of nature, and published a series of treatises which sought to emphasize the harmony which existed between scientific enquiry and Christian life. In his early days he was a member of that group of scientists which he later styled the 'Invisible College' and he took a prominent part in the formation of the Royal Society in 1662. He was active in promoting Bible translation and other evangelical enterprises, while in his will he left the sum of £50 a year for a series of eight lectures to be given in some church in London to confute unbelievers (the 'Boyle Lectures').

Boyle's collected works, with Life, were pub. by T. Birch (5 vols., London, 1744). Considerable extracts from his writings in P. E. More and F. L. Cross, *Anglicanism* (1935), nos. 56, 89, 103, 104, 124, 350, 351. Lives, besides the primary work of T. Birch, include those of R. Boulton in his edn. of Boyle's *Theological Works ... Epitomized* (3 vols., 1715), 1, pp. 1–374, R. Pilkington (London, 1959), and R. E. W. Maddison (ibid., 1969). J. R. Jacob, *Robert Boyle and the English Revolution* (Studies in the History of Science, 3; New York [1977]). R. McM. Hunt, *The Place of Religion in the Science of Robert Boyle* (Pittsburgh, 1955). J. G. Lennox, 'Robert Boyle's Defence of Teleological Inference in Experimental Science', *Isis*, 74 (Philadelphia, 1983), pp. 38–52. J. F. Fulton, *A Bibliography of the Honourable Robert Boyle* (orig. pub. in *Oxford Bibliographical Society Proceedings and Papers*, 3 (1933), pp. 1–172 and 339–65; 2nd edn., Oxford, 1961).

Brabourne, Theophilus (1590–c.1661), English *Puritan author. In early life he appears to have officiated as a clergyman at *Norwich. In 1628 and 1631 he published two pamphlets maintaining that Saturday, not Sunday, ought to be kept as the Christian Sabbath, and for the second of these, the *Defence ... of the Sabbath Day*, he was imprisoned for 18 months at Newgate. The stir thus aroused was one of the reasons for *Charles I's reissue in 1633 of the 'Book of *Sports'. Under the Commonwealth Brabourne again took up the Sabbath question in a dispute

with John Collinges, a Presbyterian writer. At the Restoration he wrote three pamphlets in defence of the royal supremacy against the *Quakers.

B. Brook, *The Lives of the Puritans*, 2 (1813), pp. 362–4. K. L. Parker, *The English Sabbath* (Cambridge, 1988), pp. 198–202. A. Gordon in *DNB* 6 (1886), pp. 139–41, s.v.

brachium saeculare. See SECULAR ARM.

Bradford, John (c.1510–55), Protestant martyr. He was a native of Manchester and for a time secretary to Sir John Harrington, paymaster of the English forces in France. He began studying law at the Inner Temple c.1547, but after hearing sermons by H. *Latimer he became conscience-stricken over his involvement in the embezzlement of military funds, made restitution, and embarked on the study of theology. He moved to St Catharine's Hall, Cambridge, where he took his MA in 1549, and shortly afterwards was elected Fellow of Pembroke Hall, where J. *Whitgift was among his pupils. He was ordained deacon in 1550 by N. *Ridley, Bp. of London, who, finding him a strong supporter of the Protestant cause and a good preacher, made him his chaplain. Soon after Mary's accession (1553) he was imprisoned on a charge of sedition in the Tower, where during 18 months he carried on an extensive correspondence, wrote *The Hurt of Hearing Mass* (posthumously pub., ?1561), and vigorously defended *predestination against the *Freewillers among his fellow-prisoners. In a trial before S. *Gardiner and others, he remained steadfast to his Protestantism and was burnt at *Smithfield on 1 July 1555.

A complete edn. of his writings was pub. by the Parker Society (2 vols., 1848, 1853). C. Hughes, 'Two Sixteenth-Century Northern Protestants: John Bradford and William Turner', *Bulletin of the John Rylands Library*, 66 (1983–4), pp. 104–38, esp. pp. 104–21. C. R. Trueman, *Luther's Legacy: Salvation and English Reformers, 1525–1556* (Oxford, 1994), pp. 27–30 and 243–88.

Bradlaugh, Charles (1833–91), free-thinker. A Londoner by birth, he was brought up in the C of E, but soon became an *atheist. He worked as a lawyer's clerk, but devoted his spare time to popular lecturing, becoming president of the London Secular Society (1858–90). From 1860 he conducted the *National Reformer* in defence of free thinking. Prosecution for its alleged sedition, followed by a legal contest as to whether Bradlaugh as an atheist could give evidence (1867–9), led to the passage of the Evidence Further Amendment Act in 1869. In 1876, together with Mrs A. Besant (1847–1933), who was his co-editor of the *National Reformer* from 1874 to 1885, he entered the lists in support of a Bristol publisher who had issued an American pamphlet, *Fruits of Philosophy*, and been lightly sentenced for its indecency. When Bradlaugh and Mrs Besant reissued the pamphlet, both were sentenced heavily, but the indictment was quashed on a technical point. He himself wrote a number of pamphlets.

In 1868 Bradlaugh stood for Parliament at Northampton, but was defeated. After two further defeats he was elected MP for Northampton in 1880. On the refusal of his plea to affirm or to be allowed to take the oath, he was several times excluded from the House of Commons and re-elected. Finally, as a result of a ruling by the Prime Minister, Sir Robert Peel, when Parliament assembled on 12 Jan. 1886 he was allowed to make the oath required by the Parliamentary Oaths Act 1866 and take his seat. In his last years he was actively interested in promoting social and political reform in *India and attended the Indian National Congress of 1889. He dissociated himself from Mrs Besant after she became a *theosophist.

Modern edn. of *Humanity's Gain from Unbelief* and Selections from other Works (Thinker's Library, 1929). H. B. Bonner (daughter), *Charles Bradlaugh: A Record of his Life and Work*, with an Account of his Parliamentary Struggle, Politics and Teachings, by J. M. Robertson (2 vols., 1894). Other Lives by A. S. Headingley (London, 1880; rev. edn., 1883) and D. Tribe (ibid., 1971). W. L. Arnstein, *The Bradlaugh Case: A Study in late Victorian Opinion and Politics* (Oxford, 1965).

Bradley, Francis Herbert (1846–1924), exponent of *Absolute Idealism. He was born at Clapham and educated at Marlborough and at University College, Oxford. From 1870 till his death he was a Fellow of Merton College, Oxford. His first important publication was his brilliant *Ethical Studies* (1876). Next followed *The Principles of Logic* (1883) and, ten years later, *Appearance and Reality* (1893), the most original work in British metaphysics in the 19th cent. Bradley argued that everywhere in the fields of natural science, ethics, religion, etc., contradictions are patent, and that therefore these realms cannot be conceived of as reality. The only true reality is to be found in an all-inclusive experience, the Absolute, wherein all contradictions, including the gulf between subject and object, are finally transcended. As the notions of personality and selfhood are riddled with contradictions, Theism and personal immortality must be rejected. In an essay on 'The Presuppositions of Critical History' (1874) he examined the foundations of historical credibility and rejected the historicity of the Gospels on the ground that their facts were without parallel in our experience. Bradley always maintained that he was indifferent to the sources of his ideas; but he was, like B. *Bosanquet, deeply indebted to G. W. F. *Hegel, partly through the medium of T. H. *Green, who had done much to encourage constructive interest in German Idealism in Oxford. Among his later works are *Essays on Truth and Reality* (1914) and a revised edition of *The Principles of Logic* (1922).

His *Essays* were collected in 2 vols., Oxford, 1935. C. A. Campbell, *Scepticism and Construction: Bradley's Sceptical Principles* (1931); R. Kagey, *The Growth of F. H. Bradley's Logic* (1931); R. Wollheim, *F. H. Bradley* (Harmondsworth, 1959); S. K. Saxena, *Studies in the Metaphysics of Bradley* (Muirhead Library of Philosophy, 1967); A. [R.]. Manser, *Bradley's Logic* (Oxford, 1983); id. and G. Stock (eds.), *The Philosophy of F. H. Bradley* (ibid., 1984). A. E. *Taylor in *DNB*, *1922–1930*, pp. 101–3.

Bradwardine, Thomas (c.1295–1349), Abp. of *Canterbury. His father lived in *Chichester, and Bradwardine was prob. born there. He was a Fellow, first of Balliol College and then of Merton College, Oxford. After becoming a master of arts in the mid-1320s, he entered the theological faculty. During this time he wrote his influential work on physics, *De proportionibus* (c.1328) and his controversial treatise on future contingents (c.1333). In 1335 he became chaplain to Richard of Bury, Bp. of *Durham, and in 1337 Chancellor of *St Paul's Cathedral. About the same time he was made confessor to Edward III, whom he

sometimes accompanied on his travels on the Continent during the wars with France. In 1346 he was one of the commissioners who tried to bring about peace between England, France, and Scotland. In 1349 he was consecrated Abp. of Canterbury at *Avignon, and, having returned to England, died in the same year of the Black Death.

Bradwardine was held in esteem by his contemporaries for his learning, esp. in mathematics and theology. His principal work, *De Causa Dei contra Pelagium* (completed by 1344), earned him the title of 'Doctor Profundus'. Under the influence esp. of St *Augustine, St *Anselm, and *Duns Scotus, he sought to build up a theological system on evident propositions, utilizing esp. the *Ontological Argument. Against the *Pelagian ideas prevalent among some contemporary theologians, he insisted on the necessity of grace and the 'irresistible' efficacy of the Divine Will, which lies behind all action, whether necessary or contingent. His writings paved the way for the predestinarian thought of John *Wycliffe. He also made original and influential contributions to a number of theoretical problems in mathematics and physics, notably in his treatment of geometry, of continuity and infinity, of proportions, and of motion.

His *De Causa Dei contra Pelagium*, ed. H. *Savile (London, 1618; photographically repr., Frankfurt, 1964), with biog. introd. (no pagination). *De proportionibus* ed. H. L. Crosby, Jun. (Madison, Wis., 1955). H. A. Oberman and J. A. Weisheipl, OP, 'The *Sermo Epinicius* ascribed to Thomas Bradwardine (1346)', *AHDLMA* 25 (for 1958; 1959), pp. 295–329, incl. text; M. L. Roure, 'La Problématique des Propositions insolubles au XIIIᵉ siècle et au début du XIVᵉ, ibid. 37 (for 1970; 1971), pp. 205–326, incl. text of Bradwardine's 'De Insolubilibus', pp. 285–326. J.-F. Genest, 'Le *De futuris contingentibus* de Thomas Bradwardine', *Recherches Augustiniennes*, 14 (1979), pp. 249–336, incl. text. S. Hahn, *Thomas Bradwardine und seine Lehre von der menschlichen Willensfreiheit* (BGPM 5, Heft 2; 1905). G. [A.] Leff, *Bradwardine and the Pelagians* (Cambridge, 1957), esp. pp. 1–124. H. A. Oberman, *Archbishop Thomas Bradwardine: A Fourteenth Century Augustinian* (Utrecht diss., 1957). Various authors in N. Kretzmann and others (eds.), *The Cambridge History of Later Medieval Philosophy* (1982), esp. pp. 374–7, 533–6, 540–2, 578–80, and 887. J. A. Weisheipl in J. I. Catto (ed.), *The Early Oxford Schools* (*The History of the University of Oxford*, 1; Oxford, 1984), esp. pp. 633–58. *BRUO* 1 (1957), pp. 244–6, with further refs. J. E. Murdoch in *Dictionary of Scientific Biography*, 2 (1970), pp. 390–7, s.v.

Brady, Nicholas (1659–1726). See TATE, NAHUM, AND BRADY, NICHOLAS.

Braga, rite of. The form of the Latin rite used in the cathedral of Braga (*Civitas Bracarensis*) in N. Portugal. There is documentary evidence for its existence from the 14th cent. and it may have owed its compilation to St Giraldus c.1100. In 1924 *Pius XI confirmed the use throughout the archdiocese of a revised form of the rite, much influenced by the then current Roman Missal. A further revision in 1971 incorporated various changes recommended by the Second *Vatican Council; at the same time its use in the archdiocese was made optional.

P. R. Rochat, *L'Office Divin au Moyen Age dans l'Église de Braga* (1980). A. A. King, *Liturgies of the Primatial Sees* (1957), pp. 155–285.

Bramhall, John (1594–1663), Abp. of *Armagh. Born near Pontefract, W. Yorks, he was educated at Sidney Sussex College, Cambridge, and ordained c.1616. In 1633 he went to Ireland as Strafford's chaplain and in 1634 became Bp. of Derry. Here he helped in strengthening episcopacy and maintaining the revenues of the Church of Ireland. In 1642 he retired to England and in 1644 to the Continent, returning for a brief spell to Ireland in 1648. On his permanent return at the *Restoration, he became Abp. of Armagh (1661) and exercised moderation in enforcing the Conformity Laws. He devoted his exile to replying to attacks upon the English Church from three quarters. In *Serpent Salve* (1643) he upheld episcopal and monarchical government against the democratic and presbyterian system of the Puritans, returning to the attack in *Fair Warning against the Scottish Discipline* (1649). His *Defence of True Liberty* (1655) was directed against the philosophical materialism and determinism of T. *Hobbes, whom he had met in *Paris; to Hobbes's *Animadversions* in reply, Bramhall answered with *Castigations of Hobbes' Animadversions* (1658), with an appendix on 'The Catching of Leviathan, the Great Whale'. In a third sphere of controversy, with Rome, he published (1653) a reply to T. B. de la Milletière's defence of *transubstantiation (1651), upholding the Anglican doctrine of the *Real Presence. His attacks on *Ultramontanism were widely welcomed by French Catholics. In 1654 he published his celebrated *A Just Vindication of the Church of England from the Unjust Aspersion of Criminal Schism*. In response to the RC reply to this by Dr Richard Smith, titular Bp of *Chalcedon, Bramhall issued his *Replication* (1656), a prayer that he might live to see the reunion of Christendom.

Collected edn. of Works, with Life by H. Vesey (Dublin, 1676); modern edn. by A. W. Haddan in the LACT (5 vols., 1842–5), with life from *Biographia Britannica* (vol. 1, pp. iii–xv). Much of Bramhall's Correspondence, with other material on his episcopate, is printed in the *Report of the Manuscripts of the late Reginald Rawdon Hastings*, ed. F. Bickley (Historical MSS Commission, 78), 4 (1947), pp. 55–152. W. J. Sparrow Simpson, *Archbishop Bramhall* (1927). F. R. Bolton, *The Caroline Tradition of the Church of Ireland with special reference to Bishop Jeremy Taylor* (1958), *passim*; H. R. McAdoo, *The Spirit of Anglicanism* (1965), pp. 368–85.

branch theory of the Church. The theory that, though the Church may have fallen into schism within itself and its several provinces or groups of provinces be out of communion with each other, each may yet be a 'branch' of the one Church of Christ, provided that it continues to hold the faith of the original undivided Church, and to maintain the *apostolic succession of its bishops. Such, it is contended by many Anglican theologians, is the condition of the Church at the present time, there being now three main branches, the Roman, the Eastern, and the Anglican Communions. The theory in this precise form was apparently first put forward in the 19th cent. under the inspiration of the *Oxford Movement. It is the basis of W. *Palmer's *Treatise on the Church of Christ* (1838), but only became general and popular later.

brasses. Monuments consisting of brass plates, engraved with images or inscriptions, set into stones in the pavement or on a wall of a church. They are more durable than incised stone slabs, and take up less room than sculptured figures. Originating in the 13th cent., they were popular until the 16th cent., esp. in England, France, Germany, and the Low Countries. In the Reformation period many were destroyed by iconoclasts; often their metal was reused elsewhere, sometimes for new brasses engraved on the reverse (known somewhat inexactly as 'palimpsests'). They enjoyed a revival in the 19th cent. They provide much valuable historical information, esp. about the costume and beliefs of the time.

H. Haines, *A Manual of Monumental Brasses* (2 vols., 1861; repr., Bath, 1970); H. Druitt, *A Manual of Costume as illustrated by Monumental Brasses* (1906; repr., Bath, 1970); M. Stephenson, *A List of Monumental Brasses in the British Isles* (1926; Appendix, 1938); H. K. Cameron, *A List of Monumental Brasses on the Continent of Europe* (1970; 2nd edn., 1973); J. Bertram, *Lost Brasses* [1976]; M. [W.] Norris, *Monumental Brasses: The Memorials* (2 vols. [1977]); id., *Monumental Brasses: The Craft* (1978); D. [G.] Meara, *Victorian Memorial Brasses* (1983); J. Coales (ed.), *The Earliest English Brasses: Patronage, Style and Workshops 1270–1350* (1987). *Transactions of the Cambridge University Association of Brass Collectors* (12 pts., 1887–93); *Transactions of the Monumental Brass Society* (1894 ff.). More popular works include M. [W.] Norris, *Brass Rubbing* [1965]; J. Page-Phillips, *Macklin's Monumental Brasses* (1969; 2nd edn., 1972).

brawling. The offence of creating a disturbance in a church or churchyard. Technically the word applies to any kind of speaking in a church other than that prescribed by the BCP. Brawling has been a punishable offence in England under ecclesiastical jurisdiction since 1551, and under civil procedure since 1860. The services of non-Anglican churches are similarly protected by the Liberty of Religious Worship Act 1855.

Bray, Thomas (1656–1730), founder of the *SPCK and of the *SPG (qq.v.). A native of Marton in Shropshire, he was educated at Oswestry School and All Souls College, Oxford. In 1690 he became Rector of Sheldon, W. Midlands. When an appeal from Maryland reached Henry *Compton, Bp. of London, for assistance in the colony's ecclesiastical organization, the Bishop selected Bray and made him his commissary; but legal complications long delayed his departure. Meanwhile Bray sought out missionaries to accompany him and (in view of the poverty of the clergy) worked out a scheme for the provision of free libraries in the colony. This last project met with such support that he determined to promote it also at home, where before his death he had been instrumental in establishing some 80 parochial libraries. Other of his educational and literary projects took shape in the foundation of the 'Society for Promoting Christian Knowledge' (1698). In 1699 he finally set sail for Maryland. Though well received by the governor, Bray soon found that he could better promote his purposes from Great Britain and before long returned home. Here the work of the SPCK had developed to such dimensions that Bray founded the 'Society for the Propagation of the Gospel' as a separate society for foreign missions (1701). His endeavours for the appointment of a bishop for New England, however, were unsuccessful. In 1706 he became Vicar of St Botolph Without, Aldgate. To put the libraries on a permanent basis he created the 'Associates of Dr Bray' (1723), which is still active. His most widely circulated work was

A Course of Lectures upon the Church Catechism (4 vols., 1696). In the American BCP (1979), feast day, 15 Feb.

H. P. Thompson, *Thomas Bray* (London, 1954). with bibl. C. T. Laugher, *Thomas Bray's Grand Design: Libraries of the Church of England in America, 1695–1785* (Association of College and Research Libraries, Publications in Librarianship, 35; Chicago, 1973). W. K. Lowther Clarke, *Eighteenth Century Piety* (1944), ch. 8, pp. 96–100. J. H. Overton in *DNB* 6 (1886), pp. 239–41.

Bray, the Vicar of. The hero of the well-known ballad whose pretended zeal for each new form of established religion from *Charles II to George I assured his tenure of his benefice. The song, which appears to date from 1720, is apparently based on an anecdote of a certain Vicar of Bray, Berks, to be read in T. *Fuller's 'Worthies' (1662. 'This vicar, being taxed by one for being a turncoat and an inconsistent changeling, "Not so", said he, "for I always kept my principle, which is this,—to live and die the Vicar of Bray" '.) Attempts to identify Fuller's cleric have not been successful. Simon Aleyn (Vicar, 1540–88) and Simon Simmonds (his predecessor, afterwards Canon of Windsor) alone seem to fit Fuller's dating; but there is no contemporary evidence that either was the sort of cleric portrayed in the song. The suggestion that he belongs to Bray, near Dublin, is a modern conjecture wholly without support. The ballad is said to have been composed by an army officer in the time of George I.

C. Kerry, *The History and Antiquities of the Hundred of Bray, in the County of Berks* (privately pr., London, 1861), with text of ballad, p. 185. An anecdote reported on p. 145 suggests that an incidental remark made by *James I to the then Vicar of Bray whom he happened to fall in with at the Bear Inn, Maidenhead ('You shall be Vicar of Bray still, I promise you'), may have been the source of the story.

brazen serpent. The image set up by *Moses in the wilderness, on looking at which those who had been bitten by serpents were healed (Num. 21: 8, 9). Acc. to 2 Kgs. 18: 4 it was destroyed by Hezekiah because the Israelites had been in the habit of burning incense to it. It is mentioned once in the NT as a type of the crucified Christ (Jn. 3: 14).

Brazil, Christianity in. The conversion of Brazil was effected by the major orders of friars (*Franciscans, *Dominicans, *Augustinians), but principally by the *Jesuits, who founded the city of São Paulo in 1554. They mastered the native languages and were pioneers in education; they worked with the indigenous people, creating communes and protecting their rights. A. *Vieira (1608–97, q.v.) was among those who took part in this enterprise. The influx of slaves from Africa, who were forcibly converted to Christianity, produced a synthesis of African religions and Catholicism as a way of preserving the language and culture of the African tribes (Afro-Brazilian rites). Brazil gained her independence from *Portugal in 1822, and the 19th cent. saw a movement for independence from *Ultramontanism among clergy and politicians. With the establishment of the Republic in 1889, the Church was disestablished and her endowments discontinued. Freedom of worship was guaranteed to all bodies. In the 40 years following the establishment of the Republic, NE Brazil saw two popular religious movements, one

led by the mystic, Antonio Conselheiro (1828–97), who preached in his holy city of Canudos (Bahia), and the other at Joaseiro (Ceará), led by the suspended RC priest Padre Cicero. In recent years Protestantism (esp. *Baptists, *Pentecostalists, and *Seventh-day Adventists), *Spiritualism, and Afro-Brazilian rites have increased their adherents. Following the Second *Vatican Council and the conferences of Latin American bishops at Medellín in 1968 and Puebla in 1979 the Brazilian conference of bishops has been active in implementing the preferential 'option for the poor' expounded at these conferences in the pastoral practice of the RC Church. Many of the pioneers of *Liberation Theology have worked within the Basic Christian communities (*comunidades eclesias de base*) in Brazil as part of a wider movement for social and political reform.

S. Leite, SJ, *Páginas de história no Brasil* (1937), esp. ch. 1, 'Influência religiosa na formação do Brasil', pp. 11–34, and *passim.* Id., *História da Companhia de Jesus no Brasil* (10 vols., Lisbon and Rio de Janeiro, 1938–50). J. [H.] Hemming, *Red Gold: The Conquest of the Brazilian Indians* (1978). R. Bastide, *Les religions africaines au Brésil: Vers une sociologie des interpénétrations de civilisations* (1960; Eng. tr. [1978]). E. da Cunha, *Os Sertões* (Rio de Janeiro, 1902; Eng. tr. as *Rebellion in the Backlands*, Chicago, 1944). A. Montenegro, *António Conselheiro* (Fortaleza, 1954). M. I. P. de Queiroz, *O Messianismo—no Brasil e no mundo* (São Paulo, 1965). T. C. Bruneau, *The Political Transformation of the Brazilian Catholic Church* (Cambridge, 1974); id., *The Church in Brazil: The Politics of Religion* (Austin, Tex., 1982). S. Mainwaring, *The Catholic Church and Politics in Brazil, 1916–1985* (Stanford, Calif., 1986). D. Regan, C.S.Sp., *Church for Liberation: A Pastoral Portrait of the Church in Brazil* (1987). J. Serrano in *DHGE* 10 (1938), cols. 565–89, s.v. 'Brésil'; M. C. Kiemen and B. Kloppenburg in *NCE* 2 (1967), pp. 762–72, s.v. L. Palacín, SJ, in *Dict. Sp.* 12 (1986), cols. 1985–95, s.v. 'Portugal et Brésil'.

bread, leavened and unleavened. In the *Eucharistic rite, the E. Churches (except the *Armenian) customarily use leavened bread, whereas Catholics in the W. use unleavened bread. The difference in practice developed gradually; but by the time of the Schism of 1054, the divergence between E. and W. was a leading cause of dissension. In the C of E the BCP of 1549 ordered the continuance of unleavened bread, while that of 1552 permitted ('it shall suffice'), without enjoining, leavened. The '*Injunctions' of Queen *Elizabeth I (1559) attempted to enforce again the use of unleavened bread, but the Book of 1661 left the rubric of 1552 practically unaltered. The *Judicial Committee of the Privy Council, however, has twice ruled that common bread is directed by the rubric. A number of modern Anglican liturgies expressly allow the use of either (e.g. those of *New Zealand and *Wales), but most make no mention of the matter. Leavened bread is generally used by Nonconformists.

Among the earliest undisputed witnesses for unleavened bread are *Alcuin (*ep.* 90, *ad fratres Lugdunenses*, AD 798; *PL* 100. 289) and his pupil, *Rabanus Maurus (*Instit. Cler.* 1. 31). J. *Sirmond, SJ, 'Disquisitio de Azymo', first pub. in his *Historia Poenitentiae Publicae* (Paris, 1651). R. M. Woolley, *The Bread of the Eucharist* (Alcuin Club Tracts, 11; 1897). M. H. Smith, *And Taking Bread . . .: Cerularius and the Azyme Controversy of 1054* (Théologie Historique, 47 [1978]). F. *Cabrol, OSB, in *DACL* 1 (pt. 2; 1907), cols. 3254–60, s.v. 'Azymes', with good bibl.

Bread of the Presence. See SHEWBREAD.

Breakspear, Nicolas. See HADRIAN IV.

Breastplate of St Patrick. An Old Irish hymn, generally familiar through Mrs C. F. Alexander's translation (1889), beginning 'I bind unto myself today The strong Name of the Trinity'. It has been dated to the early 8th cent. and was probably the 'Canticum Scotticum' mentioned in the 'Book of *Armagh' (807). Though ancient, its ascription to St *Patrick (q.v.) is impossible on linguistic grounds. The hymn belongs to the genre *loricae*. In it the author invokes the Trinity, Angels, Prophets, the powers of heaven and earth, and finally Christ Himself to protect him against the dominion of evil.

The text survives in three ancient MSS: (1) the 11th-cent. Irish *Liber Hymnorum* at *Trinity College, Dublin, (2) a 14th- or 15th-cent. copy of the Tripartite Life of St Patrick in the *Bodleian Library, Oxford (Rawl. B. 512), and (3) a MS in the British Library (Egerton 93). It was first pub., with an Eng. tr., [by J. O'Donovan] in G. Petrie, 'On the History and Antiquities of Tara Hill', *Transactions of the Royal Irish Academy*, 18 (1839), pp. 56–68; crit. edns. with metrical Eng. trs. in J. H. Bernard and R. Atkinson (eds.), *The Irish Liber Hymnorum* (HBS 13–14; 1898), 1, pp. 133–6, and 2, pp. 49–51, with notes, pp. 208–12, and W. Stokes and J. Strachan (eds.), *Thesaurus Palaeohibernicus*, 2 (1903), pp. 354–8, repr. in *The Works of St Patrick*, tr. by L. Bieler (ACW 17; 1953), pp. 67–72, incl. introd.; Eng. tr. by W. Stokes repr. in J. H. Todd, *St Patrick, Apostle of Ireland* (1864), pp. 426–9. D. A. Binchy, 'Varia III. No. 3. *Atomriug*, No. 4. The date of the so-called "Hymn of Patrick" ', *Ériu*, 20 (1966), pp. 232–6, with refs. See also works cited under PATRICK, ST.

Breda, Declaration of. The declaration made by *Charles II at Breda in the Netherlands on 4/14 Apr. 1660, immediately before the Restoration. He expressed *inter alia* his readiness to grant his subjects a 'liberty to tender consciences' in matters of religion not affecting the peace of the kingdom.

Text in Gee and Hardy, no. 114, pp. 585–8. See also general works on Charles II (q.v.).

Breeches Bible. A popular name for the *Geneva Bible of 1560 from its rendering of Gen. 3: 7, where AV has 'aprons'.

Bremond, Henri (1865–1933), French spiritual writer. He entered the Society of Jesus in 1882, and after spending his novitiate in England was ordained priest in 1892. In 1899 he was appointed editor of the *Jesuit periodical *Études*. In 1904 he left the order to devote himself entirely to literary activities. He soon experienced difficulties with the ecclesiastical authorities, notably in 1907 in connection with his essay on J. H. *Newman (pub. in 1906), and his Life of *Jane Frances de Chantal (pub. in 1912) was put on the *Index in 1913. His principal work, his voluminous *Histoire littéraire du sentiment religieux en France* (11 vols., 1916–33 + index, 1936), is a history of French spirituality, chiefly in the 17th cent., in the form of a series of essays on outstanding religious personalities. Its original and penetrating descriptions of the life of souls are illustrated by numerous quotations, often from forgotten and almost inaccessible contemporary sources. A brilliant stylist, Bremond draws captivating pictures esp. of less well-known personalities such as Mme *Acarie, J. *Surin, or the Ursuline nun Marie *Guyard. His judge-ment on representatives of a more active and ascetical type was in general less sympathetic. Among his other works is an exquisite little study, *Prière et poésie* (1926).

His *Histoire littéraire* was repr. 1967–8; index, 1971. H. Hogarth, *Henri Bremond: The Life and Work of a Devout Humanist* (1950). F. Hermans, *L'Humanisme Religieux de l'Abbé Henri Bremond 1865–1933* (1965). *Entretiens sur Henri Bremond* sous la direction de M. Nédoncelle et J. Dagens [27–31 Aug. 1965] (Décades du Centre Culturel International de Cerisy-la-Salle, NS 4 [1967]). A. Blanchet, *Histoire d'une mise à l'index: La "Sainte Chantal" de l'Abbé Bremond d'après des documents inédits* [1967]. Id., *Henri Bremond 1865–1904* (posthumously pub. [1975]). E. Goichot, *Henri Bremond historien du sentiment religieux: Genèse et stratégie d'une enterprise littéraire* [1982]. A. *Loisy, *George Tyrrell et Henri Bremond* (1936). A. Blanchet (ed.), *Henri Bremond et Maurice Blondel: Correspondance* (3 vols., 1970–1). A. Guinan, 'Portrait of a devout humanist, M. l'Abbé Henri Brémond', *HTR* 47 (1954), pp. 15–53. Polgár, 1 (1990), pp. 378–84.

Brendan, St (484–577 or 583), also 'St Brenainn', Abbot of Clonfert. In his lifetime Brendan acquired the reputation of being a navigator (as is known from St *Adomnán), and an anonymous Hiberno–Latin work, prob. of the 8th cent., the *Navigatio S. Brendani*, describes voyages made by Brendan and 12 monks to a number of mythical islands in the W. Ocean in search of an earthly paradise. Although the purpose of the *Navigatio* was the inculcation of monastic discipline, it was widely popular from the 10th cent., and was translated into many vernacular languages. The tradition that he founded the monastery of Cluain Fearta (Clonfert, in Co. Galway) may quite well be true. The churches of Brendon in Devonshire and Brancepeth in Co. Durham are dedicated to him. Feast day, 16 May. [He is to be distinguished from his contemporary St Brendan of Birr (c.490–573), whose feast is kept on 29 Nov.]

Lat. text of the 'Navigation of St Brendan' pr., with other material, by [Card.] P. F. Moran, *Acta Sancti Brendani* (Dublin, 1872); modern edn., with introd. and bibl., by C. Selmer (Publications in Mediaeval Studies, 16; Notre Dame, Ind., 1959). Modern Eng. tr. by J. J. O'Meara, *The Voyage of Saint Brendan* (Dublin, 1978). I. Short and B. Merrilees (eds.), *The Anglo-Norman Voyage of St Brendan* (Manchester, 1979); for other vernacular translations see C. Selmer, 'The Vernacular Translations of the *Navigatio Sancti Brendani*. A Bibliographical Study', *Mediaeval Studies*, 18 (1956), pp. 145–57. G. Orlandi, *Navigatio Sancti Brendani*, 1: Introduzione (Testi e documenti per lo studio dell'antichità, 38 [1968]). D. O'Donoghue, *Brendaniana: St Brendan the Voyager in Story and Legend* (Dublin, 1893); G. A. Little, *Brendan the Navigator: An Interpretation* (1945); G. Ashe, *Land to the West: St Brendan's Voyage to America* (1962), with bibl.

Brent, Charles Henry (1862–1929), Anglican '*Faith and Order' leader. Born at Newcastle, Ontario, Canada, he studied at Trinity College, Toronto, and was ordained priest in 1887. From 1888 to 1891 he was engaged in pastoral work in Boston, Mass. In 1901 he became the Protestant Episcopal Bp. of the Philippine Islands, and in 1918 of Western New York. From 1917 to 1919 he was the Chief of Chaplains of the American Expeditionary Force in Europe. From his first months in the Philippines Brent energetically combated the opium traffic. In 1909 he was President of the Opium Conference at Shanghai and in 1923 represented the USA on the League of Nations Narcotics Committee. In his later years his chief work was for the *Ecumenical (Faith and Order) Movement, in which he was one of the most ardent spirits. On returning from the *Edinburgh Conference of 1910 to the USA he induced the General Convention of the Protestant Episcopal Church to convene a 'World Conference on Faith and Order', and when the conference ultimately met at *Lausanne in 1927, Brent was its President. Feast day in the American BCP (1979), 27 Mar.

F. W. Kates, *Charles Henry Brent* (1948). R. B. Ogilby in *Dict. Amer. Biog.*, Supp. 1 (1944), pp. 115–17.

Brentano, Franz (1838–1917), Austrian philosopher. Ordained to the RC priesthood in 1864, he was appointed Privatdozent at Würzburg in 1866. In 1873, chiefly owing to intellectual difficulties about the Trinity, he separated himself from the Church. Through lectures at Vienna from 1880 to 1915 he exercised great influence on some of the leading philosophers of the next generation, among them E. Husserl and A. von Meinong. His high regard for *Scholastic and *Aristotelian doctrines, which he had inherited from his RC training, led him to be critical of all forms of Idealism, and some of the anti-idealistic currents in 20th-cent. philosophy in German-speaking countries derived directly from his teaching. His main works were *Psychologie vom empirischen Standpunkt* (vol. 1 [all issued], 1874; Eng. tr., 1973) and *Vom Ursprung sittlicher Erkenntnis* (1889; Eng. tr., 1902; also 1969).

A number of Brentano's works have been posthumously pub. under the editorship of O. Kraus, A. Kastil, and others, at Leipzig, and after the Second World War, at Berne and then Hamburg; several of these have been tr. into Eng. O. Kraus, *Franz Brentano: Zur Kenntnis seines Lebens und seiner Lehre* (Munich, 1919). A. Kastil, *Die Philosophie Franz Brentano: Eine Einführung in seine Lehre* (Berne, 1951); L. L. McAlister (ed.), *The Philosophy of Brentano* (1976). R. M. Chisholm *Brentano and Intrinsic Value* (Cambridge, 1986). P. Gregoretti, *Franz Brentano: Bibliografia Completa (1862–1982)* (Trieste, 1983). R. M. Chisholm in P. Edwards (ed.), *Encyclopedia of Philosophy*, 1 (1967), pp. 365–8, s.v.

Brenz, Johann (1499–1570), reformer of Württemberg. He was born at Weilderstadt, studied at Heidelberg under *Oecolampadius, and in 1518 came under the influence of M. *Luther. In 1522 he was appointed Preacher at the church of St Michael in Schwäbisch Hall and from now on actively supported the Reformation, preaching against the Mass and the cult of the saints. In 1525, like Luther, he refused to support the insurgents in the *Peasants' War. Against Oecolampadius he insisted in his *Syngramma Suevicum* (21 Oct. 1525) on the Real Presence in the Eucharist and thus ensured the acceptance of the Lutheran teaching over the greater part of Württemberg. He put forward a proposal for a Church Order in Hall in 1527. He participated in the *Marburg Colloquy (1529). From 1535 onwards the Hall form of Church government began to be adopted throughout Württemberg. He played an active part in the reconstitution of the University of *Tübingen (1537–8). He was present at the Disputation of Worms (1540–1) and at the Conference of *Ratisbon (1541). Obliged to flee Hall after the *Augsburg Interim (1548), he was invited to England by T. *Cranmer, but refused; he went to several German cities, compiling the *Württemberg Confession in 1552. In 1553 he became provost of the Stiftskirche in Stuttgart and adviser to Duke Christoph of Württemberg. He defended

*Ubiquitarianism in controversies with T. *Beza and H. *Bullinger. A prolific writer, he was the author of two Catechisms (1527, 1535), several biblical commentaries, sermons, and polemical treatises.

Works ed. M. Brecht and others (Tübingen, 1970 ff.). Incomplete early edn., 8 vols. fol., ibid., 1576–90. T. Pressel, *Anecdota Brentiana: Ungedruckte Briefe und Bedenken von Johannes Brenz* (Tübingen, 1868). Life by J. Hartmann and C. Jaeger (2 vols., Hamburg, 1840–2). W. E. Köhler, *Bibliographia Brentiana* (Berlin, 1904); id., *Brentiana und andere Reformatoria* (Archiv für Reformationsgeschichte, Jahrgg. 9–11, 13, 14, 16, 19, 21, 22, 24, 26; 1912–29). M. Brecht, *Die frühe Theologie des Johannes Brenz* (Beiträge zur historischen Theologie, 36; Tübingen, 1966). H.-M. Maurer and K. Ulshöfer, *Johannes Brenz und die Reformation in Württemberg* (Forschungen aus Württembergisch Franken, 9 [1973]). J. M. Estes, *Christian Magistrate and State Church: The Reforming Career of Johannes Brenz* [1982]. M. Brecht in *TRE* 7 (1981), pp. 170–81, s.v., with bibl.

Brest-Litovsk, Union of, often now called the Union of Brest. The union concluded in 1596 between the *Ukrainian (or Ruthenian) and the RC Churches, with the approbation of Pope *Clement VIII and Sigismund III of Poland. By it, the Metropolitan of Kiev, together with five of his bishops, and some millions of Christians, all of the Byzantine rite, joined the RC Church, with permission to retain their liturgy. During succeeding years the union was opposed both by Russia, which succeeded in bringing large numbers of Ruthenians back to the Orthodox Church, and also by the Latin Poles, who despised and feared Byzantine Ruthenians.

The official docs. are pr. by A. Theiner, *Vetera Monumenta Poloniae et Lithuaniae Gentiumque Finitimarum Historiam Illustrantia*, 3 (Rome, 1863), no. 185, pp.232–49; further Papal letters, pp. 269–73. E. Likowski, *Union de l'Église grecque-ruthène en Pologne avec l'Église romaine, conclue à Brest, en Lithuanie, en 1596* (1903); id., *Die ruthenisch-römische Kirchenvereinigung, genannt Union zu Brest* (1904). J. Pelesz, *Geschichte der Union der ruthenischen Kirche mit Rom von den aeltesten Zeiten bis auf die Gegenwart* (2 vols., 1881). O. [J. L.] Halecki, *From Florence to Brest (1439–1596)* (Rome, 1958), pp. 199–419; A. Jobert, *De Luther à Mohila: La Pologne dans la crise de la Chrétienté, 1517–1648* (Collection historique de l'Insitut d'Études Slaves, 21; 1974), pp. 321–43. J. Ostrowski in *DHGE* 10 (1938), cols. 615–18.

Brethren, Church of the. See TUNKERS.

Brethren of the Common Life (Lat. 'Fratres Communis Vitae'). An association founded in the 14th cent. to foster a higher level of Christian life and devotion. The original leader was G. *Groote (q.v.), a canon of Utrecht, who resigned his prebend to travel through the Netherlands and preach against clerical abuses and call men to repentance. He demanded no vows from his disciples but left them free, whether clerics or laymen, to continue in their ordinary vocations. His followers developed a lofty spirituality. They laid great stress on teaching, founding schools all over the Netherlands, and later in Germany, where a general education was offered, unsurpassed in quality and without fees. To supply books for their schools, many of their members engaged in copying MSS, and later in printing. On the death of Groote (1384), the leadership of the Brethren was assumed by *Florentius Radewijns. Before long a group of these disciples adopted a rule and organized themselves as

*Augustinian Canons. Among the 'Brethren' were I. *Busch, *Thomas à Kempis, Pope *Hadrian VI, and Gabriel *Biel. *Nicholas of Cusa and Rudolph Agricola (1443–85) also studied in their schools, and thus the movement exercised considerable influence on the New Learning. By the end of the 17th cent. the rise of modern universities and diocesan seminaries had led to their extinction. See also DEVOTIO MODERNA and WINDESHEIM.

W. J. Alberts (ed.), *Consuetudines Fratrum Vitae Communis* (Groningen, 1959). E. Barnikol, *Studien zur Geschichte der Brüder vom gemeinsamen Leben* (1917). A. Hyma, *The Christian Renaissance: A History of the 'Devotio Moderna'* (New York, 1925), with bibl. pp. 477–94; 2nd edn., with additional material (Hamden, Conn., 1965); id., *Brethren of the Common Life* (Grand Rapids, Mich., 1950). R. R. Post, *The Modern Devotion: Confrontation with Reformation and Humanism* (Studies in Medieval and Reformation Thought, 3; Leiden, 1968). C. van der Wansem, SCJ, *Het ontstaan en de geschiedenis van de Broederschap van het Gemene Leven tot 1400* (Universiteit te Leuven, Publicaties op het Gebied der Geschiedenis en der Philologie, 4e Reeks, 12; 1958). E. F. Jacob, *Essays in the Conciliar Epoch* (Manchester, 1943), pp. 121–38 ('The Brethren of the Common Life'); K. Elm, 'Die Bruderschaft vom gemeinsamen Leben', *Ons Geestelijk Erf*, 59 (1985), pp. 470–96. Pourrat, 2, pp. 381–9. W. Leesch and others (eds.), *Monasticon Fratrum Vitae Communis* (Archives et Bibliothèques de Belgique, Numéro spécial, 18; 2 vols., Brussels, 1977–9). W. Lourdaux in *DHGE* 18 (1977), cols. 1438–54, s.v. 'Frères de la vie commune'; R. Stupperich in *TRE* 7 (1981), pp. 220–5, s.v. 'Brüder vom gemeinsamen Leben', with bibl.

Brethren of the Free Spirit. Individuals who adhered to heretical views of an *antinomian nature, first identified by St *Albertus Magnus at Ries, near Augsburg, in the 1270s. They apparently believed that they could be entirely liberated from conventional moral norms through attaining perfect union with God, and were accused in particular of sexual profligacy. The heresy, which tended towards a form of speculative pantheism, was later associated with certain *Beguines and was described in two decrees of the Council of *Vienne (1311–2; 16: 'Cum de quibusdam mulieribus', and 28: 'Ad nostrum'). See also PORETTE, MARGARET.

R. Guarnieri, 'Il Movimento del Libero Spirito', *Archivio Italiano per la Storia della Pietà*, 4 (1965), pp. 351–708. G. Leff, *Heresy in the Later Middle Ages*, 1 (Manchester and New York, 1967), pp. 308–407. N. Cohn, *The Pursuit of the Millennium* (rev. edn., 1970), pp. 148–86. R. E. Lerner, *The Heresy of the Free Spirit in the Later Middle Ages* (1972). R. Guarnieri in *Dict. Sp.* 5 (1964), cols. 1241–68, s.v. 'Frères du Libre Esprit', with extensive bibl.

brethren of the Lord. References to 'the Lord's brethren', who include *James, Joseph, Simon, and *Jude, occur at Mk. 6: 3, etc., Jn. 7: 3, Acts 1: 14, 1 Cor. 9: 5. They may have been (1) sons of the Virgin *Mary and *Joseph, born after Christ. This is the most natural inference from the NT, and was accepted by *Tertullian and probably by *Hegesippus. But when put forward by *Helvidius, *c.*382, it was rejected by St *Jerome who, apparently voicing the general opinion of the Church, maintained the perpetual virginity of the Virgin Mary. Hence St Jerome held that (2) the Lord's 'brethren' were the sons of *Mary, 'the mother of James and Joses' (Mk. 15: 40), whom he identified with the wife of Clopas and sister of the Virgin Mary (Jn. 19: 25, RV). They may have been, however, (3) sons of Joseph by a former marriage

(the view of St *Epiphanius and the E. Church), or (4), acc. to a modern suggestion, sons of Mary, 'mother of James and Joses' (not here identified with the Virgin Mary's sister), and Clopas, who acc. to Hegesippus was the brother of Joseph. See MARYS IN THE NT (3) and (4), and CLEOPAS.

J. B. *Lightfoot, *St Paul's Epistle to the Galatians* (1865), pp. 241–74, with refs. to earlier lit.; T. *Zahn, 'Brüder und Vettern Jesu', *Forschungen zur Geschichte des neutestamentlichen Kanons und der altkirchlichen Literatur*, 6 (1900), 2, pp. 225–364. R. [J.] Bauckham, *Jude and the Relatives of Jesus in the Early Church* (Edinburgh, 1990), pp. 1–133. F. V. Filson in *The Interpreter's Dictionary of the Bible*, 1 (1962), pp. 470–2, s.v. 'Brothers of the Lord'.

Bretschneider, Karl Gottlieb (1776–1848), German theologian. In 1816 he became *General Superintendent at Gotha. Of his many writings, the only one of permanent interest is his *Probabilia* (1820), in which he anticipated later NT criticism by questioning the historicity of the fourth Gospel on the grounds of its divergence from the other three. In 1834 he founded the *Corpus Reformatorum*, a series of reprints of the works of the 16th-cent. Reformers, for which he himself edited the works of P. *Melanchthon.

Autobiography posthumously ed. Horst Bretscheider (Gotha, 1851); id. (ed.), *Anhang zu Karl Gottlieb Bretschneider's Selbstbiographie* (1852). E. Stöve in *TRE* 7 (1981), pp. 186 f., s.v.

Brett, Thomas (1667–1744), *Nonjuror. He was educated at Queens' and Corpus Christi Colleges, Cambridge, and ordained deacon in 1690. After holding several livings he was appointed Rector of Ruckinge in 1705. Having so far had no scruples in taking the oath, he resolved, after H. *Sacheverell's trial, never to do so again. On the accession of George I (1714) he consequently resigned his living (1715) and was received as a Nonjuror by G. *Hickes, after whose death he was consecrated bishop in 1716. From 1716 to 1725 he took part in the abortive negotiations for reunion of his party with the Greek Church. He was involved in several controversies, esp. in that on the *Usages which broke out in 1715 among the Nonjurors themselves. As an eminent liturgical scholar with a particular interest in the E. liturgies, he insisted on the explicit oblation of the Eucharistic elements to the Father and on the *Epiclesis of the Holy Spirit, but reckoned the other two controversial points (prayer for the dead and the mixed chalice) as of minor importance. His principal work is his *Dissertation on the Ancient Liturgies* (1720), which is still valuable, though it regards the so-called *Clementine Liturgy (i.e. *Apostolic Constitutions VIII) as authentic. Among his other works are *The Divine Right of Episcopacy* (1718), *Discourses concerning the Ever Blessed Trinity* (1720), a Life of J. *Johnson (posthumously pub., 1748), and answers to J. *Bingham's *History of Lay Baptism* (1712) and to B. *Hoadly's *Plain Account of the Sacrament* (1735).

His papers, including extensive correspondence, which are preserved in the *Bodleian Library, were widely used in H. Broxap, *The Later Non-Jurors* (Cambridge, 1924). W. J. Grisbrooke, *Anglican Liturgies of the Seventeenth and Eighteenth Centuries* (Alcuin Club Collections, 40; 1958), pp. 71–112 *passim*. L. Stephen in *DNB* 6 (1886), pp. 285 f., s.v.

Breviary. The liturgical book containing the Psalms, hymns, lessons, prayers, etc., to be recited in the Divine *Office of the RC Church. The various parts were originally distributed in different books, such as the *Psaltery, *Lectionary, etc., but in the 11th cent., particularly with the rise of small communities, the need was felt for an instrument with which to collate the texts necessary for the day's Offices. To meet this need the *Ordo* was developed, indicating for each day and Office the texts to be sung, with their opening words; it came to be called *Breviarium sive ordo officiorum per totam anni decursionem* ('Short Conspectus or Order for the Offices of the Whole Year'); hence prob. the term 'breviary'. It remained only for the texts themselves to be added to produce the Office book or breviary as it was henceforth called. This was done in the 12th cent. for the Papal chapel, and it was this breviary that was adopted by the *Franciscans and became widely known throughout Europe. See also OFFICE, DIVINE.

For bibl. see OFFICE, DIVINE.

Bride, St. See BRIGIT, ST.

Bridges, Robert Seymour (1844–1930), Poet Laureate. Educated at Eton and Corpus Christi College, Oxford, he practised for some years as a physician. Meanwhile he had been writing poetry, and in 1882 abandoned medicine to devote himself to literary interests and music. For most of the rest of his life he lived at Yattendon, Berks (1882–1904), and on Boar's Hill, Oxford (1907–30). In 1913 he became Poet Laureate. Already as a boy at Eton, he had been attracted to Catholic ideals through the influence of V. S. S. Coles (later Principal of Pusey House, Oxford) and D. M. Dolben. In mature life he tended to reject all rigid dogmatic belief, but retained strong Christian sympathies. His most considerable work, *The Testament of Beauty* (1929), was a philosophical poem, in 'loose Alexandrine' metre, which sought to reconcile scientific knowledge with Christian faith. He was also interested in Church music, and did much to raise the standard of hymnody in the English parish churches; in the *Yattendon Hymnal* (1895–9), which embodied his ideals, he revived many fine 16th- and 17th-cent. melodies. His hymn-book was extensively drawn on in the *English Hymnal* (1906) and the *Oxford Hymn Book* (1908). He was also one of the founders of the 'Society for Pure English'. His other publications include *The Spirit of Man* (1915), an anthology; and the first collected edition (1918) of the *Poems* of his friend G. M. *Hopkins.

Poetical Works pub., in 6 vols., London, 1896–1905; also, omitting the eight dramas, but with other new material, ibid., 1912; enlarged edn., 1936; and incl. *Testament of Beauty*, 1953. *Selected Letters*, ed. D. E. Stanford (2 vols., Newark, Del., London, and Toronto [1983–4]). E. Thompson, *Robert Bridges, 1844–1930* (1944); A. Guérard, Jun., *Robert Bridges: A Study of Traditionalism in Poetry* (Cambridge, Mass., 1942); J.-G. Ritz, *Robert Bridges and Gerard Hopkins 1863–1889: A Literary Friendship* (1960); D. E. Stanford, *In the Classic Mode: The Achievement of Robert Bridges* (Newark, Del., and London [1978]); C. Phillips, *Robert Bridges: A Biography* (Oxford, 1992). N. C. Smith in *DNB, 1922–1930* (1937), pp. 115–19. G. L. McKay, *A Bibliography of Robert Bridges* (New York and London, 1933); W. White in *NCBEL* 3 (1969), cols. 593–7.

Bridget (Birgitta) of Sweden, St (*c*.1303–73), founder of the *Bridgettine Order. The daughter of a wealthy landowner in Sweden, she is reputed to have lived a pious life and had visions as a child. She married at 13, and had eight children. In 1341 she and her husband Ulf went on a pilgrimage to *Compostela; within a year of their return her husband had died in the *Cistercian monastery of Alvastra. Shortly afterwards, she appears to have begun having a series of revelations which led her to urge the Pope's return to Rome from *Avignon, and to challenge what she saw as decay in the spiritual life of the Church. In the course of these experiences, she received detailed instructions about the foundation of a new religious order. She was helped in the foundation by the Cistercians with whom she was associated and by one of her daughters, St *Catherine of Sweden, who became the first abbess. In 1349 she went to Rome, where, except for occasional pilgrimages, she lived for the rest of her life, campaigning for the reform of the Church and the foundation of her order. Her revelations and the devotions they inspired were highly esteemed in the later Middle Ages; they are outstanding examples of the affective spirituality of the time. She was canonized in 1391. Feast day 23 July (formerly 8 Oct.).

Her 'Revelations' were pub. at Lübeck, 1492. A better and more accessible edn. is that of C. Durante (2 vols., Rome, 1628). Modern crit. edn. of the last book, *Reuelaciones Extrauagantes*, by L. Hollman (Samlingar utgivna av Svenska Fornskriftsällskapet, 2nd ser., Latinska Skrifter, 5; Uppsala, 1956); other books ed. B. Bergh and others (ibid. 7; 1967 ff. [later parts pub. Stockholm]); *Opera Minora*, ed. S. Eklund (ibid. 8; 3 vols., 1972–9). 14th-cent. Swedish tr., with other material, ed. by G. E. Klemming, *Heliga Birgittas Uppenbarelser* (5 vols. bound in 4, Samlingar utgifna af Svenska Fornskriftsällskapet, 1857–84); 15th-cent. Eng. selection of extracts ed. P. Cummings (EETS 178; 1929). Modern Eng. tr. of the Life written for her canonization procedure and selections from her 'Revelations' by A. R. Kezel, ed. M. T. Harris (Classics of Western Spirituality; Mahwah, NJ, and New York, 1990). Life by Skänning and Peter of Alvastra, her confessors, ed. C. Annerstedt, *Scriptores Rerum Suecicarum Medii Aevi*, 3, pt. 2 (Uppsala, 1871), pp. 185–206. Life by Birger, Abp. of Uppsala, ed. I. Collijn (Samlingar utgivna av Svenska Fornskriftsällskapet, 2nd ser., Latinska Skrifter, 4; 1946). Id. (ed.), *Acta et Processus Canonizationis Beate Birgitte* (ibid. 1; Uppsala, 1924–31). Best modern Life is that of a Bridgettine, H. Redpath, *God's Ambassadress—St Bridget of Sweden* (Milwaukee, 1947). B. Klockars, *Birgitta och hennes värld* (Kungl. Vitterhets Historie och Antikvitets Akademiens Handlingar, Historiska Serien, 16; 1971, with summary in Eng.), and other works of this author. Popular Life by A. Andersson (tr. from Swedish, London, 1980). F. Vernet in *Dict. Sp.* 1 (1937), cols. 1943–58, s.v. 'Brigitte de Suède'; I. Cecchetti, M. C. Celletti, and M. V. Brandi in *Bibliotheca Sanctorum*, 3 (Rome, 1956), pp. 439–533, s.v. 'Brigida di Svezia'.

Bridgettine Order (*Ordo Sanctissimi Salvatoris*), also known as the 'Brigittine Order'. It was founded by St *Bridget of Sweden, following detailed revelations which she was held to have received. Land for the mother house at Vadstena was granted in 1346 and the order approved in a bull of 1370. Its members were organized in double monasteries, originally under the direction of an abbess, with 12 priests, 4 deacons, and 8 lay brothers acting as chaplains and assistants to 60 nuns. Although strictly segregated and with different liturgical obligations, they shared a common church, the nuns' choir consisting of a raised gallery. The male branch of the order died out in 1842; the female religious still maintain a few houses. Syon Abbey, founded at Isleworth in Middlesex in 1415, was among the first religious houses in England to employ the printing press to spread its teaching; the foundation still exists in Devon. A number of attempts have been made to adapt the Bridgettine Rule, notably by the post-Reformation *Fratres Novissimi Brigittini* in Belgium and the Bridgettines of the Recollection, founded in Spain in the 17th cent.

Edns. of St Bridget's *Revelations* are listed s.v. Crit. edn. of her Rule for the order ed. S. Eklund among her *Opera Minora*, 1 (Samlingar utgivna av Svenska Fornskriftsällskapet, 2nd ser., Latinska Skrifter, 8, 1; Lund, 1975). C. Gejrot (ed.), *Diarium Vadstenense: The Memorial Book of Vadstena Abbey* (Acta Universitatis Stockholmiensis, Studia Latina Stockholmiensia, 33; 1988). B. Williamson, *The Bridgettine Order: Its foundress, history and spirit* (1922; brief). R. Ellis, *Viderunt eum filie Syon: The Spirituality of the English house of a medieval contemplative order from its beginnings to the present day* (Analecta Cartusiana, 68. 2; Salzburg, 1984). P. Debongnie, CSSR, in *DHGE* 10 (1938), cols. 728–31, s.v. 'Brigittins'; T. Nyberg in *DIP* 1 (1974), cols. 1578–93, s.v. 'Brigidini'.

Bridgewater Treatises. Eight treatises, published between 1833 and 1836, upon various aspects of 'the power, wisdom, and goodness of God, as manifested in the Creation'. They were produced under the will of F. H. *Egerton, 8th Earl of Bridgewater (1756–1829), who left a sum of £8,000 to the President of the Royal Society, to be paid to one or more authors selected by him to write and publish treatises on this subject. The eight authors chosen were: T. *Chalmers, J. Kidd, W. Whewell, Sir C. Bell, P. M. Roget, W. *Buckland, W. Kirby, W. Prout. The 'Ninth Bridgewater Treatise' (1837) by C. Babbage does not properly belong to the series.

D. W. Grundy, 'The Bridgewater Treatises and their authors', *History*, NS 31 (1946), pp. 140–52; J. M. Robson, 'The Fiat and Finger of God: The Bridgewater Treatises', in R. J. Helmstadter and B. Lightman (eds.), *Victorian Faith in Crisis* (1990), pp. 71–125.

briefs, Church. Warrants (usually royal, but sometimes issued by archbishops or bishops) for collections for specific charitable purposes. In England after the Reformation Church briefs were the successors to Papal briefs (see BULL); they were read in church during the Communion service after the Creed. They authorized collections (usually for one year) in places of worship or from house to house. They were commonly issued in favour of ecclesiastical buildings damaged by fire or storm, but secular buildings and individual sufferers might also be beneficiaries, as might persecuted groups overseas, e.g. the exiled ministers of the Palatinate (1628), the *Waldenses (1655), and Hungarian slaves (1671). The earliest printed English brief dates from 1520 and the printed broadsheet format became the norm from the 1580s. Briefs were issued with particular frequency from the Commonwealth onwards, and some 2,000 are recorded from 1624 until the suppression of the process in 1828.

W. A. Bewes, *Church Briefs or royal warrants for collections for charitable objects* (1896).

Briggs, Charles Augustus (1841–1913), OT scholar. After graduating at *Union Theological Seminary, New York, he studied in Berlin, was for some years a Presbyterian pastor, and in 1874 became Professor of Hebrew at Union Seminary. As editor (1880–90) of the *Presbyterian Review* he became known as a vigorous exponent of *Higher Criticism of the OT on the lines of W. R. *Smith in Scotland. His inaugural address as Professor of Biblical Theology in 1891 led to his trial for heresy; and though acquitted by the New York presbytery, he was suspended by the General Assembly in 1893 from clerical functions. After taking orders in the Protestant *Episcopal Church in 1899, he devoted much energy to advocating Christian reunion. He was one of the editors both of the *International Critical Commentaries* and of the standard Hebrew *Lexicon*.

Essays in Modern Theology and Related Subjects gathered and published as a Testimonial to Charles Augustus Briggs ... on the Completion of his Seventieth Year January 18, 1911 (New York, 1911), with bibl. of his chief works (to 1909) by C. R. Gillett, pp. 327–47. His lectures on the *History of the Study of Theology* (delivered at the Union Theological Seminary, New York, 1912–13) were posthumously pub. by his daughter, E. G. Briggs (2 vols., London, 1916). Obituary notices by H. P. Smith in *American Journal of Theology*, 17 (1913), pp. 497–508, and in *Expository Times*, 25 (1913–14), pp. 294–8. A. C. McGiffert in *Dict. Amer. Biog.* 3 (1929), pp. 40 f., s.v., with further bibl.

Bright, William (1824–1901), Church historian. He was Fellow of University College, Oxford, from 1847 to 1868, Tutor of Trinity College, Glenalmond, from 1851 to 1858, and (in succession to H. L. *Mansel) Regius Professor of Ecclesiastical History and Canon of Christ Church, Oxford, from 1868 until his death. He was a devoted student of the Fathers and a keen High Churchman. He wrote several well-known hymns, among them, 'And now, O Father, mindful of the love'. He was also a forceful and vivid lecturer. His historical writings include *A History of the Church, ... A.D. 313 ... A.D. 451* (1860), *Early English Church History* (1878), and *The Age of the Fathers* (2 vols., ed. W. Lock, 1903).

Selected Letters ... with a Memoir, ed. B. J. Kidd (1903). A. Clark in *DNB, 1901–1911*, 1, pp. 224 f.

Brightman, Frank Edward (1856–1932), liturgist. From 1884 to 1903 he was a librarian of Pusey House, Oxford, and from 1902 until his death a Fellow of Magdalen. A meticulously exact scholar, he issued in 1896 *Liturgies Eastern and Western*, vol. 1, 'Eastern', a new edition of the sections on the E. Church in C. E. Hammond's book (1878) on the subject. Its learned notes were the fruit of extended researches and several journeys to monasteries in the East. (Vol. 2 was never published.) His *English Rite* (1915) is a laborious and valuable edition of the different versions of the BCP, arranged in parallel columns. From 1904 to 1932 he was joint-editor of the *Journal of Theological Studies*, where his wide knowledge was constantly at the disposal of the contributors. Brightman was a strong High Churchman, whose counsel was much sought after by the leaders of the C of E.

Obituary by H. N. Bate in *Proceedings of the British Academy*, 19 (1933), pp. 345–50. S. L. Ollard in *DNB, 1931–1940*, p. 103.

Brigit, St (perhaps 5th–6th cent.), 'Bride'. Though she is regarded with great veneration in *Ireland, the traditions about her are conflicting and nothing can be said with certainty. It is even possible that she never lived, and represents the pagan goddess Brig euhemerized. Genealogical tradition has her born in the dynastic group Fothairt Laigin, and in a poem on this people written *c*.600 she is already called 'a second Mary, mother of the great Lord'. Later tradition corrupted the name to Fochart (now Faughard, nr. Dundalk), where she is often said to have been born. But all her connections are with Leinster, and esp. Cell Dara (now Kildare), where she was honoured as founder and patron. Kildare is associated with the nearby Iron Age temple site of Dún Ailinne (Knockaulin). There are two early Latin Lives and one in Old Irish (*Bethu Brigte*): the second Latin Life, written by Cogitosus (*c*.680), is closely associated with the ambitions of Kildare to achieve metropolitan status; the first Latin Life and the Old Irish Life give a more generalized picture of the national saint who after St *Patrick is the second patron saint of Ireland. Her feast day, 1 Feb., coincides with the pagan festival of Imbelc.

Fothairt poem in M. A. O'Brien, (ed.), *Corpus Genealogicarum Hiberniae*, 1 (Dublin, 1962), pp. 80–1; the best edn. of the first Latin Life is by J. Colgan, OFM, *Trias Thaumaturga* (Louvain, 1647), pp. 527–45; Cogitosus' Life in *AASS*, Feb. 1 (1658), pp. 135–41; *Bethu Brigte*, ed., with Eng. tr., by D. Ó hAodha (Dublin, 1978). Middle-Irish Life (11th cent.), ed. W. Stokes, *Three Middle-Irish Homilies* (privately pr., Calcutta, 1877), pp. 50–87, and from the Book of *Lismore by id. (Anecdota Oxoniensia, Mediaeval and Modern Series, 5; Oxford, 1890), pp. 34–53, with Eng. tr., pp. 182–200. R. Sharpe, '*Vitae S. Brigitae*: the oldest texts', *Peritia*, 1 (1982), pp. 81–106; K. McCone, 'Brigit in the seventh century: a saint with three lives?', ibid., pp. 107–45. See also J. F. Kenney, *The Sources for the Early History of Ireland*, 1 (Records of Civilization; New York, 1929), pp. 356–63.

Brigittine Order. See BRIDGETTINE ORDER.

British and Foreign Bible Society. One of the largest Bible Societies. It was founded in London in 1804 for the printing and distribution of the Bible at home and abroad, on account of representations made to the *Religious Tract Society by Thomas Charles, a *Calvinist Methodist minister of Bala. A strictly interdenominational body, by its constitution its committee is composed of 36 laymen (including 6 foreign members), the English members consisting of 15 Anglicans and 15 members of other denominations. It resisted both Bp. Herbert Marsh's wish to include the circulation of the BCP in its work, and also the Baptist bias which William *Carey sought to introduce. It has published translations of the Bible (excluding the *Apocrypha) in very many languages.

J. Owen, *The History of the Origin and First Ten Years of the British and Foreign Bible Society* (3 vols., 1816–20); W. Canton, *A History of the British and Foreign Bible Society* (5 vols., 1904–10); J. M. Roe, *A History of the British and Foreign Bible Society 1905–1954* (1965). G. Browne, *The History of the British and Foreign Bible Society, from its Institution in 1804 to its Jubilee in 1854* (2 vols., 1859). L. Howsam, *Cheap Bibles: Nineteenth-Century Publishing and the British and Foreign Bible Society* (Cambridge, 1991). T. H. Darlow and H. F. Moule, *Historical Catalogue of the Printed Editions of Holy Scripture in the Library of the British and Foreign Bible Society* (2 vols., bound in 4, 1903–11; new edn. of vol. 1, on English Bibles, by A. S. Herbert, 1968).

British Council of Churches. An organization created in 1942 to further Christian action and promote the cause of unity among the Churches of Great Britain and Ireland. On the foundation of the *World Council of Churches in 1948 it became an 'Associated Council'. Its 'Articles of Amalgamation' (23 Sept. 1943) provided for 112 members, with official representatives of the C of E, the Church of *Scotland, the *Free Churches, the Churches of *Ireland and *Wales, the *Salvation Army, the Society of *Friends, and the *Unitarian and Free Christian Churches. From 1968 the Friends and Unitarians were 'Associate Members'. Various other Churches joined the Council, including the Greek *Orthodox Church in Great Britain, and from 1965 the RC Church sent observers to its meetings. In 1985 the Council began consultation with the RC Church in England, Scotland, and Wales, and with the black-led *Pentecostal and *Holiness Churches (the 'Not Strangers but Pilgrims' Inter-Church Process), and in 1990 the Council was succeeded by the *Council of Churches for Britain and Ireland, which co-ordinates the work of the new national ecumenical bodies—Churches together in England, ACTS (Action of Churches Together in Scotland), and CYTUN (Churches Together in Wales)—and the Irish ecumenical bodies.

'Christian Aid' was originally an organ of the British Council of Churches and, along with the 'Catholic Fund for Overseas Development' (CAFOD) and the 'Scottish Catholic International Aid Fund', is an official agency of the Council of Churches for Britain and Ireland.

Articles of Amalgamation in G. K. A. *Bell, *Documents on Christian Unity*, 3rd ser., 1930–48 (1948), no. 187. E. A. Payne, *Thirty Years of the British Council of Churches 1942–1972* [1972], with Articles of Amalgamation, pp. 37–9. C. Davey and A. Dawkins, *The Story of the BCC* [1990].

British Critic, The. A mainly theological review, formed by the amalgamation of three existing periodicals (its full title was originally: 'British Critic, Quarterly Theological Review and Ecclesiastical Record'), which ran from 1827 to 1843. It supported the cause of the *Tractarian theologians, most of whom contributed articles to it. In its later years it came increasingly under the influence of those in the Tractarian Movement most in sympathy with Rome.

British Israel theory. The theory that the British people is ultimately descended from the ten Israelite tribes which were taken captive into Assyria *c*.721 BC, and thereafter wholly disappeared from Hebrew history. It was often found in conjunction with pronounced imperialist views; and though the numbers and influence of those who defend it are small, they often hold it with a persistence and enthusiasm which refuse to give a dispassionate consideration to objections urged against it. The theory meets with no support from serious ethnologists or archaeologists.

For a criticism, see H. L. Goudge, *The British Israel Theory* (1922).

Britten, Edward Benjamin (1913–76), English composer. Born at Lowestoft, Suffolk, he was encouraged by his musical mother and began writing music at an early age. After the 1927 Norwich Festival he met Frank Bridge (1879–1941); he became his pupil and rapidly espoused his pacifism. From 1930 to 1933 he studied at the rather conservative Royal College of Music in London, but in the next few years earned a somewhat unwelcome reputation as a musician committed to the Left. At this time he wrote music for documentary films, co-operating in this and other enterprises with the poet W. H. Auden (1907–73). In 1934 he met Peter Pears, the tenor (1910–86), who became his lifelong friend and collaborator. Britten went to N. America in 1939, but nostalgia for East Anglia led to his return in 1942. In 1947 he settled at Aldeburgh, Suffolk, and the next year established the famous festival for which many of his works were written. His stature as a composer, accompanist, and conductor was recognized by a series of honours, culminating in a Life Peerage in 1976.

He won early acclaim in England and on the Continent with his *Variations on a Theme of Frank Bridge* (1937). Though a brilliant imitator, Britten developed an original style, which has never inspired a 'school'. His greatest immediate successes were the opera *Peter Grimes* (1945) and the *War Requiem* written for the celebrations in connection with the dedication of *Coventry Cathedral (1962). In the *Requiem*, poems of Wilfred Owen, who died in the 1914–18 War, are juxtaposed with the traditional Latin text. *A Ceremony of Carols* for trebles and harp (1942) has remained popular. Apart from settings for the *Te Deum and *Jubilate, the attractive *Missa Brevis* for the trebles of *Westminster Cathedral (1959), and the *cantata *Rejoice in the Lamb* (1943), he wrote little music specifically for use in Church services. Nevertheless, he was preoccupied with cruelty, war, compassion, and the plight of the innocent 'outsider'; such titles as *Abraham and Isaac*, *The Burning Fiery Furnace*, and *The Prodigal Son*, given to non-liturgical works described as 'Canticles' or 'Church Parables', confirm his penchant for biblical and prophetic themes, as does that of the children's opera *Noye's Fludde* (1957).

P. [A.] Evans, *The Music of Benjamin Britten* (1979); [G.] M. [S.] Kennedy, *Britten* (Master Musicians Series, 1981); E. W. White, *Benjamin Britten: His Life and Operas* (2nd edn., 1983). A. Whittall, *The Music of Britten and Tippett* (Cambridge, 1982). C. Palmer (ed.), *The Britten Companion* (1984). J. Evans and others, *A Britten Source Book* (Aldeburgh, 1987). P. [A.] Evans in S. Sadie (ed.), *The New Grove Dictionary of Music and Musicians*, 3 (1980), pp. 293–308, s.v.

broadcasting, religious. The use of modern electronic modes of communication to transmit radio programmes dealing with religion goes back before the beginnings of regular broadcasting during the 1920s. In the late 19th cent. pioneering metropolitan telephone companies offered subscribers the opportunity of listening to religious services at a distance, and in 1912 the Canadian inventor, R. E. Fessenden, the first man successfully to broadcast radio signals in words, not morse, transmitted a Christmas eve service to ships off the E. coast of America. It included passages from St *Luke's Gospel and a violin solo of 'Holy Night' played by Fessenden himself. In Britain, in the summer of 1922, shortly before the establishment of the British Broadcasting Company, a congregation in Peckham heard the voice of their minister broadcasting from the Burndept Aerial Works in Blackheath. The transmission had a radius of *c*.100 miles.

Recognition of the religious potential of radio technology—its dangers as well as its opportunities—was strengthened when regular broadcasting began on both sides of the Atlantic. While the technology was the same, the development of Christian broadcasting in different countries was shaped by differences both of religious outlook and of institutional patterns of broadcasting. In particular, context, control, and content were markedly different in the USA and in Europe, although there were differences in Europe itself based on post-Reformation divergences in religious allegiance and history.

In the USA the first licensed radio station, KDKA, Pittsburgh, broadcast a religious service in Jan. 1921, less than two months after the station went on the air, and three years later the first radio station launched under religious auspices, KFUO ('keep forward, upward, onward') began broadcasting from the *Lutheran Concordia Seminary, St Louis. The number of such stations grew rapidly: of *c*.600 licensed radio stations in 1926, one in ten was licensed to a religious organization. Policy towards their licensing became less permissive after the setting up of the Federal Radio Commission in 1927, and the number of Church-owned stations fell sharply. When the main radio networks were established the religious broadcasts they transmitted were 'mainstream' Christian, and evangelical Protestant denominations, critical of 'liberal' religion and anxious to win converts, bought radio time from commercial stations. In the process they learned how to produce programmes that would appeal to large audiences and attract funds, making full use of radio personalities.

In Europe, where commercial stations were few in number, religious proselytizing by radio was either forbidden or frowned upon. None the less, religious broadcasting developed its own momentum. The Netherlands acknowledged 'mainstream' religious differences by creating a balanced system of public broadcasting, with four radio services based on religion: two Protestant and two RC. In Britain Christianity was afforded a special place in broadcasting, and the British Broadcasting Company, which began to operate in 1922, set up a 'Sunday Committee' in May 1923. The first religious service was broadcast from St Martin-in-the-Fields in London in Jan. 1924. The establishment of a Central Religious Advisory Committee was significant in that it included not only Anglicans and Nonconformists but also RCs, and it supervised religious broadcasting not only on Sunday but also on weekdays. In Jan. 1929 a daily service was introduced, and still survives. When the BBC became a public corporation in 1927 its charter did not mention religion, but for John Reith, General Manager of the old company and Director-General of the new corporation, religion was fundamental. Christianity, he insisted, was 'the stated and official religion of this country'.

In Italy the RC Church was strong enough to ensure that there was no Protestant religious broadcasting on state radio before 1944. In 1931 the great pioneer of radio, Guglielmo Marconi, presented the Vatican with a short-wave transmitter and introduced Pope *Pius XI delivering a greeting to the world. Protestant 'televangelism' was to deliver its own message to the world when television had supplanted radio as the major electronic medium, although radio remained a powerful force in religious broadcasting through organizations such as Trans World Radio which began as The Voice of Tangier in 1954.

Radio personalities who broadcast religious messages were sometimes drawn into political as well as religious controversy, as was Fr. Charles Coughlin, broadcasting during the 1930s from the Shrine of the Little Flower in Royal Oak, Michigan. Some broke with old traditions; others established new traditions that influenced future television broadcasters. Jerry Falwell, who became active in political as well as religious controversy during the 1970s, grew up listening to Charles Fuller's 'Old Fashioned Revival Hour' which reached an audience of over 10 million in 1937. Billy *Graham was similarly impressed. In 1950 the first telecast of Graham's 'Hour of Decision' was broadcast on a major network. The best-known early RC religious broadcaster was Mgr. Fulton J. Sheen, whose 'Life is Worth Living' was sponsored by Texaco. It was paid evangelistic broadcasting, however, that came to dominate what was increasingly thought of as a market, international as well as American.

The biggest claim for the application of new and still developing television technology was made by Ben Armstrong, Executive Director of National Religious Broadcasters, in his book, *The Electric Church* (1979), which ended with a quotation from Rev. 14: 6: 'And I saw another angel fly in the midst of heaven, having the everlasting gospel to preach unto them that dwell on the earth, and to every nation, and kindred, and tongue, and people'. The angel, he explained, could be a satellite beaming programmes to all parts of the world. Such eschatological language was bound to generate controversy, not least in Church circles. How could an 'audience' be a 'congregation'? There was also a case for arguing, as Malcolm Muggeridge did in Britain, that the effect of the media at all levels was 'to draw away from reality, which means away from Christ'. The core of such arguments generated less interest, however, than subsequent scandals affecting the reputation of some of the best-known televangelists, among them 'Jim' Bakker and Jimmy Swaggart. There has also been political controversy surrounding the role of Falwell in the emergence of the New Christian Right and other similar moral and political issues.

The advent of television in Europe opened up opportunities for religious broadcasting in a number of countries, including France, where the world's first televised RC mass was broadcast on Christmas Eve 1948 and a new 90-minute religious magazine programme, 'Le Jour du Seigneur', was launched ten months later. In West Germany a long-running bi-confessional studio sermon programme, 'Wort zum Sonntag' (the Word for Sunday), was first transmitted in prime time on Saturday evenings in 1954.

Religious broadcasting by the BBC continued to be 'mainstream' on television as on radio. Although it took time to accept its potential, the Central Religious Advisory Committee gave the BBC 'a completely free hand' in 1948 'in experimenting with different types of television acts of worship'. Progress in this direction remained slow until 1952, and it was not until 1954 that 'people's religious programmes' were introduced on television. With the advent of competition from commercial companies in 1955 the number of experiments increased. 'Stars on Sunday', introduced in 1969, in what was still a closed period reserved on Sunday evenings for religious broadcasting, was the first religious programme to achieve wide popular-ity, at its peak attracting an audience of 15 million. It also attracted criticism from those who questioned whether it could be defined as religious broadcasting at all.

The BBC made significant changes during the 1970s after the closed period was reduced in length. Increasing emphasis was placed on religious broadcasting as a forum, and in 1977 the Central Religious Advisory Committee, which after 1955 served both the BBC and the Independent Broadcasting Authority, introduced new guidelines, one of which stated that religious broadcasting should 'seek to reflect the worship, thought and action of the principal religious traditions represented in Britain, recognizing that those traditions are mainly, though not exclusively, Christian'. The Committee was also anxious to meet 'the religious interests, concerns and needs of those outside the churches'. It was the old 'mainstream' programmes, however, which attracted the largest audiences. Of these 'Songs of Praise' was the most important.

Since the 1970s technological changes have had as large an influence on patterns of religious broadcasting as Christian purposes. The development of satellite and cable systems and the challenges to public service broadcasting have influenced both the production and the distribution of religious programmes. So too has the development of video. In Europe the role of independent religious broadcasters has become more important through such bodies as the Churches Television and Radio Centre in Bushey and the World Association for Christian Communications. Yet in the Monte Carlo schedule of Trans World Radio at the end of the 1980s over 38 per cent of the religious programmes transmitted originated in the USA.

The proportion of broadcasting time devoted to religious broadcasting remains higher in Islamic countries than it does in Christian countries, except on stations run directly by religious bodies. While this contrast encourages some Christians to reach out for inter-faith broadcasting, it encourages others to proclaim a unique gospel of salvation with the help of every technological device.

A. Briggs, *The History of Broadcasting in the United Kingdom* (4 vols., Oxford, 1961–79), *passim* (see index under Religion); K. M. Wolfe, *The Churches and the British Broadcasting Corporation 1922–1956* (1984). B. Armstrong, *The Electric Church* (Nashville [1979]); W. F. Fore, *Television and Religion: The Shaping of Faith, Values and Culture* (Minneapolis, 1987); J. K. Hadden and A. Schupe, *Televangelism: Power and Politics on God's Frontier* (New York, 1988); Q. J. Schultze (ed.), *American Evangelicals and the Mass Media* (Grand Rapids, Mich., 1990). P. Elvy (ed.), *Opportunities and Limitations in Religious Broadcasting* (Edinburgh, 1991).

Broad Church. A popular term, coined on the analogy of *High Church and *Low Church, and current esp. in the latter half of the 19th cent., for those in the C of E who objected to positive definition in theology and sought to interpret the Anglican formularies in a broad and liberal sense. The expression appears to have been coined lightheartedly by A. H. Clough but gained wider currency through W. J. *Conybeare's analysis of Church parties in the 1853 *Edinburgh Review*. The existence of Broad Churchmen as a distinct party owed much to the influence of T. *Arnold and R. D. *Hampden. Characteristic representatives of the school were most of the writers for *Essays and Reviews* (1860) and A. P. *Stanley. F. D.

*Maurice, though often categorized as a Broad Church-man, disliked the designation.

The biographies of its adherents, e.g. B. *Jowett, M. *Pattison, and those named above, and works on *Essays and Reviews*, provide much useful information. W. J. Conybeare, *Essays Ecclesiastical and Social* (1855), pp. 57–164 (an expansion of his *Edinburgh Review* article). C. R. Sanders, *Coleridge and the Broad Church Movement* (Durham, NC, 1942); D. Forbes, *The Liberal Anglican Idea of History* (Cambridge, 1952); D. G. Wigmore-Beddoes, *Yesterday's Radicals: A Study of the Affinity between Unitarianism and Broad Church Anglicanism in the Nineteenth Century* (1971).

broad stole. A broad band of material formerly worn *stole-wise by the deacon during part of *High Mass in certain penitential seasons. In origin it was not a stole at all, but represented a *folded chasuble, and thus went back to the days when the deacon as well as the celebrant wore a chasuble, and folded it thus to facilitate movement. Indeed, the rubrics of the Roman Missal continued to enjoin the use of a real folded chasuble, the broad stole being permitted for reasons of convenience. It was finally given up in 1960.

Braun, *LG*, p. 150.

Brompton Oratory. The house and church of the *Oratorians in London. The first Oratory, in King William Street, was founded in 1849, principally through the efforts of J. H. *Newman. In 1854 its members moved to Brompton Road. The present church in a somewhat florid Italian style was consecrated in 1884. It is one of the most important RC centres in London.

The London Oratory, 1849–1949 (1949); H. M. Gillett, *The Story of the London Oratory Church* (1946), incl. bibl.; M. Napier and A. Laing (eds.), *The London Oratory Centenary 1884–1984* [1984]. See also Lives of FABER, F. W., cited s.v.

Brooke, Stopford Augustus (1832–1916), *Broad Church theologian and author. He was born at Glendowan, nr. Letterkenny, Co. Donegal, and educated at Trinity College, Dublin. Having been ordained in 1857, he became curate of St Mary Abbots, Kensington, in 1859, where he made a name as a preacher. His Broad views brought him into conflict with the ecclesiastical authorities, and in 1863 he went to Berlin as chaplain to the Princess Royal and to the British embassy. The post, however, proved unsatisfactory; he returned to London in 1864, and in 1865 he published his widely read *Life and Letters of Frederick W. *Robertson*. The book reflects the outlook of the Broad Church party and was sharply attacked by the Evangelicals. In 1866 he was appointed minister of the *proprietary chapel of St James, York Street, where his preaching drew large congregations. In 1867 he became chaplain-in-ordinary to the Queen. In 1876 he published his *Primer of English Literature*, which became one of the most popular works on the subject. In the same year he moved to Bedford Chapel, Bloomsbury, where he continued to engage in pastoral work even after he had left the C of E in 1880. Among the publications of this period are a *Life and Writings of Milton* (1879), a *History of Early English Literature* (1892), and volumes of sermons. In 1895 he gave up Bedford Chapel owing to ill-health, but continued his literary activities and sometimes preached in the chapels of the *Unitarians.

L. P. Jacks, *Life and Letters of Stopford Brooke* (2 vols., 1917). G. V. Jacks in *DNB, 1912–1921*, pp. 68 f.

Brooks, Phillips (1835–93), Bp. of Massachusetts. A native of Boston, he studied at Harvard and after a short period of teaching was ordained in the Protestant *Episcopal Church in 1859. From 1862 to 1869 he was Rector of Holy Trinity, Philadelphia, where he became much attracted to the liberal religious outlook of such English theologians as F. D. *Maurice and F. W. *Robertson. In 1869 he became Rector of Trinity Church, Boston, and in 1891 Bp. of Massachusetts. The most considerable American preacher of his generation, he owed his influence to his impressive personality, wide sympathies, and passionate sincerity. In 1877 he published his Yale *Lectures on Preaching* and from 1878 onwards several volumes of sermons. He was the author of the well-known carol 'O little town of Bethlehem' (1868). Commemorated in the Episcopal Church on 23 Jan.

His Life and Letters were published by A. V. G. Allen (2 vols., New York, 1901). An abridged edn. was issued in 1907. R. W. Albright, *Focus on Infinity: A Life of Phillips Brooks* (New York, 1961).

Brother Lawrence of the Resurrection (Nicolas Herman) (*c.*1614–91), *Carmelite lay brother and mystic. After being a soldier and later a hermit, he entered the Discalced Carmelite monastery at Paris in 1649, where he was given charge of the kitchen and led a life of almost constant recollection. Lawrence's writings were edited by the Abbé de Beaufort after his death in two volumes entitled *Maximes spirituelles* (1692) and *Mœurs et entretiens du F. Laurent* (1694). They recommend a very elevated form of prayer consisting in the simple practice of the presence of God, whether by the imagination or by the intellect. His maxims, which were highly appreciated by his contemporaries, were frequently quoted by *Fénelon in his *Défenses*.

Good modern edns. of selections of his prayers and letters under the title *La Pratique de la présence de Dieu*, with introd. and notes, by L. Van Den Bossche (Bruges, 1934), S. M. Bouchereaux (Paris, 1948), and C. De Meester (Paris, 1991). Convenient Eng. trs. by D. Attwater (Orchard Books, Extra Series, 3; 1926, frequently repr.) and, with introd., by J. J. Delaney (Garden City, NY, 1977). S. P. Michel in *Dict. Sp.* 9 (1976), cols. 415–17, s.v. 'Laurent (11) de la Résurrection'.

Brothers Hospitallers. The Order, whose members are for the most part laymen, developed out of the work for the sick of St *John of God (d. 1550; q.v.). It began at Granada; then with the support of *Philip II hospitals were established in Madrid, Córdoba, and elsewhere in Spain; and in 1572 *Pius V formally approved the Order, which adopted the *Augustinian rule. In the next decade the Hospital of St John Calybita, established in 1584 in Rome, became the mother-house of the Order. In addition to the three usual vows a fourth is taken to serve for life the sick in hospitals. In more recent times the Order has flourished esp. in Italy, Spain, France, and Central Europe. At present they conduct over 190 hospitals. See also HOSPITALLERS.

J. Monval, *Les Frères Hospitaliers de Saint-Jean de Dieu* (1936; rev. edn., 1950); G. Russotto, FBF, *L'ordine ospedaliero di S. Giovanni di Dio ('Fatebenefratelli')* (1950); id., *San Giovanni di*

Dio e il suo Ordine ospedaliero (2 vols., 1969); N. McMahon, OSJD, *The Story of the Hospitallers of St John of God* (Dublin, 1958). G. Antropius in *Dict. Sp.* 8 (1974), cols. 470–72, s.v. 'Jean 76: Jean de Dieu, 2. Histoire de l'Ordre'; R. Botifoll, FBF, in *DIP* 6 (1980), cols. 982–8, s.v. 'Ospedalieri di San Giovanni di Dio'.

Brothers of the Common Life. See BRETHREN OF THE COMMON LIFE.

Brown, William Adams (1865–1943), *Presbyterian theologian. From 1898 to 1930 he was Roosevelt Professor of Systematic Theology at the *Union Theological Seminary, New York. Belonging to the more liberal wing of American Presbyterianism, he took a prominent part in the *Ecumenical Movement and in Christian social work. His writings include *The Essence of Christianity* (1902), *Christian Theology in Outline* (1906), *Modern Theology and the Preaching of the Gospel* (1914), *The Church in America* (1922), and *Imperialistic Religion and the Religion of Democracy* (1923).

S. McC. Cavert and H. P. van Dusen (eds.), *The Church Through Half a Century: Essays in Honor of William Adams Brown* (1936), with biographical material pp. 3–90.

Browne, Edward Harold (1811–91), Bp. of *Winchester. Educated at Eton and Emmanuel College, Cambridge, he was ordained deacon in 1836 and priest in 1837. After some parochial charges and the Vice-Principalship of St David's College, Lampeter (1843–9), he became Norrisian Professor of Divinity at Cambridge in 1854. In 1864 he became Bp. of *Ely, and in 1873, in succession to S. *Wilberforce, Bp. of Winchester. Had he been younger he would probably have succeeded A. C. *Tait at *Canterbury in 1882. In 1890 he resigned his see. He was a moderating influence in the fierce conflicts aroused by *Essays and Reviews* (1860) and J. W. *Colenso's work on the *Pentateuch (1862–79). His theological beliefs were embodied in his *Exposition of the Thirty-Nine Articles* (2 vols., 1850–3), long a standard work among theological students. He also contributed an article on 'Inspiration' in *Aids to Faith* (1861; a reply to *Essays and Reviews*).

G. W. Kitchin, *Edward Harold Browne, D.D.* (1895).

Browne, George (d. *c.*1556), Abp. of *Dublin and promoter of the Reformation in *Ireland. An English *Augustinian friar, in 1532 he became Prior of the Augustinian house in London. Here he came into contact with T. *Cromwell. In 1534, as Provincial of his order, together with the *Dominican John Hilsey, he was charged by *Henry VIII with a general visitation of the friars which included administering the Oath of *Supremacy, and early in 1536 he was appointed Abp. of Dublin. After receiving a rebuke from the King in Sept. 1537, he endeavoured to bring about the union of the Irish Church with the C of E under the royal supremacy; he took part in the suppression of the Irish monasteries and included Protestant elements in his preaching. It seems, however, that he acted as an instrument of government policy rather than as a zealous doctrinal reformer. Under *Edward VI, the 1549 Prayer Book was used in his diocese and Browne became the leader of those members of the

Irish clergy who accepted the new religion. In 1552 he was granted the primacy of all Ireland, though on *Mary's accession the following year, this was restored to the see of Armagh. Though not sympathizing with his views, Browne consecrated J. *Bale Bp. of Ossory in 1553. In 1554 Browne was deprived of his see, presumably because he was married. Later in the year he was dispensed and allowed to hold a benefice; he almost certainly became a prebendary of St Patrick's Cathedral in Dublin.

Historical Collections of the Church in Ireland during the Reigns of Kings Henry VIII, Edward VI and Queen Mary . . . set forth in the Life and Death of George Browne (1681). B. Bradshaw, SM, 'George Browne, First Reformation Archbishop of Dublin, 1536–1554', *JEH* 21 (1970), pp. 301–26. R. W. Dixon in *DNB* 7 (1886), pp. 43–5, s.v.; *BRUO, 1501–40*, p. 76.

Browne, Robert (*c.*1550–1633), *Puritan separatist. He was a relative of William Cecil, Lord Burghley, who more than once afforded him protection. Born at Tolethorpe, nr. Stamford, Lincs, Browne studied at Corpus Christi College, Cambridge, and while there came under the influence of T. *Cartwright, then advocating a *Presbyterian polity for the Church. After nine years of increasingly radical Puritan activity in East Anglia, in 1581 Browne established an independent congregation at *Norwich and was promptly imprisoned for his schismatic act. Having been freed by Cecil's intervention, he migrated with his Norwich flock to Middelburg in the Netherlands; and there issued *A Book which sheweth the Life and Manner of all True Christians* (Middelburg, 1582) and *A Treatise of Reformation without Tarrying for Any* (ibid., 1582). Before long Browne, who was of a quarrelsome nature, fell out with many of his congregation, and left for Scotland. Not finding the welcome he had looked for from the Scottish Church, he returned to England and published *An Answer to Master Cartwright his Letter for joining with the English Churches* (London, ?1585). He then made a formal submission to the C of E, and became Master of St Olave's School, *Southwark, in 1586. His changed standpoint may be reflected in a paper, *A Reproof of Certain Schismatical Persons*, a MS copy of which is preserved at *Lambeth Palace, but argument about its authorship is inconclusive; in any case, while at Southwark he seems to have ministered to separatist congregations. In 1591 he received episcopal ordination and became Rector of Thorpe Achurch, Northants. He held the benefice until his death, though there is an unexplained period (1616–26) when the entries in the parish register are in a different hand. He died in Northampton Gaol, whither he had been committed for assaulting a police constable. Browne exercised an important influence on the beginnings of *Congregationalism, so much so that its early members were often termed 'Brownists'.

The *Reproof* mentioned in the text, a MS of 31 pages of which scattered extracts had been pub. by S. Bredwell, *The Rasing of the Foundations of Brownisme* (1588), was discovered by Champlin Burrage in 1905 and pub. as *The 'Retractation' of Robert Browne, Father of Congregationalism* (1907). A. Peel and L. H. Carlson (eds.), *The Writings of Robert Harrison and Robert Browne* (Elizabethan Nonconformist Texts, 2; 1953), pp. 150–531. C. Burrage, *The True Story of Robert Browne* (1906), with full list of Browne's writings and bibl. refs. B. R. White, *The English Separatist Tradition from the Marian Martyrs to the Pilgrim Fathers* (Oxford Theological Monographs, 1971), esp. pp. 44–90; S.

Brachlow, *The Communion of Saints: Radical Puritan and Separatist Ecclesiology 1570–1625* (ibid., 1988), *passim*. A. Jessopp in *DNB* 7 (1886), pp. 57–61.

Browne, Sir Thomas (1605–82), natural historian, antiquary, and moralist. After studying medicine at Oxford, Montpellier, and Padua, and receiving a doctorate from *Leiden, he began to practise as a physician, and in 1637 settled in *Norwich, where he spent the rest of his life. In *Religio Medici* (1642; rev. authorized edn., 1643) he expounded his personal reconciliation of devout belief in the Word of God with thoroughgoing empiricism when reading the Book of Nature, along with an unusually tolerant attitude to people of different beliefs and races. His most substantial work, *Pseudodoxia Epidemica* (1646; enlarged 1650, 1658, 1672), examined many longstanding beliefs in natural history, physiology, iconography, geography, history, and biblical and classical history in the light of reason and experience. The twin tracts *Hydriotaphia* and *The Garden of Cyrus* (pub. together, 1658) are eloquent and ingenious meditations on death and resurrection in the form of treatises on burial customs and the recurrence of quincuncial forms in ancient customs and artefacts, the natural world, and religion. Despite his learning and mildness of nature, he clung to traditional beliefs in alchemy and witchcraft, and was slow to accept the new astronomy. His other published works are *Certain Miscellany Tracts* (1683), *A Letter to a Friend upon Occasion of the Death of his Intimate Friend* (1690), and *Christian Morals* (1716; 2nd edn., with Life by S. *Johnson, 1756), whose content overlaps with that of *A Letter*, but was said by a daughter to be a continuation of *Religio Medici*.

First collected *Works*, 1686; fuller edn. with Memoir by S. Wilkin (4 vols., 1835–6); modern edn. by G. [L.] Keynes (6 vols., London, 1928–31, much corrected in 4 vols., ibid., 1964). *Religio Medici and Other Works* [*Hydriotaphia, The Garden of Cyrus, A Letter to a Friend, Christian Morals*], ed., with introd., by L. C. Martin (Oxford, 1964), *Pseudodoxia Epidemica*, ed. R. [H. A.] Robbins (2 vols., Oxford, 1981). Studies by J. S. Finch (New York [1950]), J. Bennett (Cambridge, 1962), F. L. Huntley (Ann Arbor, Mich. [1962]), and L. Nathanson (Chicago and London, 1967), and collection ed. by C. A. Patrides (Columbia and London, 1982). Bibl. by G. [L.] Keynes (Cambridge, 1924; 2nd edn., Oxford, 1968); N. J. Endicott in *NCBEL* 1 (1974), cols. 2228–33. A. H. Bullen in *DNB* 7 (1886), pp. 64–72.

Brownists. See BROWNE, ROBERT.

Bruce, Alexander Balmain (1831–99), Scottish divine. Educated at Edinburgh University, he entered the Free Church ministry, and in 1875 was appointed professor in the Free Church Hall at Glasgow. He is chiefly remembered as an exponent of the '*kenotic theory', esp. in *The Humiliation of Christ* (1876). His *Kingdom of God; or Christ's Teaching according to the Synoptic Gospels* (1889) was much criticized in the General Assembly of the Free Church for its adoption of new principles of biblical criticism, but no formal censure was passed. Among Bruce's later writings were *Apologetics; or, Christianity Defensively Stated* (1892), and two series of *Gifford Lectures for 1896–7 and 1897–8 (pub., 1897 and 1899). He also worked actively for the encouragement of Church music.

A. P. E. Sell, *Defending and Declaring the Faith* (Exeter and Colorado Springs, Colo. [1987]), pp. 89–117. E. I. Carlyle in *DNB*, Suppl. 1 (1901), pp. 321 f., s.v.

Brügglers. A small Swiss sect founded at Brügglen, near Berne, c.1745, by two brothers, Christian and Hieronymus Kohler, probably both impostors from start to finish. Of *Pietist origin, they proclaimed several fantastic doctrines, asserting, e.g., that they themselves and one of their disciples, Elizabeth Kissling, were respectively incarnations of the three Persons of the Trinity, and foretold that the world would end at Christmas 1748. Their excesses and immoralities led to their exile by the Berne government in 1749, and in 1753 Hieronymus Kohler was burnt. The sect survived for a short time in remote mountainous regions.

W. Hadorn, *Geschichte des Pietismus in den Schweizerischen Reformierten Kirchen* (Constance, 1901), pp. 243–5; id. in *PRE* (3rd edn.), 10 (1901), pp. 638–41, s.v. 'Kohler, Christian und Hieronymus', with bibl.

Brunner, Emil (1889–1966), Swiss *dialectical theologian. A native of Winterthur, from 1916 to 1922 he was a pastor at Obstalden. From 1922 to 1953, apart from several visits to America, he taught at Zurich, and then until 1956 at the International Christian University at Tokyo. He supported K. *Barth in opposing theological liberalism, but he was sharply divided from him by the influence of M. *Buber and by his acceptance of the concept of *natural theology, by which a limited knowledge of God may be gained from creation. This, though it did not, like revelation, provide a personal meeting, was a necessary condition of Christian thought. In this he was fiercely opposed by K. Barth in his pamphlet *Nein! Antwort an Emil Brunner* (1934). His writings include *Die Mystik und das Wort* (1924); *Religionsphilosophie evangelischer Theologie* (1926; Eng. tr., *The Philosophy of Religion from the Standpoint of Protestant Theology*, 1937); *Der Mittler* (1927; Eng. tr., *The Mediator*, 1934); *Das Gebot und die Ordnungen* (1932; Eng. tr., *The Divine Imperative*, 1937); *Der Mensch im Widerspruch* (1937; Eng. tr., *Man in Revolt*, 1939), *Dogmatik* (1946–60; Eng. tr., 1946–62), and *Christianity and Civilisation* (*Gifford Lectures for 1947–8; 1948–9). For a short time he professed his adherence to the *Oxford Group Movement.

Festschrift for his 60th birthday (Zurich, 1950); for his 70th birthday (Stuttgart [1959]). P. K. Jewett, *Emil Brunner's Concept of Revelation* (1954); S. Scheld, *Die Christologie Emil Brunners* (Veröffentlichungen des Instituts für Europäische Geschichte Mainz, Abteilung für abendländische Religiongeschichte, 104; Wiesbaden, 1981). C. W. Kegley (ed.), *The Theology of Emil Brunner* [1962], with list of Brunner's works to date. H. Beintker in *TRE* 7 (1981), pp. 236–42, s.v.

Bruno, St (c.925–65), Abp. of *Cologne. The third son of King Henry I of Germany (Henry the Fowler), he was educated in the circle of Bp. Balderic of Utrecht, rejoined the court in 939, was chancellor in the administration of his brother Otto I, and became archchaplain in 951. He was learned, an able administrator, and a staunch supporter of his brother. In 953 he was elevated to the see of Cologne and made Duke of Lotharingia. He exercised considerable influence in Saxon and Frankish political affairs, esp. in Lotharingia. He founded the monastery of

St Pantaleon in Cologne in 964. Feast day, 11 Oct. (though on other days in some places).

Contemporary Life by Ruotger, a monk of Cologne, is pr. in *AASS*, Oct. 5 (1786), pp. 765–86; ed. by G. H. Pertz in *MGH*, Scriptores, 4 (1841), pp. 252–75, and I. Ott (*MGH*, Scriptores Rerum Germanicarum, NS 10, 1951; new edn., 1958); Ott's text is repr., with introd. and Ger. tr. by H. Kallfelz, *Lebensbeschreibungen einiger Bischöfe des 10.–12. Jahrhunderts* (Ausgewählte Quellen zur deutschen Geschichte des Mittelalters, 22; 1973), pp. 169–261. F. Lotter, *Die Vita Brunonis des Ruotger* (Bonner historische Forschungen, 9; 1958). R. Haass, 'Bruno I. Erzbischof von Köln', *Rheinische Lebensbilder*, 1 (1961), pp. 1–11. W. Neuss and F. W. Oediger (eds.), *Geschichte des Erzbistums Köln*, 1 (1964), pp. 165–72. J. Fleckenstein, *Die Hofkapelle der deutschen Könige*, 2 (Schriften der Monumenta Germaniae historica, 16/2; 1966), esp. pp. 24–7, 49–51, and 55–60. P. Corbet, *Les Saints Ottoniens* (Beihefte der *Francia*, 15; 1986), pp. 51–8 and 74–80. J. Fleckenstein in *Lexicon des Mittelalters*, 2 (1983), cols. 753–5, s.v. 'Brun (3)', with bibl.

Bruno, St (*c*.1032–1101). The founder of the *Carthusian Order. Educated at *Cologne and Reims, he became a canon of St Cunibert's in Cologne, whence he was recalled to be 'scholasticus' of the important cathedral school of Reims (*c*.1057). Here he had among his pupils the future Pope *Urban II. He was made chancellor of the diocese in 1075 by Manasses, the new archbishop, a man of scandalous character, with whom he soon came into conflict. In the course of a long struggle Bruno was forced to leave his school (1076), but he returned in 1080 when Manasses was deposed from his see. Shortly after, Bruno turned to the religious life and for a time placed himself under the direction of St *Robert, who later founded *Cîteaux. Before long he left Robert, and with six companions went into the mountainous district near Grenoble, where, under the protection of the bishop, St *Hugh, he laid the foundations of the Carthusian Order (1084). In 1090 he was summoned by Pope Urban II to live in Italy and assist him with his counsel. He obeyed, but refusing the archbishopric of Reggio, retired to the wilds of Calabria and founded the monastery of La Torre, where he died. He was never formally canonized, but in 1514 his order obtained Papal leave to keep his festival (6 Oct.). The observance of the feast was imposed on all Westerns in communion with Rome in 1623.

His Expositions on the Psalms and on the Epp. of St *Paul have been repr. by the Carthusians of Montreuil-sur-Mer, 1891–2; also in J. P. Migne, *PL* 152 and 153; their authenticity is still a matter of dispute; see A. Stoelen, O. Carth., 'Les Commentaires scripturaires attribués à Bruno le Chartreux', *RTAM* 25 (1958), pp. 177–247; id., 'Bruno le Chartreux, Jean Gratiadei et la "Lettre de S. Anselme" sur l'Eucharistie', ibid. 34 (1967), pp. 18–83. 3 letters, with Fr. tr. and introd., in *Lettres des Premiers Chartreux*, ed. by Un Chartreux, 1 (SC 88; 1962, 2nd edn., 1988), pp. 9–93. Extracts from anon. 13th-cent. Life (*Vita Antiquior*), together with other primary material, in *AASS*, Oct. 3 (1700), pp. 491–777. [M. Laporte, OSB] *Aux Sources de la Vie Cartusienne*, 1: *Éclaircissements concernant la Vie de Saint Bruno* (St-Pierre-de-Chartreuse, 1960). A. P. F. Lefebvre, *Saint Bruno et l'ordre des Chartreux* (2 vols., 1883); H. Löbbel, *Der Stifter des Carthäuser-Ordens, der heilige Bruno aus Köln* (1899). A. Ravier, *S. Bruno, le premier des ermites de la Chartreuse* (1967). Y. Gourdel, OSB, in *Dict. Sp.* 2 (1953), cols. 705–10, s.v. 'Chartreux'; J. Dubois, OSB, in *DIP* 1 (1973), cols. 1606–15, s.v. See also works cited under CARTHUSIAN ORDER.

Bruno, Giordano (1548–1600), Italian philosopher. In 1562 he joined the *Dominican Order at Naples, but on being censured for unorthodoxy, he fled in 1576. For 17 years he moved from place to place under constant suspicion, and was in England from 1583 to 1585; during this time he seems to have acted as a spy on RC conspirators for the English government. Captured at Venice in 1592 by the emissaries of the *Inquisition, he was in confinement at Rome from 1593 till, on 17 Feb. 1600, he was burnt at the stake on the Campo dei Fiori.

Under Renaissance influences Bruno became a fierce opponent of *Aristotelian doctrines and a warm admirer of N. *Copernicus. His enthusiasm for nature, however, led him to hold an extreme form of pantheistic immanentism. God was the efficient and final cause of everything, the beginning, middle, and end, the eternal and infinite. He developed this philosophy in its many consequences in his two Italian metaphysical treatises of 1584, *De la Causa, Principio, ed Uno* and *De l'Infinito, Universo, e Mondi*. In his Latin treatises, written somewhat later, he slightly modified this extreme pantheism. In the latter half of the 19th cent. the name of Bruno came to be identified with *anticlerical elements in the movement for Italian nationalism.

Latin works ed. F. Fiorentino [F. Tocco and others] (8 vols., Florence and Naples, 1879–91); Italian works ed. G. *Gentile (2 vols., Bari, 1907–8). V. Spampanato, *Vita di Giordano Bruno* (Messina, 1921); id., *Documenti della Vita di Giordano Bruno* (Florence, 1933). A. Mercati, *Il Sommario del Processo di Giordano Bruno* (ST 101; 1942, with documents); L. Firpo, *Il Processo di Giordano Bruno* (Quaderni della *Rivista Storica Italiana*, 1; Naples, 1949). A. Corsano, *Il Pensiero di Giordano Bruno nel suo svolgimento storico* (Biblioteca storia del Rinascimento, NS 1; Florence [1940]); D. W. Singer, *Giordano Bruno: His Life and Thought*, with annotated tr. of *On the Infinite Universe and Worlds* [1950]; J. C. Nelson, *Renaissance Theory of Love: The Context of Giordano Bruno's* Eroici furori (New York, 1958); F. A. Yates, *Giordano Bruno and the Hermetic Tradition* (1964) and other arts. by this author (repr. in her *Collected Essays*, vol. 1 [1982], pp. 129–221, vol. 2 [1983], pp. 101–50); H. Védrine, *La Conception de la Nature chez Giordano Bruno* (De Pétrarque à Descartes, 14; 1967) with bibl.; J. Bossy, *Giordano Bruno and the Embassy Affair* (New Haven, Conn., and London, 1991). V. Salvestrini, *Bibliografia delle opere di Giordano Bruno* (1926; 2nd edn. by L. Firpo [to 1950], 1958).

Bruys, Pierre de. See PETER DE BRUYS.

Bryanites. See BIBLE CHRISTIANS.

Bryennios, Philotheos (1833–1914), the discoverer of the '*Didache'. A native of *Constantinople, he studied at several German universities, became professor of Church history and exegesis at Halki in 1861, director of the school in the *Phanar at Constantinople in 1867, Metropolitan of Serrae in Macedonia in 1875 and of Nicomedia in 1877. In 1873 he discovered in the library of the Hospice of the 'Jerusalem Monastery of the Holy Sepulchre' at Constantinople a MS (no. 456) written in 1056 which contained some early Christian documents of the first importance, among them the Greek texts of the Ep. of *Barnabas, the first and second Epp. of *Clement to the Corinthians, and, the most celebrated, the Didache. He published the two Clementine Epistles in 1875 and the

Didache in 1883. In 1875 he was a delegate of the E. Church at the *Bonn Reunion Conference.

Brief notice by N. Turchi in *EC* 3 (1950), col. 163. P. *Schaff, *The Oldest Church Manual called the 'Teaching of the Twelve Apostles'* (1885), pp. 279–96 (with autobiog. letter from Bryennios).

Buber, Martin (1878–1965), Jewish religious thinker. He was a native of Vienna, where he took his doctor's degree in 1900, and played an active part in the Zionist Movement, which he had joined in 1898. From 1906 onwards he devoted himself chiefly to religious studies. These led him to preoccupation with *Chasidism, whence he derived many of his ideas, e.g. those on a kind of activist mysticism and the sanctification of daily life. From 1916 to 1924 he was editor of *Der Jude*, a leading monthly of German-speaking Jewry. In 1923 he received a call to Frankfurt University, where he lectured on Jewish theology and ethics. In 1926 he started a periodical, *Die Kreatur*, with Catholic and Protestant collaborators. In 1933 he was deprived of his chair by the government, though he stayed in Germany until 1938. In that year he went to Palestine to become Professor of Sociology at the Hebrew University of *Jerusalem, where apart from lecture tours in the USA, he spent the rest of his life.

Among his more important writings are *Die Legende des Baalschem* (1908, Eng. tr., 1956), *Vom Geist des Judentums* (1916), *Die Schrift* (from 1925, translation of the Bible, with F. Rosenzweig), and *Königtum Gottes* (1932, Eng. tr., 1967), a study of the Messianic idea. The book which has exercised the greatest influence on Christian theologians as well as on the German Youth Movement is his small treatise *Ich und Du* (1923; Eng. trs., 1937 and 1970). Written in poetic language, it contrasts the 'I–Thou' relationship, in which the other is granted its full reality, with the 'I–It' relationship in which the other is subjected to my needs and purposes.

The influence of Buber's ideas, esp. on man's relationship to God, is evident in much 20th-cent. theology, both Catholic and Protestant.

Werke, 3 vols., Munich, 1962–4, incomplete; *Der Jude und sein Judentum: Gesammelte Aufsätze und Reden* (Cologne [1963]); *Briefwechsel aus sieben Jahrzehnten*, ed. G. Schaeder (3 vols., Heidelberg, 1972–5). Studies by H. Kohn (Hellerau, 1930, repr. with continuation by R. Weltsch, Cologne, 1961), M. S. Friedman (London, 1955, and 3 vols., New York, 1982–4), A. A. Cohen (ibid., 1957), H. U. von *Balthasar (Cologne and Olten, 1958; Eng. tr., 1961), M. L. Durand (New York, 1960), G. Schaeder (Göttingen [1966]), ed. P. A. Schilpp and M. [S.] Friedman (Library of Living Philosophers, 12; La Salle, Ill., and London, 1967), incl. Eng. tr. of Buber's autobiographical fragments and his replies to criticism, ed. H. Gordon and J. Bloch [New York, 1984; tr. from Heb.], and P. Vermes (London, 1988). R. Horwitz, *Buber's Way to I and Thou: An Historical Analysis and the First Publication of Martin Buber's Lectures 'Religion als Gegenwart'* (Heidelberg, 1978). P. Vermes, *Buber on God and the Perfect Man* (Brown Judaic Studies, 13; Chico, Calif. [1980]). H. Kress, *Religiöse Ethik und dialogisches Denken: Das Werk Martin Bubers in der Beziehung zu Georg Simmel* (Studien zur evangelischen Ethik, 16 [1985]), pp. 97–263. L. J. Silberstein, *Martin Buber's Social and Religious Thought* (New York and London [1989]). M. Cohn and R. Buber, *Martin Buber: A Bibliography of his Writings 1897–1978* (Jerusalem, 1980).

Bucer, Martin (1491–1551), Protestant Reformer, also spelled 'Butzer'. In 1506/7 he entered the *Dominican Order at Sélestat, moving (*c*.1516/17) to Heidelberg, where in April 1518 he heard M. *Luther dispute. In 1521 he adopted Lutheranism and by 1523, having secured Papal dispensation from his monastic vows and married, he began publicly to preach Lutheranism in Alsace. He settled in Strasbourg in 1523. In 1524 he was put in charge of the parish of Ste Aurélie; later he held that of St Thomas. While involved in polemic against RC theologians such as Conrad Treger, he also opposed *Anabaptists and other religious radicals. His doctrine of the Eucharist is normally considered half-way between that of Luther and U. *Zwingli. Although he and his colleague W. *Capito supported the Zwinglian doctrine of the Eucharist at the unsuccessful *Marburg Colloquy (1529), the *Tetrapolitan Confession, which originated in Strasbourg, expressed an intermediate position. In 1531, after Zwingli's death, Strasbourg joined the *Schmalkaldic League and in May 1536 Bucer, by signing the *Wittenberg Concord, accepted, at least ostensibly, Luther's doctrine of the Eucharist. Bucer took part in the unsuccessful conferences between Catholics and Protestants at *Hagenau (1540), *Worms (1540), and *Ratisbon (1541), and then assisted *Hermann of Wied in his vain attempt to introduce Reformed doctrines at Cologne. In 1546 when the Strasbourg Council showed itself reluctant to enforce Protestant Church discipline, Bucer introduced a system of meetings of élite groups chosen from among the faithful ('christliche Gemeinschaften') to motivate other parishioners. After unavailing opposition to the *Interim of 1548, Bucer came to England at the invitation of T. *Cranmer, and was made Regius Professor of Divinity at Cambridge. He had a marked influence on parts of the Anglican *Ordinal. He died on 28 Feb. 1551 and was buried in Great St Mary's church at Cambridge. His body was exhumed and publicly burnt in 1557. He wrote numerous theological treatises and biblical commentaries in Latin and German; his Latin style is notoriously difficult and unattractive.

Scripta Anglicana fere omnia, ed. C. Hubert (Basle, 1577). Modern edn. of his complete works in three series: (1) *Deutsche Schriften*, ed. R. Stupperich (Gütersloh, 1960 ff.); (2) *Opera latina*, ed. C. Augustijn and others (Paris, 1954–5 [vol. 15 in 2 pts.]; Leiden [Studies in Medieval and Renaissance Thought], 1982 ff.) and (3) *Correspondance*, ed. J. Rott and others (Leiden [Studies in Medieval and Renaissance Thought], 1979 ff.). Selected correspondence in J. V. Pollet, OP, *Martin Bucer: Études sur la Correspondance* (2 vols., 1958–62) and id., *Martin Bucer: Études sur les relations de Bucer avec les Pays-Bas, l'Électorat de Cologne et l'Allemagne du Nord* (Studies in Medieval and Renaissance Thought, 33; 2 vols., Leiden, 1985). Eng. tr. of *De Regno Christi* in W. Pauck (ed.), *Melanchthon and Bucer* (Library of Christian Classics, 19 [1969]), pp. 174–394. The exact corpus of Bucer's writings has been the subject of dispute; see F. Mentz, 'Bibliographische Zusammenstellung der gedruckten Schriften Butzer's', in *Zur 400jährigen Geburtsfeier Martin Butzer's* (Strasbourg, 1891), pp. 99–164; R. Stupperich, 'Bibliographia Bucerana', in H. Bornkamm, *Martin Butzers Bedeutung für die europäische Reformationsgeschichte* (Schriften des Vereins für Reformationsgeschichte, 169; 1952), pp. 37–96 (includes secondary works to 1950); P. Lardet, 'Vers une nouvelle bibliographie bucérienne: résultats d'un premier inventaire', in I. Backus and others, *Martin Bucer apocryphe et authentique* (Cahiers de la Revue de Théologie et de Philosophie, 8; Geneva, 1983), pp. 3–26. Life by H. Eells (New Haven, Conn., and London, 1931; repr. New York, 1971). J. W. Baum, *Capito und Butzer* (Elberfeld, 1860); A. Lang, *Der Evangelienkommentar*

Martin Butzers und die Grundzüge seiner Theologie (Leipzig, 1900); C. Hopf, *Martin Bucer and the English Reformation* (Oxford, 1946); G. J. van de Poll, *Martin Bucer's Liturgical Ideas* (Assen, 1954); W. P. Stephens, *The Holy Spirit in the Theology of Martin Bucer* (Cambridge, 1970); W. van't Spijker, *De Ambten bij Martin Bucer* (Kampen, 1970); I. Backus and others, *Logique et théologie au XVIᵉ siècle: aux sources de l'argumentation de Martin Bucer* (Cahiers de la Revue de Théologie et de Philosophie, 5; Geneva, 1980); G. Hammann, *Entre le secte et la cité: Le projet d'Église du réformateur Martin Bucer (1491–1551)* (Geneva [1984]). C. Krieger and M. Leinhard (eds.), *Martin Bucer and Sixteenth Century Europe: Actes du colloque de Strasbourg (28–31 août 1991)* (Studies in Medieval and Reformation Thought, 52–3; Leiden, 1993). D. F. Wright (ed.), *Martin Bucer: Reforming church and community* (Cambridge, 1994). M. Köhn, 'Bucer-Bibliographie 1951–1974', in M. de Kroon and F. Krüger (eds.), *Bucer und seine Zeit* (Veröffentlichungen des Instituts für europäische Geschichte Mainz, 80; Wiesbaden, 1976), pp. 133–64. A. W. Ward in *DNB* 7 (1886), pp. 172–7, s.v.; R. Stupperich in *TRE* 7 (1983), pp. 258–70, s.v.

Buchanan, Claudius (1766–1815), Bengal chaplain. After conversion and a period spent under the personal influence of the famous Evangelical, J. *Newton, Buchanan entered Queens' College, Cambridge, in 1791, where he made the close acquaintance of C. *Simeon. On being ordained priest in 1796, he accepted a chaplaincy in Bengal, proceeded to Calcutta shortly afterwards, and was for several years vice-provost of a cultural college which Lord Wellesley had established at Fort William. Though his official position in the East India Company restricted the amount of active mission work he could do, he used his influence to the utmost to further the cause of Christianity in native India; and it was largely through his instrumentality after his return to England (1808) that an episcopate in India was created, T. F. *Middleton, the first Bp. of Calcutta, being appointed in 1814.

Works (incomplete) in 2 pts., New York, 1812. H. N. Pearson, *Memoirs of the Life and Writings of the Rev. Claudius Buchanan* (2 vols., 1817). A. J. Arbuthnot in *DNB* 7 (1886), pp. 182–4.

Buchanan, George (1506–82), Scottish scholar and man of letters. He began his academic career as a pupil of John Major at the universities of Paris and St Andrews, and in the 1540s and 1550s held various teaching posts in France (Bordeaux and Paris) and at Coimbra in Portugal, gaining a reputation as a poet, dramatist, and classical scholar. He came under suspicion of heresy for his satires on the contemporary Church, was imprisoned for some months by the *Inquisition in Portugal, and eventually moved from humanism of the Erasmian type to alignment with the forces of Protestantism. Returning to Scotland in 1561, he took part in the counsels of the Reformed Church, became Principal of St Leonard's College, St Andrews, and served as Moderator of the General Assembly of the Kirk in 1567. Though he was tutor to both *Mary, Queen of Scots, and James VI (*James I of England), he rejected the doctrine of the *Divine Right of Kings and regarded the people as the source of political power, expounding his view in *De Jure Regni apud Scotos* (1579); in his later years he pursued the deposed Queen with implacable hostility. A Gaelic speaker and pioneer of Celtic studies, propagandist and man of affairs, he closed his many-sided career by publishing the influential but partisan *Rerum Scoticarum Histo-*

ria (1582). S. *Johnson praised him as 'the only man of genius his country produced'.

Opera Omnia, ed. T. Ruddiman (2 vols., Edinburgh, 1715). P. H. Brown, *George Buchanan: Humanist and Reformer* (ibid., 1890), id., *George Buchanan and his Times* (1906). I. D. McFarlane, *Buchanan* (1981).

Buchman, Frank (Nathan Daniel) (1878–1961), founder and director of the *Oxford Group (q.v.). Born of a *Lutheran family of Swiss descent at Pennsburg, Pa., he graduated at Muhlenberg College, studied at Mount Airy Seminary, Philadelphia, and entered the Lutheran ministry. After a year of graduate study abroad he was in charge of a parish in Philadelphia for three years and subsequently of a hostel for poor young men. In 1908 he resigned this work in a spirit of disillusionment and on a visit to England attended the *Keswick Convention, where an address on the *Atonement in a small church in the neighbourhood convinced him that his previous ministry had been wholly unprofitable and he experienced conversion. On the advice of J. R. *Mott he took up evangelistic work among the students of Pennsylvania State College. In 1915 and 1917–19 he visited *India and the Far East, and in 1920—with introductions from two Anglican missionary bishops whom he met in China—Cambridge, after which some Cambridge undergraduates joined him in a visit to Oxford. Out of this last visit the Group movement grew. In 1929 he visited South Africa with a team of supporters, and subsequently travelled widely, including tours to Canada and USA in 1932–3 and 1933–4, Scandinavia in 1934–5, Switzerland in 1935, Utrecht and the Near East in 1937. In 1938 in London he called for *Moral Re-Armament, a development of the work which stressed the role of individuals in spiritually transforming society. World Assemblies of this later movement were held at Caux, Switzerland, in 1946 and subsequent years.

Life by G. [D.] Lean (London, 1985). See also bibl. to OXFORD GROUP.

Buchmann, Theodor. See BIBLIANDER, THEODOR.

Büchner, Karl Friedrich Christian Ludwig (1824–99), German materialist philosopher. While lecturer in medicine at *Tübingen (from 1852), he published in 1855 his celebrated *Kraft und Stoff*, in which he defended a purely materialistic doctrine of the natural world, seeking on the bases of the conservation-laws of energy and of matter to reduce everything in the universe, whether mental or physical, to a single non-spiritual source. The book became a sort of Bible for the materialists and aroused such bitter opposition that Büchner was forced to retire. For the rest of his life he lived at Darmstadt, where he published several other widely read treatises. He maintained that his doctrinaire materialism was not incompatible with idealism in practical life.

R. Handy in P. Edwards (ed.), *The Encyclopedia of Philosophy*, 1 (1967), pp. 411–13, s.v.

Buckfast Abbey, Devon. The first abbey was founded in 1018 by Earl Aethelweard and was ceded to the Abbot of *Savigny in 1136. Together with a number of other Savigny houses in England it adopted the rule of Cîteaux in 1147 and remained *Cistercian until its *dissolution in

1539. In the early years of the 19th cent. a private house was built on the site and it was to this that a group of exiled French monks from the abbey of La-Pierre-qui-Vire came in 1882. Buckfast was again raised to the rank of abbey in 1902, with Dom Boniface Netter as abbot. After his death in a shipwreck in 1906 he was succeeded by Dom Anscar *Vonier, who decided to rebuild the monastic buildings. The abbey church, built by the community in Gothic style, was opened in 1922 and consecrated in 1932. The monastery was affiliated to the English *Benedictine Congregation in 1960; a preparatory school was started by the community in 1967, but closed in 1994.

W. *Dugdale, *Monasticon Anglicanum, 5 (1825 edn.), pp. 385-7. J. Stéphan, OSB, A History of Buckfast Abbey, from 1018 to 1968 (Bristol, 1970). L. H. Cottineau, OSB, Répertoire topo-bibliographique des abbayes et prieurés (Mâcon, 1935), col. 525. J. M. Canivez, O. Cist., in DHGE 10 (1938), cols. 1034-6, s.v.

Buckland, William (1784-1856), Dean of *Westminster from 1845, and geologist. He was elected to a fellowship at Corpus Christi College, Oxford, in 1808, and in 1819 became the first University reader in geology. He saw in the vestiges of the ice-age striking proof of the biblical story of the *Flood, defending his views in Reliquiae Diluvianae, or Observations on the Organic Remains attesting the Action of a Universal Deluge (1823). In 1836 he issued an ambitious contribution to the *Bridgewater Treatises on Geology and Mineralogy considered with Reference to Natural Theology.

Mrs Gordon [E. O. Buckland, daughter], The Life and Correspondence of William Buckland (1894). N. A. Rupke, The Great Chain of History: William Buckland and the English School of Geology (1814-1849) (Oxford, 1983).

Budde, Karl (1850-1935), OT scholar. He was professor of OT from 1889 to 1900 at Strasbourg and from 1900 to 1921 at Marburg. He did much to further OT criticism on the lines laid down by J. *Wellhausen. Besides many commentaries, his writings include a concise and widely read Religion of Israel (1899; Ger. edn., 1900).

Karl Budde's Schrifttum bis zu seinem 80. Geburtstage (Beiheft 54 of the ZATW, 1930).

Bugenhagen, Johann (1485-1558), 'Pomeranus', *Lutheran theologian. In early life he was a *Premonstratensian canon of Treptow (in Pomerania), where he was appointed rector of the city school in 1504. After his marriage in 1522, M. *Luther secured his appointment as pastor in *Wittenberg in 1523, and here he remained till his death, acting as Luther's confessor. He took a leading part in the organization of the Lutheran Church in N. Germany and *Denmark, and the 'Brunswick Church Order' of 1528 was mainly his work. In 1537 Bugenhagen made his way to Denmark, where his presence had been sought by King Christian III, to rearrange ecclesiastical affairs on a Protestant basis, and on 12 Aug. he crowned both King and Queen. He then proceeded to consecrate seven men to be superintendents or 'bishops', and in this way the Danish Church lost the episcopal *Apostolic Succession. He also reorganized the University of Copenhagen, arranging for lectures on St *Augustine's 'De Spiritu et Littera', Luther's 'Commentary on Galati-

ans', and the 'Loci Communes' of P. *Melanchthon. He also assisted Luther in his translation of the Bible.

Collections of sermons ed. G. Buchwald (Halle, 1885; Leipzig, 1909); Correspondence ed. O. Vogt (Stettin, 1888). The 'Brunswick Church Order' is conveniently pr. in E. Sehling (ed.), Die evangelischen Kirchenordnungen des XVI. Jahrhunderts, 16 (pt. 1; 1955), pp. 348-455. Life by H. Hering (Halle, 1888). G. Geisenhof, Bibliotheca Bugenhagiana (ibid., 1908). W. Rautenberg (ed.), Johann Bugenhagen: Beiträge zu seinem 400. Todestag [1958]. J. H. Bergsma, Die Reform der Messliturgie durch Johannes Bugenhagen (1485-1558) (Hildesheim [1966]). H. H. Holfelder, Tentatio et Consolatio: Studien zu Bugenhagens 'Interpretatio in Librum Psalmorum' (Arbeiten zur Kirchengeschichte, 45; 1974); id., Solus Christus . . . : Eine Untersuchung zur Genese von Bugenhagens Theologie (Beiträge zur historischen Theologie, 63; 1981). Id. in TRE 7 (1981), pp. 354-63, s.v.

bugia (also **scotula, palmatorium**). A portable candlestick containing a lighted candle which is sometimes held beside a RC bishop (and other prelates by special privilege) while he reads or sings certain prayers. In 1968 its use was restricted to such times as circumstances made it of practical necessity.

Bulgakov, Sergius (1871-1944), Russian theologian. The son of a Russian priest, he was intended for the priesthood but later became a philosophical and religious sceptic and active in Marxist political movements. Disillusioned after the 1905 Revolution, he slowly retraced his steps to the Church. In the Moscow Sobor of 1917, which restored the patriarchate, Bulgakov took a prominent part as a layman. He became a priest shortly afterwards. Expelled from Russia, he was Dean of the Orthodox Theological Academy at *Paris from 1925 till his death. He was a man of remarkable personality and intellectual power, well known in W. Europe and America through his participation in the *Ecumenical Movement, of which he was a warm but critical supporter. Theologically he is best known for his contributions to Sophiology, a body of thought claiming descent through V. *Solovyov and P. Florensky from the E. Fathers, which seeks to solve the problems of the relation between God and the world by the concept of the Divine Wisdom or sophia. His teaching was condemned, partly it would seem on political grounds, by the Moscow patriarchate in 1935 but without much practical result. His chief works translated into English are The Orthodox Church (1935) and The Wisdom of God (1937). His major work, in three parts called 'The Divine Wisdom and the Godmanhood', is available in Fr. tr.: Du Verbe incarné (1943), Le Paraclet (1947), and L'Épouse de l'Agneau (1984).

J. Pain and N. *Zernov (eds.), A Bulgakov Anthology (1976). K. Naumov, Bibliographie des Œuvres de Serge Boulgakov (Bibliothèque Russe de l'Institut d'Études Slaves, 68/1; Paris, 1984), with preface by C. Andronikof, pp. 7-41. N. Zernov, The Russian Religious Renaissance of the Twentieth Century (1963), pp. 138-50. S. Swierkosz, SJ, L'Église Visible selon Serge Bulgakov (Orientalia Christiana Analecta, 221; Rome, 1980), with bibl. F. C. Copleston, SJ, Russian Religious Philosophy (1988), esp. pp. 90-9.

Bulgaria, Christianity in. The official introduction of Christianity into Bulgaria occurred in 864-5, with the baptism of the Prince, Boris. Both Byzantine and German missionaries were at work in the country, and Boris wavered for a time between Constantinople and Rome, finally deciding c.870 in favour of the former. During the late 9th and early 10th cent. Clement of Ochrid (d. 916), one of the leading disciples of St *Cyril and St Methodius, laboured for several decades in Bulgaria to establish Slavonic Christianity under Byzantine auspices. Under Tsar Simeon (893–927) the Bulgarian kingdom attained great cultural brilliance, with a rich Christian literature in Slavonic; and during his reign the Bulgarian Church became *autocephalous, its head assuming the title '*Patriarch', with his seat first at Preslav and later at Ochrid. On the defeat of Bulgaria by the Byzantines in 1018, the Bulgarian Patriarchate was suppressed, but it was restored during the years 1235—1393, its seat being now at Trnovo. During the Turkish period the Bulgarian Church became increasingly subject to Constantinople, finally losing all traces of independence in 1767; and from then until 1870 the episcopate was generally filled with Greeks (compare the similar position of *Romania and *Serbia). The Bulgarians, on attaining political independence, created an autocephalous *Exarchate in 1870; but they acted without the consent of the Patriarchate of Constantinople, which excommunicated them in 1872 for the heresy of 'philetism' (nationalism), the schism remaining unhealed until 1945. In 1953 the Metropolitan of Sofia, as head of the Bulgarian Church, assumed the title 'Patriarch', being recognized as such by the *Oecumenical Patriarch in 1961. Besides the Orthodox, there is a very small RC community in Bulgaria, and a more substantial Muslim minority (c.10 per cent of the population).

M. Spinka, A History of Christianity in the Balkans: A Study in the Spread of Byzantine Culture among the Slavs (Chicago [1933]), esp. pp. 1–72 and 91–128. A. P. Vlasto, The Entry of the Slavs into Christendom (Cambridge, 1970), pp. 155–87; R. Browning, Byzantium and Bulgaria: A comparative study across the early medieval frontier (1975), pp. 140–69. [A.] M. Macdermott, A History of Bulgaria 1393–1855 (1962), pp. 143–68. I. Dujčev, Il Cattolicesimo in Bulgaria nel sec. XVII (Orientalia Christiana Analecta, 111; 1937), and other works of this author. I. Sofranov, Histoire du mouvement bulgare vers l'église catholique au XIXᵉ siècle, 1 (Bibliothèque Catholique Belge, 1960). M. Rinvolucri, Anatomy of a Church: Greek Orthodoxy Today (1966), pp. 174–83 ('Report on the Orthodox Church in Bulgaria'). P. Walters (ed.), World Christianity: Eastern Europe (Keston Book, 29; Eastbourne, 1988), pp. 271–88. R. Janin, AA, in DHGE 10 (1938), cols. 1120–94; A. de Santos Otero and F. Heyer in TRE 7 (1981), pp. 364–75, s.v. 'Bulgarien', both with bibl.

Bull (Lat. bulla, 'seal'). A written mandate of the Pope, of a more serious and weighty kind than a 'brief'. Such documents were sealed in earlier times with the Pope's signet-ring, but from the 6th cent. either seal-boxes of lead or signets stamped in wax were used. Since 1878 only the most important bulls ('consistorial bulls') are sealed in this way, others being sealed merely with a red stamp. Consistorial bulls are signed not only by the Pope, but also by the *Cardinals, and are sent out in copy, the original being retained at Rome.

For collections of bulls see BULLARIUM. N. Valois, 'Étude sur le rythme des bulles pontificales', Bibliothèque de l'École des Chartes, 42 (1881), pp. 161–98 and 257–72. R. L. Poole in DECH, pp. 72–4, s.v. 'Bulls, Papal'; G. Battelli in EC 2 (1949), cols. 1778–81, s.v. 'Bolla', with bibl.

Bull, George (1634–1710), Bp. of *St Davids and theologian. He was educated at Exeter College, Oxford, and was ordained deacon and priest on the same day in 1655. In 1659 he became Rector of Suddington, in 1686 Archdeacon of *Llandaff, and in 1705 Bp. of St Davids. In theology he was a staunch *High Churchman. His Harmonia Apostolica (1669 70) was an attack on the more Protestant theories of *justification, its thesis being that the passages where St *Paul seems to imply human incapacity for moral attainment must be interpreted in the light of St *James's Epistle. In his celebrated treatise, Defensio Fidei Nicaenae (1685; he added later several other works by way of postscript), he maintained, largely in criticism of the *Jesuit D. *Petavius, that the teaching of the pre-Nicene Fathers on the Trinity completely agreed with that of orthodox theologians of Nicene and post-Nicene times. The work greatly commended itself to J. B. *Bossuet and other contemporary French theologians, and, after the publication of one of its sequels, the Judicium Ecclesiae Catholicae, in 1694, Bull received the unusual tribute of the formal thanks of the French clergy at their synod at St Germain in 1700. In answer to their subsequent inquiries why, in view of so masterly a defence of Catholic doctrine, he did not become a RC, Bull wrote a popular and vigorous work, The Corruptions of the Church of Rome (1705). A posthumous work of Bull, popular in later times, was A Companion for the Candidates of Holy Orders, or the Great Importance of the Priestly Office (1714). His Life was written by R. *Nelson, who had been a pupil of Bull's at Suddington.

Works, ed. E. Burton (6 vols., Oxford, 1827). R. Nelson, The Life of Dr George Bull . . . with the history of those Controversies in which he was engaged (1713). L. W. Barnard, 'Bishop George Bull of St. David's: Scholar and Defender of the Faith', Journal of Welsh Ecclesiastical History, 9 (1992), pp. 37–51. J. H. Overton in DNB 7 (1886), pp. 236–8, s.v.

bullarium. A term said to have been invented by the canonist, Laertius Cherubini (d. 1626), for a collection of Papal *bulls and other similar documents. Such 'bullaria', being the collections of private individuals, have no authority beyond that attaching to their component pieces. Among the best known are those of L. Cherubini (1586); the 'Luxembourg Bullarium' (stated to have been really printed at Geneva) (1727–30); Mainardi's 'Roman Bullarium' (1733–62); and the 'Turin Bullarium' (1857–85).

T. Ortolan in DTC 2 (1905), cols. 1243–55, s.v. 'Bullaire', with bibl.; H. *Leclercq, OSB, in DACL 8 (pt. 2; 1929), cols. 2977–82, s.v. 'Lettres des papes'.

Bullinger, Heinrich (1504–75). Swiss Reformer. Born in Bremgarten in the Swiss canton of Aarau, he was educated at the monastic school in Emmerich, near Nijmegen, where he came under the influence of the *devotio moderna, and then at the University of Cologne. About 1520, hearing about M. *Luther's theology and wishing to compare it with RC teaching, he read *Gratian and *Peter Lombard, and from them was led to study the Church Fathers and the NT; he also came under the influence of P. *Melanchthon's Loci communes and some of the writings of Luther. Convinced of the primary importance of Scripture in Christian dogma, he adopted *Lutheranism and later Zwinglianism. From 1523 to 1529 he taught at the

*Cistercian school in Kappel. In 1529 he became Pastor of Bremgarten and married. Two years later he succeeded U. *Zwingli as Chief Pastor at Zurich, a post which he held until his death.

Next to J. *Calvin, Bullinger was prob. the most influential of the second-generation Reformers. Within Switzerland, he played a leading part in drawing up the first and second *Helvetic Confessions (1536 and 1566) and the *Consensus Tigurinus (1549); these provided a national basis for the Reformation and prevented it from becoming a merely cantonal phenomenon. Abroad, he combated the Lutheran doctrine of the Eucharist, in the 1560s engaging in controversy with J. *Brenz. He refuted *Anabaptist theology, notably in Von dem unverschämten Freuel (1531) and in Der Wiedertäufer Ursprung (1560), while generally maintaining an open-minded attitude to the various radical movements of the period. He was the only Continental Reformer to be consulted about the *vestiarian controversies under both *Edward VI (1550) and *Elizabeth I (1566). In 1570 he was asked by R. *Cox to prepare a reply to the bull Regnans in excelsis which excommunicated Elizabeth. The reply was published in Latin (1571), English (1572), and German (1578). The Decades, a Latin version of his Hausbuch of sermons, were translated into English in 1577 and adopted as a textbook at *Lincoln and *Canterbury. It is usually held that his chief contribution to Reformed theology is his doctrine of the *covenant; this was developed as early as his treatise De testamento (1534). Following *Marsiglio of Padua, he saw no basic distinction between the Christian State and the Christian Church and considered that the norms for a Christian society had been established by God in the OT. This doctrine had two important consequences: (1) the jurisdiction of the civil authority extended to ecclesiastical matters; and (2) the doctrine of *predestination, while still of prime importance, was less rigid than that of Calvin or T. *Beza. According to Bullinger, God's election was binding in history only in so far as men kept the conditions of the covenant. Bullinger was enormously prolific. Apart from polemical treatises, his works include histories and sermons and commentaries on the entire NT apart from Rev.

Crit. edn. of his main works by F. Büsser and others (Zurich, 1972 ff.), incl. Abteilung I: Bibliographie (2 vols., 1972–7), with details of secondary lit. to 1975. Other edns. include those of his Autobiography by J. J. Hottinger and H. H. Vögeli (3 vols., Frauenfeld, 1838–40), the Decades, by T. Harding (*Parker Society, 4 vols., 1849–52), his Diarium, by E. Egli (Quellen zur schweizerischen Reformationsgeschichte, 2; 1904), Korrespondenz mit den Graubündnern, by T. Schiess (Quellen zur Schweizer Geschichte, 23–5; 1904–6), and Ratio Studiorum, by P. Stotz (2 vols., Zurich, 1987). Modern Eng. tr. of his sermon 'Of the Catholic Church' in G. W. Bromiley (ed.), Zwingli and Bullinger (Library of Christian Classics, 24; 1953), pp. 283–325. Classic study by C. Pestalozzi (Elberfeld, 1858). A. Bouvier, Henri Bullinger . . . le successeur de Zwingli, d'après sa correspondance avec les réformés et les humanistes de langue française (1940), with bibl. F. Blanke, Der junge Bullinger 1504–1531 (Zurich, 1942). W. Hollweg, Heinrich Bullingers Hausbuch: Eine Untersuchung über die Anfänge der reformierten Predigtliteratur (Beiträge zur Geschichte und Lehre der Reformierten Kirche, 8; 1956). H. Fast, Heinrich Bullinger und die Täufer (Schriftenreihe des Mennonitischen Geschichtsvereins, 7; 1959). J. Staedtke, Die Theologie des jungen Bullinger (Zurich, 1962). S. Hausammann, Römerbriefauslegung zwischen Humanismus und Reformation: Eine Studie zu Heinrich Bullingers Römerbrief-

vorlesung von 1525 (Studien zur dogmengeschichtliche und systematische Theologie, 27; 1970). U. Gäbler and E. Herkenrath (eds.), Heinrich Bullinger 1504–1575: Gesammelte Aufsätze zum 400. Todestag (Zürcher Beiträge zur Reformationsgeschichte, 7–8; 1975). J. W. Baker, Heinrich Bullinger and the Covenant (Athens, Oh., 1980). R. C. Walton, 'Heinrich Bullinger und die Autorität der Schrift', in M. Brecht (ed.), Texte—Worte—Glaube (Arbeiten zur Kirchengeschichte, 50; 1980), pp. 274–97. H. U. Bächtold, Heinrich Bullinger vor dem Rat: Zur Gestaltung und Verwaltung des Zürcher Staatswesens in den Jahren 1531 bis 1575 (Berne, 1982). F. Büsser, Wurzeln der Reformation in Zürich (Studies in Medieval and Reformation Thought, 31; Leiden, 1985), pp. 106–98. Id. in TRE 7 (1981), pp. 375–87, s.v.

Bulteel, Henry Bellenden (1800–66), Protestant controversialist. A native of Devonshire, Bulteel was educated at Brasenose College, Oxford, and elected a Fellow of Exeter in 1824. In 1826 he became Curate of St Ebbe's church in Oxford; he resigned his fellowship on his marriage in 1829. In 1831 he preached a University Sermon on predestination and free will, in which he was outspoken about the state of the University and the C of E. Later in the year, partly on account of this sermon and partly because of his preaching in dissenting chapels, the Bp. of Oxford revoked his licence. He left the C of E and conducted services on Strict *Baptist lines in a chapel of his own. His followers were known as Bulteelers. In 1832 he attended the chapel of E. *Irving in London and for a time adopted some of his tenets. He also became convinced of the doctrine of universal redemption, which he propounded in his appendix to The Unknown Tongues by E. Irving and N. Armstrong (1832). In his Doctrine of the Miraculous Interference of Jesus on Behalf of Believers (1832) he claimed to have healed three women. His other works include an anonymous denunciation of the *Tractarians in 1845.

J. S. Reynolds, The Evangelicals at Oxford 1735–1871 (Oxford, 1953), pp. 97–9 and 162. G. C. Boase in DNB 7 (1886), p. 261.

Bultmann, Rudolf (1884–1976), NT scholar and theologian. After studying at *Marburg, *Tübingen, and Berlin he became Privatdozent at Marburg in 1912, Extraordinary Professor at Breslau in 1916, and Professor at Giessen in 1920. From 1921 until his retirement in 1951 he was Professor of NT Studies at Marburg.

A pupil of H. *Gunkel, J. *Weiss, and W. Heitmüller, and a follower of the '*Religionsgeschichtliche Schule' (esp. of W. *Wrede and W. *Bousset), Bultmann carried their history-of-traditions method (cf. *FORM CRITICISM) to the point at which any historical value in the Gospels was called radically into question. He did this notably in his Die Geschichte der synoptischen Tradition (1921; enlarged 1931, and repr. with supplement, 1957–8; Eng. tr., 1963). In his Jesus (1926; Eng. tr., Jesus and the Word, 1934), he presented the mission of Jesus as summoning His hearers to a decision (Entscheidung). This call to accept His proclamation and to obey His radical demand meant that Jesus understood Himself as the one in whom God finally and savingly present, that is to say, it implied a *Christology. Bultmann combined his biblical scholarship with the *dialectical theology of K. *Barth and the *Lutheran sola fide to make an almost complete hiatus between history and faith, leaving only the bare fact (dass) of Christ crucified as necessary for Christian faith. This kerygmatic theology, based on a Lutheran existentialist interpretation of the NT, received classic expression in his commentary on St *John's Gospel (KEK 2; 1941; Eng. tr., 1971) and *Theologie des Neuen Testaments* (1948–53; Eng. tr., 1952–5). St *Paul and the author of Jn. are treated as the only genuine theologians in the NT, because they offer an interpretation of human existence and see talk of God, Christ, and salvation in terms of the individual's changed self-understanding effected by the proclaimed Word or *kerygma. Narrowing the theological focus in this way involved criticizing the cosmological elements in the NT as 'myth' and it was his programme of '*demythologizing' the NT which in the 1940s and 1950s made Bultmann notorious. Latterly his aim to make the Christian message intelligible in the modern world has been more widely respected, and his hermeneutical concerns have been developed by RC and even conservative evangelical theologians.

After the completion of his doctoral thesis, *Der Stil der paulinischen Predigt und die kynisch-stoische Diatribe* (pub. in 1910) and his 1912 *Habilitionschrift, Die Exegese des Theodore von Mopsuestia* (posthumously pub., 1984), Bultmann developed his views on the NT and theology in a number of writings. Besides those already mentioned, they include *Das Urchristentum im Rahmen der antiken Religionen* (1949; Eng. tr., 1956), his *Gifford Lectures for 1955 entitled *History and Eschatology* (1957), *Jesus Christ and Mythology* (1958), *Die drei Johannesbriefe* (KEK 14; 1967; Eng. tr., Philadelphia [1973]), *Der zweite Brief an die Korinther*, ed. E. Dinkler (KEK 6; 1976; Eng. tr., Minneapolis [1985]), and the posthumously pub. *Theologische Enzyklopädie* (1984), as well as 27 contributions to G. *Kittel's *Theologisches Wörterbuch zum Neuen Testament* (9 vols., 1933–73; Eng. tr., 1964–76).

Bultmann pub. a collection of essays, *Glauben und Verstehen* (4 vols., Tübingen, 1933–65; Eng. tr. of most of vol. 1 as *Faith and Understanding*, 1, 1969; of vol. 2 as *Essays Philosophical and Theological*, 1955); a collection of his sermons (Tübingen, 1956; Eng. tr., 1960); and a collection of papers on the NT, *Exegetica*, ed. E. Dinkler (ibid., 1967). There are further collections of his essays ed. and tr. into Eng. by S. M. Ogden, *Existence and Faith* (Cleveland, Oh., 1960; London, 1961) and *New Testament and Mythology* (Philadelphia, 1984; London, 1985), both including some unpub. material. The correspondence between Barth and Bultmann was ed. B. Jaspert in the *Gesamtausgabe* of Barth's Works, 5.1 (Zurich [1971]; Eng. tr., Edinburgh, 1982). Other letters are available in Tübingen University Library.

C. A. Braaten and R. A. Harrisville (eds. and trs.), *Kerygma and History: A symposium on the theology of Rudolf Bultmann* (Nashville and New York, 1962); C. W. Kegley (ed.), *The Theology of Rudolf Bultmann* (1966); W. Schmithals, *Die Theologie Rudolf Bultmanns* (Tübingen, 1966, 2nd edn., 1967; Eng. tr., 1968); B. Jaspert (ed.), *Rudolf Bultmanns Werk und Werkung* (Darmstadt, 1984); M. Evang, *Rudolf Bultmann in seiner Frühzeit* (Beiträge zur historischen Theologie, 74; Tübingen [1988]), with list of Bultmann's works, pp. 341–50. [S.] G. [J.] Jones, *Bultmann: Towards a Critical Theology* (Cambridge, 1991). See also bibl. to DEMYTHOLOGIZING.

Bunsen, Christian Carl Josias von, also known as 'Chevalier Bunsen' (1791–1860), German diplomatist and amateur theologian. From 1823 to 1839 he was minister at the Prussian legation at Rome, where he proved himself a masterly diplomat and settled delicate matters connected with the relations between Germany and the Holy See. After two years as minister at Berne, he held the same office in London from 1841 to 1854. Here he was regarded as the most distinguished representative of European Prot-

estantism in England and was the chief instrument in the scheme for a joint Lutheran and Anglican bishopric in *Jerusalem. His voluminous and verbose theological writings, for the most part of little enduring value, include a treatise on the Epp. of St *Ignatius (1874); *Hippolytus and his Age* (4 vols., 1852); *Christianity and Mankind* (7 vols., 1855, an English version of some earlier writings, then first published as one work); *Gott in der Geschichte* (3 vols., 1857–8; Eng. tr., 1868–70); and *Vollständiges Bibelwerk für die Gemeinde* (9 vols., 1858–70).

Memoir by Frances, Baroness Bunsen, widow (2 vols., London, 1868). L. von *Ranke, *Aus dem Briefwechsel Friedrich Wilhelms IV. mit Bunsen* (1873). R. A. D. Owen, *Christian Bunsen and Liberal English Theology* (University of Wisconsin thesis, 1924). W. Höcker, *Der Gesandte Bunsen als Vermittler zwischen Deutschland und England* (Göttinger Bausteine zur Geschichtswissenschaft, 1; 1951). E. Geldbach (ed.), *Der gelehrte Diplomat: Zum Wirken Christian Carl Josias Bunsens* (Beihefte der Zeitschrift für Religions- und Geistesgeschichte, 21; Leiden, 1980). J. Rogerson, *Old Testament Criticism in Nineteenth Century England and Germany* (1984), pp. 121–9.

Bunting, Jabez (1779–1858), Wesleyan *Methodist minister. A native of Manchester, he was received on trial into the Methodist ministry in 1799 and admitted into full connexion in 1803 as minister at Oldham Street Chapel, Manchester. He worked in several large towns until in 1833 he was permanently attached to the Methodist headquarters in London. In 1835 he became president of the first Wesleyan Theological College, established at Hoxton. His main work was to transform the Methodist society into a Church, possessed of a sound and consolidated organization, independent of the C of E. He was anxious, however, to work in harmony with the Established Church. He also took a keen interest in foreign missions and was for 18 years secretary of the Wesleyan Missionary Society. Despite his love of political and religious freedom, he distrusted the more radical forms of democracy that commended themselves to many Nonconformists of the 19th cent.

Correspondence, 1820–9, ed. W. R. Ward (Camden Society, 4th ser. 11; 1972); Correspondence, 1830–58, ed. id. (Oxford, 1976). Life by his son, Thomas Percival Bunting (2 vols., London, 1859–87). J. [H. S.] Kent, *The Age of Disunity* (1966), pp. 44–85 and 103–26.

Bunyan, John (1628–88), author of *The *Pilgrim's Progress*. Of the external details of his life comparatively little is known. Born at Elstow in Bedfordshire, he was the son of poor parents (his father was a brazier, a trade he himself followed—hence the loose description of him as a 'tinker'), and probably acquired his knowledge and mastery of the English language from reading the Bible. He took part in the Civil War on the Parliamentary side (1644–6). About 1649 he married a woman of piety who introduced him to A. Dent's *Plain Man's Pathway to Heaven* and Bp. L. *Bayly's *Practice of Piety*, and these, together with the Bible, the BCP, and J. *Foxe's *Book of Martyrs*, seem to have been his sole reading. In 1653 he was received into an *Independent Congregation at Bedford, and after being formally recognized as a preacher in 1657, he soon became well known in that capacity. He suffered much from the repressive measures of the royalists after the Restoration of 1660, and spent most of the years 1660–72 in Bedford gaol. During and after his imprisonment he wrote extensively, including some verse compositions. Of his prose works, the chief and most famous are his autobiography, *Grace Abounding to the Chief of Sinners* (1666); *The Pilgrim's Progress* (q.v.; 1678 and 1684); and *The Holy War* (1682). For the rest of his life after his release in 1672, he worked among the Independents at Bedford, and took part in evangelistic work in other parts of the country. One of his last writings was a treatise, *Antichrist and his Ruin* (1692, posthumously pub. among his collected works), against the Church of Rome, whose influence in England under *James II he much feared. If history and biography furnish little aid in understanding the personality of Bunyan, his chief writings demonstrate that to him the world was exclusively the scene of a spiritual warfare and that nothing mattered save the salvation of the soul. In the ASB, feast day, 31 Aug.

First edn. of collected Works, vol. 1 (all pr.), London, 1692. Later edns. by G. Offer (3 vols., Edinburgh, 1852–3) and H. Stebbing (4 vols., London, 1859–60). Crit. edns. of *Miscellaneous Works* under the general editorship of R. Sharrock (13 vols., Oxford, 1976–94), of *Grace Abounding* by id. (ibid., 1962), *The Holy War* by id. and J. F. Forrest (ibid., 1980), and of *The Life and Death of Mr. Badman* by idd. (ibid., 1988). Lives by R. *Southey (London, 1830), J. A. Froude ('English Men of Letters', 1880), R. Sharrock (HUL, 1954), and G. [S.] Wakefield (London, 1992). [J. E.] C. Hill, *A Turbulent, Seditious and Factious People: John Bunyan and his Church* (Oxford, 1988). R. L. Greaves, *John Bunyan* (Courtenay Studies in Reformation Theology, 2; Appleford, Berks [1969]). N. H. Keeble, *The Literary Culture of Nonconformity in Later Seventeenth-Century England* (Leicester, 1987), *passim*; id. (ed.), *John Bunyan, Conventicle and Parnassus: Tercentenary Essays* (Oxford, 1988). A. Laurence and others (eds.), *John Bunyan and his England, 1628–88* (1990). J. F. Forrest and R. L. Greaves, *John Bunyan: A reference guide* (Boston [1982]).

Buonarroti. See MICHELANGELO.

Burchard (*c*.965–1025), Bp. of Worms from 1000. He was one of the most influential bishops of his time, and was successful in asserting episcopal authority in the secular affairs of his diocese, in building new churches, in forming new parishes, and in disciplining his clergy. Between *c*.1008 and 1012 he compiled his *Decretum*, a collection of *canon law, which exercised great influence in the 11th and 12th cents.

Decretum [ed. B. Questenburgh] (Cologne, 1548); also pr. Paris, 1549, repr. in J. P. Migne, *PL* 140. 537–1058. A Life, approx. contemporary, ed. G. Waitz in *MGH*, Scriptores, 4 (1841), pp. 829–46; repr. J. P. Migne, loc. cit., 505–36. Crit. edn. by H. Boos, *Monumenta Wormatiensia: Annalen und Chroniken* (Quellen zur Geschichte der Stadt Worms, 3; 1893), pp. 97–126, with discussion pp. xxvi f. Two later Lives ed. O. Holder-Egger in *MGH*, Scriptores, 15 (pt. 1; 1887), pp. 44–62, of which one has been re-ed. by F. J. Bendel (Paderborn, 1912). P. Fournier and G. Le Bras, *Histoire des collections canoniques en Occident depuis les Fausses Décrétales jusqu'au Décret de Gratien*, 1 (1931), pp. 364–421; H. Fuhrmann, *Einfluss und Verbreitung der pseudoisidorischen Fälschungen* (Schriften der *MGH*, 24), 2 (1973), pp. 442–85. G. Fransen, 'Le Décret de Burchard de Worms. Valeur du texte de l'édition. Essai de classement des manuscrits', *Zeitschrift der Savigny-Stiftung für Rechtsgeschichte*, 94, Kanonistische Abteilung, 63 (1977), pp. 1–19. H. Hoffmann and R. Pokorny, *Das Dekret des Bischofs Burchard von Worms* (*MGH*, Hilfsmittel, 12; 1991). C. Munier in *NCE* 2 (1967), pp. 887 f., s.v. 'Burchard, Decretum

of'; R. Kaiser and M. Kerner in *Lexikon des Mittelalters*, 2 (1983), pp. 946–51, s.v. 'Burchard (13), Bf. v. Worms'.

Burckard (or Burchard), John (d. 1506), Papal Master of Ceremonies. Born in a village near Strasbourg, he first went to Rome in Oct. 1467 and soon began to amass progressively more important benefices. He was canon of St Thomas's, Strasbourg, from 1477, a Papal Chaplain from 1478 with some duties in the Papal Chapel, and was a non-participating *Protonotary from Feb. 1481, though he seems to have had no particular canon law appointment. He was consecrated Bp. of Città Castellana and made a Cardinal in 1504, having been made Papal Master of Ceremonies in 1483.

Burckard assisted his predecessor, Agostino Patrizzi, with the revision of the *Pontificale Romanum* (1485) and with the production of a new *Caeremoniale Romanum* (completed 1488 and published in 1516). His major work was a detailed set of rubrics for *Low Mass, the *Ordo servandus per sacerdotem in celebratione Missae*, originally published at Rome in 1502. It went through several editions and was the basis of the *Ritus Celebrandi* of 1570. It was the first attempt to lay down the ceremonial for this form of Mass. Burckard's diary, begun in 1483, was a series of notes on Papal ceremonial that steadily increased in scope and which provides a primary source for the history of the Papacy in the late 15th and early 16th cents.

His *Diarium sive Rerum Urbanarum Commentarii* (1483–1506) ed. L. Thuasne (3 vols., Paris, 1883–5), with 'notice biographique' in vol. 3, pp. i–lxviii. Eng. tr. of vol. 1, 1910. Modern repr. of his *Ordo servandus per sacerdotem in celebratione Missae* in J. W. Legg, *Tracts on the Mass* (HBS 27; 1904), pp. 121–78, with introd. pp. xxv–xxviii. B. Schimmelpfenning, *Die Zeremonienbücher der römischen Kurie im Mittelalter* (Bibliothek des Deutschen Historischen Instituts in Rom, 40; 1973), pp. 136–8; M. Dykmans, SJ, *L'Œuvre de Patrizi Piccolomini ou le cérémonial papal de la première renaissance*, 1 (ST 293; 1980), pp. 70*–97*. E. Vansteenberghe in *DHGE* 10 (1938), cols. 1249–51, s.v.

Burdett-Coutts, Angela Georgina (1814–1906), heiress and philanthropist. She was a granddaughter of Thomas Coutts, the banker, from whom she inherited in 1837 nearly £2,000,000. In 1871 she was raised to the peerage. She included among her many public benefactions some munificent gifts to the C of E, building and endowing the churches of St Stephen, Rochester Row, Westminster (1847), St John, Limehouse (1853), St James, Hatcham (1854), St John, Deptford (1855), and St Stephen, *Carlisle (1865). She was led by her interest in colonial expansion and in religion to endow as dependent sees of the Church at home the Anglican bishoprics of Cape Town, South Africa (1847), and Adelaide, Australia (1847), and of British Columbia (1857).

E. Johnson (ed.), *Letters from Charles Dickens to Angela Burdett-Coutts, 1841–1865* (1953). C. B. Patterson (great-niece), *Angela Burdett-Coutts and the Victorians* (1953). Biographies by E. Healey (London, 1978) and D. Orton (ibid., 1980). J. P. Anderson in *DNB, 1901–1911*, 1, pp. 259–66.

Burgher. A member of the group in the Scottish Secession Church which defended in 1747 the lawfulness of the religious clause in the civil Burgess Oath and thus separated from the '*Antiburghers'.

Burgon, John William (1813–88), Dean of *Chichester. Educated at Worcester College, *Oxford, he became a Fellow of Oriel in 1846, Vicar of St Mary's, Oxford, in 1863, and Dean of Chichester in 1876. He was an old-fashioned *High Churchman who was famous for his support of a long series of lost causes. He fiercely denounced the disestablishment of the Irish Church in 1869, the appointment of A. P. *Stanley as a Select Preacher in 1872, and the new BCP lectionary of 1879. He was also a strenuous upholder of the *Textus Receptus of the NT, publishing in 1871 *The Last Twelve Verses of the Gospel according to St *Mark Vindicated*, and in 1883 *The Revision* [i.e. the RV] *Revised*; two further works on the subject were published posthumously. His widely read *Lives of Twelve Good Men* (1888) contained vivid sketches of 19th cent. High Churchmen, often enlivened by Burgon's provocative judgements on his contemporaries.

Life by E. M. *Goulburn (2 vols., London, 1892). A. F. Pollard in *DNB*, Suppl. 1 (1901), pp. 335–8.

Burgundio of Pisa (*c*.1110–93), lawyer. He translated the works of several Greek Fathers into Latin. His version of St *John of Damascus' *De fide orthodoxa* was the best known in the W. until 1507 and was responsible for John's popularity throughout the Middle Ages.

John of Damascus, *De fide orthodoxa: Versions of Burgundio and Cerbanus*, ed. E. M. Buytaert, OFM (Franciscan Institute Publications, text series, 8; St Bonaventure, NY, 1955), pp. 1–386, with list of his translations, p. viii. P. Classen, *Burgundio von Pisa: Richter-Gesandter-Übersetzer* (*Sb.* (Heid.), Jhg. 1974, Abh. 4). F. Liotta in *Dizionario Biografico degli Italiani*, 15 (1972), pp. 423–28, s.v.

Burial Acts. A series of enactments, passed between 1852 and 1900, giving to local authorities powers to deal with the increasing overcrowding of churchyards, and to supervise all burial grounds to secure decency of burial and adequate sanitary precautions. Authority was given for the closing of burial grounds, or their conversion to recreation grounds (in towns), and for the opening of new ones. Various provisions were also made as to the manner of burial, the fees payable, the rights and obligations of the *curate of the parish, and disinterment. By the Local Government Act 1894 permission was given to transfer the powers and duties of the Burial Boards, formerly elected by the vestry, in towns to district councils, and in rural districts to the parish councils. By the Burial Laws Amendment Act 1880, anyone with responsibility for the funeral of a parishioner was entitled to arrange burial in a churchyard or parish graveyard without the use of the Prayer Book or the attendance of a clergyman, with or without any form of Christian service. The Act also permitted C of E clergy to conduct funerals in unconsecrated burial grounds or cemeteries, and to use approved forms of service for the burial of parishioners who by rubric and canon are forbidden burial acc. to the Prayer Book rite.

On the law concerning rights to and duty of burial, see R. *Phillimore, *The Ecclesiastical Law of the Church of England*, 1 (2nd edn., 1895), pp. 650–701; H. W. Cripps, *A Practical Treatise on the Law Relating to the Church and Clergy* (8th edn. by K. M. Macmorran, 1937), pp. 564–89. For the text of the 1880 Act, see R. P. Findall, *The Church of England 1815–1948* (1972), pp. 239–41.

burial services. Burial is the traditional Christian method of disposing of the dead, and in the 4th cent., which is the earliest period of which we have information, the burials were occasions of joy, and those attending them wore white. But from about the 8th cent., when the prevalence of merely nominal Christianity made such joy not always fitting, the service became 'black', and the prayers petitions for speedy purification and for deliverance from hell. By the later Middle Ages the form had become fixed. The burial itself, at which the rite consisted of the committal prayers, was preceded overnight by *Vespers (or *Placebo), after which *Mattins and *Lauds (Dirige or *Dirge) were said in the night, and in the morning *Requiem Mass, with prayers for the absolution of the dead. Requiems were also said on the 3rd, 9th, and 30th day after death, and on anniversaries. In the RC Church the *Ordo Exsequiarum* of 1969 provides that, where it is customary, there can be a service in the house of the deceased and a procession to the church. The Requiem Mass now concludes with a final commendation in place of the absolution of the dead. The 1969 *Ordo* also provides an alternative form of service for use in a cemetery chapel and makes provision, where the *Ordinary permits, for the funeral rites, including the Mass, to take place in a house. Unless they have given signs of repentance before they died, however, none of these rites are to be conducted for notorious apostates, heretics, schismatics, public sinners, or for those who for anti-Christian reasons desired *cremation (*CIC* (1983), can. 1184). In the BCP the Dirge in a modified form (sentences, psalm, and lesson) is ordered, followed at the graveside by the committal prayers, and is to be used for all except those under (greater) excommunication, the unbaptized, and deliberate *suicides. Modern Anglican revisions make alterations of phrasing, allow other alternative psalms and different lessons. In some revisions special forms are provided for the burial of a child. (In the Irish BCP a form is given for an unbaptized child of Christian parents, as well as for an adult who had desired but not received baptism. The ASB makes no mention of any categories for whom its Funeral Service is not to be used; it has special prayers for use at the burial of a still-born or newly-born child, who would presumably be unbaptized.) Modern Anglican rites also recognize cremation, and the ASB has a Form which may be used at the Interment of Ashes. Provision for an (optional) Eucharist is made in modern Anglican burial services. In the Byzantine rite the burial service opens with various prayers and psalms, continues with the singing of the eight odes of the (hymnological) *canon, which includes the *contakion 'Give rest, O Christ, to Thy servant' (*EH* 744), and ends with an *epistle and *gospel, the whole being interspersed with litanies and prayers. The coffin is normally left open, the deceased holding an *icon of Christ and covered with a *pall; four candles are placed round the coffin and those present carry tapers. The body of the deceased is anointed, censed and blessed with *holy water, and the service ends with those present making their farewell with a kiss. A shortened form of this service (Greek: λιτή; Slavonic: *panikhida*) may be celebrated on the 3rd, 9th and 30th days after death, as well as on other occasions for all the departed. See also DEAD, PRAYERS FOR THE, and REQUIEM MASS.

W. Gresswell, *A Commentary on the Order for the Burial of the Dead* (2 vols., 1836). G. Rowell, *The Liturgy of Christian Burial* (Alcuin Club Collections, 59; 1977). D. Sicard, *La liturgie de la mort dans l'église latine des origines à la réforme carolingienne* (Liturgiewissenschaftliche Quellen und Forschungen, 63; 1978). R. Rutherford, *The Death of a Christian: The Rite of Funerals* (Studies in the Reformed Rites of the Catholic Church, 7; New York, 1980; 2nd edn., by Rutherford and T. Barr, Collegeville, Minn., 1990).

Buridan's Ass. The famous 'case', traditionally (but wrongly, it appears) ascribed to the Paris philosopher John Buridanus (*c.*1292–1358 or later), acc. to which an ass, set between two heaps of hay, absolutely equal in respect of quality and quantity, through having no motives to choose one rather than the other, died of starvation. The problem which it poses on the psychology of moral action goes back (though in another context) to *Aristotle.

Buridan's name is also connected, and here too erroneously, with the logical problem known as the *inventio medii* or 'Pons Asinorum', i.e., the bridge by which stupid scholars can find their way from the minor or major to the middle term of a syllogism. In fact the 'Pons Asinorum' is first found in the *Scotist, Peter Tartaretus (Rector of Paris University, 1490).

The problem will be found stated in Aristotle, *De Caelo*, 2. 13, p. 295 b 32. Überweg, 2, p. 597.

Burkhardt, Georg. See SPALATIN, GEORG.

Burkitt, Francis Crawford (1864–1935), NT, Semitic, and patristic scholar. He was educated at Harrow and at Trinity College, Cambridge, and from 1905 till his death he was Norrisian (from 1934 'Norris-Hulse') Professor of Divinity at Cambridge. He was esp. attracted to some of the more out-of-the-way fields in the history of early Christianity, and did important original work on the *Syriac versions of the NT, putting on a wholly new footing the study of the relation of the *Peshitta to the *Old Syriac Gospels. He also made valuable discoveries in the allied field of Syriac liturgies. Among his more important writings, nearly all of which reflect his brilliant and unconventional mind, are *The Old Latin and the Itala* (1896), *St *Ephraim's Quotations from the Gospel* (1901), the art. 'Text and Versions' in the *Encyclopaedia Biblica* (vol. 4, 1903), *Evangelion da-Mepharreshe* (2 vols., 1904), *The Religion of the Manichees* (1925), *Palestine in General History* (Schweich Lectures, 1929) and *Church and Gnosis* (1932).

E. C. Ratcliff, 'Francis Crawford Burkitt', *JTS* 36 (1935), pp. 225–53, with note by G. G. Coulton, ibid., pp. 253 f., and list of his writings pp. 337–46. J. F. Bethune-Baker in *DNB, 1931–1940* (1949), pp. 124 f., s.v.

Burma, Christianity in. Burma, formed from the Kingdoms of Ava and Pegu, came under British rule during the 19th cent. Though Ludovico di Varthema at the beginning of the 16th cent. states that there were Christian soldiers in service of the King of Pegu, it was the arrival of *Portuguese merchants that opened the way for serious attempts to convert the Burmese people to Christianity. The first RC missionary was a French *Franciscan who worked in Pegu for three years in the 1550s. Italian *Barnabites founded a mission in 1722; from 1830 this was transferred to various other religious orders. In 1807 English *Baptists began missionary work, but the first permanent Baptist mission arrived in 1813 from the *United States of America under Adoniram *Judson. Anglican missionary activity was initiated by the *SPG in 1859 and by the *BCMS in 1924; the diocese of Rangoon was formed in 1877. American *Methodists arrived in 1879 and British Methodists in 1887. Christianity gained few converts from Burmese of Buddhist background, but has had some success among the Karens, Kachins, and other tribal minorities. In the RC Church the first indigenous bishop was appointed in 1954 and a hierarchy created in 1955. The Anglican Church, formerly part of the Church of India, Burma, and Ceylon, became a separate Province in 1970. The largest Christian body in the country is the Burma Baptist Convention. For much of the period since independence in 1948, Burma has been ruled by a military-socialist government and contacts with the outside world have been restricted. In 1965–6 the government nationalized all Christian schools and hospitals; foreign missionaries were ordered to leave. In 1989 the country was renamed Myanmar. Christians comprise about 5 per cent of the population.

W. C. B. Purser, *Christian Missions in Burma* (1911); A. McLeish, *Christian Progress in Burma* (1929). P. A. Bigandet, *An Outline of the History of the Burmese Catholic Mission, 1720–1887* (Rangoon, 1887). R. L. Howard, *Baptists in Burma* (Philadelphia [1931]); H. G. Tegenfeldt, *A Century of Growth: The Kachin Baptist Church of Burma* (South Pasadena, Calif. [1974]). H. P. Thompson, *Into All Lands: The History of the Society for the Propagation of the Gospel in Foreign Parts, 1701–1950* (1950), pp. 384–93, with further bibl. p. 732. D. E. Smith, *Religion and Politics in Burma* (Princeton, NJ, 1965), esp. pp. 78–80, 244 f., and 249 f. Latourette, 6 (1944), pp. 225–35, and 7 (1945), pp. 319–23; K. S. Latourette, *Christianity in a Revolutionary Age*, 3 (1961), pp. 419 f., 5 (1963), pp. 338–42. P. Clasper in G. H. Anderson (ed.), *Christ and Crisis in Southeast Asia* (New York [1968]), pp. 13–28.

Burnet, Gilbert (1643–1715), Bp. of *Salisbury. He was a native of Edinburgh, educated at Marischal College, Aberdeen, and in 1661 became a *probationer in the ministry of the Church of Scotland. He travelled widely, was the Minister of Saltoun 1664–9, and Professor of Divinity at Glasgow University from 1669 to 1674, when he settled in England. He enjoyed influence at the English and Scottish royal courts, and from 1675 to 1684 was Chaplain to the *Rolls. In 1685 he went abroad after the collapse of the *Exclusion agitation had led to the execution and exile of some of his friends. There he was much in the confidence of William of Orange and Mary, sailed with William in 1688, and was made Bp. of *Salisbury in 1689. A staunch Whig in politics and a *latitudinarian in theology, he unsuccessfully endeavoured to carry through plans which should allow for the incorporation of the Nonconformists into the C of E. His episcopate was a model of zeal and activity, pastoral and administrative. He was also a voluminous author and a determined political controversialist, his most noteworthy writings being his *History of the Reformation in England* (3 vols., 1679–1714), his *Exposition of the XXXIX Articles* (1699), and his *History of My Own Time* (2 vols., 1723–34).

Burnet's *History of My Own Time*, ed. M. J. *Routh (6 vols., Oxford, 1823) and O. Airy (2 vols., reign of *Charles II only; ibid., 1897–1900; suppl. from unpub. MSS by H. C. Foxcroft, ibid., 1902). The Everyman edn. of 1906 (consisting of T. Stackhouse's abridgement of Bks. 1–4, orig. pub. in 1724, and the full text of Bk. 5) was reissued, with introd. by D. Allen, 1979. The best study is that of T. E. S. Clarke, H. C. Foxcroft, and C. H. Firth (Cambridge, 1907). J. J. Hughes, 'The missing "Last Words" of Gilbert Burnet in July 1687', *Historical Journal*, 20 (1977), pp. 221–7 [text of a document prepared when Burnet's life appeared to be at risk]; J. E. Drabble, 'Gilbert Burnet and the History of the English Reformation: The Historian and his Milieu', *Journal of Religious History*, 12 (1983), pp. 351–63. O. Airy in *DNB* 7 (1886), pp. 394–405.

Burney, Charles Fox (1868–1925), OT and Semitic scholar. In 1899 he was elected a Fellow of St John's College, Oxford, and in 1914 Oriel Professor of the Interpretation of Holy Scripture. He was one of the most original OT scholars of his generation. Among his more important writings are his *Notes on the Hebrew Text of the Book of Kings* (1903), his Schweich Lectures for 1917 on *Israel's Settlement in Canaan* (1918), and his commentary on *Judges* (1918). In his *Aramaic Origin of the Fourth Gospel* (1922) and his *Poetry of Our Lord* (1925), he emphasized the importance of the *Aramaic background of the Gospels for their proper understanding.

burning. Burning alive was a penalty for certain criminal offences in late Roman and early Germanic law and was subsequently adopted in the penal code of most W. European states. In medieval English Common Law burning was the penalty for women found guilty of high treason, petty treason (i.e. conspiring against the life of a husband or employer), or counterfeiting coinage.

The burning of convicted heretics was a medieval development. Although the Emp. *Diocletian had enacted in 287 that *Manichaean leaders should be burned, this law was rescinded by his Christian successors and seems to have had no influence on later practice, even though the *Cathari were known as Manichees in the Middle Ages. In 1022 Robert II of France burned some ten convicted heretics at Orléans, and burning subsequently became the normal penalty for heresy throughout the W. Initially such executions were carried out against the wishes of the Church authorities but in 1184 Pope Lucius III decreed that unrepentant heretics should be handed over to the secular authorities for punishment and this practice was followed by the *Inquisition from its inception. In 1298 *Boniface VIII in the *Sext (5. 2. 18) recommended that the heresy laws of the Emp. *Frederick II should serve as a model in all states. It is widely supposed that this refers to the constitution *Inconsutilem*, promulgated for the Sicilian Kingdom in 1231 and extended to the rest of the Empire in 1238–9, which ordered that heretics should be burned; it may, however, refer to the milder imperial constitution of 1220, which enacted banishment and confiscation of goods for heresy. Even before 1298 all rulers in fact punished heresy by burning. In England the Crown claimed the right to issue a writ to order the burning of condemned heretics, a procedure followed in 1401 by Henry IV in the case of William *Sawtree, a *Lollard. Subsequently the act *De Haeretico Comburendo* (1401) gave statutory force to the burning of heretics. It was repealed in 1533, restored by *Mary, and again repealed in 1558. The *Six Articles of 1539 imposed burning as a penalty for the denial of *transubstantiation, but they were repealed in 1547. *Elizabeth I and *James I ordered her-

etics to be burned for *Arianism and *Anabaptism. The last such burning was in 1610. The Ecclesiastical Jurisdiction Act 1677 abolished the death penalty for heresy and other doctrinal offences.

Criminal acts accomplished by *witchcraft were punishable by burning in early Germanic law. In the later Middle Ages witchcraft was equated with *apostasy as an act of treason to God and both offences, if unrepented, were punishable by burning, but the prosecution of witches was not common before the 16th cent. The penalty in Catholic countries was invariably burning, and this was also the case in some Protestant countries, such as Scotland, though in England witches were hanged. The last burning for witchcraft in the British Isles took place at Dornoch in 1727 and the death penalty for this offence was abolished in the Witchcraft Act 1735. In parts of Europe witches continued to be burned until at least the 1750s.

Burning for heresy declined in the 17th cent., and even in Spain and its dependencies where the Inquisition had the full support of the Crown the death penalty became unusual. Only four people were burned in the half-century before the Spanish Inquisition was abolished in 1808.

Burning remained a penalty for criminal offences in many European states throughout the 18th cent. (in England it was not abolished until 1790), but the offenders were often hanged first, their corpses alone being cremated.

See bibl. to INQUISITION and WITCHCRAFT.

burning bush, the. The scene of *Moses' call, where the Angel of Yahweh appeared to him 'in a flame of fire out of the midst of a bush' (Exod. 3: 2–4). The burning bush has frequently been used by Christian writers as a type of the Blessed Virgin.

Burrough, Edward (*c*.1634–63), *Quaker. Having heard G. *Fox preach in Westmorland in 1652, he determined to become a *Friend and began to preach himself, travelling up and down the country. In 1656 and 1657 he defended Quaker doctrines against an attack by J. *Bunyan. In 1661 he took up with *Charles II the cause of the Quakers in New England, who were then being persecuted by the Puritans, but without much success. In 1662 he was arrested in London for holding a meeting illegal under the Quaker Act and committed to Newgate Prison, where he died. He issued a large number of writings, most of them very brief.

His writings (mainly hortatory treatises and polemical letters) were pub. as *The Memorable Works of a Son of Thunder and Consolation*, ed. E. Hookes (1672). [F. Howgill, G. Whitehead, and others], *A Testimony concerning the Life, Death, Trials, Travels and Labours of Edward Burroughs* ('1662' [1663]). 'A Memoir of the Life and Religious Labours of that Eminent Servant of Christ and Minister of the Gospel, Edward Burrough' in W. and T. Evans (eds.), *The Friends' Library*, 14 (Philadelphia, 1850), pp. 380–491. E. Brockbank, *Edward Burrough: A Wrestler for Truth, 1634–1662* (1949). [J. E.] C. Hill, *The Experience of Defeat* (1984), pp. 143–53.

burse. A cover consisting of two squares of stiffened material in which until 1970 the rubrics of the RC Missal ordered that the *corporal should be kept. Its use became general in the 17th cent.; though no longer required, it is still widely employed both in the RC and Anglican Churches.

Braun, *LP*, pp. 215–17.

Busch, Jan (1399–c.1480). One of the principal members of the *Brethren of the Common Life. He was a native of Zwolle, and from 1420 to 1424 was professor at *Windesheim. In 1424 he was ordained priest at Bödingen, near Cologne, and thereafter filled a variety of offices in the Netherlands and Germany. His ideals were those of the Brotherhood at their best. He took a prominent part in reforming the monasteries in the spirit of the Council of *Basle and for a time worked in close cooperation with *Nicholas of Cusa, who appointed him 'Visitor Apostolic' of the *Augustinian houses of Saxony and Thuringia. He also wrote the history of the Brethren's house at Windesheim.

His *Chronicon* was first pub. by the *Bollandist, H. Rosweyde, SJ, at Antwerp, 1621, while a treatise 'De Reformatione Monasteriorum quorundam Saxoniae' first appeared in G. W. *Leibniz's *Scriptores Rerum Brunsvicensium*, 2 (1710), pp. 476–506 and 806–972. New edn. of both by K. Grube (Halle, 1886). Lives by K. Grube (Freiburg i.B., 1881) and S. van der Woude (Diss., Edam, 1947). C. Minis in *Verfasserlexikon* (2nd edn.), 1 (1978), cols. 1140–2, s.v.

Bushnell, Horace (1802–76), American *Congregational divine. Born at Bantam, nr. Litchfield, Conn., USA, he graduated at Yale University in 1827 and was assistant editor of the New York *Journal of Commerce* from 1828 to 1829. In 1829 he became a tutor at Yale, at first studying law until, throwing off his religious doubts during a college revival, he entered the theological department of Yale College in 1831. From 1833 to 1859 he was pastor to the North Congregational Church of Hartford, Conn. Owing to ill-health he held no official position in his later years, though he continued active as a writer. In 1856 he assisted in the organization of the College of California at Oakland.

Bushnell was the pioneer of liberal theology in New England. Characteristic was his restatement of the doctrine of the Trinity. On the ground that language was essentially symbolic and relative to the subject, he held that while this doctrine might be true for man in that God was experienced under three different aspects, it did not give him real information as to the inner nature of the Godhead or require the existence of eternal distinctions in His Being. He also stressed the immanence of God in creation, explaining miracles as part of the Divine law of nature, and he interpreted the *Atonement in terms of moral influence to the rejection of penal theories of satisfaction. Among his chief works were *Christian Nurture* (1847), *God in Christ* (1849), *Christ in Theology* (1851), *Nature and the Supernatural* (1858), *Work and Play* (1864), *The Vicarious Sacrifice* (1866), *Sermons on Living Subjects* (1872), and *Forgiveness and Law* (1874).

Selection of his writings, ed. H. S. Smith (Library of Protestant Thought; New York, 1965), with introd. and bibl. M. B. Cheney (his daughter), *Life and Letters of H. Bushnell* (ibid., 1880). B. M. Cross, *Horace Bushnell: Minister to a Changing America* (Chicago [1958]); W. A. Johnson, *Nature and the Supernatural in the Theology of Horace Bushnell* (Studia Theologica Lundensia, 25; 1963); J. O. Duke, *Horace Bushnell on the Vitality of Biblical Language* (Society of Biblical Literature, Centennial Publications, Chico, Calif. [1984]).

Butler, Alban (1710–73), author of *The Lives of the Saints*. Educated at *Douai, he was ordained priest in the RC Church in 1735. After long studies and many travels on the Continent in search of hagiographical material, he published in 1756–9 *The Lives of the Fathers, Martyrs and other principal Saints, compiled from original Monuments and other authentic records, illustrated with the remarks of judicious modern critics and historians*. The *Lives* (over 1,600) are arranged acc. to the Church calendar, and, though their chief purpose was edification, and history and legend are not distinguished, they remain a monument of wide research. From 1746 to 1766 Butler was a mission priest in England in the Midland District. From 1766 until his death he was President of the English College at *St-Omer, where he was a frequent counsellor of the French clergy.

Drastically rev. edn. of *The Lives of the Saints*, by H. Thurston, SJ, N. Leeson, and D. Attwater (12 vols., 1926–38). *A Dictionary of Saints* to serve also as index to the rev. edn. was compiled by D. Attwater (London, 1938), and suppl. vol., by id. (ibid., 1949). New revision of *Lives* (abbreviated, but further improved) by D. Attwater, incl. substance of *Dictionary* and of suppl. vol. (4 vols., 1956). [Charles Butler, nephew], *An Account of the Life and Writings of the Rev. Alban Butler* (1799). E. H. Burton, *The Life and Times of Bishop Challoner*, 1 (1909), pp. 166 f., 221–4, 331 f.; 2 (1909), p. 161, incl. extracts from his letters and a portrait. T. Cooper in *DNB* 7 (1886), pp. 43 f.

Butler, Joseph (1692–1752), Bp. of *Durham. A native of Wantage, Oxon, and the son of *Presbyterian parents, he studied at the dissenting academy at Tewkesbury, where T. *Secker was his fellow-student. At an early age he entered into a correspondence with S. *Clarke on his 'Boyle Lectures' which revealed his remarkable powers of reasoning. Abandoning Presbyterianism he entered Oriel College, Oxford, in 1714, was ordained deacon and, two months later, priest, at *Salisbury in 1718, and from 1718 to 1726 was preacher at the *Rolls Chapel. Here he delivered the sermons which won him his reputation. Fifteen were published in 1726, with an important preface, to which six others were added in later editions. In 1722 he had been presented to the rectory of Haughton-le-Skerne, nr. Darlington, and this he exchanged in 1726 for the wealthy benefice of Stanhope, Co. Durham. Here he lived in seclusion, engaged in pastoral duties and preparing his famous *Analogy of Religion* (1736; q.v.). In 1736, through Secker's influence, he was appointed Clerk of the Closet and from now on was constantly in attendance on Queen Caroline till her death (20 Nov. 1737). Commended to George II by the Queen on her death-bed, Butler was rewarded in 1738 with the poorly endowed see of Bristol, where he came into hostility with J. *Wesley and G. *Whitefield. To supplement his income, he was preferred in 1740 to the deanery of *St Paul's *in commendam*, and in 1750 he was translated to the bishopric of Durham. He is said (apocryphally) to have declined the see of *Canterbury in 1747 as he believed it 'too late to try to support a falling Church'.

Butler ranks among the greatest exponents of natural theology and ethics in England since the Reformation. His writings, which were esp. directed against attacks on the Christian conception of the world and the fundamental grounds of morality, stand out by their firm grasp of principle, sustained reasoning, caution, moral force, and, at times, irony. Their elevated tone is in marked contrast with that of the writings which they oppose; and, though his works make considerable demands on the reader, their moral qualities have won for them a permanent place in English literature.

Butler's moral philosophy, developed in his *Fifteen Sermons* and in the 'Dissertation on Virtue', appended to the *Analogy*, is directed esp. against the theories of T. *Hobbes, which had risen to popularity in the 18th cent. He maintained that true morality consisted in living in accordance with one's nature and that the primary constituent principles in human nature were self-love, benevolence, and conscience. Actions whose motives lie in the natural passions and instincts do not conform with the interests either of self-love or of benevolence. In criticism of the hedonists of his age, Butler argued that the desire for an object was evoked by the desired object itself, and not by any anticipation of the resulting satisfaction, and that true benevolence or love of one's neighbour was strictly disinterested. To conscience attached a supreme authority which compelled in those who admitted it an obedience which could not consider consequences. The principles of morality were intuitively evident and errors of moral judgement arose only from superstition and self-deception. Belief in Providence, however, convinced Butler that in the end the dictates of conscience and the demands of self-love will be found to have pointed to the same conclusion. (For his apologetic position, see ANALOGY OF RELIGION.)

The writings of Butler went through a number of editions in the 18th cent., but for a long time did not attract the serious attention which they merited. Throughout the 19th cent. they were widely studied by Anglican candidates for Ordination. J. H. *Newman acknowledged his great debt to the teaching of the *Analogy* on probability and the sacramentalism of nature. In the American BCP (1979), feast day, 16 June.

The best edn. of his Works is that by W. E. *Gladstone (2 vols., 1896), with a suppl. vol. of *Subsidiary Studies* (also 1896). T. Bartlett, *Memoirs of Joseph Butler* (1839); W. A. Spooner, *Bishop Butler* (1901); C. D. Broad, *Five Types of Ethical Theory* (1930), pp. 53–83; E. C. Mossner, *Bishop Butler and the Age of Reason* (New York, 1936); A. Duncan-Jones, *Butler's Moral Philosophy* (1952); P. A. Carlsson, *Butler's Ethics* (1964); J. Downey, *The Eighteenth Century Pulpit: A Study of the Sermons of Butler* [and others] (Oxford, 1969), pp. 30–57; I. [T.] Ramsey, *Joseph Butler . . .: Some Features of his Life and Thought* (Friends of Dr Williams's Library, Lecture 23; 1969); T. Penelhum, *Butler* (1985); C. Cunliffe (ed.), *Joseph Butler's Moral and Religious Thought: Tercentenary Essays* (Oxford, 1992). L. Stephen in *DNB* 8 (1886), pp. 67–72.

Butler, Josephine Elizabeth (1828–1906), social reformer. She was the daughter of John Grey of Dilston, and in 1852 married George Butler (1819–90), sometime Canon of *Winchester. Her main interest was in the reclamation of prostitutes and the suppression of the 'white slave' trade. To this end she formed in 1869 the 'Ladies' National Association for the Repeal of the Contagious Diseases Acts', and in 1875 called a meeting at Geneva which resulted in the establishment of the International Federation for the Abolition of the State Regulation of Vice. Her inspiring work can best he studied in her *Personal Reminiscences of a Great Crusade* (1896). Behind her activities as a reformer lay a life of almost continuous

prayer in which she took as her model St *Catherine of Siena (whose Life she published in 1878). In the ASB, feast day, 30 Dec.

G. W. and L. A. Johnson, *Josephine E. Butler: An Autobiographical Memoir* (1909). G. Petrie, *A Singular Iniquity: The Campaigns of Josephine Butler* (1971). Other studies by A. S. G. Butler (grandson; London, 1954), E. M. Bell (ibid., 1962) and J. Williamson (grandson; ibid., 1977). E. S. Hooper in *DNB, 1901–1911*, 1, pp. 282 f.

Butler, William John (1818–94), Dean of *Lincoln. Educated at Westminster and at Trinity College, Cambridge, he was ordained in 1841, and in 1846 became Vicar of Wantage. Here through a long incumbency he was a model parish priest of the *High Church school and trained several curates who later became famous (A. H. *Mackonochie, V. S. S. Coles, W. C. E. Newbolt, H. P. *Liddon, etc.). The Wantage diaries covering his incumbency (preserved in the Berkshire Record Office) provide one of the most detailed accounts of Tractarian parochial work in practice. In 1848 he founded in his parish St Mary's Sisterhood, which as the Community of St Mary the Virgin (CSMV) has grown into one of the largest and most active of the Anglican religious communities. In 1864 he was elected to the bishopric of Natal after J. W. *Colenso's deposition; but owing to Abp. C. T. *Longley's disapproval, declined the invitation. In 1880 he became a canon of *Worcester and in 1885 Dean of Lincoln. He remained warden of the CSMV.

Life and Letters of William John Butler [ed. by A. J. Butler (son)] (1897); [A. L. Hoare] CSMV, *Butler of Wantage: His Inheritance and his Legacy* [1948]. T. Seccombe in *DNB*, suppl. 1 (1901), pp. 359 f.

Butterfield, William (1814–1900), architect. A keen Churchman who had come under the influence of the *Oxford Movement, Butterfield was inspired by the architectural ideals of the *Cambridge Camden Society. His works include: St Augustine's College, *Canterbury (1844–8); Cumbrae College (1844–51); All Saints', Margaret Street, London (1849–59); St Alban's Holborn (1859–1862); buildings at Rugby School (1867–85); Keble College, Oxford (1867–83); and the three Anglican cathedrals at Perth (1847–90), Adelaide (1868–78), and Melbourne (1877–91) in Australia. He was also a noted designer of church furnishing.

Full study by P. [R.] Thompson, *William Butterfield* (London, 1971). *Victorian Church Art: Exhibition Catalogue, Victoria and Albert Museum* (1971), pp. 22–32. P. Waterhouse in *DNB*, suppl. 1 (1901), pp. 360–3.

Butzer, Martin. See BUCER, MARTIN.

Bye Plot (1603). Also known as the **Priests' Plot**. The lesser of two plots (the 'Main' and the 'Bye' plots) against *James I of England at his accession. William Watson and William Clarke, two RC priests, conspired with George Brooke and Lord Grey of Wilton, two Protestants out of sympathy with the new regime, to kidnap the King's person and extort concessions from him, partly on behalf of the *recusants. The plot was revealed by a Jesuit and another RC priest; Watson, Clarke, and Brooke were executed, and Lord Grey died in prison.

Byrd, William (1543–1623), English composer. Prob. born at *Lincoln and a pupil of T. *Tallis at the *Chapel Royal, he was appointed organist of Lincoln Cathedral in 1563. In 1570 he was sworn as a Gentleman of the Chapel Royal, where he became organist with Tallis. In 1575 he and Tallis were jointly granted a monopoly of printing music. He resided at Stondon Massey, Essex, from 1593.

Though he was a practising Catholic and involved in frequent litigation for recusancy, Byrd's religion never seems to have prevented him executing his duties in the Chapel Royal. Besides his three superb Masses (written *c.*1593–*c.*1595), his two books of *Gradualia* (1605 and 1607), and other music for the Latin rite, he set to music the Preces and Responses and Litany of the English liturgy and composed at least two complete Services ('Short Service' and 'Great Service') for Morning and Evening Prayer, and two other Evening Services. In addition to writing various sacred songs and setting to music Latin motets, he was one of the pioneers of the verse anthem. His many anthems include 'Sing Joyfully', 'Sing Merrily', and 'Bow Thine Ear'. He also wrote a large body of string music, keyboard music and secular choral music, esp. madrigals. His publications include *Cantiones Sacrae* (jointly with T. Tallis, 1575), *Psalms, Sonnets and Songs* (1588), *Songs of Sundry Natures* (1589), two further books of *Cantiones Sacrae* (1589 and 1591) and *Psalmes, Songs and Sonnets* (1611).

Complete Works ed. E. H. Fellowes (20 vols., London, 1937–50); new edn. by P. Brett (ibid., 1976 ff.). E. H. Fellowes, *William Byrd* (Oxford, 1936; 2nd edn., 1948); J. Kerman, *The Masses and Motets of William Byrd* (1981). Id. in S. Sadie (ed.), *The New Grove Dictionary of Music and Musicians*, 3 (1980), pp. 537–52.

Byrhtferth (d. *c.*1020), Anglo-Saxon scholar. He was a monk of Ramsey Abbey and a student of *Abbo of Fleury during the latter's time in charge of the monastic school (985–7), but little else is known of his life. He left a substantial corpus of computistical, hagiographical, and historical writings. These include a computus (principally preserved in Oxford, St John's College MS 17) and a commentary, partly in English, on this computus and known as the *Enchiridion* (written in 1011); Lives of St *Oswald (Abp. of *York and founder of Ramsey) and St Ecgwine (an early 8th-cent. Bp. of *Worcester and founder of Evesham Abbey); and a historical miscellany known as the *Historia regum* which draws heavily on earlier sources such

as *Bede and Asser's *Life of Alfred* and treats English history up to the reign of *Alfred; it was long attributed to *Simeon of Durham. Byrhtferth was clearly a scholar of exceptionally wide reading (he is the only Anglo-Saxon author whose range of interests will bear comparison with Bede's), but his writing is marred by pedantry and stylistic pretension.

The *Enchiridion* and *Computus* are ed. by P. [S.] Baker and M. Lapidge (EETS, suppl. scr. 15; 1995); *Vita S. Oswaldi*, ed. J. Raine, *The Historians of the Church of York and its Archbishops*, 1 (RS, 1879), pp. 399–475; *Vita S. Ecgwini*, ed. [J. A.] Giles, *Vita quorundam* [sic] *Anglo-Saxonum* (London, 1854), pp. 349–96 (these two Lives are both preserved uniquely in Brit. Lib. Cotton MS, Nero E. i; crit. edn., with Eng. tr. by M. Lapidge, Oxford Medieval Texts, in preparation); *Historia regum*, ed. T. Arnold, *Symeonis Monachi Opera Omnia*, 2 (RS, 1885), pp. 3–91. G. F. Forsey, 'Byrhtferth's *Preface*', *Speculum*, 3 (1928), pp. 505–22; C. [R.] Hart, 'Byrhtferth and his *Manual*', *Medium Ævum*, 41 (1972), pp. 95–109; P. S. Baker, 'The Old English Canon of Byrhtferth of Ramsey', *Speculum*, 55 (1980), pp. 22–37; id., 'Byrhtferth's *Enchiridion* and the Computus in Oxford, St John's College 17', *Anglo-Saxon England*, 10 (1982), pp. 123–42. S. J. Crawford, 'Byrhtferth of Ramsey and the Anonymous Life of St Oswald', in *Speculum Religionis: Essays and Studies in Religion and Literature . . . presented . . . to . . . Claude G. Montefiore* (Oxford, 1929), pp. 99–111; M. Lapidge, 'Byrhtferth and the *Vita S. Ecgwini*', *Mediaeval Studies*, 41 (1979), pp. 331–53. Id., 'Byrhtferth of Ramsey and the Early Sections of the *Historia Regum* attributed to Symeon of Durham', *Anglo-Saxon England*, 10 (1982), pp. 97–122.

Byzantine rite. The liturgical rite of the E. *Orthodox Church, so called because it was the rite used in *Constantinople (anciently the city of Byzantium).

Byzantine text of the NT. The form of the Greek NT text which has become the standard one in the Greek-speaking Church, now more generally known as the '*Lucianic Text' (q.v.). It is to be found in the great majority of the extant Greek MSS of the NT, and was closely followed by *Erasmus in his 'Greek Testament' (1516) and in the *Textus Receptus. It is probably in essentials the text of *Lucian of Antioch, somewhat corrupted, and perhaps also further 'revised', in the course of transmission. See also SYRIAN TEXT.

Byzantium. See CONSTANTINOPLE.

C

Cabasilas, St Nicholas (b. *c.*1322), Byzantine mystical writer. The nephew of Nilus Cabasilas, Abp. of Thessalonica (with whom he has often been confused), he appears to have remained a layman throughout his life. The date of his death is unknown. In his principal work, a set of seven discourses 'Concerning the Life in Christ' (Περὶ τῆς ἐν Χριστῷ ζωῆς), he explained how, through the three mysteries of *Baptism, *Confirmation, and the *Eucharist, spiritual union with Christ was to be achieved. He also wrote an 'Interpretation of the Divine Liturgy' ('Ερμηνεία τῆς θείας λειτουργίας). Although contemporary with the *Hesychast controversy and on friendly terms with the supporters of *Gregory Palamas, in these works he does not adopt the characteristic Palamite standpoint, and nowhere mentions the *Jesus Prayer, but he defends Palamism in a short work against Nicephoras Gregoras. He was proclaimed a saint in the Orthodox Church in 1983; feast day (in the E.), 20 June.

'Sacrae Liturgicae Interpretatio', Life in Christ, a Sermon 'Contra Feneratores', and Life of St Theodore in J. P. Migne, *PG* 150. 367–772. Three sermons on the Nativity, Annunciation, and Dormition of the BVM ed., with Lat. tr. and introd., by M. Jugie, AA, in *PO* 19 (1926), pp. 456–510. The work against Nicephoras Gregoras is ed. A. Garzya in *Byzantion*, 24 for 1954 [1956], pp. 521–32. Crit. edns. of his *Interpretation of the Divine Liturgy* by R. Bornert, OSB, and others, with Fr. tr. and notes by S. Salaville, AA (SC 4bis; 1967), and of his *Life in Christ* by M.-H. Congourdeau, with Fr. tr. (ibid. 355 and 361; 1989–90). Eng. trs. of *Interpretation* by J. M. Hussey and P. A. McNulty, with introd. by R. M. French (1960); of *Life in Christ* by C. J. deCatanzaro (New York, 1974); also, slightly abridged, by M. Lisney (Worthing, Sussex, 1989). M. Lot-Borodine, *Un Maître de la spiritualité byzantine au XIVe siècle, Nicolas Cabasilas* [1958]. W. Völker, *Die Sakramentsmystik des Nikolaus Kabasilas* (Wiesbaden, 1977). S. Salaville, AA, 'Vues sotériologiques chez Nicolas Cabasilas', *Études Byzantines*, 1 (1943), pp. 5–57. I. Ševčenko, 'Nicholas Cabasilas' "Anti-Zealot" Discourse. A Reinterpretation', *Dumbarton Oaks Papers*, 11 (1957), pp. 79–171. J. Gouillard in *DHGE* 11 (1949), cols. 14–21, and S. Salaville, AA, in *Dict. Sp.* 2 (1953), cols. 1–9, both s.v., with bibl.

Cabbala. See KABBALA.

Cabrol, Fernand (1855–1937), liturgical scholar. In 1877 he was professed a Benedictine monk at *Solesmes, and in 1896 elected prior of the projected monastery at Farnborough in Hampshire, of which in 1903 he became Abbot. In conjunction with H. *Leclercq he edited the *Dictionnaire d'archéologie chrétienne et de liturgie* (1903–53) and the *Monumenta ecclesiae liturgica* (1900–13). His own writings include *Le Livre de la prière antique* (1900; Eng. tr., *Liturgical Prayer, its History and Spirit*, 1922), *Les Origines liturgiques* (1906), and *L'Angleterre chrétienne avant les Normands* (1909). His edition of the Roman Missal, with Eng. tr. and notes [1921], was widely used.

L. Gougaud, OSB, in *RHE* 33 (1937), pp. 919–22, with refs. to other obituary notices.

Cadbury, Henry Joel (1883–1974), American NT scholar. Of *Quaker descent, he was educated at Haverford College and Harvard University; he taught at Haverford College (1910–19) and Andover Theological College (1919–26) before becoming Professor of Biblical Literature at Bryn Mawr College (1926–34) and Hollis Professor of Divinity at Harvard (1934–54). One of the founders of modern Lucan scholarship, he was a *form critic and a pioneer of *redaction criticism; both methods are reflected in *The Making of Luke-Acts* (1927). An earlier work, *The Style and Literary Method of Luke* (1919–20) virtually demolished the contention that St *Luke's writing betrayed any specifically medical knowledge or interests. He played a large part, with F. J. Foakes Jackson and K. *Lake in the production of their influential *Beginnings of Christianity* (5 vols., 1920–33). Two popular books, *The Peril of Modernizing Jesus* (1937) and *Jesus, What Manner of Man* (1947), addressed the difficulties posed by cultural change for the claim that the teaching of Christ, or 1st-cent. interpretations of Him, could be authoritative in the 20th cent. Cadbury's encyclopaedic knowledge of Greek and the Graeco-Roman world lent authority to these and his many other books and articles on biblical subjects. He was a member of the panel which produced the *Revised Standard Version* of the NT (see BIBLE (ENGLISH VERSIONS), no. 5). After his retirement he published revised editions of H. C. Braithwaite's *The Beginnings of Quakerism* (1955) and *The Second Period of Quakerism* (1961), major achievements which followed his earlier work on *George Fox's 'Book of Miracles'* (1948) and specialized articles on Quaker history. Throughout his life he played a leading role in the work of the Quakers, making several journeys to Europe on behalf of the American Friends Service Committee and accepting the Nobel Award for Peace which the Committee shared with its British counterpart in 1947.

Obituary notice by A. N. Wilder in *Harvard Magazine*, May 1975, pp. 46–52. *Then and Now: Quaker Essays: Historical and Contemporary by friends of Henry Joel Cadbury*, ed. A. Brinton (Philadelphia [1960]), with biographical sketch by M. Hoxie Jones, pp. 11–70. M. Hope Bacon, *Let This Life Speak: The Legacy of Henry Joel Cadbury* (ibid., 1987), with bibl. D. E. Nineham in *A Dictionary of Biblical Interpretation*, ed. R. J. Coggins and J. L. Houlden (1990), pp. 95–7, s.v.

Caecilian (d. before 343), Bp. of Carthage from 311, or perhaps 307 (so T. D. Barnes). His importance lies in his part in the opening stages of the *Donatist controversy. As archdeacon he had supported Mensurius, Bp. of Carthage, in his efforts to suppress the fanatical desire of many Christians for martyrdom and the uncritical veneration for *confessors, and on Mensurius' death he was elected to succeed him. The opposing rigorist party at Carthage then consecrated a rival bishop, urging that Caecilian's own consecration was invalid on the ground that he had received his orders from one Felix of Aptunga, a '*traditor'. He is the only bishop from Latin Africa who is known to have attended the Council of *Nicaea (325).

The chief sources are *Eusebius of Caesarea, St *Optatus of Milevis, and St *Augustine. P. Monceaux, *Histoire littéraire de l'Afrique chrétienne*, 4 (1913), *passim*. T. D. Barnes, 'The Beginnings of Donatism', *JTS* NS 26 (1975), pp. 13–22, repr. in id., *Early Christianity and the Roman Empire* (1984), no. 8. A. Mandouze, *Prosopographie Chrétienne du Bas-Empire*, 1: *Prosopographie de l'Afrique Chrétienne (303–533)* (1982), pp. 165–75. See also other works cited under DONATISM. For the Lat. version of the Nicene Canons which goes under his name ('Interpretatio Caeciliani', also 'Vetus Interpretatio'), see Turner, *EOMIA* (1899–1939), *passim*, and F. *Maassen, *Geschichte der Quellen und der Literatur des canonischen Rechts im Abendlande*, 1 (1870), pp. 8–11; there are no sufficient reasons, however, for the common assumption that Caecilian himself was the author of the version, cf. E. *Schwartz, 'Über die Sammlung des Cod. Veronensis LX', *ZNTW* 35 (1936), pp. 11 f.

Caedmon (d. c.680), the earliest English Christian poet. Acc. to *Bede, the source of almost all our knowledge of him, Caedmon was a labourer at the monastery at Whitby, who received in a vision the gift of composing verses in the praise of God, and as a result became a monk. He was instructed in the Scriptures, which, as Bede also tells us, he turned into verse. He was the first Anglo-Saxon writer of popular religious poetry. Prob. Caedmon's only surviving work is a hymn which he is said to have composed in a dream, and which appears in an 8th-cent. hand as an addition to the Moore MS of Bede. Many other traditional poems are ascribed to him, with doubtful justice. He was venerated as a saint at *Jarrow, and his feast kept on 11 Feb.

The principal source for his Life is Bede, *HE* 4. 22 [24]; comm. by J. M. Wallace-Hadrill (Oxford, 1988), pp. 165–7 and 240. Modern edn. of his Hymn by A. H. Smith, *Three Northumbrian Poems* (1933), pp. 38–41; it is also ed., with full comm., by U. Schwab (Messina, 1972). Eng. tr. from Junius MS by C. W. Kennedy, *The Cædmon Poems* (1916), p. 1. E. van K. Dobbie, *The Manuscripts of Cædmon's Hymn and Bede's Death Song* (New York, 1937), pp. 1–48. C. L. Wrenn, 'The Poetry of Cædmon', *Proceedings of the British Academy*, 32 ('1946' [1951]), pp. 277–95, with bibl. D. W. Fritz, 'Cædmon: a traditional Christian Poet', *Mediaeval Studies*, 31 (1969), pp. 334–7. J. Opland, *Anglo-Saxon Oral Poetry* (New Haven, Conn., and London, 1980), pp. 106–20 and 128 f. Further bibl., incl. that of Caedmon School and notes of other works attrib. to him, in *CBEL* 1 (1940), pp. 73–5; *NCBEL* 1 (1974), cols. 267–9.

Caeremoniale Episcoporum. In the RC Church, the book ordering the liturgical celebrations of a bishop. Its remote ancestors were the *Ordines Romani* produced in Carolingian times when it was necessary to adapt the rite of Rome for use elsewhere. From the 13th cent. there were various compilations dealing with the ceremonial in use at the Papal court (see the following entry); the earliest dealing specifically with episcopal ceremonial was that drawn up by Paris Grassi, Bp. of Pesaro, during the pontificate of *Julius II (1503–13) and pub. in 1564 under the title *De Cerimoniis Cardinalium et Episcoporum in eorum diœcesibus*. This work was the basis of the *Caeremoniale Episcoporum* promulgated by *Clement VIII in 1600 which, despite some changes, remained in force until the Second *Vatican Council (1962–5). A new *Caeremoniale

Episcoporum was issued in 1984. Part 1 describes the bishop's role in the diocese and provides general rules of ceremonial. Part 2 is devoted to the 'stational Mass' (no longer called 'pontifical'), when the bishop celebrates with his clergy and people in the cathedral church or elsewhere in the diocese. The other six parts cover all the occasions when the bishop officiates, incl. *ordinations, *confirmations, the blessing of *abbots and *abbesses, the *dedication or blessing of churches, and the ceremonial to be observed at *General Councils and local synods. The whole is marked by a strong pastoral sense. Unlike its predecessor, its regulations have no superiority over the liturgical books issued since the Second *Vatican Council.

For works on the *Ordines Romani*, see s.v. Comm. on the 1600 *Caeremoniale* by J. Catalani (2 vols., Rome, 1744), L. Gromier (Paris [1959]), and J. Nabuco (in Lat., ibid. [1959]).

Caeremoniale Romanum. A Latin service book dealing with the ceremonies of the Papal court. Apart from the early *Ordines Romani*, the first such book was that compiled c.1273 at the command of *Gregory X which contained the ceremonial for the election, ordination, and enthronement of a Pope (Mabillon, *Ordo* 13). A more elaborate compilation made by Card. J. Cajetan Stefaneschi c.1341 (Mabillon, *Ordo* 14) included also the ceremonial for *canonizations, a *General Council, and the coronations of emperors and kings. Other ceremonials followed, incl. that drawn up in 1488 by Augustine Patrizi, Bp. of Pienza. It was rewritten by Christopher Marcello, Abp. of Corcyra, and published at Venice in 1516 under the title *Rituum ecclesiasticorum sive sacrarum Cerimoniarum SS. Romanae Ecclesiae*. It remained in use until after the Second Vatican Council (1962–5).

J. *Mabillon, OSB, *Museum Italicum*, 2 (Paris, 1689), pp. 221–443; repr. in J. P. Migne, *PL* 78. 1105–274. Crit. edns. of the compilation made at the command of Gregory X by M. Andrieu, *Le Pontifical Romain au moyen âge*, 2 (ST 87; 1940), pp. 525–41, with introd., pp. 277–88 and 317–19, and of that of Patrizi by M. Dykmans, SJ (ST 293–4; 1980–2), also with full introd. B. Schimmelpfennig, *Die Zeremonienbücher der römischen Kurie im Mittelalter* (Bibliothek des Deutschen Historischen Instituts in Rom, 40; 1973). See further the historical introd. to the *Caeremoniale Episcoporum* (1984), pp. 7 f.

Caerularius, Michael. See MICHAEL CERULARIUS.

Caesar. The word, which was virtually a title of the Roman emperors in the 1st–3rd cents. AD, occurs several times in the NT (e.g. Mk. 12: 14–17, Jn. 19: 12, Acts 25: 8–12). To the inhabitants of Palestine and the provinces, the name denoted the Imperial throne rather than the person occupying it. The emperors contemporary with the NT were: Augustus, 27 BC–AD 14; Tiberius, AD 14–37; Gaius (Caligula), AD 37–41; Claudius, AD 41–54; *Nero, AD 54–68; Galba, AD 68–9; Otho, AD 69; Vitellius, AD 69; Vespasian, AD 69–79; Titus, AD 79–81; and *Domitian, AD 81–96.

Caesarea (Palestine). Originally known as 'Straton's Tower', the city on the coast of Palestine north of Jaffa (to be distinguished from the '*Caesarea Philippi' of Mt. 16: 13, Mk. 8: 27, the modern Banias south of Mount Hermon) was rebuilt by *Herod the Great, c.25–13 BC, prob. as a port for Sebaste (Samaria), and renamed in honour of the Emp. Augustus. It became the capital of Palestine (*c*.13 BC). In the Apostolic Church it was visited by *Philip the Evangelist (Acts 8: 40), who took up his residence here (21: 8), and by St *Peter who, in obedience to a vision, made himself known to Cornelius and was the instrument through whom the Holy Spirit was first given to the Gentiles (10: 44 f.). St *Paul was brought from *Jerusalem to Caesarea after his conversion and sent on thence to Tarsus (9: 30); he landed here on his way from *Ephesus to Jerusalem (18: 22); and he was imprisoned here for two years (23: 23, 24: 27). Under Vespasian it became a colony (AD 70). Prob. the scene of a small Council regulating the celebration of *Easter *c*.196 (*Eusebius, *HE* 5. 25), it became 'Metropolis Provinciae Syriae Palestinae' under Alexander Severus (d. 222). In consequence its bishop became metropolitan of Palestine (recognized at the Council of *Nicaea, can. 7) and held this dignity until the Council of *Chalcedon (451) subordinated him to the Patriarch of Jerusalem.

The home of *Origen from 231, Caesarea became noted as a seat of learning, with its episcopal library which contained many of Origen's works (incl. his *Hexapla*). Its most notable bishop was Eusebius (Bp., 315–*c*.340), the most learned man of his age. St *Jerome also studied here. The city suffered severely in the 7th cent. It was captured by the *Crusaders in 1101, when a chalice was found among the spoil, believed to have been used at the Last Supper. Important during the Crusades, the city was demolished in 1265 and remained in ruins until the 19th cent. In the past 40 years this has become one of the most intensively excavated sites in Israel. Both the town and the harbour installations have been studied by archaeologists and some major buildings have been partially restored.

C. T. Fritsch (ed.), *The Joint Expedition to Caesarea Maritima*, vol. 1: *Studies in the History of Caesarea Maritima* (Bulletin of the American Schools of Oriental Research, Supplemental Studies, 19; Missoula, 1975). J. Ringel, *Césarée de Palestine: Étude historique et archéologique* (Association des Publications près les Universités de Strasbourg; Paris, 1975). L. I. Levine, *Caesarea under Roman Rule* (Studies in Judaism in Late Antiquity, 7; Leiden, 1975). Id. and E. Netzer, *Excavations at Caesarea Maritima, 1975, 1976, 1979—Final Report* (QEDEM. Monographs of the Institute of Archaeology, the Hebrew University of Jerusalem, 21; 1986), with bibl. K. G. Holum and others, *King Herod's Dream: Caesarea on the Sea* (New York and London [1988]). R. Janin, AA, in *DHGE* 12 (1953), cols. 206–9, s.v. 'Césarée de Palestine'; K. G. Holum, A. Rabin and others in E. Stern and others (eds.), *The New Encyclopedia of Archaeological Excavations in the Holy Land*, 1 (Jerusalem and New York [1993]), pp. 270–91, s.v.

Caesarea Philippi. The scene of St *Peter's confession of Christ's Messiahship (Mk. 8: 27, Mt. 16: 13). It was the ancient Paneion, now Banias, at the foot of Mount Hermon. Acc. to *Eusebius (*HE* 7. 28), it was the home of the woman with the issue of blood (Mt. 9: 20), where a house was shown in his day with statues commemorating the event. The site has been thoroughly surveyed and parts of it excavated since 1967.

C. Kopp, *Die heiligen Stätten der Evangelien* (Regensburg [1959]), pp. 291–4; Eng. tr. (1963), pp. 231–5. Modern guide by J. Murphy-O'Connor, OP, *The Holy Land* (Oxford, 2nd edn., 1986), pp. 153–6. R. Janin in *DHGE* 12 (1953), cols. 209–11, s.v. 'Césarée de Philippe'; Z. U. Ma'oz in E. Stern and others (eds.), *The New Encyclopedia of Archaeological Excavations in the Holy Land*, 1 (Jerusalem and New York, [1993]), pp. 136–43, s.v. 'Banias'.

Caesarean text. A form of the Greek text of the NT (comparable with that of the *Western and *Alexandrian texts) which B. H. *Streeter claimed to have identified. In *The Four Gospels* (1924) he argued that in the early centuries distinctive forms of the text arose in different local centres, and he connected this 'local text theory' with his suggestion of a different geographical provenance for each of the four main sources underlying the Synoptic Gospels. In contrast to B. F. *Westcott and F. J. A. *Hort, Streeter identified the so-called *Neutral text as Alexandrian and distinguished this from the text of Mk. used by *Origen after his move to *Caesarea in Palestine in 231. The *Koridethi Codex (Θ) and two families of *minuscules (fam. 1 and fam. 3) are the main representatives of the Caesarean text, but even they present an impure form extensively assimilated to the *Lucianic standard. Several problems attend the local text theory, including: (1) it has proved very difficult to establish a distinctively Caesarean text in the rest of the NT apart from Mk.; (2) Origen exhibits 'Caesarean' readings even in his Alexandrian period; and (3) recent discoveries of early papyri from Egypt attest the presence of several different forms of text in the same locality. What remains of interest in Streeter's theory is the observation that there was an early form of the text of Mk. which is closer to the wording of the parallels in Mt. and Lk., and this, if original, would ease one of the difficulties for the classic 'Two Source' solution to the *Synoptic Problem.

B. H. Streeter, *The Four Gospels* (1924), ch. 4, pp. 77–108. McNeile, pp. 387–91. K. Lake, R. P. Blake, and S. New, 'The Caesarean Text of the Gospel of Mark', *HTR* 21 (1928), pp. 207–404; T. Ayuso, 'Texto cesariense o precesariense? Su realidad y su trascendencia en la critica textual del Nuevo Testamento', *Biblica*, 16 (1935), pp. 369–415; B. M. Metzger, 'The Caesarean Text of the Gospels', *Journal of Biblical Literature*, 64 (1945), pp. 457–89; repr., with additional notes, in his *Chapters in the History of New Testament Textual Criticism* (New Testament Tools and Studies, 4; 1963), pp. 42–72; E. F. Hills, 'Harmonizations in the Caesarean Text of Mark', *Journal of Biblical Literature*, 66 (1947), pp. 135–52; E. C. Colwell, 'The Significance of Grouping New Testament Manuscripts', *New Testament Studies*, 4 (1958), pp. 73–92, repr. in id., *Studies in Methodology in Textual Criticism of the New Testament* (New Testament Tools and Studies, 9; 1969), pp. 1–25; see also pp. 63–83.

Caesarius, St (*c*.470–542), Abp. of Arles from 502. About 490 he entered the monastery at *Lérins. He took a prominent part in the ecclesiastical administration of S. Gaul, and with the help of Alaric II and Theodoric the Great succeeded in establishing the claim of Arles to be the primatial see in Gaul. He was largely instrumental in securing the condemnation of *Semipelagianism at the Council of *Orange in 529. A large collection of canons, known as the '*Statuta Ecclesiae Antiqua', has, almost certainly mistakenly, been ascribed to him by many modern scholars. He was a celebrated preacher, and a considerable number of his sermons have survived; many of them are based on the works of earlier authors. He also composed two monastic rules, a brief one for monks and a longer one for nuns; as well as showing the influence of *Cassian and the monastic tradition of Lérins, they are indebted to the Rule of St *Augustine. His Life was written by St *Cyprian of Toulon in conjunction with some of his other pupils. Feast day, 27 Aug.

Several of his writings ed. J. P. Migne, *PL* 67, 39, etc. Crit. edn. G. Morin, OSB, 2 vols., Maredsous, 1937–42 (vol. 1: *Sermones*; vol. 2: *Concilia a Caesario habita, Regulae Monasticae, Opuscula Theologica, Testamentum*, with *Vita Caesarii* in appendix; 2nd edn. of *Sermones* in CCSL 103–4, 1953), which supersedes all earlier texts. *Sermones de diversis* (nos. 1–80) repr., with Fr. tr., introd., and notes, by M.-J. Delage (SC 175, 243, and 330; 1971–86). *Œuvres monastiques*, ed., with Fr. tr. and full introd., by A. de Vogüé, OSB, and J. Courreau, OSB (ibid. 345 and 398; 1988–94). Eng. tr. of his Sermons by M. M. Mueller, OSF (Fathers of the Church, 31, 47, 66; 1956–73) and of his 'Rule of Nuns' by M. C. McCarthy, SHCJ (Washington, DC, 1960). S. Cavallin, *Studien zur Vita Caesarii* (Lund, 1934); also several studies by G. Morin preparatory to his edn. M. Dorenkemper, CPPS, *The Trinitarian Doctrine and Sources of St Caesarius of Arles* (Paradosis, 9; 1953). L. de Seilhac, OSB, *L'Utilisation par S. Césaire d'Arles de la Règle de S. Augustin* (Studia Anselmiana, 62; 1974). W. E. Klingshirn, *Caesarius of Arles: The Making of a Christian Community in Late Antique Gaul* (Cambridge Studies in Medieval Life and Thought, 4th ser. 22; 1994). Bardenhewer, 5 (1932), pp. 345–56; Altaner and Stuiber (1978), pp. 475–7 and 652. *CPL* (3rd edn., 1995), pp. 329–33 (nos. 1008–19a). G. de Plinval in *DHGE* 12 (1953), cols. 186–96, s.v. 'Césaire d'Arles'; H. G. J. Beck in *NCE* 2 (1967), pp. 1046–8, s.v.; R. J. H. Collins in *TRE* 7 (1981), pp. 531–6, s.v. 'Caesarius von Arles'. See also bibl. to STATUTA ECCLESIAE ANTIQUA.

Caesarius, St, of Nazianzus (d. 369). He held various offices at court, including that of physician. There exists a set of four dialogues attributed to him, but they are much later in date. Our knowledge of him derives mainly from a panegyric delivered at his funeral by his elder brother, St *Gregory of Nazianzus. Feast day in the W., 25 Feb.; in the E., 9 Mar.

J. P. Migne, *PG* 38. 851–1190. R. Riedinger, *Pseudo-Kaisarios: Überlieferungsgeschichte und Verfasserfrage* (Byzantinisches Archiv, 12; Munich, 1969).

Caesarius of Heisterbach (*c.*1180–1240), ecclesiastical writer. Born in or near *Cologne, in 1199 he entered the *Cistercian Order at the monastery of Heisterbach (near Königswinter, on the Rhine). His best-known writings are his 'Dialogus Miraculorum' (*c.*1219–23), a collection of spiritual anecdotes for the edification of novices, full of supernatural incident, and his eight books (not all extant) 'On Miracles'. They both throw important light on the events and popular beliefs of his age, as well as on the history of the Cistercian Order. He also wrote a Life of St *Elizabeth of Hungary and a number of sermons.

Dialogus Miraculorum, ed. J. Strange (2 vols., Cologne, etc., 1851, repr., Ridgewood, NJ, 1966; Eng. tr., 2 vols., 1929). For the work *On Miracles*, see A. Hilka (ed.), *Die Wundergeschichten des Caesarius von Heisterbach*, 3 (Bonn, 1937): bks. 1–2 ed. A. Hilka, pp. 1–222; bks. 4–5 (the life and miracles of St Engelbert, murdered at Cologne in 1225) ed. F. Zschaeck, ibid., pp. 223–328. Life of St Elizabeth ed. A. Huyskens, ibid., pp. 329–90. The life and miracles of St Engelbert also ed. A. Poncelet, SJ, in *AASS*, Nov. 3 (1910), pp. 644–81. Sermons pr. Cologne, 1615; the 'exempla' (or stories) excerpted and ed. A. Hilka, op. cit., 1 (1933), with full introd. A. E. Schönback, 'Studien zur Erzählungsliteratur des Mittelalters. Teil IV: Ueber Caesarius von Heisterbach', *Sb.* (Wien), 144 (1902), Abh. 9. F. Wagner, 'Studien zu Caesarius von Heisterbach', *Analecta Cisterciensia*, 29 (1973),

pp. 79–95; B. P. McGuire, 'Written Sources and Cistercian Inspiration in Caesarius of Heisterbach', ibid. 35 (1979), pp. 227–82; id., 'Friends and Tales in the Cloister: Oral Sources in Caesarius of Heisterbach's *Dialogus Miraculorum*', ibid. 36 (1980), pp. 167–245. J. M. Canivez, O. Cist., in *Dict. Sp.* 2 (1953), cols. 430–2, s.v. 'Césaire d'Heisterbach'; K. Langosch in *Verfasserlexikon* (2nd edn.), 1 (1978), cols. 1152–68, s.v.

Caesaropapism. The system whereby an absolute monarch has supreme control over the Church within his dominions and exercises it even in matters (e.g. doctrine) normally reserved to ecclesiastical authority. The term is most generally used of the authority exercised by the Byzantine emperors over the E. patriarchates, esp. in the centuries immediately preceding the Schism of 1054.

Caiaphas. The Jewish *High Priest before whom Christ was tried (Mt. 26: 3, etc.), and at whose instigation He was condemned (Jn. 11: 49 ff.). He was appointed High Priest *c.*18 and deposed in 37. He was son-in-law of *Annas.

Cainites. A *Gnostic sect mentioned by *Irenaeus and other early writers which, regarding the God of the OT as responsible for the evil in the world, exalted those who withstood him, e.g. Cain, Esau, and Korah. They are said to have had an apocryphal Gospel of *Judas Iscariot.

St Irenaeus, *Haer.* 1. 31; St *Hippolytus, *Haer.* 8. 20; Ps.-*Tertullian, *De Praescr. Haer.* 33; St *Epiphanius, *Haer.* 38. On the Gospel of Judas, see H.-C. Puech, rev. by B. Blatz, in Schneemelcher (5th edn.), 1 (1987), pp. 309 f.; Eng. tr. (1991), pp. 386 f. G. Bareille in *DTC* 2 (1905), cols. 1307–9; G. Bardy in *DHGE* 11 (1949), cols. 226–8, s.v., both with further refs.

Caird, Edward (1835–1908), Scottish philosopher and theologian. In 1866 he became professor of moral philosophy at Glasgow and in 1893 succeeded B. *Jowett as Master of Balliol College, Oxford. He was one of the chief representatives of the Neo-*Hegelian movement in British philosophy. In *The Evolution of Religion* (1893) and *The Evolution of Theology in the Greek Philosophers* (*Gifford Lectures, 2 vols., 1904) he maintained that the religious principle was a necessary element in consciousness, and that Christianity, in that it overcame the antithesis of the real and the ideal, was the absolute religion. He also published two important works on I. *Kant, *A Critical Account of the Philosophy of Kant* (1877) and *The Critical Philosophy of Immanuel Kant* (2 vols., 1889, a recasting of the previous book) and a monograph on G. W. F. Hegel (1883).

H. Jones and J. H. Muirhead, *The Life and Philosophy of Edward Caird* (1921). Obituary note by B. *Bosanquet in *Proceedings of the British Academy* (1907–8), pp. 379–86. Study by O. Bellini (Pubblicazioni del Seminario per le Scienze Giuridiche e Politiche dell'Università di Pisa, 23; 1990). *DNB, 1901–1911*, 1, pp. 291–5 (unsigned).

Caird, John (1820–98), elder brother of the preceding, divine and philosopher. In 1845 he entered the ministry of the Church of Scotland and in 1862 was elected professor of divinity at Glasgow. In 1873 he became Principal of Glasgow University. Like his brother, he was a Neo-*Hegelian, though somewhat more orthodox. His chief writings were *An Introduction to the Philosophy of Religion* (1880) and a posthumously published set of

*Gifford Lectures on *The Fundamental Ideas of Christianity* (1899).

Memoir by E. Caird (brother) prefixed to *Fundamental Ideas of Christianity*, 1 (1899), pp. ix–cxli. C. L. Warr, *Principal Caird* (The Scottish Layman's Library, 1926). A. P. E. Sell, *Defending and Declaring the Faith* (Exeter and Colorado Springs, Colo. [1987]), pp. 64–88 and 239–42. T. Bayne in *DNB*, suppl. 1 (1901), pp. 368 f.

Caius. See GAIUS.

Cajetan, St (1480–1547), founder of the *Theatine Order. A native of Vicenza, he was ordained priest at Rome in 1516. From the first he exerted himself to spread a fresh spirit of devotion among the clergy and to that end in 1524, with Pietro Carafa (later *Paul IV) and two other priests, he founded the congregation known as the Theatines, for clerics bound by vow and living in common, but engaged in pastoral work. He was beatified in 1629 and canonized in 1671. Feast day, 8 (formerly 7) Aug.

F. Andreu, CR (ed.), *Le lettere di San Gaetano da Thiene* (ST 177; 1954). Life by Antonio Caraccioli, O. Theat., orig. pub. in Cajetan's *De Vita Pauli IV . . . Collectanea Historica* (Cologne, 1612), pp. 176–260; repr. in *AASS*, Aug. 2 (1735), pp. 282–301. Another early Life by G. B. Cataldo, O. Theat. (Rome, 1616). P. Chiminelli, *San Gaetano Thiene* (1948), with full bibl. Other modern studies incl. those by G. M. Magenis (Venice, 1726; Ger. tr., 1754), M. A. R. Maulde la Clavière ('Les Saints', 1902; Eng. tr., 1902), O. Premoli (Crema, 1910), Silvestro da Valsanzibio, OFM Cap. (Padua, 1949, with docs.), and A. Veny Ballester (Barcelona [1950], with bibl.). P. Paschini, *S. Gaetano Thiene, Gian Pietro Carafa e le origini dei chierici regolari teatini* (1926). B. Mas in *Dict. Sp.* 6 (1967), cols. 30–48, s.v. 'Gaetan de Thiene', with refs.

Cajetan, Thomas de Vio (1469–1534), theologian. He was called Gaetano ('Cajetan') from his birthplace, Gaeta. He entered the *Dominican Order in 1484, and taught philosophy and theology at Padua (where contemporary philosophical movements were represented by P. *Pomponazzi and others), Pavia, and Rome. As *General of his order (1508–18), Cardinal (1517), and Bp. of Gaeta (1519) he played an important part in ecclesiastical affairs, urging the cause of reform before the fathers of the *Lateran Council of 1512, reasoning with M. *Luther in 1518, contributing to the elections of the Emp. *Charles V (1519) and the Pope *Hadrian VI (1522), and opposing the projected divorce of *Henry VIII (1530). Except for some years during the pontificate of *Clement VII, he was seldom free from onerous duties, but he contrived to study and write continually. In philosophy and theology his acute Commentary on St *Thomas's 'Summa Theologiae' (1507–22) was the first monument of a great revival of *Thomism in the 16th cent., and remains today one of the chief classics of scholasticism. Finding that Humanists and Protestants alike were making polemical use of the Scriptures, he subsequently turned to biblical exegesis, for which he sought the assistance of scholarly philologists; and his commentaries on the Bible contain much enlightened criticism of an unexpectedly 'modern' kind.

There are modern crit. texts of many of his works, as well as some Eng. trs. Quétif and Échard, 2, pp. 14–21 and 428. The Register of his letters while Master of the Order, ed. A. de Meyer, OP (Monumenta Ordinis Fratrum Praedicatorum Historica, 17; Rome, 1935). J. F. Groner, OP, *Kardinal Cajetan* (Louvain, 1951),

with bibl. G. Hennig, *Cajetan und Luther: Ein historischer Beitrag zur Begegnung von Thomismus und Reformation* (Arbeiten zur Theologie, Reihe 2, Band 7; Stuttgart, 1966). A. Bodem, SDB, *Das Wesen der Kirche nach Kardinal Cajetan* (Trierer Theologische Studien, 25; 1971). J. Wicks, *Cajetan und die Anfänge der Reformation* (Katholisches Leben und Kirchenreform im Zeitalter der Glaubensspaltung, 43; 1983). B. Hallensleben, *Communicatio: Anthropologie und Gnadenlehre bei Thomas de Vio Cajetan* (Reformationsgeschichtliche Studien und Texte, 123; 1985). U. Horst, OP, *Zwischen Konziliarismus und Reformation* (Rome, 1985), pp. 27–54. Nos. 86–7 of the *Revue Thomiste*, NS 17 (1935), also contain arts. specially devoted to his life and teaching. D. A. Mortier, OP, *Histoire des maîtres généraux de l'ordre des Frères Prêcheurs*, 5 (1911), pp. 141–230. J. R. Volz, OP, in *CE* 3 (1908), pp. 145–8, s.v.; E. Iserloh and B. Hallensleben in *TRE* 7 (1981), pp. 538–46, s.v. 'Cajetan de Vio, Jakob', with further bibl.

Calamy, Edmund (1) (1600–66), 'the Elder', English *Presbyterian divine. Of *Huguenot descent, he was educated at Pembroke Hall, Cambridge, where he was excluded from a fellowship on account of his opposition to *Arminian teaching. From 1626 to 1636 he was lecturer at Bury St Edmunds, and from 1639 *perpetual curate of St Mary Aldermanbury in London. He took a leading part in the production of the composite work *Smectymnuus directed against J. *Hall's apology for a moderate episcopacy. As an active member of the *Westminster Assembly of 1643, he sought to defend presbyterianism as a middle course between prelacy and congregationalism. During the Commonwealth he worked for the return of *Charles II, and at the Restoration was offered as a reward for his services, but did not accept, the see of *Coventry and Lichfield. At the *Savoy Conference of 1661 he continued to take a moderate line, and hopes were entertained by the bishops of his conforming; but he refused to yield, and in 1662 he was ejected from his preferments. In 1663 he was committed for a short time to Newgate Prison for disobeying the Act of *Uniformity. Several of his sermons were published.

His Sermon preached on 17 Aug. 1662 is pr. in *Farewell Sermons of Some of the Most Eminent of the Nonconformist Divines, Delivered at the Period of their Ejection by the Act of Uniformity in the Year 1662* (1816), pp. 1–13, with biog. introd. pp. vi f. *Cromwell's Soldiers' Bible . . .* compiled by Edmund Calamy, and issued for the Use of the Commonwealth Army in 1643, was repr. in facsimile (London, 1895). C. G. Bolam and others, *The English Presbyterians* (1968), esp. pp. 50 f. and 59. A. Gordon in *DNB* 8 (1886), pp. 227–30.

Calamy, Edmund (2) (1671–1732), historian of Nonconformity, the only son of Edmund Calamy 'the Younger' (1635?–85), who was himself the son of Edmund *Calamy 'the Elder'. His works threw much light on the history of Nonconformity. Esp. valuable is a chapter (9, nearly half the first volume) in his *Abridgement of *Baxter's History* (1702; new edn., 2 vols., 1713) entitled 'A Particular Account of the Ministers, Lecturers, Fellows of Colleges, etc., who were silenced and ejected by the Act for Uniformity; with the characters and works of many of them'.

A. G. Matthews, *Calamy Revised: Being a revision of Edmund Calamy's Account of the Ministers and others ejected and silenced, 1660–2* (1934). C. G. Bolam and others, *The English Presbyterians* (1968), esp. pp. 127–35. A. Gordon in *DNB* 8 (1886), pp. 230–5.

calced (Lat. *calceatus*, 'shod'). A term applied to some branches of certain religious orders to distinguish them from their '*discalced' brethren (q.v.). Thus the unreformed *Carmelites, who wear shoes, are called 'calced' as opposed to the discalced members of the *Teresian reform, who wear sandals; the same applies to the 'calced' Conventual *Franciscans.

Calderwood, David (1575–1650), Scottish Church historian. He was educated at Edinburgh University and ordained to the charge of Crailing, Roxburgh, in 1604. A vigorous opponent of the ecclesiastical policy of *James VI and I (esp. of his attempts to reintroduce episcopacy into Scotland), in 1608 he was prohibited from attending Church courts or synods. He then devoted himself to the study of the origins of civil and ecclesiastical authority. When the King visited Scotland in 1617, Calderwood was summoned to the royal presence and put up a fearless defence of his views. He was deprived, imprisoned and subsequently exiled until after James's death. In 1641 he obtained the charge of Pencaitland in Lothian and not long afterwards co-operated with A. *Henderson in drawing up the 'Directory of Public *Worship'. His most important work, *The True History of the Church of Scotland*, was commissioned by the *General Assembly, which provided an annual pension of £800 during the last years of his life. It is characterized by anti-Erastian bias and a spirited defence of the liberties of the Church, but is still a valuable source of information on ecclesiastical history in Scotland during the 16th and 17th cents. He also wrote a number of polemical works.

Editio princeps of *The True History of the Church of Scotland*, pr. in the Netherlands, 1678, is incomplete. Fuller, but still incomplete, ed., based on MS in the British Library, by T. Thomson (Wodrow Society, 8 vols., 1842–9), with Life in final vol. [separate pagination]. Repr. of 1678 ed., with introd. by R. Peters (Menston, Leeds, 1971). W. G. Blaikie in *DNB* 8 (1886), pp. 244–6.

Caldey Island, off the S. coast of Wales, near Tenby, the seat of a monastery as far back as the 5th cent. In 1906 an abbey for Anglican Benedictines was established on the ancient ruins by Aelred Carlyle (1874–1955). In 1913 nearly the whole community transferred their allegiance to the RC Church. In 1928 they left Caldey for their present house at Prinknash, near *Gloucester, and the island was taken over by *Trappists from Chimay in Belgium.

The Benedictines of Caldey Island (Caldey, 1907). P. F. Anson, *The Benedictines of Caldey: The Story of the Anglican Benedictines of Caldey and their Submission to the Catholic Church* (1940). Id., *Abbot Extraordinary: Memoirs of Aelred Carlyle, OSB* (1958), pp. 65–179. F. L. Cross, *Darwell Stone* (1943), pp. 108–12.

calefactory (Lat. *calefactorium*, 'warming place'), the room in a medieval (esp. *Cistercian) monastery in which a fire or fires were maintained for the use of the monks. Where it existed, it was generally placed, as at *Fountains, between the refectory and the eastern range. The term survives as a designation for a communal place of recreation in modern religious houses.

calendar. The calendar in use at the time when Christianity began was the Julian, devised by Julius Caesar in 46 BC, in which the length of the years was almost but not quite accurately calculated. By AD 325 the error was enough to cause the vernal equinox to fall on 21 instead of 25 Mar., so that the 21st was then fixed as the earliest date for the Paschal full moon. The system was reformed by *Gregory XIII, who in 1582 caused ten days to be omitted from that year to balance the current error, and by altering the leap-year rules prevented its recurrence. The Gregorian Calendar was adopted in England in 1752. Certain parts of the Orthodox Church have not adopted it, and here the year now runs 13 days behind the W.

The beginning of the Christian Era with the date of the Incarnation was suggested at Rome by *Dionysius Exiguus in the 6th cent., and in due course adopted throughout Christendom. Calculation began from 25 Mar. AD 1, the supposed date of the *Annunciation, which was taken to be New Year's Day. The Gregorian Calendar restored New Year's Day to 1 Jan.

The observance of commemorations dates from early times. *Easter and *Pentecost were both observed from the very first as Jewish festivals with a new Christian significance, and like the Jewish Passover they were movable according to the moon, the calculations proving at times a source of controversy. Later the fixed festivals grew up, as well as further movable feasts depending for their date upon Easter. Of saints' days, those of the martyrs were the first and most obvious; others followed. So also the periods of fasting were gradually fixed by custom. At a very early stage the Jewish custom of a seven-day week produced regularly recurring fasts on *Wednesdays and *Fridays, an arrangement later modified but in substance preserved; while the observance of *Sunday as a festival dates from the Apostles, though it was only in 321 that an order of *Constantine forbade unnecessary Sunday work.

The new Roman Calendar of 1969 did much to bring out again the importance of the great feasts of *Christmas, Easter, and Pentecost, and to restore the primacy of Sunday over the feasts of saints; the number of saints' days was reduced, while an attempt was made to give the calendar a universal significance both in time (by including modern saints) and place. See also YEAR.

The study of chronology was put on a scientific footing for the first time by J. *Scaliger, *De Emendatione Temporum* (Paris, 1583), and D. *Petavius, SJ, *De Doctrina Temporum* (ibid., 1627). Important works of more recent date incl. the Benedictine *L'Art de vérifier les dates de faits historiques, des chartes, des chroniques et autres anciens monumens, depuis la naissance de Notre-Seigneur* [by M. F. Dantine, OSB, C. Clémencet, OSB, and U. Durand, OSB] (Paris, 1750; 2nd edn. [rev. by N. V. de Saint-Allais], 18 vols. + index, 1818–19; further continuation from 1770 to date by J. B. P. J. de Courcelles and F. d'Urban, 4 vols., 1821–38; another complete edn., 18 vols., 1821–44). C. L. Ideler, *Handbuch der mathematischen und technischen Chronologie* (2 vols., 1825–6). B. Krusch, *Studien zur christlich-mittelalterlichen Chronologie* (1880). H. Grotefend, *Zeitrechnung des Mittelalters und der Neuzeit* (2 vols., 1891–8). O. Pedersen, 'The Ecclesiastical Calendar and the Life of the Church', in G. V. Coyne, SJ, and others (eds.), *Gregorian Reform of the Calendar: Proceedings of the Vatican Conference to commemorate its 400th anniversary, 1582–1982* (Rome, 1983), pp. 17–74, with other relevant arts., pp. 3–14 and 75–134. J. Gerard, SJ, in *CE* 3 (1908), pp. 738–42, s.v. 'Chronology (General)', and H. Thurston, SJ, ibid., pp. 158–66, s.v. 'Calendar'. *The Oxford Companion to English Literature*, 5th edn. by M. Drabble (1985), pp. 1126–55, gives miscellaneous calendrical data. See also bibl. to CHRONOLOGY (BIBLICAL), YEAR (LITURGICAL), GREGORIAN CALENDAR, and PASCHAL CONTROVERSIES.

Calendar of 354. See CHRONOGRAPHER OF 354.

Calfhill (or Calfield), James (*c.*1530–70), *Calvinistic divine. Educated at Eton and at King's College, Cambridge, in 1548 he became one of the early Students of Christ Church, Oxford. In 1560 he was ordained priest, and in the same year appointed to a canonry at Christ Church. In 1564 he became Lady Margaret professor of divinity at Oxford, in 1565 Dean of Bocking, and in 1570 he was elected to the see of *Worcester, but died before consecration. One of the leading Elizabethan Calvinists, he published in 1565 his principal work, an *Answer to the 'Treatise of the Cross'* [by John Martiall, 1534–97].

His *Answer to John Martiall's Treatise of the Cross* ed. R. Gibbings for the *Parker Society, 1846, with biog. note on Calfhill, pp. vii f. Unsigned art. in *DNB* 8 (1886), pp. 252 f.

Calixtines. The moderate party of the *Hussites of Bohemia and Moravia, also known as the '*Utraquists' (q.v.). They were so named from their contention that the laity should receive Communion in both kinds—i.e. from the chalice ('*calix*') as well as under the species of bread. Both Calixtines and Subunites (*sub una specie*) received ecclesiastical recognition at the Prague Compactata of 1433 (confirmed at Iglau, 1436).

G. Constant, *Concession à l'Allemagne de la communion sous les deux espèces: Étude sur les débuts de la réforme catholique en Allemagne, 1548–1621* (Bibliothèque des Écoles Françaises d'Athènes et de Rome, 128; 2 vols., 1923).

Calixtus. For Popes of this name, see CALLISTUS.

Calixtus, Georg (1586–1656), Protestant theologian. He was educated at the University of Helmstedt, where he became an exponent of eirenic tendencies and conceived a high regard for P. *Melanchthon. He then spent four years (1609–13) travelling in RC and *Calvinist countries. On his return to Helmstedt he was appointed professor of theology (1614), and held the office till his death. He endeavoured to build up a theological system which should lead to reconciliation between *Lutherans, Calvinists, and Catholics. The basis of the proposed reunion was to be the Scriptures, the *Apostles' Creed, and the faith of the first five cents., interpreted in the light of the *Vincentian Canon. He expounded his position (which became known as '*Syncretism') in a long series of writings, of which perhaps the most important was his treatise *Judicium de controversiis theologicis quae inter Lutheranos et Reformatos agitantur, et de mutua partium fraternitate atque tolerantia propter consensum in fundamentis* (1650). He took part at the Colloquy of *Thorn in 1645.

E. L. T. Henke, *Georg Calixtus und seine Zeit* (2 vols., Halle, 1853–60). W. C. Dowding, *German Theology during the Thirty Years' War: The Life and Correspondence of George Calixtus* (1863). H. Schüssler, *Georg Calixt, Theologie und Kirchenpolitik: Eine Studie zur Ökumenizität des Luthertums* (Veröffentlichungen des Instituts für europäische Geschichte Mainz, 25; 1961), with bibl. I. Mager, *Georg Calixts theologische Ethik und ihre Nachwirkungen* (Studien zur Kirchengeschichte Niedersachsens, 19 [1969]). J. Wallmann in *TRE* 7 (1981), pp. 552–9, s.v.

Calling. As a technical theological term the word came into use in Reformation theology for the Divine act whereby those destined for salvation are persuaded to accept the Gospel. It was used in this sense, e.g., in the 'Shorter *Westminster Catechism' of 1647. *Calvinist theologians have commonly held that the Divine Calling is in itself efficacious, whereas *Lutherans have held that it requires a voluntary response. In much Evangelical Christianity of more recent times the Call of God takes a very important place in the immediate and conscious conversion which is considered normal and necessary in the religious life of every Christian.

Callistus (or Calixtus) I, St (d. *c.*222), Bp. of *Rome from *c.*217. He was apparently originally a slave. Acc. to *Hippolytus, his first appearance in history was in connection with some fraudulent banking operations, which finally led to his being sent to the mines of Sardinia. After his release at the request of Marcia, the mistress of the Emp. Commodus (180–92), he was given a pension by *Victor I. In 217 he succeeded *Zephyrinus, whose chief minister he seems to have been. His pontificate was marked by acute controversy. He was attacked by Hippolytus for countenancing *Sabellianism and for his laxity, esp. in readmitting to communion those guilty of adultery or fornication; but some of the charges against him may be discounted as based solely on the evidence of his adversary. The catacombs of 'San Callisto' on the *Appian Way are named from his having been in charge of them under Zephyrinus. Callistus himself was buried in the cemetery of Calepodius on the Aurelian Way. Feast day, 14 Oct.

Hippolytus, *Haer.* 9. 12. *LP* (Duchesne), i (1886), pp. 141 f. J. J. I. von *Döllinger, *Hippolytus und Kallistus* (1853; Eng. tr., 1876). That Callistus was the *pontifex maximus quod est episcopus episcoporum* who issued an edict on penance (*edictum peremptorium*) attacked by *Tertullian in *De pudicitia*, 81, has been maintained by many modern scholars, incl. O. *Bardenhewer and A. d'Alès, *L'Édit de Calliste* (1914); on the other side, see B. *Altaner and C. B. Daly, 'The "Edict of Callistus" ', *Studia Patristica*, ed. F. L. Cross, 3 (TU 78; 1961), pp. 176–82. J. Gaudemet, 'La decision de Callixte en matière de mariage', in *Studi in onore di Ugo Enrico Paoli* (Florence, 1956), pp. 333–44. R. E. Heine, 'The Christology of Callistus', *JTS*, NS 49 (1998), pp. 56–91. Bardenhewer, 2 (2nd edn.; 1914), pp. 636–8; Altaner and Stuiber (1978), pp. 159, 164, and 169. S. G. Hall in *TRE* 7 (1981), pp. 559–63, s.v. 'Calixtus I'.

Callistus (or Calixtus) II (d. 1124), Pope from 1119. Guido of Burgundy was a descendant of the counts of Burgundy and closely connected with almost all the royal houses of Europe. He was made Abp. of Vienne by *Urban II in 1088, became Papal legate in France in 1106, and took part in the Lateran Council of 1112, which declared null and void the *investiture privileges which the Emp. Henry V had extorted from *Paschal II. In the same year he himself presided at a Council held at Vienne, which condemned lay investiture as a heresy. Having been elected Pope at *Cluny, he excommunicated Henry at the Council of *Reims in 1119, but the intervention of the German princes, esp. Henry of Bavaria, facilitated a peaceful solution. The long-drawn-out struggle between Pope and Emperor was brought to a conclusion by the Concordat of *Worms (q.v.) in 1122, which was promulgated at the *Lateran Council of 1123, where the Pope also issued a series of decrees concerning simony, the marriage of priests, and the election of prelates. In the quarrel between his old see of Vienne and that of Grenoble,

Callistus took the side of the former and authenticated a collection of forged privileges of which, however, the larger part dates from earlier times.

U. Robert, *Bullaire du Pape Calixte II (1119–1124): Essai de restitution* (2 vols., Paris, 1891); id., *Histoire du Pape Calixte II* (1891). Studies by M. Maurer (Munich, 2 vols., 1886–9) and G. Ender (Greifswald, 1913). M. Stroll, *Symbols as Power: The Papacy following the Investiture Contest* (Brill's Studies in Intellectual History, 24; Leiden, 1991), esp. pp. 1–92. Mann, 8 (1910), pp. 139–227. É. Jordan in *DHGE* 11 (1949), cols. 424–38; G. Miccoli in *Dizionario Biografico degli Italiani*, 16 (1973), pp. 761–8, both s.v., with bibl. See also works cited under INVESTITURE CONTROVERSY.

Callistus (or Calixtus) III (1378–1458), Pope from 1455. A native of Valencia, Alfonso de Borgia enjoyed a considerable reputation as a jurist both at the University of Lérida and at the court of Alfonso V of Aragon (King, 1416–58). He originally supported the cause of *Benedict XIII (antipope 1394–1417), but eventually induced his successor Clement VIII (antipope 1423–9) to submit to Pope *Martin V in 1429. He was thereupon appointed Bp. of Valencia in the same year and created a *cardinal in 1444. The main efforts of his Papacy were directed to the organization of a crusade against the Turks, to which project he had been esp. devoted since the fall of *Constantinople in 1453. In spite of the victory of St *Giovanni Capistrano (q.v.) at Belgrade in 1456, his plans met with little success, largely owing to the unsettled state of Europe, which his attempts to arrange peace did little to allay. After the death of Alfonso V (1458), he refused to recognize the claims of his illegitimate son to the throne of Naples, of which Alfonso was overlord. His intervention in the subsequent dynastic disputes lent substance to the charge of nepotism already raised by his elevation to the cardinalate of two of his nephews (incl. the future *Alexander VI) and the appointment of a third as Duke of Spoleto. Prob. the most interesting event of his pontificate was the revision of the trial of *Joan of Arc by the annulment of the sentence and a declaration of her innocence. He was also responsible for the canonization in 1457 of *Osmund, Bp. of *Salisbury.

Regesto Ibérico de Calixto III, ed. J. Rius Serra (Consejo Superior de Investigaciones Científicas. Escuela de Estudios Medievales. Textos, 10, 29, etc.; 1948 ff.). Vita a Bartholomæo Sacho, pr. by L. A. *Muratori, *Rerum Italicarum Scriptores*, 3, pt. 2 (Milan, 1734), cols. 961–66. N. Housley, *The Later Crusades, 1274–1580* (Oxford, 1992), esp. pp. 102–5 and 293 f. Pastor, 2 (1891), pp. 317–495. E. Vansteenberghe in *DHGE* 11 (1949), cols. 438–44, s.v., incl. bibl.; M. Batllori in *NCE* 2 (1967), pp. 1081 f.; M. E. Mallet in *Dizionario Biografico degli Italiani*, 16 (1973), pp. 769–74, all s.v., with detailed bibl.

Calovius, Abraham (1612–86), German *Lutheran theologian. In 1650 he was appointed to the chair of theology at *Wittenberg, and in 1652 General-superintendent. A man of great learning, he took part in many controversies, and as a strenuous defender of rigid Lutheran orthodoxy opposed G. *Calixtus's policy of reuniting the Confessions. He also made vigorous attacks on *Socinianism and *Pietism and controverted the liberal views of H. *Grotius on biblical inspiration. In his doctrine of the 'Unio Mystica', however, he departed (probably far more than he was aware) from the

Reformation doctrine of justification. His chief dogmatic work, *Systema locorum theologicorum* (12 vols., 1655–77), is a monument of Lutheran scholasticism.

J. Wallmann in *TRE* 7 (1981), pp. 563–8, s.v. 'Calov, Abraham', incl. bibl.

caloyer (Gk. καλόγηρος, from καλός, 'fine', + γῆρας, 'old age'; i.e. 'venerable'). A designation for Greek monks.

Calvary, Mount (Lat. *Calvaria*, Gk. Κρανίον, Heb. 'Golgotha', all meaning 'skull'). The place of Christ's crucifixion, just outside *Jerusalem. It may have been originally a place of public execution where the skulls of the executed were to be seen, or the name may have been derived from a neighbouring cemetery or connected with the shape of the ground (traditionally a hill) which may have resembled a skull. Acc. to tradition it was the burial place of *Adam's skull. See also HOLY SEPULCHRE.

Calvin, John (1509–64), French reformer and theologian. Born at Noyon in Picardy, Calvin appears to have been intended for an ecclesiastical career; he obtained his first benefice and received the *tonsure at the age of 12 through the patronage of the Bp. of Noyon. Sometime between 1521 and 1523 he went to Paris, studying arts at the Collège de Montaigu, presumably with a view to proceeding to the study of theology, but from 1528 he studied civil law at Orléans and later at Bourges. Here he became familiar with the ideas of Humanism, and possibly (through the influence of Melchior Wolmar, who taught him Greek) those of M. *Luther. After the death of his father in 1531, Calvin returned to Paris to study letters, publishing his commentary on *Seneca's *De Clementia* in 1532.

Calvin's growing sympathy with the Reformation movement led to his flight from Paris in Nov. 1533, following the outcry against the address delivered by the Rector of the University of Paris, Nicholas Cop, to mark the beginning of the academic year. This oration, generally thought to have been composed by Calvin, shows obvious affinities with both *Erasmus and Luther. In 1534 Calvin resigned his ecclesiastical benefices, and, as the religious situation in France deteriorated and the threat of persecution grew, fled to Basle in 1535. The first (Latin) edition of his *Institutes (q.v.) was published there in March 1536. On passing through *Geneva in July 1536, he was persuaded by G. *Farel to remain there and assist in organizing the Reformation in the city. In Jan. 1537 Calvin and Farel drew up articles regulating the organization of the Church and worship. However, strong internal opposition to their imposition of ecclesiastical discipline arose, centring on the imposition of a confession of faith and the use of excommunication as an instrument of social policy. Meanwhile Geneva was coming under increasing pressure from its powerful neighbour and ally, Berne. On Easter Day 1538, Calvin publicly defied the city council's explicit instructions to conform to the (*Zwinglian) religious practices of Berne and was immediately ordered to leave the city.

Accepting an invitation from M. *Bucer, Calvin spent the next three years as pastor to the French congregation at Strasbourg. This period proved formative for Calvin, allowing him insights into the management of civil and ecclesiastical affairs denied him in the more provincial setting of Geneva. During this period he produced an enlarged edition of the *Institutes* (1539), in which the influence of Bucer is particularly evident in the discussion of the Church; a commentary on Romans (1539); the first French edition of the *Institutes* (1541); and the celebrated Epistle to Cardinal *Sadoleto, then endeavouring to bring Geneva back to the RC Church, in which Calvin vigorously defended the principles of the Reformation. In Aug. 1540 he married Idelette de Burc, a widow.

In Sept. 1541 Calvin accepted the invitation of the city council to return to Geneva and during the next 14 years devoted himself to establishing a theocratic regime. His 'Ecclesiastical Ordinances', which again drew heavily on the views of Bucer, were adopted by the city council in Nov. 1541. These distinguished four ministries within the Church: pastors, doctors, elders, and deacons. Other reforming measures included the introduction of vernacular catechisms and liturgy. Ecclesiastical discipline was placed in the hands of a *consistory, consisting of 12 elders and some pastors, which sought to enforce morality through the threat of temporary excommunication; among other things it prohibited such pleasures as dancing and gambling. Popular reaction against this moral control was considerable, culminating in the victory of an anti-Calvin party in the city elections of 1548. This was assisted by popular discontent arising from the large number of Protestant emigrés, largely from France, who sought refuge in Geneva. The difficulties of Calvin's public life were compounded by personal tragedy: his wife died in March 1549, leaving him to care for her two children by her previous marriage (her only child by Calvin died shortly after his birth in 1542). The trial and execution of M. *Servetus (1553), however, served to undermine the authority of the city council, and by 1555 effective opposition to Calvin had ceased.

From this time onwards Calvin was virtually unimpeded in his promotion of the Reformation in Geneva and elsewhere. His extensive commentaries on the NT were supplemented by a series dealing with OT works. The establishment of the *Genevan Academy (1559) provided an international forum for the propagation of Calvin's ideas. His influence upon the French Protestant movement (see HUGUENOTS) was enormous, Geneva being the chief source of pastors for French Protestant congregations. The publication of French editions of the *Institutes* exercised as great an influence over the formation of the French language itself as over French Protestantism. Earlier, between 1548 and 1553, Calvin addressed a series of letters to *Edward VI and Protector *Somerset, proposing a scheme for the reform of the English Church which would retain an episcopal form of government; from 1555 onwards he offered refuge in Geneva to Protestant exiles from England. In 1559 Calvin was finally made a citizen of Geneva. Until then his status had been that of a legal resident alien in the employment of the city council. He did not have access to the decision-making bodies in the city, save for the appointment of pastors and the regulation of morals. What authority he possessed appears to have derived largely from his personality and his influence as a religious teacher and preacher; even this authority, however, was constantly challenged by the city council until 1555.

Calvin was a more rigorous and logical thinker than Luther, considerably more sympathetic to the insights and methods of Humanism, and much more aware of the importance of organization, both of ideas and institutions. During his time at Geneva, his reputation and influence as an ecclesiastical statesman, as a religious controversialist, educationalist, and author was widespread. His theological insight, his exegetical talents, his knowledge of languages, his precision, and his clear and pithy style, made him the most influential writer among the reformers. His *Institutes* are still regarded as one of the most important literary and theological works of the period.

The standard edn. of Calvin's works is that by H. W. Baum, E. Cunitz, E. Reuss, P. Lobstein, and A. Erichson (Corpus Reformatorum, 29–87; 59 vols., Brunswick, 1863–1900). *Opera Selecta*, ed. P. Barth and W. Niesel (5 vols., Munich, 1926–36). Many of his works were tr. into Eng. in the 19th cent. under the auspices of the Calvin Translation Society. The collection of *Tracts and Treatises* by H. Beveridge (1844) was repr., with notes and introd. by T. F. Torrance (3 vols., 1958). Other modern trs. into Eng. incl. that of his *Theological Treatises* by J. K. S. Reid (Library of Christian Classics, 22; 1954), of a selection of his *Commentaries* by J. Haroutunian (ibid. 23; 1958), of his *Institutes* by F. L. Battles, ed. J. T. McNeill (ibid. 20–1; 1961), of his *Commentaries* on the NT by T. H. L. Parker and others, ed. D. W. Torrance and T. F. Torrance (1959 ff.), and of his Comm. on Seneca's *De Clementia* by F. L. Battles and A. M. Huglo (Leiden, 1969). The Lives of Calvin by T. *Beza, orig. prefixed to Calvin's Comm. on Joshua (posthumously pub., Geneva, 1564; Eng. tr. of the Life, London, 1564), and that prefixed to the edn. of Calvin's letters pub. Geneva, 1575, together with that attributed to Beza (the work of Nicolas Colladon) prefixed to 2nd edn. of the Comm. on Joshua (Lyons, 1565), are pr. among his works.

Modern studies dealing with Calvin generally incl. E. Doumergue, *Jean Calvin: Les hommes et les choses de son temps* (5 vols., 1899–1917; comprehensive but uncrit.); B. B. Warfield, *Calvin and Calvinism* (New York and London, 1931); Q. Breen, *John Calvin: A Study in French Humanism* (Grand Rapids, 1931; 2nd edn., 1968); R. N. Carew Hunt, *Calvin* (London, 1933); J. Rilliet, *Calvin 1509–1564* (Paris, 1963); A. Ganoczy, *Le Jeune Calvin: Genèse et évolution de sa vocation réformatrice* (Veröffentlichungen des Instituts für europäische Geschichte Mainz, 40; Wiesbaden, 1966; Eng. tr., Philadelphia, 1987; Edinburgh, 1988); T. H. L. Parker, *John Calvin: A Biography* (1975); W. J. Bouwsma, *John Calvin: A Sixteenth-Century Portrait* (New York and Oxford, 1988); A. E. McGrath, *A Life of John Calvin* (Oxford, 1990). Works on different aspects incl. E. Choisy, *La Théocratie à Genève au temps de Calvin* (Geneva [1897]); W. Niesel, *Die Theologie Calvins* (Munich, 1938; 2nd edn., 1957; Eng. tr., 1956); J. D. Benoît, *Calvin, directeur des âmes* [1949]; T. F. Torrance, *Calvin's Doctrine of Man* (1949); id., *Kingdom and Church: A Study in the Theology of the Reformation* (1956), pp. 90–164; F. Wendel, *Calvin: Sources et évolution de sa pensée religieuse* (Études d'histoire et de philosophie religieuses publiées par la faculté de théologie protestante de l'université de Strasbourg, 41; 1950; Eng. tr., 1963); E. A. Dowey, *The Knowledge of God in Calvin's Theology* (New York, 1952); P. [M.] van Buren, *Christ in Our Place: The Substitutionary Character of Calvin's Doctrine of Reconciliation* (1957); R. S. Wallace, *Calvin's Doctrine of the Christian Life* (1959); J. Boisset, *Sagesse et Sainteté dans la Pensée de Jean Calvin* (Bibliothèque de l'École des Hautes Études. Section des Sciences Religieuses, 71; 1959); W. Nijenhuis, *Calvinus Oecumenicus: Calvijn en de Eenheid der Kerk in het Licht van zijn Briefwisseling* (Kirkhistorische Studien, 3; 1959); J. *Moltmann (ed.), *Calvin-Studien 1959* (Neukirchen, 1960); H. J. Forstman, *Word and Spirit: Calvin's Doctrine of Biblical Authority* (Stanford, Calif., 1962); K. McDonnell, OSB, *John Calvin, the Church, and the Eucharist* (Princeton, NJ, 1967); B. C. Milner, Jun., *Calvin's Doctrine of the Church* (Studies in the History of Christian Thought, 5; Leiden, 1970); T. H. L. Parker, *Calvin's New Testament Commentaries* (1971); id., *Calvin's Old Testament Commentaries* (Edinburgh, 1986); H. Höfl, *The Christian Polity of John Calvin* (Cambridge, 1982); R. V.

Schnucker (ed.), *Calviniana: Ideas and Influence of John Calvin* (Kirksville, Mo., 1988). R. Peter and J.-F. Gilmont, *Bibliotheca Calviniana: Les œuvres de Jean Calvin publiées au XVI ͤ siècle* (Travaux d'Humanisme et Renaissance, 255 and 281; 1991–4). A. Erichson, *Bibliographia Calviniana: Catalogus Chronologicus Operum Calvini* (Berlin, 1900); W. Niesel, *Calvin-Bibliographie 1901–1959* (Munich, 1961); D. Kempff, *A Bibliography of Calviniana 1959–1974* (Studies in Medieval and Reformation Thought, 15; Leiden, 1975). J. N. Tylenda and P. De Klerk, 'Calvin Bibliography 1960–1970', *Calvin Theological Journal*, 6 (1971), pp. 156–93; an annual bibl. is included in subsequent issues of the Journal. See also bibls. to CALVINISM and INSTITUTES.

Calvinism. The theological system of J. *Calvin (found chiefly in his *Institutes*), esp. as formulated by T. *Beza. Accepted with varying degrees of modification by most non-Lutheran reformed Churches, it holds certain doctrines characteristic of *Lutheranism, as well as other elements peculiar to itself. Among the former are the doctrines of Scripture as the only rule of faith, of the bondage of human free will through sin, and *justification (q.v.) by grace through faith. Calvinism is distinguished from Lutheranism primarily by its more radical use of Scripture as a criterion of ecclesiastical doctrine and practice, its stress upon *predestination and divine omnipotence and on the importance of the certitude of salvation to the elect, its modification of Luther's teaching on the Church and sacraments, and its emphasis upon the necessity of discipline within the Church. Where Luther drew a sharp distinction between Law and Gospel, Calvin stressed the continuity between the OT and the NT, allowing the Law a continued role as a moral guide for believers. Whereas the origins of Lutheranism were rural and territorial, Calvinism traces its origins to highly developed urban communities, a factor reflected in the latter's advanced political, economic, and social outlooks.

Although conceding a natural knowledge of God, Calvin insisted that the Bible was the most reliable and authoritative source of knowledge of God and of the moral and religious obligations of Christians. The authority of Scripture is grounded partly objectively in its divine inspiration, and partly subjectively in the 'internal testimony of the Holy Spirit', which persuades believers of its authenticity. In the state of innocence it was possible for man to attain to beatitude through his own natural powers, but the *Fall, which was willed by God, substantially changed human nature so that now all man wills and does is sin. Hence he is no longer free but follows necessarily either the attractions of concupiscence or of grace. All human works outside the Christian faith are sins; even the good works of Christians are intrinsically evil, though covered and not counted as sins through the imputed merits of Christ. This trust ('faith' in the Protestant sense) extends not only, as in Lutheranism, to the certitude of having obtained justification but to the perfect assurance of eternal salvation, and from this follows the characteristically Calvinist doctrine of the indefectibility of grace.

The characteristic Calvinist emphasis upon the divine omnipotence is expressed in the notion of divine election and predestination, according to which God predestined some of His creatures to eternal life and others to damnation without reference to foreseen merit. The doctrine of predestination, however, is not central to Calvin's theological system, being treated rather as an intrinsically mysterious aspect of the doctrine of salvation. The growing emphasis upon deducing theology systematically from general principles, typical of Beza, led to the doctrine of predestination assuming a new importance in later Calvinism. Predestination is treated by Beza as an aspect of the doctrine of God, and the divine decrees of election as axioms from which a doctrine of salvation may be deduced. Many scholars regard this shift of emphasis as a possible distortion of Calvin's balanced discussion of the doctrine.

Calvin's attitude to the Church differs from that of Luther. He defended a theocratic polity, subjecting the State to the Church, as contrasted with Luther who upheld the supremacy of the State. In the question of the Sacraments, esp. the Lord's Supper, Calvin attempted a compromise between Luther's belief in the *Real Presence, expressed in his doctrine of *consubstantiation, and U. *Zwingli's view of a mere symbolism. His language is at times ambiguous, but his thought seems to tend more in the direction of Zwingli, sometimes regarding the Sacraments as a testimony of God's grace, confirmed by an external sign.

The most influential document of strict Calvinism is the Second *Helvetic Confession of 1566, which was accepted in many reformed countries. Calvinism gained considerable influence in *France in the early 1560s; until the Wars of Religion, it seemed possible that the *Huguenots might gain the political ascendancy in Calvin's native country. In 1622 Calvinism became the state religion in the *Netherlands. Controversy there over the issue of predestination led to the emergence of factions in the Church with competing views on this matter (*Arminians, *Gomarists, *Sublapsarians, and *Superlapsarians). Calvinism also gained considerable influence in Germany, replacing Lutheranism in several localities, e.g. in Brandenburg and the Palatinate, as it did also in parts of *Romania and *Hungary. In England, slight Calvinist influence may be discerned in the *Thirty-Nine Articles, although its greatest impact was upon *Puritanism, esp. the *Westminster Confession (1648). It had the strongest effect in Scotland (esp. through J. *Knox) and colonial N. America, where its chief representative was J. *Edwards. It suffered severe setbacks through the rationalism of the 18th and 19th cents., but in the 20th cent. re-emerged as a major theological and religious force, esp. through the writings of K. *Barth and A. *Kuyper. Its attraction for the modern religious mind probably lies partly in its intellectual coherence, and partly in its emphasis upon the sovereignty of God as a reaction against the easy humanitarianism of modern liberal Protestantism.

Dogmatic Confessions in E. F. K. Müller, *Die Bekenntnisschriften der reformierten Kirche* (Leipzig, 1903). Eng. tr. of various primary docs. in A. C. Cochrane, *Reformed Confessions of the 16th Century* (1966) and in A. Duke and others (eds.), *Calvinism in Europe 1540–1610* (Manchester and New York [1992]). Modern confessional documents ed. L. Vischer, *Reformed Witness Today* (Berne, 1982). A. Kuyper, *Calvinism* (L. P. Stone Lectures [in Eng.], Amsterdam and New York, 1899); J. T. McNeill, *The History and Character of Calvinism* (New York and London, 1954); G. L. Hunt (ed.), *Calvinism and the Political Order* (Philadelphia, 1965); J. H. Leith, *Introduction to the Reformed Tradition* (Atlanta, 1977; Edinburgh, 1978); id., *The Imperative* (Philadelphia [1988]); M. Prestwich (ed.), *International Calvinism 1541–1715* (Oxford,

1985); D. K. McKim (ed.), *Major Themes in the Reformed Tradition* (Grand Rapids [1992]).

A. Schweizer, *Die Glaubenslehre der evangelisch-reformirten Kirche dargestellt* (2 vols., Zurich, 1844–7); id., *Die protestantischen Centraldogmen in ihrer Entwicklung innerhalb der reformierten Kirche* (2 vols., ibid., 1854–6). H. Clavier, *Études sur le Calvinisme* (1936). A. A. van Schelven, *Het Calvinisme gedurende zijn bloeitijd* (3 vols., 1943–65). K. Barth, *Die christliche Lehre nach dem Heidelberger Katechismus* (Zurich, 1948). J. Orr in *HERE* 3 (1901), pp. 146–55; W. S. Reid in D. K. McKim (ed.), *Encyclopedia of the Reformed Faith* (Louisville, Ky., and Edinburgh, 1992), pp. 48–50, s.v.; R. Benedetto, ibid., pp. 50–3, s.v. 'Calvinism in America'. See also works cited under PRESBYTERIANISM, PROTESTANTISM, and REFORMATION.

Calvinistic Methodism. The Church which was established in *Wales through the revivalist preaching of Howel *Harris of Trevecca (1714–73) and Daniel Rowland of Llangeitho (1713–90). They had contacts with English *Methodists and their first joint Association with them was held in 1743 (18 months before J. *Wesley's first Conference), but among the leaders of the movement there was no wish to separate from the C of E. The English Calvinistic Methodists, led by G. *Whitefield, were eventually absorbed into *Congregationalism. At the time of the Welsh revival of 1762 Rowland, whose licence had been suspended by the Bp. of *St Davids, conducted his ministry in a meeting house at Llangeitho to which his preaching drew great numbers. However, he remained a staunch Anglican until his death. In 1770 an annotated Welsh Bible was published by Peter Williams. The movement was brought to N. Wales by Thomas Charles, who joined the Methodists in 1784. Separation from the Establishment began in 1795 as a result of persecution. Since poor preachers, hampered by heavy fines, were obliged to seek the protection of the *Toleration Act, their meeting-houses were registered as Dissenting Chapels. The first ordinations of ministers in the Connexion took place only in 1811. The Confession of Faith (based on the *Westminster Confession) was drawn up in 1823 and the *Constitutional Deed* was formally completed in 1826. The first college for candidates for the ministry was founded at Bala in 1837 with Lewis Edwards as principal, and in 1842 the South Wales Association opened a college at Trevecca, David Charles being principal. In 1905 the South Wales Association founded a college at Aberystwyth, and gradually staff and students were transferred here from both Trevecca and Bala. In 1840 a Missionary Society was formed, to work in Brittany and India. By the Calvinistic Methodist or Presbyterian Church of Wales Act 1933, the autonomy of the Church in spiritual matters was secured and a Properties Board established. This Act officially recognized as legally synonymous the alternative title which had been in use from the 1840s.

By the constitution local churches report to their district meeting, which in turn reports to the Presbytery, which is the monthly meeting of a group of districts. The Presbyteries then appoint delegates to the Associations, which are the main legislative courts of the Church. There are three Associations, the North and the South being Welsh-speaking, and the East being English-speaking. Ministers are ordained by the Associations. A General Assembly of the Associations was established in 1864; it meets annually and is a deliberative body which helps to co-ordinate the doctrinal, legislative, and financial policies of the Associations. The ministry is not now itinerant, but ministers often have several churches within their pastoral care. While deacons of a church have a certain latitude in inviting ministers to occupy the pulpit, the Presbyteries now operate a rota system, whereby all churches within their areas receive a regular ministry. Almost three-quarters of its 1,034 churches are Welsh-speaking and many of its ministers and members are zealous defenders of Welsh nationality and language. Many of its members are much involved in education, politics, and social service.

The Church was a founder member of the World Presbyterian Alliance and is a member of the World Alliance of Reformed Churches. Its membership at the beginning of 1990 was 63,214.

The *Rules of Discipline* (in Welsh) first pub. Caerleon, 1801; the *Confession of Faith* (also in Welsh), preceded by a brief history of the Movement, pub. Aberystwyth, 1824; Eng. tr. under the title *The History, Constitution, Rules of Discipline and Confession of the Calvinistic Methodists in Wales* (London, 1827; rev. Welsh edn., 1876; Eng. tr., 1877). The *Constitutional Deed* of 1826 is pr. in the *Legal Hand-Book for the Calvinistic Methodist Connexion* (2nd edn., Wrexham [1911]), pp. 57–135. The archives of two of the main Calvinistic Methodist Chapels in London, the London Tabernacle and the Spa Fields Chapel, and the Minutes of the Calvinistic Methodist Association, 1745–9, are ed. E. Welch, *Two Calvinist Methodist Chapels 1743–1811* (London Record Society Publications, 11; 1975), with introd. on Calvinistic Methodism, pp. vii–xvi. There is a considerable lit. in Welsh. Works in Eng. incl. W. Williams, *Welsh Calvinistic Methodism: A Historical Sketch of the Presbyterian Church of Wales* (London, 1872). M. W. Williams, *Creative Fellowship: An Outline of the History of Calvinistic Methodism in Wales* (Caernarvon, 1935). R. R. Williams, *Flames from the Altar: Howell Harris and his Contemporaries* (ibid., 1962). R. B. Knox, *Voices from the Past: History of the English Conference of the Presbyterian Church of Wales, 1889–1938* (1969). L. D. Morgan, *Y Diwygiad Mawr* (1981; Eng. tr., *The Great Awakening in Wales*, 1988). D. E. Jenkins, *Calvinistic Methodist Holy Orders* (Caernarvon, 1911). *Journal of the Calvinistic Methodist Historical Society* (ibid., 1916 ff.). See also Lives of H. Harris, cited s.v.

Camaldolese. St *Romuald founded a monastery at Camaldoli (Campus Maldoli), near Arezzo, between 1012 and 1023. Its ideal was the barest minimum of communal ties. A hospice which Romuald also established nearby at Fontebuona developed as a *coenobitic house; the hermitage and the monastery were intended to complement each other. Romuald left no written rule, and monastic practice has varied in the different daughter-houses. At present there are two monastic *Congregations of Camaldolese monks, one of which has since 1966 belonged to the *Benedictine Confederation. The habit is a white tunic, with hood and *scapular of the same colour. There are also houses of Camaldolese nuns.

L. Schiaparelli, F. Baldasseroni, and E. Lasino (eds.), *Regesto di Camaldoli* (Regesta Chartarum Italiae, 2, 5, 13, 14; 1907–22). M. Ziegelbauer, OSB, *Centifolium camaldulense, sive Notitia Scriptorum Camaldulensium* (Venice, 1750). J. B. Mittarelli, OSB, and A. Costadoni, OSB, *Annales Camaldulenses Ordinis Sancti Benedicti* (9 vols., Venice, 1755–73). *Cenni storici del sacro eremo di Camaldoli* (2nd edn., Florence, 1864). A. Giabbani, OSB, *L'Eremo: Vita e spiritualità eremitica nel monachismo camaldolese primitivo* (Studi e Documenti di Storia religiosa; Brescia, 1945). A. Pagnani, OSB, *Storia dei Benedettini Camaldolesi Cenobiti, Eremiti, Monache ed Oblati* (Sassoferrato, 1949). W. Kurze, 'Campus

Malduli. Die Frühgeschichte Camaldolis', *Quellen und For-schungen aus italienischen Archiven und Bibliotheken*, 44 (1964), pp. 1–34. A. Des Mazis, OSB, in *DHGE* 11 (1949), cols. 512–36, with bibl.; A. Giabbani, OSB, in *NCE* 2 (1967), pp. 1095–7, s.v.; G. Cacciamani in *DIP* 1 (1974), cols. 1718–28, s.v. See also works cited under ROMUALD, ST.

Câmara, Helder Passoa (1909–), Abp. of Olinda and Recife in Brazil. Born in Fortaleza in NE Brazil, he was ordained priest in 1931 and appointed Secretary for Education in his home state of Ceara. In 1936 he went to Rio de Janeiro, being consecrated auxiliary bishop in 1952. He was instrumental in setting up the Conference of Brazilian Bishops and the Latin American Episcopal Council (CELAM). He became increasingly concerned about the plight of the destitute (the *favelas*) in the capital and about the political and economic injustices that lay behind it. Upon his return to NE Brazil as Abp. of Olinda and Recife in 1964, his condemnation of political injustice became outspoken. Conservative interests in Church and State opposed him, and there were said to be attempts to assassinate him, but he was helped by the personal support of *Paul VI. In 1985 he was succeeded in his see by a conservative, José Cardosa Sobrinho. Câmara's writings, which were mostly occasional, gave him a world-wide reputation. They include *Revolução dentro da paz* (Rio de Janeiro, 1968; Eng. tr., 1971) and *Pour arriver à temps* (Brussels, 1970; Eng. tr., *Race against Time*, 1971).

Cambridge. The city lies where a Roman road crossed the river Granta or Cam; there was a Roman fort N. of the river on the site later occupied by the Norman castle and the modern Shire Hall. But the town grew in mid- and late Saxon times mainly S. and E. of the river; between the 10th and the early 13th cent. at least 15 parish churches were built. In the central Middle Ages Cambridge acquired a remarkable number of religious houses for a small town: *canons regular at St Giles by the Castle, *c*.1092, who later moved to Barnwell Priory; a monastic community at St Sepulchre's, the round church, *c*.1120, later a parish church; *Benedictine nuns at St Radegund's (since 1496 Jesus College), in the mid-12th cent.; *Augustinians at the Hospital of St John (since 1511 St John's College), *c*.1200; and at least six houses of friars in the 13th cent. When Cambridgeshire was split off from the large diocese of *Lincoln in 1109, its first bishop settled at *Ely, seeking the resources and the church of a rich abbey. But the link between Ely and Cambridge has always been very close, and it was prob. the bishop's learned clerks who provided hospitality in Cambridge for students escaping from riots in *Oxford in 1209, and so founded the University of Cambridge. It was certainly Hugh Balsham, Bp. of Ely, who founded the first college, Peterhouse, in 1284. The university early won royal patronage, which enabled it to survive; but until the 15th cent. it remained modest in comparison with Oxford, owing such distinction as it had largely to the peripatetic friars, including *Duns Scotus. In the early 14th cent. one great college, the King's Hall (now part of Trinity College), and a group of small colleges, academic *chantries in effect, were established; and between the 1440s, when King's College and Queens' were founded, and the mid-16th cent. the colleges in effect (as at Oxford) absorbed the student population. In the

early 16th cent. St John *Fisher was Chancellor (1504–35) and *Erasmus a celebrated visitor. The 1530s saw the suppression of the friars and of the faculty of *canon law; but it also saw T. *Cranmer of Jesus College become Abp. of *Canterbury, and H. *Latimer of Clare and N. *Ridley of Pembroke leaders of the English *Reformation; the young M. *Parker was already established at Corpus Christi College. From 1549 until 1551 M. *Bucer was Regius Professor of Divinity. Like Oxford, Cambridge produced many of the leading Anglican divines of the late 16th and 17th cents., including E. *Grindal, J. *Whitgift, J. *Donne, G. *Herbert, L. *Andrewes, J. *Cosin, and W. *Sancroft, and also some leading *Puritans, from T. *Cartwright to J. *Milton. It was also the home of the *Cambridge Platonists. It was Matthew Wren, a former Fellow of Pembroke Hall and Master of Peterhouse, who, as Bp. of Ely (1638–67), brought his nephew C. *Wren to Cambridge to build Pembroke Hall chapel for him in the 1660s; Christopher Wren went on to design Emmanuel College chapel for Sancroft and Trinity College library for I. *Barrow, the mathematician and friend of I. *Newton. Newton was pre-eminent as a mathematician, but he was also one of a small circle of unorthodox theologians, which included S. *Clarke. These apart, Cambridge was not again an eminent centre of theology until the late 19th cent., though it produced notable scholars such as R. *Bentley, notable ecclesiastical politicians such as B. *Hoadly, and the celebrated apologist W. *Paley. In the 19th cent. it played a part in the *evangelical revival, esp. through the influence of C. *Simeon, and in *High Church movements through the members of the *Cambridge Camden Society. Most celebrated perhaps of the many Cambridge theologians of the 19th cent. were the triumvirate who played a major role in translating the Revised Version (see BIBLE, ENGLISH VERSIONS, 4), J. B. *Lightfoot, B. F. *Westcott, and F. J. A. *Hort, and their younger contemporary H. B. *Swete. Biblical scholarship continued to flourish in the days of C. H. *Dodd and beyond.

R. Willis and J. W. Clark, *The Architectural History of the University of Cambridge, and of the Colleges of Cambridge and Eton* (4 vols., Cambridge, 1886). *VCH*, Cambridgeshire, ed. J. P. C. Roach, 3: *The City and University of Cambridge* (1959); *City of Cambridge* (2 vols. + map and plans, Royal Commission on Historical Monuments, 1959). *A History of the University of Cambridge*, ed. C. [N. L.] Brooke (4 vols., Cambridge, 1988 ff.). A. B. Cobban, *The Medieval English Universities: Oxford and Cambridge to c.1500* (Aldershot, 1988). C. [N. L.] Brooke, [J.] R. [L.] Highfield, and W. Swaan, *Oxford and Cambridge* (Cambridge, 1988). V. H. H. Green, *Religion at Oxford and Cambridge* (1964); C. N. L. Brooke, 'The churches of medieval Cambridge', in D. [E. D.] Beales and G. [F. A.] Best (eds.), *History, Society and the Churches: Essays in honour of Owen Chadwick* (1985), pp. 49–76. A. B. Emden, *A Biographical Register of the University of Cambridge to 1500* (Cambridge, 1963).

Cambridge Camden Society. A society founded in May 1839 by J. M. *Neale and B. *Webb for the study of ecclesiastical art. Its first president was T. Thorp, Archdeacon of Bristol and Webb's tutor at Trinity; and in 1841 it began to issue its monthly periodical, *The Ecclesiologist*. In 1846, when its headquarters removed to London, its name was altered to the 'Ecclesiological Society', under which title it survived till 1868. It greatly stimulated interest in church architecture and traditional Catholic worship, and thus assisted the liturgical and ceremonial revival in the C of E in the later 19th cent.

A *Report* containing Lists of Officers and Members, 'Laws', Lists of Churches Visited, Publications, etc., was pub. annually at Cambridge from 1840 to 1844, at less frequent intervals at London from 1845 to 1864. In all 189 numbers of *The Ecclesiologist* were issued (Nov. 1841–Dec. 1868). J. F. White, *The Cambridge Movement: The Ecclesiologists and the Gothic Revival* (Cambridge, 1962).

Cambridge Platonists. They were a group of influential philosophical divines who flourished at Cambridge between 1633 and 1688. They stood between the *Puritans and High Anglicans and consistently advocated tolerance and comprehension within the Church, basing their demand on their conception that reason was the arbiter both of natural and of revealed religion. They held that it could judge the data of revelation by virtue of the indwelling of God in the mind, since 'the spirit in man is the candle of the Lord' (B. *Whichcote). This mystical view of reason was derived principally from *Neoplatonism, though the Cambridge Platonists interpreted it not so much as ecstasy as an abiding direction of will and affection alike. They were in many ways uncritical, discovering, e.g., affinities between *Platonism and the OT. The chief modern influence on their philosophy was R. *Descartes, whose intellectualism appealed to them, though they sought to purge his doctrines of his materialist view of the inanimate world by combining with them belief in an immanent divine soul, and supplementing his mechanism by teleology. They applied their Platonism in the sphere of ethics and epistemology to establish the identity of the Will of God and the 'Summum Bonum' and of the worlds of sense and thought.

The most important of the Cambridge Platonists were B. Whichcote (1609–83), N. Culverwel (d. 1651?), John Smith (1618–52), R. *Cudworth (1617–88), and H. *More (1614–87).

Collections of extracts by E. T. Campagnac (Oxford, 1901), G. R. Cragg (Library of Protestant Thought, New York, 1968) and C. A. Patrides (Stratford-upon-Avon Library, 5; 1969; repr., Cambridge, 1980). J. Tulloch, *Rational Theology and Christian Philosophy in England in the 17th Century* (2 vols., 1872); F. J. Powicke, *The Cambridge Platonists* (1926). R. L. Colie, *Light and Enlightenment: A Study of the Cambridge Platonists and the Dutch Arminians* (Cambridge, 1957). H. R. McAdoo, *The Spirit of Anglicanism* (1965), pp. 81–155. M. Micheletti, *Animal capax religionis: Da Benjamin Whichcote a Shaftesbury* (Perugia, 1984), esp. pp. 9–109. J. Passmore in P. Edwards (ed.), *Encyclopedia of Philosophy*, 2 (1967), pp. 9–11.

camelaucum. The original name of the Papal *tiara (q.v.), found, e.g., in the Life of Pope Constantine (d. 715) in the *Liber Pontificalis*, and in the '*Donation of Constantine' (8th–9th cent.).

Camerarius, Joachim (1500–74), German classical scholar and reformer. In 1530 he sat in the Diet of *Augsburg as deputy for Nuremberg, and took part in drawing up the famous Confession. In 1535 he undertook the reorganization of the University of *Tübingen, and in 1541 that of Leipzig. A personal friend of the eirenic P. *Mel-

anchthon, whose biography he wrote in elegant Latin, he acted as a moderating influence in Lutheranism; and he discussed in 1535 with Francis I and in 1568 with Maximilian II the possibility of reunion between Catholics and Protestants. He left a large number of treatises on classical subjects and letters, a sizeable proportion of which have remained unpublished.

Study by F. Stählin (Schriften des Vereins für Reformationsgeschichte, 159; 1936). Collection of essays [several in Eng.], ed. F. Baron (Humanistische Bibliothek, Reihe 1, Bd. 24; Munich, 1978), with list of his works, pp. 231–51. T. Kolde in *PRE* (3rd edn.), 3 (1897), pp. 687–9, s.v., with bibl. Further bibl. in Schottenloher, 1 (1933), p. 104 (nos. 2545–62).

Camerlengo (Lat., *camerarius*). The chamberlain of the Papal court. He presides over the Apostolic Camera (an ancient and once important department of the Roman *Curia) and chiefly oversees economic affairs during a vacancy in the Holy See. One of his duties is to assemble and direct the *conclave. He is always a *cardinal.

N. Del Re, *La Curia Romana* (3rd edn., Sussidi Eruditi, 23; 1970), esp. pp. 295–309.

Cameron, John (d. 1446), Bp. of Glasgow and Chancellor of Scotland. In 1424 he became secretary to James I. He was provided to the see of Glasgow by Pope *Martin V at the King's request in 1426 and consecrated in Jan. 1427. He had become Chancellor by this date, and remained in office as the King's leading adviser until the murder of James in Feb. 1437. In 1427 he supported royal legislation limiting the activities of Scottish beneficeseekers in Rome; he was summoned to the Papal court to answer for this in 1429, but the King informed the Pope that he could not spare his Chancellor, who was busy with administrative and diplomatic duties. Cameron was sent as part of the official Scottish delegation to the Council of *Basle, where he was based from Feb. 1434 until mid-1437. He visited Pope *Eugenius IV at least in 1435 and perhaps again in 1436, arranging for the first visit of a Papal legate in 200 years to take steps to reform the Church in Scotland. He returned to Scotland after the King's murder, and as Chancellor was still active in the minority government of James II until he was ousted by a political change in 1439. He was still occasionally employed in the royal administration, and joined with other bishops and abbots in the parliament of 1445 in examining the claim of the Scottish bishops to make testamentary dispositions.

J. Dowden, *The Bishops of Scotland*, ed. J. M. Thomson (Glasgow, 1912), pp. 319–22. J. H. Burns, *Scottish Churchmen and the Council of Basle* (Glasgow, 1962), esp. pp. 16 f., and 38–40. T. A. Archer in *DNB* 8 (1886), pp. 293–5, s.v., with refs.

Cameron, John (c.1579–1625), Protestant theologian. He was educated at Glasgow University, and in 1600 went to France, where he taught classics at the College of Bergerac and philosophy at the University of Sedan. He later was a private tutor at Paris, Geneva, and Heidelberg, at the same time pursuing his studies. In 1608 he was appointed a minister of the Protestant Church at Bordeaux, and in 1618 he succeeded F. *Gomar as professor of divinity at Saumur. In 1620 religious conditions in France caused him to return to England, and in 1622 he was made principal of Glasgow University. He was a supporter of *James

(VI and) I and his exalted views on the prerogatives of the royal power, but the unpopularity of these views compelled him to return to Saumur in 1623. In 1624 he became professor of divinity at Montauban, where his doctrine of passive obedience to the secular authorities roused such hostility that he was assaulted in the street and his health severely injured. He died in the following year. Cameron was a very gifted linguist as well as a learned theologian. Among his writings are treatises on Grace and Free-Will (1618) and on the Satisfaction of Christ for sin (1620), in which he upheld that God's action on the will was moral, not physical, and thus was considered by stricter *Calvinists as inclining to *Pelagianism. His doctrines were accepted by a school of contemporary theologians ('Cameronites'), which included S. *Bochart and J. *Daillé.

G. B. Maury, 'John Cameron: A Scottish Protestant Theologian in France (1579–1625)', *Scottish Historical Review*, 7 (1910), pp. 325–45. A. H. Swinne, *John Cameron, Philosoph und Theologe (1579–1625)*, Bibliographisch-kritische Analyse der Hand- und Druckschriften sowie der Cameron-Literatur (Marburg, 1968; 2nd edn., Studia Irenica, 1; Hildesheim, 1972). T. F. Henderson in *DNB* 8 (1886), pp. 295 f., s.v.

Cameron, Richard (d. 1680), Scottish *Covenanting leader.

In his youth he was a schoolmaster under the episcopal incumbent of Falkland, Fife, but was won by the Covenanting cause and became a field-preacher, influencing thousands by his eloquence. In May 1678 he went to the Netherlands, where he was ordained; he returned in Oct., and in 1680 joined with a few others in the 'Sanquhar Declaration', which disowned allegiance to *Charles II and declared war upon him, attacking strongly all Covenanters who accepted the royal indulgence then offered. He fell in an affray with some royal troops at Airds Moss in Ayrshire on 22 July 1680.

Lives by J. Herkless (London [1896]) and A. Veitch (ibid., 1948).

Cameronians.

A term applied at the end of the 17th cent. to extreme *Covenanters, such as the followers of R. *Cameron (q.v.) and esp. the '*Reformed Presbyterians' who declined the settlement of the Established Church of Scotland made in 1690 under William and Mary, though they themselves repudiated the name.

J. H. Burton, *The History of Scotland from Agricola's Invasion to the Revolution of 1688*, 7 (1870), pp. 527–76 passim. J. H. S. Burleigh, *A Church History of Scotland* (1960), esp. pp. 250–3, 262 f. F. *Kattenbusch in *PRE* (3rd edn.), 3 (1897), pp. 691–3, s.v. 'Cameronianer', with bibl. See also bibl. to COVENANTERS and REFORMED PRESBYTERIAN CHURCH.

Camillus of Lellis, St (1550–1614), founder of the 'Ministers of the Sick'.

He was a native of the kingdom of Naples, and early joined the Venetian army against the Turks. His passion for gambling having reduced him to great poverty, he was employed as a labourer by the *Capuchins at Manfredonia in 1574, where, in 1575, he was converted and began to embrace a penitential life. He tried his vocation with the Capuchins and again with the *Franciscan *Recollects, but an incurable disease in his legs compelled him to leave both and he became a nurse at the hospital of St Giacomo in Rome. Under the

guidance of St *Philip Neri he grew to great holiness, and resolved to found an order for the care of the sick. He was ordained priest in 1584, and about the same time established a congregation, then called 'Camillians', who take a fourth vow to devote themselves to the service of the sick, esp. the plague-stricken. The congregation was approved by the Pope in 1586 and elevated to an order with the privileges of the *Mendicants by Gregory XIV in 1591. It expanded from Rome to a number of other Italian cities during the 1590s. Despite several painful illnesses Camillus remained its superior-general till 1607, when he resigned the government of his order to devote himself more fully to the care of the sick. His striking reforms in this field envisaged both the spiritual and the material needs of the sick, such as the separation of those afflicted with contagious diseases, well-aired wards, special diet, and, particularly, an effective spiritual assistance to the dying, whence his order is also called 'Fathers of a Good Death' or 'Agonizantes'. He was canonized in 1746, made patron of the sick by *Leo XIII in 1886, and of nurses and nursing associations by *Pius XI in 1930. Feast day, 14 (formerly 18) July.

Scritti, ed. M. Vanti (Milan and Rome, 1965). The principal authority is the Life by S. Cicatelli, for 26 years his companion and later general of the order, pub. Viterbo, 1615; Eng. tr. by F. W. *Faber, 2 vols., 1850–1. Further Life by G. B. de Rossi, SJ (Rome, 1644). M. Vanti, *S. Camillo de Lellis 1550–1614, apostolo di carità infermiera* (Turin and Rome, 1929); id., *S. Camillo de Lellis e i suoi Ministri degli Infermi* (1957; 3rd edn., 1964), and other works of this author. [A.] C. Oldmeadow, *The First Red Cross, Camillus de Lellis, 1550–1614* (1923; popular). Other Lives by C. C. Martindale, SJ (London, 1946), and H. Panneel (Mulhouse, etc., 1964). M. Vanti and P. Cannata in *Bibliotheca Sanctorum*, 3 (Rome, 1963), cols. 707–22, s.v., with bibl.; A. Prosperi in *Dizionario Biografico degli Italiani*, 17 (1974), pp. 230–4, s.v. On the order see also P. Sannazzaro, MI, in *DIP* 2 (1975), cols. 912–24, s.v. 'Chierici Regolari Ministri degli Infermi'.

Camisards.

A group of fanatical French Protestants, who rose in the revolt in the Cévennes district in 1702 against the rigorous steps taken by Louis XIV to suppress their religion and the ensuing persecution. They often fell under ecstatic inspiration and prophesied; they fought a guerilla war that neither gave nor expected quarter. Considerable cruelty was shown on both sides, and the revolt was suppressed in 1705. A further outbreak in 1709 was quickly checked. *Huguenots in England and elsewhere outside France, throughout the 18th cent., were unsympathetic to the 'inspired' prophesying and condemned a rebellion which cost 40,000 lives (counting both sides). Meanwhile Antoine Court (1696–1760), while resisting the fanaticism of the Camisards, gathered together the scattered groups into a clandestine Church (*Église du désert*); he is held to have restored the Protestant Church in France. In England, where some of them took refuge, the Camisards were known as 'French Prophets'. The name 'Camisard' is of uncertain origin; it may derive from *camisard* (a 'nocturnal attack') or *camise* (modern *chemise*; a 'shirt', worn over their clothes as a disguise).

[A. Court], *Histoire des troubles des Cevennes ou de la guerre des Camisars* (3 vols., Villefranche, 1760; repr., 2 vols., Marseilles, 1975). Smaller modern collection of primary docs. by P. Joutard, *Les Camisards* [1976]. C. Bost, *Les Prédicants protestants des Cévennes et du Bas-Languedoc, 1684–1700* (2 vols., 1912); H. Bosc, *La*

Guerre des Cévennes, 1702–1710 (6 vols., Montpellier [1985–93]). P. Joutard, La Légende des Camisards: Une sensibilité au passé [1977]. H. Schwartz, The French Prophets: The History of a Millenarian Group in Eighteenth-Century England (Berkeley, Calif., and London [1980]). R. A. *Knox, Enthusiasm (1950), pp. 356–71. C. Garrett, Spirit Possession and Popular Religion from the Camisards to the Shakers (Baltimore, 1987), pp. 15–73. F. Vernet in DTC 2 (1905), cols. 1435–43, s.v.; J. Dedieu in DHGE 11 (1949), cols. 607–14, s.v., with bibl.

campagus (Late Lat.). Originally a kind of military boot, the word came into current usage for episcopal *sandals (q.v.).

Campanella, Tommaso (baptized Giovanni Domenico) (1568–1639), Italian philosopher. In 1582 he became a *Dominican and in 1590 published his first important work, a defence of the philosopher Bernardino *Telesio (d. 1588), called Philosophia Sensibus Demonstrata. His open disavowal of the *Aristotelian philosophy aroused the suspicions of his ecclesiastical superiors, while his suspected complicity in anti-Spanish plots provoked the civil authorities of Naples. In 1603 he was sentenced to perpetual imprisonment, but he was finally released in 1629. In 1634 he withdrew to France in disguise, and spent the rest of his life at the convent of St-Honoré in Paris.

His philosophy was in the *Platonist tradition. Anticipating R. *Descartes, he held that individual consciousness was the fundamental fact of experience, and that the existence of God could be deduced from the presence of the idea of God in human consciousness. His political philosophy owed much both to *Plato and to St *Augustine. He advocated a reconstruction of the political order closely modelled on Plato's 'Republic', with society under the control of philosopher-priests who would submit the government of the state to the supreme authority of the Pope. His most important work in this field is the Civitas Solis (1623). Campanella was also a poet of some ability.

Lettere ed. by V. Spampanato (Bari, 1927); Poesie ed. G. *Gentile (Florence, 1939) and L. Firpo (Rome, 1944); Opuscoli Inediti ed. id. (Florence, 1951); Theologicorum, ed., with Ital. tr., by R. Amerio (Edizione Nazionale dei Classici del Pensiero Italiano, 10–11, 1949–51; 2nd ser. 1, 5–9, 12–16, 19–31, 33, etc., 1955 ff.); Opera Letterarie, ed. L. Bolzoni (Turin, 1977). De Praecedentia Religiosorum first ed. M. Miele, OP, in Archivum Fratrum Praedicatorum, 52 (1982), pp. 267–323. Eng. tr. of 'Apologia pro Galileo', by G. McColley in Smith College Studies in History, 22 (Northampton, Mass., 1937), nos. 3 and 4, and of Civitas Solis by D. J. Donno (Berkeley, Calif., and London, 1981). M. Baldacchini, Vita di Tommaso Campanella (Naples, 1847). L. Amabile, Fra Tommaso Campanella: La sua congiura, i suoi processi e la sua pazzia (3 vols., 1882) and other works. L. Blanchet, Campanella (Paris, 1920; repr. New York [1964]); L. Firpo (ed.), Ricerche campanelliane (Biblioteca Storica Sansoni, NS 13, 1947); G. di Napoli, Tommaso Campanella (Problemi d'Oggi, 2nd ser. 10; 1947); A. Corsano, Tommaso Campanella (Bari 1961); A. Ruschioni, Tommaso Campanella filosofo-poeta (Brunello, 1980). G. Bock, Thomas Campanella: Politisches Interesse und philosophische Spekulation (Bibliothek des Deutschen Historischen Instituts in Rom, 46; Tübingen, 1974). A. Amerio, Il sistema teologico di Tommaso Campanello (Milan, 1972). L. Firpo, Bibliografia degli scritti di Tommaso Campanella (1940). Id. in Dizionario Biografico degli Italiani, 17 (1974), pp. 372–401, s.v. with further bibl.

campanile. In general, any bell-tower or bell-steeple; but the name is esp. applied to the detached bell-tower which

originated in Italy. The earliest examples of the latter are those of San Apollinare in Classe and San Apollinare Nuovo at *Ravenna, both 10th cent. Other famous campaniles are at San Francesco, Assisi, at St-Front, Périgueux, at San Marco, *Venice, at San Zeno Maggiore, *Verona, at Siena Cathedral, and the Leaning Tower of Pisa.

Campbell, Alexander (1788–1866), co-founder, with Barton W. Stone (1772–1844), of the *Disciples of Christ. The son of Thomas Campbell (1763–1854), a Seceder *Presbyterian minister from Co. Armagh, who emigrated to the USA in 1807, Alexander followed his father in 1809 after a year at Glasgow University and settled at Bethany in what is now W. Virginia. Deeply influenced by J. *Locke and Scottish Common Sense Realism, he taught that a rational study of the biblical text revealed the essential facts of primitive Christian faith. He advocated Christian union on the basis of NT teaching, believing that it would usher in a period of Divine blessing. He and his father left the Presbyterians, holding that creeds and confessions of faith should not be made tests of fellowship. In 1812 he became convinced of the necessity for baptism by *immersion and joined the *Baptists, but his belief that baptism was for the remission of sins led eventually to his separation from them. He initiated a revival on the Western Reserve and in 1832 his movement united with Stone's Christian Connection in Kentucky. By the mid-19th cent. it was one of the largest American denominations, though two later divisions crystallized in 1906 and 1927. In 1841 he founded Bethany College. He edited and wrote nearly the whole of two periodicals, The Christian Baptist (7 vols., 1823–30) and the Millennial Harbinger (41 vols., 1830–70).

R. Richardson, Memoirs of Alexander Campbell (2 vols., Philadelphia, 1868–70). R. F. West, Alexander Campbell and Natural Religion (Yale Studies in Religious Education, 21; New Haven, Conn., and London, 1948); D. R. Lindley, Apostle of Freedom (St Louis [1957]); J. Seale (ed.) Lectures in Honour of the Alexander Campbell Bicentennial, 1788–1988 (Nashville, 1988). G. C. Boase in DNB 8 (1886), pp. 310 f.

Campbell, John McLeod (1800–72), Scottish theologian. Educated at Glasgow and Edinburgh, he was appointed in 1825 to the cure of Row (now Rhu) in Strathclyde. Here, in 1826, he became convinced of the doctrine of 'assurance of faith', which, in conjunction with his belief in the universality of the Atonement, aroused much opposition from his congregation and others as at variance with *Presbyterian principles. In 1831 the *General Assembly found him guilty of heresy and deprived him of his cure. Campbell maintained, however, a successful ministry on an independent congregation at Glasgow from 1833 until 1859, when ill-health forced his retirement. The main thesis of his principal work, The Nature of the Atonement and its Relation to Remission of Sins and Eternal Life (1856), was that the spiritual context of the sufferings of Christ, rather than their penal character, made atonement for sin.

J. McL. Campbell, Reminiscences and Reflections (ed. by his son, D. Campbell, 1873). G. M. Tuttle, So Rich a Soil: John McLeod Campbell on Christian Atonement (Edinburgh, 1986).

Campeggio, Lorenzo (1472–1539), Abp. of *Bologna. After the death of his wife (by whom he had had five children), he was ordained in 1510. He was presented with the bishopric of Feltre in 1512; and from 1513 to 1517 he was *nuncio at the Imperial court. In 1518 he was sent to England by *Leo X to try to gain *Henry VIII's support for a crusade against the Turks, but without success. He was subsequently made protector of England in the Roman *curia, and in 1524 Henry created him Bp. of *Salisbury, while in 1523 the Pope had made him Abp. of Bologna. At this time he also contended on behalf of Papal interests in Germany, but with little success. In 1528 he came back to England in the matter of Henry's projected divorce. He was provided with a document which merely defined the relevant ecclesiastical law and asserted that the question of fact must be settled in England by himself and T. *Wolsey, though the Pope had secretly pledged him to refer the matter to Rome before passing final judgement. Failing to satisfy the King, he left England in 1529 and took part in the coronation of *Charles V in the following year. In 1535 he was deprived by Act of Parliament of the see of Salisbury. He was created a cardinal in 1537.

Primary docs. concerning his part in the divorce case ed. S. Ehses, *Römische Dokumente zur Geschichte der Ehescheidung Heinrichs VIII von England, 1527–1534* (Quellen und Forschungen aus dem Gebiete der Geschichte in Verbindung mit ihrem historischen Institut in Rom herausgegeben von der Görres-Gesellschaft, 2; 1893), with introd. on Campeggio's life up to 1528, pp. xvi–xxxi; id., 'Kardinal Lorenzo Campeggio auf dem Reichstage von Augsburg, 1530', *RQ* 17 (1903), pp. 383–406; 18 (1904), pp. 358–84; and 19 (1905), pp. 129–225, with docs. G. Müller (ed.), *Legation Lorenzo Campeggios [1530–2] und Nuntiatur Girolamo Aleandros [1531–2]* (Nuntiaturberichte aus Deutschland, Abt. 1: 1533–1559, Ergänzbande 1–2; 1963–9). Early Life by C. Sigonio (Bologna, 1581). E. V. Cardinal, CSV, *Cardinal Lorenzo Campeggio, Legate to the Courts of Henry VIII and Charles V* (Boston, 1935). W. E. Wilkie, *The Cardinal Protectors of England* (Cambridge, 1974), pp. 104–238, *passim.* S. Skalweit in *Dizionario Biografico degli Italiani*, 17 (1974), pp. 454–62, s.v. 'Campeggi, Lorenzo'; E. V. Cardinal, CSV, in *NCE* 2 (1967), p. 1113, s.v., with further bibl. See also bibl. to HENRY VIII.

Campion, St Edmund (1540–81), *Jesuit. The son of a London bookseller, he was educated at the expense of the Grocers' Guild at a London grammar school, Christ's Hospital, and St John's College, Oxford, where he became a Junior Fellow in 1557. He was distinguished by his powers of leadership and his oratorical ability; in 1566 he was chosen by the university to welcome Queen *Elizabeth I to Oxford. Although already Catholic in sympathy, he was ordained deacon in the C of E in 1569, but being troubled in conscience left Oxford in 1570 for *Dublin, hoping for the revival of the university. Returning to England in disguise in 1571, he joined W. *Allen at *Douai in the same year and was received into the RC Church. Proceeding to Rome as a pilgrim, he entered the Society of Jesus in 1573 and was ordained in 1578. After a novitiate spent in Brünn, Bohemia, he taught at Prague until in 1580 he joined R. *Parsons in the first Jesuit mission to England. He preached extensively and with considerable effect in London and Lancs. In 1581 he secretly published a pamphlet entitled *Decem Rationes*, defending the RC position. He was arrested later in the year, but appears to have been offered his life if he would return to the C of E. On his refusal he was charged with conspiracy against the Crown, put on the rack and executed at Tyburn (1

Dec. 1581). He was among the *Forty Martyrs canonized in 1970.

His *Two Bokes of the Histories of Ireland*, written in 1571 and pub. in 1633, ed., with introd., by A. F. Vossen (Assen, 1963). [W. *Allen,] *A Brief History of the Glorious Martyrdom of Twelve Reverend Priests* (1582; new edn. by J. H. Pollen, SJ, 1908). H. More, SJ, *Historia Missionis Anglicanae Societatis Jesu* (St Omer, 1660), partly tr. into Eng. by F. Edwards, SJ, *The Elizabethan Jesuits* (1981), esp. pp. 41–128. R. Simpson, *Edmund Campion* (1867). Modern study by E. Waugh (London, 1935). E. E. Reynolds, *Campion and Parsons: The Jesuit Mission of 1580–1* (1980). T. M. McCoog, SJ (ed.), *The Reckoned Expense: Edmund Campion and the Early English Jesuits* (Woodridge, Suffolk, 1996). Pre-1641 edns. of works listed in A. F. Allison and D. M. Rogers, *The Contemporary Printed Literature of the English Counter-Reformation*, 1 (Aldershot, 1989), pp. 23–31 (nos. 130–204). Polgár, 1 (1990), pp. 420–3. A. De Bil in *DHGE* 11 (1949), cols. 650–6, s.v.

camp meeting. A religious *revivalist meeting held out of doors and lasting for several days, during which those taking part lived in tents or temporary huts. This kind of meeting, first tried in 1799, has on occasion been adopted by several religious bodies, but has been used most frequently by *Methodists, esp. in the USA. A one-day version was a feature of early *Primitive Methodism in England.

Canaan. The land later known as Palestine, which the Israelites occupied and conquered by degrees in the latter part of the second millennium BC or, acc. to some views, rather earlier. Of the original inhabitants (called Canaanites) some survived, and appear to have had a reactionary influence upon the development and maintenance of the Israelites' belief in Yahweh as their only God. G. E. Mendenhall argued that Israel was in fact composed, in part at least, of native Canaanites who revolted against their overlords; this idea has been developed by N. K. Gottwald.

L. H. Vincent, OP, *Canaan d'après l'exploration récente* (1907). Y. Aharoni, *The Land of the Bible* [1967; Eng. tr. of Heb. work of 1962], pp. 61–70. J. Gray, *The Canaanites* (1964). K. M. Kenyon, *Amorites and Canaanites* (Schweich Lectures, 1963; 1966). A. R. Millard, 'The Canaanites', in D. J. Wiseman (ed.), *Peoples of Old Testament Times* (Oxford, 1973), pp. 29–52. G. E. Mendenhall, 'The Hebrew Conquest of Palestine', *Biblical Archaeologist*, 25 (1962), pp. 66–87; N. K. Gottwald, *The Tribes of Yahweh: A Sociology of the Religion of Liberated Israel, 1250–1050 BCE* (Maryknoll, NY, 1979; London, 1980), esp. pp. 210–19. F. Stolz in *TRE* 17 (1988), pp. 539–56, s.v. 'Kanaan', with extensive bibl.

Canada, Christianity in. First brought to what is now Canada by Norse colonists from Greenland *c.*1001, Christianity took permanent root with the arrival of French settlers in Acadia in 1605. They soon set about evangelizing the aboriginal people. The Indian missions of New France (begun in 1610) engaged the efforts of the Franciscan *Recollects, *Jesuits, the Society of *Saint-Sulpice, and the Society of Foreign Missions of Paris. The Jesuit enterprise among the Hurons (1634–50), which culminated in several martyrdoms, left vivid historical memories. After the British conquest (formalized in 1763), *Anglicans, *Methodists, and Jesuits were prominent in eastern Canada, while from the 1840s the *CMS and the RC *Oblate Order of Mary Immaculate maintained the largest enterprises in the north and west. Work among the Inuit, begun in 1771 by *Moravians in Labrador, has been carried on elsewhere by the CMS and the Oblates.

The influence of the Jesuits, and of *Ursuline and *Augustinian hospital nuns who arrived in 1639, gave Quebec an early atmosphere of RC piety, while the pioneers of Montreal (founded in 1642) regarded their project as a holy mission. The commercialism of the fur trade thereafter tempered religious zeal, and, despite the efforts of the *ultramontane Bp. François de Laval (in Canada, 1657–88), the Church in the colony came to be governed on typically Gallican lines. Meanwhile a tradition of solid catechetical instruction was established.

American and then British immigration brought religious variety to what had been strictly a RC colony. The *SPG and other missionary societies helped to provide clergy. Frontier revivalism appealed to many, leading to the prominence of Methodists in Ontario and of *Baptists in the Maritime provinces. The Church of England enjoyed special status at first, but lost it owing to the numerical preponderance of other denominations. 19th cent. European religious movements were influential, leading to polarization between High and Low Churchmanship among Anglicans, the replication of the Scottish *Disruption among *Presbyterians, and the permeation of the RC Church by ultramontane ideas and practices. On the other hand, an impulse towards union culminated in 1925 in the formation of the United Church of Canada by Methodists, *Congregationalists, and most Presbyterians. Most provincial school systems developed along non-sectarian lines, although usually with some provision for separate RC schools; those of Quebec and Newfoundland have been strictly confessional.

During the 20th cent. cosmopolitan immigration has greatly expanded the religious spectrum. From the 1991 census it appears that 45 per cent of the population was then RC; 36 per cent was divided, in descending numerical order, among United, Anglicans, Baptists, *Lutherans, *Pentecostal, and *Orthodox. Most major denominations belong to the Canadian Council of Churches, founded in 1944, and the RC Church is now an associate member. Most of these Churches, including the RC, participate in 'coalitions' on a variety of social issues. Since the 1960s there have been a large number of new liturgies and educational curricula, and the main Protestant Churches, including the Anglican, now ordain *women. Conservative Protestant denominations are growing rapidly, however, and modernization in the RC Church has been accompanied by a massive decline in attendance at Mass and in priestly and religious vocations.

H. H. Walsh, The Christian Church in Canada (Toronto, 1956); J. W. Grant (ed.), A History of the Christian Church in Canada (3 vols., ibid. [1966–72]); R. T. Handy, A History of the Churches in the United States and Canada (Oxford History of the Christian Church, 1976), esp. pp. 116–35, 228–61, and 344–76. S. D. Clark, Church and Sect in Canada (Toronto, 1948); J. W. Grant (ed.), The Churches and the Canadian Experience (ibid., 1963); J. S. Moir (ed.), The Cross in Canada ([ibid., 1966]).

N. Voisine (ed.), Histoire du catholicisme québecois (5 vols., Montreal, 1984 ff.). R. G. Thwaites (ed.), The Jesuit Relations and Allied Documents: Travels and Explorations of the Jesuit Missionaries in France, 1610–1791 (73 vols., Cleveland, 1896–1901; selections by E. Kenton, London [1927]). A. G. Morice, OMI, History of the Catholic Church in Western Canada (2 vols., Quebec, 1910).

P. Carrington, The Anglican Church in Canada (Toronto, 1963). T. R. Millman and A. R. Kelley, Atlantic Canada to 1900: A History of the Anglican Church (ibid., 1983). T. C. B. Boon, The Anglican Church from the Bay to the Rockies: A History of the Ecclesiastical Province of Rupert's Land and its Dioceses from 1820 to 1895 (ibid. [1962]). F. A. Peake, The Anglican Church in British Columbia (Vancouver, 1959).

J. S. Moir, Enduring Witness: A History of the Presbyterian Church in Canada (Toronto [1974]). C. R. Cronmiller, A History of the Lutheran Church in Canada, 1 (all pub., 1961). G. A. Rawlyk, Ravished by the Spirit: Religious Revivals, Baptists, and Henry Alline (Kingston, Ont. [1984]). F. H. Epp, Mennonites in Canada (2 vols., Toronto [1974–82]).

J. W. Grant, Moon of Wintertime: Missionaries and the Indians of Canada in Encounters since 1534 (Toronto [1984]). J. S. Moir and C. T. McIntire (eds.), Canadian Protestant and Catholic Missions, 1820s–1960s: Historical Essays in honour of John Webster Grant (Toronto Studies in Religion, 3; New York, 1988). [A.] R. Allen, The Social Passion: Religion and Social Reform in Canada 1914–28 (Toronto [1971]). J. Hulliger, L'Enseignement social des évêques canadiens de 1891 à 1950 (Montreal [1958]). R. Cook, The Regenerators: Social Criticism in Late Victorian Canada (Toronto [1985]). J. R. Williams (ed.), Canadian Churches and Social Justice (ibid., 1984). C. E. Silcox, Church Union in Canada: Its Causes and Consequences (New York [1933]); N. K. Clifford, The Resistance to Church Union in Canada, 1904–1939 (Vancouver, 1985). R. W. Bibby, Fragmented Gods: The Poverty and Potential of Religion in Canada (Toronto [1987]).

candle. Candles are widely used in Christian worship, both in E. and W., esp. as ornaments of the *altar. They are lighted during liturgical services and at certain other times. The use of candles on the altar seems to have developed out of processional lights which were in earlier times placed beside or on the altar; and in the RC Church since 1969 it has been permissible to put the candles either on or around the altar. Votive candles are candles lit before statues in churches or shrines as personal offerings. In the C of E the use of lights is governed by the *Ornaments Rubric, the *Lincoln Judgement (1890), and the *Lambeth Opinion of 1899. The last of these condemned portable lights, but the prohibition is now seldom if ever enforced. The 1969 RC rite for the Baptism of Children provides that after the Baptism itself the father of the child shall hold a candle lit from the *Paschal Candle, and some modern liturgies (including the ASB) allow for the giving of a lighted candle to a parent or godparent to show that the candidate has passed from darkness to light. The E. Church follows a similar practice. See also ALTAR LIGHTS, CANDLEMAS, PASCHAL CANDLE.

W. Mühlbauer, Geschichte und Bedeutung der (Wachs-) Lichter bei den kirchlichen Funktionen (1874); Rohault, 6 (1888), ch. 1, pp. 1–33. D. R. Dendy, The Use of Lights in Christian Worship (Alcuin Club Collections, 41; 1959). See also bibl. to ALTAR LIGHTS.

Candlemas. The feast commemorates the purification of the BVM and the presentation of Christ in the *Temple which took place, acc. to Lk. 2: 22–39, 40 days after His birth, as the Jewish Law required (Lev. 12: 1–4). Kept locally at *Jerusalem on 14 Feb. from c.350, it is now universally kept on 2 Feb. In 542 the Emp. *Justinian ordered its observance at *Constantinople as a thanksgiving for the cessation of plague, and it thence spread throughout the E., where it was called 'The Meeting' (ὑπαπαντή), i.e. of Christ with *Simeon. Somewhat later it began to be widely kept in the W.

A procession with lighted candles is the distinctive rite in the W. Acc. to the 1970 Roman Missal, the candles are to be blessed, if possible, somewhere other than where the Mass is to be celebrated. After an antiphon, during which the candles held by the people are lighted, a short homily and the prayer of blessing, there is a procession to the church; during it the *Nunc Dimittis, with the antiphon, 'Lumen ad revelationem' (cf. Lk. 2: 32) or some other chant, is sung, commemorating Christ's entrance to the Temple. In the *Liber Pontificalis, the institution of the procession is connected with the pontificate of Pope *Sergius (687–701).

In the RC Church from 1960 onwards it has been accounted a feast of the Lord, and is now officially designated the Presentation of the Lord; its proper title in the BCP is 'the Presentation of Christ in the Temple, commonly called the Purification of Saint Mary the Virgin'.

The feast is first described by *Egeria, Peregrinatio, 26. Other early refs. are in sermons by St *Gregory of Nyssa (J. P. Migne, PG 46. 1151–82), *Theodotus of Ancyra (ibid., 77. 1389–412) and Abraham of Ephesus (6th cent.; PO 16. 448–54). It owes its introduction to Rome, with three other feasts of the BVM, to Pope Sergius I; cf. LP (Duchesne), 1, p. 376. See also L. *Duchesne, Origines du culte chrétien (1889), p. 462 (Eng. tr., 1903, p. 479), who prints the description of the Feast in the 'Ordo Romanus of St Amand'. D. De Bruyne, OSB, 'L'Origine des processions de la chandeleur et des rogations à propos d'un sermon inédit', R. Bén. 34 (1922), pp. 14–26, esp. pp. 18–26. K. [W.] Stevenson, 'The Origins and Development of Candlemas: A Struggle for Identity and Coherence?', EL 102 (1988), pp. 316–46.

The use of candles is already mentioned in the Life of Abbot Theodosius by *Cyril of Scythopolis (ed. E. *Schwartz, TU 49, Heft 2, 1939, p. 236). On the blessing of the candles, A. Franz, Die kirchlichen Benediktionen im Mittelalter, 1 (1909), pp. 445–55. H. *Leclercq, OSB, in DACL 3 (pt. 1; 1913), cols. 207–10, s.v. 'Chandeleur'; G. Löw, CSSR, in EC 10 (1953), cols. 341–5, s.v. 'Purificazione'.

Cange, Charles Dufresne, Sieur Du. See DU CANGE, CHARLES DUFRESNE.

Canisius, St Peter (1521–97), *Jesuit theologian. After studying theology at Cologne and Mainz, where he came under the influence of the Jesuit Pierre Lefèvre, he returned to Cologne. Here he founded a Jesuit colony, and attacked the Protestant views of Abp. *Hermann of Wied. From 1549 onwards he was working in Bavaria, Vienna, and Prague, preaching and lecturing against Protestantism. He secured the patronage of the Archduke, afterwards the Emperor, Ferdinand, by whom he was offered the bishopric of Vienna, an offer which the General of his Order commanded him to refuse. A vigorous exponent of the RC, and esp. the Jesuit, position, he compiled a number of catechisms of which the chief was the Summa Doctrinae Christianae (or Catechismus Major), published in 1554 with 211 questions and answers. Over 130 editions have since been issued. In 1556 he was made *Provincial of Upper Germany and was himself very largely responsible for the foundation of colleges at Augsburg, Munich, and Innsbruck, and the spread of Jesuit influence to Poland. To him, more than to any other, was due the remarkable success of the *Counter-Reformation in the S. German lands. He was canonized in 1925 and at the same time (the first occasion that such an honour had coincided with a canonization) declared to be a *Doctor of the Church. Feast day, 21 Dec. (formerly 27 Apr.).

Works listed in Sommervogel, 2 (1891), cols. 617–87, and 8 (1908), cols. 1974–83. O. Braunsberger, SJ (ed.), Beati Petri Canisii societatis Jesu Epistolae et Acta (8 vols., Freiburg i.B., 1896–1923); modern edn. of his Catechisms by F. Streicher, SJ (Societatis Jesu Selecti Scriptores, 2; 2 vols., Rome, 1933–6), and Meditationes seu Notae in Evangelicas Lectiones by id. (ibid. 3; 2 vols. in 3, Munich, 1957–'1961' [1963]). J. Brodrick, SJ, Saint Peter Canisius, SJ, 1521–1597 (1935). E. M. Buxbaum, Petrus Canisius und die kirchliche Erneuerung des Herzogtums Bayern 1549–1556 (Bibliotheca Instituti Historici S.I., 35; 1973), with full bibl. F. J. Kötter, 'Zur Eucharistiekatechese des 16. Jahrhunderts. Dargestellt an den Katechismen des Petrus Canisius und dem Cathechismus Romanus', in R. Bäumer (ed.), Reformatio Ecclesiae . . .: Festgabe für Erwin Iserloh (Paderborn, 1980), pp. 713–27. Polgár, 1 (1990), pp. 425–53. X. Le Bachelet, SJ, in DTC 2 (1905), cols. 1507–37, s.v.

Cano, Melchior (?1509–60), Spanish theologian. In 1523 he entered the *Dominican Order at Salamanca, where he studied under F. *Vitoria. By 1534 he was teaching at Valladolid; in 1543 he was appointed to the first theological professorship at Alcalá; and in 1546 he succeeded Vitoria himself at Salamanca. He took an active part in the debates on the *Eucharist and on *Penance at the Council of *Trent. In his later years he became deeply involved in Spanish ecclesiastical politics, zealously opposing the *Jesuits and defending in his Consultatio theologica (1556) *Philip II's anti-Papal policy. In 1557 he was elected Provincial of the Castile Dominicans, but his appointment was not confirmed at Rome; and when re-elected in 1559, confirmation was again refused at first, though eventually granted. Similar difficulties had arisen over his appointment as Bp. of the Canaries in 1552, but in the following year he renounced the see. As a theologian his reputation rests on his posthumous De locis theologicis (Salamanca, 1563), in which he defended the unusual thesis that the consent of the parties is merely the *matter of the sacrament of *matrimony (q.v.), the *form being the sacerdotal blessing, a view which gave rise to considerable controversy at the Council of Trent and later.

Opera pub. Cologne in 1605. Life by F. Caballero (Madrid, 1871). A. Lang, Die Loci Theologici des Melchior Cano und die Methode des dogmatischen Beweises (1925). E. Marcotte, La Nature de la théologie d'après Melchior Cano (Ottawa, 1949), with bibl. J. Sanz y Sanz, Melchior Cano: Cuestiones fundamentales de crítica histórica sobre su vida y sus escritos (1959). J. Tapia, Iglesia y teología en Melchor Cano (Publicaciones del Instituto Español de Historia Eclesiástica, Monografías, 31; Rome, 1989). C. Gutiérrez, SJ, Españoles en Trento (Corpus Tridentinum Hispanicum, 1; Valladolid, 1951), pp. 814–41. M. Andrés [Martín], La teología española en el siglo XVI (Biblioteca de Autores Cristianos, 13–14; 1976–7), esp. 2, pp. 411–23, with bibl. Quétif and Echard, 2, pp. 176–8. P. Mandonnet, OP, in DTC 2 (1905), cols. 1537–40, s.v.; V. Beltrán de Heredia, OP, in Dict. Sp. 2 (1953), cols. 73–6, s.v.; F. Courtney, SJ, in NCE 3 (1967), pp. 28 f., s.v.

canon. The Greek word κανών meant a straight rod or bar. Metaphorically the term came to be used of the rules of an art or a trade or to signify a list or catalogue. In Christian language it was adopted to denote the list of inspired books which the Church regarded as composing Holy Scripture (see CANON OF SCRIPTURE), liturgical rules, esp. that part of the Mass which includes the *consecration (see CANON OF THE MASS), and rules concerning the life and discipline of the Church. In law, the word 'canon' was gradually used exclusively of ecclesiastical enactments, and *Justinian distinguishes (civil) laws from (ecclesiastical) canons. In the Middle Ages the law of the Church came to be known as 'canon law' as distinct from 'civil law'. In the Councils of the early Church the term was usually reserved for disciplinary decisions; but since the 15th cent. Councils have more often used it for their dogmatic definitions. Generally speaking *canon law to-day covers the rules of the Church for her own organization, government, and administration.

H. Oppel, 'ΚΑΝΩΝ: Zur Bedeutungsgeschichte des Wortes und seiner lateinischen Entsprechungen', *Philologus*, Suppl. 30 (1937), pp. 1–108; L. Wenger, *Canon in den römischen Rechtsquellen und in den Papyri: Eine Wortstudie* (Sb. (Wien), 220, Abhandlungen 2; 1942).

canon (ecclesiastical title). Though first applied to all clergy on the official staff of a diocese (excluding monks, private chaplains, etc.), the word was gradually limited to those secular clergy belonging to a cathedral or collegiate church. They had a share in the revenues of the Church and were bound to a common life there, though in the early Middle Ages this was not very uniformly interpreted. Before the 11th cent., a canonry was often consistent with the holding of private property and periods of non-residence; but from then onwards those continuing to maintain this mode of life came to be known as 'secular canons' to distinguish them from the *Augustinian or 'regular' canons (q.v.) who lived under a semi-monastic rule.

'Residentiary canons' form the permanent salaried staff of a cathedral and are responsible for the maintenance of its services, fabric, etc. In the C of E a 'non-residentiary canon' (often 'honorary canon') is one who holds an unsalaried post, which may entail certain privileges and responsibilities. '*Minor canons' are clerics usually chosen for their ability to sing the services in a cathedral, and in general have no say in its government. The residentiary and non-residentiary canons, with the dean, together form the 'General Chapter', which has the right to elect or refuse to elect the Crown's nominee to a vacant episcopal see (but see CONGÉ D'ÉLIRE). See also PREBEND AND PREBENDARY.

J. Molanus, *De Canonicis Libri Tres* (Cologne, 1587). E. Amort, *Vetus Disciplina Canonicorum Regularium et Saecularium* (2 vols., Venice, 1747). The legislation governing the main duties and prerogatives of canons in the RC Church is embodied in the *CIC* (1983), cans. 503–10; the new law is much shorter than the 1917 Code as the norms have only limited applicability in different parts of the world. On canons in the C of E, H. W. Cripps, *A Practical Treatise on the Law Relating to the Church and Clergy* (8th edn. by K. M. Macmorran, 1937), esp. pp. 137–42; E. G. Moore, *Introduction to English Canon Law* (3rd edn. by T. Briden and B. Hanson, 1992), pp. 40–45, with notes p. 48. The most readily accessible discussions of the subject are in dictionary arts. D. Dunford in *CE* 3 (1908), pp. 252–5, s.v.; H. *Leclercq, OSB, in *DACL* 3 (pt. 1; 1913), cols. 223–48, s.v. 'Chanoines', with bibl.; P. Torquebiau in *DDC* 3 (1942), cols. 471–88, s.v. 'Chanoines'; id., ibid., cols. 530–95, s.v. 'Chapitres de chanoines', with bibl.; C. Dereine in *DHGE* 12 (1953), cols. 353–405, s.v. 'Chanoines', *passim* (mainly on 'canons regular'). See also bibl. to CHAPTER.

canon (hymnological). In the E. Church, the series of nine 'odes' or canticles, often acrostics, used chiefly at *Orthros. In practice there are normally only eight odes, the second being omitted except in Lent. The canon

originates from the practice of singing the nine biblical *canticles during the second part of Orthros. At first the biblical canticles were sung by themselves: then in the 7th cent. stanzas of poetry or *troparia began to be inserted between the verses of each canticle, and it is these sets of troparia that comprise the canon as we know it. In course of time the practice of reading the actual text of the canticles disappeared, being continued only in certain monasteries esp. on *Athos; and so the nine (in practice, eight) odes of the canon are now sung by themselves, with a brief refrain between the troparia. The text of the *Magnificat, however, is always included in full, except on a few great feasts. The introduction of canons is ascribed to St *Andrew of Crete. Other famous authors of canons are St *Cosmas Melodus, St *John of Damascus, and St *Theodore of Studios.

E. Wellesz, *A History of Byzantine Music and Hymnography* (Oxford, 1949), esp. pp. 168–209; 2nd edn. (1961), pp. 198–239, with refs. Krumbacher, pp. 673–9 (on Andrew of Crete, John of Damascus, and Cosmas of Jerusalem). W. Christ, 'Über die Bedeutung von Hirmos, Troparion und Kanon in der griechischen Poesie des Mittelalters', *Sb.* (Bayr.), 1870 (2), pp. 75–108. O. Heiming, OSB, *Syrische 'Eniânê und griechische Kanones* (1932). A. *Fortescue in *DACL* 2 (pt. 2, 1910), cols. 1905–10, with bibl.

Canon Episcopalis. A liturgical book for bishops, formerly used in the Latin rite; it contained the *Ordinary of the Mass, with the form of episcopal blessing and other prayers and forms used by bishops. It became obsolete after the reordering of the Mass in 1970.

canon law. The body of ecclesiastical rules or laws imposed by authority in matters of faith, morals, and discipline.

This *corpus* of law grew up very gradually. Its beginnings are to be traced to the practice of convening Councils to settle matters of uncertainty or dispute and their issue of a considerable number of *ad hoc* pronouncements on matters of doctrine and discipline. Such pronouncements had varying degrees of authority, acc. to the importance of the Council and the area of the Church which it represented. The series of 20 miscellaneous canons promulgated at *Nicaea (325) came to possess a certain primacy in both E. and W., owing to the unique authority enjoyed by this Council. To these were added the sets of canons of other Councils. As it happened, in the E. these Councils were often Arianizing assemblies (though this circumstance did not affect the orthodoxy of their canons), while in the W. the canons of the orthodox Council of *Sardica (343) were often attached to those of Nicaea and, owing to a confusion, sometimes supposed to be Nicene. The practice of the African Church of holding plenary Councils with exceptional frequency brought into being a large body of canons from its provinces. Evidence of the existence of canonical collections by the middle of the 5th cent. is provided by the citation at the Council of *Chalcedon (451) of the Antiochene canons of 330 (formerly attributed to the Council of *Antioch of 341). Notable private collectors of canons were *John Scholasticus (who arranged the Greek canons known to him under subject-headings) in the E. and *Dionysius Exiguus and the unknown author of the *Hispana Collection in the W.

Side by side with the Councils the decrees of influential bishops were another source of early ecclesiastical legislation. St *Dionysius of Alexandria, St *Gregory Thaumaturgus, St *Basil of Caesarea, and St *Amphilochius of Iconium all issued canonical letters. Special authority came to be enjoyed by the letters of the Popes (*Decretals) beginning with that of Pope *Siricius to Himerius of Tarragona (385). The 4th–5th cents. also saw the ascription of collections of canons to fictitious authors, such as the '*Apostolic Canons' (q.v.) and those attributed to St *Hippolytus and other names of repute. Under *Charlemagne much standardization took place and by the next generation, as is shown by the *Forged Decretals, a trained body of canonists had come into being.

In the Middle Ages a decisive stage was reached when *Gratian issued his *Decretum* (*c.*1140). Though in essence a private collection, the appearance of this work marked an epoch in the history of the subject and students have come to regard Gratian's work as the dividing line between *ius antiquum* and *ius novum*. (The law established later than *Trent has hence come to be termed *ius novissimum*.) The authority accorded to Gratian's *Decretum* led to its supplementation by a series of later collections (among them the *Extravagantes*), as described in the entry *Corpus Iuris Canonici* (q.v.). In the RC Church this last-named *Corpus* continued to enjoy authority right down to the present century. It was only the issue of a *motu proprio* by *Pius X on 19 Mar. 1904 which led to its being completely overhauled and codified in the *Codex Iuris Canonici* (q.v.) promulgated in 1917. This *Codex* was itself thoroughly revised and promulgated anew in 1983. A separate Code for the *Uniat Churches was issued in 1990.

Together with laws accepted as universally binding, there have always been others of only local authority. While in general the Roman canon law was binding in England in the Middle Ages, this was supplemented to some extent by the local provincial decrees of Canterbury. In 1433 the Synodal Constitutions of the province from S. *Langton (1222) to H. *Chichele (1416) were issued by W. *Lyndwood in his famous *Provinciale*. In post-Reformation times these have been modified by the canons of 1604 and 1969 (see CANONS, THE).

In the E., under the Byzantine Empire, there was a much less clear distinction between the law of the Church and State than in the W. Imperial legislation (embodied in the *Justinian Code and its supplements) dealt with such ecclesiastical matters as methods of selecting candidates for the episcopate, as well as with marriage and divorce. On the other hand, Justinian decreed that canons had the 'force of law' (*legum vicem*). The development of specifically ecclesiastical law took the form of commentary on collections of canons (esp. the *Nomocanon, q.v.). The principle of 'economy' (οἰκονομία)—following the spirit rather than the letter of the law—plays an important part in the interpretation of ecclesiastical regulations.

Older works incl. J. Pignatelli, *Consultationes Canonicae* (3 vols., Rome, 1675; and many later edns.), and the writings of *Benedict XIV (q.v.), the greatest of modern canonists. J. F. von Schulte, *Das katholische Kirchenrecht* (2 vols., 1860, 1856; 4th edn., 1876). For texts of the Conciliar canons see the *Concilia* of J. *Hardouin, SJ, J. D. *Mansi, E. *Schwartz, and C. H. *Turner (qq.v.); texts of the canons of the Oecumenical Councils, with Eng. tr., in Tanner, *Decrees* (1990). Canons of the Oecumenical Councils, local Councils of the E. Church, and the Canons of the Greek Fathers, with Fr. tr., in Joannou (2 vols. in 3; 1962–3). The most complete history of W. canon law is G. Le Bras and J. Gaudemet (eds.), *Histoire du droit et des institutions de l'Église en Occident* (1955 ff.). Briefer modern treatment by C. Van de Wiel, *History of Canon Law* (Louvain Theological & Pastoral Monographs, 5 [1991]). Still valuable is the classic F. *Maassen, *Geschichte der Quellen und der Literatur des canonischen Rechts im Abendlande*, 1 (1870; all pub.); for the later history, J. F. von Schulte, *Geschichte der Quellen und der Literatur des canonischen Rechts von Gratian bis auf die Gegenwart* (3 vols., 1875–80). P. Fournier and G. Le Bras, *Histoire des collections canoniques en occident depuis les fausses décrétales jusqu'au décret de Gratien* (2 vols., 1931–2). A. M. Stickler, SDB, *Historia Iuris Canonici Latini: Institutiones Academicae*, 1: *Historia Fontium* (Rome, 1950). S. G. Kuttner, *Harmony from Dissonance: An Interpretation of Medieval Canon Law* (Latrobe, Pa., 1960). J. A. Brundage, *Medieval Canon Law* (1995). A. van Hove, *Commentarium Lovaniense in CIC* (Malines, 1928 ff.; esp. 1. 1, 'Prolegomena', 2nd edn., 1945). The Gk. canons were collected, with comm., by St. *Nicodemus of the Holy Mountain in the *Pidalion* or 'Rudder' (Leipzig, 1800; Eng. tr., Chicago, 1957). The standard modern work on E. canon law is N. Milasch, *Das Kirchenrecht der morgenländischen Kirche*, tr. from Serbian (Zara, 1897; 2nd edn., Mostar, 1905). For a briefer account, see J. Meyendorff, *Byzantine Theology* (New York, 1974; London, 1975), pp. 79–90 and 232 (bibl.). A. Villien, E. Magnin, A. Amanien, and R. Naz (eds.), *Dictionnaire de droit canonique* (7 vols., 1935–65). C. Vogel and others in *NCE* 3 (1967), pp. 34–50, s.v. 'Canon Law, History of'.

Canon of the Mass (from Gk. κανών, 'measuring rod', 'rule', because fixed and unchanging), the ancient consecratory prayer in the Roman Mass. A prayer of this kind is found in all the Eucharistic liturgies, Gk. and Lat. It always (with the possible exception of the Liturgy of *Addai and Mari) contains the Words of *Institution (q.v.).

Though the Roman Canon presumably must be based ultimately on Gk. models, it is unlikely (despite A. *Baumstark) that it was a translation from a Gk. original. It existed as early as the 4th cent. in a nearly related form, which is quoted by St *Ambrose (d. 397) in his '*De Sacramentis' (q.v.). It received modifications at the hands of St *Gregory the Great (590–604), by whose period it had assumed virtually its present form. Some early occurrences of it are in the *Gelasian Sacramentary (q.v.), the *Bobbio Missal, and the '*Missale Francorum' (7th cent.). The variations in the text, though they attract the attention of specialists, are of relatively minor importance; the remarkable fact is the universal acceptance of a virtually identical prayer throughout the W.

The Canon of the Mass originally opened with the *Preface, and is marked as doing so in the old *Gelasian Sacramentary (Vat. Reg. 316). Later, through a misunderstanding, the Preface came to be regarded as an introduction to the Canon rather than an integral part of it, and the Canon was held to begin at the words '*Te igitur' (q.v.). It is a succession of short prayers, namely (from their opening words) 'Te Igitur', 'Memento [vivorum]', *Communicantes (intercession, slightly variable at the chief feasts), 'Hanc Igitur', 'Quam Oblationem', 'Qui Pridie' (the actual words of Consecration; accompanied since the Middle Ages by the *elevation of the Elements), 'Unde et Memores' (corresponding to the Gk. *Anamnesis, q.v.), 'Supra Quae', 'Supplices Te Rogamus' (possibly the remains of an ancient *Epiclesis, q.v.),

'Memento [defunctorum]', '*Nobis Quoque Peccatoribus', and 'Per Quem Haec Omnia' (concluding Doxology). The want of any clear sequence of thought, the existence of two separate lists of saints, and other considerations have suggested that its text was seriously dislocated at an earlier stage in its history; but none of the many modern attempts to reconstruct the original order has won wide acceptance.

From c.800 until 1967 the Canon was recited silently, only the words 'Nobis Quoque Peccatoribus' and the concluding 'Per omnia saecula saeculorum' being said aloud. In 1967, however, audible recitation of the Canon and the use of the vernacular were authorized. In 1969 some semblance of literary unity was restored to the Canon when it became permissible to omit the conclusions to each of the component prayers except that preceding the doxology; at the same time most of the names in the 'Communicantes' and 'Nobis Quoque Peccatoribus' could be left out. The Canon, in a slightly revised form, is the first of the four eucharistic prayers in the 1970 Roman Missal. For the others see EUCHARISTIC PRAYERS.

Crit. edns. by B. Botte, OSB, *Le Canon de la messe romaine* (Louvain, 1935), with notes, and L. Eizenhöfer, OSB (Rerum Ecclesiasticarum Documenta, Series Minor, 1 [Traditio textus] and 7 [Textus propinqui]; Rome, 1954–66). B. Botte, OSB, and C. Mohrmann (eds.), *L'Ordinaire de la messe* (Études Liturgiques, 2, 1953), esp. pp. 74–85. The best summary of the position at time of writing in Jungmann (1952), 2, pp. 127–340, with full bibl. refs.; Eng. tr., 2, pp. 101–274. The large lit. incl. A. Baumstark, *Liturgia romana e liturgia dell'esarcato: Il rito detto in seguito patriarchino e le origini del* Canon Missae *romano* (Rome, 1904); P. Batiffol, *Leçons sur la messe* (1920), pp. 166–275; P. Oppenheim, OSB, *Canon Missae Primitivus* (Rome, 1948); B. *Capelle, OSB, 'Innocent Ier et le Canon de la Messe', RTAM* 19 (1952), pp. 5–16, repr. in *Travaux Liturgiques*, 2 (1962), pp. 236–47, and other arts. in this vol.; G. G. Willis, *Essays in Early Roman Liturgy* (*Alcuin Club Collections, 46; 1964), pp. 111–33; special issue of *La Maison-Dieu*, no. 87 (1966), 'Le Canon de la Messe', with contributions by L. Ligier, SJ, B. Botte, OSB, and J. A. Jungmann, SJ; P. Borella, 'Evoluzione storica e Struttura letterale del Canone della Messa Romana' in L. Ligier, SJ, and others, *Il Canone* (Liturgica, NS 5; Padua, 1968), pp. 95–113; E. C. Ratcliff and A. H. Couratin, 'The Early Roman *Canon Missae*', *JEH* 20 (1969), pp. 211–24, repr. in Ratcliff's *Liturgical Studies*, ed. A. H. Couratin and D. H. Tripp (1976), pp. 91–107.

canon of Scripture (from Gk. κανών, 'measuring rod', 'rule'). The term, used also in a larger sense for a list or catalogue, gradually acquired a technical meaning for the Books which were officially received as containing the rule of the Christian faith. In this sense the words 'canon' and 'canonical', which had already been employed by *Origen, came into general use in the 4th cent.

The history of the development of the OT canon is a matter of controversy. Acc. to the legend told in the apocryphal IV *Esdras and preserved in the *Pirqe Aboth, the Hebrew canon was closed by the 'Great Synagogue' starting with Ezra after the return from Exile. Modern scholars agree that it was formed gradually at a later period but, while it seems that the process was prob. substantially completed before the beginning of the Christian era, there is no consensus about its final achievement. It was long widely accepted that the canon was finally closed in the later part of the 1st cent. AD, but Sundberg argued that there was no defined canon until considerably later, and now there is discussion as to whether the canon of the OT

formed a model for that of the NT, or whether it was perhaps the other way round. The Jews of the *Diaspora regarded several additional Greek Books as equally inspired as the Hebrew Scriptures, namely most of the Books printed in the AV and RV among the *Apocrypha. During the first three cents. these were regularly used also in the Church. In the 4th and 5th cents., however, several E. Fathers, e.g. St *Gregory of Nazianzus and St *Epiphanius, questioned their authenticity, and in the W. St *Jerome esp. would admit only the Hebrew books as canonical. Though St *Ambrose, St *Augustine, and others placed them on the same footing as the other OT Books, through St Jerome's influence doubts as to their canonicity persisted in the W. throughout the Middle Ages, though they continued to be used in the Liturgy. In the 16th cent. they were rejected by the Reformers, whereas the Council of *Trent in its Fourth Session (8 Apr. 1546) imposed their acceptance as *de fide* on all RCs, a decision confirmed by the First *Vatican Council (1870). For the attitude of the Orthodox Churches of the E., see APOCRYPHA.

The formation of the NT canon also had its vicissitudes. Each of the Four Gospels and the 13 Epistles of St Paul had been accepted, at least in some parts of the Church, as authoritative witnesses to the Apostolic teaching by c.130, though the notion of a 'canon' of the NT (i.e. a list of accepted books) only emerged later, possibly in reaction against *Marcion's truncated 'canon'. Towards the end of the 2nd cent. these NT writings came to be regarded as 'Scripture' on the same footing as the OT. The other NT writings were received more slowly; doubts persisted, esp. in the case of Heb., Jude, 2 Pet., 2 and 3 Jn., and Rev., as is shown, e.g. by a list drawn up by *Eusebius. On the other hand, certain writings, such as the Ep. of *Barnabas or the 'Shepherd' of *Hermas, were admitted by individual Churches, though rejected by the majority. St *Athanasius in his *Festal Ep.* for 367 is the earliest exact witness to the present NT canon. A Council prob. held at *Rome in 382 under St *Damasus gave a complete list of the canonical books of both the OT and the NT (also known as the '*Gelasian Decree' because it was reproduced by *Gelasius in 495) which is identical with the list given at the Council of *Trent. Notable early lists of NT Scriptures included the *Muratorian Canon (q.v.) and can. 60 of the Council of *Laodicea (4th cent.).

The canon of Scripture thus came to be defined as the collection of inspired writings, made by the tradition and authority of the Church, which contain the rule of Divine Faith. The principle that only the Church has the right to declare a Book canonical is recognized by the RC Church, the Orthodox Churches, and the Anglican Communion. The rise in recent years of the 'canonical approach' or 'canon criticism' in biblical studies represents an attempt to correct the alleged failure of historical-critical study to address the theological significance of the Bible as Scripture; its adherents hold that it is the 'final' or 'canonical' form of the biblical text that is the appropriate object of theological reflection rather than the events or experiences behind the text.

S. M. Zarb, OP, *De Historia Canonis Utriusque Testamenti* (Rome, 1934). F. V. Filson, *Which Books belong to the Bible? A Study of the Canon* (Philadelphia [1957]); H. von Campenhausen, *Die Entstehung der christlichen Bibel* (Beiträge zur historischen

Theologie, 39; 1968; Eng. tr., 1972); B. S. Childs, *Introduction to the Old Testament as Scripture* (1979); J. Barr, *Holy Scripture: Canon, Authority, Criticism* (Sprunt Lectures; Oxford, 1983), pp. 49–104. F. F. Bruce, *The Canon of Scripture* (Glasgow, 1988). H. W. Howarth, 'The Influence of St Jerome on the Canon of the Western Church', *JTS* 10 (1908–9), pp. 481–96; 11 (1909–10), pp. 321–47; 13 (1911–12), pp. 1–18. F. Schroeder in *NCE* 2 (1967), pp. 386–96, s.v. 'Bible, 3 (Canon)'; W. Künneth in *TRE* 17 (1988), pp. 562–70, s.v. 'Kanon'.

On the OT canon, H. E. *Ryle, *The Canon of the Old Testament* (1892). P. Katz, 'The Old Testament Canon in Palestine and Alexandria', *ZNTW* 47 (1956), pp. 191–217. H. H. Rowley, *The Growth of the Old Testament* (Hutchinson's University Library, 1950; 3rd edn., 1967), esp. pp. 165–9. A. C. Sundberg, *The Old Testament of the Early Church* (Harvard Theological Studies, 20; 1964). S. Z. Leiman, *The Canonization of Hebrew Scripture: The Talmudic and Midrashic Evidence* (Transactions of the Connecticut Academy of Arts and Sciences, 47, 1976, pp. 1–124; also pub. separately, Hamden, Conn. [1976]). J.-D. Kaestli and O. Wermelinger (eds.), *Le Canon de l'Ancien Testament: Sa Formation et son Histoire* [1984]. R. Beckwith, *The Old Testament Canon of the New Testament Church and its Background in Early Judaism* (1985). E. E. Ellis, *The Old Testament in Early Christianity: Canon and Interpretation in the Light of Modern Research* (Wissenschaftliche Untersuchungen zum Neuen Testament, 54; Tübingen, 1991), esp. pp. 3–74. H. L. Strack in *PRE* (3rd edn.), 9 (1901), pp. 741–68, s.v. 'Kanon des Alten Testaments'.

On the NT canon the most ambitious work is T. *Zahn, *Geschichte des neutestamentlichen Kanons* (2 vols. in 3 pts., 1888–92), to be suppl. by the same scholar's *Forschungen zur Geschichte des neutestamentlichen Kanons und der altchristlichen Literatur* (8 pts., 1881–1907). Other treatises include B. F. *Westcott, *A General Survey of the Canon of the New Testament* (1855; 4th edn., 1875). M. J. Lagrange, *Introduction à l'étude du Nouveau Testament, 1: Histoire ancienne du canon du Nouveau Testament* (1933); A. *Souter, *The Text and Canon of the New Testament* (2nd edn., rev. by C. S. C. Williams, 1954), pp. 137–220; C. F. D. Moule, *The Birth of the New Testament* (Black's NT Comm., 1962; 3rd edn., 1981); B. S. Childs, *The New Testament as Canon: An Introduction* (1984); and B. M. Metzger, *The Canon of the New Testament: Its Origin, Development, and Significance* (Oxford, 1987). J. N. Sanders in M. M. Black and H. H. Rowley (eds.), *Peake's Commentary on the Bible* (1962), pp. 679–82.

canoness. The name is first used in the 8th cent. to refer to certain communities of women who lived in common, but did not renounce their own property; they were later known as 'secular canonesses'. Membership of these communities was often restricted to noblewomen. They are all now extinct. After the 11th cent. many orders of *canons regular had a similar order for women, whose members were known as 'canonesses regular'. A number of congregations of these canonesses survive in the RC Church and undertake a variety of functions.

P. Torquebiau in *DDC* 3 (1942), cols. 488–500, s.v. 'Chanoinesses'; N. Backmund, O. Praem., in *NCE* 3 (1967), pp. 53 f., s.v.; J. B. Valvekens, O. Praem., in *DIP* 2 (1975), cols. 24–7, s.v. 'Canonichesse'; arts. by various authors on individual orders of canonesses, ibid., cols. 27–46.

canonization. In the RC Church the definitive sentence by which the Pope declares a particular member of the faithful departed, previously beatified, to have already entered into eternal glory, and ordains for the new 'Saint' a public cult throughout the whole Church. In the Orthodox Church canonizations are usually made by the synod of bishops within a particular *autocephalous Church,

though in certain instances a cultus comes to be accepted without any formal act of canonization. In the RC Church canonization is today distinguished from *beatification, which allows only a restricted public veneration of the person beatified, but in the early centuries such a distinction was almost, if not quite, unknown.

In the primitive Church, *martyrs were the first to be publicly venerated by the faithful. From the 4th cent. onwards a cultus was extended also to *confessors. Local bishops began to control the various cults in their own dioceses and councils also dealt with the subject. Frequently the veneration of certain saints spread far beyond the limits of their own diocese or country. This raised the problem of the regulation of these cults, and negligence and abuses brought about Papal intervention. The first historically attested canonization is that of *Ulrich of Augsburg by Pope John XV in 993. About 1170 *Alexander III, in a letter to King Canute of Sweden, asserted that no one should be venerated as a saint without the authority of the Roman Church; and by the inclusion of this passage in the *Decretals of *Gregory IX, it became part of W. canon law. This Papal authority is generally given nowadays only after a long legal process which was simplified by the Apostolic Constitution 'Divinus Perfectionis Magister' (25 Jan. 1983) and other legislation. The process begins at diocesan level and continues in Rome in the Congregation for the *Causes of Saints. The *Promotor Justitiae* now ensures that all the necessary investigation takes place and that the evidence is adequately tested at the diocesan level. At Rome the evidence is assessed by a body of historical consultors and then by a body of theological consultors (under the presidency of the *Promotor Fidei*) before their findings are considered by the cardinals and bishops who advise the Pope. Normally proof of one *miracle since beatification is required for canonization.

Canonization is held to confer a sevenfold honour: (1) the name is inscribed in the catalogue of saints, i.e. public recognition is enjoined; (2) the new saint is invoked in the public prayers of the Church; (3) churches may be dedicated to God in the saint's memory; (4) the Mass and Office are publicly offered to God in the saint's honour; (5) festival days are celebrated in the saint's memory; (6) pictorial representations are made in which the saint is surrounded by a heavenly light of glory; (7) the saint's relics are enclosed in precious vessels and publicly honoured.

See also RITES, CONGREGATION OF.

The Apostolic Constitution 'Divinus Perfectionis Magister' is pr. in *AAS* 75 (1983), pp. 349–55. The classic treatise on the whole subject is *Benedict XIV, *De Servorum Dei Beatificatione et Beatorum Canonizatione* (4 vols., Bologna, 1734–8). E. W. Kemp, *Canonization and Authority in the Western Church* (1948). A. Vauchez, *La Sainteté en Occident aux derniers Siècles du Moyen Âge d'après les Procès de Canonisation et les Documents Hagiographiques* (Bibliothèque des Écoles Françaises d'Athènes et de Rome, 241; 1981), esp. pp. 11–162 and 289–489. S. Wilson (ed.), *Saints and their Cults* (1983), pp. 169–216, reprinting or translating into Eng. arts. previously pub., with new bibl., pp. 315–17. K. [L.] Woodward, *Making Saints. Inside the Vatican: Who Become Saints; Who Do Not, and Why . . .* (1991 [semi-popular]). F. Veraja, *Commento alla Nuova Legislazione per le Cause dei Santi* (1983). T. J. Zubek, OFM, 'New Legislation about the Canonization of the Servants of God', *Jurist*, 43 (1983), pp. 361–75.

Canons, Apostolic. See APOSTOLIC CANONS.

Canons, the. In the C of E the principal body of canonical legislation since the Reformation was long the Book of Canons, a collection of 141 canons passed under the influence of Abp. R. *Bancroft by the *Convocation of *Canterbury in 1604 and of *York in 1606. The individual canons were based on a number of sources. Some were a reaffirmation of medieval prescriptions, others depended on M. *Parker's 'Book of *Advertisements' and the *Thirty-Nine Articles. The many subjects with which they dealt included the conduct of Divine service and the administration of the sacraments, the duties and behaviour of clerics, the furniture and care of churches, *churchwardens, the ecclesiastical courts, and marriage regulations; and several of them were directed against the *Puritans, who were endeavouring in the early 17th cent. to achieve a drastic reconstruction of the C of E. They were drawn up in Latin by Bancroft when he was still Bp. of London, and the Latin version alone has authority.

In 1939 the Abp. of Canterbury, in conjunction with the Abp. of York, appointed a 'Canon Law Commission' under the chairmanship of C. F. Garbett (Bp. of *Winchester) to consider the status of canon law in England and, if it deemed it expedient, to prepare a revised body of canons for submission to Convocation. The meetings of the Commission were delayed until 1943, but in 1947 a report was published, including a proposed set of new canons. After prolonged debate the new Code was promulged in two parts, three sections in 1964 and four in 1969. It covers much the same areas of Church life as earlier Canons and, like them, presupposes both the Common and Statute Law and the pre-Reformation Canon Law of the W. Church, except where the last has been affected by contrary statute or custom in England. All that now remains of the 1604 Book of Canons is the proviso to Canon 113 dealing with the *seal of confession, on which it was feared that new legislation might encounter difficulties with the secular authorities. The Canons are from time to time revised by the General Synod; the latest revision was in April 1993.

Lat. text pub. London, 1604; Eng. tr., ibid., 1604. There have been numerous subsequent edns. of the Eng. tr.; modern edn. of Eng. and Lat. texts by J. V. Bullard (London, 1934). *The Canon Law of the Church of England: Being the Report of the Archbishops' Commission on Canon Law, together with Proposals for a Revised Body of Canons* (1947), with bibl. The new Code was pub. under the title *The Canons of the Church of England* (1969). E. W. Kemp, *An Introduction to Canon Law in the Church of England* (1957); E. G. Moore, *Introduction to English Canon Law* (Oxford, 1967; 3rd edn. by T. Briden and B. Hanson, London, 1992); M. Hill, *Ecclesiastical Law* (1995); N. Doe, *The Legal Framework of the Church of England* (Oxford, 1996).

canons regular (Lat. *canonici regulares*). A body of canons living under rule, which originated in the 11th cent. in close connection with the Reform movement of *Gregory VII. In the 12th cent. they largely adopted the rule of St *Augustine and have since come to be known as *Augustinian (Austin) Canons (q.v.).

See bibl. to CANON (ecclesiastical title), also to AUGUSTINIAN CANONS.

canopy, processional. An awning supported by poles at the corners and carried over the Blessed Sacrament in processions, and formerly over certain high ecclesiastical dignitaries, in the RC Church.

Canossa. A castle near Reggio/Emilia in N. Italy, belonging in the 11th cent. to Countess Matilda of Tuscany. In the winter of 1076–7, King *Henry IV of Germany, deposed and excommunicated by Pope *Gregory VII in Feb. 1076, crossed the Alps to appear as a penitent before the castle where Gregory was staying. After Henry had passed three days outside it in bitter weather, on 28 Jan. 1077 Gregory acceded to the pleas of his own followers, who included Countess Matilda and St *Hugh, Abbot of Cluny, by restoring him to communion. As regards his kingship, Henry swore to abide by a Papal judgement soon to be passed. Henry was able to return to Germany and regain some of his authority, but in Mar. 1077 the German princes anticipated Gregory's decision by electing as anti-king Duke Rudolf of Swabia. The encounter at Canossa has been regarded by most modern historians as an adroit move by Henry, who thus divided his opponents, but traditionally in Germany it was perceived as a profound humiliation for the royal power by the Pope, and left a mark upon the country's political mythology: 'we will not' (Bismarck said in the *Kulturkampf) 'go to Canossa'.

The principal sources for the event are Gregory VII, *Register*, 4. 12 and 12a (ed. E. Caspar in *MGH*, Epistolae selectae, 2 (Fasc. 1; 1920), pp. 311–15), and *Lampert of Hersfeld, *Annales*, a. 1077 (ed. O. Holder-Egger in *MGH*, Scriptores rerum Germanicarum (1894), pp. 290–98). Crit. survey by G. Meyer von Knonau, *Jahrbücher des Deutschen Reiches unter Heinrich IV. und Heinrich V.*, 2 (1894), pp. 747–65. The many modern discussions incl. W. von den Steinen, *Canossa: Heinrich IV. und die Kirche* (Munich, 1957); a collection of essays of various dates ed. H. Kämpf, *Canossa als Wende* (Wege der Forschungen, 12; Darmstadt, 1963); C. Schneider, *Prophetisches Sacerdotium und Heilsgeschichtliches Regnum im Dialog 1073–1077* (Münstersche Mittelalter-Schriften, 9; 1972), pp. 201–13; H. Zimmermann, *Der Canossagang von 1077: Wirkungen und Wirklichkeit* (Abhandlungen der Akademie der Wissenschaften und der Literatur, Mainz, Geistes- und Sozialwissenschaftliche Klasse, Jahrgang 1975, Nr. 5), and C. Vogel, *Gregor VII. und Heinrich IV. nach Canossa* (Arbeiten zur Frühmittelalterforschung, 9; 1983). In Eng., see K. F. Morrison, 'Canossa: a revision', *Traditio*, 18 (1962), pp. 121–48, repr. in id., *Holiness and Politics in Early Medieval Thought* (1985), no. 4. T. Struve in *Lexikon des Mittelalters*, 2 (1983), cols. 1441–3, s.v.

cantata. Literally a form of sacred or secular musical composition designed to be sung (Lat. *cantare*) as opposed to the instrumentally performed sonata. In its sacred context it came in late-17th and early-18th cent. Germany to represent a multi-sectional work involving arias and recitatives for solo voices, as well as choral sections. In the *Lutheran service it formed a commentary on the Gospel for the day in the Communion or Ante-Communion service, and is seen in its supreme form in the c.200 surviving church cantatas of J. S. *Bach. From the 19th cent. the term has been used to describe anything between an extended *anthem (e.g. E. B. *Britten's 'Rejoice in the Lamb') to a small-scale *oratorio (e.g. R. *Vaughan Williams's 'Dona nobis pacem').

N. Fortune and others in S. Sadie (ed.), *The New Grove Dictionary of Music and Musicians*, 3 (1980), pp. 694–718.

Cantate Domino (Lat., 'O sing unto the Lord'), Ps. 98, from its first words. In the 1552 and subsequent editions of the BCP it is an alternative to the canticle '*Magnificat' at Evening Prayer. Since 1662 it has been ordered that it shall not be used here on the 19th evening, when it is read among the psalms for the day. In the American Prayer Book of 1789 the 'Magnificat' was entirely omitted and replaced by the 'Cantate'; but in the revision of 1892 the old arrangement of the English book was restored. In the main modern Anglican liturgies it is no longer used as a canticle.

Canterbury. The history of the present see begins in 597 with the arrival of St *Augustine, who with the assistance of his companions established his first church in the city. Augustine had been ordered to organize England in two ecclesiastical provinces with archbishops at London and *York. The place of London, however, was from the first taken by Canterbury, which has since then been the see of the archbishop of the southern province, who is *Primate of All England. The northern boundary of the province of Canterbury is now formed by the northern boundaries of the dioceses of *Lincoln, Leicester, Derby, and *Lichfield. In 1920 the Welsh dioceses and Monmouth (which at that time formed part of the diocese of *Llandaff) were taken from Canterbury to form the newly constituted province of the 'Church in *Wales'. From 1375 to 1558 Calais and the surrounding district formed part of the diocese of Canterbury; since 1568–9 the *Channel Islands have been in the province, being part of the diocese of *Winchester. From the time of Abp. Stephen *Langton (d. 1228), the archbishops held the title of 'legatus natus', i.e. they were recognized as *ex officio* permanent Papal legates. The struggle for precedence between the archiepiscopal sees of Canterbury and York ended in the middle of the 14th cent. with a victory for the former. The principal residence of the Abp. of Canterbury is at *Lambeth Palace in London, but he also has a palace at Canterbury. See also ANGLICAN COMMUNION; and CATHEDRALS, FRIENDS OF THE.

Acc. to *Bede (*HE* 1. 33) an already existing Roman basilica was consecrated by St Augustine as the Cathedral Church of Christ. Destroyed by a fire in 1067, the church was rebuilt by Abp. *Lanfranc, extended under Abp. *Anselm and consecrated in 1130. After a disastrous fire in 1174 the choir was rebuilt in the transitional style under the architectural direction of William of Sens and then William the Englishman. Under Abp. *Sudbury the nave was pulled down and later rebuilt in perpendicular style. The Chapter House and Cloisters are of the same period. The Chichele Steeple (also Oxford or Dunstan Steeple) was erected by Abp. *Chichele; the central Tower (Bell Harry Tower) was built between 1495 and 1503. The chief glory of the Cathedral during the Middle Ages was the shrine of St Thomas *Becket, dedicated on 7 July 1220. The former archiepiscopal throne of Purbeck marble ('St Augustine's Chair') is prob. 13th cent. The crypt is mainly Norman with Roman and Saxon fragments. Since 1575 part of the crypt has been used by Walloon and Huguenot refugees and their descendants.

In *c.*598 (acc. to Thorne and Elmham) St Augustine, with King *Ethelbert and his Queen, established a monastery to the east of the city, dedicated to Sts Peter and Paul, to accommodate the bodies of future bishops and kings of the region. In 613 the new conventual church was consecrated by Abp. Laurence (Abp. from some time between 604 and 609 to 619), the body of St Augustine being reinterred in the N. Porch. The first ten Abps. and several kings were buried there before Abp. Cuthbert (Abp. 740–60) left instructions that the tradition should be broken. The first outbreak of the chronic enmity between the monks and the Cathedral Chapter ensued. In 978 St *Dunstan rededicated the conventual church in honour of Sts Peter and Paul and St Augustine, it being commonly known thereafter by the title of the latter saint. The church was rebuilt in the 12th cent.

From its foundation the abbey was richly endowed and seems to have enjoyed a position of favour. It contended that St Augustine had granted it exemption from the jurisdiction of his successors, but the claim caused friction with the Abps., esp. during the 12th cent. About 1063 *Alexander II made to the abbots of St Augustine's the first grant of the right to wear a mitre and other episcopal insignia. Of considerable importance throughout the Middle Ages, in 1538 the monastery, then inhabited by some 30 monks and the Prior, was dissolved. In 1848 a college for the training of missionaries (named after St Augustine) was founded on the ruins. In 1952 this was reconstituted as a central house of study for the Anglican Communion. From 1969 to 1976 the buildings were occupied by a theological college associated with *King's College, London.

The archiepiscopal registers are extant from 1278 to 1326 and from 1349 onwards; description in D. M. Smith, *Guide to Bishops' Registers of England and Wales* (Royal Historical Society Guides and Handbooks, 11; 1981), pp. 1–24. The following have been pub.: that of J. *Pecham ed. C. T. Martin (RS, 3 vols., 1882–5), more complete edn. by F. N. Davis and others (Canterbury and York Society, 64–5; 1968–9); those of R. *Winchelsea ed. R. Graham (ibid. 51–2, 1952–6); of Simon Langham ed. A. C. Wood (ibid. 53; 1956); of H. Chichele ed. E. F. Jacob (ibid. 42, 45–7; 1937–47); of T. *Bourchier ed. F. R. H. Du Boulay (ibid. 54; 1957); of John Morton ed. C. Harper-Bill (ibid. 75–6; 1987–8); and of M. *Parker ed. E. M. Thompson and W. H. *Frere (ibid. 35–6, 39; 1907–33). The Acta of S. Langton ed. K. Major (ibid. 50; 1950); Acta for the period 1162–90 and 1193–1205 ed. C. R. Cheney and others, *English Episcopal Acta* 2, and 3 (1986) respectively. E. [F.] Carpenter, *Cantuar: The Archbishops in their Office* (1971; rev. edn., 1988). I. J. Churchill, *Canterbury Administration: The Administrative Machinery of the Archbishopric of Canterbury Illustrated from Original Records* (CHS NS 15; 2 vols., 1933); B. L. Woodcock, *Medieval Ecclesiastical Courts in the Diocese of Canterbury* (Oxford Historical Series, 1952). F. R. H. Du Boulay, *The Lordship of Canterbury* (1966). J. W. Lamb, *The Archbishopric of Canterbury, from its Foundation to the Norman Conquest* (1971).

On the Priory and Cathedral, *The Statutes of the Cathedral and Metropolitical Church of Christ, Canterbury* (Canterbury, 1925). J. B. Sheppard (ed.), *Literae Cantuarienses: The Letter Books of the Monastery of Christ Church, Canterbury* (3 vols., RS, 1887–9). W. *Dugdale, *Monasticon Anglicanum*, 1 (1817 edn.), pp. 81–119. R. Willis, *The Architectural History of Canterbury Cathedral* (1845). A. P. *Stanley, *Historical Memorials of Canterbury* (1855). C. E. Woodruff and W. Danks, *Memorials of the Cathedral and Priory of Christ in Canterbury* (1912). S. A. Warner, *Canterbury Cathedral* (1923). D. I. Hill, *Canterbury Cathedral* (New Bell's Cathedral Guides, 1986). P. Collinson, N. [L.] Ramsay, and M. [J.] Sparks (eds.), *A History of Canterbury Cathedral* (Oxford, 1995). C. S. Phillips, *Canterbury Cathedral in the Middle Ages* (1949). N. [P.] Brooks, *The Early History of the Church of Canterbury: Christ Church from 597 to 1066* (Leicester, 1984). C. S. Phillips,

'The Archbishop's Three Seats in Canterbury Cathedral', *Antiquaries Journal*, 29 (1949), pp. 26–36. M. H. Caviness, *The Early Stained Glass of Canterbury Cathedral, circa 1175–1220* (Princeton, NJ [1977]); id., *The Windows of Christ Church Cathedral Canterbury* (Corpus vitrearum medii aevi, Great Britain, 2; 1981). *Medieval Art and Architecture at Canterbury before 1220* (British Archaeological Association Conference Transactions for the Year 1979, 5; 1982). R. A. L. Smith, *Canterbury Cathedral Priory: A Study in Monastic Administration* (Cambridge Studies in Economic History; 1943), with bibl. R. C. Fowler in *VCH*, Kent, 2 (1926), pp. 113–21. W. Urry, *Canterbury under the Angevin Kings* (University of London Historical Studies, 19; 1967). On St Augustine's Monastery, W. Dugdale, op. cit., pp. 120–52. R. J. E. Boggis, *A History of St Augustine's Monastery, Canterbury* (1901). R. C. Fowler in *VCH*, loc. cit., pp. 126–33. M. [J.] Sparks, *St Augustine's Abbey, Canterbury, Kent* (1988). R. J. E. Boggis, *A History of St Augustine's College, Canterbury* (1907). W. A. Pantin in *DHGE* 11 (1949), cols. 785–812, s.v. 'Cantorbéry'.

Canterbury and York Society. A society founded in 1904 for the printing of episcopal registers and other ecclesiastical records.

Lists of the Society's publications are incl. in its annual reports.

Canterbury cap. A soft flat cloth cap sometimes worn by English clerical dignitaries and others. Like the college cap and the *biretta, it is simply a later form of the ordinary medieval black cloth head-dress.

canticle (Lat. *canticulum*, dim. of *canticum*, a 'song'. In the rubrics of the *Breviary, however, the non-diminutive form is used). Song or prayer (other than one of the *psalms) derived from the Bible, which is used in the liturgical worship of the Church. In the E. Church the Byzantine rite prescribes nine canticles or 'odes' for daily use at *Orthros, eight from the OT, namely the two 'Songs of *Moses' (Ex. 15: 1–19 and Dt. 32: 1–43); the 'Song of Hannah' (1 Sam. 2: 1–10); the 'Song of Habakkuk' (Hab. 3: 2–19); the 'Song of *Isaiah' (Is. 26: 1–21); the 'Song of Jonah' (Jon. 2: 2–9); the 'Song of the Three Children' (S. of III Ch. 3–22); and the *Benedicite. The ninth ode consists of two NT canticles, *Magnificat and *Benedictus. In present practice all the canticles except the Magnificat are normally omitted. The *Nunc Dimittis is used daily at *Vespers.

In the RC Divine Office, the Benedictus is said daily at *Lauds, the Magnificat at Vespers, and the Nunc Dimittis at *Compline. Varying from day to day, some 44 OT canticles are used at Lauds, and nine other NT canticles at Vespers, namely Eph. 1: 3–10; Phil. 2: 6–11; Col. 1: 12–20; 1 Tim. 3: 16; 1 Pet. 2: 21–4; Rev. 4: 11, 5: 9, 10: 12; 11: 17–18, 12: 10b–12a; 15: 3–4; 19: 1–17. The Roman Breviary also includes the *Te Deum among its canticles.

In the BCP the word 'canticle' is applied only to the Benedicite, but in common speech it is used of many of the others named above, as well as of the *Jubilate, the *Cantate, and *Deus misereatur.

J. Mearns, *The Canticles of the Christian Church, Eastern and Western, in Early and Medieval Times* (Cambridge, 1914). H. Schneider, *Die Altlateinischen Biblischen Cantica* (Texte und Arbeiten, I. Abteilung, 29–30; 1938). Id., 'Die biblischen Oden in christlichen Altertum', *Biblica*, 30 (1949), pp. 28–65, 239–72; id., 'Die biblischen Oden in Jerusalem und Konstantinopel', ibid., pp. 433–52; id., 'Die biblischen Oden im Mittelalter', ibid., pp. 479–500.

Canticle of the Sun, The (Lat. '*canticum solis*' or '*laudes creaturarum*'). A hymn of St *Francis in praise of the Divine revelation in nature, traditionally supposed to have been composed in 1225 in the garden of San Damiano at *Assisi. It receives its name from the second stanza, 'Be thou praised, my Lord, with all thy creatures, above all Brother Sun'.

Crit. edn. of text in K. Esser, OFM (ed.), *Die Opuscula des hl. Franziskus von Assisi* (Spicilegium Bonaventurianum, 13; Grottaferrata, 1976), pp. 122–33, with extensive refs. Eng. tr., with introd., in *The Writings of St Francis of Assisi*, tr. by B. Fahy, OFM (1964), pp. 127–31. J. R. H. Moorman, *The Sources for the Life of S. Francis of Assisi* (Manchester, 1940), pp. 17–19, incl. refs. to other discussions. E. Doyle, OFM, *St Francis and The Song of Brotherhood* (1980).

Canticles, Book of. See SOLOMON, SONG OF.

Cantilupe, St Thomas de (*c*.1218–82), also St Thomas of Hereford, Bp. of *Hereford. The descendant of a noble family of Hambledon in Bucks, he was educated at *Oxford, *Paris, and Orléans, and became Chancellor of Oxford University in 1261. As Chancellor he aided the barons against King Henry III, and in 1265, after the defeat of the king at Lewes, became Chancellor of England. After the collapse of the baronial power in 1265 he retired to Paris as a lecturer, but returned to Oxford, where he was Chancellor a second time in 1273. In 1275 he was elected Bp. of Hereford and became the confidential adviser of Edward I. Exercising his influence esp. against simoniacal practices and the vice of nepotism, he firmly suppressed encroachments on the rights of his see by the neighbouring lords. His later years were filled with disputes with his former teacher, John *Pecham, from 1279 Abp. of Canterbury, over questions of jurisdiction; one of these led to his excommunication by the Archbishop in 1282. He immediately appealed against the sentence at the Papal court at Orvieto, but died before judgement had been pronounced. Despite the excommunication, the fame of his sanctity and of the miracles that took place at his tomb led to his canonization in 1320. Feast day, originally 2 Oct.; in modern RC calendars, 3 Oct.

His Register, transcribed by R. G. Griffiths with introd. by W. W. Capes, pub. by the Cantilupe Society, 1906, and reissued by the *Canterbury and York Society, 2 (1907). The chief source for his Life is the Process of Canonization preserved in the Vatican MS 4015, part of which is pr. in *AASS*, Oct. 1 (1765), pp. 599–705. [E.] M. [S.] Jancey (ed.), *St Thomas Cantilupe, Bishop of Hereford: Essays in his honour* (Hereford, 1982). T. F. Tout in *DNB* 8 (1886), pp. 448–52; *BRUO* 1 (1957), pp. 347–9, s.v. 'Cantelupe, Thomas de'.

Cantilupe, Walter de (d. 1266), Bp. of *Worcester, and uncle of St Thomas de *Cantilupe. He was elected Bishop in 1236, and consecrated by *Gregory IX in person in 1237. He supported many of the actions of R. *Grosseteste, Bp. of *Lincoln; but, despite this, was held to be one of the chief 'friends of the Pope' in England. In the war between King and barons (1258–65) he took the barons' side, and this fact is said to have been the only hindrance to his canonization. He was among the greatest figures of his day both as a diocesan bishop and as a national leader.

The chief sources for his Life are the *Annales Monastici*, ed. H. R. Luard (RS, 5 vols., 1864–9, esp. 1, pp. 101–52, and 4, pp. 428–56); *Matthew Paris, *Chronica Majora*, ed. H. R. Luard (RS, 1876–82), *passim*; *The Chronicle of William of Rishanger*, ed. by J. O. Halliwell (Camden Society, os 15; 1840), and the letters of R. Grosseteste, ed. H. R. Luard (RS, 1861). H. R. Luard in *DNB* 8 (1886), pp. 452–4; *BRUO* 1 (1957), pp. 349–50, s.v. 'Cantelupe, Walter de'.

cantor. A singer who leads in the liturgical music of the Church. In cathedral and monastic churches the cantor sets the pitch of *plainsong by singing the opening words, and also performs the other solo parts of the chant. In English cathedrals he became known as the *precentor. Acc. to W. usage the number of cantors (one, two, or four) is governed by the feast or season; they may be clerics or lay persons and wear surplices or, on solemn occasions, copes. In modern RC usage the term is also used of the choir master who is enjoined to lead and encourage the people in singing their part at Mass. It is also the title of the director of music in a *Lutheran church, and usually also in the associated school. In the E. Church, the cantor, like the *lector, is one of the '*Minor Orders'.

H. *Leclercq, OSB, in *DACL* 3 (pt. 1; 1913), cols. 344–65, s.v. 'Chantres'; S. Corbin in *NCE* 3 (1967), p. 71, s.v. 'Cantor in Christian Liturgy', with further bibl.

cantoris [sc. *sedes*] (Lat.), 'the place of the cantor'. As the traditional place of the cantor is on the N. side of the choir of a cathedral or church, the term (also 'cantorial' or 'cantoral') is used to indicate those who in antiphonal singing sit on that side. The opposite side is known as '*decani'.

Capelle, Bernard (1884–1961), Abbot of Mont-César. A native of Namur, he was ordained priest in 1906 and professed a *Benedictine monk at *Maredsous in 1919. In 1928 he was elected coadjutor Abbot of Mont-César, Louvain, becoming full Abbot on his predecessor's death in 1942. In 1936 he became Maître de Conférences (History of Liturgy) in the University of Louvain. His many original and important contributions to the history of liturgy, early Christian literature and the Latin Bible, all marked by solidity and sound judgement, include *Le Texte du psautier latin en Afrique* (Collectanea Biblica Latina, 4; 1913), *Pour une meilleure intelligence de la Messe* (1946), *An Early Euchologium: The *Der-Balizeh Papyrus enlarged and re-edited* (with C. H. Roberts, 1949), and a long series of articles in *Revue Bénédictine* and other periodicals.

Collected *Travaux liturgiques de doctrine et d'histoire* (3 vols., Louvain, 1955–67). Obit. notice by F. Vandenbroucke, OSB, in *EL* 76 (1962), pp. 43–51.

Capernaum (or more correctly 'Capharnaum', as in the best Greek MSS of the NT and in the *Vulgate). A town near the Sea of Galilee, which was a centre for Christ's ministry (Mk. 2: 1), and the scene of many of His miracles. It has now been identified with Kefar Naḥum (Tell Ḥûm). The site consists of a town, largely unexplored by archaeologists, and a synagogue, usually attributed to the 3rd cent. AD, which has been excavated and partially restored. It may stand on the site of an earlier synagogue.

V. C. Corbo, OFM, and others, *Cafarnao* (Pubblicazioni dello Studium Biblicum Franciscum, 19; 4 vols., Jerusalem, 1972–5). J.

Murphy-O'Connor, OP, *The Holy Land: An Archaeological Guide from Earliest Times to 1700* (2nd edn., Oxford, 1986), pp. 188–93. S. Loffreda and V. Tzaferis in E. Stern and others (eds.), *The New Encyclopedia of the Archaeological Excavations in the Holy Land*, 1 (Jerusalem and New York [1993]), pp. 291–6.

Capistrano, St Giovanni. See GIOVANNI CAPISTRANO, ST.

capital punishment. The infliction of death following judicial sentence. St *Paul in Rom. 13 (esp. 1–5) appears to recognize its legitimacy, and no religious body as such holds it to be immoral except the Society of *Friends, although individual Christians have sometimes held that it contravenes the 6th commandment. In the C of E the 37th of the *Thirty-Nine Articles recognizes that it may be inflicted 'for heinous and grave offences'. Its abolition in many countries, however, and the great diminution since 1800 of the number of crimes punishable by death in others, may legitimately be ascribed, in part at least, to Christian enlightenment. In Great Britain the Murder (Abolition of Death Penalty) Act 1965 substituted mandatory life imprisonment for capital punishment for a trial period of five years, and on 31 Dec. 1969 this was made permanent by resolution of Parliament.

Capitilavium (Lat., 'washing of the head'). A name given to *Palm Sunday in the early Middle Ages, acc. to *Isidore of Seville in reference to the custom of washing the heads of children in preparation for the anointing which took place at Baptism on the ensuing *Holy Saturday.

Capito, Wolfgang (1478–1541), Protestant Reformer and OT scholar. His original surname was Köpfel. Educated at Ingolstadt, Heidelberg, and Freiburg i.B., he was ordained and in 1515 moved to Basle, where he came into contact with *Erasmus. From 1518 he was sympathetic to the views of M. *Luther. After a period in Mainz, in 1523 he settled in Strasbourg and became, together with M. *Bucer, the city's chief Reformer. He attempted to get the Mass abolished by peaceful means (1525–9) and was exceptionally tolerant towards *Anabaptists and other religious dissidents. With Bucer, he drew up the *Tetrapolitan Confession (1530). In 1532, in collaboration with B. *Haller, he composed the Church ordinance which consolidated the Reformation in Berne. He shared the views of U. *Zwingli on the Eucharist, though he signed the *Wittenberg Concord in 1536. His writings include a Hebrew grammar and commentaries on several Books of the OT.

Catalogue of his correspondence by O. Millet (Publications de la Bibliothèque Nationale et Universitaire de Strasbourg, 8; 1982). J. W. Baum, *Capito und Butzer* (Leben und ausgewählte Schriften der Väter und Begründer der reformierten Kirche, 3; Elberfeld, 1860). P. Kalkoff, *W. Capito im Dienste Erzbischof Albrechts von Mainz* (1907); O. E. Strasser, *Capitos Beziehungen zu Bern* (1927); id., *La Pensée théologique de Wolfgang Capiton dans les dernières années de sa vie* (Mémoires de l'Université de Neuchâtel, 11; 1938); B. Stierle, *Capito als Humanist* (Quellen und Forschungen zur Reformationsgeschichte, 42; Gütersloh, 1974), with bibl. of his works; J. M. Kittelson, *Wolfgang Capito: From Humanist to Reformer* (Studies in Medieval and Reformation Thought, 17; Leiden, 1975). M. Lienhard in *TRE* 7 (1981), pp. 636–40, s.v.

Capitular Mass. The public Mass sung or said in RC cathedrals and collegiate churches, and attended by the whole chapter. It is the parallel of the *Conventual Mass in religious communities, and is sometimes itself so described.

capitulary (Lat. *capitulare*). (1) A collection of civil statutes, esp. those made by the Merovingian and Carolingian kings. The first official use of the word in this sense is in an enactment of *Charlemagne of the year 779.

(2) A compilation of previously enacted laws made by the bishops for the practical guidance of the clergy and laity of their dioceses. These 'episcopal capitularies' also date chiefly from Frankish times.

(3) In biblical MSS a brief summary of the contents, put at the head of the several Books. These capitularies are based on classical models, and date from the 3rd cent. onwards. In some cases a single Book is prefaced by several independent capitularies. By the Greeks they were known as κεφάλαια or τίτλοι, by the Latins as *tituli, breves, breviaria, capitula*, or *capitulationes*.

cappa magna. In the RC Church, a cloak with a long train and a large hood, the use of which is now confined to bishops; in the past it was also used by all cardinals (whether bishops or not) and certain other dignitaries. Its colour is ordinarily violet, except for cardinals whose *cappa magna* is scarlet. It dates from the end of the Middle Ages, but its form has recently been much simplified.

Cappadocian Fathers, the. The three brilliant leaders of philosophical Christian orthodoxy in the later 4th cent., namely St *Basil the Great, Bp. of Caesarea in Cappadocia, St *Gregory of Nazianzus (from his birthplace, where his father was bishop), and St *Gregory, Bp. of Nyssa (qq.v.). They were the chief influence which led to the final defeat of *Arianism at the Council of *Constantinople of 381. They were all Cappadocians by birth.

Besides general patrologies, Church histories, and histories of doctrine, and works listed under the individual Fathers, see also B. Otis, 'Cappadocian Thought as a Coherent System', *Dumbarton Oaks Papers*, 12 (1958), pp. 95–124.

Capreolus, John (*c.*1380–1444), 'Thomistarum princeps', *Thomist philosopher and theologian. A native of Languedoc, he entered the *Dominican Order at Rodez. From 1407 he lectured on the *Sentences at Paris, where he was granted the licentiate in 1411. Later he was Regent of Studies at Toulouse. His principal work was a defence of St Thomas's teaching in four books ('Defensiones', 1409–32) against the attacks of *Henry of Ghent, *Duns Scotus, *Durandus of St-Pourçain, *William of Ockham, and others, which, after more than a century of eclipse, did much to revive the authority of Thomism.

Modern edn. of his Works by C. Paban and T. Pègues, OP (7 vols., Tours, 1900–8). Series of arts. by T. Pègues, OP, in *Revue Thomiste*, 7 (1899), pp. 63–81, 317–34, 507–29; 8 (1900), pp. 50–76, 288–309, 505–30; and 13 (1905), pp. 530–53. J. Ude, *Doctrina Capreoli de Influxu Dei in Actus Voluntatis Humanae secundum Principia Thomismi et Molinismi collata* (1904). U. Degl' Innocenti, OP, 'Il Capreolo e la questione sulla personalità', *Divus Thomas*, 43 (3rd ser. 17; Piacenza, 1940), pp. 27–40. M. *Grabmann, 'Johannes Capreolus OP der "Princeps Thomistarum" (†7 April 1444) und seine Stellung in der Geschichte der Thomistenschule.

Ein Gedenkblatt zu seinem fünfhundertjährigen Todestag', *Divus Thomas: Jahrbuch für Philosophie und Spekulative Theologie*, 3rd ser, 22 (1944), pp. 85–109, 145–170; repr. in *Mittelalterliches Geistesleben*, 3 (Munich, 1956), pp. 370–410. K. Forster, *Die Verteidigung der Lehre des heiligen Thomas von der Gottesschau durch Johannes Capreolus* (Münchener Theologische Studien, II. Systematische Abteilung, 9; 1955). Further bibl. in Überweg, 2, p. 788.

Captivity Epistles, the. The four epistles—Phil., Col., Eph., Philem.—generally believed to have been written by St *Paul towards the end of his life when he was in captivity at *Rome. *Caesarea and *Ephesus have also been suggested as the place of origin of one or more of the epistles. References to Paul's bondage occur, e.g. at Phil. 1: 7, Col. 4: 18, Eph. 4: 1, Philem. 9 f. See arts. on the individual epistles.

Capuchins. An offshoot of the *Franciscan Order, founded by Matteo di Bassi of Urbino (d. 1552), an *Observant Friar, who desired to return to the primitive simplicity of the order. Its members wear a pointed cowl (*capuche*), similar to that of St *Francis, sandals, and a beard. The Rule, drawn up in 1529, strongly re-emphasized the Franciscan ideals of poverty, austerity, and contemplative prayer. At first the order encountered considerable opposition from the Observant Friars, and the secession in 1541 of the third general, Bernardino *Ochino, to Protestantism nearly led to its suppression. But their enthusiastic preaching and missionary work gained them popular support and made them one of the most powerful weapons of the *Counter-Reformation. The order was until modern times the strictest of the Franciscan families, though the severity of its practices has been gradually mitigated in successive constitutions. Its members have usually been men of action rather than scholars; among the best known are St *Laurence of Brindisi, Father Joseph Leclerc du Tremblay (1577–1638; the confidant of A. M. J. du P. *Richelieu, to whom the phrase *éminence grise* was first applied, the Capuchin habit then being grey), and Theobald Mathew (1790–1856), the 'Apostle of Temperance' in Ireland and elsewhere. The official title of the order is 'Ordo Fratrum Minorum Capuccinorum' (OFM Cap.). A female branch of the order, whose members are called 'Capuchinesses', was founded in 1538.

Bullarium Ordinis FF. Minorum S. P. Francisci Capucinorum, ed. M. a Tugio, O. Cap. (7 vols., Rome, 1740–52); cont. by Petrus Damianus of Münster, O. Cap. (3 vols., Innsbruck, 1883–4). The various constitutions from 1529 to 1925 were repr. photographically (2 vols., Rome, 1980–6). Z. Boverio, O. Cap., *Annales seu Sacrae Historiae Ordinis Minorum S. Francisci qui Capucini nuncupantur* (2 vols., Lyons, 1632–9); cont. by Marcellinus of Pisa, O. Cap. (Lyons, 1676), Silvester Draghetta of Milan, O. Cap. (Milan, 1737), and P. Pellegrino of Forli, O. Cap. (Milan, 4 vols., 1882–5). Other material in Fr. Cuthbert [Hess], OSFC, *The Capuchins* (2 vols., 1928). Melchior a Pobladura, OFM Cap., *Historia Generalis Ordinis Fratrum Minorum Capuccinorum* (Bibliotheca Seraphico-Capuccina, Sectio Historica, 7–10; Rome, 1947–51), and other works of this author. T. Graf, *Die Kapuziner* (Freiburg, Switzerland, 1957). *Lexicon Capuccinum: Promptuarium Historico-Bibliographicum Ordinis Fratrum Minorum Capuccinorum (1525–1950)* (Rome, 1951). T. MacVicar, OFM Cap., in *NCE* 6 (1967), pp. 65–7, s.v. 'Franciscans, Capuchin'; Melchiorre da Pobladura, OFM Cap., in *DIP* 2 (1975), cols. 203–52, s.v.

'Cappuccini', with extensive bibl. *Analecta Ordinis Minorum Capuccinorum* pub. at Rome, 1884 ff., and *Monumenta Historica Ordinis Capuccinorum*, 1–4, Assisi, 1937–40; 4 ff., Rome, 1941 ff. See also works cited s.v. FRANCISCAN ORDER.

Carafa, Giovanni Pietro. See PAUL IV.

Carbonari (Ital., 'charcoal burners'). A secret political society in some ways resembling the Continental *Freemasons. Their existence in the chief Italian cities was reported to Napoleon in 1809, and, though their origins are unclear, their rituals suggest a connection with the French charcoal-burners ('charbonnerie') who operated in Franche-Compté and Jura before the Revolution. The Carbonari were organized in cells, each bound in obedience to a central hierarchy, but their aims and rites differed widely according to time and place. They utilized Christian symbolism, but rejected all forms of Divine revelation and looked to *natural religion as a sufficient basis for virtue and brotherhood. In politics their professed aim was the destruction of absolutism; they also aspired to free Italy from foreign rule and some sought its unification. In 1820 they and their supporters gained possession of Naples for a brief period, and in the following year *Pius VII issued a condemnation of them. The July Revolution of 1830 in France was also largely inspired by their influence. Many were absorbed in the Young Italy Movement of G. Mazzini (1831).

R. J. Rath, 'The Carbonari: Their Origins, Initiation Rites, and Aims', *American Historical Review*, 69 (1964), pp. 353–70, with extensive refs. J. M. Roberts, *The Mythology of Secret Societies* (1972), pp. 283–94. P. Pirri, SJ, in *EC* 3 (1950), cols. 765–70, s.v. 'Carboneria'; M. P. Trauth, SND, in *NCE* 3 (1967), pp. 101 f., s.v.

Cardijn, Joseph-Léon (1882–1967), Belgian cardinal, founder of the *Jocists. Himself of working-class origin, he was deeply concerned about the alienation from the Church of young workers in industrialized society. After his ordination by D. J. *Mercier in 1906, he studied political and social sciences at Louvain and became a teacher in a secondary school. He used his vacations to examine working-class conditions in various countries. In 1912 he was appointed assistant priest in a suburb of Brussels and in 1915 put in charge of the Christian social work in the city. He organized groups of young factory workers, teaching them to analyse their environment and discover their mission to evangelize those among whom they worked. His ideas spread but aroused opposition. In 1925 he appealed to Pope *Pius XI, who approved the movement, now called 'Jeunesse Ouvrière Chrétienne'. Cardijn spent much of his life organizing it on a world-wide basis. He attended the Second *Vatican Council as a *peritus*, and his book, *Laïcs en première ligne* (1963; Eng. tr., 1964) helped shape discussion on the laity. In 1965 he was made a cardinal.

M. de la Bedoyere, *The Cardijn Story* (1958); M. Fievez and J. Meert, *Cardijn* (Brussels [1969]); *Cardijn, un homme, un mouvement: Actes du Colloque de Leuven-Louvain-la-Neuve, 18–19/11/1982* (Leuven, 1983). F. Peemans in *Biographie Nationale publiée par l'Académie Royale des Sciences, des Lettres et des Beaux-Arts de Belgique*, 44 (1986), pp. 155–164. See also bibl. to JOCISTS.

cardinal (Lat., *cardo*, 'hinge'), a title first applied to any priest permanently attached to a church (in which sense it still survives in the two cardinals among the minor canons at *St Paul's Cathedral, London) and then restricted to the clergy of *Rome, i.e. the parish priests, the bishops of the *suburbicarian dioceses, and the seven (later 14) district *deacons.

The cardinals at Rome gradually formed a college, ranked as Roman princes immediately after the Pope, and became (when assembled in *Consistory) his immediate counsellors. They assumed the government of the RC Church during the vacancy of the *Holy See. In the Middle Ages they came to rank with princes of the royal blood.

The three ranks of cardinals originated at different periods. The cardinal-priests were the parish priests of various Roman churches. Cardinal-deacons had the care of the poor in the seven districts of Rome. Cardinal-bishops were created *c.* the 8th cent., when the increase of Papal business made it necessary to invoke the help of neighbouring bishops to act from time to time as the Pope's representatives. The terms 'cardinal-subdeacon' and 'cardinal-acolyte' were occasionally used of the subdeacons and acolytes at Papal ceremonies; but this usage did not persist.

The present functions of cardinals are chiefly administrative. They are nominated by the Pope. In 1586 their number was fixed at 70 by *Sixtus V, but Pope *John XXIII expressly derogated from this rule in 1958 and there is now no upper limit. Acc. to current canon law (*CIC* (1983), can. 351), all cardinals must be in priest's orders, and those not already bishops are to be given episcopal consecration. (In the last cent. E. *Consalvi and G. *Antonelli were only deacons, and it is only since 1962 that all cardinals have been made bishops.) Their duties are to reside in Rome if they hold any curial office and are not diocesan bishops, to act as heads of *curial offices and *Roman Congregations, and to preside over ecclesiastical commissions. They are given the title of 'Eminence' and have various rights, such as the faculty to hear confessions anywhere. Their insignia have traditionally included the *red hat (abolished in 1969), red *biretta (which is now used at the ceremony of admission), red skull cap, the 'sacred purple', a *ring with a sapphire stone, the *pectoral cross and, on certain occasions, the use of the *ombrellino. Every cardinal resident in Rome has the right to a revenue (*piatto cardinalizio*) if without sufficient private means.

On a vacancy in the Apostolic See they meet in secret session to elect a Pope (see CONCLAVE), a privilege that has been exclusively theirs since the Third *Lateran Council of 1179 (can. 1). Only those under 80 may now vote.

From time to time the Pope creates a cardinal *in petto*, i.e. privately, but the creation is without effect unless publication follows. The nominee, however, retains his place of seniority.

J. B. Sägmüller, *Die Thätigkeit und Stellung der Cardinäle bis Papst Bonifaz VIII.* (1896). V. Martin, *Les Cardinaux et la curie, tribunaux et offices, la vacance du siège apostolique* (1930). H. W. Klewitz, 'Die Entstehung des Kardinalkollegiums', *Zeitschrift der Savigny-Stiftung für Rechtsgeschichte*, Kanonistische Abteilung, 25 (1936), pp. 115–221; repr. in *Reformpapsttum und Kardinalkolleg* (Darmstadt, 1957), pp. 11–134. M. Belardo, *De Juribus S.R.E. Cardinalium in Titulis* (Vatican City, 1939). S. Kuttner, 'Cardinalis: The History of a Canonical Concept', *Traditio*, 3 (New

York, 1945), pp. 129–214; M. Andrieu, 'L'Origine du titre de cardinal dans l'Église romaine', *Miscellanea Giovanni Mercati*, 5 (ST 125; 1946), pp. 113–44. G. Mollat, 'Contribution à l'histoire du Sacré Collège de Clément V à Eugène IV', *RHE* 46 (1951), pp. 22–112, 566–94. K. Ganzer, *Die Entwicklung des auswärtigen Kardinalats im hohen Mittelalter: Ein Beitrag zur Geschichte des Kardinalkollegiums von 11. bis 13. Jahrhundert* (Bibliothek des deutschen historischen Instituts in Rom, 26; 1963). C. G. Fürst, *Cardinalis: Prolegomena zu einer Rechtsgeschichte des römischen Kardinalskollegiums* (Munich, 1967). A. Molien in *DDC* 2 (1937), cols. 1310–39, s.v.; P. Paschini, P. Ciprotti and V. Bartoccetti in *EC* 3 (1949), cols. 779–84, s.v. 'Cardinale'.

cardinal virtues. The four 'cardinal virtues' are prudence, temperance, fortitude, and justice. The chief Christian moral theologians, e.g. St *Ambrose, St *Augustine, and St *Thomas Aquinas, took over this classification from *Plato and *Aristotle. In Christian writers the 'cardinal' are contrasted with the '*theological' virtues of *faith, *hope, and *charity.

St Thomas, *S. Theol.* I–II, q. 61 ('De Virtutibus Cardinalibus'). F. M. Utz, OP, *De Connexione Virtutum Moralium inter se secundum Doctrinam S. Thomae Aquinatis* (Vechta, 1937). J. Pieper, *The Four Cardinal Virtues* (Notre Dame, Ind., 1966; Eng. tr. of four essays issued separately). J. Rickaby, SJ, in *CE* 3 (1908), pp. 343–5.

Cardwell, Edward (1787–1861), ecclesiastical historian. Educated at Brasenose College, Oxford, he became Camden Professor of Ancient History in 1825, and Principal of St Alban Hall in 1831, in succession to R. *Whately, an office which he held till his death. He issued through the University Press, in the administration of which he took a prominent part, several collections of documents still of great value to the student of English Church history, notably *Documentary Annals of the Reformed Church of England* (2 vols., 1839), *A History of Conferences . . . connected with the Revision of the BCP* (1840), and *Synodalia* (2 vols., 1842).

C. W. Sutton in *DNB* 9 (1887), pp. 42 f., s.v.

Carey, William (1761–1834), *Baptist missionary. Born in humble circumstances in Northamptonshire and baptized an Anglican, he was apprenticed in 1777 to a shoemaker, but, after his conversion (1779), he became convinced of Baptist teaching (1783) and spent part of his time as a preacher. For many years he continued his cobbling by night, whilst running a school by day and acting as pastor of a church. During this time he taught himself Latin, Greek, Hebrew, Dutch, and French. He believed that mission in previously unevangelized parts of the world was of prime importance, and, at the ministers' meeting at Nottingham in 1792, he promulgated the watchword, 'Expect great things from God and attempt great things for God', which led to the founding of the *Baptist Missionary Society. Sailing for India in 1793 in a Danish vessel, as the East India Company had put a ban on missionaries in British ships, he arrived in Bengal in Nov. 1793, where he was put in charge of an indigo factory at Malda, which became his mission station. In five years he translated the NT into Bengali and visited 200 villages. When the factory was closed (1799), he left for Serampore, where he was joined by four new missionaries, with whose assistance he was able to bring his Bengali New Testament

into print in 1801. At this time Fort William College was opened at Calcutta, and Carey was appointed professor of Sanskrit, Bengali, and Marathi—a position that he held for 30 years. His many labours included a translation of the whole Bible into Bengali (1809), and its translation, in whole or part, into 24 other languages and dialects. In addition, he published philological works (grammars and dictionaries) in Sanskrit, Marathi, Punjabi, and Telugu. It was his agitation that was largely responsible for the abolition in 1829 of suttee, the ancient custom that had meant the death of every widow at the time of her husband's funeral.

Lives by E. Carey (son, London, 1836), J. C. Marshman (2 vols., ibid., 1859), G. Smith (ibid., 1885), S. P. Carey (great-grandson, ibid., 1923), and M. Drewery (ibid., 1978). A. H. Oussoren, *William Carey, Especially his Missionary Principles* (Leiden, 1945). W. A. Smalley, *Translation as Mission: Bible Translation in the Modern Missionary Movement* (Macon, Ga. [1991]), pp. 40–52. B. Stanley, *The History of the Baptist Missionary Society* (Edinburgh, 1992), pp. 6–67.

Carlile, Wilson (1847–1942), founder of the *Church Army. After a successful business career (1862–78), he entered the London College of Divinity, was ordained in 1880, and served an assistant curacy in Kensington. In 1882 he founded the Church Army, and combined his work as its honorary Chief Secretary with various parochial appointments. He continued to take part in its administration until a few weeks before his death. From 1949 to 1960 his grandson, **Edward Wilson Carlile** (1915–96), was (General, 1949–51; then renamed Chief, 1951–60) Secretary of the Church Army.

E. Rowan, *Wilson Carlile and the Church Army* (1905; 5th edn. by A. E. Reffold, 1956); S. Dark, *Wilson Carlile* (1944); M. Burn, *The Pearl Divers: Pictures from the Life and Work of Prebendary Carlile* (1920); A. E. Reffold, *Seven Stars: The Story of a Fifty Years' War. A Résumé of the Life and Work of Wilson Carlile and the Church Army* (1931; reissued as 'The Audacity to Live', 1938). Id. in *DNB, 1941–1950*, pp. 134–6.

Carlisle. Acc. to *Simeon of Durham, Carlisle and an estate extending 15 miles around it was given by Ecgfrith, King of Northumberland, to St *Cuthbert when he became Bp. of *Lindisfarne in 685; there is also other evidence associating Cuthbert with Carlisle. The region seems to have remained part of the diocese of Lindisfarne/*Durham until 1101, when it passed to *York. In 1133 Carlisle became the centre of a new diocese created for the part of the former kingdom of Strathclyde south of the Solway after its annexation by William II. The first bishop was Aethelwulf, Prior of Nostell, and prob. also of the house of *Augustinian Canons, founded in Carlisle by Henry I *c.*1122. Their priory church became the new cathedral, the only one in England served by this order, but the vacancy in the see of nearly 50 years after Aethelwulf's death in 1156/7 hampered work on the building; it was completed *c.*1280 and largely destroyed by fire in 1292. Because of the impoverishment of the diocese by the Anglo-Scottish wars beginning in 1296, rebuilding was slow during the 14th cent.; the N. transept and central tower were completed by Bp. William Strickland (Bp. 1400–19). The Augustinian priory was dissolved in 1540, its lands and revenues being used to endow a new cathedral establishment. The post-Reformation bishops were

greatly concerned to extirpate RCism and improve standards of religious observance, but the cathedral fell into disrepair and five bays of the nave were demolished between
1649 and 1652. The cathedral was extensively restored in
1764 and again between 1853 and 1856. Its chief glory is
the 14th-cent. E. window. In 1856 the diocese was
enlarged by the addition of parts of southern Cumbria,
formerly in the diocese of *Chester. Notable bishops
include James *Ussher (who held the see in *commendam,
1642–56), Edward Rainbowe (1664–84), William Nicholson (1702–18), and Harvey Goodwin (1869–91).

*The Register of John de Halton, Bishop of Carlisle A.D. 1292–
1324*, transcribed by W. N. Thompson, with an introd. by T. F.
Tout (*Canterbury and York Society, 12 and 13; 1913); *The Register of John Kirkby, Bishop of Carlisle 1332–1352, and the Register
of John Ross, Bishop of Carlisle, 1325–31*, ed. R. L. Storey (ibid.
79, etc.; 1993 ff.). Extant records of the see listed in the *Ninth
Report of the Historical Manuscripts Commission*, part 1 (1863), pp.
177–97. *The Statutes of the Cathedral Church of Carlisle*, ed. with
introd. by J. E. Prescott (Carlisle, 1879). J. Nicolson and R. Burn,
*The History and Antiquities of the Counties of Westmorland and
Cumberland*, 2 (1777), pp. 243–310. C. M. L. Bouch, *Prelates and
People of the Lake Counties: A History of the Diocese of Carlisle
1133–1933* (Kendal, 1948). H. Summerson, *Medieval Carlisle: The
City and the Borders from the late eleventh to the mid-sixteenth century* (Cumberland and Westmorland Antiquarian and Archaeological Society, Extra Series, 25; 2 vols., 1993). D. R. Perriam,
'The Demolition of the Priory of St. Mary, Carlisle', *Transactions
of the Cumberland & Westmorland Antiquarian & Archaeological
Society*, 87 (1987), pp. 127–58. J. Wilson in *VCH*, Cumberland,
2, ed. id. (1905), pp. 131–51. J. E. Prescott in *DECH* (1912), pp.
95–8, s.v.; H. Dauphin, OSB, in *DHGE* 11 (1949), cols. 1050–8.

Carlstadt (*c.*1480–1541), German reformer. He was so
named from his birthplace, his real name being Andreas
Bodenstein. After studying at Erfurt and *Cologne, he
went to the newly founded University of *Wittenberg.
Here from 1505 he taught in the faculty of arts, later in
that of theology, in 1512 presiding at M. *Luther's doctoral graduation. He became known for upholding the
philosophical teaching of *Thomas Aquinas and *Duns
Scotus against the current trend towards *Nominalism. In
1516, on his return from a period in Rome, he engaged
in a spirited controversy with Luther, who asserted that
Scholasticism represented a misunderstanding of Scripture
and of St *Augustine. Soon afterwards Carlstadt changed
his position and himself became a vigorous upholder of
the Augustinian teaching on the powerlessness of the
human will and emphasis on the need for *grace. In 1517
he published 151 theses maintaining this position. In 1518
(in his 'Invectiones') he supported Luther's criticism of
*indulgences and in the following year he disputed pub-
licly with J. *Eck at Leipzig. In 1520 he was excommunicated and later in the year announced his break with the
Papacy. On Christmas Day 1521 he celebrated the
Eucharist in the vernacular, the first Reformer to do so;
he wore no vestments, abandoned the *Canon of the Mass,
made no reference to sacrifice, and communicated the laity
in both kinds. In Jan. 1522 he married. His programme
for reform at this stage was more radical than that of
Luther and he found himself in sharp conflict with him.
In 1523 he resigned his academic position and went as a
preacher to Orlamünde, where he interpreted the
Eucharist as only a memorial of Christ's death and also
refused to baptize infants. He nevertheless declined to join

T. *Müntzer in armed conflict, advocating non-violence.
He also became interested in German *mysticism. In 1524
he was expelled from Saxony. In 1525, after he had issued
an ambiguous recantation, he was allowed to live in the
vicinity of Wittenberg on certain conditions, but, fearing
imprisonment, fled in 1529, and eventually arrived in
Switzerland, where he remained for the rest of his life. In
1534, after he had abandoned his opposition to *Infant
Baptism, he was appointed preacher of the university
church and professor of Hebrew at Basle.

Karlstadts Schriften aus den Jahren 1523–25, ed. E. Hertsch (2
vols., Halle, 1956–7). His comm. on St Augustine's *De Spiritu et
Litera* (written 1518/19) and 151 Theses ed. E. Kähler, *Karlstadt
und Augustin* (Hallische Monographien, 19; ibid., 1952). O. Seitz,
Der authentische Text der Leipziger Disputation (1903). Eng. tr. of
some texts by R. J. Sider, *Karlstadt's Battle with Luther*
(Philadelphia [1978]). Full details of Carlstadt's writings by E.
Freys and H. Barge, 'Verzeichnis der gedruckten Schriften des
Andreas Bodenstein von Karlstadt', *Zentralblatt für Bibliotheks-
wesen*, 21 (1904), pp. 153–79, 209–43, 305–31; repr. separately,
Nieuwkoop, 1965, supplemented by A. Zorzin, *Karlstadt als Flug-
schriftenautor* (Göttinger Theologische Arbeiten, 48; 1990), pp.
273–307. H. Barge, *Andreas Bodenstein von Karlstadt* (2 vols.,
Leipzig, 1905); F. Kriechbaum, *Grundzüge der Theologie
Karlstadts* (Theologische Forschung, 43; Hamburg, 1967); R. J.
Sider, *Andreas Bodenstein von Karlstadt: The Development of his
Thought 1517–1525* (Studies in Medieval and Reformation
Thought, 11; Leiden, 1974); U. Bubenheimer, *Consonantia
Theologiae et Jurisprudentiae: Andreas Bodenstein von Karlstadt
als Theologe und Jurist zwischen Scholastik und Reformation* (Jus
Ecclesiasticum, 24; Tübingen, 1977); C. A. Pater, *Karlstadt as the
Father of the Baptist Movements* (Toronto, etc. [1984]). U.
Bubenheimer in *TRE* 17 (1988), pp. 649–57, s.v. 'Karlstadt,
Andreas Rudolff Bodenstein von'.

Carlyle, Thomas (1795–1881), Scottish historian, essayist, and moral teacher. Educated at Edinburgh University,
he later was elected its rector (1866). His religious influence (which alone can be referred to here) has been
widespread, for though he hated creeds, churches, and
theologies, he had a profound belief in God and was convinced that 'the Religious Principle lies unseen in the
hearts of all good men'. As an idealist who believed that
matter exists only spiritually, he was the relentless foe of
all materialistic philosophy and, through such works as
Sartor Resartus (1833–4), *On Heroes, Hero-worship, & the
Heroic in History* (1841), and *Past and Present* (1843),
which exposed worldly pleasure-seeking and money-
making, he became the religious teacher of thousands. His
independent, critical outlook rejected organized Christianity, but there was as much of the prophet as the poet in
him and he consistently preached that the 'Everlasting
Yea' is to love God.

Collected Works in 15 vols. (1857–8), in 17 vols. (1885–8), and
'Centenary Edition' by H. D. Traill in 30 vols. (1896–9). *The
Collected Letters of Thomas and Jane Welsh Carlyle* [his wife], ed.
C. R. Sanders and others (Durham, NC, 1970 ff.). There are also
collections of Thomas Carlyle's correspondence with Goethe, ed.
C. E. Norton (London, 1887); with R. W. *Emerson, ed. J. Slater
(London and New York, 1964); and with J. *Ruskin, ed. G. A.
Cate (Stanford, Calif., 1982). J. A. Froude (ed.), *Reminiscences by
Thomas Carlyle* (2 vols., 1881) and *Letters and Memorials of Jane
Welsh Carlyle* (3 vols., 1883). Id., *Thomas Carlyle, 1795–1835* (2
vols., 1882); id., *Thomas Carlyle, 1834–1881* (2 vols., 1884).
Modern Lives by D. A. Wilson (6 vols., London, 1923–34
[exhaustive but uncrit.]) and F. Kaplan (Cambridge, 1983). J.

Symons, *Thomas Carlyle: The Life and Ideals of a Prophet* (1952).
A. A. Ikeler, *Puritan Temper and Transcendental Faith: Carlyle's
Literary Vision* (Columbus, Oh. [1972]); E. M. Behnken, *Thomas
Carlyle: 'Calvinist Without the Theology'* (University of Missouri
Studies, 66; 1978); J. D. Rosenberg, *Carlyle and the Burden of
History* (Oxford, 1985); R. apRoberts, *The Ancient Dialect: Thomas
Carlyle and Comparative Religion* (Berkeley, Calif., etc., 1988).
R. L. Tarr, *Thomas Carlyle: A Bibliography of English-Language
Criticism 1824–1974* (Charlottesville, Va., 1976); id., *Thomas Car-
lyle: A Descriptive Bibliography* (Oxford, 1989).

Carmel, Mount. The high ridge in N. Palestine, immediately above the modern port of Haifa. Its caves, which
were inhabited over 150,000 years ago, are of great interest
to archaeologists. Mount Carmel was the scene of the contest described in 1 Kgs. 18 between *Elijah and the
prophets of *Baal. About AD 500 a church was built there,
and a monastery founded by Greek monks. In the Middle
Ages it became famous as the home of the *Carmelite
Order. The feast of 'Our Lady of Mount Carmel' (16 July)
is now an optional memorial.

F. M. Abel, OP, *Géographie de la Palestine*, 1 (1933), pp. 350–3.
The Stone Age of Mount Carmel, vol. 1 by D. A. E. Garrod and
D. M. A. Bate (Oxford, 1937); vol. 2 by T. D. McCown and A.
Keith (ibid., 1939). M. Avi-Yonah, 'Mount Carmel and the God
of Baalbek', *Israel Exploration Journal*, 2 (1952), pp. 118–24. O.
Eissfeldt, *Der Gott Karmel* (Sb. (Berl.), Klasse für Sprachen, Lit-
eratur und Kunst, Jahrgang 1953, Nr. 1; 1954), with refs. T. Noy
and E. Wreschner in M. Avi-Yonah (ed.), *Encyclopedia of Archae-
ological Excavations in the Holy Land*, 1 (1975), pp. 290–8, s.v.
'Carmel Caves'.

Carmelites. The 'Order of the Brothers of Our Lady of
Mount Carmel' dates from the late 12th cent. The revival
of the eremitical life in the W. Church and of *pilgrimages
to the sites associated with Christ's earthly life during the
*Crusades led many to adopt the solitary life in various
places in the Holy Land, but by the end of the 12th cent.
only those on Mt. *Carmel were securely within the
Frankish Kingdom. A group of hermits living there
accepted a rule written c.1208 by St Albert, the Latin Patr.
of *Jerusalem. They built a church dedicated to the BVM,
from which they took their title, but saw *Elijah as their
model in the contemplative life. Albert's Rule echoes the
traditional style of Palestinian *lavrae. Each hermit was
allotted a cave-dwelling, where he was to remain 'day and
night' praying continually. It also prescribed a daily
Eucharist and the recitation of the Psalter, perpetual
abstinence from meat, and an annual fast from the Feast
of the *Exaltation of the Cross (Sept. 14) to *Easter.

By the middle of the 13th cent. the instability of the
Crusader kingdom led some of the hermits to migrate to
Europe and by 1242 foundations had been made in
Cyprus, Sicily, France, and England. In 1247 Pope *Innocent IV gave permission for foundations to be made not
only in desert places, but in towns and cities, for meals to
be taken in common, and for the canonical *hours to be
recited in place of the Psalter. The undertaking of public
preaching and permission to accept alms brought the Carmelites into the class of *Mendicant Friars. They grew
rapidly. During the 14th and 15th cent. communities of
women were associated to the Order; wearing the Carmelite habit, they adopted the Rule of Albert and were formally incorporated into the Order in 1432. Also, groups of

lay people became affiliated to the Order; members of
these confraternities wore part of the Carmelite habit,
either the white mantle (from which the Carmelites were
known as Whitefriars) or the brown *scapular (on which
see SIMON STOCK, ST).

In 1432 Pope *Eugenius IV approved a second mitigation of the Rule, relaxing the abstinence from meat and
the obligation of silence. This, together with the decline
in religious observance in the later Middle Ages, led to
attempts to reform and renew the Order. Congregations
of reform included those at Mantua and Albi. Under John
Soreth (Prior General 1451–71) the existence of reformed
houses (sometimes referred to as *Observants in contrast
to the *Conventuals) was encouraged in the revised constitutions of 1456. The best known of the reforms was that
begun by St *Teresa of Avila who founded many convents
following the 'Primitive Rule' of Carmel, and her own
Constitutions for *Discalced Nuns. Her disciple St *John
of the Cross was among the first friars to follow her reform
in Spain.

After losing the French provinces during the Revolution
and suffering from the anti-monastic legislation of the
Napoleonic era, the Carmelites have rebuilt their European provinces and expanded in the New and Third
World. The Carmelite family today consists of three
orders of men; the Carmelite Friars (of the Ancient
Observance); the Discalced Carmelite Friars (who look to
the 'Teresian Reform' as their special inspiration); and the
Carmelites of Mary Immaculate (founded in India in
1831). In addition to the enclosed communities of Carmelite Nuns, there are many congregations of active Carmelite
Sisters, and *Secular Institutes of lay people. All share
in a particular devotion to the BVM, esp. to 'Our Lady
of Mt. Carmel' (feast day, 16 July). In the Middle Ages
Carmelite theologians were among the earliest defenders
of the *Immaculate Conception. Well-known Carmelites,
besides those already mentioned, include T. *Netter, St
*Mary Magdalene de' Pazzi, St *Teresa of Lisieux, and
Bl. Edith *Stein.

J. B. de Lezana, OCC, *Annales Sacri, Prophetici et Eliani Ordinis
Beatae Virginis Mariae de Monte Carmeli* (4 vols., Rome, 1645–
56). [C. de Villiers de St-Étienne,] *Bibliotheca Carmelitana: Notis
Criticis et Dissertationibus Illustrata* (2 vols., Orléans, 1752; repr.
with suppl. material by G. Wessels, OCC, Rome, 1927). Collec-
tion of texts relating to the early history ed. A. Staring, O. Carm.,
Medieval Carmelite Heritage (Textus et Studia Carmelitana, 16;
Rome, 1989). J. Smet, O. Carm., *The Carmelites: A History of the
Brothers of Our Lady of Mount Carmel* (4 vols. in 5; vols. 2–4,
Darien, Ill., 1976–88; vol. 1 first pub. Rome, 1975, but rev. [much
improved] edn., Darien, 1988) [the most authoritative history].
Id., *Cloistered Carmel: A Brief History of the Carmelite Nuns*
(Rome, 1986). Earlier general works incl. L. van den Bossche,
Les Carmes (1930) and H. Peltier, *Histoire du Carmel* [1958]. S.
Possanzini, O. Carm., *La Regola dei Carmelitani: Storia e spir-
itualità* (Florence, 1979). L. C. Sheppard, *The English Carmelites*
(1943). P. W. Janssen, OCC, *Les Origines de la réforme des Carmes
en France au XVIIe siècle* (Archives Internationales d'Histoire des
Idées, 4; The Hague, 1963). *Monumenta Historica Carmelitana*
(Lérins, 1905 ff.). *Analecta Ordinis Carmelitarum* (Rome, 1908 ff.).
B. Zimmerman, ODC, in *CE* 3 (1908), pp. 354–70, s.v.; Melchior
de Ste-Marie, OCD, in *DHGE* 11 (1949), cols. 1070–104, s.v.
'Carmel (Ordre de Notre-Dame du Mont-Carmel)', with bibl.;
Bl T. Brandsma, OCC, in *Dict. Sp.* 2 (1953), cols. 156–71, s.v.
'Carmes'. The Carmelites and their branches are comprehensively
treated by various authors in *DIP* 2 (1975), cols. 398–605, with
bibl.

On the Discalced Carmelites see also *Constitutiones Fratrum Discalceatorum Congregationis S. Eliae Ordinis Beatissimae Virginis Mariae de Monte Carmelo* (Paris, 1638). *Chroniques de l'ordre des Carmélites de la réforme de Sainte-Thérèse depuis leur introduction en France* (5 vols., Troyes, 1846–65; 2nd ser., 4 vols., Poitiers, 1888–9). Silverio de Santa Teresa, OCD, *Historia del Carmo Descalzo en España, Portugal y América* (15 vols., Burgos, 1935–52). L. Saggi, O. Carm., *Le Origini dei Carmelitani Scalzi 1567–1593: Storia et Storiografia* (Textus et Studia Carmelitana, 14; 1986). *Études carmélitaines* (Paris, 1911 ff.); *Analecta Ordinis Carmelitarum Discalceatorum* (Rome, 1926 ff.); *Ephemerides·Carmeliticae* (Florence, 1947 ff.), with supplementary *Archivum Bibliographicum Carmelitanum* (Rome, 1956 ff.). Gabriel de Sainte-Marie-Magdaleine, OCD, in *Dict. Sp.* 2 (1953), cols. 171–209, s.v. 'Carmes Déchaussés', with bibl.

carnival. Popular etymology derives the word from *caro vale*, i.e. 'good-bye flesh'; but more probable is the derivation from *carnem levare*, 'to put away flesh-meat'. It is the name given in RC countries to the period before *Lent, whether it be the three days immediately previous, or the whole period between 3 Feb. and *Ash Wednesday. Such seasons of feasting and dancing early degenerated into riots, hence the transference of the word to secular festive occasions.

carol. A song of joy, originally accompanying a dance; now applied esp. to traditional and popular songs of a religious character. The word is from the Italian *carola*, a 'ring dance' (from *carolare*, 'to sing'). Historically the carol differs from the hymn in being a popular, and often unpolished, reflection on a religious theme, composed for informal singing, whereas the hymn was written by skilled and educated churchmen for formal use in Divine Service. Modern practice in England, where the 19th and 20th cents. have seen a considerable revival of the popularity of carols, has tended to confine the singing of them to Christmastide, and also to break down the distinction between carols and hymns, carols being often sung in church, and hymns outside the liturgy. A service of carols and lessons, introduced by E. W. *Benson, Bp. of *Truro, in 1880, was adopted by King's College, Cambridge, in 1918; as modified in the following year, it has become widely popular. There are many traditional carols for seasons other than Christmas.

P. *Dearmer, R. *Vaughan Williams and M. Shaw (eds.), *The Oxford Book of Carols* (1928); H. Keyte and A. Parrott (eds.), *The New Oxford Book of Carols* (Oxford and New York [1992]); R. L. Greene (ed.), *The Early English Carols* (Oxford, 1935; 2nd edn., 1977); id. (ed.), *A Selection of English Carols* (ibid., 1962); R. Nettel (ed.), *Carols 1400–1950: A Book of Christmas Carols* (1956). E. Poston (ed.), *The Penguin Book of Christmas Carols* (Harmondsworth, 1965). E. Routley, *The English Carol* (1958), with bibl.

Caroline Books, the (*Libri Carolini*). A treatise compiled *c.*790–2, which purports to have been written by *Charlemagne, but is manifestly the work of a skilled theologian. It was an attack on the *Iconoclastic Council of 754 (for forbidding images altogether) and *Nicaea II of 787 (for allowing excessive reverence to be paid to them). Its true purpose may be explained by Charlemagne's known irritation with the Greek empress, Irene, and his wish, by discrediting Greek authority of whatever kind, to have the more justification for assuming the Imperial title. It was

long supposed that *Alcuin was its real author, but recent research has made it seem very probable that it was the work of *Theodulf of Orleans. Possibly Alcuin wrote a small part (bk. 4, chs. 14–17).

Text in J. P. Migne, *PL* 98. 989–1248; modern edn. by H. Bastgen in *MGH*, Legum Sectio III, Concilia II, Supp. (1924). Further edn. by A. Freeman in preparation. W. von den Steinen, 'Karl der Grosse und die Libri Carolini. Die tironischen Randnoten zum Codex Authenticus', *NA* 49 (1931), pp. 207–80. D. de Bruyne, 'La Composition des Libri Carolini', *R. Bén.*, 44 (1932), pp. 227–34. A. Freeman, 'Theodulf of Orleans and the Libri Carolini', *Speculum*, 32 (1957), pp. 663–705; id., 'Further Studies in the Libri Carolini', ibid. 40 (1965), pp. 203–89, and 46 (1971), pp. 597–612; id., 'Carolingian Orthodoxy and the Fate of the Libri Carolini', *Viator*, 16 (1985), pp. 65–108; id., 'Additions and corrections to the Libri Carolini: links with Alcuin and the Adoptionist controversy', in S. Krämer and M. Bernhard (eds.), *Scire litteras* (Abh. (Bayr.), NF 99; 1988), pp. 159–69. L. Wallach, *Diplomatic Studies in Latin and Greek Documents from the Carolingian Age* (Ithaca, NY, and London, 1977), pp. 43–294; cf. P. Meyvaert, 'The authorship of the "Libri Carolini" ', *R. Bén.* 89 (1979), pp. 29–57. A. Melloni, 'L' "Opus Caroli Regis contra Synodum" o "Libri Carolini" ', *Studi Medievali*, 3rd ser. 29 (1988), pp. 873–86.

Caroline Divines. The Anglican divines of the 17th cent., esp. when considered as exponents of *High Church principles. The term is not ordinarily restricted (as the word would imply) to those who wrote esp. or solely during the reigns of *Charles I (1625–49) and *Charles II (1660–85), but it is taken to include such theologians as L. *Andrewes (d. 1626). See also ANGLICANISM.

Many of their writings repr. in the *Library of Anglo-Catholic Theology*, 1841 ff. See also P. E. More and F. L. Cross, *Anglicanism: The Thought and Practice of the Church of England, illustrated from the Religious Literature of the Seventeenth Century* (1935). H. R. McAdoo, *The Structure of Caroline Moral Theology* (1949); id., *The Spirit of Anglicanism: A Survey of Anglican Theological Method in the Seventeenth Century* (1965); C. F. Allison, *The Rise of Moralism: The Proclamation of the Gospel from Hooker to Baxter* (1966).

Carolingian Schools. The reign of *Charlemagne (768–814) stimulated an intellectual Renaissance within his domains which continued throughout the 9th cent. and left its mark upon the future history of education. The responsibility for this revival largely rested with Charlemagne himself, and his advisers *Alcuin and *Theodulf of Orléans. By establishing new schools and patronizing scholars he hoped to diminish the illiteracy of the Frankish clergy. In 787 he issued a *capitulary of Baugulf, Abbot of *Fulda, ordering that in all monasteries and bishops' houses there should be study and 'let those who can, teach'. This prescription, which has been termed the 'charter of modern education', was followed in 789 by another capitulary ordering that 'there may be schools for reading-boys; let them learn psalms, notes, chants, the computus and grammar, in every monastery and bishop's house'. Further capitularies (e.g. that of 805) confirmed and elaborated Charlemagne's educational legislation. Through his initiative a Palace School was formed for the cultivation of the *seven liberal arts, which was attended by members of the court as well as the boy lectors of the royal chapel, children of the nobility, and even plebeians. It was probably the first school to give a classical education to members of the laity in any number.

During this period the chief schools were connected with cathedrals and monasteries, the school of Alcuin at Tours being the model for the rest. Of the episcopal schools, those at Orléans (under Theodulf) and at *Reims (later to be under *Hincmar and *Remigius of Auxerre) were the most distinguished. Of the schools more directly connected with monasteries, the schools at Fulda under *Rabanus Maurus, a breeding-ground for scholars, at *Corbie under Adalhard and *Paschasius Radbertus, at Ferrières under *Lupus Servatus, at St Wandrille, at St *Gall, and at St Riquier, were all notable for their scholarship.

The Carolingian Schools were not outstanding for originality of thought. Alcuin's primers, on orthography, grammar, rhetoric, and dialectic, are by modern standards very crude productions. The main purpose, for instance, why he taught mathematics was to enable pupils to calculate the dates of Church festivals. Even his interpretation of theology was quite elementary. There are many indications (e.g. decrees of the Councils of Paris, 824; of Mainz, 847; of Savonnières, 859) that the educational legislation of Charlemagne was not effectively carried out in the declining years of the Carolingian era. Nevertheless many schools (e.g. St Gall), thus stimulated by the Carolingian revival, maintained a high reputation through the early Middle Ages as educational centres. Finally the responsibility for restoring Latin to the position of a literary language and the formation of a more accurate orthography largely rests with the scholars of these schools, whilst editions and copies of the classics, both Christian and pagan, were produced which to some extent were to form in a later period the bases of Renaissance scholarship itself.

G. Monod, *Études critiques sur les sources de l'histoire carolingienne* (Bibliothèque de l'École des Hautes Études, 119; 1898), ch. 2, 'La Renaissance carolingienne', pp. 37–67; E. Patzelt, *Die karolingische Renaissance* (Vienna, 1924; 2nd edn., with additional material by C. Vogel, Graz, 1965). R. McKitterick, *The Frankish Church and the Carolingian Reforms, 789–895* (1977); id., *The Frankish Kingdoms under the Carolingians, 751–987* (1983); P. Riché, *Les Écoles et l'enseignement dans l'Occident chrétien de la fin du V⁰ siècle au milieu du XI⁰ siècle* (1979); J. [A.] Marenbon, *From the Circle of Alcuin to the School of Auxerre: Logic, Theology and Philosophy in the Early Middle Ages* (Cambridge Studies in Medieval Life and Thought, 3rd ser. 15; 1981); J. M. Wallace-Hadrill, *The Frankish Church* (Oxford History of the Christian Church, 1983), pp. 205–389. P. Godman (ed.), *Poetry of the Carolingian Renaissance* (1985; extracts, with Eng. tr. and substantial introd.), id., *Poets and Emperors: Frankish Politics and Carolingian Poetry* (Oxford, 1987). Various papers by B. Bischoff, from 1964 onwards, repr. in his *Mittelalterliche Studien*, 3 (Stuttgart, 1981), esp. pp. 1–54 and 149–212. C. R. Dodwell, *Painting in Europe 800–1200* (Pelican History of Art, 1971), esp. pp. 15–44. M. L. W. Laistner, *Thought and Letters in Western Europe, A.D. 500–900* (1931), pp. 147–325; 2nd edn. (1957), pp. 187–386. Manitius, 1, pp. 243–718. See also bibl. to ALCUIN, CHARLEMAGNE, and THEODULF OF ORLÉANS.

Carpenter, Joseph Estlin (1844–1927), English *Unitarian divine. The grandson of L. *Carpenter (q.v.), he was educated at University College, London. After some years as Unitarian minister at Clifton, Bristol (1866–1869) and Mill Hill, Leeds (1869–75), he became lecturer at Manchester New College, first at London (1875–89) and then at Oxford (1889–1906). From 1906 to 1915 he was principal of Manchester College. One of the chief figures in modern Unitarianism, he was widely respected for his extensive knowledge in comparative religion, Semitic literature, and other religious subjects. His writings include *The First Three Gospels* (1890), *The Composition of the *Hexateuch* (1902), *Comparative Religion* (in the Home University Library, 1913), and *The Johannine Writings* (1927). He was also the English translator of vols. 3 to 5 of G. H. A. *Ewald's *History of Israel*.

Joseph Estlin Carpenter: A Memorial Volume, ed. C. H. Herford (1929). J. H. Weatherall in *DNB, 1922–1930*, pp. 161 f.

Carpenter, Lant (1780–1840), *Unitarian minister. Educated at dissenting schools and at Glasgow University (1798–1801), he became a Unitarian minister, and from 1802 to 1805 was librarian of the Liverpool Athenaeum. Afterwards he was headmaster and pastor at boarding schools, first at *Exeter (1805–17) and then at Bristol (1817–29), where Harriet and James *Martineau were among his pupils. He was drowned near Naples on 5–6 Apr. 1840.

Carpenter did much to foster a more liberal spirit in English Unitarianism. In 1825, on the amalgamation of three older societies into the British and Foreign Unitarian Association, he was instrumental in expunging from the constitution of the new body a preamble branding Trinitarianism as idolatrous. He continued, however, to regard Baptism as superstitious, substituting a form of dedication of infants. Among his many works were *Unitarianism, the Doctrine of the Gospels* (1809), and *Systematic Education* (2 vols., 1815).

R. L. Carpenter (son), *Memoirs of the Life of the Rev. Lant Carpenter, LLD* (1842). A. Gordon in *DNB* 9 (1887), pp. 157–9.

Carpenter, William Boyd (1841–1918), Bp. of *Ripon. Educated at St Catharine's College, Cambridge, he held a succession of parish appointments in which he rapidly gained a great reputation as a preacher. Much liked by Queen Victoria, he was appointed a Royal Chaplain in 1879, Canon of Windsor in 1882, and Bp. of Ripon in 1884 (resigned, 1911). In 1898 he founded the Ripon Clergy College, which moved in 1919 to Oxford (where it was renamed 'Ripon Hall') and in 1933 to a site just outside Oxford on Boars Hill; in 1975 it was merged with Cuddesdon College to form Ripon College, Cuddesdon. From 1911 until his death Carpenter was a Canon of *Westminster. His influence in the later 19th cent. was far-reaching, but his prolific writings have little permanent interest.

H. D. A. Major, *The Life and Letters of William Boyd Carpenter* (1925). Id. in *DNB, 1912–1921*, p. 94.

Carpocrates (2nd cent.), *Gnostic teacher. He was probably a native of *Alexandria. His disciples, the 'Carpocratians', who survived till the 4th cent., preached a licentious ethic, the transmigration of souls, and the doctrine that Jesus was born by natural generation. His son, Epiphanes, wrote a treatise 'On Justice', in which, under the influence of *Plato's 'Republic', he advocated a community of women and goods.

*Irenaeus, *Adv. haer.* 1. 25; *Hippolytus, *Haer.* 7. 32; *Clement, *Strom.* 3. 2–6. Texts conveniently pr. in W. Völker (ed.), *Quellen zur Geschichte der christlichen Gnosis* (1932), pp. 33–8; Eng. tr. of texts in W. Foerster (ed.), *Gnosis*, 1 (Eng. tr., Oxford,

1972), pp. 36–40. H. Liboron, *Die Karpokratianische Gnosis: Untersuchungen zur Geschichte und Anschauungswelt eines spät-gnostischen Systems* (Studien zur Religionswissenschaft, 3; 1938). A. Pourkier, *L'hérésiologie chez Épiphane de Salamine* (Christianisme Antique, 4 [1992]), pp. 257–89. G. *Salmon in *DCB* 1 (1877), pp. 407–9, s.v.; E. Peterson in *EC* 3 (1949), cols. 929 f., s.v. 'Carpocrate e Carpocraziani'.

Carpzov. A family of German theologians and lawyers. Among those most distinguished in ecclesiastical affairs were:

(1) **Benedikt** (1595–1666), who founded the earliest complete system of Protestant ecclesiastical law, in his *Jurisprudentia ecclesiastica seu consistorialis* (1649).

(2) **Johann Benedikt I** (1607–57), his brother, who first systematized the *Lutheran creeds in his *Isagoge in libros ecclesiarum Lutheranarum symbolicos* (1665).

(3) **Johann Benedikt II** (1639–99) and (4) **Samuel Benedikt** (1647–1707), his sons, who were engaged in the *Pietist controversy, Johann maintaining the traditional position and Samuel supporting the Pietists, until won over by his elder brother.

(5) **Johann Gottlob** (1679–1767), son of (4), who was among the foremost orthodox OT scholars of his day in Germany, and attacked the Pietists, the *Moravians, and the first liberal Biblical critics. (See esp. *Introductio in libros Veteris Testamenti* (1714–21) and *Critica sacra* (1728).)

(6) **Johann Benedikt III** (1720–1803), grandson of (3). A classical scholar and theologian, he attacked the rationalism of W. A. Teller (1734–1804) in his *Liber doctrinalis theologiae purioris* (1768); he was also an authority on the NT and on *patristics.

Carroll, John (1735–1815), Abp. of Baltimore and first bishop of the RC hierarchy in the USA. A native of Upper Marlborough, Maryland, he was educated at *St-Omer in Flanders. He entered the *Jesuit noviciate in 1753, was ordained priest in 1769, and during the next four years taught philosophy and theology at St-Omer and Liège. After the suppression of the Jesuits in 1773 he returned to Maryland in 1774, where he led the life of a missionary, and actively supported the movement for political independence. In 1776 he took part in the embassy of B. Franklin to Canada, and, partly through Franklin's influence, was appointed by the Pope in 1784 Superior of the Missions, a step which made the Church in the USA independent of the *Vicars Apostolic in England. The priests of Maryland having petitioned *Pius VI in 1788 for a bishop for the USA, Carroll was appointed in 1789. In 1790 he was consecrated in the chapel of Lulworth Castle, Dorset, to the see of Baltimore. Here he did a great work in consolidating the RC Church. In 1808 he was made an archbishop, and his enormous diocese was divided into four sees. See also UNITED STATES OF AMERICA, CHRISTIANITY IN.

T. O'B. Hanley, SJ (ed.), *The John Carroll Papers* (3 vols., Notre Dame, Ind., and London [1976]). P. Guilday, *The Life and Times of John Carroll* (New York, 1922), incl. full bibl.; A. M. Melville, *John Carroll of Baltimore* (ibid. [1955]). J. Hennesey, SJ, 'An Eighteenth Century Bishop: John Carroll of Baltimore', *Archivum Historiae Pontificiae*, 16 (1978), pp. 171–204. Polgár, 1 (1990), pp. 462 f. R. J. Purcell in *Dict. Amer. Biog.* 3 (1929), pp. 526–8. A. M. Melville in *NCE* 3 (1967), pp. 151–4, s.v.

Carstares, William (1649–1715), statesman and Scottish *Presbyterian divine. Educated at the universities of Edinburgh (1663–7) and Utrecht (*c.*1669–72), he was probably ordained in the Dutch Reformed Church. While in the Netherlands he was introduced to William of Orange, then seeking British agents. His subsequent activities led to spells of imprisonment in both England and Scotland (1674–9 and 1683–4). In 1684 he was severely tortured and tricked into naming his associates before release and return to the Netherlands. He accompanied William to England in 1688, and conducted the thanksgiving service on the beach at Torbay. He thereafter became the King's principal adviser on Scottish affairs, acquiring a high reputation for wisdom, integrity, and fearlessness. A leading figure in the re-establishment of Presbyterianism in Scotland (1690), he became Principal of the University of Edinburgh in 1703, was four times *Moderator of the General Assembly (1705, 1708, 1711 and 1715), and played an influential part in securing Scottish acceptance of the Act of Union in 1707. Combining loyalty to the old faith with a new tolerance and sense of the possible, his life was a bridge between the *Covenanters of one century and the *Moderates of the next.

J. McCormick (ed.), *State-Papers and Letters addressed to William Carstares* (Edinburgh, 1774), with Life, pp. 3–102. A. I. Dunlop, *William Carstares and the Kirk by Law Established* (Chalmers Lectures, 1964; Edinburgh, 1967). J. B. P. Bulloch in R. S. Wright (ed.), *Fathers of the Kirk* (1960), pp. 94–106. Æ. Mackay in *DNB* 9 (1887), pp. 187–90.

Carta Caritatis. The 'Charter of Love', so called in opposition to the obligatory charters of the *Cluniac Order, was the document outlining the constitution of the *Cistercian Order, and was presented in 1119 to Pope *Callistus II. In its final form, *c.*1155, it is a masterly and novel outline of a religious order of autonomous houses forming a family; it established annual visitation of each house by the abbot of the house which founded it, and an annual General Chapter with legislative and judicial powers. There are also instructions for abbatial elections and the correction of delinquent abbots and monasteries. The Charter, short as it is, has in recent years been subjected to intensive textual criticism, and it has been divided with great probability into a nucleus, the work of *Stephen Harding, and successive additions, but controversy continues.

The official text ed. P. Guignard, *Les Monuments primitifs de la Règle cistercienne* (Dijon, 1878), pp. 76–84; crit. edn. by J. de la C. Bouton, OCR, and J. B. Van Damme, OCR *Les plus anciens Textes de Cîteaux* (Cîteaux—Commentarii Cisterciences, 2; Achel, 1974), pp. 87–106. J.-B. Auberger, OFM, *L'Unanimité cistercienne primitive: Mythe ou réalité?* (Cîteaux: Studia et documenta, 3; ibid., 1986), pp. 21–41. Account of controversy to date in [M.] D. *Knowles, *The Monastic Order in England* (2nd edn., Cambridge, 1963), pp. 752 f. P. Zakar, O. Cist., in *DIP* 2 (1975), cols. 609–13, s.v.

Carter, Thomas Thellusson (1808–1901), second generation *Tractarian divine. Educated at Eton and Christ Church, Oxford, he left Oxford before the *Oxford Movement began; but when, after a succession of parochial appointments, he became Rector of Clewer, near Windsor, in 1844, he had come deeply under Tractarian influence. In 1849 he founded at Clewer a House of Mercy for the rescue of fallen women, and in 1852 a sisterhood, the Community of St John the Baptist (CSJB), to take charge of it. Throughout the rest of his life he continued to take a prominent part in the High Church Movement, esp. through the Confraternity of the Blessed Sacrament, the *English Church Union, and the *Society of the Holy Cross. He was the author of a long series of spiritual and controversial writings, including the widely used *Treasury of Devotion* (1869).

W. H. Hutchings, *Life and Letters of Thomas Thellusson Carter* (1903). A. M. Allchin, *The Silent Rebellion: Anglican Religious Communities, 1845–1900* (1958), pp. 69–84. A. R. Buckland in *DNB, 1901–1911*, I, pp. 319–21, s.v.

Cartesianism. The set of philosophical principles embodied in the teaching of R. *Descartes (1596–1650).

Carthage, Councils of. The early ecclesiastical Councils held at Carthage fall naturally into four groups:

(1) Those under St *Cyprian in 251, 252, 254, 255, and 256. At the earlier of these Councils the chief subject was the reconciliation of those who had lapsed during the *Decian Persecution, at the later ones the dispute with Rome about the re-*baptism of heretics.

(2) Those under Gratus *c*.348 and Genethlius 390. These are the earliest African Councils of which collections of canons survive.

(3) Those under *Aurelius. There is a long series extending from 393 to 424, the most celebrated being that of May 419, when the claims of Rome to exercise jurisdiction over Africa were strongly contested (see APIARIUS). To this Council belongs the extended collection of canons (most of them taken over from earlier Councils) known as the 'Codex Canonum Ecclesiae Africanae'.

(4) Those under Boniface, Bp. of Carthage, in 525 and 534. The canons of only the former of these Councils survive.

The texts will be found in the standard collections of *Hardouin and J. D. *Mansi. For the later Councils, crit. edn. by J. Munier, *Concilia Africae A. 345—A. 525* (CCSL 149; 1974), pp. 2–19, 67–247, and 254–360, and S. Lancel, *Gesta Conlationis Carthaginiensis anno 411* (ibid. 149A; 1974), pp. 1–257; the latter is also ed., with Fr. tr., as *Actes de la Conférence de Carthage en 411* (SC 194, 195, and 224; 1972–5; complementary material in vol. 4, SC 373; 1991). F. *Maassen, *Geschichte der Quellen und der Literatur des canonischen Rechts in Abendlande bis zum Ausgange des Mittelalters*, I (1870), pp. 149–85. F. L. Cross, 'History and Fiction in the African Canons', *JTS* NS 12 (1961), pp. 227–47. J. Gaudemet, *Les Sources du Droit de l'Église en occident du IIᵉ au VIIᵉ siècle* (1985), pp. 79–83 and 104 f.

Carthusian Order. This strictly contemplative order was founded by St *Bruno, in 1084, at the *Grande Chartreuse (whence its name). At first it had no special Rule, though it demanded perfect mortification and renunciation of the world. The monks were vowed to silence and, by Bruno's orders, each lived in his own cell within the monastery, working and devoting several hours daily to mental prayer, and meeting his brethren for the *Office, for the conventual *Mass, and for meals only on feast days. Between 1121 and 1128 *Guigo I, the fifth Prior of the Grande Chartreuse, compiled as their Rule the 'Consuetudines Cartusiae', which in 1133 received the approbation of Innocent II. This with the resolutions made by the

General Chapters since *c*.1140 constituted the 'Antiquae Consuetudines' promulgated by the General Chapter in 1271. Further additions were made a century later (the 'Novae Constitutiones'), in 1509 ('Tertia Compilatio'), and in 1581 ('Nova Collectio Statutorum'). This whole body of material is known as the 'Statuta'. The elaboration of the Carthusian Rule, however, has hardly modified (except in the number of fasts) the austerity and self-denial characteristic of the order from the beginning. The basis of Carthusian custom was and is a combination of *Benedictine monachism and eremitical *asceticism.

The history of the order has been comparatively uneventful, the most notable incident being a division within the order caused by the *Great Schism (1378–1409), which was healed by the resignation of the two *Generals and the election of a third in their place. The order was one of the least affected by the decline of monasticism in the late Middle Ages. During the Reformation a number of English Carthusians were put to death by *Henry VIII, but in Spain, France, and Italy the order was prosperous. The Carthusians suffered badly during the French Revolution, and though much of their property was restored in 1816, the *anticlerical legislation of 1901 once again drove them from the Grande Chartreuse. Most of them found refuge in Spain. In 1940 they returned to the Grande Chartreuse. The headquarters of the English Carthusians is now the Charterhouse at Parkminster, W. Sussex (est. 1883). Their habit is white, with a white leather belt.

The Carthusians have numbered among their members many mystics and devotional writers. The most famous of English Carthusians is St *Hugh, from *c*.1180 the third prior of the first English Charterhouse founded at Witham in Somerset *c*.1178/9, and later Bp. of *Lincoln (1186–1200).

The order also includes a few houses of nuns who live under a similar Rule to the monks. The government of the order rests with the General, who is the Prior of the Grande Chartreuse, elected by the monks of his house, and a General Chapter, consisting of the visitors and priors, which meets every year.

Annales Ordinis Cartusiensis ab anno 1084 ad annum 1429, begun by C. Le Couteulx, Ord. Cart. (1687), ed. and cont. by Carthusians of Montreuil (8 vols., 1887–91). M. Tromby, Ord. Cart., *Storia critico-cronologica diplomatica del patriarca S. Brunone e del suo Ordine Cartusiano* (Naples, 1773–79). L. Vasseur, Ord. Cart., *Ephemerides Ordinis Cartusiensis* (ed. by Carthusians of Montreuil, 4 vols., 1890–92). V. M. Doreau, *Les Éphémérides de l'ordre des Chartreux* (4 vols., Montreuil, 1897–1900). C. Bohič, Ord. Cart., *Chronica Ordinis Carthusiensis, ab anno 1084 ad annum 1510* (4 vols., Parkminster, 1911–54). J. Hogg (ed.), *Analecta Cartusiana* (Salzburg, 1970 ff.). A. *Wilmart, OSB, 'La Chronique des premiers Chartreux', *Revue Mabillon*, 16 (1926), pp. 77–141. [M. Laporte], *Aux Sources de la vie cartusienne* (6 vols., St-Pierre-de-Chartreuse, 1960–67, incl. edn. of 'Consuetudines Cartusiae' in vol. 4). The 'Consuetudines Cartusiae' also ed., with Fr. tr., by Un Chartreux (SC 313; 1984). *Lettres des premiers Chartreux*, ed. by Un Chartreux (ibid. 88 and 274; 1962–80; 2nd edn. of vol. 1, 1988). E. Baumann, *Les Chartreux* ('Les Grands Ordres monastiques', 1928); M. Zadnikar (ed.), *Die Kartäuser: Die Orden der schweigenden Mönche* (Cologne, 1983). Anon., *Maisons de l'ordre des Chartreux: vues et notices* (4 vols., 1913–19). E. M. Thompson, *The Carthusian Order in England* (CHS NS 3, 1930); [M.] D. *Knowles, OSB, *The Monastic Order in England* (1940; 2nd edn., 1963), pp. 375–91. B. Bligny, *L'Église et les ordres religieux dans le* *royaume de Bourgogne aux XIe et XIIe siècles* (1960), pp. 245–318, with bibl., pp. 490 f. J. Dubois, OSB, 'Quelques problèmes de l'histoire de l'Ordre des Chartreux à propos de livres récents', *RHE* 63 (1968), pp. 27–54. Various other essays by id., *Histoire monastique en France au XIIe siècle* (Variorum Reprints, London, 1982), nos. 7–10. A. Gruys, *Cartusiana: Un instrument heuristique* (3 parts, 1976–8). Y. Gourdel, OSB, in *Dict. Sp.* 2 (1953), cols. 705–76, s.v. 'Chartreux'; Un Certosino and J. Dubois, OSB, in *DIP* 2 (1973), cols. 782–821, s.v. 'Certosini'. See also bibl. to BRUNO, ST, and GRANDE CHARTREUSE.

cartouche. A type of mural memorial tablet widely introduced into English churches in the 17th and 18th cents. Usually of marble, it is provided with a surface, made to resemble a somewhat bent piece of paper, for the inscription, and surrounded with ornamentation. It is often surmounted with the coat of arms of the deceased.

K. A. Esdaile, *English Church Monuments, 1510–1840* (1946), plates nos. 25, 28–30.

Cartwright, Thomas (1535–1603), *Puritan divine. Elected in 1550 a scholar of St John's College, Cambridge, which at that date strongly supported Reformation doctrines, he was forced to leave the university on *Mary's accession (1553), and did not return to Cambridge till after her death, when he became successively a Fellow of Trinity, St John's, and then Trinity once more. He took an active part in the theological disputes at the university in the early years of *Elizabeth I's reign and, apparently to escape from them, retired to Ireland from 1565 to 1567. In 1569 he was appointed Lady Margaret Professor at Cambridge, a triumph for his friends, and then began vigorously to criticize the constitution of the C of E. He was deprived of his professorship in 1570 on account of his *Presbyterian views and left Cambridge for the more congenial theological atmosphere of T. *Beza's *Geneva. In April 1572 he returned, but his defence of the *Admonition to the Parliament* involved him in a long controversy which ended with his losing his Trinity Fellowship (summer 1572). He took flight again and did not return till 1585, although from 1583 both the Earl of Leicester and Sir Francis Walsingham were giving him semi-official encouragement to write against the RC Church. On his return he took an active part in furthering Presbyterianism and the Puritan cause. When in 1590 he was arrested and tried in the Courts of *High Commission and Star Chamber, he escaped formal condemnation and was set free in 1592. On *James I's accession (1603), he took part in the Puritan petitioning of the new King, and seems to have been intended as one of the leading Puritan spokesmen at the *Hampton Court Conference, but died before it met. He was among the most gifted, able and learned of the 16th-cent. Puritans.

A. Peel and L. H. Carlson (eds.), *Cartwrightiana* (Elizabethan Nonconformist Texts, 1; 1951). A. F. Scott Pearson, *Thomas Cartwright and Elizabethan Puritanism, 1535–1603* (1925). J. F. H. New, 'The Whitgift–Cartwright Controversy', *Archiv für Reformationsgeschichte*, 59 (1968), pp. 203–11. P. [G.] Lake, *Anglicans and Puritans? Presbyterianism and English Conformist Thought from Whitgift to Hooker* (1988), esp. pp. 13–66. See also works cited under PURITANS.

Casaubon, Isaac (1559–1614), classical scholar. Born and educated at Geneva, he became professor at the uni-

versity there in 1581. In 1586 he married the daughter of the French scholar-printer H. *Stephanus [II]. In 1596 he was appointed to a professorship at Montpellier, but in 1599 he left for Paris, where King *Henry IV gave him a pension and, in 1604, appointed him his sub-librarian. His religious opinions, which were greatly influenced by patristic studies and were opposed both to RCism and extreme *Calvinism, had long been unsettled, and after Henry's death (1610) he decided to leave for England. Appointed to a prebendal stall at *Canterbury and assigned a pension of £300 a year by *James I, he determined to make England his permanent home; but he died a few years later and was buried in Westminster Abbey.

Casaubon's devotion to scholarship, both in classics and theology, was unwearied. His most important classical works were his editions of *Suetonius (which first led J. J. *Scaliger to appreciate his merits), Athenaeus, and Polybius. But if he ranks higher as a classical scholar than as a theologian, he was in fact more interested in theology than in classical literature. He wrote in defence of *Anglicanism, and in 1614 issued a severe criticism of C. *Baronius's annals. He also published (1587) a translation of the NT.

His son, **Méric Casaubon** (1599–1671), also an eminent scholar, was the editor of *Marcus Aurelius and other classical authors.

Ephemerides (Casaubon's diary, ed. J. Russell, 2 vols., 1850); M. *Pattison, *Isaac Casaubon* (1875; 2nd edn., ed. H. Nettleship, 1892). J. H. Overton in *DNB* 9 (1887), pp. 257–61.

Casel, Odo (1886–1948), liturgist. He entered the Benedictine monastery of *Maria Laach in 1905 and from 1922 until his sudden death he was spiritual director of the nuns at Herstelle. He was esp. concerned to expound the theological aspects of liturgy and saw in the Eucharist a re-enactment of the mysteries of Christ by his Church (*Mysterienlehre*). In this way he anticipated the paschal understanding of the Eucharist which was stressed a generation later during the Second *Vatican Council. He elaborated his teaching in a large number of papers, esp. in the *Jahrbuch für Liturgiewissenschaft*. His teaching is summarized in English in *The Mystery of Christian Worship* (Eng. adaptation, 1962).

A. Mayer, J. Quasten, and B. Neunheuser, OSB (eds.), *Vom Christlichen Mysterium: Gesammelte Arbeiten zum Gedächtnis von Odo Casel OSB* (Düsseldorf, 1951), with list of his works, pp. 363–75. A. Gozier, OSB, *Dom Casel* (Paris [1968]). J. Plooij, *De Mysterie-Leer van Odo Casel* (Zwolle, 1964; Ger. tr., 1965); A. Schilson, *Theologie als Sakramententheologie: Die Mysterientheologie Odo Casels* (Tübinger theologische Studien, 18; 1982). B. Neunheuser, OSB, in *NCE* 2 (1967), pp. 176 f.; id. in *TRE* 7 (1981), pp. 643–7, both s.v.

Cashel, Council of (1172). A council called by Henry II after his invasion of *Ireland and attended by Bp. Christian of Lismore as Papal legate, all the Irish hierarchy except the aged Abp. of *Armagh, and the great majority of leading churchmen, together with English clergy nominated by the King. The Irish Church was thus seen to recognize Henry II's authority. The constitutions passed by the council and intended to introduce 12th-cent. discipline to the still very irregular Irish Church have been preserved by *Giraldus Cambrensis. He also mentions a document sealed by the legate in which were set out the shortcomings of the Irish clergy and which appears to have been used by Henry II in securing letters from Pope *Alexander III confirming the subjugation of Ireland to the English Crown.

Giraldus Cambrensis, *Expugnatio Hibernica*, 1. 34 f., ed., with Eng. tr., by A. B. Scott and F. X. Martin (A New History of Ireland, Ancillary Publications, 3; Dublin, 1978), pp. 96–101, with notes, pp. 314 f.; also pr. in Giraldus' Works, 5, ed. J. F. Dimock (RS 21 E; 1867), pp. 280–3. J. A. Watt, *The Church and the Two Nations in Medieval Ireland* (Cambridge, 1970), pp. 38–41; F. X. Martin in A. Cosgrove (ed.), *A New History of Ireland*, 2 (Oxford, 1987), pp. 91–3.

Caspari, Carl Paul (1814–92), German-Norwegian theologian. Of Jewish descent, he was converted to Christianity in 1838. In 1847 he was appointed lector, and in 1857 professor, at the University of Christiania (Oslo). Here he made some important researches into the history of the early Church, esp. the development of the Baptismal *Creeds, which he published as *Quellen zur Geschichte des Taufsymbols und der Glaubensregel* (vols. 1–3, 1866–75; additional vol., 1879).

J. Belsheim in *PRE* 3 (3rd edn., 1897), pp. 737–42, s.v.

Cassander, Georg (1513–66), eirenic Catholic theologian. He was born at Pitthem, nr. Bruges, studied at Louvain, taught at Bruges c.1541 and then at Ghent, and from c.1549 lived at *Cologne. In his numerous writings he sought to mediate between the Catholics and the Protestants, advocating, for example, concessions by Catholics on giving Communion in both kinds and on clerical *celibacy. His chief work, *De Officio Pii ac Publicae Tranquillitatis vere amantis Viri in hoc Religionis Dissidio* (pub. anonymously, Basle, 1561), which took as its basis the Scriptures and the Fathers of the first six centuries, was esp. concerned to show that abuses were no sufficient reason for leaving the Catholic Church, though Cassander did not conceal his dislike of certain exaggerated Papal claims. When submitted to the Colloquy of *Poissy (1561), it gave offence to both sides. In 1564 the Emp. Ferdinand I invoked Cassander's aid in the official attempt at reunion, and to this end Cassander wrote his *Consultatio de Articulis Religionis inter Catholicos et Protestantes Controversis* (posthumously pub. in 1577), seeking to put a Catholic interpretation on the official Protestant formularies. The work met with strong disapproval from both sides. His other writings include *Hymni Ecclesiastici* (1556), *De Baptismo Infantium* (1563; against the *Anabaptists), and *De Sacra Communione Christiani Populi in utraque Panis et Vini Specie* (1564). A collected edition of his works (incomplete) was issued at Paris in 1616 and put on the *Index in the next year.

M. E. Nolte, *Georgius Cassander en zijn oecumenisch Streven* (1951), with Eng. summary. J. P. Dolan, CSC, *The Influence of Erasmus, Witzel and Cassander in the Church Ordinances and Reform Proposals of the United Duchees* [sic] *of Cleve during the Middle Decades of the 16th Century* (Reformationsgeschichtliche Studien und Texte, 83; 1957), pp. 87–111; M. Erbe, 'François Bauduin und Georg Cassander. Dokumente einer Humanistenfreundschaft', *Bibliothèque d'Humanisme et Renaissance*, 40 (1978), pp. 537–60. J. Baudot in *DACL* 2 (pt. 2; 1910), cols. 2334–40, s.v. 'Cassandre'.

Cassian, John (c.360–after 430), monk. Acc. to *Gennadius, Cassian was 'natione Scytha', i.e. born in the Roman province of Scythia Minor (modern Dobrudja); this statement is prob. correct, despite the doubts of some scholars. As a young man he joined a monastery at *Bethlehem, but left soon after (c.385) to study monasticism in Egypt, where he was much influenced by *Evagrius Ponticus. We next hear of him (c.404) as a deacon of the Church of *Constantinople, whence he was sent by St *Chrysostom on an embassy to Pope *Innocent I. After this he seems to have established himself permanently in the W. About 415 he founded two monasteries near Marseilles; and there he wrote his two books, the 'Institutes' and the 'Conferences', out of the material collected during his years in the E. The 'Institutes', which sets out the ordinary rules for the monastic life and discusses the eight chief hindrances to a monk's perfection, was taken as the basis of many W. Rules, being drawn on, e.g., by St *Benedict. The 'Conferences' take the form of conversations with the great leaders of E. monasticism. Cassian shared the unease of many of the monks of Gaul with the extremes of St *Augustine's doctrine of *grace and attacked that doctrine in *Conf.* 13; his position was later called *Semipelagianism (q.v.). He also wrote c.430 a work in seven books 'De Incarnatione Domini' at the instance of St *Leo to acquaint the W. with the teachings of *Nestorius. The E. Church treats him as a saint, but in the W. he has never been officially canonized, Marseilles only keeping his feast on 23 July. Feast day in E., 29 Feb. (when this occurs).

Cassian's 'Conferences' pr. in 1476–8 at Brussels by the *Brethren of the Common Life; other early edns., with the 'Institutes', at Basle, 1485, Venice, 1491, and Basle, 1497. Edn. of his Works by A. Gazaeus (Gazet), 2 vols. in 3, Douai, 1616, repr. J. P. Migne, *PL* 49 and 50. Crit. edn. by M. Petschenig in *CSEL* 13 ('Collations', 1886) and 17 ('Institutes' and 'De Incarnatione Domini', 1888). Petschenig's text of the 'Conferences' repr. with slight modifications, full introd. and Fr. tr. by E. Pichery, OSB (SC 42, 54, 64; 1955–9); 'Institutes' ed., with Fr. tr. by J. C. Guy, SJ (SC 109; 1965). Eng. tr. (except *Inst.* 6 and *Coll.* 12 and 22) with good prolegomena and notes by E. C. S. Gibson in NPNCF, 2nd ser. 11 (1894), pp. 161–641. [W.] O. Chadwick, *John Cassian: A Study in Primitive Monasticism* (1950; 2nd edn., much rev., 1968). A. Hoch, *Lehre des Johannes Cassianus von Natur und Gnade* (Diss., Freiburg i.B., 1895). S. Marsili, OSB, *Giovanni Cassiano ed Evagrio Pontico: Dottrina sulla carità e contemplazione* (Studia Anselmiana, 5; 1936). L. Cristiani, *Jean Cassien, ou la spiritualité du désert* (2 vols., 1946). H.-O. Weber, *Die Stellung des Johannes Cassianus zur ausserpachomianischen Mönchstradition: Eine Quellenuntersuchung* (Beiträge zur Geschichte des alten Mönchtums und des Benediktinerordens, 24; 1961); J. C. Guy, SJ, *Jean Cassien: Vie et doctrine spirituelle* (1961). V. Codina, SJ, *El aspecto cristológico en la espiritualidad de Juan Casiano* (Orientalia Christiana Analecta, 175; 1966). A. Hamman, OFM, in Quasten (cont.), *Patrology*, 4 (1986), pp. 512–23. M. Cappuyns, OSB, in *DHGE* 11 (1949), cols. 1319–48, s.v. 'Cassien, 15 (Jean)'; M. Olphe-Galliard in *Dict. Sp.* 1 (1953), cols. 214–76; [W.] O. Chadwick in *TRE* 7 (1981), pp. 650–7, s.v.

Cassinese Congregation. A monastic *Congregation of *Benedictine monks which owes its origin to a reform initiated by Ludovico Barbo at Padua in 1409. The aim of the reformers was to overcome the evil of appointing abbots *in commendam*, and the congregation was characterized until the 20th cent. by the overall authority of the General

Chapter and the centralized system of appointing abbots on a temporary basis. It spread throughout Italy and was at first called the 'Congregation of Santa Giustina' or 'of Unity' (1419). After the accession of *Monte Cassino in 1504 it became known as the Cassinese Congregation. Its system had a deep effect on the reforms initiated at this period in other countries, notably those of France, Spain, and England. At its height it had 70 houses. A decline set in during the 18th cent. At the time of the French Revolution the monks were driven out and their properties taken over by the government, but a partial restoration took place after 1815. Further confiscations of property took place in the mid-19th cent. after the unification of Italy. The Cassinese Congregation today includes a number of famous monasteries, notably Monte Cassino, Cava, *St Paul's outside the Walls. In the 19th cent. a number of monasteries separated to form the Cassinese Congregation of the Primitive Observance, now called the *Subiaco Congregation.

T. Leccisoti, OSB (ed.), *Congregationis S. Justinae de Padua O.S.B. Ordinationes Capitulorum Generalium*, pt. 1: 1424–1474 (Miscellanea Cassinese, 16–17; 1939); pt. 2: 1475–1504 (ibid. 35; 1970). P. Schmitz, OSB, *Histoire de l'Ordre de Saint-Benoît*, 3 (Maredsous, 1948), pp. 157–74; 4 (1948), pp. 148–53. A. Pantoni, OSB, in *DIP* 2 (1975), cols. 1477–85, s.v. 'Congregazione Benedettina Cassinese', with extensive bibl.

Cassiodorus, Flavius Magnus Aurelius Cassiodorus Senator (485/90–c.580), Roman statesman, author, and monastic founder. Cassiodorus belonged to a minor senatorial family, that was allied to the Aurelii and the Anicii and thus to *Boethius. He made his public career as the trusted servant and spokesman of the Ostrogothic rulers at *Ravenna, for whom he wrote the official correspondence preserved in the *Variae* and a national history, the *Historia Gothorum* (now lost). He was *quaestor* in 507, *patricius*, consul (514), *magister officiorum* (523), and praetorian prefect (533). In 537, when Ostrogothic rule had collapsed and *Justinian's armies were invading Italy, Cassiodorus withdrew from public life. He edited his *Variae*, adding as the 'thirteenth book' the philosophical *De Anima*; and he embarked on the *Expositio Psalmorum*, which may have occupied him until 548. At an undetermined date (perhaps as early as 540) he joined the Italian senatorial exiles in *Constantinople, where in 551 the *Historia Gothorum* was epitomized by Jordanes as the *Getica*. In 554 Cassiodorus returned to a pacified Italy and established the monastic community of Vivarium on his estate of Squillace near Naples. There he built up an important library, incl. much biblical commentary. He arranged for the extensive copying of manuscripts and he had Greek texts translated, including the histories of *Socrates, *Sozomen, and *Theodoret, which served as the basis of his own *Historia Ecclesiastica Tripartita*; he explained the *raison d'être* of his library—and by implication of the community which created it—in his *Institutiones Divinarum et Saecularium Litterarum*. Although Vivarium did not survive as a community beyond the 7th cent., the books written there were preserved and copied in other libraries: both *Bede's text of the Bible and the *Codex Amiatinus appear to be related to Cassiodorus' Bible (in 9 vols.) at Vivarium.

Opera Omnia ed. J. Garet (2 vols. bound in 1, Rouen, 1679), repr. in J. P. Migne, *PL* 69. 421–1334, and 70. *Variae* ed. T. *Mommsen (*MGH*, Auctores Antiquissimi, 12; 1894), and, with the *Ordo generis Cassiodororum* (the source for his relationship with Symmachus (Aurelii) and Boethius) ed. Å. J. Fridh, and *De Anima* ed. J. W. Halporn (CCSL 96; 1973); Eng. tr. of *Variae* and *Ordo generis Cassiodororum* by S. J. B. Barnish (Translated Texts for Historians, 12; Liverpool, 1992); *Expositio Psalmorum* ed., after Maurist text, by M. Adriaen (CCSL, 97–8; 1958); Eng. tr. by P. G. Walsh (ACW 51–3 [1990–1]). *Historia Ecclesiastica Tripartita* ed. W. Jacob and R. Hanslik (CSEL 71; 1952); *Institutiones*, ed. R. A. B. Mynors (Oxford, 1937); Eng. tr. by L. W. Jones (Records of Civilization, no. 40; New York, 1946). Selection of his letters ed. with introd. by T. Hodgkin (London, 1886). Monographs by G. Minasi (Naples, 1895), A. Van de Vyver in *Speculum*, 6 (1931), pp. 244–92, G. Ludwig (Frankfurt, 1967), and J. J. O'Donnell (Berkeley, Calif., and London, 1979; cf. A. Cameron in *JRS* 71 (1981), pp. 183–6). E. *Schwartz, *Zu Cassiodor und Prokop* (*Sb.* (Bayr.) 1939, Heft 2; 1939). G. Bardy, 'Cassiodore et la fin du monde ancien', *L'Année Théologique*, 6 (1945), pp. 383–425; A. Momigliano, 'Cassiodorus and Italian Culture of his Time', *Proceedings of the British Academy*, 41 (1955), pp. 207–45. J. R. Martindale, *The Prosopography of the Later Roman Empire*, 2 (1980), pp. 265–9. *CPL* (3rd edn., 1995), pp. 294–9 (nos. 896–911). M. Cappuyns, OSB, in *DHGE* 11 (1949), cols. 1349–408, s.v. 'Cassiodore'; R. Helm in *RAC* 2 (1954), cols. 915–26, s.v.; A. Momigliano in *Dizionario Biografico degli Italiani*, 21 (1978), pp. 494–504, s.v., with extensive bibl.

cassock. The long garment, now usually black (formerly of various colours), worn by the clergy. It originated in *vestis talaris* or ankle-length dress, which was retained by the clergy when, under barbarian influence in the 6th cent., shorter garments became usual for secular use. Its use was already ordered by the Council of Braga (572) and subsequent legislation has continued this tradition. The RC Church long insisted upon its use by clerics both out of church and inside, but in many countries coats of varying length have for some time been allowed for outdoor wear and now an alb may be worn in church instead of a cassock. In the C of E a cassock is still required for Morning and Evening Prayer and the Occasional Offices; either a cassock or an alb may be used for the Holy Communion. The cassocks of bishops in the W. are purple in colour, those of cardinals red, that of the Pope white, and, in England, those of royal chaplains red.

Castel Gandolfo. A small town in the Alban Hills, some 18 miles SE of Rome, not far from the Via Appia Nuova. Since the 17th cent. it has been the site of the Pope's summer residence. Under the *Lateran Treaty of 1929, the Papal palace and gardens were assigned to the extraterritorial (i.e. non-Italian) domains of the Holy See.

E. Bonomelli in *EC* 3 (1949), cols. 1014–17, s.v.

Castellio, Sebastian (1515–63), classical scholar and Protestant theologian. A native of Savoy, he was educated in Lyons. In 1540, after adopting Protestantism, he moved to Strasbourg to study under J. *Calvin. When Calvin returned to *Geneva in 1541, he procured for Castellio a post as rector of the Collège de Genève. There Castellio published the *Dialogi Sacri* (dated 1543, but issued in 1542), a school manual of Bible stories in dialogue form which remained popular until the 18th cent. In 1544 he resigned his rectorship on grounds of ill-health. His refusal to accept the canonicity of the Song of *Solomon and his unorthodox view of the descent of Christ into Hell caused a breach between him and Calvin, and he left Geneva in 1545. He worked in Basle as a proof-reader until c.1553, when he became professor of Greek in the university. In 1551 he published a controversial translation of the Bible into classical Latin, which he dedicated to *Edward VI. As well as defending the doctrine of free will in an excursus on Rom. 9: 13, the Bible contained a plea for freedom of worship which was unique among the theologians of the 16th cent. These ideas brought him into conflict with the Genevan Church, esp. with T. *Beza. He was the instigator and one of the authors (or perhaps the sole author) of the compilation *De Haereticis an sint persequendi* published in Latin and French in 1554 under the pseudonym 'Martinus Bellius'. The work, which condemned the burning of M. *Servetus, aroused a storm of opposition. In 1555 Castellio brought out a French version of his Latin Bible. As well as writing theological treatises, some of which were published only posthumously, he produced Latin translations of Xenophon, Homer, and other Greek authors. His doctrine of religious *toleration received its fullest expression in the *Conseil à la France désolée* (1562).

The 1554 Lat. edn. of *De Haereticis* was photograpically repr., with introd. by S. van der Woude (Geneva, 1954); modernized edn. of the Fr. text by A. Olivet (ibid., 1913); new Lat. and Fr. texts ed. B. Becker and M. [F.] Valkoff respectively (Travaux d'Humanisme et Renaissance, 118; 1971). Modern edns. of *Conseil à la France désolée* by M. F. Valkoff (Geneva, 1967), and of *De arte dubitandi et confidendi, ignorandi et sciendi* by E. F. Hirsch (Studies in Medieval and Reformation Thought, 29; 1981). Eng. tr. of *De Haereticis* (with excerpts from other works of Castellio and David Joris on Religious Liberty) by R. H. Bainton (Records of Civilization, 22; New York, 1935). F. Buisson, *Sébastien Castellion, sa vie et son œuvre (1515–1563)* (2 vols., 1892), with details of edns. of his works, 2, pp. 341–80. Other monographs by E. Giran (Haarlem, 1914), P. Hemmi (in Eng.) (Zurich [1937]), and C. É. Delormeau (Neuchâtel [1964]). S. Zweig, *Castellio gegen Calvin* (1936; Eng. tr., 1936); R. H. Bainton and others, *Castellioniana: Quatre études sur Sébastien Castellion et l'idée de la tolérance* (1951); B. Becker (ed.), *Autour de Michel Servet et de Sébastien Castellion* (Haarlem, 1953), pp. 142–302; H. R. Guggisberg, *Sebastian Castellio im Urteil seiner Nachwelt vom Späthumanismus bis zur Aufklärung* (Basler Beiträge zur Geschichtswissenschaft, 57; 1956). E. Droz, *Chemins de l'Hérésie: Textes et Documents*, 2 (Geneva, 1971), pp. 325–432. H. R. Guggisberg in *TRE* 7 (1981), pp. 663–5, s.v.

casuistry. The art or science of bringing general moral principles to bear upon particular cases. Its exercise is always called for in moral issues, whether the particular decision is made by individual judgement or in accordance with an established code, though the word 'casuistry' is generally restricted to the latter. The introduction of universal private *Penance was the natural cause of the rise of formal casuistry in the Church, and by the 7th cent. 'Libri Poenitentiales' were common. Later these were replaced by various 'Summae de Poenitentia' which formed complete legal digests. From the 16th cent. onwards various systems of casuistry, such as *Probabilism, *Probabiliorism, and *Equiprobabilism, developed in the RC Church in competition with each other; the first of these systems, in modified form, eventually won most popularity, largely through the advocacy of

St *Alphonsus Liguori in the 18th cent. Among *Puritan writers, W. *Perkins and W. *Ames were notable casuists, and in the Anglican tradition of the 17th cent., Jeremy *Taylor and R. *Sanderson (qq.v).

For bibl. see under MORAL THEOLOGY.

Caswall, Edward (1814–78), hymn-writer. Educated at Brasenose College, Oxford, he was Perpetual Curate of Stratford-sub-Castle, Wilts, from 1840 to 1847. In 1847 he was received into the RC Church, and in 1850 (after the death of his wife) became a member of the *Oratory at Edgbaston under J. H. *Newman. Among his many successful and popular translations of Latin hymns were 'Hark! a thrilling voice is sounding' (*AM* 47, *EH* 5), 'Bethlehem, of noblest cities' (*EH* 40), and 'Jesu, the very thought of thee' (*AM* 178, *EH* 419). He published *Lyra Catholica* (1849), besides devotional writings and other collections of poems.

T. Cooper in *DNB* 9 (1887), pp. 276 f., s.v.

catacombs. This term for subterranean burial-places is prob. derived from the Gk. κατὰ κύμβας ('at the hollows'). Applied to the Christian cemetery of St *Sebastian by the *Chronographer of 354, it was being used of similar communal burial-places c.800.

Subterranean burial was common in the ancient world, and catacombs, with their long ramifying passages, or closely related structures, can be found near *Rome and in other Italian localities, on Sicily, Malta, and Milos, in Syria, in the region of *Jerusalem, in NW Africa, and at *Alexandria. They were used by Jews, pagans, and Christians. The most famous and extensive are near Rome. Like all Roman tombs, they enjoyed legal protection, and had to be dug outside the walls. Forty-one Christian catacombs survive there; they are of great interest for the social and religious history of the early Church. Among the most important are those named after Sts *Callistus (with Papal crypt of c.230), Praetextatus, and *Sebastian, all on the Via Appia; St Domitilla Aurelia Vetus; St Commodilla on the Via Ostiensis; and Sts Marcellinus and Peter on the Via Labicana. Excavation prob. began c.150–200. Some of the earliest catacombs seem to have been dug on private ground initially, but their ownership and management soon passed to the Church; individual tombs prob. served as the nuclei for catacombs, or parts of them. It is unlikely that Christians used them for refuge, or, at first, for worship on any scale. Inhumations needed much space, and decent burial was a charitable duty. Also, while their catacombs may sometimes have included pagan mausolea, Christians needed separate cemeteries as a means of self-distinction. The proximity of *martyrs' relics was an attraction which proved a strong motive for expansion, esp. in the 4th cent.

Christian catacombs, dug by skilful and organized *fossors, consist of labyrinths of galleries, often in two to five stories with connecting stairs. Old quarries (*arenaria*) and other excavations might be exploited. Shafts (*luminaria*) admitted light and air, and let out spoil. Bodies were placed in floor-graves (*formae*) or in wall-niches (*loculi*), often holding more than one, and closed by stone slabs or tiles. These were cut in passages or in family tomb-chambers (*cubicula*), which became popular from c.300. For the more important, a large niche with a curved arch (*arcosolium), and perhaps a *sarcophagus, might be used. The numerous wall-paintings provide early examples of Christian *iconography. Highly allusive and symbolic, they owe much to Jewish and pagan motifs. Many sarcophagi and other objects of art have also been found.

Families prob. held commemorative meals at the catacombs, above or below ground, and by the 4th cent. the Eucharist was often celebrated at the grave of a martyr on the supposed anniversary of his death. The areas surrounding the graves of martyrs were enlarged and embellished; in this work Pope *Damasus (366–84) was esp. active. To accommodate the number of pilgrims attracted by the martyrs, basilicas were also built above ground in the 4th to 7th cents.; relics were sometimes moved up from the catacombs; and ground-level cemeteries developed; their effect on the religious geography of Rome was lasting. The catacombs thus expanded little after the 4th cent., but fell slowly into disuse, aided by the disturbed conditions and a declining population. In the 8th–9th cents. many of their relics were transferred to the churches of Rome, and the catacombs were largely forgotten until the 16th cent. Their investigation is still incomplete.

The fundamental works on the catacombs are those of A. *Bosio, Roma sotterranea (1632), and G. B. *de Rossi, La Roma sotterranea cristiana (3 vols., 1864–77); and on the art, J. Wilpert, Die Malereien der Katakomben Roms (2 vols., 1903). Modern works incl.: J. P. Kirsch, Le Catacombe Romane (1933; Eng. tr., Rome, 1946); P. Styger, Die römische Katakomben (1933); id., Römische Märtyrergrüfte (2 vols., 1935); P. Testini, Le Catacombe e gli Antichi Cimeteri Cristiani in Roma [Bologna, 1966]; J. Stevenson, The Catacombs (1978); H. Brandenburg, 'Überlegungen zu Ursprung und Entstehung der Katakomben Roms', in Vivarium: Festschrift Theodor Klauser zum 90. Geburtstag (Jahrbuch für Antike und Christentum, Ergänzungsband, 11; 1984), pp. 11–49. J. G. Deckers and others, Die Katakombe 'Santi Marcellino e Pietro': Repertorium der Malereien (Roma Sotterranea Cristiana, 6; 2 vols., Rome and Münster, 1987). E. R. Goodenough, 'Catacomb Art', Journal of Biblical Literature, 81 (1962), pp. 113–42; J. M. C. Toynbee, Death and Burial in the Roman World [1971], pp. 199–244; C. Pietri, Roma Christiana: Recherches sur l'Église de Rome . . . (311–440) (Bibliothèque des Écoles françaises d'Athènes et de Rome, 224; 2 vols., 1976), pp. 37–51, 69–77, 121–34, 522–57, 595–624, 659–67, and 722 f.; R. Krautheimer, Rome: Profile of a City, 312–1308 (Princeton, NJ, 1980), pp. 18 f., 24–26, and 82–6. J. Guyon, 'Dal Praedium imperiale al santuario dei martiri. Il territorio "ad duas lauros" ', in A. Giardina (ed.), Roma: Politica, Economia, Paesaggio Urbano (Società Romana e Impero Tardoantico, 2; 1986), pp. 299–332; P. Pergola, 'Le catacombe romane: mite e realtà (a proposito del cimitero di Domitilla)', ibid., pp. 333–50; C. Vismara, 'Il Cimiteri ebraici di Roma', ibid., pp. 351–92. H. *Leclercq, OSB, in DACL 2 (pt. 2; 1910), cols. 2376–486, s.v., with bibl. cols. 2447–50.

catafalque. An erection, resembling a bier and covered with a *pall, formerly used at *Requiem Masses to represent the corpse in its absence. The derivation of the word is quite uncertain, but its first syllables prob. came from the Gk. κατά, 'alongside'. The term is now also used in a more general sense of the coffin and all its appurtenances.

Cataphrygians (Gk. Καταφρυγιασταί, Καταφρύγας). An alternative title found in a few early Christian writers, e.g.

St *Epiphanius, for the *Montanists in reference to their Phrygian origin.

Epiphanius, Haer. 98. 1. 3 (PG 41. 856 B); cf. *Jerome, Comm. in Gal. 3 (PL 26. 356 C).

catechesis. Instruction given to Christian *catechumens preparing for *Baptism, esp. in the primitive Church. The word was also used of the books containing such instruction, of which the most celebrated is that of St *Cyril of Jerusalem. In the RC Church the word is now used for education in faith throughout life.

Catechetical School of Alexandria. The notion of a Christian school in *Alexandria, concerned with advanced teaching in theology and with a succession of teachers in charge of it, is found most clearly in the work of *Philip Sidetes (early 5th cent.); he speaks of such a school existing from the early 2nd cent. to the late 4th cent., giving as its first head *Athenagoras (whom he dates in the first half of the 2nd cent.). A somewhat similar conception is found in the Historia Ecclesiastica of *Eusebius; he begins rather later, with *Pantaenus (d. c.190), followed by *Clement (c.190–c.202), *Origen (c.202–31), Heraclas (231–c.233), and St *Dionysius (from c.233). After that only Achillas (who succeeded *Peter as Bp. of Alexandria, c.311) is mentioned by Eusebius as head of the school (Achillas is not mentioned by Philip). The idea of a school with a succession of teachers seems to be inspired by pagan models (e.g. the Platonic Academy in *Athens or the Museum in Alexandria), and it is difficult to be sure what historical basis it ever had. It is more probable that Pantaenus and Clement were individual teachers like St *Justin at Rome. Acc. to Eusebius, Origen was appointed by *Demetrius, Bp. of Alexandria, to give elementary ('catechetical') teaching in the Christian faith, and later (c.215) he consigned this role to Heraclas and devoted himself to more advanced teaching. Whether such an advanced school survived Origen's conflict with Demetrius and his permanent retirement to *Caesarea in 231 is uncertain. Acc. to *Rufinus, *Didymus the Blind was appointed by St *Athanasius as 'teacher of the ecclesiastical school', but the meaning of this statement is disputed. None of the other 'heads' mentioned by Philip (e.g. *Theognostus, Pierius, Peter) is designated such by anyone else in antiquity.

Primary sources: fragment of Philip Sidetes pub. by H. *Dodwell in his Dissertationes in Irenaeum (Oxford, 1689), p. 488; Eusebius, HE 5. 10, 6. 3. 3, 6. 6, 6. 15, 6. 26, 6. 29. 4, and 7. 32. 30; Rufinus, HE 2. 7. W. *Bousset, Jüdisch-christlicher Schulbetrieb in Alexandria und Rom (1915). G. Bardy, 'Aux origines de l'école d'Alexandrie', Rech. S.R., 27 (1937), pp. 65–90; id., 'Pour l'histoire de l'école d'Alexandrie' in Vivre et Penser [war-time title of R. Bibl.], 2 (1942), pp. 80–109. A. Le Boulluec, 'L'École d'Alexandrie. De quelques aventures d'un concept historiographique', in Ἀλεξανδρίνα. . . . Mélanges offerts au P. Claude Mondésert (1987), pp. 403–17. A. de La Barre in DTC 1 (1903), cols. 805–24, s.v. 'Alexandrie, IV (École chrétienne d')'; M. Simonetti in DPAC 1 (1983), cols. 117–21, s.v. 'Alessandria, II. Scuola'; Eng. tr. in Encyclopedia of the Early Church, 1 (1992), pp. 22 f.

catechism (from Gk. κατηχέω, 'to make hear', hence 'to instruct'). A popular manual of Christian doctrine. Originally the term was applied to the oral instruction on the principal Christian truths given to children and adults before Baptism. From this usage the name passed to the book containing such instructions. The term seems first to have been used in the early 16th cent., but the idea is much older. In the Middle Ages prescriptions for catechizing the faithful were frequently issued, e.g. at the Council of *Lambeth (1281), and books were produced containing explanations of the Pater Noster and the Creed, lists of mortal sins, etc., arranged preferably in groups of seven. Thus the seven petitions of the Pater Noster were connected with the seven *Beatitudes and the *seven gifts of the Holy Spirit, and the *seven deadly sins were opposed to the seven principal virtues and the seven works of mercy. One of the most active propagators of catechisms before the Reformation was J. *Gerson, whose 'ABC des simples gens' became very popular at the end of the 15th cent. Other widely used works of the type were the catechism of J. *Colet in England and the 'Christenspiegel' in Germany.

The *Reformation, with its insistence on religious instruction, brought a flood of new catechisms. The most famous is M. *Luther's Kleiner Katechismus (1529), which is still the standard book of the *Lutheran Church not only in Germany but also in other Protestant countries. The *Heidelberger Katechismus (1563) occupies a similar position in the *Calvinist communions. The short catechism of the C of E (see following entry) is printed in the BCP as a preparation for *Confirmation, and the *Presbyterian Churches generally follow the 'Humble Advice' of the *Westminster Assembly of 1647. In competition with the Protestants the RC Church, too, produced a number of new catechisms. Apart from the so-called '*Roman Catechism' (q.v.), the most famous of these is St Peter *Canisius' Summa Doctrinae Christianae (1554). During the following centuries a flood of RC catechisms appeared; in many countries, e.g. in France, there was a different one approved for each diocese; in England one superseded all others: A Catechism of Christian Doctrine, first issued in 1898, popularly called the 'Penny Catechism'. This was based on R. *Challoner's Abridgement of Christian Doctrine, first published in 1759. The desire for a modern manual of doctrine in the RC Church led to the publication in 1992 of the '*Catechism of the Catholic Church' (q.v.). Catechisms, whether Catholic or Protestant, normally contain the Creed, the *Lord's Prayer, and the Ten Commandments with explanations; RC ones also add instructions on the *Hail Mary, the three theological virtues, the *Commandments of the Church, the Sacraments, and the Virtues and Vices.

See also GENEVAN CATECHISM, HEIDELBERG CATECHISM, WESTMINSTER CATECHISMS.

T. F. Torrance, The School of Faith: The Catechisms of the Reformed Church, tr. and ed. with introd. (1959). For early Protestant Catechisms see also F. Cohrs, Die evangelischen Katechismusversuche vor Luthers Enchiridion in Monumenta Germaniae Paedagogica, ed. C. Kehrbach, vols. 20–3 and 39 (1900–7). G. Adler and G. Vogeleisen, Un Siècle de Catéchèse en France 1893–1980: Histoire—Déplacements—Enjeux (Théologie Historique, 60 [1981]). P. Tudor, 'Religious Instruction for Children and Adolescents in the Early English Reformation', JEH 35 (1984), pp. 391–413. I. Green, The Christian's ABC: Catechisms and Catechizing in England c.1530–1740 (Oxford, 1996). H.-J. Fraas and others in TRE 17 (1988), pp. 710–44, s.v. 'Katechismus', with bibl.

Catechism, Prayer Book, the 'Instruction' in the BCP in the form of a series of questions and answers 'to be learned of every person before he be brought to be confirmed by the Bishop'. The inclusion of such a body of teaching in an authorized service book was an innovation in 1549. It consisted of an explanation of the nature of *Baptism akin to that found in the service itself, the *Apostles' Creed followed by a brief explanation of the doctrine of the *Trinity, the Ten *Commandments (in abridged form in 1549, but since 1552 in full and with a prefatory introduction) followed by an explanation of man's duty to God and his neighbour, and the *Lord's Prayer with an explanation of its meaning. In 1604, in response to the Puritans' request at *Hampton Court for a clearer statement of doctrine, a section was added on the Sacraments of Baptism and Holy Communion. In 1689 it was proposed to add two further questions on the Creed and the Church, and in 1887 the Lower House of the *Convocation of Canterbury approved a considerable series of additions on the nature of the Church and Ministry, but neither of these amendments was authorized. From 1549 to 1661 the Catechism was printed at the beginning of the *Confirmation service, presumably with the intention that the bishop should ask these questions before confirming the candidates; it has since been printed as a separate item before the Confirmation service. Since 1661 the rubric has directed that instruction in the Catechism should be given after the second lesson at Evensong, but in modern times it seldom, if ever, takes place during the service. The authorship of the Catechism is a matter of dispute. The similarity it bears to the 'Small Catechism' (pub. 1573) by A. *Nowell suggests that the earlier part is his work; the 1604 addition is commonly attributed to J. *Overall, but it prob. incorporates much of Nowell's work.

The revision of the Catechism, left untouched by the proposed Prayer Book of 1928, was entrusted to a Commission of the Abps. of *Canterbury and *York in 1958. The Revised Catechism, published in 1961, was in 1962 commended by the Convocations for use during a period of seven years, which has been repeatedly extended. It widened the scope of the Prayer Book Catechism by adding material on the Church and Ministry, the Holy Spirit, the Bible, the lesser Sacraments, and *Eschatology. While the catechetical form was retained, the language was extensively modernized.

G. *Burnet, An Exposition of the Church Catechism for the Use of the Diocese of Sarum (1710). W. C. E. Newbolt, The Church Catechism (1903).

Catechism of the Catholic Church (1992). A comprehensive account of RC teaching in four sections, dealing with (1) the faith, including an exposition of the *Apostles' Creed; (2) the Sacraments; (3) life in Christ, with an exposition of the Ten *Commandments; and (4) prayer, with an exposition of the *Lord's Prayer. It includes teaching on such contemporary ethical problems as the sale of organs for transplant surgery. It was the first 'universal' catechism of the RC Church since the '*Roman Catechism' of 1566. While the latter was intended for the use of the parish clergy, this catechism was designed primarily for bishops as a point of reference in the preparation of regional catechisms. It was first suggested by the 1985

Extraordinary Synod of Bishops which called for a further implementation of the teachings of the Second *Vatican Council; in the following year Pope *John Paul II appointed a commission of bishops and cardinals which undertook the work.

An Eng. tr. appeared in 1994.

catechist. (1) In the primitive Church, a teacher of *catechumens, or a lecturer in a catechetical school.

(2) In modern usage, occasionally, a person appointed to give instruction in Christianity, e.g. to children.

(3) In the mission field, a native Christian teacher.

catechumens (Gk. κατηχούμενοι). In the early Church those undergoing training and instruction preparatory to Christian *Baptism. They were assigned a place in the church, but solemnly dismissed before the *Eucharist proper began. Since F. X. Funk's researches, the older view that they were divided into several grades, corresponding to the well-known stages of those undergoing penance, has been generally abandoned. Only those who had reached the stage of awaiting Baptism at the coming Easter formed a separate group (φωτιζόμενοι). There was an elaborate ritual of preparation, with a succession of *scrutinies, in the preceding *Lent, the candidates being finally admitted at the Paschal Mass. Illustrations of early catechetical instruction survive in St *Cyril of Jerusalem's *Lectures* (c.350) and St *Augustine's *De Catechizandis Rudibus* (c.400).

In 1962 the catechumenate was restored in the RC Church, when provision was made for the elements surviving in the *Rituale Romanum* (enrolment, exorcisms, pre-baptismal anointings) to be administered on separate occasions. The revived catechumenate was of special importance in the mission field, but the increasing number of adult Baptisms led to its establishment in other countries, e.g. France. By the Ordo 'De Initiatione Christiana Adultorum' (The Christian Initiation of Adults) of 6 Jan. 1972, the restored catechumenate became a necessary prelude to all adult Baptisms. On entering the catechumenate, candidates are marked with the sign of the cross. In the following period, which may be lengthy, they are encouraged to attend services of Bible reading and instruction. They enter the 'Time of Purification and Enlightenment' with their election for sacramental initiation; this election normally takes place on the first Sunday in Lent, and is followed by scrutinies on the third, fourth, and fifth Sundays of Lent. On appointed weekdays explanations, known as 'traditions', of the Creed and the *Lord's Prayer are given (see TRADITIO SYMBOLI), and on Holy Saturday (or earlier in Holy Week) the final ceremonies take place, namely the 'reddition' or recitation of the Creed, the *Ephphatha, and the anointing of the candidates with oil. (National conferences of bishops may, however, decide to omit the last two ceremonies.) The Baptism, Confirmation, and Communion of the candidates during the *Paschal Vigil Service is followed during Eastertide by a period of 'mystagogy', during which frequent attendance at Mass, etc., is urged.

F. X. Funk, *Kirchengeschichtliche Abhandlungen und Untersuchungen*, Bd. 1 (1897), esp. papers 6, 7, and 8; E. *Schwartz, *Bussstufen und Katechumenatsklassen* (Strasbourg, 1911). A. Dondeyne, 'La Discipline des Scrutins dans l'Église Latine avant Charlemagne', *RHE* 28 (1932), pp. 5–33, 751–87. T. Maertens, *Histoire et Pastorale du Rituel du Catéchuménat et du Baptême* (Bruges, 1962); M. Dujarier, *Le Parrainage des Adultes aux trois premiers siècles de l'Église: Recherche historique sur l'évolution des garanties et des étapes catéchuménales avant 313* (1962; Eng. tr., New York [1979]). T. Ohm, *Das Katechumenat in den katholischen Missionen* (Münster, 1959).

Catechumens, Mass of the. The Ante-Communion, or first part of the *Eucharist. It is so named because in the early Church it was the part of the service which catechumens, who were dismissed before the *Anaphora, were allowed to attend.

Categorical Imperative. In the ethical theory of I. *Kant, the absolute moral law, given in reason, and therefore unconditionally binding upon every rational being. It is contrasted with the 'hypothetical imperative', which, being either a counsel of prudence or a rule of skill, implies a hypothesis, or condition under which alone it is operative.

H. J. Paton, *The Categorical Imperative: A Study in Kant's Moral Philosophy* (1947). See also works cited s.v. KANT, I.

catena (Lat.), 'chain' (Gk. σειρά). A word applied to the biblical commentaries dating from the 5th cent. onwards, in which the successive verses of the scriptural text were elucidated by 'chains' of passages derived from previous commentators. In a wider sense the word was used of any collection of passages from different authors bearing on a single subject. Among the most celebrated of biblical catenae was St *Thomas Aquinas' 'Catena Aurea' on the Gospels.

Numerous *catenae* and frags. from *catenae* have been pub. in modern times; important collections incl. J. A. *Cramer, *Catenae Graecorum Patrum in Novum Testamentum* (8 vols., 1838–44); M. *Faulhaber, *Hohelied, Proverbien- und Prediger-Catenen* (1902); K. Staab, *Die Pauluskatenen nach den handschriftlichen Quellen untersucht* (Scripta Pontificii Instituti Biblici; Rome, 1926); id., *Pauluskommentare aus der griechischen Kirche* (Neutestamentliche Abhandlungen, 15; 1933); J. Reuss, *Matthäus-, Markus- und Johannes-Katenen* (ibid. 18, Hefte 4–5; 1941); id., *Matthäus-Kommentare aus der griechischen Kirche aus Katenenhandschriften gesammelt* (TU 61; 1957); id., *Johannes-Kommentare aus der griechischen Kirche* (ibid. 89; 1966). R. Devreesse, *Les anciens commentateurs grecques de l'Octateuque et des Rois (Fragments tirés des Chaînes)* (ST 201; 1959); id., *Les anciens commentateurs des Psaumes* (ST 264; 1970); M. Harl and G. Dorival, *La Chaîne Palestinienne sur le Psaume 118* (SC 189–90; 1972); E. Mühlenberg, *Psalmenkommentare aus der Katenenüberlieferung* (Patristische Texte und Studien, 15, 16, and 19; 1975–8); F. Petit, *Catenae Graecae in Genesim et Exodum* (CCSG 2, 15, etc.; 1977 ff.); and U. and D. Hagedorn (eds.), *Die älteren Griechischen Katenen zum Buch Hiob* (Patristische Texte und Studien, 40 etc.: 1994 ff.). M. Richard, 'Les premiers chaînes sur le Psautier', *Bulletin d'information de l'Institut de Recherche et d'Histoire des Textes*, 5, for 1956 (1957), pp. 87–98; repr. in his *Opera Minora*, 3 (Turnhout, 1977), no. 70; other arts. repr. nos 69 and 71; G. Dorival, *Les Chaînes Exégétiques grecques sur les Psaumes: Contribution à l'étude d'une forme littéraire* (SSL 43, 44, 45, etc.; 1986 ff.). G. Karo and H. *Lietzmann, 'Catenarum Graecarum Catalogus', *Nachr.* (Gött.), 1902, pp. 1–66, 299–350, and 559–620. CPG 4 (1980), pp. 185–259. R. Devreesse in *Dict. Bibl.*, Suppl. 1 (1928), cols. 1084–233, s.v. 'Chaînes exégétiques grecques'; E. Mühlenberg in *TRE* 18 (1989), pp. 14–21, s.v. 'Katenen', with further bibl.

Catesby, Robert (1573–1605), English *recusant and conspirator. In 1601 he suffered a heavy fine for his part in the conspiracy of the Earl of Essex, and allied himself with the extreme RC party, who would make no compromise with the state. He was the original mover of the *Gunpowder Plot, which he first devised in the winter of 1603–4, and with which he persevered even after he knew that it had been betrayed. After the failure of the plot he took refuge at Holbeche, near Dudley, in West Midlands, where he was killed on 8 Nov. 1605 while resisting arrest.

M. W. Jones, *The Gunpowder Plot and Life of Robert Catesby* (1909), pp. 1–53. A. Jessopp in *DNB* 9 (1887), pp. 281–4.

Cathari (or **Cathars**) (Gk. καθαρός, 'pure'). The name has been applied to several sects, e.g. to the *Novatianists by St *Epiphanius and other Greek Fathers, and, acc. to St *Augustine, in the form 'Catharistae' to a group of *Manichaeans. But it is mostly used for a large group of medieval dissenters who provided a serious challenge to the Church in the 12th and 13th cents. Traces of this way of thinking can be found in scattered places in W. Europe in the early 11th cent., beginning with a group condemned at Orléans in 1022, but it is not possible to say whether there was any real continuity between these early groups and the later fully-developed movement. From c.1140, initially in Germany, there are clear signs of influence from the *Bogomils in the E., and of the distinctive ideas and organization of the later Cathars. From this time onwards, their activity spread widely, and by 1200 they were strong in S. France and Lombardy. Contemporaries knew them under various names: Cathars, Manichaeans, *Arians, Bulgari or *Bougres*, *Albigenses (in France), and *Patarenes (in Italy). The word 'heretic' in the 13th cent. is applied almost exclusively to the Cathars, and is rarely used of other dissenting opinions. They claimed to be restoring the purity of the early Church, and there are similarities between their ideals and those of the more radical champions of reform and the apostolic life.

Their theology in its purest form was almost certainly derived from the E., and was basically dualist. They rejected the flesh and material creation as evil, affirming two principles of good and evil. There are signs in their writings of both an absolute dualism (of equal and opposite principles) and a 'mitigated' dualism (envisaging the ultimate triumph of God over the devil). The purpose of redemption was the liberation of the soul from the flesh and the end of the 'mixed' state which had been brought about by the devil. Though retaining the NT and the prophetic parts of the OT, the Cathars interpreted them as allegories, teaching that Christ was an angel with a phantom body who, consequently, did not suffer or rise again, and whose redemptive work consisted only in teaching man the true doctrine. The Catholic Church, by taking the NT allegories literally, had been corrupted and was doing the work of the devil.

Rejecting the sacraments, the doctrines of hell, purgatory, and the resurrection of the body, and believing that all matter was bad, their moral doctrine was of extreme rigorism, condemning marriage, the use of meat, milk, eggs, and other animal produce. As, however, these ideals were too austere for the majority of men and women, they distinguished two classes, the 'perfect', who received the 'consolamentum', i.e. baptism of the Holy Spirit by

imposition of hands, and kept the precepts in all their rigour, and the ordinary 'believers' who were allowed to lead normal lives but promised to receive the 'consolamentum' when in danger of death.

The Church was at first slow to react to this unaccustomed threat, but then did so by both preaching and persecution. The extensive reforms of the Fourth *Lateran Council of 1215, and the emergence of the *Dominican Order, were both in large part reactions to the threat of heresy, as was the development of the *Inquisition. By 1300 the combined effect of force and persuasion had greatly weakened the Cathars, and thereafter they did not play a major part in the history of the W. Church.

There is much primary material in the records of the Inquisition, and some valuable treatises on Catharism written by both supporters and critics. These include the *Summa de Catharis* of Rainer Sacconi, OP, and the *Liber de Duobus Principiis*, prob. by John de Lugio, both ed., with a frag. of a Catharist Ritual, by A. Dondaine, OP (Rome, 1939; the *Summa de Catharis* is also ed. by F. Šanjek, OP, in *Archivum Fratrum Praedicatorum*, 44 (1974), pp. 31–60; and the *Liber de Duobus Principiis* and the frag. of the Ritual are also ed., with Fr. tr. and introd., by C. Thouzellier, SC 198, 1973, and SC 236, 1977, respectively); Moneta of Cremona, OP, *Adversus Catharos et Valdenses*, ed. T. A. Ricchinius, OP (Rome, 1743); C. Thouzellier (ed.), *Un traité cathare inédit du début du XIIIᵉ siècle d'après le Liber contra Manicheos de Durand de Huesca* (Bibliothèque de la *RHE*, 37; 1961), and Durandus of Huesca's *Liber Antiheresis*, ed. K.-V. Selge, *Die ersten Waldenser* (Arbeiten zur Kirchengeschichte, 37; 2 vols., 1967). Eng. tr., in whole or part, of all these docs. except the last in W. L. Wakefield and A. P. Evans, *Heresies of the High Middle Ages* (Records of Civilization, Sources and Studies, 81; 1969), pp. 329–46, 511–91, 465–83, 307–29, and 494–510, with other material and extensive bibl. There are trs. of other important materials in R. I. Moore, *The Birth of Popular Heresy* (1975), esp. pp. 1–26 and 88–154, and E. [M.] Peters, *Heresy and Authority in Medieval Europe* (1980), esp. pp. 103–37. There are extensive discussions of the origin of Catharist ideas: see esp. R. I. Moore, *The Origins of European Dissent* (1977), and M. D. Lambert, *Medieval Heresy: Popular Movements from Bogomil to Hus* (1977), esp. pp. 1–150 (2nd edn., 1992, pp. 1–146), *passim*. Although there is now some more source material, the classic expositions of Catharist doctrine remain those of H. Söderberg, *La religion des Cathares* (Uppsala, 1949), and A. Borst, *Die Katharer* (Schriften der *MGH*, 12; Stuttgart, 1953). The many later works incl. J. Duvernoy, *Le Catharisme* (2 vols., Toulouse, 1976–9), and G. Rottenwöhrer, *Der Katharismus* (2 vols. in 4, Bad Honnef, 1982), with extensive bibl. For other studies, see H. Grundmann, *Bibliographie zur Ketzergeschichte des Mittelalters (1900–66)* (Sussidi eruditi, 20; Rome, 1967), and C. T. Berkhout and J. B. Russell, *Medieval Heresies: A Bibliography 1960–1979* (Subsidia Mediaevalia, 11; Toronto, 1981), esp. pp. 26–52 (nos. 290–709). *Cahiers d'Études Cathares* (Arques, 1949 ff.). D. Müller in *TRE* 18 (1989), pp. 21–30, s.v. 'Katharer', with bibl. See also works cited s.v. ALBIGENSES.

Catharinus, Ambrosius (c.1484–1553), *Dominican theologian. Lancelot Politi was born in Siena; after studying canon and civil law there he was made a doctor at the age of 17. About 1507 he left Siena to visit various universities in Italy and prob. France. By 1514 he was professor at the Sapienza in Rome. Inspired by the works of G. *Savonarola, he entered the Dominican Order at San Marco, Florence, in 1517, taking the name Ambrosius Catharinus in honour of the Sienese Dominican saints, Bl Ambrose Sansedoni and St *Catherine. His superiors soon employed him as a controversialist against *Lutheran doctrines: his *Apologia pro Veritate Catholica* appeared in 1520 and the passionate *Excusatio Disputationis contra Lutherum* in 1521. He appears not to have remained long in Florence; in 1526 he was in Pistoia and then in Siena, where he was elected prior, prob. in 1527. In Siena he became embroiled in a bitter controversy: the Sienese government was trying to force the Dominicans to celebrate the feast of the *Immaculate Conception, while the Dominican authorities were opposed to the feast and the doctrine. Catharinus, who was personally in favour of the doctrine, attempted to persuade his superiors to consent to the celebration of the feast, but he failed and incurred their bitter hostility. An attempt to win support from T. *Cajetan also failed. In 1530 Catharinus was deposed as prior. He continued to campaign in favour of the Immaculate Conception and also embarked on a critical attack (pub. at Paris, 1535) on Cajetan's exegetical works. At his request *Clement VII freed him from the control of his provincial superiors and placed him directly under the Master General. By 1535 he was living in France, where he published a volume of *Opuscula* (Lyons, 1542), which included treatises on *predestination and the Immaculate Conception. In 1545 *Paul III summoned him to the Council of *Trent as a theologian and in 1546 appointed him Bp. of Minori, though he spent little time in his see. He played a prominent part in the Council, where his views, esp. on grace, brought him into conflict with other Dominicans such as Domingo de *Soto. From 1549 he lived mainly in Rome. In 1552 his former student, *Julius III, appointed him Abp. of Conza.

On many points his teaching was at variance with the official Dominican *Thomism. He taught that it is possible in this life to know certainly whether or not one is in a state of grace, and his ideas on predestination have been seen, rather misleadingly, as foreshadowing those of L. de *Molina. He distinguished between the 'predestination' of certain special saints, such as the BVM and the Apostles, who are guaranteed by a special grace against the possibility of damnation, and the 'foreknowledge' by which God knows that some people will in fact be saved, but who remain capable of salvation or damnation throughout their lives, depending on whether or not they accept the grace which is freely offered by God to everyone. In Catharinus' view most people are not 'predestined' either to salvation or damnation, and he rejected with horror the belief that anyone is predestined to damnation. He also denied that anyone is damned simply because of *original sin.

Quétif and Échard, 2, pp. 144–51, 332, and 825, with list of his works. Photographic repr. of his *Enarrationes, Assertationes*, and various *Disputationes*, orig. pub. Rome, 1551–2, and of his *Opuscula* (2 vols., Ridgewood, NJ, 1964). Modern edn. of his *Apologia pro Veritate* by J. Schweizer (Corpus Catholicorum, 27; Münster i.W., 1956). Id., *Ambrosius Catharinus Politus (1484–1553), ein Theologe des Reformationszeitalters* (Reformationsgeschichtliche Studien und Texte, Hefte 11 and 12; 1910). F. Lauchert, *Die italienischen literarischen Gegner Luthers* (1912), pp. 30–133. D. Scaramuzzi, 'Le idee scotiste di un grande teologo domenicano del '500: Ambrogio Catarino', *Studi Francescani*, 2nd ser. 4 (1932), pp. 296–319, and 5 (1933), pp. 197–217. L. Scarina, OSB, *Giustizia primitiva e peccato originale secondo Ambrogio Catarino, OP* (Studia Anselmiana, 17; Rome, 1947). G. Bosco, OP, 'Intorno a un carteggio inedito di Ambrogio Caterino', *Memorie Domenicane*, 67 (1950), pp. 103–20, 137–66, and 233–66, incl. text. A. Duval, OP, in *Dict. Sp.* 12 (pt. 2; 1986), cols. 1844–58, s.v. 'Politi, Lancellotto'. See also works cited under TRENT, COUNCIL OF.

cathedra. Properly the bishop's chair or throne in his cathedral church. Its original position was in the centre of the apse behind the *high altar; in the Middle Ages it was often placed in the chancel, but the primitive position, which survived in some places, is again becoming common. The phrase 'ex cathedra' (i.e. 'from the throne') is used esp. of the pronouncements uttered by the Pope with the full formal weight of his office as the supposed divinely appointed guardian of Christian faith and morals, and such are held by RCs to be *infallible. No authoritative statement exists as to which particular Papal pronouncements are 'ex cathedra'.

cathedral. The church which contains the 'throne' (Gk. καθέδρα, Lat. *cathedra*) or official seat (Lat. *sedes*) of the bishop of the diocese, and hence, since the throne is one of the most important and oldest of the episcopal *insignia*, its 'mother church' (*matrix ecclesia*). Though not necessarily the largest or most splendid church in the diocese (e.g. at *Rome, where the *Vatican basilica has long outshone St John *Lateran, the cathedral church), it is usually of outstanding size and grandeur. In rare instances the bishop has two thrones and hence two cathedrals (e.g. in the Protestant diocese of *Dublin, q.v.). The original position of the bishop's chair was at the E. end of the church so that he faced W., looking over the high altar; see previous entry.

Originally the cathedral church, being in the immediate vicinity of the Bishop's residence, was served by the bishop himself and his household or *familia*. But as the bishop's pastoral and administrative responsibilities grew and became more exacting and the worship in the cathedral church also became more elaborate, the responsibility for the administration of the cathedral was gradually delegated to a separate body of clergy. The bishop, who now used his own oratory for his regular private worship, came to visit his cathedral for official worship only on greater occasions, e.g. on the chief ecclesiastical feasts. The result was that those directly responsible for the cathedral came to be a separate ecclesiastical corporation or *chapter with its own privileges and rights.

In medieval England the cathedrals were of two kinds according as their chapter was a secular or monastic body. The nine secular foundations were *Chichester, *Exeter, *Hereford, *Lichfield, *Lincoln, London, *Salisbury, *Wells, and *York; the eight religious ones were *Canterbury, *Carlisle, *Durham, *Ely, *Norwich, *Rochester, *Winchester, and *Worcester. These last were all in the custody of *Benedictine monks except Carlisle, which was served by *Augustinian Canons.

With the *Dissolution of the Monasteries under *Henry VIII, the religious foundations naturally came to an end. On these eight cathedrals new constitutions were imposed by the King; they have hence become known as the 'New Foundations' in contrast with the other nine which, retaining their medieval statutes, are known as the 'Old Foundations'. Besides these, five further 'New Foundations' survived out of the six new bishoprics which Henry VIII created from the monastic spoils, namely Bristol, *Chester, *Gloucester, *Oxford, and *Peterborough (Henry's sixth creation, that of Westminster (see WESTMINSTER ABBEY), was suppressed again in 1550). Here in every case an earlier (usually monastic) church was constituted the cathedral; and all except Oxford had a body of statutes imposed on them.

The creation of new English dioceses in modern times, beginning with *Ripon in 1836, has brought a corresponding growth of cathedrals. Here again already existing churches have been adapted to use as a cathedral, e.g. the collegiate church at Ripon, the originally monastic church at *St Albans, and parish churches at *Southwark and Bradford. New churches, however, have been built at *Truro (here, however, incorporating a small portion of the old parish church of St Mary), Guildford, *Coventry, and *Liverpool.

In the RC Church the restoration of the hierarchy in 1850 was naturally followed by the foundation of cathedrals in England. The most notable are those of *Westminster and Liverpool (qq.v.).

English cathedrals are normally governed by a body of clergy consisting of from three to six residentiary canons presided over by a dean (or, in the case of recent foundations, a provost). The degree of authority possessed by the dean in his chapter varies from place to place, in general being considerably greater in the 'New' than in the 'Old' 'Foundations'. Besides the dean and residentiary canons there is generally also a larger body of non-residentiary canons, sometimes known as *prebendaries or honorary canons. The staff of a cathedral also includes a body of *minor canons whose primary duties are to render the priest's parts of the musical service. There is also a choir to render the daily office, consisting of an organist, choirmen (sometimes known as 'lay clerks'), and choristers. In the older cathedrals there has been a long tradition of high musical performance; and the type of service now general in parish churches was borrowed in the middle of the 19th cent. from the cathedrals and hence at first known as a 'cathedral service'. In most cases the cathedral statutes make provision for all these officials, who sometimes have a considerable degree of independence accorded to them.

A. Barbosa, *Tractatus de Canonicis et Dignitatibus aliisque Inferioribus Beneficiariis Cathedralium* (3rd edn., Lyons, 1640); M. A. Frances de Urrutigoyti, *De Ecclesiis Cathedralibus, eorumque Privilegiis et Praerogativis Tractatus* (Lyons, 1665). J. de Bordenhave, *L'État des églises cathédrales et collégiales* (1643). E. A. Freeman, *History of the Cathedral Church of Wells as Illustrating the History of the Cathedral Churches of the Old Foundation* (1870). E. W. *Benson, *The Cathedral: Its Necessary Place in the Life and Work of the Church* (1878). A. H. Thompson, *The Cathedral Churches of England* (1925), with bibl. K. Edwards, *The English Secular Cathedrals in the Middle Ages* (Publications of the University of Manchester, 301; 1949; rev. edn., 1967). H. Sedlmayr, *Die Entstehung der Kathedrale* (Zurich, 1950). O. von Simson, *The Gothic Cathedral: The Origins of Gothic Architecture & the Medieval Concept of Order* (New York and London, 1956). J. Fitchen, *The Construction of Gothic Cathedrals: A Study of Medieval Vault Erection* (Oxford, 1961). P. Johnson, *British Cathedrals* [1980]; T. Tatton-Brown, *Great Cathedrals of Britain* (1989). D. Marcombe and C. S. Knighton (eds.), *Close Encounters: English Cathedrals and Societies since 1540* (Studies in Local and Regional History, 3; Nottingham, 1991); P. Barrett, *Barchester: English Cathedral Life in the Nineteenth Century* (1993).

Much information about the cathedrals of England is to be found in W. *Dugdale, *Monasticon Anglicanum* (q.v.). Among modern works dealing with Eng. cathedrals collectively are those of F. Bond (London, 1899), T. F. Bumpus (3 vols., ibid., 1905–6; rev. edn. 1922), and photographic studies incl. those of H. Bats-

ford and C. Fry (London, 1934), H. Felton and J. Harvey (ibid., 1950; rev. edn. by J. Harvey, 1974), M. Hürlimann and P. Meyer (ibid., 1950), and H. Thorold, *Collins Guide to Cathedrals, Abbeys and Priories of England and Wales* (1986). E. S. Prior, *The Cathedral Builders in England* (1905). E. H. Fellowes, *English Cathedral Music from Edward VI to Edward VII* (1941; rev. edn. by J. A. Westrup, 1969). E. G. Moore, *Introduction to English Canon Law* (3rd edn. by T. Briden and B. Hanson, 1992), pp. 40–4, with notes p. 48. M. Hill, *Ecclesiastical Law* (1995), pp. 465–97. *Heritage and Renewal: The Report of the Archbishops' Commission on Cathedrals* (1994 [recommended extensive changes in the structure of administration]).

cathedral schools. Schools established in medieval or later times for the education of the choirboys of cathedral churches. They sometimes served also the purposes of a grammar school, providing free education for poor boys living in the cathedral city. Most of these schools have in later times admitted fee-paying pupils, both day boys and boarders, and many of those which provide secondary as well as primary education are represented on the Headmasters' Conference. Several now admit girls as well as boys; in some cases girls form part of the cathedral choir. The oldest choir school is probably that at *York, which claims to have been founded in the 7th cent.

Cathedrals, Friends of the. Voluntary organizations designed to support the work and fabric of the English cathedrals. The first such society, the Friends of *Canterbury Cathedral, was founded in 1927 under the auspices of G. K. A. *Bell, then the dean; its objects were defined as 'to gather round the cathedral in association with the Dean and Chapter a body of supporters who are prepared to take some share in caring for it and in preserving it for posterity'. This precedent has since been followed in the case of many other ancient English (and esp. cathedral) churches.

Catherine, St, of Alexandria. Acc. to tradition, she was a virgin martyred at *Alexandria in the early 4th cent.; but though she is among the most widely venerated of women saints, she is not mentioned in the W. before the 8th/9th cent. Legend represents her as of a noble family and of exceptional learning, who, as a result of her protest against the persecution of Christians by Maxentius, was tied to a wheel, tortured, and finally beheaded. Her body was said to have been discovered c.800 on Mount *Sinai, whither, acc. to her *acts, it was transported by angels after her death. The monastery near the site, however, goes back to 527, and the earlier pilgrims knew nothing of its connection with St Catherine. There was great devotion to her in the Middle Ages, notably in France during the *Crusades. Her symbol is a spiked wheel; and she is patroness of young women, wheelwrights, attorneys, and scholars, and is one of the '*auxiliary saints'. Feast day, 25 Nov., suppressed in 1969.

She has sometimes been identified, but on insufficient grounds, with the unnamed woman mentioned in *Eusebius, *HE* 8. 14. 15. There are a number of versions of the legend: four Gk. texts ed. J. Viteau, *Passions des Saints Écaterine et Pierre d'Alexandrie* (1897), pp. 2–65; the legend acc. to *Simeon Metaphrastes is also pr. in J. P. Migne, *PG* 116. 276–301; further texts in H. Kunst, *Geschichte der Legende der h. Katharina von Alexandrien und der h. Maria Aegyptiaca* (1890), pp. 1–109, *passim*; two metrical Lat. versions ed. H. Varnhagen (Erlangen, 1891); A. Poncelet, SJ (ed.),

'Sanctae Catharinae Virginis et Martyris Translatio et Miracula Rotomagensia Saec. XI', *Anal. Boll.* 22 (1903), pp. 423–38; full details of edns. of Lat. MSS, to date, in *BHL* 1, pp. 250–5 (nos. 1657–700), and *novum supplementum* (1986), pp. 192–7. P. Peeters, SJ (ed.), 'Une Version arabe de la passion de Sainte Catherine d'Alexandrie', *Anal. Boll.* 27 (1907), pp. 5–32, incl. Lat. tr. R. Fawtier, 'Les Reliques rouennaises de Sainte Catherine d'Alexandrie', ibid. 41 (1923), pp. 357–68. For date of earliest Lat. Life, see H. *Delehaye, SJ, 'Les Martyrs d'Égypte', ibid. 40 (1922), pp. 5–154, esp. pp. 123 f. Life by Clemence of Barking ed. W. MacBain (Anglo-Norman Texts, 18; 1964). J. A. *Robinson, 'The Passion of Saint Catharine and the Romance of Barlaam and Joasaph', *JTS* 25 (1924), pp. 246–53. E. Weigand, 'Zu den ältesten abendländischen Darstellungen der Jungfrau und Märtyrin Katherina von Alexandria', in *Pisciculi: Studien zur Religion und Kultur des Altertums Franz Joseph Dölger . . . dargeboten (Antike und Christentum.* Ergänzungsband, 1, 1939), pp. 279–90, with refs. A. Zachou, Σινᾶ καὶ ἁγία Αἰκατερίνη (1937). On iconography, H. *Bremond, *Sainte Catherine d'Alexandrie* (L'Art et les saints, 1917). Tito da Ottone, OM Cap., *La leggenda di Santa Caterina vergine e martire di Alexandria* (Genoa, 1940), incl. information on the growth of the cult. D. Balboni and others in *Bibliotheca Sanctorum,* 3 (Rome, 1963), cols. 954–78, s.v., with further bibl.

Catherine, St, of Genoa

Catherine, St, of Genoa (1447–1510), mystic. Caterina Fieschi was of a noble Ligurian family, who at the age of 16 married Giuliano Adorno. Ten years later she was suddenly converted; and, though she found continued life with her pleasure-loving husband burdensome, she succeeded in reaching great heights of spirituality. She began to receive communion almost daily, a practice extremely rare except for priests in the later Middle Ages. Subsequently her husband too was also converted, and after this assisted her in her selfless care of the sick in a hospital in Genoa. Eventually Giuliano became a Franciscan *tertiary, but Caterina joined no order. She underwent a number of remarkable mental and at times almost pathological experiences, which were the subject of F. *von Hügel's well-known study and evaluation. Her spiritual doctrine is contained in the book published in 1551 as the *Vita e dottrina*, though perhaps she did not herself put this account of her visions and convictions into their present literary form; this is the source of her 'Dialogues on the Soul and the Body' and of her 'Treatise on Purgatory' which have often been issued separately. It used to be thought that the writings were edited by Battista *Vernazza, but recent scholarship has discredited this suggestion. In 1944 St Catherine was proclaimed by *Pius XII Patroness of the Hospitals in Italy. Feast day, 15 Sept.

Modern Eng. tr. of Catherine's 'Treatise on Purgatory' (here called 'Purgation and Purgatory') and 'Dialogue' by S. Hughes, with introd. by B. J. Groeschel, OFM Cap. (Classics of Western Spirituality, 1979). F. von Hügel, *The Mystical Element of Religion as studied in St Catherine of Genoa and her Friends* (2 vols., 1908). Von Hügel's contention that neither the 'Dialogue' nor the 'Treatise' received literary shape until a late date has been severely criticized by Umile [Bonzi] da Genova, OM Cap., in an imp. art. in *Dict. Sp.* 2 (1938), s.v. 'Catherine de Gênes', cols. 290–321, with bibl. cols. 324 f.; more recently, id., *S. Caterina Fieschi Adorno* (2 vols., 1961–62), with crit. text of 'opus Catharinianum'. G. da Pantasina, *Vita di Santa Caterina Fieschi Adorno con ricordi e documenti* (Genoa, 1929). P. Debongnie, CSSR, in *DHGE* 10 (1949), cols. 1506–15, s.v. 'Catherine de Gênes'; S. Pezella in *Dizionario Biografico degli Italiani,* 22 (1979), pp. 343–5, s.v. 'Caterina Fieschi Adorno'.

Catherine, St, de' Ricci

Catherine, St, de' Ricci (1522–90), *Dominican nun. Her baptismal name was Alessandra Lucrezia Romola. In 1535 she entered the Dominican convent of San Vincenzo, Prato, a house closely associated with the reforming movement of G. *Savonarola. From 1552 until her death she was always either prioress or subprioress. During several years she underwent periodic raptures, in which she experienced an intense union with Christ's Passion. Increasingly her reputation for sanctity and good counsel attracted to her people of all walks and stations of life, some of them becoming her 'spiritual children'. Among her correspondents were St *Charles Borromeo and St *Philip Neri and many other ecclesiastical and secular leaders. She was beatified in 1732 and canonized in 1746. Feast day, 4 Feb. (until 1971, 13 Feb.).

Modern edn. of her Letters by Guglielmo M. [later Domenico] di Agresti, OP (Collana Ricciana, Fonti, 8–12; Florence, 1973–5). Eng. tr. of Selected Letters, with introd. by id. (Dominican Sources, 3; Oxford '1985' [1986]). *Acta Canonizationis . . . Catharinae de Ricci* pub. Rome, 1749; other docs. concerned with the process pub. ibid., 1713, 1729, 1731, and 1742. The main early authority is the Life by S. Razzi, OP (Lucca, 1594; modern edn. by G. M. di Agresti in Collana Ricciana, Fonti, 3; 1965). There is much other material on St Catherine. ed. by G. M. di Agresti in other vols. of this series (12 vols., 1963–75). H. Bayonne, *Vie de Sainte Catherine de Ricci de Florence* (2 vols., 1873); G. Bertini, *Santa Caterina de' Ricci* (1935).

Catherine, St, of Siena

Catherine, St, of Siena (?1347–80), *Dominican tertiary. Caterina Benincasa was the 23rd of 25 children born to a prosperous Sienese dyer. She grew up in Christian piety, though her long hours of prayer and severe mortification at first brought her into conflict with her family. Having at the early age of 16 joined the Dominican Order of Penance (later known as the Dominican *Third Order), she lived for a further three years or so in seclusion at home until, as she believed, she received a command from Christ to leave her solitude and devote herself to the care of the sick and poor and the conversion of sinners. Before long she was being called upon to act as a mediator not only between the warring factions in and around Siena but also in such higher matters as the conflict between Florence and the Holy See. On the journeys involved in these missions, she was nearly always accompanied by some of the large band of followers, both men and women, clerical and lay, who had gathered round her, drawn by her extraordinary sanctity, attractive personality, and great spiritual wisdom. These same qualities are reflected in the 383 extant letters written or dictated by her; in the synthesis of her teaching which is usually referred to as the 'Dialogo'; and in some 26 prayers (mostly recorded from phrases she was heard to murmur in one of her frequent states of 'abstraction'). In all her writings, the central theme is that of Christ crucified, and in particular the thought of His blood, which Catherine saw as the supreme sign and pledge of divine love and the chief motive for ours. Politically her one real success was to have helped persuade *Gregory XI to transfer the Papacy from *Avignon back to Rome in 1377. Ironically, it was Gregory's premature death just over a year later that paved the way for the election of *Urban VI and then for the onset of the *Great Schism. Catherine remained unswervingly loyal to Urban, but her intense distress over the Schism tore her apart, both physically and spiritually, and she died on 29 April 1380, aged only 33. She was canonized in 1461 and declared a *Doctor of the Church in 1970. Feast day, 29 (formerly 30) April.

Works ed. G. Gigli (4 vols., Lucca, 1707–21). The best edn. of the *Dialogo* is that of G. Cavallini (Rome, 1968); this omits the chapter divisions (which do not seem to be orig.) of earlier edns., e.g. that of M. Fiorilli and S. Caramella (Scrittori d'Italia [34]; 1928). 15th cent. Eng. tr., *The Orchard of Syon*, ed. P. Hodgson and G. M. Liegey (EETS, Original Series, 258; 1966); modern trs. by A. Thorold (London, 1896; abridged edn., 1907, repr. Rockford, Ill., 1974) and S. Noffke, OP (Classics of Western Spirituality, 1980). *Lettere* ed. N. Tommaseo and P. Misciatelli (6 vols., Siena, 1913–21); crit. edn. by E. Dupré Theseider (vol. 1 only; Fonti per la Storia d'Italia, 82; 1940); good selection, with introd. and notes, by G. Cavallini, *La Verità dell'Amore* (1978). Eng. tr. of Letters by S. Noffke, OP (Medieval & Renaissance Texts and Studies, 52, etc.; Binghamton, NY, 1988 ff.); also of selections (with biog. and doctrinal introd., and extract from the *Dialogo*) by K. Foster, OP, and M. J. Ronayne, OP (London, 1980). *Orazioni* ed. G. Cavallini (Rome, 1978). Eng. tr. by S. Noffke, OP (New York, 1983). The principal sources for her Life are the *Legenda Major* by Raymond of Capua, OP, her confessor (*editio princeps* by T. Loher, Cologne, 1553, repr. in *AASS*, Apr. 3 (1675), pp. 853–959; an Eng. tr. was pub. London, prob. in 1492; modern Eng. trs. by G. Lamb, London, 1960, and C. Kearns, OP, Dublin, 1980); a Supplement to it (ed. J. Cavallini and I. Foralosso, Rome, 1974), and a *Legenda Minor* (ed. E. Franceschini, Fontes Vitae S. Catharinae Senensis Historici, 10; Milan, 1942), both by T. Caffarini; also the canonization process (ed. M.-H. Laurent, OP, ibid. 9; Milan, 1942). Further source material in Fontes, op. cit., 1 and 4 (both Florence, 1936), 15 (ibid., 1939), 20 (ibid., 1937) and 21 (ibid., 1938); the series is incomplete. Lives available in Eng. incl. those of A. T. Drane (London, 1880), E. G. Gardner (ibid., 1907), A. Curtayne (ibid., 1929), A. Levasti (Turin, 1947; Eng. tr., 1954), and M. de la Bedoyere (London, 1947; popular); see also G. Kaftan, *St Catherine in Tuscan Painting* (Oxford, 1949). Important studies include: R. Fawtier, *Sainte Catherine de Sienne: Essai de critique des sources* (Bibliothèque des Écoles françaises d'Athènes et de Rome, 121 and 135; 1921–30); id. and L. Canet, *La Double Expérience de Catherine Benincasa* (1948). E. Dupré Theseider, 'La duplice esperienza di S. Caterina da Siena', *Rivista Storica Italiana*, 62 (1950), pp. 533–74; A. Grion, OP, *Santa Caterina da Siena: Dottrina e Fonti* (Cremona, 1953); G. D'Urso, *Il Genio di santa Caterina* (1971). E. Jordan, 'La Date de naissance de Sainte Catherine de Sienne', *Anal. Boll.* 40 (1922), pp. 365–411; A. Dondaine, OP, 'Sainte Catherine de Sienne et Niccolò Toldo', *Archivum Fratrum Praedicatorum*, 19 (1949), pp. 169–207; *Congresso Internazionale di Studi Cateriniani, Siena–Rome—24–29 Aprile 1980: Atti* (Rome, 1981). L. Bianchi and D. Giunta (eds.), *Iconografia di S. Caterina da Siena* (1988 ff.). L. Zanini, *Bibliografia analitica di S. Caterina da Siena, 1901–1950* (1971); vols. covering 1951–75 and 1976–85, ed. M. C. Paterna (1985–9). M.-M. Gorce in *Dict. Sp.* 2 (1953), cols. 327–48, s.v.; E. Dupré Theseider in *Dizionario Biografico degli Italiani*, 22 (1979), pp. 361–79, s.v. 'Caterina da Siena', with detailed bibl.

Catherine, St, of Sweden (1331–81).

The daughter of St *Bridget, she herself early showed signs of great sanctity. The first abbess of Vadstena, the original house of the *Bridgettine Order, she spent the later part of her life largely in Italy, obtaining confirmation of the order, and unsuccessfully seeking her mother's canonization. Like St *Catherine of Siena, she supported the party of *Urban VI during the *Great Schism. Feast day, 22 Mar.

Life by Upho, a monk of Gotland (d. 1433), pr. in *AASS*, Mar. 3 (1668), pp. 505–17; crit. edn. by C. Annerstedt (Scriptores

Rerum Suecicarum Medii Aevi, 3, pt. 2; Uppsala, 1871), pp. 244–63. I. [G. A.] Collijn (ed.), *Processus seu Negocium Canonizacionis B. Katerine de Vadstenis* (Corpus Codicum Suecicorum Medii Aevi, 2; Copenhagen, 1943). She is also mentioned in works on St Bridget.

Catherine de' Medici

(1519–89), Queen-Consort of France from 1547, and Queen-Mother from 1559. A relative of Pope *Clement VII, she was married in 1533 to Henry, son of Francis I of France, in order that French support might free the Pope from the control of the Emp. *Charles V. Through the reigns of Francis I and her husband (Henry II), she had little influence on politics; but during those of her sons, Francis II (1559–60), Charles IX (1560–74), and Henry III (1574–89), she exercised much power, and for most of Charles's reign was the real ruler of the country. In the wars of religion then raging in France she advocated at first a policy of toleration, since she wished to use the Protestants as a check upon the dominant Catholic party, without allowing them to gain any control of affairs. Between 1567 and 1570, however, she took violent measures in face of a Protestant rebellion, and, after a brief interval of mildness in a vain effort to gain the support of *Elizabeth I of England, attempted to re-establish her position, which seemed threatened, by the murder of G. *Coligny, the Protestant leader, and the Massacre of St *Bartholomew (23 Aug. 1572), for which she must bear the chief responsibility. After 1574 she returned to a policy of compromise, but her influence on affairs grew steadily less.

Letters ed. by les Ctes Hector de la Ferrière and Baguenault de Puchesse (Paris, 10 vols., 1880–1909); Index by A. Lesort, 1943). E. [H.] Sichel, *Catherine de' Medici and the French Reformation* (1905); J. H. Mariéjol, *Catherine de Médicis (1519–1589)* (Paris, 1920; repr., 1979); P. Van Dyke, *Catherine de Medicis* (2 vols., London, 1923); J. Héritier, *Catherine de Médicis* (1959; Eng. tr., 1963); I. Cloulas, *Catherine de Médicis* (Paris, 1979); J. Orieux, *Catherine de Médicis ou la Reine noire* (2 vols., 1986). F. Watson, *The Life and Times of Catherine de' Medici* (1934); R. Roeder, *Catherine de' Medici and the Lost Revolution* (1937); J. E. Neale, *The Age of Catherine de Medici* (1943).

Catholic.

A word derived from the Gk. καθολικός, and meaning 'general' or 'universal'. It is first met with in Christian literature in St *Ignatius of Antioch (*Ep. ad Smyr.* 8. 2). In Christian terminology it has come to have various uses: (1) Of the universal Church as distinct from local Christian communities. It is applied thus to the faith of the whole Church, i.e. the doctrine believed 'everywhere, always, and by all' (see VINCENTIAN CANON). (2) In the sense of 'orthodox', as distinct from 'heretical', or (later) from 'schismatical'. (3) In historical writers, of the undivided Church before the schism of E. and W., traditionally dated in 1054. Thereafter the W. Church usually referred to itself as 'catholic', the E. preferring to describe itself as 'orthodox'. (4) Since the *Reformation RCs have come to use it of themselves exclusively. *Anglicans, and later *Old Catholics, have also adopted it to cover besides themselves and the RC Church also the E. Orthodox in the belief that these Communions together represent the undivided Church of earlier ages. (5) In general, in present-day usage, it is employed of those Christians who claim to be in possession of a historical and continuous tradition of faith and practice, as opposed to Protestants, who tend to find their ultimate standards in the Bible as interpreted on the principles of the Reformation of the 16th century.

P. M. Brlek, OFM, 'De vocis "catholica" origine et notione', *Antonianum*, 38 (1963), pp. 263–87. J. H. Maude in *HERE* 3 (1910), pp. 258–61, s.v. 'Catholicism, Catholicity'. G. W. H. Lampe (ed.), *A Patristic Greek Lexicon* (Oxford, 1968), pp. 690 f., s.v. καθολικός.

Catholic Action. Organized religious activity, esp. of a social, educational, or quasi-political kind, on the part of the RC laity, particularly when conceived as an extension of the apostolate of the hierarchy. A powerful impetus was given to such work when *Pius XI, in the encyclical 'Ubi Arcano' (23 Dec. 1922), encouraged the creation of elastic organizations for the purpose, under the direction of the clergy, in many European countries. Among such organizations are the *Jocists (q.v.), begun in Belgium, the 'Legion of Mary', founded in Ireland in 1921, and the 'Grail Movement', founded in the Netherlands in 1929. Subsequent Papal pronouncements, esp. those of *Pius XII in his later years, have insisted less on the organizational aspects of Catholic Action and more on the vocation of every member of the Church to spread the Kingdom of God on earth. After the Second *Vatican Council had encouraged initiatives and varied apostolates by the laity, the importance of the concept of Catholic Action declined.

The vast literature includes L. Civardi, *Manuale di azione cattolica secundo gli ultimi ordinamenti* (1924; Eng. tr. of vol. 1, 17th edn., by C. C. Martindale, SJ, 1935); E. Guerry, *Code de l'action catholique* (1928); J. Fitzsimons, OP, and P. McGuire, *Restoring All Things* (1939); C. K. Murphy, *The Spirit of Catholic Action* (1943); Y. J.-M. *Congar, OP, *Jalons pour une théologie du laïcat* (Unam Sanctam, 23, 1953; Eng. tr., *Lay People in the Church*, 1957; 3rd edn., 1964; Eng. tr., 1965); J. Newman, *What is Catholic Action?* (Dublin, 1958). The Second Vatican Council's Decree on the Apostolate of the Laity is pr. in *AAS* 68 (1966), pp. 837–64.

Catholic Apostolic Church. A religious body partly inspired in its origins by the teaching of E. *Irving (q.v.), its members also being known as Irvingites. It developed out of a revivalist circle which had gathered round H. *Drummond and counted Irving among its members. They believed in the near approach of the *Second Coming of Christ, in preparation for which they resolved to re-establish the primitive offices of the Church, namely those of Apostles, prophets, evangelists, pastors, and teachers, to which others, e.g. 'angels' (bishops) and deacons, were added later. J. B. Cardale, the earliest of the 'Apostles', was 'called' in 1832. In 1835 the full 'College of Apostles', numbering 12, held its first 'council' in London, and in 1836 addressed memoranda to the bishops of the C of E and to William IV stating their mission. Shortly afterwards they undertook missionary journeys to the mainland of Europe and to America, each 'Apostle' being assigned one or more countries for his activities. The effect on them of their travels, perhaps helped by the spread of *Tractarianism in England, was an increasing inclination towards Catholic doctrines and practices. It was expressed in their service book of 1842, a mixture of RC, Greek, and Anglican rites. Their 'priests' wore vestments and used incense; later Anointing of the Sick, a ceremony called 'Sealing' based on Rev. 7. 3 ff., *Reservation in the Tabernacle, and the use of *holy water were also intro-

duced. In 1853 they built a large church in Gordon Square, London (since 1963 used by the Anglican chaplaincy to London University). They carried on a vigorous though mostly secret propaganda on the mainland of Europe, esp. in the *Netherlands and Germany, where in the beginning they gained the adherence of several Catholic priests. Their chief successes, however, were obtained in the Protestant north, where they were favoured by the Prussian nobility. After the death, in 1901, of the last 'Apostle', who had been expected to survive till the Second Advent, they gradually diminished and are now virtually extinct.

E. Miller, *The History and Doctrines of Irvingism* (2 vols., 1878). P. E. Shaw, *The Catholic Apostolic Church* (New York, 1946). R. A. Davenport, *Albury Apostles: The Story of the Body known as the Catholic Apostolic Church* (1970; 2nd edn., 1973). C. G. Flegg, *'Gathered Under Apostles': A Study of the Catholic Apostolic Church* (Oxford, 1992). J. G. Simpson in *HERE* 7 (1914), pp. 422–8, s.v. 'Irving and the Catholic Apostolic Church'.

Catholic Association. An association created by D. *O'Connell for the defence of RC interests in Ireland. It was founded in May 1823, but did not come into effective existence till the following February. Through the exertions of the RC clergy a branch of it was established in nearly every parish, and it mobilized all classes of the RC community and liberal Protestants. In Feb. 1825 the government suppressed it, but its work was continued under other names. Its influence largely contributed to the passing of the Roman Catholic Relief Act 1829.

T. Wyse, *Historical Sketch of the late Catholic Association of Ireland* (2 vols., 1829). J. A. Reynolds, *The Catholic Emancipation Crisis in Ireland, 1823–1829* (Yale Historical Publications, Miscellany 60; New Haven, Conn., and London, 1954). F. O'Ferrall, *Catholic Emancipation: Daniel O'Connell and the Birth of Irish Democracy* (Dublin, 1985). See also Lives of D. O'Connell, cited s.v.

Catholic Emancipation Acts. See CATHOLIC RELIEF ACTS.

Catholic Epistles. A title used properly of the NT Epistles of Jas., 1 and 2 Pet., 1 Jn., and Jude, because they were 'general' (i.e. universal) epistles, and (unlike those of St *Paul) not addressed to specified Churches or individuals. It is usual, however, to include 2 and 3 Jn. among them, though these are addressed respectively to 'the elect lady and her children' and to Gaius. On this reckoning they thus total seven in all. The word 'catholic' may originally have been applied to some or all of these epistles for a different reason, i.e. to indicate that their *canonicity was accepted. See also arts. on separate epistles.

Catholic Majesty, His. A traditional title of the Kings of *Spain, said to have been granted by *Alexander VI to *Ferdinand of Aragon in 1494 in recognition of his conquest of Granada. In earlier times it had been borne by certain kings of France, e.g. *Pepin in 767.

The precise circumstances in which the title arose are obscure. It is the subject of a letter dated 5 Feb. 1495, by Peter Martyr (Ital. historian, 1455–1526), pr. in his *Opus Epistolarum* (Amsterdam and Paris, 1670), pp. 88 f. (no. 157). W. H. Prescott, *History of the Reign of Ferdinand and Isabella*, 2 (ed. J. F. Kirk, 1902), pp. 283 f., for note on the subject; P. de Roo, *Material for a History of Pope Alexander VI*, 5 (Bruges, 1924), pp. 2 f., with refs.; cf. J. Perez, *Isabelle et Ferdinand* [1988], pp. 7 f.

Catholic Record Society. An organization, founded in 1904, to print and circulate records bearing on the history of English RCism since the 16th cent. It has issued a long series of publications, now including the periodical *Recusant History*.

F. A. *Gasquet, Introduction to *Miscellanea*, 1 (Publications of the CRS, 1, 1905), pp. vii–xv.

Catholic Relief Acts (also **Catholic Emancipation Acts**). (1) By the Papists Act 1778 Catholics were allowed henceforward to own landed property on taking an oath not involving a denial of their religion; priests ceased to be subject to persecution at the denunciation of the common informer; and lifelong imprisonment for keeping a Catholic school was abolished. The Act was followed by the *Gordon Riots.

(2) By the Roman Catholic Relief Act 1791 those who took the prescribed oath were freed from the Statutes of Recusancy and the Oath of Supremacy; Catholic worship and schools were tolerated; and certain posts in the legal and military professions were opened to RCs.

(3) In 1793 by 33 Geo. III, c. 21 [Ireland] Catholics in Ireland were admitted to the franchise, the universities, and the professions.

(4) When the Irish situation was critical, the most decisive of the Emancipation measures, the Roman Catholic Relief Act 1829, was passed. Almost all disabilities were removed and Catholics were admitted to most public offices. The unrepealed restrictions, some of which were from the first a dead letter, included the prohibition of public celebrations and of taking the title of the ancient episcopal sees, and the invalidity of marriage before a priest.

(5) Most of these remaining disabilities were removed by the Roman Catholic Relief Act 1926. Among those still retained is the law which restrains the King or Queen of Great Britain from being a RC. The same applies to the offices of Regent, Lord Chancellor, and Keeper of the Great Seal. The disability of priests sitting in the House of Commons is shared with the clergy of the C of E (but not with ministers of the Free Churches). RCs are also still disabled from presenting or nominating to any benefice, the right passing by the Presentation of Benefices Act 1605 to the universities of Oxford and Cambridge acc. to a geographical distribution.

Catholic Truth Society. A RC society formed at the suggestion of Dr (later Cardinal) Herbert *Vaughan in 1884 for the printing of cheap literature, chiefly leaflets and tracts, of a devotional, educational, or controversial nature.

G. E. Anstruther and P. E. Hallett, *Catholic Truth Society: The First Fifty Years* (1934); C. Ralls, *The Catholic Truth Society: A New History* (1993).

Catholic University of America. The university was founded at Washington, DC, in 1889. It was originally intended for the higher education of the RC clergy; the laity were admitted in 1905. The university is governed by a board of 40 or more trustees, about evenly divided between clergy and laity, with the Abp. of Washington the *ex officio* chancellor. A number of religious orders and congregations are attached or affiliated to it with neighbouring houses of studies. It has played an important part in the educational activity of the RC Church in the USA at all levels.

J. T. Ellis, *The Formative Years of the Catholic University of America* (Washington, DC, 1946); P. H. Ahern, *The Catholic University of America, 1887–1896: The Rectorship of John J. Keane* (ibid., 1948); P. E. Hogan, SSJ, *The Catholic University of America, 1896–1903: The Rectorship of Thomas J. Conaty* (ibid., 1949); C. J. Barry, OSB, *The Catholic University of America, 1903–1909: The Rectorship of Denis J. O'Connell* (ibid., 1950); C. J. Nuesse, *The Catholic University of America: A Centennial History* (ibid., 1990). J. T. Ellis in *NCE* 3 (1967), pp. 332–4, s.v.

Catholicos (Gk. καθολικός). A title used by the *Patriarchs of the *Armenian and *Georgian Churches and the *Church of the East (in the case of the last two in the form 'Catholicos Patriarch'). In secular usage it was originally applied to certain high financial officials, and then in early Christian usage to the head of a number of monasteries in the same city. At one period it was used of certain bishops of metropolitan rank, in addition to the Patriarchs so named.

Caton, William (1636–65), one of the earliest *Quakers. He became a Quaker in 1652 under the influence of G. *Fox. He preached first in the Swarthmore district and then became an itinerant minister, working in various parts of the country; he received much harsh treatment. He spent a short time in France in 1655 and made four visits to the Netherlands, helping to build up the young Quaker community there. He wrote a good deal in a simple style and his *Journal* (edited by Fox himself, 1689) was long read among Friends.

List of his writings, among them an 'Abridgement' of *Eusebius' Chronologies (n.p., 1661), in *DNB* 9 (1887), p. 322, s.v.

Causes of Saints, Congregation for the. The Congregation was established by *Paul VI in 1969 when the Congregation of Sacred *Rites was divided. It deals with *beatification and *canonization procedures, those for declaring '*Doctors of the Church', and with the authentication and preservation of *relics. Its structure and methods of operation have been radically changed by recent legislation on canonization. While a cause is going through its diocesan stages the Congregation assists and ensures that all is done correctly. When the cause is being heard in Rome, it appoints an official (the *relator*) to oversee its progress. In due course it prepares a *positio* or report on the martyrdom or virtues of the candidate for beatification or canonization and then one on his or her alleged *miracles. Historians and theologians (headed by the *Promotor Fidei*) act as consultors. At the end of the process there is an assembly of cardinals and bishops who advise the Pope; the final decision is his alone.

For bibl. see CANONIZATION.

Caussade, Jean Pierre de (1675–1751), ascetic writer. In 1693 he joined the *Jesuits at Toulouse, was professed in 1708, and later travelled widely, being much appreciated as a preacher. From 1729 until 1740 he resided mainly in Lorraine. His last years were passed at Perpignan (1741–3), Albi (1744–6), and Toulouse (1746–51). His extensive correspondence with the *Visitandines at Nancy is a leading source of our knowledge of his doctrines.

His influence did much to rehabilitate *mysticism at a time when its claims were still suffering from the condemnation of *Quietism. Caussade tried to show that it had justification in the teaching of J. B. *Bossuet, whose authority here was of the highest in view of his part in the Quietist controversy. In addition to his letters of spiritual direction, his works include *Instructions spirituelles en forme de dialogue sur les divers états d'oraison* (1741; Eng. tr., with introd. by J. *Chapman, 1931). The treatise on abandonment to God's providence, first published by H. Ramière as *L'Abandon à la providence divine* (1867; Eng. tr., 1921), was taken from papers put together by the Visitation nuns at Nancy; it is disputed whether or not all the material can be ascribed to Caussade.

Good edn. of his *Lettres spirituelles* by M. Olphe-Galliard, SJ (2 vols., 1962–4); earlier Eng. tr. by A. Thorold (1934). His *Traité sur l'oraison du cœur* first ed., together with the second book of his *Instructions spirituelles*, by M. Olphe-Galliard, SJ [1981]. *L'Abandon à la providence divine* also ed. id. (1966; Eng. tr., 1981). M. Huillet d'Istria, *Le Père de Caussade et la querelle du pur amour* [1964], with bibl. M. Olphe-Galliard, SJ, 'Le Père Jean-Pierre de Caussade et Madame Guyon', *Bulletin de Littérature Ecclésiastique*, 82 (1981), pp. 25–56. S. [C. ff.] Tugwell, OP, *Ways of Imperfection* (1984), pp. 208–18. Polgár, 1 (1990), pp. 473–5. M. Olphe-Galliard in *Dict. Sp.* 2 (1953), cols. 354–70, incl. full bibl.

cautel. A rubrical direction for the correct administration of the Sacraments. The word is used esp. of those prefixed to the Roman *Missal of 1570 to give the celebrant guidance in the case of accidents or defects during the service.

Cave, William (1637–1713), *patristic scholar. He was incumbent successively of Islington (1662), All Hallows the Great, Thames Street, London (1679), and Isleworth (1690). His principal writings were his *Apostolici* (1677), a history of the chief figures in the first three hundred years of the Church's existence; his *Ecclesiastici* (1682), a continuation of the *Apostolici* for the 4th cent.; and his *Scriptorum Ecclesiasticorum Historia Literaria* (pt. 1, 1688; 2, 1698), a history of ecclesiastical writers down to the 14th cent. His works were all erudite and lucidly arranged.

J. H. Overton in *DNB* 9 (1887), pp. 341–3, s.v.

Caxton, William (c.1422–91), the first English printer. After spending his early years in commerce in London, Antwerp, and Bruges, where he was Governor of the English Merchant Adventurers, he entered the service of his compatriot, Margaret, Duchess of Burgundy, for whom he made several English translations. Tiring of copying these by hand, he learnt the new art of printing at Cologne (1471–2), and introduced it into Bruges in 1473–4, producing the first book ever to be printed in English, his own translation of Raoul LeFèvre's 'The Recuyell of the Histories of Troye'. In Sept. 1476 he set up his printing press at the Almonry, Westminster, and before 13 Dec. 1476 he had published an *indulgence of *Sixtus IV (the first of his known works in England). Other works printed by Caxton include *Dictes and Sayings of the Philosophers* (1477), *Ordinale secundum Usum Sarum* [1477], G. *Chaucer's *Canterbury Tales* [1477], the first *Horae ad Usum Sarum* [1477/8], *Boethius' *Consolatio Philosophiae* [1478?], the *Golden Legend* [after 20 Nov. 1485], and St *Bonaventure's *Speculum Vitae Christi* [1486]. He was not only a printer but also a translator, editor, and moralist, and an enthusiast for standardizing the English language.

Good modern reprints exist of several of Caxton's books. His important and informative Prologues and Epilogues ed. W. J. B. Crotch (EETS 176; 1928). Pioneering study by W. Blades, *The Life and Typography of William Caxton* (2 vols., 1861–3; rev. edn., 1877). N. F. Blake, *Caxton: England's First Publisher* (1976). G. D. Painter, *William Caxton: A Quincentenary Biography of England's First Printer* (1976). In 1976 the quincentenary commemorations of Caxton's coming to Westminster gave rise to a large number of works, most importantly the catalogues of exhibitions held in the British Library and Cambridge University Library, 24 Sept. 1976–31 Jan. 1977, both entitled *William Caxton* and pub. in 1976. L. Hellinga, *Caxton in Focus: The Beginning of Printing in England* [1982], with important discussion of Caxton's typefaces. P. Needham, *The Printer & the Pardoner* (Washington, DC, 1986), with a list of Caxton's work, some of which he redates from watermark evidence.

CCCS. The 'Colonial and Continental Church Society'. The name under which the Intercontinental Church Society is incorporated. The society was formed by a union in 1851 of the Newfoundland School Society (founded in 1823) with the Western Australian Missionary Society (founded in 1835). It was originally intended to enable *Evangelicals of the Church of England to take an active part in the work of Church extension in the British Empire; it later provided chaplains in many places in Continental Europe, and now supports chaplains, lay workers and teachers serving English-speaking people in all parts of the world. Altered circumstances were reflected in the changes of title to 'Commonwealth and Continental Church Society' in 1958 and to 'Intercontinental Church Society' in 1979.

Ceadda, St. See CHAD, ST.

Cecilia, St (2nd or 3rd cent.). One of the most venerated martyrs in the early Roman Church. Acc. to her acts, which are apocryphal and date from about the end of the 5th cent., she converted her pagan husband, Valerian, and his brother, Tibertius, both of whom were then martyred before her, and, after herself dying for the Christian faith, was buried in the *catacomb of St Callistus. When her relics were discovered in the catacomb of Praetextatus by Paschal I (817–24), they were moved to the church which bears her name in Trastevere in the city of Rome. Here her body is said to have been found entire and uncorrupted when the church was being repaired in 1599. She is frequently represented as playing on the organ, and is the patroness of church music. Feast day, 22 Nov.

J. P. Kirsch, *Die heilige Cäcilia in der römischen Kirche des Altertums* (Studien zur Geschichte des Altertums, 4, Heft 2; 1910). P. Franchi de' Cavalieri, *Note agiografiche*, 4 (ST 24; 1912), pp. 3–38 ('Recenti studi intorno a S. Cecilia'). H. *Delehaye, SJ, *Étude sur le légendier romain: Les saints de novembre et de décembre* (Subsidia Hagiographica, 23; 1936), pp. 77–96, incl. full bibl. refs. V. L. Kennedy, CSB, *The Saints of the Canon of the Mass* (Studi di Antichità Cristiana, 14; 1938), pp. 178–82. A.

Amore, OFM, *I Martiri di Roma* (Spicilegium Pontificii Athenaei Antoniani, 1975), pp. 144–56. H. *Quentin, OSB, in *DACL* 3 (pt. 2; 1910), cols. 2712–38, s.v.; H. *Leclercq, OSB, ibid., cols. 2738–2779, s.v. 'Cécile (Crypte et Basilique de Sainte-)'.

Cedd (or Cedda), St, Bp. of the East Saxons and brother of St *Chad (q.v.). Two of his other brothers were priests. He was brought up with St Chad at *Lindisfarne under St *Aidan and in 653 was one of the four priests sent by Oswiu, King of Northumbria, to evangelize the Middle Angles. Shortly afterwards he was recalled for a similar mission to Essex and consecrated Bp. of the East Saxons in 654. Here he founded many churches and established monasteries at West Tilbury and Ythancester (Bradwell-on-Sea, the Roman Othona). On a visit to Northumbria he also founded the abbey of Lastingham, N. Yorks, of which he became the first Abbot. At the Synod of *Whitby (664) he accepted the Roman Easter. Shortly afterwards he died of the plague at Lastingham (26 Oct. 664). He is reckoned by Florence of Worcester and *William of Malmesbury (on no sufficient grounds) the second Bp. of London. Feast day, 7 Jan.

The primary authority for his life is *Bede, *HE* 3. 21–3, 25, and 4. 3; comm. by J. M. Wallace-Hadrill (Oxford, 1988), pp. 118–20 and 233. T. F. Tout in *DNB* 9 (1887), pp. 413 f., with refs.; C. P. S. Clarke in *DECH*, pp. 102 f.

Cedron. The valley or gorge on the east of *Jerusalem, between the city and the Mount of *Olives. It was the scene of the burning of an *Asherah by Asa (1 Kgs. 15: 13) and of another by Josiah (2 Kgs. 23: 6). It is mentioned only once in the NT (Jn. 18: 1; RV, 'Kidron', NEB and RSV, 'Kedron'), as the 'brook' crossed by Christ in the night before His Passion. The spelling 'Kidron' is almost consistently that of the English versions of the OT. Since the 4th cent. AD it has been identified with the 'Valley of *Jehoshaphat' (q.v.).

Ceillier, Remi (1688–1763), ecclesiastical historian. In 1705 he joined the *Benedictine monastery of Moyen-Moutier in the Vosges, in 1718 was elected prior of that of St-Jacques de Neufchâteau, and, having moved to that of Flavigny-sur-Moselle in 1724, was prior there from 1733 till his death. His *Histoire générale des auteurs sacrés et ecclésiastiques* (23 vols., 1729–63) is a remarkably full record of what is known of Christian writers down to the middle of the 13th cent. (esp. complete for the *patristic period), though somewhat diffuse in treatment.

A. Beugnet, *Étude biographique et critique sur Dom Remi Ceillier* (Mémoires de la Société des Lettres, Sciences et Arts de Bar-le-Duc, 2nd ser. 2, 10; 1891). Id. in *DTC* 2 (1905), cols. 2049–51, s.v.

celebret (Lat.), 'let him celebrate'. In the RC Church a priest is now permitted to celebrate the Eucharist, even if he is not known to the rector of the church, provided either that he presents commendatory letters (the *celebret* document) from his own *Ordinary or Superior, or that it can be prudently judged that he is not debarred from celebrating. The *celebret* should not be more than one year old (*CIC* (1983), can. 903). In the past a *celebret* was normally required unless the priest was known.

G. F. Schorr, *The Law of the Celebret: A Historical Synopsis and a Commentary* (Catholic University of America Canon Law

Studies, 332; 1952). F. Jombart in *DDC* 3 (1942), cols. 126–31, s.v.

Celestine I, St (d. 432), Pope from 422. He continued the theological policy of his predecessor, *Boniface I, by sending *Germanus of Auxerre to Britain in 429 to combat *Pelagianism, and by writing to S. Gaul in 431 against the *Scmipelagian teaching of John *Cassian. His support of the African presbyter *Apiarius, who had appealed to Rome from the Church authorities in Africa, led a Council of *Carthage of *c*.424 to protest against what they held to be an infringement of their rights. At a Roman Synod in Aug. 430, he formally condemned *Nestorius and charged St *Cyril of Alexandria with carrying through his excommunication and deposition. Feast day, in the E., 8 Apr.; in the W., formerly 6 Apr., after 1922 27 July, and now suppressed.

Letters, mostly dealing with Nestorian conflict, collected in J. P. Migne, *PL* 50. 417–558. Crit. edn. by E. *Schwartz in *ACO* 1. 1 (pt. 7; 1929), pp. 53–7, and 1. 2 (1925–6), pp. 5–101. For the text of the spurious 'Capitula Caelestini' against Semipelagianism, from the early 6th cent. attributed to this Pope, but prob. the work of *Prosper of Aquitaine, see Denzinger-Hünermann (37th edn., 1991), pp. 113–20 (nos. 238–49); M. Cappuyns, OSB, 'L'Origine des capitula pseudo-célestiniens contre le semi-pélagianisme', *R. Bén.* 41 (1929), pp. 156–70. O. Wermelinger, *Rom und Pelagius: Die theologische Position der römischen Bischöfe im Pelagianischen Streit in der Jahren 411–432* (Päpste und Papsttum, 7; 1975), pp. 244–53. C. Pietri, *Roma Christiana: Recherches sur l'Eglise de Rome ... (311–440)* (Bibliothèque des Écoles françaises d'Athènes et de Rome, 224; 2 vols., 1976), 2, pp. 955–66, 1026–43, 1130–9, and 1357–93. H. J. Vogt, 'Papst Cölestin und Nestorius', in G. Schwaiger (ed.), *Konzil und Papst ...: Festgabe für Hermann Tüchle* (1975), pp. 85–101. On the synod of 430, Hefele and Leclercq, 2 (pt. 1; 1908), pp. 260–4 and E. Amann in *Rev. S.R.* 24 (1950), pp. 28–52. B. Studer in *DPAC* 1 (1983), cols. 638 f., s.v. 'Celestino I'; Eng. tr. in *Encyclopedia of the Early Church*, 1 (1992), p. 154.

Celestine III (*c*.1106–98), Pope from 1191. Giacinto Bobone was a member of the Roman family of the Orsini. He defended *Abelard at the Council of *Sens (1140), and, after becoming a cardinal in 1144, advocated a conciliatory policy towards *Frederick Barbarossa, and urged St Thomas *Becket to adopt a less intransigent attitude towards Henry II of England. He was elected Pope in his 85th year. His reign was marked by indecision. One of his first Papal acts was the coronation as Emperor of King Henry VI, who, having failed to conquer Sicily, oppressed the Church in Germany, and caused Richard the Lion-hearted to be imprisoned on his return from the Crusade. The aged Pope failing to take prompt action, Henry once more invaded Sicily after the death of King Tancred in 1194. Having blinded Tancred's young successor, William III, committed many other cruelties, and united Sicily with the Empire, Henry calmed the Pope with feigned promises of a *Crusade. The Pope was firmer in his dealings with the matrimonial affairs of the European princes. He forced King Alfonso IX of León to give up his plan of a marriage with a Portuguese princess within the forbidden degrees, and declared invalid a divorce conceded to King Philip Augustus by his complacent French bishops. He favoured the idea of a Crusade and approved the orders of the Knights *Templar, the *Hospitallers, and the newly founded *Teutonic Order.

His registers are lost, but 330 of his letters are pr. in J. P. Migne, *PL* 206. 867–1240, and a few further docs. in *NA* 2 (1877), p. 218; 11 (1886), pp. 398 f.; and 12 (1887), pp. 411–14. Study by J. Leineweber (Jena, 1905). V. Pfaff, 'Pro posse nostro. Die Ausübung der Kirchengewalt durch Papst Coelestin III', *Zeitschrift der Savigny-Stiftung für Rechtsgeschichte*, 74, Kanonistische Abteilung, 43 (1957), pp. 89–131, and other works of this author. Mann, 10 (1914), pp. 383–441. R. Mols in *DHGE* 12 (1953), cols. 62–77; V. Pfaff in *Dizionario Biografico degli Italiani*, 23 (1979), pp. 392–8, s.v., both incl. further bibl.

Celestine V, St

Celestine V, St (*c.*1215–96), founder of the *Celestine Order and, for some months in 1294, Pope. At the age of 17 he became a *Benedictine, but his love of solitude led him to retire to Monte Morrone in the Abruzzi, where the many disciples who collected around him became the nucleus of the Celestine Order. He became very celebrated as an ascetic and seems to have had some connections with the widespread religious movement of which the '*Spiritual Franciscans' were a part. When nearly 80 he was elected Pope on 5 July 1294, through an impasse at a Papal *conclave. His pontificate was astonishing and disastrous. Naïve and ignorant of all procedure, he became a tool in the hands of Charles II of Naples, and, after alienating his supporters, abdicated on 13 Dec. of the same year. His acts were abrogated by his ambitious successor, *Boniface VIII, who also had him arrested and imprisoned in the castle of Fumone, where he died. Partly because of his sanctity, and partly as a political move against Boniface's pontificate, Celestine was canonized by *Clement V in 1313. His baptismal name was Peter, whence he is sometimes known as 'St Peter Celestine'. Feast day, 19 May, no longer in the universal calendar.

Two versions of a 14th-cent. Life in *Anal. Boll.* 9 (1890), pp. 149–200; 10 (1891), pp. 385–92; and 16 (1897), pp. 393–487, with discussion of sources, 16, pp. 365–92; and 18 (1899), pp. 34–42. F. X. Seppelt, *Monumenta Coelestiniana* (1921); F. Baethgen, *Der Engelpapst: Idee und Erscheinung* (Leipzig, 1943); A. Frugoni, *Celestiniana* (Istituto Storico Italiano per il Medio Evo, Studi Storici, fascs. 6–7; 1954); P. Herde, *Cölestin V.* (Päpste und Papsttum, 16; 1981). Mann, 17 (1931), pp. 247–341. R. Mols in *DHGE* 12 (1953), cols. 79–101; P. Herde in *Dizionario Biografico degli Italiani*, 23 (1979), pp. 402–15, s.v.

Celestine Order

Celestine Order. A congregation of the *Benedictine Order which had its origin at Monte Morrone, not far from Sulmona in Central Italy; it was founded by Peter 'del Morrone', later *Celestine V. Established in 1259, the abbey secured the approval of Pope Urban IV in 1263, and the Order was recognized by Pope *Gregory X in 1275. Its constitution, the *Instituta beati Petri*, was based on the Rule of St *Benedict, but was highly eclectic. The severity of its discipline did not prevent the Order from numbering at one time as many as 120 monasteries. It came to an end in 1785, when the last surviving house at Calavino, near Trent, was closed.

A. Moscati, 'I monasteri di Pietro Celestino', *Bulletino d'Istituto Storico Italiano per il Medio Evo*, 68 (1956), pp. 91–163. P. Schmitz, OSB, in *DHGE* 12 (1953), cols. 102–4, s.v. 'Célestins'; V. Cattana, OSB, in *DIP* 2 (1975), cols. 732–5, s.v. 'Celestini', both with bibl. The foundation of the Order is also discussed in Lives of Pope Celestine V.

Celestius

Celestius (5th cent.), heretic. A native of Britain, he was practising as an advocate in *Rome when he met *Pelagius, who induced him to turn from secular pursuits. The two men, alarmed by the low morality of their day, became convinced that it could be reformed only by stressing the responsibility of men for their actions, and so began teaching a doctrine of free will which left no room for *grace. Celestius went so far as to deny that *Baptism is for the remission of sins, and indeed that *original sin ever existed. He was condemned in Africa (whither he had migrated *c.*410) by the Council of *Carthage of 411, and retired to *Ephesus. The condemnation was reaffirmed by the Council of Diospolis (Lydda) in 415, and by two African councils in 416. Pope *Innocent I upheld this decision, but his successor, *Zosimus (417), was inclined to favour the two friends, and reversed Innocent's decree, though he was constrained to retract his decision by an Imperial decree of banishment against them. The chief opponents of Celestius and Pelagius were St *Augustine and St *Jerome. His teachings were condemned at the Council of Ephesus (431) (cans. 1 and 4).

Convenient note by A. de Veer, 'Le Dossier de Célestius', *Œuvres de Saint Augustin*, 22 (Bibliothèque Augustinienne, 1975), pp. 691 f. For other items see bibl. to PELAGIUS.

celibacy of the clergy

celibacy of the clergy. In the E., many early councils asserted or implied the right of the clergy to be married, and this position was stabilized by the Council in *Trullo of 692 (can. 13). At the Council of *Nicaea (325) a proposal to compel all clergy to give up cohabitation with their wives was rejected, and the legal position in the E. has always been the same—priests and deacons may marry before ordination, but not after. Bishops, on the other hand, must be celibate.

In the W., a legal position was gradually reached by which all the higher clergy must be celibate. The earliest canonical enactment is can. 33 of the Council of *Elvira (*c.*306). In 386 a *decretal of Pope *Siricius ordered celibacy for 'priests and levites'; this was repeated by *Innocent I (402–17). Similar legislation was introduced in Africa, which even extended to *subdeacons. *Leo the Great (440–61) forbade men to put away their wives on receiving Holy *Orders; they were to go on living with them as brother and sister. This course was open to obvious objections, and it was not long before Gallican councils refused to ordain married men before mutual vows of continence had been exchanged between them and their wives. The wives then retired to a monastery, or were enrolled in the orders of *widows or *deaconesses. Throughout the Middle Ages there were repeated efforts to enforce celibacy on those in Holy Orders, and the Second *Lateran Council of 1139 (can. 7) made the marriage of clerics not only unlawful but invalid. This legislation was repeated at the Council of *Trent. The 1983 *Codex Iuris Canonici states that clerics are bound to celibacy and that a man who has a wife is impeded from receiving orders unless he is destined for the permanent diaconate (cans. 277 and 1042). Dispensations may, however, be granted in certain cases.

Practice has not always kept pace with legislation in this matter and there have been periods in the history of the W. Church when clerical concubinage has been rife, e.g. the 10th and 15th cents. It was a matter of debate among the Schoolmen whether celibacy was enjoined on the clergy by the law of God or the law of the Church; and was decided in favour of the latter (St *Thomas Aquinas,

Summa Theol. 2. 2, q. 88, a. 11). The relation of this law of the Church to the vow of perfect chastity required of subdeacons since the 11th cent. is still the subject of dispute among canonists. The importance of the debate lies in the degree of difficulty in granting dispensations which would follow from the answer. In practice, dispensations have in the past very rarely been given, except for deacons or subdeacons who, being at the point of death, wished for conscience' sake to have their unions ratified. In recent years, however, many dispensations have been granted to priests and deacons who, having left the ministry, wished to marry, and there has been little difficulty for subdeacons who did not propose to proceed to further orders. Since the Second *Vatican Council, which reaffirmed the need for celibacy for those in *major orders, there has been much discussion and even agitation to have the law changed so that celibacy might become a genuinely free choice. A vigorous restatement of the traditional position by Pope *Paul VI in his encyclical *Sacerdotalis Caelibatus* (of 24 June 1967) failed to halt the discussion. The traditional discipline of the *Uniat Churches (a married clergy except for bishops) was specifically exempted from the Vatican Council decree and the encyclical of 1967. Popes have also allowed priests to continue in marriage who contracted marriage during schism, e.g. *Pius VII to priests who married in the French Revolution, and *Julius III to English priests who married in the reign of *Henry VIII.

In the C of E the obligation to celibacy of the clergy was formally abolished in 1549, and thereby the marriage of Abp. T. *Cranmer was technically legalized.

H. C. Lea, *History of Sacerdotal Celibacy in the Christian Church* (2 vols., 1907; hostile and uncritical in details). F. X. Funk, *Kirchengeschichtliche Abhandlungen und Untersuchungen*, 1 (1897), pp. 121–55 ('Coelibat und Priesterehe'); E. Vacandard, *Études de critique et d'histoire religieuse* (1905), pp. 69–120 ('Les Origines du célibat ecclésiastique'); R. Gryson, *Les Origines du célibat ecclésiastique du premier au septième siècle* (Recherches et Synthèses, Section d'histoire, 2; Gembloux [1970]); G. Denzler, *Das Papsttum und der Amtszölibat* (Päpste und Papsttum, 5; 2 vols., 1973–6). The encyclical *Sacerdotalis Caelibatus* is pr. in *AAS* 59 (1967), pp. 657–97. Works in the recent debate incl. E. *Schillebeeckx, OP, *Het ambts-celibaat in de branding* (Bilthoven, 1966; Eng. tr., 1968); J. Blenkinsopp, *Celibacy, Ministry, Church* (New York, 1968; London, 1969); and R. Cholij, *Clerical Celibacy in East and West* (Leominster, 1988). E. Vacandard in *DTC* 2 (1905), cols. 2068–88, s.v. 'Célibat ecclésiastique'; H. *Leclercq, OSB, in *DACL*, 2 (pt. 2, 1910), cols. 2802–32, s.v. 'Célibat', with extensive bibl.; E. Jombart and E. Herman, SJ, in *DDC* 3 (1942), cols. 132–56, s.v. 'Célibat des clercs', also with bibl. H. Thurston, SJ, in *CE* 3 (1908), pp. 481–8, s.v.; P. Delhaye in *NCE* 3 (1967), pp. 369–74, s.v. 'Celibacy, History of'.

cell. (1) The private room or apartment of a *religious of either sex. A hermit's cell and those of monastic orders leading eremitical lives, such as the *Camaldolese, were usually separate from each other. In major orders of *Benedictines and *Augustinians the stress on common life long militated against private accommodation, though under modern social conditions it is common. The cell usually contains only bare necessities.

(2) A monastic house dependent on its mother house, e.g. in the choice of its superior and control of its personnel and property. Such establishments were generally small, though some cells of the order of *Cluny were sizeable.

(3) In quite recent times the word has come into use for small groups of Christians, mainly lay people, who have pledged themselves to intensive work for the propagation of the Christian faith in the secular surroundings in which their lot is cast. The members of such cells commonly meet together frequently for prayer, study, and mutual counsel and encouragement.

cella (also **cella cemeterialis**). A small chapel erected in cemeteries in early Christian times, and intended primarily for commemorating the departed buried there. *Cellae* were often also used as places of ordinary worship.

cellarer. One of the officials or *obedientiaries in a medieval monastic community. In theory he was responsible for the catering, and his chief duty was to see that there was always sufficient food and drink ready at hand. In practice, however, the cellarer was usually responsible for almost the whole of the monastery's dealings with outside tradesmen. Items such as coal, iron, nails, wood, or wax are frequently found in his accounts. For the performance of his duties he was allowed considerable freedom from the Rule, including non-attendance at the Divine *Office and leave of absence to visit the neighbouring markets and fairs.

Celsus (2nd cent.), pagan philosopher. His 'True Discourse' ('Ἀληθὴς Λόγος) is the oldest literary attack on Christianity of which the details have survived (*c*.178). We know of it from *Origen's reply, 'Contra Celsum', in eight books, which dates from the middle of the 3rd cent. and preserves about nine-tenths of the 'Discourse'. Celsus' attitude is that of a detached pagan observer, interested in, but with no strong feelings about, religion. He praised the *Logos doctrine and the high Christian code of morals, but he objected to the exclusive claims of the Church. Making his own some of the Jewish objections to Christianity, he criticized much in biblical history for its miracles and absurdities, and expressed his repugnance to the Christian doctrines of the Incarnation and Crucifixion. Objecting that Christians, by refusing to conform to the State, undermined its strength and powers of resistance, he made an impassioned appeal to them to abandon their religious and political intolerance. All extant MSS of the 'Contra Celsum' go back to a 13th cent. archetype in the *Vatican Library (no. 386), apart from sections of the first two books preserved in a papyrus found at Toura, near Cairo, in 1941; they derive from the same line of textual tradition.

Reconstruction of 'Ἀληθὴς Λόγος by O. Glöckner (Kleine Texte, 151; 1924); also by R. Bader (Tübinger Beiträge zur Altertumswissenschaft, 33; 1940). *Editio princeps* of the 'Contra Celsum' by D. Hoeschel, Augsburg, 1605. Crit. edns. by P. Koetschau in GCS *Origenes Werke*, 1 (Leipzig, 1899), pp. 49–374, and 2 (ibid., 1899), and with Fr. tr. by M. Borret, SJ (SC 132, 136, 147, and 150; 1967–9). Papyrus text found at Toura ed. J. Scherer (Institut français d'Archéologie orientale, Bibliothèque d'études, 28; 1956). Eng. tr. of *Contra Celsum*, with valuable introd., by H. Chadwick (Cambridge, 1953; repr. with corrections, 1965), with bibl. to date. C. Andresen, *Logos und Nomos: Die Polemik des Kelsos wider das Christentum* (Arbeiten zur Kirchengeschichte, 30; 1955); F. Mosetto, *I miracoli evangelici nel dibattito tra Celso e Origene* (Biblioteca di Scienze Religiose, 76 [1986]). J. Quasten, *Patrology*, 2 (Utrecht, 1953), pp. 52–7, with further bibl. P. Merlan in *RAC* 2 (1954), cols. 954–65, s.v.

Celtic Churches. The Churches of the areas using Celtic languages—Cumbria, *Wales, Cornwall, Brittany, *Ireland, and *Scotland—were not linked by any institutional unity, nor were there any clearly defined practices common to these Churches but distinct from those of other regional Churches in early medieval Europe. Nevertheless, they all developed from the Church in late-Roman Britain in the 100 years or so after the withdrawal of the Roman government. During the late 4th cent. most evidence for the Romano-British Church comes from the towns and villas of lowland Britain where Christian symbols on silverware and mosaics reflect the religion of a wealthy class. The account of St *Germanus of Auxerre's visit to Britain (perhaps in 429) to combat *Pelagianism, and *Victricius of Rouen's references to theological dispute in the British Church suggest that it survived for at least some decades after the end of Roman rule in Britain. It was prob. trading links with Christian communities in W. Britain that carried Christianity to Ireland, so that in 431 Pope *Celestine I could send *Palladius 'to the Irish believing in Christ' as their first bishop. Later in the 5th cent., however, when St *Patrick came from Britain, Ireland was still largely pagan, and, apart from his writings, there is no evidence of the Church there until well into the 6th cent. Meanwhile, in Britain in the 5th and 6th cents., the westward expansion of the mainly pagan Anglo-Saxons pushed back the British Churches, which are depicted by *Gildas (c.540) as wealthy, worldly, and corrupt, and in contact with Continental Europe. In the west Midlands, however, the time between the defeat of the British and the arrival of St *Augustine's mission was fairly short; by c.605 he was trying to reach agreement with the British Churches at a meeting on the R. Severn. While there is some evidence of continuity of Christian life from Roman, through British, to Anglo-Saxon times, there was also deep hostility on the part of the British towards the Anglo-Saxons and hence towards the mission sent from Rome.

As the boundaries between the British and the Anglo-Saxons moved westward, the British Church increasingly directed its attention to the west. In the 6th cent. there were Christian communities in the wilder parts of Wales, Cornwall, and Galloway. A source of inspiration and renewal in all these regions was provided by *monasticism. The desire for a more devout and ascetic life led men to leave the established churches and monasteries and to set up Christian communities in remote areas. Thus, St *Samson, in his search for a religious life, left Wales, founded churches in Ireland and Cornwall, before finally settling in Brittany. St *Columba left Ireland on a life of pilgrimage in the Hebrides and Highlands of Scotland, establishing among other churches the monastery of *Iona. During the 6th and 7th cents. the major churches of Wales and Ireland were founded, many of them by saints whose careers are known only from later Lives: *Dubricius, *Illtyd, and *David in Wales; those in Ireland included *Comgall, the founder of *Bangor, from where *Columbanus went to found monasteries at *Luxeuil and *Bobbio.

For a brief period in the 6th–7th cent. the Celtic Churches shared in a common phase of development, and a letter of Columbanus (ep. 1) implies a contrast between the Celtic Churches and those of Gaul. Certain features

have been held to characterize the Celtic Churches mainly because over these matters they came into conflict with those who followed different practices which came to prevail in the W. They adhered to a different method of calculating the date of *Easter from that used by Augustine and his successors. Pope *Honorius I urged the Irish Churches not to set themselves apart from Catholic practice in this matter and by shortly after 640 the southern Irish had adopted the Roman calendar. Some of the northern Irish Churches, however, held out longer; these included Iona. The last of the British Churches conformed in 768. A subsidiary matter was the shape of the *tonsure; conformity with Roman practice spread with the adoption of the Roman date for observing Easter.

The ecclesiastical organization of the early Churches of the Celtic lands lacked the hierarchical structure of later times. Jurisdiction was centred on the bishops, but diocesan limits were not defined and monasteries tended to be the centres of ecclesiastical administration. In Ireland powers of jurisdiction were transferred to abbots, initially in priests' orders, but from the 8th cent. lay *coarbs normally controlled the *temporalia* of even the largest churches. Here the situation was complicated by political factors and the diocesan structure remained at a rudimentary level. The boundaries of many of the dioceses which were eventually established in Ireland, Brittany, and Scotland suggest that they were based on property rights rather than political divisions. With the coming of the Normans in the 11th and 12th cents. firm diocesan and metropolitan organization was established in all these Churches. See also ANGLO-SAXON CHURCH; CHURCH OF ENGLAND; IRELAND, CHRISTIANITY IN; SCOTLAND, CHRISTIANITY IN; and WALES, CHRISTIANITY IN.

L. Gougaud, OSB, *Les Chrétientés celtiques* (1911; Eng. tr., rev., 1932). J. T. McNeill, *The Celtic Churches: A History* A.D. 200 to 1200 (Chicago and London, 1974). F. E. Warren, *The Liturgy and Ritual of the Celtic Church* (Oxford, 1881; repr., Woodbridge, Suffolk, 1987, with introd. by J. Stevenson, pp. ix–cxxviii). N. K. Chadwick, *The Age of the Saints in the Early Celtic Church* (1961). H. Williams, *Christianity in Early Britain* (1912). N. K. Chadwick and others, *Studies in the Early British Church* (Cambridge, 1958); M. W. Barley and R. P. C. Hanson (eds.), *Christianity in Britain, 300–700: Papers presented to the Conference on Christianity in Roman and Sub-Roman Britain held at the University of Nottingham 17–20 April 1967* (Leicester, 1968). [A.] C. Thomas, *The Early Christian Archaeology of North Britain* (1971 [wider than its title suggests]); id., *Christianity in Roman Britain to* AD 500 (1981). S. M. Pearce (ed.), *The Early Church in Western Britain and Ireland: Studies presented to C. A. Ralegh Radford arising out of a Conference organised in his honour by the Devon Archaeological Society and Exeter City Museum* (BAR, British Series 102; 1982). S. Victory, *The Celtic Church in Wales* (1977). K. Hughes, 'The Celtic Church: Is This a Valid Concept?', *Cambridge Medieval Celtic Studies*, 1 (1981), pp. 1–20. M. Lapidge and R. Sharpe, *A Bibliography of Celtic-Latin Literature 400–1200* (Dublin, 1985).

cemetery. A place set apart for the burial of the dead. The Gk. word (κοιμητήριον) means a 'sleeping-place', and seems to have been used exclusively of Christian burial-grounds. RC canon law still insists that, where possible, the Church should have its own cemeteries or at least an area in public cemeteries which is blessed and reserved for the faithful (*CIC* (1983), can. 1240). See also BURIAL ACTS and BURIAL SERVICES.

Cenaculum. The 'upper room' or 'cenacle' in *Jerusalem (Mk. 14: 15, Lk. 22: 12, ἀνώγεον; Acts 1: 13, ὑπερῷον) in which the *Last Supper was celebrated and the Holy Spirit descended at *Pentecost. Acc. to St *Epiphanius, a small Christian church (which appears to have been the only church in Jerusalem until the early 4th cent.) existed on the spot from the time of Hadrian (117–38). Today a complex of buildings on this site includes the Dormition Abbey (1906) and Church (1900), built beside a group of structures, including that known as 'David's tomb'; an upper room in this is supposed to be the Cenaculum.

H. Vincent, OP, and F. M. Abel, OP, *Jérusalem: Recherches de topographie, d'archéologie et d'histoire*, 2: *Jérusalem nouvelle* (1926), pp. 421–81. J. [D.] Wilkinson, *Jerusalem as Jesus Knew it: Archaeology as Evidence* [1978], pp. 168 f. and fig. 116. E. Power, SJ, in *Dict. Bibl.*, Suppl. 1 (1928), cols. 1064–84, s.v. 'Cénacle'.

cenobites. See COENOBITES.

censer. See THURIBLE.

censures, ecclesiastical. See PENALTIES.

Centre Party (Ger. *Zentrum*). The party founded by the Prussian Catholics in 1870–1 to counteract the anti-Catholic policy of the Conservatives and esp. of the National Liberals. Under the leadership of L. *Windthorst (q.v.) it was the most effective opponent of Bismarck in the '*Kulturkampf'. In the closing phases of the struggle the party had become so strong that the Chancellor could no longer be certain of a majority against it, and subsequently Chancellors frequently depended on it for support. During the war of 1914–18 the Centre Party moved with the democratic tide to the left and became a regular party of government in the Weimar Republic. As a denominationalist party, it had the flexibility to move right or left and at the end of the Weimar Republic it followed the drift to the right. Under the chancellorship of its member, H. Brüning (1930–2) it made a last effort to resist Nazism, but it governed without a majority in the Reichstag and was dependent for its powers to decree emergency legislation on the Reich President, P. von Hindenburg. In 1933 it was suppressed by A. Hitler along with the other German parties, although at the same time Hitler agreed to the Reich Concordat through which the Church hoped to be able to defend its liberties. After 1945 its place was taken by the Christian Democratic Union (*Christlich Demokratische Union*) which, unlike the Centre Party, became an interdenominational party, building on the shared experiences of Church members under the Third Reich, and rapidly established itself as the dominant party to the right of the Social Democrats and the major party of government in the Federal Republic from 1949 to 1969 and again after 1982.

K. Bachem, *Vorgeschichte, Geschichte und Politik der deutschen Zentrumspartie* (9 vols., Cologne, 1927–32). E. L. Evans, *The German Center Party 1870–1933: A Study in Political Catholicism* (Carbondale, Ill., 1981). J. K. Zeender, *The German Center Party, 1890–1906* (Transactions of the American Philosophical Society, NS 66, pt. 1; 1976); R. J. Ross, *Beleagured Tower: The Dilemma of Political Catholicism in Wilhelmine Germany* (Notre Dame, Ind., and London, 1976); D. Blackbourn, *Class, Religion and Local Politics in Wilhelmine Germany: The Centre Party in Württemberg before 1914* (New Haven, Conn., and London, 1980); R. Morsey,

Die Deutsche Zentrumspartei 1917–1923 (Beiträge zur Geschichte des Parlamentarismus und der politischen Parteien, 32; Düsseldorf, 1966); id., *Der Untergang des politischen Katholizismus: Die Zentrumspartei zwischen christlichen Selbstverständnis und 'Nationaler Erhebung' 1932/33* (Stuttgart, 1977), and other works of this author. On the Christian Democratic Union, F. Spotts, *The Churches and Politics in Germany* (Middletown, Conn. [1973]), esp. pp. 291–323; R. E. M. Irving, *The Christian Democratic Parties of Western Europe* (1979), pp. 112–63. J. K. Zeender in *NCE* 3 (1967), pp. 397–9, s.v. 'Center Party'.

Centuriators of Magdeburg. The authors of a Church history from its beginnings down to 1400, divided by 'centuries', which was pub. (in Lat.) as the *Historia Ecclesiae Christi* at Basle, 1559–74. The book, which was dominated by the rigid *Lutheranism and anti-Romanism of M. *Flacius, who co-ordinated the work, depicted the pure Christianity of the NT as coming progressively under the power of the 'Papal Antichrist' until liberated by M. *Luther. In its breadth of conception the work was a landmark in ecclesiastical history; but its inaccuracies, and esp. the liberties it took with the texts of original documents, made it an easy target for C. *Baronius in his *Annales Ecclesiastici*.

P. Polman, OFM, 'Flacius Illyricus, historien de l'Église', *RHE* 37 (1931), pp. 27–73. J. Massner, *Kirchliche Überlieferung und Autorität im Flaciuskreis: Studien zu den Magdeburger Zenturien* (Arbeiten zur Geschichte und Theologie des Luthertums, 14; 1964). H. Scheible, *Die Entstehung der Magdeburger Zenturien* (Schriften des Vereins für Reformationsgeschichte, 183; Gütersloh, 1966). See also bibl. to FLACIUS, MATTHIAS.

Cerdo (2nd cent.), Syrian *Gnostic teacher who taught in *Rome *c*.140. He maintained that the Creator God revealed in the Law of Moses and the Hebrew Prophets was to be distinguished from the Father of Jesus Christ, and also that only the soul, and not the body, will share in the resurrection. Acc. to *Irenaeus, *Marcion was one of his disciples.

The chief sources include Irenaeus, *Haer*. 1. 27 and 3. 4, *Hippolytus, *Haer*. 7. 37 and 10. 19, and *Tertullian, *Adv. Marc.* 1. 2; also (Ps.-)Tertullian, *Adv. omn. haer.* 6 (16); *Epiphanius, *Haer*. 41; these and other sources are pr. and discussed in A. *Harnack, *Marcion* (TU 45; 1921), pp. 28*–36* (Beilage 2). G. Bareille in *DTC* 2 (1905), cols. 2138 f.; E. Peterson in *EC* 3 (1950), cols. 1313 f., both s.v.

cere cloth (Lat. *cera*, 'wax'). Acc. to W. usage a cloth impregnated or smeared with wax (also known as a 'chrismale'), which is laid on the surface of the altar to prevent the linen cloths above from becoming soiled, e.g. by the holy oils used in the consecration of the *mensa.

ceremonial. In ecclesiastical usage, the performance of Divine worship with prescribed and formal actions. Strictly, 'ceremonial' is concerned with action only, the term '*ritual' being used of the form of words, but the two are often used interchangeably.

Cerinthus (*fl. c*.100), *Gnostic heretic. The source of his opinions is uncertain, but, like most Gnostics, he seems to have held that the world had been created, not by the supreme God, but either by a *Demiurge, a far less exalted being, or by angels, who had produced it out of formless matter. He taught that Jesus began His earthly life as a mere man, though at His baptism 'the Christ', a higher

Divine power, descended upon Him, only to depart from Him again before the crucifixion. His doctrines distressed the orthodox. *Polycarp, e.g., is said to have related that John, 'the disciple of the Lord', on hearing that Cerinthus was in the bath-house at *Ephesus, ran out, fearing that the house would fall on the enemy of truth (*Eusebius, *HE* 3. 28. 6). *Irenaeus (*Adv. haer.* 3. 11. 1) asserts that St John wrote his Gospel to refute Cerinthus, while the *Alogi held the curious belief that Cerinthus was himself the author of Jn. and Rev.

The chief source is Irenaeus, *Haer.* 1. 26; cf. also *Hippolytus, *Haer.* 7. 33. T. *Zahn, *Geschichte des neutestamentlichen Kanons*, 1 (1888), pp. 220–62; 2 (pt. 2; 1892), pp. 973–91. G. Bardy, 'Cérinthe', *R. Bibl.* 30 (1921), pp. 344–73. A. F. J. Klijn and G. J. Reinink, *Patristic Evidence for Jewish-Christian Sects* (Supplements to *Novum Testamentum*, 36; 1973), pp. 3–19.

Cerne, Book of. A 9th-cent. collection of non-liturgical prayers, largely Celtic in origin. The MS, which once belonged to Cerne Abbey in Dorset, is now in the Cambridge University Library (Ll. 1. 10).

The Prayer Book of Aedeluald the Bishop, commonly called the Book of Cerne, ed. A. B. Kuypers, OSB (Cambridge, 1902). Further refs. in M. Lapidge and R. Sharpe, *A Bibliography of Celtic-Latin Literature 400–1200* (Dublin, 1985), pp. 339 f. (no. 1281).

certosa. The Italian name for a *Carthusian religious house.

Cerularius. See MICHAEL CERULARIUS.

Cesarini, Julian (1398–1444), cardinal. A member of a noble Roman family, he studied at Perugia, Bologna, and Padua, where he became a friend of *Nicholas of Cusa. He later entered the service of the *Curia and was employed on several diplomatic missions. In 1419 he accompanied Branda da Castiglione on his mission against the *Hussites, and later represented Papal interests in France (1425) and England (1426). He was created cardinal *in pectore* in 1426, an appointment made public in 1430. In 1431 *Martin V made Cesarini his legate in the crusade against the Hussites and also president of the Council of *Basle. The Council was formally opened by Cesarini's deputies. When he himself returned to Basle, he solemnly inaugurated the Council on 14 Dec. 1431 and continued his leadership even when the Council had been dissolved by *Eugenius IV, though exerting himself to reconcile Pope and Council. After the transfer of the Council to Ferrara and *Florence he took a prominent part in the negotiations for the union between the Roman and Greek Churches. In 1442 he was sent to Hungary to preach the Crusade against the Turks. Through his influence King Ladislaus repudiated the Peace of Szegedin (July 1444). The war was then resumed and ended with the total defeat of the Christians at the hands of the Turks at Varna (in Bulgaria) on 10 Nov. 1444, Cesarini being killed, according to some sources, in flight after the battle.

Cesarini's correspondence with *Pius II on the Council of Basle is pr. among the latter's works (Basle, 1551). E. Hofmann, SJ (ed.), 'Ein Brief des Kardinals Julian Cesarini an Cosimo von Medici', *OCP* 5 (1939), pp. 233–5. G. Christianson, *Cesarini: The Conciliar Cardinal. The Basel Years, 1431–1438* (Kirchengeschichtliche Quellen und Studien, 10; 1979). R. Mols, SJ, in *DHGE* 12 (1953), cols. 220–49, s.v.; A. A. Strnad and K. Walsh

in *Dizionario Biografico degli Italiani*, 24 (1980), pp. 188–95, s.v., both with detailed bibl.

chaburah (cf. Heb. חֶבֶר, 'friend'). In Jewish practice a group of friends formed for religious purposes. The *Talmudic directions suggest that the chief object of such groups was to secure strict observance of the laws of ritual cleanness and of tithe, but there are indications, e.g. in the Berakôth of the *Mishnah and *Tosephta, that they also served a wider social purpose as a common weekly meal, usually on the eves of sabbaths or holy days. It has been argued that the Lord and His disciples formed such a chaburah and that the *Last Supper was a chaburah meal; the thanksgiving or blessing over the bread would then be the Jewish *berakah used when the bread was broken at the beginning of the meal, and that over the cup the berakah at the end. Further support is sought in the Gospel of St John, which avoids connecting the Last Supper with the Passover meal and asserts that the Crucifixion took place before the feast (18: 28, 19: 14), as well as in the refs. in Acts to weekly (20: 7) or daily (2: 46) Christian assemblies for the breaking of bread; these would be the continuation of the regular chaburah meal of Jesus with His disciples, but with the new significance He had given it at the Last Supper. See also KIDDUSH.

On such Jewish meals, cf. I. Elbogen, *Der jüdische Gottesdienst in seiner geschichtlichen Entwicklung* (1913). Close study of the primary sources, however, leaves it uncertain how far these groups of 'chaburoth' had any formal organization. Scholars for whom the 'chaburah' provides the setting of the Last Supper include: W. O. E. Oesterley, *The Jewish Background of the Christian Liturgy* (1925), pp. 156–93; H. *Lietzmann, *Messe und Herrenmahl* (1926), p. 250 (Eng. tr., Leiden, 1979, p. 204); R. *Otto, *Reich Gottes und Menschensohn* (1934), pp. 235 f. (Eng. tr., 1938, pp. 278 f.); and G. *Dix, OSB, *The Shape of the Liturgy* (1944), pp. 50–96. For a critique of this view, see J. Jeremias, *Die Abendmahlsworte Jesu* (3rd edn., 1960), pp. 23–5; Eng. tr. (1966), pp. 29–31.

Chad (also **Ceadda**), **St**, (d. 672), Bp. of *Lichfield and brother of St *Cedd. He was a native of Northumbria and a pupil of St *Aidan at *Lindisfarne. In 664 on his brother's death he became Abbot of Lastingham, N. Yorks. Shortly afterwards he was irregularly made Bp. of the Northumbrians, with his see at *York, by King Oswiu, the King having become impatient at the absence of St *Wilfrid, who had originally been appointed to the see but had gone to France to receive consecration. On Wilfrid's return Abp. *Theodore denied the legitimacy of Chad's appointment, and he nobly accepted this decision and in 669 retired to Lastingham. Impressed by his humility, Theodore regularized his consecration and later in the same year provided for him to be Bp. of the Mercians. Fixing his see at Lichfield, Chad was tireless in spreading the Gospel and journeyed as far afield as N. Lincolnshire, where he is said to have founded the monastery at Barrow. Feast day, 2 Mar.

The main source for his life is *Bede, *HE* 3. 23, 28, and 4. 2 f.; comm. by J. M. Wallace-Hadrill (Oxford, 1988), pp. 133 and 139–41, with refs. *AASS*, Mar. 1 (1668), pp. 143–5. R. H. Warner, *Life and Legends of St Chad, Bishop of Lichfield 669–672* [1871]. Short study by H. E. Savage (York Minster Historical Tracts, 4 [1928]). B. S. Benedikz, 'St Chad—Patron of Mercia', *Eastern Churches News Letter*, NS 4 (1977), pp. 11–20. W. R. W. Stephens in *DNB* 9 (1887), pp. 391–3, s.v. 'Ceadda'.

Chalcedon, Council of (AD 451). The Fourth *Oecumenical Council, held in the city of Chalcedon in Asia Minor, nearly opposite Byzantium. It was convoked by the Emp. *Marcian to deal with the *Eutychian heresy. At the first meeting, held on 8 Oct. 451, some 500–600 bishops were present, all of them Easterns except two bishops from the province of Africa and the two Papal legates, *Paschasinus and Boniface. The decisions of the *Latrocinium (449) were annulled and Eutyches was condemned. The Council then drew up a statement of faith, the so-called *Chalcedonian Definition, and made a large number of important enactments. All the dogmatic decisions of the Council were accepted by the W. Church, but can. 28, which made the see of *Constantinople second only to that of Rome and gave its bishop the exclusive right to ordain the metropolitans of Pontus, Asia, and Thrace (a canon which had been opposed by the Roman legates), was rejected in the W., in order (it was stated) to protect the interests of the older E. patriarchates. See also following entry.

Hardouin, 2, cols. 662–772; Mansi, 6 (1761), cols. 529–1230, and 7 (1762), cols. 1–872. Canons, Definition, and the *Tome of Leo, with Eng. tr., in Tanner, *Decrees* (1990), pp. 75–103. Crit. edn. of *Acta* ed. E. *Schwartz, *ACO* 2 (1932–8: 1. Acta Graeca. 2. Versiones Particulares. 3. Versio Antiqua a Rustico Correcta. 4. Leonis Papae I Epistolarum Collectiones. 5. Codex Encyclicus. 6. Indices). Fr. tr. of Greek text of Acts by A. J. Festugière, *Éphèse et Chalcédoine, Actes des Conciles* (1982), pp. 654–895; id., *Actes du Concile de Chalcédoine, Sessions III–VI (La Définition de la Foi)* (Cahiers d'Orientalisme, 4; Geneva, 1983), with preface by H. Chadwick, pp. 7–16. Hefele and Leclercq, 2 (2) (1908), pp. 649–857, with full bibl., pp. 650 f. E. Caspar, *Geschichte des Papsttums*, 1 (1930), pp. 511–531. A. Grillmeier, SJ, and H. Bacht, SJ (eds.), *Das Konzil von Chalcedon* (3 vols., 1951–4). R. V. Sellers, *The Council of Chalcedon* (1953). P.-T. Camelot, OP, *Éphèse et Chalcédoine* (Histoire des Conciles Œcuméniques, 2; 1962), pp. 79–182 and 209–35. S. O. Horn, *Petrou Kathedra: Der Bischof von Rom und die Synoden von Ephesus (449) und Chalcedon* (Konfessionskundliche und kontroverstheologische Studien, 45; Paderborn, 1982), pp. 143–250. *CPG* 4 (1980), pp. 82–155 (nos. 8945–9307). J. Bois in *DTC* 2 (1905), cols. 2190–208, s.v. 'Chalcédoine (Concile de)'; M. Jugie, AA, in *EC* 3 (1950), cols. 324–8; P.-T. Camelot, OP, in *NCE* 3 (1967), pp. 423–6, s.v. See also works cited under the following entry.

Chalcedon, the Definition of. The statement of the Catholic Faith made by the Council of Chalcedon of 451, and eventually accepted in both E. and W., except by the *Oriental Orthodox Churches. It reaffirms the definitions of *Nicaea and *Constantinople, asserting them to be a sufficient account of the orthodox faith about the Person of Christ, but declares that the new errors of *Nestorius and *Eutyches must be formally repudiated. It therefore expressly excluded the views (1) of those who deny the title *Theotokos ('Mother of God') to the Virgin *Mary, thereby implying that the humanity of Christ is separable from His Divine Person; and (2) of those who confuse the Divine and human natures in one, and therefore hold that the Divine nature is by this confusion passible. The synodical Epistles of *Cyril to Nestorius and to the Easterns, and the Epistle of *Leo to *Flavian (the *Tome), are reasserted; the duality of Sons, the passibility of the Godhead, any mixture or confusion of the two natures, the thesis that Christ's human nature has a different source from ours (e.g. a heavenly source), and the doctrine which holds

that the two natures existed before the union but became one at the Incarnation, are rejected. Christ is declared to be one Person in two Natures, the Divine of the same substance as the Father (ὁμοούσιος τῷ πατρί), the human of the same substance as us (ὁμοούσιος ἡμῖν), which are united unconfusedly, unchangeably, indivisibly, inseparably (ἀσυγχύτως, ἀτρέπτως, ἀδιαιρέτως, ἀχωρίστως).

It seems clear that its purpose was to define the limits of legitimate speculation rather than to make an exact and final statement of a theological position. Even so, it did not prove universally acceptable, and for two centuries after the Council Christendom was torn by the *Monophysite and *Monothelite controversies. From the end of the 7th cent., however, it has been generally received both in E. and W., except among the Oriental Orthodox Churches; and its theological standpoint was in the 8th cent. expressed in systematic form by St *John of Damascus in his 'De Fide Orthodoxa'.

The text is incl. in all edns. of the Acta (see previous bibl.). Only crit. edn. of Gk. text in *ACO* 2. 1 (2), 1933, pp. 126–30; the early Lat. versions (Versio Antiqua, Versio Rustica) are also pr. by E. Schwartz, ibid. 2 (3). F. E. *Brightman, 'Six Notes. vi: The Definition of Chalcedon', *JTS* 29 (1927–8), pp. 164 f. I. Ortiz de Urbina, SJ, 'Das Glaubenssymbol von Chalcedon. Sein Text, sein Werden, seine dogmatische Bedeutung', in A. Grillmeier, SJ, and H. Bacht, SJ, *Das Konzil von Chalcedon*, 1 (1951), pp. 389–418. On the theology of the Definition, besides histories of doctrine and several essays in A. Grillmeier and H. Bacht, op. cit., esp. A. Grillmeier, SJ, 'Die theologische und sprachliche Vorbereitung der christologischen Formel von Chalkedon', pp. 5–202; expanded by J. S. Bowden, *Christ in Christian Tradition* (1965; 2nd edn., 1975; rev. German edn., *Jesus der Christus im Glauben der Kirche*, 1, 1979), see R. V. Sellers, *The Council of Chalcedon* (1953), esp. pp. 207–350.

Chaldean Christians. The convenient, if not very appropriate, title applied to that part of the *Church of the East in communion with the see of Rome. They fall into two main groups, those of the Middle East (esp. Iraq), and those of *Malabar. As a result of dispute over succession within the Middle Eastern group, a separate line of *Uniat Patriarchs came into existence in 1553, when Simeon Sulaqa was consecrated in Rome after submitting his profession of faith to Pope *Julius III. Over the next three cents. difficulties of communication gave rise to problems. The Sulaqa line (normally with the name Simeon) remained in communion with Rome until 1672, while members of the other line (with the name Elias) briefly entered communion with Rome on several occasions. In 1681 a new Uniat line of Patriarchs at Diyarbekr was inaugurated (with the name of Joseph), to last for well over a century. In 1830 affairs were regularized and the Uniat Patriarchate was again restored, now at Baghdad, with the title 'of Babylon'. The customs and discipline of the Chaldeans have been partially assimilated to those of the Latin rite, and they follow the *Gregorian calendar. Syriac liturgical tradition and language are, however, retained. In the Middle East the Chaldeans are said to number c.800,000. For the Indian group, see MALABAR CHRISTIANS.

D. Attwater, *The Catholic Eastern Churches* (Milwaukee, Wis. [1935]), pp. 227–41, rev. as *The Christian Churches of the East*, 1 ([Leominster] 1961; London, 1963), pp. 188–98. G. Beltrami, *La chiesa caldea nel secolo dell'unione* (Orientalia Christiana, 29, fasc. 83; 1933), with bibl. S. Bello, *La Congrégation de S. Hormisdas et l'Église chaldéenne dans la première moitié du XIX' siècle* (Orientalia Christiana Analecta, fasc. 122; 1939). H. W. Codrington, 'The Chaldean Liturgy', *The Eastern Churches Quarterly*, 2 (1937), pp. 79–83, 138–52, 202–9; A. A. King, *The Rites of Eastern Christendom*, 2 (Rome, 1948), ch. 8, pp. 251–415, with bibl. J. Habbi, 'Signification de l'union chaldéenne de Mar Sulaqa avec Rome en 1553', *L'Orient Syrien*, 11 (1966), pp. 99–132, 199–230; id., 'L'Unification de la hiérarchie chaldéenne dans la première moitié du XIX' siècle', *Parole de l'Orient*, 2 (1971), pp. 121–43, 305–27. E. Tisserant in *DTC* 11 (1931), cols. 225–323, s.v. 'Nestorienne (l'Église)'; R. Rabban and C. K. von Euw in *NCE* 3 (1967), pp. 427–32, s.v. 'Chaldean Rite', with bibl. On former Chaldean canon law see J. Dauvillier in *DDC* 3 (1942), cols. 292–388, s.v. 'Chaldéen (droit)'.

Chaldee. An obsolete and misleading name for *Aramaic (the language used in a few passages in the OT). The word appears to go back to St *Jerome and probably owes its origin to an incorrect identification of the languages referred to in Dan. 1: 4 and 2: 4 respectively.

chalice (Lat. *calix*, 'cup'). In ecclesiastical usage, the cup used to contain the wine consecrated in the Eucharist. The earliest Christian chalices were commonly of glass, though other materials were sometimes used. By the 4th cent. the precious metals had become general, and valuable chalices of gold or silver set with precious stones are mentioned by St *Augustine and St *Chrysostom. The use of materials other than metal was not forbidden, however, till the 9th cent., and has again been allowed in the RC Church since 1969. The earliest form of chalice, frequently depicted in the catacombs, consists of a bowl with two handles but without stem. In Carolingian times two types were known: ministerial chalices, used for the Communion of the people at times of general Communion (corresponding to the earlier type), and sacrificial chalices, for the use of the priest. From the 14th cent. the stem was gradually elongated, and the bowl of the chalice made smaller as Communion in one kind became universal, though a chalice of unconsecrated wine was often offered to the communicant as he left the altar. In England after the Reformation the restoration of Communion in both kinds caused the chalices of the later 16th and following cents. to be made considerably larger than before.

Rohault, 4 [1887], pp. 45–153, with plates cclxx–cccxiv; Braun, *CA* (1932), pp. 17–196, with plates 1–40. C. [C.] Oman, *English Church Plate 597–1830* (1957), *passim*. V. H. Elbern, 'Der eucharistische Kelch im frühen Mittelalter', *Zeitschrift des Deutschen Vereins für Kunstwissenschaft*, 17 (1963), pp. 1–76, 117–88. W. W. Watts, *Catalogue of Chalices and other Communion Vessels* (Victoria and Albert Museum, 1922), pp. 1–38 and 47–70. H. *Leclercq, OSB, in *DACL* 2 (pt. 2; 1910), cols. 1595–645, s.v. 'Calice', with refs.

chalice veil. A square of material, usually silk, normally corresponding in colour to the Eucharistic vestments, for some cents. used in the W. to cover the *chalice and *paten during those parts of the Mass when they were not in use, i.e. until the *offertory and after the *ablutions. It was a comparatively late ornament; its use was ordered by the Missal of *Pius V (1570). Earlier in the 16th cent. the chalice was commonly brought to the altar in a 'sacculum' or small bag, and before that it was covered only with a second folded *corporal, which was spread over it after the Communion. The rubric of the BCP, ordering that the chalice be covered with a 'fair linen cloth' may reflect this usage. The rubrics of the 1970 *Missale Romanum* make no mention of the chalice veil; in many places the chalice is now covered with a large corporal, and the chalice veil is becoming obsolescent. See also HUMERAL VEIL.

N. F. Robinson, SSJE, 'Concerning Three Eucharistic Veils of Western Use', *Transactions of the St Paul's Ecclesiological Society*, 6 (1906–10), pp. 129–60, esp. pp. 140–53. Braun, *LP*, pp. 213–15.

Challoner, Richard (1691–1781), author of *The *Garden of the Soul*. Born at Lewes of *Presbyterian parents, Challoner became a RC while still a boy, and at the age of 14 was sent to *Douai to be trained for the priesthood. Here he was successively student, professor, and vice-president, and did not return to England till 1730. In 1738 he deemed it wise to leave England again for a short time, owing to Conyers Middleton's resentment at a preface in which Challoner had attacked him. In 1741 he was consecrated at Hammersmith Bishop (*in partibus*) of Debra and coadjutor to the *Vicar Apostolic, Dr Petre, whom he succeeded in 1758. Challoner was the author of many books, both controversial and devotional, including a revision of the *Douai-Reims translation of the Bible. His *Garden of the Soul*, first issued in 1740 as a prayer-book for the laity, long remained one of the favourite devotional books of English RCs, though its sober liturgical content was much diluted in some later editions. His *Meditations for Every Day of the Year* (1753) also enjoyed popularity.

Life by J. Barnard (London, 1784). E. H. Burton, *The Life and Times of Bishop Challoner, 1691–1781* (2 vols., 1909); E. Duffy (ed.), *Challoner and his Church* (1981). T. Cooper in *DNB* 9 (1887), pp. 440–3; P. Chauvin, OSB, in *DHGE* 12 (1953), cols. 282–4, s.v.

Chalmers, James (1841–1901), *Congregational missionary to New Guinea. Born in the Scottish Highlands, he intended to enter the ministry of the *United Presbyterian Church, but, after acceptance by the *LMS, he pursued his studies at Cheshunt College. After ordination, he left England in 1866 and, after a long and adventurous voyage, reached Rarotonga in the *South Pacific. There he did much to render the Church indigenous before sailing, in 1877, for New Guinea. In what was then an unknown land, he slowly won the confidence of the people, so that he was able to facilitate the establishment of British rule in the south-eastern part of the country in 1888. He vigorously opposed any move to westernize the dress or customs of the people of New Guinea. Like D. *Livingstone, Chalmers stands out as a missionary-explorer, and his books, *Work and Adventure in New Guinea* (1885) and *Pioneering in New Guinea* (1887), contained much new geographical detail. His sphere of activity was constantly extending, taking in a visit to Samoa, where he made contact with R. L. Stevenson. His last ten years were devoted to the task of establishing peaceful relations with the little-contacted peoples of the Fly River region, and to this end he sailed for Goaribari Island in the Gulf of Papua, where, at Dopima, he and his party were brutally put to death.

R. Lovett, *James Chalmers, his Autobiography and Letters* (1902). D. Langmore, *Tamate—a King: James Chalmers in New Guinea 1877–1901* (Melbourne, 1974). A. R. Buckland in *DNB, 1901–1911*, pp. 343–5.

Chalmers, Thomas (1780–1847), theologian, preacher, and philanthropist. After parish ministries in Glasgow (at Tron, 1815–19, and St John's, 1819–23), he became professor of moral philosophy at St Andrews in 1823, and in 1828 of theology at Edinburgh. He was known in his early days as an able evangelical preacher, a formidable intellectual defender of Christianity, a brilliant mathematician, and a pioneer of popular education and modern methods of poor relief. But his chief importance lies in his leadership of the movement for the choice of ministers in the Established Church of Scotland by the people, and of the Free Church schism of 1843 which followed its failure. In that year he left the Established Church with a considerable body of followers, and founded the *Free Church of Scotland, becoming in the same year principal and professor of divinity at New College, Edinburgh. His theology was Calvinistic, with the stress rather on the needs of man than on the election of God. His many writings include the first of the *Bridgewater Treatises. See also DISRUPTION.

W. Hanna, *The Life and Writings of T. Chalmers* (4 vols., 1849–52); S. J. Brown, *Thomas Chalmers and the Godly Commonwealth in Scotland* (Oxford, 1982); A. C. Cheyne (ed.), *The Practical and the Pious: Essays on Thomas Chalmers (1780–1847)* (Edinburgh, 1985). W. G. Blaikie in *DNB* 9 (1887), pp. 449–54.

Chambers, John Charles (1817–74), author of *The *Priest in Absolution* (q.v.). Educated at Emmanuel College, Cambridge, he was ordained deacon in 1842 to a curacy at Sedbergh, Cumbria. On his ordination as priest in 1846 he proceeded to Perth, where he worked till 1855. From 1856 till his death he was incumbent of St Mary's, Crown Street, and warden of the 'House of Charity', both in Soho. Here he was remarkably successful as a mission priest, working esp. among the ragged children in his cure. Besides various religious writings issued under his own name, he was the anonymous author of the celebrated *Priest in Absolution* (part 1, 1866; part 2, 1870). This work was compiled at the behest of the *Society of the Holy Cross, of which Chambers was an early member.

See W. Wroth in *DNB* 10 (1887), pp. 19 f., where, however, all reference to *The Priest in Absolution* has been avoided. J. Embry, *The Catholic Movement and the Society of the Holy Cross* (1931), ch. 5, pp. 97–127.

Chambers, Robert (1802–71), Scottish publisher and author. In 1818 he began business with a bookstall in Leith Walk, Edinburgh, and eventually joined his brother, William Chambers (1800–83), in the publishing firm of W. & R. Chambers. He was the part or sole author of a great mass of encyclopaedic works. His most famous production, the *Vestiges of the Natural History of Creation* (1844), was a popular handbook of the natural sciences (geology, zoology, etc.), defending an evolutionary (essentially Lamarckian) theory of man's origin. The work attracted much controversy; but it helped to prepare the public for the Darwinian theory. Great pains were taken to preserve anonymity—it was ascribed to the Prince Consort, Charles Lyell, and others—but in Chambers's later years his authorship was widely accepted, and publicly avowed by Alexander Ireland in a posthumous edition of 1884. Chambers himself appears to have been a man of sincere piety, and to have regarded the question at issue as purely one of science.

W. Chambers (brother), *Memoir of Robert Chambers* (1872). A. Ireland, 'Story of the authorship of the "Vestiges" told for the first time', prefixed to his edn., the 12th, of Chambers, *Vestiges of the Natural History of Creation* (1884), pp. vii–xxvii. C. H. Layman (ed.), *Man of Letters: The Early Life and Love Letters of Robert Chambers* (Edinburgh [1990]). M. Millhauser, *Just Before Darwin: Robert Chambers and* Vestiges (Middleton, Conn. [1959]). F. Watt in *DNB* 10 (1887), pp. 23–5. *NCBEL* 3 (1969), cols. 1372 f. and 1605.

chancel (Lat. *cancellus*). Originally the part of the church immediately about the altar, now called the 'sanctuary'. When further space was reserved for clergy and choir westward from the sanctuary, the word was applied to this area as well, and hence is now normally employed for the entire area within the main body of the church east of the nave and transepts. In medieval times a screen often separated chancel and nave, and some modern churches have followed this arrangement. In England, by custom the rector of an ancient parish used to be responsible for repairing only the chancel, while the liability for the nave fell on the parishioners. Now, unless there is a *lay rector, the parishioners bear the whole responsibility.

F. Bond, *The Chancel of English Churches* (1916).

chancellor. In the C of E, the diocesan chancellor is the chief representative of the *bishop in the administration of the temporal affairs of his diocese; in the diocese of Canterbury he is known as the Commissary General. He is usually the sole president of the *Consistory Court (in Canterbury the Commissary Court) in *faculty cases. The office was orig. that of a private secretary; but when the *archdeacon's responsibilities extended and he lost his personal connection with the bishop, many of his former duties passed to the chancellor, who nowadays serves as the bishop's *Official Principal and his *Vicar General. The extent of his jurisdiction varies somewhat acc. to the terms of the bishop's letters patent appointing him, but once appointed his authority derives not from the bishop but from the law. Normally his chief function is the hearing of applications for and granting of faculties and, through his *surrogates, common *marriage licences. He hears, with two clerical and two lay assessors as jury, complaints against clerics under the *Ecclesiastical Jurisdiction Measure 1963, provided that these do not involve matters of doctrine, ritual or ceremonial. Under s. 2 of the same Measure he must either hold or have held high judicial office or be a barrister or solicitor of at least seven years' standing, be at least 30 years of age and, if a layman, a communicant. If the bishop fails to appoint a chancellor, it falls to the *metropolitan to do so.

The title is also held by residentiary canons in some *cathedrals. In those of the Old Foundation the chancellor is one of the four principal dignitaries, dean, precentor, chancellor, and treasurer. He used to be responsible for the Cathedral School and also the library. In modern times he is often assigned wider educational functions.

In the RC Church the diocesan chancellor is primarily responsible for the official archives. In the past, he was invariably a priest, but he no longer needs to be (*CIC* (1983), can. 482). In practice, considerable authority is often delegated to him by the bishop.

E. G. Moore, *Introduction to English Canon Law* (3rd edn. by T. Briden and B. Hanson, 1992), pp. 115–20; T. Coningsby, 'Chancellor, Vicar-General, Official Principal—a Bundle of Offices', *Ecclesiastical Law Journal*, 2 (1992), pp. 273–85; cf. letter by A. Pearce, ibid., pp. 383–5.

On RC chancellors, J. A. Alesandro in J. A. Coriden, T. J. Green, and D. E. Heintschel (eds.), *The Code of Canon Law: A Text and Commentary* (1985), pp. 392 f.

Chancery, Papal, the name attached, in the late 12th cent., to the Pope's secretariat. Arrangements for drafting papal letters and keeping archives are traceable to the 4th cent. and to classical models, but the titles of officers changed over the centuries. In 819 the headship passed to the librarian, and late in the 11th cent. to the chancellor. He was always a *cardinal. After vacancies, 1187–91 and 1197–1205, the office lapsed in 1216 until *Pius X revived it in 1908. Instead, a vice-chancellor (after 1295 a cardinal) ruled the Chancery. The growth of papal power depended much upon the impressive muniments in its registers and the scribal and legal expertise of its secretariat. By *John XXII's time (1316–34) *Regulae cancellariae* determined the terms on which papal graces were granted and gave the Chancery quasi-legislative power. From the 15th cent. chancery control of papal correspondence diminished and its influence was restricted by the development of new offices.

H. Bresslau, *Handbuch der Urkundenlehre für Deutschland und Italien* (2 vols. + index, 1889–1960), esp. i, pp. 158–252; 2nd edn. (1912), pp. 192–352. W. [A. C.] von Hofmann, *Forschungen zur Geschichte der kurialen Behörden vom Schisma bis zur Reformation* (Bibliothek des königlich Preussischen historischen Instituts in Rom, 12–13; 1914). R. L. Poole, *Lectures on the History of the Papal Chancery down to the Time of Innocent III* (1915), incl. refs. to earlier work. P. Herde, *Beiträge zum päpstlichen Kanzlei- und Urkundenwesen im dreizehnten Jahrhundert* (Münchener Historische Studien, Abteilung Geschichtl. Hilfswissenschaften, 1; 1961, 2nd edn., 1967). C. R. Cheney, *The Study of the Medieval Papal Chancery* (Lecture; Glasgow, 1966), with bibl. refs. F. Claeys-Bouuaert in *DDC* 3 (1942), cols. 454–7, s.v. 'Chancelier (1). De la sainte Église romaine', and ibid., cols. 464–71, s.v. 'Chancellerie'.

Channel Islands, Christianity in the. Christianity was apparently introduced into the Channel Islands about the 5th–6th cent., largely by the saints who are commemorated in many of the place-names of the islands. In 933 the islands became the property of the Dukes of Normandy, but after the Norman Conquest, when England and Normandy were united under the same sovereign, it was doubtful for some time to which part of his dominions they were conceived to belong. After the separation of England and Normandy (1204) they were annexed by *John to England. Between 1482 and 1486 the islands were granted neutrality in the English–French wars; but this neutrality was annulled by William of Orange in 1689. These changes in political status affected ecclesiastical history. The islands formed part of the diocese of Coutances (on the neighbouring mainland). At the request of Henry VII (1485–1509), Papal bulls were issued in 1496 and 1500 transferring them to *Salisbury and *Winchester respectively, but neither was effective. They were finally detached from Coutances and annexed to Winchester on the orders of *Elizabeth I in 1568–9. In the 16th cent. Protestant refugees from France and elsewhere induced the islanders to adopt *Presbyterianism; but Episcopalian polity and

canons agreeable to the standards of the C of E were imposed at the end of the reign of *James I and this has been the official creed since that time, though even now *Huguenot Protestantism is strong. The two large islands of Jersey and Guernsey each have a dean, who is also a parochial incumbent.

French trs. of the BCP for use in the Channel Islands were authorized and pub. at London in 1616 and 1667, the latter being a rendering of the 1662 Book by J. Durel. P. Falle, *An Account of the Island of Jersey* (1694), pp. 115–92 (ed. E. Durell, 1837, pp. 175–262); J. Duncan, *The History of Guernsey* (1841), pp. 314–404. On the introd. of Christianity into the Channel Islands, M. Pégot-Orgier, *Histoire des îles de la Manche* (1881), pp. 37–49; E. F. Carey, *The Channel Islands* (1904), pp. 22–32. Information on ecclesiastical history is incl. in J. Uttley, *The Story of the Channel Islands* (1966) and R. Lemprière, *History of the Channel Islands* (1974). G. R. Balleine, *A History of the Island of Jersey* (1950; rev. by M. Syvret and J. Stevens, Chichester, 1981), with account of the Reformation. H. de Sausmarez, 'Considerations on the ecclesiastical position in the Channel Islands, and particularly in Guernsey', *Transactions of La Société Guernesiaise*, 10, for 1926–9 (1931), pp. 37–45. R. D. Moore, *Methodism in the Channel Islands* (1952).

Channing, William Ellery (1780–1842), American *Unitarian pastor. He graduated at Harvard in 1798, became regent there in 1802, and in 1803 was appointed pastor of the Congregational Church in Federal Street, Boston. In the schism some time later between conservative and liberal *Congregationalists in America, Channing espoused the liberal or Unitarian cause, and preached against the doctrines of the *Trinity, the *Atonement and *total depravity. From about 1820 he was considered to be a Unitarian, and is often reckoned the greatest American Unitarian theologian; but he disapproved of Unitarianism as a sect, and regarded himself as belonging 'not to a sect, but to the community of free minds'. He 'desired to escape the narrow walls of a particular church'.

Works (5 vols., Boston, 1841; 2 vols., London, 1865). *Memoir* by William Henry Channing (3 vols., London, 1848). Other Lives by E. P. Peabody (Boston, 1880), J. W. Chadwick (ibid., 1903), A. W. Brown (Syracuse, NY [1956]), and M. H. Rice (New York [1961]). R. L. Patterson, *The Philosophy of William Ellery Channing* (New York, 1952). A. Delbanco, *William Ellery Channing: An Essay on the Liberal Spirit in America* (Cambridge, Mass., and London, 1981). T. Toulouse, *The Art of Prophesying: New England Sermons and the Shaping of Belief* (Athens, Ga., and London [1987]), pp. 75–117.

Chantal, St Jane. See JANE FRANCES DE CHANTAL, ST.

chantry. An endowment for the maintenance of priests to sing or say Mass for the souls of the founder and others nominated by him (usually his kin or friends); the body of priests so endowed; and also any chapel in which such Masses were said. The chapel usually took the form either of an altar erected in a space partitioned off for the purpose within the parent building, or of a building constructed as a 'chantry chapel', annexed to the church or detached from it. In the latter case the chantry chapel, which was often close to the churchyard or at the entrance of a bridge, might have an extra storey, designed for the more secular duties of the chantry priest.

The creation of a chantry chapel in the later Middle Ages in England required a monetary endowment for its erection and upkeep, the permission of the *ordinary, the consent of the Crown for the alienation of lands held in *mortmain, and a guarantee to the priest of the parish that the chantry priest would not interfere with his rights.

Although the erection of chantries and the endowment of chantry priests dates back to the early Middle Ages, it was only in the 14th and 15th cents. that chantries became numerous. In addition to his purely ecclesiastical duties the chantry priest often had to act as schoolmaster, curate, or chaplain. At the Reformation the fate of the chantries was not long in the balance. Under *Henry VIII, owing to the financial needs of the wars being waged against France and Scotland, the Dissolution of Colleges Act 1545 was passed, stating that the possessions of chantries were generally misapplied and vesting them in the King for the term of his life; and commissioners were appointed to inquire into their property. This Act implicitly recognized that both individuals and the government were already engaged in individual suppressions; but wholesale suppression did not occur until the passing of the Dissolution of Colleges Act 1547 under *Edward VI, which widened the scope of the foundations to be dissolved. The number of chantries and guild chapels whose endowments were confiscated remains uncertain, but it was much greater than the traditionally quoted figure of 2,374. The 1547 Act provided that the money should be applied to public and charitable purposes, but much of it merely went into the pockets of Edward VI's advisers. It was laid down, however, that pensions should be paid to the chantry priests. The chantries had frequently been educational centres, and one of the chief losses was in this sphere, though in the (comparatively few) cases where there was formal provision for schooling in the chantry foundation, they were usually refounded as grammar schools, some bearing the name of Edward VI.

A large number of the chantry certificates for different counties have been pub., e.g. F. R. Raines (ed.), *A History of the Chantries within the County Palatine of Lancaster, being the Reports of the Royal Commissioners of Henry VIII, Edward VI, and Queen Mary* (Chetham Society, 59 and 60; 1862); A. Hamilton Thompson (ed.), 'The Chantry Certificates for Leicestershire returned under the Act of 37 Henry VIII., cap. iv., with an Introduction and Supplementary Documents', in *Associated Architectural Societies' Reports & Papers*, 30 (pt. 2; 1910), pp. 463–570; A. Hussey (ed.), *Kent Chantries* (Kent Archæological Society, Records Branch, 12; 1936); C. J. Kitching (ed.), *London and Middlesex Chantry Certificates 1548* (London Record Society Publications, 16; 1980). Full list to date, under counties, in E. L. C. Mullins, *Texts and Calendars: An Analytical Guide to Serial Publications* (Royal Historical Society Guides and Handbooks, 7; 1958), and id., *Texts and Calendars II: An Analytical Guide to Serial Publications 1957–1982* (ibid. 12; 1983): see index s.v. 'Chantries' and 'Chantry'. K. L. Wood-Legh, *Perpetual Chantries in Britain*, based on the Birkbeck Lectures 1954–5 (Cambridge, 1965); A. Kreider, *English Chantries: The Road to Dissolution* (Harvard Historical Studies, 97; 1979). J. J. Scarisbrick, 'Henry VIII and the dissolution of the secular colleges', in C. Cross and others (eds.), *Law and Government under the Tudors: Essays Presented to Sir Geoffrey Elton* (Cambridge, 1988), pp. 51–66. J. T. Rosenthal, 'The Yorkshire Chantry Certificates of 1546: an Analysis', *Northern History*, 9 (1974), pp. 26–47. C. [J.] Kitching, 'The Disposal of Monastic and Chantry Lands', in F. Heal and R. O'Day (eds.), *Church and Society in England: Henry VIII to James I* (London and Basingstoke, 1977), pp. 119–36. R. Whiting, *The Blind Devotion of the People: Popular Religion and the English Reformation* (Cambridge, 1989), esp. pp. 17–47 and 83–112. A. Hamilton Thompson, *The*

Historical Growth of the Parish Church (1911), ch. 2, pp. 24–50; G. H. Cook, *Mediaeval Chantries and Chantry Chapels* (1947).

chapel. The word, which is first found in Marculfus (7th cent.), seems to derive from the temporary structure in which the Kings of France housed the 'cape' (late Lat. *cappella*, dim. of *cappa*) of St *Martin (q.v.) when carrying it on their military campaigns as a sacred relic. By an extension of use it was applied to shrines containing other relics (cf. esp. the '*Sainte-Chapelle' at *Paris, built to receive the *Crown of Thorns), and then to a variety of buildings which in various ways were less than churches. They include the following:

(1) Chapels of a private institution, such as a school, college, or hospital. Such chapels are often of imposing dimensions, e.g. those of some of the colleges at Oxford and Cambridge. (2) RC and dissenting places of worship, in distinction from the English parish churches. Before the 19th cent. the word 'church' was rarely applied to such buildings. Hence 'Church and Chapel' was a common phrase for 'Members of the C of E and Nonconformists'. In Ireland the term is still current for RC churches, though these are often larger than the Protestant churches in the same town. (3) A part of a large church, or cathedral, with a separate altar. The dedication of such chapels is commonly other than that of the main church. One of them (frequently the most considerable of them) is often dedicated to the BVM and hence known as the '*Lady Chapel' (q.v.). (4) The '*Chapel Royal', which, with the Royal *Peculiars, differs from cathedral and parish churches in being under the direct jurisdiction of the Sovereign. (5) A '*chapel of ease' (q.v.), a building for the ease of parishioners who live too far from the parish church. (6) A '*proprietary chapel' (q.v.), a church in private hands; there are very few now surviving in England.

On the Continent the word is often used for the chancel of a church. It has hence come to be applied to a (musical) choir, whether religious or secular, e.g. in *Kapellmeister* ('the master of a choir').

See also ORATORY, esp. for the RC legislation on chapels, and CHANTRY.

OED (2nd edn.), 3 (1989), pp. 24–6, s.v.

chapel of ease. A chapel subordinate to a mother church, for the ease of parishioners in prayers and preaching. Many such chapels were founded from the 12th cent. onward, and a good proportion rose by custom or express licence to parochial status and were used for the administration of the Sacraments and for burials. They proved esp. useful in the vast parishes of N. England where distance and natural obstacles made attendance at the mother church difficult, if not impossible, for many parishioners, and in areas where seasonal flooding separated communities from their main parish church. The Dissolution of Colleges Act 1547, intended to suppress chantries, also put endowed chapels in peril, but nearly all the essential ones survived, and many, such as the massive Holy Trinity, Hull, became independent parish churches. In modern times chapels of ease have usually been served by the parish clergy as opportunity allows, without the appointment of a separate priest-in-charge. See also CHANTRY.

Chapel Royal. A private chapel attached to a Royal court. In England the Chapel Royal and the Royal *Peculiars are not subject to the jurisdiction of the bishop of the diocese in which they are situated, but to the 'Dean of the Chapels Royal'. They are now regularly served by priests-in-ordinary appointed by the Crown. The present English Chapels Royal are (or are situate at) St James's Palace, Hampton Court, the Chapels Royal of St John the Evangelist and St Peter *ad vincula* within HM Tower of London, and The Queen's Chapel of the Savoy. Several of these have had a distinguished tradition of choral music. The *Sainte-Chapelle at Paris was formerly a Chapel Royal of the French court.

J. H. Denton, *English Royal Free Chapels, 1100–1300: A Constitutional Study* (Manchester, 1970). D. Baldwin, *The Chapel Royal ancient and modern* (1990).

chaplain. Orig. a priest or minister who has the charge of a *chapel (q.v.). He is ordinarily a cleric who performs non-parochial duties.

Chaplains are often appointed to monarchs, to bishops, and other high ecclesiastical dignitaries; they are also appointed to serve in various institutions, such as schools, colleges, prisons, hospitals, cemeteries, and at embassies, legations, and consulates abroad. The Indian Civil Service used to appoint a number of chaplains. In the armies, navies, and air forces of most Christian countries chaplains are appointed, both permanent and temporary. In Great Britain Army and RAF chaplains are given permanent or temporary commissions, and rank equivalent to captain or above according to seniority; in the Navy they do not hold official rank; and in all the services these chaplains are drawn from all the larger religious bodies. Chaplains appointed by the State are paid by the State, those by private persons by their employers.

A. Laurence, *Parliamentary Army Chaplains 1642–1651* (Royal Historical Society Studies in History, 59; Woodbridge, Suffolk, 1990). G. Taylor, *The Sea Chaplains: A History of Chaplains of the Royal Navy* (Oxford, 1978). G. C. Zahn, *Chaplains in the RAF: A Study in Role Tension* (Manchester [1969]).

chaplet (Fr. *chapelet*, dim. of Old Fr. *chape*, 'headgear'; hence a 'crown' or 'wreath'). The name given to the three parts into which the devotion of the *Rosary is divided, each corresponding to a set of five of the 15 *Mysteries. It thus consists of five *decades, each concerned with one Mystery, and forms a complete devotion in itself. The word is also used of the string of beads constructed to count the prayers of one complete chaplet of the Rosary devotion and sometimes to denote the devotion as a whole. (*Chapelet* is the word most commonly used in France in this last sense.) The name has also been adopted for a devotion of Rosary type taught in the C of E by Fr. M. W. T. Conran, SSJE, entitled *A Chaplet of Prayer* and sanctioned by certain bishops for public use in their dioceses. It uses different prayers and Mysteries from the customary ones.

Chapman, John (1865–1933), NT and patristic scholar. He was educated at Christ Church, Oxford, and ordained deacon in the C of E in 1889. In 1890 he joined the RC Church and in 1892 entered the *Benedictine Order. In 1913 he was sent for a year as Superior to *Caldey Island

after the community there had joined the RC Church. He became Prior of *Downside in 1922 and Abbot in 1929.

In his *John the Presbyter and the Fourth Gospel* (1911) he sought to disprove the existence of a 'John the Elder' distinct from St John the Apostle, and in *Matthew, Mark and Luke* (ed. J. M. T. Barton; 1937) to show the priority of St Matthew's Gospel to the other *Synoptists. He also endeavoured to rehabilitate the supposed interpolations in the text of St *Cyprian's 'De Unitate Ecclesiae', which appear to tell in favour of the primacy of the Pope. His other writings include *Notes on the Early History of the Vulgate Gospels* (1908), *St Benedict and the Sixth Century* (1929), and his valuable *Spiritual Letters* (1935).

The Spiritual Letters of Dom John Chapman, OSB, ed. with introd. memoir by R. Hudleston, OSB (1935). Id. in *Dict. Sp.* 2 (1953), cols. 488–92, s.v.

chapter (Lat. *capitulum*). The word is in current use in a variety of ecclesiastical senses:

(1) Orig. it denoted a section of the monastic rule, such as was daily read publicly in religious houses.

(2) The assembly of the members of a religious house to listen to this reading or for similar purposes (receiving the abbot's instructions, transacting the business of the monastery, etc.). (See also CHAPTER HOUSE.) By extension the assembly of the monks or their representatives of a whole province or order came to be referred to as a 'provincial chapter' or 'general chapter'.

(3) The members of a religious house in their corporate capacity. Hence

(4) The members of any corporate body responsible for an ecclesiastical institution. In England esp. of the body responsible for the spiritual and temporal concerns of a cathedral church. In some cathedrals two capitular bodies (the Lesser and Greater Chapters) exist, with different functions, the smaller body usually consisting of the residentiary members and being included in the larger body (whose members are commonly known as 'Prebendaries' or 'Honorary Canons').

(5) The clergy of a rural deanery meeting under the chairmanship of the *rural dean (q.v.).

For chapter and verse references in the Bible, see BIBLE DIVISIONS AND REFERENCES.

The duties of cathedral chapters in the RC Church are laid down in *CIC* (1983), cans. 503–10. On chapters in the C of E, E. G. Moore, *Introduction to English Canon Law*, 3rd edn. by T. Briden and B. Hanson (1992), pp. 40–5, with notes p. 48. A. H. Thompson in *DECH* (3rd edn., 1948), pp. 103–5; L. R. Misserey, OP, in *DDC* 3 (1942), cols. 595–610. See also bibl. to CANON.

Chapter, Little. A short lesson of a verse or two of Scripture, included in each of the Breviary *Offices except the *Office of Readings. In the 1971 Breviary it is called the 'Lectio Brevis' ('Short Reading').

chapter house. A building used for meetings of a cathedral or monastic chapter. Separate buildings for such purposes appear early in the 9th cent. They are usually rectangular in shape, but a small number of polygonal ones were built in England, mainly *c.* the end of the 13th cent.

character. In the Catholic theology of the Sacraments, the indelible quality which *Baptism, *Confirmation, and

*Ordination are held to imprint on the soul. As this character is indelible and, even after the gravest sins, including apostasy, therefore remains, none of these Sacraments can be received more than once by the same person. The doctrine received explicit formulation, largely under the influence of St *Augustine, by the Schoolmen, but it was foreshadowed from an early date by such expressions as 'the Lord's seal' (σφραγὶς τοῦ Κυρίου) applied by *Clement of Alexandria to Baptism, itself based on such NT passages as Eph. 1: 13.

Chardon, Louis (1595–1651), French spiritual theologian. In 1618 he entered the *Dominican Order in Paris, where he appears to have spent most of the rest of his life. His principal writing, *La Croix de Jésus* (1649), was little known in modern times until H. *Bremond drew attention to it. Chardon here argues that just as the grace given to Christ impelled him to choose suffering and crucifixion, and even a sense of abandonment by God, so grace in the believer typically leads to crosses and desolation, even if consolations and 'mystical phenomena' may accompany the earlier stages of the spiritual life. Through desolation the soul comes to rely on God alone, not confusing the efficacy of grace with incidental feelings. Enthusiasm is thus replaced by real inner strength and the soul is united to God in a purely supernatural way. The whole work shows a pervasive influence of St *Thomas Aquinas and the current Thomistic doctrine of grace, and also a marked dependence, probably indirect, on *Eckhart and J. *Tauler. Chardon reinterpreted the contemporary mystical doctrine of the suspension of the natural operation of the powers of the soul in a Thomistic way. He published a few other writings, including a French translation of the *Dialogue* of St *Catherine of Siena (1648) and of the *Institutions* ascribed to Tauler (1650).

Modern edn. of *La Croix de Jésus* by F. Florand, OP (Paris, 1937); review by H. D. Simonin in *Archivum Fratrum Praedicatorum*, 7 (1937), pp. 337–40. Eng. tr. of *La Croix de Jésus* by R. T. Murphy, OP, and J. Thornton (2 vols., St Louis and London, 1957–9). Bremond, 8 (1928), pp. 3–77. Series of arts. by F. Florand, OP, in *La Vie spirituelle*, Suppl. 42 (1935), pp. 15–57, 108–27; 44 (1935), pp. 17–55, 85–96; 45 (1936), pp. 22–35, 100–20; 58 (1939), pp. 33–43, incl. refs. to other works. Id. in *Dict. Sp.* 2 (1953), cols. 498–503.

charge. An address delivered by a bishop, archdeacon, or other ecclesiastical person at a *visitation of the clergy under his jurisdiction. Charges are also delivered to their ordinands by bishops (and, in the Presbyterian Church, by ministers) immediately before ordination. A charge is usually more of the nature of an admonitory exhortation than a definite command, though the latter could quite properly be conveyed through a charge. See also VISITATION.

charismata (Gk. χαρίσματα, plur. of χάρισμα, 'a gift of grace'). The blessings, spiritual and temporal, bestowed on every Christian for the due fulfilment of his vocation. In a narrower sense, the word is used esp. for the supernatural graces which individual Christians need to perform the specific tasks incumbent on them in promoting the spiritual advancement of their fellows. In 1 Cor. 12: 8–11 they are enumerated as comprising the word of wisdom, the

word of knowledge, faith, the gifts of healing, working of miracles, prophecy, discerning of spirits, tongues, and the interpretation of tongues, to which are added, in verse 28, the charismata given to Apostles, prophets, teachers, and those entrusted with the government of the Church.

A. Lemonnyer, OP, in *Dict. Bibl.*, Suppl. 1 (1928), cols. 1233–43, s.v. 'Charismes'; J. H. Crehan, SJ, in *Catholic Dictionary of Theology*, 2 (1967), pp. 19–22, s.v. 'Charisms'.

Charismatic Renewal Movement or 'Charismatic Movement', also known as 'Neo-Pentecostalism'. A loosely-structured predominantly lay movement dating from *c*.1960 in the main Churches, incl. since *c*.1967 RCs. It began in N. America and is now world-wide. It has its modern origins in *Pentecostalism, and, like it, is characterized by an emphasis on group worship and the exercise of the spiritual 'gifts' ('*charismata' or 'charisms'; see previous entry), esp. divine (or *spiritual) healing and *glossolalia (but without Pentecostalism's tight correlation of glossolalia and '*baptism in the Holy Spirit'). Since the 1970s its Pentecostal origins and 'enthusiastic' features have become less evident, and its adherents have widely emphasized its orthodoxy. In the RC Church, where (in the W.) by *c*.1980 it had become one of the main lay movements and was recognized as such by the Vatican (e.g. by representation at the 1987 Rome Synod of Bishops on the Laity), it is more structured and theologically conservative than when it first appeared.

For bibl. see PENTECOSTALISM; also K. McDonnell, *Charismatic Renewal and the Churches* (New York [1976]); A. Bittlinger (ed.), *The Church is Charismatic: The World Council of Churches and the Charismatic Movement* (Geneva, 1981).

charity (Lat. *caritas*). The greatest of the '*theological virtues'. Usually, though not consistently, it is the AV translation of ἀγάπη, the virtue of which the nature and characteristics are described by St *Paul in 1 Cor. 13. It is directed primarily towards God; but it is also owed to ourselves and our neighbours as the objects of God's love. Its natural opposite is hatred, which may also take the negative form of indifference. See also AGAPE, LOVE.

Charlemagne (*c*.742–814), 'Charles the Great', first Emperor (from 800) of what was later to be called the '*Holy Roman Empire'. The son of *Pepin III, King of the Franks, and Bertrada, he was anointed with his father and Carloman, his brother, by Pope *Stephen III in 754. On Pepin's death in 768 he and Carloman divided the kingdom between them. The death of Carloman in 771 left Charlemagne sole ruler.

For the next 28 years, Charlemagne was mainly occupied with extending his kingdom in all directions. He first subdued Lombardy, perhaps at the request of *Hadrian I. Having forced the king, Desiderius, to retire to a monastery, Charlemagne assumed the Lombard crown, and was rewarded by the Pope with the title of *patricius*. Next followed (772–85) a long series of arduous campaigns against the Saxons. In 778 Bavaria was conquered and annexed in 788, and between 791 and 796 the Avar kingdom and Pannonia fell into his hands. Meanwhile dissensions among the Muslims in Spain had tempted Charlemagne over the Pyrenees. In his first expedition (778), which was a failure, Roland, Count of the Breton March, was killed; the tradition of his campaign long survived into the Middle Ages in a romantic form through *La Chanson de Roland*. The systematic conquest of northern Spain began in 785; and eventually, in 801, Barcelona was captured and made the centre of the Spanish March. On Christmas Day 800 Charlemagne was crowned Emperor by Pope *Leo III in Rome; his title thereafter suggested a renewal of the Roman Empire, a claim which met with some disfavour in Byzantium.

In addition to his conquests and wars abroad, Charlemagne brought consistency, reform, and uniformity into his government at home, building upon the firm foundations laid by his father. His creation of a strong central government, his employment of *missi dominici* (itinerant royal legates), and his legislation in the form of *capitularies, which he issued for the peoples of all the regions under his rule, reflect the vigour of his government. His encouragement of ecclesiastical reform and patronage of letters, undertaken in consultation with his lay and ecclesiastical magnates, have rightly earned for his reign and much of the succeeding cent., the description the 'Carolingian Renaissance'. He continued to promote the reform of the Frankish Church by such measures as the restoration of the metropolitans. He was personally interested in *Adoptianism and *Iconoclasm, the main theological disputes of his day, as well as in the corrected text of the Bible prepared by *Alcuin. He was anxious to achieve liturgical uniformity and sought to promote the Roman Mass; he also made provision for a standard *homiliary and an approved collection of canon law. His patronage of the scholars who formed the palace 'school' and his remarkable collection of books in the palace library did much to stimulate learning (see CAROLINGIAN SCHOOLS). It was these achievements and his encouragement of education, rather than his conquests, which form his chief claim to fame.

Official docs. ed. E. Mühlbacher in *MGH*, Diplomata Karolina, 1 (1906), pp. 77–484. The 'Codex Carolinus' (letters from Popes Gregory II, *Zacharias, Stephen II, Paul I, Constantine II, *Stephen III, and *Hadrian I to Charles Martel, Pepin, and Charlemagne), ed. W. Grundlach in *MGH*, Epistolae, 3 (1892), pp. 469–657; the latter also ed., together with various other letters, Life by *Einhard and other primary material, by P. Jaffé, *Monumenta Carolina* (Berlin, 1867). Life by Einhard also ed. O. Holder-Egger (Scriptores Rerum Germanicarum in usum scholarum, 1911), H. W. Garrod and R. B. Mowat (Oxford, 1915), and, with Fr. tr., by L. Halphen (Les Classiques d'histoire de France au moyen âge; 1923); Eng. tr. by L. Thorpe (Harmondsworth, 1969). Eng. tr. of part of the 'Codex Carolinus' in P. D. King, *Charlemagne: Translated Sources* (privately pr., Lambrigg, Cumbria, 1987), pp. 269–307. Other primary material listed in *BHL* 1, pp. 238–45 (nos. 1577–618); *Novum Supplementum* (1986), pp. 179–86. S. Abel and B. Simson, *Jahrbücher des fränkischen Reiches unter Karl dem Grossen* (Jahrbücher der deutschen Geschichte; 2 vols., 1866–83). Modern studies incl. those of A. Kleinclausz (Paris, 1934, with good introd. on sources; see also other works of this author), J. Calmette (ibid., 1945), F. Heer (London, 1975), and P. D. King (Lancaster Pamphlet, 1986). L. Halphen, *Études critiques sur l'histoire de Charlemagne* (1921); id., *Charlemagne et l'empire carolingien* (1947, repr. with suppl. bibl., 1968); K. Heldmann, *Das Kaisertum Karls des Grossen* (Quellen und Studien zur Verfassungsgeschichte des deutschen Reiches in Mittelalter und Neuzeit, 6, Heft 2; 1928). D. Bullough, *The Age of Charlemagne* (1965; 2nd edn., 1973), with useful bibl. W. Braunfels (ed.), *Karl der Grosse: Lebenswerk und Nachleben* (4 vols. + Register, Düsseldorf, 1965–8). R. Folz, *Études sur le culte liturgique de Charlemagne*

dans les églises de l'empire (Publications de la Faculté des Lettres de l'Université de Strasbourg, fasc. 115; 1951); id., *Le Couronnement impérial de Charlemagne* (1964; Eng. tr., 1974). F. L. Ganshof, *Frankish Institutions under Charlemagne* (Providence, RI, 1968; a collection of his papers tr. into Eng.). R. McKitterick, *The Frankish Church and the Carolingian Reforms 789–895* (1977), pp. 122–33; id., *The Frankish Kingdoms under the Carolingians, 751–987* (1983), pp. 59–105. J. M. Wallace-Hadrill, *The Frankish Church* (Oxford History of the Christian Church, 1983), pp. 181–204. *Karl der Grosse: Werk und Wirkung. Exhibition Catalogue* (Aachen, 1965). B. Gebhardt, *Handbuch der deutschen Geschichte*, 1 (9th edn. by H. Grundmann; Stuttgart, 1970), pp. 169–90, with further bibl. Survey of recent work by D. A. Bullough, 'Europae Pater: Charlemagne and his Achievement in the Light of Recent Scholarship', *EHR* 85 (1970), pp. 59–105. A. P. Frutaz in *EC* 3 (1950), cols. 882–6, s.v. 'Carolomagno', on the liturgical reform of his reign, with bibl. For works on the Carolingian Renaissance see bibl. to CAROLINGIAN SCHOOLS.

Charles I (1600–49), King of Great Britain and Ireland from 1625. On his accession to the throne, Charles found a considerable party among the clergy disposed to abandon the *Calvinistic views which had been predominant under *Elizabeth I and *James I, and to welcome a theological position nearer to the Catholic tradition. The King, who personally favoured the new movement (soon labelled '*Arminianism'), took steps to silence the resulting controversy, meanwhile promoting High Churchmen to important positions, and in 1633 giving the see of *Canterbury to W. *Laud, their leader. Laud's vigorous policy in enforcing a higher standard of ceremonial and favouring Arminianism earned him wide unpopularity, while the King, whose administrative, financial, and foreign policy had been as disastrous as it had been well-intentioned, suffered with him. The fact that *Henrietta Maria was a RC added to the difficulties, since Charles, torn between her demands for complete toleration of her co-religionists and the violent anti-Popery of the mass of his subjects, unsuccessfully compromised; the only result of this policy was popular indignation at the discrepancy between the half-hearted enforcement of the recusancy laws against RCs and the rigour with which the courts of Star Chamber and *High Commission, under Laud's direction, passed sentence on *Puritans, even though such sentences were lenient in comparison with those which RCs and Puritans alike suffered under Elizabeth I.

Charles's Scottish policy was similarly unfortunate. In Scotland the earlier agitation against episcopacy had died down, but between his coronation at Edinburgh in 1633 and the Prayer Book riot there in 1637 Charles did everything to inflame it. His coronation was carried out with the fullest Anglican ceremonial; he insisted that Scotland should adopt the English or a similar Prayer Book, and conform to the Laudian usages in externals; and, worst of all, the government and policy of the Church of Scotland were to be dependent upon Canterbury or upon Scottish bishops controlled by the King and Laud. The *National Covenant of 1638, which pledged Scotland to Presbyterianism, was the outcome.

The Civil War, which broke out in England in 1642, was largely caused by ecclesiastical differences. By 1648 the defeat of Charles ensured the eclipse of the C of E and the temporary triumph of Presbyterianism. The subsequent failure of Charles to negotiate successfully with his enemies owed much to his refusal to consent to a permanent sacrifice of episcopacy in order to obtain the goodwill of the Scots and the support of the victorious English Parliamentarians. His execution, an illegal act carried through by fanatical Army leaders, has been justly considered a martyrdom, for in the end it was conditioned chiefly by his resolution to defend the Church. His character, though marred by political indecision, imprudence, and faithlessness, was, in his private life, of high moral purity and beauty. His deep sense of religious principle and personal responsibility appeared to full effect in the dignity of his last hours.

On the day of his death the *Eikon Basilike, a memoir in somewhat hagiographical terms, was published, and the dead king was widely acclaimed as a martyr. From 1662 to 1859 a special service for 30 Jan., the day of his death, was annexed to the BCP by royal mandate; it ordered an annual day of national fasting. Charles I is commemorated on 30 Jan. in the ASB, and over the ages various churches have been dedicated in his name.

C. Petrie (ed.), *The Letters, Speeches and Proclamations of King Charles I* (1935). S. R. Gardiner, *History of England from the Accession of James I to the Outbreak of the Civil War* (10 vols., 1883–4), esp. vols. 6 ff.; id., *History of the Great Civil War, 1642–1649* (3 vols., 1886–91). Modern studies by P. Gregg (London, 1981) and C. Carlton (ibid., 1983). G. Albion, *Charles I and the Court of Rome* (1935); C. V. Wedgwood, *The King's Peace, 1637–1641* (1955); id., *The King's War, 1641–1647* (1958); id., *The Trial of King Charles I* (1964). A. [J.] Fletcher, *The Outbreak of the English Civil War* (1981; repr. with corrections, 1985). N. [R. N.] Tyacke, *Anti-Calvinists: The Rise of English Arminianism c.1590–1640* (Oxford, 1987), *passim*. C. Russell, *The Causes of the English Civil War* (Ford Lectures for 1987–8; ibid., 1990), esp. pp. 109–30 and 185–211. K. Sharpe, *The Personal Rule of Charles I* (New Haven, Conn., and London, 1992). J. Davies, *The Caroline Captivity of the Church: Charles I and the Remoulding of Anglicanism 1625–1641* (Oxford Historical Monographs, 1992). V. Staley, 'The Commemoration of King Charles the Martyr', in his *Liturgical Studies* (1907), no. 6, pp. 66–83; R. A. Beddard, 'Wren's mausoleum for Charles I and the cult of the Royal Martyr', *Architectural History*, 27 (1984), pp. 36–49.

Charles II (1630–85), King of Great Britain and Ireland (in exile) from 1649; restored 1660. He took the Covenant in 1650 in order to obtain Scottish aid, but abandoned it on the failure of his invasion in 1651. Thereafter he conformed to the Anglicanism dominant at the exiled court. After the Restoration political considerations, even more than personal indifference, inclined him to a policy of toleration, to which he tried to give effect in the abortive *Declarations of Indulgence of 1662 and 1672, but the exclusive Anglican sentiment of the country prevailed in parliament, as may be seen in the *Corporation Act (1661), the Act of *Uniformity (1662), the *Conventicles Act (1664) and the *Five Mile Act (1665). The Declaration of Indulgence in 1672 marked the climax of Charles's efforts to rewrite the Restoration settlement in Church and State. It provoked considerable opposition, in which Abp. G. *Sheldon played a leading part. The parliamentary defeat of Indulgence and the imposition of the *Test Act (1673) resulted in the King's finally supporting the Anglican establishment. Under Lord Treasurer Danby and, later on, in the period of Whig aggression (1679–81) he upheld the authority of the episcopate. After the dissolution of the Oxford Parliament in 1681 the hierarchy under Abp. W.

*Sancroft attempted a pastoral reformation in the parishes and dioceses of England with the support of the court and the Tory politicians of the Church party. On his deathbed the King made a formal profession of the RC faith, out of which his successor, *James II, made religious propaganda in the next reign. See also POPISH PLOT.

A. Bryant (ed.), *The Letters, Speeches and Declarations of King Charles II* (1935). Modern Lives by A. Bryant (London, 1931; rev. edn., 1955), J. R. Jones (ibid., 1987), R. Hutton (Oxford, 1989) and J. [L.] Miller (London, 1991). D. Ogg, *England in the Reign of Charles II* (2 vols., 1935). J. R. Jones (ed.), *The Restored Monarchy 1660–1688* (1979). R. [A.] Beddard, 'The Commission for Ecclesiastical Promotions, 1681–84: an Instrument of Tory Reaction', *The Historical Journal*, 10 (1967), pp. 11–40.

Charles V (1500–58), Emperor. The eldest son of Philip of Burgundy and the grandson of *Ferdinand and *Isabella, Charles soon became the most powerful man in Europe. By 1519, when he was elected Emperor, he held (besides the county of Burgundy) the Netherlands, Spain and the Spanish American Empire, the kingdom of Naples, and had a claim to the duchy of Milan. The very extent of his power was, however, his chief source of weakness; for though in Spain and the Netherlands his centralized administration was absolute, in all his other dominions his position was weakened by enemies within and without—France, the Papacy, the Turks, and the Protestant princes. The most urgent problem that confronted him was the growth of *Lutheranism. The Diet of *Worms (1521) banned M. *Luther, but for many years Charles's other difficulties only allowed him to pursue an alternating policy of concession and repression. After 1544 he managed at last to break up the *Schmalkaldic League. The Protestants, however, soon reasserted their strength, drove the Emperor out of Germany, and at the Diet of *Augsburg (1555) forced upon him the principle of '*cuius regio, eius religio'. To avoid the anomaly of persecuting Protestants in one part of his dominions and tolerating them in another, Charles abdicated in 1556, and died in retirement at the monastery of Yuste in Estremadura.

Substantial works on Charles V include those of W. Robertson and W. H. Prescott (2 vols., London, 1857), H. Baumgarten (3 vols., Stuttgart, 1885–92), and E. Armstrong (2 vols., London, 1902). The best modern Life is that of K. Brandi (2 vols., Munich, 1937–41; Eng. tr. of vol. 1, 1939 [in effect the text, vol. 2 comprising original docs.]). *Charles-Quint et son temps: Colloques internationaux du Centre National de la Recherche Scientifique, Paris 30 septembre–3 octobre 1958* (1959); P. Rassow and F. Schalk (eds.), *Karl V: Der Kaiser und seine Zeit. Kölner Colloquium 26.–29. November 1958* (Cologne, 1960). W. Friedensburg, *Kaiser Karl V und Papst Paul III, 1534–1549* (1932). R. Carande, *Carlos V y sus Banqueros* (3 vols., 1943–67; 2nd edn., vol. 1, 1965). S. A. Fischer-Galati, *Ottoman Imperialism and German Protestantism 1521–1555* (Harvard Historical Monographs, 43; 1959), *passim*. J. Lynch, *Spain under the Habsburgs*, 1 (Oxford, 1964), pp. 68–100; 2nd edn. (1981), pp. 74–108; M. Fernández Álvarez, *L'España del Emperador Carlos V (1550–1558; 1517–1556)* (*Historia de España*, ed. R. Menéndez Pidal, 18; 1966), P. Chaunu, *L'Espagne de Charles Quint* (2 vols., 1973). S. Haliczer, *The Comuneros of Castile: The Forging of a Revolution, 1475–1521* (Madison, Wis., 1981). H. E. Koenigsberger, 'The Empire of Charles V in Europe', in G. R. Elton (ed.), *New Cambridge Modern History*, 2 (1958), pp. 301–33. E. D. McShane in *NCE* 3 (1967), pp. 503–6, with useful bibl. See also works dealing with this period cited under SPAIN, CHRISTIANITY IN.

Charles Borromeo, St (1538–84), Abp. of Milan. He was one of the leaders of the *Counter-Reformation. Born of noble parentage at Arona on Lake Maggiore, he was early destined for the priesthood, and received his first benefice at the age of 12. In 1552 he went to Pavia, where he studied civil and canon law under Alciati. In 1559 his uncle, the newly elected *Pius IV, summoned him to Rome and in 1560 created him cardinal and Abp. of Milan. He had much influence on the third and last group of sessions of the Council of *Trent. On his entry into Milan he set about a radical reformation of the see, tightening up the morals and manners of clergy and laity, and making the work of the diocese more effective. He founded an order of Oblates (modelled on the *Jesuits), established seminaries for the education of the clergy, and reorganized a Confraternity of Christian Doctrine for instructing children. He took much personal interest in the sick and the poor, notably in the plague of 1576. His reforms provoked great hostility, but his influence was felt far outside his diocese, and in particular in Switzerland. He was canonized in 1610. Feast day, 4 Nov.

Federico Borromeo (1564–1631), his cousin and successor in the see of Milan from 1595, was the founder of the Ambrosiana (q.v.; 1609). Other members of his family held high office in Church and State.

Charles Borromeo's Sermons ed. J. A. Sassi (5 vols., Milan, 1747–8). His decrees and official acts are pr. in the *Acta Ecclesiae Mediolanensis*, 2–3, ed. A. Ratti [later *Pius XI] (ibid., 1890–92). *Gli Atti della Visita Apostolica di S. Carlo Borromeo a Bergamo (1575)*, ed. A. G. Roncalli [later *John XXIII] and P. Forno (Fontes Ambrosiani, 13–17; 1936–57). Modern edn. of his 'Instructiones fabricae et supellectilis ecclesiasticae' by P. Barocchi, *Trattati d'Arte del Cinquecento*, 3 (Bari, 1962), pp. 1–113. The primary authorities are the Lives by A. Valiero (Verona, 1586), C. Bascapè (Ingolstadt, 1592), and J. P. Giussano (Rome, 1610; Eng. tr., with preface by H. E. *Manning, 2 vols., 1884). A. Sala, *Documenti circa la vita e le gesta di San Carlo Borromeo* (4 vols., 1857–62). Id., *Biographia di San Carlo Borromeo* (1858). Other modern studies by M. Yeo (London, 1938; popular), A. Deroo (Paris, 1963), and H. Jedin (tr. into Ital., Rome, 1971), with useful bibl. G. Alberigo, 'Carlo Borromeo come modello di vescovo nella Chiesa post-tridentina', *Rivista storica italiana*, 79 (1967), pp. 1031–52; P. Prodi, 'Charles Borromée, archevêque de Milan, et la papauté', *RHE* 62 (1967), pp. 379–411. J. M. Headley and J. B. Tomaro (eds.), *San Carlo Borromeo: Catholic Reform and Ecclesiastical Politics in the Second Half of the Sixteenth Century* [1988]. R. Mols, SJ, in *DHGE* 12 (1953), cols. 486–534, s.v. 'Charles Borromée'; id. in *NCE* 2 (1967), pp. 710–12, s.v. 'Borromeo, Charles'; C. M. de Certeau in *Dizionario Biografico degli Italiani*, 20 (1977), pp. 260–69, s.v. 'Carlo Borromeo, santo'.

On Federico Borromeo, *Lettere del Cardinale Federico Borromeo ai Familiari*, ed. C. Marcora (1, Milan, 1971; 2, Como [1978]). F. Rivola, *Vita di Federico Borromeo Cardinale* (Milan, 1656). P. Prodi in *Dizionario Biografico degli Italiani*, 13 (1971), pp. 33–42, s.v. 'Borromeo, Federico'.

Charles Martel (*c*.690–741), Frankish ruler. He was a son of Pepin II, Mayor of the Palace to the Merovingian kings, by a concubine, Chapaida. Between 714 and 718 he fought for leadership and control of the Frankish kingdom against his father's wife Plectrud and also against the Neustrian Franks led by the Mayor Ragamfred. Having won the support of many important bishops, abbots, and aristocrats, his position as head of the Carolingian family and as *Princeps Francorum* was assured by 723. Thereafter

he consolidated his government and conducted campaigns against the Frisians, Saxons, and Bavarians. He defeated the Arab army of Abd-ar-Rahman at the famous battle of Poitiers in 732, and he attempted, unsuccessfully, to annex Aquitaine. He enjoyed good relations with the Lombards and his support was courted by the Papacy. He afforded protection to St *Boniface and continued his family's patronage of *Echternach under St *Willibrord. He was the grandfather of *Charlemagne.

T. Breysig, *Jahrbücher des fränkischen Reiches, 714–741: Die Zeit Karl Martells* (1869), with important excursus on sources, pp. 109–15. F. Lot, C. Pfister, and F. L. Ganshof, *Les Destinées de l'empire en occident de 395 à 768* (Histoire générale, ed. G. Glotz, Histoire du moyen-âge, 1, pt. 1; 1928), pp. 294–402, *passim*, esp. pp. 394–402, with refs. J. Deviosse, *Charles Martel* (Paris, 1978). J.-H. Roy and J. Deviosse, *La Bataille de Poitiers* [1966]; M. Rouche, 'Les Aquitains ont-ils trahi avant la bataille de Poitiers? Un éclairage "événementiel" sur les mentalités', *Le Moyen Age*, 74 (1968), pp. 5–26. J. Semmler, 'Zur pippinidisch-karolingischen Suksessionskrise 714–723', *Deutsches Archiv*, 33 (1977), pp. 1–36. J. M. Wallace-Hadrill, *The Frankish Church* (Oxford History of the Christian Church, 1983), pp. 132–8. See also Lives of Boniface and Willibrord, cited s.v.

Charles, Robert Henry (1855–1931), biblical scholar. He was educated at Queen's College, Belfast, and *Trinity College, Dublin. After some years as a parish priest in London and in research at *Oxford, he became professor of Biblical Greek at Dublin in 1898. From 1906 to 1913 he was again in Oxford. In 1913 he became Canon, and in 1919 Archdeacon, of *Westminster. In matters of Jewish eschatology and apocalyptic he was the greatest authority of his day, and produced numerous scholarly editions of texts, including the *Book of *Enoch* (1893, 1912), the *Book of *Jubilees* (1895), *The Apocalypse of *Baruch* (1896), and *The *Testaments of the XII Patriarchs* (1908). General surveys and conclusions of his researches were embodied in *A Critical History of the Doctrine of a Future Life . . .*, or *Hebrew, Jewish, and Christian Eschatology* (1899; 2nd edn., 1913) and *Religious Development between the Old and the New Testaments* (1914). He is best known to non-specialist readers for *The Apocrypha and Pseudepigrapha of the Old Testament* (2 vols, 1913), a comprehensive *corpus* of texts in English translation, with introductions and notes, until recently the standard reference work of its kind.

F. C. *Burkitt in *Proceedings of the British Academy*, 17 (1931), pp. 437–45. Brief memoir by C. F. D'Arcy prefixed to Charles's *Courage, Truth, Purity* (posthumous, 1931), pp. xiii–xxxv. T. W. Manson in *DNB, 1931–1940*, pp. 169 f.

Charron, Pierre (1541–1603), French preacher and philosopher. He attended the *Sorbonne and studied law at Bourges, Orléans, and Montpellier. He was ordained as a young man (the date is not known); in 1576 he became a canon of Bordeaux, in 1594 Vicar General at Cahors, and later Canon of Condom. In the 1580s he met M. de *Montaigne, who greatly influenced him. His works, which were widely read, include *Les Trois Vérités* (1593), *Discours Chrestiens* (1601), and his most famous work, *De la Sagesse* (also 1601). Charron denounced the claims of Protestants to have established rational bases for their versions of Christianity, but he did not believe the RC Church to have been any more successful in this attempt; his negative theology led him to doubt whether human reason could, unaided, reach any certainty about God or His properties. The RC Church is, however, the vehicle of revealed truth, of which it has a monopoly. In matters of morality, where the Church gives no specific guidance, wise men follow Nature and begin to discover her precepts. Charron's sceptical Catholicism is deeply indebted to Montaigne, but he has suffered from being wrongly regarded as a mere systematizer of an impoverished version of Montaigne's thought; he was opposed by the *Jesuits and by M. *Mersenne. In 1605, soon after its second edition, De la Sagesse was put on the *Index. His posthumously published Traicté de Sagesse (1606) contains a clear statement of his beliefs.

Œuvres (Paris, 1635). J. B. Sabrié, De l'humanisme au rationalisme: Pierre Charron, (1913); J. D. Charron, The 'Wisdom' of Pierre Charron: An Original and Orthodox Code of Morality (University of North Carolina Studies in the Romance Languages and Literatures, 34; Chapel Hill, NC [1961]). E. F. Rice, Jun., The Renaissance Idea of Wisdom (Cambridge, Mass., 1958), pp. 178–207; R. H. Popkin, The History of Scepticism from Erasmus to Descartes (Assen, 1960), esp. pp. 56–63.

charterhouse, Eng. version of Fr maison chartreuse, a *Carthusian religious house. The most famous house of that name was established in 1371 just W. of Aldersgate, London, and on the site of it a chapel, almshouse, and school were founded by Thomas Sutton in 1611. The school, which in 1872 was removed to near Godalming, in Surrey, is now among the most famous of English public schools.

Charter of Love. See CARTA CARITATIS.

Chartres. The town, about 50 miles S. of Paris, has been the seat of a bishop since the late 4th cent., with some intervals. The present cathedral consists of a crypt dating from the time of Bp. *Fulbert (d. 1028) and a marvellous Gothic church above it, built and decorated between c.1130 and 1230. The particular glories of Chartres are the stained glass, much of it from the 12th and 13th cents., and the stone sculpture on the west front and the porches to the north and south transepts. The 'programme' or scheme of decoration of the west door includes the *seven liberal arts, surrounding scenes from the life of the BVM. These sculptures have focused and helped to perpetuate the belief that Chartres was a major centre of learning in the 12th cent.: one of the sources of the University of *Paris. But whereas Fulbert certainly taught at Chartres, there is no evidence that 'the school of Chartres' survived (with or without interruption) until c.1150. Only *Bernard, of whom *John of Salisbury speaks warmly, is a distinctive figure in the cathedral school in the 12th cent. Other scholars and masters, such as *Thierry, taught elsewhere, notably in Paris, and were designated 'of Chartres' from their place of origin.

G. [D. S.] Henderson, Chartres (Harmondsworth, 1968). O. [G.] von Simson, The Gothic Cathedral: The Origins of Gothic Architecture & the Medieval Concept of Order (1956), pp. 183–265. W. Sauerländer, Gotische Skulptur in Frankreich 1140–1270 (1970; Eng. tr., Gothic Sculpture in France 1140–1270, 1972), passim; A. Katzenellenbogen, The Sculptural Programs of Chartres Cathedral: Christ, Mary, Ecclesia (Baltimore, 1959). Y. Delaporte and É. Houvet, Les Vitraux de la Cathédrale de Chartres (4 vols., Chartres, 1926); L. Grodecki, Le Vitrail Roman (1977), pp. 103–12. A. Cler-

val, Les Écoles de Chartres au Moyen Age (1895). E. Jeauneau, 'Lectio Philosophorum': Recherches sur l'École de Chartres (Amsterdam, 1973). N. [M.] Häring, 'Chartres and Paris revisited', in J. R. O'Donnell (ed.), Essays in honour of Anton Charles Pegis (Toronto, 1974), pp. 268–329; R. W. Southern, 'The Schools of Paris and the School of Chartres', in R. L. Benson and G. Constable (eds.), Renaissance and Renewal in the Twelfth Century (Oxford, 1982), pp. 113–37. Y. Delaporte in DHGE 12 (1953), cols. 544–74, s.v.

Chartreuse, La Grande. See GRANDE CHARTREUSE, LA.

Chasidim (also Hasidaeans). The conservative Jews in Palestine (the name means the 'pious' or 'godly') who in the 2nd cent. BC endeavoured to maintain the traditional Hebrew Law, with its scribal interpretation, against the prevalent Greek influences. When the *Maccabees revolted under Mattathias in 167/6 against the Hellenizing party, the Chasidim at first supported him, but once religious freedom had been secured (c.162), they refused to fight for national independence. The Chasidim were probably the immediate ancestors of the party of the *Pharisees. The word was used later in other senses, e.g. as a title for Jewish mystics and as the name of a Jewish sect founded in the 18th cent.

J. Morgenstern, 'The Hasidîm—Who were they?', Hebrew Union College Annual, 38 (1967), pp. 59–73. E. *Schürer, The History of the Jewish People in the Age of Jesus Christ, rev. Eng. tr. by G. Vermes and others, 1 (Edinburgh, 1973), p. 157. See also comm. to Maccabees, cited s.v.

chasuble. The outermost garment worn by bishops and priests in celebrating the *Eucharist, and in the E. Church often also at solemn celebrations of the morning and evening offices and on certain other occasions. It is derived from the 'paenula' or 'planeta', the outdoor cloak of both sexes in the later Graeco-Roman world. In shape it was originally like a tent, with a hole for the head, but gradually it was reduced in size. This took place in the W. by the cutting away of the sides, whereas in the E., where it is known as the '*phelonion', the garment was gathered up or cut away in the front. In recent years the original form has been revived in some RC churches. In the BCP of 1549 the chasuble was retained, with the cope as an alternative; in that of 1552 it was abolished; but it has been widely held that the *Ornaments Rubric of 1559, reenacted in 1662, reimposes its use. In practice, however, it seems to have been little used, if at all, in post-Reformation times in the C of E before the ceremonial revival of the 19th cent., when decisions of the civil courts against the use of Eucharistic vestments failed to check its widespread reintroduction. The *Lutheran Church in Germany retained the chasuble for some time after the Reformation, and the Scandinavian Churches still use it.

Rohault, 7 (1888), pp. 111–81, with plates dlxi–dci. Braun, LG, pp. 149–247. On the revival of the use of the chasuble in the C of E in the 19th cent., cf. F. E. *Brightman in DECH, p. 612, s.v. 'Vestments'.

Chateaubriand, François René, Vicomte de (1768–1848), French Romantic writer. He was a native of St-Malo. In 1791 he crossed to America, but soon returned, and lived from 1793 to 1800 in England. In his later life he had a distinguished career as a politician, becoming a peer, ambassador, and foreign minister. He was buried at his own request on the island of Grand Bé, near St-Malo.

His principal religious work is his *Génie du christianisme, ou beautés de la religion chrétienne*, a brilliant rhetorical defence of Catholic Christianity, which he published in 1802 on the morrow of the *Concordat. He had been converted to a living faith in Christianity by a deep emotional crisis that followed the deaths of his mother and sister (*ma conviction est sortie du cœur; j'ai pleuré et j'ai cru*). In the *Génie* he sought to lift Christianity from the discredit into which the destructive work of the 18th-cent. rationalist philosophers had brought it by transferring the debate from the plane of reason to that of feeling. He argued that the study of history proved the Christian faith to have been the main fountain of art and civilization in Europe, by the recurrent stimulus it gave to the intellectual and spiritual aspirations of mankind. His other writings of religious significance include his novel *Les Martyrs, ou le triomphe de la religion chrétienne* (1809) and a Life of de *Rancé (1844).

The edn. of his *Œuvres complètes* (12 vols., Paris [1861]) contains numerous texts not easily available elsewhere. That of his *Correspondance générale* by L. Thomas (5 vols., Paris, 1912–24) is being replaced by the edn. of B. d'Andlau and P. Riberette (ibid., 1977 ff.). There is much autobiographical material in his *Mémoires d'outre-tombe* (MS completed 1846; 20 vols., Brussels, 1848–50; 12 vols., Paris, 1849–50; Eng. tr., 6 vols., 1902), but edns. vary considerably in their text; recent ones by M. Levaillant and G. Moulinier (2 vols., Paris, 1946) and by J.-C. Berchet (ibid., 1989 ff.). C.-A. Sainte-Beauve, *Chateaubriand et son groupe littéraire sous l'empire* (2 vols., 1861), despite its personal views, remains a classic. The innumerable modern studies include J. Lemaître, *Chateaubriand* (Paris, 1912), G. Collas and others, *Chateaubriand: Le Livre du Centenaire* (ibid. [1949]; summarizing articles), P. Moreau, *Chateaubriand, l'homme et l'oeuvre* (ibid., 1956), and G. D. Painter, *Chateaubriand: A Biography*, 1 (London, 1977 [no more pub.]). G. Bertrin, *La Sincérité religieuse de Chateaubriand* (1900); V. Giraud, *Le Christianisme de Chateaubriand* (2 vols., 1925–8). P. Moreau in *NCE* 3 (1967), pp. 519–21.

Chaucer, Geoffrey (1343/4–1400), English poet. He was the son of a London merchant. After serving as a page to Elizabeth de Burgh, countess of Ulster, he fought in France and was captured at 'Retters'. Ransomed by the King, he afterwards entered his service, and during the next 30 years was employed in various diplomatic missions. Under Richard II he was Clerk of the Works at Windsor and *Westminster.

The *Canterbury Tales* were apparently begun *c.*1387 and remained unfinished at the time of Chaucer's death. *Boethius' *De Consolatione Philosophiae*, which Chaucer translated into English, was the major influence on his religious thinking; it stimulated his engagement with problems of free will, chance, destiny, and mutability in *Troilus and Criseyde*, and gave a *Stoic colouring to the *Canterbury Tales*. In the Church as an institution Chaucer apparently has little interest; the anti-ecclesiastical satire in the General Prologue to the *Canterbury Tales* is traditional in content and is not motivated by any reforming drive. It is in the saints' legends, and the Clerk's Tale of patient Griselda, that his most profound religious vision of the power of suffering is to be found.

The *Canterbury Tales* was pr. by W. *Caxton in 1477. Crit. edns. of Chaucer's Works by W. W. Skeat (7 vols., London, 1894–7)

and F. N. Robinson (Cambridge, Mass., and London, 1933; 2nd edn., 1957) with notes and bibl. Modern edn. of *Troilus and Criseyde* by B. A. Windeatt (London, 1984). M. M. Crow and C. C. Olson (eds.), *Chaucer Life-Records* (Oxford, 1966). Modern Life by M. Chute (London, 1951). Studies by T. R. Lounsbury (3 vols., London, 1892), R. K. Root (ibid., 1906), G. L. Kittredge (Cambridge, Mass., 1915), J. M. Manly (New York, 1926), G. K. *Chesterton (London, 1932), J. Livingstone Lowes (ibid., 1934), D. S. Brewer (ibid., 1953), and M. Bowden (ibid., 1965). J. M. Manly and E. Rickert, *The Text of the Canterbury Tales* (3 vols., Chicago, 1940); W. F. Bryan and G. Dempster (eds.), *Sources and Analogues of Chaucer's Canterbury Tales* (Chicago, 1941; London, 1958). W. Clemen, *Chaucers frühe Dichtung* (1963; Eng. tr., 1963). D. W. Robertson, Jun., *A Preface to Chaucer* (Princeton, NJ, and London, 1963). C. Muscatine, *Chaucer and the French Tradition* (Berkeley and Los Angeles, 1957). E. Wagenknecht (ed.), *Chaucer: Modern Essays in Criticism* (New York, 1959). R. J. Schoeck and J. Taylor (eds.), *Chaucer Criticism* (2 vols., Notre Dame, Ind., 1960–1); R. O. Payne, *The Key of Remembrance: A Study of Chaucer's Poetics* (New Haven, Conn., and London, 1963); J. Mann, *Chaucer and Medieval Estates Satire: The Literature of Social Classes and the General Prologue to the Canterbury Tales* (Cambridge, 1973). J. D. Burnley, *Chaucer's Language and the Philosophers' Tradition* (ibid., 1979). D. Brewer (ed.), *Chaucer: The Critical Heritage* (2 vols., 1978 [repr. material dating from 1385 to 1933]). H. S. Bennett, *Chaucer and the Fifteenth Century* (Oxford History of English Literature, 2; 1947), esp. pp. 1–95. E. P. Hammond, *Chaucer: A Bibliographical Manual* (New York, 1908); D. D. Griffith, *Bibliography of Chaucer, 1908–1953* (Seattle, 1955); W. R. Crawford, *Bibliography of Chaucer, 1954–63* [1967]; L. Y. Baird, *A Bibliography of Chaucer, 1964–1973* (Boston, 1977); annual bibl. in *Studies in the Age of Chaucer* (Norman, Okla., 1979 ff.).

Chelsea, Councils of. A series of synods representing the Church of all England S. of the Humber, held in Chelsea (then quite separate from London) in the late 8th and first quarter of the 9th cent.; many of the attested meetings were also attended by the King of the Mercians. Records survive of several meetings held during this period, but the most important are those of 787 and 816. The former witnessed the elevation of *Lichfield to archiepiscopal status. The latter, besides dealing with matters of ecclesiastical organization, affirmed and extended episcopal authority over monasteries; it led to a protracted dispute between Wulfred, Abp. of *Canterbury (805–32), and Cenwulf, King of Mercia (796–821).

Acts of the 816 Council in A. W. Haddan and W. *Stubbs (eds.), *Councils and Ecclesiastical Documents Relating to Great Britain and Ireland*, 3 (1871), pp. 579–84. E. B. Fryde and others (eds.), *Handbook of British Chronology* (Royal Historical Society Guides and Handbooks, 2; 3rd edn., 1986), pp. 583–9. N. Brooks, *The Early History of the Church of Canterbury* (Leicester, 1984), pp. 175–80; C. Cubitt, *Anglo-Saxon Church Councils c.650–c.850* [1995], pp. 191–203 (both on the 816 Council).

Cheltenham List. See MOMMSEN CATALOGUE.

Chemnitz, Martin (1522–86), *Lutheran theologian. After lecturing for a short time in the philosophical faculty at *Wittenberg, where in 1553 he expounded the *Loci Communes* of P. *Melanchthon, Chemnitz left for Brunswick in 1554. Here he spent the rest of his life in a pastoral capacity, refusing the many important appointments offered him. In his *Repetitio sanae doctrinae de vera praesentia* (1561) he defended the Lutheran doctrine of the real presence of Christ in the Eucharist, including Luther's teaching on ubiquity, though he deprecated further elaboration as to the mode of the presence; and in his *Examen concilii Tridentini* (1565–73) he attacked the Council of *Trent. He also wrote an important doctrinal work on the person of Christ, *De Duabus Naturis in Christo* (1570), and took a leading part in drawing up the Formula of *Concord (q.v.). He was one of the main influences in consolidating Lutheran doctrine and practice in the generation following Luther's death. His *Loci Theologici* (pub. 1591), based on his lectures, ably defend a mainly Melanchthonian theology.

Eng. tr. of his *Examen concilii Tridentini* by F. Kramer (4 vols., St Louis, 1971–86). C. G. H. Lentz, *Dr. Martin Kemnitz* (Gotha, 1866); H. Hachfeld, *Martin Chemnitz nach seinem Leben und Wirken* (Leipzig, 1867); R. Mumm, *Die Polemik des M. Chemnitz gegen das Konzil von Trient* (1905). G. Noth, 'Peccata Contra Conscientiam', in F. Hübner (ed.), *Gedenkschrift für D. Werner Elert* (1955), pp. 211–19. E. F. Klug, *From Luther to Chemnitz on Scripture and the Word* (Grand Rapids [1971]), pp. 115–248. T. Mahlmann in *TRE* 7 (1981), pp. 714–21, with extensive bibl.

Cherubicon (Gk. χερουβικόν), also 'The Cherubic Hymn'. In the E. Church, a hymn sung at the *Great Entrance by the choir, in which the worshippers are described as the mystical representatives of the *Cherubim. It is often set to very elaborate music. On *Maundy Thursday and *Holy Saturday other texts are used instead of the Cherubicon.

Cherubim. This Heb. word, which is plural in form, denotes the second of the nine orders of *angels. In the OT they appear as God's attendants, e.g. they guard His presence from profanity (Gen. 3: 24, Ezek. 28: 14, etc.), and representations of them were set up in *Solomon's *Temple at *Jerusalem, overshadowing the *Ark (cf. Ex. 25: 18–22). It is possible that Assyrian thought exercised some influence on Jewish conceptions of the Cherubim. In Christian angelology they have usually been grouped with the Thrones and the *Seraphim, though in the earliest times they were not included in the angelic lists (which were based on Eph. 1: 21 and Col. 1: 16).

P. Dhorme, OP, and L. H. Vincent, OP, 'Les Chérubins', *R. Bibl.* 35 (1926), pp. 328–58 and 481–95. W. F. Albright, 'What were the Cherubim?', *Biblical Archaeologist*, 1 (1938), pp. 1–3; M. Haran, 'The Ark and the Cherubim: Their Symbolic Significance in Biblical Ritual', *Israel Exploration Journal*, 9 (1959), pp. 30–8, 89–94; R. de Vaux, OP, 'Les Chérubins et l'Arche d'Alliance. Les Spinx gardiens et les Trônes divins dans l'Ancien Orient', *Mélanges de l'Université Saint-Joseph*, 37 (Beirut, 1960–1), pp. 91–124. J. Trinquet in *Dict. Bibl.*, Suppl. 5 (1957), cols. 161–86, s.v. 'Kerub, Kerubim'. On their representation in art, K. Künstle, *Ikonographie der christlichen Kunst*, 1 (1928), pp. 245 f.

Chester. The city was perhaps the seat of the bishops of the kingdom of Mercia; but in the Middle Ages it ceased to be a bishopric, except between 1075 and c.1100, when the present church of St John Baptist served as the cathedral. The see was refounded in 1541 by *Henry VIII, who made the church of the dissolved abbey of St *Werburg the cathedral, under a new dedication to Christ and the BVM, and Chester has remained a bishopric ever since. In 1542 the diocese was transferred from the province of *Canterbury to that of *York; it was greatly reduced in size during the 19th cent.

R. C. Christie (ed.), *Annales Cestrienses; or, Chronicle of the Abbey of S. Werburg, at Chester* (The Record Society for the Publication of Original Documents relating to Lancashire and Cheshire, 14; 1886). T. and T. C. Hughes (eds.), *The Registers of Chester Cathedral, 1687–1812* (Parish Record Society, 1904). J. Tait (ed.), *The Chartulary or Register of the Abbey of St Werburgh, Chester* (Chetham Society, 79 and 82; 1920–3). W. *Dugdale, *Monasticon Anglicanum* (1819 edn.), pp. 370–401. R. V. H. Burne, *Chester Cathedral from its Founding by Henry VIII to the Accession of Queen Victoria* (1958); id., *The Monks of Chester: The History of St Werburgh's Abbey* (1962). S. J. Lander and others in *VCH*, Chester, 3, ed. B. E. Harris (1980), pp. 1–87 on the Pre-Reformation Church and the diocese; pp. 88–123 on RCs and Protestant Nonconformists; A. J. Kettle, ibid., pp. 124–87, on the religious houses, incl. pp. 132–46 on the abbey; and B. E. Harris, ibid., pp. 188–95, on the cathedral. F. [L. M.] Bennett, *Chester Cathedral* (Chester [1925]). H. Dauphin, OSB, in *DHGE* 12 (1953), cols. 641–5, s.v. See also bibl. to WERBURG, ST.

Chester Beatty Papyri. A group of papyrus codices, most of which were acquired in 1931 by A. Chester Beatty (d. 1968); they may have formed part of the same library as the *Bodmer papyri, in which case they are likely to have been found in Panopolis (Akhmim) rather than in the Fayûm. Though they are all imperfect, several are of substantial size. They include (1) 50 leaves (of an original 66) of Genesis, 4th cent.; (2) 27 leaves (out of 84) of Genesis, 3rd cent.; (3) 50 leaves (out of 108) of Numbers and Deuteronomy, early 2nd cent.; (4) $1\frac{1}{2}$ leaves of Ecclesiasticus, 4th cent.; (5) portions of 33 leaves (out of 104) of Isaiah, 3rd cent.; (6) two small fragments of Jeremiah, 2nd cent.; (7) 50 leaves (out of 118) of Ezekiel, Daniel, and Esther, 3rd cent.; (8) portions of 30 leaves (out of 220) of the Gospels and Acts, early 3rd cent.; (9) 86 leaves (out of 99) of the Pauline epistles, early 3rd cent.; (10) 10 leaves (out of 32) of Revelation, 3rd cent.; (11) 8 leaves containing the last 11 chapters of the apocryphal Book, 1 *Enoch, and 6 containing part of the work now known as the 'Peri Pascha' by *Melito, Bp. of Sardis, 4th cent.; (12) parts of 7 leaves of the Acts of *Phileas. Of the papyri never in Chester Beatty's possession, most of the Ezekiel is at Princeton University, and 30 leaves of St Paul, with small fragments of other MSS, at Michigan University. The age of these papyri makes them very valuable evidence for the text of the Greek Bible, since they are a century or more older than the earliest vellum MSS. They are preserved in the Chester Beatty Library in Dublin.

Biblical papyri ed. by F. G. Kenyon, 8 fascs. + parallel series of plates (London and Dublin, 1933–58). Items (1) and (2) above (*P*961 and *P*962) also ed. A. Pietersma (American Studies in Papyrology, 16; 1977). On item (9) above (*P*46), also H. A. Sanders, *A Third-Century Papyrus Codex of the Epistles of St Paul* (University of Michigan Studies, Hum. Series, no. 38; 1935); on item (7) above (*P*967), A. C. Johnson, H. S. Gehman, and E. S. Kase, *The John H. Scheide Biblical Papyri: Ezekiel* (Princeton University Studies in Papyrology, 1938); on item (11), C. Bonner and H. C. Youtie, *The Last Chapters of Enoch in Greek* (Studies and Documents, 8; 1937); on item (12) A. Pietersma, *The Acts of Phileas* (Cahiers d'Orientalisme, 7; 1984). The large and scattered lit., mainly in periodicals, is summarized by E. Vogt and A. Calderini in *EC* 2 (1949), cols. 1113–15, s.v. 'Beatty, Chester, Papyri'.

Chesterton, Gilbert Keith (1874–1936), poet and essayist. After beginning a course of training in art in 1891, he abandoned it for journalism. His defence of orthodoxy and conventionality in an individual and unconventional style soon established his literary reputation. Among those of his early works which were directly or indirectly concerned with religious topics, the best known are *Heretics* (1905) and *Orthodoxy* (1908). His poems include the hymn 'O God of earth and altar'. In his novels there is less of religious interest, though his appreciation of the RC clergy appears in the 'Father Brown' stories. In 1922 he left the C of E for the RC Church; but the change of allegiance had little effect on his style or outlook. His *Autobiography* (1936) gives an illuminating picture of literary-religious circles from *c*.1895 to his death.

Collected Works, ed. D. Dooley (San Francisco, 1986 ff.). Lives by M. Ward (London, 1944; with a further study, *Return to Chesterton*, 1952), D. Barker (London, 1973), and A. S. Dale (Grand Rapids [1982]). C. Hollis, *The Mind of Chesterton* (1970). D. J. Conlon (ed.), *G. K. Chesterton: A Half Century of Views* (Oxford and New York, 1987). J. Sullivan, *G. K. Chesterton: A Bibliography* (1958; with suppl., 1968). M. Ward in *DNB, 1931–1940*, pp. 171–5.

Chevetogne. The *Benedictine community now at Chevetogne in Belgium was founded in 1925 at Amay-sur-Meuse by L. *Beauduin in response to Pope *Pius XI's request that Benedictines should pray for Christian unity (*Equidem verba*, 21 March 1924). It moved to Chevetogne in 1939. The monks seek to establish closer relations between RC and other Churches, esp. Orthodox communities; they aim at corporate reconciliation rather than individual conversions or *Uniat status. The community is divided into two groups, the Latin and the Eastern, the one following the W. rite, the other the E. (Greek and Slavonic). Since 1926 it has published *Irénikon*.

G. [W. S.] Curtis, CR, *Paul Couturier and Unity in Christ* (1964), pp. 44–51. S. A. Quitslund, *Beauduin* (New York [1973]), esp. pp. 94–145. E. Lanne, OSB, in *DIP* 2 (1975), cols. 880–2, s.v. See also other works in bibl. to BEAUDUIN, L.

Cheyne, Thomas Kelly (1841–1915), OT scholar and critic. He was the grandson of T. H. *Horne. Educated at Worcester College, Oxford, he was successively vice-principal of St Edmund Hall (1864), Fellow of Balliol (1868), rector of Tendring, Essex (1880), and Oriel Professor of the Interpretation of Holy Scripture at Oxford (1885–1908). In 1884 he became a member of the OT Company engaged on the *Revised Version. Studies at Göttingen under H. G. A. *Ewald in 1862 having led him to a critical view of the OT, he upheld as early as 1871 the 'documentary hypothesis' of Pentateuchal sources. His mind, however, went through many phases. His pastoral work at Tendring lent his writings an evangelical and homiletic colour for some years. Later he became highly, and finally recklessly, unconventional in his biblical criticism and ideas. Among his chief writings are *Prophecies of Isaiah* (1880–1), *Hosea* (1884), *Job and Solomon* (1887), *Book of Psalms* (1888), and *Founders of Old Testament Criticism* (1893). The chief production of his last period, the *Encyclopaedia Biblica* (4 vols., 1899–1903), which he edited in conjunction with J. Sutherland Black, reflects the combination of daring and originality which marked his later work.

Much autobiographical material is to be found in the prefaces to many of his books. R. H. *Charles in *Proceedings of the British*

Academy (1915–16), pp. 545–51. A. S. *Peake in *DNB, 1912–21*, pp. 119 f.

Chicago–Lambeth Articles. See LAMBETH QUADRILATERAL.

Chichele, Henry (?1362–1443), Abp. of *Canterbury. Educated under the patronage of *William of Wykeham at Winchester and New College, Oxford, he was ordained priest in 1396. His abilities as a lawyer and diplomat soon attracted the attention of both the King and the Pope, and he became Bp. of *St Davids in 1408 and Abp. of Canterbury in 1414. In 1409 he was one of the English delegates to the Council of *Pisa. When Henry V left England for the French wars in 1414, Chichele was among those appointed to assist the Duke of Bedford in administering the kingdom. He was one of the architects of the pastoral response to the *Lollard challenge undertaken by Henry V's government, and his determined resistance to *Martin V's assault on the *Provisors legislation earned him the humiliation of seeing his legatine powers suspended and the Bp. of *Winchester and the Abp. of *York created cardinals and given precedence over him. The traditional view that he encouraged the war with France to divert attention from abuses in the Church is without contemporary support. His tenacity and endurance made the English Church more independent and improved the quality of its pastoral care. His concern for learning is attested by his foundation of the college of All Souls at Oxford (1438).

The Register of Henry Chichele, Archbishop of Canterbury 1414–1443, ed. E. F. Jacob and H. C. Johnson (*Canterbury and York Society, 42, 45, 46, and 47; 1937–47; also pub. separately, 4 vols., 1938–47). E. F. Jacob, *Archbishop Henry Chichele* (1967). R. G. Davies, 'Martin V and the English Episcopate, with Particular Reference to his Campaign for the Repeal of the Statute of Provisors', *EHR* 92 (1977), pp. 309–44. *BRUO* 1 (1957), pp. 410–12.

Chichester. A town on the site of the city of Regnum. The name is held to be derived from the Saxon, Cissa (OE *Cissaceaster*, i.e. 'Cissa's camp'), one of the three sons of Aelle (alleged founder of the kingdom of Sussex in the last quarter of the 5th cent.). The see, which was founded at Selsey by St *Wilfrid during his exile from *York, was transferred to Chichester in accordance with a decree of the Council of London of 1075. Its bishops have included St *Richard (1245–53), L. *Andrewes (1605–9), R. *Montagu (1628–38), B. *Duppa (1638–41), Henry King, poet and friend of J. *Donne (1642–69), John Lake, the *Nonjuror (1685–9), and G. K. A. *Bell (1929–58). The present diocese is conterminous with E. and W. Sussex. The cathedral was built in the 12th–13th cents. A Roman inscription, the 'Pudens Stone', which is preserved outside the Town Hall, records the gift of land for a (pagan) temple by a Pudens, son of Pudentinus, whom some have attempted to identify with the Pudens of 2 Tim. 4: 21.

Three surviving medieval episcopal registers, with other primary material, incl. muniments of the Dean and Chapter, are described in *Historical Manuscripts Commission: Report of Manuscripts in Various Collections*, 1 (1901), pp. 177–204. H. Mayr-Harting (ed.), *The Acta of the Bishops of Chichester, 1057–1207* (Canterbury and York Society, pt. 130; 1964). C. Deedes (ed.), *The Episcopal Register of Robert Rede . . ., Lord Bishop of Chichester, 1397–1415* (Sussex Record Society, 8 and 11; 1908–

10); id. (ed.), 'Extracts from the Episcopal Register of Richard Praty, S.T.P., Lord Bishop of Chichester, 1438–1445', *Sussex Record Society*, 4 (1905), pp. 83–236. The episcopal registers from 1478 are continuous. F. G. Bennett, R. H. Codrington, and C. Deedes (eds.), *Statutes and Constitutions of the Cathedral Church of Chichester* (Chichester, 1904); W. D. Peckham (ed.), *The Acts of the Dean and Chapter of the Cathedral Church of Chichester, 1472–1544 (The White Book)* (Sussex Record Society, 52; 1952); id. (ed.), *The Acts of the Dean and Chapter of the Cathedral Church of Chichester, 1542–1642* (ibid., 58; 1959 [1960]); id. (ed.), *The Chartulary of the High Church of Chichester* (ibid., 46; 1944). A. S. Duncan-Jones (ed.), *The Chichester Customary* (modern observances; *Alcuin Club Collections, 36; 1948). W. R. W. Stephens, *Memorials of the South Sussex See and Cathedral Church of Chichester* (1876). T. G. Willis, *Records of Chichester* (1928), pp. 149–220. A. S. Duncan-Jones, *The Story of Chichester Cathedral* [1933]. M. Hobbs (ed.), *Chichester Cathedral: A Historical Survey* (Chichester, 1994). W. H. Godfrey and J. W. Bloe in L. F. Salzman (ed.), *VCH*, Sussex, 3 (1935), pp. 105–60. J. Warrillow in *DHGE* 12 (1953), cols. 665–74, s.v.

Childermas. An old English name for (1) the Feast of the *Holy Innocents (28 Dec.); (2) the day of the week throughout the year on which that feast fell, widely held to be a day of ill omen.

Children, Song of the Three. See SONG OF THE THREE CHILDREN.

Children's Crusade (1212). A popular movement which arose spontaneously, and with little support or sympathy from the clergy, with the intention of recovering *Jerusalem for Christian rule. Marching from *Cologne, the main party reached Genoa, but went no further, and a French party perhaps never intended to travel to the Holy Land. The details are unclear, and the movement was embellished in later legends. It is very possible that the so-called 'children' were in reality servants, shepherds, and others outside the main structures of organized society. In any event, the episode is a striking illustration of the extent of sympathy for the crusading ideal prevalent in Europe in the early 13th cent.

The contemporary evidence, and recent discussions, are summarized in P. Raedts, 'The Children's Crusade of 1212', *Journal of Medieval History*, 3 (1977), pp. 279–323. See also general works on the CRUSADES.

Chile, Christianity in. The Spanish invasion of Chile, which began in 1535, was followed by the arrival of the first missionary priest in 1541 and the establishment of the first RC diocese (Santiago) 20 years later. The conversion of the country, carried out initially by the *Franciscan friars and the *Jesuits, was not, however, completed until the end of the 17th cent. In 1818 independence from Spain was secured, but the RC Church continued to be 'protected' and state-subsidized, though other religions were tolerated; in 1925 Church and State were officially separated, but the RC Church is still an important moral and political force in the country. Some 82 per cent of the 11 million population are nominally RC, but Mass attendance declined rapidly after 1960 and is now only about 15 per cent. There are five archdioceses, 17 dioceses, and two apostolic vicarates, with just over 2,000 priests, two-thirds of whom are members of religious orders, and 5,000 nuns. In recent years a large number of lay *catechists have been

trained. The first Protestant missionary, from the *British and Foreign Bible Society, arrived in 1821. Later in the 19th cent. *Methodist and *Presbyterian missionaries came from the USA and *Lutherans and *Baptists from Germany. *Pentecostal Churches have grown phenomenally since the 1960s and have nearly 2 million members. Non-Pentecostal Protestants form about 2 per cent of the population, the largest group being the *Seventh-day Adventists. There are just over 4,000 Anglicans in the diocese of Chile.

C. S. Cotapos, *Historia eclesiástica de Chile* (Santiago, 1925), with bibl. *La provincia eclesiástica chilena: Erección de sus obispados y división en parroquias* (Freiburg i.B., 1895). R. Poblete, *La Iglesia en Chile: Estructuras eclesiásticas* (Estudios Socio-Religiosos Latino-Americanos, 6; Fribourg, Switzerland, Bogotá, and Madrid, 1962). F. Enrich, SJ, *Historia de la Compañía de Jesús en Chile* (2 vols. only [down to 1822], Barcelona, 1891). R. Lagos, OFM, *Historia de las misiones del colegio de Chillán* (Barcelona, 1908). P. Gazulla, *Los primeros mercedarios en Chile, 1536–1600* (Santiago, 1918). B. H. Smith, *The Church and Politics in Chile: Challenges to Modern Catholicism* (Princeton, NJ [1982]). R. Muñoz, *Nueva Conciencia de la Iglesia en América Latina* (Santiago, 1973; Salamanca, 1974), *passim*. T. [R.] Beeson and J. Pearce, *A Vision of Hope: The Churches and Change in Latin America* (1984), pp. 123–52, esp. pp. 142–52. J. A. de Ramón Folch in *NCE* 3 (1967), pp. 583–7.

chiliasm (Gk. χίλιοι, 'a thousand'). Another name for *Millenarianism, the theory that Christ will return to earth and reign here for a thousand years before the final consummation of all things. The belief is based on an interpretation of Rev. 20: 1–5.

Chillingworth, William (1602–44), Anglican divine. A scholar (1618) and fellow (1628) of Trinity College, Oxford, he first attracted attention when he engaged a Jesuit, 'John *Fisher', in controversy. As a result of this incident, Chillingworth was converted to the RC Church, and went to *Douai in 1630. In the following year, however, he returned to England, and in 1634 again declared himself a Protestant. His best known work was his *Religion of Protestants a Safe Way to Salvation* (1638), written as his contribution to a controversy raging between a Jesuit, Knott, and the Provost of Queen's College, Oxford, on the subject of whether Protestants could be saved. On the plea that 'the Bible only is the religion of Protestants', he defended the rights of reason and free inquiry in doctrinal matters, and denied that any Church has the gift of infallibility. He affirmed that he belonged to the C of E, because he considered her doctrine sufficiently pure to ensure salvation, and that adequate grounds were wanting to warrant disturbing the 16th-cent. settlement. During the Civil War he was a chaplain in the Royalist army, and was captured in 1643. His death in captivity at *Chichester was said to have been hastened by the efforts of the other side to convert him.

The collected edns. of Chillingworth's Works are numbered acc. to the edns. of *The Religion of Protestants a Safe Way to Salvation*, the first to bear the title *The Works of William Chillingworth* being '7th edn.', London, 1719. Life by T. Birch, prefixed to 10th edn., London, 1742, pp. ii–viii. P. Des Maizeaux, *An Historical and Critical Account of the Life and Writings of Wm. Chillingworth* (1725; ed. J. Nichols, 1863). R. R. Orr, *Reason and Authority: The Thought of William Chillingworth* (Oxford, 1967). H. Trevor-Roper, *Catholics, Anglicans and Puritans: Seventeenth Century*

Essays (1987), no. 4 ('The Great Tew Circle'), pp. 166–230, esp. pp. 166–75, 186–92, 199–209. M. *Creighton in *DNB* 10 (1887), pp. 252–7.

chimere. A gown without sleeves, worn by Anglican bishops and by doctors of divinity. It was traditionally made of silk or satin, but other materials are now sometimes used. It perhaps derives from the tabard, a medieval upper garment. It is frequently worn at liturgical functions, but also constitutes part of episcopal full dress on important civil occasions, and of the full academic dress of those entitled to wear it. It is incorrect to wear a chimere under a vestment or cope.

China, Christianity in. Legend has it that St *Thomas the Apostle preached in China as well as in India, but there is no historical evidence of this. The *Sigan-Fu stone, dated AD 781, shows that *Church of the East missionaries reached China in the 7th cent. Syriac Christianity survived till the 14th cent. The first western mission was that of John of Monte Corvino (*c.*1294). At first successful, it was brought to an end by the advent of the Ming dynasty in 1368. The celebrated mission of the *Jesuits began in 1582 with the arrival of Michele Ruggieri and Matteo *Ricci. By their skill in mathematics and astronomy, which won them the favour of influential scholars and officials, and their policy of retaining traditional Chinese ceremonies and religious terms, the Jesuits were able to establish themselves and build up a Chinese Christian community. *Franciscan, *Dominican, and other RC missionaries came in the 17th cent. Hostility to the Jesuits' method of *accommodation gave rise to the prolonged and damaging Rites Controversy, issuing in their condemnation by *Clement XI and other 18th-cent. Popes. The assertion of Papal authority in China antagonized the Emperor. This and other causes led to persecutions and to imperial decrees banning Christianity. Though not entirely stamped out, it fell into decay.

The modern missionary movement of the 19th cent., RC and Protestant, was faced by the isolationist policy of the Manchu dynasty, which sought to keep the country closed to foreigners. Robert *Morrison, the first Protestant missionary, who arrived in 1807 at Canton, where the East India Company had a precarious footing, owed his continuance there to his employment as translator by the Company. In his free time he translated the Bible and wrote a dictionary and other works. But the main development of modern missions came after the period 1839–65, during which the western powers by military action and forced treaties secured for themselves rights of residence and to some extent jurisdiction in China. This did indeed open the country to Christian missions, but the fact that they came in the wake of such action gave them an association with foreign power which was to prove a heavy liability. Once it had become possible for missionaries not only to reside at 'treaty ports' but to penetrate into the interior also, missions of all the principal denominations of Europe and America spread to every province, founding churches, schools, and hospitals. The largest single organization was the undenominational *China Inland Mission (1865). By 1895 Protestant Chinese Christians numbered over 40,000, Roman Catholics over 580,000. From time to time there were violent outbursts of anti-foreign feeling, the worst being the Boxer rising in 1900, in which thousands of Chinese Christians and many missionaries were killed.

Revolutions and wars have dominated the history of China in the 20th cent. from the overthrow of the old imperial regime in 1911 to the coming of the Communists to power in 1949, a period which included the Japanese invasion and occupation of a large part of the country, 1937–45. In spite of the turmoil Christian work went on. The period up to 1939 was notable for the development of higher education and of church organization, and for the emergence and increasing importance of Chinese leaders, such as Cheng Ching Yi and Timothy Tinfang Lew among the Protestants. In the RC Church six Chinese bishops were consecrated in 1926. The influence of Christianity seemed to be on the increase until the advent of the Communist regime.

Thereafter Christian institutions were taken over by the state, many churches were closed, and Christians became subject to pressure to make them conform to the requirements of a Communist regime. Those considered hostile to it were persecuted. Missionaries were denounced as agents of western imperialism, and when it became clear that their presence could only embarrass and even endanger local Christians, it was judged best that they should withdraw. By the end of 1952 very few remained. It was the policy of the new rulers to sever all links between the Chinese Church and the West, and to bring it under control. For this purpose they encouraged the organization among Chinese Christians of the 'Three-Self Patriotic Movement' (Three-Self refers to the ideal of a self-supporting, self-governing, and self-propagating Church). In 1957 RCs were forced to sever relations with Rome. During the Cultural Revolution (1966) all religion (not only Christianity) was virtually outlawed and driven underground. Some church buildings were used for other purposes, but many were merely closed and left undamaged. In 1979 churches began to reopen and in the 1980s restrictions on religious activities were reduced. Theological seminaries received students and Bibles and other literature were produced. International links were restored, although the breach with Rome was not mended and RCs are still divided between those loyal to the Vatican and those prepared to work within autonomous structures. In the 1980s even the tiny Orthodox community (mainly Russian) reopened churches in Urumqui in NW China. After the massacre in Beijing in June 1989 a more restrictive atmosphere prevailed, but on the other hand Christianity represented a dynamic and growing force which appealed to increasing numbers of people disillusioned with Marxism.

K. S. Latourette, *A History of Christian Missions in China* (1929), with full bibl., pp. 847–99; B. Whyte, *Unfinished Encounter: China and Christianity* (1988). M. Huc, *Le Christianisme en Chine, en Tartarie et au Thibet* (4 vols., bound in 2, 1857–8; Eng. tr., 3 vols., 1857–8); A. Launay, *Histoire des missions de Chine* (3 vols., 1903–8). P. M. D'Elia, SJ, *The Catholic Missions in China* (Shanghai, 1934); [E.] C. Cary-Elwes, *China and the Cross: Studies in Missionary History* (1957); J. Gernet, *Chine et christianisme* (1982; Eng. tr., Cambridge, 1985). J. de Moidrey, SJ, *La Hiérarchie catholique en Chine, en Corée et au Japon* (Variétés sinologiques, 38; Shanghai, 1914), esp. pp. 1–158; L. Pfister, SJ, *Notices biographiques et bibliographiques sur les Jésuites de l'ancienne mission de Chine, 1552–1773* (ibid., 59 and 60; 1932–4). C. E. Ronan, SJ, and B. B. C. Oh (eds.), *East Meets West: The Jesuits* in China 1582–1773 (Chicago [1988]); A. C. Ross, *A Vision Betrayed: The Jesuits in Japan and China 1542–1742* (Edinburgh [1994]), pp. 6–12 and 118–207. J. M. Gonzáles, OP, *Historia de las Misiones Dominicanas de China* (5 vols., 1955–67). J.-P. Wiest, *Maryknoll in China: A History, 1918–1955* (Armonk, NY, and London [1988]).

F. Bontinck, CICM, *La Lutte autour de la liturgie chinoise aux XVIIᵉ et XVIIIᵉ siècles* (Publications de l'Université Lovanium de Léopoldville, 1962). H. R. Williamson, *British Baptists in China, 1845–1952* (1957). J. Richter, *Allgemeine evangelische Missionsgeschichte*, 4, *Das Werden der christlichen Kirche in China* (1928). S. W. Barnett and J. K. Fairbank (eds.), *Christianity in China: Early Protestant Missionary Writings* (Harvard Studies in American–East Asian Relations, 9; Cambridge, Mass., and London, 1985). P. Wickeri, *Seeking the Common Ground: Protestant Christianity, the Three-Self Movement, and China's United Front* (Maryknoll, NY, 1988). D. E. MacInnis, *Religion in China Today: Policy and Practice* (Maryknoll, NY, 1989), esp. pp. 263–362. G. Hood, *Neither Bang nor Whimper: The End of a Missionary Era in China* (Singapore and London [1991]). A. Hunter and K.-K. Chan, *Protestantism in Contemporary China* (Cambridge, 1993). Latourette, 6, pp. 253–363, and 7, pp. 238–78. J. Krahl in *NCE* 3 (1967), pp. 591–602, s.v., with bibl.

China Inland Mission (CIM).
An interdenominational and international mission to the interior of *China, founded by J. H. *Taylor in 1865. After the establishment of a Communist regime, the Mission withdrew from China in 1951 and relocated its work in E. Asia. In 1965 it was renamed the '*Overseas Missionary Fellowship'. In China the work was primarily evangelistic, though it had a certain number of schools and hospitals in its care.

M. Broomhall, *The Jubilee Story of the China Inland Mission* [1915]. P. Thompson, *D. E. Hoste: ... Hudson Taylor's Successor as General Director of the China Inland Mission, 1900–1935* [c.1947]. A. J. Broomhall, *Hudson Taylor & China's Open Century* (7 vols., 1981–9). See also bibl. to TAYLOR, HUDSON.

choir (architectural).
A term generally used to describe the part of a church containing the seats of the clergy. In the Roman *basilicas these seats at first were set in a semi-circle round the *apse and behind the altar. Later they were placed in a railed-off space within the nave, or body of the church, and at its eastern end. Later still, in various parts of Christendom, *chancels replaced apses; they were much larger, and rectangular in shape, and the choir was included within the chancel, at its western end. The term 'ritual choir' is sometimes used for the seats of the clergy when these do not occupy the (architectural) choir of the church.

choir (musical).
A body of singers assisting at Divine Service. As early as the 4th cent. such bodies existed, made up of clerks in *minor orders and of boys, and, by the time of St *Gregory the Great (d. 604), the *Schola Cantorum seems to have been fully established. In the Middle Ages the choirs of cathedrals and monasteries were almost the only places where music of any kind was taught, and there, until a conventional notation came in c.1100, instruction was given orally. About the 12th cent. polyphony began to supplement the liturgical plainchant of the Church, and lay singers to augment church choirs. In all sections of W. Christendom this change reached its fullest development in the 16th–18th cents., when church music was at its most elaborate and florid, and the singers often

skilled professionals. It also became customary in this period to set the singers in a gallery, often at the W. end. The *Oxford Movement in the C of E and the *Liturgical Movement among RCs have tended to restore the choir to the *chancel, though the 1964 RC legislation laid down that it should be placed where it could best assist the people to sing their parts. This ruling confirmed the various efforts that have been made in the 20th cent. to give the congregation fuller scope for taking part in the music of the services. In recent years many churches have supplemented or replaced choirs by more informal 'music groups' utilizing both singers and instrumentalists. Mixed choirs of both sexes, though long familiar among Nonconformists, have in the 20th cent. become increasingly common in Anglican and RC churches. The traditional dress of singers is the *surplice, worn over the *cassock, though ordinary lay clothes are sometimes worn.

choir sisters.
Nuns who are under obligation to attend all choir *offices, as contrasted with lay sisters, who, though living under rule, attend only certain services. The Second *Vatican Council's Decree on the Appropriate Renewal of the Religious Life (1965) ordered that normally there should be only one class of sisters, so that the distinction is now obsolete in nearly all RC orders. See also LAY BROTHER, LAY SISTER.

chorepiscopus
(Gk. χωρεπίσκοπος; also ἐπίσκοπος τῶν ἀγρῶν). In the early Church, a bishop of a country district in full episcopal orders. The powers which he could exercise were severely restricted (cf. Conc. *Ancyr. can. 13; Conc. *Antioch. can. 10). He could ordain only to the lower ranks of the clergy and was wholly subject to the authority of his diocesan. Such chorepiscopi were very numerous in the 4th cent., esp. in Asia Minor. At the Council of *Nicaea 15 signed in their own right. But the appointment of further chorepiscopi was forbidden by the Council of *Laodicea (can. 57), which ordered that their place be taken by 'periodeutai', i.e. visiting priests (cf. Conc. *Sard. can. 6, which forbids the appointment of bishops to tiny places so that the name of bishop shall not be cheapened). At the Council of *Chalcedon (451) they signed only as representatives of their dioceses. In the E. their functions were progressively restricted to those of a modern *archdeacon, and by the 13th cent. they had disappeared. As an honorary title the word survives to the present day in the Orthodox and *Uniat Patriarchates of Antioch.

In the W. they are first mentioned in 439 at the Council of Riez. They were numerous in missionary districts in Germany in the 8th cent., but became unpopular in the 9th when they sought to extend their authority, and finally disappeared in the 12th cent. Their administrative authority passed to the archdeacon; their liturgical functions were continued by mitred abbots.

D. *Petavius, 'De Chorepiscopis', append. to *Haer.* 69, in his ed. of *Epiphanius, *Opera* (1622, 2, pp. 276–82; J. P. Migne, *PG* 42. 1045–54). H. Bergère, *Étude historique sur les chorévêques* (thesis, Paris; 1905); Hefele and Leclercq, 2 (pt. 2; 1908), pp. 1197–237 ('La Législation conciliaire relative aux chorévêques'); T. Gottlob, *Der abendländische Chorepiskopat* (Kanonistische Studien und Texte, 1; 1928). H. *Leclercq in *DACL* 3 (pt. 1; 1913), cols. 1423–52, s.v. 'Chorévêques'; J. Leclef, OSB, in

DDC 3 (1942), cols. 686–95, s.v. 'Chorévêque'; E. Kirsten in *RAC* 2 (1954), cols. 1105–14; R. Kottje in *Lexikon des Mittelalters*, 2 (1983), cols. 1884–6, both s.v. 'Chorbischof'.

chrism (Gk. χρῖσμα, from χρίω, 'anoint'; but in Greek it is usually called μύρον). A mixture of olive oil and balsam, used in the ritual of the Greek and Latin Churches. The use of special oils for liturgical functions such as the consecration of priests and kings was familiar in the OT. The practice was taken over by the early Church, and its use in the rites of Christian initiation is attested by several early Fathers, e.g. *Tertullian, St *Ambrose, and *Theodoret. St *Cyril of Jerusalem refers to it as 'the mystic chrism' (τὸ μυστικὸν χρῖσμα), and the Council of *Laodicea as 'holy chrism'. For St *Augustine the 'sacrament of chrism' refers to the inward unity of the Church, which is the bond of love, while the *Apostolic Constitutions call chrism 'the strength of confessors', and St *Gregory the Great speaks of the 'chrism of salvation'. The strength-giving richness of the oil and the fragrance of the balsam, representing the fullness of sacramental grace and the gifts of the Holy Spirit as well as the sweetness of Christian virtue, made it a favourite subject of allegorical interpretation to *Dionysius the Ps.-Areopagite and later writers. The early Schoolmen held that the chrism was a purely ecclesiastical institution, but St *Thomas Aquinas and *Duns Scotus both teach that its liturgical use, though not mentioned in the NT, goes back to Christ Himself. The *Roman Catechism (1566) followed this view, claiming for it the support of early authorities such as Pope *Fabian (d. 250). The texts adduced, however, have since been recognized as apocryphal, and the *Catechism of the Catholic Church (1992) treats chrism as an early addition.

Of the two ingredients required for the chrism oil is the older element. In the E. Church a variety of perfumes is used in addition to balsam. From at least the 4th cent. chrism was distinguished from other holy oils, e.g. that used for the unction of the sick, to which balsam is not added. Only bishops have the right to consecrate the chrism, as is already stated by the Second Council of *Carthage (390; can. 3), an injunction repeated by several later Councils. In the E. the privilege became restricted to the *Patriarchs and other heads of *autocephalous Churches. The earliest evidence for the rite of its consecration is found in Syria in the late 5th cent., by which time it had developed into a very impressive ceremony. Acc. to the present Latin usage, which dates in its essentials from the 8th cent., it is consecrated by the bishop, assisted by representative priests and deacons (when available), on *Maundy Thursday. Before 1955 the consecration took place during the Mass of the day, after the Communion, but the Ordinal of *Pius XII provided a special Mass of the Chrism to be celebrated in cathedral churches in the morning.

In the E. chrismation is part of the rite of *Baptism, and is also used for the reconciliation of apostates and the reception of converts from other Christian communions. In the W. chrism is used in the three Sacraments that confer a *character, namely at Baptism, *Confirmation, and Holy *Orders; it was also formerly used at the coronation of sovereigns (which was sometimes also thought to confer a character). In the later Middle Ages, under W. influence, chrism came to be used in the coronation of the Byzantine Emperors, and thence for the coronation of the Russian tsars. Chrism is used, in both E. and W., at the consecration of churches and altars.

P. Hofmeister, OSB, *Die heiligen Öle in der morgen- und abendländischen Kirche* (Das östliche Christentum, NF, Hefte 6–7; Würzburg, 1948). M. Dudley and [D.] G. Rowell (eds.), *The Oil of Gladness: Anointing in the Christian Tradition* (1993). For the Syriac evidence, W. Strothmann, *Das Sakrament der Myron-Weihe in der Schrift De Ecclesiastica Hierarchia des Pseudo-Dionysios Areopagitica*, 2 (Gottinger Orientforschungen, 1. Reihe, Bd. 15, Teil 2; Wiesbaden, 1978), pp. xliii–liii. A. Chavasse, 'La Bénédiction du chrême en Gaule avant l'adoption intégrale de la liturgie romaine', *Revue du Moyen-Age Latin*, 1 (1945), pp. 109–28. J. Rogues, 'La Préface consécratoire du Chrême', *Maison-Dieu*, 49 (1957), pp. 35–49. L. L. Mitchell, *Baptismal Anointing* (*Alcuin Club Collections, 48; 1966). S. Salaville, 'Un rite peu connu: la consécration du Saint Chrême au patriarcat grec de Constantinople', *L'Union des Églises*, 5 (1926), pp. 56–62. L. Eisenhofer, *Handbuch der katholischen Liturgik*, 1 (1932), pp. 308–17. P. Bernard in *DTC* 2 (1905), cols. 2395–414, s.v. 'Chrême (saint)'; F. *Cabrol, OSB, in *DACL* 6 (pt. 2; 1925), cols. 2777–91, s.v. 'Huile'.

chrismatory. A small vessel, in use since the Middle Ages, for keeping the three kinds of holy oils, namely oil of the catechumens, oil of the sick, and *chrism, from which last the name is derived. Of the vessels used for these oils one set, preserving the supply for the year, is kept in the sacristy of the cathedral. Another set containing oil for parochial use is kept in a locked cupboard in the chancel of the parish church.

chrisom. See CHRYSOM.

Christ (Gk. χριστός, lit. the 'Anointed One'). The word is the Gk. translation of the Heb. '*Messiah' (q.v. for the development of the conception among the Jews and in the early Church). Orig. a title, it very soon came to be used by the followers of the risen Jesus as a proper name for their Lord (e.g. Gal. 1: 6, Heb. 9: 11), so much so that they themselves came to be known as '*Christians' (q.v.) before long. In early Christian theology, the name was at first employed to emphasize the Lord's position as the fulfilment of the Old Israel, e.g. in St *Paul's contrast between *Adam and Christ as the 'Old' and the 'New Man'; but here again it soon lost its OT associations and was used purely as a proper name. See also JESUS CHRIST; and for the growth of the doctrine of the Person of Christ see CHRISTOLOGY.

Editors and G. F. Moore (cf. p. 346 n.) in F. J. Foakes Jackson and K. *Lake, *The Beginnings of Christianity*, 1. 1 (1920), pp. 346–68; E. de W. Burton, *Galatians* (ICC, 1921), pp. 392–9. S. V. McCasland, 'Christ Jesus', *Journal of Biblical Literature*, 65 (1946), pp. 377–83. W. Bauer, *Griechischdeutsches Wörterbuch zu den Schriften des Neuen Testaments und der übrigen urchristlichen Literatur*, 6th edn. by K. and B. Aland (1988), cols. 1768 f.; Eng. tr. of 4th edn. (Chicago, 1975), pp. 886 f. G. W. H. Lampe (ed.), *A Patristic Greek Lexicon* (Oxford, 1968), pp. 1531 f., s.v. Χριστός. A. Romeo in *EC* 4 (1950), cols. 918–21.

Christ, Disciples of. See DISCIPLES OF CHRIST.

Christ the King, Feast of. The feast observed in the RC Church in celebration of the all-embracing authority of Christ which shall lead mankind to seek the 'peace of

Christ' in the 'Kingdom of Christ'. It was instituted by *Pius XI in the encyclical *Quas primas* of 11 Dec. 1925 at the close of the *Jubilee Year, when the last Sunday in October was allotted for its observance. From 1970 it has been kept on the last Sunday before the beginning of Advent. It is also kept unofficially in some Anglican churches.

Text of *Quas primas*, in *AAS* 17 (1925), pp. 593–610.

Christ Church, Oxford. One of the largest colleges in the University of Oxford, it was founded in 1525 on the site of the monastery of St *Frideswide by T. *Wolsey as 'Cardinal College', and, seven years later, refounded as 'King *Henry the Eighth's College'. In 1545 the latter was dissolved and in 1546 reconstituted in substantially its present form as Christ Church ('Aedes Christi') by Henry VIII. At the same time the new episcopal see was moved from Oseney Abbey to the church of St Frideswide, which thus became both a cathedral and a college chapel, and the whole establishment was placed under a dean and eight canons. The number of canonries is now seven, of which four are attached to professorships in the faculty of theology. In 1867 the tutors of the college were admitted to membership of the Governing Body.

H. L. Thompson, *Christ Church* (1900); S. A. Warner, *Oxford Cathedral* (1924); E. W. Watson, *The Cathedral Church of Christ in Oxford* (1935); W. G. Hiscock, *A Christ Church Miscellany* (privately pr., Oxford, 1946). A. Hassall (ed.), *Christ Church, Oxford: An Anthology in Prose and Verse* (1911), with useful introd. E. G. W. Bill and J. F. A. Mason, *Christ Church and Reform, 1850–1867* (Oxford, 1970).

Christadelphians, a Christian sect. They were originally called 'Thomasites' after John Thomas (1805–71), who founded them in America in 1848. The name 'Christadelphians' ('Christ's brethren') was Thomas's substitute for 'Christian', which term he rejected, teaching that the beliefs and religious development which it connoted constituted an apostasy. He claimed to return to the beliefs and practice of the earliest disciples. Christadelphian doctrines include the acceptance of the Bible as inspired and infallible, and the interpretation of Hebrew prophecy and, e.g., the Book of Revelation in terms of current and future events. The doctrine of the Trinity is rejected. The core of the Gospel is belief in the return of Jesus Christ in power and great glory to set up a visible world-wide theocracy beginning at Jerusalem, and assurance of this is held to be necessary to salvation. Christadelphians also hold no form of Baptism to be valid except immersion, that the wicked will be annihilated, and that the unconverted, the ignorant, and infants will not be raised from the dead. They have no ministers or clergy. The sect publishes no statistics as to its membership.

R. Roberts, *Dr. Thomas: His Life and Work* (1884; 3rd edn., rev. by C. C. Walker and W. H. Boulton, 1954). H. Tennant, *The Christadelphians: What They Believe and Preach* (Birmingham, 1986). C. H. Lippy, *The Christadelphians in North America* (Studies in American Religion, 34; Lewiston, Lampeter, and Queenston [1989]). B. R. Wilson, *Sects and Society: A Sociological Study of Three Religious Groups in Britain* (1961), pp. 219–314, with bibl. pp. 382–5. F. J. Powicke in *HERE* 3 (1910), pp. 569–71, s.v.

Christian. The name was orig. applied to followers of

Christ by outsiders, being first used, acc. to Acts 11: 26, at *Antioch *c.* AD 40–4. In the NT it occurs in only two other places, in Acts 26: 28, where it is used by King Agrippa speaking to St *Paul, and in 1 Pet. 4: 16, where its use by enemies or persecutors is envisaged. Acc. to *Tacitus (*Annals*, 15. 44) it was already current among the populace at Rome at the time of the *Neronian persecution (AD 64) and it was always the official Roman designation of members of the Church; thus during times of persecution it was often the confession or denial of this name which was crucial, e.g. in the cases reported by *Pliny (q.v.). The form of the word, parallel to, e.g. 'Herodians' (Mk. 12: 13, etc.) and 'Caesarians' (supporters or clients of Caesar), has been thought to indicate that Christianity was considered as a quasi-political movement. Owing to its pagan origin the word was long avoided by Christian writers, except in reference to conflict with paganism. Thus in 1 Pet. 4: 16 the readers are bidden not to be ashamed of suffering on the charge of being a 'Christian', and St *Ignatius of Antioch writing of his approaching martyrdom says, 'Let me not merely be called "Christian" but be found one' (Ign., *Rom.* 3. 2). By pagans the name 'Christus' was often confused with 'chrestus' (χρηστός, good, kind) and hence the form 'Chrestiani' was used. The *Apologists (e.g. *Tertullian, *Apol.* 3 and 5) retorted that this, though a misunderstanding, was a true indication of the character of Christianity and that the name 'Christian' stood for nothing worthy of punishment. As the name for which the martyrs suffered (cf. Lk. 21: 12) and as containing the name of Christ, the term easily came to fill the obvious need for a proper name by which the Church could designate itself as distinct from Jews and pagans (and later from Muslims, etc.), rather than the earlier terms 'brethren' (Acts 1: 16), 'disciples' (Acts 11: 26), 'believers' (Acts 2: 44), and others found in the NT.

In modern times the name Christian has usually been claimed by every form of belief stemming from historic Christianity, and has tended, in nominally Christian countries, to lose any credal significance and imply only that which is ethically praiseworthy (e.g. 'a Christian action') or socially customary ('Christian name'). It was disclaimed, as too narrow, by some *Unitarians in the 19th cent., though claimed by the main Unitarian tradition. On the other hand, it has been occasionally adopted in a particular sense by sects which claim to practise mere 'New Testament Christianity' and reject denominational labels (e.g. *Bible Christians).

R. A. *Lipsius, *Ueber den Ursprung und den ältesten Gebrauch des Christennamens* (Jena, 1873). J. B. *Lightfoot, *The Apostolic Fathers*, pt. 2, S. Ignatius and S. Polycarp, 1 (1885), pp. 400–4. E. Peterson, 'Christianus', *Miscellanea Giovanni Mercati*, 1 (Studi e Testi, 121; 1946), pp. 356–72; H. B. Mattingly, 'The Origin of the Name *Christiani*', *JTS* NS 9 (1958), pp. 26–37; C. Spicq, OP, 'Ce que signifie le titre de chrétien', *Studia Theologica*, 15 (1961), pp. 68–78, with further refs. H. *Leclercq, OSB, in *DACL* 3 (pt. 1; 1913), cols. 1464–78, s.v. 'Chrétien', with bibl.; H. Karpp in *RAC* 2 (1954), cols. 1114–38, s.v. 'Christennamen', also with bibl.

Christian Aid. See BRITISH COUNCIL OF CHURCHES.

Christian Library. The collection of 50 spiritual books which J. *Wesley selected and reissued in handy form to meet the devotional and intellectual needs of his followers. It was published in 1749–55.

Christian Initiation. See BAPTISM and CONFIRMATION.

Christian Majesty, His Most (Lat. *Rex Christianissimus*). A title belonging to the Kings of France, and from 1464 invariably used by the Popes in addressing them.

Christian Science. The tenets of a religious body known chiefly for its concern with healing through prayer alone. It was founded by Mary Baker Eddy (1821–1910), a native of New Hampshire and of *Calvinistic origin. Having suffered from various ailments from her youth, for a time she believed herself cured by a mesmerist, P. P. Quimby. After a year she suffered a relapse. In 1866 she claimed to have experienced a healing while studying the account of the healing of the paralysed man in Mt. 9. She believed that she had discovered in the Bible the spiritual law and science underlying the healing work of Jesus which rendered such healing open to all who accepted the moral and spiritual discipline of His teaching. While accepting the historicity of the Gospel accounts of Jesus' birth, life, death, and bodily resurrection, she drew a distinction between Jesus the man and Christ, the divinity which He manifested. Everything that does not express the nature of God is 'unreal', a flawed and limited concept of God's kingdom. Evil and sickness have no ultimate reality and are to be destroyed by the subject's becoming aware of God's power and love (rather than by medical treatment). She set out her teaching in *Science and Health* (1875; revised, with *Key to the Scriptures*, 1883), which had an immense success. In 1877 she married Asa G. Eddy. In 1879 the 'Church of Christ, Scientist' was founded in Boston and reorganized on a permanent basis in 1892. Christian Science has subsequently spread, esp. in the English-speaking world and in Germany. Since Mrs Eddy's death, the organization, with its largely autonomous, congregationally run branches, has maintained the structure for which she provided in the *Church Manual* (1895); it is administered by a Board of five Directors who appoint their successors. *The Christian Science Monitor*, a well-informed newspaper, is one of its chief assets. Christian Science services are simple in form; those on Sunday consist chiefly of readings from the Bible and *Science and Health* and include hymns, recitation of the *Lord's Prayer (the only form of vocal prayer used), and silent prayer; mid-week meetings include accounts of healings by members of the congregation. Though Christian Scientists point to a substantial amount of testimony, the universal applicability of their methods of healing is not admitted outside their own ranks.

Modern Lives of Mary Baker Eddy by L. P. Powell (London, 1930) and R. Peel (3 vols., New York, 1966–77). N. Beasley, *The Cross and the Crown: The History of Christian Science* (Boston, 1952; London, 1953); id., *The Continuing Spirit* (Boston and Toronto, 1956; London, 1957); C. S. Braden, *Christian Science Today* (Dallas, 1958; London, 1959); R. Peel, *Christian Science: Its Encounter with American Culture* (New York, 1958); DeW. John, *The Christian Science Way of Life* (Englewood Cliffs, NJ, 1962); S. Gottschalk, *The Emergence of Christian Science in American Religious Life* (Berkeley, Calif., and London [1973]); R. A. Nenneman, *The New Birth of Christianity* (San Francisco [1992]), pp. 97–190. B. R. Wilson, *Sects and Society: A Sociological Study of Three Religious Groups in Britain* (1961), pp. 121–215, with

bibl., pp. 376–82. H. A. L. Fisher, *Our New Religion* (1933), criticizes both the life and character of the foundress and her work.

Christian Socialism. A movement for social reform initiated in the 19th cent. by members of the C of E. It was a response to the conditions of the 'Hungry Forties' and, although its leaders professed a belief in the general validity of Political Economy, its central assault was upon competitive practices in society. The movement from the start lacked internal agreement, and was educative rather than political. Its best-known leaders were J. M. F. *Ludlow, F. D. *Maurice, C. *Kingsley, and Thomas Hughes. Their short-lived periodical, *Politics for the People* (1848), though moderate in its description of the social injustices of the time, roused much opposition and soon had to be abandoned for lack of support. There were two distinct phases; the first, beginning in 1848, was an attempt to counter Chartism within the working classes by providing an alternative Christian social critique, and the second, originating with the Guild of St Matthew in 1877, was more specifically political and aimed at the permeation of the Church with social radicalism. The earlier Christian Socialists sought to apply the ideals of the French co-operatives in England, and this led to the foundation of the London Working Tailors' Association (1849) and a number of other enterprises—none of which had much contact, at least initially, with the simultaneous evolution of similar associations in the North of England. Becoming wary of the political activism of some of the members, F. D. Maurice began to dissociate himself from the co-operatives, and in 1854, with the inauguration of the Working Men's College, he sought, with some success, to divert energies into adult education instead. The eventual failure of the movement may be attributed not only to the indifference of the official C of E but also to the unresponsiveness of the workers themselves. Its work, however, marked the beginning of the modern social movement in the C of E and had much influence in the formation of the trade unions, in early co-operative legislation, and in working-class education.

C. E. Raven, *Christian Socialism, 1848–1854* (1920). G. C. Binyon, *The Christian Socialist Movement in England* (1931). M. B. Reckitt, *Faith and Society: A Study of the Structure, Outlook and Opportunity of the Christian Social Movement in Great Britain and America* (1932). Id., *Maurice to Temple: A Century of Social Movement in the Church of England* (Scott Holland Memorial Lectures, 1946; 1947). J. F. C. Harrison, *A History of the Working Men's College 1854–1954* (1954). T. Christensen, *Origin and History of Christian Socialism 1848–54* (Acta Theologica Danica, 3; Aarhus, 1962). A. R. Vidler, *F. D. Maurice and Company* (1966). P. d'A. Jones, *The Christian Socialist Revival 1877–1914: Religion, Class, and Social Conscience in Late-Victorian England* (Princeton, NJ, 1968). P. N. Backstrom, *Christian Socialism and Co-operation in Victorian England: Edward Vansittart Neale and the Co-operative Movement* (1974). E. [R.] Norman, *The Victorian Christian Socialists* (Cambridge, 1987).

Christian stewardship. See STEWARDSHIP.

Christian Year, The. The collection of poems for the Sundays and holy days of the year, by J. *Keble, published in 1827. It was very popular throughout the 19th cent., and several well-known hymns have been taken from it (e.g. *EH* 216, 370).

The phrase 'the Christian year' is also used of the liturgical *year, i.e. the year conceived as starting at *Advent Sunday.

Christina (1626–89), Queen of Sweden. The only surviving child of *Gustavus Adolphus, she succeeded to the Swedish throne in 1632 before she was 6. Until 1644 the government was in the hands of a council of regency. Christina, who was given a boy's education, received instruction in politics (from Axel Oxenstierna), ancient and modern languages, and philosophy. After assuming the direction of affairs on her 18th birthday (8 Dec. 1644), she made it her first aim to end the *Thirty Years War and was partly responsible for the Treaty of *Westphalia (1648). At home she promoted education, increasing and improving the schools and colleges founded by Gustavus and bringing into effect the first school ordinance for the whole kingdom (1649). She also sought to encourage learning by the patronage of foreign as well as Swedish scholars, artists, and scientists, among them R. *Descartes, H. *Grotius, G. J. *Voss, S. *Pufendorf, Olaf Rudbeck (discoverer of the lymphatic vessels), and J. A. *Comenius.

Interest in the RC faith, combined with dislike of the monotony of rule and her Council's repeated requests that she should marry, made her suggest abdication as early as 1651. On 6 June 1654 the Council finally accepted her resignation. In Nov. 1655 she was received into the RC Church at Innsbruck by L. *Holste and settled in Rome, first at the Palazzo Farnese and from 1668 at the Palazzo Riario. Her allegiance to her new faith, although absolute, was never blind. She made repeated attempts to lessen the penalties imposed by the *Inquisition, and criticized the Revocation of the Edict of *Nantes. At Rome she became the centre of a group of intellectuals, later known as the 'Arcadia Academy', and she pursued interests in a variety of Platonic and hermetic ideas, some far from compatible with RC dogma.

After her abdication she twice attempted (1660; 1667) to resume the Swedish crown, intrigued with J. *Mazarin to become ruler of the Spanish kingdom of Naples, and, on the abdication of John Casimir of Vasa (1668), sought the crown of *Poland; but her efforts to regain political power were unsuccessful. She died at Rome, leaving Cardinal Azzolino her chief heir. There is a monument to her in *St Peter's.

Christina left, in French highly praised by Descartes, some fragmentary writings of her own, including an autobiography. Her intellectual gifts were celebrated in verse by Andrew Marvell and J. *Milton, and she endeavoured, through Sir Bulstrode Whitelocke, to persuade Milton to visit her court. She made a collection of MSS, consisting of works on theology, Church history, philosophy, civil law, and medicine, which are deservedly famous and have been incorporated in the *Vatican Library ('Reginenses').

J. Arckenholtz, *Mémoires concernant Christine, reine de Suède* (4 vols., Amsterdam, 1751–60), incl. some of her Works and Letters, with her Autobiography in vol. 3, pp. 1–69; Eng. tr. of some of her Works (London, 1753), with account of her Life, Character, and Writings by the translator, pp. iii–xx. Numerous modern studies include those by S. Stolpe (2 vols., Stockholm, 1960–1; Eng. tr. of abridged Ger. version, 1966; and other works of this author), G. Masson (London, 1968), and the studies and docs. ed. M. von Platen (Analecta Reginensia, 1; Stockholm, 1966). W. Di Palma and others, *Cristina di Svezia: scienza ed alchimia nella Roma barocca* (Bari, 1990). S. Åkerman, *Queen Christina of Sweden and her Circle* (Brill's Studies in Intellectual History, 21; Leiden, etc., 1991), with bibl. C. N. D. de Bildt, *Christine de Suède et le cardinal Azzolino: Lettres inédites, 1666–1668, avec une introduction et des notes* (1899). G. Claretta, *La regina Cristina di Svezia in Italia, 1655–1689* (1892). C. Weibull, *Drottning Christina och Monaldesco* (1936). G. B. *Pitra and H. Stevenson, *Codices Manuscripti Graeci Reginae Suecorum et Pii PP. II* (Bibliothecae Apostolicae Vaticanae Codices Manuscripti Recensiti iubente Leone XIII; Rome, 1888). A. *Wilmart, OSB, *Codices Reginenses Latini: Codices 1–500* (all pub., Bibliothecae Apostolicae Vaticanae Codices Manu Scripti Recensiti, 2 vols., Vatican, 1937–45). *Les Manuscrits de la reine de Suède au Vatican: Réédition du catalogue de Montfaucon et cotes actuelles* (ST 238; 1964). *Christina, Queen of Sweden—a personality of European civilisation.* Exhibition arranged in collaboration with The Royal Library, the Royal Collections . . . and the National Record Office, Stockholm, Sweden (Stockholm, 1966), with preface by C. Nordenfalk.

Christkatholiken. The official name of the *Old Catholics of Switzerland. The 'Christkatholische Kirche der Schweiz' was formally founded at a synod at Olten in 1875.

Christmas. Though speculation as to the time of year of Christ's Birth dates from the early 3rd cent., *Clement of Alexandria, e.g., suggesting 20 May, the celebration of the anniversary does not appear to have been general till the later 4th cent. The earliest mention of the observance on 25 Dec. is in the *Philocalian Calendar, representing Roman practice of the year 336 (25 Dec.: *natus Christus in Betleem Judeae*). This date was prob. chosen to oppose the feast of the *Natalis Solis Invicti* by the celebration of the birth of the 'Sun of Righteousness'. Another tradition, however, derived the date of Christmas from that of the *Annunciation. The Pseudo-*Chrysostomic tractate *De solstitia et aequinoctia conceptionis et nativitatis domini nostri Iesu Christi et Iohannis Baptistae* argued that the Lord was conceived and crucified on the same day of the year, and calculated this as 25 Mar., a computation mentioned by St *Augustine (*De Trinitate*, 4. 5). Whatever the origin of the 25 Dec. date, after the accession of the Emp. *Constantine its observance in the W. seems to have spread from Rome. In the E. the closely related feast of the *Epiphany (6 Jan.), which commemorated also the Baptism of Christ, was at first the more important; but in the later 4th cent. it was connected with the Nativity, esp. in Syria, and by the middle of the 5th cent. most of the E. had adopted 25 Dec., though the Church of *Jerusalem held to 6 Jan. until 549. In the *Armenian Church 6 Jan. is still the only day devoted specifically to the celebration of the Incarnation. The controversies of the 4th to 6th cents. on the Incarnation and the Person of Christ doubtless contributed to the growth in importance of the feast.

The day is celebrated in the W. rite by three Masses, of the night (normally said at midnight), of the dawn, and of the day, which have been held to symbolize the threefold birth of Christ, eternally in the bosom of the Father, from the womb of the Virgin Mary, and mystically in the soul of the faithful.

The popular observance of the feast has always been marked by the joy and merry-making formerly characteristic of the Roman *Saturnalia* and the other pagan festivals it replaced. It developed considerably in England in the

19th cent. through the importation of German customs by the Prince Consort (e.g. Christmas trees) and the influence of Charles Dickens. The singing of *carols has become a widespread feature in both ecclesiastical and secular contexts.

L. *Duchesne, *Origines du culte chrétien* (1889), pp. 247–54 (Eng. tr. of 3rd edn., 1903, pp. 257–65). H. Usener, *Das Weihnachtsfest* (1889; 2nd edn. by H. *Lietzmann, 1911); B. Botte, OSB, *Les Origines de la Noël et de l'Épiphanie* (1932), with text of the *De solstitia*, pp. 93–105. O. *Cullmann, *Weihnachten in der alten Kirche* (Basle, 1947; Fr. tr., 1949; Eng. tr. in id., *The Early Church* (1956), pp. 17–36). J. Lemarié, OSB, *La Manifestation du Seigneur: La liturgie de Noël et de l'Épiphanie* (Lex Orandi, 23; 1957), esp. pp. 23–229. H. Frank, OSB, 'Zur Geschichte von Weihnachten und Epiphanie', *JLW* 12 ('1932'; pub. 1934), pp. 145–55; 13 ('1933'; 1935), pp. 1–38; J. Leclercq, OSB, 'Aux origines du cycle de Noël', *EL* 60 (1946), pp. 7–26; F. J. Dölger, *Antike und Christentum*, 6 (1950), pp. 23–30 ('*Natalis Solis Invicti* und das christliche Weihnachtsfest'); H. Frank, OSB, 'Frühgeschichte und Ursprung des römischen Weihnachtsfestes im Lichte neuerer Forschung', *Archiv für Liturgiewissenschaft*, 2 (1952), pp. 1–24; H. Engberding, OSB, 'Der 25. Dezember als Tag der Feier der Geburt des Herrn', ibid., pp. 25–43. J. Gaillard, 'Noël: *memoria* ou mystère?', *Maison-Dieu*, 59 (1959), pp. 37–59. R. Berger, 'Ostern und Weihnachten. Zum Grundgefüge des Kirchenjahres', *Archiv für Liturgiewissenschaft*, 8 (1963), pp. 1–20. J. Mossay, *Les Fêtes de Noël et d'Épiphanie d'après les sources littéraires cappadociennes du IVᵉ siècle* (Textes et Études Liturgiques, 3; 1965). J.-J. von Allmen, 'La Célébration de Noël d'après les livres liturgiques réformés actuels', in A.-M. Dubarle and others, *Noël-Épiphanie: ... Semaine liturgique de l'Institut Saint-Serge* [Paris] (Lex Orandi, 40; 1967), pp. 277–98, and other essays. K. Onasch, *Die Weihnachtsfest im orthodoxen Kirchenjahr* (Quellen und Untersuchungen zur Konfessionskunde der Orthodoxie, 2; 1958). A. T. Kraabel, 'The Roots of Christmas', *Dialog*, 21 (1982), pp. 274–80. G. Rietschel in *PRE* (3rd edn.), 21 (1908), pp. 47–54, s.v. 'Weihnachten'; C. Martindale, SJ, in *CE* 3 (1908), pp. 724–8; K. *Lake in *HERE* 3 (1910), pp. 601–8; H. *Leclercq, OSB, in *DACL* 12 (pt. 1; 1935), cols. 905–58 (esp. 910–34), s.v. 'Nativité de Jésus'; C. Smith in *NCE* 3 (1967), pp. 655–60, with useful bibl.

Christocentric. (1) A word originally used of systems of theology which maintain that God has never revealed Himself to man except in the Incarnate Christ. Christocentric theology bases itself on a literal interpretation of Mt. 11: 27, to the exclusion of the passages in Scripture which seem to refer to or imply a revelation in nature, and thus precludes the possibility of *natural theology altogether. Among its modern advocates are A. *Ritschl, W. *Herrmann, and K. *Barth.

(2) More generally, of any set of religious beliefs which is focused primarily on the Person of Christ.

Christology. The study of the Person of Christ, and in particular of the union in Him of the divine and human natures, and of His significance for Christian faith. In the writings of the NT, composed by those who believed in the resurrection of the crucified Jesus of Nazareth and who saw Him as the fulfilment of the ancient promises, and in particular as the *Messiah (the Christ, the 'anointed one'), reflection on Jesus is presented largely in categories drawn from current Jewish thought. He is seen as a teacher with unparalleled authority (Mk. 1: 27), a prophet (Mt. 21: 11; Lk. 24: 19; Jn. 4: 19, etc.), as Messiah (q.v.), and is regarded as standing in a peculiar filial relationship to God

(Mt. 3: 17, 11: 27; Jn. 3: 16, etc.). But rarely were merely human categories (e.g. teacher, prophet) felt to be adequate; instead of being an interpreter of the Law (or the *Torah), or of the Wisdom of God, Jesus is seen as superseding the Law (Mt. 5: 21–48) or as *Wisdom itself (1 Cor. 1: 24), and the role in the work of creation that Jewish thought had ascribed to the Torah and Wisdom is attributed to Christ, the Son of God, the Word (1 Cor. 8: 6; Heb. 1: 2; Jn. 1: 3 respectively). Some, esp. among Jewish Christians, shrank from such an interpretation of Christ and clung to the idea of Jesus as a teacher and prophet, a man inspired by the Spirit of God (the *Ebionites); others so emphasized that Jesus was a manifestation of the Divine that His humanity was felt to be a disguise, a mere appearance (the *Docetists).

The idea that in Jesus there was encountered the One through whom God had made the universe provided a starting-point for a more philosophical approach to Christology. The *Apologists of the 2nd cent. (e.g. *Justin Martyr) saw Jesus as the *Logos or Word of God, understood in line with Middle *Platonism as the source of all order and rationality; in Jesus the Logos united Himself to a human being. For the Apologists, however, the Logos was an intermediary between God and the world, and distinct from Him. When at the beginning of the 4th cent. *Arius (d. 336) held that such a subordinate Logos was not the uncreated God but part (albeit a unique part) of the created order, he met opposition from those for whom to say that Jesus was the Logos incarnate was to say in some way that He is God. At the Council of Nicaea (325), Arius was condemned and it was asserted that the Son of God who became incarnate in Jesus is 'consubstantial with the Father' (ὁμοούσιος τῷ πατρί). Such a clear affirmation of the divinity of Christ provoked much Christological reflection. The *Alexandrians emphasized that in Christ God Himself was living a human life, and they cherished the affirmation of such paradoxical self-effacement on God's part as evidence of the depth of His love for mankind. The *Antiochenes emphasized that in Christ both humanity and divinity co-operated in their integrity, and that such a conjunction of human and divine involved no encroachment on the reality of either of the two natures. In trying to work out what could be meant by the Logos becoming a man, *Apollinarius (d. *c.*390) proposed that the Logos took the place of the soul in Christ. This idea was rejected by the *Cappadocian Fathers and by the Antiochenes as impairing Christ's saving work ('the unassumed is the unhealed'), and Apollinarius was condemned at the Council of *Constantinople (381).

Alexandrian suspicions that Antiochene Christology failed to safeguard the unity of the Person of Christ were confirmed when in 428 *Nestorius, the newly elected Abp. of Constantinople (d. after 451), rejected the title of '*Theotokos' ('Mother of God') applied to the Blessed Virgin *Mary. At the Council of *Ephesus (431), Nestorius was condemned and the use of the title 'Theotokos' upheld. Shortly afterwards St *Cyril of Alexandria (d. 444) and the moderate Antiochenes led by *John of Antioch (d. 441) reached an agreement on Christology enshrined in the 'Formulary of Reunion' (433) which affirmed the unity of Christ and asserted that he is 'consubstantial (ὁμοούσιος) with the Father in Godhead and consubstantial with us in manhood'. In 447 *Eutyches (d.

454) began to teach in Constantinople that faithfulness to Cyril's teaching entailed maintaining that after the union there was one nature, and that this nature was not 'consubstantial with us'. This teaching, along with other Christological heresies, was condemned at the Council of *Chalcedon (451), which reaffirmed the teaching of the 'Formulary of Reunion' and asserted that there is 'one . . . Christ . . . in two natures, without confusion, without change, without division, without separation'. The Council also endorsed the Christological teaching of Pope *Leo (d. 461), expressed in a letter to *Flavian, the Abp. of Constantinople who had been the first to condemn Eutyches; this letter (the '*Tome of Leo'), following the teaching of St *Augustine (354–430), maintained that there is one subject in Christ to which, paradoxically, two sets of attributes, divine and human, are to be ascribed. Neither the Council of Ephesus nor that of Chalcedon secured complete agreement; those who supported Nestorius rejected Ephesus and formed a continuing schismatic Church (the *Church of the East), while many Christians in the E. felt that Chalcedon had betrayed the teaching of Cyril and so rejected the Chalcedonian Definition of Faith (the so-called '*Monophysites'). The 'Monophysites' generally rejected the teaching of Eutyches too, maintaining that Christ is consubstantial with the Father in His Godhead and consubstantial with us in His manhood, and therefore completely God, completely man, and completely one. The next two centuries saw a series of attempts, inspired by various Emperors, to secure agreement between the supporters of Chalcedon and the 'Monophysites'. The '*Henoticon' (482), which set aside the Definition of Chalcedon, secured some agreement in the East but provoked the '*Acacian schism' between the E. and W. Although the Emp. *Justinian secured Pope *Vigilius' support for his compromise involving the condemnation of the *Three Chapters, which was endorsed at the Second Council of *Constantinople (553), many Christians in the W. refused to accept it. In the 7th cent. these attempts at compromise led to the heresies of monenergism and *monothelitism, which were condemned at the Third Council of *Constantinople (680–81), after the virtual martyrdom of St *Maximus the Confessor (c. 580–662) and Pope *Martin I (d. 655), who had both opposed such attempts. Another (more successful) attempt to find common ground between the Chalcedonians and the *Oriental Orthodox Churches is found in the so-called Neo-Chalcedonianism or 'Cyrillian Chalcedonianism' of the 6th cent. In this context the doctrine of *Enhypostasia was developed; this asserts that though the humanity of Christ has no person (hypostasis) of its own, it is not on that account 'anhypostatic' (deprived of a hypostasis), but finds its hypostasis in the hypostasis of the Logos. Thus the distinguishing features of the particular man who Jesus is, as well as the essential qualities of the species (mankind) to which He belongs, are attributed to the divine hypostasis. For the Neo-Chalcedonians this notion provided a justification for the *Theopaschite formulae. These ideas are further refined in the Christological teaching of Maximus the Confessor and St *John of Damascus (d. 750).

In the W. the Council of Chalcedon's endorsement of Leo was taken to be an endorsement of the Christological teaching of Augustine that Leo represented. Later, after

*Burgundio of Pisa had translated John of Damascus' *Expositio Fidei* into Latin in the 12th cent., the fruits of Byzantine Christology became accessible in the W. Scholastic theologians introduced further refinements of their own, but they did not call in question the fundamental pattern of Christological doctrine laid down by Chalcedon and reaffirmed by later councils.

The *Reformation and the *Enlightenment were to produce pressures for a change of focus that led to developments, seen first as alternatives and then as replacements for the traditional formulations of Christological doctrines. Christological concern shifted from the question of the two natures of Christ to a more direct analysis of His work in redemption. M. *Luther's classic question at the Reformation was 'How can I find a gracious God?'. He supported his doctrine of the *Real Presence in the Eucharist with the patristic theory of *communicatio idiomatum* (exchange of divine and human attributes; see UBIQUITARIANISM). In this connection J. *Calvin stressed the divine transcendence, and more generally, in his Christology was inclined to emphasize a clear distinction between the two natures (a doctrine sometimes called the *Extra Calvinisticum*). The Lutheran tradition developed a new Christology of the two states of Christ's humiliation and exaltation in cross and resurrection, in accounting for the biblical stress on historical contingency in the Incarnation. Humiliation and condescension led to further reflection on *kenosis (self-emptying) in Jesus and in God.

Modern Christology may be said to begin in the Enlightenment, at a time when all sorts of new questions had arisen concerning the nature of man and his world in relation to God, questions to which the classical categories seemed to provide no relevant answer. To meet this challenge a new Christology was produced, that tended to see belief in the divinity of Christ as a way of articulating the conviction that the distinctive character of Christian faith in God is that this faith is focused on Jesus of Nazareth. So, following a suggestion of J. G. *Herder, it sought to look for the divinity of Jesus in the unique quality of His life on earth. F. D. E. *Schleiermacher stressed the unique quality of Jesus' consciousness of God, which He passes on to others. His successors built the methods and results of the new historical criticism of the Gospels into their Christology. For A. *Ritschl the focus is a picture of a man of pure compassion and kindness, who set a moral example in all that He did. He began the work of the *Kingdom of God, which we continue by acting in love towards our fellow men. It was in reaction to such an approach that the so-called '*dialectical theology' arose. K. *Barth's God is wholly other; in Christ He reveals Himself as and when He wishes. For R. *Bultmann Jesus is the one who confronts man with the eschatological message, demanding response in existential commitment. For Barth there is a return to the high classical Christology, for Bultmann a renewal of the attack on '*metaphysics' and concentration on obedience to God's will as revealed through Jesus' message. Bultmann's pupils, notably E. Käsemann, G. Ebeling, and E. Fuchs, developed a 'New Quest' of the historical Jesus, accepting the importance of *kerygma but seeking to relate it again to history. British Christology in the 20th cent. has been centred in large measure on the classical doctrine of the Incarnation and attempts to reinterpret it. In Anglican theology the continuing debate with the Fathers has been pursued. Traditional Incarnational Christology, however, was attacked by the authors of the *Myth of God Incarnate* symposium (1977). On the Continent of Europe J. *Moltmann and E. Jüngel see the cross of Christ as the key not just to Christology but to all legitimate talk of God. The most comprehensive treatment of Christology in Protestant theology since Barth is to be found in the work of W. *Pannenberg. RC thought has been extraordinarily fertile in the field, esp. in the work of K. *Rahner and E. *Schillebeeckx, H. *Küng, and H. U. von *Balthasar. Rahner displays an almost unique versatility in criticizing the ancient formulas, reinterpreting them radically in line with a post-Enlightenment anthropology, and then using them to interpret the central affirmations of Christology. Schillebeeckx lays stress on Jesus, the Mosaic-messianic 'eschatological prophet' as the basic NT model from which all others are derived. '*Liberation theology', produced largely in Latin America, relates the Incarnation to salvation in the most direct possible way, in its commitment to love for the poor and the dispossessed. See also HISTORICAL JESUS, QUEST OF THE; INCARNATION; HYPOSTASIS; and HYPOSTATIC UNION.

The more important modern works include I. A. *Dorner, *Entwicklungsgeschichte der Lehre von der Person Christi* (Stuttgart, 1839; 2nd edn. 2 vols., Berlin, 1845–53; Eng. tr., 5 vols., 1861–1869); R. I. *Wilberforce, *The Doctrine of the Incarnation of our Lord Jesus Christ* (1848); C. *Gore, *The Incarnation of the Son of God* (Bampton Lectures, 1891); id., *Dissertations on Subjects connected with the Incarnation* (1895); F. *Weston, *The One Christ* (1907); P. T. *Forsyth, *The Person and Place of Jesus Christ* (1909); H. M. Relton, *A Study in Christology* (1917); E. *Brunner, *Der Mittler* (Tübingen, 1927; Eng. tr., *The Mediator*, 1934); *Essays on the Trinity and the Incarnation*, ed. A. E. J. Rawlinson (1928); H. *Rashdall, *God and Man* (1930); J. K. Mozley, *The Doctrine of the Incarnation* (1936); J. M. Creed, *The Divinity of Jesus Christ* (1938); E. L. Mascall, *Christ, the Christian and the Church* (1946); D. M. Baillie, *God was in Christ* (1948); A. Grillmeier, SJ, and H. Bacht, SJ (eds.), *Das Konzil von Chalkedon* (3 vols., Würzburg, 1951–4); W. Elert, *Das Ausgang der altkirchlichen Christologie* (1957); O. *Cullmann, *Die Christologie des Neuen Testaments* (Tübingen, 1957; 2nd edn., 1958; Eng. tr., 1963); W. Pannenberg, *Grundzüge der Christologie* (Gütersloh, 1964; Eng. tr., *Jesus—God and Man*, 1968); R. H. Fuller, *The Foundations of New Testament Christology* (1965); J. Meyendorff, *Christ in Eastern Christian Tradition after Chalcedon* (Washington, DC, 1969); K. Rahner and W. Thüsing, *Christologie—systematisch und exegetisch* (Quaestiones Disputatae, 55; Freiburg, 1972; Eng. tr., 1980), and arts. by Rahner in his *Schriften zur Theologie* (Eng. tr., *Theological Investigations*); J. Moltmann, *Der gekreuzigte Gott* (Munich, 1973; Eng. tr., *The Crucified God*, 1974); J. A. T. *Robinson, *The Human Face of God* (1973); E. Schillebeeckx, OP, *Jezus, het verhaal van een levende* (1974; Eng. tr., *Jesus: An Experiment in Christology*, 1979); id., *Gerechtigheid en liefde: Genade en bevrijding* (1977; Eng. tr., *Christ: The Christian Experience in the Modern World*, 1980; both highly controversial); A. Grillmeier, *Jesus der Christus im Glauben der Kirche* (Freiburg, 1979 ff.; Eng. tr., *Christ in Christian Tradition*, 1975 ff.; vol. 1 originated as an article in Grillmeier and Bacht, op. cit., 1, pp. 5–202, of which a rev. Eng. tr. was pub. 1965); C. F. D. Moule, *The Origin of Christology* (1977); J. [H.] Hick (ed.), *The Myth of God Incarnate* (1977); E. Jüngel, *Gott als Geheimnis der Welt* (Tübingen, 1977; Eng. tr., *God as the Mystery of the World*, 1983); J. D. G. Dunn, *Christology in the Making* (1980; 2nd edn., 1989); R. Sturch, *The Word and the Christ: An Essay in Analytic Christology* (Oxford, 1991); M. Karrer, *Die Gesalbte: Die Grundlagen des Christustitels* (Forschungen zur Religion und Literatur des Alten und Neuen Testaments, 151 [1991]). A. J. Hultgren, *New Testament Christology: A Critical Assessment and Annotated Bibliography* (New York, 1988). See also works cited s.vv. CREEDS and SON OF MAN.

Christopher, St (Gk. Χριστοφόρος, 'one who bore Christ'), one of the 14 *Auxiliary Saints. Acc. to tradition, he suffered martyrdom in Asia Minor during the 3rd cent. Many legends have gathered round his name. One represents him as a powerful giant who earned his living by carrying travellers across a river, and on one occasion numbered among his passengers a small child who caused him to bow beneath his burden, since the child was none other than the Christ and His weight that of the whole world. It was a common medieval custom to place a large mural painting of the saint opposite the south door of the church, in the belief that the sight of it would safeguard the passer-by from accident that day. St Christopher is the patron of wayfarers; recently he has been adopted esp. by motorists. His feast day in the W., 25 July, was dropped from the Roman Calendar of 1969, but may be observed locally. Feast day in the E., 9 May.

Various Gk. and Lat. texts of legend in *AASS*, Jul. 6 (1729), pp. 125–49, in *Anal. Boll.* 1 (1882), pp. 121–48, and 10 (1891), pp. 393–405, and in H. Usener (ed.), *Acta S. Marinae et S. Christophori* (Bonn, 1886), pp. 54–76. H. F. [C.] Rosenfeld, *Der hl. Christophorus: Seine Verehrung und seine Legende* (Acta Academiae Aboensis, Humaniora, 10, no. 3; 1937). E. K. Stahl, *Die Legende vom heil. Riesen Christophorus in der Graphik des 15. und 16. Jahrhunderts* (1920); H. C. Whaite, *St Christopher in English Mediaeval Wallpainting* (University College (London) Monographs on English Mediaeval Art, 1; 1929). C. Johnson, *St Christopher: The Patron Saint of Travellers* (1932; enlarged 1938); A. Masseron, *Saint Christophe, patron des automobilistes* (1933). A. Lohr, OSB, 'Der heilige Christophorus und die Wandlungen im christlichen Heiligenkult', in A. Mayer, J. Quasten, and B. Neunheuser, OSB (eds.), *Vom Christlichen Mysterium: Gesammelte Arbeiten zum Gedächtnis von Odo Casel OSB* (Düsseldorf, 1951), pp. 227–59; W. Loeschcke, 'Sanctus Christophorus Canineus', in *Edwin Redslob zum 70. Geburtstag: Eine Festgabe* [1955], pp. 33–82. B. Hahn-Woernle, *Christophorus in der Schweiz: Seine Verehrung in bildlichen und kultischen Zeugnissen* (Schriften der Schweizerischen Gesellschaft für Volkskunde, 53; Basle, 1972). F. Werner in *Lexikon der christlichen Ikonographie*, 5 (1973), cols. 496–508, s.v. 'Christophorus', with bibl.

Christopherson, John (d. 1558), Bp. of *Chichester. He was one of the original Fellows of Trinity College, Cambridge, by the charter of 1546, and among the first to introduce Greek studies to the University. As an opponent of the Reformation he retired abroad during *Edward VI's reign, but his college continued to support him. When on *Mary's accession William Bill, a pronounced Protestant, was ejected from the Mastership of Trinity, Christopherson was put in to replace him; and he became chaplain and confessor to the Queen. In 1554 he was appointed Dean of Norwich and in 1557 Bp. of Chichester. For preaching an impassioned sermon on 27 Nov. 1558 after *Elizabeth's accession, against the Reformation, he was imprisoned and died shortly afterwards. He was a learned and enthusiastic patristic scholar who rendered into Latin the writings of *Philo (*Philonis Judaei Scriptoris eloquentissimi libri iv*, Antwerp, 1553) as well as the Church Histories of *Eusebius, *Socrates, *Sozomen, *Evagrius, and *Theodoret (published posthumously, Louvain, 1569). He also collected a considerable number of MSS, which he bequeathed to Trinity College.

T. Cooper in *DNB* 10 (1887), pp. 293–5, s.v., with refs.

Christophoria (Gk.), 'the carrying of Christ'. In the *Ambrosian rite, the title of a Feast observed on 7 Jan., the day following the *Epiphany, and commemorating the Return from Egypt (Mt. 2: 21).

Chrodegang, St (d. 766), Bp. of Metz prob. from 742 (possibly from 747). He was one of the chief ecclesiastical reformers of his time. Of noble birth, he became chancellor and chief minister to *Charles Martel and his successor *Pepin III, continuing in political office even after he was made Bp. of Metz. On the martyrdom of St *Boniface in 754 he assumed responsibility for the ecclesiastical affairs of the whole Frankish kingdom. In 748 he founded the abbey of *Gorze, near Metz, and continued to take a keen part in furthering monasticism throughout his diocese. He also caused the canons of his cathedral to live a community life, drawing up for them the 'rule' which bears his name (*c.*755). The picture given by this rule is that of a community consisting essentially of clerics, monastic in their common life and in the performance of the Divine Office, but unmonastic in their close connection with diocesan officials such as the bishop and archdeacon, and, above all, in their licence to hold private property. He also introduced the Roman chant and liturgy into the diocese of Metz. Feast day, 6 Mar.

'Rule' repr. from L. *d'Achery in J. P. Migne, *PL* 89. 1057–96; crit. edn. from Leiden Cod. Voss. Lat. 94 by W. Schmitz (Hanover, 1889); text, based on edn. of Schmitz, with introd. and notes, in J. B. Pelt, *Études sur la cathédrale de Metz: La liturgie* (1937), pp. 5–28. Early Eng. tr., together with Lat. text, ed. A. S. Napier in *EETS*, Original Series, 150 (1916), pp. 1–101, with introd., pp. vii–x. Life ascribed to John, Abbot of Gorze (historically valueless), ed. G. H. Pertz in *MGH*, Scriptores, 10 (1852), pp. 552–72. Of more importance is relevant section of *Paul the Deacon's *Liber de Episcopis Mettensibus*, ed. G. H. Pertz in *MGH*, Scriptores, 2 (1829), pp. 267 f. M. Buchner, 'Die "Vita Chrodegangi"—eine kirchenpolitische Tendenzschrift aus der Mitte des 9. Jahrhunderts, zugleich eine Untersuchung zur Entwicklung der Primatial- und Vikariatsidee', *Zeitschrift der Savigny-Stiftung für Rechtsgeschichte*, Kanonistische Abt., 16 (1927), pp. 1–36, with refs. to earlier studies. R. Folz and others, *Saint Chrodegang: Communications présentées au colloque tenu à Metz à l'occasion du douzième centenaire de sa mort* (Metz, 1967); E. Ewig, 'Beobachtungen zur Entwicklung der fränkischen Reichskirche unter Chrodegang von Metz', *Frühmittelalterliche Studien*, 2 (1968), pp. 67–77; repr. in id., *Spätantikes und fränkisches Gallien*, 2 (Beihefte der *Francia*, 3. 2; Munich, 1979), pp. 220–31; J. Semmler, 'Chrodegang, Bischof von Metz 747–766', in F. Knöpp (ed.), *Die Reichsabtei Lorsch: Festschrift zum Gedenken an ihre Stiftung 764*, 1 (Darmstadt, 1973), pp. 229–45, with refs. M. Parisse in *DIP* 3 (1976), cols. 314–19, s.v. 'Crodegango', with full bibl.; J. Semmler in *TRE* 8 (1981), pp. 71–4, s.v.

Chromatius, St (d. 407), Bp. of *Aquileia, N. Italy. He succeeded Valerian in the see *c.*388. A learned scholar, he conducted an active correspondence with several illustrious contemporaries, among them St *Ambrose, St *Jerome, and *Rufinus. In the *Origenistic dispute he sought to mediate between the two last named. He was a strong supporter of St John *Chrysostom, on whose behalf he interceded, without success, with the Emp. Honorius.

Eighteen of his Homilies on Mt. [3: 15–17; 5: 1–6: 24], including a separate treatise on the Eight Beatitudes, have long been known, but since 1960 many more have been identified apparently from an extensive comm. on Mt. In addition, J. Lemarié has discovered some 45 other sermons.

His works are repr., mainly from the text ed P. Braida, Udine, 1816, in J. P. Migne, *PL* 20. 247–436. Modern edn., incl. those recently ascribed to Chromatius, by R. Étaix and J. Lemarié (CCSL 9A; 2 vols., 1974–7), with bibl. to date. Sermons also ed. J. Lemarié, OSB, with Fr. tr. by H. Tardif (SC 154 and 164; 1969–71). G. Trettel, *Mysterium e Sacramentum in S. Cromazio* (Trieste, 1979). J. Lemarié, 'Chromatiana. Status Quaestionis' [in Fr.], *Rivista di Storia e Letteratura Religiosa*, 17 (1981), pp. 64–76. *Chromatius Episcopus 388–1988* (Antichità Altoadriatiche, 34; Udine, 1989). B. Studer in Quasten (cont.), *Patrology*, 4 (1986), pp. 572–4.

Chronicles, Books of. These OT Books record the history of *Israel and *Judah from the Creation to the return from *Exile after the fall of Babylon *c.*539 BC. In the Hebrew Canon they are a single Book; the division into two goes back to the *Septuagint, where they are called Παραλειπομένων α β΄, i.e. 'that which is left over', sc. from Sam. and Kgs. The term 'Chronicles' was introduced by St *Jerome, whence it made its way into the English and German versions. The work is divided into four parts. 1 Chron. 1–9 are genealogies from *Adam to the death of Saul; 10–29 describe the reign of *David; 2 Chron. 1–9 the reign of *Solomon; and 10–36 give a history of the kings of Judah.

Throughout the Books the interest concentrates on the religious aspects of the history, esp. the *Temple and its worship, to which is assigned a very large place. Thus the story of David is much concerned with his preparations for the building of the Temple, and the reign of Solomon with long descriptions of the Temple itself, its structure, liturgy, and personnel. With the same religious interest in view the less edifying episodes in the lives of David and Solomon are omitted, and the whole subsequent history of the kings of Judah is seen as a series of rewards and punishments acc. to their attitude to religion. The obvious aim of the work is to inculcate respect for the Law and to stress the advantages of its observance.

The sources used in Chron. are the canonical books, esp. Gen., Exod., Num., Jos., and Sam. and Kgs., but also extra-canonical material, among which the author names a 'History of the Kings of Israel and Judah' and a 'Midrash of the Kings of Israel and Judah'. Acc. to the list of high priests the book seems to have been written in the latter half of the 4th cent. BC. Until recently most scholars held that the Chron. formed one continuous whole with the Books of *Ezra and *Nehemiah, but whether this is so is now widely regarded as an open question. On the historical value of Chron. opinion is also divided. The older critics, such as W. M. L. *de Wette and J. *Wellhausen, refused it all credibility, whereas a number of recent scholars have argued that it used reliable information at least for the later period.

Comm. by J. W. Rothstein and J. Hänel (2 vols., KAT 18; 1927), K. Galling (Das Alte Testament Deutsch, 12; on Chron., Ez., Neh., 1954, pp. 7–185), W. Rudolph (HAT, Reihe 1, Bd. 21; 1955), F. Michaeli (Commentaire de l'Ancien Testament, 16; on Chron., Ez., Neh.; Neuchâtel, 1967, pp. 9–12, 24–250), R. J.

Coggins (New Camb. Bib., 1976), H. G. M. Williamson (New Cent. Bib., 1982), and S. Japhet (Old Testament Library; London, 1993). A. C. Welch, *The Work of the Chronicler: Its Purpose and Date* (Schweich Lectures, 1938; 1939). G. von *Rad, *Das Geschichtsbild des chronistischen Werkes* (Beiträge zur Wissenschaft vom Alten und Neuen Testament, 59, Folge 4, 3; 1930). M. *Noth, *Überlieferungsgeschichtliche Studien* (2nd edn., Tübingen, 1957), pp. 110–216 ('Die chronistische Werk (Chr)'; separate Eng. tr., *The Chronicler's History* (Journal for the Study of the Old Testament, Supplement Series, 50; Sheffield [1987]). T. Willi, *Die Chronik als Auslegung* (Forschungen zur Religion und Literatur des Alten und Neuen Testaments, 106; 1972). H. G. M. Williamson, *Israel in the Books of Chronicles* (Cambridge, 1977). S. Japhet, *The Ideology of the Book of Chronicles and its Place in Biblical Thought* (Beiträge zur Erforschung des Alten Testaments und des antiken Judentum, 9 [1989]). Eissfeldt, pp. 529–40, 769, with bibl. A. M. Brunet in *Dict. Bibl.*, Suppl. 6 (1960), cols. 1220–61, s.v. 'Paralipomènes', with bibl.

Chronicon Edessenum (Edessene Chronicle). A Syriac Chronicle extending from 133 BC to AD 540, the date of its compilation, but with very few entries before the 3rd cent. AD. Its principal interest lies in the history of *Edessa, but it sometimes supplies important incidental information on general history both East and West. L. Hallier argued that its principal sources were some early documents from *Antioch, a lost history of the Persians, and the Edessene city archives. It exists only in a single MS (Cod. Vat. syr. 163), derived from the Convent of Our Lady in the Nitrian desert.

Syr. text first pub. in J. S. *Assemani, *Bibliotheca Orientalis*, 1 (1719), pp. 387–417. Crit. edns. by L. Hallier, with Ger. tr. and comm. (TU 9. 1; 1892), and by I. Guidi (CSCO, Scriptores Syri, 3rd ser., 4, 1903, pp. 1–13, with Lat. tr. pp. 1–11). A. *Baumstark, *Geschichte der syrischen Literatur* (1922), pp. 99 f.

Chronicon Paschale. A Byzantine chronicle compiled in the first half of the 7th cent., so named from its having been based on the Easter reckoning. It contained a chronological outline of events from the creation of Adam to the 20th year of the Emp. *Heraclius (630); but not all of it has survived. The author used *inter alia* the Easter Tables of *Alexandria, the 'Fasti Consulares', Sextus *Julius Africanus, the 'Chronicon' and 'Ecclesiastical History' of *Eusebius of Caesarea, the 'Christian Topography' of *Cosmas Indicopleustes, and the 'Chronicle' of *John Malalas; and for the last 27 years he has the value of a contemporary historian. The principal MS is the *Vatican cod. gr. 1941 (10th cent.).

The document is sometimes known as the 'Chronicon Alexandrinum'; it owes the name 'Paschal Chronicle' to its first ed., C. D. *Du Cange. Best edn. by L. Dindorf in CSH Byz. (2 vols., 1832); repr. in J. P. Migne, *PG* 92. 9–1160. Eng. tr. of section covering 284–628 by M. and M. Whitby (Translated Texts for Historians, Liverpool, 1989), with introd. and bibl. G. *Mercati, 'A Study of the *Paschal Chronicle*', *JTS* 7 (1906), pp. 397–412; repr. in his *Opere minori* (ST 77; 1937), pp. 462–79.

Chronographer of AD 354, the. The name given by T. *Mommsen to the unknown compiler of an almanac drawn up for the use of Christians at *Rome in the 4th cent. The document, devoid of literary pretensions, remains an invaluable source for the study of early ecclesiastical history. All the extant MSS are fragments, but by piecing their witness together practically the whole docu-

ment can be reconstructed. Acc. to Mommsen, these are all dependent on a now lost 'Codex Luxemburgensis'. The compilation contained *inter alia* these items: (1) a calendar of Roman holidays; (2) a list of the consuls (from AUC 245 to AD 354); (3) an Easter Table (from AD 312 to 354, with an extension to AD 410); (4) a list of the city prefects at Rome from AD 254 to 354; (5) 'Depositio episcoporum', a list of the dates of death of the Bishops of Rome from AD 255 to 352; (6) a sort of primitive Roman *Martyrology; (7) a list of the Roman Bishops from St *Peter down to Pope *Liberius (see LIBERIAN CATALOGUE); (8) a chronicle based on that of St *Hippolytus, combined with (9) a chronicle of Roman secular history from early times down to the death of the Emp. Licinius (325); (10) an account of the 14 regions of the city of Rome.

Text pr., with extended comm., in T. Mommsen, 'Über den Chronographen vom Jahre 354' in *Abh.* (Sächs.), 1 (1850), pp. 547–693; and again in *MGH*, Auctores Antiquissimi, 9 (pt. 1; 1892), pp. 13–196. C. Nordenfalk, *Der Kalender vom Jahre 354 und die lateinische Buchmalerei des iv. Jahrhunderts* (Göteborg, 1936); H. Stern, *Le Calendrier de 354: Étude sur son texte et sur ses illustrations* (Institut français d'Archéologie de Beyrout. Bibliothèque Archéologique et Historique, 55; 1953). M. R. Salzman, *On Roman Time: The Codex-Calendar of 354 and the Rhythms of Urban Life in Late Antiquity* (Transformation of the Classical Heritage, 17; Berkeley, Los Angeles and Oxford [1990]). O. Seeck in *PW* 3 (1899), cols. 2477–81. See also bibl. to LIBERIAN CATALOGUE.

chronology, biblical. (1) OLD TESTAMENT. It is very difficult to date accurately the events which are narrated in the OT owing to (*a*) the absence in the ancient world of any widely recognized chronological era, (*b*) the few allusions in the OT to events outside Israel known to us from extraneous sources, and (*c*) the occasional use in the OT of chronological schemes for theological purposes. The Hebrew records are themselves sometimes inadequate, e.g. while the duration of the sojourn in Egypt is given (Gen. 15: 13, Ex. 12: 40–1), the names of the Pharaohs are not recorded. Among the important chronological data supplied in the OT are the interval between the *Exodus and the building of Solomon's *Temple (1 Kgs. 6: 1); the duration of the wandering in the wilderness (Num. 14: 33); and the lengths of the reigns of the Kings of Israel and Judah in the Books of the Kings. But the figures supplied are not always consistent even in the Hebrew text, and there are frequent divergences in the *Septuagint. However, from the 9th cent. BC onwards the dates of the events narrated can be roughly discovered by comparing them with the more detailed and accurate Assyrian and Persian chronologies.

(2) NEW TESTAMENT. The range here is shorter and the problems more circumscribed, but even so there are many difficulties. Complications are caused by the vagueness of much of the evidence and our dependence upon inferences; also by the different methods by which the years of monarchs were reckoned and the intricacies of the Jewish calendar. Acc. to Mt. 2: 1, Jesus was born 'in the days of *Herod the king' (d. *c*.4 BC), but acc. to Lk. 2: 2 during 'the first enrolment made when Quirinius was governor of Syria' (probably AD 6–9). Jesus was baptized in 'the fifteenth year of the reign of Tiberius *Caesar' (Lk. 3: 1), i.e. in AD 28 or 29, while acc. to Jn. 2: 13–20 the first *Passover after His Baptism was the 46th year of the

building of Herod's Temple (AD 27). Jesus would thus be about 30 years old when He began to teach (Lk. 3: 23). The length of Christ's ministry is difficult to determine. In the Synoptic Gospels only one Passover is explicitly mentioned, and from this fact it has sometimes been inferred that the ministry lasted only one year; in the Fourth Gospel three Passovers are recorded. The date of the Crucifixion is uncertain, the most likely years being AD 30 or 33. However, all are agreed that Jesus 'suffered under Pontius *Pilate', who was prefect of *Judaea from AD 26 to 36. With regard to the chronology of the Apostolic Age, the date of St *Paul's conversion, on which so much depends, is uncertain, in spite of the data which he supplies in Gal. 1: 18 and 2; the earliest date would be just after the Crucifixion. The concluding part of Paul's life is also obscure, as his death is not recorded. Evidence from outside the NT is scanty and sometimes ambiguous; the firmest date is supplied by an inscription which shows that Gallio, before whom Paul appeared in Corinth (Acts 18: 12–18) was proconsul of Achaea in AD 51–2. Nevertheless these uncertainties hardly affect the main outline of our picture of the course of early Christianity.

Among the first attempts to put biblical chronology on a sound basis was J. *Ussher, *Annales Veteris et Novi Testamenti* (2 parts, 1650–9); its dates gained wide currency through their frequent printing in the margins of the AV. Modern attempts to deal with the problems of biblical chronology as a whole by E. Ruffini, *Chronologia Veteris et Novi Testamenti in Aeram Nostram Collata* (Rome, 1924); J. Finegan, *Handbook of Biblical Chronology* (Princeton, NJ, 1964).
On the chronology of the OT, D. N. Freedman, 'The Chronology of Israel and the Near East. Section A. Old Testament Chronology', in G. E. Wright (ed.), *The Bible and the Ancient Near East: Essays in honor of William Foxwell Albright* (1961), pp. 203–14, with notes, pp. 225–8; A. Jepsen and R. Hanhart, *Untersuchungen zur israelitisch-jüdischen Chronologie* (Beihefte zur *ZATW*, 88; 1964); R. R. Wilson, *Genealogy and History in the Biblical World* (Yale Near Eastern Researches, 7; 1977); J. Hughes, *Secrets of the Times: Myth and History in Biblical Chronology* (Journal for the Study of the Old Testament, Suppl. Series, 66; 1990). See also bibl. to individual books.
On the NT, the classic discussion is that of C. H. *Turner in *HDB* 1 (1900), pp. 403–25, s.v. 'Chronology in the New Testament'. U. Holzmeister, SJ, *Chronologia Vitae Christi* (Scripta Pontificii Instituti Biblici, 1936); G. Ogg, *The Chronology of the Public Ministry of Jesus* (1940); J. A. T. *Robinson, *The Priority of John*, ed. J. F. Coakley (1985), pp. 123–57 ('The Chronology of the Ministry'). G. Ogg, *The Chronology of the Life of Paul* (1968); A. Suhl, *Paulus und seine Briefe: Ein Beitrag zur paulinischen Chronologie* (Studien zum Neuen Testament, 11 [1975]); R. Jewett, *A Chronology of Paul's Life* (Philadelphia, 1979; British edn., *Dating Paul's Life*, London, 1979); G. Lüdemann, *Paul, der Heidenapostel*, 1: *Studien zur Chronologie* (Forschungen zur Religion und Literatur des Alten und Neuen Testaments, 123; Göttingen, 1980; Eng. tr., 1984); N. Hyldahl, *Die Paulinische Chronologie* (Acta Theologica Danica, 19; 1986). J. Lebreton, SJ, in *Dict. Bibl.*, Suppl. 4 (1949), cols. 970–5, s.v. 'Jésus-Christ. Chronologie de la vie de Jésus', and F. Prat, ibid., 1 (1928), cols. 1299–304, s.v. See also Lives of Christ, cited under JESUS CHRIST, works on Paul, and bibl. to his various Epistles, and to Acts. For general discussions on chronology, see bibl. to CALENDAR.

Chrysippus (*c*.405–79), 'of Jerusalem', ecclesiastical writer. A native of Cappadocia, he accompanied his two brothers, Cosmas and Gabriel, to Jerusalem *c*.428 and became a monk at the laura of St *Euthymius. He was

ordained priest *c*.455 and later succeeded Cosmas as guardian of the Holy Cross at the Church of the *Holy Sepulchre ('staurophylax'). His few surviving writings include panegyrics of (1) the BVM, (2) St Theodore Tiro, (3) St *Michael the Archangel, and (4) St *John Baptist.

The chief evidences for his life are the refs. in *Cyril of Scythopolis' 'Life of St Euthymius'. For text of the four panegyrics mentioned above see: for (1), ed. M. Jugie, AA, in *PO* 19 (1926), pp. 336–43 (a repr., with corrections, of edn. of F. *Ducaeus, 1624); for (2), ed. A. Sigalas (*Byzantinisches Archiv*, 7; 1921); for (3), ed. id. in Ἐπετηρὶς Ἑταιρείας Βυζαντινῶν Σπουδῶν, 3 (Athens, 1926), pp. 85–93; for (4), ed. id. (Texte und Forschungen zur byzantinisch-neugriechischen Philologie, 20; 1937). S. Vailhé, AA, 'Chrysippe Prêtre de Jérusalem', *Revue de l'Orient Chrétien*, 10 (1905), pp. 96–9. *CPG* 3 (1979), pp. 287 f. (nos. 6705–8). P. Bruns in *L.Th.K.* (3rd edn.), 2 (1994), cols. 1190, s.v.

Chrysogonus, St. Though his cultus at *Rome dates from the 5th cent. at latest, very little is known of him. Acc. to legend, he was arrested in Rome during *Diocletian's persecution and subsequently slain at *Aquileia. From the 6th cent. onwards he was supposed to have been the spiritual director of St *Anastasia of Rome, with whom he is held to have corresponded on the behaviour of Christians towards their pagan husbands and wives. His name is included in the *Canon of the Roman Mass. Feast day in the E., 22 Dec.; in the W., formerly 24 Nov., but now suppressed.

Chief source of the legend is the 'Passio S. Anastasiae', ed. H. *Delehaye, SJ, *Étude sur le Légendier romain* (Subsidia Hagiographica, 23; 1936), pp. 221–49; cf. also pp. 151–63. On the theory that Chrysogonus was orig. the owner of a church in Rome (*titulus Chrysogoni*), the name being later misunderstood as a dedication, cf. J. P. Kirsch, *Die römischen Titelkirchen im Altertum* (1918), pp. 108–13. M. Mesnard, *La Basilique de saint Chrysogone à Rome* (Studi di Antichità Cristiana, 9; 1935); R. Krautheimer, *Corpus Basilicarum Christianarum Romae*, vol. 1, fasc. 3 (Rome, 1940), pp. 144–64; B. M. A. Ghetti, OFM, 'Nuove considerazioni sulla chiesa inferiore di S. Crisogono', *Riv. A.C.* 22 (1946), pp. 235–49. V. L. Kennedy, CSB, *The Saints of the Canon of the Mass* (Studi di Antichità Cristiana, 14; 1938), pp. 128–30, with further bibl. refs.

Chrysologus, St Peter (*c*.400–50), Bp. of *Ravenna. His episcopate coincided with the Empress *Galla Placidia's time in Ravenna. He seems to have preached before her, and shared her enthusiasm for ambitious building projects. A large collection of sermons attributed to him survives, but almost all his other writings are lost. In a letter to *Eutyches (449) he viewed his case with favour, though in a striking passage he asserted the necessity for adherence in matters of faith to the Roman see. The materials for his life are contained mainly in the historically unreliable 'Liber Pontificalis Ecclesiae Ravennatis' of Abbot *Agnellus (9th cent.). He was apparently named 'Chrysologus' (Gk. 'golden-worded') to make him a W. counterpart of '*Chrysostom' ('golden-mouthed'). In 1729 he was declared a '*Doctor of the Church'. Feast day, 30 July (formerly 4 Dec.).

Editio princeps of his Sermons by Agapitus Vincentinus, Bologna, 1534. Later edns., Bologna, 1643, and Venice, 1750; latter repr. in J. P. Migne, *PL* 52. 9–680; further sermons, with notes on authenticity of those previously pr., by A. Hamman, OFM, ibid., Supplementum, 3 (Paris, 1963), cols. 153–83. Sermons also ed. A. Olivar, OSB (CCSL 24, 24 A, 24 B; 1975–82). Id., *Los sermones de San Pedro Crisólogo* (Scripta et Documenta, 13; Montserrat, 1962), incl. some texts. Eng. tr. of Selected Sermons and Letter to Eutyches, with introd. by G. E. Ganss, SJ (Fathers of the Church, 17; 1953, pp. 3–287). Monographs by F. J. Peters (Cologne [1918]) and G. Böhmer (Paderborn, 1919). J. H. Baxter, 'The Homilies of St Peter Chrysologus', *JTS* 22 (1920–1), pp. 250–8; C. Jenkins, 'Aspects of the theology of St Peter Chrysologus', *CQR* 103 (1927), pp. 233–59. F. Sottocornola, *L'Anno liturgico nei sermoni di Pietro Crisologo* (Studia Ravennatensia, 1; Cesena, 1973). *CPL* (3rd edn., 1995), pp. 87–93 (nos. 227–37). Altaner and Stuiber (1978), pp. 458 and 648. H. Koch in *PW* 19 (pt. 2; 1938), cols. 1361–72, s.v. 'Petrus (122) Chrysologus'; A. Solignac, SJ, in *Dict. Sp.* 12 (pt. 2; 1986), cols. 1541–6, s.v. 'Pierre (18) Chrysologue'.

chrysom. The 'chrism-robe' put on a child at Baptism, as a symbol of the cleansing of its sin. Originally it may have been a cloth put over the head, to prevent the *chrism from being rubbed off. If the child died within a month of its Baptism, the chrysom was used as a shroud; hence the expression 'chrysom child'. The use of the 'whyte vesture, commonly called the Chrysome' was ordered in the BCP of 1549. It was to be put on before the unction, not after it as in the pre-Reformation English rites, and returned to the priest at the mother's *churching. In the C of E its use disappeared in 1552 and has not been officially revived, except in the Province of *Southern Africa. It survives in the RC Church.

Chrysostom, Pseudo-. A very large number of St John *Chrysostom's sermons has come down to us, and his great repute as a preacher caused many sermons to be falsely ascribed to him. Of particular interest among these pseudonymous sermons are homilies by representatives of heretical movements of the later 4th cent. from which little else survives. Three paschal homilies have been ascribed to *Apollinaris of Laodicea (Cattaneo); two homilies for the octave of *Easter seem to be *Anomoean (Liébaert), and the *Opus imperfectum in Matthaeum* (*PG* 56. 611–946) consists of a series of Latin homilies preached by an *Arian bishop of the 5th or even the 6th cent. The sermons give a rare glimpse of the spirituality of such heretical movements.

Homélies Pascales, ed., with Fr. tr., by P. Nautin and F. Floërri (SC 27, 36, and 48; 1950–7); *Deux Homélies Anoméennes pour l'octave de Pâques*, ed., with Fr. tr., by J. Liébaert (ibid., 146; 1969). Other Homilies also ed. K.-H. Uthemann and others (Turnhout, 1994 ff.). Crit. text of *Opus imperfectum* by J. van Banning, SJ (CCSL 87 B, etc.; 1988 ff.). E. Cattaneo, SJ, *Trois Homélies Pseudo-Chrysostomiennes sur la Pâque comme œuvre d'Apollinaire de Laodicée* (Théologie Historique, 58 [1981]). F. Mali, *Das 'Opus imperfectum in Matthaeum' und sein Verhältnis zu den Matthäuskommentaren von Origenes und Hieronymus* (Innsbrucker theologische Studien, 34; 1991). J. A. de Aldama, SJ, *Repertorium pseudochrysostomicum* (Documents, Études et Répertoires publiés par l'Institut de Recherche et d'Histoire des Textes, 10; 1965), limited to works already pub. *CPG* 2 (1974), pp. 540–672 (nos. 4500–5197). H. J. Sieben in *Dict. Sp.* 8 (1974), cols. 355–69, s.v. 'Jean Chrysostome (Pseudo-)', with bibl. See also bibl. to CHRYSOSTOM, ST JOHN.

Chrysostom, St John (*c*.347–407), Bp. of *Constantinople and '*Doctor of the Church'. He was educated for the law under the great pagan orator Libanius at *Antioch, where he studied theology under *Diodore of Tarsus, the leader of the *Antiochene School. He early felt a call to the monastic life. As the care of his widowed mother Anthusa prevented the immediate fulfilment of this desire, he lived for some time under rule at home, and later became a hermit (*c*.373–*c*.381), following the *Pachomian Rule with austerities which undermined his health. He was made deacon in 381, and served at Antioch under the bishop Flavian, who ordained him priest in 386, and appointed him to devote special attention to the work of preaching (a task in which his ability gained him the name of Chrysostom, 'golden-mouthed'). His powers of oratory were soon manifested in the famous series of sermons 'On the Statues' which he gave in Mar. and Apr. 387 after a riot at Antioch in which the Imperial statues had been overthrown. His preaching was directed esp. to the instruction and moral reformation of the nominally Christian society of his day. His sermons on Books of the Bible—Gen., Pss., Is., Mt., Jn., Acts, and the Pauline Epistles (incl. Heb.)—establish his title as the greatest of Christian expositors. These works combine a great facility for seeing the spiritual meaning of the author with an equal ability for immediate practical application. He was opposed, however, to the wholesale *allegorization of the Scriptures and stressed the importance of the literal sense. Against his wish, Chrysostom was made Patr. of Constantinople in 398, and immediately set about the work of reforming the city, where the corruption of court, clergy, and people alike had been encouraged by the complaisance and self-indulgence of his predecessor, St *Nectarius.

His combination of honesty, asceticism, and tactlessness, esp. in relation to the Empress Eudoxia, who with some reason took all attempts at moral reform as a censure of herself, was sufficient to work his ruin. When Chrysostom sheltered the *Tall Brothers who had fled from Egypt after the condemnation of *Origenism, *Theophilus, Patr. of *Alexandria, seized the opportunity to humiliate the see of Constantinople. At the Synod of the *Oak (403), carefully packed by Theophilus, Chrysostom was condemned on 29 charges. He was removed from his see, but shortly afterwards recalled by the court. Very soon, however, his plain speaking brought the displeasure of the Empress on him again, and his enemies saw their opportunity, and secured his banishment on a charge of unlawfully reassuming the duties of a see from which he had been canonically deposed (404). Even the support of the people of Constantinople, of the Pope (*Innocent I), and of the entire W. Church, failed to save him. He was exiled at first to near Antioch, and when it became clear that in spite of his enfeebled health he would not die there soon enough, he was moved to Pontus, and finally deliberately killed by enforced travelling on foot in severe weather. His chief claim to remembrance, apart from his personal holiness, rests on his preaching and exegesis. His early work, 'On the Priesthood', is a finely conceived description of the responsibilities of the Christian minister. Feast day in W., 13 Sept. (formerly 27 Jan., also observed in parts of the Anglican Communion); in E., 13 Nov. See also CHRYSOSTOM, PSEUDO-, and the following entries.

Collected edns. of his works, incl. much *spuria*, by F. *Ducaeus, SJ (12 vols., Paris, 1609–33), H. *Savile (8 vols., Eton, 1612, without Lat. tr.; with important prefaces and notes by I. *Casaubon and others, and generally, except for the portions ed. by F. *Field and modern edns. of individual treaties, still the best edn. of the text), and B. de *Montfaucon, OSB (13 vols., Paris, 1718–38). This last was repr. (the most convenient edn.), with revisions by G. R. L. von Sinner (13 vols., Paris, 'apud fratres Gaume', 1834–40); and, with suppls., in J. P. Migne, *PG* 47–64. Valuable edns. by F. Field of *Homm. on Matt.* (3 vols., Cambridge, 1839) and *Interpr. Omnium Epp. Paulinarum* (7 vols., Oxford, 1845–62). Other separate edns. incl. the *De Sacerdotio* ed. J. A. Nairn (Cambridge Patristic Texts, 1906) and *Contra subintroductas* ed. J. Dumortier (Nouvelle Collection des Textes et Documents, 1955).

Several treatises have been ed. in SC: by A.-M. Malingrey, *Ad eos qui scandalizati* (as *Sur la providence de Dieu*, 79; 1961), a letter to Olympias from exile (*Quod nemo laeditur*, 103; 1964), *Epp. ad Olympiadem* (13 bis; 1968), *De Incomprehensibili* (with others, 28 bis; 1970), *De inani gloria* (188; 1972), *De Sacerdotio* (272; 1980), and *Contra Anomoeos* (as *Sur l'Égalité du Père et du Fils*, 396; 1994); by J. Dumortier, *Ad Theodorum lapsum* (117; 1966), Homilies on Is. 6: 1–6 (*In illud, Vidi Dominum*) (277; 1981), and *Comm. in Isaiam* (304; 1983); by H. Musurillo, SJ, *De Virginitate* (125; 1966); by B. Grillet and G. H. Ettlinger, SJ, *Ad viduam juniorem* and *De non iterando conjugio* (138; 1968); by A. Wenger, AA, eight previously unedited baptismal homilies, from Athos MS Stavronikita 6 (50 bis., 1970); by A. Piédagnel, *De laudibus S. Pauli* (300; 1982) and three baptismal catecheses (366; 1990); by M. A. Schatkin and others, *De S. Babyla contra Iulianum et Gentiles* (362; 1990, with *De S. hieromartyre Babyla*, ed. B. Grillet and J.-N. Guinot); previously unpub. comm. on Job ed., with Fr. tr., by H. Sorlin and L. Neyrand, SJ (ibid. 346 and 348; 1988) and, with Ger. tr., by U. and D. Hagedorn (Patristische Texte und Studien, 35; 1990). Eng. tr. of sets of Homilies in LF, 16 vols., 1839–52, and NPNCF, 1st ser. 9–14, 1888–93; also of Homilies on Gen. by R. C. Hill (Fathers of the Church, 74, 82, and 87 [1986–92]); and of the eight rediscovered baptismal homilies (and four others), with valuable introd., by P. W. Harkins (ACW 31; 1963).

Life (pr. in edns. of Chrysostom) by *Palladius, entitled 'Dialogus de Vita S. Joannis Chrysostomi' (crit. edns. by P. R. Coleman-Norton, Cambridge, 1928, and, with Fr. tr., by A.-M. Malingrey and P. Leclercq, SC 341–2; 1988). Further biog. material in *Socrates, *HE* 6. 2–23, 7. 25–45, *Sozomen, *HE* 8. 2–28, and *Theodoret, *HE* 5. 27–36. Some impression of his posthumous fame emerges from F. Halkin, SJ (ed.), *Douze Récits Byzantins sur Saint Jean Chrysostome* (Subsidia Hagiographica, 60; 1977). Modern studies by A. Puech (Paris, 1891), id. ('Les Saints', 1900; Eng. tr., 1902), A. Moulard (Paris, 1941), P. Chrysostomus Baur, OSB (2 vols., Munich, 1929–1930; Eng. tr., 2 vols., 1959–60; fundamental), and J. N. D. Kelly (London, 1995). Of primary importance, esp. for chronology, L. S. de *Tillemont, *Mémoires pour servir à l'histoire ecclésiastique des six premiers siècles*, 9 (1706), pp. 1–405 and 547–626. A. Naegle, *Die Eucharistielehre des heiligen Johannes Chrysostomus* (1900). S. Verosta, *Johannes Chrysostomus, Staatsphilosoph und Geschichtstheologe* (Graz, etc., 1960). P. Stockmeier, *Theologie und Kult des Kreuzes bei Johannes Chrysostomus* (Trierer Theologische Studien, 18; 1966). T. M. Finn, *The Liturgy of Baptism in the Baptismal Instructions of St John Chrysostom* (Catholic University of America Studies in Christian Antiquity, 15; 1967). C. Kannengiesser [SJ] (ed.), *Jean Chrysostome et Augustin: Actes du Colloque de Chantilly 22–24 septembre 1974* (Théologie historique, 35 [1975]). O. Pasquato, SDB, *Gli Spettacoli in S. Giovanni Crisostomo* (Orientalia Christiana Analecta, 201; 1976). R. L. Wilken, *John Chrysostom and the Jews* (Berkeley, Calif., and London, 1983). A. Stötzel, *Kirche als 'neue Gesellschaft': Die humanisierende Wirkung des Christentums nach Johannes Chrysostomus* (Münsterische Beiträge zur Theologie, 51; 1984). F.-X. Druet, *Language, Images et Visages de la Mort chez Jean Chrysostome* (Collection d'études classiques, 3; Namur, 1990). F. van de Paverd, *St John Chrysostom, The Homilies on the Statues: An Introduction* (Orientalia Christiana Analecta, 239; Rome, 1991). J. H. W. G. Liebeschuetz, *Barbarians and Bishops* (Oxford, 1990), esp. pp. 166–227.

CPG 2 (1974), pp. 491–672 (nos. 4305–5197). Catalogue of MSS containing material ascribed to Chrysostom (incl. *dubia* and *spuria*) by M. Aubineau, R. E. Carter, SJ, and others, *Codices Chrysostomici Graeci* (Documents, Études et Répertoires publiés par l'Institut de Recherche et d'Histoire des Textes, 13, 14, 15, etc. [subsequent vols. not numbered]; 1968 ff.). B. C. Burger, *Bibliotheca Chrysostomica* (8 vols., Portland, Or., 1982 ff.); A.-M. Malingrey and others, *Indices Chrysostomici* (Hildesheim and New York, 1978 ff.); R. A. Krupp, *Saint John Chrysostom: A Scripture Index* (New York and London, 1984). E. Venables in *DCB* 1 (1877), pp. 518–35; G. Bardy in *DTC* 8 (pt. 1; 1924), cols. 660–90, s.v. 'Jean Chrysostome'; P. W. Harkins in *NCE* 7 (1967), pp. 1041–4, s.v. 'John Chrysostom, St'; A. Wenger, AA, in *Dict. Sp.* 8 (1974), cols. 331–55, s.v. 'Jean 57. Jean Chrysostome'.

Chrysostom, Liturgy of St. The normal liturgy of the E. Orthodox Church used on all days when the Eucharistic liturgy is offered except on the ten days in the year for which the Liturgy of St *Basil is prescribed. The earliest surviving text is a *Barberini MS of the 8th or 9th cent. Though there are some early elements, in its present form the Liturgy is much later than the time of St *Chrysostom, whose name it bears. Most scholars question the grounds for associating it with him at all; recently, however, many passages for which parallels can be found in Chrysostom's works have led G. Wagner to defend the connection. It probably owed its great influence to being the liturgy of the Imperial capital, and after the older liturgies of St *James (*Jerusalem and *Antioch) and St *Mark (*Alexandria) had been considerably assimilated to it, it almost entirely superseded them in the 13th cent. It is used in several different languages in the Orthodox Churches of the E.

Gk. text in F. E. *Brightman, *Liturgies Eastern and Western*, 1 (1896), pp. 309–44 (based on MS Barb., iii. 55) and 353–99 (modern text). Eng. tr., with parallel Gk. text, by A. Kokkinakis, *The Liturgy of the Orthodox Church* (1979), pp. 86–143; also in *The Divine Liturgy of . . . John Chrysostom* (Oxford, 1995). Oldest Lat. version ed. A. Strittmatter, OSB, in *Ephemerides Liturgicae*, 55 (1941), pp. 2–73, and *Traditio*, 1 (New York, 1943), pp. 79–137. Syr. vers. ed. H. W. Codrington (Rome, 1940). S. [L.] Antoniadis, *Place de la Liturgie dans la Tradition des Lettres grecques* (Leiden, 1939), esp. pp. 50–86 and 153–61. C. Kucharek, *The Byzantine–Slav Liturgy of St John Chrysostom: Its Origin and Evolution* (Allendale, NJ [1971]). G. Wagner, *Der Ursprung der Chrysostomusliturgie* (Liturgiewissenschaftliche Quellen und Forschungen, 49; 1973). J. Mateos, SJ, *La Célébration de la Parole dans la Liturgie Byzantine* (Orientalia Christiana Analecta, 191; 1971); R. F. Taft, SJ, *The Great Entrance: A History of the Transfer of Gifts and other Pre-Anaphoral Rites of the Liturgy of St Chrysostom* (ibid. 200; 1975); id., *A History of the Liturgy of St John Chrysostom*, 4: *The Diptychs* (ibid. 238; 1991), with refs. to arts. which will form parts of other vols.

Chrysostom, The Prayer of St. The familiar prayer in the BCP was drawn by T. *Cranmer from the Liturgy of St *Chrysostom (q.v., ed. F. E. *Brightman, p. 367). In the original Book (1549) it is found only in the *Litany, where it owes its presence to the fact that in 'Chrysostom' (on which Cranmer was largely dependent for the English Litany) its place was near the Deacon's Litany. It was first included among the concluding prayers at Mattins and Evensong in 1662. Its authorship is unknown.

J. Dowden, *The Workmanship of the Prayer Book* (1899), pp. 227–9.

Church. (1) TERMINOLOGY. The Eng. 'church', Ger. *Kirche*, Dutch *kerk*, etc., come ultimately from the Gk.

κυριακόν, '[thing] belonging to the Lord', which was applied orig. to a church building. The Lat. *ecclesia* and its derivatives (Fr. *église*, Ital. *chiesa*, etc., including Welsh *eglwys*), although used of the building, come from the Gk. ἐκκλησία, which in secular Greek meant an assembly, primarily of citizens in a self-governing city (e.g. that of *Ephesus, Acts 19: 39). In the *Septuagint ἐκκλησία was used of the 'assembly' or 'congregation' of the Israelites (Heb. קָהָל and esp. of those 'within the covenant' as opposed to 'the stranger in your midst' (Deut. 23: 3, Neh. 13: 1). In Acts 7: 38 the word is used with this OT ref.

In the Gospels, the word ἐκκλησία occurs only twice on the Lord's lips, at Mt. 16: 18 (the words to St *Peter, 'upon this rock [*petra*] I will build my Church'), and at 18: 17 (when a brother will not heed private remonstrance, the matter is to be told to 'the Church'). In Acts the word is first found, in its Christian sense, in 5: 11, where 'the whole Church' is to be identified with 'the Church in Jerusalem' at 8: 1. (The best MSS do not attest the word at 2: 47, where it is found in the AV.) It is uncertain whether the Jerusalem Christians applied the equivalent Aramaic word to themselves at this date; but it is clear from St *Paul's Epp. that among Greek-speaking Christians ἐκκλησία was the regular word from an early date, both for a local Christian community (e.g. 'the Churches of Galatia', 'the Church of the Thessalonians', Gal. 1: 2, 1 Thess. 1: 1) and for the whole Christian community (e.g. 1 Cor. 12: 28).

(2) NEW TESTAMENT. The origins of the Church as a sect within 1st-cent. Judaism lie in the Lord's choice of 12 disciples (called *Apostles at Mk. 6: 30, Mt. 10: 2 and in Lk.), probably representing the 12 tribes of Israel (cf. Mt. 19: 28). Their mission was initially to Israel (cf. Mt. 10: 5), but soon after the Resurrection Gentiles began to join the Hellenists, or Greek-speaking Jewish Christians, probably first at *Antioch (cf. Acts 11: 20). Paul's Gentile mission and esp. the epistles which he wrote in the 50s laid foundations for the Gentile Christianity which became dominant after the fall of *Jerusalem in 70 and the expulsion of Jewish Christians from *synagogues in the 80s. This 'parting of the ways' between Church and synagogue marked a large step in the emerging of early Catholic Christianity around 100 AD. The historical development from considerable diversity to a measure of uniformity is only partly visible because the sources are fragmentary, but the outlines of 1st-cent. life and worship can be detected. The Church's roots in Israel were all-important, and the relationship to contemporary Israel initially a vital issue (e.g. Rom. 11). Paul's fertile images (e.g. body, bride, temple) were taken up by later writers, and the experience of the Spirit was associated with a more settled ministry of *bishops, *presbyters, and *deacons.

(3) CATHOLICISM AND THE CHURCH. Though sociologically classifiable as a sect, the early Church never considered itself a merely voluntary association of individuals. From the outset its self-understanding was conditioned by its belief in God's inauguration of the new age and its imminent expectation of a new heaven and new earth (the *Kingdom of God). It constituted the faithful remnant of God's people who had recognized the coming of the *Messiah and soon understood its mission in universal terms (cf. Mt. 28: 19).

After the death of St *James (the Great), Paul and Peter in the 60s and the marginalizing of Jewish Christianity, new structures were needed and Church order developed. The memory of the Apostles was cherished and the emerging orthodoxy of the 2nd cent. aimed to be 'apostolic' in all things, repudiating as heretics those who were not. The essence of the Church was later epitomized in the traditional '*notes of the Church', namely unity, holiness, catholicity, and apostolicity. The concept is already present in Ephesians, though the term 'the *catholic church' first occurs in St *Ignatius (*Ep. ad Smyrn.*, 8. 2). As teaching the Apostles' doctrine and historically descended from them, the Church is apostolic. Its membership (at least as far as the living are concerned), its orders of ministers, and its unity are all constituted by participation in visible sacraments, i.e. those of *Baptism and *Confirmation, of Holy *Orders and of the *Eucharist, respectively. In contrast with this visible Church 'Militant here in earth', there exists the invisible Church of the faithful departed, divided into the Church Expectant (undergoing purification in *purgatory) and the Church Triumphant (already enjoying the *beatific vision in heaven). Separation from the Church Militant is the sin of *schism, and rejection of its apostolic doctrine *heresy.

In early times the doctrine of the visible unity of the Church was accepted on all sides. The schismatic bodies which arose (e.g. *Montanists, *Novatianists, *Donatists) all considered themselves the whole Church. But a theology of the Church gradually developed which gave precision to the status of those in schism. Against rigorist movements such as Donatism, St *Augustine maintained that the sacraments were everywhere to be regarded as acts of the whole Church; their *validity (q.v.) depended not on the personal qualities of the minister but only on his sacramental status. In the following period authority in the W. Church came to be increasingly concentrated in the Papacy. The *Conciliar Theory challenged the notion that the Church could not act apart from the Pope, but to little effect.

After the schism between the E. and W., the RC and the E. *Orthodox Churches each maintained that the other was in schism, and that itself was the historic manifestation of the visible Church. In 1965 the mutual excommunications were withdrawn, without, however, the fundamental claims being much affected. Anglicans and others who do not accept the exclusive claim of any Church often maintain that all parts of the Church Militant, including the RC Church, are now to some extent in schism.

(4) PROTESTANTISM AND THE CHURCH. The *Reformation led to a reformulation of the idea of the Church. It sought to proclaim its inner being in terms of the Word of God rather than in sacramental relationships. Two doctrines of the Church received wide acceptance: (*a*) the more conservative, that the Church is a visible body and in the Divine intention one throughout the world, but that in view of corruptions and errors which have arisen it is justified within a particular nation in reforming itself, even if this involves a breach of visible unity; (*b*) the more radical, that the true Church is in essence an invisible body, since the essential fact by which a man is saved and made a member of the Church is the inward fact of faith. Thus constituted, the Church is a body whose actual membership is known only to God. Most supporters of

this view of the Church held that it was desirable that it should possess an outward and visible organization, membership of which should correspond as closely as possible to the true invisible Church, though identity was impossible. In the view of some the visible organization of the Church should as far as possible be one throughout Christendom, or at least throughout reformed Christendom. In each nation or area of civil government this visible unity was to be secured by an '*established religion', determined by decree of the ruler, and on this basis the national Churches on the *Lutheran or *Calvinist model were organized. But another group of theologians held that unity of organization between Christian congregations in different places was unnecessary. The *Independents maintained that the only essential outward unity was that of each local congregation and that national Churches were undesirable.

(5) CONTEMPORARY REVIVAL. In modern times fresh interest has been taken in the theology of the Church by Catholic, Orthodox, and Protestants alike. The revived understanding of the Bible, the renewed appreciation of eschatology, the growth of the *Ecumenical Movement and the desire for reunion, the reaction from individualism in politics (at least until the 1980s), organic doctrines in philosophy, and the increased sense of history have all played their part. The Church as such is being recognized in a new sense as a fundamental fact in the Christian Revelation. In the early part of the 20th cent. this renewed vision of the Church focused on the Pauline notion of the Body of Christ. Many aspects of this teaching found expression in *Pius XII's encyclical *Mystici Corporis Christi* (29 June 1943). However, such a conception of the Church still laid great stress on its institutional character. In the second half of the 20th cent., partly as a result of the *Liturgical Movement, increased stress was laid on the Church as sacramental (as the 'primordial Sacrament' or *Ursakrament*), an idea emphasized by Orthodox theologians who see the community gathered together to celebrate the Eucharist with its bishop as the primary manifestation of the Church. It has some affinities with the conception of the Church as centred in each congregation that has characterized the *Congregational and other Protestant Churches. In the RC Church a less institutional and juridical view found expression in the Second *Vatican Council's Constitution on the Church, *Lumen Gentium* (21 Nov. 1964), in which the Church is seen primarily as the People of God; it has subsequently been developed by a number of RC theologians including H. U. von *Balthasar and E. C. F. A. *Schillebeeckx.

ON NT ECCLESIOLOGY: F. J. A. *Hort, *The Christian Ecclesia* (1897); K. L. Schmidt, 'Die Kirche des Urchristentums', in *Festgabe für Adolf Deissmann zum 60. Geburtstag* (1927), pp. 258–319; R. N. Flew, *Jesus and His Church: A Study of the Idea of the Ecclesia in the New Testament* (1938); G. Johnston, *The Doctrine of the Church of the New Testament* (Cambridge, 1943); L. Cerfaux, *La Théologie de l'Église suivant saint Paul* (Unam Sanctam, 10; 1948; enlarged edn., ibid. 54, 1965; Eng. tr., 1959); E. Best, *One Body in Christ: A Study of the Relationship of the Church to Christ in the Epistles of the Apostle Paul* (1955); P. S. Minear, *Images of the Church in the New Testament* (Philadelphia [1960]; London, 1961); R. Schnackenburg, *Die Kirche im Neuen Testament* (Quaestiones Disputatae, 14 [1961]; Eng. tr. [1966]); J. Knox, *The Church and the Reality of Christ* (1963); C. K. Barrett, *The Signs of an Apostle* (Cato lecture, 1969; 1970); W. Klaiber,

Rechtfertigung und Gemeinde: Eine Untersuchung zum paulinischen Kirchenverständnis (Forschungen zur Religion und Literatur des Alten und Neuen Testaments, 127; 1982); W. A. Meeks, *The First Urban Christians: The Social World of the Apostle Paul* (New Haven, Conn., and London [1983]); R. E. Brown, SS, *The Churches the Apostles left Behind* (New York and London, 1984), and other works of this author; J. D. G. Dunn, *The Partings of the Ways: Between Christianity and Judaism and their Significance for the Character of Christianity* (1991). K. L. Schmidt in *TWNT* 3 (1938), pp. 502–39, s.v. ἐκκλησία; separate Eng. tr., *The Church* (1949).

ON PATRISTIC ECCLESIOLOGY: E. Hatch, *The Organization of the Early Christian Churches* (1881); A. *Harnack, *Entstehung und Entwickelung der Kirchenverfassung* (1910; Eng. tr., *The Constitution & Law of the Church*, 1910); J. C. Plumpe, *Mater Ecclesia: An Enquiry into the Concept of the Church as Mother in Early Christianity* (Catholic University of America Studies in Christian Antiquity, 5; Washington, DC, 1943); G. Bardy, *La Théologie de l'Église de saint Clément de Rome à saint Irénée* (Unam Sanctam, 13; 1945); id., *La Théologie de l'Église de saint Irénée au concile de Nicée* (ibid. 14; 1947); H. von Campenhausen, *Kirchliche Amt und geistliche Vollmacht in den ersten drei Jahrhunderten* (Beiträge zur historischen Theologie, 14; Tübingen, 1953; Eng. tr., 1969); W. Elert, *Abendmahl und Kirchengemeinschaft in der alten Kirche hauptsächlich des Ostens* (Berlin, 1954; Eng. tr., St Louis [1966]); J. Ratzinger, *Volk und Haus Gottes in Augustins Lehre von der Kirche* (Münchener theologische Studien, Systematische Abt. 7; 1954); H. Rahner, [SJ,] *Symbole der Kirche: Die Ekklesiologie der Väter* (Salzburg [1964]); R. F. Evans, *One and Holy: The Church in Latin Patristic Thought* (1972); R. Murray, SJ, *Symbols of Church and Kingdom: A Study in Early Syriac Tradition* (Cambridge, 1975). H. J. Vogt, in *DPAC* 1 (1983), cols. 1049–62, s.v. 'Ecclesiologia' (Eng. tr., with some additional bibl., *Encyclopedia of the Early Church*, 1 (1992), pp. 259–62).

ON THE MIDDLE AGES: H. de *Lubac, SJ, *Corpus Mysticum: L'Eucharistie et l'Église au moyen âge* (Théologie, 3, 1944; 2nd edn., 1949); Y. M.-J. *Congar, OP, *L'Ecclésiologie du haut moyen-âge: De Saint Grégoire le Grand à la désunion entre Byzance et Rome* (1968).

MORE SYSTEMATIC DISCUSSIONS: [F. D. *Maurice,] *The Kingdom of Christ* (3 vols. [1837]); W. *Palmer, *Treatise on the Christian Church* (2 vols., 1838); D. *Stone, *The Christian Church* (1905); H. B. *Swete, *The Holy Catholic Church* (1915); A. C. *Headlam, *The Doctrine of the Church and Christian Reunion* (1920); K. *Adam, *Das Wesen des Katholizismus* (1924; 5th edn., 1928; Eng. tr., 1929); D. *Bonhoeffer, *Sanctorum Communio* (Berlin, 1930; Eng. tr., 1963); É. Mersch, SJ, *Le Corps mystique du Christ: Études de théologie historique* (Museum Lessianum, Section théologique, 28–9; 1933; Eng. tr., 1938); id., *La Théologie du Corps Mystique* (ibid. 38–9; 1944; Eng. tr., St Louis [1951]); A. M. *Ramsey, *The Gospel and the Catholic Church* (1936; 2nd edn., 1956); H. de Lubac, SJ, *Catholicisme: Les aspects sociaux du dogme* (Unam Sanctam, 3; 1938; Eng. tr., 1950); Y. M.-J. Congar, OP, *Chrétiens désunis: Principes d'un 'oecuménisme' catholique* (Unam Sanctam, 1, 1937; Eng. tr., *Divided Christendom*, 1939); id., *Esquisses du mystère de l'Église* (ibid. 8, 1941); D. T. Jenkins, *The Nature of Catholicity* (1942); C. Journet, *L'Église du Verbe incarné* (Bibliothèque de la Revue Thomiste, 2 vols., 1941–51, 2nd edn. of vol. 1, 1955; Eng. tr. of vol. 1 [only], 1955); L. S. Thornton, CR, *The Common Life in the Body of Christ* ([1942]; 4th edn., 1963); E. L. Mascall, *Christ, the Christian and the Church* (1946); E. *Brunner, *Das Missverständnis der Kirche* (Zurich, 1951; Eng. tr., 1952); O. Semmelroth, SJ, *Die Kirche als Ursakrament* (Frankfurt am Main [1953]); N. N. Afanassieff and others, *La Primauté de Pierre dans l'Église orthodoxe* (Neuchâtel [1960]; Eng. tr., J. Meyendorff and others, *The Primacy of Peter*, 1963; 2nd edn., with additional material, Crestwood, NY, 1992); G. Wingren, *Evangeliet och Kyrkan* (Lund, 1960; Eng. tr., 1964); B. C. Butler, OSB, *The Idea of the Church* (1962); H. *Küng, *Strukturen der Kirche* (Quaestiones

Disputatae, 17; 1962; Eng. tr., New York, 1964; London, 1965); id., *Die Kirche* (Freiburg, 1967; 2nd edn., 1968; Eng. tr., 1967); H. Mühlen, *Una persona mystica: Die Kirche als das Mysterium der Identität des Heiligen Geistes in Christus und den Christen* (Munich, 1964); J. Ratzinger, *Das neue Volk Gottes* (Düsseldorf [1969]); L. Bouyer, *L'Église de Dieu, corps du Christ et temple de l'Esprit* (1970); H. U. von Balthasar, *Pneuma und Institution* (Skizzen zur Theologie, 4; Einsiedeln [1974]); J. *Moltmann, *Kirche in der Kraft des Geistes* (Munich, 1975; Eng. tr., 1977); A. Acerbi, *La Chiesa nel tempo: Sguardi sui progretti di relazioni tra Chiesa e società civile negli ultimi cento anni* (Milan, 1979); R. P. McBrien, *Catholicism*, 2 (1980), pp. 565–729 (3rd edn. (one vol., 1994), pp. 569–782); J.-M.-R. Tillard, OP, *L'Évêque de Rome* (1982; Eng. tr., 1983); id., *Églises d'Églises: L'ecclésiologie de communion* (Cogitatio fidei, 143; 1987); J. D. Zizioulas, *Being as Communion: Studies in Personhood and the Church* (New York, 1985); W. Kasper, *Theologie und Kirche* (1987; Eng. tr., 1989), pt. 2. E. [C. F. A.] Schillebeeckx, OP, *Mensen als verhaal van God* (1989; Eng. tr., *The Church: The Human Story of God*, 1990).

M.-J. le Guillou and others in *Sacramentum Mundi*, 1 (1968), pp. 313–37, s.v. 'Church'; K. Berger and others in *TRE* 18 (1989), pp. 198–344, s.v. 'Kirche', with extensive bibl.

Church, Richard William (1815–90), Dean of *St Paul's. He was born at Lisbon and spent his earlier years in Florence. In 1833 he was sent to Wadham College, Oxford, because the college at that time, under B. P. Symons, had a reputation for Evangelicalism. He came under the influence of C. *Marriott of Oriel, who enlisted him in his band of translators of the Fathers, and introduced him to J. H. *Newman, E. B. *Pusey, and J. *Keble. In 1838 he was elected a Fellow of Oriel, where he remained until 1852, when he became Rector of Whatley in Somerset. As Junior Proctor he shared with H. P. Guillemard of Trinity in the dramatic vetoing of the condemnation of *Tract 90 in the university convocation (1845). He was one of the prime movers in establishing the *Guardian*, which from the first (1846) espoused High Church principles. After nearly twenty years at Whatley, Church was appointed in 1871 to the Deanery of St Paul's, where he remained until his death. In *The Gifts of Civilization* (1870, incorporating earlier work) he developed his beliefs about the relation of the Church to the world; he illustrated the same theme in his lives of St *Anselm (1870), *Spenser* (1879), and *Bacon* (1884). His book *The Oxford Movement, Twelve Years, 1833–1845* (posthumously published in 1891) is a masterpiece, as a judicious and balanced interpretation of the history of the movement.

Life and Letters of Dean Church, ed. by his daughter, M. C. Church (1894). D. C. Lathbury, *Dean Church* (1905); B. A. Smith, *Dean Church: The Anglican Response to Newman* (1965). [W.] O. Chadwick, *The Spirit of the Oxford Movement* (Cambridge, 1990), pp. 135–53 ('The Oxford Movement and its Reminiscencers'). H. C. Beeching in *DNB*, Suppl. 2 (1901), pp. 6–9.

Church Army. An Anglican society of lay *evangelists founded in 1882 by Wilson *Carlile, who brought together a number of groups already existing in some parishes. It is, to some extent, similar to the *Salvation Army. Carlile was convinced that lay people could preach the Gospel, and all officers of the Church Army are admitted to the office of evangelist at their commissioning and are licensed to their work by a diocesan bishop. The Army represents a broad spectrum of churchmanship. Its activities include diocesan and parochial evangelism, as well as varied social work (since 1889) co-ordinated with local authorities. Its officers work on chaplaincy teams in prisons, the armed forces, and in hospitals. There are independent societies in Australia, New Zealand, Canada, the USA, the Caribbean, and E. Africa.

K. [J.] Heasman, *Army of the Church* (1968). M. Turnbull, *God's Front Line* (1978); D. [MacL.] Lynch, *Chariots of the Gospel: The Centenary History of the Church Army* (Worthing, W. Sussex, 1982). See also works cited under CARLILE, W.

Church Assembly. This body, officially 'The National Assembly of the Church of England', was established by the *Convocations in 1919 'to deliberate on all matters concerning the Church of England and to make provision in respect thereof'. In 1970, as a result of the *Synodical Government Measure 1969, it was superseded by the General Synod. It was composed of a House of Bishops, comprising all the members of the two Upper Houses of Convocation; a House of Clergy, consisting of all the members of the two Lower Houses of Convocation; and a House of Laity, elected every five years by the representative electors of the Diocesan Conferences. The Assembly's most important function was to prepare ecclesiastical measures for transmission to Parliament under powers given by the Church of England Assembly (Powers) Act 1919 ('the *Enabling Act'). Parliament could either accept or reject (but not amend) such measures; if accepted they received the royal assent and became law. Measures passed by the Assembly and Parliament included the Parochial Church Councils (Powers) Measures 1921 and 1956, the Cathedrals Measures 1931 and 1963, the Parsonages Measure 1938, and the *Ecclesiastical Jurisdiction Measure 1963. Although the Revised Prayer Book was twice accepted by the Assembly, in 1927 and 1928, it was in each case subsequently rejected by Parliament. The Assembly exercised great influence, through the Central Board of Finance, on the financial affairs of the C of E.

The Reports of the Proceedings were pub. conjointly by the Church Information Board and the *SPCK. *The Church Assembly and the Church: A Book of Essays* (1930). K. A. Thompson, *Bureaucracy and Church Reform* (Oxford, 1970), pp. 179–211. *The Church Assembly News: The Official Publication of the Church Assembly* (London, 1924–69, monthly). Much contemporary information is contained in *The Official Year Book of the National Assembly of the Church of England* [from 1963 *The Church of England Year Book*] (annually).

Church Association. A society formed in 1865 during the ritual controversies by several leading Evangelical Churchmen to maintain the Protestant ideals of faith and worship in the C of E. Previously active in litigation (cf. *Church Discipline Act, *Ritual Commission), it came ultimately to rely rather on publicity. In 1950 it became (with the National Church League) the Church Society.

Church Building Society. Founded in 1818 and incorporated in 1828, the Incorporated Church Building Society has taken an important and continuous part in furthering the construction and repair of Anglican churches in England and Wales. Since 1963 it has been managed by the Historic Churches Preservation Trust (founded in 1953).

Church Commissioners for England. The body formed in 1948 by the amalgamation of the *Ecclesiastical Commissioners and *Queen Anne's Bounty. It is responsible for managing the greater part of the C of E's historic assets (stocks and shares as well as agricultural, commercial and residential property), the income of which is used to help pay, house, and provide pensions for the clergy. The Commissioners number 95: the two archbishops and 41 other diocesan bishops, three 'Church Estates Commissioners' (two appointed by the Crown and one by the Abp. of *Canterbury), 25 persons appointed formerly by the *Church Assembly and now by the General *Synod (five deans or provosts, ten other clerks in holy orders, and ten laymen), four laymen appointed by the Crown, four persons appointed by the Abp. of Canterbury, ten officers of state (see the corresponding list of former 'Ecclesiastical Commissioners'), two Aldermen of the City of London, the Lord Mayors of London and York, and one representative each of the universities of Oxford and Cambridge. The general business of the Commissioners is dealt with by its Board of Governors, which comprises no more than 30 members. In addition to their main financial responsibilities, the Commissioners have certain wider administrative duties in connection with pastoral reorganization and the future of redundant churches. They also recommend to the General Synod for submission to Parliament the scale of statutory fees to be chargeable for marriages, funerals, and other rites. After serious financial losses in the 1980s, radical changes were recommended by the Turnbull Commission.

The Church Commissioners Measure 1947, as finally approved by the Assembly, 21 June 1946, is pr. for the Church Assembly, CA 794A (1946). P. B. Wilbraham, *The First Five Years: The Story of the Church Commissioners, 1948–53* (1953). *Working as One Body: The Report of the Archbishops' Commission on the Organization of the Church of England* (1995), esp. pp. 81–95.

Church Congresses. A series of unofficial gatherings of Anglican Churchmen which were held between 1861 and 1938 (annually down to 1913, and less regularly thereafter). The first meeting (1861) was at Cambridge. Owing to other means of contact between different centres of Church life in the provinces, e.g. the setting-up of the *Church Assembly in 1920, the usefulness of the Congresses declined after the War of 1914–18.

Official reports of the Proceedings of the first 59 congresses were issued in uniform vols., 1862–1925; thereafter in the name of the editor.

Church Discipline Act 1840. This Act empowered the bishop, in cases of an alleged non-criminal offence by a cleric (e.g. irregularities in doctrine or ritual, also *simony), either to issue a Commission of Inquiry which should institute a preliminary investigation and decide whether or not there was a *prima facie* case or, alternatively, himself to transmit the case by Letters of Request to the provincial Court of Appeal. Conviction might be followed by suspension or deprivation. The Act was repealed by the *Ecclesiastical Jurisdiction Measure 1963.

R. *Phillimore, *The Ecclesiastical Law of the Church of England* (2nd edn., 1895), 2, pp. 1013–25.

Church Historical Society. A society founded in 1894 (under the presidency of Mandell *Creighton, Bp. of London) for the diffusion of historical knowledge esp. in

so far as it affected the authority and claims of the C of E. Through the *SPCK it issued a series of writings, originally of small dimensions, but all marked by a high standard of scholarship. It was wound up in 1974.

Church House, Westminster. The building in which the *Convocation of Canterbury and the General *Synod of the C of E generally sit and the headquarters of many Anglican organizations. It replaced a set of buildings erected between 1891 and 1902 on a site fronting on Dean's Yard, *Westminster. It was designed by Sir Herbert Baker, and completed and opened in 1940.

Church Hymnary, The. The authorized hymnal of most of the *Presbyterian Churches in Britain. The first edition was issued in 1898, and much revised forms in 1927 and 1973. The third edition contains nearly 700 hymns, together with *doxologies, *canticles, and a selection of psalms, both metrical and prose.

J. M. Barkley (ed.), *Handbook to the Church Hymnary Third Edition* (1979).

Church Meeting. The regular (usually monthly) assembly of all the members of a *Congregational or *Baptist Church for the purposes of Church administration, the admission of members and the election of officers, and the exercise of discipline in that particular congregation. 'The covenanted people of God' meeting in such a local unit have complete autonomy.

Church Missionary Society. See CMS.

Church's Ministry among the Jews. The 'London Society for Promoting Christianity among the Jews' was founded as an interdenominational body in 1809. It became an Anglican Society in 1815, though Christians of other denominations serve with it. Its title for official purposes is unchanged, but early in the 20th cent. it became known as the 'Church Mission to the Jews' and in 1962 as the 'Church's Ministry among the Jews'. It operates mainly in Israel and Britain, but is active in S. Africa and S. America, and there is an autonomous branch in the USA.

W. T. Gidney, *The History of the London Society for Promoting Christianity among the Jews, from 1809 to 1908* (1908). Shorter histories by G. H. Stevens, *Go Tell My Brethren* [1959] and W. Barker, *A Fountain Opened* (1983).

Church of England. It is impossible to say at what date Christianity was first planted in Great Britain, but the presence of British bishops at the Council of *Arles in 314 is evidence of the existence of an organized Church. With the coming of the Anglo-Saxon invaders, British Christianity and Christians were driven before them into the western parts of Britain and the new faith suffered a temporary eclipse. The conversion of the Teutonic pagan conquerors was effected from two sources: by the labours of *Celtic missionaries from the monasteries of Ireland and Scotland and by the mission headed by St *Augustine sent from Rome (597). To this mission the British Christians would at first pay neither obedience nor submission. The Christianization of the Heptarchy progressed slowly, and with many set-backs, for the varying fortunes of the various kingdoms involved those of the Christian bishops. Before the several local kingdoms gave place to a loosely united national kingdom the Church had first to settle down to the task of administrative unification of its scattered dioceses. Before this in turn could be attempted, the differences between the Celtic and Roman missions had to be composed. Springing from a fundamental difference of temper, the Celtic monastic tradition lacked the administrative organization of the Roman Church, and the deep divergences between the two found expression in many minor points, such as the date of Easter. At a synod held at *Whitby in 664 the conflict was at length resolved in favour of the Roman customs, and the way thereby opened for the organization of the whole Church in England under one head.

*Theodore of Tarsus, sent from Rome as Abp. of *Canterbury, undertook this vital work of unification by subdivision of dioceses, summoning of ecclesiastical councils, legislative decrees, and encouragement of learning. He was the first of a long line of statesmen-archbishops of the English Church. His work was mainly that of organizing the higher administration of the Church, for the factor of the proprietary church presented a stubborn and enduring obstacle to the assertion of episcopal control over the secular parish priests. Anglo-Saxon Christianity enjoyed a transient golden age following the vigorous primacy of Theodore, producing both scholars such as *Bede, the author of one of the greatest historical narratives of all ages, and missionaries such as *Boniface of Crediton. England, largely through its monasteries, both shared in and contributed to the renaissance of the age of *Charlemagne.

Darkness, however, supervened again upon this period of light. The plundering raids of the Northmen fell with especial devastation upon religious houses and contributed to declining standards of clerical life and learning. The reign of *Alfred provided a temporary barrier against the Danes, and saw the beginnings of a revival of religion and learning, but the confusion of the times was detrimental to the highest developments of both. Under Edgar, Abp. *Dunstan, in addition to his work as a statesman, laboured with his colleagues, St *Ethelwold and St *Oswald, to reform the monasteries and cathedral chapters in accordance with contemporary European movements. The isolation of England from the main life of the Continent, both in political and ecclesiastical affairs, could not be maintained; and the question whether these islands would pass into the orbit of a NW Scandinavian empire or become joined to the main states of W. Europe was finally settled by the Norman Conquest under *William I. The last of the old English kings, *Edward the Confessor, had assisted the introduction of Norman culture. He also refounded and rebuilt the famous abbey-church of St Peter at *Westminster.

With the Norman domination, the English Church entered into the mainstream of European religion at a time when the Hildebrandine reforming movement, associated with the pontificate of *Gregory VII, was powerfully affecting the life of the Church. *Lanfranc, the new Norman Abp. of Canterbury, assisted by a body of foreign bishops and abbots, led the way to a revival of religious life in England. The Norman age saw the removal of episcopal sees from remote villages to cities and the creation of the dioceses of *Ely and *Carlisle, the beginning of that

tremendous outburst of building of which the cathedrals constitute the finest monuments, the restoration of learning and education, and the reorganization of ecclesiastical administration. Most important of all, the separation of the ecclesiastical and civil courts opened the way for the entrance of the Roman canon law, itself the chief agent of Papal control throughout the W. Church. The English Church henceforth could not escape the ubiquitous influence of the Popes. Under kings less scrupulous than William I, relations between Church and State were not harmonious. The *investiture conflict was itself but a symbol of the attempt of the spiritual power to free itself from the control of the temporal, which in the lower orders of the clergy was typified by the proprietary church and in the episcopate by the contest between Papacy and kings over questions of electing bishops. *Anselm maintained this struggle on its highest plane of principle in his differences with Henry I, whilst Thomas *Becket's dramatic conflict with Henry II, ending in his martyrdom, was evidence of the personal passions inextricably interlocked with the assertion of principle. Henry II believed himself to be maintaining the ancient customs of the English Crown, as asserted by Henry I, but Becket was representative of the augmented prestige of the Papacy consequent on the Hildebrandine movement and the development of canon law. Behind this foreground of struggle the English Church was influenced by the several monastic revivals of Europe, an Englishman, *Stephen Harding, being the author of the nucleus of the *Carta Caritatis, the rule of the *Cistercian Order.

The 13th cent. was in many ways the culmination of the Middle Ages. In England, after the combined victory of Church and barons over King *John symbolized in Magna Carta, promising freedom to the Church from royal absolutism, the long reign of Henry III afforded wide opportunities for the Papacy and the Church. Under Henry, himself a king of deep piety and the second refounder of Westminster Abbey, the Papacy came to exercise a marked influence in episcopal appointments, esp. to the see of Canterbury, and sent representatives to England to seek financial aid for the Papal struggle against *Frederick II. During his reign, moreover, the *Friars came to England, university life was fostered, the constitutions of Otto and Ottobuono developed ecclesiastical law, and amongst the Henrician episcopate was numbered one of the most famous of all English prelates, *Grosseteste of Lincoln, distinguished alike as scholar, pastor, and administrator. *Innocent III had died very shortly before Henry's accession, but the influence of his ecclesiastical reforms, esp. as reflected in the decrees of the Fourth *Lateran Council of 1215, were felt in the English Church during his rule. There followed a period of consolidation of royal power under Edward I and, after the brief misrule of his son, under Edward III, whose reign saw the development of parliamentary institutions in England and the successful struggle of the lower clergy to avoid inclusion of their proctors in the lower parliamentary house.

With the accentuation of national self-consciousness on the one hand, and the Papal scandals of the *Babylonian captivity and *Great Schism on the other, the exactions and policy of the Roman see became the subject of increasing criticism in England. During the Hundred Years War with France many alien priories were suppressed, and their revenues diverted to the crown, whilst the statutes of *Provisors and *Praemunire attempted to curtail in the royal interest the Papal practice of diverting the revenues of English benefices to the support of foreign ecclesiastics and the payment of Papal creditors. The failure of the *Conciliar Movement, however, demonstrated the impossibility of a constitutional Papacy, and national kings found their interests better served by concordats with the Papacy through which a financial division of the spoils of the Church and a sharing of ecclesiastical appointments were effected. The chief results of the policy of concordats were to strengthen the hold of the monarchy on the Church in England and to reduce any corporate sentiment of loyalty towards the Papacy on the part of the episcopate.

When, in the 16th cent., the Tudor sovereigns deemed it expedient to measure their strength against the Papacy, they found many elements in the nation ready to lend their support. Criticism of ecclesiastical wealth, accompanied amongst the lower classes by sporadic heresy, had been prominent since the time of J. *Wycliffe. Ambitious men cast occasional glances upon the riches of monastic property. Common lawyers bore the canonists a deep grudge, and there may have been wider resentment of Papal exactions. More intangible were the evidences of religious yearnings, represented amongst the learned by the humanist revolt against Scholasticism and devotion to the study of Hebrew and Greek of which *Erasmus and J. *Colet were typical in England, and expressed amongst the literate by the purchase of newly printed religious books and the expansion of domestic piety. The occasion of the Tudor Reformation was the famous 'divorce' of *Henry VIII; but its causes lay deeper. T. *Wolsey may have weakened the affection amongst many of the bishops for Papal supremacy, whilst indicating the advantages of unified control of the English Church. Under Henry VIII the *Convocations acknowledged the King to be Supreme Head on earth of the Church of England, and a series of laws severed the financial, judicial, and administrative bonds between Rome and England. Despite the influx of *Lutheran books and ideas and the inclusion of men of reforming opinions amongst the episcopate, Henry VIII allowed only limited doctrinal changes. His order for the setting-up of the *Great Bible in all churches was an event of which the full influence and importance were not realized until later. Apart from the overthrow of Papal supremacy and the bringing of Convocation under the control of the Crown, the main events of this reign were negative, such as the *dissolution of the monasteries and the destruction of shrines. Under *Edward VI, Abp. T. *Cranmer produced the First and Second Books of *Common Prayer in 1549 and 1552, an English *Ordinal, and a statement of doctrine, the *Forty-Two Articles, and the State seized the endowments of the *chantries. This advance towards Protestantism was followed by a reaction under *Mary which restored the Papal supremacy and undid much of the work of the two previous reigns. Upon the accession of *Elizabeth I the Papal obedience was again repudiated, the Crown assumed the title of 'Supreme Governor', the Second Edwardine Prayer Book with some changes became the service book of the Church of England, the Articles of Religion were reduced to *Thirty-Nine, and the bishops, despite the caution of

Elizabeth and Abp. M. *Parker, led a campaign of Protestant evangelism.

Two bodies of critics opposed the Elizabethan settlement. Conservative sentiment remained strong among the lower clergy and the laity; Popish *recusants were sustained by missionary priests from continental colleges, and the *Roman Catholic Church in England and Wales preserved a continuous (if at times clandestine) existence. On the other side a considerable volume of Protestant opinion regarded the Prayer Book, Articles, and episcopacy as only a half-way house to a fuller and better reformation. Almost all divines of this standpoint remained within the Church, striving for changes from within, and controversy ranged over a wide ground from the wearing of the surplice to the reform of the Prayer Book and even the supplanting of episcopacy by *presbyterianism. In J. *Jewel and R. *Hooker the C of E found apologists against both Rome and Geneva, who appealed to Scripture, the Fathers, and human reason, but most educated ministers were moderate *Calvinists and there was little theological dispute. Under *James I the Convocations, by royal licence and assent, published the *Canons of 1604; but under his son, *Charles I, the ascendancy of Abp. W. *Laud and his endeavours to secure a higher standard of common order in the Church sharpened *Puritan criticism and made episcopacy and Anglicanism a subject of conflict in the Civil Wars. The victory of parliament led first to a presbyterian reform, and then, owing to the influence of the Army, to *Independency. During the Commonwealth and Protectorate the use of the BCP was prohibited, and benefices were held by episcopalian, presbyterian, and independent ministers indifferently, though clandestine BCP services continued. With the restoration of *Charles II, the C of E returned to its position as the established Church. The failure of an attempt at comprehension at the *Savoy Conference was followed by a revision of the Prayer Book, its enforcement by a new Act of *Uniformity in 1662, and by persecuting measures against dissenters. The attempts of Charles II and *James II to use the royal prerogative of indulgence to secure toleration for dissenters and Papists failed, and James II's open attack on the C of E was largely responsible for his downfall. The Protestant succession in the persons of William of Orange and later the House of Hanover delivered the Church from the dreaded danger of Popery.

After a century of fierce controversy against both Papist and Puritan, the C of E settled down from 1689 to an epoch of quiescence. A limited religious toleration pacified the dissenters; the Convocation, having lost its power of voting clerical taxation, sank into torpor; theological disputes became unpopular; and the alliance of Church and State became a mutually defensive pact against all subversive forces. The *Methodist revival was the parent both of a new Christian body and of the Anglican *Evangelical revival. *Latitudinarianism continued to dominate the intellectual atmosphere of the Georgian age, until the thoroughgoing reforms of the third decade of the 19th cent. aroused the protest of J. *Keble and effected a second administrative reformation of the Church. From this last there sprang new bishoprics and parishes, and a series of financial and administrative reforms, followed by the revival of Convocation. From Keble's protest proceeded the *Oxford Movement, which laid a new emphasis upon the catholic and apostolic character of the established Church, and upon the order of episcopacy. The Tractarian leaders, esp. J. H. *Newman and E. B. *Pusey, became the storm-centres of much controversy, and this initial period of strife culminated in the secession to Rome of Newman (1845), and at a later date of H. E. *Manning (1851).

When this revival of Church life became involved in ceremonial novelties, with consequent litigation, a generation of acute disputation set in. From another standpoint new problems of biblical interpretation and of the relation of theology to secular science produced controversies of another kind, which centred in the publication of such composite volumes as *Essays and Reviews and *Lux Mundi. Behind the dismal series of so-called ritualistic lawsuits, the Church was attempting to adjust its beliefs to a revolutionary background of human knowledge. Relations between Church and State were strained, and the 20th cent. opened with much continuation of controversy. These disputes tended to obscure the often growing and deepening activities of the Church in education and pastoral ministration. At the close of the First World War in 1919 a readjustment of the relations of Church and State was effected by the passing of the Church of England National Assembly (Powers) Act. By this measure the three houses of the Assembly, of bishops, clergy, and laity, were given powers to prepare legislation on ecclesiastical matters for the consideration of parliament. The modification worked well until, in 1927 and 1928, the House of Commons twice rejected a project for the revision of the Prayer Book, and created a deadlock in the relations between the *Church Assembly and parliament.

At the end of the Second World War (1945), the major problems facing the C of E were the need for pastoral reorganization and the provision of adequate financial resources, esp. for the stipends of the clergy. Revision of the Canons was achieved (1969). Lengthy discussions on reunion with the Methodist Church were abortive (1972; see ANGLICAN–METHODIST CONVERSATIONS), as were the subsequent attempts to establish a Covenant with the *United Reformed Church, the Methodists, *Moravians, and *Disciples of Christ (1982; see REUNION). Nevertheless, closer relations between the C of E and the Free Churches, as well as with the RC Church, have been characteristic of the post-war period; since 1972 members of other Churches have been free to receive Communion in Anglican churches. Since the 1960s there has been much discussion on the limits of theological orthodoxy. A shortage of clergy and a drop in Church membership have posed problems, and the laity has come to play an increasingly important part in the liturgical, pastoral, and governmental life of the Church. In most parts of the C of E the focus of worship is now predominantly Eucharistic. Prayer Book revision, after years of experimental services, culminated in the publication of the *Alternative Service Book (1980); it was facilitated by the *Worship and Doctrine Measure 1974, which gave the C of E liberty, under certain safeguards, to order its own worship. Church government was restructured by the *Synodical Government Measure 1969, and in 1976 the Church, through its *Crown Appointments Commission, was given a dominant voice in the choice of its bishops. Recent years have been overshadowed by the controversy surrounding the ordination of *women, which was opposed by many *Evangelicals and *Anglo-Catholics on different grounds. Nevertheless, the Deacons (Ordination of Women) Measure 1986 led to women being admitted to the diaconate and was followed by pressure for them to be made priests. This issue was even more divisive. By a small margin the Priests (Ordination of Women) Measure was passed by the General Synod in 1992 and approved by Parliament in 1993, the first women being ordained in 1994. The Measure allowed for parishes to refuse to have a woman as incumbent and accompanying legislation authorized financial compensation for most full-time stipendiary clergy who felt bound in conscience to resign in consequence of the ordination of women. An Act of Synod (the Episcopal Ministry Act) 1993 made provision for three provincial bishops who would, under the jurisdiction of the diocesan bishop, minister in those parishes which were unwilling to accept the ministrations of bishops who had been involved in the ordination of a woman.

See also ANGLICAN COMMUNION and ANGLICANISM.

The principal authority for the early history of Christianity in England is Bede, HE. Councils & Synods with other Documents Relating to the English Church: 1, A.D. 871–1204, ed. D. Whitelock, M. Brett and C. N. L. Brooke (2 vols., Oxford, 1981); 2, 1205–1313, ed. F. M. Powicke and C. R. Cheney (2 vols., ibid., 1964). General collection of docs. in Gee and Hardy. E. W. Watson, The Church of England (HUL, 1914; 3rd edn. with additional ch. by A. [T. P.] Williams, 1961). J. R. H. Moorman, A History of the Church in England (1953; 3rd edn., 1973), with bibl. D. L. Edwards, Christian England [to 1918] (3 vols., 1981–4). F. Makower, Die Verfassung der Kirche von England (1894; Eng. tr., 1895). S. C. Carpenter, The Church in England, 597–1688 (1954). [M.] D. *Knowles, OSB, The Monastic Order in England (Cambridge, 1940; 2nd edn., 1963); id., The Religious Orders in England (3 vols., 1948–59). C. H. Lawrence (ed.), The English Church and the Papacy in the Middle Ages (1965). Z. N. Brooke, The English Church and the Papacy from the Conquest to the Reign of John (1931). J. C. Dickinson, The Later Middle Ages: From the Norman Conquest to the Eve of the Reformation (An Ecclesiastical History of England, 2; 1979). J. R. H. Moorman, Church Life in England in the Thirteenth Century (1945). K. L. Wood-Legh, Studies in Church Life in England under Edward III (1934). W. A. Pantin, The English Church in the Fourteenth Century (Cambridge, 1955). E. Duffy, The Stripping of the Altars: Traditional Religion in England c.1400–c.1580 (New Haven, Conn., and London, 1992). A. G. Dickens, The English Reformation (1964; 2nd edn., 1989). J. J. Scarisbrick, The Reformation and the English People (Ford Lectures, 1982; Oxford 1984). C. [A.] Haigh, English Reformations (ibid., 1993), passim. P. Collinson, The Religion of Protestants: The Church in English Society 1559–1625 (Ford Lectures, 1979; Oxford, 1982); id., The Birthpangs of Protestant England: Religious and Cultural Change in the Sixteenth and Seventeenth Centuries (Basingstoke, 1988). F. Heal and R. O'Day (eds.), Church and Society in England: Henry VIII to James I (London and Basingstoke, 1977); D. [N. J.] MacCulloch, The Later Reformation in England 1547–1603 (ibid., 1990); S. Doran and C. Durston, Princes, Pastors and People: The Church and Religion in England 1529–1689 (1991). [J. E.] C. Hill, Economic Problems of the Church from Archbishop Whitgift to the End of the Long Parliament (Oxford, 1956). K. Fincham (ed.), The Early Stuart Church, 1603–1642 (1993). W. A. Shaw, A History of the English Church during the Civil Wars and under the Commonwealth, 1640–1660 (2 vols., 1900). R. G. Usher, The Reconstruction of the English Church (2 vols., 1910). I. M. Green, The Re-Establishment of the Church of England, 1660–1663 (Oxford Historical Monographs, 1978). J. Spurr, The Restoration Church of England 1646–1689 (New Haven, Conn., and London, 1991); J. I. A. Champion, The Pillars of

Priestcraft Shaken: The Church of England and its Enemies, 1660–1730 (Cambridge, 1992). J. W. Legg, *English Church Life from the Restoration to the Tractarian Movement* (1914); J. Walsh and others (eds.), *The Church of England c.1689–c.1833: From Toleration to Tractarianism* (Cambridge, 1993). G. F. Nuttall and [W.] O. Chadwick (eds.), *From Uniformity to Unity, 1662–1962* (1962). N. Sykes, *From Sheldon to Secker: Aspects of English Church History 1660–1768* (Ford Lectures for 1958; Cambridge, 1959). Id., *Church and State in England in the XVIIIth Century* (Birkbeck Lectures for 1931–3, 1934). S. C. Carpenter, *Eighteenth Century Church and People* (1959); id., *Church and People, 1789–1889* (1933). [E.] G. Rupp, *Religion in England 1688–1791* (Oxford History of the Christian Church, 1986). E. R. Norman, *Church and Society in England, 1770–1970: A Historical Study* (Oxford, 1976). O. J. Brose, *Church and Parliament: The Reshaping of the Church of England 1828–1860* (1959). E. R. Wickham, *Church and People in an Industrial City* (1957). [W.] O. Chadwick, *The Victorian Church* (2 vols., 1966–70). R. Lloyd, *The Church of England in the Twentieth Century* (2 vols., 1946–50; rev. as *The Church of England 1900–1965*; 1966). A. Wilkinson, *The Church of England and the First World War* (1978). K. A. Thompson, *Bureaucracy and Church Reform: The Organizational Response of the Church of England to Social Change 1800–1965* (Oxford, 1970). R. E. Rodes, *Law and Modernization in the Church of England: Charles II to the Welfare State* (Notre Dame, Ind., and London, 1991). R. P. Flindall (ed.), *The Church of England 1815–1945: A Documentary History* (1972). D. L. Edwards, *Leaders of the Church of England 1828–1944* (1971; updated, rev. edn., without notes, 1978). P. A. Welsby, *A History of the Church of England 1945–1980* (Oxford, 1984). A. Hastings, *A History of English Christianity 1920–1985* (1986), *passim*. DECH. For works on the Pre-Conquest period, see s.v. ANGLO-SAXON CHURCH; for the 15th cent., see also bibl. to LOLLARDY and WYCLIFFE, J.; for the period of the Reformation, see bibl. to CRANMER, T., CROMWELL, T., EDWARD VI, ELIZABETH I, HENRY VIII, and WOLSEY; for the 18th cent. onwards see also bibl. to EVANGEL-ICALISM; from the beginning of the 19th cent. among the most important sources are the biographies of leading churchmen such as F. *Temple, R. T. *Davidson, C. G. *Lang, W. *Temple, A. P. *Stanley, E. B. *Pusey, G. K. A. *Bell, G. F. *Fisher, A. M. *Ramsey, etc.; for this period see also bibl. to OXFORD MOVEMENT. On the whole subject see also entry ANGLICANISM, and bibl.

Church of the East

Church of the East (or *Assyrian Church of the East**). It is frequently, but misleadingly, referred to as the *Nestorian Church; its Christology, which is strictly *Antiochene, developed largely from that of *Theodore of Mopsuestia rather than from that of Nestorius. Official formulations of the 6th and 7th cent. sometimes speak of 'two natures, two *qnōmē* (corresponding to Gk. *hypostasis) and one *prosopon*' in the incarnate Christ, thus differing from the *Chalcedonian Definition which posits a single *hypostasis*.

The Church in Mesopotamia (approximately modern Iraq) lay outside the Roman Empire and took no part in the great Councils, although the Creed and Canons of the first Council of *Nicaea (325), affirming the full Divinity of Christ, were formally accepted at the Synod of Seleucia in 410. The Council of *Ephesus (431), and in particular the title of *Theotokos for the BVM, is rejected, while ambivalent attitudes have been held towards the Chalcedonian Definition, owing to a different understanding of the term hypostasis. The doctrinal position of the Church of the East was largely based on the Antiochene theology of the School of Nisibis, inherited from the 'Persian School' at Edessa (closed in 489) and propagated by *Barsumas, Bp. of Nisibis. Their most important theo-logian was Babai the Great (d. 628), author of the *Book of the Union* (sc. of the Godhead and Manhood in Christ).

By the end of Sassanian rule in Iran (651) Christians constituted an important religious minority in the country, with the seat of the Catholicos-Patriarch at Seleucia-Ktesiphon on the R. Tigris, and about ten metropolitan sees. In the 4th–5th cent. there was intermittent *persecution (usually in times of war with the Roman Empire); later there were individual martyrdoms of several high-born converts from *Zoroastrianism. One such convert was the energetic Catholicos Mar Aba I (540–52), admired (under the name of Patrikios) by *Cosmas Indicopleustes. A monastic revival in the mid 6th cent., initiated by Abraham of Kashkar (d. *c.*580) on Mt. Izla (near Nisibis), led to a large number of new monastic foundations in the course of the next few centuries; many of these are described by *Thomas of Marga in his *Book of Governors* (or *Superiors*). Monastic writers include *Sahdona, *Isaac of Nineveh, *John Saba, and Joseph the Seer (8th cent.). By the early 7th cent. missionaries from the Church of the East had reached *India (see MALABAR CHRISTIANS) and E. Asia (see SIGAN-FU STONE).

After the Arab conquests (completed in 651), the Christians met with moderately good treatment under the Caliphate, constituting an *ahl al dhimma* ('people of protection'), whose religious freedom was theoretically guaranteed in return for payment of a poll tax. Under the Abbasids (749–1258) the Patriarchate moved to Baghdad, where Syriac scholars such as Hunayn ibn Ishaq (d. 873), played an important role in the transmission of Greek philosophical and scientific literature to the Arab world.

Initially favoured by the Mongols, the Church of the East suffered drastic losses in the 14th cent. after the conversion of the Mongol dynasty to *Islam in 1295. The diary of a monk from Peking, Rabban Sauma, who was sent by the Mongols as an envoy to Europe, survives. In the mid 16th cent. the Church of the East (by now centred on the mountains of Kurdistan) was divided by the creation of a separate *Uniat Patriarchal line (see CHALDEAN CHRISTIANS). In the 19th cent. several W. missions were sent to the Church of the East. An American *Presbyterian mission set up a *Syriac printing press at Urmi, which functioned from 1841 to 1918; in 1885 the Abp. of Canterbury, E. W. *Benson, sent an educational mission (closed in 1915) which also published many Syriac biblical and liturgical texts.

The Church of the East suffered greatly as a result of political developments in the 20th century. Partly because of the influence of the 'Archbishop of Canterbury's Mission' it supported the Anglo-Russian side during the First World War; there were reprisals from both Turks and Kurds. When the war was over, after the murder of the Catholicos, most of his flock fled to the protection of the British Mandate in Iraq. At the end of the Mandate (1933), as a result of disturbances, the Catholicos was deported, eventually to settle in the USA. Members of the Church of the East are now scattered in many parts of the world, esp. in the USA; only about 30,000 remain in the Middle East (Iraq, Syria, Lebanon, and Iran). Since 1968 there has been a schism, with one Catholicos resident in Baghdad, the other in the USA.

The liturgical language of the Church of the East is

Syriac, and three anaphoras are used, attributed to Theodore of Mopsuestia, Nestorius, and *Addai and Mari. The last of these retains a number of primitive elements.

A. R. Vine, *The Nestorian Churches* (1937; popular). A. K. Arvanitis, Ἱστορία τῆς Ἀσσυριακῆς Νεστοριανικῆς Ἐκκλησίας (Athens, 1968). J. Labourt, *Le Christianisme dans l'empire perse sous la dynastie sassanide, 224–632* (1904). F. Nau, 'L'Expansion nestorienne en Asie', *Annales du Musée Guimet: Bibliothèque de Vulgarisation*, 40 [1913], pp. 193–383. J. M. Fiey, OP, *Assyrie Chrétienne* (Recherches publiées sous la direction de l'Institut des Lettres Orientales de Beyrouth, 22; 3 vols., 1965–8). Id., *Jalons pour une Histoire de l'Église en Iraq* (CSCO, Subsidia, 36; 1970); id., *Chrétiens Syriaques sous les Abbassides surtout à Bagdad (749–1258)* (ibid. 59; 1980); id., *Chrétiens Syriaques sous les Mongols (Il-Khanat de Perse, XIIIe–XIVe s.)* (ibid. 44; 1975). Id., *Pour un Oriens Christianus novus: Répertoire des diocèses syriaques orientaux et occidentaux* (Beiruter Texte und Studien, 49; 1993). W. G. Young, *Patriarch, Shah and Caliph: A Study of the Relationships of the Church of the East with the Sassanid Empire and the early Caliphates up to 820 A.D.* (Rawalpindi, 1974). G. P. Badger, *The Nestorians and their Rituals* (2 vols., 1852; descriptive account of contemporary practice as seen by a missionary, with Eng. tr. of liturgical texts). A. J. Maclean and W. H. Browne, *The Catholicos of the East and his People: Being the Impressions of Five Years' Work in the 'Archbishop of Canterbury's Assyrian Mission'* (1892). P. Kawerau, 'Die nestorianischen Patriarchate in der neueren Zeit', *ZKG* 67 (1955–6), pp. 119–31. J. F. Coakley, *The Church of the East and the Church of England: A History of the Archbishop of Canterbury's Assyrian Mission* (Oxford, 1992). J. Joseph, *The Nestorians and their Muslim Neighbors* (Princeton Oriental Studies, 20; 1961). G. Yonan, *Assyrer heute: Kultur, Sprache, Nationalbewegung der aramäisch sprechenden Christen im Nahen Osten* (Reihe Pogrom, 59; Hamburg, 1978). A. Vööbus, *History of the School of Nisibis* (CSCO, Subsidia, 26; 1965). G. Chediath, *The Christology of Mar Babai the Great* (Kottayam, 1982). S. [P.] Brock, 'The Christology of the Church of the East in the Synods of the Fifth to Early Seventh Centuries: Preliminary Considerations and Materials', in G. D. Dragas (ed.), *Aksum-Thyateira: A Festschrift for Archbishop Methodios of Thyateira and Great Britain* (1985), pp. 125–42, repr. in id., *Studies in Syriac Christianity* [1992], no. 12. J. B. Chabot (ed. and tr.), *Synodicon orientale ou recueil des synodes nestoriens* (Notices et Extraits des Manuscrits de la Bibliothèque Nationale, 38; 1902). W. de Vries, SJ, *Sakramententheologie bei den Nestorianern* (Orientalia Christiana Analecta, 133; 1947). E. A. W. Budge, *The Monks of Kûblâi Khân, Emperor of China, or The History of the Life and Travels of Rabban Swâmâ, Envoy and Plenipotentiary of the Mongol Khâns to the Kings of Europe, and Markôs who as Mâr Yahbh-Allâhâ III became Patriarch of the Nestorian Church in Asia*, tr. from the Syriac (1928). A. S. Atiyah, *A History of Eastern Christianity* (1968), pp. 237–302. E. Tisserant and É. Amann in *DTC* 11 (pt. 1; 1931), cols. 157–323, s.v. 'Nestorius. 2. L'Église nestorienne'; J. Dauvillier in *DDC* 3 (1942), cols. 292–388, s.v. 'Chaldéen, (droit)'; M. Jugie, AA, and G. de Vries, SJ, in *EC* 8 (1952), cols. 1780–7, s.v. 'Nestorio e nestorianesimo'. See also bibl. to ASSYRIAN CHRISTIANS and SYRIAC.

Church Pastoral Aid Society. See CPAS.

Church Sisters. In the Church of Scotland, women specially set apart to assist in parochial work, generally in busy industrial areas, in connection with the Women's Home Mission. They are appointed by *kirk sessions and are under the oversight of an Assembly Committee and the minister of the parish in which they labour. They have now been merged in an order of *Deaconesses.

Church Society. See CHURCH ASSOCIATION.

Church Times. A weekly religious newspaper, founded to propagate *Anglo-Catholic principles. Its first issue appeared on 7 Feb. 1863. It now occupies a position of central Churchmanship in the C of E.

B. Palmer, *Gadfly for God: A History of the Church Times* (1991).

Church Union. An Anglican association which exists 'to uphold the doctrine and discipline of the Church; to extend the knowledge of Catholic Faith and practice at home and beyond the seas; and so to bring everyone to worship the Lord as Saviour and King'. It was formed in 1934 under the presidency of the second Lord *Halifax by the amalgamation of the *English Church Union and the Anglo-Catholic Congress.

Church Unity Octave. The *octave of prayer observed annually from 18 Jan. (formerly Feast of St Peter's Chair at Rome) to 25 Jan. (Conversion of St Paul) by a group of Anglican High Churchmen and others for the visible reunion of the Church, with Rome as the central see of Christendom. It was first kept in 1908. Under P. I. Couturier (q.v.) it evolved into what became the widely-observed 'Week of Prayer for Christian Unity'.

Churches of Christ. See DISCIPLES OF CHRIST.

Churching of Women. The form of thanksgiving which Christian women make after childbirth. The custom, which is based on the Jewish rite of Purification (Lev. 12: 6), is mentioned in a letter of St *Augustine of Canterbury to St *Gregory the Great. The oldest extant forms of service, however, are medieval. The 1662 BCP office is essentially the same as that of the *Sarum rite except that psalms 116 and 127 replace 121 and 128. It is intended to precede Holy Communion. The wearing of a white veil by the woman was anciently customary and enforced by law in *James I's reign. The woman makes a thank-offering at this service.

The ASB provides new services of 'Thanksgiving for the Birth of a Child' and 'Thanksgiving after Adoption'. Both are intended to involve the whole family and include the giving of one of the Gospels to the parents. Other modern Anglican liturgies make similar provisions for a service distinct from *Baptism.

The RC office used to be closely similar to that of the BCP. It has now been replaced by a blessing of the mother at the end of the Baptismal service. If the mother is unable to attend the Baptism, a separate form of blessing is provided in the section of the *Rituale Romanum, De Benedictionibus* (1984), pt. 1, cap. 1, nos. 236–57.

In the E. Church there are various services of prayer and thanksgiving after the birth of a child. It is the child, however, who is said to be 'churched', i.e. brought to church, ideally forty days after birth. These services can be found in the *Euchologion*.

E. *Martène, *De Antiquis Ecclesiae Ritibus*, 1, cap. 9, art. 5, ordo 11. M. Righetti, *Manuale di Storia Liturgica*, 4 (2nd edn., 1959), pp. 470–2. S. Cheetham in *DCA* 1 (1875), pp. 390 f., s.v., with primary refs. C. L. Feltoe in *PBD* (1925), pp. 203 f., s.v. A. J. Schulte in *CE* 3 (1908), p. 761, s.v.

Churchmen's Union. See MODERN CHURCH PEOPLE'S UNION.

churchwardens. The election of churchwardens in the C of E is governed by the Churchwardens (Appointment and Resignation) Measure 1964 (slightly modified by the *Synodical Government Measure 1969). This preserves the arrangement of can. 89 of 1604, whereby two church-wardens are to be chosen by the incumbent and the parish-ioners, or, if they fail to agree, one is to be appointed by the incumbent, the other by the people. The election takes place annually, not later in the year than 30 April, and the persons elected are admitted to their office by the *ordinary. The duties of churchwardens are defined in the 1969 canons (can. E 1) as being 'foremost in representing the laity and in co-operating with the incumbent', encour-aging the parishioners 'in the practice of true religion', promoting unity and peace, and maintaining order and decency in the church and churchyard. They are also responsible for the movable property in the church. In the past they had also the duty of presenting offenders against ecclesiastical law, a function which they fulfilled until the 19th cent. Until the establishment of *Parochial Church Councils in 1921 they were the sole official representatives of the laity in each parish.

C. Drew, *Early Parochial Organisation in England: The Origins of the Office of Churchwarden* (St Anthony's Hall publications, 7; 1954). R. *Phillimore, *The Ecclesiastical Law of the Church of Eng-land*, 2 (2nd edn. by W. G. F. Phillimore, 1895), esp. pp. 1463–91. H. W. Cripps, *A Practical Treatise on the Law Relating to the Church and Clergy* (8th edn. by K. M. Macmorran, 1937), pp. 158–77. The 1964 Measure is pr. in K. M. Macmorran, *A Hand-book for Churchwardens and Parochial Church Councillors* (9th edn. by K. J. T. Elphinstone, E. G. Moore, and T. J. Briden, 1986), pp. 59–68; see also pp. 69–75. M. Hill, *Ecclesiastical Law* (1995), pp. 92–7.

churchyard. Properly the ground in which a church stands, though the word is often used as though equivalent to '*cemetery' (which it may or may not be). In the past such enclosures were often used as public meeting-places for the conduct of trials, markets, and other secular busi-ness.

ciborium (Gk. κιβώριον). (1) A chalice-shaped vessel, with a lid, used to contain the Sacramental Bread of the Eucharist. It apparently came into general use early in the Middle Ages. (2) The term is also sometimes applied to the canopy ('ciborium magnum') resting on four pillars over the altar of Christian *basilicas and other churches, now more usually termed in the W. the '*baldachino'.

(1) Braun, *AG*, pp. 280–347, with plates 51–9.
(2) Braun, *CA*, 2, pp. 185–261, with plates 152–8. H. *Leclercq, OSB, in *DACL* 3 (pt. 2, 1914), cols. 1588–612, s.v.

Cimabue (d. 1302 or later), the usual name of Cenni di Pepo, Florentine painter. Little is known of his life, beyond the facts that he was working in 1272 and 1302. He was, however, regarded by *Dante (*Purg.* 11. 94–6) as the most important painter in Italy before *Giotto, and G. Vasari, the 16th-cent. historian of Italian art, claimed that he was Giotto's teacher. The mosaic of St John the Evan-gelist in the apse of Pisa cathedral is the only documented work (1302), but this is now partly restored. He painted in Rome and also extensively in the church of S. Francesco, *Assisi, particularly in the transepts and apse of the Upper Church. Outstanding works on panel include the 'S. Trin-ità Madonna' (Uffizi, Florence), the 'Crucifixions' in the churches of S. Domenico, Arezzo, and S. Croce, Florence (damaged by flooding in 1966), and the 'Virgin and Child with Angels' (Louvre, Paris). The traditional attribution to Cimabue of the 'Madonna' once in the chapel of the Rucellai in S. Maria Novella, Florence (now in the Uffizi) is no longer valid; it is a documented work of 1285 by the Sienese painter Duccio di Buoninsegna (d. 1319).

A. Nicholson, *Cimabue: A Critical Study* (Princeton Mono-graphs in Art and Archaeology, 16; 1932); E. Battisti, *Cimabue* (Milan, 1963; Eng. tr., University Park, Pa., and London, 1967). U. Baldini and O. Casazza, *The Cimabue Crucifix* [1983]. J. White, *Art and Architecture in Italy 1250 to 1400* (Pelican History of Art, 1966), pp. 115–31. E. Borsook, *The Mural Painters of Tuscany* (2nd edn., Oxford, 1980), pp. 3–7.

cincture. See GIRDLE.

Circumcellions. Fanatical bands of predatory peasants who flourished in the north of Africa, esp. Numidia, in the 4th cent. They were so named because they lived or moved around (*circum*) martyrs' shrines (*cellae*) from which they drew physical sustenance, but they preferred themselves to be known as 'Agonistici', i.e. 'soldiers (of Christ)'. Though they were originally concerned only with the remedy of (probably genuine) social grievances, they became linked with the *Donatists; and as such they used great violence on behalf of the Donatist cause, taking as their battle-cry the words 'laudes Deo' ('praises be to God'). Among some Donatists at least Circumcellions who were killed on their raids were regarded as martyrs, and some seem to have sought martyrdom by suicide. The civil government tried to subdue them by force and persuasion in turn, but they survived into the 5th cent.

The chief patristic refs. include *Optatus, *De Schismate Donati-starum*, 3. 4, and St *Augustine, *Contra Gaudentium*, 1. 28. 32, and *Enarratio in Ps.*, 132. 3 and 6. Further patristic refs. in W. H. C. Frend, *The Donatist Church: A Movement of Protest in Roman North Africa* (1952), esp. pp. 172–8; id., 'The cellae of the African Circumcellions', *JTS* NS 3 (1952), pp. 87–9. H. J. Diesner, *Kirche und Staat im spätrömischen Reich* (1963), esp. chs. 1, 4, 5, with full bibl. E. Tengström, *Donatisten und Katholiken: Soziale, wirtschaftliche und politische Aspekte einer nordafrikanischen Kirchenspaltung* (Studia Graeca et Latina Gothoburgensia, 18; 1964), pp. 24–78. W. H. C. Frend, 'Circumcellions and Monks', *JTS* NS 20 (1969), pp. 542–9.

circumcision. Though circumcision had long been in use as a religious rite among the Jews, for whom it was part of the Law of *Moses (e.g. Gen. 17: 12, Ex. 12: 48), it was abandoned at an early date by nearly the whole Christian Church. At the conference at *Jerusalem *c.* AD 50 (cf. Acts 15 and Gal. 2) St *Paul and St *Barnabas gained recognition for the Church in *Antioch's practice of not circumcising Gentile converts. However, as Paul's mission spread, it attracted opposition on that account, esp. in Galatia. Only with the fall of Jerusalem and the marginalizing of Jewish Christianity was Paul's position finally victorious. From a remote date, however, the rite has been in use in the Church of *Ethiopia, where it is performed between the third and eighth day after birth, i.e. before the child is baptized. In the NT (e.g. Rom. 3:

30, Eph. 2: 11), 'the circumcision' (ἡ περιτομή) is occasionally used substantively of the Jewish people.

The Jewish Rite of Circumcision, with prayers and laws appertaining thereto. Translated into English, with an introd. essay by A. Asher (1873). R. de Vaux, OP, *Les Institutions de l'Ancien Testament*, 1 (1958), pp. 78–82; Eng. tr. (2nd edn., 1965), pp. 46–48. Arts. by L. H. Gray ('Introductory'), L. Spence ('American'), G. Foucart ('Egyptian'), D. S. Margoliouth ('Muslim'), and G. A. Barton ('Semitic') in *HERE* 3 (1910), pp. 659–80. R. Meyer in *TWNT* 6 (1959), cols. 72–83; Eng. tr. (1968), pp. 72–84, s.v. περιτέμνω, with further refs.

Circumcision, Feast of the.
The feast traditionally kept on 1 Jan., the eighth day after *Christmas, in commemoration of Christ's circumcision (cf. Lk. 2: 21: 'when eight days were accomplished'). The observance goes back to the middle of the 6th cent. It then spread, at first esp. in Spain and Gaul, but it did not become established at *Rome till the 11th cent. Its relatively late introduction into the Christian calendar has been connected with the unwillingness of the Church to introduce a festival on New Year's Day, which had been kept with great riot and licence by the pagans. Indeed, many early Missals provided a second Mass for use on that day against idolatrous practices (*ad prohibendum ab idolis*). In the *Armenian Church, the feast is observed on 13 Jan. Since it is recorded that when He was circumcised, the Lord was given the name Jesus (Lk. 2: 22), many modern Anglican liturgies call the feast the Naming of Jesus. In the RC Church there has been a tendency to observe 1 Jan. as the Octave of Christmas (as it was officially styled in 1960); in the 1969 Roman Calendar it is called the 'Solemnity of Holy Mary, the Mother of God' (*Solemnitas S. Dei Genetricis Mariae*).

F. Bünger, *Geschichte der Neujahrsfeier in der Kirche* (1910). F. *Cabrol, *Les Origines liturgiques* (1906), Appendice C, 'Le Premier des Calendes de Janvier et la Messe contre les Idoles', pp. 203–10. M. Righetti, *Manuale di Storia Liturgica*, 2 (Milan, 1955), pp. 73–77, with refs. F. Cabrol in *DACL* 3, pt. 2 (1914), cols. 1717–28, s.v., incl. further bibl.

circumincession (also circuminsession).
In Christian theology the technical term for the interpenetration of the Three Persons of the Holy Trinity. The corresponding Gk. word, περιχώρησις (lit. 'a proceeding around'), used by St *John of Damascus in this connection, was rendered into Latin *circumincessio* by *Burgundio of Pisa (d. 1193); and this later became changed into *circuminsessio* through similarity of sound.

A. Deneffe, SJ, 'Perichoresis, circumincessio, circuminsessio. Eine terminologische Untersuchung', *ZKT* 47 (1923), pp. 497–532; [G.] L. Prestige, 'Περιχωρέω and περιχώρησις in the Fathers', *JTS* 29 (1928), pp. 242–52; G. W. H. Lampe (ed.), *A Patristic Greek Lexicon* (1968), p. 1077, s.v. περιχωρέω.

Cisneros, Franceso Ximénez de.
See XIMÉNEZ DE CISNEROS, F.

Cistercian Order.
The order of White Monks, so called from the mother house at *Cîteaux, which was founded in 1098 by St *Robert of Molesme and several other brethren, incl. St *Stephen Harding, who sought to establish a form of *Benedictinism stricter and more primitive than any then existing. After some precarious years Cîteaux rose rapidly to celebrity through its connection with its most famous son, St *Bernard, who became a novice there in 1112. Its four eldest 'daughters' were founded in quick succession: la Ferté (1113), Pontigny (1114), *Clairvaux, and Morimond (1115). In the following decades the order spread very rapidly to almost every part of Europe and the Latin East. By the death of St Bernard (1153) there were 345 houses; by the end of the 13th cent. the order reached its maximum of 740; and there were still some 700 on the eve of the Reformation. There were also many houses of Cistercian nuns. The first foundation in England was at Waverley, Surrey (1128–9), soon followed by *Rievaulx (1131/2) and *Fountains (1132).

The Cistercian life was to be one of secluded communal intercession and adoration. Houses were to be erected only in remote situations, while its churches were to be plain in character and their ornaments and vestments were not made from precious materials. Strict rules on diet and silence were laid down and manual labour given its primitive prominent position. The Cistercians thus became important agricultural pioneers, playing a notable part in English sheep farming, the care of their estates being for long undertaken by *lay brothers who lived under somewhat less severe rules.

According to recent scholarship, the constitution of the Cistercian order developed gradually during the 12th cent., and its basic documents—the *Carta caritatis*, the *Exordium parvum*, and the *Exordium Cistercii*—also took shape gradually during this process. The detailed course of events remains a matter of controversy, but the order developed a constitution under which a founding abbey had permanent oversight of abbeys that it founded; this was achieved through visitation by the abbot, in principle annually but perhaps more often, to ensure observance and discipline. Daughter-abbeys could make foundations of their own; thus, lines of filiation quickly developed, often to four generations and more. Cîteaux itself was visited by the abbots of its eldest daughters (the 'proto-abbots'). All Cistercian abbots were obliged to attend an annual General Chapter at Cîteaux; if inevitably hindered they had to send a deputy. In the General Chapter was vested legislative, executive, and judicial authority over the whole order. There was no scope for the abbot of Cîteaux to develop monarchical authority, and a body of Statutes of the General Chapters was built up. No other chapters of abbots were allowed to assemble. Cistercian observances powerfully influenced those of other medieval orders, notably certain congregations of *regular canons, and after 1215 their scheme of periodic general chapters and visitations was made obligatory for other monastic orders. From the 13th cent., however, the fame of the order waned.

Starting with Castile in the 15th cent., more and more foreign houses formed national congregations, which developed outside the control of Cîteaux and the four proto-abbeys, while still remaining juridically part of the order. In France a particularly radical reform in the late 16th cent. gave rise first to a congregation and then an independent order of *Feuillants. In the 17th cent. Cistercians, like most orders, were divided between reformers (the Strict Observance), trying to return to the spirit and practice of the founding fathers by rejecting all later mitigations of the Rule, and those, led by Cîteaux, who wanted a minimum of change (the Common Observance).

The Strict Observance eventually controlled about a third of the French houses, but failed either to impose their reform on the whole order or to achieve the autonomy they sought. Those houses flourished most where austerity, as at *la Trappe, went consistently beyond the average.

In the 18th cent. Cistercians in the Austro-Hungarian Empire survived the *Josephine edicts only by undertaking major educational and pastoral responsibilities. Shortly afterwards the French Revolution destroyed not only all houses in France and neighbouring lands, but the very structure of central authority. Throughout the 19th cent. government hostility to monastic life led to massive closures and expulsions in Spain, Italy, Germany, and even Switzerland, and in the 20th cent. wars in Europe and Asia, totalitarian regimes and post-colonial turbulence have all violently, and often unpredictably, affected organisation and survival. It has been reaction to external events that has given the present Common Observance (properly the Sacred Order of Cîteaux, S. O. Cist.) its present shape, with an Abbot General and staff (finally established at Rome only in 1927), presiding over a union of about a dozen congregations, formed mainly on a national or linguistic basis. These differ widely in their pattern of life, some being responsible for high schools and universities, some in the mission field, often with parishes, and some (notably *Lérins) primarily contemplative. The largest congregations are those in Austria, Italy, and the *United States of America. The order has almost as many nuns as monks, organized in similar congregations.

The extinction of Cîteaux and the proto-abbeys in 1790/1 left la Trappe as the only French community of any male order to survive. Under the leadership of Augustin de Lestrange (elected Abbot in 1794), 24 volunteers fled to Switzerland; they soon attracted hundreds of recruits (many from other orders) and founded communities in various countries. Wartime conditions obliged Lestrange to draft regulations of excessive rigour which were only partly relaxed when peace permitted Trappists to reestablish monastic life in France; other houses, and their daughter foundations, preferred to follow A.-J. le B. de *Rancé's original reform. A fundamentally penitential view of monastic life, expressed in a uniformly strict observance, was the common aim of all the Trappist houses. It was not, however, until 1892 that the three Trappist congregations achieved union and were recognized in 1893 as a new independent order; in 1902, after the recovery of Cîteaux, which became the mother house, it was designated as the Cistercians of the Strict Observance (OCSO) or Reformed Cistercians (OCR). This order is not the continuation of the Strict Observance destroyed in 1791, but the lineal descendant of Rancé's reform of 1664 at la Trappe. Vast expansion worldwide has strained the practice of uniformity, and, with the abolition of the category of lay brothers (and sisters) after the Second *Vatican Council, major changes which were initiated, culminating in new Constitutions which were finally approved in 1990. The explicit aim is now unity, not uniformity, expressed through a pluralism which recognises cultural and regional differences. Abbots (including the Abbot General) are no longer automatically elected for life; regional conferences have much wider powers (though the General Chapter remains supreme); the Divine *Office has been simplified (but *Vigils, the Night Office, is retained);

abstention from meat is normally recommended, but detailed dietary prescriptions have been omitted; silence is normally absolute only in prescribed places and at night; contacts with family, and the outside world, are easier; and study is actively encouraged. A major change has been a much greater degree of self-government for the nuns, whose General Chapter was for the first time in 1990 given equality with that of the monks in electing the new Abbot General. There are about 80 houses of men and rather fewer of women.

Though there are now two quite separate Cistercian Orders, close and fraternal co-operation between them, at a local and also wider level, is constant.

J.-M. Canivez, OCR (ed.), *Statuta Capitulorum Generalium Ordinis Cisterciensis* (8 vols., Bibliothèque de la *Revue d'Histoire Ecclésiastique*, fascs. 9–14 B; 1933–41). J. de la C. Bouton, OCR, and J. B. Van Damme, OCR, *Les plus anciens Textes de Cîteaux* (Cîteaux—Commentarii Cistercienses, 2; Achel, 1974). A. Manrique, O. Cist., *Annales Cistercienses* (4 vols., Lyons, 1642–59; repr., Farnborough, 1970). B. Tissier, O. Cist. (ed.), *Bibliotheca Patrum Cisterciensium, id est Operum Abbatum et Monachorum Ordinis Cisterciensis qui saeculo S. Bernardi aut paulo post eius obitum floruerunt* (8 vols., bound in 3, Bonnefontaine and Paris, 1660–9). On the problems presented by the early Cistercian docs. see [M.] D. *Knowles, *Great Historical Enterprises: Problems in Monastic History* (1963), pp. 198–222; K. Hallinger, 'Die Anfänge von Cîteaux', in *Aus Kirche und Reich. . . .: Festschrift für Friedrich Kempf zu seinem 75. Geburtstag und 50. Doktorjubiläum*, ed. H. Mordek (1983), pp. 225–235. J.-B. Auberger, OFM, *L'Unanimité cistercienne primitive: mythe ou réalité?* (Cîteaux, Studia et Documenta, 3; Achel, 1986). P. Le Nain, O. Cist., *Essai de l'histoire de l'ordre de Cîteaux* (9 vols., 1695–7). L. J. Lekai, O. Cist., *The White Monks: A History of the Cistercian Order* (Okauchee, Wis., 1953); id., *The Rise of the Cistercian Strict Observance in Seventeenth Century France* (Washington, DC, 1968); id., *The Cistercians: Ideals and Reality* (Kent, Oh., 1977). A. Schneider, O. Cist., and others (eds.), *Die Cisterciense Geschichte, Geist, Kunst* (Cologne, 1974). M. Pacaut, *Les moines blancs: Histoire de l'ordre de Cîteaux* [1993].

L. Pressouyre and T. N. Kinder (eds.), *Saint Bernard et le monde cistercien: Exposition presentée par la Caisse nationale des monuments historiques et des sites à la Conciergerie de Paris du 18 décembre 1990 au 28 février 1991* (1990). L. Bouyer, Cong. Orat., *La Spiritualité de Cîteaux* (1955; Eng. tr., 1958). J. B. Mahn, *L'Ordre cistercien et son gouvernement, des origines au milieu du XIIIᵉ siècle, 1098–1265* (Bibliothèque des Écoles Françaises d'Athènes et de Rome, 116; 1945). A. A. King, *Cîteaux and her Elder Daughters* (1954), pp. 1–105. [M.] D. Knowles, *The Monastic Order in England* (Cambridge, 1940; 2nd edn., 1967), pp. 208–66, 346–62, and 632–48. J. F. O'Sullivan, *Cistercian Settlements in Wales and Monmouthshire, 1140–1540* (Fordham University Studies, History Series, 2; New York, 1947). B. D. Hill, *English Cistercian Monasteries and their Patrons in the Twelfth Century* (1968). Y. Załuska, *L'Enluminure et le Scriptorium de Cîteaux au XIIᵉ siècle* (Cîteaux, Commentarii Cistercienses, Studia et documenta, 4; Cîteaux, 1989). J.-B. Lefèvre and J.-J. Bolly, 'Monastères Bénédictins et Cisterciens dans les Albums de Croÿ (1596–1611). Histoire et Institutions des Abbayes Cisterciennes (XIIᵉ–XVIIᵉ siècles)', *R. Bén.* 100 (1990), pp. 109–238.

A. Le Bail, OSB, *L'Ordre de Cîteaux: 'La Trappe'* (Les Ordres religieux, 1924); C. Grolleau-G. Chastel, *L'Ordre de Cîteaux: La Trappe* (Les Grands Ordres monastiques et instituts religieux, 1932). Y. Estienne, *Les Trappistines: Cisterciennes de la stricte observance* (1937). M. T. Kervingant, OCSO, *Des moniales face à la Révolution française: Aux origines des Cisterciennes-Trappistines* (1989). Life in a Trappist monastery in the USA before the Second Vatican Council is depicted in the autobiography of T. *Merton, *The Seven Storey Mountain* (New York [1948]), pub. in

England as *Elected Silence* (London, 1949), and other works of this author.

The *Cistercienser-Chronik* ed. by the Cistercians of Mehrerau (1889 ff.); *Analecta Sacri Ordinis Cisterciensis* (Rome, 1945 ff.); *Collectanea Ordinis Cisterciensium Reformatorum* (Rome and Westmalle, 1934 ff.). L. J. Lekai, O. Cist., in *NCE* 3 (1967), pp. 885–9, s.v.; M. R. Flanagan, ibid. 14 (1967), pp. 261–4, s.v. 'Trappists'; L. J. Lekai, O. Cist., in *DIP* 2 (1975), cols. 1058–98, s.v. 'Cistercensi'; É. Mikkers, OCR, in *Dict. Sp.* 13 (1988), cols. 738–814, s.v. 'Robert (12) de Molesmes', 2: 'La Spiritualité Cistercienne'.

citation. A summons to appear before a court of justice, esp. an ecclesiastical court. Until the Court of Probate Act 1857 transferred jurisdiction to the temporal courts, the probate of wills was dealt with by the ecclesiastical courts, where citation is the normal method of opening proceedings. Any person may still be cited, e.g. even a *lay rector not himself a member of the C of E, for offences against ecclesiastical law, but the most common use of citation nowadays is in *faculty cases, where a citation is a notice of proceedings either publicly displayed ('general citation') or served on an interested body, e.g. English Heritage ('special citation').

Cîteaux (Lat. *Cistercium*). The mother house of the *Cistercian Order, some 16 miles S. of Dijon. Expropriated at the French Revolution, Cîteaux was acquired in 1898 by the newly independent Order formed from *Trappist congregations united in 1893. Their new Abbot General, while residing in Rome, took the title of Abbot of Cîteaux, appointing an auxiliary abbot to rule the monastery. Since 1963 the General has borne the title of Arch-Abbot and the community of Cîteaux elected its own superior, like other houses of the Order.

J. Marlier (ed.), *Chartes et documents concernant l'abbaye de Cîteaux, 1098–1182* (Bibliotheca Cisterciensis, 1; Rome, 1961). L. M. Cottineau, OSB, *Répertoire topo-bibliographique des abbayes et prieurés* (Mâcon, 1935), cols. 787–90, with extensive bibl. J.-M. Canivez, OCR, in *DHGE* 12 (1953), cols. 852–74, s.v., with bibl.; J. de la Croix Bouton and others in *Lexikon des Mittelalters*, 2 (1983), cols. 2104–7, s.v.

Cities of Refuge. In ancient Israel the six walled cities, three on each side of *Jordan, which were set aside as a protection for those who had committed accidental homicide (Deut. 4: 41–3, 19: 1–13, and Josh. 20). The existence of such places was made necessary by the primitive law which required blood vengeance from the next of kin (*goel*). In the earlier legislation of Exod. 21: 13 f. (the 'Book of the Covenant'), apparently any altar offered such asylum. Acc. to Deut. 19: 1 f., three were to be appointed when the Hebrews were established W. of Jordan and three more when the whole land was conquered (Deut. 19: 8 f.). In Josh. 20, where the selection of the cities is attributed to *Joshua (not, as in Deut. 4: 41–3, to *Moses), their names are Kedesh, Shechem, Hebron, Bezer, Ramoth in Gilead, and Golan. Asylum involved trial; and if the verdict was murder, the refuge was withdrawn.

R. de Vaux, OP, *Les Institutions de l'Ancien Testament*, 1 (1958; 4th edn., 1982), pp. 247–50; Eng. tr., *Ancient Israel* (2nd edn., 1965), pp. 160–3.

Civil Constitution of the Clergy. The legislative measures passed (12 July 1790) during the French Revolution by the Constituent Assembly to reorganize the Church in France. Since Church property was being sold and *tithe had been abolished, arrangements had to be made for paying the clergy. The Assembly was also determined to end the aristocratic monopoly of high ecclesiastical office and, in the spirit of *Gallicanism, wished to demonstrate French independence of Rome—except in the sphere of doctrine. The dioceses were reduced in number to coincide with the civil departments, the parochial structure was made more logical, the parish priests, many of them poorly paid in the past, were given fair salaries, and the bishops and *curés* were to be elected by the more prosperous of the local citizens. The Papal power of confirming nominations to the episcopate was transferred to the metropolitans. Most of the clergy, including a majority of the bishops, wished to accept the new order, however reluctantly, but they insisted that 'the Church must be consulted'. The Assembly, intoxicated by the idea of national sovereignty, would not permit the aristocratic bishops to meet in Council, and allowed only a brief period to the king in which he made covert approaches to Rome (using the threat of the annexation of Avignon). Finally, on 27 Nov. 1790, the Assembly imposed an oath to the Civil Constitution on all priests wishing to retain ecclesiastical office. About half of the parish clergy (though only four of the diocesan bishops) accepted it. Louis XVI had sanctioned the Civil Constitution on 23 May 1791, and Papal briefs condemning it reached him the following day. The condemnation had been kept secret. It was only at the beginning of May 1791 that the French clergy heard of the Papal brief 'Caritas' (of 13 April) declaring the Civil Constitution heretical, sacrilegious, and schismatic.

Text in *Archives parlementaires de 1787 à 1860. Recueil complet des débats législatifs et politiques des chambres françaises imprimé par ordre du Sénat et de la Chambre des Députés sous la direction de ... J. Mavidal ... and E. Laurent*, 1st ser., 17 (1884), pp. 55–60. The Brief 'Caritas' is pr. in A. Barlèri and R. Segreti, IC (eds.), *Bullarii Romani Continuatio ... Clementis XIII. Clementis XIV. Pii VI. Pii VII. Leonis XII. et Pii VIII.*, 9 (Rome, 1845), pp. 11–19. Eng. tr. of the main clauses of the Constitution, the decree requiring the Clerical Oath, and the brief 'Caritas' in J. H. Stewart, *A Documentary Survey of the French Revolution* (New York [1951]), pp. 169–89, and of the Constitution, with comm., in S. Z. Ehler and J. B. Morrall (eds.), *Church and State Through the Centuries* (1954), pp. 236–49. A. Mathiez, *Rome et le clergé français sous la Constituante* (1911); J. McManners, *French Ecclesiastical Society under the Ancien Régime: A Study of Angers in the Eighteenth Century* (Manchester, 1960), pp. 255–76; T. Tackett, *Religion, Revolution, and Regional Culture in Eighteenth-Century France: The Ecclesiastical Oath of 1791* (Princeton, NJ [1986]). See also bibl. to CONSTITUTIONAL CHURCH.

Civiltà Cattolica. A periodical published twice monthly by the Italian *Jesuits. At the time of the First *Vatican Council (1869–70), it actively attacked *liberalism and supported Papal infallibility.

Clairvaux (Lat. *Clara Vallis*). The fourth house of the *Cistercian Order, near Bar-sur-Aube, founded in 1115 by St *Bernard of Clairvaux. The filiation of Clairvaux soon became, and remained, the largest in the Order, of which Clairvaux was much the wealthiest house until the French

Revolution. Abbot Denis Largentier was one of the promoters (in 1615) of the Strict Observance, but after his death in 1624 Clairvaux ceased to support the movement. The community was broken up and the property confiscated by the state in 1790. Since 1808 Clairvaux has been used as a prison.

A. A. King, *Cîteaux and her Elder Daughters* (1954), pp. 207–328. A. [F.] Prévost, 'Recueil des chartes et bulles de Clairvaux', *Revue Mabillon*, 14 (1924), pp. 140–56, 233–42; 15 (1925), pp. 145–67, 258–71, 308–17; 16 (1926), pp. 49–62, 166–9, 237–48, 369–84; 17 (1927), pp. 62–71, 286–90, 421–8; 18 (1928), pp. 66–76, 158–76, 240–56, 324–37; and 19 (1929), pp. 161–72. J. Waquet (ed.), *Recueil des chartes de l'abbaye de Clairvaux*, fasc. 1 (Troyes, 1950). J. Laurent and F. Claudon, *Abbayes et prieurés de l'Ancienne France*, 12, pt. 3 (Archives de la France Monastique, 45; 1941), pp. 308–44, with full refs. J. J. Vernier (ed.), 'Inventaire du trésor de la sacristie de l'abbaye de Clairvaux de 1640', *Bibliothèque de l'École des Chartes*, 63 (1902), pp. 599–677. *La Bibliothèque de l'Abbaye de Clairvaux du XIIᵉ au XVIIIᵉ Siècle*, 1: Catalogues et Répertoires, ed. A. Vernet (1979). J.-M. Canivez, OCR, in *DHGE* 12 (1953), cols. 1050–61, s.v.; A. Dimier, OCSO, in *DIP* 2 (1975), cols. 1111 f., s.v., both with bibl.

clandestinity. The celebration of marriages without the cognizance of proper authority. The abuse became widespread in the later Middle Ages and in the 16th cent. Protestants and Catholics alike were anxious for reform. In his *Von Ehesachen* (1530) M. *Luther strongly opposed unions contracted without parental knowledge or approval, regarding such marriages (to which he esp. applied the term 'clandestine') as null and void; and he was closely followed by P. *Melanchthon, J. *Brenz, J. *Calvin, and T. *Beza. The RC canonists, though less concerned with parental consent (in which they saw a frequent danger to the liberty of the children), were at least as eager for publicity. But to insist on it as a *sine qua non* seemed to imply that the Church possessed the power of altering the matter of a sacrament. After long discussions it was laid down in Session 24 of the Council of *Trent that though clandestine marriages were true and proper marriages (*vera et rata matrimonia*), provided that they had not been rendered void by the Church, in future all such marriages in places where the ruling of the decree obtained would be held to be null. Henceforward all marriages were to be *in facie ecclesiae*, i.e. before the parish priest, local ordinary, or a priest appointed by one of them, as well as at least two other witnesses. This ruling was embodied in the decree *Tametsi*, repeated with minor modifications in *Ne Temere*, and it remains substantially unchanged in *CIC* (1983), can. 1108. Since 1970 the detailed requirements may be dispensed in the case of *mixed marriages, provided there is a public ceremony.

In the C of E publicity is secured by the publication of *banns, the issue of a *marriage licence or the certificate of a superintendent registrar, and by the requirement of proper witnesses to the ceremony. Marriages without banns were formally condemned in the 11th Canon of the Synod of *Westminster (1200). Can. 62 of the 1604 *Canons also ordered that the marriage shall take place 'in time of Divine service'. In 1754, civil legislation was introduced to prevent clandestine marriages by the Clandestine Marriages Act 1753 ('Lord *Hardwicke's Act'), while since the Marriage Act 1823 the law has required as a minimum of publicity two or more credible witnesses,

besides the minister. At the time of the service the doors of the church must not be locked, and Canon B 35 of the 1969 Canons requires all marriages to take place between 8.00 a.m. and 6.00 p.m. In the C of E clandestinity is commonly held not to void a marriage, though the 1604 Canons provided for the punishment of ministers celebrating such marriages.

Clapham Sect. An informal group of wealthy Anglican *Evangelicals, so named by Sydney Smith (1764–1840), because the majority of its members lived near Clapham and worshipped in its parish church. Among the most outstanding were J. Venn, Rector of Clapham from 1792 to 1813, Charles Grant (1746–1832), Z. *Macaulay (q.v.), Lord Teignmouth (1751–1834), James Stephen (1758–1832), Henry Thornton (1760–1815), Granville Sharp (1735–1813) and W. *Wilberforce (q.v.). Although at bottom conservative in their attitude to the social order, they shared a keen sense of moral responsibility and the belief that religion must be manifested in good works. Among the most important schemes in which they engaged were the struggle for the abolition of the *slave trade, the extension of missionary enterprise, esp. in *India, the foundation of the *British and Foreign Bible Society and the establishment of a model colony in *Sierra Leone. They also promoted such schemes for the improvement of moral standards at home as the Proclamation Society (founded 1789), the Society for Bettering the Conditions and Increasing the Comforts of the Poor (1794) and the extension of *Sunday Schools. Towards the end of her life Hannah *More (q.v.) was closely connected with the group. Mainly through the personal position of its members, many of whom were interrelated by marriage, the group was able to exercise on parliament and public opinion an influence out of all proportion to its numbers.

J. Stephen, *Essays in Ecclesiastical Biography*, 2 (1849), pp. 287–382 ('The Clapham Sect'); E. M. Howse, *Saints in Politics: The 'Clapham Sect' and the Growth of Freedom* (Toronto, 1952; London, 1953); D. Spring, 'The Clapham Sect: some social and political aspects', *Victorian Studies*, 5 (1961–2), pp. 35–48; K. Hylson-Smith, *Evangelicals in the Church of England 1734–1984* (Edinburgh, 1989), pp. 79–93. See also other works cited under EVANGELICALISM.

Clapton Sect. See HACKNEY PHALANX.

Clare, St (1193/4–1253), foundress of the '*Poor Clares'. About 1212, moved by the teaching of St *Francis of Assisi, she gave up all her possessions and joined him at the *Portiuncula. He placed her first in a *Benedictine house before moving her to San Damiano outside the walls of *Assisi. When other women wishing to live on Franciscan lines came to join her, she was made abbess (c.1215), a position she held until the end of her life. Many daughter houses were founded in Europe during the 13th cent., including 47 in Spain. The austerity of the rule went far beyond any that women had previously undertaken, and, although many of the daughter houses obtained dispensations from the original ban upon communal property, the community of 'San Damiano', with those of Perugia and Florence, obtained at St Clare's wish the 'privilegium paupertatis' from *Gregory IX, which enabled them to maintain their original state of entire poverty. She was canonized by Alexander IV in 1255. Feast day, 11 (formerly 12) Aug.

The authenticity of the rule and four letters is accepted; that of the Testament, Blessing, and another letter is contested. Eng. tr., from the edn. of I. Omaechevarria, OFM (Madrid, 1970), Francis and Clare, *The Complete Works*, tr. R. J. Armstrong, OFM Cap., and I. Brady, OFM (Classics of Western Spirituality, 1982), pp. 189–234, with introd., pp. 169–85. They are also available in Eng. trs. of primary docs. on her life cited below. Separate edn. of her writings, with Fr. tr. and introd., by M.-F. Becker and others (SC 325; 1985). Contemporary Life, attributed to *Thomas of Celano, pr. in *AASS*, Aug. 2 (1735), pp. 754–67; also ed. from MS 338 of the Bibl. Comunale of Assisi by F. Pennacchi (Assisi, 1910). Eng. tr. by P. Robinson, OFM (London, 1910); this was repr., with different introd. and notes, St Bonaventure, NY, 1953. Eng. tr. of Clare's writings and other material by R. J. Armstrong, OFM Cap., *Clare of Assisi: Early Documents* (New York, 1988), incl. the Life attributed to Thomas of Celano, pp. 184–240; also the Process of Canonization, pp. 125–75, and Bull of Canonization, pp. 176–83. B. Bughetti, OFM (ed.), 'Legenda Versificata S. Clarae Assisiensis, Saec. XIII', *AFH* 5 (1912), pp. 237–60 and 459–81; 14th cent. metrical Life ed. L. Oliger, OFM, ibid., 12 (1919), pp. 110–31. Life, written in 1494, by Ugolino Verino (1442–1505), ed., with introd. and notes, W. Seton (Chelsea, 1921). Z. Lazzeri, OFM, 'Il processo di canonizzazione di S. Chiara d'Assisi', *AFH* 13 (1920), pp. 403–507. E. Gilliat-Smith, *Saint Clare of Assisi: Her Life and Legislation* (1914). Other Lives by M. Beaufreton ('Les Saints', 1916), N. de Robeck (Milwaukee, 1951), and F. Casolini (Assisi, 1953). L. Hardick, OFM, 'Zur Chronologie im Leben der hl. Klara', *Franziskanische Studien*, 35 (1953), pp. 174–210, with other arts. on the rule and order, pp. 145–73 and 211–383. A. Fortini, 'Nuove notizie intorno a S. Chiara di Assisi', *AFH* 46 (1953), pp. 3–43. *Santa Chiara d'Assisi: Studi e cronaca del VII centenario 1253–1953* (Assisi [1954]), esp. pp. 37–310, with docs., pp. 519–42. M. Bartoli, *Chiara d'Assisi* (Bibliotheca Seraphico-Capuccina, 37; 1989; Eng. tr., 1993). L. Iriarte [OFM Cap.], 'Clara de Asís en la tipología hagiográfica femenina', *Laurentianum*, 29 (1988), pp. 416–61. P. *Sabatier, 'Le Privilège de la pauvreté', *Revue d'histoire franciscaine*, 1 (1924), pp. 1–54. R. B. and C. N. L. Brooke, 'St Clare', in D. Baker (ed.), *Medieval Women, dedicated and presented to ... Rosalind M. T. Hill* (Studies in Church History, Subsidia, 1; Oxford, 1978), pp. 275–87. F. Casolini in *Dict. Sp.* 5 (1964), cols. 1401–9, s.v. 'Frères Mineurs, 6. Sainte Claire et les Clarisses. 1. Sainte Claire', with further bibl. See also bibl. to POOR CLARES.

Clarendon, Constitutions of. A schedule of sixteen clauses, put forward by Henry II of England as a statement of English custom under his grandfather Henry I, to regulate the relations between ecclesiastical and lay jurisdiction and other matters. They were produced at the Council of Clarendon (1164) for the assent of St Thomas *Becket, Archbishop of *Canterbury, who, although he had agreed verbally to observe the customs, refused to seal the documents. Among the most important clauses were those which prohibited appeals to Rome without the king's consent (viii) and asserted the royal jurisdiction over criminous clerks (iii). Pope *Alexander III condemned these and eight other clauses, and a long dispute followed, until after Becket's murder Henry promised (1172) not to impede appeals to Rome (these came in practice to be heard in England by papal judges-delegate), and to abandon 'customs' brought in against the churches of his land in his own time—if any. However, though Henry suffered a defeat over criminous clerks (see BENEFIT OF CLERGY), he maintained other important customs, notably the right of lay courts to try actions concerning *advowsons, the con-

trol of bishoprics and royal abbeys during vacancies, and the 'election' of bishops in the King's chapel.

Text in *Councils & Synods*, 1: A.D. 871–1204, ed. D. Whitelock, M. Brett, and C. N. L. Brooke, Part 2, 1066–1204 (Oxford, 1981), pp. 877–83, with introd. pp. 852–77 and related material, pp. 883–93. Eng. tr. in Gee and Hardy, pp. 68–73 (no. 23) and, with notes, in D. C. Douglas and G. W. Greenaway (eds.), *English Historical Documents 1042–1189* (2nd edn., 1981), pp. 766–70. F. Barlow, 'The Constitutions of Clarendon', *Medieval History*, 1, no. 1 (1991), pp. 39–52. See also bibl. cited under BECKET, ST THOMAS.

Clarke, Samuel (1675–1729). A native of *Norwich, he was educated at Caius College, Cambridge, where he came under I. *Newton's influence. His ability attracted the notice of J. Moore, Bp. of Norwich, who in 1698 appointed him his chaplain. In 1704 and 1705 he delivered two sets of Boyle Lectures in defence of rational theology against the empiricism of J. *Locke. They were later published (1705–6), with the joint title (from 1716) of *A Discourse concerning the Being and Attributes of God, the Obligations of Natural Religion, and the Truth and Certainty of the Christian Revelation*. Though a critic of the *Deists, Clarke did not conceal his sympathy with some aspects of their teaching. In *A Letter to Mr. Dodwell* (1706) he defended against H. *Dodwell the natural immortality and incorporeality of the soul. In 1706 he was appointed Rector of St Benet's, Paul's Wharf, and in 1709 Rector of St James's, Piccadilly. His preaching was highly regarded by Samuel *Johnson. In 1712 he aroused the indignation, esp. of *High Churchmen, by his *Scripture-Doctrine of the Trinity*, which had marked *Unitarian leanings. He was attacked by R. *Nelson and D. *Waterland; and the Lower House of Convocation sought his condemnation. The Upper House, however, imposed no formal retractation, when Clarke promised to write no further on the subject. In the next years he entered into a correspondence with G. W. *Leibniz on space and time (pub. 1717), defending the Newtonian doctrines, and also on the nature of freewill. On Newton's death (1727) he declined an invitation to succeed him as Master of the Mint. His other writings include *Three Practical Essays, viz. on Baptism, Confirmation, Repentance* (1699); a critique of J. *Toland's *Amnyntor* (1699); *Paraphrases* on the Gospels of Mt. (1701), Mk. and Lk. (1702); and some collections of *Sermons*.

Collected ed. of his Works (4 vols., London, 1738), with Life by B. *Hoadly repr. in vol. 1, pp. i–xiv (previously prefixed to edn. of Clarke's Sermons by John Clarke, 10 vols., 1730–1, vol. 1, pp. i–l). Modern edn. of Leibniz–Clarke correspondence by H. G. Alexander (Manchester, 1956). The principal authority is the Life by his friend, W. *Whiston (London, 1730; a brief memoir by T. Emlyn is appended to 3rd edn., 1748). J. P. Ferguson, *An Eighteenth Century Heretic: Dr. Samuel Clarke* (Kineton, Warwick, 1976). J. E. Le Rossignol, *The Ethical Philosophy of Samuel Clarke* (Diss., Leipzig, 1892). L. Stephen in *DNB* 10 (1887), pp. 443–6.

Clarkson, Thomas (1760–1846), anti-slave-trade agitator. Educated at St John's College, Cambridge, he decided to devote his life to the repression of the slave trade, on which he had just written a prize essay. He was ordained deacon but hardly ever exercised his ministry. In 1787 he was involved in the establishment of a Christian settlement for poor Blacks in *Sierra Leone and also with some leading *Quakers and with W. *Wilberforce formed a group which pressed in the House of Commons for the abolition of the slave trade. Their vigorous efforts were rewarded by the Act of 1807 ending the traffic, and the emancipation of the slaves in 1833. Clarkson spent some time in France soon after the outbreak of the Revolution, urging here also the abolition of the slave trade with other abuses, and after the Peace of Vienna in 1815 propagated his views at the various European congresses. His books include *A Portraiture of Quakerism* (1806); *History of the Rise, Progress, and Accomplishment of the Abolition of the African Slave Trade by the British Parliament* (2 vols., 1808); *Memoirs of the Private and Public Life of William Penn* (2 vols., 1813); and *Researches, Antediluvian, Patriarchal and Historical, concerning the Way in which Men first acquired their Knowledge of God and Religion* (1836).

Clarkson's Correspondence with Henry Christophe, King of Haiti, ed. E. L. Griggs and C. H. Prator (Berkeley and Los Angeles, 1952). E. L. Griggs, *Thomas Clarkson: The Friend of Slaves* (1936); E. Gibson Wilson, *Thomas Clarkson: A Biography* (1989). G. F. R. Barker in *DNB* 10 (1887), pp. 454–6. See also bibl. to SLAVERY.

class meeting. A meeting, usually held weekly, of small sections of each congregation of *Methodists, under a class leader appointed by the minister, at which contributions to the Church funds are paid, and inquiry is made into the conduct and spiritual progress of individual members. This institution, peculiar to Methodism, dates from 1742.

H. D. Rack, 'The Decline of the Class-Meeting and the Problem of Church-Membership in Nineteenth-Century Wesleyanism', *Proceedings of the Wesley Historical Society*, 39 (1973–4), pp. 12–21; W. W. Dean, 'The Methodist Class Meeting: The Significance of its Decline', ibid. 43 (1981), pp. 41–8.

Claudel, Paul Louis Charles (1868–1955), French Catholic poet and diplomat. He was born at Villeneuve-sur-Fère (Aisne) and, at the age of 18 was converted from worldliness to Christian fervour. He entered the diplomatic service in 1893, and after a distinguished career, which took him to the Far East, Brazil, and many cities of Central Europe, became ambassador in Tokyo in 1921, and in 1926 in Washington. His fame rests chiefly on his plays, which revivified the French theatre; their central theme is the consecration of the world to God in Christ. *L'Annonce faite à Marie* (1912; Eng. tr., 1916) is a canticle on the religious meaning of voluntary suffering and expiation lived by the leprous young girl Violaine, who thus becomes a mediatrix of grace. His greatest play, *Le Soulier de Satin* (1929; Eng. tr., 1931), which is set in Spain in the Baroque period, extends the theme of sacrificial love and redemption to the whole world. Catholic symbolism is also apparent in his prose writings, such as *Art poétique* (1907), and *Figures et Paraboles* (1936), and in his biblical commentaries, *Les Aventures de Sophie* (1937). His poems appeared in several collections, among them *Cinq Grandes Odes* (1910; Eng. tr., 1967), *Corona Benignitatis Anni Dei* (1915), *Feuilles de Saints* (1925), and *Visages radieux* (1947). Their powerful biblical imagery, and stirring realization of the Cross as the centre of the world, rank them with the finest Christian poetry of his time, to be compared only with that of C. *Péguy.

Œuvres complètes (29 vols., 1950–86, with Suppl., 1990 ff.). Convenient edns. of: *Théâtre* (Bibliothèque de la Pléiade, 72–3;

1956; 2nd edn., 1965), *Œuvre poétique* (ibid., 125; 1957), *Œuvres en Prose* (ibid., 179; 1965), and *Journal* (ibid., 205 and 213; 1968–1969). *Jacques Rivière et Paul Claudel: Correspondance, 1907–1914,* with introd. by I. Rivière (1926; Eng. tr., *Letters to a Doubter,* 1929); *Paul Claudel et André Gide: Correspondance, 1899–1926,* ed. R. Mallet (1949; Eng. tr., 1952); *Lettres à sa fille Reine,* ed. M. Malicet (1991). J. Rivière, *Études* (1911), no. 3, pp. 61–129; J. Madaule, *Le Drame de Paul Claudel* (1936; 5th edn., 1964); J. Samson, *Paul Claudel, Poète-Musicien* (Geneva [1948]); L. Chaigne, *Vie de Paul Claudel et genèse de son oeuvre* (1961); P.-A. Lesort, *Paul Claudel par lui-même* (Écrivains de toujours, 1963); F. Varillon, *Claudel* (Les Écrivains devant Dieu [1967]); R. Griffiths (ed.), *Claudel: A Reappraisal* (1968); H. de *Lubac and J. Bastaire, *Claudel et Péguy* (1974); A. Caranfa, *Claudel: Beauty and Grace* (Lewisburg and London [1989]); D. Millet-Gérard, *Anima et la Sagesse pour une poétique comparée de l'exégèse claudélienne* (1990). *Cahiers Paul Claudel* (1959 ff.).

Claudianus Mamertus (d. *c.*474), Christian philosopher and younger brother of St *Mamertus, Bp. of Vienne. Born in the vicinity of Lyons, he became a monk and was later ordained a presbyter by his brother. He was also a close friend of *Sidonius Apollinaris. His principal work was a treatise 'De Statu Animae' (3 Books, *c.*470). In this Claudianus defended the *Neoplatonist doctrine (accepted by St *Augustine) that the soul was immaterial (against *Faustus of Riez, who, following an earlier W. tradition (*Tertullian, *Hilary), held that the soul as a created substance was of a corporeal and extended character). He also wrote a letter to the rhetorician Sapaudus in which he bemoaned the level of the arts in his age.

Works in J. P. Migne, *PL* 53. 697–786. Crit. edn. by A. Engelbrecht in (CSEL 11; 1885). Id., 'Untersuchungen über die Sprache des Claudianus Mamertus' in *Sb.* (Wien), 110 (1886), pp. 423–542. Study by R. de la Broise (Paris, thesis, 1890). P. Courcelle, *Les Lettres grecques en occident* (Bibliothèque des Écoles Françaises d'Athènes et de Rome, 159; 1943; 2nd edn., 1948), pp. 223–35; Eng. tr. (Cambridge, Mass., 1969), pp. 238–51 (on Claudianus' relation to *Porphyry). J. Madoz, SJ, *Liciniano de Cartagena y sus cartas* (Facultades de Teologia y de Filosofia del Colegio Máximo de Oña. Estudios Onienses, 1st ser. 4; 1948), pp. 28–55. E. L. Fortin, AA, *Christianisme et culture philosophique au cinquième siècle: La querelle de l'âme humaine en Occident* (Études Augustiniennes, 1959), esp. pp. 15–42 and 75–110. W. Schmid in *RAC* 3 (1957), cols. 169–79, s.v.; A. Solignac, SJ, in *Dict. Sp.* 10 (1980), cols. 186–90, s.v. 'Mamert'.

Claudius (d. after 827), Bp. of Turin. He was of Spanish birth, and became master of the royal schools of Aquitaine before his promotion to the see of Turin *c.*817. He made a series of attacks on image-worship, relics, the adoration of the Cross, and indeed every visible symbol of Christ's life, as well as on *pilgrimages and the intercession of saints. He had scant regard for the authority of the Roman see, and his views, which were regarded as heretical by many, were refuted at the request of *Louis the Pious by Dungal and Jonas of Orléans. He was also famous for his biblical commentaries, which displayed an unusually wide knowledge of the works of St *Augustine and contain extensive quotations from them. A number of works formerly attributed to other authors have been ascribed to him by Dom Paulino Bellet. Some of the older historians of the *Waldenses claimed him as their founder.

Most of his writings are still in MS; those pub. are repr. in J. P. Migne, *PL* 104. 615–928. Crit. edn. of 'Epp.' by E. Dümmler in *MGH*, Epistolae, 4 (1895), pp. 586–613. M. Ferrari, 'Note su Claudio di Torino "Episcopus ab ecclesia damnatus"', *Italia Medioevale e Umanistica*, 16 (1973), pp. 291–308, incl. text; I. M. Douglas, 'The Commentary on the Book of Ruth by Claudius of Turin', *Sacris Erudiri*, 22 (1974–5), pp. 295–320, incl. text. E. Dümmler, 'Über Leben und Lehre des Bischofs Claudius von Turin' in *Sb.* (Berl.) (1895), pp. 427–43. P. Bellet, OSB, 'Claudio de Turin, autor de los comentarios "In genesim et regum" del Pseudo Euquerio', *Estudios Biblicos*, 9 (1950), pp. 209–23; id., 'Oració de Claudi de Tori en el comentari a Hebreus del Pseudo Attó de Vercelli', in *Colligere Fragmenta: Festschrift Alban Dold*, ed. B. Fischer, OSB and V. Fiala, OSB (Texte und Arbeiten, 1. Abteilung, 2; 1952), pp. 140–3; id., 'El Liber de Imaginibus Sanctorum bajo el nombre de Agobardo de Lyon obra de Claudio de Turin', *Analecta Sacra Tarraconensia*, 26 (1953), pp. 151–94. G. Italiani, *La Tradizione esegetica nel commento ai Re di Claudio di Torino* (Florence, 1979). Manitius, 1, pp. 390–6 (with account of MS material). F. Stegmüller, *Repertorium Biblicum Medii Aevi*, 2 (Madrid, 1950), pp. 242–9 (nos. 1949–75), and 8 (ibid., 1976), pp. 379–81. P. Bellet in *NCE* 3 (1967), pp. 921 f.; G. Sergi in *Dizionario Biografico degli Italiani*, 26 (1982), pp. 158–61, both s.v.

Claudius Apollinarius. See APOLLINARIUS, CLAUDIUS.

clausura (Lat. 'closure' or, more usually, 'enclosure'). (1) The practice of separating a part of a religious house to the exclusion of those of the opposite sex to the community; and (2) the portion so enclosed. The clausura is found in all religious orders, in both E. and W., and dates from the earliest monastic rules. Permission, general or particular, is needed for religious to go outside the clausura, or for outsiders to come in, while in some cases even lay persons of the same sex as the community are held to violate the clausura by entrance. In some communities, certain parts of the house or church are neutral ground, which both the community and outsiders may enter without leave. In the RC Church an enclosure adapted to the character and mission of the Religious *Institute is required in all religious houses, with some part of the house reserved for its members. A stricter discipline applies in houses devoted to the *contemplative life; those of contemplative *nuns have to observe enclosure according to norms laid down by the Holy See (*CIC* (1983), can. 667).

Clayton, John (1709–73), one of the first '*Methodists'. Educated at Manchester Grammar School and Brasenose College, Oxford, he was a member of the '*Holy Club', founded by the *Wesleys. After ordination in 1732, he was put in charge of the Sacred Trinity Chapel, Salford, where J. Wesley and G. *Whitefield often preached for him. In 1740 he became a chaplain, and in 1760 a Fellow, of the Manchester Collegiate Church. Throughout his life he was a supporter of the Jacobites, giving great offence by his political views to the Whigs of the district. For many years he also conducted an academy at Salford.

Memoir by L. Tyerman, 'The Rev. John Clayton, M.A., the Jacobite Churchman', in *The Oxford Methodists* (1873), pp. 24–56. C. W. Sutton in *DNB* 11 (1887), pp. 13 f.

Clemens non Papa. Jacques Clement (*c.*1500–*c.*1556), a Dutch composer of Church music, who was facetiously so called to pretend to distinguish him from the contemporary Pope, *Clement VII. He was a forerunner of G. P. da *Palestrina.

Clement of Alexandria. See after Pope CLEMENT XIV.

Clement of Rome, St (*fl. c.*96), Bp. of *Rome. He appears in early succession lists as the second or third bishop after St *Peter; as, however, there is no evidence for monarchical episcopacy in Rome at so early a date, the meaning of this evidence is not clear. In primitive times he was often held to have been appointed by St Peter personally. Various writers of the 3rd and 4th cents. identify him with the Clement mentioned in Phil. 4: 3. Besides the spurious '*Clementine Literature' (q.v), two 'Epp. to the Corinthians' have been ascribed to him. The former Epistle ('I Clement') is genuine, and is his real title to fame. It was written *c.*96 in the name of the Roman Church to deal with fierce strife in the Church at Corinth, where certain presbyters had been deposed. Clement issued a call to repentance, insisting that God required due order in all things and that the deposed presbyters must be reinstated and legitimate superiors obeyed. The Apostles 'appointed bishops and deacons' in every place, and it was they who gave directions how the ministry should perpetuate itself. Clement calls the higher class of ministers indifferently 'bishops' (ἐπίσκοποι) and 'presbyters' (or elders, πρεσβύτεροι). He refers to 'offering the gifts' (*sc.* of the *Eucharist) as one of their functions, and to some or all of them as 'rulers' of the Church. Here and elsewhere he affords valuable evidence of the state of the ministry in his time, on the history of the Roman Church and (it has been held) the martyrdoms of Sts Peter and *Paul. The epistle, which was highly regarded, was being read in church at Corinth along with the Scriptures *c.*170.

The so-called 'Second Epistle of Clement' is really a homily, assigned on stylistic grounds to a separate author. The earliest surviving Christian sermon, it sets out in general terms the character of the Christian life and the duty of repentance. It probably belongs to Corinth (so J. B. *Lightfoot), though some scholars have assigned it to Rome (A. *Harnack, who attributed it to Pope Soter) or Alexandria.

In later tradition St Clement became the subject of a variety of legends. In the 'Clementine Literature' he figures as the intermediary through whom the Apostles transmit their teaching to the Church. Quite another tradition, preserved in some apocryphal *acta* (not earlier than the 4th cent.), describes how he was banished to the Crimea in the reign of Trajan and forced to work in the mines. It is said that his missionary labours in those parts met with remarkable success and that he was bound to an anchor and thrown into the Black Sea. The legend adds that his tomb, which was built by angels, was shown once a year to the inhabitants by the miraculous ebbing of the tide. Feast day in the W., 23 Nov.; in the E., 24 or 25 Nov.

Fullest collection of material, patristic and modern, in J. B. Lightfoot, *Apostolic Fathers*, pt. 1 (rev. edn., 2 vols., 1890). The two 'Epp.' survive in two MSS, the [biblical] *Codex Alexandrinus (B. Libr.; text imperfect) and the Cod. Hierosol. of AD 1056 (of *Didache fame) discovered by P. *Bryennios. They were first pr. by P. *Young ('Junius'), Oxford, 1633 (whence incorporated by J. B. *Cotelier in his *Patres Apostolici*, 1672); crit. edn. by J. B. Lightfoot, op. cit. Text also in J. P. Migne, *PG* 1 and 2 (incl. Clementines). I Clem. also ed., with Fr. tr., by A. Jaubert

(SC 167; 1971). For other edns. see APOSTOLIC FATHERS. Ancient Lat. tr. of I Clem. ed. G. *Morin, OSB, Maredsous, 1894; ancient Syr. tr. ed. R. L. Bensly and R. H. Kennett, London, 1899; Copt. frags. ed. F. Rösch, Strasbourg, 1910; Eng. tr. of 'Epp.' in J. B. Lightfoot, op. cit.; also of I Clem., with useful notes by W. K. Lowther Clarke (London, 1937). Comm. by A. Lindemann (Hb. NT 17; 1992). F. Gerke, *Die Stellung des I. Clemensbriefes innerhalb der Entwicklung der altchristlichen Gemeindeverfassung und des Kirchenrechts* (TU 47.1; 1931). L. Sanders, *Le Hellénisme de St Clément de Rome et le paulinisme* (Louvain, 1943). C. Eggenberger, *Die Quellen der politischen Ethik des I. Klemensbriefes* (Zurich, 1951); A. W. Ziegler, *Neue Studien zum ersten Klemensbrief* (1958); O. Andrén, *Rättäfärdighet och Frid: En Studie i det första Clemensbrevet* (Uppsala, 1960; with Eng. summary); O. Knoch, *Eigenart und Bedeutung der Eschatologie im theologischen Aufriss des ersten Clemensbriefes: Eine auslegungsgeschichtliche Untersuchung* (Theophaneia, 17; 1964). K. Beyschlag, *Clemens Romanus und der Frühkatholizismus: Untersuchungen zu I Clemens 1–7* (Beiträge zur historischen Theologie, 35; Tübingen, 1966). G. Brunner, *Die theologische Mitte des Ersten Klemensbriefs* (Frankfurter Theologische Studien, 11; 1972); D. A. Hagner, *The Use of the Old and New Testaments in Clement of Rome* (Supplements to *Novum Testamentum*, 34; 1973); K. P. Donfried, *The Setting of Second Clement in Early Christianity* (ibid. 38; 1974). *CPG* 1 (1983), pp. 5–7 (nos. 1001–14). Altaner and Stuiber (1978), pp. 45–7 and 551. A. Stuiber in *RAC* 3 (1957), cols. 188–97, s.v. See also bibl. to APOSTOLIC FATHERS.

Clement V (1264–1314), Pope from 1305. Bertrand de Got, a member of an influential French family, after studying at Toulouse, Orléans, and *Bologna, was appointed Bp. of Comminges in 1295 and Abp. of Bordeaux in 1299. Elected Pope in 1305 as successor to Benedict XI, he was crowned at Lyons in the presence of Philip the Fair, whose powerful influence made Clement's policy henceforward largely subservient to French interests. By fixing his residence at *Avignon in 1309 and thus inaugurating the 70 years' 'Captivity', Clement further increased his dependence on Philip, and the King insisted on a formal condemnation of Clement's predecessor, *Boniface VIII, on charges of heresy and immorality. The process, however, though actually begun in 1310, was, with Philip's assent, abandoned in 1311 when the King substituted a plan for the abolition of the *Templars, whose property he coveted. The order was suppressed at the Council of *Vienne (1311) and, though the Knights *Hospitallers received from the Pope the title to its property, the French King contrived to lay his hands on most of its possessions. As a vassal of Edward I, Clement was also brought into English affairs. In 1306 he was persuaded to suspend Robert of *Winchelsea, Abp. of *Canterbury, who was accused by the King of treason for his support of Boniface VIII, but in 1308, under Edward II, Robert was reinstalled at the request of the King. In 1306 he excommunicated Robert Bruce of Scotland for his part in the murder of the Red Comyn, and soon after deposed two bishops who had been actively in favour of the Scots rebellion. Despite his political difficulties and the discredit he brought on the Papacy by his taxation and sale of offices, Clement V did much to further scholarship, esp. the study of medicine and oriental languages, and founded the universities of Orléans (1306) and Perugia (1308). He also added to medieval Canon Law by the so-called '*Clementines' (q.v.).

Bulls ed. by the monks of *Monte Cassino, *Regestum Clementis Papae V ex Vaticanis Archetypis ... nunc primum editum cura et*

studio Monachorum Ordinis S. Benedicti (9 vols., bound in 7, with appendix, Rome, 1885–92); *Acta* ed. F. M. Delorme, OFM, and A. L. Tàutu (Pontificia Commissio ad Redigendum Codicem Iuris Canonici Orientalis. Fontes, 3rd ser., 7, tom. 1; Vatican, 1955). R. Fawtier and Y. Lanhers, *Tables des registres de Clément V publiés par les Bénédictins* (Bibliothèque des Écoles Françaises d'Athènes et de Rome, 3rd ser., 1948–57). E. *Baluze, *Vitae Paparum Avenionensium*, ed. G. Mollat (4 vols., 1916–27), esp. vol. 1, pp. 1–106 and 551–66. E. Berchon, 'L'Histoire du Pape Clément V (1305–1314)', *Actes de l'Académie Nationale des Sciences, Belles-Lettres et Arts de Bordeaux*, 55 (1893), pp. 493–535, and 56 (1894), pp. 5–171. H. G. Richardson, 'Clement V and the See of Canterbury', *EHR* 56 (1941), pp. 96–103; R. Gaignard, 'Le Gouvernement pontifical au travail. L'exemple des dernières années du règne de Clément V: 1ᵉʳ août 1311–20 avril 1314', *Annales du Midi*, 72 (1960), pp. 169–214, with refs.; J. H. Denton, 'Pope Clement V's Early Career as a Royal Clerk', *EHR* 83 (1968), pp. 303–14. L. Thier, *Kreuzzugsbemühungen unter Papst Clements V. (1305–1314)* (Franziskanische Forschungen, 24; 1973); N. Housley, 'Pope Clement V and the Crusades of 1309–10', *Journal of Medieval History*, 8 (1982), pp. 29–43. T. Schmidt, *Der Bonifaz-Prozess: Verfahren der Papstanklage in der Zeit Bonifaz' VIII. und Clemens' V.* (Forschungen zur kirchlichen Rechtsgeschichte und zum Kirchenrecht, 19; 1989), pp. 119–439. G. Mollat, *Les Papes d'Avignon* (1912; 10th edn. [1965]; Eng. tr., 1963), bk. 1, ch. 1, and *passim*. Pastor, 1 (1891), pp. 58–63. G. Mollat in *DHGE* 12 (1952), cols. 1115–29, s.v.; A. P. Bagliani in *Dizionario Biografico degli Italiani*, 26 (1982), pp. 202–15, s.v. 'Clemente V', both with full bibl.

Clement VI (1291–1352), Pope from 1342. Pierre Roger entered the *Benedictine monastery of La Chaise-Dieu at the age of 10, and later studied and taught at *Paris. He advanced rapidly in both the secular and the ecclesiastical spheres: he became successively Abbot of Fécamp in 1326, Bp. of Arras in 1328, Abp. of Sens in 1329, and Abp. of Rouen in 1330. Meanwhile he was a close and valued councillor of King Philip IV of France. Created cardinal by *Benedict XII in 1338, he was elected Pope at Avignon on 7 May 1342. His French sympathies hindered his efforts to make peace in the Hundred Years War between France and England. These and his lavish use of Papal provisions led to anti-Papal legislation in England, notably, Edward III's First Statute of *Provisors (1351). Clement appointed many cardinals, several from among his relations, which enhanced his reputation for *nepotism. In 1352 the cardinals staged a palace revolution by drawing up an unprecedented election capitulation, designed to limit the authority of the next Pope in their favour. Like his predecessors, Clement refused to confirm the election as Emperor of Louis of Bavaria, whom he regarded as a usurper, and instead appointed Charles of Bohemia (Charles IV) as King of the Romans in 1346. In Italy Clement faced many problems—the rebellious Visconti in Milan, turmoil in Naples under his ward, Queen Joanna, and popular revolution in Rome, led by Cola di *Rienzo in 1347. In 1344 the 'Holy League', formed on Clement's initiative, captured the key port of Smyrna (Izmir) from the Turks, but further crusades were prevented by the effects of plague, economic decline, and European warfare.

Despite pressure to return the Papacy to Rome, Clement strengthened its establishment at Avignon by buying the city from Joanna of Naples, and by trying to build it up as the intellectual and artistic nucleus of Christendom, both through patronage and through his spectacular extensions to the Papal palace. Clement was celebrated both for his preaching and as a theologian: his jubilee bull of 1350 is fundamental for the doctrine of *Indulgences. Although his extravagant lifestyle resembled that of the Renaissance Popes, he was a generous almsgiver to the poor, whom he befriended especially during the Black Death of 1348–9, and a protector of the Jews.

E. Déprez and others (eds.), *Clément VI (1342–1352): Lettres closes, patentes et curiales se rapportant à la France* (Bibliothèque des Écoles Françaises d'Athènes et de Rome, 3rd ser., 3 vols., 1901–61); E. Déprez and G. Mollat (eds.), *Clément VI (1342–1352): Lettres closes, patentes et curiales intéressant les pays autres que la France* (ibid., 1960–1); U. Berlière, OSB (ed.), *Lettres de Clément VI, 1342–1352*, 1 (Analecta Vaticano-Belgica, 6; 1924 [no more pub.]); id. (ed.), *Suppliques de Clément VI, 1342–1352* (ibid. 1; 1906); E. Griffe (ed.), *Lettres patentes des évêques de France, recueillies dans les registres du Pape Clément VI, 1342–1352*, 1, *Province de Bourges* (Acta Episcoporum Galliae Saeculo XIV, 1933); L. Klicman (ed.), *Acta Clementis VI Pontificis Romani, 1342–1352* (Monumenta Vaticana Res Gestas Bohemicas Illustrantia, 1; Prague, 1903). E. *Baluze, *Vitae Paparum Avenionensium* (ed. G. Mollat, esp. 1 (1916), pp. 241–308, with notes, 2 (1927), pp. 335–433). D. Wood, *Clement VI: The Pontificate and Ideas of an Avignon Pope* (Cambridge Studies in Medieval Life and Thought, 4th ser., 13; 1989). J. Gay, *Le Pape Clément VI et les affaires d'Orient (1342–1352)* (thesis, Paris, 1904). G. Mollat, 'L'Œuvre oratoire de Clément VI', *AHDLMA* 3 (1928), pp. 239–74; P. Schmitz, OSB, 'Les Sermons et discours de Clément VI, OSB', *R. Bén.* 41 (1929), pp. 15–34. A. Maier, 'Der literarische Nachlass des Petrus Rogerii (Clement VI) in der Borghesiana', *RTAM* 15 (1948), pp. 332–56, and 16 (1949), pp. 72–98. R. J. Loenertz, OP, 'Ambassadeurs grecs auprès du Pape Clément VI (1348)', *OCP* 19 (1953), pp. 178–96. F. Giunta, 'Sulla politica orientale di Clemente VI', in P. Vaccari and P. F. Palumbo (eds.), *Studi in storia medievale e moderna in onore di Ettore Rota* (Rome, 1958), pp. 149–62. G. Mollat, 'Le Saint-Siège et la France sous le pontificat de Clément VI (1342–1352)', *RHE* 55 (1960), pp. 5–24. J. E. Wrigley, 'Clement VI before his Pontificate: the early life of Pierre Roger, 1290/91–1342', *Catholic Historical Review*, 56 (1970), pp. 433–73; id., 'The Conclave and the Electors of 1342', *Archivum Historiae Pontificiae*, 20 (1982), pp. 51–81. P. E. Burnham, 'The Patronage of Clement VI', *History Today*, 28 (1978), pp. 372–81. G. Mollat, *Les Papes d'Avignon* (1912; 10th edn. [1965]; Eng. tr., 1963), esp. bk. 1, ch. 4. Id. in *DHGE* 12 (1953), cols. 1129–62, s.v.; B. Guillemain in *Dizionario Biografico degli Italiani*, 26 (1982), pp. 215–22, s.v. 'Clemente VI', both with bibl.

Clement VII (1478–1534), Pope from 1523. The son of Giuliano de' Medici and a cousin of *Leo X, he rapidly rose to a high position, becoming Abp. of Florence and cardinal in 1513. In 1523 he succeeded *Hadrian VI. Though Clement was personally of blameless character, his lack of courage led his reign to be marked by shifty diplomacy and intrigue. He attempted to steer a middle path between the conflicting aims of Francis I of France and the Emp. *Charles V, siding first with the former by the League of Cognac (1526), and then, after the sack of Rome (1527) by the Imperial armies, with the latter by the Treaty of Barcelona (1529). He pursued the same irresolute policy of procrastination in relation to the divorce of *Henry VIII from Catherine of Aragon. It was his failure to foster the movement for reform within the Church that encouraged the rapid spread of Protestant doctrine during his pontificate. In his ready patronage of scholars and artists, among the latter B. Cellini, *Raphael, and *Michelangelo, he was a true son of the house of Medici.

H. M. Vaughan, *The Medici Popes, Leo X and Clement VII* (1908), pp. 285–346; E. Rodocanachi, *Histoire de Rome: Les ponti-*

ficats d'Adrien VI et de Clément VII (1933), pp. 87–270, with bibl. pp. 281–4. G. Müller, *Die römische Kurie und die Reformation 1523–1534: Kirche und Politik während des Pontifikates Clemens' VII.* (Quellen und Forschungen zur Reformationsgeschichte, 38; 1969). Among the principal sources for the history of his relations with Henry VIII are the Calendars of the State Papers of the reign (see s.v. HENRY VIII); S. Ehses (ed.), *Römische Dokumente zur Geschichte der Ehescheidung Heinrichs VIII von England, 1527–1534* (1893). P. Crabitès, *Clement VII and Henry VIII* (1936). There is also important information in W. E. Wilkie, *The Cardinal Protectors of England* (Cambridge, 1974); see index, s.v. 'Clement VII' and 'Medici, Giulio de' '. Pastor, 9 (1910), pp. 231–67, and 10 (1910). R. Mols, SJ, in *DHGE* 12 (1953), cols. 1175–1224, s.v., with full bibl. (inaccurate); A. Prosperi in *Dizionario Biografico degli Italiani*, 26 (1982), pp. 237–59, s.v. 'Clemente VII, Papa', also with bibl.

Clement VIII (c. 1536–1605), Pope from 1592. The son of Silvestro Aldobrandini, a distinguished Italian lawyer, Ippolito Aldobrandini was a man of high personal character. He became a cardinal in 1585 and was elected Pope in 1592. It was his policy to secure the representation of all the conflicting influences in the *curia, and esp. to limit the dominance of Spanish influence. He supported the Catholic League against *Henry of Navarre, but this did not prevent his negotiating with Henry, so that in 1595 Henry was received into the Catholic Church. Clement was also largely responsible for the ensuing Treaty of Vervins (1598), which brought about peace between France and Spain. His hopes of converting *James I of England to RCism were not realized, however. In ecclesiastical matters he pursued a policy of reform. He took a keen interest in the revision of the service books, and issued new editions of the *Vulgate, the *Missal, the *Breviary, the '*Caeremoniale Episcoporum', and the *Pontifical.

K. Jaitner (ed.), *Die Hauptinstruktionen Clemens' VIII. für die Nuntien und Legaten an den Europäischen Fürstenhöfen 1592–1605* (2 vols., Tübingen, 1984), with full introd. P. Van Isacker, 'Notes sur l'intervention militaire de Clément VIII en France à la fin du XVIᵉ siècle', *RHE* 12 (1911), pp. 702–13. A. Louant, 'L'Intervention de Clément VIII dans le traité de Vervins', *Bulletin de l'Institut Historique Belge de Rome*, 12 (1932), pp. 127–86. A. O. Meyer, 'Clement VIII und Jakob I von England', *Quellen und Forschungen aus italienischen Archiven und Bibliotheken*, 7 (1904), pp. 268–306; J. Martin, PSS, 'Clément VIII et Jacques Stuart', *Revue d'Histoire Diplomatique*, 25 (1911), pp. 279–307 and 359–78. Cav. L. F. Mathaus-Voltolini, 'Die Beteiligung des Papstes Clemens VIII an der Bekämpfung der Türken in den Jahren 1592–1595', *RQ* 15 (1901), pp. 303–26 and 410–23. D. Beggiao, *La visita pastorale di Clemente VIII (1592–1600): Aspetti di riforma post-tridentina a Roma* (Corona Lateranensis, 23; 1978). Pastor, 23 (1933) and 24 (1933). R. Mols, SJ, in *DHGE* 12 (1953), cols. 1249–97, s.v., with full bibl. (inaccurate); A. Borromeo in *Dizionario Biografico degli Italiani*, 26 (1982), pp. 259–82, s.v. 'Clemente VIII', with extensive bibl.

Clement XI (1649–1721), Pope from 1700. Giovanni Francesco Albani, who was a native of Urbino, was educated at the Roman College, became a doctor of both Laws, and entered on an administrative career in the Papal States. In 1687 he was appointed Secretary of Papal Briefs and in 1690 he was created cardinal. He was an ecclesiastic of austere habits who, accepting election to the Papacy with reluctance, continued to discharge faithfully his pastoral duties. He met with ill success in the political sphere. In 1701 he protested, without effect, against the assumption of the title of King of Prussia by the Elector of Brandenburg. In the War of the Spanish Succession, having previously favoured the candidature of Philip of Anjou (1683–1746), he afterwards tried to remain neutral and procure a peaceful solution, but was forced in 1701 to recognize Philip, and in 1709, when the Imperial troops had invaded the Papal States, to abandon him in favour of the Archduke Charles; consequently in the Treaty of Utrecht (1713) his rights in Sicily, Sardinia, Parma and Piacenza were ignored. In the same year he quarrelled with the Duke of Savoy about his rights of investiture in Sicily; and when he issued an *interdict, all the clergy who accepted it were banished until the island was conquered by Philip V of Spain in 1718. On the declaration of war by the Turks on Venice in 1714, he tried, without success, to organize an alliance of princes against them.

During Clement's reign the long-drawn-out *Jansenist controversy continued within the French Church and Jansenism was once more condemned in the bull '*Vineam Domini Sabaoth' (16 July 1705). This was followed by the condemnation of P. *Quesnel's *Abrégé de la morale de l'évangile* in 1708, and, later, by the famous bull '*Unigenitus Dei Filius' (8 Sept. 1713). He also had to decide the dispute between *Dominicans and *Jesuits on the question of the Chinese rites, esp. the cult of ancestors and of Confucius, which the former condemned while the latter tolerated it. The Pope approved the decision of the *Holy Office which censured the opinion of the Jesuits, but the controversy was not finally settled until the reign of *Benedict XIV. Clement XI was a generous protector of arts and scholarship, one of the most important additions to the *Vatican Library being the MSS. collected at his instigation by J. S. *Assemani.

In 1708 he made the Feast of the *Immaculate Conception of the BVM one of obligation throughout the Church.

Works, incl. Bullarium, ed. by his nephew, Card. Albani (7 vols., Rome, 1722–4), with Life [by J. C. Battellus] prefixed to Bullarium (1723); later edn. (2 vols., Rome, 1729). [P. Polidori,] *De Vita et Rebus Gestis Clementis Undecimi* (Urbino, 1727). S. Reboulet, *Histoire de Clément XI Pape* (2 vols., Avignon, 1752). F. Pometti, 'Studii sul pontificato di Clemente XI, 1700–1721', *Archivio della R. Società Romana di Storia Patria*, 21 (1898), pp. 279–457; 22 (1899), pp. 109–179; 23 (1900), pp. 239–76, 449–515. L. Nina, *Le finanze pontificie sotto Clemente XI* (1928). A. Aldobrandini, *La guerra di successione di Spagna negli stati dell'Alta Italia dal 1702 al 1705 e la politica di Clemente XI dal carteggio di Mons* (1931). L. Just, *Clemens XI und der Code Léopold (1701–10)* (1935). [J.] Schmidlin, 'Der Konflikt der Anima mit Clemens XI', *RQ* 17 (1903), pp. 141–59 and 301–23. L. Ceyssens, 'Autour de l'Unigénitus. Le Pape Clément XI', *Bulletin de l'Institut historique Belge de Rome*, 53–4 (1983–4), pp. 253–304, repr. in id. and J. A. G. Tans, *Autour de l'Unigenitus* (Bibliotheca Ephemeridum Theologicarum Lovaniensium, 76; 1987), pp. 737–88. Pastor, 33 (1941), with bibl. R. Mols, SJ, in *DHGE* 12 (1953), cols. 1326–61, s.v.; S. Andretta in *Dizionario Biografico degli Italiani*, 26 (1982), pp. 302–20, s.v. 'Clemente XI', both with full bibl. See also other works cited under UNIGENITUS.

Clement XIII (1693–1769), Pope from 1758. Carlo della Torre Rezzonico was a native of Venice, studied with the *Jesuits at *Bologna, and became a doctor of law at Padua. Having been appointed Auditor of the *Rota for *Venice in 1728, he was made cardinal in 1737 and in 1743 Bp. of Padua, where he endeared himself to his people by his lavish almsgiving. Soon after his election to the Papacy the

storm gathered against the Society of Jesus, which came to be the chief preoccupation of his pontificate. It began in *Portugal, where the all-powerful minister, Sebastian Carvalho, afterwards Marquis de Pombal, first imprisoned and then expelled all members of the Society under pretext of their having conspired against the King, and all relations between the country and the Holy See were severed in 1760. In 1761 the Portuguese example was followed by *France, where the Parlement of Paris demanded drastic alterations in the constitutions of the Society, which Clement refused with the famous words: *Sint ut sunt aut non sint* ('Let them be as they are or not be at all'). In 1764 nearly all the French Jesuits had to go into exile, and Louis XV abolished the order by law in his kingdom. The Pope replied by the bull 'Apostolicum pascendi' of 7 Jan. 1765, giving warm praise to the Society and all its good works. In 1767 the Jesuits were expelled also from *Spain, and shipped to Civitavecchia, and soon after also from Naples and Parma. At last, in 1769, the three ambassadors of Spain, Naples, and France demanded the complete and irrevocable destruction of the Society, and the secularization of its members throughout the world, a step which is believed to have hastened Clement's death, which occurred a few days afterwards. The suppression of the Society by Papal authority was effected by his successor, *Clement XIV.

Bulls in A. Babèri (ed.), *Bullarii Romani Continuatio . . . Clementis XIII. Clementis XIV. Pii VI. Pii VII. Leonis XII. et Pii VIII.*, ed. C. A. Spetia, 1–3 (Rome, 1835–8). J. Holzwarth, *Die Verschwörung der katholischen Höfe gegen Clement den Dreizehnten* (1872). P. Dudon, 'De la suppression de la Compagnie de Jésus (1758–73)', *RQH* 132 (1938), pp. 75–107. [G. J. X.] de Lacroix de Ravignon, SJ, *Clément XIII et Clément XIV* (2 vols., 1854), vol. 1, pp. 1–236, with docs. vol. 2, pp. 1–362. A. Theiner, Orat., *Histoire du Pontificat de Clément XIV*, 1 (Fr. tr. of Germ., 1852), pp. 23–147. B. Betto, 'Papa Rezzonico attraverso le lettere inedite del confessore apostolico', *Rivista di Storia della Chiesa in Italia*, 28 (1974), pp. 388–464, incl. text of 15 letters addressed to him. C. Bellinati, *Attività Pastorale del Card. Carlo Rezzonico, Vescovo di Padova pio Clemente XIII (1743–1758)* (Padua [1969]). Pastor, 26 (1950), pp. 143–504, and 27 (1950). J. Mols, SJ, in *DHGE* 12 (1953), cols. 1381–410, s.v., with full bibl.; E. D. McShane, SJ, in *NCE* 3 (1967), pp. 937–40; L. Cajani and A. Foa in *Dizionario Biografico degli Italiani*, 26 (1982), pp. 328–43.

Clement XIV (1705–74), Pope from 1769. Giovanni Vincenzo Antonio Ganganelli was the son of a surgeon at Sant'Arcangelo, nr. Rimini, who entered the *Franciscan Order in 1723. In 1746 he was appointed Consultor of the *Holy Office by *Benedict XIV, and in 1759 created cardinal by *Clement XIII. In 1769 he was elected Pope after a stormy conclave, the Bourbon courts having decided to recognize only a Pope determined to suppress the *Jesuits.

As Pope he made it his chief aim to preserve peace with the Catholic princes in order to gain their support against the growing irreligion. He therefore restored good relations with Parma and *Spain, and esp. *Portugal, by creating cardinal the brother of the Marquis de Pombal, the Portuguese prime minister. He also suspended (1773) the annual issue of the bull '*In Coena Domini', which contained the censures reserved to the Pope. But all these concessions failed to satisfy the Bourbon courts, bent on the destruction of the Society of Jesus. After hesitating and using half-measures for some time, Clement at last yielded to the pressure of France and Spain, who threatened a schism if the order were not suppressed. In the Brief '*Dominus ac Redemptor' of 21 July 1773 which decreed its suppression, he gave as the only reason for the step the hostility which the Jesuits had incurred and the controversies in which they had been implicated. Thus the order was suppressed in all Catholic states, though Catharine II of Russia and Frederick II of Prussia (the latter only until 1780) refused to promulgate the Papal Brief, so that the Society continued to exist in their realms.

The sacrifice of the Society of Jesus did not, however, procure better relations between the Papacy and the European princes. The former Papal possessions of *Avignon and Benevento were, indeed, restored to the Holy See, but in France a royal commission for the reform of the religious orders continued its activities, suppressing religious houses without Papal approval; in Portugal the secular authorities interfered with ecclesiastical affairs and with the education of the young; and in *Poland hostile tendencies made themselves felt even among the clergy, and esp. in the Order of the *Piarists. Clement XIV introduced many measures for the development of trade and industry in the Pontifical States, but with little success, owing to the opposition of the cardinals and the Roman nobility, who could not forgive the suppression of the Jesuits.

Epistolae et Brevia Selectiora, ed. A. Theiner, Orat. (Paris, 1852). A. L. de Caraccioli, *La Vie du Pape Clément XIV* (1775; Eng. tr., 1776). A. Theiner, Orat., *Geschichte des Pontificats Clemens' XIV* (2 vols., 1853; Fr. tr., 1852). A. von Reumont, *Ganganelli: Papst Clement XIV. Seine Briefe und seine Zeit* (1847). J. A. M. Crétineau-Joly, *Clément XIV et les Jésuites* (1847); [G. J. X.] de Lacroix de Ravignon, SJ, *Clément XIII et Clément XIV* (2 vols., 1854), vol. 1, pp. 237–483, and vol. 2, pp. 363–492. L. Berra, 'Il diario del conclave di Clemente XIV del Card. Filippo Maria Pirelli', *Archivio della Società romana di Storia patria*, 85–6 for 1962–3 (1965), pp. 25–319, incl. text of journal of the conclave by Card. Pirelli, pp. 98–319. L. Szilas, SJ, 'Konklave und Papstwahl Clemens' XIV (1769). Vorspeil zur Aufhebung der Gesellschaft Jesu am 21. Juli 1773', *ZKT* 96 (1974), pp. 287–99. Pastor, 38 ('1951' [1952]); cf. L. Cicchitto, OFM Conv., in *Miscellanea Francescana*, 34 (1934), pp. 189–231. J. de la Servière, SJ, in *DTC* 3 (1908), cols. 124–34; E. Préclin in *DHGE* 12 (1953), cols. 1411–23; M. Rosa in *Dizionario Biografico degli Italiani*, 26 (1982), pp. 343–62, all s.v., with bibl.

Clement of Alexandria (*c*.150–*c*.215), theologian. Practically nothing is known of his life. Perhaps born in *Athens, after studying Christianity and philosophy in several places, he became a pupil of *Pantaenus in *Alexandria. He assumed the role of teacher himself (*c*.190), continuing after Pantaenus' death, but fled from Alexandria in the persecution *c*.202. *Eusebius (*HE* 6. 13. 1–14. 7) mentions several of his works, of which the following survive: the *Protrepticus*, or an 'Exhortation to the Greeks'; the *Paedagogus*, on Christian life and manners; eight Books of *Stromateis*, or 'Miscellanies' (though the last Book seems to be a misplaced fragment on logic); *Excerpta ex Theodoto* (extracts from the work of *Theodotus, a *Valentinian Gnostic); *Eclogae propheticae* (these two last may be material for the apparently missing eighth book of *Stromateis*); a homily (*Quis dives salvetur?*), and several fragments. Clement's work represents an attempt to meet the charge of such pagan critics of Christianity as *Celsus that it is a religion for the ignorant. He

treads a middle way between heretical *Gnosticism which had intellectual pretensions and a religion of simple faith, seeing in Christianity the fulfilment both of the OT Scriptures and of Greek philosophy. His theology is presented as a spiritual journey in the threefold work consisting of the *Protrepticus*, the *Paedagogus*, and the (projected) *Didascalus* (or 'Teacher', to which the *Stromateis* seems to bear a somewhat ambiguous relationship). In the first, the *Logos exposes the error and immorality of Greek religion and leads men, through *Baptism, to the true and pure religion of Christianity. In the second, the Logos as *paedagogus*, nurse, and physician, watches over the newly-born Christian soul, trains it in appropriate virtues, and prepares it to grasp the deeper teaching (essentially of the Scriptures) which the Logos will expound as *didascalus*. In all this Clement is deeply indebted to contemporary Middle *Platonic philosophy, and he uses many themes from the Gnostics: he applies the term 'gnostic' to the Christian who has attained the deeper teaching of the Logos. The ultimate goal of the Christian life is presented as *deification, identified both as Platonic 'assimilation to God' (*Theat.* 176 B) and as the biblical idea of imitation of God (cf. Mt. 5: 48, and the example of *Moses following God). Clement's name appears in the earlier martyrologies, where it is assigned to 4 Dec., but *Clement VIII excised it on the advice of C. *Baronius on the grounds of the doubtful orthodoxy of some of his writings. In the American BCP (1979), feast day, 5 Dec.

The *Protrepticus* and *Paedagogus* survive in the 'Arethas Codex' (Par. gr. 451 of AD 914) and some dependent MSS, the *Stromateis* in the Florence MS Laur. V. 3 (11th cent.) and a copy. *Editiones principes* by P. Victorius (Florence, 1550) and F. Sylburg (Heidelberg, 1592); good edn. by J. *Potter, 2 vols., Oxford, 1715. J. P. Migne, *PG* 8 and 9. Crit. edn. by O. Stählin in GCS 1–3, text, 1905–9; rev. by L. Früchtel and U. Treu, 1960–72; vol. 4 (very fine index), 1934–6; rev. U. Treu, 1980 ff. *Stromateis*, bk. 7, ed. F. J. A. *Hort and J. B. Mayor (London, 1902); *Protrepticus* and *Quis dives salvetur?*, with frag., ed., with Eng. tr., by G. W. Butterworth (Loeb, 1919). There are also eds., mainly based on the GCS texts, with Fr. tr. and comm., in SC: *Protrepticus*, by A. Plassart and C. Mondésert, SJ (2 bis, 1949); *Paedagogus*, by M. Harl, C. Mondésert, SJ, and H. I. Marrou (70, 108, and 158; 1960–70); *Stromateis*, bks. 1 and 2, by C. Mondésert, SJ, and others (30 and 38; 1951–4), bk. 5, by A. Le Boulluec and P. Voulet, SJ (278–9; 1981); for edns. of *Excerpta ex Theodoto* see s.v. THEODOTUS. Modern Eng. tr. of *Paedagogos* by S. P. Wood, CP (Fathers of the Church, 23; 1954) and of *Stromateis*, bks. 1–3 by J. Ferguson (ibid., 85 [1991]). Studies by E. de Faye (Paris, 1898), R. B. Tollinton (2 vols., London, 1914), G. Bardy (Paris, 1926), G. Lazzati (Milan, 1939), and C. Mondésert, SJ (Paris, 1944). C. *Bigg, *The Christian Platonists of Alexandria* (ed. F. E. *Brightman, 1913), esp. pp. 72–150. J. Munck, *Untersuchungen über Klemens von Alexandrien* (1933). E. Molland, 'Clement of Alexandria on the Origin of Greek Philosophy', *Symbolae Osloenses*, 15–16 (1936), pp. 57–85; id., *The Conception of the Gospel in the Alexandrian Theology* (Oslo, 1938), pp. 5–84. T. Camelot, OP, *Foi et gnose: Introduction à l'étude de la connaissance mystique chez Clément d'Alexandrie* (Études de théologie et d'histoire de la spiritualité, 3; 1945). F. Quatember, SJ, *Die christliche Lebenshaltung des Klemens von Alexandrien nach seinem Pädagogus* (Vienna, 1946). W. Völker, *Der wahre Gnostiker nach Clemens Alexandrinus* (TU 57; 1952). E. F. Osborn, *The Philosophy of Clement of Alexandria* (Texts and Studies, NS 3; 1957). A. Méhat, *Étude sur les 'Stromates' de Clément d'Alexandrie* (Patristica Sorbonensia, 7 [1966]). H. Chadwick, *Early Christian Thought and the Classical Tradition: Studies in Justin, Clement, and Origen* (Oxford, 1966), pp. 31–65. S. R. C. Lilla, *Clement of Alexandria: A Study in Christian Platonism and Gnosticism* (Oxford Theological Monographs, 1971). D. Wyrwa, *Die christliche Platonaneignung in den Stromateis des Clemens von Alexandrien* (Arbeiten zur Kirchengeschichte, 53; 1983). *CPG* 1 (1983), pp. 135–40 (nos. 1375–99). Altaner and Stuiber (1978), pp. 190–97 and 585–7. A. de la Barre in *DTC* 3 (1908), cols. 137–99; M. Spanneut in *NCE* 3 (1967), pp. 943 f.; A. Méhat in *TRE* 8 (1981), pp. 101–13, all s.v. See also works cited under ALEXANDRIAN THEOLOGY.

Clement I. See CLEMENT OF ROME, ST.

Clement Mary Hofbauer, St. See HOFBAUER, ST CLEMENT MARY.

Clementine Literature. The many apocryphal writings which circulated in the early Church under the name of St *Clement of Rome include, besides the so-called 'Second Ep. of Clement' (q.v.), (1) the '*Apostolic Constitutions', (2) two 'Epp. to Virgins', (3) and (4) the 'Clementine Homilies' and 'Recognitions', (5) 'Epitomes' of the last named, (6) the 'Apocalypse of Clement', more commonly known as the 'Apocalypse of St *Peter' (q.v.), (7) an unpublished Arabic Apocalypse akin to the preceding, and (8) spurious letters in the *False Decretals (q.v.). The term 'Clementines' (Κλημέντια) is by convention restricted to (3), (4), and the less important (5).

(1) The *Clementine Homilies* ('Ομιλίαι) is a religious and philosophical romance, arranged as 20 discourses, which Clement is supposed to have sent from *Rome to *James of Jerusalem, the Lord's brother, and preceded by two letters from Peter and Clement, also addressed to James, and instructions for the correct use of the work (the *Contestatio*). They describe Clement's travels in the East when he met St Peter and witnessed his conflict with *Simon Magus. The work contains much legendary matter, e.g. about Clement's family. Until A. R. M. Dressel published a complete text on the basis of Cod. Ottobon. 443 in 1853, they were only known in a defective Cod. Par. gr. 930.

(2) The *Clementine Recognitions* ('Αναγνώσεις), in 10 books, closely resembles the 'Homilies' in historical setting and theological outlook. Their narrative parts go over much the same ground, with additional details of the vicissitudes of several members of Clement's family and their final reunion after their 'recognition' (hence the title) by St Peter. The original Greek is lost; the work survives in the Lat. of *Rufinus (d. 410), who in a prefatory letter mentions that he had made various curtailments. Parts of the 'Homilies' and 'Recognitions' also survive in Syriac.

(3) The two Greek *Epitomes* ('Επιτομαί) are evidently later. They omit most of the theological discussions of the earlier works and introduce an account of Clement's martyrdom. Two Arabic epitomes also survive.

The literary and theological problems raised by the Clementines are still debated. It is undisputed that there is a literary connection between the 'Homilies' and the 'Recognitions' and it is generally thought that they both depend on a common lost source (*Grundschrift*). Some scholars think this *Grundschrift* was composed of the 'Preachings of St Peter' (not to be confused with the 'Preaching of St *Peter', q.v.) and material derived from the 'Acts of St *Peter', the former of which was prob. *Ebionite and anti-Pauline. Others hold that the *Grundschrift* is based on

a lost 'Itinerary of St Peter', an apologetic treatise displaying a rationalism akin to that of the 2nd cent. *Apologists. It is, however, generally agreed that one of the sources of the *Grundschrift* was *Bardesanes' 'Dialogue of Destiny'. This fact, combined with *Origen's quotation from some form of the Clementines in Book 3 of his 'Commentary on Genesis' (preserved in the *Philocalia*), suggests a date of composition sometime in the first third of the 3rd cent. The 'Homilies' seem to be a first reworking of the *Grundschrift*, adding a metaphysical, *Gnostic interest in *syzygies, which provides a background to the opposition of Peter and Simon Magus. They belong to the 4th cent. and betray *Arian sympathies. The 'Recognitions' seem to presuppose the 'Homilies' as well as the *Grundschrift*, but as they survive mainly in the (characteristically reworked) translation of Rufinus, it is difficult to know what their original intention was. As they stand they contain a passage expressing *Eunomian teaching (3. 2–11), which most critics think is an interpolation. In this final form, Christ is a Divine Aeon, who had previously been revealed in *Adam and *Moses. Jesus is the True Prophet and special emphasis is laid on the Jerusalem Church. There are also strong ascetic elements. Peter is a strict vegetarian and the use of water alone is allowed in the Eucharist. On the other hand there is a definite repudiation of celibacy (a mark of Jewish influence).

The documents were given a wholly disproportionate importance by the *Tübingen School, who, putting them very early, saw in the narratives of Simon Magus a reflection of the fierce conflict between 'Petrinism' and 'Paulinism' in pre-Catholic Christianity.

Homilies (1–19a only) first pr. from Par. gr. 930 by J. B. *Cotelier in his '*Apostolic Fathers' (1672), 1, pp. 546–746. A. R. M. Dressel's complete text (1853; repr. in J. P. Migne, *PG* 2. 19–468) was soon superseded by the more satisfactory edn. of P. de *Lagarde (*Clementina*, Leipzig, 1865). *Recognitions* ed. J. *Faber Stapulensis as early as 1504. Subsequent edns. by J. B. Cotelier (1672) and E. G. Gersdorf (1838; repr. *PG* 1. 1158–474). Crit. edn. of *Homilies* by B. Rehm (GCS 42; 1953; 3rd edn. by G. Strecker, 1992) and of the *Recognitions* by B. Rehm and F. Paschke (ibid. 51; 1965; 2nd edn. by G. Strecker, 1994), with concordances by G. Strecker (ibid. 58; 2 vols., 1986–9). Selections from the *Homilies*, *Recognitions*, and *Epitome* in Ger. tr., with introd., by J. Irmscher and G. Strecker in Schneemelcher, 2 (5th edn., 1989), pp. 439–88; Eng. tr., 2 [1992], pp. 483–541. W. Frankenberg, *Die syrischen Clementinen mit griechischem Paralleltext* (TU 48, Heft 3; 1937). F. Paschke, *Die beiden griechischen Klementinen-Epitomen und ihre Anhänge: Überlieferungsgeschichtliche Vorarbeiten zu einer Neuausgabe der Texte* (ibid. 90; 1966). The lit. is vast. Among the more important is H. Waitz, *Die Pseudoklementinen* (TU 25. 4; 1904); J. *Chapman, 'On the date of the Clementines', *ZNTW* 9 (1908), pp. 21–34, 147–59; O. *Cullmann, *Le Problème littéraire et historique du roman pseudo-clémentin* (1930); E. *Schwartz, 'Unzeitgemässe Betrachtungen zu den Clementinen', *ZNTW* 31 (1932), pp. 151–99; B. Rehm, 'Zur Entstehung der pseudoclementinischen Schriften', ibid. 37 (1938), pp. 77–184. G. Strecker, *Das Judenchristentum in den Pseudoklementinen* (TU 70; 1958; 2nd edn., 1981), with bibl.; W. Ullmann, 'The Significance of the *Epistola Clementis* in the Pseudo-Clementines', *JTS* NS 11 (1960), pp. 295–317; J. Rius-Camps, 'Las Pseudoclementinas. Bases filológicas para una nueva interpretación', *Revista Catalana de Teología*, 1 (1976), pp. 79–158, with Eng. summary. F. Stanley Jones, 'The Pseudo-Clementines: A History of Research', *The Second Century*, 2 (1982), pp. 1–33 and 63–96. For lexical purposes, W. C[hawner], *Index of Noteworthy Words and Phrases found in the Clementine*

Homilies (1893). *CPG* 1 (1983), pp. 8–11 (nos. 1015–21). Altaner and Stuiber (1978), pp. 134 f. and 575. B. Rehm in *RAC* 3 (1957), cols. 197–206, s.v. 'Clemens Romanus II'.

Clementines. In canon law, the collection of *Decretals, also known as the **Liber Septimus,** issued by *Clement V. It contains Decretals of *Boniface VIII, Urban IV, and Clement himself. Clement promulgated it, together with the decrees of the Council of *Vienne (1311–12), on 21 Mar. 1314 at Monteux, nr. Carpentras. Its authority being uncertain owing to Clement's having died before its general acceptance, it was promulgated afresh by *John XXII on 25 Oct. 1317. It was the last item officially embodied in the '*Corpus Iuris Canonici'.

G. Mollat in *DDC* 4 (1949), cols. 635–40, s.v. '*Corpus Juris Canonici*, IV. Les Clémentines', with refs. to lists of edns. and comm. and also bibl.

Cleopas. One of the two disciples to whom the risen Christ appeared on the road to *Emmaus on the day of the Resurrection, and made Himself known in the 'breaking of bread' (Lk. 24: 13–35). He is sometimes identified with the Clopas of Jn. 19: 25 (RV), the husband of a certain Mary, who, on the assumption that the Gk. Κλωπᾶς is the equivalent of the Aramaic חֲלְפִי (also 'Alphaeus'), has been identified with Mary, the mother of James (cf. Mk. 3: 18, 15: 40).

Clerical Disabilities Act 1870. The Act which allows a C of E cleric, after resigning all preferments, to execute a Deed of Relinquishment and thereby regain such civil rights as were lost through becoming a cleric (e.g. that of sitting in the House of Commons). However, as *Orders are indelible, the person concerned does not thereby cease to be ordained, and has since the Clerical Disabilities Act 1870 (Amendment) Measure 1934 been able to petition the Archbishop of the Province in which his Deed is recorded to vacate the enrolment of the Deed and become a cleric again without further ordination.

Clerical Subscription Act 1865. The Act amending the 36th *Canon of 1604 by changing the form of declaration made by Anglican clergymen at ordination and on accepting ecclesiastical preferment. The chief points of difference are that an Oath of *Allegiance to the Sovereign is alone required, and the acknowledgement of the Royal Supremacy is no longer imposed; and that a (general) '*assent' was demanded to the *Thirty-Nine Articles, instead of the obligation to 'acknowledge *all and every* [Article] to be agreeable to the Word of God'. The Act also provided that every beneficed clergyman, on taking up a new cure of souls, should, on the first Sunday, or on some other day appointed by the bishop, read the Articles to his congregation and make a formal assent to them and to the BCP. In 1975 the obligation to read the Articles was removed and the form of assent made less rigid. See also ASSENT, DECLARATION OF.

clericalism. A term, often used in an opprobrious sense, for an excessively professional attitude of outlook, conversation, or conduct on the part of clergymen, or for the imitation of a supposedly clerical manner by lay persons.

It is also used to describe undue clerical influence in secular affairs. See also ANTICLERICALISM.

Clericis Laicos. The bull issued by *Boniface VIII on 25 Feb. 1296 to protect the clergy of England and France against the exactions of the secular power. It forbade any cleric to pay ecclesiastical revenues to laymen without the authority of the Roman see, and any layman, under threat of excommunication, to receive such payments. The vehemence of its language aroused fierce opposition on the part of Philip the Fair and Edward I, and considerably weakened its effectiveness. It was revoked by *Clement V.

Complete text in A. Thomas, M. Faucon, and G. Digard (eds.), *Les Registres de Boniface VIII*, I (Bibliothèque des Écoles Françaises d'Athènes et de Rome, 1907), no. 1567, pp. 584 f.; Operative part of text also in Mirbt and Aland (1967), p. 457 (no. 743); Eng. tr. in Bettenson, pp. 157–9. S. Vigor, ed. by P. Dupuy, *Histoire du différend entre le Pape Boniface VIII et Philippe le Bel roy de France* (1655); J. Rivière, *Le Problème de l'Église et de l'état au temps de Philippe le Bel* (SSL 8; 1926), esp. pp. 63–70. T. S. R. Boase, *Boniface VIII* (1933), esp. ch. 5, pp. 129–56. L. Santifaller, 'Zur Original-Überlieferung der Bulle Papst Bonifaz' VIII. "Clericis Laicos" von 1296 Februar 25', *Studia Gratiana*, 11 (1967), pp. 69–90. E. J. Smyth, '*Clericis Laicos* and the Lower Clergy in England', in G. G. Steckler and D. L. Davis (eds.), *Studies in Mediaevalia and Americana: Essays in honor of William Lyle Davis, SJ* (Spokane, Wash., 1973), pp. 77–87.

Clericus. See LECLERC, JEAN.

clerk, parish. See PARISH CLERK.

Clerk in Holy Orders. A designation, chiefly legal and formal, for a bishop, priest, or deacon in the C of E, as contrasted with such clerks as 'Lay Clerks', 'Bible Clerks', etc., who execute minor ecclesiastical functions without ordination. Before the *Reformation, the word 'clerk' without qualification was applied to those in *Minor Orders, while the orders of bishop, priest, and deacon (and also the *subdiaconate from the 13th cent.) were specified as *Major, or Holy, Orders.

Clerk of the Closet. The cleric who presides over the Royal College of Chaplains. When a vacancy occurs in the list of chaplains, he is asked by the Master of the Household to suggest possible names to the Sovereign. Among his duties are the presentation of bishops to the Sovereign when they do homage after consecration, and the examination of theological books whose authors wish to present copies to the Sovereign.

J. [M.] Bickersteth and J. W. Dunning, *The Clerks of the Closet in the Royal Household* (Stroud, 1991).

clerks regular. A term applied to certain bodies of RC clergy, bound under religious vows, who live in community and engage esp. in active pastoral work. Such regular clerks originated in the 16th cent. through the efforts of various bands of clerics to perfect their pastoral work by the stimulus of ordered discipline. The first communities were largely Italian, and met with striking success at a time when the waning prestige of the Church called for such intensified effort. They included the '*Theatines' (1524), the 'Clerks Regular of the Good Jesus' founded at *Ravenna (1526), and the '*Barnabites' founded at Milan in 1530. The largest and most important member of the family is the *Jesuits or Society of Jesus (1534). Since the close of the 16th cent. there have been no official additions to the number of orders of regular clerks, but their name has been adopted by other religious congregations. The mode of life of regular clerks has greatly influenced the constitutions of various modern bodies, monastic and non-monastic, living under rule. They may be regarded as the modern counterpart of the regular *canons (q.v.).

Clermont (modern **Clermont-Ferrand**), **Collège de**, also known as the Collège Louis le Grand. The celebrated *Jesuit house at *Paris, at one time the property of G. du Prat, Bp. of Clermont (1529–60). Through the energies of J. *Sirmond and others, it acquired a celebrated collection of MSS known to scholars as the 'Claromontani'. In 1764 the College was dissolved and the MSS dispersed.

G. Dupont-Ferrier, *Du collège de Clermont au collège Louis-le-Grand* (3 vols., 1921–5). H. Fouqueray, SJ, *Histoire de la compagnie de Jésus en France*, 1 (1910), pp. 363–433.

Clermont, Council of (1095). Summoned by *Urban II for the reform of the Church and the preaching of the First *Crusade, it met at Clermont on 18–28 Nov. 1095. It was attended by some 300 clergy, predominantly French. Besides proclaiming a remission of all penances for those who travelled to Jerusalem to free the Church of God, it passed numerous canons. Their subjects included the Peace and *Truce of God, and many matters of clerical and lay discipline. The primacy of the see of Lyons was also confirmed and King Philip of France was excommunicated for adultery. Unfortunately no official record of its legislation survives; its canons must be pieced together from many sources. Urban II preached the Crusade in an open field on 27 Nov. to a great crowd of clergy and laymen.

R. Somerville, *The Councils of Urban II*, 1: *Decreta Claromentensia* (Annuarium Historiae Conciliorum, Suppl., 1; Amsterdam, 1972). Hefele and Leclercq, 5 (pt. 1; 1912), pp. 396–444. See also bibl. to CRUSADES.

Cletus, St. See ANACLETUS, ST.

Clifford, John (1836–1923), *Baptist leader. As a boy he worked in a lace factory. He experienced conversion in 1850 and was baptized in the following year. In 1858 he became the minister of the Baptist Church at Praed Street, Paddington, and when the congregation, attracted by his successful pastorate, grew too large, Westbourne Park Chapel was built for him (opened, 1877). In 1888 he became president of the Baptist Union. He was keenly interested in upholding the cause of working people and also led the movement for 'passive resistance' to A. J. *Balfour's Education Act of 1902, which he believed to be injurious to Nonconformist interests. His influence did much towards bringing about the defeat of the Unionists at the polls in 1906. He held several important offices in the Baptist Church, and from 1905 to 1911 was the first president of the Baptist World Alliance. Theologically he inclined towards a more liberal position than had been traditional in his own communion. His many writings exercised great influence on his generation.

Life and Letters of Dr. John Clifford, ed. J. Marchant (1924). G. W. Byrt, *John Clifford* (1947). J. H. Rushbrooke in *DNB, 1922–1930*, pp. 188–90.

Climacus, St John. See JOHN CLIMACUS, ST.

Clinici. See under BAPTISM (p. 150, col. 2).

Clitherow, St Margaret (c.1556–86), the 'martyr of *York'. The daughter of a Sheriff of York, she was converted to the Roman obedience at the age of 18, and became an ardent friend of the persecuted RCs. In 1586 she was arrested and charged at the York Assizes with harbouring priests. To save her children from being forced to witness against her, she refused to plead, and was barbarously crushed to death. She was one of the *Forty Martyrs canonized by *Paul VI in 1970; feast day, previously 2 Apr. See also FORTY MARTYRS OF ENGLAND AND WALES.

Life by John Mush, her confessor (first pub. London, 1849). Modern studies by K. M. Longley (under the name of 'Mary Claridge', London, 1966) and under her own name, (Wheathampstead, Herts, 1986).

cloister. An enclosed space which in the Middle Ages and in modern times has normally formed the central part of a monastery or other religious building. It consists of a garth or open plot surrounded on all four sides by broad covered alleys with roofs supported on their inner sides by arcades (orig. open but later often glazed) and on their outer sides by the walls of the church or other major building. The term is also used in general for a Religious House, or the Religious Life. See also CLAUSURA.

J. C. Dickinson, *Monastic Life in Medieval England* (1961), esp. pp. 28–31. P. Meyvaert, 'The Medieval Monastic Claustrum', *Gesta*, 12 (1973), pp. 53–59; repr. in Meyvaert's *Benedict, Gregory, Bede and Others* (1977), no. 16.

Close, Francis (1797–1882), Dean of *Carlisle. He was educated at Merchant Taylors' School and St John's College, Cambridge, and became incumbent of Cheltenham in 1826. His sermons, modelled on those of C. *Simeon, soon won him a large following, and made him one of the best known of Evangelical preachers. By his opposition to the theatre, horse-racing, and esp. 'Sabbath-breaking', he exercised great influence on the public life of Cheltenham. A spokesman of the Evangelicals on education, in 1847 he founded the colleges of St Paul and St Mary in the town. He was hostile to *Tractarianism and saw in 'Popery', whether Anglican or Roman, one of the chief dangers of the age. From 1856 to 1881 he was Dean of Carlisle. His long series of books (largely sermons) and tracts were of great influence in their day. The Dean Close School was founded at Cheltenham as a public school for boys in his memory.

'Contem Ignotus' [Richard Glover], *The Golden Decade of a Favoured Town: Being Biographical Sketches and Personal Recollections of the Celebrated Characters who have been connected with Cheltenham from 1843 to 1853* (1884), pp. 10–69; *Memorials of Dean Close*, ed. by one who knew him (Carlisle, 1885). G. Berwick, 'Close of Cheltenham: Parish Pope', *Theology*, 39 (1939), pp. 193–201 and 276–85. M. [M.] Hennell, *Sons of the Prophets: Evangelical Leaders of the Victorian Church* (1979), pp. 104–21. G. C. Boase in *DNB* 11 (1887), pp. 123 f.

Clotilde, St (474–545), Frankish queen. By birth a Burgundian princess, she married *Clovis, King of the Salian Franks, in 492 or 493. She at once endeavoured to convert him to Christianity, and partly as a result of a great victory over the Alemanni, he and many of his followers were baptized by St *Remigius, Bp. of Reims. *Gregory of Tours gives 496 as the date of Clovis' baptism, but in recent years historians have come to think that it may have been as late as *c*.503, or even 508. After her husband's death in 511 Clotilde's life was saddened by internecine struggles between her sons and the tragic fate of her daughter, and she retired to the abbey of St *Martin at Tours, where her reputation for piety and good works continued undimmed. In later times the events of her life were much embroidered in the interests of epic. Feast day, 3 June.

Crit. edn. of a Life, prob. 10th cent., by B. Krusch in *MGH*, Scriptores Rerum Merovingicarum, 2 (1888), pp. 349–51; Eng. tr. in *Sainted Women of the Dark Ages*, ed. and tr. J. A. McNamara and others (Durham, NC, and London, 1992), pp. 38–50. G. Kurth, *Sainte Clotilde* ('Les Saints', Paris, 1897; Eng. tr., 1898). For works on the baptism of Clovis and the date of his conversion, see bibl. to CLOVIS.

Cloud of Unknowing, The. An anonymous 14th-cent. English mystical treatise. There has been much inconclusive discussion about the identity of the author, who was prob. contemporary with Walter *Hilton. The most important of his other works are *The Book of Privy Counselling* and *An Epistle of Discretion of Stirrings*. The author was deeply influenced by the anti-intellectualist interpretation of *Dionysius the Pseudo-Areopagite, as found in *Thomas Gallus, and insists that, in this life, God as He is in Himself cannot be grasped by the intellect; between Him and us there is always a 'cloud of unknowing', which can be pierced only by 'a sharp dart of love'. He is, however, the proper object of our wills, which should be directed towards Him with a 'naked entent', as free from any admixture of creatures as possible. Those who are called to 'the higher part of the contemplative life' should abandon discursive and affective meditation in favour of this 'naked entent', in which our being is simply offered, unanalysed, to God, whom we cannot think. This 'entent' may be sustained with the help of monosyllabic 'meditation' or very brief ejaculatory prayer. The author warns against adopting the 'work' of contemplatives unless one is called to it by God.

Crit. edns. by P. Hodgson, with introd. and bibl., of *The Cloud of Unknowing* and *The Book of Privy Counselling* (EETS, Orig. Ser. 218, 1944; repr. with corrections and new bibl., 1958); of *Deonise Hid Diuinite and Other Treatises on Contemplative Prayer related to The Cloud of Unknowing* (ibid., 231; 1955); and of *The Cloud of Unknowing and related Treatises* (Analecta Cartusiana, 3; Salzburg, 1982); Latin versions of *The Cloud*, ed. J. [P. H.] Clark (ibid., 119; 2 vols., 1989). Modern trs. of *The Cloud* by C. Wolters (Penguin Classics, 1961; repr. with *The Book of Privy Counselling* and other works, 1978) and J. Walsh, SJ (Classics of Western Spirituality, 1981). W. Riehle, *Studien zur englischen Mystik des Mittelalters* (Anglistische Forschungen, 120; 1977; Eng. tr., 1981). A. J. Minnis, 'The Sources of *The Cloud of Unknowing*: A Reconsideration', in *The Medieval Mystical Tradition in England: Papers Read at Dartington Hall, July 1982*, ed. M. Glasscoe (Exeter, 1982), pp. 63–75. S. [C. ff.] Tugwell, OP, *Ways of Imperfection* (1984), pp. 170–86. V. M. Lagorio and R. Bradley, *The 14th-*

Century English Mystics: A Comprehensive Annotated Bibliography (New York and London, 1981), pp. 81–90.

Clovesho, Councils of. A series of synods representing the Church of all England south of the Humber, held between the late 7th and the first quarter of the 9th cent.; many of the attested meetings were also attended by the King of the Mercians. A decision of the Council of *Hertford in 672 or 673 laid down that the clergy should meet annually at Clovesho (on 1 Aug.), and records of varying degrees of authenticity—survive of the meetings which were held in 716, 742, 747, 792, 794, 798, 803, 824, and 825. Those of 747 and 803 are the most important. The former dealt with ecclesiastical discipline and liturgy, ordering in the later strict adherence to the Roman rite. The latter was the occasion of the abolition of the archiepiscopal status of *Lichfield, set up in 787, and the restoration of the Mercian sees to the province of *Canterbury. The site of Clovesho is unknown.

Acts of the Councils of 747 and 803, with other primary material, in A. W. Haddan and W. *Stubbs (eds.), *Councils and Ecclesiastical Documents Relating to Great Britain and Ireland*, 3 (1871), pp. 360–76 and 541–8. C. Cubitt, *Anglo-Saxon Church Councils c.650–c.850* [1995], pp. 99–152 (on the Council of 747). E. B. Fryde and others (eds.), *Handbook of British Chronology* (Royal Historical Society Guides and Handbooks, 2; 3rd edn., 1986), pp. 583–9.

Clovis (*c*.466–511), King of the Franks. The son of Childeric I, he became King of the Salian Franks in 481 and forthwith began to expand his domain. He attacked and defeated his rival, the Roman general Syagrius, at Soissons, and incorporated into his dominions much of Roman Gaul and other territories, including those of the Ripuarian Franks and the Thuringians. The decisive event in his career was his conversion to Catholic Christianity and his baptism (see CLOTILDE). The date, 496, given by *Gregory of Tours, has been disputed, with 503, 506, and even 508 suggested. The chronology of Clovis's reign is of crucial importance for the interpretation of his career. A link is usually made between his Catholicism and his success, notably the overthrow of the *Arian King Alaric II and the Visigothic forces at the battle of Vouillé in 507, and the consolidation of his dominions, since he gained the aid of the Catholic bishops and Roman officials in governing the country. In 508 the E. Emp. Anastasius conferred on him the title of 'Proconsul'. Ruthless and cruel, Clovis was a man of consummate ability. The oldest redaction of the Salic law was drawn up during his reign.

G. Kurth, *Clovis* (Tours, 1896; 3rd edn., 2 vols., Brussels, 1923). A. van de Vyver, 'La Victoire contre les Alamans et la conversion de Clovis', *Revue Belge de Philologie et d'Histoire*, 15 (1936), pp. 859–914, and 17 (1937), pp. 35–94; id., 'Clovis et la politique méditerranéenne', in *Études d'histoire dédiées à la mémoire de Henri Pirenne* [ed. F. L. Ganshof, E. Sabbe, and F. Vercauteren] (1937), pp. 367–87; id., 'La Chronologie du règne de Clovis d'après la légende et d'après l'histoire', *Le Moyen Age*, 53 (1947), pp. 177–96. F. Oppenheimer, *Frankish Themes and Problems* (1952), pp. 17–63 ('The Place and Date of Clovis' Baptism'). J. M. Wallace-Hadrill, *The Long-Haired Kings and other Studies in Frankish History* (1962), esp. pp. 163–85. G. Tessier, *Le Baptême de Clovis* (1964); id., 'La Conversion de Clovis et la christianisation des Francs', *Settimane di Studio del Centro Italiano di Studi sull' Alto Medioevo*, 14 (1967), pp. 149–89. R. Weiss, *Chlodwigs Taufe: Reims 508. Versuch einer neuen Chronologie für die*

Regierungszeit des ersten christlichen Frankenkönigs unter Berücksichtigung der politischen und kirchlich-dogmatischen Probleme seiner Zeit (Geist und Werken der Zeiten, 29; 1971). M. Reydellet, *La Royauté dans la littérature latine de Sidoine à Isidore de Séville* (Bibliothèque des Écoles françaises d'Athènes et de Rome, 243; 1981), pp. 94–113. I. N. Wood, 'Gregory of Tours and Clovis', *Revue Belge de Philologie et d'Histoire*, 63 (1985), pp. 249–72. H. *Leclercq, OSB, in *DACL* 3 (pt. 2; 1914), cols. 2037–74, s.v. 'Clovis (Baptême et sépulture de)'.

Cluny, Cluniacs. The influential monastery of Cluny, near Mâcon in Burgundy, was founded by William the Pious, Duke of Aquitaine, in 909/10. The high standard of monastic observance set by Berno of Baume, its first Abbot (909/10–927), was adopted before Berno's death in some five or six neighbouring monasteries. The real founder of Cluny's influence, however, was Berno's successor, St *Odo (927–42), under whose encouragement many monasteries in the S. of France, and even some of the most important Italian houses (*Monte Cassino, Santa Maria on the Aventine, *Subiaco) reformed themselves after the Cluniac model. Under Odo's gifted successors Aymardus (942–*c*.954; d. *c*.963 [perh. 964]), Majolus (*c*.954–94) and St *Odilo (994–1048; q.v.) an ever-growing number of houses, old and new, adopted the reform. Its objects included a return to the strict *Benedictine rule, esp. as expounded by St *Benedict of Aniane, cultivation of the personal spiritual life, stress on the choir office (which tended to grow to excessive length) and the splendour and solemnity of worship generally, with a corresponding reduction in manual labour. Great attention was also paid to sound economic organization and independence of lay control. It now seems clear that in the 10th cent. the Cluniac houses were not yet welded into a system, which only developed under Odilo and his successor *Hugh (1049–1109). Under Hugh, when the influence of Cluny reached its height, the number of Cluniac houses was well over 1,000. Then the centralization was such that the heads of the subject-houses were ordinarily priors, not abbots.

Esp. in the 11th and early 12th cents. Cluny exercised decisive influence on the life of the Church. Its leading figures came from noble families who increasingly enjoyed the confidence of sovereigns and popes. Their ideals were widely admired by the secular clergy and largely inspired the reforms (repression of *simony, *celibacy of clergy) of *Gregory VII. The new church at Cluny (begun in 1088), of which *Urban II consecrated the high altar in person on 25 Oct. 1095 and Innocent II the whole church (except the *narthex) in 1131–2, was then the largest church in Europe (555 ft. long).

After Hugh's death the next abbots were Pontius (1109–22), Hugh II (1122), and *Peter the Venerable (1122–56). From the beginning of the 13th cent., the Cluniacs became organized as an Order on the *Cistercian model, with General Chapters and a system of visitations. In the later Middle Ages the influence of Cluny greatly declined, but the monastery survived until 1790. The *Hôtel de Cluny* in Paris (since 1833 a museum) was formerly the town-house of the Abbots of Cluny.

The first English Cluniac house was St Pancras at Lewes, founded by William de Warenne in 1077. Others soon followed at Wenlock (*c*.1081), Bermondsey (*c*.1085), Castle Acre (1089), and Thetford (1104), and, in Scotland,

at Paisley (1163). By the middle of the 12th cent. their number had risen to 36. As alien priories they were frequently sequestered by the Crown during the French Wars. In the later Middle Ages the control from Cluny was in fact slight. At the Dissolution there were eight greater and nearly 30 lesser Cluniac houses.

Bibliotheca Cluniacensis, ed. M. Marrier, OSB, and A. Quercetanus (Paris, 1614); *Bullarium Sacri Ordinis Cluniacensis*, ed. P. Simon, OSB (Lyons, 1680). *Consuetudines Cluniacensium Antiquiores cum redactionibus derivatis*, ed. K. Hallinger, OSB (Corpus Consuetudinum Monasticarum, 7, pt. 2; Siegburg, 1983; see also introd., ibid., 7, pt. 1; 1984); *Liber Tramitis Aevi Odilonis Abbatis*, ed. P. Dinter (ibid., 10; 1980); for Abbot Hugh's reign, 'Ordo Cluniacensis Bernardi monachi' in [M. Herrgott, OSB (ed.)] *Vetus Disciplina Monastica* (Paris, 1726), pp. 133–364, and 'Antiquiores Consuetudines Cluniacensis Monasterii collectore S. Udalrico' in L. *d'Achery, OSB, *Spicilegium*, ed. S. *Baluze and E. *Martène, 1 (1723), pp. 641–703, repr. in J. P. Migne, *PL* 149. 635–778. *Statuts, chapitres généraux et visites de l'ordre de Cluny* with preface and notes by G. Charvin, OSB (9 vols. in 11, 1965–82). G. de Valous, *Le Monachisme clunisien des origines au XV*[e] *siècle: Vie intérieure des monastères et organisation de l'ordre* (Archives de la France monastique, 39–40; 1935; 2nd edn., 2 vols., 1970). G. F. Duckett, *Charters and Records among the Archives of the ancient Abbey of Cluni* (2 vols., 1888); E. Sackur, *Die Cluniacenser* (2 vols., 1892–4). L. M. Smith, *The Early History of the Movement of Cluny* (1925). K. Hallinger, OSB, *Gorze-Kluny: Studien zu den monastischen Lebensformen und Gegensätzen im Hochmittelalter* (2 vols., Studia Anselmiana, 22–25; 1950–1951). J. Wollasch, H. E. Mager, and A. Diener, *Neue Forschungen über Cluny und die Cluniacenser*, ed. G. Tellenbach (Freiburg, 1959). H. E. J. Cowdrey, *The Cluniacs and the Gregorian Reform* (Oxford, 1970). M. Pacaut, *L'Ordre de Cluny (909–1789)* (1986). J. Evans, *Monastic Life at Cluny, 910–1157* (1931). N. Hunt, *Cluny under St Hugh, 1049–1109* (1967). K. J. Conant, *Cluny: Les Églises et la Maison du Chef d'Ordre* (Mâcon, 1968). *A Cluny: Congrès scientifique, fêtes et cérémonies liturgiques en l'honneur des saints Abbés Odon et Odilon 9–11 juillet 1949. Travaux du congrès . . . publiés par la Société des Amis de Cluny* (Dijon, 1950). A number of essays are collected and tr. into English in N. Hunt (ed.), *Cluniac Monasticism in the Central Middle Ages* (1971). [M.] D. *Knowles, OSB, *The Monastic Order in England* (1940; 2nd edn., 1963), esp. chs. 8 and 16. E. M. Wischermann, *Marcigny-sur-Loire: Gründungs- und Frühgeschichte des ersten Cluniacenserinnenpriorates (1055–1150)* (Münstersche Mittelalter-Schriften, 42; 1986). P. Racinet, *Les Maisons de l'Ordre de Cluny au Moyen Âge: Evolution et permanence d'un ancien ordre bénédictin au nord de Paris* (Bibliothèque de la *RHE* 76; 1990). G. de Valous in *DHGE* 13 (1956), cols. 35–174, with extensive bibl. N. Bulst and others in *Lexikon des Mittelalters*, 2 (1983), cols. 2172–94, s.v. 'Cluny, Cluniazenzer'. See also works cited under ODILO and PETER THE VENERABLE.

CMS. The 'Church Missionary Society', originally called the 'Society for Missions in Africa and the East', was founded in 1799 with Thomas *Scott (q.v.) as its first secretary. Though later in date than the *SPCK and the *SPG, it became the first C of E society to send missionaries to the indigenous populations of Africa and Asia. It did pioneering work in West, and later East, Africa, many parts of India, Pakistan and Bangladesh, Sri Lanka, China, Japan, and the Middle East. It also worked in its early years in Canada and New Zealand. The CMS of Australia, New Zealand, and Ireland are sister societies. The CMS fostered the development of autonomous Churches and now works in partnership with them. In 1993 it had *c*.200 mission partners in 27 countries and an annual budget of just over £4 million. From its earliest days its theology has been consistently *Evangelical. See also BCMS.

E. Stock, *The History of the Church Missionary Society* (3 vols., 1899; suppl. vol. 4, 1916). C. Hole, *The Early History of the Church Missionary Society for Africa and the East to the end of A.D. 1814* (1896). *The Centenary Volume of the Church Missionary Society for Africa and the East, 1799–1899* (1902). J. Murray, *Proclaim the Good News: A Short History of the Church Missionary Society* (1985). [G. H.] G. Hewitt, *The Problems of Success: A History of the Church Missionary Society 1910–1942* (2 vols., 1971–77). S. M. Johnstone, *A History of the Church Missionary Society in Australia and Tasmania* (Sydney, 1925). F. E. Bland, *How the Church Missionary Society came to Ireland* (Dublin, 1935). E. Elbourne, 'The foundation of the Church Missionary Society: the Anglican missionary impulse', in J. Walsh and others (eds.), *The Church of England c.1689–c.1833* (Cambridge, 1993), pp. 247–64. *The CMS News-Letter*, periodically from Dec. 1939. There is also a Register of Missionaries from 1804 to 1904, and Annual Reports of the Society from 1801 to 1970.

coadjutor-bishop. A bishop appointed to assist a diocesan bishop in his duties, often with the right of succession to the see at the next vacancy. The practice of appointing coadjutor-bishops is much followed in the RC Church, but seldom in the Anglican Communion, except in certain dioceses outside England, and in the *Episcopal Church of America, where it is a common practice.

coarb (Irish *comarba*, in early medieval Latin texts *heres*, but later *cuverbus* and variants). In Ireland, the 'heir' or successor of a saint who founded a church. Until *c.* the 12th cent. the coarb was head of the church and controlled the temporalities. He sometimes also held the office of abbot or bishop but was more often a layman. After the institution of the hierarchy in the 12th cent., the coarbial family generally remained as hereditary occupants of former ecclesiastical estates.

St J. D. Seymour, 'The coarb in the medieval Irish Church (*circa* 1200–1550)', *Proceedings of the Royal Irish Academy*, 41 (1932–4), C, pp. 219–31. J. Barry, 'The Appointment of Coarb and Erenagh', *Irish Ecclesiastical Record*, 5th ser. 93 (1960), pp. 361–5, with refs. to earlier arts.

Coat of Christ, Holy. See HOLY COAT.

Cocceius, Johannes (1603–69), Johann Koch, dogmatic theologian. Born in Bremen, where he studied under Matthias Martinius, in 1629 he moved to Franeker, where William *Ames and Sixtius Amama were amongst his teachers. He taught at Bremen from 1630 to 1636, when he returned to Franeker as Professor of Hebrew, adding a Chair in Theology in 1643. In 1650 he moved to *Leiden. In his works, which were grounded in considerable knowledge of oriental languages, he sought to expound dogmatic theology on a purely biblical basis; but although professedly a *Calvinist, he objected both to the Calvinist spirit and to the scholastic orthodoxy of his day. He interpreted the relation between God and man in terms of a personal covenant and his system thus became known as *Föderaltheologie*. After his death his followers were openly accused of unorthodoxy, and there seems little doubt that his teaching was a factor leading to the later growth of *Pietism. His most important treatise was his *Summa doctrinae de Foedere et Testamento Dei* (1648).

Collected works ed., with brief Life, by his son, J. H. Cocceius (8 vols., Amsterdam, 1673–5). G. Schrenk, *Gottesreich und Bund im älteren Protestantismus, vornehmlich bei Johannes Coccejus* (Beiträge zur Föderung christlicher Theologie, Reihe 5, Bd. 5; Gütersloh, 1923); H. Faulenbach, *Weg und Ziel der Erkenntnis Christi: Eine Untersuchung zur Theologie des Johannes Coccejus* (Beiträge zur Geschichte und Lehre der Reformierten Kirche, 36; Neukirchen [1973]). C. S. McCoy, 'Johannes Cocceius: Federal Theologian', *Scottish Journal of Theology*, 16 (1963), pp. 352–70. H. Faulenbach in *TRE* 8 (1981), pp. 132–40, s.v.

Cochlaeus, Johannes (1479–1552), RC controversialist. His real name was Dobeneck. He went to *Cologne in 1504, where he developed a distaste for *Scholasticism and a strong sympathy for the *Platonist and humanist revival of the Renaissance. In 1521 and the following years he was engaged in writing against M. *Luther, but the bitter tone of his polemic gained little favour even from his own side. In 1526 he accepted a canonry at Mainz, *c.*1534 at Meissen, and in 1539 at Breslau. He attended many of the conferences of the period, at which the points of difference between Catholics and Protestants were argued, but on these occasions his services were little used. His best-known works are *Historiae Hussitarum Libri XII* (1549) and *Commentaria de Actis et Scriptis M. Lutheri, 1517–1546* (1549). In 1525 he had made every endeavour to prevent the printing of W. *Tyndale's English New Testament at Cologne.

Life by M. Spahn (Berlin, 1898). H. Jedin, *Des Johannes Cochlaeus Streitschrift de libero arbitrio hominis (1525): Ein Beitrag zur Geschichte der vortridentinischen katholischen Theologie* (Breslauer Studien zur historischen Theologie, 9; 1927); A. Herte, *Die Lutherkommentare des Johannes Cochläus* (Reformationsgeschichtliche Studien und Texte, Heft 33; 1935); id., *Das katholische Lutherbild im Bann der Lutherkommentare des Cochläus* (3 vols., Münster, 1943); R. Bäumer, *Johannes Cochlaeus (1479–1552): Leben und Werk in Dienst der katholischen Reform* (ibid., 1980), with bibl. Id. in *TRE* 8 (1981), pp. 140–6, s.v.

co-consecrator. A bishop who assists the chief consecrator in the laying-on of hands at the making of a bishop. There should be at least two (cf. Conc. *Nic. [325], can. 4), though in the West the absence of an assistant is not deemed to invalidate the consecration. It is also a widely held belief among dogmatic theologians that all who lay hands are consecrators, so that, even assuming some defect in the chief consecrator, the consecration might still be valid.

Code of Holiness. See HOLINESS, CODE OF.

Codex Alexandrinus ('A'). The early 5th-cent. MS of the Greek Bible, written on vellum in two columns to the page, which Cyril *Lucar, then Patr. of *Constantinople, offered to *James I (1603–1625) through the English Ambassador, Sir Thomas Roe (d. 1644). The MS (now Royal MS 1 D. v–viii) did not reach England until after James's death. In 1757 it passed with the rest of the Royal Library to the newly founded British Museum, whence (1973) to the British Library. Its earlier history is obscure, but it was probably brought to *Alexandria from *Constantinople in 1308. In the Gospels the Codex is the earliest example of a *Byzantine text; in Acts and the Pauline Epistles it is late *Alexandrian. The order of the biblical Books is Gen., Exod., Lev., Num., Deut., Jos., Jgs., Ruth, 1 and 2 Sam., 1 and 2 Kgs., 1 and 2 Chron., the *Minor Prophets, Is., Jer., Bar., Lam., Epistle of Jeremy,

Ezek., Dan., Est., Tob., Judith, 1 and 2 Esd., 1–4 Macc., Pss., Job, Prov., Eccles., Song of Songs, Wisd., Ecclus.; Mt., Mk., Lk., Jn., Acts, Jas., 1 and 2 Pet., 1–3 Jn., Jude, Rom., 1 and 2 Cor., Gal., Eph., Phil., Col., 1 and 2 Thess., Heb., 1 and 2 Tim., Tit., Philem., and Rev. They are followed by the two (so-called) Epp. of *Clement.

The Codex Alexandrinus was one of the earliest of the uncial MSS to be made available to scholars. The first Ep. of Clement was ed. from it by P. *Young (Oxford, 1633). It was used by B. *Walton in the *Biblia Polyglotta* (6 vols., London, 1655–7). The OT was ed. J. E. *Grabe (2 vols., Oxford, 1707–20) and by H. H. Baber (3 vols., London, 1816–21). NT ed. C. G. Woide (ibid., 1786). Photographic edn. by E. M. Thompson (4 vols., ibid., 1879–83), with introd. in vol. 1, pp. 3–12; reduced photographic edn. by F. G. Kenyon, H. J. M. Milne, and T. C. Skeat (5 vols., ibid., 1909–1957), introd. to NT vol., pp. 5–11, and to OT, vol. 4, pp. 1–4. H. J. M. Milne and T. C. Skeat, *Scribes and Correctors of the Codex Sinaiticus* (1938), pp. 91–3 (app. 2) and pls. 10–43. B. M. Metzger, *The Text of the New Testament* (Oxford, 1964; 3rd edn., 1992), pp. 46 f.; K. and B. Aland, *Der Text des Neuen Testaments* (1982; 2nd edn., 1989; Eng. tr., Grand Rapids and Leiden, 1987; 2nd edn., 1989), *passim*.

Codex Amiatinus. The oldest extant MS of the Latin *Vulgate and a primary witness to the text. It was one of three Bibles written at either *Wearmouth or Jarrow under Abbot Ceolfrith between *c*.690 and 700. It has been calculated that the three copies required the skins of some 1,550 calves. In 716 Ceolfrith set out with the codex for Rome, intending to present it to *Gregory II, but he died at Langres on the way. From the 9th or 10th cent. the MS was in the monastery of Monte Amiata, hence its name. After the suppression of the monastery in 1782 it was transferred to the Laurentian Library at Florence. Fragments of one of the sister Bibles were discovered in 1909 and 1937 and are now in the British Library (Add. MSS 37777 and 45025 respectively); a further leaf discovered at Kingston Lacy House in Dorset in 1982 is on permanent deposit in the British Library (Loan MS 81; the 'Bankes Leaf').

The MS was used for the revision of the Vulgate for the Sixtine edn., pub. Rome, 1590, and its readings are noted in the Vatican edn. of 1926 ff. For the NT F. F. Fleck noted its readings in his edn. of the Vulgate NT (Leipzig, 1840), and it is the basis of the edn. of J. *Wordsworth, H. J. White, etc. (3 vols., Oxford, 1889–1954). The complete text of the NT was pub. by C. *Tischendorf (Leipzig, 1850; reissued, 1854). There is no complete edn. of the OT, but much of it is pr. in T. Heyse and C. Tischendorf (eds.), *Biblia Sacra Latina* (Leipzig, 1873). G. B. *de Rossi, *La Bibbia offerta da Coelfrido abbate al sepolcro di S. Pietro* (1888). P. Corssen, 'Die Bibeln des Cassiodorus und der Codex Amiatinus', *Jahrbücher für Protestantische Theologie*, 9 (1883), pp. 619–33. H. J. White, 'The Codex Amiatinus and its Birthplace', *Studia Biblica et Ecclesiastica*, 2 (Oxford, 1890), pp. 273–309. G. Schmid, 'Zur Geschichte des Codex Amiatinus', *Th.Q.* 89 (1907), pp. 577–84; A. Mercati, 'Per la storia del Codice Amiatino', *Biblica*, 3 (1922), pp. 324–8. B. Fischer, OSB, 'Bibelausgaben des frühen Mittelalters', *Settimane di Studio del Centro italiano di Studi sull'Alto Medioevo*, 10 (1963), pp. 519–600, esp. pp. 559–61. R. L. S. Bruce-Mitford, 'The Art of the Codex Amiatinus', *Journal of the British Archaeological Association*, 3rd ser. 32 (1969), pp. 1–25. E. A. Lowe, *English Uncial* (Oxford, 1960), pp. 8–13, with plates viii–x. Id., *Codices Latini Antiquiores*, 3 (ibid., 1938), p. 8 (no. 299); J. J. Alexander, *Insular Manuscripts, 6th to the 9th century* (A Survey of the Manuscripts Illuminated in the British Isles, 1; 1978), pp. 32–5 (no. 7), with bibl. See also bibl. to VULGATE.

Codex Bezae ('D'). This bilingual (Latin and Greek) MS of the Gospels (in the order Mt., Jn., Lk., Mk.,) and Acts, with a fragment of the Latin of 3 John, is important as the main uncial representative of the so-called *Western text (q.v.). Its peculiarity is its combination of certain omissions with extensive additions, esp. in Acts. The MS was written between the 4th and 6th cent. but little is known of its subsequent history. Some of its readings were reported to R. *Stephanus and included in the 3rd edition of his Greek New Testament of 1550. It came into the possession of T. *Beza, after whom it is named, and who in turn donated it to the University of Cambridge, where it is still. It is a small codex (10 in. by 8 in.) with Latin and Greek texts facing each other, arranged in 'sense lines' to facilitate comparison. The Latin is not, however, a direct translation of the Greek text. The Greek itself contains many blunders, and the work of several later correctors is evident. It is likely, therefore, to have come from a predominantly Latin-speaking area, but there is no certainty as to exact provenance; S. France, N. Africa, Italy, Sicily, and Phoenicia are possibilities.

Text first pub. by T. Kipling (2 vols., fol., Cambridge, 1793). Crit. edn., with introd. and notes, by F. H. A. *Scrivener (Cambridge, 1864). Photographic edn. in 2 vols., Cambridge, 1899. The readings of the Codex Bezae are noted by C. *Tischendorf in his edns. of the NT (Leipzig, 1841, etc.). J. R. *Harris, *A Study of the Codex Bezae* (Texts and Studies, 2, no. 1; Cambridge, 1891). F. H. Chase, *The Old Syriac Elements in the Text of the Codex Bezae* (1893). K. *Lake, 'On the Italian Origin of Codex Bezae. 1. Codex Bezae and Codex 1071', *JTS* 1 (1900), pp. 441–5. J. R. Harris, *The Annotators of the Codex Bezae* (1901). E. J. Epp, *The Theological Tendency of Codex Bezae Cantabrigiensis in Acts* (Cambridge, 1966). D. C. Parker, *Codex Bezae: An early Christian manuscript and its text* (ibid., 1992). J. D. Yoder, *Concordance to the Distinctive Greek Text of Codex Bezae* (New Testament Tools and Studies, 2; 1961).

Codex Canonum Ecclesiae Universae. Under this title C. Justel (1580–1649) published in 1610 an eclectic text which he believed to represent the 'official' canon law collection of the early Church, sanctioned by the Council of *Chalcedon (451) and later by the Emp. *Justinian (d. 565). It contained the canons of *Nicaea, *Ancyra, *Neocaesarea, *Gangra, *Antioch, *Laodicea, *Constantinople, *Ephesus, and *Chalcedon in a continuous sequence of 207 items in Greek, with his own Latin translation. It exercised some influence on later scholars, but rested on a number of misconceptions about the nature of the earliest canonical collections.

F. *Maassen, *Geschichte der Quellen und der Literatur des canonischen Rechts im Abendlande*, 1 (1870), pp. xxxix–xlii; J. Gaudemet, *Les Sources du droit de l'église en occident du ii⁰ au vii⁰ siècle* (1985), pp. 73–9.

Codex Ephraemi ('C'). A 5th-cent. Greek MS of the Bible now at *Paris (Bibl. Nationale, Gr. 9). In the 12th cent. it was converted into a *palimpsest by a covering of some of the writings of St *Ephraem Syrus. Only portions of the original MS have survived, and the text is not always decipherable; but every book of the NT except 2 Thess. and 2 Jn. is represented to some extent. In the

Gospels the text is fundamentally *Alexandrian, but it also contains a *Western element.

Text of NT (as much as could be deciphered) ed., with introd. by C. *Tischendorf, Leipzig, 1843; of OT, ibid., 1845. F. G. Kenyon, *Our Bible and the Ancient Manuscripts* (1895), pp. 137–9; rev. by A. W. Adams (1958), pp. 206 f. R. W. Lyon, 'A Re-examination of Codex Ephraemi Rescriptus', *New Testament Studies*, 5 (1959), pp. 260–72. B. M. Metzger, *The Text of the New Testament* (Oxford, 1964; 3rd edn., 1992), pp. 12 and 48 f. K. and B. Aland, *Der Text des Neuen Testaments* (1982; 2nd edn., 1989; Eng. tr., Grand Rapids and Leiden, 1987; 2nd edn., 1989), *passim*.

Codex Fuldensis. The Latin MS of the NT (*Fulda, Landesbibliothek, Bonifatianus I), written in 541–6 at the order of *Victor, Bp. of Capua. The four Gospels are arranged in a harmony, in the manner and order of *Tatian's '*Diatessaron', though the text has been revised to agree with that of the *Vulgate. Its early presence at Fulda and the identification of an annotating hand which is thought to be that of St *Boniface have led to the suggestion that it was once owned by him.

Text ed. E. Ranke (Marburg and Leipzig, 1868). H. J. Vogels, *Beiträge zur Geschichte des Diatessaron im Abendland* (Neutestamentliche Abhandlungen, 8, Heft 1; 1919), pp. 1–34. E. A. Lowe, *Codices Latini Antiquiores*, 8 (Oxford, 1959), p. 49 (no. 1196). M. B. Parkes, 'The Handwriting of St Boniface: A Reassessment of the Problems', *Beiträge zur Geschichte der Deutschen Sprache und Literatur*, 98 (1976), pp. 161–79. K. and B. Aland, *Der Text des Neuen Testaments*, (1982; 2nd edn. 1989; Eng. tr., Grand Rapids and Leiden, 1987; 2nd edn., 1989), *passim*.

Codex Iuris Canonici (CIC). The code of *canon law in force in the (Latin) RC Church at the present day. By the end of the 19th cent. the material of Roman canon law had become so unwieldy that in 1904 *Pius X appointed a commission under the direction of Cardinal Gasparri to collect and redact the canon law and produce a codex. The result of their labours, a comparatively small volume divided into five books and 2,414 canons, was promulgated by *Benedict XV on 27 May 1917, and came into force at *Pentecost in the following year. During the Second *Vatican Council a commission was set up to revise the 1917 codex; its work was much influenced by the Council. The codex promulgated by *John Paul II on 25 Jan. 1983 consists of seven books divided into 1,752 canons. On 2 Jan. 1984 a commission was set up to interpret the codex authoritatively. A separate codex for the *Uniat Churches was promulgated on 18 Oct. 1990, to come into force on 1 Oct. 1991. See also CANON LAW; CORPUS IURIS CANONICI.

Among the many comm. on the 1917 Codex, those in Eng. incl. Charles Augustine [Bachofen], OSB, *A Commentary on the New Code of Canon Law* (8 vols., St Louis and London, 1918–22); A. G. Cicognani, *Ius Canonicum* (Rome, 1925; rev. Eng. tr., *Canon Law*, Westminster, Md. [1934]); T. L. Bouscaren and A. C. Ellis, *Canon Law: A Text and Commentary* (Milwaukee [1946]; 4th edn., with F. N. Korth [1963]). J. A. Abbo and J. D. Hannan, *The Sacred Canons: A Concise Presentation of the Disciplinary Norms of the Church* (2 vols., St Louis and London, 1952; 2nd edn. [1960]). A. Vetulani and R. Naz in *DDC* 3 (1942), cols. 908–40, s.v., with bibl. D. Staffa in *EC* 3 (1949), cols. 1911–19, s.v., with further bibl.

The official text of the 1983 Codex is in *AAS* 75 (1983), part 2 (25 Jan.), with corrections in Appendix, 22 Sept. (separate pagination). An Eng. tr., prepared by the Canon Law Society of Great Britain and Ireland, in association with others, was pub. in 1983.

Comm. by J. A. Coriden, T. J. Green, and D. E. Heintschel (eds.), *The Code of Canon Law: A Text and Commentary* (1985). Further comm. ed. E. Caparros, M. Thériault, and J. Thorn, *Code of Canon Law Annotated* (Montreal, 1993; based on the Sp. comm. prepared under the auspices of the Instituto Martín de Azpilcueta of the University of Navarra in Pamplona, 5th edn., 1992). G. Sheehy and others (eds.), *The Canon Law: Letter & Spirit* (1995). The text of the 'Codex Canonum Ecclesiarum Orientalium' is pr. in *AAS* 82 (1990), pp. 1045–363. V. Pospishil, *Eastern Catholic Church Law according to the Code of Canons of the Eastern Churches* (Brooklyn, N.Y., 1993). A valuable account of the work of revision and authoritative interpretations are contained in the periodical *Communicationes* issued by the commission, now a council (Rome, 1969 ff.).

Codex Sinaiticus (ℵ). The celebrated MS of the Greek Bible (British Library, Add. MS 43725), discovered by C. *Tischendorf in the monastery of St Catherine on Mount *Sinai. On a visit in 1844 he found some leaves of the OT Books, and instantly recognized its great value. He was given 43 leaves which are now in Leipzig. On his third visit in 1859 he borrowed the MS and presented it to the Tsar of Russia. In 1869 this 'donation' was regularized. The Soviet Government sold it to the British Museum in 1933 for £100,000, nearly half of which was paid by public subscription. In 1975 15 leaves of Gen. were discovered in St Catherine's. Besides half the OT (1 Chron., Neh., Est., Tob., Judith, 1 Macc., 4 Macc., Is., Jer., Lam., Joel–Mal., Pss., Prov., Eccles., Song of Songs, Wisd., Ecclus., and Job), the MS contains the whole of the NT as well as the 'Ep. of *Barnabas' and part of the 'Shepherd' of *Hermas. It is written on vellum, four columns to the page (two columns in Pss., Prov., Eccles., Song of Songs, Wisd., Ecclus., and Job), and in quires of eight leaves. Three hands took part in the original writing, and the text has been revised by a number of correctors. Although the text seems to be Egyptian, it is quite uncertain where it was written, though it was in *Caesarea in Palestine in the 6th cent. Its date is probably about the middle of the 4th cent.

The NT text of the codex is closely allied to that of *Codex Vaticanus, together with which it is the chief witness to the *Neutral or *Alexandrian text. The MS exercised a decisive influence on the text of the '*Revised Version' of the NT of 1881, but less on recent editions.

Text ed. C. Tischendorf (4 vols., St Petersburg, 1862): two further frags. ed. id., *Appendix Codicum Celeberrimorum Sinaitici Vaticani Alexandrini* (Leipzig, 1867), pp. 3–6. Photographic edn. by H. and K. *Lake (2 vols., Oxford, 1911–22), with introd. by K. Lake. H. J. M. Milne and T. C. Skeat, *Scribes and Correctors of the Codex Sinaiticus* (1938). I. Ševčenko, 'New Documents on Constantine Tischendorf and the *Codex Sinaiticus*', *Scriptorium*, 18 (1964), pp. 55–80. *The British Library, Catalogue of Additions to the Manuscripts, 1931–1935* (1967), pp. 207–12. B. F. *Westcott and F. J. A. *Hort, *The New Testament in the Original Greek: Introduction* (1882), pp. 210–30 and 246–71. B. M. Metzger, *The Text of the New Testament* (Oxford, 1964; 3rd edn., 1992), pp. 42–6; K. and B. Aland, *Der Text des Neuen Testaments* (1982; 2nd edn., 1989; Eng. tr., Grand Rapids and Leiden, 1987, 2nd edn., 1989), *passim*. Popular account of its discovery in J. Bentley, *Secrets of Mount Sinai: The Story of Codex Sinaiticus* (1985).

Codex Vaticanus ('B'). The 4th-cent. MS of the Greek Bible, now in the *Vatican Library (Vat. gr. 1209), where its presence is certainly vouched for in the 1481 catalogue, ('Biblia in tribus columnis ex membranis in rubeo'), and probably in the 1475 catalogue ('Biblia ex membranis in rubeo'). Its earlier history is unknown. It was extensively restored in the 15th cent. Most of Gen. was copied from Chis. R VI 38 in the Vatican Library. Ps. 105: 27–137: 6, Heb. 9. 14–13: 25, and Rev. were copied from an unidentified MS. The *Pastorals are totally missing. T. C. Skeat conjectures that the restoration, which is unusual, was for presentation to a Pope, and the Council of *Florence would have been a suitable occasion for the Greeks to make such a presentation. With its nearest relative, P75 (see BODMER PAPYRI), and *Codex Sinaiticus, it is the chief witness to the *Neutral or *Alexandrian text.

The MS was the basis of the Sixtine edn. of the *Septuagint pub. Rome, 1587, and its successors. The complete text was ed. A. *Mai (5 vols., Rome, 1857); also ed., under the auspices of Pope *Pius IX, by C. Vercellone and J. Cozza (6 vols., Rome, 1869–1881). The NT was also ed., after Mai, by C. *Tischendorf (Leipzig, 1867, with appendix, 1869). Photographic edn. by J. Cozza-Luzi (5 vols. Rome, 1889–90); also in 4 vols., ibid., 1904–1907; NT in Codices e Vaticanis selecti, 30 (1968). H. J. M. Milne and T. C. Skeat, Scribes and Correctors of the Codex Sinaiticus (1938), pp. 87–91 (App. 1). J. Šagi, SJ, 'Problema historiae codicis B', Divus Thomas, 75 (Piacenza, 1972), pp. 3–29; T. C. Skeat, 'The Codex Vaticanus in the Fifteenth Century', JTS NS 35 (1984), pp. 454–65; B. F. *Westcott and F. J. A. *Hort, The New Testament in the Original Greek: Introduction (1882), pp. 210–46 and 250–70; B. M. Metzger, The Text of the New Testament (Oxford, 1964; 3rd edn., 1992), pp. 47 f.; K. and B. Aland, Der Text des Neuen Testaments (1982; 2nd edn., 1989; Eng. tr., Grand Rapids and Leiden, 1987; 2nd edn., 1989), passim.

Codrington, Christopher (1668–1710), soldier, poet, and colonial administrator. In 1690 he became a probationer-fellow of All Souls, Oxford, and varied his life in Oxford with military expeditions to Flanders. In 1699 he was appointed to succeed his father as Captain-General of the Leeward Islands, but he resigned his post after the failure of an expedition against Guadeloupe in 1703, and lived in retirement in Barbados until his death, studying Church history and metaphysics. In his will he left £10,000 and a large library to All Souls, and also bequeathed two estates, with part of Barbuda, to found in Barbados a college of physic and divinity, where the members were to live under vows of poverty, chastity, and obedience, and do missionary work in the West Indies. The provision for the threefold vow was disregarded, but Codrington Missionary Training College was built in 1714–42. From 1955 to 1969 it was run by the *Community of the Resurrection, which trained candidates for Ordination in the College.

V. T. Harlow, Christopher Codrington 1668–1710 (1928, repr., 1990). N. Langley, Christopher Codrington and his College (1964). A. Dobson in DNB 11 (1887), pp. 203 f.

Coelestis Urbs Jerusalem. Breviary hymn for the office of the dedication of a church. See URBS BEATA HIERUSALEM.

Coemgen, St. See KEVIN, ST.

Coenaculum. See CENACULUM.

coenobite (Gk. κοινόβιος, 'living in a community', from κοινός, 'common', and βίος, 'life' or 'way of life'). A religious in vows who lives in a community (as opposed to a *hermit). The word is by extension also used in a technical sense of *anchorites who occupy separate dwellings and observe a rule of silence, but live otherwise as a community of *monks in a common enclosure. This latter way of life originated in the desert and is now followed in the W. chiefly in the *Carthusian Order. See also LAVRA.

Coffin, Charles (1676–1749), hymn-writer. In 1712 he became principal of the Collège Dormans-Beauvais at Paris, and in 1718 rector of the University. In 1727 he published a collection of Latin hymns, many of which were adopted in the Paris Breviary of 1736. Several are well known in their English versions, e.g. 'On Jordan's bank the Baptist's cry', 'The Advent of our God', and 'O Holy Spirit, Lord of Grace'.

The majority of Coffin's hymns were pub. in his Hymni Sacri (Paris, 1736) and in the Hymnes du nouveau bréviaire de Paris (ibid., 1736, to which he was one of the contributors; this was ed. J. H. *Newman, Oxford, 1838). Collected edn. of his works pub. in 2 vols., Paris, 1755. Bremond, 10 (1932), pp. 70–7, 90 f., and 159–63.

cogito ergo sum (Lat., 'I think, therefore I am'). The primary datum of truth accepted by R. *Descartes in his method of doubt, on the ground that, however much a man doubted, he could never think away himself as the doubting subject.

Coke, Thomas (1747–1814), pioneer of *Methodist missions and bishop of the American Methodist Church. Driven out of his curacy at South Petherton in Somerset for his Methodist leanings in 1777, he became J. *Wesley's assistant and after his death (1791) a leading figure in the Wesleyan connexion. In 1784 Wesley 'ordained' him as Superintendent (or 'Bishop') of the Methodist Episcopal Church formed at a conference in Baltimore later that year. He divided his time thereafter between the rapidly growing American Church and the earliest *West Indian missions, which he initiated and sustained. He died at sea on his way to launch a mission to *India.

Collected edn. of his Journals (Dublin, 1816), with Life by J. Sutcliffe, pp. 1–32. Authorized Life by S. Drew (London, 1817). Full modern study by J. [A.] Vickers, Thomas Coke, Apostle of Methodism (1969).

Colbertine Breviary. A breviary compiled for the household of J. B. Colbert, Louis XIV's finance minister, and printed between 1675 and 1680. It had close affinities with the breviary of Cardinal F. de *Quiñones. It appears to have been the work of the Abbé J. Gallois (1632–1707).

Ed. from the British Library copy (C. 35. f. 21) by T. R. Gambier-Parry (HBS 42–43; 1912–13).

Colenso, John William (1814–83), Bp. of Natal. Born at St Austell, Cornwall, he was educated at St John's College, Cambridge, where he was elected a Fellow in 1837. In 1836 he became a mathematics master at Harrow, in 1842 returned to St John's as a tutor, and in 1846 became vicar of Forncett St Mary, Norfolk. In 1853 he was appointed the first Bishop of the newly constituted see of Natal, where he soon became keenly interested in the native problem and provoked criticism from the orthodox by his leniency in not insisting on the divorce of the wives of polygamists on their baptism. In 1861 he issued a Commentary on the Epistle to the Romans which by its denial of eternal punishment and rejection of much traditional sacramental theology aroused a storm of protest; still greater opposition was provoked by his papers on *The Pentateuch and the Book of Joshua Critically Examined* (in parts, 1862–79), challenging the traditional authorship and historical accuracy of these Books; and in 1863 he was declared deposed by his Metropolitan, Robert *Gray of Cape Town (Bp. 1847–72). Colenso, however, denied the Bp. of Cape Town's jurisdiction. He appealed to the *Judicial Committee of the Privy Council, which delivered sentence in his favour (20 Mar. 1865), on the ground that the Letters Patent appointing him preceded those appointing Gray. Hence, although solemnly excommunicated in 1866 by Gray, who in 1869 consecrated W. K. Macrorie (1831–1905) as Bp. of Maritzburg and Natal with a jurisdiction conterminous with that of Natal, Colenso maintained his position and by a series of judicial decisions secured the cathedral and endowments of the see. Though his attitude to the native question and some of his practical activities on their behalf (which were carried on after his death by his daughter Harriette, 1847–1932) continued to alienate many, esp. in Great Britain, he retained the affection of his diocese.

On his death his followers, styled 'the Church of England in Natal', applied to the Abps. of *Canterbury and *York for the consecration of a successor. In 1891 Macrorie resigned and after protracted negotiations all parties agreed that the Abp. of Canterbury should appoint a Bishop of Natal; and in 1893 the Archbishop consecrated A. H. Baynes (1854–1942). On his failure to reconcile the Church of St Paul's, Durban, Baynes resigned (1901), though the Vestry agreed to reunion in the following year. The schism in Natal was formally ended in 1911, when the Bp. of Natal recovered the endowments of which Colenso had been registered proprietor.

Much relevant material in the correspondence of his wife, F. Colenso, *Colenso Letters from Natal* arranged with comments by W. Rees (Pietermaritzburg, 1958). Life by G. W. Cox (2 vols., London, 1888). Modern study by P. [B.] Hinchliff (ibid., 1964). J. [J.] Guy, *The Heretic: A Study of the Life of John William Colenso 1814–1883* (Johannesburg and Pietermaritzburg, 1983). J. [W.] Rogerson, *Old Testament Criticism in the Nineteenth Century: England and Germany* (1984), pp. 220–37. See also bibl. to SOUTH AFRICA, CHRISTIANITY IN.

Coleridge, John Taylor (1790–1876), the biographer of J. *Keble. He was a nephew of S. T. *Coleridge. In 1809 he was elected a scholar of Corpus Christi College, Oxford, and from 1812 to 1818 was a Fellow of Exeter. After leaving Oxford he became a barrister of the Middle Temple. In 1832 he was appointed Recorder of *Exeter and from 1835 to 1858 was a Justice of the King's Bench. A keen Churchman, he published in 1869 his biography of J. Keble (d. 1866), whose lifelong friend he had been.

[B. J. S.] Coleridge, *The Story of a Devonshire House* (1905), esp. chs. 10–19.

Coleridge, Samuel Taylor (1772–1834), poet and thinker. He was born at Ottery St Mary, Devonshire, where his father was vicar. He was educated at Christ's Hospital and Jesus College, Cambridge, but left the university in 1793, probably on account of debts and a love affair. After a short-lived attempt to join the 15th Dra-

goons, he returned to Cambridge for a time but took no degree. In 1795 he married Sarah Fricker, and in the same year made the acquaintance of W. *Wordsworth. After some unsuccessful publishing ventures he thought of taking up the career of a *Unitarian minister, with which sect he had come into contact at Cambridge, but gave up the plan when Josiah and Thomas Wedgwood settled an annuity on him. In 1798 he published, in conjunction with Wordsworth, the *Lyrical Ballads*, his most famous contribution being 'The Ancient Mariner'. In the same year he went to Germany to study the *Kantian philosophy. The chief fruit of the journey was his brilliant translation of F. Schiller's *Wallenstein* (1800). During the next years he wrote his last great poems, among them the second part of 'Christabel' (1800) and the 'Ode to Dejection' (1802). From that time his poetic powers declined, possibly under the influence of his growing addiction to opium. After travelling in Malta (1804) and Italy (1805–6), he lectured in London on Shakespeare and other poets with considerable success (1810–13), and in 1813 had his tragedy 'Remorse' produced at Drury Lane. In 1816 he made a partly successful effort at conquering the opium habit, and in the same year published a volume of poems containing 'Christabel', 'Kubla Khan', and 'Pains of Sleep'. Also in 1816 appeared his *Lay Sermons* and in 1817 *Sibylline Leaves* and *Biographia Literaria*. *On the Constitution of Church and State* (1830) and the popular *Aids to Reflection* (1825) are among his most important religious publications. They were followed by the posthumous *Confessions of an Enquiring Spirit* (1840).

Coleridge's religious development partly reflects the trends of his time. After the rationalistic influences of his school-days and the Unitarian leanings of his early manhood he came under the sway of the *pantheism of J. *Boehme and B. *Spinoza, which had been revived by J. W. Goethe and other German thinkers. It was so congenial to his nature that he never seems to have really abandoned it, even in his avowedly Christian period, dating from *c*.1810. He preached the need of man for a spiritual interpretation of life and the universe against a fossilized Protestant orthodoxy as well as against the materialistic and rationalist trends of his time; but his thirst for freedom in every department of life frequently led him beyond the boundaries of the Christian revelation. His denial of any inherent opposition between the development of modern science and the essence of Christianity showed an insight rare in his time; but he refused to admit metaphysical proofs of religious truth and only conceded the pragmatic test of its beneficent influence on human life. This conviction, that Christianity is primarily ethical, led him to believe in the possibility of a unification of Christendom on a wide basis of common tenets; it earned him the title of 'Father of the Broad Church Movement'.

Complete Works, ed. W. G. T. Shedd (7 vols., New York, 1853); modern edn. by K. Coburn and others (16 vols., London and New York, 1969 ff.). The best edns. of his *Poetical Works* are those of J. D. Campbell (London and New York, 1893) and E. H. Coleridge (grandson, 2 vols., Oxford, 1912). *Collected Letters*, ed. E. L. Griggs (6 vols., Oxford, 1956–71); *Notebooks*, ed. K. Coburn (3 vols. in 6, London, 1957–73). The standard biography is the Life by J. D. Campbell (London, 1894). Other Lives and studies by E. K. Chambers (Oxford, 1938), L. Hanson (on his early years, London, 1938), H. House (ibid., 1953), M. Carpenter (ibid., 1954), J. B. Beer (ibid., 1959 and 1977),

J. Colmer (Oxford, 1959), M. Suther (New York, 1960), N. Fruman (ibid., 1971, London, 1972), and B. Willey (London, 1972). R. W. Armour and R. F. Howes (eds.), *Coleridge the Talker: A Series of Contemporary Descriptions and Comments* (Ithaca, NY, and London, 1940). E. Blunden and E. L. Griggs (eds.), *Coleridge: Studies by Several Hands on the Hundredth Anniversary of his Death* (1934); J. [B.] Beer (ed.), *Coleridge's Variety: Bicentenary Studies* (1974). R. Holmes, *Coleridge: Early Visions* (1989). J. Livingston Lowes, *The Road to Xanadu* (1927). T. McFarland, *Coleridge and the Pantheist Tradition* (Oxford, 1969). C. R. Sanders, *Coleridge and the Broad Church Movement* (Durham, NC, 1942), pp. 19–88; J. D. Boulger, *Coleridge as Religious Thinker* (New Haven, Conn., 1961); J. R. Barth, SJ, *Coleridge and Christian Doctrine* (Cambridge, Mass., 1969), and other works of this author. G. N. G. Orsini, *Coleridge and German Idealism: A Study in the History of Philosophy with Unpublished Materials from Coleridge's Manuscripts* (Carbondale, Ill., and London [1969]). E. S. Shaffer, *'Kubla Khan' and The Fall of Jerusalem: The Mythological School in Biblical Criticism and Secular Literature, 1770–1880* (1975), esp. pp. 17–190; S. Prickett, *Romanticism and Religion: The Tradition of Coleridge and Wordsworth in the Victorian Church* (Cambridge, 1976), pp. 9–69; L. S. Lockridge, *Coleridge the Moralist* (Ithaca, NY, and London, 1977); C. Welch in N. Smart and others (eds.), *Nineteenth Century Religious Thought in the West*, 2 (1985), pp. 1–28. G. [C. D.] Davidson, *Coleridge's Career* (1990). R. Gravil and M. Lefebure (eds.), *The Coleridge Connection: Essays for Thomas McFarland* (1990). J. L. Haney, *A Bibliography of Samuel Taylor Coleridge* (Philadelphia, 1903); T. J. Wise, *A Bibliography of the Writings in Prose and Verse of Samuel Taylor Coleridge* (London, 1913); id., *Coleridgeana: Being a Supplement to the Bibliography of Coleridge* (ibid., 1919; the two works are repr. in one vol., 1970); R. Haven and others, *Samuel Taylor Coleridge: An Annotated Bibliography of Criticism and Scholarship* (Boston, Mass., and London, 1976 ff.). L. Stephen in *DNB* 11 (1887), pp. 302–16.

Colet, John (1466?–1519), Dean of *St Paul's. The son of Sir Henry Colet, who had been twice Lord Mayor of London, he studied probably at Magdalen College, *Oxford, and later in Paris and Italy, where he learned Greek. He returned *c.*1497 to Oxford, where he delivered a series of lectures on St Paul's Epistles, notable for their critical spirit and their plea for a return to the discipline of the primitive Church. From this time onwards he constantly inveighed against the worldliness of the higher clergy, pluralities, and non-residence, and, though he never challenged the traditional dogmas of the Church, he was frequently suspected of heresy. His opinions were very sympathetically received by his two famous friends, *Erasmus (to whom he later paid an annuity) and Sir Thomas *More. From 1504 till his death he was Dean of St Paul's. On his father's death he received a large fortune, part of which he spent, in the face of opposition, in re-founding St Paul's School, where 153 boys, without restriction of nationality, could gain the rudiments of education, be brought up in a sound Christian way, and learn Greek as well as Latin (first High Master of the School, William Lilly).

His *Opus de Sacramentis Ecclesiae* ed. as 'A Treatise on the Sacraments of the Church' (1867), *Super Opera Dionysii* as 'Two Treatises on the Hierarchies of Dionysius' (1869), *Enarratio in Epistolam S. Pauli ad Romanos* as 'An Exposition on St Paul's Epistle to the Romans' (1873), *Enarratio in Primam Epistolam S. Pauli ad Corinthios* as 'An Exposition on St Paul's First Epistle to the Corinthians' (1874), *Opuscula Quaedam Theologica* as 'Letters to Radulphus on the Mosaic Account of the Creation, together with other Treatises' (1876), all ed. for the first time with Eng. tr., introd., and notes by J. H. Lupton. Edn. and Eng. tr. of his

marginal comm. to the first edn. of M. *Ficino's *Epistolae* (1495), letters and certain other material by S. Jayne (Oxford, 1963). Comm. on 1 Cor. also ed., with Eng. tr. and introd., by B. O'Kelly and C. A. L. Jarrott (Medieval and Renaissance Texts and Studies, 21; Binghamton, NY, 1985). J. H. Lupton (ed. and tr.), *The Lives of Jehan Vitrier . . . and John Colet . . . written . . . by Erasmus in a Letter to Justus Jonas* (1883). Id., *A Life of John Colet* (1887); id., *The Influence of Dean Colet upon the Reformation of the English Church* (1893). J. A. R. Marriott, *The Life of John Colet* (1933); E. W. Hunt, *Dean Colet and his Theology* (1956); L. Miles, *John Colet and the Platonic Tradition* (La Salle, Ill., 1961; London, 1962); J. B. Gleason, *John Colet* [1989]. *BRUO* 1 (1957), pp. 462–4. S. L. Lee in *DNB* 11 (1887), pp. 321–8.

Colettines. A branch of the *Poor Clares founded by St Colette (1381–1447), a native of *Corbie in Picardy who was canonized in 1807 (Feast day, 6 Mar.). She established seventeen convents in her lifetime. Today the Colettine Sisters are found mainly in France.

U. d'Alençon, OM Cap. (ed.), 'Documents sur la Réforme de Ste. Colette en France', *AFH* 2 (1909), pp. 447–56, 600–12; 3 (1910), pp. 82–97; id. (ed.), 'Lettres inédites de Guillaume de Casal à Sainte Colette de Corbie et notes pour la biographie de cette sainte', *Études Franciscaines*, 19 (1908), pp. 460–81, 668–91. J. [G. A.] Goulven, *Rayonnement de Sainte Colette* (1952), esp. pt. 2; E. Lopez, *Culture et sainteté: Colette de Corbie (1381–1447)* (Saint-Etienne, 1994). S. Roisin in *DHGE* 13 (1956), cols. 238–46, s.v. 'Colette de Corbie'; G. Odoardi, OFM, in *DIP* 2 (1975), cols. 1211–7, s.v. 'Colettani', both with bibl.

Coligny, Gaspard de (1519–72), *Huguenot leader. A member of one of the greatest families in France, he spent much of his life at court and in the service of the French Army. He was converted to *Calvinism in 1560, and after the death of the Prince de Condé in 1569 became the recognized leader of the Huguenot cause. His influence at court over the young King, Charles IX, led France to aid the Netherlands in their revolt against the Duke of Alva. The queen mother, *Catherine de' Medici, who was a keen Catholic and also jealous of Coligny's position, tried to have him assassinated on 22 Aug. 1572; and when that had failed, provoked the Massacre of St *Bartholomew two days later, in which he was killed.

J. Delabore, *Gaspard de Coligny, amiral de France* (3 vols., 1879–82); A. W. Whitehead, *Gaspard de Coligny, Admiral of France* (1904). J. Shimizu, *Conflict of Loyalties: Politics and Religion in the Career of Gaspard de Coligny* (Travaux d'Humanisme et Renaissance, 114; Geneva, 1970). *Actes du Colloque l'Amiral de Coligny et son temps (Paris, 24–28 octobre 1972)* (1974). M. Prévost in *DHGE* 13 (1956), cols. 248 f., s.v. See also works cited s.v. BARTHOLOMEW, MASSACRE OF ST.

collation. The word is used in several senses, secular and ecclesiastical. Among the latter are: (1) the light meal allowed on days of *fasting in addition to the one full meal (the 'comestio'); (2) the lives of the *Fathers, esp. as arranged for reading in monasteries. This usage perhaps derives from the title of John *Cassian's 'Collationes Patrum', a record of his conversations with the hermits of the Egyptian deserts; and (3) *institution to an ecclesiastical benefice when the *ordinary is himself the patron (i.e. when presentation and institution are one and the same act).

collect (Lat. *oratio*, also *collecta*). The short form of prayer, constructed (with many varieties of detail) from (1) an invocation, (2) a petition, and (3) a pleading of Christ's name or an ascription of glory to God; and one of the most characteristic items in the W. liturgy. The prayers later known as *Secrets and *Postcommunions are structurally indistinguishable, though the term 'collect' is normally confined to the prayer (or prayers) in the Eucharistic rite which immediately precedes the lections. The writings of Pope *Leo I show that such prayers were familiar in the middle of the 5th cent. They are fully developed in the earliest Latin *Sacramentaries (*Leonine, *Gelasian, *Gregorian). They also secured an established place in the daily *offices as well as in the Eucharist. Early collects were always directed to the Father; but since the Middle Ages collects addressed to the Son have been regularly admitted to the liturgy.

The term 'collect' (*collecta*) was orig. a title in the *Gallican rite. It denoted, as B. *Capelle (after *Walafrid Strabo) has shown, the 'collecting' of the petitions of the several members of the congregation into a single prayer (cf. Synod of *Agde, AD 506, can. 30). This sense of the word is thus not connected with the use of *collecta* for the assembly ('collection') of the congregation for worship, as has often been supposed.

Since the Middle Ages it has been the practice on certain days other than the Greater Feasts to recite more than one collect in the liturgy. In the Latin rite the choice and number of the additional collects followed elaborate rules: e.g. when two feasts of not widely different rank occurred on the same day, the inferior feast was normally commemorated by a second collect, while on days of relatively less importance, there were usually three collects. The Secrets and Postcommunions always corresponded in number and in general content with the collects. In the revisions of the liturgy after the Second *Vatican Council, however, all *commemorations have been abolished.

The collects in the BCP mostly derive from the medieval sources, esp. the *Sarum Missal and Breviary. Several, however, were T. *Cranmer's original compositions (e.g. those for Advent 1 and 2), while the wording of many which have a Latin basis was freely modified and adapted, to give a good English rhythm. In 1662 a few further collects were provided (e.g. those for Epiphany 6, for which the earlier forms of the BCP had made no provision, and Advent 3). At Mattins and Evensong two unalterable collects are provided for recitation after the collect for the day daily throughout the year.

Jungmann (1949), 1, pp. 445–81; Eng. tr. (1951), pp. 359–90 (full discussion with bibl. refs.). B. Capelle, OSB, 'Collecta', *R. Bén.* 42 (1930), pp. 197–204, repr. in his *Travaux liturgiques*, 2 (1962), pp. 192–203; O. Casel, OSB, 'Beiträge zu römischen Orationen', *JLW* 11 (1931), pp. 35–45; G. G. Willis, *Further Essays in Early Roman Liturgy* (Alcuin Club Collections, 50; 1968), pp. 91–131 ('The Variable Prayers in the Roman Mass'), esp. pp. 91–121. B. Capelle, OSB, in *RAC* 1 (1957), cols. 243–5, s.v. 'Collecta'.

On the collects in the BCP, M. R. Dudley, *The Collect in Anglican Liturgy: Texts and Sources 1549–1989* (Alcuin Club Collections, 72; Collegeville, Minn. [1994]).

Collectar (Lat. *Collectarium*). A medieval liturgical book containing the collects used in the Divine *offices.

Collegialism. A term applied (prob. first by J. H. Boehmer of Halle, d. 1745) to the thesis esp. associated

with H. *Grotius (1583–1645) and S. *Pufendorf (1632–94) that Church and State are both purely voluntary associations (*collegia*) in which supreme authority rests with the body of the members, and that the civil magistrate has no other relations with the Church than those which he enjoys with every other voluntary association within his territory.

collegiality. A word used in a theological context to signify that bishops constitute a body, of which each is a part, and not a mere collection of individuals. The term *collegium* was applied to bishops corporately by *Cyprian (*Ep.* 68), and the idea was prominent in writings on the *Conciliar theory. The Dogmatic Constitution *Lumen Gentium* of the Second *Vatican Council states that the bishops form an *ordo* analogous to the single apostolic college of *Peter and the other apostles. This *ordo* includes within it the Roman Pontiff, whose primacy, as the successor of St Peter, remains intact. To some extent the concept found expression in the establishment of the Synod of Bishops by *Paul VI in *Apostolica Sollicitudo* (15 Sept. 1965). The Synod, which consists predominantly of representatives of national episcopal conferences, is charged with advising the Pope on matters of importance to the whole Church; assemblies are normally summoned by the Pope at about three-yearly intervals.

J. Lécuyer, C.S.Sp., *Études sur la collégialité épiscopale* (1964); Y. M.-J. *Congar, OP (ed.), *La Collégialité épiscopale: Histoire et théologie* (Unam Sanctam, 52; 1965). M. J. Le Guillou, OP, 'L'expérience orientale de la collégialité épiscopale et ses requêtes', *Istina*, 10 (1964), pp. 111–24.

Collegiants. An obscure offshoot of the *Remonstrants (q.v.), founded in the *Netherlands *c.*1619, and so called because they termed their communities 'colleges'. They were also known as 'Rynsburgers' from Rynsburg, near *Leiden, where they held their early meetings. They held that the Church was an invisible society and every externally constituted Church a corruption. Apart from the belief that Christ was the Messiah and the Bible inspired Scripture, they admitted no confession of faith or organized ministry. Their theology in general was very liberal and their ethics pietistic. *Baptism was generally administered by *immersion when each year the whole sect met at Rynsburg for prayer, study and a commemoration of the Last Supper. At the end of the 17th cent. they were influenced by the views of B. *Spinoza (who resided at Rynsburg 1661–4), over whose teaching there were divisions within the sect. The sect seems to have died out towards the end of the 18th cent., when most of its adherents were absorbed in the Remonstrants or the *Mennonites.

J. C. Van Slee, *De Rijnsburger Collegianten* (1895). A. Fix, 'Radical Reformation and Second Reformation in Holland', *Sixteenth Century Journal*, 18 (1987), pp. 63–80. N. van der Zijpp in H. S. Bender and others (eds.), *The Mennonite Encyclopedia*, 1 (1955), pp. 639 f., s.v.

Collegiate Church. A church which is endowed for a body of canons and/or prebendaries (the 'chapter'), but is not, like a *cathedral, a bishop's see. Instances in the C of E are *Westminster Abbey and St George's Chapel, *Windsor.

Collier, Jeremy (1650–1726), English *Nonjuror. In 1685 he was made lecturer of Gray's Inn. He was detained in Newgate without trial for some months in 1689 for writing one of the earliest and most influential attacks on the Revolution, *The Desertion Discuss'd*, and in 1692 his refusal to accept bail led to a further period of imprisonment on the charge of corresponding with *James II. In 1696 he was outlawed for giving absolution on the scaffold to two attempted assassins of William III, but returned to London in 1697. For some years he wrote frequent attacks on the stage of his day, the best known being *A Short View of the Immorality and Profaneness of the English Stage* (1698; facsimile repr. 1971); these provoked angry replies from W. Congreve and others. In 1713 he was consecrated as a 'bishop of the Nonjurors', and joined in their attempt at reunion with the Orthodox Church. He was also largely responsible for the production of the Nonjurors' Communion Office of 1718. This rite, which in some matters followed that of 1549, influenced the Scottish Liturgies of 1764 and 1929. His many writings include *An Ecclesiastical History of Great Britain* (2 vols., fol., 1708–14).

Life by T. Lathbury in his edn of *An Ecclesiastical History of Great Britain*, 9 (1852), pp. i–xlviii. R. Anthony, SC, *The Jeremy Collier Stage Controversy, 1698–1726* (Milwaukee, Wis., 1937); K. Ressler, 'Jeremy Collier's Essays', in *Seventeenth Century Studies*, ed. R. Shafer, 2nd ser. (Princeton, NJ, 1937), pp. 179–285. W. Hunt in *DNB* 11 (1887), pp. 341–7.

Collins, Anthony (1676–1729), *Deist. He was a native of Heston, Greater London, and educated at Eton and King's College, Cambridge. He subsequently lived in London until 1715, when he settled in Essex and became deputy-lieutenant. He was greatly influenced by J. *Locke, of whom he was an intimate friend, and his works are an epitome of English freethinking. In his first important publication, an *Essay Concerning the Use of Reason* (1707), he opposed the traditional distinction between things that are above and those that are against human reason. In *Priestcraft in Perfection* (1709) he tried to prove that the clause in Art. 20 of the *Thirty-Nine Articles on the power of the Church to decree rites and ceremonies and to decide religious controversies had been inserted by fraud. His principal work, *A Discourse of Freethinking* (1713), contains bitter attacks on the ministers of all denominations. It argued that free inquiry was the only means of attaining to the truth and was commanded by Scripture. The book, which was designed as a defence of Deism, was attacked by many Churchmen, among them R. *Bentley, B. *Hoadly, J. *Swift, and W. *Whiston. In 1715 he published his *Inquiry Concerning Human Liberty*, a concise and able statement of *Determinism, which was sharply attacked by S. *Clarke. In his *Discourse of the Grounds and Reasons of the Christian Religion* (1724) he denied that the OT contains prophecies of Christ. As he held fulfilled prophecies to be the only valid proof of the truth of Christianity, the book was intended as an implied rejection of it. He also denied the canonicity of the NT, as well as the immateriality and immortality of the soul.

Study by J. O'Higgins, SJ (International Archives on the History of Ideas, 35; The Hague, 1970). L. Stephen in *DNB* 11 (1887), pp. 363 f. See also DEISM.

Colloquy of Marburg. See MARBURG, COLLOQUY OF.

Colluthus (4th cent.), schismatic priest of *Alexandria. During the episcopate of St *Alexander (312–28) he assumed the power of conferring orders, though only a presbyter. In 324 he was deposed at the Council convened at Alexandria by *Hosius to deal with the *Arian issue (though Colluthus himself does not seem to have supported Arius). Nothing is known of his subsequent history. Some scholars have found in his career support for the view that in its early days ordination in the Alexandrian Church was conferred by presbyters.

The authorities include *Athanasius, *Apol. c. Arianos*, 12 and 75; *Epiphanius, *Haer.* 69. 2; *Theodoret, *HE* 1. 8; and *Augustine, *Haer.* 65. B. I. Pheidas, Τὸ Κολλουθιανὸν σχίσμα καὶ αἱ ἀρχαὶ τοῦ 'Αρειανισμοῦ (Athens, 1973). Brief art. by G. *Salmon in *DCB* 1 (1877), p. 596, s.v.

Collyridians. A 4th-cent. sect, mentioned by St *Epiphanius (*Haer.* 79). Acc. to him it originated in Thrace and consisted mostly of women, who offered an idolatrous cult to the BVM. They sacrificed cakes (κολλυρίς, hence the name) to her, which they afterwards consumed. The custom may have originated in connection with the popularization of the title '*Theotokos', and been influenced by the pagan habit of offering cakes to the goddess Ceres.

Brief notice by G. Bareille in *DTC* 3 (1908), cols. 369 f., s.v.

Colman, St (d. 676), leader of the *Celtic party in Northumbria. A native of Ireland, he became a monk of *Iona, and later (661) succeeded St *Finan as Bp. of *Lindisfarne. Here he supported the king, Oswiu, in maintaining Celtic customs against the Romanizing party in the court, headed by Eanfleda, Oswiu's Kentish queen. To settle the quarrel, Oswiu summoned the Synod of *Whitby in 664, at which Colman pleaded for the retention of such customs as the Celtic time of keeping Easter and the Celtic tonsure and appealed to the authority of St *Columba. St *Wilfrid, however, who claimed for the Roman practices the authority of St Peter, finally won the king over to his side. Colman then left Lindisfarne and passed the rest of his life at the monastery of Innisboffin, Co. Mayo. Feast day, 18 Feb.

The primary authority is *Bede, *HE* 3. 25 f., and 4. 4; comm. by J. M. Wallace-Hadrill (Oxford, 1988), pp. 125 f. and 128–30. W. Hunt in *DNB* 11 (1887), pp. 389 f.

Cologne. The see was founded in or before the reign of *Constantine (d. 337), and the city occupied by the Franks at intervals from 330 onwards. In the 11th–12th cents. the Abps. of Cologne became important secular princes and later (1356) were recognized as imperial electors. The see remained politically important until 1801, when its property was secularized, though the archbishopric was restored in 1821. The present cathedral dates from the 13th–15th and the 19th cents., and contains the shrine of the *Magi. Among other famous churches of the town are St Maria in Kapitol and St Gereon's, both built in the 11th cent. (both badly damaged in the Second World War; since largely restored).

There is a very large literature on the subject in its many aspects—topography, archbishopric, cathedral, churches, university, and schools. Modern works on the archbishopric incl. R. Knipping and others (eds.), *Die Regesten der Erzbischöfe von Köln im Mittelalter* (Publikationen der Gesellschaft für Rheinische

Geschichtskunde, 21; 4 vols., Bonn, 1901–61); W. Neuss (ed.), *Geschichte des Erzbistums Köln* (1964 ff.; 2nd edn. by F. W. Oediger and others, 1972 ff.). R. Haass and J. Hoster (eds.), *Zur Geschichte und Kunst im Erzbistum Köln: Festschrift für Wilhelm Neuss* (Studien zur Kölner Kirchengeschichte, 5; Düsseldorf, 1960), and other vols. in this series (1952 ff.). P. Berglar and O. Engels (eds.), *Der Bischof in seiner Zeit: Bischofstypus und Bischofsideal im Spiegel der Kölner Kirche. Festgabe für Joseph Kardinal Höffner, Erzbischof von Köln* (1986). A. Franzen in *DHGE* 13 (1956), cols. 275–311, s.v.; R. Lill in *NCE* 3 (1967), pp. 1013–18, s.v.; W. Janssen and others in *TRE* 19 (1990), pp. 289–305; P. Noelke and others in *Lexikon des Mittelalters*, 5 (1991), cols. 1254–68, these last both s.v. 'Köln'.

Colombini, Bl Giovanni (1304–67), founder of the *Gesuati. A wealthy wool-merchant who came from an old patrician family of Siena, he was deeply moved by reading the Life of St *Mary of Egypt when he was about 50. From that time he devoted himself to the service of the poor and the sick, many of whom he received into his house. After eight years of this life he persuaded his wife to accept a separation, settled an annuity on her, distributed the rest of his property to several religious institutions, and, together with his friend Francisco Mini, led a life of evangelical poverty, prayer, and works of mercy. When his example was imitated by many young men from noble Sienese families, the authorities of the city exiled him. With 25 followers he visited several Italian towns, and by his preaching and example effected a great number of conversions. When soon afterwards an epidemic broke out in Siena, it was regarded as a punishment, and Colombini was called back. In 1367 he and his disciples were formally constituted by *Urban V into the congregation of the Gesuati, and he died shortly after. He was beatified by *Gregory XIII. Feast day, 31 July.

Letters ed. A. Bartoli (Lucca, 1856); later ed. P. Cherubelli (Siena, 1957). Short Life by Bl John Tossignano (d. 1446), pr. by J. D. *Mansi (ed.), *Stephani Baluzii ... Miscellanea*, 4 (Lucca, 1764), pp. 566–71. Life by F. Belcari (Florence [*c.*1480]), ed. R. Chiarini (Arezzo, 1904); Eng. tr. from edns. of 1541 and 1832 (London, 1874). Life by J. B. Rossi, SJ (Rome, 1646), pr. in *AASS*, Jul. 7 (1731), pp. 354–98. Modern Life by the Comtesse de Rambuteau (3rd edn., Paris, 1893). G. Pardi, 'Della vita e degli scritti di Giovanni Colombini da Siena', *Bullettino Senese di Storia Patria*, 2 (1895), pp. 1–50 and 202–30, with docs.; id., 'Il Beato Colombini da Siena', *Nuova Rivista Storica*, 11 (1927), pp. 287–336. A. M. Piazzoni in *Dizionario Biografico degli Italiani*, 27 (1982), pp. 149–53, s.v. See also bibl. to GESUATI.

Colonial and Continental Church Society. See CCCS.

Colonial Clergy Act 1874. The Act which regulated the conditions under which those ordained to the Anglican ministry in the British colonies could receive preferment or officiate in public in Great Britain. The written permission of the archbishop of the English province and a Declaration of *Assent in terms similar to that provided for in the *Clerical Subscription Act 1865 were required. It was superseded by the *Overseas and Other Clergy (Ministry and Ordination) Measure (No. 3) 1967.

Colonna family. A distinguished Roman family which has played a considerable part in Papal and European politics, esp. between the 12th and 18th cents. The Colonnas were vassals of the Pope, but their political leanings in the Middle Ages were mostly Ghibelline and pro-Imperial. They were the hereditary adversaries of the Orsini family. The Colonnas gave a number of cardinals to the Church, the first being the Benedictine monk, Giovanni Colonna (d. 1216), who was created cardinal in 1193 by Pope *Celestine III. A protector of the *Franciscan Order, he was praised for his virtues by St *Bonaventure. His nephew, also called Giovanni (d. 1245), was made cardinal in 1212. He took part in the conquest of Damietta (1219) during the Fifth Crusade, and later assisted the Emp. *Frederick II against the Pope. His nephew Giacomo (d. 1318) was created cardinal in 1278 by Nicholas III, of the house of Orsini, who hoped by this step to reconcile the two hostile families. Together with his nephew Pietro he bitterly opposed *Boniface VIII, who in 1297 deprived both cardinals of their dignity, excommunicated the whole family, and seized their property. They were reinstated by *Clement V in 1305. The family, which continued to be given cardinalates by the Popes in the 14th cent., received fresh distinction through the election of one of its members, Oddo, to the Papacy (1417), who, as *Martin V, ended the W. schism in 1429. After continued strife with the Orsini in the latter half of the 15th cent., a reconciliation was effected in the 16th, for the perpetuation of which *Sixtus V arranged a marriage between the two houses. The most famous woman of the family was Vittoria Colonna (1490–1547); remarkable alike for her literary talents and for her gift of attracting the finest spirits of her time, among them esp. *Michelangelo. She was deeply interested in the reform of the Church, and probably at one time leant towards the Reformation, but her connection with Card. R. *Pole kept her faithful to the Catholic Church. Among the later members of the family were Marcantonio (d. 1584), who took part in the victory of *Lepanto (1571), and his learned namesake (d. 1597), who was appointed head of the Commission of the *Vulgate by Sixtus V and librarian of the Vatican by *Clement VIII.

P. Colonna, *I Colonna dalle origini all'inizio del secolo XIX* (1927); P. Paschini, *I Colonna* (Rome, 1955). 29 members of the family are treated by G. Mollat and others in *DHGE* 13 (1956), cols. 328–40, s.v., and 76 members of the family in *Dizionario Biografico degli Italiani*, 27 (1982), pp. 253–457.

colophon. The paragraph often found at the end of MSS and early printed books giving information about authorship, title, printer, place of printing, date, and sometimes (in the case of MSS) the scribe himself. The use of the colophon tended to decline when many of these particulars were transferred to the title page. The word used in this special sense does not seem to be earlier than 1749.

A. W. Pollard, *An Essay on Colophons* (Chicago, 1905), with introd. by R. Garnett. Benedictines of Le Bouveret, *Colophons de manuscrits occidentaux des origines au XVI* siècle* (Spicilegii Friburgensis Subsidia, 2–7; 1965–82).

Colosseum. The name by which the 'Flavian Amphitheatre' at *Rome has been known since about the 8th cent. The largest arena in the world, it was completed by Titus *c.*80, and has long been venerated as the scene of many martyrdoms in the early Church, though the truth of this tradition has been questioned by modern scholars, notably H. *Delehaye. Its present imperfect state is due partly to destruction by earthquakes and partly to its use as a quarry for stone until *Benedict XIV forbade its further demolition. The Cross erected in the centre of the arena in the 18th cent. was removed in 1874, but replaced in 1927. Excavation and restoration has been undertaken intermittently in recent generations and continues.

R. Rea and others, *Anfiteatro Flavio: Immagine, Testimonianze, Spettacoli*, ed. A. M. Reggiani (Archeologia e Storia a Roma [1988]), with bibl. G. Lugli, *The Flavian Amphitheatre* (Rome, 1960 [pamphlet]). M. E. Blake, *Roman Construction in Italy from Tiberius through the Flavians* (Washington, DC, 1959), pp. 91–96, with refs. H. Delehaye, 'L'Amphithéâtre flavien et ses environs dans les textes hagiographiques', *Anal. Boll.* 16 (1897), pp. 209–52.

Colossians, Epistle to the.

A letter included in the NT, traditionally held to have been written by St *Paul when he was in prison, prob. at *Rome, but possibly at *Ephesus. In modern times an increasing number of scholars have attributed it to an early follower, but Pauline authorship has been equally strongly defended, esp. on the ground of the similarities of the personal details with those in *Philemon (which virtually all critics regard as authentic). The Church at Colossae, a city on the Lycus (*Churuk Su*), had been founded not by St Paul in person, but by Epaphras (1: 7), apparently when St Paul was working at Ephesus. The primary purpose of the epistle is to recall its readers to faith in Christ as their all-sufficient Redeemer and Lord. After a solemn statement of Christ's position in relation to God, creation, and the Church (1: 3 ff.), a warning is given against a certain 'philosophy' which was making converts at Colossae (2: 1 ff.). In the course of the epistle St Paul refers to certain features of the Hellenistic and Judaic religion of the period, e.g. the 'rudiments' or 'elements' (τὰ στοιχεῖα) of the world, angelic mediators, law-keeping, and asceticism, which later filled a prominent place in *Gnosticism. The epistle has important passages dealing with the Person of Christ (1: 15), the redeemed life (3: 1 ff.), and Christian morals (3: 5–4: 6). There are many close verbal parallels with the Ep. to the *Ephesians (q.v.).

Comm. by J. B. *Lightfoot (London, 1875; with Philemon), C. F. D. Moule (Cambridge Greek Testament Comm., 1957; with Philemon), F. F. Bruce (New London Commentary on the NT, 1957; with E. K. Simpson on Eph.; rev. 1984, with Philemon and Eph.), E. Lohse (KEK, 1968; Eng. tr., Philadelphia, 1971; with Philemon), R. P. Martin (New Cent. Bib., 1974; with Philemon), E. Schweizer (Evangelisch-Katholischer Kommentar zum Neuen Testament, 1976; Eng. tr., 1982), J.-N. Aletti, SJ (Études Bibliques, 1993), M. Barth and H. Blanke, tr. into Eng. by A. B. Beck (Anchor Bible [1994]), and J. D. G. Dunn (New International Greek Testament Commentary, Carlisle, 1996; with Philemon). E. Percy, *Die Probleme der Kolosser- und Epheserbriefe* (Acta Reg. Soc. Human. Litt. Lundensis, 39; Lund, 1946). H. J. Gabathuler, *Jesus Christus: Haupt der Kirche—Haupt der Welt. Der Christushymnus Colosser 1, 15–20 in der theologischen Forschung der letzten 130 Jahre* (Abhandlungen zur Theologie des Alten und Neuen Testaments, 45; 1965). Kümmel, pp. 335–48. P. Benoît, OP, in *Dict. Bibl.*, Suppl. 7 (1966), cols. 157–70, s.v. 'Paul, Colossiens (Épître aux)', with bibl. See also bibl. to EPHESIANS, EPISTLE TO THE.

colours, liturgical.

A sequence of colours at different seasons of the ecclesiastical year for vestments and other liturgical objects is first found in the use of the *Augustinian Canons at *Jerusalem at the beginning of the 12th cent. They are mentioned by Pope *Innocent III in his *De Sacro Altaris Mysterio*. But it is not until much more recent times that a standard sequence in general use in the W. Church became established. The colours prescribed by the modern Roman service books are five—white (*albus*), red (*rubeus*), green (*viridis*), purple (*violaceus*), and black (*niger*). White is used e.g. on *Trinity Sunday, on the Feasts of Christ (so far as they are not memorials of His Passion) and of the BVM, on *Corpus Christi, and on the feasts of virgins and confessors, and since 1970 also in some countries for funerals; red, e.g. at *Whitsun and on the feasts of apostles (except St John) and of martyrs, and since 1970 also on *Palm Sunday and *Good Friday; green on the Sundays and *ferial days between the *Epiphany and *Lent and between Trinity Sunday and *Advent, both exclusive; purple, e.g. in Lent and Advent, and often for funerals; and black (which was formerly obligatory on these occasions) is still sometimes used in Masses and offices of the dead (also, until 1969, on Good Friday). Rose pink may be used on *Gaudete and *Laetare Sundays. In the *Sarum use, red was commonly used on the days for which the Roman books prescribe green, and in a few Anglican churches the Sarum sequence has been introduced in modern times, though the Roman sequence is that usually followed. It has recently been permitted in the RC Church to use the best vestments, of whatever colour, on more important feast days. Of the Eucharistic vestments, the *stole and *chasuble are usually of the appropriate colour, as are also the *chalice veil and *burse, and the *altar hangings. In the 14th cent., the custom of veiling statues, pictures, etc., in linen or other white material during Lent was in many places extended to the use of such material for vestments and altar-hangings; hence the so-called 'Lenten array' adopted in some Anglican churches in modern times. In the E. Church there are no definite rules about colours, though there is a natural tendency to use more sombre colours at penitential seasons, while white (or red in some Russian Churches) is used at all services, including funerals, from Easter to Ascensiontide.

J. W. Legg, *Notes on the History of the Liturgical Colours* (1882); W. St J. Hope and E. G. C. F. Atchley, *English Liturgical Colours* (1918). Braun, *LG*, pp. 728–60.

Columba, St

(*c*.521–97), known in Irish as Colum Cille, 'dove of the Church', Abbot of *Iona and missionary. He came of Irish royal lineage, but from an early age preferred the religious life. He was trained in Irish monasteries by some of the leading teachers of his day, incl. St *Finnian. After the battle of Cúl-drebene (561), for which he was held in part responsible, in 563 he sailed from Ireland to Britain as 'a pilgrim for Christ', and founded a monastery at Iona. He made at least one journey to the King of the Picts, Bridei, whom, acc. to *Bede, he converted, though his biographer, St *Adomnán is equivocal on the point. In 574 Columba anointed Aedán mac Gabráin as King of the Scots of Dalriada, and in the following year attended the convention of the kings at Druim Cett in Ireland. He founded the monastery of Durrow in Ireland (in 585 or later acc. to Adomnán, though Bede says before 565). He is said to have established many other churches in Ireland and Scotland and is widely venerated. Feast day, 9 June.

Crit. edn. of the 'Altus Prosator', the best known of the poems attributed to St Columba, by C. Blume in *AHMA* 51 (1908), pp. 275–83: other hymns, pp. 283–8 and 325 f. For lit. on St Columba's authorship of various other works, see Kenney, below. The principal sources for his career are Bede, *HE* 3. 4 (comm. by J. M. Wallace-Hadrill, Oxford, 1988, pp. 92–4, 128–9, and 229) and the Life by Adomnán (for edns. and discussions, see s.v.). Other sources are listed by J. F. Kenney, *The Sources for the Early History of Ireland*, 1 (Records of Civilizations; New York, 1929), pp. 422–48, with details of works attributed to Columba, pp. 263–5. M. Herbert, *Iona, Kells, and Derry: The History and Hagiography of the Monastic Familia of Columba* (Oxford, 1988), incl. crit. edn. and Eng. tr. of Middle Irish homiletic Life, pp. 218–86; also extensive bibl. Other modern discussions incl.: D. A. Bullough, 'Columba, Adomnan and the Achievement of Iona', *Scottish Historical Review*, 43 (1964), pp. 111–30 and 44 (1965), pp. 17–33; J. Bannerman, *Studies in the History of Dalriada* (1974), esp. pp. 79–85; and A. P. Smyth, *Warlords and Holy Men: Scotland, AD 80–1000* (The New History of Scotland, 1; 1984), pp. 84–115. More devotional studies incl. those of J. Smith (Edinburgh, 1798), L. Menzies (London, 1920), and W. I. R. Finlay (ibid., 1979); also C. R. F. *Montalembert, *Les Moines d'Occident*, 3 (1866), pp. 101–331 (Eng. tr., 3, 1867, pp. 97–313).

Columbanus, St (d. 615), abbot and missionary. An Irishman and monk of the community of St *Comgall in *Bangor, *c.*590 Columbanus left Ireland on perpetual pilgrimage and sailed to Gaul. Here he set up monasteries with strict rules at Annegray and *Luxeuil, in the Vosges. His religious fervour and his encouragement of private *Penance did much to respiritualize barbarized areas of Gaul, where Christianity was at a low ebb. However, he aroused opposition from the episcopate by his uncompromising adherence to the traditions of the Irish Church. He vigorously defended these in letters to Popes and to a Gallic synod (603), but later he lost royal protection through his outspoken attacks on the king's polygamy, and he was expelled from the country with his closest followers (610). They began missionary work among the heathen Alamanni near Lake Constance, but were driven out by political upheavals in 612, though St *Gall stayed on. Finally Columbanus and his companions settled at *Bobbio, which later became a great centre of learning. Feast day, 23 Nov.

Columbanus' surviving works include letters, 13 sermons, and the Monks' Rule; the Communal Rule and the Penitential ascribed to him are also substantially his work, but controversy continues about the poetry.

Crit. edn. of his *Opera*, by G. S. M. Walker (Scriptores Latini Hiberniae, 2; Dublin, 1957), with bibl. to date; cf. A. Mundó, OSB, in *Scriptorium*, 12 (1958), pp. 289–93. 'Penitential' ed. J. Laporte, OSB (Monumenta Christiana Selecta, 4; Tournai, 1961). Life by Jonas of Susa and other material ed. B. Krusch in *MGH*, Scriptores Rerum Merovingicarum, 4 (1902), pp. 1–156, and 7, pt. 2 (1920), pp. 822–7; also pr. in *Ionae Vitae Sanctorum Columbani, Vedastis, Iohannis* (Scriptores Rerum Germanicarum, 1905), pp. 1–294. Eng. tr. by D. C. Munro (Translations and Reprints from the Original Sources of European History, no. 7; Philadelphia, 1895). 'Miracula Sancti Columbani', ed. H. Bresslau in *MGH*, Scriptores, 30, pt. 2 (1934), pp. 993–1015. Full bibl. details of sources in M. Lapidge and R. Sharpe, *A Bibliography of Celtic-Latin Literature 400–1200* (Dublin, 1985), pp. 165–8, 171 f., and 331 (nos. 639–42, 650–6, and 1251).
Mélanges Colombaniens: Actes du Congrès International de Luxeuil 20–23 juillet 1950 (Bibliothèque de la Société d'Histoire Ecclésiastique de la France [1951]); *San Colombano e la sua opera in Italia* (Convegna Storico Colombaniano, Bobbio, 1–2 settembre 1951; Bobbio, 1953). J. W. Smit, *Studies on the Language and Style of Columba the Younger (Columbanus)* (Amsterdam, 1971); M.

Lapidge, 'The Authorship of the Adonic Verses "ad Fidolium" attributed to Columbanus', *Studi Medievali*, 3rd ser. 18 (1977), pp. 815–80; H. B. Clarke and M. Brennan (eds.), *Columbanus and Merovingian Monasticism* (BAR International Series, 113; Oxford, 1981); K. Schäferdiek, 'Columbans Wirken im Frankenreich', in H. Löwe (ed.), *Die Iren und Europa im früheren Mittelalter*, 1 (Stuttgart, 1982), pp. 171–201; P. C. Jacobsen, 'Carmina Columbani', ibid., pp. 434–67; D. Schaller, 'Die Siebensilberstrophen "de mundi transitu"—eine Dichtung Columbans?', ibid., pp. 468–83. M. Lapidge, 'Columbanus and the Antiphonary of Bangor', *Peritia*, 4 (1985), pp. 104–16. Id. (ed.), *Columbanus* (forthcoming). J. M. Wallace-Hadrill, *The Frankish Church* (Oxford History of the Christian Church, 1983), pp. 63–73. D. Bullough in *Dizionario Biografico degli Italiani*, 27 (1982), pp. 113–29, s.v. 'Colombano'.

Colvill, John. See COVEL, JOHN.

Combefis, François (1605–79), *patristic scholar. A native of Aquitaine, he entered the *Dominican Order in 1624. He published first editions of the Greek text of several of the Fathers, among them *Amphilochius of Iconium, *Methodius of Olympus, and *Andrew of Crete (all in one vol., 1644), and also an excellent edition of *Maximus the Confessor (1675). He also produced an edition (1679) of St *Basil the Great, though this was superseded by the still better *Maurist edition (1721–30).

Quétif and Échard, 2, pp. 678–87, incl. list of his works. R. Coulon in *DTC* 3 (1908), cols. 385–7, s.v.

Comber, Thomas (1645–99), Dean of *Durham from 1691. He was the author of *A Companion to the Temple and Closet; or a Help to Publick and Private Devotion, in an Essay upon the Daily Offices of the Church* (1672–6), written with the intention of reconciling Protestant dissenters to the services of the C of E. Comber strongly resisted *James II's attempts to fill Anglican benefices with RCs, and unreservedly welcomed William and Mary.

C. E. Whiting (ed.), *The Autobiographies and Letters of Thomas Comber* (Surtees Society, 156–157, for 1941–2; 1946–1947), incl. list of MS sources for life.

Comboni, Bl [Antonio] Daniele (1831–81), first RC Bishop of Central Africa and founder of the *Verona Fathers. Born near Brescia, he was ordained priest for the African mission in 1854 in the Institute founded at Verona by Nicholas Mazza, and joined its Nile expedition three years later. In 1861 he was sent to Aden to bring ransomed Black slaves to Verona for education, and was then appointed Vice-Rector of the Mazza Institute's African colleges. In Rome in 1864 he conceived his 'Plan for the Regeneration of Africa', the basic idea of which was to 'save Africa with Africa', and in the following year he went again to Egypt to study its feasibility. In 1867, after the Mazza Institute abandoned its African work, Comboni founded the Missionary Institute for Africa, now officially called the Comboni Missionaries of the Sacred Heart, but commonly known as the Verona Fathers. Between further journeys to Egypt, he presented a stirring 'Petition on behalf of the Black Populations of Central Africa' to the First *Vatican Council in 1870, and was entrusted by *Pius IX with the mission to Central Africa. In 1872 he founded the Institute of the Missionary Sisters of Verona (Comboni Missionary Sisters). After starting missionary work in the *Sudan, he was appointed *Vicar Apostolic of Central Africa in 1877 and died at Khartoum in 1881. Comboni was deeply involved in the struggle against *slavery and he travelled extensively in Europe to bring the plight of Africans to the attention of statesmen and philanthropists. He was beatified in 1996. Feast day, 10 Oct.

Comboni pub. his 'Plan', *Piano per la Rigenerazione dell'Africa* at Turin, 1864. M. Grancelli, *Mons. Daniele Comboni e la Missione dell'Africa Centrale* (Verona, 1923); *Il Servo di Dio, Mons. Daniele Comboni* [by A. Capovilla, MCCJ] (ibid., 1928). P. Chiochetta [MCCJ], *Daniele Comboni: Carte per l'Evangelizzazione dell'Africa* (Bologna, 1978). O. Branchesi, *Safari for Souls: Bishop Daniel Comboni, Founder of the Sons of the Sacred Heart (Verona Fathers) and of the Missionary Sisters of Verona* (Cincinatti [1951]). B. Ward, *A Heart for Africa* (pamphlet issued by Comboni Missionary Publications, London, etc., 1989).

Comboni Missionaries. See VERONA FATHERS.

Comenius, Johannes Amos (in Czech, Jan Amos Komensky) (1592–1670), Bohemian educationist. He belonged to the *Bohemian Brethren (Moravian), and studied theology at the *Calvinist universities of Herborn and Heidelberg, where he came under the influence of *millenarianism. From 1618 to 1621 he was a Moravian minister at Fulnek, and later at Lissa in Poland where he wrote his most important educational works, *Didactica Magna* (published 1657) among them. From 1641 onwards he travelled in England, Sweden, and Germany, collecting material for further educational writings and promoting the international Protestant cause. He returned to Lissa in 1648 and became first senior of the Brethren; and from 1650 to 1654 he lived in Hungary, where he founded a school on his principles at Sárospatak. After Lissa had been destroyed by Polish Catholics in 1656, Comenius found a refuge in the Netherlands, where he finished his last work, the *Unum Necessarium*, in 1668.

His educational ideals were deeply influenced by his personal religious experience. Hoping for a Utopian Church which would unite all religions in Christian love, the 'unum necessarium', he regarded education as the surest way to its fulfilment. In numerous schools men were to be formed into images of Christ by means of the 'pansophia', i.e. an organic development of all elements of Divine wisdom. The methods he advocated were far in advance of the ordinary practice of his time. Coercion was to be avoided; the senses were to be employed wherever possible; and everything to be learnt was first to be properly understood. Not much learning, but the development of the character on Christian lines, was to be the ultimate aim. His ideas have had considerable influence on modern pedagogy. Since the 1890s a wider interest in Comenius' religious and philosophical ideas has revived, and institutes for the study of them exist both in Germany and in the Czech Republic, where he occupies a prominent place in the national pantheon.

His main works are collected as *Vybrané spisy* (8 vols. + index, Prague, 1958–78) and repr. in facsimile as *Ausgewählte Werke*, ed. D. Tschiżewskij and K. Schaller (4 vols. in 6 parts, Hildesheim, 1973–83). A complete edn. of his *Opera Omnia* is being pub. at Prague, 1969 ff. His rediscovered pansophic testament, *De rerum humanarum emendatione consultatio catholica* was first ed. in full by J. Červenka and V. T. Miškovská-Kozáková (2 vols., Prague,

1966). Eng. tr. of pt. 4 of this work, *Pampaedia*, by A. M. O. Dobbie (Dover [1986]). Other modern Eng. trs. of *Didactica Magna* (London, 1896; 2nd edn. with additions, 1910), *Labirynt Swěta a Lusthauz Srdce* ... ('The Labyrinth of the World and the Paradise of the Heart', London, 1901; repr., 1950), *Via Lucis* (London, 1938), *Angelus Pacis* (New York [1944]), and *Didactica Analytica* (Chicago, 1953). Facsmile repr. of the London, 1672, edn. of *Orbis Sensualium Pictus*, with introd. by J. Bowen (Sydney, 1967). Studies on his educational significance by A. Heyberger (Travaux publiés par l'Institut d'Études Slaves, 8; Paris, 1928) and J. E. Sadler (London, 1966). The fullest Life is M. Blekastad, *Comenius* (Oslo and Prague, 1969 [in Ger.]). J. F. Young, *Comenius in England* (1932); J. Needham (ed.), *The Teacher of Nations* (1942); M. Spinka, *John Amos Comenius: That Incomparable Moravian* (Chicago, 1943); W. Rood, *Comenius and the Low Countries* (Amsterdam, 1970); E. Földes and I. Mészáros (eds.), *Comenius and Hungary: Essays* (Budapest, 1973).

Comes (Lat., *Liber comitis, Liber comicus,* or *Liber commicus*), a book containing the passages to be read at Mass as *Epistles, or containing both the Epistles and *Gospels. Originally a collection of complete readings, the terms came to be used for lists containing only references to the passages to be read, usually the opening words of each reading. The word 'comes' used to be thought to come from the Latin meaning of 'companion' but perhaps derives from *comma*, a section or *pericope.

W. H. *Frere, *Studies in Early Roman Liturgy*, 3, The Roman Epistle-Lectionary (*Alcuin Club Collections, 32; 1935), esp. pp. 1–25 (text of 'Liber Comitis' from Corbie lectionary at St Petersburg) and pp. 45 f., 49–61, and 73–84. T. Klauser, *Das römische Capitulare Evangeliorum*, 1 (Liturgiewissenschaftliche Quellen und Forschungen, 28; 1935), esp. pp. xv f. and xix. A Mundó, OSB, 'Frammenti palinsesti del "Liber commicus" visigoto', in *Studi sulla Chiesa Antica e sull'Umanesimo: Studi presentati nella Sezione di Storia Ecclesiastica del Congresso Internazionale per il IV Centenario della Pontificia Università Gregoriana, 13–17 ottobre 1953* (Analecta Gregoriana, 70; 1954), pp. 101–6. Vogel, *Sources*, p. 392, note 138. H. *Leclercq, OSB, in *DACL* 9 (pt. 1, 1930), cols. 220–43, s.v. 'Liber Comicus'.

Comfortable Words, the. Four passages from the NT (Mt. 11: 28, Jn. 3: 16, 1 Tim. 1: 15, 1 Jn. 2: 1 f.) recited by the celebrant at the Holy Communion in the C of E after the Absolution of the people, to confirm the pardon just given. They are based on Abp. *Hermann's 'Consultatio' (1543), where (with the exception of the first, which was added by the Anglican Reformers) they appear between the Confession and Absolution. They were prescribed first by the Order of the *Communion (1548) and subsequently in all editions of the BCP. In the ASB their use is optional.

A short 'Pastoral and Theological Commentary' by W. W. S. March (London, 1961).

Comforter, the. The title of the Holy Spirit found in the AV, RV, and some modern English translations of Jn. 14: 16 and 26; 15: 26, and 16: 7. The Greek word (παράκλητος) means 'advocate' at 1 Jn. 2: 1, where, however, it refers to Christ. The earlier Latin versions rendered it by 'advocatus' in the Gospels also, but the functions assigned are wider than judicial, and the *Vulgate left it untranslated as *paracletus*. The more general word 'helper' is now widely favoured. The translation *consolator*, which first appeared in the 7th cent., gave rise through the French to the rendering 'Comforter'.

Comgall, St (d. *c*.600), abbot of *Bangor (Co. Down), is one of the best attested founders of monastic churches in 6th-cent. Ireland. The 7th-cent. Life of St *Columbanus by Jonas of Bobbio describes Columbanus' years of study with Comgall, and his virtues are praised in a hymn preserved in the later 7th-cent. Antiphonary of *Bangor. His name was known on the Continent, probably as a result of the activity of Columbanus' disciples; he is praised, for example, in the martyrology by *Notker Balbulus, and a copy of his rule appears in a 9th-cent. booklist from *Fulda. None of the Latin Lives now preserved is older than the early 13th cent., though a text was known in the 12th cent. to Jocelin of Furness. Feast day, 10 May.

The older of two Lat. Lives (as revised in the 13th cent.) is ed. C. Plummer, *Vitae Sanctorum Hiberniae*, 2 (Oxford, 1910), pp. 3–21; the other (based on it) is ed. W. W. Heist, *Vitae Sanctorum Hiberniae ex codice olim Salmanticensi nunc Bruxellensi* (Subsidia Hagiographica, 28; Brussels, 1965), pp. 332–4; they are complemented by P. Grosjean, SJ (ed.), 'S. Comgalli Vita Latina. Accedunt duae narrationes Gadelicae', *Anal. Boll.* 52 (1934), pp. 343–56. J. F. Kenney, *The Sources for the Early History of Ireland*. 1: *Ecclesiastical* (Records of Civilization, New York, 1929), pp. 396 f.

Comma Joanneum. See JOHANNINE COMMA.

commandery. Among the *Hospitallers, an estate or manor in the charge of a member of the order. In 1540 all commanderies which survived in England were seized by the Crown. The corresponding institution among the *Templars was the '*preceptory'.

Commandments, the Ten, also called the 'Decalogue' (from Gk. δέκα, 'ten', and λόγος, 'word'), the precepts divinely revealed to *Moses on Mt. *Sinai and engraved on two tables of stone. Acc. to Exod. 32: 19, the tables were broken by Moses on coming down from the mountain because of the idolatry of the people, but later replaced by another pair (Exod. 34: 1) which were deposited in the *Ark. The text of the Commandments is preserved in the OT in two closely similar versions (Exod. 20: 1–17 and Deut. 5: 6–21). The chief differences are that whereas in Exod. the observance of the *Sabbath is motivated by a religious reason, namely Yahweh's rest on the seventh day of Creation, in Deut. the ground is humanitarian. Also, in the prohibition of covetousness, Exod. classes a man's wife with his other domestic property, whereas Deut. treats her separately. These differences are perhaps to be explained in terms of the less developed social teaching of the writer of the Exod. account. As regards the origin of the Decalogue, many of the older critical scholars, e.g. F. *Delitzsch, R. Kittel, and S. R. *Driver, held it to be of the Mosaic age. J. *Wellhausen, C. H. *Cornill, R. Smend, and others argued that it legislates not for wandering nomads but for a settled agricultural community, and that its moral teaching reflects the ideals of the 8th and 7th cent. Prophets; they therefore dated it in the 7th cent. More recently there has been some reaction against this view, and the dating of the Decalogue is now regarded as an open question among scholars, with many again accepting the possibility that the code in its primitive form may go back to Moses himself.

There is another and, acc. to many OT critics, older version of the 'Ten Words' preserved in Exod. 34: 11–28, where much more emphasis is laid on ritual prescriptions.

The Ten Commandments, as we have them today, form an organic body of religious and moral principles, based on the Hebrew monotheistic conception of God. They are clear and succinct; and, apart from the prohibition of images and the precept of observing the Sabbath, they contain only rules of life that are the common property of mankind. Hence they were never abrogated in the New Dispensation, but rather deepened and supplemented by the Lord's teaching in the *Sermon on the Mount, and summed up by Him in the double precept of love towards God and one's neighbour (Mk. 12: 29–31 and parallels). This summary of the Law draws together Deut. 6: 4–5 and Lev. 19: 18. Acc. to *Tertullian the Divine precepts were engraven on the hearts of men even before being written on the tables of stone (cf. Jer. 31: 31–4), an opinion later found also in St *Augustine and St *Gregory the Great. Acc. to St *Thomas Aquinas, St *Bonaventure, and other Schoolmen, all precepts of the Old Law belong to the *Natural Law, and hence the Commandments were given only to remind men of their obligations which had been obscured by sin.

By the time of St Augustine the Ten Commandments had gained a prominent place in the instruction of catechumens. They were esp. used to counteract the moral errors of the *Manicheans, who alleged the Decalogue to be the work of the evil principle. They came to the fore again in the development of the penitential system in the 9th cent., and from the 13th cent. have kept their central place in Christian instruction. They received an esp. prominent place in the popular systems of teaching of the *Reformers, and were fully commented on by M. *Luther in his 'Grosser' and 'Kleiner Katechismus'. There is a difference in the enumeration in the different Churches. In the C of E as well as in the Greek and the Reformed (Calvinist and Zwinglian) Churches the prohibitions relating to false worship are reckoned as two, whereas the RC Church and the Lutherans count them as one. Thus the enumeration of the subsequent Commandments differs, e.g. the fourth (Anglican, etc.) Commandment on the sanctification of the Sabbath is reckoned as the third by those following the RC method. The number ten is made up by the latter splitting up the last Commandment forbidding covetousness into two. In the 1552 BCP the recitation of the Ten Commandments was introduced into the Communion Office, where they are to be regarded as a substitute for the lessons from the OT in ancient liturgies or, more probably, for the *Kyrie Eleison of the medieval rite. The rubric requiring their recitation at every Celebration remains in the BCP, though in modern practice they are often omitted, replaced by the Kyrie Eleison or summed up in the Lord's two Great Commandments (Mk. 12: 29–31); provision is made for either of the last alternatives in the ASB.

S. *Mowinckel, *Le Décalogue* (Études d'Histoire et de Philosophie religieuses publiées par la Faculté de Théologie protestante de l'Université de Strasbourg, 16; 1927). H. H. Rowley, 'Moses and the Decalogue', *Bulletin of the John Rylands Library*, 34 (1952), pp. 81–118. J. J. Stamm, *Die Dekalog im Lichte der neueren Forschung* (Berne, 1958; 2nd edn., 1962; Eng. tr., with additions, by M. E. Andrew, Studies in Biblical Theology, 2nd ser., 2; 1967).

A. C. J. Phillips, *Ancient Israel's Criminal Law: A New Approach to the Decalogue* (Oxford, 1970). E. W. Nicholson, 'The Decalogue as the Direct Address of God', *Vetus Testamentum*, 27 (1977), pp. 422–33. P. Delhaye, *Le Décalogue et sa place dans la morale chrétienne* (2nd edn., 1963). G. Bourgeault, SJ, *Décalogue et morale chrétienne* (1971). F. E. Vokes, 'The Ten Commandments in the New Testament and in First Century Judaism' in F. L. Cross (ed.), *Studia Evangelica*, 5 (TU 103; 1968), pp. 146–54. A. Eberharter in *Dict. Bibl.*, Suppl. 2 (1934), cols 341–51, s.v. 'Décalogue'; L. Perlitt and others in *TRE* 8 (1981), pp. 408–30, s.v. 'Dekalog'; R. F. Collins in *Anchor Bible Dictionary*, 6 (1992), pp. 383–7, s.v. 'Ten Commandments' each with bibl. See also comm. on EXODUS and DEUTERONOMY.

Commandments of the Church (also **Precepts of the Church**). Certain moral and ecclesiastical precepts, imposed by the RC Church on all her members. They were tabulated in the Middle Ages, and later more strictly classified. Thus St Peter *Canisius in his *Summa Doctrinae Christianae* (1555) mentions five and St Robert *Bellarmine in his *Doctrina Christiana* (1589) lists six, though the '*Roman Catechism' (1566) does not speak of them. The *Catechism of the Catholic Church* (1992) lists five, namely (1) to attend Mass on Sundays and *Feasts of Obligation; (2) to go to Confession (see PENANCE) at least once a year; (3) to receive Holy Communion during the *Easter season; (4) to keep holy the Feasts of Obligation; (5) to observe the days of *fasting and *abstinence; to these is added the duty of providing for the material needs of the Church (nos. 2042–3).

J. W. Melody in *CE* 4 (1908), pp. 154 f., s.v.; E. Dublanchy in *DTC* 3 (1908), cols. 388–93, s.v. 'Commandements de l'Église', both with bibl.

Commemoration. Acc. to traditional W. liturgical custom, when two feasts fell on the same date, that of lesser rank was commonly only 'commemorated'. This was done, e.g. at Mass, by its *collect, *secret, and *postcommunion being read after the corresponding prayers of the feast of greater rank which was being observed. See also OCCURRENCE, CONCURRENCE.

commendam (Med. Lat. *commenda*, a 'trust' or 'custody'). An individual was said to hold an ecclesiastical benefice *in commendam* when its revenues were granted to him temporarily during a vacancy. The person so provided might be a layman, in which case he would *ipso facto* be debarred from performing the duties. Gradually the word came to be restricted, esp. to benefices which a bishop or other dignitary held more or less permanently along with his see. The first reference to the custom is in the writings of St *Ambrose, who mentions a Milanese church which he had 'commended'. The practice not unnaturally led to great abuses. The holding of benefices *in commendam* in the C of E is prohibited by the Ecclesiastical Commissioners Act 1836.

Commendatio Animae (Lat., 'Commendation of the soul'). The prayers formerly prescribed in the *Rituale Romanum to be said at the bedside of a dying person. The 1972 'Order for the Anointing of the Sick and their Pastoral Care' (*Ordo Unctionis Infirmorum eorumque Pastoralis Curae*) calls the corresponding section *Commendatio morientium* ('Commendation of the dying'). Both plead that the soul may go forth in the name of God, but the 1972 rite provides a wider choice of biblical readings, psalms and prayers.

L. Gougaud, OSB, 'Étude sur les "Ordines Commendationis Animae" ', *EL* 49 (1935), pp. 3–27. R. Rutherford, *The Death of a Christian* (Studies in the Reformed Rites of the Catholic Church, 7; New York, 1980), pp. 65–9; 2nd edn. (Collegeville, Minn., 1990), pp. 67–71.

commendation, final. See ABSOLUTIONS OF THE DEAD.

Commination service. The service drawn up by the compilers of the BCP for use on *Ash Wednesday (as a substitute for earlier penitential discipline) and on other days appointed by the *ordinary. It consists of an exhortation, clearly intended for use by a non-preaching clergy (during which the Curses are solemnly recited), Psalm 51, suffrages, and prayers. It first appeared in the BCP of 1549, and has, with various modifications, been included in all subsequent revisions. It is now seldom used.

Commodian, Christian Latin poet. He is generally held to have flourished in Africa in the middle of the 3rd cent., despite the doubts of some scholars, who put him later, e.g. in the 5th cent. in S. Gaul. He was certainly a convert from paganism. Two of his poems have survived, 'Instructiones adversus Gentium Deos pro Christiana Disciplina' and 'Carmen Apologeticum adversus Judaeos et Gentes'. Although altogether wanting in literary style, his work is a landmark in the history of Latin verse, as his rhythm is based on accent alone, without attention to quantities. Theologically he was a *Chiliast and *Patripassianist, and in the *Decretum Gelasianum his works were reckoned as apocryphal.

Editio princeps of 'Instructiones' by N. Rigaltius, Toul, 1649, repr. in J. P. Migne, *PL* 5. 201–62; of 'Carmen Apologeticum' by J. B. *Pitra in *Spicilegium Solesmense*, 1 (1852). Crit. edns. of Works by E. Ludwig (Teub., 1877–8), B. Dombart (CSEL 15; 1887), and J. Martin in CCLS 128 (1960), pp. 1–122, with bibl. A. F. van Katrijk, *Lexicon Commodianeum* (Amsterdam, 1934); P. Courcelle, 'Commodien et les invasions du V\ siècle', *Revue des Études Latines*, 24 (1946), pp. 227–46; J. Martin, 'Commodianus', *Traditio*, 13 (1957), pp. 1–71. J. Perret, 'Prosodie et Métrique chez Commodien', *Pallas*, 5 (1957), pp. 27–42; L. Callebat, 'Tradition et novation dans la poésie de Commodien', ibid. 13 (1966), pp. 85–94; A. Salvatore, *Interpretazioni Commodianee: Nuove ricerche sul Carme Apologetico* (Naples, 1974). J. *Daniélou, SJ, *Les Origines du christianisme latin* (Histoire des doctrines chrétiennes avant Nicée, 3; 1978), pp. 93–111 and 224–34; Eng. tr. (1977), pp. 99–125 and 273–88. J. Fontaine, *Naissance de la poésie dans l'Occident chrétien* (Études Augustiniennes, 1981), pp. 39–52 and 292 (bibl.). A. di Berardino, OSA, in Quasten (cont.), *Patrology*, 4 (1986), pp. 259–65, with bibl. L. Krestan in *RAC* 3 (1957), cols. 248–52, s.v.

Common Life, Brethren of the. See BRETHREN OF THE COMMON LIFE.

Common of the Saints (Lat. *Commune Sanctorum*). In the W. Church, those parts of the *Missal and *Breviary containing the office for such saints as do not have a complete individual office (a '*proper') of their own.

Common Order, Book of. (1) The directory of worship drawn up by J. *Knox in 1556 for the English Protestant congregations in Geneva. It is also known as 'The Order of Geneva' and as 'Knox's Liturgy'. It was appointed for use in Scotland by the General Assembly in 1562; revised and enlarged in 1564; and continued in general use among the *Calvinists of Scotland until 1645, when it was replaced by the Directory of Public *Worship compiled by the *Westminster Assembly.

(2) In modern times the title has been revived for various service-books, none of them mandatory, used in Scotland by Churches of the *Presbyterian tradition. After the union of the Church of Scotland and the *United Free Church in 1929, the Committee on Public Worship and Aids to Devotion prepared the 1940 *Book of Common Order*, which was authorized by the *General Assembly; this drew extensively on two earlier books, *Prayers for Divine Service* (1923, 1929) from the pre-Union Church of Scotland, and the *Book of Common Order* (1928), from the United Free Church. The 1979 *Book of Common Order* was essentially a revision of the 1940 *Book* carried out by the Committee on Public Worship and Aids to Devotion under the supervision of the General Assembly. It attracted considerable criticism, and in 1994 a new book, entitled simply *Common Order*, and following the 1940 rather than the 1979 model, was published by the Assembly's Panel on Worship. *Common Order* (1994) contains orders for Morning and Evening Worship (five each); Baptism; 'Public Profession, Confirmation, and Admission to the Lord's Supper' (one service); Communion (five, in which classical, Celtic, Reformed and modern ecumenical patterns are evident); and Marriage (three); together with orders for daily and occasional services, funerals and private devotions, and prayers for the seasons of the Christian Year. The *Revised English Bible* is used throughout; the lectionary is the *Revised Common Lectionary*; and ample provision is made for congregational participation, e.g. through responses. The language (which is inclusive, and replaces 'thou' with 'you') aims at simplicity and directness, and the layout is in short lines, like verse, rather than in paragraphs.

(1) G. W. Sprott and T. Leishman (eds.), *The Book of Common Order of the Church of Scotland . . . and the Directory for the Public Worship of God, agreed upon by the Assembly of Divines at Westminister* (1868), pp. 1–253, with introd. pp. xiii–lxvii.
(2) D. B. Forrester, 'Worship since 1929', in id. and D. M. Murray (eds.), *Studies in the History of Worship in Scotland* (Edinburgh, 1984), pp. 156–70. J. A. Whyte in J. G. Davies (ed.), *A New Dictionary of Liturgy and Worship* (1986), pp. 446–8, s.v. 'Presbyterian Worship'.

Common Prayer, The Book of. The official service book of the C of E containing the daily offices of Morning and Evening Prayer, the forms for administration of the *Sacraments and other public and private rites, the *Psalter and (since 1552) the *Ordinal. The book was compiled originally through the desire of T. *Cranmer and others to reform, simplify and condense the Latin services of the medieval Church and to produce in English a single, convenient, and comprehensive volume as an authoritative guide for priest and people. A printed edition of the (Latin) Sarum *Breviary (1543) and the issue of the *Litany in English (1544) and of the Order of the *Communion (1548), which was an English supplement to the Latin Mass, paved the way for the complete reform.

In 1548 Cranmer discussed the draft of a new Prayer Book with a conference of scholars, and in 1549 Parliament had the 'First Prayer Book of Edward VI' printed, and by the first Act of *Uniformity enforced it as the national Use. An Ordinal was issued in 1550. In doctrine and ritual this First BCP was a compromise between the old and the new schools, and it failed to please either. The criticisms of the latter, represented by e.g. *Peter Martyr and M. *Bucer, were concerned chiefly with *vestments, prayers for the *dead, and the invocation of the Holy Spirit in the Prayer of Consecration. Revision in the light of these criticisms led to the issue in 1552 of the 'Second Prayer Book of Edward VI', authorized by another Act of Uniformity. This added the present introduction to Morning and Evening Prayer, recast the Holy Communion office, radically reordered the burial service, excluding all prayers for the dead, ordered the use of the surplice instead of other vestments, and omitted all reference to 'Mass' and 'Altar'. The *Black Rubric was added without the sanction of the Act of Uniformity. *Mary's Act of Repeal (1553) restored the ancient services. As the 'Elizabethan BCP' (1559) the 1552 book was reissued with a few slight alterations, and, except for a few minor details, it remained unchanged for the rest of the 16th cent. The part played by Convocation in the issue of these three books is obscure; so also is the origin of the *Ornaments Rubric which was attached to *Elizabeth I's book.

Puritan objections to the BCP, which had been accumulating under Elizabeth, were ventilated on the accession of *James I by the *Millenary Petition. Hence 1604 saw the *Hampton Court Conference between bishops and Puritan divines, and a further minor revision in which the most important change was the addition of the second part of the *Catechism. After the 16 years in which the Book was officially superseded by the Directory of Public *Worship (1645), the *Restoration of *Charles II was followed by the re-establishment of the Church's episcopal structure, and in 1661 the *Savoy Conference met to consider afresh Puritan grievances. On its proving abortive, Convocation took over the task of yet another revision, and the Act of Uniformity of 1662 authorized the BCP as revised (see DURHAM BOOK). The re-insertion, with modification, of the Black Rubric, omitted in Elizabeth's BCP, was the principal concession to Puritans. The most important change was the introduction of the AV of 1611 for the Epistles and Gospels.

Despite further proposals, most notably in 1689, the 1662 BCP has remained almost unchanged. The *lectionary (q.v.) has been revised a number of times since 1871, and the Shortened Services Act (1872) allowed a more elastic interpretation of some of the rubrics. There were, however, persistent ritualistic controversies in the late 19th cent., and these led to the appointment in 1904 of a Royal Commission on *Ecclesiastical Discipline which in 1906 recommended that 'Letters of Business' be issued to the *Convocations with a view to Prayer Book revision. After nearly two decades the Convocations decided to retain the 1662 Book and to incorporate all changes in a new book, which should include the 1662 texts with alternatives whose use would be wholly permissive. The new Book, which represented a compromise, permitted *Reservation of the Sacrament and in its (Alternative) Eucharistic rite approximated more closely to the medieval services than the 1662 Book had done. Though passed by the Convocations and the *Church Assembly, it was rejected by the House of Commons on 15 Dec. 1927. An amended form was again rejected by the Commons in 1928. In response to this rejection the bishops issued a unanimous statement that the Church must retain its inalienable right to order its forms of worship, and in July 1929 the Upper House of the Convocation of Canterbury resolved that bishops should be guided by the proposals of 1928. The legal basis of these actions is unclear.

Despite fairly widespread use in some quarters of individual services, such as *Baptism and *Matrimony, the 1928 Book did not win general acceptance. Dissatisfaction and doubts about the legal position led to the adoption of the *Interim Rite by many *Anglo-Catholics, while *Evangelicals tended to be uninterested in, or even opposed to, a revision of the 1662 Book which they valued as a doctrinal safeguard. Nearly all churchmen, however, departed to a considerable extent from the strict observance of the 1662 Book, and the desire for a generally acceptable liturgy found expression in the convening of the Lambeth Round Table Conference of 1938 and elsewhere. In 1955 the Abps. of *Canterbury and *York appointed a Liturgical Commission to prepare a revision which, after a period of authorized experiment with individual services from 1965, led to the publication in 1980 of the *Alternative Service Book (q.v.).

Outside England, the BCP has undergone numerous revisions, beginning with the Scottish BCP of 1637, issued under the influence of W. *Laud; this was abortive at the time, but historic in its influence on later revisers. Revisions by the *Nonjurors had no legal force, but led to the first effective Scottish (Episcopalian) Eucharistic rite of 1764, which in turn, through S. *Seabury, influenced the first American BCP of 1789 (revised 1892). Elsewhere the English 1662 Book was used until the Church of *Ireland, freed by disestablishment from the Act of Uniformity, in 1877 produced its own BCP, a conservative revision in a Protestant direction. In the early 20th cent., parallel to the English revision of 1928, but free from parliamentary control, new editions of the BCP were issued in *Canada (1922), the *United States of America (1928), and Scotland (1929). In other parts of the Anglican Communion the BCP or parts of it were generally translated into the local languages, though in several areas different forms of the Communion Service in particular appeared in book or pamphlet form in the first half of the 20th cent. Until 1948 the Lambeth Conferences viewed the BCP as a bond of the Anglican Communion, and it was only from 1958 that encouragement was given for provincial revisions; this change of attitude stemmed partly from appreciation of the rites of the Church of *South India. The last of the revisions which closely followed the 1662 BCP were the (alternative) Book of *South Africa (1954) and those of *India, Pakistan, Burma and Ceylon (1960), and of Canada (1962).

In the 1960s modern English was introduced into the Anglican liturgy and new experimental rites began to address God as 'you' rather than 'Thou'. One influence here was the choice of modern English for the RC vernacular liturgy after the Second *Vatican Council; for a while it met with considerable resistance. As in the C of E, the revision of individual services was widely followed by the issue of a single Book. In a few cases, where some provision for the use of traditional language was included

in the Book, its use was made mandatory, e.g. the American BCP (1979) or that of Wales (1984). More often the new Books are alternative to the BCP, e.g. those of *Australia (1978), Ireland (1984), Canada (1985), Southern Africa and *New Zealand (both 1989), though in practice they often seem to be tending to replace it.

The privilege of printing the BCP is confined to the Queen's Printer and the University Presses of Oxford and Cambridge, to which an Order in Council from the Privy Council Office is transmitted on the occasion of any necessary change (e.g. of names in the State Prayers). The various edns. of the BCP, with sources, are set out in parallel columns, with meticulous accuracy, in F. E. *Brightman, The English Rite (2 vols., 1915), with important introd. E. C. Ratcliff, The Booke of Common Prayer of the Churche of England: Its Making and Revisions M.D.XLIX–M.D.CLXI (with 80 illustrations, 1949). More recent rites pr. in W. J. Grisbrooke (ed.), Anglican Liturgies of the seventeenth and eighteenth centuries (Alcuin Club Collections, 40; 1958); T. J. Fawcett (ed.), The Liturgy of Comprehension, 1689: An abortive attempt to revise the Book of Common Prayer (ibid. 54; 1973); B. [J.] Wigan (ed.), The Liturgy in English (ibid. 43; 1962); C. O. Buchanan (ed.), Modern Anglican Liturgies 1958–1968 (1968); id. (ed.), Further Anglican Liturgies 1968–1975 (Nottingham, 1975); id (ed.), Latest Anglican Liturgies 1976–1984 (1985). Among the classic comm. on the BCP are those of A. *Sparrow (1661), R. *Sanderson (1674), and C. *Wheatly (1710). F. Procter, A History of the Book of Common Prayer (1855; new edn. by W. H. Frere, CR, 1901); W. K. Lowther Clarke (ed.), Liturgy and Worship: A Companion to the Prayer Books of the Anglican Communion (1932). D. E. W. Harrison, The Book of Common Prayer (1946; 3rd edn. as Common Prayer in the Church of England, 1969). G. J. Cuming, A History of Anglican Liturgy (1969). E. C. Whitaker, Martin Bucer and the Book of Common Prayer (Alcuin Club Collections, 55; 1974). G. [J.] Cuming, The Godly Order: Texts and Studies relating to the Book of Common Prayer (ibid. 65; 1983). F. A. *Gasquet and E. *Bishop, Edward VI and the Book of Common Prayer (1890). P. N. Brooks, Thomas Cranmer's Doctrine of the Eucharist (2nd edn., 1992), pp. 112–62. S. Brook, The Language of the Book of Common Prayer (1965). R. C. D. Jasper, Prayer Book Revision in England 1800–1900 (1954). J. Dowden, The Scottish Communion Office, 1764 (Oxford, 1922). M. J. Hatchett, The Making of the First American Book of Common Prayer, 1776–1789 (New York, 1982); id., Commentary on the American Prayer Book (ibid., 1980). G. Harford, M. Stevenson, and J. W. Tyrer (eds.), Prayer Book Dictionary (1912; rev. edn., 1925).

Commonwealth and Continental Church Society. See CCCS.

Communicantes. The section of the *Canon of the Roman Mass, so named from its first word, which comes shortly before the Words of *Institution. Like the 'Hanc igitur' and 'Qui pridie', it is subject to some modification acc. to the ecclesiastical calendar, having variant forms for *Christmas, *Epiphany, *Maundy Thursday, *Easter, *Ascensiontide, and *Pentecost. It consists of a memorial of the saints, mentioning by name the BVM, St *Joseph, the eleven Apostles and St *Paul, eleven Roman martyrs, and one African (St *Cyprian). In earlier times local saints were sometimes added in particular districts, but since 1570 the prayer has been recited everywhere in the same form as at Rome, though since 1969 it has been permissible to omit all but the first five names.

Jungmann (1952), 2, pp. 213–25; Eng. tr., 2, pp. 170–9. V. L. Kennedy, CSB, The Saints of the Canon of the Mass (Vatican City, 1938), passim. A. *Baumstark, 'Das Communicantes und seine Heiligen-Liste', JLW 1 (1921), pp. 5–33; C. Callewaert, 'S. Léon, le *Communicantes* et le *Nobis quoque peccatoribus'*, *Sacris Erudiri*, 1 (1948), pp. 123–64; B. *Capelle, OSB, 'Problèmes du "Communicantes" de la Messe', *Rivista Liturgica*, 40 (1953), pp. 187–95, repr. in his *Travaux liturgiques*, 2 (Louvain, 1962), pp. 269–75; L. Eizenhöfer, OSB, '*Te igitur* und *Communicantes* im römischen Messkanon', *Sacris Erudiri*, 8 (1956), pp. 14–75.

communicatio idiomatum (Lat., 'interchange of the properties'; Gk. ἀντίδοσις τῶν ἰδιωμάτων). The doctrine propounded by several of the Fathers, e.g. *Cyril of Alexandria, that while the human and Divine natures in Christ were distinct, the attributes of the one may be predicated of the other in view of their union in the one Person of the Saviour. The doctrine received conciliar authority by its inclusion in the '*Tome' of St *Leo (449). The term, in its Greek form, was first regularly used in the 6th cent. by theologians who defended the *Chalcedonian Definition; the Latin form, which derived from it, seems to have become a technical phrase in the Middle Ages. *Communicatio idiomatum* played an important part in *Lutheran Eucharistic theology, where it was held to establish the ubiquity of Christ's body (hence 'ubiquitarianism', q.v.).

Communion, frequency of. On a possible interpretation of Acts 2: 46, the apostolic community communicated daily, and from such passages as Acts 20: 7 and various 2nd cent. writers, it seems that the members of the local churches all communicated at the Sunday Eucharist. But in later times, even though attendance at the Liturgy was general, communion became very infrequent. The Fourth *Lateran Council (1215) (cap. 21) provided that all Christians should communicate at least once a year, and this minimum was the normal later medieval practice. In postmedieval times, nearly all religious revivals, both Catholic and Protestant, have aimed at increasing frequency of communion; the BCP in 1549 and later editions fixed the minimum at three times a year; the Restoration Church witnessed a concerted effort by the hierarchy to provide monthly communion in all cathedral churches; the *Wesleys communicated two or three times a week; the leaders of the *Oxford Movement urged frequent communion; and in 1905 Pope *Pius X strongly pressed it upon RCs (Decree of 20 Dec. 1905). The relaxation in the rules about the *Eucharistic fast (q.v.) was directed to the same end, and in the second half of the 20th cent. communion has been allowed for a second time on the same day in some circumstances, e.g. at a *Nuptial Mass. At present weekly communion is fairly common among the laity of the RC Church and the C of E; in religious communities and among a small proportion of the laity in both Churches daily communion is normal, but the majority of people adopt a standard of less frequent communion. The same change from infrequent communion (not more often than once a month) to weekly (or even more frequent) communion has occurred in the E. Orthodox Churches and many Protestant non-episcopal bodies in the course of the 20th cent., though in both cases there have been earlier, isolated attempts to restore the ancient practice of weekly communion.

P. Browe, SJ, *De Frequenti Communione in Ecclesia Occidentali usque ad annum Christi 1000: Documenta Varia* (Rome, 1932); id., *Die häufige Kommunion im Mittelalter* (1938). H. Bohl, *Kommunionempfang der Gläubigen: Probleme seiner Integration*

in der Eucharistiefeier (Frankfurt etc. [1980]). R. Taft, 'The Frequency of the Eucharist throughout History', *Concilium*, 152 (1982), pp. 13–24. E. Dublanchy in *DTC* 3 (1908), cols. 515–52, s.v. 'Communion eucharistique (fréquente)', with bibl.; J. Dühr, SJ, in *Dict. Sp.* 2 (1953), cols. 1234–92, s.v. 'Communion fréquente'.

Communion, The Order of the (1548). A form for administering Holy Communion, drawn up in English for use in conjunction with the *Sarum (Latin) Mass. It was the first step towards the English Communion Service, and it came into use on *Easter Day 1548. Its essential parts were an exhortation, a brief address to the intending communicants, the *General Confession followed by the Absolution, the *Comfortable Words, the Prayer of *Humble Access, the Words of Administration (for both kinds), and the Blessing; and it was interpolated into the Latin Mass between the communion of the priest and that of the people. The whole of its contents found a place in the later Anglican BCPs, though the position of its several items has varied. An early copy sent to Frankfurt was translated into German by Miles *Coverdale.

The interpolation of this Order into the rest of the Eucharistic rite in the 1549 BCP bore the title 'The Supper of the Lord and the Holy Communion, commonly called the Mass', which in turn became 'The Order of the Administration of the Lord's Supper, or Holy Communion' in 1552 and later revisions. Hence the origin of the most commonly used title for the Eucharist in the C of E.

A facsimile of the British Library copy C. 25, f. 15 was ed. for the *Henry Bradshaw Society by H. A. Wilson (1908). See also bibl. to COMMON PRAYER, BOOK OF.

Communion anthem or **antiphon** (Lat. *Communio*). In the Roman Mass the short passage said or sung during the administration of the communion. It was formerly said by the priest, but is now usually recited by the reader, choir or people. If there is music, it is sung by the choir with a psalm, between the verses of which the antiphon is interpolated. It may be replaced by a hymn or other chant. The practice of singing a chant during the communion of the people is recorded in the *Apostolic Constitutions* (4th cent.) and elsewhere. It came to be reduced to merely the antiphon of the Psalm and was placed after the communion until the earlier practice was restored in 1958. It would seem that Ps. 34 was commonly chosen, doubtless because of the appropriateness of verse 8.

Jungmann (1952), 2, pp. 486–96; Eng. tr., 2, pp. 391–400. H. *Leclercq, OSB, in *DACL* 3 (pt. 2; 1914), cols. 2427–36, s.v. 'Communion (rite et antienne de la)'; M. Huglo in *NCE* 4 (1967), pp. 39–41, s.v. 'Communion Antiphon'; H. Hucke and M. Huglo in S. Sadie (ed.), *The New Grove Dictionary of Music and Musicians*, 4 (1980), pp. 591–4, s.v. 'Communion'.

Communion in both kinds. The custom of receiving Holy Communion under the two species of bread and wine was general until about the 12th cent. There were, however, exceptions. *Tertullian and St *Cyprian, e.g., attest the widespread African custom of the laity taking the consecrated bread home with them for private Communion. This usage, which had probably sprung up during the persecutions, is attested in the 4th cent. for Egypt and *Alexandria by St *Basil and for *Rome by St *Jerome. In the E. it seems to have survived till the 8th cent. Another exception to the rule was the practice of the 3rd-cent. anchorites of communicating with the reserved Eucharistic bread alone. The sick and the children seem also to have been habitually communicated under one species only, in the case of infants usually that of wine. The Mass of the *Presanctified, too, presupposed, for priests and people alike, Communion under the species of bread only. From the 7th cent. the 'intinctio panis', i.e. the dipping of the bread into the consecrated wine, became a widespread usage. Forbidden by the Third Council of Braga (675), the custom again became popular in the 11th cent., chiefly because it prevented the spilling of the Precious Blood. It was again forbidden, e.g. by the Council of Westminster in 1175. In the E. the 'intinctio' seems to have been unknown during the first nine centuries, but acc. to the testimony of Card. *Humbert (d. 1061), was generally practised before the 11th. By the 13th cent. the practice of communicating under the species of wine had almost universally disappeared in the W., the Synod of *Lambeth of 1281, e.g., restricting in can. 1 the consecrated wine to the celebrant. The legitimacy of this practice was denied by the *Hussites, esp. the party of the *Calixtines, who were condemned by the Council of *Constance in 1415. The chalice was conceded to them, however, by the Council of *Basle (1437), but the decision, which had never been confirmed by the Pope, was revoked in 1462. See also INTINCTION, UTRAQUISM.

The subject again became a matter of acute controversy in the 16th cent. The Reformers insisted that Communion in both kinds alone had scriptural warrant. In reply the Council of *Trent ruled that there was no Divine precept to communicate under the two species and that existing practice was justified by the doctrine of concomitance (q.v.). Hence, in the RC Church, Communion in both kinds was restricted to the celebrating priest. During the Second *Vatican Council, however, there was evidence of a strong desire to restore the chalice to the laity, particularly on special occasions such as marriage and religious professions, and the Constitution on the Sacred Liturgy envisaged the reception of Communion in both kinds in some instances. On 7 March 1965 the Congregation of Rites listed the instances in which bishops could permit reception in both kinds and published the rite to be observed; it provided for the four alternatives of drinking from the chalice, using a tube or a spoon, or by intinction. The occasions when it is allowed have since been much extended, and it has become more general. In the E. it is the almost general practice to give Communion from a spoon containing the Eucharistic Bread, which has previously been placed in the Wine. The C of E and all the reformed Churches have always administered Communion in both kinds.

The Tridentine doctrine was formulated in Session 21 (16 July 1562); the relevant canons are pr., with Eng. tr., in Tanner, *Decrees* (1990), pp. 726–8. Classic discussion by J. B. *Bossuet, *Traité de la communion sous les deux espèces* (1682). J. J. Megivern, CM, *Concomitance and Communion: A Study in Eucharistic Doctrine and Practice* (Studia Friburgensia, NS 33; Fribourg and New York, 1963). E. Dublanchy in *DTC* 3 (1908), cols. 552–72, s.v. 'Communion eucharistique (sous les deux espèces)'. See also bibl. to EUCHARIST, and works cited under CALIXTINES.

Communion of Saints (Lat. *Communio Sanctorum*). Part of the ninth article of the *Apostles' Creed. It has been interpreted in several senses: (1) The spiritual union existing between each Christian and Christ, and so between each and every Christian, whether in *Heaven (the 'Church *Triumphant'), in *Purgatory (the 'Church *Expectant'), or on earth (the 'Church *Militant'). J. *Pearson (*On the Creed*, s.v.) expounds this communion as the communion of holy persons on earth with the Holy Trinity, with the Angels, with nominal Christians (e.g. in Baptism), with other holy persons, and with the saints in Heaven. He does not mention the Church Expectant. (2) The fellowship of Christians upon earth only. (3) The sharing of holy *things*, i.e. the share which all Christians have in the Sacraments, esp. the *Eucharist, *sanctorum* here being taken as neuter. Of these, (1) is the traditional view.

J. P. Kirsch, *Die Lehre von der Gemeinschaft der Heiligen im christlichen Altertum* (1900; Eng. tr., 1911); G. *Morin, OSB, 'Sanctorum Communionem', *Revue d'Histoire et de Littérature Religieuses*, 9 (1904), pp. 209–36; J. N. D. Kelly, *Early Christian Creeds* (1950; 3rd edn., 1972), pp. 388–97; A. Michel, *La Communion des Saints* (Doctor Communis, 9, fasc. 1; Rome, 1956); S. Benko, *The Meaning of Sanctorum Communio* (Studies in Historical Theology, 3; 1964). P. Bernard in *DTC* 3 (1908), cols. 429–54, s.v. 'Communion des saints, son aspect dogmatique et historique', with bibl.; R. S. Bour, ibid., cols. 454–80, s.v. 'Communion des saints d'après les monuments de l'antiquité chrétienne', with bibl.

Communion plate. In the RC Church, a plate of silver or metal gilt held under the chin of the communicant at the reception of Holy Communion. It may be held either by the communicant himself or by a server. Its use was directed by an instruction of the Congregation of the Sacraments (26 Mar. 1929) but has become obsolescent.

The term is also applied collectively to the vessels used for the celebration of the Eucharist, which are often plated with gold.

Communion Sunday. A Sunday on which the Holy Communion is celebrated. The phrase was in common use in England until the general revival in the latter part of the 19th cent. of celebrations in the C of E at least every Sunday.

Communion table. The table at which the Holy Communion is celebrated. In the C of E the word is used esp. by *Low Churchmen, *High Churchmen commonly preferring the word 'altar' as better expressive of the Eucharistic sacrifice, which they believe is offered upon it. Since in 'high' churches the altar (for the same doctrinal reason) is often of stone and not of wood, there is a further reason in such cases against its being described as a 'table'. In Latin theology the word *mensa*, however, is of widespread and ancient usage for the 'altar'. In the E. Church it is called the 'Holy Table'.

The placing of the communion table at the E. end of the church, richly covered and railed in, became almost universal in the 17th cent. This reversion to pre-Reformation practice reflected the changing emphasis within Anglican sacramental theology. In modern times there has been a tendency to bring the communion table forward and adopt a *westward position.

G. W. O. Addleshaw and F. Etchells, *The Architectural Setting of Anglican Worship* (1948), pp. 108–244.

Communion tokens. Metal tokens stamped with such devices as texts, initials, chalices, and the *Good Shepherd, which were used as certificates of fitness for admission to the Communion. There is evidence of the employment of '*houselling tokens' in England in 1534. In the Church of *Scotland, where they have been most generally used, they were common from the first, and the institution has survived, their place being taken today by printed cards on which the communicants' names are written. As these cards are distributed previously by the elders and collected at the service, a check is kept on those who do not communicate. In isolated Presbyterian churches in Scotland and other parts of the Commonwealth, however, the old metal tokens are still retained.

Communion under both kinds. See COMMUNION IN BOTH KINDS.

Community of the Resurrection. This Anglican community was founded at *Oxford in 1892 by C. *Gore, then principal of Pusey House. Its original members were, besides C. Gore, its first superior: J. O. Nash, J. Carter, M. C. Bickersteth, G. Longridge, and W. H. *Frere. In 1893 the Community moved to Radley, Oxon, and five years later to Mirfield, Yorks. From the beginning one of the chief aims of the Community was to adapt the religious life to the changed circumstances of the modern age. Most of the original members continued to combine the scholarly, educational, and evangelistic work in which they had been engaged before profession with common life; but with growing numbers the Community began to develop work of its own, notably the College of the Resurrection at Mirfield for the training of ordinands, and pastoral and educational work in South Africa.

A. Wilkinson, *The Community of the Resurrection: A Centenary History* (1992). G. P. H. Pawson, CR, *Edward Keble Talbot: His Community and his Friends* (1954); N. Mosley, *The Life of Raymond Raynes* (1961).

Comnena, Anna. See ANNA COMNENA.

Company of Jesus. See JESUITS.

comparative religion. A modern name, not (as its form would imply) for a particular kind of religion, but for the branch of study which investigates by scientific and historical methods the religions of the world in their mutual relations. Its development dates from the later 19th cent., under the influence of evolutionary ideas and the greatly increased factual knowledge of other religions through the researches of anthropologists. Its successful pursuit as a science rests on the universality of religion among primitive as well as civilized peoples and the frequent recurrence of certain patterns of religious experience and activity in widely separated ethnological and social groupings. In scope, comparative religion studies the conditions under which these various forms of religious behaviour manifest themselves, the processes of their growth and the part which they play in the cultures and traditions to which they belong. On the other hand, questions relating to the ultimate philosophical and theological validity of the various religions are beyond its purview, its avowed purpose being to describe and classify phenomena and their functional purposes rather than to evaluate them.

None the less, despite this theoretical exclusion of questions of validity, the discipline has raised various pressing questions for the Christian faith, notably by its recognition that much in the Christian tradition is not, as was long supposed, exclusive to it, but is held in common with other world religions. It is at this point that comparative religion and *philosophy of religion (q.v.) overlap. The recognition of these parallels has acutely raised the question of the 'Absoluteness' of Christianity (E. *Troeltsch). On the other hand, Christian students of the subject have argued with great cogency that the study has emphatically brought out the distinctiveness of certain elements in the Christian religion which, judged even by purely historical criteria, indicate its pre-eminence above all other religions. Among these are its conceptions of God and of human personality and certain features of the Christian ethic. On the practical side the study has brought Christian apologists a deeper understanding of other religions and exercised a far-reaching influence on missionary methods. It is also reflected in the Second *Vatican Council's 'Declaration on the Relationship of the Church to Non-Christian Religions' (*Nostra Aetate*).

J. G. Frazer, *The Golden Bough: A Study in Comparative Religion* (2 vols., 1890; 3rd edn., 12 vols., 1907–15); E. Durkheim, *Les Formes élémentaires de la vie religieuse* (1912; Eng. tr., 1915); H. Pinard de la Boullaye, SJ, *L'Étude comparée des religions* (2 vols., 1922–5); W. Schmidt, *Handbuch der vergleichenden Religionsgeschichte* (Münster, 1930; Eng. tr., 1931); G. van der Leeuw, *Phänomenologie der Religion* (Tübingen, 1933; Eng. tr., *Religion in Essence and Manifestation*, 1938); E. O. James, *Comparative Religion* (1938; revised edn., 1961); A. C. Bouquet, *Comparative Religion* (1941); M. Éliade, *Traité d'histoire des religions* (1949; Eng. tr., 1958); R. C. Zaehner, *At Sundry Times: An Essay in the Comparison of Religions* (1958); W. A. Lessa and E. Z. Vogt (eds.), *Reader in Comparative Religion* (Evanston, Ill., 1958; 2nd edn., New York and London, 1965); M. Eliade and J. M. Kitagawa (eds.), *The History of Religions: Essays in Methodology* (Chicago, 1959); H. Kraemer, *World Culture and World Religions: The Coming Dialogue* (1960); [E.] G. [S.] Parrinder, *Comparative Religion* (1962); H. D. Lewis and R. L. Slater, *World Religions: Meeting Points and Major Issues* (1966); R. C. Zaehner, *Concordant Discord: The Interdependence of Faiths* (Gifford Lectures for 1967–9; Oxford, 1970); E. J. Sharpe, *Comparative Religion: A History* (1975); W. C. Smith, *Towards a World Theology: Faith and the Comparative History of Religion* (1981); J. Hick, *An Interpretation of Religion* (Gifford Lectures, 1986–7; 1989). J. Finegan, *The Archaeology of World Religions* (Princeton, NJ, 1952). On the relation of Christianity to the non-Christian religions, H. Kraemer, *The Christian Message in a non-Christian World* (1938); S. [C.] Neill, *Christian Faith and Other Faiths: The Christian Dialogue with other Religions* (Moorhouse Lectures, 1960; 1961); E. O. James, *Christianity and Other Religions* (1968); G. D'Costa, *Theology and Religious Pluralism* (Oxford, 1986). Much valuable material in J. *Hastings (ed.), *Encyclopaedia of Religion and Ethics* (12 vols., and index, 1908–26), esp. art. by S. A. Cook, ibid. 10 (1918), pp. 662–93, s.v. 'Religion'; R. C. Zaehner (ed.), *The Concise Encyclopaedia of Living Faiths* (1959); S. G. F. Brandon (ed.), *A Dictionary of Comparative Religion* (1970); M. Eliade and others (eds.), *Encyclopedia of Religion* (15 vols. + index [1987]), esp. art. by S. Cain, E. J. Sharpe, and T. L. Benson, vol. 14, pp. 64–92, s.v. 'Study of Religion'. *Numen: International Review for the History of Religions* (Leiden, 1954 ff.); *History of Religions: An International Journal for Comparative Historical Studies* (Chicago, 1961 ff.). See also bibl. to ANIMISM, ANTHROPOLOGY, and THEOLOGY OF RELIGIONS.

competetes (Lat., 'those qualified'). In the early Church *catechumens admitted to the final stage of preparation for *Baptism. They were also known as 'electi', or, in the E., as 'those being illuminated' (φωτιζόμενοι).

Compline (Lat. *Completorium*). The last of the canonical day-hours (see OFFICE) in the W. Church, said before retiring for the night. There is evidence that St *Basil compiled an office approximating to Compline, and in the W., before the time of St *Benedict, who incorporated Compline in his Rule, there were forms used in the city of Rome which influenced the offices of the early medieval secular churches. All probably formalized less structured prayers customarily said in the evening. The corresponding service in the E. Church is known as *Apodeipnon (ἀπόδειπνον, Gk. 'after supper'). Ps. 91 occurs in most forms of Compline, and usually also Pss. 4 and 134 (with the addition of Ps. 31: 1–6 in medieval secular breviaries). Other elements, such as the hymn *Te lucis ante terminum* and the '*Nunc Dimittis' (not taken into the Benedictine rite until 1977) were soon added to the earliest core. The details of the service varied greatly in the different W. breviaries; since 1912 the Roman breviary has included a wider selection of Psalms than in the past. The essential parts of the office were incorporated into the *Evensong of the BCP. A form of Compline was included in the proposed 1928 revision of the BCP as a separate service to be used 'when Evensong has previously been said'. Several of the more recent revisions of the Prayer Book in other parts of the Anglican Communion include Compline, either under that name (e.g. the American BCP of 1979) or under a different title (e.g. 'Prayer at the End of the Day' in the Australian Prayer Book of 1978).

In the RC Church *Novum Rubricarum* (1960; sect. 147) strongly recommended that Compline be recited as the final office of the day, even if for a just cause Mattins of the following day had already been anticipated. The 1971 Breviary allows that it be said before or after midnight, so long as it is recited before retiring for the night.

N. Gihr, *Prim und Komplet des römischen Breviers, liturgisch und aszetisch erklärt* (Theologische Bibliothek, 1907). J. Pargoire, 'Prime et Complies', *Revue d'Histoire et de Littérature Religieuses*, 3 (1898), pp. 281–8 and 456–67. C. Callewaert, JCD, 'De Completorio ante s. Benedictum', *Collationes Brugenses*, 30 (1930), pp. 225–30, repr. in id., *Sacris Erudiri* (Steenbrugge, 1940), pp. 127–30. V. Raffa, FDP, 'Alcuini problemi relativi a Compieta', *EL* 82 (1968), pp. 315–34. O. Klesser in *LW* 1 (1965), cols. 443–6, s.v. See also appropriate parts of works cited under OFFICE, DIVINE.

Complutensian Polyglot. The first polyglot edition of the whole Bible, begun in 1502 at the expense of Card. F. *Ximénes de Cisneros, who assembled a group of scholarly editors at the university which he had founded at Alcalá (Lat. 'Complutum'), where the Bible was finely printed in six folio volumes, 1514–17. The OT has the Hebrew, Latin *Vulgate, and Greek *Septuagint (with interlinear Latin) in parallel columns; in the *Pentateuch only, the Chaldee paraphrase, printed in Hebrew characters with a Latin translation beside it, is added at the foot of the page. Vol. 6 (1515) is a Hebrew and Chaldee vocabulary, with a short Hebrew grammar. The NT Greek in vol. 5 was the earliest ever printed (1514), but prob. it was the four-year privilege granted to the Greek Testament of *Erasmus

(1516) that held up the circulation of the whole Complutensian Bible until c.1522. The large Greek type, used here only in the NT and based on an early book-hand, is justly much admired.

J. P. R. Lyell, *Cardinal Ximenes . . . with an account of the Complutensian Polyglot Bible* (1917), pp. 24–52. B. Hall, *Humanists and Protestants 1500–1900* (Edinburgh, 1990), pp. 1 51 ('Cardinal Jiménez de Cisneros and the Complutensian Bible'). Darlow and Moule, 2, pp. 2–6.

Compostela. A city in NW Spain, properly Santiago [i.e. 'St James'] de Compostela, traditionally supposed to be the place of burial of St *James the Apostle. The seat of the bishops of the ancient see of Iria from the 9th cent., Compostela was raised to metropolitan status in 1120. The military Order of *Santiago, founded in 1170, played a role in the reconquest of Spain from the Muslims. The shrine of St James is a centre for pilgrimages from all over Spain, and from many other parts of the world.

Liber Sancti Jacobi: Codex Calixtinus, ed. W. M. Whitehill, G. Prado, OSB, and Jesús C. Garcia (3 vols., Santiago de Compostela, 1944). P. David, *Étude sur le Livre de Saint-Jacques attribué au Pape Calixte II* (4 parts, Lisbon, 1946–9; repr. from the *Bulletin des Études Portugaises*); M. C. Díaz y Díaz, *El Códice Calixtino de la Catedral de Santiago* (Centro de Estudios Jacobeos, Monografías de *Compostellanum*, 2; 1988). A. López Ferreiro, *Historia de la Santa A[postólica] M[etropolitana] Iglesia de Santiago de Compostela* (11 vols., Santiago de Compostela, 1898–1911). R. A. Fletcher, *Saint James's Catapult: The Life and Times of Diego Gelmírez of Santiago de Compostela* [Bp. of Santiago, 1100–40] (Oxford, 1984), with survey of the earlier history of the city and the cult of St James, pp. 1–101. K. J. Conant, *The Early Architectural History of the Cathedral of Santiago de Compostela* (Cambridge, Mass., 1926). See also bibl. to SPAIN, CHRISTIANITY IN.

comprecation. The word is used esp. of the intercession which the saints are believed to make on behalf of the rest of the Church. Some Anglican theologians (e.g. J. *Bramhall) have maintained that, though direct *invocation of the saints is an unwarranted practice, it is legitimate to request God for their prayers; and such requests for the saints' intercessions have also loosely been called comprecation.

Compton, Henry (1632–1713), Bp. of London. He was educated at Queen's College, *Oxford, and in early life served in the army. After ordination in 1662, he held various preferments, was appointed Bp. of Oxford in 1674, and translated to London in 1675. As Dean of the Province of Canterbury, he was responsible for supervising the 'Compton Census' of 1676, a detailed record of the number of RCs and Protestant Dissenters in each parish and now an important demographic source. A friend of Danby, the Lord Treasurer, Compton was tutor to the princesses Mary and Anne, and officiated at the marriages of both of them. His stoutly anti-Papist attitude and his friendliness towards Protestant Dissenters failed to commend him to *James II, and he was restrained by the Ecclesiastical Commission from the exercise of his spiritual functions, nominally on the ground of his refusal to suspend J. *Sharp, then Rector of St Giles'-in-the-Fields, for his anti-Roman sermons. Having signed the invitation to William of Orange, he took an active part in the events which led to James II's deposition and he officiated in place of W. *Sancroft, at the coronation of William and Mary. He strongly supported the project for comprehension and the *Toleration Act. For some not very clearly known reason, he was twice passed over when the primacy was vacant, in favour of J. *Tillotson and T. *Tenison successively; and during the reign of *Anne he became regarded as a High Churchman, if not a Tory, since he voted for the *Occasional Conformity Bill and in favour of the resolution that the Church was in danger. In 1686 he published under the title *Episcopalia* a set of addresses to his clergy.

Anon. Life, perh. by N. Salmon, London, c.1715. New edn. of his *Episcopalia*, with brief memoir of Compton by S. W. Cornish, Oxford, 1842. [E.] A. [O.] Whiteman (ed.), *The Compton Census of 1676* (Records of Social and Economic History, NS 10; 1986). E. [F.] Carpenter, *The Protestant Bishop* (1956). D. H. Hosford, 'Bishop Compton and the Revolution of 1688', *JEH* 23 (1972), pp. 209–18. S. L. Lee in *DNB* 11 (1887), pp. 443–7.

Comte, Auguste (1798–1857), founder of French *Positivism and of the 'Religion of Humanity'. He was a native of Montpellier and educated at the École Polytechnique, *Paris, where he studied esp. science and mathematics. Having lost his religious faith he came under the influence of H. *Saint-Simon, whose disciple he was from 1816 to 1824. His *Système de politique positive* (1822; Eng. tr., 1875–7) contains in germ most of his later ideas. His principal work was his *Cours de la philosophie positive* (6 vols., 1830–42; condensed Eng. tr. by H. Martineau, 2 vols., 1853). The foundation of his system is the law of the three stages—the theological, the metaphysical, and the 'positive'—which constitute the phases of development of the human race as a whole as well as of its individual members. Whereas in the theological and metaphysical stages the human mind seeks a cause or essence to explain phenomena, in the third or positive phase explanation is discovered in a law. Comte advocated the organization of mankind in one vast system in which altruism was to conquer egoism. Conceiving this to be possible only on a religious basis, he constructed a new kind of religion, with humanity, the 'great being', in the place of God. He introduced an elaborate cultus, borrowed chiefly from Catholicism, with its priests and sacraments, and even produced a 'Positivist Calendar' in which the names of scientists and scholars replaced those of the saints. His revolutionary ideas lost him his post as examiner in mathematics at the École Polytechnique, which he had held from 1837 to 1844, and from this time he was supported chiefly by the generosity of his disciples, among whom, with reservations, was J. S. Mill. In 1848 he founded the 'Positive Society' which aimed at applying the principles of Positivism to the reconstruction of society. In his chief sociological work, *Système de politique positive*, he attempted to apply his utilitarian ethical principles to social and political questions.

Crit. edns. of *Correspondance générale et Confessions* by P. E. de Berrêdo Carneiro and others (Archives Positivistes, 8 vols., 1973–90) and of *Écrits de jeunesse 1816–1828* by idd. (ibid., 1970). Life by H. Gouhier (Paris, 1931; rev. edn., 1965). The numerous studies include those of J. F. E. Robinet (Paris, 1860), [M. P.] E. Littré (ibid., 1863; photographically repr., Farnborough, 1971), J. S. Mill (London, 1865; repr. from the *Westminster Review*; repr., Ann. Arbor, Mich., 1961), E. *Caird (Glasgow, 1885), L. Lévy-Bruhl (Paris, 1900; Eng. tr., 1903), H. Gouhier (3 vols.,

ibid., 1933–41), F. S. Marvin (London, 1936), P. Arnaud (Paris, 1969), E. E. Evans-Pritchard (lecture; Manchester [1970]), C. Rutten (Paris, 1972), and S. de Acevedo and others (Lyons [1988]). T. R. Wright, *The Religion of Humanity: The Impact of Comtean Positivism in Victorian Britain* (Cambridge, 1986).

concelebration. The joint celebration of the *Eucharist by a number of priests. This was prob. usual in the early Church, when the bishop was normally the celebrant. In the W. the practice gradually gave way to separate celebrations, each priest saying Mass at a different time or place, except at *Ordinations, when the newly ordained priests regularly concelebrated with the bishop. In 1963 the 'Constitution on the Liturgy' of the Second *Vatican Council restored the practice of concelebration in the W. Church, and it is now widespread, esp. in religious communities. It is required that all concelebrating priests recite the central part of the Canon together (normally silently). In the E. concelebration by a number of priests survived, though in modern times in most E. rites the Canon is actually said by the celebrant alone.

A. A. King, *Concelebration in the Christian Church* (1966). Articles by B. Botte, OSB, A. Raes, SJ, and others, in *Maison-Dieu*, 35 (1953), pp. 9–75. A. G. Martimort, 'Le Rituel de la concélébration eucharistique', *EL* 77 (1963), pp. 147–68. R. Taft [SJ], 'Ex Oriente Lux? Some Reflections on Eucharistic Concelebration', *Worship*, 54 (1980), pp. 308–25; revised in id., *Beyond East and West: Problems in Liturgical Understanding* (Washington, DC [1984]), pp. 81–99. R. Cabié in A. G. Martimort, *L'Église en Prière* (1983–4 edn.), 2, pp. 238–46; Eng. tr. (1986), pp. 221–30, with bibl. P. de Puniet, OSB, in *DACL* 3 (pt. 2; 1914), cols. 2470–88, s.v. with bibl.

Concentus. See ACCENTUS.

Conception of the BVM. See IMMACULATE CONCEPTION OF THE BVM.

'Concerning the Service of the Church.' The present title of the preface to the original (1549) edition of the BCP. When the present 'Preface' was added in 1662 (immediately before the 1549 preface) it was necessary to give the original preface a new name, and it then received the above title. Its contents were based on the preface to the reformed Roman *Breviary of F. de *Quiñones, and it is probably the work of T. *Cranmer. Its object was to explain the merits of the new Book over its Latin predecessors.

Conciliar theory. The doctrine that supreme authority in the Church lies with a *General Council. The movement associated with this theory culminated in the 15th cent., but the foundations of it were laid in the early years of the 13th, when canonists found difficulty in reconciling the increasing claims of Papal authority with the theoretical possibility of a heretical Pope. Hugh of Pisa (d. 1210), for instance, in his *Summa super Decreta* taught that a heretical Pope could err, and sought to maintain the inerrancy of the Church by distinguishing between the local Roman Church and the Catholic Church as a whole. In the following century, with the further growth of Papal power, the movement gained increasing support and its principles were invoked in the dispute between Philip IV of France and *Boniface VIII in an attempt to depose the latter. John of Paris (d. 1306), the most important advocate of the theory at the time, in his treatise *De Potestate Regia et Papali* (1302) taught that the Pope was the steward of God in matters spiritual and temporal; as such he could be deposed for injustice by those who had elected him, who had themselves acted as representatives of the whole Christian people. *Marsiglio of Padua in his *Defensor Pacis* (1324) maintained the supremacy of the state in all matters, spiritual as well as temporal. *William of Ockham, attacking the indefectibility of both Pope and General Council, sought the fulfilment of the Lord's promise of the inerrancy of the Church in the survival of truth in any part of it, however obscure.

The outbreak of the *Great Schism in 1378 raised the question of the supremacy of authority in an acute form. In 1380 *Conrad of Gelnhausen in his *Epistola Concordiae* advocated the summoning of a General Council, arguing that the absence of a single recognized Pope left the duty of convoking it to the *cardinals. The success of the Council of *Constance in ending the schism to some extent undermined the position of the conciliarists, though the Council in its 4th and 5th sessions had already declared that any Christian, including the Pope, was bound by the decisions of a General Council, which derived its authority directly from God. In 1418 *Martin V prepared a prohibition of appeals from the Pope to a future General Council; *Pius II, who before becoming Pope had been an exponent of the Conciliar theory, in 1460 promulgated the bull 'Execrabilis' formally forbidding such appeals. Although the *De Concordantia Catholica* of *Nicholas of Cusa embodied a balanced scheme for the reform of the Church, the failure of the conciliar theory to win general acceptance after the 15th cent. may be taken as one of the factors at least indirectly leading to the *Reformation, and within the RC Church to such movements as *Gallicanism. It is of interest that the Second *Vatican Council has again emphasized the corporate authority of the episcopate, though not over against the Papacy. See also COLLEGIALITY.

Eng. tr. of various primary docs., with introd., by C. M. D. Crowder, *Unity, Heresy and Reform, 1378–1460: The Conciliar Response to the Great Schism* (1977). V. Martin, 'Comment s'est formée la doctrine de la supériorité du Concile sur le Pape', *Rev. S.R.* 17 (1937), pp. 121–43, 261–89, 405–27. B. Tierney, *Foundations of the Conciliar Theory* (Cambridge Studies in Medieval Life and Thought, NS 4, 1955). P. de Vooght, *Les Pouvoirs du Concile et l'autorité du Pape au Concile de Constance* (Unam Sanctam, 56; 1965). F. Oakley, *Council over Pope? Towards a Provisional Ecclesiology* (New York, 1969). A. J. Black, *Monarchy and Community: Political Ideas in the Later Conciliar Controversy 1430–1450* (Cambridge Studies in Medieval Life and Thought, 3rd ser., 2; 1970). G. Alberigo, *Chiesa Conciliare: Identità e significato del conciliarismo* (Brescia, 1981). H. J. Sieben, *Traktate und Theorien zum Konzil von Beginn des Grossen Schismas bis zum Vorabend der Reformation, 1378–1521* (Frankfurter theologische Studien, 30; 1983). W. Brandmüller, *Papst und Konzil im Grossen Schisma (1378–1431): Studien und Quellen* (1990). See also works cited under writers mentioned in the article.

conclave (Lat. *cum clave*, 'with a key'). The closed apartment in which the college of *cardinals is shut up during the entire process of electing a new Pope. The custom of keeping the cardinals enclosed was adopted in 1271 to hasten a Papal election which was still not made after nearly three years, and this practice has been followed ever since. The word 'conclave' is also applied to the meeting itself, either on this particular occasion or, more loosely, of the cardinals for any purpose.

L. Lector [really Mgr. J. Guthlin], *Le Conclave, origines, histoire, organisation, législation ancienne et moderne* (1894); A. Ceccaroni, *Il conclave: Storia, costituzioni, cerimonie* (1901). E. Ruffini Avondo, 'Le origini del conclave papale', *Atti della Reale Accademia delle Scienze di Torino*, 27 (1927), pp. 409–31. The procedure for the election of a Pope is now governed by Pope *Paul VI's Apostolic Constitution 'Romano Pontifici Eligendo' (*AAS* 67 (1975), pp. 609–45), modified by Pope *John Paul II's Apostolic Constitution 'Universi Dominici Gregis' (*ASS* 88 (1996), pp. 305–43. Further bibl., with refs. to doc. sources, in F. Cerroti, *Bibliografia di Roma medievale e moderna*, 1 (1893), esp. pp. 544–52. A. Molien in *DDC* 3 (1942), cols. 1319–42, s.v.

concomitance. The doctrine that in the Eucharist the Body and Blood of Christ are present in each of the consecrated species. It implies that the fullness of communion is to be had in either element alone, and it has been held, esp. among RCs, to justify the withdrawal of the chalice from the laity. In a more extended sense, the word is also used for the doctrine that in virtue of the *hypostatic union of God and man in Christ, the Godhead and the human soul of Christ are also present in the Eucharistic elements after their consecration. See also COMMUNION IN BOTH KINDS.

J. J. Megivern, CM, *Concomitance and Communion: A Study in Eucharistic Doctrine and Practice* (Studia Friburgensia, NS 33; Fribourg and New York, 1963), esp. pp. 51–257. See also works cited s.v. EUCHARIST.

Concord, Formula (1577) and Book (1580) of. The 'Formula of Concord', the last of the classical *Lutheran formulae of faith, was drawn up in Mar. 1577, by a number of theologians, among them Jacob *Andreae, M. *Chemnitz, and Nikolaus Selnecker (1530–92). Internal disagreements within Lutheranism over the proper interpretation of the *Augsburg Confession (1530) followed the external peace established with the Peace of *Augsburg (1555). In 1567 Andreae was commissioned to produce a union formula. Initially unsuccessful, he later preached a series of six sermons which were summarized in 11 theses, known as the Swabian Concord of 1573 (revised by Chemnitz in the Swabian-Saxon Concord of 1575). Other Lutherans produced the Maulbronn Formula in 1576. The Elector of Saxony then assembled theologians to work on a common statement. The result was the Torgau Book, which was produced in 1576, combining the Swabian-Saxon Concord and the Maulbronn Formula. Andreae was asked to edit the results of these efforts and to provide a summary of their content. Thus the Solid Declaration (the Bergen Book of 1577) was produced along with an Epitome, which together constitute the Formula of Concord. The Formula treats various topics, such as *original sin and free will, the relationship between law and gospel, the Person of Christ, *adiaphora (things 'nonessential' to salvation), and eternal foreknowledge and Divine election. It denies that human merit and free will have any role in the justification of man and just as resolutely rejects *antinomianism; it upholds the bodily presence of Christ in the Lord's Supper irrespective of the faith of the recipient, affirms the Divine majesty of the man Jesus and thus also the omnipresence of the human as well as the Divine nature of Christ, stresses the necessity of resistance when a declaration of faith is demanded, and closely links Divine election to the word of the gospel. It appeals first to Scripture as the only 'rule and norm' of doctrine, followed by the early Church Fathers, the *Apostles', *Nicene, and *Athanasian Creeds, the Augsburg Confession of 1530 (to which P. *Melanchthon's 'Treatise on the Power and Primacy of the Pope' was appended in 1537) and its Apology (1531), the *Schmalkaldic Articles (1537) and M. *Luther's two catechisms (1529). These documents consequently became the basis for the Book of Concord (*Konkordienbuch*), published in German at Dresden in 1580 (the Latin edition appeared in 1584). Finally, an extensive 'catalogue of testimonies' (*catalogus testimoniorum*) from Scripture and the writings of the early church appeared in an appendix, testifying to the avowed ecumenical character of Lutheran doctrine, particularly its Christology. Thus while the Book of Concord represents a definitive collection of the principal confessional documents of Lutheranism, a certain hierarchy of authorities among the documents is recognised, the Augsburg Confession and Luther's Small Catechism assuming pride of place.

Crit. text by H. *Lietzmann and others, *Die Bekenntnisschriften der evangelisch-lutherischen Kirche, herausgegeben im Gedenkjahr der Augsburgischen Konfession 1930* (10th edn., Göttingen, 1986). Eng. tr. by T. G. Tappert and others (Philadelphia, 1959). E. Schlink, *Theologie der lutherischen Bekenntnisschriften* (1940; 3rd edn., 1948; Eng. tr., Philadelphia [1961]). [G.] F. Bente, *Historical Introductions to the Book of Concord* (St Louis, 1965). L. W. Spitz and W. Lohff (eds.), *Discord, Dialogue, and Concord: Studies in the Lutheran Reformation's Formula of Concord* (Philadelphia [1977]); W. Lohff and L. [W.] Spitz (eds.), *Widerspruch, Dialog und Einigung: Studien zur Konkordienformel der Lutherischen Reformation* (Stuttgart, 1977). R. Preus and W. Rosin (eds.), *A Contemporary Look at the Formula of Concord* (St Louis, 1978). See also works cited s.v. LUTHERANISM.

Concord of Wittenberg. See WITTENBERG, CONCORD OF.

concordance. An alphabetical list of words in the Bible giving, for each appearance of a word, its location and a brief context. The first such list, a concordance to the *Vulgate, was the product of efforts by the *Dominican Order in the 13th cent. to provide preachers with the tools necessary for writing sermons. Compiled at St Jacques in Paris and related to the compilation of collections of biblical distinctions for use in preaching, the development of the concordance can be seen in at least three stages. The first, completed under the direction of Hugh of St Cher some time between 1230 and 1240, provided only locations without context. Before mid-century, there were various efforts to make the concordance easier to use. The multi-volume concordance associated with Richard of Stavensby and other English Dominicans working at St Jacques provided an eight- to ten-word context for each entry, which proved to be too cumbersome for efficient use. A third version, in one volume and with briefer contexts, was produced at St Jacques before 1286. This concordance, published in Strasbourg in 1474 and adapted by F. P. Dutripon (Paris, 1838), has remained in use until modern times.

Concordances to the Hebrew Old Testament and the Greek Septuagint were both products of W. Europe, made in imitation of the Latin concordance. A Hebrew concordance, compiled 1437–45 by Rabbi Isaac b. Kalonymus, was pub. at Venice in 1523 and tr. into Lat. 1556; it was revised by M. de Calasio, OFM (Rome, 1621). A *Hebrew Concordance adapted to the English Bible* was pub. by John *Taylor (2 vols., 1754–7). A concordance to the *Septuagint was compiled by C. Kircher (3 vols., Frankfurt, 1607); the standard modern work is that of E. *Hatch and H. A. Redpath (3 vols., Oxford, 1892–1906). The pioneer concordance to the Gk. NT was that of S. Birck, pub. at Basle, 1546; in 1638 it was followed by the Ταμεῖον of Erasmus Schmidt (pub. Wittenberg), which was ed. by C. H. Bruder (Leipzig, 1842; rev., with readings of S. P. *Tregelles, and B. F. *Westcott and F. J. A. *Hort, Leipzig, 1888). This was generally replaced among English scholars by the concordance of W. F. *Moulton and A. S. Geden (Edinburgh, 1897). The standard concordance to the Gk. NT is now that of K. Aland and others (Berlin, 1978–83). A more concise concordance based on this was issued in 1987.

The first concordance in English was that to M. *Coverdale's translation of the NT by T. Gybson (1535); that to the whole Bible was made by J. *Merbecke (1550). Others followed but all were superseded by A. *Cruden's (1737), which in its later editions is extremely detailed and complete. The most significant revision of it was made by J. Eadie and others (Glasgow, 1840). The chief later concordance to the English Bible is R. Young's *Analytical Concordance to the Bible* (Edinburgh, 1879). A concordance incl. refs. to the RV was pub. in 1894 (ed. J. Strong, London); a concordance to the translation of J. *Moffatt appeared in London, 1950. More recently there have been published concordances to the RSV in 1957, with a concise concordance by B. M. Metzger in 1962, and a concordance to the main English versions of the NT by M. Darton in 1976. There are separate concordances to most modern translations of the Bible (often produced by computer assisted methods).

A. Kleinhans, OFM, 'De Prima Editione Catholica Concordantiarum Hebraico-Latinarum Sacrorum Bibliorum' [1621 edn.], *Biblica*, 5 (1924), pp. 39–48. On concordances to the Vulgate, R. H. and M. A. Rouse, 'The Verbal Concordance to the Scriptures', *Archivum Fratrum Praedicatorum*, 44 (1974) pp. 5–30; idd., 'Concordances et index', in H.-J. Martin and J. Vezin (eds.), *Mise en page et mise en texte du livre manuscrit* [1990], pp. 218–28. S. L. Greenslade (ed.), *The Cambridge History of the Bible*, [3] *The West from the Reformation to the Present Day* (1963), pp. 526–8 ('Concordances'). E. Mangenot in *Dict. Bibl.* 2 (1899), cols. 892–905, s.v. 'Concordances de la Bible'. See also bibl. to CRUDEN, A.

concordat. An agreement between the civil and ecclesiastical authorities upon some matter of vital concern to both parties. See also, besides the following entry, LATERAN TREATY (1929).

Concordat of 1801. The agreement concluded, on 16 July 1801, between *Pius VII and Napoleon Bonaparte, then First Consul, which led to the formal restoration of the Catholic Church in France. By its terms the French government recognized the Catholic religion as that of the great majority of French citizens. All existing bishops were to resign their sees; fresh dioceses were mapped out; and the state was given the right of nominating new bishops. Napoleon insisted on having an amalgam of the old

*Constitutional bishops (12 of them) and the old orthodox bishops who had been dispossessed by the state in 1791 (16 of them), together with 32 priests from both parties. Alienated Church property was to remain in the hands of those who had acquired it, but the government agreed to ensure a fitting maintenance to the bishops and parish priests. The expected benefits of these terms to the Church were considerably reduced by Napoleon's subsequent publication of the *Organic Articles (q.v.).

Le Cte Boulay de La Meurthe (ed.), *Documents sur la négociation du concordat et sur les autres rapports de la France avec le saint-siège* (6 vols., 1891–1905), with Texte Définitif du Concordat in Lat. and Fr., no. 645, vol. 3, pp. 213–19; the Fr. version, lacking the preamble, also pr. in Mirbt, no. 558, pp. 419 f. Le Cte Boulay de La Meurthe, *Histoire de la négociation du concordat de 1801* (Tours, 1920). [F. D.] Mathieu, *Le Concordat de 1801: Ses origines—son histoire* (1903). H. H. Walsh, *The Concordat of 1801: A Study of the Problem of Nationalism in the Relations of Church and State* (New York, 1933). J. Leflon, *Étienne-Alexandre Bernier, évêque d'Orléans, 1762–1806* (2 vols., 1938), vol. 1, pp. 121–313, vol. 2, pp. 1–169; id., *Monsieur Emery: L'Église concordataire et impériale* [1946], esp. pp. 39–199. S. Delacroix, *Le Réorganisation de l'Église de France après la Révolution (1801–1809)*, 1 (1962). See also bibl. to CONSTITUTIONAL CHURCH.

Concordia Regularis. See REGULARIS CONCORDIA.

concupiscence. In moral theology the inordinate desire for temporal ends which has its seat in the senses. The notion of concupiscence has its biblical foundations esp. in the teaching of St *Paul (Rom. 7: 7 ff., etc.) and was developed by St *Augustine in his struggle against *Pelagianism. Acc. to Augustine the cause of concupiscence is the *Fall of *Adam, who, having lost *Original Righteousness, transmitted to us a nature in which the desires of the flesh are no longer subordinated to reason. St *Thomas Aquinas, elaborating the Augustinian teaching, regards it as the material (i.e. passive, because residing in the senses) element of Original Sin, the formal (active, residing in the will) element being loss of Original Righteousness. From the moral point of view it is *materia exercendae virtutis*, for it provides reason and will with opportunities for resisting the disordered movements of the senses. Orthodox Protestant theology, on the other hand, both in its *Lutheran and in its *Calvinist forms, regards concupiscence itself as sin and its very existence as an offence against God; and the *Jansenists held a similar view. The Council of *Trent (sess. 5) followed St Thomas's teaching against the Reformers, and in post-Tridentine theology it is usually regarded as a consequence of Original Sin rather than as part of it.

K. *Rahner, SJ, 'Zum theologischen Begriff der Konkupiszenz', *ZKT* 65 (1941), pp. 61–80, repr. in his *Schriften zur Theologie*, 1 (1954), pp. 377–414; Eng. tr. (1961), pp. 347–82. R. Biot and C. Baumgartner in *Dict. Sp.* 2 (1953), cols. 1334–73; L. Scheffczyk in *Sacramentum Mundi*, 1 (1968), pp. 403–5, both s.v.

concurrence. The falling on consecutive days of ecclesiastical feasts or other days to be observed, so that Second *Vespers or *Evensong of the first coincided with First Vespers or Evensong of the second. The complicated rules which used to govern the use of collects, etc., in such situations in the RC Church no longer apply; First Vespers of a *Solemnity cancels all other observances.

concursus divinus (Lat., 'Divine concourse'). A technical theological term for the co-operation of the *grace of God with the actions of finite creatures.

Catholic theologians are in general agreement that it is of two forms, namely (1) *mediate*, such as God's gift of capacities to His creatures appropriate to the performing of certain tasks, and (2) *immediate*, such as the direct dependence of man on God in the actual exercise of these capacities; but the exact manner in which the concursus takes place has been much disputed. *Thomists have held that immediate concursus precedes the action (*praemotio physica*), whereas *Molinists have maintained that the concursus and the action are simultaneous (*concursus simultaneus*). Among Protestant theologians, the fact of the 'Divine concourse' was allowed by *Lutherans and rejected by *Calvinists. The two facts which the several accounts of the 'Divine concourse' have been concerned to maintain are man's own responsibility for his sinful acts and the universality of God's sovereign rule.

condignity. In the Scholastic theology of *grace, those actions which fallen man performs as a Christian in conscious reliance on the Holy Spirit are held to merit the grace of God 'by condignity' (*gratia de condigno*), i.e. as from a debtor. NT support is found in the case of Cornelius, whose prayers and alms are said to have come up for a memorial before God. (Cf. Acts 10: 31, esp. *Vulgate text.)

conditional Baptism. See BAPTISM.

conditional immortality (also known as **annihilationism**). A theory acc. to which immortality is not a necessary attribute of the immaterial soul but conditional on its behaviour during its life in the body. Though this opinion had a solitary representative in the 4th-cent. African Christian author *Arnobius, it was never held in Christendom until recent times, except in isolated cases of philosophical speculation, and it was formally condemned at the Fifth *Lateran Council in 1513. In the 19th cent., however, it found favour with many thinkers as a possible way of accounting for the fate of the impenitently wicked without accepting either the orthodox doctrine of eternal punishment or the *Origenistic theory of universalism. It was elaborated by Edward White, a *Congregational minister, in his *Life in Christ* (1846; expanded and wholly recast, 1875), which attempted to prove from Scripture that 'Immortality is the peculiar privilege of the regenerate', and it found some acceptance among English and American as well as Continental thinkers. It was restated in a milder form by J. *Martineau, acc. to whom the wicked are not annihilated, but lose their personal being, and this belief was admitted to be tolerable by C. *Gore. The teaching of the mortality of the soul is generally considered to be opposed to the Christian doctrine of man and to the dignity and responsibility of the human soul. It has, however, been recently revived by some *Evangelical theologians, who hold that annihilation follows a period of torment in *Hell.

E. W. Fudge, *The Fire that Consumes. A Biblical and Historical Study of Final Punishment* (Houston [1982]; 2nd edn., revised by P. Cousins, *The Fire that Consumes. The Biblical Case for Conditional Immortality*, Carlisle [1994]). H. W. Fulford in *HERE* 3

(1901), pp. 822–5, s.v.; G. C. Joyce, ibid. 1 (1908), pp. 544–9, s.v. 'Annihilation'; both with bibl.; B. J. Warfield in the *New Schaff-Herzog Encyclopedia of Religious Knowledge*, 1 (1908), pp. 183–86, s.v. 'Annihilationism'.

Condren, Charles de (1588–1641), French theologian and spiritual director. Though intended by his father for a military career, an early vocation to a life of prayer led him to study theology at the *Sorbonne. He was ordained priest in 1614, entered the *Oratory in 1617, and succeeded P. de *Bérulle as Superior-General in 1629. He founded houses in Nevers, Langres, and Poitiers. His spirituality was centred on an intense devotion to the mysteries of the Incarnate Christ and on the sacrifice of the Mass, related to the eternal sacrifice of Christ. His pessimistic outlook saw in man only his sinfulness. Although he was much sought after as a spiritual director, he published nothing in his lifetime. His letters were posthumously issued in 1642 and *L'Idée du sacerdoce et du sacrifice de Jésus-Christ*, put together by his disciples, in 1677. He had considerable influence on J.-J. *Olier. In Britain his Eucharistic teaching came to be appreciated through the *Tractarians; an Eng. tr. of *L'Idée* was issued in 1906.

The best collected edn. of his Works is that of L. M. Pin (2 vols., Paris, 1857–8); crit. edn. of his Letters by P. Auvray, Cong. Orat., and A. Jouffrey, Cong. Orat. (ibid., 1943). The primary source for his life is the biog. by D. Amelote (anon, 2 pts., Paris, 1643). Study (in Eng.) by M. V. Woodgate (Dublin, 1949), with bibl. Bremond, 3, pp. 283–340; Pourrat, 3, pp. 521–5 and 551–67; L. Cognet, *La Spiritualité Moderne*, 1 (1966), pp. 382–90. A. Molien, Cong. Orat., in *Dict. Sp.* 2 (1953), cols. 1373–88, s.v., with further bibl. See also bibl. to ORATORIANS.

conduct. A name formerly in general use for any priest who was engaged to read the prayers in the chapel of a college of which he was not on the foundation. The chaplains at Eton College are still so described.

Confessing Church (*Bekennende Kirche*), also known as the 'Confessional Church' (*Bekenntnis-Kirche*). The group of German Evangelical Christians most actively opposed to the '*German Christian' Church Movement sponsored by the Nazis between 1933 and 1945. It consisted of the 'Pastors' Emergency League' founded in Nov. 1933 under the leadership of M. *Niemöller, the Lutheran *Landeskirchen* which had not succumbed to the German Christians, and a strong parish movement particularly in the W. provinces of Germany. In 1934 the Church opposition began to set up its own canonical authorities (esp. the Councils of the Brethren, *Bruderräte*) at all levels in those regions where the official administration was 'German Christian'; the Synod of Barmen in May 1934 issued the *Barmen Declaration (q.v.) which laid the foundation for subsequent resistance to all attempts to make the Evangelical Churches an instrument of Nazi policy. Persecution of clergy and laity failed to prevent the opposition of the Confessing Church until the outbreak of War in 1939 brought open resistance to an end. Many of the younger confessional pastors were conscripted and fell in battle.

At the end of the War, in 1945, leaders of the Confessing Churches met a delegation of the Provisional *World Council of Churches under G. K. A. *Bell at Stuttgart and made to them a 'Declaration of Guilt'. This action opened the way to a restoration of fellowship between the German Churches and the World Council of Churches, which gave considerable assistance to the Confessing Church. In 1948 the '*Evangelical Church in Germany' was founded from a federation of all the regional Lutheran, Reformed and United Churches in Germany. The 'Confessing Church' continued to be an active movement, though no longer claiming to be the only Church government.

In its earlier days the adherents of the movement generally called themselves the 'Confessional Church' to emphasize that their opposition was primarily religious (based on confessions of faith) and not political; later this name was felt to be no longer appropriate and they came to prefer 'Confessing Church', with the sense of being a Church of confessors for the faith rather than those who owed allegiance to a formal dogmatic Confession.

H. Hermelink (ed.), *Kirche im Kampf: Dokumente des Widerstands und des Aufbaus in der Evangelischen Kirche Deutschlands von 1933 bis 1945* (Tübingen, 1950); C. Nicolaisen and G. Kretschmar (eds.), *Dokumente zur Kirchenpolitik des dritten Reiches* (vols. 1–2, Munich, 1971–5; vol. 3, Gütersloh, 1994). K. D. Schmidt (ed.), *Die Bekenntnisse und grundsätzlichen Äusserungen zur Kirchenfrage* (3 vols., Göttingen, 1934–6). W. Niemöller, *Kampf und Zeugnis der Bekennenden Kirche* (Bielefeld, 1948); id., *Die Evangelische Kirche im Dritten Reich: Handbuch des Kirchenkampfes* (ibid., 1956). J. S. Conway, *The Nazi Persecution of the Churches, 1933–45* [1968]. K. Meier, *Die evangelische Kirchenkampf* (3 vols., Göttingen, 1976–84). K. Scholder, *Die Kirchen und das Dritte Reich* (2 vols. [1977–85], incomplete; Eng. tr., 1987–8). A. Boyens, *Kirchenkampf und Ökumene 1933–1939: Darstellung und Dokumentation* (Munich [1969]; id., *Kirchenkampf und Ökumene 1939–45* (ibid. [1973]). V. Conzemius, 'Églises chrétiennes et totalitarisme national-socialiste', *RHE* 63 (1968), pp. 437–503 and 868–948, esp. pp. 437–58, repr. as Bibliothèque de la *RHE*, 48 (1969), esp. pp. 5–26. O. Diehn, *Bibliographie zur Geschichte des Kirchenkampfes 1933/1945* (Arbeiten zur Geschichte des Kirchenkampfes, 1; Göttingen, 1958), and other specialized studies in the same series (*Registerband*, ed. G. Grünzinger-Siebert and others, the final vol. 30; 1984).

Confessio Augustana. See AUGSBURG CONFESSION.

Confessio Helvetica. See HELVETIC CONFESSION.

Confessio Scotica. See SCOTTISH CONFESSION.

confession. (1) A tomb of a *martyr ('*confessor'). The term is used also of the structure built over such a tomb, and of a crypt or shrine under the *High Altar of a church in which relics are placed. In the Middle Ages the word was further applied to the entire church in which a martyr was buried. The *confessio* of St Peter in the *Vatican is perhaps the most celebrated of all such tombs.

(2) The profession of faith made by a martyr or confessor (e.g. 1 Tim. 6: 13, 2 Cor. 9: 13), and so in general a declaration of religious belief. In this sense the word has been occasionally applied to the ancient ecumenical *creeds, but it is more generally used of the Protestant professions of faith in the 16th and 17th cents., of which the Confession of *Augsburg (1530) was the earliest. From this sense derives its use for a communion, or religious body.

(3) An acknowledgment of sin, made either in general terms by a congregation in the course of liturgical worship, or specifically by an individual penitent in public confes-

sion, or more usually in private or *auricular confession. See also ABSOLUTION and PENANCE.

confession rooms. In some RC churches small rooms have been set aside for the administration of *Penance because of the emphasis laid on the importance of the dialogue between penitent and confessor in the 1973 *Ordo Poenitentiae*. Such rooms, usually furnished with two chairs, a table, and a kneeler, make it possible for difficulties to be discussed face to face in a way precluded by the use of the confessional 'box' which became common in the 16th cent.

Confessions of St Augustine, The. A prose-poem ostensibly addressed to God, written *c.*398–400, soon after the author had become Bp. of Hippo and when some critics were anxious about his *Manichaean past. The title means both 'confessing' in the biblical sense of praising God, and also avowal of faults; there is an undercurrent of self-vindication and pervasive anti-Manichaean polemic. The main theme is announced in the opening paragraph: 'You have made us for yourself, and our heart is restless until it rests in you'. Books 1–9 are autobiographical, describing his loss of faith, his decade of adherence to Mani, succeeded by deep scepticism, and a conversion to *Neoplatonism which led to the recovery of his childhood faith and to baptism. The climaxes are the description of his decision in a Milan garden in July 386 (how far this is factual is controversial), the vision shared with St *Monica at Ostia, and the account of her death. The last four books deal with memory (10), time (11), creation (12), and an allegory of the Church in Gen. 1 (13); they portray on a cosmic scale the theme of return to and rest in the ultimate ground of being in God.

Modern edns. by E. B. *Pusey (Oxford, 1838; inaugurating the *Tractarian *Bibliotheca Patrum*), P. Knöll (CSEL 33; 1896), J. Gibb and W. Montgomery (Cambridge Patristic Texts, 1908), P. de Labriolle (2 vols., Paris, 1925–7), A. C. Vega, OSA (Escurial, 1930), F. Skutella (Teub., Leipzig, 1934; rev. H. Juergens and W. Schaub, ibid., Stuttgart, 1969, with further corrections, 1981; rev. L. Verheijen, CCSL 27; 1981) and, with comm., by J. J. O'Donnell (3 vols., Oxford, 1992). Eng. trs. by Sir Tobie Matthew (St-Omer, 1620; mod. edn. by R. Huddleston, OSB, London, 1923), W. Watts (ibid., 1631; repr. in Loeb, 2 vols., 1912), E. B. Pusey (LF 1, 1838; rev. of tr. of W. Watts), F. J. Sheed (London, 1943), J. K. Ryan (Garden City, NY, 1960), R. S. Pine-Coffin (Harmondsworth, 1961), R. Warner (New York, 1963), and H. Chadwick (Oxford, 1991).

The more important works on the *Confessions* include P. Alfaric, *L'Évolution intellectuelle de saint Augustin* (thesis, Paris, 1918); R. L. Ottley, *Studies in the Confessions of St Augustine* (1919); C. Boyer, SJ, *Christianisme et néoplatonisme dans la formation de saint Augustin* (thesis, Paris, 1920); K. *Holl, *Augustins innere Entwicklung* (*Abh.* (Berl.), Jg. 1922, Heft 4; 1923), repr. in Holl's *Gesammelte Aufsätze zur Kirchengeschichte*, 3 (1928), pp. 54–116; K. Nörregaard, *Augustins Bekehrung* (1923); M. Zepf, *Augustins Confessiones* (Heidelberger Abhandlungen zur Philosophie und ihrer Geschichte; 9; 1926); W. J. Sparrow Simpson, *St Augustine's Conversion* (1930); K. *Adam, *Die geistige Entwicklung des heiligen Augustinus* (1931; Eng. tr., *Saint Augustine: The Odyssey of his Soul*, 1932); P. Henry, SJ, *La Vision d'Ostie: Sa place dans la vie et l'œuvre de saint Augustin* (1938; Eng. tr., *The Path to Transcendence*, Pittsburgh Theological Monograph Series, 37; 1981); M. Verheijen, OESA, *Eloquentia Pedisequa: Observations sur le style des Confessions de saint Augustin* (Latinitas Christianorum Primaeva, 10; Nijmegen, 1949); P. Courcelle, *Recherches sur*

les *Confessions de saint Augustin* (1950; 2nd edn., 1968); J. M. Le Blond, *Les Conversions de saint Augustin* (1950); J. O'Meara, *The Young Augustine* (1954); G. N. Knauer, *Die Psalmenzitate in Augustins Konfessionen* (1955); M. Pellegrino, *Le 'Confessioni' di Sant'Agostino: Studio introduttivo* (1956; Fr. tr., 1961); F. Bolgiani, *La conversione di S. Agostino e l'VIII° Libro delle 'Confessioni'* (Università di Torino. Pubblicazioni della Facoltà di Lettere e Filosofia, 8, fasc. 4; 1956); P. Courcelle, *Les Confessions de Saint Augustin dans la tradition littéraire: antécédents et postérité* (1963); R. J. O'Connell, *St Augustine's Confessions* (Cambridge, Mass., 1969); C. [J.] Starnes, *Augustine's Conversion: A Guide to the Argument of* Confessions *I–IX* (Waterloo, Ont. [1990]). See also works cited under AUGUSTINE.

confessor. (1) In the early Church one who suffered for confessing his or her faith, but only to an extent which did not involve martyrdom. Later the term was applied loosely to markedly holy men, and ultimately to those pronounced to be such by the Pope. King *Edward (d. 1066) was declared a Confessor by *Alexander III in 1161.

(2) A priest who hears (esp. private) confessions.

Confirmation. In Sacramental theology, the rite whereby the grace of the Holy Spirit is conveyed in a new or fuller way to those who have already received it in some degree or fashion at *Baptism. Though the rite goes back to very early times, there have been wide differences as to its method of administration, as well as to the theological interpretation put upon it. It has been held, at least among Catholic theologians, to imprint a *character on the recipient, so that the same person cannot be confirmed more than once.

Many theologians have found early instances of Confirmation in the imposition of hands by the Apostles, e.g. by St *Peter and St *John on the converts of Samaria (Acts 8: 14–17) and by St *Paul on the disciples at *Ephesus (19: 1–7). Other NT passages which may refer to it are the 'laying on of hands', as distinct from the 'teaching of baptisms', in Heb. 6: 2, or again the frequent mention in the NT of the 'sealing with the Spirit' (e.g. 2 Cor. 1: 20 f., Eph. 1: 13, 4: 30), though perhaps these belong with more probability to Baptism. The difficulty of fitting the NT references into a wholly unified pattern becomes clear when we observe that, whereas in many places the full imparting of the Holy Spirit is closely linked with the actual Baptism, e.g. in the Baptism of the Lord Himself (Mk. 1: 10) and of the first converts on the Day of *Pentecost (Acts 2: 38), in others the Spirit is given prior to, and seemingly independently of, Baptism (Acts 9: 17 f.).

In the sub-Apostolic age, a similar variety of practice is met with. Washing with water, anointing with oil, and the laying on of hands all come to be associated with initiation into the fullness of Christian life, and the aggregate spiritual effect which flowed from these outward observances was held to include the removal of sin, admission to the Church of the Redeemed, 'sealing' to eternal life, and the imparting of the Spirit. There was, however, very considerable variety alike of practice and interpretation.

The laying on of hands appears as an integral part of the Baptismal liturgy in *Tertullian (*De Baptismo* 8, and *De Res. Carnis* 8) and, together with anointing, in the *Apostolic Tradition*. It is distinguished from the actual Baptism by St *Cyprian (*Epp.* 70, 74) and by Pope *Cornelius (ap. *Eusebius, *HE* 6. 43). By the 4th cent. 'Confirmation', whether conferred by anointing or laying on of hands, was in the W. frequently a distinct rite separated from Baptism. In the course of time the number of candidates seeking admission to the Church meant that the bishop could no longer baptize them all in person; the parish clergy came regularly to administer Baptism and the part of the bishop in the initiation ceremonies was deferred until the next episcopal visitation. What had once been scarcely distinguishable elements in the Baptismal complex were performed at different times by different ministers.

The practice, however, became stereotyped in different ways in the E. and W. In the E. the primitive custom of conferring 'Confirmation' in immediate relation to Baptism was retained. This was achieved by confining the bishop's part to the consecration of the oil used for the anointing. This was then conveyed to the parish priest, who performed the actual rite of Confirmation as occasion required. After anointing, it was the regular custom in the E. to dispense Holy Communion at once, so that the infant received all three Sacraments in a single service. Such has remained the practice in the E. down to the present day.

In the W., on the other hand, the bishop retained his function as the regular minister of the rite (as he had been originally also of Baptism). Confirmation was therefore deferred until an opportunity arose of presenting the candidate to the bishop in person. One result was that, owing to difficulties of communication and the manifold duties apt to claim the attention of the bishop, Confirmation became very irregular in the Middle Ages and later. But, at least until the 16th cent., the separation was accidental and the ideal of the two rites being conferred together never lost. *Elizabeth I was brought by *Henry VIII to Baptism and Confirmation when but three days old.

The precise theological significance of the rite has been, and still is, disputed. Some regard it as an integral part of, and in its effects indistinguishable from, Baptism. Others regard it as conveying a new gift of the Spirit, esp. the grace necessary to strengthen the candidate in his conflict with evil. The latter view, elaborated in a homily by *Faustus of Riez (formerly attributed to *Eusebius of Emesa), gained wide currency through its incorporation in the *Forged Decretals and it is still widely held in the W. In the Middle Ages Confirmation came to be accounted one of the *Seven Sacraments. St *Thomas Aquinas (*Summa Theol.* 3, q. 72) and other *Dominican theologians held that it was immediately instituted by Christ; St *Bonaventure (for whom it was 'the sacrament of warriors') believed that it was instituted by the Holy Spirit under the 'successors of the Apostles' (*In Sent.* 4, dist. 7, art. 1); while the *Summa* (4, q. 9) of *Alexander of Hales expressed the curious view that it was constituted a Sacrament by the Council of Meaux of 845. The *Tridentine theologians were remarkably reticent on the subject. In the RC Church there have been wide differences as to wherein the 'matter' of the Sacrament consists. Acc. to some (J. *Sirmond, D. *Petavius), it was the laying on of hands; acc. to others (St Thomas Aquinas, Card. *Bellarmine), anointing with chrism; acc. to still others (J. *Morinus), the two together, a view reflected in the *Catechism of the Catholic Church* (1992).

Since the later Middle Ages the usual practice in the RC Church has been to confer Confirmation as soon as convenient after the seventh birthday, but since 1971 it has been open to national Conferences of bishops to decide on a later age. According to the 1971 rite, Confirmation is normally administered during Mass. After the homily the candidates renew their Baptismal promises. The bishop then extends his hands over them and prays that they may receive the Holy Spirit; he then traces the sign of the Cross with *chrism (oil blessed on *Maundy Thursday) on the forehead of each candidate. The Mass continues, ending with the special blessing provided. Priests may also confirm with the bishop, provided that the chrism is given to them by the bishop. Faculties for priests to confirm on their own with chrism blessed by the bishop have long been given in exceptional cases; in cases of candidates *in articulo mortis* they were given to all parish priests in 1947 and later to other priests; and in 1971 they were widely extended, so that a priest can confirm adults whom he baptizes or receives into the RC Church from another communion.

At the Reformation, the C of E continued the medieval practice; but the use of oil ceased in 1549 and the sign of the Cross in 1552. The 1552 BCP introduced the formula of administration, recited by the bishop while laying his hand on the head of each candidate: 'Defend, O Lord, this [Thy] child with Thy heavenly grace, that he may continue Thine for ever; and daily increase in Thy Holy Spirit more and more, until he come unto Thy everlasting kingdom. Amen.' In 1662 a solemn ratification of the Baptismal vows was introduced, serving to emphasize the primitive link between the two rites, giving expression to the truth that we have not experienced all that the NT means by Baptism until we have publicly made a personal confession of our faith, and thereby going some way to meeting *Baptist objections to Infant Baptism. The *Alternative Service Book provides a much shorter formula for the Bishop including the name of each candidate, while the 1552 prayer is recited for all the candidates by the bishop and people. Acc. to a rubric in the BCP (taken over from the *Sarum rite) no one is to be admitted to Communion until he is confirmed or 'ready and desirous to be confirmed'. The usual practice is for a course of instruction in Christian faith and practice to precede Confirmation, which is administered at various ages; the title of the *Catechism states that it shall be learnt of every child before he be brought to Confirmation. Hence in the C of E Confirmation provides a regular opportunity for giving young people systematic instruction in the Christian faith. The rite is also in general use, and with similar pastoral purposes, among *Lutherans and some other Protestant bodies.

In modern times there has been much discussion among Anglican theologians about the nature of the gift conveyed by Confirmation. Acc. to one group (D. *Stone, G. W. H. Lampe, and E. C. Whitaker) the fullness of the Holy Spirit is imparted to the Christian in Baptism, and to ascribe to Confirmation a special objective giving of the Spirit is to detract from the grace offered in Baptism. Another school (F. W. Puller, SSJE, A. J. Mason, and L. S. Thornton, CR) regards the gift of the Holy Spirit in Confirmation to be of such fundamental importance that without it Baptism is virtually incomplete. This view seems to many to detract from the grace conferred in Baptism. The form of words used by the bishop in the ASB Confirmation ('Let your Holy Spirit rest upon them') is acceptable both to those who emphasise the action of God (in bestowing the Holy Spirit) and those who stress the part of the candidate in making a personal commitment. The latter group tend to favour a later age for Confirmation and are often not averse to giving Communion to the young before they are confirmed; the former, seeking to preserve the traditional sequence of Baptism, Confirmation, Communion, often wish to allow children to be confirmed at an earlier age.

The main RC legislation is contained in *CIC* (1983), cans. 879–96. Among the classical RC works are J. Morin, Cong. Orat., *De Sacramento Confirmationis* (part of his *Opera Posthuma*; Paris, 1703); cf. also L. *Holste, *De forma Sacramenti Confirmationis apud Graecos* (orig. ed. in Holste's *Annotationes*, Rome, 1666). Anglican works incl. J. *Hall, Χειροθεσία, *or the Apostolic Institution of Imposition of Hands* (1649); H. *Hammond, *De Confirmatione* (1661); J. *Taylor, Χρῖσις Τελειωτική. *A Discourse of Confirmation* (1663); cf. also R. *Baxter, *Confirmation and Restauration* (1658). Among modern treatises should be mentioned F. W. Puller, SSJE, *What is the Distinctive Grace of Confirmation?* (1880); M. Heimbucher, *Die heilige Firmung* (Augsburg, 1889); A. J. Mason, *The Relation of Confirmation to Baptism* (1891; 2nd edn., 1893); A. T. Wirgman, *The Doctrine of Confirmation considered in Relation to Holy Baptism as a Sacramental Ordinance of the Catholic Church* (1897); A. C. A. Hall, *Confirmation* (Oxford Library of Practical Theology, 1900); F. Dölger, *Das Sakrament der Firmung* (Theologische Studien der Leo-Gesellschaft, 15; 1906); F. H. Chase, *Confirmation in the Apostolic Age* (1909); J. B. Umberg, SJ, *Die Schriftlehre vom Sakrament der Firmung* (1920); J. Coppens, *L'Imposition des mains et les rites connexes dans le Nouveau Testament et l'Église ancienne* (Louvain diss., Wetteren and Paris, 1925); G. *Dix, OSB, *Confirmation or the Laying on of Hands?* (Theology Occasional Papers no. 5; 1936); id., *The Theology of Confirmation in Relation to Baptism* (lecture; 1946); G. W. H. Lampe, *The Seal of the Spirit: A Study of the Doctrine of Baptism and Confirmation in the New Testament and the Fathers* (1951; 2nd edn., 1967), with bibl.; L. S. Thornton, CR, *Confirmation: Its Place in the Baptismal Mystery* (1954); B. Neunheuser, OSB, *Taufe und Firmung* (Handbuch der Dogmengeschichte, 4, Heft 2; 1956; 2nd edn., 1983; Eng. tr., 1964); M. Thurian, *La Confirmation: Consécration des laïcs* (Collection Communauté de Taizé, 1957); K. B. Cully (ed.), *Confirmation: History, Doctrine and Practice* (Greenwich, Conn., 1962); J. D. C. Fisher, *Christian Initiation: Baptism in the Medieval West. A Study in the Disintegration of the Primitive Rite of Initiation* (*Alcuin Club Collections, 47; 1965); L. A. van Buchem, OP, *L'Homélie pseudo-Eusébienne de Pentecôte: L'Origine de la confirmatio en Gaule Méridionale et l'interprétation de ce rite par Fauste de Riez* (Nijmegen, 1967), esp. pp. 87–205; J. P. Bouhot, *La Confirmation: Sacrement de la communion ecclésiale* (Lyons, 1968); A. Hamman, OFM, *Le Baptême et la Confirmation* (1969); E. C. Whitaker, *Sacramental Initiation Complete in Baptism* (Grove Liturgical Study, 1; Bramcote, 1975). There was also a special issue of *La Maison-Dieu*, no. 54 (1954), with arts. by B. Botte, OSB, T. Camelot, OP, and others. Comprehensive discussions in A. *Tanquerey, *Synopsis Theologiae Dogmaticae*, 3 (25th edn., 1947), pp. 383–412; *Confirmation, or the Laying on of Hands*, vol. 1; *Historical and Doctrinal*; vol. 2: *Practical* (1926–7). P. Fransen in *Sacramentum Mundi*, 1 (1968), pp. 405–10. On its liturgical aspects see E. *Martène, OSB, *De Antiquis Ecclesiae Ritibus* (1699), I. 1. 2; F. Procter and W. H. *Frere, *A New History of the Book of Common Prayer* (1901), esp. pp. 602–7. J. D. C. Fisher, *Christian Initiation: The Reformation Period. Some Early Reformed Rites of Baptism and Confirmation and other Contemporary Documents* (Alcuin Club Collections, 51; 1970), pp. 159–260; id., *Confirmation, Then and Now* (ibid. 60; 1978);

P. J. Jagger, *Christian Initiation 1552–1969: Rites of Baptism and Confirmation since the Reformation Period* (ibid. 52; 1970). J. Behrens, *Confirmation, Sacrament of Grace: The theology, practice and law of the Roman Catholic Church and the Church of England* (Leominster, 1995). On the current RC rite, see J. D. Crichton, *Christian Celebration: The Sacraments* (1973), esp. pp. 88–113. J. Ysebaert, *Greek Baptismal Terminology* (Graecitas Christianorum Primaeva, 1; Nijmegen, 1962). Various writers in *DTC* 3 (1908), cols. 975–1103; H. J. Lawlor and H. Thurston, SJ, in *HERE* 4 (1911), pp. 1–10; P. de Puniet, OSB, and H. *Leclercq, OSB, in *DACL* 3 (pt. 2; 1914), cols. 2515–51; T. Camelot, OP, in *NCE* 4 (1967), pp. 145–50, s.v. See also bibl. to BAPTISM.

Confiteor (Lat., 'I confess'). One of the forms of confession of sins (so named from its first word) used in the RC Church, e.g. at *Mass and *Compline. In its usual form confession used to be made to God, to the BVM, to St *Michael, St *John the Baptist, St *Peter, St *Paul, and 'all the saints'; from 1969 confession has been addressed to God and those present, and prayers asked of the BVM, angels and saints. The RC forms have been widely adopted in the C of E, though not contained in the BCP, where there are several other forms provided for liturgical use.

confraternity. See FRATERNITIES.

Congar, Georges-Yves (1904–95), theologian. Born at Sedan in the French Ardennes, he trained for the priesthood in Paris and in 1925 entered the *Dominican Order, taking the names Marie-Joseph, which he added to Yves in many of his works. At Le Saulchoir (in Belgium) he developed his passionate interests in ecclesiology and *ecumenism, making contact with L. *Beauduin, P. I. *Couturier, and various Protestant and *Orthodox theologians. After publishing a controversial article in which he ascribed the alienation of French culture from the Church to the latter's 'disfigured visage', in 1936 he announced a series of ecclesiological studies under the title 'Unam Sanctam'. The first of these was his own *Chrétiens désunis* (1937; Eng. tr., *Divided Christendom*, 1939), in which he sought to work out 'principles for Catholic ecumenism' in the light of the different conceptions of unity, and so of ecumenism, among liberal Protestants, Anglicans, and the Orthodox. As a prisoner-of-war at Colditz (1940–45), he came into contact with typical members of other Churches and became aware of their hostility to RCism, and shortly after the end of the war in *Vraie et fausse réforme dans l'Église* (1950) he made a courageous appeal for a reform of the Church's structures by a 'return to the sources', a reform which would neither disrupt the continuity of the Church's history nor disturb the peace and charity of her members. Following earlier warnings about 'false eirenicism', the publication of an article in support of the 'worker-priest' movement in France led to Congar's being forbidden to teach in 1954. He was sent first to the École Biblique at Jerusalem and then to Cambridge, where he found the restrictions on his contacts with Anglicans burdensome. In Dec. 1955 he was able to move to Strasbourg. With the election of Pope *John XXIII in 1958, the situation changed radically. Congar was appointed theological consultor to the preparatory commission of the Second *Vatican Council, he helped to write the 'Message to the World' given at its opening, and he influenced a number of its most important documents. In 1965 he became a member of the Catholic–Lutheran commission of dialogue, in 1969 *Paul VI added his name to the newly founded Pontifical International Theological Commission, and in 1985 *John Paul II invited him to attend the Extraordinary Synod convoked to consider the fruits of the Council; infirmity prevented his acceptance. He was created a *cardinal in 1994. His other works include *Esquisse du mystère de l'Église* (1941; Eng. tr., 1960); *L'Ecclésiologie du haut moyen âge* (1968); *L'Église: De saint Augustin à l'époque moderne* (1970); and *Je crois en l'Esprit Saint* (3 vols., 1979–80; Eng. tr., 1983), a full-scale treatment of the doctrine of the Holy Spirit, to which his attention turned in his later years.

There is a list of Congar's many works by P. Quattrocchi in J.-P. Jossua, OP, *Le Père Congar: La Théologie au service du peuple de Dieu* [1967], pp. 213–72 (Eng. tr., Chicago, 1968, pp. 185–241); A. Nichols, OP, 'An Yves Congar Bibliography 1967–1987', *Angelicum*, 66 (1989), pp. 422–66. Id., *Yves Congar* (London, 1989); M.-M. Wolff, *Gott und Mensch: Ein Beitrag Yves Congars zum ökumenischen Dialog* (Frankfurter Theologischer Studien, 38; 1990). A. Nichols, OP, in D. F. Ford (ed.), *The Modern Theologians*, 1 (Oxford, 1989), pp. 219–36.

congé d'élire (Fr. 'permission to elect', *sc.* a bishop). Royal nomination of bishops was an ancient practice in England. Henry II felt it necessary to define the procedure in the Constitutions of *Clarendon. In 1214 King *John agreed that bishops should be elected by the Dean and Chapter of the cathedral, but that royal permission to proceed to the election, the *congé d'élire*, was to be first secured, and the election to be confirmed by Royal Assent afterwards. This settlement, later confirmed by Edward I and again by Edward III, remained in force until the Reformation. Under *Henry VIII, by the Appointment of Bishops Act 1533, the appointment of bishops was from 1534 vested in the Crown. When a bishopric fell vacant a *congé d'élire*, that is, a licence under the Great Seal, was granted to the Dean and Chapter, who were required to elect the person named by the King in the accompanying 'letter missive'. Failure to elect the royal nominee rendered the Dean and Chapter subject to the penalties of *Praemunire, and the King was then empowered to appoint to the see by letters patent. Under *Edward VI a fresh Act (1547) substituted for the *congé d'élire* nomination by letters patent in all cases, but this Act was repealed under *Mary. The Act of 1533 was revived in 1559 by the Act of *Supremacy 1558; it remains substantially in force, though the penalties of Praemunire have been abolished by the Criminal Law Act 1967.

The Appointment of Bishops Act 1533 is pr. in *Halsbury's Statutes of England and Wales* (4th edn., 1986) 14, pp. 138–42; see also E. G. Moore, *Introduction to English Canon Law* (3rd edn. by T. Briden and B. Hanson, 1992), pp. 18 and 26, and bibl. s.v. BISHOP.

Congo, Democratic Republic of the. See ZAIRE.

Congo, Kingdom of, Christianity in. A *Portuguese expedition reached the ancient Congo kingdom in 1483. In 1491 the king, Nzinga Nkuvu, was baptized, receiving the name of João, that of the reigning king of Portugal. One of his sons, Mvemba Nzinga, governor of the province of Nsundi, was baptized as Afonso. King João soon reverted to paganism, but Afonso did not, and in 1506, on the death of his father, he defeated a pagan brother, with some Portuguese assistance, and became king. Afonso I (1506–43) remains an extraordinary figure: as seen through

his surviving letters he was consistent in a policy of Christianization, and his capital, San Salvador, was endowed with a number of churches. His son Henry, sent to Lisbon for education, was there made a bishop in 1521 and returned to Africa, but died a few years later. Afonso continued to appeal for more priests and to complain of the effect of the slave trading of the Portuguese.

No subsequent king had the moral qualities of Afonso, but for centuries all of them regarded themselves as Christian and regularly appealed both to Portugal and Rome for assistance. In 1596 Pope *Clement VIII made San Salvador into a diocese but effectively the diocesan centre soon moved to the Portuguese colonial town of Luanda. A *Jesuit college was opened in San Salvador in 1625 and a catechism in Kikongo was printed at the same time (by far the earliest literary work in any Bantu language). A number of local priests (mostly *mesticos*) were ordained in this period. In 1645 a *Capuchin mission, mostly Italian, arrived in the Congo and over the next 150 years hundreds of Capuchins worked in the country.

In 1665 Antonio I and most of his nobility were killed in a crushing defeat by a Portuguese army at the Battle of Ambuila. The kingdom largely disintegrated and San Salvador was abandoned for some decades. In 1704 a young woman named Kimpa Vita (or Beatrice) claimed to be possessed by St *Antony [of Padua] and begged the king, Pedro IV, to return to San Salvador. When he failed to do so, she led the return herself, taking up residence by the ruined cathedral where the bishop formerly lived. Under Capuchin influence, she was tried for heresy and burnt at the stake in 1706. In this period Church life continued to flourish in the almost independent western coastal province of Soyo, but in the course of the 18th cent. the supply of missionaries faded away and without a local priesthood Christian life slowly disappeared almost everywhere, though it was sustained to some extent by the *maestri*, trained catechist interpreters, who led the Church in the absence of a priest. Fra Cherubino da Savona in the 1770s was the last priest to reside in the country for any length of time, but when the British *Baptist missionaries arrived at San Salvador in the 1870s, Pedro V, who welcomed them, still thought of himself as a Christian king. For later history see ANGOLA and ZAIRE.

The largest collection of material is A. Brásio, C.S.Sp. (ed.), *Monumenta Missionaria Africana* (20 vols., Lisbon, 1952–88). More convenient collections of docs. in Fr. tr.: L. Jadin and M. Dicorato (eds.), *Correspondance de Dom Afonso, roi du Congo 1506–1543* (Académie royale des Sciences d'Outre-Mer, Classe des Sciences morales et politiques, NS 41, no. 3; Brussels, 1974); J. Cuvelier and L. Jadin (eds.), *L'ancien Congo d'après les archives romaines (1518–1640)* (Académie royale des Sciences coloniales, section des Sciences morales et politiques, Mémoires, Collection in-8°, 36, fasc. 2; ibid., 1954); and L. Jadin (ed.), *L'ancien Congo et l'Angola 1639–1655 d'après les archives Romaines, Portugaises, Néerlandaises et Espagnoles* (Bibliothèque de l'Institut historique Belge de Rome, 20–22; 1975). The earliest account by a Capuchin, Giovanni Francesco da Roma, *Breve Relatione* (Rome, 1648), was tr. into Fr. by F. Bontinck, CICM, *Brève Relation de la Fondation de la mission des Frères Mineurs Capucins . . . au Royaume de Congo* (Publications de l'Université Lovanianum de Leopoldville, 13; 1964). Later accounts incl. G. A. Cavazzi, Capuchin, *Istorica Descrizione de' tre' Regni Congo, Matamba, et Angola*, ed. F. Alamandini, Cap. (Bologna, 1687); R. Rainero, *Il Congo agli Inizi del Settecento nella Relazione di P. Luca da Caltanissetta* (Florence [1974]); and C.

Piazza, *La Missione del Soya (1713–1716) nella relazione inedita di Giuesppe da Modena, OFM Cap.* (Rome, 1973).

Good general account by A. Hilton, *The Kingdom of Kongo* (Oxford, 1985). A. Hastings, *The Church in Africa 1450–1950* (Oxford History of the Christian Church, 1994), pp. 71–129. T. Filesi, *Le Relazioni tra il Regno del Congo e la Sede Apostolica nel XVI Secolo* (Pubblicazioni dell'Istituto Italiano per l'Africa, 1st ser., no. 10; Como [1968]). Id., 'Nazionalismo e Religione nel Congo all'Inizio del 1700: la Setta degli Antoniani', *Africa: Rivista trimestrale di studi e documentazione dell'Istituto Italiano per l'Africa*, 26 (1971), pp. 267–303, 463–508; 27 (1972), pp. 645–68, incl. Eng. summary. R. Gray, '*Come Vero Prencipe Catolico*: the Capuchins and the Rulers of Soyo in the late seventeenth century', *Africa, Journal of the International African Institute*, 53, no. 3 (1983), pp. 39–54. Comprehensive survey of lit. by T. Filesi and I. de Villapadierna, *La 'Missio Antiqua' dei Cappuccini nel Congo (1645–1835): Studio Preliminare e Guida delle Fonti* (Subsidia Scientifica Franciscalia, 6; 1978).

Congregation of the Lord (also **Congregation of Christ** or simply the **Congregation**). The title was assumed in *Mary's reign by the Scottish Reformers who supported J. *Knox. It appears to derive from the language of the *National Covenant (1557), where the word 'congregation', in the sense of a religious community, occurs eight times.

Congregational Council for World Mission. See COUNCIL FOR WORLD MISSION.

Congregationalism. Congregationalism is that form of Church polity which rests on the independence and autonomy of each local church. It professes to represent the principle of democracy in Church government, a polity which is held to follow from its fundamental belief in Christ as the sole head of His Church. All the members of the Church, being Christians, are 'priests unto God'. Where two or three such meet in Christ's name He is in their midst guiding their thoughts and inspiring their actions, and each such community, duly constituted with its officers, is regarded as an outcrop and representative of the Church Universal. It has been held that the system is primitive in that it represents the earliest form of Church order. It requires a very high standard of Christian devotion to maintain it, though it is admitted that in practice it has fallen sometimes sadly below that ideal.

Modern Congregationalism begins with the Reformation. M. *Luther himself taught the priesthood of all believers, though he never carried the doctrine to what Congregationalists consider to be its logical conclusion. As early as 1550 there is evidence of bodies of men and women meeting together to preach the pure Word of God and administer the Sacraments as *Separatists from the national Church. When it became apparent that *Elizabeth I did not intend any drastic reformation of the Church, the number of these companies increased. When, therefore, R. *Browne, in 1582, wrote *A Book which sheweth the Life and Manners of all true Christians* and *A Treatise of Reformation without tarrying for any and of the Wickedness of those Preachers which will not reform till the Magistrate command or compel them*, the little books found a public prepared to receive them. Browne maintained that 'the Kingdom of God was not to be begun by whole parishes, but rather of the worthiest, were they never so few', and, in insisting that these 'gathered Churches', bound under God by cov-

enant, should be independent of the state and have the right to govern themselves, he laid down the lines of essential Congregationalism. He was followed by H. *Barrow, J. *Greenwood, and J. *Penry. In 1589 Barrow wrote *A true Description out of the Word of God of the visible Church* which set forth a doctrine of the Church practically identical with that of Browne.

From the 1580s there is evidence that Brownists (as outsiders generally called them) increased in numbers, particularly in southern England. Somewhat amorphous Separatism gradually became more clearly defined Congregationalism, and Churches were formed in *Norwich, London, and elsewhere. Under persecution, the movement was driven underground, with some Separatists emigrating to regroup in Amsterdam, *Leiden, and ultimately in the *United States of America, esp. in New England. There Congregationalism played a great part in shaping both the religion and the politics of the new country. But in England also the leaven continued to work and the Independents, as they were then called, became leaders in the struggle against *Charles I and W. *Laud, and ultimately formed the backbone of O. *Cromwell's army. At the *Westminster Assembly in 1643, the Five Dissenting Brethren stoutly defended the Congregationalist cause and the *Savoy Declaration (q.v.) of 1658 laid down their polity afresh in the light of experience gained in the Netherlands and America.

The Act of *Uniformity 1662 made Nonconformists of Independents and Presbyterians alike, but the *Toleration Act 1688 restored to them at least the right to exist. Attempts at fusion between these two types of Church were not successful mainly because of theological differences. Independents, in spite of their *Calvinism, were the broader in outlook and the more evangelical in tone. They grew in numbers and influence, and being excluded from the ancient universities, set up Dissenting Academies of their own which did fine educational work, and they played a leading role in the foundation of London University. As R. W. *Dale pointed out in 1891, 'Congregationalists for many generations were accustomed to assert the claims of the intellect in religion far more earnestly than other evangelical Churches'. At the same time they were evangelistic in practice, as is witnessed by their founding of the London Missionary Society (*LMS). An independent product of the 18th cent. evangelical revival was the indigenous growth of Congregationalism in Scotland, largely due to the activities of two brothers, Robert (1764–1842) and Alexander (1768–1851) Haldane.

The independency of Congregational Churches did not involve them in complete isolation. From the first they recognized the bond of a common faith and order, and the stronger among them used to help the weaker. In time they came to form County Associations of Churches for mutual intercourse and support. The Congregational Union of Scotland was formed in 1812 and that of England and Wales in 1832. The basis of such Unions was a full recognition of the distinctive principle of Congregationalism, characteristically expressed by the 1832 Union of England and Wales, namely, 'the scriptural right of every separate church to maintain perfect independence in the government and administration of its own particular affairs'. They had therefore no legislative authority, but served to advise, encourage, and help the Churches and to express their common mind. In 1966 the Assembly of the Union of England and Wales agreed that the Churches of the Union should covenant together in the Congregational Church in England and Wales, in which the local autonomy of the Church is practised alongside a mutual concern and care. In 1972 the greater part of the Congregational Church in England and Wales united with the *Presbyterian Church of England to form the *United Reformed Church. Continuing Congregational Churches outside the union include the Fellowship of Evangelical Congregational Churches (founded in 1966) and the Congregational Federation (founded in 1972). In the USA most of the Congregational Christian Churches in 1957 joined with the Evangelical and Reformed Churches to form the *United Church of Christ (q.v.), and Congregationalists have been involved in modern unions in many other parts of the world (see REUNION).

R. W. Dale, *A Manual of Congregational Principles* (1884). J. Waddington, *Congregational History* (5 vols., 1869–80). R. W. Dale (ed. A. W. Dale), *History of English Congregationalism* (1907). D. [T.] Jenkins, *Congregationalism: A Restatement* (1954). E. [R.] Routley, *The Story of Congregationalism* (1961). G. F. Nuttall, *Visible Saints: The Congregational Way 1640–1660* (Oxford, 1957). R. Tudur Jones, *Congregationalism in England 1662–1962* (1962). A. Peel, *These Hundred Years: A History of the Congregational Union of England and Wales, 1831–1931* (1931); id. (ed.), *Essays Congregational and Catholic issued in commemoration of the Centenary of the Congregational Union of England and Wales* [1931]. R. W. Cleaves, *Congregationalism 1960–1976: The Story of the Federation* (Swansea, 1977). B. D. Spinks, *Freedom or Order? The Eucharistic Liturgy in English Congregationalism, 1645–1980* (Pittsburgh Theological Monographs, NS 8; Allison Park, Pa., 1984). A. P. F. Sell, *Saints: Visible, Orderly and Catholic: The Congregational Idea of the Church* (Princeton Theological Monograph Series, 7; Allison Park, Pa., 1986). H. Escott, *A History of Scottish Congregationalism* (Glasgow, 1960). W. Walker, *A History of the Congregational Churches in the United States* (New York, 1894); G. G. Atkins and F. L. Fagley, *History of American Congregationalism* (Boston and Chicago [1942]). J. Corrigan, *The Prism of Piety: Catholick Congregational Clergy at the Beginning of the Enlightenment* (New York and Oxford, 1991). *Transactions of the Congregational Historical Society* (21 vols., London, 1901–72), cont. as *Journal of the United Reformed Church History Society* (ibid., 1973 ff.). See also bibl. to HALF-WAY COVENANT and SEPARATISTS.

Congregations, Monastic. A group of monasteries united under a superior, usually known as Abbot President or Abbot General. The purpose of the union is to foster good discipline, but individual monasteries retain their independence. Examples in the *Benedictine Order are the *Cassinese Congregation, named after the central house at *Monte Cassino, as well as various national Congregations, e.g. the English and the Swiss. Most Monastic Congregations are unions of monasteries of monks but there are a few Congregations of nuns, e.g. the Polish Congregation.

V. Dammertz, OSB, *Das Verfassungsrecht der Benediktinischen Mönchskongregationen in Geschichte und Gegenwart* (Kirchengeschichtliche Quellen und Studien, 6; St Ottilien, 1963).

Congregations, Religious. Those Religious *Institutes within the RC Church in which members take simple *vows were, until the promulgation of the *Codex Iuris Canonici of 1983, officially designated Religious Congregations, and they were subject to different rules from those applied to Religious Orders, in which solemn vows are

taken. The terminology, no longer officially recognized, is still in general use. The earliest Religious Congregations trace their origins back to the Middle Ages, but they developed strongly only after the *Counter-Reformation. During the 20th cent. the differences between the rules of canon law governing Religious Congregations and those governing Religious Orders have gradually been reduced. See also INSTITUTES OF CONSECRATED LIFE.

Congregations, Roman. See ROMAN CONGREGATIONS.

Congruism. The doctrine that God confers *grace for the performance of good works ('gratia de congruo') in accordance with such human circumstances as He foresees will be most favourable to its use. The doctrine is an attempt to reconcile the dependence of human moral action upon Divine grace with the freedom of the human will. It was strongly advocated c.1580 by certain *Jesuits, esp. the *Molinists, and imposed upon all schools of the Society of Jesus in 1613 by C. *Aquaviva, then its General. The 13th of the Anglican *Thirty-Nine Articles denies that works done before justification 'as the School-authors say, deserve grace of congruity'.

The classical expositions of Congruism are to be found in the writings of F. *Suárez, SJ (d. 1617), and of St Robert *Bellarmine (d. 1621). For Aquaviva's decree ('De Observanda Ratione Studiorum, deque Doctrina S. Thomae Sequenda'), issued 14 Dec. 1613, see *Praepositorum Generalium Selectae Epistolae et Documenta ad Superiores* (Besançon, 1877), pp. 54–60. H. Quilliet in *DTC* 3 (1908), cols. 1120–38, s.v.; F. Courtney, SJ, in *A Catholic Dictionary of Theology*, 2 (1967), pp. 95–9, s.v.

Connolly, Richard Hugh (1873–1948), *patristic scholar. Born at Carcoar in Australia, he was educated at *Downside and at Christ's College, Cambridge. He made his solemn profession at Downside Abbey in 1896, was ordained priest in 1899, and became Head of Benet House, Cambridge (1904–16), where he was closely associated with some outstanding patristic scholars in the university (J. A. *Robinson, F. C. *Burkitt, J. F. Bethune-Baker). His main work lay in the field of early Syrian Christianity. He co-operated with J. F. Bethune-Baker in introducing *Nestorius' 'Bazaar of Heracleides' to the notice of European scholars (1908), edited the *Liturgical Homilies of Narsai* (1909; important appendix by E. *Bishop), made out a strong case for the Hippolytean authorship of the '*Apostolic Tradition' (*The So-called Egyptian Church Order*, 1916), edited (in English) the *Didascalia Apostolorum* (1929), and established the *Ambrosian authorship of the *De Sacramentis* (1942). He also contributed frequent papers to the *Journal of Theological Studies*, among them some important articles on the *Didache.

Conrad of Gelnhausen (c.1320–90), theologian. He studied in *Paris, taking his first degree in 1344, then in *Bologna, where he became Doctor decretorum in 1375. After this he became Provost of Worms. Returning to Paris in 1378, he wrote his two principal works, the *Epistola Brevis* and the *Epistola Concordiae*. He left Paris in 1382 to become the first Chancellor of the University of Heidelberg at the invitation of Ruprecht I of the Palatinate, to whom he had addressed the *Epistola Concordiae*. He died as Chancellor in 1390, and the 200 books he left behind became the basis of the new Heidelberg University library. Heavily influenced by *Marsiglio of Padua and *William of Ockham, he was, along with his co-patriot Henry of Langenstein, one of the first publicists of the *via concilii* (see CONCILIAR THEORY) since the outbreak of the *Great Schism. The foundation of his thought lay in his appeal to the underlying authority of the Church understood as the whole congregation of the faithful as opposed simply to the Pope and his immediate curia. This gave him sufficient reason to argue for the summoning of a General Council by the cardinals on behalf of the universal Church even without the convocation of the Pope.

His 'Epistola Concordiae' was ed. F. P. Bliemetzrieder, *Literarische Polemik zu Beginn des grossen abendländischen Schismas* (Publikationen des Österreichischen Historischen Instituts in Rom, 1; 1910), pp. 111–40. A. Kneer, *Die Entstehung der Konziliaren Theorie: Zur Geschichte des Schismas und der Kirchenpolitischen Schriftsteller Konrad von Gelnhausen († 1390) und Heinrich von Langenstein († 1397)* (*RQ*, Suppl. 1; 1893); K. Wenck, 'Konrad von Gelnhausen und die Quellen der konziliaren Theorie', *HZ* 76 (1896), pp. 6–61. G. [G. B.] Ritter, *Die Heidelberger Universität*, 1 (1936), pp. 46 f., 50–2, 56–60, and 261–9. R. N. Swanson, *Universities, Academics and the Great Schism* (Cambridge Studies in Medieval Life and Thought, 3rd ser. 12; 1979), pp. 59–63, 66–8, and 211 f. G. Kreuzer in *Verfasserlexikon* (2nd edn.), 5 (1985), cols. 179–81, s.v. 'Konrad von Gelnhausen', with further bibl.

Conrad of Marburg (*c.*1180–1233), Papal *Inquisitor. He was prob. a native of Marburg and his title 'Magister' shows that he studied at one of the universities, perhaps *Paris or *Bologna. A man of strong force of character and much learning and severely ascetic, in 1213 he appeared as an ardent preacher of the *Crusade of *Innocent III. Soon afterwards he was charged with various reforming missions in Germany, including the visitation of certain convents. These tasks won him the confidence of the Landgrave Ludwig IV of Thuringia, who entrusted him with important ecclesiastical appointments in his dominions. In 1225 he became the spiritual director and confessor of St *Elizabeth (q.v.), Ludwig's wife, whom he treated, esp. in her later years, with excessive severity; and after her death (19 Nov. 1231) he was appointed as one of the witnesses in the cause of her canonization. Meanwhile he proved himself a zealous opponent of heresies (*Cathari, *Waldenses) and on 11 Oct. 1231 *Gregory IX (1227–41) nominated him the first Papal Inquisitor in Germany, with absolute authority over heretics. He exercised his authority ruthlessly, often condemning persons on insufficient evidence and handing them over for punishment to the secular arm. When he charged Henry II, Count of Sayn, with heresy (1233) he was publicly denounced at a court of bishops and princes at Mainz and murdered on his way back to Marburg on 30 July 1233.

B. Kaltner, *Konrad von Marburg und die Inquisition in Deutschland* (Prague, 1882); A. Hausrath, *Kleine Schriften* (1883), pp. 137–233 ('Der Ketzermeister Konrad von Marburg'). P. Braun, 'Der Beichtvater der heiligen Elisabeth und deutsche Inquisitor Konrad von Marburg (†1233)', *Beiträge zur Hessischen Kirchengeschichte*, 4 (1911), pp. 248–300 and 331–64. A. Patschovsky, 'Zum Ketzerverfolgung Konrads von Marburg', *Deutsches Archiv*, 37 (1981), pp. 641–93. P. Segal in *Neue Deutsche Biographie*, 12 (1980), pp. 544–6, s.v. 'Konrad von Marburg', with bibl. See also works cited under ELIZABETH, ST.

Consalvi, Ercole (1757–1824), Italian statesman. He entered the Papal service at an early age, and was thrown into prison as a declared anti-Revolutionary after the French occupation of the Papal States in 1798. On recovering his freedom he joined the new Pope, *Pius VII, and in 1800 was created a cardinal and made Secretary of State. In this office he was chiefly responsible for the negotiation of the *Concordat with Napoleon, and for fostering opposition to the *Organic Articles. Though Napoleon managed to secure his dismissal, Consalvi would not be intimidated, and became the leader of the 'black cardinals' in Paris until he was forcibly retired to *Reims. On Napoleon's abdication (1814) he was immediately reappointed as Secretary, and, after a short visit to England, represented the Pope at the Congress of Vienna (1815). Here he secured the restoration of the Papal States, the reorganization of which occupied his remaining years.

Mémoires du Cardinal Consalvi . . . Avec une introduction et des notes par J. Crétineau-Joly (2 vols., Paris, 1864; enlarged edn. by J. E. B. Drochon [*c.*1896]); M. N. Rocca di Corneliano (ed.), *Memorie del cardinale Ercole Consalvi* (1950); A. Roveri and others (eds.), *La Missione Consalvi e il Congresso di Vienna* (Fonti per la Storia d'Italia pubblicate dall'Istituto Storico Italiano per l'Età Moderna e Contemporanea, 105, 115, 127, etc.; 1970 ff.). E. L. Fischer, *Cardinal Consalvi: Lebens und Charakterbild des grossen Ministers Papst Pius VII* (1899); M. Petrocchi, *La restaurazione, il cardinale Consalvi e la riforma del 1816* (1941). J. T. Ellis, *Cardinal Consalvi and Anglo-Papal Relations, 1814–1824* (Washington, DC, 1942). A. Roveri, *La Santa Sede tra Rivoluzione Francese e Restaurazione: Il Cardinale Consalvi 1813–1815* (Biblioteca di Storia, 16; Florence, 1974). Life by J. M. Robinson (London, 1987). L. von *Ranke, *Historisch-Biographische Studien* (1877), pp. 1–180 ('Cardinal Consalvi und seine Staatsverwaltung unter dem Pontificat Pius VII'). G. Mollat in *DHGE* 13 (1956), cols. 509–23, s.v.; A. Roveri in *Dizionario Biografico degli Italiani*, 28 (1983), pp. 33–43, s.v.

consanguinity, blood-relationship. By Scripture and *canon law, consanguinity within certain degrees is a *diriment impediment to marriage; that is, it makes the marriage of the persons concerned not only unlawful but null and void. See also under KINDRED AND AFFINITY, TABLE OF, and PROHIBITED DEGREES.

Current RC legislation is contained in *CIC* (1983), can. 1091. G. Oesterlé in *DDC* 4 (1949), cols. 232–48, s.v., with full bibl.

conscience (Lat. *conscientia*, 'knowledge with another', 'knowledge within oneself'). The word has followed its Lat. predecessor in acquiring a moral significance, and now denotes the capacity for judging the rightness of actions, either considered generally, or actually proposed or already performed. Christians agree that it is unique to man and that its effectiveness is increased by experience and through *grace.

NT writers adopted the equivalent term 'syneidesis' from Hellenistic Greek philosophers, who seem to have understood it mainly as an index of moral failings or as a moral dissuasive; on this view it never gives positive encouragement: a good conscience is a quiet conscience. The NT associates the good conscience with *faith and with the *Holy Spirit.

In medieval Western thought it became usual to distinguish between the general knowledge of moral principles (termed *synteresis after a copyist's error for syneidesis) and its application to particular cases, called *conscientia* in a stricter sense. The former presupposed a moral discernment left untouched by the *Fall, and opinions differed as to whether its source lay in the affections and the will, as the *Franciscans held, or in the practical reason, as St *Thomas Aquinas and the *Dominicans taught. (Some modern writers suggest that the affections, will, and reason are all involved, as in much other mental activity.) The Reformers reacted strongly against the theory of an uncorrupted natural power to discern good and evil, and emphasized the dependence of the Christian conscience upon faith.

More recent thinkers have been sharply divided on the reality and authority of conscience. English writers on ethics influenced by T. *Hobbes and D. *Hume have tended to discard the concept and speak simply of moral judgement; others, esp. Bp. J. *Butler, have seen in conscience a kind of moral sense, in the exercise of which man becomes aware of a Being higher than himself. Such an idea was reinforced by Protestant teaching on the 'internal witness' of the Holy Spirit. In the teaching of I. *Kant conscience is the awareness of the universal claim of the moral dictates of reason (the '*Categorical Imperative'). Religion is the recognition of this claim as the will of God, but, since the ground on which the claim is recognized is that it is rational, man, as a rational being, remains (or becomes) autonomous in submitting himself to it. From such a point of view conscience can be considered as a mediator between the Law of God and the will of man, or even as the voice of God (an influential idea found in the writings of some of the early Fathers and in much popular teaching); it is also by following the dictates of conscience that man realizes his independence of purely conventional and social codes. Such ideas have been seriously challenged by modern psychology (esp. the teaching of S. Freud) which regards conscience as the activity of the super-ego, which is formed in childhood and represses drives that are socially unacceptable.

In much modern philosophy it is suggested that where conscience passes beyond moral judgement it is simply an internalized moral habit formed in response to social pressures. Nevertheless, a critical attitude to such social pressures (and an increased awareness of their relativity), combined with the sense that man's freedom implies some kind of ultimate autonomy, has meant that the notion of conscience has seemed useful where an individual's sense of value conflicts with those imposed by the state or society. Moral theologians have stressed the need for conscience to be informed by attention to the teaching of Scripture and the Church; conscience, thus informed, is to be followed. If the resulting action is faulty as a result of *invincible ignorance, the imperfection in conscience is excusable. Nevertheless, it is wrong for a person to do what he thinks wrong, even if apparently legitimate authority seems to require it. To follow one's conscience in such circumstances (e.g. conscientious objection to military service; see WAR, CHRISTIAN ATTITUDE TO), is now increasingly regarded as legitimate. Since the *Enlightenment, freedom of religious belief and practice has also come to be seen as a matter of conscience which the state has no right to restrict; the Virginia Bill of Rights of 1776, for instance, insists that 'all men are equally entitled to the free exercise of religion, according to the dictates of

conscience' (§ 16), and the same right is embodied in the Universal Declaration on Human Rights adopted by the United Nations in 1949 (Art. 18). In contrast to much earlier teaching of the RC Church (e.g. in the *Syllabus Errorum, 1864), the Second *Vatican Council in 1965 affirmed the rights of conscience in matters of religion (*Dignitatis Humanae Personae*, 3).

H. *Rashdall, *The Theory of God and Evil* (2 vols., 1907), esp. 1, pp. 164–8 and 175 f.; cf. also id., *Conscience and Christ* (1916). K. E. *Kirk, *Conscience and its Problems* (1927). E. D'Arcy, *Conscience and its Right to Freedom* (1961); P. Delhaye, *La Conscience morale du chrétien* [1964]; O. [M. T.] O'Donovan, *Resurrection and Moral Order* (Leicester and Grand Rapids, 1986), esp. pp. 114–20 and 190–97. C. A. Pierce, *Conscience in the New Testament* (Studies in Biblical Theology, 15; 1955). On the classical roots and biblical and patristic understanding, H. Chadwick in *RAC* 10 (1978), cols. 1025–107, s.v. 'Gewissen'. Useful collection of texts, in Eng. tr., with introd. by T. C. Potts, *Conscience in Medieval Philosophy* (Cambridge, 1980); cf. also id. in N. Kretzmann, A. Kenny and J. Pinborg (eds.), *The Cambridge History of Later Medieval Philosophy* (1982), pp. 687–704. The basic work on medieval theories is O. Lottin, OSB, *Psychologie et morale aux XIIe et XIIIe siècles* (6 vols., Louvain, 1942–60), esp. vol. 2. [R.] P. Ramsey, *War and the Christian Conscience* (Durham, NC, 1961).

consecration. The separation of a thing or person for Divine service. In Christian theology the term has commonly been used: (1) Of the Eucharist, for the act whereby the bread and wine become the Body and Blood of Christ. (2) Of the making of bishops. In the RC Church, however, bishops are now usually said to be ordained rather than consecrated; this terminology is also used in the ASB. See ORDERS and ORDINAL. (3) Of clergy or laity professing the *counsels of perfection through vows or other sacred bonds recognized by the Church. Acc. to the 1983 *CIC* (can. 207) such persons are said to be 'consecrated to God in their own special way'. (4) Of churches and altars. The permanent setting apart of these things for the service of God was formerly described as their consecration; in official documents it is now more usually called their dedication. See DEDICATION OF CHURCHES.

Consecration, the Prayer of. The central prayer in the Eucharistic Rite of the BCP, corresponding to the middle of the *Canon in the Roman Mass and (to a lesser extent) of the *Anaphora in E. rites. In the 1662 form of the BCP it consists of: (1) a 'memorial' of the death of Christ; (2) a prayer that in the reception of the Sacrament the faithful may partake of the Body and Blood of Christ; (3) a recital of the narrative of institution, with a performance of the *manual acts; (4) *Amen*, said by the congregation.

Consensus Genevensis (also known as the **De aeterna Dei Praedestinatione**). J. *Calvin's elaborate reformulation of his teaching on *Predestination. Directed primarily against A. *Pighi, it was also intended to combat H. H. *Bolsec and other theologians who had attacked Calvin's doctrine. After obtaining the support of the ministers of Geneva on 18 Dec. 1551, Calvin presented it to the City Council of Geneva on 1 Jan. 1552.

The text, besides being pr. among Calvin's works, is pr. in H. A. Niemeyer (ed.), *Collectio Confessionum in Ecclesiis Reformatis Publicatarum* (Leipzig, 1840), pp. 218–310; part is repr. in Kidd, pp. 643–5 (no. 314). Eng. tr., with introd., by J. K. S. Reid (London, 1961). See also bibl. to CALVINISM.

Consensus Tigurinus (Lat., 'the Zurich Agreement'). The formula of faith agreed upon in May 1549 by J. *Calvin and G. *Farel, representing the Protestants of French Switzerland, and H. *Bullinger (H. *Zwingli's successor in the town of Zurich), representing those of German Switzerland. Its 26 arts. were primarily concerned to set forth a doctrine of the Eucharist which conformed to *Calvinist principles and was free from the objections which, in the eyes of the Zwinglians, attached to *consubstantiation. The Consensus contributed to widening the breach between Calvinism and *Lutheranism.

The text, besides being pr. among Calvin's works, is pr. in *Registres de la Compagnie des Pasteurs de Genève au temps de Calvin*, ed. R.-M. Kingdon and J.-F. Bergier, 1: 1546–1553, ed. J.-F. Bergier (Travaux d'Humanisme et Renaissance, 55; 1964), pp. 64–70; also in Kidd, pp. 652–6 (no. 319). U. Gäbler in *TRE* 8 (1981), pp. 189–92, s.v., with further bibl. See also bibl. to CALVINISM.

Conservative Evangelicalism. See under EVANGELICALISM.

consignatorium (also known as the **chrismarium** or **locus chrismatis**). The room or building sometimes adjoining the *baptistery in which the bishop on *Holy Saturday or the Vigil of *Pentecost (the two days on which Baptism was solemnly conferred in the early Church) used to confirm the newly baptized by 'signing' them with the *chrism. Some fine examples of such 'consignatoria' have been discovered in N. Africa.

F. J. Dölger, 'Die Firmung in den Denkmälern des christlichen Altertums', *RQ* 19 (1905), pp. 1–41, esp. pp. 26–41, with refs. F. Sühling in *RAC* 3 (1957), cols. 303–6, s.v., with bibl. refs.

consistory (Lat. *consistorium*). Orig. the ante-chamber of the Imperial palace at Rome where the Emperor administered justice from a seat on a tribunal with others standing around him (*consistentes*). The word is now used of certain ecclesiastical courts.

In the C of E the Consistory Court is the bishop's court for the administration of ecclesiastical law within his own diocese, except in the diocese of Canterbury where it is known as 'the Commissary Court'. The judge is styled the '*Chancellor' (in Canterbury, the Commissary General). In *faculty cases, except when the bishop in his letters patent appointing the Chancellor reserves to himself the power to try certain cases, the Chancellor is the sole judge. Since the *Ecclesiastical Jurisdiction Measure 1963, when the Chancellor gives a conclusive certificate that a case involves a point of doctrine, ritual or ceremonial, it becomes a 'reserved matter', and in faculty cases appeal from the Consistory Court then lies to the *Court of Ecclesiastical Causes Reserved. Under the same Measure the Consistory Court is the court of first instance in cases against clerics not involving doctrine, ritual or ceremonial (known as 'conduct cases'). In these cases the Chancellor sits with two clerical and two lay assessors. In both faculty and conduct cases not involving doctrine, ritual or ceremonial, appeal from the Consistory Court lies first to the Provincial Court (the *Arches Court of Canterbury or the Chancery Court of York), and thence to the *Judicial Committee of the Privy Council. Consistory Courts lost much of their former importance when their jurisdiction in matrimonial and testamentary matters was removed by the Matrimonial Causes Act 1857 and the Court of Probate Act 1857, and their powers have been even further curtailed by the 1963 Measure.

In the RC Church the Consistory is an assembly of *cardinals convoked by the Pope and meeting under his presidency. Acc. to current legislation (*CIC* (1983), can. 353), consistories are of two kinds: 'ordinary' and 'extraordinary'. An ordinary consistory, to which only those cardinals resident in Rome need be summoned, is held when the Pope wishes to consult them about some serious matter or perform some solemn act, such as conferring the *pallium, or the public celebrations when a new cardinal is created. On these occasions representatives of civil states and other invited persons may attend. Extraordinary consistories, to which all cardinals are summoned, take place when the special needs of the Church or more serious matters suggest it.

In many *Presbyterian Churches (Switzerland, the Netherlands, USA), the Consistory Court is the name given to the court corresponding to the *Kirk session (q.v.) in *Scotland.

On the C of E Consistory Court, E. G. More, *Introduction to English Canon Law* (3rd edn. by T. Briden and B. Hanson, 1992), pp. 114–22.
On the RC Consistory, A. Boudinbon in *EB* (11th edn.), 6 (1910), pp. 978 f., s.v.; H. Papi, SJ, in *CE* 4 (1908), pp. 285 f., s.v.; J. Raffalli in *DDC* 4 (1949), cols. 354–6, s.v. See also bibl. to CURIA.

Consolata Missionaries, Institute of the Consolata for Foreign Missions (IMC). RC missionary congregation of men and women founded by Bl Giuseppe *Allamano at Turin. The Consolata Fathers were founded in 1901, the Sisters in 1910. The Institute received final, official approval in 1923. The Consolata Missionaries are characterized by devotion to the BVM 'Consolata' (Virgin of Consolation), and by the spirituality of bringing the consolation of the Gospel to the world. Allamano sent his missionaries to *Kenya, *Ethiopia, Tanzania, and Mozambique. Since his death (1926) houses and missions have been opened in many other countries of Africa, in Latin America, Europe, and N. America.

V. Merlo Pich, IMC, in *DIP* 5 (1978), cols. 138–42, s.v. 'Istituto Missioni Consolata'; M. Gatti, ibid., cols. 1526 f., s.v. 'Missionarie della Consolata'; U. Viglino, IMC, in *NCE* 4 (1967), p. 217, s.v. See also works on ALLAMANO, cited s.v.

Constance, Council of (1414–18). The Council was convoked in 1414 by *John XXIII at the instigation of the Emp. Sigismund. Its purpose was to end the *Great Schism and also to reform the Church and combat heresy.

In 1414 there were three Popes: Gregory XII, in the line of *Urban VI; *Benedict XIII, the successor of Clement VII of Avignon; and John XXIII, who was in the line inaugurated at the Council of *Pisa. At Constance, since John had summoned the Council, only his obedience was represented, but it far outnumbered that of his rivals. This fact, together with the presence of a large number of Italian bishops, gave him a feeling of security, which was soon shaken by the general movement to secure ecclesiastical peace by the removal of all three Popes in favour of a fourth. When, in order to neutralize the Italian preponderance, the Council decided to vote by Nations (Italian, German, French, and English), and when accusations were being circulated against his personal behaviour, John became frightened and offered to resign if his rivals would do the same. He then left Constance in disguise on 20 March 1415. The Council was thrown into confusion, but was rallied by Sigismund. Besides summoning John to return, in order to give itself judicial standing in the absence of its Papal convenor, in its fifth session (15 April 1415) the Council enacted the decree 'Haec Sancta', declaring that 'this Council holds its power direct from Christ; everyone, no matter his rank or office, even if it be Papal, is bound to obey it in whatever pertains to faith, to the extirpation of the above-mentioned schism, as well as to the reform of the Church in its head and in its members'. This decree was the apex of *Conciliar Theory. John was brought back, condemned for scandalous conduct (but not for heresy) and deposed on 29 May.

Gregory XII abdicated on 4 July, but only after his representative, Cardinal Dominici, had convoked the Council anew. (Gregory did not recognize the earlier convocation, and the Council acquiesced in this action.) His cardinals then joined the assembly. Gregory himself was nominated permanent legate at Ancona and died on 18 Oct. 1417.

Benedict XIII with the King of Aragon met Sigismund at Perpignan on 18 Sept. 1416, but they failed to reach an agreement. Sigismund then signed a pact with the Spanish kings and their allies at Narbonne, whereby the assembly (not the Council) at Constance would invite the Spaniards to a council in Constance, and in the course of the next year various Spanish and Portuguese delegates arrived. Meantime Sigismund tried to restore peace between England and France, but because of his alliance with the English the French left the English–German combination at the Council and voted with the Italians and Spanish.

On 27 Jan. 1417 Sigismund returned to the Council, determined to effect ecclesiastical reform before electing a new Pope. There were serious divisions on the question, the Italians demanding an election first. On 26 July 1417 Benedict was deposed. A compromise on the reform-election issue was accepted whereby such reform decrees as had so far been agreed upon should be promulgated, and the Pope elected by a conclave of all the cardinals, with six additional members from each Nation, the successful candidate to need two-thirds of the votes of the cardinals and of each separate Nation. After a conclave of three days, Oddo *Colonna, a cardinal deacon, was elected on 11 Nov. 1417 and took the name of *Martin V.

Apart from the healing of the schism, reform of the Church had been demanded from the beginning. There were, however, numerous obstacles, esp. the diversity of interests of the different Nations and the desire of the various bodies, including the Universities, to preserve their own advantages. Apart from a decree concerning the *Franciscan Order (23 Sept. 1415), the first five reforming decrees were promulgated on 9 Oct. 1417. The first of these, 'Frequens', enacted that there should be a General Council after 5, 7, and then every 10, years, each one announced by the preceding one. The other four decrees concerned regulations for schisms, the profession to be made by a Pope, translation of bishops and the prohibition

of *spolia*. A list of 18 points needing reform (*avisamenta*) was drawn up (30 Oct. 1417). After the election of Martin V a commission endeavoured to devise decrees on the lines of these *avisamenta*, but no unanimity was achieved. Then each Nation and the Pope proposed decrees, which resulted in seven enactments concerned mainly with exemptions and taxes. Many of the aspirations of the individual Nations were settled by *concordats, a term which seems to have been used here for the first time.

The Council also dealt with contemporary heresies, esp. those of J. *Wycliffe and J. *Huss. It condemned over 200 propositions of the former, and ordered his body to be removed from consecrated ground. The latter, who had taught doctrines allegedly similar to those of Wycliffe, came to Constance under safe-conduct from the Emperor. He was, however, imprisoned, and refusing to recant, he was condemned as a heretic on 6 July 1415 and handed over to the secular authorities to be burned at the stake. In the next year *Jerome of Prague, his follower and friend, suffered the same fate. The affairs of the French Franciscan, John Parvus (Jean Petit), and the Dominican, John Falkenberg, who had taught the legality of tyrannicide, were also treated at the Council, but not finally decided. The Council was dissolved on 22 Apr. 1418.

The Council of Constance is usually reckoned as the Sixteenth *Oecumenical Council, but opinions differ as to whether its oecumenicity dates from its beginning, Gregory's reconvocation or Martin's election. Consequently some hold the decree 'Haec Sancta' to be oecumenical, others not. Among the former, some hold it to be of permanent validity, others as conciliar but intended only as a temporary expedient to meet a transient situation. The Council's importance lay in its ending of the schism and in its crystallizing and diffusing of ideas about authority in general and especially about authority in the Church which were to have far-reaching effects.

Hardouin, 8, cols. 209–944; Mansi, 27 (1784), cols. 519–1240, and 28 (1785), cols. 1–958. Indispensable collection of sources by H. von der Hardt, *Magnum Oecumenicum Constantiense Concilium* (6 vols., Frankfurt and Leipzig, 1697–1700; indices, etc., 1742). Crit. edn. of the *Acta Concilii Constantiensis* by H. Finke (4 vols., Münster, 1896–1928). Text of the decrees, with Eng. tr. and introd., in Tanner, *Decrees* (1990), pp. 403–51. Eng. trs. of contemporary sources by L. R. Loomis, *The Council of Constance*, ed. and annotated by J. H. Mundy and K. M. Woody (Records of Civilization, Sources and Studies, 63; 1961), with full introd., and of main docs. by C. M. D. Crowder, *Unity, Heresy and Reform, 1378–1460: The Conciliar Response to the Great Schism* (1977), pp. 65–138, with introd., pp. 7–28. U. Richental (d. 1436/7), *Das Konzil zu Konstanz* (reprod. in facsimile and ed. with comm. by O. Feger, 2 vols., Constance, 1964), with text, 2, pp. 149–278. Hefele and Leclercq, 7 (pt. 1; 1916), pp. 71–584. H. Jedin, *Bischöfliches Konzil oder Kirchenparlament? Ein Beitrag zur Ekklesiologie der Konzilien von Konstanz und Basel* (Vorträge der Aeneas Silvius Stiftung an der Universität Basel, 2; 1963). A. Franzen and W. Müller (eds.), *Das Konzil von Konstanz: Beiträge zu seiner Geschichte und Theologie. Festschrift ... Dr. Hermann Schäufele* (1964). J. Gill, SJ, *Constance et Bâle-Florence* (Histoire des Conciles Œcuméniques, 9; 1965), esp. pp. 41–115. P. de Vooght, *Les Pouvoirs du Concile et l'autorité du Pape au Concile de Constance: Le décret Haec Sancta Synodus du 6 avril 1415* (Unam Sanctam, 56; 1965). T. E. Morrissey, 'The Decree "Haec Sancta" and Cardinal Zabarella', *Annuarium Historiae Conciliorum*, 10 (1978), pp. 145–76. Collection of arts. of various dates ed. R. Bäumer, *Das Konstanzer Konzil* (Wege der Forschung, 415; Darmstadt, 1977). W. Brandmüller, *Das Konzil von Konstanz*

1414–1418 (1991 ff.). E. Delaruelle, E. R. Labande, and P. Ourliac in Fliche and Martin, 14 (1962), pp. 167–215. L. Cristiani in *DDC* 4 (1949), cols. 390–424; B. Tierney in *NCE* 4 (1967), pp. 219–23, s.v.; W. Brandmüller in *TRE* 19 (1990), pp. 529–35, s.v. 'Konstanz, Konzil von', with bibl. See also bibl. to D'AILLY, PIERRE; GERSON, JEAN LE CHARLIER; HUSS, JOHN; and WYCLIFFE, JOHN.

Constance Missal. See MISSALE SPECIALE.

Constantine the Great

Constantine the Great (d. 337), Roman emperor. The date of his birth is unknown; it has been variously placed between 272 and 288. The son of the Emp. Constantius Chlorus and St *Helena, he was sent in 293 to the court of *Diocletian, the senior emperor, under whose influence he learned the new Byzantine ideas of absolute sovereignty, which were rapidly replacing the Roman conception of the principate. In 306, on the death of Constantius, he was proclaimed Emperor at *York, and became senior ruler of the empire in 312, after defeating his rival Maxentius at the *Milvian Bridge. At that battle, following instructions received (according to *Lactantius) in a dream on the previous night, Constantine fought under the sign of the Cross, which was subsequently modified into the *Labarum standard. He attributed his victory to the Christian God, and shortly afterwards toleration and imperial favour were given to Christianity. In 313 he agreed with his fellow-emperor Licinius on a policy of religious freedom enshrined in the so-called Edict of *Milan.

Since Constantine's policy was to unite the Christian Church to the secular State by the closest possible ties, it was natural that even before he formally professed Christianity himself he should be concerned with the internal affairs of the Church. In 313 the *Donatist schismatics in Africa appealed to him to settle their controversy with the Church of that province, and at their request he referred the matter first to a commission of bishops, then to a synod of Gaul and Italy (*Arles, 314), and finally in 316 heard the case himself. In each trial the verdict went against the Donatists, who thereupon attacked not only their ecclesiastical opponents but also the State, encouraging rioting and brigandage. Constantine was therefore constrained to reinforce his verdict with repressive measures; he was, however, unable to end the schism, and in 321 he abandoned the Donatists to the judgement of God.

A similar appeal from the contending parties led Constantine to summon the Council of *Nicaea (325) to settle the *Arian dispute about the Person of Christ. The Emperor took an active part, though unbaptized, a circumstance which foreshadows the Byzantine theory of the emperors as supreme rulers of Church and State alike. The victory of orthodoxy which the creed of the council symbolized did not prevent Constantine from banishing prominent orthodox leaders in later years (e.g. St *Athanasius in 336) at the instance of their enemies. Constantine came under the influence of men of various beliefs, esp. *Hosius, Bp. of Córdoba, and Lactantius (in the W.), then *Eusebius, Bp. of Caesarea, and *Eusebius, Bp. of Nicomedia (in the E.).

The breach with the old traditions of Rome was complete when, after the victory at Chrysopolis (324) which had made him sole emperor, Constantine fixed his capital at Byzantium (rebuilt and inaugurated as 'Constantinople' in 330). As Roman emperor he had to deal cautiously with paganism, which remained important and influential among his subjects; yet throughout his reign his commitment to Christianity is clear, even though he was not baptized until just before his death (deferment of baptism was common in those days). His policy and legislation, though not free from grave blemishes, show a strongly Christian tendency from the first. He humanized the criminal law and the law of debt, mitigated the conditions of slavery, made grants to support poor children, thus discouraging the exposure of unwanted babies, freed celibates and unmarried persons from special taxation, legislated against incontinence, and exempted Christian clergy from the burden of the decurionate. In 321 he ordered that *Sunday should become a public holiday. He liberally endowed Christian church building, esp. at the Holy Places in Palestine, Rome, and Constantinople.

If the centralization of the empire at Constantinople led to an increasing Imperial control of the E. Church, it had also the consequence, perhaps unforeseen, of making the bishops of Rome more prominent than any other figure, lay or ecclesiastical, in the W.; and it is from the 4th cent. that the Papacy begins to assume its secular importance and the position which it held in the Middle Ages.

Legend has added much to history. A tradition going back to the 5th cent. asserts that he was baptized at the *Lateran by Pope *Sylvester, and his connections with the Pope are further embellished in the *Donation of Constantine (q.v.). In the E. Church he has been named the 'Thirteenth Apostle' and is venerated as a saint. Feast day in the E., 21 May (with St *Helena).

The chief primary sources are several official edicts of Constantine; some contemporary panegyrics by pagan orators; Lactantius, *De Mortibus Persecutorum*; and Eusebius, *Vita Constantini*. Useful collection of documents concerning the Donatist controversy pr. as an appendix to the works of *Optatus, ed. C. Ziwsa (CSEL 26; 1893), pp. 183–216. Eng. tr. of primary sources by P. R. Coleman-Norton, *Roman State & Christian Church*, 1 (1966), pp. 27–215. Crit. edn. of Eusebius' *Vita* by F. Winkelmann (GCS, 1975; 2nd edn., 1991). H. Grégoire, 'Eusèbe n'est pas l'auteur de la "Vita Constantini" dans sa forme actuelle et Constantin n'est pas "converti" en 312', *Byzantion*, 13 (1938), pp. 561–83, denied the genuineness of the whole work, but he has had little following. On the discovery of a papyrus containing a contemporary copy of one of the docs. in the Life, see A. H. M. Jones and T. C. Skeat, 'Notes on the Genuineness of the Constantinian Documents in Eusebius's Life of Constantine', *JEH* 5 (1954), pp. 196–200. F. Halkin, SJ (ed.), 'Une Nouvelle Vie de Constantin dans un Légendier de Patmos', *Anal. Boll.* 77 (1959), pp. 63–107; with refs. to other legends; id., 'L'Empereur Constantin converti par Euphratas', ibid. 78 (1960), pp. 5–17; A. Linder, 'The Myth of Constantine the Great in the West: Sources and Hagiographic Commemoration', *Studi medievali*, 3rd ser. 16 (1975), pp. 43–95.

The modern study of Constantine may be said to begin with J. Burckhardt, *Die Zeit Konstantins des Grossen* (1853). The problem posed here as to the genuineness of Constantine's acceptance of Christianity has been the subject of a large and important literature, notably N. H. Baynes's Raleigh Lecture, 'Constantine the Great and the Christian Church', *Proceedings of the British Academy*, 15 (1929), pp. 341–442.

Other works incl. F. J. Dölger (ed.), *Konstantin der Grosse und seine Zeit: ... Festgabe zum Konstantinsjubiläum* (*RQ*, Suppl. 19; 1913); E. *Schwartz, *Kaiser Konstantin und die christliche Kirche* (1913; 2nd edn., 1936); A. Piganiol, *L'Empereur Constantin* (1932); A. Alföldi, *The Conversion of Constantine and Pagan Rome* (1948); A. H. M. Jones, *Constantine and the Conversion of Europe* (1948);

J. Vogt, *Constantin der Grosse und sein Jahrhundert* (Munich, 1949); P. Franchi de' Cavalieri, *Constantiniana* (ST 171; 1953); H. Dörries, *Das Selbstzeugnis Kaiser Konstantins* (*Abh.* (Gött.), Dritte Folge, 34; 1954); H. Kraft, *Kaiser Konstantins religiöse Entwicklung* (Beiträge zur historischen Theologie, 20; 1955); H. Dörries, *Konstantin der Grosse* (Urban-Bücher, 29 [1958]; Eng. tr., 1972); id., *Constantine and Religious Liberty*, tr. by R. Bainton (D. H. Terry Lectures, 1958; New Haven, Conn., 1960); R. MacMullen, *Constantine* (New York, 1969; London, 1970); T. D. Barnes, *Constantine and Eusebius* (1981), esp. pp. 3–77 and 191–275; id., *The New Empire of Diocletian and Constantine* (1982). R. Lane Fox, *Pagans and Christians* (1986), pp. 609–62; R. Leeb, *Konstantin und Christus* (Arbeiten zur Kirchengeschichte, 58; 1992); J. Bleicken, *Constantin der Grosse und die Christen* (Historische Zeitschrift, Beihefte, NF 15; 1992). There is also a useful collection of specialized papers in *Dumbarton Oaks Papers*, 21 (1967). Modern summaries, with further bibl., *C. Anc. H.* 12. J. Vogt in *RAC* 3 (1957), cols. 306–79, s.v., with bibl. On the cult of Constantine, see esp. H. *Leclercq, OSB, in *DACL* 3 (pt. 2, 1914), cols. 2622–95, s.v.

Constantinople. In AD 330 *Constantine inaugurated Constantinople as his capital on the site of the Greek city of Byzantium. The town, which was later considerably enlarged, remained the capital of the E. Empire until 1453, except from 1204 to 1261 when, after capture by the *Crusaders, it was the capital of a Latin empire. From 1453 it was the Turkish capital until this was transferred to Ankara in 1923.

Byzantium had a Christian community at least from the 2nd cent., and Constantinople was a Christian city from its inauguration. The Bishop was at first subject to the see of Heraclea; but before long, as the Bishop of the 'New Rome', he took his place beside the Bps. of *Alexandria, *Antioch, and *Rome. At the council in the city in 381 he was given honorary pre-eminence after the Bp. of Rome, and in 451, though the Pope objected, patriarchal powers were formally conferred upon him (can. 28). Meanwhile Alexandria had striven with Constantinople for supremacy in the E., and *Theophilus and *Cyril of Alexandria obtained respectively the depositions of *Chrysostom (in 403) and *Nestorius (in 431). Finally Rome and Constantinople were left to struggle for pre-eminence. A gradual estrangement ensued: the final breach between the Catholic W. and the Orthodox E. is usually assigned to the year 1054, but the beginning of the schism cannot in fact be exactly dated. Since the 6th cent. the Patr. (as the Bp. was now designated) of Constantinople has been recognized in the E. as the *Oecumenical Patriarch.

Since the city has come under Turkish domination, most of its many ancient churches have become mosques, including the celebrated church of *Sancta Sophia (more recently, converted into a museum). By the Treaty of Lausanne (1923) the Turkish Republic is bound to protect the Greek Christians in Constantinople; but the Patriarch may be chosen only from Turkish citizens.

Les Regestes des Actes du Patriarcat de Constantinople, 1: *Les Actes des Patriarches*, fascs. 1–3 [381–1206], ed. V. Grumel, AA (Constantinople, 1932–47; 2nd edn., Paris, 1972–89); fasc. 4 [1208–1309] ed. V. Laurent, AA (Paris, 1971); fascs. 5–6 [1301–1410], ed. J. Darrouzès, AA (ibid., 1977–9); fasc. 7 [1410–53] ed. id. (ibid., 1991), with index to fascs. 1–7. Id. (ed.), *Notitiae Episcopatuum Ecclesiae Constantinopolitanae* (Géographie Ecclésiastique de l'Empire Byzantin, 1; 1981). *Das Register des Patriarchats von Konstantinopel* [14th cent.], ed., with Ger. tr., by H. Hunger, O. Kresten, and others (Corpus Fontium Historiae Byzantinae,

19/1 etc.; Vienna, 1981 ff.). C. D. *Du Cange, *Constantinopolis Christiana* (Paris, fol., 1680; still useful). C. Diehl, *Constantinople* (Paris, 1912). R. Janin, AA, *Constantinople byzantine: Développement urbain et répertoire topographique* (Archives de l'Orient Chrétien, 4; 1950; 2nd edn., 1964); J. Ebersolt, *Constantinople: Recueil d'études, d'archéologie et d'histoire* (1951). P. Sherrard, *Constantinople: Iconography of a Sacred City* (1965). D. Talbot Rice, *Constantinople: Byzantium—Istanbul* (1965). M. Maclagan, *The City of Constantinople* (Ancient Peoples and Places, 1968). G. Dagron, *Naissance d'une Capitale: Constantinople et ses institutions de 330 à 451* (Bibliothèque Byzantine, Études, 7; 1974); C. [A.] Mango, *Le Développement urbain de Constantinople (IVᵉ au VIIᵉ siècles)* (Travaux et mémoires du centre de recherche d'histoire et civilisation de Byzance, Collège de France, Monographies, 2; 1985). G. Every, SSM, *The Byzantine Patriarchate 451–1204* (1947; rev. edn., 1962). G. Downey, *Constantinople in the Age of Justinian* (Norman, Okla., 1960). S. Runciman, *The Fall of Constantinople* (1965). R. Janin, AA, *Les Églises et les monastères* [de Constantinople] (Géographie Ecclésiastique de l'Empire Byzantin, 3; 2nd edn., 1969). T. F. Mathews, *The Early Churches of Constantinople: Architecture and Liturgy* [1971]; id., *The Byzantine Churches of Istanbul: A Photographic Survey* [1976]. Valuable study, with full bibl., by S. Vailhé, AA, in *DTC* 3 (1908), cols. 1307–519, s.v. 'Constantinople (Église de)'; more recent study by R. Janin, AA, in *DHGE* 13 (1956), cols. 626–754. G. Downey in *NCE* 4 (1967), pp. 231–7, s.v., with further bibl.

Constantinople, First Council of (381). It was convened by the Emp. *Theodosius I to unite the E. Church at the end of the lengthy *Arian controversy on the basis of the *Nicene faith. It met under the presidency of *Melitius, Bp. of Antioch (who died during the Council) and was attended by 150 orthodox bishops and 36 bishops of *Pneumatomachian sympathies who later withdrew. Although neither W. bishops nor Roman legates were present, its achievement was sufficiently significant for it to come to be regarded as the Second *General Council in both E. and W. The work of the Council of *Nicaea with regard to the doctrine of Christ was ratified, and the humanity of Christ safeguarded by condemning *Apollinarianism. The so-called Niceno-Constantinopolitan Creed, traditionally ascribed to this Council, was probably not drawn up by it, though it may well have been endorsed by it in the course of its deliberations (so A. M. Ritter, followed by J. N. D. Kelly; see NICENE CREED). In ecclesiastical matters the Council (*a*) appointed *Nectarius as Bp. of Constantinople, in place of St *Gregory of Nazianzus; (*b*) granted to Constantinople honorary precedence (τὰ πρεσβεῖα τῆς τιμῆς) over all Churches save Rome; and (*c*) misguidedly appointed as Bp. of *Antioch Flavian rather than Paulinus, who, by an agreement of the schismatic parties, should have succeeded Melitius.

Hardouin, 1, cols. 807–26; Mansi, 3 (1759), cols. 521–600; Tanner, *Decrees* (1990), pp. 21–35. Hefele and Leclercq, 2 (pt. 1; 1908), pp. 1–48. Crit. edn. of Lat. versions of canons in *EOMIA* 2. 3 (1929), pp. 401–72. Gk. text of canons with names of Bishops ed. from two Patmos MSS by C. H. Turner in *JTS* 15 (1914), pp. 161–78. W. *Bright, *Notes on the Canons of the First Four General Councils* (2nd edn., 1892), pp. 90–128. I. Ortiz de Urbina, SJ, *Nicée et Constantinople* (Histoire des Conciles Œcuméniques, 1; 1963), esp. pp. 139–242. A. M. Ritter, *Das Konzil von Konstantinopel und sein Symbol: Studien zur Geschichte und Theologie des II. Ökumenischen Konzils* (Forschungen zur Kirchen- und Dogmengeschichte, 15; 1965). N. Q. King, 'The 150 Holy Fathers of the Council of Constantinople 381 A.D. Some notes on the Bishoplists', in K. Aland and F. L. Cross (eds.), *Studia Patristica*, 1 (TU 63; 1957), pp. 635–41. *CPG* 4 (1980), pp. 25–7 (nos. 8598–8601).

J. Bois in *DTC* 3 (1908), cols. 1227–31, s.v.; R. Janin, AA, in *DHGE* 13 (1956), cols. 754–7, s.v.

Constantinople, Second Council of (553).

This, the Fifth General Council, was convoked by the Emp. *Justinian to decide the prolonged controversy over the *Three Chapters: whether *Theodore of Mopsuestia, *Theodoret of Cyrrhus, and *Ibas of Edessa should be condemned as tainted with *Nestorianism, or whether, following the attitude of the Council of *Chalcedon, they should be accepted. The Emperor, who wished to reconcile moderate *Monophysite opinion, was opposed to any toleration of Theodore, Theodoret, and Ibas. Justinian's first decree condemning the Three Chapters (543/4) met with W. opposition, though Pope *Vigilius himself vacillated, first condemning *Menas, the Patriarch of *Constantinople, and the Emperor's supporters (547), but then withdrawing his anathema. The Emperor's second decree against the Three Chapters (551) met with the same W. opposition, and again Vigilius first condemned Menas (552), but then retracted his condemnation. The Council was convoked to resolve the matter.

It was convened on 5 May 553 under the presidency of Eutychius, the new Patr. of Constantinople. The 165 bishops who signed the acts were almost all Easterns. The Three Chapters were condemned and their authors anathematized. During its course Vigilius, who refused to attend for fear of violence as well as in protest against the preponderance of E. bishops present, drew up the so-called 'Constitutum', signed by himself and 16 W. bishops, in which, while condemning 60 propositions of Theodore of Mopsuestia, he refused to anathematize his person on the grounds that he had not been condemned at *Ephesus (431) or Chalcedon (451) and that it was not the custom of the Church to condemn the dead. The Council replied by erasing the Pope's name from the diptychs in the 7th session. Vigilius was for a short time exiled, but as the Emperor had nothing to gain from a rupture with the Pope he used every means to bring about a reconciliation. Vigilius finally agreed to accept the Council and annulled his former decisions in favour of the Three Chapters.

Of the 14 anathemas pronounced by the Council the first 12 are directed chiefly against Theodore of Mopsuestia, the 13th against Theodoret of Cyrrhus, and the 14th against Ibas. In the 11th anathema the name of *Origen occurs in a list of heretics, but there are grounds for believing this to be an interpolation. Despite the Papal acceptance the Council was not at once recognized as oecumenical in the W. Milan and *Aquileia even broke off communion with Rome, and relations were not restored with Milan until the end of the 6th, and with Aquileia until the end of the 7th, cent. The Council, unlike the four preceding General Councils, issued no canons.

Hardouin, 3, cols. 1–328; Mansi, 9 (1743), cols. 157–658; crit. edn. by J. Straub, *ACO*, Tomus 4, vol. 1 (Berlin, 1971). Acts conveniently pr., with Eng. tr. and introd., in Tanner, *Decrees* (1990), pp. 105–22. H. *Noris, *Dissertatio Historica de Synodo Quinta Oecumenica* (1673; repr. in Noris's *Opera*, 1, Verona, 1729, cols. 550–820). F. Diekamp, *Die origenistischen Streitigkeiten im sechsten Jahrhundert und das fünfte allgemeine Konzil* (1899), pp. 77–98. R. Haacke, OSB, 'Die kaiserliche Politik in den Auseinandersetzungen um Chalkedon (451–553)', in A. Grillmeier, SJ, and H. Bacht, SJ (eds.), *Das Konzil von Chalkedon*, 2 (Würzburg, 1953), pp. 95–177, esp. pp. 141–77. F.-X. Murphy, CSSR, and P. Sherwood, OSB, *Constantinople II et Constantinople III* (Histoire des Conciles Œcuméniques, 3; 1974), pp. 13–130. Hefele and Leclercq, 3 (pt. 2; 1909), pp. 1–156. *CPG* 4 (1980), pp. 159–66 (nos. 9332–66). J. Bois in *DTC* 3 (1908), cols. 1231–59, s.v.; R. Janin, AA, in *DHGE* 13 (1956), cols. 757–60, s.v., both with bibl. See also bibl. to MONOPHYSITISM, THEODORE OF MOPSUESTIA, and THREE CHAPTERS.

Constantinople, Third Council of (680–81).

This, the Sixth General Council, was convoked at the demand of the Emp. Constantine IV (Pogonatus) to settle the prolonged *Monothelite controversy in the E. Church. Pope *Agatho, having held a Synod at *Rome (680) in which the doctrine of the Two Wills in Christ was again affirmed, sent his delegates to the Emperor with a letter expounding this teaching. On their arrival the Emperor called a Council of the bishops of the patriarchates of *Constantinople and *Antioch. The debates of its 18 sessions, conducted chiefly by the Papal envoys, were concerned solely with the Monothelite question. Macarius, the Patr. of Antioch, was condemned as a Monothelite, and in the 13th session the principal leaders of the heresy, among whom the Council included the former Pope *Honorius, were anathematized.

The Dogmatic Decree of the Council is principally a reproduction of the profession of faith drawn up at *Chalcedon, affirming the doctrine of the Two Natures, to which is added, as a necessary consequence, the statement of the reality of the Two Wills (θελήματα) and the Two Operations (ἐνέργειαι). The Council rejected all natural unity of the two wills, but admitted the existence of a moral unity, resulting from the complete harmony between the Divine and the human will in the God-man. The same position was affirmed regarding the duality of operations. The decree concluded with a résumé of the Christological teaching of the various Councils. This Council issued no canons.

Hardouin, 3, cols. 1043–644; Mansi, 11 (1765), cols. 189–922. Crit. edn. by R. Riedinger (ACO, 2nd ser. 2; 2 parts, 1990–92). Tanner, *Decrees* (1990), pp. 123–30. Hefele and Leclercq, 3 (pt. 1; 1909), pp. 472–538. F.-X. Murphy, CSSR, and P. Sherwood, OSB, *Constantinople II et Constantinople III* (Histoire des Conciles Œcuméniques, 3; 1974), pp. 133–260. P. Conte, 'Il significato del primato papale nei padri del VI concilio ecumenico', *Archivum Historiae Pontificiae*, 15 (1977), pp. 7–111. L. Bréhier in Fliche and Martin, 5 (1938), pp. 183–91. *CPG* 4 (1980), pp. 178–84 (nos. 9416–42). J. Bois in *DTC* 3 (1908), cols. 1259–73; R. Janin, AA, in *DHGE* 13 (1956), cols. 760–3, s.v. See also bibl. to MONOTHELITISM.

Constantinopolitan Creed.

See NICENE CREED.

Constitutional Church.

The State Church set up in the French Revolution by the *Civil Constitution of the Clergy (q.v.). Its clergy were those who took the oath of 27 Nov. 1790 as prescribed by the Constituent Assembly. When the Papal condemnation became known, some retracted, but most stayed on in office accepting the inevitability of schism. Under the pressure of war, invasion and civil strife the Revolution turned to the cruelties of Terror, and the clergy became regarded as traitors. On 23 Sept. 1793 the registration of births, marriages, and deaths was taken from them, and in Oct. 1793 the Christian calendar was abolished in favour of a revolutionary one. Having stayed in France and in public office, the Constitutional clergy were available for victimization, and were subject to grim pressures to renounce their orders. Forty-seven of their bishops saved their lives by giving up their episcopal functions, though only 23 actually apostasized. When the Terror ended and the decree of 21 Feb. 1795 allowed a limited toleration, the Constitutional Church was resurrected by Henri Grégoire, Bp. of Blois, and held a national Council in 1797. Its end came with the *Concordat of 1801.

There is an extensive lit. on the Catholic Church in France at the time of the Revolution. L. Sciout, *Histoire de la constitution civile du clergé, 1790–1801* (4 vols., 1872–81). P. de La Gorce, *Histoire religieuse de la Révolution française* (5 vols., 1909–23), esp. vol. 1, pp. 349–506. H. *Leclercq, OSB, *L'Église constitutionnelle, juillet 1790–avril 1791* (1934). A. Latreille, *L'Église Catholique et la Révolution française* (2 vols., 1946–50). J. McManners, *The French Revolution and the Church* (1969), with bibl. A. Dansette, *Histoire religieuse de la France contemporaine*, 1 (1948), pp. 76–187. See also bibl. to CIVIL CONSTITUTION OF THE CLERGY and CONCORDAT OF 1801.

Constitutions of Clarendon. See CLARENDON, CONSTITUTIONS OF.

consubstantial. Of one and the same substance or being. The word is used esp. of the eternal relationship which subsists between the three Persons of the Holy Trinity. The Latin *consubstantialis* is the W. counterpart of the Greek ὁμοούσιος (see HOMOOUSION), the test-word of theological orthodoxy in the *Arian controversy.

consubstantiation. In the doctrine of the *Eucharist, the belief, esp. associated with the name of M. *Luther, that, after the consecration, the substances both of the Body and Blood of Christ and of the bread and wine coexist in union with each other. Luther illustrated it by the analogy of the iron put into the fire whereby both fire and iron are united in the red-hot iron and yet each continues unchanged. The doctrine was formulated in opposition to the medieval doctrine of *transubstantiation, acc. to which the substances of the bread and wine were no longer present after consecration, but only their '*accidents' persisted.

J. H. Crehan, SJ, in *A Catholic Dictionary of Theology*, 2 (1967), pp. 114–17. See also works cited under EUCHARIST.

Consuetudinary. See CUSTOMARY.

Consultation on Church Union (COCU). A Church union negotiating committee of American Churches of Protestant and Anglican tradition seeking a form of union which would be at once 'truly catholic, truly evangelical, and truly reformed'. The Consultation began in 1962 in response to a sermon by Eugene C. Blake of the former United *Presbyterian Church in the USA. Its original members were the United Presbyterian Church, the (then Protestant) *Episcopal Church, the *United Church of Christ, the Christian Church (*Disciples of Christ), the *Methodist Episcopal Church, and the Evangelical United Brethren. It has subsequently been joined by the African Methodist Episcopal Church, the African Methodist Episcopal Zion Church, the Christian Methodist Episcopal Church, the Presbyterian Church in the United States, and the International Council of Community Churches (formerly known as the National Council of Community Churches). It thus includes both Black and White Churches. (Mergers between the Methodist Episcopal Church and the Evangelical United Brethren to form the United Methodist Church in 1968, and between the United Presbyterian Church in the USA and the Presbyterian Church in the United States to form the Presbyterian Churches (USA) in 1983, reduced the number of Churches participating, but not the range.) Other Churches which have observer-participant status include the Evangelical *Lutheran Church in America, the Reformed Church in America, and the RC Church. In 1970 a draft *Plan of Union* was put forward for consideration; it described a plan of full and organic union among the Churches. The responses to this proposal, which was dropped in 1973, led the participating Churches to redefine their ecumenical goal as a relationship of full communion among the various continuing traditions, Church union now being understood as communion in faith, sacraments, ministry, and mission. The *COCU Consensus* (1984), which is the theological basis for this second plan of union, has been approved as a whole or in part by the governing bodies of the participating Churches. The plan itself, *Churches in Covenant Communion* was in 1988 approved by a plenary session of the Consultation and has been referred to the participating Churches; they are expected to have completed voting upon it by 1998.

G. F. Moede in N. Lossky and others (eds.), *Dictionary of the Ecumenical Movement* [1991], p. 227, s.v. See also bibl. to ECUMENICAL MOVEMENT.

contakion (Gk. κοντάκιον, from κοντός, 'pole' or 'shaft'; hence a vellum roll wound round a piece of wood). In the E. Church, a hymn composed in a series of strophes and intended for liturgical use. Contakia, esp. those of St *Romanos, enjoyed very wide popularity during the 6th–7th cents., but from the 8th cent. onwards they came to be largely replaced by a new form of liturgical hymnography, the *canon. In modern editions of the service books, usually only the first strophe of the contakion is included; this is read or sung after the sixth ode of the canon, after the *Little Entrance in the Liturgy, and at most offices.

P. Maas, 'Das Kontakion', *Byzantinische Zeitschrift*, 19 (1910), pp. 285–306, repr. in id., *Kleine Schriften*, ed. W. Buchwald (1973), pp. 368–91. E. Wellesz, *A History of Byzantine Music and Hymnography* (Oxford, 1949), esp. pp. 152–67; 2nd edn. (1961), pp. 179–97, with refs.

Contarini, Gasparo (1483–1542), cardinal. He belonged to one of the foremost families of Venice. After education at the University of Padua, where he was won for the New Learning, he served as Venetian ambassador at the court of *Charles V (attending in this capacity the Diet of *Worms of 1521), in England, in Spain, and at the Papal court. He soon became famous as a theologian. In 1516 he published a treatise defending (against P. *Pomponazzi) the immortality of the soul, and *c.*1530 a book against M. *Luther, *Confutatio Articulorum seu Quaestionum Lutheri*. His popularity at Rome led him, though only a layman, to be created a cardinal by *Paul III in 1535. In 1536 he was put on the commission which was to prepare the way for the Council (of *Trent) and in 1536–7 he issued the 'Consilium de emendanda ecclesia', proposing many radical reforms. In 1536 he became Bp. of Belluno. At the Conference of *Ratisbon (1541), where he championed the doctrine of '*double justice', he took an active part in this last attempt at reunion with the Lutherans, before the influence of the *Counter-Reformation ideals finally closed the possibility of reconciliation. It was while searching at Ratisbon for a common formula on justification that he wrote his 'Epistola de justificatione' (25 May 1541), a profession of faith in which Contarini was believed in many quarters to have compromised the Catholic doctrine. His own mystical experience of 1511, which led him to put his trust in the merits of Christ rather than religious observances, antedated Luther's *Turmerlebnis* by several years.

Opera [ed. by L. Contarini, with a Life by G. della Casa] (Paris, 1571). *Gegenreformatorische Schriften* (c.1530–42) ed. F. Hünermann (Corpus Catholicorum, 7; 1923). F. Dittrich (ed.), *Regesten und Briefe des Cardinals Gasparo Contarini, 1483–1542* (1881). Id., *Gasparo Contarini, 1483–1542: Eine Monographie* (1885). G. Bianchini, *Un magistrato-cardinale del secolo XVI* (1895); H. Rückert, *Die theologische Entwicklung Gasparo Contarinis* (1926); H. Hackert, *Die Staatsschrift Gasparo Contarinis und die politischen Verhältnisse Venedigs im sechzehnten Jahrhundert* (Heidelberger Abhandlungen zur mittleren und neueren Geschichte, Heft 69; 1940). H. Jedin, *Kardinal Contarini als Kontroverstheologe* (Katholisches Leben und Kämpfen im Zeitalter der Glaubensspaltung, 9; 1949). Id., 'Ein "Turmerlebnis" des jungen Contarini', *Hist. J.* 70 (1951), pp. 115–30, repr. in id., *Kirche des Glaubens—Kirche des Geschichte*, 1 (1966), pp. 167–80; id., 'Contarini und Camaldoli', *Archivio Italiano per la Storia della Pietà*, 2 (1959), pp. 51–118, incl. text of 30 letters. P. Matheson, *Cardinal Contarini at Regensburg* (Oxford, 1972). G. Fragnito, *Gasparo Contarini* (Bibliotheca della Rivista di Storia e Letteratura Religiosa, Studi e Testi, 9; 1988). D. Fenlon, *Heresy and Obedience in Tridentine Italy: Cardinal Pole and the Counter Reformation* (Cambridge, 1972), esp. pp. 6–11, 45–50, and 55–68. K. Ganzer, 'Gasparo Contarini', in E. Iserloh (ed.), *Katholische Theologen der Reformationszeit*, 1 (Katholisches Leben und Kirchenreform im Zeitalter der Glaubensspaltung, 44; 1984), pp. 107–15, with bibl. H. Jedin in *DHGE* 13 (1956), cols. 771–84; G. Fragnito in *Dizionario Biografico degli Italiani*, 28 (1983), pp. 172–92, s.v.

contemplation, contemplative life. The Lat. *contemplatio*, like its Gk. equivalent (θεωρία), primarily means looking at things, whether with the eyes or with the mind; in either sense it can be contrasted with doing things (πρᾶξις). On this basis a distinction can be made between practical and speculative kinds of science, and practical and speculative elements in a human life. *Aristotle surmised that a purely contemplative (i.e. intellectual) life would be the best, should it be possible, but this was disputed by others, such as the *Stoics. The Stoics and *Epicureans subordinated speculation to practical ethics, but the Middle and *Neo-Platonists maintained the superiority of contemplation, whose goal was stated to be knowledge of, or union with, God. On this basis a 'contemplative life' could be identified as one devoted to God rather than to any kind of activity.

Many of the Greek Fathers adopted the ideal of the 'contemplative life', proceeding through the philosophical study of creatures to the knowledge of God. But θεωρία also retains the important sense of 'study of the Scriptures', with particular emphasis on the spiritual sense.

St *Augustine maintained that there is a contemplative element (namely faith) and a practical element (morals) in every Christian life, but he came to be doubtful about the propriety of a purely contemplative life. St *Gregory the Great gave a classic definition of the contemplative life as one devoted exclusively to the love of God (*Hom. in Ez.* 2. 2. 8; *PL* 76. 953 AB); he also argued that we know God precisely in loving Him (*Hom. in Evang.* 2. 27. 4; *PL* 76. 1207 A). In later tradition there is a bifurcation in the use of contemplative words: some writers continued to use them with reference to the intellectual life (*Thomas Aquinas defining the 'contemplative life' as that of the person whose bias is speculative rather than practical), while others began to contrast 'contemplation' with the intellectual life.

In the latter part of the Middle Ages there was a tendency to conflate the notions of meditation, prayer and contemplation around the idea of an intense love of God, felt in the affections. This eventually led to the notion of contemplation as a form of prayer, and so to 'contemplative prayer', distinguished by St *Teresa of Avila and St *John of the Cross from '*mental prayer' or meditation. They defined it as being a supernatural state of prayer, in which the exercise of the natural powers of the mind and will is suspended. Since the 17th cent. some writers have distinguished between this kind of strictly supernatural contemplation ('infused contemplation') and 'acquired contemplation', in which the working of the natural powers is not entirely suspended. Various states have been designated as 'acquired contemplation', chiefly (a) a simplified intellectual gazing, (b) simplified affective prayer, and (c) a state in which the soul receives a supernatural illumination, but without its natural powers ceasing to operate (also called 'active contemplation'). Other writers have insisted that 'acquired contemplation' is a contradiction in terms.

Inasmuch as the goal of the Christian life is the vision of God in heaven, Augustine and others maintain that the 'contemplative life' is the eschatological goal of all Christians, the fruit and reward of the entire Christian life. 'Contemplation' on earth can thus be seen as a foretaste of heaven.

In modern times 'contemplative life' has been equated with the life of members of strictly enclosed religious orders, such as the *Carthusians and *Carmelite nuns.

Contemplation is discussed in books on the spiritual life: see bibl. to PRAYER. M. E. Mason, OSB, *Active Life and Contemplative Life: A Study of the Concepts from Plato to the Present* (Milwaukee, Wis., 1961). J. Lebreton, SJ, and others, in *Dict. Sp.* 2 (1953), cols. 1643–2193, s.v.

contemplative life. See previous entry.

Contestatio (Lat.). In *Gallican service books, the usual name for the *Preface at the *Eucharist.

contingency. A property of entities, events, or propositions. Contingent entities are things which do not have to exist. Contingent events are ones which do not have to occur. Contingent propositions are those which do not have to be true. In metaphysics it has been held that created things are contingent and that God, by contrast, is 'necessary'. The idea here is that God alone exists of necessity, i.e. He has the quality of *aseity. In St *Thomas Aquinas and other medieval thinkers 'contingent' means 'able to be generated and able to perish in the course of nature'. This account allows for there being created necessary things (e.g. heavenly bodies, angels, human souls). The concept of contingency has been invoked in versions of the *Ontological Argument and the *Cosmological Argument (qq.v.).

contraception, procreation, and abortion, ethics of. The fundamental principles applied by Christians in reflecting on moral problems associated with procreation are the sacredness of human life, love of neighbour, and respect for the sovereignty and providence of God. On the basis of these principles early Christian thinkers (including the authors of the *'Didache' and Epistle of *Barnabas, *Athenagoras, *Clement of Alexandria, *Tertullian, Sts *Ambrose, *Chrysostom, *Jerome, and *Augustine) were united in their condemnation of infanticide and abortion, in contrast to their pagan contemporaries. Abortion was forbidden at the Council of *Elvira (c.306, can. 61). The general patristic teaching against contraception was related to this set of attitudes and was shaped by an insistence against *Gnostics and *Manichees on the integrity of OT teaching that procreation within marriage was good, combined with reasoning (paralleled in *Stoic thought) which asserted the unnaturalness of a sexual act which did not have procreation as its end.

These early established prohibitions predominated in Christian teaching until recent times when there has been some questioning of traditional attitudes to contraception and abortion. The 1930 *Lambeth Conference declared that where there is 'a clearly felt moral obligation to limit or avoid parenthood, and where there is a morally sound reason for avoiding complete abstinence, . . . other methods may be used' (Resolution 15). This qualified acceptance in the Anglican Communion of the propriety of artificial contraception was a sign of the change of view on this topic which has prevailed in the mainstream Protestant Churches and finds some support among RC moralists. It was reinforced by the 1958 Lambeth Conference's commendation of 'responsible parenthood' (Res. 115). The official teaching of the RC Church, however, remains that affirmed in *Pius XI's encyclical *Casti Connubii* (1930) condemning any use of marriage 'in the exercise of which the act, by human effort, is deprived of its natural power of procreating life'. This document in passing acknowledges the legitimacy of intercourse during the infertile period; the so-called 'rhythm method', positively accepted by *Pius XII in 1951 and approved in *Paul VI's encyclical *Humanae Vitae* (1968), is the only form of birth-control, other than abstinence, apparently allowed to RCs. The teaching of *Humanae Vitae* on contraception was specifically repudiated by the 1968 Lambeth Conference (Res. 22) and within the RC Church it has been found difficult by the laity and is criticized by some priests, esp. in the developing world where there are grave problems of over-population. It was nevertheless reiterated in *John Paul II's encyclical *Evangelium Vitae* (1995). In the E. Church various local Church authorities have issued statements condemning artificial contraception, but there have been no modern pronouncements on the subject endorsed

by the Orthodox Church, and it appears that individually given advice varies in different areas.

The underlying differences in Christian thought about the proper use of sexual intercourse within marriage which are expressed in disagreement over contraception are reflected in the different responses to recent technological advances aimed at the alleviation of infertility and which have made possible artificial insemination by husband or (an anonymous) donor (AIH and AID), egg donation, and *in vitro* fertilization (where sperm and egg are united in the laboratory). Against artificial insemination by the husband and *in vitro* fertilization Pope Pius XII objected that these techniques, contrary to *natural law, separated the procreative and unitive meanings or aspects of sexual intercourse, a point which is central to the condemnation of artificial contraception in the encyclical *Humanae Vitae* (1968) and to the elaboration of Pius's teaching by the Congregation of the Doctrine of the Faith in *Donum Vitae* (1987); this last also emphasized that they failed to respect the dignity of the human and personal act that procreation ought to be. Additional grounds for rejecting artificial insemination by donor and *in vitro* fertilization which employs donated material are found in the invasive nature of each in relation to the exclusive covenant between husband and wife. Other moralists, including some RCs, have argued that, while a Christian marriage must be open to the goods for which it was ordained (the W. theological tradition identified these as the procreative, unitive, and sacramental goods), it can be so even if each individual act of sexual intercourse is not. Thus the separation of the meanings of intercourse which is alleged to occur when contraception is used and to which the traditional RC teaching objects, is judged to be morally acceptable, provided there is no outright rejection of the procreative good of marriage but only a temporary concern for considerations of, e.g., responsible parenthood. This position, implicit in the report of the Lambeth Conference of 1930, opens the way for a different approach to the problems of the treatment of infertility, though it does not necessarily entail conclusions markedly different from those defended by the RC Church. According to this approach, artificial insemination by the husband and *in vitro* fertilization is judged to be in principle acceptable in enabling marriage to achieve one of its goods, though in so far as the practice of *in vitro* fertilization normally involves the production of spare embryos to increase the likelihood of success of this uncertain intervention, it is open to serious criticism. In the case of procedures using donated material, many have regarded as decisive the objection that they allow procreation to take place outside marriage. Surrogacy (where a fertilized egg is carried to term on behalf of a couple who have contributed one or both parts of the genetic material) is acceptable to few, if any, moral theologians of any denomination. It separates from marriage not only the act of procreation but the entire pregnancy and delivery, and is thought to entail a view of children as transferable commodities. Indeed concern has been voiced that all technological manipulation of procreation leads to our viewing children as products of human ingenuity, with the danger that those so regarded will be used as objects and not honoured as sharing our nature.

The development of techniques for combating infertility have involved the use of human embryos, and debates on the legitimacy of such research have become linked with questions of abortion. Though by no means as widespread as those relating to contraception, there have been changes in attitude here. The advent of modern surgery renders it possible in certain circumstances, by aborting the foetus, to save a woman whose life would be endangered by the birth of a child, and some Christians, including a number of Anglicans and Orthodox, regard abortion as permissible in such cases, while maintaining that the foetus is usually deserving of protection. A minority of W. Christians go further and accept abortion where the mother's interests or the interests of her family are seriously threatened and it is in this direction that the civil law in many countries has changed. In Britain the Abortion Act 1967 allowed legal termination of pregnancy prior to the 28th week in order to avoid injury to the 'physical or mental health' of the mother or 'any existing child of her family', or 'where there is a substantial risk that if the child were born it would suffer such physical and mental abnormalities as to be seriously handicapped'. The Act specifically exempts conscientious objectors from any obligation to take part in the treatment authorized except where it is necessary 'to save the life or to prevent grave permanent injury to the physical or mental health' of the mother. The judgement of the Supreme Court of the USA in Roe v. Wade in 1973 was more radical in holding that the prohibition of abortion prior to viability was unconstitutional, thereby denying the foetus the *prima facie* protection which the English law enshrines. However, the 1967 Act has been applied in such a way that there has been little difference in practice between the two countries. These legal changes have gone too far in the view of probably a majority of Christians. The RC Church maintains that any abortion as an end in itself ('direct abortion') is always unlawful, though an operation which will result in the destruction of a foetus may be licit, since it is permissible, for sufficient reason, to perform an action in itself good or indifferent from which two results, one good and one bad, may follow. Thus the removal of a womb which is cancerous may be considered an indirect and licit abortion. Even among those Christians who do not subscribe to the RC position, there is widespread unease over a situation in which abortion is virtually available 'on demand', an unease reflected for example in the resolution of the General *Synod of the C of E in 1983 accepting abortion only when the mother's life was endangered. In the USA a woman's right to an abortion as defined in Roe v. Wade was limited by the decision of the Supreme Court in 1989 in Webster v. Reproductive Health Services and it is likely that there will be other challenges to the earlier decision. In Britain the 1967 Act was amended in the Human Fertilisation and Embryology Act 1990. Termination of pregnancy may now take place no later than the 24th week, except where there is a risk of handicap to the child or a grave threat to the health of the mother, in which case there is no limit on when an abortion may occur. The same Act introduced regulations on experimentation on embryos which is allowed during the first 14 days of development, but not thereafter. The controversy surrounding the passing of this legislation demonstrates the importance and the difficulty of the question of when a human life begins and an embryo must be judged to be a person. The RC belief that 'from the time that the ovum is fertilized, a human life is

begun', is the basis of its repeated condemnation of direct abortion, and, more recently, of 'the use of human embryos or foetuses as an object of experimentation' or 'as providers of organs or tissue for transplants in the treatment of certain diseases' (*Evangelium Vitae*, 1995). For all Christians, a clear answer to the question of when a human life begins would be decisive, and the balancing of benefits and harms secondary. But differing answers are put forward by Christians as well as others, as is the view that no clear answer is to be had.

The Papal encyclicals *Casti Connubii* are pr. in *AAS* 22 (1930), pp. 539–92, and *Humanae Vitae*, ibid. 60 (1968), pp. 481–503; the statement of the Congregation of the Doctrine of the Faith 'On Respect for Human Life in its Origins and on the Dignity of Procreation' (*Donum Vitae*), ibid. 80 (1988), pp. 70–102; the encyclical *Evangelium Vitae*, ibid. 87 (1995), pp. 401–522. The Report of *The Lambeth Conference 1930* [1930] includes, besides the resolution (pp. 43 f.), the findings of the relevant committee, pp. 89–92; *The Lambeth Conference 1958* (1958), resolution 115, pt. 1, p. 57, with committee report on 'Family Planning', pt. 2, pp. 146–50. There is a full survey of the subject, incl. patristic references, in J. T. Noonan, *Contraception: A History of its Treatment by the Catholic Theologians and Canonists* (Cambridge, Mass., 1965; enlarged edn., ibid. and London, 1986). See also bibl. to HUMANAE VITAE.

Pius XII's views on artificial insemination and on *in vitro* fertilization are contained in addresses to conferences of RC doctors, pr. in *AAS* 41 (1949), pp. 557–61; 43 (1951), pp. 835–54; and 48 (1956), pp. 467–74, the second of these incidentally containing the first positive Papal endorsement of the use of the infertile period as a means of birth-control. For text of *Humanae Vitae*, *Donum Vitae*, and *Evangelium Vitae*, see above. *Personal Origins: The Report of a Working Party on Human Fertilisation and Embryology of the Board for Social Responsibility of the C of E* (1985) was a response to the *Report of the Committee of Inquiry into Human Fertilisation and Embryology*, commissioned by the Department of Health and Social Security and pub. by the Stationery Office [Cmnd. 9314; 1984], the so-called Warnock report, which was repr. with preface by M. Warnock, *A Question of Life* (1985). [*Personal Origins*, which carries no authority beyond that of group which compiled it, holds that Christians may judge that the protection due to human life need not be afforded to the early embryo.] The many other works dealing with these problems incl. B. Häring, *Medical Ethics* (Slough, 1972), pp. 65–94; J. Mahoney, *Bioethics and Belief: Religion and Medicine in Dialogue* (1984); and G. R. Dunstan and M. J. Seller (eds.), *The Status of the Human Embryo: Perspectives from Moral Tradition* [1988]. The concern that the new technologies encourage us to relate to children as products is expressed by K. *Rahner, 'Zum Problem der genetischen Manipulation', *Schriften der Theologie*, 8 [1967], pp. 286–321; Eng. tr. in *Theological Investigations*, 9 (1972), pp. 225–52; [R.] P. Ramsey, *Fabricated Man: The Ethics of Genetic Control* (New Haven, Conn., and London, 1970); and O. M. T. O'Donovan, *Begotten or Made?* (Oxford, 1984).

The RC ruling of the Congregation of the Doctrine of the Faith 'On Procured Abortion' is pr. in *AAS* 66 (1974), pp. 730–47. *Abortion: An Ethical Discussion. The Report of a Committee established by the C of E Board for Social Responsibility* (1965), countenances therapeutic abortion where there is a threat to the 'physical and mental health of the mother'; it carries no authority beyond that of the body which compiled it. J. T. Noonan, (ed.), *The Morality of Abortion* (Cambridge, Mass. [1970]), incl. a historical account by the ed., pp. 1–59; B. Häring, op. cit., pp. 94–119; [R.] P. Ramsey, *Ethics at the Edges of Life* (New Haven, Conn., and London, 1978), pp. 1–142; M. Tooley, *Abortion and Infanticide* (Oxford, 1983); G. R. Dunstan and M. J. Seller, op. cit.

Contra-Remonstrantie. The counter-declaration in which the more rigid Dutch *Calvinists stated their objections to the *Arminian '*Remonstrance' (q.v.). It was drawn up for the Conference which met at The Hague on 11 Mar. 1611. Its main points were: (1) Unconditional and absolute predestination of some souls to damnation. (2) Children as well as adults may be among the elect. (3) Election is not acc. to works or belief, but only at God's pleasure. (4) Christ died only for the elect. (5) The Holy Spirit speaks in Scripture only to the elect. (6) The elect can never lose the true belief. (7) This preservation does not lead to carelessness of life, but to positive virtue.

The text is in G. J. Hoenderdaal, 'Remonstrantie en Contra-remonstrantie', *Nederlands Archief voor Kerkgeschiedenis*, NS 51 (1970–1), pp. 49–92 (the seven articles on pp. 85–7).

contrition (Lat. *contritio*, 'a wearing away of something hard'). Contrition is a form of interior repentance, defined by the Council of *Trent as 'sorrow of heart and detestation of sin committed, with the purpose of not sinning in future' (sess. 14, cap. 4). Moral theologians commonly hold that to be real it must have its grounds in the love of God, and hence distinguish it from *attrition (q.v.), an imperfect form of sorrow for sin, inspired by such lower motives as the fear of punishment. The classic utterance of the contrite heart in the OT is the *Miserere (Ps. 51). In the Gospels the need for contrition is taught esp. in the Parables of the Prodigal Son (Lk. 15: 11–32) and of the Pharisee and the Publican (Lk. 18: 9–14).

*Leo X replied to M. *Luther's attack on the medieval notions of contrition in his bull, *Exsurge, Domine* (15 June 1520; list of heresies condemned repr. in Denzinger and Hünermann (37th edn., 1991), pp. 488–92, nos. 1451–92). H. Dondaine, OP, *L'Attrition suffisante* (Bibliothèque Thomiste, 25; 1943). C. R. Meyer, *The Thomistic Conception of Justifying Contrition* (Mundelein, Ill., 1949). P. de Letter, SJ, 'Perfect Contrition and Perfect Charity', *Theological Studies*, 7 (1946), pp. 507–24; id., 'Two Concepts of Attrition and Contrition', ibid. 11 (1950), pp. 3–33. T. Ortolan in *DTC* 3 (1908), cols. 1671–94; P. de Letter, SJ, in *NCE* 4 (1967), pp. 278–83, s.v. See also works cited s.v. PENANCE.

convent. The name 'convent' is derived from the Lat. *conventus*, a meeting or association of men for some purpose. In ecclesiastical usage it can refer either to the buildings in which a body of religious live together, or to the religious community itself. Historically it has been applied to the domicile of religious of either sex, though in English it tends now to be restricted to houses of women religious.

Conventicles Acts 1664 and 1670. The 1664 Act declared illegal all meetings in private houses or elsewhere of more than five persons (in addition to the household) for worship other than that prescribed in the BCP, while the 1670 Act mitigated the penalties laid down in 1664, but gave wider powers to those employed in suppressing conventicles. The penalties were suspended by the *Toleration Act 1688 ('Declaration of Indulgence'), but the Acts themselves were not finally repealed until the 19th cent.

The 1670 Act is pr. in Gee and Hardy, pp. 623–32 (no. 119). A. Fletcher, 'The Enforcement of the Conventicle Acts 1664–1679', in W. J. Sheils (ed.), *Persecution and Toleration* (Studies in Church History, 21; Oxford, 1984), pp. 235–46.

Conventual Mass. The public Mass sung (or occasionally said) in religious communities where public choir *office is recited. This Mass is attended by the whole community. In cathedrals and collegiate churches the conventual Mass is properly known as a *Capitular Mass, though the more general term 'conventual' is sometimes used.

Conventuals. The branch of the *Franciscan Order which allowed adaptations and mitigations to the Rule of St *Francis and the use of Papal privileges, including those permitting the accumulation of property. In reaction to their policy there arose the reform of the *Observantines. *Leo X favoured the Observantines and only reluctantly allowed the Conventuals to continue to exist. The term is also used of a similar division in the *Carmelite Order.

The position of the Conventuals is defended by R. M. Huber, OFM Conv., *A Documented History of the Franciscan Order, 1182–1517* (Milwaukee and Washington, DC, 1944). G. Odoardi, OFM Conv., in *DIP* 3 (1976), cols. 1–94, s.v. 'Conventuali', and cols. 94–106, s.v. 'Conventuali Riformati', with extensive bibl. See also other works cited under FRANCISCAN ORDER.

conversi, a name widely used of *lay brothers (q.v.) in monasteries. Their exact relation in medieval times to the other members of the community is a matter of considerable obscurity.

Conversion of St Paul, Feast of. The feast, kept on 25 Jan., is peculiar to the W. and of *Gallican origin, as contrasted with that of Sts Peter and Paul (29 June), which originated in *Rome. In some early *martyrologies it is called the *translatio* of St Paul, a fact which suggests that the date in the calendar was connected with the *translation of the relics of the Apostle (to his *basilica outside Rome?), though this still leaves its non-Roman origin unexplained.

Convocations of Canterbury and York. The two ancient provincial assemblies of the clergy of the C of E. Traces of Church assemblies of the nation are already met with in *Bede, but their history properly begins with the ecclesiastical reorganization under Abp. *Theodore (668–90). In 735 began the separate provincial authority of *York, which henceforth remained a separate body.

Originally the assemblies consisted only of prelates, but in 1225 Stephen *Langton summoned in addition *proctors for the cathedral and monastic chapters. In 1258 archdeacons were also convoked with letters of proxy from their clergy. The future form of the Convocation of Canterbury was finally reached under Abp. *Pecham in 1283; it consisted of the bishops, abbots, deans, and archdeacons, together with two representatives from the clergy of each diocese and one representative from each chapter. At first the bishops and lower clergy sat together and the whole body of clergy still constitute what is properly one assembly; but since the 15th cent. the convocations have sat as two Houses—the 'Upper' and 'Lower' Houses. The Abp. of Canterbury (or York) presides in the Upper House and in Full Synod (which consists of both Houses sitting together). At the beginning of each Convocation the Lower House is directed to elect one of its members *Prolocutor or Referendary; he presides over the Lower House when it sits separately, is responsible for communications between the Houses, and ascertains the opinion of the Lower House when a vote is taken in Full Synod. Business is normally initiated in the Upper House and sent down to the Lower House for its concurrence, which may be refused. It is possible to initiate business in the Lower House and send it for consideration by the President and Upper House either by a motion of the Lower House or by a process known as *gravamen et reformandum*; in this a schedule is introduced in the Lower House stating a grievance and usually proposing a remedy. If a grievance is adopted by the Lower House as an *articulus cleri*, it is transmitted to the Upper House as a united complaint of the inferior clergy. Since the Reformation the heads of religious houses have not sat in Convocation. From 1936 to 1970 the older Universities (Oxford, Cambridge, and London) were represented in the Province of Canterbury, the electors being the clerks in Holy Orders resident or holding offices in the Universities concerned. In 1970 the representation of the Universities was broadened to include more recent foundations.

From a very early date these assemblies were the means through which the clergy taxed themselves. Edward I's attempt under the '*praemunientes* clause' (1295) to summon representatives of the clergy to Parliament and thus compel the clergy to grant their taxes in this body failed, and it was not until after the Restoration that Convocation surrendered the right of making its own grants to the King (1664).

In the Middle Ages and later the legislative powers of Convocation varied considerably. The normal method of legislation was by canons. The King was always on the look-out for any infringement of the Royal prerogative; and in 1532 *Henry VIII extorted from Convocation the '*Submission of the Clergy' (q.v.), later embodied in an Act of Parliament (1534). This Act severely limited the powers of Convocation and had a far-reaching effect on its subsequent fortunes. After the Reformation Convocation was both summoned and dissolved at the same time as Parliament, and the validity of the canons enacted by Canterbury Convocation in 1640, after the dissolution of Parliament, has been called in question. The Church of England Convocations Acts 1966, however, laid down that from 1970 there should be quinquennial elections to Convocation, which should meet without reference to Parliamentary sessions.

With the return of the Church of England following the Stuart Restoration in 1660 care was taken to ensure the revival of the Convocations. In 1661 and 1662 a number of projects, including schemes for the reform of Church courts, discipline and clerical income, were debated, but only one item of business was perfected, namely the revision of the BCP in 1662. After 1664 the Convocations ceased to be licensed for business, a seemingly unforeseen consequence of Abp. *Sheldon's surrender of the clergy's right to tax themselves independently of the laity. The next two decades saw repeated attempts to secure a working Convocation, but without success. Its suspension was a major obstacle to the reforming zeal of the episcopate under Sheldon and *Sancroft.

After the Revolution of 1688 the Convocations entered upon a stormy period, when they were drawn into the current disputes about *Divine Right, Non-Resistance, and Passive Obedience. But while the majority of the clergy were *High Churchmen and often Jacobite in sym-

pathy, the Government secured in the early 18th cent. a Whiggish Bench of Bishops, so that the Upper House of Convocation was often in disagreement on important questions with the High Church clergy of the Lower House. This conflict was brought to an end with the *Bangorian Controversy in 1717, when, to prevent the condemnation of a sermon and book by Bp. B. *Hoadly, the Convocations were prorogued by Royal Writ. For nearly a century and a half the powers of the Crown under the Act for the Submission of the Clergy were interpreted as making it inexpedient for the Convocations to discuss any business whatever, and its meetings were purely formal. It was not until 1852, under the combined influence of the *Evangelical and *Oxford Movements, that the Convocation of Canterbury took the bold step of discussing business again. York followed the example of Canterbury in 1861.

The Houses of Convocation have always been, and still are, exclusively clerical assemblies. But from 1885 there was associated with Convocation a 'House of Laymen' in each Province chosen by the Diocesan conferences. At the beginning of the 20th cent. the practice of joint sittings of the two Convocations was also initiated, and in 1904 a Representative Council consisting of the members of both the Convocations together with the two Houses of Laymen, sitting conjointly, was begun. This Representative Council, however, had no legal position or authority until 1920, when it was superseded by the *Church Assembly (q.v.), whose powers were defined in the Church of England Assembly (Powers) Act 1919, commonly known as the *Enabling Act. By the *Synodical Government Measure 1969, practically all the functions of Convocation, including the power to legislate by canon, were transferred to the General Synod, consisting of three Houses of Bishops, Clergy and Laity. Provision was made, however, for each Convocation to meet separately in its own Province and matters before the General Synod concerning doctrine and worship can be referred to them for separate consideration if they exercise their right to require this. Apart from this provision, and a few other minor exceptions, the Convocations may transact formal business only.

E. *Gibson, *Synodus Anglicana, or the Constitution and Proceedings of an English Convocation, shown from the Acts and Registers thereof to be Agreeable to the Principles of an Episcopal Church* (1702; ed. E. *Cardwell, 1854), with numerous primary docs.; E. Cardwell (ed.), *Synodalia: A Collection of Articles of Religion, Canons, and Proceedings of Convocations in the Province of Canterbury, from the Year 1547 to the Year 1717*, 2 (1842). The proceedings of the Convocation of Canterbury are pub. in the *Chronicle of Convocation* (London, 1859 ff.); those of the Convocation of York in the *York Journal of Convocation* (London, 1874 ff.). A. F. Smethurst and H. R. Wilson (eds.), *Acts of the Convocations of Canterbury and York (together with certain other resolutions) passed since the reform of the Convocations in 1921* (1948; enlarged edn. to end of 1970, 1971). T. Lathbury, *A History of the Convocation of the Church of England* [to 1742] (1842); J. W. Joyce, *England's Sacred Synods: A Constitutional History of the Convocations of the Clergy, from the Earliest Records of Christianity in Britain to the date of the Promulgation of the Present Book of Common Prayer* (1855). D. B. Weske, *Convocation of the Clergy: A Study of its Antecedents and its Rise with special emphasis upon its Growth and Activities in the Thirteenth and Fourteenth Centuries* (CHS, 1937). E. W. Kemp, *Counsel and Consent: Aspects of the Government of the Church as Exemplified in the History of the English Provincial*

Synods (*Bampton Lectures for 1960; 1961). E. Barker, *The Dominican Order and Convocation* (1913), pp. 31–76. N. Sykes, *From Sheldon to Secker* (1959), pp. 36–67. A. F. Smethurst, *Convocation of Canterbury: What it is; what it does; how it works* (1949). G. Crosse in *DECH* (3rd edn. 1948), pp. 144–50, s.v.

Convulsionaries. Adherents of a movement initiated by supposedly miraculous phenomena in 1731 at the tomb of the *Jansenist François de Paris (1690–1727) at Saint-Médard, Paris, that evolved into a prophetic and mystical sect. Its members, who came from a diversified background, were mostly Jansenist *Appellants against the bull '*Unigenitus' (1713). Their prophetical behaviour ('convulsions') and association of pain with spiritual experience is interpreted as an extreme expression of the uneasiness produced in French society by the Jansenist crisis, both in religion and politics. The sect disappeared at the beginning of the 19th cent.

Primary sources collected and ed. by C.-L. Maire, *Les convulsionnaires de Saint-Médard: Miracles, convulsions et prophéties à Paris au XVIIIe siècle* (Collection Archives, 95 [1985]). R. A. *Knox, *Enthusiasm* (1950), esp. ch. 16, 'The Convulsionaries of Saint-Médard', pp. 372–88. B. R. Kreiser, *Miracles, Convulsions, and Ecclesiastical Politics in Early Eighteenth-Century Paris* (Princeton, NJ, 1978). D. Vidal, *Miracles et convulsions jansénistes au XVIIIe siècle* (1987). L. Loevenbruck in *DTC* 3 (1908), cols. 1756–62, s.v. 'Convulsionnaires', with refs. See also works cited s.v. JANSENISM.

Conybeare, Frederick Cornwallis (1856–1924), *Armenian scholar. He was a Fellow of University College, Oxford, from 1881 to 1887, and spent much of his life travelling in search of Armenian MSS. Among his works were a *Collation with the Ancient Armenian Versions of the Greek Text of Aristotle's Categories* (1892), and editions of important early documents of the Armenian Church, some of which he published in his *Rituale Armenorum* (1905). His discovery of an Armenian MS in which the concluding verses of St Mark's Gospel (16: 9–20) were assigned to the 'Presbyter Ariston' (whom he identified with *Aristion), attracted much attention. For several years he was a member of the Rationalist Press Association, and his *Myth, Magic and Morals, a Study of Christian Origins* (1909), written as an attack on Christianity, evoked a reply from W. *Sanday under the title *A New Marcion* (1909).

L. Mariès, 'Frederick Cornwallis Conybeare (1856–1924). Notice biographique et bibliographie critique', *Revue des Études Arméniennes*, 6 (1926), pp. 185–332. D. S. Margoliouth in *DNB, 1922–1930*, pp. 210 f.

Conybeare, William John (1815–57), joint author with J. S. *Howson of *The Life and Epistles of St Paul* (1852). From 1842 to 1848 he was first principal of the Liverpool Collegiate Institute, where he was joined in 1845 by Howson. After resigning on account of poor health, he became Vicar of Axminster, Devon (1848–54). See also HOWSON, J. S.

Unsigned art. (based on information from his son) in *DNB* 12 (1887), pp. 62 f.

Cook, Stanley Arthur (1873–1949), biblical critic and Semitic historian. A native of King's Lynn, he was educated at Wyggeston School, Leicester, and at Gonville and Caius College, Cambridge, where he was afterwards Fellow and lecturer (1904–32). From 1932 to 1938 he was Regius Professor of Hebrew. His extensive writings were marked by a wide knowledge, esp. of early Semitic customs and archaeology, which he interpreted with freshness and imagination, though the unconventionality of his conclusions set his work somewhat apart from the main stream of OT discussion. From 1896 to 1903 he was a member of the editorial staff of the *Encyclopaedia Biblica*, and from 1902 to 1932 edited the journal of the *Palestine Exploration Fund. His writings include *The Study of Religions* (1914), *The Religion of Ancient Palestine in the Light of Archaeology* (Schweich Lectures, 1930), *The Old Testament: A Reinterpretation* (1936), and *The 'Truth' of the Bible* (1938).

Select bibl. of his works in D. W. Thomas (ed.), *Essays and Studies Presented to Stanley Arthur Cook . . . in Celebration of his Seventy-fifth Birthday 12 April 1948* (Cambridge Oriental Series, no. 2, 1950), pp. 1–13. Id. in *DNB, 1941–1950*, pp. 174 f.

Cooper, Thomas (d. 1594), also 'Cowper', Bp. of *Winchester. In 1531 he became a chorister at Magdalen College, Oxford, where he was a Fellow (1540–45) and later Master of Magdalen College School. His Protestant beliefs led him to abandon his project of ordination on *Mary's accession (1553), but he fulfilled his intention shortly after her death (1558). He was a man of great learning, and among his works were a Latin Dictionary (1548), a Chronicle ('Cooper's Chronicle', 1549, a continuation of an unpublished chronicle of Thomas Lanquet, d. 1545), and a *Thesaurus Linguae Romanae et Britannicae* (1565). In 1562 he wrote *An Answer in Defence of the Truth against the Apology of Private Mass* directed against an attack on Bp. J. *Jewel's *Apology*. In 1567 he became Dean of *Christ Church, Oxford, in 1569 Dean of *Gloucester, in 1571 Bp. of *Lincoln, and in 1584 Bp. of Winchester. In the latter capacity he wrote against the *Marprelate tracts and was then himself attacked, esp. in *Hay any Work for Cooper*.

Cooper's *Admonition to the People of England* [against Martin Marprelate] (orig. pub. 1589), ed. J. Petherham (London, 1847) and E. Arber (English Scholar's Library, 15; Birmingham, 1882); his *Answer in Defence of the Truth against the Apology of Private Mass* ed. W. Goode (*Parker Society, 1850), with list of Cooper's works, pp. xi–xv. C. W. Foster (ed.), *Lincoln Episcopal Records in the Time of Thomas Cooper* (Publications of the Lincoln Record Society, 2; 1912; repr. by the *Canterbury and York Society, 9; 1913). *BRUO, 1501–1540*, pp. 135 f.

Coornhert, Dirck Volckertszoon (1522–90), Dutch theologian. Born in Amsterdam of a wealthy family, he was sent for a time to Spain and Portugal, but soon returned and settled in Haarlem. Here he practised as an engraver in copper and, self-educated, also published translations of the Latin classics into Dutch. As a civic official he became one of the leading supporters of William the Silent suffering exile (1568–72). He defended liberalism against the strongly *Calvinist doctrines then current in the Netherlands, advocating toleration, opposing capital punishment for heretics, and criticizing the *Heidelberg Catechism esp. on the issue of predestination. Influenced by the writings of S. *Castellio, and esp. by the *Theologia Germanica, he urged the necessity of interior piety and the inward dominion of the Holy Spirit. He rejected the idea of a visible Church and maintained the sufficiency of a faith inspired by the Bible and the Apostles' Creed. Rejecting the notion of original sin and stressing the freedom of the human will, the strongly ethical nature of his thought is especially evident in his *Zedekunst dat is Wellevenskunste* (1586). The *Arminians and the *Pietists owed something to his influence. A Dutch version of the NT on which he was engaged was incomplete at his death.

Works pub. at Amsterdam (3 vols., 1630). Studies by B. Becker (Rijks Geschiedkundige Publicatiën, Kleine Serie, 25; 1928) and H. Bonger (Amsterdam, 1978). J. A. L. Lancée in *Biografisch Lexicon voor de Geschiedenis van het Nederlandse Protestantisme*, 3 (1988), pp. 78–83.

cope. A semicircular cloak worn at certain liturgical functions when the *chasuble is not used. Both vestments took their origin in the Roman *paenula* or *pluviale*, the cope gradually reaching its present form by being opened in front. It has been held that it did not become a liturgical vestment until the 9th cent. or later, but H. *Leclercq has collected a large number of examples from primitive frescoes and mosaics which suggest that it was regarded as typical of the clergy at least by the 6th cent. The term *cappa* first appears in *Gregory of Tours (d. 594). In the Middle Ages it was widely used as a ceremonial choir habit by whole communities on feasts, while the 'cappa nigra', a cloak of thick black material serving the same purpose as the original *pluviale*, was worn in choir as a protection against the cold. The hood of the original garment survives as an ornament (often triangular) on the back of the cope.

In the BCP of 1549 the celebrant at the Holy Communion was ordered to wear a cope or vestment (i.e. chasuble), but in 1552 the rubric was withdrawn. The use of a cope by the celebrant at the Communion in cathedral and collegiate churches was prescribed by can. 24 of 1604. Probably its use never wholly died out in the C of E. It has been extensively revived in England since the middle of the 19th cent. Copes made for the coronation and funeral of *Charles II are still in use in *Westminster Abbey.

Braun, *LG*, pp. 306–58. E. *Bishop, 'The Origins of the Cope as a Church Vestment', *Dublin Review*, 120 (1897), pp. 17–37, repr. in id., *Liturgica Historica* (1918), ch. 11. H. *Leclercq, OSB, and E. Mombert in *DACL* 3, pt. 1 (1913), cols. 365–81, s.v. 'Chape'.

Copernicus, Nicholas (1473–1543), astronomer. He studied first at the University of Cracow and then read law and medicine in *Bologna and Padua. Owing to the early death of his father, he grew up under the influence of his uncle, Lucas Walzelrode, Bp. of Warmia (in NE Poland), who secured ecclesiastical preferments for him. After serving for some time in his uncle's immediate entourage, he spent the latter part of his life (from 1510) in Frauenburg (the cathedral city of the diocese of Warmia), in which he had held a canonry since 1495 (confirmed in 1497). By 1514 Copernicus had written a short treatise known as the *Commentariolus* (first published in 1878), sketching out a new system of astronomy in which the sun rather than the earth was the centre of the universe, and the earth became one of the planets revolving round it. This was given mature expression in his *De revolutionibus orbium caelestium* (1543). The arguments for

this at the time were by no means conclusive, but after developments by J. *Kepler, G. *Galileo, I. *Newton and others the system became astronomical orthodoxy. At first theological objections were muted, but when the issues were popularized though the work of Galileo, religious debate became intense, and in 1616 the *De revolutionibus* was placed on the *Index pending correction. An anonymous preface to the work, written without Copernicus' knowledge by the Lutheran pastor A. *Osiander, and asserting that the system should be treated as merely hypothetical, had probably been intended to ward off theological controversy. Copernicus himself dedicated his book to the Pope and included in it both an appreciative letter from Card. Nicolaus von Schönberg and a brusque dismissal of those who might cavil with it on scriptural grounds.

Crit. edns. of *De Revolutionibus* [by M. Curtze] for the Societas Copernicana Thorunensis (Toruń, 1873), by F. and C. Zeller (vol. 2 of projected edn. of his works, Munich, 1949), and by R. Gansiniec and others for the Polish Academy of Sciences (Warsaw and Cracow, 1975). Eng. tr. of his Complete Works sponsored by the Polish Academy of Science (3 vols., London, Warsaw, and Cracow, 1972–85: vol. 1 being a facsimile repr. of the MS of *De Revolutionibus*; vol. 2, Eng. tr. of *De Revolutionibus* with comm. by E. Rosen; vol. 3, Minor works by id.). Eng. tr. of *De Revolutionibus* also by A. M. Duncan (London, etc., 1976), and of the *Commentariolus*, Copernicus' 'Letter against Werner' (a minor astronomical work), and a letter of George Joachim von Lauchen, known as Rheticus, giving a summary of Copernicus' views, with introd. and notes, by E. Rosen, *Three Copernican Treatises* (Records of Civilization, Sources and Studies, 30; New York, 1939; 3rd edn., with rev. Life of Copernicus and bibl. to 1970, 1971). The *Commentariolus* is also tr., with comm., by N. W. Swerdlow in the *Proceedings of the American Philosophical Society*, 117 (1973), pp. 423–512. The standard Life is L. Prowe, *Nicolaus Coppernicus* (2 vols., Berlin, 1883–4). Other works incl. J. L. E. Dreyer, *History of Planetary Systems from Thales to Kepler* (Cambridge, 1906; repr. as *A History of Astronomy from Thales to Kepler*, New York [1953]), pp. 305–44; A. Armitage, *Copernicus: The Founder of Modern Astronomy* (1938); T. S. Kuhn, *The Copernican Revolution* (Cambridge, Mass., 1957); A. Koyré, *La Révolution Astronomique* [1961], pp. 13–115; Eng. tr. (1973), pp. 13–116; O. Pedersen and M. Phil, *Early Physics and Astronomy* (1974), esp. pp. 299–319; R. S. Westman, 'The Melanchthon Circle, Rheticus, and the Wittenberg Interpretation of the Copernican Theory', *Isis*, 66 (1975), pp. 165–93; id. (ed.), *The Copernican Achievement* (UCLA Center for Medieval and Renaissance Studies, Contributions, 7; 1975); N. M. Swerdlow and O. Neugebauer, *Mathematical Astronomy in Copernicus's De Revolutionibus* (New York, etc., 1984). H. Baranowski, *Bibliografia Kopernikowska 1509–1955* (Warsaw, 1958); cont. for 1956–71 (ibid., 1973); and for 1972–5 in *Studia Copernica*, 17 (1977), pp. 179–201.

Copleston, Edward (1776–1849), Bp. of *Llandaff. A fine classical scholar, he was elected a Fellow of Oriel College, Oxford, in 1795 and Provost of the college in 1814. In 1826 he became Dean of *Chester, and in 1827 both Bp. of Llandaff and Dean of *St Paul's, holding the offices in plurality. While at Oxford he played a large part in instituting the Honours School with its system of examinations which in essence still survives, and in raising his college to its position of intellectual pre-eminence in the earlier half of the 19th cent., thus providing the setting for the *Oxford Movement. In his theological views Copleston was a '*Noetic', who, despite his scant sympathy with the *Tractarians, counted himself a *High Churchman. His writings, which are few, included some brilliant replies to attacks made on Oxford in the *Edinburgh Review*.

Copleston's *Advice to a Young Reviewer with a Specimen of the Art*, orig. pub. Oxford, 1807, was repr. ibid., 1926; also ed. G. [S.] Gordon, *Three Oxford Ironies* (1927), pp. 49–73, with introd., pp. 7–17 and 37–44. Memoir by W. J. Copleston (London, 1851), with selections from his diary and correspondence. Further extracts from his works pr. by R. *Whately, *Remains of the late Edward Copleston* (1854), with introd. reminiscences, pp. 1–98. W. Tuckwell, *Pre-Tractarian Oxford* (1909), pp. 17–50. T. E. Kebbel in *DNB* 12 (1887), pp. 174–6. See also bibl. to NOETICS.

Coptic (language).

'Copt' is a European form of the Arabic 'Kibt', which is itself derived from the Gk. Αἰγύπτιοι ['Egyptians']. Coptic was the language usually spoken by the 'Copts', the native populace of Egypt, from about the 3rd to the 10th cents. AD. After the 10th cent. the language was gradually supplanted by Arabic; but it appears to have survived in a few places down to the end of the 17th cent., and is still that of the liturgy of the *Coptic Church. In essence it was the language of ancient Egypt, into which a large number of Greek words had been incorporated, and was written in an alphabet closely akin to that of the Greeks. It occurs in four main dialects, namely *Sahidic, *Bohairic, *Fayumic, and Akhmimic. The NT was translated into all four, first into the Sahidic, the dialect used in the south of Egypt, where the need was greatest as the influence of Greek culture was least. Of the extensive remains of early Christian literature in Coptic, much the greater part consists in translations from the Greek. This applies also to the large number of Gnostic writings now known, some of which show little or no Christian influence (see NAG HAMMADI). Among the surviving works originally composed in Coptic are the writings of *Shenoute, some homilies and legends of the saints.

Coptic grammars by J. M. Plumley (Sahidic; London, 1948), A. Mallon, SJ (Fr.; Beirut, 1904; 4th edn. by M. Malinine, 1956, with valuable bibl., pp. 254–401), G. Steindorff (Berlin, 1894; rev. edn., Chicago, 1951), and T. O. Lambdin (Sahidic; Macon, Ga., 1983). W. Till, *Achmîmisch-koptische Grammatik* (1928); id., *Koptische Dialektgrammatik* (1931; 2nd edn., 1961); id., *Koptische Grammatik, saïdischer Dialekt* (1955; 3rd edn., 1966). W. E. Crum, *A Coptic Dictionary* (1929–39); R. Kasser, *Compléments au dictionnaire copte de Crum* (Publications de l'Institut Français d'Archéologie Orientale. Bibliothèque d'Études Coptes, 7; Cairo, 1964); id., *Dictionnaire auxiliaire, étymologique et complet de la langue copte* (Geneva, 1967 ff.). W. Kammerer, *A Coptic Bibliography* (Ann Arbor, Mich., 1950). W. C. Till, 'Coptic and its Value', *Bulletin of the John Rylands Library*, 40 (1958), pp. 229–58. A. S. Atiya (ed.), *The Coptic Encyclopedia*, 8 ('Linguistics') (New York, etc. [1991]). R.-G. Coquin, 'Langue et littérature coptes', in M. Albert and others, *Christianismes orientaux* (1993), pp. 167–217.

Crit. edns. of Coptic NT by G. Horner: in Bohairic dialect, 4 vols., Oxford, 1898–1905; in Sahidic dialect, 7 vols., ibid., 1911–24. Coptic OT ed. very incompletely and in scattered places; cf. A. Vaschalde, 'Ce qui a été publié des versions coptes de la Bible', *R. Bibl.*, 28 (1919), pp. 220–43, 513–31; 29 (1920), pp. 91–106, 241–58; 30 (1921), pp. 237–46; 31 (1922), pp. 81–8 and 234–58; cont. in *Le Muséon*, 43 (1930), pp. 409–31; 45 (1932), pp. 117–58; 46 (1933), pp. 299–313. G. Mink, 'Die koptischen Versionen des Neuen Testament', in K. Aland (ed.), *Die alten Übersetzungen des Neuen Testaments, die Kirchenväterzitate und Lektionare* (Arbeiten zur Neutestamentlichen Textforschung, 5; 1972), pp. 160–299; B. M. Metzger, *The Early Versions of the New Testament* (Oxford, 1977), pp. 99–141. G. Mink and S. P. Brock in *TRE* 6 (1980), pp. 196–200, s.v. 'Bibelübersetzungen, 1. 5'; S. Emmel in *Anchor Bible Dictionary*, 4 (1992), pp. 180–88, s.v. 'Languages (Coptic)', with recent. bibl.

Coptic Church.

One of the *Oriental Orthodox Churches. *Eusebius (*HE* 2. 16) records the tradition that the Church in Egypt was founded by St *Mark the Evangelist, and *Alexandria ranked with *Antioch and *Rome as one of the chief sees of the early Church. The Egyptian Church suffered severely in the persecution under *Diocletian, and it has ever since reckoned its era from AD 284, the year of his accession. In the early 4th cent. Christian *monasticism was founded in Egypt by St *Antony and others, and the fame of the monasteries of *Nitria and *Scete spread throughout Christendom.

The theological controversies of the 5th cent. on the Nature of Christ were embittered by opposition between Alexandria and *Constantinople. At the Council of *Chalcedon (451), *Dioscorus, Patr. of Alexandria, was deposed; the majority of the Copts, however, rejected the Council and its Definition of the two natures in the incarnate Christ and became increasingly isolated from the rest of Christendom. The Orthodox (*Melchite) body established in Alexandria received little support from the native population, and bitter disputes persisted. In Upper Egypt, however, the rapid development of monasticism is attested by the many Coptic 'Lives of the Saints' and 'Sayings of the Fathers' and abundant ruins of their buildings. In 616 the Copts passed for a time under Persian domination. In 642 they were conquered by the Arabs, whose rule in varying form has lasted to the present day. Long periods of comparative peace would be suddenly broken by persecution, e.g. under the Caliph el Hakim (996–1021), who is said to have destroyed 3,000 churches and caused large numbers to apostatize.

In the course of centuries their numbers gradually declined. They are now said to total about 4 million. Their hierarchy consists of a Patriarch, over 60 bishops, and priests and deacons. Outside Egypt there are Coptic dioceses at Jerusalem, in the Sudan, Kenya, France, and the USA. The *Ethiopian Church is a daughter Church of Egypt, and since 1959 has been autonomous and *autocephalous. The Coptic language is found only in the service-books, which are equipped with an Arabic text in parallel columns. The normal liturgy is that of St *Basil. Five important fasts are observed: (1) The pre-Lenten 'Fast of *Nineveh'; (2) The Great Fast of Lent (55 days); (3) The Fast of the Nativity, before *Christmas (28 days); (4) The Fast of the Apostles, after the Ascension; and (5) The Fast of the Virgin, before the Assumption (15 days). Since *c*.1960 there has been a remarkable revival of monastic life, esp. in the Nitrian Desert.

There is also a small *Uniat Coptic Church, dating from 1741, when Athanasius, the Coptic Bishop of Jerusalem, joined the RC Church. It is said to number *c*.105,000.

J. M. Wansleben, *Histoire de l'Église d'Alexandrie, fondée par S. Marc* (1677). A. J. Butler, *The Ancient Coptic Churches of Egypt* (2 vols., 1884). M. Roncaglia, *Histoire de l'Église copte* (6 vols., Dar Al-Kalima, 1966 ff.). J. Maspero (posthumous), *Histoire des patriarches d'Alexandrie depuis la mort de l'empereur Anastase jusqu'à la réconciliation des Églises jacobites, 515–616* (Bibliothèque de l'École des Hautes Études, fasc. 237; 1923); R. Strothmann, *Die koptische Kirche in der Neuzeit* (Beiträge zur historischen Theologie, 7; 1932). M. Cramer, *Das Christlich-Koptische Ägypten einst und heute: Eine Orientierung* (Wiesbaden, 1959). P. Verghese (ed.), *Koptisches Christentum: Die orthodoxen Kirchen Ägyptens und Äthiopiens* (Die Kirchen der Welt, 12; Stuttgart, 1973), pp. 11–129. C. Cannuyer, *Les Coptes* (Turnhout [1990]). S. C. Malan (ed. and tr.), *Original Documents of the Coptic Church* (3 pts., 1872–3); R. M. Woolley (ed. and tr.), *Coptic Offices* (1930); A. A. King, *The Rites of Eastern Christendom*, 1 (Rome, 1947), ch. 5, pp. 337–495, with bibl. O. H. E. Burmester, *The Egyptian or Coptic Church: A Detailed Description of her Liturgical Services and the Rites and Ceremonies observed in the Administration of her Sacraments* (Cairo, 1967); id. (ed. and tr.), *Ordination Rites of the Coptic Church* (Publications de la Société d'Archéologie Copte, Textes et documents, 16; Cairo, 1985). H. Quecke, *Untersuchungen zum koptischen Stundengebet* (Publications de l'Institut Orientaliste de Louvain, 3; 1970), with texts. O. F. A. Meinardus, *Monks and Monasteries of the Egyptian Deserts* (Cairo, 1961; rev. edn., 1989); id., *Christian Egypt Ancient and Modern* (ibid., 1965), and other works of this author. A. *Fortescue, *The Lesser Eastern Churches* (1913), pp. 163–290; D. Attwater, *The Dissident Eastern Churches* (Milwaukee [1937]); id., *The Catholic Eastern Churches* (ibid. [1935]), pp. 135–49, both rev. as *The Christian Churches of the East* (2 vols., [Leominster] 1961; London, 1963), 1, pp. 128–37, 2, pp. 184–92; A. S. Atiya, *A History of Eastern Christianity* (1968), pp. 11–145. M. Jugie, AA, *Theologia Dogmatica Christianorum Orientalium ab Ecclesia Catholica Dissidentium*, 5 (Paris, 1935), pp. 349–787 *passim*, esp. pp. 458–64. Id. in *DTC* 10 (pt. 2; 1929), cols. 2251–306, s.v. 'Monophysite (Église Copte)', with bibl.; C. D. G. Müller in *TRE* 1 (1977), pp. 512–33, s.v. 'Ägypten IV'; T. Orlandi in *TRE* 19 (1990), pp. 595–607, s.v. 'Koptische Kirche'; A. S. Atiya in M. Eliade (ed.), *Encyclopedia of Religion*, 4 (1987), pp. 82–6, s.v.

Corban ('oblation'). A Heb. word (קָרְבָּן), peculiar to *Ezekiel and the Priestly material of the *Pentateuch, for altar offerings, either the fixed obligatory dues, or free-will votive gifts. It is probably to this latter kind of gift that Christ refers in Mk. 7: 11 when He objects to the practice of letting 'Corban' take precedence over the duty of maintaining one's parents.

K. H. Rengstorf in *TWNT* 3 (1938; Eng. tr., 1966), pp. 860–66, s.v. Κορβᾶν, with further bibl., ibid. 10 (pt. 2; 1979), pp. 1146 f. See also comm. on Mark, Gospel of St, cited s.v.

Corbie. This celebrated monastery, some 10 miles E. of Amiens, was founded from *Luxeuil *c.*660. It possessed a very fine library from which more early MSS have survived than from any other abbey; they played an important part in the transmission of Latin classical and patristic texts. It also had one of the most important *Carolingian theological schools. In 1624 a selection of its books were transferred to *Saint-Germain-des-Prés. At the time of the Revolution (1794) some of these passed to the Bibliothèque Nationale; others were taken to Russia and are now at St Petersburg.

P. Héliot, *L'Abbaye de Corbie: Ses églises et ses bâtiments* (Bibliothèque de la Revue d'histoire ecclésiastique, 29; 1957). *Corbie Abbaye Royale: Volume du XIIIᵉ Centenaire* (Lille, 1963). D. Ganz, *Corbie in the Carolingian Renaissance* (Beihefte der Francia, 20; Sigmaringen, 1990). L. Delisle, *Le Cabinet des MSS. de la Bibliothèque Nationale*, 2 (1874), pp. 104–41, 427–40. O. Dobiaš-Roždestvenskaïa, *Histoire de l'atelier graphique de Corbie de 651 à 830 reflétée dans les Corbeienses Leninopolitani* (St Petersburg, 1934). B. Bischoff, 'Hadoardus and the Manuscripts of Classical Authors from Corbie', *Didascaliae: Studies in honor of Anselm M.*

Albareda, ed. S. Prete (New York, 1961), pp. 39–57; Ger. text in his *Mittelalterliche Studien*, 1 (Stuttgart, 1966), pp. 49–63. C. de Merindol, *La Production des Livres peints à l'abbaye de Corbie au XIIᵉ siècle* (Paris thesis, 3 vols., Lille, 1976). E. A. Lowe, *Codices Latini Antiquiores*, 6 (Oxford, 1953), pp. xxii–xxvi. A. *Wilmart, OSB, in *DACL* 3 (pt. 2, 1914), cols. 2913–58, s.v. 'Corbie (Manuscrits liturgiques de)'. H. Peltier in *DHGE* 13 (1956), cols. 809–24; M. Rouche in *Lexikon des Mittelalters*, 3 (1986), cols. 224–8, both s.v. with bibl.

Cordeliers. A name sometimes given in France to the Franciscan *Observantines from the knotted cord which they wore round the waist. The word was also assumed by a political club during the French Revolution, as the convent in which it met had once belonged to the Cordeliers.

Corinth. In NT times Corinth was the capital of the Roman province of Achaia. It lay on the great trade route between *Rome and the E. and occupied a very important site for the propagation of the Christian Gospel on account of its political and geographical position, its cosmopolitan population, and its commercial supremacy. The Church was established here by St *Paul *c.*50, and included many prominent Jewish converts (Acts 18: 4 and 8; 1 Cor. 9: 20), but it appears, both from Acts and the two Epp. of Paul to Corinth, that the Christian community consisted largely of Gentiles. It seems to have contained some who prided themselves on their intellect, and certainly many from the poorer classes (1 Cor. 1: 26), including slaves (who were often well-educated). The Corinthian Church took a leading part in the collection for the saints (2 Cor. 9: 2–5). Paul was helped by *Silas and *Timothy and, in spite of Jewish opposition, 'he dwelt there a year and six months' (Acts 18: 11). During his stay, the proconsul *Gallio dismissed a charge against Paul of worshipping contrary to the Jewish Law, a decision which in effect amounted to permission to preach in the province. Paul left behind him a flourishing community, but the pagan antecedents of his converts seriously affected the life of the Church, as is seen in the Epistles to the *Corinthians. In fact the city was noted for its profligacy and moral laxity. In later Christian history Corinth took a relatively minor part.

See also CLEMENT OF ROME.

Good summary by W. M. *Ramsay in *HDB* 1 (1898), pp. 479–83, s.v. Reports of the modern excavations carried out under the direction of the American School of Classical Studies at Athens have been pub. by H. N. Fowler and others, *Corinth* (Cambridge, Mass., 1929–43; Princeton, NJ, 1948 ff. [17 vols. in 35 parts to 1985]). R. Carpenter, *Ancient Corinth: A Guide to the Excavations* (1928; 4th edn. by O. Broneer, 1949). L. Cerfaux, *L'Église des Corinthiens* (1946). F.-J.[-M.] de Waele, *Corinthe et Saint Paul* (Les Hauts Lieux de l'Histoire, 15 [1961]). J. Murphy-O'Connor, OP, *St Paul's Corinth: Texts and Archaeology* (Good News Studies, 6; Wilmington, Delaware, 1983). T. Lenschau and others in *PW*, Suppl. 4 (1924), cols. 991–1036, s.v. 'Korinthos'; J. Finegan in *The Interpreter's Dictionary of the Bible*, 1 (1962), pp. 682–8, s.v.; C. L. Thompson, ibid., Suppl. Vol. (1976), pp. 179 f., s.v. See also bibl. to following entry.

Corinthians, Epistles to the. These two Epistles of St *Paul to his converts were prob. written from *Ephesus and Macedonia, *c.*52–6.

1 Cor. was occasioned by news which St Paul had received from the Church at Corinth. The subjects dealt with include party-feeling among the Corinthian Chris-

tians, and their tendency to think too highly of a certain kind of human 'wisdom' (1: 10–4: 21); his own position as an apostle (4: 1–13; 9); a sexual scandal at Corinth and the treatment of a particular offender (5 and 6); the question of litigation between Christians (6: 1–8); and certain points on which they had consulted him in a letter, namely marriage and celibacy in relation to the Christian gospel (7), problems regarding the relations of Christians with the surrounding paganism (8), behaviour at Christian worship (10 and 11), 'spiritual gifts' such as prophecy and speaking with tongues (12), and the *resurrection of the dead (15). The sections on the *Eucharist (10: 16 ff., 11: 20 ff.), on love (*agape) as the highest of spiritual gifts (13), and on the Resurrection (15), are among the most important in the NT.

In 2 Cor. the principal topic is apostleship, negatively defined in chs. 10–13, positively in 2: 14–7: 4. Paul's own status as an *apostle had been challenged and his conduct attacked. In the earlier chapters he defends his conduct, setting out at length the authority and ministry of the Christian apostle, which is derived from Christ's New *Covenant, far superior to the *Torah and the Old Covenant of Sinai in both glory and efficacy, in that it effects the reconciliation of humanity with God by the atoning death of Christ (3: 4–6: 10). He rejoices that he and the Corinthians are now one again (7: 8 ff.). Chs. 8–9 deal with the collection for the Church at *Jerusalem which Paul was organizing. Both seem so loosely attached to what proceeds that some think they were originally separate letters. The passage 6: 14–7: 1 may also be a separate fragment, possibly from an earlier epistle (cf. 1 Cor. 5: 9), but conceivably not even written by Paul. Ch. 10 starts afresh with a new treatment of Paul's relations with the Church at Corinth and a severe condemnation of his opponents (ψευδαπόστολοι, 'false apostles'). The content and tone are so different from the earlier celebration of reconciliation that many critics believe they stem from a different epistle, possibly that referred to at 2: 4. Hypotheses about several fragments being combined are common, but many scholars defend the integrity of this epistle and most accept that of 1 Cor. Apart from 2 Cor. 6: 14–7: 1 and 1 Cor. 14: 34–5 the authenticity of neither is seriously questioned today.

Ancient commentators incl. *Chrysostom (Gk.), *Theodoret (Gk.), *Ambrosiaster (Lat.), and *Pelagius (Lat.). Modern comm. on 1 Cor. by H. *Lietzmann (Hb. NT, 1907; 4th edn., with 2 Cor., by W. G. Kümmel, 1949), J. *Weiss (KEK, repr. 1970), A. *Robertson and A. Plummer (ICC, 1911), E.-B. Allo, OP (Études Bibliques, 1934), C. Spicq, OP (La Sainte Bible, 11, pt. 2, 1948, pp. 161–306), J. Héring (Commentaire du Nouveau Testament, 7, 1949; Eng. tr., 1962), C. K. Barrett (Black's NT Comm., 1968), H. Conzelmann (KEK, 1969; Eng. tr., Philadelphia [1975]), F. F. Bruce (New Cent. Bib., 1971, with 2 Cor.), W. F. Orr and J. A. Walther (Anchor Bible, 32; 1976), and G. D. Fee (New International Comm. on the NT, 1987); on 2 Cor. by A. Plummer (ICC, 1915), E.-B. Allo, OP (Études Bibliques, 1937), C. Spicq, op. cit., pp. 307–99, W. G. Kümmel, op. cit., J. Héring (Commentaire du Nouveau Testament, 8, 1958; Eng. tr., 1967), F. F. Bruce, op. cit., C. K. Barrett (Black's NT Comm., 1973), R. *Bultmann, ed. E. Dinkler (KEK, 1976), V. P. Furnish (Anchor Bible, 32 A; 1984), R. P. Martin (Word Biblical Comm., 40; Waco, Texas, 1986), and M. E. Thrall (ICC, 2 vols., 1994 ff.). W. Schmithals, Die Gnosis in Korinth: Eine Untersuchung zu den Korintherbriefen (Forschungen zur Religion und Literatur des Alten und Neuen Testaments, NF 48; 1956; 2nd edn., 1965; Eng. tr., Nashville [1971]). G. Bornkamm, Die Vorgeschichte des sogenannten Zweiten Korintherbreifes (Sb. (Heid.), 1961, Abh. 2; summary in Eng., 'The History of the Origin of the so-called Second Letter to the Corinthians', New Testament Studies, 8 (1962), pp. 258–64). J. C. Hurd, Jun., The Origin of I Corinthians (1965). G. Theissen, The Social Setting of Pauline Christianity, tr. from essays in various places and ed. J. H. Schütz (1982).

Corinthians, Third Epistle to the. An apocryphal letter written in reply to an equally apocryphal letter from the Church of Corinth. The two are sometimes incorporated in the 'Acts of *Paul' (c.170). The Gk. originals survive only in a papyrus codex (containing inter alia the Nativity of Mary) of the 3rd cent. in the *Bodmer collection. The text also survives, as a separate entity, in the biblical *canon of the *Armenian Church as well as in two *Vulgate Latin MSS (one at Milan, the other at Laon) and in a Coptic version of the 'Acts of Paul', while St *Ephraem Syrus (c.360) commented on it as though it were a genuine Pauline document. The author insists on the authority of the OT prophets, the resurrection of the flesh, the birth of Christ from Mary, and the creation of man, facts which show that its purpose was anti-*Gnostic.

M. Testuz (ed.), Papyrus Bodmer x–xii (Geneva, 1959), pp. 9–45 (Gk. text with Fr. tr. and introd.). Coptic text in C. Schmidt's crit. edn. of the 'Acta Pauli' (1936, q.v.). Armenian recension in Ger. tr. and two Lat. texts in P. Vetter, Der apokryphe dritte Korintherbrief (1894). Eng. tr. in J. K. Elliott, The Apocryphal New Testament (Oxford, 1993), pp. 380–2. A. F. J. Klijn, 'The Apocryphal Correspondence between Paul and the Corinthians', VC 17 (1963), pp. 2–23. Bardenhewer, 1, pp. 601–5; Altaner and Stuiber (1978), pp. 136 f.

Cornelius (d. 253), Bp. of *Rome. He was elected Pope in April 251, when, owing to the *Decian persecution and the martyrdom of *Fabian, the see of Rome had been vacant for 14 months. He found himself faced with strong opposition from the *Novatianist schismatics, who objected to his relatively lenient policy towards those who had lapsed during the persecutions; but he had the support of synods at Rome and *Carthage (251–2). Several of his letters, written in a colloquial 'vulgar Latin', have survived, including a correspondence with St *Cyprian. He died in exile, traditionally as a martyr, at Centum Cellae (Civitavecchia), and was buried at Rome in the crypt of Lucina in the 'Coemeterium Callisti', where his tomb is still to be seen with the Latin inscription 'Cornelius Martyr'. Feast day, 16 Sept.

His Epp. to Cyprian are pr. inter Epp. Cypr., nos. 49 and 50. P. *Coustant, Epistolae Romanorum Pontificum, 1 (1721), cols. 123–206; M. J. *Routh, Reliquiae Sacrae, 3 (2nd edn., 1846), pp. 11–89. G. Mercati, D'alcuni nuovi sussidii per la critica del testo di S. Cipriano (1899), pp. 72–86 ('Le lettere di S. Cornelio papa'). M. Bévenot, 'Cyprian and his Recognition of Cornelius', JTS NS, 28 (1977), pp. 346–59. L. Reekmans, La tombe du pape Corneille et sa région cémétériale (Roma Sotterranea Cristiana, 4; Vatican City, 1964). G. Bardy in DHGE 13 (1956), cols. 891–4, s.v. 'Corneille (Saint)'.

Cornelius a Lapide (1567–1637), Cornelis Cornelissen van den Steen, Flemish biblical exegete. He was born at Bocholt nr. Liège, and educated at the *Jesuit colleges of Maastricht and *Cologne. In 1592 he entered the Society of Jesus, and was professor of exegesis at Louvain from 1596. In 1616 he was called to Rome, where he taught the same subject and finished his celebrated commentaries, comprising all the Canonical Books except Job and the Psalms, though several of them were published only after his death. His works have owed their enduring popularity, esp. among preachers, to their clarity, deep spirituality, and allegorical and mystical exegesis, buttressed by a wide erudition which enabled the author to draw extensively on the Fathers and on medieval theologians.

Complete edns. of his Comm. on the Bible pub. in 10 vols., Amsterdam, 1681; 11 vols., Venice, 1717; 11 vols., Cologne, etc., 1732; 11 vols., Venice, 1740; and several later edns. Eng. tr. by T. W. Mossman of his Comm. on the Gospels (5 vols., 1876–86) and by W. E. Cobb of his Comm. on 1 Cor. (1896) and on 2 Cor. and Gal. (1897). S. Pagano, OMI, 'Analysis Notionis Inspirationis S. Scripturae apud Cornelium a Lapide', *Revue de l'Université d'Ottawa*, 15 (1945), pp. 65*–85*. G. Boss, *Die Rechtfertigungslehre in den Bibelkommentaren des Kornelius a Lapide* (Katholisches Leben und Kämpfen im Zeitalter der Glaubensspaltung, 20; 1962). Sommervogel, 4 (1893), cols. 1511–26; 9 (1900), col. 573; Polgár, 2 (1990), pp. 379–81. G. Heinrici in *PRE* (3rd edn.), 4 (1898), pp. 289–91, s.v.

Cornill, Carl Heinrich (1854–1920), OT scholar. He was professor of OT exegesis at Königsberg (1888), Breslau (1898), and Halle (1910). In the main he was a disciple of J. *Wellhausen. He wrote several books, notably an *Introduction to the Canonical Books of the OT* (1891) (Eng. tr. of 5th edn., 1907) and a *History of the People of Israel* (1898, Eng. tr. also 1898), which through their wide circulation did much to spread Wellhausen's methods of criticism and exegesis.

K. v. Rabenau in *Neue Deutsche Biographie*, 3 (1957), pp. 367 f.

Coronation of our Lady. The final triumph of the Blessed Virgin in heaven, wherein she was crowned by her Divine Son. It is the subject of the fifth *Glorious Mystery of the *Rosary. The octave-day of the *Assumption of the BVM was observed in a few places as the feast of her Coronation, and the calendar introduced in 1969 has a *memoria of the BVM as Queen on this day (22 Aug.).

Coronation Rite in England. The rite for the coronation of English kings falls into three parts: (1) the promises made by the king and his acclamation by the people; (2) the consecration and anointing of the king; (3) the vesting, coronation, and enthronement of the king (and coronation of the queen consort), followed by the homage and the king's Communion. These three divisions appear throughout the history of the rite.

The earliest surviving rite for the coronation of an English king (based on texts of both English and Continental origin) dates from the 9th cent. It was amplified thereafter, prob. in the early 10th cent., and was used, for example, at the coronation of King *Edgar in 973. In the course of time it underwent various further modifications, the most elaborate form of it being that in the *Liber Regalis*, which was used in 1308 for Edward II. For the coronation of *James I in 1603 it was translated into English, the penitential psalms were omitted, and the Eucharist was conformed, with certain variations, to that in the BCP. A drastic rearrangement and curtailment was made in 1685 by Abp. W. *Sancroft to suit current ideas, and since *James II, being a RC, could not communicate, the Communion Service was omitted. For the coronation of William and Mary in 1689 the Eucharist was reinstated

in its central position, and among other changes Parliament caused an oath to be added for the defence of *Protestantism. Since 1689 the only changes have been minor abbreviations.

The most useful collection of docs. is L. G. Wickham Legg, *English Coronation Records* (1901). Much interesting material is assembled in A. Taylor, *The Glory of Regality* (1820). Texts of the rite in J. Wickham Legg (ed.), *Three Coronation Orders* (HBS 19; 1900; contains the Order of William III and Mary, an Anglo-French version of the English Coronation Order, and the Consecration of the Anglo-Saxon King; C. Wordsworth (later Subdean of Salisbury), *The Manner of the Coronation of King Charles the First* (HBS 2; 1892); F. Sandford, *The History of the Coronation of . . . King James II . . . and Queen Mary* (1687). *The Coronation Service of her Majesty Queen Elizabeth II*. With a short historical Introduction, Explanatory Notes, and an Appendix by E. C. Ratcliff (1953).

Modern studies include R. M. Woolley, *Coronation Rites* (Cambridge Handbooks of Liturgical Study, 1915); E. C. Ratcliff, *The English Coronation Service* (1936; with text of Rite used in 1911); R. H. Murray, *The King's Crowning* (1936), with bibl. P. E. Schramm, *A History of the English Coronation* (Eng. tr. by L. G. Wickham Legg, 1937). E. Eichmann, *Königs- und Bischofsweihe* (*Sb.* (Bayr.), 1928, Abh. 6); id., *Der Kaiserkrönung im Abendland* (2 vols., Würzburg, 1942). C. A. Bouman, *Sacring and Crowning: The Development of the Latin Ritual for the Anointing of Kings and the Coronation of an Emperor before the Eleventh Century* (Bijdragen van het Instituut voor Middeleeuwse Geschiedenis der Rijks-Universiteit te Utrechts, 30; 1957). P. L. Ward, 'The Coronation Ceremony in Mediaeval England', *Speculum*, 14 (1939), pp. 160–78, with refs. C. Dawson, *Beyond Politics* (1939), pp. 93–115 ('Considerations on the Coronation of an English King'). H. G. Richardson, 'The Coronation in Medieval England', *Traditio*, 16 (1960), pp. 111–202. J. L. Nelson, 'The Earliest Royal *Ordo*: Some Liturgical and Historical Aspects', in B. Tierney and P. Linehan (eds.), *Authority and Power: Studies on Medieval Law and Government Presented to Walter Ullmann* (Cambridge, 1980), pp. 29–48, repr. in her *Politics and Ritual in Early Medieval Europe* (1986), pp. 341–60; id., 'The Second English *Ordo*', ibid., pp. 361–74; see also nos. 10–14 and 17. A. Hughes, 'The Origins and Descent of the Fourth Recension of the English Coronation', in J. M. Bak (ed.), *Coronations: Medieval and Early Modern Monarchic Ritual* (Berkeley, Los Angeles, and Oxford [1990]), pp. 197–216.

corporal (from Lat. *corpus*, 'body', since it holds the Body of the Lord). In W. liturgical usage, a square piece of linen on which the bread and wine are placed and consecrated in the *Eucharist. Such a cloth was used in the 4th cent., but there was no distinction between the corporal and the ordinary linen altar cloth now used under the corporal before the 9th cent. Formerly it was large enough to cover the chalice also (as it still is among the *Carthusian monks), but later a second folded corporal (now called the *pall) was introduced for this purpose. See also ANTIMINSION, EILETON, and BURSE.

Braun, *LP*, pp. 205–9. E. G. C. F. Atchley, 'On Certain Variations from the Rule Concerning the Material of the Altar Linen', *Transactions of the St Paul's Ecclesiological Society*, 4 (1900), pp. 147–60, esp. pp. 156–60. N. F. Robinson, SSJE, 'Concerning Three Eucharistic Veils of Western Use', ibid. 6 (1906–10), pp. 129–60, esp. pp. 129–40. H. Thurston, SJ, in *CE* 4 (1908), pp. 386 f., s.v.

corporal works of mercy. There are traditionally seven: (1) feeding the hungry; (2) giving drink to the thirsty; (3) clothing the naked; (4) harbouring the stranger; (5) visiting the sick; (6) ministering to prisoners; (7) burying the dead. Cf. Mt. 25: 35 f. See also SPIRITUAL WORKS OF MERCY.

Corporation Act 1661. The Act of the 'Cavalier Parliament' requiring all members of municipal corporations to take an oath abjuring rebellion against the king, declaring the *Solemn League and Covenant null and unlawful, and affirming that they had received the Sacrament of Communion acc. to the rites of the C of E within the year preceding their election. It was repealed in 1828.

Text repr. in Gee and Hardy, pp. 594–600 (no. 116).

Corpus Christi, Feast of, officially called 'Festum Corporis et Sanguinis Christi' in the RC Church since 1970. The feast commemorating the institution and gift of the Holy *Eucharist, observed in the W. Church on the Thursday after *Trinity Sunday. The natural day in the Christian calendar for this commemoration would be *Maundy Thursday, on which the Eucharist was instituted; but the memory of the Passion on that day made a separate day for the Eucharist desirable, and the Thursday after Trinity Sunday was chosen as the first free Thursday after Eastertide. The institution of the feast was largely due to the influence of Blessed *Juliana (d. 1258), a devout nun of Liège who was led to take action in the matter c.1230 in response to a vision. In 1264 its observance was commanded by the bull 'Transiturus' of Urban IV, and in the 14th cent. the keeping of the feast became universal in the W. The services of the day have traditionally been attributed to St *Thomas Aquinas; though modern scholarship has challenged the authenticity of the material on which this ascription is based, it is defended on internal evidence. Outdoor processions with the Bl Sacrament are common in some countries.

See also LAUDA SION and PANGE LINGUA.

P. Browe, SJ (ed.), *Textus antiqui de Festo Corporis Christi* (Münster, 1934). E. Dumoutet, *Corpus Domini: Aux sources de la piété eucharistique médiévale* (1942). C. Lambot, OSB, and I. Fransen, OSB, *L'Office de la Fête-Dieu primitive: Textes et mélodies retrouvés* (Maredsous, 1946). *Studia Eucharistica: DCC Anni de Condito Festo Sanctissimi Corporis Christi 1246–1946* (Antwerp, 1946). L. M. J. Delaissé, 'A la recherche des origines de l'office du Corpus Christi dans les manuscrits liturgiques', *Scriptorium*, 4 (1950), pp. 220–39; P.-M. Gy [OP], 'L'Office du Corpus Christi et S. Thomas d'Aquin: État d'une recherche', *RSPT* 64 (1980), pp. 491–507. M. Rubin, *Corpus Christi: The Eucharist in Late Medieval Culture* (Cambridge, 1991), pp. 164–212.

Corpus Iuris Canonici. The chief collection of *canon law in the W. Church before the promulgation of the *Codex Iuris Canonici in 1917. It was composed of: (1) the 'Decretum' of *Gratian, a collection of canons of Councils, decrees of Popes, and other material put together in the middle of the 12th cent. This collection had no authority other than that of the individual canons which composed it; (2) the collection of *Decretals of *Gregory IX, compiled at the command of that Pope by St *Raymond of Peñafort, and intended as a supplement to the 'Decretum' of Gratian. It was divided into five books and promulgated in 1234. In addition to the authority already possessed by its component parts, it received the further authority of Gregory IX; (3) the *Sext. A sixth book added to the Decretals of Gregory by *Boniface VIII in 1298; (4) the '*Clementines', a further collection compiled by *Clement

V and promulgated after his death by *John XXII in 1317; (5) the '*Extravagantes' of John XXII, namely the decrees of that Pope collected by a private person and published in 1325; (6) the 'Extravagantes Communes', the decrees of various Popes between 1261 and 1484. These several items, the last two of which were unofficial insertions, are found in a single collection in printed editions from 1499 onwards, though the name did not come into general use till after Gregory XIII's bull 'Cum pro munere' (1 July 1580).

Best edn. by E. Friedberg (2 vols., Leipzig, 1879–81). Crit. edn. of the Extravagantes of John XXII by J. Tarrant (Monumenta Iuris Canonici, 8th ser., vol. 6; Vatican City, 1983). P. Torquebiau and G. Mollat in *DDC* 4 (1949), cols. 610–64 s.v., incl. bibl.

correctoria (Lat., 'correctories'). The term is applied to two kinds of medieval works:
(1) Books containing sets of variant readings for 'correcting' the corrupted text of the Latin *Vulgate Bible. The *Dominican and *Franciscan friars took an active part in the composition and diffusion of such books.
(2) Polemical writings between Franciscans and Dominicans, criticizing or defending the teachings of St *Thomas Aquinas, after the Paris and Oxford condemnations of 1277 and the *Correctorium Fratris Thomae* (1278) of the English Franciscan, William de la Mare.

(1) R. Loewe in G. W. H. Lampe (ed.), *The Cambridge History of the Bible*, 2 (1969), pp. 148–52.
(2) D. A. Callus, OP, in *NCE* 4 (1967), pp. 349–52, s.v., both with further refs.

corrody. Originally the right possessed by some benefactors of religious houses or their nominees to board and lodging within them. The term came also to be applied to pensions and other similar allowances (mostly in kind) made by the monastery to those who served its various needs or who, by the payment of a lump sum, had secured a corrody as a kind of annuity for life. Their prevalence was one of the causes of monastic impoverishment in the later Middle Ages.

On the etymology of the word see *OED*, s.v. J. R. H. Moorman, *Church Life in England in the Thirteenth Century* (1945), pp. 46 and 269–71; J. M. Tillotson, 'Pensions, Corrodies and Religious Houses: An Aspect of the Relations of Crown and Church in Early Fourteenth-Century England', *Journal of Religious History*, 8 (1974–5), pp. 127–43; B. Harvey, *Living and Dying in England 1100–1540: The Monastic Experience* (Oxford, 1993), pp. 179–209.

Cosin, John (1594–1672), Bp. of *Durham. He was a member of a wealthy family of *Norwich and educated at Caius College, Cambridge. After holding several other benefices he was collated to a canonry at Durham in 1625 and became rector of Brancepeth in Co. Durham in 1626. He was a personal friend of W. *Laud and R. *Montague, and as such incurred the hostility of the *Puritan party. This was increased when he published, in 1627, his famous *Collection of Private Devotions*, a book of prayers compiled at the instigation of *Charles I for the use of Queen *Henrietta Maria's English maids of honour. In 1635 he was elected master of Peterhouse, whose chapel he decorated acc. to High Church principles, and in 1640 he was appointed Dean of *Peterborough. The Long Parliament deprived him of all his benefices and in 1644 he was ejected from the mastership of Peterhouse. In the same year he went to *Paris, where he became chaplain to the C of E members of the Queen's household. He showed sympathy for the *Huguenots, and engaged in bitter controversy with the RCs, disinheriting his son on his reception into the RC Church. After the Restoration he returned to England and was made Bp. of Durham in 1660. He attended the *Savoy Conference in 1661 and had considerable influence on the subsequent revision of the BCP. This included his new translation of several of the collects, and his translation of the '*Veni Creator' was incorporated into the *Ordinal. A diligent administrator and pastor, as bishop he used all the powers at his command to induce both Puritans and RCs to conform to the C of E. He was also a keen business man who sanctioned the sale of offices in his patronage, and he was one of the three bishops who advocated divorce in cases of adultery. Most of his literary works are of a controversial nature, being directed esp. against RC doctrine. He attacked *transubstantiation in his *Historia Transubstantiationis Papalis* (written 1656, pub. 1675), and the inclusion of the so-called Apocrypha in the RC Canon of the Scriptures in *A Scholastical History of the Canon of Holy Scripture* (1657). See also DURHAM BOOK.

Works pub. in the Library of Anglo-Catholic Theology (5 vols., 1843–55), with Life in vol. 1, pp. xiii–xx; G. Ornsby (ed.), *The Correspondence of John Cosin* (Surtees Society, 52 for 1868, and 55 for 1870; 1869–72). Crit. edn. of *A Collection of Private Devotions* by P. G. Stanwood and D. O'Connor (Oxford, 1967). Modern Life by P. H. Osmond (London, 1913). J. G. Hoffman, 'The Puritan Revolution and the "Beauty of Holiness" at Cambridge', *Proceedings of the Cambridge Antiquarian Society*, 72 (for 1982–3; 1984), pp. 94–105, and other arts. by this author there mentioned. C. W. Dugmore, *Eucharistic Doctrine in England from Hooker to Waterland* (1942), pp. 102–10. J. H. Overton in *DNB* 12 (1887), pp. 264–71.

Cosmas and Damian, Sts, the patron saints of physicians. Nothing precise as to their lives seems discoverable, though it is unnecessary to suppose that their legend has a mythological basis founded on that of the 'Dioscuri'. Acc. to later tradition, the twin brothers practised their profession without claiming reward from their patients, and were hence known as the 'moneyless' (ἀνάργυροι). Both are also supposed to have suffered martyrdom. Their Passion, which exists in several forms and languages, is late and historically valueless. Their cultus was firmly established in the E. in the 5th cent., and at *Rome a church was constructed in their honour on the edge of the Forum out of a temple of Romulus, by Felix IV (526–30), with the saints depicted in mosaics. The two saints are mentioned in the *Canon of the Roman Mass. Feast day, in the E., 1 July (also 1 Nov.); in the W., 26 (previously 27) Sept.

The Gk. and Lat. recensions of the Acta and Passio are listed in *BHG* (3rd edn., 1957), 1, pp. 126–36, and in *BHL* 1 (1898–9), pp. 297 f., and Novum Supplementum (1986), pp. 227–9. Discussion and extracts in *AASS*, Sept. 7 (1760), pp. 430–77. L. Deubner, *Kosmas und Damian: Texte und Einleitung* (1907). The oldest Greek text, discovered in 1907, ed. E. Rupprecht (Neue Deutsche Forschungen. Abteilung Klassische Philologie, 1; Berlin, 1935). Evidence for growth of the cult in *AASS*, Nov. 2, pt. 2 (1931), pp. 528 f. M.-L. David-Danel, *Iconographie des saints médecins Côme et Damien* (Lille, 1958), A. Wittmann, *Kosmas und*

Damian: Kultausbreitung und Volksdevotion (1967). M. van Esbroeck, SJ, 'La diffusion orientale de la légende des saints Cosme et Damien', *Hagiographie, Cultures et Sociétés, IVᵉ–XIIᵉ siècles: Actes du Colloque organisé à Nanterre et à Paris (2–5 mai 1979)* (1981), pp. 61–77. V. L. Kennedy, CSB, *The Saints of the Canon of the Mass* (Studi di Antichità Cristiana, 14; 1938), pp. 137–40. R. Krautheimer, *Corpus Basilicarum Christianarum Romae*, 1, fasc. 3 (Rome [1946]), pp. 137–43.

Cosmas Indicopleustes (Κοσμᾶς Ἰνδικοπλεύστης, i.e. 'Cosmas, the Indian navigator'; mid-6th cent.), geographer. He was a merchant of *Alexandria who may have become a monk. His 'Christian Topography' (Χριστιανικὴ τοπογραφία), in 12 books c.547, attacks the Ptolemaic system in favour of various fantastic astronomical doctrines intended to harmonize with a literal understanding of the Bible. The chief value of the book lies in its geographical information (esp. on *Sri Lanka) and its witness to the spread of the Christian Church at his time. In exegesis Cosmas follows *Theodore of Mopsuestia; he was probably a *Nestorian.

Editio princeps by B. *Montfaucon, OSB, *Collectio Nova Patrum*, 2 (1707), pp. 113–345, from Vat. gr. 699, the oldest MS (8th–9th cent.); repr. in J. P. Migne, *PG* 88. 9–476. Crit. edns. by E. O. Winstedt, Cambridge, 1909, and, with Fr. tr., by W. Wolska-Conus (SC 141, 159, 197; 1968–74). Eng. tr., with notes, by J. W. McCrindle (Works issued by the Hakluyt Society, 98; 1897). W. Wolska, *La Topographie chrétienne de Cosmas Indicopleustès: Théologie et Science au VIᵉ siècle* (Bibliothèque Byzantine, 3; 1962); T. Hainthaler in A. Grillmeier, *Jesus der Christus im Glauben der kirche*, 2/4 (1990), pp. 150–65; Eng. tr. (1996), pp. 147–61. E. Peterson, 'Die alexandrinische Liturgie bei Kosmas Indicopleustes', *EL* 46 (1932), pp. 66–74. M. V. Anastos, 'The Alexandrian Origin of the *Christian Topography* of Cosmas Indicopleustes', *Dumbarton Oaks Papers*, 3 (1946), pp. 73–80. Krumbacher, pp. 412–14; Bardenhewer, 5, pp. 95–8. H. *Leclercq, OSB, in *DACL* 8 (pt. 1; 1928), cols. 820–49, s.v. 'Kosmas Indicopleustès'.

Cosmas Melodus, St (c.675–c.751) also 'Cosmas of Jerusalem' and 'Cosmas of Maïuma', author of Greek liturgical hymns. He was adopted by the father of St *John of Damascus and educated by a monk, also called Cosmas, who also wrote poetry, whence a certain confusion regarding the authenticity of some of the poetry of the younger author. Early in the 8th cent. he entered the *Laura of St *Sabas nr. *Jerusalem, and in 735 became Bp. of Maïuma nr. Gaza. The most famous of his works are his '*canons' (κανόνες), odes in honour of the great Christian feasts such as the *Nativity, the *Epiphany, and *Exaltation of the Cross, of which 14 were incorporated in the liturgical books of the E. Church. He also wrote ἰδιόμελα, which are smaller poems, also dealing with religious subjects. His poetry is brilliant in form and metrical design, inspired by the language of the Bible and the doctrine of the Church, though the clarity of thought and expression is frequently impaired by the artificial structure of the verse. Cosmas is also most probably the author of a Commentary on the poems of St *Gregory of Nazianzus, first pub. by A. *Mai in *Spicilegium Romanum*, 2. 2 (1839), pp. 1–306. Feast day in E., 14 Oct.

His 14 canons are pr. in W. Christ and M. Paranikas (eds.), *Anthologia Graeca Carminum Christianorum* (Leipzig, 1871), pp. 161–204. His Comm. on the Carmina of St Gregory of Nazianzus repr. from A. Mai in J. P. Migne, *PG* 38. 339–680. Comm. on these canons by Theodore Prodromus (early 12th cent.; cf. Krumbacher, pp. 87 f., 749–60), pub. in part by H. M. Stevenson (Rome, 1888); further comm., based on that of Theodore Prodromus, by *Nicodemus of the Holy Mountain, Ἑορτοδρόμιον (Venice, 1836; subsequently repr.). T. E. Detorakis, Κοσμᾶς ὁ Μελωδός. Βίος καὶ ἔργο (Thessalonica, 1979; with summary in Fr.). On the canon on the Recovery of the Cross cf. H. J. W. Tillyard, 'A Canon by Saint Cosmas', BZ 28 (1928), pp. 25–37 (with edn. of music).

Cosmocrator (Gk. κοσμοκράτωρ, lit. 'Ruler of the World'). The word, taken from pagan religious vocabulary, is used in the NT (Eph. 6: 12) in the plural for the devil and his demons (cf. Jn. 12: 31; 2 Cor. 4: 4). In Hellenistic writers, it was esp. employed of the supposed rule of malignant spirits over the powers of nature, and thus came to be used as a technical term for Satan, e.g. by the *Gnostics and *Marcion. In the system of *Valentinus the Cosmocrator was contrasted with the *Demiurge.

cosmogony (Gk. κοσμογονία). A doctrine or myth about the origin of the universe. The word is used esp. of the speculations of the early Greek philosophers and also of the pagan mythologies.

Cosmological Argument (from Gk. κόσμος, 'world'). The name is used to refer to a family of arguments all of which hold that the existence of the world or universe (as opposed to its character) must be caused by God. In some forms the argument maintains that God must be postulated as a cause of the world's beginning (this form of the argument is sometimes called 'the kalām cosmological argument', after the Arabic school of thought which advocated it). Other forms of the argument suggest that the existence of the world implies the existence of God whether or not the world had a beginning. The philosophical roots of the argument lie in the work of ancient Greek philosophers such as *Plato and *Aristotle. More developed versions can be found in Jewish, Islamic and Christian writers including *Maimonides, Al-Ghazali (1056–1111), St *Anselm, St *Thomas Aquinas, *Duns Scotus, R. *Descartes, J. *Locke, and G. W. *Leibniz. The argument has been subjected to much philosophical criticism (notably by D. *Hume and I. *Kant). It is, however, still probably the most popular theistic argument with those who believe that the existence of God can be proved or in some sense rationally supported.

The subject regularly finds a place in philosophical discussions of belief in God as well as in works on the philosophers mentioned above. Works specifically devoted to it incl. W. L. Rowe, The Cosmological Argument (Princeton, NJ, and London [1975]); A. [G. N.] Flew, 'What are Cosmological Arguments?', in id. (ed.), The Presumption of Atheism and Other Philosophical Essays on God, Freedom and Immortality (1976), pp. 53–60; and W. L. Craig, The Cosmological Argument from Plato to Leibniz (1980).

cosmology (Gk. κόσμος, 'the world' + λόγος, 'a doctrine'). The part of *metaphysics which deals with the world, considered as a totality of phenomena in time and space. It was one of the accepted divisions of philosophy among thinkers of the *Enlightenment, and the word was adopted thence by I. *Kant, who denied, however, that its conclusions were capable of ultimate justification by the speculative intellect.

Cotelier, Jean Baptiste (1627–86), French *patristic scholar. In 1667 he was appointed by J. B. Colbert to assist with the cataloguing of the Greek MSS in the Royal Library at Paris. His writings include a celebrated edition of the *Apostolic Fathers published in 1672, as well as Ecclesiae Graecae Monumenta (3 vols., 1677–86).

J. B. Martin in DTC 3 (1908), cols. 1922–4.

cotta. A shortened form of the *surplice reaching to the waist or a little lower, with less ample sleeves, and a square-cut yoke at the neck. In comparatively modern times it virtually ousted the medieval shape of surplice in the RC Church. More recently, however, the surplice has sometimes been preferred.

Braun, LG, pp. 136–46.

Cottonian Library. The large collection of MSS, state papers, and books brought together by Sir Robert (Bruce) Cotton (1571–1631). It was in the possession of his descendants until an Act of Parliament (the British Museum Act 1770) brought it under public control. In 1731, while housed at Ashburnham House, part of the collection was destroyed by fire. When the British Museum was founded in 1753, it was transferred to Bloomsbury, its present home. Among its many MSS of theological and religious interest are the 'Cottonian Genesis' (Otho B. vi; a MS of the *Septuagint text but now surviving only in fragments) and the 'Lindisfarne Gospels' (Nero D. iv). The curious shelf-marks with the names of the Roman emperors were introduced when the books were arranged under a series of Imperial busts.

A Catalogue of the Manuscripts in the Cottonian Library deposited in the British Museum (1802). K. Sharpe, Sir Robert Cotton 1586–1631 (Oxford, 1979), esp. pp. 48–83. On Cotton's early life, see also H. Mirrlees, A Fly in Amber (1962).

Council. A formal meeting of bishops and representatives of several churches convened for the purpose of regulating doctrine or discipline. General or *Oecumenical Councils are assemblies of the bishops representing the whole Church. The decrees of such General Councils are held to possess the highest authority which the Church can give, and RCs assert that such councils must be summoned, and their decrees confirmed, by the Pope. Local or 'particular' councils represent the various units—e.g. *provinces, *patriarchates, *exarchates—of the Church, but these are now more often called by other names, e.g. 'synods'. Acc. to Acts 15, the first Council of the Church was held at Jerusalem. See also CONCILIAR THEORY.

Of the many edns. of the Acta of Ecclesiastical Councils, the first was that of J. Merlin (2 vols., Paris, 1524). Later important collections incl. those of J. *Hardouin, J. D. *Mansi, C. H. *Turner, and E. *Schwartz (qq.v.). Fullest ed. of British Councils by D. *Wilkins (q.v.), now partially superseded by Councils & Synods with other Documents Relating to the English Church: 1. A.D. 871–1204, ed. D. Whitelock, M. Brett, and C. N. L. Brooke (2 vols., Oxford, 1981); 2. 1205–1313, ed. F. M. Powicke and C. R. Cheney (2 vols., ibid., 1964). C. J. *Hefele and H. *Leclercq, OSB, Histoire des conciles (11 vols. in 22 parts, 1907–52); W. Brandmüller (ed.), Konziliengeschichte (Paderborn, etc., 1979 ff.). On early Greek Councils, CPG 4 (1980), pp. 1–184 (nos. 8500–9444). Annuarium Historiae Conciliorum (Amsterdam, 1969 ff.). See also bibl. to OECUMENICAL COUNCILS.

Council for World Mission. In 1966 the Congregational Council for World Mission was formed to succeed the *LMS and the Commonwealth Missionary Society. Its members were the *Congregational Churches of the United Kingdom, Australia, New Zealand, and South Africa. Though a Congregational Council, it encouraged Churches 'to assume for themselves such form of church order as to them shall appear most agreeable to the Word of God'. When the *United Reformed Church was formed in 1972, the Council was enlarged, and in 1973 its name was changed to Council for World Mission (Congregational and Reformed). In 1977 the Council was fully internationalized, with 22 member Churches in all continents, but principally those Churches which had been associated with the LMS or *Presbyterian missionary work. Since some of these (e.g. the Church of *South India) are episcopal in form, it was agreed to call the Council simply the Council for World Mission.

Council of Churches for Britain and Ireland. The organization which in 1990 succeeded the *British Council of Churches (q.v.). It has the same basis, but a new commitment to the search for unity and to common evangelism and service. It embraces a wider spectrum of Christian traditions, including among its members the RC Church in England, Wales, and Scotland, *Pentecostal and *Holiness Churches, and the Russian, Greek, and Oriental *Orthodox Churches, as well as the *Anglican and mainstream Protestant Churches. It co-ordinates the work of the new national ecumenical bodies—Churches Together in England, ACTS (Action of Churches Together in Scotland), CYTUN (Churches Together in Wales)—and the Irish ecumenical bodies. It is directed and managed by an Assembly, Church Representatives Meeting, and a Steering Committee. It has six Presidents.

The Next Steps for Churches Together in Pilgrimage, pub. by the British Council of Churches and the *Catholic Truth Society [1989].

Counsels of Perfection. Traditionally three, i.e. poverty, or renunciation of private property (in some cases even of communal property); chastity, or renunciation of marriage; and obedience to the lawful commands of lawful superiors (sometimes regarded as involving the interior submission of the mind and will as well). Since the late Middle Ages, they have been regarded as forming the basis of religious life in nearly all its forms.

Counter-Reformation. The revival of the RC Church in Europe, usually considered as extending from about the middle of the 16th cent. to the period of the *Thirty Years War (1618–48). Both the conception and the term itself have their dangers, since, though greatly stimulated by Protestant opposition, reform movements within the RC Church had begun almost simultaneously with the Lutheran schism, and the two reforming movements may be regarded with some justification as streams proceeding in reverse directions but from the same source. F. *Ximénez de Cisneros, G. *Savonarola, and M. *Luther himself, in his early career as a Catholic reformer, represent early stirrings of conscience within the Church against the abuses of the Renaissance age, but the new religious orders of the 1520s (*Capuchins, *Theatines, *Barnabites)

should probably be regarded as the first organic signs of the Counter-Reformation. These orders preceded by some years St *Ignatius Loyola's foundation of the *Jesuits, but soon after its confirmation by *Paul III in 1540 the latter organization became the spearhead of the movement both within Europe and as a missionary force in America and the East. The definitions of doctrine and various internal reforms accomplished in the last session of the Council of *Trent (1562–3) sealed the triumph of the Papacy both over those Catholics, like the Emp. Ferdinand I and Charles IX of France, who wished for conciliation with the Protestants, and over those French and Spanish bishops who had opposed Papal claims. The Popes of the later 16th cent., notably *Paul IV, *Pius V, and *Sixtus V, took advantage of peace in Italy to improve discipline and efficiency within the *Curia and amongst the episcopate. With the *Inquisition they paralleled a Spanish conception of ecclesiastical discipline at least in Italy, while Spain under *Philip II, the strongest military power of the day, constituted itself the secular arm of the Counter-Reformation throughout Europe. If, however, the movement in its later stages appears increasingly a product of Spanish hegemony and national ideals, there can be no question regarding the apostolic zeal which continued to mark such leaders as St *Francis de Sales and St *Charles Borromeo, or regarding the spiritual qualities of the Spanish mystics. The all-pervasive zeal of the Jesuits, the co-operation of the Papal nuncios, the *Index Librorum Prohibitorum*, the skilful manipulation of the constitutional machinery of the Holy Roman Empire, and the conversion of several important princes were but a few of the factors making for success during the late 16th and early 17th cents. Within Europe the greatest triumph of the movement was the reconquest to the Roman obedience of S. Germany and Poland. In Central Europe the position was scarcely stabilized until the Peace of *Westphalia (1648).

M. Philippson, *Les Origines du catholicisme moderne: La contre-révolution religieuse au XVIᵉ siècle* (Brussels, etc., 1884); P. Janelle, *The Catholic Reformation* (Milwaukee, 1949); H. O. Evennett, *The Spirit of the Counter-Reformation* (Birkbeck Lectures, 1951, ed. J. Bossy; Cambridge, 1968); A. G. Dickens, *The Counter Reformation* (1968); M. R. O'Connell, *The Counter Reformation 1559–1610* (New York and London, 1974); A. D. Wright, *The Counter Reformation: Catholic Europe and the Non-Christian World* (1982); L. Châtellier, *L'Europe des dévots* (1987; Eng. tr., *The Europe of the Devout: The Catholic Reformation and the Formation of a New Society*, Cambridge, 1989). J. Delumeau, *Le Catholicisme entre Luther et Voltaire* (Nouvelle Clio, 30 bis; 1971; Eng. tr., 1977). H. Jedin, *Katholische Reformation oder Gegenreformation? Ein Versuch zur Klärung der Begriffe nebst einer Jubiläumsbetrachtung über das Trienter Konzil* (Lucerne, 1946). P. Broutin, *L'Évêque dans la tradition pastorale du XVIᵉ Siècle* ([Fr. adaptation of an essay by H. Jedin, orig. pub. 1942], 1953). J. Bossy, 'The Counter-Reformation and the People of Catholic Europe', *Past and Present*, 47 (1970), pp. 51–70. D. Fenlon, *Heresy and Obedience in Tridentine Italy: Cardinal Pole and the Counter Reformation* (Cambridge, 1972). W. Reinhard, 'Gegenreformation als Modernisierung? Prolegomena zu einer Theorie des konfessionellen Zeitalters', *Archiv für Reformationsgeschichte*, 68 (1977), pp. 226–52. E. Iserloh, J. Glazik, and H. Jedin, *Reformation, Katholische Reform und Gegenreform* (Handbuch der Kirchengeschichte, ed. H. Jedin, 4, 1967), pp. 449–686 (Eng. tr., *History of the Church*, ed. H. Jedin and J. Dolan, 5; 1980, pp. 431–645). J. O'Malley, SJ (ed.), *Catholicism in Early Modern History: A Guide to Research* (Reformation Guides to Research, 2; St Louis [1988]). L. Cristiani in Fliche and Martin, 17 (1948), and L. Willaert, SJ, ibid. 18

(1960). T. M. Parker in *New Cambridge Modern History*, 3, ed. R. B. Wernham (1968), pp. 44–71. There is also much material in the histories of the Popes by L. von *Ranke and L. *Pastor. J. H. Pollen, SJ, in *CE* 4 (1905), pp. 437–44, s.v., with bibl.; E. L. Lamp in *NCE* 4 (1967), pp. 384–9, s.v., with more recent bibl. See further bibl. to TRENT, COUNCIL OF.

Countess of Huntingdon's Connexion. See HUNTINGDON, SELINA, COUNTESS OF.

Courayer, Pierre François Le (1681–1776), French theologian. He became a *canon regular of St-Geneviève at Paris in 1697, professor of theology in 1706, and librarian of St-Geneviève in 1711. While at Paris he corresponded with Abp. W. *Wake on the subject of the episcopal succession in the English Church. In 1721 he completed a treatise defending the validity of *Anglican Ordinations, but the censorship caused publication to be delayed till 1723, when it was issued at Nancy in Lorraine (with the name of a Brussels bookseller on the title-page), as *Dissertation sur la validité des ordinations des Anglais et sur la succession des évêques de l'église anglicane, avec les preuves justificatives des faits avancés* (Eng. tr. by D. Williams, 1725). In 1726 Courayer issued a reply to his many (esp. *Jesuit) critics. His thesis was then formally condemned by the French bishops, and in 1728 he was excommunicated and fled to England. He received for the rest of his life generous hospitality in England, though he never joined the C of E. In his will he professed his continued adherence to the Church of Rome, though dissociating himself from some of her tenets.

Courayer later pub. a new Fr. tr. of P. *Sarpi's *History of the Council of Trent* (2 vols., London, 1736; new edn., Amsterdam, 3 vols., 1751). His *Dissertation on the Validity of the Ordinations of the English* was issued in a rev. tr. at Oxford, 1844, with a memoir of the author. *Relation historique et apologétique des sentimens et de la conduite du P. Le Courayer* (2 vols., Amsterdam, 1729). E. Préclin, *L'Union des Églises gallicane et anglicane: Une tentative au temps de Louis XV. P. F. Le Courayer (de 1681 à 1732) et Guillaume Wake* (1928). G. G. Perry in *DNB* 12 (1887), pp. 328–30.

Court of Delegates. See DELEGATES, COURT OF.

Court of Ecclesiastical Causes Reserved. A court in the C of E established by the *Ecclesiastical Jurisdiction Measure 1963. It has original jurisdiction over offences by clergy involving doctrine, ritual, or ceremonial ('a reserved matter'), and suits of *Duplex Querela; it also hears appeals from the *Consistory Courts in *faculty cases involving matters of doctrine, ritual, or ceremonial. It consists of five judges appointed by the Sovereign, of whom two are communicants who hold or have held high judicial office, and three are or have been diocesan bishops. Appeal lies to a Commission of Review.

Court of Faculties. See FACULTIES, COURT OF.

Court of High Commission. See HIGH COMMISSION, COURT OF.

Courtenay, William (c.1342–96), Abp. of *Canterbury. The fourth son of Hugh, Earl of Devon, and through his mother great-grandson of Edward I, he rose rapidly to high position in Church and State. In 1367 he was appointed Chancellor of Oxford and proved himself a vigorous upholder of the University's independence. In 1369 he was appointed Bp. of *Hereford, in 1375 Bp. of London, and in 1381 Abp. of Canterbury. As Archbishop he was a strong opponent of J. *Wycliffe and John of Gaunt and a supporter of Papal authority, save when national interests were directly attacked. He was responsible for the calling of the Blackfriars Council of 1382, which condemned Wycliffe's doctrines.

Register of William de Courtenay, Bp. of Hereford (A.D. 1370–5), ed. by W. W. Capes (Cantilupe Society, 1913; also in *Canterbury and York Society, 15; 1914). J. H. Dahmus, *The Metropolitan Visitations of William Courteney, Archbishop of Canterbury 1381–1396: Documents transcribed from the original manuscripts of Courtenay's Register, with an Introduction describing the Archbishop's Investigations* (University of Illinois Studies in the Social Sciences, 31, 2; 1950). Id., *William Courtenay, Archbishop of Canterbury 1381–1396* (University Park, Pa., and London, 1966). K. B. McFarlane, *John Wycliffe and the Beginnings of English Nonconformity* (1952 [1953]), pp. 70–80, 105–16, and *passim*. W. Hunt in *DNB* 12 (1887), pp. 342–7; *BRUO* 1 (1957), pp. 502–4.

Coustant, Pierre (1654–1721), French patristic scholar. He was a native of Compiègne, where he was educated at the *Jesuit College. After entering in 1671 the *Benedictine monastery of the *Maurist congregation of Saint-Rémi at *Reims, he was sent in 1681 to the abbey of *Saint-Germain-des-Prés in *Paris to help T. Blampin with the edition of St *Augustine. His principal achievement, however, was his edition of the works of St *Hilary (1693). It contains an elaborate preface, defending the orthodoxy of Hilary's doctrine, followed by a detailed biography of the saint, as well as separate prefaces to the various treatises. After a three-years' term as prior at Nogent-sous-Courcy he returned to Saint-Germain, where he was entrusted with the monumental undertaking of editing a complete collection of Papal letters from St *Clement of Rome to *Innocent III. After more than 20 years of work the first volume of the *Epistolae Romanorum Pontificum*, covering the period from AD 67 to 440, appeared in 1721, with erudite introductions and notes. Coustant also wrote two treatises, *Vindiciae Manuscriptorum Codicum* (1706) and *Vindiciae Veterum Codicum* (1715), in defence of the Maurist editions of the Fathers against the *Jesuit, B. Germon, who had questioned the genuineness of several of their sources.

M. Ott in *CE* 4 (1908), pp. 454 f., s.v.; M. Lalmant, OSB, in *DDC* 4 (1949), cols. 729–31, s.v., with bibl. See also works cited under MAURISTS.

Couturier, Paul Irénée (1881–1953), French priest and worker for Christian unity. Educated at Lyons, he was ordained priest in 1906, and after spending three years studying science he joined the staff of the Institut des Chartreux at Lyons, where he remained until 1951. During the 1920s he came in touch with the Russian refugees in the area and learnt much of their spiritual background. In 1932, when he was staying at the priory of Amay-sur-Meuse (see CHEVETOGNE), an introduction to the work of Cardinal *Mercier aroused his interest in the *Ecumenical Movement. The following year he introduced a Triduum or three-day period of prayer for Church unity at Lyons, followed in 1934 by an octave of prayer from 18 to 25 Jan. This was a development of the

*Church Unity Octave founded by two Anglicans in 1908, but from the first prayer was specifically offered for the unity of all baptized Christians 'as and how Christ wills'; Orthodox and other religious bodies as well as Anglicans were included. From 1939 the octave was observed as the 'Week of Universal Prayer'. He also arranged interdenominational conferences at the monastery of *La Trappe des Dombes and at Presinge. He engaged in a vast correspondence in connection with his ecumenical work, produced and distributed innumerable tracts on prayer for unity, and was in close touch with leaders of the *World Council of Churches. In 1952 he was given the title of honorary Archimandrite by Maximus IV, the Greek *Melchite (RC) patriarch of Antioch.

A collection of his writings, ed. M. Villain, SM, as Œcuménisme spirituel, pub. Tournai, 1963. A la mémoire de l'Abbé Paul Couturier (Témoignages) (Lyons, 1954), incl. essay by M. Villain, pp. 9–42, sep. tr. into Eng. (Haywards Heath, 1959). M. Villain, L'Abbé Paul Couturier (Tournai, 1957); G. [W. S.] Curtis, CR, Paul Couturier and Unity in Christ (1964).

Covel, John (1638–1722), also 'John Colvill', master of Christ's College, Cambridge. Born at Horningsheath, Suffolk, he was educated at Bury St Edmunds and Christ's College, Cambridge, where he delivered a Latin oration on the return of the Stuarts. Appointed chaplain to the British Embassy at *Constantinople in 1669, he there amassed material for his unpublished diaries and future publications. On his return to England (1679) he was appointed Lady Margaret Preacher of Divinity at Cambridge, and in 1681 chaplain to the Princess of Orange at The Hague. He was master of Christ's from 1688 till his death, and vice-chancellor of Cambridge University in 1689 and 1708. His chief work on the Greek Church, Some Account of the present Greek Church, with Reflections on their present Doctrine and Discipline, particularly in the Eucharist and the rest of their seven Pretended Sacraments (1722), was published after many delays just before his death. Though not widely noticed, it was one of the few books that gave information on the Greek Church till the 19th cent. Covel's Diaries and Collections are preserved in the British Library.

'Extracts from the Diaries of Dr John Covel, 1670–1679', ed. J. T. Brent, Early Voyages and Travels in the Levant (Hakluyt Society, 87; 1893), pp. 101–287. W. Hunt in DNB 12 (1887), pp. 355 f.

covenant. A bond entered into voluntarily by two parties by which each pledges himself to do something for the other. The notion was employed in a range of secular senses (in association with marriages, commercial contracts, etc.) before it was used as a theological model for the relationship between Yahweh and His people Israel. As such, the idea of covenant (Heb. בְּרִית) became central to the religion of the OT. The *Ark was an important symbol of Yahweh's presence and covenant. The Prophets press the truth that the perfect relation between God and man is based on the inward righteousness of the heart, and *Jeremiah (31: 31 ff.) looks forward to a 'new covenant'. St *Paul sees this eschatological conception realized in the sacrificial death of Christ represented in the Eucharist (1 Cor. 11: 25), whereas the tradition found in Mk. 14: 24 and in the best MSS of Matt. 26: 28 echoes Exod. 24: 8 and probably sees the sacrificial death of Christ in terms

of that foundational covenant with Israel. The Ep. to the *Hebrews quotes Exod. 24 in ch. 9 but contrasts that *Mosaic convenant with the new and better covenant foretold by Jeremiah and inaugurated by Christ's life, death, and exaltation (7: 22 and 12: 24)

E. W. Nicholson, God and his People: Covenant and Theology in the Old Testament (Oxford, 1986). J. Barr, 'Some Semantic Notes on the Covenant', in Beiträge zur Alttestamentlichen Theologie: Festschrift für Walter Zimmerli zum 70. Geburtstag, ed. H. Donner and others (Göttingen, 1977), pp. 23–38. J. Behm and G. Quell in TWNT 2 (1935), pp. 105–37 (Eng. tr., 2, 1964, pp. 104–34), with further bibl. ibid. 10 (pt. 2, 1979), pp. 1041–6, s.v. διατίθημι, διαθήκη; E. Kutsch in E. Jenni (ed.), Theologisches Handwörterbuch zum Alten Testament, 1 (1971), cols. 339–52, s.v. בְּרִית.

Covenant, National. See NATIONAL COVENANT.

Covenanters. The bodies of *Presbyterians in Scotland who in the 16th and 17th cents. bound themselves by religious and political oaths to maintain the cause of their religion. Various small covenants were signed between 1556 and 1562, leading up to the *King's Confession of 1581, which was signed by Scotsmen of all classes. In the next cent. the attempt of *Charles I to introduce the Scottish Prayer Book of 1637 prompted the *National Covenant of 1638, which was very widely signed, and even professed loyalty to the Crown. After the outbreak of civil war, the English Parliament made an alliance with the rebel Scots in the terms of a *Solemn League and Covenant (1643; often known simply as 'the Covenant'), which carried with it the attempt to force Presbyterianism on England, but, though temporarily successful, it led in the end to divisions among the Covenanters themselves. The persecution of the Presbyterians in Scotland between 1661 and 1688 gave rise to further new Covenants. With the collapse of the Stuart regime in December 1688 the Presbyterians reasserted themselves, and successfully called for the abolition of episcopacy. In the western shires there took place a series of incidents known as the 'Rabbling'; over Christmas some 200 episcopalian clergy were forcibly evicted from their livings. Even with the re-establishment of the Presbyterian Kirk these extreme Covenanters remained dissatisfied, and formed the *Cameronian sect, which was joined to the *Free Church in 1876.

J. K. Hewison, The Covenanters: A History of the Church in Scotland from the Reformation to the Revolution (2 vols., 1908). J. Dodds, The Fifty Years' Struggle of the Scottish Covenanters, 1638–88 (1860). W. L. Mathieson, Politics and Religion: A Study in Scottish History from the Reformation to the Revolution (2 vols., 1902). J. Barr, The Scottish Covenanters (Glasgow, 1946). I. B. Cowan, The Scottish Covenanters, 1660–1668 (1976). D. Stevenson, The Scottish Revolution 1637–1644: The Triumph of the Covenanters (Newton Abbot, Devon [1973]). W. Makey, The Church of the Covenant 1637–1651: Revolution and Social Change in Scotland (Edinburgh [1979]). J. [S.] Morrill (ed.), The Scottish National Covenant in its British Context (ibid. [1990]). A. I. Macinnes, Charles I and the Making of the Covenanting Movement 1625–1641 (ibid. [1991]). See also general works on the history of Scotland.

Coventry, W. Midlands. A Benedictine house was founded at Coventry in 1043 by Leofric, Earl of Mercia, and his wife, the famous 'Lady Godiva'. On the death of the Abbot in 1095, custody of the Abbey was granted to Bishop Limesey of *Chester, who transferred his see to

Coventry; the title of *abbot was vested in the bishop as at *Worcester and *Winchester. During the episcopate of Hugh Nonant (1188–98) the double title of Bishop of Coventry and *Lichfield was adopted. Although this title stood until 1836, when the archdeaconry of Coventry was transferred to the diocese of Worcester, it was only during the 12th cent. that Coventry was the place of residence of the bishop and a genuine see town.

In 1918 the see was reconstituted with the archdeaconries of Coventry and Warwick. The collegiate church of St Michael (originally a parish church, completed in 1433) became the cathedral, but was largely destroyed during an air raid in 1940. A new cathedral, designed by Sir Basil Spence and built at right angles to the ruins of the old cathedral, was consecrated in 1962. Essentially modern in design, it is constructed of stone; its slender pillars cause attention to be focused on the 72-foot-high tapestry of Christ in Glory behind the altar. The tapestry was designed by Graham Sutherland and woven near Aubusson in France. The rich colouring of the huge stained glass windows is visible only from the north (altar) end of the nave, since the sides of the church are built on a zig-zag pattern to allow a clear light only on the altar. Other features of the church include the star-shaped Chapel of Unity attached to the cathedral (administered by a joint council of Anglican and Free Churches), the Chapel of Industry (symbolizing the close relationship of the cathedral with the city), the bronze sculpture of St Michael and the Devil by Jacob Epstein on the exterior of the east wall of the nave, the baptistery window designed by John Piper, and the huge glass screen at the south end of the nave, engraved with figures designed by John Hutton and allowing an uninterrupted view of the old cathedral ruins. The Charred Cross in the old ruins remains an emblem of the work of reconciliation with Germany, and the Cathedral authorities have fostered a number of initiatives, including the rebuilding of part of the Deaconesses' Hospital at Dresden in 1965–7.

For works on the diocese of Coventry and Lichfield, see s.v. LICHFIELD. On the Priory, J. C. Cox in VCH, Warwick, 2, ed. W. Page (1908), pp. 52–9. On the Cathedral, B. [U.] Spence, Phoenix at Coventry: The Building of a Cathedral (1962); id. and H. Snoek, Out of the Ashes: A Progress Through Coventry Cathedral (1963); J. Thomas, Coventry Cathedral (New Bell's Cathedral Guides, 1987). W. E. Rose, Sent from Coventry: A Mission of International Reconciliation (1980). H. Dauphin, OSB, in DHGE 13 (1965), cols. 994–1001, s.v., with further bibl.

Coverdale, Miles (1487 or 1488–1569) translator of the Bible. Ordained priest in 1514, he entered the house of the *Augustinian friars at Cambridge, where, under the influence of the prior, Robert Barnes (1495–1540), he became an enthusiast for ecclesiastical reform. After preaching against confession and images, he was forced to reside abroad, and in 1535 he produced on the Continent the first complete English Bible, a translation made from the *Vulgate, M. *Luther's Bible, W. *Tyndale's Pentateuch and NT, and other sources, and probably printed at Zurich. In 1538 he made a translation of the NT conforming more closely to the Vulgate, and in 1539 he issued with R. *Grafton the '*Great Bible'. After serving as pastor at Bergzabern, he returned to England, took part in the suppression of the W. Rebellion, and in 1551 became

Bp. of *Exeter. He went into exile again in Mary's reign, returning in 1559. He assisted at M. *Parker's consecration, and for the rest of his life was a leader of the Puritan party. See also BIBLE (ENGLISH VERSIONS).

G. Pearson (ed.), Writings and Translations of Myles Coverdale, Bishop of Exeter (*Parker Society, 1844); id. (ed.), Remains of Myles Coverdale (ibid., 1846), with biog. notice, pp. vii–xxiii. Memorials of Myles Coverdale (1836). J. F. Mozley, Coverdale and his Bibles (1953). R. A. Leaver, 'Goostly psalmes and spirituall songes': English and Dutch metrical Psalms from Coverdale to Utenhove 1535–1566 (Oxford, 1991), esp. pp. 62–86 and 286–99. H. R. Tedder in DNB 12 (1887), pp. 364–72, s.v.

cowl. A monastic garment which derives from the Roman hooded cloak. By the 10th cent. the cuculla or froccus had developed into the full, wide-sleeved robe (similar to an academic gown), often without a hood, worn over the tunic and *scapular by modern *Benedictines and *Cistercians during the liturgy. The hood (usually unattached) which forms part of the habit of most religious orders is sometimes called a 'cowl' (e.g. by the *Augustinian Friars, the *Franciscans, and the *Servites). The *Capuchins derive their name from their pointed cowls.

K. Hallinger, OSB, Gorze-Kluny: Studien zu den monastischen Lebensformen und Gegensätzen im Hochmittelalter, 2 (Studia Anselmiana, 24–5; Rome, 1951), pp. 661–96. H. *Leclercq, OSB, in DACL, 2 (1910), cols. 2127–34, s.v. 'Capuchon'.

Cowley Fathers, the. A colloquial name for the priests of the *Society of St John the Evangelist, founded in the neighbourhood of Cowley, near Oxford.

Cowper, Thomas. See COOPER, THOMAS.

Cowper, William (1731–1800), poet and hymn-writer. Born at Great Berkhamstead, where his father was rector, he was a pupil at Westminster School from 1741 to 1747. In 1748 he was entered at the Middle Temple and in 1754 called to the Bar. In 1759 he moved to the Inner Temple and was appointed Commissioner of Bankrupts; he was, however, more interested in literature than law. From this period his attacks of depression appear to date. Fear of an examination for a disputed appointment to the clerkship of the House of Lords in 1763 provoked a suicidal mania, prob. aggravated by a frustrated love for his cousin. His delusions began to take a religious colouring, and he was sent to a private lunatic asylum near *St Albans. His terrors at first increased, but were gradually soothed by Dr Nathaniel Cotton (1705–88), who was himself something of a poet. In 1765 he moved to Huntingdon to be near his brother, eventually residing with the Revd Morley Unwin and Mary, his wife. He accompanied the latter to Olney on the death of her husband in 1767. Having become intensely devout since his illness, he worked as a lay assistant to the *Evangelical incumbent, John *Newton, at whose request he began composing hymns. A further attack of insanity (1773–6) prevented his marriage with Mary Unwin, who encouraged him to write secular poetry. In 1786 they moved to Weston Underwood and in 1795 to East Dereham. He does not seem entirely to have recovered from an attack of insanity in 1787, and suffered a serious relapse in 1794.

Cowper contributed his finest hymns to the 'Olney Collection', published in conjunction with J. Newton in 1779.

They include 'God moves in a mysterious way' (written as a period of madness approached; first pub. 1774), 'Hark, my soul! it is the Lord' (first pub. 1768; transl. into Italian by W. E. *Gladstone), 'Oh for a closer walk with God' (first pub. 1772), and 'Jesus, where'er Thy people meet' (first pub. in the *Olney Hymns*). His secular poetry, much of which has a religious bent, is marked by a love of nature and a tenderness which foreshadows the romantics. This includes *The Task* (1785), the famous ballad of John Gilpin (pub. 1783) and *The Loss of the Royal George*. He also published a translation of Homer (1791) and began to translate J. *Milton's Latin and Italian poems (posthumously pub., 1808).

Collected Works, ed. J. Newton (10 vols., London, 1817). Later edns. incl. those of R. Southey (15 vols., ibid., 1835–7, and 8 vols., Bohn's Standard Library, 1853–5) and of W. Hayley and T. S. Grimshawe (8 vols., London, 1835). Cowper first issued his (collected) *Poems* in 2 vols., London, 1782–5; many later edns., incl. those of H. S. Milford ('Oxford Edition', 1905; 4th edn., 1934, repr. with revisions 1967) and J. D. Baird and C. Ryskamp (Oxford, 1980 ff.). *Life and Posthumous Writings*, ed. W. Hayley (3 vols., Chichester, 1803–4); *Life and Letters*, ed. id. (4 vols., ibid., 1809). *Letters and Prose Writings*, also ed. J. King and C. Ryskamp (5 vols., Oxford, 1979–86); *Selected Letters*, ed. idd. (ibid., 1989). Lord David Cecil, *The Stricken Deer* (1929); G. Thomas, *William Cowper and the Eighteenth Century* (1935); M. J. Quinlan, *William Cowper: A Critical Life* (Minneapolis, 1953); C. Ryskamp, *William Cowper of the Inner Temple, Esq.: A Study of his Life and Works to the Year 1768* (Cambridge, 1959); V. Newey, *Cowper's Poetry: A Critical Study and Reassessment* (Liverpool English Texts and Studies, 20; 1982); J. King, *William Cowper: A Biography* (Durham, NC, 1986). Bibl. to 1837 by N. [H.] Russell (Oxford Bibliographical Publications, NS 12; 1963) and of works from 1895 to 1960, by L. Hartley (Chapel Hill, NC, 1960). N. H. Russell in *NCBEL* 2 (1971), cols. 595–603.

Cox, Richard (*c*.1500–81), Bp. of *Ely. He was educated at Eton and King's College, Cambridge, and held a number of ecclesiastical appointments. He sat on the commission which drew up the *King's Book (1543). On the accession of *Edward VI, to whom he had been tutor from 1540 and almoner from 1544, his reforming zeal came to the fore. He helped in compiling the 'Order of the *Communion' of 1548, and the Prayer Books of 1549 and 1552; and he was also on the commission appointed in 1551 for reforming the *canon law. As first Dean of *Christ Church (1546–53) and Chancellor of Oxford University (1547–52), he was mainly responsible for introducing *Peter Martyr and other foreign divines into the university, and his alteration of statutes, diversion of funds, and destruction of books, ornaments, and MSS in order to eradicate Popery won him the name of 'Cancellor' of the university. On *Mary's accession he was imprisoned for a time and deprived of preferments, and then went into exile at Frankfurt, where his successful disputes with J. *Knox gave rise to the names 'Coxians' and 'Knoxians'. Under *Elizabeth I he became Bp. of Ely in 1559, but he refused to minister in the Queen's chapel on account of its crucifix and lights. He contemplated resigning in 1580, but the formal document was never completed. He was an honest but narrow-minded ecclesiastic; he was severe on Romanists, and impatient of *Puritans.

Several of Cox's letters are pr. in the *Correspondence of Matthew Parker*, ed. H. Bruce for the *Parker Society (1853), pp. 151 f. and 281 f.; in *The Zürich Letters*, ed. H. Robinson for the Parker

Society, 1 (1842), pp. 26–8, 65–7, 112 f., 207 f., 220 f., 234–8, 243–5, 268 f., 279–82, 282–6, 297–300, 306–9, 314–19, 328–30; 2 (1845), pp. 41 f., 192–5; and in *Original Letters Relative to the English Reformation written during the Reigns of King Henry VIII, King Edward VI, and Queen Mary, chiefly from the Archives of Zürich*, ed. id. for the Parker Society, 1 (1846), pp. 119–24. C. H. Garrett, *The Marian Exiles* (Cambridge, 1938), pp. 134–6. *BRUO, 1501–1540*, pp. 146 f.

CPAS, the 'Church Pastoral Aid Society'. A society founded in 1836 to assist the home mission work of the Anglican Church by making grants of money for the stipends of curates and men and women lay workers. Its sympathies are markedly Evangelical.

Crakanthorpe, Richard (1567–1624), *Anglican divine. He was educated at Queen's College, Oxford, where he was elected Fellow in 1598. Hence he became a disciple of J. *Rainolds and a learned defender of *Calvinist principles. Early in the reign of *James I he accompanied the ambassador, Lord Evers, to the court of the Emp. Rudolph II. In 1605 he was appointed rector of Black Notley, nr. Braintree, Essex, and in 1617 rector of Paglesham. He interested himself esp. in the Romanist controversy. His principal work, *Defensio Ecclesiae Anglicanae* (1625; posthumous), was an answer to the *Sui Reditus ex Anglia Consilium* of M. A. *de Dominis, in which the Abp. of Spalato had defended his recantation. It was a learned work and written in excellent Latin, but its tone was ferocious and the argument too closely dependent on de Dominis's text to allow Crakanthorpe to develop his own views. His other writings include books on metaphysics (1619) and logic (1622) and a *Defence of Constantine with a Treatise of the Pope's Supremacy* (1621).

Modern edn. of his *Defensio Ecclesiae Anglicanae* [by C. Wordsworth] in LACT (1847). His treatise 'Of the Pope's Temporal Monarchy' is pr. in J. Brogden, *Catholic Safeguards Against the Errors, Corruptions and Novelties of the Church of Rome*, 3 (1851), pp. 44–109. G. G. Perry in *DNB* 13 (1888), p. 2 f.

Cramer, John Antony (1793–1848), Dean of *Carlisle. Educated at Christ Church, he became Principal of New Inn Hall, Oxford, in 1831, Regius professor of modern history in 1842 (in succession to T. *Arnold), and Dean of Carlisle in 1844. Besides several classical writings he published the '*Catenae' of many of the Greek fathers on the NT (8 vols., 1838–44).

[He is to be distinguished from **Johann Andreas Cramer** (1723–88), who translated St *Chrysostom's Homilies into German (1748–51).]

List of works in *DNB* 13 (1888), pp. 4 f.

Cranach, Lucas (1472–1553), 'the Elder', German painter. In his youth he was celebrated as a painter of altar-pieces and all his life of portraits. In the very early days of the *Reformation he espoused the *Lutheran cause, and was a friend and admirer of M. *Luther and the other reforming leaders, several of whom he painted. He also produced many woodcuts of religious subjects. His zeal for the new ideas is shown in a picture now at Leipzig, and dated 1518, which shows the soul of a dying man rising to meet the Trinity, in illustration of the doctrine of *justification by faith alone.

M. J. Friedländer and J. Rosenberg (eds.), *Die Gemälde von Lucas Cranach* (1932; 2nd edn., in Eng. tr., London, 1978), with extensive bibl.; J. Rosenberg (ed.), *Die Zeichnungen Lucas Cranach d. Ä.* (1960). E. Ruhmer, *Cranach* (Cologne, 1963; Eng. tr., 1963); W. Schade, *Die Malerfamilie Cranach* (Dresden, 1974); D. Koepplin and T. Falk, *Lukas Cranach: Gemälde, Zeichnungen, Druckgraphik* (2 vols., Basle and Stuttgart, 1974–6). F. Ohly, *Gesetz und Evangelium: Zur Typologie bei Luther und Lucas Cranach* (Schriftenreihe der Westfälischen Wilhelms-Universität Münster, NF 1 [1985]).

Cranmer, Thomas (1489–1556), Abp. of *Canterbury. Born at Aslockton, the second son of a Nottinghamshire squire, he was educated at Jesus College, Cambridge, and ordained when he became a Fellow in 1523. From the marginal notes in his copy of J. Merlin's *Quattuor conciliorum generalium* (Paris, 1524) it appears that Cranmer was soon convinced that specifically English matters were not properly any concern of the Pope, and when in 1529 it seemed likely that *Henry VIII's 'divorce' proceedings against Catherine of Aragon were unlikely to succeed, Cranmer played an active part in marshalling University opinion on behalf of the King. Henry employed him on an unsuccessful embassy to the Emp. *Charles V (during which he secretly married Margaret Osiander, the niece of Andreas *Osiander), and when William *Warham died in the summer of 1532, the King quickly arranged for Cranmer to be elected as his successor.

Cranmer was consecrated Abp. of Canterbury on 30 Mar. 1533. If he accepted the office with reluctance, it was soon clear that he was to be Henry's chief instrument in overthrowing the Papal supremacy in England. In 1533 he annulled Catherine's marriage with Henry and three years later pronounced a similar judgement on the King's marriage with *Anne Boleyn. He also married Henry to and divorced him from Anne of Cleves. But despite this apparent subordination and subservience to the King's will, he acted not only at the behest of Henry but in conformity with his own opinions, based on his understanding of patristic and conciliar precedent. He was partly responsible for the '*Ten Articles' and, with Thomas *Cromwell, for the dissemination of the Bible in the vernacular. On the other hand, he took relatively little part in the *dissolution of the monasteries and opposed the '*Six Articles' of 1539, under which, indeed, he had to banish his own wife (whom he already kept in seclusion).

After Henry's death (1547), under *Edward VI Cranmer was able to achieve his ambition to revise Church services in the 'tongue understanded of the people', a process begun with the issue of the *Litany in English in 1544. His developing theology embraced the latest ideas of the Continental *Reformation, a fact discernible in his understanding of the Eucharist and his determination in the BCP of 1549 and that of 1552 to 'turn the Mass into a Communion'. On his initiative a number of continental theologians, among them *Peter Martyr and M. *Bucer, were invited to England, and Cranmer continued in other ways to push forward his project for union with the reforming Churches of Europe. He was largely responsible for the abolition of the old Church ceremonies, for the destruction of images and other relics, for the '*Forty-Two Articles', and, with Peter Martyr, for an attempt at *canon law revision (*Reformatio Legum Ecclesiasticarum). He disagreed with Northumberland,

Edward's unscrupulous adviser, and with reluctance acknowledged Lady Jane Grey as Edward's successor.

On the accession of *Mary Tudor (1553), Cranmer, who had been partly responsible for the tragedy of her mother's life, was accused of high treason, tried, and sentenced, but the Queen spared his life. He was, however, imprisoned and finally tried for heresy. He was sentenced and degraded, and then under duress and acute depression signed several recantations. On the day of his death he renounced his recantations and was burnt at the stake in Oxford on 21 Mar. 1556, putting his hand into the flames and saying 'This hand hath offended'. However his behaviour may be judged, his belief in the 'godly prince' placed him in a serious moral dilemma when the sovereign accepted Papal supremacy. To Cranmer the C of E owes not only the masterly English style of the liturgy in use almost universally for some 400 years, but also its essentially scriptural spirituality for which he was largely responsible. Feast day in the ASB, 21 Mar.; in the American BCP (1979), 16 Oct. (with H. *Latimer and N. *Ridley).

Works ed. H. Jenkyns, *The Remains of Thomas Cranmer* (4 vols., Oxford, 1833). *Miscellaneous Writings and Letters* also ed. E. Cox (*Parker Society, 1846); *Writings and Disputations . . . Relative to the Sacrament of the Lord's Supper*, ed. id. (ibid., 1844). Annotated extracts from his writings by P. N. Brooks, *Cranmer in Context* (Cambridge, 1989). Cranmer's *Defence of the True and Catholic Doctrine of the Last Supper* also ed. [C. H. H. Wright] (London, 1907). A MS showing his early attempts to frame the offices of *Mattins and *Evensong ed. J. W. Legg, *Cranmer's Liturgical Projects* (HBS 50; 1915), with introd. The principal source for his Life, apart from the *Letters and Papers, Foreign and Domestic, of the Reign of Henry VIII* (see bibl. to HENRY VIII), is the biography by J. *Strype (London, 1694; later edns., 3 vols., Oxford, 1848–54, and 2 vols., London, 1853, both with docs. re-edited). The MS which forms the basis of the account by J. *Foxe, and other material, are ed. J. G. Nichols, *Narratives of the Days of the Reformation* (Camden Society [1st ser.], 77; 1859), pp. 218–75. Modern Lives by H. J. Todd (2 vols., London, 1831), A. F. Pollard (New York and London, 1904), A. C. Deane (London, 1927), G. W. Bromiley (ibid., 1956), J. [C.] Ridley (Oxford 1962) and D. [N. J.] MacCulloch (New Haven and London [1996]). C. H. Smyth, *Cranmer and the Reformation under Edward VI* (Cambridge, 1926); F. E. Hutchinson, *Cranmer and the English Reformation* (1951); G. W. Bromiley, *Thomas Cranmer, Theologian* (1956). P. [N.] Brooks, *Thomas Cranmer's Doctrine of the Eucharist* (1965; 2nd edn., 1992). P. Ayris and D. Selwyn (eds.), *Thomas Cranmer, Churchman and Scholar* (Woodbridge, Suffolk, 1993). E. C. Ratcliff, 'The Liturgical Work of Archbishop Cranmer', *JEH* 7 (1956), pp. 189–203. J. *Gairdner in *DNB* 13 (1888), pp. 19–31.

Crashaw, Richard (*c.*1613–49), English lyrical and religious poet. The son of a *Puritan divine, he was educated at Charterhouse and at Pembroke Hall, Cambridge, where he came under the influence of many High Church friends, esp. N. *Ferrar, whom he often visited at *Little Gidding. He was elected to a fellowship at Peterhouse in 1637, but expelled in 1644 owing to his refusal to subscribe to the *National Covenant. He then fled to France, where he was received into the RC Church. In 1646 his friend, A. Cowley, found him in great destitution at Paris and persuaded Queen *Henrietta Maria to exert her influence on his behalf. As a result he went to Italy, where he became an attendant to Card. Palotta. Owing to his denunciation of some persons of the cardinal's household he had to leave Rome for *Loreto in 1649 where he had obtained a small benefice. He died there soon afterwards. His sacred poetry, collected in *Steps to the Temple* (1646) and *Carmen Deo Nostro* (1652), is filled with a devotion nourished on the Song of Solomon and the mysticism of St *Teresa, and shows his talent in composing liturgical verses for sacred occasions. His style, though often somewhat heavy and diffuse, is vivid with unusual imagery, as in the famous 'Wishes to his Supposed Mistresse' and notorious 'The Weeper'. The ardour of his religious feeling is conveyed by the musical qualities of his verses. A few striking expressions in '*Paradise Lost', bks. 1 and 2, suggest that J. *Milton was indebted to 'Sospetto d'Herode', Crashaw's free rendering of G. Marino's poem. Alexander Pope's letter to Henry Cromwell (17 Dec. 1710) provides early and acute criticism of Crashaw's rhetoric; Shelley is believed to have read Crashaw; and 'Christabel', part 2, shows S. T. *Coleridge's fascination with some lines in the 'Hymn to St Teresa'.

Modern edns. of his Poems by L. C. Martin (Oxford, 1927; 2nd edn., 1957) and by G. W. Williams (Garden City, NY, 1970). G. W. Williams, *Image and Symbol in the Sacred Poetry of Richard Crashaw* (Columbia, SC, 1963); M. F. Bertonasco, *Crashaw and the Baroque* (University, Ala. [1971]); R. V. Young, *Richard Crashaw and the Spanish Golden Age* (Yale Studies in English, 191; New Haven, Conn., and London [1982]); T. F. Healy, *Richard Crashaw* (Medieval and Renaissance Authors, 8; Leiden, 1986). J. R. Roberts (ed.), *New Perspectives on the Life and Art of Richard Crashaw* (Columbia, Mo., and London [1990]). A. D. Cousins, *The Catholic Religious Poets from Southwell to Crashaw* (1991), pp. 126–76. J. R. Roberts, *Richard Crashaw: An Annotated Bibliography of Criticism, 1632–1980* (Columbia, Mo., 1985).

Creation. In theology, the notion that the Universe was brought into being out of nothing by the free act of God, hence termed the Creator.

This doctrine, esp. characteristic of the Judaeo-Christian tradition, is to be contrasted with such theories as *pantheism and emanationism on the one hand and *dualism on the other. Since it finds a place at once for Divine Transcendence and Divine Immanence, it is closely linked with the philosophical position known as *Theism (q.v.), with its insistence on Personality in God. Its corollary is belief in the contingency of the world. And since on this view creatures owe their being to God, they partake of His goodness and hence are to be accounted 'very good' (Gen. 1: 31).

When fully elaborated the belief is clearly incompatible with the view that in constructing the universe God made use of pre-existing matter (*Plato). Certain Fathers, however, notably *Justin (*Apol.* 1. 59) and *Clement of Alexandria (*Strom.* 5. 14), accepted this Platonic view, finding support for it in Wisd. Sol. 11: 17. But it was rejected in favour of the view of creation 'out of nothing', e.g. by *Theophilus of Antioch (*Apol. ad Autolycum*, 2. 4); and it received its death-blow in the conflict with *Gnosticism. Hence from the end of the 2nd cent. the thesis of creation *ex nihilo* was almost universally accepted in the Church. It was dogmatically formulated at the Fourth *Lateran Council of 1215, and reaffirmed by the First *Vatican Council of 1870.

Though a doctrine of Creation does not as such require that the world took its beginning in or with time, Christian theologians in general have decisively rejected the eternity of the universe. But they have commonly held that its tem-poral origin is capable of being established only through revelation (cf. Gen. 1). St *Thomas Aquinas, e.g., asserted that it was incapable of rational proof, being 'credible, but not demonstrable or knowable' (*credibile, non autem demonstrabile vel scibile, Cont. Gent.* 2. 38). Similarly in the 18th cent. I. *Kant, in his famous section on the 'Antinomies' in the *Critique of Pure Reason*, upheld the incompetence of reason to prove either the creation of the world in time or the contrary.

The changes in the traditional picture of creation brought about by increased scientific knowledge (astronomical, geological, palaeontological, biological) since the beginning of the 19th cent. have at times caused much religious unsettlement to orthodox Christians. But though they must radically affect our view of the order, dating, and character of the events (and hence also whether the OT can be conceived as a scientific book), they hardly touch the fundamental philosophical questions which surround the notion of creation. Nevertheless, the traditional picture of creation often suggested an event at the beginning of time (although St *Augustine had spoken of creation *cum tempore* rather than *in tempore*), and such a view has become increasingly untenable. Not only does the theory of evolution, involving the emergence of new species within the created order, demand an understanding of creation as a continuous process through time rather than as having been completed by a single Divine *fiat* once in the remote past, but developments in modern physics (relativity, quantum theory, etc.) make it difficult to see what could be meant by creation other than an affirmation of the dependence of the created order on God's sustaining and preserving power. These considerations are reflected in most modern theology.

Classical medieval discussion by St Thomas Aquinas, *Cont. Gent.* 2, qq. 6–38, and *Summa Theol.* 1, qq. 44–46. F. *Suárez, SJ, *De Opere Sex Dierum* (2 vols., Lyons, 1621); D. *Petavius, SJ, *Theologica Dogmatica*, 3 (Paris, 1644), pp. 220–585 ('De Opificio Sex Dierum'). Modern RC doctrine was summarized by the First Vatican Council, Sess. 3, can. 1 ('De Deo Rerum Omnium Creatore'). The doctrine figures prominently in the dogmatic works of K. *Barth and E. *Brunner (qq.v.). A. D. Sertillanges, OP, *L'Idée de création et ses retentissements en philosophie* (1945). L. Scheffczyk, *Schöpfung und Vorsehung* (Handbuch der Dogmengeschichte, ed. M. Schmaus and A. Grillmeier, SJ, 2, Fasz. 2a, 1963; Eng. tr., 1970), with bibl. K. *Rahner, SJ, and others in *Mysterium Salutis*, ed. J. Feiner and M. Löhrer, 2 (Einsiedeln [1967]), pp. 405–558. A. Ehrhardt, *The Beginning: A Study in the Greek Philosophical Approach to the Concept of Creation from Anaximander to St John* (Manchester, 1968). G. May, *Schöpfung aus dem Nichts: Die Entstehung der Lehre von der Creatio ex nihilo* (Arbeiten zur Kirchengeschichte, 48; 1978; Eng. tr., 1994). A. R. Peacocke, *Creation and the World of Science* (*Bampton Lectures, 1978; Oxford, 1979). J. *Moltmann, *God in Creation* (*Gifford Lectures, 1984–5; 1985). K. Tanner, *God and Creation in Christian Theology* (Oxford, 1988). H. Pinard in *DTC* 2 (1908), cols. 2034–201, s.v.; J. Strahan in *HERE* 4 (1911), pp. 226–31, s.v.; P. F. Harris and E. A. Sillem in *A Catholic Dictionary of Theology*, 2 (1967), pp. 137–48, s.v., all with bibl. See also bibls. to META-PHYSICS, THEISM, and comm. on GENESIS.

Creationism (also **Creatianism**), the doctrine that God creates *ex nihilo* a fresh soul for each human individual at or after its conception. It is opposed to *Traducianism (q.v.), which maintains that the soul is generated with the body, as well as to any doctrine of the soul's pre-existence (e.g. that upheld by *Origen and some of his followers). It was vigorously defended by St *Jerome as alone compatible with Catholic theology, though he admitted that W. tradition (*Tertullian, etc.) was in favour of Traducianism. St *Augustine was undecided in the matter. Creationism was supported by medieval theologians generally, who accepted *Peter Lombard's formula *catholica ecclesia animas docet in corporibus infundi et infundendo creari* (*Sent.* lib. 2, d. 18, n. 8); and St *Thomas Aquinas (*Summa Theol.*, q. 118, a. 2) held the contrary doctrine heretical.

The word is occasionally used also for the doctrine that the world was created (as opposed, e.g., to *monism and *pantheism), and also for a literal reading of the biblical accounts of creation (as opposed to the theory of evolution).

P. B. T. Bilaniuk in *NCE* 4 (1967), pp. 428 f., s.v., with refs.

credence. A small side table, also known as a 'credence table', usually placed conveniently in the sanctuary near the altar, to hold the bread, wine, and water to be used at the Eucharist, and other accessories of the service. The name (from Lat. *credo*, I believe, trust) seems to have developed from the use of the word for any side table on which meats were placed for tasting or assaying.

Crediton. Acc. to tradition, St *Boniface was born in Crediton, but the earliest authority for the belief is John Grandison, Bp. of *Exeter 1327–69, and it has generally been abandoned by scholars. About 909 Abp. Plegmund divided the diocese of *Sherborne and Crediton became the see of a new bishopric covering Devon and Cornwall. Before 931 King *Athelstan set up a separate diocese of Cornwall at St Germans, but on the death of Brihtwold, Bp. of St Germans (*c*.1027), Cornwall again became part of the see of Crediton. In 1050 (owing to its exposure to pirates) Leofric, Bp. of Crediton from 1046, with the approval of *Leo IX, moved the see to Exeter (q.v.). The church of Holy Cross at Crediton is a fine, mainly perpendicular, medieval building.

Since 1897 Crediton has provided the title of a *suffragan bishop.

credo ut intelligam (Lat., 'I believe so that I may understand'). A formula in which St *Anselm summarized his conception of the relations between faith and knowledge (*Proslogion*, ch. 1). In essence it was the teaching of St *Augustine.

creed. A creed is a concise, formal, and authorized statement of important points of Christian doctrine, the classical instances being the *Apostles' Creed and the *Nicene Creed. Originally, candidates for baptism accepted a short formula of belief which varied in detail in different localities. By the 4th cent. these baptismal confessions had become more uniform and were everywhere tripartite in structure, following Mt. 28: 19. Finally, the Apostles' Creed in the W. and the Nicene Creed in the E. became the only baptismal confessions in use until the liturgical changes in the W. Church in the 1960s. The Council of *Nicaea (325) put in a credal form the profession of faith which it promulgated as a general standard of orthodoxy; and the use of creeds for this purpose rapidly spread in the 4th cent. The present practice of reciting the (Nicene)

Creed at the Eucharist did not begin until the 5th cent., when it was introduced as a local custom in the E. It was not included in the Roman Mass until 1014. See also RULE OF FAITH.

Texts in A. Hahn, *Bibliothek der Symbole und Glaubensregeln der alten Kirche* (3rd edn., rev. G. L. Hahn, 1897). The best single handbook on the whole subject is J. N. D. Kelly, *Early Christian Creeds* (1950; 3rd edn., 1972). P. *Schaff, *The Creeds of Christendom, with a History and Critical Notes* (3 vols., New York, 1877). C. P. *Caspari, *Ungedruckte, unbeachtete, und wenig beachtete Quellen zur Geschichte des Taufsymbols und der Glaubensregel* (3 vols., Christiania, 1866–75); id., *Alte und neue Quellen zur Geschichte des Taufsymbols und der Glaubensregel* (ibid., 1879). C. H. *Turner, *The History and Use of Creeds and Anathemas in the Early Centuries of the Church* (CHS, 1906). C. H. *Dodd, *The Apostolic Preaching and its Developments* (1936). D. van den Eynde, *Les Normes de l'enseignement chrétien* (1933). O. Cullmann, *Die ersten christlichen Glaubensbekenntnisse* (1943; Eng. tr., *The Earliest Christian Confessions*, 1949). R. P. C. Hanson, *Tradition in the Early Church* (1962), pp. 52–74. A. M. Ritter, 'Creeds' in I. Hazlett (ed.), *Early Christianity: Origins and Evolution to AD 600: In Honour of W. H. C. Frend* (1991), pp. 92–100. H. Lietzmann, 'Symbolstudien, I–XIV', *ZNTW* 21 (1922), pp. 1–34; 22 (1923), pp. 257–79; 24 (1925), pp. 193–202; and 26 (1927), pp. 75–95. See also bibls. to APOSTLES' CREED; ATHANASIAN CREED; NICENE CREED.

Creed, Apostles'. See APOSTLES' CREED.

Creed, Nicene. See NICENE CREED.

Creed of Pius IV. The formula, often called the **Professio fidei Tridentinae**, published by *Pius IV in the bull 'Injunctum nobis' of 13 Nov. 1564, and until 1967 imposed on holders of all the principal ecclesiastical offices in the RC Church. The Creed contains a summary of the doctrines promulgated at the Council of *Trent, among them the Tridentine doctrines of the relation between Scripture and ecclesiastical traditions, of original sin and justification, of the Mass and the *seven sacraments, of the saints, of *indulgences, and of the primacy of the Roman see. The form of it was slightly modified in 1877 so as to include subscription also to the decrees of the First *Vatican Council. It was replaced in 1967 by a shorter and less explicit formula.

The Creed, which is pr. in the main collections of conciliar decrees, is repr. in Denzinger and Hünermann (37th edn., 1991), pp. 587–9 (nos. 1862–70). Eng. tr. in Bettenson (2nd edn., 1963), pp. 375–7.

Creed of St Athanasius. See ATHANASIAN CREED.

Creeping to the Cross. See VENERATION OF THE CROSS.

Creighton, Mandell (1843–1901), Bp. of London. Educated at Merton College, Oxford, of which he became a Fellow and Tutor, he devoted himself to historical work, delivering lectures on ecclesiastical, Italian, and Byzantine history. In 1870 he was ordained to the diaconate and in 1875 was appointed Vicar of Embleton, Cumbria, where he became friendly with the Greys of Howick and Fallodon. In 1884 he was elected to the Dixie professorship of ecclesiastical history at Cambridge and to a fellowship at Emmanuel College. During his tenure of the professorship he continued his great but uncompleted work on the *History of the Papacy* (5 vols., London, 1882–94), a clear, dispassionate, and erudite study, and acted as first editor of the *English Historical Review* on its foundation in 1886. In 1891 he succeeded W. C. Magee as Bp. of *Peterborough and six years later was translated to London. His episcopate was marked by statesmanship, scrupulous efficiency, and tact, esp. in dealing with the conflicts between *Ritualists and *Kensitites.

Mandell Creighton, his Life and Letters, by Mrs [Louise] Creighton [widow] (2 vols., 1904). W. G. Fallows, *Mandell Creighton and the English Church* (1964). [W.] O. Chadwick, *Creighton on Luther* (Inaugural Lecture; Cambridge, 1959). G. W. Prothero in *DNB*, Suppl. 2 (1901), pp. 82–8.

cremation. Disposal of the dead by reducing the body to ashes. The practice was not common in primitive times, but in the ancient civilized world it was the normal custom except in Egypt, Judaea, and China. Belief in the *resurrection of the body made cremation repugnant to the early Christians, whose use of burial is attested by the evidence of the *catacombs at *Rome. By the 5th cent. Christian influence had caused it to be abandoned throughout the Roman Empire. It was revived in the 19th cent., largely in free-thinking circles, though among some Christians it has now come into favour. The RC Church used to forbid its members to dispose of their dead in this way, mainly on account of the associations of the practice. It was, however, generally permitted by an instruction of the *Holy Office issued on 5 July 1963 and a form of service is now provided for use in a crematorium, though burial is still recommended (cf. *CIC* (1983), cans. 1176, § 3 and 1184, § 1. 2). In the C of E the legitimacy of cremation is recognized by the 1969 Canons (B 38), which add that 'save for good and sufficient reason the ashes of a cremated person should be interred or deposited . . . in consecrated ground'. Cremation is normally forbidden in the Orthodox Church.

E. Valton in *DTC* 3 (1908), cols. 2310–23, s.v. 'Crémation'; H. *Leclercq, OSB, in *DACL* 7 (pt. 1; 1926), cols. 502–8, s.v. 'Incinération'; P. Palazzini in *EC* 3 (1950), cols. 838–42, s.v. 'Cremazione'; A. Closs and M. B. Walsh in *NCE* 4 (1967), pp. 439–41, s.v., all with bibl.

Cremer, Hermann (1834–1903), German Protestant theologian. In 1870 he was elected to a professorship at Greifswald (an office he combined with a pastorate in the city until 1890), and held this till his death, refusing further preferment. He strongly resisted the liberalizing movement in theology, and in *Die paulinische Rechtfertigungslehre* (1899) reaffirmed a traditionalist interpretation of St Paul's teaching about redemption. His best-known work is his lexicon to the NT (Eng. tr., *Biblico-Theological Lexicon of NT Greek*, 1878), a forerunner of G. *Kittel's *Theologisches Wörterbuch zum Neuen Testament*.

Briefwechsel und Dokumente, ed. R. Stupperich (Mitteldeutsche Forschungen, 97; 1988). K. M. A. Kaehler, *Wie Hermann Cremer wurde? Erinnerungen eines Genossen* (Beiträge zur Förderung christlicher Theologie, Jahrg. 8, Heft 1; 1904); E. Cremer, *Hermann Cremer: Ein Lebens- und Charakterbild* (1912). W. Koepp, 'Die antithetische Paradoxtheologie des späten A. H. Cremer', *Zeitschrift für Systematische Theologie*, 24 (1955), pp. 290–341. H. Beintker in *TRE* 8 (1981), pp. 230–6, s.v.

crib, Christmas. By popular custom in the W. Church, a representation of the crib (or manger) in which Jesus was laid at His birth (Lk. 2: 7), containing a model of the Holy Child, is placed on Christmas Eve (24 Dec.) in church; it was usual for it to remain until the octave day of the *Epiphany (13 Jan.), but since the abolition of octaves in 1969 the day of its removal has become less uniform. Figures of the BVM and St *Joseph, cattle, angels, and shepherds are usually included, and figures of the *Magi are added on the Epiphany (6 Jan.). St *Francis of Assisi is thought to have made the first model of the crib at Greccio in 1223. The traditional site of Christ's birth is crowned with the Church of the Nativity at *Bethlehem, and the reputed remains of His crib are preserved at *Santa Maria Maggiore in Rome.

R. Berliner, *Die Weihnachtskrippe* (Munich [1955]). N. de Robeck, *The Christmas Crib* [1938]. H. *Leclercq, OSB, in *DACL* 1 (pt. 2; 1907), cols. 2047–59, s.v. 'Âne'; 2 (pt. 1; 1910), cols. 966–71, s.v. 'Bœuf', and 3 (pt. 2; 1914), cols. 3022–9, s.v. 'Crèche'; R. F. McNamara in *NCE* 4 (1967), pp. 447 f., s.v.

Crisis, Theology of. Another name for the *Dialectical Theology of K. *Barth and his disciples, based on a triple set of associations of the Greek word κρίσις, namely: (1) 'separation', i.e. the sharpness of the dialectical distinction between temporal history and God's Eternity; (2) 'judgement', i.e. God's sentence of condemnation on all human effort and achievement; and (3) 'catastrophe', i.e. the suddenness and finality of that Divine verdict.

crisom. See CHRYSOM.

Crispin and Crispinian, Sts (*c*.285), martyrs. Acc. to the purely legendary account of their martyrdom, they were two Christian brothers who came of a noble Roman family. During the persecution of *Diocletian they fled to Soissons, where they set up as shoemakers, taking for their work only such money as was freely offered them, and finally were put to death. They are held to be the patrons of shoemakers, cobblers, and other leather-workers. Another tradition connects them with Faversham in Kent. Feast day, 25 Oct.

Martyrium and other material, with full comm., in *AASS*, Oct. 11 (1864), pp. 495–540. A. *Butler, *The Lives of the Saints*, ed. H. Thurston, SJ, and D. Attwater (rev. edn.), 4 (1956), pp. 197 f.

critical apparatus (Lat. *apparatus criticus*). In printed editions of texts (e.g. of the Greek NT), a list of MS readings differing from those in the accepted text. The apparatus is commonly printed at the foot of the page. The first edition of the Greek NT to contain a critical apparatus was that of Robert *Stephanus I (1550). See also TEXTUAL CRITICISM.

Critique of Pure Reason, The. The treatise in which I. *Kant set out for the first time the principles of the 'Critical Philosophy'. It was published at Riga in 1781. A much-altered 2nd edition appeared in 1787. Its difficulties and apparent contradictions are probably to be largely explained by the fact that its composition was extended over a period of 10 or 11 years and that it incorporates drafts representing several stages in the development of the philosopher's beliefs.

The best Eng. tr. is that of N. K. Smith (London, 1929). The standard comm. are those of H. Vaihinger (2 vols., Stuttgart, 1881–2) and, in Eng., by N. K. Smith (London, 1918; 2nd edn., 1923). Comm. for students by T. E. Wilkerson (Oxford, 1976). T. D. Weldon, *Introduction to Kant's Critique of Pure Reason* (Oxford, 1945; 2nd edn., 1958); P. F. Strawson, *The Bounds of Sense: An Essay on Kant's* Critique of Pure Reason (1966). See also bibl. to KANT, I.

Critopulos, Metrophanes. See METROPHANES CRITO-PULOS.

Croce, Benedetto (1866–1952), Italian philosopher. He came under the influence of *Hegelianism while a law student at Rome and from 1886 onwards devoted himself to philosophical studies at Naples. His philosophy is a form of 'Creative Idealism' which concentrates on the forms taken by the life of the Spirit. Of these forms Croce recognizes four, namely, 'Intuition' (art), 'Concept' (science, philosophy, and history), 'Individuality' (economics), and 'Universality' (ethics). Religion he held to be a sub-form of Intuition, and Theology an illicit application of Concept, and both only transitory manifestations of the Spirit. His principal writings are the series collectively entitled *Filosofia dello spirito*, namely, 1, *Estetica come scienza dell'espressione linguistica generale* (1902); 2, *Logica come scienza del concetto puro* (1909); 3, *Filosofia della practica: Economica ed etica* (1909); 4, *Teoria e storia della storiografia* (1917). Many of his writings have been translated into English.

Cinquant' anni di vita intellettuale italiana, 1896–1946: Scritti in onore di Benedetto Croce (ed. C. Antoni and R. Mattioli, 2 vols., Naples, 1950). Bibliography of his writings by S. Borsari, *L'opera di Benedetto Croce* (Naples, 1964). Studies by R. Piccoli (London, 1922), M. Abbate (Turin, 1955), A. R. Caponigri (London, 1955), G. N. G. Orsini (Carbondale, Ill., 1961), A. Bausola (Milan, 1965 and 1966), and G. Galasso (Milan, 1990). A. Caracciolo, *L'estetica e la religione di Benedetto Croce* (Arona, 1958). F. Capanna, *La religione in Benedetto Croce* (Bari, 1964). A. Momigliano, 'Reconsidering B. Croce (1866–1952)' [Memorial Lecture], *Durham University Journal*, 59 (1966), pp. 1–12, repr. in his *Quarto Contributo alla Storia degli Studi Classici e del Mondo Antico* (1969), pp. 95–115, with valuable discussion of literature. C. Boulay, *Benedetto Croce jusqu'en 1911* (Travaux d'histoire éthico-politique, 37; Geneva, 1981), with extensive bibl. D. D. Roberts, *Benedetto Croce and the Uses of Historicism* (Berkeley, Calif., and London [1987]). H. S. Harris in P. Edwards (ed.), *Encyclopedia of Philosophy*, 2 (1967), pp. 263–7; P. Craveri and G. Patrizi in *Dizionario Biografico degli Italiani*, 31 (1985), pp. 181–205, both s.v.

Crockford's Clerical Directory. A biographical handbook of Anglican clergy, founded by Edward William Cox (1809–79), whose position as serjeant-at-arms obliged him to name the work after his clerk, John Crockford. Apart from the (then Protestant) *Episcopal Church of the USA, it included all the clergy of the *Anglican Communion (except for Japan from 1947 and China from 1955), but in 1985 was restricted to those of England (including the diocese of Gibraltar in *Europe), *Wales, and *Scotland, together with *Ireland from 1987; in 1985 responsibility for its publication was taken over by the *Church Commissioners and the Central Board of Finance of the C of E. The first edition appeared in 1858, entitled 'The Clerical Directory', Crockford's name being added only in 1860. Publication was at first occasional, and then annual

between 1876 and 1948, except between 1916 and 1919, in 1921 and 1928, and between 1942 and 1946. (Attenuated *Supplements* came out in 1928, 1942, 1943, and 1945.) Since 1949 it has usually been biennial. The *Clergy List*, begun in 1841, has been incorporated in *Crockford* since 1917. The anonymous prefaces, which appeared until 1987, developed into essays on topics of current ecclesiastical interest.

Extracts from prefaces between 1922 and 1944 were collected in *Crockford Prefaces: The Editor Looks Back* (1947).

Cromwell, Oliver (1599–1658), Lord Protector. Born at Huntingdon, he entered Sidney Sussex College, Cambridge, in 1616, married Elizabeth Bourchier, the daughter of a City merchant, in 1620, and was elected MP for Huntingdon in 1628.

The turning-point of his career was his election as MP for Cambridge in the Short Parliament of 1640, a position which he retained during the ensuing momentous Long Parliament. Henceforth he vehemently asserted the religious and political views of the *Puritan party which he combined with the fervent spirituality of the *Independents. Thus, when the Civil War broke out (1642), it appeared to him no less than to *Charles I as a religious struggle. He built up a magnificently trained and disciplined fighting force—the 'New Model Army'—which he used with startling effect on the battlefields of Marston Moor (1644) and Naseby (1645). In politics he exercised his influence on behalf of the Independents against the rigid intolerance of the Presbyterians. After the defeat of the Scots (who had supported the King in the Second Civil War) at Preston (1648), he foresaw that the Puritan cause could not be finally successful without the removal of the King, and accordingly he now urged the necessity for his execution. Cromwell's name stands fourth among the signatures on Charles I's death warrant.

Thereafter Cromwell used his army to repress any attempts at insurrection. The Irish revolt was crushed with a ruthlessness which can be understood only in the light of contemporary fears that Ireland might be used as a base for foreign intervention on behalf of the Stuarts. Cromwell defeated the insurgent Scots on 3 Sept. 1650 at Dunbar and a year later to the day at Worcester. He had long been dissatisfied with the inefficiency and oligarchical ways of the Long Parliament, and on 20 Apr. 1653 he forcibly dismissed it.

Henceforth Cromwell, who was installed as 'Lord Protector' on 16 Dec. 1653 under the *Instrument of Government*, ruled England by a series of constitutional experiments—from 'Barebones' Parliament' of 140 'Saints' to the Major-Generals—none of which really proved successful. Yet his rule was firm, efficient, and moderate. Bishops, deans, and cathedral chapters were removed from the life of the C of E, and the use of the BCP was discountenanced; the parishes survived, but under a miscellaneous ministry of ordained and non-ordained pastors. A committee of *Triers was set up to eject unfit clergy. Attempts were also made to improve public morals and manners, to further education, to reform the law, and to instil 'true godliness'. His government, never truly popular, rested on military force, and was opposed by one party or another.

It fell apart at his death on 3 Sept. 1658, the anniversary of the battles of Dunbar and Worcester. He was buried in *Westminster Abbey. At the Restoration his body was disinterred and hung at Tyburn.

Cromwell's character, a combination of religious inspiration and practical efficiency, is not easy to interpret, nor have historians past or present reached agreement about it. 'A great bad man' was Clarendon's final verdict. Cromwell believed that he was the instrument of a Divine providence: 'I have not sought these things; truly I have been called unto them by the Lord'. His conception of government was that of a 'constable set to keep the peace of the parish'. He was not without ambition, but refused to take the title of king urged upon him in the *Humble Petition and Advice* in 1657. At times ruthless and at others magnanimous, he was undoubtedly the presiding genius of the Commonwealth.

Letters and Speeches, ed. T. *Carlyle (2 vols., London, 1845; rev. edn. by S. C. Lomas, with introd. by C. H. Firth, 3 vols., ibid., 1904); new edn. by W. C. Abbott (4 vols., Cambridge, 1937–47). The best modern Lives are those of S. R. Gardiner (London, 1899), J. Morley (ibid., 1900), C. H. Firth (New York and London, 1900), G. R. S. Taylor (London, 1928), C. V. Wedgwood (ibid., 1939; rev. edn., 1973), and A. Fraser (ibid., 1973). M. [P.] Ashley, *Oliver Cromwell* (1937); id., *The Greatness of Oliver Cromwell* (1957); id., *Oliver Cromwell and the Puritan Revolution* (1958). D. Underdown, *Royalist Conspiracy in England 1649–1660* (New Haven, Conn., 1960). [J. E.] C. Hill, *God's Englishman: Oliver Cromwell and the English Revolution* (1970). R. C. Richardson (ed.), *Images of Oliver Cromwell: Essays for and by Roger Howell* (Manchester [1993]). H. Kittel, *Oliver Cromwell: Seine Religion und seine Sendung* (Arbeiten zur Kirchengeschichte, ed. H. Lietzmann, 9; 1928); R. S. Paul, *The Lord Protector: Religion and Politics in the Life of Oliver Cromwell* (1955); H. F. L. Cocks, *The Religious Life of Oliver Cromwell* (1960). H. R. Trevor-Roper, 'Oliver Cromwell and his Parliaments', in R. Pares and A. J. P. Taylor (eds.), *Essays Presented to Sir Lewis Namier* (1956), pp. 1–48; repr. in I. Roots (ed.), *Cromwell: A Profile* (1973), pp. 91–135. C. H. Firth in *DNB* 13 (1888), pp. 155–86.

Cromwell, Thomas (*c*.1485–1540), Earl of Essex. After an adventurous and probably ill-spent early life, he returned to England from the Continent, where he may have served in the French army in Italy, and took up his father's trade as a cloth-dresser. For some time he seems to have combined this with legal work. Through the latter he gained the favour of T. *Wolsey and in 1523 he entered the House of Commons. From 1524 Wolsey made use of him for the suppression of a number of small monasteries to provide the endowment of his two proposed colleges at Ipswich and Oxford. On Wolsey's disgrace (1529), he entered the King's service and became a strong advocate of Protestantism and the royal supremacy in Church and State. His rise was rapid and in 1535 he was appointed Vicar General and Vice-Gerent in Spirituals, thus becoming the chief adviser and instrument of the King in all ecclesiastical affairs. It was he who arranged for the visitation, and finally the *dissolution, of the monasteries between 1536 and 1540. He also acted as the chief intermediary between Henry and the Reformation Parliament, in which he sat as MP for Taunton. In 1536 and 1538 he issued *Injunctions, ordering that a Bible should be provided in every church, that the clergy should perform certain definite duties, and that a register of births, marriages, and deaths should be kept. In his foreign policy he endeavoured to bring about the alliance of England with the Protestant princes of Germany, and with this in view he arranged a marriage between Henry VIII and Anne of Cleves. The King's disgust at the marriage and persistent intrigue by Cromwell's conservative enemies were the causes of his undoing; for though Cromwell had only recently been created Earl of Essex (17 Apr. 1540) and was the recipient of landed estates confiscated from the monasteries, he was arrested, sentenced for treason, and beheaded on 28 July 1540.

R. B. Merriman, *Life and Letters of Thomas Cromwell* (2 vols., Oxford, 1902). *Letters to Cromwell and others on the Suppression of the Monasteries*, ed. G. H. Cook (1965). A. G. Dickens, *Thomas Cromwell and the English Reformation* (1959). G. R. Elton, *The Tudor Revolution in Government: Administrative Changes in the Reign of Henry VIII* (Cambridge, 1953); id., *Policy and Police: The Enforcement of the Reformation in the Age of Thomas Cromwell* (ibid., 1972); id., *Reform and Renewal: Thomas Cromwell and the Common Weal* (ibid., 1973); id., *Reform and Reformation: England 1509–1558* (1977), pp. 126–295; A. Fox and J. Guy, *Reassessing the Henrician Age: Humanism, Politics and Reform 1500–1550* (Oxford, 1986), pp. 151–220. G. Redworth, *In Defence of the Church Catholic: The Life of Stephen Gardiner* (Oxford, 1990), pp. 105–29 ('The Fall of Thomas Cromwell'). See also works cited under HENRY VIII.

crosier. The bishop's staff, sometimes carried also by abbots and abbesses. It is now normally crook-shaped, but in earlier times was often in the shape of the letter T. Its origin has been traced by some to the rod used by Roman augurs in their divination, by others to the ordinary walking-stick. It is mentioned in Spanish documents of the 7th cent. as a symbol of the bishop's jurisdiction. In the E. Church the crosier is surmounted by a cross between two serpents. The familiar W. form resembling a shepherd's crook is due to later symbolism. In the 19th cent. antiquaries often applied the term wrongly to the archiepiscopal cross.

C. Rohault de Fleury, *La Messe: Études archéologiques sur ses monuments*, 8 (1889), pp. 75–110, with plates DCXLI–DCLIII. P. Hofmeister, OSB, *Mitra und Stab der wirklichen Prälaten ohne bischöflichen Charakter* (Kirchenrechtliche Abhandlungen, Heft 104; 1928), *passim*. P. Salmon, 'Aux origines de la crosse des évêques', in *Mélanges en l'honneur de Monseigneur Michel Andrieu* (*Rev. S.R.*, volume hors série; 1956), pp. 373–83. H. *Leclercq, OSB, and L. Gougaud, OSB, in *DACL* 3 (pt. 2; 1914), cols. 3144–59, s.v. 'Crosse'; R. Berger in *L.Th.K.* (3rd edn.), 2 (1994), cols. 501 f., s.v. 'Bischofsstab', both with bibl. On the Eng. word 'Crosier', cf. *OED* (2nd edn.), 4 (1989), p. 46, s.v.

Cross, Devotion to the. See EXALTATION OF THE CROSS; INVENTION OF THE CROSS; VENERATION OF THE CROSS.

Crowland Abbey. This monastery was founded on an island in the Fens by King Ethelbald in 716 in honour of St *Guthlac, who had lived as a hermit on the site. After a fire in 1091 it was rebuilt, and added to in the succeeding centuries. At the *Dissolution (1539), the E. part of the church and the transepts were demolished, but the nave and aisles were used as a parish church until the end of the 17th cent. Then the roof and S. aisle fell, and since that date the N. aisle only has been so used. The Early English W. front survives in a ruined state. The form 'Croyland Abbey' is also found.

The earliest account of the history of Crowland Abbey to the late 11th cent. is given by *Orderic Vitalis, *Historia Ecclesiastica*, bk. 4 (ed. with Eng. tr. by M. Chibnall, 2 (Oxford Medieval Texts, 1969), pp. 338–51; see also introd., pp. xxiv–xxix). *Ingulfi Croylandensis Historia* [ed. W. Fulman] (Rerum Anglicarum Scriptorum Veterum, 1 (1684), pp. 1–107); *Historiae Croylandensis Continuatio* (ibid., pp. 451–593). W. *Dugdale, *Monasticon Anglicanum* (ed. J. Caley, H. Ellis, and B. Blandinel, 2, 1819), pp. 90–126. R. Gough, *The History and Antiquities of Croyland Abbey in the County of Lincoln* (1783). F. M. Page, *The Estates of Crowland Abbey* (1934). R. Graham in *VCH*, Lincoln, 2, ed. W. Page (1906), pp. 105–18. H. Dauphin, OSB, in *DHGE* 13 (1956), cols. 1066–71, s.v.

Crown Appointments Commission. Under a convention agreed with the leaders of the main political parties in 1976, when a diocese in the C of E becomes vacant the Crown Appointments Commission submits to the Prime Minister, on whose advice the Sovereign appoints diocesan bishops, the names of two candidates, which may be given in order of preference. The Prime Minister retains the right to recommend to the Sovereign either of these candidates or to ask the Commission for one or more further names. The Commission consists of 12 voting members: the Abps. of *Canterbury and *York, three members elected by and from the House of Clergy and three elected by and from the House of Laity of the General *Synod, and four appointed by and from the *Vacancy-in-See Committee of the vacant diocese. The Abp. of the province in which the vacancy occurs is chairman. In the case of a vacancy in the archbishopric of Canterbury, the chairman is a communicant lay member of the C of E appointed by the Prime Minister; in the case of the archbishopric of York such a lay person is appointed by the Standing Committee of the General Synod. The appointment of the Bp. of Gibraltar in *Europe falls outside the scope of the Commission.

The General Synod's regulations on the composition and powers of the Crown Appointments Commission constitute Standing Order 159.

Crown of Thorns. One of the instruments of Christ's Passion (Jn. 19: 2). Its supposed preservation as a relic is first mentioned in the 5th cent., and in the 6th *Cassiodorus refers to it as one of the glories of the earthly *Jerusalem. It is said to have been moved later to *Constantinople. In 1239 the Constantinople relic came into the possession of St *Louis IX, King of France, who built the *Sainte-Chapelle at Paris (completed 1248) to house it. Successive kings of France gave individual thorns to churches in various countries.

F. de Mély, *Exuviae Sacrae Constantinopolitanae* (Paris, 1904), pp. 165–440. J. E. A. Gosselin, *Notice historique sur la sainte couronne d'épines de Notre-Seigneur Jésus-Christ, et sur les autres instruments de sa passion, qui se conservent dans l'église métropolitaine de Paris* (1828); C. Rohault de Fleury, *Mémoire sur les instruments de la passion de N.-S. J.-C.* (1870), bk. 2, ch. 3, pp. 199–224. H. St J. Hart, 'The Crown of Thorns in John 19, 2–5', *JTS* NS 3 (1952), pp. 66–75. J. Kopeć and A. Rayez, SJ, in *Dict. Sp.* 7 (pt. 2; 1971), cols. 1825 f., s.v. 'Instruments de la Passion', 3: 'La Couronne d'Épines'.

Crowther, Samuel Adjai (or Ajayi) (*c.*1809–91), African bishop. As a boy of about 13, Ajayi, who was a member of the Egba section of the Yoruba people (now

W. *Nigeria), was captured in a Fulani attack and sold as a slave. The ship transporting him was arrested and brought to *Sierra Leone, where he came under the care of the *Church Missionary Society in 1822. At baptism he took the name of a CMS committee member. He was among the first students of the Fourah Bay Institution, served as a teacher in Sierra Leone, and was a CMS representative on the government's Niger Expedition of 1841. After studying at Islington College (the CMS training college in London), he was ordained in 1843 and was one of the foundation members of the CMS Yoruba mission. From 1857 he led the Niger Mission with an all African staff, covering the area from the Upper Niger to the Delta, and from 1864 he was Bishop of Western Africa beyond the Queen's jurisdiction (jurisdiction over White clergy being avoided). In his closing years his authority was bypassed, his staff superseded, and the African Niger mission effectively dismantled by European missionaries.

Crowther was the first African Anglican bishop, the exemplar of the younger H. *Venn's indigenous Church policy, and the victim of a more ethnocentric missionary approach in the imperial period. He was also the principal influence on the orthography of and translation into Yoruba, introducing the marking of tone, and he encouraged vernacular translation by his clergy. He conducted what was perhaps the first positive Christian dialogue with African Muslims.

Journals of the Rev. James Frederick Schön and Mr. Samuel Crowther, who . . . accompanied the Expedition up the Niger in 1841 (1842; repr., with introd. by J. F. A. Ajayi, Missionary Researches and Travels, 18; 1970), pp. 257–385; Crowther's *Journal of an Expedition up the Niger and Tshadda Rivers . . . in 1854* (1855; also repr. with introd. by J. F. A. Ajayi, ibid. 15; 1970); his journal of the Niger Expedition of 1857–9, *The Gospel on the Banks of the Niger* (1859; repr., Colonial History Series, 1968), pp. 1–239. J. Page, *The Black Bishop: Samuel Adjai Crowther* (London, 1908). P. R. McKenzie, *Inter-religious Encounters in West Africa: Samuel Ajayi Crowther's Attitude to African Traditional Religion and Islam* (Leicester Studies in Religion, 1 [1976]). G. O. M. Tasie, *Christian Missionary Enterprise in the Niger Delta 1864–1918* (Studies on Religion in Africa, 3; Leiden, 1978), esp. pp. 30–137. T. E. Yates, *Venn and Victorian Bishops Abroad* (Studia Missionalia Upsaliensia, 33; Uppsala and London, 1978), esp. pp. 114–17, 134–6, and 140–63. See also works cited under NIGERIA.

crozier. See CROSIER.

crucifix. A model of the cross, bearing an image of the crucified Lord. Crucifixes are widely used as objects of private and public devotion in the W. In the E. their place is taken by crosses with flat likenesses, i.e. a form of *icon. In pre-Reformation times the crucifix was common throughout the W. Church, esp. as the central object of the rood-screen, which ran across the entrance to the *chancel of many churches. As the central ornament of the altar it began to come into general use in the 13th cent., though it had occasionally been so used earlier. This use was until recently almost universal in RC churches. Since 1969 it has sometimes been replaced by a crucifix hung above the altar or on the wall behind it, or even by a processional cross in the vicinity. In the C of E a crucifix was occasionally used on the altar after the Reformation, e.g. in Queen *Elizabeth I's private chapel, but instances are very rare until the liturgical revival in the 19th cent.

Among Protestants, the sole body which habitually uses the crucifix is the *Lutheran Church.

L. Bréhier, *Les Origines du crucifix dans l'art religieux* (1904); E. Sandberg-Vavalà, *La Croce dipinta italiana e l'iconografia della Passione* (Verona [1929]); L. H. Grondijs, *L'Iconographie byzantine du Crucifié mort sur la croix* (Bibliotheca Bruxellensis, 1 [1941]; 2nd edn. [1947]); J. E. Hunt, *English and Welsh Crucifixes 670-1550* (1956); P. Thoby, *Le Crucifix des Origines au Concile de Trent: Etude iconographique* (Nantes, 1959, with suppl., 1963); E. [J.] Hürkey, *Das Bild des Gekreuzigten im Mittelalter* (Worms, 1983); B. C. Raw, *Anglo-Saxon Crucifixion Iconography and the Art of the Monastic Revival* (Cambridge, 1990). Braun, *AG*, pp. 466–92, with plates 88–92. G. Schiller, *Ikonographie der christlichen Kunst*, 2 [1968], pp. 98–176; Eng. tr., 2 (1972), pp. 88–164. R. Scheider Berrenberg, *Kreuz, Kruzifix: Eine Bibliographie* (Munich, 1973). O. *Marucchi, F. *Cabrol, OSB, and H. Thurston, SJ, in *CE* 4 (1908), pp. 517–39, s.v. 'Cross and Crucifix'; H. *Leclercq, OSB, in *DACL* 3 (pt. 2; 1914), cols. 3045–131, s.v. 'Croix et crucifix'.

crucifixion. Infliction of death by nailing or binding to a cross. It arose in the E., and was also frequently used by the Carthaginians. By the Romans it was much used as the extreme punishment for slaves, but it might also be inflicted upon any person who could not prove Roman citizenship. It was preceded by scourging. From the reign of Galba (AD 68–9) the lower orders among Roman citizens might also suffer this penalty. *Constantine abolished crucifixion as a legal punishment, but isolated instances are recorded later in the 4th cent. Some of the Christian martyrs under the Roman Empire suffered in this way; and (acc. to tradition) some, as St *Peter, were crucified head downwards or, as St *Andrew, on an X-shaped cross.

The crucifixion of Jesus Christ between two thieves is recorded by all four Evangelists (Mt. 27: 35–8, Mk. 15: 24–7, Lk. 23: 33, Jn. 19: 18). He was offered and tasted, but declined to drink, the potion of medicated wine provided by a group of charitable women in Jerusalem for such sufferers. The Ep. of *Barnabas, which compares the cross with the letter T, implies that the Lord's Cross was of the shape known as a 'crux commissa'. But the more general view, held e.g. by St *Augustine (*Enn. in Ps.* 103. 14) on the basis of Eph. 3: 18, was that it was a 'crux immissa', with the upright extending above the transom.

M. Hengel, 'Mors turpissima Crucis', in *Rechtfertigung: Festschrift für Ernst Käsemann*, ed. J. Friedrich and others (1976), pp. 125–84; enlarged Eng. tr., *Crucifixion* (1977), repr. in id., *The Cross of the Son of God* (1986), pp. 91–185. D. Smith in *DCG* 1 (1917), pp. 397–9, s.v.; H.-W. Kuhn in *TRE* 19 (1990), pp. 713–25, s.v. 'Kreuz II'.

Cruden, Alexander (1701–70), compiler of the 'Biblical Concordance'. Born in Aberdeen, he was educated on strict *Presbyterian principles, taking his degree from Marischal College, c.1720. His subsequent life was marked by eccentricities bordering on insanity, apparently caused by disappointments in love; and he was several times put in confinement. Moving to London c.1726, he was employed successively as a private tutor, a proof-corrector, and French reader to the Earl of Derby. On dismissal from this last post, he established a bookshop in London in 1732 and was appointed bookseller to Queen Caroline in 1735. In 1736 he began to compile his Concordance (OT and NT), a task for which he was pre-eminently qualified by

long study of the Scriptures, an ingrained conscientiousness, and esp. a habit of tracing words through the Bible for amusement. He completed the work in some 18 months and presented a copy to Queen Caroline in Nov. 1737. Later editions of this work remain the standard concordance for users of the AV. In later life Cruden set himself to reform the morals of the country. Calling himself 'Alexander the Corrector', a title prob. suggested by his work for the press, he even made application to Parliament (1755) for official nomination to the office. He published two further editions of the Concordance (1761 and 1769), as well as religious pamphlets.

E. Olivier, *The Eccentric Life of Alexander Cruden* (1934). The earliest Life is that by A. Chalmers (8 pp.) prefixed to the 6th edn. of the Concordance (1810). W. D. Macray in *DNB* 13 (1888), pp. 249–51.

cruets. Vessels of glass or precious metal in which the wine and water for the *Eucharist are brought to the altar.

Braun, *CA*, pp. 414–40, with illustrations, plates 80–6.

Crusades. The primary use of the term is to describe the series of expeditions from W. Europe to the E. Mediterranean, beginning in 1095, designed to recover the *Holy Land from Islam and then to retain it in Christian hands, and later to counteract the expanding power of the Ottoman Empire. The word itself was slow to evolve, the expeditions often being known at first as '*pilgrimages'; terms such as *crux* and *croiserie* were introduced c. the middle of the 13th cent., doubtless derived from the cross worn on the clothing of Crusaders and pilgrims to the Holy Land.

Many forces, ideological and social, combined to produce the Crusades. The long tradition of pilgrimages to the Holy Land was strengthened at this time by the growing devotion to the Lord's historical life, and hence to the places where He had lived. The W. Church had progressively abandoned the original Christian hostility to *war, and had come to a *rapprochement* with the military aristocracy. Crusaders were encouraged by the grant of *indulgences and by the status of *martyr in the event of death. At the same time, the prospect of acquiring land in the E., and the pressure of an expanding population, helped to persuade both the nobility and the peasantry to participate in the movement. However, the actual form and date of the First Crusade can be explained by the collapse of the E. frontier of the Byzantine Empire in the face of attack by the Seljuk Turks after the Battle of Manzikert in 1071, and the political consequences which arose from this in E. and W. Europe. The Crusades took the form of a series of expeditions among which the largest are numbered in a conventional order. The Crusades developed a characteristic pattern of devotion, but the participants on occasions behaved with extreme brutality, both towards the Jews at home and the subjected people in the East.

The history of the Crusades may be roughly divided into three periods.

(1) 1095–1204. The *First Crusade* was solemnly proclaimed by Pope *Urban II at the Council of *Clermont on 27 Nov. 1095, with the double object of relieving the pressure of the Seljuk Turks on the E. Empire and of

freeing the church of *Jerusalem from Muslim control. Several armies proceeded from France and S. Italy across the Balkans and Asia Minor, under the leadership of *Adhémar, Bp. of Le Puy, Raymond of Toulouse, *Godfrey of Bouillon, Robert of Normandy, and *Bohemond and Tancred of Apulia. Antioch was captured in June 1098, and Jerusalem on 15 July 1099. Godfrey was appointed as the first Latin ruler of Jerusalem, and on his death his brother Baldwin succeeded him and was crowned King of Jerusalem on Christmas Day 1100. The following 20 years were occupied in extending the precarious hold of the conquerors and in establishing a series of Latin states (Antioch, Tripoli, and Jerusalem) extending along the whole coast-line of Syria and Palestine, with a fourth, *Edessa, to the east of Antioch.

In face of steady resurgence of Muslim power, the new states proved difficult to defend. The *Second Crusade* of 1147, provoked by the fall of Edessa (1144), was preached by St *Bernard of Clairvaux and led by Louis VII of France and Conrad III, King of the Romans. It failed to relieve the situation in the Frankish East, and in 1187 Saladin wholly overcame the army of the Kingdom of Jerusalem, captured the city and overran a great part of the Latin possessions. This disaster provoked the *Third Crusade* of 1189–1192, in which the Emp. *Frederick Barbarossa, Richard I of England, and Philip II of France all took part. Considerable territory along the coast was recovered, but Jerusalem itself remained in the hands of Saladin. In 1202 the *Fourth Crusade* set out in an attempt to improve the situation, but under the influence of Boniface of Montferrat and the Venetians it was deflected from its original objective of Egypt to Constantinople, where a Latin Empire was established in 1204. Although this achieved a temporary reunion of the E. and W. Churches under the authority of *Innocent III, its long-term effect was to increase the bitterness of the division, and further to weaken the E. Empire as a defence against Muslim expansion.

(2) 1204–91. Attempts continued in the 13th cent. to defend the remaining Frankish possessions in Syria. Several expeditions went to the Holy Land, and Jerusalem was recovered through negotiation by *Frederick II and was once again in Latin hands from 1229 to 1244. The two largest Crusades (the international one of 1217–21 and the French one under *Louis IX) were directed against Egypt, but both failed after a promising beginning. The Latin states were slowly overrun, and in 1291 the last remaining possessions on the mainland fell. Public opinion in the W. was becoming critical of Papal conduct of Crusading, partly because the concept had been extended to cover expeditions against non-Christians in Europe (such as the Muslims of Spain or the pagan Slavs), against heretics (as in the Crusade against the *Albigensians) or against the political enemies of the Papacy (such as the Hohenstaufen in 13th-cent. Italy). At the same time attempts were made, esp. by the friars, to spread the Gospel by preaching. The establishment of Mongol rule over a great part of Asia presented a threat to E. Europe, but at the same time offered the prospect of trade, of contact with the '*Church of the East' throughout central Asia, and of bringing the Gospel to nations previously unknown.

(3) AFTER 1291. The final loss of the Latin states made it unlikely that Jerusalem would ever be recovered for Christendom, but W. powers continued to discuss plans for its reconquest, and the expansion of Ottoman power into E. Europe in the 14th cent. provoked a long series of attempts to organize expeditions against it. Major expeditions to the Balkans were defeated by the Turks at Nicopolis in 1396 and at Varna in 1444. Christian resistance to the Turks continued, clearly in the Crusading tradition, long after the fall of Constantinople in 1453. Crusading ideas helped to shape the Portuguese and Spanish oceanic expansion in the early 16th cent., and the history of the Crusades was thus interwoven with early colonialism. Islamic critics count the Crusades (along with colonialism and the foundation of the State of Israel) among the historical injustices which the West has perpetrated against Islam. In the W. world in the 19th and 20th cents. the titles 'Crusade' and 'Crusader' have been used for a variety of enterprises, usually in a favourable sense.

See also CHILDREN'S CRUSADE, HOSPITALLERS, TEMPLARS, WAR, CHRISTIAN ATTITUDE TO.

The standard collection is *Recueil des historiens des croisades publié par les soins de l'Académie Royale des Inscriptions et Belles-Lettres: Historiens occidentaux* (5 vols. bound in 6, 1844–89); *Historiens grecs* (2 vols., 1875–81); *Documents arméniens* (2 vols., 1869–1906); *Historiens orientaux* (5 vols. bound in 6, 1872–1906); *Lois* (2 vols., 1841–3). Only a few texts have been re-edited, but there are numerous Eng. trs., incl. L. and J. Riley-Smith, *The Crusades: Idea and Reality, 1095–1274* (Documents of Medieval History, 4; 1981); also J. A. Brundage, *The Crusades: A Documentary Survey* (Milwaukee, 1962) and A. C. Krey, *The First Crusade* (Princeton, NJ, and London, 1921). General histories of the movement include S. Runciman, *A History of the Crusades* (3 vols., 1951–4); K. M. Setton (ed.), *A History of the Crusades* (vols. 1–2, Philadelphia, 1955–62; 2nd edn. of vols. 1 and 2, and vols. 3–6, Madison, Wis., 1969–89), with extensive bibl.; H. E. Mayer, *Geschichte der Kreuzzüge* (1965, and later edns.; Eng. tr. of 2nd edn., Oxford, 1972; rev. Eng. tr., 1988); and J. Riley-Smith, *The Crusades: A Short History* (1987). On Frankish Syria there is J. L. La Monte, *Feudal Monarchy in the Latin Kingdom of Jerusalem 1100 to 1291* (Cambridge, Mass., 1932); J. Richard, *Le Royaume latin de Jérusalem* (1953; Eng. tr., 2 vols., Amsterdam etc., 1979); M. Benvenisti, *The Crusaders in the Holy Land* (Jerusalem, 1970); J. Prawer, *The Latin Kingdom of Jerusalem* (1972); and id., *Crusader Institutions* (Oxford, 1980). The military problems are analysed in R. C. Smail, *Crusading Warfare (1097–1193)* (Cambridge, 1956) and C. Marshall, *Warfare in the Latin East, 1192–1291* (ibid., 1992). For Crusading ideology, see C. Erdmann, *Die Entstehung des Kreuzzugsgedankens* (Forschungen zur Kirchen- und Geistesgeschichte, 6; 1935; Eng. tr., Princeton, NJ, 1977); J. Riley-Smith, *What were the Crusades?* (1977); É. [E. H.] Delaruelle, *L'idée de croisade au moyen âge* (Turin, 1980); and the controversial P. Alphandéry and A. Dupront, *La Chrétienté et l'idée de croisade* (2 vols., 1954–9). The legal aspects of the movement are discussed in J. A. Brundage, *Medieval Canon Law and the Crusader* (Madison, Wis., and London, 1969). The reasons for the collapse of the defence of Latin Syria are discussed by P. A. Throop, *Criticism of the Crusade: A Study of Public Opinion and Crusade Propaganda* (Amsterdam, 1940), and E. Siberry, *Criticism of Crusading 1095–1274* (Oxford, 1985). On the thinking behind the 'diversion' of the Crusaders from the Holy Land, see E. Christiansen, *The Northern Crusades: The Baltic and the Catholic Frontier 1100–1525* (1980), and N. Housley, *The Italian Crusades: The Papal-Angevin Alliance and the Crusades against Christian Lay Powers, 1254–1343* (Oxford, 1982); see also bibl. to ALBIGENSIANS. The continuation of the Crusades after 1300 is examined in J. Muldoon, *Popes, Lawyers and Infidels: The Church and the Non-Christian World 1250–1550* (Liverpool [1979]), N. Housley, *The Later Crusades, 1270–1580* (Oxford, 1992), and C. Tyerman, *England and the Crusades 1095–1588* (Chicago and London, 1988).

Many of these works contain bibls., but full details can be found in H. E. Mayer, *Bibliographie zur Geschichte der Kreuzzüge* (Hannover, 1960; 2nd edn., 1965).

Crusius, Christian August (1715–75), German theologian. He became professor of philosophy at Leipzig in 1744, and of theology in 1750. He attacked the philosophies of G. W. *Leibniz and C. *Wolff as anti-Christian, and urged that their determinist doctrines were dangerous to morality. He also objected strongly to the view, which first became common in his time, that the Books of the Bible should be studied on the same principles of criticism as other literature. His chief writings were his *Entwurf der notwendigen Vernunftwahrheiten* (1745) and his *Hypomnemata ad theologiam propheticam* (3 vols., 1764–68). He was held in high regard by I. *Kant, whose ethical doctrines he probably influenced.

A. Marquardt, *Kant und Crusius* (Diss., Kiel, 1885); A. Seitz, *Die Willensfreiheit in der Philosophie des C. A. Crusius* (1899); M. Benden, *Christian August Crusius: Wille und Verstand als Prinzipien des Handelns* (Abhandlungen zur Philosophie, Psychologie und Pädagogik, 73; Bonn, 1972). G. Röwenstrunk in *TRE* 8 (1981), pp. 242–4.

crutched friars (fratres cruciferi). A general name given to several religious congregations, mostly of *canons regular, whose history is very obscure; they derive their name from their custom of carrying a cross in their hands or having one sewn on the front of their habit. The oldest body of crutched friars may be that founded in the Holy Land from Crusading times, of which practically nothing is known. Another order in Italy secured Papal confirmation in 1187, having been founded a little earlier; it was suppressed in 1650. A congregation of crutched brethren from Bohemia and Poland was established as a military order in 1234 at Prague. More permanent was the community founded in Flanders *c.*1210 by Theodore of Celles (d. 1236), which secured Papal confirmation in 1248. It had daughter houses not only in modern Belgium and the Netherlands, but also in France, Germany, and England. Most of its houses were suppressed at the time of the French Revolution or Napoleon, but a revival took place. The order now has houses in the Netherlands, Belgium, the United States of America, Brazil, Germany, and Austria, as well as an international college in Rome and a number of mission stations.

A. van de Pasch, OSC, *De tekst van de constituties der Kruisheren van 1248* (Brussels, 1952). C. R. Hermans, *Annales Canonicorum Regularum S. Augustini, Ordinis S. Crucis* (3 vols., 's Hertogenbosch, 1858). H. van Rooijen, *Theodorus van Celles* (Cuyk, 1936); id., *De Oorsprong van de Orde der Kruisbroeders of Kruisheren* (Drest, 1961). H. F. Chettle, 'The Friars of the Holy Cross in England', *History*, NS 34 (1949), pp. 204–20. D. M. *Knowles and R. N. Hadcock, *Medieval Religious Houses: England and Wales* (1953), pp. 204–5. H. Vinken in *DHGE* 13 (1956), cols. 1042–62, s.v. 'Croisiers'; J. W. Rausch in *NCE* 4 (1967), pp. 472 f., s.v. 'Crosier Fathers'; H. L. M. van Rooijen in *DIP* 3 (1976), cols. 303 f., s.v. 'Crocigeri', and cols. 304–11, s.v. 'Crocigeri belge', with extensive bibl.

crypt. A chamber or vault beneath a church, either partly or wholly below ground, often used as a chapel or a burying-place. These functions date from the earliest ages of the Church, when Christian services sometimes took place in the *catacombs or underground burying-places in Rome, the tombs of martyrs often serving as altars, and later as centres of pilgrimage. Anglo-Saxon crypts, such as those at *Hexham and *Ripon, were often modelled on the *confessio* of *St Peter's, Rome.

A. Grabar, *Martyrium: Recherches sur le culte des reliques et l'art chrétien antique*, 1 (1946), pp. 436–87. H. M. Taylor, 'Corridor Crypts on the Continent and in England', *North Staffordshire Journal of Field Studies*, 9 (1969), pp. 17–52.

Crypto-Calvinism. A term used by the *Gnesio-Lutherans to denigrate the teachings, esp. the Eucharistic teachings, of P. *Melanchthon. In the interests of conciliation with the *Calvinists, Melanchthon softened M. *Luther's dogmatism on the *Real Presence and unworthy reception of the Sacrament ('manducatio impiorum'), and was in consequence attacked by *Flacius Illyricus and his party. The resulting *Adiaphorist Controversy introduced those endless disputes among Lutherans which were to be a major cause of their political weakness in the next generation.

H. Junghans in *TRE* 20 (1990), pp. 123–9, s.v. 'Kryptocalvinisten', with bibl.; G. Hintzen in *L.Th.K.* (3rd edn.), 6 (1997), cols. 496 f., s.v. 'Kryptocalvinismus'.

Cudworth, Ralph (1617–88), *Cambridge Platonist. Born at Aller in Somerset, where his father was rector, he became successively Fellow of Emmanuel College, Cambridge (1639), Master of Clare Hall (to which he was appointed by the Parliamentary visitors, 1645), Regius Professor of Hebrew (also 1645), and Master of Christ's College (1654). In addition he held the livings of North Cadbury from 1650, of Ashwell from 1662, and a prebendal stall at *Gloucester from 1678. Perhaps the most distinguished representative of the Cambridge Platonists, he was an opponent both of religious dogmatism and of atheism of the T. *Hobbes type. In his chief work, *The True Intellectual System of the Universe* (1678), a cumbrous composition which he never completed, he argued that the only real source of knowledge is the Christian religion. Religious truth was embodied in three great principles: the reality of the supreme Divine intelligence and the spiritual world which that intelligence has created, the eternal reality of moral ideas, and the reality of moral freedom and responsibility. It was in this way that Cudworth, who, as his conception of a 'Plastic Medium' indicates, was very strongly influenced by Platonic ideas, attempted to assert the necessity for a revealed religion against the atheism of his day. His ethical beliefs were worked out in his *Treatise concerning Eternal and Immutable Morality* (not published till 1731).

Cudworth's *True Intellectual System of the Universe* was tr. into Lat. by J. L. *Mosheim (2 vols., Jena, 1733); partly from this Lat. tr. the Eng. was ed. by T. Birch, along with Cudworth's *Discourse concerning the true Notion of the Lord's Supper* (orig. pub. 1642) and two Sermons, as *The Works of Ralph Cudworth* (4 vols., Oxford, 1829), with account of his life and writings in vol. 1, pp. 7–37. J. A. Passmore, *Ralph Cudworth: An Interpretation* (Cambridge, 1951). G. Aspelin, *Ralph Cudworth's Interpretation of Greek Philosophy* (Göteborgs Högskolas Årsskrift, 49, pt. 1; 1943); L. Gysi, *Platonism and Cartesianism in the Philosophy of Ralph Cudworth* (Berne, 1962); id. (now 'Mother Maria'), *Ralph Cudworth: Mystical Thinker* (Newport Pagnell [1973; brief]). F. J.

Powicke, *The Cambridge Platonists* (1926), pp. 110–29. L. Stephen in *DNB* 13 (1888), pp. 271 f.

cuius regio, eius religio (Lat., 'In a [prince's] country, the [prince's] religion'). The formula adopted at the Religious Peace of *Augsburg (1555), by which the princes of the Empire were to be permitted to settle whether the religion of their own lands should be RC or Lutheran.

Culdees. The name *céle Dé*, 'companion of God', was used in the 8th and 9th cents. of Irish religious who sought a life of stricter devotion in certain churches. The movement is particularly associated with Tallaght, Co. Dublin, in the time of its abbot St Máel Rúain (d. 792). Later the word was used of the clergy forming the permanent establishment at certain churches in Ireland and Scotland until, during the 12th cent. and later, they were replaced by *canons regular, as at *Armagh and St Andrews. The name, Latinized as *Keledeus*, in this period came to be derived from *colo*, 'I worship'; the English form goes back to Hector Boece (1526), 'Culdei, i.e. cultores Dei'. By this date it was used in a debased sense, esp. in Scotland, to mean any religious of Celtic observance in the loosest sense; during the 18th and 19th cents. it was used more narrowly of the religious of *Iona.

W. Reeves, *The Culdees of the British Isles, as they appear in History* (Dublin, 1864), repr. (apart from the preface and index) in *The Transactions of the Royal Irish Academy*, Antiquities, 24 (1873), pp. 119–263. A 12th-cent. Litany of the Culdees in use at Dunkeld is pr. in A. W. Haddan and W. *Stubbs (eds.), *Councils and Ecclesiastical Documents Relating to Great Britain and Ireland*, 2 (pt. 1; 1873), pp. 278–85. E. J. Gwynn and W. J. Purton, 'The monastery of Tallaght', *Proceedings of the Royal Irish Academy*, 29 (1911), pp. 115–79; E. [J.] Gwynn (ed.), *The Rule of Tallaght* (*Hermathena*, Suppl. 2 to no. 40; 1927). G. W. S. Barrow, 'The Cathedral Chapter at St Andrews and the Culdees in the Twelfth and Thirteenth Centuries', *JEH* 3 (1952), pp. 23–39; repr. in id., *The Kingdom of the Scots* (1973), pp. 212–32. P. O'Dwyer, O. Carm., *Céli Dé: Spiritual reform in Ireland 750–900* (Dublin, 1977; 2nd edn., 1981). J. F. Kenney, *The Sources for the Early History of Ireland*, 1 (Records of Civilization, Sources and Studies, New York, 1929), esp. pp. 468–77. C. McGrath in *NCE* 4 (1967), pp. 520 f., s.v., with bibl.

Cullmann, Oscar (1902–), NT scholar and theologian. Born at Strasbourg, he studied at the universities of Strasbourg and *Paris, and in 1930 he became professor in the former. In 1938 he became professor at Basle and from 1948 to 1972 he was simultaneously also professor in the Protestant faculty of the University of Paris. Cullmann's work lay in the area of *Biblical Theology, and he was specially concerned in developing a theory of *Heilsgeschichte*. This was expounded in *Christus und die Zeit* (1946; Eng. tr., *Christ and Time*, 1951). According to Cullmann, what is most distinctive in the NT is its view of time and history. Running through the whole course of world history there has been a relatively narrow stream of sacred history. This sacred history, the midpoint of which was Jesus Christ, provides the clue to the understanding of general history, which is seen to be linear in form and to run from creation to consummation. Cullmann stressed the objectivity of this sacred history as against the existential interpretation favoured by R. *Bultmann. In *Heil als Geschichte* (1965; Eng. tr., *Salvation in History*, 1967) Cullmann restated his views and tried to meet some of the

objections to his earlier work. Another important contribution to Biblical Theology was *Die Christologie des Neuen Testaments* (1957; Eng. tr., 1959). His *ecumenical interests were demonstrated in his important study on the place of St *Peter in the primitive Church, *Petrus: Jünger, Apostel, Märtyrer* (1952; Eng. tr., 1953). He was invited to be an observer at the Second *Vatican Council and has been active in developing relations between Protestants and RCs on the Continent of Europe.

J. Frisque, *Oscar Cullmann: Une théologie de l'histoire du salut* (Cahiers de l'actualité religieuse, 11; 1960), with bibl., incl. list of his works, pp. 263–76. Festschriften for Cullmann's 60th birthday, *Neotestamentica et Patristica* (Supplements to *Novum Testamentum*, 6; 1962), repr. list of his works, brought up to date by W. Rordorf, pp. ix–xix; for his 65th birthday, *Oikonomia: Heilsgeschichte als Thema der Theologie*, ed. F. Christ (Hamburg, 1967); and for his 70th birthday, *Neues Testament und Geschichte*, ed. H. Baltensweiler and B. Reiche (Zurich and Tübingen, 1972), with bibl. for 1962–71 by H. Heck, pp. 329–44. H.-G. Hermesmann, *Zeit und Heil: Oscar Cullmanns Theologie der Heilsgeschichte* (Konfessionskundliche und kontroverstheologische Studien, 43 [1979]). K.-H. Schlaudraff, 'Heil als Geschichte'? Die Frage nach dem heilsgeschichtlichen Denken, dargestellt anhand der Konzeption Oscar Cullmanns* (Beiträge zur Geschichte der biblischen Exegese, 29 [1988]).

Cum Occasione. The constitution of *Innocent X, dated 31 May 1653, condemning five propositions which embodied the dogmatic substance of *Jansenism.

Text in *Bullarum, Diplomatum et Privilegiorum Sanctorum Romanorum Pontificum Taurinensis Editio*, 15 (Turin, 1868), pp. 720 f. The condemned propositions repr. in Denzinger and Hünermann (37th edn., 1991), pp. 614 f. (nos. 2001–7).

Cumberland, Richard (1632–1718), Bp. of *Peterborough and moral philosopher. Having turned from the study of medicine and anatomy to that of theology, he became Vicar of Brampton (Northants) in 1658, and of All Hallows, Stamford, *c*.1667. In 1691, though little known as an ecclesiastic, he was appointed to the see of Peterborough, which he administered faithfully, though without special distinction, for the rest of his life. His principal work, *De legibus naturae disquisitio philosophica* (1672), which, through being commended by S. *Pufendorf, established Cumberland's reputation abroad, was designed as a reply to T. *Hobbes. In it Cumberland maintained that the laws of nature are ethical and immutable, and that their root-principle was that of 'Universal Benevolence' (which he opposed deliberately to the 'Egoism' of Hobbes). He was the real founder of English *Utilitarianism.

S. Payne, *A Brief Account of the Life, Character and Writings of . . . Richard Cumberland* (1720). E. Sharp, 'The Ethical System of Richard Cumberland and its Place in the History of British Ethics', *Mind*, NS 21 (1912), pp. 371–98. L. Kirk, *Richard Cumberland and Natural Law: Secularisation of Thought in Seventeenth-Century England* (Cambridge, 1987). L. Stephen in *DNB* 13 (1888) pp. 289 f.

cuneiform (Lat. *cuneus*, 'wedge'). The characters of wedge-shaped or arrow-headed components in which the ancient Akkadian, Persian, and other inscriptions were written. It was probably invented by the Sumerians, who developed it out of what was originally a pictorial form of writing, and was widely used throughout the ancient Near East.

The name is said to have been first used by Thomas Hyde, Regius Professor of Hebrew at Oxford (d. 1703). For sign lists see R. Labat, *Manuel d'épigraphie akkadienne: Signes, syllabaire, idéogrammes* (1948; rev. edn. by F. Malbran-Labat, 1976); M. Dietrich and O. Loretz, *Die Keilalphabete* (Abhandlungen zur Literatur Alt-Syrien-Pälestinas, 1; Münster, 1988). G. R. *Driver, *Semitic Writing: From Pictograph to Alphabet* (Schweich Lectures for 1944; 1948; 3rd edn. by S. A. Hopkins, 1976), pp. 1–77; C. B. F. Walker, *Cuneiform* [1987], repr. in J. T. Hooker and others, *Reading the Past: Ancient Writing from Cuneiform to the Alphabet* [1990], pp. 15–73.

curate. Properly, a clergyman who has the care ('cure') of a parish, i.e. in England a *rector, *vicar, or *perpetual curate. Such a clergyman is also known as the 'incumbent'. He is chosen by the 'patron' (the person or body having the right to nominate a clergyman for the parish in question), and is admitted to the cure of souls ('instituted' or 'collated') by the bishop of the diocese. He can be removed only by resignation, exchange of cure, promotion to another benefice involving the cure of souls, or deprivation either as a 'censure' in a conduct case under the *Ecclesiastical Jurisdiction Measure 1963 or automatically following a conviction in the temporal courts for some disgraceful offence.

In general speech, however, the word is now used to denote an assistant or unbeneficed clergyman, i.e. one appointed to assist the incumbent in the performance of his duties, or to take charge of a parish temporarily during a vacancy or while the incumbent is unable to perform his duties ('curate in charge'). Assistant curates are nominated by the incumbent or the bishop, and licensed by the bishop. The licence may be revoked by the bishop after due notice.

From 1662 to 1688 the episcopalian incumbents of Scottish parishes were styled curates.

A. T. Hart, *The Curate's Lot: The Story of the unbeneficed English Clergy* (1970).

Cur Deus Homo (Lat., 'Why [did] God [become] man?'). The title of St *Anselm's famous treatise on the *Atonement (1097–8), in which he rejected the theory that the death of Christ could be explained in terms of a ransom from the devil and interpreted it in the light of the justice and mercy of God. See SATISFACTION.

Lat. text repr. from edn. of Anselm's works by F. S. Schmitt, OSB, 2 (Edinburgh, 1946), pp. 37–133, with Fr. tr. and full introd. and notes, by R. Roques (SC 91; 1963). There have been various Eng. trs. See also bibl. to ANSELM.

Curé d'Ars, the, St Jean-Baptiste Marie Vianney (1786–1859). He was born at Dardilly, near Lyons, and intended for the priesthood from an early age. His education and training were interrupted by his conscription for the army, from which he deserted, and again considerably lengthened by his inability to learn Latin. After ordination at last in 1815, he was for three years assistant priest at Écully, and then appointed in Feb. 1818 parish priest at Ars. In this remote village he achieved almost worldwide fame. First from the neighbouring parishes, then from all France, finally from other countries too, came men and women, of all sorts and conditions, to seek his counsel. By

1855 the number of his visitors was computed at 20,000 a year, and during his last few years he was forced to spend 16 to 18 hours a day in the confessional. He was beatified in 1905, canonized in 1925, and in 1929 created the patron of parish priests. Feast day, 4 (formerly 9) Aug.

Sermons (4 vols., Lyons, 1883). A. Monnin, SJ, *Le Curé d'Ars: Vie de M. Jean-Baptiste Vianney* (2 vols., 1861; Eng. trs., 1907 and 1924); J. Vianney, *Le Saint Curé d'Ars, 1786–1859* ('Les Saints', 1905; Eng. tr., 1906); F. Trochu, *Le Curé d'Ars: Saint Jean-Marie-Baptiste Vianney (1786–1859) d'après toutes les pièces du procès de canonisation et de nombreux documents inédits* (1925; Eng. tr., 1927); id., *L'Admirable Vie du Curé d'Ars* (1932; Eng. tr., 2 vols., 1934–6). Other Lives by J. Darche (Paris, 1865), H. *Ghéon (ibid., 1928; Eng. tr., 1929), L. C. Sheppard (London, 1958), M. Trouncer (ibid., 1959), D. Pézeril (Paris, 1959; Eng. tr., 1961) and R. Fourrey (ibid., 1981). J. Genet, *L'Énigme des sermons du Curé d'Ars* (1961). B. Nodet in *Dict. Sp.* 8 (1974), cols. 840–4, s.v. 'Jean-Marie Vianney'.

Cureton, William (1808–64), *Syriac scholar. Educated at Christ Church, Oxford, he was ordained in 1831, became a sub-librarian of the *Bodleian Library in 1834, and from 1837 to 1849 was on the staff of the British Museum. There it was Cureton's task to catalogue the Syriac MSS brought back from the *Nitrian monasteries by H. *Tattam. Among his discoveries were the Syriac text of three of St *Ignatius's Epistles (to *Polycarp, to the Eph., and to the Rom.; published 1845), which he argued were the only genuine ones (a position no longer held); the 'Curetonian' *Old Syriac text of the Gospels (published 1858); and the 'Festal Letters' of *Athanasius (published 1848).

His *Ancient Syriac Documents relative to the earliest Establishment of Christianity in Edessa and the neighbouring Countries* was posthumously pub. by W. Wright (1864), with preface, pp. i–ix. S. Lane-Poole in *DNB* 13 (1888), pp. 325 f., s.v.

Curia. The Papal court and its functionaries, esp. those through whom the government of the RC Church is administered. It includes the *Roman Congregations, Tribunals, and Pontifical Councils, and acts with the delegated authority of the Pope. General reforms of its structure and functioning were introduced by Pope *Paul VI in 1967 and then by Pope *John Paul II's Apostolic Constitution 'Pastor Bonus' of 28 June 1988. The current internal Regulations received Papal approval on 4 Feb. 1992. The term is also used in the RC Church of the court of diocesan officials (esp. legal officials) who act on behalf of an individual diocesan bishop. In medieval times the word was commonly used of any court, ecclesiastical or lay. Current RC canon law on the Roman and diocesan Curia is contained in *CIC* (1983), cans. 360–61 and 469–94.

There is an extensive specialized literature. More general modern works include F. M. Cappello, *De Curia Romana iuxta Reformationem a Pio X sapientissime inductam* (2 vols., Rome, 1911–'1912' [1913]); N. del Re, *La Curia Romana: Lineamenti storico-giuridici* (1941; 3rd edn., Sussidi Eruditi, 23; 1970), with bibl.; C. M. Berutti, OP, *De Curia Romana: Notulae historico-exegetico-practicae* (Rome, 1952). K. Jordan, 'Die Entstehung der römischen Kurie', *Zeitschrift der Savigny-Stiftung für Rechtsgeschichte*, 72, Kanon. Abt., 28 (1939), pp. 97–152, with refs. The Apostolic Constitution 'Pastor Bonus' is pr. in *AAS* 80 (1988), pp. 841–934; the Regulations are pr. ibid. 84 (1992), pp. 201–67. B. Ojetti, SJ, in *CE* 13 (1912), pp. 147–54, s.v. 'Roman Curia'; P. Torquebiau in *DDC* 4 (1939), cols. 971–1008, s.v. 'Curie romaine', and on the diocesan synod see id., ibid., cols. 961–71, s.v. 'Curie diocésaine'. See also bibls. to ROMAN CONGREGATIONS (also under the sep. headings) and CARDINAL.

cursive script was the basis of what became a formal book-hand, properly called 'Greek minuscule', which used small, rounded ('lower-case') letters, joined together for speed of writing. Its letter-forms are first found in Egyptian documentary hands of the 7th and 8th cents. AD. At the beginning of the 9th cent. the fully developed minuscule replaced *uncial (except in large volumes for liturgical use) as the only book-hand for copying Greek literary works. The earliest dated example is the Uspensky Gospels (St Petersburg MS 219) of AD 835. It continued in use, with only minor modifications, until the invention of printing.

Cursor Mundi. An early English poem on the history of the world, probably dating from the early 14th cent. It is based on the Bible, but incorporates much that is legendary. The first four books extend from the Creation to the successors of *Solomon, the fifth deals with the early life of Jesus and the BVM, the sixth with Christ's later life and the Apostles, and the seventh with the Last Judgement. It is in a northern dialect and seems to have been written in one of the large northern monasteries, but the author is unknown.

There is an edn. by R. Morris in four parallel columns from different MSS (EETS 57, 59, 62, 66, 68, 99, 101; 1874–93); see also *The Southern Version of Cursor Mundi,* ed. S. M. Horrall and others (Ottawa Medieval Texts and Studies, 5, 13, 14, 16, etc.; 1978 ff.). S. M. Horrall, ' "For the commun at understand". *Cursor Mundi* and its Background', in M. G. Sargent (ed.), *De Cella in Seculum: Religious and Secular Life and Devotion in Late Medieval England. An Interdisciplinary Conference in Celebration of the Eighth Centenary of the Consecration of St Hugh of Avalon . . . 20–22 July, 1986* (Cambridge, 1989), pp. 97–107. A. E. Hartung (ed.), *A Manual of the Writings in Middle English, 1050–1500,* 7 (New Haven, Conn., 1986), pp. 2276–8, with bibl. pp. 2503–7.

Cusanus, Nicolaus. See NICHOLAS OF CUSA.

Customary (also known as a **Consuetudinary** or **Liber Ordinarius**). The book containing (1) the rites and ceremonies for the services, and/or (2) the rules and customs of discipline, of a particular monastery, cathedral, or religious order. In the Middle Ages, when local differences were great, they were of considerable practical use; but the greatly increased standardization of worship and discipline in more recent times, e.g. by the Congregation of *Rites (founded in 1588), led to their disappearance. The medieval customaries are of great value as source-books for the historian and the liturgiologist.

Cuthbert, St (*c.*636–87), Bp. of *Lindisfarne. In 651 Cuthbert became a monk at Melrose. Somewhat later he went with his abbot, Eata, to found a monastery at *Ripon; but when they refused to conform to Roman usages as the sub-king Alhfrith demanded, they were expelled and returned south. Shortly afterwards the Synod of *Whitby (664) pronounced in favour of the Roman Easter and *tonsure, and they conformed. In 664 Cuthbert became Prior of Melrose, where he was a zealous pastor of the surrounding countryside. After some years he felt called

to the solitary life, but Eata appointed him Prior of Lindisfarne; later he was allowed to become a hermit on Farne Island, where many had recourse to his spiritual counsel. In 684 he was reluctantly elected Bp. of *Hexham; but after agreeing to exchange sees with Eata, he was consecrated Bp. of Lindisfarne at Easter 685. After a brief but active episcopate, Cuthbert, aware that he had not long to live, withdrew again as a solitary to Farne, where he died on 20 Mar. 687. He was buried on Lindisfarne. In 698 his body was exhumed, apparently incorrupt, and his cult developed rapidly, with the Lindisfarne Gospels and also three Lives being produced in his honour before 720. In the 9th cent. the Scandinavian threat prompted the Lindisfarne community to take his body to a safer site; in 883 they settled at Chester-le-Street, moving thence to Durham in 995. Important *sanctuary rights developed early around Cuthbert's body, and his cult, surviving both the Scandinavian and Norman conquests, emerged as one of the most important in medieval England. His *pectoral cross, portable altar, coffin-reliquary, and other objects survived the destruction of his shrine in 1539–40, and were recovered when his tomb in Durham Cathedral was opened in 1827. Feast day, 20 Mar.

Life by an anonymous monk of Lindisfarne (written between 699 and 705) and *Bede's prose Life are ed., with Eng. tr., by B. Colgrave, *Two Lives of Saint Cuthbert* (Cambridge, 1940; repr. 1985). Bede's metrical Life ed. W. Jaager (Palaestra, 198; Leipzig, 1935). Further information in Bede's *Ecclesiastical History,* 3. 25 and 4. 26–32 (edns. and comm. listed under Bede). Further Eng. tr. of Bede's prose Life by J. F. Webb, *Lives of the Saints* (Penguin Classics, 1965), pp. 69–129; rev. edn. as *The Age of Bede,* ed. D. H. Farmer (ibid., 1983), pp. 41–102. Various 10th–12th-cent. works on the posthumous miracles and translations of Cuthbert are included in T. Arnold's edn. of *Simeon of Durham's *Opera Omnia* (2 vols., RS, 1882–5). J. Raine, *Saint Cuthbert* (Durham, 1828); C. F. Battiscombe (ed.), *The Relics of Saint Cuthbert* (Oxford, 1956). G. Bonner, D. [W.] Rollason, and C. [E.] Stancliffe (eds.), *St Cuthbert, his Cult and his Community to AD 1200* (Woodbridge, Suffolk, 1989). Useful brief introd. ed. D. W. Rollason, *Cuthbert, Saint and Patron* (Durham, 1987).

Cynewulf (early 9th cent.), Anglo-Saxon poet. His name, spelled out in runic letters, is found in the epilogues of four Anglo-Saxon poems which are therefore certainly his work. They are all religious in content. The second part of *Christ,* the only part by Cynewulf, celebrates the mystery of the Ascension; *Juliana* is the account of the martyrdom of the saint; *Elene,* which many scholars consider his masterpiece, tells the story of the finding of the true Cross by St *Helena, and *The Fates of the Apostles* is a fragment incorporating legends about the apostles after their dispersal. The poems, which are obviously inspired by great devotion to the mysteries of the Christian faith and to the saints, have many passages of great beauty. Besides the authentic four, others have been attributed to Cynewulf, but these assignations are conjectural. Of the author himself nothing is known; he has been identified with Cynewulf, Bp. of *Lindisfarne (d. 783), and also with Cynwulf, an otherwise unknown priest whose signature is appended to the decrees of the Council of *Clovesho (803). The first identification is chronologically impossible; the second incapable of proof. See also DREAM OF THE ROOD.

C. W. Kennedy, *The Poems of Cynewulf translated into English Prose* (1910), with important introd., pp. 1–83, and bibl., pp. 335–

47. Good crit. edns., with full notes, by A. S. Cook of 'The Christ' (Boston, 1900), of 'Elene', with the 'Phoenix' and 'Physiologus' (New Haven, Conn., and London, 1919); by R. Woolf of 'Juliana' (London, 1955); by P. O. E. Gradon of 'Elene' (ibid., 1958); and by K. R. Brooks of 'Andreas' and 'The Fate of the Apostles' (Oxford, 1961). C. Schaar, *Critical Studies in the Cynewulf Group* (Lund Studies in English, 17; 1949), with bibl. K. Sisam, 'Cynewulf and his Poetry', *Proceedings of the British Academy*, 18 (1932), pp. 303–31. D. G. Calder, *Cynewulf* (Boston, 1981). S. B. Greenfield and F. C. Robinson, *A Bibliography of Publications on Old English Literature to the end of 1972* (Toronto and Manchester, 1980), pp. 207–10 (nos. 3368–408).

Cyprian, St (d. 258), Bp. of Carthage. Thascius Caecilianus Cyprianus was a pagan rhetorician converted to Christianity *c*.246. Within two years he was elected Bp. of Carthage, having by that time acquired a profound knowledge of the Scriptures and the writings of *Tertullian. A few months later the *Decian persecution broke out (autumn 249), and he was forced to flee, but continued to rule his Church from exile by letter. He returned in 251. Large numbers of Christians had lapsed from their faith, and many more had become *libellatici*. The confessors, i.e. those who had stood firm, were reconciling the lapsed on easy terms, by virtue of the merits of the martyrs. Cyprian was strongly opposed to their practice and two councils (251, 252) decided that the lapsed should be reconciled after suitable penance and delay. In 252 there occurred an outbreak of the plague in Carthage, which was ascribed to the crimes of the Christians. In spite of their charitable works, organized by Cyprian, hatred of them, and esp. of their leader, increased. Meanwhile the schism of *Novatian, arising out of the question of the lapsed, gave rise to the rebaptism controversy. Cyprian received the support of the African bishops in two councils (255–6) in demanding the rebaptism of schismatics, on the ground that no one outside the Church could administer her sacraments. As the Church at Rome held that both schismatics and heretics could validly administer baptism, there followed a violent correspondence between Cyprian and *Stephen, Bp. of Rome, which has also acquired significance for later controversy concerning the Papal claims. But for the moment the controversy was cut short by the persecution of the Emp. Valerian. Cyprian having been banished, an attempt was made in 258 to arrest him. For the time being he hid himself, in order that he might suffer in his own city; but on the second attempt he gave himself up, and was martyred in Carthage on 14 Sept. 258.

Cyprian's writings, mainly short treatises and letters, enjoyed great popularity from the first. He had none of the brilliance of his predecessor, Tertullian, but his sober judgement and pastoral instincts gained him his hearing. Some of his works are also of theological importance, esp. those dealing with the Church, the ministry, and the Sacraments. They include: (1) *Ad Quirinum* or *Testimonia* (*c*.248), a collection of biblical proof-texts in three books, arranged under subjects; (2) *De Habitu Virginum* (*c*.249), in praise of virginity; (3) *De Lapsis* (*c*.251), dealing with the conditions for reconciling the lapsed; (4) *De Catholicae Ecclesiae Unitate* (251), a treatise held in special esteem, on the nature of true unity in the Church in its relation to the episcopate ('habere non potest Deum patrem qui ecclesiam non habet matrem', cap. 6). Acc. to M. Bévenot, SJ, Cyprian issued this work in two recensions; (5) *De*

Dominica Oratione (*c*.252); and (6) *De Opere et Eleemosynis* (*c*.253), on almsgiving as a means of obtaining grace.

A like importance attaches to his correspondence, some of his letters (e.g. *Ep*. 63, on the Eucharist) being virtually short treatises. The *corpus* consists of 81 items (65 Cyprian's own and 16 replies). Here again the subjects are practical rather than dogmatic, and we gain a clear picture of his ideals as a bishop.

Though slain on 14 Sept., he is commemorated in the BCP calendar on 26 Sept. (by confusion with a converted magician of Antioch venerated on that day; see foll. entry) and in the Roman Missal on 16 Sept. (to avoid *Holy Cross Day and the former *Octave of the *Nativity of the BVM). The proposed 1927–8 revision of the BCP had another date, 13 Sept., adopted in the ASB and elsewhere.

Editio princeps of Cyprian's works by J. Andreas (Rome, 1471). Important later edns. by *Erasmus (Basle, 1520), J. *Fell and J. *Pearson (Oxford, 1682), and S. *Baluze and P. *Maran (Paris, 1726). This last repr. in J. P. Migne, *PL* 4 (unsatisfactory). Crit. edns. by W. Hartel in CSEL (3 vols., 1868–71), and by R. Weber and others (CCSL, 3 3A, etc.; 1972 ff.). Letters also ed., with Fr. tr., by L. Bayard ('Collection des Universités de France', 2 vols., 1925; 2nd edn., 1961); *De Dominica*, ed., with Fr. tr., by M. Réveillaud (Études d'histoire et de philosophie religieuses, 58; 1964); *De Lapsis* and *De Ecclesiae Catholicae Unitate*, ed., with Eng. tr., by M. Bévenot, SJ (Oxford Early Christian Texts, 1971); *Ad Demetrianum*, ed., with Ital. tr., by E. Gallicet (Corona Patrum, 4; 1976); *Ad Donatum* and *De Bono Patientiae*, ed., with Fr. tr., by J. Molager (SC 291; 1982). Eng. tr. by R. E. Wallis in ANCL (2 vols., 1868–9); also of his Letters by G. W. Clarke (ACW 43, 44, 46, and 47 [1984–9]), with useful introds. There survive a contemporary Life (not wholly reliable), acc. to St *Jerome by Cyprian's deacon *Pontius, and the official description of his martyrdom ('Acta Proconsularia'); convenient edn. of the 'Acta', with Eng. tr., by H. Musurillo, *The Acts of the Christian Martyrs* (Oxford, 1972), pp. 168–75. Modern Lives by E. W. *Benson (London, 1897), and P. Hinchliff (ibid., 1974). Also P. Monceaux, *Histoire littéraire de l'Afrique chrétienne*, 2: *Saint Cyprien et son temps* (1902). H. von Soden, *Die Cyprianische Briefsammlung: Geschichte ihrer Entstehung und Überlieferung* (TU 25, Heft 3; 1904). On the variant texts of the *De Catholicae Ecclesiae Unitate*, the fullest study is that of M. Bévenot, SJ, *St Cyprian's De Unitate, chap. 4, in the Light of the Manuscripts* [1939]; id., *The Tradition of Manuscripts: A Study in the Transmission of St Cyprian's Treatises* (Oxford, 1961). A. d'Alès, *La Théologie de S. Cyprien* (1922); H. Koch, *Cathedra Petri: Neue Untersuchungen über die Anfänge der Primatslehre* (Beihefte zur ZNTW, 11; 1930), and other works of this author; B. Poschmann, *Ecclesia Principalis: Ein kritischer Beitrag zur Frage des Primats bei Cyprian* (1933). I. Schrijnen and C. Mohrmann, *Studien zur Syntax der Briefe des heiligen Cyprian* (2 vols., Nijmegen, 1936–7); G. S. M. Walker, *The Churchmanship of St Cyprian* (Ecumenical Studies in History, 9; 1968); M. A. Fahey, SJ, *Cyprian and the Bible* (Beiträge zur Geschichte der Biblischen Hermeneutik, 9; 1971); U. Wickert, *Sacramentum Unitatis: Ein Beitrag zum Verständnis der Kirche bei Cyprian* (Beihefte zur ZNTW, 41; 1971); H. Gülzow, *Cyprian und Novatian: Der Briefwechsel zwischen den Gemeinden in Rom und Karthago zur Zeit der Verfolgung des Kaisers Decius* (Beiträge zur historischen Theologie, 48; 1975); C. Saumagne, *Saint Cyprien, évêque de Carthage, 'Pape' d'Afrique* (Études d'Antiquités Africaines, 1975); S. Deléani, *Christum sequi: Étude d'un thème dans l'œuvre de Saint Cyprien* (1979). Altaner and Stuiber (1978), pp. 172–81 and 582 f. CPL (3rd edn., 1995), pp. 11–20 (nos. 38–67). M. Bévenot, SJ, in *TRE* 8 (1981), pp. 246–54, s.v.

Cyprian, St (*c*.300), a converted magician of *Antioch. Acc. to a prob. worthless legend which apparently influenced the legend of Faust, Cyprian was a pagan magician and astrologer who, when using his arts to ensnare a Christian virgin, Justina, was converted to her faith. Cyprian eventually became a bishop and Justina the head of a convent. In the *Diocletianic Persecution both were apprehended, brought to the Imperial residence at Nicomedia, and beheaded. Their reputed relics are in the Baptistery of St John *Lateran at Rome. Feast day, with St Justina, in the E. 2 Oct.; in the W., formerly 26 Sept., dropped from the calendar of the RC Church in 1969; the date, 26 Sept., was wrongly allotted to St *Cyprian of Carthage, q.v., in the BCP.

In an early form the legend was known to St *Gregory of Nazianzus (d. 389/90) and *Prudentius (d. c.410). Gk. and Lat. text of Legend, with comm., in *AASS*, Sept. 7 (1750), pp. 195–246. H. *Delehaye, SJ, 'Cyprien d'Antioche et Cyprien de Carthage', *Anal. Boll.* 39 (1921), pp. 314–32. T. *Zahn, *Cyprian von Antiochien und die deutsche Faustsage* (1882). R. *Reitzenstein, 'Cyprian der Magier', *Nachr.* (Gött.), 1917, pp. 38–79. L. Radermacher, *Griechische Quellen zur Faustsage, Sb.* (Wien), 206, Abh. 4; 1927, pp. 1–41 ('Der Zauberer Cyprianus'). L. Krestan and A. Hermann in *RAC* 3 (1957), cols. 467–77, s.v. 'Cyprianus II (Magier)'.

Cyprian, St

(d. by 549), Bp. of Toulon. He was the principal author of the first book of a Life of his friend, *Caesarius of Arles. In 529 at the Council of *Orange he took an active part in combating *Semipelagianism. A letter to Maximus of Geneva is extant in which Cyprian shows knowledge of the '*Te Deum', and defends himself against the charge of *Theopaschitism. Feast day, 3 Oct.

Book 1 of the Life of St Caesarius of Arles in *AASS*, Aug. 6 (1743), pp. 64–75, and in J. P. Migne, *PL* 67. 1001–24. Crit. edns. by B. Krusch in *MGH*, Scriptores Rerum Merovingicarum, 3 (1896), pp. 457–83, and by G. *Morin, OSB, *Sancti Caesarii . . . Opera Omnia*, 2 (Maredsous, 1942), pp. 296–323. Cyprian's letter to Maximus ed. W. Gundlach in *MGH*, Epistolae, 3 (1892), pp. 434–6, and with introd. by C. Wawra in *Th. Q.* 85 (1903), pp. 576–94. S. Cavallin, *Literarhistorische und text-kritische Studien zur Vita S. Caesarii Arelatensis* (Lunds Universitets Årsskrift, NF, Avd. 1, Bd. 30, Nr. 7; 1934). Discussion of material for his life in *AASS*, Oct. 2 (1768), pp. 164–78.

Cyprus, Christianity in.

Cyprus was evangelized by Sts *Paul and *Barnabas (Acts 13). The many Cypriot saints mentioned in Byzantine *Synaxaria point to the firm hold Christianity secured in the island at an early date. At the Council of *Nicaea (325), Cyprus was represented by three bishops, including St *Spyridon, while later in the century St *Epiphanius (d. 403) was a distinguished Bp. of Salamis. About this time definite claims to independence of the patriarchates, esp. of *Antioch, were made by the Church of Cyprus, and in spite of the adverse view of Pope *Innocent I (402–17), the Council of *Ephesus in 431 formally recognized the claims of the Cypriot bishops in its 7th Session. A subsequent decision by *Acacius, Patr. of *Constantinople, confirmed this independence when it was challenged in 488 by *Peter the Fuller, Patr. of Antioch. Since then the archbishop, or *exarch, has been held to rank immediately after the five patriarchs. Arcadius and Sergius, Abps. of Constantia (Salamis) in the 7th cent., are famous as opponents of the Emp. *Heraclius.

The Cypriots passed under Arab rule, but were set free in the 10th cent., and at this time the great monasteries of the island were built. The Crusaders were welcomed, but soon caused trouble by introducing in 1196 a Latin hierarchy, which with unrelenting cruelty took control of Church affairs, so that the history of the next four centuries contains in Church events nothing but Greco-Latin strife. But the Latin Church was completely extinguished when the Turks took the island in 1571. The Greeks were more fortunate. Though many were massacred, they were permitted eventually to reconstitute their Church in four dioceses. In 1821, at the beginning of the Greek War of Independence, all four Cypriot bishops were executed. After the establishment of British rule in 1878, the bishops and clergy occasionally found relations strained with the authorities because they tended to be nationalist leaders. In 1960 Abp. Makarios became first President of the Republic of Cyprus. The Church in Cyprus is governed by the Holy Synod of the four dioceses. After the Turkish invasion in 1974, nearly 40 per cent of the island was occupied; most of the Greeks were expelled from the area and the churches and monasteries closed, demolished, or turned into mosques. In the whole of Cyprus there are a very few RCs, who are under the spiritual care of *Franciscan friars, and also some *Uniats.

J. Hackett, *A History of the Orthodox Church of Cyprus from the Coming of the Apostles Paul and Barnabas to the Commencement of the British Occupation (A.D. 45–A.D. 1878) together with Some Account of the Latin and other Churches existing in the Island* (1901). H. T. F. Duckworth, *The Church of Cyprus* (1900). There is much information and extensive refs. in G. Hill, *A History of Cyprus* (4 vols., Cambridge, 1940–52). A. and J. A. Stylianou, *The Painted Churches of Cyprus* (Stourbridge, 1964; 2nd edn., London, 1985). R. Janin, AA, in *DHGE* 12 (1953), cols. 791–820, s.v. 'Chypre', with full bibl.

Cyril, St

(c.315–87), Bp. of *Jerusalem from about 349. In 357 *Acacius, the extreme *Arian Bp. of *Caesarea, who claimed ecclesiastical jurisdiction over Jerusalem, had Cyril banished from his see on the ground of his opposition to Arianism, but the Council of *Seleucia recalled him in 359. Two further banishments followed. Meanwhile Cyril's beliefs on the burning question of the Godhead of Christ had been suspect in the opposite quarter, since he disliked the *Homoousios (the watchword of the Nicene faith) as being a man-made term. Accordingly the Council of *Antioch in 379 sent St *Gregory of Nyssa to Palestine to report on the situation. He brought back word that though the life of the Jerusalem Church was morally corrupt and full of factions, its faith was sound. It has been suggested that Cyril, to prove his orthodoxy, recited the creed traditionally in use at Jerusalem (which like the *Nicene Creed contained the Homoousios) at the Council of *Constantinople in 381, and that its adoption by the Council fixed it in its present form.

The most important surviving work of Cyril is a series of catechetical instructions delivered to the candidates for Baptism on *Holy Saturday: a pre-Lenten 'Procatechesis', 18 'Catecheses' delivered during Lent, and 5 'Mystagogic Catecheses' delivered in Easter week after Baptism. The Procatechesis and the Catecheses were delivered about 350. The 'Mystagogic Catecheses' must be placed at the end of Cyril's episcopate, if indeed they are by him. If, as many think, they are by his successor, John, they may well reflect Cyril's own teaching. They give a full and very illuminating picture of the preparation for Baptism then in use and much material for reconstructing the Palestinian liturgy of the 4th cent. Cyril does not mention the Words of *Institution in the Eucharist, perhaps because they were too familiar, perhaps because they were too sacred; but it is just possible that his rite did not contain them. He speaks of non-communicating attendance at the Eucharistic rite, and stresses the Real Presence. He strongly affirms the value and efficacy of Baptism with its anointing, renunciations, washing-away of sins, and laying on of hands. Feast day, 18 Mar.

Early edns. by J. Prévost (Paris, 1608) and T. Milles (London, 1703). Much improved edn. by the *Maurists, A. A. Touttée and P. *Maran (Paris, 1720), repr. in J. P. Migne, PG 33. More recent edns. by W. K. Reischl and J. Rupp, 2 vols., Munich, 1848–60, (of Procatechesis and Mystagogical Lectures only) by F. L. Cross, London, 1951, with bibl., and of the Mystagogical Lectures by A. Piédagnel, Cong. Orat., with Fr. tr. by P. Paris, PSS (SC 126; 1966; 2nd edn., 1988). Eng. tr. by R. W. *Church in LF, with pref. by J. H. *Newman (Oxford, 1838); rev. by E. H. Gifford in NPNCF 7 (1894), pp. 1–157; and by L. P. McCauley, SJ, and A. A. Stephenson (Fathers of the Church, 61 and 64; 1969–70). Eng. tr. of selections in W. Telfer, Cyril of Jerusalem and Nemesius of Emesa (Library of Christian Classics, 4; 1955), pp. 19–199. Important 'Dissertationes' by A. A. Touttée, op. cit. J. Lebon, 'La Position de St Cyrille de Jérusalem dans les luttes provoquées par l'arianisme', RHE 20 (1924), pp. 181–210 and 357–86; B. Niederberger, Die Logoslehre des hl. Cyrillus von Jerusalem (Paderborn, 1923). The ascription of the five Mystagogical Catecheses to Cyril has been challenged by W. J. Swaans, 'A propos des catéchèses mystagogiques attribuées à St Cyrille de Jérusalem', Le Muséon, 40 (1942), pp. 6–43. J. H. Greenlee, The Gospel Text of Cyril of Jerusalem (Texts and Studies, 17; 1955). A. Paulin, Saint Cyrille de Jérusalem Catéchète (Lex Orandi, 29; 1959). P. Nautin, 'La date du "De Viris Inlustribus" de Jérôme, de la mort de Cyril de Jérusalem et celle de Grégoire de Nazianze', RHE 56 (1961), pp. 33–35. P. W. L. Walker, Holy City, Holy Places? Christian Attitudes to Jerusalem and the Holy Land in the Fourth Century (Oxford Early Christian Studies, 1990), esp. pp. 31–4, 116–30, and 311–46. CPG 2 (1974), pp. 289–96 (nos. 3585–618). Altaner and Stuiber (1978), pp. 312 f. and 614, with further bibl. X. Le Bachelet in DTC 3 (1908), cols. 2527–77; E. J. Yarnold, SJ, in TRE 8 (1981), pp. 261–6, s.v.

Cyril, St

Cyril, St (d. 444), Patr. of *Alexandria. In 412 he succeeded his uncle Theophilus in the patriarchal see. He soon opened warfare with impartial vigour upon *Novatianism, *Neoplatonism, the Jews, and the Imperial prefect, Orestes, and if he himself bore no personal responsibility for the death of the distinguished philosopher *Hypatia, her murder was certainly the work of his supporters. The chief contest of his life, however, came c.430. It arose out of the support given by *Nestorius, Patr. of *Constantinople, to his chaplain, Anastasius, who had preached against the application of the word *Theotokos to the BVM on the ground that she was the mother of only the humanity of Christ. The rivalry of the patriarchal sees, the antipathy of *Alexandrian to *Antiochene theological thought, and a personal love of conflict, made Cyril the obvious champion of the contested word, and he defended it in his Paschal letter for 429. He then persuaded Pope *Celestine to summon a synod at *Rome in 430 and condemn Nestorius, had the condemnation repeated in his own synod at Alexandria, and sent notice of both decrees to Nestorius with a covering letter and 12 anathemas. This letter, which epitomized Cyril's

faith, was formally approved by the councils of *Ephesus (431) and *Chalcedon (451; after Cyril's death), but at the latter council his anathemas were omitted. At the Council of Ephesus, Cyril himself assumed control and had Nestorius condemned before the Antiochene bishops had arrived. On their arrival the Antiochenes held a separate council, and Cyril in turn was pronounced deposed. The Emperor at first confirmed both depositions, though that of Cyril was quickly reversed. In 433 an agreement was reached by Cyril and the more moderate Antiochenes.

Whatever may be thought of some of the methods adopted by Cyril in his controversies, his distinction and ability as a theologian are beyond dispute. The most brilliant representative of the Alexandrian theological tradition, he put into systematic form, on the basis of the teaching of St *Athanasius and the *Cappadocian Fathers, the classical Greek doctrines of the Trinity and of the Person of Christ. Where, in points of detail, his Christology appears to differ from that of the Council of Chalcedon, the divergence is partly, if not wholly, terminological. He appears to have used the Greek word φύσις as almost if not quite the equivalent of ὑπόστασις ('person'), and not in its later sense of 'nature'; and it was this use of language which gave a ready handle to those who later sought to claim his authority for *Monophysitism.

His writings reflect Cyril's outstanding qualities as a theologian. They are marked by precision in exposition, accuracy in thought, and skill in reasoning, though they lack elegance in style. They include a large collection of letters (among them, 29 'Paschal homilies'); many exegetical books, e.g. commentaries on Jn. and Lk., and many other Books of both the OT and the NT, much of which survives in fragments or versions; several treatises on dogmatic theology; an Apology against *Julian the Apostate; and a rather meagre (in view of Cyril's celebrity as a preacher) collection of sermons. Feast day in E., 9 June; in W., 27 June (formerly 9 Feb.).

The only collected edn. of Cyril's Opera is due to J. Aubert, Canon of Notre-Dame, Paris (6 vols., Paris, 1638; repr., with additions, J. P. Migne, PG 68–77). Further texts ed. A. *Mai, Rome, various dates. New edn. of certain treatises, mainly comm., by P. E. *Pusey (7 vols., Oxford, 1868–77). Crit. edns. of several of Cyril's letters in E. *Schwartz, ACO 1: Consilium Ephesinum (5 parts, Berlin, 1922–30) passim, and of Select Letters, with Eng. tr., by L. R. Wickham (Oxford Early Christian Texts, 1983); also of 'De Incarnatione Unigeniti' and 'Quod unus sit Christus', with Fr. tr., by G. M. de Durand, OP (SC 97; 1964); of 'De sancta trinitate', with Fr. tr., by id. (ibid. 231, 235, and 246; 1976–8); of 'Contra Iulianum', with Fr. tr., by P. Burguière and P. Évieux (ibid. 322, etc.; 1985 ff.), and of his Festal Letters, by W. H. Burns, with introd. by P. Évieux and Fr. tr. by id. and others (ibid. 372, 392, etc.; 1991 ff.). Syr. text of his Comm. on Luke, pt. 1, ed. J. B. Chabot in CSCO, Scriptores Syri, 4th ser. 1 (1912); Lat. tr. by R. M. Tonneau (ibid. 70; 1953). Eng. tr. of selected writings, Oxford, 1872 and 1881. J. Kopallik, Cyrillus von Alexandrien: Eine Biographie (Mainz, 1881). E. Schwartz, Cyrill und der Mönch Viktor (Sb. (Wien), 208, Abh. 4; 1928). Kyrilliana: Études variées à l'occasion du XVᵉ centenaire de saint Cyrille d'Alexandrie (various authors, Cairo, 1947). H. du Manoir de Juaye, SJ, Dogme et spiritualité chez S. Cyrille d'Alexandrie (1944). M. Richard, 'Les Traités de Cyrille d'Alexandrie contre Diodore et Théodore et les fragments dogmatiques de Diodore de Tarse', Mélanges dédiés à la mémoire de Félix Grat, 1 (1946), pp. 99–116. N. Charlier, CSSR, 'Le Thesaurus de Trinitate de Saint Cyrille d'Alexandrie', RHE 45 (1950), pp. 25–81. J. Liébaert, La Doctrine christologique de saint Cyrille d'Alexandrie avant la Querelle nestorienne (1951). A. Kerrigan, OFM, St Cyril of Alexandria, Interpreter of the Old Testament (Analecta Biblica, 2; Rome, 1952). L. M. Armendáriz, SJ, El Nuevo Moisés: Dinámica cristocéntrica en la tipología de Cirilo Alejandrino (Estudios Onienses, 3rd ser. 5; 1962); R. L. Wilken, Judaism and the Early Christian Mind: A Study of Cyril of Alexandria's Exegesis and Theology (Yale Publications in Religion, 15; 1971). R. M. Siddals, 'Logic and Christology in Cyril of Alexandria', JTS NS 38 (1987), pp. 341–67. CPG 3 (1979), pp. 1–57 (nos. 5200–438). Altaner and Stuiber (1978), pp. 283–8 and 605 f., with bibl. J. Mahé in DTC 3 (1908), cols. 2476–527, s.v.; M. Jugie, AA, in EC 3 (1950), cols. 1715–24, s.v. 'Cirillo d'Alessandria'; W. J. Burghardt, SJ, in NCE 4 (1967), pp. 571–6, s.v.

Cyril, St (826–69), **and Methodius, St** (c.815–85), the 'Apostles of the Slavs'. They were brothers who came of a Greek family of *Thessalonica, with a tradition of public service. The younger brother, originally 'Constantine', did not assume the name of Cyril until he became a monk in 868. Methodius, the elder, after holding the post of governor of a Slav province of the Empire, became a monk on Mount Olympus in Asia Minor. Constantine, after completing his studies in *Constantinople, was appointed to a chair of philosophy there. In 860–1 both brothers went on an imperial diplomatic mission to the Khazars, north of the Caucasus. In 862 the Emp. Michael III sent them as missionaries to what is now Moravia, where they taught in the vernacular. Before leaving Constantinople, Constantine invented an alphabet called *Glagolitic (see also CYRILLIC), and thus became the founder of Slavonic literature, adopting Slavonic also for the celebration of the Liturgy and circulating a Slavonic version of the Scriptures. A few years later they journeyed to Rome. Here Cyril died in a monastery shortly after taking his vows and was solemnly buried in the church of San Clemente. Methodius was then consecrated bishop and returned to Moravia. But, though he was fortified with full Papal authority, he was opposed by the German bishops and imprisoned for over two years. Pope John VIII secured his release, but deemed it expedient for a time to withdraw his permission to use Slavonic as the regular liturgical language. Acc. to some sources, it was Constantine who brought the reputed remains of St *Clement to Rome from the Crimea. Feast day in the E., 11 May; in the W., now 14 Feb. (formerly 9 Mar. and later 7 July). In 1980 *John Paul II declared them 'Patrons of Europe'.

Their anonymous, and almost contemporary biographies, are of great historical value. The principal Slavonic texts are ed., with Lat. tr., by F. Grivec and F. Tomšič (Radovi Staroslavenskog Instituta, 4; Zagreb, 1960). Eng. tr. by M. Kantor and R. S. White of The Vita of Constantine and the Vita of Methodius (Michigan Slavic Materials, 13 [1976]). Further material in the Greek Life of St Clement of Ochrid (one of their principal disciples), ascribed to *Theophylact, conveniently pr. in J. P. Migne, PG 126. 1193–240; Eng. tr. by S. Nikolov in I. Duichev (ed.), Kiril und Methodius (East European Monographs, 172; Boulder, Colo. [1985]), pp. 93–123. F. Dvornik, Les Légendes de Constantin et de Méthode vues de Byzance (Byzantinoslavica, 1; 1933), with bibl.; F. Grivec, Konstantin und Method: Lehrer der Slaven (Wiesbaden, 1960); P. Duthilleul, L'Évangélisation des Slaves: Cyrille et Méthode (Bibliothèque de Théologie, série IV. Histoire de la Théologie, 5; 1963). Cyrillo-Methodiana: Zur Frühgeschichte des Christentums bei den Slaven 863–1963. Im Auftrage der Görres-Gesellschaft, herausgegeben von M. Hellmann and others (Slavistische Forschungen, 6; Cologne, 1964). I. Dujčev, 'Problèmes cyrillométhodiens', Byzantion, 37 (1968), pp. 21–56, with

bibl. F. Dvornik, Byzantine Missions among the Slavs: SS. Constantine-Cyril and Methodius (New Brunswick, NJ, 1970). A. P. Vlasto, The Entry of the Slavs into Christendom (Cambridge, 1970), esp. pp. 29–81. D. Obolensky, 'Sts Cyril and Methodius, Apostles of the Slavs', St Vladimir's Seminary Quarterly, 7 (1963), pp. 1–11, repr. in id., Byzantium and the Slavs: Collected Studies (1971), no. 9; see also nos. 10 and 11. Id., The Byzantine Commonwealth: Eastern Europe, 500–1453 (1971), pp. 73 and 136–53. A.-E. N. Tachiaos, Cyril and Methodius of Thessalonica: The Acculturation of the Slavs (Thessaloniki [1989]), with sumptuous illustrations. P. Devos in NCE 4 (1967), pp. 579–81, s.v.

Cyril Lucar. See LUCAR, CYRIL.

Cyril of Scythopolis (b. c.525), Greek monk and hagiographer. Born at Scythopolis, the ancient Bethshan, of parents who kept a hospice for travelling monks, Cyril, while still a child, came under the influence of St *Sabas (q.v.; d. 532). In 543 he received the *tonsure and made his way to Jerusalem, where St John the Hesychast sought to win him for his monastery. Cyril, however, at first determined to live the life of an anchorite on the banks of the *Jordan. Before long (544) he attached himself to the monastery of St *Euthymius (d. 473). The *Origenist controversies having brought this community to an end (555), Cyril entered the neighbouring monastery of St Sabas two years later. He was the author of the Lives of seven Palestinian abbots (St Euthymius, St Sabas, St John the Hesychast, St Cyriacus, St Theodosius, St Theognius, St Abraham). They are among the best of the Greek hagiographical productions, being remarkable for their accurate detail. Written in popular Greek, they also have considerable philological interest.

Collected edn. of the 'Lives' by E. *Schwartz (TU 49, Heft 2; 1939), but for critique of Schwartz's datings of them cf. E. Stein in Anal. Boll. 62 (1944), pp. 169–86. Eng. tr. by R. M. Price, with notes and introd. by J. Binns (Cistercian Studies series, 114; Kalamazoo, Mich., 1991). Fr. tr. by A.-J. Festugière, OP, Les Moines d'Orient, 3, parts 1–3 (1962–3). The Georgian text of his Life of St Cyriacus ed., with Lat. tr., by G. Garitte in Muséon, 75 (1962), pp. 339–440, with refs. to edns. and MSS of Georgian versions of other Lives. F. Diekamp, Die origenistischen Streitigkeiten im sechsten Jahrhundert (1899), pp. 1–25. T. Hermann, 'Zur Chronologie des Kyrill von Skythopolis', ZKG 45 (1926), pp. 318–39. B. Flusin, Miracle et Histoire dans l'Œuvre de Cyrille de Scythopolis (Études Augustiniennes, 1983). CPG 3 (1979), pp. 405–8 (nos. 7535–43). Beck, pp. 408–10; Altaner and Stuiber (1978), p. 241. I. Hausherr, SJ, in Dict. Sp. 2 (1953), cols. 2687–90.

Cyrillic. The alphabet used by the Slavonic peoples of the E. Church. It is so named from its attribution to St *Cyril, one of the two 'Apostles of the Slavs' (9th cent.), though in fact *Glagolitic and not 'Cyrillic' is generally believed to be the alphabet Cyril devised. Cyrillic dates, however, from about the same time. It differs from Glagolitic in being based on Greek *uncial writing, whereas Glagolitic seems to be of composite origin.

Czechoslovak Church, the. The origins of the so-called Czech National Church (Československá Církev) lie in long-standing Bohemian traditions of national Catholicism (see HUSS, J.) and go back to an association of Catholic priests in 1890, called 'Jednota'. It aimed at the introduction of the Czech language into the Liturgy, the abolition of compulsory celibacy for the priesthood, and the participation of the laity in the government of the Church. In 1919, when Czechoslovakia became an independent state, these demands were submitted to Rome. On their rejection the Jednota, whose main inspiration was nationalist, decided to form an independent religious body in 1920. Within a few months it had won many adherents and was recognized by the government.

The Czechoslovak Church was constituted on Presbyterian lines, though with four bishops. These were elected, but not consecrated, and there is no belief in the *Apostolic Succession. In doctrine the Church was strongly rationalistic, owing to the influence of its first patriarch, Karel Farský. The Divine Sonship of Christ and the Eucharist were interpreted on modernist lines, and the doctrines of *Original Sin, *Purgatory, and the Veneration of Saints were rejected. Scriptural exegesis rested on the principles of reason, experience, and the results of scholarship. After Farský's death (1927) the doctrines became more conservative. When the first attraction was past, numbers remained static; the Czechoslovak Church has prob. never included much more than 5 per cent of the population. In 1971 it adopted the title 'Czechoslovak Hussite Church', emphasizing its affinities with the teaching of J. Huss.

F. M. Hník, A. Spisar, and F. Kovář, *The Czechoslovak Church* (Prague, 1937). R. Urban, *Die Tschechoslowakische Hussitische Kirche* (Marburg, 1973). L. Nemec, *The Czechoslovak Heresy and Schism: The Emergence of a National Czechoslovak Church* (Transactions of the American Philosophical Society, NS 65, pt. 1; 1975). G. A. Procházka, 'Die tschechoslowakische Nationalkirche', in F. Siegmund-Schultze (ed.), *Ekklesia*, 5, Lfg. 20 (1937), pp. 175–85, with bibl.

D

'D'. A symbol used by scholars who follow the 'documentary hypothesis' of the origins of the *Pentateuch; it denotes the source most characteristically represented by the Book of Deut. (nearly all of which is assigned to 'D'). In contrast with the precisely expressed ritual and ceremonial interests of '*P' and the more simple narrative style of '*J' and '*E', it is predominantly hortatory. From its apparent points of contact with the provisions of 'the book of the law' said to have been found in the Temple in the reign of Josiah (2 Kgs. 22 f.), it is by many associated, if not identified, with that 'book' and its composition generally assigned to the early 7th cent. See DEUTERONOMY, BOOK OF.

d'Achery, Jean Luc (1609–85), historian and patristic scholar. He was professed at the *Maurist abbey at Vendôme in 1632. In 1637 he became librarian of the abbey of *Saint-Germain-des-Prés, where he helped to put in order the large collection of books and manuscripts and initiated scholarly work among the Maurists. Among his most important publications are an edition of the works of *Lanfranc (1648) and the 13 vols. of his *Veterum aliquot Scriptorum . . . Spicilegium* (1655–77). Among those he trained was J. *Mabillon, with whom he shared in the production of the first volume of the *Acta Sanctorum Ordinis S. Benedicti*.

J. Fohlen, 'Dom Luc d'Achery (1609–1685) et les débuts de l'érudition mauriste', *Revue Mabillon*, 55 (1965), pp. 149–75; 56 (1966), pp. 1–30, 73–98; 57 (1967), pp. 17–41 and 56–156. Y. Chaussy, OSB, *Les Bénédictins de Saint-Maur*, 1 (Études Augustiniennes, 1989), pp. 67–72. B. Heurtebize in *Dict. Sp.* 1 (1937), cols. 175–7, s.v. 'Achery, Luc d' '. See also other works cited under MAURISTS.

Daillé, Jean (1594–1670), French Reformed theologian and controversialist. He was born at Châtellerault, studied at Poitiers and Saumur, and in 1612 became tutor to P. *du Plessis-Mornay's grandsons, with whom he travelled in Italy and England. In 1625 he became pastor in Saumur, and from 1626 until his death was pastor at Charenton, where the Reformed Church of Paris held its services. He had a great reputation as a preacher and theologian. In his *Traité de l'employ des saints Pères* (1632; Eng. tr., 1651) he rejected the authority of the Fathers as irrelevant for his time and was attacked by both Protestant and Catholic theologians. He followed up the controversy in *La Foi fondeé sur les saintes écritures* (1634), in which he attempted to prove that all Christian doctrines are either explicitly stated in Scripture or can be deduced from it. In *De Scripturis quae sub Dionysii Areopagitae et Ignatii Antiocheni nominibus circumferuntur* (Geneva, 1666) he compiled 66 objections to the genuineness of the *Ignatian literature; his main contentions were refuted by J. *Pearson (1672). As a friend and fellow-minister, he defended the teaching of Moïse *Amyraut (1596–1664), in particular his belief that Christ died for all men and not only for the elect. He

was moderator of the last national synod of the French Reformed Church at Loudun in 1659. His other works include *Apologie des Églises Réformées* (1633; Eng. tr., 1653), *De Pseudepigraphis Apostolicis* (1653), *Adversus Latinorum de Cultus Religiosi Objecto Traditionem* (1664), and *De Cultibus Religiosis Latinorum* (1671).

Abbrégé de la vie de Mr Daillé [by Jean Daillé, son] pr. with *Les Deux Derniers Sermons de Mr Daillé* (Paris, 1670). Study by E. Mettey (Strasbourg, 1863). A. [R.] *Vinet, *Histoire de la prédication parmi les Réformés de France au dix-septième siècle* (1860, posthumously pub.), pp. 182–216; P. [J.] Bayley, *French Pulpit Oratory 1598–1650* (Cambridge, 1980), esp. pp. 117–21 and 225–30. B. G. Armstrong, *Calvinism and the Amyraut Heresy* (Madison, Wis., and London, 1969), esp. pp. 12 f. E. and E. Haag, *La France Protestante*, 4 (1853), pp. 180–6; 2nd edn. by H. Bordier, 5 (1886), pp. 23–38, incl. list of his works. J. de la Servière, SJ, in *DTC* 4 (1911), cols. 3–5.

d'Ailly, Pierre (1350 or 1351–1420), French cardinal and theologian. He was a native of Compiègne, and in 1363 or 1364 entered the College of Navarre in *Paris, then a stronghold of *Nominalism, where he became master of arts in 1368 and doctor of theology in 1381. During this period he commented on the 'Sentences' of *Peter Lombard and wrote several scientific, philosophical, and theological treatises which show the great influence of R. *Bacon and esp. of *William of Ockham. Having become canon at Noyon in 1381, he was made Rector of the College of Navarre in 1384, Chancellor of the University of Paris in 1389, and soon afterwards confessor and almoner to Charles VI. In 1391 he obtained the archdeaconry of Cambrai in addition to many other benefices which he held in plurality. After the death of *Clement VII he became a favourite with his successor *Benedict XIII, who appointed him Bp. of Le Puy in 1395. He never entered this diocese, and in 1397 was translated to the more important see of Cambrai. The chief concern of his life was to find a means of healing the *Great Schism. With this end in view he broke with Benedict XIII in 1408 and in 1409 attended the Council of *Pisa, where he supported the newly elected third Pope, *Alexander V. In 1412 he assisted at the Council of Rome, convoked by Alexander's successor, *John XXIII, for which he outlined a programme of reforms entitled 'Capita Agendorum'. In the same year John XXIII created him cardinal in the hope of retaining his support, and shortly afterwards he was made Papal Legate to the German Emperor Sigismund. From 1414 to 1418 he attended the Council of *Constance, where he supported the theory of the supremacy of the General Council over the Pope, without, however, entirely approving the famous 'Decrees of Constance'. In 1416 he published his 'Tractatus super Reformatione Ecclesiae', the third part of an elaborate work 'De Materia Concilii Generalis'. Its first part was published among the works of his friend and disciple J. *Gerson, the second was published in full only in 1964. Several of its suggestions for ecclesiastical reforms were later adopted by the Council of *Trent. The 'Tractatus' had a great influence esp. in England and Germany.

In his doctrinal teaching he most frequently accepted the views of Ockham. He held that the existence of God was not a rationally demonstrable truth, and that sin was not as such inherently evil but sinful only because God wills it to be so. He maintained that bishops and priests received their jurisdiction directly from Christ and not mediately through the Pope, and that neither Pope nor Council was infallible. These and other of his opinions were later adopted and developed by M. *Luther and the other Reformers; and his teaching on the Church exercised a decisive influence on *Gallicanism. D'Ailly is also notable for his studies concerning astronomy, astrology, and geography; his *Imago Mundi*, in which he suggested that the Indies could be reached from the W., was known to Columbus.

Most of his Latin sermons were pr. by the *Brethren of the Common Life under the title *Tractatus et Sermones* (Brussels, c.1484). Nine French sermons ed. É. Brayer, *Notices et extraits des Manuscrits de la Bibliothèque Nationale et autres bibliothèques*, 43 (1965), pp. 248 325. Modern edn., with Fr. tr., of *Imago Mundi* by E. Buron (3 vols., Paris, 1930), with valuable introd. in vol. 1, pp. 5–113, and bibl., pp. 113–24. Facsimile of a collection of autograph texts, with introd. by G. Ouy (Umbrae codicum occidentalium, 9; Amsterdam, 1966). Studies by L. Salembier (Lille, 1886; also other works by this author incl. important posthumously pub. synthesis of his earlier works, Tourcoing, 1932) and P. Tschackert (Gotha, 1877). M. Patronnier de Gandillac, 'De l'usage et de la valeur des arguments probables dans les questions du Cardinal Pierre d'Ailly sur le "Livre des Sentences" ', *AHDLMA* 8 (1933), pp. 43–91. G. Lindbeck, 'Nominalism and the Problem of Meaning as illustrated by Pierre d'Ailly on Predestination and Justification', *HTR* 52 (1959), pp. 43–60. B. Meller, *Studien zur Erkenntnislehre des Peter von Ailly* (Freiburger theologische Studien, 67; 1954); F. Oakley, *The Political Thought of Pierre d'Ailly* (Yale Historical Publications, Miscellany, 81; 1964), with text of the *De Materia Concilii Generalis*, pp. 252–342. P. Glorieux, 'La vie et l'œuvre de Pierre d'Ailly', *Mélanges de science religieuse*, 22 (1965), pp. 61–78; id., 'Les années d'études de Pierre d'Ailly', *RTAM* 44 (1977), pp. 127–49. W. Courtenay, 'Covenant and Causality in Pierre d'Ailly', *Speculum*, 46 (1971), pp. 94–119, repr. in id., *Covenant and Causality in Medieval Thought* (1984), no. 9, with refs. A. E. Bernstein, *Pierre d'Ailly and the Blanchard Affair: University and Chancellor of Paris at the Beginning of the Great Schism* (Studies in Medieval and Reformation Thought, 24; Leiden, 1978). B. Guenée, *Entre l'Église et l'État* [1987], pp. 125–299, with notes pp. 461–77; Eng. tr., *Between Church and State* (Chicago and London, 1991), pp. 102–258, with notes pp. 388–405. L. Thorndike, *A History of Magic and Experimental Science*, 4 (New York, 1934), pp. 101–13. L. Salembier in *DHGE* 1 (1912), cols. 1154–65, s.v. 'Ailly, Pierre de'. See also bibl. to CONSTANCE, COUNCIL OF, and GERSON, JEAN LE CHARLIER DE.

Dair Balaizah Fragments. See DER BALYZEH FRAGMENTS.

Dale, Robert William (1829–95), *Congregational preacher, theologian, and educational reformer. From 1853 until his death he was pastor (co-pastor 1853–9) of Carr's Lane Chapel, Birmingham. He came to take a leading part in municipal affairs in Birmingham, co-operating closely with Joseph Chamberlain, and in 1870 he keenly supported W. E. Forster's Education Bill. In 1891 he was President of the International Congregational Council. He stood for progressive, but in fundamentals orthodox, Evangelicalism. In *The Atonement* (1875), his most influential work, he strongly maintained a penal doctrine against the liberal views of such men as B. *Jowett and H. *Bushnell. But his orthodoxy here differed from that of traditional *Protestantism. He sought to put the emphasis on the ethical rather than the forensic, and in some respects his teaching on the Atonement has points of contact with that of H. *Grotius. His other writings include sets of lectures on *Preaching* (1877) and on *Ephesians* (1882).

Biography by his son, A. W. W. Dale (London, 1898). A. Gordon in *DNB*, Suppl. 2 (1901), pp. 104–6.

D'Alembert, Jean Le Rond (1717–83), French mathematician, philosopher, and *Encyclopaedist. A foundling discovered near the church of St Jean le Rond, *Paris (hence his name), he was educated by the *Jansenists at the Mazarin College. He soon showed remarkable mathematical talents and, after short-lived attempts to train as a lawyer and a physician, resolved to devote himself wholly to mathematics. In 1741 he was admitted a member of the Academy of Sciences. In 1743 in his *Traité de dynamique* he developed the mechanical principle henceforward known as 'D'Alembert's Principle'. Several important other works and papers on mathematics followed. He was drawn into various religious disputes by his extensive collaboration for some years in *Diderot's *Encyclopédie* and his association with the 'philosophic' circle of freethinkers that produced it. D'Alembert contributed the *Discours préliminaire*, which dealt, along lines laid down by F. *Bacon and J. *Locke, with the rise, progress, and affinities of the several sciences, as well as many articles on literary, and esp. mathematical, subjects. His article on 'Geneva' provoked the *Calvinists to a lively controversy. Among his other writings were an attack on the *Jesuits (1765) and a collection of biographies of members of the Academy who died between 1700 and 1772.

Collected Works, 18 vols., Paris, 1805. Unpub. items ed. M. C. Henry (Paris, 1887). Eng. tr. of 'Miscellaneous Pieces' (London, 1764). Studies by J. Bertrand (Paris, 1889), R. Grimsley (Oxford, 1963), and T. L. Hankins (ibid., 1970). M. Muller, *Essai sur la philosophie de Jean d'Alembert* (1926). G. J. Van Treese, *D'Alembert and Frederick the Great* (Philosophical Questions Series, 9; Louvain and Paris, 1974). M. Emery and P. Monzani (eds.), *Jean d'Alembert, savant et philosophe: Actes du Colloque organisé par Centre International de Synthèse-Fondation pour la Science, Paris, 15–18 juin 1983* [1989]. A special number of the periodical *Dix-Huitième Siècle*, 16 (1984) is devoted to D'Alembert, with Eng. summaries. See also bibl. to ENCYCLOPAEDISTS.

Dalgairns, Bernard (baptismal names John Dobree) (1818–76), priest of the *Oratory. He was a supporter of the *Oxford Movement in its earliest days, but in 1845, after spending some time in retirement with J. H. *Newman at Littlemore, was, like him, received into the RC Church. While at Littlemore he wrote the Life of St *Stephen Harding for the series 'Lives of the English Saints' (1844). In 1849, after some months in France and Italy, he joined Newman and F. W. *Faber in the Oratory, and was later caught up in the tensions between the London and Birmingham houses. A member of the

*Metaphysical Society, he wrote various devotional and theological works.

A letter of Newman about him pr. in *Newman the Oratorian*, ed. P. Murray, OSB (Dublin, 1969), pp. 349–59; cf. [L.] M. Trevor, *Newman* (2 vols., 1962), *passim*. H. N. Oxenham, *Short Studies in Ecclesiastical History and Biography* (1884), pp. 309–17. T. Cooper in *DNB* 13 (1888), pp. 388 f.; S. Bowden in *CE* 4 (1908), pp. 604 f., s.v. See also other works on Newman and Faber, cited s.vv.

Dallæus, Johannes. See DAILLÉ, JEAN.

Dalman, Gustaf Herman (1855–1941), biblical scholar. In 1895 he was appointed professor of the Institutum Delitzschianum (see DELITZSCH, FRANZ) at Leipzig. From 1902 to 1917 he was Director of the German Evangelical Institute for Archaeology in Palestine, and afterwards professor at Greifswald. In 1925 he went out again to Palestine as director of the Gustaf Dalman-Institut für Palästinawissenschaft. He conducted many important researches into the language, ideas, and customs of 1st-cent. *Judaism, and his work may be said to have established that Christ spoke ordinarily in Aramaic and not in Greek. His writings include *Grammatik des jüdisch-palästinischen Aramäisch* (1894); *Christentum und Judentum* (1898; Eng. tr., 1901); *Die Worte Jesu* (1898; Eng. tr., 1902); *Orte und Wege Jesu* (1919; Eng. tr., 1935); *Jesus-Jeschua* (1922; Eng. tr., 1929); *Arbeit und Sitte in Palästina* (1928–39).

A. Alt in *Palästinajahrbuch des deutschen evangelischen Instituts für Altertumswissenschaft des heiligen Landes zu Jerusalem*, Jahrg. 37 (1941), pp. 5–18. List of his works by K. H. Rengstorf in *Wissenschaftliche Zeitschrift der Ernst Moritz Arndt-Universität Greifswald*, 4 (1955), pp. 209–32.

dalmatic. An over-tunic reaching to the knees worn in the W. Church at *High Mass by *deacons, and on certain occasions also by bishops. The E. bishop's 'sakkos' is almost identical. Perhaps of Dalmatian origin, it became a popular garment among the upper classes in Rome in the 2nd cent. Till the 10th cent. it was invariably white and made of linen or wool; later it was coloured and of silk. It is ornamented with two *clavi* or coloured strips running from front to back over the shoulders, which at one time were invariably red. The dalmatic is bestowed upon the deacon at his ordination in the Latin Rite. In England, the sovereign wears a dalmatic at his (or her) coronation. See also TUNICLE.

Braun, *LG*, ch. 12, 'Dalmatik und Tunicella', pp. 247–305. H. *Leclercq, OSB, in *DACL* 4 (1921), cols. 111–19, s.v. 'Dalmatique'.

Damascus. The ancient capital of Syria. Mentioned as far back as the early 15th cent. BC by the Egyptian king Thutmoses III, it is frequently referred to in the OT, owing to the conflicts and alliances between Syria, Israel, and Judah in the earlier days of the Hebrew monarchy. After its fall in 732 BC to the Assyrian king Tiglath Pileser III, it lost most of its importance for several centuries. In the Seleucid period it was overshadowed by the new Syrian capital of *Antioch. It was on the road from *Jerusalem to Damascus that St *Paul was converted to the Christian faith (Acts 9). A Christian community has existed here continuously from Apostolic times. It is now the seat of the Greek Orthodox, the Greek Catholic (*Melkite), and *Syrian Orthodox Patriarchs of Antioch.

C. Watzinger and K. Wulzinger, *Damascus* (2 vols., 'Die Antike Stadt' and 'Die Islamische Stadt', Wissenschaftliche Veröffentlichungen des Deutsch-Türkischen Denkmalschutz-Kommandos, Hefte 4–5; 1921–4). J. Sauvaget, *Les Monuments historiques de Damas* (Beirut, 1932). W. T. Pitard, *Ancient Damascus: A Historical Study of the Syrian City-State from Earliest Times until its Fall to the Assyrians in 732 B.C.E.* (Winona Lake, Ind., 1987). L. Jalabert in *DACL* 4 (pt. 1; 1920), cols. 119–45; R. Janin, AA, in *DHGE* 14 (1960), cols. 42–7, both s.v. 'Damas'; N. Elisséeff in *Encyclopaedia of Islam* (2nd edn.), 2 (1965), pp. 277–91, s.v. 'Dimashk'.

Damascus Fragments. See DEAD SEA SCROLLS.

Damasus, St (c.304–84), Pope from 366. Of Spanish descent, he entered the service of his predecessor, Pope *Liberius, who appointed him a deacon. On Liberius' death (24 Sept. 366), a fierce conflict broke out between the supporters of Damasus and those of his rival, Ursinus (or Ursicinus). Ursinus was elected Pope in the basilica of Julius (S. Maria in Trastevere), while Damasus was chosen by the great majority of the clergy and people of *Rome in S. Lorenzo in Lucina. In the ensuing struggle, during which the supporters of Ursinus gained possession of the Liberian Basilica (S. Maria Maggiore), acc. to Ammianus Marcellinus 137 persons (acc. to the *Gesta inter Liberium et Felicem*, 160) were killed. The Emp. Valentinian I intervened in support of Damasus and banished Ursinus for a time to *Cologne, though it was not until c.381 that the troubles ceased.

Damasus was very active, by synods and with the help of the Imperial power, in suppressing heresy (*Arianism, *Donatism, *Macedonianism, *Luciferians). From 371 he was engaged in protracted dealings with St *Basil of Caesarea with a view to the overthrow of Arianism; and at Antioch he supported the party of *Paulinus. Damasus did much to strengthen the position of the see of Rome (Decree of Gratian, 378), made provision for the proper housing of the Papal archives, and was keenly interested in the monuments of the martyrs, adorning their tombs with the series of famous marble inscriptions engraved by Filocalus. He also erected the titular church of S. Lorenzo in Damaso, and a church on the Via Ardeatina at the catacombs of Sts Marcus and Marcellianus. At a Council prob. held at Rome in 382 he promulgated a Canon of Scriptural Books and commissioned his secretary, St *Jerome, to revise the biblical text (see VULGATE). In the Middle Ages he was erroneously held to be the author of the *Liber Pontificalis*. See also FIDES DAMASI and TOME OF DAMASUS. Feast day, 4 (formerly 11) Dec.

Works in J. P. Migne, *PL* 13. 109–424. Crit. edn. of the docs. on the Ursinian schism in CSEL 35 ('Collectio Avellana'), pp. 48–58. *LP* (Duchesne), I, pp. 212–15. M. Ihm (ed.), *Damasi Epigrammata* (Leipzig, 1895); A. Ferrua, SJ, *Epigrammata Damasiana* (Sussidi allo studio delle antichità cristiane, 2, 1942; 59 Epigrams are here recognized as genuine). A. Salvatore, *L'epigramma damasiano 'in Laudem Davidis'* (Naples, 1960), with anthology of epigrams. C. Pietri, *Roma Christiana: Recherches sur l'Église de Rome . . .(311–440)* (Bibliothèque des Écoles françaises d'Athènes et de Rome, 224; 2 vols., 1976), I, pp. 405–884 *passim*; and see index. H. M. Shepherd, Jun., 'The Liturgical Reform of Damasus I', in P. Granfield and J. A. Jungmann (eds.), *Kyriakon: Festschrift Johannes Quasten*, 2 (Munich, 1970), pp. 847–63. J. Fontaine, *Naissance de la Poésie dans l'Occident Chrétien* (Études Augustiniennes, 1981), pp. 111–25. A. Di Berardino in Quasten (cont.), *Patrology*, 4 (1986), pp. 273–8. A. Van Roey in *DHGE* 14 (1960), cols. 48–53, with bibl.

Damian, St. See COSMAS AND DAMIAN, STS.

Damian, St Peter. See PETER DAMIAN, ST.

Damien, Father (1840–89), leper missionary. Joseph de Veuster, the son of a small farmer, became a member of the Picpus Society (Fathers of the Sacred Hearts of Jesus and Mary) in 1859, taking the religious name 'Damien'. Sent to the Hawaiian Islands in 1863, he was ordained priest at Honolulu in the following year, and later put in charge of several districts in the islands of Hawaii and Molokai, where he converted the natives and built them chapels. In 1873 he was sent at his own request to a settlement of lepers at Molokai who were without any attendance. Here he ministered single-handed to the spiritual and physical needs of 600 lepers, dressing their wounds, building them houses, and digging their graves. Even after he had caught the disease himself he continued his work, now assisted by other members of his order and Sisters of Charity, until he became helpless.

Letters ed. by his brother, Father Pamphile [A. P. de Veuster] (London, 1889), with introd. V. Jourdan, SSCC, *Le Père Damien de Veuster* (Braine-le-Comte [1931]). Other lives include those by I. Caudwell (London, 1931), P. Compton (ibid., 1933), J. V. Farrow (ibid., 1937), and O. Englebert (Paris, 1940; Eng. tr., Derby, NY [1955]).

damnation. In general, 'condemnation', but esp. to eternal loss (*damnum*) in hell. Some theologians have distinguished the loss of the *Beatific Vision, the attainment of which constitutes the joy of heaven, from positive retributive punishment for the sins done on earth, and asserted that both are present in the sufferings of the damned; others have held that the deprivation and conscious loss of heaven and of God is itself the natural and sufficient consequence of persistence in sin. The eternity of damnation for those who finally reject the will of God appears to follow from various sayings of Christ, e.g. Mt. 25: 46.

Dance of Death. An allegorical subject in European art, in which the figure of Death, usually represented as a skeleton, is shown meeting various characters in different states of life and leading them all in a dance to the grave. The cycle in the Cemetery of the Innocents in Paris (1425; destroyed in the 16th cent.) served as a model for numerous similar series of wall-paintings in graveyards throughout Europe in the later Middle Ages. Examples survive chiefly in engravings, e.g. the series by the Paris printer G. Marchant and by H. Holbein (the younger). It was called in German *Totentanz* and in French *Danse macabre*.

Modern facsimile edn. of *The Dance of Death* by Hans Holbein (1497–1543), with introd. and notes by J. M. Clark (London, 1947). G. Buchheit, *Der Totentanz: Seine Entstehung und Entwicklung* (Leipzig, 1926). J. M. Clark, *The Dance of Death in the Middle Ages and Renaissance* (Glasgow, 1950), with bibl.; H. Rosenfeld, *Der mittelalterliche Totentanz* (Beihefte zum Archiv für Kulturgeschichte, 3; 1954; 2nd edn., 1968); S. Cosacchi, *Makabertanz: Der Totentanz in Kunst, Poesie und Brauchtum des Mittelalters* (Meisenheim am Glan, 1965); R. Hammerstein, *Tanz und Musik*

des Todes: Die mittelalterlichen Totentänze und ihr Nachleben (1980); A. Breeze, 'The Dance of Death', *Cambridge Medieval Celtic Studies*, 13 (1987), pp. 87–96.

Daniel, Book of. The Book falls into two main divisions:
1. A narrative section describing the experiences of Daniel and his three companions under Nebuchadnezzar (1–4) and Belshazzar (5), kings of Babylon, and Darius the Mede (6). These include their refusal to eat unclean meats (1), Daniel's successful interpretation of Nebuchadnezzar's dream (2), the miraculous release of the three companions from the fiery furnace (3), Nebuchadnezzar's madness (4), the supernatural writing on the wall ('Mene, Mene, Tekel, Upharsin') at Belshazzar's feast (5), and Daniel's preservation in the lions' den (6).
2. A series of visions granted to Daniel in the reigns of Belshazzar (7, 8), Darius the Mede (9), and Cyrus (10–12), which reveal the future destinies of the Jewish people. Several of the passages in these later chapters bear all the characteristics of *Apocalyptic literature.

The traditional belief that the Book was written in the 6th cent. BC by Daniel, one of the Jewish exiles in Babylon, is now almost universally regarded as untenable. A number of historical errors make it next to impossible to believe that it dates from the period of the Exile, and a much later date is borne out also by its doctrinal standpoint, by its position in the *canon of Scripture, and by its language (the section 2: 4–7: 18 is written in *Aramaic, not Hebrew, and even Greek loan-words occur). The consensus of modern critical opinion is that it was written between 167 and 164 BC. On this hypothesis the purpose of the Book was to encourage the reader during the persecution of the Jews at the hands of *Antiochus Epiphanes (175–164 BC).

There is only one passage where Daniel is directly quoted in the NT, namely, the reference to the 'abomination of desolation' in Mk. 13: 14 and parallels. But there are many points where its teaching has been taken up and developed, e.g. the use of the figure of the *Son of Man (7: 13), the conception of angels mediating between a transcendent God and man, and above all the doctrine of the *resurrection of the dead in 12: 2.

In the *Apocrypha there appear three 'books', viz. 'The Song of the Three Holy Children', 'The History of Susanna', and 'The History of the Destruction of Bel and the Dragon', all of which are found in the Gk. text of Daniel, though not in the Heb.; and all seem to be Gk. writings, later than the Book itself. On these, see the separate entries.

Commentaries by S. R. *Driver (Camb. Bib., AV, 1900), J. A. Montgomery (ICC, 1927), with bibl. pp. xv–xxvi, R. H. *Charles (Oxford, 1929), A. Bentzen (HAT, Reihe 1, Bd. 9; 1937; 2nd edn., 1952), E. W. Heaton ('Torch Bible' Comm., 1956), N. W. Porteous (Das Alte Testament Deutsch, 23; 1962, 2nd edn., 1968; Eng. tr., 1965, 2nd edn., 1979), O. Plöger (KAT 18; 1965), M. Delcor (Sources Bibliques, 1971), A. Lacocque (Commentaire de l'Ancien Testament, 15b; 1976; Eng. tr., 1979), and L. F. Hartman, CSSR, and A. A. di Lella, OFM (Anchor Bible, 23; 1978). P. R. Davies, *Daniel* (Old Testament Guides, Sheffield [1985]). Among the older writers, upholding the conservative view, the best known is E. B. *Pusey, *Daniel the Prophet: Nine Lectures* (1864). H. L. Ginsberg, *Studies in Daniel* (New York, 1948). H. H. Rowley, 'The Unity of the Book of Daniel', *Hebrew Union College Annual*, 23 (pt. 1, 1952), pp. 233–73; repr. in *The Servant of the Lord and Other Essays on the Old Testament* (1952), pp. 235–

68; rev. edn. with further bibl. (Oxford, 1965), pp. 249–80. Id., *Darius the Mede and the Four World Empires in the Book of Daniel* (1935). [P.] M. Casey, *Son of Man: The Interpretation and Influence of Daniel 7* (1979). R. Bodenmann, *Naissance d'une Exégèse: Daniel dans l'Église ancienne des trois premiers siècles* (Beiträge zur Geschichte der Biblischen Exegese, 28; 1986).

Daniel, St (409–93), *Stylite. He was the most famous of the disciples of St *Simeon Stylites, whose cowl he received. After spending his early years at Samosata and other monasteries in the E., at the age of 51 he took up his position on a pillar four miles from *Constantinople, on which he was ordained priest by St *Gennadius and lived for thirty-three years. Generally regarded as an oracle, he only once left his pillar (*c*.476), to rebuke the Emp. Basiliscus for supporting *Monophysitism. Feast day, 11 Dec.

Early Gk. Life, ed. H. *Delehaye, SJ, in *Anal. Boll.* 32 (1913), pp. 121–229; repr. in id. (ed.), *Les Saints stylites* (Brussels, 1923), pp. 1–94. Eng. tr. in E. [A. S.] Dawes and N. H. Baynes, *Three Byzantine Saints* (1948), pp. 1–71, with notes, pp. 72–84. On this Vita cf. N. H. Baynes in *EHR* 40 (1925), pp. 397–402. Other Lives listed in *BHG* (3rd edn., 1957), pp. 150 f. V. Laurent, AA, in *DHGE* 14 (1960), col. 73, s.v. 'Daniel (11), (Saint) le Stylite'.

Daniélou, Jean (1905–74), *Jesuit theologian. Born at Neuilly-sur-Seine, he became a Jesuit in 1929. He then studied in Jersey, at Lyons (where he came under the influence of H. de *Lubac), and at Mongré, and he received a doctorate from the *Sorbonne for a thesis, *Platonisme et théologie mystique* (1944), on the spiritual theology of St *Gregory of Nyssa in whom he had an abiding interest. From 1943 he was a professor at the Institut Catholique in Paris. A *peritus* at the Second *Vatican Council, he was made a cardinal in 1969. His importance as a theologian rests mainly on his patristic scholarship. In addition to monographs on *Origen (1948) and *Philo (1958), his work in this field includes his *Histoire des Doctrines Chrétiennes avant Nicée* (1958–78; Eng. tr., 1964–77). In the first volume and in several other works he explored the Jewish roots of Christianity. Closely connected with this interest was his work on patristic *exegesis, notably in *Sacramentum Futuri* (1950; Eng. tr., 1960), in which he popularized the distinction between *allegory and types (see TYPES). He also contributed to the patristic revival of the 20th cent. by his promotion of a number of publishing ventures; these included the collection of 'Sources Chrétiennes', an important series of patristic and medieval texts, with French translation, of which the first volume (because of wartime difficulties containing only the French translation) was issued in 1942.

Epektasis: Mélanges patristiques offerts au cardinal Jean Daniélou, ed. J. Fontaine and C. Kannengiesser (1972), incl. 'bibliographie patristique', pp. 675–89. M.-J. Rondeau and others, *Jean Daniélou 1905–1974* [1975]. A 'Société des Amis du Cardinal Jean Daniélou' was founded in Paris in 1975 to collect material on his activities and to promote the study of his writings and the continuance of his influence. It issues an annual bulletin. Polgár, 1 (1990), pp. 549–53.

Dante Alighieri (1265–1321), Italian poet and philosopher. Little is known of his early life except that he was born in Florence, lost his parents before he was 18, was betrothed at the age of 12 and married in 1293. In 1274

he first met his Beatrice (prob. Bice Portinari, the daughter of a Florentine citizen and wife of Simone dei Bardi), and he became her poet nine years later. Her death in 1290 led to a crisis, resolved by writing the *Vita nuova* (prob. in 1292, possibly later) in which he promised her a poem 'such as had been written for no lady before', a promise fulfilled in the *Divina Commedia. He then turned to the study of philosophy, prob. under the *Dominicans at Florence, and wrote a series of allegorical *Canzoni* or odes on the Lady Philosophy and literal ones on Courtesy, Nobility, Liberality, and Justice. In 1294 he entered politics but, having supported the opponents of Pope *Boniface VIII, he was exiled from Florence in 1301 and travelled widely in Italy. He returned to the study of philosophy and wrote the incomplete *De Vulgari Eloquentia* in Latin and began the *Convivio* (Banquet), which was designed to comment freely on his earlier philosophical *Canzoni*. In the course of the fourth book he became aware of the significance of the Roman Empire; the appearance of the Emp. Henry VII in Italy at the same time (1310) converted Dante into an ardent supporter of the Emperor, for whom he wrote in Latin the treatise *De Monarchia* (1312–14?). This work, which was condemned as heretical (*Averroist) in 1329, argued the need for a universal monarchy to achieve the temporal happiness of mankind and the independence of the Empire from the Pope and the Church, which should abandon all temporal authority and possessions and concentrate on happiness in the world to come. Dante's political prospects were shattered by the death of Henry VII in 1313, and in 1315 his native city of Florence renewed its sentence against him. He spent some years at *Verona and from *c*.1316 lived at *Ravenna, where he died. The last period of his life was devoted to the completion of the *Divina Commedia* (q.v.), which established him as one of the few poets who belong to all times and all nations.

Best collected edn. of *Opere* by the Società Dantesca Italiana, ed. M. Barbi, E. G. Parodi and others (Florence, 1921; appendix, 1922; 2nd edn., 1960). Crit. edn. of *Vita nuova* by M. Barbi (Florence: Edizione Nazionale delle Opere di Dante, 1; 1932); of *Rime (Canzoni)* by G. Contini (Turin, 1939; 2nd edn., 1946); Eng. tr. and comm. by K. Foster and P. Boyde, *Dante's Lyric Poetry* (2 vols., Oxford, 1967); *De Vulgari Eloquentia* ed. A. Marigo (Florence: Nuova Edizione diretta da M. Barbi, 6; 1938; 2nd edn. by P. G. Ricci: Edizione sotto auspici della Fondazione Giorgio Cini, 6; 1957); *Convivio* ed. G. Busnelli and G. Vandelli (Florence: Nuova Edizione diretta da M. Barbi, 4–5; 1934–7); *De Monarchia* ed. P. G. Ricci (Verona: Edizione Nazionale, 5; 1965); *Il Fiore* and *Il Detto d'Amore* ed. G. Contini (Milan: Edizione Nazionale, 8; 1984); *Letters* ed. P. Toynbee (Oxford, 1920; 2nd edn., 1966); and *Eclogue* ed. P. H. Wicksteed and E. G. Gardner (London, 1902). Edns., with comm. by various authors, of all minor works in *Opere Minori* (La Letteratura Italiana, Storia e Testi, 5; 2 vols., Milan and Naples [1979–84]). A. Solerti (ed.), *Le vite di Dante, Petrarca e Boccaccio* (Storia Litteraria d'Italia; Milan, 1904), pp. 3–236. E. Moore, *Studies in Dante* (4 series, Oxford, 1896–1917); P. Toynbee, *Dante Alighieri* (1900; 4th edn., 1910); N. Zingarelli, *Dante* (Storia Litteraria d'Italia, 1903; rev. edn., 2 vols., Milan, 1944); K. Vossler, *Die Göttliche Komödie* (4 pts., Heidelberg, 1907–10; Eng. tr., 2 vols., 1929); B. *Croce, *La poesia di Dante* (Bari, 1921; Eng. tr., 1922); B. Nardi, *Saggi di filosofia dantesca* (Milan, 1930; 2nd edn., Florence, 1967); id., *Dante e la cultura medievale* (Bari, 1942); id., *Nel mondo di Dante* (1944); E. *Gilson, *Dante et la philosophie* (1939; Eng. tr., 1948); U. Cosmo, *Guida a Dante* (Turin, 1947; Eng. tr., Oxford, 1950);

C. S. Singleton, *Dante Studies* (2 vols., Cambridge, Mass., 1954–8); U. Limentani (ed.), *The Mind of Dante* (Cambridge, 1965); K. Foster, OP, *The Two Dantes, and other Studies* [1977]; P. Boyde, *Dante, Philomythes and Philosopher* (Cambridge, 1981); J. Freccero, *Dante: The Poetics of Conversion*, ed. R. Jacoff (Cambridge, Mass., and London, 1986). Introduction by G. [A.] Holmes, *Dante* (Past Masters; Oxford, 1980). P. Toynbee, *A Dictionary of Proper Names and Notable Matters in the Works of Dante* (Oxford, 1898; rev. by C. S. Singleton, 1968). *Enciclopedia Dantesca* (5 vols., Rome, 1970–6, + Appendix, 1978). See also bibl. to DIVINA COMMEDIA.

Darboy, Georges (1813–71), Abp. of *Paris. He was ordained priest in 1836, and after holding some teaching and other appointments became Bp. of Nancy in 1859 and Abp. of Paris in 1863. In his first year at Paris he consecrated the newly restored cathedral of *Notre-Dame. His *Gallican sympathies and claims to episcopal independence brought him into conflict with Rome, and before and during the First *Vatican Council he was one of the chief opponents of the definition of Papal infallibility, although he eventually subscribed to it. During the siege of Paris in 1870–1, he devoted himself wholeheartedly to the care of the destitute and helpless. When in 1871 the Commune secured control of the city, he was seized and shot in cold blood on 24 May 1871, blessing his executioners. His writings include a Life of St Thomas *Becket (2 vols., 1858).

Œuvres pastorales de Mgr Darboy, comprenant ses mandements et ses allocutions, depuis son élévation au siège de Nancy jusqu'à sa mort (2 vols., 1876). 'Monseigneur Darboy et le saint-siège. Documents inédits', *Revue d'Histoire et de Littérature religieuses*, 12 (1907), pp. 240–81; Diary kept during the Vatican Council, ed. A. Duval and Y. *Congar in *RSPT* 54 (1970), pp. 417–52. J. A. Foulon, *Histoire de la vie et des œuvres de Mgr Darboy, archevêque de Paris* (1889). Further Life by J. A. Guillermin (Paris, 1888). M. O'Gara, *Triumph in Defeat: Infallibility, Vatican I, and the French Minority Bishops* (Washington, DC [1988]), *passim*. F. Guédon in *DHGE* 14 (1960), cols. 83–6, s.v. See also works cited under GALLICANISM.

Darby, John Nelson (1800–82), *Plymouth Brother and founder of the 'Darbyites'. He was ordained to a title in Wicklow *c*.1826, but resigned in 1827, and shortly after joined a sect called the 'Brethren', then newly founded by A. N. Groves, which rejected all Church order and outward forms. In 1845 a quarrel within this body caused a local schism at Plymouth, and in 1847 at Bristol; and Darby became the leader of the stricter Brethren, who were organized as a separate body ('Darbyites'). Both before and after this time Darby made many tours abroad to lecture and preach, visiting France, Switzerland, Germany, Canada, the USA, the West Indies, and New Zealand between 1830 and his death. Darby wrote countless controversial, doctrinal, and devotional works. He was also a hymn-writer, and edited the hymn-book generally used by the Plymouth Brethren.

Collected Writings ed. by W. Kelly (London, 32 vols. and index [1867–83]). Modern Life by W. G. Turner (London, 1926). A. Reese, *The Approaching Advent of Christ: An Examination of the Teaching of J. N. Darby and his Followers* [1937]. C. B. Bass, *Backgrounds to Dispensationalism: Its historical genesis and ecclesiastical implications* (Grand Rapids, Mich. [1960]).

D'Arcy, Martin Cyril (1888–1976), *Jesuit philosophical theologian. Educated at *Stonyhurst, *Oxford,

and the *Gregorian University at Rome, he entered the Society of Jesus and was ordained priest in 1921. From 1933 to 1945 he was Master of Campion Hall, Oxford, and from 1945 to 1950 Provincial of the English Province of the Jesuits. He expounded Catholic principles and philosophy to a public with less narrowly theological interests. His larger works include *St Thomas Aquinas* (1930); *The Nature of Belief* (1931), an analysis of faith which, following J. H. *Newman's *Grammar of Assent*, emphasized its affective and non-logical elements; and *The Mind and Heart of Love* (1945), an assessment of the Christian conception of love (*agape, as contrasted with eros and philia), strongly influenced by D. Saurat and A. Nygren. Much of his most characteristic writing was in essays, articles, and contributions to collective works.

Reminiscences recorded in Georgetown University (1960–1) were pub. under the title *Laughter and Love of Friends*, ed. W. S. Abell (Westminster, Md., 1991).

Dark Ages, the. A term in current use for the period in W. Europe extending from the decay of classical culture *c*. the 5th cent. to the beginning of medieval culture *c*. the 11th cent. It was formerly in common usage to cover also the medieval period down to the Renaissance.

Darwinism. The form of the theory of evolution put forward by Charles Darwin (1809–82), esp. in his works *The Origin of Species* (1859) and *The Descent of Man* (1871). He held that species of living beings evolve by natural selection, the individuals best adapted to their circumstances in any generation being those most likely to survive and propagate. He became gradually more and more of an agnostic in religion.

G. Himmelfarb, *Darwin and the Darwinian Revolution* (1959); M. Banton (ed.), *Darwinism and the Study of Society* (1961); N. C. Gillespie, *Charles Darwin and the Problem of Creation* (Chicago and London, 1979); J. R. Moore, *The Post-Darwinian Controversies: A Study of the Protestant Struggle to come to terms with Darwin in Britain and America 1870–1900* (1979); J. Durant (ed.), *Darwinism and Divinity: Essays on Evolution and Religious Belief* (Oxford, 1985); A. Desmond and J. Moore, *Darwin* (London, 1991).

d'Aubigné, Jean Henri Merle. See MERLE D'AUBIGNÉ, JEAN HENRI.

Davenport, Christopher (in religion **Franciscus a Sancta Clara**) (*c*.1595–1680), English RC theologian. There has been some confusion about his early life. Probably while studying at *Oxford, he was converted to the RC faith and by 1616 he was in *Douai. He entered the *Franciscan Order at Ypres in 1617, and later returned to England, where he became chaplain successively to Queens *Henrietta Maria and Catherine of Braganza. He was on good terms with many of the Anglican clergy, and in his *Paraphrastica Expositio Articulorum Confessionis Anglicanae* (published separately in 1634, afterwards as an appendix to his *Deus, natura, gratia*) he endeavoured to show that the *Thirty-Nine Articles could be interpreted in conformity with Catholic tradition.

Collected edn. of his works (corrected), Douai, 2 vols., 1665–7. *Paraphrastica Expositio Articulorum Confessionis Anglicanae* was repr. from the Lat. edn. of 1646, with Eng. tr., ed. F. G. *Lee (London, 1865), with sketch of the author's life, pp. xix–xxx. J. B. Dockery, OFM, *Christopher Davenport, Friar and Diplomat* (1960). R. I. Bradley, SJ, 'Christopher Davenport and the Thirty-Nine Articles', *Archiv für Reformationsgeschichte*, 52 (1961), pp. 205–28. G. G. Perry in *DNB* 14 (1888), pp. 108 f.; H. Dauphin, OSB, in *DHGE* 14 (1960), cols. 109–11, s.v.

Davenport, John (1597–1670), *Puritan divine. Prob. the uncle (rather than the brother, as used to be thought) of Christopher Davenport (see preceding entry), he was educated at Merton and Magdalen Colleges, Oxford, and in 1624 became Vicar of St Stephen's, Coleman Street, in London. He incurred the hostility of W. *Laud, who nevertheless called him 'a most religious man', through a 'feoffment scheme' for the purchase of lay impropriations and his efforts to raise money for distressed ministers in the Palatinate. In 1633 he resigned his living and became co-pastor of the English church in Amsterdam. In 1637 he sailed to Boston with other well-known refugees, and in 1638 founded at Quinnipiac the colony of New Haven. In the colony, which was governed by 'The Seven Pillars of the State' (of which he was one), Church membership was obligatory for electors and civil officers, until in 1665 the colony was absorbed in Connecticut. In 1662 he became involved in a controversy over Baptism, connected with the '*Half-Way Covenant'. In 1668 he was ordained a minister, and set over the first church at Boston. He was the author of many works, including *A Catechism containing the chief Heads of the Christian Religion* (1659) and *The Power of Congregational Churches Asserted and Vindicated* (1672). In 1642 there appeared *The Profession of the Faith of the Reverend and Worthy Divine, Mr. John Davenport*.

Letters ed. I. McB. Calder (New Haven, Conn., 1937), with short biog. sketch, pp. 1–12. J. T. Adams in *Dict. Amer. Biog.* 5 (1930), pp. 85–7.

David (d. prob. *c.*970 BC), first king of the Judaean dynasty. His reign is recounted in 1 Sam. 16–1 Kgs. 2 and in the idealized description in 1 Chron. 2 f. and 10–29.

David, the youngest son of Jesse, a Judaean of *Bethlehem, first appears when at God's command he is anointed by Samuel to the future kingship (1 Sam. 16: 13). Acc. to one tradition (1 Sam. 16: 14–23), he was summoned to the court of Saul as a skilful player upon the harp and eventually appointed the king's armour-bearer. Acc. to another, he appears to have first attracted Saul's attention when as an untried youth he gained his victory over Goliath, the Philistine giant (1 Sam. 17: 12–18: 4). He was promoted by Saul, won the affection of Jonathan, Saul's son, and married Michal, Saul's daughter. Then, however, he excited the king's jealousy and came in danger of his life. He fled to Nob (1 Sam. 21: 1) and thence prob. to the territory of western *Judah; here he gathered a band of supporters. After defeating a body of Philistines near Keilah (1 Sam. 23: 1–5), he established himself at Ziklag as a vassal of Achish, King of Gath (1 Sam. 27: 6). He was saved from taking part in a campaign against the Israelites only by the distrust of the Philistine lords (1 Sam. 29).

On the death of Saul on Mt. Gilboa (*c.*1010 BC), David, prob. still under Philistine patronage, set himself up at

*Hebron as king of the Judaean tribes (2 Sam. 2: 1–4). Seven and a half years later, when Ishbosheth, Saul's son, had been murdered, he was accepted also by the Israelites (2 Sam. 4 f.). As soon as he had captured *Jerusalem from the Jebusites, he established it as his capital (2 Sam. 5) and brought the *Ark to the city (2 Sam. 6). Acc. to tradition, David planned to build a temple, but was told by the prophet Nathan that this would be achieved by his son (2 Sam. 7). In a series of battles David broke the supremacy of the Philistines and secured ascendancy over the neighbouring tribes (2 Sam. 8). He was undoubtedly an outstanding general and politician; he established *Israel as an independent power with a small but significant empire. Concerning his reign of 33 years in Jerusalem relatively little information survives, though we have an extended account of the struggles over the succession among his sons (Absalom, *Solomon, etc) and their supporters (2 Sam. 9–20; 1 Kgs. 1–2).

Our portrait of David, one of the most lifelike in the OT, is that of a ruler who both gave and inspired deep affection, not least through the magnanimity which he frequently showed to his personal enemies. The narrative reports, with striking honesty, his lapses into sin (adultery with Bathsheba and murder of Uriah; 2 Sam. 11), but also gives a moving picture of his repentance (2 Sam. 12).

David has traditionally been regarded as the author of the *Psalms (q.v.), many of which have been associated in later times with particular incidents in his life, e.g. the *Miserere (Ps. 51) with his repentance after the Bathsheba incident. But the tendency of modern OT scholarship is against assigning to David more than a small fraction of the Psalter. It is possible, however, that he composed the dirges over Saul and Jonathan (2 Sam. 1: 19–27) and Abner (2 Sam. 3: 33 f.).

In Hebrew tradition, the name of David came to occupy a central position. He was the king whose house and dominion were to stand for ever (2 Sam. 7: 12–16). But though his dynasty continued to reign in Judah, it lost the allegiance of the northern tribes (Israel) on the death of Solomon (*c.*930 BC) and after frequent misfortunes and attacks fell to the Babylonians *c.*586 BC. These calamities led the Prophets to look to the re-establishment of the full sovereignty of 'David' (i.e. of the house of David) as part of the deliverance of the nation (e.g. Amos 9: 11, Hos. 3: 5, Is. 16: 5, Jer. 30: 9, and Ezek. 37: 24) to be achieved through a future prince of the house (Is. 9: 6 f.), a 'Branch' from the stock of Jesse (Is. 11: 1–10; Jer. 33: 14–26). As the hope of the *Messiah grew, the deliverer was awaited from among the descendants of David, while David himself was conceived as a *type of the expected Messiah on the basis of such references as Ps. 110.

In the NT the Evangelists assume the Davidic descent of the Messiah (see GENEALOGIES OF CHRIST). It is as the 'Son of David' (e.g. Mt. 21: 9) that the Lord is welcomed to Jerusalem before His Passion. His Davidic ancestry is also stressed in Rom. 1: 3, 2 Tim. 2: 8 and Rev. 5: 5, 22: 16.

In the Fathers the idea of David as the type of Christ is a commonplace. St *Augustine draws a parallel between David's victory over Goliath and that of the Lord over Satan; St *Cyril of Alexandria explains that David's sling foreshadows the Cross of Christ; while in both St Augustine and St *Gregory the Great the victory of David in his weakness foreshadows that of the Church and the Christian martyrs. In Christian art he is regularly depicted with a crown and a harp. His role as the ancestor of Christ is graphically represented in the *Jesse windows (q.v.).

L. Rost, *Die Überlieferung von der Thronnachfolge Davids* (Beiträge zur Wissenschaft vom Alten und Neuen Testaments, Dritte Folge, 6; 1926; Eng. tr., *The Succession to the Throne of David*, Sheffield, 1982); R. N. Whybray, *The Succession Narrative: A Study of II Samuel 9–20 and 1 Kings 1 and 2* (Studies in Biblical Theology, 2nd ser. 9; 1968). D. M. Gunn, *The Story of King David: Genre and Interpretation* (Journal for the Study of the Old Testament, Supplement Series, 6; Sheffield, 1978). H. Steger, *David Rex et Propheta: König David als vorbildliche Verkörperung des Herrschers und Dichters im Mittelalter, nach Bilddarstellungen des achten bis zwölften Jahrhunderts* (1961). J. M. Myers in *Interpreter's Dictionary of the Bible*, 1 (New York, etc., 1962), pp. 771–82, s.v. See also comm. to Sam. and Kings, cited s.vv., and histories of Israel.

David, St (d. *c*.601), patron saint of *Wales. Though he is one of the most famous British saints, there is no reliable biography of him. His earliest Life, that by Bp. Rhygyfarch or Ricimas, which dates from the second half of the 11th cent., was written with a view to supporting the claims of the Welsh bishops to independence of *Canterbury. Acc. to the legend, he belonged to a noble family; after having become a priest, he lived for a time in retirement; later he became the founder of 12 monasteries; finally he settled at Mynyw or Menevia, where he established an abbey whose religious led a life of extreme asceticism modelled on that of the Egyptian monks. About 560 he is said to have attended the Synod of Brefi (the modern Llanddewi Brefi), apparently one of the few historically established facts of his life; but the story that he spoke there with such eloquence that he was chosen primate of the Cambrian Church seems to be legendary, as well as the assertion that he transferred the episcopal see from Caerleon to Menevia, now *St Davids. He is related to have called in 569 a Council, generally styled the 'Synod of Victory', because held at a place the Latin name of which is given as 'Lucus Victoriae' (Caerleon). Other features of St David's life, such as his pilgrimage to *Jerusalem and his consecration as archbishop by its patriarch, are mere inventions. St David's cult seems to have been approved by Pope *Callistus II *c*.1120; in 1398 Abp. *Arundel ordered his feast to be kept throughout the province of Canterbury. Feast day, 1 Mar.

St David is mentioned in the 'Martyrology of St *Oengus' (*c*.800) and in the 'Catalogue of the Saints of Ireland' (9th–10th cent.), but without any details of his life being given. Text of Rhygyfarch's Life ed. A. W. Wade-Evans, *Y Cymmrodor*, 24 (1913), pp. 4–28. The same author pub. an Eng. tr. with copious notes, *The Life of St David* (1923). It is also ed., with Eng. tr., by J. W. James (Cardiff, 1967). See also D. S. Evans (ed.), *The Welsh Life of St David* (ibid., 1988). S. M. Harris, *Saint David in the Liturgy* (ibid., 1940). N. K. Chadwick in id. and others, *Studies in the Early British Church* (Cambridge, 1958), pp. 134–57.

David of Augsburg (*c*.1200–72), German preacher and spiritual writer. Prob. a native of Augsburg, he entered the *Franciscan Order at Regensburg, where he became novice-master. Later he was transferred to the newly founded house at Augsburg, where, with his friend Berthold of Regensburg (d. 1273), also a great preacher, he carried on active evangelism. His principal Latin writings, which have frequently been ascribed to St *Bernard and to St *Bonaventure, are a major three-part work 'De Exterioribus et Interioris Hominis Compositione' (usually referred to as 'De Compositione'), which is much influenced by *William of St-Thierry, and two letters. The authenticity of 'De Inquisitione Haereticorum' and various other Latin works has been disputed. He is generally regarded as the first author to publish spiritual treatises in German. Of those usually regarded as genuine 'Die sieben Staffeln des Gebetes' is a free rendering of 'Septem Gradus Orationis' (an anonymous work, thought by many to be by David himself); 'Die sieben Vorregeln der Tugend' is based on chapters in 'De Compositione'; and even independent compositions, such as 'De Spiegel der Tugend' and his commentary on the *Lord's Prayer, betray close affinities with 'De Compositione'. His teaching was eminently practical. He inculcated perfect obedience and humility, warned against illusions, and though enlarging more on the active than the contemplative life, kept in view the mystic union of the soul and its three faculties of memory, understanding, and will with God. His works continued to be used in the later Middle Ages, especially in the Netherlands.

David's 'De Compositione Hominis Exterioris' and other Lat. works for novices ed. Quaracchi, 1899; 'De Inquisitione Haereticorum' first ed. W. Preger, *Abh.* (Bayr.), 14 (1879), Abteilung 2, pp. 181–235; 'Septem gradus Orationis' first ed. J. Heerinckx, OFM, *Revue d'ascétique et de mystique*, 14 (1933), pp. 146–70; his German works in F. Pfeiffer (ed.), *Deutsche Mystiker des vierzehnten Jahrhunderts*, 1 (1845), pp. 309–405. Crit. edn. of 'Die sieben Staffeln des Gebetes' by K. Ruh (Kleine deutsche Prosadenkmäler des Mittelalters, 1; 1965). Eng. tr. of various Lat. works by D. Devas, OFM, under the title *Spiritual Life and Progress* (2 vols., 1937), with introd. D. Stöckerl, *Bruder David von Augsburg* (Veröffentlichungen aus dem kirchenhistorischen Seminar München, 4, Heft 4; 1914). K. Ruh, 'David von Augsburg und die Entstehung eines Franziskanischen Schrifttums in deutscher Sprache', in H. Rinn (ed.), *Augusta 955–1955: Forschungen und Studien zur Kultur- und Wirtschaftsgeschichte Augsburg* (Augsburg, 1955), pp. 71–82. F. M. Schwab, OCD, *David of Augsburg's 'Paternoster' and the Authenticity of his German Works* (Münchener Texte und Untersuchungen zur deutschen Literatur des Mittelalters, 32; 1971), incl. text. C. Rüegg, *David von Augsburg* (Deutsche Literatur von den Anfängen bis 1700, 4 [1989]). K. Ruh in *Verfasserlexikon* (2nd edn.), 2 (1980), cols. 47–58, s.v.

David of Dinant (*fl.* 1200), naturalist and philosopher. He prob. came from Dinant in Belgium. He is given the title 'Magister', which implies study in a school; he described himself as a physician, mentioned a stay in Greece, and said that he wrote a work *De anatomia venarum et arteriarum et nervorum totius corporis* (identified by B. Lawn with the *De iuvamento anhelitus* which circulated under the name of Galen). In a letter of Pope *Innocent III of 1206 he is called 'capellanus noster'. In 1210 a Council of the Province of Sens ordered that his writings (*Quaternuli*) should be brought to the Bp. of Paris and burnt. These writings have until recently been known only from fragments quoted by others, chiefly *Albertus Magnus. In 1933 A. Birkenmajer and R. de Vaux independently identified fragments of his work, and these were edited by M. Kurdziałek in 1963. The fragments, which contain passages reproduced by Albertus Magnus, apparently come from an incomplete work in various stages of elaboration. They show considerable knowledge of the physical works of *Aristotle derived from a reading of the original text. Together with discussion of natural phenomena (including natural explanations for some biblical miracles), some startling doctrines are set forth. David taught that all distinctions in real being (*ens in actu*) are to be explained by a primal possible being (*materia prima*), which he identified with the Divine Being. All things, material, intellectual, and spiritual, have one and the same essence, that is, God. The sources for David's views have been much discussed, but G. Théry is prob. right in maintaining that the preponderant influence is Aristotle. We do not know whether David taught in Paris, but the circulation of such views there led to the condemnation of the study of the *Metaphysics* of Aristotle and of his works on natural philosophy in Paris. Albertus Magnus attacked David's writings mercilessly. He was concerned to show that the materialistic view of David not only found no support in Aristotle, but that Aristotle's philosophy, rightly understood, was a condemnation of David's interpretation. David's position was entirely different from that of *Amalric of Bène, who was condemned at the same time.

'Quaternulorum Fragmenta' ed. M. Kurdziałek (Studia Mediewistycne, 3; Warsaw, 1963). G. Théry, OP, *Autour du Décret de 1210*: I. David de Dinant (Bibliothèque Thomiste, 6; 1925), with text of extracts from Albertus Magnus and Thomas Aquinas, and refs. to earlier works. A. Birkenmajer, 'Découverte de fragments manuscrits de David de Dinant', *Revue Néo-scolastique de Philosophie*, 35 (1933), pp. 220–9; R. de Vaux, OP, 'Sur un texte retrouvé de David de Dinant', *RSPT* 22 (1933), pp. 243–5. B. Lawn, *I Quesiti Salernitani* (rev. Ital. tr., 1969), pp. 100–5, identifying further fragments. M.-T. d'Alverny, 'Les nouveaux apports dans les domaines de la science et de la pensée au temps de Philippe Auguste: La Philosophie', in R.-H. Bautier (ed.), *La France de Philippe Auguste: Le Temps des mutations* (Colloques Internationaux du Centre National de la Recherche Scientifique, 602; 1982), pp. 863–80, esp. pp. 867–70.

Davidson, Andrew Bruce (1831–1902), Scottish OT scholar. He belonged to the *Free Church of Scotland and was educated at Marischal College, Aberdeen, and at New College, Edinburgh. At the latter he became assistant professor of Hebrew in 1858 and professor of Hebrew and Oriental languages in 1863. He was one of the first to introduce historical methods of OT exegesis into Scotland, and though his own dogmatic orthodoxy was seldom challenged, that of several of his pupils, who carried his principles a stage further, notably W. R. *Smith, was fiercely contested. His writings include *An Introductory Hebrew Grammar* (1874); commentaries on *Job* (1884), *Ezekiel* (1892), and *Nahum, Habakkuk, Zephaniah* (1896), in the 'Cambridge Bible'; *The Theology of the Old Testament*, ed. S. D. F. Salmond (1904); and a large number of articles in J. *Hastings's *Dictionary of the Bible*. He was also a member of the OT Revision Committee.

J. Strahan, *Andrew Bruce Davidson* (1917). Also biog. introd. by A. T. Innes to A. B. Davidson, *The Called of God*, ed. J. A. Paterson (1902), pp. 3–58. Complete list of his works in *The Expository Times*, 15 (1904), p. 453. R. A. Riesen, *Criticism and Faith in late Victorian Scotland* (Lanham, Md. [1985]), pp. 252–376. S. R. *Driver in *DNB*, 1901–1911, I, pp. 471 f.

Davidson, Randall Thomas (1848–1930), Abp. of *Canterbury. The son of Scottish Presbyterian parents, he was educated at Harrow (where he was confirmed) and at

Trinity College, Oxford, and then trained for holy orders by C. J. *Vaughan. He was ordained deacon in 1874 to the curacy of Dartford, Kent, where he remained until in 1877 he became resident chaplain to the Abp. of Canterbury, A. C. *Tait, whose second daughter he married. An interview with Queen Victoria, on the occasion of Tait's death in 1882, greatly impressed her with his personality, and in 1883 he was appointed Dean of Windsor. In 1891 he became Bp. of *Rochester, in 1895 of *Winchester, and in 1903 Abp. of Canterbury. He resigned in 1928, the first Abp. of Canterbury to do so.

As the confidential adviser of Queen Victoria, and afterwards as Primate, Davidson exercised an exceptional influence upon the life of Church and nation. He endeavoured esp. to maintain the comprehensiveness of the C of E and to strengthen the Church as a spiritual and moral witness in national life. His primacy was a period of special difficulty, requiring him to take action with regard to such varied questions as the disestablishment of the Church in *Wales, the *Kikuyu Controversy, the *Enabling Act, the *Malines Conversations, the Coal Strike (1926), Prayer Book Revision, and relations with various E. Churches. Having been present at every *Lambeth Conference since 1878, when he was Tait's chaplain, he presided over those of 1908 and 1920. As episcopal secretary to the 1897 Conference he was instrumental in establishing the Lambeth Consultative Committee, and in 1908 he chaired some of the sessions of the first Pan-Anglican Congress in London. He was the first Abp. of Canterbury to make an official visit to the United States of America and Canada (1904). Though suffering from lifelong ill-health owing to an accident in boyhood, he was an indefatigable worker. He possessed the courage necessary in a leader, even if he more often preferred to exercise the caution of a chairman. His elevation to the peerage as 'Baron Davidson of Lambeth', after his resignation of the primacy, was the recognition of one whose service to the Church was also, in a high degree, service to the nation.

G. K. A. *Bell, *Randall Davidson* (2 vols., 1935; 3rd edn., 1952). Id. in *DNB*, 1922–1930, pp. 240–8.

Day Hours. Traditionally the services of the *Breviary other than *Mattins (which constituted the 'night office'), i.e. *Lauds, *Prime, *Terce, *Sext, *None, *Vespers, and *Compline. The office-book containing these services is known as the *Diurnal. For the arrangement of offices in the 1971 Breviary, see under OFFICE, DIVINE.

Day of Atonement. See ATONEMENT, DAY OF.

Day's Psalter. A popular name (which does not appear on any title page) for the *metrical edition of the Psalms by Thomas *Sternhold (d. 1549) and John Hopkins (d. ?1570). It applies to the early complete editions of this Psalter, which were printed by John Day (1522–84) from 1562 onwards. More commonly called the *Old Version*, it had been in use, in incomplete form, since 1549. Reissued by other printers, it continued to circulate widely for over a hundred years.

deacon (Gk. διάκονος, 'servant', 'minister'; cf. διακονέω, 'I serve'), the rank in the Christian ministry next below the presbyter (priest) and bishop. The institution of the diaconate is traditionally seen in the ordination of the 'seven men of honest report' (including *Stephen and *Philip), by the imposition of hands for the service of the poor and the distribution of alms (Acts 6: 1–6), though the word διάκονος is not found here. Where it occurs in the NT in a technical sense (Phil. 1: 1, 1 Tim. 3: 8) it is in conjunction with 'bishop' (ἐπίσκοπος); deacons seem to be assistants to the bishops. In the *Pastoral Epp. the deacons are a separate class of Church officers, charged chiefly with material duties.

In post-NT times deacons continued to exercise similar functions. They are mentioned in *Clement of Rome's Ep. to the Corinthians, and in the Epp. of *Ignatius they appear for the first time in the third place, after bishops and presbyters. In the patristic age, when the office was normally held for life, their functions varied from place to place. While the celebration of the Eucharist was reserved for the bishop or priest (along with the giving of *absolution and pronouncement of the *blessing), deacons commonly read or chanted the *Epistle and *Gospel at the Eucharist, received the offerings of the faithful and inscribed the names of the donors in the *diptychs, assisted the bishop (and later the priest) in the distribution of the consecrated elements to the people or distributed them themselves, directed the prayers of the laity during the service, and gave the signal for *penitents and *catechumens to leave the Church before the beginning of the *Eucharistic Prayer. These liturgical functions were considerably curtailed in the W. when, in 595, *Gregory the Great transferred many of their musical functions to the *cantors.

Their original office of collecting and distributing the alms gave them considerable importance and the *archdeacon, the chief deacon of a given place, became the bishop's principal administrative officer. In Rome their influence was esp. marked through their association with the Pope; here their number was long restricted to seven, a tradition which was perpetuated in the seven *Cardinal Deacons. It gave rise, however, to abuses. Already at *Nicaea (325; can. 18) their powers were curbed and the Council of *Toledo in 633 and the *Trullan Synod of 692 had to stress their hierarchical inferiority to the priesthood. Their influence diminished considerably during the Middle Ages, and in most W. episcopal Churches in modern times the diaconate has become merely a necessary stage in preparation for the priesthood. The E. Church, however, has always retained a permanent diaconate. Candidates for the diaconate cannot be ordained until they have reached the canonical *age. The characteristic vestments of the deacon in the W. are the *dalmatic, and *stole worn over the left shoulder; in the E. the *orarion.

In the post-Tridentine RC Church the deacon had hardly any functions beyond his ministrations at High Mass and *Benediction. Only with special permission was he allowed to preach or administer Solemn Baptism, though he retained the right to chant the Gospel, to present the offerings to the celebrant, to invite the congregation to pray, and to chant the '*Ite, missa est' at Mass; to expose the Bl Sacrament and put it back in the Tabernacle at Benediction; and to sing the *Exultet. Because of the short time normally spent in the diaconate and hence the fewness of deacons, the liturgical functions proper to a

deacon came to be frequently performed by a priest. The Second *Vatican Council (1962–5) envisaged the possibility of the restoration of a permanent diaconate; following the procedure envisaged, bishops in some countries have ordained older married men as deacons, though young men ordained deacon are still bound to *celibacy. The Council's Constitution 'On the Church' (Lumen Gentium, 29) also defined the duties of a deacon, allowing him, when authorized, to baptize solemnly, administer Communion, assist at and bless weddings, give *Viaticum to the dying, instruct and exhort the people, and officiate at funerals.

At the Reformation the C of E retained the order of deacon, though, as it abolished the *minor orders, this then became the lowest rank of ecclesiastical minister. In 1986 the order became open to women as well as men, as was already the case in certain other Provinces of the Anglican Communion. The functions of Anglican deacons are similar to those of their modern RC counterparts. Men who are to be made priests normally remain deacons for one year.

In many of the Protestant Churches the name is applied to the holders of an office in the ministry. In the *Lutheran Church the word 'deacon' is applied to assistant parochial ministers, even though they are in full Lutheran orders. J. *Calvin's Institutes (4. 3. 9) recognized two classes of deacons, those who administered the alms and those who cared for the poor and sick. These remain the functions of deacons in *Presbyterianism, where there is also provision for a deacons' court, directly responsible to the presbytery and concerned with the proper distribution of Church goods. Where such a court does not exist, the deacons' functions are performed by *elders. In the *Baptist and *Congregational Churches more definitely spiritual functions are assigned to the deacons, who assist the pastor and also distribute the elements at the Communion. See also the following entry.

H. Krimm (ed.), Das Diakonische Amt der Kirche (Stuttgart, 1953; 2nd edn., 1965); id. (ed.), Quellen zur Geschichte der Diakonie (2 vols., ibid. [1960–64]). J. Colson, La Fonction diaconale aux origines de l'Église (Textes et Études Théologiques, 1960). K. *Rahner, SJ, and H. Vorgrimler (eds.), Diaconia in Christo: Über die Erneuerung des Diakonates (Quaestiones Disputatae, 15–16; 1962), with bibl. P. Winninger and Y. [M.-J.] *Congar, (eds.), Le Diacre dans l'Église et le Monde d'Aujourd'hui (Unam Sanctam, 59; 1966). J. N. Collins, Diakonia: Re-interpreting the Ancient Sources (New York, 1990). Deacons in the Ministry of the Church: A Report to the House of Bishops of the General Synod of the Church of England (General Synod Paper 802; 1988). H. W. Beyer in TWNT 2 (1935; Eng. tr., 1963), pp. 88–93, s.v. διάκονος. S. Cheetham in DCA 1 (1875), pp. 526–32, s.v.; J. Forget in DTC 4 (1911), cols. 703–31, s.v. 'Diacres'; H. *Leclercq, OSB, in DACL 4 (pt. 1; 1920), cols. 738–46, s.v. 'Diacre'; F. Claeys-Bouuaert in DDC 4 (1949), cols. 1198–206, s.v. 'Diacre'; T. Klauser in RAC 3 (1957), cols. 888–909, s.v. 'Diakon'.

deaconess. A woman officially charged with certain functions in the Church. The practice of a woman fulfilling the office of *deacon goes back to the Apostolic age. St *Paul's mention of Phoebe 'deaconess (οὖσαν διάκονον) of the Church that is at Cenchreae' (Rom. 16: 1), as well as 1 Tim. 3: 11 are usually held to refer to a special office; and *Pliny, in his letter to Trajan, speaks of two 'ancillae quare ministrae dicebantur'. However, the term διακόνισσα (Lat. diaconissa) did not come into use until the 4th cent. Earlier documents use 'diacona', 'vidua', or 'virgo canonica', and the distinction between *widows and deaconesses is rather obscure.

The office, which developed greatly in the 3rd and 4th cents., is described in the '*Didascalia' and the '*Apostolic Constitutions'. The age of entry, fixed at 50 by the 'Didascalia', was reduced to 40 by the Council of *Chalcedon. The deaconess devoted herself to the care of the sick and the poor of her sex; she was present at interviews of women with bishops, priests, or deacons; instructed women catechumens, and kept order in the women's part of the church. Her most important function was the assistance at the baptism of women, at which, for reasons of propriety, many of the ceremonies could not be performed by the deacons. When, therefore, adult baptism became rare, the office of deaconess declined in importance. This process was helped by abuses which had crept in, when deaconesses undertook ministerial functions, e.g. in the *Oriental Orthodox Churches and the *Church of the East, where they administered Holy Communion to women. The Councils of Epaon (517) and of Orléans (533) abrogated the office, but it is found in other places till the 11th cent. In the E., where the prerogatives of deaconesses were more marked, including the investiture with the stole and the distribution of the chalice, the process was somewhat slower. The reception of stole and maniple by the *Carthusian nuns at their profession would seem to be a survival of the ancient office.

In the 19th cent. the office was revived in a modified form. The first Protestant community of deaconesses was that established by the German pastor, T. Fliedner, at *Kaiserswerth (q.v.) in 1836. From there it spread to other countries, notably England and the USA. In the C of E, the Deaconess Community of St Andrew was founded in 1861 and the first deaconess (Miss Elizabeth Ferard) was set apart for her work the following year by A. C. *Tait, Bp. of London. Diocesan institutes on the model of Kaiserswerth were founded in many parts of the country, and rules drawn up for them in 1871. The example was followed by the *Methodists in America in 1888, and in the same year deaconesses were established in the Church of Scotland.

In the C of E the order of deaconess was described in the 1969 Canons (can. D. 1) as 'the one order of ministry ... to which women are admitted by prayer and the laying on of hands by the bishop'; at the same time it was stated that it was 'not one of the holy orders of the Church of England'. Acc. to the revised Canons, the main duties of the deaconess are 'to lead the people in public worship, to exercise pastoral care, to instruct the people in the Christian faith, and to prepare them for the reception of the sacraments'. She may be authorized to say Morning and Evening Prayer (except the Absolution), to read the Epistle and Gospel at the Holy Communion, and to distribute the Sacrament. At the invitation of the minister, she may also preach, in the absence of the minister baptize, and, with the goodwill of the persons concerned, conduct funerals. Under the Deacons (Ordination of Women) Measure 1986, women were admitted to the diaconate. Existing deaconesses could be ordained deacons. There were to be no further admissions to the order of deaconesses, but those already admitted who did not wish to become deacons remained deaconesses.

J. Mayer (ed.), *Monumenta de Viduis, Diaconissis, Virginibusque Tractantia* (Florilegium Patristicum, 42; Bonn, 1938), with refs. C. H. *Turner, 'Ministries of Women in the Primitive Church: Widow, Deaconess and Virgin in the First Four Christian Centuries', *The Constructive Quarterly*, 7 (1919), repr. in *Catholic and Apostolic*, ed. H. N. Bate (1931), no. 11, pp. 316–51, esp. pp. 328–43; A. Kalsbach, *Die altkirchliche Einrichtung der Diakonissen bis zu ihrem Erlöschen* (Römische Quartalschrift, Supplementheft 22; 1926); J. G. Davies, 'Deacons, Deaconesses and the Minor Orders in the Patristic Period', *JEH* 14 (1963), pp. 1–15, esp. pp. 1–6; R. Gryson, *Le Ministère des femmes dans l'Église ancienne* (Recherches et Synthèses, Section d'Histoire, 4; Gembloux [1972]); A. G. Martimort, *Les Diaconesses: Essai historique* (Bibliotheca Ephemerides Liturgicae, Subsidia, 24; Rome, 1982; Eng. tr., San Francisco, 1986); M.-J. Aubert, *Les Femmes diacres: Un nouveau chemin pour l'Église* (Le Point théologique, 47 [1987]). C. Robinson, *The Ministry of Deaconesses* (1898); *The Ministry of Women: A Report by a Committee Appointed by the Abp. of Canterbury* (1919); J. Grierson, *The Deaconess* (1981) [on deaconesses in the C of E]. A. Kalsbach in *RAC* 3 (1957), cols. 917–28, s.v. 'Diakonisse'.

dead, prayers for the. The custom of praying for the dead is a traditional practice independent of any biblical support: 'If you look in Scripture for a formal law governing these and similar practices, you will find none. It is tradition that justifies them, custom that confirms them, and faith that observes them' (*Tertullian, *de cor.*, 4. 1). The only scriptural text where such prayer is clearly recorded is 2 Macc. 12: 40–5. There is, however, ample evidence for its use in the inscriptions of the *catacombs, with their constant prayers for the peace and refreshment of the souls of the departed, and the early liturgies commonly contain commemorations of the dead. Of the early Fathers, Tertullian, *Cyprian, and others are witnesses of the regular practice of praying for the dead, and in the 4th cent. one of the counts against the heretic *Aerius was that he denied its efficacy and legitimacy.

In the E. Church no limits are placed on such prayer. In the Liturgy of St *Chrysostom, the Eucharistic sacrifice is offered for (ὑπέρ) the saints and martyrs, and there is authority for praying for those 'bound in *Hades' (Service of Kneeling, *Pentecostarion, Rome, 1883, p. 414) and for pagans (cf. *Apophthegmata Patrum, Macarius, 38). In the W. prayer for the dead was closely connected with the development of the doctrine of *purgatory (q.v.); gradually such prayer was limited to prayer for the 'holy souls', i.e. the souls in purgatory. The W. Church does not pray for the martyrs, because they are believed to be in full possession of beatitude immediately after death, a refusal later extended to all canonized saints. Nor, it is held, can the damned, i.e. those who have died in unrepented mortal sin, be assisted by our prayers, though who they are is known to God alone. Thus the public offering of Mass for the excommunicate (and even for those outside the RC Church) was long forbidden, though private prayers and Masses for the Dead might be said for them. Acc. to modern RC Canon Law, unless they gave some sign of repentance before death, Masses for the Dead and funeral rites are not to be conducted for notorious apostates, heretics, schismatics, public sinners, or for those who for anti-Christian reasons desired *cremation. If, however, their own minister is not available, baptized persons belonging to another Church or ecclesial community may be given

RC funeral rites, unless it is established that they did not wish this (*CIC* (1983), cans. 1183–5).

At first the Protestant Reformers continued the traditional custom of praying for the dead. But before long they came to denounce it, partly because they believed it to be without biblical foundation (2 Macc. 12: 40–5 was dismissed, since the 'Apocrypha' no longer ranked as Scripture), partly through their rejection of the doctrine of purgatory and the practices associated with it. In the C of E express prayers for the dead have been absent from the BCP since 1552 and the practice is denounced as unprofitable in the *Homily 'On Prayer' (part 3) on the ground that it is useless to intercede for the dead, who are already either in heaven or hell. The liturgy of the *Nonjurors, however, included prayers for the dead, and since the middle of the 19th cent. the practice has been increasingly adopted in the C of E. Prayers for the dead were included in an authorized 'Form of Intercession' put out in 1900 on behalf of the forces serving in South Africa and since then in other official forms of service. In a veiled form they were inserted for optional use in the proposed revision of the BCP in 1927–8; they are allowed in the ASB and some (though not all) other modern Anglican liturgies. Prayer for the dead is still avoided by those of marked *Evangelical belief and in the Free Churches. See also BURIAL SERVICES and REQUIEM.

The traditional Catholic teaching was reasserted at the Council of *Trent, sessions 22 (cf. can. 3) and 25 (for both, see Denzinger and Hünermann (37th edn., 1991), nos. 1743, 1753, 1820), as well as in the Decree of Union subscribed at the Council of *Florence of 1439 (ibid., no. 1304). *Prayer and the Departed: A Report of the Archbishops' Commission on Christian Doctrine* (1971). F. S. Paxton, *Christianizing Death: The Creation of a Ritual Process in Early Medieval Europe* (Ithaca, NY, and London, 1990). See also PURGATORY.

Dead Sea. The inland sea to the SE of Palestine into which the *Jordan flows. It is much the lowest lake in the world, being nearly 1,300 feet below sea-level. Acc. to Hebrew tradition, it was formed when the cities of the plain, Sodom and Gomorrah, were overthrown for their wickedness (cf. Gen. 13: 13 and 19: 24–8). There are several refs. to it in the OT (e.g. Zech. 14: 8), though never as the 'Dead Sea' by name. The vision of Ezek. 47 looks forward to a day when a river issuing from the *Temple at Jerusalem will flow into the sea and make its stagnant waters fresh. In the NT there is no mention of it. The designation 'Dead Sea' (θάλασσα νεκρά) is first found in Pausanias and Galen.

G. A. *Smith, *The Historical Geography of the Holy Land* (25th edn.; 1931), ch. 23, pp. 497–530, with bibl. refs. F. M. Abel, OP, *Géographie de la Palestine*, 1 (1933), pp. 167–9. Modern guide by J. Murphy-O'Connor, OP, *The Holy Land* (2nd edn., Oxford, 1986), pp. 197–201.

Dead Sea Scrolls. The term denotes scrolls and fragments discovered for the most part between 1947 and 1960 at seven sites on the NW and W. shores of the Dead Sea: eleven caves near *Qumran, two caves in Wadi Murabba'at, the caves of Nahal Hever, Nahal Mishmar, and Nahal Ṣe'elim, and at Khirbet Mird and Masada. Commonly it is used only in reference to the writings from the caves near Qumran. These writings are referred to by cave number, site, and abbreviated title; e.g. 1QH = cave

number 1, Qumran, *Hodayot* (= Hymns of Thanksgiving).

From the Qumran caves there are remains of over 750 documents, in *Hebrew, *Aramaic, and *Greek, mostly written on skin, many of which remain largely unedited. Most of the Hebrew MSS are written in square script, though a few of the biblical ones are written in palaeo-Hebrew. Palaeographers assert that some of the texts may be as old as the 3rd cent. BC, but most of the MSS are written in the styles of script now labelled as Hasmonean (c.130–50 BC) or Herodian (c.50 BC to AD 50). In view of the fact that practically no other MS material in Hebrew and Aramaic has survived from this period, the scrolls are of great importance palaeographically.

About the origins of the scrolls all that can be said is that probably they once belonged to the library of the Jewish community which was based on a large building at Qumran. Many scholars have identified the community to whom the scrolls belonged with the *Essenes.

Among the biblical MSS nearly all the books of the canonical OT are represented. These MSS are important for aiding in the reconstruction of the history of the OT text. Not all of them were copied at Qumran. Some scholars group the biblical MSS in families according to the place of the supposed origin of the text-type; those that agree predominantly with the *Massoretic text are linked with Babylonian Judaism, those closer to the *Septuagint with *Alexandria, and those closer to the *Samaritan Pentateuch with Palestine. Other scholars draw attention to the variety of text-types in the OT quotations in the NT and reserve judgement on theories of textual families, especially since all the biblical MSS show affinities with more than one family.

The non-biblical MSS include copies of several *apocryphal and pseudepigraphical books already known (e.g. *Enoch, *Jubilees) as well as many not previously known. Some MSS seem to relate more specifically to the Qumran community; among these are the Manual of Discipline (1QS, a community rule akin to the *Didache), the pesharim (eschatological commentaries on prophetic texts), the War Scroll (1QM), and various liturgical texts (e.g. 1QH). Some texts, such as the Damascus Document (also known as the Zadokite Documents or Cairo Damascus Covenant), may have been composed elsewhere, then copied and extensively edited at Qumran.

Despite claims to the contrary, it is almost certain that no copies of any NT book have been found at Qumran. However, the wealth of evidence that the scrolls provide for Jewish life and thought at the time when Christianity was born mean that they are a source of information which no student of Christian origins can afford to ignore.

Principal edns. incl. M. Burrows (ed.), *The Dead Sea Scrolls of St. Mark's Monastery* (2 vols., New Haven, Conn., 1950–1); E. L. Sukenik, *The Dead Sea Scrolls of the Hebrew University* (Jerusalem, 1954; with introd. and notes in Eng., 1955); D. Barthélemy, OP, J. T. Milik, and others (eds.), *Discoveries in the Judaean Desert* (Oxford, 1955 ff.: about 30 vols. planned; 10 pub. to 1994); N. Avigad and Y. Yadin, *A Genesis Apocryphon* (Jerusalem, 1956); J. P. M. van der Ploeg, OP, and A. S. van der Woude, *Le Targum de Job de la Grotte XI de Qumrân* (Leiden, 1971); J. T. Milik, *The Books of Enoch: Aramaic Fragments of Qumrân Cave 4* (Oxford, 1976); Y. Yadin (ed.), *The Temple Scroll* (3 vols. with suppl. vol. of plates, Jerusalem, 1977 (Heb.); Eng. tr. of vols. 1 and 2, 1983); D. N. Freedman and K. A. Mathews, *The Paleo-Hebrew Leviticus Scroll (11QpaleoLev)* (Winona Lake, Ind. [1985]); C. Newsom,

Songs of the Sabbath Sacrifice (Atlanta, Ga. [1985]); E. M. Schuller, *Non-Canonical Psalms from Qumran: A Pseudepigraphic Collection* (ibid. [1986]). B. Z. Wacholder and M. G. Abegg, *A Preliminary Edition of the Unpublished Dead Sea Scrolls: The Hebrew and Aramaic Texts from Cave Four* (Washington, DC, 1991 ff.). E. Tov, *The Dead Sea Scrolls on Microfiche*, with pr. catalogue by S. A. Reid (Leiden, 1993). Selected Heb. pointed texts ed., with Ger. tr., by E. Lohse (Munich, 1964; 2nd edn., 1971); selected texts in Eng. tr. by G. Vermes (Harmondsworth, 1962; 3rd edn., 1987) and by M. Knibb, *The Qumran Community* (Cambridge, 1987). Eng. tr. of nearly all the non-Biblical material in F. García Martínez, *The Dead Sea Scrolls Translated: The Qumran Texts in English* (Leiden [1994]; an expanded Eng. tr. of *Textos de Qumrán*, 1992). Comm. with Heb. text and trs. incl. Y. Yadin, *The Scroll of the War of the Sons of Light against the Sons of Darkness* [= War Scroll] (Jerusalem, 1955; Eng. tr., Oxford, 1962; incl. text and Eng. tr.); S. Holm-Nielsen, *Hodayot: Psalms from Qumran* (Acta Theologica Danica, 2; Aarhus, 1960; Eng. tr. only); A. R. C. Leaney, *The Rule of Qumran and its Meaning* (1966; Eng. tr. only); W. H. Brownlee, *The Midrash Pesher of Habakkuk* (Society of Biblical Literature, Monograph Series, 24; Missoula, Mont. [1979]); M. P. Horgan, *Pesharim: Qumran Interpretations of Biblical Books* (Catholic Biblical Quarterly Monograph Series, 8; Washington, DC, 1979); P. R. Davies, *The Damascus Covenant: An Interpretation of the 'Damascus Document'* (Journal for the Study of the Old Testament, Supplement Series, 25; Sheffield, 1983).

The extensive literature incl. J. T. Milik, *Dix ans de découvertes dans le Désert de Juda* (1957; Eng. tr., Studies in Biblical Theology, 26; 1959); F. M. Cross, *The Ancient Library of Qumrân and Modern Biblical Studies* (1958); G. R. *Driver, *The Judaean Scrolls* (Oxford, 1965); F. M. Cross and S. Talmon (eds.), *Qumran and the History of the Biblical Text* (Cambridge, Mass., and London [1975]); L. H. Schiffman, *The Halakhah at Qumran* (Studies in Judaism in Late Antiquity, 16; Leiden, 1975); G. Vermes, *The Dead Sea Scrolls: Qumran in Perspective* (1977; 2nd edn., 1982); G. J. Brooke, *Exegesis at Qumran: 4QFlorilegium in its Jewish Context* (Journal for the Study of the Old Testament, Supplement Series, 29; Sheffield [1985]); P. R. Callaway, *The History of the Qumran Community* (Journal for the Study of the Pseudepigrapha, Supplement Series, 3; Sheffield [1988]). Works specifically on the relationship between the Dead Sea Scrolls and the NT include M. Black, *The Scrolls and Christian Origins* [1961]; J. Murphy-O'Connor, OP (ed.), *Paul and Qumran* (1968); J. H. Charlesworth (ed.), *John and Qumran* (1972); B. E. Thiering, *The Qumran Origins of the Christian Church* (Sydney, 1983). E. *Schürer, *The History of the Jewish People in the Age of Jesus Christ*, rev. Eng. tr. by G. Vermes and others, 3 (pt. 1; Edinburgh, 1986), pp. 380–469. J. A. Fitzmyer, SJ, *The Dead Sea Scrolls: Major Publications and Tools for Study* (Society of Biblical Literature, Resources for Biblical Study, 20; rev. edn., Atlanta, Ga. [1990]). P. W. Skehan and others in *Dict. Bibl.*, Suppl. 9 (1979), cols. 805–1014, s.v. 'Qumran', sections 4–6.

Deadly Sins, Seven. See SEVEN DEADLY SINS.

De Aleatoribus (or *Adversus Aleatores*). A short homily, written in somewhat uncouth Latin, which vigorously denounces dice-players and all games of chance. Its authorship has been much disputed. At one time it was believed to be a work of *Cyprian (d. 258), but this view has now been almost universally abandoned. In 1888 A. *Harnack ascribed it to Pope *Victor I (189–99), thus making it the earliest piece of Christian Latin literature. Subsequently the parallels with Cyprian's writings suggested that it drew on them and thus could not be earlier than the middle of the 3rd cent.; Harnack himself came to believe that it was the work of a *Novatianist antipope at

Rome. More recently J. *Daniélou has revived the case for an early date (late 2nd cent.).

Crit. edn. of text in Cyprian's *Opera*, ed. W. Hartel, CSEL 3 (1), pp. 92–104; text also in J. P. Migne, *PL* 4. 827–36. A. Harnack, *Der pseudocyprianische Tractat De Aleatoribus, die älteste lateinische Schrift, ein Werk des römischen Bischofs Victor I. (saec. II)* (TU 5, Heft 1; 1888); id., 'Zu Pseudocyprian, Adv. Aleat. 1 (p. 93, 1 f., ed. Hartel)' in TU 20, Heft 3 (1900), pp. 112–16. H. Koch, 'Zur Schrift *adversus aleatores*', in *Festgabe für K. Müller* (1922), pp. 58–67. J. Daniélou, *Histoire des doctrines chrétiennes avant Nicée*, 3: *Les Origines du Christianisme latin* (1978), pp. 87–91; Eng. tr. (1977), pp. 93–8. Bardenhewer, 2, pp. 496–9.

dean (Lat. *decanus*, from *decem*, 'ten'). The title of various, originally minor, officials, e.g. a monk supervising ten novices.

(1) *Rural deans assist the *bishop in administering a subdivision of an *archdeaconry. In the 9th cent. this office replaced the archpresbyterate. The modern RC equivalent of the rural dean is technically known as a 'vicar forane' but in England is commonly described merely as a dean.

(2) The dean of a *cathedral (also formerly an archpresbyter) controls its services and, with the *chapter, supervises its fabric and property. He ranks next to the bishop, of whom in the Anglican, but not the RC, Church he is considerably independent. In some recent foundations, however, the bishop is also dean, and decanal functions are largely discharged by a *provost under his authority.

(3) The heads of the *collegiate churches of *Westminster, *Windsor, and other *peculiars which are governed by deans (and chapters) are independent of episcopal authority.

(4) The 'Dean of the Province of *Canterbury' is the Bp. of London *ex officio*. He summons the Bishops of the Southern Province to meet in *Convocation under a mandate from the Abp. of Canterbury.

(5) For *Dean of the Arches, see following entry.

(6) In the RC Church, the Dean of the Sacred College is one of the *Cardinal Bishops, since 1965 elected by the suburbican cardinals from among their number.

(7) The *Lutheran superintendent and *Calvinist overseer are sometimes styled dean.

The title of dean of a college or of a university faculty, very often held by a layman, should not be confused with the ecclesiastical title; but the Dean of *Christ Church, Oxford, is both head of the college and dean of the cathedral.

Dean of the Arches and Auditor. The judge in the *Arches Court of Canterbury, who also holds the parallel post of Auditor in the Chancery Court of York. Formerly *Bow Church ('Sta. Maria de Arcubus'), from which he derived his title, was, with twelve other parishes, exempt from the jurisdiction of the Bp. of London, and the Dean exercised *peculiar jurisdiction over the 13 parishes. The original office is now extinct, because the parishes have been incorporated into the see of London, but the legal functions that gradually came to be attached to it are still performed by a judge who retains the title. He has to be a barrister of at least ten years' standing or a person who has held high judicial office, and, if a layman, a communicant. See also ARCHES COURT OF CANTERBURY.

I. J. Churchill, *Canterbury Administration* (2 vols., 1933), esp 1, pp. 436–46, and 2, pp. 186–92, with list of Deans, pp. 238–40. E. G. Moore, *Introduction to English Canon Law* (3rd edn. by T. Briden and B. Hanson, 1992), pp. 112, 119, 122, 124 f.

Dearmer, Percy (1867–1936), writer on ceremonial subjects and religious music. He was educated at Westminster and at *Christ Church, Oxford, where he was much influenced by James Adderley and C. *Gore and became one of the first members of the Christian Social Union. Ordained deacon in 1891 and priest in 1892, he set himself to popularize the adaptation of medieval English ceremonial to the Prayer Book rite, setting out his ideals in *The Parson's Handbook* (1899), a widely used manual, and putting them into practice as Vicar of St Mary's, Primrose Hill, Hampstead (1901–15), where he attracted the interest of many leading artists. From 1919 to 1936 he was Professor of Ecclesiastical Art at *King's College, London, and in 1931 he became a Canon of *Westminster. He was co-editor of *English Hymnal* (1906), *Songs of Praise* (1925), and the *Oxford Book of Carols* (1928); to these collections he contributed several hymns and translations. He also wrote many popular books on ecclesiastical, topographical, and other subjects.

The Parson's Handbook was extensively rev. and rewritten in an abbreviated form for the 13th edn. by C. E. Pocknee (1965). Life by his wife, N. Dearmer (1940, with bibl.). F. R. Barry in *DNB*, *1931–1940*, pp. 216 f.

'Death of God' Theology. A movement that had considerable vogue in the 1960s, esp. in the *United States of America. The phrase 'God is dead' has been used in a number of ways. It occurs in a Good Friday hymn by M. *Luther with reference to the death of Christ, an extreme example of *communicatio idiomatum*. G. W. F. *Hegel quoted the words, but gave them a new sense, namely that Absolute Spirit has given up its transcendence in order to enter the finite reality of history. Other German writers (e.g. the poet H. Heine and the novelist Jean Paul) spoke of the death of God in a cultural sense, meaning that man had now entered on a stage of civilization to which the concept of God had no relevance (see ATHEISM). This atheistic meaning was taken up by F. W. *Nietzsche, who proclaimed the death of God as a human act: to achieve their full stature as autonomous beings, men must abolish God and become responsible for the world and creators of moral values. These differences of meaning are reflected in the 'death of God' theologies. G. Vahanian in a book entitled *The Death of God* (1961) claimed that in contemporary W. culture God had ceased to be a meaningful factor. Ideas from D. *Bonhoeffer's posthumously published *Widerstand und Erbegung* (Eng. tr. as *Letters and Papers from Prison*), esp. his talk about 'religionless Christianity', were drawn into the debate, and a number of theologians sought to produce a variety of versions of Christianity without God. Paul van Buren believed that analytical philosophy had shown discourse about God to be incoherent; T. J. J. Altizer taught a quasi-Hegelian theory that God had entirely dispersed Himself among finite beings; and W. Hamilton, like many 19th-cent. atheists, held that a transcendent God was incompatible with

human freedom. J. A. T. *Robinson's *Honest to God* (1963) was much less extreme than the writings of the Americans mentioned, but it did call in question the traditional doctrine of a transcendent deity. This dissatisfaction with traditional theism has been largely incorporated in more recent attempts to work out a doctrine of *God (q.v.).

G. Vahanian, *The Death of God: The Culture of Our Post-Christian Era* (New York, 1961); W. Hamilton, *The New Essence of Christianity* (New York, 1961; London, 1966); P. M. van Buren, *The Secular Meaning of the Gospel Based on an Analysis of its Language* (New York and London, 1963); T. J. J. Altizer, *The Gospel of Christian Atheism* (Philadelphia [1966]; London, 1967); id. and W. Hamilton (eds.), *Radical Theology and the Death of God* (Indianapolis, 1966; Harmondsworth, 1968); C. W. Christian and G. R. Wittig (eds.), *Radical Theology: Phase Two. Essays on a continuing discussion* (New York [1967]); S. M. Daecke, *Der Mythos vom Tode Gottes* [1969]; E. Jüngel, *Gott als Geheimnis der Welt* (3rd edn., Tübingen, 1978), esp. pp. 55–137; Eng. tr., *God as the Mystery of the World* (1983), pp. 43–104.

de Auxiliis. In 1597 *Clement VIII appointed the 'Congregatio de Auxiliis' to deal with the contemporary disputes on the manner in which Divine *grace operated. Though Reformation controversies had forced the subject on the attention of RC theologians, the Council of *Trent (1546–63) had left many of the issues unsettled, and towards the end of the 16th cent. division of opinion had become very acute. A fresh stage was reached when the *Jesuit theologian, L. de *Molina, published his *Concordia liberi arbitrii cum gratiae donis* (1588), and the *Dominican theologian, D. *Báñez, vigorously controverted his teaching. The 'Congregatio' reported for the first time on 19 Mar. 1598, advising that the circulation of Molina's book be forbidden and 90 propositions extracted from it condemned; but the Pope declined to ratify the decision. A second attempt to secure Papal confirmation when the number of offending propositions had been reduced to 20 was equally unsuccessful. Yet a further attempt, under *Paul V, to achieve the same object failed. Finally, on 5 Sept. 1607, in an attempt to satisfy both sides, the Pope decreed that the Dominicans could not justly be accused of *Calvinism nor the Jesuits of *Pelagianism, and that neither side should pronounce the contrary teaching heretical.

de Bruys, Pierre. See PETER DE BRUYS.

decadary cult. The system of worship instituted during the French Revolution on the basis of a 10-day 'week' (ending with 'Décadi', the day of rest) to supplant that associated with the Christian calendar.

decade (Lat. *decem*, 'ten'). The name technically used for each of the five divisions into which each *chaplet of the Rosary is subdivided, because each contains ten *Hail Marys, together with the *Lord's Prayer and a *Gloria Patri. As each decade is associated with one of the 15 *Mysteries of the Rosary, they form unities in themselves and are sometimes recited as such, without the whole chaplet being said.

decalogue. See COMMANDMENTS, THE TEN.

decani [sc. *sedes*] (Lat.), 'the place of the dean' (*decani*). As the dean's stall is on the south side of the cathedral, the term 'decani' is used to indicate those who in antiphonal singing sit on the decanal side of the choir. It is now in common usage for other churches, besides cathedrals. The opposite side is known as '*cantoris'.

de Cantilupe, St Thomas and **Walter.** See CANTILUPE, ST THOMAS DE and WALTER DE.

Decapolis, the. A region consisting of ten allied cities E. of the *Jordan in N. Palestine. It included the towns of *Damascus, Gerasa, and Gadara, and contained a Greek-speaking population. Cf. Mt. 4: 25, Mk. 5: 20 and 7: 31.

G. A. *Smith, *The Historical Geography of the Holy Land* (25th edn. 1931), ch. 29, pp. 621–38; A. H. M. Jones, *The Cities of the Eastern Roman Provinces* (2nd edn. by A. Avi-Yonah and others, Oxford, 1971), pp. 259 and 279 f. C. H. Kraeling (ed.), *Gerasa, City of the Decapolis* (New Haven, Conn., 1938) [account of excavations, 1928–34]. J.-P. Rey-Coquais in *Anchor Bible Dictionary*, 2 (1992), pp. 116–21, s.v.

de Caussade, Jean Pierre. See CAUSSADE, JEAN PIERRE DE.

Deceased Wife's Sister's Marriage Act 1907. The provisions of this Act, though enjoying full civil sanction, were in conflict with the ecclesiastical law of the C of E, which, until the *Canons were amended by *Convocation in 1946, disallowed the marriage of a widower with his wife's sister or a widow with her husband's brother. A corresponding Deceased Brother's Widow's Marriage Act was passed in 1921. The provisions, extended to include aunts, nieces, uncles, and nephews of the deceased party, are now contained in the Marriage (Enabling) Act 1960. Both classes of marriage were prohibited in M. *Parker's 'Table of *Kindred and Affinity', but they do not figure in the corresponding table in the 1969 Canons. An incumbent of the C of E who has scruples is not compelled to solemnize such a marriage, but he is not entitled to exclude from Communion anyone married under the statutory provisions as 'an open and notorious evil liver'. See also AFFINITY.

Decius (d. 251), Roman Emperor from 249. C. Messius Quintus Decius was appointed by the Emp. *Philip the Arabian to take command on the Danube against the Goths. After some military success, in 249 he was proclaimed Emperor by the troops, defeated Philip, and was accepted by the Senate. In 249 he commanded all subjects to sacrifice and obtain certificates of their obedience. What was perhaps intended as a general act of solidarity with the ancient religion caught the Christians and led to the first persecution of them on an imperial scale. Some Christians stood firm and were martyred, incl. *Fabian, Bp. of Rome, Alexander, Bp. of Jerusalem, and *Babylas, Bp. of Antioch. Others gave way or through bribery obtained false certificates (see LIBELLATICI). The intensity of the persecution waned by the beginning of 251; it ended when Decius was killed in battle in June of that year. The defections raised in an acute form the question whether penance was possible for the *lapsed and led to the conflict between St *Cyprian and the *Novatianists over their treatment.

See St Cyprian's works *passim*, and *Eusebius, *HE* 4–7. W. H. C. Frend, *Martyrdom and Persecution in the Early Church* (Oxford, 1965), pp. 404–13; G. W. Clarke in his Eng. tr. of *The Letters of St Cyprian of Carthage*, 1 (ACW 43 [1984]) pp. 21–39; R. Lane Fox, *Pagans and Christians* (Harmondsworth, 1986), pp. 450–62; H. A. Pohlsander, 'The Religious Policy of Decius', in *Aufstieg und Niedergang der römischen Welt*, 2. 16. 3, ed. W. Haase (1986), pp. 1826–42. See also PERSECUTIONS, EARLY CHRISTIAN.

Declaration against Transubstantiation. The Declaration imposed in 1673 by the Popish Recusants Act 1672 (commonly called the *Test Act) on all persons holding civil or military office. It ran as follows: 'I, *AB*, do . . . declare that I do believe that in the sacrament of the Lord's Supper there is not any transubstantiation of the elements of bread and wine . . . at or after the consecration thereof by any person whatsoever'. See also DECLARATION OF THE SOVEREIGN.

Declaration of Assent. See ASSENT, DECLARATION OF.

Declaration of the French Clergy. See GALLICAN ARTICLES.

Declaration of the Sovereign. Also known as the 'Royal Declaration'. The Declaration repudiating the RC faith which was imposed on William III and Mary when they came to the throne in 1689 by Parliament in the Bill of Rights 1688. It has been taken by all subsequent sovereigns. In its original form it was based on the *Declaration against Transubstantiation (q.v.), but included also a repudiation of the Roman doctrines of the *Invocation of Saints and of the *Sacrifice of the Mass, and a 'long rigmarole' wherein the sovereign affirmed that he was not being dispensed by the Pope from taking the Oath in its plain meaning. The Oath survived the repeal of the Test Act by the Roman *Catholic Relief Act 1829; but to remove offence it was altered by the Accession Declaration Act 1910 to 'I, *N*, do solemnly and sincerely in the presence of God profess, testify, and declare that I am a faithful Protestant, and that I will, according to the true intent of the enactments which secure the Protestant succession to the Throne of my Realm, uphold and maintain the said enactments to the best of my powers according to law'.

Declarations of Indulgence. These were statements of government policy issued on the authority of the royal prerogative, and were the means chosen by *Charles II and *James II to give a lead to public opinion in the matter of religious *toleration. On 25 Oct. 1660 Charles II published his 'Declaration Concerning Ecclesiastical Affairs' (known as the Worcester House Declaration), in which he announced his intention of calling a conference to implement the Declaration of *Breda giving a 'liberty to tender consciences', and granting indulgence in certain matters, mainly ceremonial (the Cross in Baptism, bowing at the Holy Name, use of surplices), at least until after the projected (*Savoy) Conference (1661).

There were four Declarations of Indulgence, properly so called: (1) On 26 Dec. 1662 Charles II issued a Declaration, proclaiming his continued intention of honouring his promises at Breda and of placing before Parliament a bill allowing him to exercise more freely the power of suspending the penal laws against dissenters from the C of E.

But in Feb. 1663 the Commons petitioned for the stern enforcement of the Act of *Uniformity and the bill for toleration was defeated in the Lords.

(2) On 15 Mar. 1672 Charles II issued a further Declaration, suspending the execution of the penal laws in matters ecclesiastical against all nonconformists and recusants. This was a more serious attempt at toleration, and from it may be dated the existence of organized *nonconformity. Licences were issued to dissenting ministers and meeting-places. Anglican opposition was led by G. *Sheldon, and in 1673 Parliament resolved that 'penal statutes in matters ecclesiastical cannot be suspended but by Act of Parliament'. The Declaration and the licences were withdrawn.

(3) On 4 Apr. 1687 James II issued a Declaration allowing full liberty of worship. It suspended the operation of the penal laws, allowed peaceable meetings of nonconformists provided that the Justices of the Peace were notified, ordained that the oaths of supremacy and allegiance should not be required of those employed in the royal service and remitted all penalties pending for ecclesiastical offences. This endangered the Anglican monopoly in Church and State.

(4) On 27 Apr. 1688 James II issued a further Declaration of Indulgence, which was followed on 4 May by an Order in Council requiring that it be read in all churches on two successive Sundays (20 and 27 May in London, 3 and 10 June elsewhere). It provoked fierce Anglican opposition which led to the arrest and trial of the *Seven Bishops. The Order in Council was almost universally disobeyed.

The text of the Worcester House Declaration pr. in E. *Cardwell, *Documentary Annals of the Reformed Church of England*, 2 (Oxford, 1839), pp. 234–50; the 1662 Declaration, ibid., pp. 260–69; of 1672, pp. 282–6, and those of 1687 and 1688, pp. 308–15. The Worcester House Declaration is also pr. in A. Browning, *English Historical Documents 1660–1714* (1953), pp. 365–70; the Declaration of 1662, ibid., pp. 371–4; that of 1672, pp. 387 f.; of 1687, pp. 395–7; of 1688, pp. 399 f.; and the Order in Council of 1688, ibid., p. 83. The 1688 Declaration is also pr. in Bettenson, pp. 407–10; 2nd edn. (1963), pp. 420–3. F. Bate, *The Declaration of Indulgence 1672* (1908).

Declaratory Acts. Two Acts in Scottish *Presbyterian Churches relieving ministers from their obligation to subscribe to every item of the subordinate standards of faith, esp. the *Westminster Confession. (1) The Declaratory Act of 1879, passed by the *United Presbyterian Church, proclaimed the central doctrines of 'the love of God to all mankind, His gift of His Son to be the propitiation for the sins of the whole world, and the free offer of salvation to men without distinction' as 'vital in the system of Gospel truth', but went on to affirm that the damnation of infants and the heathen is not necessarily involved in *election and that total depravity and foreordination to death must allow for human responsibility. It disapproved of anything in the standards supposed to over-exalt the civil magistrates and asserted the Church's obligation to maintain *voluntaryism. It explicitly upheld liberty of opinion on such matters as the 'six days' in the creation story in Genesis. (2) The Declaratory Act of the *Free Church of Scotland of 1892 followed similar lines, but refrained from reference to voluntaryism and any implied attack on a

State Church as such. This latter Act was rejected by a small conservative body, chiefly Highland, which formed themselves into the 'Free Presbyterian Church'. In the Church of Scotland its Act on the Formula of 1910 had an effect similar to that of the Declaratory Acts and freedom of opinion on non-fundamental matters was recognized. In the Basis and Plan of Union (1929), the two Declaratory Acts and the Act on the Formula are included among 'leading documents setting forth the constitution' of the reunited Church of Scotland.

Texts of the two Acts in J. T. Cox, *Practice and Procedure in the Church of of Scotland*, 6th edn. by D. F. M. MacDonald (Edinburgh, 1976), pp. 435–7. A. L. Drummond and J. Bulloch, *The Church in Late Victorian Scotland* (ibid., 1978), pp. 35–9 and 263–73, also incl. texts.

Decollation of St John the Baptist. The feast celebrated on 29 Aug. in commemoration of the martyrdom of St *John the Baptist at the hands of *Herod Antipas, as related in Mt. 14: 3–12 and Mk. 6: 14–30. It is already mentioned in the *Hieronymian Martyrology and the *Gelasian Sacramentary. It has been observed in England at least since 668. In the 1969 Roman Calendar it is called 'the Passion of St John the Baptist'. References in the Martyrology of *Ado and elsewhere indicate that it originally commemorated the translation of the head of John the Baptist from a monastery near Emesa known as the Spelaion to a church in the city. In the E. Church the date is observed as a fast-day.

*Augustine, *Sermones*, 307 and 308 (ed. Ben.).

de Condren, Charles. See CONDREN, CHARLES DE.

decretals. Papal letters, strictly those in response to a question. They have the force of law within the Pope's jurisdiction. The first decretal was prob. that sent in 385 by Pope *Siricius to Himerius, Bp. of Tarragona. The earliest influential collection was that made in about 520 by *Dionysius Exiguus. About 850 appeared the '*False Decretals' (q.v.), containing many forged letters of popes before Siricius. After *Gratian had systematized existing *canon law in his 'Decretum' (*c.*1140), authoritative collections of later decretals were published by *Gregory IX (1234), *Boniface VIII (1298), and *Clement V (1317).

Decretales ineditae saeculi XII, ed. from the papers of the late Walther Holtzmann by S. Chodorow and C. Duggan (Monumenta Iuris Canonici, Series B, vol. 4; Vatican City, 1982). A. van Hove, *Commentarium Lovaniense in Codicem Iuris Canonici*, vol. 1, tom. 1 (Mechlin and Rome, 1928; 2nd edn., 1945). C. Duggan, *Twelfth-Century Decretal Collections and their Importance in English History* (1963). G. Le Bras, C. Lefebvre, and J. Rambaud in G. Le Bras, *Histoire du droit et des institutions de l'Église en Occident*, 7: *L'Âge classique 1140–1378: Sources et théorie du droit* (1965). G. Fransen, *Les Décrétals et les Collections de Décrétales* (Typologie des Sources du Moyen Âge Occidental, 2; Turnhout, 1972). *Studies in the Collections of Twelfth-Century Decretals* from the papers of the late Walther Holtzmann, ed., rev., and tr. C. R. and M. C. Cheney (Monumenta Iuris Canonici, Series B, vol. 3; Vatican City, 1979). A. Van Hove in *CE* 4 (1908), pp. 670–3, s.v.; C. Duggan in *NCE* 4 (1967), pp. 707–9, s.v. See also bibl. to DIONYSIUS EXIGUUS and FALSE DECRETALS.

Decretals, False. See FALSE DECRETALS.

Decretum Gelasianum. An early Latin document, handed down most frequently under the name of Pope *Gelasius (492–6), but in some MSS as the work of *Damasus (366–84) or *Hormisdas (514–23), containing *inter alia* a Latin list of the Books of the Bible. Acc. to E. von Dobschütz, it is not a Papal work at all, but a private compilation which was composed in Italy (but not at *Rome) in the early 6th cent. Other scholars, while accepting this date, think it originated in Gaul. The document is in five parts, dealing with: (1) Christ and the Holy Spirit; (2) the Canonical Scriptures; (3) the Roman Church and its dependent sees; (4) the orthodox Councils and Fathers; (5) the 'Books to be Received' (works of the Fathers) and the *Apocryphal writings (biblical and patristic). The last item (*De libris recipiendis et non recipiendis*) gives the usual title to the whole work.

Text in J. P. Migne, *PL* 19. 787–94 (pts. 1–3) and 59. 157–64 (pts. 2–5). Crit. edn. by E. von Dobschütz (TU 38, Heft 4; 1912). J. *Chapman, OSB, 'On the *Decretum Gelasianum* De Libris recipiendis et non recipiendis', *R. Bén.* 30 (1913), pp. 187–207 and 315–33. E. *Schwartz, 'Zum *Decretum Gelasianum*', *ZNTW* 29 (1930), pp. 161–8. Bardenhewer, 4, pp. 626 f. H. *Leclercq, OSB, in *DACL* 6 (pt. 1; 1924), cols. 722–47, s.v. 'Gélasien (Décret)', with extensive bibl.; G. Bardy in *Dict. Bibl.*, Suppl. 3 (1938), cols. 579–90, s.v. 'Gélase (Décret de)'.

Dedication, Jewish Feast of the. The feast instituted by *Judas Maccabaeus in 165 BC, to commemorate the purification of the Temple and its altar after their defilement by *Antiochus Epiphanes (1 Macc. 4: 59; 2 Macc. 10: 6). It was ordered to be observed on the 25th day of Chislev each year and kept for 8 days. A special feature of the feast, apart from the fact that it could be celebrated outside Jerusalem, was the lighting of lamps; hence it was sometimes called the 'Feast of the Lights'. Modern Jews observe the feast as 'Hanukkah'; it falls in late Nov. or Dec. The only reference to it in the NT is at Jn. 10: 22.

O. S. Rankin, *Origins of the Festival of Hanukkah* (1930). S. Zeitlin, 'Hanukkah, its Origin and Significance', *JQR* NS 29 (1938), pp. 1–36; J. Morgenstern, 'The Chanukkah Festival and the Calendar of Ancient Israel', *Hebrew Union College Annual*, 20 (1947), pp. 1–136, and 21 (1948), pp. 365–496. R. de Vaux, OP, *Les Institutions de l'Ancien Testament*, 2 (1960), pp. 420–25, with bibl. p. 460; Eng. tr. (2nd edn., 1965), pp. 510–14, with bibl. p. 552. M. D. Herr in *Encyclopaedia Judaica*, 7 (Jerusalem, 1972), cols. 1280–8, s.v. 'Hanukkah'.

dedication of churches. The earliest recorded instance of the dedication of a Christian church is that of the cathedral at Tyre in 314, described in the 'oratio panegyrica' of *Eusebius (*HE* 10. 3 f.). There is a 7th-cent. formulary in the *Gelasian Sacramentary consisting of prayers, blessings, and sprinkling with *holy water. In the following cents. the ceremonies increased in number, and by the 13th cent. the ritual had reached in essentials the form used until modern times, as is witnessed by the '*Pontifical' of *Durandus. It already contained the six principal parts—the blessing outside, the blessing in the middle of the church, the preparation for the consecration of the altar, the actual consecration of the altar, the procession of the relics, and the blessing of the altar vessels, ornaments, etc.—followed finally by the Mass. The 1977 *Ordo Dedicationis Ecclesiae et Altaris* places the whole ceremony within the Mass. The first part consists of the solemn

entry into the church (or *introit), sprinkling the walls with holy water, scriptural readings, homily, and Creed; the second part includes the actual rite of dedication, i.e. the *Litany of the Saints, the placing of the relics of a saint under the altar, if there are any relics to be so placed (see ALTAR), the Prayer of Dedication, the anointing of the altar and walls of the church (in 12 or 4 places) with *chrism, followed by their censing, and the lighting of candles at the altar and on the walls; the third part consists of the central portion of the Mass, ending with the inauguration of the Blessed Sacrament chapel, blessing, and dismissal.

Acc. to modern practice the dedication of churches is restricted to buildings that are exclusively and permanently set aside for public worship; it may normally be performed only by a bishop, though in very extraordinary circumstances a priest may be mandated to act. Other buildings, incl. private and public chapels, may be blessed by a simple rite. The walls are sprinkled with holy water at the beginning of the Mass, and after the Creed the altar is blessed and censed. In non-permanent buildings, altars, even if movable, may also be blessed. This rite may be performed by a priest.

The distinction between the dedication and blessing of churches and altars in current RC liturgical texts seems to replace the earlier distinction between their consecration and blessing. Consecration came to require the deposition of relics, but, as a letter of Pope *Vigilius (*c.*538: J. P. Migne, *PL* 69. 18) makes clear, the celebration of Mass was the essential element in the hallowing of a church, other items being of secondary importance. Although dedication is intended to be permanent, acc. to canon law (*CIC* (1983), can. 1222), where a church cannot be used for worship, the diocesan bishop may allow it to be used for a secular but not unbecoming purpose. Desecrated churches must be reconciled by a special rite.

The Feast of the Dedication is the annual celebration of the day of the dedication of the church, and is to be kept, strictly speaking, only by consecrated churches. It is to be distinguished, of course, from the Patronal Feast. The first recorded observance of such a feast is that of the dedication of the Church of the *Anastasis (see HOLY SEPULCHRE) in *Jerusalem, described by *Egeria. In 1536 the English Convocations ordered that the Feast of Dedication 'throughout this realm' should be kept on the first Sunday in October, and this practice is commonly followed in England where the date of consecration is not known, though no such feast is contained in the calendar of the BCP. The Revised Book of 1928, however, proposed the first Sunday in October, 'if the day of consecration be not known'. In the RC Church the dedication festival of the *Lateran is kept throughout the Church on 9 Nov.; the observance of those of the other three principal Roman *basilicas, those of Sts Peter and Paul (S. Pietro in Vaticano and S. Paolo fuori le mura; 18 Nov.) and *Santa Maria Maggiore (5 Aug.), is optional.

E. *Martène, *De Antiquis Ecclesiae Ritibus*, 3 (1702), pp. 232–327, Lib. 2, cap. 13. R. W. Muncey, *A History of the Consecration of Churches and Churchyards* (1930). D. Stiefenhofer, *Die Geschichte der Kirchweihe vom 1.–7. Jahrhundert*, (Veröffentlichungen aus dem kirchenhistorischen Seminar München, 3. Reihe, No. 8; 1909). J. Baudot, OSB, *La Dédicace des églises* (1909). S. Benz, OSB, 'Zur Geschichte der römischen Kirchenweihe nach den

Texten des 6. bis 7. Jahrhunderts', in H. Emonds, OSB (ed.), *Enkainia: Gesammelte Arbeiten zum 800jährigen Weihengedächtnis der Abteikirche Maria Laach* (Düsseldorf, 1956), pp. 62–109. M. Andrieu, *Les* Ordines Romani *du Haut Moyen Age*, 4 (SSL 28; 1956), pp. 359–84 ('La Dédicace des églises à Rome et la déposition des reliques'). C. Vogel and R. Elze (eds.), *Le Pontifical romano-germanique du dixième siècle*, 1 (ST 226; 1963), pp. 82–194. W. H. *Frere, *Pontifical Services Illustrated from Miniatures of the XVth and XVIth Centuries* (*Alcuin Club Collections, 3 and 4; 1901), 'Pontifical Services not included in the Book of Common Prayer. 1. The Consecration of Churches', vol. 1, pp. 1–54, and vol. 2, pls. vii and xi, figs. 33 and 34. J. Wickham Legg (ed.), *English Orders for Consecrating Churches in the Seventeenth Century, together with Forms for the Consecration of Churchyards, the First Stone of a Church, the Reconciliation of a Church and the Consecration of Altar Plate* (HBS 41; 1911). J. *Wordsworth, *On the Rite of Consecration of Churches, especially in the Church of England . . . together with the Form of Prayer and Order of Ceremonies in use in the Diocese of Salisbury* (CHS Tract 52; 1899). J. D. Crichton, *The Dedication of a Church* (Dublin, 1980). P. Jounel in A. G. Martimort, *L'Église en prière*, 1, new edn. by I. H. Dalmais and others [1984], pp. 223–34; Eng. tr. (1987), pp. 215–25, with further bibl. P. de Puniet in *DACL* 4 (1921), cols. 374–404, s.v. 'Dédicace des églises', with refs. J. E. Swallow in *PBD* (1912), pp. 241–4, s.v. 'Consecration of Churches and Churchyards'. F. Arnold-Forster, *Studies in Church Dedications or England's Patron Saints* (3 vols., 1899); F. Bond, *Dedications and Patron Saints of English Churches* (1914); K. E. *Kirk, *Church Dedications of the Oxford Diocese* (Oxford, 1946).

de Dominis, Marco Antonio (*c.*1560–1624), 'Spalatrensis', Abp. of Spalato. He entered the Society of Jesus as a youth, became famous as a professor of mathematics at Padua and of rhetoric and logic at Brescia, left the *Jesuits in 1596, and was Abp. of Spalato and Primate of Dalmatia from 1602 to 1616. Political conflicts between Rome and *Venice, to whose territory his see belonged, and personal difficulties with his clergy led him to resign his office and go to England. On his way there he wrote a bitter pamphlet against Rome, *Scogli del cristiano naufragio*. He was warmly welcomed by *James I, received as a member of the C of E, and made Dean of *Windsor and Master of the Savoy in 1617. In the same year he assisted at the consecration of G. Montaigne (d. 1628) as Bp. of *Lincoln and published the first part of his main work *De Republica Ecclesiastica*, an attack on the monarchical government of Rome and a defence of national Churches. He edited P. *Sarpi's *Historia del Concilio Tridentino* (1619), which he dedicated to James I; his anti-papal additions displeased the author. But his pride and avarice soon lost him his English friends, and fearing for his security when negotiations began for the Spanish marriage of Prince *Charles, he sought reconciliation with Rome. He left England in 1622, and now attacked the C of E as violently as formerly the Church of Rome, in *Sui Reditus ex Anglia Consilium* (1623; Anglican reply by R. *Crakanthorpe, 1625). After the death of Gregory XV, however, he came into conflict with the *Inquisition and was confined to the castle of Sant'Angelo at Rome as a relapsed heretic, where he died soon after.

H. Newland, *The Life and Contemporary Church History of Antonio de Dominis* (1859). D. Cantimori, 'Su M. A. De Dominis', *Archiv für Reformationsgeschichte*, 49 (1958), pp. 245–58. W. B. Patterson, 'The Peregrinations of Marco Antonio de Dominis, 1616–24', in D. Baker (ed.), *Religious Motivation: Biographical and Sociological Problems for the Church Historian* (Studies in Church

History, 15; Oxford, 1978), pp. 241–57, with bibl. N. Malcolm, *De Dominis (1560–1624): Venetian, Anglican, Ecumenist and Relapsed Heretic* (1984). Polgár, 1 (1990), pp. 558–62. S. Cavazza in *Dizionario Biografico degli Italiani*, 33 (1987), pp. 642–50, s.v., with full bibl.

deduction. In logic, the process of reasoning whereby a conclusion is reached from an already known or accepted premiss. The opposite process is termed '*induction'.

Deer, Book of. A 9th–10th cent. MS which formerly belonged to the monastery of Deer in Buchan (Aberdeen). It contains a corrupt text of St John's Gospel, with portions of the other Gospels, the *Apostles' Creed, a fragment of a service for the *Visitation of the Sick (with Gaelic rubrics), and a series of grants to the monastery, the last being in a later hand. The Visitation of the Sick agrees in character with the Irish Books of Dimma and Mulling, while the grants throw important light on the social structure of *Scotland at the time. The MS, which was formerly in the library of John Moore, successively Bp. of *Norwich and *Ely (d. 1714), is now in Cambridge University Library (Ii. 6. 32).

Ed. J. Stuart for the Spalding Club (Edinburgh, 1869). K. [H.] Jackson, *The Gaelic Notes in the Book of Deer* (Osborn Bergin Memorial Lecture, 1970; Cambridge, 1972). K. Hughes, *Celtic Britain in the Early Middle Ages: Studies in Scottish and Welsh Sources*, posthumously ed. D. Dumville (Woodbridge, Suffolk, 1980), pp. 22–37.

Defender of the Faith (Lat. *Fidei Defensor*). A title conferred at his own request on *Henry VIII in 1521 by Pope *Leo X in recognition of his treatise *Assertio Septem Sacramentorum*, in which, with the assistance of various leading theologians, he had defended the doctrine of the *seven sacraments against M. *Luther. In 1544 Parliament recognized the style as an official title of the English monarch and it has been borne since that date by all British sovereigns. It may be compared with the titles 'Christianissimus' and 'Catholicus' formerly taken by the kings of France and Spain respectively.

Text of bull conferring title in T. Rymer, *Foedera*, 13 (1712), pp. 756–8, with facsimile. J. M. Brown, 'Henry VIII's Book, "Assertio Septem Sacramentorum," and the Royal Title of "Defender of the Faith" ', *Transactions of the Royal Historical Society*, 8 (1880), pp. 242–61. R. Rex, 'The English Campaign against Luther in the 1520s', ibid., 5th ser. 39 (1989), pp. 85–106. See also studies of Henry VIII, cited s.v.

Defender of the Matrimonial Bond (Lat. *Defensor Vinculi Matrimonialis*). A person whose duty is to uphold the marriage bond when cases in which the nullity or dissolution of particular marriages is in dispute are heard in the RC ecclesiastical courts. The office was constituted by Pope *Benedict XIV in his *bull 'Dei Miseratione' (3 Nov. 1741).

R. Naz in *DDC* 4 (1949), cols. 1069–71, s.v. 'Défenseur du lien'; T. J. McNicholas in *NCE* 4 (1967), p. 717, s.v. 'Defender of the Bond', with further bibl.

Defenestration of Prague. The incident which precipitated the *Thirty Years War. On 23 May 1618 the Bohemian Protestant insurgents broke up a meeting of the Imperial Commissioners in the Hradschin Palace at Prague by throwing two of the Catholic councillors, Wilhelm von Slawata and Jaroslav von Martinitz, and their secretary out of the window.

C. V. Wedgwood, *The Thirty Years War* (1938), pp. 78–80, with refs. to sources. See also other works cited s.v. THIRTY YEARS WAR.

Defensor (late 7th cent.), monk of Ligugé, near Poitiers. He was the compiler of the 'Liber Scintillarum', an ascetical compilation which had a very wide circulation throughout the Middle Ages, often in a modified form, and was attributed to *Bede and others. The compiler drew on the Bible and on a considerable range of *patristic writers. He marked the extracts with the names of their authors, but sometimes derived them from indirect sources.

'Liber Scintillarum' pr. in J. P. Migne, *PL* 88. 598–718; crit. edn. by H. M. Rochais, OSB (CCSL 117, 1957, pp. 1–308; also, with Fr. tr., SC 77 and 86, 1961–2). Id. in *Dict. Sp.* 3 (1957), cols. 88–90, s.v., with bibl.

de fide. In Catholic theology, a proposition is said to be *de fide* (or *de fide catholica*) if it has been expressly declared and defined by the Church to be true and that to contradict it would be heretical. The expression is used e.g. by F. *Suárez and John de *Lugo, and constantly by modern Catholic apologists.

de Foucauld, Charles Eugène (1858–1916), French explorer and 'Hermit of the Sahara'. After an easy and dissipated life as a lieutenant of cavalry, he became seized with a passion for Africa and in 1883–4 undertook a dangerous expedition through Morocco, the results of which he published in the fundamental work, *Reconnaissance au Maroc* (1888). A period of spiritual unrest followed this expedition, but he was brought back to the Catholic faith under the experienced direction of the Abbé *Huvelin (1886). After making a pilgrimage to the Holy Land in 1888–9, in 1890 he entered the *Trappist monastery of Notre-Dames-des-Neiges, and was sent to the daughter house at Akbès in Syria. Desirous of a life of even greater solitude and austerity, he left the order when the period of his temporary vows was completed in 1897, lived as a servant of the *Poor Clares at *Nazareth and *Jerusalem until 1900, and returned to France to be ordained priest in 1901. A few months later he went to Algeria, where he led a hermit's life, first in the oasis of Beni Abbès and, from 1905, in the still more remote Hoggar Mountains and at the oasis of Tamanrasset. Here, besides studying the language of the Tuaregs and composing dictionaries and translations, he made his chief occupations prayer, penance, and works of charity which won him the admiration and love of the French soldiers as well as of the Muslim desert tribes, though he did not obtain conversions. In 1916 he was assassinated for reasons which remain obscure, but probably in connection with the Holy War of the Senoussi. The cause of his beatification was introduced at Rome in 1927.

Although he composed rules for communities of 'Little Brothers' and 'Little Sisters', no companions joined him during his lifetime. In 1933, however, René Voillaume and four other priests, inspired by his writings, settled at El Abiodh Sidi Cheikh, on the edge of the Sahara, and

adopted a monastic way of life based on his first rule. They were scattered during the Second World War, but returned in 1945 and with other recruits established themselves in small fraternities which are now to be found in most parts of the world. While maintaining a deeply contemplative element in their lives, these 'Little Brothers of Jesus' seek to conform to the economic and social milieu in which they live; they mostly earn their living, wearing ordinary clothes, and working in factories, farms, fisheries, etc., exercising their influence by sharing the life of those around them. With similar aims, the Little Sisters of the Sacred Heart were founded near Montpellier in 1933, the Little Sisters of Jesus at Touggourt in the Sahara in 1939, to be followed by the Little Brothers and Little Sisters of the Gospel in 1958 and 1965 respectively. In addition, there are associations of priests and lay people inspired by the life of de Foucauld.

Œuvres spirituelles, ed. B. Jacqueline (Paris, 1973 ff.). Earlier selections ed. R. Bazin (ibid., 1923; Eng. tr., 'Meditations of a Hermit', 1930) and ed. D. Barrat (ibid. [1958]). Various collections of his correspondence have been pub., incl. that with the Abbé Huvelin, ed. J.-F. Six (Tournai [1957]). Other collections listed by R. Quesnel (see below). R. Bazin, *Charles de Foucauld, explorateur du Maroc, ermite au Sahara* (1921; Eng. tr., 1923). M. Carrouges, *Charles de Foucauld, explorateur mystique* (1954; Eng. tr., 1956); id., *Foucauld devant l'Afrique du Nord* (1961); J.-F. Six, *Itinéraire spirituel de Charles de Foucauld* (1958); M. M. Preminger, *The Sands of Tamanrasset* (New York, 1961; London, 1963); R. Quesnel, *Charles de Foucauld: Les étapes d'une recherche* (1966), with details of his works, pub. and unpub., pp. 297–302. Popular study by E. Hamilton, *The Desert my Dwelling* (1968). R. Aubert in *DHGE* 17 (1971), cols. 1394–1402, s.v. 'Foucauld, Charles-Eugène de'.

On the Little Brothers, see R. Voillaume, *Au cœur des masses: la vie religieuse des Petits Frères du Père de Foucauld* (1952; Eng. adaptation as *Seeds of the Desert*, 1955). On the Little Sisters, G. Rocca, SSP, in *DIP* 6 (1980), cols. 1620–2, s.v. 'Piccole Sorelli di Gesú', cols. 1624 f., s.v. 'Piccole Sorelle del Sacro Cuore', and cols. 1625 f., s.v. 'Piccole Sorelli del Vangelo'.

de Groot, Hugo. See GROTIUS, HUGO.

De Haeretico Comburendo. The Latin title of the Suppressions of Heresy Act 1400, passed in 1401, which was the first step taken by Parliament to suppress *Lollardy. By it persons holding heretical views were to be arrested and tried by canon law. If the diocesan pronounced sentence of heresy, they were to be handed over to the secular courts, who would 'cause [them] to be burnt that such punishment may strike fear to the minds of others'. Its provisions were not altogether new. It had long been the custom that after degradation by an ecclesiastical council the state carried out the penalty of burning prescribed by canon law, and the execution of the Lollard William *Sawtrey was hurried through before the passing of this Act to maintain the principle. The Act was repealed by *Henry VIII, revived by *Mary, and finally repealed in 1559 by the Act of *Supremacy 1558 under *Elizabeth I.

Eng. tr. of text in Gee and Hardy, no. 42, pp. 133–7; repr. in Bettenson, pp. 251–5. F. W. *Maitland, *Roman Canon Law in the Church of England* (1898), pp. 158–79 ('The Deacon and the Jewess'), esp. pp. 176–9. K. B. McFarlane, *John Wycliffe and the Beginnings of English Nonconformity* [1953], pp. 149–56.

de Hauranne, Duvergier. See SAINT-CYRAN, ABBÉ DE.

deification (Gk. θέωσις or θεοποίησις), 'becoming God', the normal term for the transforming effect of *grace in Greek patristic and E. *Orthodox theology. The only explicit biblical support for the notion of deification is provided by 2 Pet. 1: 4 ('that you might be partakers of the Divine nature'), but it is closely allied to the Pauline doctrine that through the Spirit we are sons of God (cf. Rom. 8) and to the Johannine doctrine of the indwelling of the Holy Trinity (cf. Jn. 14–17). St *Irenaeus develops the idea that as God shared our life in the Incarnation, so we are destined to share the Divine life and 'become what he is' (*Adv. Haer.* 5, *praef.*). *Clement of Alexandria links this conception with the *Platonic ideal of assimilation to God, ὁμοίωσις θεῷ. The concept of deification involves the belief that through grace man can overcome the effects of the *Fall and acquire 'Divine' attributes, notably incorruptibility and immortality, but its central tenet is that God through the Incarnation of His Son has called men to share the Divine life in the Son. As St *Athanasius put it, 'the Word became flesh . . . that we, partaking of His Spirit, might be deified (θεοποιηθῆναι)' (*De Decretis*, 14), or *Cyril of Alexandria: 'For we have all become partakers of Him, and have Him in ourselves through the Spirit. For this reason we have become partakers of the divine nature and are called sons' (*In Joan.* 9). In the W. such language became less popular. It was retained in the E. and the traditional teaching received its definitive formulation in the work of St *Gregory Palamas, who held that man can be united with the Divine energies, though not with the Divine essence. Although the language of deification is less prominent in W. theology, it remained in liturgical prayers and in the teaching of the mystics where it led to suspicions of *pantheism. The patristic revival in the *Oxford Movement led to a recovery of the concept of deification.

J. Gross, *La Divinisation du Chrétien d'après les pères grecs* (1938); V. *Lossky, *Vision de Dieu* (Bibliothèque Orthodoxe; Neuchâtel, 1962; Eng. tr., 1963); M. Lot-Borodine, *La Déification de l'homme selon la doctrine des pères grecs* (Bibliothèque œcuménique, 9; 1970). G. I. Mantzaridis, *The Deification of Man: St Gregory Palamas and the Orthodox Tradition* (Crestwood, NY, 1984; Eng. tr. of a work orig. pub. in Gk. in 1963). G. Bonner, 'Augustine's Conception of Deification', *JTS* NS 37 (1986), pp. 369–86. A. Louth, 'Manhood into God: The Oxford Movement, the Fathers and the Deification of Man', in K. Leech and R. [D.] Williams (eds.), *Essays Catholic and Radical* (1983), pp. 70–80. Brief account of the doctrine in the C of E by A. M. Allchin, *Participation in God* (1988).

Deiniol, St (d. *c.*584), Welsh saint. He is honoured as the founder of the monastery of *Bangor Iscoed and is alleged to have been consecrated first Bp. of Bangor by St *Dubricius in 516, but very little is known of him. Among the Welsh churches dedicated to him is that at Hawarden in Clwyd. St Deiniol's Library, Hawarden, a residential library for students in the arts, was founded by W. E. *Gladstone in 1896, and of the 100,000 books, some 30,000 are from Gladstone's own collection. Feast day, 11 Sept.

Brief note with refs. by C. Hole in *DCB* 1 (1877), p. 802, s.v.; T. F. Tout in *DNB* 14 (1888), pp. 18 f., s.v. 'Daniel'.

Deir Balyzeh Fragments. See DER BALYZEH FRAGMENTS.

Deism (from Lat. *Deus*, 'God'). The term, orig. interchangeable with *Theism (q.v.), i.e. belief in one Supreme Being as opposed to *atheism and polytheism, is now generally restricted to the system of natural religion which was first developed in England in the late 17th and 18th cents. Among its precursors are P. *Charron, J. Bodin (*c.*1530–96), and esp. Lord *Herbert of Cherbury (q.v.), who in his *De Veritate* (1624) set out five truths common to all religions. J. *Locke, though himself objecting to the title of 'Deist', also profoundly influenced subsequent developments through his *Reasonableness of Christianity* (1695). The classic exposition of Deism is J. *Toland's *Christianity not Mysterious* (1696), which argues against revelation and the supernatural altogether. S. *Clarke, in his *Demonstration of the Being and Attributes of God* (1704–6), distinguished four classes of Deists. For the first, God is only the Creator, with no further interest in the world; the second group admit a Divine Providence, but only in the material, not in the moral and spiritual, order; the third believe in certain moral attributes of God, but not in a future life; and the fourth accept all the truths of natural religion, including belief in a life to come, but reject revelation. A. *Collins's *Discourse on Freethinking* (1713) argued that freedom of thought was sufficient for the discovery of truth, while the authority of the biblical records was doubtful. M. *Tindal in *Christianity as Old as Creation* (1730) maintained that the religion of nature is the common element of all creeds. As it developed, the negative elements in Deism received greater emphasis. Belief in Divine Providence, as well as in rewards and punishments, was gradually abandoned. The chief mark of later Deism was belief in a Creator God whose further Divine intervention in His creation was rejected as derogatory to His omnipotence and unchangeableness.

Deism, which was never widely accepted in this country, had a great influence in *France, where *Voltaire, J.-J. *Rousseau, and the *Encyclopaedists were its chief exponents. In Germany the movement became widespread during the reign of Frederick II of Prussia; Tindal's work, which was translated by J. L. Schmidt in 1741, was drawn upon by H. S. *Reimarus, whose fragments were published by G. E. *Lessing (1773–8); I. *Kant's *Die Religion innerhalb der Grenzen der blossen Vernunft* (1793) states the Deist position from the point of view of transcendental Idealism.

Deism, which by its separation of the Creator from His creatures undermined all personal religion, soon found vigorous critics. Among its most influential refutations was Bp. J. *Butler's *Analogy of Religion* (1736), which argued that the difficulties in the way of accepting Revealed Religion are no more formidable than those confronting the advocate of the Natural Religion proposed by Deism.

J. Leland, *A View of the Principal Deistical Writers* (2 vols., 1754–6); G. V. Lechler, *Geschichte des englischen Deismus* (2 vols., 1841); A. S. Farrar, *A Critical History of Free Thought* (*Bampton Lectures, 1862); L. Stephen, *History of English Thought in the Eighteenth Century*, 1 (1876), chs. 2–4, pp. 74–277, with bibl. pp. 276 f. H. M. Morais, *Deism in Eighteenth Century America* (New York, 1934). H. Reventlow, *Bibelautorität und Geiste der Moderne* (Forschungen zur Kirchen- und Dogmengeschichte, 30; 1980), pp. 470–671; Eng. tr., *The Authority of the Bible and the Rise of the Modern World* (1984), pp. 289–410. R. E. Sullivan, *John Toland and the Deist Controversy: A Study in Adaptations* (1982). C. Gestrich in *TRE* 8 (1981), pp. 392–406, s.v.

Deissmann, Adolf (1866–1937), Protestant theologian. In 1897 he became professor of the NT at Heidelberg, and in 1908 at Berlin. He did distinguished pioneer work in biblical philology, making full use of the material from the recently discovered *papyri. His many writings include two series of *Bibelstudien* (1895, 1897; Eng. tr. as *Bible Studies*, 1901), *Licht vom Osten* (1908; Eng. tr. as *Light from the Ancient East*, 1910), and *The Religion of Jesus and the Faith of Paul* (1923). In 1930 he edited (in conjunction with G. K. A. *Bell) *Mysterium Christi*, a collection of papers on Christology by British and German theologians. He also took a prominent part in the *Ecumenical Movement.

To mark his 60th birthday, there appeared a *Festgabe für Adolf Deissmann* (Tübingen, 1927), with a portrait. E. Plümacher in *TRE* 8 (1981), pp. 406–8, s.v. with further refs.

de La Bigne, Marguerin (*c*.1546–89), French patristic scholar. His chief work was *Sacra Bibliotheca Sanctorum Patrum* (8 vols., 1575; index vol., 1579), in which a vast number of patristic works were published, some of them for the first time.

J. P. Migne, *PL* 81. 209–12 ('Epistola Dedicatoria').

de Lagarde, Paul Anton. See LAGARDE, PAUL ANTON DE.

de la Taille, Maurice (1872–1933), *Jesuit theologian. A native of Semblançay, he was educated at St Mary's College, Canterbury, where he entered the Society of Jesus in 1890. From 1905 to 1916 he taught theology at the Catholic university of Angers, and from 1916 to 1918 was military chaplain to the Canadian army. From 1919 onwards he taught dogmatic theology at the *Gregorian university at Rome. His principal work, *Mysterium Fidei* (1921; Eng. tr. of first 2 of the 3 books, 2 vols., 1941–50), is an original and comprehensive study of the Mass. Divided into three books, dealing with the Sacrifice once offered by Christ Himself, with the Mass as the Sacrifice of the Church, and with the Eucharist as a Sacrament, its dominating thought is the unity of the Redeemer's sacrifice begun in the oblation of the Last Supper, consummated in the Passion, and continued in the Mass. Acc. to de la Taille there is only one real immolation, that on Calvary, to which the Supper looks forward and on which the Mass looks back. He uses a wealth of material, chiefly patristic and scholastic, to support his thesis, and to defend his doctrine against theologians who hold that there must be a real immolation in the Mass. In several minor writings occasioned by this controversy, among them *The Last Supper and Calvary* (1924) and *The Mystery of Faith and Human Opinion* (1930), the author defended himself against his critics.

J. Lebreton, SJ, 'Le Père Maurice de la Taille', *Rech. S.R.* 24 (1934), pp. 5–11; B. Leeming, SJ, 'A Master Theologian: Father Maurice de la Taille', *Month*, 163 (1934), pp. 31–40. M. Lepin, *L'Idée du sacrifice de la messe d'après les théologiens depuis l'origine jusqu'à nos jours* (1926), pp. 659–720. For his work on *grace and the whole supernatural order, see R. Del Colle, *Christ and the Spirit: Spirit-Christology in Trinitarian Perspective* (New York and Oxford, 1994), esp. pp. 64–90. Polgár, 2 (1990), pp. 388 f., s.v. 'La Taille'. M. J. O'Connell, SJ, in *NCE* 4 (1967), pp. 726 f., s.v.

Delegates, Court of. In England, under the Submission of the Clergy Act 1533 commissioners were appointed to hear, and pronounce final sentence upon, appeals from the Archbishops' courts, which until the passing, in Mar. 1533, of the Ecclesiastical Appeals Act 1532 had gone to Rome. These commissioners came to be known as the Court of Delegates, even though a fresh commission, consisting usually of three puisne judges and four civilians, was appointed for each separate case. The powers of the Court were transferred to the King in Council in 1832, and in 1833 its place was taken by the *Judicial Committee of the Privy Council.

H. C. Rothery (ed.), 'Introduction with Appendix to the Return of all Appeals in Causes of Doctrine and Discipline made to the High Court of Delegates' as Hist. App. 9 to the *Report of the Commissioners appointed to inquire into the Constitution and Working of the Ecclesiastical Courts* [Cd. 3760], pp. 253–66 of the MS pagination. The best historical account of the court is that drawn up by W. *Stubbs for the Hist. App. 1, ibid., pp. 46–9 (pr. among the Parliamentary Papers, 1883, 24, pp. 120–3 of the MS pagination). G. I. O. Duncan, *The High Court of Delegates* (Cambridge Studies in English Legal History, 1971).

Delehaye, Hippolyte (1859–1941), *Bollandist. A native of Antwerp, he entered the Society of Jesus (*Jesuits) in 1879. After studying philosophy at Louvain (1879–82), teaching mathematics at the Collège St-Barbe at Ghent (1882–6), and studying theology at Innsbruck (1886–7), he settled in Brussels in 1887. In 1891 he joined the Bollandists and for the rest of his life was actively engaged in hagiographical studies. In 1912 he became President of the Bollandists.

Delehaye contributed regularly to the *Acta Sanctorum [*AASS*] from 1894 until his death. He was joint editor of, and among the principal contributors to, the *Propylaeum ad AASS Novembris* (1902), the *AASS*, Nov. 3 (1910), Nov. 4 (1928), and Nov. 2 (2) (1931), and the *Propylaeum ad AASS Decembris* (1940); and for Nov. 2 (2) he prepared (with H. *Quentin) the important text and study of the *Hieronymian Martyrology. Under the influence of C. Smedt he undertook the cataloguing of scattered hagiographical MSS (*Bibliotheca Hagiographica Graeca*, 1895), and he assisted in the cataloguing of hagiographical MSS in various important libraries. His books, all based on wide erudition but many of them directed to a non-specialized public, include *Les Légendes hagiographiques* (1905; Eng. tr., 1907), *Les Légendes grecques des saints militaires* (1909), *Les Origines du culte des martyrs* (1912), *Les Passions des martyrs et les genres littéraires* (1921; posthumous rev. edn., 1966), *Les Saints Stylites* (1923), *Sanctus* (1927), and *Étude sur le Légendier Romain* (1936). He was also a constant contributor to the *Analecta Bollandiana*.

Collection of his articles orig. pub. outside Bollandist sources to mark the 25th anniversary of his death under the title *Mélanges d'Hagiographie grecque et latine* (Subsidia Hagiographica, 42; 1966). *L'Ancienne Hagiographie Byzantine* (lectures given in 1935), ed. B. Joassart and X. Lequeux (ibid. 73; 1991), with list of his works, pp. xxi–xxxvii (240 items). 'Le R. P. Hippolyte Delehaye', *Anal. Boll.* 60 (1942), pp. i–lii, incl. list of works and refs. to other notices; repr., with additions, in P. Peeters, SJ, *L'Œuvre des Bollandistes* (2nd edn.; Académie Royale de Belgique. Classe des Lettres et des Sciences Morales et Politiques. Mémoires. Collection in-8°, 54, fasc. 5; 1961), pp. 103–49. Eng. tr. of memoir by Peeters in D. Attwater's tr. of Delehaye's *Legends of the Saints* (1962), pp. 187–244. R. Aubert, 'Le Père H. Delehaye et le Cardinal Mercier', *Anal. Boll.* 100 (1982), pp. 740–80, with docs.

de Lisle, Ambrose Lisle March Phillipps (1809–78), English RC writer. Born of Anglican parents, he was converted to Roman Catholicism in 1824. In 1835 he gave 230 acres of Charnwood Forest to the *Trappist Order for the building of the monastery of Mount St Bernard and in 1838 founded the 'Association of Universal Prayer for the Conversion of England'. Over much of his life he was active in furthering reunion between the C of E and Rome, and was on friendly terms with the leaders of the *Oxford Movement. In 1857 he joined in founding the 'Association for Promoting the Unity of Christendom' (*APUC), which included Anglicans and Orthodox as well as RCs, withdrawing, however, when it was condemned by Rome in 1864. In 1862 he assumed the name of de Lisle (signing prior to that date Ambrose Lisle Phillipps).

E. S. Purcell, *Life and Letters of Ambrose Phillipps de Lisle* (2 vols., 1900). M. Pawley, *Faith and Family: The Life and Circle of Ambrose Phillipps de Lisle* (Norwich, 1993). T. Cooper in *DNB* 14 (1888), pp. 321 f.

Delitzsch, Franz Julius (1813–90), OT scholar and orientalist. A native of Leipzig, where he taught for some years, he later held professorships at Rostock (1846–50), Erlangen (1850–67), and Leipzig (1867–90). Of a pietistic *Lutheran background and Jewish descent, he esp. sought to combat anti-Semitism and foster the conversion of the Jews, editing a periodical *Saat auf Hoffnung* from 1863, founding a Jewish missionary college, establishing at Leipzig an 'Institutum Judaicum' (1886; later 'Institutum Delitzschianum') and translating the NT into Hebrew (pub. 1877). He published a long series of Commentaries on the OT, conservative and practical in tendency, but displaying increasing understanding of the critical view of the OT. In 1857 he issued a commentary on Heb. (Eng. tr., 2 vols., 1868–70). He also wrote extensively on Rabbinic subjects, edited in conjunction with S. Baer the Heb. text of the OT (except Ex.–Deut.; 1861–97), and published some devotional works. As a final apology he issued *Der tiefe Graben zwischen alter und moderner Theologie: Ein Bekenntnis* (1888).

D. W. Volck (ed.), *Theologische Briefe der Professoren Delitzsch und von Hofmann* (1891); O. Eissfeldt and K. H. Rengstorf (eds.), *Briefwechsel zwischen Franz Delitzsch und Wolf Wilhelm Graf Baudissin 1866–1890* (Abhandlungen der Rheinisch-Westfälischen Akademie der Wissenschaften, 43; Opladen [1973]). 'Memorial Tribute' by S. I. Curtiss (Edinburgh, 1891), with bibl. K. H. Rengstorf, *Die Delitzsch'sche Sache: Ein Kapitel preussischer Kirchen- und Fakultätspolitik im Vormärz* (Arbeiten zur Geschichte und Theologie des Luthertums, 19; 1967). S. Wagner, *Franz Delitzsch: Leben und Werke* (Beiträge zur evangelische Theologie, 80; 1978). J. W. Rogerson, *Old Testament Criticism in the Nineteenth Century: England and Germany* (1984), pp. 111–20. A. Köhler in *PRE* (3rd edn.), 4 (1898), pp. 565–70; F. Vigouroux in *Dict. Bibl.* 2 (1899), cols. 1341 f., with complete list of Delitzsch's writings.

Delitzsch, Friedrich (1850–1922), German Assyriologist. He was the son of F. J. *Delitzsch, and held professorships at Leipzig (1878), Breslau (1893), and Berlin (1899). He published various works on oriental subjects, among them *Prolegomena eines neuen hebräisch-aramaischen Wörterbuchs zum Alten Testament* (1886), *Assyrische Grammatik* (1889), and *Geschichte Babyloniens und Assyriens* (1891). His most celebrated book, however, was his *Babel*

und Bibel (2 parts, 1902–3; Eng. tr., 1903), based on lectures delivered before the Emp. Wilhelm II, which claimed that several OT narratives were of Babylonian origin and that Judaism was essentially dependent on Babylonian culture. He reviewed the controversy aroused by this book in *Babel und Bibel: Ein Rückblick und Ausblick* (1904). Among his later writings, all hostile to Christian orthodoxy, were *Mehr Licht* (1907) and *Die grosse Täuschung* (2 vols., 1920–1).

Obituary notice by I. M. Price in *Beiträge zur Assyriologie*, 10, Heft 2 (1927), pp. i–xii [in Eng.], with refs. E. G. Kraeling, *The Old Testament since the Reformation* (1955), pp. 149–63.

della Robbia, Florentine family of artists. The two most celebrated are:

(1) **Luca della Robbia** (1399/1400–1482). His early works were sculptures, of which the singing and dancing boys (1431–8), done in marble, for the organ gallery of the cathedral of Florence, is the most famous (now in the Museo dell'Opera del Duomo). His principal work in bronze is the north sacristy door of the cathedral (1446–69), which is divided into several panels representing the Madonna, St John the Baptist, the Evangelists, and Doctors of the Church. From 1442 he began to work chiefly in enamelled terracotta, a technique which he greatly improved. These reliefs show most often white figures on a pale-blue ground, framed by brilliantly coloured borders of fruits and flowers. His Madonnas of the Rose-Garden and of the Apple in the Bargello at Florence are of exquisite charm and real dignity, and the Chapel of the Crucifix at San Miniato, the Tabernacles at Impruneta, and other decorative works, belong to the finest specimens of Italian enamelled terracotta.

(2) **Andrea della Robbia** (1435–1525), nephew of Luca. He continued the tradition of his uncle and ran a large and highly productive family workshop. He did the fine series of medallions with infants for the front of the Foundling Hospital at Florence (1487) and a large number of Madonnas. Many of these are of great charm. The most elaborate work he executed was the series of altars for the Franciscan church at La Verna.

A. Marquand, *Luca della Robbia* (Princeton Monographs in Art and Archaeology, 3; 1913); id., *Andrea della Robbia* (2 vols., ibid. 11; 1922). On other members of the family, see id., *Giovanni della Robbia* (ibid. 8; 1920); id., *The Brothers of Giovanni della Robbia* (ibid. 13; 1928), all with illustrations and detailed bibl. M. Cruttwell, *Luca and Andrea della Robbia and their Successors* (1902). L. Planiscig, *Luca della Robbia* (Florence, 1948); J. Pope-Hennessy, *Luca della Robbia* (Oxford, 1980), with full bibl. C. Seymour, Jun., *Sculpture in Italy 1400 to 1500* (Pelican History of Art, 1966), pp. 92–7, 119–21, and 141 f. (Luca), and 166 f. (Andrea).

de Lubac, Henri. See LUBAC, HENRI DE.

Deluge, the. See FLOOD, THE.

de Lugo, John. See LUGO, JOHN DE.

de Maistre, Joseph (1753–1821), French *Ultramontane writer. He was born at Chambéry in Savoy and educated by the *Jesuits. At first influenced by the 18th-cent. rationalists, after the Revolution of 1789 he became a reactionary, who saw in the Church the safeguard of political stability. In 1802 he was appointed Sardinian minister at St Petersburg, where he remained until 1817, when he returned to Savoy. In his principal work, *Du pape* (1819), he argued that the only true basis of society lay in authority, which took the double form of spiritual authority vested in the Papacy and temporal authority committed to human kings. The religious basis of history, which was to be understood as throughout under the direction of Divine Providence, was manifested in the redemptive power of suffering and blood. His other writings include *De l'Église gallicane* (1821) and *Soirées de St-Pétersbourg, ou Entretiens sur le gouvernement temporel de la Providence* (1821). De Maistre has been called the 'Prophet of the Past' (P. S. Ballanche, 1776–1847), but his ideas did much to further the overthrow of *Gallicanism and assist the rise of Ultramontanism (F. R. de *Lamennais, C. R. F. *Montalembert, the First *Vatican Council) in the later 19th cent.

Œuvres (7 vols., Brussels, 1838); *Œuvres complètes* (14 vols., Lyons, 1884–7), incl. his posthumous works and unpub. correspondence, with 'Notice biographique' by his son, R. de Maistre, in vol. 1, pp. v–xliii, orig. pub. in the latter's edn. of his father's *Lettres et opuscules inédits* (2 vols., 1851), vol. 1, pp. v–xxvi. *Œuvres* also ed. J.-L. Darcel and others (Geneva, 1980 ff.). Eng. tr. of selections from his works by J. Lively (London, 1965). F. Vermale, *Joseph de Maistre émigré* (Société Savoisienne d'Histoire et d'Archéologie, 64; 1927); C. J. Gignoux, *Joseph de Maistre, prophète du passé, historien de l'avenir* (1963); R. Triomphe, *Joseph de Maistre: Étude sur la vie et sur la doctrine d'un matérialiste mystique* (Geneva, 1968); R. A. Lebrun, *Joseph de Maistre: An Intellectual Militant* (Kingston, Ont., and Montreal [1988]), with bibl. C. Latreille, *Joseph de Maistre et la papauté* (1906); G. Goyau, *La Pensée religieuse de Joseph de Maistre* (1921); M. Jugie, AA, *Joseph de Maistre et l'Église gréco-russe* [1922]; E. Dermenghem, *Joseph de Maistre mystique* (1923; 2nd edn., 1946, repr., 1980). G. Breton, '*Du pape' de Joseph de Maistre: Étude critique* (1931). F. Bayle, *Les Idées politiques de Joseph de Maistre* (1945). I. Berlin, *The Crooked Timber of Humanity*, ed. H. Hardy (1990), pp. 91–174 ('Joseph de Maistre and the Origins of Fascism' [written by 1960]).

de Marca, Pierre. See MARCA, PIERRE DE.

Demetrius. The name of two persons in the NT. (1) A silversmith of *Ephesus, who led an unsuccessful riot against St *Paul, on the ground that the Apostle's preaching would endanger the trade in silver images (Acts 19: 24 ff.). (2) A disciple commended by St *John, of whom nothing else is known (3 Jn., verse 12).

Demetrius, St (d. 231 or 232), Bp. of *Alexandria from 189. The interest in him centres in his relations to *Origen. As Bp. of Alexandria he began by supporting Origen, whom he recognized as head of the *Catechetical School in the city *c.*202. Later, however, when the Bps. of *Jerusalem and *Caesarea allowed him to preach in spite of his being a layman, Demetrius recalled him to Alexandria and censured his conduct. At a synod in 231 he finally banished him for having been ordained priest irregularly at Caesarea, and shortly afterwards deprived him of the priesthood. It is possible that there were doctrinal reasons behind the breach between Origen and Demetrius. He is greatly venerated in the Coptic Church. Feast day, in E., 26 Oct.; in W., 9 Oct.

*Eusebius, *HE* 5. 22; 6. 3, 8, 19, and 26. Bardenhewer, 2, pp. 194 f.; L. *Duchesne, *Histoire ancienne de l'Église*, 1 (1906), pp.

341–6. Brief note, with refs., by B. F. *Westcott in *DCB* 1 (1877), p. 803; V. Grumel in *DHGE* 14 (1960), cols. 198 f., both s.v.

Demiurge. This, the English form of a Greek word (δημιουργός) meaning 'craftsman', was used of the Divine Being by *Plato in his account of the formation of the visible world, and so by Greek Christian writers simply of God as the Creator of all things. The *Gnostics used the word disparagingly of the inferior deity to whom they ascribed the origin of the material universe, distinguishing him from the supreme God. In its English form the word is commonly used in reference to this Gnostic doctrine.

demythologizing (Ger. *Entmythologisierung*). A term employed from 1941 by R. *Bultmann (q.v.) for his proposal to interpret the NT critically in order to express the theological meaning of its mythological language. Bultmann claimed that the biblical three-storied universe, belief in *miracles, *angels, demons, etc., was incredible in the modern world, and that the Gospel message could be freed from these false stumbling-blocks and expressed instead through an appropriate language, descriptive of human existence, such as that which he himself borrowed from M. *Heidegger's *Sein und Zeit* (1927; Eng. tr., 1962). In the ensuing controversy, the roots of Bultmann's position were often lost sight of in disputes about the definition of myth and modernity, and, despite his insistence that he was interpreting rather than simply eliminating myth, his slogan has come to be attached to a variety of reductionist interpretations of Christianity.

R. Bultmann, 'Neues Testament und Mythologie', incl. in his *Offenbarung und Heilsgeschehen* (Beiträge zur evangelischen Theologie, Bd. 7; 1941). H. W. Bartsch and others (eds.), *Kerygma und Mythos* (Theologische Forschung, 1–2, 5, 8–9, 19, 23, 30–1, 40, 44, 45, 52, and 56; 1948–75), with repr. of Bultmann's paper, 1, pp. 15–53; Eng. tr. of selections from vol. 1 by R. H. Fuller (1953), with Bultmann's paper pp. 1–44, and bibl. pp. 224–8; of selections from vols. 2–5 by id. (1962), with bibl. pp. 357 f. Revised Eng. tr. of Bultmann's orig. essay by S. M. Ogden in his collection of Bultmann's papers, *New Testament and Mythology and Other Basic Writings* (Philadelphia, 1984; London, 1985), pp. 1–43. J. Macquarrie, *The Scope of Demythologizing* (1960). R. A. Johnson, *The Origins of Demythologizing: Philosophy and Historiography in the Theology of Rudolf Bultmann* (Studies in the History of Religion, 28; Leiden, 1974).

Denifle, Heinrich Seuse (1844–1905), Church historian. Born at Imst in the Tyrol, he entered the *Dominican Order in 1861, was ordained priest in 1866, and taught philosophy and theology at Graz from 1870 to 1880. Called to Rome in 1880 as associate to the General of the Order, he became a collaborator in the projected new edition of the works of St *Thomas Aquinas, travelling all over Europe in search of MSS. In 1883 he was appointed sub-archivist at the *Vatican. In 1885 he founded, with F. *Ehrle, the *Archiv für Litteratur- und Kirchengeschichte des Mittelalters*, and in 1887 he was appointed editor of the records of Paris University.

His writings include his monumental *Chartularium Universitatis Parisiensis*, written in conjunction with A. Chatelain (Paris, 4 vols., 1889–97); several works on the German mystics of the 14th cent., Meister *Eckhart, J. *Tauler, and *Henry Suso; and an unfinished work on M. *Luther and Lutheranism. This last is a brilliant, but wholly unsympathetic, exposition of Luther's teaching and methods, based on a wide study and acute analysis of contemporary sources.

J. P. Kirsch, 'Le R. P. Denifle, OP', *RHE* 6 (1905), pp. 665–76. A. Walz, OP, 'Analecta denifleana', *Antonianum*, 32 (1955), pp. 124–40, 220–52, 317–58, with further refs. M. D. *Knowles, 'Denifle and Ehrle', *History*, 54 (1969), pp. 1–12. O. Spiess, OP, in *Dict. Sp.* 3 (1954), cols. 238–41; A. Walz, OP, in *DHGE* 14 (1960), cols. 221–45.

Denis. See DIONYSIUS.

Denison, George Anthony (1805–96), Archdeacon of Taunton from 1851. Ordained deacon and priest in 1832, he was Vicar of East Brent from 1845 till his death. He was throughout his life a vigorous defender of rigid *High Church principles. Between 1854 and 1858 he was unsuccessfully prosecuted in the civil courts for teaching the doctrine of the *Real Presence in the *Eucharist. From 1839 to 1870 he strongly supported the cause of Church education against the movement for universal and compulsory education in state schools, a cause which was largely lost when the Education Act of 1870 was passed.

G. A. Denison, *Notes of My Life, 1805–1878* (1878). L. E. Denison (his niece), *Fifty Years at East Brent* (1902). J. Coombs, *George Anthony Denison: The Firebrand 1805–1896* (1984). J. M. Rigg in *DNB*, Suppl. 2 (1901), pp. 127–9.

Denmark, Christianity in. After one or two unsuccessful missions to Denmark, the Christian faith gained a firm footing in the 9th cent., when the Danish chief, Harold, was baptized on a visit to *Louis the Pious, the Frankish king, and on his return brought with him St *Anskar. Under Sven I (985–1014) and Cnut the Great (1014–35) Christianity became generally accepted. In 1104 the Church in Denmark was separated from the metropolitan see of Hamburg-Bremen, to which it had been united since the time of St Anskar, and its seven bishops placed under the primacy of the Bp. of *Lund. During the later Middle Ages the bishops acquired considerable temporal power and became correspondingly unpopular.

The Reformation in Denmark took place between 1520 and 1540. The chief events were the formal proclamation of religious freedom at the Diet of Odense in 1527, the adoption of a *Lutheran creed (the *Confessio Hafnica*) in 1530, the expropriation of the hierarchy and the monasteries in the following years, and the visit of J. *Bugenhagen to set up a Lutheran episcopate and introduce a new liturgy in 1537. The Danish Bible appeared in 1550. Restrictions upon RCs were milder than in other Protestant countries, but in 1624 the death penalty was imposed by royal rescript upon any RC priests found performing their official duties, while the *Danske Lov* of 1683 ordered that converts to RCism should lose all their property.

In common with the rest of Lutheranism, Danish Christianity suffered from the dry intellectualism of Lutheran 'orthodoxy' in the 17th cent. and experienced the *Pietist reaction in the late 17th and early 18th. A revival of orthodox Lutheranism, in which the *Libri Symbolici*, or ecclesiastical creeds, were restored to honour, was largely due to N. F. S. *Grundtvig (1783–1872), whose view of Scripture and tradition inclined towards the Catholic standpoint. To him also was due the idea of the Folk High

Schools (*Folkehöjskoler*), which have since proved a strong Christian influence. In contrast to him was S. *Kierkegaard (1813–55), who opposed both the State Church and the harmonizing theology of H. L. *Martensen (q.v.). By laws of 1849 and 1852, which gave complete religious liberty to Denmark, the Evangelical Lutheran Church was officially disestablished, but continued to receive state grants, and remained entirely subordinate to the state in all matters of legislation. In 1947 Parliament legislated for women pastors, despite resistance from all but one of the bishops. A commission to reform the liturgy sat from 1953 to 1963, but its proposals, after experimentation, were not accepted; a further commission was established in 1970, and in 1987 new rites for consecrating bishops and ordaining priests were adopted. About 90 per cent of all Danes are nominally Lutherans, though there is a small RC minority and a number of Baptists. The Lutheran primate, who ordains the other bishops, is the Bp. of Zealand; he resides at Copenhagen, but his cathedral church is at Roskilde. Danish missions abroad began in 1814, and have been established in various parts of the world; their most extensive and successful work has been done in Greenland.

A. Krarup (ed.), *Bullarium Danicum: Pavelige Aktstykker Vedrørende Danmark, 1198–1316* (2 halvbind, Copenhagen, 1931–3); *Acta Pontificum Danica: Pavelige Akstykker Vedrørende Danmark, 1316–1536*, ed. L. Moltesen and others (7 vols., ibid., 1904–43). A. Krarup and W. Norvin (eds.), *Acta Processus Litium inter Regem Danorum et Archiepiscopum Lundensem* (ibid., 1932). M. C. Gertz (ed.), *Vitae Sanctorum Danorum* (ibid., 1908–12). L. N. Helveg, *Den danske Kirkes Historie* (5 vols., 1870); L. P. Fabricius, *Danmarks Kirkehistorie* (2 vols., 1934–5); H. Koch and others (eds.), *Den Danske Kirkes Historie* (8 vols., 1950–66). M. S. Lausten, *Danmarks Kirkehistorie* (1983), with bibl. P. Hartling (ed.), *The Danish Church* (Denmark in Print and Pictures, Copenhagen [1964]); L. S. Hunter (ed.), *Scandinavian Churches: A Picture of the Development of the Life of the Churches of Denmark, Finland, Iceland, Norway and Sweden* (1965). P. G. Lindhardt, *Skandinavische Kirchengeschichte seit dem 16. Jahrhundert* (Die Kirche in ihrer Geschichte. Ein Handbuch, ... Ad. B. Moeller, Band 3, Lieferung M3; Göttingen [1982]), pp. 236–63, with bibl. pp. 308–10. E. H. Dunkley, *The Reformation in Denmark* (CHS, 1948), with bibl. J. O. Andersen, *Der Reformkatholizismus und die dänische Reformation* (1954); M. S. Lausten, *Reformationen i Danmark* (1987). J. Schnell, *Die dänische Kirchenordnung von 1542 und der Einfluss von Wittenberg* (1927). M. S. Lausten and L. C. Brøndum in *TRE* 8 (1981), pp. 300–19, s.v. 'Dänemark'.

Denney, James (1856–1917), Scottish *Free Church theologian. Educated at Glasgow University and Glasgow Free Church College, he was made minister of East Free Church, Broughty Ferry, in 1886. From 1897 till his death he taught theology at the Glasgow Free Church College. In his later years he became actively involved in the administration of the *United Free Church, becoming in 1913 convener of its Central Fund. He also took a prominent part in the movement for reunion with the Established Church of *Scotland. As a theologian he moved doctrinally from a liberal to an evangelical position. In his *Christology he asserted firmly the traditional doctrine of the Person of Christ. He held the Atonement to have a purely substitutionary character. His main works were *The Death of Christ* (1902), *Jesus and the Gospel* (1908), *The Christian Doctrine of Reconciliation* (1917), and editions of

I and II Thessalonians (1892), *II Corinthians* (1894), and of the Greek text of *Romans* (1900).

Letters of Principal James Denney to W. Robertson Nicoll, 1893–1917 [1920], with 'Appreciation' by W. R. *Nicoll (pp. xiii–xxvii) and 'Memoirs of a Student', by J. A. Robertson (pp. xxxi–xliii). J. *Moffatt (ed.), *Letters of Principal James Denney to his Family and Friends* [1922]. T. H. Walker, *Principal James Denney, D.D.: A Memoir and a Tribute* (1918). J. R. Taylor, *God Loved Like That! The Theology of James Denney* (1962). A. P. E. Sell, *Defending and Declaring the Faith* (Exeter and Colorado Springs, Colo. [1987]), pp. 195–220 and 264–71. A. S. *Peake in *DNB*, 1912–1921, pp. 153 f.

de Noailles, Louis Antoine (1651–1729), Abp. of *Paris. Born in the Auvergne, he was educated at the *Jesuit college of Aurillac and then at the Collège du Plessis in Paris. Ordained in 1675, he became Doctor of Theology in 1676, was made Bp. of Cahors in 1679, and translated to Châlons-sur-Marne in 1680. He became Abp. of Paris in 1695 through the influence of Mme de Maintenon. He was created a cardinal by Innocent XII in 1700, and made head of the *Sorbonne in 1710. He was a zealous and devoted pastor, and an ardent reformer of clerical discipline (obligatory residence in seminaries before ordination, annual retreats, courses on moral theology). In accordance with *Gallican ideals, he fostered a renewal of the traditional French liturgical books (Breviary, Missal, Ritual, Ceremonial). He became involved in most of the controversies of the age, notably in 1699 over F. *Fénelon's *Maximes des saints*. His repeated commendation in 1695 and 1699 of P. *Quesnel's *Réflexions morales* caused him to be suspected of *Jansenism, even though he condemned certain intrinsic Jansenist doctrines in 1698. A staunch Gallican, by defending the rights of the French bishops in the *Assemblies of the Clergy over which he presided in 1700, 1704, and 1713, he incurred the antagonism of the *Ultramontanes. Similarly his objections to '*Vineam Domini' in 1705 and his opposition to '*Unigenitus' met with widespread disfavour. He formally appealed against the latter in Sept. 1718; though he was forced to sign an acceptance of it in 1728, he had previously prepared a recantation which was circulated later. He published two volumes of pastoral instructions in 1718–19. See also APPELLANTS.

E. de Barthélemy, *Le Cardinal de Noailles, évêque de Châlons, archevêque de Paris, d'après sa correspondance inédite, 1651–1728* (1886). M. Fosseyeux, 'Le Cardinal de Noailles et l'administration du diocèse de Paris (1695–1729)', *Revue Historique*, 114 (1913), pp. 261–84; 115 (1914), pp. 34–54. L. Ceyssens, 'Autour de l'Unigenitus. Le cardinal de Noailles (1651–1728)', *Lias*, 11 (1984), pp. 169–252; repr. in id. and J. A. G. Tans, *Autour de l'Unigenitus* (Bibliotheca Ephemeridum Theologicarum Lovaniensium, 76; 1987), pp. 649–733. J. Carreyre in *DTC* 11 (pt. 1; 1931), cols. 678–81, s.v. 'Noailles', with notes on sources.

de Nobili, Robert (1577–1656), *Jesuit missionary. He was born in Rome, entered the order in 1596, and set out for *India in 1603. Observing the religious influence of the Brahmins in Hindu society, he adopted the penitent lifestyle of a Brahmin Sanyasi in the hope of winning public credibility. In response to objections from his fellow missionaries and from the Abp. of Goa, he defended this strategy in several theological treatises and in canonical proceedings. Once Pope Gregory XV had approved his

method in 1623, de Nobili was able to work widely and successfully in S. India. A considerable theologian and linguist, he left writings in Latin, Italian, Portuguese, Sanskrit, Tamil, and Telugu, both on the Christian faith in general and on specific issues arising in India.

Of his works on missiology, written in Latin, that on Indian Customs (dating from 1615), ed., with Eng. tr., by S. Rajamanickam, SJ (Palayamkottai, 1972); on Adaptation (dating from 1619) ed., with Eng. tr., by id. (ibid., 1971). Fr. tr., with notes, of what is called his 'First Apology' (dating from 1610), by P. Dahmen, SJ (Paris, 1931). Various Tamil works ed. S. Rajamanickam, SJ (Tamil Literary Society, Tuticorin, 1963–8). P. Dahmen, SJ, *Robert de Nobili S. I.: Ein Beitrag zur Geschichte des Missionsmethode und der Indiologie* (Münster, 1924; Fr. tr., Brugge, 1924; Eng. tr. serialized in *Catholic Herald of India*, 23 (1925; details in Polgár, cited below); V. Cronin, *A Pearl to India* (1959); S. Rajamanickam, SJ, *The First Oriental Scholar* (Tirunelveli, 1972); P. R. Bachmann, *Roberto Nobili 1577–1656: Ein missionsgeschichtlicher Beitrag zum christlichen Dialog mit Hinduismus* (Bibliotheca Instituti Historici S.I., 32; Rome, 1972). S. Arokiasamy, SJ, *Dharma, Hindu and Christian, according to Robert de Nobili* (Rome, 1986). Sommervogel, 5 (1894), cols. 1779 f.; Polgár, 1 (1990), pp. 578–83. V. Cronin in *NCE* 10 (1967), pp. 477–9, s.v. 'Nobili, Roberto de'.

Denys. See DIONYSIUS.

deodand (Lat. *Deo dandum*, 'to be given to God'). In old English law, a personal chattel or thing which had been the cause of the death of a person, and as such was forfeit to the Crown to be applied to pious uses, e.g. given in alms. The law regulating deodands was formally abolished in 1846.

Deo gratias (Lat., 'Thanks be to God'). A liturgical formula in constant use in the services of the W. Church. In the Roman Mass it (or its vernacular version) is said by the people after each of the first two lessons and as a response to *Ite, missa est or other form of dismissal. The Rule of St *Benedict requires its use by the doorkeeper in receiving a stranger or a beggar (cap. 66). During the *Donatist controversy in *Africa it was a mark of orthodoxy as contrasted with the 'Deo laudes' used by the schismatics. Instances are met with of 'Deogratias' as a Christian proper name.

deontology. A term used first by J. Bentham in 1826 for the science of ethics or moral obligation, esp. as distinct from jurisprudence.

deosculatorium (Lat., from *deosculor*, 'to kiss feelingly'). Another name for the object known as the *pax brede, sometimes used in the *Mass.

Deprecatio Gelasii (Lat., 'Intercession of Gelasius'). A Latin litany for the Church universal (pro ecclesia universali). Both the form and much of the content are of E. origin. The ascription to Pope *Gelasius (492–6) is now generally accepted. The litany appears to have been introduced by him into the Roman Mass, possibly at the place where the *Kyrie became established. The text has come down to us in collections of prayers for private use put together in France in the 9th cent.

B. *Capelle, OSB, 'Le Kyrie de la messe et le Pape Gélase', *R. Bén.* 46 (1934), pp. 126–44, with crit. text; repr. in *Travaux* *liturgiques*, 2 (Louvain, 1962). pp. 116–34. C. Callewaert, 'Les Étapes de l'histoire du Kyrie', *RHE* 38 (1942), pp. 20–45. P. De Clerck, *La 'Prière Universelle' dans les liturgies latines anciennes* (Liturgiewissenschaftliche Quellen und Forschungen, 62; 1977), pp. 166–87, incl. text and full bibl.

De Profundis (Lat., 'Out of the deep'). A title of Ps. 130, from its opening words. The psalm is one of the fifteen '*Gradual Psalms*' as well as one of the '*Seven Penitential Psalms*'. Its appeal for help from the misery of sin, and its expression of trust in deliverance, have led to its traditional use in the W. Church, esp. in the Office for the Departed. In *Ireland it used to be regularly recited at Mass after the *Last Gospel for the victims of former religious persecution.

H. Thurston, SJ, 'The *De Profundis*', *The Month*, 132 (1918), pp. 358–68; repr. in id., *Familiar Prayers*, ed. P. Grosjean, SJ (1953), no. 10, pp. 164–77.

de Rancé, Armand-Jean Le Bouthillier. See RANCÉ, ARMAND-JEAN LE BOUTHILLIER DE.

Der Balyzeh Fragments. A few incomplete pages of a Gk. papyrus codex containing liturgical prayers and a Creed (*c*. 6th cent.), discovered by W. Flinders Petrie and W. Crum at Der Balyzeh (Dair Balaizah), S. of Assiout, in 1907. They throw important light on the history of Christian worship in Egypt, e.g. the existence (cf. the liturgies of St *Serapion and of St *Mark, also Egyptian) of a Eucharistic *Epiclesis before the Words of *Institution. The compilation of the prayers has been variously dated (T. Schermann and P. Drews, *c*.225; F. E. *Brightman, *c*.350; B. *Capelle, *c*.575). The Creed has affinities with the short Creed in the *Apostolic Tradition* of St *Hippolytus. The papyrus is preserved in the *Bodleian Library, MSS Gr. liturg. c. 3(P) and d. 4(P).

Earlier edns. of the text superseded by that of C. H. Roberts and B. Capelle, OSB, *An Early Euchologium* (Bibliothèque du *Muséon*, 23; Louvain, 1949). P. E. Kahle, Jun. (ed.), *Bala'izah: Coptic texts from Deir Bala'izah in Upper Egypt* (2 vols., 1954). J. Van Haelst, 'Une nouvelle reconstruction du papyrus liturgique der Dèr-Balizeh', *Ephemerides Theologicae Lovanienses*, 45 (1969), pp. 444–55.

de' Ricci, Scipione. See RICCI, SCIPIONE DE'.

de Rossi, Giovanni Battista (1822–94), archaeologist and epigrapher. Born and educated in Rome, he was appointed a Scriptor of the Vatican Library in 1844, Prefect of the Museo Cristiano del Vaticano in 1878, and Secretary of the Pontificia Commissione di Archaeologia Sacra in 1884. In 1841 Giuseppe Marchi, SJ (d. 1860), fired his interest in the Roman *catacombs, to whose excavation and study he devoted the rest of his life. He made systematic use, as none of his predecessors had done, of literary sources (itineraries, *martyrologies, the *Liber Pontificalis), *iconography, and brick-stamps to find and interpret archaeological data. He put the catacombs into their legal and social context. He examined later materials and contents of rubble, as well as the original galleries and their monuments. He had strong support from *Pius IX, and numerous friends and pupils, including O. *Marucchi and G. Wilpert, continued his work. He contributed much to the study of pagan as well as Christian Rome,

and to the preservation of Rome's monuments. At the First *Vatican Council, he used his learning to attest the priority of the *Apostolic See and so to defend *infallibility.

Of primary importance among his many publications were *Inscriptiones Christianae Urbis Romae septimo saeculo antiquiores* (1, 1861; 2.1, 1888), *La Roma sotterranea cristiana* (3 vols., 1864–77), *Musaici cristiani e saggi dei pavimenti della chiesa di Roma anteriori al secolo XV* (27 fascs., 1872–99), and *Piante iconografiche e prospettiche di Roma anteriori al secolo XVI* (1879). With G. Henzen and E. Bormann he collected the *Corpus Inscriptionum Latinarum*, 6, pts. 1–5 (*Inscriptiones Latini Urbis Romae*, 1876–94), with H. Stevenson catalogued the *Codices Palatini Latini bibliothecae Vaticanae* (1886), and with L. *Duchesne edited the *Hieronymian Martyrology for the *Acta Sanctorum* (Nov. 2.1; 1894). His memorandum on the *ampullae sanguinis*, circulated privately in 1862, was ed. by A. Ferrua in 1944. In 1863 he founded the *Bulletino di Archaeologia Cristiana*, which he edited for 30 years.

There is a list of his works up to 1892 in *Mélanges G. B. de Rossi* (Supplément aux *Mélanges d'Archéologie et d'Histoire*, 12; 1892), pp. 1–27, and to 1894 by H. *Leclercq (see below), cols. 92–9. P. M. Baumgarten, *Giovanni Battista de Rossi, der Begründer der christlich-archäologischen Wissenschaft: Eine biographische Skizze* (Cologne, 1892; Ital. tr., enlarged, 1892); O. Marucchi, *Giovanni Battista de Rossi: Cenni Biografici* [1901]; G. Ferretto, *Note Storico-bibliografiche di Archeologia Cristiana* (1942), pp. 318–71. E. Kirschbaum, SJ, 'P. Giuseppe Marchi SJ (1795–1860) und Giovanni B. De Rossi (1822–1894)', *Gregorianum*, 21 (1940), pp. 564–606. H. Leclercq, OSB, in *DACL* 15 (pt. 1; 1950), cols. 18–100, s.v. 'Rossi, J.-B. de', with extensive bibl.; N. Parise in *Dizionario Biografico degli Italiani*, 39 (1991), pp. 201–5, s.v.

De Sacramentis. A short liturgical treatise on the Sacraments, almost certainly the work of St *Ambrose (d. 397). Its six homilies ('Books'), addressed to the newly baptized in Easter week, treat of *Baptism, *Confirmation, and the *Eucharist. Its special interest is that it is the earliest witness to the Roman *Canon of the Mass in substantially its present form; also granted its Milanese provenance, it attests the influence of Roman usage in N. Italy. The author insists that it is the word of Christ which consecrates (*conficit*) the Eucharist; and in his canon he refers to the species as an unbloody offering (*incruentam hostiam*) and a figure (*figura*) of the Body and Blood of Christ (cf. *Serapion's ὁμοίωμα). In the 16th cent. doubts about its Ambrosian authorship were expressed by the *Zwinglians who disliked its strongly conversionist doctrine, and its authenticity was a point at issue at the *Marburg Colloquy of 1529. The Benedictine editors of Ambrose (1690) also had hesitations, which were shared by subsequent scholars, some of whom attributed it to *Maximus of Turin, and a date in the 5th or 6th cent. came to be commonly assumed. R. H. *Connolly, however, following hints in F. *Probst and G. *Morin, showed that the biblical text in *De Sacramentis* coincides with the idiosyncratic text used by Ambrose elsewhere and so put its Ambrosian authorship virtually beyond question.

J. P. Migne, *PL* 16. 409–62. Crit. edns. by O. Faller in *Sancti Ambrosii Opera*, 7 (CSEL 73, 1955), pp. 13–85, and by B. Botte, OSB (SC 25; 1950; 2nd edn., 1961), with important introd. Eng. tr. by T. Thompson (London, 1919), with introd. by J. H. Srawley; new and extensively rev. edn., 1950. G. Morin, OSB, 'Pour l'authenticité du *De Sacramentis* et de l'*Explanatio Symboli* de S. Ambroise', *JLW* 8 (1928), pp. 86–106; R. H. Connolly, OSB, *The De Sacramentis a Work of Ambrose: Two Papers* (*Downside Abbey, 1942). K. Gamber, *Die Autorschaft von de Sacramentis: Zugleich ein Beitrag zur Liturgiegeschichte der römischen Provinz Dacia mediterranea* (Studia patristica et liturgica, 1; Regensburg, 1967) [attributes the *De Sacramentis* to *Nicetas of Remesiana: a view not generally accepted]. Further bibl. in Altaner and Stuiber (1978), pp. 383 and 630 f., and in Quasten (cont.), *Patrology*, 4 (1986), pp. 172 f.

Descartes, René

Descartes, René (1596–1650), philosopher. Born near Tours, he was educated at the *Jesuit college at La Flèche and at the University of Poitiers. As a young man he travelled widely and in 1619, after a day's meditation in a 'stove-heated room' in Bavaria, became convinced that he was destined to found a new philosophical system. After further travels, and some years spent in Paris, he settled in the Netherlands in 1629. On hearing of the condemnation of *Galileo in 1633, he suppressed his treatise on physics, *Le Monde* (pub. 1664), but his *Discours de la Méthode* (with essays on optics, meteorology, and geometry) appeared anonymously in 1637. The definitive statement of his metaphysics, *Meditationes de Prima Philosophia*, was published in 1641, and the mammoth philosophical and scientific textbook, *Principia Philosophiae*, in 1644. The *Passions de l'âme*, on physiology and psychology, appeared in 1649. The same year Descartes accepted an invitation to act as tutor to Queen *Christina of Sweden; he died in Stockholm the following February.

From the start Descartes was attracted by the clarity and certainty of mathematics, and aimed to extend its methods to the whole of human knowledge. To this end he devised his method of doubt, 'rejecting everything in which one can imagine the least doubt', so as to arrive at an unshakeable foundation for philosophy. This he finds in the famous '*Cogito ergo sum*' ('I am thinking, therefore I exist'). He then proceeds to reconstruct human knowledge, establishing the existence first of God and then of an external world whose nature we can understand provided we restrict ourselves to the (God-given) 'clear and distinct perceptions' of the intellect.

Descartes's proof of God's existence starts from the idea of God which he finds within himself: whatever caused this idea must have all the perfections that are represented in the idea. Descartes adds the supplementary argument that he could not exist, possessing, as he does, the idea of God, unless he derived his existence from God. He also offers an *a priori* demonstration that God's existence cannot be separated from His essence (see ANSELM, ST, and ONTOLOGICAL ARGUMENT).

Descartes's most controversial doctrine is his mind/body 'dualism'—the claim that the mind is an unextended incorporeal substance entirely distinct from the body. He also contributed importantly to the 17th-cent. scientific revolution by arguing for the elimination of 'real qualities' from physics in favour of explanations involving only 'the divisions, shapes, and motions of matter'.

Standard edn. of his *Œuvres* by C. Adam and P. Tannery (12 vols., 1897–1910, + index, 1913; rev. edn., 1964–76). Eng. tr. of his more important *Philosophical Writings* by J. Cottingham, R. Stoothoff, and D. Murdoch (2 vols., Cambridge, '1984'–1985 [both vols. 1985]). Eng. tr. of his *Philosophical Letters* by A. [J.] Kenny (Oxford, 1970). M. Gueroult, *Descartes selon l'ordre des raisons* (Philosophie de l'Esprit, 2 vols., 1953); F. Alquié, *Descartes: L'Homme et l'œuvre* (1956); H. Gouthier, *La Pensée métaphysique de Descartes* (Bibliothèque d'histoire de la philosophie, 1962) and other works of this author; A. [J.] Kenny, *Descartes: A Study of his Philosophy* (New York, 1968); B. Williams, *Descartes: The Project of Pure Enquiry* (Harmondsworth, 1978); M. D. Wilson, *Descartes* (London, 1978); J. Cottingham, *Descartes* (Oxford, 1986). W. Doney (ed.), *Descartes: A Collection of Critical Essays* (1968). G. Sebba, *Bibliographia Cartesiana: A Critical Guide to the Descartes Literature, 1800–1960* (The Hague, 1964). L. J. Beck in *NCE* 4 (1967), pp. 784–8, s.v., with bibl.

Descent of Christ into Hell, the

Descent of Christ into Hell, the. This belief is based on such biblical passages as Mt. 27: 52 f., Lk. 23: 43, 1, and Pet. 3: 18–20, though various opinions have been held as to their exact meaning. Some have thought that the descent into hell refers to the victory over the powers of evil, others have connected it with the Dereliction on the Cross and the full bearing by Christ of the fruits of sin in our stead. Most Christian theologians, however, believe that it refers to the visit of the Lord after His death to the realm of existence, which is neither heaven nor hell (qq.v.) in the ultimate sense, but a place or state where the souls of pre-Christian people waited for the message of the Gospel, and whither the penitent thief passed after his death on the cross (Lk. 23: 43).

The earliest known occurrences of the article in the Creeds are in 4th-cent. *Arian formularies, namely, the Fourth Creed of *Sirmium of 359 and those of Nike and Constantinople of 360. Thence it found its way into the Aquileian Creed of *Rufinus (it is not found in the *Old Roman Creed), gradually spread over the W., and found a place in the *Apostles' Creed. It also occurs in the *Athanasian Creed and is the subject of Art. 3 of the *Thirty-Nine Articles, but is absent from the *Nicene Creed. See also HELL.

J. Monnier, *La Descente aux Enfers: Étude de pensée religieuse d'art et de littérature* (Paris thesis, 1904); C. Schmidt, 'Der Descensus ad inferos in der alten Kirche', appended to his edn. of *Gespräche Jesu mit seinen Jüngern der nach der Auferstehung* [Epistula Apostolorum] (TU 43; 1919), pp. 453–576 (Excurs 2); J. A. MacCulloch, *The Harrowing of Hell: A Comparative Study of an Early Christian Doctrine* (1930); J. Kroll, *Gott und Hölle: Der Mythos vom Descensuskampf* (Studien der Bibliothek Warburg, 20; 1932). B. Reicke, *The Disobedient Spirits and Christian Baptism: A Study of 1 Pet. III. 19 and its Context* (Acta Seminarii Neotestamentici Upsaliensis, 13; 1946). W. Bieder, *Die Vorstellung von der Höllenfahrt Jesu Christi* (Abhandlungen zur Theologie des Alten und Neuen Testaments, 19; 1949). A. Grillmeier, SJ, 'Der Gottessohn in Totenreich. Soteriologische und christologische Motivierung der Descensuslehre in der älteren christlichen Überlieferung', *ZKT* 71 (1949), pp. 1–53, 184–203, with extensive refs. W. J. Dalton, SJ, *Christ's Proclamation to the Spirits: A Study of 1 Peter, 3: 18–4: 6* (Analecta Biblica, 23; Rome, 1965). W. Maas, *Gott und die Hölle: Studien zum Descensus Christi* (Sammlung Horizonte, NS 14; Einsiedeln [1979]). J. N. D. Kelly, *Early Christian Creeds* (1950; 3rd edn., 1972), pp. 378–83. See also comm. on 1 Pet. 3: 18–20 (esp. E. G. Selwyn, pp. 314–62), on the Apostles' Creed (among older works, esp. J. *Pearson), and on the Thirty-Nine Articles. F. *Loofs in *HERE* 4 (1911), pp. 654–63, s.v. 'Descent into Hades (Christ's)'; J. Chaîne in *Dict. Bibl.*, Suppl. 2 (1934), cols. 395–431, s.v. 'Descente du Christ aux Enfers'; E. Koch in *TRE* 15 (1986), pp. 455–61, s.v. 'Höllenfahrt Christi', with extensive bibl.; J. Kremer and others in *L.Th.K.* (3rd edn.), 5 (1996), cols. 237–40, s.v. 'Höllenabstieg Christi'.

Determinism. The view that all events (including human actions) are somehow inevitable or necessitated. Versions of Determinism were defended by ancient thinkers such as Democritus (*c.*460–*c.*370 BC) and *Stoic philosophers; later defenders of deterministic positions included T. *Hobbes, A. *Schopenhauer, and numerous writers reacting to the scientific developments of the 17th and 18th cent. An influential argument urged in favour of Determinism is that all events must be caused and causes necessitate their effects. Other arguments include logical ones (e.g. that the truth value of statements about the future cannot be altered—an argument famously discussed by *Aristotle) and theological ones (e.g. that God foreknows all human actions, which must therefore occur in accordance with His knowledge—an argument considered by St *Augustine, *Boethius, and St *Thomas Aquinas). The most frequently raised objections to Determinism as a theory of human action are: (1) that it makes nonsense of praise and blame; (2) that belief in Determinism is incompatible with belief in the propriety of deliberating; (3) that people can be directly aware of their power to choose other than as they do; and (4) that causation does not imply necessitation. Arguments to this effect can be found in such authors as Aristotle, Thomas Aquinas, R. *Descartes, Thomas Reid (1710–96), and W. *James. See also PREDESTINATION.

De Thou, Jacques Auguste (1553–1617), historian and book-collector. Coming from a family of magistrates, De Thou ('Thuanus') held high legal office, and helped to enact the Edict of *Nantes (1598). His Latin history of contemporary France, *Historiae sui temporis* (5 vols., 1604–20), describes the religious wars in detail. It was placed on the *Index, though its author remained a (very *Gallican) Catholic. He built up an important library which was doubled in size by his son, **Jacques Auguste De Thou** (1609–77). The MSS from it came eventually to the Bibliothèque Royale in 1732 and 1754; the printed books were dispersed at the De Soubise sale in 1789.

For edns of his works see H. Hauser, *Les Sources de l'histoire de France: XVI*ᵉ *siècle (1494–1610)*, 2 (1909), p. 35, no. 775. *Catalogus Bibliothecae Thuanae* (Paris, 1679). H. Harrisse, 'Les De Thou et leur célèbre Bibliothèque 1573–1680–1789', *Bulletin du Bibliophile*, 1903 and 1904. Further studies by J. Collinson (London, 1807) and S. Kinser (International Archives of the History of Ideas, 18; The Hague, 1966). A. Soman, *De Thou and the Index* (Geneva, 1972).

Deusdedit, St (before consecration known as **Frithuwine**) (d. 664), Abp. of *Canterbury. He was the first Anglo-Saxon to hold this position, to which he was consecrated in 655. Hardly anything is known of the events of his primacy. Feast day, 14 July.

The principal authority is *Bede, *HE* 3. 20, 28, and 4. 1; comm. by J. M. Wallace-Hadrill (Oxford, 1988), p. 116. N. Brooks, *The Early History of the Church of Canterbury* (Leicester, 1984), pp. 67 f.

Deus Misereatur. The Psalm (67) provided in the BCP of 1552 and later editions as an optional alternative to the *Nunc Dimittis at *Evensong, except on the 12th day of the month.

Deuterocanonical Books, the. An alternative name for the Books contained in the Greek (*Septuagint) version of the OT, but not in the Hebrew. They are more commonly known as the *Apocrypha.

Deutero-Isaiah. The name commonly given to the unknown author of most or all of the later chapters of the Book of Is. Earlier OT critics, e.g. S. R. *Driver, G. A. *Smith, in the belief that Is. 40–66 was a unity, applied the term to the author of all these chapters; it is now usually restricted to the author of 40–55 (56–66 being probably of later date). Deutero-Isaiah was active in the later years of the Babylonian Exile (*c.*550–539 BC). See also ISAIAH and TRITO-ISAIAH; and, esp. for bibl., SERVANT SONGS.

Deuteronomistic History. The name given by M. *Noth and others to the Books Deut.–2 Kgs., all of which appear to have been compiled on the same editorial principle, i.e. originally independent units of material, such as collections of laws, stories about the Judges, the so-called 'Court History' (2 Sam. 9–1 Kgs. 2), and the Elijah and Elisha 'cycles', have been assembled together and set in a framework by an editor or editors who believed that obedience to the Divine commands led to success and disobedience to disaster. The Divine commands are set out in Deut. with appropriate warnings, and in the subsequent Books Israel's history is recounted and commented on in the light of this retributive theory. The editor's purpose is thus not so much to record history as to draw out its religious lessons, with the particular intention of giving a theological explanation for the conquest of *Judah by the Babylonians in the early 6th cent BC. As examples of his method, style, and outlook may be cited the farewell speeches of Moses (Deut. 31), Joshua (Jos. 24) and Samuel (1 Sam. 12), and also the comments on the fall of Samaria (2 Kgs. 17: 7–23) and of Jerusalem (2 Kgs. 23: 26–7 and 24: 2–4).

M. Noth, *Überlieferungsgeschichtliche Studien*, 1 (Halle/Salle, 1943; 2nd edn., Tübingen, 1957), pp. 3–110; Eng. tr., *The Deuteronomistic History* (Journal for the Study of the Old Testament, Supplement Series, 15; Sheffield, 1981); R. D. Nelson, *The Double Redaction of the Deuteronomistic History* (ibid. 18; 1981). A. D. H. Mayes, *The Story of Israel between Settlement and Exile: A Redactional Study of the Deuteronomistic History* (1983). See also recent comm. to DEUTERONOMY cited s.v.

Deuteronomy, Book of. The fifth and last Book of the *Pentateuch. Its English title comes via the Lat. *Deuteronomium* from the Gk. Δευτερονόμιον ('repetition of the law'), a *Septuagint mis-rendering of Deut. 17: 18 where the Heb. means 'a copy of the law'. In Heb. tradition the Book is commonly referred to by its two opening words אֵלֶּה הַדְּבָרִים ('These are the words').

The Book, which contains *Moses' final utterances on the E. side of the *Jordan before his death, consists essentially of seven mainly legislatory and hortatory addresses as follows: (1) After a brief introduction (1: 1–5), a survey of the journey from Mount Sinai to the Promised Land with its lessons (1: 6–4: 40). (2) Exhortations to serve Yahweh as the only true God, with certain laws interspersed (4: 45–11: 32); 5: 6–21 contains the Ten *Commandments in their Deuteronomic form and 6: 4–9 the principal section of the *Shema. (3) The central core of the legislation in the Book, the so-called 'Deuteronomic Code' (12: 1–28: 68). 12–16 deal mainly with religious duties (Law of the One Sanctuary; *Tithes; Feasts of *Passover, of Unleavened Bread, and of *Weeks, etc.); 17–20 with civil enactments (Monarchy; *Cities of Refuge; Laws of War; etc.); and 21–5 with social and domestic regulations (aliens, usury, vows, etc.). (4) Exhortations to keep the Covenant with Yahweh, with the threat of punishment for disobedience and the promise of restoration for repentance (29 f.). (5) The appointment of Joshua as Moses' successor and the giving of the custody of the 'Book of the Law' to the *Levites (31: 1–29). (6) The 'Song of Moses', with an appendix (31: 30–32: 52). (7) The 'Blessing of Moses' (33), followed by an account of Moses' death (34). Some scholars have argued that the ordering of the Book reflects the pattern of a (postulated) Covenant Renewal Ceremony.

The distinctive style and diction of Deut. mark it off from the other Pentateuchal Books. Throughout, emphasis is laid on the fact that Yahweh is the only true God, that His love for His peculiar people Israel is unbounded, and that Israel must love Him in return.

Acc. to the traditional view, the Book was written by Moses. Most modern critics, however, have sought to bring it to a much later date. The view most widely held assigns it to the 7th cent. BC. Stress is laid on the close contact with, and apparent dependence of its theology on, the teaching of the 8th-cent. Prophets, e.g. its emphasis on the love of God (esp. characteristic of *Hosea), its monotheism, and its humane modifications of the supposedly earlier laws of the 'Book of the Covenant' (Ex. 20: 22–23: 33). On the other hand its apparent identification of 'the sons of Aaron' with 'the Levites' (two classes later distinguished) and the absence of ref. to the Day of *Atonement and the Levitical system in general, indicate a date earlier than the 'Priestly Code' (6th cent. or later). It has hence commonly been supposed that the Book of the Law found in the Temple which was the basis of Josiah's Reformation (621 BC; cf. 2 Kgs. 22 f.) is to be identified with some form of the central section of Deuteronomy with which it shares a concern for the concentration of worship in one sanctuary (cf. Deut. 12). If so, it was not improbably compiled shortly before this date, perhaps in the reign of Manasseh (c.690–643) or even in the early part of that of Josiah himself (640–609 BC). Some critics, however, have argued for a date even as early as the 10th or 11th cent.; others have favoured an exilic or post-exilic setting. The tendency of much recent scholarship has been to concern itself with the tradition which the Book embodies and to emphasize that in its present form it exhibits evidence of a lengthy literary history.

Comm. by S. R. *Driver (ICC, 1895), G. von *Rad (Das Alte Testament Deutsch, 8; 1964; Eng. tr., 1966), A. D. H. Mayes (New Cent. Bib., 1979), and E. Nielsen (HAT, Reihe 1, Bd. 6; 1995). G. Hölscher, 'Komposition und Ursprung des Deuteronomiums', ZATW 40 for 1922 (1923), pp. 161–255. A. C. Welch, The Code of Deuteronomy: A New Theory of its Origin [1924]; id., Deuteronomy: The Framework of the Code (1932). G. von Rad, Deuteronomium-Studien (1947; Eng. tr., Studies in Biblical Theology, 9; 1953). E. W. Nicholson, Deuteronomy and Tradition (Oxford, 1967). M. Weinfeld, Deuteronomy and the Deuteronomic School (Oxford, 1972). J. G. McConville, Law and Theology in Deuteronomy (Journal for the Study of the Old Testament, Supplement Series, 33; Sheffield, 1984). N. Lohfink (ed.),

Das Deuteronomium: Entstehung, Gestalt and Botschaft (Bibliotheca Ephemeridum Theologicarum Lovaniensium, 68; 1985). M. Weinfeld in Anchor Bible Dictionary, 2 (1992), pp. 168–83.

Deutsche Christen. See GERMAN-CHRISTIANS.

Deutsche Theologie (Ger.). The vernacular title of Theologia Germanica (q.v.).

Deutscher Orden. See TEUTONIC ORDER.

de Veuster, Joseph. See DAMIEN, FATHER.

devil (Gk. διάβολος, 'calumniator', 'accuser'). In theological terminology the chief of the fallen angels. He is mentioned very rarely in the older books of the OT, where a clear contrast between good and evil on a cosmic scale is lacking. In the narrative of the *Fall (Gen. 3) the serpent, which seduces *Eve and is thus the cause of man's first sin, has traditionally been considered an embodiment of the devil, through whom, acc. to the Book of *Wisdom (2: 24), 'death entered into the world'. The evil spirit tormenting Saul (1 Sam. 18: 10) has also traditionally been regarded as a devil, as also the lying spirits that deceive the prophets of Ahab (1 Kgs. 22: 21–3). In the Book of Job, *Satan acts as a tempter and tormentor, always, however, in submission to the will of Yahweh. In 1 Chron. 21: 1 *David's decision to number Israel is attributed to Satan (though 2 Sam. 24: 1 provides a different explanation), and in the vision of *Zechariah Satan acts as the accuser of the high priest Joshua (Zech. 3: 1–2). In the pseudepigraphical Jewish literature there is a much more developed demonology with many traces of pagan influence. 1 *Enoch 6–16 interprets the narrative of Gen. 6: 1–4 about the 'sons of God' whose intercourse with women produced a race of giants, as fallen angels, and says that they were condemned to eternal punishment. Similar stories are reported in the Book of *Jubilees, the *Testaments of the Twelve Patriarchs, and other Jewish writings of the period between OT and NT.

The NT embodies and develops the later Jewish teaching on the devil. He tempts the Lord at the beginning of His public ministry (Mk. 1: 13, Mt. 4: 1–11, Lk. 4: 1–13), presenting himself as the master of the world (Mt. 4: 8–9), and Christ shows by His teaching and example his powerlessness over those who resist him. Later Satan renews his attacks in the persons of the demoniacs, thus manifesting the enmity between his kingdom and the kingdom of God, which is also taught in several parables, e.g. that of the tares among the wheat (Mt. 13: 24–30). He has wanted the disciples, esp. St *Peter, but the Lord has prayed for him, that his faith might not fail (Lk. 22: 31–2); for the power of Satan, whom Jesus saw 'fallen as lightning from heaven' (Lk. 10: 18), is already broken. Being 'a murderer from the beginning' (Jn. 8: 44), he is the 'prince of the world' but has no power over Christ (Jn. 14: 30), for he is already judged (Jn. 16: 11), and at the Last Judgement he and all those who belong to him will depart into eternal fire (Mt. 25: 41). St *Paul and the other Apostles follow this teaching. 1 Peter recommends sobriety and vigilance as the chief means of resisting him (5: 8–9), and in Jude we find a brief allusion to the fall of the angels (1: 6; cf. 2 Pet. 2: 4). A fuller account of the angels' fall is given in Rev. 12: 7–9, which chapter also contains a detailed description of the devil's persecution of the Church under the figure of the Woman clothed with the sun.

In *patristic times there was no fixed teaching on the subject. Great influence was exercised by the apocryphal literature, esp. by the Books of Enoch. The view that demons are the sons of the fallen angels and human mothers is reproduced by many early Fathers, e.g. St *Justin Martyr, and similar opinions were held by *Tertullian and St *Cyprian. Others, e.g. St *Irenaeus and *Clement of Alexandria, distinguish between the serpent, the seducer of Eve, and the other fallen angels, and most of them hold that the fall of the angels was caused by their envy of man. *Origen, however, rejects the tales in 1 Enoch 6–16 about the carnal intercourse between angels and women and attributes the fall of the former not to envy but to pride. His view was accepted first in the E., e.g. by St *Athanasius and also by St *Basil, who affirms that the devil is a spiritual being fallen from heaven through pride, and later also in the W., though the idea of angelic marriage was not at once rejected. St *Augustine held that the devil fell through pride, because he would not submit to God, and that his envy of man was only a later consequence of his first sin. Though refusing to explain the fall of the angels by concupiscence, he assumed that they have bodies. He rejected the opinion advanced by Origen that the devils may finally be reconciled to God (*Apocatastasis).

In the Middle Ages there was much speculation on the subject, represented esp. by the *Dominican and the *Franciscan schools. Acc. to the former, following St *Albert the Great and St *Thomas Aquinas, all angels were created in a state of grace, though not of beatitude. The initial sin of the devil, which fixed him in evil, was committed after the first instant of his creation had passed. It consisted in pride, manifesting itself in the desire not for equality with God, which the angelic intellect knows to be impossible, but for a natural beatitude obtained by his own powers. The fall of the other angels was caused by their consent to his sin. The Franciscans, on the other hand, following *Duns Scotus, held that the devils committed various kinds of sin before becoming obstinate in evil, that *Lucifer, their chief, desired equality with God, and that his sin consisted in an immoderate love of his own excellence. From the 15th cent. Latin theologians have in general followed either the Thomist or the Scotist view. A compromise was attempted by F. *Suárez, who advanced the novel opinion that the sin of the devil consisted in the desire of being himself hypostatically united to the Word. Since the 16th cent. the traditional teaching in its main outlines has been accepted by the majority of Christians, but there has been a marked reaction against the speculative elaborations of the Middle Ages.

There have been very few doctrinal decisions on the subject. The Council of Braga (561) defined against the *Priscillianists that the devil was created good and could not himself create; and the 4th *Lateran Council (1215) affirmed that he became evil by his own will.

G. Roskoff, *Geschichte des Teufels* (2 vols., Leipzig, 1869). L. Coulange [pseud. for J. Turmel], *The Life of the Devil* (1929; Eng. tr. of work pub. under his own name, *Histoire du diable*, 1931). G. Bazin and others, *Satan* (Études carmélitaines, 1948), with full bibl.; Eng. tr. of part, with additional essays and introd., by C. Moeller, *Satan* (1951). H. A. Kelly, *Towards the Death of Satan: The Growth and Decline of Christian Demonology* (1968). J. B. Russell, *The Devil: Perceptions of Evil from Antiquity to Primitive Christianity* (Ithaca, NY, and London, 1977); id., *Satan: The Early Christian Tradition* (ibid., 1981); id., *Lucifer: The Devil in the Middle Ages* (ibid. [1984]). N. Forsyth, *The Old Enemy: Satan and the Combat Myth* (Princeton, NJ, 1986). G. *Papini, *Il Diavolo* (Florence, 1954; Eng. tr. 1955). E. Mangenot and T. Ortolan in *DTC* 4 (1911), cols. 321–409; S. Lyonnet, SJ, J. *Daniélou, SJ, and others in *Dict. Sp.* 3 (1957), cols. 141–238, both s.v. 'Démon', with bibl. W. Foerster and K. Schäferdiek in *TWB* 7 (1964). pp. 151–65 (Eng. tr., 7, 1971, pp. 151–65), s.v. σατανᾶς.

Devil's Advocate. See PROMOTOR FIDEI.

Devotio Moderna (Lat., 'Modern Devotion'). The term is applied to the revival and deepening of the spiritual life which, from the end of the 14th cent., spread from the Netherlands to parts of Germany, France, and Italy. It originated in the circle round G. *Groote, and found its classic expression in *Thomas à Kempis's '*Imitation of Christ'. It laid great stress on the inner life of the individual and encouraged methodical meditation, esp. on the Life and Passion of Christ. St *Augustine, St *Bernard, and St *Bonaventure were among its acknowledged spiritual guides. The Modern Devotion made its way among the people chiefly through free associations of secular priests and lay people, called '*Brethren of the Common Life' (q.v.), whereas among the religious the *Windesheim Canons were its principal representatives.

The Lives of G. Groote, *Florentius Radewijns, and their followers by Thomas à Kempis tr. into Eng. by J. P. Arthur (London, 1905). A. Hyma, *The Christian Renaissance: History of the 'Devotio Moderna'* (New York, 1925; repr., with additional chs., as 2nd edn., Hamden, Conn., 1965). S. Axters, OP, *Geschiedenis van de Vroomheid in de Nederlanden*, 3: *De Moderne Devotie 1380–1550* (Amsterdam, 1956). R. R. Post, *The Modern Devotion: Confrontation with Reformation and Humanism* (Studies in Medieval and Reformation Thought, 3; Leiden, 1968), with extensive refs. G. Epiney-Burgard, *Gérard Grote (1360–1384) et les débuts de la dévotion moderne* (Veröffentlichungen des Instituts für europäische Geschichte Mainz, 54; Wiesbaden, 1970); J. Andriessen and others (eds.), 'Geert Grote & Moderne Devotie', *Ons Geestelijk Erf*, 59 (1985), pp. 113–505 (also issued separately, Nijmegen, 1985); P. Bange and others (eds.), *De doorwerking van de Moderne Devotie Windesheim 1387–1987* (Hilversum, 1988). P. Debongnie, CSSR, in *Dict. Sp.* 3 (1957), cols. 727–47, s.v. 'Dévotion moderne'.

Devout Life, Introduction to the. The celebrated treatise on the spiritual life by St *Francis de Sales. It is one of the earliest guide books of its period for people living in the world. It grew out of the spiritual direction which Francis gave to his cousin's wife, Mme de Charmoisy. It deals, in a style full of imagery, with the practical problems of people of social standing and their obligations, but its teaching is of universal application. The first edition appeared at Lyons in 1609, but Francis frequently revised it until 1619, the date of the definitive edition. Jeremy *Taylor's *Holy Living* is much influenced by it.

In addition to the many popular editions there are good crit. edns. by C. Florisoone (Collection Guillaume Budé, 2 vols., 1930; 2nd edn., 1961) and by E.-M. Lajeune, OP (Collection Livre de Vie [1962]). The numerous Eng. trs. include that by R. *Challoner (London, 1762). Convenient modern Eng. tr. by

M. Day, Cong. Orat. (Orchard Books, 1956). See also bibl. to FRANCIS DE SALES.

de Wette, Wilhelm Martin Leberecht (1780–1849), German theologian. He was born at Ulla, near Weimar, studied at Jena, and held theological chairs at Heidelberg (1809) and Berlin (1810). From 1806 he published works on biblical criticism and from 1813 on systematic theology. His radical rationalism raised a storm of opposition and, nominally because he had supported the murderer of A. F. F. von Kotzebue, he was deprived of his professorship and had to leave Berlin (1819). After a short stay at Weimar he accepted the theological chair at Basle (1822). In his later years he became more conservative. Under the influence of J. F. Fries and F. D. E. *Schleiermacher, he sought to do justice to the transcendent by faith and to the finite by scientific knowledge, to emphasize the importance of religious experience, to spiritualize dogma, and to construct a theology without a metaphysical basis. But his condemnation of cold reason displeased the rationalists, and his doubts regarding biblical miracles and his reduction of the stories of the Birth, Resurrection, and Ascension of Christ to myths offended the *Pietists. His numerous writings include *Kommentar über die Psalmen* (1811), *Lehrbuch der historisch-kritischen Einleitung in die kanonischen und apokryphischen Bücher des AT* (1817), *Christliche Sittenlehre* (1819–23), *Einleitung ins NT* (1826; Eng. tr., 1858), and *Das Wesen des christlichen Glaubens* (1846).

A. F. J. Wiegand, *W. M. L. de Wette, 1780–1849* (1879). E. Staehelin, *Dewettiana* (Basle, 1956); R. Smend, *Wilhelm Martin Leberecht de Wettes Arbeit am Alten und am Neuen Testament* (ibid., 1958); P. Handschin, *Wilhelm Martin Leberecht de Wette als Prediger und Schriftsteller* (ibid., 1958); J. W. Rogerson, *W. M. L. de Wette, Founder of Modern Biblical Criticism* (Journal for the Study of the Old Testament, Supplement Series, 126; Sheffield [1992]).

d'Hulst, Maurice (1841–96), French scholar and priest. He played a prominent part in founding the Catholic University of Paris (1875), and in 1881 he became first rector of the newly constituted *Institut Catholique. Throughout his life he laboured for the higher education of the French clergy. In his first years at the Institut Catholique he was closely associated with many of those who later became *Modernists, but after the encyclical ''*Providentissimus Deus' (18 Nov. 1893), he became more conservative. His *Question biblique* (1893) represented his earlier attitude. D'Hulst was also much esteemed as a preacher and spiritual director.

A. Baudrillart, *Vie de Mgr d'Hulst* (2 vols., 1912–14). [C.] Cordonnier, *Monseigneur d'Hulst: Sa vie, ses luttes, son rayonnement* (1952). Y. Marchasson in *Dict. Sp.* 7 (pt. 1; 1969), cols. 944–7, s.v. 'Hulst, Maurice d' '.

diaconicon (Gk., 'appertaining to the deacon'). The area to the south of the sanctuary in a Byzantine church, so called because it is in the charge of the deacons. In it the sacred vessels are kept and cleansed, and the vestments, service-books, and other necessaries of Divine service are stored. It thus corresponds with the *sacristy in the W. The corresponding area to the north of the sanctuary is termed the *prothesis. The word is also used of the book containing the deacon's part in the Liturgy.

G. Bandmann, 'Über Pastophorien und verwandte Nebenräume im mittelalterlichen Kirchenbau', in W. Braunfels (ed.), *Kunstgeschichtliche Studien für Hans Kauffmann* [1957], pp. 19–58. H. *Leclercq, OSB, in *DACL* 4 (1921), cols. 733–5, s.v.

Diadochus (mid-5th cent.), Bp. of Photike after 451. Hardly anything is known of his life. He was the author of 100 'Capita Gnostica' (κεφάλαια γνωστικά) on the means of attaining spiritual perfection, which enjoyed great popularity in succeeding generations and were cited by St *Maximus the Confessor, in the *Doctrina Patrum*, and by *Photius. He fashions an orthodox synthesis from both *Messalian and *Evagrian ideas, basing his understanding of the spiritual life on Baptism. He is one of the earliest witnesses to the devotion which found expression in the *Jesus Prayer (q.v.). Besides a homily on the Ascension, which has long been known, Diadochus is also very prob. the author of a work entitled the 'Vision', which takes the form of a dialogue with *John the Baptist. Some late MSS also ascribe to him a series of questions and answers, called by E. des Places a catechism; this work is elsewhere attributed to *Simeon the New Theologian.

Works ed., with Fr. tr., by E. des Places, SJ (SC 5 bis, 1955; repr., with additional material, ibid. 5 ter, 1966). Eng. tr. of 'Capita Gnostica' by G. E. H. Palmer, P. Sherrard, and K. [T. R.] Ware, *The Philokalia*, 1 (1979), pp. 251–96. F. Dörr, *Diadochus von Photike und die Messalianer: Ein Kampf zwischen wahrer und falscher Mystik im fünften Jahrhundert* (Freiburger theologische Studien, 47; 1937). P. Chrestos, Διάδοχος ὁ Φωτικῆς (Thessalonica, 1952). H. Dörries, *Wort und Stunde*, 1 (1966), pp. 352–422 ('Diadochos und Symeon'). E. des Places, SJ, 'Diadoque de Photicé et le Messalianisme', in *Kyriakon: Festschrift Johannes Quasten*, ed. P. Granfield and J. A. Jungmann, 2 (1970), pp. 591–5. K. [T. R.] Ware, 'The Jesus Prayer in St Diadochus of Photice', in *Aksum-Thyateira: A Festschrift for Archbishop Methodios of Thyateira and Great Britain*, ed. G. D. Dragas (1985), pp. 557–68. E. des Places, SJ, in *Dict. Sp.* 3 (1957), cols. 817–34; D. Stiernon, AA, in *DHGE* 14 (1960), cols. 374–8, with further bibl.

Dialectical Theology. A title applied to the theological principles of K. *Barth (q.v.) and his school on the ground that, in distinction from the dogmatic method of ecclesiastical orthodoxy, which treats of God as a concrete Object (*via dogmatica*), and the negative principles of many mystics, which forbid all positive affirmations about God (*via negativa*), it finds the truth in a dialectic apprehension of God which transcends the 'Yes' and the 'No' of the other methods (*via dialectica*). Its object is to preserve the Absolute of faith from every formulation in cut-and-dried expressions.

After the publication of Barth's *Römerbrief* in 1919 the Dialectical Theology rapidly spread, at first esp. in Continental Protestantism. Rejecting the whole liberal tradition in modern theology, whose spirit it saw classically embodied in F. D. E. *Schleiermacher, it sought to go back to the principles of the Reformers, esp. J. *Calvin, and drew its inspiration from thinkers in revolt against the humanist ideal, notably S. *Kierkegaard, F. M. *Dostoevsky, and the *Blumhardts. Its principal exponents (with varying degrees of emphasis) include E. *Brunner, F. *Gogarten, and E. *Thurneysen (qq.v.). Before long its stress on the Divine transcendence commended it also to many theologians of other traditions. In Great Britain its influence has been greatest in the Church of *Scotland; but it has also been considerable in the

C of E, esp. since E. C. *Hoskyns's translation of the *Römerbrief* in 1933. The rise of *Existentialism (q.v.) in the RC Church also owed much to its influence.

For bibl., see BARTH, K.

Dialogue of the Redeemer. A fragmentary document, sometimes called the 'Dialogue of the Saviour', found in Codex III of the *Nag Hammadi library. It presents a conversation between Christ (possibly after His Resurrection) and His disciples, particularly *Matthew, Judas, and *Mary [Magdalene]. There are parallels with Mt., Lk., and Jn., and also with the Gospel of *Thomas, but literary dependence appears unlikely.

Coptic text and Eng. tr., ed. S. Emmel, *Nag Hammadi Codex III, 5* (Nag Hammadi Studies, 26; Leiden, 1984), with introd. by H. Koester and E. H. Pagels. Eng. tr., with brief introd., also in J. M. Robinson (ed.), *The Nag Hammadi Library in English* (3rd edn., Leiden, 1988), pp. 244–55. B. Blatz in Schneemelcher, 1 (5th edn., 1987), pp. 244–55; Eng. tr., 1 (1991), pp. 300–12.

Diamper, Synod of (1599). A diocesan synod of the native (St Thomas) Church of *India, held under Alexis Menezes, Abp. of Goa, at Diamper (now Udiyamperūr, some 12 miles SE of Cochin). It brought the *Malabar Uniat Church (q.v.) into being. *Nestorianism was renounced, complete submission to Rome imposed, and many westernizing reforms were made. Continuity of worship and practice was preserved, including the use of the (Syriac) Liturgy of *Addai and Mari, though with several modifications. For a long time Portuguese authority enforced the decisions of the synod, but as its influence waned the Church began to disintegrate and there were many secessions, notably in 1653. In recent years there have been various moves to restore the Syro-Malabar liturgy.

[C. J. *Hefele and H. *Leclercq] *Histoire des conciles d'après les documents orginaux*, 11: C. de Clercq, 'Conciles des Orientaux catholiques', pt. 1 (1949), pp. 36–67. J. Thaliath, TOCD, *The Synod of Diamper* (Orientalia Christiana Analecta, 152; 1958). S. [C.] Neill, *A History of Christianity in India*, 1 (Cambridge, 1984), pp. 208–19. A. Thazhath, *The Juridical Sources of the Syro-Malabar Church* (Kottayam, 1987), pp. 133–44 (with bibl.). J. Vellian, *Syro-Malabar Liturgy*, 1: *Raza: The Most Solemn Qurbana* (Syrian Churches Series, 14; 1989), pp. 21–57. C. de Clercq in *DDC* 4 (1949), cols. 1207–10, s.v.

Diario Romano ('The Roman Daybook'). An official annual publication giving particulars of all feasts and fasts to be observed, of the special ceremonies celebrated in particular churches, and of the days on which they are celebrated, in the diocese of Rome.

Diaspora, Jewish. The Dispersion (διασπορά) of the Jews had its beginnings in the Assyrian and Babylonian deportations (*c*.721 and *c*.597 BC). Originally confined to parts of Asia, esp. Armenia and Iran, it later spread throughout the Roman Empire to Egypt, Asia Minor, Greece, and Italy. By NT times, acc. to *Philo, there were not less than a million Jews in *Alexandria. The Jews of the Diaspora remained in close touch with their home country, paying the *Temple taxes and keeping their religion. The Jewish *synagogues in Asia and Asia Minor were the first scenes of Christian preaching (cf. Acts); in the 4th cent. the missionary activities of the Jews in the

Roman Empire were eliminated by the growing power of Christianity. Henceforth the Jews of the W. Diaspora became more and more cut off from the surrounding Gentile civilization, and the E. Diaspora, with its centre in Babylon, became increasingly important. The Hebrew for 'diaspora' (גלות, גולה, *galuth* or *golah*) strictly means 'exile', an ancient conception which in modern times has surfaced prominently in the ideology of Zionism.

In Germany the word 'diaspora' is used of members of any religious body living as a minority among those of other beliefs, and esp. of Protestants living in Catholic parts and vice versa.

E. *Schürer, *The History of the Jewish People in the Age of Jesus Christ*, rev. Eng. tr. by G. Vermes and others, 3 (pt. 1; Edinburgh, 1986), pp. 1–176. M. Stern, 'The Jewish Diaspora' in S. Safrai and M. Stern (eds.), *The Jewish People in the First Century*, 1 (Compendia Rerum Iudaicarum ad Novum Testamentum, Section 1, vol. 1; Assen, 1974), pp. 117–83; S. Safrai, 'Relations between the Diaspora and the Land of Israel', ibid., pp. 184–215; S. Appelbaum, 'The Legal Status of the Jewish Communities in the Diaspora', ibid., pp. 420–63; id., 'The Organization of the Jewish Communities in the Diaspora', ibid., pp. 464–503. See also works cited under JUDAISM.

Diatessaron. The edition of the four Gospels in a continuous narrative, compiled by *Tatian about 150–60. From an early date it circulated widely in *Syriac-speaking Churches, where it became the standard text of the Gospels down to the 5th cent., when it gave way to the four separate Gospels. Its original language may have been Syriac, Greek, or (so F. C. *Burkitt) even Latin. Its publication in the 2nd cent. is a notable witness to the authority already enjoyed by the Four Gospels.

Our knowledge of its structure is derived principally from six sources: (1) The 'Commentary' on it made by St *Ephraem Syrus in the 4th cent. This survives in its entirety only in an *Armenian version, first published by the *Mechitarist Fathers in 1836; a considerable part of the Syriac text was acquired by the *Chester Beatty Library and published in 1963. (2) An Arabic harmony, available in five MSS, which is more valuable for the sequence than the text (which has been adapted to the *Peshitta). (3) A Persian harmony, also translated from Syriac, preserved in a single MS. (4) The Latin *Codex Fuldensis, where the order of the Diatessaron has been preserved, though the text has been assimilated to that of the *Vulgate. (5) A number of medieval harmonies of the Gospels, of which the most important is that in medieval Dutch, known as the 'Liège Diatessaron'. (6) A short Greek papyrus fragment of 14 imperfect lines containing the account of the request for the body of Christ made by *Joseph of Arimathaea. This fragment, which was found at *Dura Europos and identified at Yale in 1933, has strengthened the case for the Diatessaron's having been originally compiled in Greek.

Crit. edn. of the Armenian version of Ephraem's comm. by L. Leloir, OSB (CSCO 137: Scriptores Armeniaci, 1; 1953; with Lat. tr., ibid. 145: Scriptores Armeniaci, 2; 1954); Syriac text in Chester Beatty MS 709 ed., with Lat. tr., by id. (Chester Beatty Monographs, 8; Dublin, 1963; additional pages, also Chester Beatty Monographs, 8: Louvain, 1990). Fr. tr. from Syriac and Armenian texts by id. (SC 121; 1966). Arab. text ed. P. A. Ciasca, Rome, 1888 (2nd edn., 1934); also by A. S. Marmardji, OP, Beirut, 1935. Eng. tr. of Arab. text pub. by J. H. Hill as *The Earliest Life of

Christ ever compiled from the Four Gospels (1894). Persian text ed., with introd. and Ital. tr., by G. Messina, SJ (Biblica et Orientalia, 14; Rome, 1951). The Liège Diatessaron ed. by D. Plooij, C. A. Phillips, and A. H. A. Bakker, with Eng. tr. by A. J. Barnouw (8 pts., Verhandelingen der Koninklijke [Nederlandse] Akademie van Wetenschappen [te Amsterdam], Afd. Letterkunde, Nieuwe Reeks, 29 and 31; 1929–70), and, repr. the Eng. tr., but with less crit. app., by C. C. de Bruin (Corpus Sacrae Scripturae Neerlandicae Medii Aevi, Series Minor, Tomus 1: Harmoniae Evangeliorum, 1; Leiden, 1970); other Dutch harmonies (ibid. 2–4; 1970). 13th–14th cent. Ital. version ed. V. Todesco, A. Vaccari, SJ, and M. Vattasso (ST 81; 1938). C. H. Kraeling, *A Greek Fragment of Tatian's Diatessaron from Dura* (Studies and Documents, 3; 1935). Syriac text reconstructed from comm. and other early material, with Sp. tr., by I. Ortiz de Urbina, SJ, *Vetus Evangelium Syrorum et exinde excerptum Diatessaron Tatiani* (Biblia Polyglotta Matritensia, 6; Madrid, 1967), pp. 207–99, with introd. pp. ix–xv; cf. R. Murray, SJ, in *Heythrop Journal*, 10 (1969), pp. 43–9. F. C. Burkitt (ed.), *Evangelion Da-Mepharresche: The Curetonian Version of the Four Gospels, with the readings of the Sinai Palimpsest and the early Syriac Patristic Evidence*, 2 (1904), esp. pp. 173–212. S. Lyonnet, SJ, *Les Origines de la Version arménienne et le Diatessaron* (Biblica et Orientalia, 13; Rome, 1950). L. Leloir, OSB, 'Le Diatessaron de Tatien', *L'Orient Syrien*, 1 (1956), pp. 208–31 and 313–34; id., *L'Évangile d'Éphrem d'après les œuvres éditées: Recueil des textes* (CSCO 180: Subsidia, 12; 1958): id., *Le Témoignage d'Éphrem sur le Diatessaron* (ibid. 227: Subsidia 19; 1962). W. Henss, *Das Verhältnis zwischen Diatessaron, christlicher Gnosis und 'Western Text'* (Beiheft zur ZNTW 33; 1967). W. L. Petersen, *Tatian's Diatessaron: Its Creation, Dissemination, Significance, and History in Scholarship* (Supplement to *VC* 25; 1994). B. M. Metzger, *The Early Versions of the New Testament* (Oxford, 1977), pp. 10–36. T. Baarda, *Early Transmission of Words of Jesus: Thomas, Tatian and the Text of the New Testament*, ed. J. Helderman and S. J. Noorda (Amsterdam, 1983), esp. pp. 65–78, 'In Search of the Diatessaron text'.

Dibelius, Martin (1883–1947), NT scholar. A native of Dresden, he was educated at Neufchâtel, Leipzig, Tübingen, and Berlin. From 1910 to 1915 he was a Privatdozent at Berlin. In 1915 he succeeded J. *Weiss as Professor of NT Exegesis and Criticism at Heidelberg, holding office until his death. He was an active supporter of the *Ecumenical Movement and a leader of the *Faith and Order Commission.

At first interested esp. in the study of Semitic languages and of comparative religion, he concentrated increasingly on the NT. Here he was a pioneer of the *Formgeschichtliche* method (q.v.), the technique of which he applied to the Epistles as well as the Gospels. Working on the foundations of Weiss, he laid great emphasis on preaching as a medium of transmission of the Lord's words; and in general his attitude to the Gospel traditions was more conservative than that of most members of the school. His most considerable work in this field was *Die Formgeschichte des Evangeliums* (1919; 2nd edn., 1933; Eng. tr., *From Tradition to Gospel*, 1934).

Dibelius's other publications include *Die Geisterwelt im Glauben des Paulus* (1909), *Die Isisweihe bei Apuleius und verwandte Initiations-Riten* (1917), *Geschichtliche und übergeschichtliche Religion im Christentum* (1925), *Geschichte der urchristlichen Literatur* (1926; Eng. tr., 1936), *Die Botschaft von Jesus Christus* (1935; Eng. tr., 1939), *Gospel Criticism and Christology* (1935), *Jesus* (Sammlung Göschen, 1939). He also contributed to the *Handbuch zum Neuen Testament* (ed. H. *Lietzmann) commentaries on 1 and 2 Thess.

and Phil. (1911), Col., Eph., and Philem. (1911), 1 and 2 Tim. and Tit. (1913), and *Hermas (1923), and to the H. A. W. *Meyer series (*Kritisch-exegetischer Kommentar über das N.T.*) that on James (1921; Eng. tr., 1976).

List of his works in 'Bibliographia Dibeliana atque Bultmanniana', in *Coniectanea Neotestamentica*, ed. A. Fridrichsen, 8 (1944), pp. 1–22. M. Dibelius, *Gesammelte Aufsätze zur Apostelgeschichte* (ed. H. Greeven, 1951). Further collected papers, *Botschaft und Geschichte*, ed. G. Bornkamm (2 vols., 1953–6).

Dibelius, Otto (1880–1967), Bp. of Berlin. The cousin of M. *Dibelius, he was born in Berlin, and, after several other pastoral cures in the *Lutheran Church, was appointed to the church 'Zum Heilsbronnen' in Berlin in 1915. In 1921 he was given responsibility for education and minority questions in the Berlin *Konsistorium*, and this led him to travel to *Sweden and the *United States of America. In 1925 he became *General Superintendent of the Kurmark. Although conservative and nationalist in his political views, he consistently advocated that the Church should be independent of the State. His books were widely read and he was active in promoting religious journalism. He was on friendly terms with Abp. N. *Söderblom and G. K. A. *Bell and took part in various early conferences of the *Ecumenical Movement. He was dismissed from his post in 1933 and, though put under restraint by the Nazis, worked with the *Bruderrat* of the *Confessing Church in Berlin. Accused of treason by the '*German-Christians' for his earlier defence of the rights of conscientious objectors, he took them to court in a celebrated trial in 1934–6 and won his case. In 1937 he circulated an open letter to Hitler's Minister for Church Affairs, Hanns Kerrl, attacking his attempt to interfere in matters of belief. Kerrl brought a libel suit against Dibelius, but again Dibelius won. In 1945 he became Bp. of Berlin and in 1949 Presiding Bishop of the *Evangelical Church in Germany, in which capacity he vigorously upheld religious freedom in the face of Communistic atheism. In 1954 he became a President of the *World Council of Churches. His works include *Das Vaterunser: Umrisse zu einer Geschichte des Gebets in der alten und mittleren Kirche* (1903), *Das Jahrhundert der Kirche: Geschichte, Betrachtung, Umschau und Ziele* (1926), *Friede auf Erden? Frage, Erwägungen, Antwort* (1930) and *Grenzen des Staates* (1949).

His autobiography was pub. under the title *Ein Christ ist immer im Dienst* (1961; Eng. tr., New York, 1964; London, 1965). Life by R. Stupperich (Göttingen, 1989). Id. (ed.), *Otto Dibelius: Sein Denken und Wollen. Eine Gedenkschrift zu seinem 90. Geburtstag* (1970). C. Nicolaisen in *TRE* 8 (1981), pp. 729–31, s.v., with further bibl.

didache (Gk. διδαχή, 'teaching'). The elements in primitive Christian apologetic of an instructional kind, as contrasted with *kerygma or 'preaching'.

Didache (Διδαχὴ Κυρίου διὰ τῶν δώδεκα ἀποστόλων), a short early Christian manual on morals and Church practice. Of its 16 brief chapters, chs. 1–6 describe the 'Two Ways', the 'Way of Life' and the 'Way of Death'; they include quotations from the *Sermon on the Mount. Chs. 7–15 contain instructions on *Baptism, *fasting, *prayer, the *Eucharist, and how to treat *apostles and *prophets, *bishops, and *deacons. Ch. 16 is a prophecy of the

*Antichrist and the *Second Coming. The treatise contains much of interest to the student of early Christian liturgy. The *Lord's Prayer is given in full. Baptism is by *immersion if possible, otherwise by threefold *affusion. Fasting on *Wednesdays and *Fridays is ordered. Two Eucharistic Prayers, of an unusual and primitive kind, are given. The ecclesiastical organization described is underdeveloped. An itinerant ministry of 'apostles and prophets' is of great importance; they are described as 'your chief priests' and may celebrate the Eucharist. At the same time a local ministry of bishops and deacons is also envisaged and seems to be taking the place of the itinerant ministry.

The author, date, and place of origin are unknown. The work was quoted as Scripture by *Clement of Alexandria, and is mentioned by *Eusebius of Caesarea and by *Athanasius. It is the earliest of the series of 'Church Orders', and forms the basis of the 7th Book of the '*Apostolic Constitutions'. Although in the past many English and American scholars (J. A. *Robinson, R. H *Connolly) tended to assign it to the late 2nd cent., most scholars nowadays place it in the 1st cent., including J.-P. Audet, OP, who dates it *c.* AD 60. It describes the life of a Christian community, prob. in Syria. The author knew the tradition of Christ's teaching which lies behind the Gospels. The 'Two Ways' section is closely paralleled in the Ep. of *Barnabas (18 ff.) and the Latin *Doctrina Apostolorum* (once thought to be a translation of the Didache); it seems likely that they are all based on an earlier Jewish source.

The only known MS (written in 1056) was discovered by P. *Bryennios at the 'Jerusalem Monastery of the Holy Sepulchre' at *Constantinople in 1873 and published by him in 1883.

The publication of the 'Didache' in 1883 evoked a vast literature. Ed., with facsimile, by J. R. *Harris (Baltimore and London, 1887). Other edns. by A. *Harnack (TU 2, Hefte 1–2; 1884). P. *Schaff (New York and London, 1885), H. *Lietzmann (Kleine Texte, 6; 1936), T. Klauser (Florilegium Patristicum, 1; Bonn, 1940), as well as in the modern edns. of the *Apostolic Fathers (q.v.). Text also ed., with crit. comm. by J.-P. Audet, OP (Études Bibliques, 1958) and by W. Rordorf and A. Tuilier (SC 248; 1978). Eng. tr. by C. *Bigg (1898; rev. by A. J. Maclean, 1922). *Doctrina Apostolorum*, ed. J. Schlecht from Cod. Monac. 6264 (11th cent.) at Freiburg i.B., 1900; cf. B. *Altaner, 'Zum Problem der lateinischen Doctrina Apostolorum', *VC* 6 (1952), pp. 160–7; repr. in his *Kleine patristische Schriften* (TU 83; 1967), pp. 335–42. Coptic frag. in Brit. Lib. (MS Or. 9271), ed. G. Horner, *JTS* 25 (1923–4), pp. 225–31; cf. C. Schmidt in *ZNTW* 24 (1925), pp. 81–99. J. A. Robinson, *Barnabas, Hermas and the Didache* (Donnellan Lectures for 1920; 1920); R. H. Connolly, OSB, 'The Didache in Relation to the Epistle of Barnabas', *JTS* 33 (1932), pp. 237–53. F. E. Vokes, *The Riddle of the Didache* (1938), with bibl. E. Peterson, 'Ueber einige Probleme der Didache-Ueberlieferung', *Riv. A.C.* 27 (1951), pp. 37–60. B. C. Butler, OSB, 'The Literary Relations of Didache, Ch. xvi', *JTS* NS 11 (1960), pp. 265–83; id., 'The "Two Ways" in the Didache', ibid. 12 (1961), pp. 27–38. L. Clerici, *Einsammlung der Zerstreuten: Liturgiegeschichtliche Untersuchung zur Vor- und Nachgeschichte der Fürbitte für die Kirche in Didache 9, 4 und 10, 5* (Liturgiewissenschaftliche Quellen und Forschungen, 44; 1965); A. Vööbus, *Liturgical Traditions in the Didache* (Stockholm, 1968). S. Giet, *L'Énigme de la Didachè* (posthumously pub., 1970); G. Schöllgens, 'Die Didache als Kirchenordnung', *Jahrbuch für Antike und Christentum*, 29 (1986), pp. 5–26. C. N. Jefford (ed.), *The* Didache *in Context: Essays on its Text, History and Transmission* (Supplements to *Novum Testamentum*, 77; 1995). On the Eucharistic Prayers, see also Jungmann, 1 (1958 edn.), pp. 15–17; Eng. tr., 1, pp. 11–13, and lit. cited. *CPG* 1 (1983), pp. 225 f. (nos. 1735 f.). J. Quasten, *Patrology*, 1 (Utrecht, 1950), pp. 29–39; Altaner and Stuiber (1978), pp. 79–82 and 557.

Didascalia Apostolorum. An early 'Church Order', professedly 'the Catholic Teaching of the Twelve Apostles and holy Disciples of our Redeemer' (Syriac title). Its author, prob. a physician who had been converted from Judaism, seems to have composed it in N. Syria in the earlier half of the 3rd cent. The work is addressed to readers in various states of life, esp. married persons (chs. 2–3), and deals with such subjects as the Bishop's duties, penance, liturgical worship, behaviour during persecution, widows and deaconesses, the settlement of disputes and the administration of offerings; but the arrangement is unmethodical and disorderly. A double anointing precedes Baptism; none follows. It is esp. directed against Christians who regard the Jewish ceremonial law as still binding. The author is far more lenient than his W. contemporaries (*Tertullian, *Cyprian) in allowing repentant sinners back to Communion. A six-days' fast before Easter is enjoined.

The work, orig. in Gk., survives complete only in a Syriac version, with substantial portions in Latin. As it was worked over and embodied in the *Apostolic Constitutions, much of the Greek text can be reconstructed with tolerable certainty. Among the sources used are the '*Pericope Adulterae' (Jn 7: 53–8: 11), the *Didache, the *Ignatian Epp., *Hermas, and the *Sibylline Oracles (Book 4); the author prob. also made use of other 2nd-cent. sources.

Syr. text ed. P. de *Lagarde, Leipzig, 1854; crit.edn., with Eng. tr., by A. Vööbus (CSCO 401–2 and 407–8, Scriptores Syri, 175–6 and 179–80; 1979). Lat. text, partly constructed by Funk, in F. X. Funk (ed.), *Didascalia et Constitutiones Apostolorum*, 1 (Paderborn, 1905), pp. 2–384, with introd., pp. iii–xiv. R. H. *Connolly, OSB, *Didascalia Apostolorum: The Syriac Version translated and accompanied by the Verona Latin Fragments* (Oxford, 1929). Lat. version ed. E. Tidner (TU 75; 1963). Gk. frags. ed. J. V. Bartlet, 'Fragments of the Didascalia Apostolorum', *JTS* 18 (1916–17), pp. 301–9. Convenient Eng. tr. by S. [P.] Brock and M. Vasey, *The Liturgical Portions of the Didascalia* (Grove Liturgical Study, 29; 1982). P. Galtier, SJ, 'La Date de la Didascalie des Apôtres', *RHE* 13 (1947), pp. 315–51. K. *Rahner, SJ, 'Busslehre und Busspraxis der Didascalia Apostolorum', *ZKT* 72 (1950), pp. 257–81., repr. in revised form in id., *Schriften zur Theologie*, 11 (1973), pp. 327–59 (Eng. tr., 15, 1983, pp. 225–45). *CPG* 1 (1983), p. 229 (no. 1738). J. Quasten, *Patrology*, 2 (Utrecht, 1953), pp. 147–52; Altaner and Stuiber (1978), pp. 84 f. and 558, both with bibl.

Diderot, Denis (1713–84), French *Encyclopaedist. A native of Langres in Burgundy, he studied there with the *Jesuits and in Paris, but soon gave up ideas of a career in the Church or the law, and after a bohemian youth worked as a translator from English. He published two controversial works, *Pensées philosophiques* (1746), a defence of rational *deism against atheism, and *Lettre sur les aveugles* (1749), whose materialist and anti-religious implications earned him a spell in prison. A publisher's suggestion in 1746 that he should translate Ephraim Chambers's *Cyclopedia* developed into a project to edit, with the help of J. Le R. *D'Alembert, a new and more ambitious French encyclopaedia, which became the source of Diderot's livelihood and his chief occupation for some 20 years (see

ENCYCLOPAEDISTS). His initial estrangement from the Church can perhaps be attributed primarily to impatience with the sexual restraints which it imposed, but intellectual obstacles increased it. Influenced by the natural religion of the third Earl of Shaftesbury (whose *Inquiry Concerning Virtue* he had translated in 1745), the epistemology of J. *Locke, and contemporary scientific enquiry, Diderot moved from rationalist deism to a materialist empiricism on *Epicurean lines, which dispensed with belief in a deity. Atheism, however, confronted him with severe moral difficulties. His original work as a dramatist and art critic is permeated with a desire to see the stage and picture gallery take over from the pulpit; and his later creative writings, often in dialogue form and all intended only for posthumous publication, show a striking preoccupation with ethical problems. The trio of dialogues usually known as *Le Rêve de D'Alembert* (1769, pub. 1830) is a brilliant presentation of his boldest philosophical and scientific ideas and their moral implications. *La Religieuse* (1760, pub. 1796) is an attack, in a vivid fictional narrative, not only on the contemporary social abuse of forced religious vows, but on the physical and psychological unnaturalness of the monastic life itself. *Le Neveu de Rameau* (begun *c.*1761, pub. 1823) presents a picture of a cynical parasite which involves discussion of the nature of social morality and of the place of genius in society. *Jacques le fataliste* (1773, pub. 1796) explores the conflict between materialist *determinism and moral freedom in a mock-picaresque tale influenced by Sterne's *Tristram Shandy*.

The old standard edn. of his collected works (ed. J. Assézat and M. Tourneux, 20 vols., Paris, 1875–7) is being superseded by that ed. H. Dieckmann and others (Paris, 1975 ff. [33 vols. projected]). Correspondence, ed. G. Roth and J. Varloot (16 vols., ibid., 1955–70). Studies by J. Morley (2 vols., London, 1878), H. Gillot (Paris, 1937), F. Venturi (tr. into Fr., Paris, 1939), L. G. Crocker (East Lansing, Mich., 1954; London, 1955; 2nd edn., 1966), R. Pomeau (Paris, 1967), and A. M. Wilson (New York, 1972). P. Hermand, *Les Idées morales de Diderot* (Bibliothèque de la Faculté des Lettres de l'Université de Paris, 2nd ser. 1; 1923); J. Thomas, *L'Humanisme de Diderot* ([1932]; 2nd edn., 1938); J. R. Loy, *Diderot's Determined Fatalism: A Critical Appreciation of Jacques le Fataliste* (New York, 1950); G. May, *Diderot et 'La Religieuse'* (New Haven, Conn., and Paris, 1954). Collection of arts. from various sources ed. J. Schlobach, *Denis Diderot* (Wege der Forschung, 655; 1992). See also bibl. to ENCYCLOPAEDISTS.

Didymus (the Gk. form of the Heb. 'Thomas', i.e. 'twin'). An alternative name in Jn. 11: 16, 20: 24, 21: 2 for the Apostle *Thomas.

Didymus the Blind (*c.*313–98), *Alexandrian theologian. He was blind from infancy. Of immense erudition, he was, acc. to *Rufinus, entrusted by St *Athanasius with the direction of the '*Catechetical School' at Alexandria, where he numbered St *Jerome and Rufinus among his pupils. Though a staunch *Nicene in trinitarian theology, he was regarded by Jerome as too deeply influenced by *Origen, and indeed he was condemned as an Origenist at the Council of *Constantinople in 553. As a result of this condemnation much of his vast literary output (mainly scriptural commentaries, but also incl. a commentary on Origen's *De Principiis*) has perished. His 'On the Holy Spirit' (in Jerome's translation) and a mutilated text of 'Against the Manichees' have long been known, as well as

many fragments of his exegesis. In the 18th cent. J. A. Mingarelli claimed 'On the Trinity' for Didymus, though doubts have been cast on this attribution in modern times. Books 4 and 5 of St *Basil's *Contra Eunomium* have been attributed to him, and (less plausibly) St *Gregory of Nyssa's *Adversus Arium et Sabellium*. An accidental discovery of a group of 6th- or 7th-cent. papyrus codices near Toura, south of Cairo, in 1941 (which also includes some works of Origen) brought to light his commentaries on Job, Zechariah, and Genesis, as well as commentaries on Ecclesiastes and Psalms 20–44, the authenticity of which is uncertain. These discoveries confirm Origen's influence on his writings and provide much greater insight into his methods of scriptural exegesis which significantly develop the Origenist heritage.

Editio princeps of *De Trinitate*, by J. A. Mingarelli, Bologna, 1769; repr., with other writings of Didymus, in J. P. Migne, *PG* 39. 131–1818 (the only collected edn.). Crit. edn. of *De Trinitate*, with Ger. tr., by J. Hönscheid and I. Seiler (Beiträge zur klassischen Philologie, 44, 52, etc.; Meisenheim am Glam, 1975 ff.). Many exegetical frags. in a crit. edn. by K. Staab, *Pauluskommentare aus der griechischen Kirche* (Neutestamentliche Abhandlungen, 15; 1933), pp. 1–45; frags. of comm. on Psalms ed. E. Mühlenberg, *Psalmenkommentare aus der Katenenüberlieferung*, 1 (Patristische Texte und Studien, 15; 1975), pp. 119–375, and 2 (ibid. 16; 1977). Comm. on Job ed. A. Henrichs and others (Papyrologische Texte und Abhandlungen 1, 2, 3, 31/1, etc.; 1968 ff.); that on Zech. ed. with full introd., notes, and Fr. tr., by L. Doutreleau, SJ (SC 83–5; 1962); that on Gen., with Fr. tr., by P. Nautin and L. Doutreleau, SJ (ibid. 233 and 244; 1976–8). Comm. on Eccles. ed. G. Binder, L. Liesenborghs, and others (Papyrologische Texte und Abhandlungen, 9, 13, 16, 22, 24–6; 1969–83) and on Pss. by M. Gronewald and others (ibid. 4, 6, 7, 8, 12; 1968–70), with suppl. by id. in B. Kramer, *Kleine Texte aus dem Tura-Fund* (ibid. 34; 1985), pp. 121–35, with other frags. from Toura in the same vol. G. Bardy, *Didyme l'Aveugle* (1910). J. Lebon, 'Le Ps.-Basile (Adv. Eunom., iv–v) est bien Didyme d'Alexandrie', *Muséon*, 1 (1937), pp. 61–83; W. M. Hayes, SJ, 'Didymus the Blind is the Author of *Adversus Eunomium* IV/V', in E. A. Livingstone (ed.), *Studia Patristica*, 17 (Oxford, 1982), pp. 1108–14, with survey of earlier lit. L. Doutreleau, SJ, 'Le *De Trinitate* est-il l'œuvre de Didyme l'Aveugle?', *Rech. S.R.* 45 (1957), pp. 514–57; L. Béranger, 'Sur deux énigmes du *De Trinitate* de Didyme l'Aveugle', ibid. 51 (1963), pp. 255–67. W. A. Bienert, *'Allegoria' und 'Anagoge' bei Didymos dem Blinden von Alexandria* (Patristische Texte und Studien, 13; 1972). J. [H.] Tigcheler, *Didyme l'Aveugle et l'Exégèse allégorique: Étude sémantique de quelques termes exégétiques importants de son commentaire sur Zacharie* (Graecitas Christianorum Primaeva, 6; Nijmegen, 1977). *CPG* 2 (1974), pp. 104–11 (nos. 2544–72). Altaner and Stuiber (1978), pp. 280 f. and 604 f. F. M. Young, *From Nicaea to Chalcedon* (1983), pp. 83–91, 341, and 367 f. W. *Bright in *DCB* 1 (1877), pp. 827–9, s.v.; A. Van Roey in *DHGE* 14 (1960), cols. 416–27, s.v. 'Didyme l'Aveugle'.

Dies Irae (Lat., 'Day of wrath'), the opening words, and hence the name, of the *sequence in the Mass for the Dead in the W. Church. It is now thought to go back to a rhymed prayer of late 12th-cent. *Benedictine origin. To this prayer, depicting the soul awaiting judgement, a *Franciscan (possibly *Thomas of Celano) has added a greater sense of urgency, reflecting the eschatological mood of the mid-13th cent. The first printed Missal containing it as the sequence for Requiem Masses is that of Venice, 1485. Until 1969 its use was obligatory in Masses on *All Souls' Day, on the day of decease or burial of the person for whom the Mass was offered, and on the anniversary of the death, though it could be omitted on other days. It may now also be omitted in all Masses of the Dead. Many translations into English have been made (e.g. *EH* 351), but the vigour of the concise Latin original is usually lost.

F. Ermini, *Il Dies Irae e l'innologia ascetica nel secolo decimo-terzo: Studi sulla litteratura latina del medio evo* (1903). Raby, pp. 443–50, incl. orig. text, p. 448, and note of trs., p. 449, with bibl., p. 485. J. C. Payen, 'Le *Dies Irae* dans la prédication de la mort et des fins dernières au Moyen-Age', *Romania*, 86 (1965), pp. 48–76. K. Vellekoop, *Dies irae, dies illa: Studien zur Früh-geschichte einer Sequenz* (Utrecht diss., Bilthoven, 1978).

Dietrich of Nieheim (or of 'Niem') (*c.*1340–1418), Papal notary and historical writer. Entering the service of the curia he became Abbreviator and Scriptor, and pub-lished two treatises on curial administration. He was appointed Bp. of Verden by Boniface IX in 1395 without, however, receiving consecration, and was deprived of the office four years later. After the election of Gregory XII he took a prominent part in the efforts to end the *Great Schism. He was present at the Council of *Constance (1415), where he renounced *John XXIII and vigorously upheld the *conciliar standpoint. His historical works, though one-sided, are an invaluable source for contempor-ary events, esp. 'Nemus Unionis' (1408) and 'De Schismate' (1409/10). Of his writings advocating reform the most important is 'Avisamenta edita in Concilio Con-stanciensi' (1414/15), in which he asserted the plenary powers of a General Council including its right to depose the Pope, attacked clerical abuses, and put forward schemes for ecclesiastical reform.

Crit. edns. of 'De Schismate' by G. Erler (Leipzig, 1890); of 'Avisamenta' in the *Acta Concilii Constanciensis*, ed. H. Finke, 4 (1928), pp. 584–636; of 'De Modis uniendi et reformandi eccle-siam in concilio universali' by H. Heimpel (Quellen zur Geistes-geschichte des Mittelalters und der Renaissance, 3; 1933); id., 'Eine unbekannte Schrift Dietrichs v. Niem über die Berufung der Generalkonzilien (1413/1414)', *Sb.* (Heid.), 1929/30, Abh. 1. Political and historical writings which have come to light since 1948, ed. A. Lhotsky and others (*MGH*, Staatsschriften des späteren Mittelalters, 5; 2 parts, 1956–80), with introd. by K. Colberg in pt. 2, pp. vii–lvii, and list of his works with edns., p. lviii. G. Erler, *Dietrich von Nieheim* (Leipzig, 1887); H. Heimpel, *Dietrich von Niem* (Westfälische Biographien, Bd. 2; 1932); K. Pivec and H. Heimpel, *Neue Forschungen zu Dietrich von Niem* (*Nachr.* (Gött.), 1951, Heft 4). E. F. Jacob, 'Dietrich of Niem. His Place in the Conciliar Movement', *Bulletin of the John Rylands Library, Manchester*, 19 (1935), pp. 388–410; repr. in id., *Essays in the Conciliar Epoch* (Manchester, 1943), pp. 24–43, with additional notes in 3rd edn. (1963), pp. 241–4. K. Colberg in *Lexikon des Mittelalters*, 3 (1986), cols. 1037 f., s.v. See also works cited under CONCILIAR THEORY

digamy. In the early Church, second marriages were gen-erally looked upon with disfavour (cf. 1 Cor. 7: 39 f.). *Athenagoras went so far as to regard them as 'a specious adultery' (*Legat.* 33), and this view became part of the official teaching of certain heretical bodies (*Montanists, *Novatianists). Even the orthodox Council of *Neocaesa-rea (314) presupposed the imposition of a slight penance on digamists (can. 7). The Council of *Nicaea (325), how-ever, in providing for the reconciliation of Novatianists,

insisted (can. 8) that those who had married twice should not be excluded from Christian fellowship.

The E. Church has always been more severe in this matter than the W. Second marriages were often held not to be marriages at all, and even now the nuptial blessing is not given in the same form as for a first marriage. Even more suspect were third marriages, and since the 10th cent. fourth marriages have been forbidden altogether.

St Paul's words that a bishop must be the husband of one wife (1 Tim. 3: 2: μιᾶς γυναικὸς ἄνδρα) were widely held, e.g. by *Innocent I and St *Augustine, to make digamy a disqualification for Ordination, though St *Jerome held the contrary view (*Ep.* 69). In RC canon law, the impediment, still retained in the 1917 Code (*CIC*, can. 984, § 4), no longer persists.

diggers. See FOSSORS.

Diggers (17th cent.). A section of the *Levellers, founded in 1649 by Gerrard Winstanley. Its adherents held that Christian principles required a communistic mode of life and the cultivation of crown property and common land with the spade. Work was started in April 1649 on waste land at St George's Hill and Oatlands, Surrey. Winstanley expounded his principles and schemes in several pamph-lets and other camps were set up briefly in the Home Counties and Midlands, but the movement was suppressed within a year.

G. H. Sabine (ed.), *The Works of Gerrard Winstanley*, with appendix of docs. relating to the Digger Movement (New York, 1941); [G.] Winstanley, *The Law of Freedom, and other Writings*, ed., with introd., [J. E.] C. Hill (Penguin Classics, 1973; reissued, with postscript, 1983). A hitherto unknown pamphlet by Winstan-ley, 'England's Spirit Unfoulded', was ed. G. E. Aylmer in *Past and Present*, 40 (1968), pp. 3–15; 'A Declaration of the grounds and Reasons, why we the poor Inhabitants of the Parrish of Iver in Buckinghamshire, have begun to digge . . .' (issued 1 May 1650) was ed. K. Thomas, ibid. 42 (1969), pp. 57–68. O. Lutaud, *Winstanley, Socialisme et Christianisme sous Cromwell* (1976); [J. E.] C. Hill, *The Religion of Gerrard Winstanley* (Past and Present, Suppl. 5; 1978); T. W. Hayes, *Winstanley the Digger: A Literary Analysis of Radical Ideas in the English Revolution* (Cambridge, Mass., 1979); G. E. Aylmer, 'The Religion of Gerrard Winstanley', in J. F. McGregor and B. Reay (eds.), *Rad-ical Religion in the English Revolution* (Oxford, 1984), pp. 91–119. N. Baxter, 'Gerrard Winstanley's Experimental Knowledge of God (The Perception of the Spirit and the Acting of Reason)', *JEH* 39 (1988), pp. 184–201.

dikirion, trikirion (Gk. δικήριον, τρικήριον). Candles, held in candlesticks with two and three branches respect-ively, used by E. bishops when giving the blessing during a pontifical Liturgy. They symbolize the two Natures of Christ and the three Persons of the Trinity.

Dillmann, Christian Friedrich August (1823–94), German biblical scholar and orientalist. He studied at Tübingen under H. *Ewald and F. C. *Baur, and later worked on Ethiopic MSS in Paris, London, and Oxford, producing catalogues of the Ethiopic MSS in the British Library and the Bodleian Library (1847–8). In 1848 he returned to Tübingen, where in 1853 he obtained a pro-fessorship, and later he held chairs at Kiel (1854), Giessen (1864), and Berlin (1869). To him more than any other scholar is due the revival of Ethiopic studies in the 19th cent. He was also a capable OT critic. Among his works were a grammar (1857; 2nd edn., 1899; Eng. tr., 1907) and lexicon (1865) of Ethiopic, and editions of Ethiopic texts of the OT down to Kings, of the Apocrypha, and of some non-canonical books, while late in life he produced commentaries on the *Hexateuch (1875–86; Eng. tr. of Genesis by W. B. Stevenson, 1897) and on Isaiah (1890).

Dillmann's *Handbuch der alttestamentlichen Theologie*, posthumously ed. R. Kittel (1895). Portrait and very brief Life prefixed to vol. 5 of Dillmann's edn. of the Ethiopic OT (*Libri Apocryphi*, Berlin, 1894; no pagination). W. Baudissin in *PRE* (3rd edn.), 4 (1898), pp. 662–9, s.v., with list of obituary notices.

Dilthey, Wilhelm (1833–1911), German philosopher of history and culture. Born at Biebrich, nr. Wiesbaden, he was professor successively at Basle (1866), Kiel (1868), Breslau (1871), and Berlin (1882, in succession to H. Lotze). He was also a leading member of the Prussian Academy and entrusted with its edition of I. *Kant (1902 ff.). In the front rank of historians of modern culture and ideas and also the virtual creator of the philosophy of history in its present form, Dilthey stressed the fundamental differences between the methods of the humanities or 'human sciences' (*Geisteswissenschaften*), employed in the study of culture, art, religion, etc., and those adapted to the natural sciences (*Naturwissenschaften*). He worked out his position in his *Einleitung in die Geisteswissenschaften* (vol. 1, 1883) which, like many of Dilthey's other works, was never completed. His belief that the current methods of empirical psychology failed to reach the real spiritual life of persons as studied in the humanities issued in his *Ideen über eine beschreibende und zergliedernde Psychologie* (1894), in which he elaborated the ideal of a 'descriptive and analytic' psychology. He was much influenced by F. D. E. *Schleiermacher, on whom he wrote a massive *Life* (Part 1, 1870; Part 2, pub. 1966); like him, he saw the act of understanding as an attempt to recreate the creative process of the writer or artist. He was critical, however, of the possibility of a philosophy of history in the traditional sense, as well as of a systematic sociology, holding that the spiritual life was too complex to be comprehended in formulae. Dilthey's own studies in religion were esp. directed to it as an element in human culture. The religious *Weltanschauung*, unlike the philosophical, was restricted in that it did not aim at universality. His doctrines on history have exercised influence on Christian thought, esp. through E. *Troeltsch. His extended studies in hermeneutics, which, however, take the word in a very wide sense, are very relevant to the problems of biblical exegesis.

Dilthey's works, most of which were orig. pub. in the *Abh.* (Berl.), were collected and ed. G. Misch and others (Berlin, 1914 ff.; the first 12 vols. were repr. and the edn. cont. by M. Redeker and others, Göttingen, 1957 ff.; 20 vols. to 1990). Diary and letters for 1852–70 ed. C. Misch (Leipzig and Berlin, 1933); further collections of correspondence ed. S. von der Schulenburg (Halle, 1923) and E. Weniger (*Abh.* (Berl.), 1936, no. 9). Eng. tr. of various extracts, with introd., by H. P. Rickman, *Meaning in History: W. Dilthey's Thought on History and Society* (1961), and *Selected Writings*, tr. by id. (Cambridge, 1976). *Selected Works* [in Eng. tr.] also ed. R. A. Makkreel and F. Rodi (6 vols., Princeton, NJ, 1985 ff.). Separate Eng. tr. of *Einleitung in die Geisteswissenschaften (Introduction to the Human Sciences)*, with introd., by R. J. Betanzos [1988]. H. A. Hodges, *Wilhelm Dilthey: An Introduction* (1944); id., *The Philosophy of Wilhelm Dilthey* (1952), both with

detailed bibl.; H. Diwald, *Wilhelm Dilthey: Erkenntnistheorie und Philosophie der Geschichte* (Göttingen, 1963); R. A. Makkreel, *Dilthey: Philosopher of the Human Studies* (Princeton, NJ [1975]); M. Ermarth, *Wilhelm Dilthey: The Critique of Historical Reason* (Chicago and London, 1978); H. P. Rickman, *Wilhelm Dilthey: Pioneer of Human Studies* (1979); T. Plantinga, *Historical Understanding in the Thought of Wilhelm Dilthey* (Toronto, etc. [1980]). H. P. Rickman in P. Edwards (ed.), *Encyclopedia of Philosophy*, 2 (1967), pp. 403–7.

diocese. In ecclesiastical use, normally the territorial unit of administration in the Church. In the RC Church a diocese is now defined as 'a portion of the people of God entrusted for pastoral care to a bishop' (*CIC* (1983), can. 369), but in practice a diocese normally comprises a particular area. It is governed by a bishop, with the assistance of the lower clergy, and sometimes one or more other bishops; it is usually divided into parishes, which may be grouped into *rural deaneries and *archdeaconries (though the latter have not survived in the RC Church). Dioceses are commonly associated to form a *province, over which one of the diocesan bishops presides, with varying powers of intervention in the affairs of other dioceses. Traditionally the bishop is supreme in his diocese and possesses *ordinary jurisdiction.

In the early days of the Church, when Christianity was chiefly an urban religion, dioceses covered only the principal towns and cities. As the new religion spread, the limits of the various dioceses were extended and new rural dioceses were created, until now there is hardly any part of the world which is not within the jurisdiction of some diocesan bishop.

The word 'diocese' (Gk. διοίκησις) only gradually established itself in its current Christian sense. The original word for a local group of Christians was simply a 'church' (ἐκκλησία). Later, e.g. in the *Apostolic (cans. 14, 15) and *Nicene (can. 16) Canons, it was 'parish' (παροικία), and in the E. Church this word is still retained for the territory subject to a bishop, διοίκησις being used for the *patriarch's area of control. In the W., however, the word was in use in Africa in its modern sense at the end of the 4th cent., though *parochia* continued to be employed down to the 9th cent. and even later. The word also had a long secular history for the larger administrative units of the later Roman Empire. Meaning primarily 'administration', it was first used in Cicero's time of a territorial area over which supervision was exercised, namely of the three regions of Cibyra, Apamea, and Synnada added to Cilicia (Cic., *Ep. ad Fam.* 3. 8. 4; 13. 67. 1). Under *Diocletian it was adopted for the 12 new regions into which the Empire was divided for the purposes of civil government, the largest of these dioceses being 'Oriens' (16 provinces) and the smallest Britain (4 provinces). Its ecclesiastical use was of slow growth. As late as *Anastasius Bibliothecarius it was applied to the ecclesiastical province, as distinct from the area governed by a single bishop.

On the history of the word, see C. D. *Ducange, *Glossarium*, s.v.; J. *Bingham, *Origines Ecclesiasticae*, 9, esp. cap. 2, sect. 2; W. *Bright, *The Canons of the First Four General Councils* (2nd edn., 1892), pp. 101–5. See also G. Hill, *English Dioceses: A History of their Limits* (1900).

Diocletian (Gaius Aurelius Valerius Diocletianus) (245–313), Roman Emperor from 284 to 305. Diocles, who was born of humble parents at Salona in Dalmatia, took up a military career, serving with distinction under Probus and Aurelian. On 17 Sept. 284, on the murder of Numerian, the army proclaimed him Emperor at Chalcedon. He was defeated in the ensuing hostilities against Carinus, Numerian's joint-Emperor; but as Carinus was promptly slain by his own officers, Diocletian (as he now chose to call himself) became undisputed master. Endowed with immense energy, great gifts of organization, and a mind dominated by logic, he made it his main purpose to stabilize and reform the Empire. To this end, he created an absolute monarchy, centring all power in himself as the semi-Divine ruler, and making his palace the *domus divina* and his own person sacred; and henceforth the Senate was to be permanently in a subordinate position. In 286 he associated Maximian in the government as co-Augustus, taking the Eastern Empire for himself and giving Maximian the West. In 293 he turned the 'imperial college' into a tetrarchy by the creation of two 'Caesars', Constantius Chlorus and Galerius. He further divided the Empire into twelve *dioceses, each consisting of several provinces, which, from the 4th cent., formed the basis of the territorial organization of the Church. With this strong organization, the Empire was consolidated and somewhat extended. Diocletian also introduced far-reaching military, administrative, fiscal, and economic reforms, including the celebrated Edict on Maximum Prices ('De pretiis rerum venalium') of 301. On 1 May 305 he formally abdicated at Nicomedia, compelling his reluctant colleague Maximian to take the same step. He lived his last years in retirement at his large palace at Spalato (Split).

For the greater part of his reign the Christians seem to have enjoyed the tranquillity which had been theirs since the Rescript of Gallienus (260). Only the *Manichees were repressed, by an edict of *c.*298 (dated 31 March but without the year), as a sect lately originating in Persia. It was in 303 that the Great *Persecution broke out. An edict issued at Nicomedia on 23 Feb. enjoined the demolition of churches and the burning of Christian books. Some incidents which followed (fires in the palace at Nicomedia, reports of unrest at Melitene and in Syria) led to further edicts. The next two were directed solely against the clergy. The punishment inflicted for resistance was imprisonment, torture, and, in some cases, death. A fourth edict issued early in 304 enjoined sacrifice to the gods on all subjects. The persecution brought a considerable number of martyrs. Its severity varied in different parts of the Empire acc. to the changing fortunes of the Imperial rulers in the next decade. Its final collapse was due to *Constantine's defeat of Maxentius at the *Milvian Bridge on 28 Oct. 312 and the 'Edict of *Milan' (q.v.) early in the next year.

Good discussion in *C. Anc. H.* 12 (1939), esp. chs. 9 (by H. Mattingly), 10, and 11 (by W. Ensslin); and, for the Persecution, ch. 19 (by N. H. Baynes). W. Ensslin, *Zur Ostpolitik des Kaisers Diokletian, Sb.* (Bayr.), 1942, Heft 1; W. Seston, *Dioclétien et la tétrarchie. 1. Guerres et réformes, 284–300* (Bibliothèque des Écoles Françaises d'Athènes et de Rome, 162; 1946); S. Williams, *Diocletian and the Roman Recovery* (1985). T. D. Barnes, *The New Empire of Diocletian and Constantine* (Cambridge, Mass., and London, 1982), *passim*. A. H. M. Jones, *The Later Roman Empire 284–602* (3 vols., Oxford, 1964), 1, pp. 37–76, with refs. in 3, pp. 2–10. W. Ensslin in *PW*, Zweite Reihe, 7 (1948), cols. 2419–95, s.v. 'Valerius (142) Diocletianus'; W. Seston in *RAC* 3 (1957),

cols. 1036–53, s.v. For works on the Persecution, see bibl. to PERSECUTIONS, EARLY CHRISTIAN.

Diocletianic Era. The reckoning of time from the year of *Diocletian's accession (AD 284). It is also known as the **Era of the Martyrs** (though in fact the *persecution of the Christians did not break out till 303; see previous entry). It is still followed by the *Ethiopians and *Copts.

Diodore (d. *c.*390), Bp. of Tarsus. A native of *Antioch, Diodore studied at *Athens and then ruled a monastery near Antioch until the strength of *Arianism drew him into the city to combat it. He also opposed *Julian the Apostate. Banished to Armenia in 372, he later returned and became Bp. of Tarsus in 378. In 381 he was named by *Theodosius I one of the bishops communion with whom was a test of orthodoxy.

As a teacher, he followed the *Antiochene tradition in theology, insisting on literal and historical exegesis and, against *Apollinarius, on the complete humanity of Christ. His pupils included St John *Chrysostom and *Theodore of Mopsuestia. Apart from the recently published Comm. on the Psalms, only fragments of his very extensive writings (largely biblical commentaries) survive. Many were destroyed by Arians, while others perished when the condemnation of his pupil Theodore made Diodore himself suspect of Christological heresy.

Comm. on Psalms, ed. J.-M. Olivier (CCSG 6, etc.; 1980 ff.). Considerable frags. of his 'De Fato' are preserved in *Photius, *Bibl. cod.* 233; cf. ibid. 102 and also 18, where Photius asserts, apparently by an error, that Diodore was condemned by the Fifth General Council of 553. Frags. ed. by B. Corderius (Antwerp, 1643–6) and by A. *Mai; repr. in J. P. Migne, *PG* 33. 1545–1628. Syriac frags. ed. P. [A.] de *Lagarde, *Analecta Syriaca* (Leipzig, 1858), pp. 91–100. Further frags. in K. Staab (ed.), *Pauluskommentare aus der griechischen Kirche* (Neutestamentliche Abhandlungen, 15; 1933), pp. 82–112, and R. Devreesse, *Les Anciens Commentateurs grecs de l'Octateuque et des Rois* (ST 201; 1959), pp. 155–67. M. Brière, 'Quelques Fragments syriaques de Diodore, évêque de Tarse (378–394?)', *Revue de l'Orient Chrétien*, 30 (1946), pp. 231–83, incl. text and Fr. tr.; R. Abramowski, 'Der theologische Nachlass des Diodor von Tarsus', *ZNTW* 42 (1949), pp. 19–69, with text. A. *Harnack, *Diodor von Tarsus: Vier pseudojustinische Schriften als Eigentum Diodors nachgewiesen* (TU 21. 4; 1901). M. Richard, 'Les Traités de Cyrille d'Alexandrie contre Diodore et Théodore et les fragments dogmatiques de Diodore de Tarse', in *Mélanges dédiés à la mémoire de Félix Grat*, 1 (1946), pp. 99–116, repr. in his *Opera Minora*, 2 (Turnhout and Louvain, 1977), no. 51; R. Abramowski, 'Untersuchungen zu Diodor von Tarsus', *ZNTW* 30 (1931), pp. 234–62; E. Schweizer, 'Diodor von Tarsus als Exeget', ibid. 40 (1941), pp. 33–75. *CPG* 2 (1974), pp. 342–4 (nos. 3815–22). J. Quasten, *Patrology*, 3 (Utrecht and Westminster, Md., 1960), pp. 397–401; Altaner and Stuiber (1978), pp. 318 f. and 615, with further bibl. L. Abramowski in *DHGE* 14 (1960), cols. 496–504, s.v. 'Diodore (4) de Tarse'; C. Schäublin in *TRE* 8 (1981), pp. 763–7, s.v. 'Diodor von Tarsus'.

Diognetus, the Epistle to. A letter written by an unknown Christian to an otherwise unknown inquirer. It probably dates from the 2nd, or perhaps the 3rd, cent. Answering three questions (ch. 1), the author explains why paganism and Judaism cannot be tolerated (2–4), describes Christians as the soul of the world (5–6), and insists that Christianity is the unique revelation of God, whose love works man's salvation (7–10). Chs. 11 f., which contain a *Logos-doctrine and a comparison of the Church to Paradise, are widely regarded as a fragment of another work. The letter survived antiquity in a single 13th–14th-cent. MS (which was destroyed at Strasbourg in 1870), in which it followed certain treatises wrongly ascribed to St *Justin Martyr.

Ed. princeps, by H. *Stephanus (Paris, 1592). The Epistle is commonly included in edns. of the *Apostolic Fathers; also repr. in J. P. Migne, PG 2. 1167–86. Good modern edns., with introd. and notes, by H. G. Meecham (Manchester, 1949) and by H. I. Marrou (SC 33; 1951; 2nd edn., 33 bis, 1965). Eng. trs. by L. B. Radford (1908) and in collected trs. of Apostolic Fathers. G. N. Bonwetsch and E. *Schwartz have argued that chs. 11 f. are to be ascribed to *Hippolytus. R. Brändle, Die Ethik der 'Schrift an Diognet' (Abhandlungen zur Theologie des Alten und Neuen Testaments, 64; Zurich [1975]). T. Baumeister, 'Zur Datierung der Schrift an Diognet', VC 42 (1988), pp. 105–11. M. Rizzi, La questione dell' unità dell' 'Ad Diognetum' (Studia Patristica Mediolanensia, 16; 1989), with summary in Eng. CPG 1 (1983), p. 55 (no. 1112). J. Quasten, Patrology, 1 (Utrecht, 1950), pp. 248–53; Altaner and Stuiber (1978), pp. 77 f., and 556 f. S. Zincone in DPAC 1 (1983), cols. 969–71, s.v. 'Diogneto'; Eng. tr. in Encyclopedia of the Early Church, 1 (1992), p. 237.

Dionysius (1) the Areopagite. His conversion by St Paul at Athens is recorded in Acts 17: 34. Dionysius (2) of Corinth calls him the first bishop of the Church at Athens. Later, confusion was caused by the attempt to identify Dionysius (3) of Paris with him, and to assign to him the writings on mystical theology described below under (6).

Dionysius (2) (c.170), Bp. of *Corinth. He wrote several letters briefly described by *Eusebius (HE 4. 23), in one of which he thanks the Roman Church for assisting Corinth and mentions that *Clement's letter was habitually read in their Church. Feast day in the E., 8 Apr.

Four frags. of Dionysius' Ep. to Rome are preserved in Eusebius (HE 4. 23. 10–12, and 2. 25. 8), who also records that Dionysius wrote an Ep. to the Nicomedians directed against *Marcion (4. 23. 4). Frags. collected in M. J. *Routh, Reliquiae Sacrae, 1 (2nd edn., 1846), pp. 175–201. W. Bauer, Rechtgläubigkeit und Ketzerei im ältesten Christentum (1934), esp. pp. 110–12 and 128–31 (Eng. tr., 1972, pp. 106–8 and 124–7). P. Nautin, Lettres et écrivains chrétiens des IIᵉ et IIIᵉ siècles (Patristica, 2; 1961), pp. 13–32 ('Denys de Corinthe et ses correspondants'). Id. in DHGE 14 (1960), cols. 261 f., s.v. 'Denys (9) de Corinthe'.

Dionysius (3) of Paris, St (c.250), also **St Denys**, patron saint of France. Acc. to *Gregory of Tours (6th cent.), he was one of seven 'bishops' sent to convert Gaul and, after becoming Bp. of Paris, suffered martyrdom. In 626 his remains were translated to King Dagobert's foundation at *St-Denis, near Paris. In the 8th cent. it was believed that he had been sent by *Clement of Rome, c. AD 90; and in the 9th-cent. Life by Hilduin, Abbot of St-Denis (d. 840), he was further identified with Dionysius the Areopagite (1), and consequently believed to be the author of the Pseudo-Dionysian writings (6). Feast day, 9 Oct. (when he is commemorated with Sts Rusticus and Eleutherius).

Gregory of Tours, Hist. Franc. 1. 30. AASS, Oct. 4 (1780), pp. 865–987. BHL 1 (1898–9), nos. 2171–89. Good survey of problem in Eng., with refs. to lit. to date, by S. McK. Crosby, The Royal Abbey of Saint Denis from its Beginnings to the Death of Suger, 475–1151, ed. P. Z. Blum (New Haven, Conn., and London, 1987), pp. 3–12 ('Saint Denis, Legend and History'). R. J. Loenertz, OP,

'La Légende parisienne de S. Denys l'Aréopagite. Sa genèse et son premier témoin', Anal. Boll. 69 (1951), pp. 217–37. G. M. Spiegel, 'The Cult of Saint Denis and Capetian Kingship', Journal of Medieval History, 1 (1975), pp. 43–69; repr. in S. Wilson (ed.), Saints and their Cults (1983), pp. 141–68. J. Semmler, 'Saint-Denis: von der bischöflichen Coemeterialbasilika zur königlichen Benediktinerabtei', in H. Atsma (ed.), La Neustrie: Les pays au nord de la Loire de 650 à 850, 2 (Beihefte der Francia, 16/2; Sigmaringen, 1989), pp. 75–123. A. Patschovsky and G. Binding in Lexikon des Mittelalters, 3 (1986), cols. 1077–9, s.v.

Dionysius (4) the Great, St (d. c.264), Bp. of *Alexandria. Acc. to *Eusebius, Dionysius was a pupil of *Origen and became head of the *catechetical school in Alexandria, c.233; both assertions have been questioned by some modern scholars. He became Bp. of Alexandria in 248. During the *Decian persecution (250) he fled from the city, was captured, escaped, and lived in hiding. He returned (?251), but was banished during the persecution of Valerian (257). Again he returned to face civil war, famine, and plague, and died an old man, c.264. Feast day, 17 Nov.

His importance as a theologian rests on the writings evoked by the many controversies in which he was engaged. He decided to readmit the lapsed to the Church (see CYPRIAN) and, with Pope *Stephen, not to rebaptize heretics and schismatics, though he refused to break with the Churches which did so. He attacked *Sabellianism, but was himself accused of tritheism by *Dionysius of Rome (5, below), who, however, accepted his defence. Later, *Athanasius defended, but *Basil rejected, his orthodoxy. He also opposed *Paul of Samosata. He showed notable independence as a biblical critic, setting out strong arguments for denying the common authorship of the Fourth Gospel and Rev. His treatise De Natura is the earliest extant Christian refutation of *Epicureanism.

His writings have survived mainly in extracts preserved by Eusebius, Athanasius, and others.

Frags. ed. S. de Magistris (Rome, 1796); also in J. P. Migne, PG 10. 1233–344 and 1575–602. Crit. edn. by C. L. Feltoe (Cambridge Patristic Texts, 1904). Eng. tr. also by C. L. Feltoe [1918]. W. A. Bienert, Dionysius von Alexandrien (Patristische Texte und Studien, 21; 1978). P. Nautin, Lettres et écrivains chrétiens des IIᵉ et IIIᵉ siècles (Patristica, 2; 1961), pp. 151–65. C. Andresen, ' "Siegreiche Kirche" im Aufstieg des Christentums. Untersuchungen zu Eusebius von Caesarea und Dionysius von Alexandrien', in Aufstieg und Niedergang der Römischen Welt, 2. 23. 1 (1979), pp. 387–459. CPG 1 (1983), pp. 187–99 (nos. 1550–612). J. Quasten, Patrology, 2 (Utrecht, 1953), pp. 101–9. Altaner and Stuiber (1978), pp. 210 f. and 590. B. F. *Westcott in DCB 1 (1877), pp. 850–2; A. Van Roey in DHGE 14 (1960), cols. 248–53, s.v. 'Denys (4) Le Grand'; W. A. Bienert in TRE 8 (1981), pp. 767–71, s.v. 'Dionysius von Alexandrien'.

Dionysius (5), St (d. 268), Bp. of *Rome from 259. Little is known of him except his controversy on *subordinationism with *Dionysius (4) of Alexandria. *Basil of Caesarea (Ep. 70) records that he sent help to the Church of Caesarea when it was invaded by barbarians (perh. 264). Feast day, 26 Dec.

Genuine and spurious writings in J. P. Migne, PL 5. 99–136. The chief authorities are scattered refs. in Eusebius, HE 7, and in *Athanasius, De Decretis, 25 and 26, and De Sententiis Dionysii, passim. J. N. D. Kelly, The Oxford Dictionary of Popes (1986), pp. 22 f., s.v.

Dionysius (6) the Pseudo-Areopagite (*c*.500), mystical theologian. The name given to the author of a *corpus* of theological writings to which the supporters of *Severus (Patr. of Antioch, 512–18) appealed at a colloquy at Constantinople in 533, attributing them to Dionysius (1) of Athens. Though at an early date Hypatius, Bp. of Ephesus (*c*.520–40), rejected the attribution, it was normally accepted until, and even after, the 16th cent. Since the author draws on *Proclus (410/2–85) and is first cited by Severus, he is believed to have written in the early 6th cent. (perhaps as late as the 520s), probably in Syria.

His extant writings, which combine *Neoplatonism with Christianity, are the following: (1) The 'Celestial Hierarchy' (Περὶ τῆς οὐρανίας ἱεραρχίας), which explains how the nine orders of angels mediate God to man. (2) The 'Ecclesiastical Hierarchy' (Περὶ τῆς ἐκκλησιαστικῆς ἱεραρχίας), which deals with the Sacraments and the orders of clergy and laity. (3) The 'Divine Names' (Περὶ θείων ὀνομάτων), which examines the being and attributes of God. (4) The 'Mystical Theology' (Περὶ μυστικῆς θεολογίας), which describes the ascent of the soul to union with God. There also survive ten letters, and Dionysius mentions other parts of an elaborate theological system, probably never achieved.

The aim of all Dionysius' works is the union of the whole created order with God, which union is the final stage of a threefold process of purification, illumination, and perfection or union: a triad which has been vastly influential in the Christian mystical tradition. The way to such union (ἔνωσις) with God, or *deification (θείωσις) as Dionysius is fond of calling it, has several aspects. One aspect is concerned with the use of the sensible created order in achieving deification; this embraces both the use of images as metaphors in theology (e.g. 'God is a consuming fire') and the use of material elements in sacramental action: Dionysius calls this aspect 'symbolic' (συμβολική) theology. In pursuit of it he develops a view of the cosmos as hierarchically ordered with the Trinity at the top, descending through nine choirs of angels, to the terrestrial order, where three sacraments (*Baptism, *Eucharist, and the consecration of *Chrism) are administered by three orders of clergy (bishops, priests and deacons) to the three ranks of those who receive their ministrations (monks, ordinary laity, and those excluded from communion). Another aspect concerns the perfecting of our intellectual concepts in their application to God (or in our praise of God, as Dionysius puts it): this is called 'cataphatic' (καταφατική) theology. But both of these reveal that God is beyond symbols and concepts, and this discovery points to '*apophatic' (ἀποφατική) theology, in which the soul, passing beyond the perceptions of the senses as well as the reasoning of the intellect, is united with the 'ray of divine darkness' and comes to know God through unknowing.

The supposed apostolic authority of these writings, added to their intrinsic value, caused them to exercise a profound influence on medieval theology both in the E. and the W. In the E. Church they were commented on by, among others, John of Scythopolis, St *Maximus the Confessor, and George Pachymeres. In the W. the approval of St *Gregory the Great and *Martin I, and esp. that of the *Lateran Council of 649 which quoted

them against the *Monothelites, established the authority of the Dionysian writings. The 9th-cent. translations into Latin by Hilduin and John Scotus *Erigena had little influence in the W., but in the 12th cent. renewed interest in Dionysius, manifest among the *Victorines and in the translation by John the Saracen, led to the adoption of the Dionysian works as one of the bases of medieval theology. They were the subject of commentaries by such doctors as *Hugh of St-Victor, Robert *Grosseteste, St *Albert the Great, St *Thomas Aquinas, and St *Bonaventure; and the medieval mystics, e.g. Meister *Eckhart, John *Tauler, and the author of 'The *Cloud of Unknowing', are deeply indebted to them. A great change in the earlier estimate of them took place in the 16th cent., when not only the Reformers but a few Catholic scholars such as T. *Cajetan, J. *Sirmond, and D. *Petavius contested their authenticity, which was warmly defended by C. *Baronius, St Robert *Bellarmine, L. *Lessius, and others. Only the researches of modern scholars, esp. J. Stiglmayr and H. Koch, have definitely established their 5th-6th cent. date and the relations of the author with Syria and those who showed their opposition to the Definition of *Chalcedon by ignoring it.

The edn. of his works by B. Corderius, SJ (2 vols. fol., Antwerp, 1634) has frequently been repr., e.g. in J. P. Migne, *PG* 3 and 4 (incl. Lat. tr. and comm. on Dionysius. Crit. edn. by B. R. Suchla ('Divine Names'), G. Heil ('Celestial Hierarchy' and 'Ecclesiastical Hierarchy'), and A. M. Ritter ('Mystical Theology' and Letters) (Patristische Texte und Studien, 33 and 36; 1990–1). Earlier edn. of the 'Celestial Hierarchy' by G. Heil, with notes and Fr. tr. by M. de Gandillac and introd. by R. Roques (SC 58; 1958). For Lat. versions see P. Chevallier, OSB (ed.), *Dionysiaca: Recueil donnant l'ensemble des traductions latines des ouvrages attribués au Denys de l'Aréopage* (2 vols., Paris, 1937). Eng. tr. of his works by C. Luibheid and P. Rorem (Classics of Western Spirituality, 1987). Fr. tr. of his works, with introd. and bibl., by M. de Gandillac (Bibliothèque Philosophique, 1945). J. Stiglmayr, SJ, 'Der Neuplatoniker Proclus als Vorlage des sog. Dionysius Areopagita in der Lehre vom Übel', *Hist. J.* 16 (1895), pp. 253–73 and 721–48. H. Koch, *Pseudo-Dionysius Areopagita in seinen Beziehungen zum Neuplatonismus und Mysterienwesen* (Forschungen zur christlichen Litteratur- und Dogmengeschichte, 1, Hefte 2–3; 1900). R. Roques, *L'Univers dionysien: Structure hiérarchique du monde selon le Pseudo-Denys* (Théologie, 29; 1954); id., *Structures théologiques de la gnose à Richard de Saint-Victor* (Bibliothèque de l'École des Hautes Études, Section des Sciences Religieuses, 72; 1962), pp. 61–240. W. Völker, *Kontemplation und Ekstase bei Pseudo-Dionysius Areopagita* (Wiesbaden, 1958). J. Vanneste, SJ, *Le Mystère de Dieu: Essai sur la structure rationnelle de la doctrine mystique du Pseudo-Denys l'Aréopagite* (Museum Lessianum, Section Philosophique, 45 [1959]). S. Gersh, *From Iamblichus to Eriugena: An Investigation of the Prehistory and Evolution of the Pseudo-Dionysian Tradition* (Studien zur Problemgeschichte der antiken und mittelalterlichen Philosophie, 8; Leiden, 1978). P. Rorem, *Biblical and Liturgical Symbols within the Pseudo-Dionysian Synthesis* (Pontifical Institute of Mediaeval Studies, Studies and Texts, 71; Toronto, 1984). A. Louth, *Denys the Areopagite* (1989). H. U. von *Balthasar, *Herrlichkeit*, 2 (1962), pp. 147–214 (Eng. tr., *The Glory of the Lord*, 2, 1984, pp. 144–210). I. P. Sheldon-Williams in A. H. Armstrong (ed.), *The Cambridge History of Later Greek and Early Medieval Philosophy* (1967), pp. 457–72, with select bibl. p. 685. A van Daele, SJ, *Indices Pseudo-Dionysiani* (Louvain, 1941). Altaner and Stuiber (1978), pp. 501–5 and 657 f. R. Roques in *RAC* 3 (1957), cols. 1075–121, s.v. 'Dionysius Areopagita'; id. and others in *Dict. Sp.* 3 (1957), cols. 244–429, s.v. 'Denys (2), l'Aréopagite (Le Pseudo-)', with bibl.; R. Roques, M. Cappuyns, OSB, and R. Aubert in *DHGE* 14 (1960), cols. 265–310, s.v. 'Denys (14) le Pseudo-Aréopagite'.

Dionysius (7) Exiguus (5th–6th cent), Scythian monk, famous for his contributions to ecclesiastical chronology and canon law. Very little is known of his life. He seems to have arrived in Rome shortly after the death of Pope *Gelasius I (496); he was certainly alive in 526 and clearly dead by c.556. Acc. to *Cassiodorus he dubbed himself 'Exiguus' out of humility. When called upon to construct a new Easter cycle, he abandoned the era of *Diocletian, and dated the first year in his Easter cycle from the (supposed) year of the Incarnation, making the 248th year from the accession of Diocletian (AD 284) the year 532 'from the incarnation of our Lord Jesus Christ'. This 'Christian Era' was adopted in England at the Synod of *Whitby, 664, and later became widespread on the Continent. His *corpus* of canon law was the first collection to gain wide influence. In its second edition, which was its classic form, it contained the *Apostolic Canons; the canons of the Councils of *Nicaea, *Ancyra, *Neocaesarea, *Gangra, *Antioch, *Laodicea, *Constantinople, *Chalcedon and *Sardica, and of *Carthage, 419; and 41 Papal decretals from *Siricius (384–98) to Anastasius II (496–8). This collection was in general use in the 6th and 7th cents., and, somewhat augmented, was sent by Pope *Hadrian to *Charlemagne in 774. This form circulated in the Frankish Church, even into the 12th cent. Dionysius also translated many important Greek patristic writings into Latin; some of these reflect his support for the *Theopaschites.

Works in J. P. Migne, *PL* 67. 9–520. The Dionysian Canons are pr. in all early canonical collections; most accessible in J. P. Migne, loc. cit., 139–316. Crit. text in *EOMIA* (under each council). 'First Recension' of Canons ed. A. Strewe, *Die Canonensammlung des Dionysius Exiguus in der ersten Redaktion* (1931). F. *Maassen, *Geschichte der Quellen und der Literatur des canonischen Rechts*, 1 (1870), pp. 132–6, 422–40, 960–5. H. Wurm, *Studien und Texte zur Dekretalensammlung des Dionysius Exiguus* (1939). W. M. Peitz, SJ, *Dionysius Exiguus-Studien*, ed. H. Foerster (Arbeiten zur Kirchengeschichte, 33; 1960 [much criticized]). C. W. Jones, 'The Victorian and Dionysiac Paschal Tablets in the West', *Speculum*, 9 (1934), pp. 408–21, esp. pp. 413–21. B. Krusch, *Studien zur christlichmittelalterlichen Chronologie*, pt. 2: *Dionysius Exiguus, der Begründer der christlichen Ära* (Abh. (Berl.), 1938, no. 8), pp. 59–87. Mordek, pp. 241–9. J. Rambaud-Buhot in *DDC* 4 (1949), cols. 1131–52, s.v. 'Denys le Petit'; id. in *NCE* 4 (1967), pp. 877 f., s.v.; H. Mordek in *Lexikon des Mittelalters*, 3 (1986), cols. 1088–92, s.v. 'Dionysius (3) Exiguus', with extensive bibl.

Dionysius (8) the Carthusian (Denys van Leeuwen, Denys Ryckel) (1402–71), theologian and mystic. He was educated by the *Brethren of the Common Life at Zwolle in the Netherlands, studied at *Cologne University, and entered the Charterhouse at Roermund in 1424/5. He compiled a series of very extensive commentaries on the OT and NT, edited or commented on the works of *Boethius, *Peter Lombard, *John Climacus, and *Dionysius the Pseudo-Areopagite (by whom he was much influenced), and also wrote books on moral theology, ecclesiastical discipline, homilies, and a tract against the Muslims. His writings became very popular in the centuries succeeding his death, though Dionysius has little real claim to be considered an original writer. His mystical experiences gained for him the title of 'Doctor Ecstaticus'. In 1451–2 he accompanied Cardinal *Nicholas of Cusa to

Germany in the cause of Church reform and to preach a crusade against the Turks.

His works were ed. in various formats by D. Loer and others at Cologne between 1530 and 1559. New edn. by the Carthusians, Montreuil-sur-Mer and (later) Tournai, and Parkminster, 42 vols. in 44, 1896–1935 [vols. 1–14, comm. on whole Bible; 15 f., on Dionysius the Pseudo-Areopagite; 17 f., 'Summa Fidei' and 'Dialogion'; 19–25 bis, comm. on *Sentences + separate index; 26–8, on Boethius, *Cassian, and John Climacus; 29–32, Sermons; 33–42, 'Opera Minora' + additional index vol. Vol. 1 also contains a Life by D. Loer (orig. pub. 1532) and a list by Dionysius of his 187 writings and of the writers he had studied]. *Opera Selecta*, ed. K. Emery (CCCM 121, 121A, etc.; 1991 ff.), with important introd. K. Krogh Tonning, *Der letzte Scholastiker* (Freiburg i.B., 1904). P. Teeuwen, *Dionysius de Karthuizer en de philosophisch-theologische Stroomingen aan de Keulsche Universiteit* (Brussels, 1938). M. Beer, *Dionysius' des Kartäusers Lehre vom Desiderium Naturale des Menschen nach der Gottesschau* (Münchener Theologische Studien, 2. Systematische Abteilung, 28; 1963); N. Maginot, *Der Actus Humanus Moralis unter dem Einfluss des Heiligen Geistes nach Dionysius Carthusianus* (ibid. 35; 1968). R. Macken, OFM, *Denys the Carthusian: Commentator on Boethius's 'De Consolatione Philosophiae'* (Analecta Cartusiana, 118; Salzburg, 1984). Useful summary in English by A. Stoelin, 'Denys the Carthusian', *Month*, NS 25 (1961), pp. 218–30. Id. in *Dict. Sp.* 3 (1957), cols. 430–49, s.v. 'Denys le Chartreux'.

Dioscorus (d. 454), Patr. of *Alexandria. During St *Cyril's patriarchate he became Archdeacon of Alexandria, and on his death in 444 succeeded to the see. When c.448 *Eutyches began to attract attention by his Christological doctrines Dioscorus gave him his support, and in 449 presided over the so-called '*Latrocinium' Council at Ephesus, in which *Flavian, Bp. of Constantinople, was deposed. Dioscorus' fortunes changed with the reversal of theological policy on the death of the Emp. *Theodosius II in 450. At the Third Session of the Council of *Chalcedon in 451, he was deposed, and he was banished by the civil authorities to Gangra in Paphlagonia. A few of his letters, and a legendary panegyric of his life by the deacon Theopistus, have survived in Syriac. He is accounted a saint in the *Coptic Church; feast day, 4 Sept.

Our most reliable source on Dioscorus is the 'Acta' of the Council of Chalcedon (q.v.). Syr. text of 'Life' by Theopistus, with Fr. tr., ed. F. Nau in *Journal Asiatique*, 10th ser. 1 (1903), pp. 5–108 and 241–310. F. Haase, 'Patriarch Dioskur I von Alexandrien nach monophysitischen Quellen', in M. Sdralek (ed.), *Kirchengeschichtliche Abhandlungen*, 6 (1908), pp. 141–233. J. Lebon, *Le Monophysisme sévérien* (1909), pp. 84–93 ('Les Écrits de Dioscore I d'Alexandrie'). Id., 'Autour du cas de Dioscore d'Alexandrie', *Muséon*, 59 (1946), pp. 515–28, incl. Syriac text, with Fr. tr., of doc. in defence of Dioscorus. Bardenhewer, 4, pp. 78 f. W. *Bright in *DCB* 1 (1877), pp. 854–62; N. Charlier in *DHGE* 14 (1960), cols. 508–14, with extensive bibl.

Dippel, Johann Konrad (1673–1734), German *Pietist and alchemist. The son of a *Lutheran pastor, he was educated at Giessen university, became a private tutor, and in the controversy between Lutheran orthodoxy and Pietism at first upheld the former, but later, under G. *Arnold's influence, himself became a Pietist. He wrote many controversial works in defence of his new convictions, the best known being *Orthodoxia Orthodoxorum* (1697) and *Papismus Protestantium Vapulans* (1698). They emphasized the alleged contrast between Christianity and the Church, between ethics and dogma, and between right living and right doctrine, maintaining that the development of Christianity from *Constantine onwards was a gradual declension from the high ideals of primitive times. His opposition to Protestant orthodoxy aroused the hostility of the Lutheran ecclesiastical authorities, who forbade him to issue further theological publications. He now turned to chemistry, becoming the inventor of the Prussian Blue, and also occupied himself with alchemy. In 1704 he went to Berlin, but he had to leave it in 1707 because of his continued Pietist activities and found refuge in the Netherlands. Here he took his medical degree at *Leiden (1711), but he again had to leave because of his theological views. In 1714 he went to Altona, which at that time belonged to Denmark, but becoming embroiled with the government in 1719 he was condemned to lifelong captivity on the island of Bornholm. Having been freed and expelled from Denmark in 1726, he went to Sweden, where, through his influence, Pietism began to gain ground, so that the orthodox Lutheran clergy brought about his expulsion. He now went back to Germany, where he finally found a refuge at Berleburg. The main inspiration of his life was his belief that the Christian religion consisted not in a dogmatic creed but in the practice of charity and self-sacrifice.

His Works were ed. (3 vols.) at Berleburg in 1747. Life by W. Bender (Bonn, 1882). K.-L. Voss, *Christianus Democritus: Das Menschenbild bei Johann Conrad Dippel* (Zeitschrift für Religions- und Geistesgeschichte, Beiheft; 12; 1970). Id. in M. Greischat (ed.) *Orthodoxie und Pietismus* (Gestalten der Kirchengeschichte, 7; 1982), pp. 277–85.

diptychs. The lists of names of living and departed Christians for whom special prayer is made in the Greek and Latin Eucharistic Liturgies. Though until recently read secretly in the W., in early times the diptychs were recited publicly, and the inclusion or exclusion of a name was held to be a sign of communion or of excommunication. The term is derived from the two-leaved folder (Gk. δίπτυχον) within which the lists were written. See also BOOK OF LIFE.

A. F. Gori, *Thesaurus Veterum Diptychorum Consularium et Ecclesiasticorum* (3 vols., Florence, 1759; with full discussion and reproductions of 'Consular Diptychs', i.e. diptychs, usually with elaborately incised covers, which were distributed by consuls on taking office and became the artistic model for ecclesiastical diptychs). E. *Bishop in R. H. *Connolly, *The Liturgical Homilies of Narsai* (Texts and Studies, 8, no. 1; 1909), pp. 97–114. R. F. Taft, SJ, *A History of the Liturgy of St John Chrysostom*, 4: *The Diptychs* (Orientalia Christiana Analecta, 238; 1991). F. *Cabrol, OSB, in *DACL* 4 (pt. 1; 1920), cols. 1045–94, s.v. 'Diptyques (Liturgie)', and H. *Leclercq, OSB, ibid., cols. 1094–170, s.v. 'Diptyques (Archéologie)'; O. Stegmüller in *RAC* 3 (1957), cols. 1138–49, s.v. 'Diptychon'.

Directory of Church Government, A (1645). An English translation of a Book of *Discipline (*Disciplina Ecclesiae Sacra*) compiled by W. *Travers; the Latin original was completed by 1587. It was divided into 'Disciplina Sacra' and 'Disciplina Synodica'. In both Latin and English the work circulated in manuscript among the *Puritans, many of whom formally subscribed its articles. The English version was published early in 1645 in the interests of the projected introduction of the *Presbyterian system into England.

A facsimile of the 1645 edn. of the Directory (dated '1644' old style) pub., with introd. by P. Lorimer, in 1872. The *Disciplina*, with other related material, pub. by F. *Paget, *Introduction to the Fifth Book of Hooker's Ecclesiastical Polity* (Oxford, 1899; 2nd edn., 1907), Appendices 3 and 4. P. Collinson, *The Elizabethan Puritan Movement* (1967), esp. pp. 291–302 and 317–29.

Dirge (Lat. *Dirige*). A traditional name for the *Office for the Dead. The office, which dates from the Middle Ages, is contained in the ancient *breviaries and in the early English *primers. The name, deriving from the former antiphon, 'Dirige Domine Deus meus in conspectu tuo viam meam' (Ps. 5: 8), was originally confined to the morning office; but it later came to include the *Vespers (the '*Placebo') sung on the evening before. It has often been set to music, one of its most famous settings being the *Mattutino di Morti* of David Perez of Lisbon (1752). The term has for some time been obsolete except in figurative use.

diriment impediment. In *canon law, a fact or circumstance relating to a person that makes him or her incapable of contracting a valid marriage. It used to be distinguished from an 'impedient impediment', which only rendered a marriage unlawful, but not null and void. Acc. to present RC canon law, the existing diriment impediments include insufficient age, impotency, an already existing marriage, abduction, a public perpetual *vow of chastity in a religious *institute, holy orders, disparity of religion, affinity, and consanguinity; but such of the impediments as are not of Divine Law may be dispensed by the ecclesiastical authorities for good reason.

J. Freisen, *Geschichte des canonischen Eherechts bis zum Verfall der Glossenlitteratur* (1888), esp. pp. 221–7. O. D. Watkins, *Holy Marriage* [1924], pp. 68–71. G. H. Joyce, SJ, *Christian Marriage* (1933; 2nd edn., 1948), *passim*. T. P. Doyle, OP, in J. A. Coriden and others (eds.), *The Code of Canon Law: A Text and Commentary* (1985), pp. 757–74. A. Bride in *DDC* 5 (1953), cols. 261–322, s.v. 'Empêchements de mariage', *passim*.

discalced (from Lat. *discalceare*, 'to make unshod'). The term is applied to certain religious orders and congregations whose members wear sandals, e.g. the Discalced *Carmelites, *Trinitarians, and *Passionists. The custom was followed by the primitive E. monks, who went barefooted, after Mt. 10: 10. It was introduced into the W. by St *Francis of Assisi, and was followed in its most rigorous form, i.e. without any kind of footwear, by the Discalced *Franciscans, founded by St *Peter of Alcántara. Today sandals are always worn, either with or without socks, though in the latter case exceptions are usually made in particularly severe climates.

Disciples of Christ (or **Churches of Christ**). A religious body which began in the *United States of America among *Presbyterians concerned for evangelism on the American frontier in the early 19th cent., particularly Thomas Campbell (1763–1854), his son Alexander *Campbell and Barton W. Stone (1771–1844). Under the influence of the ideas of John *Glas, the brothers Robert (1764–1842) and Alexander (1768–1851) Haldane, and the Scotch Baptists, it aimed at achieving the unity of all Christians through the restoration of New Testament Christianity and rejected credal formulae as tests of fellowship. It became a separate communion in 1832. The Churches are congregationally organized, regard the Scriptures as the exclusive basis of faith, practise believers' baptism and celebrate the Lord's Supper as the chief act of worship every Sunday. Parallel movements developed in Great Britain in the 1830s, and subsequently in *Australia, *New Zealand, and *Canada as a result of emigration, and in *India, *China, *Japan, Thailand, the *Philippines, *Malawi, *Zimbabwe, *Zaire, *South Africa, Jamaica, Puerto Rico, and elsewhere in Latin America as a result of missionary activity. Theological differences, particularly over instrumental music and congregational autonomy, enhanced by sociological differences, led to the formation of three main groups in the USA after 1906: (1) the Christian Church (Disciples of Christ), (2) the Christian Churches/Churches of Christ, and (3) the Churches of Christ. These divisions were reflected to a certain extent elsewhere, but without the same distinction of name. Disciples have also been active in the *Ecumenical Movement and have joined in Church unions in Japan, *North India, Zaire, South Africa, Jamaica and Great Britain (where the majority of Churches of Christ joined the *United Reformed Church in 1981). Remaining outside the last union are the Fellowship of Churches of Christ (formed in 1980) and those Churches which left the Association of Churches of Christ in Great Britain in the early 20th cent. because of differences over biblical interpretation and instrumental music.

W. E. Garrison, *Religion follows the Frontier* (New York, 1931); R. Butchart, *The Disciples of Christ in Canada since 1830* (Toronto, 1949); R. G. Nelson, *Disciples of Christ in Jamaica, 1858–1958* (St Louis [1958]); D. E. Harrell, *Quest for a Christian America: The Disciples of Christ and American Society to 1866* (Nashville, 1966); id., *The Social Sources of Division in the Disciples of Christ, 1865–1900* (Atlanta [1973]); W. E. Tucker and L. G. McAllister, *Journey in Faith: A History of the Christian Church (Disciples of Christ)* (St Louis [1975]); D. M. Thompson, *Let Sects and Parties Fall: A Short History of the Association of Churches of Christ in Great Britain and Ireland* (Birmingham, 1980). See also bibl. to CAMPBELL, A.

Disciplina Arcani (Lat., 'Discipline of the Secret'). The practice ascribed to the early Church of concealing certain theological doctrines and religious usages from *catechumens and pagans. The term is said to have been coined by the Calvinist J. *Daillé (d. 1670); but in 1614 I. *Casaubon had already explained certain silences of the early Fathers on the supposition that they imitated the secrecy of the mystery religions. Daillé himself held that the practice was mainly educational, to give catechumens a greater desire and reverence for the Sacraments. A third explanation was put forward by E. *Schelstrate, who held that it was of Dominical institution and practised by the Apostles, and that its application extended not only to *Baptism and the *Eucharist, but also explained the scarcity or absence of early Christian evidences on such subjects as the *Trinity, the *Mass, the number of the *Sacraments, *transubstantiation, and the cult of the *saints. The discussion continued through the 18th and 19th cents., RC theologians generally defending Schelstrate's theory, whereas most Protestant scholars followed Casaubon in tracing the practice to a pagan model.

In recent times the traditional theories have been generally abandoned. Acceptance of theological development makes them largely superfluous. It is unnecessary to assume direct borrowing from the mysteries; but early Christians were moved by similar religious feelings to a restricted acceptance of a widespread practice. It was adopted partly through the reticence necessary in an age of persecution, partly through the natural human instinct to withdraw the most intimate and sacred elements of faith from the knowledge of outsiders; and it was reflected in the custom of not admitting catechumens to the central part of the Eucharist. Allusions to it are found in *Tertullian, St *Cyprian, and *Origen, and more definitely in 4th- and 5th-cent. writers, among them St *Cyril of Jerusalem, *Egeria, and St John *Chrysostom for the E., and St *Ambrose, *Innocent I, and St *Augustine for the W. By the 6th cent. the practice seems to have disappeared.

I. Casaubon, *De Rebus Sacris et Ecclesiasticis* (London, 1614), Exercitio 16, pars 43, 'Mysterium' (pp. 541–67). E. A. Schelstrate, *De Disciplina Arcani* (Rome, 1685). P. *Batiffol, *Études d'histoire et de théologie positive* (1902), pp. 3–41; F. X. Funk, 'Das Alter der Arkandisziplin', repr. in his *Kirchengeschichtliche Abhandlungen und Untersuchungen*, 3 (1907), pp. 42–57. G. Mensching, *Das heilige Schweigen* (Religionsgeschichtliche Versuche und Vorarbeiten, 20, Heft 2; 1926), pp. 125–33. H. Clasen, *Die Arkandisziplin in der Alten Kirche* (Heidelberg Diss., cyclostyled, 1956; noted in *TLZ* 82, 1957, cols. 153 f.). P. Batiffol in *DTC* 1 (1903), cols. 1738–58, s.v. 'Arcane'; E. Vacandard in *DHGE* 3 (1924), cols. 1497–513, s.v. 'Arcane'; O. Perler in *RAC* 1 (1950), cols. 667–76, s.v. 'Arkandisziplin'; V. Recchia in *DPAC* 1 (1983), cols. 315–17, 'Arcano (disciplina dell')'; Eng. tr. in *Encyclopedia of the Early Church*, 1 (1992), p. 242, s.v., all with bibl.

discipline. The word has several religious connotations.

(1) The totality of ecclesiastical laws and customs regulating the religious and moral life of the Church. In this sense it comprises all Church activities not regulated by Divine law, such as the administration of the Sacraments, offices, feasts, devotions, etc.

(2) In a more restricted sense, a system of mortification, e.g. that involved in the religious life (monastic discipline).

(3) A scourge of knotted cords, chain, or other instrument used for penitential beating.

(4) As a technical term, the word is applied esp. to the *Calvinist polity, which, in contrast with that of M. *Luther, was built up on rigid principles. Its object is the good of the offender, the purity of the Church, and the glory of God. It is the duty of the consistories, formed by elders and pastors, to fix penalties for neglect of religious duties, culminating in excommunication. In grave cases, offenders were formerly handed over to the state. This practice was taken up by the *Presbyterians, who laid down their principles in the *Book of *Common Order* and the *First Book of *Discipline* (qq.v.). In the past disciplinary measures were often taken in the face of the congregation. Nowadays cases are generally dealt with by the minister. Processes against a minister are begun before his presbytery and appeal can be made to the *General Assembly.

W. Dürig, 'Disciplina. Eine Studie zum Bedeutungsumfang des Wortes in der Sprache der Liturgie und der Väter', *Sacris Erudiri*, 4 (1952), pp. 245–79, with refs.

Discipline, Books of. The 'First Book of Discipline' (1560), drawn up at Edinburgh at the government's request by J. *Knox and five of his fellow-Reformers as a plan for the ordering and maintenance of the new Scottish Church, was an adaptation of the Genevan 'Ordonnances' to the needs of a nation. Its nine heads were: (1) Doctrine; (2) Sacraments; (3) Abolishing of Idolatry; (4) Ministers and their Lawful Election; (5) Provision for the Ministers; (6) Rents and Patrimony of the Kirk; (7) Ecclesiastical Discipline; (8) Election of Elders, Deacons, etc.; and (9) The Policy of the Church. Knox's more ardent supporters welcomed its rigid discipline, but parts of the Book were obnoxious to the nobility, esp. the proposed system of national education, which threatened the newly possessed landlords with the loss of their revenues. Hence, civil authority being needed for its enforcement, the Book remained a dead-letter.

The so-called 'Second Book of Discipline' (1578), chiefly the work of A. *Melville, was prepared as a manifesto of the stricter Presbyterians against efforts to restore a modified episcopacy. It was endorsed by the General Assembly in 1581, though this Book also never obtained complete civil recognition.

The First Book was ed., with introd. and comm., by J. K. Cameron (Edinburgh, 1972); the Second Book by J. Kirk (ibid., 1980). J. H. S. Burleigh, *A Church History of Scotland* (1960), pp. 163–76 and 198–201. J. Kirk, ' "The Polities of the Best Reformed Kirks": Scottish achievements and English aspirations in church government after the Reformation', *Scottish Historical Review*, 59 (1980), pp. 22–53; G. Donaldson, ' "The Example of Denmark" in the Scottish Reformation' in id., *Scottish Church History* (Edinburgh, 1985), pp. 60–70.

discus (Gk. δίσκος, δισκάριον). In the E. Church, the plate on which the bread of the Eucharist is offered and consecrated, corresponding to the *paten in the W. It is commonly somewhat larger and more concave and normally stands on a central foot. It is never placed on the chalice. The *Last Supper is sometimes represented on its inner surface.

Dismas. The traditional name of the Good Thief (Lk. 23: 39–43) crucified with Christ. The name of the other is said to have been Gestas.

The name, from the Gk. δυσμή, 'dying', is found in the 'Gospel of *Nicodemus', ch. 10; cf. C. *Tischendorf, *Evangelia Apocrypha* (2nd edn., 1876), pp. 192 f., 362. A. Bessières, *Le Bon Larron, Saint Dismas* [1937]. H. Lesêtre in *Dict. Bibl.* 4 (1908), cols. 94–6, s.v. 'Larron'; H. *Leclercq, OSB, in *DACL* 8 (pt. 1; 1928), cols. 1402–4, s.v. 'Larrons (Les Deux)'.

dismissal. The traditional form of dismissal at the conclusion of the Eucharist is the '*Ite, missa est', from which the term '*Mass' derives. In the Roman Missal of 1970 alternative forms of dismissal are provided.

dispensations. Licences granted by ecclesiastical authority to do some act otherwise canonically illegal, or for the remittance of a penalty for breaking such a rule. The practice of granting dispensations began very early. By the 5th cent. the bishops of Rome were employing the dispensing power, and a similar power was also used on occasion by other bishops, councils, and even (in minor matters) parish priests. By the later Middle Ages the dispensation had become more or less a prerogative of the Pope, and this position, with the elimination of certain minor abuses, was maintained by the Council of *Trent. The Second

*Vatican Council, in its decree on the Office of Bishops (*Christus Dominus*, 1965), however, gave diocesan bishops ordinary power to dispense from general laws of the Church in particular cases, except in matters specially reserved for the Pope. These last were further defined by Pope *Paul VI in 1966.

All writers on the subject are agreed that there must be an adequate reason for the use of the dispensing power. Thus St *Basil urges that the needs of the time and the advantages of the Church are the two main requisites for a just dispensation and this has been the consistent teaching of later canonists. The chief objects of the dispensing power are in relation to the ordination of clergy, the translation of bishops, vows, marriage, and divorce. The Church can suspend or abrogate, however, only laws of its own making, and not such as are natural (*ius naturale*) or Divine (*ius divinum*).

In England in 1534 the Ecclesiastical Licences Act 1533 transferred the Pope's dispensing power to the Abp. of *Canterbury. It is now used mainly in the granting of special *marriage licences. The Clergy (Ordination) Measure 1990 empowers the Abps. of Canterbury and *York to allow a divorced person whose former spouse is still living to be ordained.

Among Nonconformists, the *Methodist Conference sometimes grants dispensations allowing a lay person to preside at Holy Communion when the shortage of ordained ministers is such that the people would otherwise be deprived of regular sacramental ministry.

Early treatment of the subject by *Ivo of Chartres, 'Prologue in *Decretum*' (*PL* 161. 47–60). Classical discussions by F. *Suárez, SJ, *Tractatus de Legibus* (Antwerp, 1613), pp. 449–95 (lib. 6, capp. 10–24), and P. de *Marca, *De Concordia Sacerdotii et Imperii* (Paris, 1641), pp. 512–56 (lib. 3, capp. 13–15). Current RC legislation is contained in *CIC* (1983), cans. 85–93. W. J. Sparrow Simpson, *Dispensations* (1933), with bibl. A. van Hove, *Commentarium Lovaniense in Codicem Iuris Canonici*, vol. 1, tom. 5: De Privilegiis, De Dispensationibus (Mechlin and Rome, 1939), pp. 293–459. J. Brys, *De Dispensatione in Iure Canonico praesertim apud Decretistas et Decretalistas usque ad Medium Saeculum Decimum Quartum* (Louvain thesis, 1925). *Dispensation in Practice and Theory with special reference to the Anglican Churches: Being the Report of a Commission appointed by the Archbishop of Canterbury in 1935 under the Chairmanship of E. J. Palmer* (1944). E. G. Moore, *Introduction to English Canon Law*, 3rd edn. by T. Briden and B. Hanson (1992), pp. 131–6. D. S. Chambers, *Faculty Office Registers 1534–1549: A Calendar of the first two Registers of the Archbishop of Canterbury's Faculty Office edited with introduction and index* (Oxford, 1966). R. Naz in *DDC* 4 (1949), cols. 1284–96. s.v. 'Dispense'.

Dispersion, the. See DIASPORA.

Disruption, the (1843). The great split in the Established Church of *Scotland, when the *Free Church of Scotland (at first, 'Free Protesting Church of Scotland') was formed by the secession of 474 (out of 1,203) ministers on 18 May 1843. The dispute centred in the demand of the presbyteries for a voice ('veto') in matters of patronage. In 1833 legislation (the 'Veto Act') had been introduced into the *General Assembly to secure the right to object to a presentee to a benefice on reasonable grounds. After being thrown out in that year, the Act passed in 1834, largely through the exertions of T. *Chalmers (q.v.). The consequence was a succession of conflicts in the next decade between the General Assembly and the civil court ('Court of Session'), culminating in the Disruption. At first the destinies of the Free Church were in the hands of T. Chalmers, who was elected the first moderator and organized the Church with great ability. He created a Sustentation Fund for the support of the clergy by imposing a subscription of one penny a week from every member of the Church. The schism was not finally healed until 1929.

R. Buchanan, *The Ten Years' Conflict* (2 vols., 1849); T. Brown, *Annals of the Disruption; with Extracts from the narratives of ministers who left the Scottish Establishment in 1843* (1884). G. D. Henderson, *Heritage: A Study of the Disruption* (1943); H. Watt, *Thomas Chalmers and the Disruption* (1943); S. J. Brown, *Thomas Chalmers and the Godly Commonwealth in Scotland* (Oxford, 1982), esp. pp. 282–349. J. H. S. Burleigh, *A Church History of Scotland* (1960), pp. 334–69; G. I. T. Machin, *Politics and the Churches in Great Britain 1832 to 1868* (1977), pp. 112–47. See also works cited under CHALMERS, T.

Dissenters. In a religious context, those who separate themselves from the communion of the Established Church. Originally the term included RCs, but it is now usually restricted to Protestant Dissenters. It is occasionally used in contradistinction to 'Nonconformists' of those who not only dissent from the national Church as at present established, but disagree with the principle of established Churches.

Dissenters' Marriage Act. The common designation of the Marriage Act 1836, which relieved Nonconformists of the need to be married in an Anglican church, allowing marriages to be solemnized in any registered place of religious worship, in a registrar's office, or acc. to the usages of *Jews and *Quakers. By the Marriage Act 1898, the presence of the registrar at the chapel, required since 1836, was no longer demanded. The law was consolidated by the Marriage Act 1949.

Dissolution of the Monasteries. The wealth of the English monasteries, a certain moral laxity, and what many regarded as their undue stress on the contemplative aspect of the religious life, had made them in the later Middle Ages an object of criticism. Spasmodic attempts at reform had met with little success and various small suppressions had taken place. It was, however, from personal motives that *Henry VIII effected the complete abolition of the system; among these were the need to replenish his treasury. He decided first on the suppression of the smaller monasteries. A biased report (based on a hurried visitation of a fraction of the monasteries involved) declared the evil condition of the houses, and the Suppression of Religious Houses Act 1535 was passed in 1536. It ordered the suppression of all religious houses having an annual value of less than £200, some 250 in all being involved. It is unlikely that at this stage a total dissolution was contemplated; some smaller houses were reprieved, and the King sponsored some refoundations which were technically new monasteries. However, the popularity of monasteries, particularly in the north, coupled with economic and other grievances, led to the popular risings collectively known as the *Pilgrimage of Grace (1536–7). Although a real threat, these were quickly put down, and their defeat provided a powerful incentive to begin a vigorous campaign of total monastic dissolution. Royal agents toured the country to obtain individual surrenders of the remaining monasteries and nunneries, while in 1538 two separate campaigns sup-

pressed all the remaining friaries and removed the shrines which had been so prominent in many monastic churches. The Suppression of Religious Houses Act 1539 completed the process by vesting in the Crown all monasteries that had been or should be surrendered; the last houses surrendered in the spring of 1540. The King's principal adviser throughout was Thomas *Cromwell (q.v.).

Effected in a brutal and highly unscrupulous manner, the Dissolution of the Monasteries met with small resistance. Care was taken to observe the letter of the law, and the subsequent economic and social dislocation is now known to have been considerably less than used to be thought. Most religious, with the exception of the friars, were pensioned, and a considerable number in due course obtained benefices as secular clergy. Nuns, debarred from ecclesiastical office and, until the reign of *Edward VI, marriage, had mostly to subsist on very meagre pensions. The incidental losses to charity, art, and learning were considerable, many precious MSS and church furnishings perishing through destruction and decay.

Most of the spoils of the Dissolution sooner or later passed from the Crown to the Tudor nobility and gentry, but part of the proceeds went to the foundation of the six new sees of Bristol, *Chester, *Gloucester, *Oxford, *Peterborough, and *Westminster (the last soon suppressed). Where the local parishioners had their altar in the conventual church, this was spared, the old places of worship (usually the nave) continuing in use. In some dozen cases the parishioners bought the rest of the church concerned, e.g. at Christchurch, Dorset.

The *Valor Ecclesiasticus (q.v.) is an important source for the financial state of the monasteries immediately prior to the Dissolution. The principal authority for the actual Dissolution is the material calendared in *Letters and Papers, Foreign and Domestic, of the Reign of Henry VIII* (details in bibl. to HENRY VIII). T. Wright (ed.), *Three Chapters of Letters Relating to the Suppression of the Monasteries* (Camden Society, 26; 1843); selections repr. in G. H. Cook (ed.), *Letters to Cromwell and others on the Suppression of the Monasteries* (1965); J. [A.] Youings, *The Dissolution of the Monasteries* (1971). G. Baskerville, *English Monks and the Suppression of the Monasteries* (1937); [M.] D. *Knowles, OSB, *The Religious Orders in England*, 3 (Cambridge, 1959), esp. pp. 195–417; G. W. O. Woodward, *The Dissolution of the Monasteries* (1966). A. Savine, *English Monasteries on the Eve of the Dissolution* (Oxford Studies in Social and Legal History, 1; 1909). J. C. Dickinson, 'Early Suppressions of English Houses of Austin Canons', in *Medieval Studies presented to Rose Graham*, ed. V. Ruffer and A. J. Taylor (Oxford, 1950), pp. 54–77. G. A. J. Hodgett, 'The Unpensioned Ex-religious in Tudor England', *JEH* 13 (1962), pp. 195–202; C. Kitching, 'The Disposal of Monastic and Chantry Lands', in F. Heal and R. O'Day (eds.), *Church and Society in England: Henry VIII to James I* (1977), pp. 119–36, with bibl. on pp. 184 f.; E. M. Hallam, 'Henry VIII's Monastic Refoundations of 1536–7 and the Course of the Dissolution', *Bulletin of the Institute of Historical Research*, 51 (1978), pp. 124–31. List of monasteries dissolved in J. *Gairdner, *The English Church in the Sixteenth Century from the Accession of Henry VIII to the Death of Mary* (1902), pp. 419–30, and S. M. Jack, 'Dissolution Dates for the Monasteries Dissolved under the Act of 1536', *Bulletin of the Institute of Historical Research*, 43 (1970), pp. 161–181. Information on individual houses at the time of the Dissolution in [M.] D. Knowles and R. N. Hadcock, *Medieval Religious Houses: England and Wales* (1953; rev. edn., 1971).

dittography (Gk. διττός, 'double', and γράφω, 'I write'). The repetition by a copyist, through carelessness, of the same letter(s) or word(s), e.g. in the text of Acts 2: 4 in the Codex Laudianus (*et repleti sunt et repleti sunt omnes spiritu sancto*). It is a frequent source of corruption in the transmission of MSS. The opposite error is known as '*haplography'.

Diurnal. The service-book containing the '*Day Hours' (*horae diurnae*), i.e. all the traditional canonical hours except *Mattins.

Dives (Lat., 'rich'). A word which has become a convenient, almost a proper, name for the unnamed rich man in the parable, Lk. 16: 19–31. He was condemned not for his wealth but for his selfish enjoyment of it.

Divina Commedia, La. The name commonly given to *Dante's sacred poem describing his vision of the three realms of the world to come, *Inferno*, *Purgatorio*, and *Paradiso*. Dante himself may have described the trilogy as a comedy; the epithet divine is a later addition. The poem describes a vision in which Dante travels for a week at Easter 1300 from a dark forest on this side of the world down through Hell to Satan at the centre of the Earth and up the seven terraces of the mount of Purgatory, an island in the Antipodes opposite Jerusalem, to its summit, the Earthly Paradise, where Adam and Eve were created. So far *Virgil has been his guide, but now he meets Beatrice, who conducts him through the nine planetary and stellar spheres to the Empyrean, where St *Bernard of Clairvaux takes her place. St Bernard presents Dante to the BVM, at whose intercession the poet is granted a glimpse of the *Beatific Vision.

The date, purpose and detailed interpretation of the poem are widely disputed. Dante may have begun writing in 1305 or possibly not until after 1310. The work was circulated in batches of Cantos before its completion and is mentioned early in 1314. The fictional date, 1300, means that many subsequent events are presented as prophecies, though some prophecies seem to remain unfulfilled. Virgil is commonly said to represent Natural Reason and Beatrice Faith, Revelation, Theology, or the Church, though it is clear that she is also the Florentine girl, jealous of the honours Dante has paid to other women. St Bernard is not merely a symbol but a man who in contemplation has been granted a glimpse of the Beatific Vision. The poem is not just a version of scholasticism; it interprets a personal vision and a story of individual salvation in which Dante claims the rare privilege of the vision of God's Essence in this life. He accepts the authority of the Church and the office of the Pope, however severe his comments on the persons of individual popes and other churchmen whom he depicts in Hell. The poem has survived in a large number of MSS, been the subject of commentaries from an early date, widely translated and has exercised a deep influence, esp. on 19th-cent. English literature and art (e.g. on drawings of W. *Blake).

Edns. of Dante's collected works are listed s.v. Crit. edn. of *Divina Commedia*, with introd., by G. Petrocchi (Opere di Dante Alighieri, Edizione Nazionale, 7; 4 vols., 1966–7). Eng. trs. incl. those of D. L. *Sayers (Harmondsworth, 1949–62), G. L. Bickersteth (Aberdeen, 1955), and in prose, with comm., by J. D. Sinclair (3 vols., London, 1939–46; rev. edn., 1948), and, with best comm. in Eng., by C. S. Singleton (Bollingen Series, 80; 6

vols., Princeton, NJ [1970–5]; vols. 1–2, *Inferno*, also pub. London, 1971). Comm. in Ital. by N. Sapegno (3 vols., Florence, 1955–7) and U. Bosco and G. Reggio (3 vols., ibid., 1979). J. Tambling, *Dante and Difference: Writing in the 'Commedia'* (Cambridge Studies in Medieval Literature, 2; 1988). E. H. Wilkins and T. G. Bergin, *A Concordance to the Divine Comedy of Dante Alighieri* (Cambridge, Mass., and London, 1965). G. F. Cunningham, *The Divine Comedy in English: A Critical Bibliography: 1782–1900* (1965); *1901–66* (1966).

Divine Praises, the. A series of praises, beginning with the words 'Blessed be God, Blessed be His Holy Name', sometimes said or sung after *Benediction of the Blessed Sacrament (usually in the vernacular) before the Host is replaced in the tabernacle. They are thought to have been compiled *c*.1779 by Louis Felici, SJ, to be used in reparation for blasphemy and profanity. In 1801 they were indulgenced by *Pius VII. The original Praises have been extended by the addition of Praise to the *Immaculate Conception in 1856, the *Sacred Heart in 1897, St *Joseph in 1921, the *Assumption of the BVM in 1950, the *Precious Blood in 1960, and the Holy Spirit in 1964.

H. T[hurston, SJ], 'The Divine Praises', *The Month*, 131 (1918), pp. 510–13, incl. refs. to earlier discussions.

Divine Right of Kings. The doctrine that monarchy is God's chosen form of government, and that rebellion against the monarch is always a sin. Where active obedience to an evil ruler is morally impossible, it is held that passive obedience (i.e. the willing acceptance of any penalty imposed for non-compliance) is demanded.

From the NT, St *Paul's injunction to obey 'the powers that be' (Rom. 13: 1–2) reverberated through the centuries, providing the mainstay of Christian political quietism, although it was constantly modified by the overriding need to 'obey God rather than man' (Acts 5: 29). The Divine Right of Kings involves also the larger claim that monarchy is ordained by God. This dates from the Christianization of the Roman Empire. While both the OT and the NT contain passages which make it hard to discern a consistent attitude to kingship or the secular power, generally the early Fathers (and esp. *Tertullian) regarded the pagan state as Babylonish, echoing the hostility found in Rev. But this attitude gave way to a triumphalist celebration of the Roman *imperium* as being God's instrument. The panegyrics of *Eusebius (*c*.330) upon the first Christian Emperor were crucial, and permanently established *Constantine as the model of the Godly Prince, deployed, for instance, in the 'caesaropapal' propaganda of *Henry VIII's Reformation in England. Eusebius also claimed that Christ's Incarnation at the time when Augustus was 'lord of the world' providentially allowed the fulfilment of the command to 'go and teach all nations', a view echoed in *Dante's *Monarchy* (*c*.1310).

Perhaps under the influence of *Neoplatonism, Greek theories of divine kingship became Christianized: the emperor was the earthly image of God's ruling wisdom. Divine attributes were used to describe kings, and, in parallel, imperial vocabulary used to describe Christ's Kingship. Jewish precedents also served: monarchs were to emulate the rulership of *Moses and *David. The Platonic ideal of hierarchy, the Great Chain of Being in the divine, human, and animal kingdoms, was transmitted through the Middle Ages by the writings of *Dionysius the

Pseudo-Areopagite (c.500). Elaborate 'body politic' metaphors proliferated. To the monarch's Godlike nature was added his Christ-like nature; as Christ has a natural and mystic body, so the king had two bodies, natural and fictive; Christ and the king embody the Church and the State. Monarchs were quasi-sacerdotal, they were lay 'bishops' or 'priests' of the law. This 'liturgical' idea of kingship predominated in the Byzantine empire, in Anglo-Saxon kingship, and in the Carolingian and Ottonian empires of the early Middle Ages. Sacramental *anointings became a normal feature of coronations, and many Anglo-Saxon kings were venerated as saints. The practice of 'touching for the *King's evil' (q.v.) arose, persisting in France and England until the 18th cent.

With the revival of knowledge of *Aristotle and of Roman law from the 12th cent., the notion of liturgical kingship gave way to a more legalistic style of argument. The theory of Divine Right became a theological gloss upon Roman jurisprudence, and later upon ideas of absolute sovereignty. The absolutist tendency was mitigated, e.g. in the 'Mirror for Princes' books (13th–16th cents.), by stress on the royal duty to cultivate the virtues. God's power and the king's power were unlimited, but since God consults His reason and His goodness when legislating, so the king should emulate Him. Divine Right kingship confronted, and was provoked by, two opposing traditions: the claims to supreme authority by the Church and by popular representative institutions.

Scholastic emphasis on the naturalness of political communities encouraged a 'patriarchalist' theory of the king as father of his people, as inheritor of Adam's authority, and as one object of the commandment to 'Honour thy father'. This is exemplified in the books of King *James I of England (esp. The True Law of Free Monarchies, 1598), and in Sir Robert Filmer's Patriarcha (written c.1640; posthumously pub., 1680), which J. *Locke attacked in his Two Treatises of Government (written c.1680; pub. '1690' [in fact 1689]). Under the Stuarts the doctrine was widely accepted by Anglican divines and, although *James II's attack on the C of E eroded support for the doctrine, it continued to be loyally upheld by the *Nonjurors. Those who opposed it accepted that sovereign authority was ordained by God, but they insisted that God left people free to choose the form of government, whether monarchy or not. Thus they dislodged the special divinity of kingship, although the idea had a final resurgence at the beginning of the 19th cent. in the Romantic reaction against the French Revolution (e.g. in F. R. de *Chateaubriand).

P. Laslett (ed.), Patriarcha and Other Political Works of Sir Robert Filmer (Oxford, 1949). J. N. *Figgis, The Theory of the Divine Right of Kings (Cambridge Historical Essays, 9; 1896; 2nd edn., with additional essays, 1914). N. H. Baynes, Byzantine Studies and Other Essays (1955), esp. pp. 47–66. E. [M.] A. Isiche, Political Thinking and Social Experience: Some Christian Interpretations of the Roman Empire from Tertullian to Salvian (Christchurch, New Zealand [1964]). E. H. Kantorowicz, The King's Two Bodies: A Study in Mediaeval Political Theology (Princeton, NJ, 1957); W. Ullmann, Principles of Government and Politics in the Middle Ages (1961), pp. 117–211.

Divine service. A title which, like the Lat. servitium divinum from which it is derived, would seem properly to belong only to the Divine *Office, and hence to Mattins

and Evensong, and not to be applicable, e.g., to the Holy Communion. Cf. the preface to the BCP which since 1662 has been headed '*Concerning the Service of the Church' and refers only to these offices. It was customary for English church notice-boards in the 19th cent. to distinguish between the times for Divine service and those for Holy Communion. The expression is, however, often used more loosely for any form of religious service.

F. E. *Brightman, 'Common Prayer', JTS 10 (1908–9), pp. 515–18.

Divine Word, Society of the (SVD), RC religious and missionary congregation of priests and lay brothers. It was founded in 1875 at Steyl in the Netherlands by Bl Arnold Janssen (1837–1909), a German priest who made his foundation outside Germany because of the *Kulturkampf. Originally a foreign mission society of German secular priests, it soon recruited lay brothers and by 1884 had become a religious congregation with public vows. It was officially approved in 1905. Foundations were made in *Argentina, *West Africa, the *United States of America, Papua New Guinea, *Japan, and the *Philippines, as well as in Britain and other European countries. Acc. to its 1983 constitutions, the Society understands its work to be focused 'first and foremost where the Gospel has not been preached at all, or only insufficiently, and where the local Church is not viable on its own'. It has been deeply involved in secondary and tertiary education, in promoting popular appreciation of Scripture, and in disseminating religious literature, for these purposes maintaining its own printing works. Notable achievements were made in the field of social anthropology, esp. by Wilhelm Schmidt (1868–1954) and the Anthropos Institute (now at St Augustin, near Bonn), which continues his work. In the USA Divine Word missionaries founded the first RC foreign missionary seminary in 1909 at Techny, Illinois, and pioneered the lay *retreat movement. They also initiated the Catholic apostolate to Black Americans, founding a special seminary to train Black priests, one of whom, Joseph Bowers, became Bp. of Accra, *Ghana, in 1953. The congregation has over 5,000 members.

H. Fischer, SVD, Arnold Janssen: Gründer des Steyler Missionswerkes (Steyl [1919]; Eng. tr., Techny, Ill., 1925); F. Bornemann, Arnold Janssen, der Gründer des Steyler Missionswerkes (Steyl, 1969; Eng. tr., Manila [1975]). V. J. Fecher, SVD, in NCE 4 (1967), pp. 923 f., s.v.; C. Pape, SVD, and P. Sessolo, SVD, in DIP 8 (1988), cols. 1601–8, s.v. 'Società del Divin Verbo'.

Divine Worship, Congregation for. See RITES, CONGREGATION OF SACRED.

Divino Afflante Spiritu. See BIBLICAL COMMISSION.

Divino Afflatu (Lat., 'by God's inspiration'). The constitution of Pope *Pius X, issued on 1 Nov. 1911, which introduced important reforms into the manner of reciting the Divine Office and celebrating Mass. Among many other changes, it provided for the regular recitation of the whole Psalter each week, and also laid down revised rules for the Office when two or more feasts occurred on the same day.

Text in *AAS* 3 (1911), pp. 633–8, with 'Rubricae in Recitatione Divini Officii et in Missarum Celebratione Servandae ad Normam Constitutionis Apostolicae "Divino Afflatu" ', pp. 639–51. E. Burton and E. Myers, *The New Psalter and its Use* (1912), incl. text of constitution, pp. 2–8, and Eng. tr., pp. 8–14.

divorce. The word is used in two senses: (1) *a vinculo*, i.e. as a dissolution of the marriage bond, and (2) *a mensa et thoro*, i.e. legal separation. Since W. *canon law has always insisted upon the principle of indissolubility, divorce in sense (1) is contrary to the canons and formularies of the C of E. In the RC Church the position is different. A sacramental and consummated marriage can be dissolved only by death, but marriages which are not sacramental (i.e. those not between two baptized persons), or are sacramental but not consummated, may be dissolved under various headings, incl. the *Pauline Privilege. In the E. Church, the civil legislation begun by the Emp. *Justinian has been tolerated, if not approved, and divorce is allowed on a wide number of grounds. Civil legislation in England, by a series of Acts of Parliament culminating in the Matrimonial Causes Act 1973, has extended the grounds on which a decree of divorce may be obtained; the irretrievable breakdown of marriage is now the sole criterion. In sense (2) W. canon law permits divorce for grave causes, the chief of which is adultery. In this case the separation granted is permanent. In all other cases the right to live apart holds good only for so long as the cause remains. RC legislation is contained in *CIC* (1983), cans. 1151–5. See also MATRIMONY and NULLITY.

R. Phillips, *Putting Asunder: A History of Divorce in Western Society* (Cambridge, 1988), with refs. to earlier works. See also bibl. to MATRIMONY, esp. the works of G. H. Joyce, SJ, K. E. *Kirk, T. A. *Lacey and R. C. Mortimer, and O. D. Watkins. L. G. Wrenn, 'Some Notes on the Petrine Privilege', *The Jurist*, 43 (1983), pp. 394–405. T. P. Doyle, OP, in J. A. Coriden and others (eds.), *The Code of Canon Law: A Text and Commentary* (1985), pp. 811–22. A. Villien in *DTC* 4 (1911), cols. 1455–78, s.v.

Dix, Gregory (1901–52), Anglican *Benedictine monk and liturgical scholar. Educated at Westminster School and Merton College, Oxford, from 1924 to 1926 he was a lecturer in modern history at Keble College, Oxford. He was ordained priest in 1925, entered Nashdom Abbey, Bucks, in the following year, and took his final vows in 1940. In 1946 he was appointed Select Preacher in the University of Cambridge and proctor in *Convocation for the diocese of Oxford. In 1948 he was elected Prior of Nashdom.

Dix, who became in his later years one of the best-known figures in the C of E, owed his influence to his brilliance, unconventionality, and good humour as a controversialist. These qualities largely contributed to the success of *The Shape of the Liturgy* [1945], his most considerable work; it did much to revive and popularize liturgical studies in the C of E. His other writings include *The Treatise on the Apostolic Tradition of St Hippolytus of Rome* (Church Historical Society, vol. 1 [all pub.], 1937; 2nd edn. by H. Chadwick, 1968), *A Detection of Aumbries* (notes on the history of *Reservation, 1942) and *The Question of Anglican Orders: Letters to a Layman* (1944), besides contributions to *The Parish Communion* (1937), to *The Apostolic Ministry* (ed. K. E. *Kirk, 1946) and to *Laudate* and other periodicals. *Jew and Greek: A study in*

the primitive Church, was posthumously ed. by H. J. Carpenter (1953).

K. W. Stevenson, *Gregory Dix 25 Years on* (Grove Liturgical Study, 10; 1977). S. Bailey, *A Tactful God* (Leominster, 1995). A. H. Couratin in *DNB, 1951–1960*, pp. 301 f.

Dobeneck, Johann. See COCHLAEUS, JOHANNES.

Docetism (Gk. δοκέω, 'I seem'). In the early Church, a tendency, rather than a formulated and unified doctrine, which considered the humanity and sufferings of the earthly Christ as apparent rather than real. Evidence for its existence is to be found in the NT (1 Jn. 4: 1–3; 2 Jn. 7; cf. Col. 2: 8 f.), but it reached its zenith in the next generation, esp. among the *Gnostics. In some forms it held that Christ miraculously escaped the ignominy of death, e.g. by *Judas Iscariot or *Simon of Cyrene changing places with Him just before the Crucifixion. Docetic doctrines were vigorously attacked by St *Ignatius and all the leading anti-Gnostic writers. Among those esp. charged with Docetism was *Cerinthus. *Serapion, Bp. of Antioch (190–203), who is the first to use the name 'Docetists' (Δοκηταί), and some others wrote of them as a distinct body.

A. Orbe, SJ, *Cristología gnóstica: Introducción a la soteriología de los siglos II y III*, 1 (Biblioteca de Autores Cristianos, 384; 1976), pp. 380–412. G. *Salmon in *DCB* 1 (1877), pp. 867–70, s.v.; A. *Fortescue in *HERE* 4 (1911), pp. 832–5, s.v.; G. Bardy in *Dict. Sp.* 3 (1957), cols. 1461–8, s.v. 'Docétisme', all with patristic refs. See also bibl. to GNOSTICISM.

Doctors, Scholastic. In later medieval times, the outstanding Scholastic teachers and others were given distinguishing epithets, of which the following are among the better known:

Doctor angelicus (or *communis* or *sanctus*)	St *Thomas Aquinas
Doctor authenticus	*Gregory of Rimini
Doctor christianissimus	John *Gerson
Doctor ecstaticus	Jan van *Ruysbroeck (also of *Dionysius the Carthusian)
Doctor invincibilis (or *singularis*)	*William of Ockham
Doctor irrefragabilis (or *doctorum*)	*Alexander of Hales
Doctor mellifluus	St *Bernard of Clairvaux
Doctor mirabilis (or *admirabilis*)	Roger *Bacon
Doctor profundus	Thomas *Bradwardine (also of Jacobus de Esculo)
Doctor seraphicus (or *devotus*)	St *Bonaventure
Doctor solidus (or *copiosus*)	*Richard of Middleton
Doctor subtilis	*Duns Scotus
Doctor universalis (or *venerabilis* or *expertus*)	St *Albertus Magnus

F. *Ehrle, *Die Ehrentitel der scholastischen Lehrer des Mittelalters* (*Sb.* (Bayr.), 1919, Abhandlung 9; 1919); F. Lehmann, 'Mittelalterliche Beinamen und Ehrentitel', *Hist. J.* 49 (1929), pp. 215–39. J. C. Vansteenkiste in *NCE* 4 (1967), pp. 935–8, s.v., with more extensive list.

Doctors' Commons. A society of ecclesiastical lawyers founded in the late 15th cent., though not incorporated until 1768. It served as a college of advocates for those practising in the ecclesiastical courts, as also in the Court of Admiralty. The judges of the Abp. of *Canterbury's courts were usually selected from this college. From 1565 its headquarters were in Knightrider Street, near *St Paul's Cathedral. The advocates lost their exclusive rights of audience under the Court of Probate Act 1857 and the Matrimonial Causes Act 1857; in consequence the members sold the property and divided the proceeds among themselves, but the college remained in legal existence until the last member died in 1912.

G. D. Squibb, *Doctors' Commons: A History of the College of Advocates and Doctors of Law* (Oxford, 1977), with bibl.

Doctors of the Church (Lat. *Doctores Ecclesiae*). A title regularly given since the Middle Ages to certain Christian theologians of outstanding merit and acknowledged saintliness. Originally the W. theologians, *Gregory the Great, *Ambrose, *Augustine, and *Jerome, were held to be the 'four doctors' *par excellence*; but in later times the list has been gradually increased to over 30.

*Benedict XIV, *De Servorum Dei Beatificatione*, 4 (Bonn, 1738), pt. 2, cap. 11, no. 8–cap. 12, no. 9, pp. 96–107. Bardenhewer, 1, pp. 42–6; J. de Ghellinck, SJ, 'Les Premières Listes des "Docteurs de l'Eglise" en Occident', *Bulletin d'ancienne Littérature et d'Archéologie chrétienne*, 2 (1912), pp. 132–4; rev. as appendix 3 of *Le Mouvement théologique du XIIᵉ siècle* (2nd edn., 1948), pp. 514–17; C. A. Kneller, SJ, 'Zum Verzeichnis der Kirchenlehrer', *ZKT* 40 (1916), pp. 1–47. V. Pugliese, G. Löwe, CSSR, and G. Carandente in *EC* 4 (1950), cols. 1901–7, s.v. 'Dottori della chiesa', with list of doctors and bibl.; H. Smolinsky in *L.Th.K.* (3rd edn.), 6 (1997), cols. 20–22, s.v. 'Kirchenlehrer.'

Doctrina Apostolorum. See DIDACHE.

Doctrine in the Church of England (1938). The Report of the Commission on Doctrine set up in 1922 by the Abps. of *Canterbury and *York. The Commission consisted of Anglican theologians of moderate *Catholic, *Evangelical, and *Modernist beliefs under the chairmanship first of H. M. Burge, Bp. of *Oxford, and, after his death in 1925, of W. *Temple, then Bp. of Manchester. Its terms of reference were 'to consider the nature and grounds of Christian doctrine with a view to demonstrating the extent of existing agreement within the C of E and with a view to investigating how far it is possible to remove or diminish existing differences'.

The body of the Report is in three parts. The first, on 'the Doctrine of God and of Redemption', contains a summary statement of some of the chief elements in the Christian doctrine of God and of the world, followed by detailed discussion of the fact of sin and of the Person and Work of Christ, esp. His Birth and Resurrection. In the second and longest part, which deals with the Church and Sacraments, the Ministry and the Eucharist are the chief subjects of discussion. The third part on Eschatology was added because of the widespread confusion, arising in part from the tendency to interpret literally the apocalyptic symbolism of the NT.

On its presentation to the *Convocations, the Report met with much hostile criticism, partly perhaps through a misunderstanding of its character and purpose. It did not claim to be an authoritative epitome of the doctrine of the C of E, but simply an examination of beliefs actually held. Theological perspectives had also changed since the time when the Commission was appointed.

The Report was repr. in 1982, with new introd. by G. W. H. Lampe, 'The 1938 Report in Retrospect', pp. ix–lx.

Doctrine of the Faith, Congregation of the. See HOLY OFFICE.

Dodd, Charles Harold (1884–1973), NT scholar and theologian. After studying at University College and Mansfield College, Oxford, and at Berlin, Dodd was ordained minister of Warwick *Congregational Church in 1912. In 1915 he was appointed Yates Lecturer in NT at Mansfield College, Oxford, in 1930 Rylands Professor at Manchester, and from 1935 to 1949 he was Norris-Hulse Professor of Divinity at Cambridge. Dodd's earlier works include *The Authority of the Bible* (1928), *The Epistle to the Romans* (*Moffatt NT Comm., 1932) and *The Bible and the Greeks* (1935). In *The Parables of the Kingdom* (1935), *The Apostolic Preaching and its Developments* (1936) and *History of the Gospel* (1938) he put forward his much discussed conception of 'realized eschatology', viz. that the OT promises of, and Christ's authentic words on, the coming of the *Kingdom of God (q.v.) received their realization in the Incarnation and its consequences for mankind. His study on *The Interpretation of the Fourth Gospel* (1953) and *The Historical Tradition in the Fourth Gospel* (Sarum Lectures, 1954–5; pub. 1963) argue that the tradition underlying St John's Gospel has greater claim to historical value than has often been thought. From 1950 Dodd was General Director and from 1965 Joint Director of what was to be the New English Bible (see BIBLE, ENGLISH VERSIONS, 5). He played a major part in the translation of the NT (pub. 1961).

Collections of his essays issued as *New Testament Studies* (Manchester, 1953) and *More New Testament Studies* (ibid., 1968). *The Background of the New Testament and its Eschatology: In Honour of C. H. Dodd*, ed. W. D. Davies and D. Daube (1956), with bibl. of Dodd's works, pp. xiii–xviii. Life by F. W. Dillistone (London, 1977).

Doddridge, Philip (1702–51), *Dissenting divine and hymn-writer. The twentieth child of his parents, after their death he owed much to the Dissenting minister at St Albans, Samuel Clark (1684–1750). Declining an offer from the Duchess of Bedford of university education if he would conform, and against the advice of E. *Calamy, he entered the Dissenting Academy at Kibworth, Leics, under John Jennings, and after Jennings's death in 1723 succeeded him as minister there. In 1729 the Academy was reconstituted at Northampton under Doddridge, who became minister of an important Dissenting congregation in the town. Both in Northampton, where he established a Charity School and was among the founders of the County Infirmary, and more widely, through his writings and his Academy, Doddridge's stature and influence quickly grew. In 1736 he received a DD from the university of Aberdeen. He died prematurely in 1751 at Lisbon, after a breakdown in his health.

'Ordained a presbyter' in 1730 by eight ministers, five of them *Presbyterians, Doddridge early opposed *Calvinist rigidity and throughout his ministry sought to obliterate party lines in the interests of reconciliation and unity; in 1748 he suggested to Abp. T. *Herring an interchange of pulpits between clergy of the C of E and Dissenting ministers. Following his friend and patron I. *Watts, he wrote a large number of hymns, many of which are still in use, e.g. 'O God of Bethel' and 'Hark the glad sound'. Acquainted with the *Wesleys, G. *Whitefield, the Countess of *Huntingdon, and the *Moravian N. L. von *Zinzendorf, he welcomed the first stirrings of the Evangelical Revival both in England and overseas, and was among the pioneers of the modern missionary enterprise. Of his many writings, which comprised sermons, commentaries, devotional pieces, and theological treatises (several of them translated into Dutch), *The Rise and Progress of Religion in the Soul* (1745) is perhaps the most effective.

Works, incl. Memoir by [J.] Orton, in 10 vols. (1802–5) and in 5 vols. (1803–4). J. D. Humphreys (great-grandson, ed.), *The Correspondence and Diary of Philip Doddridge* (5 vols. 1829–31). G. F. Nuttall, *Calendar of the Correspondence of Philip Doddridge, DD* (Historical Manuscripts Commission Joint Publications, 26, and Northampton Record Society, 29; 1979). J. Orton, *Memoirs of the Life, Character and Writings of the late Reverend Philip Doddridge* (1766; ed. D. Russell, 1825). C. Stanford, *Philip Doddridge* (1880). M. Deacon, *Philip Doddridge of Northampton, 1702–51* (Northampton, 1980). G. F. Nuttall (ed.), *Philip Doddridge 1702–51: His Contribution to English Religion* (1951); J. van den Berg and G. F. Nuttall, *Philip Doddridge (1702–1751) and the Netherlands* (Publications of the Sir Thomas Browne Institute, Leiden, NS 8; 1987). A. Gordon in *DNB* 15 (1888), pp. 158–64.

Dodwell, Henry (1641–1711), 'the elder', English theologian. Educated at *Trinity College, Dublin, of which he became a Fellow, he resigned his fellowship in 1666 from reluctance to take holy orders. Settling in London, he soon established a reputation as a patristic scholar; he later edited the posthumous works of J. *Pearson. In 1688 he was appointed Camden praelector of ancient history at Oxford. He contended that the replacement of the *Nonjuring bishops was uncanonical and was deprived of his post in 1691 when he declined to take the Oath of Allegiance. He retired to Shottesbrooke in Berkshire, where for a time the antiquary T. *Hearne was his pupil. In 1710 he rejoined the established Church.

Dodwell was one of the foremost of the Nonjuring apologists. In *A Vindication of the Deprived Bishops* (published anonymously, 1692) he anticipated many of the fears of *Erastianism and heresy that were to be debated in the *Convocation and *Bangorian controversies. His other works include *Separation of Churches from Episcopal Government as practised by the present Nonconformists proved Schismatical* (1679), *Dissertationes Cyprianicae* (1682), *Occasional Communion fundamentally Destructive of the Discipline of the Primitive Catholic Church* (1705), and *A Case in View* (1705), suggesting that when the last of the Nonjuring Bishops died, there would be no reason to maintain the schism.

His son, **Henry Dodwell** 'the younger' (d. 1784), was a *Deist, who secured some notoriety from his *Christianity not founded on Argument* (1742).

F. Brokesby, *The Life of Henry Dodwell, with an Account of his Works* (1715). M. Goldie, 'The Nonjurors, Episcopacy, and the

Origins of the Convocation Controversy', in E. Cruickshanks (ed.), *Ideology and Conspiracy: Aspects of Jacobitism, 1689–1759* (Edinburgh [1982]), pp. 15–35, *passim*. J. H. Overton in *DNB* 15 (1888), pp. 179–82 (on both Dodwells).

dogma (Gk. δόγμα, 'opinion', from δοκεῖν). The original meaning of the word was 'that which seems good', and hence it was applied by classical authors as a technical term either to the distinctive tenets of the various philosophical schools or to the decrees of public authorities. In this second sense it is used in the *Septuagint and the NT, e.g. Dan. 2: 13, Acts 16: 4, Eph. 2: 15, etc., whereas the patristic use developed from the first. 'Dogma', in the Christian sense as opposed to the teachings of the philosophers, soon acquired a definite theological significance. In the accepted Christian meaning the term signifies a religious truth established by Divine Revelation and defined by the Church.

Dold, Alban (1882–1960), liturgical scholar. Born at Villingen in the Black Forest, he was professed at the Benedictine monastery of *Beuron in 1903. He applied himself esp. to the study of liturgical *palimpsests; he elaborated new techniques and extended a photographic process, originally invented by Fr. Raphael Kögel, OSB, for reading difficult texts by fluorescence. By this means he was able to read a number of early liturgical pieces, incl. a *lectionary dating from the 5th or 6th cent. Most of the texts which he recovered were published in the series *Texte und Arbeiten*, which he founded in 1917.

B. Fischer and V. Fiala (eds.), *Colligere Fragmenta: Festschrift A. Dold zum 70. Geburtstag am 7.7.1952* (Texte und Arbeiten, Beiheft 2; 1952), with bibl. [122 items], pp. i–xx; suppl. in K. Gamber, *Sakramentartypen* (Texte und Arbeiten, 49/50; 1958), pp. viii–x. P. Gordan, OSB, 'P. Alban Dold zum Gedächtnis', *Benediktinische Monatschrift*, 36 (1960), pp. 467–70; K. Gamber, 'Kurze Biographie und Bibliographie von Pater Alban Dold OSB', *EL* 75 (1961), pp. 244 f.

Dolling, Robert William Radclyffe, 'Father Dolling' (1851–1902), *Anglo-Catholic missioner. A nephew of William Alexander, who became Abp. of *Armagh, Dolling was an Irishman by birth, though not by descent. Educated at Harrow and Trinity College, Cambridge, in 1878 he came to London, where he soon fell under the influence of A. H. *Stanton at St Alban's, Holborn. Dolling in turn played a seminal part in the religious development of G. *Tyrrell. His work as warden of a fellowship for postmen (the 'St Martin's Postmen's League') earned him the name of 'Brother Bob'. In 1885, two years after his ordination, he was put in charge of St Agatha's, Landport, the Winchester College Mission, where for ten years he fought very successfully against the evils of slum life. The remarkable transformation that was achieved in the parish under his influence is vividly set out in his *Ten Years in a Portsmouth Slum* (1896). Though without any intrinsic interest in ceremonial, he refused to modify his practice where change might seem to imply concession in matters of faith. In consequence, following opposition from R. T. *Davidson, then Bp. of Winchester, he resigned from Landport in 1896. From 1898 till his death he was Vicar of St Saviour's, Poplar.

Life by C. E. Osborne (London, 1903); shorter memoir by J. Clayton (ibid., 1902). W. B. Owen in *DNB, 1901–1911*, 1, pp. 512 f.

Döllinger, Johann Joseph Ignaz von (1799–1890), Bavarian Church historian. Ordained priest in 1822, he was from 1823 to 1826 professor of Church history at Aschaffenburg and from 1826 until 1873 at Munich. At first he held strong *Ultramontane opinions, and his early writings show few signs of the independence which characterized his later work. Contact with the newer tendencies of Church history in other countries, and his friendship with such men as J. H. *Newman and Lord *Acton, gradually aroused his critical sense. Before 1840 he had developed his notion of a German Church free from state control, but in full communion with Rome, and this project he defended in the National Parliament of Frankfurt, as well as in several of his writings, notably his *Reformation* (3 vols., 1845–8) and *Luther* (1851).

In the 1850s he wrote several important works on Church history, among them *Hippolytus und Kallistus* (1853), *Heidenthum und Judenthum* (1857), and *Christentum und Kirche* (1860). He gradually came to be distrustful of Roman influence, and in 1861, in two published lectures, he attacked the temporal power of the Pope, thereby arousing hostility esp. among the *Jesuits. In 1863 he took the leading part at the Congress of Munich, where a liberal form of Catholicism was defended. The publication of the '*Syllabus' in 1864 and the calling of the First *Vatican Council with the avowed intention of suppressing Liberalism further increased his disagreement with Roman policy. The *Letters of *Janus* (in conjunction with others; 1869) and *Letters of *Quirinus* (1869–70) revealed him as a formidable critic of the Council and of the doctrine of *infallibility. After refusing to submit to the Conciliar decisions, he was excommunicated in 1871 by Abp. G. v. Scherr of Munich. In his later years he largely identified himself with the *Old Catholic Churches, and worked for reunion (see BONN REUNION CONFERENCES). As a mark of general esteem, he was appointed in 1873 president of the Bavarian Royal Academy of Sciences in succession to J. von Liebig.

Döllinger's other writings included *Die Papstfabeln des Mittelalters* (1863), *Geschichte der Moralstreitigkeiten in der römisch-katholischen Kirche seit dem 16. Jahrhundert* (2 vols., 1889; with F. H. Reusch) and *Briefe und Erklärungen über die vatikanischen Dekrete* (1890). His publications showed that a background of dogmatic orthodoxy could produce work of no less brilliance and calibre than the destructive criticism of the *Tübingen School. His capacity for work was almost limitless and his personal life simple. He was also a great teacher.

Many of his works have been tr. into Eng. H. Schörs (ed.), *Ignaz von Döllinger's Briefe an eine junge Freundin* (1914). Correspondence with Acton, 1850–1890, ed. V. Conzemius (3 vols., Munich, 1963–71); vol. 4 of correspondence (with Charlotte, Lady Blennerhassett), ed. id. (ibid., 1981). A. Plummer, *Conversations with Dr. Döllinger 1870–1890*, ed. R. Boudens (Bibliotheca Ephemeridum Theologicarum Lovaniensium, 67; 1985). J. *Friedrich, *Ignaz von Döllinger: Sein Leben auf Grund seines schriftlichen Nachlasses* (3 vols., 1899–1901). E. Michael, SJ, 'Döllinger. Ein Charakterbild', *ZKT* 15 (1891), pp. 401–76, 577–666; 16 (1892), pp. 1–81, 193–230, 385–427, rev. and reissued as *Ignaz von Döllinger: Eine Charakteristik* (2nd edn., 1892). L. von Kobell,

Ignaz von Döllinger: Erinnerungen (1891; Eng. tr., 1892). S. Lösch, *Döllinger und Frankreich* (1955). J. Speigl, *Traditionslehre und Traditionsbeweis in der historischen Theologie Ignaz Döllingers* (Beiträge zur neueren Geschichte der katholischen Theologie, 5; Essen, 1964). J. Finsterhölzl, *Die Kirche in der Theologie Ignaz v. Döllingers bis zum ersten Vatikanum* (Studien zur Theologie und Geistesgeschichte des Neunzehnten Jahrhunderts, 9; 1975). W. Brandmüller, *Ignaz v. Döllinger am Vorabend des I. Vatikanums* (Kirchengeschichtliche Quellen und Studien, 9; 1977). Lord Acton, 'Doellinger's Historical Work', *EHR* 5 (1890), pp. 700–44; repr. in *The History of Freedom and Other Essays*, ed. J. N. *Figgis and R. V. Laurence (1907), pp. 375–435. V. Conzemius, 'Aspects ecclésiologiques de l'évolution de Döllinger et du Vieux Catholicisme', *Rev. S.R.* 34 (1960), pp. 247–79. W. Müller in *DHGE* 14 (1960), cols. 553–63, s.v.

DOM, i.e. **Deo Optimo Maximo** (Lat., 'to God, the Best and Greatest'). Originally a pagan formula addressed to Jupiter, it came to be widely used with a Christian application over the doors of churches and on sepulchral monuments. The celebrated temple of Jupiter on the Capitol at *Rome was pre-eminently that to Jupiter 'Optimus Maximus', and this was no doubt the immediate source of the Christian application of the phrase.

Dom (abbreviation of *Dominus*, 'Master'). A title given to professed monks of the *Benedictine, *Cistercian, and *Carthusian orders, as well as to certain *canons regular. In the *Cassinese Congregation of the Benedictines it is also given to novices. The corresponding Italian 'Don' is used in a wider sense, e.g. of Don *Bosco.

Dome of the Rock (Arab. *Kubbet es-Sakhra*). The Muslim shrine in *Jerusalem, built in the area of the Jewish *Temple. It was completed in AD 691/2. The rock from which it takes its name is believed by Muslims to be that from which Muhammad ascended to heaven, and by Jews to be that on which *Abraham prepared to sacrifice *Isaac. Both are also held to be on the site of Araunah the Jebusite's threshing-floor (2 Sam. 24: 18) and of the altar of burnt sacrifice of *Solomon's Temple. The shrine is also known as the 'Mosque of Omar', a name given to it in the belief that it was the work of the second Caliph, Omar (581–644).

R. Hartmann, *Der Felsendom in Jerusalem und seine Geschichte* (Zur Kunstgeschichte des Auslandes, Heft 69; 1909). K. A. C. Creswell, *The Origin and Plan of the Dome of the Rock* (British School of Archaeology in Jerusalem, Supplementary Papers, 2; 1924), with full refs. Id., *A Short Account of Early Muslim Architecture*, rev. J. W. Allan (Aldershot, 1989), pp. 18–42.

Domine quo vadis? (Lat., 'Lord, whither goest thou?'). Acc. to the apocryphal *Acta Petri* (see PETER, ACTS OF), St *Peter was persuaded by the Church towards the end of his life to flee from Rome to escape persecution. Meeting the Lord on the way, he addressed to Him the question 'Domine quo vadis?' and received the answer, 'I go to Rome to be crucified,' whereupon St Peter turned back and gave himself up for crucifixion. Legend connects the incident with the site of the '*Quo Vadis' chapel on the *Appian Way, half a mile from the Porta San Sebastiano.

Dominic, St (*c.*1174–1221), founder of the Order of Friars Preachers, known as the *Dominican Order. Born in Caleruega, Old Castile, he studied arts and theology at

Palencia. During a famine he sold his possessions, including his annotated books, to help the poor. Shortly afterwards he joined the canons at Osma, where the bishop, Martín Bazán (1190–1201), was trying to restore full regular life under the Rule of St *Augustine. By 1201 Dominic was subprior of the community. In 1203–5 he accompanied Diego of Acebes, the new Bp. of Osma, on two embassies to N. Europe; in the course of these he and Diego became interested in missionary work to pagans. *Innocent III refused Diego's request to resign his see, but on their way back to Spain Diego and Dominic became involved in the mission against the *Albigensians. On Diego's advice, a new style of itinerant, mendicant preaching was adopted in imitation of the *Apostles. Dominic became a regular member of the mission, and in 1215 he was put in charge of its new base in Toulouse. With the support of Bp. Fulk of Toulouse he founded a permanent community of preachers there. On the advice of Innocent III, the preachers adopted the Rule of St Augustine, and between 1216 and 1218 they were progressively recognized by *Honorius III as a new religious order, the Order of Preachers. In 1217 Dominic began to disperse his friars to other parts of the world, and they made an important foundation in *Paris, attached to the University. He himself travelled in Italy, Spain, and France, preaching and making foundations. In 1220 he summoned a General Chapter at *Bologna, where the Order's first constitutions were completed; they emphasized the priority of preaching and the good of souls. The second General Chapter was held in 1221; it dispatched groups of Dominicans in all directions, including England.

In addition to the friars, Dominic also laid the foundations of an order of Dominican nuns. From 1207 he was responsible for a community of women established by Diego at Prouille, in Albigensian territory. In 1219 he took charge of a Papal project for establishing a reformed monastery of women at San Sisto, Rome. He also established a house of nuns at Madrid; his only surviving literary work is a letter to this community. He was particularly keen to set up another house in Bologna, though this was not actually founded until 1223.

Dominic was remarkable for the intensity of his zeal for souls and for his dedication to prayer, for his fearlessness, and for his friendliness. His single-minded determination to be a preacher and to send out preachers on the apostolic model made him refuse three bishoprics which he was offered. He is traditionally, but wrongly, held to have instituted the *Rosary. He died on 6 Aug. 1221. He was canonized in 1234. Feast day, 8 Aug.; formerly 5 Aug. until 1558, then 4 Aug. (as still in the ASB).

Gerald de Frachet, OP, *Vitae Fratrum Ordinis Praedicatorum*, ed. B. M. Reichert, OP (Monumenta Ordinis Fratrum Praedicatorum Historica, 1; Rome, 1897); M.-H. Laurent, OP, and others (eds.), *Monumenta Historica Sancti Patris Nostri Dominici*, fasc. 2 (ibid. 16; 1935); V. J. Koudelka, OP, and R. J. Loenertz, OP (eds.), *Monumenta Diplomatica S. Domini* (ibid. 25; 1966). Crit. edn. of 'The Nine Ways of Prayer of St. Dominic' by S. [C. ff.] Tugwell, OP, *Mediaeval Studies*, 47 (1985), pp. 1–124, and of Dominic's letter to the Madrid nuns by id., *Archivum Fratrum Praedicatorum*, 56 (1986), pp. 5–13. Useful Fr. tr. of primary docs. ed. M.-H. Vicaire, OP, *Saint Dominique de Caleruega d'après les documents du XIIIe siècle* (1955; 2nd edn. as *Saint Dominique: La Vie Apostolique*, 1965, and *Saint Dominique et ses Frères: Evangile ou Croisade?*, 1967). Eng. trs. of primary material ed. F. C.

Lehner, OP, *Saint Dominic: Biographical Documents* (Washington, DC, 1964); S. [C. ff.] Tugwell, OP (ed.), *Early Dominicans: Selected Writings* (Classics of Western Spirituality, 1982), pp. 51–119; Jordan of Saxony, OP, *On the Beginnings of the Order of Preachers*, ed. and tr. S. [C. ff.] Tugwell, OP (Dominican Sources [1]; Parable, Ill., and Dublin, 1982). *AASS*, Aug. 1 (1733), pp. 358–658. P. Mandonnet, OP, *Saint Dominique: L'idée, l'homme et l'œuvre* (1921; 2nd edn., much enlarged, with notes by M. H. Vicaire, OP, and R. Ladner, OP, 2 vols. [1937]; Eng. tr., St Louis, 1944); M.-H. Vicaire, OP, *Histoire de saint Dominique* (2 vols., 1957; 3rd edn., rev., 1982; Eng. tr., 1964); id., *Dominique et ses Prêcheurs* (Studia Friburgensia, NS 55; 1977; 2nd edn., 1979). G. Bedouelle [OP], *Dominique ou la Grâce de la Parole* (1982; rev. Ger. tr., *Dominikus: Von der Kraft des Wortes*, 1984; Eng. tr., San Francisco, 1987). V. J. Koudelka [OP], *Dominikus* (Olten and Freiburg, 1983; Eng. tr., 1997). S. [C. ff.] Tugwell, OP, 'Notes on the life of St Dominic', *Archivum Fratrum Praedicatorum*, 65 (1995), pp. 5–169; 66 (1966), pp. 5–200; 67 (1997), pp. 27–59. See also works cited under DOMINICAN ORDER.

Dominica in albis. In the W. Church, the name formerly given to *Low Sunday as that on which those newly baptized at *Easter put aside their white robes. The expression is an abbreviation of 'Dominica in albis deponendis' or 'depositis'. The previous Saturday was correspondingly known as 'Sabbatum in albis'. In 1969 it was designated 'Dominica in Octava Paschae seu Dom. II Paschae'.

Dominical Letter. See SUNDAY LETTER.

Dominican Order (Ordo Praedicatorum, OP), known in Britain also as **Black Friars** (from the black mantle worn over a white habit) and in France as **Jacobins** (from their first house in *Paris, the priory of St Jacques). The Dominicans are officially dedicated to preaching and the good of souls, and from the outset study has occupied a central position. Founded by St *Dominic, the order took definite shape at the General Chapter at *Bologna in 1220. At St Dominic's desire, the order adopted not only individual, but corporate poverty, owning nothing but its actual houses and churches; communities, as well as individual friars, were to be supported only by alms, not by properties or revenues. The order spread rapidly throughout Europe and into Asia, and in the great age of exploration Dominicans followed close upon the Portuguese and Spanish explorers in both the E. and W. hemispheres. During the Reformation and later during successive political upheavals they lost many of their houses and even provinces, but since the revival of the order in the 19th cent. it has again spread throughout the world.

The intellectual side of the order's work expanded greatly during the 13th cent., and a complex educational system was established, culminating in the '*Studia Generalia', usually associated with universities. Several Dominican houses contained public schools of theology. The adaptation of *Aristotle to Christian philosophy was the work esp. of the Dominicans, chiefly St *Albertus Magnus and St *Thomas Aquinas.

Although the Dominicans maintained elements of monastic observance, from the outset they abandoned manual labour, to facilitate preaching and study, and in 1220 they made constitutional provision for an unusually wide use of dispensations from conventual observances. These dispensations and the frequent absence of friars from the community (and slightly later, the setting up of houses where friars could live outside the community), together with the needs of the increasing number of academics in the order, led to a weakening of community life and to a privatizing of the control of funds. The tendency towards laxity of observance was reinforced by indiscriminate recruiting to restore the losses caused by the Black Death. During the 14th cent. there were attempts to reform the order, leading to the eventual establishment of reformed priories and later reformed congregations and provinces. In spite of the constitutional difficulties these posed, the reform succeeded in revitalizing conventual life in the order. But the law of corporate poverty was increasingly found to be unworkable and, after being progressively whittled away, it was finally abolished by *Sixtus IV in 1475, a move which was accepted even by most of the Dominican reformers.

The constitutional government of the order has been much admired, and it has been claimed that it influenced the development of *Convocation and even of Parliament in England and the Constitution of the USA. There is a balance between central government, under the Master of the Order and a bi-cameral system of General Chapters, and local government in the provinces and priories. All superiors are now elected for fixed terms of office.

In the Middle Ages the Dominicans were used extensively by the Papacy for such missions as the preaching of *Crusades, the collecting of monetary levies, visitations, diplomatic missions, and, in many places, the *Inquisition. They were also used by secular rulers and provided many royal confessors.

There are also cloistered nuns (the Second Order) and fraternities of lay Dominicans (the *Third Order (q.v.) or Tertiaries) under the jurisdiction of the Master of the Order; together with the numerous autonomous *congregations of Dominican sisters engaged in various active works, and 12 Secular *Institutes, these form the non-juridical 'Dominican Family'.

Works of individual Dominican writers in J. Quétif, OP, and J. Echard, OP, Scriptores Ordinis Praedicatorum Recensiti (2 vols., Paris, 1719–21); a continuation covering the period 1701–50 was compiled by R. Coulon, OP, and A. Papillon, OP (12 parts, Paris and Rome, 1910–34); T. Kaeppeli, OP, Scriptores Ordinis Praedicatorum Medii Aevi (4 vols., Rome, 1970–93). A. Walz, OP, Compendium Historiae Ordinis Praedicatorum (Rome, 1930; 2nd edn., 1948); W. A. Hinnebusch, OP, The History of the Dominican Order [to 1500] (2 vols., Staten Island, NY [1966–73]); A. D'Amato, OP, L'Ordine dei Frati Predicatori (Rome [1983]); B. M. Ashley, OP, The Dominicans (Collegeville, Minn. [1990]). A. H. Thomas, OP, De Oudste Constituties van de Dominicanen (Bibliothèque de la RHE, 42; 1965 [with resumé in Fr.]). W. R. Bonniwell, OP, A History of the Dominican Liturgy (New York, 1944); A. Gonzalez Fuente, OP, La Vida Liturgica en la Orden de Predicadores (Institutum Historicum FF. Praedicatorum Romae ad S. Sabinae, Dissertationes Historicae, 20; 1981). Bede Jarrett, OP, The English Dominicans (1921; rev. and abridged by W. Gumbley, OP, 1937), S. [C. ff.] Tugwell, OP (ed.), Early Dominicans: Selected Writings [in Eng. tr.] (Classics of Western Spirituality, 1982). W. A. Hinnebusch, OP, The Early English Friars Preachers (Institutum Historicum FF. Praedicatorum Romae ad S. Sabinae, Dissertationes Historicae, 14; Rome, 1951). B. Smalley, English Friars and Antiquity in the Early Fourteenth Century (Oxford, 1960). G. Anstruther, OP, A Hundred Homeless Years: English Dominicans 1558–1658 (1958). W. Gumbley, OP, Obituary Notices of the English Dominicans from 1552 to 1952 (1955). B. *Altaner, Die Dominikanermissionen des 13. Jahrhunderts (Breslauer Studien zur historischen Theologie, 3; Habelschwerdt, 1924); W. J. Loedding, OP, Die schwarz-weisse Legion: Missionsgeschichte des Domini-

kanerordens (Cologne, 1974); M. A. Medina, OP, Una Comunidad al Servicio del Indio: La Obra de Fr. Pedro de Cordoba, OP (1482–1521) (Madrid, 1983). M. Andrés Martín, Los Recogidos: Nueva visión de la mística española (1500–1700) (1975), pp. 392–449 ('Trayectoria del Recogimiento entre los Dominicos'). G. G. Meersseman [OP] and G. P. Pagini, Ordo Fraternitatis: Confraternite e Pietà dei Laici nel Medioevo (Italia Sacra, 24–6; 1977), pp. 578–1270 ('Le Antiche Confraternite Domenicane', i.e. vol. 2 and part of vol. 3). Monumenta Ordinis Praedicatorum (Rome, 1897 ff.). Dominican Sources: New Editions in English (Parable, Ill., and Dublin, 1982 ff.). Archivum Fratrum Praedicatorum (Rome, 1931 ff.). There are also a number of series and journals issued in different provinces. P. Mandonnet, OP, in DTC 6 (1920), cols. 863–924, s.v. 'Frères Prêcheurs'; A. Duval, OP, in Catholicisme, ed. G. Jacquemet and others, 3 (1952), cols. 984–93, s.v. 'Dominicaines'; id. and P. M. Gy, OP, ibid. 4 (1956), cols. 1618–28, s.v. 'Frères Prêcheurs'; H.-D. Simonin, OCR, and others in Dict. Sp. 5 (1964), cols. 1422–524, s.v. 'Frères Prêcheurs'; W. A. Hinnebusch, OP, in NCE 4 (1967), pp. 971–82, s.vv. 'Dominican Spirituality' and 'Dominicans'; H.-M. Vicaire, OP, and A. Duval, OP, in DHGE 18 (1977), cols. 1369–426, s.v. 'Frères Prêcheurs'. See also bibl. to DOMINIC, ST.

Dominis, Marco Antonio de. See DE DOMINIS, MARCO ANTONIO.

Dominus ac Redemptor. The brief of *Clement XIV of 21 July 1773, which suppressed the *Jesuit Order. It was issued mainly at the instigation of Joseph Moniño, the Spanish ambassador, to whom it probably owes most of its provisions. As its execution was left mainly to the local bishops, the treatment meted out to the Jesuits varied widely in different localities.

Text in A. Barbèri and A. Spetia (eds.), Bullarii Romani Continuatio, 4 (Rome, 1841), pp. 607–18; the main clauses are repr. in Mirbt, pp. 404–11 (no. 546), with refs. See also works cited under JESUITS.

Dominus vobiscum. A Latin liturgical salutation, meaning 'The Lord be with you', to which the response is Et cum spiritu tuo, 'And with thy spirit'. Both formulae are probably as old as Christianity. The salutation occurs in Ruth 2: 4; the closest scriptural approximation to the response is in 2 Tim. 4: 22. Both the salutation and response are found in the *Apostolic Tradition of St *Hippolytus.

It was the subject of a short treatise by St *Peter Damian, pr. in J. P. Migne, PL 145. 231–52. W. C. van Unnik, 'Dominus vobiscum: The Background of a Liturgical Formula', in A. J. B. Higgins (ed.), New Testament Essays: Studies in Memory of Thomas Walter Manson (Manchester, 1959), pp. 270–305. H. Ashworth, OSB, 'Et cum spiritu tuo. An Inquiry into its Origin and Meaning', Clergy Review, 51 (1966), pp. 122–30. F. J. van Beeck, SJ, 'A Note on Two Liturgical Greetings and the People's Reply', EL 103 (1989), pp. 519–22. Jungmann (ed. 1958), i, pp. 463–9; Eng. tr., i, pp. 361–6. A. Heinz in L. Th. K. (3rd edn.,) 3 (1995), col. 324, s.v.

Domitian, Titus Flavius (AD 51–96), Roman Emp. from 81. The son of Vespasian, he succeeded his brother Titus. He was assassinated in 96. Roman historians ranked him as a tyrant; Christian tradition (*Eusebius, HE 3. 13 ff.) held him to have been a persecutor, a view prob. confirmed by I Clement 7. Under his successor, Trajan, being a Christian was already a capital offence, but this may have been the case continuously since *Nero. Acc. to a very widespread tradition, it was during Domitian's reign that the Apostle *John, in exile at *Patmos, received the revelations recorded in the Apocalypse. See also the following entry and PERSECUTIONS, EARLY CHRISTIAN.

The principal authorities include *Suetonius, 'Domitianus' in *De Vita Caesarum*, 8; Dio Cassius, *Hist. Rom.* 67 (ed., with Eng. tr. by E. Cary, Loeb edn. 8, 1925, pp. 316–59); and Eusebius, *HE* 3. 13–20. A. Garzetti, *From Tiberius to the Antonines* (rev. Eng. tr., 1974), pp. 265–95, with bibl. pp. 645–58, 750 f. and 754 f. B. W. Jones, *The Emperor Domitian* (1992). E. M. Smallwood, 'Domitian's Attitude toward the Jews and Judaism', *Classical Philology*, 51 (1956), pp. 1–13; P. Keresztes, 'The Jews, the Christians, and the Emperor Domitian', *VC* 27 (1973), pp. 1–28. See also bibl. s.v. PERSECUTIONS, EARLY CHRISTIAN.

Domitilla, Flavia (d. *c.* AD 100), Roman matron of the Imperial family, regarded since the 4th cent. as a Christian martyr. She was the daughter of the Emp. Vespasian (reigned 69–79) and married to Titus Flavius Clemens, *Domitian's cousin. Domitian banished her to the island of Pandateria when he put Clemens to death in 95. Acc. to the Roman historian Dio Cassius, both were accused of 'atheism', a charge which has sometimes been thought to imply either Judaism or Christianity. Domitilla is specifically said to have suffered as a Christian by *Eusebius; Clemens is not so described until some 400 years later by *George Syncellus. Both claims are open to serious doubt, though the 'Coemeterium Domitillae' on the Via Ardeatina outside Rome was used in her time as a place of burial by Christians, presumably of her household. See also GLABRIO and NEREUS AND ACHILLEUS, STS.

Dio Cassius, *Hist.* 67. 14; Eusebius, *HE* 3. 18. 4, and *Chron.* Dom. 16; George Syncellus, *Chronographia*, ed. W. Dindorf, p. 650. *Prosopographia Imperii Romani*, 3 (2nd edn., Berlin and Leipzig, 1943), pp. 142 f. (no. 240), s.v. 'Flavius Clemens', and pp. 188 f. (no. 418), s.v. 'Flavia Domitilla'. E. M. Smallwood, 'Domitian's Attitude toward the Jews and Judaism', *Classical Philology*, 51 (1956), pp. 1–13; P. Keresztes, 'The Jews, the Christians, and the Emperor Domitian', *VC* 27 (1973), pp. 1–28. H. *Leclercq, OSB, in *DACL* 4 (1921), cols. 1401–42, svv. 'Domitille (Flavie)' and 'Domitille (Cimetière de)'. See also works cited under PERSECUTIONS, EARLY CHRISTIAN.

Donatello (*c.*1385/6–1466) **(Donato di Niccolò di Betto Bardi)**, Italian sculptor. He was born and died in Florence, and worked on its cathedral on and off for 30 years. In contrast to his contemporaries Lorenzo Ghiberti (under whom he briefly worked), Fra *Angelico, or Luca *della Robbia (who also worked on the cathedral), he realized that Christian pathos can be expressed by distortion and ugliness, and that physical and spiritual beauty are not the same; his ravaged *Magdalen* (*c.*1455; Florence, Baptistery) and to a lesser degree his *St John the Baptist* (1438; Venice, Frari) or the *Baptist* (*c.*1457; Siena Cathedral), all have an emotional impact far greater than that of their usual gentle imagery. His previous study, in Rome, of later antique and early Christian art—esp. portraits and *sarcophagi—taught him to use dramatic gesture and strong characterization, which he combined with the perspective then being evolved by his friend Filippo Brunelleschi. His low reliefs, such as the *Ascension, with the Giving of the Keys* (London, Victoria and Albert Museum) or *Herod presented with the Head of the Baptist* (1427; Siena, Baptistery) exploit perspective, as do the reliefs for the High Altar in the Basilica of St Antony

at Padua (1443–*c.*1450; the altar has since been reconstructed). His works in Padua (his headquarters, 1443–53) were decisive in the formation of the Paduan and Venetian schools of painting, influencing esp. A. *Mantegna and Giovanni Bellini. Every later sculptor, including *Michelangelo, was deeply indebted to him.

H. W. Janson, *The Sculpture of Donatello* (2 vols., Princeton, NJ, 1957). Other studies by G. Castelfranco (Florence [1981]), M. Greenhalgh (London, 1982), and B. A. Bennett and D. G. Wilkins (Oxford, 1984).

Donation of Constantine (Constitutum or Donatio Constantini). A document which was fabricated in the second half of the 8th cent. (perhaps in the interests of the church of St Saviour at the *Lateran, or possibly in the curia of Pope *Stephen II), and certainly before *c.*850, when it was incorporated in the *False Decretals. It purports to be a record by the Emp. *Constantine of his conversion, the profession of his new faith, and the privileges he conferred upon Pope *Sylvester I (314–35), his clergy, and their successors. These included primacy over all other Churches, particularly those of *Antioch, *Alexandria, *Constantinople, and *Jerusalem, and dominion over Rome and 'all the provinces, places, and *civitates* of Italy and the Western regions'. The Pope was also made supreme judge of the clergy, the chief of whom were to have the rank of Senators, and he was even offered the Imperial crown (which, however, he refused). These grants were prob. first used to support the universal claims of the Papacy in a letter written in 1053 by *Leo IX to *Michael Cerularius, and were frequently cited for the same purpose by his successors. The effect of the Donation, and even its authenticity, were occasionally challenged earlier, but its falsity was demonstrated in the 15th cent. by *Nicholas of Cusa, Bp. R. *Pecock, and L. *Valla.

Crit. edn. by H. Fuhrmann (*MGH*, Fontes Iuris Germanici Antiqui in Usum Scholarum, 10; 1968). Eng. tr., omitting the profession of faith, in S. Z. Ehler and J. B. Morrall (eds.), *Church and State through the Centuries* (1954), pp. 15–22. D. Maffei, *La Donazione di Constantino nei giuristi medievali* (Milan, 1964), with bibl. T. F. X. Noble, *The Republic of St Peter: The Birth of the Papal State, 680–825* (Philadelphia [1964]), pp. 134–7, with bibl. to date. W. Levison, 'Konstantinische Schenkung und Silvester-Legende', *Miscellanea Francesco Ehrle*, 2 (ST 38; 1924), pp. 159–247, repr. in Levison's *Aus rheinischer und fränkischer Frühzeit* (1948), pp. 390–465. H. Fuhrmann, *Einfluss und Verbreitung der pseudoisidorischen Fälschungen*, 2 (Schriften der *MGH*, 24/2; 1973), pp. 354–407, with refs. N. Huyghebaert, 'Une légende de fondation: le *Constitutum Constantini*', *Moyen Âge*, 85 (1979), pp. 177–209. H. Fuhrmann in *TRE* 8 (1981), pp. 196–202, s.v. 'Constitutum Constantini' with full refs., esp. to his own earlier papers; J. Van Engen in *Dictionary of the Middle Ages*, 4 [1984], pp. 257–9, s.v.; H. Fuhrmann in *Lexikon des Mittelalters*, 5 (1991), cols. 1385–7, s.v. 'Konstantinische Schenkung'.

Donatism. The Donatists were a schismatic body in the African Church who became divided from the Catholics through their refusal to accept *Caecilian, Bp. of Carthage (consecrated most prob. in 311), on the ground that his consecrator, Felix of Aptunga, had been a *traditor* during the *Diocletianic *persecution. The Numidian bishops, supporting the objectors, consecrated Majorinus as a rival to Caecilian, and he was soon afterwards succeeded by Donatus, from whom the schism is named.

A commission under *Miltiades, Bp. of Rome, investigated the dispute in 313. It decided against the Donatists, who thereupon appealed unsuccessfully, first to the Synod of *Arles (314) and then to the Emperor (316). But the schism prospered, for theologically (with doubtful justification) it claimed St *Cyprian's authority, while politically it drew upon African regional feeling, since the Catholics were supported by Rome. It also relied upon Numidian jealousy of Carthage and on economic unrest. The Emperor began coercion in 316, but abandoned it in 321. When, later, the Donatist leaders associated themselves with violent bands of marauders, called *circumcelliones, state repression began again (347) under Constans, but was relaxed under *Julian (361–3).

The theological attack on the Donatists was led first by St *Optatus, and later by St *Augustine. The efforts of their own more moderate supporters, such as the orator *Tyconius, probably did more harm than good to their cause. In 405 the state again intervened against them, and at a large conference at Carthage in 411 the Imperial commissioner pronounced finally against Donatism. The schism, though greatly weakened, persisted until the African Church was destroyed by the Arabs in the 7th–8th cent.

Theologically the Donatists were rigorists, holding that the Church of the saints must remain 'holy' (cf. *Novatianism), and that sacraments conferred by traditores were invalid. Apart from their denial that Felix of Aptunga was in fact a traditor, the Church maintained that the unworthiness of the minister did not affect the *validity of sacraments, since, as Augustine insisted, their true minister was Christ. The Donatists, on the other hand, went so far as to assert that all those who communicated with traditores were infected, and that, since the Church is one and holy, the Donatists alone formed the Church. Converts to Donatism were rebaptized, a proceeding repeatedly condemned by orthodox synods.

The chief sources are Optatus, *De Schismate Donatistarum* (c.368), and the anti-Donatist writings of Augustine (edn. Ben., vol. 9). Useful introd. by Y. M.-J. *Congar to the anti-Donatist writings in the edn. of Augustine pub. under the direction of the Études augustiniennes, Œuvres de Saint Augustin, 28 (1963), pp. 9–133, with refs. Collection of docs. in Fr. tr. by J.-L. Maier, *Le Dossier du Donatisme* (TU 134–5; 1987–9). P. Monceaux, *Histoire littéraire de l'Afrique chrétienne*, 4–6 (1912–22). G. G. Willis, *Saint Augustine and the Donatist Controversy* (1950). W. H. C. Frend, *The Donatist Church: A Movement of Protest in Roman North Africa* (1952), with useful preface to 3rd printing (1985), pp. v–vii. S. L. Greenslade, *Schism in the Early Church* (1953; 2nd edn., 1964), passim. J. P. Brisson, *Autonomisme et Christianisme dans l'Afrique romaine de Septime Sévère à l'invasion vandale* (1958). E. Tengström, *Donatisten und Katholiken: soziale, wirtschaftliche und politische Aspekte einer nordafrikanischen Kirchenspaltung* (Studia Graeca et Latina Gothoburgensia, 18; 1964). R. Crespin, *Ministère et sainteté: Pastorale du clergé et solution de la crise donatiste dans la vie et la doctrine de saint Augustin* (1965). B. Kriegbaum, *Kirche der Traditoren oder Kirche der Märtyrer? Die Vorgeschichte des Donatismus* (Innsbrucker theologische Studien, 16; 1986). P. [R. L.] Brown, 'Christianity and Local Culture in Late Roman Africa', *Journal of Roman Studies*, 58 (1968), pp. 85–95, repr. in id., *Religion and Society in the Age of Saint Augustine* (1972), pp. 279–300, with other relevant arts., pp. 237–78 and 301–31. A. Schindler in *TRE* 1 (1977), pp. 654–68, s.v. 'Afrika I. 3. 4: Der Donatismus', with bibl. pp. 690–700.

Donne, John (1571/2–1631), *Metaphysical poet and

Dean of *St Paul's. He was a member of a RC family, his mother being the sister of the *Jesuit missionary priest Jasper Heywood, and a granddaughter of a sister of Sir Thomas *More. He entered Hart Hall, Oxford, in 1584 and possibly studied after this at Cambridge, or perhaps abroad. He entered Thavies Inn in 1591 and transferred to Lincoln's Inn in 1592. During this period he was much exercised over the problem of his religious allegiance and for a time, according to I. *Walton, 'betrothed himself to no Religion that might give him any other denomination than *a Christian*'. By 1598 he had certainly conformed to the Church of England. In 1596 he accompanied Essex and Raleigh to Cadiz and in 1597 to the Azores; and in 1598 became private secretary to the Lord Keeper, Sir Thomas Egerton, a post from which he was dismissed four years later owing to his secret marriage to Ann More, his master's wife's niece, in 1601. During the next years he and his growing family lived in poverty and dependence on the charity of friends. He found employment in controversial writing and in 1610 wrote the *Pseudo-Martyr* to persuade Catholics that they might take the Oath of Allegiance. In the next year he wrote a witty satire on the Jesuits, *Ignatius his Conclave*. Around this period he composed but did not publish *Biathanatos*, a casuistic discussion and defence of suicide. After repeated failures to find secular employment he at last complied with the wish of the King and was ordained in 1615. The reason he himself gave for delay was scruple at accepting orders as a means of making a living. In 1621 he became Dean of St Paul's, where he preached on all great festivals. He was also a regular preacher at court and a favourite with both James and Charles. During a serious illness in 1623 he wrote his *Devotions upon Emergent Occasions* (1624), and the famous 'Hymn to God the Father'. He died in 1631 and was buried in St Paul's. His monument, showing him standing in his shroud, survived the Great Fire. In the American BCP (1979), feast day, 31 Mar.

Donne's secular poetry was mainly written in his youth: satires, love-elegies, and lyrics, though the date of these last is questionable. His religious poetry belongs mostly to his troubled and unhappy middle years of poverty and discouragement. After his ordination his genius found expression in preaching. His fame as a poet suffered eclipse after the Restoration but had a striking revival in the 20th century. His vigorous, dramatic style, his capacity for introspection, and the subtle blend of argument and passion in his love poems and religious poems attracted poets in revolt against the Romantic tradition, most notably T. S. *Eliot. His sermons are masterpieces of the old formal style of preaching, packed with patristic learning and adorned with brilliant images and striking rhetorical effects, but his great strength is as a moral theologian, preaching as a sinner who has found mercy to other sinners. Although the contrast between Jack Donne, the youthful rake, and Dr John Donne, the divine, has been overdrawn, there is no doubt that he was haunted by an intense consciousness of the gravity of sin as he was by the thought of physical death. His great theme as a love-poet was the bliss of union; his great theme as a preacher was God's mercy. Both themes are given singular force coming from one who wrote so often of a love that was 'rage' and not 'peace'; and knew in experience the meaning of working out one's salvation with fear and trembling.

Poems, orig. pub. 1633; enlarged edn., 1635; modern edns. of *Divine Poems* by H. Gardner (Oxford, 1952; 2nd edn., 1978); *Elegies and Songs and Sonnets*, ed. id. (ibid., 1965); *Epithalamions, Anniversaries, and Epicedes*, ed. W. Milgate (ibid., 1978); *Satires, Epigrams, and Verse Letters*, ed. id. (ibid., 1967). There are separate modern edns. of *Biathanatos* (pr. 1644, pub. 1647) by M. Rudick and M. P. Battin (New York, 1982) and E. W. Sullivan (Newark, Del., etc. [1984]); of *Ignatius His Conclave* by T. S. Healy, SJ (Oxford, 1969), and *Essays in Divinity* (orig. pub. 1651) by E. Simpson (ibid., 1952); facsimile repr. of *Pseudo-Martyr* (Delmar, NY, 1974). Collections of *LXXX Sermons* (1640), *Fifty Sermons* (1649), and *XXVI Sermons* (1660); modern edns. of *Sermons* by G. R. Potter and E. M. Simpson (10 vols, Berkeley and Los Angeles, Calif., 1953–62); of *Sermons on the Psalms and Gospels, with a Selection of Prayers and Meditations* by E. M. Simpson (ibid., 1963); of *Prebend Sermons* by J. M. Mueller (Cambridge, Mass., 1971). Modern edns. of *Devotions upon Emergent Occasions* by A. Raspa (Montreal and London, 1975) and E. Savage, SSJ (Salzburg Studies in English Literature, Elizabethan & Renaissance Studies, 21–2; 1975). Donne's *Letters to Several Persons of Honour* were pub. in 1651, and a further *Collection of Letters* made by Sir Tobie Mathews (1660). *Life* by I. Walton (1640, successively enlarged 1658, 1670, and 1675); modern Life by R. C. Bald (Oxford, 1970). W. R. Mueller, *John Donne: Preacher* (Princeton, NJ, and London, 1962); W. Schleiner, *The Imagery of John Donne's Sermons* (Providence, RI, 1970); B. A. Doebler, *The Quickening Seed: Death in the Sermons of John Donne* (Salzburg Studies in English Literature, Elizabethan & Renaissance Studies, 30; 1974); J. S. Chamberlin, *Increase and Multiply: Arts-of-Discourse Procedure in the Preaching of John Donne* (Chapel Hill, NC, 1976); J. Carey, *John Donne: Life, Mind and Art* (1981; 2nd edn., 1990); M. T. Hester, *Kinde Pitty and Brave Scorn: John Donne's Satyres* (Durham, NC, 1982); P. G. Stanwood and H. [A.] R. Asals, *John Donne and the Theology of Language* (Columbia, Mo., 1986). A. J. Smith (ed.), *John Donne: The Critical Heritage* (1975). T. D. Reeves (ed.), *An Annotated Index to the Sermons of John Donne* (Salzburg Studies in English Literature, Elizabethan & Renaissance Studies, 95; 3 vols., 1979–81). G. [L.] Keynes, *A Bibliography of Dr John Donne* (Publications of the Baskerville Club, 2; 1914; 4th edn., Oxford, 1973); J. R. Roberts, *John Donne: An Annotated Bibliography of Modern Criticism, 1912–1967* (University of Missouri Studies, 60; 1973); id., *John Donne: An Annotated Bibliography of Modern Criticism, 1968–78* (Columbia, Mo., and London, 1982); R. D. Dunn and J. Horder in *NCBEL* 1 (1974), cols. 1169–86.

doorkeeper. The doorkeepers, or *ostiarii*, constituted the lowest of the *Minor Orders of the W. Church. Their functions, as stated in the *Pontifical, were similar to those of the modern verger; in antiquity they were particularly responsible for excluding unauthorized persons from attending the Eucharist. The order, which was probably established at Rome during the first half of the 3rd cent., is first attested in a letter of Pope *Cornelius written in 251. It is no longer recognized in the E. Churches, though doorkeepers (θυρωροί) are mentioned in the canons of *Laodicea (can. 24). In the RC Church the office was abolished in 1972.

A. Michel in *DTC* 12 (pt. 2; 1935), cols. 2600–2, s.v. 'Portier', with bibl.; H. *Leclercq, OSB, in *DACL* 14 (pt. 2; 1948), cols. 1525–33, s.v. 'Portier'; A. Piolanti in *EC* 9 (1952), cols. 435–7, s.v. 'Ostiariato'.

Dorchester, Oxon. Originally a Roman station, it was conquered by the West Saxons *c.*560. In 635 St *Oswald, King of Northumbria, and Cynegils, King of the West Saxons, concurred in establishing it as a see, with St *Birinus as bishop. The diocese covered an area stretching

from Dorset to Bucks and from Surrey to the Severn, part of which was for centuries disputed between the kingdoms of Wessex and Mercia. In later pre-Conquest times the diocese extended north to the Humber. About 1072–3, when the importance of the place had declined, Bp. Remigius, formerly a monk of Fécamp (consecrated 1067, d. 1092), transferred the see to *Lincoln. In 1140 Alexander, Bp. of Lincoln, founded an abbey of *Augustinian Canons, which was suppressed in 1536. By the 16th cent. the abbey church was the only notable feature of the village. In 1939 the Bishopric of Dorchester was re-created suffragan to *Oxford. Until 1956 it was held in conjunction with the Archdeaconry of Oxford.

J. H. Parker (ed.), *The History of Dorchester, Oxfordshire, British Earthworks—Roman Camp—Bishopric, and the Architectural History of the Church* (Oxford, 1882). J. Cook and T. Rowley (eds.), *Dorchester through the Ages* (ibid., 1985), with bibl.

Dordrecht, Synod of. See DORT, SYNOD OF.

Dormition of the BVM. In the E. Church, the Feast of the Falling Asleep (*dormitio*) of the Blessed Virgin, corresponding to the *Assumption in the West. It is observed on 15 Aug. and accounted one of the *Twelve Great Feasts. See also ASSUMPTION OF THE BVM.

Dorner, Isaak August (1809–84), German *Lutheran theologian. The son of a Lutheran pastor, he was educated at *Tübingen. He became professor of theology successively at Tübingen in 1838, at Kiel in 1839, at Königsberg in 1843, at Bonn in 1847, at Göttingen in 1853, and finally at Berlin in 1862. In theology he sought to interpret the *Kantian and post-Kantian systems in terms of the traditional Lutheran faith. He also took a prominent part in the ecclesiastical life of his time. The best known of his many writings was his treatise on the history of the doctrine of the Person of Christ, first published in 1839 (Eng. tr. in 5 vols., 1861–9). In 1867 he issued his *Geschichte der protestantischen Theologie* (Eng. tr., 2 vols., 1871). He was the founder, and for many years the editor, of the *Jahrbücher für deutsche Theologie* (1856 ff.).

His son, **August Dorner** (1846–1920), later became a distinguished theologian, holding professorial chairs at *Wittenberg and Königsberg.

I. A. Dorner's *System der christlichen Sittenlehre* was pub. posthumously by A. Dorner (1885); Eng. trs. by C. M. Mead and R. T. Cunningham (1887) and of extracts by C. Welch, *God and Incarnation in Mid-Nineteenth Century German Theology* (New York, 1965), pp. 115–284, both with introd. Correspondence of H. L. *Martensen, Bp. of Zealand, with I. A. Dorner (2 vols., Berlin, 1888). I. Bobertag, *Isaak August Dorner* (Gütersloh, 1906). J. Rothermundt, *Personale Synthese: Isaak August Dorners dogmatische Methode* (Forschungen zur systematischen und ökumenischen Theologie, 19 [1968]). C. Axt-Piscalar, *Der Grund des Glaubens: Eine theologiegeschichtliche Untersuchung zum Verhältnis von Glaube und Trinität in der Theologie Isaak August Dorners* (Beiträge zur Historischen Theologie, 79; 1990). J. Rothermundt in *TRE* 9 (1982), pp. 155–8, s.v. On August Dorner, W. Herms, ibid., pp. 150–5.

Dorotheus, St (6th cent.), ascetical writer. He entered a Palestinian monastery near Gaza, where he came under the influence of *Barsanuphius and *Evagrius, and *c.*540 he founded a monastery of his own, also near Gaza, of which he became *archimandrite. For the use of its members he wrote a series of 'Instructions' (Διδασκαλίαι Ψυχωφελεῖς) on the religious life, though not all the 24 items in the edition made in the 9th cent. are by Dorotheus himself. A number of letters also survive, and modern editors regard some of the traditional 'Instructions' as letters. In his spiritual doctrine Dorotheus gives an exceptionally high place to humility, not only maintaining that it was the cement of all other virtues but even putting it above love. His writings are an important source for earlier ascetic writers ('fathers'), on whose doctrines he frequently draws. They were highly esteemed by A. J. de *Rancé, who translated them into French for use by his *Trappists.

Works attributed to Dorotheus repr. from A. *Gallandi in J. P. Migne, *PG* 88. 1611–842. Modern edn., with Fr. tr., by L. Regnault, OSB, and J. de Préville, OSB (SC 92; 1963). Eng. tr. of [21] 'Instructions' entitled *Discourses and Sayings* by E. P. Wheeler (Cistercian Studies, 33; 1977), with introd. *CPG* 3 (1979), pp. 373–7 (nos. 7352–60). Altaner and Stuiber (1978), pp. 519 and 660. J. M. Szymusiak, SJ, and J. Leroy, OSB, in *Dict. Sp.* 3 (1957), cols. 1651–64, s.v. 'Dorothée (Saint)'.

Dorothy, St, also **Dorothea**, virgin and martyr. *Eusebius mentions a Christian lady of *Alexandria exiled in the *persecution under *Diocletian, whose name *Rufinus gives as Dorothea in his translation (*HE* 8. 14. 15). The '*Hieronymian Martyrology' commemorates a virgin and martyr called Dorothea, who is usually taken to be the same person, together with a 'Theophilus'. Acc. to the later legendary *Acta* she was martyred at Caesarea in Cappadocia; on her way to martyrdom a young lawyer, Theophilus, mocked her, asking her to send him fruits from the garden to which she was going. At the place of execution she knelt to pray, when an angel appeared with a basket of apples and roses, which she sent to Theophilus. When he had tasted of the fruit he, too, became a Christian and a martyr. Her martyrdom was made the subject of one of the charming *Sieben Legenden* of Gottfried Keller, the Swiss novelist. Feast day, 6 Feb., suppressed in 1969.

Discussion and text of 'Acta ex tribus MSS codicibus' in *AASS*, Feb. 1 (1658), pp. 772–6. Further recensions listed in *BHL* 1 (1898–9), pp. 349 f. (nos. 2321–5), and *Novum Supplementum* (1986), pp. 286 f. G. Keller, *Sieben Legenden* (1872), pp. 123–35. R. Van Doren in *DHGE* 14 (1960), col. 684, s.v. 'Dorothée (1)'; A. Amore and M. C. Celletti in *Bibliotheca Sanctorum*, 4 (1964), cols. 820–6, s.v.

dorsal (also **dossal**). A piece of cloth, often embroidered, which is sometimes hung at the back of an altar in place of a *reredos. It is apparently a survival of the curtains which in earlier times were hung between the four columns of the *ciborium.

Dort, Synod of (1618–19). The assembly of the Dutch Reformed Church, convened at Dort (Dordrecht) by the States-General to deal with the *Arminian Controversy. Although primarily a national gathering of Dutch theologians, several foreign delegates from Switzerland, the Palatinate, Great Britain, and other states took part; the British delegation comprised G. Carleton (Bp. of *Llandaff), J. *Hall (following illness replaced by T. Goad), J. Davenant, S. Ward, and W. Balcanquall. The Synod, which met in 154 formal sessions, sat from

13 Nov. 1618 to 9 May 1619, though the Arminians ('*Remonstrants'), led by S. *Episcopius, were not introduced till 6 Dec. 1618. The most important decision taken before their arrival was that which approved the proposal for an official Dutch translation of the Bible. John Bogerman of Leeuwarden, a strict *Calvinist, was elected president. The Synod, supported by Prince Maurice of Orange, was biased against Arminianism from the start and its decisions were a foregone conclusion. Five sets of articles passed on 23 Apr. 1619 asserted: (1) unconditional election, (2) a limited atonement, (3) the total depravity of man, (4) the irresistibility of grace, and (5) the final perseverance of the saints. At a final session on 9 May 1619 the Synod drew up 93 canonical rules and confirmed the authority of the *Belgic Confession and the *Heidelberg Catechism. This victory for Calvinist principles led to some 200 Remonstrant clergy being deprived, H. *Grotius being sentenced by the States-General to perpetual imprisonment, and J. van Oldenbarnevelt, the aged Advocate of Holland, being beheaded on a false charge of high treason.

Lat. text of canons, orig. pub. 6 May 1619, pr. in P. *Schaff, *The Creeds of Christendom*, 3 (1877), pp. 550–80, with abridged Eng. tr., pp. 581–97; introd. in vol. 1 (1877), pp. 512–15. H. H. Kuyper, *De Post acta . . . van de Nationale Synode van Dordrecht* (Amsterdam [1899]); H. Kaajan, *De Pro-acta der Dordtsche Synode in 1618* (Rotterdam, 1914). Id., *De groote Synode van Dordrecht in 1618–1619* (Amsterdam [1918]). A. W. Harrison, *The Beginnings of Arminianism to the Synod of Dort* (1926), pp. 300–83. P. Y. De Jong (ed.), *Crisis in the Reformed Churches: Essays in Commemoration of the Great Synod of Dort, 1618–1619* (Grand Rapids, 1968). N. Tyacke, *Anti-Calvinists: The Rise of English Arminianism c.1590–1640* (Oxford Historical Monographs, 1987), pp. 87–105.

dorter. A dormitory, esp. in a monastery. It was sometimes of great length, e.g. that at *Durham (1398–1404) 194 ft. long (now a library and museum). From Norman times, and possibly earlier, it was usually on the first floor of the E. range of the cloister, and thus adjacent to one of the transepts of the conventual church, to which direct access for the night office was provided by a flight of steps.

J. C. Dickinson, *Monastic Life in Medieval England* (1961), p. 33.

Dositheus (2nd cent.), Judaeo-*Gnostic heretic. He belonged to *Samaria, but very little is known of him. Acc. to *Hegesippus (*Eusebius, *HE* 4. 22), he was one of four original founders of sects in Palestine. *Origen, who mentions him several times, states that he set himself up as the Messiah foretold in Deut. 18: 18 (*Contra Celsum*, 1. 57) and insisted on strict observance of the Sabbath (*De Princ.* 4. 3. 2). Acc. to the *Clementine Recognitions (2. 8–11; cf. Hom. 2. 24), *Simon Magus first belonged to the circle of Dositheus and later ousted him. His followers (Dositheans) never seem to have been more than a very small body (Origen, *Contra Celsum*, 6. 11, mentions 'scarcely thirty' as surviving in his day), but they survived down to the 10th cent.

Among the writings discovered at *Nag Hammadi is a short work which begins 'The revelation of Dositheus about the three steles of Seth'. It relates what Dositheus 'saw and understood', but it is not clear whether it claims to be the work of this Dositheus or some unknown namesake.

S. J. Isser, *The Dositheans: A Samaritan Sect in Late Antiquity* (Studies of Judaism in Late Antiquity, 17; Leiden, 1976), with Eng. tr. of the primary sources and survey of modern discussion. 'The Three Steles of Seth' ed., with Fr. tr., by P. Claude (Bibliothèque Copte de Nag Hammadi, 'Textes', 8; Quebec, 1983). Eng. tr. in J. M. Robinson (ed.), *The Nag Hammadi Library in English* (3rd edn., Leiden, 1988), pp. 396–401. G. *Salmon in *DCB* 1 (1877), pp. 902 f.; A. *Jülicher in *PW* 10 (1905), cols. 1608 f.

Dositheus (1641–1707), Patr. of *Jerusalem from 1669. A native of the Peloponnese, prob. of humble family, on the death of his father at the age of 8 he was placed by the Abp. of *Corinth in a neighbouring monastery. He was ordained deacon three years later, and prob. educated at Athens under N. Kerameus (d. 1663). Before 1657 he entered the service of the Patr. of Jerusalem and in 1661 became Archdeacon of Jerusalem and in 1666 Abp. of *Caesarea. On the resignation of *Nectarius Pelopides (1661–69) he was appointed Patr. of Jerusalem by a synod held at *Constantinople. His best-known achievement was the Synod of *Jerusalem (q.v.) held in 1672 and intended to combat the influence of Protestantism in the Greek Church; Dositheus was the principal author of its decrees and confession. His patriarchate was also marked by the inauguration of various monastic and financial reforms, and more esp. by his vigorous defence of the Greeks against the Latins, as in the dispute with the *Franciscans over their rights to the Holy Places. He tried to extend the influence of Hellenism in Russia by adroit intervention in the disputes aroused by the patriarchate of *Nikon, by joining with Callixtus II (Patr. of Constantinople, 1689–93) in condemning the *Calvinistic teaching of J. Karophyllis on the *Eucharist in 1691, and by opposition to the *Uniat Churches in his writings against L. *Allatius and R. *Bellarmine. To combat W. influence in theology he established a printing press at Jassy in *Romania in 1680. His many theological works, characterized by wide erudition rather than original thought, include an Ἐγχειρίδιον against Calvinism (Bucharest, 1690). He edited a trilogy of three large volumes, Τόμος Καταλλαγῆς (Jassy, 1694), Τόμος Ἀγάπης (Jassy, 1698), and Τόμος Χαρᾶς (Rîmnicu Vîlcea, 1705), containing material relating to *Photius and works by *Gregory Palamas, together with more recent anti-Latin treatises. He also compiled a history of the Patriarchate of Jerusalem in twelve [really thirteen] books (ed. anonymously by P. Kerameus; posthumously published, Bucharest, 2 vols., 1715).

Dositheus pub. many other writings, most of them at Jassy. C. Notaras, his nephew, inserted a Life of his uncle into Dositheus's posthumous 'History of the Jerusalem Patriarchate' (Ἱστορία περὶ τῶν ἐν Ἱεροσολύμοις Πατριαρχευσάντων; also, from its division into twelve books, known as the Δωδεκάβιβλος; Bucharest, 1715). A. Palmieri, OSA, *Dositeo patriarca greco di Gerusalemme* (Florence, 1909). I. V. Doura, Ὁ Δοσίθεος Ἱεροσολύμων καὶ ἡ προσφορὰ αὐτοῦ εἰς τὰς Ῥουμανικὰς χώρας καὶ τὴν ἐκκλησίαν αὐτῶν (Athens, 1977). [J. C.] S. Runciman, *The Great Church in Captivity* (Cambridge, 1968), esp. pp. 350–3. G. Podskalsky, *Griechische Theologie in der Zeit der Türkenherrschaft (1453–1821)* (Munich, 1988), pp. 282–95. A. Palmieri, OSA, in *DTC* 4 (1911), cols. 1788–1800, with full bibl.; additional bibl. by V. Grumel in *DHGE* 14 (1960), col. 700; M. Jugie, AA, in *EC* 4 (1950), cols. 1890 f., s.v. 'Dositeo'.

Dostoevsky, Fedor Mikhailovitch (1821–81), Russian novelist. He was the son of a retired military Russian sur-

geon of *Orthodox or *Uniat priestly ancestry, born at Moscow, where he was educated at a private boarding-school. From 1838 to 1843 he attended the Military Engineering College at St Petersburg, but resigned his commission after three years. In 1849 he was arrested for revolutionary activities and eight months later condemned to death. Although he was eventually reprieved, this imminence of death made a deep impression on him. During four years' forced labour in Siberia, he gained an intimate knowledge and deep affection for the ordinary Russian people. In 1854 he was transferred as a private in an infantry battalion to Semipalatinsk, where he was able to resume his writing. In 1856 he formed an unhappy marriage terminated by the death of his wife in 1863. He returned to St Petersburg in 1859, and with his elder brother in 1861 founded the review *Vremya* (suppressed 1863), in which he defended Slavophil democratic ideas. Deeply in debt through gambling and general mismanagement, in 1867 he married his secretary, who later became his publisher. In 1873 he was invited by Prince Meshchersky to edit the newspaper *Grazhdanin*, to which he contributed his *Author's Diary* (published separately, 1876). Although known chiefly as a journalist in his lifetime, his more enduring works were the novels in which he penetrated the deep recesses of the human mind. They include (all written in Russian) *Memoirs from the Underworld* (1864), *Crime and Punishment* (1865–6), *The Idiot* (1869), *The Possessed* (1871), and *The Brothers Karamazov* (1880).

The centre of Dostoevsky's religious experience is the consciousness of salvation as the free gift of God to the weak and miserable and the refusal to admit any co-operation between God and man. There is no way from man to God, only one from God to man, who is united to his fellows by the common bond of sin. The result is a complete absence from religion of reason and will, and the moral effort that flows from them. The heroes and heroines of Dostoevsky's novels live entirely by their emotions, of which the foremost is boundless and irrational compassion. In the short story 'The Grand Inquisitor', incorporated in *The Brothers Karamazov*, the institutional Church is represented as the great tyrant and falsifier of Christ whom she would crucify again if He came back to earth. Dostoevsky's writings have had a profound influence, not only among Russian Orthodox (esp. those who left Russia after the Revolution) but also on the *Dialectical Theology of K. *Barth.

The standard Eng. tr. of Dostoevsky's novels is that by C. Garnett (12 vols., 1912–20). The principal works have also been tr. by D. Magarshack in Penguin Classics. There is a very extensive literature, mainly in Russ. More important studies available in Eng. include works by E. H. Carr (London, 1931), E. J. Simmons (New York, 1940), K. Mochulsky (in Russ., Paris, 1947; Eng. tr., 1967), R. Wellek (ed.) (Englewood Cliffs, NJ, 1962), E. Wasiolek (Cambridge, Mass., 1964), A. Steinberg (London, 1966), J. Frank (Princeton, NJ, 1976 ff.; London, 1977 ff.), and J. Catteau (Paris, 1978; Eng. tr., Cambridge, 1989). G. Steiner, *Tolstoy or Dostoevsky: An Essay in Contrast* (New York, 1959; London, 1960). J. Coulson, *Dostoevsky: A Self Portrait* (1962), incl. Eng. tr. of extensive extracts of letters. P. Evdokimov, *Dostoïevsky et le problème du mal* (Lyons, 1942). A. B. Gibson, *The Religion of Dostoevsky* (1973); S. Hackel, 'The Religious Dimension: Vision or Evasion? Zosima's discourse in *The Brothers Karamazov*', in M. V. Jones and G. M. Terry (eds.), *New Essays on Dostoyevsky* (Cambridge, 1983), pp. 139–68. W. J. Leatherbarrow, *Fedor*

Dostoevsky: A Reference Guide (Boston, Mass. [1990] [bibl. 1846–1988]).

Douai, NE France. Formerly part of the Spanish Netherlands, Douai from 1562 was the seat of a university founded by *Philip II, and it came to house several colleges founded for the benefit of RC students from the British Isles. The most important was that founded by W. *Allen in 1568. This was intended to supply a learned clergy in England when the RC faith should be re-established, but it soon became a seminary for mission priests in England, and many of its *alumni* suffered death for their faith. Members of the college translated the *Douai-Reims Bible. Except for a brief period when it was removed to Reims (1578–93), the college remained at Douai until it was suppressed during the French Revolution. Its work was then transferred to England, where it was carried on at Crook Hall, near Ushaw, and at St Edmund's Old Hall, Ware. A similar college for Scottish students was founded at Douai in 1580, followed in 1607 by an English Benedictine community (which transferred to England in 1795 and has been settled at *Downside Abbey since 1814).

The First and Second Diaries of the English College, Douay, ed. by the Fathers of the Congregation of the London Oratory with hist. introd. by T. F. Knox, Cong. Orat. (Records of the English Catholics under the Penal Laws, 1; 1876); E. H. Burton and T. L. Williams (eds.), *The Douay Diaries, Third, Fourth and Fifth, with the Rheims Report 1597–80* (*Catholic Record Society, 10 and 11; 1911); E. H. Burton, *The Douay College Diaries: The Seventh Diary, 1715–1778, preceded by a Summary of Events, 1691–1715* (ibid. 28; 1928). P. Guilday, *The English Catholic Refugees on the Continent, 1558–1795*, 1 (1914), chs. 4 and 9, 'The English College at Douai', pp. 63–120 and 307–45, incl. full bibl. notes to date. J. H. Baxter, 'The Scots College at Douai', *The Scottish Historical Review*, 24 (1927), pp. 251–7; H. Chadwick, SJ, 'The Scots College, Douai, 1580–1613', *EHR* 56 (1941), pp. 571–85. C. Lefebvre in *DHGE* 14 (1960), cols. 703–32, s.v. See also bibl. s.v. DOWNSIDE.

Douai Abbey, Woolhampton, Berks. The English *Benedictine community of St *Edmund the Martyr was founded in Paris in 1615. It became an important Jacobite centre, and *James II was buried in the monastic church. Many of its members served on pastoral missions in England. One of them, Charles Walmesley, who was *Vicar Apostolic of the Western District from 1770 to 1797, in 1790 consecrated John *Carroll, the first RC Bishop in the USA. The community experienced serious difficulties at the time of the French Revolution and in the following years when France and Britain were at war, and in 1818 the remaining monks moved to the buildings of St Gregory's, at Douai (see previous entry), vacated by the community which settled at *Downside. A school was established and benefited from the bursaries given by the French government to English RC bishops and other superiors for the education of students in France. For much of the 19th cent. the community supplied bishops for Port Louis, Mauritius. In 1903 the monks were expelled from France. Taking the name of Douai, they settled at Woolhampton; the vast abbey church was completed in 1993. The monks run a large public school, and parishes throughout England.

F. C. Doyle, OSB (ed.), *Tercentenary of St Edmund's Monastery* (1917). S. Marron, OSB, 'The Foundation of St Edmund's, Paris', *Douai Magazine*, NS 3 (1924), pp. 99–108; id., 'The Early Years at St Edmund's, Paris', ibid., pp. 258–65; id., 'St Edmund's; A Prison in the Reign of Terror', ibid., NS 1 (1920), pp. 20–9; id., 'Paris to Douai: A Chapter of our History', ibid., pp. 173–80.

Douai-Reims Bible. The version of the Bible in use among English-speaking RCs for more than three centuries. It was the work of members of the English College at *Douai, of whom the chief were G. *Martin (d. 1582), Thomas Worthington, Richard Bristow, and William *Allen, all of them formerly from Oxford. It claimed to provide a version free from the heretical renderings in the earlier English Bibles. The work was begun at Douai, but owing to the migration of the college to Reims in 1578, the NT was completed in that city and published there in 1582. The OT, which did not appear till 1609–10, was published at Douai, whither the college had returned in the meantime. The translation, which was made not from the original languages but from the Latin *Vulgate, was painstaking and reached a high standard of consistency, but was often too literal to be suitable for use in public worship or private devotional reading. There was also a strong tendency to retain technical words (e.g. 'pasch', 'parasceve', 'azymes') without alteration, and many passages are more an Anglicization than a translation of the Latin, e.g. Phil. 2: 7 (8): 'He exinanited Himself'. The dogmatic intentions of its authors found expression in the prologue and in the notes that accompany the text. Its language exercised considerable influence on the text of the *Authorized Version. Modern editions of this translation are based on the revision made by R. *Challoner in 1749–50. The Reims NT was vigorously attacked in 1589 by W. *Fulke.

Facsimile repr. of orig. edn. (English Recusant Literature 1558–1640, vols. 265 f. (OT) and 267 (NT); 1975), with introds. by D. M. Rogers. J. G. Carleton, *The Part of Rheims in the Making of the English Bible* (1902). A. W. Pollard, *Records of the English Bible* (1911), pp. 33–7, with docs., pp. 298–313. J. Isaacs in H. Wheeler Robinson (ed.), *The Bible in its Ancient and English Versions* (1940), pp. 190–5. H. Pope, OP, and S. Bullough, OP, 'The History of the Rheims-Douai Version', in B. Orchard, OSB, and others (eds.), *A Catholic Commentary on Holy Scripture* (1953), pp. 34–9, with bibl. S. L. Greenslade in id. (ed.), *The Cambridge History of the Bible*, [3] *The West from the Reformation to the Present Day* (1963), pp. 161–3; F. J. Crehan, SJ, ibid., pp. 211–13. Darlow and Moule, ed. A. S. Herbert, 1 (1968), pp. 95 f., 127 f. For background, see also Douai diaries and other works cited s.v. DOUAI, and Letters and Memorials of W. Allen s.v. ALLEN, W.

Double Feasts. The name formerly given, in the Roman *Missal and *Breviary, to the more important feasts. They were distinguished as (ordinary) Doubles, Greater Doubles, Doubles of the Second Class, and Doubles of the First Class. The use of the term is of uncertain origin.

double justice. A distinction between two kinds of righteousness drawn by some 16th-cent. theologians in an attempt to explain the mystery of *justification. In the Middle Ages and the Renaissance such writers as *Alexander of Hales, St *Thomas Aquinas, and *Erasmus, had distinguished between the justice acquired through *grace and that acquired through good works. This traditional distinction lay behind M. *Luther's early work *De duplici iustitia* (1519). In the 1530s and 1540s the distinction was developed in a different form by such Catholic writers as J. *Gropper, G. *Contarini, and G. *Seripando. Recognizing some truth in Luther's doctrine of justification by faith, they now distinguished between (1) inherent justice acquired through sanctifying grace and/or good works performed in co-operation with grace, and (2) imputed justice acquired through faith when the merits of Christ were imputed to the believer. Consciousness of the continuing influence of *concupiscence and the impossibility of complete certainty of one's state of grace led the Christian to place his trust in the second kind of justice rather than the first. A version of the theory was discussed at the Conference of *Ratisbon in 1541. The Council of *Trent declined to support the theory, but did not condemn it.

A. E. McGrath, *Iustitia Dei: A History of the Christian Doctrine of Justification* (Cambridge, 1986), vol. 2, pp. 57–61 and 74–7. E. [J.] Yarnold, '*Duplex iustitia*. The Sixteenth Century and the Twentieth', in G. R. Evans (ed.), *Christian Authority: Essays in Honour of Henry Chadwick* (Oxford, 1988), pp. 204–23.

double monastery. A religious house for both men and women. The two sexes dwelt in separate but contiguous establishments, worshipped in distinct parts of a common church, and were ruled by a common superior. Such monasteries are first found in the E. in the later generations of the Roman Empire. They were numerous in 6th- and 7th-cent. France, England, and through the Anglo-Saxon missions, in Germany. In the W. double monasteries women (often from families of high social standing) frequently had a dominant role— as e.g. at Whitby, ruled in the 7th cent. by St *Hilda, or *Ely, under St *Etheldreda. Most of them disappeared in the disorders of the 9th and 10th cents., but they were revived (generally only for a short time) by certain of the smaller monastic orders of the 12th cent., including that of St *Gilbert of Sempringham.

M. Bateson, 'Origin and Early History of Double Monasteries', *Transactions of the Royal Historical Society*, NS 13 (1899), pp. 137–98. U. Berlière, OSB, *Les Monastères doubles aux XIIe et XIIIe siècles* (Académie Royale de Belgique. Classe des Lettres et des Sciences Morales et Politiques. Mémoires, 2nd ser. 18; 1923). M. J. L. G. Aliette, Marquise de Maillé, *Les Cryptes de Jouarre* (1971), pp. 13–57 ('Les Monastères Colombaniens de Femmes'). M. Parisse in *Lexikon des Mittelalters*, 3 (1986), cols. 1257–9, s.v. 'Doppelkloster'. See also bibl. to GILBERT OF SEMPRINGHAM, ST, and esp. the introd. to *The Book of St Gilbert*, pp. xlii–lii.

Double Procession of the Holy Spirit, the doctrine of the W. Church acc. to which the Holy Spirit proceeds from the Father and the Son. Support for it is found in several NT passages, notably Jn. 16: 13–15, where Christ says of the Holy Spirit 'He shall take (λήψεται) of Mine and shall shew it unto you'. It is urged that in the Inner-Trinitarian relations one Person cannot 'take' or 'receive' (λήψεται) anything from either of the others except by way of Procession. Among other texts adduced for the doctrine are Gal. 4: 6, where the Holy Spirit is called 'the Spirit of the Son', Rom. 8: 9 'the Spirit of Christ', Phil. 1: 19 'the Spirit of Jesus Christ', and the Johannine texts on the sending of the Holy Spirit by Jesus (14: 16, 15: 26, 16: 7). Among the Greek Fathers St *Cyril of Alexandria is usually considered one of the most important witnesses to the doctrine. He develops it in his struggle against *Nestorianism, speaking of the Holy Spirit as belonging to the Son, τὸ ἴδιον τοῦ Υἱοῦ. He also uses several times the characteristic Latin formula 'and the Son' side by side with the Greek phrase 'through the Son', the former indicating the equality of principle, the latter the order of origin. The doctrine was expressly denied, on the other hand, by *Theodore of Mopsuestia and *Theodoret. Among the Latin Fathers, St *Jerome, St *Ambrose, and esp. St *Augustine are representatives of the teaching summed up in the '*Filioque' (q.v.). But the doctrine did not become a matter of controversy until the time of *Photius (864), who asserted it to be contrary to the teaching of the Fathers and even suspected the relevant passages as interpolations. At the Council of *Florence (1439), Mark of Ephesus repeated this theory; but today most theologians of the E. Church recognize that St Augustine and other Latin Fathers taught the Double Procession, but only as a private opinion. The objection urged by E. theologians against the doctrine is that there must be a single Fount of Divinity (πηγὴ θεότητος) in the Godhead. The consideration urged by W. theologians in its support is that, as both Latins and Greeks attribute everything as common to the Father and the Son except the relation of Paternity and Filiation, the Spiration of the Holy Spirit, in which this relation is not involved, must also be common to both.

H. B. *Swete, *On the History of the Doctrine of the Procession of the Holy Spirit from the Apostolic Age to the Death of Charlemagne* (1876). Preface to P. E. *Pusey's Eng. tr. of Cyril's *Commentary on the Gospel according to S. John* (LF 43; 1874), pp. ix–lx. M. Jugie, AA, *Theologia Dogmatica Christianorum Orientalium ab Ecclesia Catholica Dissentium*, 1 (Paris, 1926), esp. pp. 286–311, and 2 (1933), pp. 296–535. Id., *De Processione Spiritus Sancti ex Fontibus Revelationis et secundum Orientales Dissidentes* (Lateranum, NS 2, nos. 3–4; 1936), with refs. Eng. tr. of V. *Lossky, 'The Procession of the Holy Spirit in the Orthodox Triadology', *Eastern Churches Quarterly*, 7 (1948), suppl. issue, 2, pp. 31–53. R. Haugh, *Photius and the Carolingians: The Trinitarian Controversy* (Belmont, Mass., 1975). H. J. Marx, SVD, *Filioque und Verbot eines anderen Glaubens auf dem Florentinum* (Veröffentlichungen des Missionspriesterseminars St Augustin bei Bonn, 26; 1977). J.-M. Garrigues, *L'Esprit qui dit 'Père!': L'Esprit-Saint dans la vie trinitaire et le problème du Filioque* [1981]. See also bibl. s.v. FILIOQUE.

Doukhobors (Russ.), 'Spirit-fighters'. A Russian sect of unknown origin. It seems to have arisen among Russian peasants in the district of Kharkov *c.*1740, and spread rapidly. Under Paul I (d. 1801) the Doukhobors came into conflict with the government and were banished to Siberia and other places; under Alexander I (d. 1825) they settled in Taurida as an agricultural community run on communist lines. Owing to the intolerance of the Orthodox clergy and their own growing moral laxity, they were again banished and sent to Transcaucasia in 1841. In 1895, having come under the influence of L. *Tolstoy, they refused to serve in the army and burnt their weapons. Being once more expelled they found themselves reduced to starvation, when the assistance of Tolstoy and the *Quakers enabled most of them to emigrate to Cyprus and, more successfully, to Canada. Here they became a nuisance to the government because they refused to own land as individuals and to register births, deaths, and marriages. After various upheavals, the majority of the Canadian Doukhobors, now centred in the western provinces of Canada, in 1938 were organized into the Union of Spiritual Communities in Christ, known also as the Orthodox Doukhobors; a tiny splinter group, the Sons of Freedom, are thought to practise subversion. Those Doukhobors who remained in Russia continued to suffer persecution, many being deported to Siberia and Central Asia. The Doukhobors believe that God is present in all human beings, who are thus equal; that Christ was one of a succession of inspired leaders, amongst whom are numbered the leaders of the Doukhobors. They reject the Bible, hierarchy, sacraments, and Christian dogma.

J. Elkinton, *The Doukhobors: Their History in Russia. Their Migration to Canada* (Philadelphia, 1903); A. Maude, *A Peculiar People: The Doukhobors* (1904). J. F. C. Wright, *Slava Bohu: The Story of the Dukhobors* (New York, 1940). H. B. Hawthorn (ed.), *The Doukhobors of British Columbia* (1955). G. Woodcock and I. Avakumovic, *The Doukhobors* (1968). F. C. *Conybeare, *Russian Dissenters* (Harvard Theological Studies, 10; 1921), pp. 266–87. A. Palmieri in *DTC* 4 (1908), cols. 1802–11; A. A. Stamouli in *HERE* 4 (1911), pp. 865–7.

dove. As a Christian symbol, the dove has many meanings. (1) From the dove with the olive branch in its beak in the story of the Flood (Gen. 8: 11), it is a sign of peace and reconciliation. (2) In the primitive Church, from the ref. to His descent upon Christ at His baptism under the form of a dove (Mk. 1: 10), it was esp. a type of the Holy Spirit. This symbol is found esp. in the vaults of early churches and frequently in conjunction with pictorial representations of the other two Persons of the Trinity. (3) From the Song of Solomon, where the Bride is called a dove (e.g. 2: 14, 5: 2), the symbol has been applied either to the Church, e.g. by *Tertullian, St *Ambrose, and St *Augustine, or to the individual soul regenerated by baptism, e.g. by St *Hilary of Poitiers. (4) Other meanings of the dove are to denote inspired theological knowledge in the case of many saints, e.g. St *Gregory the Great, St *Dominic, St *Thomas Aquinas, and St *Teresa of Ávila; and (5) to represent certain Christian virtues, notably purity and humility.

The 'Eucharistic Dove' is a hollow receptacle in the shape of a dove to contain the Blessed Sacrament. Its use was formerly believed, apparently wrongly, to go back to Tertullian. There are references to its use in a 9th-cent. Life of St *Basil and in the 'Consuetudines Cluniacenses' of Udalric. It was popular in the 12th and 13th cents., and more than 30 such receptacles of this period are extant. Eucharistic doves are now used mainly in churches of the Byzantine rite.

F. Sühling, *Die Taube als religiöses Symbol im christlichen Altertum* (Römische Quartalschrift, Suppl. 24; 1930), with full refs. Id., 'Taube und Orante. Ein Beitrag zum Orantenproblem', *RQ* 39 (1931), pp. 333–54. W. Stengel, *Das Taubensymbol des Heiligen Geistes* (1904). J. P. Kirsch in *DACL* 3 (pt. 2; 1914), cols. 2198–231, s.v. 'Colombe'.
On the Eucharistic Dove, F. Raible, *Der Tabernakel einst und jetzt* (1908), pp. 131–52; H. R. Kaufmann, 'Eucharistic Doves', in *Eucharistic Vessels of the Middle Ages* (Exhibition Catalogue, Busch-Reisinger Museum, Harvard University, Cambridge, Mass., 1975), pp. 86–96. Braun, *CA* 2, pp. 608–16, with pls. 353–5; id., *AG*, pp. 319–23.

Downside Abbey. St Gregory's Abbey, Downside, near Bath, is the premier house of the English *Benedictine Congregation. It traces its origin to a small settlement of English monks begun at *Douai in 1607, for which a monastery was built in 1611 with a school attached for the education of English RC boys. Expelled from Douai in the French Revolution, the monks found refuge in England, where Sir Edward Smythe put his Shropshire country seat at their disposal. In 1814 the community moved to Downside. In 1899 it was raised from the status of a priory to that of an abbey. It is today one of the centres of RC life in England, maintaining in its own buildings its large and important school. The Abbey church, consecrated in 1935, is one of the finest examples of modern Gothic in England. The monks, who carry on the Benedictine liturgical tradition, edit a quarterly periodical, *The Downside Review*, chiefly devoted to Church history, esp. monastic interests and philosophy. Scholars of distinction at Downside in recent times include F. A. *Gasquet, E. C[uthbert] Butler (1858–1934), J. *Chapman, R. H. *Connolly, B. C[hristopher] Butler (1902–86), and [M.] D. *Knowles.

H. N. Birt, OSB, *Downside: The History of St Gregory's School from its Commencement at Douay to the Present Time* (1902). [R.] H. Connolly, OSB, *Some Dates and Documents for the Early History of our House*, 1 [all pub.] (privately pr., 1930). H. van Zeller, OSB, *Downside By and Large* (1954). Arts. in *The Downside Review*, 33 (1914). *Downside Abbey: Church Guide* (1905 and subsequent edns.). Life of Henry Edmund Ford, Abbot 1900–1906, by B. Hicks, OSB (London [1947]). [M.] D. Knowles, OSB, 'Abbot Butler: a memoir' and 'The Works and Thought of Abbot Butler', *Downside Review*, 52 (1934), pp. 347–465, with a list of his works, pp. 466–72, repr. (without list of works) in *The Historian and Character and other Essays* (Cambridge, 1963), pp. 264–362; A. Bellenger, OSB, 'The English Benedictines: the Search for a Monastic Identity 1880–1920', in J. Loades (ed.), *Monastic Studies* [1] (Bangor, 1990), pp. 299–321, with refs. B. Sankey, OSB, in *DHGE* 14 (1960), cols. 767–9, s.v.

Dowsing, William (1596–1668), Puritan iconoclast. He is remembered for his energy in carrying out the order of Parliament of 1643 for the destruction of the ornaments in churches. He was employed on this task under the Earl of Manchester in Cambridgeshire (1643–4) and in Suffolk (6 Jan.–1 Oct. 1644), and his journal testifies to the zeal and completeness of his work. At the Restoration Dowsing was left unpunished, and he died in obscurity.

The orig. MS of the Journal is lost. Sections were first pub. by R. Loder (1786) from a transcript made in 1704 when the orig. was sold with the rest of Dowsing's library. A transcript of the Cambridge section survives in the Baker MSS, vol. 38 (c.1738), pp. 455–8 and 471–3, in the Cambridge University Library. There are modern edns. of the Suffolk sections by C. H. E. White (Ipswich, 1885) and of the Cambridgeshire section by A. C. Moule (Cambridge, 1926). The supposed account of destruction at Gorleston (now Norfolk) is a forgery. J. S. Morrill, 'William Dowsing: the Bureaucratic Puritan' in id. and others (eds.), *Public Men and Private Conscience in Seventeenth-Century England: Essays presented to G. E. Aylmer* (Oxford, 1993), pp. 173–203.

Doxology. An ascription of glory (Gk. δόξα) to the Persons of the Holy Trinity. (1) The Greater Doxology is the *Gloria in Excelsis*. (2) The Lesser Doxology is the *Gloria Patri*. (3) Metrical forms, in some cases with special reference to a particular mystery of Christ or season of the Church, were appended to the hymns of the *Breviary, and in later times to other hymns also. Among the most familiar of these in English is the verse which begins 'Praise God from Whom all blessings flow', written by T. *Ken.

J. A. Jungmann, SJ, *Die Stellung Christi im liturgischen Gebet* (Liturgiegeschichtliche Forschungen, 7–8; 1925; 2nd edn., ibid. 19–20; 1962), pp. 151–68; Eng. tr. (1965), pp. 172–90, with refs. J. M. Hanssens, SJ, *La Liturgie d'Hippolyte* (Orientalia Christiana Analecta, 155; 1959), pp. 343–70 ('Les Doxologies de la liturgie hippolytienne'). A. *Fortescue in *CE* 5 (1909), pp. 150 f.; H. *Leclercq, OSB, in *DACL* 4 (1921), cols. 1525–36; A. Stuiber in *RAC* 4 (1959), cols. 210–26, all s.v.

Dragonnades (1683–6). The persecutions, so named from their being carried out by mounted troops ('dragoons'), who were quartered on the *Huguenots under the direction of Louis XIV with a view to crushing their independence and forcing them to accept the Catholic religion. They brought financial ruin on the Huguenots and their alleged success in inducing the great majority of them to accept the faith was made a pretext for revoking the Edict of *Nantes on 18 Oct. 1685.

J. Orcibal, *Louis XIV et les Protestants* (Bibliothèque de la Société d'Histoire Ecclésiastique de la France, 1951), esp. chs. 3 and 4; W. C. Scoville, *The Persecution of Huguenots and French Economic Development, 1680–1720* (Berkeley, Calif., 1960), esp. pp. 61 f. and 76–8. Y. Krumenacker, 'Les dragonnades de Poitou: leur écho dans les mémoires', *Bulletin de la Société de l'Histoire du Protestantisme français*, 131 (1985), pp. 405–22. See also works cited under NANTES, EDICT OF.

drama, Christian. In the first centuries of the Christian era drama existed only in the form of *spectacula*, which necessarily incurred the deep hostility of the Church. All plays, in the remote historical origins of the dramatic art, were acts of religious worship; and even the sterilizing degeneration of Classical and post-Classical polytheism had not destroyed the superficially liturgical character of the public shows. To take part, even as a spectator, in such a performance was to make an overt act of paganism, whether or not any definitely idolatrous ceremony was involved in it. This is the chief foundation of *Tertullian's invective in his *De Spectaculis* (c.200). Besides, the moral tendency of the pagan shows was wholly inconsistent with the Christian character, as two examples—the gladiatorial combats and the obscene comedies—sufficiently prove. Tertullian used this argument, but it was more thoroughly developed by *Cyprian (3rd cent.) and *Chrysostom (4th cent.). The pagans themselves acknowledged the demoralizing effect of their spectacles; the Emp. *Julian forbade pagan priests to go to the theatre (363); and *Augustine's friend, Alypius, though a heathen, abhorred all such 'deadly amusements' in his first youth (c.370). A third cause of the antagonism of the early Church towards *spectacula* in general lay in the supposed opposition between that asceticism implicit in the Christian profession and the pursuit of secular pleasures.

The destruction of the Roman Empire and of the Imperial religion involved the disappearance of the traditional pagan shows, and although plays of a kind were certainly performed in various places throughout the Dark Ages, drama ceased to present an important problem for the Christian conscience. In the 10th cent. two significant documents indicate a new development. The Saxon nun *Hrosvit wrote a number of edifying 'comedies' in imitation of Terence, and the English monk, *Ethelwold, described the 'praiseworthy custom' of celebrating the death and resurrection of Christ by a representation, with mime and dialogue, to be performed in church during or after the liturgical rites. Hrosvit may have been ignorant of the Classical conditions of performance, but there is a growing recognition of the theatricality of her plays. Those who devised the earliest Resurrection 'plays', using the *trope *Quem quaeritis*, were developing a representational or dramatic tendency implicit in all liturgical worship, and especially marked in the *Gallican rite. The Resurrection play provided the model for other liturgical dramas, which were widely disseminated in Europe until the 16th cent. Vernacular religious drama intended for popular audiences existed as early as the 12th cent. (in the *Mystère d'Adam*), but was chiefly represented in the 14th and 15th cents. by the English Corpus Christi or '*Mystery' cycles, the French Passion plays, and the *Morality genre.

Side by side with the elaboration of the mysteries and morality plays, there took place a great development of purely secular drama in all parts of Christendom. The attitude of the medieval Church towards stage plays in general was not wholly consistent, and individual instances of intolerance can be found; but since most of the plays were at least ostensibly edifying, and the players organized in ostensibly pious confraternities, the traditional hostility of the early Fathers to the *spectacula* had no longer any direct relevance to the changed situation. Since the 16th cent. drama has been once more released from its ecclesiastical connection. The more puritanical of the Reformers and their followers, e.g. W. *Prynne, tended to repudiate the stage altogether, though T. *Beza wrote mystery plays for a Protestant public. But on the whole, Christian people, while exhibiting a certain mistrust of the moral effects of play-going and esp. of acting, have acquiesced in the establishment of drama as a normal part of social life. The traditional religious plays have survived in various parts of the world (see OBERAMMERGAU), and there have been numerous civic, academic, and commercial revivals of the medieval mysteries and moralities during the 20th cent.

Anthology of medieval texts by D. Bevington, *Medieval Drama* (Boston [1975]); P. Meredith and J. E. Tailby, *The Staging of Religious Drama in Europe in the Later Middle Ages: Texts and Documents in English Translation* (Kalamazoo, Mich., 1983). A. C. Cawley and others, *Medieval Drama* (The Revels History of Drama in English, 1; 1983). E. K. Chambers, *The Mediaeval Stage* (2 vols., Oxford, 1903); K. Young, *The Drama of the Medieval Church* (2 vols., ibid., 1933); W. L. Smoldon, *The Music of the Medieval Church Dramas*, ed. C. Bourgeault (1980). O. B. Hardison, *Christian Rite and Christian Drama in the Middle Ages* (Baltimore [1965]); R. [P.] Axton, *European Drama of the Early Middle Ages* (1974). W. Tydeman, *The Theatre in the Middle Ages: Western European Stage Conditions, c.800–1576* (Cambridge, 1978). E. K. Chambers, *English Literature at the Close of the Middle Ages* (Oxford History of English Literature, 1945), pp. 1–65; F. P. Wilson, *The English Drama 1485–1585* (ibid., 1969), pp. 1–77 and 85–101. M. Roston, *Biblical Drama in England from the Middle Ages to the Present Day* (1968). V. A. Kolve, *The Play called Corpus Christi* (1966); R. [E.] Woolf, *The English Mystery Plays* (1972); R. Potter, *The English Morality Play* (1975). I. Lancashire, *Dramatic Texts and Records of Britain: A Chronological Topography to 1558* (Toronto and Cambridge, 1984). G. Frank, *The Medieval French Drama* (Oxford, 1954), pp. 1–206. N. D. Shergold, *A History of the Spanish Stage from Medieval Times to* the *End of the Seventeenth Century* (ibid., 1967), pp. 1–112 and 415–504. W. F. Michael, *Das deutsche Drama des Mittelalters* (Grundriss der germanischen Philologie, 20; 1971). V. de Barth-olomaeis, *Origini della Poesia Drammatica Italiana* (Nuova Bib-lioteca Italiana, 7; 2nd edn., Turin, 1952). C. J. Stratman, CSV, *Bibliography of Medieval Drama* (2nd edn., 2 vols., New York [1972]).

Dream of the Rood, The. An Old English poem of some 156 lines which, in the form of a dream-vision, represents the feelings of the Cross (expressed partly in the Cross's *persona*) during the Crucifixion; as such, the Cross becomes the object of mystical contemplation and a power-ful symbol of personal salvation. No source for the poem has been identified (although it draws to some extent on the Latin tradition of *enigmata*), and it is best regarded as the individual creation of a poet of genius. The poet is unknown (although the poem was formerly attributed to *Cynewulf), as are the date and origin of the poem. Some 15 of its lines were carved on the 8th-cent. Ruthwell Cross, and an inscription reminiscent of two of its verses appears on the famous Brussels Cross (a lavish silver *reliquary of the late 10th or early 11th cent. in the Cathedral at Brussels), but the complete text is preserved only in the late 10th cent. Vercelli Book (Vercelli Chapter Library, Codex CXVII).

Crit. edns., with full notes, by A. S. Cook, *The Dream of the Rood: An Old English Poem attributed to Cynewulf* (Oxford, 1905); B. Dickins and A. S. C. Ross (London, 1934; 4th edn., 1954); and M. Swanton (Manchester, 1970). H. R. Patch, 'Liturgical Influ-ence in *The Dream of the Rood*', *Publications of the Modern Lan-guage Association of America*, 34 (1919), pp. 233–57; R. Woolf, 'Doctrinal Infuences on *The Dream of the Rood*', *Medium Ævum*, 27 (1958), pp. 137–53; J. V. Fleming, ' "The Dream of the Rood" and Anglo-Saxon Monasticism', *Traditio*, 22 (1966), pp. 43–72; B. C. Raw, '*The Dream of the Rood* and its Connections with Early Christian Art', *Medium Ævum*, 39 (1970), pp. 239–56; C. B. Pas-ternack, 'Stylistic Disjunctions in *The Dream of the Rood*', *Anglo-Saxon England*, 13 (1984), pp. 167–86. Further bibl. in S. B. Greenfield and F. C. Robinson, *A Bibliography of Publications on Old English Literature to the End of 1972* (Toronto and Manches-ter, 1980), pp. 214–17 (nos. 3482–3527).

Drews, Arthur (1865–1935), German anti-Christian apologist. A disciple of E. von *Hartmann (q.v.), he taught from 1896 onwards at the Technical High School at Karlsruhe. Identifying God and world in a 'concrete monism', he held that religion consisted in a man's con-sciousness of himself as a supra-individual being and that true religion was based solely on reason, not on history. Hence he explained Christianity as a form of *Gnosticism and in *Die Christusmythe* (2 vols., 1909–11; Eng. tr., 1911) he challenged the historical existence of the Person of Christ. This denial caused a considerable stir. He wrote a large number of other works.

List of his writings in W. Ziegenfuss (ed.), *Philosophen-Lexikon*, 1 (1949), p. 256. J. Macquarrie in P. Edwards (ed.), *Encyclopedia of Philosophy*, 2 (1967), pp. 417 f., s.v.

Drexelius, i.e. **Jeremias Drexel** [not 'Drechsel'] (1581–1638), spiritual writer. In 1598 he entered the Society of Jesus (*Jesuits), and for many years was Professor of the Humanities at Augsburg. He is remembered chiefly as the author of a long series of devotional treatises which went through numerous editions and translations and circulated

equally among Protestants and Catholics. Among the most popular of them were his *Heliotropium; seu conformatio humanae voluntatis cum divina* (1627) and his *Noe archi-tectus arcae, in diluvio navarchus, descriptus et morali doc-trina illustratus* (1642).

His works are enumerated in Sommervogel, 3 (1892), cols. 181–205, and 9 (1900), cols. 243–5. K. Pörnbacher, *Jeremias Drexel: Leben und Werk eines Barockpredigers* (Beiträge zur altbayerischen Kirchengeschichte, 24, Heft 2; Munich, 1965). Polgár, 1 (1990), p. 607. P. Bailly in *Dict. Sp.* 3 (1957), cols. 1714–17, s.v.

Driver, Sir Godfrey Rolles (1892–1975), OT scholar and Semitic philologist. The son of S. R. *Driver, he was educated at Winchester and New College, Oxford. He was elected a Fellow of Magdalen College in 1919 and held the title of Professor of Semitic Philology from 1938 to 1962. He was intimately concerned with the New English Bible (see BIBLE, ENGLISH VERSIONS, 5), translating several Books and acting as Convener of the Old Testament Panel from 1957 and Joint Director (with C. H. *Dodd) from 1965. He was knighted in 1968.

His works include *Grammar of the Colloquial Arabic of Syria and Palestine* (1925), *Semitic Writing* (Schweich Lec-tures for 1944; 1948), and *The Judaean Scrolls* (1965), and editions, which have become standard texts, of *Assyrian Laws* (1935) and *Babylonian Laws* (1952–5), both with J. C. Miles, and *Aramaic Documents of the Fifth Century B.C.* (1954) and *Canaanite Myths and Legends* (1956).

Select bibl. of his writings in *Hebrew and Semitic Studies pre-sented to Godfrey Rolles Driver … in celebration of his seventieth birthday 20 August 1962*, ed. D. W. Thomas and W. D. McHardy (Oxford, 1963), pp. 191–206., with suppl. in *Vetus Testamentum*, 30 (1980), pp. 185–91. J. A. Emerton, 'Godfrey Rolles Driver 1892–1975', *Proceedings of the British Academy*, 63 (for 1977; 1978), pp. 345–62. J. Barr in *DNB, 1971–1980*, pp. 252 f.

Driver, Samuel Rolles (1846–1914), OT and Hebrew scholar. Of *Quaker descent, he was educated at Winches-ter and New College, Oxford, and in 1870 elected a Fellow of New College. From 1883 until his death he was Regius Professor of Hebrew and Canon of *Christ Church (in succession to E. B. *Pusey). His wide and exact knowledge of the OT, combined with sound judgement, caution, and a strong Christian faith, did much to foster the spread of the critical view of the OT in Britain. His *Treatise on the Use of the Tenses in Hebrew* (1874) established his reputa-tion as a Semitic scholar; and his *Introduction to the Literat-ure of the Old Testament* (1897) remained a standard work for some fifty years. Before his death he had issued com-mentaries of one kind or another on about half the OT, the more notable being those on *Deuteronomy (1895), *Joel and *Amos (1897), *Daniel (1900), and *Genesis (1904). His other writings included *Notes on the Hebrew Text … of the Books of Samuel* (1890), *The Parallel Psalter* (1904), *Modern Research as illustrating the Bible* (Schweich Lectures, 1909), and *Ideals of the Prophets* (ed. G. A. Cooke, 1915). He also collaborated with F. Brown and C. A. Briggs in the preparation of the Oxford Hebrew Lexicon (1891–1905) and contributed extensively to J. *Hastings's *Dictionary of the Bible* and other reference works.

W. *Sanday, *The Life-Work of Samuel Rolles Driver: A Sermon Preached in Christ Church on March 8, 1914* (1914); G. A. Cooke,

'Driver and Wellhausen', *HTR* 9 (1914), pp. 249–57. Bibl. of his pub. works in Driver's *Ideals of the Prophets* (ed. by G. A. C[ooke], 1915), Appendix A, pp. 213–34. J. [W.] Rogerson, *Old Testament Criticism in the Nineteenth Century: England and Germany* (1984), esp. pp. 273–5 and 282 f. G. A. Cooke in *DNB, 1912–1921*, pp. 162 f.

Droste-Vischering, Clemens August von (1773–1845), Abp. of *Cologne. A native of Münster i.W., he was the descendant of a devout Catholic family of the Westphalian nobility. In 1827 he became Auxiliary Bp. of Münster, and in 1835 he was elected Abp. of Cologne at the suggestion of the Prussian government, who hoped by this step to reconcile the Catholic nobility of Westphalia and the Rhineland as well as the clergy and laity to their policy. Soon, however, he came into conflict with the government through refusing his approbation to theological lectures and publications propagating the doctrines of G. *Hermes, which had been condemned by *Gregory XVI in 1835. The final break occurred over mixed marriages, which led to the Archbishop's imprisonment in the fortress of Minden in 1837 under pretext of treasonable activities. Gregory XVI protested; but the most powerful defence of the Archbishop was J. J. von *Görres's *Athanasius* (1838), which roused the support even of hitherto lukewarm Catholics. The effect of the conflict was a considerable increase in the vigour of Catholic life in Germany. Droste-Vischering was freed in 1839 and retired to Münster. After the accession of Frederick William IV, in 1841 the struggle ended in a compromise, the Archbishop retaining his dignity but leaving the government of his diocese to a coadjutor more acceptable to Prussia. His writings included *Über die Religionsfreiheit der Katholiken* (1817), written on the occasion of the tercentenary of M. *Luther's Ninety-Five Theses, and *Über den Frieden unter der Kirche und den Staaten* (1843).

H. J. Kappen, *Clemens August, Erzbischof von Köln: Ein Lebensbild* (1897). Short study by H. Kipper (Frankfurter Zeitgemässe Broschüren, NS 27, Heft 2; 1907). J. Will, 'Die achtzehn Thesen des Erzbischofs Klemens August von Köln in ihrer dogmatischen Berechtigung', *Theologie und Glaube*, 21 (1929), pp. 316–28. H. Richtering (ed.), *Die Nachlässe der Gebrüder Droste zu Vischering* (Westfälische Quellen und Archivverzeichnisse, 12; Münster, 1986), pp. 121–94. W. Müller in *DHGE* 14 (1960), cols. 815–20, s.v. 'Droste-Vischering (1)', with extensive bibl.

Drummond, Henry (1786–1860), politician and *Irvingite leader. After some years in business he entered Parliament in 1810, and although ostensibly a Tory, voted throughout his life independently on the merits of individual measures, giving esp. support to those directed against RCs and Jews, but also taking a vigorous part in secular debates. In 1817 he went to Geneva, and there carried on a campaign against *Socinianism which split the local Protestant Church. From 1826 onwards he took a leading part in founding the Irvingite body (*Catholic Apostolic Church, q.v.), in which he held the rank of apostle, evangelist, and prophet, and which he helped greatly to finance. In 1834 he was ordained 'angel for Scotland' by the Irvingites, and continued to preach until 1856.

Short Introductory Notice by Lord Lovaine to his edn. of H. Drummond's *Speeches in Parliament and Some Miscellaneous Pamphlets*, 1 (1860), pp. iii–ix. C. G. Flegg, *'Gathered Under Apostles': A Study of the Catholic Apostolic Church* (Oxford, 1992),

esp. pp. 34–41, 392–5, and 481 f. J. A. Hamilton in *DNB* 16 (1888), pp. 28 f.

Drummond, Henry (1851–97), theological writer and revivalist. Brought up in the *Free Church of Scotland, he was educated at New College, Edinburgh, and at *Tübingen. In 1874–5 he assisted D. L. *Moody and I. D. Sankey in their mission in Ireland and England and worked with Moody on a similar undertaking in 1882. In 1883 he published his *Natural Law in the Spiritual World*, a work which sought to interpret the spiritual in terms of the principle of continuity evident in the natural order. In his later years Drummond conducted successful missions to several universities of Great Britain. He was also well known as a geologist and explorer in N. America and Central Africa. His other writings include *Tropical Africa* (1888) and *The Ascent of Man* (1894).

Lives by G. A. *Smith (London, 1899) and C. Lennox (ibid., 1901). Anthology ed. J. W. Kennedy (New York, 1953), with biog. introd., pp. 19–62. Brief sketches by J. Y. Simpson ('Famous Scots Series', London, 1901) and A. H. Walker (London, 1913). T. Seccombe in *DNB*, Suppl. 2 (1901), pp. 157 f.

Drummond, James (1835–1918), *Unitarian divine. Educated at Trinity College, Dublin, and at Manchester New College, London, he became in 1860 assistant pastor of Cross Street Chapel, Manchester. From 1885 to 1906 he was Principal of Manchester New College, first in London and later (from 1889) at Oxford. In his books he attempted to write without bias either for or against orthodoxy, and valued Unitarianism rather for its encouragement of theological freedom than for its own particular dogmatic negations. This outlook led sometimes to unexpected and unconventional conclusions. Thus he maintained that the Resurrection and the nature miracles of the Gospels were not *a priori* impossible, though the evidence for affirming them was insufficient, and that, though the Apostle *John was the author of the Fourth Gospel, the gospel was of only very limited historical value. Among his works were: *The Jewish Messiah* (1877), *Philo Judaeus* (2 vols., 1888), *Via, Veritas, Vita* (*Hibbert Lectures for 1894; 1894), *An Inquiry into the Character and Authorship of the Fourth Gospel* (1903), and *Studies in Christian Doctrine* (1908).

A Memorial Introduction by E. Drummond (daughter) and G. D. *Hicks is prefixed to his *Pauline Meditations* (1919), pp. vii–lxii. A. S. *Peake in *DNB, 1912–1921*, pp. 163 f.

Dry Mass (*Missa sicca*). An abbreviated form of Mass which became customary esp. in the late Middle Ages. It was not properly a Mass at all, since the *Offertory, *Canon, and Communion were omitted, but it was used on a variety of occasions, e.g. when the priest wished to say a second Mass on a particular day (the prescriptions against *bination prohibiting a proper Mass); on the occasion of pilgrimages, when a priest who had not broken his fast was not available; in rough sea on board ship (then called a *missa nautica* or *missa navalis*); or on hunting expeditions (*missa venatoria, missa venatica*). The celebration of Dry Masses was particularly widespread in France, and made its way even to Rome. It survives among the *Carthusians, who may say a Dry Mass of Our Lady in their cells after *Prime or *Terce; the practice is now optional. In the RC Church the pre-1955 Blessing of Palms on Palm Sunday, and in the C of E the *Ante-Communion service when ended with the 'Prayer for the Church Militant', may be regarded as forms of it.

J. Pinsk, 'Die *Missa sicca*', *JLW* 4 (1924), pp. 90–118.

Dryden, John (1651–70), poet, dramatist, and controversial writer. Of *Puritan upbringing, he served in a civilian capacity under O. *Cromwell, whose death he commemorated in *Heroic Stanzas* (1659). *Astrea Redux* (1660), written to celebrate the return of *Charles II, included a plea for clemency for those such as his family who had served under the Protectorate. His next major poem, *Annus Mirabilis* (1666), published in the aftermath of the Great Fire and in the middle of an unpopular war, established his skill as an advocate of royal policy. *Religio Laici* (1682) was inspired by the *Deists' sceptical use of R. *Simon's *Histoire critique du Vieux Testament*, which Dryden defended as compatible with Anglican freedom of inquiry. He depicted the C of E as providing a *via media* between Popery and fanaticism, at the same time reflecting severely on *Calvinist tenets on the legitimacy of resistance, which he likened to Catholic claims to the right to depose a heretical monarch. Presbyterians were prominent among the Whigs who sought to exclude the future *James II on grounds of his RCism, and Dryden, as poet laureate and historiographer royal, sought to elaborate on the parallel between Rome and Geneva in such works as the verse satire *Absalom and Achitophel* (1681) and the tragedy *The Duke of Guise* (1683). After James's accession Dryden became a RC (1686) and defended his new Church as the 'milk white hind' in the allegorical *Hind and the Panther*, published in 1687 after the first *Declaration of Indulgence. Dismissed from office at the Revolution of 1688, he turned to theatre and verse translation.

The standard edn. of his Works is that of W. Scott (18 vols., London, 1808), with Life as vol. 1; rev. edn. by G. Saintsbury (18 vols., Edinburgh, 1882–93); more recent edn. by E. N. Hooker and others (Berkeley and Los Angeles, 1956 ff.). *Letters*, also ed. C. E. Ward (Durham, NC, 1942) and *Poems*, ed. J. Kinsley (4 vols., Oxford, 1958). M. van Doren, *The Poetry of John Dryden* (New York, 1920; 3rd edn., 1946); J. M. Osborn, *John Dryden: Some Biographical Facts and Problems* (New York, 1940; rev. edn., Gainsville, Fla, 1965); D. N. Smith, *John Dryden* (Clark Lectures, 1948–9; Cambridge, 1950); C. E. Ward, *The Life of John Dryden* (Chapel Hill, NC, and London [1961]); B. King (ed.), *Dryden's Mind and Art* (Edinburgh, 1969); S. N. Zwicker, *Politics and Language in Dryden's Poetry* (Princeton, NJ [1984]); J. A. Winn, *John Dryden and his World* (New Haven, Conn., and London [1987]). H. Macdonald, *John Dryden: A Bibliography of Early Editions and Drydeniana* (1939); D. J. Latt and S. H. Monk, *John Dryden: A Survey and Bibliography of Critical Studies, 1895–1974* (Minneapolis [1976]). J. Barnard in *NCBEL* 2 (1971), cols. 439–63.

dryness. See ARIDITY.

dualism. (1) A philosophical doctrine which holds that mind and matter are distinct, equally real, and not essentially related, as opposed to *monism, which asserts that all that exists has a single ultimate nature.

(2) A metaphysical system which holds that good and evil are the outcome or product of separate and equally ultimate first causes.

(3) The view, attributed to the *Nestorians by their enemies, but repudiated by themselves, that in the Incarnate Christ there were not merely two natures but two persons, a human and a Divine.

S. Pétrement, *Le Dualisme chez Platon, les Gnostiques et les Manichéens* (Bibliothèque de Philosophie Contemporaine, 1947), and other works of this author; U. Bianchi, *Il dualismo religioso: Saggio storico ed etnologico* (1958). J. Duchesne-Guillemin and H. Dörrie in *RAC* 4 (1959), cols. 334–50, s.v. 'Dualismus'; U. Bianchi in M. Eliade (ed.), *Encyclopedia of Religion*, 4 [1987], pp. 506–12, s.v.

Dublin (*Dubh-linn*, 'the black pool'). Dublin grew up as a Norse town during the 9th cent. The population was mixed Hiberno-Irish by the 11th cent., when, prob. at the instigation of the Norse king Sihtric of Dublin (d. 1036), the city received a bishop. Dúnájn, or Donatus, the first known bishop, died in 1074. His early successors were trained in England, and, like the Bps. of Waterford and Limerick, the Bps. of Dublin made profession of allegiance to the Abp. of *Canterbury. These dioceses were more a part of the English Church than the Irish, as letters to and from Canterbury show. In 1152 at the Synod of Kells *pallia were conferred on the bishops of Dublin and Tuam as well as on the Abps. of *Armagh and Cashel, and Dublin was integrated into the Irish hierarchy. The first Abp., Patrick, was succeeded by St Laurence O'Toole (Abp. 1162–80), who made the cathedral chapter a community of *canons regular. During his archiepiscopate the English invasion of Ireland took place. Dublin was established as the bridgehead and later the capital of English government, and subsequent Abps. down to the *Reformation were exclusively Englishmen nominated by the Crown. John Comyn (Abp. 1182–1212) pursued a strongly pro-English policy. He also laid the foundations of St Patrick's Cathedral and secured privileges for his see at the expense of Armagh. This rivalry continued throughout the Middle Ages, and was not finally settled in the RC succession until 1893.

In 1536 *Henry VIII appointed as Abp. George *Browne, who, under *Edward VI, introduced the BCP and was deposed under *Mary in 1554. Under *Elizabeth I the (Protestant) Church of *Ireland was finally established, with possession of the two cathedrals of Holy Trinity (now Christ Church) and St Patrick's, and in 1591 *Trinity College was founded to support the settlement. The majority of the population, however, remained RC, despite spasmodic persecution during the next two centuries; during this period there were but few resident archbishops, Dublin frequently being governed by *Vicars General. John Carpenter (Abp. 1770–86) reorganized the RC diocese, and normal life was resumed at the end of the 18th cent. under the Dominican Thomas Troy (Abp. 1786–1823). Under him *Maynooth College was founded, the pro-cathedral, dedicated to Our Lady, was begun in 1815, and many schools and religious houses were established. Since 1929 Dublin has been the seat of a Papal *nuncio.

Notable Protestant Abps. in modern times include R. *Whately (1831), R. C. *Trench (1864), J. H. *Bernard (1915), C. F. D'Arcy (1919; translated to Armagh in 1920), a considerable philosopher, and G. O. Simms (1956; translated to Armagh, 1969).

There is much primary material ed. J. T. Gilbert, *Historical and Municipal Documents of Ireland, A.D. 1172–1320* (Rolls Series, 1870). H. Cotton, *Fasti Ecclesiæ Hibernicæ: The Succession of the Prelates and Members of Cathedral Bodies in Ireland*, 2 (1848), pp. 1–212; 5 (1860), pp. 77–139. J. T. Gilbert, *A History of the City of Dublin* (3 vols., 1854–9); D. A. Chart, *The Story of Dublin* (Medieval Towns Series, 1907; rev. edn., 1932). A. Gwynn, SJ, 'The Origins of the See of Dublin', *Irish Ecclesiastical Record*, 5th ser. 57 (1941), pp. 40–55, 97–112. M. V. Ronan, *The Reformation in Dublin 1536–1558* (1926). [P. F.] Moran, *History of the Catholic Archbishops of Dublin, since the Reformation*, 1 (Dublin, 1864). W. Butler, *The Cathedral of Holy Trinity, Dublin: Christ Church* (1901); W. M. Mason, *The History and Antiquities of the Collegiate and Cathedral Church of St Patrick, near Dublin, from its foundation in 1190, to the Year 1819* (Dublin, 1820). J. H. Bernard, *The Cathedral Church of St Patrick* (Bell's Cathedral Series, 1903). N. Donnelly, *Short History of Some Dublin Parishes* (1906). C. Mooney, OFM, in *DHGE* 14 (1960), cols. 830–936, s.v., with bibl.; R. D. Edwards in *NCE* 4 (1967), pp. 1076–9, s.v., also with bibl. For ecclesiastical history see also bibl. s.v. IRELAND, CHRISTIANITY IN.

Dublin Review. This quarterly RC review owes its origin to M. J. Quin (1796–1843), an Irishman who practised at the English bar. The first issue appeared in May 1836. It has exercised from the first a great influence both within and outside the RC Church. For its success in its earliest years, N. *Wiseman and D. *O'Connell were largely responsible; and it was a quotation from St *Augustine—*securus iudicat orbis terrarum*—in an article by N. Wiseman in the issue for Aug. 1839, that encouraged J. H. *Newman's first serious doubts about the Catholicity of the C of E. From 1863 to 1878, under the editorship of W. G. *Ward, it strongly supported the cause of Papal Infallibility and attacked theological liberalism. In 1961 its name was changed to *The Wiseman Review*, but it reverted to its original title in 1965. In 1969 it was incorporated into *The Month*.

Arts. in *Dublin Review*, 198 (1936), pp. 187–321. T. Corbishley, SJ, 'Marriage of True Minds', *Month*, NS 42 (1969), pp. 4–7.

Dubourg, Anne (*c.*1520–59), French Protestant martyr. In 1547 he became professor of civil law at Orléans. It was prob. here that he was first drawn towards the Reformed faith, though he remained formally a Catholic until after becoming *conseiller-clerc* to the Parliament of *Paris in 1557. At Easter 1559 he professed his faith by receiving communion with the *Huguenots. A provocative speech in defence of the Huguenots delivered in Parliament before Henry II on 10 June 1559 led to his arrest and trial for heresy. He was burnt at the stake on 23 Dec. 1559.

M. Lelièvre, 'Anne du Bourg avant son incarcération à la Bastille', *Bulletin de la Société de l'Histoire du Protestantisme Français*, 36 (1887), pp. 569–90; id., 'Le procès et le supplice d'Anne du Bourg', ibid. 37 (1888), pp. 281–95 and 337–55; id., 'Les derniers jours d'Anne du Bourg', ibid., pp. 506–29; id., *Anne du Bourg, conseiller au Parlement de Paris et martyr* (Toulouse, 1903). R. d'Amat in *Dictionnaire de Biographie Française*, 11 (1967), pp. 1035 f., s.v.

Dubricius, St (6th cent.), also 'Dyfrig', reputed Bp. of *Llandaff. None of the traditions about him seems to merit credence. He is said to have been a pupil of St *Germanus of Auxerre (chronologically impossible); to have had his headquarters at Henllan near Ross and at Moccas,

whence he established many other monastic settlements; and to have spent his last years as a hermit on the island of Bardsey (Ynys Enlli). He was the subject of many medieval legends, *Geoffrey of Monmouth making him Abp. of Caerleon and asserting that he crowned King Arthur. Tradition also makes him the consecrator of St *Samson of Dol and of St *Deiniol. Feast day, 14 Nov.

Apart from passing reference in the Life of St Samson, the sources are all late: *The Liber Landavensis* (Book of Llandaff; ed. J. G. Evans and J. Rhys, 'Old Welsh Texts', 4; Oxford, 1893, pp. 68–86); Geoffrey of Monmouth, *Historia Regum Britanniae*, 8. 12, 9. 4, 12, and 15 (ed. A. Griscom, New York and London, 1929, pp. 413, 432, 437, 453, and 458); late 12th-cent. Life by Benedict of Gloucester pr. in H. *Wharton, *Anglia Sacra*, 2 (London, 1691), pp. 654–61. Hardy, 1, pp. 40–4. S. Baring-Gould and J. Fisher, *The Lives of British Saints*, 2 (1908), pp. 359–82. G. H. Doble, *Saint Dubricius* ('Welsh Saints', 2; Guildford and Esher, 1943); rev. edn., *Lives of the Welsh Saints*, ed. D. S. Evans (Cardiff, 1971), pp. 56–87. T. F. Tout in *DNB* 16 (1888), pp. 82 f.

Ducaeus, Fronto (1559–1624), Fronton du Duc, *patristic scholar. He became a *Jesuit in 1577 and was librarian at the College of Clermont at Paris from 1604. He edited many Greek patristic writings, including those of *Chrysostom (12 vols., 1609–36), *Gregory of Nyssa (2 vols., 1615), and *Basil the Great (3 vols., 1618–38). He also issued an extended reply to *du Plessis-Mornay's book on the Eucharist.

Sommervogel, 3 (1892), cols. 233–49, and 9 (1900), col. 254. P. Lejay in *CE* 5 (1909), p. 181, s.v. 'Duc, Fronton du'; P. Bernard in *DTC* 6 (1920), cols. 930–3; suppl. note in *DHGE* 19 (1981), cols. 188 f., both s.v. 'Fronton du Duc'.

Du Cange, Charles Dufresne (1610–88), French historian and philologist. He was educated as a lawyer, but becoming dissatisfied with that profession, purchased in 1645 the position of Treasurer of France. His interest in history led him to a special study of Byzantine Greek and Low Latin, of which languages he soon became master. In 1678 he published his *Glossarium ad scriptores mediae et infimae latinitatis* (3 vols., fol.), which remains the principal complete dictionary of Late Latin. It is a work of immense erudition based on a great variety of sources. This was followed in 1688 by a similar work on Low Greek (2 vols., fol.). Du Cange is also the author of important works on Byzantine and French history.

The Lat. 'Glossary' has frequently been ed. and much expanded. An edn. in 6 vols. was issued by the *Maurists, Paris, 1733–6; standard edn. by L. Favre (10 vols., Niort, 1883–7), with 'Notice sur la vie et les ouvrages de Charles Dufresne Du Cange' appended to vol. 9 (separate pagination; it is followed by a detailed list of his works, pub. and unpub.). A photographic repr. of the Gk. 'Glossary' was issued at Paris, 1943. M. Esposito in *DACL* 4 (1921), cols. 1654–60, s.v., with detailed bibl.; H. *Leclercq, OSB, ibid. 8 (pt. 1; 1928), cols. 1422–52, s.v. 'Latin, 1. Le Glossarium'; J. H. Baxter in *NCE* 4 (1967), pp. 1086 f., s.v.

Duchesne, Louis (1843–1922), French Church historian. After being ordained priest in 1867, he continued his theological studies in Rome and subsequently travelled in Greece and Asia Minor. In 1877 he was appointed professor of Church history at the *Institut Catholique at Paris, a position he resigned in 1885 owing to the opposition aroused by his lectures on the history of doctrine. For the next ten years he held a chair at the École Supérieure des Lettres. From 1895 to his death he was director of the French school at Rome; in 1910 he became a member of the French Academy. He was eminent esp. in the field of Christian archaeology and the history of the early Church, though his sharp critical sense and negative attitude towards traditional legends aroused opposition. His works include an edition of the *Liber Pontificalis (2 vols., 1886–92), Origines du culte chrétien (1889; Eng. tr. by M. L. McClure under the title Christian Worship, 1903), Fastes épiscopaux de l'ancienne Gaule (3 vols., 1894–1915), L'Histoire ancienne de l'Église chrétienne (3 vols., 1906–10, put on the *Index in 1912; Eng. tr., 3 vols., 1909–24), and L'Église au sixième siècle (1925).

Duchesne's Scripta Minora: Études de topographie romaine et de géographie ecclésiastique (Collection de l'École Française de Rome, 13; 1973), with bibl. by J.-C. Picard, pp. ix–l. E. Dupont, Mgr Duchesne chez lui en Bretagne (Rennes, 1923). C. d'Hablorville, Grandes Figures de l'Église contemporaine (1925), pp. 1–177. Monseigneur Duchesne et son temps: Actes du Colloque organisé par l'École Française de Rome (Palais Farnèse, 23–25 mai 1973) (Collection de l'École Française de Rome, 23; 1973). B. Waché, Monseigneur Louis Duchesne (1843–1922): Historien de l'Église, Directeur de l'École Française de Rome (ibid. 167; 1992). H. *Leclercq, OSB, in DACL 6 (1925), cols. 2680–735, s.v. 'Historiens du christianisme. 38'; P. d'Espezel in DHGE 14 (1960), cols. 965–84.

du Duc, Fronton. See DUCAEUS, FRONTO.

duelling, Christian attitude to. Despite the protest of the Church, the recognition of the judicial duel by civil law continued till the later Middle Ages; and until the early 19th cent. in England, and much later abroad, the duel, though forbidden by law, was a recognized court of appeal in questions of 'honour' among the upper classes. In the *Codex Iuris Canonici of 1917 (can. 2351) automatic *excommunication was decreed for all in any way concerned with a duel. The subject is not specifically mentioned in the 1983 Code.

J. G. Millingen, The History of Duelling (2 vols., 1841). V. G. Kiernan, The Duel in European History (Oxford, 1988). F. Billacois, Le Duel dans la société française des XVIe–XVIIe siècles [1986]. V. Cathrein, SJ, in CE 5 (1909), pp. 184–7, s.v.; P. Fourneret in DTC 4 (1911), cols. 1845–56, s.v. 'Duel'; L. Falletti in DDC 5 (1953), cols. 3–40, s.v. 'Duel'.

Duff, Alexander (1806–78), Scottish *Presbyterian missionary. The first missionary of the Established Church of Scotland to India, he arrived at Calcutta in 1830, after twice being shipwrecked. At once he opened a school there, which later developed into a college that became a centre of W. education in India. From 1834 till 1840 he was engaged in stirring up the Church of Scotland to support his work; but shortly after his return to India in 1840 came the Schism of 1843, and Duff, joining the *Free Church, lost all his mission property. He nevertheless continued his work, until in 1849 he had to return home. In 1851 (and again in 1873) he was elected Chairman of the General Assembly of the Free Church. During his last stay in India (1856–64) he was largely occupied with the foundation of the University of Calcutta. In 1864 he visited S. Africa and on his return to Scotland spent much of the rest of his life working for the missionary cause.

Life by G. Smith (2 vols., London, 1879). Memorials of Alexander Duff (1890) by his son. W. Paton, Alexander Duff (1923). W. G. Blaikie in DNB 16 (1888), pp. 125–8, s.v.

Dufresne, Charles, Sieur Du Cange. See DU CANGE, CHARLES DUFRESNE.

Dugdale, William (1605–86), author of the *Monasticon Anglicanum (q.v.). He spent nearly all his life in antiquarian research. His share in the Monasticon Anglicanum began with his meeting in 1638 with Roger Dodsworth, then engaged in collecting documents illustrating the history of Yorkshire and the foundation of monasteries in the N. of England. A little later, in view of the dreaded war, he was commissioned by Sir Christopher Hatton to make exact drafts and records of monuments in the principal churches of England. During the Civil War he was employed by *Charles I in the delivery of royal warrants demanding the surrender of castles held by rebel garrisons. Besides the Monasticon, of which the first volume appeared in 1655, his writings included Antiquities of Warwickshire (1656), History of St Paul's Cathedral (1658), and The Baronage of England (1675–6). In 1677 Dugdale was created Garter Principal King of Arms.

His Visitation of the County of Yorks was pr. in The Surtees Society, 36 (1859), with index by G. J. Armytage (London, 1872), and ed. J. W. Clay (3 vols., Exeter, 1894–1917); that of Lancs ed. F. R. Raines (Chetham Society, 84, 85, and 88; 1872–3); that of Staffs ed. H. S. Grazebrook in The William Salt Archaeological Society, 2 (pt. 2; 1881), pp. 23–65, and by G. J. Armytage and W. H. Rylands (The Publications of the Harleian Society, 64; 1912); that of Derbys pub. London, 1879; that of Durham ed. J. Foster (London, 1887) and pr. in The Newcastle upon Tyne Record Series, 5 (1925), pp. 1–84; that of Cumberland and Westmorland ed. J. Foster (Carlisle, 1891); that of Northumberland ed. id. (Newcastle upon Tyne, 1891) and pr. in The Newcastle upon Tyne Record Series, 4 (1924), pp. 1–102. W. Hamper (ed.), The Life, Diary and Correspondence of Sir William Dugdale (1827). Short anon. Life (London, 1713); Life in Heraldic Miscellanies (London [1793]), pp. 1–24; W. F. S. Dugdale, 'Sir William Dugdale', in A. Dryden (ed.), Memorials of Old Warwickshire (1908), pp. 219–230. D. C. Douglas, English Scholars (1939), pp. 31–59; 2nd edn. (1951), pp. 30–51. F. Maddison, D. Styles, and A. Wood, Sir William Dugdale 1605–1686: A List of his printed works and of his portraits with notes on his life and the manuscript sources (Warwick, 1953). L. Fox (ed.), English Historical Scholarship in the Sixteenth and Seventeenth Centuries: A record of the papers delivered at a Conference arranged by the Dugdale Society to commemorate the tercentenary of the publication of Dugdale's Antiquities of Warwickshire (1956), esp. pp. 88–91.

Duhm, Bernhard (1847–1928), OT scholar. He was born at Bingum in Ostfriesland and received his schooling in Aurich and his theological education at Göttingen, where he became professor extraordinarius in 1877. In 1888 he was appointed professor ordinarius at Basle, where he remained till his death. It was above all as an interpreter of the Prophets that Duhm excelled. His first book, Die Theologie der Propheten als Grundlage für die innere Entwicklungsgeschichte der israelitischen Religion dargestellt (1875), laid a sound foundation for the best of his later work. It also gave an impulse from the side of prophetic criticism to the great contemporary movement in *Pentateuchal criticism, which led to the establishment of the 'documentary hypothesis' associated with J. *Wellhausen. Duhm held that the completed Law was later than the 8th- and 7th-cent. Prophets. His reconstruction of the development of Israelite religion was a counterpart to what J. Wellhausen was to present in his *Prolegomena*. Further, Duhm sought to understand the Prophets as great religious personalities. His commentary on Isaiah (1892) exercised a far-reaching influence. Of special interest were his separation of Is. 56–66 from 40–55 (*Deutero Isaiah) as a later composition (*Trito-Isaiah) and his view that the four *Servant Songs (42: 1–4, 49: 1–6, 50: 4–9, and 52: 13–53: 12) were not the work of Deutero-Isaiah. The whole commentary was marked by discerning exegesis and poetic appreciation, but also at times marred by apparently arbitrary textual emendation. In *Israels Propheten* (1916; 2nd edn., 1922) he presented his interpretation of the Prophets again in more popular form. He also published commentaries on Job (1897), Psalms (1899; 2nd edn., 1922) and Jeremiah (1901), and a number of short studies, mainly on aspects of OT religion.

Biog. foreword by W. Baumgarten to his edn. of Duhm's comm. on Isaiah, *Das Buch Jesaja* (5th edn., 1967), pp. v–xiii. H. J. Kraus, *Geschichte der historisch-kritischen Erforschung des Alten Testaments von der Reformation bis zur Gegenwart* (Neukirchen, 1956), pp. 250–7; 3rd edn. (1982), pp. 275–83. J. Ebach in *TRE* 9 (1982), pp. 214 f., s.v., with further refs.

Dukhobors. See DOUKHOBORS.

dulia (Latinized form of Greek δουλεία, 'service'). The reverence which, acc. to Orthodox and RC theology, may be paid to the saints, as contrasted with *hyperdulia* (ὑπερδουλεία), which may be paid only to the BVM, and *latria* (λατρεία), which is reserved for God alone. In classical as contrasted with ecclesiastical usage δουλεία is a stronger term than λατρεία.

du Moulin, Pierre (1568–1658), 'Molinaeus', French Reformed theologian. The son of a Protestant preacher, Joachim du Moulin, whose family had settled at Sedan, Pierre became tutor in 1588 to the young Earl of Rutland. In 1592 he returned from England to the Continent and was appointed professor of philosophy and Greek in the university of *Leiden. From 1599 to 1620 he was minister of the Reformed Congregation at Charenton, and from 1620 till his death minister and professor at Sedan. He took a prominent part in religious controversy, upholding a mediating position which irritated Catholics and Calvinists alike; and more than 80 writings flowed from his pen. Over a long period he kept up relations with many Anglicans, including *James I. P. *Jurieu (1637–1713) was his grandson.

His Autobiog. was pub. in the *Bulletin de la Société de l'Histoire du Protestantisme français*, 7 (1858), pp. 170–82, 333–44, and 465–77. Eng. tr. of his *Nouveauté du papisme, opposée à l'antiquité du vray christianisme* by his son, P. du Moulin (London, 1662), with Life by id. (no pagination). L. Rimbault, *Pierre du Moulin 1568–1658* (De Pétrarque à Descartes, 10; 1966), incl. Life by his son, repr. pp. 195–234, and various unpublished docs. G. Bonet Maury in *PRE* (3rd edn.), 5 (1898), pp. 56–60, s.v.

Dunkards, Dunckers. See TUNKERS.

Duns Scotus, Bl Johannes (*c*.1265–1308), 'Doctor Subtibilis' or 'Doctor Marianus', medieval philosopher and theologian. Little is known of his life. He was prob. born near Duns in Berwickshire. He took the *Franciscan habit, perhaps at Dumfries *c*.1280, and was ordained priest in Northampton in 1291. He was then apparently studying in *Oxford, where he read both arts and theology and lectured on the *Sentences* of *Peter Lombard, prob. in 1298–9. He is known to have been in Oxford in 1300–1. It is possible that he lectured in Cambridge (1301–2), but the evidence is weak. Though the idea that he studied in Paris *c*.1293–6 is improbable, it is certain that he completed his doctoral requirements there and became regent master in 1305. In 1307 he moved to *Cologne, where he died the following year.

His principal work is the commentary on the *Sentences*. This survives in three forms: copies of his own lecture notes (*Lectura*) for the Oxford commentary; copies of students' notes (*Reportatae*) taken from the various lectures; copies of his own final revision of the various notes. This last and most important version (the *Ordinatio*) was left incomplete at his death. His other writings include commentaries on some of *Aristotle's and *Porphyry's works on logic, a set of *quaestiones* on Aristotle's *Metaphysics*, a *Tractatus de Primo Principio*, and *Quodlibeta*.

Writing after the condemnation of a number of Aristotelian positions (including some opinions of St *Thomas Aquinas) by the Abp. of Paris in 1277, Scotus attempts to mediate between Aristotelianism and the Augustinianism associated with his main opponent, *Henry of Ghent. Scotus definitively rejects the Aristotelian principle of plenitude (no genuine possibility can remain forever unrealized), and posits instead the radical contingency (non-necessity) both of created entities and of God's action. He believes that for human will to be genuinely free, it must be really able to will what it does not in fact choose to will. The intellect offers a strong guidance to the will, inclining it to the right act; but the will is able to go against the suggestion of reason. Thus, Scotus denies the universal applicability of Aristotle's principle, 'everything which is moved is moved by some other agent', on the grounds that the will is freely capable of moving itself to an action. God's will is free in the sense that God can freely desire opposite objects and effects: thus, human actions are given moral value only if God commands them. The exception is the act of loving God. It is impossible to understand the word 'God' without also understanding that God should be loved. For this reason, God cannot will that creatures hate Him.

Scotus' proof of the existence of God attempts to show that one necessary cause is required in order to explain the existence of contingent entities. Creatures do not exist necessarily, and have essentially only the possibility of existence. But if the existence of some creature is really possible, then the creature must be capable of being caused; and if a creature is capable of being caused, there must be some agent able to cause it. Thus, in order to explain the existence of creatures, it is necessary to posit some being that exists necessarily.

Scotus rejects St Thomas Aquinas's position that individuation is by matter, and holds instead that the unity and individuality of each created thing is given by its own form of individuality (*haecceitas*) added to its matter and form. Unlike some of his contemporaries, he does not think that all substances—including God and the *angels—are material. He also believes that not every complete individual thing is a person: Christ's human nature is a complete individual thing that is not a human person. Individuals are properly called persons by virtue of the negative qualification of not being united to a divine person. Scotus rejects the Aristotelian position that the intellect can know only the universal ideas that it abstracts from sense data, and allows instead a certain intuitive knowledge of individual things. On the other hand, he rejects Henry of Ghent's Augustinian position that certitude follows only from divine illumination, and holds, like Aquinas, that certitude derives from necessary principles that are known naturally by the intellect.

In his theology Scotus lays stress on the primacy of Christ as the supreme manifestation of God's love; it follows that Christ's coming was not conditioned by any other historical events, and in particular that the Incarnation would have taken place irrespective of the *Fall. For Scotus this also entailed the doctrine of the *Immaculate Conception of the BVM, a doctrine that he was the first well-known theologian to defend.

The thought of Scotus exercised a profound influence in the Middle Ages and beyond; in particular it was the principal element in the Franciscan theological tradition well into the 18th cent. Though the rise of *Nominalism in the 14th cent. reduced the impact of Scotus' *Realist metaphysics in the later Middle Ages, in modern times there has been renewed sympathy with his appreciation of the non-intellectual elements in man. The word 'dunce', used by humanists and the Reformers to ridicule the subtleties of the Schools, is a curious testimony to his popularity. He was beatified in 1993. Feast day, 8 Nov.

Collected edns. of his works [by L. *Wadding, OFM, and others] (12 vols., Lyons, 1639; with repr. of his Life by Wadding from the *Annales*) and F. Vivès (26 vols., Paris, 1891–5; repr., Farnborough, 1969); crit. edn. of his *Opera [Theologica]*, by C. Balić, L. Modrić, and others (Rome, 1950 ff.); an edn. of his *Opera Philosophica* by the Franciscan Institute of St Bonaventure, NY, is in preparation. *De Primo Principio*, ed., with Eng. tr., by A. [B.] Wolter, OFM (Chicago, 1966; 2nd edn., with comm. [1982]). *Quodlibetal Questions*, ed., with Sp. tr., by F. Alluntis, OFM (Biblioteca de Autores Cristianos, 1968); Eng. tr. from this text by F. Alluntis, OFM, and A. B. Wolter, OFM, *God and Creatures* (Princeton, NJ, and London [1975]). Selection of his *Philosophical Writings* ed., with Eng. tr., by A. [B.] Wolter, OFM (Nelson Philosophical Texts, 1962; 2nd edn., Indianapolis and Cambridge [1987]). Eng. tr. of some texts *On the Will and Morality* by id. (Washington, DC, 1986). Fr. tr., with comm., of his *Commentary on the Sentences*, Ordinatio 1. 3. 1, 1. 8. 1, and Collatio 24, by O. Boulnois, as *Sur la connaissance de Dieu et l'univocité de l'étant* [1988].

A. Bertoni, *Le Bienheureux Jean Duns Scot: sa vie, sa doctrine, et ses disciples* (Levanto, 1917); E. Longpré, *La Philosophie du B. Duns Scot* (1924; repr. from *Études franciscaines*); [C. Balić,] *Les Commentaires de Jean Duns Scotus sur les quatre livres des sentences: Étude historique et critique* (Bibliothèque de la *RHE*, 1; 1927); E. Bettoni, OFM, *Duns Scoto* (Brescia, 1946; Eng. tr., Washington, 1961); id., *Duns Scoto Filosofo* (Milan, 1966); A. [B.] Wolter, OFM, *The Transcendentals and their Function in the Metaphysics of Duns Scotus* (Catholic University of America, Philosophical Series, 96; Washington, 1946); id., *The Philosophical Theology of John Duns Scotus* [Collected Papers], ed. M. McC. Adams (Ithaca, NY, and London, 1990); E. *Gilson, *Jean Duns Scot: Introduction à ses positions fondamentales* (Études de philosophie médiévale, 42; 1952); R. R. Effler, OFM, *John Duns Scotus and the Principle 'Omne Quod Movetur ab Alio Movetur'* (St Bonaventure, NY,

1962); J. K. Ryan and B. M. Bonansea (eds.), *John Duns Scotus, 1265–1965* (Studies in Philosophy and the History of Philosophy, 3; Washington, 1965); F. Wetter, *Die Trinitätslehre des Johannes Duns Scotus* (BGPM 41, Heft 5; 1967); L. Honnefelder, *Ens Inquantum Ens: Der Begriff des Seienden als solchen als Gegenstand der Metaphysik nach der Lehre des Johannes Duns Scotus* (ibid., NF 16; 1979); C. Bérubé, *De l'homme à Dieu selon Duns Scot, Henri de Gand et Olivi* (Bibliotheca Seraphico-Capuccina, 27; Rome, 1983), esp. pp. 113–223 and 241–390; B. M. Bonansea, OFM, *Man and his Approach to God in John Duns Scotus* (Langham, Md., etc. [1983]). The series 'Studia Scholastico-Scotistica', pub. by the Societas Internationalis Scotistica (Rome, 1968 ff. [8 vols. to 1984]) contains papers read at Scotistic conferences, 1966 ff. F. Copleston, SJ, *A History of Philosophy*, 2 (1950), pp. 476–551. O. Schäfer, OFM, *Bibliographia de Vita Operibus et Doctrina Iohannis Duns Scoti . . . Saec. XIX–XX* (Rome, 1955); S. Gieben, 'Bibliographia scotistica recentior (1953–1965)', *Laurentianum*, 6 (1965), pp. 492–522; D. A. Cress, 'Toward a Bibliography on Duns Scotus on the Existence of God', *Franciscan Studies*, 35 (1975), pp. 45–65. *BRUO*, 1 (1957), pp. 607–10; *BRUC*, pp. 198–201 and 674–5, with bibl. to 1961. P. Raymond, OFM Cap., in *DTC* 4 (1911), cols. 1865–947; C. Balić, OFM, in *NCE* 4 (1967), pp. 1102–6; W. Dettloff and L. Honnefelder in *TRE* 9 (1982), pp. 218–40.

Dunstan, St (*c*.909–88), Abp. of *Canterbury. After being attached for some time to the court of King *Athelstan, he made his profession as a monk at *Glastonbury (where he had earlier received the tonsure) and *c*.940 became abbot. He was a strict ascetic who completely reformed the monastery, insisting on the full observance of the *Benedictine Rule, and under him the monastery became famous for its learning. He became a royal counsellor under King Eadred (946–55), but during the next reign had to migrate to Flanders. After his recall in 957 by *Edgar, King of Mercia and Northumbria, he was made Bp. of *Worcester and London; after Edgar had become King of all England in 959, Dunstan was made Abp. of Canterbury the same year. The King and the Archbishop together planned and carried out a thorough reform of Church and State. After the death of Edgar, Dunstan and his friend St *Oswald secured the election of King *Edward the Martyr, who continued his predecessor's policy. Edward, however, ruled for only a short time, and under his successor Dunstan's influence began to decrease. The restoration of regular monastic life, which seems to have been virtually extinct in England by the middle of the 10th cent., was in the first instance Dunstan's work; but as it got under way in Edgar's reign (959–75) much of the initiative passed to his colleagues St *Ethelwold and St Oswald. He zealously supported the cause of learning and himself achieved fame as musician, illuminator, and metalworker. In the political field his most important work was his support of King Edgar. Feast day, 19 May. See also REGULARIS CONCORDIA.

W. *Stubbs (ed.), *Memorials of Saint Dunstan, Archbishop of Canterbury* (Rolls Series, 1874). Crit. edn., with Eng. tr., by M. Winterbottom and M. Lapidge of Lives by 'B' (unidentified) and Adalhard (Oxford Medieval Texts, in preparation). Books belonging to St Dunstan, possibly incl. specimens of his handwriting, reprod. with introd. by R. W. Hunt, *Saint Dunstan's Classbook from Glastonbury* (Umbrae Codicum Occidentalium, 4; Amsterdam, 1961). F. A. *Gasquet and E. *Bishop, *The Bosworth Psalter* (1908), Appendix by L. A. St L. Toke, 'Some Notes on the Accepted Date of St Dunstan's Birth', pp. 131–43. J. A. *Robinson, *The Times of St Dunstan* (Ford Lectures, 1922; 1923), esp. no. 4, pp. 81–103. D. [J.] Dales, *Dunstan: Saint and Statesman* (Cambridge, 1988). N. [L.] Ramsay and others (eds.), *St Dunstan: His Life, Times and Cult* (Woodbridge, Suffolk, 1992). [M.] D. *Knowles, OSB, *The Monastic Order in England* (Cambridge, 1940; 2nd edn., 1963), pp. 31–56. M. Lapidge, 'St Dunstan's Latin Poetry', *Anglia*, 98 (1980), pp. 101–6. N. Brooks, *The Early History of the Church of Canterbury* (Leicester, 1984), ch. 10, esp. pp. 243–53. [D.] H. Farmer in *DHGE* 14 (1960), cols. 1063–8, s.v.

duomo (cf. Lat. *domus*, 'a house'). The Italian name for a cathedral, as pre-eminently the house of God's people in the diocese.

Dupanloup, Félix Antoine Philibert (1802–78), Bp. of Orléans from 1849. A native of Savoy, he was educated in *Paris, and, on being ordained priest in 1825, was appointed *vicaire* of the Madeleine, whence he was transferred to the church of St-Roch in 1834. He instituted the method of teaching children known as the 'Catechism of *St-Sulpice', and became one of the foremost Catholic educationists of France. As superior of the seminary of St-Nicolas-du-Chardonnet (1837–45) he tried his new educational methods with the greatest success. As Bp. of Orléans, Dupanloup exerted strong pressure on public policy, esp. in education, and was active in securing for the Church the right, conceded by the 'Loi Falloux' of 1850, to conduct voluntary schools. Later he was an ardent advocate of the Pope's claims against the House of Savoy. At the First *Vatican Council (1870) he strongly advised the minority, of whom he was one, to abstain from voting and to withdraw, but he loyally accepted the decision of the Council when promulgated. His published works included *La Haute Éducation intellectuelle* (1850), *La Femme studieuse* (1869) and several panegyrics and pastoral letters.

Selected Letters ed. F. Lagrange (2 vols., Paris, 1888). Standard Life by id. (3 vols., ibid., 1883–4; Eng. tr., 2 vols., 1885); cf. [M.] U. Maynard, *Monseigneur Dupanloup et M. Lagrange son historien* (1884). Other Lives by M. M. F. Trench (anon., London, 1890) and E. Faguet (Paris, 1914). C. Marcilhacy, *Le Diocèse d'Orléans sous l'épiscopat de Mgr Dupanloup 1849–1878* (Histoire des mentalités [1962]), esp. part 1. S. Lösch, *Döllinger und Frankreich* (Munich, 1955), esp. pp. 247–342. R. Aubert, 'Monseigneur Dupanloup et le Syllabus', *RHE* 51 (1956), pp. 79–142, 471–512, 837–915, incl. orig. docs.; id., 'Mgr Dupanloup au début du concile du Vatican', in *Miscellanea Historiae Ecclesiasticae: Congrès de Stockholm, août 1960* (Bibliothèque de la *RHE* 38; 1961), pp. 96–116. *Mgr Dupanloup et les problèmes politiques de son temps, colloque 1978* (Société archéologique et historique de l'Orléanais, nº horssérie, 1980); *Education et images de la femme chrétienne en France au début du XXᵐᵉ siècle à l'occasion du centenaire de la mort de Mgr. Dupanloup*, ed. F. Mayeur and J. Gadille (Lyons, 1980), pp. 15–78 ('Monseigneur Dupanloup éducateur et ses disciples'). R. Aubert in *DHGE* 8 (1960), cols. 1070–122, s.v., with bibl.; id. in *NCE* 4 (1967), pp. 1108 f., s.v. For works dealing with his relations with the First Vatican Council, see also bibl. to the latter.

Du Perron, Jacques Davy (1556–1618), French cardinal, statesman, and controversialist. He was the son of a *Calvinist minister at Saint-Lô, a member of the minor nobility, who gave him a grounding in classical languages. In 1576 Du Perron went to Paris and was presented to Henry III. After wide reading, he was converted to RCism in 1577/8 and came to be much influenced by St Robert

*Bellarmine. Du Perron was appointed reader to the King and made a name for himself with funeral orations for P. de Ronsard in 1586 and *Mary, Queen of Scots, in 1587. Under *Henry IV he was made Bp. of Évreux in 1591. He helped to instruct Henry IV before his reception into the RC Church (1593) and was sent to Rome to secure Papal absolution from heresy for him in 1595. He was involved in a number of controversies, of which the best known is that with P. *du Plessis-Mornay in 1600; his refutation of him and his *Traité de l'Eucharistie* were published in the same volume in 1622. He was created a cardinal in 1604 and soon sent as ambassador to Rome, where he took part in the election of Popes Leo XI and *Paul V. In 1606 he was appointed Abp. of Sens; installed in 1609, he introduced a number of reforms in his archdiocese. After Henry's assassination (1610), he was appointed a member of the Regency. During 1611–12 he carried on a controversial correspondence with *James I (initially through I. *Casaubon) on the meaning of catholicity; this culminated in his *Replique à la Response du . . . Roi de la Grand Bretagne* (pub. 1620). He was also involved in the conflict between the *Gallicans and the *Ultramontanists. He attacked E. Richer's *De Ecclesiastica et Politica Potestate* (1611), which defended Gallican principles, and in his famous 'Harangue' at the Estates General in 1615 he again defended an Ultramontanist position against that favoured by the *tiers état*. The 'Harangue' provoked a reply from James I, upholding the power of kings as Divine but independent of the Pope. Du Perron was a member of the Académie des Valois and a poet of some renown.

Diverses Œuvres, ed. by his brother, Jean Davy Du Perron, who succeeded him as Abp. of Sens, and his nephew, Jacques Le Noël Du Perron, Bp. of Angoulême (Paris, 1622), with Life, pp. 1–36; *Ambassades et négotiations*, ed. by C. de Ligny, his secretary (ibid., 1623). Crit. edn. of his funeral oration for Ronsard by M. Simonin (Textes littéraires français, Geneva, 1985). Facsimile of a collection of his poems, orig. pub. Paris, 1622 (ibid., 1988). There are also facsimile reprs. of the Eng. trs. of his Refutation of du Plessis-Mornay, orig. pub. c.1601 (Ilkley, Yorks., 1978); of his Letter to Casaubon, orig. pub. 1612 (Menston, Yorks., 1971); of his Reply to James I, orig. pub. 1630 (Ilkley, 1975); and of his 'Harangue', orig. pub. 1616 (ibid., 1977). Further Life by [J. L.] de Burigny (Paris, 1768). P. Féret, *Le Cardinal Du Perron . . .: Étude historique et critique* (1877). *Le Cardinal Jacques Davy Du Perron: Mélanges publiés à l'occasion du IVᵉ Centenaire de la naissance par la Société d'Archéologie et d'Histoire Naturelle de la Manche* (Saint-Lô, 1956), with bibl. F. A. Yates, *The French Academies of the Sixteenth Century* (Studies of the Warburg Institute, 15; 1947), *passim* (see index s.v. 'Davy Du Perron'); R. Snoeks, *L'Argument de tradition dans la controverse eucharistique entre catholiques et réformés français au XVIIᵉ siècle* (Louvain and Gembloux, 1951), esp. pp. 76–129. C. Grente in *Dictionnaire des Lettres Françaises. Le XVIᵉ Siècle* (1951), pp. 271–6, s.v.; R. Snoeks in *DHGE* 14 (1960), cols. 1130–6, s.v., with extensive bibl.; T. de Morembert in *Dictionnaire de Biographie Française*, 12 (1970), cols. 339–41, s.v.

Dupin, Louis Ellies (1657–1719), a prolific and influential *Gallican theologian. The first volumes of his *Nouvelle Bibliothèque des Auteurs ecclésiastiques* (some 60 vols., 1686–1719) were considered too critical of the early Christian centuries and aroused opposition, notably from J. B. *Bossuet and R. *Simon. He was censured by the Abp. of Paris (1693), but continued writing the *Bibliothèque*, which was put on the *Index in 1757. Banished from Paris in 1704 for alleged *Jansenism, he was removed from his Regius professorship, but remained a respected member of the *Sorbonne. He was involved in the religious affairs of his age, esp. in opposition to the Bull *Unigenitus. Ecumenically minded, he took part in a project for union between the Russian and French Churches in 1717, and in Feb. 1718 he entered into correspondence with Abp. W. *Wake in an equally unsuccessful attempt to achieve union between the Churches of England and France. Besides his historical writings, his main works are theological and biblical: De Antiqua Ecclesiae Disciplina (1686), Traité de la doctrine chrétienne (1703), put on the Index respectively in 1688 and 1704, and Prolégomènes sur la Bible (1699). He also edited the works of St *Optatus (1700) and J. *Gerson (1706).

J. Gres-Gayer (ed.), Paris-Cantorbéry (1717-1720): Le Dossier d'un premier œcuménisme [1989]. Id., 'Un théologien gallican, témoin de son temps: Louis Ellies Du Pin (1657-1719)', Revue d'Histoire de l'Église de France, 72 (1986), pp. 67-121; id., 'Un théologien gallican et l'Écriture sainte: Le "Projet biblique" de Louis Ellies Du Pin (1657-1719)', in J.-R. Armogarthe (ed.), Le Grand Siècle et la Bible [1989], pp. 255-75; id., 'Le gallicanisme de Louis Ellies Du Pin (1657-1719)', Lias, 18 (1991), pp. 37-82. N. Sykes, William Wake, 1 (Cambridge, 1957), pp. 254-95 and 302-14. J. Carreyre in DTC 12 (pt. 2; 1935), cols. 2111-15, s.v. 'Pin'; A. Dodin in Dict. Sp. 3 (1957), cols. 1825-31, s.v.

du Plessis-Mornay, Philippe (1549-1623), French statesman and *Huguenot leader. He was a native of Normandy. After the death of his father (1559), his family became Protestants. He studied in Paris and then went on a tour through Europe. On his return, he served for a time with de Condé in the second War of Religion. After escaping from the St *Bartholomew's Day Massacre (1572) he fled to England, where he was befriended by Sir Philip Sidney. For the next ten years he acted as a military leader in the Huguenot cause and as diplomatic agent to William of Orange and *Henry of Navarre. In 1578 he published in London his Traité de l'Église (Eng. tr., 1579) and in 1579 finished writing De la Vérité de la religion chrétienne (pub. Antwerp, 1581; Eng. tr., 1587). He actively furthered the proceedings of the general synods of the French Reformed Churches and cherished the ideal of a union of all Protestant Churches, possibly under the aegis of *James I. In 1589 he became governor of Saumur, where he built a Protestant church and founded (1593) a Protestant academy. The conversion of Henry IV (1593), whose trusted counsellor he had been, came as a blow; but he continued to work for religious toleration and on behalf of his co-religionists, and helped to secure the Edict of *Nantes (1598). In 1598 he issued a treatise on the Eucharist, De l'Institution, usage et doctrine du saint sacrement de l'eucharistie en l'Église ancienne, the fruit of many years' study. J. D. *Du Perron charged him with innumerable misquotations from the Fathers, and at a public disputation before Henry IV, at Fontainebleau on 4 May 1600, du Plessis was defeated, though few actual misquotations were found. His Mysterium Iniquitatis seu Historia Papatus (Saumur, 1611; also pub. in French; Eng. tr., 1612) was an attack on C. *Baronius and R. *Bellarmine. In 1621, after the renewal of persecution under Louis XIII, he was deprived of the governorship of Saumur and retired to his castle, La Fôret-sur-Sèvre (Poitou), where he died.

The best edn. of his Mémoires et correspondance is that in 12 vols., Paris, 1824-5. This includes a memoir of his life by his widow (vol. 1, pp. 5-503), which is also ed., with some additional correspondence, by Mme de Witt-Guizot (Société de l'Histoire de France, 2 vols., 1868-9; partial Eng. tr. of the Life by L. Crump [1926]). [David de Licques and others], Histoire de la vie de Messire Philippes de Mornay (Leiden, 1647). R. Patry, Philippe du Plessis-Mornay (Paris, 1933). M. Richter, Il 'Discours de la Vie et de la Mort' di Philippe du Plessis-Mornay (Pubblicazioni dell'Università Cattolica del S. Cuore, Saggi e Ricerche, 3rd ser. 4; Milan, 1964), incl. text. J. Leclerc, SJ, Histoire de la tolérance au siècle de la réforme, 2 [1955], pp. 90-1 and 181-4; Eng. tr. (1960), pp. 104-6 and 213-15. E. Haag, La France Protestante, 7 (1857), pp. 512-42, s.v. 'Mornay, Philippe de'; R. Snoeks in DHGE 14 (1960), cols. 1136-41, s.v., with extensive bibl.

Duplex Querela. In the C of E the form of action open to a cleric whom the Bishop refuses to institute to a benefice to which he has been presented. Unlike the patron's corresponding action, *Quare Impedit, it takes place in an ecclesiastical court, viz. the *Court of Ecclesiastical Causes Reserved. Appeal lies to a Commission of Review, appointed by the Crown in Chancery. Where the cleric is himself the patron he may sue the bishop either under Duplex Querela or Quare Impedit but not in both actions at the same time.

duplication. An alternative term for *binination.

Duppa, Brian (1588-1662), Bp. of *Winchester. In 1629 he became Dean of *Christ Church, Oxford. A *High Churchman, he was in favour with the court. On W. *Laud's recommendation he was appointed tutor to the Prince of Wales (later *Charles II) and the Duke of Gloucester, with the former of whom he retained much influence all his life. In 1638 he became Bp. of *Chichester, and in 1641 of *Salisbury. From 1645 to 1660 Duppa was one of the leaders of the persecuted Church. He remained in close touch with *Charles I till his death, and during the Commonwealth did his utmost to keep the extruded clergy together and held private ordinations as opportunity offered. From 1653 to 1660, in conjunction with Edward Hyde at the exiled Court, he was making plans to preserve the episcopal succession, though without success. As W. *Juxon's representative, he was the chief consecrator at the first consecration after the Restoration. In 1660 he was translated to Winchester.

A spiritual manual by Duppa, Holy Rules and Helps to Devotion, both in Prayer and Practice (1673), was ed. by B. Parry (1675); it was frequently repr. in the 17th cent. G. Isham (ed.), The Correspondence of Bishop Brian Duppa and Sir Justinian Isham, 1650-1660 (Northamptonshire Record Society, 17 [1955]), with memoir of Duppa, pp. xix-xxxi. N. Pocock in DNB 16 (1888), pp. 242 f.

Dura Europos. This ancient city (the 'Pompeii of the Syrian desert') on the right bank of the Euphrates, half way between Aleppo and Baghdad, first attracted attention in 1920 through the accidental discovery of some paintings here by a British army officer. A preliminary survey was made by J. H. Breasted (1920), and the site systematically excavated by F. Cumont (1922-3) and later jointly by Yale University and the French Academy of Inscriptions (1928-37). The city, which was earlier a Seleucid fortress and then a Parthian caravan city, came into Roman hands c. AD 165, when it was again made a fortress. It was held until *c*.256, when it was abandoned. It has yielded a rich harvest of discoveries, among them: (1) a 3rd-cent. Gk. fragment of *Tatian's *Diatessaron; (2) the earliest known certain Jewish synagogue, AD 245, with notable paintings of events from OT history; and (3) an early Christian church. This was constructed from two rooms of a private house by removing the partition wall. It had a raised platform, doubtless for the altar, at the E. end, while a third room of the house was converted into the *baptistery. At first it appeared that the conversion of the building into a church dated from *c*.232, but in the Final Report of the Excavations it is argued that the building itself dates from *c*.232 and the conversion from the 240s.

F. Cumont, *Fouilles de Doura-Europos, 1922–1923* (Paris, 1926). P. V. C. Baur, M. I. Rostovtzeff and others, *The Excavations at Dura-Europos* (preliminary reports of excavations undertaken Oct. 1928–36 in annual sessions issued in 10 vols., New Haven, Conn., 1929–52; final report pub. ibid., 1943 ff., incl. vol. 8, part 1: *The Synagogue* by C. H. Kraeling, 1956 (repr., with additional material, incl. index, New York, 1979), and part 2: *The Christian Building*, by id., 1967), with bibl. General survey in M. I. Rostovtzeff, *Dura Europos and its Art* (Oxford, 1938); R. Wischnitzer, *The Messianic Theme in the Paintings of the Dura Synagogue* (Chicago, 1948). J. Gutmann (ed.), *The Dura-Europos Synagogue: A Re-Evaluation* (Missoula, Mont., 1973). C. Hopkins, *The Discovery of Dura-Europos*, ed. B. Goldman (1979). O. Eissfeldt in *RAC* 4 (1959), cols. 358–70, s.v., with extensive bibl.; J. A. Fischer in *NCE* 4 (1967), pp. 1112 f., s.v.

Durandus of Saint-Pourçain (*c*.1275–1334), scholastic philosopher, 'Doctor Modernus', also (by later writers) 'Doctor Resolutissimus'. He became a *Dominican and taught at *Paris, where he lectured on the Sentences and in 1312 became 'magister in theologia'. In 1313 he was summoned to be Lector at the Papal Court at *Avignon. Later he became Bp. successively of Limoux (1317), Le Puy-en-Velay (1318), and Meaux (1326). He was one of the earliest exponents of what came to be called *Nominalism, which he developed in directions distinct from the teaching of St *Thomas Aquinas. Rejecting the current doctrine on intelligible and sensible species, he held that the only real entities were individuals and that the search for a principle of individuation was meaningless. In theology he stood for a sharp contrast between faith and reason, holding e.g. that rational argument could not disprove that the doctrine of the Trinity did not contain impossibilities. He also held that the presence of Christ in the Eucharist did not preclude the continuing existence of the bread and wine. His principal work, a 'Commentary on the Sentences', survives in three recensions: (1) before 1308, (2) 1310–13, (3) 1317–27. In deference to the criticisms of his superiors he modified certain passages in the first recension, but the second recension was no less sharply criticized. He replied in three disputations (*Quodlibets) held at *Avignon. By the time of the third recension, Durandus as a bishop was free from the jurisdiction of the Dominican Order. His other writings include *De paupertate Christi et Apostolorum* (1322), *De Origine Potestatum et Jurisdictionum* (1329), and a treatise on the condition of human souls after their separation from the body (*c*.1333). Eleven articles in the last-named work were censured by a Papal Commission set up by *John XXII (1333), but the censure was lifted by *Benedict XII. Durandus was highly esteemed in the later Middle Ages.

Comm. on the Sentences (3rd recension) pub. Paris, 1508; several other edns. in the 16th cent.; crit. edn. of the *Quaestio de Natura Cognitionis* (II Sent. (A) d. 3, qu. 5) by J. Koch (Opuscula et Textus Historiam Ecclesiae eiusque Vitam atque Doctrinam illustrantia, 6; Münster, 1929). *De Origine Potestatum et Jurisdictionum*, pub. Paris, 1506. *Tractatus de Habitibus* ed. J. Koch (Opuscula et Textus Historiam Ecclesiae eiusque Vitam atque Doctrinam illustrantia, 8; Münster, 1930). *De Visione Dei quam habent Animae Sanctorum ante Iudicium Generale*, pr. in part in O. Raynaldus, *Annales Ecclesiastici*, 15 (Cologne, 1652), under the year 1333, nos. 49–57; brief extract from *De Paupertate Christi et Apostolorum*, ibid., under the year 1322, nos. 59–61. *Quodlibeta Avenionensia tria* ed. P. T. Stella (Textus et Studia in Historiam Scholasticae cura Pontificii Athenaei Salesiani, 1; Zurich, 1965). J. Koch, *Durandus de S. Porciano, O.P.: Forschungen zum Streit um Thomas von Aquin zu Beginn des 14. Jahrhunderts*, Teil 1, *Literargeschichtliche Grundlegung* (*BGPM* 26, Heft 1; 1927). P. Fournier, 'Durand de Saint-Pourçain, théologien', *Histoire littéraire de la France*, 37 (1938), pp. 1–38, with refs. J. Koch, 'Jakob von Metz, O.P., der Lehrer des Durandus de S. Porciano, O.P.', *AHDLMA* 4 (1929–30), pp. 169–232, repr. in his *Kleine Schriften*, 1 (Rome, 1973), pp. 133–200; see also 'Die Magister-Jahre des Durandus de S. Porciano, O.P. und der Konflikt mit seinem Orden', ibid. 2 (1973), pp. 7–118. M. D. Philippe, OP, 'Les Processions divines selon Durand de Saint-Pourçain', *Revue Thomiste*, 47 (1947), pp. 244–88. B. Decker, *Die Gotteslehre des Jakob von Metz: Untersuchungen zur Dominikanertheologie zu Beginn des 14. Jahrhunderts*, ed. R. Haubst (BGPM 42, Heft 1; 1967), *passim*. Kaeppeli, 1 (1970), pp. 339–50. J. A. Weisheipl, OP, in *NCE* 4 (1967), pp. 1114–16, s.v.

Durandus of Troarn (*c*.1010–88), Abbot of Troarn in Normandy from 1059. A monk of Fécamp, who was crossbearer to John (Abbot, 1028–78; a spiritual counsellor and writer of note), Durand presents in his 'Liber de corpore et sanguine Domini' the Eucharistic doctrine that was approved at Fécamp in the 1050s. Squarely based on the Fathers, his treatise concedes nothing to the radical methodology of *Berengar of Tours.

His 'Liber de Corpore et Sanguine Domini', orig. pr. by J. L. *d'Achery in an appendix to his edn. of Lanfranc (1648), is repr. in J. P. Migne, *PL* 149. 1375–1424. R. Heurtevent, *Durandus de Troarn et les origines de l'hérésie bérengarienne* ('Études de Théologie historique', 5; 1912), with bibl. G. Poras in *DHGE* 14 (1960), cols. 1159 f., s.v. 'Durand (6) de Troarn', with further refs.

Durandus, William (*c*.1230–96), Bp. of Mende from 1285. Born in France, he taught at Modena and possibly at *Bologna, where he had studied. He was one of the chief medieval canonists. A legal official of the Roman *Curia, he attended Pope *Gregory X at the second Council of *Lyons (1274), and prob. helped to draft its decrees. Among canon lawyers his *Speculum iudicale* was widely influential and led to his being known as 'the Speculator'; centred on legal procedure, it drew on his judicial and administrative experience. Also much acclaimed was his *Rationale divinorum, a compendium of liturgical knowledge with allegorical interpretation. His *Pontifical was taken, for contents and arrangement, as a model, and is the direct ancestor of that in use until recent times.

He is to be distinguished from his nephew and successor in the bishopric of Mende of the same name (d. 1330), to whom the authorship of the Pontifical is sometimes accredited.

Crit. edns. of his Pontifical by M. Andrieu, *Le Pontifical romain du moyen-âge*, 3 (ST, 88; 1940), with important introd., and of his *Rationale* by A. Davril, OSB, and T. M. Thibodeau (CCCM, 140, 140A, etc.; 1995 ff.). J. Berthelé and M. Valmary (eds.), 'Les Instructions et Constitutions de Guillaume Durand, le Spéculateur, d'après le manuscrit de Cessenon', *Académie des Sciences et Lettres de Montpellier. Mémoires de la Section des Lettres*, 2nd ser. 3 (1900), pp. 1–148. Eng. trs., with notes, of the first book of his *Rationale*, with introd. by J. M. *Neale and B. *Webb, *The Symbolism of Churches and Church Ornaments* (1843), and of the third book by T. H. Passmore, *The Sacred Vestments* (1899). V. Le Clerc, 'Guillaume Duranti, évêque de Mende, surnommé le Spéculateur', *Histoire littéraire de la France*, 20 (1842), pp. 411–97, with notes of edns. of his works to date. P.-M. Gy, OP (ed.), *Guillaume Durand: Évêque de Mende* (v. 1230–1296). *Canoniste, liturgiste et homme politique. Actes de la Table Ronde du C.N.R.S., Mende 24–27 Mai 1990* (1992). L. Falletti in *DDC* 5 (1953), cols. 1014–75, s.v. 'Guillaume Durand', with bibl.; S. Kuttner in *NCE* 4 (1967), p. 1117, s.v. 'Duranti, William, the Elder'. On William Durandus, his nephew, also Bp. of Mende, see P. Viollet, 'Guillaume Durant le Jeune, évêque de Mende', *Histoire littéraire de la France*, 35 (1921), pp. 1–139.

Dürer, Albrecht (1471–1528), German painter and engraver. A native of Nuremberg, at first he entered his father's goldsmith business, but in 1486 began the study of wood-cutting under Michael Wolgemut. After travelling abroad, particularly to *Venice (1494/5 and 1505–7), he settled down at Nuremberg. Of his religious paintings, the best known are the Paumgärtner altar-piece (the *Nativity between St George and St Eustace*; before 1505) and the *Four Apostles* (1526), both at Munich, and the *Adoration of the Magi* (1504) at Florence; of his woodcuts, the series known as the *Large Passion*, the *Small Passion*, and the *Life of the Virgin* (all pub. in 1511); and of his engravings (which are characterized by closely observed landscape backgrounds), the *Virgin with the Monkey* (c.1498), *St Eustace* (c.1501), and *St Jerome in his Study* (1514).

Dürer provided links between Italian art and the Gothic North; a prime example of this interchange is the *Feast of the Rose Garlands* altar-piece (Prague), painted in Venice in 1506 for German clients. His woodcuts had much influence on Italian painters and were widely used as illustrations to Bibles in various languages, esp. his scenes of the Apocalypse (1498). Although he never renounced his Catholic faith, he felt sympathetic towards the *Reformation, and after his death he was eulogized by M. *Luther. He enjoyed the friendship of the Emp. Maximilian, *Erasmus, and many of the chief statesmen, humanists, and reformers of his day, some of whom he recorded in vivid portraits.

The three best collections of Dürer's drawings are in the Albertina in Vienna, the Staatliche Museum in Berlin, and the British Museum in London. F. Winkler, *Die Zeichnungen Albrecht Dürers* (4 vols., 1936–9); W. L. Strauss, *The Complete Drawings of Albrecht Dürer* (6 vols., New York, 1974, with suppl. [1977]), both listing and reproducing his drawings. F. Anzelewsky, *Albrecht Dürer: Das malerische Werk* [1971], listing and illustrating his paintings. There are also catalogues, with illustrations: of his paintings, drawings, and prints from an exhibition at Nuremberg, *Albrecht Dürer 1471–1971* (Munich, 1971) and of his graphic work in American collections from an exhibition held at the National Gallery of Art, Washington, DC, *Dürer in America*, ed. C. W. Talbot (1971); of his drawings and prints in the British Museum by J. Rowlands (London, 1971); of his drawings in the Albertina in Vienna by W. Koschatzky and A. Strobl [Salzburg, 1971], and

of his drawings in the Staatliche Museum, Berlin, by F. Anzelewsky and H. Mielke (Berlin, 1984). F. W. H. Hollstein, *German Engravings, Etchings and Woodcuts*, 7: *Albert and Hans Dürer*, ed. K. G. Boon and R. W. Scheller (Amsterdam [c.1962]), pp. 1–259. Dürer's *Schriftlicher Nachlass* [Letters, Diaries, etc.], ed. H. Rupprich (3 vols., 1956–69). The large number of monographs include those by E. Panofsky (Princeton, NJ, 2 vols., 1943; 3rd edn., 1948; with full list of Dürer's works and useful select bibl., 1, pp. 287–96), M. Levey (London, 1964), C. White (ibid., 1971), F. Anzelewsky (Stuttgart, 1980), J. C. Hutchison (Princeton, NJ, 1990), and P.-K. Schuster (2 vols., Berlin, 1991). J. Białostocki, *Dürer and his Critics 1500–1971* (Saecula Spiritalia, 7; Baden-Baden, 1986).

Durham. At the end of the 10th cent. the see of *Lindisfarne was removed to Durham, and a cathedral was begun as a shrine for the relics of St *Cuthbert. Bp. Carilef began to build the present cathedral in place of the older one in 1093, and replaced the secular clergy by a *Benedictine community, which lasted till the *Dissolution in 1540. The Galilee chapel, projecting from the W. end, was built at the end of the Norman era, and the celebrated Chapel of Nine Altars, with its rose windows and elaborate carving, is Early English. The medieval bishops held immense civil jurisdiction (mainly in County Durham), ranking as Counts Palatine; this dignity, which became less important at the Reformation period, was attached to the see down to the time of W. *van Mildert, bishop from 1826 to 1836. In his episcopate the University of Durham was founded (1832). The see was comprised mainly of the counties of Durham and Northumberland until the separation of the diocese of Newcastle (covering Northumberland) in 1882. It still shares with the sees of London and *Winchester a rank inferior only to *Canterbury and *York, and superior to all others in the two provinces; and the bishop is entitled to sit in the House of Lords immediately he takes possession of his see, irrespective of his seniority of consecration. A hall at Oxford for students from Durham, established c.1300 by Prior Richard de Hoton and refounded in 1380 by Bp. Hatfield as 'Durham College', was re-established in 1555 as Trinity College, Oxford.

H. S. Offler (ed.), *Durham Episcopal Charters, 1071–1152* (Surtees Society, 179; 1968). T. D. Hardy (ed.), *Registrum Palatinum Dunelmense: The Register of Robert de Kellawe, Lord Palatine and Bishop of Durham 1311–1316* (4 vols., Rolls Series, 1873–8); G. W. Kitchin (ed.), *Richard d'Aungerville of Bury: Fragments of his Register and other Documents* (Surtees Society, 119; 1910); R. L. Storey (ed.), *The Register of Thomas Langley, Bishop of Durham 1406–1437* (ibid. 164, 166, 169, 170, 177, and 182; 1956–70); M. P. Howden (ed.), *The Register of Richard Fox, Lord Bishop of Durham, 1491–1501* (ibid. 147; 1932); G. Hinde (ed.), *The Registers of Cuthbert Tunstall, Bishop of Durham 1530–59 and James Pilkington, Bishop of Durham 1561–76* (ibid. 161; 1952). J. Raine (ed.), *Historiae Dunelmensis Scriptores Tres: Gaufridus de Coldingham, Robertus de Graystanes, et Willielmus de Chambre* (ibid. 9; 1839). *Sanctuarium Dunelmense* pr. in *The Publications of the Surtees Society*, 5 (1837), pp. 1–90. J. Stevenson (ed.), *Liber Vitae Ecclesiae Dunelmensis* (ibid. 13; 1841). J. Raine (ed.), *The Durham Household Book: or The Accounts of the Bursar of the Monastery of Durham from Pentecost 1530 to Pentecost 1534* (ibid. 18; 1844). Id., *Depositions and other Ecclesiastical Proceedings from the Courts of Durham extending from 1311 to the Reign of Elizabeth* (ibid. 21; 1845). Id., *The Obituary Roll of William Ebchester and John Burnby, Priors of Durham* (ibid. 31; 1856). W. Greenwell (ed.), *Bishop Hatfield's Survey: A Record of the Possessions of the See of*

Durham, made by order of Thomas de Hatfield, Bishop of Durham (ibid. 32; 1856). J. T. Fowler (ed.), *Extracts from the Account Rolls of the Abbey of Durham* (ibid. 99, 100, 103; 1898–1901). Id. (ed.), *The Rites of Durham: Being a Description or Brief Declaration of all the Ancient Monuments, Rites and Customs belonging or being within the Monastical Church of Durham before the Suppression. Written 1593* (ibid. 107; 1903). J. M. Falkner and A. H. Thompson (eds.), *The Statutes of the Cathedral Church of Durham* (ibid. 143; 1929). F. Barlow (ed.), *Durham Annals and other Documents of the Thirteenth Century* (ibid. 155; 1945). Id., *Durham Jurisdictional Peculiars* (Oxford Historical Series, British Series, 1950). G. T. Lapsley, *The County Palatine of Durham* (Harvard Historical Studies, 8; 1900). R. A. B. Mynors, *Durham Cathedral Manuscripts to the End of the Twelfth Century* (1939); W. A. Pantin, *Report on the Muniments of the Dean and Chapter of Durham* (privately pr., 1939). W. Dugdale, *Monasticon Anglicanum*, 1 (1817 edn.), pp. 219–52. R. B. Dobson, *Durham Priory 1400–1450* (Cambridge Studies in Medieval Life and Thought, 3rd ser. 6; 1973). B. Willis, *A Survey of the Cathedrals of York, Durham, Carlisle, etc.*, 1 (1727), pp. 221–83. R. W. Billings, *Architectural Illustrations and Description of the Cathedral Church at Durham* (1843). C. J. Stranks, *This Sumptuous Church: The Story of Durham Cathedral* (1973). *Medieval Art and Architecture at Durham Cathedral* (British Archaeological Association Conference Transactions, 3, for the year 1977; 1980). C. R. Peers, J. Queckett, and F. H. Cheetham in *VCH*, Durham, 3, ed. W. Page (1928), pp. 93–114. D. Rollason, M. Harvey, and M. Prestwich (eds.), *Anglo-Norman Durham 1093–1193* (Woodbridge, Suffolk, 1994). M. [E.] James, *Family, Lineage, and Civil Society: A Study of Society, Politics, and Mentality in the Durham Region, 1500–1640* (Oxford, 1974). W. A. Pantin in *DHGE* 14 (1960), cols. 1179–99, s.v. See also works cited s.v. CUTHBERT, ST.

Durham Book, the. One of the primary documents lying behind the 1662 Book of *Common Prayer. It is a folio copy of the BCP printed in 1619 with MS annotations in the margin and between the lines. These MS notes, by J. *Cosin (q.v.) and his chaplain, W. *Sancroft, were designed as a first draft for the revision of 1662. They appear to have been begun c.1626/7, but for the most part they belong to the winter of 1660–61; and they include the proposals of the *Savoy Conference (Apr.-July 1661). The Book is preserved in the Cosin Library, Durham (formerly D. 3. 5, now in a special safe). A fair copy was made by W. Sancroft later in 1661 in another copy of the BCP (printed in 1634); this is now in the Bodleian Library (Auct. v. 3. 16). Most of the proposals in Sancroft's 'Fair Copy' were taken over into the 'Convocation Book' and the '*Annexed Book' (q.v.) and thus found their way into the 1662 BCP.

Text, with full introd., notes, and bibl., ed. G. J. Cuming (London, 1961).

Durie (or Dury), John (1596–1680), Scottish Protestant divine. Appointed in 1625 minister to the English Company of Merchants at Elbing in Prussia, he devised plans for the reunion of the non-RC Churches, esp. the *Lutherans and *Calvinists, and between 1630, when his appointment ceased, and 1633 visited various dignitaries in England and on the Continent on behalf of his designs. In 1634 he was ordained priest in the C of E and made a chaplain to the King, and down to 1641 he again travelled widely in the cause of religious unity. In the Civil War he was at first a royalist, and tutor at The Hague to Princess Mary of Orange, but in 1643 he took up a chaplaincy at Rotterdam, and in 1645 returned to London to take part in

drawing up the *Westminster Confession and Catechisms. From 1645 to 1654 he was in England, but made another tour for negotiation from 1654 to 1657, meeting with nothing but acrimony from the Lutherans. His bases of reunion were too vague to win enthusiasm. Being out of favour at the Restoration, he left England again in 1661, and settled at Cassel, where he died.

Durie's pamphlet, *A Case of Conscience: whether it be lawful to admit Jews into a Christian Commonwealth* (orig. pub. c.1650), is repr. from the edn. of 1656 in *The Harleian Miscellany*, 7 (1811), pp. 251–5; *The Reformed Librarie-Keeper* (1650) was ed. by R. S. Grannis (Chicago, 1906), with biog. sketch, pp. 9–36. Studies by K. Brauer (Marburg, 1907) and J. M. Batten (Chicago, 1944), with list of his works. G. H. Turnbull, *Hartlib, Dury and Comenius* (1947), pp. 127–341. G. Westin, *Negotiations about Church Unity, 1628–1634* (Uppsala Universitets Årsskrift, 1932, Teologi 3). R. Rouse and S. C. Neill (eds.), *A History of the Ecumenical Movement 1517–1948* (2nd edn., 1967), pp. 97–9 and 134–6. J. Westby-Gibson in *DNB* 16 (1888), pp. 261–3.

Dury, John. See DURIE, JOHN.

Duvergier de Hauranne. See SAINT CYRAN, ABBÉ DE.

Dyfrig, St. See DUBRICIUS, ST.

dying, care of the. The spiritual care of the dying has always been a central concern of the Church, and from an early date provision was made for reconciliation through *Penance and for sacramental anointing (see UNCTION), while there have long been special provisions for the administration of Communion to those facing death (see VIATICUM). The physical care of the sick and dying was one of the characteristic activities of the religious orders, and the work done by Mother *Teresa in seeking out the destitute and dying is in this tradition. In the W. the physical care of the sick and dying largely passed to secular institutions. It was partly in reaction to the limitations of such care, in which the main thrust of medicine was directed to prolonging life, that the modern hospice movement developed. This owes much to the vision of Dame Cecily Saunders (b. 1918) and St Christopher's Hospice in South London, opened in 1967. The movement is founded on the view that by the proper control of physical pain and distressing symptoms, dying patients are enabled to value and find meaning in what remains of their lives and perhaps even accept death when it becomes inevitable. The work of St Christopher's Hospice has had international influence both through the founding of other hospices and through the incorporation of the basic principles of hospice care into medical and nursing practice.

The modern hospice movement has developed at a time when there has been an increasing advocacy of so-called euthanasia. Etymologically euthanasia means an easy or gentle death (Gk. εὐθανασία), but in modern usage it has come to denote the termination of life on humanitarian grounds, as in the case of incurable illness. Like *suicide, such action is incompatible with a proper respect for the sacredness of human life and God's sovereignty over it and with a Christian attitude to suffering; Christian moralists regard it as illicit, though there is said to be no obligation to pursue burdensome or extraordinary means to preserve life. Euthanasia was condemned by the RC Church in 1940, 1980, and 1995 and by the General *Synod of the C of E in 1976. Bodies such as the Voluntary Euthanasia

Legislation Society, founded in England by C. K. Millard in 1932, have argued for the legalization of euthanasia, but bills presented to Parliament in 1936, 1969, and 1976 have been defeated. While not legalizing euthanasia as such, the state of California in the USA in 1976 made it legally possible there for terminally ill patients to authorize, by prior directive, the withholding or withdrawal of life-sustaining procedures when death is believed to be imminent. In the Netherlands, provided certain strictly defined criteria are met, prosecutions are not normally brought against doctors bringing about the death of terminally ill patients who so desire it, though the action remains technically illegal.

The RC judgement of the *Holy Office condemning euthanasia and its successor's 'Declaration on Euthanasia' are pr. in *AAS* 32 (1940), pp. 553 f., and ibid. 72 (1980), pp. 542–52; John Paul II's encyclical 'Evangelium Vitae', ibid. 87 (1995), pp. 401–522. A Report of a Working Party of the C of E Board for Social Responsibility, *On Dying Well: An Anglican Debate on Euthanasia* (1975) was strongly influenced by the work of Dame Cecily Saunders and was welcomed by the General Synod in 1976. The Report of a Working Party of the Linacre Centre for the Study of health care, *Euthanasia and Clinical Practice: Trends, Principles and Alternatives* (1982) treats similar questions. See also [R.] P. Ramsey, *The Patient as Person: Explorations in Medical Ethics* (New Haven, Conn., and London, 1970); id., *Ethics at the Edges of Life* (ibid., 1978), pp. 143–332; R. M. Veatch, *Death, Dying, and the Biological Revolution: Our Last Quest for Responsibility* (ibid., 1976); and R. F. Weir (ed.), *Ethical Issues in Death and Dying* (New York, 1977).

Dykes, John Bacchus (1823–76), writer of hymn-tunes. He was *precentor of *Durham cathedral (1849–62) and then, from 1862, vicar of St Oswald's, Durham, where his High Church sympathies led to a long and unhappy conflict with his Bishop (Charles Baring). His melodic hymn-tunes, of which many were included in *Hymns, Ancient and Modern*, became very popular. Among them were *Hollingside* ('Jesu, Lover of my soul'), *Dominus regit me* ('The King of Love my Shepherd is'), *Nicaea* ('Holy, Holy, Holy!'), and *St Cross* ('O come and mourn').

J. T. Fowler (ed.), *Life and Letters of John Bacchus Dykes* (1897).

Dyophysites (Gk. δυοφυσῖται, from δύο, 'two', and φύσις, 'nature'; the form διφυσῖται is also found). A title given by the *Monophysites to the Catholics in reference to the orthodox belief that in the Person of Christ there coexist the two distinct natures of God and man, and not one composite nature. In modern times it was used by F. *Loofs as a distinguishing mark of the Christology of the *Antiochene school of theologians.

Dyothelites (Gk. δύο, 'two', θέλημα, 'will'). Those who, as against the *Monothelites, hold the orthodox doctrine that in the Person of Christ there are two distinct wills, the one human and the other Divine.

dysteleology. A term introduced by E. Häckel to denote 'purposelessness of nature' (the opposite of 'teleology'). It is also used of the study of certain rudimentary organs, thought by some to be purposeless in the evolution of species.

E

'E'. A symbol widely used by scholars who follow the 'documentary hypothesis' of the origins of the *Pentateuch; it denotes the Elohistic (Heb. אֱלֹהִים, 'elohim, 'God') source. This consists largely of narrative, and together with '*J' (q.v.) comprises most of the famous stories of the Patriarchs and Exodus; it is distinguished from 'J' by its regular use of 'elohim ('God') where 'J' uses the divine name Yahweh (Jahveh or Jehovah). It is commonly thought to embody the traditions current in the Northern Kingdom of Israel and to date from a period somewhat later than 'J' (perhaps 9th cent. BC).

For bibl. see PENTATEUCH.

Eadmer (c.1060–c.1128), English historian and theologian. He was brought up from childhood at the monastery of Christ Church, *Canterbury. During the whole of the period when St *Anselm was Abp. of Canterbury (1093–1109), Eadmer was a member of his household, sharing in his wanderings in exile; for much of the time he took notes on which his *Historia Novorum* and his Life of Anselm were largely based. In 1120 he was offered the Bishopric of St Andrews, but he was never consecrated. Besides his valuable *Vita Anselmi*, he wrote the Lives of various early English saints (incl. *Wilfrid and *Dunstan). His *Historia Novorum*, covering the period from c.1066 to c.1122, is an important source for the English history of its times. The *Tractatus de conceptione S. Mariae*, formerly attributed to St Anselm, and one of the earliest systematic treatises on the doctrine of the *Immaculate Conception of the BVM, which it defends, is also his work.

Collected edn. of his works appended to those of St Anselm ed. G. Gerberon, OSB (Paris, 1675; sep. pagination); repr. from the Paris edn. of 1721 in J. P. Migne, *PL* 159. 345–808, with refs.; Life of Anselm, ibid. 158. 49–118. Eadmer's *Historia Novorum* and *Vita Sancti Anselmi* also ed. M. Rule (RS, 1884, with introd.); crit. edn. of the latter, with Eng. tr., by R. W. Southern (London, 1962; repr., with corrections, Oxford, 1972); his Life of St Dunstan, ed. W. *Stubbs, *Memorials of Saint Dunstan* (RS, 1874), pp. 162–249; his Life of St Wilfrid, ed. J. Raine, *The Historians of the Church of York and its Archbishops* (2 vols., RS, 1879–86), 1, pp. 161–226, together with a 'Breviloquium Vitae Sancti Wilfridi', perhaps by Eadmer, pp. 227–37; his Life of St *Oswald, ed. id., ibid. 2, pp. 1–59; his Life of Bregwine, Abp. of Canterbury 761–4, ed. B. W. Scholz in *Traditio*, 22 (1966), pp. 127–48. *Tractatus de conceptione Sanctae Mariae*, ed. H. Thurston, SJ, and T. Slater, SJ (Freiburg i.B., 1904). 'Nova Opuscula de Sanctorum Veneratione et Obsecratione', ed. A. *Wilmart, OSB, in *Rev. S.R.* 15 (1935), pp. 184–219 and 354–79. Eng. tr. of his *Historia Novorum* by G. Bosanquet (1964). R. W. Southern, *Saint Anselm and his Biographer* (Birkbeck Lectures, 1959; Cambridge, 1963), pp. 227–374. See also bibl. to IMMACULATE CONCEPTION OF THE BVM.

Earle, John (c.1601–65), Bp. of *Salisbury. He was born at *York, educated at *Christ Church and Merton College, Oxford, and early secured literary fame by his *Microcosmography, or A Piece of the World* (1628), a pleasing and popular collection of character studies modelled on those of Theophrastus. He attracted royal favour by his pleasing

manners and was appointed tutor to Charles, Prince of Wales. In 1643 he became Chancellor of Salisbury Cathedral, but was soon deprived by the *Puritans. He accompanied *Charles II in his exile, and at the Restoration was appointed in quick succession Dean of *Westminster (1660), Bp. of *Worcester (1662), and Bp. of Salisbury (1663). In the administration of his diocese he showed himself tolerant towards Nonconformists and a critic of the *Conventicles and *Five Mile Acts.

Modern edns. of Earle's *Microcosmography* by P. Bliss (London, 1811) and by A. S. West (Cambridge, 1897); also later edns. Facsimile of author's holograph MS preserved in the *Bodleian Library, Oxford, pub. Leeds, 1966. List of edns. in *NCBEL* 1 (1974), cols. 2044 f. A. G. Matthews (ed.), *Walker Revised, being a Revision of John Walker's* Sufferings of the Clergy during the Great Rebellion 1642–60 (Oxford, 1948), p. 372. G. G. Perry in *DNB* 16 (1888), pp. 320 f.

Earthquake Synod. During the spring and summer of 1382 a Synod was held at Blackfriars, London, under Abp. W. *Courtenay; in the course of one meeting, dated by most historians as that of 21 May when 24 theses from the writings of J. *Wycliffe were condemned as heretical or erroneous, the city was shaken by an earthquake. The name is sometimes extended to all the meetings of 1382 at which various actions were taken against heresy. The 1382 condemnation added various articles, including three dealing with the Eucharist, to those mentioned in earlier edicts against Wycliffe.

Primary account of the Council, with a list of its members, in *Fasciculi Zizaniorum*, ed. W. W. Shirley (RS, 1858), pp. 272–91; see also pp. 493–500. Modern account, drawing on this and other sources, by J. H. Dahmus, *The Prosecution of John Wyclif* (New Haven, Conn., and London, 1952), pp. 89–128.

Easter. The Feast of the Resurrection of Christ, being the greatest and oldest feast of the Christian Church. Its importance is emphasized liturgically by the long preparation of *Lent and *Passiontide, by the special ceremonies of *Holy Week, and by the following *Paschaltide, marked in the W. Church by the frequent reiteration of *Alleluia at the *Mass and in the Divine *Office, as the expression of Easter joy. In the ancient Church the *catechumens, after watching all Saturday night, were baptized early on Easter Day and received Communion. The night before Easter was celebrated by the illumination of the churches and even whole cities. In the W. Church the ceremonies were put back to the afternoon in the 10th cent. and to the morning of *Holy Saturday in the 14th, so that in the RC Church the Vigil, with the first Easter Mass, came to be celebrated on Saturday. A similar development took place in the E. Church, though here in addition Mattins of Easter Day begins at midnight on Saturday–Sunday, followed by the Liturgy of Easter Day. In the RC Church in 1951 it became permissible to offer the first Mass of Easter during the night of Saturday–Sunday, and in 1955 such celebration became obligatory. (For details of the service, see PASCHAL VIGIL SERVICE.) The BCP provides special anthems for use on Easter Day in place of the *Venite.

The derivation of the name 'Easter' is uncertain. Acc. to *Bede, it is connected with an Anglo-Saxon spring goddess 'Eostre'. At any rate it seems clear that, as in the case of Christmas (q.v.), the Christian feast of Easter has superseded an old pagan festival. The popular custom of exchanging 'Easter eggs' is of very ancient origin.

The date of the Easter feast is determined by the Paschal Full Moon, its extreme limits being 21 Mar. and 25 Apr. In the early Church, the two principal methods of computation were those of *Alexandria (owing to its astronomical resources) and *Rome. For the various disputes on the subject see PASCHAL CONTROVERSIES.

The principal texts are set out in H. A. P. Schmidt, SJ, *Hebdomada Sancta* (2 vols. in 3, Freiburg, etc., 1956-7), *passim*. Texts also ed., with Ital. tr. and introd. by R. Cantalamessa, *La Pasqua nella Chiesa antica* (Traditio Christiana, 4; 1978; Eng. tr. Collegeville, Minn. [1993]). B. Fischer and J. Wagner (eds.), *Paschatis Sollemnia: Studien zu Osterfeier und Osterfrömmigkeit* (1959). G. Bertonière, *The Historical Development of the Easter Vigil and Related Services in the Greek Church* (Orientalia Christiana Analecta, 193; Rome, 1972). On the early history of the feast, cf. also H. Schürmann, 'Die Anfänge christlicher Osterfeier', *Th.Q.* 130 (1951), pp. 414-25; O. *Casel, OSB, 'Art und Sinn der ältesten christlichen Osterfeier', *JLW* 14 (1938), pp. 1-78; C. Mohrmann, 'Pascha, Passio, Transitus', *EL* 66 (1952), pp. 37-52; W. Huber, *Passa und Ostern: Untersuchungen zur Osterfeier der alten Kirche* (Beiheft zur *ZNTW* 35; 1969); R. Cantalamessa, *La Pasqua della nostra salvezza: Le tradizioni pasquali della Bibbia e della primitiva Chiesa* [Turin, 1971]. T. J. Talley, *The Origins of the Liturgical Year* (New York [1986]), pp. 1-57. On the religious and theological significance of the observance, L. Bouyer, Cong. Orat., *Le Mystère pascal* (Lex Orandi, 6; 1945; Eng. tr., 1951). F. L. Cross, *I Peter: A Paschal Liturgy* (1954). P. Jounel in A. G. Martimort and others, *L'Église en Prière* (new edn.), 4 (1983), pp. 45-69; Eng. tr. (1986), pp. 33-56. H. *Leclercq, OSB, in *DACL* 13 (pt. 2; 1938), cols. 1521-74, s.v. 'Pâques'; J. D. Crichton in *A Catholic Dictionary of Theology*, 2 (1967), pp. 202-4, s.v. See also bibl. to PASCHAL CONTROVERSIES.

Easter Litany. The principal confession of faith of the *Bohemian Brethren. It takes the form of the *Apostles' Creed with considerable expansions, mainly from Scripture, though it is conceived more as an act of worship than as a dogmatic formulary and is designed primarily for use in church on Easter morning. It dates from 1749.

The text (Ger. and Eng.) is pr. in P. Schaff, *The Creeds of Christendom*, 3 (1877), pp. 799-806.

Eastern Catholics. See UNIAT CHURCHES.

Eastern Orthodox Church. See ORTHODOX CHURCH.

eastward position. In connection with liturgy, the term designates the position of the celebrant of the Eucharist standing on the same side of the altar as the people, with his back to them; because of the normal *orientation of churches, in this position he usually faces E. The adoption of this position was introduced at *Rome from the Frankish Empire in the 8th or 9th cent. Before that the celebrant had stood on the far side of the altar, facing the people, in what was later called the *westward position. Until the middle of the 20th cent. the so-called eastward position

became universal in the W., even when, as in the Papal basilicas, it involved facing W. It is still always used in the E. Church.

In the C of E, authority for the use of the eastward position depends on the interpretation of three rubrics in the BCP, i.e. the fourth rubric at the beginning of the service, the rubric before the absolution, and the rubric before the prayer of consecration. The first of these, which dates from 1552, legislated for the time when the altar-table was placed, at the time of a celebration of the Communion, in the body of the church or chancel. Since the traditional altar-wise position came back in the 17th cent., the rubric, although retained in the 1662 BCP, has strictly ceased to be applicable, though in 1890 Abp. E. W. *Benson pronounced the eastward position to be a legitimate interpretation of this rubric. The second rubric is less precise. The third rubric has been interpreted legally as permitting either position, provided the 'manual acts' are visible to the congregation. In practice, except in extreme Evangelical churches where the *north end is taken, the eastward position had become almost universal in the C of E until the RC Church gradually again adopted a westward position, now found also in many C of E churches.

See bibl. s.v. ORIENTATION.

Ebedjesus (Abdisho' bar Berikha) (d. 1318). The last important theological writer of the *Church of the East. He became Bp. of Sigar and Bêt Arabâye in 1284/5, and about five years later Metropolitan of Armenia. He wrote extensively in Syriac, but several of his works are lost. Those which survive include a valuable catalogue of Syriac authors, two important compendia of canon law (the *Collectio canonum synodicorum* and the *Ordo iudiciorum ecclesiasticorum*), a theological work entitled *Margaritha* (the *Pearl*), and the *Paradisus Eden*, a series of 50 poems.

His collection of Canons, his 'Epitome Canonum Apostolicorum', and 'Margaritha', with a Lat. tr. by [J.] A. *Assemani, are pr. by A. *Mai, *SVNC* 10 (Rome, 1838), pt. 1, pp. 1-331. Selections of the *Paradisus* poems ed., with Lat. tr., H. Gismondi, SJ (Beirut, 1888); the first 25 ed. P. Cardahi (ibid., 1899). Eng. tr. of his 'Catalogue' and 'Margaritha' in G. P. Badger, *The Nestorians and their Rituals*, 2 (1852), pp. 361-422. Lat. tr. of his *Ordo iudiciorum ecclesiasticorum* by J.-M. Vosté, OP (Codificazione Canonica Orientale, Fonti, 2nd ser., fasc. 15; Rome, 1940). A. *Baumstark, *Geschichte der syrischen Literatur* (1922), pp. 323-5, incl. full refs. J. Dauvillier in *DDC* 5 (1953), cols. 91-134, s.v.

Eberlin, Johannes (*c*.1468-1533), popular Reformation polemical writer. Born in Günzburg (Bavaria), he became a *Franciscan. He encountered the writings of M. *Luther while at Freiburg im Breisgau in 1520, and in 1521 he published a series of 15 pamphlets (the *Bundsgenossen*). The earliest of these reflect Luther's criticism of the contemporary Church and society, whereas the later ones show the more radical influence of *Carlstadt. The radical social ideas expressed in the later pamphlets contributed significantly to the popular discontent which was to manifest itself in the *Peasants' War. Entering the University of *Wittenberg in 1522, he came under the direct influence of Luther and P. *Melanchthon; this led to a moderation of his more extreme views, already evident in *Vom Misbrauch christlicher Freiheit* (1522). From 1525 he was preacher to Count George II of Wertheim. As a diversion he produced a German translation of *Tacitus' *Germania*.

Ausgewählte [sämtliche] Schriften, ed. L. Enders (3 vols., Neudrucke deutscher Litteraturwerke des xvi. und xvii. Jahrhunderts, nos. 139–41, 170–2, and 183–8; 1896–1902). His tr. of Tacitus' *Germania*, ed. A. Masser (Innsbrucker Beiträge zur Kulturwissenschaft, Germanistische Reihe, 30; 1986). M. Radlkofer, *Johann Eberlin von Günzburg und sein Vetter Hans Jakob Wehe von Leipheim* (1887). Studies on his *Bundsgenossen* by J. H. Schmidt (Leipzig, 1900) and W. Lucke (Halle, 1902). Full bibl. in Schottenloher, 1 (1933), pp. 205 f. (nos. 5144–67), and 7 (1966), p. 65 (nos. 54180–84). T. Kolde in *PRE* (3rd edn.), 5 (1898), pp. 122–5; R. Weijenborg, OFM, in *DHGE* 14 (1960), cols. 1306 f., both s.v.

Ebionites (Heb. אֶבְיוֹנִים 'poor men'). A sect of Jewish Christians which flourished in the early cents. of the Christian era. The several scattered sources from which our knowledge of them is derived cannot easily be harmonized and related. It seems clear, however, that the sect flourished esp. on the E. of the *Jordan and that two of their principal tenets were (1) a 'reduced' doctrine of the Person of Christ, to the effect, e.g., that Jesus was the human son of Joseph and Mary and that the Holy Spirit in the form of a dove lighted on Him at His baptism, and (2) over-emphasis on the binding character of the Mosaic Law. They are said to have rejected the Pauline Epistles and to have used only one Gospel; on this see following entry. A poor community, they appear to have adopted a severely ascetic mode of life and to have remained outside the main stream of Christian development. It is difficult to state exactly what their relation was to such sects as the *Nazarenes; A. *Harnack and F. J. A. *Hort identified the two bodies, while J. B. *Lightfoot and T. *Zahn distinguished them.

The sources are scattered. They include *Justin, *Dial. c. Tryph.* 47; *Irenaeus, *Adv. Haer.* 1. 26. 2; 3. 11. 7; 3. 21. 1; and 5. 1. 3; *Tertullian, *De Praescr.* 33; *Hippolytus, *Haer.* 7. 34 and 9. 13–17; *Eusebius, *HE* 3. 27; *Epiphanius, *Haer.* 30. H. J. Schoeps, 'Ebionite Christianity', *JTS* NS 4 (1953), pp. 219–24; J. A. Fitzmyer, SJ, 'The Qumran Scrolls, the Ebionites and their Literature', *Theological Studies*, 16 (1955), pp. 335–72, with refs. J. Daniélou, SJ, *Théologie du judéo-christianisme*, 1 (1958), pp. 68–76; Eng. tr. (1964), pp. 55–66. A. F. J. Klijn and G. J. Reinink, *Patristic Evidence for Jewish Christian Sects* (Supplement to *Novum Testamentum*, 36; 1973), pp. 19–43. A. Orbe, SJ, *Cristología gnóstica: Introducción a la soteriología de los siglos II y III*, 1 (Biblioteca de Autores Cristianos, 384; 1976), pp. 351–79. J. M. Fuller in *DCB* 2 (1880), pp. 24–8; W. Beveridge in *HERE* 5 (1912), pp. 139–45, with bibl.; G. Strecker in *RAC* 4 (1959), cols. 487–500, s.v.; H. J. Schoeps in *DHGE* 14 (1960), cols. 1314–19, s.v., with bibl.; J. H. Crehan, SJ, in *A Catholic Dictionary of Theology*, 2 (1967), pp. 204–6, s.v.

Ebionites, Gospel according to the. The name given by modern scholars to the Jewish-Christian *apocryphal Gospel supposed to have been used by the *Ebionites (q.v.). *Irenaeus says that the Ebionites use the 'Gospel according to Matthew' (*Adv. Haer.* 1. 26. 2 and 3. 11. 7), though from the the beliefs he ascribes to them (ibid. 3. 21. 1 and 5. 1. 3) it seems that this cannot be identified with the canonical Mt. *Eusebius (*HE* 3. 27. 4), on the other hand, says that they use the 'Gospel according to the Hebrews'. The principal authority is *Epiphanius (*Haer.* 30). He not only states that the Ebionites 'receive the Gospel according to Matthew' and 'call it the Hebrew Gospel', but he quotes passages from the Gospel used by

the Ebionites. These show that it was written in Greek. The relationship between this Gospel and the 'Gospel of the Nazarenes' and the 'Gospel according to the *Hebrews' is unclear; they are perhaps quite distinct.

Text of the Epiphanian frags., with notes, in A. *Hilgenfeld, *Novum Testamentum extra Canonem Receptum*, fasc. 4 (1866), pp. 32–8. Eng. tr. in J. K. Elliott, *The Apocryphal New Testament* (Oxford, 1993), pp. 14–16; Ger. tr., with notes by P. Vielhauer and G. Strecker in Schneemelcher, 1 (5th edn., 1987), pp. 138–42; Eng. tr., 1 (1991), pp. 166–71, and discussion of the whole question of Jewish Christian Gospels (with bibl.), pp. 114–28; Eng. tr., pp. 134–53. H. Waitz, 'Neue Untersuchungen über die sogen. judenchristlichen Evangelien', *ZNTW* 36 (1937), pp. 60–81; M. É. Boismard, OP, 'Évangile des Ébionites et problème synoptique', *R.Bibl.* 73 (1966), pp. 321–52. W. L. Petersen in *Anchor Bible Dictionary*, 2 (1992), pp. 261 f., s.v.

Ecce Homo (Lat., 'Behold the Man!'). The title of the Life of Christ, published (orig. anonymously) by Sir John *Seeley in 1865. It was a typical expression of the phase in 19th-cent. liberal thought which was more interested in the 'historic' Jesus than in the 'metaphysical Christ of the Creeds'. In it Seeley presented in an easy style an attractive picture of Christ as a moral reformer. So much, however, that belonged to the traditional conception of Christ was passed over in silence that the orthodoxy of its author was widely challenged, among others by J. H. *Newman, A. P. *Stanley, and W. E. *Gladstone. The work secured an immense circulation.

There is an edn. in the 'Everyman Library', with introd. by Sir Oliver Lodge.

Ecchellensis. See ABRAHAM ECCHELLENSIS.

Ecclesia docens (Lat., 'the teaching Church'). A term traditionally used by some Catholic writers of the clergy, who are commissioned to teach the Christian faith, as contrasted with the laity, who are called *ecclesia discens*, 'the learning Church'. Since the Second *Vatican Council, however, the distinction has become less rigid.

Ecclesiastes, Book of. The main theme of the Book, traditionally ascribed to *Solomon, is the worthlessness and vanity of human life. The title 'Ecclesiastes' found in the Greek and Latin versions is an attempted rendering of the Hebrew title 'Qoheleth'; English versions generally translate this as 'the Preacher', though the probable meaning of the Hebrew word is 'a speaker in an assembly'. In the Hebrew Bible it was the last of the five '*Megilloth' or Rolls, and was read publicly in the Synagogue on the Feast of *Tabernacles. It belongs to the so-called *Wisdom Literature, a fact which explains its association with the name of Solomon, who is no longer seriously held to be the author. Considerations of subject-matter and linguistic style make it clear that the book is the product of a late age in OT history, and it is known that it was one of the latest books to be admitted to the Hebrew canon. Like *Job, it questions the confident assumptions of much of the earlier Wisdom literature, but adopts a more detached and even cynical tone. The occasional passages which are out of harmony with its general pessimism are treated by many scholars as later interpolations in the interests of orthodoxy and canonicity, although others remain satisfied with the unity of the Book. There have been attempts, both Jewish and Christian, to interpret the Book so as to bring its teaching into accord with orthodox ethical principles. No direct quotations of it occur in the NT.

Comm. by H. W. Hertzberg (KAT 16. 4; 1932; 2nd edn., 17. 4–5, on Eccles. and Est., 1963, pp. 19–238), W. Zimmerli (Das Alte Testament Deutsch, 16. 1, on Prov. and Eccles., 1962; 2nd edn. on Prov., Eccles., Song of Songs, Lam., and Est., 1967, pp. 123–253), A. Lauha (Biblischer Kommentar, Altes Testament, 19; Neukirchen, 1978), G. Ogden (Sheffield, 1987), J. L. Crenshaw (Old Testament Library, 1988), and R. N. Whybray (New Cent. Bib., 1989). H. L. Ginsberg, *Studies in Koheleth* (Texts and Studies of the Jewish Theological Seminary of America, 17; New York, 1950); R. Gordis, *Kohelet—the Man and his World* (ibid. 19; 1951; 2nd edn., 1968). O. Loretz, *Qohelet und die alte Orient: Untersuchungen zu Stil und theologischer Thematik des Buches Qohelet* (Freiburg, etc. [1964]). R. Braun, *Kohelet und die früh-hellenistische Popularphilosophie* (Beiheft zur *ZATW* 130; 1973). C. F. Whitley, *Koheleth: His Language and Thought* (ibid. 148; 1979). M. V. Fox, *Qohelet and his Contradictions* (Journal for the Study of the Old Testament, Supplement Series, 71; 1989). H. Gese, 'Die Krisis der Weisheit bei Koheleth', in *Les Sagesses du Proche-Orient ancien: Colloque de Strasbourg, 17–19 mai 1962* (Paris, 1963), pp. 139–51; Eng. tr. in J. L. Crenshaw (ed.), *Theodicy in the Old Testament* (Issues in Religion and Theology, 4; 1983), pp. 141–53. G. von *Rad, *Weisheit in Israel* (Neukirchen [1970]), pp. 292–308; Eng. tr. (1972), pp. 226–39. R. N. Whybray, *Ecclesiastes* (Old Testament Guides, Sheffield, 1989). Eissfeldt, pp. 491–500, with bibl. A. Barucq in *Dict. Bibl.*, Suppl. 9 (1977), cols. 609–74, s.v. 'Qohéleth'; J. L. Crenshaw in *Anchor Bible Dictionary*, 2 (1992), pp. 271–80, s.v.

Ecclesiastical Commissioners. The body which from 1835 to 1948 managed the estates and revenues of the C of E. In 1835 two commissions were appointed to consider reforms in the allotment of Church revenues; and in the following year an Act of Parliament (the Ecclesiastical Commissioners Act) was passed, establishing a permanent body of Ecclesiastical Commissioners, who were constituted a corporation with power to hold and purchase lands and to prepare schemes for the alteration and redistribution of ecclesiastical revenues. Its constitution was several times amended. In 1948 it consisted of the archbishops and bishops of England, the deans of *St Paul's, *Westminster, and *Canterbury, the Lord Chancellor, the Lord President of the Council, the First Lord of the Treasury, the Chancellor of the Exchequer, one of the principal Secretaries of State, the Lord Chief Justice, the Master of the Rolls, and certain lay members of the C of E appointed by the Crown and the Abp. of Canterbury. The joint treasurers were three lay 'Church Estates Commissioners', two of them appointed by the Crown and the third by the Abp. of Canterbury. The Commission presented an annual report to Parliament. In 1948 the Ecclesiastical Commissioners and *Queen Anne's Bounty united in a new body, the *Church Commissioners for England (q.v.).

G. F. A. Best, *Temporal Pillars: Queen Anne's Bounty, the Ecclesiastical Commissioners, and the Church of England, 1704–1948* (1964), pp. 296–514. [W.] O. Chadwick, *The Spirit of the Oxford Movement* (Cambridge, 1990), pp. 63–85.

Ecclesiastical Courts Commissions. There were two Parliamentary Commissions on the English Church courts in the 19th cent.

(1) That set up under the influence of Lord Brougham, originally appointed on 28 Jan. 1830 and reappointed with additional members on 5 July 1830. It included Abp. W. *Howley and five Bishops. Under pressure from Brougham, it recommended (25 Jan. 1831) the replacement of the Court of *Delegates by the Privy Council as the final court of appeal in ecclesiastical matters; this led to the establishment of the *Judicial Committee of the Privy Council in 1833. The full report, issued in Feb. 1832, advocated many drastic changes, including trial by jury in ecclesiastical cases and the abolition of the provincial courts of *York. Some of its less revolutionary recommendations were adopted later in the 19th cent.

(2) That appointed by the Prime Minister (W. E. *Gladstone) and Lord Chancellor (R. *Palmer, first Earl of Selborne), at the request of the Abp. of Canterbury (A. C. *Tait), on 16 May 1881 'to inquire into the constitution and working of the Ecclesiastical Courts as created or modified under the Reformation Statutes of the 24th and 25th years of King Henry VIII and any subsequent Acts'. Its immediate object was to find some new and better way of dealing with the ritual controversies. It consisted of 25 members, among them both Archbishops (Tait and W. Thomson), Bp. E. W. *Benson, Lord Penzance, R. J. *Phillimore, E. A. Freeman, and W. *Stubbs. It recommended in its report (July 1883) a radical revision of the courts, the final court to consist of five lay judges appointed by the Crown, who had formally affirmed that they belonged to the C of E. Only nine of the commissioners signed the report without qualifications and Convocation objected to the constitution proposed for the final court. No legislation followed. Several of the appendices to the report, esp. those of Stubbs, are of great historical value.

(1) *The Special and General Reports made to his Majesty by the Commissioners appointed to Inquire into the Practice and Jurisdiction of the Ecclesiastical Courts in England and Wales* (Parliamentary Papers, 1831–2, vol. 24 [C. 199]). (2) *Report of the Commissioners Appointed to Inquire into the Constitution and Working of the Ecclesiastical Courts* (2 vols.; Parliamentary Papers, 1883, vol. 24 [C. 3760 and 3761]).

Ecclesiastical Discipline, Royal Commission on. The Commission was appointed in 1904 as a result of pressure by Members of Parliament on the new Abp. of Canterbury, R. T. *Davidson, to take effective action against Ritualism. Its brief was to inquire into 'breaches or neglect of the Law relating to the conduct of Divine Service in the Church of England and to the ornaments and fittings of Churches' and to devise remedies. Its members were mainly laymen, but all were churchmen. After taking evidence from 164 witnesses and consulting the bishops, the Commissioners reported unanimously on 21 June 1906 that the law of public worship was too narrow, and that the machinery for discipline had broken down. They recommended that practices significant of teaching repugnant to the doctrine of the C of E should be made to cease, if necessary by force of law; that *Letters of Business should be issued to the *Convocations to regularize the vestments of the minister, and to provide greater elasticity in public worship; that the recommendations of the *Ecclesiastical Courts Commission of 1883 should in the main be carried out, with the replacement of the *Judicial

Committee of the Privy Council as the final court of appeal; that the *Public Worship Regulation Act 1874 should be repealed; and that dioceses should be divided to secure greater supervision. The Letters of Business envisaged were duly issued on 10 Nov. 1906, thus initiating the long project of Prayer Book revision (defeated in the House of Commons in 1927 and 1928); see COMMON PRAYER, BOOK OF.

The Report of the Royal Commission on Ecclesiastical Discipline [Cd. 3040] and the Minutes of Evidence taken before the Royal Commission on Ecclesiastical Discipline [Cd. 3069 and Cd. 3070] are pr. among the Parliamentary Papers, 1906, vol. 33. G. K. A. *Bell, Randall Davidson (1935), pp. 454–73; A. R. Vidler, The Church in an Age of Revolution (Pelican History of the Church, 5; 1961), pp. 162–4.

Ecclesiastical Jurisdiction Measure 1963. A Measure intended to simplify the ecclesiastical law and jurisdiction in the C of E in accordance with the recommendations of the Archbishops' Commission on Ecclesiastical Courts of 1954. It repealed a large number of existing enactments, including the *Church Discipline Act 1840, the *Public Worship Regulation Act 1874, the Clergy Discipline Act 1892 and the Incumbents (Discipline) Measure 1947.

By the Measure, the *Consistory Court is the court of first instance against clerics for offences not involving doctrine, ritual or ceremonial ('conduct cases'), and retains its existing *faculty jurisdiction. A new court, the *Court of Ecclesiastical Causes Reserved, has jurisdiction of first instance in matters involving doctrine, ritual, or ceremonial, and also hears appeals from the Consistory Court in faculty cases involving any of these matters. A Royal Commission consisting of three Lords of Appeal and two Bishops who are members of the House of Lords hears appeals from that court. The appellate jurisdiction of the *Judicial Committee of the Privy Council has ceased, except for certain faculty cases.

Conduct cases include conduct unbecoming the office and work of a clerk in holy orders and persistent neglect of duty, and there is a limitation period of three years. A complaint is first considered by the Bishop, who may refer it to an examiner, who decides whether a prima facie case is established. If so, the accused is tried in the Consistory Court by the *Chancellor sitting with two clerical and two lay assessors. The procedure in general follows the practice of the criminal law, so the Chancellor is judge in matters of law, and the assessors in matters of fact, and appeal lies to the Provincial Court. Where the complaint concerns doctrine, ritual or ceremonial, there is an informal hearing before a Bishop, who may veto proceedings, or refer it to a Committee of the Convocation. If a prima facie case is established, the accused is tried before the Court of Ecclesiastical Causes Reserved, whence an appeal lies to a Commission of Review appointed by the Crown. Neither of these courts is bound by a previous decision of the Judicial Committee of the Privy Council, or by its own precedents if fresh evidence is adduced.

The censures that may be inflicted are deprivation, *inhibition, suspension, monition, and a new penalty of rebuke. Deposition from holy orders may follow deprivation. Deprivation also follows certain convictions and orders in the secular court. Similar proceedings are employed in the case of Bishops, who are liable to the same censures. The Measure makes provision for the costs of both prosecution and defence to be paid by the Church Commissioners, in some cases jointly with the Central Board of Finance. The expense can be considerable, and this alone, quite apart from the complexity of the procedures, makes prosecutions rare.

Halsbury's Laws of England and Wales (4th edn., 1986), 14, pp. 275–336; E. G. Moore, Introduction to English Canon Law (3rd edn. by T. Briden and B. Hanson, 1992), pp. 111–30.

Ecclesiastical text of the NT. A name occasionally given to the *Byzantine text on the ground that it was the text which established itself for official use in the Greek-speaking Church.

Ecclesiastical Titles Act 1851. The Act, passed at the time of the '*Papal Aggression', forbidding the assumption by RCs of territorial titles within the United Kingdom under penalty of a fine, and rendering void all bequests or donations made to persons under such titles. It was introduced as a counter-measure to the reinstitution of the RC hierarchy by *Pius IX in 1850, but, being a dead letter from the first, was repealed by the Ecclesiastical Titles Act 1871, which none the less preserves the principle that only the Crown can validly confer rank or title in the Realm, and is still in force.

ecclesiasticism. A word, commonly used in a depreciatory sense, for (1) over-attention to the external details of ecclesiastical practice and administration, or (2) the point of view which is formed and guided solely by the interests of the Church as an organization.

Ecclesiasticus. A Book of the *Apocrypha, orig. 'the Wisdom (or 'Proverbs') of Jesus the son of Sirach', also known as 'Ben-Sira' or 'Sirach'. The name 'Ecclesiasticus' is already found in *Cyprian; it is referred by *Rufinus to the Book's pre-eminence among the *deuterocanonical writings as a 'Church Book' (liber ecclesiasticus) for the purposes of moral instruction; but this explanation is doubtful, since (1) the name is earlier than the distinction between the deuterocanonical ('Apocryphal') Books and the rest of the OT, and (2) other evidence is wanting that the Book occupied this position of pre-eminence in the patristic period, the Apocryphal Book most quoted by the Fathers being Wisd. Sol. The origin of the name therefore remains uncertain.

Ecclus. is generally reckoned among the so-called Wisdom writings. Ch. 24 contains an important passage in which the personified figure of Wisdom is identified with the Law of Moses (v. 23). The Book was written or compiled in Hebrew by Jesus (i.e. Joshua) the son of Sirach of Jerusalem (prologue, cf. 50: 27). The translator's prologue (or preface) states that the translation into Greek was made by the author's grandson in Egypt after 132 BC. (The first prologue printed in the AV is spurious.) The historical catalogue of famous men (44–50) ends with Simon the son of Onias the High Priest, who appears to be the High Priest of this name who held office c.225–200 BC (not his earlier namesake, c.300–270 BC). The author also apparently knew nothing of the conflict between faithful Jews and Hellenists which dominates the literature of the *Maccabaean period (c.170 BC onwards). Internal evidence thus confirms a date about two generations before 132 BC for the original writing. It was presumably composed wholly or mainly in Palestine, though the author was aware of the larger Hellenistic world (cf. 10: 8) and his ideal scribe is represented as travelling abroad and appearing before rulers (39: 4).

In modern times the Book was known until comparatively recently only in its Greek translation, translations derived from the Greek, and a Syriac translation based on the Hebrew original. A Hebrew text, however, was known to *Jerome and is quoted in the *Talmud. Since 1896 extensive fragments of the Hebrew have been identified among the MSS discovered in the *geniza of an ancient synagogue in Cairo; further, much smaller fragments have been found in the area of the *Dead Sea.

Hebrew text ed., with Fr. tr. and comm., by I. Levi (Bibliothèque de l'École des Hautes Sciences, Sciences religieuses, 10; 2 vols., 1898–1901); also ed., with Ger. tr., by R. Smend (Berlin, 1906). Separate Eng. tr. of rev. text by W. O. E. Oesterley (Translations of Early Documents, 1st ser., Palestinian Jewish Texts (Pre-Rabbinic), 2; 1916). A. A. Di Lella, OFM, *The Hebrew Text of Sirach: A Text-Critical and Historical Study* (Studies in Classical Literature, 1; 1966), with extensive bibl. to 1964. Comm. by R. Smend (Berlin, 1906), G. H. Box and W. O. E. Oesterley in R. H. *Charles (ed.), *The Apocrypha and Pseudepigrapha of the Old Testament*, 1 (Oxford, 1913), pp. 268–517, J. G. Snaith (Camb. Bib., NEB, 1974), and P. W. Skehan and A. A. Di Lella, OFM (Anchor Bible, 1987). J. Haspecker, SJ, *Gottesfurcht bei Jesus Sirach: Ihre religiöse Struktur und ihre literarische und doktrinäre Bedeutung* (Analecta Biblica, 30; 1967). J. T. Sanders, *Ben Sira and Demotic Wisdom* (Society of Biblical Literature, Monograph Series, 28; Chico, Calif. [1983]). R. Smend, *Griechisch-syrisch-hebräischer Index zur Weisheit des Jesus Sirach* (1907); D. Barthélemy and O. Rickenbacher (eds.), *Konkordanz zum Hebräischen Sirach* (Göttingen, 1973). E. *Schürer, *The History of the Jewish People in the Age of Jesus Christ*, rev. Eng. tr. by G. Vermes and others, 3 (pt. 1; Edinburgh, 1986), pp. 198–212. A. A. Di Lella in *Anchor Bible Dictionary*, 6 (1992), pp. 931–45, s.v. 'Wisdom of Ben-Sira'.

ecclesiology (Gk. ἐκκλησία, a 'church'). The science of the building and decoration of churches. The word was first used in the 19th cent., when interest in ecclesiastical buildings was much increased by such groups as the *Cambridge Camden Society. This Society published *The Ecclesiologist*, until it was later taken over by the Ecclesiological Society, 29 vols. in all (1841–68). Nowadays the term more commonly refers to the theology of the Church (q.v.).

Echternach. The monastery of Echternach in Luxembourg was founded in 698 by St *Willibrord. A Roman villa on the site had been occupied as a royal or aristocratic residence in the 5th and 6th cents.; half of this, together with other lands, was given to Willibrord in 697/8, the other half in 706. The abbey remained in the Carolingian sphere of influence for the next two centuries; it was taken under royal protection by *Pepin III and in 751 granted immunity from secular interference of any kind. A community of canons at Echternach is recorded in 848–50, and it was not until 973 that the Rule of St *Benedict was adopted. In the early 8th cent. the scriptorium produced a large number of fine MSS, most of them in insular script. There was another spate of book production in the 11th cent., and the monastery became the court atelier of

the Salian Emperors of Germany through the connection of Abbot Humbert (1028–51) and the Emp. Henry III and his mother. The fortunes of the abbey declined in the later Middle Ages. It was dissolved in 1797. Remains of the later Merovingian church and the three-aisled Carolingian church of c.800 are still visible. A dancing procession to the tomb of St Willibrord takes place on the Tuesday after *Whitsunday.

[H.] C. Wampach, *Geschichte der Grundherrschaft Echternach im Frühmittelalter* (Publications de la section historique de l'institut royal grand-ducal de Luxembourg, 63; 2 vols., 1929–30), and other works of this author; N. Gauthier, *L'évangélisation des pays de la Moselle* (1980), pp. 316–28; M. Werner, *Adelsfamilien im Umkreis der frühen Karolinger* (Sigmaringen, 1982), pp. 60–98; J. Krier and R. Wagner, 'Zur Frühgeschichte des Willibrordus-Kloster in Echternach', *Hémecht*, 37 (1985), pp. 15–51; H. Hoffmann, *Buchkunst und Königtum im ottonischen und frühsalischen Reich*, 1 (Schriften der Monumenta Germaniae Historica, 30/1; 1986), pp. 509–16; R. McKitterick, 'The Diffusion of Insular Culture in Neustria between 650 and 850: The Implications of the Manuscript Evidence', in H. Atsma (ed.), *La Neustrie: Les pays au nord de la Loire de 650 à 850*, 2 (Beiheft der *Francia*, 16/2; Sigmaringen, 1988), pp. 395–431, esp. pp. 421–9; G. Kiesel and J. Schoeder (eds.), *Willibrord, Apostel der Niederlande, Gründer der Abtei Echternach* (Saint-Paul, Luxembourg, 1989), esp. pp. 127–70 and 271–307. [H.] C. Wampach in *DHGE* 14 (1960), cols. 1365–75, s.v.

Eck, Johann (1486–1543), **Johann Maier 'of Eck'** (his birthplace, Egg an der Günz), hence **Eckius**, German theologian. From 1510 till his death he was professor of theology at Ingolstadt. He came under humanist influences, and his early writings, which included commentaries on *Aristotle and Petrus Hispanus (Pope *John XXI), were almost anti-Scholastic in their theology. In 1514 he attacked the medieval prohibition of interest, defending a return on capital up to 5 per cent, and won support for his thesis at *Bologna and Vienna. Until the controversy over *indulgences broke out, he was on good terms with M. *Luther; but in the public debate at Leipzig in 1519 he opposed *Carlstadt and Luther, and was largely responsible for procuring the latter's excommunication by the bull '*Exsurge Domine' at Rome in 1520. About this time he wrote an extended defence of the Papal position in *De primatu Petri adv. Ludderum libri III* (Paris, 1521), besides shorter works against Luther; and for the rest of his life he took a prominent part in organizing Catholic opposition to German Protestantism. In 1530 he was the champion of the Catholic attack on the *Augsburg Confession. In 1537 he published a German-dialect version of the Bible for Catholic use. He was one of the Catholic participants in the Conference of *Ratisbon (1541).

J. Metzler, SJ (ed.), *Tres Orationes Funebres in Exequiis Ioannis Eckii habitae* (Corpus Catholicorum, 16; 1930), with full introd., list of his works and modern edns. to date. His *Enchiridion locorum communium adversus Lutherum et alios hostes ecclesiae* (1525–1543), ed. P. Fraenkel (ibid. 34; 1979); *De Sacrificio missae* (1526), ed. E. Iserloh, V. Pfnür, and P. Fabisch (ibid. 36; 1982); other texts in P. Fabisch and E. Iserloh (ed.), *Dokumente zur Causa Lutheri (1517–1521)*, 1 (ibid. 41; 1988), pp. 376–447. J. Greving, *Johann Eck als junger Gelehrter: Eine literar- und dogmengeschichtliche Untersuchung über seinen Chrysopassus Praedestinationis aus dem Jahre 1514* (Reformationsgeschichtliche Studien und Texte, 1; 1906); id., *Johann Ecks Pfarrbuch für U. L. Frau in Ingolstadt* (ibid. 4 and 5; 1908), with text; A. Brandt, *Johann Ecks Predigttätigkeit an*

U. L. Frau zu Ingolstadt, 1525–42 (ibid. 27 and 28; 1914), with text; H. Schauerte, *Die Busslehre des Johannes Eck* (ibid. 38 and 39; 1919); E. Iserloh, *Die Eucharistie in der Stellung des Johannes Eck* (ibid. 73 and 74; 1950); id., *Johannes Eck (1486–1543): Scholastiker, Humanist, Kontroverstheologe* (Katholisches Leben und Kirchenreform im Zeitalter der Glaubensspaltung, 41; 1981); K. Rischar, *Johann Eck auf dem Reichstag zu Augsburg 1530* (Reformationsgeschichtliche Studien und Texte, 97; 1968); W. Klaiber, *Ecclesia militans: Studien zu den Festtagspredigten des Johannes Eck* (ibid. 120; 1982). M. Ziegelbauer, *Johannes Eck: Mann der Kirche im Zeitalter der Glaubensspaltung* [1987]); E. Iserloh (ed.), *Johannes Eck (1486–1543) im Streit der Jahrhunderte: Internationales . . . aus Anlass des 500. Geburtstages des Johannes Eck vom 13. bis 16. November 1986 in Ingoldstadt und Eichstätt* (Reformationsgeschichtliche Studien und Texte, 127; 1988). J. P. Kirsch in *CE* 5 (1909), pp. 271–3, s.v.; F. Zoepfl in *Dict. Sp.* 4 (pt. 1; 1960), cols. 86–93, s.v.

Eckhart, Meister (*c*.1260–*c*.1328), German theologian and preacher. Born at Hochheim in Thuringia, he entered the *Dominican convent of Erfurt as a youth and was sent to study in *Paris. He prob. also studied under St *Albertus Magnus at *Cologne. He returned to Paris as a lecturer (1293–4) and as a Master in Theology (1302–3 and 1311–13). In between he was prior of Erfurt and vicar of Thuringia (1294–*c*.1300) and provincial of the new Dominican province of Saxony (1303–11). After his last period in Paris he lived in Strasbourg until 1323, and then in Cologne.

As a scholastic theologian, Eckhart conceived an ambitious and original speculative and exegetical project, the *Opus Tripartitum*, only parts of which survive. He became famous as a vernacular preacher, esp. to nuns, and prob. also to *beguines. His brilliant, creative use of German makes him an author at once attractive and difficult. His readiness to exploit verbal ambiguities and dramatic paradoxes left him open to widely differing interpretations. When he was accused of heretical teaching in 1326 and tried before the court of the Abp. of Cologne, he appealed to the Pope but died during the proceedings. In 1329 *John XXII condemned 28 propositions as heretical or misleading, but declared that Eckhart had recanted before his death, in terms which prob. reflect Eckhart's insistence that he never had any heretical intentions. Up to modern times he has been claimed by numerous ideologies (incl. the Nazis in the 20th century), but recent scholarship, building on the work of H. S. *Denifle, has attempted a more scientific interpretation, based equally on his Latin and German writings.

Eckhart teaches that we should 'break through' the complexity of all the particulars which confront us, to reach the simple 'ground' of all reality, where God and the soul are inseparably one, by abstracting from all that is 'this' or 'that', both metaphysically and ascetically. 'Abstractedness' (*Abgescheidenheit*) is, for Eckhart, the highest virtue, subsuming both humility and charity, because it produces the most intimate union with God, from which the Christian life flows as spontaneously as God's own life. The Word is thus born in the soul; indeed, the soul gives birth to the Word. This doctrine skirts round the conventional dichotomy between the active and contemplative lives. In spite of the condemnation, Eckhart's writings continued to be copied and studied in and beyond the Dominican Order. Among those influenced by

him were *Henry Suso, J. *Tauler, and *Nicholas of Cusa.

Crit. edn. for the 'Deutsche Forschungsgemeinschaft' of his Ger. works by J. Quint and others and of his Lat. works, with Ger. tr., by K. Weiss, J. Koch, E. Benz, and others (Stuttgart, 1936 ff., nearing completion). Lat. works also ed., with Fr. tr., by F. Brunner, A. de Libera, and others (Paris, 1984 ff.). The edn. of his Ger. works by F. Pfeiffer (Leipzig, 1857, repr. 1924 and 1962) contains much spurious and doubtful material. Eng. trs. of his Ger. works by M. O'C. Walshe (vols. 1–2, London, 1979–81; vol. 3, Shaftesbury, 1987); of a selection of his Lat. and Ger. works by E. Colledge, OSA, and B. McGinn (Classics of Western Spirituality, 1981); and of *Parisian Questions and Prologues* by A. A. Maurer, CSB (Toronto, 1974).

H. Denifle, OP, 'Meister Eckeharts lateinische Schriften, und die Grundanschauung seiner Lehre', *Archiv für Litteratur- und Kirchengeschichte des Mittelalters*, 2 (1886), pp. 417–652. G. Théry, OP, 'Édition critique des pièces relatives au procès d'Eckhart contenues dans le manuscrit 33ᵇ de la Bibliothèque de Soest', *AHDLMA* 1 (1926), pp. 129–268. J. Quint, *Die Überlieferung der Deutschen Predigten Meister Eckeharts* (Bonn, 1932). J. Ancelet-Hustache, *Maître Eckhart et la Mystique Rhénane* (1956; Eng. tr., 1957). J. Koch, 'Kritische Studien zum Leben Meister Eckharts', *Archivum Fratrum Praedicatorum*, 29 (1959), pp. 5–51, 30 (1960), pp. 5–52; repr. in his *Kleine Schriften*, 1 (Rome, 1973), pp. 247–347; also other arts. in this vol. U. M. Nix, OP, and R. Öchslin, OP (eds.), *Meister Eckhart der Prediger: Festschrift zum Eckhart-Gedenkjahr* (Freiburg, etc., 1960). V. *Lossky, *Théologie négative et connaissance de Dieu chez Maître Eckhart* (Études de philosophie médiévale, 48; 1960). I. Degenhardt, *Studien zum Wandel des Eckhartbildes* (Studien zur Problemgeschichte der antiken und mittelalterlichen Philosophie, 3; Leiden, 1967). R. Schürmann, *Maître Eckhart ou la joie errante: Sermons allemands traduits et commentés* ([1972]; expanded Eng. version, Bloomington, Ind., and London, 1978). C. F. Kelly, *Meister Eckhart on Divine Knowledge* (New Haven, Conn., and London, 1977). A. M. Haas, *Meister Eckhart als normative Gestalt geistlichen Lebens* (Einsiedeln, 1979); id., *Sermo Mysticus: Studien zur Theologie und Sprache der deutschen Mystik* (Dokimion, 4; 1979), esp. pp. 186–254. É. Zum Brunn and A. de Libera, *Maître Eckhart: Métaphysique du Verbe et Théologie Négative* (Bibliothèque des Archives de Philosophie, NS 42; 1984). É. Zum Brunn and others, *Maître Eckhart à Paris: Une critique médiévale de l'ontothéologie: Les Questions parisiennes n° 1 et n° 2 d'Eckhart* (Bibliothèque de l'École des Hautes Études, section des sciences religieuses, 86; 1984), incl. text and Fr. tr. K. Ruh, *Meister Eckhart, Theologe, Prediger, Mystiker* (Munich, 1985). F. [J.] Tobin, *Meister Eckhart: Thought and Language* (Philadelphia, 1986). W. Trusen, *Der Prozess gegen Meister Eckhart* (Rechts- und Staatswissenschaftliche Veröffentlichungen der Görres-Gesellschaft, NF 54; 1988). O. Davies, *Meister Eckhart: Mystical Theologian* (1991). H. Stirnimann and R. Imbach (eds.), *Eckardus Theutonicus, homo doctus et sanctus: Nachweise und Berichte zum Prozess gegen Meister Eckhart* (Freiburg, 1992). B. McGinn, 'Meister Eckhart', in P. Szarmach (ed.), *An Introduction to the Medieval Mystics of Europe* (Albany, NY, 1984), pp. 237–57. N. Largier, *Bibliographie zu Meister Eckhart* (Neue Schriftenreihe zur Freiburger Zeitschrift für Philosophie und Theologie, 9; 1989). Kaeppeli, 1 (1970), pp. 354–8. R.-L. Oechslin, OP, in *Dict. Sp.* 4 (pt. 1; 1960), cols. 93–116, s.v.; F. Vandenbroucke, OSB, in *DHGE* 14 (1960), cols. 1385–403, s.v. 'Eckhart (1)'; id., in *NCE* 5 (1967), pp. 38–40, s.v., all with bibl.

eclecticism. Any system of theology or philosophy which, rather than adhere to one school or tradition, selects such elements as seem the best in several systems, and combines them.

ecphonesis (Gk. ἐκφώνησις). Esp. in the E. Church, the concluding words, uttered in an audible voice, of a prayer the rest of which has been recited quietly (μυστικῶς).

ecstasy. The Greek word ἔκστασις, with its cognate forms, is used to refer to any state of powerful emotion, such that one is 'beside oneself'. Although often employed pejoratively, the idea of being 'taken out of oneself', suggested by the word's etymology, could be applied in a good sense to someone being raised above himself to consort with the divine (*Plato, *Phdr.* 249c), and it was often used of poetic inspiration, regarded as transcending the ordinary powers of the mind. In this sense it is applied to prophetic inspiration by *Philo (*Quis heres* 249) and by the *Apologists (*Justin, *Dial.* 115. 3; *Athenagoras, *Leg.* 9. 1). However, the orthodox reaction to the ecstatic prophesying of the *Montanists made 'ecstasy' a bad word (*Clement of Alexandria, *Strom.* 1. 85. 3; *Origen, *Cels.* 7. 3), and later theology took it as axiomatic that, whereas diabolical possession does disrupt the ordinary workings of the mind, divine inspiration enhances them without suspending them (*Thomas Aquinas, *Super Matt.* 849). *Plotinus used 'ecstasy' in a positive sense to refer to a union with God in which the individual, having passed beyond his own mental powers, is no longer quite 'himself' (*Enn.* 6. 9. 11). Subsequent Platonism distinguished between good and bad senses of the word (*Iamblichus, *Myst.* 3. 25), and this is followed by *Dionysius the Pseudo-Areopagite (*Ep.* 9. 5), who connects 'ecstasy' in a good sense both with love, which takes us out of ourselves towards the objects of our love (*DN* 4. 13), and with faith (*DN* 7. 4), by which we surrender ourselves to the inspiration of God and become one with Him (*DN* 2. 9, 3. 2). With the growth in the later Middle Ages of an interest in paranormal phenomena associated with intense absorption in spiritual things, ecstasy came to be associated with 'rapture', and both tended to become more technical terms, referring to a state of more or less complete abstraction from the senses. Under the influence of St *Teresa of Ávila and St *John of the Cross, ecstasy and rapture were given a specific place in the scheme of spiritual progress, the two words often being effectively identified, though more precise theologians continue to distinguish between them, the latter term being used only when someone is carried out of himself quite helplessly by some influx of special grace. It is generally believed that the heart and mind of the recipient of this grace are supernaturally enflamed with love and enlightened with knowledge.

M. de Goedt, J. Kirchmeyer, SJ, and others in *Dict. Sp.* 4 (pt. 2; 1961), cols. 2072–171, s.v. 'Extase (B), mystique chrétienne', with extensive bibl. refs.

ectene (Gk. ἐκτένεια, 'earnest prayer'; cf. Acts 12: 5, προσευχὴ δὲ ἦν ἐκτενῶς γινομένη, 'prayer was made without ceasing'). In the E. Church, a prayer constructed like a *litany for use in the Liturgy and other services. It consists of short petitions said by the *deacon to which choir or congregation respond with *Kyrie Eleison.

Ecthesis (Gk. ἔκθεσις, 'a statement of faith'). The formula issued in 638 by the Emp. *Heraclius forbidding the mention of 'energies' (ἐνέργειαι), whether one or two, in the Person of Christ and asserting that the two Natures were united in a single Will (*Monothelitism, q.v.). It had been drafted earlier in the year by *Sergius, Patr. of *Constantinople, after consultation with Pope *Honorius (q.v.). It was accepted by Councils held at Constantinople in 638 and 639, but soon disowned by Heraclius as well as by Honorius' two successors in the Roman see (Severinus, 638–40; John IV, 640–2).

The text is preserved among the acts of the Lateran Council of 649, sess. 3; pr., with Lat. tr., in Hardouin, 3, cols. 791–6, and Mansi, 10 (1764), cols. 991–8. The condemnation in can. 18 of this council is repr. in Denzinger and Hünermann (37th edn., 1991), pp. 237 f. (nos. 518 f). Hefele and Leclercq, 3 (pt. 1; 1909), pp. 387–99, with full refs. F.-X. Murphy, CSSR, and P. Sherwood, OSB, *Constantinople II et Constantinople III* (Histoire des Conciles Œcuméniques, 3 [1974]), pp. 163–73. See also bibl. to HERACLIUS and MONOTHELITISM.

Ecumenical Councils. See OECUMENICAL COUNCILS.

Ecumenical Movement (formerly more usually Oecumenical, from Gk. οἰκουμένη, 'the whole inhabited world'). The movement in the Church towards the recovery of the unity of all believers in Christ, transcending differences of creed, ritual, and polity. This aspiration can be traced in various forms from NT times, but has never been so potent as in the 20th cent. The modern ecumenical movement may be dated from the *Edinburgh Missionary Conference of 1910, though this itself owed much to earlier movements which prepared the way. They included the *Evangelical revivals of the 18th and 19th cents., which crossed national and denominational frontiers, the great missionary expansion of the 19th cent., with its emphasis on interdenominational co-operation, the work of the Bible Societies which drew on the resources of many different Churches, and the *Student Christian Movement, which was interdenominational in membership and world-wide in scope. The Edinburgh Conference of 1910 led immediately to the establishment of the International Missionary Council, and thence to the creation in 1925 of the Universal Christian Conference on *Life and Work, which was concerned with the application of Christianity to social, economic, and political life. It was followed in 1927 by the first World Conference on *Faith and Order at *Lausanne, which addressed itself to the theological basis of the Church and its unity. The next decades were marked by the establishment of many national Councils of Churches (e.g. the Canadian Council of Churches, formed in 1944) and by the continued development of the Life and Work and Faith and Order movements. After a lengthy period of preparation these joined in 1948 to form the *World Council of Churches.

The initiative between 1910 and 1927 came mainly from within W. Protestantism, though it was reinforced in 1920 by an Encyclical Letter from the *Oecumenical Patriarch of Constantinople appealing to 'all the Churches of Christ' for 'closer intercourse and mutual co-operation'. This was paralleled by the Appeal for Reunion issued by the 1920 *Lambeth Conference. Both E. *Orthodox (incl. the Church of Greece) and *Oriental Orthodox (incl. the Malankara *Syrian Orthodox Church in India) have been in the World Council of Churches from its beginning. The Russian Orthodox Church, overcoming earlier reservations, joined in 1961, by which time nearly all the Orthodox Churches had become members. During the 1950s there was increasing contact between certain RCs and leaders of the World Council of Churches, as well as unofficial co-operation in some areas, esp. in prayer for

Christian unity. This changed atmosphere was reflected in the visit of G. F. *Fisher, Abp. of Canterbury, to Pope *John XXIII in 1960. In 1961 for the first time official observers were permitted by the Vatican to attend the World Council of Churches' Third Assembly in New Delhi. The Pope's decision to invite observers from non-RC Churches to the Second *Vatican Council the following year was of great significance; this was heightened in 1964 by the Council's Decree on Ecumenism, which described members of other communions as 'separated brethren' rather than outside the Church. Within this new climate the historic severance between the E. Church and W. Catholicism began to be bridged and in 1965 Pope *Paul VI and the Oecumenical Patriarch *Athenagoras nullified the anathemas which had been in force since 1054 (see GREAT SCHISM).

Signs of the continuing vitality of the ecumenical movement include the numerous organic unions achieved (esp. in the 1960s and 1970s) among Protestant Churches in many parts of the world, with more being negotiated (see REUNION). Of particular significance were those (as in *South and *North India and in *Pakistan) which incorporated episcopally and non-episcopally ordered Churches. The multilateral discussions on issues dividing the Churches carried on by the Faith and Order Commission of the World Council of Churches are now paralleled by the many bilateral dialogues between World Christian Communions (the world-wide organizations representing each of the major denominations), e.g. between the *Anglican Communion and the *World Alliance of Reformed Churches. Also striking is the continued development of Councils of Churches at regional (as in the All Africa Conference of Churches, formed in 1958), national, and local levels, now normally including the Orthodox, with RCs belonging to some 35 national and one regional Council.

Among the trends that have marked the ecumenical movement since the late 1960s has been the dramatically increased participation of non-Western Churches and women. Official ecumenical activity has become professionalized, with many Churches having staff specializing in the field. At the same time there has been a widespread development of 'unofficial' ecumenism as Christians have gathered, across denominational lines (and often in advance of the official positions of the Churches to which they belong), for common worship or to make a common witness on social issues. Major questions now include how to involve more Evangelical, Charismatic, and *Pentecostal Churches which (except in Latin America) have so far taken little part in the ecumenical movement, and whether Councils of Churches are purely the servants of their member Churches, or also have a prophetic role in challenging them to take further steps towards visible unity and to increase their co-operation in Christian witness and service.

See also REUNION and WORLD COUNCIL OF CHURCHES.

G. K. A. *Bell (ed.), Documents on Christian Unity 1920–4 (1924); id., 2nd ser. [1920–30] (1930); id., 3rd ser. 1930–48 (1948); id., 4th ser. 1948–57 (1958). L. Vischer (ed.), A Documentary History of the Faith and Order Movement 1927–1963 (St Louis [1963]); G. Gassmann (ed.), Documentary History of Faith and Order 1963–1993 (Faith and Order Paper, 159; Geneva [1993]). H. Meyer and L. Vischer (eds.), Growth in Agreement: Reports and Agreed Statements of Ecumenical Conversations on a World Level (Faith and Order Paper, 108; New York and Geneva [1984]). C. G. Patelos (ed.), The Orthodox Church in the Ecumenical Movement: Documents and Statements 1902–1975 (Geneva [1978]); P. McPartlan (ed.), One in 2000? Towards Catholic-Orthodox Unity. Agreed Statements and Parish Papers (Slough, 1993).

Studies incl. K. [D.] Mackenzie (ed.), Union of Christendom (1938); R. Rouse and S. C. Neill (eds.), A History of the Ecumenical Movement, 1517–1948 (1954; 2nd edn., with rev. bibl., 1967; vol. 2: The Ecumenical Advance, 1948–1968, ed. H. E. Fey, 1970; both vols. repr., Geneva [1986], with bibl. covering the period 1968–85 in vol. 2, pp. 509–53); N. Goodall, The Ecumenical Movement: What it is and what it does (1961; 2nd edn., 1964); id., Ecumenical Progress: A Decade of Change in the Ecumenical Movement 1961–71 (1972); S. [C.] Neill, The Church and Christian Union (Bampton Lectures for 1964; 1968); W. A. Visser 't Hooft, Memoires: een leven in de oecumene (Amsterdam, 1971; Eng. tr., 1973); B. Till, The Churches Search for Unity (Harmondsworth, 1972); R. Beaupère, L'Oecuménisme (1991). N. Lossky and others (eds.), Dictionary of the Ecumenical Movement (1991). There are also a number of periodicals concerned with the ecumenical movement incl. Irénikon (Amay s.Meuse and then *Chevetogne, 1926 ff.), Eastern Churches Quarterly (16 vols., 1936–64), cont. as One in Christ (various places, 1965 ff.), Una Sancta (Meitingen, 1946 ff.), The Ecumenical Review (Geneva, 1948 ff.), Oekumenische Rundschau (Frankfurt, 1952 ff.), Istina (Paris, 1954 ff.), Mid-Stream (Indianapolis, 1962 ff.).

Ecumenical Society of the Blessed Virgin Mary. An interdenominational society founded in London in 1966 'to advance the study at various levels of the place of the BVM in the Church under Christ and to promote ecumenical devotion'. Its inauguration was inspired by the vision of Martin Gillett (d. 1980) that the BVM, usually regarded as a source of division between the Churches, should become an agent of ecumenism; Gillett himself had been ordained as a deacon in the C of E and later received into the RC Church. Members of the society include clergy and laity of the RC, Anglican, Orthodox, and Free Churches; it has branches in England, Ireland, and the USA, and holds meetings both regional and international.

A. Stacpoole, OSB (ed.), Mary's Place in Christian Dialogue. Occasional Papers of the Ecumenical Society of the Blessed Virgin Mary, 1970–1980 (Slough, 1982). Papers of conferences held at Chichester in 1986 and Liverpool in 1989 ed. id., Mary and the Churches (Dublin, 1987) and Mary in Doctrine and Devotion (ibid., 1990).

Eden, Garden of. The original home of *Adam and *Eve (Gen. 2: 8–3: 24), translated in the LXX by a word meaning '*Paradise'. From it issued the four rivers Pishon, Gihon, Hiddekel, and Euphrates (ibid.). The name is prob. connected with the Babylonian edinu, 'a plain' (such as would be made very fertile by irrigation), but would suggest in Heb. 'delight'. The writer of the Gen. narrative may have had in mind the well-watered country of Mesopotamia (cf. 2: 14), but the geographical ideas implied are very primitive or even mythological. Elsewhere, in Is. 51: 3, Ezek. 28: 13 and 31: 9, and Joel 2: 3, Eden is mentioned as a place of extreme fertility and magnificent trees. Older biblical scholars frequently made attempts to identify the site, e.g. Friedrich *Delitzsch put it some 100 miles N. of Baghdad.

F. Delitzsch, Wo lag das Paradies? (1881). A. Schulz, 'Eden', ZATW 51 (1933), pp. 222–6. A. Brock-Utne, Der Gottesgarten: Eine vergleichende religionsgeschichtliche Studie (Avhandlinger utgitt av det Norske Videnskaps-Akademie i Oslo, II. Hist.-Filos.

Klasse, 1935, no. 2; 1936). J. W. Rosenberg, 'The Garden Story Forward and Backward: The Non-Narrative Dimension of Gen. 2–3', *Prooftexts: A Journal of Jewish Literary History*, 1 (Baltimore, 1981), pp. 1–27. E. Cothenet in *Dict. Bibl.* Suppl. 6 (1960), cols. 1177–1220, s.v. 'Paradis'; H. N. Wallace in *Anchor Bible Dictionary*, 2 (1992), pp. 281–3, s.v. See also comm. cited s.vv. GENESIS (esp. that of C. Westermann), EZEKIEL, etc.

Edersheim, Alfred (1825–89), biblical scholar. An Austrian of Jewish parentage and upbringing, he was converted to Christianity at Pest by a Scottish *Presbyterian, John Duncan, and accompanied him to Edinburgh. After studying theology at Edinburgh and Berlin, he entered the Presbyterian ministry in 1846, but later joined the C of E (1875), and from 1876 to 1882 was Vicar of Loders in Dorset. He made an intensive study of the doctrines, practices, and conditions of *Judaism in the centuries preceding and following the beginning of the Christian era. Of his writings the most widely read was his *Life and Times of Jesus the Messiah* (2 vols., 1883), a work of great erudition written in an easy style, but somewhat lacking in critical judgement.

Tohu-Va-Vohu ['*Without Form and Void*']: *A Collection of Fragmentary Thoughts and Criticisms*, ed. with a memoir by E. Edersheim [daughter] (1890; memoir, pp. vii–xxxii). S. R. *Driver in *DNB*, Suppl. 2 (1901), pp. 175 f.

Edessa. The site has probably been inhabited from remote times, but the present city (now Urfa) was founded by Seleucus I in 304 BC. After the fall of Seleucid power it was the centre of an independent kingdom from *c.*132 BC until AD 214, and then a Roman colony. It was from a very early date the centre of Syriac-speaking Christianity. The church there, destroyed in 201 after a flood, may be the oldest known Christian edifice. Edessa is prob. the home both of the *Old Syriac and *Peshitta versions of the NT, and possibly also of the *Diatessaron. Its fame was enhanced by its claim to possess from AD 394 onwards the relics of the Apostle St *Thomas. It was the home of the 'Persian School' until that was closed in 489 on account of its alleged *Nestorian tendencies, and has always been an important centre of opposition to the Christological teaching of the Council of *Chalcedon (it remained the residence of a *Syrian Orthodox metropolitan until the beginning of the 20th century). In 641 it fell into the hands of the Arabs, but continued to be an important Christian centre for several centuries. It fell to the Byzantines in 944, and later became the capital of a small crusader principality, until its capture by Zengi in 1144. See also ABGAR, LEGEND OF, and CHRONICON EDESSENUM.

W. *Cureton (ed.), *Ancient Syriac Documents relative to the Earliest Establishment of Christianity in Edessa and the Neighbouring Countries, from the Year After Our Lord's Ascension to the Beginning of the Fourth Century* (1864). L. J. Tixeront, *Les Origines de l'église d'Édesse et la légende d'Abgar: Étude critique suivie de deux textes orientaux inédits* (1888). J. B. Segal, *Edessa: 'The Blessed City'* (Oxford, 1970), with bibl. Id., 'When did Christianity come to Edessa?', in B. C. Bloomfield (ed.), *Middle East Studies and Libraries: A Felicitation Volume for ... J. D. Pearson* (1980), pp. 179–91. R. Duval, 'Histoire politique, religieuse et littéraire d'Édessa jusqu'à la première croisade', *Journal asiatique*, 8th ser. 18 (1891), pp. 87–133, 201–78, 381–439; 19 (1892), pp. 5–102. F. C. *Burkitt, *Early Eastern Christianity* (1904), pp. 1–38. A. *Baumstark, 'Vorjustinianische kirchliche Bauten in Edessa', *Oriens*

Christianus, 4 (1904), pp. 164–83; K. E. McVey, 'The Domed Church as Microcosm', *Dumbarton Oaks Papers*, 37 (1983), pp. 91–121 [on the 6th-cent. church at Edessa]. H. J. W. Drijvers in *Aufstieg und Niedergang der Römischen Welt*, II. Principat, 8 (1977), pp. 863–96, with bibl., pp. 902–4. W. Bauer, *Rechtgläubigkeit und Ketzerei im ältesten Christentum* (1934), pp. 6–48; Eng. tr. (1972), pp. 1–43. H. J. W. Drijvers in *TRE* 9 (1982), pp. 277–88, s.v., with bibl.; K. E. McVey in *Anchor Bible Dictionary*, 2 (1992), pp. 284–7, s.v.

Edgar (*c.*943–75), King of England from 959. The younger son of King Edmund, he became King of Mercia (and Northumbria) in 957, and, on the death of his brother Eadwig, King of all England in 959. He lent his support to the work of monastic reform, appointing St *Dunstan Abp. of *Canterbury in 959, St *Ethelwold Bp. of *Winchester in 963, and St *Oswald Bp. of *Worcester in 961 and Abp. of *York in 971. In 964 he was instrumental in driving the secular clergy from the Old and New Minsters at Winchester, and from other houses; and it was on his initiative that a synodal council was convened at Winchester *c.*970, resulting in the promulgation of the *Regularis Concordia*. In 973 his establishment of firm rule throughout England, and his wider authority in Britain, was marked by his (second) coronation, at Bath; but after his death in 975, the succession was disputed between his sons St *Edward the Martyr and Ethelred the Unready, and resentment of his policies found expression in widespread disturbances. Edgar's reign was remembered by Churchmen as a period of great order and prosperity, and he came to be known as Edgar the Peaceful.

The chief authorities are the Anglo-Saxon Chronicle and Lives of Sts Dunstan, Ethelwold, and Oswald; see also the tract on King Edgar's establishment of monasteries, attributed to Ethelwold, conveniently pr. in *Councils & Synods ... 1, A.D. 871–1204*, ed. D. Whitelock, M. Brett, and C. N. L. Brooke, 1 (Oxford, 1981), pp. 142–54 (no. 33); Eng. tr. also in D. Whitelock (ed.), *English Historical Documents c.500–1042* (2nd edn., 1979), pp. 920–3 (no. 238); and the King's charters, listed in P. H. Sawyer, *Anglo-Saxon Charters* (Royal Historical Society Guides and Handbooks, 8; 1968), pp. 223–60 (nos. 667–827). F. M. Stenton, *Anglo-Saxon England* (Oxford History of England; 3rd edn., 1971), pp. 367–72; E. John, *Orbis Britanniae and other Studies* (Leicester, 1966), *passim*.

Edict of Milan. See MILAN, EDICT OF.

Edict of Nantes. See NANTES, EDICT OF.

Edinburgh Conference (1910), World Missionary Conference. Convened as a consultative gathering to study missionary endeavour in the light of the circumstances of the day, the Conference was significant esp. for its presentation of the ideal of world-evangelization and as a forerunner of the *Ecumenical Movement. Through the creation of the International Missionary Council, it also led to much greater co-operation among Missionary Societies. Some 1,200 delegates, representative of many Christian bodies and some 160 Missionary Boards or Societies, took part. J. R. *Mott was chairman of the Committee and J. H. *Oldham general secretary of the Conference.

World Missionary Conference, 1910 (Report, 9 vols. [1910]). W. H. T. *Gairdner, *Edinburgh 1910: An Account and Interpretation of the World Missionary Conference* (1910).

Edinburgh Conference (1937). The second World Conference on *Faith and Order, which continued the work of *Lausanne (q.v.). Its subjects were Grace, the Word of God, the Communion of Saints, the Ministry and Sacraments, and the Church's Unity in Life and Worship. The Report issued by the Conference stated the agreements as well as the differences. Grace, equated with the manifestation of God's love in the creation and redemption of man, is given in the Church through the Word and the Sacraments. Scripture is the principal rule of Christian doctrine and worship, but there was dissension as to the authority of the Church to interpret it, on the place assigned to Tradition, and on the nature, visibility, and membership of the Church. The Communion of Saints was interpreted in various ways as synonymous with the Holy Catholic Church, as the way of life of Christians in the state of grace, or, esp. by the Orthodox, as including also the angels and the Saints in heaven. There was considerable division on the number and efficacy of the Sacraments and on the ministry, the Presbyterians and other Protestants rejecting episcopacy as taught in the Orthodox Church and in the C of E. The union visualized by the Conference was largely one of co-operative action, confederation, and intercommunion, founded on essential unity in faith. The principal obstacle in the way of its achievement was the opposition between two main types of the conception of the Church as 'authoritarian' and 'personal' respectively. The Conference approved the proposal of a '*World Council of Churches' (q.v.). See also ECUMENICAL MOVEMENT.

The Second World Conference on Faith and Order, held at Edinburgh, August 3–18, 1937, ed. L. Hodgson (1938).

Edmund, St, of Abingdon (also wrongly **Edmund Rich**) (*c.*1180–1240), Abp. of *Canterbury. Born at Abingdon, Oxon, of pious parents, Edmund early obtained a reputation for austerity and sanctity. Before 1222 he became Treasurer of *Salisbury Cathedral, and in 1233 he was elected Abp. of Canterbury. During his short tenure of the primacy he boldly, though ineffectually, attempted to check royal mismanagement and Papal exactions. When the legate, Cardinal Otto, whom Henry III had induced the Pope to appoint, arrived, Edmund protested against the infringement of his archiepiscopal rights; but he failed to stop the exploitation of ecclesiastical wealth and patronage, and retired to Pontigny in self-imposed exile. In his earlier years he had taught the new logic at Oxford, and his association with the University is commemorated in St Edmund Hall, the one surviving medieval Hall in Oxford. He wrote a devotional treatise *Speculum Religiosorum*; the vulgate Latin text, which is a translation from one of the Anglo-Norman versions and commonly known as the *Speculum Ecclesie*, had a wide circulation. He was canonized by *Innocent IV in 1247. Feast day, 16 Nov.

Speculum Religiosorum and *Speculum Ecclesie* ed. H. P. Forshaw, SHCJ (Auctores Britannici Medii Aevi, 3; London, 1973), with refs. to earlier edns. of the latter. The chief authorities are the Monastic Chroniclers, esp. *Matthew Paris, and several early biographies. Modern Lives by W. Wallace (London, 1893), B. Ward (ibid. 1903), and C. H. Lawrence (Oxford, 1960), incl. texts of early material. A. B. Emden, *An Oxford Hall in Medieval Times* (1927). C. H. Lawrence, 'Edmund of Abingdon', *The Month*, NS 29 (1963), pp. 213–29. *BRUO* 1 (1957), pp. 6 f., s.v. 'Abingdon,

Edmund of'. T. A. Archer in *DNB* 16 (1888), pp. 405–10; C. H. Lawrence in *Dict. Sp.* 4 (pt. 1; 1960), cols. 293–5, s.v.

Edmund Campion, St. See CAMPION, ST EDMUND.

Edmund the Martyr, St (*c.*840–69), King of East Anglia. Born of Saxon stock, Edmund had become King of the East Angles by 865. His equitable rule was cut short in 869 by the invasion of the Danes under Inguar and Hubba. After the defeat of his army, he was captured; but though the invaders promised him his life if he would share his kingdom with Inguar, he refused as a Christian to associate himself thus with a pagan, and was condemned to be made the target of the Danes' archery practice, and finally beheaded. The cult of the martyr started almost immediately, and his body was translated in the 10th cent. to the present Bury St Edmunds, where the abbey rapidly became a great place of pilgrimage. Feast day, 20 Nov.

T. Arnold (ed.), *Memorials of St Edmund's Abbey*, 1 (RS, 1980), incl. 'Passio Sancti Edmundi' of *Abbo of Fleury (pp. 3–25), 'De Infantia Sancti Edmundi' of Gaufridus de Fontibus (pp. 93–103), and other material on the miracles attributed to Edmund. The Life by Abbo of Fleury is also ed. M. Winterbottom, *Three Lives of English Saints* (Toronto Medieval Latin Texts, 1972), pp. 67–87. *Corolla Sancti Edmundi*, ed. with a preface by Lord Francis Hervey (1907; with Eng. tr. of chief sources). Id. (ed.), *The History of King Eadmund the Martyr and of the Early Years of his Abbey: Corpus Christi College, Oxford MS. 197* (Oxford, 1929). *La Vie de Seint Edmund le Rei*, an Anglo-Norman poem of the Twelfth Century by Denis Piramus also ed. by F. L. Ravenel (Philadelphia, 1906), and, with useful introd., by H. Kjellman (Göteborgs Kungl. Vetenskaps- och Vitterhets-Samhälles Handlingar, Femte Földjen, Ser. A, 4. 3; 1935). G. Loomis, 'The Growth of the Saint Edmund Legend', *Harvard Studies and Notes in Philology and Literature*, 14 (1932), pp. 83–113. D. Whitelock, 'Fact and Fiction in the Legend of St. Edmund', *Proceedings of the Suffolk Institute of Archaeology*, 31 (for 1969; 1970), pp. 217–33; and other arts. in this issue commemorating St Edmund; R. M. Thomson, 'Two Versions of a Saint's Life from St. Edmund's Abbey', *R. Bén.* 84 (1974), pp. 383–408. S. J. Ridyard, *The Royal Saints of Anglo-Saxon England* (Cambridge, 1988), pp. 211–33 ('The Cult of St Edmund').

Edward, St (*c.*962–78), king and martyr. He was the eldest son of *Edgar the Peaceful, King of England, whom, contrary to the wishes of his stepmother, Queen Elfrida, but with the support of Abp. *Dunstan, he succeeded on his death in 975. Three years later he was murdered. Acc. to the details in *William of Malmesbury, this took place near Corfe in Dorset at the instigation of Elfrida, who had him stabbed while drinking by one of her attendants. His body was buried in the church of Wareham and a year later translated to Shaftesbury. In 1008 he was officially decreed a martyr and miracles were reported at his tomb. Feast day, 18 Mar.; of his translation, 20 June.

The chief authorities are William of Malmesbury, Florence of Worcester and the Anglo-Saxon Chronicle, and the *Vita S. Oswaldi*. See also *Memorials of St Dunstan* (ed. W. *Stubbs, RS, 1874). D. J. V. Fisher, 'The Anti-Monastic Reaction in the Reign of Edward the Martyr', *Cambridge Historical Journal*, 10 (1950–52), pp. 254–70. C. E. Fell, *Edward, King and Martyr* (Leeds Texts and Monographs, 1971), incl. text of *Passio* or Life of Edmund, in its present form dating from late 11th or early 12th cent.

Edward the Confessor, St (*c*.1005–66), English king. The son of Ethelred II and Emma, the daughter of Duke Richard I of Normandy, he was sent to Normandy in 1013 and educated there in Norman ways. On the death of his half-brother, Hardicanute, in 1042, he was acclaimed King. He owed the throne largely to the support of the powerful Earl Godwin, whose daughter, Eadgyth (or Edith), he married later in 1045. His reign was outstandingly peaceful, seriously disturbed only by the abortive rebellion of Earl Godwin and his sons in 1051 against Edward's turning to other favourites, including Normans. Though banished at the time, Godwin returned by force in 1052, and the subsequent dominance of his family led to the succession of Harold Godwinson, Edward's brother-in-law, in 1066. Edward, always a martial figure and great hunter, in his later years re-endowed and rebuilt St Peter's Abbey at *Westminster (the church was re-consecrated on 28 Dec. 1065) as his mausoleum. His reputation for sanctity developed after the Norman Conquest. Some Westminster monks, led by Osbert of Clare, maintained that as King he had been mild and merciful, had loved and fostered the Church; although married, had remained a virgin; and that in life as in death had performed miracles. On the petition of King Henry II and the English Church he was canonized by *Alexander III in 1161 and his relics translated on 13 Oct. (his feast day) in both 1163 and 1269.

The earliest, anonymous, Life, attributed to a monk of St Bertin, was almost certainly written before *c*.1100; it is dated 1065-6 by F. Barlow (see below). The Life by Osbert of Clare was completed in 1138. H. R. Luard (ed.), *Lives of Edward the Confessor* (RS, 1858), incl. text of anon. Life (pp. 389–435); it is also ed., with Eng. tr., by F. Barlow (London, 1962, 2nd edn., 1992), incl. full refs. and notes, and appendix on the development of Edward's cult. M. Bloch, 'La Vie de S. Édouard le Confesseur par Osbert de Clare', *Anal. Boll.* 41 (1923), pp. 5–131, incl. text, pp. 64–131; F. Barlow, *Edward the Confessor* (1970; 2nd edn., 1979). L. E. Tanner, 'Some Representations of St. Edward the Confessor in Westminster Abbey and Elsewhere', *Journal of the British Archaeological Association*, 3rd ser. 15 (1952), pp. 1–12. See also works cited s.v. ANGLO-SAXON CHURCH.

Edward VI (1537–53), King of England. The son of *Henry VIII and Jane Seymour, he was a precocious and studious boy. He was provided by his father with consistently Protestant tutors, and succeeded to the throne in 1547, at a time which was critical for the C of E. Having delegated his royal authority to the Privy Council, dominated first by the Protector, *Somerset, and then by the Duke of Northumberland, he was himself of little account politically. His one important intervention in politics occurred in 1553: when he realized that tuberculosis threatened his life he joined with Northumberland in an attempt to alter the succession in favour of his cousin Lady Jane Grey in place of his half-sisters *Mary and *Elizabeth. His reign is outstanding ecclesiastically for numerous reforms and alterations often forced on the Church by an *Erastian government; they reflected the influence of Continental theologians, particularly of *Peter Martyr Vermigli and M. *Bucer, but also of the *Zwinglian tradition of Zurich. It was marked by the publication (1547) of a Book of *Homilies, drawn up by T. *Cranmer; by the *Injunctions (1547) condemning pictures and all lights except the two before the Blessed Sacrament, providing a copy of the *Great Bible and of the paraphrase of *Erasmus in every parish church, and enforcing the reading in English of the Epistle and Gospel at *High Mass; by the Acts of Parliament (1547) imposing penalties on those who spoke irreverently of the Sacrament of the Altar, and enjoining that Communion be given in both kinds, abolishing the **congé d'élire* and repealing the *Lollard heresy laws and the Act of *Six Articles; by the Privy Council's Proclamations (1548) enumerating ceremonies no longer to be enforced, abolishing all images, and enforcing the use of the newly drawn up order in English for the giving of Communion in both kinds; by the recognition (1549) of clerical marriages; by the Act of *Uniformity passed in 1549, imposing by penal legislation the use of the First BCP; by the new *Ordinal (1550); by the destruction of altars (1550) and the substitution of wooden tables; by the attack on the doctrine of the *Real Presence; by the Second and more Protestant BCP (1552); the *Forty-Two Articles of Religion (1553), and the *Catechism and *Primer of 1553.

J. G. Nichols (ed.), *Literary Remains of King Edward the Sixth* (Roxburghe Club, 2 vols., 1857). R. H. Brodie (ed.), *The Calendar of the Patent Rolls preserved in the Public Record Office: Edward VI, 1547–1553* (6 vols., 1924–9); other calendars of the papers of his reign issued by the Master of the Rolls in their respective series. W. K. Jordan (ed.), *The Chronicle and Political Papers of King Edward VI* (1966). P. F. Tytler, *England under the Reigns of Edward VI and Mary* (2 vols., 1839), vol. 1, and vol. 2, pp. 1–187. C. H. [E.] Smyth, *Cranmer & the Reformation under Edward VI* (Cambridge, 1926). H. W. Chapman, *The Last Tudor King: A Study of Edward VI [October 12th, 1537–July 6th, 1553]* (1958). W. K. Jordan, *Edward VI: The Young King. The Protectorship of the Duke of Somerset* (1968); id., *Edward VI: The Threshold of Power. The Dominance of the Duke of Northumberland* (1970). M. L. Bush, *The Government Policy of Protector Somerset* (1975). D. E. Hoak, *The King's Council in the Reign of Edward VI* (1976). G. Constant, *La Réforme en Angleterre, 2. Introduction de la Réforme en Angleterre, Édouard VI (1547–1553)* (1939; Eng. tr., 1942); A. G. Dickens, *The English Reformation* (1964), esp. chs. 9–10; 2nd edn. (1989), chs. 10–11. See also bibl. to REFORMATION.

Edwards, Jonathan (1703–58), American evangelical preacher and *Calvinist theologian. He was nurtured in the piety of New England *Puritanism and educated at the newly founded Yale College. After several years as a supply minister and tutor, he was ordained to the ministry of the *Congregational church at Northampton, Massachusetts, in 1727. There he maintained an intense programme of study and meditation reflected in his private writings at the same time that he was drawn into the public arena by his congregation's participation in a series of revivals beginning in 1734. His *Faithful Narrative of the Surprising Works of God* (1737) brought him into the limelight, both in the American colonies and abroad. During the *Great Awakening of the 1740s he emerged as the champion of evangelical religion; he preached the necessity of a 'new birth' and in his *Treatise Concerning Religious Affections* (1746) he defended the role of both the will and the intellect in the religious life, thereby averting charges of rationalism and enthusiasm. As a conservative Reformed theologian, he opposed *Arminianism with insights derived from the Bible, the theological tradition, and the *Enlightenment. He defended the evangelical revivals as the work of the Holy Spirit and sought to rekindle them when they dissipated in later years. In 1750 he was dismissed from his congregation because he insisted on strict standards for admission to Communion. Subsequently he served as a missionary to the Indians at Stockbridge, Massachusetts. There he wrote a philosophical treatise on the bondage of the will (*Freedom of the Will*, 1754), an exposition of the traditional notion of human depravity (*Original Sin*, posthumous) and a speculative essay on ethics (*Nature of True Virtue*, also posthumous). Freedom, as popularly understood, he rejected, maintaining that self-determination was 'unphilosophical, self-contradictory, and absurd', and that the essence of virtue and vice lay 'not in their cause but in their nature'. In theology he was an orthodox Calvinist and it was his desire to defend the extreme position of 'election' that inspired his metaphysical account of freedom. In 1757 he became president of the College of New Jersey (later Princeton), where he died of smallpox after only three months in office. Regarded as the foremost American theologian and philosopher of the colonial period, Edwards has exercised influence through his voluminous writings, through a school of disciples known as the 'New England Theologians', and through the expansion of the evangelical movement during the 19th and 20th cents.

See also GREAT AWAKENING.

Works, ed. E. Williams and E. Parsons (8 vols., Leeds, 1806–11; 2 suppl. vols., Edinburgh, 1847); by S. Austin (8 vols., Worcester, Mass., 1808–9; repr. Boston, 1843); by S. E. Dwight, incl. Memoir (10 vols., New York, 1829–30); and by P. [G. A.] Miller and J. E. Smith (New Haven, Conn., and London, 1957 ff.). Lives by A. V. G. Allen (Edinburgh, 1889), O. E. Winslow (New York, 1940) and P. [G. A.] Miller (ibid., 1949); on the period to 1750, P. J. Tracy, *Jonathan Edwards, Pastor: Religion and Society in Eighteenth-Century Northampton* (ibid., 1980). C. C. Cherry, *The Theology of Jonathan Edwards: A Reappraisal* (Garden City, NY, 1966); R. A. Delattre, *Beauty and Sensibility in the Thought of Jonathan Edwards: An Essay in Aesthetics and Theological Ethics* (New Haven, Conn., and London, 1968); C. A. Holbrook, *The Ethics of Jonathan Edwards: Morality and Aesthetics* (Ann Arbor, Mich. [1973]); W. J. Scheick (ed.), *Critical Essays on Jonathan Edwards* (Boston [1980]); N. Fiering, *Jonathan Edwards's Moral Thought and its British Context* (Chapel Hill, NC [1981]); B. Kuklick, *Churchmen and Philosophers from Jonathan Edwards to John Dewey* (New Haven, Conn., and London [1985]), esp. pp. 15–42. M. Vetö, *La Pensée de Jonathan Edwards* (1987); S. H. Lee, *The Philosophical Theology of Jonathan Edwards* (Princeton, NJ [1988]); N. O. Hatch and H. S. Stout, *Jonathan Edwards and the American Experience* (New York and Oxford, 1988); A. C. Guelzo, *Edwards on the Will: A Century of Theological Debate* (Middletown, Conn. [1989]). The most useful bibl. is M. X. Lesser, *Jonathan Edwards: A Reference Guide* (Boston [1981]). See also H. T. Johnson, *The Printed Writings of Jonathan Edwards 1703–1758* (Princeton, NJ, and London, 1940).

Edwin (*c.* 585–633), Northumbrian king. The son of Ælla, King of Deira (i.e. S. Northumbria), Edwin was banished by the King of Bernicia (N. Northumbria) who had seized his father's kingdom. After taking refuge, first in N. Wales, then in Mercia, and finally with Redwald, King of E. Anglia, he was restored to the throne through Redwald's victory over the Bernician king, Ethelfrith, in 616. He proved an able ruler, and in 625 married Ethelburga, the sister of the Kentish king, Eadbald, and daughter of King *Ethelbert, a Christian woman who was accompanied to Northumbria by her chaplain, *Paulinus.

Edwin's victory over the West Saxons, which made him the most powerful monarch in England, was followed by his Baptism at Paulinus' hands (627). He then appointed Paulinus Bp. of *York and set about building a stone church there, but his plans were foiled by the invasion of his kingdom by Penda, the heathen King of Mercia, and his ally, Cadwallon of N. Wales. His defeat and death at the battle of Hatfield Chase, 12 Oct. 633, was followed by the break-up of his kingdom. He was long venerated as a saint, his festival being kept on 12 Oct.

The primary authority is *Bede, *HE* 2. 9–20. Notes to edn. by C. Plummer, 2 (Oxford, 1896), pp. 93–117; further refs. in index, s.v. 'Aeduini', pp. 401 f.; comm. by J. M. Wallace-Hadrill (ibid., 1988), pp. 52, 59 f., 65–75, 80, 84 f., 122, 222, and 226, with refs.

Effeta. See EPHPHATHA.

efficacious grace. In the RC theology of *grace, grace to which free consent is given by the will so that it always produces its effect (*effectum*). In the controversy between the *Dominicans (D. *Báñez) and the *Jesuits (L. de *Molina), the former held the efficacy of such grace to be dependent on the character of the grace itself, the latter on the fact that it is given under circumstances which God foresees to be congruous with the dispositions of the recipient. Both parties were agreed that, although the result was inevitable, the grace did not necessitate the will and destroy freedom. Both sufficient and efficacious grace are regarded as different forms of 'actual grace'.

Egbert (d. 766), Abp. of *York. A member of the Northumbrian royal house, he was educated in a monastery, ordained deacon at *Rome, and appointed Bp. of York *c.*732. In 735, on the advice of the Ven. *Bede (in a letter still surviving), he applied for the *pallium from Pope Gregory III. Owing to this increase of dignity and the harmonious relations with the King which ensued when his brother ascended the Northumbrian throne in 738, he was able to carry out many reforms. His most important work was the foundation of the cathedral school, where he himself taught theology and numbered *Alcuin among his pupils. Of the literary works connected with his name the best known is the compilation of canons known as the 'Excerptiones e dictis et canonibus SS. Patrum' (the *Excerptiones Egberti*) or in some MSS as the 'De Jure Sacerdotali'; in its present form, however, this cannot be earlier than the 11th cent. The 'Dialogus Ecclesiasticae Institutionis', a treatise on various points of Church discipline, and the 'Poenitentiale' (or 'Confessionale'), which exists in Latin and the vernacular, have been much added to from later sources. The 'Pontificale', which goes under Egbert's name is a later compilation having no connection with him; it is, however, of great value as an early source for the history of the liturgy and of the English *Coronation Rite. A letter from St *Boniface to Egbert has also survived.

The 'Excerptiones', 'Dialogus Ecclesiasticae Institutionis', and 'Poenitentiale', repr. from G. D. *Mansi, with introd., in J. P. Migne, *PL* 89. 377–451; better text of the 'Poenitentiale', which more probably represents the genuine work of Egbert, repr. from F. W. H. Wasserschleben, *Die Bussordnungen der abendländischen Kirche* (1851), pp. 231–47, in A. W. Haddan and W. *Stubbs (eds.), *Councils and Ecclesiastical Documents Relating to Great*

Britain and Ireland, 3 (1871), pp. 416–31, with important note on Egbert's works, pp. 413–416. Anglo-Saxon text of the 'Poenitentiale' ed. J. Raith (Bibliothek der angelsächsischen Prosa, 13; 1933) and R. Spindler (Leipzig, 1934). 'Pontificale' ed. W. Greenwell (Surtees Society, 27; 1853). The letter of Bede is pr. among his *Opera Historica*, ed. C. Plummer, 1 (Oxford, 1896), pp. 405–23, with notes, 2 (1896), pp. 378–88; also in A. W. Haddan and W. Stubbs, op. cit., pp. 314–26; Eng. tr. in D. Whitelock (ed.), *English Historical Documents c.500–1042* (English Historical Documents, ed. D. C. Douglas, 1; 2nd edn., 1979), pp. 799–810 (no. 170). The letter from St Boniface is pr. in A. W. Haddan and W. Stubbs, op. cit., pp. 358–60; Eng. tr. in D. Whitelock, op. cit., pp. 823 f. On the 'Excerptiones', P. Fournier and G. Le Bras, *Histoire des collections canoniques en occident*, 1 (1931), pp. 316–20. On the 'Poenitentiale', A. J. Frantzen, *The Literature of Penance in Anglo-Saxon England* (New Brunswick, NJ, 1983), pp. 69–78 and 107–10. On the 'Pontificale', F. *Cabrol, OSB, in *DACL* 4 (1921), cols. 2211–20, s.v. 'Egbert (Pontifical de)', with full bibl. J. Raine in *DCB* 2 (1880), pp. 50–2, s.v. 'Egbert (6)'; H. Dauphin, OSB, in *DHGE* 14 (1960), cols. 1476–8, s.v. 'Egbert (8)'.

Egbert, St (d. 729), Northumbrian hermit. He was a monk of *Lindisfarne who crossed to *Ireland in search of learning and sanctity, where during a plague he vowed that if his life were spared he would never go back to his native land. He was largely instrumental in organizing the evangelization of Germany and arranged the mission of St *Willibrord and others. About 716, or slightly earlier, he came to *Iona, where he played a large part in persuading the monks to observe the Roman method of calculating the date of Easter (see PASCHAL CONTROVERSIES). He remained there, living a life of great devotion, until his death. News of his death may have inspired *Bede to start work on his *Ecclesiastical History*. Feast day, 24 Apr.

The principal authority is Bede, *HE* 3. 4, 27; 4. 3, 26; 5. 9 f., 22–4; comm. by J. M. Wallace-Hadrill (Oxford, 1988), pp. 94, 132, 141, 181 f., and 196–8. W. Levison, *England and the Continent in the Eighth Century* (Ford Lectures for 1943; 1946), pp. 52 f., 271. A. A. M. Duncan, 'Bede, Iona, and the Picts', in R. H. C. Davis and J. M. Wallace-Hadrill (eds.), *The Writing of History in the Middle Ages: Essays Presented to Richard William Southern* (Oxford, 1981), pp. 1–42, esp. pp. 41 f. T. F. Tout in *DNB* 17 (1889), pp. 146 f., s.v., with refs.

Egede, Hans (1686–1758), *Lutheran missionary from Norway to Greenland, the 'Apostle of the Eskimos'. From 1707 to 1717 he ministered at Vaagen, in the Lofoten Islands. In 1717 he went to Bergen to get support for a scheme for a mission to Greenland and in 1721 he set out. After many difficulties, but much success, he returned to Copenhagen in 1736, where he founded a seminary for missionaries to Greenland. His work among the Eskimos was carried on after 1736 by his sons Poul (1708–89), who succeeded him as Bp. of Greenland, and Niels (1710–82).

H. M. Fenger, *Bidrag til Hans Egedes og dem grønlandske Missions Historie 1720–60* (1879); L. T. A. Bobé, *Hans Egede, Grønlands Missionær og Kolonisator* (Copenhagen, 1941; Eng. tr., ibid., 1952); O. G. Myklebust (ed.), *Hans Egede: Studier til 200-Årsdagen for hans Død 5. November 1958* (Studies of the Egede Institute, 8; Oslo, 1958). E. Garnett, *To Greenland's Icy Mountains: The Story of Hans Egede, Explorer, Coloniser, Missionary* (1968) [orig. written for children, but useful]. M. Lidegaard in *TRE* 14 (1985), pp. 259 f., s.v. 'Grönland', with bibl., p. 263.

Egeria, Pilgrimage of. A treatise narrating the journey of a devout woman to Egypt, the *Holy Land, *Edessa, Asia Minor, and *Constantinople, prob. in 381–4. She is traditionally thought to have been a nun or abbess, perhaps from Spain or more probably Gaul; she certainly had considerable intelligence and powers of observation. In the first part, she records her identification of various places and scenes *en route* with the sites of biblical events, e.g. *Moses' brook, the place where the Golden Calf was made, the city of *Melchizedek ('Sedima'). In the latter part the descriptions are mainly of liturgical matters, esp. the services at *Jerusalem and in the neighbourhood. They include accounts of the daily and Sunday offices, *Epiphany (including the Night Station at *Bethlehem), *Holy Week and *Easter (including the procession with palms to the Mount of *Olives and the *Veneration of the Cross), and *Whitsuntide, in all of which Egeria had evidently taken part. It becomes clear that in her time in Egypt and at Jerusalem the Feast of the Nativity was kept on 6 Jan. She is also the earliest writer to mention the Feast of the *Purification (here 14 Feb.).

The text is preserved (apart from a few fragments also contained in a Madrid MS) in a single 11th cent. MS which was discovered by F. Gamurrini at Arezzo in 1884. Gamurrini held the writer to be St Silvia, the sister of the Roman prefect, Rufinus, and hence the document came to be known as the 'Peregrinatio Silviae'. In 1903, however, Dom M. Férotin argued that she was very probably to be identified with one Egeria (or, as he thought, Etheria), referred to by Valerius, a 7th cent. monk of the region of El Bierzo in N. Spain, and this identification is now very widely accepted. The 'Peregrinatio' is written in a curious Latin dialect, though how far this is a local form is disputed.

Edns. by J. F. Gamurrini (Rome, 1887), J. H. *Bernard (London, 1891), P. Geyer (CSEL, 1898), H. Pétré (SC 21; 1948), O. Prinz (Heidelberg, 1960), A. Franceschini and R. Weber, OSB, in *Itineraria et Alia Geographica* (CCSL 175; 1965), pp. 29–103, and, with Fr. tr., by P. Maraval (together with letter of Valerius, ed. and tr. M. C. Díaz y Díaz, SC 296; 1982), with bibl. Eng. trs., with notes, by G. E. Gingras (ACW 38 [1970]) and J. [D.] Wilkinson (London, 1971; rev. edn., Jerusalem and Warminster, 1981). F. *Cabrol, *Étude sur la Peregrinatio Silviae* (1895); M. Férotin, 'Le Véritable Auteur de la *Peregrinatio Silviae*. La vierge espagnole Éthéria', *RQH* 74 (1903), 2, pp. 367–97; A. Bludau, *Die Pilgerreise der Aetheria* (1927); P. Devos, SJ, 'La Date du Voyage d'Égérie', *Anal. Boll.* 85 (1967), pp. 165–94; id., 'Égérie à Bethléem. Le 40ᵉ jour après Pâques à Jérusalem, en 383', ibid. 86 (1968), pp. 87–108; E. D. Hunt, 'St. Silvia of Aquitaine. The Role of a Theodosian Pilgrim in the Society of East and West', *JTS* NS 32 (1972), pp. 351–73; E. Lamirande, 'La pélerine Égérie', *Église et Théologie*, 15 (1984), pp. 259–91; H. Sivan, 'Who was Egeria? Pilgrimage and Piety in the Age of Gratian', *HTR* 81 (1988), pp. 59–72. *Atti del Convegno Internazionale sulla Peregrinatio Egeriae nel centenario della pubblicazione del Codex Aretinus 405 . . .: Arezzo 23–25 ottobre 1987* (Arezzo [1990]). M. Starowieyski, 'Bibliografia Egeriana', *Augustinianum*, 19 (1979), pp. 297–318. A. Hamman in Quasten (cont.), *Patrology*, 4 (1986), pp. 558–62.

Egerton, Francis Henry (1756–1829), 8th Earl of Bridgewater and founder of the *Bridgewater Treatises. He was educated at Eton and *Christ Church, Oxford, and elected a Fellow of All Souls in 1780. He became a Prebendary of Durham and collected other ecclesiastical preferments which he retained to the end of his life, performing his duties by proxy. In 1823 he succeeded his brother as Earl of Bridgewater. He was a great patron of learning and a good scholar, if eccentric. His own works, largely on family history, were mainly privately printed. Under the terms of his will he left to the President of the Royal Society £8,000, which financed the production of the Bridgewater Treatises, and he left to the British Museum his MSS and £12,000, of which the interest was partly for the custodian and partly to augment his collection, which came to be known as the 'Egerton MSS'. Money from this fund was used to purchase the '*Egerton Papyrus' (see following entry).

C. W. Sutton in *DNB* 17 (1889), pp. 154–6.

Egerton Papyrus. Two imperfect leaves and a scrap of papyrus in the British Library (numbered 'Egerton Papyrus 2') containing passages from a Greek writing akin to, but distinct from, the canonical Gospels. On palaeographical grounds the papyrus, which was part of a codex (not a roll), used to be dated *c.* AD 150 or even earlier; it was thus regarded as the oldest known specimen of Christian writing, with the possible exception of the *Rylands St John. This dating has been called in question by the identification as part of Egerton 2 of a fragment in Cologne (P. Köln VI 255) which is dated nearer 200. The surviving leaves of Egerton 2 contain four incomplete narratives, all relating to the period of Christ's Ministry. Their closeness to the canonical Gospels may imply that the author was acquainted with them; on the other hand, it seems likely that he had access to independent historical material derived from genuine tradition. The actual date of the 'unknown Gospel' is presumably earlier than that of the codex, as there is no reason to suppose it is an autograph.

The text was first pub., with Eng. tr., by H. I. Bell and T. C. Skeat as *Fragments of an Unknown Gospel and other early Christian Papyri* (1935), with facsimiles. Idd., *The New Gospel Fragments* (more popular, with rev. text, 1935). Eng. tr. also in J. K. Elliott, *The Apocryphal New Testament* (Oxford, 1993), pp. 37–40. The Cologne papyrus is ed. by M. Gronewald in id. and others, *Kölner Papyri*, 6 (Abhandlungen der Rheinisch-Westfälischen Akademie der Wissenschaften, Sonderreihe Papyrologica Coloniensia, 7 [1987]), pp. 136–45. C. H. *Dodd, 'A New Gospel', *Bulletin of the John Rylands Library*, 20 (1936), pp. 56–92. G. Mayeda, *Das Leben Jesu—Fragment Papyrus Egerton 2 und seine Stellung in der urchristlichen Literaturgeschichte* (1946). H. I. Bell, 'The Gospel Fragments P. Egerton 2', *HTR* 42 (1949), pp. 53–63. J. Jeremias and W. Schneemelcher in Schneemelcher, 1 (5th edn.; 1987), pp. 82–5; Eng. tr., 1 (1991), pp. 96–9.

Eginhard. See EINHARD.

Egypt, Christianity in. See COPTIC CHURCH.

Egyptian Church Order. The early liturgical treatise which, as a result of the researches of Dom Hugh *Connolly and E. *Schwartz, is now commonly identified as the '*Apostolic Tradition' of St *Hippolytus (q.v.). It was so described by H. Achelis (1891), when it was known to exist in *Ethiopic, *Coptic, and Arabic versions, 'merely to give it a name, which so far it lacks'.

Egyptians, Gospel according to the. An apocryphal gospel, probably written in Egypt in the first half of the

2nd cent., which seems to have circulated widely since it was known to *Clement of Alexandria, *Theodotus (his *Gnostic adversary), and *Origen. Its standpoint is markedly ascetic (apparently *Encratite). Only a few quotations from it survive. This text has nothing to do with the 'Gospel of the Egyptians' found in the *Nag Hammadi Library (NHC III. 2 and IV. 2), also called 'The Holy Book of the Great Invisible Spirit'.

Clement Al., *Strom.* 3. 9 (63–6); 3. 13 (92); *Hippolytus, *Haer.* 5. 7; *Epiphanius, *Haer.* 62. 2. Eng. tr., with introd., in J. K. Elliott, *The Apocryphal New Testament* (Oxford, 1993), pp. 16–19. Bardenhewer, pp. 521–4. W. Schneemelcher in Schneemelcher, 1 (5th edn., 1987), pp. 174–9; Eng. tr., 1 (1991), pp. 209–15.

Egyptian Versions of the Bible. See BOHAIRIC, FAYUMIC, SAHIDIC.

Ehrle, Franz (1845–1934), medievalist. A native of Isny in Württemberg, he was educated by the *Jesuits of Feldkirch and entered their novitiate at Gorheim in 1861. Driven from Germany by the *Kulturkampf, he lived from 1873 to 1877 at Ditton Hall, Lancs, where he was ordained priest in 1876. After travelling on the Continent for some years and examining a great number of medieval MSS, he went to Rome in 1880, where he remained till his death, except during the war years of 1915–19, which he spent at Feldkirch and later at Munich. In 1885 he started, in conjunction with H. *Denifle, the *Archiv für Litteratur- und Kirchengeschichte des Mittelalters*, and in 1890 published the first volume of his *Historia Bibliothecae Romanorum Pontificum*. From 1895 to 1914 he was prefect of the *Vatican Library, which he reorganized on modern lines, attaching to it a reference library and a department for the restoration of MSS. He was created cardinal in 1922. In 1924, on the occasion of his 80th birthday, he was presented with the 5 vols. of *Miscellanea Francesco Ehrle*, containing essays by many scholars of European reputation on a large variety of subjects. His *Der Sentenzenkommentar Peters von Candia* (1924) was an important study in 14th-cent. Scholasticism and his *I più antichi statuti della facoltà teologica dell'Università di *Bologna* (1932) important for its introduction. With Denifle, Ehrle was the founder of the scientific study of the history of Scholasticism.

The 'Album' appended to the *Miscellanea Francesco Ehrle* (ST 37–42; 1924) incl. 'Cenni biografici' (pp. 12–16) and list of his publications to date; *Gesammelte Aufsätze zur englischen Scholastik*, ed. F. Pelster, SJ (Storia e Letteratura, 50; Rome, 1970), with biographical introd., pp. xxi–xxix. M. *Grabmann, 'Heinrich Denifle O.P. und Kardinal Franz Ehrle S.J. Ein nachträgliches Gedenken zu ihrem hundertsten Geburtstag', *Philosophisches Jahrbuch*, 56 (1946), pp. 9–26, esp. pp. 16–26, with bibl. p. 16. F. Pelster, SJ, 'Franz Kardinal Ehrle und seine Verdienste um die Geschichte der Scholastik', appended to his edn. of Ehrle's comm. on the encyclical *Aeterni Patris* (Sussidi Eruditi, 6; 1954), pp. 191–202. M. D. *Knowles, 'Denifle and Ehrle', *History*, 54 (1969), pp. 1–12. Polgár, 1 (1990), pp. 625–8.

Eichhorn, Johann Gottfried (1752–1827), biblical scholar and orientalist. He studied at Göttingen (1770), and became professor of oriental languages at Jena in 1775. From 1788 he was professor of philosophy at Göttingen. He was one of the first commentators to make a scientific comparison between the biblical books and other Semitic writings. He was also among the earliest critics to divide

*Genesis between the 'Yahwist' and 'Elohist' sources, and to distinguish the priestly law in *Exodus–*Leviticus–*Numbers from the popular code in *Deuteronomy. His most important works include his *Einleitung ins Alte Testament* (3 vols., 1780–3); *Einleitung in die apokryphischen Bücher des AT* (1795); *Einleitung in das NT* (2 vols., 1804–12). His work, though inaccurate, was popular and did much to encourage biblical study and criticism.

H. C. A. Eichstaedt, *Oratio de Jo. Godofredo Eichhornio* (Jena [1827]). E. Sehmsdorf, *Die Prophetenauslegung bei J. G. Eichhorn* (Göttingen, 1971). J. C. O'Neill, *The Bible's Authority* (Edinburgh, 1991), pp. 78–94. H.-J. Zobel in *TRE* 9 (1982), pp. 369–71, s.v., with further bibl.

Eighteen Benedictions, the (Heb. *Shemoneh 'Esreh*, 'eighteen'; also *Tephillah*, 'prayer', or *'Amidah*, 'standing'). A group of prayers, now numbering 19, which are recited on weekdays at each of the three services of the Jewish synagogue. The first three, which are benedictions, and the last three, which are thanksgivings, are used also on *Sabbaths and festivals, but the middle group, consisting of petitions, is then replaced by other prayers. Their contents date in part from pre-Christian times; but apparently they were for long not written down and varied in number and wording, esp. in the middle section.

The current Orthodox text is in the 'Morning Service' in S. Singer, *The Authorised Daily Prayer Book of the United Hebrew Congregations of the British Empire* (1949), pp. 44–54. They are also pr., with a variant text and Eng. tr., in C. W. Dugmore, *The Influence of the Synagogue upon the Divine Office* (1944), pp. 114–25; Eng. tr., with brief discussion and full bibl. refs., also in E. *Schürer, *The History of the Jewish People in the Age of Jesus Christ*, rev. Eng. tr. by G. Vermes and others, 2 (Edinburgh, 1979), pp. 455–63. K. G. Kuhn, *Achtzehngebet und Vaterunser und der Reim* (Wissenschaftliche Untersuchungen zum Neuen Testamentum, 1; 1950). J. Heinemann, *Prayer in the Talmud: Forms and Patterns* (Eng. tr. from Heb. [orig. pub. in 1964], Studia Judaica, 9; Berlin and New York, 1977), esp. pp. 13–76 and 218–27.

Eikon Basilike, 'The Portraiture of His Sacred Majesty in His Solitudes and Sufferings'. An influential royalist work, secretly published just before the death of *Charles I in 1649, and purporting to be the King's own work. It has long been attributed to J.*Gauden, later Bp. of Exeter; he prob. created the book, using genuine materials written, and later corrected, by the King. It provoked a reply in John *Milton's *Eikonoklastes* (1649).

Text ed., with introd., by P. A. Knachel (New York, 1966). C. Wordsworth, *Who Wrote EIKΩN BAΣIΛIKH?* (1824), and later writings by the same author; H. J. Todd, *Bishop Gauden, the Author of Icôn Basilikè* (1829). The fullest treatment is by F. F. Madan, *A New Bibliography of the Eikon Basilike of King Charles I with a Note on the Authorship* (Oxford Bibliographical Society, NS 3, for 1949; 1950); cf. H. Trevor-Roper, ' "Eikon Basiliké". The problem of the King's Book', *History Today*, 1, pt. 9 (Sept. 1950), pp. 7–12, repr. in id., *Historical Essays* (1957), pp. 211–20.

eileton (Gk. εἰλητόν; lit. 'something wrapped' or 'wound'). In the E. Church, a cloth spread on the altar during the Liturgy. It is the real counterpart of the W. *corporal, though the functions of the latter are now partly filled by the *antiminsion. It is interpreted as symbolizing the linen cloth wrapped around Christ's head during His entombment.

Einhard (c. 770–840), also 'Eginhard', Frankish historian. He was educated at the school of *Fulda, and later became a member of *Charlemagne's palace school at Aachen and one of the Emperor's most trusted friends. He was a craftsman as well as a scholar and teacher, and is credited with responsibility for overseeing the building works at Aachen. On Charlemagne's death Einhard continued in the favour of his successor, *Louis I, and was presented by him with numerous abbeys and the estates of Michelstadt and Mulinheim (Seligenstadt), where he retired c.830 and founded a monastery to which the relics of Sts Marcellinus and Peter were brought. He was the author of several works, one of which, the 'Life of Charlemagne', was among the most remarkable biographies of the Middle Ages. It is modelled on the *Vitae* of *Suetonius, and thereby freed from the annalistic methods of its contemporaries, and distinguished for its fresh and accurate presentation of the Emperor's character and rule. He may also have written an epic poem about Charlemagne, of which only one book survives (known by the title of 'Karolus Magnus et Leo Papa'). His authorship of the so-called 'Annales Einhardi' (attributed to him by G. H. Pertz) is no longer accepted.

For edns. and trs. of Life of Charlemagne, see bibl. to CHARLEMAGNE. *Translatio et Miracula Sanctorum Marcellini et Petri* ed. G. Waitz, *MGH*, Scriptores, 15 (pt. 1; 1887), pp. 238–64; Eng. tr. by B. Wendell (Cambridge, Mass., 1926). *Epistolae* ed. K. Hampe in *MGH*, Epistolae, 5 (1899), pp. 105–45. *Karolus Magnus et Leo Papa*, ed., with Ger. tr., by F. Brunhölzl, and essays by H. Beumann and others (Studien und Quellen zur Westfälischen Geschichte, 8; Paderborn, 1966). The so-called 'Annales Einhardi' are ed. G. H. Pertz in *MGH*, Scriptores, 1 (1826), pp. 174–218. A. Kleinclausz, *Éginhard* (Annales de l'Université de Lyon, 3rd ser., fasc. 12; 1942), with full refs. F. L. Ganshof, 'Éginhard, biographe de Charlemagne', in *Bibliothèque d'Humanisme et Renaissance: Travaux et Documents*, 13 (1951), pp. 217–30; Eng. tr., id., *The Carolingians and the Frankish Monarchy* (1971), pp. 1–16. M. Bondois, *La Translation des saints Marcellin et Pierre: Étude sur Einhard et sa vie politique de 827 à 834* (Bibliothèque des Écoles des Hautes Études, 160; 1907). H. Beumann, 'Topos und Gedankengefüge bei Einhard', *Archiv für Kulturgeschichte*, 33 (1951), pp. 337–50; id., 'Einhard und die karolingische Tradition im ottonischen Corvey', *Westfalen*, 30 (1952), pp. 150–74, both repr. in his *Ideengeschichtliche Studien zu Einhard und anderen Geschichtsschreibern des früheren Mittelalters* (Darmstadt, 1962), pp. 1–39. K. Hauck (ed.), *Das Einhardkreuz: Vorträge und Studien über Münsteraner Diskussion zum arcus Einhardi* (Abh. (Gött.), Dritte Folge, 87; 1974). D. Schaller, 'Das Aachener Epos für Karl den Kaiser', *Frühmittelalterliche Studien*, 10 (1976), pp. 134–68. H. Löwe, 'Die Einstehungszeit der Vita Karoli Einhards', *Deutsches Archiv*, 39 (1983), pp. 85–103. E. S. Duckett, *Carolingian Portraits* (Ann Arbor, Mich. [1962]), pp. 58–91. J. Fleckenstein in *Lexikon des Mittelalters*, 3 (1986), cols. 1737–9, with bibl.

Einsiedeln, *Benedictine abbey and place of pilgrimage in Switzerland. Previously the dwelling-place of the hermit, St *Meinrad (q.v.), the abbey was founded by St Benno, Bp. of Metz, and Eberhard in 934. The present church is a fine baroque building of enormous dimensions, and in the abbey library is a large collection of valuable MSS.

'Annales Einsidlenses' ed. G. H. Pertz in *MGH*, Scriptores, 3 (1839), pp. 137–49. Calendar of docs. by G. Morel, OSB, *Die Regesten der Benedictiner-Abtei Einsiedeln* (Regesten der Archive in der schweizerischen Eidgenossenschaft ed. T. v. Mohr, 1; Chur, 1848). Profession book ed. R. Henggeler, OSB, (Einsiedeln, 1934).

G. Meier, OSB, *Catalogus Codicum Manuscriptorum qui in Biblio-theca Monasterii Einsidlensis OSB servantur* (1899). O. Ringholz, OSB, *Geschichte des fürstlichen Benediktinerstiftes U.L.F. von Einsiedeln, seiner Wallfahrt, Propsteien, Pfarreien und übrigen Besit-zungen*, vol. 1 (no more pub.; Einsiedeln, 1904). Id., *Die Kultur-arbeit des Stiftes Einsiedeln* (ibid., 1913). R. Henggeler, OSB, *Das Stift Einsiedeln und die französische Revolution: Ein Beitrag zur Ein-siedler Klostergeschichte von 1730–1808* (ibid., 1924). J. Salzgeber, OSB, *Die Klöster Einsiedeln und St Gallen im Barockzeitalter: Historisch-soziologische Studie* (Beiträge zur Geschichte des alten Mönchtums und des Benediktinerordens, 28; Münster [1967]). Id. in *Helvetia Sacra*, 3. 1, pt. 1 (Berne [1986]), pp. 517–94, with full refs. R. Henggeler, OSB, in *DHGE* 15 (1963), cols. 95–7, s.v. See also works cited under MEINRAD, ST.

Ekphonesis. See ECPHONESIS.

Ekthesis. See ECTHESIS.

Eldad and Modad, Book of. An apocryphal book, forged on the basis of Num. 11: 26–9. Though it no longer survives, it was quoted by *Hermas (*Vis.* 2. 3) and perhaps also (J. B. *Lightfoot) by *Clement of Rome (1 Clem. 23. 3 f.; cf. also '2 Clem.' 11. 2 f.).

A.-M. Denis, *Introduction aux pseudépigraphes grecs d'Ancien Testament* (Studia in Veteris Testamenti Pseudepigrapha, 1; Leiden, 1970), pp. 142–4; E. G. Martin in J. H. Charlesworth (ed.), *The Old Testament Pseudepigrapha*, 2 (1985), pp. 463–5. J. B. Lightfoot (ed.), *S. Clement of Rome: The Two Epistles to the Corinthians* (1869), notes on pp. 91 f. and 205 f.

elder. A Church officer in the *Presbyterian Church. Elders are of two kinds: (1) 'Teaching elders', whose function is pastoral; (2) 'Ruling elders', i.e. laymen often set apart by ordination who assist the pastor in the administration and government of the Church. Biblical support for the distinction was found by J. *Calvin and others in 1 Tim. 5: 17. When the word is used without further specification, the latter class is commonly meant.

For the history of the office in the early Church, see PRESBYTER.

election (Gk. ἐκλογή, 'choice'). In the vocabulary of theology, an act of the Divine Will exercising itself on creatures, among which it chooses some in preference to others. In the OT the Divine election bears esp. on Israel, the 'Chosen People', and among them in particular on those who do the will of God and remain faithful in time of trial. In the NT the place of the Old Israel is taken by the members of the new Christian community. The number of the elect is small (Mt. 22: 14), but Satan cannot prevail against them and they will be gathered together 'from the uttermost part of the earth' (Mk. 13: 22 and 27) on the Last Day. In St Paul the term 'election' usually signifies vocation acc. to the Divine predilection, e.g. in Rom. 9: 11 and 11: 5, 7, 28, and 1 Thess. 1: 4. In the teaching of the Fathers and Schoolmen the term plays an important part in connection with *predestination (q.v.). St *Augustine's belief that gratuitous predestination to eternal salvation presupposes an act of election on the part of God deeply influenced subsequent W. theology, though it left the E. very largely untouched. The Fathers frequently use the terms 'election', and 'predestination' without distinction, but some later theologians, e.g. St *Thomas Aquinas, give 'election', as an act of the will, a

logical priority over predestination, as an act of the intelligence, because God must first will the end, i.e. salvation, for a creature, i.e. elect it, before ordaining it towards this end, i.e. predestining it. Most *Jesuit theologians, however, reject the Thomist distinction and use the terms 'election' and 'predestination' indifferently, as was done by the Fathers.

The doctrine of election filled a central place in the *Institutes* of J. *Calvin, who affirmed that certain persons are elected by God wholly without relation to faith or works. This belief was everywhere held by Calvinist theologians till questioned by the school of *Arminius, for whom election was God's choice of those who believe and persevere by grace in faith and works. An even wider interpretation was given to it in the works of F. D. E. *Schleiermacher, who maintained that election includes all humanity, but that, on earth, only certain men and women are, through historical circumstances, elect. In the theology of K. *Barth, the idea of election was central; he focused on the assertion that it is primarily in Jesus Christ that election (and reprobation) is realized.

It is to be observed that, while a natural consequence of belief in election might be expected to be to weaken or destroy moral effort, history in fact does not bear out this deduction, even in the case of those holding an extreme form of the doctrine.

Elephantine Papyri. A collection of *Aramaic documents from the reigns of Xerxes, Artaxerxes I, and Darius II (485–404 BC), found in 1904–8 on the site of an ancient Jewish military colony which had settled at Elephantine in the far south of Upper Egypt some time before the conquest of Egypt by the Persians. The papyri throw valuable light on the organization, law, and religious beliefs and practices of the colony, and indirectly of the Jewish *Diaspora in the 5th cent. BC. They provide evidence for the existence of a syncretistic form of Judaism which is in sharp contrast with the orthodox Judaism of *Ezra and *Nehemiah.

Plates, with Eng. tr. and notes, ed. A. H. Sayce and A. E. Cowley, *Aramaic Papyri Discovered at Assuan* (1906). Crit. edns. of the text by E. Sachau, *Aramäische Papyrus und Ostraka aus einer jüdischen Militär-Kolonie zu Elephantine* (1911, with Ger. tr. and notes), and, with Eng. tr. and full notes, by A. [E.] Cowley, *Aramaic Papyri of the Fifth Century B.C.* (1923). Separate Eng. tr. by A. [E.] Cowley, *Jewish Documents of the Time of Ezra* (Translations of Early Documents, Series 1, Palestinian Jewish Texts (Pre-Rabbinic), 1919). Further papyri from Elephantine, purchased in 1893 by Charles Edwin Wilbour (d. 1896) which remained unknown until they were bequeathed by his daughter to the Brooklyn Museum in 1947, ed., with Eng. tr. and useful introd., by E. G. Kraeling, *The Brooklyn Museum Aramaic Papyri: New Documents of the Fifth Century B.C. from the Jewish Colony at Elephantine* (New Haven, Conn., and London, 1953). Fr. tr., with introd. and notes, by P. Grelot, *Documents Araméens d'Égypte* (Littératures Anciennes du Proche-Orient, 1972), esp. pp. 398–423. B. Porten, *Archives from Elephantine: The Life of an Ancient Jewish Military Colony* (Berkeley, Calif., 1968); M. H. Silvermann, *Religious Values in the Jewish Proper Names at Elephantine* (Alter Orient und Altes Testament, 217; 1985). B. Porten in *Anchor Bible Dictionary*, 2 (1992), pp. 445–55, s.v.

Elevation. At the Eucharist, the lifting of the sacred elements in turn by the celebrant immediately after he has recited the Words of *Institution over them, its purpose being to exhibit them for the people's adoration. The practice of elevating the *Host apparently originated in France early in the 13th cent., possibly in response to a growing popular desire to see the Host at the moment of consecration, which was believed to take place at this point and not, as some theologians argued, only after the Words of Institution had been pronouced over the wine also. The elevation of the chalice was added later. A second, more ancient, elevation of the Host and chalice together (formerly known as the 'lesser elevation') is made at the end of the *Canon or other *Eucharistic Prayer in the Roman and *Ambrosian rites.

H. Thurston, SJ, 'The Elevation', *The Tablet*, 110 (1907), pp. 603–5, 643–5, 684–6. E. Dumoutet, *Le Désir de voir l'hostie et les origines de la dévotion au saint sacrement* (1926). P. Browe, SJ, 'Die Elevation in der Messe', *Jahrbuch für Liturgiewissenschaft*, 9 (1929), pp. 20–66; id., *Die Verehrung der Eucharistie im Mittelalter* (1933), ch. 2, pp. 26–69. V. L. Kennedy, CSB, 'The Moment of Consecration and the Elevation of the Host', *Mediaeval Studies*, 6 (1944), pp. 121–50, with full refs.; id., 'The Date of the Parisian Decree on the Elevation of the Host', ibid. 8 (1946), pp. 87–96. H. B. Meyer, SJ, 'Die Elevation im deutschen Mittelalter und bei Luther', *ZKT* 85 (1963), pp. 162–217. Jungmann (1958 edn.), 1, pp. 158–60; 2, pp. 256–62 and 331–3 (Eng. tr., 1, pp. 120 f.; 2, pp. 206–10 and 266–8).

Eleven Thousand Virgins. See URSULA, ST.

Elgar, Sir Edward (1857–1934), English composer. The son of a Worcester music seller and RC organist, he was largely self-taught musically. After much early hardship he rose to international fame *c.* 1900 as a composer of choral and orchestral music. He was knighted in 1904, became Master of the King's Music in 1924, and created a baronet in 1931. Among his works of a religious nature are his setting of J. H. *Newman's *Dream of Gerontius* (1900), and the *oratorios *The Apostles* (1903) and *The Kingdom* (1906).

Letters . . . and Other Writings, ed. P. M. Young (1956); *Letters to Nimrod: Edward Elgar to August Jaeger 1897–1908*, ed. id. (1965); *Elgar and his Publishers: Letters . . .*, ed. J. N. Moore (2 vols., Oxford, 1987); *Letters of a Lifetime*, ed. id. (ibid., 1990). [G.] M. [S.] Kennedy, *Portrait of Elgar* (1968; rev. edn., 1982); J. N. Moore, *Edward Elgar: A Creative Life* (Oxford, 1984). C. Kent, *Edward Elgar: A Guide to Research* (New York and London [1993]).

El Greco (1541–1614), properly Domenicos Theotocopoulos, painter and sculptor. A native of Crete, he went to Italy some time before 1570 and prob. studied under *Titian in Venice before going to Rome. His works from this period include two paintings of the *Healing of the Blind* and two of the *Purification of the Temple*. By 1577 he was in Toledo, where he seems to have spent the rest of his life interpreting religious themes in the spirit of the *Counter-Reformation. His *Martyrdom of St Maurice*, commissioned for the Escorial, failed to please *Philip II, and El Greco thenceforward worked mainly for churches and religious houses. The works of his Spanish period are marked increasingly by a quality of mysticism as well as by personal idiosyncrasies. Formal modelling is abandoned as human forms and facial expressions are exaggerated and even distorted to produce an emotional rather than a literal likeness. In colour, too, his elongated sinuous forms are matched by the startling effects of his cold, ashen hues, often painted on to a dark background. As a portrait painter, he stands comparison with Titian and Rubens. His work also exhibits an early interest in landscape. His major works include *The Disrobing of Christ* in the sacristy of Santo Domingo, Toledo, *The Burial of Count Orgaz* for the church of Santo Tomé, Toledo, and the altar-pieces for the Hospital of San Juan Bautista extra Muros, Toledo. He was also responsible for the entire scheme of decoration (incl. the sculpture) in the Capilla Mayor of the Hospital de la Caridad, Ilescas.

M. B. Cossío, *El Greco* (3 vols., Madrid, 1908); A. L. Mayer, *Dominico Theotocopuli El Greco* (Munich, 1926); H. E. Wethey, *El Greco and his School* (2 vols., Princeton, NJ, 1962); D. Davies, *El Greco* (Oxford, 1976). E. Waterhouse and E. Baccheschi, *El Greco: The Complete Paintings* (1980). *El Greco of Toledo: Catalogue of an exhibition organized by the Toledo Museum of Art and other institutions*, with contributions by J. Brown and others (Eng. lang. edn., Boston, 1982). R. G. Mann, *El Greco and his Patrons: Three Major Projects* (Cambridge Studies in the History of Art, 1986).

Elias. See ELIJAH.

Elias of Cortona (*c.* 1180–1253), General of the *Franciscan Order. A native of *Assisi and one of the earliest of the companions of St *Francis, he soon rose to prominence. In 1219 he became first Provincial of Syria, and in 1221 Vicar-General of the order. On Francis' death (1226) he was mainly instrumental in the erection of the basilica at Assisi as a burial-place for the saint. In 1232 he became the third General of the order, but his government was marked by repeated crises, as he acted in a despotic manner towards all those, and esp. the '*Spiritual Franciscans', who opposed his princely way of life. In 1239 he was deposed from his office by Pope *Gregory IX. Thenceforth he supported the Emp. *Frederick II in his anti-Papal policy, and later was excommunicated and expelled from the order. For the small body of friars who followed him, he erected a monastery at Cortona. On his deathbed he is said to have made his submission to the Pope. A man of remarkable gifts, he was possessed of a character which was a strange combination of piety and pride.

His 'Epistola Encyclica de Transitu S. Francisci . . . ad omnes Provincias Ordinis Missa', pr. in *Analecta Franciscana*, 10 (1941), pp. 525–8. I. Affò, OFM, *Vita di Frate Elia, ministro generale de' Francescani* (Parma, 1783). E. Lempp, *Frère Élie de Cortone: Étude biographique* (1901). P. *Sabatier, *Examen de la vie de Frère Élie du Speculum Vitae, suivi de trois fragments inédits* (Opuscules de Critique historique, 11; 1904). D. Sparacio, *Fra Elia compagno, vicario e successore di S. Francesco Serafico* (2nd edn., 1923). S. Attal, *Frate Elias compagno di Francesco* (1936; rev. edn., Geneva, 1953). A. Pompei, OFM Conv., 'Frate Elia d'Assisi nel Giudizio dei Contemporanei e dei Posteri', *Miscellanea Francescana*, 54 (1954), pp. 539–635. R. B. Brooke, *Early Franciscan Government: Elias to Bonaventure* (Cambridge, 1959), pp. 3–177. L. di Fonzo, OFM Conv., in *DHGE* 15 (1963), cols. 167–83, s.v. 'Élie (12) d'Assise'; G. Odoardi, OFM Conv., in *DIP* 3 (1976), cols. 1094–1110, s.v. 'Elia, di Assisi', both with refs. to primary sources.

Eligius, St (*c.* 590–660), Fr. 'Éloi', Bp. of Noyon and patron saint of metalworkers. He was born at Chaptelat near Limoges. Through his skill in working in precious metals, he was given positions at the courts of the Frankish kings, Clothair II (d. 629), who made him Master of the

Mint at Marseilles, and his son Dagobert I (d. 639), whose chief councillor he became. Under Dagobert he was instrumental in ransoming captives, founding monasteries, and building churches. In 641 he was consecrated Bp. of Noyon (on the same day as his close friend St *Ouen was consecrated Bp. of Rouen) and became a zealous pastor, evangelizing Flanders, esp. the territories round Antwerp, Ghent, and Courtrai. An early Life of Eligius incorporates the substance of two early homilies attributed to him, one attacking superstition and the other on the Last Judgement. The other homilies ascribed to him are almost certainly not authentic. Feast day, 1 Dec.

'Vita Eligii Episcopi Noviomagensis', pr. in J. P. Migne, *PL* 87. 479–594; crit. edn. by B. Krusch in *MGH*, Scriptores Rerum Merovingicarum, 4 (1902), pp. 634–741 (with homily on the Last Judgement pr. separately, pp. 751–61). His letter to Pope Desiderius in J. P. Migne, op. cit. 259; also ed. W. Arndt in *MGH*, Epistolae, 3 (1892), p. 206, repr. in *CCSL* 117 (1957), p. 330. The other homilies attributed to him are pr. in J. P. Migne, op. cit. 593–654. É. Vacandard, 'Les Homélies attribuées à saint Éloi', *RQH* 64 (1898), pp. 471–80; F. Plaine, OSB, 'Nouvelles remarques sur les homélies attribuées à saint Éloi', ibid. 65 (1899), pp. 235–42; É. Vacandard, 'Réponse aux remarques de Dom Plaine', ibid., pp. 243 55. P. Parsy, *Saint Éloi, 590–659* ('Les Saints', 1907); J. Duquesne, *Saint Éloi* [1985]. P. Fouracre, 'The Work of Audoenus of Rouen and Eligius of Noyon in extending episcopal influence from the town to the country in seventh-century Neustria', in D. Baker (ed.), *The Church in Town and Countryside* (Studies in Church History, 16; Oxford, 1979), pp. 77–91. *CPL* (3rd edn., 1995), p. 689 (nos. 2094–6). É. Vacandard in *DTC* 4 (1911), cols. 2340–9; É. Brouette in *DHGE* 15 (1963), cols. 260–3, both s.v. 'Éloi', with further bibl.

Elijah (Gk. form, 'Elias') (9th cent. BC). Traditionally held to be the greatest Hebrew prophet, and certainly a forerunner of the classical prophets (Amos, Isaiah, etc.). He maintained the ascendancy of the worship of Yahweh in the face of Canaanite and Phoenician cults (1 Kgs. 18) and upheld the claims of moral uprightness and social justice (1 Kgs. 21). With *Enoch he shared the glory of not seeing death but of translation into heaven (2 Kgs. 2: 1–18); and such was the impression which he made on the people that his return was held to be a necessary prelude to the deliverance and restoration of Israel (Mal. 4: 5 f.). In the NT (e.g. Mk. 9: 4) he appears as the typical representative of the OT prophets. He is regarded with particular devotion by the *Carmelites. Feast day, 20 July.

The main material is to be found in comm. on Kings, cited s.v. Modern works devoted to Elijah incl. *Élie le prophète* (Études Carmélitaines, 2 vols., 1956), G. Fohrer, *Elia* (Abhandlungen zur Theologie des Alten und Neuen Testaments, 31; 1957; 2nd edn., ibid. 53; 1968), and L. Bronner, *The Stories of Elijah and Elisha as Polemics against Baal Worship* (Pretoria Oriental Series, 6; Leiden, 1968). H. H. Rowley, 'Elijah on Mount Carmel', *Bulletin of the John Rylands Library*, 43 (1961), pp. 190–219. J. T. Walsh in *Anchor Bible Dictionary*, 2 (1992), pp. 463–6, s.v.

Eliot, Thomas Stearns (1888–1965), poet and critic. Born in St Louis, Missouri, he was educated at the Smith Academy, St Louis, Harvard (1906–9 and again 1911–13), the *Sorbonne (1910–11), and Merton College, Oxford (1914–15). He taught for a short time in Highgate Grammar School, London, and worked for Lloyds Bank; from this period his main interests appear to have been literary. Assistant editor of *The Egoist* from 1917 to 1919 and a

frequent contributor to *The Athenaeum*, in 1922 he became the first editor of *The Criterion*, which he made a leading organ of literary expression until it ceased in 1939. In 1925 he joined the board of Faber, the publisher. He received many honours, including the Order of Merit and the Nobel Prize for literature (both in 1948).

Brought up in the American *Unitarian tradition, Eliot passed through a period of agnosticism reflected in his earlier poetry, e.g. *Prufrock* (1917) and *Poems 1920* (1920). The expression of his sense of the emptiness of life reached its climax in *The Waste Land* (1922) and is also seen in *The Hollow Men* (1925). These early poems rejected the poetical tradition as it had developed in England since the 18th cent. and found inspiration in the 17th-cent. *Metaphysical poets and the 19th-cent. French symbolists. In 1927 Eliot was baptized in the parish church at Finstock, Oxon, and in 1928 he declared his viewpoint to be 'classicist in literature, royalist in politics, and *anglo-catholic in religion' (Preface to *For Lancelot Andrewes*). Henceforth much of his poetry, culminating in *Four Quartets* (1935–42), expressed his religious search, his struggle with faith and doubt, and his attempt to find fresh meaning in tradition; here he turned notably to *Dante, as well as to such mystics as St *John of the Cross and *Julian of Norwich. His influence as a poet was immense. His attempts at poetical drama were less successful, but also sought to communicate something of the dilemmas of faith, explicitly in *Murder in the Cathedral* (1935; written for the *Canterbury Festival of that year), but no less genuinely in his later plays, *The Family Reunion* (1939), *The Cocktail Party* (1950), *The Confidential Clerk* (1954), and *The Elder Statesman* (1959). He was also influential as a critic; many of his early essays were published in *Selected Essays* (1932; 3rd edn., enlarged, 1951), and his later essays collected in *On Poetry and Poets* (1957) and *To Criticize the Critic* (1965). He was deeply interested in the social implications of Christianity and discussed these in *The Idea of a Christian Society* (1939) and *Notes towards a Definition of Culture* (1948).

Complete Poems and Plays (1969). A facsimile and transcript of the original drafts of *The Waste Land*, incl. the annotations of Ezra Pound, ed. by V. Eliot (widow) (1971). *Letters*, ed. id. (1988 ff.). Biographies by L. Gordon (2 vols., Oxford, 1977–88) and P. Ackroyd (London, 1984). The many symposia on Eliot and his work include those ed. by R. March and Tambimuttu (London, 1948), A. Tate (ibid., 1967), and J. Olney (Oxford, 1988). F. O. Matthiesen, *The Achievement of T. S. Eliot: An Essay on the Nature of Poetry* (1935; 3rd edn., 1958); H. [L.] Gardner, *The Art of T. S. Eliot* (1949); id., *The Composition of Four Quartets* (1978); G. [C.] Smith, *T. S. Eliot's Plays and Poetry: A Study in Sources and Meaning* (Chicago [1956]); H. Kenner, *The Invisible Poet* (New York, 1959; London, 1960); C. H. Smith, *T. S. Eliot's Dramatic Thought and Practice* (Princeton, NJ, and London, 1963); H. Howarth, *Notes on Some Figures Behind T. S. Eliot* (1965); E. M. Browne, *The Making of T. S. Eliot's Plays* (Cambridge, 1969); M. Lojkine-Morelec, *T. S. Eliot: Essai sur la génèse d'une écriture* (Publications de la Sorbonne, 2nd ser. 17; 1985); C. Ricks, *T. S. Eliot and Prejudice* (1988); P. Murray [OP], *T. S. Eliot and Mysticism: The Secret History of Four Quartets* (1991). D. Gallup, *T. S. Eliot: A Bibliography* (2nd edn., 1969); B. Ricks, *T. S. Eliot: A Bibliography of Secondary Works* (1980). R. Ellmann in *DNB*, 1961–1970, pp. 325–9.

Elipandus (717–802), Abp. of Toledo. He was the originator and chief exponent of the *Adoptianist heresy in

Spain, though his capacities as a theologian were much inferior to those of his supporter, *Felix of Urgel. He seems to have been led to his theological position by opposition to the unorthodox Trinitarian views of a certain *Migetius, which he had condemned at a council at Seville in 782. Though his doctrines were proscribed as heretical in synods at Ratisbon (792), *Frankfurt (794), Rome (798), and Aachen (799), the Arab domination enabled him to retain possession of his see till his death. A few of his letters survive.

Elipandus' letters are pr. in J. P. Migne, *PL* 96. 859–82; crit. edn. by J. Gil, *Corpus Scriptorum Muzarabicorum*, 1 (Manuales y Anejos de 'Emerita', 28; Madrid, 1973), pp. 67–78, 80–111. His creed is ed. by J. Gil, ibid., pp. 78–80. The attack on his doctrine by Beatus of Liebana and Etherius of Osma is pr. in Migne, loc. cit. 893–1030; crit. edn. by B. Löfstedt (CCCM 59; 1984). J. F. Rivera [Recio], *Elipando de Toledo: Nueva aportación a los estudios mozárabes* (Toledo, 1940), with bibl. Id. in *DHGE* 15 (1963), cols. 204–14, s.v.; K. Schäferdiek in *Lexikon des Mittelalters*, 3 (1986), cols. 1830 f., s.v.

Elisha (Gk. form, 'Eliseus') (9th cent. BC), Hebrew prophet and the successor of *Elijah. Various stories of his life are told in 1 Kgs. 19–2 Kgs. 13, but he had not the individuality or strength of character of his predecessor. It has been argued that the Elisha cycle of stories merely represents a more primitive version of the tradition about the prophet whom we know as Elijah, but most critics regard Elisha as an actual historical figure. He appears as the head of a band of enthusiasts called the 'sons of the prophets'.

See bibl. S.V. ELIJAH.

Elizabeth, St. The mother of *John the Baptist and 'cousin' (Lk. 1: 36) of the BVM. The visit of the Blessed Virgin to her shortly before the birth of Christ is commemorated in the Feast of the *Visitation. According to a few MSS of the NT, it was she, and not Mary, who spoke the words called the '*Magnificat'. Feast day in the W., 5 Nov.; in the E., 5 Sept.

Elizabeth, St, of Hungary (now more generally known as **Elizabeth of Thuringia**) (1207–31). She is to be distinguished from Elizabeth of Hungary, the *Dominican nun (1293–1337). The daughter of King Andrew II of Hungary, she was born at Pressburg. In 1211, with a view to a future marriage for political purposes, she was sent to Thuringia and did not again leave Germany; and in 1221 she married Ludwig IV, the Landgrave of Thuringia. From an early age she showed a desire for the ascetic life, and, esp. in the first years after her early marriage, came under the influence of the *Franciscans, who had recently arrived in Germany. On her husband's death on the *Crusade in 1227, she was driven from the court by his brother, Henry Raspe, on the pretext that her charities were exhausting the state finances, and this determined her to renounce the world completely. In 1228 she settled at Marburg, where she came under the absolute rule of *Conrad of Marburg, who had been her spiritual director since 1225. Under his orders, which seem to have been quite unsuited to Elizabeth's devout and delicate nature, she gave up her children, submitted to physical chastisement at his hands, and amid a life of great austerity, spent

all her energies in visiting and caring for the sick and poor. After her early death in 1231, numerous miracles at her tomb were recorded, and she was canonized in 1235. The fine Gothic Elizabethskirche at Marburg was built to enshrine her relics, where they remained till removed by *Philip of Hesse in 1539. Feast day, 17 (formerly 19, and so in the American BCP, 1979) Nov.

Early Lives and miracles (incl. the *Summa vite* by Conrad of Marburg), ed. A. Huyskens, *Quellenstudien zur Geschichte der hl. Elisabeth Landgräfin von Thüringen* (Marburg, 1908); *Libellus de dictis quatuor ancillarum S. Elisabeth confectus*, ed. id. (Kempten and Munich, 1911); the Life by *Caesarius of Heisterbach, ed. id. in A. Hilka (ed.), *Die Wundergeschichte des Caesarius von Heisterbach*, 3 (1937), pp. 329–90; that by Theodoric of Apolda, OP (b. 1228), ed. H. Canisius, *Antiquae Lectiones*, 5 (Ingolstadt, 1604), pp. 147–217. Further anonymous Life ed. D. Henniges, OFM, in *AFH* 2 (1909), pp. 240–68. K. Wenck, 'Quellenuntersuchungen und Texte zur Geschichte der heiligen Elisabeth. I. Über die Dicta Quatuor Ancillarum Sanctae Elisabeth', *NA* 34 (1909), pp. 427–502. Modern Lives by C. R. F. *Montalembert (Paris, 1836; Eng. tr., 1904), E. Busse-Wilson (Munich, 1931), and J. Ancelet-Hustache (Paris, 1946; Eng. tr., Chicago, 1963). P. Braun, 'Der Beichtvater der heiligen Elisabeth und deutsche Inquisitor Konrad von Marburg (†1233)', *Beiträge zur Hessischen Kirchengeschichte*, 4 (1911), pp. 248–300 and 331–64. *Sankt Elisabeth: Fürstin, Dienerin, Heilige. Aufsätze, Dokumentation, Katalog. Austellung zum 750. Todestag der hl. Elisabeth, Marburg, Landgrafenschloss und Elisabethkirche, 19. November 1981–6. Januar 1982* (Sigmaringen [1982]). U. Arnold and H. Leibing, *Elisabeth, der Deutsche Orden und ihre Kirche* (Quellen und Studien zur Geschichte des Deutschen Ordens, 18; 1983). F. Schmoll, *Zur Ikonographie der heiligen Elisabeth im 13. bis 16. Jahrhundert* (1914). J. Ancelet-Hustache in *DHGE* 15 (1963), cols. 225–8, s.v. 'Élisabeth, 10 (Sainte) de Thuringe'.

Elizabeth I (1533–1603), Queen of England from 1558. She was the daughter of *Henry VIII and *Anne Boleyn, declared illegitimate by statute in 1536. In 1544 the Succession to the Crown Act 1543 placed her next in succession after *Edward and *Mary. She was tutored by reforming Cambridge scholars, and learnt French, Greek, Latin, Italian, and perhaps Spanish. In her youth she cultivated an image of godly austerity and behaved with prudence in the face of the unwelcome advances in 1548 of Lord Thomas Seymour, the widowed husband of her stepmother, Catherine Parr. In the reign of her half-sister Mary (1553–1558), she conformed outwardly to Catholicism, but was often suspected of involvement in plots against Mary.

After her accession, Elizabeth attempted to break away from the policies which had made Mary unpopular. Her own sympathies and supporters were Protestant, and she immediately appointed Protestant preachers for public occasions. In the Parliament of 1559, she sought to achieve a royal supremacy and the restoration of the 1552 Book of *Common Prayer; after resistance in the House of Lords she accepted supreme governorship and an amended Prayer Book which made a few concessions to Catholics. Though she appointed Protestant bishops, led by M. *Parker, she made some further attempts to conciliate conservative opinion: she reintroduced a *crucifix in her chapel, contemplated a prohibition of clerical marriage, tried to insist on traditional *vestments, and was probably responsible for last-minute modifications in the *Thirty-Nine Articles of 1563. Later she attempted to limit Protestant preaching, a course of action which brought about a clash with Abp. E. *Grindal in 1576. Her refusal to consider further structural changes in the Church led to tensions with leading Protestants, including her own bishops and councillors.

Although political realities often made her cautious, Elizabeth posed as the restorer of the Gospel and the patron of Protestants. She sent military aid to Protestant rebels in Scotland in 1560, France in 1562, and the Netherlands in 1585. The Netherlands involvement soon brought open war with Spain which continued for the rest of the reign, and during the 1590s her government was also embroiled in serious difficulties with national and Catholic movements in Ireland. In 1569 she faced a conservative revolt in northern England, and in 1570 she was excommunicated by *Pius V; these attacks confirmed her public status as a Protestant heroine, which was stressed in ballads, portraits, and sermons. In 1579–80 she considered marriage to the Catholic Duke of Anjou, but abandoned the idea after a popular outcry. Her collection of private prayers suggests a genuine Protestant piety, hatred of superstition, and commitment to the doctrine of *justification by faith alone.

From 1583 Elizabeth turned more decisively against English Catholics, partly for fear of plots and partly as the growth of popular Protestantism made conservative concessions less necessary. Persecution of Catholics was vigorous in 1585–91, and in 1587 Elizabeth reluctantly allowed the execution of her cousin Mary Stuart (*Mary, Queen of Scots), who had been a focus of Catholic plotting. The defeat of the Spanish *Armada in 1588 was presented by Elizabeth's propagandists as evidence of Divine favour, and she claimed that her successes showed that she had been chosen to rule by God. Her image as Protestant protectress helped her to overcome suspicion of female rule, and made anti-popery a powerful national ideology.

The principal primary material for the reign is to be found in the Calendars of the State Papers, Domestic and Foreign. Useful collections of docs. repr. in G. W. Prothero (ed.), *Select Statutes and other Constitutional Documents Illustrative of the Reigns of Elizabeth and James I* (1894; 4th edn., 1913, pp. 1–249), and G. R. Elton (ed.), *The Tudor Constitution: Documents and Commentary* (Cambridge, 1960; 2nd edn., 1982). G. B. Harrison (ed.), *The Letters of Queen Elizabeth* (1935, with refs. to earlier collections). Collection of docs. in C. Cross, *The Royal Supremacy in the Elizabethan Church* (1969). The most important modern studies are those by M. *Creighton (London, 1896), J. E. Neale (ibid., 1934), J. Hurstfield ('Teach Yourself History', 1960; Pelican, 1971), and P. [B.] Johnson (London, 1974). Other studies by M. Waldman (ibid., 1952), and [M.] E. [H.] Jenkins (ibid., 1958), C. Erickson (ibid., 1983), and C. A. Haigh (ibid., 1988). W. [T.] MacCaffrey, *The Shaping of the Elizabethan Regime* (Princeton, NJ, 1968; London, 1969); id., *Queen Elizabeth and the Making of Policy, 1572–1588* (Princeton, NJ, 1981); id., *Elizabeth I: War and Politics 1588–1603* (ibid., 1992). W. P. Haugaard, *Elizabeth and the English Reformation* (Cambridge, 1968). C. [A.] Haigh (ed.), *The Reign of Elizabeth I* (Basingstoke and London, 1984). D. [N. J.] MacCulloch, *The Later Reformation in England 1547–1603* (ibid., 1990). D. M. Dean and N. L. Jones (eds.), *The Parliaments of Elizabethan England* (Oxford, 1990).

Elkesaites. A Jewish sect which arose *c.* AD 116 in Mesopotamia. They took their name from their sacred writing, the 'Book of Elkesai', which professed to contain the revelation given to Elkesai ('hidden power') by an angel 96 miles high. In the early 3rd cent. this book was taken over by Judaeo-Christians who held beliefs similar to those of the *Ebionites, insisting on a very strict observance of the rites and teaching of the Mosaic Law, rejecting sacrifices and certain biblical books, esp. the Pauline Epistles, maintaining a *Docetic view of the Person of Christ, and placing great emphasis on the redemptive nature of Baptism. Their ethical and social teaching was ascetic in character. Almost all our knowledge of them derives from references in St *Hippolytus' *Refutatio omnium haeresium* (9. 13–17; 10. 29) and St *Epiphanius' *Haereses* (19; 30. 17; 53). It is disputed whether Alchasaios, the leader of a baptist sect, mentioned in the Greek life of *Mani, is to be identified with Elkesai.

Frags. of 'Book of Elkesai' collected by A. *Hilgenfeld in *Novum Testamentum extra Canonem Receptum*, fasc. 3 (Leipzig, 1866), pp. 153–67. W. Brandt, *Elchasai: Ein Religionsstifter und sein Werk* (1912). J. Thomas, *Le Mouvement baptiste en Palestine et Syrie* (Gembloux, 1935), esp. pp. 140–56. A. Heinrichs and L. Koenen, 'Mani und die Elchasaiten', *Zeitschrift für Papyrologie und Epigraphik*, 5 (1970), pp. 141–60. G. P. Luttikhuizen, *The Revelation of Elchasai* (Texte und Studien zum Antiken Judentum, 8; 1985). J. Irmscher in Schneemelcher, 2 (5th edn., 1989), pp. 619–23; Eng. tr., 2 [1992], pp. 685–90.

Ellerton, John (1826–93), English hymn-writer. Educated at Trinity College, Cambridge, he was ordained in 1850 and held a succession of parochial appointments. He is esp. remembered for his many hymns, both original compositions and translations, among them being 'The day Thou gavest, Lord, is ended', 'Saviour, again to Thy dear Name we raise', and 'O Strength and Stay, upholding all creation'.

H. Housman, *John Ellerton: Being a Collection of his Writings on Hymnology together with a Sketch of his Life and Works* (1896; Life, pp. 15–181).

Ellicott, Charles John (1819–1905), English divine. Educated at St John's College, Cambridge, of which he became a Fellow (1845), he subsequently occupied the chair of divinity at King's College, London (1858–61), and the Hulsean professorship at Cambridge (1860–1). In 1861 he became Dean of *Exeter and two years later Bp. of *Gloucester and Bristol. On the division of the see into two parts in 1897, he became Bp. of Gloucester, resigning in 1904. He sat on many commissions, being chairman of the British New Testament Revision Company 1870–81, of which he missed only 2 out of the 407 sittings. He edited a considerable number of the Pauline Epistles (Gal., 1854; others 1855–8; 1 Cor., 1887) and wrote several other theological and religious books.

His *Addresses on the Revised Version of Holy Scripture* (1901), forming the Charge to the Archdeaconry of Cirencester at the Visitation in Oct. 1901, were repr. in 1933. R. Bayne in *DNB*, 1901–1911, 1, pp. 618 f.

Elmo, St, in Spain known as 'San Telmo'; since at least the 15th cent. the popular name for the Bl Peter Gonzalez (*c.* 1190–1246). Born in Castile, Peter became a canon, then dean, of Palencia, where his uncle was bishop. Soon afterwards he joined the *Dominicans in the same city. He became a tireless itinerant preacher. Called to the service of Ferdinand III, for a time he accompanied the King's campaign against the Moors in Andalucia. He spent his last ten years preaching in NW Spain and northern Portugal, concerning himself not only with the spiritual needs of the people, but also with their temporal needs, particularly the provision of bridges. He died in Tuy, which soon became the centre for his cult. He was regarded as a special patron of seafarers; this is prob. the reason he was given the name of an earlier patron of theirs, St Erasmus, known as Ermo or Elmo, one of the 14 *Auxiliary Saints and a martyr in the *Diocletianic persecutions (feast day, 2 June). The electrical discharge often seen at the mastheads and yard-arms of ships, known as St Elmo's fire, was interpreted as a sign of his protection. The cult of Peter Gonzalez was confirmed by *Benedict XIV in 1741. Feast day, 14 Apr.

The anonymous 13th-cent. 'Legenda B. Petri', together with a collection of miracles made in 1258, an office, and the decree confirming his cult, are pr. in H. Florez, OSA, *España sagrada*, 23 (Madrid, 1767) pp. 245–89. 16th-cent. Life by Stephanus Sampayo, OP, in *AASS*, Apr. 2 (1675), pp. 391–8. J. Gómez Sobrino, 'Documentos sobre San Telmo existentes en el Archivo de la Catedral de Tuy', *Arquivo Histórico Dominicano Português*, 3/1 (Porto, 1984), pp. 317–26. H. Sancho, *S. Pedro González* (Vergara, 1921); L. Galmés, OP, *El Bienaventurado Fray Pedro González O.P. San Telmo* (Biblioteca Dominicana, 13; Salamanca, 1991). A. Dávila, *San Telmo: Notas sobre el desarrollo de su culto en las Antillas* (Santo Domingo, 1983). On St Erasmus, *AASS*, Jun. 1 (1695), pp. 211–19.

Elohim (Heb. אֱלֹהִים, lit. 'gods'). Used occasionally in the OT of heathen gods, supernatural beings, or earthly judges, but generally of the God of Israel, for whom it is a very frequent term, esp. in what has often been reckoned the second oldest *Pentateuchal source (the supposed writer of which is therefore referred to by critics as '*E', or 'the Elohist'). The use of the plural form to describe the one God is frequently explained as a 'plural of majesty', though it may reflect a background in polytheistic culture.

Éloi, St. See ELIGIUS, ST.

Elphege, St. See ALPHEGE, ST.

Elvira, Council of. A Spanish Council held at the beginning of the 4th cent., traditionally dated *c.* 306, almost certainly at Granada. It passed 81 canons whose interest lies in the severe disciplinary penalties enforced for apostasy and adultery. It also required continence of all the clergy under pain of deposition (can. 33). Several of the canons order lifelong excommunication without reconciliation even at death.

Hardouin, 1 (1715), cols. 247–58; Mansi, 2 (1759), cols. 1–406. Crit. text in G. Martinez Diez, SJ, and F. Rodriguez, SJ (eds.), *La Coleccion Canonica Hispana*, 4 (1984), pp. 233–68. Hefele and Leclercq, 1 (1; 1907), pp. 212–64. A. W. W. Dale, *The Synod of Elvira and Christian Life in the Fourth Century: A Historical Essay* (1882). L. *Duchesne, 'Le Concile d'Elvire et les Flamines chrétiens', *Mélanges Renier* (1886), pp. 159–74; V. C. de Clercq, CICM, *Ossius of Cordova* (Washington, DC, 1953), esp. pp. 85–117. S. Laeuchli, *Power and Sexuality: The Emergence of Canon Law at the Synod of Elvira* (Philadelphia, 1972), with Eng. tr. of the canons, pp. 126–35. M. Meigne, 'Concile ou Collection d'Elvire', *RHE* 70 (1975), pp. 361–87. D. Ramos-Lissón in J. Orlandis and D. Ramos-Lissón, *Die Synoden auf der Iberischen Halbinsel bis zum Einbruch des Islam* (1981), pp. 3–30. J. Gaudemet in *DHGE* 15

(1963), cols. 317–48, s.v. 'Elvire II. Le Concile d'Elvire', with extensive bibl.

Ely. In 673 St *Etheldreda (Audrey) founded a *double monastery here for monks and nuns, endowing it with the principality of the Isle. After her death in 679, her shrine became a place of pilgrimage and the importance of Ely grew. In 870 the monastery was destroyed by the Danes, but in 970 it was restored, for monks only, by King Edgar and *Ethelwold, Bp. of *Winchester, and about 100 years later a new church, now the cathedral, was begun by Abbot Simeon (1082–93). In 1109 Henry I and Abp. *Anselm formed the see of Ely out of the large diocese of *Lincoln, and the prior and monks became the cathedral chapter. At the *Dissolution the prior became the dean, and eight canonries were founded (1541). In 1848 two of the canonries were attached to the Regius Professorships of Hebrew and Greek at Cambridge; by an Act of 1877 the latter was severed at the next vacancy in 1889 and joined to a new professorship of a theological character known as the Ely Professorship of Divinity (suppressed in 1980); the other chair was dissociated from the canonry in 1932. The cathedral, which contains every style of architecture from early Norman to late Perpendicular, is famous for its central octagon (1322–8), with its domed roof (known as 'The Lantern', completed in the 1340s), and other 14th cent. work including the magnificent Lady Chapel. Much of the monastic building has survived. The Grammar School was founded in 1541, and the Theological College in 1876 (opened in 1881 but closed in 1964).

Liber Eliensis ed. E. O. Blake (Camden Society, 3rd ser. 92; 1962). F. R. Chapman (ed.), *Sacrist Rolls of Ely* (2 vols., Cambridge, 1907). S. J. A. Evans (ed.), *Ely Chapter Ordinances and Visitation Records, 1241–1515* (Camden Miscellany, 17; 1940). W. E. Dickson (ed.), *A Catalogue of Ancient Choral Services and Anthems, preserved . . . in the Cathedral Church of Ely* (1861). W. *Dugdale, *Monasticon Anglicanum*, 1 (1817 edn.), pp. 457–500. J. Bentham, *The History and Antiquities of the Conventual and Cathedral Church of Ely from the Foundation of the Monastery, A.D. 673, to the Year 1771* (Cambridge, 1771; 2nd edn., 1812, with suppl. by W. Stevenson, Norwich, 1817). T. D. Atkinson, *An Architectural History of the Benedictine Monastery of Saint Etheldreda at Ely* (Cambridge, 1932, with a vol. of plates). British Archaeological Association Conference Transactions for the Year 1976, 2: *Medieval Art and Architecture at Ely Cathedral* (1979). G. Zarnecki, *The Early Sculpture of Ely Cathedral* (1958). D. [M.] Owen, 'The Muniments of Ely Cathedral Priory', in C. N. L. Brooke and others (eds.), *Church and Government in the Middle Ages: Essays Presented to C. R. Cheney on his 70th Birthday* (Cambridge, 1976), pp. 157–76. S. J. A. Evans, 'Ely Almonry Boys and Choristers in the Later Middle Ages', in C. J. Davies (ed.), *Studies presented to Sir Hilary Jenkinson* (1957), pp. 155–63. E. Miller, *The Abbey and Bishopric of Ely: The Social History of an Ecclesiastical Estate from the Tenth to the Early Fourteenth Century* (Cambridge Studies in Medieval Life and Thought, NS 1; 1951). M. D. Ellis and L. F. Salzman in *VCH*, Cambridge and the Isle of Ely, 2, ed. L. F. Salzman (1948), pp. 199–210. *Ely Cathedral Monographs* (Ely, 1973 ff.). D. M. Owen and D. Thurley (eds.), *The King's School, Ely: A Collection of Documents relating to the History of the School and its Scholars* (Cambridge Antiquarian Records Society, 5; Cambridge, 1982). H. Dauphin, OSB, in *DHGE* 15 (1963), cols. 348–66, s.v.

Elzevir (or Elsevier), 16th–17th cent. Dutch family of printers at *Leiden and Amsterdam, celebrated for the neatness and accuracy of their editions, esp. their pocket texts. In 1624 they issued their first edition of the Greek NT, which, though it was little more than a reprint of T. *Beza's text of 1565, at once won favour and was accepted for some two centuries as the *Textus Receptus.

A. C. J. Willems, *Les Elzévier* (1880); G. Berghman, *Études* (1885) and *Nouvelles Études* (1897) *sur la bibliographie elzévirienne*; H. B. Copinger, *The Elzevier Press* (1927); D. W. Davies, *The World of the Elzeviers, 1580–1712* (The Hague, 1954); S. L. Hartz, *The Elseviers and their Contemporaries: An Illustrated Commentary* (Amsterdam, 1955). H. J. de Jonge, *Daniel Heinsius and the Textus Receptus of the New Testament: A Study of his Contribution to the Editions of the Greek Testament Printed by the Elzeviers at Leiden in 1624 and 1633* (Leiden, 1971).

Ember Days. Four groups each of three days, in the Church year, namely the Wednesday, Friday, and Saturday after St *Lucy (13 Dec.), *Ash Wednesday, *Whitsunday, and *Holy Cross Day (14 Sept.) respectively, which have been observed as days of fasting and abstinence in the Churches of the W. Their early history and original purpose are obscure. At first there were apparently only three groups, perhaps taken over from the pagan religious observances connected with harvest, vintage, and seed-time; in this form they traditionally date back to the time of Pope *Callistus I (*c.*220) and were certainly well established at Rome in the time of Pope *Leo (440–61), who preached a series of Embertide sermons. From Rome their observance spread through W. Christendom. In 1969 in the RC Church the traditional Ember days were replaced by days of prayer for various needs at times to be determined by regional conferences of bishops. From at least the 5th cent. the Ember seasons were recognized as esp. appropriate for *Ordinations, and the BCP provides prayers for those 'to be admitted into Holy Orders' to be said every day in the Ember Weeks. The association of Ember days with prayer for ordination candidates is preserved in modern Anglican liturgies, even when the usual times for Ordinations has changed. Thus the ASB places two groups of Ember days in the weeks before the Sundays nearest the feasts of St *Peter and St *Michael and All Angels.

G. *Morin, OSB, 'L'Origine des Quatre Temps', *Rev. Bén.* 14 (1897), pp. 337–46. L. Fischer, *Die kirchlichen Quatember: Ihre Entstehung, Entwicklung und Bedeutung* (Veröffentlichungen aus dem Kirchenhistorischen Seminar München, 4, 3; 1914). K. *Holl, *Gesammelte Aufsätze zur Kirchengeschichte*, 2 (1928), no. 9, 'Die Entstehung der vier Fastenzeiten in der griechischen Kirche' [1923], pp. 155–203. G. G. Willis, *Essays in Early Roman Liturgy* (Alcuin Club Collections, 46; 1964), pp. 49–98. T. J. Talley, 'The Origin of the Ember Days. An Inconclusive Postscript', in P. De Clerck and E. Palazzo (eds.), *Rituels: Mélanges offerts à Pierre-Marie Gy, O.P.* (1990), pp. 465–72. A. Molien in *DTC* 13 (pt. 2; 1937), cols. 1447–55, s.v. 'Quatre-Temps'; R. E. McNally in *NCE* 5 (1967), pp. 296–8, s.v.

Embolism (Gk. ἐμβολισμός, 'intercalation'). The name given to the prayer in the Roman Mass inserted between the *Lord's Prayer and the Prayer for Peace. Its opening words, 'Libera nos, quaesumus, Domine, ab omnibus malis', take up the final words of the Lord's Prayer ('Libera nos a malo') which has just preceded it. Many E. liturgies have a similar prayer at this point. The word is also used (not in a specifically religious sense) to denote the difference of days in the calendar between the lunar year of 354 days and the solar year of $365\frac{1}{4}$ days, also known as the '*epact'.

Jungmann (1958 edn.), 2, pp. 352–63; Eng. tr., 2, pp. 284–93, with full refs.

Embury, Philip (1728–75). One of the earliest *Methodist preachers in America. A native of Ireland, he was converted by J. *Wesley in 1752, and began to preach soon afterwards. In 1760 he emigrated to America, but did not begin to preach there till 1766. In 1768 he built the first Methodist church in America, in New York, but in 1770 he removed to Camden, where he founded a Methodist society.

F. Baker, *From Wesley to Asbury* (Durham, NC, 1976), esp. pp. 40–4. H. E. Starr in *Dict. Amer. Biog.* 6 (1931), pp. 125 f.; A. B. Moss in N. B. Harmon (ed.), *The Encyclopedia of World Methodism*, 1 (Nashville [1974]), p. 772, s.v.

Emerson, Ralph Waldo (1803–82), American essayist, philosopher, and poet. The son of a *Unitarian minister of Boston, he was educated at Boston Latin School and Harvard College, and trained for the Unitarian ministry at the Divinity School, Cambridge, Mass. He was 'approbated to preach' in 1826 and ministered at Boston from 1829 to 1832, when he resigned owing to his extremely unconventional views on the *Eucharist; he continued to preach until 1847. On a visit to Europe in 1833 he met T. *Carlyle, S. T. *Coleridge, and W. *Wordsworth, with the first of whom he formed a close friendship. Returning to America the same year, he settled at Concord, Mass., where, with the exception of the period of a second visit to Britain in 1847–8, he remained for the rest of his life as a lecturer on literature and philosophy.

Emerson's philosophy was founded on a combination of rationalism and mysticism. Although he disowned the name, it appears that he fundamentally believed in 'Transcendentalism'—the doctrine that 'the highest revelation is that God is in every man'. It follows that man contains all that is needful in himself and that everything that happens to him has its origin within him. In his lecture on *The Defects of Historical Christianity* (delivered 1835) he went so far as to maintain that even redemption was to be sought within the soul. In spite, however, of the exalted position which he accorded to man philosophically, he had little liking for democracy and was only reluctantly led (by 1856) to support the cause of the abolition of slavery. At least from the 1840s he enjoyed a wide influence and popularity enhanced by the freshness and imagination of his style. From 1840 to 1844 Emerson was editor of *The Dial*, a Transcendentalist periodical in which some of his poetry was published. His prose works, of which the majority were based on his lectures, include *Nature* (1838), two series of *Essays* (1841, 1844), *Representative Men* (1850), *English Traits* (1856), *Conduct of Life* (1860), *Society and Solitude* (1870) and *Letters and Social Aims* (1876). They are mainly ethical in purpose, but are possessed of an underlying religious tone. His poetry, though attractive in its inspiration, lacks the polish of his prose.

Complete Works, ed. by E. W. Emerson (Centenary Edition, 12 vols., Boston, New York, and London, *c.* 1903–4); also ed. A. [R.] Ferguson and others (Cambridge, Mass., 1971 ff.); *Journals*, ed. E. W. Emerson and W. E. Forbes (10 vols., Boston and New York, 1909–14); also ed. W. H. Gilman and others (16 vols., Cambridge, Mass., 1960–82); *Letters*, ed. R. L. Rusk (6 vols., New York, 1939); *Early Lectures*, ed. S. E. Whichter, R. E. Spiller, and W. E. Williams (3 vols., Cambridge, Mass., 1959–72); *Complete Sermons*, ed. A. J. von Frank and others (4 vols., Columbia, Mo., 1989–92). Selections ed. F. I. Carpenter (New York [1934]) and C. Bode and M. Cowley, *The Portable Emerson* (Harmondsworth, 1981). J. E. Cabot, *A Memoir of Ralph Waldo Emerson* (2 vols., 1887). J. Benton, *Emerson as a Poet* (New York, 1883); O. W. Holmes, *Ralph Waldo Emerson* (1885); G. E. Woodberry, *Ralph Waldo Emerson* (New York, 1907); K. W. Cameron, *Emerson the Essayist* (2 vols., Raleigh, NC, 1945); R. L. Rusk, *The Life of Ralph Waldo Emerson* (New York, 1949; London, 1957); J. Bishop, *Emerson on the Soul* (Cambridge, Mass., and London, 1964); G. W. Allen, *Waldo Emerson: A Biography* (New York, 1981); B. L. Packer, *Emerson's Fall: A New Interpretation of the Major Essays* (New York, 1982); J. Myerson (ed.), *Emerson Centenary Essays* (Carbondale, Ill. [1982]); J. McAleer, *Ralph Waldo Emerson: Days of Encounter* (Boston [1984]); A. D. Hodder, *Emerson's Rhetoric of Revelation: Nature, the Reader and the Apocalypse Within* (University Park, Pa., and London [1989]). F. O. Matthiessen, *American Renaissance: Art and Expression in the Age of Emerson and Whitman* [1941], pp. 3–75. M. R. Konvitz (ed.), *The Recognition of Ralph Waldo Emerson: Selected Criticism since 1837* (Ann Arbor, Mich. [1972]). J. Myerson, *Ralph Waldo Emerson: A Descriptive Bibliography* (Pittsburgh, 1982); R. E. Barkholder and J. Myerson, *Emerson: An Annotated Secondary Bibliography* (ibid., 1985).

Eminence. A title of honour given to a *cardinal of the RC Church. Until a decree of *Urban VIII in 1630 confined its use to the cardinals, the Imperial electors and the Grand Master of the Hospital of St John of Jerusalem (who still retains it), it had been more widely used. Before that date cardinals were entitled 'Illustrissimi' or 'Reverendissimi'.

Emmanuel. See IMMANUEL.

Emmaus. The village in which the Lord made His Resurrection appearance to two of the disciples (Lk. 24: 13–35). It was 60 furlongs from *Jerusalem (Lk. 24: 13; but acc. to a variant reading 160, perhaps an accommodation to the ancient identification of this Emmaus with that mentioned in 1 Macc. 3: 40, etc.). Among suggested sites are Kuloniyeh ('Colony') to the W, Khamasah to the SW, and Amwas, some 19 miles WNW of Jerusalem.

L. H. Vincent, OP, and F. M. Abel, OP, *Emmaüs: Sa basilique et son histoire* (1932). P. Duvignau, *Emmaüs: Le Site—le mystère* (1937). J. Murphy-O'Connor, OP, *The Holy Land: An Archaeological Guide from Earliest Times to 1700* (2nd edn., Oxford, 1986), pp. 133, 270 f., and 320. M. Avi-Yonah and M. Gichon in E. Stern and others (eds.), *The New Encyclopedia of Archaeological Excavations in the Holy Land*, 2 (Jerusalem and New York [1993]), pp. 385–9, s.v.

Emmerick, Anna Katharina (1774–1824), ecstatic. She entered an *Augustinian house at Agnetenberg, Dülmen, Westph., in 1802, where she aroused the dislike of some of the laxer members by the fervour of her spiritual life. In 1812 the house was closed by order of the civil authorities, and she took refuge in a private house, where she had a serious illness. At about this time she received the *Stigmata of the Passion on her body. Her 'Meditations on the Passion' (*Das bittere Leiden unseres Herrn und Heilandes Jesus Christ*) were taken down by Clemens Brentano (1778–1842) and published in 1833 (Eng. tr., 1862). Other

visions were collected by Brentano and published after his death as *Leben der heil. Jungfrau Maria* (1852; Eng. tr., 1954) and a further collection of Brentano's notes were edited by K. E. Schmöger, CSSR, *Das Leben unsers Herrn und Heilandes Jesu Christi* (3 vols., 1858–60).

Crit. edns. of *Das bittere Leiden*, both based on Brentano's notes, by A. Michelitsch (Graz, 1935) and D. K. Bücher (Munich, 1937). W. Hümpfner, OESA, *Clemens Brentanos Glaubwürdigkeit in seinen Emmerick-Aufzeichnungen* (Würzburg, 1923). Biog. by K. E. Schmöger (2 vols., Freiburg i.B., 1867–70; Eng. tr., New York, 1885), and many others. Best modern Life is H. J. Seller, *Im Banne des Kreuzes: Lebensbild der stigmatisierten Augustinerin Anna Katharina Emmerick* (Würzburg, 1940). J. Adam, SCJ, *Clemens Brentanos Emmerick-Erlebnis* (Freiburg i.B., 1956). O. Katann, 'Die Glaubwürdigkeit von Clemens Brentanos Emmerick-Berichten. Zum gegenwärtigen Stand der Quellen und der Forschung', *Literaturwissenschaftliches Jahrbuch*, NF 7 (1966), pp. 145–94. H. Thurston, SJ, 'The Problem of Anne Catherine Emmerich', *Month*, 138 (1921), pp. 237–48, 344–56, 429–39, 519–30, repr. in *Surprising Mystics* ed. J. H. Crehan, SJ (1955), pp. 38–99. W. Hümpfner in *Dict. Sp.* 4 (1960), cols. 622–7, s.v.

Ems, Congress of. A conference attended by representatives of the four archbishops of Mainz, Trier, *Cologne, and Salzburg, which was held at Bad Ems in Hesse-Nassau in 1786. Its object was to carry into effect the teachings of 'Justinus Febronius' (J. N. von *Hontheim), which repudiated Papal interference in all but purely spiritual matters. It issued on 25 Aug. the 'Punctation of Ems' (*Emser Punktation*), proposing, *inter alia*, that in future appeals to Rome in Germany should be restrained, the bishops should have the control of matrimonial dispensations, and Papal bulls and other official Roman decisions should not be binding until accepted by the German episcopate. The project failed to secure the support of the German bishops, who interpreted the plan as a device of the archbishops to aggrandize their own position.

L. *Pastor, *The History of the Popes from the Close of the Middle Ages* (Eng. tr.), 40 (1953), pp. 43–65. M. Höhler (ed.), *Des kurtrierischen Geistlichen Rats Heinrich Aloys Arnoldi Tagbuch über die zu Ems gehaltene Zusammenkunft der vier Erzbischöflichen ... Deputierten, 1786* (Mainz, 1915). C. Mirbt in *PRE* (3rd edn.), 5 (1898), pp. 342–50; H. Raab in *DHGE* 15 (1963), cols. 441–4; F. Maass in *NCE* 5 (1967), p. 329, all s.v.

Emser, Hieronymus (1478–1527), editor of earlier writers, secular essayist, and controversialist. From about 1504 he was secretary to Duke George of Saxony. He is chiefly remembered for his controversy with M. *Luther, which lasted from 1519 till his death, and was popular and scurrilous in character. He disliked Luther's 'December Bible' of 1522, and published a counter-edition in 1527, made to resemble it as much as possible, with introduction and notes added. In 1530 the *Brethren of the Common Life settled at Rostock issued it in a Low German translation. Emser's Bible went into over 100 editions in the 16th, 17th and 18th cents.

His first writings against Luther ed. F. Thurnhofer in the *Corpus Catholicorum*, 4 (1921); his writings in support of the Mass ed. T. Freudenberger, ibid. 28 (1959). Life by G. Kawerau (Halle, 1898). H. Smolinsky, *Augustin von Alveldt und Hieronymus Emser: Eine Untersuchung zur Kontroverstheologie der frühen Reformationszeit im Herzogtum Sachsen* (Reformationsgeschichtliche Studien und Texte, 122; 1983). E. Iserloh in

DHGE 15 (1963), cols. 445 f., s.v., with detailed refs.; J. Steinruck in *TRE* 9 (1982), pp. 576–80, s.v.

Enabling Act. The commonly used name for the Church of England Assembly (Powers) Act 1919, which gave the C of E a general power, subject to the control of Parliament and the Act of *Uniformity 1662, to legislate for itself. Its provisions closely followed recommendations in the *Report on the Relations of Church and State* (1916), and incorporated as a schedule the Appendix to the Addresses made by the *Convocations of Canterbury and York to the King in May 1919. It conferred legislative powers on the *Church Assembly, established an Ecclesiastical Committee consisting of 15 members of each of the Houses of Parliament, nominated by the Lord Chancellor and the Speaker respectively, to which its measures were to be submitted before proceeding to Parliament, which could pass or reject (but not amend) them. It also gave legal status to *Parochial Church Councils.

Enarxis (Gk. Ἔναρξις, lit. 'beginning'). In the Byzantine liturgy, the section between the *Proskomide and the *Little Entrance. It consists of three Diaconal Litanies, each followed by Psalms or antiphons sung by the choir, and ending (on some occasions) with the *Beatitudes. The celebrant meanwhile silently recites the prayers known as the 'Prayers of the Antiphon' (Εὐχαὶ Ἀντιφώνου); the third of these is the 'Prayer of St *Chrysostom' found in the BCP. The Enarxis was prob. first introduced into the Liturgy in the 9th cent.

9th cent. text in Brightman, *LEW*, pp. 310–12; current text, pp. 362–7.

encolpion (Gk. ἐγκόλπιον), also known as the *panagia. An oval medallion worn by bishops in the E. Church, suspended from the neck by a chain. The figure of Christ or the BVM is normally depicted upon it, and relics are sometimes placed inside it. Certain prelates have the privilege of wearing two encolpia.

enclosure. See CLAUSURA.

Encratites. A title applied to several groups of early Christians who carried their ascetic practice and doctrine to extremes which were in most cases considered heretical. They are referred to by *Irenaeus, *Clement of Alexandria, and *Hippolytus, who respectively call them ἐγκρατεῖς, ἐγκρατηταί, and ἐγκρατῖται. The name, however, seems never to have been used very precisely, but to have been applied in a general sense to many of the *Gnostic, *Ebionite, and *Docetic sects. They commonly rejected the use of wine and flesh-meat, and often also of marriage. It was largely in Encratite circles that the *Apocryphal Gospels and Acts were produced.

Irenaeus, *Adv. Haer.* 1. 28; Clement Al., *Strom.* 7. 17 (108. 2), etc.; Hippolytus, *Haer.* 8. 20; cf. also *Epiphanius, *Haer.* 46, 47. A certain Julius Cassian, the author of a book Περὶ Εὐνουχίας, was reckoned a leading exponent of Encratite doctrines, while St *Jerome (*Ep.* 48. 2) names *Tatian as the *princeps encratitarum.* G. Blond, 'L'"Hérésie" encratite vers la fin du quatrième siècle', *Rech. S.R.* 31 (1944), pp. 159–210; F. Bolgiani, 'La tradizione eresiologica sull'encratismo', *Atti della Accademia delle Scienze di Torino*, II. Classe di Scienze Morali, Storiche et Filologiche, 91 (1957), pp. 343–419; U. Bianchi (ed.), *La Tradizione dell'Enkrateia:*

... *Atti del Colloquio Internazionale, Milano, 20–23 aprile 1982* (1985). H. Chadwick in *RAC* 5 (1962), cols. 343–65, s.v., with bibl. See also bibl. s.v. TATIAN.

encyclical. A circular letter sent to all the churches of a given area. In early times the word might be used of a letter sent out by any bishop, but in modern RC usage the term is restricted to such letters as are sent out worldwide by the Pope. It has also been used from the first (1867) of the letters issued by the Anglican bishops at the end of the *Lambeth Conferences.

Encyclopaedists. The name given to contributors to the French *Encyclopédie*, a large collaborative work (28 vols., 1751–72). Edited by D. *Diderot and (initially) J. Le R. *D'Alembert, with some 160 contributors, it developed out of a project to translate the *Cyclopedia* of Ephraim Chambers. The first two volumes appeared with official approval in 1751–2, but the next five volumes aroused growing clerical opposition, and the *Encyclopédie* was formally banned in 1759. Diderot nevertheless continued his editorial work, and in 1765 was able to publish the remaining ten volumes of text under a false imprint; publication of the eleven volumes of plates were completed in 1772. Other editors published four supplementary volumes of text and one of plates at Paris and Amsterdam in 1776–7, followed by two volumes of tables issued in 1780.

The *Encyclopédie* sets out to review the full extent of human achievement in the arts and sciences from a purely secular standpoint. Many articles on religious topics were prudently entrusted to sound theologians, but the general tone of the works is that of rationalist humanism, and anticlerical opinions, scepticism concerning the claims of revealed religion, and pleas for religious, intellectual, and political liberty are everywhere insinuated into the vast mass of accurate and up-to-date scholarly and practical information. The religious views of the editors and major contributors (who included C. L. J. de S. *Montesquieu, *Voltaire, and J.-J. *Rousseau) ranged from *deism to militant atheism, but they were united in their opposition to Catholic orthodoxy and in their demand for toleration. The *Encyclopédie* became a rallying-point for opponents of established beliefs and practices (the 'philosophes'), in the political and social as well as the religious spheres.

J. Lough (ed.), *The Encyclopédie of Diderot and D'Alembert: Selected Articles* (1954). J. Morley, *Diderot and the Encyclopaedists* (2 vols., 1878); F. Venturi, *Le origini dell'Enciclopedia* (1946; 2nd edn., 1963); N. N. Schargo, *History in the Encyclopédie* (New York, 1947). D. H. Gordon and N. L. Torrey, *The Censoring of Diderot's* Encyclopédie *and the Re-established Text* (New York, 1947). P. Grosclaude, *Un Audacieux Message: L'Encyclopédie* (1951); J. Proust, *Diderot et l'*Encyclopédie (1962; 2nd edn., 1967); J. Lough, *Essays on the* Encyclopédie *of Diderot and d'Alembert* (1968); id., *The* Encyclopédie (1971), and other works of this author. R. [C.] Darnton, *The Business of Enlightenment: A Publishing History of the* Encyclopédie *1775–1800* (Cambridge, Mass., 1979). R. N. Schwab and others, *Inventory of Diderot's* Encyclopédie (Studies on Voltaire and the Eighteenth Century, 80, 83, 85, 91–3, and 223; Geneva and later Oxford, 1971–84). F. A. and S. L. Kafker, *The Encyclopedists as Individuals: A Biographical Dictionary of the Authors of the* Encyclopédie (ibid. 257; 1988). See also bibl. to DIDEROT, D'ALEMBERT, etc.

energumen (Gk. ἐνεργούμενος). In ancient Christian literature a term used of demoniacs and others possessed of abnormal mental and physical states, esp. insanity. Following the example of the Lord, the Church treated them with special pity and care. They received the ministrations of *exorcists. At the Eucharist they were normally dismissed at the end of the *Missa Catechumenorum with prayer and blessing, though if not violent they might be admitted to communion. They were debarred from ordination, even after cure.

E. *Martène, OSB, *De Antiquis Ecclesiae Ritibus*, 3 (1702), cap. 9, pp. 497–530. H. *Leclercq, OSB, in *DACL* 5 (pt. 1, 1922), cols. 964–78, s.vv. 'Exorcisme', 'Exorciste'; T. Klauser in *RAC* 5 (1962), cols. 51–3, s.v. 'Energumenoi'.

England, Church of. See CHURCH OF ENGLAND (for history); ANGLICANISM (for theological outlook).

English Church Music, School of. See ROYAL SCHOOL OF CHURCH MUSIC.

English Church Union. A society formed in 1859 as the 'Church of England Protection Society', and renamed in 1860 the 'English Church Union', when it incorporated various local Church societies. Its object was to defend, and further the spread of, *High Church principles in the C of E. The Union championed many priests during the ritual prosecutions, and frustrated many attacks upon Catholic practices. In 1934 the ECU was united with the Anglo-Catholic Congress to form the '*Church Union'. In 1868 Charles Lindley Wood, afterwards Viscount *Halifax, was elected president and was for many years its dominating personality.

G. Bayfield Roberts, *The History of the English Church Union, 1859–1894* (1895). J. G. Lockhart, *Charles Lindley, Viscount Halifax*, 1 (1935), pp. 137–56, 173–91; 2 (1936), pp. 113–24.

English College, Rome. The seminary for English candidates for the RC priesthood. Originally founded in 1362 as a hospice for English pilgrims, it was refounded as a seminary in 1579 by *Gregory XIII; its students had to take an oath to go to England when it should seem good to their superiors. Soon afterwards its direction was entrusted to the *Jesuits, who were in charge of it until the suppression of the Society in 1773. It then passed into the hands of Italian secular priests, under whose direction it remained till it was closed during the invasion of the French. In 1818 it was restored by *Pius VII, and since then its rectors have always been members of the English secular clergy, the most famous of them being N. P. S. *Wiseman, afterwards cardinal.

Liber Ruber Venerabilis Collegii Anglorum de Urbe, ed. by W. Kelly, assisted by O. Littledale, S. Roxburgh, and I. Vaughan, I. (1) Annales Collegii; Nomina Alumnorum (*Catholic Record Society, 37 and 40; 1940–3), incl. bibl., 1, p. xiv, note i. Incomplete Eng. tr. by H. Foley, SJ, *Records of the English Province of the Society of Jesus*, 6 (1880), pp. 1–540, with other material from the College archives. *The Responsa Scholarum of the English College, Rome, 1598–1685*, ed. A. Kenny (Catholic Record Society, 54–55; 1962–3). *The English Hospice in Rome*, with preface by G. W. Tickle (*The Venerabile*, 21; 1962; also other arts. in this periodical). M. E. Williams, *The Venerable English College Rome: A History, 1579–1979* (1979). See also Lives of W. *Allen, R. *Parsons, and N. P. S. Wiseman.

English Hymnal, The. This widely used Anglican hymnal, pub. in 1906, was the result of a considered attempt by a group, mainly of Anglo-Catholic sympathies, to eradicate banalities and generally to raise the quality of English hymnody, in the matter both of words and music. The editorial committee responsible for the words included W. J. Birkbeck, P. *Dearmer, and T. A. *Lacey, while the musical editor was R. *Vaughan Williams. It included *Office Hymns and *Propers for the Sung Eucharist, both taken mainly from the *Sarum books. A new edition, with extensive revision of the plainchant music by J. H. Arnold, was issued in 1933. The *English Hymnal Service Book*, pub. 1962, contains hymns from the *English Hymnal*, the Psalter pointed for chanting, J. *Merbecke's setting of the Holy Communion, the versicles and responses at Mattins and Evensong, and other material which obviates the need to provide copies of the BCP. In 1975 *English Praise*, a supplement to *English Hymnal*, was pub., containing 106 hymns not in the parent book. A new version of the original book, designed to meet the needs occasioned by liturgical revision and changes in custom and feeling, was issued in 1986 under the title *New English Hymnal*. It includes a congregational setting for the Rite A Communion Service of the ASB, a number of responsorial psalm settings, and other liturgical matter.

English Ladies (Ger. *Englische Fräulein*). A popular name, esp. in Germany, for the 'Institute of the Blessed Virgin Mary' founded by Mary *Ward, q.v.

Enhypostasia (Gk. ἐν 'in', and ὑπόστασις, 'person'). The doctrine that, in the Incarnate Christ, though the humanity has no 'person' (*hypostasis*) of its own, it is not on that account 'anhypostatic' (deprived of a *hypostasis*), but finds its *hypostasis* in the *hypostasis* of the Logos. Thus the distinguishing features of the particular man who Jesus is, as well as the essential qualities of the species (mankind) to which He belongs, are attributed to the Divine *hypostasis*. The notion occurs in the work of *Leontius of Byzantium, but is fully exploited only by *Leontius of Jerusalem and the *Neo-Chalcedonians (or Cyrilline Chalcedonians), who used it to give fuller expression to the human side of Christ's work without endangering the unity of His person. It was taken up in later Byzantine theology, notably by St *John of Damascus. In modern times the doctrine has been defended by H. M. Relton (*A Study in Christology*, 1917). The noun ἐνυποστασία is apparently not found in the ancient writers, though the theologians mentioned make abundant use of its cognates.

A Patristic Greek Lexicon, ed. G. W. H. Lampe (Oxford, 1968), pp. 485–6, s.v. ἐνυπόστατος.

Enlightenment, the. Though the term originated as a translation of the German *Aufklärung*, it is now applied more generally to the movement of ideas which characterized much of 18th-cent. Europe. In many ways it was a continuation of the scientific spirit of the previous age, esp. of the thought of R. *Descartes, J. *Locke, and I. *Newton. Its adherents distrusted all authority and tradition in matters of intellectual inquiry, and believed that truth could be attained only through reason, observation, and experiment. On the whole, however, they were more socially committed than their predecessors. They sought

to diffuse knowledge as much as to create it and where possible to use their scientific method in the service of their humanitarian ideals of tolerance, justice, and the moral and material welfare of mankind. The more scientific among them (e.g. J. Bentham and other *Utilitarians) tried to discover 'Newtonian' laws governing man and his social relationships, believing that if these could be found, man would be in a position to control his destiny. Others, such as C. L. J. de S. *Montesquieu, D. *Hume, and Adam Smith (1723–90), attempted a more open-minded investigation of the nature of society. A third group (esp. French writers such as P. H. D. d'Holbach (1723–89) and J.-J. *Rousseau) were more revolutionary in their programme. The movement embraced a wide spectrum of views and aims, incl. *Voltaire's defence of the victims of religious persecution, the encouragement of technology in D. *Diderot's Encyclopédie, and attempts to improve legal practice in Italy and the economy in Spain, but its adherents were united by a common belief in 'reason' and zeal for human welfare. In general, with notable exceptions such as Hume and I. *Kant, they were propagandists rather than philosophers. But their activity transformed the intellectual map of Europe.

The thinkers of the Enlightenment often came into conflict with the Church. Some, such as d'Holbach, were dogmatic atheists; others, such as Hume and Diderot, rejected religion less vehemently. The majority were prob. *deists. Yet, though the movement as a whole was undoubtedly hostile to orthodox Christianity, there were many exceptions to this generalization. Even in relatively intolerant Catholic countries, such as France and Spain, it was possible for men such as A. R. J. Turgot (1727–81) and G. M. de Jovellanos (1744–1811) to reconcile their faith with 'enlightened' ideas. In Protestant lands, where 'rational theology' was developing within the Churches, there was more co-operation; and in Scotland, e.g., many of the leaders of the Enlightenment were also ministers of the Kirk.

See also AUFKLÄRUNG.

There is a very extensive lit. E. Cassirer, Die Philosophie der Aufklärung (Tübingen, 1932; Eng. tr., Princeton, NJ, 1951); P. Hazard, La Crise de la conscience européenne (3 vols., 1935; Eng. tr., 1953); id., La Pensée européenne au XVIIIᵉ siècle de Montesquieu à Lessing (3 vols., 1946; Eng. tr., 1954). P. Gay, The Party of Humanity: Studies in the French Enlightenment (New York and London, 1964); id., The Enlightenment: An Interpretation (ibid., 1967); L. G. Crocker, An Age of Crisis: Man and World in Eighteenth Century French Thought (Baltimore, 1959); id., Nature and Culture: Ethical Thought in the French Enlightenment (ibid., 1963). R. J. White, The Anti-Philosophers: A Study of the Philosophes in Eighteenth-Century France (1970). G. R. Cragg, Reason and Authority in the Eighteenth Century (Cambridge, 1964). Collection of previously pub. arts. by R. Mortier, Le Cœur et la Raison (Oxford, Brussels, and Paris, 1990). A. Richardson, History Sacred and Profane (Bampton Lectures for 1962; 1964), pp. 41–5, 90–103. E. Hegel in NCE 5 (1967), pp. 435–9, s.v., with further bibl.

Ennodius, St, Magnus Felix (c.473–521) Christian rhetorician and Bp. of Pavia. Born at Arles, he was brought up probably at Pavia (possibly at Milan). After ordination as deacon c.493 by St Epiphanius, Bp. of Pavia, he went to Milan, where he taught rhetoric until consecrated Bp. of Pavia c.514. In the dispute about the succession to Pope Anastasius II (d. 498), he defended

*Symmachus and wrote a libellus against those who challenged the synod of 502, maintaining that the Papal office was de jure exempt from all interference from the secular power. He was twice sent by Pope *Hormisdas on missions to Anastasius, Patr. of *Constantinople, to effect a reconciliation with the E. His abundant writings suffer from a turgid style, but are valuable through the incidental light they throw on the happenings and cultural ideals of his age. They include an account of his own religious experiences ('Eucharisticon de Vita Sua'), a long panegyric on the Arian King *Theodoric (507), a Life of St Epiphanius of Pavia, several discourses ('Dictiones'), many epitaphs and epigrams, and a considerable collection of hymns, modelled on those of St *Ambrose. His work reflects an attempt to combine a fundamentally pagan culture with the profession of the Christian creed. His epitaph survives in the church of S. Michele in Pavia. Feast day, 17 July.

His writings, ed. by J. *Sirmond (Paris, 1611), are repr. in J. P. Migne, PL 63. 13–364. There are good critical edns. by W. Hartel (CSEL, 1882) and F. Vogel (MGH, 1884, with full prolegomena). G. Bardy, 'Saint Ennodius de Pavie', in J. R. Palanque (ed.), Le Christianisme et l'Occident barbare (1945), pp. 229–64; L. Navarra, 'Contributo storico di Ennodio', Augustinianum, 14 (1974), pp. 315–42. Altaner and Stuiber (1978), pp. 478 f. and 653. E. M. Young in DCB 2 (1880), pp. 123 f.; J. Fontaine in RAC 5 (1962), cols. 398–421, s.v.

Enoch, OT patriarch. The OT records nothing of Enoch except that he was the father of Methuselah and that 'he walked with God and he was not; for God took him' (Gen. 5: 24). In Jewish tradition many legends became attached to him and in the NT his ascension is referred to at Heb. 11: 5. For the pseudepigraphical books ascribed to Enoch, see the following entry.

Enoch, Books of. (1) 1 Enoch, or 'Ethiopic Enoch' as it is sometimes called from the fact that it survives in its most complete form in Ethiopic, is one of the most important Jewish *Pseudepigrapha. It embodies a series of revelations, of which Enoch is the professed recipient, on such matters as the origin of evil, the angels and their destinies, and the nature of *Gehenna and *Paradise. Apart from the continuous Ethiopic text, several Greek fragments have come to light (some of them extensive), a single Latin fragment, and a number of fragments in *Aramaic and Hebrew (representing the remains of ten or more separate MSS) from *Qumran. The original language of the work appears to have been Aramaic, or possibly Hebrew.

As it is preserved in Ethiopic, the work is clearly composite. About the precise divisions and their dates there is some disagreement. R. H. *Charles divided it as follows into five sections composed at different dates: Section 1 (chs. 1–36) incorporates portions of 'The Book of Noah' and was written before 170 BC; 2 (chs. 37–71) contains the 'Parables' or 'Similitudes', c.105–64 BC; 3 (chs. 72–82), 'The Book of the Heavenly Luminaries', before 110 BC; 4 (chs. 83–90), 'The Dream Visions', c.165–161 BC; and 5 (chs. 91–104), incorporating an 'Apocalypse of Weeks', contains material of various dates.

The passages on 'the Son of Man' in the 'Parables' or 'Similitudes' (chs. 37–71) have been widely held to have influenced the NT writings; and other NT titles, such as 'the Righteous One' and 'the Elect One' have been said to have appeared here first as Messianic designations. But this view has been increasingly questioned, especially since the discovery of the Qumran fragments; for although all the other sections of 1 Enoch are well represented in these fragments, chs. 37–71 are not represented at all. Nor are they represented in the Greek and Latin fragments. It is probable, therefore, that they are a later (Christian) inscription into the Book, and that it was the NT which influenced them rather than vice versa. But about the value of the other sections of the Book for understanding the NT there can be no doubt. 1 En. 1: 9 is explicitly quoted as Enoch's in the Ep. of Jude (vv. 14–15), and themes appear to be taken up elsewhere, e.g. in 2 Peter 2. 1 En. 79: 56 is quoted as 'Scripture' in the Ep. of *Barnabas (16: 4; cf. 4: 3); and *Tertullian also regarded the Book as Scripture, although he admitted that he knew of 'some' who did not (*Cult. Fem.* 1. 3. 1).

(2) 2 Enoch, or 'Slavonic Enoch', or 'The Book of the Secrets of Enoch' (a title based on the titles in some of the MSS), has many points of contact with 1 Enoch, although there are no literary parallels. It survives only in Old Church Slavonic, the language of the Russian Church, and first came to knowledge of W. scholars in the last part of the 19th cent. Of the Slavonic text there are two recensions, of which the shorter is undoubtedly the earlier. About its origin, date, authorship, and original language, opinions have differed widely. At one extreme, R. H. Charles thought that it was written about the beginning of the Christian era, by an Alexandrian Jew, and in Greek (though certain parts of it 'were founded on Hebrew originals'); at the other extreme, it has been argued that it is a *Bogomil work, written in Bulgarian between the 12th and 15th cents. As an intermediate view may be instanced that of A. Vaillant, that the author was a Jewish Christian, who was concerned to produce a Christian counterpart to the Jewish 1 Enoch, and wrote in Greek, prob. in the 2nd or early 3rd cent.

(3) 3 Enoch, a Jewish work, dating from well within the Christian era (perhaps the 4th or 5th cent. AD), has gradually come to light, mainly in fragments, from c.1870 onwards. The continuous Hebrew text was first published by H. Odeberg in 1928 from a *Bodleian MS of c. AD 1511. Its subjects include the destinies of 'Metatron' (i.e. the Divine servant who is identified with Enoch), many descriptions of angels and their operations, and an account of *Sheol. It appears to betray traces of an anti-Christian polemic.

(1) Ethiopic text ed. A. *Dillmann (Leipzig, 1851), J. Flemming (TU 22, Heft 1; 1902), R. H. Charles (Anecdota Oxoniensia. Semitic Series, pt. 11; 1906) and, with Eng. tr., by M. A. Knibb (2 vols., Oxford, 1978). Greek texts conveniently pr. in H. B. *Swete, *The Old Testament in Greek according to the Septuagint*, 3 (4th edn., Cambridge, 1912), pp. 789–809, and C. Bonner (ed.), *The Last Chapters of Enoch in Greek* (Studies and Documents, 8, 1937); all the available frags. ed. M. Black, *Apocalypsis Henochi Graece* (Pseudepigrapha Veteris Testamenti Graece, 3; Leiden, 1970). J. T. Milik and M. Black (eds.), *The Books of Enoch: Aramaic Fragments of Qumrân Cave 4*, (Oxford, 1976, incl. Eng. tr.). Eng. tr. of Dillmann's text by R. H. Charles (Oxford, 1893) and of his own edn. (ibid., 1912). The latter is repr., with introd., in R. H. Charles (ed.), *The Apocrypha and Pseudepigrapha of the Old Testament*, 2 (Oxford, 1913), pp. 163–281; Knibb's tr. is repr., with introd., in H. F. D. Sparks (ed.), *The Apocryphal Old Testament* (Oxford, 1984), pp. 169–319. Further Eng. trs. by E. Isaac in J. H. Charlesworth (ed.), *The Old Testament Pseudepigrapha*, 1 (1983), pp. 5–89, and by M. Black (Studia in Veteris Testamenti Pseudepigrapha, 7; Leiden, 1985), with comm. and textual notes. E. Sjöberg, *Der Menschensohn im Äthiopischen Henochbuch* (Acta Reg. Societatis Humaniorum Litterarum Lundensis, 41; 1946); C. P. van Andel, *De Structuur van de Henoch-Traditie en het Nieuwe Testament* (Studia Theologica Rheno-Traiectina, 2; Utrecht, 1955, with Eng. summary). J. Theisohn, *Die auserwählte Richter: Untersuchungen zur traditionsgeschichtlichen Ort der Menschensohngestalt der Bilderreden des Äthiopischen Henoch* (Göttingen [1975]). J. C. VanderKam, *Enoch and the Growth of an Apocalyptic Tradition* (Catholic Biblical Quarterly Monograph Series, 16; Washington, DC, 1984). S. Uhlig, *Das Äthiopische Henochbuch* (Jüdische Schriften aus hellenistisch-römischer Zeit, Band 5, Lieferung 6; 1984). M. Barker, *The Older Testament* (1987), pp. 8–80; id., *The Lost Prophet: The Book of Enoch and its Influence on Christianity* (1988). E. *Schürer, *The History of the Jewish People in the Age of Jesus Christ*, rev. Eng. tr. by G. Vermes and others, 3 (pt. 1, Edinburgh, 1986), pp. 250–77. G. W. E. Nickelsburg in *Anchor Bible Dictionary*, 2 (1992), pp. 508–16. See also bibl. to SON OF MAN.

(2) Slavonic text, with Fr. tr., ed. A. Vaillant (Textes publiés par l'Institut d'Études slaves, 4; 1952). Eng. trs. by W. R. Morfill, with introd. by R. H. Charles (Oxford, 1896); by N. Forbes and R. H. Charles in R. H. Charles (ed.), *The Apocrypha and Pseudepigrapha of the Old Testament*, 2 (Oxford, 1913), pp. 425–69; by F. I. Andersen in J. H. Charlesworth (ed.), *The Old Testament Pseudepigrapha*, 1 (1983), pp. 91–221; and by A. [A.] Pennington in H. F. D. Sparks (ed.), *The Apocryphal Old Testament* (Oxford, 1984), pp. 321–62. E. Schürer, op. cit. 3 (pt. 2, 1987), pp. 746–50. F. I. Andersen in *Anchor Bible Dictionary*, 2 (1992), pp. 516–22.

(3) Heb. text ed., with Eng. tr., by H. Odeberg (Cambridge, 1928; repr., New York, 1973, with prolegomenon by J. C. Greenfield). Eng. tr. by P. [S.] Alexander in J. H. Charlesworth (ed.), *The Old Testament Pseudepigrapha*, 1 (1983), pp. 223–315. Id. in *Anchor Bible Dictionary*, 2 (1992), pp. 522–6.

enthronization. The rite by which a newly consecrated archbishop, bishop, or sovereign is put into possession of his throne. It is normally performed by ceremonially leading him to it and seating him thereon; in the case of a sovereign it forms part of the rite of *Coronation (q.v.). Since a bishop's throne was the earliest emblem of his office, his enthronement prob. orig. signified his assumption of power to govern the Church; it would seem to have been performed in silence by the consecrating bishop immediately after the candidate's consecration and before the celebration of the Mass. By the time of the earliest English Pontificals (10th cent.) enthronization was accompanied by the recitation of a prayer (prob. of *Gallican origin) and a blessing of the new bishop, prob. by the consecrator. In the late 12th cent., owing to the growing custom of consecrating bishops outside their cathedral churches, it became a separate rite, which was accompanied by prayers and performed by a third bishop appointed by the metropolitan. In the 13th cent. various changes in the wording of the rite gave ground to the legal interpretation of the ceremony as parallel to the *induction of a clerk, i.e. it was understood as the formal assumption (*possessio*) of the see; at the same time metropolitans began to assign the task to their *archdeacons. In the later Middle Ages the increase in the practice of translation gave the ceremony an added importance; a new and more precise formula became customary; and, as the legal aspects were emphasized, cathedral chapters used the occasion to demand from the new bishop, who needed access to the cathedral for the purpose, an oath of loyalty to the Church and pledges to preserve its rights. Until the *Reformation the ceremony was performed at *Canterbury by the Prior and at *York by the Dean. In the C of E, the Archdeacon of Canterbury normally enthrones bishops in that Province, but in the Province of York the duty is undertaken by the Dean or Provost of the cathedral of the diocese. In the RC Church enthronization is usually performed by the consecrating bishop if the candidate is consecrated in his own cathedral church; but it is no longer of any juridical significance. The enthronement of the Pope in the Church of *St Peter, Rome, was formerly a ceremony of considerable importance, because, until 1059, it was deemed to confer on him the power of administering the Church.

The term is also applied to the sealing up of relics in a new altar and in the E. Church to induction to a cure of souls.

E. C. Ratcliff, 'On the Rite of the Inthronization of Bishops and Archbishops', *Theology*, 45 (1942), pp. 71–82. N. Gussone, *Thron und Inthronisation des Papstes von den Anfängen bis zum 12. Jahrhundert* (Bonner Historische Forschungen, 41; 1978).

enthusiasm (Gk. ἐνθουσιασμός). The original meaning of the word, the 'being possessed by a god', was current in the 17th cent. Later it took on the sense of fancied inspiration, S. *Johnson defining it as 'a vain confidence of Divine favour or communication'; and in the 18th cent. it was widely used for extravagance in religious devotion.

R. A. *Knox, *Enthusiasm: A Chapter in the History of Religion* (1950).

Entrance, Great; Little. See GREAT ENTRANCE; LITTLE ENTRANCE.

Enurchus, St (4th cent.), Bp. of Orléans. Hardly anything is known with certainty of him. Feast day, 7 Sept. In 1604 a mention of the feast was included, probably (via the *Preces Privatae* of 1564) from the Calendar of the *York Breviary, in that of the BCP, to mark Queen *Elizabeth I's birthday. The form 'Evurtius' found in modern Prayer Books is the correct one; 'Enurchus' appears to derive from a misreading in the York Breviary (printed 1524), which reads 'Euurcius'.

The highly legendary 'Vita' by Lucifer the Subdeacon, pr. in *AASS*, Sept. 3 (1750), pp. 52–8, with discussion by J. Stilting, SJ, pp. 44–52, is based on an earlier work, pr. in *Catalogus Codicum Hagiographicorum Latinorum Antiquorum Saeculo XVI qui asservantur in Bibliotheca Nationali Parisiensi*, 2 (1890), pp. 312–19; both Lives can be dated to the first half of the 9th cent. L. S. Le Nain de *Tillemont, *Mémoires pour servir à l'histoire ecclésiastique des six premiers siècles*, 8 (2nd edn., 1713), pp. 555 f. On the commemoration in Anglican calendars, see V. Staley, *The Liturgical Year* (1907), pp. 43–5.

epact (Gk. ἐπακτός, 'brought in'). (1) The excess of days in the solar year over the lunar year of 12 months. (2) The age in days of the moon on 1 Jan. of a given year. In the latter sense the epact is used in ecclesiastical calculations of the date of Easter.

epanokamelavchion (Gk. ἐπανωκαμηλαύχιον, ἐπικαλυμμαύχιον). The veil placed on top of the *kamelavchion and hanging down at the back, worn by monks and bishops in the E. Church. It is normally of black material, except in the case of metropolitans of the Russian Church, who wear a veil of white.

Epaphroditus. A 'brother, and fellow-worker, and fellow-soldier' of St *Paul, mentioned only in Phil. (2: 25 and 4: 18; and perhaps also 4: 3). He carried a gift from Philippi to Paul and returned, probably bearing the Ep. to the Philippians. There is no reason to identify Epaphroditus with the Epaphras of Col. 4: 12.

eparchy (Gk. ἐπαρχία). In the E. Church, the name for an ecclesiastical *province. It is a subdivision of the civil diocese or 'exarchate'. The word is of frequent occurrence in the canons of E. councils, e.g. in those of *Nicaea (325) and *Chalcedon (451). Its ecclesiastical head is the 'eparch', often called the 'metropolitan', who has a veto on the election of the bishops of the dioceses in his eparchy. In the Council of Chalcedon (can. 17), however, the phrase 'eparch of the [civil] diocese' (ἔπαρχος τῆς διοικήσεως) is used to describe what is more commonly and accurately called the '*exarch' (ἔξαρχος).

Ephesians, Epistle to the. The NT Epistle opens with an exposition of God's eternal purpose to redeem Jews and Gentiles alike in Christ, and their common destiny of being built up into the Church 'upon the foundation of the apostles and prophets, Jesus Christ Himself being the chief corner-stone' (1: 3–2: 22). These promised glories for the Church are echoed through the whole Epistle. The author then proceeds to speak of his own position as Apostle of the Gentiles (3: 1–13), and to dwell on the spiritual (3: 14–21) and moral (4: 1–6: 9) implications of conversion, with particular instructions on the duties of the married life (5: 22–33), of children and parents (6: 1–4), and of slaves and their masters (6: 5–9). There is a concluding section exhorting his readers to 'put on the whole armour of God' in their spiritual struggle (6: 10–20).

The Epistle raises many critical questions. It was apparently written when the author was in prison. Considerations of style and theological emphasis, compared with those of the other epistles of St *Paul, have led an increasing number of modern scholars to question its genuineness. The original destination of the Epistle is uncertain. The words 'in Ephesus' in 1: 1 are wanting in some early MSS (B ℵ P⁴⁶), a circumstance which, combined with the absence of all personal references, has led some scholars to suppose it was a circular letter addressed largely to Christians whom the author had not met (cf. 1: 15, 3: 2), and that a blank was left in the original and the appropriate place-name inserted in the copy sent to each Church. There are close literary and theological parallels with Col., which are almost certainly to be explained by direct connection between the two, e.g. that Eph. is a working up of Col. into a more systematic doctrinal treatise, or even an orderly exposition of the Gospel as preached by Paul, designed to provide a suitable introduction to the first collection of his letters.

Modern comm. by H. Schlier (Dusseldorf, 1957), J. Gnilka (Herders Theologischer Kommentar zum Neuen Testament, 10, Fasc. 2; 1971), M. Barth (Anchor Bible, 2 vols. [1974]), C. L. Mitton (New Cent. Bib., 1976), G. B. Caird (New Clar. Bib., RV, on Eph., Phil., Col., and Philem., 1976, pp. 9–94), H. Conzelmann (Das Neue Testament Deutsch, 8; 14th edn., by J. Becker and others, on Gal., Eph., Phil., Col., Thess., and Philemon, 1976, pp. 86–124), R. Schnackenburg (Evangelisch-Katholischer Kommentar zum Neuen Testament, 10; Zurich, etc. [1982]; Eng. tr., Edinburgh, 1991), A. T. Lincoln (Word Biblical Comm. 42; Dallas, Tex. [1990]), and E. Best (ICC, 1998). E. J. Goodspeed, *The Meaning of Ephesians* (Chicago, 1933). E. Percy, *Die Probleme der Kolosser- und Epheserbriefe* (Skrifter utgivna av kungl. Humanistika Vetenskapssamfundet i Lund, 39; 1946), pp. 179 474. C. L. Mitton, *The Epistle to the Ephesians: Its Authorship, Origin and Purpose* (1951). E. J. Goodspeed, *The Key to Ephesians* (Chicago, 1956). J. C. Kirby, *Ephesians, Baptism and Pentecost: An inquiry into the structure and purpose of the Epistle to the Ephesians* (1968). A. van Roon, *The Authenticity of Ephesians* (Supplements to *Novum Testamentum*, 39; 1974 [Eng. tr. of work pub. in Dutch in 1969]). E. Best, *Ephesians* (New Testament Guides, Sheffield, 1993). V. P. Furnish in *Anchor Bible Dictionary*, 2 (1992), pp. 535–42.

Ephesus. In NT times, Ephesus, one of the largest cities of the Roman world, was the capital of the Proconsular Province of Asia and, although its harbour was then silting up, was still a great port and commercial centre. Its fame was due largely to its great temple, dedicated to Artemis, or 'Diana' as the Romans called her. This, the fifth on the site, had been erected *c.*330 BC and counted as one of the 'Seven Wonders of the World'; and Ephesus's proudest title was that of 'temple warden' ($νεωκόρος$) to the goddess (Acts 19: 35).

In early Christian times Ephesus was the scene of important labours of St Paul (see esp. Acts 18 and 19), the traditional home of the aged St *John, and the scene of the Third General Council of the Church in AD 431. During St Paul's three years' residence in the city, the great riot took place in the theatre so graphically described in Acts 19: 21–41. The belief that St John the Apostle lived in Ephesus in his old age is widespread, though disputed. An ancient tradition makes the city the scene of his encounter with the heretic *Cerinthus, and the ruins of a large Byzantine church built by *Justinian mark his traditional burial place. Ephesus was one of the 'Seven Churches' addressed by the Seer in the Apocalypse (Rev. 2: 1–7), the Ephesians being commended for their hatred of the works of the *Nicolaitans (2: 6). The ruins of a double church near the theatre are almost certainly those of the church in which the Council met in AD 431. About a mile from the theatre is a cave where the *Seven Sleepers of Ephesus are reputed to have taken refuge during the *Diocletianic persecution. See also EPHESIANS, EPISTLE TO THE; POLYCRATES, ST.

D. G. Hogarth, with others, *Excavations at Ephesus: The Archaic Artemisia* (British Museum Publication, 1908; atlas in separate vol., 1908). *Forschungen in Ephesos veröffentlicht vom Österreichischen archäologischen Institute* (Vienna, 1906 ff.). J. Keil, *Ephesos: Ein Führer durch die Ruinenstätte und ihre Geschichte* (Vienna, 1915; 5th edn., 1964). C. Picard, *Éphèse et Claros: Recherches sur les sanctuaires et les cultes de l'Ionie du nord* (Bibliothèque des Écoles Françaises d'Athènes et de Rome, 123; 1922). F. Miltner, *Ephesos: Stadt der Artemis und des Johannes* (Vienna, 1958). C. Foss, *Ephesus after Antiquity: A Late Antique, Byzantine and Turkish City* (Cambridge, 1979). W. M. *Ramsay, *The Letters to the Seven Churches in Asia* (1904), pp. 210–50; C. J. Hemer, *The Letters to the Seven Churches of Asia Minor in their Local Setting* (Journal for the Study of the New Testament, Supplement Series, 11; Sheffield [1989]), pp. 35–56. R. Tonneau, OP,

'Éphèse au temps de saint Paul', *R. Bibl.* 38 (1929), pp. 5–34 and 321–63. P. Antoine in *Dict. Bibl.*, Suppl. 2 (1934), cols. 1076–104, s.v.; R. Janin, AA, in *DHGE* 15 (1963), cols. 554–61, s.v. 'Éphèse (1)'; J. Finegan in *The Interpreter's Dictionary of the Bible*, 2 (1962), pp. 114–18, s.v.; D. Boyd, ibid., Suppl. Vol. (1976), pp. 269–71. D. Knibbe and others in *PW*, Suppl. 12 (1970), cols. 248–364 and 1588–1704, s.v. 'Ephesos'.

Ephesus, Council of (431). The third General Council, summoned by *Theodosius II in the hope of settling the *Nestorian controversy. With the support of Memnon, Bp. of Ephesus, St *Cyril of Alexandria, who was the chief opponent of *Nestorius, opened the council on 22 June 431, without waiting for the arrival either of the Syrian bishops, headed by John of *Antioch, who formed the party most likely to take a sympathetic view of Nestorius, or of the legates of the Pope, *Celestine. Nestorius was deposed from his see of *Constantinople and excommunicated, his doctrines condemned, and the Creed of *Nicaea reaffirmed. When they had arrived, the Syrian bishops, joined by *Theodoret and a considerable group who had protested against Cyril's action, held a rival meeting at which Cyril and Memnon were excommunicated. A reconciliation between John and Cyril was finally effected in 433. The council passed eight canons, the first seven dealing with matters arising out of the doctrinal question (in which the Pelagian *Celestius was condemned, along with Nestorius) and the eighth with the jurisdictional rights of *Cyprus. In its rejection of Nestorianism, the council gave formal approval to the title *Theotokos (q.v.).

Earlier texts of 'Acta' pr. in Hardouin, 1, cols. 1271–722; Mansi, 4 (1760), cols. 567–1482; 5 (1761), cols. 7–1022. These are now superseded by the crit. edn. of E. *Schwartz, *ACO* 1 (5 parts, 1922–30); Fr. tr. of parts 1–3 by A. J. Festugière, *Éphèse et Chalcédoine, Actes des Conciles* (1982), pp. 11–650. Coptic Acts (of little historical value), ed. W. Kraatz (TU 26, Heft 2; 1904). I. Rucker, *Ephesinische Konzilsakten in armenische-georgischer Überlieferung* (*Sb.* (Bayr.), 1930, Heft 3). Canons and some other material, with Eng. tr., in Tanner, *Decrees* (1990), pp. 37–74. A. d'Alès, *Le Dogme d'Éphèse* (1931). I. Rucker, *Studien zum Concilium Ephesinum zur 1500-Jahrfeier des dritten ökumenischen Konzils* (5 Hefte, privately pub., Oxenbronn bei Günzburg a.D., 1930–5). P.-T. Camelot, OP, *Éphèse et Chalcédoine* (Histoire des Conciles Œcuméniques, 2; 1962), pp. 13–75 and 191–209. L. I. Scipioni, *Nestorio e il concilio di Efeso* (Studia Patristica Mediolanensia, 1; 1974), esp. pp. 201–98. Hefele and Leclercq, 2 (pt. 1; 1908), pp. 287–377. Fliche and Martin, 4 (1939), pp. 163–96. A. Grillmeier, SJ, in id. and H. Bacht, SJ (eds.), *Das Konzil von Chalkedon*, 1 (1951), esp. pp. 159–64; expanded Eng. tr., *Christ in Christian Tradition* (2nd edn., rev., 1971), pp. 443–87. *CPG* 4 (1980), pp. 30–69 (nos. 8620–8867). M. Jugie, AA, in *DTC* 5 (1913), cols. 137–63, s.v. 'Éphèse (Concile de)'; id. in *EC* 5 (1950), cols. 114–19, s.v. 'Efeso II, Concilio di', with refs. to series of arts. in *Échos d'Orient* and other bibl.; J. Liébaert in *DHGE* 15 (1963), cols. 561–74, s.v. 'Éphèse (2), Concile de', with extensive refs.; J. H. Crehan, SJ, in *A Catholic Dictionary of Theology*, 2 (1967), pp. 217–20, s.v., with bibl.

Ephesus, Robber Council of 449. See LATROCINIUM.

Ephesus, Seven Sleepers of. See SEVEN SLEEPERS OF EPHESUS.

ephod. An ancient Israelite liturgical vestment of linen and beaten gold, most probably in the form of a waistcloth with shoulder-straps. It is described in Ex. 28: 6–12 and 39: 2–5. It was worn apparently only by the high priest, but a similar garment entirely of linen was worn by other persons, as by Samuel when serving before the tabernacle at Shiloh (1 Sam. 2: 18), and by *David when performing a prophetic dance (2 Sam. 6: 4). The same word was also applied to a certain kind of image (frequently in Jgs., 8: 27 and 17: 5).

K. Budde, 'Ephod und Lade', *ZATW* 39 (1921), pp. 1–42. J. Morgenstern, 'The Ark, the Ephod, and the "Tent of Meeting" ', section 7: 'The Ephod', *Hebrew Union College Annual*, 18 (1943–1944), pp. 1–17. K. Elliger, 'Ephod und Choschen. Ein Beitrag zur Entwicklungsgeschichte der hohepriestlichen Ornats', *Vetus Testamentum*, 8 (1958), pp. 19–35. R. de Vaux, OP, *Les Institutions de l'Ancien Testament*, 2 (1960), pp. 201–4, with bibl. pp. 464 f.; Eng. tr. (2nd edn., 1965), pp. 349–52, with bibl. p. 544.

ephor (Gk. ἔφορος). In the E. Church, a lay guardian or protector in whose charge monastic property was often vested from the 10th cent. onwards. The practice was much abused, as such property was apt to be diverted to secular purposes, e.g. the enrichment of the ephor himself. The word is used also of the holders of various ecclesiastical offices.

Ephphatha. The ceremony in the Roman Baptismal rite in which the celebrant in pronouncing the words 'Ephphatha, that is Be opened' (Mk. 7: 34) touches the ears and mouth of the candidate, praying that he may hear and preach the faith. It is found from an early date in the Baptismal service for Easter Eve at Rome and Milan.

Ephraem Syrus, St (*c.*306–73), Syrian biblical exegete and hymn-writer. Acc. to late Syriac sources he was the son of a pagan priest at Nisibis, his native town; but from indications in his own writings most modern scholars believe that his parents were Christians. He was ordained deacon, perhaps by St *James of Nisibis; but it is unlikely that he accompanied him to the Council of *Nicaea (325). After the cession of Nisibis to Persia in 363 Ephraem withdrew into the Roman Empire and settled at *Edessa, where most of his extant works were written. Later very unreliable legends report journeys to Egypt, where he is said to have spent eight years and confuted the *Arians, and to the Cappadocian Caesarea, where he is stated to have visited St *Basil. He became famous for the austerity and sanctity of his life as well as for his learning.

Ephraem's voluminous exegetical, dogmatic, controversial, and ascetical writings are mostly in verse. Their inspiration is scriptural throughout and they make abundant use of typology and symbolism. Although Ephraem abhors any systematic presentation, his theological vision is nevertheless a coherent one. His poetry is divided into hymns (*madrāshē*) and verse homilies (*mēmrē*). Over 500 genuine hymns survive, often of great beauty and insight; they were arranged after his death into hymn cycles, of which the most famous are those on Faith (including the five 'On the Pearl'), on Paradise, and on Nisibis (the second half of this cycle, however, is concerned with the *Descent of Christ into Hell). Several of his works, verse as well as prose, were written to counter heretics, esp. *Marcion, *Bardesanes, and *Mani, as well as the Arians and *Anomoeans. Of the biblical commentaries those on Gen. and the *Diatessaron are the most important. He wrote exclusively in Syriac, but his works were translated into Armenian and Greek at a very early date,

and via the latter into Latin and Slavonic; many of the works attributed to him in these languages, however, are not genuine. His liturgical poetry had a great influence on the development of both Syriac and Greek hymnography. Feast day in the E., 28 Jan.; in the W., formerly 1 Feb.; from 1920, when he was declared a Doctor of the Church, 18 June; from 1969, 9 June (10 June in American BCP, 1979). See also CODEX EPHRAEMI.

The collection of Ephraem's works by J. S. and S. E. *Assemani and P. B. Mobarek, SJ (3 vols. of Syriac texts (Rome, 1737–46) and 3 vols. of Greek texts (ibid. 1732–46)), is very unsatisfactory. Crit. edn. of Gk. text begun by S. J. Mercati (vol. 1, fasc. 1, Rome, 1915; all pub.). T. J. Lamy (ed.), *S. Ephraem Syri Hymni et Sermones* (4 vols., Malines, 1882–1902) contains only works not pub. in the Rome edn. Crit. edn., with Ger. tr., of his hymns, by E. Beck: those *De Fide* (CSCO 154, with tr. 155; 1955), *Contra Haereses* (ibid. 169, with tr. 170; 1957), *De Paradiso* with *Contra Julianum* (ibid. 174, with tr. 175; 1957), *De Nativitate* (ibid. 186, with tr. 187; 1959), *De Virginitate* (ibid. 223, with tr. 224; 1962), *De Ieiunio* (ibid. 246, with tr. 247; 1964), and of his *Paschahymnen* (ibid. 248, with tr. 249; 1964); also by id. of his *Carmina Nisibena* (ibid. 218 and 240, with tr. 219 and 241; 1961–3), of his *Sermones de Fide* (ibid. 212, with tr. 213; 1961) and his *Sermo de Domino Nostro* (ibid. 270, with tr. 271; 1966); and of his *Homiliae de Nicomedia*, by C. Renoux, with Fr. tr. (PO 37, fascs. 1–2; 1975); C. W. Mitchell (ed.), *St Ephrem's Prose Refutations of Mani, Marcion and Bardaisan* (Text and Translation Society, 2 vols., 1912–21); commentaries on Gen. and Ex. ed. R. M. Tonneau (CSCO 152, with Lat. tr. 153; 1955) and on the Diatessaron, with Lat. tr., by L. Leloir, OSB (Chester Beatty Monographs, 8; Dublin, 1963; with additional pages, also Chester Beatty Monographs, 8; Louvain, 1990); Eng. tr. by C. McCarthy (Journal of Semitic Studies Supplement, 2; Oxford, 1993). Comm. on Acts and Epp. survive only in Armenian. Eng. trs. of 'Metrical Hymns and Homilies' by H. Burgess (2 vols., 1835), of Selections by J. Gwynn in *NPNCF*, 2nd ser., vol. 13, pt. 2 (1898), with introd. Dissertation, and of Selected Prose Works' by E. G. Matthews and J. P. Amar (Fathers of the Church, 91 etc., 1994 ff.); also by S. [P.] Brock of 12 Poems, *The Harp of the Spirit* (London, 1975; enlarged to 18 Poems, 1983) and *Hymns on Paradise* (Crestwood, NY, 1990), and by K. E. McVey of Hymns ['On the Nativity', 'Against *Julian the Apostate', and, 'On Virginity'] (Classics of Western Spirituality [1989]).

E. Beck, *Ephräms Polemik gegen Mani und die Manichäer im Rahmen der zeitgenössischen griechischen Polemik und der des Augustinus* (CSCO, Subsidia, 55; 1978). P. Yousif, *L'Eucharistie chez saint Éphrem de Nisibe* (Orientalia Christiana Analecta, 224; 1984). S. [P.] Brock, *The Luminous Eye: The Spiritual World Vision of St Ephrem* (Rome, 1985; revised repr., Cistercian Studies Series, 124; Kalamazoo, Mich., 1992). T. Bou Mansour, *La pensée symbolique de saint Ephrem le Syrien* (Bibliothèque de l'Université Saint-Esprit, 16; Kaslik, 1988). M. P. Roncaglia, 'Essai de bibliographie sur saint Ephrem', *Parole de l'Orient*, 4 (1973), pp. 343–70; suppl. by S. [P.] Brock, ibid. 10 (1981/2), pp. 320–7, and 14 (1987), pp. 305–8. A. *Baumstark, *Geschichte der syrischen Literatur* (1922), pp. 31–52. I. Ortiz de Urbina, SJ, *Patrologia Syriaca* (2nd edn.; Rome, 1965), pp. 56–83. E. Beck in *Dict. Sp.* 4 (1960), cols. 788–800, s.v. 'Éphrem le Syrien' and D. Hemmerdinger-Iliadou and J. Kirchmeyer, SJ, ibid., cols. 800–22, s.v. 'Éphrem (2) (Les Versions)'; R. M. Murray, SJ, in, *A Catholic Dictionary of Theology*, 2 (1967), pp. 220–3; id., in *TRE* 9 (1982), pp. 755–62, both s.v., with bibl.

epiclesis (Gk. ἐπίκλησις). Although the term originally meant 'invocation' and subsequently 'prayer' in general, it has long been commonly used in Christian writings only for the petition for the consecration of the bread and wine in the Eucharist, and it is usually restricted to the form of this petition which asks the Father to send the Holy Spirit upon the bread and wine to make them into the Body and Blood of Christ. Its history and theological significance are highly controversial.

Early *Eucharistic Prayers, such as that in the *Apostolic Tradition* (early 3rd cent.), have petitions for the illapse of the Holy Spirit on the Church's offering, asking that those who receive the elements may profit thereby; a particular fruit of blessing sought is the gathering into one of all present in the hope of the Kingdom of God. The connection between the epiclesis and the unity of God's people remains in later prayers, but from the 4th cent. the petition is more explicitly for the consecration and transformation of the gifts of bread and wine. Thus the Liturgies of St *James and St *Basil pray that the Holy Spirit might descend 'upon us and upon these gifts'. The Liturgy of St *Chrysostom and the commentary on the liturgy in the *Catechetical Lectures* of St *Cyril of Jerusalem (*c*.350) are even more explicit in praying for a change in the elements. During the 4th cent. a form of epiclesis which prayed for both the unity and eschatological good of the communicants and for the change of the bread and wine into the Body and Blood of Christ, became common in E. liturgies. In the Egyptian tradition, a very vague epiclesis (originally of the *Logos (or Word) rather than the Holy Spirit) preceded the Words of *Institution. The Greek Liturgy of St *Mark contained a vague epiclesis that the Holy Spirit might 'fill' the Sacrifice, but also petitioned for consecration of the elements after the Words of Institution.

In the W. a petition in epicletic form appears in some of the ancient Hispano-Gallican rites; it comes sometimes before and sometimes after the Institution Narrative, explicit invocations of the Holy Spirit being rather more frequent in the latter position. The Roman *Canon of the Mass contains no such explicit mention of the Holy Spirit, though some scholars have sought to detect traces of an epiclesis in the prayer (*Quam oblationem*) that the bread and wine may be changed into the Body and Blood of Christ which comes before the Institution Narrative. There is an older tradition of seeking such traces in the *Supplices*, asking for the acceptance of the earthly sacrifice in heaven that it may be beneficial for us. Rather, the whole sequence from *Quam oblationem* to the end of *Supplices* is a unified act of oblation and prayer for that oblation's acceptance. The modern RC Eucharistic Prayers contain a double epiclesis; both prayers are explicitly for the operation of the Holy Spirit, the first that the elements may be changed and the second in connection with the fruits of communion.

T. *Cranmer introduced a reference to the action of the Holy Spirit into the invocation before the Words of Institution in the BCP of 1549 ('With Thy Holy Spirit and Word vouchsafe to bless and sanctify these Thy gifts and creatures of Bread and Wine'). It was removed in 1552 and not reintroduced in 1662. It was restored in the Scottish Prayer Book of 1637, and was used by the *Nonjurors. All the Eucharistic rites in the American BCP (1979) include an epiclesis before or after the Words of Institution, mostly using a form of words based on the 1764 Scottish liturgy, and most of the rites in the ASB have some form of double epiclesis. Many other modern Anglican liturgies contain a double or single epiclesis, in varying positions, some invoking the operation of the Holy

Spirit on the elements, some on the communicants, and some more generally on, or through, the Eucharistic action. Rites such as those of the Church of *South India, the *United Reformed Church (1989), and the *Common Order of the Church of Scotland (1994), all provide single epicleses that pray both for the consecration of the elements and for the benefits of communion; such petitions usually come after the Institution Narrative.

J. Brinktrine, *De Epiclesis Eucharisticae Origine* (Rome, 1923). G. *Dix, OSB, 'The Origins of the Epiclesis', *Theology*, 28 (1934), pp. 125–37 and 187–202. E. G. C. F. Atchley, *On the Epiclesis of the Eucharistic Liturgy and in the Consecration of the Font* (*Alcuin Club Collections, 31; 1935). M. Jugie, AA, *De Forma Eucharistiae: De Epiclesibus Eucharisticis* (Rome, 1943). B. Botte, OSB, 'L'Épiclèse de l'Anaphore d'Hippolyte', *RTAM* 14 (1947), pp. 241–51; B. *Capelle, OSB, 'L'Anaphore de Sérapion. Essai d'exégèse', *Muséon*, 59 (1946), pp. 425–43, repr. in his *Travaux liturgiques*, 2 (Louvain, 1962), pp. 344–58. E. Stommel, *Studien zur Epiklese der römischen Taufwasserweihe* (Theophaneia, 5; 1950). C. Kern, 'En marge de l'épiclèse', *Irénikon*, 24 (1951), pp. 166–94. G. S. Smit, 'Épiclèse et théologie des sacrements', *Mélanges de Science Religieuse*, 15 (1958), pp. 95–136. J. H. McKenna, CM, *Eucharist and Holy Spirit: The Eucharistic Epiclesis in Twentieth Century Theology (1900–1966)* (Alcuin Club Collections, 57; 1975); id., 'The Eucharistic Epiclesis in Twentieth Century Theology (1900–1966)', *EL* 90 (1976), pp. 289–328 and 446–82; id., 'The Epiclesis Revisited. A Look at Modern Eucharistic Prayers', ibid. 99 (1985), pp. 314–36. J. H. Crehan, SJ, 'Eucharistic Epiklesis: New Evidence and a New Theory', *Theological Studies*, 41 (1980), pp. 698–712; R. Albertine, MM, 'The Epiclesis Problem—The Roman Canon (Canon I) in the Post-Vatican Liturgical Reform', *EL* 99 (1985), pp. 337–48. W. R. Crockett, *Eucharist: Symbol of Transformation* (New York [1989]), pp. 54–63. S. Salaville, AA, in *DTC* 5 (1913), cols. 194–300, s.v. 'Épiclèse eucharistique'; F. *Cabrol, OSB, in *DACL* 5 (pt. 1, 1922), cols. 142–84; M. Jugie, AA, in *EC* 5 (1951), cols. 409–13; J. Laager in *RAC* 5 (1962), cols. 583–99, s.v. 'Epiklesis, II. Liturgische'.

Epictetus (*c*.50–*c*.130), *Stoic philosopher. He was probably born at Hierapolis in Phrygia. A slave in the household of *Nero, he attended the lectures of the Stoic Musonius Rufus and later became a freedman. He taught in Rome till expelled by *Domitian *c*.90, when he settled at Nicopolis in Epirus. Though he wrote nothing, his discourses were taken down by his disciple, Flavius Arrianus, and issued in two treatises, the longer 'Discourses of Epictetus' (Ἐπικτήτου Διατριβαί), of which four Books survive, and a shorter and more popular 'Enchiridion'. They reveal him as a religious thinker earnestly seeking for truth and concerned to uphold moral righteousness. His conception of God as the Father of men is more in keeping with belief in a personal and transcendent God than with the Stoic pantheism which he inherited. He stressed the kinship of God and man, the brotherhood of men, and the obligation of moral perfection, to be attained by resignation and renunciation (ἀνέχου καὶ ἀπέχου). The influence of Christian ideas on Epictetus or vice versa has often been discussed, but the resemblances hardly go beyond a striking similarity of moral temper. Only once are the Christians ('Galileans') mentioned in his writings, and then contemptuously. He was, however, valued in Christian ascetic circles.

Best edns. of the Discourses are those of J. Schweighäuser (5 vols., Leipzig, 1799–1800, with other works, incl. Christian reworking of Epictetus), H. Schenkl (Teubner edn., 1894; 2nd edn., 1916), and J. Souilhé, with Fr. tr. (Collection des Universités de France, 4 vols., 1943–65; rev. edn., 1975 ff.); edn. based on Schenkl, with Eng. tr., by W. A. Oldfather (Loeb, 2 vols., 1926–8); Enchiridion, ed. J. Schweighäuser (Leipzig, 1798); also repr. in H. Schenkel, op. cit., and, with Eng. tr., in W. A. Oldfather, op. cit. A. Bonhoeffer, *Epictet und die Stoa* (Stuttgart, 1890); id., *Die Ethik des Stoikers Epictet* (ibid., 1894); id., *Epiktet und das Neue Testament* (Religionsgeschichtliche Versuche und Vorarbeiten, 10; 1911); D. S. Sharp, *Epictetus and the New Testament* (1914). E. Riondato, *Epitteto* (Padua, 1965 ff.). W. A. Oldfather, *Contributions toward a Bibliography of Epictetus* (Urbana, Ill., 1927; suppl. ed. M. Harman, ibid., 1952). A. Jagu, M. Spanneut, and J.-E. d'Angiers, OFM Cap., in *Dict. Sp.* 4 (1960), cols. 822–54; M. Spanneut in *RAC* 5 (1962), cols. 599–681, s.v. 'Epiktet'.

Epicureanism. The system of philosophical ethics founded by the Greek thinker Epicurus (342–270 BC). Epicurus held that the senses, as the one and only source of all our ideas, provided the sole criterion of all truth. On this basis he reasserted the materialistic atomism of Democritus and denied immortality. He did not reject the existence of gods, but refused to concede their interference in human affairs. The goal of human conduct he sought in pleasure, which he equated with freedom from pain and from fear. During and after his lifetime his doctrines proved very attractive. Among later Epicureans were Apollodorus, Zeno of Sidon, and (the most famous) the Roman Lucretius. In the NT, Epicureans are referred to in Acts 17: 18. Fragments of many of Epicurus' writings have been recovered from the charred papyri of Herculaneum.

Fragments of Epicurus ed. H. Usener (Leipzig, 1887), C. Bailey with Eng. tr. (Oxford 1926), and G. Arrighetti (Turin, 1960; rev. edn., 1973). 'Ethica' ed. W. Schmid from Pap. Herc. 1251 (Studia Herculanensia, 1; 1939), and by C. Diano (Florence, 1946). Diogenes Laertius, *Lives and Opinions of Eminent Philosophers*, 10 (ed. with Eng. tr. by R. D. Hicks, Loeb, 1925, 2, pp. 528–677; ed. H. S. Long, Oxford Classical Texts, 2, 1964, pp. 494–565). C. Bailey, *The Greek Atomists and Epicurus: A Study* (1928); E. Bignone, *L'Aristotele perduto e la formazione filosofica di Epicuro* [1936]; A.-J. Festugière, OP, *Épicure et ses dieux* (1946; 2nd edn., 1968; Eng. tr., Oxford, 1955); N. W. DeWitt, *Epicurus and his Philosophy* (Minneapolis, 1954); P. Merlan, *Studies in Epicurus and Aristotle* (Klassisch-Philologische Studien, 22; Wiesbaden, 1960), pp. 1–72; B. Farrington, *The Faith of Epicurus* (1967); J. M. Rist, *Epicurus: An Introduction* (Cambridge, 1972); D. Lemke, *Die Theologie Epikurs: Versuch einer Rekonstruktion* (Zetemata, 57; 1973). H. Jones, *The Epicurean Tradition* (1989). W. Schmid in *RAC* 5 (1962), cols. 681–819, s.v. 'Epikur'.

epigonation (Gk. ἐπιγονάτιον, from ἐπιγουνίς, 'thigh'). In the E. Church, a lozenge-shaped vestment, formed of cardboard covered with cloth and decorated with a cross (and sometimes also with elaborately embroidered icons), hanging from the right side. Its use was originally confined to bishops, but in more recent times it has also come to be worn by *archimandrites and *archpriests.

Braun, *LG*, pp. 550–4.

epiklesis. See EPICLESIS.

epimanikion (Gk. ἐπί, 'on'; Lat. *manica*, 'sleeve'). The epimanikia are cuffs, usually of embroidered silk, now worn in the E. Church by bishops and priests over the ends of the sleeves of the *sticharion, and by deacons over the ends of the sleeves of the cassock. Their use, which

dates at least from the 11th cent., was in the 12th cent. still confined to bishops, and hence they may be a development of the cuffs of the bishop's sticharion itself. They seem to have a W. counterpart in the 'manica' referred to in the description of the *Gallican rite in the Letters attributed to St *Germanus of Paris.

Epiphanius, St (*c*.315–403), Bp. of Salamis. A native of Palestine, he became an enthusiastic supporter of the monastic movement and founded *c*.335 a monastery near Eleutheropolis in Judaea. His reputation for earnestness and organization was such that in 367 he was elected by the bishops of Cyprus to become their metropolitan, as Bp. of Salamis (at that time called Constantia). He continued throughout his life an ardent upholder of the faith of *Nicaea, and was intolerant of all suspicion of heresy. Of his writings in defence of orthodox belief, the most important was his 'Panarion', commonly known as the 'Refutation of all the Heresies', in which he described and attacked every heresy known to him from the beginning of the Church. Though, like all his works, it is badly constructed and far too receptive of statements and legends which support his position, it preserves much invaluable historical material. In his later life he took an active part in the *Apollinarian and *Melitian controversies, and after meeting St *Jerome in Rome in 382, joined forces with him in his attack on *Origenism. A visit to *Jerusalem for the purpose in 394 led to serious friction with the bishop, John, in which Jerome also became involved. In 400 he travelled to *Constantinople on behalf of *Theophilus, Bp. of Alexandria, who had expelled the Origenist monks; but, seeing that he was being used as a tool against John *Chrysostom, he set out again for Salamis and died at sea on the way back. Besides the 'Panarion' he also wrote a doctrinal treatise, the 'Ancoratus' ('Ἀγκυρωτός), in the MSS of which the *Nicene-Constantinopolitan creed appears perhaps for the first time; treatises 'On Measures and Weights' and 'On Gems'; and also against the use of *images in Christian worship. Feast day, 12 May.

Editio princeps of Epiphanius' chief works by J. Oporinus, Basle, 1544. Much improved text ed. D. *Petavius, SJ, 2 vols., Paris, 1622; repr. in J. P. Migne, *PG* 41–3. More recent text by W. Dindorf, 5 vols., Leipzig, 1859–62. Crit. text of 'Ancoratus' and 'Panarion' (or 'Haereses'), ed. K. *Holl (GCS, 3 vols., 1915–33); 'Panarion' revised by J. Dummer (ibid., 1980 ff.). Eng. tr. of 'Panarion', by F. Williams (Nag Hammadi Studies, 35 and 36; Leiden, 1987–94); Eng. tr. of selected passages by P. R. Amidon, SJ (New York and Oxford, 1990). Syr. text of 'De Mensuris et Ponderibus', ed. J. E. Dean (Chicago, 1935); Georg. text ed., with Fr. tr., by M.-J. van Esbroeck, SJ (CSCO, 460–1; Scriptores Iberici, 19–20; 1984); Georg. text of 'De Gemmis', by R. P. Blake and H. de Vis (Studies and Documents, ed. K. *Lake, 2; London, 1934). K. Holl, 'Die Schriften des Epiphanius gegen die Bilderverehung', *Sb.* (Berl.), 1916, pp. 828–68, repr. in his *Gesammelte Aufsätze zur Kirchengeshichte*, 2 (Tübingen, 1928), pp. 351–87. J. F. Dechow, *Dogma and Mysticism in Early Christianity: Epiphanius of Cyprus and the Legacy of Origen* (Patristic Monograph Series, 13; Louvain and Macon, Ga. [1988]). A. Pourkier, *L'hérésiologie chez Épiphane de Salamine* (Christianisme Antique, 4 [1992]). *CPG* 2 (1974), pp. 324–41 (nos. 3744–807). Altaner and Stuiber (1978), pp. 315–18 and 614 f. F. M. Young, *From Nicaea to Chalcedon* (1983), pp. 133–42, 347, and 383 f. W. Schneemelcher in *RAC* 5 (1962), cols. 909–27; P. Nautin in *DHGE* 15 (1963), cols. 617–31, s.v. 'Épiphane (10), Saint de Salamine'.

Epiphany (Gk. ἐπιφάνεια, 'manifestation'; later τὰ Ἐπιφάνια is used of the feast). Feast of the Church on 6 Jan. It originated in the E., where it was celebrated in honour of the Baptism of Christ (sometimes also in connection with the Nativity) from the 3rd cent. onwards. *Clement of Alexandria (d. c.215) reports that the *Gnostic sect of the *Basilideans observed a feast in honour of the Baptism of Christ around this time of year (*Strom.* 1. 21), and from the 4th cent. there is ample evidence for the feast, which then ranked with *Easter and *Pentecost as one of the three principal festivals of the Church. One of its main features in the E. is the solemn blessing of water.

It was introduced into the W. Church in the 4th cent. but here lost its character as a feast of the Baptism of Christ, which it has retained in the E. Church down to the present day. Instead it became associated with the manifestation of Christ to the Gentiles in the person of the *Magi, as is borne out by the Homilies of *Leo I on the 'Theophania' (an alternative name of the feast). In the Mass and Office the Magi were given the chief place, though mention is also made of the Baptism of Christ and of the miracle at Cana. In 1955 both the Octave and Vigil of the Epiphany were abolished, but the Sunday after Epiphany was made a separate feast of the Baptism, which had figured largely in the liturgy of the Octave. In England the Sovereign makes offerings of gold, frankincense, and myrrh in the *Chapel Royal on the feast.

For the main lit. dealing with Christmas and the Epiphany see under CHRISTMAS. On the Epiphany only, John, Marquess of Bute and E. A. W. Budge, *The Blessing of the Waters on the Eve of the Epiphany: The Greek, Latin, Syriac, Coptic, and Russian Versions Edited or Translated from the Original Texts* (1901). K. *Holl, 'Der Ursprung des Epiphanienfestes', *Sb.* (Berl.), 1917, pp. 402–38, repr. in Holl's *Gesammelte Aufsätze zur Kirchengeschichte*, 2 (1928), pp. 123–54. C. Mohrmann, *Epiphania* (lecture; Nijmegen and Utrecht, 1953). R. H. Bainton, *Collected Papers in Church History*, 1 (Boston [1962]), pp. 22–38 ('The Origins of the Epiphany'). A. J. Vermeulen, 'Le Développement sémasiologique d'Ἐπιφάνεια et la fête de l'Épiphanie', *Græcitas Christianorum Primæva*, Suppl. 1 (1964), pp. 7–44. J. *Daniélou, SJ, 'Les Origines de l'Épiphanie et les Testimonia', in A.-M. Dubarle and others, *Noël–Épiphanie: . . . Semaine liturgique de l'Institut Saint-Serge [Paris]* (Lex Orandi, 40; 1967), pp. 65–84; R.-G. Coquin, 'Les Origines d'Épiphanie en Egypte', ibid., pp. 139–70; A. Renoux, OSB, 'Épiphanie à Jérusalem au IVᵉ et au Vᵉ siècles', ibid., pp. 171–93, and other essays. F. Nikolasch, 'Zum Ursprung des Epiphaniefestes', *EL* 82 (1968), pp. 393–429, with bibl. C. C. Martindale, SJ, in *CE* 5 (1909), pp. 504–6; C. Smith in *NCE* 5 (1967), pp. 480 f., s.v.; E. Pax in *RAC* 5 (1962), cols. 899–909, s.v. 'Épiphanie, e. Liturgie'; F. Mann and H.-C. Schmidt-Lauber in *TRE* 9 (1982), cols. 762–70, s.v. 'Epiphaniasfest'.

episcopacy (Gk. ἐπίσκοπος, lit. 'overseer'), the system of Church government by bishops. Where it prevails it is commonly related to the institution of the *Apostolate by Christ. In the NT the word ἐπίσκοπος (AV, 'bishop') appears to be used of the same office as πρεσβύτερος ('presbyter'). See BISHOP.

Episcopal Church in the United States of America. The Church in the *United States of America in communion with the see of *Canterbury. Previously known as the Protestant Episcopal Church in the United States of America, it adopted the new title as an alternative in 1967 and as its official designation in 1979.

The first Anglican church in America was built at Jamestown, Virginia, in 1607; many other congregations were established in different parts of the Continent, all under the jurisdiction of the Bp. of London; and from 1701 onwards the spread of the Anglican Church was vigorously furthered by the *SPG, founded in that year. But it was only after the War of Independence that the Protestant Episcopal Church was established as an autonomous organization. S. *Seabury (q.v.) was elected by the clergy of Connecticut as their bishop, and, after legal difficulties had prevented his consecration in England, he received episcopal *orders in 1784 at the hands of the bishops of the Episcopalian Church in *Scotland. Further bishops were consecrated in England, however, in 1787 and 1790. At a General Convention in 1789 a constitution and canons were drawn up and the Book of *Common Prayer revised. The Church for a long time met with considerable prejudice on account of its British connections, but gradually this feeling lessened.

The Church was a pioneer in the foundation of theological seminaries and established the *General Theological Seminary in New York as early as 1817 (there are now ten others). During the Civil War of 1861–5 the Church in the southern states formed itself into a separate body, but reconciliation followed the peace in 1865. After that date the Church expanded both at home and abroad, and missionary dioceses were set up in such places as Alaska, Hawaii, the *Philippines, Puerto Rico, Cuba, *China, *Japan, Liberia, and *Brazil. Since 1867 the American Church has taken a prominent part in all the *Lambeth Conferences. Further revisions in the Prayer Book were made in 1892 and in 1928–9; a new Prayer Book, based on rites authorized in 1967 and 1976, became official in 1979. It includes services in both traditional and contemporary language. There is also a single, official hymnal, the latest revision being that of 1982.

The constitution of the Church provides for the laity a major role both in all the legislative bodies and in the vestries of individual churches. Bishops are elected, by majority vote of both clerical and lay order, in diocesan conventions. The ultimate governing body of the Church is the General Convention, which meets every three years. There are no archbishops, but there is a Presiding Bishop: until 1919 the senior bishop by consecration, but now elected by the General Convention. An Executive Council, composed of elected members representing bishops, other clergy, and laity, is the continuing executive organ between meetings of the General Convention.

Theological and ecclesiastical parties run in some measure upon similar lines to those in the C of E. Opposition to the decision of the General Convention in 1976 to permit the ordination of women to the priesthood, and to a lesser degree to the new Prayer Book, led to the formation of several small schismatic bodies. The consecration early in 1989 of the first woman to become a bishop in the Anglican Communion (as suffragan in the diocese of Massachusetts) aroused further controversy. Nevertheless, a woman was elected as diocesan bishop in Vermont in 1993. The generally liberal social programmes established by recent General Conventions have also provoked strong opposition.

The Church has long taken a prominent part in ecumenical activities. Modern developments include the *Consultation on Church Union (COCU), Anglican–RC negotiations, and official joint commissions with *Lutheran and *Orthodox theologians. In 1990 preliminary agreement was reached with the Evangelical Lutheran Church in America to establish full eucharistic communion: the final Concord of Agreement was, however, rejected by the Evangelical Lutheran Church in 1997.

Membership of the Church declined markedly between 1966 and 1990. In the latter year there were just under 2.5 million members (nearly 3.5 million in 1966), with about 1.75 million communicants.

See also UNITED STATES OF AMERICA, CHRISTIANITY IN.

W. S. Perry [Bp. of Iowa] (ed.), *Historical Collections relating to the American Colonial Church* (5 vols. in 4, relating to Virginia, Pennsylvania, Massachusetts, Maryland, and Delaware; privately pr. at Hartford, Conn., 1870–8). W. White, Bp. of Pennsylvania, *Memoirs of the Protestant Episcopal Church in the United States of America* (Philadelphia, 1820), with orig. docs. W. S. Perry, *The History of the American Episcopal Church, 1587–1883* (2 vols., Boston, 1885); C. C. Tiffany, *A History of the Protestant Episcopal Church in the United States of America* (American Church History Series, 7; New York, 1895); W. W. Manross, *A History of the American Episcopal Church* (ibid., 1935; 2nd edn., 1950); R. W. Albright, *A History of the Protestant Episcopal Church* (New York and London, 1964). P. M. Dawley, *The Episcopal Church and its Work* (Greenwich, Conn., 1955). J. T. Addison, *The Episcopal Church in the United States, 1789–1931* (New York, 1951). G. E. DeMille, *The Catholic Movement in the American Episcopal Church* (Philadelphia, 1941; 2nd edn., enlarged, 1950); id., *The Episcopal Church since 1900* (New York, 1955). D. E. Sumner, *The Episcopal Church's History, 1945–1985* (Wilton, Conn. [1987]). R. W. Prichard, *A History of the Episcopal Church* (Harrisburg, Pa. [1991] [multicultural approach]). W. S. Perry, *The Episcopate in America: Sketches, Biographical and Bibliographical, of the Bishops of the American Church* (New York, 1895). A. L. Cross, *The Anglican Episcopate and the American Colonies* (Harvard Historical Studies, 9; 1902). E. C. Chorley, *Men and Movements in the American Episcopal Church* (Hale Lectures for 1943; New York, 1946). E. L. Parsons and B. H. Jones, *The American Prayer Book: Its Origins and Principles* (New York, 1937). M. J. Hatchett, *The Making of the First American Book of Common Prayer, 1776–1789* (New York, 1982); id., *Commentary on the American Prayer Book* (New York, 1980). C. R. Barnes, *The General Convention: Offices and Officers, 1785–1950* (Philadelphia, 1951). E. A. White, *Annotated Constitution and Canons for the Government of the Protestant Episcopal Church in the United States of America, adopted in General Convention 1789–1922* (New York, 1924; rev. and cont. to 1981 by J. A. Dykman, 2 vols., Greenwich, Conn., 1984). Also important arts. in the *Historical Magazine of the Protestant Episcopal Church* (Austin, Tex., 1932 ff.; since 1987 called *Anglican and Episcopal History*). See also bibl. to UNITED STATES OF AMERICA, CHRISTIANITY IN.

Episcopalian. Properly a member of any Church ruled by bishops (*episcopi*), but esp. of the *Anglican Communion as opposed to non-episcopal bodies, e.g. the Church of *Scotland.

episcopi vagantes (Lat., 'wandering bishops'). The name given to persons who have been consecrated bishop in an irregular or clandestine manner or who, having been regularly consecrated, have been excommunicated by the Church that consecrated them and are in communion with no recognized see. A man is also included in this group when the number in communion with him is so small that

his sect appears to exist solely for his own sake. W., but not E., theology is generally ready to admit that such consecrations are valid. In modern times the main streams of succession deriving from 'episcopi vagantes' are those founded by A. H. *Mathew, J. R. *Vilatte, and an Armenian, Leon Chechemian, and the principal sects founded and governed by them are the 'American Catholic Church' (Vilatte), the '*Old Roman Catholic Church' (Mathew), the 'Negro Orthodox Church' (Vilatte), and the 'Free Protestant Church of England' (Chechemian). In addition to these are smaller sects and stray bishops whose orders have been obtained by dubious means or come from doubtful sources, as well as certain *Theosophist bishops who trace their orders to Mathew.

A. J. Macdonald, *Episcopi Vagantes in Church History* (1945); H. R. T. Brandreth, *Episcopi Vagantes and the Anglican Church* (1947; rev. edn., 1961); P. F. Anson, *Bishops at Large* (1964).

Episcopius. The assumed name of Simon Bisschop (1583–1643), who systematized the typical tenets of *Arminianism. Born at Amsterdam, he studied at *Leiden (1600–6), where he came under the influence of J. Arminius. He was one of the signatories to the *Remonstrance (1610) and in 1612 succeeded F. *Gomar as professor of theology at Leiden. Episcopius was the chief spokesman for the group of thirteen Remonstrants summoned to appear at the Synod of *Dort which condemned and banished them in 1619. He then went to the Spanish Netherlands where he drew up a confession of faith (pub. in Dutch, 1621; in Lat., 1622) for the newly founded Remonstrant Brotherhood. After a few years in France (1621–6), where he continued the exposition of his views, he became minister of the Remonstrant Church in Rotterdam and ultimately (1634) was appointed as the first professor of theology in the Remonstrant seminary at Amsterdam. Laying great stress upon the importance of scholarly scriptural exegesis after the manner of *Erasmus, he emphasized the practical nature of Christianity, affirmed that the Church is based upon a minimum of speculative beliefs, remonstrated against current Calvinist dogmas of *predestination and *original sin, stressed the responsibility of man, not God, for sin, and taught a reduced view of the divinity of Christ and a *subordinationist doctrine of the Trinity.

Opera Theologica, ed. posthumously by S. Curcellaeus and P. van Limborch (2 vols., Amsterdam, 1650–65). Life by P. van Limborch (ibid., 1701). F. Calder, *Memoirs of Simon Episcopius* (1835). A. H. Heantjens, *Simon Episcopius als Apologeet van het Remonstrantisme* (Leiden, 1889). H. C. Rogge in *PRE* (3rd edn.), 5 (1898), pp. 422–4; J. Dutilleul in *DTC* 5 (1913), cols. 367–9; G. J. Hoenderdaal in *Biographish Lexicon voor de Geschiedenis van het Nederlandse Protestantisme*, 2 (1983), pp. 191–5. See also works cited under ARMINIANISM.

epistemology (Gk. ἐπιστήμη, 'knowledge'), also known as **Theory of Knowledge**. The philosophical discipline which examines the nature and validity of human cognition.

Epistle. In Christian worship it was long customary for two passages of Scripture to be read or sung at the Eucharist; the former came to be known as the 'Epistle', doubtless because it was normally taken from the NT

Epistles, though sometimes from Acts, and in the W. occasionally from the OT or Rev. In early times, both in the E. and W., the Gospel was preceded by several lessons, of which the Epistle was the last. In the Roman rite, with certain exceptions, only the Epistle survived until 1969; OT readings were then restored on many days, and it is now fairly common on weekdays to have no lesson from the non-Gospel parts of the NT. Until the 8th cent. the reading of the Epistle was assigned to the *lector; it then fell to the *subdeacon and came to be regarded as his special function; in modern times the duty is very often undertaken by a lay person, or by the celebrant himself. The Epistle was formerly read from the *ambo or rood-*screen where such existed. In early times the selection of Epistles was made to provide continuity from Sunday to Sunday; traces of this 'lectio continua' survived, and the principle has been partially restored in the RC Church. The series of Epistles in the BCP was largely taken over from the *Sarum Missal. In the C of E the ASB provides an OT lesson, Epistle, and Gospel throughout the year, but allows the OT lesson or the Epistle to be omitted. The reader or chanter of the Epistle has sometimes been known as the 'Epistoler'; in the *Canons of 1604 (can. 24), the form 'Epistler' occurs. The 'Epistolary' was the medieval name for the book containing the Epistles. In the E. Church an Epistle (called '*Apostle') and Gospel are chanted not only at the Eucharistic liturgy, but at any sacramental celebration (including the *burial service).

Jungmann (1958 edn.), 1, pp. 501–38; Eng. tr., 1, pp. 391–421, with refs. W. H. *Frere, *Studies in Early Roman Liturgy*, 3, The Roman Epistle-Lectionary (*Alcuin Club Collections, 32; 1935). G. Godu in *DACL* 5 (pt. 1; 1922), cols. 245–344, s.v. 'Épîtres'. F. E. *Brightman, *The English Rite* (2 vols., 1915), *passim*. See also works cited s.v. LECTIONARY.

Epistle of the Apostles. See TESTAMENT OF OUR LORD IN GALILEE.

Epistolae Obscurorum Virorum. The famous pamphlet in the dispute between J. *Reuchlin and the *Dominicans of Cologne. It appeared in two parts (1515 and 1517), the first written chiefly by Crotus Rubianus (1486–1540), the second almost entirely by Ulrich von *Hutten (1488–1523). The title is a parody of the collection of genuine letters to Reuchlin published by him in 1514 and entitled *Clarorum virorum epistolae*. These imaginary letters are supposed to be addressed to a real person, Ortwin Gratius, who, though a humanist, belonged to the party of the Dominicans. Written in a style parodying the most monkish Latin, they are a witty and bitter satire on the methods of later *Scholasticism, on the religious practices of their age, and on many ecclesiastical institutions and doctrines. Their great popularity contributed much to discredit the old theological learning and its representatives.

Epistolae Obscurorum Virorum: The Latin Text with an English Rendering, Notes and an historical Introduction by F. G. Stokes (1909); Stokes's Eng. tr. (only) repr. under the title *On the Eve of the Reformation*, with new introd. by H. Holborn (New York and London, 1964). R. P. Becker, *A War of Fools: The Letters of Obscure Men. A Study of the Satire and the Satirized* (Berne, 1981).

Epistula Apostolorum. See TESTAMENT OF OUR LORD IN GALILEE.

epitaphion (Gk. ἐπιτάφιον, 'belonging to burial'). In the E. Church, a richly embroidered veil, on which is represented the scene of Christ's burial. It is carried in procession at the end of *Vespers on *Good Friday and is then placed in the centre of the church, decorated with flowers. At the end of *Orthros of *Holy Saturday it is again carried in procession. In the Greek use, it is then placed on the altar; in the Russian, it is returned to the centre of the church and only placed on the altar at the end of the Midnight Office, immediately before the *Mattins of *Easter Day. It remains on the altar until the eve of *Ascension Day.

epitrachelion (Gk. ἐπιτραχήλιον; from τράχηλος, 'neck'), also **peritrachelion**. The form of the stole worn by the priest in the E. Church. It is a long strip of material fastened in front and decorated with crosses and a fringe. It is to be distinguished from the *orarion, which is the liturgical garment of the deacon.

Equiprobabilism. The moral system defended by St *Alphonsus Liguori (q.v.). It sought to steer a mid-course between *Probabiliorism and *Probabilism, holding that the stricter course should be followed if the question concerns the cessation of the law, while the laxer course may be pursued if the question is whether the law ever existed.

Era of the Martyrs. See DIOCLETIANIC ERA.

Erasmus, St. See ELMO, ST.

Erasmus, Desiderius (1466/9–1536), 'Roterodammensis' or 'Roterodamus', humanist. There is still doubt about the date of his birth, but he was probably the (illegitimate) son of Rogerius Gerardus. Christened 'Herasmus'; he took in adult life the name of 'Desiderius' as a Latinized form of 'Erasmus', itself a supposed Greek equivalent of his baptismal name. He went to school first at Gouda and then at Deventer, where the humanist, Alexander Hegius, was one of his masters and where he came under the influence of the '*Brethren of the Common Life'. Despite considerable reluctance, he became an *Augustinian Canon at St Gregory's, Steyn, nr. Gouda, in 1487, and eagerly began to read the Classics and the Fathers. In 1492 he was ordained priest. Finding about this time a protector in Henry of Bergen, Bp. of Cambrai, with the agreement of his superiors he left his monastery. In 1495 he began to study at Paris, residing at first at the College of Montaigu. In 1499 he accompanied his pupil, William Blount, 4th Baron Mountjoy (d. 1534), who afterwards became his patron, to England. At Oxford he was deeply influenced by J. *Colet, who encouraged his dislike of *Scholasticism and directed him to the study of the NT. Having returned to the Continent in 1500, he went to Paris and Louvain, where he refused a professorship, and instead began a profound study of Greek. After another visit to England, he made his way to Italy, where he received a doctorate in theology at Turin on 4 Sept. 1506. He continued his Greek studies at *Bologna and in 1507 got in touch with Aldus Manutius, who published his Latin translation of Euripides. Erasmus joined Aldus' 'New Academy' in *Venice, and while there he published the revised version of his *Adagia*, the *Adagiorum chiliades*, with which he finally achieved international fame. He visited Rome on three occasions in 1509 and established important friendships with Giovanni de' Medici (later *Leo X), Cardinal Domenico Grimani, and Tomasso Fedra Inghirami, the Librarian of the *Vatican. On the accession of *Henry VIII (1509), Mountjoy induced him to return to England and Erasmus stayed for a time in T. *More's house, where he wrote his witty Μωρίας Ἐγκώμιον. Drawn to Cambridge by St John *Fisher, Erasmus was the first teacher of Greek there, and also lectured in divinity, possibly succeeding Fisher in the newly created Lady Margaret professorship of theology. The promises of financial support which had made Erasmus leave Italy for England never materialized, and in 1514 he left for Basle, where he prepared his translation of the NT for the press of J. *Froben. In 1516 he accepted an invitation to Brussels to the court of the future *Charles V, who made him a royal councillor. Having been freed from all his obligations to his monastery by a Papal brief in 1517, he resumed his wanderings, but in 1521 made his permanent abode at Basle, in Froben's house. In order to keep his freedom he refused many brilliant offers, including one from Francis I at Paris, another from the Archduke Ferdinand at Vienna, and a third from Henry VIII to return to England. When, in 1529, the Reformation was introduced at Basle, he fled to Freiburg im Breisgau, where he lived till 1535, continually advocating religious peace. He died at Basle, whither he had gone to supervise the printing of his edition of *Origen.

Among Erasmus' earliest works are the Adagia (1500), a collection of Greek and Latin proverbs, successively enlarged in later editions, and the Enchiridion Militis Christiani (1504), in which he shows the usefulness of scholarship for the formation of the Christian. His well-known Μωρίας Ἐγκώμιον, seu Laus Stultitiae (1509), is a bitter satire on monasticism and the corruptions of the Church and helped to prepare the way for the Reformation. In 1516 appeared his celebrated edition of the Greek NT with his own translation into classical Latin. Though based on insufficient MS material and not without bias, it exercised a profound influence on theological studies and was several times revised during Erasmus' lifetime, most notably in 1519. In 1524 he entered the Reformation controversy by his Diatribe de Libero Arbitrio, in which he emphasized the importance of human free-will against M. *Luther. Luther replied in his De Servo Arbitrio (1525), which Erasmus answered in its turn by his Hyperaspistes (1526). Next to his Greek NT, his most important work was probably his attempt to put into print reliable texts of the Fathers, among them his favourite St *Jerome (9 vols., 1516), St *Cyprian (1520), *Arnobius (1522) St *Hilary (1523), St John *Chrysostom (various works at different dates), St *Irenaeus (1526), St *Ambrose (1527), St *Augustine (1528-9), St *Basil (1532), and a Latin version of Origen (1536), though in a few of these Erasmus' own share probably did not go much further than writing the prefaces.

The most renowned scholar of his age, Erasmus was a man of vast if not always deep erudition, of uncommon intellectual powers, but averse to metaphysical speculation, esp. in its medieval and Scholastic forms. Though he had himself paved the way for the Reformation by his merciless satires on the doctrines and institutions of the Church,

his scholarly character, which abhorred violence and sought tranquillity, prevented him from joining the Protestants, and threw him back on the tradition of the Church as the safeguard of stability. In the later years of his life he became suspect to both parties. Luther inveighed against him as a sceptic and Epicurean, and on the other side, though the Popes, esp. Leo X, had been favourable to him, the University of Paris censured various writings of his between 1525 and 1542. After his death his writings were forbidden by *Paul IV in 1558; this prohibition was partly modified by the Council of *Trent, but reimposed in toto by *Sixtus V in 1590. Later editions of the *Index long continued to forbid certain works and to permit others only if expurgated.

The editio princeps of his Opera Omnia was prepared by his friend and disciple Beatus *Rhenanus (9 vols., Basle, 1540-1). Crit. edns. of his Opus epistolarum by P. S. Allen, H. M. Allen, and H. W. Garrod (11 vols., Oxford, 1906-47, + index by B. Flower and E. Rosenbaum, 1958) and of his Opera Omnia by an international committee of scholars (Amsterdam, 1969 ff.; c.30 vols. expected). The edn. of his Opera Omnia by J. *LeClerc (10 vols., Leiden, 1703-6) remains standard for ref. to works not contained in the two modern edns. Eng. trs. of his works and letters are being pub., in Collected Works of Erasmus (Toronto, 1974 ff.). His valuable prefaces to his editions of the Fathers, the NT, and certain other works have been collected by R. Peters and repr. in facsimile (Menston, Yorks, 1970). The 1535 edn. of his Annotations on New Testament has also been reproduced in facsimile, with variants from the earlier edns., ed. A. Reeve and M. A. Screech: vol. 1, The Gospels (London, 1986), vol. 2, Acts–2 Cor. (Studies in the History of Christian Thought, 42; Leiden, 1990) [the apparatus is, however, incomplete]. His early impact on England can be studied from E. J. Devereux, Renaissance English Translations of Erasmus: A Bibliography to 1700 (Toronto, etc., 1983).

There is a vast lit. on Erasmus. Major modern studies available in Eng. incl. those of J. Huizinga (Haarlem, 1924; Eng. tr., New York and London, 1924; also with tr. of some letters, London, 1952), R. H. Bainton (New York, 1969; London, 1970), C. Augustijn (Munich, 1986; Eng. tr., 1991) and L. E. Halkin (Paris [1987]; Eng. tr., Oxford, 1993). M. M. Phillips, Erasmus and the Northern Renaissance (1949; 2nd edn., Woodbridge, Suffolk, 1981). A. Flitner, Erasmus im Urteil seiner Nachwelt: Das literarische Erasmus-Bild von Beatus Rhenanus bis zu Jean LeClerc (Tübingen, 1952); B. Mansfield, Phoenix of His Age: Interpretations of Erasmus c.1550–1750 (Toronto, etc. [1979]); id., Man on his Own: Interpretations of Erasmus c.1750–1920 (ibid. [1992]). E. E. Reynolds, Thomas More and Erasmus [1965]. E.-W. Kohls, Die Theologie des Erasmus (Theologische Zeitschrift, Sonderband 1; 2 vols., Basle, 1966). E. Rummel, Erasmus' Annotations on the New Testament: From Philologist to Theologian (Toronto, etc. [1986]); id., Erasmus and his Catholic Critics (Bibliotheca Humanistica & Reformatorica, 45; 2 vols., Nieuwkoop, 1989). P. Walter, Theologie aus dem Geist der Rhetorik: Zur Schriftauslegung des Erasmus von Rotterdam (Mainz, 1990). R. J. Schoek, Erasmus of Europe: The Making of a Humanist 1467–1500 (Edinburgh, 1990); A. G. Dickens and W. R. D. Jones, Erasmus the Reformer (1994). A. J. Brown, 'The Date of Erasmus' Latin Translation of the New Testament', Transactions of the Cambridge Bibliographical Society, 8 (1984), pp. 351–80. Contemporaries of Erasmus, ed. P. G. Bietenholz and T. B. Deutscher (3 vols., Toronto, etc. [1985–7]), contains biogs. of some 1,900 contemporaries mentioned by Erasmus in his works and correspondence. Bibls. of Erasmian studies by J.-C. Margolin: for 1936–49 (Paris, 1969), for 1950–61 (ibid., 1963), and 1962–70 (ibid. and Toronto, 1977), with excellent Fr. summaries of the works listed. Works after 1970 are recorded in the annual Bibliographie internationale de l'Humanisme et de la Renaissance (Geneva, 1966 ff.) and in Archiv für Reformationsgeschichte. C. Augustijn in TRE 10 (1982), pp. 1–18, s.v., with bibl.

Erastianism. The ascendancy of the State over the Church in ecclesiastical matters, so named from the Swiss theologian, Thomas Erastus (Ger. Lieber or Lüber; 1524–83).

Born at Baden in Switzerland, Erastus studied philosophy and medicine and was appointed professor of medicine at Heidelberg in 1558. When the extreme *Calvinists endeavoured to introduce their 'Holy Discipline' in the Palatinate, Erastus wrote against them his *Explicatio Gravissimae Quaestionis*, which, however, was not published until 1589 in London. In Erastus' view, the civil authorities in a state which professes but one religion have the right and the duty to exercise jurisdiction in all matters whether civil or ecclesiastical, and to punish all offences; and even such purely ecclesiastical sanctions as *excommunication are subject to their approval.

The book was translated into English under the title *The Nullity of Church Censures* in 1659, but its ideas had begun to take root in this country from the end of the 16th cent. Erastian tenets influenced R. *Hooker, who defended the supremacy of the secular power in his *Ecclesiastical Polity* (1594), and they came to the fore in the *Westminster Assembly (1643). They were somewhat modified when applied to the modern secularized state as visualized, e.g., by T. *Hobbes. In this case the representatives of the state, though themselves professing any or no religion, assert their right to legislate on religious matters concerning the Established Church, e.g., when, in 1928, the revised Prayer Book was rejected by Parliament. In this modified sense the term is now generally understood. See also ESTABLISHMENT.

J. N. *Figgis, 'Erastus and Erastianism', *JTS* 2 (1901), pp. 66–101. A. Bonnard, *Thomas Éraste, 1524–1583, et la discipline ecclésiastique* (thesis, Lausanne, 1894); R. Wessel-Roth, *Thomas Erastus: Ein Beitrag zur Geschichte der reformierten Kirche und zur Lehre der Staatssouveränität* (Veröffentlichungen des Vereins für Kirchengeschichte in der evang. Landeskirche Badens, 15; 1954). J. N. Figgis in *DECH*, pp. 206 f., s.v.

Erconwald (d. *c*.693), Bp. of London. Born of a princely family, he devoted his fortune to the founding of two religious houses, over one of which, that at Barking, he placed his sister, St *Ethelburga, and over the other at Chertsey he himself acted as abbot. In 675 he succeeded Wini as Bp. of London and proved himself a pious and able prelate. He was buried in *St Paul's Cathedral, where his tomb soon became a centre of veneration. Feast day, 30 Apr.

The principal authority is *Bede, *HE* 4. 6; comm. by J. M. Wallace-Hadrill (Oxford, 1988), pp. 145–7. D. Whitelock, *Some Anglo-Saxon Bishops of London* (1975), pp. 5–10. W. *Stubbs in *DCB* 2 (1880), pp. 177 f., s.v. 'Erkenwald'.

Eric of Auxerre. See HEIRIC OF AUXERRE.

Erigena (or more correctly **Eriugena**), John the Scot (*c*.810–*c*.877), philosopher. An Irishman, he went abroad and gained the patronage of Charles the Bald, who gave him charge of the palace school at Laon. So far as is known, he held no ecclesiastical appointment, but was a scholar in attendance on the king. The latter years of his life are very obscure. The tradition that he was invited to England by *Alfred and taught in the abbey of

*Malmesbury rests on a mistaken identification with a later John made by *William of Malmesbury.

Erigena's philosophy, which was suspected of heterodoxy only at a much later date, is an attempted reconciliation of the *Neoplatonist idea of emanation with the Christian idea of creation. In his greatest work, *Periphyseon* or *De Divisione Naturae*, he urged that Nature should be divided into four categories. First, Nature which is not created but creates, i.e. God; secondly, Nature which is created and which creates, i.e. the world of primordial causes or Platonic ideas; thirdly, Nature which is created and which does not create, i.e. things perceived through the senses; and lastly, Nature which neither creates nor is created, i.e. God, to whom all things must in the end return. Thus the world was held to begin and end with God. There is a strong savour of pantheism about his teaching; and the treatise was condemned at *Paris in 1210 and again by *Honorius III at Sens in 1225. In his *De Divina Praedestinatione*, written against *Gottschalk, he argued that in reality, i.e. for God, evil is non-existent, and in consequence sin and its punishment are corollaries, the sin bearing the punishment in itself.

Erigena was a deeply original thinker and a great scholar, with a knowledge of Greek which was quite exceptional for his time. He did an important work in translating the writings of *Dionysius the Ps.-Areopagite into Latin and writing a commentary on his *Celestial Hierarchy*. He also translated the *Ambigua* and the *Quaestiones ad Thalassium* of St *Maximus the Confessor and the *De Hominis Opificio* of St *Gregory of Nyssa (which he called *De Imagine*), and wrote a number of exegetical works.

Collected Works, ed. H. J. Floss for J. P. Migne, *PL* 122. 125–1244. Crit. edns. of *Periphyseon* (*De Divisione Naturae*), bks. 1–3, with Eng. tr. I. P. Sheldon-Williams and L. Bieler [Scriptores Latini Hiberniae, 7, 9, and 11; Dublin, 1968–81); bk. 4, ed. É. A. Jeauneau, with Eng. tr. by J. J. O'Meara and I. P. Sheldon-Williams, ibid., 13; 1995); of his *Carmina*, with Eng. tr., by M. W. Herren (ibid. 12; 1993); of his *De Divina Praedestinatione*, by G. Madec (CCCM 50; 1978); of his *Expositiones in Hierarchiam Caelestem* by J. Barbet (ibid. 31; 1975); of his tr. of Maximus the Confessor's *Quaestiones ad Thalassium* by C. Laga and C. Steel (CCSG 7 and 22; 1980–90); of his comm. on the prologue to Jn., with Fr. tr., by É. Jeauneau (SC 151; 1969) and of his (incomplete) comm. on Jn. by id. (ibid. 180; 1972); two letters, ed. E. Dümmler, *MGH*, Epistolae, 6 (1925), pp. 158–62; full text of his comm. on the *De nuptiis Philologiae et Mercurii* of Martianus Capella first ed. C. E. Lutz (Mediaeval Academy of America Publication 34; Cambridge, Mass., 1939); his tr. of Gregory of Nyssa's *De Imagine* ed. M. Cappuyns, OSB, in *RTAM* 32 (1965), pp. 205–62. Eng. tr. of *Periphyseon* by I. P. Sheldon-Williams, rev. by J. J. O'Meara (Cahiers d'études médiévales, Cahier spécial, 3; Montreal, 1987). The comm. on *Boethius' *Opuscula Sacra* attributed to Erigena ed. E. K. Rand (Quellen und Untersuchungen zur lateinischen Philologie des Mittelalters, 1, Heft 2; 1906); the authenticity of the ascription of this work to Erigena has been challenged by M. Cappuyns, OSB, 'Le plus ancien commentaire des "Opuscula sacra" et son origine', *RTAM* 3 (1931), pp. 237–72; H. Silvestre, 'Le Commentaire inédit de Jean Scot Érigène au mètre ix du livre III du "De Consolatione Philosophiae" de Boèce', *RHE* 47 (1952), pp. 44–122; E. K. Rand, 'The Supposed Autograph of John the Scot', *University of California Publications in Classical Philology*, 5 (1920), pp. 135–41, with plates [fasc. 8].

M. Cappuyns, OSB, *Jean Scot Érigène: Sa vie, son œuvre, sa pensée* (Universitas Catholica Lovaniensis. Dissertationes . . . 2nd ser. 26; 1933); J. J. O'Meara, *Eriugena* (Oxford, 1988), incl. Eng. tr. of homily on prologue of Jn. (pp. 158–76), and bibl. M.

Cappuyns, 'Glose inédite de Jean Scot sur un passage de Maxime', *RTAM* 31 (1964), pp. 320–4, with text; id., 'Les "Bibli Vulfadi"' et Jean Scot Érigène', ibid. 33 (1966), pp. 137–9. D. Moran, *The Philosophy of John Scottus Eriugena* (Cambridge, 1989); W. Otten, *The Anthropology of Johannes Scottus Eriugena* (Brill's Studies in Intellectual History, 20; Leiden, 1991). Proceedings of various international conferences on Erigena, esp. R. Roques (ed.), *Jean Scot Érigène et l'histoire de la Philosophie* (Colloques Internationaux du Centre National de la Recherche Scientifique, 561; 1977), W. Beierwaltes (ed.), *Eriugena: Studien zu seinen Quellen* (Abh. (Heid.), 1980, Abh. 3); G.-H. Allard (ed.), *Jean Scot Écrivain* (Cahiers d'études médiévales, Cahier spécial, 1; Montreal and Paris, 1986); and W. Beierwaltes (ed.), *Eriugena Redivivus* (Abh. (Heid.), 1987, Abh. 1). M. Brennan, 'A Bibliography of Publications in the Field of Eriugenian Studies, 1800–1975', *Studi Medievali*, 3rd ser. 18 (1977), pp. 401–47. R. Roques in *Dict. Sp.* 8 (1974), cols. 735–61, s.v. 'Jean Scot (Érigène)'.

Ernesti, Johann August (1707–81), German *Lutheran theologian. For the first part of his career he was chiefly engaged in classical teaching, and brought out several famous editions of ancient authors. After holding professorships in Leipzig in non-religious subjects, he became in 1759 a theological professor there. His chief importance lies in his attempt to reconcile the theological tradition of his Church with historical criticism of the Bible, in opposition alike to uncritical rationalism and to mystical and allegorical interpretation. He insisted that the meaning of Scripture must be determined by philological and grammatical considerations and not by dogmatic presuppositions. His principal work was his *Institutio interpretis Novi Testamenti* (1761).

Collected works in *Opuscula Oratoria, Orationes, Prolusiones et Elogia* (Leipzig, 1762), *Opuscula Philologica Critica* (ibid., 1764; 2nd edn., 1776), *Opuscula Theologica* (ibid., 1773) and *Opuscula Varii Argumenti* (ibid., 1794). Eulogy by A. W. Ernesti is appended to the *Opusculorum Oratoriorum Novum Volumen* (ibid., 1791), pp. 253–72. G. Heinrici in *PRE* (3rd. edn.), 5 (1898), pp. 469–74.

Errington, George (1804–86), titular RC Abp. of Trebizond. A native of Yorkshire, he attended St Cuthbert's College, Ushaw (1814–21) and then entered the *English College in Rome. He was appointed its vice-rector in 1832, but a breakdown in his health forced him to resign the post. Eight years later, in 1840, he returned to England with N. P. S. *Wiseman. He was president of St Mary's College, Oscott (1843–7) and then served as a mission priest in Liverpool and Salford. After the re-establishment of the RC hierarchy (1850), he was made Bp. of Plymouth in 1851, but left his diocese in 1855, when he was appointed coadjutor to Wiseman and titular Abp. of Trebizond, with the right of succession to the see of *Westminster. During the following years his relations with Wiseman became strained owing to his coolness towards converts from the *Oxford Movement, and esp. towards H. E. *Manning, and in 1860 the cardinals advised Errington's removal. After he rejected a proposal of *Pius IX that he should resign, his connection with Westminster was severed by the Pope in 1862. Though twice offered sees elsewhere, Errington refused to leave England, still hoping to secure succession to Westminster after Wiseman's death. In 1869–70 he took part in the First *Vatican Council, where he was one of the signatories of the Anti-Infallibility Petition. He spent his remaining years as tutor of the theological students at St Paul's College, Prior Park.

W. Ward, *The Life and Times of Cardinal Wiseman*, 2 (1897), pp. 253–88, 321–94, and 587–637. E. [R.] Norman, *The English Catholic Church in the Nineteenth Century* (Oxford, 1984), esp. pp. 131–8, 259–62, and 307 f. C. Kent in *DNB* 17 (1889), p. 398.

Erskine, Ebenezer (1680–1754), leader of the most important 18th-cent. secession from the Church of *Scotland (those who seceded are sometimes referred to as the 'Secession Church'). Minister at Portmoak from 1703 and at Stirling from 1731, he was fervently loyal to the Reformed and Covenanting tradition, deploring the inroads allegedly being made upon it by the authorities of his day. He thus declined to take the Oath of Abjuration of the Pretender imposed by Act of Parliament in 1712 on grounds of its *Erastian form, though certainly not because of any personal allegiance to the Stuart cause. A sermon which he preached in 1732 against 'respect for persons' (upholding the rights of ordinary Church members) in ministerial settlements ('God's promise of guidance is given not to heritors or patrons but to the Church, the Body of Christ') brought him into conflict with the socially deferential General Assembly. He and three other ministers felt obliged to 'make a secession' from the 'prevailing party' in the Established Church, forming themselves into an 'associate presbytery' in Dec. 1733. In 1736 he issued a 'judicial testimony' against the Established Church, and in 1740 he was formally deposed from his charge. Within a few years, and despite internal divisions, the Seceders had become a powerful Evangelical force in the religious life of Scotland. They divided in 1747 over the *Burgher Oath but came together again in the *United Secession Church in 1820. Erskine's sermons have been described as 'probably the finest religious literature that Scottish Protestantism has generated'.

Sermons and Discourses (4 vols., Edinburgh, 1761). A. R. McEwen, *The Erskines* [1900]. J. M'Kerrow, *History of the Secession Church* (1839; rev. edn., 1841), esp. pp. 37–67 and 810–19; J. H. Leckie, *Secession Memories: The United Presbyterian Contribution to the Scottish Church* (Edinburgh, 1926), pp. 13–66. P. H. van Harten, *De Prediking van Ebenezer en Ralph Erskine* (Utrecht thesis; The Hague [1987]), with summary in Eng. A. Gordon in *DNB* 17 (1889), pp. 404–7.

Erskine, Thomas (1788–1870), Scottish religious thinker. Erskine trained as a lawyer and was admitted as a member of the Faculty of Advocates in Edinburgh in 1810. When he succeeded to the family estates at Linlathen, Angus, in 1816, he gave up the bar and devoted himself to the study of theology, making personal contact with religious and philosophical thinkers of diverse views in many countries, and publishing a number of books. He developed very liberal opinions, finding the true meaning of Christianity mainly in its conformity with man's spiritual and ethical needs. In 1831 he warmly took up the cause of J. McLeod *Campbell after his deposition by the General Assembly for teaching the universal atonement. In England he was attracted to the teaching of F. D. *Maurice. Erskine never severed formal connection with the Church of Scotland, though he used to read the service of the BCP.

W. Hanna, *Letters of Thomas Erskine of Linlathen* (2 vols., 1877). H. F. Henderson, *Erskine of Linlathen: Selections and Biography* (1899). N. R. Needham, *Thomas Erskine of Linlathen: His Life and Theology 1788–1837* (Rutherford Studies, 1st ser. 3; Edinburgh [1990]). W. Benham in *DNB* 17 (1889), pp. 444 f.

eschatology (from Gk. ἔσχατος, 'last', and λόγος, 'discourse'), the doctrine of the last things, that is the ultimate destiny both of the individual soul and the whole created order. The term first appears in English in the 19th cent., but the topic forms the subject of the final section of the creeds and systematic theologies. When the end of the world did not come as expected in the early Church, it became peripheral to most Christian theology, but the imminent expectation of it erupted from time to time in sectarian circles (see MILLENARIANISM). Meanwhile, the concept was gradually individualized. The author of Ecclus. 7: 36 had advised his readers to 'remember your last things' (LXX: τὰ ἔσχατά σου), i.e. 'the end of your life' (RSV) and the 'Four Last Things', death, judgement, heaven, and hell, formed the subjects of *Advent preaching. In the 19th cent. ideas of historical development fuelled the secularized eschatologies of G. W. F. *Hegel and Karl Marx, and the discovery of early Jewish *Apocalypses drew the attention of biblical scholars to the eschatological material in Scripture. In the OT it is sometimes associated with *Messianic hopes (e.g. Jer. 23: 5–6), but usually not (e.g. Jer. 31). Apocalypses from Daniel to Revelation are often strongly eschatological, as is the *Qumran material, whereas Rabbinic material contains proportionately much less. Mk. 13, Mt. 24, and the writings of St *Paul show how important this expectation of the end of this age was for early Christianity, but it was above all the claim of J. *Weiss in 1892 that Christ Himself spoke primarily of God's final intervention that made systematic theologians aware of the centrality of eschatology. A. *Schweitzer popularized this view of Christ and saw in it the key to His whole strategy. Others, notably C. H. *Dodd (following R. *Otto) eliminated this futuristic aspect of the phrase '*kingdom of God' by describing His teaching as 'realized eschatology'. The extent of the eschatological element in Christ's teaching is disputed among exegetes (see JESUS CHRIST), but most feel that Schweitzer failed to do justice to His moral teaching. K. *Barth and R. *Bultmann reinterpreted the concept, stressing its relationship to Christ, but eliminating its future scope. Recent attempts to retrieve this, like those of J. *Moltmann and the *liberation theologians, owe much to Marxism but have a strongly biblical character. See also PAROUSIA.

The large number of studies on the subject generally incl. F. *von Hügel, *Eternal Life* (1912); [A. W. H.] P. Althaus, *Die letzten Dinge* (Gütersloh, 1922; 5th edn., 1949); J. *Baillie, *And the Life Everlasting* (1934); A. E. *Taylor, *The Christian Hope of Immortality* (1938); M. Werner, *Die Entstehung des christlichen Dogmas* (Berne, 1941; 2nd edn., Tübingen, 1954; Eng. tr., 1957); J. A. T. *Robinson, *Jesus and His Coming: The Emergence of a Doctrine* (1957); R. Bultmann, *History and Eschatology* (Gifford Lectures, 1955; Edinburgh, 1957); J. Moltmann, *Theologie der Hoffnung* (1964; Eng. tr., 1967). On the biblical teaching, besides the works of A. Schweitzer and K. Barth (qq.v.), important studies incl. H. *Gunkel, *Schöpfung und Chaos in Urzeit und Endzeit* (1895; Eng. tr. of part in B. W. Anderson (ed.), *Creation in the Old Testament* (Issues in Religion and Theology, 6; 1984), pp. 25–52); H. Gressmann, *Die Ursprung der israelitisch-jüdischen Eschatologie* (Forschungen zur Religion und Literatur des Alten und Neuen Testaments, 6; 1905); S. [O. P.] *Mowinckel, *Han som kommer* (1951; Eng. tr., *He That Cometh*, Oxford, 1956); H. P. Müller, *Ursprünge und Strukturen alttestamentlicher Eschatologie* (Beihefte zur *ZATW*, 109; 1969); D. E. Gowan, *Eschatology in the Old Testament* (Edinburgh, 1987); and a collection of essays of various dates ed. H. D. Preuss, *Eschatologie im Alten Testament* (Weg der Forschung, 480; Darmstadt, 1978). R. H. *Charles, *A Critical History of the Doctrine of a Future Life in Israel, in Judaism and in Christianity* (Jowett Lectures for 1898–9; 1899; 2nd edn., 1913). J. Weiss, *Die Predigt Jesu vom Reiche Gottes* (1892; 2nd edn., 1900; Eng. tr. of 1st edn., 1971); R. Otto, *Reich Gottes und Menschensohn* (1934; Eng. tr., 1938); C. H. Dodd, *The Parables of the Kingdom* (1935); id., *The Apostolic Preaching and its Developments* (1936), esp. Appendix on 'Eschatology and History', pp. 193–240; A. N. Wilder, *Eschatology and Ethics in the Teaching of Jesus* (New York, 1939; rev. edn., 1950); W. G. Kümmel, *Verheissung und Erfüllung: Untersuchungen zur eschatologischen Verkündigung Jesu* (Abhandlungen zur Theologie des Alten und Neuen Testaments, 6; 1945; 2nd edn., 1953; Eng. tr., 1957); N. Perrin, *The Kingdom of God in the Teaching of Jesus* (1963); A. T. Lincoln, *Paradise Now and Not Yet: Studies in the Role of the Heavenly Dimension in Paul's Thought with Special Reference to his Eschatology* (Society for New Testament Studies Monograph Series, 43; Cambridge, 1981); and a collection of essays of various dates ed. B. Chilton, *The Kingdom of God* (Issues in Religion and Theology, 5; 1984). On patristic eschatology, B. E. Daley, *The Hope of the Early Church* (Cambridge, 1991). A. Feuillet in *Dict. Bibl.*, Suppl. 6 (1960), cols. 1331–419, s.v. 'Parousie'; D. L. Petersen and others in *Anchor Bible Dictionary*, 2 (1992), pp. 575–609, s.v. See also bibl. to APOCALYPTIC LITERATURE.

Esdras, Books of. 'Esdras' is the Greek and Latin form of *Ezra. In the *Septuagint there are two books of this title—Esdras A, a Greek book based on parts of 2 Chron., Ez., and Neh., with an interpolated story not extant in Hebrew; and Esdras B, a straightforward rendering of the Hebrew Ezra-Neh. (treated as one book). In the current form of the *Vulgate these are increased to four, namely: I and II Esdras, i.e. St *Jerome's rendering of Ezra and Neh., treated as separate books; III Esdras, the *Old Latin version of Esdras A; and IV Esdras, another book not extant in Greek (see below). For the original Vulgate Jerome deliberately confined himself to the first two of these, rejecting the other two as uncanonical (*Praef. in Esd., c. Vigil.* 7); but all four books are commonly included (with some confusion in the numbering) in Latin biblical MSS. In 1546 the Council of *Trent (sess. 4) finally rejected III and IV Esdras from the RC *Canon, and in subsequent editions of the Vulgate they appear (with the Prayer of *Manasses) as an Appendix following the NT. In the *Geneva Bible (1560) and subsequent English Versions, I and II Esdras of the Vulgate are entitled 'Ezra' and 'Nehemiah', while III and IV Esdras are the '1' and '2' Esdras of the Apocrypha.

1 ESDRAS (i.e. Esdras A of the LXX, III Esdras of the Vulgate, or *The Greek Ezra*) recounts the story of Israel from Josiah to Ezra. It is mainly composed of matter taken from the Heb. canonical books:

(a) 1–2 are taken from 2 Chron. 35 and 36, Ez. 1 and 4: 7–24, and contain nothing original. The material from Ez. 4: 7–24 is here placed in a different context (1 Esd. 2: 16–30); it is possible that 1 Esdras here gives a more reliable chronology than the canonical Ezra.

(*b*) 3: 1–5: 6: a story of the competition of three young men of the bodyguard of Darius in solving the riddle 'What thing is strongest?' The victory is found to rest with neither 'wine' nor 'the king' nor 'women', but with 'truth'. This leads on to a speech by Zerubbabel (see ZECHARIAH), in favour of monotheism as the worship of the God of Truth. Adjudged the winner, Zerubbabel receives as his prize from Darius royal assistance for the Jews in their rebuilding of the Temple. This story finds no parallel in the Heb. canonical books.

(*c*) 5: 7–9: 55: a list of the returning exiles (Ez. 2) and subsequent narrative concerning Ezra, taken from Ez. 3: 1–4: 5 and 5–10, Neh. 7: 73–8: 13.

There is no agreement about the origin of the work. Some have argued that 'the Greek Ezra' was a re-editing of Esdras B found in the Septuagint, i.e. the straightforward Greek version of Ezra-Neh. (E. *Schürer), or of some other Greek translation (H. *Ewald); others have claimed that it was derived independently from the Heb. (H. St J. Thackeray). From the Lat. of 4: 41 comes the often cited sentence *Magna est veritas et praevalet* (frequently misquoted as *praevalebit*), 'Great is truth and it prevails' (or 'will prevail'). The book is generally dated between *c*.200 and *c*.50 BC.

2 ESDRAS (IV Esdras of the Vulgate, or *The Ezra-Apocalypse*) is composite, viz.:

(*a*) 1–2: an introductory section beginning *Liber Esdrae Prophetae Secundus*, extant only in Latin. This is a denunciation of the sins of Israel, largely following in phraseology and content the OT prophets. Part of it (esp. 2: 10–48) is also based on the NT and Christian belief, e.g. the vision of the multitude of the redeemed and of the Son of God in 2: 42–8 (the only definitely Christian passage in the Apocrypha).

(*b*) 3–14: the 'Ezra-Apocalypse' proper. This Jewish work is the oldest part of the composite 2 Esdras. The writer, speaking in the name of Salathiel ('who am also Ezra'), relates his visions and discourses with an angel. Ch. 13 contains a vision of the Messiah described as a Man, seen rising from the depths of the sea (i.e. from somewhere inaccessible to human knowledge, 13: 51–2), who destroys a hostile multitude by the breath of his mouth (cf. 2 Thess. 2: 8) and gathers to himself a peaceable multitude (explained as the *Ten Tribes, 13: 39 f.).

This central section of the book (3–14) was probably written in Hebrew. It is extant in Syriac, Ethiopic, Arabic, Armenian, Sahidic, and Georgian versions as well as in Latin; a Greek version (not recovered) is quoted by *Clement of Alexandria (*Strom.* 3. 16) and in the *Apostolic Constitutions* (8. 7). The visions of the Eagle (chs. 11–12) and of the Man, and the story of Ezra and the scriptural canon (ch. 14), were believed by G. H. Box to be of different authorship from the rest of the 'Ezra-Apocalypse'. The Apocalypse proper is dated by most scholars after the fall of Jerusalem (AD 70) and reasons are advanced for placing it not later than the reign of Hadrian (117–38).

(*c*) 15–16. These chapters, which are no part of the Ezra-Apocalypse, were apparently written as a Christian appendix to 2 Esdras (IV Esdras of the Vulgate) and in some MSS are separately reckoned as 'V Esdras', or sometimes (where chs. 1–2 are reckoned as 'V Esdras') 'VI Esdras', but they never appear to have been separately current.

On 1 Esdras, S. A. *Cook in R. H. *Charles (ed.), *The Apocrypha and Pseudepigrapha of the Old Testament*, 1 (Oxford, 1913), pp. 1–58. C. C. Torrey, *Ezra Studies* (Chicago, 1910); id., 'A Revised View of First Esdras', in *Louis Ginzberg Jubilee Volume on the Occasion of his Seventieth Birthday* (New York, 1945), pp. 395–410. Modern comm. by J. M. Myers (Anchor Bible, 1974, on 1 and 2 Esd., pp. 1–104) and R. J. Coggins (New Camb. Bib., 1979, on 1 and 2 Esd., pp. 4–75).

On 2 Esdras, Lat. text ed. R. L. Bensly, with introd. by M. R. James (Texts and Studies, 3, no. 2; Cambridge, 1895); also by A. F. J. Klijn (TU 131; 1983). Syriac text ed. R. J. Bidawid, *The Old Testament in Syriac according to the Peshitta Version*, pt. 4, fasc. 3 (Leiden, 1973), 2nd item. Lat. text, with Fr. trs. of Syriac and Ethiopic versions, and comm. by L. Gry (2 vols. Paris, 1938). Eng. tr., with comm. and Lat. text in appendix, by G. H. Box, *The Ezra-Apocalypse: Being Chapters 3–14 of the Book commonly known as 4 Ezra, or II Esdras* (1912); further Eng. tr. of the same section, with comm., by id. in R. H. Charles, *The Apocrypha and Pseudepigrapha of the Old Testament*, 2 (Oxford, 1913), pp. 542–624; Eng. tr. of the whole of 2 Esdras (chs. 1–16) by B. M. Metzger in J. H. Charlesworth (ed.), *The Old Testament Pseudepigrapha*, 1 (1983), pp. 517 59. Modern comm. on the whole of 2 Esdras by J. M. Myers (Anchor Bible, 1974, on 1 and 2 Esdras, pp. 105–354), M. A. Knibb (New Camb. Bib., 1979, on 1 and 2 Esd., pp. 76–305), and J. Schreiner (Jüdische Schriften aus hellenistisch-römischer Zeit, Band 4, Lieferung 4; 1981). T. A. Bergren, *Fifth Ezra: The Text, Origin and Early History* (Society of Biblical Literature, Septuagint and Cognate Studies Series, 25; Atlanta [1990]).

Espen, Zeger Bernhard Van. See VAN ESPEN, ZEGER BERNHARD.

Espousals of the Blessed Virgin Mary (*Desponsatio BVM*). A feast of the Latin Church. Its institution in honour of St *Joseph was advocated by P. *d'Ailly and J. *Gerson, but its existence as a feast of Mary is first attested in 1517, when *Leo X permitted its celebration to the Nuns of the Annunciation. Since then it has spread to several countries, notably Germany and Spain, but its observance has never been extended to the Universal Church. It is usually kept on 23 Jan.

Essays and Reviews (1860). A collection of essays by seven authors who believed in the necessity of free inquiry in religious matters. Among them were M. *Pattison's 'Tendencies of Religious Thought in England, 1688–1750', B. *Jowett's 'The Interpretation of Scripture', and F. *Temple's 'The Education of the World'. The volume at first attracted little notice and the *Guardian* reviewed it in a temperate although hostile manner, but when Bp. S. *Wilberforce denounced its liberalism in violent terms in the *Quarterly*, general interest was aroused. A meeting of the bishops at Fulham condemned the book in Feb. 1861, and the archbishop issued this condemnation as an encyclical. The Lower House of *Convocation proposed a synodical condemnation, and legal action was taken against two of the essayists (H. B. Wilson and R. Williams), who were condemned to deprivation for a year, although they secured the reversal of this verdict by the *Judicial Committee of the Privy Council. As a protest against the minimizing spirit of the volume, 11,000 clergymen declared their belief in the inspiration of the Scriptures and the eternity of punishment, and the book was at length synodically condemned in 1864.

H. P. *Liddon, *Life of Edward Bouverie Pusey*, esp. 4 (1897), pp. 38–62 and 68–81. I. Ellis, *Seven against Christ: A Study of 'Essays and Reviews'* (Studies in the History of Christian Thought, 23; Leiden, 1980).

Essays Catholic and Critical (1926). An influential volume of fifteen essays by a group of *Anglo-Catholic scholars on leading themes of Christian belief, with special attention to the issues raised by recent biblical studies and philosophy. The editor was E. G. Selwyn (1885–1959; later Dean of *Winchester), the other contributors E. O. James, A. E. *Taylor, A. E. J. Rawlinson, W. L. Knox, L. S. Thornton, E. C. *Hoskyns, J. K. Mozley, E. J. Bicknell, K. E. *Kirk, E. Milner-White, A. H. Thompson, N. P. *Williams, and W. Spens. The essayists maintained that the terms 'catholic' and 'critical' were not antithetical, but stood for two movements which in union led to a deeper understanding of historic Christianity. Typical of the book are essays seeking to reconcile religion with primitive anthropology and the fact of the *Fall with psychological theories of human nature, and to reinterpret the Person and Work of Christ in the light of contemporary criticism of the *Synoptic Gospels.

Essenes. A Jewish ascetic sect, mentioned neither in the Bible nor the *Talmud, but referred to by *Philo, *Josephus, and the elder Pliny. The name may mean 'the pious ones' or (perhaps more likely) 'the healers'. They seem to have originated in the 2nd cent. BC, and come to an end in the 2nd cent. AD, and never to have passed beyond the limits of Palestine. At the beginning of the Christian era they numbered about 4,000. Their manner of life was highly organized and communistic; they imposed on candidates for membership a three-year novitiate, with oaths of obedience and secrecy; and they abstained from all but the simplest forms of earning their livelihood. Their piety was in some respects akin to that preached by *Judaism of a *Pharisaic type, though it is possible that details of their worship and teaching came from non-Jewish sources. The suggestions, occasionally made, that various figures in the early Church, including even Christ Himself, had Essene connections, remain unsubstantiated. The '*therapeutae' mentioned by Philo are very similar to the Essenes, but are prob. not identical. Many scholars have identified the Essenes with the community of the Dead Sea Scrolls (q.v.).

The chief sources are Josephus, *Jewish Antiquities*, 13. 5. 9; 15. 10. 4 f.; 18. 1. 5; id., *Jewish War*, 2. 8. 2–13; Philo in *Eusebius, *Praeparatio Evangelica*, 8. 11, and Pliny, *Natural History*, 5. 17. Convenient collection of texts by A. Adam, *Antike Berichte über die Essener* (Kleine Texte, 182; 1961; 2nd edn. by C. Burchard, 1972). Texts also ed., with Eng. tr. and introd., by G. Vermes and M. D. Goodman, *The Essenes according to the Classical Sources* (Sheffield, 1989). J. B. *Lightfoot, *St Paul's Epistles to the Colossians and to Philemon* (1875), pp. 83–95 and 114–79. S. Wagner, *Die Essener in der wissenschaftlichen Diskussion vom Ausgang des 18. bis zum Beginn des 20. Jahrhunderts: Eine wissenschaftsgeschichtliche Studie* (Beiheft zur *ZATW*, 79; 1960). E. *Schürer, *The History of the Jewish People in the Age of Jesus Christ*, rev. Eng. tr. by G. Vermes and others, 2 (Edinburgh, 1979), pp. 555–74 and 583–90, with bibl. B. Rigaux, OFM, in *DHGE* 15 (1963), cols. 1013–35; J. J. Collins in *Anchor Bible Dictionary*, 2 (1992), pp. 619–26, both s.v., with bibl.

Establishment. In ecclesiastical usage the term is applied to the recognition by the state of a particular Church as that of the state. It implies a relationship of the two bodies, but the closeness of that relationship varies widely from the *theocracy of 16th cent. *Geneva to the situation in *Scotland, where the *Presbyterian Church, though established, is virtually independent of state control. Whether a Church is established or not, ultimate power inevitably rests with the secular authority. In OT Judaism and in much of the ancient world, religious observance was a part of the civil order, but the first move towards the establishment of the Christian Church must be dated from the time of the Emp. *Constantine (d. 337); he not only granted toleration to Christianity but gave the Church a favoured position in the Empire and exercised considerable control over its affairs. The Emp. *Theodosius (379–95) took the process a stage further, making heresy a legal offence as well as using the power of the state to combat paganism. Imperial control of the Church was far greater in the E. than in the W., but as Christianity spread throughout Europe, it was the conversion of the rulers which was the key factor, and esp. among the Germanic tribes, those who provided the endowments for the Church claimed rights of patronage. During the Middle Ages there were numerous disputes between lay rulers and the Papacy (e.g. the *Investiture Controversy); despite the growth and centralization of Papal power, there were determined efforts to restrict its exercise, e.g. in Sicily, where *Ferdinand the Catholic in 1514 proclaimed himself responsible for both spiritual and temporal affairs. After the Reformation the RC Church remained as the established religion in much of Europe (as recently as 1953 it was recognized as 'the only religion of the Spanish nation'), but elsewhere, most notably in *France, the Church was largely under the controlling influence of the Crown. In Protestant states, as the jurisdiction of the Pope was repudiated, national Churches were established. '*Cuius regio, eius religio' was a natural extension of Germanic principles and only took a stage further the claims of medieval emperors and kings to have an authority parallel to that of the Pope, and of equally Divine origin. The establishment of national Churches completely rejecting the authority of the Pope, while asserting their continuity with the primitive Church, involved some adjustments; these normally included financial support for the established Church by the state and more direct control over appointments and other matters. By the 18th cent., however, the whole idea of established Churches was being challenged. The American constitution forbade an establishment of religion, on grounds of principle. In *Ireland and *Wales the Anglican Church was disestablished in 1869 and 1919 respectively, mainly because it was not the Church of the majority of the Christian inhabitants. More generally the secularization of society in the 19th and 20th cents. has led to the separation of Church and state and the consequent disestablishment of the Church in parts of Europe, e.g. in the *Netherlands in 1848 and in France in 1910. In South America, Asia, and Africa the establishment of independent states normally involved the separation of Church and state and the disestablishment of Churches set up by the former colonial powers.

In England the C of E is the established Church. Its peculiar position is reflected in the fact that 26 of its bishops have seats in the House of Lords, while no other ecclesiastical body is so represented *ex officio*. In turn a measure of control over its affairs is exercised by the state. This balance is immediately due to what is known as the 'Royal Supremacy'. The Act of *Supremacy of 1534, which was one of the key elements in the English Reformation, declared *Henry VIII 'the only supreme head in earth of the Church of England'. When the Act (repealed under *Mary) was restored under *Elizabeth I, she was more modestly described as 'the only supreme governor of this realm . . . as well in all spiritual or ecclesiastical things or causes as temporal'. This distinction was continued by *Charles II in the Declaration which forms a preface to the *Thirty-Nine Articles and is echoed in Article 37. What, however, began under Henry VIII as an exclusively royal supremacy (aimed at excluding Papal jurisdiction and claiming authority for the *divine right of kings derived from the status of the kings of Judah in the OT) was, with the general constitutional shift, to become by the end of the 17th cent. mainly a Parliamentary Supremacy. After the Reformation the only way of enacting new legislation for the Church was by authority of Act of Parliament. This situation was somewhat modified by the *Enabling Act (1919) which conferred power on the *Church Assembly (now superseded by the General *Synod) of the C of E to legislate on any matter by Measure. Parliament, however, retained ultimate control in that no Measure is effective until it receives the Royal Assent, which can be given only if the Measure is presented to the Sovereign with the approval of both Houses of Parliament. A further step towards independence was achieved with the approval by Parliament of the Church of England (*Worship and Doctrine) Measure (1974), which gave the General Synod power to legislate by Canon on forms of worship. Canons (formerly passed only by *Convocation) are of limited effect, being binding only on ecclesiastical *personae*, and of no effect if in any way contrary to the general law of the land, and therefore unable to modify the BCP, which had the statutory authority of the Acts of *Uniformity. In addition, since the Reformation, Canons have required, and still require, the Royal Assent. The Crown has also a wide measure of patronage. Some of this (e.g. *advowsons) is little different from that vested in individuals and corporations, but much derives from the Act of Supremacy whereby the Crown appoints all bishops and deans, albeit, in the case of diocesan bishops, after considerable consultation with representatives of the Church. (For current practice see CROWN APPOINTMENTS COMMISSION.) A further aspect of the Royal Supremacy can be seen in the fact that the Church's Courts are, like all courts of law, the Queen's Courts, whose decisions are binding on everyone. See also ERASTIANISM.

On the establishment of the C of E, E. G. Moore, *An Introduction to English Canon Law* (Clarendon Law Series, Oxford, 1967), pp. 10–16; 3rd edn. by T. Briden and B. Hanson (London, 1992), pp. 10–15; *Halsbury's Laws of England* (4th edn.), 14 (1975), pp. 163–71 (paras. 345–60). E. T. Davies, *Episcopacy and Royal Supremacy in the Church of England in the XVIth Century* (Oxford,

1950), pp. 59–137; C. Cross, *The Royal Supremacy in the Elizabethan Church* (Historical Problems, Studies and Documents, 8; 1969); id., 'Churchmen and the Royal Supremacy' in F. Heal and R. O'Day (eds.), *Church and Society in England: Henry VIII to James I* (1977), pp. 15–34. H. Chadwick, 'Royal ecclesiastical supremacy' in B. Bradshaw and E. Duffy (eds.), *Humanism, Reform and Reformation: The Career of Bishop John Fisher* (Cambridge, 1989), pp. 169–203.

Esther, Book of. This Book relates an episode in the reign of Xerxes I (here called 'Ahasuerus'), King of Persia from 486 to 465 BC. It tells how Esther, a kinswoman of the Jew, Mordecai, attained a position of influence and honour as the royal consort, and used it to save her fellow-countrymen when they were in danger of extermination by the grand-vizier, Haman. Although there may be an historical basis for the story, in its present form it seems to be a popular romance; it contains indeed very little of a directly religious purport, and no mention is made in the Book of the name of God. The probable reason for its inclusion in the *canon of the OT was that it described the institution of *Purim (q.v.), a feast still kept as one of the annual commemorations of the Jewish year. Nothing is known of the author. The Greek Bible contains certain additional chapters, which appear in the English Bible in the *Apocrypha; they supply further detail not found in the Hebrew version as we have it today. There are no quotations from Esther in the NT nor, so far, have any fragments of the Book been found among the biblical MSS at *Qumran.

Comm. by L. B. Paton (ICC, 1908), H. *Gunkel (Tübingen, 1916), M. Haller (HAT, Reihe 1, 18, on Ruth, Song of Songs, Est., Lam., 1940), pp. 114–36, repr., with introd. by E. Würthwein in 2nd edn. (1969), pp. 165–96; H. Ringgren (Das Alte Testament Deutsch, 16, on Song of Songs, Lam., Est., 1958, pp. 113–44), H. Bardtke (KAT 17. 4/5, on Eccles. and Est., 1963, pp. 239–408), C. A. Moore (Anchor Bible, 1971), A. Meinhold (Zürcher Bibelkommentare, AT 13; 1983), and D. J. A. Clines (New Cent. Bib., on Ezr., Neh., and Est., 1984, pp. 251–333). Id., *The Esther Scroll: The Story of the Story* (Journal for the Study of the Old Testament, Supplement Series, 30; Sheffield [1984]). Series of important arts. repr. in *Studies in the Book of Esther*, ed., with substantial introd., by C. A. Moore (New York [1982]), incl., pp. 130–41, B. W. Anderson, 'The Place of the Book of Esther in the Christian Bible', orig. pr. in *Journal of Religion*, 30 (1950), pp. 32–43. Eissfeldt, pp. 505–12 and 767, with further bibl. See also bibl. to PURIM.

Estienne, Henri; Robert. See STEPHANUS.

Estius (1542–1613), Latinized name of Willem Hessels van Est, exegete and hagiographer. He was a native of Gorcum in S. Holland and studied at Louvain, where one of his masters was M. *Baius. He became a doctor of theology in 1580, and professor at *Douai in 1582. In 1595 he was made chancellor of the university of Douai, the theological faculty of which at that time ranked among the foremost in Europe. His *Historia Martyrum Gorcomiensium* (1603) was a well-documented history of the *Gorcum Martyrs, to one of whom his family was related, and considered the most important piece in the process of their beatification. His principal work, the *Commentarii in Omnes Divi Pauli et Catholicas Epistolas* (1614–16), is valuable esp. for its careful exegesis of the literal sense and its judicious choice of *patristic material, following the *Antiochene rather than the *Alexandrian school. It was frequently reprinted down to the end of the 19th cent. Estius, who was considered a saint by his friends and pupils, took part in the controversies of his time, esp. in that on *Molinism, in which he opposed the *Jesuits. He also left extensive notes for a new edition of St *Augustine. He was called 'Doctor Fundatissimus' by *Benedict XIV.

All Estius' publications, except the *Historia Martyrum Gorcomiensium*, were posthumous. Collected edn. of his biblical works, 3 vols., Venice, 1659. J. Ferrer, *Pecado original y justificación en la doctrina de Guillermo Estio* (Madrid, 1960). L. Salembier in *DTC* 5 (1913), cols. 871–8, with bibl.

Eternal City, the (Lat. *Urbs Aeterna*). A designation of Rome found in classical writers such as Ovid and Tibullus, as well as in official documents of the period of the Empire. As applied to Christian Rome, it emphasizes the continuous and pervasive influence of the see in the history of (esp. W.) Christendom.

eternal life. In Christianity, not only a life of endless duration but the fullness of life of which the believer becomes possessed here and now through participation in God's eternal being. It unites the strong sense of historical process characteristic of Hebrew thought with elements from the Greek (*Platonic) belief that man's true life lies in a timeless world in which he is freed from the impediments of material and temporal existence. The modern appreciation of its implications owes much to F. D. *Maurice, for whom eternal life was sharing in the life of God and eternal death refusal to share in that life ('Eternity has nothing to do with time or duration'), and also to F. *von Hügel, notably his book *Eternal Life* (1912). In the NT its conditions are esp. emphasized in St John's Gospel.

J. Baillie, *And the Life Everlasting* (1934). F. D. Maurice, *Theological Essays* (1853), pp. 436 f. See also bibl. to IMMORTALITY.

Ethelbert, St (d. 616), King of Kent. A descendant of Hengist, the legendary ancestor of the Jutish royal house of Kent, he became king *c.*560 and is stated by *Bede to have extended his power to all England south of the Humber. His marriage with Bertha, daughter of Charibert, the Frankish king, marks the first introduction of Christianity into Anglo-Saxon England, since Charibert insisted that she should be free to practise her Christian faith (Bede, *HE* 1. 25). Probably through Bertha's influence, he welcomed St *Augustine and the Roman mission in 597, was himself converted in the same year, and thenceforward gave his full support to the cause of Christianity in his realm. He was thus the first Christian English king. Feast day, 24 Feb.; in modern calendars, 25 Feb.

Almost the sole authority is Bede, *HE* 1. 25 f. and 32 f., and 2. 3–5; the refs. in the Anglo-Saxon Chronicle, s. 565 and 568, introduce chronological difficulties. See comm. to Bede's *HE* by J. M. Wallace-Hadrill (Oxford, 1988), pp. 32–4, 36 f., 44–6, 54 f., and 59–61, with further bibl. The best edn. of his 'Dooms' (or law code), with Ger. tr., by F. Liebermann, *Die Gesetze der Angelsachsen*, 1 (ed. Savigny-Stiftung, 1903), pp. 3–8; also ed., with Eng. tr., by F. L. Attenborough, *The Laws of the Earliest English Kings* (Cambridge, 1922), pp. 4–17.

Ethelbert, St (d. 794), King of the East Angles and martyr. He is said to have been treacherously killed by

*Offa of Mercia or his wife, Cynethryth, to whose daughter he was to have been betrothed. He was buried at *Hereford, where the cathedral is placed under his patronage, jointly with that of the BVM. Feast day, 20 May.

An unreliable Life, abridged from that in the *Speculum Historiale de Gestis Regum Angliae* of Richard of Cirencester (ed. J. E. B. Mayor, RS 1, 1863, pp. 262–94), is repr. from J. Brompton, *Historiae Anglicanae Scriptores Decem* (1652), cols. 748–54, in the *AASS*, Mai. 5 (1685), pp. 241*–6*, with certain miracles from a Life by Giraldus (Cotton MS Vitell. E. VII, destroyed 1731), pp. 246* f. Summary, with other MS Lives, in Hardy, 1, pt. 2 (1862), pp. 494–6. Giraldus' Life ed. M. R. James in *EHR* 32 (1917), pp. 214–44. W. *Stubbs in *DCB* 2 (1880), pp. 215 f., s.v. 'Ethelbert (3)'.

Ethelburga, St (d. *c.*676), Abbess of Barking. She was the sister of St *Erconwald, Bp. of London, and the first abbess of his *double monastery at Barking in Essex. The dedication of the church at Bishopsgate is perhaps to be ascribed to her, but there were a number of other prominent women of the same name in Anglo-Saxon Christianity. Feast day, 11 Oct.

The chief authority is *Bede, *HE* 4. 6–9; notes in edn. of C. Plummer, 2 (Oxford, 1896), pp. 217–9, and comm. by J. M. Wallace-Hadrill (ibid., 1988), pp. 146 f.; 11th-cent. Life by *Goscelin, largely based on Bede, ed. M. L. Colker in *Studia Monastica*, 7 (1965), pp. 398–417, with introd. pp. 383–97. 'Acta' by J. Capgrave pr. in *AASS*, Oct. 5 (1786), pp. 649–52.

Etheldreda, St (d. 679), founder of the *double monastery at *Ely. The daughter of Anna, a Christian king of the East Angles, she was married at an early age to an earldorman of the South Gyrwe, but retained her virginity. On his death, three years later, she withdrew to the Isle of Ely for a life of prayer. After five years, at the request of her relatives, she returned to the world to marry Egfrith of Northumbria, but refused to consummate this marriage also. After another 12 years she obtained Egfrith's consent to become a nun and *c.*672 received the veil from St *Wilfrid at Coldingham, where her aunt, Ebbe, was abbess. About a year later she founded the double monastery of Ely, of which she was abbess until her death. From another form of her name, 'St Audrey', the word 'tawdry' is derived through the cheap finery exposed for sale at St Audrey's fair. Feast day, 23 June; of her translation, 17 Oct.

The chief authority is *Bede, *HE* 4. 3, 19 f.; comm. by J. M. Wallace-Hadrill (Oxford, 1988), pp. 159–61; see also pp. xxviii f. *Liber Eliensis* (ed. E. O. Blake, Camden Society, 3rd ser. 92; 1962, esp. pp. 1–40, *passim*). *William of Malmesbury, *Gesta Pontificum*, ed. N. E. S. A. Hamilton (RS, 1870), pp. 323 ff. C. W. Stubbs, *Historical Memorials of Ely Cathedral: Two Lectures* (1897), Lecture 1, with notes, 'The Shrine of St Audrey', pp. 1–94. C. J. Stranks, *St Etheldreda Queen and Abbess* (Ely Cathedral Monographs [7]; 1975).

Ethelhard (d. 805), Abp. of *Canterbury. (He is to be distinguished from Ethelhard, Bp. of *Winchester, d. 759.) He was prob. Abbot of 'Hlud' (? 'Lydd' or 'Louth') when, in 791, he was elected to the archbishopric, apparently as *Offa's nominee. He was not consecrated until two years later. The opposition of the Kentish people to a Mercian archbishop, which probably caused this delay, broke out openly in 796, when Eadbert Praen, a cleric and member of the royal house of Kent, headed the rebellion of the Kentish nobility and forced the archbishop to flee. After Eadbert's capture, in 798, Ethelhard recovered his see, and now strove to restore it to its old power which it had lost when Offa had obtained archiepiscopal status for *Lichfield from *Hadrian I. This was abolished in 802 after a visit of Ethelhard to *Leo III at Rome, and the Papal decision in favour of Canterbury was acknowledged by the Council of *Clovesho in 803, which marked an important step towards national unity. Throughout his life Ethelhard enjoyed the friendship of *Alcuin, who gave him active support in his difficulties.

Docs. relating to his episcopate in A. W. Haddan and W. *Stubbs (eds.), *Councils and Ecclesiastical Documents Relating to Great Britain and Ireland*, 3 (1871), pp. 467–535. Two of Alcuin's letters to him, with other information, are given by *William of Malmesbury, *Gesta Pontificum*, ed. N. E. S. A. Hamilton (RS, 1870), pp. 17–19. N. Brooks, *The Early History of the Church of Canterbury* (Leicester, 1984), pp. 179 f.

Ethelwold, St (*c*.908–84). Bp. of *Winchester. Like St *Dunstan, with whom he was closely associated all his life, he was one of the leaders of the reform movement in the English Church in the late 10th cent. He was first a monk at *Glastonbury, then Abbot of Abingdon, and from 963 Bp. of Winchester. Together with St Dunstan and St *Oswald of Worcester he effected the revival of English monasticism, which had fallen on evil days during the anarchy and confusion of the Danish invasions; he took as his model Continental usages, including those of the abbey of *Fleury. The *Regularis Concordia* was partly, perhaps mainly, his work. He is very probably the author of an account of the monastic revival of his time ('King Edgar's Establishment of the Monasteries'). He was also responsible for translating the 'Rule of St *Benedict' into English; his concern for precision and clarity was a factor in establishing the Winchester dialect as the standard literary language in the late Old English period. Feast day, 1 Aug.

[M. M.] A. Schröer (ed.), *Die angelsächsischen Prosabearbeitungen der Benedictinerregel* (Bibliothek der angelsächsischen Prosa, 2; Kassel, 1885; repr. with additional material by H. Gneuss, Darmstadt, 1964). The Proem to the *Regularis Concordia* and 'An Account of King Edgar's Establishment of Monasteries' are conveniently pr. in *Councils & Synods ... I*, A.D. 871–1204, ed. D. Whitelock, M. Brett, and C. N. L. Brooke, 1 (Oxford, 1981), pp. 133–41 and 142–54. Lives by Wulfstan, monk of Winchester, and *Aelfric, ed., with Eng. tr., by M. Lapidge and M. Winterbottom, *Wulfstan of Winchester: The Life of St Æthelwold* (Oxford Medieval Texts, 1991). D. J. V. Fisher, 'The Early Biographies of St Ethelwold', *EHR* 67 (1952), pp. 381–91. J. A. *Robinson, *The Life and Times of St Dunstan* (1923), pp. 104–22. E. John, 'The Beginning of the Benedictine Reform in England', *R. Bén.* 73 (1963), pp. 73–87. H. Gneuss, 'The Origin of Standard Old English and Æthelwold's School at Winchester', *Anglo-Saxon England*, 1 (1972), pp. 63–83; M. Gretsch, 'Æthelwold's Translation of the *Regula Sancti Benedicti* and its Latin Exemplar', ibid. 3 (1974), pp. 125–51. B. Yorke (ed.), *Bishop Æthelwold: His Career and Influence* (Woodbridge, Suffolk, 1988). D. Parsons (ed.), *Tenth-Century Studies: Essays in Commemoration of the Millennium of the Council of Winchester and Regularis Concordia* (1975). See also other works cited under REGULARIS CONCORDIA.

Etheria. See EGERIA.

Ethical Movement. In 1876 an association, the 'Society for Ethical Culture', was founded in the USA by Felix Adler (1851–1933), to unite those who hold that morality is the fundamental element in religion. It is, in Adler's own words, 'based upon three tacit assumptions, sex purity, the principle of devoting the surplus of one's income beyond that required for one's own genuine needs to the elevation of the working classes, and, finally, continued intellectual development'. Adler originally professed the Jewish faith, but the movement quickly broke off relations with both Judaism and Christianity. A corresponding movement for Great Britain, begun in 1887 by Stanton Coit, did not meet with corresponding support, though certain prominent British philosophers (e.g. J. H. Muirhead, B. *Bosanquet, S. Alexander, and J. S. Mackenzie) expressed sympathy with it.

Ethics and Religion: A Collection of Essays by Sir John Seeley, Felix Adler, and Others (1900). F. Adler, *The Religion of Duty* (1905); id., *An Ethical Philosophy of Life* (1918). W. M. Salter, *Ethical Religion* (Boston, 1889); W. L. Sheldon, *An Ethical Movement* (1896). S. Coit (ed.), *Ethical Democracy: Essays in Social Dynamics*. H. J. Bridges (ed.), *Aspects of Ethical Religion: Essays in honor of Felix Adler* (New York, 1926). H. B. Radest, *Toward Common Ground: The Story of the Ethical Societies in the United States* (New York [1969]). B. Kraut, *From Reform Judaism to Ethical Culture: The Religious Evolution of Felix Adler* (Cincinnati, 1979). G. Spiller in *HERE* 5 (1912), pp. 412–14, s.v.; B. Kraut in M. Eliade (ed.), *The Encyclopedia of Religion*, 5 (1987), pp. 171–3, s.v. 'Ethical Culture'.

Ethiopian (or Abyssinian) Church, one of the *Oriental Orthodox Churches. Christianity was introduced into Ethiopia in the 4th cent. by St *Frumentius (q.v.) and Edesius of Tyre, but it is disputed whether King Azanas, known to have been Christian from a Greek inscription found in 1969, was the same person as King Ezana (Aizanas) to whom the Emp. Constantius wrote concerning Frumentius. The arrival of the 'Nine Saints', perhaps from Syria, in the late 5th cent. helped to spread Christianity, and in the first half of the 6th cent. the kingdom of *Axum in N. Ethiopia became an important Christian power under King Kaleb, who avenged the Jewish King Dhu Nuwas's persecution of Christians in Himyar. During the Axumite period the Bible and various patristic writings (notably the collection known as the 'Qerellos') were translated into Ethiopic (Ge'ez).

The advent of *Islam led to the rapid decline of the Ethiopian kingdom from the 7th cent. onwards and to its isolation from the rest of the Christian world. Little is known of its history until the rise of the Zagwe dynasty (1137–1270), to one of whose kings, Lalibela, the construction of the rock-hewn churches at Roha (Lalibela) is attributed. Only after the restoration in 1270 of the Solomonic dynasty (claiming descent from the Queen of Sheba and Menelik, her son by *Solomon) do historical sources become plentiful. At this time the Church was revitalized by the reforms of Tekla Haymanot, the founder of the influential monastery, Debra Libanos, and missionary work was undertaken in the south. Under King Amda Sion (1314–44), the national saga, called the 'Kebra Nagast' or 'Glory of Kings', was written. During the 14th–15th cent. many theological texts were translated from Arabic, sometimes incorporating material ultimately of W. origin (e.g. the 'Miracles of the Virgin'). The reign of the energetic King Zar'a Ya'qob (1434–68) witnessed several ecclesiastical reforms. In 1441–2 some Ethiopian monks from Jerusalem attended the Council of *Florence. During the Muslim incursions (1520–51) there was widespread destruction of churches and books.

In the 16th and 17th cents. there were extensive contacts with the Portuguese, who sent both military help and missionaries. The *Jesuits enjoyed particular success and in 1626 King Susenyos gave his formal obedience to the Papacy and abjured '*Monophysitism' on behalf of his people. Public outcry at this action, however, led to his abdication and the expulsion of the Jesuits (1632). The country became closed to missionary work until the 19th cent. Theological debate with the Jesuits gave rise to internal disputes concerning the meaning of the 'Unction' of Christ, the 'Unctionists' holding that the Holy Spirit provided the unction, and the 'Unionists' that the Son was both anointer and anointed.

From the time of Frumentius until 1959 the head of the Ethiopian Orthodox Church was a metropolitan bishop, or '*Abuna', normally a *Copt, appointed by the Coptic Orthodox Patriarch. In 1959, the Church became fully independent and its head now has the title of Patriarch.

The language of the liturgy (and of all literature until the 19th cent.) is Ge'ez, which died out as a spoken language in the early Middle Ages. There is now also a considerable Christian literature in Amharic. A distinctive feature of Ethiopian Christianity lies in its many Judaic features.

There is a small *Uniat Ethiopian Catholic Church, governed (since 1961) by a metropolitan bishop, and generally following the rites of the Ethiopian Orthodox Church.

M. *Lequien, *Oriens Christianus*, 2 (Paris, 1750), cols. 641–60. H. M. Hyatt, *The Church of Abyssinia* (Oriental Research Series, 1928). A. Hastings, *The Church in Africa 1450–1950* (Oxford History of the Christian Church, 1994), esp. pp. 130–69. J. S. Trimingham, *The Christian Church and Missions in Ethiopia* (1950). E. Ullendorff, *The Ethiopians* (1960; 2nd edn., 1965), esp. pp. 97–115. M. Chaîne, *La Chronologie des temps chrétiens de l'Égypte et de l'Éthiopie* (1925). T. Tamrat, *Church and State in Ethiopia, 1270–1527* (Oxford, 1972). S. Kaplan, *The Monastic Holy Man and the Christianization of early Solomonic Ethiopia* (Studien zur Kulturkunde, 73; 1984). P. [G.] Caraman, *The Lost Empire: The Story of the Jesuits in Ethiopia 1555–1634* (1985). D. Crummey, *Priests and Politicians: Protestant and Catholic Missions in Orthodox Ethiopia, 1830–1868* (Oxford, 1972). S. A. B. Mercer, *The Ethiopic Liturgy* (Hale Lectures for 1914–15; Milwaukee, 1915). E. Hammerschmidt, *Studies in the Ethiopic Anaphoras* (Berliner Byzantinistische Arbeiten, 25; 1961); id., *Stellung und Bedeutung des Sabbats in Äthiopien* (Studia Delitzschiana, 7; 1963). T. Uqbit, *Current Christological Positions of Ethiopian Orthodox Theologians* (Orientalia Christiana Analecta, 196; 1973). E. Littmann, 'Geschichte der äthiopischen Litteratur' in C. Brockelmann, *Geschichte der christlichen Litteraturen des Orients* (1907), pp. 185–269; J. M. Harden, *An Introduction to Ethiopic Christian Literature* (1926); E. Cerulli, *Storia della letteratura etiopica* (Milan, 1956; 3rd edn., Florence, 1968). A. *Fortescue, *The Lesser Eastern Churches* (1913), pp. 293–322; D. Attwater, *The Catholic Eastern Churches* (Milwaukee; rev. edn., 1937), pp. 150–60; rev. as *The Christian Churches of the East*, 2 (London, 1961), pp. 193–203; P. Verghese (ed.), *Koptisches Christentum: Die orthodoxen Kirchen Ägyptens und Äthiopiens* (Die Kirchen der Welt, 12; Stuttgart, 1973), pp. 133–207. E. Hammerschmidt and others in J. Assfalg and P. Kruger (eds.), *Kleines Wörterbuch des Christlichen Orients* (Wiesbaden, 1975), pp. 53–73. E. Coulbeaux in *DTC* 5 (1913), cols. 922–69,

s.v. 'Éthiopie (Église d)'; C. Santi, OFM, and others in *EC* 5 (1951), cols. 684–708, s.v. 'Etiopia'; B. Velat in *Dict. Sp.* 4 (pt. 2; 1961), cols. 1453–77, s.v. 'Éthiopie'; F. Heyer in *TRE* 1 (1977), pp. 572–96, s.v. 'Äthiopien'; G. Haile in M. Eliade (ed.), *Encyclopedia of Religion*, 5 (1987), pp. 173–7, s.v., all with bibl.

Ethiopic Versions of the Bible. Bible translation into Ethiopic (Ge'ez) prob. began in the 4th–5th cent., basically from Greek, but with some influence from Syriac and possibly also Hebrew. From the 14th cent. there were revisions based on *Arabic texts. Almost all Ethiopic biblical MSS date from the 13th/14th cent. or later. The extent of the canon of the Ethiopian Orthodox Church is unclear in detail, but most lists of books said to comprise the canon include (in addition to the OT, NT, and most of the *Deuterocanonical Books) various other items such as *Jubilees, 1 *Enoch, and the Ethiopic *Didascalia.

There is no satisfactory complete edn., though most Books of the OT have been pub., and the NT was first ed. by Petrus Aethiops (Tesfa Sion) (Rome, 1548). Edns. of Ethiopic biblical texts to date are cited in E. Ullendorff, *Ethiopia and the Bible* (Schweich Lectures, 1967; 1968); there are more recent edns. of Rev. by J. Hofmann (CSCO 281–2, Scriptores Aethiopici, 55–6; 1967, incl. Lat. tr.; with crit. discussion, ibid. 297, Subsidia, 33; 1969); of Mic. by H. F. Fuhs (Bonner Biblische Beiträge, 28; 1968); of Hos. by id. (ibid. 38; 1971); and of 1 Enoch by M. A. Knibb (2 vols., Oxford, 1978, incl. Eng. tr.). B. M. Metzger, *The Early Versions of the New Testament* (Oxford, 1977), pp. 215–56. R. [T.] Beckwith, *The Old Testament Canon of the New Testament Church and its Background in Early Judaism* (1985), pp. 478–505. R. W. Cowley, *The Traditional Interpretation of the Apocalypse of St John in the Ethiopian Orthodox Church* (Cambridge, 1983); id., *Ethiopian Biblical Interpretation* (University of Cambridge Oriental Publications, 38; 1988). B. Botte, OSB, in *Dict. Bibl.*, Suppl. 6 (1960), cols. 825–9, s.v. 'Orientales de la Bible (Versions)', IV. 'Versions Éthiopiennes'; G. Mink and S. P. Brock in *TRE* 6 (1980), pp. 205–7, s.v. 'Bibelübersetzungen' I. 8., 'Die Übersetzungen ins Äthiopische'; R. Zuurmond in *Anchor Bible Dictionary*, 6 (1992), pp. 808–10, s.v. 'Versions, Ancient (Ethiopic)'.

Eucharist. (1) NAME. The title 'Eucharist' (Gk. εὐχαριστία, 'thanksgiving') for the central act of Christian worship is to be explained either by the fact that at its institution Christ 'gave thanks' (1 Cor. 11: 24, Mt. 26: 27, etc.) or by the fact that the service is the supreme act of Christian thanksgiving. Early instances of its occurrence are in the *Didache* (9. 1), in St *Ignatius (*Philad.* 4, etc.), and in St *Justin (*Apol.* 1. 66). Other names for the service are the 'Holy Communion', the '*Lord's Supper', the '*Mass' (qq.v.), and, in the E. Church, the 'Divine Liturgy'.

(2) ORIGIN. In the NT there are four accounts of its institution, one by St *Paul in 1 Cor. 11: 23–5, and three in the *Synoptic Gospels (Mt. 26: 26–8, Mk. 14: 22–4, Lk. 22: 17–20). It is recorded that it was celebrated by the early Christian community at *Jerusalem (Acts 2: 42, 46) and by St Paul on his visit to Troas (Acts 20: 7). These passages show that from a very early date the service was a regular part of Christian worship, and was held to have been instituted by Christ. There is no record of the institution in the Fourth Gospel, but its existence is suggested in Jn. 6: 32–58. Traditionally it has been held that there was preparation for it in the OT, e.g. in the presentation of bread and wine by *Melchizedek, King of Salem (Gen. 14: 18), in the offerings of fine flour and wine (e.g. Lev.

2, 23: 13), in the descriptions of the meal to which Wisdom invites in Prov. (9: 1–5) and Ecclus. (24: 19–21), in the *Passover, and in the '*Kiddush'; and it has sometimes been held that the Divine preparation for it included some pagan sacramental rites as well. The main background in the NT, however, is Jewish and not pagan.

(3) DOCTRINE. The development of Eucharistic doctrine was gradual. In the *patristic period there was remarkably little in the way of controversy on the subject, but the emphases were different in different parts of the Church.

(a) That the Eucharist conveyed to the believer the Body and Blood of Christ was universally accepted from the first, and language was very commonly used which referred to the Eucharistic elements as themselves the Body and Blood. Even where the elements were spoken of as 'symbols' or 'antitypes' there was no intention of denying the reality of the Presence in the gifts. From the 4th cent., language about the transformation of the elements began to become general; but both before and after this, while some theologians wrote as if they believed in the persistence of the bread and wine after consecration, others wrote as though they held them to be no longer there. In the later part of the patristic period, the same lines of thought are continued uncontroversially, though there is a tendency towards a division between the precursors of *transubstantiation on the one side and those who emphasized the continued reality of the bread and wine (as well as the presence of the Body and Blood) in the consecrated elements on the other. Later, as the earlier conception of a 'symbol' as that which conveys and is what it represents gave way to the understanding of it as being other than what it represents, the description of the bread and wine as symbols dropped out or was denied. But hardly anywhere is there any attempt at precise formulation. The Fathers who made important contributions to the early development of Eucharistic doctrine include St *Cyril of Jerusalem, St *Chrysostom, St *Gregory of Nyssa, St *Cyril of Alexandria, *Theodoret, St *Ambrose, St *Augustine, and St *John of Damascus.

The first controversies on the nature of the Eucharistic Presence date from the earlier Middle Ages. In the 9th cent. *Paschasius Radbertus raised doubts as to the identity of Christ's Eucharistic Body with His Body in heaven, but won practically no support. Considerably greater stir was provoked in the 11th cent. by the teaching of *Berengar, who denied that any material change in the elements was needed to explain the Eucharistic Presence. These controversies had the effect of making some more precise definition desirable. The Fourth *Lateran Council (1215) used the current term 'transubstantiation' to assert the Real Presence against the *Cathari. Later in the century this teaching was worked out in much detail, with the assistance of the newly recovered philosophy of *Aristotle, notably by St *Thomas Aquinas. It was maintained that consecration effected a change in the 'substance' of the Bread and Wine, whereas the 'accidents' (i.e. the outward appearance) remained. Concurrently with this development went a great increase in Eucharistic devotion and the institution by Urban IV (1261–4) of the Feast of *Corpus Christi (1264).

At the Reformation, great controversies on the subject took place. M. *Luther defended a doctrine of *consubstantiation, acc. to which after the consecration both the bread and wine and the Body and Blood of Christ coexisted. U. *Zwingli, on the other hand, affirmed that the Lord's Supper was primarily a memorial rite, and that there was no change in the elements whatever. It was this deep-rooted divergence of Eucharistic belief that prevented the union of the forces of the German and Swiss Reformers, despite the attempt to heal the breach at the Colloquy of *Marburg (1529). J. *Calvin and his followers held a view of the Eucharist intermediate between these two. They denied that any change in the elements took place, but maintained that the faithful received the power or virtue of the Body and Blood of Christ, a doctrine which thus became known as *virtualism; and this or a very similar doctrine was held by some of the chief Anglican Reformers. At the Council of *Trent (sess. 13, 11 Oct. 1551), where recent disputes had made some formulation desirable, the doctrine of transubstantiation was reaffirmed in language more explicit than in 1215, but care was taken to avoid any formal definition of it in terms of accidents and substance, despite the general acceptance of this explanation among the leading RC theologians of the time.

Since the 16th cent. great attention has continued to be paid to Eucharistic doctrine in all parts of W. Christendom. It has been the subject of many refinements in the RC Church, e.g. in the writings of M. *Cano, F. *Suárez, J. de *Lugo, J. B. *Franzelin. Apart from transubstantiation, which on the *prima facie* reading of the 28th of the *Thirty-Nine Articles is excluded, a large variety of doctrines has been held in the C of E. The ambiguous, if not actually divergent, language of the BCP has encouraged the coexistence of these doctrines. It has been maintained that the consecrated elements are the Body and Blood of Christ, or that they possess the virtue of the Body and Blood, or that the faithful communicant receives with them the Body and Blood, or that they are merely symbols in the modern sense of the word. There has also been considerable variety of teaching in the Nonconformist Churches.

Since the Second *Vatican Council various RC theologians have explored the use of the notions of 'transignification' and 'transfinalization' as expressing the mode of the Eucharistic Presence. The encyclical 'Mysterium Fidei' of Pope *Paul VI in 1965, while it emphasized the doctrine of transubstantiation which the Pope held to be in danger, explicitly asserted that 'as a result of transubstantiation the species of bread and wine undoubtedly take on a new significance and a new finality'.

(b) From at least the end of the 1st cent. it was also held that the Eucharist is in some sense a sacrifice, though here again definition was gradual. The suggestion of sacrifice is contained in much of the NT language. In Judaism bread and wine were sacrificial elements, and the words at the institution, 'covenant' (διαθήκη), 'memorial' (ἀνάμνησις), 'poured out' (ἐκχυννόμενον), all have sacrificial associations. In early post-NT times the constant repudiation of animal sacrifice and emphasis on life and prayer at Christian worship did not hinder the Eucharist from being described as a sacrifice from the first. This aspect of Eucharistic doctrine, rather than any precise understanding of the Eucharistic Presence, was the centre of discussion in the E. Church, and a Council at *Constantinople in 1157 upheld the teaching that the Liturgy makes present the Sacrifice of Christ that is 'eternally celebrated' upon the 'altar on high'. It was long, however, before any attempt was made, either in the E. or W., to define more closely the nature of the sacrifice, though from the 14th cent. onwards a vast literature on the subject developed. Among the Reformation theologians there arose a strong tendency either to deny the sacrifice or to explain it in an unreal sense. The Council of Trent, on the other hand, dealt fully with the doctrine of the Sacrifice of the Mass. It affirmed that the Sacrifice of the Mass was propitiatory (*propitiatorium*), that it availed for the living and the dead, that it did not detract from the sufficiency of the Sacrifice of *Calvary. It embodied its teaching on the sacrifice in nine canons (sess. 22; 17 Sept. 1562).

During the 20th cent. a good deal of attention has been paid to the nature of the Eucharistic Sacrifice. Many modern writers have stressed the close relation between what takes place on the earthly altar and the perpetual Sacrifice of Christ in Heaven. In this connection F. C. N. Hicks and others have urged that the purpose of all sacrifice is life, the victim being slain not for its death as such but to liberate its blood, which is pre-eminently its life. M. *de la Taille (q.v.) elaborated the parallelism between the Oblation at the Last Supper and that on the Christian altar, holding that both were integrally related to the one immolation on Calvary. Another development (A. *Vonier, OSB; E. Masure) has been to interpret the Eucharistic Sacrifice in terms of sacrament, setting out from the conviction that it is of the essence of a sacrament to be meaningful and significant. More recently, theologians have emphasized the element of *anamnesis (or memorial) as central to an understanding of the Eucharist. This thinking is reflected in the Report of the *Anglican–Roman Catholic International Commission (q.v.) which achieved a measure of agreement on the nature of the Eucharistic Sacrifice by stressing the notion of anamnesis, understood as 'the making effective in the present of an event in the past'. The Eucharist is thus presented as 'a means through which the atoning work of Christ on the cross is proclaimed and made effective in the Church'.

In a less theoretical direction the *Liturgical Movement emphasized that the Eucharist is the commemoration of the whole paschal mystery, the passion, death, resurrection, and ascension of Christ, and brought out its relationship to the corporate nature of the Church and the role of the laity in its celebration. The Constitution of the Second Vatican Council on the Sacred Liturgy, while primarily concerned with liturgical reform, took up some of these insights. It lays stress on the corporate nature of the Eucharist, on the function of the laity in the Church's Eucharistic life, and on the sociological significance of Eucharistic worship, expressed in the active participation of the people. It declares that 'at the Last Supper . . . our Saviour instituted the Eucharistic Sacrifice of His Body and Blood' and that 'He did this in order to perpetuate the sacrifice of the Cross throughout the centuries until He should come again and so to entrust to His beloved spouse, the Church, a memorial of His death and resurrection'. It does not, however, go into detail about the precise nature of the sacrifice.

See also EUCHARISTIC PRAYERS.

On the history of the Eucharist: C. *Gore, *The Body of Christ* (1901); P. *Batiffol, *Études d'histoire et de théologie positive*, 2nd ser., *L'Eucharistie* (1905); D. *Stone, *A History of the Doctrine of the Holy Eucharist* (2 vols., 1909); J. Betz, *Eucharistie in der Schrift und Patristik* (Handbuch der Dogmengeschichte, 4, Heft 4a; 1979); B. Neunheuser, OSB, *Eucharistie in Mittelalter und Neuzeit* (ibid. 4, Heft 4b; 1963); H. B. Meyer, SJ, *Eucharistie: Geschichte, Theologie, Pastoral* (Gottesdienst der Kirche, 4; Regensburg, 1989). A. *Schweitzer, *Das Abendmahl in Zusammenhang mit dem Leben Jesu und der Geschichte des Urchristenthums* (1901; Eng. tr., Macon, Ga. [1982]); M. Goguel, *L'Eucharistie des origines à Justin Martyr* (1909); H. *Lietzmann, *Messe und Herrenmahl* (1926; Eng. tr., Leiden, 1953–79). J. Jeremias, *Die Abendmahlsworte Jesu* (1935; 3rd edn., 1960; Eng. trs., 1955 and 1966). H. Schürmann, *Eine quellenkritische Untersuchung des Lukanischen Abendmahlsberichtes Lk. 22, 7–38* (Neutestamentliche Abhandlungen, 19, Heft 5; 20, Hefte 4–5; 1953–7). R. Feneberg, *Christliche Passafeier und Abendmahl: Eine biblisch-hermeneutische Untersuchung der neutestamentliche Einsetzungsberichte* (Studien zum Alten und Neuen Testament, 27; 1971). X. Léon-Dufour, SJ, *Le partage du pain eucharistique selon le Nouveau Testament* ([1982]; Eng. tr., New York [1987]). E. B. *Pusey, *The Doctrine of the Real Presence as contained in the Fathers* (1855); C. Gore, *Dissertations on Subjects connected with the Incarnation*, Diss. 3: 'Transubstantiation and Nihilianism' (1895); J. [R.] Geiselmann, *Die Eucharistielehre der Vorscholastik* (Forschungen zur Christlichen Literatur- und Dogmengeschichte, 15, Hefte 1–3; 1926); G. Macy, *The Theologies of the Eucharist in the Early Scholastic Period: A Study of the Salvific Function of the Sacrament according to the Theologians c.1080–c.1220* (Oxford, 1984); B. J. Kidd, *The Later Medieval Doctrine of the Eucharistic Sacrifice* (1898); M. Rubin, *Corpus Christi: The Eucharist in Late Medieval Culture* (Cambridge, 1991). T. G. A. Hardt, *Venerabilis et adorabilis Eucharistia: Eine Studie über die lutherische Abendmahlslehre im 16. Jahrhundert* (Forschungen zur Kirchen- und Dogmengeschichte, 24; 1988). C. W. Dugmore, *Eucharistic Doctrine in England from Hooker to Waterland* (1942); id., *The Mass and the English Reformers* (1958). F. Clark, SJ, *Eucharistic Sacrifice and the Reformation* (Oxford, 1960; 2nd edn., 1967). P. [N.] Brooks, *Thomas Cranmer's Doctrine of the Eucharist: An Essay in Historical Development* (1965; 2nd edn., 1992). J. C. Bowmer, *The Sacrament of the Lord's Supper in Early Methodism* (1951).

On the theology of the Eucharist: R. I. *Wilberforce, *The Doctrine of the Holy Eucharist* (1853); J. B. Franzelin, *Tractatus de SS. Eucharistiae Sacramento et Sacrificio* (1868); W. *Sanday (ed.), *Different Conceptions of Priesthood and Sacrifice* (1900); M. de la Taille, *Mysterium Fidei* (1921; Eng. tr. of books 1 and 2, 2 vols., 1941–50); A. Vonier, OSB, *A Key to the Doctrine of the Eucharist* (1925); F. C. N. Hicks, *The Fullness of Sacrifice* (1930); E. Masure, *Le Sacrifice du Chef* (2nd edn., 1932; Eng. tr., *The Christian Sacrifice*, 1944). Y. [T.] Brilioth, *Eucharistic Faith and Practice, Evangelical and Catholic* (Eng. tr. by A. G. Hebert, 1930). E. L. Mascall, *Corpus Christi: Essays on the Church and the Eucharist* (1953; 2nd edn., 1965). G. *Aulén, *För eder utgiven* (Stockholm, 1956; Eng. tr., *Eucharist and Sacrifice*, Philadelphia, 1958; Edinburgh, 1960). M. Thurian, *L'Eucharistie: Mémorial du Seigneur, Sacrifice d'action de grâce et d'intercession* (Collection Communauté de Taizé; Neuchâtel, 1959; Eng. tr., *The Eucharistic Memorial*, Ecumenical Studies in Worship, 7–8; 1960–1). O. *Casel, *The Mystery of Christian Worship* (1962), and other works of this author. E. *Schillebeeckx, OP, *Christus Tegenwoordigheid in de Eucharistie* (1967; Eng. tr., *The Eucharist*, 1968). J. M. Powers, SJ, *Eucharistic Theology* (New York, 1967; London, 1968), with bibl. [on recent RC thinking]. G. Wainwright, *Eucharist and Eschatology* (1971). *Report of the Anglo-Catholic Congress, 1927* (subject: The Holy Eucharist); *Thinking about the Eucharist* (essays by members of the Archbishops' Commission on Christian Doctrine, with a Preface by I. T. Ramsey; 1972). J. Betz in *Mysterium Salutis*, ed. J. Feiner and M. Löhrer, 4 (pt. 2; Einsiedeln [1973]), pp. 185–313. C. J. Cocksworth, *Evangelical Eucharistic Thought in the Church of England* (Cambridge, 1993). P. J. Fitzpatrick, *In Breaking of Bread: The Eucharist and Ritual* (ibid., 1993).

On the liturgy of the Eucharist: G. *Dix, OSB, *The Shape of the Liturgy* [1945]; J. A. Jungmann, SJ, *Missarum Sollemnia: Eine* *genetische Erklärung der römischen Messe* (2 vols., 1948; 4th edn., 1958; Eng. tr. of 1949 edn., New York, 1951–5) and other works of this author; J. D. Crichton, *Christian Celebration: The Mass* (1971). Various authors in C. [P. M.] Jones, G. Wainwright, and E. J. Yarnold, SJ (eds.), *The Study of Liturgy* (1978), pp. 147–288; rev. edn. (1992), pp. 184–338. A. G. Martimort, *L'Église en Prière* (new edn.), 2: R. Cabié, *L'Eucharistie* (1983; Eng. tr., 1986).

C. Ruch and others in *DTC* 10 (pt. 1; 1928), cols. 795–1316, s.v. 'Messe'.

Eucharistic Congresses. International congresses organized by the RC Church for promoting devotion to the Blessed Sacrament. Their ancestor, a local gathering arranged through the exertions and enthusiasm of Mgr Gaston de Ségur, met at Lille in 1881. In succeeding years the Congresses have gradually developed to their present international character. That of 1908 which met in London was the first occasion on which a Papal *legate had entered England since Cardinal R. *Pole (d. 1558).

Reports of some of the Congresses have been pub. shortly afterwards. J. Vaudon, *L'Œuvre des congrès eucharistiques, ses orgines* (1911); M. L. Paladini, *Die eucharistischen Kongresse: Ursprung und Geschichte* (1912). Current RC directions are contained in the section of the *Rituale Romanum, *De Sacra Communione et de Cultu Mysterii Eucharistici extra Missam* (1973), nos. 109–12 (pp. 44 f.), Eng. tr., *Holy Communion and Worship of the Eucharist Outside Mass*, 1, Rites (1978), pp. 57 f. N. Mitchell, OSB, *Cult and Controversy: The Worship of the Eucharist Outside Mass* (Studies in the Reformed Rites of the Catholic Church, 4; New York, 1982), esp. pp. 342 f. T. F. Meehan in *CE* 5 (1909), pp. 592–4, s.v.; J. C. Willke in *NCE* 5 (1967), pp. 617 f., s.v.

Eucharistic fast. By this is commonly understood complete abstinence from food and drink for a period preceding the reception of Holy Communion. Unlike other forms of fasting, it is designed less as a form of asceticism than to do honour to the Eucharistic Gifts.

The traditional period of the fast was from the previous midnight. The practice appears to have developed gradually. The earliest express legislation on the subject is in the Council of *Hippo of 393 (can. 28), which allowed, however, an exception on *Maundy Thursday; this decree was re-enacted at Carthage in 397 (can. 29). St *Augustine (*ep.* 54, *ad Januarium*; *c.*400) advocates the fast, believing it to be of universal observance and dating back to Apostolic times. Throughout the Middle Ages its observance was virtually universal. It was also taken over by the Reformers, who tended to stress esp. its disciplinary value. Among Protestants, however, it gradually died out; in England it also seems to have almost disappeared in the 18th cent. In the 19th cent. the observance was assiduously encouraged by the *Tractarians and their followers. It led to the institution of the early morning Celebration and the discouragement of communicating at the mid-morning High Celebration, except by the (still fasting) celebrant. Another consequence was that *Evening Communions (q.v.) were originally deprecated by High Churchmen. By the end of the 19th cent. the practice had become widespread in the C of E and was a strong devotional influence. The proposed BCP of 1928 contained the rubric: 'It is an ancient and laudable custom of the Church to receive this Holy Sacrament fasting. Yet for the avoidance of all scruple it is hereby declared that such preparation may be used or not used, according to every man's conscience in the sight of God.' Any mention of the subject seems to be absent from modern liturgies and it seldom figures even in devotional literature of recent times. The practice of the RC Church (see below) has influenced many Anglicans.

Since the beginning of the 20th cent. the RC Church has shown an increasing tendency to relax and curtail the discipline. Influences in this direction have been the encouragement of more frequent Communion (see COMMUNION, FREQUENCY OF) and the disorganization of social habits, especially during the Second World War. Special relaxations were gradually introduced for those in sickness and on active service, and for others for whom a rigid fast would have been burdensome. These dispensations were standardized in *Pius XII's Apostolic Constitution 'Christus Dominus' (16 Jan. 1953) and the accompanying instruction. His *motu proprio* 'Sacram Communionem' of 19 March 1957 laid down that the consumption of water at any time did not break the natural fast; in future a three-hour fast from solid food and alcoholic drink and a one-hour fast from non-alcoholic liquid was to be observed before the reception of Holy Communion; the celebrating priest was to reckon the period of the fast from the beginning of Mass. On 21 Nov. 1964 †Paul VI reduced the period of the Eucharistic fast to one hour before the reception of Holy Communion. Acc. to the *CIC* (1983), can. 919, 'Whoever is to receive the blessed Eucharist is to abstain for at least one hour before holy Communion from all food and drink, with the sole exception of water and medicine'. There are, however, exceptions for priests celebrating a second or third Mass on the same day, the elderly and sick, and for those caring for them.

In the E. Church a strict Eucharistic fast is observed from bedtime on the previous day.

H. T. Kingdon, *Fasting Communion* (1873; 2nd edn., 1875, much extended); F. W. Puller, SSJE, *Concerning the Fast before Communion* (1903); J. Wickham Legg (ed.), *Papal Faculties allowing Food before Communion* (CHS, no. 87; 1905). P. *Dearmer, *The Truth about Fasting, with special Reference to Fasting Communion* (1928). J. M. Frochisse, SJ, 'A propos des origines du jeûne eucharistique', *RHE* 28 (1932), pp. 594–609; G. R. Dunstan, 'The Fast before Communion', *Theology*, 53 (1950), pp. 11–19 and 57–64. The Ap. Const. 'Christus Dominus' is pr. in *AAS* 45 (1953), pp. 15–24, with the accompanying Instruction, ibid., pp. 47–51. Both are repr., with Eng. tr. and comm., in W. Conway, *The New Law on the Eucharistic Fast* (Dublin, 1954). 'Sacram Communionem' is pr. in *AAS* 49 (1957), pp. 177 f.; the 1964 regulation ibid. 57 (1965), p. 186. A. Bride in *DDC* 6 (1957), cols. 142–81, s.v. 'Jeûne eucharistique'. A. M. Carr in *NCE* 5 (1967), p. 847, s.v. 'Fast, Eucharistic'.

Eucharistic Prayers, forms of the central prayer of the Eucharist (q.v), known in the E. as the *Anaphora. From at least the 6th cent., the Roman rite knew only one form, the *Canon of the Mass. As the word *Eucharist* implies, a major theme of such prayers is thanksgiving. Their origin is prob. to be found in the Jewish prayers of blessing at meals and synagogue blessings, prayers that blessed God for creation, gave thanks for redemption, and made supplication. Many of the early Christian prayers were not so much one single prayer as a series of short prayers, a form apparently preserved in the Roman Canon. Until well into the 3rd cent., and possibly later, the bishop as the normal leader at the Eucharist, would have improvised the prayer, and the forms that survive from this early period are probably only possible models (e.g. the Eucharistic prayer in the *Apostolic Tradition*; cf. also St Polycarp's prayer before his martyrdom in the *Martyrdom of Polycarp*, 14; the *Didache* may provide another example). The 4th and 5th cents. saw the composition of the great prayers in the liturgies attributed to St *Basil, St John *Chrysostom, and others. In the *Gallican, old Spanish (*Mozarabic) and *Ambrosian rites the prayer continued to be in the form of several short prayers. The composition of Eucharistic prayers continued in *Syrian Orthodox areas until well into the Middle Ages, but in the W. the suppression of the Gallican rites and the severe restriction of other local liturgies left the Roman Canon virtually the only Eucharistic Prayer in use. At the Reformation *Lutherans suppressed all of the Canon except the *Preface and the Words of *Institution; *Reformed Church orders often used those words as a warrant for celebration and had no equivalent to a Eucharistic Prayer. In the C of E the 1552 BCP retained the Preface but separated the Prayer of *Humble Access from the prayer containing the institution narrative (called the Prayer of Consecration from 1662), itself separated from the rest of the Eucharistic Prayer after the Words of Institution by the Communion.

Eucharistic Prayers usually contain the following elements: a thanksgiving for creation and redemption, at some point in which the *Sanctus* almost invariably occurs; the words of Christ at the *Last Supper (seen as exclusively consecratory in W. theology from the Middle Ages until modern times); the *Anamnesis or prayer of Oblation; the *Epiclesis or invocation of the Holy Spirit (upon the elements and upon the communicants); and usually some form of intercession, in union with the saints, for the living and departed, and a final doxology. Some ancient prayers did not contain all these elements; the original Anaphora of *Addai and Mari may not have had the Words of Institution, and the Epiclesis is undeveloped in the Roman Canon.

In 1968 the Congregation of Sacred *Rites provided three Eucharistic Prayers for use in the RC Church as alternatives to the Roman Canon, which in a slightly revised form became Eucharistic Prayer I. Prayer II is an adaptation of the prayer in the *Apostolic Tradition*, with the addition of the *Sanctus* and the rearrangement of sections, esp. the Words of Institution which, for pastoral reasons, are the same in all three new prayers. Prayer III is a modern composition more in the tradition of the Canon, but with elements from other sources. Prayer IV is related to an ancient prayer once current in Egypt and later adapted to form what is known as the Anaphora of St Basil; new intercessions have been added. All three have an Epiclesis before and after the consecration, and intercessions in which there is a brief invocation of the BVM and the saints. Further Eucharistic Prayers have subsequently been authorized, beginning with those for Reconciliation and for Children in 1975. By this time the different Provinces of the Anglican Communion had devised a variety of Eucharistic Prayers, and since then liturgical revision has proceeded apace in most Churches. Rite A of the ASB has four Eucharistic Prayers, as has the American *Lutheran Book of Worship* of 1983, while the 1989 *United Reformed Church order has three. The Eucharistic rite of the Church of *South India (1962), which has been widely influential, was based on the *Apostolic Tradition*.

A. Hänggi and I. Pahl (eds.), *Prex Eucharistica: Textus e variis liturgiis antiquioribus selecti* (Spicilegium Friburgense, 12; 1968); I. Pahl (ed.), *Coena Domini*, 1: *Die Abendmahlsliturgie der Reformationskirchen im 16./17. Jahrhundert* (ibid. 29; 1983). R. C. D. Jasper and G. J. Cuming (eds.), *Prayers of the Eucharist: Early and Reformed* (1975; 2nd edn., New York, 1980).

H. *Lietzmann, *Messe und Herrenmahl* (1926), esp. pp. 125–32; Eng. tr. (Leiden, 1979), pp. 102–8; G. *Dix, OSB, *The Shape of the Liturgy* [1945], pp. 50–5. J. P. Audet, 'Literary Forms and Contents of a Normal Εὐχαριστία in the First Century', in K. Aland and others (eds.), *Studia Evangelica*, 1 (TU 73; 1959), pp. 643–62. L. Bouyer, *Eucharistie: Théologie et spiritualité de la prière eucharistie* ([1966]; Eng. tr., 1968). L. Ligier, SJ, 'The Origins of the Eucharistic Prayer: From the Last Supper to the Eucharist', *Studia Liturgica*, 9 (1973), pp. 161–85. C. Giraudo, *La Struttura letteraria della preghiera eucaristica* (Analecta Biblica, 92; 1981). A. Bouley, OSB, *From Freedom to Formula: The Evolution of the Eucharistic Prayer from Oral Improvisation to Written Texts* (Catholic University of America Studies in Christian Antiquity, 21; Washington, DC [1981]). E. Mazza, *Le Odierne Preghiere Eucaristiche* (1984; Eng. tr., *The Eucharistic Prayers of the Roman Rite*, New York [1986]). F. C. Senn (ed.), *New Eucharistic Prayers: An Ecumenical Study of their Development and Structure* (ibid. [1987]).

Eucharistic vestments. In the W. the traditional vestments of the priest celebrating Mass are the *alb, *amice, *chasuble, *girdle, *maniple, and *stole. They derive from the ordinary secular clothing of Roman citizens in the 2nd cent., the alb being a development of the *tunica*, the chasuble of the *paenula*, and the maniple of the *mappula*. In the E. Church the vestments are fundamentally the same but differ in shape. In the RC Church the celebration of the Mass without vestments is normally forbidden. In the C of E since the *Reformation their history is complex. The 1549 BCP ordered a 'white alb plain, with a vestment or cope', but in the 1552 BCP they were abolished. The *Ornaments Rubric in the 1662 BCP, however, at least on a *prima facie* interpretation, orders their use. After falling into complete disuse for over two centuries, they were restored on the authority of the Rubric in the 19th cent., being first worn at Wilmcote in Warwickshire in 1845. From that time controversy on the subject raged violently. In 1908 a sub-committee of five bishops reported to the Upper House of Convocation that their use was permitted, if not commanded, by the Ornaments Rubric; they were tolerated by the rubrics of the proposed Prayer Book of 1927–8, and can. B 8 of the 1969 Canons permits 'an alb with the customary vestments'. See also COPE and VESTMENTS.

For bibl., see under separate vestments and also under VESTMENTS and ORNAMENTS RUBRIC.

Euchelaion (Gk. εὐχέλαιον). In the Greek Church, the regular term for the Sacrament of Holy *Unction.

Eucherius, St (d. *c.*450), Bp. of Lyons. Accompanied by his wife and two sons, he entered the famous monastery of *Lérins and became a keen exponent of the ascetic way of life. He was elected to the see of Lyons at some time between 432 and 441 (when he attended the Synod of *Orange), but of his administration we know very little. His extant writings comprise two exegetical works (*Formulae Spiritalis Intelligentiae* and *Instructiones ad Salonium*), a *Passio Agaunensium Martyrum* (on the

*Theban Legion) and two small ascetic treatises (*De Laude Heremi* and *De Contemptu Mundi*). Acc. to *Gennadius of Marseilles he made a summary of the writings of John *Cassian, though it is uncertain whether any of this survives. Feast day, 16 Nov.

Authentic works in J. P. Migne, *PL* 50. 701–832 (with account of earlier edns., cols. 687–98). Crit. edn. (unfinished) by K. Wotke (CSEL 31; 1894). Gennadius, *De Viris Ill.* 63 [64]. N. K. Chadwick, *Poetry and Letters in Early Christian Gaul* (1955), esp. pp. 151–60. S. Pricoco, *L'Isola dei santi: Il cenobio di Lerino e le origini del monachesimo gallico* (1978), *passim*. A. Hamman in Quasten (cont.), *Patrology*, 4 (1986), pp. 504–7. L. R. Wickham in *TRE* 10 (1982), pp. 522–5; S. Pricoco in *DPAC* 1 (1983), cols. 1270–2 (Eng. tr. in *Encyclopedia of the Early Church*, 1 (1992), p. 295), both s.v., with bibl.

Euchites (Gk. εὐχῆται or εὐχῖται). The heretical sect also known as the *Messalians (q.v.). The Greek, like the Syriac, title means 'those who pray'.

Euchologion (Gk. εὐχολόγιον). In the E. Church, the liturgical book containing the text and rubrics of the three Eucharistic rites in current use (of St *Chrysostom, of St *Basil, and the Liturgy of the *Presanctified), the invariable parts of the Divine *Office, and the prayers required for the administration of the *Sacraments and *Sacramentals. It thus combines the essential parts of what in the W. is contained in the *Missal, *Pontifical, and *Rituale.

Among the earliest MSS of the Euchologion are the 'Barberini Codex S. Marci III. 55 (77)', now Vat. gr. 366; the Cod. Porphyr., formerly of the Imperial Library at St Petersburg; and the Cod. Sin. 957; all 8th–9th cent. The earliest pr. texts come from Venice (1526, 1544, 1550, etc.). A collection of texts, with crit. discussion, in J. *Goar, OP, Εὐχολόγιον, sive Rituale Graecorum (Paris, 1647; 2nd edn., Venice, 1730). P. de Meester, OSB, *Studi sui sacramenti amministrati secondo il Rito Bizantino* [1947], pp. 189–240. Id. in *EC* 5 (1951), cols. 784–6, s.v.

eudemonism. The ethical theory which defines the end of right action as εὐδαιμονία, 'well-being'. The classical exponent of this system is *Aristotle. St *Thomas Aquinas, who uses St. *Augustine's term *beatitudo* ('blessedness') for εὐδαιμονία, found a place for it in Christian moral philosophy; but in his account the 'well-being' of man is discovered in the vision of God. This Christian eudemonism has been criticized, especially by the *Quietists, on the ground that it leaves no room for the pure disinterested love of God, which should be the foundation of Christian morals. Among Anglican moral philosophers, H. *Rashdall defended a form of eudemonism.

R. A. Gauthier in *Dict. Sp.* 4 (1960), cols. 1660–74, s.v., with refs.

Eudes, St John (1601–80), French missioner. Born at Ri in Normandy and educated at the *Jesuit college at Caen, he was accepted by the Superior General of the *Oratory in 1623 and priested in 1625. After heroic service in plagues in 1627 and 1631, he spent ten years in conducting missions. In 1641 he founded the 'Order of our Lady of Charity', dedicated to the heart of Mary, to care for fallen women, which in 1644 was entrusted to the *Visitandines of Caen. In 1643 he withdrew from the Oratory and

founded at Caen the 'Congregation of Jesus and Mary', dedicated to the hearts of Jesus and Mary, an association of priests whose object was to conduct seminaries. In 1657 the Caen sisters set up an independent community ('Sisters of our Lady of Charity of the Refuge'), with a fourth vow, to care for fallen women.

St John Eudes shares with St *Margaret Mary Alacoque the claim to have initiated devotion to the *Sacred Heart of Jesus. He sought to give it a theological foundation and wrote several offices of the feast. He also fostered devotion to the heart of Mary, introducing in his congregation a feast in its honour in 1648, and publishing in 1670 *Le Cœur admirable de la Mère de Dieu*. The best known of his other writings is *La Vie et le royaume de Jésus* (1637). He was beatified in 1909 and canonized in 1925. Feast day, 19 Aug.

The 'Congregation of Jesus and Mary', whose members are commonly known as 'Eudists', was almost extinguished by the Revolution. It was reconstituted in 1826 and is now chiefly concerned with secondary education. In recent times it has been active in South America, the *United States, and esp. *Canada. In 1835 a separate congregation, the Sisters of our Lady of Charity of the Good Shepherd, was formed to establish reformatories.

Œuvres complètes pub. with introd. and notes, 12 vols., Paris, 1905–9; *Lettres choisies et inédites* ed. C. Berthelot du Chesnay, CJM (Namur, 1958). The primary Life by P. Hérambourg, CJM (1661–1720) was ed. by A. Le Doré (Paris, 1869) and, more accurately, by D. Boulay, CJM (ibid., 1925; Eng. tr., Westminster, Md., and Dublin, 1960). Modern Lives by D. Boulay (4 vols., Paris, 1905–8), H. Joly ('Les Saints', 1907; Eng. tr., 1932), E. Georges (Paris, 1925), and A. Pioger (Paris, 1940). Bremond, 3 (1921), pp. 583–671. C. Lebrun, CJM, *La Spiritualité de S. Jean Eudes* (1933; Eng. tr., 1934). C. Berthelot du Chesnay, *Les Missions de Saint Jean Eudes* (1967). P. Milcent, CJM, in *Dict. Sp.* 8 (1974), cols. 488–501, s.v. 'Jean (90) Eudes'. E. Georges, *La Congrégation de Jésus et Marie, dite des Eudistes* (1933). Heimbucher, 2, pp. 592–5. C. Berthelot du Chesnay in *DHGE* 15 (1963), cols. 1331–5, s.v. 'Eudistes', with further bibl.

Eudists. See previous entry.

Eudoxius (*c*.300–370), *Anomoean leader. A native of *Armenia, in the later 330s he was made by his *Arian friends Bp. of Germanicia and took part in many of the Arian councils. In 357 he secured possession of the see of *Antioch; and though soon forced to withdraw, he became Bp. of *Constantinople in 360. Of his writings only a few fragments survive.

M. Tetz, 'Euxodius-Fragmente?', in F. L. Cross (ed.), *Studia Patristica*, 3 (TU 78; 1961), pp. 314–23. *CPG* 2 (1974), pp. 253 f. (nos. 3405 and 3410). M. Jugie, AA, in *DTC* 5 (1913), cols. 1484–7; M. Spanneut in *DHGE* 15 (1963), cols. 1337–40, both s.v.

Eugenius III (d. 1153), *Cistercian, Pope from 1145. Bernardo Pignatelli of Pisa entered the Cistercian abbey of *Clairvaux under St *Bernard in 1135 and was subsequently made Abbot of San Anastasio at Rome. Elected Pope in 1145, he had to flee before his consecration, owing to his refusal to recognize the sovereignty of the Roman Senate. He went to Farfa, where he was consecrated, and from there to Viterbo, and in 1147 to France, where he worked for the Second *Crusade, which he commissioned St Bernard to preach. He held synods at *Paris (1147),

Trier (1147), *Reims (1148), dealing chiefly with matters of doctrine, esp. the heresy of *Gilbert de la Porrée and the visions of St *Hildegard, and at Cremona (1148), where he excommunicated *Arnold of Brescia, who had become the leader of the rebellious Roman Senate. In 1149 he returned to Rome but had to leave it again. In 1153 he concluded the Treaty of Constance with *Frederick I (Barbarossa), who guaranteed the rights of the Church. Early in the same year Eugenius had re-entered Rome, where he died seven months later. An ardent reformer of the morals of the clergy and of monastic observance, he had formed his life on the spiritual counsels of St Bernard, who had written for him his famous ascetical treatise 'De Consideratione'. His cult was approved by *Pius IX in 1872. Feast day, 8 July.

592 of Eugenius' letters in J. P. Migne, *PL* 180. 1013–614, with refs. Jaffé, 2 (2nd edn., 1888), pp. 20–89. The principal sources are the Life by Card. Boso in *LP* (Duchesne, 2, 1892, pp. 386 f.) and the account of *John of Salisbury, *Historia Pontificalis* (ed. M. Chibnall, 1956, repr., Oxford, 1986, *passim*; see index). H. Gleber, *Papst Eugen III., 1145–1153, unter besondere Berücksichtigung seiner politischen Tätigkeit* (Beiträge zur mittelalterlichen und neueren Geschichte, ed. F. Schneider, 6; 1936). G. del Guerra and others, *Il Beato Eugenio III*, a cura del Capitolo della Primaziale di Pisa (Pisa, 1954). M. Maccarrone, *Papato e Impero dalla elezione di Federico I alla morte di Adriano IV (1152–1159)* (Lateranum, NS 25; 1959), pp. 11–103. E. Caspar, 'Die Kreuzzugsbullen Eugens III', *NA* 45 (1924), pp. 285–305, with text. Mann, 9 (1914), pp. 127–220. M.-A. Dimier in *DHGE* 15 (1963), cols. 1349–55, s.v. 'Eugène III'; I. Daniele in *Bibliotheca Sanctorum*, 5 (1964), cols. 196–201, s.v. 'Eugenio III'.

Eugenius IV (1383–1447), Pope from 1431. Gabriele Condulmaro was born of a wealthy Venetian family, and at an early age entered an *Augustinian monastery. In 1408 he was appointed Cardinal-Priest of San Clemente by his uncle, Gregory XII. He was elected Pope in 1431, one of his first acts being to dismiss the Council of *Basle (q.v.), which had met in the summer of the same year. The Council refused to dissolve, however, and reasserted the theory of *conciliar supremacy, which had been defended at *Constance. In 1433 Eugenius gave way and recognized the Council as canonical. A year later a revolt in Rome forced the Pope to flee to Florence, where he remained until 1443. His relations with the Council remained tense. In 1438, against the wishes of the majority, he transferred the Council to Ferrara and in the following year to Florence. The union of the Greek and Roman Churches at Florence in 1439, though not permanent, greatly increased his authority. Meanwhile the continuing Council of Basle deposed him and elected an antipope, Felix V (Amadeus VIII, Duke of Savoy) in 1439. In 1443 Eugenius returned to Rome. In the following year the *Crusade against the Turks in which he was deeply concerned ended with the defeat of the Christians at Varna. With France relations had become strained owing to the semi-schismatic *Pragmatic Sanction of Bourges (1438), but through the skill of his envoy, Aeneas Sylvius Piccolomini (later *Pius II), the Pope secured a diplomatic success which brought the Empire over to his side (1447). See also FLORENCE, COUNCIL OF.

Eugenius was a Pope of austere piety, a vehement opponent of nepotism, but often imprudent in his policy. His residence at Florence brought him into contact with the Italian Renaissance, and he showed himself a patron of art and literature.

F. P. Abert, *Papst Eugen der Vierte* (1884). J. Gill, SJ, *Eugenius IV: Pope of Christian Union* (Westminster, Md., 1961; London [1962]). E. v. Ottenthal, 'Die Bullenregister Martins V und Eugens IV', *Mittheilungen des Instituts für oesterreichische Geschichtsforschung*. Ergänzungsband 1 (1885), pp. 401–589. P. Paschino, *Roma nel rinascimento* (Storia di Roma, 12; 1940), pp. 120–65. J. W. Stieber, *Pope Eugenius IV, the Council of Basel and the Secular and Ecclesiastical Authorities in the Empire* (Studies in the History of Christian Thought, 13; Leiden, 1978). C. M. de Witte, 'Les Bulles pontificales et l'expansion portugaise au XVᵉ siècle', *RHE* 48 (1953), pp. 683–718, esp. pp. 697–718, incl. texts. Pastor, 1 (1891), pp. 281–361. E. Delaruelle, E. R. Labande, and P. Ourliac in Fliche and Martin, 14 (parts 1–3; 1962), pp. 229–447, *passim*. P. de Vooght in *DHGE* 15 (1963), cols. 1355–9, s.v. 'Eugène IV'.

Eugippius (*c*.455–*c*.535), Abbot of Lucullanum, near Naples. He wrote a Life of St *Severinus of Noricum (*c*.511) and a monastic Rule, recently discovered. He also compiled a collection of extracts from the writings of St *Augustine which was much read in the Middle Ages. He was prob. involved in the revision of the *Vulgate text of the Gospels.

Works pr. J. P. Migne, *PL* 62. 549–1200. Crit. edn. by P. Knoell (CSEL 9; 2 pts., 1895–6). Rule ed. F. Villegas and A. de Vogüé (CSEL 87; 1976). M. Cappuyns in *DHGE* 15 (1963), cols. 1376–8; V. Pavan in *DPAC* 1 (1983), cols. 1278 f. (Eng. tr. in *Encyclopedia of the Early Church*, 1 (1992), p. 296), both s.v. For edns. and works on the Life of St Severinus see SEVERINUS, ST.

Euhemerism. The theory that the ancient beliefs about the gods originated from the elaboration of traditions of actual historical persons. The name is derived from Euhemerus, a Sicilian writer (*c*.315 BC), who developed this thesis in a book, Ἱερὰ Ἀναγραφή. Christian apologists, like *Lactantius, saw in this theory the true explanation of the origins of the Greek gods.

F. Jacoby, *Die Fragmente der griechischen Historiker*, 1 (1923), pp. 300–13 (no. 63). H. F. van der Meer, *Euhemerus van Messene* (Amsterdam thesis, 1949); J. W. Schippers, *De Ontwikkeling der Euhemeristische Godencritiek in de Christelijke Latijnse Literatuur* (Utrecht thesis; Groningen, 1952), with summary in Eng. J. D. Cooke, 'Euhemerism: A Mediaeval Interpretation of Classical Paganism', *Speculum*, 2 (1927), pp. 396–410; T. S. Brown, 'Euhemerus and the Historians', *HTR* 39 (1946), pp. 259–74. J. Geffcken in *HERE* 5 (1912), pp. 572 f.; K. Thraede in *RAC* 6 (1966), cols. 877–90, s.v., with bibl.

eulogia (Gk. εὐλογία, 'a blessing'). The word was used in early times both actively for a 'benediction' and passively for 'something blessed'. In the latter sense it was applied to the blessed bread which was distributed to *catechumens and others after the Mass was ended, for consumption either before leaving the church or at home later. See also PAIN BÉNIT.

A. Stuiber in *RAC* 6 (1966), cols. 900–28, s.v., with bibl.

Eunan, St. See ADOMNÁN, ST.

Eunomius (d. 394), *Arian Bp. of Cyzicus in Mysia. Of Cappadocian peasant origin, he went to *Alexandria, where he became a pupil of *Aetius (q.v.) *c*.356. He returned with him to Antioch, attending the Arian synod summoned there by *Eudoxius, and was made deacon. With Eudoxius and Aetius, he was delated to the Emp. Constantius by *Basil of Ancyra on charges of conspiracy and banished to Phrygia. After the deposition of Basil in 360, however, Eudoxius was made Bp. of Constantinople and Eunomius was consecrated Bp. of Cyzicus. He accepted the see only when Eudoxius promised to restore Aetius, a promise never fulfilled. The clergy were hostile and after a successful defence of his doctrine at a synod in Constantinople, Eunomius resigned a few months later. Uncompromising support for Aetius led to an abortive arraignment for heresy by *Acacius in 361. Constantius' death and the accession of *Julian gave the party breathing-space, but under *Jovian and later Valens, the breach with Eudoxius became final. Banished and recalled under Valens, under *Theodosius Eunomius was again banished, ultimately to Dakora, where he died.

Eunomius' principal work, an Ἀπολογητικός (known as his 'First Apology'), was composed c.360, and is prob. the defence of his doctrine which he made at Constantinople. It was answered by St *Basil of Caesarea, whose reply survives. Eunomius issued a rejoinder, Ὑπὲρ τῆς Ἀπολογίας Ἀπολογία (his 'Second Apology') in three books, prob. in 378. St *Gregory of Nyssa's Contra Eunomium (c.382) was a reply to this work and constituted an elaborate attack on the whole system. Eunomius also wrote two further books on the same controversy and a commentary on Romans, which, like his letters, are now lost, and another treatise Ἔκθεσις πίστεως (383), to which Gregory replied in his Refutatio Confessionis Eunomii.

Eunomius' doctrine was *Anomoean. He taught a single supreme Substance whose simplicity is opposed to all, even virtual, distinction whether of properties or attributes. This Substance, which he called ἀγεννησία ('ungenerated Being'), he held to be absolutely intelligible. He denied that the generation of the Son took place within the Divine Nature, but regarded Him as a being immediately produced by the Father, from whom He received the creative power which caused Him to resemble the Father. Among the beings created by the Son the Holy Spirit held the first place. He is the Son's instrument for the sanctification of souls. Scripture plays a more significant role in Eunomius' system than in the writings of his forerunner Aetius, but the most prominent feature of his teaching is its stress on the importance of exactitude of doctrine for the life of faith. His views met with no lasting success and were soon forgotten. His chief importance for the history of theology lies in the reaction his theses provoked, esp. from the *Cappadocian Fathers, whose doctrine of God and of human knowledge of God largely took shape as a critique of Eunomius.

Extant Works ('First Apology', Ἔκθεσις, and Fragments pr. in full, with Eng. tr., and summary of the 'Second Apology'), ed. R. P. Vaggione (Oxford Early Christian Texts, 1987). Basil's reply, together with Eunomius' 'First Apology' ed., with Fr. tr., by B. Sesboüé, SJ, and others (SC 299 and 305; 1982–3) (Eunomius' Apology, SC 305, pp. 179–299). Frags. of the 'Second Apology' are preserved in Gregory's Contra Eunomium; best edn. by W. Jaeger, Gregorii Nysseni Opera, 1–2 (Leiden, 1960). Ancient sources incl. *Photius, Cod. 138, and *Jerome, De Vir. Ill. 120. *Socrates, HE 4. 7, *Philostorgius, HE 10. 6, and passim. E. Cavalcanti, Studi Eunomiani (Orientalia Christiana Analecta, 202; 1976). J. *Daniélou, SJ, 'Eunome l'Arien et l'exégèse néoplatonicienne du Cratyle', Revue des Études grecques, 69 (1956),

pp. 412–32. R. Mortley, From Word to Silence, 2 (Theophaneia, 31; Bonn, 1986), pp. 135–59. M. [F.] Wiles, 'Eunomius: Hair-Splitting Dialectician or Defender of the Accessibility of Salvation?', in R. [D.] Williams (ed.), The Making of Orthodoxy: Essays in Honour of Henry Chadwick (Cambridge, 1989), pp. 157–172. F. Diekamp, 'Literargeschichtliches zu der eunomianischen Kontroverse', BZ 18 (1909), pp. 1–13; L. R. Wickham, 'The Date of Eunomius' Apology: A Reconsideration', JTS NS 20 (1969), pp. 231–40. J. Quasten, Patrology, 3 (Utrecht and Westminster, Md., 1960), pp. 306–9. CPG 2 (1974), pp. 260 f. (nos. 3455–60). E. Venables in DCB 2 (1880), pp. 286–90, s.v.; M. Spanneut in DHGE 15 (1963), cols. 1399–405, s.v. 'Eunomius (2) de Cyzique'; L. Abramowski in RAC 6 (1966), cols. 936–47, s.v.; A. M. Ritter in TRE 10 (1982), pp. 525–8, s.v.

Euphemia, St (perhaps 4th cent.), virgin and martyr. She was greatly venerated in the E., esp. as patroness of the church where the Council met at *Chalcedon in 451; but the legends are all late and unreliable. There is a church dedicated to her in *Rome which was restored by Pope *Sergius (687–701). Her name occurs in the *Ambrosian Canon of the Mass. Feast day, 16 Sept.

AASS, Sept. 5 (1755), pp. 255–86, F. Halkin, SJ (ed.), Euphémie de Chalcédoine: Légendes byzantines, with appendix by P. Canart (Subsidia Hagiographica, 41; 1965), with refs. A. M. Schneider, 'Sankt Euphemia und das Konzil von Chalkedon', in A. Grillmeier, SJ, and H. Bacht, SJ (eds.), Das Konzil von Chalkedon, 1 (1951), pp. 291–302. R. Janin, AA, in DHGE 15 (1963), cols. 1409 f., s.v. 'Euphémie (3)'.

Europe, Diocese in. A diocese of the C of E, created in 1980 by the union of the jurisdiction of the Bp. of London in Northern and Central Europe with the former diocese of Gibraltar. It is officially known as the Diocese of Gibraltar in Europe. In 1633 jurisdiction over Anglican congregations outside the British Isles was vested in the Bp. of London; from the 19th cent. dioceses and provinces were established in all parts of the world. These included the extra-provincial diocese of Gibraltar, created in 1842, with responsibility for territories bordering on the Mediterranean, incl. Turkey, and other parts of Southern Europe. The Bp. of London retained jurisdiction over Northern and Central Europe; from 1883 he delegated this responsibility to a *suffragan bishop, from 1925 styled Bp. of Fulham. In 1970 the Bp. of Fulham was also given charge of the diocese of Gibraltar. In 1980 a single diocese in Europe was formed. It is attached to the Province of *Canterbury and subject to the metropolitan jurisdiction of the Archbishop with the Bp. of London as the episcopal Visitor of the diocese. The diocesan bishop is appointed by the Abp. of Canterbury, the Bp. of London, and an episcopal member of the Standing Committee of the Anglican Consultative Council acting jointly; he himself, acting jointly with the Abp. of Canterbury and the Bp. of London, appoints his suffragan bishop. The cathedral church of the Holy Trinity in Gibraltar is the cathedral of the diocese; the collegiate church of St Paul at Valletta is a pro-cathedral, as also, since 1981, is the church of the Holy Trinity, Brussels.

Eusebian Canons and Sections. The system of tables (κανόνες) devised by *Eusebius of Caesarea to enable the reader of the Gospels to turn up passages ('sections') in the other Gospels that are parallel to the one before him or contain similar subject-matter. These tables are often the table to consult. Sometimes the table was elaborately illuminated. Eusebius himself explained the system in his epistle to Carpianus, mentioning the pioneer work of *Ammonius Saccas, to whom the numbering of the sections was formerly ascribed. They were of great use in identifying passages before the now current division into chapters and verses became established.

The Canons and Eusebius' letter to Carpianus are conveniently pr. in E. *Nestle and K. Aland (eds.), *Novum Testamentum Graece* (27th edn., Stuttgart, 1993), pp. 84*–89*, with note, p. 79*. J. W. *Burgon, *The Last Twelve Verses of the Gospel according to St Mark* (1871), pp. 125–32, 295–312. E. Nestle, 'Die eusebianische Evangelien-Synopse', *Neue Kirchliche Zeitschrift*, 19 (1908), pp. 40–51, 93–114, 219–32. C. Nordenfalk, 'The Eusebian Canon-Tables: Some Textual Problems', *JTS* NS 35 (1984), pp. 96–104.

Eusebius (*c*.260–*c*.340), Bp. of *Caesarea, the 'Father of Church History'. He was a pupil of the scholar and martyr *Pamphilus, who trained him in the tradition of *Origen and imbued him with a hatred of *Sabellianism which remained with him all his life. After Pamphilus' death (310), he fled from the persecution to *Tyre, and then into Egypt, where he spent some months in prison. By 315 he was Bp. of Caesarea. During the *Arian controversy he supported Arius and was condemned by the Council of Antioch (324/5). At the Council of *Nicaea he was reinstated by the Emp. *Constantine when he produced the baptismal creed of Caesarea as evidence of his orthodoxy. But (despite what Eusebius says) this creed cannot have formed the basis of the *Nicene Creed (q.v.), which Eusebius ultimately accepted. His acceptance was, however, half-hearted, and he continued as one of the opponents of *Athanasius. About 327 he was offered the bishopric of Antioch, but refused it. In 335 he attended the Council of Tyre and the dedication of the church of the Resurrection at *Jerusalem, and was afterwards summoned by Constantine to advise on the case of Athanasius. He delivered the 'Tricennial Oration' in honour of the 30th anniversary of Constantine's accession to power in 336 and was active until he died.

Of Eusebius' many writings the most celebrated is his 'Ecclesiastical History', the principal source for the history of Christianity from the Apostolic Age till his own day. As with all Eusebius' writings, its literary style is poor. But it contains an immense range of material on the E. Church (he has little to say about the W.), largely in the form of long extracts taken over bodily from earlier writers. If Eusebius' interpretation of these documents was sometimes in error, this is to be explained by his want of critical judgement and not by conscious perversion of the facts. The 'History' consists of ten books, of which the last three deal in great detail with the events of his own time. Indeed, it is widely (though not universally) held that the 'History' had originally ended before 303 with book 7, and that the later books were added in successive editions, the final edition with book 10 being revised as late as *c*.325. Besides the original Greek, it survives in *Latin, *Syriac, and *Armenian versions.

Among his other historical writings are: 'The Martyrs of Palestine', an account of the *Diocletianic persecution between 303 and 311, of which he was an eye-witness; a 'Chronicle' in two books, i.e. a summary of universal history with a table of dates; and a 'Life of Constantine', a panegyric which, though excessive in its flattery, contains

invaluable historical matter. His apologetic writings include a defence of Christianity 'Against Hierocles' (a pagan governor of Bithynia), and a pair of treatises, the 'Preparation for the Gospel' and the 'Demonstration of the Gospel'. The former of these (in 15 books) shows why Christians accept the Hebrew and reject the Greek tradition, while the latter (in 20 books, only partly extant) attempts to prove Christianity by the OT. The 'Preparation' contains many quotations from classical authors now lost. His other extant writings are a work on the Incarnation called 'The Theophany', two books against *Marcellus of Ancyra, a collection of OT passages foretelling the coming of Christ, commentaries on the Psalms and Isaiah (which employ the allegorical methods of Origen), a book on Problems of the Gospels, a treatise on 'Easter' (*De solemnitate Paschali*) in which he expounds the Eucharistic *Sacrifice, and a valuable work on Biblical topography called the *Onomasticon*.

His writings are repr., from various sources, in J. P. Migne, *PG* 19–24; crit. edn. by I. A. Heikel and others (GCS, 9 vols. in 11, 1902–75). *Editio princeps* of *HE* by R. *Stephanus (Paris, 1544); much improved text by H. *Valesius (ibid., 1659); crit. text, with Rufinus' version, by E. *Schwartz and T. *Mommsen in the GCS edn. of his works (2 vols., 1903–8); this is repr., with notes and Fr. tr. by G. Bardy, and index by P. Périchon, SJ (SC 31, 41, 55, and 73; 1952–60). Crit. edns., with Fr. tr., of the 'Preparation for the Gospel' by É. des Places, SJ, and others (ibid. 206, 215, 228, 262, 266, 292, 307, 338, and 369; 1974–91), and of 'Against Hierocles' by id. (ibid. 333; 1986). Eng. trs. of *HE* by K. *Lake and J. E. L. Oulton (2 vols., Loeb, 1926–32), H. J. Lawlor and J. E. L. Oulton (2 vols., London, 1927–8), R. J. Deferrari (Fathers of the Church, 19 and 29; 1953–5), and G. A. Williamson (Harmondsworth, 1965; rev. by A. Louth, 1989).

H. J. Lawlor, *Eusebiana* (1912); J. Stevenson, *Studies in Eusebius* (1929); D. S. Wallace-Hadrill, *Eusebius of Caesarea* (1960). H. Berkhof, *Die Theologie des Eusebius von Caesarea* (Amsterdam, 1939); R. Farina, *L'Impero e l'Imperatore cristiano in Eusebio di Cesarea: La prima teologia politica del cristianesimo* (Bibliotheca Theologica Salesiana, Series I: Fontes, 2; Zurich, 1966). R. M. Grant, *Eusebius as Church Historian* (Oxford, 1980). C. Luibhéid, *Eusebius of Caesarea and the Arian Crisis* (Dublin, 1981). T. D. Barnes, *Constantine and Eusebius* (1981), esp. pp. 81–188. É. des Places, *Eusèbe de Césarée Commentateur* (Théologie historique, 63 [1982]). P. W. P. Walker, *Holy City, Holy Place? Christian Attitudes to Jerusalem and the Holy Land in the Fourth Century* (Oxford Early Christian Studies, 1990), esp. pp. 3–130 and 347–410. H. W. Attridge and G. Hata (eds.), *Eusebius, Christianity, and Judaism* (Studia Post-Biblica, 42; Leiden, etc., 1992). *CPG* 2 (1974), pp. 262–75 (nos. 3465–507). Bardenhewer, 3 (1912), pp. 240–62; Altaner and Stuiber (1978), pp. 217–24 and 591 f. J. Quasten, *Patrology*, 3 (Utrecht and Westminster, Md., 1960), pp. 309–45. J. B. *Lightfoot in *DCB* 2 (1880), pp. 308–48; E. Schwartz in *PW* 6 (pt. 1; 1907), cols. 1370–439; J. Moreau in *DHGE* 15 (1963), cols. 1437–60, s.v. 'Eusèbe (17) de Césarée de Palestine'; id. in *RAC* 6 (1966), cols. 1052–88, s.v., with bibl.; J. Stevenson in *NCE* 5 (1967), pp. 633–6, s.v.; D. S. Wallace-Hadrill in *TRE* 10 (1982), cols. 537–43, s.v. See also bibl. to CONSTANTINE.

Eusebius, Bp. of Dorylaeum. See after EUSEBIUS, ST, BP. OF VERCELLI.

Eusebius (d. *c*.359), Bp. of Emesa (Homs) in Syria. He was a native of *Edessa, a biblical exegete and writer on doctrinal subjects, of *Semiarian sympathies, and prob. a disciple of *Eusebius of Caesarea. Having declined to fill the see of *Alexandria when *Athanasius was deposed in 339, he became Bp. of Emesa shortly afterwards. Until modern times only fragments of his writings (mainly in exegetical catenae) were known. A collection of some 14 homilies (in Latin translation) of his Caesarean namesake (first pub. by J. *Sirmond, SJ, in 1643) had been conjecturally ascribed to him; this ascription was confirmed when A. *Wilmart, OSB, and later E. M. Buytaert, OFM, demonstrated that Eusebius was indeed the author of 17 homilies, also in Latin translation, ascribed to him in a Troyes MS (523), which contains two homilies of the Sirmond collection. A collection of sermons in Armenian which is ascribed to him also contains some which are held to be authentic. A collection of Latin sermons of Gallican provenance has long gone under the name of 'Eusebius'; these are believed to be derived from *Faustus of Riez (q.v.).

Crit. text of his sermons (in Latin) ed. E. M. Buytaert, OFM, in SSL, fasc. 26 (1, La Collections de Troyes; Discours 1–17), 1953; fasc. 27, 1957 (2, La Collection de Sirmond; Discours 18–29). Armenian collection ed. N. Akinian in *Handes Amsorya*, 70–72 (1956–8; for details see *CPG* 2 (1974), pp. 279 f. (no. 3531). Part of an encomium on Eusebius by *George of Laodicea is preserved in *Socrates, *HE* 2. 9, and *Sozomen, *HE* 3. 6. A. Wilmart, OSB, 'Le Souvenir d'Eusèbe d'Émèse', *Anal. Boll.* 38 (1920), pp. 241–84 (text, pp. 263–84). E. M. Buytaert, OFM, 'L'Authenticité des dix-sept opuscules contenus dans le MS. T. 523 sous le nom d'Eusèbe d'Émèse', *RHE* 43 (1948), pp. 1–89; id., *L'Héritage littéraire d'Eusèbe d'Émèse: Étude critique et historique* (Bibliothèque du Muséon, 24; 1949). D. Amand de Mendieta, 'La Virginité chez Eusèbe d'Émèse et l'ascétisme familial dans la première moitié du IVᵉ siècle', *RHE* 50 (1955), pp. 777–820. O. Perler, 'Pseudo-Ignatius und Eusebius von Emesa', *Hist. J.* 77 (1958), pp. 73–82. H. J. Lehmann, *Per Piscatores: Studies in the Armenian Version of a Collection of Homilies of Eusebius of Emesa and Severian of Gabala* (Århus, 1975). *CPG* 2 (1974), pp. 276–82 (nos. 3525–43). Altaner and Stuiber (1978), pp. 224 and 592 f. For the sermons of Eusebius 'Gallicanus', see *CPL* (3rd edn., 1995), pp. 312–14 (nos. 966–966a). They are ed. J. Leroy and F. Glorie (CCSL 101, 101A and 101B; 1970–1).

Eusebius (d. *c*.342), Bp. of Nicomedia. He was the leader of the Arian party in the first half of the 4th cent. In early life he had been a disciple of *Lucian of Antioch, with *Arius as his fellow-pupil. His first see was Berytus (modern Beirut), but when Arius turned to him after his condemnation by *Alexander, Bp. of *Alexandria, Eusebius was already Bp. of Nicomedia, the imperial capital in Asia Minor. There he used his influence at court on Arius' behalf. Although at the Council of *Nicaea (325), he signed the Creed, shortly afterwards he was exiled because of his support for Arius. On his return in 328/9 he led the struggle against *Athanasius, securing his deposition at the Synod of Tyre (335). In 337 he baptized the dying *Constantine. He was translated from Nicomedia to *Constantinople in 339, and in 341 he assembled the Dedication Council at *Antioch which marked the beginning of the ascendancy of Arianism in the Councils of the Church. His followers were commonly known by his name (οἱ περὶ Εὐσέβιον).

A. Lichtenstein, *Eusebius von Nikomedien: Versuch einer Darstellung seiner Persönlichkeit und seines Lebens unter besonderer Berücksicht seiner Führerschaft im arianischen Streite* (1903). G. Bardy, *Recherches sur Saint Lucien d'Antioche et son école* (Études de

Théologie Historique, 1936), pp. 296–315. J. Quasten, *Patrology*, 3 (Utrecht and Westminster, Md., 1960), pp. 190–3. *CPG* 2 (1974), pp. 7 f. (nos. 2045–56). G. Bareille in *DTC* 5 (1913), cols. 1539–51, s.v. 'Eusèbe (6) de Nicomédie'; M. Spanneut in *DHGE* 15 (1963), cols. 1466–71, s.v. 'Eusèbe (24) de Nicomédie'.

Eusebius, St (d. 380), Bp. of Samosata by 360. He supported the election of *Melitius to the see of *Antioch and shared his subsequent opposition to *Arianism. Later he became closely associated with St *Basil of Caesarea, from whom he was the recipient of several letters, and St *Gregory of Nazianzus. In 374 he was exiled for his orthodoxy to Thrace, but four years later recalled by the Emp. Gratian. He was killed by an Arian woman who threw a brick at his head. Feast day in E., 22 June; in W., 21 June.

Theodoret, *HE* 5. 4. 8. *AASS*, Jan. 4 (1707), pp. 235–42. Syr. Life, perh. based on Gk. sources, in P. Bedjan (ed.), *Acta Martyrum et Sanctorum*, 6 (1896), pp. 335–77. F. Halkin, SJ, 'Une Vie grecque d'Eusèbe de Samosate', *Anal. Boll.* 85 (1967), pp. 5–15; P. Devos, SJ, 'Le Dossier syriaque de S. Eusèbe de Samosate', ibid., pp. 195–240, incl. Fr. tr. of Syr. Life. H. R. Reynolds in *DCB* 2 (1880), pp. 369–72, s.v. 'Eusebius (77), bishop of Samosata'; M. Spanneut in *DHGE* 15 (1963), cols. 1473–5, s.v. 'Eusèbe (29) de Samosate'.

Eusebius, St (d. 371), Bp. of Vercelli from 340. He was born in Sardinia. A strong supporter of orthodoxy in the *Arian conflict, at the request of Pope *Liberius he accompanied St *Lucifer of Cagliari on his embassy to Constantius in 354. After the Synod of Milan (355) he was exiled to the E., whence he did not return until the reign of *Julian (362). He lived with his clergy at Vercelli under rule and has hence been sometimes regarded by the *canons regular as one of their founders (with St *Augustine of Hippo). Three of his letters have survived, and the ancient *Old Latin Gospel Codex in the cathedral library of Vercelli (cod. *a*) is ascribed, though improbably, to Eusebius' own hand. He also made a Lat. trans. of *Eusebius of Caesarea's 'Commentary on the Pss.', now lost. A treatise, *De Trinitate*, traditionally attributed to St *Athanasius, has been ascribed to him, though this ascription has been widely contested. Feast day, 2 Aug. (until 1969, 16 Dec.).

J. P. Migne, *PL* 12. 9–972 (on the Codex, 9–948; text of Epistolae, 947–54). Crit. edn. of his three letters, of certain letters addressed to Eusebius, the *De Trinitate*, and other material, by V. Bulhart (CCSL 9, 1957, pp. 1–205). J. S. Ferrerius, *S. Eusebii Vercellensis . . . ejusque in Episcopatu Successorum Vita* (Rome, 1602). *CPL* (3rd edn., 1995), pp. 34–6 (nos. 105–11e). Altaner and Stuiber (1978), pp. 366 f. and 626. V. C. De Clercq in *DHGE* 15 (1963), cols. 1477–83, s.v. 'Eusèbe (33) de Verceil', with bibl.

Eusebius (mid-5th cent.), Bp. of Dorylaeum. He was an ardent advocate of theological orthodoxy. In 429, at that time a lawyer of *Constantinople, he made a public protest against the teaching of *Nestorius in a 'Contestatio' (Διαμαρτυρία) addressed to the clergy of Constantinople. By 448 he had become Bp. of Dorylaeum in Phrygia Salutaris, in which year he led the attack on the heresy of *Eutyches at the 'Home Synod' at Constantinople. In 449 he was deposed and exiled by the '*Latrocinium' of *Ephesus. After the accession of the Emp. *Marcian (450), the theological policy of the court was reversed. Eusebius was reinstated in his see and took a prominent part at the

Council of *Chalcedon (451), where he assisted in drafting its Definition of the Faith.

His *Contestatio* in Mansi, 4 (1740), cols. 1007–12. Early Lat. version in J. P. Migne, *PG* 84. 581–3. Crit. edn. of Gk. in E. *Schwartz, *ACO* I. 1. 1 (1927), pp. 101 f. *CPG* 3 (1979), pp. 152 f. (nos. 5940–44). G. Bareille in *DTC* 5 (1913), cols. 1532–7, s.v., with bibl.

Eustace, St, also 'Eustachius', early Christian martyr. His very existence is doubtful. Acc. to 7th-cent. legends he was a Roman general under Hadrian and converted by a vision of a stag with a crucifix between its antlers, which occurred at Guadagnolo near Praeneste (Palestrina). (Details from the story were later incorporated in the legend of St *Hubert, q.v.) He and his family are said to have been later roasted to death in a brazen bull. Some of his relics appeared in the 12th cent. in *Paris, where they were destroyed by the *Huguenots in 1567. He is one of the 14 so-called *Auxiliary Saints and is the patron of the city of Madrid and (with St Hubert) of hunters. Feast day, 20 Sept. (dropped in the W. in 1969).

Legends of St Eustace and his family in *AASS*, Sept. 6 (1757), pp. 106–37. A. Monteverdi, *La leggenda di S. Eustachio* (Bergamo, 1909); id., *I testi della leggenda di S. Eustachio* (ibid., 1910). H. *Delehaye, SJ, 'La Légende de saint Eustache', *Académie Royale de Belgique. Bulletins de la Classe des Lettres et des Sciences Morales et Politiques*, Brussels, 1919, pp. 175–210, with full bibl. refs.; repr. in *Mélanges d'hagiographie grecque et latine* (Subsidia Hagiographica, 42; 1966), pp. 212–39. O. Engels, 'Die hagiographischen Texte Papst Gelasius' II. in der Überlieferung der Eustachius-, Erasmus- und Hypolistuslegende', *Hist. J.* 76 (1957), pp. 118–33, esp. pp. 119–25, with refs. R. Aubert in *DHGE* 16 (1967), cols. 6 f., s.v. 'Eustache (1)', with bibl.

Eustathius, St, Bp. of *Antioch from *c.*324 to *c.*327. A native of Side, he was Bp. of Beroea (modern Aleppo) before his translation to Antioch. At the Council of *Nicaea (325) he was given a position of honour, and on his return to his diocese banished many of his clergy suspected of *Arianism. His uncompromising support for the Nicene position brought him into conflict with, among others, *Eusebius of Caesarea, who charged him with *Sabellianism. Eustathius' deposition was secured at a council in Antioch (perhaps as early as 326) and he was banished by *Constantine to Thrace, where he remained until his death (see MELITIAN SCHISMS (2)). He was famed for his eloquence. Of his writings only 'de Engastrimutho' (against *Origen) survives complete, but there are several fragments of, and references to, Eustathius' other works. He criticized Arian Christology for denying Christ's human soul, thereby foreshadowing later Antiochene objections to *Apollinarianism. Feast day, 16 July.

Collection of texts and frags. in J. P. Migne, *PG* 17. 609–1066. The sermon pr. in F. Cavallera, *S. Eustathii Episcopi Antiochensis in Lazarum, Mariam et Martham Homilia Christologica* (Paris, 1905; with useful collections of frags.), is prob. not the work of Eustathius. More recent edn. of frags., with discussion, in M. Spanneut, *Recherches sur les écrits d'Eustathe d'Antioche, avec une édition nouvelle des fragments dogmatiques et exégétiques* (Mémoires et Travaux publiés par des professeurs des Facultés Catholiques de Lille, 55; 1948). Crit. edn. of 'De Engastrimutho' in E. Klostermann, *Origenes, Eustathius und Gregor von Nyssa über die Hexe von Endor* (Kleine Texte, 83; 1912), pp. 16–62. Crit. reconstruction of his Ep. to *Alexander of Alexandria on the subject of *Melchizedek in B. *Altaner, 'Die Schrift Περὶ τοῦ Μελχισεδέκ

des Eustathios von Antiocheia', *BZ* 40 (1940), pp. 30–47, repr. in his *Kleine patristische Schriften* (TU 83; 1967), pp. 343–62. F. Scheidweiler, 'Die Fragmente des Eustathios von Antiocheia', *BZ* 48 (1955), pp. 73–85. H. Chadwick, 'The Fall of Eustathius of Antioch', *JTS* 49 (1948), pp. 27–35, repr. in his *History and Thought of the Early Church* (1982), no. 13. On his theology, R. V. Sellers, *Eustathius of Antioch and his Place in the Early History of Christian Doctrine* (1928). M. Spanneut, 'La Position théologique d'Eustathe d'Antioche', *JTS* NS 5 (1954), pp. 220–4. *CPG* 2 (1974), pp. 243–53 (nos. 3350–98). Altaner and Stuiber (1978), pp. 309 f. and 613. M. Spanneut in *DHGE* 16 (1967), cols. 13–23, s.v. 'Eustathe (2) d'Antioche'.

Eustathius (*c.*300–after 377), Bp. of Sebaste in Pontus from *c.*357. In his youth he was a pupil of *Arius at *Alexandria, and throughout his life vacillated in his attitude to the *Nicene cause. At the synods of *Ancyra (358) and Lampsacus (364) he defended *homoiousian doctrines. His main interests, however, esp. in his earlier years, were in the *monastic movement, in the organization of which he took a prominent part. In this connection he seems to have greatly influenced St *Basil the Great, with whom for a time he was on terms of close friendship, in the foundation of his rule. In his later years he became the leading spirit in Asia Minor in furthering the *Macedonian heresy.

F. *Loofs, *Eustathius von Sebaste und die Chronologie der Basilius-Briefe: Eine patristische Studie* (1898); J. Gribomont, OSB, 'Le Monachisme au IVᵉ s. en Asie Mineure: de Gangres au Messalianisme', in K. Aland and F. L. Cross (eds.), *Studia Patristica*, 2 (TU 64; 1957), pp. 400–15; id., 'Eustathe le Philosophe et les voyages du jeune Basile de Césarée', *RHE* 54 (1959), pp. 115–24. S. Salaville, AA, in *DTC* 5 (1913), cols. 1565–71, s.v., with bibl.; J. Gribomont in *DHGE* 16 (1967), cols. 26–33, s.v. 'Eustathe (7) de Sébaste'; id., in *Dict. Sp.* 4 (pt. 2; 1961), cols. 1708–12, s.v. 'Eustathe (2) de Sébaste'.

Eustochium, St Julia (370–*c.*419), a Roman virgin of noble descent. With her mother, St *Paula, she came under the influence of St *Jerome, who counselled them in an attempt to lead the life of the Egyptian hermits in the midst of Rome. A letter (Jerome, *Ep.* 22) which he addressed to her on the subject of virginity created such a stir that they were obliged to leave the city (385). After visiting Syria and Egypt on the way, they settled in *Bethlehem, where they built four monasteries, of which Eustochium assumed the direction on her mother's death in 404. Feast day, 28 Sept.

In addition to *Ep.* 22 (*PL* 22. 394–425), St Jerome addressed to Eustochium *Epp.* 31 (ibid. 445 f.) and 108 (ibid. 878–906); a letter from Paula and Eustochium is pr. among Jerome's *Epp.* (no. 46; ibid. 483–92); further refs. incl. those in *Epp.* 54 (ibid. 550–60) and 66 (ibid. 639–47). *AASS*, Sept. 7 (1760), pp. 630–45. W. H. Fremantle in *DCB* 2 (1880), p. 392, s.v., with further refs.; P. Antin, OSB, in *Dict. Sp.* 4 (pt. 2; 1961), cols. 1715–18, s.v.

Euthalius. The reputed author of a collection of editorial material found in many MSS of the Greek NT. The editor's work, which consisted of (1) an arrangement of the text in short lines as an aid to reading it aloud, (2) a system of references to quotations from other parts of the Bible, and (3) a division of the Books into chapters, with summary headings of their contents, extended over the Pauline Epp., the Acts, and the Catholic Epp. Attached to the Euthalian prologue to the Pauline Epp. is a 'Martyrium Pauli' which appears to date from either 458 (L. A. Zacagni) or 396 (F. C. *Conybeare); but the reasons for identifying the author of this item with that of the rest of the Euthalian material now seem insufficient, and J. A. *Robinson has argued that Euthalius is to be dated in the middle of the 4th cent. Virtually nothing further is known of him beyond the fact that he is described as 'a deacon'. Adequate grounds for identifying him with the author of a long confession of faith (7th cent.), ascribed to 'Euthalius, Bp. of Sulce', are wanting.

L. A. Zacagni, *Collectanea Monumentorum Veteris Ecclesiae Graecae et Latinae*, 1 (Rome, 1698), pp. 401–708, mostly repr. in J. P. Migne, *PG* 85. 619–790. J. A. Robinson, 'Euthaliana', *Texts and Studies*, 3. 3 (Cambridge, 1895); E. von Dobschütz, 'Euthaliusstudien', *ZKG* 19 (1899), pp. 107–54; F. C. Conybeare, 'The Date of Euthalius', *ZNTW* 5 (1904), pp. 39–52; G. Zuntz, 'Euthalius = Euzoius?', *VC* 7 (1953), pp. 16–22; J. W. Marchand, 'The Gothic Evidence for "Euthalian Matter"', *HTR* 49 (1956), pp. 159–67. S. [P.] Brock, 'The Syriac Euthalian Material and the Philoxenian Version of the NT', *ZNTW* 70 (1979), pp. 120–30. J. N. Birdsall, 'The Euthalian material and its Georgian versions', *Oriens Christianus*, 68 (1984), pp. 170–95. *CPG* 2 (1974), p. 301 (nos. 3640–2).

euthanasia. See DYING, CARE OF THE.

Euthymius, St (377–473), monk. A native of Melitene in Lesser Armenia, where he was ordained priest, he came to *Jerusalem in 405. After living as a monk and solitary in several places near Jerusalem, he finally established c.426 a *lavra at Khan-el-Ahmar. In the period immediately following *Chalcedon (451), he was one of the very few in Palestine who remained unwavering in his support of the Council. He exercised a formative influence upon Palestinian monasticism, and among his many disciples was St *Sabas. Feast day, 20 Jan.

The principal authority is the Life by *Cyril of Scythopolis; crit. edn. by E. *Schwartz, in *TU* 49 (pt. 2; 1939), pp. 3–85; Fr. tr. by A.-J. Festugière, *Les Moines d'orient*, 3. 1 (1962). R. Génier, OP, *Vie de Saint Euthyme le Grand* (1909). S. Vailhé, AA, 'Saint Euthyme le Grand', *Revue de l'Orient Chrétien*, 12 (1907), pp. 298–312, 337–55; 13 (1908), pp. 181–91, 225–46; 14 (1909), pp. 189–202, 256–63. D. J. Chitty, *The Desert a City* (Oxford, 1966), esp. pp. 83–100. J. Darrouzès in *Dict. Sp.* 4 (pt. 2; 1961), cols. 1720–2, s.v. 'Euthyme (2)'.

Euthymius (mid-11th cent.), monk of the Περίβλεπτον monastery at *Constantinople. He wrote a polemical work against the Phundagiagitae, a sect of the *Bogomils, which was prob. known to *Euthymius Zigabenus, under whose name it survived, and with whom he has long been confused. He was prob. also the author of the so-called 'First Invective' against the Armenians.

The text of his 'Contra Phundagiagitas' in J. P. Migne, *PG* 131. 47–58, is incomplete; better edn. in G. Ficker, *Die Phundagiagiten* (Leipzig, 1908), pp. 3–86. The 'First Invective' is pr. in J. P. Migne, *PG* 132. 1155–1218, under the name of 'Isaac the Catholicos'. V. Grumel, 'Les Invectives contre des Arméniens du "Catholicos Isaac"', *Revue des études byzantines*, 14 (1956), pp. 174–91. Beck (1959), pp. 532 f.

Euthymius Zigabenus (early 12th cent.), Byzantine theologian. Nothing is known of his life, except that at the command of the Emp. Alexis Comnenus, he wrote a work against all heresies, the Πανοπλία Δογματική. In this the old heresies are refuted by an array of patristic texts; the new ones, comprising the last 6 of 28 chapters, are treated more independently. The most interesting is the section (27) on the *Bogomils, our knowledge of whom rests almost entirely on this and the account by Euthymius, monk of the Peribleptos (see previous entry). The work was supplemented later by the Θησαυρὸς Ὀρθοδοξίας of *Nicetas Acominatos (d. c.1217). Euthymius' other important works are his extensive commentaries on the Psalms, the Four Gospels, and the Epp. of St Paul, in which he utilizes mainly patristic sources, esp. St *Chrysostom. His works are remarkable esp. for the account they take of the literal sense of the Bible, an achievement unusual among the later Greek exegetes.

The Gk. text of his 'Panoplia Dogmatica', was first pub. by Metrophanes Gregoras (Tergovist, 1710); of his Comm. on Pss. by A. Bongiovanni (Venice, 1763); of his Comm. on Gospels by C. F. Matthaei (3 vols. bound in 4, Leipzig, 1792); and of his Comm. on Pauline Epp. by N. Kalogeras, Abp. of Patras (2 vols., Athens, 1887). Collected edn. in J. P. Migne, *PG* 128–131. More complete text of 'Panoplia Dogmatica', 27, in G. Ficker, *Die Phundagiagiten* (Leipzig, 1908), pp. 87–111. J. Wickert, 'Die Panoplia Dogmatica des Euthymios Zigabenos', *OC* 8 (1911), pp. 278–388. M. Jugie, AA, 'La Vie et les œuvres d'Euthyme Zigabène', *ÉO* 15 (1912), pp. 215–25. Modern study (in Greek) by A. N. Papavassiliou (2nd edn., Nicosia, 1979). Krumbacher, pp. 82–4; Beck (1959), pp. 614–16, with bibl. refs. M. Jugie, AA, in *DTC* 5 (1913), cols. 1577–82; G. Podskalsky in *TRE* 10 (1982), pp. 557 f., both s.v.

Eutyches (c.378–454), heresiarch. He was *archimandrite of a large monastery at *Constantinople, with great influence at court through the eunuch Chrysaphius. His keen opposition to *Nestorianism led him to be accused in 448 by *Eusebius of Dorylaeum of the opposite heresy of confounding the two natures in Christ (see CHRISTOLOGY). Deposed by *Flavian, Abp. of Constantinople, after synodical action, he then appealed to Pope *Leo for support, and by court influence secured a retrial and acquittal at the *Latrocinium at Ephesus in 449. Meanwhile, Leo repudiated his doctrines in his '*Tome'. A change of emperor in 450 turned the scales against him, and at the Council of *Chalcedon in 451 he was deposed and exiled. Eutyches affirmed that there was only one 'nature' (φύσις) in Christ 'after the union', and denied that His manhood was consubstantial with ours, a view which was held to be incompatible with our redemption through Him. Although the *Oriental Orthodox Churches share his language of 'one nature after the union', they explicitly condemned him for his denial that Christ's human nature was consubstantial with ours. See also MONOPHYSITISM.

E. *Schwartz, 'Der Prozess des Eutyches', *Sb.* (Bayr.) Jhrg. 1929, Heft 5 [texts with notes and comm.]. R. Draguet, 'La Christologie d'Eutychès d'après les Actes du Synode de Flavien (448)', *Byzantion*, 6 (1931), pp. 441–57; B. Emmi, OP, 'Leone ed Eutiche', *Angelicum*, 29 (1952), pp. 3–42. T. Camelot, OP, in A. Grillmeier, SJ, and H. Bacht, SJ (eds.), *Das Konzil von Chalkedon*, 1 (Würzburg, 1951), pp. 229–42, and H. Bacht, ibid. 2 (1953), pp. 197–222 and 224–8. M. Jugie in *DTC* 5 (1913), cols. 1582–609, s.v. 'Eutychès et eutychianisme', with full bibl.; J. H. Crehan, SJ, in *A Catholic Dictionary of Theology*, 2 (1967), pp. 243–6, s.v.; L. R. Wickham in *TRE* 10 (1982), pp. 558–65, s.v. For further bibl., see s.v. MONOPHYSITISM.

Eutychianism. See MONOPHYSITISM.

Evagrius Ponticus (346–99), spiritual writer. A native of Pontus, he was ordained deacon by St *Gregory of Nazianzus and became a noted preacher at *Constantinople. In 382 he departed to the *Nitrian desert, where he became a friend and disciple of St *Macarius of Egypt. Here he spent the rest of his life. From 553 onwards he was condemned several times for *Origenistic views.

Recent studies show that he occupies a central place in the history of Christian spirituality. The first monk to write extensively, he deeply influenced *Palladius, *Cassian, *Diadochus of Photike, and *Maximus the Confessor. Influenced by, and developing, Origenistic metaphysics, he worked out an account of the progress of the monk (or hermit) through ἀπάθεια (see APATHEIA) to contemplation, showing great psychological insight. His writings (largely lost or extant only in Lat. or Syr. translations) include his 'Monachos' or 'Practicos' (on the spiritual life of the monk); 'Gnostic Chapters' (a more advanced treatment of the same subject), prefaced by a brief work called *The Gnostic*; a treatise 'On Prayer' (at one time attributed to *Nilus of Ancyra); a collection of Apophthegms; and several letters. He also produced *scholia on Pss., Prov., and other biblical Books, which have only been discovered (sometimes only in part) in modern times.

Works (incomplete) in J. P. Migne, *PG* 40. 1213–86; also ibid. 79. 1165–1200 (*De Oratione* of 'Nilus'). W. Frankenberg, *Evagrius Ponticus* in *Abh.* (Gött.), NF 13. 2, 1912, pp. 49–635 (Syr. texts, with new Gk. retranslation). J. Muyldermans, *Evagriana Syriaca: Textes inédits du British Museum et de la Vaticane* (Bibliothèque du *Muséon*, 31; 1952), with Fr. tr.; Syr. text and Fr. tr. of *Kephalaia Gnostica* ed. A. Guillaumont (*PO* 28. 1; 1958). Crit. edns. of *Monachos*, with introd. and Fr. tr., by A. and C. Guillaumont (SC 170–1; 1971); of *The Gnostic*, with Fr. tr., by idd. (ibid. 356; 1989); and of *scholia* on Prov., with Fr. tr., by P. Géhin (ibid. 340; 1987). Eng. trs. of *Monachos* and 'On Prayer' by J. E. Bamberger, OCSO (Cistercian Studies Series, 4; '1970' [1972]). R. Melcher, *Der 8. Brief des hl. Basilius ein Werk des Evagrius Ponticus* (1923). J. Muyldermans, *A travers la tradition manuscrite d'Évagre le Pontique: Essai sur les manuscrits grecs conservés à la Bibliothèque Nationale de Paris* (Bibliothèque du *Muséon*, 3; 1932), and other works of this author. S. Marsili, OSB, *Giovanni Cassiano ed Evagrio Pontico: Dottrina sulla carità e contemplazione* (Studia Anselmiana, 5; 1936). I. Hausherr, 'Le Traité de l'oraison d'Évagre le Pontique', *Revue d'Ascétique et de Mystique*, 35 (1959), pp. 121–46, 241–65, 361–85; 36 (1960), pp. 3–35, 137–87, repr. as *Les Leçons d'un Contemplatif* (1960). A. Guillaumont, *Les 'Képhalaia Gnostica' d'Évagre le Pontique et l'histoire de l'origénisme chez les Grecs et chez les Syriens* (Patristica Sorbonensia, 5; 1962). J. Driscoll, OSB, *The 'Ad Monachos' of Evagrius Ponticus: Its Structure and a Select Commentary* (Studia Anselmiana, 104; 1991). D. J. Chitty, *The Desert a City* (Oxford, 1966), esp. pp. 49–53; A. Louth, *Origins of the Christian Mystical Tradition* (ibid., 1981), pp. 100–13. *CPG* 2 (1974), pp. 78–97 (nos. 2430–82). Altaner and Stuiber (1978), pp. 265–7 and 601 f. J. Lemaître, R. Roques, and M. Villier in *Dict. Sp.* 2 (1953), cols. 1775–85, s.v. 'Contemplation'; A. and C. Guillaumont ibid. 4 (1960), cols. 1731–44, s.v.; idd. in *RAC* 6 (1966), cols. 1088–107, s.v.

Evagrius Scholasticus (*c.*536–600), Church historian. A native of Coele-Syria, he was a lawyer by profession. His 'History', which is in six books, extends from the Council of *Ephesus (431) to 594, and thus continues the Histories of *Eusebius and his successors. Though a poor theologian and a credulous gatherer of legends, he made use of several excellent sources and, like Eusebius of Caesarea, incorporated extracts from them.

'Ecclesiastica Historica' with Lat. tr., ed. H. *Valesius and W. Reading in *Historiae Ecclesiasticae*, 3 (Cambridge, 1720), pp. 249–473; repr. in J. P. Migne, *PG* 86 (2). 2415–906. Crit. edn. by J. Bidez and L. Parmentier ('Byzantine Texts', London, 1898). Eng. tr., with short account of Evagrius and his writings, together with *Theodoret, in Bohn's Ecclesiastical Library (1854), pp. 251–467. Fr. tr., with notes, by A.-J. Festugière, OP, in *Byzantion*, 45 (1975), pp. 188–488. P. Allen, *Evagrius Scholasticus, the Church Historian* (SSL 41; 1981). *CPG* 3 (1979), p. 398 (no. 7500). Bardenhewer, 5 (1932), pp. 119 f.; G. Moravcsik, *Byzantinoturcica*, 1 (2nd edn., Berliner Byzantinistische Arbeiten, 10; 1958), pp. 257–9. A. de Halleux in *DHGE* 16 (1967), cols. 1495–8, s.v. [in Suppl.]; M. J. Higgins in *NCE* 5 (1967), p. 645, s.v.

Evangeliary. (1) A book containing the complete text of the Four Gospels. (2) The liturgical book containing the portions of the Four Gospels which are read as the 'Gospel' at the *Eucharist, arranged acc. to their place in the ecclesiastical calendar. When in the 10th cent. the practice of incorporating the text of the 'Gospel' into the *Sacramentaries began to become general, the Evangeliaries lost much of their importance, though in recent years they have in some places been brought back into prominence. The 1969 *Ordo Missae* recommended that the Gospel Book be carried in procession and placed on the lectern before the Gospel was read.

W. H. *Frere, *Studies in Early Roman Liturgy*, 2. *The Roman Gospel Lectionary* (Alcuin Club Collections, 30; 1934).

Evangelical Alliance. An interdenominational body, formed in London in 1846, to 'associate and concentrate the strength of an enlightened *Protestantism against the encroachments of *Popery and *Puseyism, and to promote the interests of a Scriptural Christianity'. Those responsible for its foundation included E. *Bickersteth and the Congregational minister John Angell James (1795–1859). It was the only definitely ecumenical organization which arose out of the evangelical movement of the 19th cent. It received support in varying degrees from almost the whole of the Protestant world, though the keen controversy on *slavery at its first meeting delayed the institution of a branch in the USA till 1867. Friedrich Wilhelm IV, who strongly favoured it, summoned a large meeting to Berlin in Sept. 1857; but it never gained a real hold in Germany, where its place was taken by the '*Evangelische Bund' (q.v.). Much work was done by the Alliance in the 19th cent. for oppressed religious minorities in Europe. In the 20th cent. its influence greatly declined and the American branch was dissolved in 1944. In 1951, however, the American National Association of Evangelicals and the British Evangelical Alliance held a joint conference at Woodschoten in the Netherlands. At this meeting the World Evangelical Fellowship was founded. It is composed of national interdenominational bodies of evangelical background, and has a statement of faith close to that of the Evangelical Alliance. From the first the Evangelical Alliance has observed a week early in January as an annual week of prayer.

J. A. Arnold, 'These Fifty Years. A Brief Epitome of the History of the Evangelical Alliance', in *Jubilee of the Evangelical Alliance: Proceedings of the Tenth International Conference held in London June–July 1896* (1897), pp. 43–64. J. W. Ewing, *Goodly Fellowship: A Centenary Tribute to the Life and Work of the World's Evangelical Alliance, 1846–1946* [1946]; J. E. Orr, *The Second*

Evangelical Awakening in Britain (1949). R. Rouse and S. C. Neill, *A History of the Ecumenical Movement*, 1 (2nd edn., 1967), esp. pp. 255–7 and 318–24. J. Cochlovius in *TRE* 10 (1982), pp. 650–6, s.v. 'Evangelische Allianz'. Reports of the General Conferences were usually issued under the title *The Religious Condition of Christendom*.

Evangelical Association. See following entry.

Evangelical Church. A small Protestant religious body, sometimes known as the **Albright Brethren** from their founder Jacob Albright (1759–1808), a native of Pennsylvania and a member of the *Lutheran Church. After an experience of conversion in 1791, Albright associated himself with the Methodist Episcopal Church and in 1796 began to preach among the Germans living in his state. Failing to win the support of his Methodist leaders, he created for his followers an independent organization. At a conference in 1809, his followers agreed to be known as the 'So-called Albright People', and from 1816 as the 'Evangelical Association'. About 1890 internal controversies led to a schism, but this was healed in 1922, and the reunited body called itself the 'Evangelical Church'. In 1946 it joined with another Church of similar background in the USA, the United Brethren in Christ, to form the Evangelical United Brethren Church; this itself merged with the Methodist Church in 1968 to form the United Methodist Church.

W. W. Orwig, *Geschichte der Evangelischen Gemeinschaft*, 1 [to 1845] (all pub., Cleveland, Oh. 1857; Eng. tr., ibid., 1858); R. Yaekel, *Albright and his Co-Labourers* (ibid., 1883); id., *History of the Evangelical Association* (2 vols., ibid., 1892–5). S. P. Spreng, 'History of the Evangelical Association', in *The American Church History Series*, 12 (New York, 1894), pp. 383–439. A. Stapleton, *Annals of the Evangelical Association of North America and History of the United Evangelical Church* (Harrisburg, Pa., 1900); R. W. Albright, *A History of the Evangelical Church* (ibid., 1942). F. A. Norwood, *The Story of American Methodism* (Nashville and New York [1974]), esp. pp. 111–18 and 419–25. R. Kücklich, *Die evangelische Gemeinschaft in Europa: Ill. Festschrift zum 75-jähr. Jubiläum ihres Bestehens, 1850–1925* (1925).

Evangelical Church in Germany (*Evangelische Kirche in Deutschsland*). The federation of autonomous Protestant territorial Churches (*Landeskirchen*) in Germany.

A precursor of the federation may be seen in the Eisenach Conference of the governing bodies of the territorial Churches (1852–1903); in 1903 the regional Churches formed a closer link through the German Evangelical Churches Committee, in 1922 changed into the German Evangelical Church Federation, which existed until Nazi pressure in 1933 led to the establishment of the German Evangelical Church and the conflict between the *German-Christians and the *Confessing Church over its government. Leaders of the Confessing Church played a prominent part in the establishment of the Evangelical Church in Germany after the end of the Second World War.

Seven of the 27 member Churches were already united in the Evangelical Church of the Union, which owed its origin to the attempt of King Frederick William III of Prussia in 1817 to unite the Lutheran and Reformed Churches in his province. Within these Churches, which form the largest single unit in the Evangelical Church in Germany, there is full sacramental fellowship, but the strictly Lutheran Churches are not yet officially in full communion with them or with the other smaller Reformed bodies. In 1948 the Lutheran regional Churches formed the United Evangelical Lutheran Church of Germany within the Evangelical Church in Germany. In 1969 the 8 *Landeskirchen* of E. Germany were forced to withdraw from the Evangelical Church in Germany and formed their own League of Evangelical Churches. A fresh attempt was then made to reach a greater measure of unity between the remaining (W. German) members of the Evangelical Church in Germany. This was based on the so-called *Leuenberg Concord of 1973 which was adopted by the Protestant Churches in E. and W. Europe. However, although the central bodies of the Evangelical Church in Germany passed the reform, it failed to achieve ratification in all the member Churches. Following the unification of Germany in 1990, steps were taken to unite the two Evangelical Churches, and in 1991 the *Landeskirchen* of the former German Democratic Republic rejoined those of the Evangelical Church in Germany.

The Evangelical Church in Germany is governed by a Council, a Conference of Churches, and a Synod. These central bodies have discussed major matters of public policy ever since 1945, incl. German rearmament, nuclear weapons, and reconciliation with Germany's eastern neighbours. The legacy of the 1930s has made the question of the proper political role of the Church an acute one. The Evangelical Church in Germany has been at the centre of political controversy but has reaffirmed its belief that the Church should not be bound to a particular political view.

H. Brunotte, *Die Evangelische Kirche in Deutschland: Geschichte, Organisation und Gestalt der EKD* (Gütersloh, 1964). F. Spotts, *The Churches and Politics in Germany* (Middletown, Conn., 1973), *passim*. H. Rudolph, *Evangelische Kirche und Vertriebene 1945 bis 1972* (Arbeiten zur kirchlichen Zeitgeschichte, Reihe B, 11–12; 1984–5). R. F. Goeckel, *The Lutheran Church and the East German State: Political Conflict and Change under Ulbricht and Honecker* (Ithaca, NY, and London, 1990). E. Wilkens in *Evangelisches Staatslexikon*, ed. H. Kunst and others (2nd edn., 1975), cols. 639–50; W.-D. Hauschild in *TRE* 10 (1982), pp. 656–77, both s.v. 'Evangelische Kirche in Deutschland'. Annual reports on the Evangelical Church in Germany (and until 1990 on the League of Evangelical Churches in the GDR) appear in *Kirchliches Jahrbuch für die Evangelische Kirche in Deutschland* (formerly *Kirchliches Jahrbuch für die evangelischen Landeskirchen Deutschlands*) (Gütersloh, 1948 ff.).

Evangelical Counsels. See COUNSELS OF PERFECTION.

Evangelicalism. (1) In a wider sense the term 'Evangelical' has been applied since the Reformation to the Protestant Churches by reason of their claim to base their teaching pre-eminently on the 'Gospel'. The Church created in Prussia in 1817 by the union of *Lutheran and *Reformed was officially known as the 'Evangelical Church' (*Evangelische Kirche*). A more recent instance is the inclusive designation of all the Protestant Churches of Germany as the 'Evangelische Kirche in Deutschland' (see EVANGELICAL CHURCH IN GERMANY).

(2) In Germany and Switzerland, the word 'Evangelical' (*evangelisch*) was long in use, esp. of the Lutheran group of Protestant Churches as contrasted with the *Calvinist ('Reformed') bodies.

(3) In the C of E the term is currently applied to the school which lays special stress on conversion and salvation by faith in the atoning death of Christ. The group originated in the 18th cent. to bring reality into religion when a low tone pervaded English life and many clergy were negligent and worldly. It has several points of contact with the *Methodist movement, esp. in the more Calvinistic form of G. *Whitefield. The most influential leaders of the early period were H. *Venn (1725–97) and J. *Newton (1725–1807); they encouraged the Evangelical clergy to respect parochial boundaries and not to separate from the C of E. To a rather later period belonged C. *Simeon (1759–1836). He made Evangelicalism a force at *Cambridge and indirectly at the other universities, and prepared clergy and laity for work in the parishes and overseas; those who came under his influence included H. *Martyn (1781–1812). Simeon also bought livings, esp. in towns, and founded a body of trustees to administer Church patronage in accordance with Evangelical principles. At the same time the Elland Society built up a large fund to finance Evangelical ordinands. Various clerical societies kept Evangelicals together. Dislike of their religious earnestness led to much opposition, but the piety and humanity of the Evangelicals gradually won them a large following. In parliament W. *Wilberforce (1759–1833) led a group known as 'the Saints'; they campaigned vigorously for the abolition of the *slave trade and the extension of missionary enterprise in *India. The Church Missionary Society (*CMS) and the Colonial (later Commonwealth) and Continental Church Society (*CCCS) both owe their origin to the Evangelicals. They were also involved in the early growth of the *British and Foreign Bible Society.

From about 1830 Anglican Evangelicalism narrowed and there were divisions between the extreme and moderate Evangelicals, esp. over belief in the return of Christ before the millennium. There was a general acceptance of belief in the verbal inspiration of the Bible and resistance to the findings of science and biblical criticism. The more extreme views found expression in the *Record, under the control of Alexander Haldane (1810–82); its contributors included H. McNeile (1795–1879) of Liverpool, H. Stowell (1799–1865) of Salford, and F. *Close (1797–1882) of Cheltenham. More moderate views were found in the Christian Observer (1802–77), whose first editor was Z. *Macaulay. E. *Bickersteth (1786–1850) and H. *Venn (1796–1873) of the CMS were among the leaders of moderate Evangelicalism. On the positive side the first Evangelical bishops, H. *Ryder (1777–1836), J. B. *Sumner (1780–1862), and C. R. *Sumner (1790–1874), raised the standard of episcopal care in their dioceses, esp. in the administration of *Ordination and *Confirmation. Scripture readers from the London City Mission (founded in 1835) and the *CPAS worked effectively in the inner cities. Lord *Shaftesbury (1801–85) initiated the Factory Acts. The centre of Evangelicalism is the home and family, and from Evangelical families came many Christian leaders, not all of whom remained Evangelical. Early rising and family prayers have been at the heart of Evangelical piety.

Anglican Evangelicalism changed direction again under the American influence of the revivalist movements of the 1870s and 1880s and of the *Keswick Convention. Foreign missions became the priority. With the stress on personal consecration and world evangelism, social and political reform disappeared from the Evangelical programme and was discouraged in university Christian unions. The most important Evangelical figure of this period was Bp. J. C. *Ryle (1816–1900).

In the 20th cent. there has been a deep division among Evangelicals. *Liberal Evangelicals accepted the findings of biblical criticism and in 1923 formed the *Anglican Evangelical Group Movement. Conservative Evangelicals, on the other hand, stood firm on the authority of Scripture and its verbal inspiration, and in 1922 the *BCMS broke away from the CMS on this issue. Max Warren (1904–77), who in 1942 became secretary of the CMS, did all that he could to liberalize Evangelical attitudes in the face of the growing influence of the more *Fundamentalist American Evangelicals; he sought to promote Evangelical research and writing on a broad basis by the formation of the 'Evangelical Fellowship for Theological Literature' (1942–72). In the post-war period the Conservative Evangelicals, under the leadership of John Stott (b. 1921), have experienced a revival which has made them one of the most influential elements in the C of E. The 'crusades' of Billy *Graham, the Charismatic Movement, a serious interest in academic theology, and experiments in new forms of worship and evangelism have all contributed to this growth. The first National Evangelical Anglican Conference at Keele in 1967 broke the isolation of a century. Since then Conservative Evangelicals have played a full part in the General *Synod and other councils of the C of E, often working with *Anglo-Catholics in opposition to liberalism. They now take part in the *Ecumenical Movement, and there has been a new concern for politics and social justice and a more positive attitude towards the enjoyment of culture.

D. W. Bebbington, Evangelicalism in Modern Britain: A History from the 1730s to the 1980s (1989); K. Hylson-Smith, Evangelicalism in the Church of England 1734–1984 (Edinburgh, 1989). L. E. Binns, The Early Evangelicals: A Religious and Social Study (1953); C. I. Foster, An Errand of Mercy: The Evangelical United Front, 1780–1837 (Chapel Hill, NC [1960]); F. K. Brown, Fathers of the Victorians: The Age of Wilberforce (Cambridge, 1961). K. [J.] Heasman, Evangelicals in Action: An Appraisal of their Social Work in the Victorian Era (1962); [W.] O. Chadwick, The Victorian Church, 1 (1966), pp. 440–55; I. [C.] Bradley, The Call to Seriousness: The Evangelical Impact upon the Victorians (1976); M. [M.] Hennell, Sons of the Prophets: Evangelical Leaders of the Victorian Church (1979); P. Toon, Evangelical Theology 1833–1856: A Response to Tractarianism (1979); E. Jay, The Religion of the Heart: Anglican Evangelicalism and the Nineteenth-Century Novel (Oxford, 1979); D. M. Rosman, Evangelicals and Culture [1984]; R. Manwaring, From Controversy to Co-Existence: Evangelicals in the Church of England 1914–1980 (Cambridge, 1985); E. [G.] Rupp, Religion in England 1688–1791 (Oxford History of the Christian Church, 1986), pp. 325–490; B. Hilton, The Age of Atonement: The Influence of Evangelicalism on Social and Economic Thought, 1785–1865 (Oxford, 1988); M. A. Noll and others (eds.), Evangelicalism: Comparative Studies of Popular Protestantism in North America, the British Isles, and Beyond, 1700–1900 (New York and Oxford, 1994).

Evangelical Union. A religious denomination formed in Scotland in 1843. In 1841 James *Morison (1816–93), minister of a United Secession congregation in Kilmarnock and a close biblical student, was suspended by his presbytery for his anti-Calvinistic views. He affirmed that Christ made atonement for all and condemned the doctrine of unconditional election. In 1843, along with three other ministers, he founded the 'Evangelical Union', which was soon joined by a number of Scottish Congregationalists. The Union was an association of independent Churches over which it exercised no jurisdiction. Its members were commonly called 'Morisonians'. In 1897 most of the Churches in the Union joined with the Congregational Union of Scotland.

H. Escott, *A History of Scottish Congregationalism* (Glasgow, 1960), pp. 116–34, 165–82.

Evangelische Bund (Ger., 'Evangelical League'). An alliance of German Protestants founded in 1886–7 by Prof. W. *Beyschlag and others for the defence of Protestant interests against the growing power of Catholicism. It furthered its purposes by contacts with the secular press and through the issue of literature of its own, as well as by other methods. The movement, which took on a strongly nationalistic colour in the years immediately preceding the War of 1914–1918, had gained by 1914 a membership of 540,000, though its influence decreased subsequently. After 1933 a greater emphasis on the theological basis led to a better understanding of Catholic thinking. The headquarters of the Evangelische Bund in Berlin, with its library and archives, were destroyed in 1942, but in 1947 it established an institute for confessional research at Bensheim in Hessen. This has provided a centre specializing in the study of non-Protestant Churches, in particular the RC Church and its attitude to social and political questions. Contact is maintained with similar organizations in W. and E. Europe and there are frequent conferences.

H. Hüttenrauch, *Der evangelische Bund: Sein Werden, Wachsen und Wirken* (1911). W. Beyschlag, *Zur Entstehungsgeschichte des evangelischen Bundes* (1926). G. Maron (ed.), *Evangelisch und Ökumenisch: Beiträge zum 100jährigen Bestehen des Evangelischen Bundes* (Kirche und Konfession, 25; Göttingen, 1986). W. Fleischmann-Bisten and H. Grote, *Protestanten auf dem Weg: Geschichte des Evangelischen Bundes* (Bensheimer Hefte, 65; ibid., 1986). W. Beyschlag in *PRE* (3rd edn.), 3 (1897), pp. 549–53, s.v. 'Bund, Evangelischer'; H. Grote in *TRE* 10 (1982), pp. 683–6, s.v.

Evangelische Kirche in Deutschland. See EVANGELICAL CHURCH IN GERMANY.

evangelist (Gk. εὐαγγελιστής, 'a proclaimer of the εὐαγγέλιον or Gospel').
(1) In the NT the word is thrice used of a travelling missionary (Acts 21: 8; Eph. 4: 11; 2 Tim. 4: 5). Probably no special office is designated, but the evangelist ordinarily combined his duty of proclaiming the Gospel with such offices as those of *bishop or *deacon. *Philip, e.g., was both a 'deacon' and an 'evangelist' and the Apostles are also said to have 'evangelized'. In modern usage the word is applied to certain laymen in Protestant Churches who undertake popular preaching.
(2) In a more technical sense, the author of one of the canonical Gospels, i.e. exclusively St *Matthew, St *Mark, St *Luke, and St *John. This usage established itself in the 3rd cent. Traditionally the four evangelists are symbolized respectively by a man, a lion, an ox, and an eagle, on the basis of Rev. 4: 6–10.

Evangelistarium (Gk. εὐαγγελιστάριον). In the Orthodox Church, a book of tables indicating the Gospel lections for each year in accordance with the varying date of *Easter.

Evangelium Veritatis. A *Gnostic treatise included among the Coptic texts discovered at *Nag Hammadi, which opens with the words 'The Gospel of Truth'. 'Gospel' here seems to bear the non-technical sense of 'good news', and the phrase is not given separately as a title. The work expounds the mission of Jesus as 'the Word' or 'the Name' of the Father, alludes briefly to His teaching ministry, and comments on His death on the Cross and its significance. There are numerous similarities with the New Testament, but also some unusual features, such as the attribution of evil to Error, personified as a female figure (Planē). *Irenaeus (*Adv. Haer.* 3. 11. 9) mentions a work produced by the disciples of *Valentinus, which was composed not long before the time of writing (*c.* AD 180) and 'presumptuously' entitled 'Veritatis Evangelium' (Gospel of Truth), though quite unlike the other gospels; it has been suggested that the present work is in question, that it was written by Valentinus, and represents the less unorthodox thought of his early years (*c.* AD 140). The work certainly shows little trace of the elaborate speculations which are usually associated with the Valentinian system; some scholars, however, believe that they are presupposed, though not emphasized, in order to conciliate orthodox opinion; others that the work has no connection with Valentinus.

Facsimile, with edn. of Coptic text and translations into Fr., Ger. and Eng., by M. Malinine, H.-C. Puech, and G. Quispel, *Evangelium Veritatis* (Zurich, 1956, with suppl., 1961). Coptic text also pr., with Eng. tr., introd. and bibl., by H. W. Attridge and G. W. MacRae, SJ, in H. W. Attridge (ed.), *Nag Hammadi Codex I* (Nag Hammadi Studies, 22–3; 1985), 1, pp. 55–122, with notes, 2, pp. 39–135. Eng. tr. also in J. M. Robinson (ed.), *The Nag Hammadi Library in English* (3rd edn., Leiden, 1988), pp. 38–51. J.-É. Ménard, *L'Évangile de Vérité* (Nag Hammadi Studies, 2; Leiden, 1972). H.-C. Puech in Schneemelcher, 1 (1959), pp. 160–6; Eng. tr., 1 (1963), pp. 233–41. *CPG* 1 (1983), pp. 71–3 (no. 1177).

Evanson, Edward (1731–1805), divine. After becoming Vicar of *Tewkesbury in 1769, and of Longdon in Worcestershire in 1770, he developed views with *Unitarian affinities, advocating the removal of the *Nicene and *Athanasian creeds from the BCP. A prosecution instituted against him in 1775 before the Bp. of *Gloucester failed on a technical point, but in 1778 he resigned his living and became a schoolmaster at Mitcham. Here he held occasional services and administrations of the Lord's Supper, which he considered the only Sacrament. Besides some controversial writings against J. *Priestley, he published *The Dissonance of the Four Generally Received Evangelists* (Ipswich, 1792), in which he accepted only the Gospel of Luke. His book was the earliest formal attack on the traditional authorship of St John's Gospel.

His Sermons were issued in 2 vols. in 1807, prefixed by a Life. T. Falconer replied to his book on the Gospels in his *Bampton Lectures for 1810 (pub. 1811). F. Strachotta, *Edward Evanson, 1731–1805* (Theologische Arbeiten zur Bibel-, Kirchen-, und Geistesgeschichte, 12; Halle, 1940). *DNB* 18 (1889), pp. 78 f. (unsigned).

Evanston, Illinois. The Second Assembly of the *World Council of Churches met at Evanston in 1954.

The Evanston Report, ed. W. A. Visser 't Hooft (1955).

Eve. The first woman, the wife of *Adam. Acc. to Gen. 3: 20 she was so named because she was the mother of all living beings; but the Hebrew word (חַוָּה) for Eve may have meant 'serpent', and her name thus been associated with the primitive myth that all life originated in a primeval serpent. Eve is tempted by the serpent to eat of the fruit of the tree of knowledge; she and Adam disobey, '*fall', and are driven out from *Eden; and Eve is punished with the pain of childbirth. In the NT (1 Cor. 11: 9 f., 1 Tim. 2: 13 ff.) the relationship of Adam and Eve is used by St *Paul to support his teaching about the relative status of man and woman in Christian worship. It was a common medieval conceit that the Latin form of her name ('Eva'), spelled backwards, was the first word of the angel's address to the BVM ('Ave') and symbolized the reversal of Eve's fall through the Incarnation. Recently the figure of Eve has become important for *Feminist Theology.

The principal discussions are to be found in comm. on GENESIS, cited s.v. A. M. Dubarle, OP, 'Les Fondements bibliques du titre marial de Nouvelle Ève', Mélanges Jules Lebreton, 1 (Rech. S.R. 39; 1951), pp. 49–64. M. Leisch-Kiesl, Eva als Andere: Eine exemplarische Untersuchung zu Frühchristentum und Mittelalter (Cologne, 1992). E. Mangenot in DTC 5 (1915), cols. 1640–55; M. Planque, SJ, in Dict. Sp. 4 (pt. 2; 1961), cols. 1772–88, both s.v.

Evelyn, John (1620–1706), Anglican diarist. Born at Wotton in Surrey, he was educated at Southover free school, near Lewes, and at Balliol College, Oxford. In 1641 he visited the Netherlands and later (1643–5) travelled extensively in France and Italy. In 1647 at Paris he married Mary, the daughter of Sir Richard Browne (1605–1683), a girl of not more than 12 years. In 1649, after the King's execution, he went abroad again. After his final return (Feb. 1652) he settled at Sayes Court, a large estate near Deptford. Here he interested himself in rural pursuits until the *Restoration, carrying on a friendly correspondence with John *Wilkins, then Warden of Wadham, and Robert *Boyle, with both of whom he was closely associated in the creation of the Royal Society. He also became connected with Jeremy *Taylor, whom, among other dispossessed clergy, he befriended under the Commonwealth. He enjoyed the favour of *Charles II and *James II and was on intimate terms with many leading personalities of the time. He held several royal appointments, nobly remaining at his post when one of these required his residence in London during the Great Plague. He played a prominent part in Church affairs, esp. in the rebuilding of *St Paul's Cathedral, and continued to take an active interest in the Royal Society. After the Revolution he lived in comparative retirement.

Evelyn's wide interests made him a prolific writer. The Diary, if it lacks the liveliness of that of Pepys (1633–1703), is a true reflection of his character and an important document for social history. It reveals him as a man of scholarly temperament and wide culture, which he combined with a firm devotion, and a strong loyalty to the royalist cause even though he disapproved of much of the life of the Court. His best-known works include Fumifugium (1661), Sculptura (1662), and Sylva (1664). Of more specifically religious interest are his Mystery of Jesuitism (1664), The Pernicious Consequences of the New Heresie of the Jesuites Against the King and the State (anon., 1666) and his translation of The Golden Book of St John Chrysostom concerning the Education of Children (1659); and two posthumous publications, The Life of Mrs. [Margaret] Godolphin (ed. S. *Wilberforce, 1847) and The History of Religion (ed. R. M. Evanson, 2 vols., 1850).

Extracts from his Diary and some letters first pub. by W. Bray (2 vols., London, 1818). The complete text ed., with comm., by E. S. de Beer (6 vols., Oxford, 1955); repr., with some omissions and no comm. (Oxford Standard Authors, 1959). Modern Life by A. Ponsonby (London, 1933); short study by F. Higham (ibid., 1968). W. G. Hiscock, John Evelyn and Mrs. Godolphin (1951); id., John Evelyn and his Family Circle (1955). J. Bowle, John Evelyn and his World (1981). G. [L.] Keynes, John Evelyn: A Study in Bibliophily with a Bibliography of his Writings (Cambridge, 1937; 2nd edn., Oxford, 1968).

evening Communion. There are possible references to evening celebrations of the Eucharist in the NT (e.g. 1 Cor. 11: 21), but it would appear that an early hour of the day soon became the usual time. After the *Reformation certain Protestant Churches, which held the service to be mainly commemorative, celebrated the Lord's Supper in the morning or evening indiscriminately. In the C of E the practice of evening Communion appears to date from the middle of the 19th cent. It was introduced by W. F. *Hook at Leeds in 1852 in order to meet the needs of his industrial parish. From the first it met with much opposition (notably from H. P. *Liddon) as in conflict with the traditional rule of fasting from the previous midnight, and until the middle of the present cent. it was a mark of *Low Churchmanship. In the RC Church rules about the *Eucharistic Fast were relaxed and evening Masses permitted in military establishments during the Second World War. In 1953 *Pius XII's encyclical 'Christus Dominus' permitted evening Masses generally on *Feasts of Obligation, *First Fridays, and certain other occasions. The *Maundy Thursday Mass was restored to an evening hour in 1955 and two years later in the motu proprio 'Sacram Communionem' permission for an evening Mass was extended to every day when pastoral reasons demanded it. Since then celebrations of the Eucharist in the evening have become generally accepted in the RC Church in both parish churches and religious houses, and are also now found in both *High and Low Church circles in the C of E.

The practice was deprecated in many episcopal charges in the 19th cent., notably by S. *Wilberforce, Bp. of *Oxford. [H. P. Liddon], 'Evening Communion', The Christian Remembrancer, 40 (1861 for 1860), pp. 191–214; repr., with additions and notes [by W. *Bright; also anon.], as Evening Communion Contrary to the Teaching and Practice of the Church in all Ages (1872); J. Hughes-Games, Evening Communion: The Argument for the Practice Stated and the Objections against it Answered (1894). E. Dekkers, OSB, 'L'Église ancienne a-t-elle connu la messe du soir?', in Miscellanea Liturgica in Honorem L. Cuniberti Mohlberg, 1 (Bibliotheca 'Ephemerides Liturgicae', Sect. Hist., 22; 1948), pp. 231–57, with refs. See also bibl. to EUCHARISTIC FAST.

Evening Prayer. See EVENSONG. The term is also sometimes used of the evening Office (*Vespers) provided in the 1971 *Breviary.

Evensong. The name given in medieval England to the canonical hour of *Vespers. It is now in common use for the BCP service of Evening Prayer. The structure of this latter is closely related to the traditional type of Divine service. After preparatory prayers the service proper opens with the versicles and responses, 'O Lord, open thou, etc.', and the *Lord's Prayer. This is followed by certain Psalms varying acc. to the day of the month, a reading from the OT, the *Magnificat, a further reading from the NT, and the *Nunc Dimittis. After the recitation of the *Apostles' Creed follow the *Kyrie Eleison, the Lord's Prayer, versicles and responses, the Collect for the day, two invariable collects, 'in quires and places where they sing' the *anthem, and further prayers. In substance it is a conflation of the *Sarum services of Vespers and *Compline. The name 'Evensong', found in the 1549 BCP, was replaced by 'Evening Prayer' in 1552, but came back again (in the Table of Proper Lessons) in 1662.

In the ASB, Ps. 134, the *Phos Hilaron, or the Easter Anthems precede the Psalms of the day; the recitation of the Psalter at Mattins and Evensong may be spread over about ten weeks; and there are alternative canticles to the Magnificat and Nunc Dimittis. If the Eucharist is to follow, the service is drastically curtailed. There is also a Shorter Form, with one biblical reading and one canticle, which varies according to the day of the week. Other modern Anglican liturgies have made similar modifications.

Evergetinos, Paul (d. 1054), compiler of an influential monastic *florilegium. After founding a monastery called Theotokos Evergetis near *Constantinople, around 1050 he put together a selection of spiritual texts in four books, each containing 50 chapters. It was entitled by him *Synagoge*, but is usually referred to as the *Evergetinon*. It draws on a relatively small library of authors (e.g. John *Cassian, *Barsanuphius, *Diadochus, *Ephraem Syrus, *Isaac of Nineveh, *Mark the Hermit, and *Maximus the Confessor), but it is remarkable for the wealth of its anonymous hagiographical material (drawn mainly from the *Menologion and monastic collections) and the solidity of its teaching. Frequently copied in the Middle Ages, its publication by *Nicodemus of the Holy Mountain (Venice, 1783) won for it an immense influence in modern Greek Orthodox spirituality.

There is no crit. edn. of the *Evergetinon*, but the 1783 text has often been reissued, e.g. 4 vols., Athens, 1977. The basic modern study is that of M. Richard in *Dict. Sp.* 5 (1964), cols. 502 f., s.v. 'Florilèges spirituels grecs, 3. Florilèges monastiques, 20, L'Évergétinon', repr. in his *Opera Minora*, 1 (Turnhout and Louvain, 1976), first item. I. Hausherr, SJ, 'Paul Évergétinos a-t-il connu Syméon le Nouveau Théologien?', *OCP* 23 (1957), pp. 58–79; repr. in his *Études de Spiritualité Orientale* (Orientalia Christiana Analecta, 183; 1969), pp. 262–83. Beck (1959), p. 587. A. Solignac, SJ, in *Dict. Sp.* 12 (pt. 1; 1984), cols. 562–4, s.v. 'Paul Évergétinos'.

On the monastery, R. Janin, AA, *La Géographie ecclésiastique de l'empire byzantin*, première partie, *Le Siège de Constantinople et le patriarcat œcuménique*, 3, *Les églises et les monastères* (2nd edn., 1969), pp. 178–84.

Evurtius, St (4th cent.), Bp. of Orléans. The correct form of St *Enurchus (q.v.).

Ewald, Heinrich Georg August (1803–75), OT theologian and orientalist. He was educated at the University of Göttingen, where he taught from 1827 to 1837. In 1838 he went to *Tübingen and joined in the attack on F. C. *Baur and the Tübingen School. From 1847 to 1867 he was back in Göttingen. He was the author of a long series of books. His 'Hebrew Grammar' (1827) was a landmark in the history of OT philology, but of even greater influence was his *Geschichte des Volkes Israel* (5 vols., 1843–55; two further vols. on the Apostolic Age were added to the 2nd edn. in 1858–9). In its English translation (vol. 5, 1865; the rest, 1867–86) it much influenced British scholarship. Ewald exercised a restraining influence on some of the negative tendencies of the OT criticism of his day.

Life by T. Witton Davies (London, 1903). T. K. *Cheyne, *Founders of Old Testament Criticism* (1893), pp. 66–118. J. Rogerson, *Old Testament Criticism in the Nineteenth Century: England and Germany* (1984), pp. 91–103.

Exaltation of the Cross. The feast in honour of the Cross of Christ, observed on 14 Sept. It is also known as 'Holy Cross Day'. In the W. Church, the *Martyrology and *Offices commemorate on this day the exposition of the supposed true Cross at *Jerusalem in 629 by the Emp. *Heraclius, after his recovery of it from the Persians into whose hands it had fallen in 614. Actually this event in Jerusalem took place in the spring, and the date, 14 Sept., has become attached to it through confusion with a much earlier commemoration kept in Jerusalem on that day, namely of the dedication in 335 of the basilica built by the Emp. *Constantine on the site of the *Holy Sepulchre. It seems likely that the '*Invention' of the Cross, formerly observed on 3 May, was commemorated on this day before the celebration of the incident of 629.

The first clear mention of the Feast in the W. is in the notice of Pope *Sergius (687–701) in the *LP* (ed. Duchesne), 1, p. 374; cf. Duchesne's note, pp. 378 f. There is an early ref. to the adoration of the Cross at Jerusalem in the *Pilgrimage of *Egeria* (chs. 48 f.); but Egeria does not record its date of observance in the calendar. Cf. A. Bludau, *Die Pilgerreise der Aetheria* (Studien zur Geschichte und Kultur des Altertums, 15, Hefte 1–2; 1927), pp. 185–90. I. de Combes, *Études sur les souvenirs de la Passion: La Vraie Croix perdue et retrouvée* (1902; Eng. tr., 1907). H. Thurston, SJ, 'Relics, Authentic and Spurious' [The Cross and Title], *The Month*, 155 (1930), pp. 420–9. H. *Leclercq, OSB, in *DACL* 3 (pt. 2; 1914), cols. 3131–9, s.v. 'Croix (Invention et exaltation de la vraie)'; A. Bugnini, in *EC* 4 (1950), cols. 960–3, s.v. 'Croce VII'. See also bibl. to INVENTION OF THE CROSS.

examining chaplains. The duty of examining candidates for holy orders belongs properly to the *archdeacon, as the BCP Ordinal shows. But can. C 7 of the 1969 Canons requires further that candidates be diligently examined by the archdeacons 'and other ministers appointed for this purpose', regarding their knowledge of Holy Scripture and the doctrine, discipline, and worship of the C of E. Can. 35 of the 1604 Canons specified that examining chaplains should be at least three in number; should be members of the cathedral church, if possible, or at any rate of the diocese; and should assist at the laying-on of hands. These requirements no longer apply.

S. C. Gayford in *PBD* (1912), pp. 326 f., s.v. 'Examination'.

exapostilarion (Gk. ἐξαποστειλάριον, from ἐξαπο- στέλλω, 'dismiss'). A *troparion occurring at the end of the *canon at *Orthros in the E. Church.

exarch. The title of: (1) certain civil governors in the later Roman Empire, notably the Exarch of *Ravenna; (2) certain bishops lower in rank than *patriarchs but having rights over the *metropolitans of one civil diocese (though the title has sometimes been given to patriarchs and metropolitans themselves).

excardination (Lat. *cardo*, 'hinge'; hence *excardinare*, 'to unhinge'). In W. canon law, the liberation of a cleric from his present *Ordinary with a view to fresh enlistment ('incardination') under a new superior. For details see INCARDINATION.

ex cathedra. See CATHEDRA.

Exceptions. The long list of objections made by the *Puritans at the *Savoy Conference (1661) to the existing Prayer Book (of 1604) with a view to its revision. They were directed against certain of the Book's doctrinal affirmations and ceremonial prescriptions, as well as minor matters where no question of principle was involved. The Puritans pressed for such changes as the omission of *Lent and of saints' days with their vigils, the use of the AV instead of the text of the *Great Bible (1539) for all scriptural passages in the Book, the substitution of the word 'minister' for 'priest' and 'curate', and of 'Lord's Day' for 'Sunday'. Of a few of these 'Exceptions' account was taken in the revised Book of 1662, but for the most part they were disallowed.

Text in E. *Cardwell, *A History of Conferences . . . connected with . . . the Book of Common Prayer* (1840), ch. 7, § S.

Exclusion, Right of (Lat. *Ius Exclusionis* or *Ius Exclusivae*). The right formerly claimed by the heads of certain Catholic states to name a particular candidate whom they desired to exclude from being elected Pope. The claim goes back to the 16th cent., and the last occasion on which it was exercised was by the Austrians in 1903 (against Cardinal Rampolla). The right was finally annulled by *Pius X in *Commissum Nobis* (20 Jan. 1904) and *Vacante Sede Apostolica* (25 Dec. 1904).

Exclusion Controversy. The crisis caused by the attempt of the Whigs, led by the first Earl of Shaftesbury, to exclude James, Duke of York (later *James II), from the succession to the throne after his brother *Charles II. Liberties, religion, and property were held to be in danger from the RC views and absolutist inclinations of the Duke. The crisis was set in motion by T. *Oates's announcement of the *Popish Plot, and the question of Exclusion dominated elections to and sessions of three successive Parliaments in 1679–81. A Bill to exclude James failed to pass beyond the Commons in 1679, and another was rejected by the Lords next year; at the Oxford Parliament of 1681 Charles II took advantage of fears of another civil war and scored a complete triumph over the Whigs, which he followed up with various successful counter-measures against them in the next two years. The controversy gave rise to

much polemical writing (e.g. by J. *Dryden and J. *Locke) and to violent anti-Catholic feeling.

J. R. Jones, *The First Whigs: The Politics of the Exclusion Crisis, 1678–1683* (1961). K. H. D. Haley, *The First Earl of Shaftesbury* (Oxford, 1968), *passim*. T. Harris, *London Crowds in the Reign of Charles II: Propaganda and Politics from the Restoration until the Exclusion Crisis* (Cambridge, 1987), esp. pp. 62–188. See also bibls. to CHARLES II and JAMES II.

excommunication. An ecclesiastical censure imposed by competent authority which excludes those subjected to it from the communion of the faithful and imposes on them other deprivations and disabilities. It does not profess to extend to the union of the soul with God, since that union is held to depend on the immediate effect of sanctifying grace and to be unaffected by any act of the Church. Hence it is not impossible for a man to be excommunicated and yet to be and remain in a state of grace.

In early times excommunication could be either 'greater' or 'less'. Basically, the greater deprived a man of his right to administer or receive the Sacraments and of all intercourse, private or public, with his fellow Christians, and of all rights and privileges in the Church. The lesser deprived him only of the right to receive the Sacraments and to hold ecclesiastical office. In the modern RC Church a related distinction between those excommunicate '*vitandi' and '*tolerati' survived until recently, supported by an elaborate legal structure. This has been radically changed by the 1983 *Codex Iuris Canonici*. Excommunication is now one of the censures or 'medicinal' *penalties; it is either declared or imposed by an ecclesiastical authority, or it is incurred automatically, e.g. by procuring an *abortion. All excommunicated persons are forbidden to celebrate the Sacraments or to receive them (except when in danger of death), to take any ministerial part in ceremonies of public worship, or to exercise any ecclesiastical offices, ministries, functions, or acts of government. If the excommunication has been imposed or declared, some additional consequences follow: if the excommunicated person tries to take a ministerial part in public worship, he is to be prevented from doing so or the liturgical action is to stop, unless there is a serious reason to the contrary; acts of governance which would otherwise have been valid, though illicit, are invalidated; and no income from offices connected with the Church may be enjoyed (can. 1331).

In the Anglican Church the use of excommunication is implied in the rubrics of the BCP and was openly threatened in the canons of 1604. In the 17th cent. it was fairly commonly applied for a variety of misdemeanours, but after the *Restoration its frequent use brought it into discredit with both the laity and the spiritual authorities, and it became increasingly rare in the C of E. The 1969 Canons, however, still envisage the possibility of dying after being 'declared excommunicate for some grievous and notorious crime', and excommunication is more common in the Anglican Churches overseas, esp. in missionary dioceses. Except in the case of heathen converts, it is usually confined to 'minor excommunication'.

W. Doskocil, *Der Bann in der Urkirche: Eine rechtsgeschichtliche Untersuchung* (Münchener theologische Studien, 3. Kanonistische Abteilung, 11; 1958). F. D. Logan, *Excommunication and the Secular Arm in Medieval England* (Pontifical Institute of Medieval

Studies, Studies and Texts, 15; Toronto, 1968). E. Vodola, *Excommunication in the Middle Ages* (Berkeley, Calif., and London [1986]). A. Boudinhon in *CE* 5 (1909), pp. 678–91, s.v.; É. Jombart in *DDC* 5 (1953), cols. 915–27, s.v.; W. Doskocil in *RAC* 7 (1969), cols. 1–22, s.v. 'Exkommunikation', with extensive bibl. See also comm. to CODEX IURIS CANONICI, cited s.v.

exegesis (from Gk. ἐξηγέομαι, 'I narrate', 'explain'). The act of explaining a text, in theology usually a sacred text. The explanation may include translation, paraphrase, or commentary on the meaning. Its purpose may be either to describe the author's meaning or to apply that meaning to a contemporary situation. Its rules are governed by the science of *hermeneutics (q.v.).

On account of the obscurities of Scripture, biblical exegesis has been practised from early times, both by Jews and Christians. In the time of Christ it was practised by *Philo, the *Qumran community and the Rabbis, according to different methods. These were also employed by the writers of the NT, who likewise presupposed the Divine inspiration of the OT. In conflict with *Gnostic exegetes, Christian writers, esp. St *Irenaeus and *Tertullian, insisted that the meaning of Scripture be elucidated in conformity with apostolic tradition. A chiefly allegorical mode of interpretation was fostered esp. in the *Alexandrian school, whose earliest exponents were *Clement and *Origen. By contrast, the school of *Antioch, represented, among others, by St John *Chrysostom and *Theodore of Mopsuestia, cultivated the explanation of the literal sense of the Bible. The most important exegetes among the W. Fathers were St *Jerome and St *Augustine, who sought to combine the two kinds of exegesis, though the former emphasized the literal, the latter the allegorical, sense. Among the later Greek Fathers the science of exegesis was represented esp. by *Hesychius of Jerusalem, St *John of Damascus, and *Euthymius Zigabenus. In the W. many of the Schoolmen were concerned with the methods of exegesis, notably *Peter Lombard, *Alexander of Hales, and St *Thomas Aquinas. They favoured the fourfold method of literal, allegorical, moral, and anagogical (or mystical) exegesis; their chief contribution was an increase in the systematization of materials and in logical order.

At the *Reformation, many Protestant theologians, esp. J. *Calvin, rejected the authority of the Church's tradition as a criterion for exegesis, substituting the interior witness of the Holy Spirit. Such teaching made possible a variety of individual interpretations, although in practice *Lutheran, *Reformed, and *Anglican orthodoxy maintained the traditional exegesis of, e.g., Christological and Trinitarian passages. Since, for Protestants, the Bible became the supreme norm of doctrine, biblical study was accorded a position of high value. It was, therefore, in Protestantism that literary and historical criticism, undermining the traditional doctrine of inspiration, was practised by English *Deists, and emerged strongly in Germany in the 18th cent. J. S. *Semler, J. J. *Wettstein, and J. A. *Ernesti were among the earliest biblical critics. From the beginning of the 19th cent. much attention was given to the origin, nature, and history of the individual biblical documents and to reconstructions of biblical history, including the life of Jesus. These investigations, esp. the work of the *Religionsgeschichtliche Schule, claimed freedom from the guidance of theology in presenting a descriptive explanation of the texts in their own historical context. The conclusions yielded sometimes conservative, sometimes radical, results. In England, under the influence of *Methodism in the 18th cent. and of the *Oxford Movement in the 19th, exegesis developed along mainly conservative lines. With notable exceptions among the *Modernists, RC exegesis until fairly recent times largely ignored or reacted against critical scholarship. Although from 1902 the work of RC biblical critics has been guided by the decisions of the *Biblical Commission, the encyclical 'Divino Afflante Spiritu' (1943) of Pope *Pius XII, with its cautious encouragement of the use of modern critical techniques and its affirmation of the freedom of scholarly research, has fostered work marked by a new openness and independence. This openness to modern critical methods has been further developed since the Second *Vatican Council.

The prestige of descriptive biblical exegesis created many problems for a doctrinal theology built upon the older theory of inspiration. Among 20th-cent. theologians and exegetes, K. *Barth was prominent in maintaining the independence of Church Dogmatics from a merely descriptive exegesis. R. *Bultmann, by contrast, held that biblical criticism emphasizes the need to reinterpret the meaning of the whole biblical message in a modern framework. His call for *demythologization precipitated a renewed interest in hermeneutics.

F. W. *Farrar, *History of Interpretation* (*Bampton Lectures for 1885; 1886); W. *Sanday, *Inspiration* (Bampton Lectures for 1893; 1893). R. M. Grant, *The Bible in the Church* (New York, 1948; rev. edn. as *A Short History of the Interpretation of the Bible*, 1965); J. D. Wood, *The Interpretation of the Bible* (1958); J. D. Smart, *The Interpretation of Scripture* (1961). R. *Simon, *Histoire critique des principaux commentateurs du Nouveau Testament* (Rotterdam, 1693). J. G. Rosenmüller, *Historia Interpretationis Librorum Sacrorum in Ecclesia Christiana* (5 parts, Heidelberg and Leipzig, 1795–1814). J. Bonsirven, SJ, *Exégèse rabbinique et exégèse paulinienne* (1939). B. de Margerie, SJ, *Introduction à l'histoire de l'exégèse* (4 vols., 1980–90 [up to St *Bernard]). M. Simonetti, *Profilo Storico dell'Esegesi Patristica* (1981; Eng. tr., Edinburgh, 1994); T. Finan and V. Twomey (eds.), *Scriptural Interpretation in the Fathers: Letter and Spirit* (Dublin [1995]). B. Smalley, *The Study of the Bible in the Middle Ages* (1941; 3rd edn., 1983); C. Spicq, OP, *Esquisse d'une histoire de l'exégèse latine au Moyen Age* (Bibliothèque Thomiste, 26; 1944); B. Bischoff, 'Wendepunkte in der Geschichte der lateinische Exegesis im Frühmittelalter', *Sacris Erudiri*, 6 (1954), pp. 189–281; repr. in id., *Mittelalterliche Studien*, 1 (Stuttgart, 1966), pp. 205–73; H. de *Lubac, SJ, *Exégèse médiévale* (Théologie, 41, 42, 59; 1959–64). W. G. Kümmel, *Das Neue Testament: Geschichte der Erforschung seiner Probleme* (Orbis academicus, 3. 3; 1958; Eng. tr., 1973). S. [C.] Neill, *The Interpretation of the New Testament 1861–1961* (Firth Lectures, 1962; 1964; 2nd edn., *The Interpretation of the New Testament 1861–1986* by Neill and T. Wright, Oxford, 1988). G. Vermes and R. P. C. Hanson in *The Cambridge History of the Bible*, 1, ed. P. R. Ackroyd and C. F. Evans (1970), pp. 199–231 and 412–53 respectively; G. W. H. Lampe, J. Leclercq, OSB, B. Smalley, S. J. P. van Dijk, OFM, and E. J. J. Rosenthal, ibid. 2, ed. G. W. H. Lampe (1969), pp. 102–279. See also bibl. to HERMENEUTICS.

exemplarism. The view of the *Atonement (sometimes also known as the 'moral' or 'subjective' theory) which holds that the value of the Death of Christ for us lies purely in the moral example which it sets us of complete love and self-surrender, thus moving our imagination and will to repentance and holiness. Those who object to this view criticize it rather as inadequate than as erroneous. One of its chief supporters in recent times was H. *Rashdall, in *The Idea of Atonement* (1919), but exemplarist ideas can be traced as far back as the works of P. *Abelard (d. 1142/3), if not further.

exemption. In an ecclesiastical sense, freedom from control by one's normal superior (usually the bishop of the diocese) and hence in general immediate subjection either to the superior of one's religious house or order, or to the Pope. The term 'exempt' is also applied to dioceses which are not subject to a metropolitan but are directly under the Holy See. The earliest known instance of monastic exemption is that granted by Pope *Honorius I in 628 to the Abbey of *Bobbio. Such exemptions, which from the 11th cent. became common and from the 12th cent. the normal rule, were the cause of much friction between the bishops and the religious orders in the Middle Ages. Other corporations (e.g. cathedral chapters) or private persons were also increasingly granted exemptions, and by the 16th cent. the practice had been carried to an extreme. One of the chief reforms effected by the Council of *Trent was the restoration to the bishop of his proper ordinary jurisdiction. The 1983 *Codex Iuris Canonici* changed the legal impact of exemption by making it subordinate to the rightful autonomy of life, especially of governance, enjoyed by all *Institutes of Consecrated Life. This autonomy means that each Institute has its own discipline in the Church and can preserve whole and entire its spirit, character, and sound traditions; local bishops are charged to safeguard and protect this autonomy (can. 586). In certain circumstances the Pope can withdraw ('exempt') Institutes from the governance of local bishops and subject them to himself or another ecclesiastical authority (can. 591).

J. D. O'Brien, SJ, *The Exemption of Religious in Church Law* (Milwaukee, Wis. [1943]). D. *Knowles, OSB, 'Essays in Monastic History, 4: The Growth of Monastic Exemption', *Downside Review*, 50 (1932), pp. 201–31 and 396–436. K. Pennington, *Pope and Bishops: The Papal Monarchy in the Twelfth and Thirteenth Centuries* [Philadelphia, 1984], pp. 154–89. R. Ombres, OP, '*Iusta Autonomia Vitae*. Religious in the Local Church', *Clergy Review*, 69 (1984), pp. 310–19, with bibl. E. Fogliasso in *DDC* 5 (1953), cols. 637–46, s.v.; id., ibid., cols. 646–65, s.v. 'Exemption des religieux', with bibl.

exequatur (Lat., 'he may perform'). The right, also known as the 'Regium Placet', claimed by certain governments to prevent ecclesiastical enactments of the Roman see from taking automatic effect in their territories. In the 17th and 18th cents. the *Jansenists and the *Gallicanists, e.g. Z. B. *Van Espen in his *De Promulgatione Legum Ecclesiasticarum* (1712), were the chief supporters of these claims from the ecclesiastical standpoint. The attempts of the Papacy in more recent times to restrain it, e.g. that of *Pius IX in his *Syllabus* of 1864, have met with varying success, and certain modern governments have continued to exercise some controlling power of this kind.

H. Papius, 'Zur Geschichte des Placets', *Archiv für katholisches Kirchenrecht*, 18 (1867), pp. 161–237. A. Bertola in *EC* 5 (1950), cols. 917–19, s.v.; R. Naz in *DDC* 7 (1965), cols. 10–14, s.v. 'Placet'; C. B. du Chesnay in *NCE* 5 (1967), pp. 717 f., s.v.

Exeter (in Roman times, Isca Dumnoniorum). By *c.*680 English settlers had established within the walls a monastery which was refounded or restored by Kings *Athelstan in 932, *Edgar in 968, and Canute in 1019. But it was once more a decayed minster by 1050, when Bp. Leofric of *Crediton, who combined the dioceses of Devon and Cornwall, converted it into a new see safe from Viking attack. The boundaries of the diocese remained practically unchanged until the formation of the see of *Truro in 1876. It is now almost conterminous with the county of Devon.

Although Leofric organized a secular cathedral following the Rule of St *Chrodegang, the monastic buildings remained until William Warelwast (Bp. 1107–37) began to erect a Norman cathedral of which only the towers remain. The present structure was begun by Walter Bronescombe (Bp. 1258–80). Peter Quivel (or Quinel, Bp. 1280–91) introduced the decorated style in which most of the cathedral is built and transformed the towers into transepts. The building was dedicated by John Grandison (1327–69) and completed by Thomas Brantingham (1370–94). Under the Commonwealth it was temporarily divided by a brick wall and used as two dissenting chapels. The interior was restored under the direction of G. G. *Scott between 1870 and 1877. Notable are its *miserere seats dating from the episcopate of William Briwere (1224–44), a clock made at *Glastonbury in 1285 and brought to Exeter in 1314, the Bishop's throne installed by Walter de *Stapeldon (1308–26), and the magnificent 14th- and 15th-cent. image screen across the west front. In the library are preserved *Edward the Confessor's charter confirming the changes he and Leofric had made and granting the new see to Leofric, the 10th-cent. 'Exeter Book' presented by Leofric, and the Exon Domesday. Edmund Lacy (Bp. 1420–55) was honoured as a popular saint. Other famous bishops include R. *Foxe (1487–92), M. *Coverdale (1551–3), J. *Hall (1627–41), H. *Phillpotts (1831–69), and F. *Temple (1869–85).

The University of Exeter received its charter in 1955.

The fullest account is to be found in the learned works of George Oliver (1781–1861), the chief of which are *The History of Exeter* (1821; 2nd edn., 1861); *Ecclesiastical Antiquities of Devon* (1828; '2nd edn.', really a new work, 3 vols., 1839–42); *Monasticon Diœcesis Exoniensis* (1846); and *Lives of the Bishops of Exeter and a History of the Cathedral* (1861). Selection of Episcopal Registers, ed. F. C. Hingeston-Randolph (9 vols., 1886–1909); that of E. Lacy (Bp. of Exeter, 1420–55), ed. G. R. Dunstan (*Canterbury and York Society, parts 129, 132, 134, 137, and 139; 1963–72). Facsimile reprod. of the Exeter Book, with introductory chs. by R. W. Chambers, M. Förster, and R. Flower (Exeter and London, 1933). R. J. E. Boggis, *A History of the Diocese of Exeter* (Exeter, 1922). F. Barlow and others, *Leofric of Exeter: Essays in Commemoration of the Foundation of Exeter Cathedral Library in A.D. 1072* (Exeter, 1972). V. Hope and J. Lloyd, *Exeter Cathedral: A Short History and Description* (ibid., 1973); F. Kelly (ed.), *Medieval Art and Architecture at Exeter Cathedral* (British Archaeological Association Conference Transactions, no. 11; 1991); W. Swanton (ed.), *Exeter Cathedral: A Celebration* (Exeter, 1991). N. Orme, *Exeter Cathedral as it was 1050–1550* (ibid., 1986). C. Brooks and D. Evans, *The Great East Window of Exeter Cathedral* (ibid., 1988). N. [B. L.] Pevsner, *South Devon* (The Buildings of England; Harmondsworth, 1952), pp. 128–55. H. Dauphin, OSB, in *DHGE* 16 (1967), cols. 223–52, s.v.

Exeter Hall. A building in the Strand, London, which was erected *c.*1830 and used for religious and philanthropic assemblies, esp. by those of Evangelical sympathies, down to 1907. 'Exeter Hall' thus came to be used allusively as a title for a certain type of *Evangelicalism.

Exile, the. A term commonly used, esp. by OT scholars, for the *Babylonian Captivity (q.v.).

Existentialism. The term, which derives from S. *Kierkegaard (d. 1855, q.v.), is usually applied to certain types of modern philosophical thinking which share a practical concern for the individual existing person and his freedom. Such thinking stands in radical opposition to objective philosophy (e.g. the thought of R. *Descartes), positivist science, and mass society. Although such thinkers as St *Augustine and B. *Pascal have been claimed as ancestors of Existentialism, the contemporary movement goes back mainly to Kierkegaard, F. W. *Nietzsche, and E. Husserl (1859–1938): Kierkegaard with his emphasis that 'God is a subject and therefore exists only for subjectivity in inwardness' (e.g. in his *Concluding Unscientific Postcript*, 1846), Nietzsche with his stress on man not as a combination of mind and body, but as one who possesses a will (e.g. *Der Wille zur Macht*, 1901; Eng. tr., *The Will to Power*, 1909–10), and Husserl, whose *Phenomenology provided a systematic method of describing the universal elements in human consciousness (e.g. in his article 'Phenomenology' in *EB* 14th edn., 1927). The main body of Existentialist writings appears to derive from the discovery of Kierkegaard in Germany in the early 20th cent., esp. by theologians in opposition to Liberal Protestantism, and from the shattering of cultural values in Europe after the First World War.

Attempts have been made to divide Existentialist authors into two groups, namely the secular—among whom are included M. *Heidegger, M. Merleau-Ponty (1908–61), and J. P. Sartre (1905–80)—and the religious, e.g. Kierkegaard, G. Marcel (1889–1973) and K. *Jaspers. But there are differences within each group and sometimes real affinities between them.

Heidegger in *Sein und Zeit* (1927; Eng. tr., *Being and Time*, 1962) explored the 'nature of Being' as philosophy's major theme. Access to this theme is gained only by considering man in his historical, temporal sense. In his later, semi-oracular writings Heidegger claimed that poetry could announce, and expose us to, Being. Sartre's principal early work, *L'Être et le Néant: Essai d'ontologie phénoménologique* (1943; Eng. tr., *Being and Nothingness*, 1957), stresses being-for-itself, that is, human consciousness with personal, chosen values, as man faces an apparently absurd world with feelings of anguish and disgust. Sartre's ideas also found expression in plays and novels, e.g. *La Nausée* (1938; Eng. tr., 1962). His later *Critique de la raison dialectique*, vol. 1 (1960; Eng. tr., 1976), signals the eclipse of individualism in favour of Marxism.

Marcel became a RC in 1929. He abandoned idealist philosophy to embrace a Christian personalism whose keynote is hope. This position is expressed in *Être et avoir* (1935; Eng. tr., *Being and Having*, 1949). Jaspers' philosophy dealt with being-as-self rather than being-as-object. In his *Philosophie* (1932; Eng. tr., 3 vols., 1969–71) he set out the limits of scientific knowledge, explored Existence as the possibility of self-determination, and in his metaphysics sought to relate Existence to an elusive Transcendence described only through ciphers or symbols.

The question of a Christian Existentialism has been a prominent element in Protestant theological debate for over 50 years. With its origins in Kantianism and modern research on M. *Luther, and stimulated by the *Dialectical Theology of the 1920s, it was taken up by R. *Bultmann, who drew on Heidegger's analysis. Opponents have claimed that Existentialism, which is anti metaphysical and anti-cosmological in character, reduces theology to anthropology, dissolves the historical foundations of Christianity, and treats salvation as no more than a self-generated decision in favour of authentic existence. Supporters have claimed that an Existential standpoint is implicit in the NT, that to acknowledge the salvation event as part of history only serves to confirm the radical nature of faith, locating salvation not in external events but in an encounter between the hidden God and our personal existence.

Existentialism was condemned by the encyclical '*Humani Generis' (1950), but it has continued to exercise an important influence on some RC theologians (e.g. K. *Rahner). There are signs, however, that theological Existentialism is losing some of its appeal, as theologians concern themselves with social problems and again explore metaphysical questions.

J. Wahl, *Études kierkegaardiennes* (1938); id., *Existence humaine et transcendance* (1944); P. Foulquier, *L'Existentialisme* (1946); E. Mounier, *Introduction aux existentialismes* (1947); J. Hessen, *Existenzphilosophie* (Essen, 1948); H. J. Blackham, *Six Existentialist Thinkers* ('1951' [1952]); F. H. Heinemann, *Existentialism and the Modern Predicament* (1953); J. Macquarrie, *An Existentialist Theology: A Comparison of Heidegger and Bultmann* (1955); id., *Existentialism* (1972), with bibl.; D. E. Roberts, *Existentialism and Religious Belief* (New York, 1957); W. Barrett, *Irrational Man: A Study in Existential Philosophy* (New York, 1958; London, 1961); M. Warnock, *Existentialism* (Oxford, 1970).

Exodus, Book of. The second Book of the *Pentateuch. The English title follows the Gk. and Lat. versions, the Heb. title (וְאֵלֶּה שְׁמוֹת 'And these are the names') being the first words of the text. The Book records the events attending the 'Exodus' (i.e. the release of the Israelites under *Moses from their Egyptian bondage) and Yahweh's subsequent giving of the Law on Mount *Sinai. It describes the oppression of the Israelites, who had settled in Egypt in the time of Joseph, at the hands of a new king (1); the birth and preservation of Moses from slaughter, and his Divine commission to deliver his fellow-slaves (2–4); the refusal of the Pharaoh to release the Israelites, even in the face of the 'plagues' (the waters turned to blood; frogs; swarms of flies; etc.), until the loss of his first-born made him relent, and the institution of the *Passover (5: 1–12: 36); the escape of the Israelites through the miraculous parting of the *Red Sea and the destruction of their Egyptian pursuers in its returning waters (12: 37–18: 27); the encampment of the Israelites at Mount Sinai and Moses' ascent to the summit of the mount, where he received from Yahweh the Ten *Commandments and a large body of other legislation, moral, ceremonial, and religious (19–40).

The authorship of the Book has, like that of the Pentateuch as a whole, traditionally been ascribed to Moses. Modern biblical scholars are divided between those who agree that the Book forms part of a unified composition but assign the whole to a later time than that of Moses, and those who believe the Book, and indeed the rest of the Pentateuch, to be a composite work, its strata prob. having been written between the 9th and the 5th cent. BC. Perhaps the earliest item is the couplet ascribed to Miriam in 15: 21, which may well be one of the oldest fragments of the OT. Critical scholarship has been much exercised about the date of the Exodus. The extreme limits seem to be 1580 BC and 1215 BC, and at present most scholars favour either the first or second third of the 13th cent. BC.

Elsewhere in the Bible, frequent and fervent references to the Exodus occur (e.g. Ps. 78: 43–53, Is. 51: 10, Mic. 6: 4–5, Heb. 11: 27–9). Indeed the deliverance has throughout Jewish history been regarded as the outstanding instance of God's favour to His chosen people. Christian writers from NT times have used the imagery of the Passover in ch. 12 with reference to the sacrifice of Christ on Calvary and mediately to the Christian sacrifice of the *Eucharist. In modern times, the Exodus has become an important symbol of liberation for many groups, from Black Christians in the United States of America to so-called *Liberation theologians of Latin America.

Comm. by S. R. *Driver (Camb. Bib., RV, 1911), J. *Weiss (Graz and Vienna, 1911), G. Beer (HAT, Reihe 1, Abt. 3, 1939), M. *Noth (Das Alte Testament Deutsch, 5; 1959; Eng. tr. 1962), J. P. Hyatt (New Cent. Bib., 1971), B. S. Childs (Old Testament Library, 1974), and J. I. Durham (Word Biblical Comm., Waco, Tex. [1987]). W. Beyerlin, *Herkunft und Geschichte der ältesten Sinaitraditionen* (Tübingen, 1961; Eng. tr., Oxford [1966]); G. Fohrer, *Überlieferung und Geschichte des Exodus: Eine Analyse von Ex. 1–15* (Beihefte zur ZATW, 91; 1964). R. W. L. Moberly, *At the Mountain of God: Story and Theology in Exodus 32–34* (Journal for the Study of the Old Testament, Supplement Series, 22; Sheffield, 1983). H. Cazelles, PSS, *Autour de l'Exode (Études)* (1987). On the Exodus, C. F. *Burney, *Israel's Settlement in Canaan: The Biblical Tradition and its Historical Background* (Schweich Lectures for 1917; 1918). H. H. Rowley, *From Joseph to Joshua: Biblical Tradition in the Light of Archaeology* (Schweich Lectures for 1948; 1950). S. Herrmann, *Israels Aufenthalt in Ägypten* (Stuttgarter Bibelstudien, 40 [1970]; Eng. tr., Studies in Biblical Theology, 2nd ser. 27; 1973). R. de Vaux, OP, *Histoire ancienne d'Israël*, 1 (Études Bibliques, 1971), pp. 339–421; Eng. tr. (1978), pp. 359–452. E. W. Nicholson, *Exodus and Sinai in History and Tradition* (Oxford, 1973). J. J. Bimson, *Redating the Exodus and Conquest* (Journal for the Study of the Old Testament, Supplement Series, 5; Sheffield, 1978; 2nd edn., 1981); G. I. Davies, *The Way of the Wilderness: A Geographical Study of the Wilderness Itineraries in the Old Testament* (Society for Old Testament Study, Monograph Series, 5; Cambridge, 1979). On the Exodus theme in later tradition, B. van Iersel and A. Weiler (eds.), *Exodus—A Lasting Paradigm* (Concilium, 189; 1987). Brief introd. by W. Johnstone, *Exodus* (Old Testament Guides; Sheffield, 1990). J. *Daniélou, SJ, in *RAC* 7 (1969), cols. 22–44, s.v., with bibl.; W. Johnstone in *A Dictionary of Biblical Interpretation*, ed. R. J. Coggins and J. L. Houlden (1990), pp. 222–6, s.v.

exomologesis (Gk. ἐξομολόγησις). Properly a full or public *confession of sin. In the early Church the word was applied to the whole process of confession, satisfaction, and forgiveness by which a penitent sinner was reconciled to the Church.

ex opere operato. A term in use among theologians at least since the early 13th cent. to express the essentially objective mode of operation of the sacraments, and its independence of the subjective attitudes of either the minister or the recipient. The 'opus operatum' ('act done') is contrasted with the doing of the act, whether the 'opus operans' ('act doing') or the 'opus operantis' ('act of the doer'). To say, therefore, that a sacrament confers grace 'ex opere operato' is to assert in effect that the sacrament itself is an instrument of God, and that so long as the conditions of its institution are validly fulfilled, irrespective of the qualities or merits of the persons administering or receiving it, grace is conferred. It is this property of being effective 'ex opere operato' which Catholic theologians hold to differentiate the sacraments from other channels of Divine grace. The doctrine, which does not deny that right dispositions are necessary on the part of the recipient if grace is to be really effectual, was formally approved at the Council of *Trent (sess. 7, *de sacramentis in genere*, can. 8).

exonarthex (Gk. ἐξωνάρθηξ). The outer *narthex or porch in E. churches.

exorcism. The practice of expelling evil spirits by means of prayer or set formulas was common among the Jews and pagans, and was taken over by the Christian Church after the example of Christ and His Apostles (cf. Mt. 10: 1 ff., Lk. 11: 14 ff., Acts 16: 18, 19: 13 ff., etc.). Exorcism has been practised on persons possessed with an evil spirit from NT times onwards. It has always been applied to catechumens; and the BCP of 1549 preserved one such prayer in the Baptismal Office. In the Latin rite three exorcisms were long included in the Baptismal rite before the actual Baptism. The 1969 RC Order for the Baptism of Infants, however, includes only one exorcism, which may be omitted, while the 1972 Order for Adult Initiation provides exorcisms at various stages of the restored catechumate, but none in the Baptismal rite. The Baptismal exorcisms do not presuppose a state of possession, but are prayers asking for the restraint of the powers of evil.

An elaborate rite for the exorcism of evil spirits is contained in the *Rituale Romanum*; its use is restricted to priests who have episcopal permission; and the rite itself is under review. In England in the 1960s and 1970s interest in the occult and the spread of the *Charismatic Movement led in many Churches to concern with demon possession and to a revival of the practice of exorcism in the C of E. The report of a commission, appointed in 1963 by R. Mortimer, Bp. of *Exeter, was published in 1972; it recommended the appointment of an exorcist in each diocese. After a tragic case in 1974 attracted publicity, in 1975 the Abp. of *Canterbury issued some guidelines, namely that exorcism should be carried out only in collaboration with the resources of medicine, in the context of prayer and sacrament, with a minimum of publicity, by experienced persons authorized by the diocesan bishop, and that it must be followed by continuing pastoral care. Following these guidelines, individual diocesan bishops formulated appropriate policy for their dioceses.

J. *Martène, OSB, *De Antiquis Ecclesiae Ritibus* (3 vols., Rouen, 1700–2), vol. 1, pp. 32 f., 52 f., 81, 159–61; 2, pp. 259, 302 f., 307 f., 347, 359, 371, 390, 394, 400, 427, 431 f., 446, 451, 465, 474, 488 f.; 3, pp. 498 and 517–20. F. *Probst, *Sakramente und Sakramentalien in den drei ersten christlichen Jahrhunderten* (1872), pp. 16–62. F. J. Dölger, *Der Exorzismus im altchristlichen Tauf-*

ritual (Studien zur Geschichte und Kultur des Altertums, 3, Hefte 1–2; 1909). L. Delatte, *Un Office byzantin d'exorcisme (Ms. de la Lavra du Mont Athos,* Θ 20) (Académie royale de Belgique, Classe de Lettres, Mémoires, Collection in-8°, 2nd ser. 52; 1957), with introd., text, and comm. R. M. Woolley, *Exorcism and the Healing of the Sick* (CHS, 1932). *Exorcism: The Report of a Commission convened by the Bishop of Exeter,* ed. R. Petitpierre, OSB (1972). Id., *Exorcising Devils* (1976). The guidelines of the Abp. of Canterbury were issued in response to a question in the General Synod; they are pr. in *Report of the Proceedings of the General Synod,* 6 (1975), p. 361. J. Richards, *But deliver us from evil: An Introduction to the Demoniac Dimension in Pastoral Care* (1974). J. Forget in *DTC* 5 (1913), cols. 1762–80, s.v. 'Exorcisme'; H. *Leclercq, OSB, in *DACL* 5 (1922), cols. 964–78, s.v. 'Exorcisme, exorciste'. See also bibl. s.v. EXORCIST.

exorcist. The second of the traditional *Minor Orders. The power of exorcizing evil spirits, however, was never confined to the members of a particular order (cf. preceding entry). Bishops and priests from the earliest times assumed the primary responsibility for the sick and possessed, and even laymen are known to have exercised the gift of healing. The office of 'exorcist' is first mentioned in a letter of Pope *Cornelius (d. 253). Its duties came to include the imposition of hands on '*energumens' and the exorcizing of *catechumens. In the RC Church these functions of the exorcist have long been practically extinct, and the office only a step to the priesthood. It was finally suppressed in 1972.

T. Bischofberger, *Die Verwaltung des Exorcistats nach Massgabe des römischen Benediktionale* (1884; rev. edn. by C. Wehrmeister, 1927). F. Wieland, *Die genetische Entwicklung der sog. Ordines Minores in den drei ersten Jahrhunderten* (RQ, Suppl., 7; 1897), pp. 114–32 and 172–4. See also bibl. to previous entry and works cited under MINOR ORDERS.

Exoucontians. The extreme *Arians of the 4th cent., so called from their doctrine that the Son was created out of non-being (ἐξ οὐκ ὄντων). Their leader was *Aetius. They were also known as 'Aetians' and '*Anomoeans'.

expectant. A name formerly used of a candidate for the *Presbyterian ministry in *Scotland before he had received a licence to preach the Gospel.

expectant, the Church. The body of Christians waiting between earth and heaven, in what is traditionally called *Purgatory, and thus distinguished from the Church in *Heaven (*triumphant) and that still on earth (*militant).

Expectation Sunday. A title occasionally given to the Sunday between *Ascension Day and *Whitsunday. The name is in reference to the Apostles' 'expectation' of the Descent of the Holy Spirit after Christ's Ascension (Acts 1: 4 f.).

expiation. The atoning or making up for an offence committed against God or one's neighbour. Christianity claims that the only sufficient expiation of human sin is the offering made by Jesus Christ of His earthly life and death, and that of this offering the merits are infinite. Acc. to Catholic theology, its effects are applied to the soul in baptism and (for sins thereafter committed) in absolution. In virtue of its all-sufficiency the performance by Christians of good or pious works, done as penance, has value only through their being effected in union with the perfect expiation offered by Christ. See also ATONEMENT.

Expiation, Day of. An alternative name for the Jewish feast usually known as the Day of *Atonement (Tisri 10).

Exposition of the Blessed Sacrament. For more than a thousand years of the Church's history it was not customary to show public devotion to the *Reserved Sacrament. From *c.* the 11th cent., however, in the W. there were the beginnings of a public manifestation of faith and love of the sacramental presence of Christ in the Eucharist. This showed itself in the desire of the people to look at the Host when elevated during Mass (see ELEVATION); to have it exposed for veneration outside Mass, and carried in solemn processions. Exposition of the Blessed Sacrament as a service apart from Mass is first found in the late 14th cent.

In modern practice there are two forms of exposition: (1) the solemn form when a large Host is exposed to view in a *monstrance, placed on or above the altar, surrounded by lights and often by flowers, and censed; and (2) the simple form in which the *ciborium containing Hosts for Communion is shown at the open doors of the *tabernacle. Since 1967 in the RC Church exposition may always be by either form; it takes place in accordance with the regulations of the bishop. In either case there are biblical readings, hymns, prayers, and a time of silence, and sometimes a homily. The rite concludes with the blessing of the people with the Host (veiled in the simple form of exposition). In the past the blessing was often given after only a brief period of exposition, in a form of the service popularly known as '*Benediction of the Blessed Sacrament'; it is now forbidden to give the blessing on its own. See also FORTY HOURS' DEVOTION.

J. B. Thiers, *Traité de l'exposition du St Sacrement de l'autel* (Paris, 1673). F. Raible, *Das Tabernakel einst und jetzt: Eine historische und liturgische Darstellung der Andacht zur aufbewahrten Eucharistie* (1908), pp. 150–316 passim. H. Thurston, SJ, 'Our Popular Devotions', no. 4, 'Benediction of the Blessed Sacrament: Part II, Exposition', *The Month,* 98 (1901), pp. 58–69; id., 'Exposition of the Blessed Sacrament', ibid. 99 (1902), pp. 537–40. E. Dumoutet, *Le Désir de voir l'Hostie et les origines de la dévotion au Saint Sacrement* (1927), pp. 75–98. The current RC legislation on Exposition and Benediction is contained in the section of the *Rituale Romanum, *De Sacra Communione et de Cultu Mysterii Eucharistici extra Missam* (1973), nos. 82–100 (pp. 38–42); Eng. tr., *Holy Communion and Worship of the Eucharist Outside Mass,* 1, Rites (1978), pp. 44–54, with supplementary appendix on the 'Rite of Eucharistic Exposition and Benediction', pp. 64–95. N. Mitchell, OSB, *Cult and Controversy: The Worship of the Eucharist Outside Mass* (Studies in the Reformed Rites of the Catholic Church, 4; New York, 1982), esp. pp. 176–81, 211–13, 337–40. H. Thurston, SJ, in *CE* 5 (1909), pp. 713 f., s.v., with bibl.

Exsurge, Domine. The bull issued by *Leo X on 15 June 1520 threatening to excommunicate M. *Luther, the 'new *Porphyry' (*novus Porphyrius*). It listed 41 propositions, attributed to Luther, which it condemned as 'heretical or scandalous or false or offensive to pious ears, or seductive to simple minds and standing in the way of the Catholic faith'. They dealt with such matters as *indulgences, *penance, *purgatory, sacramental *grace, and the Pope's teaching authority. Its promulgation in Germany was entrusted to J. *Eck, whose unpopular and provocative methods met with fierce opposition both at Leipzig (29 Sept.) and at *Wittenberg (3 Oct.). After an unsuccessful appeal for a *General Council on 17 Nov., Luther finally broke with the Papacy by publicly burning the bull at Wittenberg on 10 Dec. 1520.

For the text (somewhat abbreviated), see Kidd, no. 38; propositions also in Denzinger and Hünermann (37th edn., 1991), pp. 487–92 (nos. 1451–92). P. Kalkoff, 'Die Übersetzung der Bulle "Exsurge" ', *ZKG* 45 (1926), pp. 382–99, with refs. to earlier arts. by this author; H. Roos, SJ, 'Die Quellen der Bulle "Exsurge Domine" (15.6.1520)' in J. Auer and H. Volk (eds.), *Theologie in Geschichte und Gegenwart: Michael Schmaus zum sechzigsten Geburtstag dargebracht* (Munich, 1957), pp. 909–26. See also works cited under LUTHER.

extra-liturgical services. Services for which no fixed form is provided in the authorized liturgical formularies. For the form of such functions the person conducting them is responsible, subject to the directions of the bishop and parish priest.

Extravagantes. The term, at one time applied to certain officially recognized Papal *decretals which had 'wandered outside', i.e. were not included in, the 'Decretum' of *Gratian ('extra decretum vagantes'), is now used almost exclusively of the two concluding sections of the *Corpus Iuris Canonici*, viz. the 'Extravagantes Ioannis XXII' (on which see JOHN XXII) and the 'Extravagantes Communes'. The latter is a collection of decretals of various Popes from Urban IV (d. 1264) to *Sixtus IV (d. 1484). Down to 1917, when the *Codex Iuris Canonici* was issued, the official authority of many items in the Extravagantes was allowed, though it belonged to them only as individual documents, and not because of any authority attaching to these two collections as a whole.

Crit. text by E. Friedberg in his edn. of *Corpus Iuris Canonici*, 2 (1881), cols. 1201–312; cf. also Friedberg's Prolegomena, ibid., cols. lxiv–lxviii. 'Extravagantes Iohannis XXII', also ed. J. Tarrant (Monumenta Iuris Canonici, Series B, vol. 6; Vatican City, 1983). G. Le Bras, C. Lefebvre, and J. Rambaud, *Histoire du droit et des institutions de l'Église en Occident*, 7, L'Age Classique (1965), pp. 254–6, with refs. P. Torquebiau in *DDC* 4 (1949), cols. 640–3, s.v. 'Corpus Juris Canonici, V. Les Extravagantes'.

Extreme Unction. See UNCTION.

Exultet. In the W. liturgy, the 'Paschal Proclamation' (*praeconium paschale*) or 'Paschal Praise' (*laus paschalis*) sung by the deacon standing near the *Paschal Candle on *Holy Saturday, and so named from its opening word, 'exultet'. It seems that originally it was the practice for the deacon to compose his own *praeconium*; but the form which came into general use can be traced back to 7th/8th-cent. Gaul and had generally displaced other forms by the 9th cent. There were local variations and some parts fell out of use during the Middle Ages. The chant to which it is sung is one of the finest in the Latin liturgy.

In S. Italy, from the early 10th to the 14th cent., it was customary to write out this *Prose (sometimes in the local, or *Vetus Itala*, form), with appropriate musical directions, on rolls known as 'Exultet Rolls'. The text, finely written in Beneventan script, was divided into sections interspersed with illuminated pictures disposed in the reverse way from the text, so that the pictures might be the right

way up for the congregation when the section of the roll which had been read had been slipped over the back of the *ambo. About 30 such rolls are known to survive.

The principal documents are pr. in H. A. P. Schmidt, SJ, *Hebdomada Sancta*, 2 (pt. 1; Rome, 1957), pp. 627–50. L. *Duchesne, *Les Origines du culte chrétien* (1889), pp. 242–6; Eng. tr. of 3rd edn. (1903), pp. 252–6. H. M. Bannister, 'The *Vetus Itala* Text of the *Exultet*', *JTS* 11 (1910), pp. 43–54. P. *Capelle, OSB, 'L'"Exultet" pascal, œuvre de Saint Ambroise', *Miscellanea Giovanni Mercati*, 1 (Studi e Testi, 121; 1946), pp. 219–46; reply by M. Huglo, OSB, 'L'Auteur de l'*Exultet* pascal', *VC* 7 (1953), pp. 79–88. Id. in S. Sadie (ed.), *The New Grove Dictionary of Music and Musicians*, 6 (1980), pp. 334–6, s.v., with bibl.

On the Exultet Rolls, A. M. Latil, OSB (ed.), *Le miniature nei rotoli dell'Exultet* (Monte Cassino, 1899; coloured plates); M. Avery, *The Exultet Rolls of South Italy*, vol. 2 (plates; all pub.; Princeton, NJ, 1936). G. Cavallo, *Rotoli de Exultet dell'Italia meridionale* (Bari, 1973). There is also a facsimile edn. of an 11th-cent. Exultet Roll from Monte Cassino (of great artistic merit) in the British Library (Add. MS 30337), with introd. by J. P. Gilson (London, 1929).

Exuperius, St (d. after 410), Bp. of Toulouse. He was renowned for his liberality to the poor and also to monks, and for having finished the basilica of St Saturninus at Toulouse. St *Jerome dedicated to him his Commentary on Zech. Feast day, 28 Sept.

For the text of Pope *Innocent I's Ep. to Exuperius (Ep. 6; 20 Feb. AD 405), with its important list of the Canonical Books of Scripture, prescriptions on clerical celibacy, etc., see J. P. Migne, *PL* 20. 495–502. *AASS*, Sept. 7 (1760), pp. 623–30. H. Crouzel, 'Saint Jérôme et ses Amis Toulousains', *Bulletin de littérature ecclésiastique*, 73 (1972), pp. 125–46, esp. pp. 129–38. G. Bareille in *DTC* 5 (1913), cols. 2022–7.

Eyck, Hubert and Jan Van. See VAN EYCK, HUBERT and JAN.

Ezekiel, Book of. One of the three 'Major' Prophetic Books of the OT, the other two being *Isaiah and *Jeremiah. The Book falls into five main divisions: (1) Chs. 1–24. The message here is one of denunciation and the main theme the forthcoming destruction of *Jerusalem and *Judah at the hands of the Babylonians. (2) Chs. 25–32. A series of prophecies directed against foreign nations, namely Ammon (25: 1–7), Moab (25: 8–11), Edom (25: 12–14), Philistia (25: 15–17), *Tyre and Sidon (26–8), and Egypt (29–32). (3) Chs. 33–7. Prophecies relating to the redemption and restoration of the Jewish people. Ch. 37 describes the forthcoming restoration under the vivid image of the raising of dry bones to new life. (4) Chs. 38–9. The dramatic account of an assault upon the land of *Israel by *Gog and the overthrow of him and his forces by *Yahweh. (5) Chs. 40–8. A detailed vision of the ideal theocracy and esp. the form and worship of the reconstructed *Temple.

Ezekiel was a Jerusalem priest, prob. carried captive to *Babylonia by Nebuchadnezzar in the first deportation in 597 BC. There he appears to have experienced a call to *prophecy in 593 BC; this call is heard in the context of a vision of the Glory of God moving across the plain as though on a chariot (chs. 1–3). Some scholars have held that Ezekiel had a ministry in Jerusalem as well as in Babylonia, and a few that he was never in Babylonia at all, but the commonest view is that the whole of his ministry was spent in Babylonia. His experience, shared by his fellow-exiles, seems to have convinced him of the universality of the rule of Yahweh, present in Babylonia as in Palestine. Traditionally the entire Book was regarded as the work of Ezekiel, but in the 20th cent. some have held that only a relatively small part of it goes back to the Prophet himself. Today the majority would regard the bulk of the Book as coming from Ezekiel, with most of the rest deriving from prophetic circles influenced by the tradition of his words.

The theology of Ezekiel is characterized by a strong emphasis on the majesty of Yahweh, the God of Israel. Yahweh's holiness is manifested in the rigorous judgement upon His people which is the theme of the first part of the Book (chs. 1–24); later it is because of Yahweh's own holiness that He restores His people, acting for the sake of his 'holy name', lest the nations should misunderstand Israel's suffering as evidence that Yahweh is a weak God. Israel does not deserve restoration but Yahweh will nevertheless give her a 'new heart' and a 'new spirit' and so enable her to respond positively to Him (ch. 36). These themes may be seen as anticipating the emphasis on freely given *grace characteristic of St *Paul.

Many scholars have found a marked stress on the responsibility of the individual in Ezekiel, though others have given less weight to this theme. Such individualistic features as do occur are balanced by a complementary belief in the corporate nature of the religious community, seen in the detailed provision for the future life of the restored nation. Some features of the language of the Book appear to point the way towards the rise of the *Apocalyptic literature. The combination of both Priestly and Prophetic themes is striking. The Book had great influence in post-exilic Israel and Ezekiel (like *Ezra) has sometimes been called 'The Father of Judaism'.

Comm. by C. H. *Cornill (Heb. text, Ger. tr. and comm., Leipzig, 1886), A. B. *Davidson (Camb. Bib., AV, 1892; rev. for RV text by A. W. Streane, 1916), J. Herrmann (KAT 11; 1924), G. A. Cooke (ICC, 1936). G. Fohrer and K. Galling (HAT, Reihe 1, Bd. 13; 1955), W. Eichrodt (Das Alte Testament Deutsch, 22; 2 vols., 1959–66; Eng. tr., 1970), W. Zimmerli (Biblischer Kommentar, Altes Testament, 13; 18 parts, 1955–69; 2nd edn., 2 vols., 1979; Eng. tr. of 1st edn., 2 vols., Philadelphia, 1979–83). D. M. G. Stalker (Torch Bib. Comm., 1968), J. W. Wevers (New Cent. Bib., 1969). M. Greenberg (Anchor Bible, 1983 ff.), and W. H. Brownlee and L. A. Allen (Word Biblical Comm., 28–29; Waco, Tex., and Dallas [1986–90]). G. Hölscher, *Hesekiel: Der Dichter und das Buch* (Beihefte zur ZATW, 39; 1924); C. C. Torrey, *Pseudo-Ezekiel and the Original Prophecy* (Yale Oriental Series, Researches, 18; 1930); V. Herntrich, *Ezechielprobleme* (Beihefte zur ZATW, 61; 1932); H. W. *Robinson, *Two Hebrew Prophets* (1948), pp. 63–125; C. G. Howie, *The Date and Composition of Ezekiel* (Journal of Biblical Literature Monograph Series, 4; 1950); H. H. Rowley, 'The Book of Ezekiel in Modern Study', *Bulletin of the John Rylands Library*, 36 (1953–4), pp. 146–90; J. Garscha, *Studien zum Ezechielbuch: Eine redaktionskritische Untersuchung von Ez 1–39* (Berne, 1974); K. W. Carley, *Ezekiel among the Prophets* (Studies in Biblical Theology, 2nd ser. 31; 1975); F. Hossfeld, *Untersuchungen zu Komposition und Theologie des Ezechielbuches* (Forschung zur Bibel, 20; Würzburg, 1977); B. Lang, *Ezechiel: Der Prophet und das Buch* (Erträge der Forschung, 153; Darmstadt, 1981); P. [M.] Joyce, *Divine Initiative and Human Response in Ezekiel* (Journal for the Study of the Old Testament, Supplement Series, 51; Sheffield [1989]); K.-F. Pohlmann, *Ezechielstudien: Zur Redaktionsgeschichte des Buches und zur Frage*

nach den ältesten Texten (Beihefte zur ZATW, 202; 1992). H. McKeating, *Ezekiel* (Old Testament Guides; Sheffield, 1993).

Eznik (5th cent.), Bp. of Bagrevand in *Armenia. A native of Kolb and a disciple of St *Mesrob, he was one of the most polished and learned of early Christian Armenian writers. His principal surviving work is a treatise, *The Confutation of the Sects* (c.441–8), in four books, directed respectively against (1) the pagans, (2) the religion of the Persians, (3) the Greek philosophers, and (4) the *Marcionites. He also took part in translating the Armenian version of the Bible, and, acc. to native tradition, wrote some homilies which have perished.

The Confutation of the Sects has been pub. (in Armenian) at Smyrna (1762) and Venice (1826, 1863). Crit. edn. by L. Mariès, SJ, and C. Mercier (PO 28, fasc. 3, with literal Fr. tr. and notes, fasc. 4; 1959). Earlier Fr. tr. by Le Vaillant de Florival (Paris, 1853); Ger. trs. by J. M. Schmid (Vienna, 1900) and S. Weber, *Ausgewählte Schriften der armenischen Kirchenväter*, 1 (Munich, 1927), pp. 1–180. L. Mariès, SJ, 'Le *De Deo* d'Eznik de Kołb, connu sous le nom de "Contre les sectes"', *Revue des Études Arméniennes*, 4 (1924), pp. 113–205; 5 (1925), pp. 11–130. C. F. J. Dowsett, 'On Eznik's Refutation of the Chaldean Astrologers', ibid., NS 6 (1969), pp. 45–65. Bardenhewer, 5, pp. 209–16; Altaner and Stuiber (1978), pp. 352 and 623, with bibl. V. Inglisian in RAC 7 (1969), cols. 118–28, s.v.

Ezra. The Jewish priest and scribe, who played a central part in the reform of *Judaism in the 5th or 4th cent. BC. His activities are recorded in the Books of *Ezra and Nehemiah, and of 1 *Esdras. On his arrival in *Jerusalem from Persia 'in the seventh year of Artaxerxes the king' (Ez. 7: 7), he set about his purposes on the basis of a royal warrant. His work marks the stage in the history of Judaism at which the distinction between the universalist and exclusivist attitudes to the Gentiles became clearly defined, and as a champion of the latter Ezra took strict measures to secure the racial purity and distinctiveness of the Jewish people. Ezra (like *Ezekiel) has sometimes been called 'the Father of Judaism'. After his establishment in Jerusalem, he promulgated a code of laws (Neh. 8: 1–12); one of the first responses to this act was a solemn observance of the Feast of *Tabernacles. The chronology of the period is obscure and there is considerable confusion in the OT record. The traditional date of Ezra's arrival in Jerusalem is 458 BC. This date is supported by some scholars; others favour 428 (arguing that in Ez. 7: 7 'the seventh year' should read 'the thirty-seventh year') or 398 (on the assumption that Artaxerxes II was the king mentioned). If this last date is correct, Ezra belonged to a later generation than *Nehemiah, who arrived in Jerusalem in 444.

For bibl. see the following entry.

Ezra and Nehemiah, Books of. These Books continue the history of the Hebrew people begun in the Books of *Chronicles, extending the narrative from the end of the Babylonian Exile (c.539 BC) down to the latter half of the 5th, or perhaps the beginning of the 4th, cent. BC; the greater part of it is concerned with the work of Ezra and Nehemiah. Ez. 1–6 relates the return of the exiles from Babylon, the efforts made to rebuild the *Temple at *Jerusalem and the encouragement given to the project by the prophets *Haggai and *Zechariah; 7–10 deals with Ezra's mission to Jerusalem and the reforms he introduced, notably in the matter of mixed marriages. Neh. 1–7 contains Nehemiah's plans for the restoration of Jerusalem; 8–10 record the reading and acceptance of the Law; 11 and 12 describe arrangements for the occupation of the city; and 13 narrates a further series of Nehemiah's reforms.

It is generally supposed by modern scholars that the compiler of the Books wrote at a date considerably later even than the time of Ezra and Nehemiah, though opinion is divided as to whether he was also the author of the Books of Chronicles. There are a number of apparent historical inaccuracies in the Books, e.g. in the chronological details of the Persian kings, the foundation of the Temple, and the arrival of Ezra in Jerusalem (see preceding entry). These have been accounted for by the insufficient data and the preconceived ideas of a compiler of much later date. Some critics, however, have recently defended the historical reliability of much of the material. The compiler clearly drew his matter from several sources. Certain sections (written in the first person) appear to be derived from the 'Memoirs of Ezra' and the 'Memoirs of Nehemiah'. Ez. 4: 8–6: 18 and 7: 12–26 are written in *Aramaic, not Hebrew, and may therefore have been taken from a collection of official Aramaic documents; the various catalogues of names which occur may also derive from official sources. See also ESDRAS, BOOKS OF.

Comm. by H. E. *Ryle (Camb. Bib., RV, 1893), W. Rudolph (HAT, Reihe 1, Bd. 20; 1949), K. Galling (Das Alte Testament Deutsch, 12; on Chron., Ezra, and Neh., 1954, pp. 186–255), J. M. Myers (Anchor Bible, 1965), R. J. Coggins (Camb. Bib., NEB, 1976), D. J. A. Clines (New Cent. Bib., on Ezra, Neh., and Est., 1984, pp. 1–249), H. G. M. Williamson (Word Biblical Comm., 16; Waco, Tex., 1985), and J. Blenkinsopp (London, 1989). H. G. M. Williamson, *Ezra and Nehemiah* (Old Testament Guides, Sheffield [1987]).

C. C. Torrey, *The Composition and Historical Value of Ezra-Nehemiah* (Beihefte zur ZATW, 2; 1896). Id., *Ezra Studies* (Chicago, 1910). H. H. Schaeder, *Esra der Schreiber* (1930). G. von *Rad, 'Die Nehemia-Denkschrift', ZATW 76 (1964), pp. 176–87. S. *Mowinckel, *Studien zu dem Buche Ezra-Nehemia* (Skrifter utgitt av Det Norske Videnskaps-Akademi i Oslo, Hist.-filos. Klasse, NS 3, 5, 7; 1964–5). J. A. Emerton, 'Did Ezra go to Jerusalem in 428 BC?', *JTS*, NS 17 (1966), pp. 1–17, with refs. U. Kellermann, *Nehemia: Quellen, Überlieferung und Geschichte* (Beihefte zur ZATW, 102; 1967). S. Japhet, 'The Supposed Common Authorship of Chronicles and Ezra-Nehemiah investigated anew', *Vetus Testamentum*, 18 (1968), pp. 330–71. J. Bright, *A History of Israel* (3rd edn., 1981), pp. 391–402 (Excursus II: 'The Date of Ezra's Mission to Jerusalem', with full bibl. on this subject).

F

Faber, Frederick William (1814–63), *Oratorian and hymn writer. Born at Calverley, a small town in W. Yorkshire, he was educated at Shrewsbury and Harrow and at Balliol and University Colleges, Oxford. In 1837 he was elected to a Fellowship at the latter college. His upbringing was *Calvinist; but at Oxford he came under the influence of J. H. *Newman and collaborated in the work on the *Library of the Fathers*. In 1837 he was ordained deacon and in 1839 priest. In 1842 he was appointed Rector of Elton, Cambs. Two years later he published a short *Life of St Wilfrid* which created a sensation from its RC sympathies. On 17 Nov. 1845 he was received into the RC Church, a few weeks after Newman. With other converts he formed a small community, the 'Brothers of the Will of God', at Birmingham; in 1847 he was ordained priest; and in 1848, with his companions, joined the Oratory of St *Philip Neri, recently introduced into England by Newman. In 1849 Faber became the head of the London branch, at first established in King William Street, Strand, and from 1854 on its present site in the Brompton Road. Relations between the London and Birmingham Oratories were not always happy, with Newman disapproving of Faber's florid devotion and *Ultramontane attitudes.

Faber was the author of many hymns and devotional books. His writings owe their popularity to a combination of fervent spirituality and a lucid style. They have been translated into many languages. Among the better known are *All for Jesus* (1853), *Growth in Holiness* (1854), and *The Creator and the Creature* (1858). Perhaps the most popular of his hymns is 'My God, how wonderful Thou art'.

Life and Letters, ed. J. E. Bowden (1869; new edn., 1888). F. A. Faber (brother), *A Brief Sketch of the Early Life of F. W. Faber* (1869). Life by R. [G.] Chapman (London, 1961). D. Gorce, *Faber: Un Anglican à l'âme franciscaine (années d'avant sa conversion) 1814–1845* [1967]. G. M. Gozzelino, *La Vita Spirituale nel Pensiero di Federico Guglielmo Faber* (Bibliotheca Theologica Salesiana, 1st ser. 4; Zurich, 1969). J. F. Quinn, 'Newman, Faber and the Oratorian Separation: A Reappraisal', *Recusant History*, 20 (1990–1), pp. 106–26. T. Cooper in *DNB* 18 (1889), pp. 108–11; L. Cognet in *Dict. Sp.* 5 (1964), cols. 3–13, s.v. 'Faber (3), Frédéric-William', with further bibl.

Faber, Jacobus (*c.*1455–1536), also known as **Lefèvre d'Étaples** or **Stapulensis**, early French humanist. A native of Étaples, after ordination to the priesthood he devoted himself to the study of the classics at *Paris, where he made the acquaintance of some of the leading humanists. In 1492 he went to Italy and there became keenly interested in the ancient philosophers, esp. Aristotle. In 1507 Guillaume Briçonnet, then abbot of *St-Germain-des-Prés and later Bp. of Meaux, appointed him librarian of the monastery. Exchanging his secular for religious studies, he published in 1512 a Latin commentary on St Paul's Epistles. Two critical essays on St *Mary Magdalene (1517 and 1518) were followed by his formal

condemnation by the *Sorbonne for heresy in 1521. As he was by then involved in a diocesan programme of reform at Meaux (instigated by Briçonnet), the government, fearing an infiltration of *Lutheranism, also condemned him and in 1525 he was forced to flee to Strasbourg. Later he was taken under the protection of the Queen of Navarre. He never accepted the Reformation doctrines on grace, justification, and predestination, and his attitude to the Reformation has been compared with that of *Erasmus. His other writings include the first printed text of the (Lat.) *Ignatian Epp. (Paris, 1498) and a translation of the NT into French (1523; from the *Vulgate), followed by the Pss. in 1525 and the OT complete in 1528.

Prefatory Epistles and Related Texts, ed. E. F. Rice, Jun. (New York and London, 1972). The *Epistres et Évangiles pour les cinquante et deux dimenches de l'an*, written by Faber and his followers [or pupils], ed. G. Bedouelle and F. Giacone (Leiden, 1976). Studies by C. H. Graf (Strasbourg, 1842) and J. Barnaud (Paris, 1900). A. Renaudet, *Préréforme et humanisme à Paris pendant les premières guerres d'Italie (1494–1517)* (2nd edn., 1953), *passim*. E. F. Rice, Jun., 'The Humanist Idea of Christian Antiquity: Lefèvre d'Étaples and his Circle', *Studies in the Renaissance*, 9 (1962), pp. 126–60, incl. list of patristic texts ed. Faber, pp. 142–7. R. M. Cameron, 'The Charges of Lutheranism brought against Jacques Lefèvre d'Étaples', *HTR* 63 (1970), pp. 119–49, with refs. G. Bedouelle, *Lefèvre d'Étaples et l'Intelligence des Écritures* (Travaux d'Humanisme et de Renaissance, 152; 1976); id., *Le Quincuplex Psalterium de Lefèvre d'Étaples: Un guide de lecture* (ibid. 171; 1979), incl. repr. of 1513 edn. of the *Quincuplex Psalterium* (first pub., 1509). G. Bedouelle in *TRE* 10 (1982), pp. 781–3, s.v., with bibl.

Faber, Johann (1478–1541), German theologian. A native of Leutkirch in Württemberg, he studied at *Tübingen and Freiburg, and in 1530 became Bp. of Vienna. Ferdinand I employed him on several important missions, including a visit to England to engage *Henry VIII's help against the Turks. His lifelong friendship with *Erasmus led him at first to sympathize with P. *Melanchthon and U. *Zwingli in their desire to reform the Church; but as the underlying doctrinal cleavage manifested itself, he withdrew his support from the Reformation programme and became a zealous defender of Catholic orthodoxy, earning the title 'the hammer of the heretics'. His works consist chiefly of controversial treatises and a few collections of sermons.

Faber's *Malleus in Haeresim Lutheranam* was first pub. Cologne, 1524; modern edn. by A. Naegele, Corpus Catholicorum, 23–26; Münster i.W., 1941–52; 'Opuscula', ed. J. *Cochläus, Leipzig, 1537; 'Opera' (mostly sermons, letters, and diaries), ed. Cologne, 3 vols., fol., 1537–41. A. Horawitz, 'Joh. Heigerlin (genannt Faber), Bischof von Wien, bis zum Regensburger Convent' in *Sb.* (Wien), 107 (1884), pp. 83–220. Further study by L. Helbling (Reformationsgeschichtliche Studien und Texte, Hefte 67–8; Münster i.W., 1941). J. Wodka in *DHGE* 16 (1967), cols. 329–34, s.v. 'Fabri (2), Johannes'; H. Immenkötter in *TRE* 10 (1982), pp. 784–8, s.v. 'Fabri, Johann', both with bibl.

Fabian, St (d. 250), Bp. of Rome from 236. Little is known of his pontificate beyond the fact that when the *Decian Persecution broke out early in 250, he was among the first to suffer martyrdom. Acc. to the *Liber Pontificalis*, it was he who divided the city of Rome into seven ecclesiastical regions, each of them in the charge of a deacon. His body was buried in the *catacomb of San Callisto and later moved to the church of San Sebastiano, where it was discovered in 1915. Feast day, 20 Jan.

*Cyprian, *Ep.* 9; *LP* (Duchesne), 1 (1885), pp. 148 f. P. Styger, 'Scavi a San Sebastiano', *RQ* 29 (1915), pp. 73–110 (esp. 'La scoperta del corpo di S. Fabiano', pp. 100–5); F. Grossi-Gondi, SJ, *S. Fabiano, papa e martire dopo le scoperte sull'Appia* (1916). H. *Leclercq, OSB, in *DACL* 5 (pt. 1; 1922), cols. 1057–64, s.v.; P. Nautin in *DHGE* 16 (1967), cols. 316 f., s.v. 'Fabien (1)'.

Fabiola, St (d. 399), Roman matron. She belonged to the patrician *gens Fabia*. Having divorced her first husband for his vicious life, she remarried (contrary to the Church canons). After the death of her second 'husband', she did public penance before the *Lateran and entered on a life of great austerity, distributing her immense wealth to the poor and tending the sick. In 395 she went to *Bethlehem, where she stayed with St *Paula and St *Eustochium and put herself under the direction of St *Jerome. The tensions created by the *Origenistic controversy, her personal distaste for the isolated convent life at Bethlehem, and finally the incursion of the Huns into Palestine, led her to return to Rome, where she continued her charitable works until her death. Feast day, 27 Dec.

To St Fabiola St Jerome addressed two letters: *Epp.* 64 and 78; the principal source is the letter which Jerome wrote on her death, *Ep.* 77. W. H. Fremantle in *DCB* 2 (1880), pp. 442 f., with refs. See also bibl. to JEROME.

Fabri, Felix (1438–1502), a learned *Dominican, from 1468 based at Ulm, who in his *Evagatorium* left a vivid account of his journeys in 1480 and 1483–4 to Egypt and the Holy Land, where he visited *Jerusalem. He wrote many other works.

Evagatorium, ed. G. D. Hassler (Stuttgart, 1843–9); Eng. tr. by A. Stewart (Palestine Pilgrims' Text Society, 7–10; 1892–3). H. F. M. Prescott, *Friar Felix at Large: A Fifteenth-century Pilgrimage to the Holy Land* (New Haven, Conn., 1950); id., *Once to Sinai: The Further Pilgrimage of Friar Felix Fabri* (1957). P. S. Allen, *The Age of Erasmus* (1914), pp. 238–51. A. Duval in *DHGE* 16 (1967), cols. 326–9, s.v. 'Fabri (1), Félix'; K. Hannemann in *Verfasserlexikon* (2nd edn.), 2 (1980), cols. 682–9, s.v., with bibl.

Fabri, Johannes. See FABER, JOHANN.

Fabricius, Johann Albert (1668–1736), *Lutheran classical scholar and bibliographer. Born at Leipzig and educated there and at Quedlinburg, in 1693 he settled in Hamburg as a private librarian. From 1699 until his death he taught rhetoric and ethics and was rector of the Johanneum from 1708 to 1711.

Fabricius was an indefatigable student whose monumental bibliographical work, if lacking in scientific accuracy, laid the foundations for all subsequent histories of literature. His *Bibliotheca Graeca* (14 vols., 1705–28; revised and continued by G. C. Harles, 1790–1812) covered the period from Homer to the fall of

*Constantinople (1453). His other compilations include the *Bibliotheca Latina* (1697; revised and enlarged, 3 vols., 1721–2), *Bibliotheca Latina Mediae et Infimae Aetatis* (5 vols., 1734–6; vol. 6, in collaboration with C. Schoettgen, 1746). He also did important work on the Apocrypha, publishing the *Codex Apocryphus Novi Testamenti* (2 vols., 1703, enlarged with 3rd vol., 1719) and the *Codex Pseudepigraphus Veteris Testamenti* (1713). He also produced the first collected edition of the works of St *Hippolytus (2 vols., 1716–18), and editions of Sextus Empiricus (1718), St *Philaster of Brescia (1721) and Dio Cassius (completed by H. S. *Reimarus, 1750–1).

H. S. Reimarus (son-in-law), *De Vita et Scriptis Joannis Alberti Fabricii Commentarius* (Hamburg, 1737). There is also a brief introd. on Fabricius's life and works prefixed to the edn. of his *Bibliotheca Latina* (6 vols. bound in 3, Florence, 1858), vol. 1, pp. xx–xxiv. B. Heurtebize in *DTC* 5 (1913), cols. 2063–5; H. Reincke in *Neue Deutsche Biographie*, 4 (1959), pp. 732 f., both s.v.

Faculties, Court of. The court of the Abp. of *Canterbury which grants faculties (see FACULTY). Its judge, who is called the 'Master of the Faculties', is usually the same person as the *Dean of the Arches and Auditor. After it had been enacted by the Ecclesiastical Licences Act 1533 that dispensations, licences, and faculties which had previously been granted by the Pope were henceforth to be granted by the Abp. of Canterbury in the provinces both of Canterbury and of *York, the Court of Faculties was established in 1534 to take over this jurisdiction.

D. S. Chambers (ed.), *Faculty Office Registers 1534–1549: A Calendar of the first two Registers of the Archbishop of Canterbury's Faculty Office* (Oxford, 1966), with valuable introd. See also bibl. to foll. entry.

faculty. A dispensation or licence from an ecclesiastical superior permitting an action to be done or a position to be held which without it could not lawfully be done or held. Thus the Preface to the *Ordinal in the BCP forbids anyone to be admitted a deacon under 23 years of age 'unless he have a Faculty'. Under the Ecclesiastical Licences Act 1533 the Court of *Faculties was created to restrain persons from suing for dispensations from Rome. As in every diocese the consecrated lands and buildings, with their contents, are in the ultimate guardianship of the Bishop, faculties are necessary for additions or alterations to churches and churchyards. They are normally issued by the Bishop's *Chancellor or, since the Care of Churches and Ecclesiastical Jurisdiction Measure 1991, in uncontested cases by the *Archdeacon, and without a faculty the erection of, e.g., an altar, a statue, or a memorial tablet in a church is illegal. When once erected (whether with or without a faculty), a fresh faculty is needed for the removal of such objects, even temporarily. Where there is litigation over matters involving faculties, the case is first heard in the *Consistory Court. If the Chancellor gives a conclusive certificate that a point of doctrine, ritual, or ceremonial ('a reserved matter') is involved, an appeal lies from there to the *Court of Ecclesiastical Causes Reserved, while if he certifies that no such point is involved, it lies to the *Arches Court of Canterbury or to the Chancery Court of York, and thence to the *Judicial Committee of the Privy Council.

In the academic world a faculty is the organization for the teaching of a particular subject, so called because it can grant a faculty to receive or to supplicate for a degree. The traditional faculties are those of theology, canon and civil law, medicine, and arts.

G. H. Newsom, *Faculty Jurisdiction of the Church of England* (1988; 2nd edn. by G. L. Newsom, 1993). M. Hill, *Ecclesiastical Law* (1995), pp. 384–464.

Facundus (6th cent.), Bp. of Hermiane in the province of Byzacena in Africa. In the *Monophysite controversy he was one of the chief supporters of the *Three Chapters. In view of the dispute he made his way to *Constantinople, and in 547–8 completed there an apology for the accused in his treatise 'Pro Defensione Trium Capitulorum', in which he upheld the orthodoxy of each of the three theologians concerned—*Ibas, *Theodore of Mopsuestia (in this case with some reserves), and *Theodoret—and argued forcibly that to condemn the Three Chapters meant to reject the Christology of *Chalcedon (451). After his return to Africa, and the anathematization of the Three Chapters at the Second Council of Constantinople (553), he and his supporters were excommunicated for a time by Pope *Vigilius. He defended himself in two further writings, both of them dating from *c.*571—'Contra Mocianum Scholasticum' and 'Epistola fidei catholicae in defensione trium capitulorum'.

Works ed. J. *Sirmond, SJ, Paris, 1629; repr. in J. P. Migne, *PL* 67. 527–878; crit. edn. by J.-M. Clément, OSB, and R. Vander Plaetse (CCSL 90A; 1974). Study (in Russian) by A. Dobroklonskij (Moscow, 1880; discussed by A. *Harnack in *TLZ*, 1880, cols. 632–5). R. B. Eno, 'Doctrinal Authority in the African Ecclesiology of the Sixth Century: Ferrandus and Facundus', *Revue des Études Augustiniennes*, 22 (1976), pp. 95–113, esp. pp. 100–13; M. Simonetti, '*Haereticum non facit ignorantia*. Una nota su Facondo di Ermiane e la sua difesa dei Tre Capitoli', *Orpheus*, NS 1 (1980), pp. 76–105. Bardenhewer, 5, pp. 320–4; M. Pellegrino in *EC* 5 (1950), cols. 954 f., s.v. 'Facondo di Ermiana'.

Fairbairn, Andrew Martin (1838–1912), *Congregational theologian. Of Covenanting ancestry, Fairbairn was born at Inverkeithing in Fife and studied at Edinburgh University. He was successively minister of the *Evangelical Union churches at Bathgate (1860–72) and St Paul's Street, Aberdeen (1872–7), principal of the (Congregational) Airedale Theological College at Bradford (1877–86), and first principal of Mansfield College, Oxford (1886–1909). Through visits to Germany he came under the influence of I. A. *Dorner, F. A. G. *Tholuck, and E. W. *Hengstenberg, and warmly advocated theological liberalism. His eloquence, learning, and personal character won him a unique position among Congregational ministers in his generation. His writings include *Studies in the Philosophy of Religion and History* (1876), *The Place of Christ in Modern Theology* (1893), *Catholicism, Roman and Anglican* (1899), and *The Philosophy of the Christian Religion* (1902). He also took an active part in religious and political controversy, notably in connection with the Education Act of 1902.

W. B. Selbie, *Life of Andrew Martin Fairbairn* (1914). P. [B.] Hinchliff, *God and History: Aspects of British Theology 1875–1914* (Oxford, 1992), pp. 185–97. W. B. Selbie in *DNB*, *1912–1921*, pp. 179 f.

faith. The term is used in at least two quite distinct senses in a Christian context.

(1) It is applied objectively to the body of truth ('the Christian faith') to be found in the *Creeds, in the definitions of accredited *Councils, in the teachings of doctors and saints, and, above all, in the revelation contained in the Bible. This complex of doctrine is held to embody or else follow from the teaching of Christ Himself, and as God's supreme revelation to mankind to be wilfully rejected by man only at the peril of his salvation. Technically it is known as 'the faith believed in' (*fides quae creditur*).

(2) To this objective faith is opposed 'subjective' faith. Faith thus understood is the first of the three '*theological virtues', set by St *Paul side by side with 'hope' and 'love' (1 Cor. 13: 13). It is the human response to Divine truth, inculcated in the Gospels as the childlike and trusting acceptance of the *Kingdom and its demands, and known as 'the faith whereby belief is reached' (*fides qua creditur*). Acc. to orthodox theologians, faith in this latter sense is a supernatural, not a natural, act. The Christian can make an act of faith only in virtue of God's action in his soul.

Such clarity was, however, reached only gradually. The Greek word for faith (πίστις) was already current in philosophical circles in contrast to knowledge (ἐπιστήμη, γνῶσις); it signified intellectual assent based on unspecifiable grounds, understood either disparagingly (as by *Plato), or as the grasp of first principles (as by *Aristotle). The NT, prob. influenced by Hebrew usage, understood by faith less intellectual assent than personal trust: it is this that is the foundation of the Christian's relationship to God and Christ, and it is often correlated with knowledge (e.g. Jn. 17 and 1 Cor. 13). *Clement of Alexandria was the first to draw these traditions together, defending the Christian stress on faith against pagan (Platonic) criticism by invoking the Aristotelian understanding, so that faith is seen as a divinely given assent to the fundamental principles of Christianity. Clement's synthesis gradually established itself among Christian theologians. At the same time, though apparently independently, the Platonic tradition revalued πίστις, so that for *Proclus it is ranked with truth and love.

With St *Augustine the classic understanding of faith was achieved. Faith demands an act of the will, and is thus more than intellectual. He defined it as 'thinking with the giving of assent' (*cum assentione cogitare*). This voluntaristic moment in the act of faith accounts for the moral quality which it is held to possess and the conviction that wilful unbelief, as a misdirection of the will, merits the censure of God. To express this twofold element in the full act of faith, *Peter Lombard distinguished between (a) 'unformed faith' (*fides informis*), i.e. pure intellectual assent to a proposition, and (b) 'faith formed by love' (*fides formata caritate*), i.e. the developed faith, e.g. of St Paul in Gal. 5: 6. It is in the light of this distinction that the apparent opposition between the teaching of the author of the Epistle of St *James and that of St Paul about faith has been held to be capable of reconciliation.

As a supernatural act, faith is a higher faculty than reason. In the developed teaching of the Middle Ages, a distinction (which can be traced back to *Boethius) was drawn between those truths accessible to the human intellect by the light of natural reason, e.g. the existence of

God, and those which could be appropriated only by faith, e.g. belief in the Trinity. There was difference of opinion as to whether there were any truths which could in a full sense be the objects of both faith and reason; in so far as any overlap was conceded, it was held by the most reputable theologians that the truths of reason and of faith were coincident. Only in the later and decadent Scholasticism was it maintained that one and the same proposition could be proved untrue by reason and accepted as true by faith.

At the Reformation, the part of faith in the Christian religion received a new emphasis. M. *Luther's teaching on *justification by 'faith alone' stressed the voluntaristic side of faith, in so far as faith was allowed to be a human act at all. The chief moment in it was trust (*fiducia*), and supremely personal trust and confidence in the atoning work of Christ. The Lutheran theologians of the next generation analysed the act of faith into its three components of knowledge (*notitia*), assent (*assensus*), and trust (*fiducia*), though they held that the two former were subordinate to *fiducia*. The Anglican *Thirty-Nine Articles, while by referring favourably to justification by faith only (Art. XI) and denying merit to works done before justification (Art. XIII) they guard against ascribing virtue to human effort apart from divine grace, assert, nevertheless, that works which are the fruit of faith are pleasing to God (Art. XII). The ancient opposition between faith and knowledge re-emerged in the wake of the *Enlightenment in such thinkers as I. *Kant and S. *Kierkegaard, for whom faith is so contrasted with knowledge as to be a subjective attitude without objective content.

The Second *Vatican Council both exemplified and initiated a new phase in the inter-confessional exploration of faith. In the first place it did not conceive the 'truth' of 'the Gospel' in such exclusively propositional terms as previous theologians had done. Scriptural truth is that 'which, for the purpose of our salvation, God wished to be consigned to Holy Writ'. That is to say, the truth is Christ Himself, and what He has done for men, not a series of theological or anthropological propositions. Further, in expounding this 'truth' that is Christ and His work, the RC Church now acknowledges in a new way that Scripture and Tradition form a single source of revelation, and is willing to distinguish between the deposit of truth itself and the mode in which this truth is communicated. There are contingent elements in doctrinal definitions, and therefore doctrines may be, and indeed must be, reformulated, as they undergo development.

Secondly, RC theologians have shown a remarkably profounder grasp of the 'Protestant' principle of justification by faith alone, an understanding richer in many ways than that of many Protestants. The Second Vatican Council also recognized the importance of conscience as a gift to the human person that must never be overridden, but always called to the affirmations of faith willingly.

Classic discussion in St *Thomas Aquinas, *Summa Theologiae*, II (2), qq. 1–7. J. *Butler, *The *Analogy of Religion* (1736); J. H. *Newman, *An Essay in Aid of a Grammar of Assent* (1870; ed., with introd. and notes, by I. T. Ker, Oxford, 1985). From the vast modern literature, the foll. may be mentioned: M. C. *D'Arcy, SJ, *The Nature of Belief* (1931; 2nd edn., 1958); J. *Oman, *The Natural and the Supernatural* (1931); D. M. Emmet, *Philosophy and Faith* (1936); B. Mitchell (ed.), *Faith and Logic: Oxford Essays in Philosophical Theology* (1957); id., *The Justifica-*

tion of Religious Belief (1973); J. [D.] Hick, *Faith and Knowledge* (Ithaca, NY, 1957; 2nd edn., London, 1967); id. (ed.), *Faith and the Philosophers* (1964); J. Pieper, *Über den Glauben* (Munich, 1962; Eng. tr., 1964); W. Cantwell Smith, *Faith and Belief* (Princeton, NJ, 1979). S. Harent in *DTC* 6 (1920), cols. 55–514, s.v. 'Foi'; A. de Bovis, SJ, in *Dict. Sp.* 5 (1964), cols. 529–619, s.v. 'Foi'; C. H. Pickar and others in *NCE* 5 (1967), pp. 792–804, s.v.

Faith, Defender of the. See DEFENDER OF THE FAITH.

Faith, Promoter of the. See PROMOTOR FIDEI.

Faith, St (d. *c.*287), virgin and martyr. Acc. to the legend which dates from the 8th or 9th cent., she suffered for the faith at Agen in Aquitaine, under Maximian Hercules and the procurator Dacian, together with St Caprasius. Dulcidus, Bp. of Agen (5th cent.), translated her relics to a basilica which he built in honour of St Faith and St Caprasius, and many miracles are believed to have taken place at her shrine. Her relics were brought *c.*855 to the abbey of Conques, which became a famous place of pilgrimage, visited e.g. by the Emp. *Frederick Barbarossa. Her cult was very popular in the Middle Ages, and many churches were dedicated to her, among them that of Farringdon Ward Within, London. This was pulled down in 1240 to make room for the choir of *St Paul's Cathedral, a chapel of which was then dedicated to St Faith. This dedication survives in the 'St Faith's Chapel' in the crypt of the present cathedral. Feast day, 6 Oct.

AASS, Oct. 3 (1770), pp. 263–329, incl. text of Acta, pp. 288 f.; other versions of the Acta listed in *BHL* 1 (1898–1899), pp. 441–4 (nos. 2928–65), and *Novum Supplementum* (1986), pp. 334–6. The *Liber Miraculorum Sancte Fidis*, ed. A. Bouillet (Paris, 1897). On the 11th-cent. *Chanson de Sainte Foi* (ed., with modern Fr. tr., by A. Thomas, Paris, 1925), see E. Hoepffner and P. Alfaric, *La Chanson de Sainte Foy* (Publications de la Faculté des Lettres de l'Université de Strasbourg, 32 and 33; 1926). A. Bouillet and L. Servières, *Sainte Foy, vierge et martyre* (1900). L. *Duchesne, *Fastes épiscopaux de l'ancienne Gaule*, 2 (2nd edn., 1910), pp. 144–6. J. Daoust in *DHGE* 17 (1971), cols. 1358–64, s.v. 'Foy (Sainte)'.

Faith and Order. The branch of the *Ecumenical Movement of which the chief object has been to bring about the reunion of the Christian Churches, and by which the Conferences at *Lausanne in 1927 and *Edinburgh in 1937 were organized. It is now absorbed in the *World Council of Churches.

L. Vischer (ed.), *A Documentary History of the Faith and Order Movement, 1927–1963* (St Louis [1963]); G. Gassmann (ed.), *Documentary History of Faith and Order 1963–1993* (Faith and Order Paper, 159; Geneva [1993]).

Faithful, Mass of the (Lat. *Missa Fidelium*). The part of the *Mass which extends from the *Offertory to the end. It contains all the most essential parts of the service. It is so named because in early times the (unbaptized) *catechumens were dismissed before the Offertory and only the baptized (the 'fideles') remained to join in the Eucharistic offering.

falda. A white vestment formerly worn over the alb and reaching from the hips to the ground. Its use was confined to the Pope, who, until recently, wore it on solemn occasions.

E. Dante in *EC* 5 (1950), col. 962, s.v., with ill., col. 961.

faldstool (Lat. *faldistorium*). In the RC Church the folding stool used in the *sanctuary by bishops and other prelates when they do not occupy the throne. The absence of a back enables it to be used both for sitting on and as a *prie-dieu. Unlike the throne, it may be used not only by the bishop of the diocese but also by prelates who have no *ordinary jurisdiction in the place.

Falk, Paul Ludwig Adalbert (1827–1900), German Liberal politician. In 1872 he was appointed Minister of Public Worship and Education by Bismarck with explicit instructions to defend the rights of the state against the Church in the *Kulturkampf. In this he succeeded only in two points, namely in excluding the Church from the supervision of schools and from civil marriage. His *May Laws, designed to put the relations between Church and state on an entirely new basis, were a failure owing to the uncompromising resistance not only of the Catholic Church but also of orthodox Protestantism to a measure destructive of all positive Christian education. Bismarck's consequent change of policy in 1879 caused Falk's resignation and also marked the end of the Kulturkampf.

Short study by H. R. Fischer (Hamm, 1901); full Life by E. Foerster (Gotha, 1927). R. Ruhenstroth-Bauer, *Bismarck und Falk im Kulturkampf* (Heidelberger Abhandlungen, 70; 1944). K. Kupisch in *RGG* (3rd edn.), 2 (1958), cols. 862–4, s.v. 'Falk (1), Adalbert', with further refs. See also works cited under KULTURKAMPF.

Fall, the. The first act of disobedience of *Adam and *Eve whereby humanity lost its primal innocence and entered upon its actual condition of sin and toil. As described in Gen. 2 f., Eve, tempted by the serpent, ate of the forbidden fruit of the 'tree of the knowledge of good and evil' in the Garden of *Eden, and then induced Adam to follow her example. The punishment was expulsion from Paradise, the imposition of toilsome work on Adam and the pains of childbirth on Eve, and the decree of perpetual enmity between the serpent, which would 'bruise [man's] heel', and the man, who would 'bruise [the serpent's] head' (Gen. 3: 15). Acc. to traditions as old as the *Apocrypha, Eve's sin involved mankind in the loss of immortality (cf. Ecclus. 25: 24), and the serpent was identified with the Devil (cf. Wisd. 2: 23 f.). These conclusions are not drawn elsewhere in the OT. The story itself suggests rather that Adam and Eve were not originally possessed of immortality (though they might have obtained it; cf. Gen. 3: 22 f.). What the biblical narrative teaches positively is that sin arose by free human choice, and that all human life has been thereby radically altered for the worse, so that its actual state is very different from that purposed for it by the Creator. The doctrine of evil which it inculcates is, as against every form of dualism (which makes evil as well as good of Divine origin), pantheism (which denies the distinction between Creator and creation), or determinism (which denies human free will), that sin arose through free human agency; and this belief is integral to Christianity and Judaism alike.

Other questions, often more prominent in theological debate but really subordinate to this fundamental doctrine, concern (1) the ultimate origin of the evil manifested in Eve's and Adam's sin, (2) the historicity of the story of Gen. 2 f., and (3) the nature and extent of the consequences of the Fall for mankind. These issues are closely intertwined.

The common Christian belief down to modern times considered the Fall of Adam and Eve as an historical event. The serpent, which is represented in the Gen. narrative quite naïvely as a talking animal, was identified with the Devil or Satan, a spiritual being, who must have been created good and himself previously fallen, and hence the original Fall was inferred to be that of Satan rather than that of Adam and Eve. Adam and Eve being considered as historical persons and all subsequent humanity as their descendants, the consequences of the Fall were held to affect all mankind by inheritance, or even by a theory of 'seminal identity' by which an ancestor's act may involve all his descendants also (cf. Heb. 7: 9 f.). Acc. to the view expressed in Wisd. and Ecclus. (cf. above) and strongly endorsed by St *Paul (Rom. 5: 12 ff., 1 Cor. 15: 22), it was Adam's sin that 'brought death into the world' because 'in Adam all sinned' and therefore became liable to death. It is noteworthy that, as St Paul appeals to this belief as a premiss accepted by his readers, it appears to have been generally accepted in the early Church, at least among Gentile Christians, and the Fall thus to have been, from the first, part of the background against which the Christian doctrine of Redemption was expounded. Until the rise of *Pelagianism it was not a subject of controversy. The Greek Fathers, however, tended to minimize the evil done to man by the sin of Adam, laying more stress on the responsibility of each individual, while the Latins (esp. St *Augustine), emphasizing the enormity of Adam's transgression and the magnitude of its consequences for mankind, developed the doctrine of *Original Sin (q.v.), which Pelagius opposed by denying the reality of any evil consequences from the Fall to subsequent mankind. *Origen (q.v.), almost alone among the Fathers, found the ultimate source of evil in a pre-mundane Fall or falls of equal created spirits who, by voluntarily declining to a greater or less degree from the goodness in which they were created, became respectively demons, men, or angels. For him the human fall took place in a spiritual pre-natal existence (*De Princ.* 2. 8 f.) and the story of Eden was to be interpreted allegorically (*De Princ.* 4. 3).

In modern times the whole concept of the Fall has often been rejected as inconsistent with the facts of man's development known to science, esp. with evolution. The biblical story itself belongs to the realm of myth and is told with much anthropomorphic and metaphorical detail. Orthodox Christian apologists insist, however, that man possesses a power of moral choice not shared with the animals; that at some stage in human development this God-given power began to be misused; and that once begun, such wrong use has necessarily affected subsequent generations and given rise to the vast accumulated power of sin in the world. They would say that it was this fact which made necessary the redemption of the world by Christ. Since it was in close connection with the doctrine of Redemption that Christian thought about the Fall developed, the Church has seen in the story of Gen. 2 f. a fundamental truth about man in his relation to God, even if the truth is held to be there conveyed in legendary form.

Belief in the fall of Adam is defined as *de fide* by the Council of *Trent, Sess. V, Can. 1 (AD 1546). F. R. Tennant, *The Sources of the Doctrines of the Fall and Original Sin* (1903); id., *The Origin and Propagation of Sin* (Hulsean Lectures, 1902). N. P. *Williams, *The Ideas of the Fall and of Original Sin* (Bampton Lectures for 1924, 1927). L. Ligier, *Péché d'Adam et péché du monde* (Théologie, 43 and 48; 1960–1), with extensive refs. J. [H.] Hick, *Evil and the God of Love* (1966). J. Denney, J. A. MacCulloch, and D. S. Margoliouth in *HERE* 5 (1912), pp. 701–15, s.v. See also comm. on Gen. and bibl. to ORIGINAL SIN.

False Decretals. A collection of canon law documents said in the text to be the work of '*Isidore Mercator' (q.v.), but in fact compiled *c.*850, prob. in France in the circle of the opponents of *Hincmar, Abp. of Reims. In its fullest form it contains three sections, the second and third of which are based on the genuine canons of councils and *decretals of the 7th-cent. *Collectio *Hispana*, though much adapted and interpolated. The first section consists of letters in the names of pre-Nicene Popes from *Clement I to *Miltiades (d. 314), and includes the *Donation of Constantine; all are spurious. A shorter form, containing only the decretals from Clement to *Damasus (d. 384), circulated independently. The forgeries deal with many issues, but show a special concern for the protection of the rights of diocesan bishops against their metropolitans and the laity, and for the Papal supremacy as their guarantee. The compiler or compilers produced a number of related works, based on very wide reading, though the False Decretals are by far the most influential. They were drawn on extensively in the canon law collections of the reform associated with *Gregory VII, and so many of them reappear in the *Decretum* of *Gratian. They seem to have been known to Pope *Nicholas I by 865; although some of his contemporaries asserted that they were forgeries, throughout the rest of the Middle Ages they were generally assumed to be historical. Both T. *More and J. *Fisher, unaware of their true character, used them to defend the claims of the Papacy. Their genuineness was systematically attacked by the Magdeburg *Centuriators in 1559, and is now universally rejected.

Editio princeps in J. Merlin, *Concilia* (Paris, 1524 ['1523']); they are also pr. in subsequent edns. of the *Concilia*. The 2nd edn. of Merlin's text (Cologne, 1530) is repr. in J. P. Migne, *PG* 130. P. Hinschius (ed.), *Decretales Pseudo-Isidorianae et Capitula Angilramni* (Leipzig, 1863), has a valuable preface, but is only partly based on the manuscripts and has many limitations. P. Fournier and G. Le Bras, *Histoire des collections canoniques en occident*, 1 (1931), pp. 127–233. E. Seckel, *Die erste Zeile Pseudoisidors, die Hadriana-Rezension* In nomine domini incipit praefatio libri huius *und die Geschichte der Invokationen in den Rechtsquellen*, posthumously ed. by H. Fuhrmann (*Sb.* (Berl.), Klasse für Philosophie, Geschichte, Staats-, Rechts- und Wirtschaftswissenschaften, Jahrgang 1959, no. 4; 1959), with detailed bibl. S. Williams, *Codices Pseudo-Isidoriani* (Monumenta Iuris Canonici, Series C, 3; New York, 1971). H. Fuhrmann, *Einfluss und Verbreitung der pseudoisidorischen Fälschungen* (Schriften der *MGH*, 24; 3 vols., 1972–4), with discussion of bibl. to date. J. Richter, 'Stufen pseudoisidorischer Verfälschung', *Zeitschrift der Savigny-Stiftung für Rechtsgeschichte*, Kanonistische Abteilung, 64 (1978), pp. 1–72. E. Seckel in *PRE* (3rd edn.), 16 (1905), pp. 265–307, s.v. 'Pseudoisidor', retains much of its value. H. Fuhrmann in *NCE* 5 (1967), pp. 820–4, s.v.

Familists. The members of a sect called the 'Family of Love', founded by H. *Nicholas (q.v.) in Emden in 1540. Though opposed to *solifidianism, they believed in the '*Inner Light' and the birth of Christ in their own souls; they rejected the services and sacraments of the official Churches, but were advised by their founder to conform outwardly to the religion of the State. The sect won supporters in Germany, the Netherlands, France, and England. On the Continent of Europe it all but disappeared soon after 1600, but in England, despite Queen *Elizabeth I's 'Proclamation against the Sectaries of the Family of Love' in 1580 and the arrest of a number of its members, it survived until the end of the 17th cent. Nicholas's books were reprinted under O. *Cromwell and were widely read by the *Quakers and the English admirers of J. *Boehme.

Chronica, Ordo Sacerdotis, Acta HN: Three Texts on the Family of Love, ed., with Eng. summaries, by A. [A. H.] Hamilton (Leiden, 1988). G. H. Williams, *The Radical Reformation* (Philadelphia [1962]), esp. pp. 477–82; 3rd edn. (Sixteenth Century Essays & Studies, 15; Kirksville, Mo. [1992]), pp. 723–9. H. de la Fontaine Verwey, 'The Family of Love', *Quaerendo*, 6 (1976), pp. 219–71. A. [A. H.] Hamilton, *The Family of Love* (Cambridge, 1981). J. D. Moss, "*Godded with God*": Hendrik Niclaes and his Family of Love (Transactions of the American Philosophical Society, 71, pt. 8; 1981). N. Smith, *Perfection Proclaimed: Language and Literature in English Radical Religion 1640–1660* (Oxford, 1989), pp. 144–84.

fan, liturgical (Lat. *flabellum*, Gk. ῥιπίδιον or ἑξαπτέρυγον, 'six-winged', so called because the figure of a seraph appears upon it). From the 4th cent. at latest, fans were sometimes used at the Eucharist for keeping flies and other insects away from the oblations, and the practice continued in the W. down to the 14th cent. Their use survives in the *Byzantine, *Armenian, *Coptic, and *Syrian Orthodox rites, though their significance now is purely symbolic. As a mark of honour, until recently two fans were used whenever the Pope was carried in procession on the '*sedia gestatoria'.

Braun, *AG*, pp. 624–60, with plates 140–2. H. *Leclercq, OSB, in *DACL* 5 (pt. 2; 1923), cols. 1610–25, s.v. 'Flabellum', with extensive bibl. to date.

Fanar, the. See PHANAR, THE.

fanon. Of uncertain derivation, the word has been applied to several accessories of religious worship, apparently common to all being the fact that they are made from an embroidered piece of stuff. Among them are the *maniple; the white linen cloth in which the congregation formerly brought their Eucharistic offerings; the strings of the *mitre; the *humeral veil of the *subdeacon; and processional banners. In modern usage the word is confined to the collar-shaped liturgical garment (Ital. *fanone*) until recently worn by the Pope over his *amice when celebrating a solemn pontifical Mass. This garment was at one time known as the 'orale'.

Braun, *LG*, pp. 52–7.

Farel, Guillaume (1489–1565), Reformer of French Switzerland. While studying in Paris (*c.*1509–17), he came under the influence of J. *Faber (Stapulensis). He adopted Protestantism in the early 1520s and became involved with a group of scholars and theologians of Protestant sympathies (incl. Faber) who were active in Meaux under the leadership of its Bishop, Guillaume Briçonnet. After the group's dispersal, in 1524 Farel moved to Basle, where he disputed with the opponents of the Reformation. He was banished a few months later, prob. at the instigation of *Erasmus. He prepared the first Protestant liturgy in French (*La maniere et fasson*) prob. in 1528, though the earliest known copy dates from 1533, and in 1529 he published his famous *Sommaire*, a declaration of Protestant belief. He introduced the Reformation in Neuchâtel in 1530. Together with P. *Virct, he established the Reformation in the Canton of Vaud and in 1534–6 in Geneva. It was he who persuaded J. *Calvin to stay in Geneva, and the two were expelled together in 1538. Farel then returned to Neuchâtel, where he put into practice the Genevan Reformation model. Later, he was active in bringing about the *Consensus Tigurinus (1549).

Farel's *Le Pater Noster et le Credo en Françoys* [devotional expositions] was repr. from the first edn. [1524], with slight emendations and introd. by F. [M.] Higman (Geneva, 1982). Modern Lives by M. Kirchhofer (2 vols., Zurich, 1831–4; Eng. tr., 1837), S. Delattre (Paris, 1931), the monumental composite vol., *Guillaume Farel, 1489–1565: Biographie nouvelle écrite d'après les documents originaux par un groupe d'historiens, professeurs et pasteurs de Suisse, de France et d'Italie* (by C. Schnetzler and others), ed. by the Comité Farel (Neuchâtel and Paris, 1930), and D. Nauta (Amsterdam, 1978). *Actes du Colloque Guillaume Farel, Neuchâtel, 29 septembre–1ᵉ octobre 1980*, ed. P. Barthel and others (Cahiers de la *Revue de Théologie et de Philosophie*, 9; 2 vols., Geneva, etc., 1983), with catalogue of Farel's correspondence, 2, pp. 13–104, and bibl. of his works, pp. 105–45. H. Heyer, *Guillaume Farel: Essai sur le développement des idées théologiques* (thesis, Geneva, 1872; Eng. tr., Texts and Studies in Religion, 54; Lewiston, Queenston, and Llandaff [1990]). E. Jacobs, *Die Sakramentslehre Wilhelm Farels* (Zürcher Beiträge zur Reformationsgeschichte, 10; 1978). O. Fatio in *TRE* 11 (1983), pp. 30–6, s.v.

farmery, also 'fermery', another form of 'infirmary', esp. of a monastery. It was usually a separate building in the charge of the *infirmarian (q.v.). In it the normal monastic discipline as to food and other matters was greatly relaxed.

Farrar, Frederic William (1831–1903), Dean of *Canterbury. He was educated at *King's College, London, where he was influenced by F. D. *Maurice, and at Trinity College, Cambridge, and became in turn housemaster at Harrow (1855), headmaster of Marlborough (1871), Canon of Westminster and Rector of St Margaret's (1876), and Dean of Canterbury (1895). A 'Broad Church Evangelical', he had great influence on the religious feeling and culture of the Victorian middle classes, esp. through his *Life of Christ* (1874), which went through 12 editions in a year, and his *Life and Works of St Paul* (1879). In these he expressed devout faith interpreted by wide scholarship and set out in a popular style. His *Eternal Hope* (1877), a collection of sermons in which he questioned the doctrine of eternal punishment for the wicked, provoked great controversy. Besides other theological works, Farrar wrote fiction. *Eric; or Little by Little* (1858), a school tale partly autobiographical, was long popular.

Life by R. Farrar, son (London, 1904), with list of his works, pp. xiii–xxii. R. Bayne in *DNB, 1901–1911*, 2 (1912), pp. 9–12.

fast. See FASTS AND FASTING.

Fastidius (early 5th cent.), British ecclesiastical writer. *Gennadius (*De vir. ill.* 56) calls him 'Britannorum epis-

copus' and attributes to him two works, 'De vita christiana' and 'De viduitate servanda'. Their identity is much disputed. The 'De vita christiana' has sometimes been held to be the work of the same title preserved among the works of St *Augustine; this is certainly *Pelagian, but there are substantial objections to the attribution to Fastidius. Other scholars have sought to identify his 'De vita christiana' with the first work in the 'Corpus Pelagianum' printed by C. P. *Caspari. If this hypothesis were correct, it would follow that Fastidius left Britain for Sicily *c.*410, was converted to Pelagianism by a 'noble lady', intended to visit Rome (perhaps to meet Pelagius), and returned to Britain as bishop *c.*430. The attempts to attribute to Fastidius a work beginning 'Audi, filia', preserved among the writings of *Caesarius of Arles, and the other items in Caspari's 'Corpus Pelagianum' are even more speculative.

C. P. Caspari, *Briefe, Abhandlungen und Predigten aus den zwei letzten Jahrhunderten des kirchlichen Altertums und dem Anfange des Mittelalters* (Oslo, 1890), pp. 3–167, with notes pp. 223–389; texts, mainly repr. in J. P. Migne, *PL*, Suppl. No 1, with notes pp. 223–389; texts, 1 (1958), cols. 1375–505 and 1687–94. The pseudo-Augustinian 'De vita christiana' is repr. from the Benedictine edn. of Augustine in J. P. Migne, *PL* 40. 1031–46; 'Audi, filia' is repr. ibid. 67. 1094–8. All these works are repr., with Eng. tr. (except for the Ps.-Augustinian 'De vita christiana') in R. S. T. Haslehurst, *The Works of Fastidius* (1927; inaccurate). G. Morin, OSB, 'Le *De vita christiana* de l'évêque breton Fastidius et le livre de Pélage "ad viduam" ', *R. Bén.* 15 (1898), pp. 481–93; id., 'Fastidius ad Fatalem? Pages inédites du Vᵉ siècle d'après le manuscrit CCXXI de Reichenau', ibid. 46 (1934), pp. 3–17, with refs. to earlier arts. I. Kirmer, OSB, *Das Eigentum des Fastidius im pelagianischen Schrifttum* (Diss., Würzburg, 1937), attributing 12 works to Fastidius; R. F. Evans, 'Pelagius, Fastidius, and the Pseudo-Augustinian *De Vita Christiana*', *JTS* NS 13 (1962), pp. 72–98, with full history of the controversy; J. Morris, 'Pelagian Literature', ibid. 16 (1965), pp. 26–60. G. de Plinval in *DHGE* 16 (1967), cols. 676 f., s.v. See also bibl. to PELAGIANISM.

fasts and fasting. Fasting, which was rigorously practised in Judaism and by the disciples of St *John the Baptist, was apparently recommended by Christ both by example and teaching (Lk. 4: 2, Mt. 6: 16–18 and Mk. 2: 20). It was observed by the Apostles (Acts 13: 2, 14: 23, 2 Cor. 11: 27), and in the early Church regular weekly fast days soon developed, *Wednesday and *Friday being mentioned in the *Didache. In the W. *Saturday was later substituted for Wednesday (*c.*400), but again abolished in more recent times. The fast of *Lent (q.v.), which was from the beginning connected with the feast of *Easter, lasted originally only two days, but it had been extended to 40, at least in many places, by the 4th cent. (*Athanasius, *Festal Epp.*). The E. Church added three further periods of fasting, *Advent (from 15 Nov.), from the Monday after *Pentecost to Sts *Peter and *Paul, and the fortnight before the *Assumption. The W. only developed the *Vigil fasts before the great feasts and the fasts of the *Ember Days.

In early times fasting meant entire abstention from food for the whole or part of the fast day and, in the latter case, a restricted diet. In the E. Church it is still observed with considerable strictness: during the whole of Lent, for example, the ancient rules continue to be followed by many, no meat being eaten, nor animal products (eggs, milk, butter, cheese), and fish only on certain days. In principle, during Lent only one meal is taken, in the middle of the afternoon (after *Vespers), but this discipline is generally confined to monastic circles. In modern RC practice fasting generally means one chief meal at midday and a small 'collation' in the morning and in the evening; in the past, it also included *abstinence from flesh meat, though Days of Abstinence have been distinguished from Fast Days since 1781. The quantity and quality of food to be taken on Fast Days is now simply to conform with approved local custom. The only two universally obligatory Fast Days in the RC Church are *Ash Wednesday and *Good Friday (CIC (1983), can. 1251). The obligation to fast binds those who have attained their majority until they are 60 (can. 1252). In the C of E the BCP contains a 'Table of the Vigils, Fasts and Days of Abstinence' to be observed in the year, but no specific directions are given as to their mode of observance. They were generally kept in the 16th and 17th cents., and as late as the primacy of G. *Sheldon (1663–77) dispensations were taken out for setting aside the Lenten fasts. Their observance was revived in the 19th cent. under the influence of the *Oxford Movement, and the 1969 Canons (B 6. 3), referring to the Days of Fasting etc., listed in the BCP, notes that 'the forty days of Lent, particularly Ash Wednesday and the Monday to Saturday before Easter, ought specially to be observed'.

As a penitential practice, fasting is designed to strengthen the spiritual life by weakening the attractions of sensible pleasures. The early Church continued the Jewish custom of linking fasting and prayer, and in the lives of the saints the two almost always go together. More or less rigorous fasts are practised in all the more austere religious orders, e.g. by the *Carthusians, *Cistercians, and *Carmelites. See also ABSTINENCE and EUCHARISTIC FAST.

A. Linsenmayr, *Entwicklung der kirchlichen Fastendisziplin bis zum Konzil von Nicäa* (1877); J. Schümmer, *Die altchristliche Fastenpraxis: Mit besonderer Berücksichtigung der Schriften Tertullians* (Liturgiegeschichtliche Quellen und Forschungen, Heft 27; 1933). Useful introd. on the nature and purpose of fasting, with details of Orthodox practice, by K. [T.] Ware in *The Lenten Triodion*, tr. by Mother Mary and K. [T.] Ware (The Service Books of the Orthodox Church, 1978), esp. pp. 13–28 and 35–37. V. Staley, *The Fasting Days Appointed to be Observed in the English Church* (2nd edn., 1899). A. J. Maclean, 'Fasting and Abstinence', in W. K. L. Clarke (ed.), *Liturgy and Worship* (1932), pp. 245–56, with bibl. Id. and A. R. Whitman in *PBD* (1912), pp. 333 f., s.v. F. *Cabrol, OSB, in *DACL* 7 (pt. 2; 1927), cols. 2481–501, s.v. 'Jeûnes'; P. M. J. Clancy in *NCE* 5 (1967), pp. 847–50, s.v. 'Fast and Abstinence'. J. Muddiman in *Anchor Bible Dictionary*, 2 (1992), pp. 773–6, s.v. See also bibl. to ABSTINENCE, LENT, EMBER DAYS, VIGILS, and EUCHARISTIC FAST.

Father (Lat. *Pater*). Originally the title of bishops (cf. the BCP *Ordinal, where the bishop is addressed as 'Reverend Father in God'), it was later applied esp. to confessors, called in medieval English 'ghostly fathers'. As a title of religious the term properly belongs only to *Mendicant Friars, whereas monks and *canons regular are called *Dom (Lat. *Domnus* or *Dominus*). In England, however, all RC priests, whether regular or secular, are now called 'Father', a custom introduced apparently from Ireland in the latter half of the 19th cent. and favoured by H. E. *Manning and others. It has also come into widespread currency among Anglo-Catholics. On the Continent other terms are used for the secular clergy, e.g. 'Monsieur le

Curé' (or 'Monsieur le Vicaire') in French, or 'Don' in Italian. 'The Holy Father' is a popular title of the Pope.

Fathers, Apostolic. See APOSTOLIC FATHERS.

Fathers, White. See WHITE FATHERS.

Fathers of the Church. From an early date the title (πατήρ) was applied to bishops as witnesses to the Christian tradition, but from the end of the 4th cent. it was used in a more restricted sense of a more or less clearly defined group of ecclesiastical authors of the past whose authority on doctrinal matters carried special weight. St *Basil and St *Gregory of Nazianzus are among the first to prove the orthodoxy of their teaching by appealing to the agreement of series of patristic texts, later known by the technical term 'consensus Patrum'. In the great Christological controversies of the 5th cent. all parties claimed the authority of the Fathers for their teaching, e.g. St *Cyril of Alexandria and the Council of *Ephesus (431) as well as *Theodoret. By the end of the 5th cent. the term had come to be applied also to teachers who were not bishops, e.g. to St *Jerome. The so-called '*Gelasian Decree' gives a list of works of the 'Holy Fathers' which includes even those of the layman *Prosper of Aquitaine. Acc. to the commonly accepted teaching, the Fathers of the Church were characterized by orthodoxy of doctrine, holiness of life, the approval of the Church, and antiquity. This last condition was variously interpreted till the 18th cent. From that time the patristic period is generally held to be closed with St *Isidore of Seville in the W. and St *John of Damascus in the E. Among the E. Orthodox, however, no such limitation is found, and many Orthodox theologians hold the witness of the Fathers to be an abiding mark of the Church.

The authority of the Fathers was held by the older Catholic theologians to be infallible only when they taught a doctrine unanimously. The teaching of individual Fathers, on the other hand, though not lightly to be set aside, was admittedly liable to error. In modern usage *Tertullian, *Origen, and a few other ancient authors, though not of unimpeachable orthodoxy, are usually numbered among the Fathers of the Church. In any case, it is a popular rather than an exact title and, unlike '*Doctor of the Church', not formally conferred.

Bardenhewer, 1, pp. 37–50 ('Kirchenvater, Kirchenschriftsteller und Kirchenlehrer'). G. *Florovsky, 'The Authority of the Ancient Councils and the Tradition of the Fathers', in *Glaube, Geist, Geschichte: Festschrift für Ernst Benz*, ed. G. Müller and W. Zeller (Leiden, 1967), pp. 177–88; repr. in id., *Bible, Church and Tradition: An Eastern Orthodox View* (Belmont [1972]), pp. 93–103. É. Amann in *DTC* 12 (pt. 1; 1933), cols. 1192–215, s.v. 'Pères de l'Église'.

Fatima. A small town in the middle of Portugal, famous as a place of pilgrimage to the Basilica and Shrine of Our Lady of Fatima.

On 13 May 1917 three illiterate children, between the ages of 10 and 13, saw a vision of a lady, who reappeared on five subsequent occasions. On the last she declared herself to be 'Our Lady of the Rosary', told them to recite the Rosary daily, and asked for a chapel to be built in her honour. Two of the children died in 1919, but the third,

Lucia Santos (still alive in 1995), became a *Carmelite nun at Coimbra. She wrote two accounts of the visions, in 1936–7 and 1941–2, and by permission of authority she was allowed to reveal a part of the 'secret'. It is thus that we learn the 'Threefold Message of Fatima', namely the practice of Penance, the recitation of the Rosary, and Devotion to the Immaculate Heart of Mary. Publication of the full 'secret', which could not be unsealed until 1960, has been postponed indefinitely. The end of Communist rule in the Soviet Union has been seen by some as a fulfilment of the promise of the lady on her third appearance that 'if my requests are heeded Russia will be converted'.

There is a vast literature; the more important works include L. Fischer, *Fátima: Das portugiesische Lourdes* (1930), and other works of this author; L. Gonzaga da Fonseca, SJ, *Le meraviglie di Fatima* (2nd edn., 1932; many subsequent edns.); W. T. Walsh, *Our Lady of Fátima* (1949). There is also a popular account by F. Ryan, OP, *Our Lady of Fatima* (Dublin, 1939), and an attractive record of a pilgrimage to Fatima by C. C. Martindale, SJ, *Portuguese Pilgrimage* (1949), with bibl., p. 148. E. Dhanis, SJ, 'À propos de "Fatima et la critique"', *Nouvelle Revue Théologique*, 74 (1952), pp. 580–606. R. Aubert in *DHGE* 16 (1967), cols. 679–82, s.v.

Faulhaber, Michael von (1869–1952), German cardinal. A native of Franconia, he was ordained priest in 1892, spent the years from 1895 to 1898 in Rome, taught theology at Würzburg University from 1899 to 1903, and was appointed professor of OT theology at Strasbourg in 1903. In 1910 he became Bp. of Speyer, and in 1917 Abp. of Munich; he was created cardinal in 1921. In his earlier years Faulhaber made some important contributions to *patristics, notably in his edition in *Die Prophetenkatenen nach römischen Handschriften* (1889), and in assigning to St *Hesychius of Jerusalem a commentary on the Psalms formerly attributed to St *Athanasius (1901). Later he became the leader of the right-wing German Catholics, and, though originally impressed by A. Hitler after his accession to power (1933), he soon became one of the most courageous and outspoken critics of the Nazis. He also published several books dealing with contemporary problems, e.g. the emancipation of women.

L. Volk (ed.), *Akten Kardinal Michael von Faulhabers 1917–1945* (Veröffentlichungen der Kommission für Zeitgeschichte, Reihe A, 17, 26 [1975–8]). *Episcopus: Studien über das Bischofsamt . . . zum 80. Geburtstag dargebracht* (1949); *Festschrift Kardinal Faulhaber zum achtzigsten Geburtstag dargebracht* [1949]. A. Martini, SJ, 'Il Cardinale Faulhaber e l'enciclica "Mit Brennender Sorge"', *Archivum Historiae Pontificiae*, 2 (1964), pp. 303–20. G. Schwaiger, 'Kardinal Michael von Faulhaber', *ZKG* 80 (1969), pp. 359–74. V. Conzemius in *DHGE* 16 (1967), cols. 692–711, s.v.

Faustinus and Jovita, Sts (2nd cent.), martyrs of Brescia. Acc. to the legend, they were brothers of noble birth whose faith excited the wrath of their fellow-townsmen of Brescia. They were taken prisoner under Trajan, and then tortured and transported to Milan, Rome, and Naples, making innumerable converts on the way. Owing to their persistence Hadrian, who happened to pass through Brescia, ordered their execution. Several cities (incl. Brescia, Rome, and *Bologna) claim to possess their relics. It is very doubtful if any of the incidents in the legend is historical, and no mention of them is made by the two best-

known early ecclesiastical writers of Brescia, *Philaster and *Gaudentius. Feast day, 15 Feb., suppressed in 1969.

'Acta' with discussion in *AASS*, Feb. 2 (1658), pp. 805–21. Further discussion and texts ed. F. Savia, SJ, 'La Légende des SS. Faustin et Jovite', *Anal. Boll.* 15 (1896), pp. 5–72, 113–59, and 377–99. A. Rimoldi in *DHGE* 16 (1967), cols. 735 f., s.v.

Faustus of Milevis (late 4th cent.), *Manichaean propagandist. A native of Milevis, he won fame as a rhetorician at Rome. When Faustus visited Carthage in 383, *Augustine, himself still a Manichee, put himself under his direction; but he found Faustus a fraud, and thus the way was prepared for his acceptance of the Catholic faith. Faustus' teachings can be partly reconstructed from Augustine's *Contra Faustum Manichaeum* (c.400).

For bibl., see AUGUSTINE, ST.

Faustus of Riez, St (d. c.490), monastic teacher and theologian. Probably of British or Breton origin, he entered the monastery of *Lérins and in 433 succeeded Maximus as abbot. About 460 he became Bp. of Riez (in Provence), but was later driven from his see by the Visigothic king, Euric, on account of his opposition to Euric's *Arianizing policy. His treatise *De Gratia* was written c.472 to refute the *Predestinarian doctrines condemned by recent councils of Arles and Lyon (and elsewhere ascribed by Faustus to a certain Lucidus). In this work he adopted a *Semipelagian position, insisting even more strongly than John *Cassian on the necessity of human co-operation with Divine grace, and on the initial free will of men, even when in sin, for the acceptance of that grace. His prowess as a preacher is attested by *Sidonius Apollinaris and *Gennadius of Marseilles; a collection of Gallic sermons transmitted under the name of *Eusebius (of Emesa) may be partly based on a corpus of his homiletic works. Though his teaching on grace was condemned at the Second Council of *Orange in 529, he is revered as a saint in the S. of France. Feast day, 28 Sept.

Opera [excluding sermons of Pseudo-Eusebius, but including several others now not regarded as authentic], ed. A. G. Engelbrecht (CSEL 21, 1891, pp. 1–348). J. P. Migne, PL 58. 783–870. Suppl. ed. A. Hamman, OFM, 3 (1963), cols. 492–709, incl. sermons attributed to Eusebius. Crit. edn. of these last by J. Leroy and F. Glorie (CCSL 101, 101A, and 101B; 1970–1). L. A. van Buchem, OP, *L'Homélie pseudo-eusébienne de Pentecôte: L'Origine de la* Confirmatio *en Gaule Méridionale et l'interprétation de ce rite par Fauste de Riez* (Nijmegen, 1967), incl. text. G. Weigel, SJ, *Faustus of Riez; an historical introduction* (Philadelphia, 1938 [rare]). T. A. Smith, *De Gratia: Faustus of Riez's Treatise on Grace and its Place in the History of Theology* (Christianity and Judaism in Antiquity, 4; Notre Dame, Ind. [1990]), with bibl. E. L. Fortin, AA, *Christianisme et Culture philosophique au cinquième siècle* (Études Augustininennes, 1959), pp. 43–74. CPL (3rd edn., 1995), pp. 311–16 (nos. 961–77). Altaner and Stuiber (1978), pp. 473 f. and 651. P. Viard in *DHGE* 16 (1967), cols. 731–4, s.v.; R. J. H. Collins in *TRE* 11 (1983), pp. 63–7, s.v.; M. Simonetti in *DPAC* 1 (1983), cols. 1336–8; Eng. tr. in *Encyclopedia of the Early Church*, 1 (1992), pp. 320 f., s.v.

Fawkes, Guy (1570–1606). The most famous member of the *Gunpowder Plot conspiracy. Born in Yorkshire, he was brought up a Protestant, but becoming a Papist he sold his English property and joined the Spanish Army in

1593. In 1604 he was brought into the Plot by R. *Catesby and given the task of firing the gunpowder. While keeping watch on the cellar he was arrested (5 Nov. 1605), but disclosed the conspiracy only under torture. In company with his fellow-conspirators, T. Winter, A. Rokewood, and R. Keyes, he was executed on 31 Jan. 1606. See also GUN-POWDER PLOT.

[R. Davies], *The Fawkes's of York in the Sixteenth Century: including notices of the Early History of Guye Fawkes, the Gunpowder Plot Conspirator* (1850), esp. pp. 27–47. D. Carswell (ed.), *The Trial of Guy Fawkes and Others: The Gunpowder Plot* ('Notable British Trials', 1934). H. Garnett, *Portrait of Guy Fawkes: An Experiment in Biography* (1962); E. N. Simons, *The Devil of the Vault: A Life of Guy Fawkes* (1963). A. J. Loomie, SJ, *Guy Fawkes in Spain: The 'Spanish Treason' in Spanish Documents* (Bulletin of the Institute of Historical Research, Special Supplement, 9; 1971). See also bibl. to GUNPOWDER PLOT.

Fayûm Gospel Fragment. A brief papyrus fragment, written in the 3rd cent. AD, discovered in Egypt in 1882, which contains an imperfect account of the prediction of St *Peter's denial, closely akin to Mk. 14: 27–30. It is probably an extract from a lost gospel abbreviating and reworking synoptic material; it is less likely to be a fragment of some early ecclesiastical writer who was making a free quotation from the canonical gospels. It is preserved at Vienna among the Rainer Papyri.

The text was pub. by G. *Bickell in *ZKT* 9 (1885), pp. 498–504. A. *Harnack, 'Das Evangelienfragment von Fajjum', appended to A. Resch, *Agrapha* (TU 5, Heft 4; 1889), pp. 481–97. W. Schneemelcher in Schneemelcher, 1 (5th edn., 1987), p. 87; Eng. tr., 1 (1991), p. 102. J. van Haelst, *Catalogue des Papyrus Littéraires Juifs et Chrétiens* (1976), p. 588 (no. 589). H. Y. Gamble in *Anchor Bible Dictionary*, 2 (1992), pp. 778 f.

Fayumic. A dialect of *Coptic spoken in early Christian times in Middle Egypt. The NT was translated into it, probably from *Sahidic, but only a few fragments of the version exist. It was formerly known (incorrectly) as 'Bashmuric', from a province in the Delta.

feasts, ecclesiastical. These come under three chief headings: (1) SUNDAYS. The weekly commemoration of the Resurrection, which falls on the first day of every week. Sundays have been kept by Christians from Apostolic times as days of worship, and in 321 the Emp. *Constantine proclaimed that Sunday should be a general holiday.

(2) MOVABLE FEASTS. Of these the most important are (a) *Easter, the annual commemoration of the Resurrection, and (b) *Pentecost or Whitsunday, the 7th Sunday after Easter, the commemoration of the descent of the Holy Spirit upon the Church. These commemorate events which took place at the times of the Jewish *Passover and Feast of *Weeks, and like them vary with the Paschal full moon. Certain other feasts, and also the fast of *Lent, vary with the date of Easter.

(3) IMMOVABLE FEASTS. Of these the earliest were probably the anniversaries of martyrs, which were kept at Rome from the 3rd cent., and in Asia Minor as early as the 2nd. Later, other saints were commemorated either on their death-day or the day of translation of their relics, or occasionally on other days. By the 4th cent. various fixed festivals of the Lord, esp. *Christmas and the *Epiphany, became generally observed, and later various feasts of the BVM, with other feasts of the Lord, were added.

Ecclesiastical feasts are observed by a '*Proper' in the *Eucharist and *Offices. The fullest calendars in present use are those of the RC and Orthodox bodies; the BCP provides a list of days to be observed, and a further list without specific instructions that they must be kept. Both together are of modest dimensions, and many modern Anglican liturgies provide an enlarged calendar.

The term *festum* (commonly translated 'feast' in English) is one of the classifications in the current RC calendar. *Festa* are of less importance than *solemnitates* ('solemnities') and of greater significance than *memoriae* ('memorials'). They usually commemorate less important events in the life of the Lord or saints.

See bibl. to YEAR, LITURGICAL.

Feasts of Obligation. In the RC Church, feast days of outstanding importance which the laity as well as the clergy are obliged to observe by hearing Mass on the day itself or the evening of the previous day and by abstaining from 'work or business that would inhibit the worship to be given to God, the joy proper to the Lord's Day, or the due relaxation of mind and body'. The 1983 *CIC* (can. 1246) lists, besides all *Sundays, *Christmas Day (25 Dec.), the *Epiphany (6 Jan.), the *Ascension, *Corpus Christi, the Solemnity of the BVM (1 Jan.), her *Assumption (15 Aug.) and *Immaculate Conception (8 Dec.), the feasts of St *Joseph (1 May), Sts *Peter and *Paul (29 June), and *All Saints (1 Nov.). Since, however, Episcopal Conferences, may, with the approval of the Holy See, suppress certain of these days or transfer them to a Sunday, the list is likely to vary in different countries.

Feathers Tavern Petition (1772). A petition to Parliament signed at the Feathers Tavern, Strand, London, by *c.*250 liberal Christians for the abolition of subscription to the *Thirty-Nine Articles, and its replacement by a simple declaration of belief in the Bible. Among its principal sponsors were Francis Blackburne, Archdeacon of Cleveland (1705–87), Theophilus *Lindsey, and John Jebb (1736–86). The petition was presented to the Commons by Sir William Meredith and debated on 6 February 1772. Largely through the influence of a speech of E. Burke it was defeated on a division by 217 votes to 71.

The text of the petition is pr. among *The Works . . . of Francis Blackburne*, ed. by his son, F. Blackburne, vol. 7 (1805), pp. 15–19, with various associated docs. in the same vol. The greater part of Burke's speech on the subject, which he preserved with a view to possible pub., is in his *Works*, 1st edn., vol. 5 (1812), pp. 323–36 (ed. F. H. Willis and F. W. Raffety, 6 vols., World's Classics, vol. 3 (1906), pp. 291–303). G. M. Ditchfield, 'The Subscription Issue in British Parliamentary Politics, 1772–79', *Parliamentary History*, 7 (1988), pp. 45–80, esp. pp. 48–51.

Febronianism. The movement in the RC Church in Germany in the 18th cent. against the claims of the Papacy, esp. in the temporal sphere. It may be considered from some points of view as the German counterpart of *Gallicanism. In 1742 the three Archbishop-Electors invited J. N. von *Hontheim (q.v.), suffragan Bp. of Trier, to investigate their existing grievances against Rome, and in 1763 he published his findings in *De statu ecclesiae et legitima potestate Romani pontificis*, under the pen-name of 'Justinus Febronius'. The book, while recognizing that the Pope was the head of the Church and the supervisor of Church administration and (subject to the Universal Church or a General Council) of faith and morals, attacked the medieval accretions of temporal power. It advocated that Church affairs should be kept as far as possible in episcopal and civil hands, and that all Papal claims based on the *False Decretals should be annulled. In 1764 it was put on the *Index, but in 1769 it received the approval of the Archbishop-Electors, who drew up a list of thirty objections against the Papal claims. The Archbishop-Electors attempted to assert their claims at Bad *Ems (q.v.) in 1786, but without success. The outbreak of the French Revolution and lack of support from other German bishops caused the movement to collapse. See also WESSENBERG, I. H. VON.

O. Meyer, *Febronius, Weihbischof Johann Nicolaus von Hontheim und sein Widerruf* (Tübingen, 1880); J. Küntziger, *Fébronius et le fébronianisme* (Mémoires couronnés et autres mémoires publiés par l'Académie Royale des Sciences, des Lettres et des Beaux-Arts de Belgique. Collection in-8°, 44; 1891; présenté à la Classe des Lettres dans la séance du 6 mai, 1889). V. Pitzer, *Justinus Febronius: Das Ringen eines katholischen Irenikers und die Einheit der Kirche im Zeitalter der Aufklärung* (Kirche und Konfession, 20; Göttingen, 1976). A. *Fortescue in *HERE* 5 (1912), pp. 807–9, s.v.; T. Ortolan in *DTC* 5 (1913), cols. 2115–24, s.v. 'Febronius'; V. Pitzer in *TRE* 11 (1983), pp. 67–9, s.v. 'Febronius/Febronius-mus', all with bibl.

Fechner, Gustav Theodor (1801–87), psychologist and spiritualistic philosopher. He spent nearly all his life at Leipzig, where he held a professorship from 1834 to 1839. He became well known as a psychologist by his law ('Fechner's Law') of the mathematical relation between the intensity of a sensation and the corresponding stimulus. In philosophy he expounded an extreme form of '*animism', contending that all existents in the universe were endowed with consciousness, and that everything was enclosed by the all-pervasive Being of God. His writings include *Elemente der Psychophysik* (2 vols., 1860) and *Die Tagesansicht gegenüber der Nachtansicht* (1879).

There is an Eng. tr. of Fechner's *Das Büchlein vom Leben nach dem Tode* (orig. pub. under name of Dr Mises; 1836) by H. Wernekke (London, 1882). Selections of his Works in Eng. tr. by W. Lowrie, *Religion of a Scientist* (New York and London, 1946), with bibl. Life by J. F. Kuntze (nephew; Leipzig, 1892). K. Lasswitz, *Gustav Theodor Fechner* (1896). J. Brožek and H. Gundlach (eds.), *G. T. Fechner and Psychology: International Gustav Theodor Fechner-Symposium, Passau, 12–14 June, 1987* (Passauer Schriften zur Psychologiegeschichte, 6; 1988). A. Zweig in P. Edwards (ed.), *Encyclopedia of Philosophy*, 3 (1967), pp. 184–6, s.v.

Felicity, St (2nd cent.), Roman martyr. She is one of the seven Roman martyrs named in the *Depositio Martyrum* of the '*Liberian Catalogue' for 10 July. Acc. to the *acta* (not later than 6th cent.), she was martyred with her seven sons. Acc. to F. C. *Burkitt and V. L. Kennedy, she is the Felicity referred to in the *Canon of the Roman Mass. Feast day, 23 Nov. She has also been commemorated with her sons ('The Seven Brothers') on 10 July.

Acta in T. *Ruinart, *Acta Primorum Martyrum Sincera et Selecta* (Paris, 1689), pp. 21–3. Further sources listed in *BHL*, pp. 429 f.

(nos. 2853–5), and *Novum Supplementum* (1986), pp. 325 f. F. C. Burkitt, 'St Felicity in the Roman Mass', *JTS* 32 (1930–1), pp. 279–87; V. L. Kennedy, CSB, *The Saints of the Canon of the Mass* (Studi di antichità cristiana, 14; 1938), pp. 164–8. H. *Leclercq, OSB, in *DACL* 5 (pt. 1; 1922), cols. 1259–98, s.v. 'Félicité (Passion et cimetière de)'; R. Aubert in *DHGE* 16 (1967), cols. 864–6, s.v. 'Félicité (3)', with bibl.

Felicity, St (d. 203), African martyr. She was one of the companions of St *Perpetua (q.v.), with whom she was martyred. Feast day, 7 Mar. (formerly 6 Mar.).

For the contemporary *acta*, see PERPETUA.

Felix, St (d. c.648), Bp. of Dunwich. He was a native of Burgundy. After converting the East Anglian prince, Sigeberht, then in exile, to Christianity, he made his way to England where, under the direction of Honorius, Abp. of *Canterbury, he successfully preached the Gospel to the heathen in East Anglia. He fixed his episcopal see at the seaport town of Dunwich in Suffolk (now mainly submerged) and acc. to *Bede (*HE* 2. 15) ruled his diocese for 17 years. His name survives in Felixstowe in Suffolk and Felixkirk in N. Yorks. His relics were preserved at Ramsey Abbey. Feast day, 8 Mar.

The chief authority is Bede, *HE* 2. 15; 3. 18, 20, 25; comm. by J. M. Wallace-Hadrill (Oxford, 1988), pp. 77 f., 111 f., 115, and 223, with further refs. Short account also in *William of Malmesbury, *De Gestis Pontificum Anglorum*, 2. 74 (ed. N. E. S. A. Hamilton, RS, 1870, p. 147). M. *Creighton in *DNB* 18 (1889), pp. 291 f.

Felix (d. 818), Bp. of Urgel in Spain. With *Elipandus, Bp. of Toledo, he was one of the leaders of the *Adoptianist heresy. He was charged as a heretic at the Council of Ratisbon (792) in the presence of *Charlemagne, but, on being vanquished in debate, solemnly recanted and a little later publicly renounced his error before *Hadrian I at Rome. Shortly afterwards, however, he became convinced of his heresy again. He professed to be unconvinced by a criticism that *Alcuin wrote of his doctrines and, on his refusal to give way, he was formally accused at the Councils of *Frankfurt (794) and Aachen (799 or 800). At the latter Alcuin apparently persuaded him that his teaching was at variance with Christian tradition, notably as expressed in St *Cyril of Alexandria and St *Leo, and he recanted a second time. But his orthodoxy was not considered altogether irreproachable, and he remained until his death under the supervision of the Abp. of Lyons.

Confessio repr. in J. P. Migne, *PL* 96. 881–8. The *Liber de Variis Quaestionibus adversus Judaeos seu ceteros Infideles vel plerosque Haereticos*, ed. A. C. Vega and A. E. Anspach (Escurial, 1940), who ascribed it to St *Isidore of Seville, has been claimed as the work of Felix, by J. Madoz, SJ, 'Una obra de Félix de Urgel, falsamente adjudicada a San Isidoro de Sevilla', *Estudios eclesiásticos*, 23 (1949), pp. 147–68; the attribution has not won general assent. O. Engels in *Lexikon des Mittelalters*, 4 (1989), col. 342. See also works cited s.v. ADOPTIANISM.

Fell, John (1625–86), Bp. of *Oxford. He was educated at *Christ Church, Oxford, where he became a Student at the early age of 11. His loyalty to the Crown caused his ejection in 1648, but he contrived with a small group of friends to maintain the C of E service in a private house, and at the Restoration he was rewarded with a canonry at Christ Church and, in Nov. 1660, with the deanery. He took the keenest interest in the spiritual and intellectual life of the college, to which he attracted an impressive array of scholars and noblemen. He regularly went to service four times daily. In 1676 he became Bp. of Oxford, retaining the deanery. His own writings include Lives of H. *Hammond (1661) and R. *Allestree (1684) and a valuable critical edition (the so-called 'Oxford text') of the writings of St *Cyprian (1682). In addition, his patronage of young divines and his labours in re-establishing the University Press did much for the strength of patristic learning in the restored C of E. As the local diocesan, a firm vice-chancellor, and the head of one of the most powerful colleges, Fell largely brought about the re-imposition of Anglican orthodoxy on the University after 1660. He was resolute in opposing Popery, an enemy to Nonconformity and a staunch Tory. He it was who expelled J. *Locke from his Studentship at Christ Church at the order of *Charles II in his time of triumph. He is the subject of the well-known epigram beginning 'I do not love thee, Dr. Fell' (a translation prob. by Thomas Brown, a Christ Church undergraduate, of Martial, *Epigrams*, 1. 32).

S. Morison and H. Carter, *John Fell, the University Press, and the 'Fell' types* (Oxford, 1967), esp. pp. 3–58. M. Clapinson (ed.), *Bishop Fell and Nonconformity: Visitation Documents from the Oxford Diocese, 1682–83* (Oxfordshire Record Society, 52; 1980). H. L. Thompson, *Christ Church* ('University of Oxford, College Histories', 1900), pp. 82–104. G. G. Perry in *DNB* 18 (1889), pp. 293–5. See also works cited under CHRIST CHURCH.

Fellowship of St Alban and St Sergius. See ALBAN, ST, AND ST SERGIUS, FELLOWSHIP OF.

Feminist Theology. A theological movement of various strands which are united in a determination to secure change for the better in terms of social justice for women. Its origins may be traced to 19th-cent. social campaigns, such as that against slavery, and the suffragette movement, but it was only after the end of the Second World War (1945), and particularly in the 1980s, that it posed a serious challenge within the Christian tradition. The catalysts were RC women responding to the work of the Second *Vatican Council, most notably Mary Daly, Rosemary Radford Ruether, and Elisabeth Schüssler Fiorenza.

The central issue for feminist theology is the unease within the Christian tradition about associations of the female or feminine with the godlike. Feminist theologians (men as well as women) argue that the female/feminine can image God in as full (and as limited) a way as God is imaged by the male/masculine. Since it is agreed that God transcends both sex and gender, feminist theologians urge the need for a humanly inclusive theology, the 'envisioning' of God in a gender-inclusive way. They argue that since it is as normal a part of the human experience to be female as male, theology needs to come to terms with this reality in a way that it has not previously done. The insights and experiences of women are as important in theology as those of men, and this claim requires re-evaluation of the language of doctrine and liturgy at least. (They sometimes speak of the*alogy* rather than theology.)

The differences between men and women are, they argue, purely biological in function, but what a particular tradition or society makes of these differences is of importance, and it is held that the Christian tradition has fostered a disabling gender construction for women. The central stumbling-blocks to attributing the full 'image of God' to women have been fourfold. First, the failure to find the feminine in God, already mentioned. The others are the insistence that woman is wholly derivative and hence secondary to man; the assumption that woman is characterized by passivity; and the tendency to identify women with bodiliness as opposed to the transcendent mind. While men have been traditionally characterized as active, intelligent, and strong—qualities which are attributed *par excellence* to God—the religiously sanctioned gender construction of women is that they are passive, emotional, weak, and particularly responsible for sin and evil. With this view is linked an assumption about the role of men and women in procreation. Whereas women are now held to have at least an equal part in human reproduction, the earlier belief was that it was the male who is primarily creative and that the child originates essentially only from one source. This view is regarded as entrenched in Christian symbolism and is held to exert influence on discussions over the ordination of *women and of marriage and family life, as well as the appropriate language for God, notably metaphors of mother/father.

Feminist theologians are not concerned to pretend that the differences between the sexes can be obliterated, since there is no necessary connection between the perception of the differences and the devaluation of women on theological grounds. The meaning of other and same sex relationships is, however, of importance to them, given the experience of heterosexuality and such devaluation. They are also increasingly attentive to the complications which race, class, and particular contexts add to the theological enterprise, and they are aware of the importance of global inter-religious dialogue for women. Central also to feminist theology is the integration of ethics with theology, not only in the interests of women themselves, and in paying attention to neglected areas of men's lives, so transforming relationships between the sexes, but also in the interests of children, who are normally perceived as the responsibility of their mothers rather than of both parents. Attention is therefore paid to the values of which women are culturally the bearers, such as care, interdependence, etc., and the fact that one reason why (universally) women are poor is that they not only bear children, but also do most of the work in rearing them. This is regarded as another area of disjunction between the language of 'fathering' for God and the experience of women. Issues about pregnancy-termination, the use of fetal tissue, artificially assisted human reproduction and ethical questions arising from developments in human genetics are integral to the feminist theological-ethical agenda. Feminist theology is established as a discipline in many higher educational institutions and is influential in ecclesiastical life as a movement in active lay theology and spirituality.

A collection of representative articles was ed., with comm. and bibl., by A. Loades, *Feminist Theology: A Reader* (1990). Other works by feminist theologians incl. V. Saiving Goldstein, 'The Human Situation: A Feminine View', *Journal of Religion*, 40 (1960), pp. 100–12; M. Daly, *The Church and the Second Sex* (1968; repr., with new afterword, Boston [1985]); id., *Beyond God the Father: Toward a Philosophy of Women's Liberation* (Boston

[1973]; London, 1986); M. A. Farley, 'Sources of Sexual Inequality in the History of Christian Thought', *Journal of Religion*, 56 (1976), pp. 162–76; J. Plaskow, *Sex, Sin and Grace: Women's Experience and the Theologies of Reinhold Niebuhr and Paul Tillich* (Washington, DC [1980]); E. Schüssler Fiorenza, *In Memory of Her: A Feminist Theological Reconstruction of Christian Origins* (New York and London, 1983); R. R. Ruether, *Sex and God-Talk* (1983); id., *Women-Church: Theology and Practice of Feminist Liturgical Communities* (San Francisco [1985]); G. Lloyd, *The Man of Reason: 'Male' and 'Female' in Western Philosophy* (1984), pp. 28–37 (on Augustine and Aquinas); P. Trible, *Texts of Terror: Literary-Feminist Readings of Biblical Narratives* (Overtures to Biblical Theology, 13; Philadelphia [1984]); id., *God and the Rhetoric of Sexuality* (ibid. [1987]); M. Hayter, *The New Eve in Christ: The Use and Abuse of the Bible in the Debate about Women in the Church* (1987); A. Loades, *Searching for Lost Coins: Explorations in Christianity and Feminism* (1987); G. Ramshaw, *Worship: Searching for Language* (Washington, DC, 1988), pp. 151–87 ('Naming God'); U. King, *Women and Spirituality: Voices of protest and promise* (1989), with bibl.; J. M. Soskice (ed.), *After Eve* (1990); and D. Hampson, *Theology and Feminism* (Oxford, 1990).

Fénelon, François de Salignac de la Mothe (1651–1715), Abp. of Cambrai. He was born in Périgord, of an ancient and distinguished, but impoverished, family. He studied at *St-Sulpice, was ordained *c.*1675, and served in the parish. In 1678 he became superior of the *Nouvelles Catholiques*, an institution for the education of girls and women recently converted from Protestantism. In 1685–6 he took part in a mission in the Saintonge to instruct those forcibly converted through the *Dragonnades; he was strict on orthodoxy, but humane in his approach. In 1687 he published his *Traité de l'éducation des filles*, written at the request of the Duchess of Beauvillier. Two years later he was appointed tutor to Louis XIV's grandson, the Duke of Burgundy, for whom he wrote the educational novel *Télémaque* (pub. 1699, but not in its complete form until 1717). In this work, intended for a future king, he wrote in favour of a limited absolutism, rejected wars of aggression, and held that kings and their policies are subject to moral law in the true interest of the state. The implied criticism of Louis XIV hindered his career. In the autumn of 1688 he met Mme *Guyon; he was impressed by her account of her spiritual experiences (which he regarded as authentic), and esp. by her doctrine of pure love and 'passive' prayer, though he did not apparently care for her voluminous writings in the *Quietist vein. He defended her for a long time and was therefore implicated when she was censured in 1694. In 1693 he was elected a member of the French Academy. In 1695 he became Abp. of Cambrai and later in the same year signed the Thirty-Four Articles of *Issy which condemned Quietism. In 1697, however, he published his *Explication des maximes des saints sur la vie intérieure* (Eng. tr., 1698), defending the concept of disinterested love and citing the works of recognized (esp. canonized) spiritual writers in support of his position. The book was attacked by J. B. *Bossuet and a long and bitter controversy ensued, sustained by intrigues in Rome. Fénelon was banished from court in the summer of 1679 and spent the rest of his life in his diocese. Here his charitable giving mitigated suffering, esp., but not only, during the War of Spanish Succession. When, under pressure from Louis XIV, Pope Innocent XII condemned 23 propositions from Fénelon's book (Brief of 12 Mar. 1699), he submitted unreservedly, and when the *Jansenist controversy

broke out again, he wrote in defence of the orthodox teaching on grace and other matters. He developed his spiritual teaching in his *Traité sur l'existence de Dieu* (part pub. in 1712; Eng. tr., 1713; the whole not until 1718; Eng. tr., 1720). He was much sought after as a spiritual director. He had considerable influence in the 18th cent., both inside and outside France, and among Protestants (esp. on J. *Wesley), partly because of the Life written by Ramsay.

Œuvres complètes pub. in 35 vols., Versailles and Paris, 1820–30 ('Édition de Versailles'), and 10 vols., Paris, 1848–52 ('Édition de Saint-Sulpice'), repr. Geneva, 1971; modern edn. by J. Le Brun (Paris, 1983 ff.). *Œuvres spirituelles*, also ed. F. Varillon, SJ (Paris [1954]); *Correspondance*, ed. J. Orcibal and others (vols. 1–5, Paris, 1972–6; vols. 6 ff., Geneva, 1987 ff.). Eng. tr. of selection of his letters by D. Sandford (London, 1957) and J. McEwen, with introd. by T. *Merton (ibid. [1964]), and of his *Traité de l'éducation des filles*, with introd. and notes, by H. C. Barnard (Cambridge, 1966). A. M. Ramsay, *Histoire de la vie de Mess' François de Salignac de la Motte-Fénelon* (La Haye, 1723; Eng. trs., 1723 and 1897). Introductory studies by K. D. Little (New York [1951]), M. Raymond (*Les écrivains devant Dieu*, Bruges, 1967), and J. H. Davis (Boston [1979]). H. *Bremond, *Apologie pour Fénelon* (1910); É. Carcassonne, *Fénelon: I.'Homme et l'œuvre* [1946]; *Dix-septième siècle*, nos. 12–14 (1951–2), special issue devoted to Fénelon; J.-L. Goré, *L'Itinéraire de Fénelon: Humanisme et spiritualité* (1957); F. Varillon, *Fénelon et le pur amour* (Maîtres spirituels [1957]); L. Cognet, *Crépuscule des mystiques: Fénelon, Bossuet* (Tournai [1958]); B. Dupriez, *Fénelon et la Bible: Les origines du mysticisme Fénelonien* (Travaux de l'Institut Catholique de Paris, 8 [1961]); R. Spaemann, *Reflexion und Spontaneität: Studien über Fénelon* (Stuttgart, 1963); H. Hillenaar, *Fénelon et les Jésuites* (Archives internationales d'histoire des idées, 21; The Hague, 1967); M. Haillant, *Fénelon et la Prédication* (Publications de la Faculté des Lettres et Sciences Humaines de Paris-Nanterre, Série A, vol. 6; 1969); id., *Culture et imagination dans les œuvres de Fénelon* (1982–3); H. Gouhier, *Fénelon philosophe* (Bibliothèque d'histoire de la philosophie, 1977). L. Ceyssens, 'Autour de la bulle Unigenitus: Fénelon', *Antonianum*, 59 (1984), pp. 482–540, repr. in id. and J. A. G. Tans, *Autour de l'Unigenitus* (Bibliotheca Ephemeridum Theologicarum Lovaniensium, 76; 1987), pp. 521–79. Popular account by M. de la Bedoyere, *The Archbishop and the Lady* (1956). L. Cognet in *Dict. Sp.* 5 (1964), cols. 151–70; id. in *DHGE* 16 (1967), cols. 958–87, both s.v. *Revue Fénelon* (Paris, 1911 ff.).

Feophan the Recluse, St. See THEOPHAN THE RECLUSE, ST.

Ferdinand II (1578–1637), Holy Roman Emperor. Educated by the *Jesuits at Ingolstadt University, Ferdinand was one of the chief upholders of the *Counter-Reformation. As ruler of Inner Austria since 1596, he had already done much to re-establish Catholicism there when he became Emperor in 1619. He then set about extirpating Protestantism from all the Habsburg domains. Anticipating his repressive measures, the Protestants of Bohemia rebelled and attempted to replace him as king with the *Calvinist Elector Palatine *Frederick III. Although Ferdinand suppressed this revolt, his decision to punish Frederick broadened the conflict into the *Thirty Years War. Continued Catholic successes in the 1620s culminated when his generals, Wallenstein and Tilly, forced the Protestant leader, Christian of Denmark, to agree to the Treaty of Lübeck (1629). Under the influence of his Jesuit confessor, William Lamormaini, Ferdinand published the 'Edict of Restitution', ordering Protestants to restore to the Catholics all appropriated ecclesiastical property within their dominions. Once again the Protestants rebelled, and for a time under *Gustavus Adolphus they almost overthrew the Emperor. Gustavus's death in battle (1632) saved Ferdinand, and for the rest of his reign the Thirty Years War pursued its desultory and disastrous course.

F. C. Khevenhiller, *Annales Ferdinandei* (9 vols., Regensburg, 1640–6). F. Hurter, *Geschichte Kaiser Ferdinands II und seiner Eltern* (11 vols., Schaffhausen, 1850–64). J. Loserth (ed.), 'Akten und Korrespondenzen zur Geschichte der Gegenreformation in Innerösterreich unter Ferdinand II', *Fontes Rerum Austriacarum: Österreichische Geschichts-Quellen.* Abt. 2, Diplomataria et Acta, 58 (1906) and 60 (1907). H. Sturmberger, *Kaiser Ferdinand II. und das Problem des Absolutismus* (Österreich Archiv; 1957); J. Franzl, *Ferdinand II: Kaiser im Zwiespalt der Zeit* (Graz, 1978); R. Bireley, SJ, *Religion and Politics in the Age of the Counterreformation: Emperor Ferdinand II, William Lamormaini, SJ, and the Formation of Imperial Policy* (Chapel Hill, NC [1981]).

Ferdinand V (1452–1516), 'the Catholic', King of Castile and León and II of Aragon. The son of John II of Aragon, in 1469 he married his cousin, *Isabella, the disputed heiress of the Castilian throne. Together they defeated the rival candidate, who was aided by the Portuguese and various Castilian noble families. Ferdinand and Isabella ruled jointly both in Castile and later in Aragon, where Ferdinand inherited his father's throne in 1479. Here they resolved internal social revolts and countered the French threat to the northern border. Isabella's death in 1504 was followed in 1506 by that of their daughter's consort Philip the Handsome; this allowed Ferdinand to resume authority in Castile as governor in his daughter's name. He is known primarily as a skilful politician abroad and for making Spain a dominant power in Italian politics through a reorganized and efficient army. He recovered Roussillon and Cerdagne from the French in 1493, conquered Orán in North Africa in 1509, and helped to bring Lower Navarre under Castilian control in 1512. As a consequence of his political skills, he was enshrined in Machiavelli's *Prince*. For his conquest of the Moors of Granada in 1492 and his zeal for the Spanish *Inquisition he and Isabella were called the '*Catholic Kings' by *Alexander VI.

W. H. Prescott, *History of the Reign of Ferdinand and Isabella* (3 vols., '1838' [1837], and many later edns.); R. B. Merriman, *The Rise of the Spanish Empire in the Old World and the New*, 2 (New York, 1918; repr. 1962); J. M. Doussinagne, *La política internacional de Fernando el Católico* (1944); J. A. Maravall and others, *Pensamiento político, política internacional y religiosa de Fernando el Católico* (V Congreso de Historia de la Corona de Aragón. Estudios, 2; Saragossa, 1956); J. Vicens Vives, *Historia crítica de la vida y reinado de Fernando II de Aragón* (vol. 1 only [to 1481], 1962); J. H. Elliott, *Imperial Spain 1469–1716* (1963), pp. 5–135; J. Pérez, *L'Espagne des Rois Catholiques* [1971]; id., *Isabelle et Ferdinand: Rois Catholiques d'Espagne* [1988]. F. [F. R.] Fernández-Armesto, *Ferdinand and Isabella* [1975]. L. Suárez Fernández, *Los Reyes Católicos: La Expansión de la Fe* (Forjadores de Historia, 16 [1990]), and other works of this author. J. N. Hillgarth, *The Spanish Kingdoms 1250–1516*, 2 (Oxford, 1978), pp. 349–628, with bibl. pp. 667–84 ('The Catholic Monarchs 1474–1516'). J. M. Batista i Roca in *The New Cambridge Modern History*, 1, ed. G. R. Potter (1957), pp. 316–42. Tarsicio de Azcona, OFM Cap., in *DHGE* 16 (1967), cols. 1027–42, s.v. 'Ferdinand (5) le Catholique', with extensive bibl.

feretory (Lat. *feretrum*, from Gk. φέρειν, 'to carry').

Another name for a *shrine (q.v.), in which a saint's relics are deposited and venerated.

feria. While in classical Latin the word means 'feast day' or 'holiday', in ecclesiastical language it is applied to such days (other than Saturdays and Sundays) on which no feast falls. The history of this change of meaning is involved and somewhat obscure. Since 1969 in the RC Church, lessons have been supplied for every day in the year, but apart from those days (e.g. in *Advent) with special collects, the rest of the Mass is normally taken from that of the previous Sunday. Before 1969, on ferias with no office of their own, the Sunday Mass was resumed *in toto*, unless a *Votive Mass was substituted. Under present arrangements, the ferial Masses of Ash Wednesday and Holy Week take precedence over all other celebrations; on other days the 'Ritual Masses' (e.g. those for weddings and ordinations) may be substituted for the ferial Mass and, except on the weekdays of Lent and the last week of Advent (which take precedence over obligatory memorials), Votive Masses and 'Masses for Various Occasions' may also be substituted. The BCP provides that 'the Collect, Epistle and Gospel appointed for the Sunday shall serve all the week after, where it is not in this book otherwise ordered'; the ASB provides lessons for every day.

'Feria' is applied to weekdays already in *Tertullian (*De jejunio*, 2). For some suggestions as to how the word changed its meaning, see art. by R. Sinker in *DCA* 1 (1875), pp. 667 f., s.v.

Fermentum (Lat., 'leaven'). In *Rome (5th cent.), the fragments of the Bread of the Eucharist sent on Sundays from the Papal Mass to the presbyters in the parish churches (*tituli*) to typify the unity of the faithful in Christ. The practice is attested by Pope *Innocent I (*Ep. xxv ad Decentium*, 5). In a modified form it survived on *Maundy Thursday down to the 8th cent.

Innocent's letter to Decentius, ed. R. Cabié (Bibliothèque de la *RHE* 58; 1973), pp. 26–8, with Fr. tr., pp. 27–9, and note on Fermentum, pp. 50–3. M. Andrieu, *Les Ordines Romani du Haut Moyen Age*, 2 (SSL 23; 1948), pp. 61–4; J. A. Jungmann, SJ, '*Fermentum*. Ein Symbol kirchlicher Einheit und sein Nachleben im Mittelalter', in *Colligere Fragmenta: Festschrift A. Dold*, ed. B. Fischer and V. Fiala (Beuron, 1952), pp. 185–90. F. *Cabrol, OSB, in *DACL* 5 (1922), cols. 1371–4, with patristic refs.

Ferrandus (d. before Apr. 548), deacon of the Church of Carthage (the traditional praenomen 'Fulgentius' is prob. mistaken). His 'Breviatio canonum' is an important epitome, systematically arranged, of canons of the early councils, Greek and African. There survive also his Life of St *Fulgentius, and some letters, two of them bearing on the *Theopaschite Controversy.

Works ed. P. F. Chifflet, Dijon, 1649; repr. in J. P. Migne, *PL* 67. 877–962, and ('Vita Fulgenti') ibid. 65. 117–50; some further letters in *PL*, Suppl. 4 (1967), cols. 22–39. Crit. edn. of the 'Breviatio' by C. Munier, *Concilia Africae A.345–A.525* (CCSL 149; 1974), pp. 284–311. Life of Fulgentius also ed., with Fr. tr. and introd. on life and works of Ferrandus, by G. G. Lapeyre (Paris, 1929). M. Simonetti, 'Ferrando di Cartagine nella controversia Teopaschita', in H. J. Auf der Maur and others (eds.), *Fides Sacramenti, Sacramentum Fidei: Studies in Honour of Pieter Smulders* (Assen, 1981), pp. 219–32. A. Mandouze, *Prosopographie Chrétienne du Bas-Empire, 1: Prosopographie de l'Afrique Chrétienne*

(303–533) (1982), pp. 446–50. M. Jourjon in *Dict. Sp.* 5 (1964), cols. 181–3, s.v. 'Ferrand (1)'. See also bibl. to FULGENTIUS.

Ferrar, Nicholas (1592–1637), founder of *Little Gidding. A native of London, in 1605 he entered Clare Hall, Cambridge, where he was one of the most brilliant of his generation, and in 1610 was elected a Fellow. In 1613 he had to leave Cambridge on account of his health and during the next five years travelled on the Continent, chiefly in Germany, Italy, and Spain. Having returned to England in 1618 he was employed by the Virginia Company, of which he became Deputy-Treasurer in 1622. Shortly before the dissolution of the Company, in 1624, he was returned to Parliament, but the sombre political prospect as well as his religious aspirations determined him to give up the brilliant career which was opening before him. In 1625 he settled at Little Gidding, an estate 11 miles NW of Huntingdon, bought by his mother in the preceding year. There he was joined by his brother and brother-in-law with their families in order to establish a kind of community life in accordance with the principles of the C of E. In 1626 he was ordained deacon by W. *Laud, and under his direction this household of some 30 persons lived a life of prayer and work under a strict rule. Ferrar himself played a full part in the life of the community. His austerity was exemplified in a very sparing diet, little sleep, and an almost complete absence of recreation. His piety and ideals, essentially biblical and founded on the BCP, were warmly approved by the Bp. of Lincoln, J. *Williams. In 1633 *Charles I visited Little Gidding and was greatly impressed by their life. The community incurred, however, the hostility of the *Puritans, and after Ferrar's death was denounced in a pamphlet entitled *The Arminian Nunnery* (1641) as an attempt to introduce RC practices in the country. Most of Ferrar's manuscripts were destroyed in a Puritan raid in 1646, which also brought the community to an end. His only publications are translations of J. de *Valdés' *Divine Considerations* and L. *Lessius's treatise *On Temperance.* Feast day in the ASB, 2 Dec.; in the American BCP (1979), 1 Dec.

See also LITTLE GIDDING.

A full Life was compiled by his brother John Ferrar (d. 1657), but was never printed. Part of this survives in a copy made by the Cambridge antiquary, T. Baker (d. 1740), now in the Cambridge University Library. Another Life by F. Peck (d. 1743), who used all the Ferrar papers, was also not printed. A good short Life by F. Turner, Bp. of Ely (d. 1700), based on the work of J. Ferrar, is in the British Library (Add. MS 34656); it was copied by S. Jebb (d. 1772), whose MS is in Cambridge University Library. Both J. Ferrar's and Peck's works were used in P. Peckard, *Memoirs of the Life of Mr. Nicholas Ferrar* (Cambridge, 1790); subsequently the MSS of both disappeared. Baker's copy of J. Ferrar's Life and Turner's Life ed. J. E. B. Mayor, *Nicholas Ferrar: Two Lives* (Cambridge, 1855; misleadingly describing the latter as the 'Life of Nicholas Ferrar by Doctor Jebb'). A crit. text of Baker's MS, supplemented where possible by selections from Turner and Peckard, ed. B. Blackstone, *The Ferrar Papers* (1938), pp. 3–94, with 'A Selection of Family Letters', pp. 223–312. T. T. *Carter (ed.), *Nicholas Ferrar: His Household and his Friends* (1892); H. P. K. Skipton, *The Life and Times of Nicholas Ferrar* (1907); A. L. Maycock, *Nicholas Ferrar of Little Gidding* (1938). M. *Creighton in *DNB* 18 (1889), pp. 377–80. See also bibl. to LITTLE GIDDING.

Ferrar MSS. A group of NT *minuscule MSS (nos. 13, 69, 124, 346, 543, 1689, and some half-dozen others), the common origin of the first four of which was established in 1868 by W. H. Ferrar, Trinity College, Dublin. They are also known as 'Family 13'. They date from the 11th to the 15th cent. They were prob. written in Calabria or are descendants of a Calabrian archetype. They have affinities with the *Caesarean type of text. A peculiarity of them is the placing of the '*pericope adulterae' (Jn. 7: 53–8: 11) after Lk. 21: 38.

K. *Lake and S. Lake, *Family 13 (The Ferrar Group): The Text according to Mark* (Studies and Documents, 11; 1941); J. Geerlings, *Family 13—The Ferrar Group: The Text according to Matthew* (ibid. 19; 1961); id., *Family 13 (The Ferrar Group): The Text according to Luke* (ibid. 20; 1961); id., *Family 13 (The Ferrar Group): The Text according to John* (ibid. 21; 1962). Id., *The Lectionary Text of Family 13 according to Cod. Vat. Gr. 1217* (ibid. 18; 1959).

Ferrara–Florence, Council of. See FLORENCE, COUNCIL OF.

festivals, ecclesiastical. See FEASTS, ECCLESIASTICAL.

festum. See FEASTS, ECCLESIASTICAL.

Fête-Dieu ('Feast of God'). The French title for the Feast of *Corpus Christi.

Fetter Dienstag (Ger., 'Fat-Tuesday'). An old German name for *Shrove Tuesday, now *Fastendienstag* or *Fastenabend*, from the practice of consuming on that day the eggs and fat prohibited during Lent. (Fr. *mardi gras*.)

Fetter Donnerstag (Ger., 'Fat-Thursday'). The Thursday preceding *Ash Wednesday, traditionally observed, like the following Monday and (*Shrove) Tuesday, as a day of feasting. (Fr. *jeudi gras*.)

Feuardent, François (1539–1610), French *patristic scholar and controversialist. A native of Coutances, he studied at Bayeux and *Paris, and after becoming a *Franciscan was ordained priest in 1561. For some years he devoted himself wholeheartedly to the cause of the Catholic League, preaching extensively in Paris and the Low Countries. The chief of his numerous writings against *Calvinism is his *Theomachia Calvinistica* (1604), in which he claimed to refute 1,400 errors of his Calvinist adversaries. His patristic writings, the most valuable part of his work, include editions of St *Ildefonsus of Toledo (1576), St *Irenaeus (1576; reissued, Cologne, 1596), Michael *Psellus (1577), St *Ephraem Syrus (1579), *Arnobius (1596), and *Lactantius (never published). He also commented on several Books of the Bible and produced a new edition of the *postils of *Nicholas of Lyra.

Édouard, OFM Cap., in *DTC* 5 (1913), cols. 2262–5.

Feuerbach, Ludwig Andreas (1804–72), German philosopher. He began as a student of theology at Heidelberg. In 1824 he went to Berlin, where he came under the personal influence of G. W. F. *Hegel and decided to exchange theology for philosophy. In 1828 he began teaching at Erlangen, but for the greater part of his life held no public office. He sought to recast Hegel's teaching in a positivistic sense openly hostile to Christianity. Rejecting all belief in transcendence, he held that theology and philosophy were properly concerned only with the nature of man, who was the true *ens realissimum*. Christianity was but an illusion, in Hegelian language the 'dominance of subjectivity' (*die Allmacht der Subjektivität*). Of his many writings the most celebrated was his *Wesen des Christentums* (1841; Eng. tr. by George Eliot as *The Essence of Christianity*, 1854). He exercised a far wider influence than the intrinsic merits of his writings deserved, notably on F. *Nietzsche and R. Wagner, and esp. on K. Marx and the whole Communist school in Germany. His other writings include *Grundsätze der Philosophie der Zukunft* (1843), *Das Wesen der Religion* (1845), *Theogonie* (1857), and *Gottheit, Freiheit und Unsterblichkeit* (1866; vol. 10 of *Sämmtliche Werke*).

Collected Works in 10 vols., Leipzig, 1846–66; new edn. by W. Bolin and F. Jodl, 10 vols., Stuttgart, 1903–11; also ed. W. Schuffenhauer and others, 16 vols., Berlin, 1967 ff. Selected Letters, ed. W. Bolin (2 vols., Leipzig, 1904) and W. Schuffenhauer (ibid., 1963). The first draft of *Das Wesen der Religion* was reconstructed by F. Tomasoni (Pubblicazioni della Facoltà di Lettere e Filosofia dell'Università di Milano, 119; Florence, 1986). K. Grün, *Ludwig Feuerbach* (2 vols., 1874). F. Engels, *Ludwig Feuerbach und der Ausgang der klassischen deutschen Philosophie* (1888; Eng. trs., Chicago, 1903, and London [1934]). S. Rawidowicz, *Ludwig Feuerbachs Philosophie: Ursprung und Schicksal* (1931). G. Nüdling, *Ludwig Feuerbachs Religionsphilosophie: Die Auflösung der Theologie in Anthropologie* (Paderborn, 1936; 2nd edn., 1961). K. E. Bockmühl, *Leiblichkeit und Gesellschaft: Studien zur Religionskritik und Anthropologie im Frühwerk von Ludwig Feuerbach und Karl Marx* (Forschungen zur systematischen Theologie und Religionsphilosophie, 7; 1961). E. Schneider, *Die Theologie und Feuerbachs Religionskritik* (Studien zur Theologie und Geistesgeschichte des Neunzehnten Jahrhunderts, 1; Göttingen, 1972). A. Philonenko, *La Jeunesse de Feuerbach 1828–1841: Introduction à ses Positions Fondamentales* (Bibliothèque d'histoire de la philosophie, 2 vols., 1990). V. A. Harvey, *Feuerbach and the Interpretation of Religion* (Cambridge, 1995). J. Salaquarda in *TRE* 11 (1983), pp. 144–57, s.v.

Feuillants. The reformed *Cistercians of Le Feuillant (formerly Fulium) in the neighbourhood of Toulouse, founded in 1577 by Abbot J. de la Barrière (1544–1600). After expelling from his house, which had grown lax and corrupt, those who would not accept his reform, the Abbot established a new rule stricter than the original. *Gregory XIII approved his action in 1581 and in 1589 *Sixtus V established the independence of the order. In 1588 a similar order for women, the 'Feuillantines', was begun. The Feuillants spread to Italy, where they were called 'Reformed Bernardines', and both the French and Italian branches produced some distinguished men, among them Cardinal J. Bona (d. 1674). In the 17th cent. the rigours of the original rule were somewhat relaxed. The order came to an end during the Napoleonic wars. Some *martyrologies describe de la Barrière as 'Venerable', and keep his feast on 25 Apr.

C. J. Morotius, O. Cist., *Cistercii Reflorescentis seu Cong. cistercio-monasticarum B. Mariae Fuliensis in Gallia et reformatorum in Italia Chronologica Historia* (Turin, 1690). G. Crucifix-Bultingaire, *Feuillants & Feuillantines* (privately pr., Paris, 1911). *Gallia Christiana*, 13 (1785), cols. 216–21. [P. Helyot,] *Histoire des ordres monastiques, religieux et militaires, et des congrégations séculières*, 5 (1718), pp. 401–20; Heimbucher, 1, pp. 374–6. Life of Jean de la Barrière by A. Bazy (Toulouse, 1885). E. M. Obrecht,

OCR, in *CE* 6 (1909), pp. 64 f., s.v.; M. Standaert in *Dict. Sp.* 5 (1964), cols. 274–87, s.v.; L. Ferrando in *DHGE* 16 (1967), cols. 1338–44, s.v., both with bibl.

Fichte, Johann Gottlieb (1762–1814), German Idealist philosopher. He was educated at Schulpforta and at the universities of Jena and Leipzig, where he studied Protestant theology. In 1790 he became acquainted with I. *Kant's philosophical system. His 'attempt at a critique of all revelation' (*Versuch einer Kritik aller Offenbarung*, 1792) showed his great powers, and he was appointed professor of philosophy at Jena in 1794, but dismissed in 1799 for atheism. In 1807–8 he delivered his famous *Reden an die deutsche Nation* which had great influence on the development of German nationalism and the overthrow of Napoleon. From 1809 till his death he was professor at the newly founded university of Berlin.

Fichte claimed that his philosophical doctrines were implicit in those of I. Kant, which he sought to develop on the lines of 'spontaneity' and 'autonomy'. Acc. to him the objects of our knowledge are the products of the consciousness of the ego as regards both their matter and their form. This ego, however, is not the individual 'I', but the Absolute Ego, which can be known only by philosophical intuition. It develops in three phases. In the first it posits itself, in the second it posits a non-ego against itself, and in the last it posits itself as limited by the non-ego. Acc. to Fichte God is the Absolute Ego, 'the living operative moral order'; but He is not to be conceived as personal. True religion consists in 'joyously doing right'. When society will have reached a condition in which morality is the norm, the existence of the Church will be unnecessary.

Fichte expounded his doctrines, which have been summed up as 'ethical pantheism', in a long series of works. Among the more important were *Grundlage der gesamten Wissenschaftslehre* (1794–5), *Grundlage des Naturrechts* (1796), *Erste* and *Zweite Einleitung in die Wissenschaftslehre* (both 1797), *System der Sittenlehre* (1798), *Der geschlossene Handelsstaat* (1800), *Die Bestimmung des Menschen* (1800), *Grundzüge des gegenwärtigen Zeitalters* (1806), and *Anweisung zum seligen Leben* (1805), the last his chief contribution to the philosophy of religion.

Sämmtliche Werke (ed. I. H. Fichte, son), 8 vols., Berlin, 1845–6. *Nachgelassene Werke*, ed. id., 3 vols., Bonn, 1834–5. Crit. edn. of *Werke*, incl. *Nachgelassene Schriften* and *Briefe*, under the auspices of the Bayerische Akademie by R. Lauth and others (Stuttgart, 1962 ff.). Eng. tr. of 'Popular Works', 2 vols., London, 1848–9. Modern Eng. trs. include: *Early Philosophical Writings* by D. Breazeale (Ithaca, NY, and London, 1988); *Attempt at a Critique of all Revelation* by G. Green (Cambridge, 1978), with introd., pp. 1–30; *Foundations of Transcendental Philosophy* by D. Breazeale (Ithaca, NY, and London, 1992); *Science of Knowledge, with the First and Second Introductions*, ed. and tr. by P. Heath and J. J. Lachs (New York, 1970; Cambridge, 1982); and *The Vocation of Man*, with introd., by P. Preuss (Indianapolis and Cambridge [1987]). *J. G. Fichte im Gespräch: Berichte der Zeitgenossen*, ed. E. Fuchs and others (Specula, 1; 6 vols. in 7, Stuttgart, etc., 1978–92). Lives by I. H. Fichte (2 Thle., Sulzbach, 1830–31), K. Fischer (*Geschichte der neueren Philosophie*, 5, Heidelberg, 1869; 4th edn., vol. 6, ibid., 1914), R. Adamson (Knight's Philosophical Classics, 1881), F. Medicus (Leipzig, 1914). X. Léon, *La Philosophie de Fichte* (1902); id., *Fichte et son temps* (3 vols., 1922–7). G. H. Turnbull, *The Educational Theory of J. G. Fichte* (Liverpool, 1926; with translations). M. Wundt, *Fichte-Forschungen* (1929). W. Ritzel, *Fichtes Religionsphilosophie*

(Forschungen zur Kirchen- und Geistesgeschichte, NF 5 [1956]). M. Buhr (ed.), *Wissen und Gewissen: Beiträge zum 200. Geburtstag Johann Gottlieb Fichtes 1762–1814* (1962). A. Philonenko, *La Liberté humaine dans la philosophie de Fichte* (Bibliothèque d'histoire de la philosophie, 1966). T. Rockmore, *Fichte, Marx, and the German Philosophical Tradition* (Carbondale, Ill., and London [1980]). J. Widmann, *Johann Gottlieb Fichte: Einführung in seine Philosophie* (Sammlung Göschen, 2219; 1982). F. Neuhouser, *Fichte's Theory of Subjectivity* (Cambridge, 1990). H. M. Baumgartner and W. G. Jacobs, *J. G. Fichte-Bibliographie* (Stuttgart, 1968). R. Adamson in *EB* (11th edn.), 10 (1910), pp. 313–16; W. Janke in *TRE* 11 (1983), pp. 157–71, both s.v.

Ficino, Marsilio (1433–99), Italian humanist and philosopher. Born at Figlione near Florence, he was intended by his father to be a physician. At some stage, however, he came under the patronage of Cosimo de' Medici (1398–1464), who, under the influence of *Gemisthus Plethon (who had come to Florence for the Council, 1439), had conceived the idea of founding a Platonic Academy, of which Ficino became head. As a result of Cosimo's patronage he had applied himself to Greek literature and language, and before long he had made himself a competent Greek scholar. He undertook a complete fresh translation of Plato, a task which, by leading him to consult many of the chief scholars of the day, did much to promote the study of Plato and philosophy generally. By the death of Cosimo (1464) ten of the Dialogues were finished and the whole was completed and published at Florence in 1484.

Meanwhile, Ficino's original mind, with its love of nature and its bent towards mysticism, gained him a wide influence. In 1473, after some hesitation, he sought ordination to the priesthood and became exemplary in his new duties. He continued to defend his 'Platonic philosophy', which meant for him not only the teachings of the *Neoplatonists but all the nobler elements in Greek thought. This synthesis of Christianity and Greek mysticism he expounded in *De Religione Christiana* (1476; dedicated to Lorenzo de' Medici, d. 1492), in immediate intention directed esp. against the critics of Christianity among the contemporary *Averroists. In 1487 he was appointed a Canon of Florence, where his expositions of the Gospels and Epistles formed the basis of his 'Commentaries'. His principal philosophical work, *Theologia Platonica de Immortalitate Animorum* (written between 1469 and 1474), largely based on Plato's *Phaedo*, appeared in 1482. In his later years he translated into Latin *Plotinus, *Porphyry, and *Dionysius the Ps.-Areopagite. Shortly before his death he was charged with magic, on the grounds of his belief in planetary influences, but he succeeded in purging himself.

Though he lacked critical judgement and had little sense of history, his erudition, wide sympathies, and enthusiasm gave him a far-reaching influence. He was sought out by scholars from all over Europe, among them J. *Colet and J. *Reuchlin, and kept up a large correspondence. His Florentine 'Academy' did not survive him, but his version of Plato remained the standard Latin text for the next hundred years.

Letters pub. Venice, 1495. Collected Works pub. in 2 vols., Basle, 1561, 1576, and Paris, 1641. *Supplementum Ficinianum: Marsilii Ficini Florentini Philosophi Platonici Opuscula Inedita et Dispersa*, ed. P. O. Kristeller (2 vols., Florence, 1937). Modern edns. of his Comm. on Plato's *Symposium*, with Eng. tr., by S. R. Joyce (University of Missouri Studies, 19, no. 1; Columbia, 1944; 2nd edn., Dallas, Tex., 1985) and, with Fr. tr., by R. Marcel (Les Classiques de l'humanisme. Collection publiée sous le patronage de l'Association Guillaume Budé, 1956); of his *Theologia Platonica de Immortalitate Animorum* by id. (2 vols., ibid., 1964); of the Comm. on the *Philebus*, with Eng. tr., by M. J. B. Allen (Publications of the Center for Medieval and Renaissance Studies, University of California, Los Angeles, 9; 1975); of passages on the soul in the *Phaedrus*, by id. (ibid. 14; 1981); of the Comm. on the *Sophist*, with Eng. tr., by id. (Berkeley, Los Angeles, and Oxford [1989]); of *De triplici vita* (orig. pub. Florence, 1489), with Eng. tr., by C. V. Kaske and J. R. Clark (Medieval & Renaissance Texts & Studies, 57; Binghamton, NY, 1989); and of his Letters by S. Gentile (Florence, 1990 ff.). Eng. tr. of Letters, by members of the Language Department of the School of Economic Sciences, London (1975 ff.). [A. M.] J. Festugière, *La Philosophie de l'amour de Marsile Ficin et son influence sur la littérature française au XVIe siècle* (Études de Philosophie Médiévale, 31. 3; 1941). P. O. Kristeller, *The Philosophy of Marsilio Ficino* (New York, 1943; rev. edn. of Italian tr., Florence, 1988, with recent bibl.). R. Marcel, *Marsile Ficin* (Paris, 1958). F. A. Yates, *Giordano Bruno and the Hermetic Tradition* (1964), *passim*; A. Field, *The Origins of the Platonic Academy of Florence* (Princeton, NJ, 1988). G. C. Garfagnini (ed.), *Marsilio Ficini e il Ritorno di Platone* (Istituto Nazionale di Studi sul Rinascimento, Studi e Testi, 15; 2 vols., 1986), incl. P. O. Kristeller, 'Marsilio Ficino and his Work after Five Hundred Years', vol. 1, pp. 15–196, with extensive bibl.

Fidei Defensor. See DEFENDER OF THE FAITH.

Fideism. A term applied to a variety of doctrines which hold in common belief in the incapacity of the intellect to attain to knowledge of divine matters and correspondingly put an excessive emphasis on faith. Though such systems have a long history, the word itself was apparently coined (for their own doctrines) by the Paris Protestant theologians, A. *Sabatier and E. Ménégoz (1838–1921), whose irrationalism derived from I. *Kant and F. D. E. *Schleiermacher. Later it came to be used much more widely and for the most part in a hostile sense. Scholastic theologians regularly charged the *Modernists with 'Fideism' in their theories of knowledge.

Fidelium, Missa. See FAITHFUL, MASS OF THE.

Fides Damasi (or Faith of Damasus). An important credal formula which was formerly attributed to St *Damasus or St *Jerome, but which, in view of its MS tradition, its influence on other creeds, and some of its theological expressions, is now generally thought to have originated in S. Gaul towards the end of the 5th cent. It is closely related in structure to the *Athanasian Creed, consisting like it of an exposition of Trinitarian doctrine (probably including the *Filioque) followed by a carefully reasoned Christological statement. It should not be confused with the *Tome of Damasus (*Tomus Damasi*).

The text is conveniently pr. in Denzinger and Hünermann (37th edn., 1991), pp. 48 f. (nos. 71–2); A. E. Burn, *An Introduction to the Creeds* (1899), pp. 244–8, incl. text; J. N. D. Kelly, *The Athanasian Creed* (Paddock Lectures, 1962–3; 1964), pp. 10 f., with text pp. 134 f. J. A. de Aldama, SJ, 'El Simbolo "Clemens Trinitas" ', *Gregorianum*, 14 (1933), pp. 485–500, esp. pp. 495–500; id., *El Simbolo Toledano I* (Analecta Gregoriana, 7; 1934), esp. pp. 127 f.

Fides Hieronymi. An early form of the *Apostles' Creed, prob. late 4th cent. Ascribed in the manuscripts to St *Jerome, it has also been attributed to St *Gregory of Elvira; but there is no consensus. Attention was drawn to its existence in several MSS (St Mihiel 28; Oxford, Bod. 147; Cambridge, Trinity College, O. 5. 5; London, B. Lib., Royal 6. B. XIII) by Dom G. *Morin. It is one of the earliest Latin Creeds with the words 'descended into hell' ('descendit ad inferna') and 'the *communion of saints' ('sanctorum communionem').

G. Morin, OSB, 'Un Symbole inédit attribué à saint Jérôme', *R. Bén.* 21 (1904), pp. 1–9, incl. text. A. *Wilmart, OSB, 'La Lettre de Potamius à Saint Athanase', ibid. 30 (1913), pp. 257–85, esp. pp. 274 f. Text also pr. by V. Bulhart in works ascribed to Gregory of Elvira (CCSL 69; 1967), pp. 273–5.

Field, Frederick (1801–85), biblical and patristic scholar. Educated at Christ's Hospital and Trinity College, Cambridge, he was elected a Fellow of his college in 1824, and from 1842 to 1863 was rector of Reepham in Norfolk. In the latter year he resigned his living and moved to *Norwich in order to devote his entire time to scholarship. In 1870 he became a member of the OT Revision Company. Field was one of the most learned and accurate patristic scholars of the 19th cent. His editions of St *Chrysostom's 'Homilies on St Matthew' (3 vols., 1839) and 'on St Paul's Epistles' (1849–62) marked the first attempt at establishing a critical text since the time of H. *Savile and B. de *Montfaucon. His splendid edition of *Origen's *Hexapla (2 vols., 1867–75) embodied the results of many years' research. He was also a keen student of the Greek text of the OT and NT, which he sought to understand in the light of a wide knowledge of classical literature; and many of his results in this field were contained in his *Otium Norvicense* (3 parts, 1864–81; part 3 republished posthumously, with additions by the author, 1897).

W. A. Greenhill in *DNB* 18 (1889), pp. 402–4, s.v.

Field, John (1545–88), *Presbyterian propagandist. Little is known of his early life, but he was described as a Bachelor of Arts of *Christ Church, Oxford, when he was ordained priest, uncanonically early, by E. *Grindal in 1566. From 1568 he worked as lecturer, curate and schoolmaster in his native London, where he was soon a leading member of an extreme *Puritan group. He was debarred from preaching for eight years (1571–9), and in 1572, after the failure of a move to moderate the Act of *Uniformity in the Puritan interest, he wrote the bitter and pungent 'View of Popish Abuses yet remaining in the English Church' which appeared with Thomas Wilcox's *Admonition to the Parliament. Both were sentenced to one year's imprisonment for breach of the Act of Uniformity, but had set the pattern for a succession of Presbyterian manifestos. Field's aim, especially in face of Abp. *Whitgift's energetic campaign for conformity, was the further reform of the Church of England by the imposition of a hierarchy of Presbyterian synods and by the substitution of a more austere form of public prayer, with greater provision for preaching. As corresponding secretary of the London conference of extreme Puritan ministers he showed himself an adept propagandist and organizer; however, he failed in his attempt to impose a Presbyterian uni-

formity on English Puritans, and became ready to rely on 'the multitude and people' to achieve the introduction of the new discipline. Though again suspended from preaching after 1585 he was protected from worse penalties by sympathizers on the Queen's Council. He probably provided material for the *Marprelate Tracts; but as the organizing genius of extreme Elizabethan Puritanism Field had no successor.

Field's activities (esp. in connection with elections to and proceedings in Parliament) are still shrouded in some obscurity; little of his correspondence has been pr. (his letters to Anthony Gilby are in Cambridge University Library, Baker MS 32), his works are scattered, and the 'Register' of evidences for the Puritan controversy which he compiled has not been pr. in full. P. Collinson, 'John Field and Elizabethan Puritanism', in S. T. Bindoff and others (eds.), *Elizabethan Government and Society: Essays presented to Sir John Neale* (1961), pp. 127–62, repr. in id., *Godly People* [1983], pp. 335–70. Id., *The Elizabethan Puritan Movement* (1967), passim. A. Gordon in *DNB*, Suppl. 2 (1901), pp. 205 f.

Field, Richard (1561–1616), Dean of *Gloucester. He was educated at Magdalen College, Oxford, and became Divinity Reader at *Winchester Cathedral in 1592, Rector of Burghclere c.1595, chaplain in ordinary to Queen *Elizabeth I in 1598, and Prebendary of Windsor in 1604. In 1604 he took part in the *Hampton Court Conference and in 1609 he was appointed Dean of Gloucester (where, however, he rarely resided). His principal work, his treatise *Of the Church* (Bks. 1–4, 1606; Bk. 5, 1610), was primarily conceived as an apology for the C of E against Rome, though controversy was subordinated to the exposition of principles. The notes of the true Church were (1) Antiquity, (2) Succession, (3) Unity, (4) Universality, and (5) the name 'Catholic'; and Field argued that the counterpart of the modern RC Church was to be found in early times in the *Donatists, with their claims to exclusiveness and purity. Field held that the Protestant bodies on the Continent were also part of the Church of Christ. The intimate friend of R. *Hooker, H. *Savile, and other noted scholars, Field was one of the most learned and acute theologians of his age.

There is a modern repr. of his treatise *Of the Church*, pub. by the Eccl. Hist. Soc., 4 vols., 1847–52. *Some Short Memorials concerning the Life of . . . Richard Field . . . by his son N. Field . . . published by John *Le Neve (1717). R. Hooper in *DNB* 18 (1889), pp. 410–12.

Fifth Monarchy Men. A fanatical sect of the middle of the 17th cent. whose members aimed at bringing in the 'Fifth Monarchy' (Dan. 2: 44) which should succeed the four empires of Assyria, Persia, Greece, and Rome. During it, Christ was to reign with His saints for a thousand years (Rev. 20: 4). For a time they supported O. *Cromwell, in the belief that the Commonwealth was a preparation for the Fifth Monarchy, but when they found their theocratic hopes unlikely to be realized they turned against him. After unsuccessful risings in 1657 and 1661, the leaders were beheaded and the sect died out.

E. Rogers, *Some Account of the Life and Opinions of a Fifth-Monarchy-Man: Chiefly extracted from the Writings of John Rogers, Preacher* (1867); C. H. Firth, *The Life of Thomas Harrison* (from Proceedings of the American Antiquarian Society, at the Semi-Annual Meeting, April 26, 1893; Worcester, Mass., 1893). L. F. Brown, *The Political Activities of the Baptists and Fifth Monarchy Men in England During the Interregnum* (Washington, DC, and

London, 1912); W. M. Lamont, *Godly Rule: Politics and Religion 1603–60* (1969); B. S. Capp, *The Fifth Monarchy Men: A Study in Seventeenth-century Millenarianism* (1972); R. L. Greaves, *Deliver Us From Evil: The Radical Underground in Britain, 1660–1663* (New York and Oxford, 1986), *passim*.

Figgis, John Neville (1866–1919), Anglican historian and theologian. The son of a Brighton minister of 'Lady *Huntingdon's Connexion', he was educated at St Catharine's College, Cambridge, where he came under the influence of F. W. *Maitland and M. *Creighton. After being received into the C of E, in 1894 he was ordained to a curacy at Kettering. In 1896 he published *The Divine Right of Kings*, an original attempt to exhibit the permanent religious significance of the doctrine from a study of its development. From 1896 to 1902 he was lecturer at St Catharine's and chaplain to Pembroke College, and from 1902 to 1907 rector of Marnhull in Dorset. In the meantime he had become an ardent disciple and correspondent of Lord *Acton, some of whose writings he later edited. In 1907 appeared *From Gerson to Grotius*, a useful contribution to the history of political thought. In the same year he entered the *Community of the Resurrection at Mirfield. In 1908–9 he delivered the *Hulsean Lectures on *The Gospel and Human Needs* (1909). His other writings include *Civilisation at the Cross Roads* (1912), and *The Political Aspects of St Augustine's 'City of God'* (1921; posthumous). Figgis's brilliance and depth of thought, clothed in an easy style, made him an unusually effective apologist. In his conception of the Christian State, he was a resolute opponent of the idea of absolute sovereignty and was among the first Christian thinkers alive to the dangers to religion and human freedom of the modern omnicompetent State.

Part of his *Churches in the Modern State* (1913) is repr. in P. Q. Hirst (ed.), *The Pluralist Theory of the State* (1989), pp. 111–27, with introd. pp. 1–47, *passim*. M. G. Tucker, *John Neville Figgis: A Study* (1950). An introd. by G. R. Elton to a 1965 repr. of Figgis's *The Divine Right of Kings* is repr. in Elton, *Studies in Tudor and Stuart Politics and Government*, 2 (Cambridge, 1974), pp. 193–214. D. [G.] Nicholls, *The Pluralist State* (1975), *passim*. A. Wilkinson, *The Community of the Resurrection* (1992), esp. pp. 118 f., 139–41. W. H. *Frere in *DNB, 1912–1921*, p. 181.

Filaret. See PHILARET.

Filaster. See PHILASTER.

Filioque (Lat., 'And the Son'). The dogmatic formula expressing the *Double Procession of the Holy Spirit (q.v.), added by the W. Church to the Nicene-Constantinopolitan *Creed immediately after the words 'the Holy Spirit . . . who proceedeth from the Father'. It is no part of the original Creed, but is first met with as an interpolation (acc. to the usual texts) at the Third Council of *Toledo (589). In 796 its use was defended by *Paulinus of Aquileia at the Synod of Friuli and from *c.*800, when the Creed began to be generally chanted at the Mass throughout the Frankish Empire, the words became widely familiar. Its introduction by Frankish monks in 807 into their monastery at *Jerusalem on the Mount of *Olives aroused strong but easily understandable opposition from the E. monks of St *Sabas, and when the matter was referred to *Leo III he tried to suppress the addition

to the formula while approving the doctrine. He caused the Creed in its original form to be engraved on two silver tables deposited at the tomb of St *Peter. The 'Filioque', however, continued to be sung, and soon after 1000 had been adopted also at Rome. Since the time of *Photius, who violently denounced it, the 'Filioque' has been made the chief ground of attack by the Orthodox Church on the Church of Rome. At the Reunion Councils of *Lyons (1274) and *Florence (1439), the acceptance of the doctrine, though not of the addition to the Creed, was imposed on the Greeks as a condition of the short-lived union. English theologians, following the *Thirty-Nine Articles, have generally accepted the W. tradition, e.g. R. *Hooker, J. *Pearson, and E. H. *Browne, and it was vigorously upheld by E. B. *Pusey in *On the Clause 'And the Son'* (1876). Discussions on the formula took place between Anglicans, *Old Catholics, and the E. Church at *Bonn in 1874 and 1875, and again at St Petersburg in 1912 in the conversations between F. W. Puller, SSJE, and Russian Orthodox theologians, but in both cases without positive results. More recent discussion (between the Orthodox and RCs, Anglicans and others, and in the *World Council of Churches) have been similarly fruitless, though Anglican theologians participating in such discussions are often disposed to agree to dropping the Filioque from the Creed. See also DOUBLE PROCESSION.

The history of the phrase is discussed in all works on the Creed, its doctrinal significance in treatises on the Holy Spirit. J. N. D. Kelly, *Early Christian Creeds* (1950; 3rd edn., 1972), pp. 358–67. G. B. Howard, *The Schism between the Oriental and Western Churches, with special references to the addition of the Filioque to the Creed* (1892). P. de Meester, OSB, 'Études sur la théologie orthodoxe', 4, 'Le Filioque', *R. Bén.* 24 (1907), pp. 86–103. A. E. Burn, 'Some Spanish MSS. of the Constantinopolitan Creed', *JTS* 9 (1908), pp. 301–3. M. Jugie, AA, 'Origine de la controverse sur l'addition du *Filioque* au symbole', *RSPT* 28 (1939), pp. 369–85. B. *Capelle, OSB, 'Le Pape Léon III et le "Filioque"', in *1054–1954: L'Église et les églises. Études et travaux . . . offerts à Dom Lambert *Beauduin*, 1 (Chevetogne, 1954), pp. 309–22; repr. in his *Travaux liturgiques*, 3 (1967), pp. 35–46. L. Vischer (ed.), *Spirit of God, Spirit of Christ: Ecumenical Reflections on the Filioque Controversy* (*Faith and Order Paper, 103; 1981). A. Palmieri in *DTC* 5 (1913), cols. 2309–43, s.v., with full bibl.; J. Gill, SJ, in *NCE* 5 (1967), pp. 913 f., s.v. See also bibl. to DOUBLE PROCESSION.

Finan, St (d. 661). The successor of St *Aidan as Bp. of *Lindisfarne. He was an Irishman by birth, and in his earlier life a monk of *Iona. He vigorously and consistently upheld the Celtic ecclesiastical traditions against the successors of St *Augustine of Canterbury, who, coming from the South, strove to bring English customs into closer conformity with those of Rome. He was a keen missionary and baptized Peada, ruler of the Middle Angles, and Sigebert, King of Essex. Feast day, 9 or 17 Feb.

The principal authority is *Bede, *HE* 3. 17, 21 f., and 25–7; notes *ad loc.*, ed. C. Plummer, 2 (1896), pp. 176–8 and 188 f.

Finding of the Cross. See INVENTION OF THE CROSS.

Finland, Christianity in. The origins of Christianity in Finland are obscure. It seems clear, however, that by the 12th cent. Finland had received Christianity from *Sweden and *Russia. Henry, Bp. of Uppsala, an Englishman murdered c.1160, took part in the conversion of the Finns. In 1220 an independent Church organization, centred on the episcopal see of Turku (Åbo) was established under Bp. Thomas (prob. also an Englishman). In the 15th cent. the Church of Finland had sufficient eminence for its divines to hold prominent positions in the world of learning, the best known being Olaus Magni, Bp. of Turku from 1450 to 1460, who was twice rector of the *Sorbonne.

*Lutheranism' was introduced into Finland in 1523 by Peter Särkilax (d. 1530); Michael Agricola (1512–57) was later prominent in the Reform Movement. The latter gained a ready hearing through his issue of popular Finnish religious writings, while his translation of the NT (1548) virtually created the Finnish written language. Severe measures were taken for the extermination of RCism. In Karelia (E. Finland), however, the population remained Orthodox, though it suffered persecution when the land fell to Sweden in 1617. In 1809 Finland came under Russian rule, and the Orthodox Church of Finland then rapidly increased in numbers and influence. By Acts of 1869 and 1889 RCism was tolerated for the first time since 1523, but the RCs form a very small minority. The National Church of Finland is a Lutheran body. Like other Lutheran Churches it was influenced by *Pietism in the 18th cent. Episcopal succession was lost in 1884, when all three sees became vacant simultaneously and their successors were consecrated by the (non-episcopal) Dean of Turku, but it has gradually been recovered with the help of the Church of Sweden. In 1934 the Church of Finland and the C of E negotiated mutual Eucharistic hospitality; the Porvoo Agreement of 1992 provides for common membership of the Churches and an interchangeable ministry. The Church of Finland is much the largest Church, to which over 90 per cent of the population belong. It has long had women theologians and since 1987 has ordained women. The Orthodox Church in Finland is a second established State Church. When Finland gained independence from Russia in 1917–18, the Finnish Orthodox Church declared itself autonomous; this autonomy was recognized by Patr. *Tikhon in 1921, but after the Church joined the jurisdiction of the Patr. of *Constantinople in 1923 recognition by Moscow was withdrawn in 1924 and only restored in 1957. In 1980 the General Assembly decided to seek autocephalous status. About 1 per cent of the population belong to the Orthodox Church. There are also a number of *Pentecostals. The percentage of the population overtly practising Christianity is high in Finland, though since 1923 it has been possible to register with the state as of no religion.

G. Sentzte, Die Kirche Finnlands (Helsinki, 1963; abbreviated Eng. tr., ibid., 1963). M. Sinnemäki, The Church in Finland (Helsinki, 1973). L. S. Hunter (ed.), Scandinavian Churches: A Picture of the Development of the Life of the Churches of Denmark, Finland, Iceland, Norway and Sweden (1965), esp. pp. 68–75. P. G. Lindhardt, Skandinavische Kirchengeschichte seit dem 16. Jahrhundert (Die Kirche in ihrer Geschichte: Ein Handbuch, . . . ed. B. Moeller, Band 3, Lieferung M3; Göttingen [1982]), pp. 302–7. A. Malin, Der Heiligenkalendar Finnlands: Seine Zusammensetzung und Entwicklung (Suomen Kirkkohistoriallisen Seuran, 20; Helsingfors, 1925). V. Purmonen (ed.), Orthodoxy in Finland, Past and Present (Kuopio, Finland, 1981; 2nd edn., 1984). J. H. Wuorinen, A History of Finland (New York and London, 1965), esp. pp. 31–42 and 60–6. W. A. Schmidt, 'Recent Research in Ecclesiastical History in Finland', JEH 7 (1956), pp. 226–37. W. Schmidt and others in RGG (3rd edn.), 2 (1958), cols. 960–99, s.v.; J. Gallén in DHGE 17 (1971), cols. 217–31, s.v.; B. Krug in TRE 11 (1983), pp. 185–92, s.v. 'Finnland, II'.
The Church of England and the Church of Finland: A Summary of the Proceedings at the Conferences held at Lambeth Palace, London, on October 5 and 6, 1933, and at Brändö, Helsingfors, on July 17 and 18, 1934 (1935). G. K. A. *Bell (ed.), Documents on Christian Unity, 3rd ser., 1930–48 (1948), nos. 188–92, pp. 146–53.

Finney, Charles Grandison (1792–1875), American evangelist. Born in Connecticut, he moved with his family to the western part of New York State in 1794. In 1821 he underwent a powerful conversion experience. Giving up the profession of law, he was ordained by the *Presbytery of Oneida, NY, in 1824, and began his spectacular, and controversial, rise to prominence as an itinerant revivalist preacher. Beginning in villages, by 1827 he was preaching in cities on the E. coast. In 1829 he preached his first revival meeting in New York City and soon settled there as a pastor. In 1835 he was appointed Professor of Theology in the recently founded Oberlin College, Oberlin, Ohio. Abandoning Presbyterianism for *Congregationalism, in 1837 he became pastor of the First Church (Congregational) in Oberlin, while remaining Professor of Theology at the College. In 1851 he became its President. He continued to hold revival meetings in various cities until 1860, visiting Great Britain in 1849–51 and again in 1859–60.

Finney almost singlehandedly transformed *revivalism in America. He popularized so-called 'new measures': 'protracted meetings' (with the cessation of all non-religious activities over a period of several days), the 'anxious bench', prayer meetings, public prayer for individuals by name, and a dramatic, even confrontational, pulpit style. He became a staunch opponent of *Calvinism and *predestination, espousing a theology of human responsibility and agency in conversion. He argued that successful revivals (and conversions) were not the results of divine grace alone; they were the result of 'the right use of constituted means'. Finney, along with Oberlin's first President, Asa Mahan, was a proponent of Oberlin Perfectionism, which affirmed that 'obedience to the moral law, or a state of entire consecration to God in this life' were states of moral perfection attainable by individuals. Finney was also an advocate of coeducation and the abolition of *slavery. His writings include Lectures on Revivals of Religion (1835) and Lectures on Systematic Theology (1846).

An expurgated edn. of his Memoirs pub., New York and London, 1876; complete restored text ed. G. M. Rosell and R. A. G. Dupuis (Grand Rapids, Mich., 1989). His Lectures on the Revivals of Religion, ed., with introd., by W. G. McLoughlin (Cambridge, Mass., 1960). Life by G. F. Wright (New York, 1891). Modern study by K. J. Hardman (Syracuse, NY, 1987; Darlington, Co. Durham, 1990). W. J. McLoughlin, Modern Revivalism: Charles Grandison Finney to Billy Graham (New York [1959]), pp. 3–121.

Finnian, St (6th cent.). Irish annals and genealogies distinguish two saints, Finnian of Clonard (d. 549) and Finnian of Moville (d. 579). One or other is likely to be the Vennianus auctor who wrote to St *Gildas about matters of monastic discipline and who composed the Poenitentiale Vinniani used by St *Columbanus. *Adomnán's 'Life of St *Columba' also mentions a St 'Uinnianus', 'Finnio' or

'Findbarr'. The early forms of the name suggest that the saint was a Briton who settled in Ireland, but identifications with the cults at Moville and Clonard are disputed, and it has been suggested that there may have been only one person. By the 8th cent. Finnian of Clonard had an established reputation as a teacher and there is an undated Latin Life of him. Finnian of Moville remained obscure. Feast day, Finnian of Clonard, 12 Dec.; Finnian of Moville, 10 Sept.

Poenitentiale Vinniuni, ed., with Eng. tr., by L. Bieler, *The Irish Penitentials* (Scriptores Latini Hiberniae, 5; Dublin, 1963), pp. 74–95. Frags. of Gildas's answer to Finnian are among those pr., with Eng. tr., by H. Williams in his edn. of Gildas, *De Excidio Britanniae* (Cymmrodorion Record Series, 3; 1899–1901), pp. 255–71. L. Fleuriot, 'Le "saint" breton *Winniau* et le Pénitentiel dit "de *Finnian*" ', *Études celtiques*, 15 (1976–8), pp. 607–14; P. Ó Riain, 'St Finnbarr: A Study in a Cult', *Journal of the Cork Historical and Archaeological Society*, 82 (1977), pp. 63–82; D. N. Dumville, 'Gildas and Uinniau', in M. Lapidge and D. N. Dumville (eds.), *Gildas: New Approaches* (Studies in Celtic History, 5; Woodbridge, 1984), pp. 207–14.

The Life of St Finnian of Clonard is ed. W. W. Heist, *Vitae Sanctorum Hiberniae* (Subsidia Hagiographica, 28; Brussels, 1965), pp. 96–107, and discussed by K. Hughes in *EHR* 69 (1954), pp. 352–72, and in *Anal. Boll.* 73 (1955), pp. 342–62, 75 (1957), pp. 337–9.

Fioretti. See LITTLE FLOWERS OF ST FRANCIS.

firmament (lit. 'something made solid'). In the OT (Gen. 1: 6, etc.), the word commonly refers to the dome or canopy of heaven, which was supposed by the Hebrews to be a solid vault dividing the upper or celestial from the lower or terrestrial waters. It was conceived that the upper waters came down as rain through opened sluices, and that above these waters Yahweh sat enthroned. In Ezek. (1: 26, etc.) the word appears to denote the base supporting God's moving throne.

Firmicus Maternus, Julius (d. after 360), rhetorician. Little is known of him beyond the facts that he was prob. of Sicilian origin and converted to Christianity in adult life. While still a pagan, he wrote his *Mathesis* in eight books, a compendium of astrology interwoven with moral reflections. His most important work, the *De errore profanarum religionum* (written at Rome *c*.347), is an appeal to the emperors Constantius and Constans to destroy the pagan idols by force. A treatise in three books, *Consultationes Zacchaei et Apollonii*, has been ascribed to him, prob. mistakenly, by Dom G. *Morin.

The *Consultationes* and *De Errore*, pr. in J. P. Migne, *PL* 20. 1071–166, and 12. 971–1050. Crit. edns. of *Mathesis* by W. Kroll, F. Skutsch and K. Ziegler (2 vols., Teub., 1898–1913), *De Errore* by K. Ziegler (ibid., 1907, and, with Ger. tr., Munich, 1953) and, with Fr. tr., by R. Turcan (Collection des Universités de France, 1982), and of the *Consultationes* by G. Morin, OSB (Florilegium Patristicum, 39; 1935). Eng. trs. of *De Errore* by C. A. Forbes (ACW 37 [1970]) and of *Mathesis* by J. R. Bram (Park Ridge, NJ [1975]). P. Courcelle, 'Date, source et genèse des "Consultationes Zacchaei et Apollinii" ', *Revue de l'histoire des religions*, 146 (1954), pp. 174–93. B. Studer in Quasten (cont.), *Patrology*, 4 (1986), pp. 569–72. P. Hadot in *Dict. Sp.* 5 (1964), cols. 384–8, s.v.; K. Ziegler in *RAC* 7 (1969), cols. 946–59, s.v., with extensive bibl.

Firmilian, St (d. 268), Bp. of Caesarea in Cappadocia from *c*.230. A great admirer of *Origen, Firmilian once summoned him to the Cappadocian Caesarea for instruction and later went himself to Origen's *Caesarea (in Palestine) to sit at his feet. He supported St *Cyprian against Pope *Stephen I in his doctrine that baptism could be validly performed only within the confines of the Church, and that heretics on joining the Church must therefore be 'rebaptized'. His only extant writing is a letter on the subject addressed to Cyprian (Cyp., *Ep.* 75). In 264 he was president of the first of the synods of Antioch held to consider the case of *Paul of Samosata, and died on his way to the second. Feast day in the E., 28 Oct.

Our chief source of information about Firmilian is *Eusebius, *HE* 6. 27; 6. 46. 3; 7. 5. 1; 7. 14; 7. 28. 1; 7. 30. 4 f. *Opera Cypriani*, ed. W. Hartel (CSEL 3 (2); 1871), pp. 810–27 (the Lat. tr. is apparently the work of Cyprian himself; there are no sufficient grounds for holding it to be interpolated). B. Bossue, SJ, 'De Firmiliano ... Commentarius Historicus', *AASS*, Oct. 12 (1867), pp. 470–510. G. A. Michell, 'Firmilian and Eucharistic Consecration', *JTS* NS 5 (1954), pp. 215–20. Bardenhewer, 2, pp. 312–14. J. *Chapman, OSB, in *CE* 6 (1909), pp. 80 f., s.v.; P. Nautin in *DHGE* 17 (1971), cols. 249–52, s.v.

First Fridays. The special observance of the first Friday in each month in the RC Church is based on the promise which Christ is supposed to have made to St *Margaret Mary Alacoque (1647–90) that unusual graces and favours would be given to all who received Holy Communion on the first Friday of nine consecutive months. Those who fulfilled this obligation could rest in the assurance that they would have the grace of full repentance, that they would not die in sin or without the sacraments, and that the *Sacred Heart would be their refuge at the hour of death. Though still observed, the devotion receives less emphasis than it formerly did now that more frequent Communion is general.

J. O'Connell, *The Nine First Fridays: The 'Great Promise' of the Sacred Heart of Jesus to Saint Margaret Mary. Its Origin, Authenticity and Meaning* (1934), incl. bibl.

first-fruits. See ANNATES.

fish (Gk. ἰχθύς). In Christian art and literature the fish is a symbol of Christ, also sometimes of the newly baptized and of the Eucharist. It came into use in the 2nd cent., but neither its origin nor its meaning have so far been completely elucidated. It occurs in *Tertullian's 'De Baptismo', where the writer compares the neophytes to little fishes, following the Fish, in connection with the idea of the second birth in the waters of Baptism. This image is found also in the 'Shepherd' of *Hermas, in the Inscription of *Abercius, in *Clement of Alexandria, and in many other old Christian documents; but it is doubtful whether the symbol is exclusively Christian or influenced by Babylonian and Indian mythology. Opinions are also divided as to whether the symbol is derived from the acrostic ΙΧΘΥΣ = Ἰησοῦς Χριστός Θεοῦ Υἱὸς Σωτήρ ('Jesus Christ, Son of God, Saviour'), or the acrostic from the symbol. The acrostic is frequently held to have originated in *Gnostic circles, since it is found in the '*Sibylline Oracles'. In the 4th and 5th cents. the fish became an emblem also of the Eucharist, and is frequently found in the paintings of the *catacombs in combination with bread and wine. In recent years, in some parishes of the C of E certain associations willing to help those in need have adopted the symbolism of a fish.

From early times fish, esp. in a dried condition, has taken the place of meat on days of fasting and abstinence. See FAST.

J. B. *Pitra, OSB, *Spicilegium Solesmense*, 3 (Paris, 1855), pp. 499–543 ('IΧΘΥΣ, sive de Pisce Allegorico et Symbolico'); J. B. *de Rossi, ibid., pp. 545–84 ('De Christianis Monumentis IΧΘΥΝ exhibentibus'); H. Achelis, *Das Symbol des Fisches und die Fischdenkmäler der römischen Katakomben* (Marburg, 1888); R. Pischel, 'Der Ursprung des christlichen Fischsymbol', *Sb.* (Berl.), 1905 (1), pp. 506–32; C. R. Morey, 'The Origin of the Fish-Symbol', *Princeton Theological Review*, 8 (1910), pp. 93–106, 231–46, and 401–32; 9 (1911), pp. 268–89; 10 (1912), pp. 278–98. I. Scheftelowitz, 'Das Fisch-Symbol im Judentum und Christentum', *Archiv für Religionswissenschaft*, 14 (1911), pp. 1–53. F. J. Dölger, *IΧΘΥΣ* (vol. 1, *RQ*, Suppl. 17; 1910; 2nd edn., Münster i.W., 1928; vols. 2–5, ibid., 1922–43). L. Werhahn-Stauch, 'Christliche Fischsymbolik von den Anfängen bis zum hohen Mittelalter', *Zeitschrift für Kunstgeschichte*, 35 (1972), pp. 1–68. R. St J. Tyrwhitt in *DCA* 1 (1880), pp. 673 f., s.v., and pp. 625–8, s.v. 'Eucharist (in Christian Art)'; F. Cumont in *PW* 9 (pt. 1; 1914), cols. 844–50, s.v. 'Ichthys'; H. *Leclercq, OSB, in *DACL* 7 (pt. 2; 1927), cols. 1990–2086, s.v. *IΧΘΥΣ*; J. Quasten in *NCE* 5 (1967), pp. 943–6, s.v. 'Fish, Symbolism of'; J. Engemann in *RAC* 7 (1969), cols. 1021–97, s.v. 'Fisch, B. Christlich'.

Fisher, Geoffrey Francis (1887–1972), Abp. of *Canterbury. Born at Higham-on-the-Hill, Leics., he was educated at Marlborough and Exeter College, Oxford. He was successively assistant master of Marlborough (1911), Headmaster of Repton (1914, succeeding W. *Temple), and Bp. of *Chester (1932). His translation to London in 1939 gave wider scope for his administrative ability, which he showed in his attempt to establish some ritual conformity by the issue of Bishops' Regulations, and more markedly by his chairmanship of the *Church Assembly Committee set up to deal with pastoral reorganization required by war damage, and of the Churches' Main War Damage Committee. He became involved in the '*Sword of the Spirit' movement in 1940; his careful diplomacy ensured continued ecumenical participation in it at a difficult time. In 1945 he was translated to Canterbury. In 1946 he preached the influential Cambridge sermon on *reunion, a subject in which he displayed great interest during his archiepiscopate; he was chairman of the *World Council of Churches at its inauguration in 1948, and in 1960, when he travelled to meet the Orthodox Patriarch of Jerusalem, the Oecumenical Patriarch of Constantinople, and Pope *John XXIII, he was the first Archbishop of Canterbury to visit the Vatican since 1397. The second Anglican Congress took place in Minneapolis with his encouragement in 1954. He presided over the *Lambeth Conferences of 1948 and 1958, which owed their representative character partly to his careful preparation, especially in America, and partly to the establishment of new provinces among the emergent nations, among them *West Africa (1951), Central Africa (1955), and East Africa (1959). He also set up the East Asian Episcopal Conference in 1954 and raised the Bishopric in *Jerusalem to metropolitan rank in 1957. He thus divested himself of authority over the African and Asian parts of the Anglican

Communion. At home his support ensured the amalgamation of *Queen Anne's Bounty with the *Ecclesiastical Commissioners to form the *Church Commissioners for England in 1948. From 1946 onwards he devoted considerable time to what he regarded as one of his most important tasks, the revision of the Canon Law, though new *Canons were not authorized until 1969. The most widely travelled Archbishop of Canterbury to date, because of television he was also the most widely seen. He resigned in 1961, and was granted a life barony.

E. [F.] Carpenter, *Archbishop Fisher: His Life and Times* (Norwich, 1991). Shorter study by W. Purcell (London, 1969). P. A. Welsby, *A History of the Church of England 1945–1980* (Oxford, 1984), pp. 3–108 and 177 f. I. H. White-Thomson in *DNB, 1971–1980*, pp. 316–18.

Fisher, St John (1469–1535), Bp. of *Rochester. Educated at Michaelhouse, *Cambridge, he became a doctor of divinity and was elected vice-chancellor in 1501. The following year he was appointed to the theology lectureship founded by Lady *Margaret Beaufort at Cambridge, and some time between 1497 and 1504 he became her confessor. Encouraging her patronage of his university, he assisted in her two foundations of Christ's and St John's Colleges. In 1504 he was appointed Bp. of Rochester and Chancellor of Cambridge University, and from 1505 to 1508 he was also President of Queens' College. Fisher was one of the greatest scholars of his day. His library was said to be the finest in England, and he was a friend of *Erasmus, whom he persuaded to teach Greek at Cambridge. He was also devoted to the welfare of his diocese, and even in his lifetime he was regarded as a model bishop. He enjoyed a high reputation as a preacher, and was chosen in 1509 to preach at Henry VII's funeral and at the memorial service of the Lady Margaret. Despite a later attribution, he was not the author of *Henry VIII's *Assertio Septem Sacramentorum*, but when Protestant doctrines became prominent in the 1520s Fisher emerged as one of the leading defenders of Catholicism. His *Assertionis Lutheranae Confutatio* (1523) was one of the most popular Catholic attacks on M. *Luther of the decade; his *De Veritate Corporis et Sanguine Christi in Eucharistia* (1527) mounted a major defence of Catholic Eucharistic doctrine against J. *Oecolampadius. Both these works heavily influenced polemicists and even the Council of *Trent. When Henry VIII began to seek a divorce from Catherine of Aragon in 1527, Fisher soon became her foremost defender, writing several books on her behalf. From that time his relations with Henry deteriorated. He strenuously opposed Henry's attacks on the liberties of the English Church, securing the mitigation of Convocation's first submission to the King as Supreme Head by the insertion of the saving clause 'as far as the law of Christ allows' (1531). Because of his opposition to the King he was included in the Act of Attainder against Elizabeth *Barton (1534), although his sentence of imprisonment was commuted to a fine. After refusing to take the oath required by the Act of Succession, he was imprisoned in the Tower (Apr. 1534), where he wrote a 'spiritual consolation' for his sister Elizabeth, a *Dominican nun. On 7 May 1535 he was tricked into denying the royal supremacy by a messenger who claimed that the King wanted Fisher's opinion in confidence for his conscience's sake. Fisher was given six weeks to reconsider the matter, during which time news arrived that *Paul III had created him a cardinal. At his trial on 17 June, his defence that he had not denied the supremacy maliciously was dismissed by a ruling that all denials were malicious. He was found guilty of treason and condemned to death; he was beheaded on 22 June 1535. He was beatified in 1885 and canonized in 1935. Feast day, formerly 9 July; now, with Thomas *More, 22 June.

Opera collected by his fellow English RCs and pub. at Würzburg, 1597, various works written by him in Eng. being tr. into Lat. for the purpose. Facs. repr., Farnborough, 1967. *The English Works of John Fisher*, ed. J. E. B. Mayor (EETS, Extra Series, 27; 1876; repr. 1935 with text of additional sermon, pp. 429–76). J. Rouschausse (ed.), *Erasmus and Fisher: Their Correspondence 1511–1524* (De Pétrarque à Descartes, 16; Paris, 1968), prints 18 surviving letters, with notes and Eng. tr. Modern edn. of his *Sacri Sacerdotii Defensio contra Lutherum* (1525) by H. K. Schmeink (Corpus Catholicorum, 9; Münster i.W., 1925); Eng. tr. by P. E. Hallett (London, 1935). The *Spirituall Consolation* (first pub. *c*.1578) and the *Treatise of Prayer* in the Eng. tr. by St A[lban] R[oe], OSB (Paris, 1640), repr. in facs. (English Recusant Literature 1558–1640, 11; Menston, Leeds, 1969). Pre-1641 edns. of his works in languages other than Eng. are listed in A. F. Allison and D. M. Rogers, *The Contemporary Printed Literature of the English Counter-Reformation*, 1 (Aldershot, 1989), pp. 62–5 (nos. 415–40). The earliest Life, a composite production chiefly written between 1567 and 1576, was first ed. by T. Bailey, *The Life and Death of John Fisher* (1655); a more accurate edn. by F. van Ortroy, SJ, in *Anal. Boll.* 10 (1891), pp. 121–365, and 12 (1893), pp. 97–281. One MS (BL Harleian MS 6382), ed. R. Bayne (EETS, Extra Series, 117; 1921). Modernized edn. by P. Hughes (London, 1935). T. E. Bridgett, CSSR, *Life of Blessed John Fisher* (1888); E. E. Reynolds, *Saint John Fisher* (1955; rev. edn., 1972); M. Macklem, *God Have Mercy: The Life of John Fisher of Rochester* (Ottawa [1967]); E. L. Surtz, SJ, *The Works and Days of John Fisher* (Cambridge, Mass., 1967); J. Rouschausse, *La Vie et l'Œuvre de John Fisher* (Nieuwkoop [1972]); B. Bradshaw and E. Duffy (eds.), *Humanism, Reform and Reformation: The Career of Bishop John Fisher* (Cambridge, 1989); R. Rex, *The Theology of John Fisher* (ibid., 1991). *BRUC*, pp. 229–30. J. K. McConica in P. G. Bietenholz and T. B. Deutscher (eds.), *Contemporaries of Erasmus*, 2 (1986), pp. 36–39, s.v.

Fisher, Samuel (1605–65), *Quaker. Educated at Trinity College and New Hall, Oxford, he was a *Puritan lecturer and then a *Baptist minister in Ashford before he joined the *Friends in 1655. Apart from a tour of the Netherlands, Germany, and Italy in 1657–8, he preached mainly in Kent and later in London, where he was imprisoned in 1661 and again in 1662. His numerous works include *Rusticus ad Academicos . . . The Rustick's Alarm to the Rabbies, or The Country Correcting the University and Clergy* (pub. in 1660, after the Restoration); it is considered the most important piece of Quaker controversial writing of the Commonwealth period.

Collected works repr. as *The Testimony of Truth Exalted* (1679). A. C. Bickley in *DNB* 19 (1889), pp. 70–2.

Fisher the Jesuit (1569–1641), i.e. **John Fisher**, RC controversialist. His real name was Percy. Born in Co. Durham, he was converted to the RC faith as a young man. After studying abroad, he joined the *Jesuits in 1594 and served many years on the English mission, where he made a name for himself in private disputations and public controversy and won (among others) W. *Chillingworth and the Countess of Buckingham to the Roman faith.

Among his Anglican opponents were *James I and Bps. F. *White and W. *Laud. Laud published in 1639 a lengthy *Relation* of his conference with Fisher, and this was several times reprinted. Fisher himself published several controversial and apologetical works.

Modern edn. of W. Laud, *A Relation of the Conference between William Laud, late Archbishop of Canterbury, and Mr. Fisher the Jesuit*, with introd. and notes, by C. H. Simpkinson ('The English Theological Library', 1901). T. H. Wadkins, 'King James I meets John Percy, SJ (12 May, 1622). An unpublished manuscript from the religious controversies surrounding the Countess of Buckingham's conversion', *Recusant History*, 19 (1988), pp. 146–54. H. Foley, SJ, *Records of the English Province of the Society of Jesus*, 1 (1877), pp. 521–42. A. F. Allison and D. M. Rogers, 'A Catalogue of Catholic Books in English printed abroad or secretly in England, 1558–1640', *Biographical Studies*, 3 (1956), pp. 242–4 (nos. 603–10). T. Cooper in *DNB* 19 (1889), pp. 63 f.

fistula. A tube, usually of gold or silver, through which the laity occasionally received communion from the chalice at the Eucharist in the Middle Ages. Its use came to be confined to solemn Papal Masses, when the Pope and his deacon received communion in this way. Since 1969 in the RC Church both celebrant and laity have been permitted to receive communion through a *calamus* or reed; nothing is laid down about the material from which it should be made.

Braun, *AG*, pp. 247–65, and plate 48. H. J. Hotham in *DCA* 1 (1875), p. 675, s.v.; W. Henry in *DACL* 2 (pt. 2; 1910), col. 1583, s.v. 'Calamus', with bibl.

FitzRalph, Richard (*c*.1295–1360), Abp. of *Armagh. He became Chancellor of *Oxford University in 1332 and of *Lincoln Cathedral in 1334, Canon of *Lichfield in 1335, Dean of Lichfield in 1337, and Abp. of Armagh in 1347. He was a celebrated preacher, deeply imbued with scholasticism, and an eager promoter of learning among his clergy. From 1334 to 1336 he visited the Papal court at *Avignon and became involved in the controversy over the *Beatific Vision arising from the pronouncements of *John XXII. From 1337 to 1344 he was again at Avignon and engaged in a controversy with emissaries of the *Armenian Church; this led to the composition of his attack on the Greek and Armenian standpoint in his 'Summa de Questionibus Armenorum' (pub. 1511). His final visit to Avignon started in 1357 and was concerned with his attack on the *Mendicant Orders, maintaining that voluntary begging was against the teaching of Christ. He formulated his opinion in the treatise 'De Pauperie Salvatoris', in which he dealt with the question of evangelical poverty and the connection of dominion, possession, and use with the state of grace; it later greatly influenced J. *Wycliffe. His position was not officially condemned, and he died three years later at Avignon.

Modern edn. of his 'De Pauperie Salvatoris' appended to R. L. Poole's edn. of Wycliffe's *De Dominio Divino* (Wyclif Society, 1890), pp. 273–476. L. L. Hammerich, *The Beginning of the Strife between Richard FitzRalph and the Mendicants, with an edition of his autobiographical Prayer and his Proposition Unusquisque* (Copenhagen, 1938). G. Leff, *Richard FitzRalph, Commentator on the Sentences: A Study in Theological Orthodoxy* (Manchester [1963]). K. Walsh, *A Fourteenth Century Scholar and Primate: Richard FitzRalph in Oxford, Avignon, and Armagh* (Oxford, 1981), with bibl. G. Meersseman, OP (ed.), 'La Défense des ordres mendiants contre Richard Fitz Ralph, par Barthélemy de

Bolsenheim O.P. (1357)', *Archivum Fratrum Praedicatorum*, 5 (1935), pp. 124–73. A. Gwynn, SJ, 'The Sermon Diary of Richard FitzRalph, Archbishop of Armagh', *Proceedings of the Royal Irish Academy*, 44 (1937–8), section C, pp. 1–57. J.-F. Genest, 'Contingence et Révélation des Futurs: La *Quaestio Biblica* de Richard FitzRalf', in J. Jolivet and others (eds.), *Lectionum Varietates: Hommage à Paul Vignaux* (Études de philosophie médiévale, 65; 1991), pp. 199–246, incl. text. R. L. Poole in *DNB* 19 (1889), pp. 194–8. *BRUO* 2 (1958), pp. 692–4, s.v., with refs.

Five Mile Act. The common name for the Nonconformists Act 1665, which was one of the penal statutes, part of the so-called Clarendon Code, passed to secure the position of the C of E at the Restoration. It specifically dealt with those clergymen who had refused to conform to the Act of *Uniformity 1662. It prohibited Nonconformist ministers from preaching, teaching, or coming within five miles of a city, or corporate town, or parish where they had previously officiated, unless they had taken the nonresistance oath, declaring that they would not 'at any time endeavour any alteration of Government either in Church or State'. The Act gave the informer legal status by empowering the Justices of the Peace to commit offenders upon the sworn testimony of a third party. Its effects were severely felt by the Dissenters, as their congregations were chiefly situated in the towns, but indirectly it contributed to the spread of Nonconformity in the countryside.

Text in Gee and Hardy, pp. 620–3 (no. 118); mainly repr. in Bettenson (2nd edn., 1963), pp. 416–18.

flabellum. See FAN, LITURGICAL.

Flacius, Matthias (1520–75), from his birthplace also known as **Illyricus**, *Lutheran theologian. He was born in the Venetian town, Albona (now Labin in Croatia), and attended the school of San Marco in *Venice. He was sent to Germany on the advice of the Franciscan Provincial, Baldo Lupetina, his uncle, who was later judicially put to death by drowning for his sympathies for the Reformation. Flacius studied Greek with Simon Grynaeus in Basle and with Matthias Garbitius in *Tübingen, where he also studied Hebrew with the radical Lutheran Johannes Forster. Having arrived in *Wittenberg in 1541, he was appointed professor of Hebrew in 1544. He became an outstanding Hebraist. While apparently not a close personal friend of M. *Luther, he supported the so-called *Gnesio-Lutheran tendency and after Luther's death defended Lutheran teaching against what he regarded as concessions to RCs. In 1548 he tried in vain to unite the theological faculty at Wittenberg against the *Augsburg Interim and had to leave for Magdeburg, where he stayed until 1557. From there he wrote against the *Adiaphorists, marking his distance from P. *Melanchthon's conciliatory line. He was the leading force behind the work of the *Centuriators of Magdeburg, but probably not one of the authors. His *Catalogus Testium Veritatis* (1556) seeks out historical support for Lutheran doctrine and displays wide learning. In 1557 he became professor of NT at Jena. Here his view of free will, which in the 1580s was to make T. Heshusius accuse him of *Manichaeism, led him into conflict with V. *Strigel and other defenders of *synergistic doctrines, and he lost his post in Dec. 1561. He then went to Regensburg, where he worked on his *Clavis Scripturae Sacrae* (1567). This outlines a method of biblical exegesis

in part based on philological work, and in part on the manuals of rhetoric by P. Melanchthon and Andreas Hyperius. After the fall of his protector, the count of Ortenberg, Flacius rapidly lost support and left Regensburg for Antwerp (1566–7), Strasbourg (1567–73), where he dedicated his *Glossa Compendiaria in Neuen Testamentum* (1570) to the city council, and finally Frankfurt am Main, where he died in the care of the *Magdalenes. See also MISSA ILLYRICA.

Lives by J. B. Ritter (Frankfurt, 1725) and W. Preger (Erlangen, 2 parts, 1859–61). L. Haikola, *Gesetz und Evangelium bei Matthias Flacius Illyricus* (Studia theologica Lundensia, 1; 1952); R. Keller, *Der Schlüssel zur Schrift: Die Lehre vom Wort Gottes bei Matthias Flacius Illyricus* (Arbeiten zur Geschichte und Theologie des Luthertums, NF 5 [1984]). P. Polman, OFM, 'Flacius Illyricus, historien de l'Église', *RHE* 27 (1931), pp. 27–73. O. K. Olson, 'Matthias Flacius Illyricus', in J. Raitt (ed.), *Shapers of Religious Traditions in Germany, Switzerland, and Poland, 1560–1600* [1981], pp. 1–17. J. F. Gilmont in *DHGE* 17 (1971), cols. 311–26; O. K. Olson in *TRE* 11 (1983), pp. 206–14, with bibl.

flagellants. The bands of men who in later medieval times scourged themselves in public procession, often to the accompaniment of psalms, in penance for the sins of the world. The anarchy and famine caused by war in North and Central Italy, and perhaps the prophecies of *Joachim of Fiore, combined to produce a conviction of the Divine displeasure; in 1260, prob. originating at Perugia, there was an outbreak of such manifestations throughout Italy. The movement was spontaneous and embraced all classes; it was not originated by the clergy or the religious orders. Its adherents engaged in processions, scourgings, and observances in churches; devotion to the BVM was a prominent feature, and social reconciliation and moral reform were strongly promoted. The movement may be regarded as an aspect of the long history of *fraternities. It quickly spread across the Alps to Germany, France, and the Low Countries. In 1348–9, the Black Death led to a revival of the movement, particularly in Northern Europe and above all in Flanders and N. France. When the University of *Paris was asked to pass judgement on it, it referred the matter to the Papacy at *Avignon, where Pope *Clement VI in 1349 called for its suppression by ecclesiastical and secular authorities. However, it survived into the 15th cent., esp. in Thuringia. In Italy, processions of flagellants, orthodox in belief, continued to be held at intervals until the 19th cent. In some missionary areas such observances have persisted, subject to ecclesiastical regulation and restraint, until more recent times.

For the main sources see Segl, cited below. P. Runge (ed.), *Die Lieder und Melodien der Geissler des Jahres 1349 nach der Aufzeichnung Hugo's von Reutlingen* (1900); U. Berlière, OSB, 'Trois Traités inédits sur les flagellants de 1349', *R. Bén.* 25 (1908), pp. 334–57. L. A. *Muratori, *Antiquitates Italicae Medii Aevi*, 6 (Milan, 1742), pp. 446–82, diss. 75, 'De Piis Laicorum Confraternitatibus earumque Origine, Flagellantibus, et Sacris Missionibus'. *Il movimento dei Disciplinati nel settimo centenario dal suo inizio (Perugia—1260): Convegno internazionale: Perugia, 25–28 Settembre 1960* (Deputazione di Storia Patria per l'Umbria, Appendice al Bollettino 9; 1962). A. Hübner, *Die deutschen Geisslerlieder* (1931). N. Cohn, *The Pursuit of the Millennium* (rev. edn., 1970), pp. 127–47. G. [A.] Leff, *Heresy in the Later Middle Ages*, 2 (1967), pp. 485–93, with bibl. R. Kieckhefer, 'Radical tendencies in the flagellant movement of the mid-fourteenth century', *Journal of Medieval and Renaissance Studies*, 4 (1974), pp. 157–76; id., *Repression of Heresy in Medieval Germany* (Liverpool, 1979), pp. 79–82 and 96 f. L. A. St L. Toke in *CE* 6 (1909), pp. 89–92, s.v.; P. Bailly in *Dict. Sp.* 5 (1964), cols. 392–407, s.v., sections 1–3; G. Alberigo in *DHGE* 17 (1971), cols. 327–37, s.v.; G. Cecchini in *DIP* 4 (1977), cols. 60–72, s.v. 'Flagellanti'; P. Segl in *TRE* 12 (1984), pp. 162–9, s.v. 'Geissler'.

flags on church towers.

Acc. to a ruling given in 1938 by the Earl Marshal, the proper flag to fly on a church tower in England is the red Cross of St *George, with an escutcheon of the Arms of the See in which the church is ecclesiastically situate in the first quarter; but, where this flag cannot be obtained, custom sanctions the use of the plain St George's Cross. No rules have been laid down as to the occasions on which the flag is to be flown, but it is usual for this to be done on important Church festivals, on special occasions of rejoicing, and sometimes on days of national observance.

Flavia Domitilla.

See DOMITILLA, FLAVIA.

Flavian, St

(d. 449), Patr. of *Constantinople from 446. He is remembered for the important part which he took in the *Monophysite struggle. In 448 he had excommunicated *Eutyches at a synod at Constantinople (the so-called σύνοδος ἐνδημοῦσα) for heretical teaching about the Person of Christ. In the following year Imperial pressure secured the reversal of this decision at the *Latrocinium at Ephesus, and the maltreatment that Flavian suffered here is said to have caused his death a few days later. His remains were subsequently brought solemnly to Constantinople by the Empress *Pulcheria. He was vindicated at the Council of *Chalcedon, which regarded him as a martyr. Feast day in the E., variously 16, 17, 18 Feb. and 12 Nov.; in the W., 18 Feb.

Flavian's *libellus appellationis*, written immediately after the Latrocinium and directed to Pope *Leo, was found in 1874 by G. Amelli, the librarian of the *Ambrosiana, in the Novara Capitular MS 30 and first pub. by Amelli in *S. Leone Magno e l'Oriente* (1882). It was reissued by T. *Mommsen, *NA* 11 (1886), pp. 362–4. A subsequent edn., with an important introd., was pub. by T. A. *Lacey, *Appellatio Flaviani: The Letters of Appeal from the Council of Ephesus, A.D. 449, addressed by Flavian and Eusebius to St Leo of Rome* (Church Historical Society, 70; 1903). V. Grumel, AA (ed.), *Les Regestes des Actes du Patriarcat de Constantinople*, 1 (fasc. 1, 2nd edn., 1972), pp. 75–84 (nos. 94–110a). H. Chadwick, 'The Exile and Death of Flavian of Constantinople: A Prologue to the Council of Chalcedon', *JTS* NS 6 (1955), pp. 17–34. *CPG* 3 (1979), pp. 150–2 (nos. 5930–8). J. Liébaert in *DHGE* 17 (1971), cols. 390–6, s.v. 'Flavien (13)'.

Fléchier, Esprit

(1632–1710), French preacher and man of letters. After studying at Tarascon, he was ordained and went to *Paris where, in 1671, he was appointed *lecteur* (tutor) to the Dauphin. He was chiefly known and admired for his sermons, in particular his funeral orations (most notably that on Turenne). In 1673 he was elected a member of the French Academy. In 1685 he became Bp. of Lavaur and in 1687 of Nîmes, where he exerted a conciliatory influence in the aftermath of the revocation of the Edict of *Nantes (1685).

Œuvres complètes, ed. by G. M. Ducreux (10 vols., Nîmes, 1782) and by J. P. *Migne (2 vols., Paris, 1856). A. E. Delacroix,

Histoire de Fléchier d'après les documents originaux (1865). Modern Life by G. [F. X. M.] Grente (Paris, 1934). A. Fabre, *La Jeunesse de Fléchier* (2 vols., 1882); id., *De la correspondance de Fléchier avec Mme Deshoulières* (1872); id., *Fléchier, orateur* (1872). Notice by C. A. Sainte-Beuve prefixed to M. Chéruel (ed.), *Les Mémoires de Fléchier sur les Grands-Jours d'Auvergne* (1856), pp. iii–xxxix. G. Grente in *Dictionnaire des Lettres Françaises: Le Dix-Septième Siècle* (1954), pp. 427–32.

Fleming, Richard

(d. 1431), Bp. of *Lincoln and founder of Lincoln College, Oxford. Educated at University College, Oxford, he became a Prebendary of *York in 1406. In 1407 he was Junior Proctor at Oxford. At this period he had *Wycliffite sympathies, which brought him into conflict with T. *Arundel, Abp. of *Canterbury, then attempting to eradicate *Lollard doctrine from the university. In 1408 he became rector of Boston, Lincs, and in 1420 Bp. of Lincoln. In 1423 Fleming represented the English nation at the Councils of Pavia and Siena, where he made an eloquent speech before *Martin V championing the Papacy. In 1424 Martin V promoted him to the see of York, but the Chapter having already elected the Bp. of *Worcester, the King's ministers refused to confirm the appointment. In 1427 Fleming founded Lincoln College, Oxford, primarily as a school for opponents of Wycliffite teaching (which he himself had long since forsworn).

His Episcopal Register, ed. N. H. Bennett (*Canterbury and York Society, 73; 1984 ff.). V. [H. H.] Green, *The Commonwealth of Lincoln College 1427–1977* (Oxford, 1979), pp. 2–6. For his supposed Lollard sympathies, *Snappe's Formulary and Other Records*, ed. H. E. Salter (Oxford Historical Society, 80; 1924), pp. 95–100 and 121–8. R. L. Poole in *DNB* 19 (1889), pp. 282–4. *BRUO* 2 (1958), pp. 697–9, s.v. 'Flemyng, Richard'.

Fletcher, John William

(1729–85), Vicar of Madeley in Salop from 1760. (His original name was de la Fléchère.) A Swiss by birth and education, he arrived in England in 1750. Prob. late in 1753 he joined the *Methodist movement (then still within the C of E) and underwent a 'conversion' experience in Jan. 1754. In 1757 he was ordained deacon and priest on two successive Sundays, and in 1760 he accepted the living of Madeley as a benefice providing more work and less income than another which he had been offered and declined. From 1768 to 1771 he also exercised, so far as his parochial duties allowed, a general supervision over Lady *Huntingdon's college at Trevecca for the training of ministers. Although he resisted John *Wesley's desire to designate him as his successor in the leadership of the Methodists, his sanctity won him a strong personal influence in the movement as well as among the colliers in his parish. He was a prominent advocate of Wesley's doctrine of 'Christian *perfection'. His theological works include six 'Checks to Antinomianism' (1771–5), which was occasioned by the disputes between the '*Arminians' and the '*Calvinists'. He also controverted the *Unitarian doctrines of J. *Priestley.

Collected works, 9 vols., London, 1800–4; 7 vols., ibid., 1826; and 2 vols., Shebbear, Devon, and London, 1835. Lives by J. Wesley (London, 1786) and J. Benson (ibid., 1805). L. Tyerman, *Wesley's Designated Successor* (1882). G. Lawton, *Shropshire Saint: A Study in the Ministry and Spirituality of Fletcher of Madeley* (1960). P. P. Streiff, *Jean Guillaume de la Fléchère, John William Fletcher, 1729–1785: Ein Beitrag zur Geschichte des Methodismus* (Basler und Berner Studien zur historischen und systematischen

Theologie, 51 [1984]). J. H. Overton in *DNB* 19 (1889), pp. 312–14.

Fleury (Lat. *Floriacum*). The place owed its celebrity to the (real or supposed) transference hither in the 7th cent. of the remains of Sts *Benedict and *Scholastica from *Monte Cassino after the Lombards had ravaged Italy, and the large monastery that was erected to house them. It is also known as Saint-Benoît-sur-Loire. Its most famous monk was *Abbo; the reign of his successor, Abbot Gauzlin (1004–30), was also a high point of its monastic and architectural history. Fleury played a considerable part in the monastic revival in England in the 10th cent. In 1790 the abbey was suppressed and most of the buildings demolished, the only part to survive being the magnificent Romanesque basilica, which became the parish church. In 1944 monks from the abbey of La Pierre-qui-Vire returned to Fleury, and a new abbey has been built.

M. Prou and A. Vidier (eds.), *Recueil des chartes de l'Abbaye de Saint-Benoît-sur-Loire* [up to 1245] (Documents publiés par la Société historique et archéologique du Gâtinais, 5–6; 1900–37). *Vita Gauzlini*, written by Andrew, a monk of Fleury who had made his profession under Gauzlin, ed., with Fr. tr., by R.-H. Bautier and G. Laboury (Sources d'histoire médiévale, 2; 1969). A. Vidier, *L'Historiographie à Saint-Benoît-sur-Loire et les miracles de saint Benoît* (posthumously pub., 1965). Various papers on Fleury in *Studia Monastica*, 21 (1979), an issue devoted to the Cult and Relics of St Benedict and St Scholastica; cf. *Il Sepolcro di San Benedetto*, 2 (Miscellanea Cassinese, 45; 1982), pp. 293–310. D. W. Rollason, 'The Miracles of St Benedict: A Window on Early Medieval France', in H. Mayr-Harting and R. I. Moore (eds.), *Studies in Medieval History presented to R. H. C. Davis* (1985), pp. 73–90. E. A. Lowe, *Codices Latini Antiquiores*, 6 (Oxford, 1953), pp. xviii–xxi. M. Mostert, *The Library of Fleury: A Provisional List of Manuscripts* (Middeleeuwse Studies en Bronnen, 3; Hilversum, 1989). L. H. Cottineau, OSB, *Répertoire topo-bibliographique des abbayes et prieurés* (Mâcon, 1935), cols. 2610–13, s.v. 'St-Benoît-sur-Loire', with extensive bibl. J. Laporte, OSB, in *DHGE* 17 (1971), cols. 441–76, s.v.

Fleury, Claude (1640–1723), ecclesiastical historian. Born in Paris, he was educated by the *Jesuits at the Collège de *Clermont. In 1658 he was called to the bar and practised there until 1667. In 1668 he met J. B. *Bossuet and under his influence took Holy Orders in 1669. In 1672 he was appointed tutor to the young Princes de Conti and in 1680 to the Duc de Vermandois (an illegitimate son of Louis XIV). From 1689 he acted, together with F. de S. de la M. *Fénelon, as tutor to Louis XIV's grandsons. He was given the Cistercian abbey of Loc-Dieu (in the region of Aveyron in S. France) *in *commendam in 1684. In connection with his teaching he composed a *Traité du choix et de la méthode des études* (1686; Eng. tr., 1695), with a chapter on the education of women. In 1694 he was elected a member of the French Academy. In the *Quietist controversy Fleury, as a friend of both opponents, tried to assess the theological errors without renouncing his loyalty to either, even though he somewhat favoured Fénelon's position. Bossuet, in the end, vouched for his orthodoxy. In 1706 he became Prior of Notre-Dame-d'Argenteuil, near Paris. After Louis XIV's death (1715), he was chosen confessor to the young Louis XV, as one who was 'neither *Jansenist nor *Molinist nor *Ultramontane, but Catholic'.

Fleury's chief work is his *Histoire ecclésiastique* (20 vols., 1691–1720), the first large-scale history of the Church, which is deservedly held in repute for its learning and judgement. He enlisted the help of the *Maurist historians J. *Mabillon and B. de *Montfaucon. Before his death Fleury had reached the year 1414; it was continued to 1778 by J. C. Fabre and others. It was censured for its *Gallican views, but Pope *Benedict XIV prevented its being put on the *Index in 1740. Fleury's ninth *Discours sur l'histoire ecclésiastique*, the *Discours sur les libertés de l'Église Gallicane* (1733), however, was put on the Index, as were some of his other works. Besides treatises on secular law, his other writings include *Institution du droit ecclésiastique* (1677), *Les Mœurs des Israélites* (1681), *Les Mœurs des Chrétiens* (1682; Eng. tr., 1698), and *Grand Catéchisme historique* (1683; Eng. tr., 1726).

Several collections of Fleury's sermons and treatises were issued posthumously, incl. *Discours* (2 vols., Paris, 1752) and *Opuscules* (5 vols., Nîmes, 1780). J. *Wesley incorporated an Eng. tr. of extracts from *Les Mœurs des chrétiens* in his 'Christian Library' (3rd edn., 1767). Eng. tr. of portions of the *Histoire ecclésiastique*, by J. H. *Newman (3 vols., 1842–44). F. Gaquère, *La Vie et les œuvres de Claude Fleury, 1640–1723* (Paris, 1925). R. E. Wanner, *Claude Fleury (1640–1723) as an Educational Historiographer and Thinker* (International Archives of the History of Ideas, 76; The Hague, 1975). A. Dodin in *Dict. Sp.* 5 (1964), cols. 412–19, s.v.; D. Gorce in *DHGE* 17 (1971), cols. 479–89, s.v. 'Fleury (3) Claude'.

Flight into Egypt, the. As recorded in Mt. 2: 13 f., St *Joseph and the BVM journeyed from *Bethlehem into Egypt, taking the infant Jesus out of danger from *Herod the Great after the visit of the *Magi. After Herod's death they returned to *Nazareth (Mt. 2: 23). A reflection of the career of *Moses is clear; any historical basis for the story is, however, often questioned.

Flood, the. Acc. to Gen. 6: 5–9: 17, God brought a 'flood of waters' upon the earth 'to destroy all flesh' (Gen. 6: 17), because of the wickedness of the human race; only *Noah and his family, with specimens of each species of animal life, were preserved in the *Ark to repeople the earth. Scholars who support the 'documentary hypothesis' of the origin of the *Pentateuch claim to discern within the biblical text a conflation of two sources, '*J' and '*P'. The account is related to Mesopotamian traditions of a great flood. There is a Sumerian flood story and allusions to this flood in the Sumerian King List (both on tablets of c.1900–1700 BC). The Babylonian Epic of Atra-hasīs offers the fullest account, in which the flood is the gods' answer to the problem of human noise after previous attempts to diminish their numbers had failed. It survives in incomplete copies dating from c.1650 to c.500 BC. No surviving copy contains the episode of the sending out of three birds from the Ark, which closely parallels Gen. 8: 6–12, but the flood story, including reference to the birds, is incorporated in the Babylonian *Gilgamesh Epic 11, and Berossus, a Babylonian priest c.300 BC, also summarizes it. There can be little question that the biblical version ultimately depends on a Babylonian source, and this no doubt drew on memories of exceptional floods in Sumer in the first half of the third millennium BC. Archaeological evidence of such floods has been found at several sites.

W. G. Lambert and A. R. Millard (eds.), *Atra-ḥasīs: The Baby-lonian Story of the Flood*, with *The Sumerian Flood Story*, ed. M. Civil (Oxford, 1969), incl. Eng. tr. On the material parallel to the Gen. account, also W. G. Lambert in *TRE* 5 (1980), pp. 67–79, s.v. 'Babylonien und Israel'. J. P. Lewis, *A Study of the Interpreta-tion of Noah and the Flood in Jewish and Christian Litera-ture* (Leiden, 1968), esp. pp. 42–120, 156–80. W. M. Clark, 'The Flood and the Structure of Pre-patriarchal History', *ZATW* 83 (1971), pp. 184–211; R. Oberforcher, *Die Flutprologe als Komposi-tionsschlüssel der biblischer Urgeschichte* (Innsbrucker theologische Studien, 8; 1981). J. P. Lewis in *Anchor Bible Dictionary*, 2 (1992), pp. 798–803, s.v. See also comm. on GENESIS, cited s.v., and bibl. to ARK and NOAH.

Florence, Council of (1438–45). This was a continua-tion of the Council at *Basle, which Pope *Eugenius IV transferred first to Ferrara in 1438, to Florence in 1439, and to Rome in 1443; the whole is reckoned by RCs as the 17th *Oecumenical Council. The chief object of the Coun-cil of Florence was reunion with the Greek Church, which sought support from the W. against the Turks, who were nearing *Constantinople. After a majority of the members assembled at Basle had refused to move to a place more convenient to the Greeks, Eugenius IV transferred the Council to Ferrara, where it opened on 8 Jan. 1438. Among its most distinguished members were the Greek Emperor, John VIII Palaeologus, and Joseph, Patr. of Con-stantinople. Its leading theologians included, on the Latin side, Card. J. *Cesarini and the *Dominican, John of Montenero; on the Greek the unionist *Bessarion, Metro-politan of Nicaea and later cardinal, and the anti-unionist Mark, Metropolitan of *Ephesus. The Council was form-ally inaugurated on 9 April, but delay caused by the Emperor led to the formation of a commission of 10 Latins and 10 Greeks to decide which were the principal points of controversy. These were the *Double Procession of the Holy Spirit, the use of unleavened *bread for the *Eucharist, the doctrine of *purgatory and the primacy of the Pope. The next two months were spent in informal discussion on purgatory. The first public session (on 8 Oct. 1438) debated, on the choice of the Greeks, the *Filioque clause as an addition to the Creed. The Greeks asserted that any addition to the Nicene Creed, even of a single word, whether it was doctrinally correct or not, was, according to the prohibition enacted at the Council of *Ephesus, illegal, and its perpetrators excommunicated. The Latins claimed that the prohibition referred to mean-ing, not words. Discussion, without agreement, continued in 13 sessions until 13 Dec., by which time the Papal exchequer was empty.

On 10 Jan. 1439 the Council was transferred to Flor-ence, the city having agreed, against future repayment, to finance it. From 2 to 24 Mar. in eight sessions it debated the Filioque clause as doctrine—whether the Holy Spirit proceeds from the Father only, acc. to the Greeks, or from the Father and the Son, acc. to the Latins—without agree-ment. Public sessions having thus failed, various expedi-ents were tried to lead to union, in the course of which Bessarion addressed to the Greek synod his 'Oratio Dog-matica', urging that the Double Procession was taught more or less explicitly by both Greek and Latin Fathers. The Latins gave the Greeks a precisely worded statement of doctrine, which the Greeks modified, and then would not clarify the resulting ambiguities. In the prevailing

atmosphere of defeat, as a last resort, on 27 May the Pope addressed the Greeks. Thereupon the unionists among the Greeks urged with renewed energy what to all Greeks was axiomatic, that saints cannot err in faith, so that, though Latin saints and Greek saints expressed their faith differ-ently, substantially they were in agreement. The argument prevailed. By 8 June the Greeks had accepted the Latin statement of doctrine. On 10 June Patriarch Joseph died. Statements on the Eucharist and on Papal primacy, which caused some difficulty, on purgatory and on the legitimacy of the Filioque clause were presented to the Greeks and eventually accepted. These were incorporated into the Decree of Union, beginning with the words '*Laetentur Coeli', which was eventually signed on 5 July 1439 and solemnly promulgated the following day. Mark of Ephesus was the only Greek bishop to refuse his signature.

After the departure of the Greeks the Council remained in session to deal with the continuing Council of Basle and the union with other E. Churches. All members of the Council of Basle were declared heretics and excommunic-ated, and the superiority of the Pope over the Councils was affirmed in the bull 'Etsi non dubitemus' of 20 Apr. 1441. Union was established with the *Armenians in 1439 and with the *Copts of Egypt in 1442. In 1443 the Council was transferred to Rome. Little is known of its further activities, except that unions were effected with several other E. Churches, such as the *Syrians (1444) and certain *Chaldeans and *Maronites of Cyprus. There is no record of any official closing of the Council.

The union of the Greeks was challenged by popular sentiment in Constantinople, and many of the older bishops recanted. Mark of Ephesus throughout remained against the union, though Bessarion and other of the younger prelates continued in favour. Constantinople was captured by the Turks in 1453 and the union ceased. That with Armenia lasted until the fall of Caffa to the Turks in 1475. Exact information about the other unions is lacking.

The importance of the Council of Florence lies in its definition of doctrine and in the principle it established for Church union—unity of faith with diversity of rite—a principle followed in several subsequent unions and still valid.

Hardouin, 9, cols. 1–1080; Mansi, 31 (1798), cols. 459–1120, and in suppl. to vol. 31 (1801), cols. 1121–998. Crit. edn. of relev-ant material in *Concilium Florentinum: Documenta et Scriptores. Editum consilio et impensis Pontificii Instituti Orientalium Studiorum* (11 vols., Rome, 1940–77, esp. vol. 5, the *Acta Graeca*, ed. with Lat. tr. by J. Gill, SJ (1953), and vol. 6, the *Acta Latina*, ed. G. Hofmann, SJ (1955)). Text of decrees, with Eng. tr., in Tanner, *Decrees* (1990), pp. 513–91, with introd., pp. 453 f. Eng. tr. of various primary docs. in C. M. D. Crowder, *Unity, Heresy and Reform 1378–1460: The Conciliar Response to the Great Schism* (1977), pp. 165–81. E. Cecconi, *Studi storici sul concilio di Firenze* (Naples, 1869, with docs.). Hefele and Leclercq, 7 (pt. 2; 1916), pp. 951–1106. G. Hofmann, SJ, *Papato, conciliarismo, patriarcato, 1438–1439: Teologi e deliberazioni del Concilio di Firenze* (Miscellanea Historiae Pontificiae edita a Facultate Historiae Ecclesiasticae in Pontificia Universitate Gregoriana, 2 (pt. 1; col-lectionis totius n. 2; 1940)). J. Gill, SJ, *The Council of Florence* (Cambridge, 1959); id., *Personalities of the Council of Florence* (Oxford, 1964). J. Décarreaux, *Les Grecs au Concile de l'Union, Ferrare-Florence 1438–1439* [1970]. J. M. Hussey, *The Orthodox Church in the Byzantine Empire* (Oxford History of the Christian Church, 1986), pp. 267–86. G. Alberigo (ed.), *Christian Unity: The Council of Ferrara-Florence 1438/39–1989* (Bibliotheca

Ephemeridum Theologicarum Lovaniensium, 97; 1991). P. De Vooght, OSB, in *DHGE* 17 (1971), cols. 561–8, s.v. J. Gill, SJ, in *TRE* 5 (1980), pp. 289–96, s.v. 'Basel-Ferrara-Florenz, Konzil von. II. Das Konzil von Florenz', both with bibl. See also bibl. to BASLE, COUNCIL OF and EUGENIUS IV.

Florentius Radewijns (1350–1400). One of the earliest members of the *Brethren of the Common Life. He belonged to the group which had come under the influence of G. *Groote, and on Groote's death in 1384 became the head of the community which he had founded at Deventer in the Netherlands. His house here was the first settled establishment of the Brethren, who seem previously not to have lived under a common roof. Under his influence the monastery at *Windesheim was founded in 1387.

The principal authority is the Life by *Thomas à Kempis, pr. among the latter's works (Nuremberg, 1494, fol. 38ʳ–fol. 44ʳ, and in all later edns.); Eng. tr. by J. P. Arthur, *The Founders of the New Devotion* (1905), pp. 81–162. A. Hyma, *The 'Devotio Moderna' or Christian Renaissance* (Grand Rapids, Mich. [1925]), esp. pp. 49–58, virtually repr. in his *The Brethren of the Common Life* (ibid., 1950), pp. 55–63; R. R. Post, *The Modern Devotion* (Studies in Medieval and Reformation Thought, 3; Leiden, 1968), esp. pp. 317–25. M. van Woerkum, SCJ, 'Florentius Radewijns: Leven, Geschriften, Persoonlijkheid en Ideeën', *Ons Geestelijk Erf*, 24 (1950), pp. 337–64. Id. in *Dict. Sp.* 5 (1964), cols. 427–34, s.v. 'Florent (4) Radewijns'; G. Epiney-Burgard in *Verfasserlexikon* (2nd edn.), 7 (1989), cols. 967–72, s.v. 'Radewijns, Florens'. See also other works cited under BRETHREN OF THE COMMON LIFE; DEVOTIO MODERNA; GROOTE, G.; and WINDESHEIM.

florilegium (Lat. *flos*, 'a flower', and *lego*, 'I gather', by extension 'I read'). A collection of selected passages from the writings of previous authors. Special interest attaches to the Greek *patristic florilegia. Besides those composed of excerpts from commentaries on the Bible and known as *catenae, a considerable number of dogmatic florilegia compiled from the 5th cent. onwards have survived. Such collections of passages (χρήσεις) were often drawn up to establish the orthodoxy or heterodoxy of individual theologians, and many became incorporated into the *Acta* of the ecclesiastical councils. For the historian they are often of much value, esp. when they preserve passages from works of which the bulk has been lost. A patristic florilegium of a non-dogmatic kind is the collection of extracts made by *Gregory of Nazianzus and *Basil of Caesarea from the writings of *Origen and known as the *'Philocalia'.

Latin florilegia are well established from the 5th cent. onwards. Their material is patristic, later supplemented by excerpts from Carolingian authors such as Haymo of Auxerre (d. *c*.865), and later still by excerpts from major 12th-cent. writers such as *Hugh of St-Victor and St *Bernard. The early florilegia were dogmatic and ascetic, as, for example, the Augustinian florilegium by *Prosper of Aquitaine and the widely known ascetic florilegium by *Defensor of Ligugé. In the later Middle Ages florilegia became preaching tools, a notable example, well organized and indexed, being the *Manipulus Florum* of Thomas of Ireland (d. before 1338).

Among the more important dogmatic florilegia are the 'Doctrina Patrum de Incarnatione Verbi' (preserved in MSS Vat. gr. 2200, Bodl. Misc. 184, etc.; ed. F. Diekamp, Münster i.W., 1907; 2nd edn. by B. Phanourgakis and E. Chrysos, ibid., 1981) and the 'Anti-Chalcedonian Collection in Vat. gr. 1431' (ed. E.

*Schwartz, *Abh.* (Bayr.), 32, Heft 6, 1927; with valuable discussion of florilegia generally). M. Richard, 'Notes sur les Florilèges dogmatiques du Vᵉ et du VIᵉ siècle', in *Actes du VIᵉ Congrès International d'Études Byzantines*, 1 (1950), pp. 307–18; id., 'Les Florilèges diphysites du Vᵉ et du VIᵉ siècle', in A. Grillmeier, SJ, and H. Bacht, SJ (eds.), *Das Konzil von Chalkedon*, 1 (Würzburg [1951]), pp. 721–48; R. H. and M. A. Rouse, *Preachers, Florilegia and Sermons: Studies on the Manipulus florum of Thomas of Ireland* (Studies and Texts, 47; Toronto, 1979). Krumbacher, pp. 206–18. M. *Grabmann, *Die Geschichte der scholastischen Methode*, 1 (1909), pp. 114–16 and 183–8; J. de Ghellinck, SJ, *Patristique et Moyen-Age*, 2 (1947), pp. 289–98. H. M. Rochais, P. Delhaye, and M. Richard in *Dict. Sp.* 5 (1964), cols. 435–512, s.v. 'Florilèges spirituels'; H. M. Rochais in *NCE* 5 (1967), pp. 979 f.; H. Chadwick in *RAC* 7 (1969), cols. 1131–60; esp. cols. 1143–60; E. Mühlenberg and F. Brunhölzl in *TRE* 11 (1983), pp. 215–21, all s.v., with bibl.

Florovsky, George (1893–1979), Russian theologian. The son of a Russian priest, he graduated in arts at Odessa University (1916), subsequently lecturing there in philosophy (1919–1920). Leaving Russia in 1920, he went first to Sofia and then to Prague, where he was made lecturer in the faculty of law (1922–6). In 1926 he became Professor of Patristics at the Orthodox Theological Institute of St Sergius in Paris, and later Professor of Dogmatics. He was ordained priest in 1932. Moving to the USA in 1948, he became successively Professor and Dean at St Vladimir's Russian Orthodox Seminary, New York (1948–55), Professor of Eastern Church History at Harvard Divinity School (1956–64), and Visiting Professor at Princeton University (from 1964). He wrote extensively on the Greek Fathers (mainly in Russian), urging the necessity for a 'neo-Patristic synthesis', and he published an elaborate study of Russian religious thought, *Ways of Russian Theology* (in Russian, Paris, 1937; Eng. tr. in *Collected Works*, 5–6). He played a leading part in the *Ecumenical Movement, from 1937 serving regularly as a delegate at assemblies of the *Faith and Order movement and of the *World Council of Churches.

Collected Works [in Eng.], after his death ed. R. S. Haugh, vols. 1–5 (incomplete, Belmont, Mass., 1972–9); complete edn., incorporating reissue of earlier edn. (14 vols. + index, ibid., 1987 ff.). D. Neiman and M. Schatkin (eds.), *The Heritage of the Early Church: Essays in honor of . . . Georges Vasilievich Florovsky* (Orientalia Christiana Analecta, 195; Rome, 1973), with list of his works, pp. 437–51. G. H. Williams, 'Georges Vasilievich Florovsky: his American career (1948–1965)', *The Greek Orthodox Theological Review*, 11 (1965), pp. 7–107. Y. N. Lelouvier, *Perspectives russes sur l'Église: Un théologien contemporain, Georges Florovsky* (1968). C. Künkel, *Totus Christus: Die Theologie Georges V. Florovskys* (Forschungen zur systematischen und ökumenischen Theologie, 62 [1991]).

Florus (d. *c*.860), deacon of Lyons. Little is known of his life, but he was prob. born in the region of Lyons. He served successive Abps. of Lyons, *Agobard, Amolo, and Remigius, and was a canon of the cathedral church. His works on canon law, liturgy, and theology, which he appears never to have signed, were written in their service. When *Amalarius was made administrator of the see of Lyons and tried to make changes in the liturgy, Florus attacked him in a series of works, one of which, the 'Expositio Missae', continued to be read. He took part in the controversy on predestination, defending *Gottschalk and attacking Johannes Scottus *Erigena. He was deeply versed in patristic writings, and the manuscripts at Lyons contain many traces of his editorial work. He compiled various Expositions on the Pauline Epistles, based on the writings of different Fathers; the one based on works of St *Augustine circulated widely under the name of *Bede.

Works collected in J. P. Migne, *PL* 119. 11–424, incl. analysis (only) of the Exposition based on Augustine; the text is pr among the works of Bede (e.g. *Bedae Opera*, 6 (Cologne, 1688), cols. 31–823). Presentation of other Expositions on the Pauline Epistles attributed to Florus, by P.-I. Fransen, OSB, in *R. Bén.* 87 (1977), pp. 349–71 (extracts from St *Ephraem); 94 (1984), pp. 195–228 (St *Jerome); 98 (1988), pp. 278–317 (St *Gregory the Great); and of a collection of patristic and conciliar excerpts 'De fide' by C. Charlier, OSB, in *Traditio*, 8 (1952), pp. 81–109. Crit. edn. of the 'Expositio Missae' by P. Duc, *Étude sur l'Expositio Missae de Florus de Lyon* (Belley, 1937). Martyrology ed. J. Dubois, OSB, and G. Renaud, *Édition pratique des martyrologes de Bède, de l'anonyme lyonnais et de Florus* (1976). Three letters ed. E. Duemmler in *MGH*, Epistolae, 5 (1899), pp. 206–10, 267–74, and 340–3. Crit. edn. of his verse by id. in *MGH*, Poetae, 2 (1884), pp. 509–66, and by K. Strecker, ibid. 4 (1923), pp. 930 f. C. Charlier, OSB, 'Les Manuscrits personnels de Florus de Lyon et son activité littéraire', in *Mélanges E. Podechard* (Lyons, 1945), pp 71–84; id., 'La Compilation augustinienne de Florus sur l'Apôtre. Sources et authenticité', *R. Bén.* 57 (1947), pp. 132–67. A. Cabaniss, 'Florus of Lyons', *Classica et Mediaevalia*, 19 (1958), pp. 212–32. C. Charlier in *Dict. Sp.* 5 (1964), cols. 514–26, s.v.; M. Cappuyns, OSB, in *DHGE* 17 (1971), cols. 648–54, s.v. 'Florus (6) de Lyon'.

Flüe, Nikolaus von. See NICHOLAS OF FLÜE.

Focolare, the (Ital., 'hearth'). A lay movement, predominantly RC, but with ecumenical membership and aspirations. Officially styled 'Opera di Maria' ('Work of Mary'), it was founded during the Second World War by Chiara Lubich (b. 1920) in Trent, N. Italy, when the city was under bombardment; it dates its foundation to 7 Dec. 1943. It received papal approval from *John XXIII in 1962 and its statutes were sanctioned by *John Paul II in 1990. The Focolare includes both celibate and married people, as well as children, priests, and religious. It sees its spirituality as containing the whole Gospel, interpreted from the angle of Christ's prayer 'May they all be one' (Jn. 17: 21) and works to this end through dialogue between the Churches, with other religions, and with contemporary culture. It is active in almost every country, with members from most Christian denominations, as well as people of other faiths and non-believers. It has its own publishing houses, training centres, and small townships. In 1977 Chiara Lubich was awarded the Templeton Prize for progress in Religion.

L'Unità è la nostra avventura: Il movimento dei Focolari [ed. S. Veronesi and others] (Rome, 1986; Eng. tr., Brooklyn, NY [1987]). E. [H.] Robertson, *Chiara* ([Belfast] 1978); id., *The Fire of Love: A Life of Igino Giordani 'Foco'* (1989), esp. pp. 157–251.

folded chasuble. A form of the *chasuble pinned up in front (*planeta plicata*) formerly worn in the W. Church by the *deacon and *subdeacon at *High Mass in penitential seasons. Its use at a normal High Mass was dropped in 1960, though it survived at *Ordinations until 1968. The so-called *broad stole worn by the deacon at the reading

of the Gospel is in origin also a 'folded chasuble', but folded in another way.

Braun, *LG*, pp. 166–9 ('Anlegungsweise der Kasel bei den Diakonen, Subdiakonen und Akolythen. Die Planeta Plicata').

Foliot, Gilbert (*c.*1110–87), Bp. of London. Born into the lower ranks of the English aristocracy, he was a clerk and a pupil of Robert *Pullen, perhaps at Oxford. Before 1130 he became a monk at *Cluny. On account of the respect inspired by his austerity, learning, and social connections, his rise was swift; he became one of the claustral priors of Cluny, Prior of Abbeville, and in 1139 Abbot of *Gloucester. King Stephen appointed him to the abbacy, prob. at the instigation of Miles, castellan of Gloucester, Foliot's cousin. Gradually he came to play an important, although usually controversial, part in ecclesiastical and political affairs. A friend of *Theobald, Abp. of *Canterbury, he was elected Bp. of *Hereford at the Council of Reims (1148) through Angevin influence, but he made his peace with Stephen. A disappointed candidate for the Archbishopric of Canterbury in 1162, with Thomas *Becket's support he was translated to London in 1163. When Henry II quarrelled with Becket in Oct. 1163, Foliot supported the King, esp. at Becket's trial at Northampton (Oct. 1164) and became one of the Archbishop's greatest enemies, refusing to repeat the profession of obedience to Canterbury which he had already made in 1148, advancing London's claim to metropolitan status, and orchestrating the royalist bishops' opposition to the 'traitor'. After Becket's flight into exile (Nov. 1164), in his capacity as Dean of the Province of Canterbury, Foliot operated as its acting-head until Becket excommunicated him for recalcitrance on Palm Sunday 1169. On his appeal to Rome, the Pope empowered the Bp. of *Exeter and the Abp. of Rouen to absolve him (Easter 1170). On 29 Nov., however, on the authority of Papal letters dated 16 Sept., Becket reanimated the excommunication, now reinforced by suspension, because Foliot had taken part in the coronation of the King's son on 14 June in derogation of the rights of the Church of Canterbury. When Becket on his return to England refused to absolve him, Foliot crossed to the King's court in Normandy and took part in the discussions which led to Becket's murder. After successfully purging himself of complicity, he was released from excommunication on 1 Aug. 1171 and from suspension on 1 May 1172. Thereafter he resumed a leading position in the English Church. Among his theological works are commentaries on the Lord's Prayer and on the Song of Songs. Many of his letters and *acta* have survived.

The Letters and Charters of Gilbert Foliot, Abbot of Gloucester (1139–48), Bishop of Hereford (1148–63) and London (1163–87). An edn. projected by Z. N. Brooke, completed by [S.] A. Morey, OSB, and C. N. L. Brooke (Cambridge, 1967); earlier edn. of letters repr. in J. P. Migne, *PL* 190. 739–1068, index, 1500–6. 'Expositio in Cantica Canticorum', ed. P. Young (London, 1638), repr. in J. P. Migne, *PL* 202. 1147–304. [S.] A. Morey, OSB, and C. N. L. Brooke, *Gilbert Foliot and his Letters* (Cambridge Studies in Medieval Life and Thought, NS 11; 1965). [M.] D. *Knowles, *The Episcopal Colleagues of Archbishop Thomas Becket* (Ford Lectures for 1949, 1951), esp. pp. 37–49. G. G. Perry in *DNB* 19 (1889), pp. 358–60.

Folkestone Ritual Case. See RIDSDALE JUDGEMENT.

font (Lat. *fons*, 'spring of water'). Receptacle for baptismal water, normally made of stone, more rarely of metal. In early times, when adult Baptism by immersion was the rule, it was a large basin below ground-level in which the neophyte stood while the water was poured over him. When infant Baptism came to be the norm, the font, still rather large, was raised slightly above the ground so that the child could conveniently be immersed by the minister. Later still, when *affusion became the prevalent form of Baptism in the West, fonts became smaller and higher, being frequently richly ornamented, and gradually took on their present cup shape. They also came to be covered by a lid that was sometimes locked to preserve the purity of the baptismal water and to guard it from profanation. In some churches the font stands either in a separate chapel (*baptistery) or is railed off in a locked enclosure. The 1969 (RC) *Ordo Baptismi* lays down that the font may be in any convenient part of the church to allow the congregation to assemble for Baptisms. In the Orthodox Church it is now customary to employ a portable font, made of metal and kept in the sacristy when not in use.

F. Simpson, *A Series of Ancient Baptismal Fonts Chronologically Arranged* (1828); [T. Combe], *Illustrations of Baptismal Fonts* (1844), with introd. by F. A. Paley. F. Bond, *Fonts and Font Covers* (1908); C. J. Wall, *Porches and Fonts* (1912), pp. 175–338; E. Tyrrell-Green, *Baptismal Fonts* (1928); G. Pudelko, *Romanische Taufsteine* (1932); G. Zarnecki, *English Romanesque Lead Sculpture: Lead Fonts of the twelfth century* (1957). J. G. Davies, *The Architectural Setting of Baptism* (1962). H. *Leclercq, OSB, in *DACL* 14 (pt. 1, 1939), cols. 1080–119, s.v. 'Piscine'.

Fontevrault, Order of. A 'double order' of monks and nuns, living under the rule of one abbess, though in separate convents. In 1100 Bl Robert d'Arbrissel (d. 1116) founded an abbey at Fontevrault, SE of Saumur in France, on the basis of the *Benedictine Rule, with certain more rigorous additions, and in *c*.1115 gave it a constitution with Petronilla as its first abbess. Dependent houses were soon established in many parts of France, and a few in England and Spain. In the 13th cent. the Order was very poor, but considerably prospered in the 14th, and after a period of decadence in the 15th was reformed by successive abbesses between 1475 and 1502. It disappeared in the Revolution of 1789, but was revived as an order for women only by Mme Rose in 1806, certain modifications being then made to the original Rule.

[H. Nicquet, SJ], *Histoire de l'ordre de Fontevrault* (Angers, 1586; Paris, 1642). Edouard [pseudonym of A. Biron], *Fontevrault et ses monuments ou histoire de cette royale abbaye depuis sa fondation jusqu'à sa suppression, 1100–1793* (2 vols., 1873–4); L. F. Bossebœuf, *Fontevrault: Son histoire et ses monuments* (Tours [1890]). *Histoire de l'ordre de Fontevrault, 1100–1908*, by the Religious of Sainte-Marie-de-Fontevrault-de-Boulaur now located in Vera in Navarre (3 vols., Auch, 1911–15). L. A. Picard, *L'Ordre de Fontevrault de 1115 à 1207* (Saumur [1933]). S. Poignant, *L'Abbaye de Fontevrault et les filles de Louis XV* (1966). J. Dalarun, *L'Impossible Sainteté: La vie retrouvée de Robert d'Arbrissel (v.1045–1116), fondateur de Fontevraud* (1985); id., *Robert d'Arbrissel, fondateur de Fontevraud* (1986). J. Daoust in *DHGE* 17 (1971), cols. 961–71, s.v.; J.-M. Bienvenu in *Dict. Sp.* 13 (1988), cols. 704–13, s.v. 'Robert (2) d'Arbrissel', both with bibl.

fool in Christ. See SALOS.

Fools, Feast of. A mock religious festival which was widely celebrated in the Middle Ages on or about 1 Jan., esp. in France. It may have grown out of a 'festival of the *subdeacons', sometimes kept on 1 Jan. The feast was an occasion of much buffoonery and extravagance, often approaching the blasphemous, and several ecclesiastical reformers (e.g. R. *Grosseteste, Bp. of Lincoln) made attempts to suppress it. In 1435 very severe penalties were imposed by the Council of *Basle for its observance, and it seems to have finally disappeared in the middle of the 16th cent. See also MISRULE, LORD OF; BOY BISHOP; ASSES, FEAST OF.

E. K. Chambers, *The Mediaeval Stage* (1903), 1, pp. 274–335; J. Heers, *Fêtes des fous et Carnavals* [1983], esp. pp. 105–89. H. Thurston, SJ, in *CE* 6 (1909), pp. 132 f., s.v.

foot-pace. See PREDELLA.

foot-washing. See PEDILAVIUM.

Forbes, Alexander Penrose (1817–75), Bp. of Brechin, the 'Scottish Pusey'. Originally in the East India Company, he entered Brasenose College, Oxford, in 1840. Here he came under the influence of the *Oxford Movement, gave up his intention of returning to India and decided to be ordained. On the nomination of E. B. *Pusey, he became Vicar of St Saviour's, Leeds, in 1847, but a few months later he was elected Bp. of Brechin, where he remained for the rest of his life and laboured to further Tractarian principles in Scotland. His defence of the doctrine of the Real Presence in his primary charge, delivered on 5 Aug. 1857, led to his censure in 1860 by the college of bishops. Later he became keenly interested in the cause of the *Old Catholics. A close friend of R. M. *Benson, he took a particular interest in the foundation of the *Society of St John the Evangelist. His writings, mainly practical, but with a sound scholarly (esp. *patristic) basis, included *A Commentary on the Seven Penitential Psalms* (1847), *A Short Explanation of the *Nicene Creed* (1852; 2nd edn., much enlarged, 1866), a translation of Part I of Claude Arvisenet's *Memoriale Vitae Sacerdotalis* (1853), and *An Explanation of the Thirty-Nine Articles* (2 vols., 1867–8; written at Pusey's suggestion). He also published, partly in conjunction with his brother (see following entry), several liturgical and hagiographical texts.

D. J. Mackey, *Bishop Forbes: A Memoir* (1888); W. Perry, *A. P. Forbes* (1939); R. Strong, *Alexander Forbes of Brechin: The First Tractarian Bishop* (Oxford, 1995). M. [C.] Lochhead, *Episcopal Scotland in the Nineteenth Century* [1966], pp. 106–38. A. Vian in *DNB* 19 (1889), pp. 378 f.

Forbes, George Hay (1821–75), *patristic scholar. Brother of the preceding, he was hampered throughout his life by severe paralysis of the legs. At an early age he developed keen liturgical interests, while his High Church beliefs brought him into relation with the *Tractarians. In 1848, despite his infirmity, he was ordained deacon by Patrick Torry, Bp. of St Andrews (1844–52), and in the same year started an Episcopal mission at Burntisland. Ordained priest by his brother in 1849, he worked as a model pastor, building a church at Burntisland and setting up his own printing press. The liturgical texts which he edited, mostly from his own press, included *The Ancient Liturgies of the Gallican Church* (with J. M. *Neale, 3 parts,

1855–67) and the *Arbuthnott Missal (with A. P. *Forbes, 1864). The edition of the *Sarum Missal, by F. H. Dickinson, published at Burntisland in 1861–83, also embodied much of his work. All his publications reflected his meticulous accuracy, and he was described by E. *Bishop as 'facile princeps among those who have dealt with Western Liturgy in the last century'.

W. Perry, *George Hay Forbes: A Romance in Scholarship* (1927). M. [C.] Lochhead, *Episcopal Scotland in the Nineteenth Century* [1966], pp. 154–60.

Forbes, William (1585–1634), first Bp. of Edinburgh. A native of Aberdeen, he was educated at Marischal College in the town, where he was for a time professor of logic. After holding various offices, he was appointed by *Charles I Bp. of Edinburgh in 1634, but died two months later. He is remembered esp. for his erudite *Considerationes modestae et pacificae controversiarum de Justificatione, Purgatorio, Invocatione Sanctorum, Christo Mediatore et Eucharistia*, published posthumously in 1658. It shows Forbes as a strong *High Churchman, keen on reconciliation with Rome and zealous for episcopacy. In his treatment of the *Eucharist he defended a doctrine of the Real Presence; and though he criticized the doctrine of *transubstantiation, he denied that it was heretical. He also held that the Eucharist was a propitiatory sacrifice.

The *Considerationes Modestae* were reissued, with Eng. tr., by G. H. *Forbes (LACT, 2 vols., 1850–6).

Forged Decretals. See FALSE DECRETALS.

Form. The word 'form', taken literally, is synonymous with 'shape', but it is used by philosophers in a wider sense. For *Plato a form (εἶδος or ἰδέα) was an eternal transcendent prototype which acted as a pattern for each sort of earthly reality. *Aristotle held that forms existed only within things themselves, making them what they are and (in living things) controlling their development. St *Augustine followed Plato, but, like many other Christians, he adopted the Middle *Platonic understanding of the forms as thoughts of the divine mind which find expression in created reality. In the Middle Ages Aristotle's distinction of form and matter was revived and given a much extended use.

Medieval thinkers distinguished several kinds of 'forms', the more important being: (1) 'substantial forms', which are the principles determining prime matter to a particular nature, e.g. man or horse; (2) 'accidental forms', which determine substances to some accidental mode of being, e.g. whiteness or greatness; (3) 'separated forms', which exist apart from matter, thus the angels and human souls after death. Acc. to St *Thomas Aquinas there can be only one substantial form for every being, whereas the Franciscan school admits several. The concept of the substantial form was used in the question of the relations between soul and body. Acc. to the Thomist teaching, approved by the Council of *Vienne in 1312 and the Fifth *Lateran Council in 1513, the rational soul is the form of the human body which gives it its human condition. The idea that reality is constituted by form and matter (*hylomorphism) was also employed in connection with the theology of the *Sacraments. The form was held to consist of the words which give significance to the sacra-

mental use to which the matter was put. Thus in Baptism the matter of the sacrament was water, whereas its form consisted of the Trinitarian formula employed.

The notion of form has continued to play an important role. G. W. *Leibniz saw forms as part of reality; his 'monads' were a kind of pure form. I. *Kant used the word 'form' in a subjective sense independent of the Platonic tradition, to denote the basic characteristics of human experience. He therefore distinguished between the two forms of perception (*Anschauungsformen*), i.e. space and time, and the forms of thought (*Verstandesformen*) arranged in 12 'categories' of unity, plurality, totality, etc., which are valid *a priori*. G. W. F. *Hegel saw the forms of being as controlled by a single form-giving principle, the Absolute Idea. In E. Husserl's (1859–1935) *Phenomenology, the form is understood neither metaphysically nor subjectively, but is grasped by the perceiving subject. Modern *Existentialism tends to depreciate the notion of form as a purely human convention which impairs our freedom.

formalism. The word is used in religious contexts in at least three senses. (1) Undue insistence on the outward observances of religion or the prescriptions of a moral code, with a corresponding neglect of the inner spirit or significance which the 'forms' were designed to safeguard. (2) In the 17th cent. the word was used of readiness to support the religious body or party in power at the moment, i.e. for religious time-serving. This sense is now obsolete. (3) Of theories of ethics which look for the ground of moral action in the form of the moral law alone (e.g. in the '*Categorical Imperative' of I. *Kant), without reference to any specific purposes or values which it is desired through the action to achieve or realize. An elaborate criticism of the Kantian form of this doctrine is contained in Max Scheler's *Der Formalismus in der Ethik und die materiale Wertethik* (1913–16).

formal sin. A sinful act which is both in itself wrong and known by the person committing it to be wrong. See also MATERIAL SIN.

Form Criticism (Ger. *Formgeschichte*). As applied esp. to the Bible, the attempt to discover the origin and trace the history of particular passages by analysis of their structural forms. It entails three distinct processes: (1) the analysis of the material into the separate units, the form of each of which is held to have been gradually fixed in the process of transmission from mouth to mouth; (2) the recovery of the earlier history of these forms; and (3) the ascertainment of the historical setting which determined the various forms.

The method was first applied by H. *Gunkel to the narratives of Gen. (1901) and extended by H. Gressmann to the narratives about *Moses (1903) and the other Books of the *Pentateuch. Gunkel's principal application of Form Criticism, however, was in the study of the Psalms; he concluded that Hebrew religious poetry had a long history, that its forms had taken shape in oral tradition at a comparatively early date and had become fully developed before the Exile (*c.*586 BC). So fruitful was the technique that it has since been widely applied to the rest of the OT.

The most notable use of Form Criticism has been upon the oral traditions behind the *Synoptic Gospels. J. *Weiss pointed the way in his article in *Religion in Geschichte und Gegenwart* (1st edn., 1912) and in 1919 M. *Dibelius published his analysis of the Gospels into various literary forms, assigning them to preachers, teachers, and narrators, and assuming that the earliest original form to which we can get back is the short sermon, such as we find in Acts. A little later, R. *Bultmann (1921) produced a still more detailed analysis, while M. Albertz (1921) argued that the Gospel discourses were in part modified by early 'community debates', and G. Bertram (1922) that the form of the narrative of Christ's Passion (which most Form-Critics regard as much more primitive than the rest of the Gospel) was influenced by the liturgical needs and practices of the early Church. The main classes of form which emerge are: (1) *Paradigms (i.e. models for preachers) or *Apophthegms. These are short stories culminating in a saying of Jesus, such as that of the Tribute Money (Mk. 12: 13–17); (2) *Miracle Stories*; (3) *Sayings*; and (4) *Historical Narratives* and *Legends* (i.e. narrative material). It is widely agreed that the needs of the Church helped to preserve and mould the traditions about Jesus; more controversial is the claim that they were created in this context or that their use in the Church can be inferred from their literary form (*Sitz im Leben).

In so far as the method has been applied to the remaining books of the NT, attention has tended to be concentrated on the identification of catechetical material and liturgical formulae, such as 'baptismal' phrases, and lists of virtues and vices. It is held that the isolation of these categories of material behind the NT Epistles throws light on the life of the early Church, and in particular that it may be used to explain the parallels between various Epistles without supposing their authors to have been dependent on one another.

M. Dibelius, *Die Formgeschichte des Evangeliums* (1919; 3rd edn., 1959; Eng. tr., *From Tradition to Gospel*, 1934); R. Bultmann, *Die Geschichte der synoptischen Tradition* (1921; 2nd edn., 1931; Eng. tr., 1963); V. Taylor, *The Formation of the Gospel Tradition* (1933); R. H. *Lightfoot, *History and Interpretation in the Gospels* (1935); P. Carrington, *The Primitive Christian Catechism: A Study in the Epistles* (Cambridge, 1940); E. G. Selwyn, *The First Epistle of St Peter* (1946), pp. 363–466; B. Gerhardsson, *Memory and Manuscript: Oral Tradition and Written Transmission in Rabbinic Judaism and Early Christianity* (Acta Seminarii Neotestamentici Upsalensis, 22; 1961); id., *Evangeliernas Förhistoria* (Lund, 1977; Eng. tr., *The Origins of the Traditions*, 1979); K. Koch, *Was ist Formgeschichte? Neue Wege der Bibelexegese* (Neukirchen, 1964; 2nd edn., 1967; Eng. tr., 1969); E. Güttgemanns, *Offene Fragen zur Formgeschichte des Evangeliums* (Beiträge zur evangelischen Theologie, Theologische Abhandlungen, 54; 1970; Eng. tr., *Candid Questions concerning Gospel Form Criticism*, Pittsburgh, 1979); G. M. Tucker, *Form Criticism of the Old Testament* (Philadelphia [1971]); J. H. Hayes (ed.), *Old Testament Form Criticism* (Trinity University Monograph Series in Religion, 2; San Antonio, Tex. [1974]); W. H. Kelber, *The Oral and Written Gospel* (Philadelphia [1983]); J. Barton, *Reading the Old Testament: Method in Biblical Study* (1984), pp. 30–44; K. Berger, *Formgeschichte des Neuen Testaments* (Heidelberg, 1984). J. Barton and V. K. Robbins in *Anchor Bible Dictionary*, 2 (1992), pp. 938–44, s.v.

Formgeschichte. See FORM CRITICISM.

Formosus (*c.*816–96), Pope from 891. He became Cardinal-Bp. of Porto in 864, and was employed by successive Popes on several diplomatic missions. As Pope he acted constructively towards the E. Church, in 892 proposing a compromise solution to the vexed question of *Photius' ordinations. After his death the party opposed to him in Imperial politics charged him with usurpation of the Holy See, and a synod convened by Pope Stephen VI (896–7) in Jan. 897 exhumed, stripped, and mutilated his body, and declared him deposed. Succeeding Popes, however, reversed the decisions of this synod.

His Letters (8) in J. P. Migne, *PL* 129. 837–48; crit. edn. of four letters by G. Laehr in *MGH*, Epistulae, 7 (1928), pp. 366–70. Hefele and Leclercq, 4 (2; 1911), pp. 708–19, with bibl. J. Duhr, 'Le Concile de Ravenne en 898. La Réhabilitation du Pape Formose', *Rech. S.R.* 22 (1932), pp. 541–79; id., 'Humble Vestige d'un grand espoir déçu. Épisode de la vie de Formose', ibid. 42 (1954), pp. 361–87. Fliche and Martin, 7 (1940), pp. 20–6, 113 f. F. Vernet in *DTC* 6 (1920), cols. 594–9, with suppl. bibl. by P. Viard in *DHGE* 17 (1971), cols. 1093 f.; J. N. D. Kelly, *The Oxford Dictionary of Popes* (1986), pp. 114 f.

Formula Missae et Communionis. The reformed Communion Service, prepared for N. Hausmann, Pastor of Zwickau, which M. *Luther put out in Dec. 1523. The Latin language was kept, and as far as the Creed the traditional form of the Roman Mass was scarcely altered. The 'Mass of the *Faithful', however, underwent drastic revision. The *Offertory was made into a mere preparation of the elements, without any prayers; the Words of *Institution were included in the *Preface; then followed immediately the singing of the *Sanctus and the '*Benedictus qui venit', during which the *Elevation took place; and the rest of the *Canon was omitted altogether. During the giving of Communion, which was to be in both kinds, the *Agnus Dei was sung. The purpose of this unprecedented arrangement was to avoid any suggestion of the doctrine of the Eucharistic sacrifice. The form of service, moreover, was intended only to give general guidance to the celebrant, who was left free to modify it as he wished. It was upon this rite that Luther's 'German Mass' of 1526 and the majority of the later Lutheran liturgies were modelled.

Text ed. H. *Lietzmann in his Kleine Texte für theologische und philologische Vorlesungen und Übungen, no. 36 (Bonn, 1909). A. L. Richter, *Die evangelischen Kirchenordnungen des sechszehnten Jahrhunderts*, 1 (1846), pp. 1–17, incl. text, pp. 2–7. Text and further refs. in E. Sehling, *Die evangelischen Kirchenordnungen des XVI. Jahrhunderts*, 1 (pt. 1; 1902), pp. 3–9. Extracts in Kidd, pp. 127–32 (no. 66). F. E. *Brightman, *The English Rite*, 1 (1915), pp. xxxi f.

Formula of Concord. See CONCORD, FORMULA OF.

Forsyth, Peter Taylor (1848–1921), *Congregational minister and theologian. After holding five pastorates, he became principal of Hackney College, Hampstead, in 1901. In early life he was a liberal in theology, largely through the influence of G. W. F. *Hegel and A. *Ritschl; but he later radically modified his attitude to liberalism through a deep sense of need of Atonement through the Cross. By the freshness of his approach to the fact of Redemption, combined with a study of all recent work on the subject, he gave a new significance to such words as 'substitution', 'penalty', and 'satisfaction'. If his many published writings did not pretend to scholarship in the narrower sense, they were full of penetrating discussions. They include *The Cruciality of the Cross* (1909); *The Person and Place of Jesus Christ* (1909), in which a form of *kenoticism is linked with a doctrine of progressive Incarnation; *The Work of Christ* (1910), where it is argued that, in the Atonement, God is both reconciler and reconciled; *The Christian Ethic of War* (1916); *The Justification of God* (1916); and *The Soul of Prayer* (1916). Since his death, he has been recognized as one of Britain's foremost Nonconformist theologians.

Selections from his practical writings, ed. H. Escott, *Peter Taylor Forsyth (1848–1921), Director of Souls* (1948), with biog. and bibl. notes, pp. xvii–xx, and 'An Appraisement', pp. 3–33. Memoir by J. Forsyth Andrews (daughter) prefixed to 2nd edn. of his *Work of Christ* (1938), pp. vii–xxviii. His *Positive Preaching and Modern Mind* (1908) was repr., with 'A Contemporary Assessment' by D. G. Miller and others, *P. T. Forsyth: The Man, the Preachers' Theologian, Prophet for the 20th Century* (Pittsburgh, 1981), pp. 1–112. W. L. Bradley, *P. T. Forsyth: The Man and his Work* (1952); J. H. Rodgers, *The Theology of P. T. Forsyth* (1965); T. Hart (ed.), *Justice the True and Only Mercy: Essays on the Life and Theology of Peter Taylor Forsyth* (Edinburgh, 1995).

Fortescue, Adrian (1874–1923), writer on liturgical and historical subjects. Educated at the Scots College at Rome (1891–4) and at Innsbruck University (1894–9), he was ordained priest in 1898. After serving several parishes and missions in England he became the RC parish priest at Letchworth in 1907, where he built a church which he made a centre of liturgical life. Apart from his pastoral work he devoted himself to writing on a variety of subjects, esp. on Liturgy and on the E. Churches. *The Orthodox Eastern Church* (1907), *The Lesser Eastern Churches* (1913), and *The Uniate Eastern Churches* (1923) all cover a wide range of historical material. *The Mass* (1912) was a useful summary of modern studies in the Roman rite. *The Ceremonies of the Roman Rite* (1918; 12th edn., rev. by J. B. O'Connell, 1962) was until recently a widely used directory of ceremonial practice.

J. G. Vance and J. W. Fortescue (distant cousin), *Adrian Fortescue: A Memoir* (1924), with list of main works, pp. 61 f. H. *Leclercq, OSB, in *DACL* 9 (pt. 2; 1930), col. 1739, s.v. 'Liturgistes' (critical).

Fortunatus, Venantius. See VENANTIUS FORTUNATUS.

Forty Hours' Devotion (also known as the **Quarant' Ore** or **Quarantore**). A modern Catholic devotion in which the Blessed Sacrament is exposed (see EXPOSITION) for a period of *c.* 40 hours, and the faithful pray before it by turns throughout this time. Since 1967 the Exposition has been interrupted for the celebration of Mass unless the celebration takes place in a chapel apart from the exposition area. In its present form the devotion began in Italy in the 16th cent. The period of 40 hours was probably fixed as that during which Christ's body rested in the tomb. The 1918 *Codex Iuris Canonici* (can. 1275) ordered that the devotion should be held annually in all RC churches where the Bl Sacrament was habitually reserved; the 1983 Code (can. 942) simply recommends an annual exposition for an appropriate time (which is not defined),

and then only if a fitting attendance of the faithful is expected.

H. Thurston, SJ, *Lent and Holy Week: Chapters on Catholic Observance and Ritual* (1904), pp. 114–48, incl. bibl. notes; J. A. Jungmann, SJ, 'Die Andacht der vierzig Stunden und das heilige Grab', *Liturgisches Jahrbuch*, 2 (1952), pp. 184–98. N. Michell, OSB, *Cult and Controversy: The Worship of the Eucharist Outside Mass* (New York [1982]), pp. 311–18. C. Cargnoni, OFM Cap., in *Dict. Sp.* 13 (pt. 2; 1986), cols. 2702–23, s.v. 'Quarante-Heures'.

Forty Martyrs of England and Wales. Forty English and Welsh RCs put to death by the State between 1535 and 1680. The heightened standards of proof demanded by the RC Church for *canonization, and the consequent increase in time and money needed for gathering and presenting evidence, in 1960 led the promoters of the causes of those who had been executed between 1535 and 1680 to concentrate their attention on a select number, termed the Forty Martyrs. The faithful were encouraged to ask favours in the name of the whole group, and the Roman authorities agreed to accept proof of two resulting miracles (the number prescribed by *Canon Law) for the whole group instead of each member of it. The group is representative of all the 357 martyrs whose causes are still formally in progress, these 40 being drawn from the most popular among the 199 who were beatified in 1886, 1895, or 1929; it comprises 13 secular priests (incl. Cuthbert *Mayne), 3 *Benedictines, 3 *Carthusians, 2 *Franciscans, 1 *Augustinian Friar, 1 *Bridgettine, 10 *Jesuits (incl. Edmund *Campion and Robert *Southwell), and 7 layfolk, of whom 3 are women (incl. Margaret *Clitherow). The Forty Martyrs were canonized by Pope *Paul VI on 25 October 1970. Feast day, 25 Oct.

A general pamphlet, *Forty Martyrs*, and 24 others describing the lives of all the martyrs have been pub. since 1960 by the Office of the Vice-Postulation, 114 Mount Street, London. C. Tigar, *Forty Martyrs of England and Wales* (Osterley, 1961). G. F. Nuttall, 'The English Martyrs 1535–1680: a statistical review', *JEH* 22 (1971), pp. 191–7.

Forty Martyrs of Sebaste. See SEBASTE, FORTY MARTYRS OF.

Forty-Two Articles. The collection of Anglican doctrinal formulae which were issued in 1553. They were accompanied by a Royal Mandate, dated 19 June 1553, requiring all clergy, schoolmasters, and members of the universities on taking their degrees, to subscribe to them. They were, for the most part, drafted by T. *Cranmer, not later than the spring of 1552; final minor changes were made in the autumn. It is very doubtful, despite the assertion on their title that they had been 'agreed on by the bishops and other learned men in the Synod at London, in the year of our Lord God MDLII', whether they ever received the authority of *Convocation. Owing to the restoration of the RC faith under Mary (1553–8), they were never enforced, but they formed the basis of the later *Thirty-Nine Articles.

The text (both Lat. and Eng.) is pr. in E. C. S. Gibson, *The Thirty-Nine Articles of the Church of England*, 1 (1896), pp. 70–89, with introd. pp. 12–29. G. *Burnet, *The History of the Reformation of the Church of England*, ed. N. Pocock, 5 (Oxford, 1865), pp. 314–29, prints the Eng. text with notes of the differences between the Forty-Two and the Thirty-Nine Articles.

forty-two line Bible. See MAZARIN BIBLE.

forum (Lat., 'place of public assembly', hence 'judicial tribunal'). In *moral theology the term is applied to the exercise by the Church of her judicial power. A distinction is made between the 'internal forum', where, esp. in the Sacrament of *Penance, judgement is given on matters which relate to the spiritual good of the individual, and the 'external forum', e.g. the ecclesiastical courts, where the public good of the Church and her members is in question. The term 'forum of conscience' (*forum conscientiae*) is also used of the decisive authority of conscience over every individual soul.

Fosdick, Harry Emerson (1878–1969), American divine. He was ordained to the *Baptist ministry in 1903. From 1904 to 1915 he was pastor at Montclair, NJ, and from 1908 also taught homiletics at the *Union Theological Seminary, New York. In 1918 he was called to a *Presbyterian pulpit, but owing to *Fundamentalist pressure requiring his acceptance of traditional Presbyterian standards of doctrine, he withdrew in 1925. From 1926 to 1946 he was minister of the Baptist Riverside Church, New York. In his later years his approach to dogma was more positive. He wrote many books from the evangelical liberal point of view, among them *The Manhood of the Master* (1913), *The Meaning of Prayer* (1915), *The Modern Use of the Bible* (1924), *A Pilgrimage to Palestine* (1928), *Successful Christian Living* (1937), *Living under Tension* (1941), and *A Faith for Tough Times* (1952).

A collection of Fosdick's *Riverside Sermons*, with introd. by H. P. Van Dusen (New York, 1958), was issued in honour of his 80th birthday. His autobiog., *Living of These Days* (New York, 1956; London, 1957). R. M. Miller, *Harry Emerson Fosdick: Preacher, Pastor, Prophet* (New York, 1985).

fossors (Lat. *fossores* or *fossarii*, from *fodere*, 'to dig'), grave-diggers. In very early Christian times they were regarded as inferior clergy, and in the latter part of the 4th and earlier part of the 5th cent. became powerful corporations, with the management of the *catacombs in their hands. They had power to sell grave-spaces, and numerous inscriptions survive in which such sales are recorded. Included in their corporations were the artists who adorned Christian tombs. Burial in the catacombs at Rome becoming impossible after the fall of the city in 410, the inscriptions of the *fossores* virtually cease, but a chronicle as late as the 6th cent. includes them among the *clerici*. They were also called *lecticarii* from their habit of carrying the corpse on a *lectica* ('bier'), as well as *copiatae* (probably from the Gk. κόπος, 'labour').

F. Wieland, *Die genetische Entwicklung der sog. Ordines Minores in den drei ersten Jahrhunderten* (*RQ*, Supplementheft 7; 1897), pp. 57–60 and 163–5. E. Conde Guerri, *Los 'Fossores' de Roma Paleocristiana* (Studi di Antichità Cristiana, 33; 1979) with bibl. J. Stevenson, *The Catacombs* [1978], pp. 20–3. H. *Leclercq, OSB, in *DACL* 5 (pt. 2; 1923), cols. 2065–92, s.v. 'Fossoyeurs', with refs.

Foucauld, Charles de. See DE FOUCAULD, CHARLES.

Foundations. A theological symposium, published in 1912. It professed to be a 'statement of Christian belief in terms of modern thought', and consisted of nine essays, with an introduction by B. H. *Streeter. The contributors, who were all Oxford men, were, in addition to Streeter, N. S. Talbot, R. Brook, A. E. J. Rawlinson, R. G. Parsons, W. *Temple, and W. H. Moberly. The book marked a definite stage in current theological debate and it exercised much immediate influence, but its optimistic liberalism and immanental standpoint proved increasingly unacceptable in succeeding decades. On its publication the book created much controversy, notably over some of Streeter's conclusions in his essay on the Historic Christ.

See the contemporary religious journals. R. A. *Knox, 'Absolute and Abitofhell' (orig. pub. 1912; repr. in *Essays in Satire*, 1928), is a brilliant satire 'in the manner of Mr. John Dryden'. Cf. also R. A. Knox, *Some Loose Stones* (1913). F. A. Iremonger, *William Temple* (1948), ch. 9 (pp. 155–66); P. [B.] Hinchliff, *God and History* (Oxford, 1992), pp. 232–47.

Fountains Abbey. A *Cistercian abbey, three miles SW of Ripon, which was founded in 1132 by monks from the *Benedictine abbey of St Mary's, *York; it became a daughter house of *Clairvaux the following year. Numbers increased so rapidly that by 1150 it was itself able to found 12 daughter-houses. At the Reformation the monastery was surrendered to the Crown by Abbot M. Bradley, on 26 Nov. 1539. It was the richest of the Cistercian houses at the time of the *Dissolution. The extensive remains of the church and cloister buildings are without parallel; the most conspicuous structure of the ruins is the great tower, built by Abbot Huby *c*.1500, a splendid example of Perpendicular work.

Main primary material in J. R. Walbran (ed.), *Memorials of the Abbey of St Mary of Fountains* (Surtees Society, 42 and 67; 1863–78). W. H. St John Hope, 'Fountains Abbey', *Yorkshire Archaeological Journal*, 15 (1900), pp. 269–402. D. Nicholl, *Thurstan, Archbishop of York* (York, 1964), pp. 151–91. L. G. D. Baker, 'The Genesis of English Cistercian Chronicles. The Foundation History of Fountains Abbey', *Analecta Cisterciensia*, 25 (1969), pp. 14–41; and 31 (1975), pp. 179–212. R. Gilyard-Beer, *Fountains Abbey, Yorkshire* (Ministry of Public Buildings and Works Official Guidebook; HMSO, 1970). J. Solloway in *VCH*, York, 3 (1913), pp. 134–8. J. Lefèvre in *DHGE* 17 (1971), cols. 1318–27, s.v.

Four Causes, the. Acc. to *Aristotle, there are four kinds of cause, viz.: 'material' (that of which a thing is made); 'formal' (what a thing is, i.e. the genus, species, etc., which distinguishes it from other things); 'efficient' (the effective or motive force which brings it into being); and 'final' (the end or purpose of its existence). St *Thomas Aquinas, who attempted to set the Aristotelian philosophy in a Christian context, associates the second cause with God (conceived as exemplary cause) and refers the third, and fourth causes directly to God, who is at once the origin of the separate and individual being of everything, the effective creative force, and the reason and end of the being of all that exists (*Summa Theol.* 1. 44).

Four Crowned Martyrs. See QUATTRO CORONATI.

Four Gallican Articles. See GALLICAN ARTICLES.

Fourteen Holy Helpers. See AUXILIARY SAINTS.

Fox, George (1624–91), founder of the Society of *Friends (q.v.). He was born at Drayton-in-the-Clay (now

Fenny Drayton) in Leicestershire, where his father was a weaver. While he was apprenticed to a shoemaker, he looked after the latter's sheep. In 1643 he felt the call to give up all ties of family and friendship and spent the next years travelling in search of enlightenment. In 1646 he abandoned attendance at church, relying increasingly on the *Inner (or Inward) Light of the living Christ. The following year he began to preach, teaching that truth is primarily to be found in the inner voice of God speaking to the soul. He was frequently imprisoned, first at Nottingham in 1649, but his enthusiasm and moral earnestness soon attracted followers whom he began to form into a stable organization. From 1652 he was based at Swarthmoor Hall, near Ulverston, the house of Judge Thomas Fell, whose widow Margaret (1614–1702) he married in 1669. To promote the growth of the Society of Friends he undertook frequent missionary journeys—to Ireland in 1669, to the West Indies and N. America in 1671–3, to the Netherlands and Germany in 1677, and to the Netherlands again in 1684. He was a magnetic personality of great spiritual power, selfless devotion, and patience in persecution, and of remarkable organizing abilities. He died on 31 Jan. 1691. His famous *Journal*, prepared for publication by Thomas Ellwood, was first issued in 1694.

A collection of his doctrinal writings was pub. under the title *Gospel-Truth Demonstrated* (1706). There is an (incomplete) edn. of his *Works* (8 vols., Philadelphia, 1831; repr., New York, 1975). Complete edn. of his *Journal* by N. Penney (2 vols., Cambridge, 1911); his *Short Journal and Itinerary Journals*, also ed. id. (ibid., 1925); good edn. for general readers by J. L. Nickalls (ibid., 1952; repr., London, 1975). Pastoral Letters, ed. T. C. Jones, '*The Power of the Lord is Over All*' (Richmond, Ind., 1989). A lost work was reconstructed by H. J. *Cadbury as *George Fox's 'Book of Miracles'* (Cambridge, 1948). T. Hodgkin, *George Fox* (1896); A. N. Brayshaw, *The Personality of George Fox* (1918; repr., 1919; rev. edn., 1933); H. E. Wildes, *Voice of the Lord: A Biography of George Fox* (Philadelphia, 1965); H. L. Ingle, *First among Friends: George Fox and the Creation of Quakerism* (New York and Oxford, 1994). A. Gordon in *DNB* 19 (1889), pp. 117–22.

Foxe, John (1516–87), martyrologist. He went to Brasenose College, *Oxford, at an early age, and was Fellow of Magdalen from 1539 to 1545. On the accession of Queen *Mary he fled to the Continent, and stayed successively at Strasbourg, Frankfurt, and Basle, where he met other Protestant refugees, notably J. *Knox and E. *Grindal. At this period he wrote a history of the Christian persecutions, first issued in Latin at Strasbourg in 1554. An expanded English edition appeared in 1563 as the *Acts and Monuments of matters happening in the Church*, commonly known as 'Foxe's Book of Martyrs'. The book, which was approved and officially publicized by the bishops, went through four editions in Foxe's lifetime. Its chief object was to extol the heroism and endurance of the Protestant martyrs of Mary's reign. Its homely style, combined with its vivid descriptions of the sufferings imposed on the victims of Papist tyranny, gained it great popularity. It still retains major historical value, particularly in preserving early Protestant oral tradition and documents, despite the obvious bias which Foxe's commentary displays. By 1559 he had returned to England and in 1560 he was ordained priest by E. Grindal, Bp. of London. Though he subsequently received a prebendal stall both at *Salisbury and *Durham, he lived mainly in London, working on successive revisions of his *Acts and Monuments* and writing other historical, polemical, and devotional works.

Source material for his work ed. J. Gough Nichols, *Narratives of the Days of the Reformation, chiefly from the manuscripts of John Foxe* (Camden Society [1st ser.], 77; 1859). Earliest Life, pr. in Eng. and Lat. in vol. 2 of the 1641 edn. of his *Acts and Monuments* (no pagination); it professes to be the work of his son. *Acts and Monuments*, ed. G. Townsend (8 vols., 1843–9), contains a further Life (1, pp. 1–160) and a defence of the veracity of the work (pp. 161–236). J. F. Mozley, *John Foxe and his Book* (1940); W. Haller, *Foxe's Book of Martyrs and the Elect Nation* (1963); V. N. Olsen, *John Foxe and the Elizabethan Church* (1973). J. Facey, 'John Foxe and the Defence of the English Church', in P. [G.] Lake and M. Dowling (eds.), *Protestantism and the National Church in Sixteenth Century England* (1987), pp. 162–92. *BRUO, 1501–1540*, pp. 212–14.

Foxe, Richard (? 1448–1528), Bp. of *Winchester and founder of Corpus Christi College, *Oxford. He appears to have been educated at Magdalen College, Oxford, and also studied at Cambridge and Paris. After Henry VII's accession (1485), as a reward for earlier services, he was appointed bishop successively of *Exeter (1487), *Bath and Wells (1492), *Durham (1494), and Winchester (1501), preferments intended primarily to provide him with financial means while engaged in important diplomatic work. Under *Henry VIII (1509–47) he at first retained his ascendancy, but from 1511 onwards he was gradually superseded by T. *Wolsey. Only in the later years of his life did he seriously concern himself with his episcopal duties. His sympathies for the New Learning found expression in his foundation of Corpus Christi College, at Oxford, in 1515–16.

The Register of Richard Fox while Bishop of Bath and Wells, A.D. MCCCCXCII–MCCCCXCIV, ed. E. C. Batten (1889), incl. Life (pp. 1–142); part of this Register is ed. with that of Robert Stillington by H. C. Maxwell-Lyte (Somerset Record Society, 52; 1937), pp. 174–200; *The Register of Richard Fox Lord Bishop of Durham 1494–1501*, ed. M. P. Howden (Surtees Society, 147; 1932). *Letters of Richard Fox, 1486–1527*, ed. P. S. and H. M. Allen (1929). J. Greatrex, 'On Ministering to "Certayne Devoute and Religiouse Women": Bishop Fox and the Benedictine Nuns of Winchester Diocese on the Eve of the Dissolution', in W. J. Sheils and D. Wood (eds.), *Women in the Church* (Studies in Church History, 27; 1990), pp. 223–35. T. Fowler in *DNB* 19 (1889), pp. 150–6. *BRUO* 2 (1958), pp. 715–19; *BRUC*, pp. 239–41.

Fra Angelico, Fra Bartolommeo. See ANGELICO, BL FRA, BARTOLOMMEO FRA.

Fraction. The formal breaking of the bread which in all Eucharistic liturgies takes place before the Communion. It goes back to Christ's action at the *Last Supper (Mt. 26: 26 and parallels) and was a sufficiently striking element in the primitive rite to make the 'breaking of bread' (Acts 2: 42; cf. 20: 7) a regular name for the Eucharist.

The precise moment of the Fraction varies. In the Roman rite it has traditionally come immediately after the Lord's Prayer, where the rubrics required that the Host be divided into three parts and one of them dropped into the chalice (the 'commixture'). Since 1969, however, the celebrant has broken a small portion from the Host and placed it in the chalice immediately after the *Kiss of Peace; during the *Agnus Dei which follows he divides the Host into a number of portions which are used for the communion of the people. In other rites the Fraction is considerably more elaborate. Thus in the *Byzantine rite the Host is divided into four portions, which are arranged on the paten in the form of a cross, and one of them is then put into the chalice. In the *Mozarabic rite the Host is divided into nine portions, seven of which are then arranged in the form of a cross. A rubric in the 1662 BCP orders the breaking of the bread immediately before it is consecrated, a most unusual position. At the time of the Fraction, the Koinonikon is sung in the Byzantine Liturgy, the Confractorium in the Ambrosian, and the Agnus Dei in the Roman rite.

'Fractio Panis' as a title is used of the early 2nd-cent. fresco which perhaps depicts an early Eucharist in the Cappella Greca in the *Catacomb of St *Priscilla, uncovered by J. Wilpert in 1893.

L. *Duchesne, *Origines du culte chrétien* (1889), pp. 62, 79 f., 175–7, 208–12 (Eng. tr., 1903, pp. 63, 85, 184–6, 218–22). T. Schermann, 'Das "Brotbrechen" im Urchristentum', *Biblische Zeitschrift*, 8 (1910), pp. 33–52 and 162–83. B. *Capelle, OSB, 'Le Rite de la fraction dans la messe romaine', *R. Bén.* 53 (1941), pp. 5–40; id., 'Fraction et commixtion', *La Maison Dieu*, 35 (1953), pp. 79–94; both repr. in his *Travaux liturgiques*, 2 (1962), pp. 287–331. R. Cabié in A. G. Martimort, *L'Église en prière* (édition nouvelle), 2 [1983], pp. 128–31 and 182 f.; Eng tr. (1986), pp. 109–13 and 214 f. W. E. Scudamore in *DCA* 1 (1875), pp. 686–9, s.v.; F. *Cabrol, OSB, in *DACL* 5 (pt. 2; 1923), cols. 2103–16, s.v. 'Fractio Panis'.

On the fresco mentioned above, cf. J. Wilpert, *Fractio Panis: Die älteste Darstellung des Eucharistischen Opfers in der 'Cappella Greca'* (1895).

France, Christianity in. Christianity appears to have been introduced into Gaul as early as the 2nd cent. by missionaries from Asia Minor. The Christian community at Lyons suffered persecution in 177 and St *Irenaeus, its bishop, was a man of more than local stature as an apologist and theologian. From the 3rd cent. contacts with Rome had been formed, and a Gallic episcopate, with many new sees, geographically based on the Roman administrative divisions of Gaul, was established between *c.*250 and 313. A synod of the W. Church at *Arles in 314 included among its participants 14 Gallic bishops and the following century saw the definitive organization of the Gallo-Roman Church. Among the most illustrious saints and scholars of the period were St *Martin of Tours, St *Hilary of Poitiers, St *Paulinus of Nola and St *Germanus of Auxerre. Their writings and those of their contemporaries show that Gaul was as aware as other parts of the W. Church of the major controversies, such as *Novatianism, *Arianism, *Priscillianism, and *Semipelagianism. In the adjustment to new rulers and the gradual transformation of the old Roman forms of government in the 5th and early 6th cents., the bishops, such as St *Sidonius Apollinaris of Clermont and St *Caesarius of Arles, acquired a new prominence as leaders and spokesmen of the people. This aspect of the bishop's role continued throughout the Merovingian period, as is clear from the career of St *Gregory of Tours. The occupation of S. Gaul by Arian Visigoths seems to have done little to disrupt the life of Catholic bishops. With the conversion of the Frankish king *Clovis to Catholicism and his conquest of Gaul, however, the way was prepared for a fruitful, if

tense, relationship between the Church and the secular rulers, exemplified in the relations between Clovis and St *Remigius of Reims, and between the rulers of Burgundy and St *Avitus of Vienne. Clovis convened the council of Orléans in 511 and many Church synods were held subsequently in Gaul, the canons of which were embodied in later classical collections, notably the *Vetus Gallica*, produced in the region of Lyons *c.*600 and subsequently disseminated from Autun *c.*700. The liturgy of the early Gallic Church (the so-called *Gallican rite) appears to have had affinities with the *Ambrosian rite of Milan, but Roman usage gained prominence during the 7th and 8th cents. The Gallo-Roman bishops and their Frankish successors supported missionary enterprises, such as those of St *Amandus, in the peripheral regions of the Frankish kingdom, esp. to the north and east. Such work was given a new impetus with the inspiration provided by the followers of the Irishman, St *Columbanus. Many new monasteries, such as *Luxeuil and *Corbie, were founded, often in close conjunction with the landed aristocracy. Thus a new stratum of monastic life was added to the earlier foundations inspired by Martin, John *Cassian, and the monks of the Rhône–Saône river valley.

A new phase in the history of the Frankish Church was inaugurated by the Carolingian rulers, *Pepin III, who secured the throne definitively in 751, his son *Charlemagne, and his successors. In close conjunction with the Englishman, St *Boniface, Carloman, Pepin's brother, convened Church councils which set out to reform and reorganize the Church in Frankish Gaul. Pepin, aided by St *Chrodegang, did likewise, and Charlemagne was able to build on their achievements by means of legislation touching on all aspects of the Church's life. His son, *Louis the Pious, continued the work, his most notable achievement in this sphere being the promotion of the Rule of St *Benedict. In due course the clergy took up the royal initiative and their work is apparent in the range of synodal and episcopal statutes produced in the 9th and 10th cents. As well as dealing with doctrinal affairs, such as *Iconoclasm, *Adoptianism, *predestination, the dispute over the *Filioque* clause in the *Nicene Creed, and matters of ecclesiastical discipline such as Christian marriage and divorce, the Frankish Church was notable for its regularization of the liturgy and use of the *Gregorian Sacramentary, its formulations of standardized Gospel and Epistle *lectionaries and *homiliaries, its promotion of the Dionysio-Hadriana collection of *canon law, the development of ecclesiastical chant, and an influential revision of the *Vulgate text of the Bible. Many notable theologians contributed to the intellectual debates of the day, among them *Theodulf of Orléans, *Alcuin, *Agobard of Lyons, *Gottschalk, and *Hincmar of Reims. From the time of Pepin III's accession a close relationship was established between the Frankish rulers and the Papacy, which was expressed dramatically by the coronation of Charlemagne as Emperor in 800.

In 987 Hugh Capet succeeded the last Carolingian ruler of France (a political area whose boundaries had been largely determined in 843, although the achievement of political and national unity was a long and gradual process). Hugh was loyally supported by the Abp. of Reims, and the Capetians and the Church usually worked closely together to their common benefit. Under the earlier kings the period of the *Investiture Controversy saw no open clash with the Papacy over the king's claim to confer on bishops the *ring and *crosier, while two reforming Popes, *Urban II and *Callistus II, were Frenchmen, and France stood out as the homeland of the *Crusades. A number of 12th-cent. Popes came to France as a refuge from political difficulties at Rome; the title 'most Christian king' became a regular formula in Papal letters to the Capetians. In the 10th and 11th cents. the reformed monastic connection of *Cluny increasingly provided the Capetian monarchy with a model for centralization; *Suger, Abbot of *St-Denis, was a devoted and politically skilful servant of Kings Louis VI (reigned 1108–37) and Louis VII (reigned 1137–80), as well as a pioneer of Gothic architecture. During the 12th cent. France saw the development of *Cistercian monasticism with its outstanding representative in St *Bernard of Clairvaux, as well as of *canons regular. The growth of cathedral schools and then of universities, esp. that of *Paris, made France a country of great writers and theologians such as Peter *Abelard and *Peter Lombard; in the 13th cent. St *Thomas Aquinas taught for a time at Paris. In the 12th cent. the *Albigensians spread widely in S. France; beginning under Philip II Augustus (reigned 1180–1223) the Albigensian Crusades (1209–29) were promoted under Pope *Innocent III and enabled the Capetian monarchy to assimilate Languedoc into the Frankish kingdom. Under St *Louis IX feudal and Christian monarchy in France reached its apogee, although Louis was far from being a supporter of the political plans and wishes of Pope *Innocent IV.

Philip IV ('the Fair') (reigned 1285–1314) brought about the completion of the development of Capetian monarchy from suzerainty to virtual sovereignty. The power of the feudal lords was curtailed, and the imprisonment of Pope *Boniface VIII at Anagni in 1303 by Philip's agents was a severe blow to Papal power and prestige. The election to the Papacy in 1305 of *Clement V was followed by its emigration to *Avignon, within the French dominion. So far from being a French captivity of the Papacy, it was France that was most thoroughly raided for benefices in a period of great expansion in Papal 'provisions'. In both matters of benefices and finance a tacit agreement between the Popes and the Kings of France allowed each to pillage the Church. *Gallicanism took form as Church Councils sought to deprive the Pope of his control over benefices and taxation as a means to end the *Great Schism of 1378. However the apparent alternation between Gallicanism, expressed, e.g., in the *Pragmatic Sanction of Bourges of 1438, and submission to the Papacy (e.g. in the concordat of 1472) concealed a continuation of complicity. While French power suffered military defeat, royal propaganda enhanced the position of the King of France as second head of the Gallican Church.

The Concordat of 1516 between *Leo X and Francis I (reigned 1515–47) was essentially a diplomatic agreement in the context of the Italian wars, but it had considerable impact on Christianity in France. By conceding to the French Crown the right to nominate to major benefices, it disposed her monarchs to seek accommodation rather than a break with Rome. It also dictated the (unsuccessful) strategy of J. *Calvin and T. *Beza, which aimed to capture the support of the Crown, and thus of the bishops, so

that with the backing of ecclesiastical authority the entire Gallican Church could be transformed on Protestant principles. Until the adoption of the RC faith in 1593 by *Henry IV the *Huguenots kept alive the hope that this might be achieved. In the event they obtained only a limited measure of protection in the Edict of *Nantes (1598). The Gallican hierarchy persisted in regarding the reformed religion as heretical, and systematic attempts were made to undermine its teachings and persuade its adherents to return to the traditional faith. The protection offered by the law was steadily eroded in the course of the 17th cent. and finally removed in 1685 with the Revocation of the Edict of Nantes. By this time the number of French Protestants had long been in decline; north of the Loire they had never recovered their vigour after the Massacre of St *Bartholomew's Day in 1572.

The 15th and early 16th cent. in France was a time of active piety, manifested in much construction and elaboration of churches, chantry chapels and oratories, cults of the BVM and of the saints, purchases of *indulgences and endowing of private Masses. These features testified to lively collective devotion but also to individual anxiety provoked by the doctrine of *purgatory and by fears about the after-life. For some educated men traditional forms of piety came to look like superstitions, rationally unacceptable because they had lost their power to reassure. They sought security in the scrutiny of texts, turning to the Bible and to the works of such commentators as *Erasmus, J. *Faber and M. *Luther, all of whose writings provoked debate and elicited a diversity of response. Search for spiritual reassurance was common to Protestantism and to the revitalized Catholic devotion of which it was at the outset itself a part.

Later in the 16th cent. RC Christianity in France was invigorated by post-*Tridentine piety. Florid expressions of penitential fervour gave way to devotion of a contemplative character in the Compagnie du Saint-Sacrement and among the French *Oratorians, both strong at Court. In the 17th cent. the French Church was illuminated by the lives of St *Francis de Sales and St *Vincent de Paul, and by the eloquence and leadership of prelates such as J. B. *Bossuet and F. *Fénelon. It saw the foundation of *seminaries to train the parochial clergy, while Louis XIV (reigned 1643–1715) initiated the rule that promotion to the episcopate required an apprenticeship in diocesan administration. The King affirmed the power of his Crown, not only against the Protestants, but also against Rome, inducing the clergy to publish the *Gallican Articles in 1682. He also struck against the *Jansenists. Their movement, which in France stemmed from Antoine *Arnauld, was opposed by the *Jesuits, and Louis, believing it to be 'republican', destroyed their spiritual centre at *Port-Royal and encouraged the designs of the Jesuits leading to the bull '*Unigenitus' (1713). The bull was ridiculed by men of the *Enlightenment, and the Jansenist clergy appealed to a future General Council against it. In the mid-18th cent. the Abp. of Paris debarred dying Jansenists from the Last Sacraments, provoking a wave of *anticlerical bitterness. The Parlement defended the Jansenists and forced Louis XV to expel the Jesuits from France in 1764.

Except in large cities, religious practice was almost universal. The parish clergy were well-educated and the splendour of the liturgical observances in the great collegiate churches unsurpassed. The education of children was in ecclesiastical hands and the care of the sick and poor was dependent on the dedicated work of women in the religious orders. But intellectually the Church could make only a halting reply to criticism (as from *Voltaire and J.-J. *Rousseau) and it was the target of anticlericalism, partly because of its intolerance (only in 1787 did Protestants receive a grudging toleration), but chiefly on account of its wealth. This was largely in the hands of the aristocracy, who monopolized practically all the bishoprics and well-paid canonries and held the abbatial revenues of the monasteries in *commendam, while a third of the parish priests were on subsistence wages.

In the Revolution of 1789, Church property was sold to pay off the national debt, *tithe was abolished, and the taking of monastic vows ended. The *Constitutional Church, set up by the *Civil Constitution of the Clergy (1790), was a new ecclesiastical order. After the National Assembly imposed an oath to the Civil Constitution on priests who wished to retain office, about half accepted, though some later revoked their oath when they learned that Rome had condemned the settlement. When the Revolutionary Government went to war against the kings of Europe, the clergy were regarded as a fifth column, and during the terror of 1793–4, they suffered cruel victimization. The *Concordat of 1801 (q.v.), between Napoleon and *Pius VII, 'restored the altars' by creating a new episcopate which included 16 bishops of the pre-revolutionary Church, 12 from the Constitutional Church, and 32 newly consecrated. Despite the provisions of the *Organic Articles (1802), the Concordat increased the prestige of Rome and weakened the old independent Gallican spirit of the French clergy, especially in the light of Pius VII's reaction to Napoleon's conduct. From then onwards *Ultramontanism became a force, moving to its major triumph at the First *Vatican Council (1870). Meanwhile the years following 1801 saw the founding of numerous religious orders at home and the intensification of missionary activity to all parts of the world. The names of '*Lourdes' and the '*Curé d'Ars' (qq.v.) are indicative of a widespread growth in personal piety.

The various political changes in France during the 19th cent. did not disturb the position of the RC Church. Meanwhile Calvinism revived in some measure, and French Evangelicals took a prominent part in missionary work in Africa and elsewhere. The split in 1872 between orthodox, moderates, and liberals weakened the Calvinist community considerably.

The identification of so many Churchmen with the régime of Napoleon III and, later, with proposals for a royalist restoration, led the politicians of the Third Republic to adopt anticlerical policies, and towards the end of the 19th cent. various acts were passed to weaken the influence of the Church. The most significant of these was the Education Act of 1882 which completely secularized primary education, and subsequent acts which placed restrictions on religious teaching in secondary education. Pope *Leo XIII's call to French Catholics to rally in support of the Republic in 1892 was little heeded and the Church's involvement in politics led to a sharp reaction on the part of succeeding governments. In the early years of the 20th cent. most religious orders were expelled from France, and in 1905, after a series of quarrels between the French government and the Holy See, the entire severance of Church and State took place. The State grant to the Church ceased and all recognition of the Church as an institution ceased with it. Henceforth no distinction was made between clergy and others in regard to liability for military service and no pious bequests, except to individuals, were legally valid. On the other hand, Catholics and Protestants alike had their rights of assembly as private persons guaranteed by the State.

In the same period some of the most radical thinking in ecclesiastical circles had been taking place in France. The *Modernist movement included the attempts of A. *Loisy to bring biblical exegesis into line with modern scientific discoveries and the attempts of the philosophical thinkers (notably M. *Blondel and L. *Laberthonnière) to bring dogma into line with modern philosophical systems and the modern mind. The first decades of the 20th cent. also witnessed the growth in importance of 'social catholicism', which was marked by concern for the fate of the poor in a capitalist society.

During the First World War the French clergy fought side by side with the laity, and in this way the estrangement of many of the French laity from the Church was much diminished. Unobtrusively the religious orders returned and the inter-war period was marked by moderation in the relations between the Church and State. At the same time French Catholic scholarship flourished under the leadership of J. *Maritain and É. *Gilson. It remained vigorous for some time after the end of the Second World War, exemplified in the publications of G.-Y. *Congar, H. de *Lubac, P. *Teilhard de Chardin, and J. *Daniélou, while French Dominicans in Jerusalem produced the first Catholic scholarly translation of Scripture (1948–54; Eng. tr., the 'Jerusalem Bible', 1966). The basis for a new social and political orientation among Christians in France had been laid by the philosophy of Emmanuel Mounier (1905–50). In the periodical Esprit, which he founded in 1932, he propounded a spiritual humanism, with socialist leanings, which was gradually accepted by the hierarchy; at the same time he introduced a revived personal and spiritual dimension into socialist thought. The loss of the working classes to the Church in the 19th cent. has lent particular importance to social issues in French ecclesiastical thinking. The publication in 1943 of a book by A. Godin and Y. Daniel entitled La France, pays de mission?—the question mark was included at the request of the ecclesiastical authorities—spurred attempts to tackle the problem. These included the activities of worker priests in the region of Marseilles in the 1940s and 1950s and the fostering of *Catholic Action as the dominant instrument of pastoral work among every class of society. Consequently, in the period of unrest which followed the 'events' of May 1968, many of the clergy found themselves allied to the students and workers. Meanwhile, the political party, the Mouvement Républicain Populaire, represented social Catholicism after the Second World War, and in 1984 Catholics were able to defeat the plans of the socialist government to integrate Church schools in the state system. Despite the reactionary movement led by Abp. M. Lefèvre, the changes introduced by the Second *Vatican Council were absorbed at parish level. In 1966 the huge diocese of Paris was divided into four separate, but closely linked dioceses, in a pattern which has been followed in other parts of the world. In the 1980s the Church established two *broadcasting stations, Radio Notre-Dame in Paris and Radio Fourvière in Lyons. Protestants, Orthodox and Jews now also use these stations. In 1988 c.80 per cent of the population described themselves as RC, though only 10 per cent practised their religion.

A large mass of documentary material is contained in *Gallia Christiana (q.v.). Much information on the history of the Church will be found in all histories of France, e.g. F. Lavisse, Histoire de France depuis les origines jusqu'à la Révolution (9 vols., 1900–11); id., Histoire de France contemporaine, depuis la Révolution jusqu'à la paix de 1919 (10 vols., 1920–2), both with detailed bibls. [R. F. W.] Guettée, Histoire de l'Église de France (12 vols., 1847–56). G. Goyau, Histoire religieuse de la France (1922; new edn., with continuation by G. Hanotaux, 1942). C. Poulet, OSB, Histoire de l'Église de France (3 vols., 1944). A. Latreille, E. Delaruelle, J. R. Palanque, and R. Rémond, Histoire du catholicisme en France (3 vols., 1957–62). J. Le Goff and R. Rémond (eds.), Histoire de la France religieuse (4 vols., 1988–92).

L. *Duchesne, Fastes épiscopaux de l'ancienne Gaule (3 vols., 1894–1915). É. Griffe, La Gaule Chrétienne à l'époque romaine (3 vols., 1947–65; 2nd edn. of vols. 1–2, 1964–6). R. W. Mathisen, Ecclesiastical Factionalism and Religious Controversy in Fifth-Century Gaul (Washington, DC [1989]). J. M. Wallace-Hadrill, The Frankish Church (Oxford History of the Christian Church, 1983); R. McKitterick, The Frankish Church and the Carolingian Reforms 789–895 (1977). J. Chélini, L'Aube du Moyen Age: Naissance de la chrétienté occidentale. La vie religieuse des laïcs dans l'Europe carolingienne (750–900) (1991). F. Prinz, Frühes Mönchtum im Frankenreich (Munich, 1965; 2nd edn., Darmstadt [1988]). V. Martin, Les Origines du gallicanisme (2 vols., 1939). E. M. Hallam, Capetian France, 987–1328 (1980), esp. pp. 99–110, 190–203, 230–9, and 310–24. P. E. Schramm, Der König von Frankreich: Das Wesen der Monarchie vom 9. zum 16. Jahrhundert (2 vols., Weimar, 1939; 2nd edn., 1960). F. Lot and R. Fawtier, Histoire des Institutions Françaises au Moyen Âge, 3: Institutions Ecclesiastiques (1962). J. Rivière, Le Problème de l'Église et de l'état au temps de Philippe le Bel (SSL 8; 1926). N. Valois, La France et le grand schisme d'occident (4 vols., 1896–1902).

F. Lebrun (ed.), Histoire des Catholiques en France du XVᵉ siècle à nos jours [1980]. [P. G. J. M.] Imbart de La Tour, Les Origines de la réforme (4 vols., 1905–35). J. K. Farge, Orthodoxy and Reform in Early Reformation France: The Faculty of Theology of Paris, 1500–1543 (Studies in Medieval and Reformation Thought, 32; Leiden, 1985). R. M. Kingdon, Geneva and the Consolidation of the French Protestant Movement 1564–1572 (Geneva and Madison, Wis., 1967). D. R. Kelley, The Beginning of Ideology: Consciousness and Society in the French Reformation (Cambridge, 1981). Selection of docs. ed. A. Duke and others, Calvinism in Europe, 1540–1620 (Manchester and New York [1992]), pp. 57–128; M. Prestwich, 'Calvinism in France, 1559–1629' in id. (ed.), International Calvinism 1541–1715 (Oxford, 1985), pp. 71–107. A. N. Galpern, The Religions of the People in Sixteenth-Century Champagne (Harvard Historical Studies, 92; Cambridge, Mass., 1976). N. M. Sutherland, Princes, Politics and Religion 1547–1589 (1984) [collected essays incl. some not previously pub.]. D. Crouzet, Les Guerriers de Dieu: La violence au temps des troubles de religion, vers 1525—vers 1610 (2 vols. [1990]).

L. N. Prunel, La Renaissance catholique en France au XVIIᵉ siècle (1921). J. McManners, French Ecclesiastical Society under the Ancien Régime: A Study of Angers in the 18th century (Manchester, 1960). T. Tackett, Religion, Revolution and Regional Culture in 18th-Century France: The Ecclesiastical Oath of 1791 (Princeton, NJ, 1986). J. McManners, The French Revolution and the Church (1969).

A. Dansette, Histoire religieuse de la France contemporaine (2 vols., 1948–51; rev. edn., 1965; Eng. tr., 2 vols., 1961). G. Constant, L'Église de France sous le consulat et l'empire, 1800–1814

(1928). C. S. Phillips, The Church in France, 1789–1848: A Study in Revival (1929); id., The Church in France, 1848–1907 (CHS publications, NS, no. 19; 1936). A. Gough, Rome and Paris: The Gallican Church and the Ultramontane Campaign 1843–1853 (Oxford, 1986). B. Reardon, Liberalism and Tradition: Aspects of Catholic Thought in Nineteenth-Century France (Cambridge, 1975). S. Mours, Un Siècle d'évangélisation en France (1815–1914) (2 vols., 1963). E. Lecanuet, Cong. Orat., L'Église de France sous la Troisième République (2 vols., 1907–10). J. McManners, Church and State in France, 1870–1914 (1972). A. R. Vidler, A Century of Social Catholicism, 1820–1920 (1964), pp. 3–78 and 112–40. É. Poulat, Intégrisme et catholicisme intégral: Un réseau secret international antimoderniste: La 'Sapinière' (1909–1921) (1969). Id., Naissance des prêtres-ouvriers (1965). M. Kelly, Pioneer of the Catholic Revival: The Ideas and Influence of Emmanuel Mounier (1979). [J. Loew], Journal d'une mission ouvrière, 1941–1959 (1959). H. Godin and Y. Daniel, La France, pays de mission? ([1943]; partial Eng. tr., with other material, M. Ward, France Pagan? The Mission of Abbé Godin, 1949). W. Bosworth, Catholicism and Crisis in Modern France: French Catholic Groups at the Threshold of the Fifth Republic (Princeton, NJ, 1962).

E. Mâle, L'Art religieux du 12ᵉ siècle en France (1922); id., L'Art religieux du 13ᵉ siècle en France (1898; Eng. tr., 1913); id., L'Art religieux de la fin du moyen-âge en France (1908). J Evans, Monastic Architecture in France, from the Renaissance to the Republic (Cambridge, 1964). R. [M.] Griffiths, The Reactionary Revolution: The Catholic Revival in French Literature 1870–1914 (1966). Bremond. G. Goyau, La France missionnaire dans les cinq parties du monde (2 vols., 1948). J. Fontaine and others in Dict. Sp. 5 (1964), cols. 785–997, s.v.; E. Delaruelle and others in NCE 6 (1967), pp. 2–25, s.v.; J.-R. Palanque and others in DHGE 18 (1977), cols. 1–157, s.v. See also bibls. to ACTION FRANÇAISE, CONCORDAT, CONSTITUTIONAL CHURCH, GALLICANISM, HUGUENOTS, JANSENISM, MODERNISM, and QUIETISM.

Frances of Rome, St (1384–1440), Sta Francesca Romana, foundress of the *Oblates of St Benedict of Tor de' Specchi. Born at Rome, she was married in 1397 to Lorenzo de' Ponziani, although she desired to enter religion. She was an exemplary wife and mother, at the same time living a life under rule with her husband's brother's wife, Vannozza. She and her family suffered much when Ladislas of Naples took Rome in 1408. In 1425 she realized her long-cherished plan of founding a society of pious women, not under strict vows, to help the poor. At first called the Oblates of Mary, they later became known as the Oblates of Tor de' Specchi from the house in which they lived. After Lorenzo's death (1436) Francesca entered the community and became Superior. An account of her visions and spiritual struggles was taken down by Giovanni Mattiotti, her confessor, and forms the main part of his Life of her. She was canonized in 1608 and *Pius XI declared her a patroness of motorists. Feast day, 9 Mar.

Lat. recension of Life by Giovanni Mattiotti pr. in AASS, Mar. 2 (1668), pp. *92–*176; It. recension (prob. the earlier) ed. M. Armellini (Rome, 1882); modern It. tr. by M. Scarpini (Florence, 1923). Life by M. M. Anguillaria (Rome, 1641) adds little; Lat. tr. in AASS, loc. cit., pp. *176–*211. Account of canonization, ibid., pp. *212–*216; introd., pp. *88–*92. P. T. Lugano, OSB (ed.), I processi inediti per Francesca Bussa dei Ponziani (Santa Francesca Romana), 1440–1453 (ST 120; 1945), with refs. to earlier works, esp. p. xxxiv; see esp. arts. in Rivista storica benedettina. G. M. Brasó, OSB, 'Identificazione delle fonti autografe della biographia di Santa Francesca Romana', Benedictina, 21 (1974), pp. 165–87. Modern Lives by G. Fullerton (London, 1855), J. Rabory (Paris, 1884), Ctesse de Rambuteau (ibid., 1900), Berthem-Bontoux (ibid., 1931), and C. Albergotti (Rome, 1940). E.

Vaccaro and M. L. Casanova in *Bibliotheca Sanctorum*, 5 (Rome [1965]), cols. 1011–28, s.v. 'Francesca Romana', with extensive bibl.

Francis of Assisi, St (1181/2–1226), founder of the *Franciscan Order. The son of Pietro Bernardone, a rich cloth merchant of Assisi, and his wife, Pica, Francis assisted his father in his business until he reached the age of 20. Gallant, high-spirited, and generous, he lived as a youth the life usual for one of his station. In 1202, during a border dispute between Perugia and Assisi, he was taken prisoner and held captive for a year. After his release he returned to Assisi and his old ways and endured a long illness. Setting off again for war in 1204, he was directed by a vision to return to Assisi, where he began to lose all taste for his former life. On a pilgrimage to Rome, he was moved to compassion by the beggars outside *St Peter's and, exchanging his clothes with one of them, spent a day himself begging for alms. This experience affected him deeply. When he returned to Assisi, he broke with his old companions, was disowned by his father, then overcame his fear of leprosy by embracing a leper, and devoted himself to repairing churches, starting with S. Damiano. One morning *c*.1208, while attending Mass in the church of the *Portiuncula in the plain below Assisi, he heard the Lord's words read, bidding His disciples leave all (Mt. 10: 7–19), and at once understood them as a personal call. He discarded staff and shoes, put on a long dark garment girded with a cord, and set out to save souls. Before long he gathered round him a band of like-minded men.

When the number of his followers reached 12, Francis drew up a short and simple rule for them ('Regula Primitiva') and on a visit to Rome in 1209 secured for it the oral approval of *Innocent III. On his return he spent some time at Rivo Torto near Assisi and from there he sent out friars two by two to preach. They called themselves 'friars minor' (fratres minores), and increased rapidly. In 1212 his ideals were accepted by St *Clare (q.v.), a noble lady from Assisi, who founded a similar society for women centred on the church of S. Damiano. In 1214–15 Francis tried to reach Africa by way of S. France and Spain, but illness forced him to return to Italy. In 1215 he was probably at the Fourth *Lateran Council where his new rapidly growing Order somehow escaped the command to adopt an existing rule. According to one tradition, he obtained the '*Portiuncula Indulgence' (q.v.) from *Honorius III in 1216. At the Chapter at Assisi at Pentecost 1217 the Order was divided into provinces and ministers were appointed to supervise them. In 1219 Francis went to Egypt; he was present at the siege and capture of Damietta (Nov. 1219) and afterwards visited the Ayyubid sultan al-Kamil.

During his absence in the E., Francis put two vicars in charge of the Order, but owing to their mismanagement he had to return to correct abuses. He was helped in this task by his friend Card. Ugolino of Segni, the future *Gregory IX. Francis codified his rather amorphous rule into what is known as the 'Regula Prima', but withheld submitting it for approval. Continuing disagreements among the friars and the opposition of prelates to their way of life led him, against the wishes of some friars, to rewrite and shorten the rule and to submit it for Papal approval. On 29 Nov. 1223 Honorius III solemnly

approved his rule, hence known as the 'Regula Bullata', the first rule to receive Papal approbation. It was during these years that Francis resigned as Minister General of the Order and handed over its day-to-day running to a friar whom he called the Minister General—first to Peter Cathanii (d. 1221), then to *Elias of Cortona—but without relinquishing real leadership of the Order. It was about this time that lay people began to associate themselves with his Order to form a '*Third Order'. In 1223 Francis arranged for apparently the first Christmas *crib to be made. The evidence that he was a *deacon derives mainly from the account of this incident. In Sept. 1224 he received on Mount La Verna, a retreat in the Apennines granted to him and his friars by the Lord of Chiusi, the gift of the *Stigmata. He died at the Portiuncula on 3 Oct. 1226. Less than two years later, on 16 July 1228, he was canonized by Gregory IX. In 1230 his body was moved to the newly built church on the edge of Assisi. Feast day, 4 Oct. (Commemoration of the Stigmata, 17 Sept.).

Francis's generosity, his simple and unaffected faith, his passionate devotion to God and man, his love of nature and his deep humility have made him one of the most cherished saints in modern times. The revival of interest in him among the more educated owes much to the study of P. *Sabatier, the Calvinist pastor at Strasbourg, who combined original research into the early Franciscan documents with warm sympathy for, and a fascinating presentation of, his ideals.

See also FRANCISCAN ORDER, CANTICLE OF THE SUN, and LITTLE FLOWERS OF ST FRANCIS.

The authentic writings of Francis are all quite short and their canon is still not fixed. They include two Rules (the 'Regula Prima' and the 'Regula Bullata'), the Rule for those living in hermitages ('Regula pro Eremitoriis'), the Testament, 28 Admonitions, 8 letters, the 'Salutation of the BVM' and other liturgical works, and the 'Canticle of the Sun'. The earliest collected edn. is that of L. *Wadding, OFM (Antwerp, 1623, often repr.). Crit. edn. by K. Esser, OFM (Spicilegium Bonaventurianum, 13; Grottaferrata, 1976; also, with less full apparatus, Bibliotheca Franciscana Ascetica Medii Aevi, 12; ibid., 1978). Earlier edn. of works in Lat. by the Franciscans at Quaracchi (ibid. 1; 1904; 3rd edn., 1949) and H. Boehmer and others (Tübingen and Leipzig, 1904; 3rd edn., 1961). Esser's text is repr., with Fr. tr., introd. and notes by T. Desbonnets, OFM, and others (SC 285; 1981). Eng. trs. by P. Robinson, OFM (London, 1906), J. Meyer, OFM (Chicago, 1952), L. Sherley-Price (London, 1959), B. Fahy, OFM (ibid. [1964]), and in Francis and Clare, *The Complete Works*, tr. R. J. Armstrong, OFM Cap., and I. C. Brady, OFM (Classics of Western Spirituality, 1982), pp. 25–166.

Friars began writing about Francis soon after his death. The attempt to determine the authors of the different medieval Lives, their date and importance comprises what is known to scholars as the 'Franciscan Question'. The earliest Life is the 'Vita Prima' of *Thomas of Celano, commissioned by Pope Gregory IX on the canonization of Francis. Next in date is the so-called 'Legenda Trium Sociorum' and possibly the 'Anonymus Perusinus', which may be the memoirs of Brothers Bernard and Giles. In 1246 Thomas of Celano wrote a 'Vita Secunda', based on the reminiscences of the companions of Francis and other early friars, and supplemented it with a 'Tractatus de miraculis'. In 1260 the General Chapter commissioned St *Bonaventure to write a new Life of Francis and in 1266 made this 'Legenda Major' the 'authorized Life', ordering the destruction of all earlier Lives. This led to the growth of oral legends which culminated in the 'Actus Beati Francisci et Sociorum Eius', which became in the later Italian condensation, 'I Fioretti di San Francesco' ('The Little Flowers of St Francis', q.v.). The earlier material, notably the writings of Brother Leo, had not, however, entirely perished and has been recovered in modern times, with much controversy. P. Sabatier mistakenly believed that the 'Speculum Perfectionis', a collection of stories about St Francis based on this material, was written at the Portiuncula in 1227, whereas the true date is 1318. A better candidate is the collection of stories in Perugia MS 1046 brought to light in 1922 by F. Delorme, OFM, and known by various names, incl. the 'Legenda Perusina' and 'Compilatio Assisiensis'. It almost certainly predates 1246. A work of a different kind, but with its own special value, is the 13th-cent. allegory about St Francis and Lady Poverty, the 'Sacrum Commercium'. In the later Middle Ages the most important work was Bartholomew of Pisa's 'Liber de Conformitate Vitae b. Patris Francisci ad Vitam Domini Nostri Jesu Christi', presented by its author to the General Chapter of the Franciscans in 1399.

There are crit. edns. of the Lives and 'Tractatus de miraculis' by Thomas of Celano and the 'Legenda Major' of Bonaventure, with other material, by the Franciscans of Quaracchi (Analecta Franciscana, 10; 1926–41); of the 'Legenda Trium Sociorum' by T. Desbonnet, OFM, in *Archivum Franciscanum Historicum*, 67 (1974), pp. 38–144; the 'Anonymus Perusinus' by L. Di Fonzo, OFM Conv., in *Miscellanea Franciscana*, 72 (1972), pp. 117–483; the 'Legenda Perusina' by R. B. Brooke as *Scripta Leonis, Rufini et Angeli Sociorum S. Francisci* (Oxford Medieval Texts, 1970, with Eng. tr.), and by M. Bigaroni, OFM, as *Compilatio Assisiensis* (Pubblicazioni della Biblioteca Francescana Chiesa Nuova—Assisi, 2; Assisi, 1975); of 'Speculum Perfectionis' by P. Sabatier (British Society of Franciscan Studies, 13 and 17; 1928–31); of the 'Actus Beati Francisci et Sociorum Eius' by J. Cambell, M. Bigaroni, and G. Boccali, all OFM (Pubblicazioni della Bibliotheca Francescana Chiesa Nuova—Assisi, 5; Assisi, 1988); the 'Little Flowers' by G. Pagnani, OFM (Rome [1959]), and the 'Sacrum Commercium' by S. Brufani (Medioevo Francescano, Testi, 1; Assisi, 1990). All of these, except the 'Anonymus Perusinus', have been tr. into Eng., some many times. Most of them have been conveniently, though uncritically, collected by M. A. Habig, OFM, *St Francis of Assisi: Writings and Early Biographies* (Chicago [1973]; 3rd edn., 1979, also pub. in London). Modern edn. of Bartholomew of Pisa's 'Liber de Conformitate' by the Franciscans of Quaracchi (Analecta Franciscana, 4–5; 1906–12).

Among modern Lives special importance attaches to that of P. Sabatier (Paris, 1893; Eng. tr., 1894), which inaugurated modern Franciscan studies. It was preceded by those of K. Hase (Leipzig, 1856) and Mrs [M. O. J.] Oliphant (London, c.1870). The more important Lives since that of Sabatier include those of J. Jörgensen (Copenhagen, 1907; Eng. tr., 1912), Fr. Cuthbert [Hess], OSFC (London, 1912), O. Englebert (Paris, 1947; rev. edn., 1982; Eng. trs., 1950 and Chicago [1965]), and A. Fortini (4 vols. in 5 [Assisi, 1959]; abbreviated Eng. tr., New York, 1981). Good popular studies by G. K. *Chesterton (London [1923]), T. S. R. Boase (ibid., 1936), J. R. H. Moorman (ibid., 1950), M. de la Bedoyere (ibid., 1962), R. Manselli (Rome, 1980), and J. Green (Paris, 1983; Eng. tr., 1985). Pictorial biog. by L. von Matt and W. Hauser (Zurich, 1952; Eng. tr., 1956). W. Seton (ed.), *St. Francis of Assisi, 1226–1926: Essays in Commemoration* (London, 1926); M. W. Sheehan, OFM Cap. (ed.), *St Francis of Assisi: Essays in Commemoration, 1982* (St Bonaventure, NY, 1982). J. R. H. Moorman, *The Sources for the Life of S. Francis of Assisi* (Publications of the University of Manchester, 274, Historical Series, 79; 1940); R. Manselli, *Nos qui cum eo fuimus: Contributo alla questione Francescana* (Bibliotheca Seraphico-Capuccina, 28; 1980). L. Di Fonzo, OFM Conv., 'Per la cronologia di S. Francesco. Gli anni 1182–1212', *Miscellanea Francescana*, 82 (1982), pp. 1–115. Id. in *DHGE* 18 (1977), cols. 683–98, s.v. 'François (8) d'Assise'; id. in *DIP* 4 (1977), cols. 513–27, s.v. 'Francesco, di Assisi', both with further bibl. See also works cited under STIGMATIZATION.

Francis Borgia, St. See BORGIA, ST FRANCIS.

Francis of Paola, St (1416–1507), founder of the Order of *Minims. Coming from a modest, deeply religious family, he spent a year with the *Franciscans as a boy in fulfilment of a vow of his parents. Here he developed a great love of austerity, and in 1431 began to lead a strictly ascetic life as a hermit, first in a cave near the Tyrrhenian Sea, then in a nearby forest. About 1435, the date held to be that of the foundation of his order, he was joined by others, and before long he was the spiritual guide of a group of hermits, with whom from c.1452 he began to live in community. Other foundations followed later. He became renowned for his holiness throughout Italy and beyond its frontiers, and many miraculous cures were attributed to him. His fame was such that Louis XI of France, in terror of death after an apoplectic fit, sent for him; while his son, Charles VIII, kept him near him as his spiritual director and built him two monasteries. The last three months of his life St Francis spent preparing himself for death in his cell in complete solitude. He was canonized in 1519 and declared 'Patron of Italian Seafarers' in 1943. His emblem is the word CARITAS in a circle of rays. Feast day, 2 Apr.

AASS, Apr. 1 (1685), pp. 103–234. The 'anonymous Life' [by L. Clavense] also ed. G. M. Perrimezzi (2 vols., Rome, 1707). Modern Life by G. M. Roberti (Rome, 1915). A. [M.] Galuzzi, OM, *Origini dell'Ordine dei Minimi* (Corona Lateranesis, 11; 1967). R. Fiot, *Saint François de Paule à Amboise* (pamphlet for the Association des Amis de Saint François de Paul; Chambray-les-Tours [1975]). The apostolic letter of Pope *Pius XII appointing him patron of Italian seafarers is pr. in *AAS* 35 (1943), pp. 163 f. F. Russo, MSC, *Bibliografia di San Francesco di Paola* (Supplemento al 'Bollettino Ufficiale dell'Ordine dei Minimi', 3, no. 1; 1957). R. Fiot in *Dict. Sp.* 5 (1964), cols. 1040–51, s.v. 'François (19) de Paule'; A. Galuzzi, OM, in *DHGE* 18 (1977), cols. 742–5, s.v. 'François (50) de Paule', with further bibl.

Francis de Sales, St (1567–1622), Bp. of Geneva from 1602, and one of the leaders of the *Counter-Reformation. Born at the castle of Sales in Savoy, he was educated at Annecy, Paris (1578–88; first at the Collège de *Clermont and then at the *Sorbonne), and Padua (1588–92), reading theology and law. Despite attractive offers of a position by the Duke of Savoy, he felt a strong vocation to holy orders, and in 1593 was ordained priest and made Provost of Geneva. He undertook a mission in the largely Protestant Chablais and, in the face of personal danger and suffering, he won many *Calvinists to Catholicism by his unfailing spirit of charity and his engagement in controversy in a conciliatory spirit. In 1599 he was nominated Coadjutor-Bp. of Geneva, though he was not consecrated until he succeeded to the see in 1602. During that year he went to Paris and met P. de *Bérulle, the circle around Mme *Acarie, and St *Vincent de Paul. He administered his diocese from Annecy in a reforming spirit, also continuing regularly to preach and minister as confessor. In 1604 he met St *Jane Frances de Chantal in Dijon; he became her director and with her founded the *Visitation Order in Annecy in 1610. His most famous writings, the *Introduction to the *Devout Life* (1609; q.v.) and the *Treatise on the Love of God* (1616; Eng. tr. 1630), designed for those more advanced in the spiritual life, were adapted for publication from instructions given to individuals. Both works had considerable influence on later spiritual writings. He was beatified in 1661, canonized in 1665, and declared a '*Doctor of the Church' in 1877 and 'Patron of Catholic Journalists' in 1923. Feast day, 24 (formerly 27) Jan. See also BOSCO, ST JOHN, and SALESIANS.

The best edn. of his *Œuvres complètes* is that pub. by the Visitandines of Annecy (26 vols., Annecy, 1892–1932 + vol. 27, 'table analytique' by A. Denis, 1964); Eng. tr. by H. B. Mackey, OSB, and others, under the direction of J. C. Hedley, OSB (6 vols., 1883–1908). Crit. edn. of his *Œuvres* [*Introduction à la Vie Dévote, Traité de l'Amour de Dieu*, and *Recueil des Entretiens spirituels*], by A. Ravier and R. Devos (Bibliothèque de la Pléiade [1969]) and of his *Correspondance: Les Lettres d'amitié spirituelle*, by A. Ravier, SJ (Bibliothèque Européenne [1980]). Selected letters tr. into Eng., with introd., by E. [C. V.] Stopp (1960). The primary contemporary authority is C.-A. de Sales (nephew), *De Vita et Rebus Gestis . . . Francisci Salesii* (Lyons, 1634; mod. Fr. tr., 2 vols., 1857). J. P. Camus, *L'Esprit du bien-heureux François de Sales* (6 vols., 1639–41; abridgement by P. Collot, 1727, frequently repr.; Eng. trs. of this abridgement, 1872, 1910, and New York, 1952). A. J. M. Hamon, *Vie de Saint François de Sales* (2 vols., 1854; Eng. tr., 2 vols., 1925–9); F. Trochu, *Saint François de Sales* (2 vols., Paris, 1946); E. J. Lajeunie, OP, *Saint François de Sales: L'Homme, la pensée, l'action* (2 vols., posthumously pub. [1966]). Other modern studies incl. those of M. de la Bedoyere (London, 1960), E.-M. Lajeunie ('Maîtres spirituels', 1962), R. Murphy (Paris, 1964), R. Bady ('Les écrivains devant Dieu' [1970]), and C. H. Palmer (Ilfracombe, 1974). P. Serouet, *De la vie dévote à la vie mystique: Saint Thérèse d'Avila, Saint François de Sales* [1958]. R. Kleinman, *Saint François de Sales and the Protestants* (Travaux d'Humanisme et Renaissance, 52; Geneva, 1962). H. Lemaire, *Les Images chez Saint François de Sales* (1962). R. Devos, *Saint François de Sales, par les témoins de sa vie: Textes extraits des procès de béatification* (Annecy, 1967). *Mémorial du IVe Centenaire de la Naissance de Saint François de Sales 1567–1967* (ibid. [1968]). Julien-Eymard d'Angers, OFM Cap., *L'Humanisme Chrétien au XVIIe Siècle: St François de Sales et Yves de Paris* (International Archives of the History of Ideas, 31; The Hague, 1970), pp. 1–78. H. Bordes and J. Hennequin (eds.), *L'Unidivers Salésien: Saint François de Sales hier et aujourd'hui. Actes du Colloque International de Metz, 17–19 septembre 1992* (1994). V. Brasier, E. Morganti, and M. St Durica, *Opera e scritti riguardanti San Francesco di Sales: Repertorio bibliografico 1623–1955* (Biblioteca del 'Salesianum', 44; 1956); J. Struś, SDB, 'San Francesco di Sales 1567–1622. Rassegna bibliografica dal 1956', *Salesianum*, 45 (1983), pp. 635–71. Bremond, 1 (1916), pp. 68–127; Eng. tr., 1 (1928), pp. 55–100. P. Serouet in *Dict. Sp.* 5 (1964), cols. 1057–97, s.v. 'François (25) de Sales'; R. Devos in *DHGE* 18 (1977), cols. 753–60, s.v. 'François (63) de Sales', both with extensive bibl.

Francis of Vitoria. See VITORIA, FRANCESCO DE.

Francis Xavier, St (1506–52), 'Apostle of the Indies' and 'of *Japan'. He was one of the greatest of Christian missionaries, and an original member of the *Jesuits. The son of an aristocratic Spanish-Basque family, he was born in Navarre. While studying at the University of Paris, he met St *Ignatius of Loyola, and on 15 Aug. 1534 with him and five others made a vow of lifelong poverty and service either in the Holy Land or wherever the Pope should send them. He was ordained priest in 1537. In 1540 Pedro de Mascarenhas, Portuguese ambassador to the Papal court, petitioned *Paul III for Jesuits to evangelize the East. At two days' notice, Xavier, then secretary of the Society, left Rome and sailed from Lisbon on 7 Apr. 1541. In May 1542 he reached Goa, which he made his headquarters. From there he went on to Travancore, Malacca, the Molucca Islands, and *Sri Lanka. In 1549 he landed in Japan, the language of which he studied, and founded there a Church which endured through great persecutions. He returned to Goa in 1552, but left in the same year for a mission to China. On the way, at the island of Sancian (Changchuan; S. of Canton), he fell ill and died before he could enter the country. His body was brought to the church of the Good Jesus at Goa, where it lies magnificently enshrined. His work is remarkable for the extent of his journeys (in spite of his invariable seasickness) and the large number of his converts. The Jesuits have attributed to him more than 700,000 conversions. Wherever he preached he left organized Christian communities. His methods have sometimes been attacked, e.g. he has been criticized for not attempting to understand the oriental religions, for invoking the help of the *Inquisition, for approving the persecution of the *Church of the East, and for using the government at Goa as a means of proselytizing. The well-known hymn, 'O Deus, ego amo Te' ('My God, I love Thee, not because', tr. E. *Caswall), long ascribed to Xavier, appears to be a Latin rendering of a Spanish sonnet by an unknown 17th-cent. author. He was canonized in 1622, and *Pius X named him patron of the work of the Congregation for the *Propagation of the Faith. Feast day, 3 Dec.

Monumenta Xaveriana (Monumenta Historica Societatis Jesu, 2 vols., Madrid, 1899–1912); letters also ed. G. Schurhammer, SJ, and J. Wicki, SJ (ibid., vols. 67 and 68; Rome, 1944–5). Eng. tr. of *Letters and Instructions* by M. J. Costelloe, SJ (St Louis, 1992). H. Tursellini, SJ, *De Vita Francisci Xaverii* (Rome, 1594; Eng. tr., Paris, 1632). Modern Lives by J. Brodrick, SJ (London, 1952), G. Schurhammer (2 vols. in 4, Freiburg, 1955–73; Eng. tr., 4 vols., Rome, 1973–82), and J. M. Recondo, SJ (Madrid, 1988). Various papers by Schurhammer assembled in his *Gesammelte Studien*, 3. *Xaveriana* (Bibliotheca Instituti Historici S.I., 22; 1964). A. C. Ross, *A Vision Betrayed: The Jesuits in Japan and China 1542–1742* (Edinburgh [1994]), pp. 13–51. Polgár, 3 (1990), pp. 675–731. G. Schurhammer in *Dict. Sp.* 5 (1964), cols. 1099–1107, s.v. 'François (28) de Xavier'; J. Wicki in *NCE* 4 (1967), pp. 1059 f., s.v. 'Xavier, Francis, St', both with bibl.

Franciscan Order. The Order of Friars Minor was founded by St *Francis of Assisi (q.v.) in 1209, when he gave his followers their first rule, now lost. This rule was recast in 1221 and brought into its final form in 1223, when *Honorius III confirmed it by bull, whence it is known as 'Regula bullata'. Its distinguishing mark is the insistence on complete poverty not only for individual friars but corporately for the whole order. The friars were to live by the work of their hands or, if need be, by begging, but were forbidden to own any property or to accept money. With the rapid spread of the order and the need for settled houses, this ideal soon proved unworkable if taken literally. Thus two schools of thought developed in the order. The one, whose members were called '*Spirituals', insisted on interpretation acc. to the letter; the other, followed by the majority, preferred a more moderate view in accordance with the requirements of the times. From 1245 onwards the discussion grew violent and endangered the unity of the order, though it temporarily abated under the conciliatory influence of St *Bonaventure, who was General from 1257 to 1274. From 1310 to 1312 the question was debated before the Pope, and in 1317–18 decided against the stricter party by two bulls of *John XXII which permitted the order corporate ownership. Many of the Spirituals fled and became schismatics under the name of '*Fraticelli'. In 1321 the problem of poverty arose again, this time in the theoretical form as to whether Christ and the Apostles had owned property, and a heated scholastic discussion between Franciscans and *Dominicans developed. These futile disputes, together with the Black Death (1348–52) and the *Great Schism (1378–1417), led to a general decline of the order in the 14th cent. Laxity also increased as their material prosperity grew. But during this period many efforts at reform were made, and a return to poverty was brought about by the so-called '*Observants', who opposed the lax '*Conventuals'. The 'Observants' gained ecclesiastical recognition when in 1415 the Council of *Constance granted their French province special provincials, and in 1443 *Eugenius IV provided them with a separate Vicar General. In 1517 they were finally separated from the Conventuals and declared the true Order of St Francis. Early in the 16th cent. another reform, introduced by Matteo di Bassi (1495–1552), led to the establishment of the *Capuchins (q.v.), whose rule was drawn up in 1529.

During the 17th and 18th cents. reform parties sprang up again. Of these the chief were the 'Reformati', the *Recollects and the *Discalced, who lived after their own statutes, though remaining under the same General. Besides these internal differences, the political events of the 18th and 19th cents., esp. the French Revolution, the secularization of *Joseph II, the revolutions in Spain (1834), Poland (1831), Italy, and the *Kulturkampf in Prussia, did great harm to the order. At the end of the 19th century, however, it regained new vigour by the reunion of its different branches, which was confirmed by *Leo XIII in 1897.

The order, which has always cultivated popular preaching and missionary activities, has given a great number of saints to the Church, the best known being St *Antony of Padua, popular as a miracle-worker. Though not primarily instituted as a learned order, it has produced many celebrated scholars, among them St Bonaventure, *Duns Scotus, and *William of Ockham. Among the popular devotions they promoted are the *Angelus, the *crib, and the *Stations of the Cross. Franciscans were among the chief defenders of the *Immaculate Conception in the Middle Ages.

To the Franciscan friars are attached a Second Order of contemplative nuns (the *Poor Clares, q.v.) and a *Third Order (q.v.), now divided into Regular and Secular Tertiaries.

In 1224 the first Franciscans to establish themselves in England arrived under *Agnellus of Pisa and settled at once at *Canterbury, London, and *Oxford. Their piety and learning won them a ready hearing, and by the middle of the century there were some 50 friaries and over 1,200 friars in England. Their early history (down to c.1258) was vividly described by Thomas of Eccleston ('De Adventu Fratrum Minorum in Angliam'). John *Pecham, one of their number, held the see of Canterbury from 1279 to 1292. In the 14th cent., when they no longer possessed the same moral and intellectual qualities, they became the object of J. *Wycliffe's attacks. The Observants were introduced by Henry VII and acted as confessors to *Henry VIII and Catherine of Aragon; but they were scattered before the *Dissolution. Since the middle of the 19th cent., many Franciscan houses have been re-established.

In the C of E a group inspired by Franciscan ideals settled near Batcombe (Cerne Abbas) in Dorset in 1921, to minister in the first place to the unemployed who tramped the roads. In 1931 they took vows and were constituted a religious community. They have grown considerably in numbers and influence and have been active in evangelistic work, esp. in the universities. A small Anglican community for women has also been started with its headquarters at Freeland, Oxon.

The most important source for the order as a whole, apart from its official docs., is L. *Wadding, OFM (q.v.), *Annales Minorum* (8 vols., Lyons, 1625–54; later edns. much extended); id., *Scriptores Ordinis Minorum* (Rome, 1650; suppl., with corrections, by J. H. Sbaralea, OFM, 1806). *Bullarium Franciscanum* (4 vols., ed. J. H. Sbaralea, OFM, Rome, 1759–68; 3 further vols. ed. C. Eubel, OFM, ibid., 1898–1904, + Epitome et Supplementum by id., Quaracchi, 1908; NS ed. U. Hüntemann, OFM, and J. M. Pou y Marti, OFM, 3 vols., ibid., 1929–49). *Analecta Franciscana, sive Chronica aliaque varia Documenta ad Historiam Fratrum Minorum Spectantia*, ed. by the Franciscans of Quaracchi (11 vols. to date, Quaracchi, 1885–1970). Useful collection of sources for the history of the order in England ed. J. S. Brewer and R. Howlett, *Monumenta Franciscana* (2 vols., RS, 1858–82). For details of edns. of early constitutions and other sources see A. G. Little, *A Guide to Franciscan Studies* (Helps for Students of History, 23; 1920). G. Golubovich, OFM, and others, *Bibliotheca Bio-Bibliografica della Terra Santa e dell'Oriente Francescano*: Serie Prima: Annali (5 vols., Quaracchi, 1905–27); Nuova Serie: Documenti (14 vols., ibid., 1921–39; further vols. in preparation, Cairo); Serie Terza: Documenti (2 vols., Ethiopia Francescana, Quaracchi, 1928–48); Serie Quarta: Studi (Cairo, 1954 ff.). Docs. on the Chinese Mission pr. in *Sinica Franciscana* (Rome, 1929 ff.). H. Holzapfel, OFM, *Handbuch der Geschichte des Franziskanerordens* (1909). A. Masseron, *Les Franciscains* ('Les Grands Ordres monastiques et instituts religieux', 1931; Eng. tr., 1931). A. Gemelli, OFM, *Il francescanesimo* (2nd edn., Vita e pensiero, 1932; Eng. tr., 1934). [M. Badin, in religion] Père Gratien de Paris, OFM Cap., *Histoire de la fondation et de l'évolution de l'ordre des Frères Mineurs au XIIIᵉ siècle* (1928). F. de Sessevalle, of the Third Order, *Histoire générale de l'ordre de Saint François, la premiere partie, le moyen-âge, 1209–1517* (2 vols., 1935–7). R. M. Huber, OFM Conv., *A Documented History of the Franciscan Order, 1182–1517* (Milwaukee, Wis., and Washington, DC, 1944). J. [R. H.] Moorman, *A History of the Franciscan Order from its origins to the year 1517* (Oxford, 1968). R. B. Brooke, *Early Franciscan Government: Elias to Bonaventure* (Cambridge, 1959). M. D. Lambert, *Franciscan Poverty: The Doctrine of the Absolute Poverty of Christ and the Apostles in the Franciscan Order, 1210–1323* (CHS, 1961). D. Nimmo, *Reform and Division in the Medieval Franciscan Order from Saint Francis to the Foundation of the Capuchins* (Bibliotheca Seraphico-Capuccina, 33; Rome, 1987). A. G. Little, *Studies in English Franciscan History* (Ford Lectures for 1916; Publications of the University of Manchester, 113, Historical Series, 29; 1917) and other works; [M.] D. *Knowles, OSB, *The Religious Orders in England* [1] (1948), pp. 114–45, 171–93, 205–52. J. R. H. Moorman, *The Franciscans in England* (1974). Father Cuthbert [Hess], OFM Cap., *The Friars and How They Came to England* (1903; Eng. tr. of Thomas of Eccleston's 'De Adventu FF. Minorum in Angliam', with pref. essay, 'On the Spirit and Genius of the Franciscan Friars', pp. 1–128). L. Lemmens, OFM, *Geschichte der Franziskanermissionen* (Missionswissenschaftliche Abhandlungen und Texte, ed. J. Schmidlin, 12; 1929). The many collections of studies and periodicals devoted to the affairs of the order incl. the pubs. of the British Society of Franciscan Studies (19 vols., Aberdeen, 1908–37), *Études franciscaines* (Paris, 1899 ff.), *La Verna* (Florence, 1903–14; then called *Studi Francescani*, ibid., 1914 ff.), *Archivum Franciscanum Historicum* (Quaracchi, 1908 ff.), *Franziskanische Studien* (Münster i.W., 1914 ff.), *Revue d'Histoire Franciscaine* (Paris, 1924 ff.), and *Fran-*

ciscan Studies (New York, 1941 ff.). Heimbucher, 1, pp. 656–814, with detailed bibl. M. Bihl, OFM, and Z. Engelhardt, OFM, in *CE* 6 (1909), pp. 281–302, s.v. 'Friars Minor, Order of'; Édouard d'Alençon, OFM Cap., in *DTC* 6 (1920), cols. 809–63, s.v. 'Frères Mineurs'; E. Longpré, OFM, and others in *Dict. Sp.* 5 (1964), cols. 1268–401, s.v. 'Frères Mineurs'; L. di Fronzo, OFM Conv., in *DIP* 4 (1977), cols. 464–511, s.v. 'Francescani (1209–1517)'; E. Frascadore, OFM, and others, ibid., cols. 839–911, s.v. 'Fratri Minori simpliciter dicti'; K. S. Frank, OFM, in *L.Th.K.* (3rd edn.), 4 (1995), cols. 30–5, s.v. 'Franziskaner', all with bibls. See also bibls. to CAPUCHINS, OBSERVANTS, RECOLLECTS, and SPIRITUAL FRANCISCANS.

Franciscus a Sancta Clara. See DAVENPORT, CHRISTOPHER.

Franck, Sebastian (*c.*1499–*c.*1542), German humanist and radical reformer. After studying at Ingolstadt and Heidelberg, he was ordained priest. He became a *Lutheran in the 1520s, and held pastoral appointments from 1526 in Ansbach-Bayreuth and then in Gustenfelden. Becoming disenchanted with this work, he moved to Nuremberg and worked in the printing trade. His increasingly radical ideas damaged his reputation with the city magistrates and he moved to Strasbourg, from which he was expelled in 1531. After brief stays at Kehl and Esslingen, he came to Ulm in 1533. Despite tense relations with the civic authorities, he was not expelled until 1539. He spent his final years in Basle. Franck promoted a form of undogmatic Christianity which was equally offensive to Catholics and Protestants. His varied writings are largely secular, but his historical compilation *Chronica* (3 vols., 1531) expressed his radical religious views. His more specifically theological works include a German edition of A. Althamen's *Diallage* (1528; a treatise against the *Anabaptists) and an index to the Bible (1539). He also produced German translations of S. Fish's *Supplication of Beggars* (1529) and of *Erasmus' *Moriae Encomium* with *Agrippa's *De Vanitate Scientiarum* (1534).

Life by C. A. Hase (Leipzig, 1869). Modern study by W. E. Peuckert (Munich, 1943). H. Weigelt, *Sebastian Franck und die lutherische Reformation* (Schriften des Vereins für Reformationsgeschichte, 186; 1972). S. Ozment, *Mysticism and Dissent* (New Haven, Conn., and London, 1973), pp. 137–67; G. H. Williams, *The Radical Reformation* (Philadelphia, 1957; London, 1962), pp. 264–7, 457–65, and 499–504; 3rd edn. (Sixteenth Century Essays & Studies, 15; Kirksville, Mo. [1992]), pp. 394–8, 694–703 and 747–50. Bibliography by K. Kaczerowsky (Wiesbaden, 1976). A. Séguenny in *TRE* 11 (1983), pp. 307–12, s.v., with extensive bibl.

Francke, August Hermann (1663–1727), German *Pietist and educationalist. He was born at Lübeck, and after studying philosophy and theology at Erfurt and Kiel became a lecturer at Leipzig in 1685. He was attracted to a pietistic form of religion and held 'Collegia Philobiblica' in which the Bible was expounded on devotional lines. Through P. Anton he came into contact with P. J. *Spener, whose spirituality deeply impressed him and who became his mentor. In 1691 he was appointed professor of Greek and Oriental languages at the newly founded University of Halle and pastor of Glaucha, nr. Halle, where his sermons and pastoral activities soon attracted a large congregation. In 1695 he laid the foundation of his famous

Institutes, later known as 'Franckesche Stiftungen', by opening a poor-school in his house. In 1696 he founded his 'Paedagogium' and his orphanage. Both grew rapidly, and during the next years other institutions, such as a publishing house and a dispensary, were added. In 1698 he became professor of theology; this appointment strengthened his position. In his struggles with his orthodox opponents, as well as with representatives of *Enlightenment thought, he was supported by the Prussian king, Frederick William I, who in 1723 at Francke's suggestion removed the philosopher Christian *Wolff from Halle. Francke's theology was similar to that of Spener, but he placed more emphasis on the need for an inner religious struggle ('Busskampf'). At the same time the strict ethical code which he tried to impose gave his form of Pietism a legalist turn which influenced the development of Pietism, esp. in North and Central Germany.

His works, which are mainly of a devotional and practical character, ed. E. Peschke (Texte zur Geschichte des Pietismus, Abt. II; 1981 ff.). Life by G. Kramer (2 vols., Halle a.S., 1880–2). A. Nebe, *Neue Quellen zu August Hermann Francke* (1927). E. Beyreuther, *August Hermann Francke 1663–1727: Zeuge des lebendigen Gottes* (Marburg [1956]); id., *August Hermann Francke und die Anfänge der ökumenischen Bewegung* (Leipzig, 1957). E. Peschke, *Studien zur Theologie August Hermann Franckes* (2 vols., 1964–6); id., *Bekehrung und Reform: Ansatz und Wurzeln der Theologie August Hermann Franckes* (Arbeiten zur Geschichte des Pietismus, 15; 1977). K. Deppermann, *Der hallesche Pietismus und der preussische Staat unter Friedrich III. (I.)* (Göttingen [1961]). Id. in M. Greschat (ed.), *Orthodoxie und Pietismus* (Gestalten der Kirchengeschichte, 7; Stuttgart, 1982), pp. 241–60, with bibl. E. Beyreuther in *RGG* (3rd edn.), 2 (1958), cols. 1013–15, s.v. 'Francke (1), August Hermann'; F. de Boor in *TRE* 11 (1983), pp. 312–20, s.v. See also bibl. to PIETISM.

Frankfurt, Councils of. Frankfurt am Main was the scene of some 16 Imperial councils during the Carolingian epoch. The best known of them was called by *Charlemagne in 794 to condemn the *Adoptianist heresy. It was attended by bishops from all over the Frankish kingdoms, including Aquitaine and Italy. Besides repudiating Adoptianism it condemned the decree of the Second Council of *Nicaea (787) on the worship of *icons, probably through a misunderstanding of the distinction made between λατρεία and προσκύνησις.

On the Council of 794, Hardouin, 4, cols. 865–912; Mansi, 13 (1767), cols. 829–56; crit. edn. by A. Werminghoff in *MGH*, Concilia, 2 (pt. 1; 1906), pp. 108–71. Hefele and Leclercq, 3 (pt. 2; 1910), pp. 1045–60 and 1240–6. C. de Clercq, *La Législation religieuse franque de Clovis à Charlemagne*, 1 (Louvain, 1936), pp. 184–91; F. L. Ganshof, 'Observations sur le Synode de Francfort de 794', in *Miscellanea Historica in Honorem Alberti de Meyer*, 1 (Université de Louvain, Recueil de travaux d'histoire et de philologie, 3rd ser. 22; 1946), pp. 306–18. L. Wallach, *Alcuin and Charlemagne: Studies in Carolingian History and Literature* (Cornell Studies in Classical Philology, 32; 1959), pp. 147–77 *passim*. S. Anton in *DHGE* 18 (1977), cols. 561 f.; W. Hartmann in *Lexicon des Mittelalters*, 4 (1989), cols. 740 f., with bibl.

Franzelin, Johann Baptist (1816–86), Austrian cardinal and theologian. He entered the Society of Jesus in 1834, and in 1857 was appointed professor of dogmatic theology at the Roman College. He took a prominent part in preparing the First *Vatican Council, where he acted as one of the leading theologians. In 1876 he was raised to the cardinalate. A theologian of great learning and accuracy of mind, he wrote a long series of dogmatic works of which the chief was his *De Divina Traditione et Scriptura* (1870). In his treatise on the Eucharistic Sacrifice (1868) he followed J. de *Lugo in teaching that the immolation in the Sacrifice consisted in the reduction to a lower state of Christ's human nature by being clothed in the species of bread and wine. Franzelin took an active part in the controversy with Greek Orthodox and Protestant scholars on the procession of the Holy Spirit, setting forth the traditional W. doctrine in his *Examen doctrinae Macarii Bulgakov* (1876).

'Commentarius de Vita Eminentissimi Auctoris' prefixed to his posthumous *Theses de Ecclesia Christi* (1887), pp. v–xxxi. N. Walsh, SJ, *John Baptist Franzelin, SJ . . .: A Sketch and a Study* (Dublin, 1895). F. Gaar, *Das Prinzip der göttlichen Tradition nach Joh. Baptist Franzelin* (Ratisbon [1973]). P. Walter, *Johann Baptist Franzelin (1816–1886): Jesuit, Theologe, Kardinal* (Bolzano, 1987). Polgár, 1 (1990), pp. 674 f. P. Bernard in *DTC* 6 (1920), cols. 765–7; supplementary bibl. in *DHGE* 18 (1977), col. 1032, s.v.

Fraser, Alexander Campbell (1819–1914), idealist philosopher. He was a pupil of Sir William Hamilton at Edinburgh, and in 1844 was ordained in the *Free Church of Scotland, which had been created by the schism in the previous year, to the charge of Cramond, nr. Edinburgh. On Hamilton's death in 1856, he succeeded to his professorship at the University and held the chair till 1891. His main philosophical interest was the study of G. *Berkeley, whose writings he twice edited for the Clarendon Press (1871, 1901). The earlier edition was accompanied by a volume of Berkeley's *Life and Letters* incorporating much new material, and in 1881 he contributed the volume *Berkeley* to Blackwood's Philosophical Classics. He also published a set of *Gifford Lectures on *The Philosophy of Theism* (1895–6). Though his own philosophical position was greatly influenced by the doctrines of Berkeley, Fraser did not follow him slavishly; and his success as a teacher owed more to his ability to stimulate interest in the issues of philosophy than to the inculcation of any particular conclusions. He described the course of his philosophical development in his *Biographia Philosophica* (1904).

J. Kellie, *Alexander Campbell Fraser: A Sketch of his Life and Philosophical Position* (1909). A. S. Pringle-*Pattison, 'Alexander Campbell Fraser, 1819–1914', *Mind*, 24 (1915), pp. 289–325; id. in *DNB, 1912–1921* (1927), pp. 195–7.

frater, the hall of a monastery or friary used for meals or refreshment. The word is in origin related to 'refectory' (*refectorium*) through the Old French *refraitour*.

J. C. Dickinson, *Monastic Life in Mediaeval England* (1961), pp. 34 f.

fraternities. During and after the Middle Ages, fraternities of many kinds were founded in the Church to meet the religious and social needs of clergy and laity. Their primary purpose was to secure for their members mutual support in death through Masses, prayers, and alms, as well as intercessions in sickness and other religious benefits. They also provided in financial and material ways for such contingencies as death, sickness, and natural disasters, and by social gatherings such as corporate meals they promoted fellowship and recreation. They aspired to foster peace and concord among their members by providing a forum for the resolving of disputes. Through their almsgiving they made a considerable contribution to the relief of poverty. Their distant origins lay in the *collegia* of the classical world and in early Germanic *Schutzgilden*; they developed rapidly from Carolingian times when *Hincmar of Reims already attested their multiplication in his concern to safeguard their religious as well as their convivial character. The Abbotsbury Guild Statutes (dating from between c.1025 and c.1050) are a good early example of the statutes by which they came to be governed. Such fraternities, with the features of being locally based, having their own officials and statutes, and assembling periodically for religious and social purposes, should be distinguished from the looser spiritual confraternities of monasteries and from monastic unions of prayers and benefits, as well as from specifically trade associations. Until the 13th cent., fraternities may usefully be classified as rural or parish, abbatial (i.e. affiliated to an abbey), and urban (esp. in towns with episcopal sees); clerical, or mixed clerical and lay, fraternities were not uncommon. Thereafter, fraternities increasingly catered for burgeoning forms of lay piety; increasing lay self-awareness sometimes gave rise to fraternities exhibiting zeal against sinful clergy and even radical anticlericalism. Italy saw particularly significant developments, esp. the emergence from c.1260 of the so-called *disciplinati* or *flagellants, who were much concerned to counter heresy and sodomy, as well as to appease civil strife and to relieve poverty. Many fraternities were associated with the orders of *Mendicant Friars, and these were often not specifically attached to any particular territory; the most striking example was the *Dominican confraternity of the BVM which evolved into the world-wide Confraternity of the *Rosary.

In the modern RC Church, fraternities are governed by canon law covering public and private associations of the faithful (*CIC* (1983), cans. 298–329). Each has to have its own statutes, defining its purposes, government, and membership.

L. A. *Muratori, *Antiquitates Italicae Medii Aevi*, 6 (Milan, 1742), pp. 446–82, diss. 75, 'De Piis Laicorum Confraternitatibus earumque Origine, Flagellantibus, et Sacris Missionibus', incl. some primary docs. Hincmar's Synodical Capitula of 852, chs. 14–16, are pr. in J. P. Migne, *PL* 125. 777–8. The Abbotsbury Guild Statutes are pr., with Eng. tr. in *Councils & Synods with Other Documents Relating to the English Church*, 1: A.D. 871–1204, ed. D. Whitelock, M. Brett, and C. N. L. Brooke, 1 (Oxford, 1981), pp. 516–20. The extensive modern lit. includes J. Wollasch, 'Gemeinschaftsbewusstsein und soziale Leistung im Mittelalter', *Frühmittelalterliche Studien*, 9 (1975), pp. 268–86; G. G. Meersseman and G. P. Pacini, *Ordo fraternitatis: Confraternite e pietà dei laici nel medioevo* (Italia Sacra. Studi e documenti di storia ecclesiastica, 24–6; 1977); N. J. Housley, 'Politics and Heresy in Italy: Anti-Heretical Crusades, Orders and Confraternities, 1200–1500', *JEH* 33 (1982), pp. 193–208; and *Le Mouvement Confraternel au Moyen Age: France, Italie, Suisse. Actes de la table ronde . . . Lausanne 9–11 Mai 1985* (Collection de l'École française de Rome, 97; 1987). Collections of papers on 'Le confraternite in Italia tra Medioevo e Rinascimento', ed. G. De Rosa, *Ricerche di Storia Sociale e Religiosa*, NS 9, nn. 17–18 (1980); on 'La Sociabilità Religiosa nel Mezzogiorno: le confraternite laicali', ed. V. Paglia (ibid. 19, nn. 37–8; 1990). P. Horden, 'The Confraternities of Byzantium', in W. J. Sheils and D. Wood (eds.), *Voluntary Religion*

(Studies in Church History, 23; Oxford, 1986), pp. 25–45, with other arts. on fraternities in the W. Church, pp. 85–109. G. Le Bras in Fliche and Martin, 12 (pt. 1 [1964]), pp. 414–17. C. Lefebvre in *DIP* 2 (1973), cols. 1442–5, s.v. 'Confraternità'.

Fraticelli. Originally a term of contempt for heretical *Franciscans, it was applied to two groups, both confined mainly to Italy. The *Fraticelli de Paupere Vita* were followers of Angelo Clareno (d. 1337); some of them were reconciled to the Order in the 15th cent. The *Fraticelli de Opinione* were followers of Michael of Cesena (d. 1342; hence 'Michaelites'); they were organized as a Church with their own bishops, priests, and women preachers. Both groups were extinct by 1500. See also SPIRITUAL FRANCISCANS.

D. L. Douie, *The Nature and the Effect of the Heresy of the Fraticelli* (Publications of the University of Manchester, 220; Historical Series, 61; 1932).

Frederick I (Barbarossa) (*c.*1122–90), German King and Emperor. On the death of his uncle, Conrad III, in 1152, the German princes elected Frederick of Swabia King, partly because he was on his mother's side a Guelph, as well as being a Hohenstaufen on his father's. He secured peace in the German kingdom by the gradual introduction of a new system of quasi-regal duchies which replaced the old tribal units, and by allowing his Guelph cousin, Henry the Lion, Duke of Saxony and Bavaria, a virtually free hand in the north-east. In Italy, however, the treaty of Constance, which he concluded with Pope *Eugenius III in 1153 and renewed with *Hadrian IV in 1155, gave less freedom of movement to him than to the curia, and after his coronation as Emperor in 1155 he was unable to move south against the Normans. His aggressive policy towards the Lombard communes sought not only to reclaim regalian rights but to administer them for his own profit. Similar plans further south threatened the temporal lordship of the Papacy, and the growing tension between Frederick and Hadrian IV was aggravated by questions of protocol at their first meeting. At the Diet of Besançon in 1157 he and his chancellor, Rainold of Dassel, took exception to Hadrian's description of the empire as a Papal gift (*beneficium*), and insisted that the 'holy empire' (*sacrum imperium*; see HOLY ROMAN EMPIRE) was a 'free crown' governed by the sacred Roman law. The law students were put under the Emperor's protection at Roncaglia in 1158. When, at the Papal election of 1159, two popes emerged, Frederick at the Council of Pavia in 1160 recognized the candidate of the minority of cardinals, Victor IV, against *Alexander III. The schism, which lasted for 17 years, was mainly a conflict of interests, but it isolated Frederick and the German bishops who supported him from the clerical élite of France and the Anglo-Norman world. A military solution proved impossible. After Frederick had suffered heavy losses at Rome through malaria in 1167, the resistance of the communes revived. He was faced with the need to make concessions either to the Lombard League or to Alexander III and after his defeat at Legnano in 1176 he preferred to submit to the Pope. He was able to gain much from Alexander and his successors without forcing a final settlement of the territorial conflict in central Italy. His long absences in Italy weakened his position in Germany, where Henry the Lion rebelled and revived the old Guelph–Hohenstaufen feud. After Henry's overthrow in 1181, however, Frederick became an awe-inspiring figure, and his power was increased by the marriage in 1186 of his son and heir, Henry, to Constance, the heiress of the Norman kingdom of Sicily. His piety was conservative: he wanted to resemble *Charlemagne, whom he had had canonized by one of his antipopes in 1165. He saw in the *Crusade the culmination of his strivings and in 1189 he set out at the head of a large host by the land route through Hungary. He considered an attack on *Constantinople, but the submission of Isaac Angelus was enough to deflect the army across the Dardanelles, and Frederick was drowned in the river Saleph in Cilicia.

'Constitutiones', ed. L. Weiland in *MGH*, Constitutiones et Acta Publica Imperatorum et Regum, 1 (1893), pp. 191–463. 'Diplomata', ed. H. Appelt and others (*MGH*, Diplomata Regum et Imperatorum Germaniae, 10; 5 vols., 1975–90). The central narrative source until 1160 is *Otto of Freising and Rahewin's *Gesta Frederici*, ed. G. Waitz and B. de Simson (*MGH*, Scriptores Rerum Germanicarum in Usum Scholarum, 1912) and F. J. Schmale (Ausgewählte Quellen zur deutschen Geschichte des Mittelalters, 17; 1965). Eng. tr. by C. C. Mierow (Records of Civilization, Sources and Studies, 49; 1953). For the later period, *Ottonis de Sancto Blasio Chronica*, ed. A. Hofmeister (*MGH*, Scriptores Rerum Germanicarum in Usum Scholarum, 1912). For the Crusade, see A. Chroust (ed.), *Quellen zur Geschichte des Kreuzzuges Kaiser Friedrichs I* (*MGH*, Scriptores Rerum Germanicarum, NS 5; 1928). W. von Giesebrecht, *Geschichte der deutschen Kaiserzeit*, 5 (2 pts., Leipzig, 1880–8) and 6 (ed. B. von Simson, ibid., 1895); H. Simonsfeld, *Jahrbücher des Deutschen Reiches unter Friedrich I*, 1: *1152–1158* (Jahrbücher der Deutschen Geschichte, 1908). Modern studies by R. Wahl (Munich, 1941; 3rd edn., 1950), K. Jordan (Persönlichkeit und Geschichte, 13; 1959), M. Pacaut ([Paris] 1967; Eng. tr., 1970), P. Munz (London, 1969), and F. Oppl (Darmstadt, 1990). Cf. also K. Jordan, *Heinrich der Löwe* (Munich, 1979; Eng. tr., Oxford, 1986), *passim*. H. Heimpel in *Neue Deutsche Biographie*, 5 (1961), pp. 459–78, s.v., with bibl.

Frederick II (1194–1250), Holy Roman Emperor and King of Sicily. His father, the Hohenstaufen Emp. Henry VI, died at Messina in 1197 and his mother Constance the following year, so that the young Frederick grew up in Palermo, the victim of intrigues and struggles which damaged not only the rights of his crown but also his personality. His guardian, Pope *Innocent III, tried to keep him and the *regno* (S. Italy and Sicily) under his tutelage, but he needed Frederick's help against the Guelph Emp. Otto IV, who, after Innocent had crowned him in 1209, broke his engagements to the Papacy in Italy. Frederick was thus able to regain his lost family position north of the Alps; when in 1220 the German princes and bishops were induced to elect his son Henry VII King of the Romans, the empire and the *regno* once more had a single ruler of the Hohenstaufen dynasty, a situation which both the Papacy and the Lombard cities had reason to fear. Already in 1215, at his coronation at Aachen, Frederick had taken the cross, but he needed time to rebuild the government of his S. Italian kingdom and postponed his departure more than once. Excommunicated by Pope *Gregory IX, he set out in 1228 and by agreement with the Sultan al-Kamil he regained Jerusalem for the Latins and crowned himself King in the Church of the *Holy Sepulchre. Here also he uttered the first of his great manifestos, exalting his majesty by presenting himself as the instrument of God in the place of David. Back in Italy he reconquered his invaded provinces and with many concessions wrested absolution and peace from the reluctant Pope by the Peace of San Germano in 1230. In Germany he crushed a rebellion of his son Henry and astonished the princes with his exotic Saracen guards and oriental spendour. Yet in 1236, at the translation of his recently canonized kinswoman, St *Elizabeth, he wore the cowl of a *Cistercian monk. Shortly afterwards he opened his long delayed offensive against the Lombard communes, and the inevitable and final breach with the Papacy followed. Gregory IX again excommunicated Frederick and released his subjects from obedience to him on 20 March 1239. Although Frederick was subsequently able to secure the election of *Innocent IV in 1243, Innocent at the General Council of *Lyons on 17 July 1245 declared Frederick guilty of *heresy and *sacrilege and deposed him from both the emperorship and the Sicilian kingship. Frederick's propaganda yielded nothing to the Papacy's in grandeur of style and struck a new note of warning against the curia's greed and ambition. His emperorship became increasingly messianic and eschatological, while his enemies branded him as *antichrist. The military strength of the anti-imperial cities and conspiracy and treachery in his entourage exposed the narrow base of his regime and its ruthless fiscal severity in the south, but when he died at Castel Fiorentino in 1250 the conflict was not yet clearly decided in Italy or in Germany. Frederick could charm and dazzle, but suspicion, pride, and obstinacy marred his judgement. An accomplished linguist, fluent in Arabic and interested in the sciences no less than the occult, he transcended the conventions of W. Christian kingship, not always to his advantage. He has been wrongly hailed as the prophet, if not the founder, of the modern state. His actions and the rhetoric of his chancery only took the ideas of sacred emperorship to their furthest limits. They remained unfulfilled, but neither the culture of his court nor the tenor of his anti-papal propaganda perished with him.

Principal official docs. pr. in J. L. A. Huillard-Bréholles (ed.), *Historia Diplomatica Friderici Secundi* (6 vols. in 11, Paris, 1852–61, with important introd. in prefatory vol., ibid., 1859). E. Winkelmann, *Kaiser Friedrich II.* (Jahrbücher der deutschen Geschichte, 2 vols. [1218–33]; 1889–97). H. Conrad and others (eds.), *Die Konstitutionen Friedrichs II. von Hohenstaufen für sein Königreich Sizilien* (Studien und Quellen zur Welt Kaiser Friedrichs II., 2; 1973); H. Dilcher, *Die Sizilische Gesetzgebung Kaiser Friedrichs II.: Quellen der Constitutionen von Melfi und ihrer Novellen* (ibid. 3; 1975). The standard modern work, despite its visionary and transcendent cast, is the Life by E. Kantorowicz (Berlin, 1927; suppl. vol., 1931; Eng. tr., 1931). In Eng. there is also a modern study by T. C. van Cleve (Oxford, 1972). Other studies include those of 'Georgina Masson' [Marion Johnson] (London, 1957), H. M. Schäller (Persönlichkeit und Geschichte, 34; 1964), and S. Abulafia (London, 1988). A collection of papers pub. 1939–1965, ed. G. Wolf, *Stupor Mundi: Zur Geschichte Friedrichs II. von Hohenstaufen* (Wege der Forschung, 101; Darmstadt, 1966); J. Fleckenstein (ed.), *Probleme um Friedrich II.* (Studien und Quellen zur Welt Kaiser Friedrichs II., 4; 1974). N. Cohn, *The Pursuit of the Millennium* (rev. edn., 1970), pp. 108–126. K. J. Leyser, *Medieval Germany and its Neighbours 900–1256* (1982), pp. 269–76. Id., 'Frederick Barbarossa and the Hohenstaufen Polity', *Viator*, 19 (1988), pp. 153–76, repr. in id., *Communications and Power in Medieval Europe: The Gregorian Revolution and Beyond*, ed. T. Reuter (1994), pp. 115–42, with other relevant material, pp. 143–55. C. A. Willemsen, *Bibliographie zur*

Geschichte Kaiser Friedrichs II. und der letzten Staufer (MGH, Hilfsmittel, 8; 1986). See also bibl. to CRUSADES.

Frederick III (1463–1525), Elector of Saxony, surnamed 'the Wise' (not be confused with Frederick II (1482–1556), Elector of the Palatinate, also known as 'the Wise'). Succeeding his father Ernst as Elector in 1486, from the outset Frederick was interested in humanist education and Church reform. In 1502 he founded the University of *Wittenberg and later invited M. *Luther and P. *Melanchthon to teach there. When Luther was cited to Rome in 1518, Frederick's attempts to have the matter settled in Germany led to Luther's interview with Card. T. de V. *Cajetan at Augsburg later that year and to C. von *Miltitz's mission to Saxony. Frederick consistently sought to protect Luther, refusing to implement the bull '*Exsurge Domine' in 1520 and arranging safe custody for him at the *Wartburg after the Diet of *Worms had outlawed him in 1521. How far he himself accepted Lutheran doctrine is disputed. A devout Catholic in his earlier years, he supported Luther and permitted Lutheran changes in Wittenberg. Yet, while he acceded to Luther's request to abandon the annual display of his collection of relics (one of the largest collections in Europe), he could not bring himself to part with them, and he protested against the iconoclastic tendencies of some of Luther's followers. See also SPALATIN, GEORG.

G. *Spalatin's historischer Nachlass und Briefe: Aus dem Originalhandschriften* hrsg. von C. G. Neudecker and L. Preller, 1: *Friedrichs des Weisen Leben und Zeitgeschichte* (1851). I. Ludolphy, *Friedrich der Weise, Kurfürst von Sachsen, 1463–1525* (Göttingen [1984]), with extensive bibl. P. Kirn, *Friedrich der Weise und die Kirche* (Beiträge zur Kulturgeschichte des Mittelalters und der Renaissance, 30; 1926). I. Ludolphy in *TRE* 11 (1983), pp. 666–9, s.v. 'Friedrich der Weise', with extensive bibl.

Frederick III (1515–76), Elector Palatine of the Rhine, surnamed 'the Pious'. Through his wife Maria (d. 1567), the daughter of Casimir of Bayreuth, whom he married in 1537, Frederick became well disposed towards the Reformation, though she was more inclined to *Lutheranism, he to *Calvinism. In 1559 he succeeded to the Electorate. At first he sought to compromise between Calvinism and Lutheranism, but from the start he favoured the Reformed wing, and in 1563 his publication of the *Heidelberg Catechism put the Palatinate firmly in the Calvinist camp. He welcomed Calvinist refugees from *France and the *Netherlands, and supplied aid to the Calvinist rebels in those countries. He also supported Calvinism in many parts of Germany outside his own lands, and constantly intrigued against the Catholic princes to secure the abrogation of the 'ecclesiastical reservation' in the 1555 Peace of *Augsburg. His son, Louis VI, who succeeded him in 1576, abandoned Calvinism for Lutheranism; on his death in 1583, policy was reversed again by Frederick's second son, John Casimir, who restored Calvinism and brought up in that faith his young nephew Frederick IV, in whose name he ruled until his own death in 1594.

Letters ed. A. Kluckhohn (2 vols. in 3, Brunswick, 1868–72); id., *Friedrich der Fromme, Kurfürst von der Pfalz, der Schützer der reformirten Kirche, 1559–1576* (Nördlingen, 1879). D. Visser (ed.), *Controversy and Conciliation: The Reformation and the Palatinate 1559–1583* (Pittsburg Theological Monographs, NS 18; Allison

Park, Pa., 1986). [W.] O. Chadwick, 'The Making of a Reforming Prince: Frederick III, Elector Palatinate', in R. B. Knox (ed.), *Reformation, Conformity and Dissent: Essays in Honour of Geoffrey Nuttall* (1977), pp. 44–69. H. J. Cohn, 'The Territorial Princes in Germany's Second Reformation, 1559–1622', in M. Prestwich (ed.), *International Calvinism 1541–1715* (Oxford, 1985), pp. 135–65, esp. pp. 148–54. Further bibl. in Schottenloher, 3 (1936), pp. 376–8 (nos. 32124–48).

Free Church Federal Council. Following a congress in Manchester in 1892 a National Free Church Council was formed to which was affiliated a loose network of local councils. Membership was not grounded on any representative principle and the annual assembly dealt with a wide range of public questions as well as theological and ecclesiastical matters. Hugh Price *Hughes, a *Methodist, and John *Clifford, a *Baptist, played notable parts in the movement. In 1919, under the leadership of J. H. *Shakespeare of the Baptist Union, the Federal Council of Evangelical Free Churches was organized. There was a declaratory statement of common faith and practice, which excluded *Unitarians, and membership was put on an officially approved representative basis. In 1940 the National Free Church Council united with the Federal Council in the Free Church Federal Council. The National Free Church Women's Council has now also been amalgamated. The present body brings together 18 Free Church Denominations or Councils for common thought and action, and seeks to offer to the wider ecumenical life of the Churches a distinctive Free Church contribution.

E. K. H. Jordan, *Free Church Unity: History of the Free Church Council Movement 1896–1941* (1956). J. Munson, *The Nonconformists* (1991), pp. 157–84.

Free Church of England. A small Protestant body which traces its beginnings to a dispute in 1843 between H. *Phillpotts, Bp. of *Exeter, and one of his clergy, James Shore, in charge of Bridgetown chapel-of-ease, Totnes. Shore's cause was taken up by T. E. Thoresby (d. 1883), a Minister of the Countess of *Huntingdon's Connexion, and eventually in 1863 the Free Church of England received definite shape in association with the latter. It accepted the *Thirty-Nine Articles and recognized the legitimacy of episcopacy, though its ministry at first was presbyterian. Later in the century it became affiliated to a similar group, which had separated in 1873 from the Protestant Episcopal (Anglican) Church in USA under G. D. Cummins, formerly Assistant Bp. of Kentucky, and known as the 'Reformed Episcopal Church'. This association enabled the English body to obtain episcopal orders. In 1927 the two bodies were legally united.

F. Vaughan [Bishop Primus], *A History of the Free Church of England, otherwise called the Reformed Episcopal Church* (Bath [1938]; 2nd edn. [Wallasey], 1960). G. H. Jones in *HERE* 10 (1918), pp. 629–31, with bibl., p. 632, s.v. 'Reformed Episcopal Church'.

Free Church of Scotland. The religious body formed at the *Disruption (1843) by the separation of nearly a third of the ministers and members of the established Church of *Scotland. In 1900 it united with the *United Presbyterian Church to form the *United Free Church (q.v.).

Free Churches. See NONCONFORMITY.

Free from Rome Movement. See LOS VON ROM.

Free Spirit, Brethren of the. See BRETHREN OF THE FREE SPIRIT.

Freemasonry, Christianity and. The origins of the Freemasons go back probably to the 12th cent., when the English masons established a religious fraternity under the protection of St *John the Baptist, to guard the secrets of their craft. In the later Middle Ages this brotherhood came to be concerned almost exclusively with the moral and religious education of its members. It was abolished by *Edward VI in 1547, but later reorganized for social and educational purposes, and in the 18th cent. became a stronghold of *Deism. Freemasonry spread from England to many other countries. In France, Italy, and the other Latin countries the Masonic Lodges were openly hostile to the Church and to religion in general, whereas in England, Germany, and the Germanic countries they professed for the most part an undoctrinal Christianity. The hostility of Latin Freemasonry to religion led to its repeated condemnation by the Church and the prohibition of membership by RCs under pain of excommunication. The subject was dealt with by many Popes, among them Clement XII (1738), *Benedict XIV (1751), *Pius VII (1814), *Pius IX (1864), and *Leo XIII (1884), and acc. to the 1917 Code of Canon Law (*CIC* (1917), can. 2335) Freemasons automatically incurred excommunication reserved to the Holy See. The 1983 Code makes no specific mention of Freemasonry, but on 26 Nov. 1983 the Congregation for the Doctrine of the Faith declared that membership of Masonic associations was still forbidden to RCs on pain of being in grave sin and of exclusion from Holy Communion. In Great Britain as well as in the USA Freemasonry, though undogmatic, demands belief in God from its members and is not hostile to religion as such. It is concerned chiefly with philanthropic and social activities and has the support of royalty and the nobility, many of whom it counts among its members. Members of the E. Orthodox Church are forbidden to become Freemasons under pain of excommunication.

Freer Logion. A passage added to the text of Mk. 16: 14 in the 5th-cent. Greek Codex 'W' (now in the Freer Museum at Washington) which includes a saying attributed to the Risen Christ. In response to a plea that He should reveal His righteousness, He is reported as saying: 'The limit of the years of the power of Satan is fulfilled; but other fearful things draw near even upon them for whom, because they had sinned, I was delivered unto death that they may return unto the truth and sin no more; that they may inherit the spiritual and incorruptible glory of righteousness in heaven. But go ye into all the world', etc. [as in Mk. 16: 15]. Though the saying forms no part of the original text, as the whole of Mk. 16: 9–20 is a later addition to the gospel, its language is in agreement with its context, and it may well be of the same *provenance* and date. It appears to have been known to St *Jerome.

Text in H. A. Sanders, *The Washington Manuscript of the Four Gospels* (University of Michigan Studies, Humanistic Series, 9; 1912), p. 246; repr. in V. Taylor, *The Gospel According to St Mark*

(1952), with Eng. tr., pp. 614 f.; Eng. tr. also in Schneemelcher (5th edn.), 1 (Eng. tr., 1991), pp. 248 f. C. R. Gregory, *Das Freer Logion* (Versuche und Entwürfe; 1; 1908).

freewill offerings. In ancient *Israel's sacrificial system, one of the three forms of peace offering (Lev. 7: 11–18) was so named because it went beyond what legal demands required. It resembled the 'votive offering' in being made in connection with a prayer for particular blessings, but differed in being offered whether the blessing was granted or not. The Feast of *Weeks was customarily accompanied by such a freewill offering (Deut. 16: 10). In modern times the term has been applied to a method of Church finance whereby members of the congregation agree to pay regular contributions to a 'freewill offering fund' over and above, or in place of, the usual collections made in times of Divine service.

Freewillers. A small group of religious radicals who were active in SE England from the 1540s to the 1560s. Led by one Henry Hart or Harte (d. by 1557), they resisted the growing trend of English Protestant thought towards *predestination, proclaimed the importance of human free will in gaining salvation, and advocated religious *toleration. Persecuted by *Mary and opposed by other Protestants, notably J. *Bradford, they dispersed and have no traceable links with the later English *Arminians.

J. W. Martin, 'English Protestant Separatism at its Beginnings: Henry Hart and the Free-Will Men', *Sixteenth-Century Journal*, 7, no. 2 (1976), pp. 55–74; id., 'The First that Made Separation from the Reformed Church of England', *Archiv für Reformationsgeschichte*, 77 (1986), pp. 281–312. M. T. Pearse, 'Free Will, Dissent, and Henry Hart', *Church History*, 58 (1989), pp. 452–9. D. A. Penny, *Freewill or Predestination: The Battle over Saving Grace in mid-Tudor England* (Royal Historical Society Studies in History, 61; 1990).

French Protestants. See HUGUENOTS.

frequency of Communion. See COMMUNION, FREQUENCY OF.

Frere, Walter Howard (1863–1938), Bp. of *Truro. Educated at Trinity College, Cambridge, and Wells Theological College, he was ordained in 1887. He was a *High Churchman, and in 1892 joined the *Community of the Resurrection, Mirfield, of which he was Superior from 1902 to 1913, and again from 1916 to 1922. In 1923 he became Bp. of Truro. He was a leading authority on liturgical matters, and, in matters of practice, an advocate of 'English' rather than 'Roman' forms of ceremonial. His writings in this field include *The Use of Sarum* (2 vols., 1898, 1901); *A New History of the Book of Common Prayer* (based on F. Procter's earlier work; 1901); and *The Principles of Religious Ceremonial* (1906). He was also actively interested in promoting the reunion of Christendom, esp. between the Anglican and E. Orthodox Churches; and he took part in the *Malines Conversations. In 1935 he resigned the see of Truro and ended his life at Mirfield.

J. H. Arnold and E. G. P. Wyatt (eds.), *Walter Howard Frere: A Collection of his Papers on Liturgical and Historical Subjects* (*Alcuin Club Collections, 35; 1940); R. C. D. Jasper (ed.), *Walter Howard Frere: His Correspondence on Liturgical Revision and Reconstruction* (ibid. 39; 1954). Memoir ed. C. S. Phillips

(London, 1947). A. Wilkinson, *The Community of the Resurrection* (1992), *passim*. A. H. Thompson in *DNB, 1931–1940*, pp. 296 f.

friar. The popular title of a brother (*frater*) or member of one of the Mendicant Orders founded during the Middle Ages. The Latin *frater* was originally used for all religious, but as the Mendicant Orders dropped other terms, such as *dominus* and *monachus*, *frater* or 'friar' came to designate their members in particular. In England these orders were chiefly distinguished by the colours of their mantles, the four chief being the 'Grey Friars' (*Franciscans), the 'Black Friars' (*Dominicans), the 'White Friars' (*Carmelites), and the '*Augustinian Friars'. Among others were the 'Trinity' or 'Red Friars', and the '*Crutched' or 'Crossed Friars'.

Friday (Old Engl. *frigedæg*, 'day of [the goddess] Frig', the wife of Odin). In the Christian Church, Friday is widely kept as a weekly commemoration of the Passion of Christ, being traditionally observed by *abstinence from meat (*Christmas Day, if it falls on a Friday, is excepted by the rubrics of the BCP, and, in the RC Church, certain other great festivals also) or by other acts of penitence or charity. The *Wednesday and Friday fasts were probably derived from the Jewish bi-weekly fast. The primitive practice was to keep a complete fast until 3 p.m., when a service took place, which in some places was the *Eucharist, and elsewhere in essentials an *Ante-Communion. Friday is the Muslim sabbath, in commemoration of the creation of *Adam on this day (Gen. 1: 24–31). See also FIRST FRIDAYS, GOOD FRIDAY, and PAENITEMINI.

Early refs. to the observance of Friday in *Didache*, 8. 1, and *Hermas, *Simil.* 5. 1. For the Friday abstinence, see *CIC* (1983), cans. 1250–53. G. Schreiber, *Die Wochentage im Erlebnis der Ostkirche und des christlichen Abendlandes* (Wissenschaftliche Abhandlungen der Arbeitsgemeinschaft für Forschung des Landes Nordrhein-Westfalen, 11; 1959), pp. 168–206.

Fridays, First. See FIRST FRIDAYS.

Frideswide, St (d. traditionally 735, but 727 acc. to the oldest source), patron saint of the city and University of *Oxford. The little that is known of her depends on a brief account by *William of Malmesbury and two 12th-cent. Lives. Acc. to the oldest of these, she was the daughter of Didanus, 'King of Oxford', she was consecrated a virgin and became the first abbess of a convent founded by her father in Oxford. Sought in marriage by Algar, 'King of Leciester', the Life reports that she was transported miraculously to Bampton, Oxon, where she hid for three years; Algar meanwhile tried to enter Oxford, but was struck dead at the town gate. Frideswide also spent some time in retreat at Binsey, near Oxford, where a holy well appeared in answer to her prayers. She returned to Oxford before her death. A monastery bearing her name and occupied by secular canons is known to have existed in Oxford in 1002. Its occupants were succeeded by *Augustinian Canons in or before 1122. Her relics were translated on 12 Feb. 1180 and again in 1289; the shrine became a place of pilgrimage until its spoliation in 1538. Twice a year it was solemnly visited by the University and in 1434 Abp. H. *Chichele ordered her feast (19 Oct.) to be observed as that of the patroness of the University. In 1525 St Frideswide's monastery was suppressed by T. *Wolsey as part of his plan for Cardinal College; and in 1546 the monastic church became the cathedral of the new diocese of Oxford. In 1561 the relics of St Frideswide were mixed by J. *Calfhill with the remains of the wife of *Peter Martyr (Vermigli) which had been buried in the cathedral under *Edward VI. Her festival was abolished in 1549, but it appears in the Latin BCP of 1560 and in the Oxford University Calendar. A service attended by University and civic dignitaries is held on or near 19 Oct.

AASS, Oct. 8 (1853), pp. 533–90. F. M. Stenton, 'St Frideswide and her Times', Oxoniensia, 1 (1936), pp. 103–12; repr. in Preparatory to Anglo-Saxon England, ed. D. M. Stenton (Oxford, 1970), pp. 224–33; J. Blair, 'Saint Frideswide Reconsidered', Oxoniensia, 52 (1987), pp. 71–127. Id. (ed.), 'Saint Frideswide's Monastery at Oxford: Archaeological and Architectural Studies', ibid. 53 (1988), pp. 1–275, repr. separately, Gloucester, 1990. The Cartulary of the Monastery of St Frideswide at Oxford was ed. S. R. Wigram (Oxford Historical Society, 28 and 31; 1895–6).

Friedrich. See also FREDERICK.

Friedrich, Johannes (1836–1917), Church historian. Born at Poxdorf in Upper Franconia, he was educated at Bamberg and Munich, and taught at Munich from 1862. He soon gained a great reputation for sound historical judgement and in 1869 J. A. Hohenlohe (1823–96), Abp. of Ephesus (in partibus) and afterwards (1876) Cardinal, a leading German prelate, took him as his secretary to Rome for the First *Vatican Council. He joined his former mentor J. J. I. von *Döllinger (to whom he sent much of the material for *Quirinus's Letters from Rome) and others in resisting the definition of Papal Infallibility, believing it to be historically indefensible. He left Rome before the Council ended, but he refused to accept the decrees and in April 1871 he was excommunicated. The Bavarian Government offered him protection and in 1872 he was nominated professor of church history at Munich. He was at first a leading member of the *Old Catholic communion in Germany, but withdrew when it ceased to uphold clerical celibacy. His writings, which were many, include Johann Wessel (1862); Die Kirchengeschichte Deutschlands (2 vols., 1867–9); Tagebuch während des vatikanischen Concils (1871), followed by a Verteidigung (1872); a large-scale Geschichte des vatikanischen Konzils (3 vols., 1877–87); Beiträge zur Geschichte des Jesuitenordens (1881); Johann Adam *Möhler (1894); and Ignaz von Döllinger (3 vols., 1899–1901).

F. Hacker, 'Johannes Friedrich als Führer der altkatholischen Bewegung', Internationale kirchliche Zeitschrift, 8 (1918), pp. 252–74.

Friends, Society of, commonly known as *Quakers (q.v.). A body with Christian foundations, originally called 'Children of the Light', 'Friends in the Truth', 'Friends of the Truth', or 'Friends'. The present official title, 'Religious Society of Friends', came into general use in the 19th cent.; in some parts of the USA the style 'Friends' Church' has been employed since the late 19th cent.

The Quaker movement arose out of the religious ferment of the mid-17th cent. G. *Fox, its leader, emphasized the immediacy of Christ's teaching within each person and held that to this ordained ministers and consecrated buildings were irrelevant. By 1655, when Quakers were mentioned in a proclamation of O. *Cromwell, they had spread throughout Britain and Ireland and to the Continent of Europe, and in 1682 W. *Penn founded Pennsylvania as a 'Holy Experiment' on Quaker principles. In their meetings Friends waited silently upon the Lord without a pre-arranged order of worship, believing that God would use any one of those present, man or woman, to minister. Their refusal to take *oaths or pay *tithes, or to accept any authority which they felt conflicted with their inner guidance, and their testimony against 'hat honour' and flattery of language and manner, led to persecution under the Commonwealth, intensified after the Restoration (1660). Over 20,000 of them were fined or imprisoned, and at least 450 died in gaol, before the *Toleration Act 1688 ended widespread persecution.

During the 18th cent. Quakerism was influenced by *Quietism, and in the 19th cent. by the *Evangelical Movement, both in Britain and in the USA. In America a split occurred in 1827–8 as a result of the teaching of E. *Hicks, whose emphasis on 'Christ within' seemed to undervalue the authority of Scripture and the historic Christ. Beginning in 1845 there were further secessions by conservative groups maintaining mystical emphases and stressing the traditional 'plainness of speech, behaviour and apparel'. In Britain there were three minor secessions: that following the evangelical 'Beacon' controversy of the 1830s, so named from the book, A Beacon to the Society of Friends (1835) by Isaac Crewdson (1780–1844), which criticized Hicks's views, and those of the conservative Fritchley Friends and a small group of 'rationalist' Friends in Manchester, both by the early 1870s.

Between 1667 and 1671 Fox, with other Friends, established a series of Meetings for Church Affairs. The primary meeting was, and still is, the Monthly Meeting, in Britain covering several congregations which may have Preparatory Meetings. Monthly Meetings were grouped into Quarterly Meetings, covering larger areas, and in 1668 a Yearly Meeting was established for the whole of Britain. The Monthly Meeting still retains its central position, with responsibility for membership, pastoral care, and matters of discipline. In Britain General Meetings have now replaced Quarterly Meetings. Each of the world's Yearly Meetings is autonomous, but through the Friends World Committee for Consultation (established in 1937), all Quakers have opportunities to reach a better understanding of their varying backgrounds. In 1675 the London Yearly Meeting established a Meeting for Sufferings, primarily to consider ways of securing redress from persecution and other sufferings. This still meets regularly as a standing representative committee entrusted between Yearly Meetings with the care of matters affecting the Society in Britain. In other Yearly Meetings the titles Representative Meeting or Permanent Board are generally used for similar bodies.

The religious tenets of 17th-cent. Friends are set out in the classic work of R. *Barclay, Theologiae Verae Christiana Apologia (1676). Modern Friends continue to affirm their belief in the *Inner (or Inward) Light and the direct experience of God's Spirit, guiding, saving, and empowering them for action as well as growth. Like Barclay, they value the Bible, but regard it as 'a secondary rule subordinate to the Spirit'. Relying on the leadings of the Spirit, they have no set liturgy or creeds, and, believing that all life can be sacramental, they have no *Sacraments as such, though they believe in a spiritual baptism and communion. There is no ordained ministry in the Society and all members are encouraged to contribute to the Meeting according to their gifts, but certain officers accept specific duties for limited periods. 'Elders' are responsible for the nurture of the spiritual life of the Meeting and 'overseers' for the pastoral care of its members. In their Meetings for Church Affairs, Friends seek to discern God's will, and the 'clerk' records the 'sense of the Meeting'; no decision is taken by voting. The Society's discipline, corporately agreed by the members, is recorded in a *Book of Discipline*, which is regularly revised. In parts of the USA silent worship with spontaneous ministry has been replaced by prearranged forms, often led by a paid pastor. Such structured worship is also found in other parts of the world where Friends have had missions.

Friends' opposition to oaths and military service early brought them into conflict with the civil authorities, and during the 20th cent. many have been imprisoned for their witness against war. Until the middle of the 19th cent., like other Nonconformists, they were excluded from the universities in England, and many sought to express their convictions in commerce, industry, and banking. Friends have become widely known for their commitment to social and educational progress, penal reform, the promotion of peace and justice, and, esp. in the 20th cent., international relief. In 1947 the Nobel Peace Prize was given jointly to the (British and Irish) Friends Service Council and the American Friends Service Committee. The Friends World Committee for Consultation is recognized as a non-governmental organization with consultant status at the United Nations, and Friends have established a Quaker Council for European Affairs in Brussels. They are involved in the *Ecumenical Movement and work closely with members of other Churches and faiths. Their former attitude to music and the theatre has changed considerably and many Quakers are now enthusiastic supporters of the arts.

Besides Barclay's *Apology* (see above) the classic work on the Society of Friends is W. Sewel, *The History of the Rise, Increase, and Progress of the Christian People called Quakers* (1722; his own Eng. tr. of a work orig. pub. in Dutch, 1717). W. C. Braithwaite, *The Beginnings of Quakerism* (1912; 2nd edn. by H. J. *Cadbury, Cambridge, 1955); id., *The Second Period of Quakerism* (1919; 2nd edn. by H. J. Cadbury, Cambridge, 1961); R. M. Jones, *The Later Periods of Quakerism* (2 vols., 1921); A. N. Brayshaw, *The Quakers* (1921; 3rd edn., 1938); R. M. Jones, *The Faith and Practice of the Quakers* (1927); E. Russell, *The History of Quakerism* (New York, 1943, repr., Richmond, Ind., 1979); H. Brinton, *Friends for 300 Years* (New York [1952]; London, 1953); E. Vipont, *The Story of Quakerism* (1954; repr., with additional chapter, Richmond, Ind., 1977); J. Sykes, *The Quakers: A New Look at their Place in Society* (1958); J. Punshon, *Portrait in Grey: A Short History of the Quakers* (1984); H. Barbour and J. W. Frost, *The Quakers* (New York, etc., 1988). H. Barbour, *The Quakers in Puritan England* (1964); E. Isichei, *Victorian Quakers* (Oxford, 1970); J. O. Greenwood, *Quaker Encounters* (3 vols., York, 1975–8); R. Bauman, *Let your Words Be Few: Symbolism of Speaking and Silence among Seventeenth-Century Quakers* (Cambridge Studies in Oral and Literate Cultures, 8; 1983); M. J. Sheeran, SJ, *Beyond Majority Rule: Voteless Decisions in the Religious Society of Friends* (Philadelphia [1983]). *Journal of the Friends' Historical Society* (1903 ff.); *Bulletin of the Friends Historical Society* (later *Association*; then *Quaker History*) (Philadelphia, 1906 ff.).

Friends of Cathedrals. See CATHEDRALS, FRIENDS OF.

Friends of God. See GOTTESFREUNDE.

Frith, John (*c.*1503–33), Protestant martyr. He was educated at Eton and graduated from King's College, Cambridge. In 1525 T. *Wolsey made him a junior canon of his newly founded 'Cardinal College' (Christ Church), Oxford. In 1528 he was imprisoned for heresy, but escaped to the Continent, where he assisted W. *Tyndale with his work on the Bible. On his return in 1532 he was arrested, and after a book of his on the Eucharist (written for a friend and not intended for publication) had come into the hands of T. *More, he was condemned to death for denying that *purgatory and *transubstantiation were necessary dogmas, and burned at Smithfield on 4 July 1533. Ostensibly at Marburg, but in fact at Antwerp, he had published *A Pistle to the Christen Reader: Antithesis wherein are compared together Christ's Acts and our Holy Father the Pope's* (1529) and *A Disputation of Purgatory* (1531).

The Whole Works of W. Tyndall, John Frith and Doct. Barnes, ed. by J. *Foxe ('1572'), incl. short Life (separately paginated). Frith's Works, largely reproduced from the edn. of T. Russell (London, 1831), with variants noted at the foot of each page, and other primary material, ed., with full introd., by N. T. Wright (Courtenay Library of Reformation Classics, 7; copyright, 1978 [pub. 1983]). W. A. Clebsch, *England's Earliest Protestants 1520–1535* (Yale Publications in Religion, 11; 1964), pp. 78–136; C. R. Trueman, *Luther's Legacy: Salvation and English Reformers, 1525–1556* (Oxford, 1994), esp. pp. 121–55. *BRUO 1501–1540*, pp. 218–20. A. C. Bickley in *DNB* 20 (1889), pp. 278–80.

Froben, Johann (*c.*1460–1527), 'Frobenius', printer and scholar. A native of Hammelburg, Bavaria, Froben started a press in Basle in 1491. After working in close association with Johannes Amerbach (1443–1513) and Johannes Petri (d. 1512), Froben started publishing on his own account in 1512. His press was renowned throughout Europe for the excellent quality of its type and high standards of scholarship and accuracy. *Erasmus moved into his house *c.*1513 and prepared a long series of editions for his press, the most famous being the *editio princeps* of the Greek NT (1516). Among the Church Fathers whose works Erasmus edited through Froben were *Jerome (1516), *Cyprian (1520), and *Hilary of Poitiers (1523). After Froben had issued some of M. *Luther's Latin writings in 1518, he published nothing further by any of the authors of the Protestant Reformation. After his death the press was carried on by his son, Jerome Froben, and his son-in-law, Nicolaus Episcopius.

Various of his letters are pr. among the correspondence of Erasmus, ed. P. S. Allen (11 vols., Oxford, 1906–47; for details see index vol., 1958) and in *Die Amerbachkorrespondenz*, ed. A. Hartmann, vols. 1–3 (Basle, 1942–7). I. Stockmeyer and B. Reber, *Beiträge zur Basler Buchdruckergeschichte* (1840), pp. 85–115, incl. list of books pub. by him. P. S. Allen, 'Erasmus' Relations with his Printers', *Transactions of the Bibliographical Society*, 13 (1916), pp. 297–321, repr. in id., *Erasmus: Lectures and Wayfaring Sketches* (Oxford, 1934), pp. 109–37. E. Hilgert, 'Johann Froben and the Basel University Scholars, 1513–1523', *Library Quarterly*, 41 (1971), pp. 141–69. P. G. Bietenholz in id. and T. B. Deutscher (eds.), *Contemporaries of Erasmus*, 2 (Toronto, etc. [1986]), pp. 60–3, with bibl. A. Pfister in *Neue Deutsche Biographie*, 5 (1960), pp. 638–40.

Froissart, Jean (*c.*1335–*c.*1404), French chronicler. He was a native of Valenciennes, and at an early age visited the English court, whither he returned in 1361. The consort of Edward III, Philippa of Hainault, became his benefactress, and he travelled to Scotland, Gascony, and Milan. He returned to Hainault in 1368. From 1373 to 1382 he was parish priest at Lestinnes-au-Mont, and from 1382 until his death private chaplain of Guy de Châtillon, Count of Blois, and canon of Chimay. These offices, however, did not prevent him from undertaking lengthy journeys over much of Europe collecting first-hand information for his work. These famous 'Chroniques' relate in four books the history of the more considerable European countries between 1325 and 1401, most of it being based on eye-witness accounts. The work presents a remarkably lively picture of the times of the Hundred Years War, though it is unreliable in chronological and geographical details. Up to 1361 much of it is derived from a similar work by Jean le Bel, a canon of St-Lambert, Liège. Froissart also wrote poems of love and adventure in the style of his time.

Œuvres de Froissart: Chroniques ed. Baron [J.] Kervyn de Lettenhove (25 vols. in 26 parts, Brussels, 1867–77, with rev. edn. of id., *Froissart: Étude littéraire sur le XIVme siècle* (2 vols. bound in one, 1857) in vol. 1) and *Poésies* ed. A. Scheler (3 vols., ibid., 1870–72). Best edn. of the *Chroniques*, pub. by the Société de l'Histoire de France, ed. S. Luce, G. Raynaud, L. and A. Mirot (1869 ff.: 15 vols. to 1975). Eng. tr. by Sir John Berners (London, 1523), ed. W. P. Ker (6 vols., 1901–3). Eng. tr. of selected passages by G. Brereton (Penguin Classics, 1968). F. S. Shears, *Froissart: Chronicler and Poet* (1930); G. G. Coulton, *The Chronicler of European Chivalry* (1930); J. J. N. Palmer (ed.), *Froissart: Historian* (Woodbridge, Suffolk [1981]); P. F. Ainsworth, *Jean Froissart and the Fabric of History: Truth, Myth, and Fiction in the Chroniques* (Oxford, 1990).

frontal (Lat. *antependium, pallium altaris*). The panel of embroidered cloth, or in some cases of wood or metal, ornamented with carving or enamel, placed in front of the altar. It is most usual for the frontal to be changeable, and its colour to agree with the liturgical colour of the season or day; and a *rubric in the 1570 *Missal ordered this practice to be followed 'where possible' (quoad fieri potest; Rubr. Gen. 20). There is no ruling on the subject in the 1970 Missal. The Anglican Canons of 1604 ordered that the Lord's Table should be 'covered, in time of Divine Service, with a carpet of silk or other decent stuff, thought meet by the Ordinary of the place' (can. 82); the requirement is repeated in the 1969 Canons (F 2).

Froude, Richard Hurrell (1803–36), *Tractarian. The elder brother of James Anthony Froude, the historian, he was educated at Eton and Oriel College, Oxford, where he became a Fellow (1826) and shortly afterwards (1827) a tutor, of his college. Intimacy with his colleague, J. H. *Newman, greatly influenced both. After travels with Newman in the Mediterranean in the winter of 1832–3, he took part in the conference on Church reform at Hadleigh Rectory (July 1833), and collaborated closely with Newman and J. *Keble in the early stages of the Tractarian Movement, though symptoms of consumption caused him to spend much of his remaining years out of England. His *Remains*, which were edited posthumously, with a preface by Newman (part 1, 2 vols., 1838; part 2, 2 vols., 1839), and which were largely extracts from his pri-

vate diary, provoked a storm. His strictures on the Reformers, the more exaggerated of them written half jestingly, were thought disloyal by those who had not known Froude personally, while the records of his spiritual and ascetic practices, which even his close friends had not suspected to lie behind his handsome appearance and lively manner, and his praise of clerical celibacy and devotion to the BVM, startled his readers.

The primary source is his *Remains*, referred to above. J. H. Newman, *Apologia pro Vita Sua* (ed. M. J. Svaglic, Oxford, 1967, pp. 33–5). R. W. *Church, *The Oxford Movement* (1891), ch. 3 (with some recollections by Lord Blachford appended, pp. 50–56). L. I. Guiney, *Hurrell Froude: Memorials and Comments* (1904). W. J. Baker, 'Hurrell Froude and the Reformers', *JEH* 31 (1970), pp. 243–59. P. Brendon, *Hurrell Froude and the Oxford Movement* (1974). P. Gauthier, *La Pensée religieuse de Richard Hurrell Froude, 1803–1836* [1977].

Fructuosus, St (d. 259), Bp. of Tarragona. With two deacons, Augurius and Eulogius, he was arrested in the *persecution under Valerian and burnt at the stake in the amphitheatre. The *acta* of his passion seem certainly authentic. His martyrdom is referred to by *Prudentius (*Peristephanon*, hymn 6) and St *Augustine (*serm.* 273). Feast day, 21 Jan.

AASS, Jan. 2 (1643), pp. 339–42. P. F. de' Cavalieri, *Note agiografiche*, 8 (ST 65; 1935), 'Gli atti di S. Fruttuoso di Tarragona', pp. 127–99, incl. text, pp. 182–94; this text is adapted, with Eng. tr., in H. Musurillo, *The Acts of the Christian Martyrs* (Oxford, 1972), pp. 176–85. J. den Boeft and J. Bremmer, 'Notiunculae Martyrologicae', *VC* 35 (1981), pp. 43–56, esp. pp. 49–52.

Fruits of the Holy Spirit. These, based on Gal. 5: 22 f. (AV, RV), are 'love, joy, peace, long-suffering, gentleness, goodness, faith, meekness, temperance', to which the *Vulgate text adds 'modesty, continence, chastity', making 12 in all. That the correct number of the fruits is 12 is defended on theological grounds by St *Thomas Aquinas, *Summa Theol.* II. 1, q. 70, a. 3.

A. Gardeil, OP, in *DTC* 6 (1920), cols. 944–9; C. A. Bernard, SJ, in *Dict. Sp.* 5 (1964), cols. 1569–75, both s.v. 'Fruits du Saint-Esprit'.

Frumentius, St (*c.*300–*c.*380), 'Apostle of the Abyssinians'. Acc. to *Rufinus (*HE* 1. 9 f.), Aedesius and Frumentius were the two young companions of a Tyrian merchant, Meropius. After all three were captured by 'barbarians' on the way back from a voyage to 'India', Meropius was executed, but the other two, who were both Christians, were taken before their captors' king, whom they later assisted in the government of his country. Frumentius took advantage of the opportunity to carry on mission work, and on reporting the fruits of his work at *Alexandria, he was consecrated Bp. of *Axum by St *Athanasius (*Apol. ad Constantium*, 31). He appears to have been a strong opponent of *Arianism. Feast day, among the Greeks, 30 Nov.; among the *Copts, 18 Dec.; in the W., 27 Oct.

Frumentius is also mentioned in the 5th-cent. histories of *Socrates (1. 19), *Sozomen (2. 24), and *Theodoret (1. 22). F. Thelamon, *Païens et Chrétiennes au IVe Siècle: L'apport de l' "Histoire ecclesiastique" de Rufin d'Aquilée* (Études Augustiniennes, 1981), pp. 37–83. B. W. W. and F. A. Dombrowski, 'Frumentius/

Abbā Salāmā: zu den Nachrichten über die Anfänge des Christentums in Äthiopien', *OC* 68 (1984), pp. 114–69. J. Doresse in *DHGE* 14 (1960), cols. 1416–20, s.v. 'Edesius (2) et Frumentius' and ibid. 19 (1981), col. 242, s.v. 'Frumence', with bibl.

Fry, Elizabeth (1780–1845), *Quaker prison reformer. Born at Norwich, the third daughter of John Gurney, banker, in 1800 she married Joseph Fry, a London merchant and a 'Plain Quaker', by whom she had a large family. In 1808 she established a girls' school at Plashet, nr. East Ham. In 1811 she was recorded as an approved 'minister' in the Society of Friends and became a noted speaker. In 1813 her interest was aroused in the appalling state of the prisons and, at the instigation of William Forster (1784–1854) and Stephen Grellet (1773–1855), she devoted herself to the welfare of female prisoners in Newgate. Here her Bible readings made a deep impression. In 1817 she formed an Association for the Improvement of the Female Prisoners in Newgate 'to provide for the clothing, instruction, employment of the women; to introduce them to a knowledge of the Holy Scriptures, and to form in them as much as possible those habits of order, sobriety and industry which may render them docile and peaceable while in prison, and respectable when they leave it'. She also campaigned for the separation of the sexes in prison, classification of criminals, and female supervision of women, and in 1818 she gave evidence on the state of the prisons to a committee of the House of Commons. Between that time and her final illness in 1843 she visited every convict ship that carried women prisoners to the colonies. She also devoted herself to other classes of the helpless, taking part in the formation of a night shelter in London (1820) and instituting visiting societies in Brighton and elsewhere to deal with mendicancy. In her later years she travelled extensively in Europe, fostering prison reform. Behind all her philanthropic work there was a strong Christian impulse and she never ceased to combine it with active evangelization.

Her writings include *Observations on the Visiting, Superintendence and Government of Female Prisoners* (1827), *Texts for Every Day in the Year* (1831) and a report, issued jointly with her brother, J. J. Gurney, on Irish social conditions (1827). In 1846 an asylum was founded in her memory in Mare Street, Hackney, for women discharged from prison under the name of the 'Elizabeth Fry Refuge'.

Memoir, with extracts from her journal and letters, ed. by two of her daughters (2 vols., 1847; rev. and enlarged edn. 1848; abridged edn. by Mrs F. Cresswell, daughter, 1856). R. B. Johnson (ed.), *Elizabeth Fry's Journeys on the Continent 1840–1841, from a Diary kept by her Niece, Elizabeth Gurney* (1931). Other Lives by T. Timpson (London, 1847), S. Corder (ibid., 1853), J. Whitney (Boston, 1936; London, 1937), J. [H. S.] Kent (London, 1962), and J. Rose (ibid., 1980). W. G. Blaikie in *DNB* 20 (1889), pp. 294–6.

Fulbert, St (*c*.970–1028), scholar and Bp. of *Chartres. Born in N. France—perhaps in Picardy—he studied the liberal arts under Gerbert of Aurillac (later Pope *Sylvester II), probably at *Reims. By 1004 he was a deacon at Chartres cathedral and teaching in the cathedral school. As Bp. of Chartres (1006–28) Fulbert encouraged sound learning, advised both his metropolitan, Abp. Leutheric of Sens, and King Robert the Pious on practical and legal questions, and took diligent pastoral care of his diocese.

He began the rebuilding of Chartres cathedral after the fire of 1020; the undercroft of the present building is Fulbert's work. His principal extant writing is a collection of over 100 letters and 24 poems; the former are concerned mainly with politics and administration, the latter range from schoolroom mnemonics and anecdotes to autobiography and prayers. Also attributed to Fulbert, with varying degrees of security, are a long prayer to the BVM, several Marial and other sermons, and further poems, including the Easter hymn, 'Chorus Novae Ierusalem' ('Ye choirs of New Jerusalem'). Feast day, 10 Apr.

Opera Varia ed. C. de Villiers (Paris, 1608); works repr. mainly from the 'Magna Bibliotheca Patrum' with additions and introd. notices in J. P. Migne, *PL* 141. 163–374. Crit. edns. of his *Letters and Poems*, with Eng. tr., by F. Behrends (Oxford Medieval Texts, 1976), and of his hymns by G. M. Dreves in *AHMA* 50 (1907), pp. 280–9. C. Pfister, *De Fulberti Carnotensis Vita et Operibus* (Paris thesis; Nancy, 1885). L. C. MacKinney, *Bishop Fulbert and Education at the School of Chartres* (Texts and Studies in the History of Mediaeval Education, 6; Notre Dame, Ind., 1957). Y. Delaporte, 'Fulbert de Chartres et l'École Chartraine de Chant liturgique au XIᵉ siècle', *Études grégoriennes*, 2 (1957), pp. 51–81. J. M. Canal, CMF, 'Los sermones marianos de San Fulberto de Chartres (†1028)', *RTAM* 29 (1962), pp. 33–51; id., 'Texto critico de algunos sermones marianos de San Fulberto de Chartres o a él atribuibles', ibid. 30 (1963), pp. 55–87, with 'Adición', pp. 329–33; id., 'Los sermones marianos de san Fulberto de Chartres. Conclusión', ibid. 33 (1966), pp. 139–47. H. Barré, *Prières anciennes de l'Occident à la Mère du Sauveur* [1963], pp. 150–62. Manitius, 2, pp. 682–94. Raby, pp. 258–63, with bibl., p. 478. A. Clerval in *DTC* 6 (1920), cols. 964–7; F. Behrends in *NCE* 6 (1967), pp. 216 f., with illustration of contemporary MS, both s.v.

Fulda. The *Benedictine abbey of Fulda in Hesse Nassau was founded in 744 by St Sturmius, a disciple of St *Boniface, to assist missionary work among the Saxons. Boniface's tomb made it a great pilgrimage centre, and it became a rich and powerful corporation with lands all over Germany. Under *Rabanus Maurus (abbot, 822–42), it was one of the foremost centres of Christian culture in Europe. It possessed a very fine library, of great importance for the transmission of classical and patristic texts, which disappeared during the *Thirty Years War. In the 16th cent. the *Lutherans gained control for a time, but mainly through the work of the *Jesuits the abbey was again firmly established in Catholic hands shortly after the beginning of the 17th cent. In 1803 the abbey was finally secularized, but from 1821 Fulda has been an episcopal see.

Annales Fuldenses conveniently ed. F. Kurze (*MGH*, Scriptores Rerum Germanicarum in usum scholarum, 7; 1891). *Urkundenbuch des Klosters Fulda*, 1, ed. E. E. Stengel (Veröffentlichungen der Historischen Kommission für Hessen und Waldeck, 10; 3 parts, 1913–58). *Die Klostergemeinschaft von Fulda im früheren Mittelalter*, ed. K. Schmid (Münstersche Mittelalter-Schriften, 8; 3 vols. in 5 parts; 1978); useful summary by M. Parisse, 'La communauté monastique de Fulda', *Francia*, 7 (for 1979; 1980), pp. 551–65. P. Lehmann, *Fuldaer Studien* (*Sb.* (Bayr.), 1925, Abh. 3, and 1927, Abh. 3); id., 'Die alte Klosterbibliothek Fulda und ihre Bedeutung', *Aus der Landesbibliothek Fulda*, 2 (1928), pp. 5–12, repr. in id.; *Erforschung des Mittelalters*, 1 (Leipzig, 1941), pp. 213–31, with further refs. K. Christ, *Die Bibliothek des Klosters Fulda im 16. Jahrhundert: Die Handschriften-Verzeichnisse* (Zentralblatt für Bibliothekswesen, Beiheft 64; 1933). K. Lübeck, *Fuldaer Studien* (Veröffentlichung des Fuldaer Geschichtsvereins, 27–9; 1949–51), and other works of this author. E. E. Stengel,

Abhandlungen und Untersuchungen zur Geschichte der Reichsabtei Fulda (Fulda, 1960). A. Brall (ed.), *Von der Klosterbibliothek zur Landesbibliothek: Beiträge zum zweihundertjährigen Bestehen der Hessischen Landesbibliothek Fulda* (Bibliothek des Buchwesens, 6; 1978), with bibl. H. Hoffmann, *Buchkunst und Königtum im ottonischen und frühsalischen Reich* (Schriften der *MGH*, 30/1; 1986), pp. 132–80. U. Hussong, 'Studien zur Geschichte der Reichsabtei Fulda bis zur Jahrtausendwende', *Archiv für Diplomatik*, 31 (1985), pp. 1–225; 32 (1986), pp. 129–304, with extensive bibl. J. Semmler in *NCE* 6 (1967), pp. 218–20; J. Leinweber and R. Aubert in *DHGE* 19 (1981), cols. 339–66; M. Sandmann in *Lexikon des Mittelalters*, 4 (1989), cols. 1020–2, all s.v.

Fulgentius, St (468–533 or perhaps, as recent scholars have argued, *c.*462–527), Bp. of Ruspe in N. Africa. He abandoned the Roman civil service for the monastic life, and suffered constant persecution from the *Arian king, Thrasamund. Soon after becoming Bp. of Ruspe *c.*507 (or 502), he was banished to Sardinia with 60 other Catholic bishops, returned to Africa *c.*515 (or 510) for a public debate with the Arian clergy, was banished again two years later, and finally allowed by King Hilderic to return in 523. This last date is fixed by the death of Thrasamund, and it is known that Fulgentius died at the age of 65, but the rest of the chronology of his life is disputed. It is, however, clear that he was of a scholarly disposition, that he knew some Greek, and that he was a thoroughgoing follower of St *Augustine. He wrote many treatises, of little originality, against Arianism and *Pelagianism. A few letters survive, but of the many sermons ascribed to him, about eight are certainly authentic. His Life was written by his friend *Ferrandus of Carthage. Feast day, 1 Jan.

Works ed. by the Maurist L. Mangeant (Paris, 1684) repr. in J. P. Migne, *PL* 65. 103–1020; crit. edn. by J. Fraipont, OSB (CCSL 91 and 91A; 1968). Life by Ferrandus ed., with Fr. tr., by G. G. Lapeyre (Paris, 1929). H.-J. Diesner, *Fulgentius von Ruspe als Theologe und Kirchenpolitiker* (Stuttgart [1966]). M. Simonetti, 'Note sulla "Vita Fulgentii"', *Anal. Boll.* 100 (1982), pp. 277–89. C. Tibiletti, 'Polemiche in Africa contro i teologi provenzali', *Augustinianum*, 26 (1986), pp. 499–517. A. Mandouze, *Prosopographie Chrétienne du Bas-Empire*, 1 (1982), pp. 507–13. Bardenhewer, 5 (1932), pp. 303–16; Altaner and Stuiber (1978), pp. 489 f. and 655. P. Langlois in *RAC* 8 (1972), cols. 632–61, with extensive bibl.

Fulgentius Ferrandus. See FERRANDUS.

Fulke, William (1538–89), *Puritan theologian. He was educated at St John's College, Cambridge, where he was elected Fellow in 1564. He soon became involved in the *Vestiarian Controversy; indeed his zeal in persuading nearly 300 members of his college to abandon the use of the surplice in chapel led to his expulsion for a time. However, he benefited from the patronage of the Earl of Leicester, and, after receiving other preferment, he was elected Master of Pembroke Hall in 1578. He continued to take a prominent part in the Puritan cause and in 1581 disputed with the *Jesuit, St Edmund *Campion. His many treatises in defence of extreme Protestant principles were learned and effective, though their language was often coarse and virulent. By a strange irony, it was largely his polemical attack on the *Reims version of the NT (the text of which Fulke printed side by side with that of the '*Bishops' Bible') that led to its becoming widely known in England and opened the way for its influence on the

language of the AV. He also wrote extensively on astronomy.

Modern edns. of his *Defence of the Sincere and Holy Translations of the Holy Scriptures ... against the Cavils of Gregory Martin* (1583) by C. H. Hartshorne (*Parker Society, 1843), with biographical memoir, pp. i–xi, and of his refutations of works by T. *Stapleton, J. Martiall, and N. *Sanders by R. Gibbings (ibid., 1848). W. McKane, *Selected Christian Hebraists* (Cambridge, 1989), pp. 76–110, with notes pp. 226–31 and bibl. pp. 249 f. E. Venables in *DNB* 20 (1889), pp. 305–8.

Fuller, Andrew (1754–1815), *Baptist divine. A native of Cambridgeshire, he was ordained pastor of the Baptist congregation at Soham in 1775, and in 1782 became minister at Kettering. While at Soham he published *The Gospel worthy of all Acceptation* [1785], a book directed against the extreme form of *Calvinism which allowed 'nothing spiritually good to be the duty of the unregenerate'. The book greatly impressed W. *Carey, and when in 1792 the Baptist Missionary Society was founded, with Fuller as its first secretary, Carey spoke of him as 'holding the rope' while he himself 'went down into the mine'. In 1793 he published a defence of Calvinistic Baptist teaching against some *Socinian charges that free grace implies moral relaxation, and against *Deism he wrote *The Gospel its own Witness* (1799). He also published collections of expository and other sermons.

Complete Works, with a Memoir of his life by A. G. Fuller (son), in 23 parts (London [*c.* 1831–] 1846). J. Ryland, *The Work of Faith, the Labour of Love, and the Patience of Hope illustrated; in the Life and Death of the Reverend Andrew Fuller* (1816). Further Memoirs of his Life and Writings by J. W. Morris (London, 1815) and T. E. Fuller, grandson (ibid., 1863). G. Laws, *Andrew Fuller: Pastor, Theologian, Ropeholder* (1942). B. Stanley, *The History of the Baptist Missionary Society 1792–1992* (Edinburgh, 1992), pp. 4–35 *passim*. W. G. Blaikie in *DNB* 20 (1889), pp. 309 f.

Fuller, Thomas (1608–61), Anglican historian. Educated at Queens' College, Cambridge, he was later Curate of St Benet's, Cambridge (1630–3), Rector of Broadwindsor, Dorset (1634–1641), Curate of Waltham Abbey (from *c.*1649; where he was summoned before O. *Cromwell's *Triers, though he managed to escape deprivation), and Rector of Cranford (1658–61). His witty and popular style won him a wide reputation. Of his historical writings, the most renowned are his *Church-History of Britain* (1655) and his *Worthies of England* (posthumous, 1662), on both of which Fuller worked for a great part of his life, collecting some of his material during his campaigns with the royalist forces in the Civil War. Of a more popular kind was *The Holy State and the Profane State* (1642), a series of 'characters' illustrating the Christian moral ideal. He also wrote a *History of the Holy War* (1639), on the *Crusades, besides other works.

Full Life, with bibl., by J. E. Bailey (1874). *Collected Sermons*, ed. J. E. Bailey and W. E. A. Axon (1891); *Selections*, ed. E. K. Broadus (1928). W. Addison, *Worthy Dr. Fuller* (1951). S. Gibson, 'A Bibliography of the Works of Thomas Fuller, D.D.', with introd. by G. [L.] Keynes, in *Oxford Bibliographical Society Proceedings and Papers*, 4 (1936), pp. 63–161.

Fullo, Petrus. See PETER THE FULLER.

Fundamentalism. A movement in various Protestant bodies which began in the late 19th cent. and developed after the First World War (1914–18), esp. in the USA. It has roots in the Bible itself, the Reformation, Protestant orthodoxy, and evangelical *revivalism, but it arose in the late 19th cent. in reaction against evolutionary theories, liberal theology, and biblical criticism. A series of Bible Conferences of Conservative Protestants was held in various parts of America; that of Niagara in 1895 issued a statement of belief containing what later came to be known as the 'five points of fundamentalism', namely the verbal inerrancy of Scripture, the Divinity of Jesus Christ, the *Virgin Birth, a substitutionary theory of the *Atonement, and the physical and bodily return of Christ. The term 'fundamentalism', however, appears to derive from a series of tracts entitled *The Fundamentals*, published between 1910 and 1915. In 1919 the World's Christian Fundamentals Association was founded; it organized rallies in many American cities and during the following decade several Protestant denominations, esp. *Baptists, *Presbyterians, and *Disciples of Christ, were divided into Fundamentalist and Modernist wings. Some leading scholars were condemned and rival seminaries established. The controversy attracted widespread public attention in 1925 when William Jennings Bryan (1860–1925), the American Democratic leader, assisted in the prosecution of J. T. Scopes, a schoolteacher of Dayton, Tennessee, who was convicted on the charge of violating the state law by teaching the doctrine of biological evolution in the so-called 'monkey trial'.

The word is applied in a broader sense to other religious and political groups (e.g. 'Muslim Fundamentalism') and since 1950 these have grown in strength, generally supporting conservative social positions and adding aggression to the so-called 'moral majority' in America. In some areas it has been reinforced by a *charismatic tendency and has sometimes been associated with *Millenarianism. It now often has little connection with denominational boundaries, but remains hostile to the *Ecumenical Movement. In Britain it is found within conservative Protestant denominations, but the term is rejected as pejorative.

J. I. Packer, *'Fundamentalism' and the Word of God* (1958); E. R. Sandeen, *The Roots of Fundamentalism: British and American Millenarianism 1800–1930* (1970); G. M. Marsden, *Fundamentalism and American Culture: The Shaping of Twentieth-Century Evangelicalism: 1870–1925* (New York and Oxford, 1980); J. Barr, *Fundamentalism* (1977; 2nd edn., 1981); id., *Escaping from Fundamentalism* (1984).

funeral services. See BURIAL SERVICES.

G

Gabbatha. Acc. to Jn. 19: 13, the place in *Jerusalem where *Pilate sat down in judgement on Christ. The 'Hebrew' (more accurately, the *Aramaic) word is stated in the Gospel to be the equivalent of the Greek Λιθόστρωτος, 'Pavement'. The site of the official residence (*praetorium*) of Pilate, where Gabbatha was, has not been conclusively identified by archaeologists. However, Gabbatha is now thought more likely to have been in the huge 'upper' palace in the Upper City built by *Herod the Great between the site of the modern Citadel at the Jaffa Gate and the Armenian Garden than in the much less elaborate Antonia, at the NW corner of the Temple Area, where a stone pavement, of uncertain Roman date, exposed beneath the Ecce Homo convent of the Sisters of Sion, is popularly referred to as the *Lithostroton*.

Le Père Barnabè, d'Alsace, OFM, *Le Prétoire de Pilate et la Forteresse Antonia* (1902). L. H. Vincent, OP, and F. M. Abel, OP, *Jérusalem*, 2 (1922), pp. 562–86. L. H. Vincent, OP, 'L'Antonia et le prétoire', *R. Bibl.* 42 (1933), pp. 83–113; id., 'Autour du prétoire', ibid. 46 (1937), pp. 563–70; id., 'Le Lithostrotos évangélique', ibid. 59 (1952), pp. 513–30; P. Benoit, OP, 'Prétoire, Lithostroton et Gabbatha', ibid., pp. 531–50, repr. in his *Exégèse et Théologie*, 1 (1961), pp. 316–39. M. Aline de Sion, *La Forteresse Antonia à Jérusalem et la question du Prétoire* (Paris thesis; Jerusalem, 1957). P. Benoit, OP, 'L'Antonia d'Hérode le Grand et le Forum Oriental d'Aelia Capitolina', *HTR* 64 (1971), pp. 135–67, repr., with revisions, in *Exégèse et Théologie*, 4 (1982), pp. 311–46. J. Wilkinson, *Jerusalem as Jesus knew it: Archaeology as Evidence* [1978]), pp. 137–42.

Gabirol, Solomon Ibn. See AVICEBRON.

Gabriel (Heb.), 'man of God'. One of the seven *archangels. He is mentioned in Dan. 8: 15 f. and 9: 21 f., where he assists Daniel in the understanding of his visions. In the NT he foretells the birth of St *John the Baptist to his father, *Zachariah, and announces the conception of the Lord to the BVM (Lk. 1: 11 f., 1: 26). As the messenger of Divine comfort, he is accorded in Jewish theology the place of highest rank after *Michael. Feast day in the E., 26 Mar.; in the W., formerly 24 Mar. (i.e. the day before the *Annunciation); now, with Michael and *Raphael, on 29 Sept.

E. B. *Pusey, *Daniel the Prophet* (1864), pp. 520 f. O. *Bardenhewer, *Mariä Verkündigung: Ein Kommentar zu Lk. 1, 26–38* (Biblische Studien, 10, Heft 5; 1905), pp. 48–59. J. Michl in *RAC* 5 (1962), cols. 239–43, s.v. 'Engel VI (Gabriel)'. See also general commentaries on St Luke's Gospel (s.v.).

Gabriel Severus (c.1540–1616), theologian. A native of the Morea, Gabriel was consecrated Metropolitan of Philadelphia, now Ala-Shehr, in Asia Minor, in 1577. The see being in Turkish hands and its duties slight, Gabriel migrated to Venice to act as bishop for the Greek Christians in the Venetian Republic. There he acquired a reputation as a theologian and anti-Latin controversialist: but

while opposing the RC Church, at the same time he borrowed heavily from the methods and terminology of Latin Scholasticism. His best-known work is a defence of the Greek practice of venerating the eucharistic elements at the *Great Entrance on the ground that, being dedicated for consecration, they are no longer common bread and wine, but have become 'holy' and 'honourable' by participation (μετοχικῶς), and therefore deserve a reverence only second in order to the adoration due to the consecrated Eucharist. Some of his writings were translated into Latin by R. *Simon and published by him at Paris in 1671 as *Fides Ecclesiae Orientalis seu Gabrielis Metropolitae Philadelphiensis Opuscula*.

M. Jugie, AA, 'Un théologien grec du XVIᵉ siècle, Gabriel Sévère et les divergences entre les deux Églises', *ÉO* 16 (1913), pp. 97–108, with bibl. D. *Stone, *A History of the Doctrine of the Holy Eucharist*, 1 (1909), pp. 173–5. G. Podskalsky, *Griechische Theologie in der Zeit der Türkenherrschaft (1453–1821)* (Munich, 1988), pp. 118–24. M. Jugie, AA, in *DTC* 6 (1920), cols. 977–83, s.v., with bibl.

Gaetano da Thiene. See CAJETAN, ST.

Gairdner, James (1828–1912), English historian. In 1846 he entered the Public Record Office. His many writings include editions of the *Calendar of Letters and Papers of the reign of *Henry VIII* (London, 1862–1905) and of the *Paston Letters* (1872–5), as well as *Henry VII* (1889), *The English Church in the Sixteenth Century* (1902), and *Lollardy and the Reformation in England* (4 vols., 1908–13). A diligent and accurate historian, he wrote particularly on the period of the *Reformation in England, where he believed that modern historians had commonly done less than justice to the Catholic case.

Preface by W. Hunt in his edn. of Gairdner's *Lollardy and the Reformation*, 4 (posthumous, 1913), pp. v–xii. R. H. Brodie in *DNB, 1912–1921*, p. 206; D. M. Loades in J. Cannon and others (eds.), *The Blackwell Dictionary of Historians* (1988), pp. 146 f.

Gairdner, William Henry Temple (1873–1928), Anglican missionary. Educated at Rossall and Trinity College, Oxford, he went to Cairo as a *CMS missionary in 1898, was ordained priest in 1901, and worked in co-operation with his friend Douglas Thornton, whose biography he wrote (1908), until the latter's death in 1907. After prolonged study of Arabic and Islamics, he threw himself into the reorganization of the Arabic Anglican Church, with the determination to make it a living spiritual home for converted Muslims. He became the apostle of Arabic Christian scholarship and a pioneer teacher of the colloquial language, producing a Conversation Grammar of *Egyptian Colloquial Arabic* (1917), *The Phonetics of Arabic* (1925), besides hymns and versified Gospel stories in the vernacular. He also published many other works, devotional, exegetical, doctrinal, musical, and linguistic, in

Arabic and in English, the *Reproach of Islam* (1909) being the best known.

C. E. Padwick, *Temple Gairdner of Cairo* (1929). M. D. Gairdner (widow; ed.), *W. H. T. G. to his Friends: Some Letters and Informal Writings of Canon W. H. Temple Gairdner of Cairo, 1873–1928* [1930].

Gaisford, Thomas (1779–1855), Dean of *Christ Church, Oxford, from 1831. Educated at Christ Church, he became Regius Professor of Greek in 1812. In 1829 he was offered the bishopric of Oxford on the death of C. *Lloyd, but refused it. His reputation rests chiefly on his contributions to the study of the Greek classics (e.g. Hephaestion, Herodotus, Stobaeus). In the field of *Patristics, he prepared critical editions of *Eusebius of Caesarea's *Praeparatio* (1843) and *Demonstratio Evangelica* (1852), as well as of the Byzantine lexicographer *Suidas (1834).

H. R. Luard in *DNB* 20 (1889), pp. 370–2, s.v. H. L. Thompson, *Christ Church* (1900), pp. 193–202.

Gaius, also **Caius** (early 3rd cent.), Roman presbyter. Acc. to *Eusebius (*HE* 2. 25. 6; cf. 6. 20. 3), he was an orthodox Churchman (ἐκκλησιαστικὸς ἀνήρ). Under *Zephyrinus (198–217) he held a debate with a Montanist, Proclus. He accepted the 13 Epp. of St Paul, but rejected the Gospel and Rev. of St John, holding them to be the work of *Cerinthus (see ALOGI). *Photius describes him as 'Bishop of the Gentiles' (ἐθνῶν ἐπίσκοπος), but this is probably due to confusion with *Hippolytus, with whom, as we learn from a Commentary of the Jacobite, Dionysius Bar-Salibi (12th cent.), Gaius also had a controversy. His reference to the 'trophies of the apostles' (τὰ τρόπαια τῶν ἀποστόλων, Eusebius, *HE* 2. 25. 7) has been one of the key texts in the discussions about the excavations under *St Peter's, Rome.

E. Prinzivalli, 'Gaio e gli Alogi', *Studi Storico Religiosi*, 5 (1981), pp. 53–68. In Eng. there is a useful note to their tr. of Eusebius, *Ecclesiastical History* by H. J. Lawlor and J. E. L. Oulton, 2 (1928), p. 208.

Galatians, Epistle to the. St *Paul apparently wrote this letter from *Ephesus or Macedonia to his Galatian converts on receiving news of a movement requiring them to keep all the commands of the Jewish Law, and thereby (as he thought) endangering the whole value of their faith in Christ. Though J. H. *Ropes and others have suggested that he was at the same time opposing a different group which called for the total rejection of the Jewish Law and even of moral standards, this theory has never been established.

The Epistle opens with an account of Paul's career from his conversion onwards, intended to show (1) that he had received his commission directly from God; (2) that no human teacher had authority to change the Gospel that he, Paul, had preached; and (3) that the original *Apostles at Jerusalem, i.e. *Peter, *James, and *John, had recognized the rightfulness of his mission to the Gentiles. He then emphasizes the futility of trying to live by 'works of the law' and maintains that the way in which a person is justified in the sight of God is not that of 'law' but of 'faith'. This is argued from the case of *Abraham, who was justified by faith in God's promises. As these promises

to Abraham were fulfilled in Christ, all external considerations, such as whether a believer is a Jew or a Greek, are transcended; Christians are one in Christ Jesus. They receive the gift of the Spirit, and it is the Spirit which is the source of the Christian life, yielding its fruit in 'love, joy, peace, long-suffering, kindness, goodness, faithfulness, meekness, temperance' (5: 22). The Epistle ends with a further warning to the readers not to put their trust in Jewish observances.

The Epistle was written with a passionate intensity and is universally recognized as genuine. Traditionally it has been held that it was addressed to Christians in the country of Galatia in the interior of Asia Minor, which had been peopled by Gauls in the 3rd cent. BC (the 'N. Galatian theory'). Many scholars, however, have argued that 'Galatia' means the Roman province of Galatia, which covered a much wider area in Asia Minor, and of which the S. part included the cities of Pisidian Antioch, Iconium, Derbe, and Lystra, mentioned in Acts 13 f. (the 'S. Galatian theory'). On either theory there are complex problems as to how to relate the events in Paul's life as recorded in Gal. 1 f. with those in Acts. Older scholars were almost unanimous in identifying the journey to Jerusalem in Gal. 2: 1–10 with that in Acts 15. But some biblical students, among them J. *Calvin, but esp. exponents of the 'S. Galatian theory', have equated it with the journey in Acts 11: 29 f. and have thereby explained the absence of references to the 'decrees' of Acts 15: 20 on the hypothesis that the Epistle was written before the Council had taken place; that would be in AD 50 or a little earlier, and Galatians would then be the earliest of the Pauline Epistles. Most scholars, however, prefer a later date in the mid-50s because of the contacts with the language and subject-matter of Romans, and some reconcile Paul's record with Acts by supposing that Acts 11 and 15 stem from different sources but refer to the same visit.

Modern comm. by J. B. *Lightfoot (Cambridge and London, 1865), W. M. *Ramsay (London, 1899), E. de W. Burton (ICC, 1921), G. S. Duncan (Moff. Comm., 1934), H. Schlier (HKNT, Siebente Abteilung; 10th edn., 1949), P. Bonnard (Commentaire du Nouveau Testament, 9, with Eph., 1953, pp. 9–132), H. N. Ridderbos, tr. into Eng. by H. Zylstra (New London Commentary, Grand Rapids, 1953; 2nd edn., London, 1954), J. Bligh, SJ (London, 1969), D. Guthrie (New Cent. Bib., 1969), F. Mussner (Herders Theologischer Kommentar zum Neuen Testament, 9; 1974), D. Lührmann (Züricher Bibelkommentar, NT 7; 1978), H. D. Betz (Hermeneia; Philadelphia [1979]), F. F. Bruce (New International Greek Testament Commentary; Exeter, 1982), R. N. Longenecker (Word Biblical Comm., 41; Dallas, Tex. [1990]), and J. D. G. Dunn (Black's NT Comm., 1993). J. H. Ropes, *The Singular Problem of the Epistle to the Galatians* (Harvard Theological Studies, 14; 1929). E. P. Sanders, *Paul, the Law, and the Jewish People* (Philadelphia [1983]), *passim*. C. K. Barrett, *Freedom and Obligation: A Study of the Epistle to the Galatians* (1985); J. M. G. Barclay, *Obeying the Truth: A Study of Paul's Ethics in Galatians* (Edinburgh, 1988). Kümmel, pp. 294–304. H. D. Betz in *Anchor Bible Dictionary*, 2 (1992), pp. 872–5.

Gale, Thomas (*c*.1635–1702), antiquary. After studying at Trinity College, Cambridge, he became successively Regius Professor of Greek at Cambridge (1666), High Master of St Paul's School (1672), and Dean of *York (1697). A versatile scholar of European reputation and a correspondent of J. *Mabillon, he was the editor of *Historiae Anglicanae Scriptores Quinque* (1687) and *Historiae*

Britannicae Scriptores (1691), the latter of which contained as its first three items the texts of *Gildas, Nennius, and Eddi. The *Rerum Anglicarum Scriptores* (1684), often attributed to Gale, was in fact the work of William Fulman, who collaborated with Gale in some of his other writings. These three folios, which were all published anonymously at Oxford, contained the monastic chronicles of several of the lesser houses such as Burton and Margam, and are a valuable source, not only for local history, but also for the study of the history of medieval England in general. He was also the author of several other works, including an unpublished edition of *Origen's '*Philocalia'.

J. E. B. Mayor, *Cambridge in the Time of Queen Anne* (1911), pp. 448–50, incl. sources and list of MSS. D. C. Douglas, *English Scholars* (1939), esp. pp. 69–72 and 213–21; 2nd edn. (1951), pp. 59–61 and 168–74. G. Goodwin in *DNB* 20 (1889), pp. 378–80.

Galerius (d. 311), Roman Emperor. An Illyrian of humble birth, he rose in the army and in 293 was appointed by *Diocletian as his co-adjutor ('Caesar') in the E.; on Diocletian's abdication in 305 he succeeded him as Augustus. According to Christian writers his influence had inspired the persecution initiated in 303. Unable to enforce his dominance in the W., and suffering from an illness gloatingly described by *Lactantius (*De Mortibus Persecutorum*, 33), he finally issued an edict of toleration in 311 (see PERSECUTIONS). He died soon afterwards.

The chief Christian sources are Lactantius, *De Mortibus Persecutorum*, 9–35, and *Eusebius, *HE* 8. 16 f. T. D. Barnes, *Constantine and Eusebius* (1981), pp. 8–34, 39, and 159. W. Ensslin in *PW* 14 (1930), cols. 2516–28, s.v. 'Maximianus (Galerius)'.

Galgani, St Gemma (1878–1903), Italian *stigmatic. She was born of poor parents at Camigliano in Tuscany and lived most of her life at Lucca. Ill-health frustrated her desire of becoming a *Passionist nun, though she took the three vows privately and, in addition, a vow of perfection. She enjoyed frequent ecstasies, and received the stigmata and marks of scourging intermittently between 1899 and 1901. Apart from her conviction of occasional diabolical possession, her spiritual life was normally peaceful. She was beatified in 1933 and canonized in 1940. Feast day, 11 Apr.

Lettere, ed. by the Passionists, with preface by E. Pellegrinetti (Isola del Liri, 1941); *Estasi, diario, autobiografia*, ed. idd., also with preface by E. Pellegrinetti (ibid., 1943). The principal secondary authority is the Life by her confessor, Germano di S. Stanislao (Rome, 1907; many subsequent edns.). Substantial modern studies by E. Zoffoli, CP (Rome, 1957) and J.-F. Villepelée (3 vols., Hauteville, Switzerland, 1971–8); in Eng. there are Lives by B. Williamson (London [1932]) and [C. C.] Amedeo della Madre del Buon Pastore, CP (Rome, 1933; Eng. tr., 1935). Federico dell'Addolorata, CP, in *Dict. Sp.* 6 (1967), cols. 183–7, s.v. 'Gemma Galgani', with detailed bibl., with additional bibl. in *DHGE* 20 (1984), col. 337, s.v. 'Gemma Galgani'.

Galilee (Heb. הַגָּלִיל). (1) Originally the term was applied only to part of the tribe of Naphtali, but in NT times it was given to all the district in N. Palestine extending from the Mediterranean to the *Jordan, and the word is now generally used in this sense. It constituted one of the four Roman divisions of Palestine. Its position on the main trade routes between Egypt and Syria had made it from early times a cosmopolitan province. It was the scene of almost all the Lord's earlier life and of a great part of His ministry and included such places as *Nazareth, *Capernaum, *Bethsaida, and Magdala. Many of its chief towns were situated on the 'Sea of Galilee', a lake some 680 ft. below the level of the Mediterranean through which the R. Jordan flows.

(2) In medieval cathedrals, an outer porch or chapel to which penitents are said to have been admitted on *Ash Wednesday, before being brought into church to do their *penance.

S. Klein, *Beiträge zur Geographie und Geschichte Galiläas* (1909); id., *Neue Beiträge zur Geschichte und Geographie Galiläas* (Palästina-Studien, Heft 1; 1923). A. Alt, 'Die Stätten des Wirkens Jesu in Galiläa territorialgeschichtlich betrachtet', *Beiträge zur biblischen Landes und Altertumskunde*, 68 (1951), pp. 51–71; separate Eng. tr. as *Where Jesus Worked* (1961). M. Goodman, *State and Society in Roman Galilee*, A.D. 132–212 (Totowa, NJ, 1983). G. A. *Smith, *The Historical Geography of the Holy Land* (25th edn.; 1931), pp. 413–63. S. Freyne in *Anchor Bible Dictionary*, 2 (1992), pp. 895–9, s.v. 'Galilee' (Hellenistic/Roman); A. Ronen and others in E. Stern and others (eds.), *The New Encyclopedia of Archaeological Excavations in the Holy Land*, 2 (Jerusalem and New York [1993]), pp. 449–58, s.v.

Galilei, Galileo (1564–1642), Italian mathematician and scientist, usually known simply as 'Galileo'. An early attempt to enter the monastic life was foiled by his father, the musical theorist Vincenzio Galilei, who envisaged a medical career for his son. Nevertheless Galileo did not complete his medical course at the University of Pisa, but turned to mathematics and in 1589 became professor of mathematics at Pisa; in 1592 he was appointed to the more lucrative chair at Padua. At this time he developed ideas on a new science of motion that eventually found mature expression in his *Discorsi e Dimostrazioni Matematiche intorno à Due Nuove Scienze* (1638). By asking, not about the causes of motion, but rather how they would occur in certain ideal situations, he concluded that an unimpeded horizontal motion would continue indefinitely at uniform speed, and an unimpeded vertical motion would be uniformly accelerated—ideas that can be seen as leading towards Newtonian physics. In 1609 Galileo heard of a new optical instrument, later known as the telescope; he soon had exemplars made for himself and embarked on a systematic observation of the heavens. His results, which he used for supporting a heliocentric *Copernican cosmology, were published in *Sidereus Nuncius* (1610) and *Istoria e Dimostrazioni intorno alle Macchie Solari* (1613). In 1610 he moved to Florence as Chief Mathematician and Philosopher to the Grand Duke of Tuscany, and soon the theological implications of Copernicanism became a matter of great concern (which they had not been hitherto). Galileo in 1615 composed a long letter (pub. in 1636, *Lettera a Madama Cristina di Lorena, Granduchessa di Toscana*) on the relation of astronomy to Scripture, in which he advocated a liberal use of the principle of *accommodation in interpreting biblical passages seemingly inconsistent with the motion of the earth. Matters came to a head in 1615 and early 1616 when the theologians of the *Holy Office asserted that to maintain the immobility and centrality of the sun as opposed to that of the earth was heretical, and soon Copernicus' *De revolutionibus orbium caelestium* (pub. in 1543) was placed on the *Index, pending correction.

Galileo was informed of the decision and was reported to have acquiesced in it. For some years he was publicly silent about Copernicanism, but when his friend Maffeo Barberini became Pope *Urban VIII in 1623, he gained the impression that he could discuss the new system, provided that he treated it as hypothetical and did not introduce biblical arguments. The result was his *Dialogo sopra i Due Massimi Sistemi del Mondo* (1632), which was more faithful to the letter than the spirit of this understanding, and contained an apparent insult to the Pope. Galileo was summoned before the *Inquisition, made to recant, and spent the rest of his life under house arrest. His famous words *Eppur si muove* (None the less it does move) seem to be legendary. The 'Galileo Affair' has been a continuing leitmotif in accounts of the meeting of science and religion, and Pope *John Paul II in 1981 appointed a commission to study the case and in 1992 endorsed its report admitting the 'subjective error' of Galileo's judges.

The standard edn. of his works is the 'Edizione nazionale' by A. Favaro (20 vols., Florence, 1890–1909; repr. 1968). Eng. trs. include *Discoveries and Opinions of Galileo*, tr. S. Drake (Garden City, NY, 1957; tr. of *Siderius Nuncius* and *Lettera a Madama Cristina di Lorena*, with extracts from other works); *Siderius Nuncius*, tr. A. van Helden (Chicago, 1989); *Dialogo sopra i Due Massimi Sistemi del Mondo*, tr. S. Drake (Berkeley, Calif., etc., 1953); and *Discorsi e Dimostrazioni*, tr. id. (Madison, Wis., 1974). The secondary bibl. is vast; E. McMullin (ed.), *Galileo: Man of Science* (New York and London [1967]) incl. convenient updating of bibls. of Carli, Favaro and Boffito (see below). Useful biogs. by J. Brodrick, SJ (London [1964]), L. Geymonat (Turin, 1957; Eng. tr., New York and London, 1965), S. Drake, *Galileo at Work: His Scientific Biography* (Chicago and London, 1978), and, on an introductory level, id., *Galileo* (Past Masters, Oxford, 1980). S. M. Pagano (ed.), *I Documenti del Processo di Galileo Galilei* (Collectanea Archivi Vaticani, 21; 1984). Eng. tr. of various primary docs., with introd., by M. A. Finocchiaro, *The Galileo Affair: A Documentary History* (Berkeley, Calif., etc. [1989]). Secondary works dealing with Galileo's relations with the Church include G. de Santillana, *The Crime of Galileo* (1958); J. J. Langford, *Galileo, Science and the Church* (New York, 1966); P. Poupard (ed.), *Galileo Galilei: 350 ans d'histoire 1633–1983* (Tournai [1983]); O. Pedersen, 'Galileo and the Council of Trent: The Galileo Affair Revisited', *Journal for the History of Astronomy*, 14 (1983), pp. 1–29; G. V. Coyne, SJ, and others (eds.), *The Galileo Affair: A Meeting of Faith and Science. Proceedings of the Cracow Conference, 24 to 27 May 1984* (Vatican City, 1985); R. S. Westfall, 'The Trial of Galileo: Bellarmino, Galileo, and the Clash of Two Worlds', *Journal for the History of Astronomy*, 20 (1989), pp. 1–23, repr., with other material, *Essays on the Trial of Galileo* (Vatican City, 1989). P. Redondi, *Galileo eretico* (1983; Eng. tr., Princeton, NJ, 1987; London, 1988), argues provocatively that the underlying cause of Galileo's condemnation was his espousal of an atomism that was seen as inconsistent with the doctrine of *transubstantiation. Comprehensive bibl. covering the period 1568–1895 by A. Carli and A. Favaro (Rome, 1896), 1896–1940 by G. Boffito (ibid., 1943); and 1942–1964 by E. Gentili (Milan, 1966). S. Drake in *Dictionary of Scientific Biography*, 5 (1981 edn.), pp. 237–49, s.v.

Gall, St (*c*.550–*c*.650), missionary. It is unclear whether he was of Frankish or Alemannian origin, but he was certainly one of the followers of St *Columbanus, from whom he separated in 612 when the latter went to Italy. Gall remained in that part of Swabia which is now Switzerland, living mainly as a hermit. He is symbolically represented in art by a bear. Feast day, 16 Oct.

The famous monastery of St Gallen was founded *c*.719 on the site of Gall's hermitage. From the end of the 8th cent. its '*scriptorium' and collection of MSS were long among the most famous in Europe; the library is still housed in the monastic building.

(1) SAINT. In addition to contemporary refs. in Jonas, 'Vita S. Columbani', three Lives are extant: the earliest dates from the late 7th cent., the second, by Wetti, *c*.820, and the third, by *Walafrid Strabo, *c*.833/4; modern edn. by B. Krusch in *MGH*, Scriptores Rerum Merovingicarum, 4 (1902), pp. 229–337, incl. comm. Eng. tr. of Walafrid Strabo's Life by M. Joynt (Translations of Christian Literature, 5th ser., 1927). Frags. of metrical Life by *Notker in *MGH*, Poetae Latinae, 4. 2 (1923), pp. 1093–1108. F. Blanke, *Columban und Gallus: Urgeschichte des schweizerischen Christentums* (Zurich, 1940). B. and H. Helbling, 'Der heilige Gallus in der Geschichte', *Schweizerische Zeitschrift für Geschichte*, 12 (1962), pp. 1–62. K.-U. Jäschke, 'Kolumbanus von Luxeuil und sein Wirken im alemannischen Raum', in A. Borst (ed.), *Mönchtum, Episkopat und Adel zur Gründungszeit des Klosters Reichenau* (Vorträge und Forschungen, 20; Sigmaringen, 1974), pp. 77–130. A. Borst, *Mönche am Bodensee 610–1525* (Sigmaringen, 1978), pp. 19–32, with notes pp. 539 f. ('Gallus, Eremit an der Steinach').

(2) ABBEY. H. Wartmann [contd. by P. Bütler, T. Schiess, and others], *Urkundenbuch der Abtei St Gallen* (6 vols., 1863–1955). W. Horn and E. Born, *The Plan of St Gall: A Study of the Architecture and Economy of, and Life in a Paradigmatic Carolingian Monastery* (3 vols., Berkeley, Calif., 1979); W. Jacobsen, *Der Klosterplan von St Gallen und die karolingische Architektur* [1992]. J. Dunft and others in E. Gilomen-Schenkel (ed.), *Helvetia Sacra*, Abteilung 3, Band 1, Teil 2 (Berne, 1986), pp. 1180–369, with bibl. J. M. Clark, *The Abbey of St Gall as a Centre of Literature and Art* (1926), with bibl.; W. Vogler (ed.), *Die Kultur der Abtei Sankt Gallen* (1990; Eng. tr. by J. C. King, Stuttgart and Zurich [1991]). E. Ehrenzeller, *Geschichte der Stadt St Gallen* (St Gall, 1988), esp. pp. 3–124 passim. E. A. Lowe, *Codices Latini Antiquiores*, 7 (Oxford, 1956), pp. 18–44 [nos. 893–997]. R. Sprandel, *Das Kloster St Gallen in der Verfassung des Karolingischen Reiches* (Forschungen zur Oberrheinischen Landesgeschichte, 7; Freiburg i.B., 1958). R. McKitterick, *The Carolingians and the Written Word* (Cambridge, 1989), pp. 77–126.

Galla Placidia (*c*.390–450), Roman Empress. The daughter of *Theodosius I, she was carried off by *Alaric the Goth, when he captured *Rome in 410, and in 414 married his successor, King Ataulf. After his murder in 415, she rejoined Honorius, her brother, and on the accession of her son, Valentinian III, in 425 she acted as regent. An important influence in the religious struggles of the time, she was an uncompromising Catholic and gave her support to Pope *Leo I in the *Eutychian controversy. She built several famous churches at *Ravenna, among them her own mausoleum, which is adorned with splendid mosaics.

V. A. Sirago, *Galla Placidia e la trasformazione politica dell'Occidente* (Université de Louvain, Recueil de Travaux d'Histoire et de Philologie, 4th ser. 25; 1961); S. I. Oost, *Galla Placidia Augusta: A Biographical Essay* (Chicago and London, 1968), with bibl. T. Hodgkin, *Italy and her Invaders*, 1. 2 (1892), pp. 817–88. C. Ricci, *Il mausoleo di Galla Placidia in Ravenna* (1914). Also H. *Leclercq, OSB, in *DACL* 6 (pt. 1; 1924), cols. 248–75; V. A. Sirago in *DHGE* 19 (1981), cols. 807–11, s.v. For works on her churches, see also bibl. s.v. RAVENNA.

Gallandi, Andrea (1709–79), *patristic scholar. An *Oratorian priest who lived at Venice, he is best known for his *Bibliotheca veterum patrum antiquorumque scriptorum *ecclesiasticorum Graecorum* (14 vols., 1765–81), a collection of treatises drawn from 380 writers of the first seven cents. of the Christian era, in which special attention was paid to the less-known authors. It is still a work of great service to students of the Fathers. He also published *De vetustis canonum collectionibus sylloge* (1778), an important collection of writings on the history of canon law.

P. Godet in *DTC* 6 (1914), col. 1095, with bibl.

Gallia Christiana. A documentary account of the bishoprics, bishops, abbeys, and abbots of France. It derives from a work under this title first published by Claude Robert in 1626. A later edition issued in 1656 was approved by the *Assembly of the French Clergy, but only after a passage suspected of *Jansenism had been removed. Since the beginning of the 18th cent., when a thorough revision was undertaken by the *Maurist, Denys de Sainte-Marthe (1650–1725), the work has been continued chiefly by Benedictine scholars, among them, Félix Hodin, Étienne Brice, and Jacques Taschereau. For students of the detailed history of France, it remains indispensable.

Work partly repr., with some minor changes, by P. Piolin, OSB (Paris, 1870–77). A not very satisfactory revision was begun as *Gallia Christiana Novissima* by U. Chevalier (Montbéliard, 7 vols., 1899–1920). V. Fouqué, *Du Gallia Christiana et de ses auteurs: Étude bibliographique* (1857). A. Degert, 'Pour refaire la *Gallia Christiana*', *Revue d'Histoire de l'Église de France*, 8 (1922), pp. 281–301. H. *Leclercq, OSB, in *DACL* 6 (1924), cols. 277–310.

Gallican Articles, the Four (1682). The rights and privileges claimed by the French clergy at an assembly of 36 bishops and 34 deputies held at Paris on 19 March 1682. The demands arose from the dispute between Louis XIV and *Innocent XI over the appointment of bishops and the revenues of vacant sees. The document was drawn up by J. B. *Bossuet (q.v.).

The first denied that the Pope had dominion (*puissance*) over things temporal, and affirmed that kings are not subject to the authority of the Church in temporal and civil matters or to deposition by the ecclesiastical power, and that their subjects could not be dispensed by the Pope from their allegiance. The second upheld the decrees of the Council of *Constance (1414–18), and thus reaffirmed the authority of General Councils over the Pope. The third insisted that the ancient liberties of the Gallican Church were inviolable. The fourth asserted that pending the consent of the Church (i.e. until a General Council was convened), the judgement of the Pope is not irreformable. The Articles were quashed by the constitution 'Inter multiplices' of *Alexander VIII of 4 Aug. 1690, and by Louis XIV in a letter to the Pope on 14 Sept. 1693, but for over a decade they were taught in the French theological schools and made a test for admission to academic degrees and public office. See also GALLICANISM.

C. Gérin, *Recherches historiques sur l'assemblée du clergé de 1682* (1869; 2nd edn., rev., 1870), with text of Articles, pp. 317 f. of 2nd edn.; J.-T. Loyson, *L'Assemblée du clergé de France de 1682* (1870), with text of Articles, pp. 349–51, and of Louis's letter, pp. 520 f. The constitution 'Inter Multiplices' is pr. in the *Bullarum, Diplomatum et Privilegiorum Sanctorum Romanorum Pontificum Taurinensis Editio*, 20 (Naples, 1883), pp. 67–70, with refs. to earlier Papal declarations. The main clause of the constitution, together with the text of the Articles, is repr. in Denzinger and Hünermann (37th edn., 1991), pp. 656–8 (nos. 2281–5). Eng. tr.

of the Articles in S. Z. Ehler and J. B. Morrall, *Church and State Through the Centuries* (1954), pp. 207 f. P. Blet, SJ, *Les Assemblées du clergé et Louis XIV de 1670 à 1693* (Analecta Gregoriana, 189; 1972), pp. 312–580. See also bibl. to GALLICANISM.

Gallican chant. The music of the early *Gallican rite has not survived; there are neither notated chants nor even chant books without music. A few non-Roman pieces from MSS of the 10th cent. and later have been identified as 'Gallican' (such as the chants for the *Reproaches on Good Friday); and in some cases they may indeed go back to the period before the general adoption of the Roman rite in Gaul; but they are mere straws in the wind. More recently it has been argued that certain Gregorian *Offertories may enshrine Gallican music. However, the rite and its music may well have varied considerably from one locality to another; it was suppressed before the chant had become the exclusive property of trained singers, and nothing certain of its nature is known. The neo-Gallican liturgy in the 17th and 18th cents. gave rise to a musical repertory which differed from the Roman, but it can have no link with the early Gallican chant; it has been little studied.

A. Gastoué, *Le Chant Gallican* (Grenoble, 1939; orig. pub. in the *Revue du chant grégorien*, 41–3; 1937–9). K. Levy, 'Toledo, Rome and the Legacy of Gaul', *Early Music History*, 4 (1984), pp. 49–99. M. Huglo in S. Sadie (ed.), *The New Grove Dictionary of Music and Musicians*, 7 (1980), pp. 113–25, s.v. 'Gallican rite, music for the'.

Gallican Confession. The *Confession de foi* or *Confessio Gallicana*, adopted in the First National Synod of Protestants at Paris in 1559. The first draft was the work of J. *Calvin, but it was revised, chiefly by his pupil Antoine de la Roche Chandieu (1534–91), before its formal acceptance. It was written in French and contained 35 articles, and in substance was an epitome of Calvin's central doctrines. A modified form of it, with 40 articles, was ratified at the Synod of La Rochelle in 1571. The Confession has often been attached to editions of the French Bible.

P. *Schaff, *Creeds of Christendom* (1877), 1, pp. 490–8; 3, pp. 356–82 (text). Eng. tr., with introd., also in A. C. Cochrane, *Reformed Confessions of the 16th Century* (1966), pp. 137–58, with bibl. p. 140. J. Pannier, *Les Origines de la Confession de Foi et la discipline des Églises réformées de France* (Études d'histoire et de philosophie religieuses publiées par la faculté de théologie protestante de l'Université de Strasbourg, 32; 1936).

Gallican Psalter. St *Jerome's revision of the Latin Psalter made *c*.392 on the basis of the *Hexaplaric Greek text of the LXX. Possibly under the influence of *Gregory of Tours, this version became very popular in Gaul (hence the name 'Gallican'), where it was adopted for use in the liturgy. Under the influence of *Alcuin it came to displace the Hebrew Psalter in almost all subsequent biblical MSS of the Vulgate and is the version normally found in printed editions of the Latin Bible. Its use for public recitation spread throughout the W. Church, though in Italy it did not displace the *Roman Psalter until the time of Pope *Pius V (1566–72). See also PSALTER.

Gallican rite. This term is used with three meanings: (1) for the liturgical forms in use in Gaul before the adoption of the Roman rite under *Charlemagne; (2) loosely, for all the non-Roman rites of the early W. Church; (3) for the 'Neo-Gallican' liturgies of the 17th and 18th cents. What follows relates only to (1).

It is not known why in early times the rites of N. Italy, Gaul, Spain and the *Celtic Churches differed from that of Rome, nor are scholars agreed as to their *provenance*. The two problems are closely linked. Several explanations are offered. (1) The older theory was that the non-Roman rites could be traced back to Apostolic origin in *Ephesus, whence they spread to the W. via Lyons (see IRENAEUS). The insuperable objection to this theory, as L. *Duchesne pointed out, is that no rite of the 2nd cent. could be so elaborate and so dependent upon the calendar as the Gallican rite was. (2) Others, e.g. Dom P. Cagin, have held that this 'non-Roman' type of rite represents the primitive Roman rite; but this theory assumes, without evidence, that the Roman rite was revised into its present form under Pope *Damasus (c.384). (3) Another widely accepted view, e.g. that of Duchesne, was that the liturgies came from Milan, which at the turn of the 4th and 5th cents. was very influential. This view can no longer be maintained since R. H. *Connolly's vindication of the Ambrosian authorship of the *De Sacramentis*, which includes the Roman Canon. (4) Perhaps the least unsatisfactory view is that it was indigenous to Gaul and that it developed with the introduction of variable prayers controlled by the Church calendar. The earliest evidence for this theory comes from Marseilles, c.450, when the priest Musaeus is said by *Gennadius to have first chosen lections and responsories appropriate to feast days, and a little later to have composed a large and excellent volume of Masses (*sacramentorum*) containing in separate sections the 'proper' of 'offices and seasons'. The composition of Masses came to be a literary activity in Gaul and Spain; *Sidonius Apollinaris is known to have composed many. The extant Mass books are not earlier than the 8th cent. and are already partly 'Romanized', except for the eleven *Mone Masses of the 7th cent. The letters once believed to be by *Germanus of Paris have been shown by A. *Wilmart to be dependent in some passages on *Isidore of Seville and can no longer be used as evidence for the Gallican rite of the 6th cent. They do, however, provide the only full description of a 7th–8th cent. rite used in Gaul.

Many of the surviving Gallican Masses are more prolix and oratorical than the austere forms of the Roman sacramentaries, while others are concise. The structure of the services, however, is in certain respects remarkably different. Some of the characteristics are shared by the *Mozarabic, Celtic, and even *Ambrosian rites. The main differences of the Gallican rite, as we have it, are (1) THE *MASS. (*a*) The *Trisagion was regularly sung in Greek and Latin before the *Kyries (which were in threefold form) and before and after the *Gospel. (*b*) The *Benedictus Dominus followed the Kyries, and the *Benedicite was sung after the OT Lesson. (*c*) The *diptychs and the *Kiss of Peace occurred before the *Canon. (*d*) The Canon, with the exception of the *Institution, varied with the season. (*e*) The Institution, in many extant Masses, was followed by a prayer *post pridie*, which was sometimes a form of *epiclesis. (*f*) The Fraction took place, accompanied by its own *antiphon, *before* the *Pater Noster. (*g*) A Trinitarian hymn (the *Trecanum) was sung during the *Communion. (2) *BAP-

TISM. The most notable points of contrast with the Roman rite are the placing of the profession of faith before the actual baptism and the addition of the rite of '*Pedilavium'. (3) *ORDINATION. The Gallican rite seems to have included a public ceremony for the minor orders which has been borrowed by Rome. And in many ways the Gallican Ordination services have influenced the Roman. See STATUTA ECCLESIAE ANTIQUA.

In the reign of *Pepin III the Gallican rite was already conflated with the Roman in some places, and Charlemagne actively sought to achieve uniformity with Roman usage (see GREGORIAN SACRAMENTARY). He was not, however, entirely successful and the present Roman rite still bears marks of its conflation with that of Gaul.

For the Mass the chief texts are the *Bobbio Missal, the *Missale Francorum*, the *Missale Gothicum*, the *Missale Gallicanum Vetus*, and the Mone Masses. K. Gamber (ed.), *Ordo antiquus Gallicanus: Der gallikanische Messritus des 6. Jahrhunderts* (Textus patristici et liturgici, 3 [1965]). Editions of the letters attributed to Germanus, and bibl. on these texts, cited s.v. See also J. *Mabillon, OSB, *De Liturgia Gallicana* (Paris, 1685; repr. in J. P. Migne, *PL* 72. 101–448); J. M. *Neale and G. H. *Forbes, *The Ancient Liturgies of the Gallican Church* (3 parts, Burntisland, 1855–67); L. Duchesne, *Origines du culte chrétien* (2nd edn., 1893; Eng. tr., 1903), esp. ch. 7; P. Cagin, OSB, 'Avant-propos à l'antiphonaire ambrosien', *Paléographie Musicale*, 5 (1896), pp. 70–97. J.-B. Thibaut, *L'Ancienne Liturgie Gallicane: Son origine et sa formation en Provence aux ve et vi^e siècles* [1929]; E. Griffe, 'Aux origines de la Liturgie Gallicane', *Bulletin de Littérature Ecclésiastique*, 52 (1951), pp. 17–43; H. Ashworth, OSB, 'Gregorian Elements in Some Early Gallican Service Books', *Traditio*, 13 (1957), pp. 431–43; W. S. Porter, *The Gallican Rite* (1958), with bibl. [by F. L. Cross], pp. 57–61; A. A. King, *Liturgies of the Past* (1959), pp. 77–185; J. Pinell, OSB, 'Anámnesis y Epíclesis en el antiguo rito galicano', *Didaskalia*, 4 (1974), pp. 3–130. J. Quasten in *NCE* 6 (1967), pp. 258–62, s.v. 'Gallican Rites'; J. Pinell in *DPAC* 1 (1984), cols. 1425–31, s.v. 'Gallicana (liturgia)'; Eng. tr. in *Encyclopedia of the Early Church*, 1 (1992), pp. 334–6.

Gallicanism. The collective name for the body of doctrine which asserted the more or less complete freedom of the RC Church, esp. in France, from the ecclesiastical authority of the Papacy. During the *Great Schism, such theologians as J. *Gerson and P. *d'Ailly had ably represented a primitive form of Gallican doctrine which had been taught in the *Sorbonne almost from the time of its foundation (1257). At this period the chief question at issue was the claim of the French Church to a privileged position in relation to the Papacy, these *libertés de l'Église gallicane* (whence the name Gallicanism) being based upon supposed prerogatives of the French Crown (prerogatives which a sober view of history scarcely warranted). In 1516 the *Pragmatic Sanction of Bourges (1438) was superseded by the Concord of *Bologna in which the French king's right of nomination to bishoprics and other high ecclesiasical offices was conceded. The constitutional decisions of the Council of *Trent (1545–63) were not received in France, and such writers as P. *Pithou, Edmond Richer (1559–1631), and P. de *Marca popularized a theory of Church government which minimized in various ways the authority claimed by the Papacy over the national Churches ('royal Gallicanism') and over the individual bishops ('episcopal Gallicanism'). In 1663 the Sorbonne published a declaration, the substance of which was reaffirmed by the *Assembly of the French clergy in 1682 in the formula known as the Four *Gallican Articles (q.v.). This declaration, though solemnly withdrawn by king and clergy in 1693, remained the typical Gallican manifesto. Gallican principles were preached throughout the 18th cent. by the opponents of the bull '*Unigenitus', and once more officially codified and proclaimed for the use of other national Churches at the synod of *Pistoia in 1786. The *Organic Articles added to Napoleon's concordat of 1801 included Gallican provisions, and Napoleon himself favoured the Gallican party among his clergy. After the Restoration, however, the work of the *Jesuits, and of such writers as J. *de Maistre and F. R. de *Lamennais, bore fruit in a renascence of *Ultramontanism in France, so that F. *Dupanloup, H. Maret (1805–84), and A. J. A. *Gratry found little support for their moderate Gallican positions at the time of the First Vatican Council (1869–70). The definition of Papal *Infallibility at the Council had the effect of making Gallican principles, at least in the field of dogma, incompatible with the profession of *Roman Catholicism. Although the main aims of Gallicanism in the 19th cent. concerned matters of administration (the freedom of bishops from undue interference by the Curia) and liturgy (the preservation of local rites, such as that of *Lyons) rather than belief, after the Council Gallicanism had only a historical importance. See also FEBRONIANISM.

L. Mention (ed.), *Documents relatifs aux rapports du clergé avec le royauté de 1682 à 1705* (Collection de Textes pour servir à l'Étude et à l'Enseignement de l'Histoire, 1893). N. Valois, *La France et le grand schisme en occident* (4 vols., 1896–1902), *passim.* V. Martin, *Les Origines du gallicanisme* (2 vols., 1939); id., *Le Gallicanisme et la réforme catholique: Essai historique sur l'introduction en France des décrets du concile de Trente (1563–1615)* (1919); id., *Le Gallicanisme politique et le clergé de France* (Université de Strasbourg, Bibliothèque de l'Institut de Droit Canonique, 3; 1929). A.-G. Martimort, *Le Gallicanisme de Bossuet* (Unam Sanctam, 24; 1953). A. Gough, *Paris and Rome: The Gallican Church and the Ultramontane Campaign 1848–1853* (Oxford, 1986). M. O'Gara, *Triumph in Defeat: Infallibility, Vatican I, and the French Minority Bishops* (Washington, DC [1988]). J. Lecler, 'Qu'est-ce que les libertés de l'Église Gallicane?', *Rech. S.R.* 23 (1933), pp. 385–410, 542–68; 24 (1934), pp. 47–85; G. Mollat, 'Les Origines du gallicanisme parlementaire aux XIVᵉ et XVᵉ siècles', *RHE* 43 (1948), pp. 90–147; R. Thysman, 'Le Gallicanisme de Mgr Maret et l'influence de Bossuet', ibid. 52 (1957), pp. 401–65. H. Dubruel and H. X. Arquillière in A. d'Alès, SJ (ed.), *Dictionnaire apologétique de la foi catholique*, 2 (1911), cols. 193–273, with full bibl. refs.; M. Dubruel in *DTC* 6 (1920), cols. 1096–137, s.v.; R. Laprat in *DDC* 6 (1957), cols. 426–525, s.v. 'Libertés de l'Église gallicane (Gallicanisme)'. J. Turmel in *HERE* 6 (1913), pp. 156–63, s.v.; C. Berthelot du Chesnay in *NCE* 6 (1967), pp. 262–7, s.v.

Gallio, Lucius Junius. The brother of *Seneca, he was the Proconsul of Achaia before whom St *Paul was accused at *Corinth (Acts 18: 12). That he held office in AD 52 is established by an inscription found at Delphi in 1905; this is an important fixed date in NT chronology.

Prosopographia Imperii Romani (2nd edn.), 4, ed. A. Stein and L. Petersen (Berlin, 1966), pp. 335 f. (no. 757), s.v. 'L. Iunius Gallio Annaeanus', which cites the literary and epigraphic evidence of his career. Convenient summary in M. Black and H. H. Rowley (eds.), *Peake's Commentary on the Bible* (1962), p. 914. K. Haacker in *Anchor Bible Dictionary*, 2 (1992), pp. 901–3.

Gallus, Thomas. See THOMAS GALLUS.

Gamaliel. The great Jewish rabbi, 'had in reputation among all the people' (Acts 5: 34), who was the teacher of St *Paul in his pre-Christian days (Acts 22: 3). He was a grandson of the liberal *Hillel, and his broad, tolerant views were well exemplified in his attitude to St *Peter and his companions (Acts 5: 34–40). It has been doubted, but on insufficient grounds, whether so fiery and intolerant a character as St Paul could have sat at the feet of such a tolerant master. Acc. to a late and prob. worthless tradition in the *Clementine Recognitions (1. 65), Gamaliel afterwards became a Christian.

E. *Schürer, *The History of the Jewish People in the Age of Jesus Christ*, rev. Eng. tr. by G. Vermes and others, 2 (Edinburgh, 1979), pp. 367 f., with refs. H. L. Strack and P. Billerbeck, *Kommentar zum Neuen Testament aus Talmud und Midrasch*, 2 (1924), pp. 636–9; H. L. Strack, *Einleitung in Talmud und Midrasch*, 7th edn., rev. by G. Stemberger [1982], p. 74 f.; Eng. tr. (Edinburgh, 1991), p. 73. See also comm. to ACTS.

gambling. See BETTING AND GAMBLING.

Gams, Pius Bonifatius (1816–92), Church historian. A native of Württemberg, he became a professor at Hildesheim in 1847, and in 1855 a *Benedictine at St Boniface's monastery at Munich. His two chief works are a history of the Church of Spain (*Kirchengeschichte von Spanien*, 3 vols., 1862–79), a massive compilation, but somewhat uncritical in its treatment of sources; and an invaluable *Series Episcoporum* (Ratisbon, 1873; supplement, 1886; the whole photographically repr., Graz, 1957), which contains, arranged acc. to their sees, the names of all the known bishops in communion with Rome down to that date.

F. Lauchert, 'Die kirchengeschichtlichen und zeitgeschichtlichen Arbeiten von P. B. Gams in Zusammenhang gewürdigt', *Studien und Mitteilungen aus dem Benediktiner- und dem Cistercienser-Orden*, 27 (1906), pp. 634–49; 28 (1907), pp. 53–71, 299–305, with list of his works, pp. 305–15.

Gandolphy, Peter (1779–1821), *Jesuit preacher. Born in London and educated abroad, he attained fame as a preacher at the Spanish Chapel in Manchester Square, London, where he made many converts. In 1812 he issued *A Liturgy, or Book of Common Prayers and Administration of Sacraments . . . for the Use of all Christians in the United Kingdom of Great Britain and Ireland*, which was modelled upon the Anglican Prayer Book. This publication, together with his sermons, caused him to be accused by his ordinary, Bp. W. Poynter (d. 1827), of heresy. Although vindicated by the Congregation of *Propaganda in Rome (1817), he gave up his work in London (1818) and retired to his family home at East Sheen.

Sommervogel, 3 (1892), cols. 1181 f., s.v.; T. Cooper in *DNB* 20 (1889), pp. 400 f., s.v., with further refs.

Gang-Days. An obsolete title of the three *Rogation Days (the Monday, Tuesday, and Wednesday before *Ascension Day) from the ancient practice of perambulating the parish bounds on those days. The forms 'Gang-Monday' 'Gang-Week', are also met with.

Gangra, Council of. A Council held at Gangra in Paphlagonia *c.*341. It passed 20 canons, directed against a false asceticism (led by *Eustathius, Bp. of Sebaste) which condemned marriage and avoided the ordinary services of the Church. To these canons are added an epilogue, often called 'canon 21', explaining the true nature of asceticism. The canons are not in themselves important; but, as they were included in the first Greek *corpus* translated into Latin, they attained a very wide circulation.

Hardouin, 1, cols. 529–40; Mansi, 2 (1759), cols. 1095–122; crit. edn. of Lat. texts in *EOMIA* 2. 2 (1913), pp. 145–214; Lat. and Gk. texts also pr., with Fr. tr., in Joannou, 1, pt. 2 (1962), pp. 83–99. Hefele and Leclercq, 1 (pt. 2; 1907), pp. 1029–45. J. Gribomont, OSB, 'Le Monachisme au IVᵉ s. en Asie Mineure: de Gangres au Messalianisme', in K. Aland and F. L. Cross (eds.), *Studia Patristica*, 2 (TU 64; 1957), pp. 400–15, esp. pp. 400–7. T. D. Barnes, 'The Date of the Council of Gangra', *JTS* NS 40 (1989), pp. 121–4 [argues for *c*.355]. *CPG* 4 (1980), pp. 13 f. (nos. 8553 f.). G. Bardy in *DDC* 5 (1953), cols. 935–8, s.v. 'Gangres (Concile de)'.

Gansfort, Wessel. See WESSEL.

Garden of Eden. See EDEN, GARDEN OF.

Garden of Gethsemane. See GETHSEMANE, GARDEN OF.

Garden of the Soul, The. The 'Manual of Spiritual Exercises and Instructions for Christians who, living in the world, aspire to Devotion' compiled by R. *Challoner and first published in 1740. It at once became a favourite with English RCs and has remained in continuous use until recent years, though in the course of 200 years parts of it have been modified almost out of recognition. The influence exercised by the earlier editions in moulding the deep but sober piety of English RCs, before more Italian forms of devotion became popular, led the older school sometimes to be called 'Garden-of-the-Soul Catholics'.

See bibl. to CHALLONER, R.

Gardiner, Stephen (*c*.1497–1555), Bp. of *Winchester. From 1525 to 1549 he was master of Trinity Hall, Cambridge, and took an active interest in promoting Greek studies in the university. He was employed by *Henry VIII and T. *Wolsey on diplomatic business, notably in the negotiations with Rome for annulling the marriage with Catherine of Aragon, and in 1533 acted as an assessor in the court which finally declared the marriage null and void. In 1531 he had been given the see of Winchester. He accepted, at least for a time, the royal supremacy over the Church, arguing in his *De Vera Obedientia* (1535) that the Pope had no legitimate power over national Churches. He was strongly opposed to the Reformist influences of T. *Cromwell, but prob. was not personally responsible for the *Six Articles. By the end of Henry's reign he was regarded as the chief opponent in England of the Reformation doctrines. In *Edward VI's reign he was imprisoned in the Tower (1548) and deprived of his bishopric (1551), but was restored to his see by *Mary, and became Lord High Chancellor. He approved of the submission of England to Rome, but was instrumental in securing the retention of the property of the dissolved monasteries by their lay owners. The mediating course which he followed in the reign of Henry VIII has led his character to be variously judged.

H. Chitty and H. E. Malden (eds.), *Registra Stephani Gardiner et Johannis Poynet, Episcoporum Wintoniensium* (*Canterbury and

York Society, 37; 1930), pp. 1–91; J. A. Muller (ed.), *Letters of Stephen Gardiner* (1933). P. Janelle (ed.), *Obedience in Church and State: Three Political Tracts by Stephen Gardiner* (1930). Second (1553) edn. of Eng. tr. of *De Vera Obedientia*, repr. Leeds, 1966. J. S. Brewer (ed.), *State Papers*, 7–11 (1849–52), *passim*. J. A. Muller, *Stephen Gardiner and the Tudor Reaction* (1926). G. Redworth, *In Defence of the Church Catholic: A Life of Stephen Gardiner* (Oxford, 1990).

Garnet or Garnett, Henry (1555–1606), English *Jesuit. He became a RC while a boy, went to Rome, and studied under R. *Bellarmine. In 1586 he set out to work on the English Mission, of which he became Superior in 1587. He was arrested and executed, some months after the *Gunpowder Plot, for complicity in it. Though he certainly had some knowledge of it beforehand, it is disputed whether his information was entirely gained through a confessional case, referred to him under the *seal, or whether he had independent evidence. In support of the latter view is the fact that, although English law gave no protection to the confessional, the prosecution apparently preferred not to use evidence based upon it. In any case, it was not suggested that Garnet personally took part in the plot; he was condemned and executed for not having revealed his knowledge of it.

Life in H. Foley, SJ, *Records of the English Province of the Society of Jesus*, 4 (1878), pp. 35–192. P. Caraman, *Henry Garnet 1555–1606 and the Gunpowder Plot* (1964). A. F. Allison, 'The Writings of Fr. Henry Garnet, SJ', *Biographical Studies*, 1 (1951), pp. 7–21. See also works cited s.v. GUNPOWDER PLOT.

Garnier, Jean (1612–81), *Jesuit patristic scholar. A native of *Paris, he entered the Society of Jesus at Rouen in 1628 and taught theology at the Collège de *Clermont at Paris from 1653 to 1679. In 1673 he published his edition of *Marius Mercator (in J. P. *Migne, *PL* 48) with valuable treatises on *Pelagianism and *Nestorianism which were the basis of all subsequent research on both subjects. In 1680 he edited the 'Liber Diurnus' of the Roman pontiffs, adding historical, doctrinal, and critical notes esp. on the ordinations and professions of faith of the Popes, and a treatise on the orthodoxy of Pope *Honorius I (also reproduced in Migne, *PL* 105, but without the treatise on Honorius). He also completed J. *Sirmond's edition of *Theodoret (1684; posthumous), with critical essays on his works and doctrine. He published, besides, several works on Scholastic philosophy and on moral and doctrinal theology.

He is not to be confounded with Julien Garnier, OSB (1670–1725), the *Maurist editor of St *Basil.

Sommervogel, 3 (1892), cols. 1228–32; 9 (1900), col. 398. H. Foerster (ed.), *Liber Diurnus Romanorum Pontificum* (Berne, 1958), pp. 15–20. P. Bernard in *DTC* 6 (1920), cols. 1160–3.

Gascoigne, Thomas (1403–58), English scholar and theologian. He was born at Hunslet, nr. Leeds, and educated at *Oxford, probably at Oriel, where he continued to live for the rest of his life. He was frequently either chancellor or vice-chancellor of the university. Ordained priest in 1427, he held the rectory of Kirk Deighton for a short time; but with the exception of a prebendal stall in *Wells Cathedral, he declined nearly all other ecclesiastical offices, including the chancellorship of *York Minster, to devote himself to scholarly pursuits. He was also very active as a preacher and, though hostile to *Wycliffite influences, severe in his denunciations of pluralities, appropriations, and other ecclesiastical and monastic abuses. His principal work was the 'Liber Veritatum' or 'Dictionarium Theologicum' (written between 1431 and 1457), a theological dictionary which is both an important guide to the political and religious history of the time and an interesting revelation of Gascoigne's own views.

'Collectanea Historica' from Gascoigne's *Dictionarium Theologicum* pr. in T. *Hearne's edn. of Walter Hemingford (*fl.* 1300), *Historia de Rebus Gestis Edwardi I, Edwardi II et Edwardi III*, 2 (1731), pp. 509–50, with Life, pp. 504–8; J. E. T. Rogers (ed.), *Loci e Libro Veritatum: Passages Selected from Gascoigne's Theological Dictionary Illustrating the Condition of the Church and State, 1403–1453* (1881). W. A. Pronger, 'Thomas Gascoigne', *EHR* 53 (1938), pp. 606–26; 54 (1939), pp. 20–37. R. L. Poole in *DNB* 21 (1890), pp. 41–4; *BRUO* 2 (1958), pp. 745–8.

Gasquet, Francis Aidan (1846–1929), cardinal and historian. Born in London of an old Provençal family, he was educated at *Downside and entered the *Benedictine Order in 1866. Elected Prior of Downside in 1878, he raised the standard of both priory and school and considerably enlarged their scope. From 1885 he carried on research at the British Library and Public Record Office. In 1896 he went to Rome, where he played an important part as a member of the Commission on *Anglican Ordinations. On his return he became chairman of the commission for the reform of the English Benedictine Congregation, whose abbot-president he was from 1900 to 1914. In 1907 *Pius X made him president of the International Commission for the Revision of the *Vulgate. In 1914 he was created cardinal, and henceforward resided in Rome. On the death of Pius X he took part in the conclave, countering anti-British propaganda, and negotiated for the appointment of a British minister to the Vatican. He became Prefect of the Archives of the Holy See in 1917, and two years later *Vatican Librarian. In most of his historical work Gasquet was closely associated with Edmund *Bishop. His writings increased knowledge of medieval English monasticism, though in his later years his inaccuracy was exposed by G. G. Coulton and others. His works include *Henry VIII and the English Monasteries* (2 vols., 1888–9), which caused a great stir, *Religio Religiosi* (1918), and *Monastic Life in the Middle Ages* (1922).

Notes by J. C. Fowler, OSB, B. Kuypers, OSB, and U. Butler, OSB, in *The Downside Review*, 47 (1929), pp. 123–56, incl. bibl. of his works, pp. 147–9. S. Leslie, *Cardinal Gasquet: A Memoir* (1953). M. D. *Knowles, *Cardinal Gasquet as an Historian* (Creighton Lecture; 1957); repr. in *The Historian and Character and Other Essays* (Cambridge, 1963), pp. 240–63. E. C. Butler, OSB, in *DNB, 1922–1930*, pp. 330–2.

Gauden, John (1605–62), Bp. of *Worcester. He was educated at St John's College, Cambridge, studied later also at Wadham College, Oxford, and in 1640 became Vicar of Chippenham, Cambs. In the early days of the Civil War his sympathies were with Parliament, and for a short time in 1643 he was a member of the *Westminster Assembly. Later he changed his opinions, but was able none the less to retain his living throughout the Commonwealth period. At the Restoration in 1660 he was made Bp. of *Exeter, and in 1662 was translated, not, as he had hoped, to *Winchester, but to Worcester. He published

several controversial works against the *Puritans, including his monumental *Ecclesiae Anglicanae Suspiria* (1659), and defences of the Anglican ministry and liturgy. He was probably the author of the *Eikon Basilike* (q.v.), alleged to have been written by *Charles I in prison.

See bibl. s.v. EIKON BASILIKE. R. Hooper in *DNB* 21 (1890), pp. 69–72.

Gaudentius, St (4th–5th cent.), Bp. of Brescia. A friend of St *Ambrose, he succeeded *Philaster in the see of Brescia before 397. In 404–5 he journeyed to Constantinople to plead with the Emperor on behalf of St *Chrysostom, but without avail. Twenty-one of his sermons survive, including a set of 10 delivered in Easter week which have many references to the Eucharist. Feast day, 25 Oct.

Sermons pr. in J. P. Migne, *PL* 20. 827–1002; crit. edn. by A. Glueck (CSEL 68; 1936). J. Wittig, *Filaster, Gaudentius und Ambrosiaster* (Kirchengeschichtliche Abhandlungen, no. 8; Breslau, 1909), pp. 1–56. C. R. Norcock, 'St Gaudentius of Brescia and the *Tome* of St Leo', *JTS* 15 (1913–14), pp. 593–6; Y. M. Duval, 'Saint Léon le Grand et saint Gaudence de Brescia', ibid. NS 11 (1960), pp. 82–4. F. Trisoglio, *San Gaudenzio da Brescia scrittore* (Turin, 1960); id., 'Appunti per una ricerca delle Fonti di S. Gaudenzio da Brescia', *Rivista di Studi Classici*, 24 (1976), pp. 50–125. M. Simonetti in Quasten (cont.), *Patrology*, 4 (1986), pp. 133–5. P. Viard in *Dict. Sp.* 6 (1967), cols. 139–43, s.v., with bibl.

Gaudete Sunday. The Third in *Advent, from the opening word of the *Introit. As on Mid-Lent Sunday (*Laetare) rose-coloured vestments may be worn.

Gaume, Jean Joseph (1802–79), theological writer. Ordained priest in 1825, he spent his earlier years in teaching and pastoral work at Nevers. Later he was Vicar General successively of *Reims and Montauban. He came to notice through his advocacy of excluding the pagan classics from all Christian schools and substituting patristic texts; he was supported by L. *Veuillot but controverted by F. *Dupanloup among others. His extensive writings (of unequal value) include *Le Manuel des confesseurs* (1837; 11th edn., 1880), *Catéchisme de persévérance* (8 vols., 1838), *L'Europe en 1848* (1848), *Lettres à Monseigneur Dupanloup, évêque d'Orléans, sur le paganisme dans l'éducation* (1852), *Bibliothèque des classiques chrétiens* (30 vols., 1852–5), *La Révolution* (12 vols., 1856–9), and *Pie IX et les études classiques* (1875). The first named, pub. in an adapted Eng. tr. for the use of Anglican confessors by E. B. *Pusey (1877), was also widely used in England.

A. Ricard, *Étude sur Mgr Gaume: Ses œuvres, son influence, ses polémiques* (1872). H. P. *Liddon, *Life of E. B. Pusey*, 4 (1897), pp. 303–6. E. Mangenot in *DTC* 6 (1920), cols. 1168–71; J. Guerber, SJ, in *Dict. Sp.* 6 (1967), cols. 147 f.; supplementary material (unsigned) in *DHGE* 20 (1984), cols. 65 f., s.v.

Gaunilo, Count. The 11th-cent. Benedictine monk of Marmoutier, near Tours, who, in the guise of the 'fool' (cf. Ps. 14: 1), criticized in his *Liber pro insipiente* the validity of the *Ontological Argument for the existence of God which St *Anselm had formulated in his *Proslogion*. Anselm replied with his *Liber apologeticus adversus respondentem pro insipiente*.

Gavanti, Bartolommeo (1569–1638), *Barnabite liturgical scholar. He took an important part in the reform of the *Breviary and *Missal under Popes *Clement VIII and *Urban VIII. In his *Thesaurus sacrorum rituum, seu Commentaria in rubricas Missalis et Breviarii Romani* (Rome, 1628), his most considerable work, he brings together much historical information on the origin and mystical significance of W. liturgical practice.

Opera Theologico-Canonica (2 vols., bound in 1, Venice, 1760). O. Premoli, Barnabite, *Storia dei Barnabiti nel seicento* (1922), pp. 178–82; G. Boffito, Barnabite, *Scrittori barnabiti*, 2 (1933), pp. 132–48. P. Rippa, Barnabite, in *DHGE* 20 (1984), cols. 130–4, s.v.

Geddes, Jenny. Acc. to tradition, the name of a vegetable-seller who, on Sunday, 23 July 1637, threw her folding stool at the head of David Lindsay, Bp. of Edinburgh, in St Giles' Cathedral when the new and hated Scottish Prayer Book was used for the first time.

The occurrence of a tumult on the introduction of the Scottish BCP is recorded in the contemporary annals. The name of 'Jane or Janot Gaddis (yet living at the time of this relation)' is apparently first mentioned in Richard Baker, *A Chronicle of the Kings of England from the Time of the Romans Government unto the Death of King James*. Continuation [by F. Phillips], 5th impression (1670), p. 478.

Gehenna (Gk. γέεννα). Lit. 'the Valley of Hinnom' (Heb. גֵּי הִנֹּם); the meaning of Hinnom is unknown. It was orig. used purely topographically, prob. for the Wady er-Rababi to the SW and S. of Jerusalem, which joined at the SE of the city with the valley of the *Cedron, though it has sometimes (e.g. by Sir Charles Warren) been identified with the Cedron. In this sense the 'Valley of Hinnom' is mentioned at Jos. 15: 8 and 18: 16. From early times it was a place of human sacrifice, esp. to Moloch at Topheth (cf. 2 Kgs. 16: 3, 21: 6), and as such was polluted by Josiah (2 Kgs. 23: 10–12); *Jeremiah warned that a time would come when it would be renamed the 'Valley of Slaughter' (Jer. 7: 32, 19: 6). In later Jewish thought it was increasingly looked upon as a Divinely appointed place of punishment for apostates and other great sinners (e.g. 1 *Enoch 27: 2 f.; 90: 26 f.; 2 *Esdras 7: 36–8). Hence in the NT the word is used for the final place of torment for the wicked after the Last Judgement (Mt. 5: 29, 10: 28, 18: 9; Jas. 3: 6; EVV 'hell'). The statement of Kimchi (c. AD 1200) that fires were continually kept burning in the Valley of Hinnom has commonly been accepted by modern commentators; but it seems to be without earlier authority.

H. Vincent, OP, *Jérusalem*, 1 (1912), pp. 123–34. H. L. Strack and P. Billerbeck, *Kommentar zum NT aus Talmud und Midrasch*, 4 (1928), pp. 1029–1118. J. Jeremias in *TWNT* 1 (1933), pp. 655 f.; Eng. tr., 1 (1964), pp. 657 f., s.v. γέεννα, with bibl. refs.; J. Chaine in *Dict. Bibl.*, Suppl. 3 (1938), cols. 563–79, s.v.; D. F. Watson in *Anchor Bible Dictionary*, 2 (1992), pp. 926–8, s.v.

Geiler von Kaisersberg, Johann (1445–1510), 'the German *Savonarola', preacher. Born at Schaffhausen on the Rhine, Geiler (also 'Geyler') was educated at Ammersweiher, nr. Kaisersberg (also 'Kaysersberg') in Alsace, and Freiburg University. He was ordained priest in 1470. From 1465 to 1471 he lectured on *Aristotle at Freiburg and from 1471 to 1476 on theology at Basle, where he also preached in the cathedral. In 1476 he

returned to Freiburg as professor, becoming rector of the university in the same year. But his reforming interests soon led him to abandon academic work; and after declining an invitation to a pulpit at Würzburg on grounds of patriotism he accepted a special office of preacher created for him in the cathedral of the neighbouring Strasbourg in 1478. Except for a short interval he remained here for the rest of his life.

Geiler was an uncommonly forceful and impressive preacher. In spite of his austere moral ideals and his denunciation of the vices of all classes, his freshness, vivacity, apt illustration, and knowledge of the human heart won and held his hearers. Although he demanded reform, he never seems to have contemplated abandoning the Church. Personally something of a mystic, he is said to have enjoyed preaching but been haunted by fears arising from his work in the confessional.

He did not publish his own sermons, which survive in texts taken down by his hearers or elaborated by others from his notes. Among the most interesting is the series based on Sebastian Brant's *Narrenschiff* ('Ship of Fools'). His other works include an edition of the works of J. *Gerson (4 vols., 1488–1502).

Ausgewählte Schriften, ed. P. de Lorenzi (4 vols., Trier, 1881–3); *Älteste Schriften*, ed. L. Dacheux (Freiburg i.B., 1882); *Sämtliche Werke*, ed. G. Bauer (Ausgaben deutscher Literatur des XV. bis XVIII. Jahrhunderts, 129, 139, 149, etc.; 1989 ff.). C. Schmidt, *Histoire littéraire de l'Alsace à la fin du XVe et au commencement du XVIe siècle*, 2 (1879), pp. 373–90, for details of the early edns. of his works. His Life by Beatus *Rhenanus was pub. at Strasbourg, 1510; modern edn., with extensive notes on Geiler by Jacob Wimpfeling, ed. O. Herding, *Jacobi Wimpfeling Opera Selecta*, 2. 1 (Munich, 1970). L. Dacheux, *Un Réformateur catholique à la fin du XVe siècle* (1876). C. Schmidt, op. cit., 1 (1879), pp. 337–461. E. Breitenstein, OMI, 'Die Quellen der Geiler von Kaysersberg zugeschriebenen Emeis', *Archiv für Elsässische Kirchengeschichte*, 13 (1938), pp. 149–202. E. J. D. Douglass, *Justification in late medieval preaching: A Study of John Geiler von Keisersberg* (Leiden, 1966). H. Kraume, *Die Gerson-Übersetzungen Geilers von Kaysersberg: Studien zur deutschsprachigen Gerson-Rezeption* (Münchener Texte und Untersuchungen zur deutschen Literatur des Mittelalters, 71; 1980), with extensive bibl. F. Rapp in *Dict. Sp.* 6 (1967), cols. 174–9; id. in *TRE* 12 (1984), pp. 159–62, both s.v.

Geisshäussler, Oswald. See MYCONIUS.

Gelasian Decree, the. See DECRETUM GELASIANUM.

Gelasian Sacramentary. Considerable confusion arises from the fact that the term is applied both to a particular MS (Vat. Reg. Lat. 316) and to the class of Sacramentaries to which it belongs. The Vatican MS, which dates from the mid-8th cent., is the oldest known Roman Sacramentary in which the Feasts are arranged acc. to the ecclesiastical year. Acc. to B. Bischoff, it was written by the nuns of Chelles in the neighbourhood of Paris. It contains certain Gallican elements, e.g. mention of *Francorum imperium* in the *Good Friday prayers.

Vat. Reg. Lat. 316 and other like MSS (Gelasians in the broader sense, sometimes known as 'Gelasians of the 8th century') contain the Roman *Canon of the Mass in nearly its traditional form. This Frankish Gelasianum, which embodied other Roman material as well as Gallican elements, circulated widely in Gaul later in the 8th cent. The ascription of the text in any of these forms to Pope *Gelasius (492–6) has been shown by B. *Capelle to be mistaken.

Vat. Reg. Lat. 316 was first pr. by G. M. *Tommasi, *Codices Sacramentorum Nongentis Annis Vetustiores* (Rome, 1680), pp. 13–262. Modern edns., incl. collations with other MSS, by H. A. Wilson (Oxford, 1894) and L. C. Mohlberg, OSB (Rerum Ecclesiasticarum Documenta, Series Maior, Fontes, 4; Rome, 1960). Photographic edn. of Vat. Reg. Lat. 316, with essays by L. M. Tocci and B. Neunheuser, OSB (2 vols., Vatican City, 1975). E. Bourque, *Études sur les sacramentaires romains*, pt. 2, vol. 1: *Le Gélasien du VIIIᵉ siècle* (Bibliothèque théologique de Laval; Quebec, 1952). A. Chavasse, *Le Sacramentaire Gélasien (Vaticanus Reginensis 316): Sacramentaire presbytéral en usage dans les titres romains au VIIᵉ siècle* (Bibliothèque de Théologie, 4th ser. 1; 1958). B. Capelle, OSB, 'L'Œuvre liturgique de S. Gélase', *JTS* NS 2 (1951), pp. 129–44, repr. in his *Travaux liturgiques*, 2 (Louvain, 1962), pp. 146–60; B. Bischoff, 'Die Kölner Nonnenhandschriften und das Skriptorium von Chelles', in *Karolingische und Ottonische Kunst*, ed. F. Gerke and others (Forschungen zur Kunstgeschichte und christlichen Archäologie, 3; Wiesbaden, 1957), pp. 395–411, repr. in his *Mittelalterliche Studien*, 1 (Stuttgart, 1966), pp. 16–34. [M.] B. Moreton, *The Eighth-Century Gelasian Sacramentary* (Oxford, 1976). Vogel, *Sources*, pp. 64–78. H. Ashworth, OSB, in *NCE* 12 (1967), pp. 794 f., s.v. 'Sacramentaries', with bibl. pp. 799 f. See also following entry.

Gelasius, St (d. 496), Pope from 492. Acc. to his own account he was 'Romanus natus', but the *Liber Pontificalis* asserts that he was 'natione Afer'. On his accession to the Papacy he continued the policy of his predecessor, Felix III, in tenaciously upholding the primacy of the Roman see against *Constantinople during the *Acacian schism. His genuine writings include a treatise on the Two Natures in Christ (*Adversus Eutychen et Nestorium*), other works on the Acacian conflict, and a large collection of Letters on practical matters arising out of *Arianism, *Pelagianism, and *Manichaeism, and various disciplinary subjects. To rebut the Manichaean abhorrence of wine, he insisted on the Eucharist being received in both kinds. He also laid down (*Ep.* 15) the long established rule that ordinations should be at what were later called the *Ember Seasons. A famous passage on the superiority of the ecclesiastical to the civil power in *Ep.* 12 (ad Imp. Anastasium) influenced much medieval political doctrine. Although it is now agreed that the *Gelasian Sacramentary, as well as the *Decretum Gelasianum* are wrongly attributed to him, some scholars have traced his work in the *Leonine Sacramentary (q.v.). The famous letter to the senator Andromachus concerning the *Lupercalia, and two Masses in the Gelasian Sacramentary related to it, may be the work of his predecessor. Feast day, 21 Nov.

His *Epp.* (many, esp. in relation to his brief pontificate) are listed in Jaffé, pp. 83–95. Text of his letters, and other docs., in J. P. Migne, *PL* 59. 13–190; further material in *Supplementum*, ed. A. Hamman, OFM, 3 (1963), cols. 739–87. Crit. edn. of 'Adversus Andromachum contra Lupercalia' and the Masses in the Leonine Sacramentary attributed to Gelasius by G. Pomarès (SC 65; 1959). *LP* (Duchesne), 1, pp. 255–7. W. Ullmann, *Gelasius I. (492–496): Das Papsttum an der Wende der Spätantike zum Mittelalter* (Päpste und Papsttum, 18; 1981), with bibl. H. Koch, *Gelasius im kirchenpolitischen Dienste seiner Vorgänger, der Päpste Simplicius, 468–483, und Felix III, 483–492* (Sb. (Bayr.), 1935, Heft 6). A. K. Ziegler, 'Pope Gelasius I and his Teaching on the Relation of Church and State', *Catholic Historical Review*, 27 (1942), pp. 412–37. On his liturgical work, see B. *Capelle, OSB, 'Messes du pape S. Gélase dans le sacramentaire léonien', *R. Bén.* 56 (1945–6), pp. 12–41;

id., 'Retouches gélasiennes dans le sacramentaire léonien', ibid. 61 (1951), pp. 3–14; id., 'L'Œuvre liturgique de S. Gélase', *JTS* NS 2 (1951), pp. 129–44; all repr. in his *Travaux liturgiques*, 2 (Louvain, 1962), pp. 79–115 and 146–60; C. Coebergh, OSB, 'Le Pape Saint Gélase Iᵉʳ auteur de plusieurs messes et préfaces du soi-disant Sacramentaire léonien', *Sacris Erudiri*, 4 (1952), pp. 46–102. Altaner and Stuiber (1978), pp. 462 f., and 649. J. Chapin in *NCE* 6 (1967), pp. 315 f.

Gelasius (d. 395), Bp. of *Caesarea in Palestine from *c.*367. He was the son of St *Cyril of Jerusalem's sister. A convinced *Nicene, Gelasius was ousted from his see during the reign of Valens (when Euzoïus was intruded), returning on the accession of *Theodosius in 379. He wrote: (1) a continuation of *Eusebius' 'Ecclesiastical History'. Possibly (so A. Glas, P. Heseler) this was the basis of *Rufinus' last two books, but more probably (P. van den Veen, P. Peeters, SJ) the latter was an original work; (2) A treatise against the *Anomoeans; (3) An 'Expositio Symboli', a work prob. akin to Cyril's 'Catechetical Lectures', of which fragments survive.

He is praised by *Jerome, *De Vir. Ill.* 130, and *Theodoret, *HE* 5. 8. Coll. of frags., with introd., by F. Diekamp, *Analecta Patristica* (Orientalia Christiana Analecta, 117; 1938), pp. 16–49 (frags., pp. 44–9). A. Glas, *Die Kirchengeschichte des Gelasios von Kaisareia* (Byzantinisches Archiv, 6; 1914); F. Winkelmann, *Untersuchungen zur Kirchengeschichte des Gelasios von Kaisareia* (Sb. (Berl.), Klasse für Sprachen, Literatur und Kunst, Jahrgang 1965, no. 3; 1966). *CPG* 2 (1974), p. 276 (nos. 3520 f.). Altaner and Stuiber (1978), pp. 225 f. and 593, with full bibl.

Gelasius of Cyzicus (*fl.* 475), ecclesiastical historian. He wrote a 'Syntagma', or collection of the *Acta* of the *Nicene Council (325), to refute the *Monophysite claim that their faith was identical with that professed by the Nicene Fathers. It has been shown that Gelasius made use of good sources such as *Eusebius, *Rufinus, *Socrates, and *Theodoret, but his book has little, if any, independent historical value. Its existence has sometimes been supposed (prob. wrongly) to lend support to the view that an official record of the *Acta* of Nicaea was current in the early Church.

J. P. Migne, *PG* 85. 1191–1360. Crit. edn. by G. Loeschcke and M. Heinemann (GCS, 1918). G. Loeschcke, 'Das Syntagma des Gelasius Cyzicenus', *Rheinisches Museum*, 60 (1905), pp. 594–613, and 61 (1906), pp. 34–77. C. H. *Turner, 'On Gelasius of Cyzicus', *JTS* 1 (1899), pp. 125 f. F. Winkelmann, 'Die Quellen der Historia Ecclesiastica des Gelasius von Cyzicus (nach 475)', *Byzantinoslavica*, 27 (1966), pp. 104–30.

Gellert, Christian Fürchtegott (1715–69), German poet. He spent most of his life at Leipzig, where he became a teacher at the university. He wrote, besides fables on the model of La Fontaine, many Church hymns which became very popular among both *Lutherans and Catholics. They include the familiar Easter hymn, 'Jesus lives! thy terrors now'. Some of them were set to music by L. van Beethoven.

Sämtliche Schriften, ed. J. A. Schlegel and G. L. Heyer (10 vols., Leipzig, 1769–74), with Life by J. A. Cramer as vol. 10. *Gesammelte Schriften* also ed. B. Witte and others (Berlin and New York, 1988 ff.); *Briefwechsel* ed. J. F. Reynolds (ibid., 1983 ff.). B. Witte (ed.), 'Ein Lehrer der ganzen Nation': Leben und Werk Christian Fürchtegott Gellerts (Munich, 1990). Eng. Life in Mrs Douglas's tr. of Gellert's *Moral Lessons delivered . . . in the University of Leipzig* (3 vols., 1805), vol. 1. R. Mohr in *TRE* 12 (1984), pp. 298–300, s.v., with bibl.

Gellone, Sacramentary of. An early Sacramentary of the *Gelasian ('of the 8th cent.') type, written not earlier than 790, and a primary authority for the history of the early Roman liturgy. It formerly belonged to the *Benedictine abbey of Gellone, near Aniane, whence it passed in the 17th cent. to *St-Germain-des-Prés and in 1795 to the Bibliothèque Nationale, where it is now Par. lat. 12048.

Text ed. A. Dumas, OSB, with introd. by J. Deshusses, OSB (CCSL 159–159A; 1981). E. Bourque, *Études sur les sacramentaires romains*, pt. 2, vol. 1 (Bibliothèque Théologique de Laval; Quebec, 1952), pp. 3–6, 47–80.

Gemara. A name used of the Rabbinic commentary on the *Mishnah to be found in the *Talmud. The Gemara of the Babylonian Talmud is written in E. Aramaic (a language closely allied to *Syriac), that of the Palestinian Talmud in W. Aramaic.

Gematria. A method of interpretation employed by the Rabbis to extract hidden meanings from words. The name 'Gematria', which is Hebrew, is perhaps a corruption of the Greek word γεωμετρία ('geometry'). As in Hebrew every letter possessed a numerical value, it was possible, by counting up the values of the letters in a Hebrew word, to assign to it a numerical value; and on this basis the method operated. Thus the Rabbis argued that Eliezer, the steward of *Abraham (Gen. 15: 2), must be worth all the servants of Abraham put together, on the ground that Abraham had 318 servants (Gen. 14: 14), and 318 is the numerical equivalent of the word Eliezer.

This strange method of interpretation was also occasionally used by Babylonians and by Greeks in the Hellenistic period, and by early Christians. In Rev. 13: 18 the number of the Beast is given as 666, and this is the numerical equivalent of the two Hebrew words for 'Nero Caesar'. In the Ep. of Barnabas (c. 9) gematria is applied on the basis of the corresponding number of the Greek numerals, to give a mystical significance to the number of Abraham's servants. 300 = τ = the Cross, and 18 = ιη the first two letters of the name Jesus. Therefore the number of servants typifies Jesus and the Cross.

S. Waldberg, *Darkhe ha-shinnuyim* [in Heb.] (Lwów, 1870). F. Dornseiff, *Das Alphabet in Mystik und Magie* (Στοιχεῖα, 7; 1922), pp. 91–118. G. Scholem in *Encyclopaedia Judaica*, 7 (Jerusalem, 1971), cols. 369–74, s.v. See also bibl. to KABBALA.

Gemistus Plethon, Georgius (*c.*1355–1452), Renaissance scholar. A native of *Constantinople, from the beginning of the 15th cent. he lived in Mistra in the Peloponnese, involving himself in matters of state and enjoying a reputation for wisdom. He conceived a great veneration for the doctrines of *Plato, and exchanged his original name for that of 'Plethon', apparently through its similar sound with that of his master. In 1438–9, when, as one of the E. spokesmen, he attended the Council of *Florence, he was welcomed with enthusiasm by some of the Italian humanists, notably Cosimo de' Medici, though it is difficult to assess the extent of his influence in the W. He set forth his philosophical doctrines in his 'Laws' (Νόμοι), a

work (of which only fragments survive) written on the model of the 'Laws' of Plato. He was less interested in theology than in philosophical speculation; but he wrote in defence of the E. doctrine of the *Procession of the Holy Spirit.

Although much of his work survives in autograph, until recently little had been ed. in accordance with modern standards; cf. A. Diller, 'The Autographs of Georgius Gemistus Pletho', *Scriptorium*, 10 (1956), pp. 27–41. Works collected in J. P. Migne, *PG* 160. 805–1020. Frags. of the 'Laws', ed. C. Alexandre, with Fr. tr. by A. Pellissier (Paris, 1858). B. Lagarde, 'Le "De Differentiis" de Pléthon d'après l'autographe de la Marcienne', *Byzantion*, 43 (1973), pp. 312–43 (incl. text); L. G. Benakis, 'Πλήθονος, Πρὸς Ἡρωτημένα ἄττα Ἀπόκρισις', Φιλοσοφία, 4 (1974), pp. 330–76 (incl. text). Crit. ed., with Fr. tr., of his treatise 'On the Virtues' (Περὶ ἀρετῶν) by B. Tambrun-Krasker (Corpus Philosophorum Medii Aevi, 3; Leiden, etc., 1987). *Contra Scholarii pro Aristotele Objectiones*, ed. E. V. Maltese (Teub., 1988); *Opuscula de Historia Graeca*, ed. id. (ibid., 1989). I. P. Mamalakis, Γεώργιος Γεμιστὸς-Πλήθων (Texte und Forschungen zur byzantinisch-neugriechischen Philologie, 32; Athens, 1939). M. V. Anastos, 'Pletho's Calendar and Liturgy', *Dumbarton Oaks Papers*, 4 (Cambridge, Mass., 1948), pp. 183–305. F. Masai, *Pléthon et le platonisme de Mistra* (1956). T. S. Nikolaou, Αἱ περὶ πολιτείας καὶ δικαίου ἰδέαι τοῦ Γ. Πλήθωνος Γεμιστοῦ (Byzantine Texts and Studies, 13; Thessalonica, 1974). C. M. Woodhouse, *George Gemistos Plethon: The Last of the Hellenes* (Oxford, 1986), incl. Eng. tr. of *De Differentiis*. E. Stéphanou in *DTC* 12 (1933), cols. 2393–404, s.v. 'Pléthon', with further bibl.

Gemma Galgani, St. See GALGANI, ST GEMMA.

genealogies of Christ. The gospels of Mt. and Lk. both contain a genealogy of Christ, the former (1: 2–17) tracing His descent from *Abraham and the latter (3: 23–38) carrying it back to '*Adam, the son of God'. The genealogies are intended in both cases to emphasize that Christ belonged to the house of *David. The differences between them are probably to be explained by the 'Jewish' and 'Gentile' interests of the respective Evangelists.

M. D. Johnson, *The Purpose of the Biblical Genealogies with special reference to the Setting of the Genealogies of Jesus* (Society for New Testament Studies, Monograph Series, 8; Cambridge, 1969; 2nd edn., 1988); R. E. Brown, SS, *The Birth of the Messiah* [1977], pp. 57–95, with bibl. See also comm. to MATTHEW, ST, and LUKE, ST, GOSPEL OF.

General. The usual name for the head of a religious order or congregation, now officially known as *institutes of consecrated life. The necessity for the office arose out of the centralized government required by the *Mendicant orders and the later congregations. The term is usually combined with a noun. Thus, the *Franciscans and *Capuchins have a 'Minister General', the *Carmelites a 'Prior General', and the *Jesuits, *Redemptorists, and others a 'Superior General'. The head of the *Dominicans was formerly known as the 'Master General', but is now the 'Master'. Since 1893 the *Benedictine congregations, too, have a General in the 'Abbot Primate', whose rights, however, are restricted by the independence of the individual monasteries prescribed by the rule. The General is normally elected by the 'General Chapter' for a set period, but in the case of the Jesuits for life. Heads of international religious institutes tend to reside in Rome.

General Assembly. The highest court of a Church in *Presbyterianism. It consists of ministers and elders elected to represent the whole Church, over which it exercises supreme jurisdiction.

General Baptists. As contrasted with the *Particular Baptists (q.v.), those *Baptists whose theology was *Arminian and whose polity allied with that of the *Presbyterians. To this group belonged the earliest English Baptists, led by T. *Helwys. After many General Baptist Churches had moved towards *Unitarianism, a New Connexion was formed in 1770 under the influence of the Evangelical revival. This group united with the Particular Baptists in 1891.

General Chapter. A canonical meeting of the heads and representatives of a religious order or congregation esp. for the purpose of electing new superiors and dealing with business concerning the whole order. They were introduced in the *Cistercian Order in 1119 and made compulsory for all orders by the Fourth *Lateran Council in 1215. Their frequency varies, but today they are normally held every three or four years. The *Jesuits, however, hold a General Chapter (known as a 'General Congregation') only as need arises, e.g. when their General dies. Apart from the Pope, General Chapters constitute the highest authority for their respective religious.

General Confession. (1) In the BCP the Confession at the beginning of *Mattins and *Evensong 'to be said of the whole congregation after the minister, all kneeling'. It is in three parts—a confession of sin, a supplication for forgiveness of past misdeeds, and a prayer for grace to live righteously in the future. It was first added to the BCP in 1552 and has remained virtually unchanged.

(2) The term is also applied to a private confession where the penitent (exceptionally) resolves to confess, so far as he is able, all his past sins and not only those since his last confession. General confessions are sometimes recommended when the penitent is entering on a new state of life, e.g. marriage, Holy Orders, or the religious life, or leaving for a foreign land.

General Councils. See OECUMENICAL COUNCILS.

General Judgement, the. Also the Last Judgement. In Christian theology, the final judgement on mankind after the Resurrection of the Dead. In contrast with the so-called *Particular Judgement (q.v.) on souls only immediately after death, the General Judgement is held to be the occasion of God's final sentence on humanity as a whole, as well as His verdict on both the soul and body of each individual.

General Superintendent. Formerly the highest ecclesiastical office in many of the German Protestant Churches. The General Superintendent exercised his authority in conjunction with the provincial consistory and synod. The number varied in the different provinces, e.g. there were four in Brandenburg, three in Saxony, two in Pomerania. In recent times the title has been replaced, often after much controversy, in the W. provinces by that of Präses; and in the E. provinces there has now been set up a Bishop of Berlin over the General Superintendents. The appointment is purely ecclesiastical and does not receive confirmation from the State.

General Thanksgiving. In the BCP the first of the Thanksgivings 'to be used before the two final prayers of the Litany or of Morning and Evening Prayer', so named to distinguish it from the *particular* thanksgivings ('for rain', etc.) which follow. It was composed in 1661 by Bp. E. *Reynolds and revised by Bp. R. *Sanderson.

W. W. S. March, *Ground of the Heart* (1963). G. [J.] Cuming, *The Godly Order* (Alcuin Club Collections, 65; 1983), pp. 161–5.

General Theological Seminary, New York City. The largest training centre for clergy of the *Episcopal Church of USA. It was founded in 1817 in answer to a demand within the Church for a more thorough, systematic, and disciplined training for the ministry, and it seeks to cater for the needs of the Church in all parts of the country. Assisted by bequests, the seminary has been able to erect several fine buildings. Training is now given to over a hundred students in both academic and practical subjects by a large and scholarly faculty. The 'Paddock Lectures' are delivered regularly by noted visitors.

P. M. Dawley, *The Story of the General Theological Seminary: A Sesquicentennial History 1817–1967* (New York, 1969).

Genesis, Book of. The opening Book of the OT, and the first of the five Books of the *Pentateuch. The English title follows that of the *Septuagint (Greek) version, the Hebrew title (בְּרֵאשִׁית, 'Bereshith', i.e. 'in the beginning') being the first word of the text. The Book contains the story of the beginnings of the universe and of the early history of the human race. Chs. 1–11 contain the so-called 'primeval history', including accounts of the *Creation (1–2), the *Fall (3), Cain and *Abel (4), the *Flood (6–9), and the Tower of *Babel (11). With the call of Abram (*Abraham), the ancestor of the people of *Israel, in 12: 1–3, the so-called 'salvation history' begins. Chs. 12–35 recount the stories of the *Patriarchs, Abraham (12–25: 18), *Isaac (25: 19–26: 35), and *Jacob (27–35) (chs. 5, 10, and 36 contain genealogies). The final section of the Book (chs. 37–50) tells the story of Joseph's captivity in Egypt and the eventual prosperity of his family there.

Both in Jewish and Christian tradition the Book has long been held to be the work of *Moses. However, most modern scholars believe either that it is a composite structure made up of material from various sources which can also be traced in other Books of the Pentateuch (q.v.) or that, together with the rest of the Pentateuch, it forms in essence a unified composition from a period considerably later than that of Moses. For the Christian theologian it is of value as containing the biblical basis of much Christian doctrine, e.g. of the Creation and the Fall. Upon the promise made to Abraham and his seed (17: 7, etc.) depends the covenant relationship between God and the chosen nation of Israel, a conception prominent within the OT as a whole.

Comm. by H. *Gunkel (KHAT 1; 1901; Eng. tr. of introd. as *The Legends of Genesis*, Chicago, 1901; repr., New York, 1964), S. R. *Driver (West. Comm., 1904; 12th edn., with appendix by G. R. *Driver, 1926), J. Skinner (ICC 1910; 2nd edn., 1930), O.

Procksch (KAT 1; 1913; 2nd edn., 1924), U. Cassuto (2 vols. (Heb.), Jerusalem, 1944–9, on Gen. 1: 1–11: 32; with appendix in 2nd edn., 1953, on 12: 1–13: 5; Eng. tr., 2 vols., ibid., 1961–4), G. von *Rad (Das Alte Testament Deutsch, 2–4, 1949–53; 9th edn., 1972; Eng. tr., 1972), E. A. Speiser (Anchor Bible, New York [1964]), R. Davidson (Camb. Bib., NEB, 2 vols., 1973–9), C. Westermann (Biblischer Kommentar, Altes Testament, 1; 3 vols., 1974–82; Eng. tr., Minneapolis, 1984–6; London, 1984–7), and G. J. Wenham (Word Biblical Comm., 1; Waco, Tex. [1987]; 2, Dallas [1994]). J. Chaine, Le Livre de la Genèse (1949). O. Eissfeldt, Die Genesis der Genesis: Vom Werdegang des ersten Buches der Bibel (Tübingen, 1958; 2nd edn., 1961). B. Vawter, On Genesis: A New Reading (Garden City, NY, 1977). P. D. Miller, Genesis 1–11: Studies in Structure & Theme (Journal for the Study of the Old Testament, Supplement Series, 8; Sheffield, 1978). W. Eichrodt, 'In the Beginning: A Contribution to the Interpretation of the First Word of the Bible', in B. W. Anderson and W. Harrelson (eds.), Israel's Prophetic Heritage: Essays in Honor of James Muilenburg (New York and London, 1962), pp. 1–10, repr. in B. W. Anderson (ed.), Creation in the Old Testament (Issues in Religion and Theology, 6; 1984), pp. 65–73. See also works cited under PATRIARCH and PENTATEUCH.

Geneva. The foundation of a Christian community in Geneva dates from c. AD 350. By the end of the 4th cent. it was the centre of a diocese which extended into the neighbouring territory of Savoy (now part of France). The cathedral was built about this time. In 1162 the Emp. *Frederick I conferred secular authority on Ardutius de Faucigny, Bp. of Geneva, and from then the Genevan bishops bore the title of 'prince-bishop'. Increasing prosperity in the 13th and 14th cents. led to pressure from the merchants for Geneva to be constituted a city-state, and in 1387 Bp. Adhémar Fabri granted the city its franchise, while retaining the basic powers of the prince-bishop. In 1444 a Papal privilege declared that all bishops of Geneva must be drawn from the ducal house of Savoy. The annexation of the city by Savoy was, however, avoided by a 'combourgeoisie' concluded in 1477 between Geneva and the Swiss cantons of Berne and Fribourg.

The beginnings of the Genevan Reformation are linked with a purely political rebellion against the remaining powers of the prince-bishop from 1513 onwards; the last bishop, Pierre de la Baume, left the city in 1533. It was the preaching of G. *Farel, P. *Viret, and Antoine Froment (1510–84) which gave a confessional basis to the movement and led to the abolition of the Mass on 10 Aug. 1535. The Reformation was officially adopted by an edict of 21 May 1536; the city-state was separated from the RC diocese which continued to bear its name until 1819. J. *Calvin did not arrive in Geneva until July 1536 and effected most of his reforms in 1541/2. He was responsible for introducing the *Presbyterian system of Church government. The Genevan Church was ruled by the Company of Pastors, headed by Calvin. The Consistory, a mixed body of clergy and laymen, shared with the civil magistrates in the policing of morals and was charged with settling questions of Church discipline. In 1559 Calvin founded the *Genevan Academy, whose chief object was to train clergy of all nationalities. His successor, T. *Beza, made few changes.

In the late 16th cent. threat of invasion by the RC Duchy of Savoy was the main concern in Geneva; in 1602 the city was attacked, but the Savoy troops were repelled. By the early 17th cent. there was a degree of theological

stagnation. The Genevan Academy was facing competition from other Protestant seminaries, and the theology of Calvin and Beza became frozen into a rigid pattern. Theologians from Geneva defended F. *Gomar's teaching on *predestination at the Synod of *Dort (1618) and in 1647 candidates for the ministry were required to accept the articles of Dort, Calvin's original teaching being considered too vague. Between 1678 and 1706 all ministers had to sign the conservative Consensus helveticus, a confession of faith drawn up by all the Swiss Protestant Churches in 1675. In the 18th cent. however, more liberal tendencies were manifest in the teaching at the Genevan Academy, and Jean-Alphonse Turrettini, Professor of History from 1697 to 1707, engaged in ecumenical discussions with *Lutherans and *Anglicans. In 1707 Lutherans were granted freedom of worship in Geneva.

The revolutions of 1791 and 1794, which followed in the wake of the French Revolution, had little effect on the religious life of the city, but its annexation by Napoleon in 1799 led to the official recognition of RC worship for the first time since 1535. After the withdrawal of French troops in 1815 Geneva's frontiers were modified and the city with its dependencies became a canton of the Swiss Confederation. In 1819 the RC parishes were incorporated into the diocese of Lausanne and have so remained.

The years 1815–31 were marked by a series of Protestant *revivalist movements which were probably a reaction to 18th-cent. rationalism. In 1831 the 'Société évangélique', modelled on British Evangelical Societies (see EVANGELICALISM), was founded. All these movements were critical of the established Calvinist Church which was made more directly dependent on the State as a result of new constitutions in 1842 and 1847. In 1907, however, after a referendum, the Church was separated from the State and became known as the 'Église nationale protestante' (ENP). Its basic structure has altered little since Calvin's time. The Consistory, on which laymen (elders) form a majority, nowadays fulfils the same role as a *Presbytery. There are no other Church courts, but the Company of Pastors survives and can influence the Consistory's decisions.

Geneva is the seat of several international ecclesiastical organizations such as the *World Council of Churches, the *World Alliance of Reformed Churches, and the Lutheran World Federation. In a historical context, Geneva is regarded as the centre of Presbyterianism and is used to denote the system in the same way as Rome is used to designate the RC Church or Constantinople the Orthodox.

P. Guichonnet (ed.), Histoire de Genève (Toulouse and Lausanne [1974]). L. Binz, Vie religieuse et réforme ecclésiastique dans le diocèse de Genève ... (1378–1408), 1 (Mémoires et Documents publiés par la Société d'Histoire et d'Archéologie de Genève, 46; 1973). H. Heyer, L'Église de Genève 1535–1909 (Geneva, 1909). H. Naef, Les Origines de la Réforme à Genève (1936; repr., with additional vol. 2, Travaux d'Humanisme et Renaissance, 100 (1 and 2); Geneva, 1968); E. W. Monter, Calvin's Geneva (New York and London [1967]). M.-C. Pitassi, De l'Orthodoxie aux Lumières: Genève 1670–1737 (Histoire et Société, 24; Geneva, 1992). R. Stauffenegger, Église et Société: Genève au XVIIe siècle (Mémoires et Documents publiés par la Société d'Histoire et d'Archéologie de Genève, 49; 2 vols., 1983–4). O. Fatio (ed.), Genève Protestante en 1831 (Publication de la Faculté de Théologie de l'Université de Genève, 6 [1983]). L. Binz, J. Emery, and C. Santschi, 'Le Diocèse de Genève', Helvetia Sacra, 1. 3 (Berne [1980]), pp. 5–329.

Registres de la Compagnie des Pasteurs de Genève, ed. R. M. Kingdon, J.-F. Bergier, and others (Travaux d'Humanisme et Renaissance, 55, 107, 137, 153, 180, 198, 215, 236, 252, 274, 291, etc.; 1962 ff.). The Register of the Company of Pastors of Geneva in the Time of Calvin, ed. and tr. P. E. Hughes (Grand Rapids, Mich. [1966]). P.-F. Geisendorf, Bibliographie raisonnée de l'histoire de Genève des origines à 1798 (Mémoires et Documents publiés par la Société d'Histoire et d'Archéologie de Genève, 43; 1966); later bibl. listed annually in the Bulletin d'histoire et d'archéologie de Genève (1966 ff.). L. Binz in DHGE 20 (1984), cols. 422–53, s.v.; R. M. Kingdon in TRE 12 (1984), pp. 368–75, s.v. 'Genf'.

Geneva Bible. This translation of the Bible, popularly known as the 'Breeches Bible' from its rendering of Gen. 3: 7 ('they . . . made themselves breeches'; AV 'aprons'), was first published as a whole at Geneva in 1560. It was the first English edition to introduce verse numeration. Issued in a handy form, instead of in folio, with compendious notes of a *Calvinist flavour, it was the Bible most widely read in private use in England for about a century. For further details, see BIBLE, ENGLISH VERSIONS.

Facsimile of the 1560 edn., with introd. by L. E. Berry and full bibl. (Madison, Wis., and London, 1969). C. Eason, The Geneva Bible: Notes on its Production and Distribution (1937). A. W. Pollard, Records of the English Bible (1911), pp. 24–8, 43–5, with docs., pp. 279–86. L. Lupton, A History of the Geneva Bible (25 vols., c.1966–94). D. G. Danner, 'The Contribution of the Geneva Bible of 1560 to the English Protestant Tradition', Sixteenth Century Journal, 12, no. 3 (1981), pp. 5–18; M. S. Betteridge, 'The Bitter Notes: The Geneva Bible and its Annotations', ibid. 14 (1983), pp. 41–62. Darlow and Moule, ed. A. S. Herbert, 1 (1968), pp. 61–3; for further edns. of Geneva Bible, see pp. 65 f., 74 f., and passim.

Geneva gown. The black preaching-gown worn by the early *Reformed ministers, loose fitting, with full sleeves. It was almost universally replaced by a surplice for Anglican preachers in the 19th cent. after some controversy, and is now worn by *Presbyterians and other Calvinists. Its use was held to emphasize the ministry of the Word, over against belief in a sacrificing priesthood.

Genevan Academy. This celebrated school was founded in 1559 by J. *Calvin with the support of the City Council and under the guidance of the Compagnie des Pasteurs, primarily for the education of theologians. Students were attracted in large numbers from all over Europe, and Geneva soon became the centre of international Protestantism. The first Rector was T. *Beza, and among early members were T. *Cartwright, who lectured in theology in 1571, J. *Arminius, and J. Uytenbogaert (1557–1644), the leader of the Dutch Arminians. The scope of studies, at first purely theological, was gradually widened. In 1872 a Faculty of Medicine was created and the Academy transformed into the modern university. See also GENEVA.

Le Livre du Recteur de l'Académie de Genève (1559–1878), ed. S. Stelling-Michaud (Travaux d'Humanisme et Renaissance, 33; 6 vols., 1959–80). C. Borgeaud and P. E. Martin, Histoire de l'Université de Genève (5 vols. in 6; Geneva, 1900–59). M. Marcacci, Histoire de l'Université de Genève 1559–1986 (ibid., 1987).

Genevan Catechism. A name applied to two quite distinct formulae of J. *Calvin:

(1) Catechismus Genevensis Prior. A compendium of doctrine (Instruction et confession de foi dont on use en l'Église

de Genève), based on the *Institutes. Issued early in 1537, it is associated with the Articles concernant l'Organisation de l'Église (dated 16 Jan. 1537), which were compiled by Calvin and G. *Farel, and with the formal Confession written by Farel, but the precise relationship of the documents is not clear. The Latin version of the Catechism appeared in 1538. The Confession was imposed on the inhabitants of *Geneva. As yet the Trinity was not made a doctrine of faith.

(2) Catechismus Genevensis. A catechism in the form of question and answer, first published in French in 1542 and formally reissued with a Latin translation in 1545. It became one of the basic documents of the Genevan ecclesiastical state. Its five sections are on Faith, the Law, Prayer, the Word of God, and the Sacraments.

(1) The text of the first Catechism and the Confession are pr. among Calvin's works, ed. W. Baum and others, 22 (Corpus Reformatorum, 50; Brunswick, 1880), cols. 25–96; Lat. tr. of the Catechism, ibid. 5 (Corpus Reformatorum, 33; 1866), cols. 313–62; the Articles, ibid. 10, pt. 1 (Corpus Reformatorum, 38, pt. 1; 1871), cols. 5–14; all three docs. are also in Calvin's Opera Selecta, ed. P. Barth and W. Niesel, 1 (Munich, 1926), pp. 369–426. Fr. text of the Catechism repr., with notes by R. Rilliet and T. Dufour (Geneva, 1878). The Confession is repr., with introd. by C. Chimelli in I. Backus and C. Chimelli (eds.), 'La Vraie Piété': Divers traités de Jean Calvin et Confession de foi de Guillaume Farel (Histoire et Société, 12; Geneva [1986]), pp. 41–53. Eng. tr. of the Confession in A. C. Cochrane, Reformed Confessions of the 16th Century (1966), pp. 117–26.

(2) No copies of the 1542 edn. are known. From the 1545 edn. the Lat. and Fr. texts are pr. among Calvin's works, edn. cit., 6 (Corpus Reformatorum, 34; 1867), cols. 1–160. Lat. also in Calvin's Opera Selecta, edn. cit., 2 (1942), pp. 59–151; Fr. text (modernized), with historical introd., in O. Fatio and others (eds.), Confessions et Catéchismes de l'Église reformée (Publications de la Faculté de Théologie de l'Université de Genève, 11; 1986), pp. 26–89. An Eng. tr. was pub. at Geneva, 1556; also in T. F. Torrance, The School of Faith: The Catechisms of the Reformed Church (1959), pp. 3–65. See also works cited under CALVIN.

Geneviève, St, or **Genovefa** (c.422–c.500), Virgin and chief Patroness of the city of *Paris. Acc. to the ancient Life, she consecrated herself to God at the age of 7, and was specially blessed by St *Germanus of Auxerre. At 15 she took the veil, and from then onwards devoted herself to a life of mortification. The great power attributed to her intercession was seen in her influence with the Frankish conquerors of Paris, and in the diversion from the city in 451 of the hordes of Huns under *Attila II. After her death, her intercession continued to be invoked, and to it was attributed the cessation of a fierce pestilence in 1129. The historicity of her Life, at one time fiercely contested, has recently been defended by competent scholars. Feast day, 3 Jan.

Of the five recensions of her Life: 'Text A' (prob. the earliest), ed. B. Krusch in MGH, Scriptores Rerum Merovingicarum, 3 (1896), pp. 204–38; 'Text B' ed. C. Kohler, Étude critique sur le texte de la vie latine de Sainte Geneviève (Bibliothèque de l'École des Hautes Études, 48; 1881), pp. 1–47, with variants from 'Text D' (not otherwise edited) in the second apparatus under the heading 'IIIᵐᵉ Famille'; 'Text C' ed. C. Künstle, Vita Sanctae Genovefae (Teub., 1910); 'Text E' ed. C. Kohler, op. cit., pp. 48–72. Eng. tr. of Text A in Sainted Women of the Dark Ages, ed. and tr. by J. A. McNamara and others (Durham, NC, and London, 1992), pp. 17–37. M. Heinzelmann and J.-C. Poulin, Les Vies anciennes de sainte Geneviève de Paris (Bibliothèque de l'École des

Hautes Études, 4ᵉ section, 329; 1986), with refs. Modern Lives by C. H. Lesêtre ('Les Saints', 1900) and by J. Dubois, OSB, and L. Beaumont-Maillet (Paris, 1982). R. Amiet, *Le Culte liturgique de sainte Geneviève* (1984). J. Dubois, OSB, in *DHGE* 20 (1984), cols. 455–64, s.v. 'Geneviève (2)'.

geniza (from Heb. גנז, 'to hide'). The chamber attached to a *synagogue used to house MS books unfit for use in worship, e.g. worn-out copies of the Scriptures and also heretical books. Valuable fragments of biblical and other Jewish MSS were discovered in the 19th cent. in the geniza of an ancient synagogue at Cairo, which dates from AD 882, among them portions of the Hebrew text of *Ecclesiasticus and the text published as *Fragments of a Zadokite Work*. The majority of these fragments now constitute the Taylor–Schechter Collection in Cambridge University Library. See also DEAD SEA SCROLLS.

P. [E.] Kahle, *The Cairo Geniza* (1947; 2nd edn., Oxford, 1959); S. D. [F.] Goitein, *A Mediterranean Society: The Jewish Communities of the Arab World as Portrayed in the Documents of the Cairo Geniza*, 1 (Berkeley, Calif., etc., 1967), pp. 1–28. S. C. Reif (ed.), *Published Material from the Cambridge Genizah Collections: A Bibliography, 1896–1980* (Cambridge, 1988).

Gennadius I (d. 471), Patr. of *Constantinople. In his earlier years he vigorously opposed the Christological teaching of St *Cyril of Alexandria (d. 444). In 458 he succeeded Anatolius (449–58) as Patriarch and in 460 he received a letter from St *Leo (*Ep.* 170), warning him against *Timothy Aelurus. Gennadius was the author of many Commentaries, notably on Gen., Dan., and the Pauline Epp.; considerable sections of these have survived, mainly in *catenae*. A few fragments of his dogmatic writings have also been preserved, among them extracts from a work against Cyril's 'Twelve Anathemas' and of a treatise 'Ad Parthenium'. He also wrote an encomium on the *Tome of St Leo and an encyclical against *simony (from a Synod at Constantinople, prob. 459). Feast day in the E., 17 Nov.; commemorated in the Roman Martyrology on 25 Aug.

Frags. collected in J. P. Migne, *PG* 85 (2). 1613–1734; others in K. Staab, *Pauluskommentare aus der griechischen Kirche* (1933), pp. 352–418. F. Diekamp, *Analecta Patristica* (Orientalia Christiana Analecta, 117; 1938), sect. 6, 'Gennadius von Konstantinopel', pp. 54–108. R. Devreesse, *Les Anciens Commentateurs grecs de l'Octateuque et des Rois* (ST 201; 1959), pp. 183–5. V. Grumel, AA, *Les Regestes des Actes du Patriarcat de Constantinople*, 1, fasc. 1 (2nd edn., 1972), pp. 103–9 (nos. 143–7). A. Grillmeier, *Jesus der Christus im Glauben der Kirche*, 2 (pt. 1; 1986), pp. 189–96; Eng. tr. (1987), pp. 166–72. *CPG* 3 (1979), pp. 158–61 (nos. 5970–86). C. H. *Turner in *HDB* 5 (extra vol., 1904), pp. 517–19, s.v. 'Patristic Commentaries'.

Gennadius II. See GEORGE SCHOLARIUS.

Gennadius of Marseilles (*fl.*470), presbyter and ecclesiastical historian. His chief surviving work, the 'De Viris Illustribus', is a continuation of St *Jerome's book of the same name. Completed about 480, it contains 101 notices (10 of them apparently added by a later hand) of ecclesiastical writers, E. and W., mostly of the 5th cent. While biographical detail is slight, the bibliographical information is invaluable. The account of Gennadius himself (no. 100 [101]) mentions several other works of which only fragments remain. He is almost certainly the author of an early

recension of the *Liber ecclesiasticorum dogmatum*, a theological compendium which circulated widely in the Middle Ages. C. Munier attributed to him the 'Statuta Ecclesiae Antiqua' (q.v.). He is usually regarded as a *Semipelagian.

J. P. Migne, *PL* 58. 1059–1120; Suppl. ed. A. Hamman, OFM, 3 (1963), cols. 722–5. Modern edns. of *De Vir. Illust.* by E. C. Richardson (TU 14 (1); 1896) and W. Herding (Teub., 1924). Text of *Liber Ecclesiasticorum Dogmatum*, ed. C. H. *Turner in *JTS* 7 (1905–6), pp. 78–99; 8 (1906–7), pp. 103–14. B. Czapla, *Gennadius als Litterarhistoriker* (Kirchengeschichtliche Studien, 4, Heft 1; Münster, 1898). Studies by A. Feder, SJ, in *Scholastik*, 2 (1927), pp. 481–514; 3 (1928), pp. 238–43; and 8 (1933), pp. 217–32 and 380–99. G. *Morin, OSB, 'Le Liber Dogmatum de Gennade de Marseille et problèmes qui s'y rattachent', *R. Bén.* 24 (1907), pp. 445–55. S. Pricoco, 'Storia ecclesiastica e storia letteraria; il *De viris inlustribus* di Gennadio di Marsiglia', in *La storiografia ecclesiastica nella tarda antichità: Atti del convegno tenuto in Erice (3–8 XII 1978)*, ed. S. Calderone (Centro di Studi Umanistici, Facoltà di Lettere e Filosofia, Università di Messina, 1980), pp. 241–73. Bardenhewer, 4, pp. 595–9; Altaner and Stuiber (1978), pp. 8, 474, and 651, for further bibl. C. Munier in *Dict. Sp.* 6 (1967), cols. 205–8, s.v.; C. Pietri in *TRE* 12 (1984), pp. 376–8, s.v.

Gennesaret. A district on the W. shore of the Sea of *Galilee, which is hence called also the Lake of Gennesaret (Lk. 5: 1). Christ landed there after the Feeding of the Five Thousand (Mk. 6: 53).

Gentile, Giovanni (1875–1944), Italian philosopher and educationist. A native of Castelvetrano, he studied at Palermo. He then taught at Naples (1898–1906), and was professor of the history of philosophy at Palermo (1906–14), Pisa (1914–17), and Rome from 1917. Shortly after this last appointment he was made a senator. He was one of the earliest supporters of Fascism, which he regarded as the incarnation of Idealism, and on B. Mussolini's accession to power became Minister of Education (1922–4). As such, he carried out important paedagogic reforms and reintroduced the teaching of the Catholic religion into the schools. He was assassinated by anti-Fascists at Florence in 1944.

Gentile developed his idealist philosophy in conjunction with B. *Croce (from whom he later parted on political grounds) under the influence of G. B. *Vico, I. *Kant, and G. W. F. *Hegel. Reality, which was fundamentally historical, was the idea as realized in the human mind, so that philosophy was the supreme form of self-consciousness, in which the process of self-formation culminated. God was the 'transcendent pure thinking', which overcomes all mental differences and antagonisms. The significance of religion was that it promoted the awareness of objective ideas, and in particular of the reality to which all others were subordinate. It was a complete intuition of life, and the Catholic form of it was esp. suited to the needs of the Italian people.

Gentile was a prolific writer. His most important philosophical work was *Teoria generale dello spirito* (1916; Eng. trans., 1922).

The standard edn. of his *Opere complete* is that a cura della Fondazione Giovanni Gentile per gli Studi Filosofici (55 vols., Florence, 1942 ff. + Letters, 1969 ff.). Eng. tr. of *Genesi e struttura della società* (1946) by H. S. Harris (Urbana, Ill., 1960), with introd. pp. 1–52 and bibl. of works in Eng., pp. 53–63; and of *Filosofia d'Arte* (1931) by G. Gullace (1972), with introd., pp. xi–c. *Giovanni Gentile: La vita e il pensiero*, a cura della Fondazione Giovanni Gentile per gli Studi Filosofici (1948 ff.), incl. bibl. of his writings, vol. 3. Istituto della Enciclopedia Italiana, *Il Pensiero di Giovanni Gentile*, ed. S. Betti and F. Rovigatti (2 vols., 1977), with bibl., 2, pp. 913–1000. Life by M. di Lalla (Florence, 1975). E. Chiocchetti, *La filosofia di G. Gentile* (1922); V. La Via, *L'idealismo attuale di G. Gentile* (1925); R. W. Holmes, *The Idealism of G. Gentile* (1937); B. Bianchi, *Il problema religioso in Giovanni Gentile* (Problemi filosofici, 5; 1940); S. Romano, *Giovanni Gentile: La Filosofia al Potere* (1984). S. Natoli, *Giovanni Gentile filosofo europeo* (Turin, 1989 [slight]).

Gentiles. A biblical term (Heb. גּוֹיִם, 'nations'; Gk. ἔθνη, 'nations', or Ἕλληνες, 'Greeks') usually applied to non-Jews. The meaning of the corresponding Lat. word, *gentiles*, used in the *Vulgate to translate the Heb. and Greek, has changed during the centuries. In post-Augustan Latin it meant 'fellow-countrymen' and in still later Latin more generally 'foreigners'.

genuflectentes (Lat., 'those who kneel'). In the ancient Church a class of *penitents who were permitted to be present at the first part of the liturgy, kneeling at the west end of the nave. They were dismissed, together with the *catechumens and *energumens, before the Mass of the *Faithful.

genuflexion. A momentary kneeling on the right knee, with the body erect, used in the W. Church as a ceremonial reverence when passing before the Blessed Sacrament, or before the unveiled cross on *Good Friday, and formerly invariably at the *incarnatus* in the *Nicene Creed (now only on *Christmas Day and the feast of the *Annunciation), and on certain other occasions. Until 1967, a double genuflexion, made by kneeling on both knees and bowing the head, was used before the Blessed Sacrament exposed.

L. Gougaud, OSB, 'Some Liturgical and Ascetic Traditions of the Celtic Church. I. Genuflexion', *JTS* 9 (1908), pp. 556–61. H. *Leclercq, OSB, in *DACL* 6 (pt. 1; 1924), cols. 1017–21; E. Bertaud, OSB, in *Dict. Sp.* 6 (1967), cols. 213–26, s.v. 'Génuflexions et Métanies', with refs.

Geoffrey of Monmouth (d. 1154), Bp. of *St Asaph and pseudo-historian. He presumably came from Monmouth; he was for a time a canon of the collegiate church of St George in the Castle at Oxford; he died as Bp. of St Asaph. His fame rests on the *Historia Regum Britanniae*, a work of historical fiction, claiming to trace the history of Britain from Brutus, great-grandson of Aeneas, to Cadwaladr, in the 7th cent. AD. It enshrines the Prophecies of Merlin and a substantial (and imaginary) account of the reign of King Arthur. Whether his aims were primarily literary, or whether there were deeper political motives, his achievement was to establish Arthur as a subject of 'serious history', and so he played a role in the history of romance. It is a mainly secular narrative, but his fabulous account of ecclesiastical affairs in the court of Arthur, and of the archbishoprics of London, York, and Caerleon, had some influence on 12th-cent. ecclesiastical politics, esp. in encouraging at least one Bp. of London to claim independence of Canterbury. He also wrote a *Life of Merlin* in verse.

The best edn. of the *Historia Regum Britanniae* is that by N. Wright and others (Cambridge, 1985 ff); other modern edns. by

A. Griscom (London, 1929) and E. Faral (see below). Eng. trs. by S. Evans (London, 1904; rev. by C. W. Dunn, 1963) and L. Thorpe (Penguin Classics, 1966). Modern edn., with Eng. tr., of *Life of Merlin* by J. J. Parry (University of Illinois Studies in Language and Literature, 10, no. 3; 1925); also, with new Eng. tr., by B. Clarke (Cardiff, 1973). E. Faral, *La Légende arthurienne*, pt. 1 (Bibliothèque de l'École des Hautes Études, 255–7; 1929, with text of both works in last vol.). V. I. J. Flint, 'The *Historia Regum Britanniae* of Geoffrey of Monmouth: Parody and its Purpose. A Suggestion', *Speculum*, 54 (1979), pp. 447–68; C. N. L. Brooke, *The Church and the Welsh Border in the Central Middle Ages* (Studies in Celtic History, 8; Woodbridge, 1986), pp. 95–106, 'Geoffrey of Monmouth as a Historian'. M. J. Curley, *Geoffrey of Monmouth* (New York, etc., 1994).

George, St, patron saint of England and martyr. Very little is known of his life, or even of his martyrdom; but his historical existence, though still sometimes disputed, is now generally accepted. Despite E. *Reynolds' and E. *Gibbon's identification of the two, he seems to have nothing to do with *George of Cappadocia. A not improbable view is that he suffered at or near Lydda before the time of *Constantine (d. 337). He is perhaps referred to (though not by name) in *Eusebius (*HE* 8. 5); but not until the 6th cent. did his cultus become popular and the legends of his exploits receive elaboration. The slaying of the dragon is first credited to him in the latter part of the 12th cent. and the belief became popular from its appearance in the 13th-cent. '*Golden Legend'. It may have derived from the myth of Perseus' slaying of the sea monster at Arsuf or Joppa, both cities in the neighbourhood of Lydda. In the E. he is distinguished as a great martyr (μεγαλόμαρτυς). Feast day, 23 Apr. He is reckoned one of the *Auxiliary Saints.

The circumstances in which St George became the patron saint of England, where he appears to have been known at least from the 8th cent., are obscure. His *acta* were translated into Anglo-Saxon, and pre-Conquest churches (e.g. one at Doncaster, 1061) are dedicated to him. In 1222 St George's Day was made a lesser holy day at the Synod of Oxford. From the 14th cent. the red cross on a white background ('St George's arms') became a kind of uniform for soldiers and sailors. His rank as patron of England (in place of St *Edward the Confessor) prob. dates from the reign of Edward III, who founded the Order of the Garter under St George's patronage (*c*.1347). In 1415 the Constitution of Abp. H. *Chichele made his feast one of the chief holy days of the year. W. *Caxton's translation and printing of the 'Golden Legend' did much to popularize the story.

AASS, Apr. 3 (1675), pp. 100–63. Widely variant Acts of St George exist in many recensions (Gk., Lat., Syriac, Coptic, Ethiopic, Armenian, etc.). Gk. Acts ed., with discussion, by K. Krumbacher and A. Ehrhard (*Abh.* (Bayr.), 25, Heft 3; 1911); crit. edn. of Ethiopic Acts by V. Arras, OFM (CSCO 138, 1953; Lat. tr. CSCO 139, 1953). Ethiopic text also reproduced from MSS in the British Library with Eng. tr. and useful introd. by E. A. W. Budge (London, 1930); Syriac Acts, also with Eng. tr., by E. W. Brooks in *Muséon*, 38 (1925), pp. 67–115. M. Huber, OSB, 'Zur Georgslegende', in *Festschrift zum XII. Allgemeinen Deutschen Neuphilologentage in München, Pfingsten 1906* (Erlangen, 1906), pp. 175–235 (with Lat. texts, pp. 194–235). H. *Delehaye, SJ, *Les Légendes grecques des saints militaires* (1909), pp. 45–76. J. B. Aufhauser, *Das Drachenwunder des heiligen Georg in der griechischen und lateinischen Überlieferung* (Byzantinisches Archiv, 5; 1911). F. Cumont, 'La Plus Ancienne Légende de saint Georges', *Revue* d'Histoire des Religions, 114 (1936), pp. 5–41, with further Lat. text, pp. 42–51. Popular account in G. J. Marcus, Saint George of England (1939); also I. H. Elder, George of Lydda (1949). D. Balboni and M. C. Celletti in Bibliotheca Sanctorum, 6 (1965), cols. 512–531, s.v. 'Georgio, santo, martire'.

George (c.640–724), 'Bp. of the Arabians'. He was born in the neighbourhood of *Antioch and in 686 became bishop of the Arabian nomads in Mesopotamia, with his see at Akula. His writings are one of the principal authorities for the history of *Syriac Christianity and literature. They include a translation of, and commentaries on, a number of *Aristotle's works, additions to the 'Hexaemeron' of *Jacob of Edessa, and a long series of letters on matters of doctrine, liturgy, and ascetic practice.

His verse treatises on the consecration of *chrism and the Lives of the hermits ed. V. Ryssel in Atti della Reale Accademia dei Lincei, Classe di Scienze morali, storiche e filologiche, 9 (1892), pp. 45–93. Selected works tr. into Ger. by id., Georgs des Araberbischofs Gedichte und Briefe (1891). 'An Exposition on the Rites of Baptism, the Eucharist and the Consecration of the Chrism' ed. R. H. *Connolly and H. W. Codrington, Two Commentaries on the Jacobite Liturgy (Text and Translation Society, 1913), pp. 3–15 (of the Syriac), with Eng. tr. pp. 11–23. Syriac texts of his trs. of Aristotle ed. G. Furlani in Atti della Reale Accademia Nazionale dei Lincei, Memorie della Classe di Scienze morali, storiche e filologiche, 6th ser., vol. 5 (1933–6), pp. 3–68 [Categories and De Interpretatione]; pp. 143–230 [Prior Analytics, bk. 1]; 6th ser., vol. 6 (1937–40), pp. 231–87 [Prior Analytics, bk. 2]. W. Wright, A Short History of Syriac Literature (1894), pp. 156–9; I. Ortiz de Urbina, SJ, Patrologia Syriaca (Rome, 2nd edn., 1965), pp. 183 f., with further bibl. C. D. G. Müller in TRE 12 (1984), pp. 378–80, s.v. 'Georg der Araberbischof'.

George of Cappadocia (4th cent.), *Arian bishop who was intruded into the see of *Alexandria. Our knowledge of him, though derived almost exclusively from hostile sources, leaves little doubt of his grasping and violent character. He took possession of the see of Alexandria in the Lent of 357, i.e. about a year after Athanasius' retirement in Feb. 356, and held it till he was murdered by the rabble on 24 Dec. 361. As a member of the extreme Arian party, he was opposed by the *Semiarians no less than the orthodox. Some features of his martyrdom passed into the legends about St *George; it was this fact which formed the basis of the mistaken view of E. *Gibbon that he was the historical character around whom the legends of the saint originated.

W. *Bright in DCB 2 (1880), pp. 638–40, s.v. 'Georgius (4)'.

George Hamartolos (9th cent.), 'George the Sinner', also 'George the Monk', Byzantine chronicler. He flourished under Michael III (842–67). He wrote a 'Chronicon Syntomon' in four Books, extending from the Creation down to AD 842. Though coloured by its bitter hatred of *Iconoclasm, it is an important source for the period immediately preceding *Photius. Its main interests are those of the more educated members of a Byzantine monastery. In the MSS it is carried on to 948 by 'The Logothete' (perhaps *Simeon Metaphrastes, q.v.), and to the 12th cent. by other writers. It was translated at an early date into Old Church Slavonic and Georgian.

Editio princeps of complete chronicle by E. de Muralt (St Petersburg, 1857, unsatisfactory; repr. in J. P. Migne, PG 110). Crit. edn. by C. de Boor (2 vols., Teub., 1904; repr., with correc-

tions by P. Wirth, 1978). [The 'Vitae Recentiorum Imperatorum' in PG 109. 823–984, is only an extract from the Chronicon, repeated from 110. 979–1194.] Slavonic text ed. V. M. Istrin (3 vols., St Petersburg, 1920–30); Georgian text ed. S. Kauchtschischwili (Tiflis, 1910–16). Krumbacher, pp. 352–8; G. Moravcsik, Byzantinoturcica, 1 (2nd edn., Berlin, 1958), pp. 277–80, with extensive bibl. J. Mossay and C. Gérard in DHGE 20 (1984), cols. 642 f., s.v. 'Georges (54) le Moine'.

George of Laodicea (4th cent.), *Semiarian bishop. A native of Alexandria, he became a strong supporter of the Arian party which followed *Eusebius of Nicomedia, and c.335 was appointed Bp. of Laodicea in Syria. Later, however, he opposed the *Anomoeanism of *Eudoxius, and became one of the chief exponents of the *Homoiousian theology. In defence of his position he composed in 359, in conjunction with *Basil of Ancyra and others, a statement of his faith which is preserved by *Epiphanius (Haer. 73. 12–22). He appears to have died shortly after 360.

CPG 2 (1974), pp. 283 f. (nos. 3555–8). P. Nautin in DHGE 20 (1984), cols. 629 f., s.v. 'Georges (46), évêque de Laodicée'.

George Scholarius (c.1405–c.1472), Patr. of *Constantinople. In early life he became a teacher of philosophy and then a civil court judge in Constantinople. He attended the Council of *Florence (1439), where he supported the scheme for reunion in opposition to his fellow-Greek, *Gemistus Plethon. On returning to the E., however, he gradually became the enemy of all projects of union. Around 1450 he entered a monastery and took the name of 'Gennadius'. After the capture of the city he was made Patriarch as 'Gennadius II' in 1454 by the Sultan Muhammad II, who himself invested him with his crozier and mantle, and established with him the *concordat which in effect governed the relations between the Orthodox Church and the Muslim power until 1923. After one (or possibly two) years in office he resigned, spending the rest of his life in a monastery, apart from two more short reigns as Patriarch (not of his choice, but by order of the Sultan). He was a prolific writer. In philosophy he was an enthusiastic admirer of *Aristotle. He learnt Latin in youth, and translated works by St *Thomas Aquinas into Greek: despite his later opposition to the Union of Florence, he retained his interest in Thomism to the end of his life.

Crit. edn. of his Works by L. Petit, AA, X. A. Siderides, and M. Jugie, AA (8 vols., Paris and Athens, 1928–36), with full introd. Older edns. repr. in J. P. Migne, PG 160. 319–774. Speeches at the Council of Florence ed. J. Gill, SJ (Concilium Florentinum, Documenta et Scriptores, 8, fasc. 1; Rome, 1964). The first satisfactory study of George Scholarius is by M. Jugie, AA, in DTC 14 (pt. 2; 1941), cols. 1521–70, with bibl. M. Pharantos, Ἡ Θεολογία Γενναδίου τοῦ Σχολαρίου (1969). T. N. Zissis, Γεννάδιος Β' Σχολάριος (Analecta Vlatadon, 30; Thessalonica, 1980). J. Gill, Personalities of the Council of Florence and other Essays (Oxford, 1964), pp. 79–94; C. J. G. Turner, 'George-Gennadius Scholarius and the Union of Florence', JTS NS 18 (1967), pp. 83–103. Beck, pp. 760–3. J. Gill in NCE 6 (1967), pp. 333 f., s.v. 'Gennadius II Scholarius', with further refs.

George Syncellus (fl. c.800), Byzantine historian. Little is known of him beyond the facts that he lived for some time in Palestine and was later the '*syncellus' of Tarasius, Patr. of *Constantinople (784–806). He wrote an important 'Chronicle' from the Creation to the time of

*Diocletian, which after his death was brought down by his friend, Theophanes the Confessor, to AD 813. The treatment of biblical times is much fuller than that of the later period. His sources included (either directly or indirectly) *Eusebius, *Julius Africanus, Anianus of Alexandria (5th cent.), Panodorus (c.400), and other writers. He possessed some critical insight into the value of his material and preserves some important fragments, but his use of his sources is dull and unimaginative.

Crit. edn. of his Chronicle by A. A. Mosshammer (Teub., 1984). G. L. Huxley, 'On the Erudition of George the Synkellos', *Proceedings of the Royal Irish Academy*, Section C, 81 (1981), pp. 207–17. W. Adler, *Time Immemorial: Archaic History and its Sources in Christian Chronography from Julius Africanus to George Syncellus* (Dumbarton Oaks Studies, 26; 1989), pp. 132–234. Krumbacher, pp. 339–42.

Georgia, Church of. The origins of Christianity in Georgia (also known as Iberia; in the S. Caucasus) extend back to the 4th cent., if not earlier. The preaching of a Christian slave woman from Cappadocia, St Nino, led to the conversion of the Iberian royal house c.350, and so to the adoption of the Christian faith as the religion of the country. At first dependent upon the Patriarchate of *Antioch, the Georgian Church became *autocephalous in the 8th cent., its independence being reaffirmed at a Council of Antioch c.1057. The Georgians developed a rich Christian literature in their own tongue, above all during the 11th–13th cents. In 1811 the Georgian Church was absorbed by the Church of *Russia; it regained its autocephalous status in 1917, but was not recognized by the Soviet authorities or the Russian Church until 1943. The Georgian Church was a focus of nationalist opposition and suffered severe persecution; sees were left vacant and parishes without pastoral oversight. After the accession of the *Catholicos Patriarch Ilya II in 1977 there was a revival, and links were established with the Papacy and the Abp. of *Canterbury. Eduard Shevardnadze, former foreign minister of the USSR, who became chairman of the State Council of Georgia in 1992, was baptized in the same year.

M. Tamarati, *L'Église géorgienne des origines jusqu'à nos jours* (Rome, 1910). S. C. Malan (ed.), *A Short History of the Georgian Church*, tr. from the Russian of P. Ioselian (1866). C. Toumanoff, *Studies in Christian Caucasian History* (Washington, DC, 1963). F. Thélamon, 'Histoire et structure mythique: la conversion des Ibères', *Revue historique*, 247 (1972), pp. 5–28. W. E. D. Allen, *A History of the Georgian People from the beginning down to the Russian Conquest in the Nineteenth Century* (1932). M. Tarchnišvili, *Geschichte der kirchlichen georgischen Literatur* (ST 185; 1955). D. M. Lang, *Lives and Legends of the Georgian Saints* (1956). R. Janin, AA, in *DTC* 6 (1920), cols. 1239–89; G. Garitte in *Dict. Sp.* 6 (1967), cols. 244–56, s.v. 'Géorgienne (Littérature spirituelle)'; C. Toumanoff in *NCE* 6 (1967), pp. 361–9, s.v. 'Georgia, Church in Ancient'; J. Assfalg and D. M. Lang in *TRE* 12 (1984), pp. 389–96, s.v. 'Georgien'.

Georgian Version. The earliest version of the New Testament in the Georgian language, which like *Armenian traditionally owes its alphabet to St *Mesrob (5th cent.), dates from the 6th cent. The translation was apparently made from the Armenian, though from better texts than any now surviving Armenian MS. R. P. Blake has observed that certain MSS of the Georgian Gospels represent a type of the *Caesarean text, which in the

Adysh MS of the Gospels (897) has been preserved in relative purity, though in most MSS it has been more or less completely 'corrected' to the *Lucianic type. The Gospels and the Pauline Epp. were always written until modern times in distinct MSS, so that their textual traditions are independent.

Ed. princeps of OT by Prince Vakhusht, Moscow, 1742–3. Modern edns. of Mt. and Mk. by B. V. Beneševič (St Petersburg, 1909–11), of Mk. and Mt. by R. P. Blake in *PO* 20, fasc. 3 [pp. 437–574] (1928), and 24, fasc. 1 [pp. 1–168] (1933), of Jn. by id. and M. Brière, ibid. 26, fasc. 4 [pp. 453–599] (1950), and of Lk. by M. Brière, ibid. 27, fasc. 3 [pp. 275–457] (1955), incl. corrections to the edns. of Mt., Mk., and Jn. B. M. Metzger, *The Early Versions of the New Testament* (Oxford, 1977), pp. 182–98. K. *Lake and R. P. Blake, 'The Caesarean Text of the Gospel of Mark', *HTR* 21 (1928), pp. 207–404, esp. pp. 286–307. J. N. Birdsall in *Anchor Bible Dictionary*, 6 (1992), pp. 810–13, s.v. 'Versions, Ancient (Georgian)'.

Gerald de Barri. See GIRALDUS CAMBRENSIS.

Gerald of Wales. See GIRALDUS CAMBRENSIS.

Gerbert of Aurillac. See SYLVESTER II.

Gerhard, Johann (1582–1637), *Lutheran theologian. Born in Quedlingburg, where J. *Arndt was pastor, he studied medicine at *Wittenberg and theology at Jena, and taught theology at Jena from 1616 until his death. A prolific writer, Gerhard's great dogmatic work is his massive *Loci Theologici* (9 vols. in 10, 1610–22), which became a standard compendium of Lutheran orthodoxy. It reintroduced scholastic methodology and terminology into Reformation dogmatics, while at the same time exhibiting a lively practical interest in ethics and culture. An ardent controversialist, Gerhard's principal polemical work is his *Confessio Catholica* (1634–7), which, with M. *Chemnitz's *Examen concilii Tridentini* (1565–73) and Gerhard's own *Bellarminus ὀρθοδοξίας testis* (1631–3), became a popular anti-Catholic Lutheran apology. Gerhard also demonstrated a keen interest in biblical and patristic study. He completed a harmony of the Gospels begun earlier by Chemnitz and P. Leyser, the *Harmonia Evangelistarum Chemnitio-Lyseriana* (1626–7), and after his death his son published a *Patrologia* (1653) assembled from material in his writings. His devotional masterpiece, *Meditationes Sacrae* (1606) went through many editions in several languages, incl. an English translation in 1631. J. B. *Bossuet considered him the third most important Protestant theologian after Luther and Chemnitz.

The standard edn. of his *Loci Theologici* by I. F. Cotta (20 vols. + index in 2 parts, Tübingen, 1762–89). [F.] A. [G.] *Tholuck (ed.), *Spicilegium ex Commercio Epistolico Johannis Gerhardi* (Halle, 1864). Life (in Latin) by E. R. Fischer (Leipzig, 1723). J. Wallmann, *Der Theologiebegriff bei Johann Gerhard und Georg Calixt* (Beiträge zur historischen Theologie, 30; 1961), pp. 5–84; R. Schröder, *Johann Gerhards lutherische Christologie und die aristotelische Metaphysik* (ibid. 67; 1983). R. P. Scharlemann, *Thomas Aquinas and John Gerhard* (Yale Publications in Religion, 7; New Haven, Conn., and London, 1964). M. Honecker, 'Die Kirchengliedschaft bei Johann Gerhard und Robert Bellarmin', *Zeitschrift für Theologie und Kirche*, NF 62 (1965), pp. 21–45. R. Kirste, *Das Zeugnis des Geistes und das Zeugnis der Schrift: Das testimonium spiritus sancti internum als hermeneutisch-polemischer Zentralbegriff bei Johann Gerhard in der Auseinandersetzung mit Robert Bellarmins Schriftverständnis* (Göttinger Theologische Arbeiten, 6; 1976). W.

Elert, *Morphologie des Luthertums*, 1 (1931; Eng. tr., St Louis, 1962); R. D. Preus, *The Theology of Post-Reformation Lutheranism* (2 vols., St Louis [1970–2]), *passim*. J. Baur, 'Johann Gerhard', in M. Greschat (ed.), *Orthodoxie und Pietismus* (Gestalten der Kirchengeschichte, 7; Stuttgart, 1982), pp. 99–119. M. Honecker in *TRE* 12 (1984), pp. 448–53, s.v.

Gerhard Zerbolt of Zutphen (1367–98), member of the *Brethren of the Common Life. After studying at various places he became a priest and librarian of the Brethren of the Common Life at Deventer. He became a close friend of *Florentius Radewijns. He was remarkable for his learning, esp. in moral theology and canon law as well as in ascetic and mystical theology, and an excellent director of souls. Of his writings the best known are 'De reformatione virium animae' and 'De spiritualibus ascensionibus', which influenced the '*Spiritual Exercises' of St *Ignatius Loyola. His authorship of two treatises on prayer and the reading of Scripture in the vernacular is uncertain.

His 'Scriptum pro quodam Inordinate Gradus Ecclesiasticos et Praedicationis Officium Affectante', ed. A. Hyma, *Nederlandsch Archief voor Kerkgeschiedenis*, NS 20 (1927), pp. 179–232. Life by *Thomas à Kempis in *Opera et Libri Vite Fratris Thomae de Kempis* [Nuremberg, 1494], fols. xxix–xxxviii. J. van Rooij, O. Carm., *Gerard Zerbolt van Zutphen*, 1. *Leven en Geschriften* (1936). G. H. Gerrits, *Inter Timorem et Spem: A Study of the Theological Thought of Gerard Zerbolt of Zutphen (1367–1398)* (Studies in Medieval and Reformation Thought, 37; Leiden, 1986), with bibl. S. D. van Veen in *PRE* (3rd edn.), 21 (1908), pp. 735–7, s.v. 'Zütphen, Gerhard Zerbolt van'; W. Lourdaux in *Dict. Sp.* 6 (1967), cols. 284–9, s.v. 'Gérard (19) Zerbolt de Zutphen'.

Gerhardt, Paul (1607–76), German *Lutheran hymnwriter. After studying theology at *Wittenberg and spending some years as a private tutor at Berlin he became provost at Mittelwalde in 1651 and pastor at the St Nikolaikirche at Berlin in 1657. He resigned this post in 1666 through unwillingness to sign a declaration submitting to the *syncretist edicts of the Elector of Brandenburg. In 1668 he was appointed archdeacon at Lübben, where he remained to his death. Though in his theology he was an uncompromising Lutheran, he was susceptible to the influence of Catholic mysticism, esp. that of St *Bernard, and one of his most beautiful hymns, 'O sacred head, sore wounded', is based on the 'Salve caput cruentatum' attributed to the saint. Combining a deep personal piety and filial trust in God with the love of nature of the true poet, as expressed, e.g., in the fine verses of 'The duteous day now closeth' (Eng. tr., R. *Bridges), his hymns have become widely known, esp. in Germany. He ranks as one of the greatest hymn-writers of German Protestantism.

P. Wackernagel (anon. ed.), *Paulus Gerhardts geistliche Lieder* [1843]; modern edn. of his *Dichtungen und Schriften* by E. von Cranach-Sichart (Munich [1957]). H. Petrich, *Paul Gerhardt* (1914). R. Eckart, *Paul Gerhardt: Urkunden und Aktenstücke zu seinem Leben und Kämpfen* (1919). T. B. Hewitt, *Paul Gerhardt as a Hymnwriter and his Influence on English Hymnology* (New Haven, Conn., and London, 1919), with bibl. H. Hoffmann (ed.), *Paul Gerhardt: Dichter, Theologe, Seelsorger, 1607–1676. Beiträge der Wittenberger Paul-Gerhardt-Tage 1976* (1978). R. Eckart, *Paul Gerhardt-Bibliographie* (1909). E.-H. Pältz in *TRE* 12 (1984), pp. 453–7, s.v.

Gerhoh of Reichersberg (1092/3–1169), *Augustinian Canon, theologian, and exegete. Born at Polling, in Ba-

varia, he studied at Freising, Moosburg, and Hildesheim. He became 'magister scholarum' of the cathedral school at Augsburg *c.*1118, but he had to leave this post some three years later owing to his opposition to his simoniacal bishop, Hermann of Augsburg, and found refuge in the house of Augustinian Canons at Rottenbuch (in the diocese of Freising), where he was converted to the ideal of a *vita apostolica* of poverty, prayer, and service. After their reconciliation in 1123, Gerhoh accompanied Hermann to the First *Lateran Council. Upon his return to Augsburg Gerhoh's zeal for reform found no favour among his fellow cathedral clergy; therefore in 1124 he entered Rottenbuch as an Augustinian Canon and as such lived an exemplary life. But he soon differed from the community about the duty of propagating reform outside the cloister and, after a brief period as a parish priest at Cham, from 1128 to 1132 he resided in Regensburg. His ideas on clerical life and Church discipline were set out in his 'Liber de aedificio Dei' (1128–9). In 1132 he was appointed provost of the house of Augustinian Canons at Reichersberg (in the diocese of Passau), to the great spiritual and material advantage of the community. He was often sent on embassies to Rome, where he came into contact with St *Bernard of Clairvaux; but his zeal for reform gained him much hostility. He was even accused of heresy, though he had always defended the orthodox teaching, esp. against the *Christological errors of *Abelard and *Gilbert de la Porrée. In 1166 he was banned by the Emp. *Frederick I and forced to flee from his monastery because he refused to support the Imperialist antipope. His ideas on the schism were laid down in his famous work 'De Investigatione Antichristi' (1160/2), in which he advocates a clearer definition of the spheres of Papal and Imperial power. In addition to his controversial writings, Gerhoh wrote a discursive commentary on the Psalms, in which he draws extensively on contemporary sources, esp. *Anselm of Laon, *Rupert of Deutz, *Hugh of St-Victor, and Gilbert de la Porrée.

Opera Omnia in J. P. Migne, *PL* 193. 461–1814, and 194. 9–1490; F. Scheibelberger (ed.), *Gerhohi . . . Opera Hactenus Inedita* (Linz a.d. Donau, 1875); much of his work also ed. E. Sackur in *MGH*, Libelli de Lite Imperatorum et Pontificum Saeculis XI. et XII., 3 (1897), pp. 131–525; *Opera Inedita*, ed. D. Van den Eynde, OFM, and others (Spicilegium Pontificii Athenaei Antoniani, 8–10; 1955–6). Crit. edn. of his *Liber de novitatibus huius temporis*, addressed in 1156 to Pope *Hadrian IV, by N. M. Häring, SAC (Pontifical Institute of Mediaeval Studies, Studies and Texts, 24; 1974). J. Günster, *Die Christologie des Gerhoh von Reichersberg: Eine dogmengeschichtliche Studie zu seiner Auffassung von der hypostatischen Union* (1940). D. Van den Eynde, OFM, *L'Œuvre littéraire de Géroch de Reichersberg* (Spicilegium Pontificii Athenaei Antoniani, 11; 1957). E. Meuthen, *Kirche und Heilsgeschichte bei Gerhoh von Reichersberg* (Studien und Texte zur Geistesgeschichte des Mittelalters, 6; Leiden, 1959). P. Classen, *Gerhoch von Reichersberg* (Wiesbaden, 1960). W. Beinert, *Die Kirche-Gottes Heil in der Welt: Die Lehre von der Kirche nach den Schriften des Rupert von Deutz, Honorius Augustodunensis und Gerhoch von Reichersberg* (BGPM NF 13; 1973), incl. introd. on his life and work, pp. 50–68. A. M. Lazzarino del Grosso, *Armut und Reichtum im Denken Gerhohs von Reichersberg* (Zeitschrift für Bayerische Landesgeschichte, Beiheft (Reihe B) 4; 1973); id., *Società e Potere nella Germania del XII Secolo: Gerhoch di Reichersberg* ('Il Pensiero Politico' Biblioteca, 6; 1974). J. Mois, *Das Stift Rottenbuch in der Kirchenreform des XI.–XII. Jahrhunderts* (Beiträge zur Altbayerischen Kirchengeschichte, 3rd ser. 19;

1953), pp. 114–43. R. W. and A. J. Carlyle, *A History of Mediaeval Political Thought in the West*, 4 (1922), pp. 342–83. P. Classen in *Dict. Sp.* 6 (1967), cols. 303–8, s.v.

Germain, St. See GERMANUS, ST.

Germain-des-Prés, St-. See ST-GERMAIN-DES-PRÉS.

German Baptists. See TUNKERS.

German-Christians (*Deutsche Christen*). A Protestant group which, during the Hitler régime, tried to bring about a synthesis between Nazism and Christianity. Its more extreme adherents wished to eliminate the OT, St *Paul ('the Rabbi'), and the doctrines of St *Augustine (with their 'Jewish' sense of sin), and to eradicate from the Gospels everything Jewish or 'servile'. Finding their Holy Land not in Palestine, but in Germany, they held that the law of God was embodied in Hitler. It was their professed purpose to 'complete' M. *Luther's Reformation. Concealment of their more extreme aims, coupled with a broadcast by Hitler urging all Nazis to vote, gained them a large majority at the Church elections in July 1933; and L. *Müller (q.v.), the most influential figure in the group, was elected *Reichsbischof of the German Evangelical Church. Müller's extreme measures, notably his attempt to introduce an 'Aryan paragraph' (excluding Jews from being clergymen or Church officials, on the model of the state legislation) into Reich Church law and his incorporation of the Evangelical Youth into the 'Hitler Jugend', wholly alienated the embryonic '*Confessing Church' and he was virtually superseded by the appointment of Hanns Kerrl as Minister for Church affairs in 1935. None the less, the 'German-Christians' retained the official leadership of more than half the German *Landeskirchen* during the Second World War. After it the more extreme members disappeared from public view, while others seceded from the official *Landeskirchen* to join in a free Church.

K. Meier, *Die Deutschen Christen: Das Bild einer Bewegung in Kirchenkampf des Dritten Reiches* (Göttingen, 1964). R. Gutteridge, *Open thy mouth for the dumb! The German Evangelical Church and the Jews 1879–1950* (Oxford, 1976), esp. pp. 69–313.

Germanus, St (d. 437/48), Bp. of Auxerre, in the 420s and 430s (perhaps 407–37, 412–42, or 418–48). *Prosper of Aquitaine (*Chron.* s.a. 429) records Pope *Celestine I's sending of Germanus to quell *Pelagianism in Britain at the instigation of *Palladius. Otherwise, we depend heavily upon the Life written by Constantius of Lyons between *c*.460 and 490. This tells of Germanus' training as a lawyer, promotion to provincial rule, popular acclamation as bishop of Auxerre, two visits to Britain to combat Pelagianism, and final journey to Ravenna, where he died. His body was brought back to Auxerre for burial. Constantius' portrayal of an ascetic bishop of considerable standing, who intervened with secular authorities, is convincing; but he knows little about Germanus' visits to Britain apart from reports of miracle stories. It is possible that the second visit to Britain is simply a hagiographical doublet of the first. Germanus may have had links with Palladius' mission to Ireland. Muirchú's later association of St *Patrick with Germanus is of very dubious authenticity. Feast day, 31 July. See also GENEVIÈVE, ST.

For edns. of Prosper's Chronicle, see under PROSPER. Constantius' *Vita Germani* was first pr., in a corrupt text, by B. Mombritius, *Sanctuarium seu Vitae Sanctorum*, 1 (Milan, 1480), fols. 318–25. Crit. edns. by W. Levison in *MGH*, Scriptores Rerum Merovingicarum, 7 (pt. 1; 1919), pp. 225–83, and, with Fr. tr., by R. Borius (SC 112; 1965). Eng. tr. by F. R. Hoare, *The Western Fathers* (1954), pp. 281–320. Metrical and prose Lives were also written in the 9th cent. by *Heiric of Auxerre (q.v.). W. Levison, 'Bischof Germanus von Auxerre und die Quellen zu seiner Geschichte', *Neues Archiv*, 29 (1904), pp. 95–175. *Saint Germain d'Auxerre et son temps: Communications présentées à l'occasion du XIXe Congrès de l'Association Bourguignonne des Sociétés Savantes réuni à Auxerre . . . pour commémorer le XVe centenaire de la mort de saint Germain d'Auxerre*, with introd. by G. Le Bras (Auxerre, 1950). N. K. Chadwick, *Poetry and Letters in Early Christian Gaul* (1955), pp. 240–74 and 285–8. I. Wood, 'The End of Roman Britain: Continental Evidence and Parallels', in *Gildas: New Approaches*, ed. M. Lapidge and D. Dumville (Studies in Celtic History, 5; Woodbridge, Suffolk, 1984), pp. 1–25, esp. pp. 6–17. E. A. Thompson, *Saint Germanus of Auxerre and the End of Roman Britain* (ibid. 6; 1984); cf. review by C. E. Stancliffe in *JTS* NS 37 (1986), pp. 603–8.

Germanus, St (*c*.496–576), Bp. of *Paris. A native of Autun (Augustodunum), he was ordained priest in 530 and rose to become abbot of the monastery of St Symphorian in his own city, where he exercised great generosity to the poor. In 555 he became Bp. of Paris. Here he sought to check the licence of the Frankish kings and stop the perpetual civil wars; and he won considerable influence over Childebert, son of *Clovis. He took part in several Councils, among them Paris III (561/2?), Tours II (567), and Paris IV (573). His prophecy that death would overtake Sigebert if he did not desist from invoking the trans-Rhenish barbarians against his brother, Chilperic, was fulfilled when Sigebert was murdered by assassins. The church of *St-Germain-des-Prés stands on the site of an elaborate 7th-cent. tomb over his remains (destroyed, 1793). His Life, written by *Venantius Fortunatus, abounds in miraculous legends. Feast day, 28 May; of his translation, 25 July.

Two letters attributed to him are of great importance for the history of the *Gallican liturgy. Older scholars, accepting their genuineness, used them in the reconstruction of the Gallican rite; but A. *Wilmart, following up doubts expressed by H. Koch and E. *Bishop, made out a strong case against their authenticity. He maintained that they were written in the S. of France *c*.700, and represent a rite as much Spanish as French, which had already absorbed a number of foreign elements. This view is now widely accepted.

Crit. edn., with introd., of the 'Vita' by Venantius Fortunatus, by B. Krusch in *MGH*, Scriptores Rerum Merovingicarum, 7 (1919) pp. 337–418; another brief Life, together with the account of the translation of his relics, ibid., pp. 419–28. These three items also pr. in *AASS*, Mai. 6 (1688), pp. 774–806; the Life by Venantius Fortunatus, also in J. P. Migne, *PL* 72. 55–78. O. Holder-Egger, 'Zur Translatio S. Germani', *NA* 18 (1893), pp. 274–81. R. Aubert in *DHGE* 20 (1984), cols. 927–9, 'Germain (22)', with bibl.

The two letters mentioned above are preserved in an 8th-cent. MS at Autun. They were first pr. by E. *Martène, OSB, in his *Thesaurus Novus Anecdotorum*, 5 (Paris, 1717), pp. 91–100; repr. in J. P. Migne, *PL* 72. 89–98; crit. edn. by E. C. Ratcliff (posthumously pub., HBS, 98; 1971). On their authenticity, see A. Wilmart, OSB, in *DACL* 6 (pt. 1; 1924), cols. 1049–102, s.v.

'Germain de Paris (Lettres attribuées saint)'; Wilmart's conclusions have been challenged by A. van der Mensbrugghe, 'L'Expositio Missæ Gallicanæ est-elle de saint Germain de Paris (†576)?', *Messager de l'Exarchat du Patriarche Russe en Europe Occidentale*, 8 (1959), pp. 217–49 (partly repeated by id., 'Pseudo-Germanus Reconsidered' in F. L. Cross (ed.), *Studia Patristica*, 5 (TU 80; 1962), pp. 172–84) but reasserted by R. Cabié, 'Les lettres attribuées à saint Germain de Paris et les origines de la liturgie gallicane', *Bulletin de Littérature Ecclesiastique*, 73 (1972), pp. 183–92.

Germanus, St (*c*.640–*c*.733), Patriarch of *Constantinople. Descended from a noble Byzantine family, Germanus received a careful education. After the fall and execution of his father, he was made a eunuch (prob. in 669) and became one of the clergy of *Sancta Sophia, of which he was later the head. He prob. played some part in the Sixth Oecumenical Council (the Third Council of *Constantinople, 680) and in the *Trullan Synod (692), but there is no certain evidence as to his role. It seems that at the synod convoked by the Emp. Philippicus in 712 to restore the *Monothelite heresy, Germanus, by then Metropolitan of Cyzicus, yielded to the threats of the Emperor and signed the declaration against the Sixth Oecumenical Council. If he actually did so, a fact which has been contested, he soon returned to orthodoxy. He was elected Patriarch in 715 and at a synod called shortly afterwards officially proclaimed the Catholic faith and anathematized the Monothelites. In 725 the Emp. *Leo III, the Isaurian, issued his first edict against the veneration of icons (see *ICONOCLASTIC CONTROVERSY), and during the four subsequent years of his patriarchate Germanus was the soul of resistance against Iconoclasm. He was forced to resign in 730 and retired to Platonium. He is known to have written three treatises: 'De haeresibus et synodis', his only extant historical work, 'De vitae termino', a work of philosophical theology, and 'De vera et legitima retributione' (the *Antapodotikos*), which has not survived. Among his other writings, many of which perished at the hands of the Iconoclastic Emperors, there remain four dogmatic letters, three of them bearing on the Iconoclastic Controversy, and seven homilies on the BVM, of whose cult he was one of the most ardent promoters. Mary's incomparable purity, foreshadowing the doctrine of the *Immaculate Conception, and her universal mediation in the distribution of supernatural blessings, are his two frequently recurring themes. He is very probably also the author of the 'Historia mystica ecclesiae catholicae', an interpretation of the contemporary Byzantine Liturgy, as well as of several fine liturgical poems. Feast day, 12 May.

Works in J. P. Migne, *PG* 98. 9–454. Crit. edn., with Eng. tr., of *De vitae termino* by C. Garton and L. G. Westerink (Arethusa Monographs, 7; Buffalo, NY, 1979). For the *Historia Mystica*, see F. E. *Brightman, 'The *Historia Mystagogica* and other Greek Commentaries on the Byzantine Liturgy', *JTS* 9 (1907–8), pp. 248–67 and 387–97, incl. text, and N. Borgia, 'La ''Εξήγησις' di S. Germano e la versione latina di Anastasio Bibliotecario', *Roma e l'oriente*, 2 (1911), pp. 144–56, 219–28, 286–96, and 346–54, incl. reconstructed text. This text is repr. in St Germanus of Constantinople, *On the Divine Liturgy*, with Eng. tr. and comm. by P. Meyendorff (Crestwood, NY, 1984). Lat. version by *Anastasius Bibliothecarius ed. S. Pétridès, AA, in *Revue de l'Orient Chrétien*, 10 (1905), pp. 309–13 and 350–63. V. Grumel, AA (ed.), *Les Regestes des Actes du Patriarcat de Constantinople*, 1, fascs. 2–3 (2nd edn., rev. by J. Darrouzès, AA, 1989), pp. 1–10 (nos. 325–42). L. Lamza, *Patriarch Germanos I. von Konstantinopel (715–730)*

(Das östliche Christentum, NF 27; Würzburg, 1975; incl. ed. and Ger. tr. of Gk. *Vita*, dating from the 9th, or perhaps the 11th, cent.). J. List, *Studien zur Homiletik Germanos I. von Konstantinopel und seine Zeit* (Texte und Forschungen zur byzantinisch-neugriechischen Philologie, 29; 1939: philological). R. Bornert, OSB, *Les Commentaires Byzantins de la Divine Liturgie du VIIᵉ au XVᵉ Siècle* (Archives de l'Orient Chrétien, 9; 1966), pp. 125–80. W. Lackner, 'Ein hagiographisches Zeugnis für den Antapodotikos des Patriarchen Germanos I. von Konstantinopel', *Byzantion*, 38 (1968), pp. 42–104. *CPG* 3 (1979), pp. 503–10 (nos. 8001–33). Beck, pp. 473–6; Altaner and Stuiber (1978), pp. 525 and 661. F. Cayré in *DTC* 6 (1920), cols. 1300–9, s.v., with full bibl.; J. Darrouzès, AA, in *Dict. Sp.* 6 (1967), cols. 309–11, s.v. 'Germain (2) I de Constantinople', also with bibl.

Germany, Christianity in. See CONFESSING CHURCH; EVANGELICAL CHURCH IN GERMANY; GERMAN-CHRISTIANS; HOLY ROMAN EMPIRE; LUTHERANISM; REFORMATION; and THIRTY YEARS WAR.

Gerontius, The Dream of. This celebrated poem by J. H. *Newman was first published in the periodical, *The Month*, for April and May 1865, and in book form in 1866. It is a vision of a just soul leaving a body at death and of its subsequent intercourse with the angels. It has been set to music by E. *Elgar, and two of the poems in it are well known as hymns—'Firmly I believe and truly' and 'Praise to the Holiest in the height'.

Gerson, Jean le Charlier de (1363–1429), French Churchman and spiritual writer, the 'doctor christianissimus'. He was born nr. Rethel in the Ardennes. In 1377 he entered the College of Navarre at *Paris, then the centre of *Nominalism, where he studied under Pierre *d'Ailly, who remained his lifelong friend. He was made doctor of theology *c*.1394, and in 1395 succeeded d'Ailly as Chancellor of Notre-Dame and of the University. From the beginning of his career he worked for the reform of the Church from within, which he endeavoured to bring about chiefly by a renewal of the spirit of prayer and sacrifice, and for the abolition of the *Great (Western) Schism. In 1397 he fled from the strain of the life in Paris to Bruges, where he held the benefice of Dean of the Church of St Donatian. While there he wrote his famous treatise 'On the Manner of Conducting oneself in a Time of Schism', exhorting clergy and laity of both obediences to recognize each other's Sacraments and urging charity in their judgements. In 1398 he did not vote for the refusal of obedience to the *Avignon Pope, and the later return of France to the obedience of *Benedict XIII was largely his work, due esp. to his treatise 'De Restitutione Obedientiae'. After his return to Paris (1401) he resumed his office as Chancellor and was instrumental in bringing back the *Dominicans (1403), who had been expelled from the University for their teaching on the *Immaculate Conception. He approved the decisions of the Councils of *Pisa (1409) and Rome (1412–13), though not taking part in them himself. In 1415 he attended the Council of *Constance, which he encouraged to continue its sessions after the flight of *John XXIII. He asserted the superiority of a General Council over the Pope and demanded that the doctors of theology should have a deliberative and definitive voice in it together with the bishops. He also took an important part in the drawing-up of the famous Four

Articles of Constance, the future charter of *Gallicanism. He had a share in the condemnation of J. *Huss, and denounced the propositions advanced by Jean Petit in favour of tyrannicide. This earned him the hostility of the Duke of Burgundy, Jean sans Peur, who had had the Duke of Orléans assassinated, and in whose defence Jean Petit had drawn up his theses. The hatred of Burgundy prevented Gerson from returning to Paris after the conclusion of the Council, and he went to the Benedictine abbey of Melk, nr. Vienna, where he wrote his treatise 'De Consolatione Theologiae', modelled on *Boethius. After the death of Jean sans Peur he returned to France (1419), where he spent the last ten years of his life in seclusion at Lyons, devoting himself entirely to the practice of the spiritual life and pastoral work.

Among his writings dealing with the position of the Church are 'De Unitate Ecclesiae', 'De Auferibilitate Papae ab Ecclesia', and 'De Potestate Ecclesiae' (1417), in which he developed the *Conciliar theory but without rejecting the primacy of the Pope. In moral theology he accepted the extreme Nominalist doctrine, then generally taught in the schools, acc. to which nothing was sinful in itself but the sinfulness or goodness of an act depended solely on the Will of God. Among the large number of his treatises devoted to the spiritual life are 'The Mountain of Contemplation' (1397, his principal work), 'Mystical Theology', 'Perfection of the Heart', and Commentaries on the *Magnificat and on the Song of *Solomon. His mystical teaching, which has marked *Augustinian tendencies, is a synthesis of much that is best in Catholic mysticism from *Dionysius the Pseudo-Areopagite to J. *Ruysbroeck, his particular sympathies being with St *Bernard, the *Victorines, and St *Bonaventure. He consciously opposed this spiritual teaching of the 'antiqui' to the dry intellectualist activities of the Nominalist 'moderni', who threatened to convert theology into mere dialectics. Gerson was also a zealous advocate of frequent *Communion and was deeply concerned over the religious education of children.

Gerson's influence has been deep and lasting mainly in two directions: his Conciliar views found an echo in Gallicanism, of which he is sometimes called the father, and his mystical teaching was admired by *Nicholas of Cusa and by the *Brethren of the Common Life, as well as by St *Ignatius Loyola, St Robert *Bellarmine, and St *Francis de Sales. His writings were also greatly valued by M. *Luther in his early years. The '*Imitation of Christ' has sometimes been ascribed to him, esp. by French scholars, but it is now generally admitted that both internal and external evidence are against this attribution.

Editio princeps of his collected works, 4 vols., Cologne, 1483–4; the best complete edn. is that of L. E. *Dupin (5 vols., Antwerp, 1706, with Life); modern edn. by [P.] Glorieux (10 vols., Paris, 1960–73), with useful introd. in vol. 1. Notulae super quaedam verba Dionysii de Caelesti Hierarchia, ed. A. Combes (Études de philosophie médiévale, 30; 1940); six sermons in the vernacular, ed. L. Mourin (Études de théologie et d'histoire de la spiritualité, 8; 1946). J. B. Schwab, Johannes Gerson (Würzburg, 1858); J. L. Connolly, John Gerson, Reformer and Mystic (Louvain, 1928). A. Combes, Jean de Montreuil et le Chancelier Gerson (Études de philosophie médiévale, 32; 1942); id., Essai sur la critique de Ruysbroeck par Gerson (Études de théologie et d'histoire de la spiritualité, 4 and 5 (1); 1945–8); id., La Théologie mystique de Gerson: Profil de son évolution (2 vols., 1963–5), with refs. to other studies

by this author. L. Mourin, Jean Gerson, prédicateur français (Rijksuniversiteit te Gent, Werken uitgegeven door de Faculteit van de Wijsbegeerte en Letteren, 113; 1952). L. B. Pascoe, SJ, Jean Gerson: Principles of Church Reform (Studies in Medieval and Reformation Thought, 7; Leiden, 1973). G. H. M. Posthumus Meyjes, Jean Gerson et l'assemblée de Vincennes (1392): Ses conceptions de la juridiction temporelle de l'Église (ibid. 26; 1978), with text of 'De jurisdictione spirituali et temporali', pp. 121–31. C. Burger, Aedificatio, Fructus, Utilitas: Johannes Gerson als Professor der Theologie und Kanzler der Universität Paris (Beiträge zur historischen Theologie, 70; Tübingen, 1986). D. C. Brown, Pastor and Laity in the Theology of Jean Gerson (Cambridge, 1987). M. S. Burrows, Jean Gerson and De Consolatione Theologiae (1418) (Beiträge zur historischen Theologie, 78; Tübingen, 1991). L. Salembier in DTC 6 (1920), cols. 1312–30; A. Combes, L. Mourin, and F. Simone in EC 6 (1952), cols. 185–91; P. Glorieux in Dict. Sp. 6 (1967), cols. 314–31; additional bibl. in DHGE 20 (1984), cols. 1056 f.; C. Burger in TRE 12 (1984), pp. 532–8; in English, P. Glorieux in NCE 6 (1967), pp. 449 f.; all s.v.

Gertrude, St (1) (626–59), abbess.

She was the daughter of Pepin the Elder (d. 640). On her father's death, her mother, Blessed Ida, founded a convent at Nivelles in Belgium, and on Ida's death Gertrude became its first abbess. She ruled the convent well, but her personal austerities so weakened her that c.656 she resigned her office and gave herself wholly up to devotion until her death three years later. She is widely venerated in the Netherlands and Belgium, and is invoked as patroness of travellers; also against plagues of mice and rats, with which creatures she is often depicted. Feast day, 17 Mar.

A contemporary Vita is printed in AASS, Mar. 2 (1668), pp. 592–99; critical edn. of two recensions by B. Krusch in MGH, Scriptores Rerum Merovingicarum, 2 (1888), pp. 447–74. Eng. tr. in Sainted Women of the Dark Ages, ed. and tr. J. A. McNamara and others (Durham, NC, and London, 1992), pp. 220–34. BHL (1898–1901), nos. 3490–504, pp. 520–2. J. J. Hoebanx, L'Abbaye de Nivelles des Origines au XIVᵉ siècle (Mémoires de l'Académie Royale de Belgique, Collection in-8°, 46, pt. 4; 1952), pp. 22–61. M. van Uytfanghe in Lexikon des Mittelalters, 4, (1989), cols. 1356 f., s.v. 'Gertrud v. Nivelles', with bibl.

Gertrude, St (2), 'the Great' (1256–c.1302),

German mystic. She is to be distinguished from the Abbess Gertrude of Hackeborn (1232–92), with whom she was long confused in older works and in the Breviary. At the age of 5 she was entrusted to the *Cistercian-inspired convent of Helfta in Thuringia, where she received a sound education. She experienced a conversion at the age of 25, and from that time led a life of contemplation. She was closely associated with other visionary women, notably *Mechthild of Magdeburg and St Mechthild of Hackenborn. Her 'Legatus Divinae Pietatis', of which only the Second Book was written by herself (the other four being based on her notes), is one of the major literary products of Christian mysticism. Most of her mystical experiences took place during the liturgical offices of the Church which were the mainspring of her spirituality. St Gertrude was one of the first exponents of devotion to the *Sacred Heart, which she believed was revealed to her in several visions, described in her book with great beauty and simplicity. She also wrote a collection of prayers, 'Exercitia Spiritualia', some of which have become very popular in RC piety. She was never formally canonized, but her cult was first authorized in 1606 and extended to the entire RC

Church by *Clement XIII in 1738, and since 1677 she has been included in the *Roman Martyrology. Feast day (since 1932), 16 Nov. She is the patroness of the West Indies.

Her Revelations were first pub., in a partial Ger. tr., along with those of Mechtild of Hackeborn, by M. von Weida, OP [Leipzig, 1505]. The Lat. text was ed. J. Lansperger, O. Cart. (Cologne, 1536). Good edns. of her works by the monks of *Solesmes, *Revelationes Gertrudianae ac Mechtildianae*, 1 (Poitiers and Paris, 1875) and her *Œuvres Spirituelles*, ed., with Fr. tr., by J. Hourlier, OSB, and others (SC 127, 139, 143, 255, and 331; 1967–86), with valuable introd. by P. Doyère, OSB, in vol. 2, pp. 9–91, and bibl. pp. 93–8. There are numerous Eng. tr. of her Revelations; that under the title 'Herald of Divine Love' by M. Winkworth (Classics of Western Spirituality, New York, etc. [1993]) translates bks. 1 and 2 and most of bk. 3. K. Ruh, 'Gertrud von Helfta: Ein neues Gertrud-Bild', *Zeitschrift für deutsches Altertum und deutsche Literatur*, 121 (1992), pp. 1–20. G. J. Lewis, *Bibliographie zur deutschen Frauenmystik des Mittelalters* (Bibliographien zur deutschen Literatur des Mittelalters, 10; 1989), pp. 196–218 (nos. 1616–808). P. Doyère, OSB, in *Dict. Sp.* 6 (1967), cols. 331–9, s.v., with detailed bibl.; id. in *NCE* 6 (1967), pp. 450 f.; K. Grubmüller in *Verfasserlexikon* (2nd edn.), 3 (1981), cols. 7–10, s.v., with bibl.

Gervasius and Protasius, Sts, the proto-martyrs of Milan. When, in 386, St *Ambrose was about to dedicate his new church at Milan, the predecessor of the present S. Ambrogio, he obeyed 'a presentiment' (*cuiusdam ardor praesagii*) and dug in the church of Sts Felix and Nabor in search of relics. Two large skeletons were discovered, perfect except that the heads had been severed. These were recognized as the remains of two early martyrs, Gervasius and Protasius, and were transferred to the new church, whereat, it is recorded, miraculous healings took place, to the discomfiture of the *Arians and the edification of the orthodox. Of Gervasius and Protasius nothing certain is known, though later tradition declared that they had been martyred in the latter half of the 2nd cent. Feast day, 19 June.

Ambrose, *Ep.* 22 (PL 16. 1019–26) [*Ep.* 77 in ed. M. Zelzer, CSEL 82, pt. 3 (1982)]. *AASS*, Jun. 3 (1701), pp. 817–46. H. *Delehaye, 'Quelques dates du martyrologe hiéronymien', *Anal. Boll.* 49 (1931), pp. 22–50, esp. pp. 30–4. J. Doignon, 'Perspectives ambrosiennes: SS. Gervais et Protais, génies de Milan', *Revue des Études Augustiniennes*, 2 (1956), pp. 313–34. M. C. de Azevedo, 'Appunti sulla relazione di S. Ambrogio circa lo scavo del Sepolcro dei SS. Gervasio e Protasio', *Notizie dal Chiostro del Monastero Maggiore: Rassegna di Studi del Civico Museo Archeologico e del Civico Gabinetto Numismatico di Milano*, Anno 1968, pp. 1–9. E. Dassmann, 'Ambrosius und die Märtyrer', *Jahrbuch für Antike und Christentum*, 18 (1975), pp. 49–68, esp. pp. 52–7. U. Zanetti, SJ, 'Les passions des SS. Nazaire, Gervais, Protais et Celse', *Anal. Boll.* 97 (1979), pp. 69–88. V. Zangara, 'L'*inventio* dei corpi dei martiri Gervasio e Protasio. Testimonianze d'Agostino su un fenomeno di religiosità popolare', *Augustinianum*, 21 (1981), pp. 119–33. H. *Leclercq, OSB, in *DACL* 6 (pt. 1; 1924), cols. 1232–9; A. Rimoldi in *Bibliotheca Sanctorum*, 6 (Rome, 1965), cols. 298–302, s.v.

Gesenius, Heinrich Friedrich Wilhelm (1786–1842), orientalist and biblical scholar. From 1811 till his death he was professor of theology at Halle, where he concentrated his attention on problems of Semitic philology and became the most outstanding Hebraist of his generation. In 1810–12 he issued the earliest edition of his celebrated *Heb-*

räisches und chaldäisches Handwörterbuch, which went through many revisions, and formed the basis of the Hebrew Lexicon (1906) of C. A. *Briggs, S. R. *Driver, and F. Brown. This was followed in 1813 by the first edition of his 'Hebrew Grammar' (standard Eng. tr., 1910), and in 1820–1 by his commentary on Isaiah.

T. K. *Cheyne, *Founders of Old Testament Criticism* (1893), pp. 53–65. E. F. Miller, *The Influence of Gesenius on Hebrew Lexicography* (Contributions to Oriental History and Philology, no. 11; New York, 1927). J. [W.] Rogerson, *Old Testament Criticism in the Nineteenth Century: England and Germany* (1984), pp. 50–7. J. Hahn in *TRE* 13 (1984), pp. 39 f., s.v.

Gess, Wolfgang Friedrich (1819–91), German theologian. From his earliest years he possessed a deep faith, built upon an intensive study of the Bible. In 1850 he became professor at the Protestant 'Missionshaus' at Basle, in 1864 ordinary professor of systematic theology at Göttingen, and in 1871 professor at Breslau. From 1880 to 1885 he was *General Superintendent of the province of Posen. He was among the earliest defenders of a *kenotic doctrine of the Incarnation, which he expounded in *Die Lehre von der Person Christi* (1856), his most important work. He claimed to base this teaching (as, indeed, all his theology) on the Bible alone, without reference to the Creeds or other post-biblical authority.

Gess elaborated his views on the Person of Christ further in *Christi Selbstzeugnis* (Basle, 1870) and several later works. W. Schmidt in *PRE* (3rd edn.), 6 (1899), pp. 642–6.

Gestas. See DISMAS.

Gesuati (or, officially, **Clerici apostolici S. Hieronymi**). A congregation of laymen, founded *c.*1360 by Bl John *Colombini (1304–67). They devoted themselves esp. to prayer, mortification, and works of charity, and followed at first the *Benedictine, later the *Augustinian Rule. Their popular name derived from their frequent use of the ejaculations 'Praised be Jesus', or 'Hail Jesus', esp. at the beginning and end of their sermons. Originally a very loosely knit group, they received Papal approbation from *Urban V in 1367 on condition that they established proper monasteries. At the same time they adopted a uniform habit, consisting of a white tunic with a square hood and a greyish-brown cloak. They took only *Minor Orders till 1606, when they were allowed to have one or two priests in each of their convents. After Colombini's death (1367) they spread throughout Italy, and in 1425 founded houses also in Toulouse. They were dissolved by Clement IX in 1668 because they had lost the spirit of their order.

They also had a female institute of contemplative nuns, the 'Jesuatesses' or 'Sisters of the Visitation of Mary', founded *c.*1367 by Colombini's cousin, Catherine Colombini (d. 1367). They led a very austere life and existed as a congregation till 1872.

G. Dufner [OSB], *Geschichte der Jesuaten* (Uomini e Dottrine, 21; Rome, 1975). Id. in *Dict. Sp.* 8 (1974), cols. 392–404, s.v. 'Jean (65) Colombini de Sienne'.

Gethsemane, Garden of. The garden to which the Lord retired with His disciples after the Last Supper and which was the scene of His agony and betrayal (Mt. 26:

36, etc.). It is in the valley between *Jerusalem and the Mount of *Olives, just across the brook *Cedron. The traditional site is now in *Franciscan hands.

G. Orfali, OFM, *Gethsémani, ou Notice sur l'Église de l'Agonie de la Prière, d'après les fouilles récentes accomplies par la custodie franciscaine de Terre Sainte, 1909 et 1920* (1924); [L.] H. Vincent, OP, and F. M. Abel, OP, *Jérusalem*, 2 (1914–26), pp. 301–27, with appendix on 'L'Église primitive de Gethsémani', pp. 1007–13. C. Kopp, *Die heiligen Stätten der Evangelien* (Regensburg, 1959), pp. 387–99; Eng. tr. (1963), pp. 335–50. E. Power, SJ, in *Dict. Bibl.*, Suppl., 3 (1938), cols. 632–59, s.v.

Geulincx, Arnold (1624–69), Belgian philosopher. A native of Antwerp, he studied philosophy and theology at Louvain (1641–6), where he became professor of philosophy in 1646. In 1658 he was deprived of his chair on account of his attacks on Scholasticism and monasticism. In the same year he went to *Leiden, where he became a *Calvinist. In 1662 he was made a lecturer on logic, and professor of philosophy in 1665. Among the works that appeared during his lifetime are *Quaestiones Quodlibeticae* (1653), *Logica* (1662 and 1668), *Methodus* (1663), and *Ethica* (1666). His more important works, however, namely the Γνῶθι σεαυτόν, *sive Ethica* (1675), and the *Metaphysica Vera* (1691), were posthumous.

Starting from R. *Descartes's distinction between body and thought, Geulincx was led to develop the theory known as '*Occasionalism', denying any action of bodies on bodies or bodies on spirits or spirits on bodies, and consequently all movements produced by our will. God is the sole cause of all movement and of all thought, all secondary causes, acc. to Geulincx, being illusory. As man is incapable of exercising any activity whatever on the outside world or on his own body, on each 'occasion' of a bodily event God causes the corresponding feeling in the soul and vice versa, and thereby everything is immediately subjected to God. The human will, which is capable of making a voluntary effort towards the good, has only an appearance of freedom, for the resulting activity, whether it be success or failure, depends on God alone. Man can thus in fact achieve nothing of himself. He is a spectator of what God works in him, the greatest virtue being a resigned and humble submission to all that happens. God himself, however, is wholly inaccessible to man, and in order to lead the moral life man must turn to the Divine in himself, i.e. the human reason by which he participates in the Divine nature. This combination of a rigorous determinism with an almost pantheistic exaltation of reason, which was one of the main features of Geulincx's thought, was later developed by N. *Malebranche and B. *Spinoza.

Complete Works, ed. J. P. N. Land (3 vols., The Hague, 1891–3). V. van der Haeghen, *Geulincx: Études sur sa vie, sa philosophie et ses œuvres* (Ghent, 1886); J. P. N. Land, 'Arnold Geulincx and his Works', *Mind*, 16 (1891), pp. 223–42; id., *Arnold Geulincx und seine Philosophie* (1895). E. Pfleiderer, *Arnold Geulinx als Hauptvertreter der okkasionalistischen Metaphysik und Ethik* (1882); E. Terraillon, *La Morale de Geulincx dans ses rapports avec la philosophie de Descartes* (1912). G. Schmitz, 'Geulincx und die Bewegung des Pur Amour', *Zeitschrift für Religions- und Geistesgeschichte*, 3 (1951), pp. 209–19. W. Doney in P. Edwards (ed.), *The Encyclopedia of Philosophy*, 3 (1967), pp. 323–5, s.v.

Geyler von Kaisersberg. See GEILER VON KAISERSBERG.

Ghana, Christianity in. The name 'Ghana' was taken on independence in 1957 by the former British colonial territory of Gold Coast in W. Africa. This had been constituted by successive 19th-cent. annexations: the coastal Fante states, the inland confederation of states known as Ashante, and various territories northward, augmented in 1918 by part of the German colony of Togo.

Christian activity dates from the arrival of the Portuguese on the coast in 1471. Despite periodic conversions, RCs were still a small community when the Dutch took over Portuguese interests in 1642. For the next two centuries several European powers had coastal trading sectors. Among chaplains appointed to these were two Fante ministers: J. E. J. Capitein (1717–47) of the Dutch Reformed Church and the Anglican Philip Quaque (1741–1816). Following transient *Pietist and *Moravian missions, sustained missionary work began when the Swiss-based Basel Mission entered the Danish sector in 1828. In 1835 a Bible-reading group formed by a pupil of Quaque invited the *Wesleyan Methodists. The North German (Bremen) Mission followed in 1847. Missions, favoured by the increasingly dominant British, prospered in the Fante south. Ashante was more resistant, and British conquest in 1896 prob. stiffened opposition to Christianity. The Basel Mission, which introduced West Indian missionaries, stimulated agricultural and commercial development and did excellent linguistic work. Western education, provided by all missions, produced active Church leadership and, increasingly, articulate criticism of colonial rule. RC missions returned: the Society of *African Missions in 1880 and the *White Fathers (esp. interested in the Northern territories) in 1913. During the First World War the missionaries from continental Europe were expelled, and the *United Free Church of Scotland provided a partial substitute. Education and other institutions suffered, but Church membership increased under local leadership. In addition, preachers without missionary tutelage, emulating Prophet W. W. *Harris, caused large movements towards Christianity; Sampson Oppong (1890?–1965) deeply affected parts of Ashante and John Swatson (*fl.* 1914–24) much enlarged the small Anglican mission. Where Christianity was longer established, Churches stressing prophecy and healing (e.g. the Musama Disco Cristo Church and the Church of the Twelve Apostles) developed, incorporating elements of traditional culture.

The pioneers of Ghanaian independence were mostly influenced by Christianity, and the Churches have been able to resist several acts of state power. Contemporary Ghanaian Christianity (strong in the South, very limited in the North) is diversified, with new denominations and *charismatic and para-church movements in addition to the historic Churches deriving from the older missions.

W. H. Debrunner, *A History of Christianity in Ghana* (Accra, 1967). R. M. Wiltgen, SVD, *Gold Coast Mission History 1471–1880* (Techny, Ill., 1956). W. Schlatter, *Geschichte der Basler Mission, 1815–1915* (3 vols., Basle, 1916; vol. 4, *Geschichte der Basler Mission, 1914–1919*, posthumously ed. H. W. Witschi [1965]), vol. 1 *passim*; vol. 3, pp. 19–195; vol. 4, esp. pp. 40–6 and 162–95. F. L. Bartels, *The Roots of Ghana Methodism* (Cambridge, 1965). N. Smith, *The Presbyterian Church of Ghana, 1835–1900* (Accra, 1966). C. G. Baëta, *Prophetism in Ghana: A Study of some 'Spiritual' Churches* (London, 1962); D. M. Beckmann, *Eden Revival: Spiritual Churches in Ghana* (St Louis and London [1975]). S. G. Williamson, *Akan Religion and the Christian Faith*, ed. K. A.

Dickson (Accra, 1965), esp. pp. 3–82. W. H. Mobley, *The Ghanaian's Image of the Missionary: An analysis of the published critiques of Christian missionaries by Ghanaians 1897–1965* (Studies on Religion in Africa, 1; Leiden, 1970).

Ghéon, Henri, pseudonym of Henri Léon Vangeon (1875–1944), French Catholic writer. The son of a chemist, he became a doctor by profession. He was brought up as a Catholic by his mother, but at the age of *c*.15 appears to have lost all faith, until the death of his niece and other friends precipitated his reconciliation (1914). He published his first collection of verse in 1897 and in 1909 he was among the founders of the *Nouvelle Revue Française. Le Pain*, his first play to be publicly performed (8 Nov. 1911), was a popular tragedy written in verse. His first two specifically Christian dramas, however, *Trois Miracles de sainte Cécile* and *Le Pauvre sous l'escalier*, both 1921, were failures, a fact which convinced him of the need to appeal to a wider Catholic public. He devoted himself to the task of building up a Christian theatre, producing his own plays and working with a company of young Catholics founded by himself in 1924 under the title 'Les Compagnons de Notre-Dame' and from 1931 with their successors 'Les Compagnons de Jeux'. Many of his works had kinship with the 15th-cent. *Mystery Plays. Their subject was the Lives of the Saints and other sacred themes and their deliberate *naïveté* of tone was an attempt to reproduce the atmosphere of medieval hagiography. They include *La Vie profonde de S. François d'Assise* (written 1925), *Le Mystère du Roi S. Louis* (1931), *Le Mystère de l'invention de la Croix* (1932; Eng. tr., 1956), *Mystère des prodiges de Notre-Dame de Verdun* (1937), and *Le Jeu de S. Laurent de Fleuve* (1938). Henri Ghéon's biographies, which combined the freshness of his plays with a higher standard of authenticity, appealed to a wide public; they included Lives of the *Curé d'Ars (1928; Eng. tr., 1929), of St *Teresa of Lisieux (1934; Eng. tr., 1935), of St John *Bosco (1935; Eng. tr., 1935), of St *Vincent Ferrer (1939; Eng. tr., 1939), and of St *Martin of Tours (1941; Eng. tr., 1946). He also wrote the script for a film on John Bosco (1936), novels and literary criticism.

H. Ghéon and A. Gide, *Correspondance 1897–1944*, ed. J. Tipsy (2 vols., Paris, 1976). M. Deléglise, *Le Théâtre d'Henri Ghéon: Contribution à l'étude du renouveau théâtral* (Sion, 1947).

ghetto. In former times the street or quarter of a city in which the Jewish population customarily lived. The word is perhaps a shortened form of the Ital. diminutive *borghetto*, 'small borough'. The earliest ghettos were found in the Italian cities of the 11th cent., but they became common in the later Middle Ages, and in 1556 *Paul IV established a ghetto in Rome which was not finally abolished until 1870. As a general rule the Jews were not allowed to leave the ghetto, which was commonly surrounded by walls and gates, at night or on Christian holy days. The ghettos were often self-governing. Ghettos of great importance existed at *Venice, Frankfurt, Prague, and Trieste. In modern times the word has often been used loosely of any close settlement of a minority group.

Gibbon, Edward (1737–94), historian of the later Roman Empire. He was born at Putney. His weak constitution prevented normal schooling, but he was an omnivorous

reader. He was educated at Westminster and in 1752, at the early age of 15, sent to Magdalen College, Oxford, where he was converted to the RC Church (1753). To detach him from Catholicism, his father placed him with M. Pavilliard, a *Calvinist minister at Lausanne, where by wide and systematic reading of the Latin classics and French literature Gibbon laid the foundations of his vast erudition. He reverted to Protestantism in 1754 and returned to England in 1758. In 1761 he published his *Essai sur l'étude de la littérature*, defending the study of classical literature. From 1763 to 1765 he travelled on the Continent, visiting France, Switzerland, and Italy. On 15 Oct. 1764, at Rome, as he 'sat musing amidst the ruins of the Capitol', he conceived the plan of the *Decline and Fall of the Roman Empire*, which was to occupy him for almost all the rest of his life. Vol. 1, which was published in 1776, had an immediate success. Vols. 2 and 3 followed in 1781. Gibbon was MP for Liskeard (1774–80) and Lymington (1781–3). In 1783 he returned to Lausanne, where by 1787 he had completed the last three volumes (pub. 1788). In 1788–9 he began his *Memoirs* (posthumously pub. 1796). Returning to England in 1793, he died on 16 Jan. 1794.

The *Decline and Fall* remains unchallenged as a history of the later Roman Empire on the grand scale. It is based on a wide study of original sources, supplemented by the researches of such French and Italian historians as L. S. Le N. de *Tillemont, J. *Mabillon, B. *Montfaucon, and L. A. *Muratori. Its breadth of treatment, large perspectives, meticulous accuracy, and its author's mastery of style are among its principal merits. In chs. 15 and 16 of vol. 1, the rapid growth of early Christianity is ascribed to five causes, namely the intolerant zeal of its adherents, the doctrine of an afterlife, the miraculous powers ascribed to the early Church, the pure morals of its members, and the discipline it enforced; and the violent controversy provoked by Gibbon's hostile attitude echoes still. The history of the Byzantine Empire is a medley of superstition and crime, while the Middle Ages are the 'triumph of barbarism and religion'. All supernatural considerations are treated with bitter irony and ridicule; but Gibbon's indirect method avoided the prosecution to which an open attack on Christianity would have exposed him.

The best edn. of the *Decline and Fall* is that of J. B. Bury (7 vols., 1896–1900). *Miscellaneous Works of Edward Gibbon with Memoirs of his Life and Writings* (3 vols., 1796–1815). Crit. edns. of his *Memoirs* by G. A. Bonnard (1966) and of his *Letters* by J. E. Norton (3 vols., 1956). Studies by H. H. *Milman (London, 1839), G. M. Young (ibid., 1932), and J. W. Swain (ibid., 1966); also introd. by J. W. Burrow, *Gibbon* (Past Masters, Oxford, 1985). P. B. Craddock, *Young Edward Gibbon* (Baltimore and London [1982]); id., *Edward Gibbon, Luminous Historian 1772–1794* (ibid. [1989]). S. T. McCloy, *Gibbon's Antagonism to Christianity* (1933). H. L. Bond, *The Literary Art of Edward Gibbon* (Oxford, 1960). P. Ducrey (ed.), *Gibbon et Rome à la lumière de l'historiographie moderne* (Université de Lausanne, Publications de la Faculté des Lettres, 22; Geneva, 1977); G. W. Bowersock and others (eds.), *Edward Gibbon and the Decline and Fall of the Roman Empire* (Cambridge, Mass., and London, 1977); [J.] L. Gossman, *The Empire Unpossess'd: An Essay on Gibbon's* Decline and Fall (Cambridge, 1981); R. Porter, *Edward Gibbon: Making History* (1988). D. Womersley, *The Transformation of* The Decline and Fall of the Roman Empire (Cambridge Studies in Eighteenth-Century English Literature and Thought, 1; 1988). J. E. Norton, *A Bibliography of the Works of Edward Gibbon* (Oxford, 1940); G. [L.] Keynes, *The Library of Edward Gibbon: A Catalogue of his*

Books (1940), with introd., pp. 11–36. P. B. Craddock, *Edward Gibbon, A Reference Guide* (Boston [1987]). L. Stephen in *DNB* 21 (1890), pp. 250–6.

Giberti, Gian Matteo (1495–1543), Bp. of *Verona. He was one of the leading advocates in Italy of ecclesiastical reform who prepared the way for the Council of *Trent. Patronized by Cardinal Giulio de' Medici (the future *Clement VII), whose secretary he became, in 1521 he was sent as envoy to *Charles V and in 1524 became Bp. of Verona. He was a trusted counsellor of Clement VII and *Paul III, and in 1536 was appointed to sit on the reforming commission known as the 'consilium de emendanda ecclesia'. He also produced some good editions of various patristic writings (e.g. of *Chrysostom and *John of Damascus).

Works (Constitutiones Gibertinae, Costituzioni per le monache, Monitiones generales, Edita selecta, Lettere scelte, etc.), ed. P. and H. *Ballerini (Verona, 1733). Life by G. B. Pighi (ibid., 1900; 2nd edn., 1924). A. Grazioli, *Gian Matteo Giberti, vescovo di Verona, precursore della riforma del Concilio di Trento* (ibid., 1955). A. Prosperi, *Tra Evangelismo e Controriforma: G. M. Giberti (1495–1543)* (Uomini e Dottrine, 16; 1969).

Gibraltar in Europe, Diocese of. See EUROPE, DIOCESE IN.

Gibson, Edmund (1669–1748), Bp. of London. A native of Bampton, Cumbria, he was educated at Queen's College, Oxford, where he was elected a taberdar in 1690. His early publications included editions of the Anglo-Saxon Chronicle (1692), of Quintilian's *De Institutione Oratoria* (1693), and of W. Camden's *Britannia* (1695). In 1696 he was appointed by T. *Tenison *Lambeth Librarian, and in 1697 ordained priest. In 1698 he edited the posthumous works of Sir Henry Spelman (*Reliquiae Spelmannianae*) on the laws and antiquities of England. He entered the lists against F. *Atterbury in the *Convocation controversy, upholding the archbishop's prerogatives over both Houses. A fruit of the controversy was his standard manual *Synodus Anglicana; or the Constitution and Proceedings of an English Convocation* (1702; new edn. by E. *Cardwell, 1854). In 1703 he became Canon of *Chichester and rector of Lambeth. After prolonged studies he issued in 1713 his *magnum opus*, the *Codex Iuris Ecclesiastici Anglicani* (2nd edn., 1761), still the most complete collection of English ecclesiastical documents. On W. *Wake's translation to *Canterbury, Gibson succeeded him as Bp. of *Lincoln (1716), himself being translated to London in 1723. A *High Church Whig, he laboured to reconcile the clergy, nearly all Tories, to the house of Hanover, and he was the driving force behind the foundation of the Regius Professorships in Modern History at Oxford and Cambridge. Until 1736 he was constantly consulted over ecclesiastical appointments by Robert Walpole, but his opposition to the Quakers' Relief Bill (designed to reform the method of collecting tithe and Church rate from *Quakers) lost him Walpole's sympathy and any chance of the primacy on Wake's death in 1737. Theologically Gibson upheld orthodoxy, writing against the *Latitudinarians and the *Deists. At first he was relatively tolerant of the *Methodists, but later he became bitterly antipathetic and denounced them. He ruled his two dioceses energetically and efficiently, and

actively promoted the religious welfare of the American colonists, then under the jurisdiction of the see of London. His later publications include *A Preservative against Popery* (3 vols., 1738), a collection of controversial treatises, mainly from the time of *James II.

N. Sykes, *Edmund Gibson: A Study in Politics and Religion in the Eighteenth Century* (1926). Id., *From Sheldon to Secker* (Ford Lectures, 1958; Cambridge, 1959), esp. pp. 192–210.

Gichtel, Johann Georg (1638–1710), German sectarian. A native of Ratisbon in Bavaria and of Protestant upbringing, he came under the influence of Dutch visionaries and, exiled from Ratisbon, spent most of his life in Amsterdam. Here he read the writings of J. *Boehme, which he esteemed as highly as the Bible and of which he made the first complete edition in 1682. He himself became the founder of a small sect which condemned marriage and Church services, and which had followers in the Netherlands and Germany until modern times.

The 1779 edn. of Gichtel's *Theosophia Practica* (orig. pub. as *Eine kurze Eröffnung und Anweisung der drei Prinzipien und Welten im Menschen*, 1696) was repr., with introd. by G. Wehr (Freiburg i.B., 1979). B. Gorceix, *Johann Georg Gichtel: Théosophe d'Amsterdam* [Lausanne, 1975]. A. W. Hegler in *PRE* (3rd edn.), 6 (1899), pp. 657–60, s.v.

Gidding, Little. See LITTLE GIDDING.

Gideon Bibles. Bibles placed in hotel bedrooms and other places by an organization of Christian business and professional men and their wives. The Gideons were founded by a small group of commercial travellers in Janesville, Wisconsin, in 1899; they took their name from Gideon, whose victory against overwhelming odds is recorded in Jgs. 6: 11–7: 25, and adopted as their badge a gold circle with a white pitcher on a blue background, with a red flame coming out of the top of the pitcher. This badge enabled the Gideons to recognize each other and was later incorporated on to the Bibles they distributed. The idea of distributing Bibles came from a Christian Association for Commercial Travellers in Britain which had been placing wholesome literature, including Bibles, in the hotels frequented by its members for some 30 years. In 1908 the Gideons pledged themselves to the task of placing Bibles in every hotel in the USA. The Bibles they distributed contained a page of notes on suggested reading as well as the address in Chicago (later Nashville) of the headquarters of the Gideons who were willing to follow up inquiries through their local members. In 1947 the Gideons International Extension Committee was formed. The British Gideons were launched in 1949 (with headquarters at Lutterworth since 1974) and Gideons have been established throughout the English-speaking world. Until 1974 the AV was used exclusively, but now the New International Version and the New King James Version are also available. Bibles are now widely distributed in prison cells, schools, hospitals, and the Armed Forces, as well as to hotels.

P. Thompson, *The Gideons: The story of The Gideons International in the British Isles* (1984).

Gifford Lectures. The series of lectures delivered in the Scottish universities under the foundation of Adam Gifford, Lord Gifford (1820–87), 'for promoting, advancing, teaching, and diffusing the study of natural theology, in the widest sense of that term, in other words, the knowledge of God' and 'of the foundation of ethics'. The first course was delivered in 1888. Notable Gifford Lecturers (with their years of tenure) include J. Ward (1896–8), R. B. Haldane (1902–4), B. *Bosanquet (1911–12), A. S. Pringle-*Pattison (1912–13), A. J. *Balfour (1914 and 1922–3), S. Alexander (1916–18), W. R. *Inge (1917–18), C. C. J. *Webb (1918–20), F. *von Hügel (1924–6), É. *Gilson (1931–2), E. R. Bevan (1932–4), W. *Temple (1932–4), K. *Barth (1937–8), R. *Niebuhr (1939), C. Dawson (1947–8), G. Marcel (1949–50), V. A. Demant (1956–8), H. D. Lewis (1966–8), E. L. Mascall (1968–70), and R. W. Southern (1970–2).

S. L. Jaki, *Lord Gifford and his Lectures: A Centenary Retrospect* (Edinburgh and Macon, Ga., 1986).

Gilbert Foliot. See FOLIOT, GILBERT.

Gilbert de la Porrée (Porreta) (d. 1154), biblical commentator and early scholastic theologian. Born *c*.1080 or slightly later, he was a pupil of *Bernard of Chartres and of *Anselm of Laon. He became chancellor of *Chartres and an influential master in Paris, before becoming Bp. of Poitiers in 1142. His earliest works were his commentaries on the Psalter, undertaken in the school of Laon, and on the Pauline Epistles. These commentaries were sometimes cited as the middle gloss (*media glosatura*), i.e. between those of Anselm of Laon and *Peter Lombard. The work for which he is chiefly remembered is his commentary on the theological *opuscula* of *Boethius. The language used in this work on the question of reconciling the statements 'God is one' and 'God is three' aroused violent opposition, and Gilbert was summoned to appear before the Council of Reims in 1148. Despite strong pressure from St *Bernard of Clairvaux, there was no formal condemnation. Gilbert, like many of his contemporaries, was deeply interested in language and logic. He was attempting to make his distinctions clear, and was not so much concerned to show that they were verified in reality. In some fields of theology this had fruitful results, e.g. in the development of methods of theological inquiry, and in clarifying concepts, such as the power of the sacraments, but for the consideration of the doctrine of the Trinity it led to serious misunderstandings. Gilbert was clearly a very inspiring teacher, and the views of his followers, the Porretani, are often cited by 12th cent. theologians. As late as the third quarter of the 12th cent. a small group of writers, of whom the chief was Adhémar, canon of St Ruf, was obstinately searching for materials to justify Gilbert's statements on the Trinity. The second canon of the Fourth *Lateran Council (1215), in which the formulation of Peter Lombard was promulgated, put an end to these attempts. Gilbert has in the past been credited with the authorship of the 'Liber sex Principiorum', which is found in MSS of the 13th cent. onwards incorporated in *Aristotle's 'Organon'; it is now clear that it is not his work.

Gilbert's comm. on four of Boethius' *Opuscula Sacra* first pr. among Boethius' works, Basle, 1570, pp. 1119–273; repr. J. P. Migne, *PL* 64. 1255–412; crit. edn. by N. M. Häring, SAC (Pontifical Institute of Mediaeval Studies, Studies and Texts, 13; Toronto, 1966). Comm. on 1 Cor. ed. A. M. Landgraf (ST 117;

1945). A set of *Sententie* ed. N. M. Häring in *AHDLMA* 45, for 1978 (1979), pp. 83–180, and 46 for 1979 (1980), pp. 45–105. The 'Liber Sex Principiorum' is pr. by L. Minio-Paluello (*Aristoteles Latinus*, Ser. 1, 6–7, Bruges and Paris, 1966, pp. 33–59, with index pp. 123–32). *John of Salisbury, *Historia Pontificalis*, 8–14 (ed., with Eng. tr., by M. Chibnall, Nelson's Medieval Texts, 1956, pp. 15–41). A. Hayen, SJ, 'Le Concile de Reims et l'erreur théologique de Gilbert de la Porrée' in *AHDLMA* 10 (1936), pp. 29–102; M. E. Williams, *The Teaching of Gilbert Porreta on the Trinity, as found in his commentaries on Boethius* (Analecta Gregoriana, 56; 1951); H. C. van Elswijk, OP, *Gilbert Porreta: Sa vie, son œuvre, sa pensée* (SSL 33; 1966), with bibl. L. O. Nielsen, *Theology and Philosophy in the Twelfth Century: A Study of Gilbert Porreta's Thinking and the Theological Expositions of the Doctrine of the Incarnation during the Period 1130–1180* (Acta Theologica Danica, 15; Leiden, 1982). J. Marenbon in [E.] P. [M.] Dronke (ed.), *A History of Twelfth-Century Western Philosophy* (Cambridge, 1988), pp. 328–57. A. Dondaine, OP, *Écrits de la 'Petite École' Porrétaine* (Conférence Albert le Grand, 1962; Montreal and Paris, 1962). N. M. Haring in *NCE* 6 (1967), pp. 478 f., s.v.

Gilbert of Sempringham, St (*c*.1083–1189), founder of the Gilbertine Order. While parish priest of his native *Sempringham, he encouraged seven women of his flock to adopt a rule of life on a *Cistercian model, and about a year later, with the support of Alexander, Bp. of *Lincoln, received their profession. He soon associated with them companies of lay sisters and lay brothers to assist with the manual work of the community. Their numbers grew; in 1139 a second foundation was established; and further foundations followed. In 1147 Gilbert journeyed to Cîteaux, seeking the incorporation of his nuns in the Cistercian Order; but when the chapter declined to govern communities of women, Gilbert returned and arranged for the spiritual direction of his communities by *Canons Regular who followed the *Augustinian Rule. Henceforward his communities took the form of a double order. In 1148 Gilbert had received Papal approbation of his work. The only purely English order, it rapidly grew, and at the time of Gilbert's death numbered nine double monasteries and four of canons only. King Henry II was a friend and supporter of Gilbert, and English kings continued to favour the Order throughout the Middle Ages. At the Dissolution they possessed some 25 houses, which were surrendered to the Crown without resistance. Feast day, 4 Feb.

The Life, miracles, and canonization dossier compiled by an unknown canon of the Order in the early 13th cent. was known as the 'Book of St Gilbert'; ed., with modern Eng. tr. and full introd., by R. Foreville and G. Keir (Oxford Medieval Texts, 1987). Gilbertine Rule in W. *Dugdale, *Monasticon Anglicanum*, 6 (pt. 2; ed. 1830), pp. *xxix–*xcix (between pp. 946 and 947). R. Graham, *S. Gilbert of Sempringham and the Gilbertines* (1901), esp. pp. 1–28; B. Golding, *Gilbert of Sempringham and the Gilbertine Order c.1130–c.1300* (Oxford, 1995), esp. pp. 1–70. G. Constable, 'Aelred of Rievaulx and the Nun of Watton: an episode in the early history of the Gilbertine Order', in D. Baker (ed.), *Medieval Women* (Studies in Church History, Subsidia, 1; Oxford, 1978), pp. 205–26. B. Golding, 'The Distortion of a Dream: Transformations and Mutations of the Rule of St Gilbert', *Word and Spirit*, 11 (1989), pp. 60–78. R. Foreville in *Dict. Sp.* 6 (1967), cols. 374–6, s.v. 'Gilbert (4) de Sempringham'.

Gildas, St (6th cent.), British monk and historian. Little is known of his life and background; recent research has sought such information in the text of his own work rather than in the much later, and unreliable, Lives (though one of these plausibly indicates that he came from Strathclyde). It appears that he received his education in late-Roman schools, and he was expert in the literary fashions of his time; his complex and often convoluted word order and a correct but frequently tortuous late-Latin style sometimes make his meaning difficult to discern.

His famous history, *De Excidio et Conquestu Britanniae ac flebili Castigatione in Reges, Principes et Sacerdotes* was written (apparently in S. Wales) primarily as a denunciation of the evils (notably British treachery and the destruction of towns and killing of clergy) which accompanied the subversion of sub-Roman Britain by the invading pagan English between *c*.450 and *c*.550, but it has been used in efforts to discover the sequence and manner in which that subversion took place. He was the only contemporary writer who attempted, within the confines of the hortatory genre, a general survey of British history from the latter days of Roman rule until *c*.550, and he is a valuable, though difficult, witness for the background of society in Britain (mainly in the west) in the century following the third consulship of Aetius (446–53); faith in his reliability for contemporary events has been undermined by his obvious ignorance and errors about past events of which he had no direct knowledge. He may have had access to official documents, but he preserves a partial account of only one, gives only one, muddled, indication of the chronology of his own life, and names (with insufficient detail) only five of the 'tyranni' under whom sub-Roman Britain and whatever ecclesiastical institutions it possessed collapsed. It is not now thought that he wrote the Penitential attributed to him, but fragments of letters by him survive. Feast day, 29 Jan.

Crit. edn. of Gildas's 'De Excidio' by T. *Mommsen in *MGH*, Auctores Antiquissimi, 13 [= Chronica Minora, 3] (1896), pp. 25–85; other works, pp. 86–90. The 'De Excidio' and fragments of letters are repr. from this edn., with variants and Eng. tr. by M. Winterbottom (London and Chichester, 1978), which also repr. the edn. and Eng. tr. of the so-called Penitential of Gildas from the edn. of the Irish Penitentials by L. Bieler (see PENITENTIAL BOOKS). The 11th-cent. Life of Gildas by a monk of Ruys in Brittany, ed. T. Mommsen, loc. cit., pp. 91–106; 12th cent. Life by Caradoc of Llancarvan ibid., pp. 107–10; introd., pp. 3–24. C. E. Stevens, 'Gildas Sapiens', *EHR* 56 (1941), pp. 353–73; T. D. O'Sullivan, *The De Excidio of Gildas: Its Authenticity and Date* (Columbia Studies in the Classical Tradition, 7; Leiden, 1978). M. Lapidge and D. Dumville (eds.), *Gildas: New Approaches* (Studies in Celtic History, Woodbridge, Suffolk, 1984). F. Kerlouégan, *Le De Excidio Britanniae de Gildas* (1987). A. Gransden, *Historical Writing in England c.550 to c.1307* (1974), pp. 1–5. J. N. L. Myres, *The English Settlements* (Oxford History of England, 1986), pp. 8–20. T. F. Tout in *DNB* 21 (1890), pp. 344–6, s.v.

Giles, St (? 8th cent.), Lat. *Aegidius*. One of the 14 *Auxiliary Saints. Acc. to a 10th-cent. biography, St Giles was an Athenian who fled to France from the admiration of his countrymen and made himself a hermitage in a forest near the mouth of the Rhône, where he lived on herbs and the milk of a hind. Once when Flavius Wamba, King of the Visigoths, was hunting in the forest, the monarch chased the hind to the abode of the hermit and was so impressed by Giles's holiness that he built him a monastery. Though the medieval account, which makes him an Athenian and connects him with persons as far apart in

time as St *Caesarius of Arles (d. 542) and *Charlemagne (d. 814), is clearly unhistorical, it may contain a basis of real fact. A 9th-cent. Papal bull mentions Wamba as having founded an abbey for him, to which a charter was given by Benedict II (684–5). Later on, the town of St Gilles, which grew up near his grave, became a famous place of pilgrimage. He was one of the most popular medieval saints, and in England alone 160 churches were dedicated to him. He was invoked as their patron by cripples, beggars, and blacksmiths. Feast day, 1 Sept.

The principal authority is an anonymous Lat. Life pr. in *AASS*, Sept. 1 (1746), pp. 299–304, with introd. and brief extracts of his miracles (see below), pp. 284–99; another recension of the Life is pr., with introd., in *Anal. Boll.* 8 (1889), pp. 102–20. The *Liber Miraculorum Sancti Aegidii*, written before 1124, ed. in full by P. Jaffé in *MGH*, Scriptores, 12 (1861), pp. 316–23; also pr. in *Anal. Boll.* 9 (1890), pp. 393–422. *BHL* 1, pp. 17 f. (nos. 93–8); *novum suppl.* (1986), pp. 13 f. E. Rembry, *Saint Gilles: Sa vie, ses reliques, son culte en Belgique et dans le nord de la France* (2 vols., bound in 1, Bruges, 1881–2); E. C. Jones, *Saint Gilles: Essai d'histoire littéraire* (Paris thesis, 1914). F. Brittain, *Saint Giles* (Cambridge, 1928). J. Pycke in *DHGE* 20 (1984), cols. 1352–6, s.v. 'Gilles (2)', with extensive bibl.

Giles of Rome (d. 1316; born *c*.1243–7), otherwise 'Aegidius Romanus', medieval philosopher. He was born at Rome, perhaps descended from the *Colonna family. At an early age he became an *Augustinian Hermit at *Paris and attracted attention by his intellectual gifts, which later won him the surname of 'doctor fundatissimus'. From 1269 to 1271 he had as his teacher St *Thomas Aquinas. In 1292 he was elected *General of his order, which he strove to extend by the foundation of many convents. In 1295 *Boniface VIII made him Abp. of Bourges.

Giles was a very fertile author whose writings include commentaries on *Aristotle's 'Physics', the 'De Anima', and the '*Liber de Causis', and on *Peter Lombard's 'Sentences'; treatises against the *Averroists, on *angels, and on *Original Sin; and exegetical writings on several Pauline Epp. and on St John's Gospel. His most popular work, which was translated into many languages, was the 'De Regimine Principum' written for his pupil, the future King Philip the Fair. His treatise 'De Summi Pontificis Potestate' may have been the foundation of Boniface VIII's famous bull '*Unam Sanctam' (q.v.). In his teaching Giles of Rome followed St Thomas on such points as the unity of the substantial form and the real distinction between essence and existence in creatures, but against him he maintained the primacy of will over reason and denied that before the Fall *Adam possessed sanctifying grace. His teaching, both past and future (*sententias scriptas et scribendas*), was prescribed to be followed in the schools of the Augustinian Order in 1287.

His writings were widely pr. in the 15th and 16th cents. For bibl. details, see G. Boffito, *Saggio di bibliografia egidiana* (Florence, 1911), G. Bruni, *Le opere di Egidio Romano* (1936), and id., 'Saggio bibliografico sulle opere stampate di Egidio Romano', *Analecta Augustiniana*, 24 (1961), pp. 331–55. Crit. edn. of his *Opera Omnia* by F. del Punta and others (Unione Accademica Nazionale, Corpus Philosophorum Medii Aevi, Testi e Studi, 4–8, 10–11, etc.; Florence, 1985 ff.). Separate modern edns. of 'De Ecclesiastica Potestate' by R. Scholz (Weimar, 1929); 'Theoremata de Esse et Essentia', with introd., by E. Hocedez, SJ (Museum Lessianum, Section Philosophique, 12; 1930); and 'De Erroribus Philosophorum' by J. Koch, with Eng. tr. (Milwaukee, 1944).

Eng. tr. of 'De Ecclesiastica Potestate', with introd. and notes, by R. W. Dyson (Woodbridge, Suffolk, and Dover, NH, 1986). E. Hocedez, SJ, 'La Condamnation de Gilles de Rome', *RTAM* 4 (1932), pp. 34–58; P. W. Nash, SJ, 'Giles of Rome on Boethius' "Diversum est esse et id quod est" ', *Mediaeval Studies*, 12 (1950), pp. 57–91, with full notes; id., 'The Accidentality of Esse according to Giles of Rome', *Gregorianum*, 38 (1957), pp. 103–15. M. A. Hewson, *Giles of Rome and the Medieval Theory of Conception: A Study of the* De formatione corporis humani in utero (1975). J. F. Wippel, 'The Relationship between Essence and Existence in Late-Thirteenth-Century Thought: Giles of Rome, Henry of Ghent, Godfrey of Fontaines, and James of Viterbo', in P. Morewedge (ed.), *Philosophies of Existence, Ancient and Medieval* (New York, 1982), pp. 131–64, esp. pp. 134–41 and 152–8. N. Merlin in *DTC* 6 (1920), cols. 1358–65, s.v. 'Gilles de Rome'; A. Trape in *EC* 5 (1951), cols. 138–41, s.v. 'Egidio Romano', with good bibl.; D. Gutiérrez in *Dict. Sp.* 6 (1967), cols. 385–90, s.v. 'Gilles (3) de Rome'; P. W. Nash in *NCE* 6 (1967), pp. 484 f.

Gilgamesh, Epics of. The Babylonian Gilgamesh Epic is a long, composite narrative poem known from tablets and fragments dating from *c.*1800 to *c.*300 BC. These come from several editions, none of them surviving complete. A single edition circulated in the first millennium BC. This is divided into twelve tablets, though the final one does not belong with the others, but is the second half of a Sumerian Gilgamesh Epic in Babylonian translation. The Babylonian versions were preceded by five Sumerian Gilgamesh Epics, each devoted to a single episode. Two of these form the basis of the Babylonian text, preceded and followed by other material (incl. the *flood story) and elaborated with considerable literary skill. The story centres on Gilgamesh's fear of death, which he first counters by performing a heroic deed (to achieve the immortality of fame). Then the death of his close friend Enkidu intensifies his fear and he resolves to achieve personal immortality. In this he fails and has to be content that his fame will survive him. Two scenes from the stories are depicted in ancient art. Gilgamesh was certainly a historical figure who ruled the Sumerian city of Uruk (Erech/Warka) in the first half of the third millennium BC. He was deified shortly after his death and continued in tradition as a netherworld god. Apart from the flood story, no other parts of this tradition are related to the Bible, though the opening episode, the civilizing of Enkidu, deals with questions which are also taken up in the story of the Garden of *Eden. However, the name 'Gilgamesh' occurs in the *Dead Sea Scrolls in a context of giants.

Best edn. of the Babylonian text, with transliteration and notes, by R. Campbell Thompson (Oxford, 1930). Crit. edn. of all the texts by A. R. George is in preparation. Eng. trs. by A. Heidel, *The Gilgamesh Epic and Old Testament Parallels* (Chicago, 1946), pp. 16–101, and by M. G. Kovacs (Stanford, Calif., 1989). P. Garelli (ed.), *Gilgameš et sa légende: Études recueillies . . . à l'occasion de la VIIe Rencontre Assyriologique Internationale* (Cahiers du Groupe François-Thureau-Dangin, 1; 1960), with bibl. pp. 1–27; J. H. Tigay, *The Evolution of the Gilgamesh Epic* (Philadelphia, 1982), with bibl. pp. 304–33. On the reference to Gilgamesh in the Dead Sea Scrolls, see J. T. Milik, *The Books of Enoch* (Oxford, 1976), p. 313.

Gill, Arthur Eric Rowton (1882–1940), sculptor, letterist, and wood-engraver. The son of a minister in the Countess of *Huntingdon's Connexion who became an Anglican priest, he joined the RC Church in 1913 and became a *Dominican tertiary. After training in an architect's office, he studied lettering under Edward Johnston. His best-known works are the *Stations of the Cross in *Westminster Cathedral (finished 1918), ten panels in the New Museum, Jerusalem (1934–7), and the bas-reliefs of 'The Re-creation of Man' with the words of G. M. *Hopkins, 'Thou mastering me God', inscribed above it (1935–8) in the League of Nations Council Hall at Geneva. In his art he sought to express a Christian vision of the created order (his appreciation of which included an unembarrassed celebration of erotic love); he was also a social philosopher, a pacifist, and a writer. As a stone-carver who revived the art of working directly upon the stone, he excelled as a carver of inscriptions and a maker of small stone objects such as crucifixes and holy-water stoups.

Eric Gill, *Autobiography* (1940); W. Shewring (ed.), *Letters of Eric Gill* (1947). R. Speaight, *The Life of Eric Gill* (1966); D. Attwater, *A Cell of Good Living: The Life, Works and Opinions of Eric Gill* (1969); M. Yorke, *Eric Gill: Man of Flesh and Spirit* (1981); F. MacCarthy, *Eric Gill* (1989). E. R. Gill, *Bibliography of Eric Gill* (1953); id., *The Inscriptional Work of Eric Gill: An Inventory* (1964). W. Shewring in *DNB, 1931–1940*, pp. 339–41, s.v.

Gilpin, Bernard (1517–84), 'Apostle of the North'. He was a great-nephew of C. *Tunstall, Bp. of *Durham. Born at Kentmere in Cumbria, he was educated at Queen's College, Oxford, where he came under the spell of *Erasmus' writings. After *Henry VIII's refoundation of Cardinal College as *Christ Church, Gilpin was elected one of its first Students. Disapproving of the Edwardian doctrinal changes, he had serious scruples about abandoning Catholicism. When he preached at Court on 8 Jan. 1553, he expressed his final rejection of Papal supremacy, as well as his disgust at lay plundering of Church lands. Leaving England later in 1553 to arrange for the printing of Tunstall's work on the Eucharist, he returned only when Tunstall made him Archdeacon of Durham, almost certainly in 1556. The following year Tunstall also granted him the rich living of Houghton-le-Spring. However, his continuing attacks on clerical corruption led to trouble with the Marian Church authorities. On the accession of *Elizabeth I he was offered, but declined, both the bishopric of *Carlisle (1559) and the provostship of Queen's (1560). His scruples about the doctrinal changes soon revived and, horrified by E. *Sandys's views on the Eucharist, he accepted the new order with some reluctance. In the next years he made many long and successful missionary journeys in the N. of England, during which his unbounded liberality and unsparing denunciation of abuses brought him a very large following, including some of the *Puritans.

Gilpin's sermon at Court [dated '1552' old style, i.e. 1553] is pr. in 4th edn. of Carleton's Life, 1636 (see below), and in 1752 with W. Gilpin's Life. The primary authority is the Life by G. Carleton, Bp. of *Chichester (London, 1628, in Lat.; Eng. version, ibid., 1629); more substantial Life by William Gilpin, a collateral descendant (London, 1752). D. Marcombe, 'Bernard Gilpin: Anatomy of an Elizabethan Legend', *Northern History*, 16 (1980), pp. 20–39. *BRUO, 1501–1540*, pp. 232 f.

Gilson, Étienne (1884–1978), French *Thomist philosopher. He was educated at the *Sorbonne, where he came under the influence of H. *Bergson and L. Lévy-Bruhl.

At the latter's suggestion he embarked on a study of the Scholastic influence on R. *Descartes and thus became conversant with medieval thought. In 1913 he was appointed professor at Lille and subsequently held chairs at Strasbourg (1919–20), the Sorbonne (1921–32), and the Collège de France (1932–51). After his retirement he became a full-time professor at the Pontifical Institute of Mediaeval Studies at Toronto, of which he had been one of the founders in 1929 and had remained director of studies ever since. From 1959 he lived mainly in France.

The first-fruits of the studies suggested by Lévy-Bruhl were the *Index scolastico-cartésien* (1912) and *La Liberté chez Descartes et la théologie* (1913). These were followed by *La Philosophie au moyen âge* (2 vols., 1922; revised 1944), a popular manual which showed the systems of the Middle Ages as achievements in their own right. He published an English version, which was not a straight translation, as *History of Christian Philosophy in the Middle Ages* (1955). His other important works on medieval philosophy include *Le Thomisme* (1919; Eng. tr. 1924), an outline of St Thomas's metaphysics; *La Philosophie de saint Bonaventure* (1924; Eng. tr. 1938), on St *Bonaventure's conception of philosophical and mystical experience; *Introduction à l'étude de saint Augustin* (1929; Eng. tr. 1960); *L'Esprit de la philosophie médiévale* (*Gifford Lectures, 1932; Eng. tr. 1936); *La Théologie mystique de saint Bernard* (1934; Eng. tr. 1940) on the special characteristics of *Cistercian mysticism; *Héloïse et Abélard* (1938; Eng. tr. 1953); *L'Être et l'Essence* (1948; Eng. version, *Being and some Philosophers*, 1949); and *Jean Duns Scot, introduction à ses positions fondamentales* (1952). He was one of the founders of the *Archives d'histoire doctrinale et littéraire du moyen âge*, to which he contributed some of his most significant work, including articles on St Thomas Aquinas's criticism of Augustine and *Avicenna's influence on Duns Scotus in the first two volumes. In his later years he wrote on art.

Gilson's letters to H. de *Lubac, SJ, were ed. by the latter (Paris, 1986); his correspondence with J. *Maritain was ed. G. Prouvost (Bibliothèque des Textes Philosophiques, 1991). J. Maritain and others, *Étienne Gilson: Philosophie de la chrétienté* (Rencontres, 30; 1949). L. K. Shook, *Etienne Gilson* (Etienne Gilson Series, 6; Toronto, 1984). M. McGrath, *Etienne Gilson: A Bibliography* (ibid. 3; 1982). A. Maurer in *NCE* 14 (1967), pp. 137 f., s.v. 'Thomism', with further bibl.

Gioberti, Vincenzo (1801–52), Italian politician and religious philosopher. He was born and educated at Turin and ordained priest in 1825. Under the influence of Giuseppe Mazzini (1805–72), he made it his chief ambition to free Italy from foreign political and intellectual domination. On resigning a chaplaincy which he held at court (1833), he was arrested on suspicion of political intrigue and banished from Italy (1834). For the next eleven years he taught at Brussels, where he published most of his philosophical works. Returning to Italy in 1847, he became President of the Chamber of Deputies and in 1849 a member of the Cabinet of Victor Emmanuel II (1820–78). After unsuccessful negotiations in Paris, he relinquished his political position shortly afterwards and lived in France for the rest of his life.

Gioberti's philosophical ideas were in substance *Ontologistic. He held that there was an exact correspondence between the orders of being and knowing and that

the human mind directly perceived the absolute necessary Being, God, the creative cause of all existence and the source of human knowledge. The pantheistic character of some of his later teaching, in which he came to regard creation as the essential function of thought, caused some of his treatises to be put on the *Index. Despite the affinities of his doctrines with those of A. *Rosmini, the two philosophers wrote against each other. His principal writings include *Teoria del sovrannaturale* (Brussels, 1838), *Introduzione allo studio della filosofia* (ibid., 1840), *Degli errori filosofici di Antonio Rosmini* (3 vols., ibid., 1841–4), and *Del primato morale e civile degli Italiani* (2 vols., ibid., 1843).

Among Gioberti's posthumous writings were *Meditazioni filosofiche inedite di Vincenzo Gioberti* (ed. E. Solmi, Florence, 1909), *Epistolario* (ed. G. *Gentile and G. Balsamo-Crivelli, 11 vols., Turin, 1927–37), and *Cours de philosophie, 1841–42* (ed. G. Calò and M. Battistini, Milan, 1947). Anthology by G. Gentile entitled *Nuova protologia* (Bari, 1912). 'National Edition' of his complete works (Milan, 1938–47; Rome, 1969; Padua, 1970 ff.). Modern studies by L. Stefanini (Milan, 1947), G. Bonafede (Palermo, 1950), G. de Crescenzo (Brescia, 1964), and G. Derossi (Milan, 1971). B. M. G. Reardon, *Religion in the Age of Romanticism* (Cambridge, 1985), pp. 147–56. L. Stefanini in *EC* 6 (1951), cols. 414–22.

Giotto (*c*.1267–1337), the usual name of Ambrogiotto di Bondone, Florentine painter. Acc. to G. Vasari, the 16th-cent. historian of Italian art, he was a pupil of *Cimabue; *Dante (*Purg*. 11. 94–6) linked them as the most important painters in Italy to date. Little is known of his life: in Rome he was patronized by Card. Stefaneschi; from *c*.1329–33 he was in the employ of King Robert of Naples; and in 1334 he was appointed surveyor of the cathedral at Florence, where he initiated the building of the campanile. His work is important in the development of modern painting; he broke away from the rigid formality and stereotyped formulas characteristic of late Byzantine art in Italy and introduced a new sense of dramatic realism. Though it is a matter of dispute whether he designed the cycle of frescoes in the Upper Church at *Assisi—which include some of the most familiar images in the life of St *Francis—he was certainly responsible for those in the Arena Chapel at Padua and the Peruzzi and Bardi Chapels of Santa Croce in Florence; all demonstrate his concern for naturalism and his genius for narrative and characterization. In Rome his most spectacular work was the huge mosaic of the *Navicella* (the Ship of the Church, with Christ walking on the waters) in the old *St Peter's, which was reworked in the 17th cent. Other works include the *Ognissanti Madonna* in the Uffizi in Florence.

Reproductions of his paintings, largely in colour, with notes by E. Baccheschi (Classici dell'Arte, 3; Milan, 1966; with Eng. tr. of notes and new introd. by A. Martindale, Classics of World Art [1969]). C. Gnudi, *Giotto* (Milan [1958]; Eng. tr. [1959]). G. Previtali, *Giotto e la sua bottega* (Milan [1967]); *Giotto e il suo tempo: Atti del Congresso Internazionale per la celebrazione del VII Centenario della nascita di Giotto, 24 settembre–1 ottobre 1967* [1971]. J. H. Stubblebine, *Giotto: The Arena Chapel Frescoes* (1969); A. Smart, *The Assisi Problem and the Art of Giotto* (Oxford, 1971). S. Y. Edgerton, *The Heritage of Giotto's Geometry: Art and Science on the Eve of the Scientific Revolution* (Ithaca, NY, and London, 1991). J. [E.] C. T. White, *Art and Architecture in Italy 1250 to 1400* (Pelican History of Art, 1966), pp. 203–32; 2nd edn. (1987), pp. 309–48. Bibl. by R. Salvini (R. Istituto d'Archeologia e Storia dell'Arte, Bibliografie e Cataloghi, 4; Rome, 1938), with further vol. covering the period 1937–70, by C. de Benedictis (1973).

Giovanni Capistrano, St (1386–1456), *Franciscan friar. He was born at Capistrano in the Abruzzi and studied law at Perugia, where in 1412 he was made governor by King Ladislaus of Naples and married. Taken prisoner in a war with the family of the Malatestas, he experienced a vision of St *Francis while in captivity, which fired him with a desire to enter the religious life. On his release he obtained a dispensation from the impediment of matrimony and in 1416 sought admission to the novitiate of the Friars Minor. He was professed in 1417, priested in 1420, and immediately undertook a series of missions throughout Italy. In 1429, with other *Observant Friars, he was charged at Rome with heretical teaching on the poverty of Christ but acquitted. He took part in the General Chapter of the order which met at *Assisi in 1430 to secure the union of the Conventuals and the Observants, and assisted his old master, St *Bernardino of Siena (d. 1444), in the reform of the order. On several occasions he was vicar-general of the order. In 1451 he was sent by Pope *Nicholas V to Austria in response to an appeal by the Emp. Fredcrick III for help against the *Hussites. His successful labours all over E. Europe were ended by the advance of the Turks after the capture of *Constantinople (1453). After failing to arouse Bavaria and Austria to the danger, he went to Hungary, where early in 1456 the Turks were preparing to attack Belgrade. Together with Hunyady he raised an army which completely defeated the Turks on 22 July, but he died of plague on 23 Oct. of the same year. He was beatified in 1694, canonized in 1724; the feast was made of general observance in 1890, when it was transferred to 28 Mar.; in 1969 it was restored to 23 Oct.

The primary authorities, besides his own writings, are the contemporary Lives by his companions in the order (arranged chronologically): Jerome of Utino, pr. in *AASS*, Oct. 10 (1861), pp. 483–91; Nicholas of Fara, pr. ibid., pp. 439–83, with variant MS of the preface ed. E. Hocedez, SJ, in *Anal. Boll.* 23 (1904), pp. 320–4; Christopher of Varese, pr. in *AASS*, loc. cit., pp. 491–545; the Hungarian, Peter of Oedenburg (completed by 1489), pub. Vienna, 1523. Seven of his letters are pr. in *AASS*, loc. cit., pp. 546–52, with important introd. by J. van Hecke, SJ, pp. 269–439. Considerable material also in the works of L. *Wadding (q.v.). A. Hermann, *Capistranus Triumphans* (Cologne, 1700). D. van Andrichem, OFM, 'Explicatio Primae Regulae S. Clarae auctore S. Joanne Capistranensi (1445)', *AFH* 22 (1929), pp. 336–57, 515–28, incl. text. J. Łuszczki, OFM, *De Sermonibus S. Ioannis a Capistrano: Studium Historico-Criticum* (Studia Antoniana, 16; Rome, 1961). J. Hofer, CSSR, *Johannes von Capistrano* (Innsbruck [1936]; rev. edn. by O. Bonmann, OFM, 2 vols., Heidelberg, 1964–5; Eng. tr., St Louis, 1943; the best modern work). H. Lippens, OFM, 'S. Jean de Capistran en mission aux états bourguignons, 1442–1443', *AFH* 35 (1942), pp. 113–32 and 254–95, with docs. O. Bonmann, OFM, in *Dict. Sp.* 8 (1974), cols. 316–23, s.v. 'Jean de Capestrano'; id. in *DIP* 4 (1977), cols. 1212–23, s.v.

Giraldus Cambrensis (*c.*1146–1223), **Gerald de Barri**, historian. A native of Pembrokeshire, he studied at Paris, and from *c.*1175 to 1203 was Archdeacon of Brecon. He was elected Bp. of *St Davids in 1176 and again in 1199, but on each occasion failed to obtain consecration to the see, as the English feared that a Welshman would seek to make his Church independent again of *Canterbury. After protracted negotiations at Rome, his election was cancelled by Pope *Innocent III in 1203. He filled, however, several other important offices, and in 1188 preached the Third *Crusade in Wales, on which he would have gone himself had not Henry II dissuaded him. Among his more important writings are 'Topographia Hibernica', 'Expugnatio Hibernica', 'Itinerarium Kambriae', and 'De iure et statu Menevensis Ecclesiae'. They are amusing and vivid, though at times much influenced by personal and party feeling and their facts exaggerated.

Works ed. J. S. Brewer and others (RS, 8 vols., 1861–91). Crit. edn. of *De Invectionibus* by W. S. Davies (Y Cymmrodor, 30; 1920); of *Speculum Duorum* by Y. Lefèvre and others (Cardiff, 1974, incl. Eng. tr.); and of *Expugnatio Hibernica* by A. B. Scott and F. X. Martin (New History of Ireland, Ancillary Publications, Irish Medieval Texts, 1; Dublin, 1978, with Eng. tr.). Eng. tr. of Historical Works by T. Forester, R. C. Hoare, and T. Wright (Bohn's Antiquarian Library, 1863); of his Autobiography by H. E. Butler (London, 1937), with introd. by C. H. Williams, pp. 9–21; of the first version of 'Topographia Hibernica' by J. J. O'Meara (Dundalk, 1951; rev. edn., Penguin Classics, 1982); and of 'Itinerarium Kambriae' by L. Thorpe (ibid., 1978). M. Richter, *Giraldus Cambrensis: The Growth of the Welsh Nation* (Aberystwyth, 1972; 2nd edn., 1976). R. [J.] Bartlett, *Gerald of Wales 1146–1223* (Oxford Historical Monographs, 1982). B. F. Roberts, *Gerald of Wales* (Cardiff, 1982). F. M. Powicke, 'Gerald of Wales', *Bulletin of the John Rylands Library*, 12 (1928), pp. 389–410, repr. in his *Christian Life in the Middle Ages and other Essays* (1935), pp. 107–29. M. Lapidge and R. Sharpe, *A Bibliography of Celtic-Latin Literature 400–1200* (Dublin, 1985), pp. 22–8 (nos. 52–75). Y. Lefèvre in *DHGE* 20 (1984), cols. 1484 f., s.v. 'Giraud de Barri'.

girdle (Lat. *cingulum*, Gk. ζώνη). As an article of liturgical attire, a normal accompaniment of the *alb, and hence one of the six Eucharistic vestments. It is held to typify sacerdotal chastity and, in ref. to Lk. 12: 35–8, spiritual watchfulness. In the E. Church, where it takes the form of a broad band of material rather than a simple cord, its use is confined to bishops and priests, the deacon's alb being worn ungirdled.

Braun, *LG*, pp. 101–17.

Glabrio, Manius Acilius, consul in AD 91. Ordered by the Emp. *Domitian to fight with the wild beasts in the amphitheatre at Albano, he was banished after a successful contest, and finally executed about the same time as the husband of *Domitilla in 95. The nature of the charges against him is unclear; it is likely that he was a victim of Domitian's suspicions of the high aristocracy. The idea that he was himself a Christian is prob. mistaken, though the family grave shows that some servants of the household were, if not necessarily in his generation.

The main authorities are Dio Cassius, *Hist.* 67. 13 f., and *Suetonius, *Domitianus*, 10. *Prosopographia Imperii Romani*, 1 (2nd edn.), ed. E. Groag and A. Stein (Berlin and Leipzig, 1933), pp. 9 f. (no. 67), s.v. 'M'. Acilius Glabrio'. E. M. Smallwood, 'Domitian's Attitude toward the Jews and Judaism', *Classical Philology*, 51 (1956), pp. 1–13, esp. pp. 6 f. and 9. G. B. *de Rossi, 'L'ipogeo degli Acilii Glabrioni nel cimitero di Priscilla', *Bullettino di Archeologia Cristiana*, 4th ser. 6 (1888–9), pp. 15–66 and 103–33. See also H. *Leclercq, OSB, in *DACL* 6 (1924), cols. 1259–74, s.v.

Gladstone, William Ewart (1809–98), British statesman. Under the influence of his ardently *Evangelical mother he early showed religious inclinations. He was educated at Eton and Christ Church, Oxford. As an undergraduate he considered taking holy orders but, mainly on his father's advice, opted for 'public service' and entered Parliament in 1832. Though he left Oxford before the beginning of the *Oxford Movement, he was brought into contact with it by his friends James Robert Hope[-Scott] (1812–73) and H. E. *Manning. His study of Richard *Hooker and other 16th- and 17th-cent. English divines and of the 'Occasional Offices' of the BCP convinced him of the soundness of the *High Church doctrines, which he succeeded in combining with the tenets of his Evangelical education, and for the defence of which he frequently used his political position. In 1838 he published *The State in its Relations with the Church*, written from the point of view of the politician and in favour of the establishment of the Church, not without pungent criticisms of the RC position. In *Church Principles considered in their Results* (1840) he upheld the visibility of the Church, the certainty of the apostolic succession, and the efficacy of the Sacraments as well as the Divine institution of the C of E. In 1845 he resigned from Peel's Cabinet over the proposed grant to the RC college of *Maynooth, though he later defended the grant in the House of Commons. His High Church views led him to address an Open Letter to the Bp. of London (C. J. *Blomfield) after the *Gorham case, in which he maintained the compatibility of the royal supremacy with the intrinsic jurisdiction of the Church. In 1854 he supported Archdeacon G. A. *Denison, who was prosecuted for teaching the *Real Presence, a doctrine to which Gladstone was deeply attached. Owing to these convictions he was sometimes suspected of sympathy with the RC Church, which, however, he strongly repudiated, mainly on the ground that it was a regime of tyranny. He was much involved in the controversies of the Scottish Episcopal Church.

After having been several times Chancellor of the Exchequer he became in 1865 for the first time leader of the House of Commons, and in 1867 leader of the Liberal Party, which, though predominantly Anglican in leadership, drew strong support from Nonconformist votes. He was responsible for the law abolishing compulsory Church rates and fought the next election on the issue whether the Irish Church was to be disestablished. Having abandoned his earlier view, he defended disestablishment in his *Chapter of Autobiography* (1868) and carried it through as Prime Minister in 1869. In 1871 his government passed the *Universities Tests Act. In 1873 he brought in a bill proposing a combined Catholic and Protestant university for Ireland, which was defeated. In the next year he opposed Abp. A. C. *Tait's *Public Worship Bill in the interests of the liberty of the C of E, and in the same year published several bitter attacks on the Church of Rome, esp. on recent *Vatican decrees, which were answered by J. H. *Newman and H. E. Manning. In 1896 he pleaded in a letter to Card. M. Rampolla for the recognition of *Anglican Ordinations. Though he kept close to Tractarian principles throughout his life, he defended the doctrine of *conditional immortality in his *Studies Subsidiary to the Works of Bishop Butler* (1896). Gladstone in his private life lived up to the tenets of his religion: he was a weekly communicant, lavish in almsgiving and frugal in his habits, esp. in matters of sleep and food. He was

responsible for the founding of many new sees in the growing British Empire, and maintained his keen and sympathetic interest in all theological and ecclesiastical questions until his death. Much of his legislation was controversial, not least to Churchmen, but he was widely recognized as an outstanding example of a Victorian Christian statesman.

Diaries ed. M. R. D. Foot and others (14 vols., Oxford, 1968–94). *Correspondence on Church and Religion of W. E. Gladstone*, ed. D. C. Lathbury (2 vols., 1910). Some of Gladstone's political correspondence has also been pub. There is an important collection of Gladstone's theological articles in his *Later Gleanings* (1897). The extensive lit. incl. J. Morley, *The Life of W. E. Gladstone* (3 vols., 1903); G. W. E. Russell, *W. E. Gladstone* (1891); H. C. G. Matthew, *Gladstone 1809–1874* (Oxford, 1986); id., *Gladstone 1875–1898* (ibid., 1995). J. [D.] Bastable (ed.), *Newman and Gladstone: Centennial Essays* (Dublin, 1978). A. R. Vidler, *The Orb and the Cross: A Normative Study in the Relations of Church and State with Reference to Gladstone's Early Writings* (1945); P. Butler, *Gladstone: Church, State, and Tractarianism. A Study of his Religious Ideas and Attitudes, 1809–1859* (Oxford Historical Monographs, 1982). P. J. Jagger, *Gladstone: The Making of a Christian Politician* (Princeton Theological Monograph Series, 28; Allison Park, Pa. [1991]). H. C. G. Matthew, 'Gladstone, Vaticanism, and the Question of the East', in D. Baker (ed.), *Religious Motivation: Biographical and Sociological Problems for the Church Historian* (Studies in Church History, 15; 1978), pp. 417–42; A. Ramm, 'Gladstone's Religion', *Historical Journal*, 28 (1985), pp. 327–40.

Glagolitic. The medieval Slavonic alphabet, still used in the liturgical books of the *Uniats in Dalmatia, etc. It is generally thought that it was devised by St *Cyril, the Apostle of the Slavs, in the 9th cent. Other surviving literature in the alphabet includes translations of the Gospels and collections of Homilies. In modern Glagolitic *Missals (since 1927), only the *Canon is printed in Glagolitic letters, the rest being in Latin type. See also CYRILLIC.

L. Jelic (ed.), *Fontes Historici Liturgiae Glagolito-Romanae a XIII ad XIX saeculum* (Krk, 1906). S. Smržik, SJ, *The Glagolitic or Roman-Slavonic Liturgy* (Series Cyrillomethodiana, 2; Cleveland, Oh., and Rome, 1959). A. P. Vlasto, *The Entry of the Slavs into Christendom* (Cambridge, 1970), pp. 38–44.

Glanvill, Joseph (1636–80), religious writer. Educated at Exeter and Lincoln Colleges, Oxford, he became rector of the Abbey Church, Bath, in 1666. Throughout his life he took a keen interest in natural phenomena, esp. in their bearing on religion, and he was an early member of the Royal Society (elected in 1664). In several of his many treatises he endeavoured to prove that the evidence derived from the most varied physical phenomena lent support to religious belief. Like most of his scientific contemporaries, he was an ardent believer in the *Cartesian philosophy. In his *Saducismus Triumphatus* (1681) he defended belief in witchcraft. A passage in his *Vanity of Dogmatizing* (1661) suggested to Matthew *Arnold his poem 'The Scholar-Gipsy'.

Facsimile repr. of the 1689 edn. of *Saducismus Triumphatus* with introd. by C. O. Parsons (Gainesville, Fla., 1966), of Glanvill's *Plus Ultra or The Progress and Advancement of Knowledge since the Days of Aristotle* (1668) with introd. by J. I. Cope (ibid., 1958), and of *The Vanity of Dogmatizing*, with introd. by S. Medcalf (Hove, Sussex, 1970). Life prefixed to *Saducismus Triumphatus*, 4th edn., 1726. J. I. Cope, *Joseph Glanvill, Anglican Apologist* (St Louis, 1956), with bibl.; S. Talmor, *Glanvill: The Uses and Abuses of Scepticism* (Oxford, etc., 1981). N. H. Steneck, ' "The Ballad of Robert Crosse and Joseph Glanvill" and the Background to *Plus Ultra*', *British Journal for the History of Science*, 14 (1981), pp. 59–74. B. Willey, *The Seventeenth Century Background* (1934; repr. 1986), ch. 9, pp. 170–204. H. S. and I. M. L. Redgrove, *Joseph Glanvill and Psychical Research in the Seventeenth Century* (1921). L. Stephen in *DNB* 21 (1890), pp. 408 f.; W. H. Austin in *Dictionary of Scientific Biography*, 5 (1981 edn.), pp. 414–17, s.v.

Glasites (also **Sandemanians**), a small Scottish sect named after John Glas (1695–1773) and his son-in-law, Robert Sandeman (1718–71). Their founder, John Glas, the son of the (*Presbyterian) minister at Auchtermuchty, Fife, was ordained in 1719 as minister of Tealing, near Dundee. By the mid-1720s he had come to the conclusion that the existence of a State Church was unscriptural and he challenged the whole basis of the Presbyterian establishment. He gave public expression to his views in *The Testimony of the King of Martyrs concerning His Kingdom* (1727); he was accordingly suspended from his ministerial duties in 1728 and deposed in 1730. He established independent congregations among his (mainly poor) followers, for whom non-ordained elders conducted communion services, and Glasite meeting houses were set up in Dundee, Perth, Edinburgh, and other urban centres in Scotland. Their unusual custom of celebrating the *agape with broth attracted attention.

Gradually leadership of the movement passed to Robert Sandeman, who had abandoned plans to pursue a professional career and became a weaver; in 1744 he was elected a Glasite elder. In his *Letters on Theron and Aspasio* (1757) Sandeman attacked the *Calvinist teaching that God imputes the righteous acts of Christ to individual Christians, holding rather that a reasoned faith was the only basis for a proper relationship with God and the attainment of salvation. The publication of this book provided links which resulted in the formation of meeting houses in the NW Pennines, in London, and in New England, where Sandeman died. The Sandemanians, never more than *c*.1,000 in number, included the scientist Michael Faraday from 1821 until his death in 1867.

The *Works* of Glas, who was a man of considerable erudition, were pub. at Edinburgh (4 vols., 1761) and again at Perth (5 vols., 1782–3). Full treatment of the Glasites in G. [N.] Cantor, *Michael Faraday: Sandemanian and Scientist* (1991), esp. pp. 11–85, with bibl. refs. pp. 305–6. A. Gordon in *DNB* 21 (1890), pp. 417 f. and 50 (1897), pp. 255 f.

Glastonbury Abbey. Probably the oldest and one of the most influential of English monasteries. Orig. a *Celtic foundation believed to date from the 7th cent., it was refounded by King Ine of Wessex *c*.705. It was destroyed in the 9th cent. by the Danes. Later it seems to have been served by a small group of clerks until, *c*.940, King *Edmund made St *Dunstan its abbot. From his time dates the great revival of the monastery, which was organized acc. to the *Benedictine Rule, and which became one of the main educational and religious centres in the country. About 970 it adopted the '*Regularis Concordia', designed to unify English monastic life. It continued to flourish under the Normans, and became a famous place of pilgrimage, owing to the tombs of King Arthur and St Dunstan, which it was believed to contain. Between 1129 and 1139 *William of Malmesbury wrote its history, 'De Antiquitate Glastoniensis Ecclesie': in a version of this

revised in the mid-13th cent. are recorded the legends which associate it with *Joseph of Arimathaea (q.v.), King Arthur, and St *Patrick. Under Richard I a long drawn-out dispute arose between the abbey and the Bp. of *Bath and Wells, who claimed its revenues. It was eventually settled by the Pope in favour of the monks. The monastery was suppressed in 1539 and its last abbot, Bl Richard Whiting, executed. Since 1908 the ruins have been the property of Diocesan Trustees; adjoining is an Anglican Retreat House.

Around the 'Glastonbury Thorn', a kind of Levantine hawthorn which flowered twice a year, about Christmas and in May, several legends collected. It was cut down by one of O. *Cromwell's soldiers, but descendants of it remain to the present day.

A. Watkin, OSB (ed.), *The Great Cartulary of Glastonbury* (Somersetshire Record Society, 59, 63, and 64; 1947–56). Modern edns. of William of Malmesbury, *De Antiquitate Glastoniensis Ecclesie*, with Eng. tr., by J. Scott (Woodbridge, Suffolk, 1981), and of John of Glastonbury (14th cent.), *Cronica sive Antiquitates Glastoniensis Ecclesie*, by J. P. Carley (British Archaeological Report 47. 1–2; 1978; rev. edn., with Eng. tr, by D. Townsend, Woodbridge, 1985). W. *Dugdale, *Monasticon Anglicanum*, 1 (ed. 1817), pp. 1–79. R. Willis, *The Architectural History of Glastonbury Abbey* (Cambridge, 1866). J. Parker, 'Glastonbury: The Abbey Ruins', *Somersetshire Archaeological and Natural History Society*, 26 (1881), pp. 25–106; the excavations under the direction of C. R. Peers, A. W. Clapham, and E. Horne, OSB, begun in 1929, are reported ibid. 75 (1930), and foll. vols. W. Newell, 'William of Malmesbury and the Antiquities of Glastonbury', *Publications of the Modern Language Association of America*, 18 (1903), pp. 459–512. J. A. *Robinson, *Two Glastonbury Legends: King Arthur and St Joseph of Arimathea* (1926); G. Ashe, *King Arthur's Avalon: The Story of Glastonbury* (1957); R. F. Treharne, *The Glastonbury Legends: Joseph of Arimathea, The Holy Grail and King Arthur* (1967). A. Gransden, 'The Growth of the Glastonbury Traditions and Legends in the Twelfth Century', *JEH* 27 (1976), pp. 337–58.

glebe. In English and Scots ecclesiastical law, the land devoted to the maintenance of the incumbent of the parish. Since Norman times, every church has been required to have a house and glebe (together included in the *manse) before it can be consecrated by the bishop. The glebe now excludes the parsonage house and the land occupied with it. Glebe can be either cultivated by the incumbent himself or leased to tenants. Since the Ecclesiastical Leasing Act 1858 it can also be sold outright, with the consent of the *Church Commissioners (until 1948 the *Ecclesiastical Commissioners), after three months' prior notice to the bishop. On 1 April 1978 the ownership of all glebe land was transferred, under the Endowments and Glebe Measure 1976, s. 15, from the incumbent to the Diocesan Board of Finance, which now manages it for the benefit of the diocesan stipends fund. In Scotland, all glebe was vested in the General Trustees of the Church by the Church of Scotland (Property and Endowments) Act 1925.

Gloria in Excelsis. The initial words in Latin, and hence the common designation, of the hymn 'Glory be to God on high', etc. It is also known as the 'Greater *Doxology' and the 'Angelic Hymn'. A Greek Christian 'private psalm', i.e. a hymn composed upon the model of the canonical Psalms, its authorship and age are alike unknown. In the 4th cent. it formed part of morning prayers, and is still recited in the Byzantine *Orthros. In the Roman Mass it is sung after the *Kyries on Sundays (except those of *Advent and *Lent) and on certain feast days, a usage the beginning of which appears in the *Gregorian Sacramentary. In the English BCP of 1549 the hymn followed the Kyries as in the Roman Mass. In later editions of the BCP it was moved to the conclusion of the service, where it immediately precedes the Blessing. The ASB provides for it to be used in either position. The American Prayer Book of 1928 allowed its use at the end of the Psalms for the day in Evening Prayer.

C. Blume, 'Der Engelhymnus *Gloria in Excelsis Deo*', *Stimmen aus Maria Laach*, 73 (1907), pp. 43–62; A. *Baumstark, 'Die Text-überlieferung des Hymnus Angelicus', in *Hundert Jahre Marcus-und-Weber Verlag* (Bonn, 1909), pp. 83–7; J. Brinktrine, 'Zur Entstehung und Erklärung des *Gloria in Excelsis*', *RQ* 35 (1927), pp. 303–15; B. *Capelle, OSB, 'Le Texte du *Gloria in excelsis*', *RHE* 44 (1949), pp. 439–57; repr. in his *Travaux liturgiques*, 2 (1962), pp. 176–91. Jungmann (1958 edn.), 1, pp. 446–61; Eng. tr., 1, pp. 346–59. J. Gaillard, OSB, *Catholicisme*, 5 [1963], cols. 56–8, s.v.

Gloria Patri. The first words of the Lesser *Doxology ('Glory be to the Father', etc.), an ascription of praise to the Holy Trinity. It probably originated as an adaptation of the Jewish 'blessings' addressed to God, early Christian examples being Rom. 16: 27, Phil. 4: 20, Rev. 5: 13, but its form was no doubt influenced by the Trinitarian Baptismal formula of Mt. 28: 19. Variations are found, esp. in connection with the *Arian controversy. The use of the Gloria Patri at the end of Psalms dates from the 4th cent., and it is found quite early in metrical form at the end of hymns in the Offices. Until recent times it was omitted in *Requiem Masses and in the Office for the Dead, at Mass during the last two weeks of Lent and in the Psalms of the Office on the last three days of Holy Week, but it is now retained on all these occasions. The English Puritans forbade its use as unscriptural, but it was restored with the BCP at the Restoration.

H. Thurston, SJ, 'Notes on Familiar Prayers: 9, The "Gloria Patri" ', *The Month*, 131 (1918), pp. 406–17; repr. in Thurston's *Familiar Prayers*, ed. P. Grosjean, SJ (1953), pp. 178–92. J. A. Jungmann, SJ, *Die Stellung Christi im liturgischen Gebet* (Liturgiegeschichtliche Forschungen, 7/8; 1925), pp. 151–77. Jungmann (1958 edn.), 1, pp. 423 f.; Eng. tr., 1, pp. 328 f. J. Gaillard, OSB, in *Catholicisme*, 5 [1963], cols. 59–61, s.v.

Glorious Mysteries, the Five. The third *chaplet of the *Rosary (q.v.), consisting of (1) the Resurrection; (2) the Ascension; (3) the Descent of the Holy Spirit at Pentecost; (4) the *Assumption of the BVM; and (5) the *Coronation of the BVM.

Glos(s)a Ordinaria, the standard medieval commentary on the Bible, also known as the **Glos(s)a Communis** or simply the **Glos(s)a**. It was drawn up chiefly from extracts from the Fathers, and was arranged in the form of marginal and interlinear glosses. Its history has until recently been obscured because it was believed that the marginal gloss was the work of *Walafrid Strabo, and the interlinear gloss the work of *Anselm of Laon. In fact one is never found without the other, and the same compiler was responsible for both. Its composition was begun in the school of Anselm of Laon. Anselm was responsible for the Gloss on the Psalter, the Pauline Epistles, and on the Gospel of St John, his brother Ralph for the Gloss on

the Gospel of St Matthew. Gilbert the Universal, who taught at Auxerre before becoming Bp. of London (1128–34), was responsible for the Pentateuch and prob. Joshua, Judges and the four Books of Kings, and also the Great Prophets and Lamentations. The compilers of the Gloss on the other Books are either uncertain or unknown, but the whole Bible was covered by *c.* the middle of the 12th cent. The history of the Gloss varies from Book to Book. For example, the Gloss on the Pauline Epistles has a long and complicated pre-history. The Gloss on Acts is almost entirely compiled from *Rabanus Maurus and *Bede.

The term is also used of the standard commentaries on the *canon law texts.

The *editio princeps*, pub. at Strasbourg, 1480/1, is repr. in facsimile, with introd. by K. Froehlich and M. T. Gibson (4 vols., Turnhout, 1992). The edn. in J. P. Migne, *PL* 113–114 incl. only the marginal gloss. The text pr. with the works of *Nicholas of Lyre is complete, but is to some extent interpolated with later additions. S. Berger, *Histoire de la Vulgate pendant les premiers siècles du moyen-âge* (1893), pp. 132–6; B. Smalley, 'Gilbertus Universalis, Bishop of London (1128–34) and the Problem of the "Glossa Ordinaria" ', *RTAM* 7 (1935), pp. 235–62; 8 (1936), pp. 24–60; id., 'La Glossa Ordinaria. Quelques prédécesseurs d'Anselme de Laon', ibid. 9 (1937), pp. 365–400; J. de Ghellinck, SJ, *Le Mouvement théologique du XII* siècle* (2nd edn., Museum Lessianum, Section Historique, 10; 1948), pp. 104–12; R. Wasselynck, 'L'Influence de l'exégèse de S. Grégoire le Grand sur les commentaires bibliques médiévaux (VIIᵉ–XIIᵉ s.)', *RTAM* 32 (1965), pp. 157–204, esp. pp. 183–92; E. Bertola, 'La "Glossa ordinaria" biblica ed i suoi problemi', ibid. 45 (1978), pp. 34–78; R. Wielockx, 'Autour de la "Glossa Ordinaria" ', ibid. 49 (1982), pp. 222–8. B. Smalley, *The Study of the Bible in the Middle Ages* (3rd edn., Oxford, 1983), pp. x f., and 46–66. M. T. Gibson, 'The Place of the *Glossa ordinaria* in Medieval Exegesis', in M. D. Jordan and K. Emery (eds.), *Ad Litteram: Authoritative Texts and their Medieval Readers* (Notre Dame, Ind., and London [1992]), pp. 5–27, repr. in Gibson, '*Artes' and Bible in the Medieval West* (Aldershot, 1993), no. 15. B. Smalley in *TRE* 13 (1984), pp. 452–7, s.v. On the canon law gloss, H. Kantorowicz in B. Smalley, *The Study of the Bible in the Middle Ages* (2nd edn., Oxford, 1952), pp. 55 f., with refs.

glossolalia. Speaking in tongues, a form of ecstatic speech. The term was coined in the 19th cent. from the Gk. γλῶσσα, 'tongue', + λαλιά, 'talking', to denote the phenomena reported in 1 Cor. 14: 6, 23, etc. In psychological terms it can be understood as an abandoning of conscious control of the speech organs to the subconscious. For long some people have believed the resulting speech to be supernaturally initiated. Glossolalia was a common phenomenon in NT times (cf. Acts 10: 46; 1 Cor. 14), but St *Paul did not regard it as one of the greatest gifts (cf. 1 Cor. 13: 8; 14: 9). What most authorities believe to be a similar or identical experience has been encountered in many religious revivals and plays a prominent part in modern *Pentecostalism and in the *Charismatic Renewal Movement. Christians differ about the spiritual value or significance of praying 'in tongues', but scientific opinion does not now hold that it is necessarily harmful or evidence of psychological disturbance.

W. J. Samarin, *Tongues of Men and Angels: The Religious Language of Pentecostalism* (New York and London, 1972); C. G. Williams, *Tongues of the Spirit: A Study of Pentecostal Glossolalia and related Phenomena* (Cardiff, 1981). H. N. Malony and A. A. Lovekin, *Glossolalia: Behavioral Science Perspectives on Speaking in Tongues* (New York and Oxford, 1985). W. E. Mills (ed.),

Speaking in Tongues: A Guide to Research on Glossolalia (Grand Rapids, Mich., 1986). L. T. Johnson in *Anchor Bible Dictionary*, 6 (1992), pp. 596–600, s.v. 'Tongues, Gift of', with further refs.

Gloucester. Until 1541 Gloucester was in the diocese of *Worcester. The abbey-church of St *Peter, the present cathedral, is on the site of an earlier religious house, established in 681 by Osric, under-king of the Hwicce, and converted into a college of secular priests in 823. This college was refounded as a *Benedictine monastery by *Wulfstan, Abp. of York, in 1017. In 1088 a fire destroyed the old monastic buildings, and in 1089 Serlo, the first Norman Abbot (1072–1104), began the present church. This Norman structure was constantly added to and embellished in the Middle Ages. Specially notable are the early Perpendicular panelling superimposed on the Norman pillars in the choir (begun after 1337); the great E. window, a war memorial to Gloucester knights slain at Crécy (1346) and the siege of Calais (1347); the magnificent cloisters with the earliest example of fan tracery (before 1377); and the remarkably fine central tower (mid-15th cent.). In the N. ambulatory is the tomb of Edward II, whose body was brought here after his murder at Berkeley Castle, 21 Sept. 1327; it became an important place of pilgrimage for a time and the wealth of the abbey greatly increased. The most notable person connected with the abbey was Gilbert *Foliot (Abbot 1139–48).

In 1540 the monastery was suppressed and in 1541 John Wakeman, the last Abbot of *Tewkesbury became the first Bishop of the newly founded see of Gloucester. The diocese covered most of Gloucestershire, with parts of Herefordshire and Worcestershire. In 1836 it was united with the see of Bristol, but separated again in 1897. From 1713 to 1937 one of the canonries was attached to the Mastership of Pembroke College, Oxford. Notable Bps. of Gloucester have been J. *Hooper (1551–5), burnt in St Mary's Square outside the Abbey gates; R. Frampton (1681–91), *Nonjuror, who just missed joining the *Seven Bishops; W. *Warburton (1760–79); C. J. *Ellicott (1863–1905); and E. C. S. Gibson (1905–22), who published notable works on the *Thirty-Nine Articles and the *Creeds. Deans have included W. *Laud (1616–21) and the economist Josiah Tucker (1758–99). Every third year the Three Choirs Festival is held at Gloucester.

W. H. Hart (ed.), *Historia et Cartularium Monasterii Sancti Petri Gloucestriae* (3 vols., RS, 1863–7). H. P. R. Finberg, *The Early Charters of the West Midlands* (Leicester, 1961), pp. 153–66. H. G[ee] (ed.), *The Statues of Gloucester Cathedral* (1918). 'The Records of the Dean and Chapter of Gloucester' are described by W. H. Stevenson in the *Twelfth Report of the Historical Manuscripts Commission*, Appendix, pt. 9 (1891), pp. 397–9. W. *Dugdale, *Monasticon Anglicanum*, 1 (1817 edn.), pp. 531–66. D. Verey and D. Welander, *Gloucester Cathedral* (Gloucester, 1979); D. Welander, *The History, Art and Architecture of Gloucester Cathedral* (Stroud, 1991). S. Eward, *No Fine but a Glass of Wine: Cathedral Life at Gloucester in Stuart Times* ([Wilton] 1985). N. M. Herbert, 'Gloucester Cathedral and the close', *VCH*, Gloucester, 4, ed. id. (1988), pp. 275–88.

gloves, liturgical (Lat. *chirothecae*). In the W. Church, the privilege of wearing liturgical gloves ordinarily belonged to the Pope, the cardinals, and the bishops, though it has sometimes been conferred on abbots and others by the Holy See. They may be worn during a *Pontifical Mass, though since 1968 they have ceased to be obligatory. They used to follow the liturgical colour of the day, and may still do so, or may be white. Apparently first used in France at about the end of the 9th cent., they made their way thence to Rome a little later.

X. Barbier de Montault, *Les Gants pontificaux* (Tours, 1877). Braun, *LG*, pp. 359–84; Braun, *LP*, pp. 154–7

Gnesio-Lutherans. A modern name for the party of strict *Lutherans who opposed the Leipzig Interim (a temporizing form of the *Augsburg Interim) put forward by Duke Maurice of Saxony. Their first campaign was against P. *Melanchthon and his followers, the *Philippists, who accepted the Interim on the grounds that its concessions towards Catholicism involved only 'adiaphora' (see ADIAPHORISTS). But the antagonisms thus aroused outlived the Interim. The Gnesio-Lutherans, led by N. von *Amsdorf and M. *Flacius, harried the Philippists in a series of controversies from their base in Jena, where the Ernestine Dukes of Saxony founded a university in the 1550s to make up for the loss of *Wittenberg (and their electoral status) to Duke Maurice of the Albertine branch of the family. They interpreted the Philippists' concessions towards Catholics or Calvinists as a betrayal of M. *Luther's legacy, accusing them of crypto-catholic soteriology in the *Majoristic, *synergist, and *Osiandrist controversies, and of *crypto-Calvinism in their eucharistic doctrine. These controversies reverberated through the 1550s and 1560s, despite several attempts to restore unity at religious colloquies, notably at Worms in 1557 and Naumburg in 1561. In the 1570s, as many of the leaders on both sides died, peace moves met with greater success, culminating in the Formula of *Concord (1577).

R. Kolb, 'Dynamics of Party Conflict in the Saxon Late Reformation. Genesiolutherans vs Philippists', *Journal of Modern History*, 49 (1977), on-demand suppl., pp. D1289–D1305. R. Keller in *TRE* 13 (1984), pp. 512–19, s.v., with bibl. See also works cited under AMSDORF, N. VON, and FLACIUS, M.

Gnosticism. The name, derived from the Greek word γνῶσις ('knowledge'), given to a complex religious movement which in its Christian form comes into clear prominence in the 2nd cent. Whether Gnosticism was an erratic development of Christian teaching (as the Fathers thought) or whether Christian Gnosticism had its origins in trends of thought already present in pagan religious circles, is still a matter of dispute among scholars. In Christianity, the movement appeared at first as a school (or schools) of thought within the Church, but by the end of the 2nd cent. the Gnostics had mostly become separate sects. In some of the later books of the NT, e.g. 1 John and the *Pastoral Epistles, forms of false teaching are denounced which appear to be similar to, though less developed than, the Gnostic systems of teaching referred to by 2nd-cent. writers.

Gnosticism took many different forms, commonly associated with the names of particular teachers, e.g. *Valentinus, *Basilides, and *Marcion (qq.v.). But though Marcion and his community stand somewhat apart, certain features are common to the movement as a whole. A central importance was attached to 'gnosis', the supposedly revealed knowledge of God and of the origin and destiny of mankind, by means of which the spiritual element in man could receive redemption. The source of this special 'gnosis' was held to be either the Apostles, from whom it was derived by a secret tradition, or a direct revelation given to the founder of the sect. The systems of teaching range from those which embody much genuine philosophical speculation to those which are wild amalgams of mythology and magical rites drawn from all quarters, with the most slender admixture of Christian elements. The OT Books and many of the NT Books were used and expounded by the greater sects, and a central place was assigned to the figure of Jesus, but on a number of fundamental points the interpretation of these Christian features differed widely from that of orthodox Christianity.

Characteristic of Gnostic teaching was the distinction between the *Demiurge or 'creator god' and the supreme remote and unknowable Divine Being. From the latter the Demiurge was derived by a longer or shorter series of emanations or 'aeons'. He it was who, through some mischance or fall among the higher aeons, was the immediate source of creation and ruled the world, which was therefore imperfect and antagonistic to what was truly spiritual. But into the constitution of some men there had entered a seed or spark of Divine spiritual substance, and through 'gnosis' and the rites associated with it this spiritual element might be rescued from its evil material environment and assured of a return to its home in the Divine Being. Such men were designated the 'spiritual' ($\pi\nu\epsilon\nu\mu\alpha\tau\iota\kappa\omicron\iota$), while others were merely 'fleshly' or 'material' ($\sigma\alpha\rho\kappa\iota\kappa\omicron\iota$ or $\upsilon\lambda\iota\kappa\omicron\iota$), though some Gnostics added a third intermediate class, the 'psychic' ($\psi\upsilon\chi\iota\kappa\omicron\iota$). The function of Christ was to come as the emissary of the supreme God, bringing 'gnosis'. As a Divine Being He neither assumed a properly human body nor died, but either temporarily inhabited a human being, Jesus, or assumed a merely phantasmal human appearance.

The principal anti-Gnostic writers, such as *Irenaeus, *Tertullian, and *Hippolytus, emphasized the pagan features of Gnosticism. They appealed to the plain sense of Scripture as interpreted by the tradition of the Church and insisted on the identity of the Creator and the supreme God, on the goodness of the material creation, and on the reality of the earthly life of Jesus, esp. of the Crucifixion and the Resurrection. Man needed redemption from an evil will rather than an evil environment. These writers' excerpts and descriptions of the Gnostic systems were until recently our main source of information. The study of Gnosticism entered a new phase, however, with the discovery of a large collection of Coptic texts at *Nag Hammadi (q.v.) in 1945–6. It comprised over 40 separate treatises, of which very few were previously known. The writings vary widely in date and style; some are thought to date from the 2nd cent. or even earlier, though the actual copies are not earlier than the 4th cent. Most of the writings are at least superficially Christian and display Gnostic tendencies in varying degrees.

The discovery of the Nag Hammadi texts promises to throw fresh light on the origins of Gnosticism, though many details are still unclear. It has generally been thought that while some of the important ideas used by the Gnostics, e.g. the light-symbolism and the religious use of the word 'gnosis' itself, are pre-Christian, the sects themselves and their elaborate mythologies are not; though some German scholars, such as R. *Reitzenstein, W. *Bousset

and R. *Bultmann, have strongly supported the conception of pre-Christian Gnosticism. It is at least clear that pre-Christian Jewish sects provided a fertile soil for Gnostic ideas. The Jews had developed a tradition of speculative interpretation of the OT (see MIDRASH) which gave rise to a large extra-canonical literature which was influenced by Iranian religious thought (see ZOROASTRIANISM). On the other hand Greek-speaking Jews such as *Philo attempted to explain their faith in terms of Greek philosophy; Egyptian religious writers of the Hermetic school borrowed both from the Greeks and from the Book of *Genesis (e.g. in the *Poimandres), and cultivated Greeks such as Plutarch discussed philosophical adaptations of the Egyptian myth of Isis. Finally, specifically Christian themes were introduced into this amalgam of ideas, whether as a dominant force or as a mere superficial decoration. The Nag Hammadi texts probably show all these influences, though that of philosophy is less evident than in already known Valentinian texts.

Gnosticism in various forms persisted for several centuries. The sect of the *Manichees, founded by Mani the Persian in the 3rd cent., spread as far as Turkestan and survived there until the 13th cent.; meanwhile the possibly related sects of the *Albigenses and *Cathari had appeared in France, Germany, and Italy. One sect of Gnostics, the *Mandaeans, has survived in Mesopotamia until the present day. See also DOCETISM.

The main anti-Gnostic texts of the Christian Fathers are Irenaeus, *Adversus Haereses*, *Clement of Alexandria, *Excerpta ex Theodoto*, Tertullian, *Adversus Marcionem*, etc., Hippolytus, *Refutatio Omnium Haeresium*, and *Epiphanius, *Panarion*. See also the criticisms of *Plotinus, *Enneads*, 2. 9. A useful selection of Gk. texts, incl. many frags. of Gnostic writings, is W. Völker, *Quellen zur Geschichte der christlichen Gnosis* (Tübingen, 1932). The Ep. of Ptolemy to Flora was re-edited by G. Quispel (SC 24; 1949; 2nd edn., 1966). Coptic Gnostic texts known before 1946 are contained in the Askew Codex (see PISTIS SOPHIA), the Bruce Codex (ed. C. Schmidt, TU 8, Hefte 1–2, 1892; repr., with Eng. tr. and notes by V. MacDermot, *The Books of Jeu and the Untitled Text in the Bruce Codex*, Nag Hammadi Studies, 13; Leiden, 1978), and the Berlin Codex 8502 (ed. W. C. Till, TU 60, 1955, 2nd edn. by H.-M. Schenke, 1972; partial Eng. tr. in R. M. Grant, *Gnosticism: An Anthology* (1961), pp. 65–85). Larger collection of texts in English, *Gnosis*, ed. W. Foerster, Eng. tr. ed. R. McL. Wilson (2 vols., Oxford, 1972–4; tr. from *Die Gnosis*, 2 vols., Zurich, 1969–71) and B. Layton, *The Gnostic Scriptures* (1987). For texts found at Nag Hammadi, see s.v.

Some older studies of Gnosticism are still valuable, including F. C. *Baur, *Die christliche Gnosis oder die christliche Religionsphilosophie in ihrer geschichtlichen Entwicklung* (Tübingen, 1835); R. A. *Lipsius, *Die Quellen der ältesten Ketzergeschichte neu untersucht* (Leipzig, 1875; on the literary relations between the early anti-Gnostic writers); A. *Hilgenfeld, *Die Ketzergeschichte des Urchristenthums, urkundlich dargestellt* (ibid., 1884; with text of chief frags.); W. Bousset, *Hauptprobleme der Gnosis* (Göttingen, 1907); E. de Faye, *Gnostiques et gnosticisme* (1913; 2nd edn., 1925). The best and most comprehensive recent survey is K. Rudolph, *Die Gnosis: Wesen und Geschichte einer spätantiken Religion* (Leipzig, 1977; Eng. tr., 1983). See also H. Jonas, *Gnosis und spätantiker Geist*, 1 (Göttingen, 1934; rev. edn., with suppl., 1964); 2. 1 (1954; rev. edn., 1966); id., *The Gnostic Religion* (Boston, 1958; 2nd edn., 1963); G. Scholem, *Major Trends in Jewish Mysticism* (Jerusalem, 1941; 3rd edn., London, 1955); H. J. Schoeps, *Theologie und Geschichte des Judenchristentums* (Tübingen, 1949); id., *Urgemeinde—Judenchristentum—Gnosis* (ibid., 1956); G. Quispel, *Gnosis als Weltreligion* (Zurich, 1951); J. Doresse, *Les Livres secrets des gnostiques d'Égypte*, 1 (1958; Eng. tr., 1960); R. McL. Wilson, *The*

Gnostic Problem (1958); id., *Gnosis and the New Testament* (Oxford, 1968); R. M. Grant, *Gnosticism and Early Christianity* (New York, 1959; 2nd edn., 1966); E. Peterson, *Frühkirche, Judentum und Gnosis* (1959); U. Bianchi (ed.), *Le origini dello gnosticismo* (Studies in the History of Religions, 12; Leiden, 1967); W. Eltester (ed.), *Christentum und Gnosis* (Beihefte zur *ZNTW*, 37; 1969); E. M. Yamauchi, *Pre-Christian Gnosticism: A Survey of the Proposed Evidence* (1973; 2nd edn., Grand Rapids, Mich. [1983]); K.-W. Tröger (ed.), *Gnosis und Neues Testament: Studien aus Religionswissenschaft und Theologie* (Gütersloh [1973]); id. (ed.), *Altes Testament—Frühjudentum—Gnosis* (ibid. [1980]); S. Pétrement, *Le Dieu séparé: Les origines du gnosticisme* (1984; Eng. tr., 1991); A. H. B. Logan, *Gnostic Truth and Christian Heresy: A Study in the History of Gnosticism* (Edinburgh, 1996). R. McL. Wilson in A. Richardson and J. Bowden (eds.), *A New Dictionary of Christian Theology* (1983), pp. 226–30, s.v.; K. Berger and R. McL. Wilson in *TRE* 13 (1984), pp. 519–50, s.v. 'Gnosis/Gnostizismus', with extensive bibl.; K. Rudolph in *Anchor Bible Dictionary*, 2 (1992), pp. 1033–40, s.v.

Goar, Jacques (1601–54), French liturgiologist. He was a native of Paris, and after studying Greek and Latin entered the *Dominican Order in 1619. Having been lecturer at the convent at Toul, he went to Greece in 1631 as prior of the convent of St Sebastian in Chios in order to perfect himself in the language and to study the rites of the Greek Church. In 1637 he went to Rome as prior of San Sisto, and in 1644 settled at Paris, where he brought out a series of works, the most important being his celebrated Εὐχολόγιον *sive Rituale Graecorum* (Paris, 1647; 2nd edn., much improved, Venice, 1730). It contains the rites of the Greek Liturgy, Offices, Sacramentaries, etc., based on MSS as well as on printed sources, and gives Latin translations and valuable notes. It is still the classic work for Greek liturgical studies, and has served as a basis for all subsequent research on the subject. Among his other works are editions of the *Compendium Historiarum* of George Cedrenus (1647), the *De Officiis Magnae Ecclesiae* of the so-called Codinus Curopalata (1648), and of the *Chronographia* of George Monachus and the Patr. Tarasius (1652).

Quétif and Échard, 2, pp. 574 f. A. Strittmatter, OSB, 'The "Barberinum S. Marci" of Jacques Goar', *EL* 47 (1933), pp. 329–67. R. Coulon, OP, in *DTC* 6 (1920), cols. 1467–9.

God. The Greek word for God (θεός) is used both as a common noun, as in polytheism, where a number of supposed existences claim belief, worship, and service, and as a proper name, e.g. in *monotheism, where there is and can be but one such existence. *Judaism, *Islam, and Christianity all proclaim belief in one God. Christianity alone affirms that God is a trinity in unity, a 'Tri-unity', consisting of 'three persons in one substance', the Father being the Source of all existence, the Son the Eternal Object of the Father's love and the Mediator of that love in creation and redemption, and the Holy Spirit the Bond of Union between the Father and the Son.

In the OT account of the Divine revelation to *Moses on *Sinai (Ex. 3: 2–15 and 6: 2–8) God makes Himself known in the name '*Yahweh' ('I am who I am') as the unique God (Ex. 20: 3, 5), who tolerates no rival and is alone Lord of the earth (Ex. 9: 29), omnipotent and holy (Ex. 15: 3–18), merciful and faithful to His word (Ex. 34: 6 f.) and demanding obedience to His commandments (Ex. 20: 1–17). This exalted conception of the Creator-God was affirmed by all the greatest religious leaders of Israel. The prophets esp. developed the different aspects of God acc. to their character and special mission. *Amos preached the righteousness of God, limited by no national barriers, while *Hosea stressed God's love and mercy towards Israel, using as analogies the human relationships of husband and wife, father and child. *Isaiah, and later *Ezekiel, exalt His incomparable holiness and transcendence. Particularly during the Exile, there emerged the conviction that God would grant His people the ability to do His will (Jer. 31: 31–4; Ezek. 36: 26 f.). Whilst for many in Israel Yahweh remained pre-eminently a national God, the idea of God as saviour of the Gentiles as well as the Jews had an important place, esp. during and after the Exile (e.g. Is. 49: 6; Jonah). This universality is reflected in some of the Psalms, in which Book all the strands of Jewish monotheistic piety are gathered.

It was to make patent the fullness of truth about God that (acc. to Christian belief) a new revelation was given. This was made through the Incarnate Son, who revealed God as the Father of all men, whose infinite goodness has no need to manifest itself in material recompenses. It was in the light of this new knowledge that the author of the Fourth Gospel conceived God as light, life, and love; but no epitome can convey the richness and extent of the several aspects of the revelation contained in the NT. Above all, it was a revelation of God through the facts of history. Certain events of an historic order were perceived to possess a unique status and significance for those to whom the truth was committed. There resulted a conception of God which, while safeguarding the legitimacy of natural theology (cf. Rom. 1: 18 ff.) within certain limits, recognized His character as *sui generis*.

In the patristic age three principal factors determined the development of the doctrine of God: (1) the *data* of Scripture, (2) the controversies with pagans, Jews, and heretics; and (3) the Greek philosophy which was the foundation of the education of most of the Fathers. In seeking to make their case for Christianity in the cultured world around them, the *Apologists of the 2nd and 3rd cents. made extensive use of reason and philosophy. Thus *Justin Martyr, who was much influenced by *Platonist teaching, stressed the ineffability, omnipotence, and impassibility of God. This attitude was shared by *Tatian and many others, whereas *Athenagoras and *Theophilus elaborated His simplicity, indivisibility, and universal providence. St *Irenaeus developed his doctrine esp. against the *Gnostics, to whose dualism and emanationism he opposed the absolute self-sufficiency and perfection of God. The theology of the early Alexandrian Fathers, *Clement and *Origen, is characterized by their vigorous affirmation of the Divine transcendence, incomprehensibility, and ineffability. Despite this emphasis, however, they upheld the natural knowability of God through creation. This is also stressed by *Tertullian, who adds to it the testimony of the human soul and deduces from the conception of God as the First Cause His possession of all perfections. Thus by the time of *Nicaea (325) the great lines of Christian thought were fixed, and such Divine attributes as eternity, immutability, omniscience, and omnipotence had become the undisputed belief of all Christians.

The doctrine of the pre-Nicene age was deepened by the great speculative theologians of Alexandria, esp. St

*Athanasius, St *Didymus, and St *Cyril. They insist that God, though incomprehensible in His inner Being, can be known through the human soul, made in His image, and through the visible creation. St *Cyril of Jerusalem deals with the subject implicitly in his 'Catecheses', esp. with the unity, sovereign dominion, and creative action of God. The *Cappadocians were led to an explicit examination of the Divine nature and our knowledge of it in their call to reply to *Eunomius, who had asserted that the full Being of God is adequately expressed by the word 'Unoriginate' (ἀγέννητος), to which all other designations can be reduced. Against him St *Gregory of Nazianzus maintained that negative attributes are not enough, and that such positive names as love, wisdom, justice, etc., should be added, though the most suitable name for God is Being.

The speculations of the Fathers were gathered up into a powerful synthesis in the various works of St *Augustine. He gives several proofs for the existence of God, e.g. from contingency, from the order and beauty of the world, from the eternal principles of human reason, and the moral argument from conscience. These proofs, however, were not yet elaborated with the systematic methods of the Middle Ages. The influence of Plato shows itself in Augustine's idea of God as the First Principle, cause of all truth and of all goodness. Though God is above all human thought and language, He is not abstract and indeterminate being, but concrete and actual, 'above whom, outside whom, and without whom nothing exists' (*Soliliquia* 1.1.4). Using *Neoplatonic categories, *Dionysius the Pseudo-Areopagite developed an elaborate understanding of our knowledge of God. Through concepts and images we gain some understanding of God and communion with Him as the cause of all beings, but Dionysius stresses the Divine transcendence perhaps more than any other of the Fathers; he sees God as beyond Being and more surely reached by *apophatic theology, where one denies concepts and images and knows God by unknowing. This negation is by way of transcendence, and Dionysius signalled this by a fondness for Divine epithets prefixed by ὑπερ- ('hyper-'): ὑπερούσιος ('beyond being'), ὑπεράγαθος ('more than good'), and even ὑπέρθεος ('more than Divine') (see esp. *Ep.* 2).

The ideas of Dionysius were taken over, with some modifications, by his translator, John Scottus *Erigena. Acc. to Erigena, God is known by reason as the cause of things, but not as what He is. A higher knowledge of Him is possible by contemplation, but even here and in the *Beatific Vision He is not seen Himself, but only through theophanies which He grants to angels and believers. This fundamental agnosticism led to reiterated condemnations of his doctrine; but the stress he laid on philosophy constitutes a link between the patristic age and the Scholasticism that was to follow.

One of the principal concerns of the Schoolmen was to investigate the Divine Nature by the method of rational proof, without direct appeal to revelation. St *Anselm of Canterbury was the author of the *Ontological Argument (q.v.) for His Being. Under the influence of the newly discovered *Aristotle, St *Thomas Aquinas introduced some radical changes and developments. He rejected the Ontological Argument; but on the principle that only something itself in the state of 'act' can move anything from the state of 'potentiality' to the state of 'act', he elab-

orated his famous fivefold proof for the existence of God (*Quinque Viae*). Starting with creation, he argued from its visible effects to the conception of God as the First Immovable Mover, the First Efficient Cause, the necessary Being, the most perfect Being, and the Ordainer of the universe. He endeavoured to hold the balance between an anthropomorphic conception of God and an exaggerated transcendence. In God, as self-subsistent Being, essence was identical with existence, and as 'Actus purus' without any admixture of potentiality He was Himself all perfections. In this way Thomas develops the idea that there are three ways of conceiving God—by affirmation, negation, and eminence. Thus while His goodness (way of affirmation) is asserted, He may also be called 'not good', i.e. not good in the way that man is good (way of negation; see APOPHATIC THEOLOGY), and 'super-good', i.e. above all ideas of goodness (way of eminence). Though Thomas was not immediately followed in his rejection of the Ontological Argument, which continued to be upheld by theologians of the *Franciscan school, e.g. St *Bonaventure and *Duns Scotus, his doctrine of God became the officially accepted basis of the teaching of post-*Tridentine Catholic theology.

The shattering personal experiences of the Reformers were reflected in their intensely personal conceptions of God. M. *Luther directed a fierce tirade against the speculative theology of the Schools. J. *Calvin esp. emphasized the Divine Majesty and transcendence. And even in Catholic quarters the *Nominalism of the late Middle Ages had contributed to the disintegration of the Thomistic synthesis. *Nicholas of Cusa (d. 1464) believed that God, as the *coincidentia oppositorum*, lies beyond all rational categories, but because He is in all things and all things are in Him, the universe mirrors on the finite level something of the Divine nature. The fundamental unity of God and the world was stated even more forcibly in the next century by G. *Bruno, for whom God was the world-soul. In contrast to these pantheistic conceptions, R. *Descartes endeavoured to uphold the transcendence of the Divine Being. In his former argument in his *Meditations* for the existence of God, he urged that the human mind can conceive an infinite and perfect Being only because the idea of the Other exists in our minds and this idea has a proportionate cause. His other argument was essentially a reformulation of the Ontological Argument. The pantheistic trend of modern philosophy was resumed by B. *Spinoza, who elaborated the threefold notion of God as thought, as substance, and nature. There are no two separate terms of Creator and creature, but a complex series of stages from God to the universe, so that the exact transition from the Divine to the finite is incapable of definition. Descartes's Ontological Argument for the existence of God was reasserted, with an attempt at greater stringency, by G. W. *Leibniz. If a perfect and necessary Being is not a contradictory and fictitious object, such a Being must exist, because existence is one of its attributes.

A decisive attack on natural theology was made in the 18th cent. by I. *Kant, who, in his *Critique of Pure Reason* (1781), attempted to prove the impossibility of any rational proof of the existence of God. This was a consequence of his attack on speculative metaphysics in all its forms. He also urged that in any case the arguments from causality and teleology would be insufficient to prove what Christian Theism means by God without the assistance of the Ontological Argument. The only valid proof of the existence of God is that from morality. 'I had to remove knowledge (*Wissen*) to make way for faith (*Glauben*).' The reality of moral obligation required the postulate of a wise, holy, and omnipotent Being, who would ensure the future harmony between the accomplishment of duty and happiness. The step from the refusal of any metaphysical basis for the belief in God to resting the belief on feeling (*Gefühl*), which was supposed to include intuition (*Anschauung*), was made by F. D. E. *Schleiermacher. All religious statements must be derived not from deductive logic but from personal experience, and the origin of belief in God be sought in the feeling of dependence, common to human beings. Among British thinkers of the 19th cent. Sir W. Hamilton and H. L. *Mansel sought to uphold the traditional conception of God on a basis of agnosticism which had affinities with the teaching of Kant.

But the 19th cent. also witnessed under the stimulus of G. W. F. *Hegel a powerful movement in speculative theology. In a grandiose system, Hegel fused evolutionary conceptions with the pantheism of Spinoza and thereby, while doing violence to the Christian doctrine of creation, put philosophical theology into relationship with modern physical, biological, and historic conceptions. His work exercised great influence in England through its presentation, in a much modified form, by T. H. *Green, F. H. *Bradley, and B. *Bosanquet, as well as subsequently, with much greater reserve, by A. S. Pringle-*Pattison, C. C. J. *Webb, and W. *Temple.

The main trend in the early part of the 20th century was against immanentism, with a reaffirmation of the Divine transcendence. The beginnings of the movement are probably to be sought in the reaction against the anti-intellectualism of such movements as *Pragmatism (W. *James, H. *Bergson, F. C. S. Schiller's 'Humanism') and also RC *Modernism (M. *Blondel, A. *Loisy). After 1914 the movement was esp. associated in Protestant theology with the names of K. *Barth and, in a less extreme form, E. *Brunner. In Catholic theology this movement had its counterpart in a revival of the Scholastic teaching about a Divine Being at once rigidly traditional in its fundamental principles and yet anxious to take full account of the changed position of secular thought. This Scholastic movement, which may be said to take its origin with the constitution 'Dei Filius' of the First *Vatican Council (1870), was fostered by *Leo XIII and the Louvain School (D. J. *Mercier). Among its later exponents were É. *Gilson, R. Garrigou-Lagrange, J. *Maritain, M. C. *D'Arcy, and E. L. Mascall. Also keen to develop Thomist insights in the contexts of modern philosophical trends were the 'transcendental Thomists', of whom the most prominent were K. *Rahner and E. Coreth. Their thought was a development of that of J. Maréchal, who, back in the 1920s, produced a massive version of the transcendental critique of knowledge which claimed to be free from the 'agnosticism' characterizing the critique of Kant; their philosophical idiom was influenced by the *Existentialism of M. *Heidegger. Of the same outlook, but uninfluenced by Heidegger, was the Canadian B. J. F. Lonergan (d. 1984).

The so-called '*death of God' theology (q.v.) had a considerable vogue in the 1960s, esp. in the United States of America. Although it seems to have been no more than a passing fashion, it reflected widespread dissatisfaction with traditional philosophical Theism, some of which was inspired by reflection on the 'silence of God' during the Nazi attempt in the Second World War to exterminate the Jewish people (the *Holocaust). This dissatisfaction has been enduring, and for some led to the embracing of some form of *panentheism. Schubert Ogden, arguing that theology without God is a contradiction, sought to reconstruct the concept of God on the basis of the philosophies of A. N. Whitehead and C. Hartshorne (*Process Theology). This view revives the notion of a *coincidentia oppositorum* and presents God as both transcendent and immanent, eternal and temporal, impassible and passible. It has attracted a large following in the United States of America. Reflection on the silence of God during the Holocaust lies behind the doctrine of a God who suffers in the theology of J. *Moltmann (who also uses the term 'panentheism') and in that of E. Jüngel, who both ground this teaching directly on the doctrines of the Trinity and the Incarnation rather than on philosophical notions.

See also TRINITY, DOCTRINE OF THE.

On the OT, W. Eichrodt, *Theologie des Alten Testaments*, esp. 1 (Leipzig, 1933), pp. 86–150; 2 (ibid., 1935), pp. 1–45; Eng. tr., 1 (1967), pp. 178–288; 2 (1967), pp. 15–92; G. von *Rad, *Theologie des Alten Testaments* (2 vols., Munich, 1957–60; Eng. tr., Edinburgh, 1962–5), *passim*. More popular: A. [C. J.] Phillips, *God B.C.* (Oxford, 1977); C. Westermann, *What Does the Old Testament Say About God?*, ed. F. W. Golka (Atlanta and London, 1979). Also S. E. Balentine, *The Hidden God: The Hiding of the Face of God in the Old Testament* (Oxford Theological Monographs, 1983).

On the NT, R. *Bultmann, *Theologie des Neuen Testaments* (3 parts, Tübingen, 1948–53; Eng. tr., 2 vols., 1952–5); J. Jeremias, *Neutestamentliche Theologie* (vol. 1 only pub., Gütersloh [1971]; Eng. tr., 1971), both *passim*; H. Moxnes, *Theology in Conflict: Studies in Paul's Understanding of God in Romans* (Novum Testamentum, Supplement 53; Leiden, 1980).

On the Fathers, G. L. Prestige, *God in Patristic Thought* (1936); R. M. Grant, *The Early Christian Doctrine of God* (Charlottesville, Va., 1966); [G.] C. Stead, *Divine Substance* (1977).

The vast modern lit. includes C. C. J. Webb, *Studies in the History of Natural Theology* (1915); id., *God and Personality* (Gifford Lectures, 1918; 1918); R. Garrigou-Lagrange, OP, *Dieu, son existence et sa nature* (1914; 5th edn., 1928; Eng. tr., 2 vols., 1934–6); A. S. Pringle-Pattison, *The Idea of God in the Light of Recent Philosophy* (Gifford Lectures, 1912–13; Oxford, 1917); F. *von Hügel, *Essays and Addresses on the Philosophy of Religion* (2 series, 1921–6); id., *The Reality of God and Religion and Agnosticism*, ed. E. G. Gardner (1931); J. Maréchal, SJ, *Le Point de départ de la métaphysique* (5 vols., 1922–47); J. Maritain, *Distinguer pour unir, ou Les degrés du savoir* (1932; Eng. tr., *The Degrees of Knowledge*, 1959); W. Temple, *Nature, Man and God* (Gifford Lectures, 1932–4; 1934); K. Barth, *The Knowledge of God and the Service of God according to the Teaching of the Reformation* (Gifford Lectures, 1937–8; 1938); J. *Baillie, *Our Knowledge of God* (1939); K. Rahner, SJ, *Geist in Welt: Zur Metaphysik der endlichen Erkenntnis bei Thomas von Aquin* (Innsbruck [1939]; 2nd edn., Munich [1957]; Eng. tr., *Spirit in the World*, 1968); A. E. Taylor, *Does God Exist?* (1945; see also his art. 'Theism' in HERE 12 (1921), pp. 261–87); E. L. Mascall, *He Who Is* (1943); B. J. F. Lonergan, SJ, *Insight: A Study of Human Understanding* (1957); E. Coreth, SJ, *Metaphysik* (Innsbruck [1961]; abridged Eng. tr., with critique by B. J. F. Lonergan, New York, 1968); H. Zahrnt, *Die Sache mit Gott: Die protestantische Theologie im 20. Jahrhundert* (Munich, 1968; Eng. tr., *The Question of God*, 1969); J. Moltmann, *Der gekreuzigte Gott* (Munich [1972]; Eng. tr., *The Crucified God*, 1974); J. Macquarrie, *Thinking about God* (1975); id., *In Search of Deity*

(Gifford Lectures, 1983–4, 1984); E. Jüngel, *Gott als Geheimnis der Welt* (Tübingen, 1977; Eng. tr., *God as the Mystery of the World*, Edinburgh, 1983); H. *Küng, *Existiert Gott?* (Munich and Zurich [1978]; Eng. tr., *Does God Exist?*, 1980); [J. S.] K. Ward, *Rational Theology and the Creativity of God* (Oxford, 1982); W. Kasper, *Der Gott Jesu Christi* (Mainz, 1982; Eng. tr., 1984); B. [E. A.] Davis, OP, *Thinking about God* (1985); H. McCabe, OP, *God Matters* (1987), esp. pp. 2–51; P. Helm, *Eternal God* (1988); R. [G.] Swinburne, *The Christian God* (Oxford, 1994). See also bibl. to PROCESS THEOLOGY and 'DEATH OF GOD' THEOLOGY.

God Save the King/Queen, British National Anthem. The origins of both words and tune are obscure; and as regards the words it is also uncertain whether the Eng. or Lat. version is the older. The opening words of the Lat. are 'O Deus optime, salvum nunc facito, Regem nostrum'.

The phrase 'God save the King' occurs in the Eng. Bible at 1 Sam. 10: 24, 2 Sam. 16: 16, and 2 Kgs. 11: 12, both in the *Coverdale version (1535) and in the AV of 1611, while as early as 1545 'God save the King' was a watchword in the Navy, with 'Long to reign over us' as a counter-sign. It seems probable that the anthem arose from a series of common loyal phrases being gradually combined into one national hymn; and there is some evidence that the words were put into substantially their present form for use in the RC chapel of *James II. Among individuals of later date to whom the authorship of the Anthem has sometimes (prob. wrongly) been attributed are Henry Carey (*c.*1685–1743), author of 'Sally in our Alley', and James Oswald (*c.*1710–69), a Scotsman who had settled in London. It was certainly much used in its present form in London theatres in 1745 (the year of the landing of the Young Pretender); the three stanzas were printed in the *Gentleman's Magazine* for Oct. of the same year; and its general popularity dates from that time.

In a similar way the tune seems to be a 17th-cent. recasting of earlier phrases. We find the earliest elements in the medieval plainsong notation to the antiphon to the *Magnificat for the Saturday before the Seventh Sunday after Pentecost ('Unxerunt Salamonem'). The same rhythm occurs in a 16th-cent. Genevan folk-song. In the tune of a Christmas carol, dated 1611, and attributed to John Bull (*c.*1562–1628), it begins to take the familiar form. In the USA, where the tune goes by the name of 'America', it is sung to the words 'My country, 'tis of thee'.

W. H. Cummings, *God Save the King: The Origin and History of the Music and Words of the National Anthem* (1902); P. A. Scholes, '*God Save the King!' Its History and its Romance* (1942). Id., *God Save the Queen! The History and Romance of the World's First National Anthem* (1954; the most substantial work on the subject).

godchildren. See GODPARENTS.

Godescalc. See GOTTSCHALK.

Godfrey of Bouillon (d. 1100), *Crusader. A member of the family of the counts of Boulogne and duke of Lower Lorraine, he departed on the First Crusade in August 1096 and led the assault which captured *Jerusalem on 15 July 1099. He was elected first Christian ruler of the city as prince and began the process of extending the conquests of the Crusade into a viable political unit. He died on 18

July 1100 and was succeeded by his brother Baldwin I as king. Although Godfrey was only one of several important princes on the Crusade, the chronicler Albert of Aix represented him as its hero, and later epics depicted him as a type of the ideal Christian knight.

The account of Albert of Aix is pr. in *Recueil des Historiens des Croisades: Historiens occidentaux,* 4 (1879), pp. 265–713. Modern works incl. M. Lobet, *Godefroid de Bouillon: Essai de biographie antilégendaire* (Brussels [1943]); H. Glaesener, 'Godefroid de Bouillon, était-il "un médiocre"?', *RHE* 39 (1943), pp. 309–41; J. C. Andressohn, *The Ancestry and Life of Godfrey of Bouillon* (Indiana University Publications, Social Science Series, 5; Bloomington, 1947); H. Dorchy, 'Godefroid de Bouillon, Duc de Bas-Lotharingie', *Revue Belge de Philologie et d'Histoire,* 26 (1948), pp. 961–99; G. Waeger, *Gottfried von Bouillon in der Historiographie* (Geist und Werk der Zeiten, 18; Zurich, 1969), and G. H. Hagspiel, *Die Führerpersönlichkeit im Kreuzzug* (ibid. 10; 1963). On his status as ruler of Jerusalem, see J. Riley-Smith, 'The Title of Godfrey of Bouillon', *Bulletin of the Institute of Historical Research,* 52 (1979), pp. 83–6. E. Barker in *EB* (11th edn.), 12 (1910), p. 172, s.v. For main bibl. see works cited under CRUSADES.

godparents, also sponsors. Witnesses, in person or by proxy, to a Christian baptism, who take on themselves special responsibilities for the Christian upbringing of the newly baptized. These responsibilities are most serious in the case of infant baptism, at which the godparents also make the promises of renunciation, faith, and obedience in the child's name. The number of godparents required varies. In the RC Church one is sufficient, though there may be one of each sex. Traditionally the Anglican formularies have stated that each child should have three godparents, of whom two are to be of the same sex as the child, but modern rites tend to be less specific. In most Anglican Churches parents may stand, usually provided there is one other sponsor. Parents are barred in the RC Church and in some Protestant communions.

D. S. Bailey, *Sponsors at Baptism and Confirmation: An Historical Introduction to Anglican Practice* (1952). J. H. Lynch, *Godparents and Kinship in Early Medieval Europe* (Princeton, NJ, 1986).

Goerres, J. J. von. See GÖRRES, J. J. VON.

Gog and Magog. In Rev. 20: 8 Gog and Magog are two powers under the dominion of Satan. In the OT they appear together in Ezek., chs. 38–9. There Gog is described as the chief prince of various national groups which invade the land of Israel but are eventually to be vanquished by *Yahweh. Gog is said to be 'of the land of Magog' (38: 2). The identity of Gog and Magog in these chapters is obscure; some scholars have found reference to Scythians or other northern invaders, while others have seen in the word 'Magog' a cryptic allusion to Babylon. In the later *apocalyptic and *rabbinic literature Gog and Magog are conventional figures for those opposed to the people of God. Acc. to a medieval legend, formerly embodied in statues of Gog and Magog at the Guildhall, London (destroyed by fire in 1940), they were two giants who were made porters at 'Troynovant' (London) by 'Brutus the Trojan'.

J. G. Aalders, *Gog en Magog in Ezechiël* (Kampen, 1951), with Eng. summary. A. van den Born, 'Étude sur quelques toponymes bibliques, I. Le Pays du Magog', *Oudtestamentische Studiën,* 10 (1954), pp. 197–201. See also comm. on Ezekiel cited s.v., esp.

that of W. Zimmerli (Biblischer Kommentar, Altes Testament, 13; 2nd edn., vol. 2, 1979, pp. 940–75; Eng. tr., 2, Philadelphia, 1983, pp. 281–324, with extensive bibl.).

Gogarten, Friedrich (1887–1967), Protestant theologian. A native of Dortmund, he became pastor at Stelzendorf in Thuringia in 1917 and at Dorndorf in 1925. From 1931 to 1935 he was Professor of Systematic Theology at Breslau and from 1935 to 1953 at Göttingen. In reaction from E. *Troeltsch's historicism, Gogarten formulated a fresh interpretation of culture and civilization in the spirit of K. *Barth's *Dialectical Theology and much influenced by the thought of M. *Buber. Real historical happenings take place only in the obedience of faith when the Ego accepts the unconditional claims of a concrete 'Thou'. His writings include *Fichte als religiöser Denker* (1914), *Religion und Volkstum* (1915), *Von Glauben und Offenbarung* (1923), *Ich glaube an den dreieinigen Gott* (1926), and *Entmythologisierung und die Kirche* (1953; Eng. tr., 1955). He also contributed extensively to the Barthian periodical *Zwischen den Zeiten* (1923 onwards).

H. Fischer, *Christlicher Glaube und Geschichte: Voraussetzungen und Folgen der Theologie Friedrich Gogartens* (Gütersloh, 1967); A. V. Bauer, *Freiheit zur Welt: Zum Weltverständnis und Weltverhältnis des Christen nach der Theologie Friedrich Gogartens* (Konfessionskundliche und Kontroverstheologische Studien, 25; Paderborn, 1967); J. Vohn, *Sittliche Erkenntnis zwischen Rationalität und Glauben: Ein Aspekt der Säkularisierung im Licht der Theologie Friedrich Gogartens* (ibid. 37; 1977); R. Weth, *Gott in Jesus: Der Ansatz der Christologie Friedrich Gogartens* (Forschungen zur Geschichte und Lehre des Protestantismus, Reihe 2, Band 36; 1968), with list of his works, pp. 312–21; C. Naveillan, *Strukturen der Theologie Friedrich Gogartens* (Beiträge zur Ökumenischen Theologie, 7; 1972). P. Henke in *TRE* 13 (1984), pp. 563–7, s.v.

Golden Calf (עֵגֶל, the Heb. word translated 'calf', would be more properly rendered 'young bull'). An object of worship set up (*a*) by the Israelites in the wilderness (Ex. 32); (*b*) by King Jeroboam I (*c*.930–910 BC) at Bethel and Dan for the worship of the *Ten Tribes (1 Kgs. 12: 28).

Golden Legend. A collection of saints' lives and short treatises on the Christian festivals, compiled by *James of Voragine (q.v.). It was completed by 1265. Intended as a source-book for preachers, it had a mixed reception in James's own order, the *Dominicans, but it became enormously popular with a wider audience and was translated into many languages; some 1,000 medieval MSS of the Latin text survive. In the course of the 16th cent. its popularity declined sharply and it was attacked by some Catholics, such as J. L. Vives and M. *Cano, as well as by Protestant writers, on the grounds that its accumulation of historically implausible tales would endanger true religion. In modern times it has been the subject of renewed interest.

Editio princeps, Cologne, 1470; crit. edn. by T. Graesse (Dresden and Leipzig, 1846; 3rd edn., 1890). Caxton's tr. was repr. by W. *Morris and F. S. Ellis (3 vols., London, 1892). Modern Eng. trs. by [W.] G. Ryan and H. Ripperger (2 vols., New York and London, 1941), and by W. G. Ryan (2 vols. Princeton, NJ, 1993). M. von Nagy and N. C. de Nagy, *Die Legenda aurea und ihr Verfasser Jacobus de Voragine* (Berne and Munich, 1971); A. Boureau, *La Légende Dorée: Le système narratif de Jacques de Voragine (†1298)* (1984); S. L. Reames, *The Legenda Aurea*

(Madison, Wis., 1985). B. Fleith, *Studien zur Überlieferungsgeschichte der lateinischen Legenda Aurea* (Subsidia Hagiographica, 72; 1991). R. Rhein, *Die Legenda Aurea des Jacobus de Voragine* (Beihefte zum Archiv für Kulturgeschichte, 40; 1995). G. P. Maggioni, *Ricerche sulla composizione e sulla trasmissione della 'Legenda Aurea'* (Biblioteca di *Medioeva Latino*, 8; 1995). Sister Mary Jeremy, 'Caxton's *Golden Legend* and Voragine's *Legenda Aurea*', *Speculum*, 21 (1946), pp. 212–21. See also bibl. to JAMES OF VORAGINE.

Golden Number. The number of any year in the Metonic cycle (devised in 432 BC by the Athenian astronomer Meton) and adopted in the ecclesiastical calendar since the time of St *Hippolytus. The calculation rests on the assumption (very nearly correct) that 235 lunations ('lunar months') correspond with 19 solar years. As stated in the tables at the beginning of the BCP, the Golden Number of any given year is found by adding 1 to the number of the year of our Lord, and then dividing by 19; the remainder is the Golden Number of the year in question (or, if there is no remainder, it is 19). It was the value of the number for computing the date of *Easter that led it to be termed in the Middle Ages the Golden Number (*aureus numerus*). The view sometimes found that it was so named because it was printed in calendars in letters of gold is without authority.

Golden Rose. An ornament of wrought gold and gems in the form of a rose which is blessed by the Pope on the Fourth Sunday in *Lent ('Rose Sunday') and afterwards presented as a mark of special favour to some distinguished individual or community. In recent times it has often been sent to the queens of Catholic countries. If there is no worthy recipient, the rose is laid up in the *Vatican, where it is blessed every year until distribution is made. The origin of the custom is obscure; but as early as 1049 *Leo IX speaks of it as an ancient institution. That sent by *Clement V to the city of Basle is preserved in the Musée de Cluny at Paris.

C. Cartari, *La rosa d'oro pontificia* (Rome, 1681). E. Cornides, *Rose und Schwert im päpstlichen Zeremoniell von den Anfängen bis zum Pontifikat Gregors XIII.* (Wiener Dissertationen aus dem Gebiete der Geschichte, 9; 1967), with bibl. C. Burns, *Golden Rose and Blessed Sword: Papal Gifts to Scottish Monarchs* (Glasgow, 1970), incl. general introd. J. Kreps, OSB, 'La Rose d'or', *Les Questions liturgiques et paroissiales*, 11 (1926), pp. 71–104 and 149–78. P. M. J. Rock in *CE* 6 (1909), pp. 629 f., s.v.

Golden Rule. A (modern) name for the precept in the Sermon on the Mount: 'All things whatsoever ye would that men should do to you, do ye even so to them' (Mt. 7: 12; cf. Lk. 6: 31). In a negative form it is found in the *Western text of Acts 15: 29, and in a saying attributed to *Hillel in the Talmud (b. Shabbath, 31a).

A. Dihle, *Die Goldene Regel: Eine Einführung in die Geschichte der antiken und frühchristlichen Vulgärethik* (1962).

Golden Sequence. The *Sequence for *Whitsunday, '*Veni, Sancte Spiritus' (q.v.).

Golgotha. See CALVARY, MOUNT.

Gomar, Francis (1563–1641), Dutch *Calvinist leader. A native of Bruges, he studied at Strasbourg, Neustadt, *Oxford, *Cambridge, and Heidelberg. In 1586 he became pastor of the Dutch community at Frankfurt and in 1594 was appointed professor of theology at *Leiden. Here he became an upholder of strict Calvinist principles, and engaged in a prolonged controversy with J. *Arminius, esp. after the latter became his fellow-professor in 1603. After Arminius' death (1609) the bitterness of the controversy was increased by the appointment of the liberal C. *Vorstius as Arminius' successor. Accordingly in 1611 Gomar resigned and became minister of the Reformed congregation at Middleburg and lecturer at the theological school there. From 1615 to 1618 he taught at Saumur and from 1618 till his death held a professorship at Groningen. At the Synod of *Dort (1618–19) he was among the principal opponents of Arminianism but failed to win majority support for his *Supralapsarian view of Predestination. A keen student of the Semitic languages, he was one of the official revisers of the Dutch OT. The bulk of his theological work was devoted to scriptural exegesis where, despite his convinced Calvinism, he had the highest regard for the scholarship of *Erasmus.

Works pub. in 3 vols., fol., Amsterdam, 1644. G. P. van Itterzon, *Franciscus Gomar* [in Dutch] (The Hague, 1929). J. Forget in *DTC* 6 (1920), cols. 1477–86, s.v.; G. P. van Itterzon in *Biografisch Lexicon voor de Geschiedenis van het Nederlandse Protestantisme*, 2 (1983), pp. 220–5. See also works cited under DORT, SYNOD OF.

Gonzales, St Peter. See ELMO, ST.

Good Friday ('Feria sexta in Parasceve'). The Friday before Easter on which the anniversary of the Crucifixion is kept. It is a day of fast, abstinence, and penance, and in the RC Church Good Friday, together with (after 1955) *Holy Saturday, are the only days in the year on which no Celebration of the Mass takes place.

The present Latin Rite goes back to the early days of Christianity. It consists of three parts: (1) the lessons and prayers, which are virtually the old 'Mass of the *Catechumens', with the singing of the Passion acc. to St John; (2) the ceremonial *Veneration of the Cross, described already in the 'Peregrinatio *Egeriae', with the chanting of the *Reproaches and the *Trisagion; and (3) the Communion with Hosts reserved on Maundy Thursday (see Mass of the *Presanctified). Since 1955 this has included a General Communion of the people. The liturgical colour of the day, which was formerly black, is now red. The hour of the service, which since the 16th cent. had customarily taken place in the morning, was moved in 1955 to the afternoon (about 3 p.m., the traditional hour of Christ's death) or later. *Tenebrae of Holy Saturday, which until the 1955 reform was sung on Good Friday evening, has now been restored to the morning of Holy Saturday.

Most of the medieval practices were abolished by the Churches of the Reformation. The C of E provides for the normal celebration of the Eucharist, but until recently this very rarely happened, and in modern Anglicanism a form of service akin to that of the current RC rite has been fairly widely adopted. (*Lent, Holy Week, Easter: Services and Prayers commended by the House of Bishops of the General Synod of the Church of England* (1986) provides for both.) In some Nonconformist Churches the day is kept as a feast rather than a fast; in Continental Protestantism it is customary to have the usual services with sermons, and often Good Friday is a special day for the administra-

tion of the Lord's Supper. In the RC Church popular devotions developed beside the liturgical services. The best known is the *Three Hours Service from noon to 3 p.m., a post-Reformation devotion propagated by the *Jesuits and widely taken over in the C of E.

In the *Orthodox Church the day is known as the 'Great Friday' (ἡ μεγάλη παρασκευή). The liturgical celebrations consist of the Divine *Office, each office being extended. Mattins (anticipated on the evening of Maundy Thursday) includes the chanting of the 'Twelve Gospels' (i.e. 12 passages drawn from the Passion narratives of all four Gospels). On the Good Friday morning the Little Hours (known as the 'Royal Hours' from the customary attendance of the Emperor or Tsar) follow one immediately after another; each includes a lesson from the Prophets, an Epistle and a Gospel. Vespers ends with the solemn veneration of the *epitaphion. Compline includes a lamentation placed on the lips of the BVM. Mattins of Holy Saturday, on Good Friday night, finishes with a symbolic burial service of Christ.

H. A. P. Schmidt, SJ (ed.), *Hebdomada Sancta*, 1 (Rome, 1956), pp. 92–116; 2, part 1 (1957), *passim*; 2, part 2 (1957), pp. 778–808. H. Thurston, SJ, *Lent and Holy Week* (1904), pp. 326–403; J. W. Tyrer, *Historical Survey of Holy Week: Its Services and Ceremonial* (Alcuin Club Collections, 29; 1932), esp. pp. 116–42. G. G. Willis, *Essays in Early Roman Liturgy* (ibid. 46; 1964), pp. 1–48 ('The Solemn Prayers of Good Friday'). S. Janeras, *Le Vendredi-Saint dans la tradition liturgique byzantine* (Studia Anselmiana, 99; 1988). T. P. Gilmartin in *CE* 6 (1909), pp. 643–5, s.v.; W. J. O'Shea in *NCE* 6 (1967), pp. 621–4, s.v.

Good Samaritan. The Samaritan of the parable in Lk. 10: 30–7 who, in contrast to the priest and Levite who 'passed by on the other side', tended the traveller who had fallen among thieves on his way from *Jerusalem to *Jericho and provided hospitality for him at an inn. His action illustrates the Christian response to the question: 'Who is my neighbour?' (Lk. 10: 29).

W. Monselewski, *Der barmherzige Samariter: Eine auslegungsgeschichtliche Untersuchung zu Lukas 10, 25–37* (Beiträge zur Geschichte der biblischen Exegese, 5; Tübingen, 1967). See also comm. on LUKE, GOSPEL OF ST.

Good Shepherd. The title of Christ based esp. on His discourse in Jn. 10: 7–18 and the parable of the Good Shepherd in Lk. 15: 3–7 (cf. Mt. 18: 12–14). The theme, which rests partly upon OT imagery (esp. Is. 40: 11 and Ezek. 34), is taken up later in the NT, e.g. in Heb. 13: 20 and 1 Pet. 2: 25 and 5: 4. In early Christian art Christ was frequently represented (e.g. in the *catacombs) as the Good Shepherd with a lamb upon His shoulders. The Second Sunday after *Easter has sometimes been known as 'Good Shepherd Sunday', on account of the traditional Gospel for the day, which in the RC Church is now used in only one year out of three.

Gorcum Martyrs. A group of 19 religious and secular priests who were put to death by *Calvinists at Briel on 9 July 1572, after the capture of Gorcum (or Gorinchem, S. Holland) by the *Gueux (26 June 1572). Eleven of the martyrs were friars of the *Franciscan convent at Gorcum. They were beatified by Clement X in 1675 and canonized by *Pius IX on 29 June 1867. Feast day, 9 July.

W. *Estius, *Historia Martyrum Gorcomiensium* (Douai, 1603), repr. in *AASS*, Jul. 2 (1721), pp. 736–847. J. Meerbergen, *Die HH. Martelaren van Gorcum* (Tongerloo, 1928); D. de Lange, *De Martelaren van Gorcum* (Utrecht [1954]). G. Hesse, 'De oudere Historiografie der HH. Martelaren van Gorcum', *Collectanea Franciscana Neerlandica*, 2 (1931), pp. 447–98; W. Lampen, OFM, 'Notae de SS. Nicolao et Sociis O.F.M. Martyribus Gorcomiensibus', *Collectanea Franciscana*, 28 (1958), pp. 404–11. J.-F. Gilmont in *DHGE* 21 (1986), cols. 731–3, s.v. 'Gorcum (Martyrs de)'.

Gordon Riots (also **No Popery Riots**). The riots that broke out on 2 June 1780 when a mob, headed by Lord George Gordon, an eccentric and fanatic, marched to Parliament with a petition for the repeal of the *Catholic Relief Act of 1778. The huge procession of demonstrators carried flags with the legend 'No Popery', and, after pillaging the houses of Catholics, the rioters became completely out of hand and held the City of London until, at the personal command of George III, they were dispersed by the military. 210 persons were killed in the streets and another 75 died of wounds. Lord George Gordon, after being acquitted on a charge of high treason (1781), became a Jew and finally (1793) died insane in Newgate prison.

J. P. de Castro, *The Gordon Riots* (1928), with bibl. G. F. E. Rudé, 'The Gordon Riots: A Study of the Rioters and their Victims', *Transactions of the Royal Historical Society*, 5th ser. 6 (1956), pp. 93–114. C. Hibbert, *King Mob: The Story of Lord George Gordon and the Riots of 1780* (1958). The proceedings of the trial of Gordon for high treason on 5 and 6 Feb. 1781, taken in shorthand by S. Gurney, are repr. in *A Complete Collection of State Trials and Proceedings for High Treason and other Misdemeanours*, ed. T. R. Howell, 21 (1814), cols. 485–652; the trial of H. J. Maskell, also connected with the riot, is pr. ibid., cols. 653–88. *The Life of Lord George Gordon* by his friend and admirer, Robert Watson (1795). Modern Life by P. Colson, *The Strange History of Lord George Gordon* (1937). L. Stephen in *DNB* 22 (1890), pp. 197 f., s.v. 'Gordon, Lord George'.

Gordon's Calvary. The site outside the Damascus Gate in the north wall of *Jerusalem which is held by some modern archaeologists to be the place of Christ's Crucifixion. As against the traditional site of the *Holy Sepulchre, this place was first proposed by O. Thenius in 1849. It derives its usual name from General C. G. Gordon, a strong advocate of it. It is a cliff with weathermarks which have a certain likeness to the features of a human countenance (cf. Jn. 19: 17: 'the place of a skull'), but the shape of the rock in this area is largely due to later quarrying. Since there is now archaeological evidence that the traditional site was outside the walls of Jerusalem at the time of the Crucifixion, Gordon's Calvary cannot claim credence on the ground that it alone was 'without the gate' (Heb. 13: 12). Nearby is a tomb, known as the 'Garden Tomb', which advocates of Gordon's Calvary hold to have been the site of Christ's burial.

C. G. Gordon, *Reflections in Palestine 1883* (1884), pp. 1–3. See further general works, s.v. CALVARY and JERUSALEM.

Gore, Charles (1853–1932), Bp. of *Oxford. Educated at Harrow and Balliol College, Oxford, he was elected a Fellow of Trinity College, Oxford, in 1875. From his schooldays he had been a *High Churchman, and in 1884, on H. P. *Liddon's recommendation, was appointed first principal of Pusey House, Oxford. His independent mind, combined with an almost prophetic strength of character, brought a new strand into the Anglo-Catholic Movement. In his concern to bring Catholic principles to bear on social problems and to come to terms with OT criticism, he exercised great influence on the younger generation at Oxford. When in 1889 *Lux Mundi (q.v.) appeared under Gore's editorship, his own essay on 'The Holy Spirit and Inspiration' caused disquiet among many of the older and more conservative school of High Church theologians. In *The Ministry of the Christian Church* (1888; new edn., 1919), by C. H. *Turner) he upheld Catholic teaching about episcopacy, largely in criticism of E. *Hatch's *Bampton Lectures. His own Bampton Lectures (1891) on 'The Incarnation of the Son of God' were a popular exposition of the *kenotic theory of the Incarnation. They were supplemented by his *Dissertations* on allied subjects in 1895.

Meanwhile Gore had been actively concerned with the foundation of the *Community of the Resurrection (now at Mirfield), and in 1893 he became vicar of Radley, Oxon, settling the community in the vicarage. From 1894 to 1902 he was a Canon of *Westminster. Here he became widely known as a preacher and exegete, and several series of his NT expositions were afterwards issued as books. In his *Body of Christ* (1901), a work on the Eucharist, he set out the place of the Sacrament in the Christian life and also sought to reformulate the doctrine of the Real Presence without *transubstantiation.

In 1902 he was consecrated Bp. of *Worcester and when, largely through his initiative, the diocese of Birmingham was established in 1905 he became its first bishop. Here in the civic life of Birmingham he was highly successful. In 1911 he was translated to Oxford. He was far less happy in this large rural diocese and became increasingly conscious of isolation through the trend of various theological controversies (*Foundations, *Reservation, etc.) and the absence of Catholic support in the Convocations. In 1919 he resigned his see. In his later years he continued to write in defence of the Christian faith. His trilogy, *Belief in God* (1921), *Belief in Christ* (1922), and *The Holy Spirit and the Church* (1924)—the three works being subsequently reissued in a single volume as *The Reconstruction of Belief*—was very widely read and appreciated. After 1920 his attitude towards certain developments in Anglo-Catholicism became increasingly critical, and in 1925 he summarized his position in *The Anglo-Catholic Movement To-day*; but he remained a fervent apologist for High Church principles until his death. His other writings include *The Question of Divorce* (1911), *The Religion of the Church* (1916), and *Jesus of Nazareth* (Home University Library, 1929).

G. L. Prestige, *The Life of Charles Gore: A Great Englishman* (1935). J. Carpenter, *Gore: A Study in Liberal Catholic Thought* (1960). J. [F.] Gore [nephew], *Charles Gore, Father and Son: A Background to the Early Years and Family Life of Bishop Gore* (1932). G. Crosse, *Charles Gore* (1932); A. Mansbridge, *Edward Stuart Talbot and Charles Gore* (1935). R. Ekström, *The Theology of Charles Gore* (Lund, 1944). P. [D. L.] Avis, *Gore: Construction and Conflict* (Worthing, 1988). A. Wilkinson, *The Community of the Resurrection* (1992), *passim*. W. R. *Inge, 'Bishop Gore and the Church of England' (anon.), *Edinburgh Review*, 207 (1908), pp. 79–104; repr. in Inge's *Outspoken Essays*, 1 (1919), pp. 106–36. A. T. P. Williams in *DNB*, 1931–1940, pp. 349–53.

Gorgonia, St (d. *c.*370), sister of St *Gregory of Nazianzus (q.v.) and St *Caesarius. She is known almost exclusively through St Gregory's panegyric (*Orat.* 8), which represents her as of a pious and generous disposition. An incident in her life has sometimes (but probably wrongly) been taken as an early instance of devotion to the Reserved Sacrament. In acc. with contemporary custom she was not baptized until the end of her life. Feast day in E., 23 Feb.; in W., 9 Dec.

Gregory's *Oratio* is repr. in J. P. Migne, *PG* 35. 787–818. H. Thurston, SJ, 'The Early Cultus of the Reserved Eucharist', *JTS* 11 (1909–10), pp. 275–9. D. Gorce in *DHGE* 21 (1986), cols. 762–5, s.v.

Gorham Case. In 1847 the Revd G. C. Gorham was presented by the Lord Chancellor to the vicarage of Brampford Speke in the diocese of *Exeter. The Bp. of Exeter, H. *Phillpotts, who suspected his orthodoxy, examined him, found him unsound on the doctrine of *baptismal regeneration, and refused to institute him to the living. After a complicated lawsuit, Gorham appealed to the recently formed *Judicial Committee of the Privy Council, which, attributing to him a view which he did not hold, declared it to be not contrary to the doctrine of the C of E. The decision gave great offence to High Churchmen and aroused a storm of controversy. Over 60 books and pamphlets were published, and many seceded to the RC Church, including H. E. *Manning and R. I. *Wilberforce. As the Bp. of Exeter still refused to institute, Gorham was eventually instituted by Abp. J. B. *Sumner. The case had the result of drawing attention to the limitations of the Privy Council as an ecclesiastical court of appeal.

J. C. S. Nias, *Gorham and the Bishop of Exeter* (1951), with full bibl. details of pamphlets and other contemporary literature.

Görres, Johann Joseph von (1776–1848), German Catholic author. A native of Coblenz, he was educated under the deep influence of the rationalism of the 18th cent. As a youth he was an enthusiastic supporter of the French Revolution, but a stay at Paris in 1799–1800 disillusioned him. In 1800–6 he taught natural science at Coblenz. The study of J. G. *Herder and F. W. J. von *Schelling awakened his religious interests, which found expression in his *Glaube und Wissen* (1805), a work of largely pantheistic character. In 1806–8 he lectured at Heidelberg University, mainly on historical and literary subjects. Here he came into contact with the leaders of German Romanticism, whose love of the religious history of the past inspired his *Mythengeschichte der asiatischen Welt* (2 vols., 1810). During the Napoleonic wars he took up the cause of German independence and was for a time an immensely popular figure. In 1814 he started the first great German newspaper, the *Rheinischer Merkur*. After the Peace of Paris (1815) he met with increasing hostility from the reactionary Prussian government and his paper was suppressed in 1816. In *Teutschland und die Revolution* (1819) he demanded liberty and a fuller place for the Catholic Church in public life. An order of arrest followed, but Görres escaped by flight to Strasbourg. In 1824 he formally returned to the faith of the RC Church. In 1827 Ludwig I of Bavaria offered him a professorship at Munich University, where he became the centre of a circle of famous Catholic scholars, among whom were J. J. I. von *Döllinger and J. A. *Möhler. From 1828 to 1832 they

published the influential periodical *Eos*, which opposed Catholic ideals to the contemporary rationalism. There followed his *Christliche Mystik* (4 vols., 1836–42), which, though uncritical in the use of sources and sometimes fanciful, gave a strong impulse to the study of the mystics. When, in 1837, the Abp. of Cologne, Clemens August von *Droste-Vischering, was deposed and imprisoned by the Prussian government, Görres took up his cause in his tract *Athanasius* (1838), which brought all Catholic Germany to the defence of the Church. Another treatise, *Die Triarier* (1838), directed against the defenders of the government, received special Papal approval. His last years were darkened by the scandal round Lola Montez which resulted in the deposition of several professors belonging to his circle. A brilliant writer, he devoted himself unstintingly to the cause he had at heart. His work contributed considerably to the spread of Catholic ideas in modern Germany.

The 'Görres-Gesellschaft zur Pflege der Wissenschaft im katholischen Deutschland' was founded at Coblenz on the centenary of Görres's birth (25 Jan. 1876) to promote scientific and historical studies on Catholic principles. Suppressed by the Nazis in 1941, when its property was confiscated, it was reconstituted in 1948. It publishes, *inter alia*, two important periodicals, the *Historisches Jahrbuch* and *Oriens Christianus*. Collected edn. of Görres's writings, Munich, 9 vols., 1854–74; crit. edn. by W. Schellberg and others under the auspices of the Görres-Gesellschaft (Cologne, 1926 ff., with suppl. vol. containing biog. information, ed. H. Raab, 1985). Selected Works ed. W. Frühwald (2 vols., Freiburg, etc., 1978). Lives by J. Galland (Freiburg i.B., 1876), J. N. Sepp (Nördlingen, 1877; 2nd edn., Dresden, 1896), W. Schellberg (Cologne, 1926), R. Saitschick (Olten and Freiburg i.B., 1953), and H. Raab (Paderborn, 1978). The *Historisches Jahrbuch*, 96 (1976), Heft 1, was devoted to studies of his thought, marking the 200th anniversary of his birth. H. Jaeger, SJ, in *Dict. Sp.* 6 (1967), cols. 572–8; B. Wacker in *L.Th.K.* (3rd edn.), 4 (1995), cols. 841 f., both s.v., with bibl.

Gorton, Samuel (*c*.1592–1677), founder of the 'Gortonites'. Born in Lancashire, he worked as a clothier in London for some time before he sailed *c*.1636 for Boston, Mass., in the hope of enjoying complete religious freedom. Of a fiery and difficult temperament, he found himself engaged in continual conflict with the civil authorities in America. He gradually came to hold many unorthodox doctrines, e.g. he denied that of the Trinity and professed faith in *conditional immortality. Further difficulties with the civil powers led him to return to England in 1644, where he published an attack on what he held to be the repressive policy of the Massachusetts government, *Simplicitie's Defence against Seven-Headed Policy* (1646). He died in America. His followers survived as a sect till the middle of the 18th cent.

His *Simplicitie's Defence* and a letter to Nathaniel Morton are repr. in P. Force (ed.), *Tracts and Other Papers Relating Principally to the Origin, Settlement and Progress of the Colonies in North America*, 4 (1846); further letters in *Collections of the Massachusetts Historical Society*, 4th ser. 7 (1865), pp. 601–31. Lives by J. M. Mackie in J. Sparks (ed.), *Library of American Biography*, 2nd ser. 5 (Boston, 1845), pp. 317–411, and by A. Gorton (Philadelphia, 1907). P. F. Gura, 'The Radical Ideology of Samuel Gorton: New Light on the Relation of English to American Puritanism', *William and Mary Quarterly*, 3rd ser. 36 (Williamsburg, 1979), pp.

78–100. C. Goodwin in *DNB* 22 (1890), pp. 251–3; J. T. Adams in *Dict. Amer. Biog.* 7 (1931), pp. 438 f.

Gorze, *Benedictine monastery in the diocese of Metz, not far from the city. It was founded in 748 by St *Chrodegang, who acquired the relics of the Roman martyr St Gorgonius for the house. Like other Lotharingian communities, it went through a difficult period with lay abbots in the 9th cent. After 933, however, it was revived and built up by Adalbero I, Bp. of Metz (929–62), and became one of the chief seats of monastic reform; it acquired great influence and many adherents, esp. in the Empire. Not only was the abbey itself a centre of monastic revival based on rigorous conventual discipline, common life and efficient estate management, in the area E. of the Rhine, but it has become customary to describe a variety of observances and their propagation as 'Gorzian' in contrast with those of *Cluny. The Gorzian reform worked within the traditions of St *Benedict of Aniane. One of its salient features was that its leaders, such as Abbots Arnold (d. *c.*968), John (d. 974) and Immo (d. *c.*1015) put themselves at the disposal of patrons, both lay and episcopal, who invited them to take charge of and reform monasteries in their domains. *Reichenau and St *Gall were among the houses reformed in this way. Ecclesiastical and secular control remained with the bishops, lordship and advocacy with the lay rulers who had called in the abbots of Gorze or their disciples. They did not form a network of institutions permanently subject to a mother house and their association found expression chiefly in the bonds of confraternity and mutual prayer.

Historians of monasticism have distinguished between the original currents of reforming enterprise from Gorze and St Maximin, Trier, and a new impulse, the so-called neo-Gorzian (*Junggorze*) movement of the 11th cent. In this the influence of Cluny on the internal life of the communities was more marked, but the constitutional arrangements were left unchanged. The chief agents of this observance were St William of Dijon (Abbot of Gorze *c.*1016–31) and two monks of the house, Ekkebert, later Abbot of Schwarzach (in the diocese of Würzburg), and Herrand of Ilsenburg, nr. Halberstadt, who became bishop in 1090. In distant abbeys such as Tegernsee, traces of the Gorzian customs, introduced in the 10th cent., remained until well into the 12th.

The importance of Gorze declined after the 11th cent., but the monastery continued in existence until its secularization in 1572. In 1580 canons took the place of monks until the chapter was suppressed in 1790.

The Cartulary of Gorze was ed. A. d'Herbomez (Mettensia, 2; Mémoires et documents publiés par la Société Nationale des Antiquaires de France, Paris, 1898); the Necrology of Gorze was ed. M. Parisse (Annales de l'Est publiées par l'Université de Nancy II, Mémoire, 40; 1971). The principal narrative sources are the Life of Abbot John written by John of St Arnulf between 974 and 984, ed. H. G. Pertz in *MGH*, Scriptores, 4 (1841), pp. 335–77, and the 'Miracula S. Gorgonii' of *c.*964, ibid., pp. 238–47. K. Hallinger, OSB, *Gorze-Kluny: Studien zu den monastischen Lebensformen und Gegensätzen im Hochmittelalter* (Studia Anselmiana, 22–5; Rome, 1950–1). N. Reimann, 'Beitrag zur Geschichte des Klosters Gorze im Spätmittelalter (1270–1387)', *Studien und Mitteilungen zur Geschichte des Benediktiner-Ordens*, 81 (1970), pp. 337–89. N. Bulst, *Untersuchungen zu den Klosterreformen Wilhelms von Dijon (962–1031)* (Pariser historische Studien, 11; Bonn,

1973). J. Schneider in *DHGE* 21 (1986), cols. 811–17; M. Parisse in *Lexikon des Mittelalters*, 4 (1989), cols. 1565–7, both s.v.

Goscelin (d. after 1107), English hagiographer. He is believed to have been born at or near Thérouanne, in France, and entered the *Benedictine monastery of St Bertin at St Omer. Herman, then Bp. of Ramsbury (later Bp. of Sherborne and then *Salisbury), came there in exile, and on his return to England in 1058 took Goscelin into his service. Goscelin was also, for a time, one of the chaplains to the nuns of Wilton, and *c.*1080 wrote the Life of St Edith. At Wilton he was the director of Eve, one of the nuns, who became a recluse at Angers. To her he wrote his 'Liber Confortatorius' (1082–3), a work of spiritual direction. Before it was written Goscelin had fallen into disfavour with Herman's successor, *Osmund, and he seems to have stayed in a succession of monastic houses (among them *Peterborough, *Ely, Ramsey, and the nunnery of Barking), writing the Lives of local saints, usually based on earlier material. About 1090 he came to St Augustine's, *Canterbury, where he remained for the rest of his life. He wrote Lives of many Canterbury saints, the chief being a longer and shorter Life of St *Augustine and an account of the translation of his relics. The date of Goscelin's death is unknown, but he was still alive in 1107. He was a skilful writer, but his rhymed prose and high-flown vocabulary are an obstacle to the modern reader's enjoyment. His Lives were the means by which the memory of many Anglo-Saxon saints survived the Norman Conquest.

The longer of his Lives of St Augustine (the *Historia Major*) is repr. in J. P. Migne, *PL* 80. 43–94; the shorter (the *Historia Minor*) is repr. ibid. 150. 743–64, with the account of the translation of his relics, 155. 13–46. Of the other Lives collected in Migne, *PL* 155. 47–116, that of St *Swithun (47–80) is spurious; those of St *Ives, St *Werburg, St Edith, and St Laurence, Abp. of Canterbury, are genuine. The Life of St Edith is pr. in full by A. *Wilmart, OSB, in *Anal. Boll.* 56 (1938), pp. 5–101, 265–307; Life of St Wulfhild of Barking ed. M. Esposito, ibid. 32 (1913), pp. 10–26; that of St Wulsin (or Wulfsige), Bp. of Sherborne, ed. C. H. Talbot in *R. Bén.* 69 (1959), pp. 68–85; that of St *Mildred, ed. D. W. Rollason, *The Mildrith Legend* (Leicester, 1982), pp. 105–43, and her translation ed. id. in *Mediaeval Studies*, 48 (1986), pp. 139–210; M. L. Colker, 'Texts of Joscelyn of Canterbury which relate to the History of Barking Abbey', *Studia Monastica*, 7 (1965), pp. 383–460, with introd.; the Life of St *Justus is pr. in *AASS*, Nov. 4 (1925), pp. 535–7. For the Life of St Milburg, H. P. R. Finberg, *The Early Charters of the West Midlands* (Leicester, 1961), pp. 197–216. It is possible that Goscelin was the author of the anonymous Life of *Edward the Confessor, ed., with Eng. tr., by F. Barlow, *The Life of King Edward . . . attributed to a Monk of St Bertin* (1962), who gives the best account of his works, pp. 91–111, with further refs. The 'Liber Confortatorius' was ed. C. H. Talbot in *Studia Anselmiana*, 37 (Rome, 1955), pp. 1–117. A. Wilmart, OSB, 'Ève et Goscelin', *R. Bén.* 46 (1934), pp. 414–38; 50 (1938), pp. 42–83.

Gospel (Gk. εὐαγγέλιον, Old Eng. *godspel*, 'good news'). (1) The central content of the Christian revelation, the glad tidings of redemption. It is St *Paul's epistles that have given to this Greek noun such an important position in Christian vocabulary, but the way he uses it without explanation in writing to believers in *Rome whom he did not know suggests that the Christian sense was already current. St *Mark follows Paul's usage but can also on occasion extend it to refer to the contents of Christ's own preaching (1: 14 f.). The cognate verb εὐαγγελίζομαι, to bring glad tidings, is found in religious contexts in the *Septuagint. Is. 52: 7 is quoted at Rom. 10: 15, with reference to the Christian message, and Is. 61: 1 at Mt. 11: 5 (par. Lk. 7: 22) on the lips of Christ, with reference to His own preaching. The centrality of the noun in Paul and Mk. probably derives from the Septuagintal verb which Paul and later St *Luke use frequently. But the noun also has a pagan background and usage evidenced in an inscription from Priene (9 BC), where Augustus' birthday is said to have been 'for the world the beginning of things which owing to him are *glad tidings*'.

(2) During the 2nd cent. the word came to be used as a title for the written books in which the Christian Gospel was set forth. This usage may have been drawn from the ambiguous title line of Mk. (1: 1). As there can properly be only one Gospel (cf. Gal. 1: 7), 2nd-cent. superscriptions called the Church's books 'The Gospel *according to* Matthew' (τὸ εὐαγγέλιον κατὰ Μαθθαῖον), etc. The unique authority belonging to the four Gospels of Matthew, Mark, Luke, and John was becoming established in the second half of the century. It is asserted by St *Irenaeus, but already in effect presupposed by *Tatian's *Diatessaron.

(3) The word is also used to refer to the so-called *apocryphal Gospels written in the 2nd cent. and later outside the emerging Church, even though some of them lack the narrative framework normally considered characteristic of the genre. The Gospel of *Thomas provides parallels to a few Synoptic sayings and parables and some scholars have argued that these may derive from the oral tradition rather than being dependent on the Synoptic Gospels. But in general these writings, including Thomas, are clearly later and historically inferior to the canonical Gospels whose authority they never seriously challenged in the Church. They are of interest rather to the general historian of religion.

There is a general introd. by G. N. Stanton, *The Gospels and Jesus* (Oxford, 1989); see also R. A. Burridge, *What are the Gospels? A Comparison with Graeco-Roman Biography* (Society for New Testament Studies, Monograph Series, 70; 1992) and arts. on separate Gospels. A number of the apocryphal Gospels are listed, with lit. on them, s.v. APOCRYPHAL NEW TESTAMENT; Eng. tr. of main texts in Schneemelcher (5th edn.), 1 (Eng. tr., 1991), and in J. K. Elliott, *The Apocryphal New Testament* (Oxford, 1993), pp. 1–225; Eng. tr. of the *Nag Hammadi material also in J. M. Robinson, *The Nag Hammadi Library in English* (Leiden, 1977; 3rd edn., 1988). The non-canonical material is given prominence in E. Pagels, *The Gnostic Gospels* (New York, 1979; London, 1980); J. D. Crossan, *Four Other Gospels: Shadows on the Contours of Canon* (Minneapolis [1985]); and H. Koester, *Ancient Christian Gospels: Their History and Development* (1990); judicious evaluation by C. M. Tuckett, *Nag Hammadi and The Gospel Tradition* (Edinburgh, 1986).

Gospel (in the Liturgy). In the Eucharistic rite, the lection from the Gospels proper to each Mass. It varies greatly in length, from one or two verses to a whole chapter or more. It always occupies the last place (i.e. after the *Epistle and other lections, if any) as the position of honour. Traditionally it is the privilege of the deacon to read it, though at one time it was read at *Constantinople on Easter Day by the bishop and at *Alexandria by the

archdeacon (*Sozomen, *HE* 7. 19). In early times it was prob. read from the *ambo by the deacon facing south; nowadays in the W., wherever the Gospel is read, the reader always faces the people, though in the E., a deacon (if not in the pulpit) faces east, and bishops (and usually priests) face west. In the Byzantine rite Gospels are solemnly chanted at various other services, notably at Mattins on Sundays and major feast days.

In the current W. rite, the deacon, bearing the book, goes in procession to the appointed place, accompanied by *thurifer and *acolytes, and before beginning to read says 'Dominus vobiscum', announces the place, makes the *sign of the cross on the book and on himself and censes the book. He then reads the Gospel in its proper tone. The use of lights at the Gospel is already mentioned by St *Jerome (*Bethlehem, AD 378). The early custom of the congregation standing was retained for the reading of the Gospel even when different postures became usual for other parts of the service; cf. the rubric in the BCP (inserted by J. *Cosin in 1661). See also LAST GOSPEL.

Jungmann (1958 edn.), 1, pp. 565–83; Eng. tr., pp. 442–55, with refs. See also bibl. to EVANGELIARY and LECTIONARY.

Gospel Music. Religious music of a *revivalist nature, originating in the *United States of America in the second half of the 19th cent. Its texts, involving much use of the first person, tend to emphasize the themes of personal salvation and the anticipation of heavenly joys, while the music is largely derived stylistically from popular secular music. Developing from the *spirituals and *Sunday School hymnody, it fully manifested itself in the hymn-singing and other music associated with the crusades of D. L. *Moody and I. D. Sankey, and was disseminated in such publications as Sankey's *Sacred Songs and Solos* (1873; much altered in numerous later editions). The music, unsophisticated in both melody and harmony, owed much to the parlour and theatre songs of the time, and was often coupled to words of a sentimental nature. Its most characteristic feature is the use of a refrain at the end of each verse. 'Blessed assurance' and 'The old rugged Cross' are typical examples. The music of the *Salvation Army and other *Evangelical groups was strongly influenced by the style. In the *Black Churches from the early 20th cent. Gospel Music took a more radical form, incorporating elements of ragtime, jazz, blues, and similar styles, with considerable florid embellishment of simple melodies and much 'call and response' interaction between those leading the singing and the congregation. Its performance may involve anything from a solo singer with guitar or instrumental group (electronic *organ, drums, and tambourine are esp. favoured) to full-scale 'gospel choirs', with or without congregational participation. Hand-clapping, dancing, and other physical movements are a common accompaniment, and in its more extreme forms it can induce trance-like states and be associated with 'speaking in tongues' (*glossolalia). This Black style of Gospel Music has spread throughout the *Pentecostal and other charismatically inspired Churches world-wide. It has also had considerable commercial appeal, often independent of its religious context; with professional performers, it enjoys a significant place in the popular music recording market, where it is usually known simply as 'Gospel'.

T. Heilbut, *The Gospel Sound: Good News and Bad Times* (New York [1971]); S. S. Sizer, *Gospel Hymns and Social Religion: The Rhetoric of Nineteenth-Century Revivalism* (Philadelphia, 1978); D. Cusic, *The Sound of Light: A History of Gospel Music* (Bowling Green, Oh. [1990]). J. H. Hall, *Biography of Gospel Song and Hymn Writers* (New York [1914]); J. R. Baxter, *Gospel Song Writers Biography* (Dallas, 1971); R. Anderson and G. North, *Gospel Music Encyclopedia* (New York and London [1979]). I. V. Jackson, *Afro-American Religious Music: A Bibliography and a Catalogue of Gospel Music* (Westport, Conn , and London, 1979). H. Eskew and P. Oliver in S. Sadie (ed.), *The New Grove Dictionary of Music and Musicians*, 7 (1980), pp. 549–59, s.v.; rev. and expanded version by H. Eskew and others in H. W. Hitchcock and S. Sadie (eds.), *The New Grove Dictionary of American Music*, 2 (1986), pp. 248–61, s.v.

Gospel of Truth. See EVANGELIUM VERITATIS.

Gospeller. The person who reads or sings the Gospel at the *Eucharist. The word is used esp. of the deacon who is selected by the bishop from among the newly ordained to perform this function at an Ordination Mass.

Gother (more correctly **Goter**), **John** (d. 1704), RC controversialist. A native of Southampton, he came from a *Presbyterian family and was converted to the RC faith at an early age. In 1668 he entered the English College at Lisbon, where he was ordained priest and later became prefect and supervisor of studies. Being sent to England in 1682, he defended the RC cause during the controversies under *James II. In 1685 he published the first part of his famous work, *A Papist Misrepresented and Represented*, the second and third parts following in 1687. It evoked a long line of answers from E. *Stillingfleet and other Anglican divines. After the Revolution of 1689 Gother became chaplain at Warkworth Castle, where he taught the future Bishop, R. *Challoner. He wrote several treatises on doctrinal subjects such as *transubstantiation and the use of *images, as well as devotional books on hearing Mass, Confession, and other religious duties. His translation of the Roman Missal (posthumously pub. in 1718) was apparently the first English version of the complete Latin text; from 1737 it was entitled *The Roman Missal for the Use of the Laity*.

His writings ed. by W. Crathorne, *Spiritual Works* (16 vols., 1718–36). G. Every, 'John Goter with Laborious Christians 1680–1704', *Heythrop Journal*, 23 (1982), pp. 30–45.

Gothic Version. Acc. to *Philostorgius (*HE* 2. 5), *Socrates (*HE* 4. 33), and *Sozomen (*HE* 6. 37), the Greek Bible was translated into the Gothic language by the *Arian bishop *Ulphilas (d. 383). Of the NT only 2 Cor. and considerable portions of the four Gospels and the other Pauline Epp. survive. Of the OT only three short fragments of Ezra and Neh. exist. Among the NT MSS is the celebrated 'Codex Argenteus', written in gold and silver letters upon purple vellum, and now at Uppsala; it contains more than half of the text of the Gospels.

All the surviving MSS derive from the period of the Gothic settlement in N. Italy and of contact with the Latin-speaking Church. This provides the most likely explanation for the W. readings of Old-Latin type which are found in the text, as also for the Gospels being in the *Western order—Matthew, John, Luke, Mark. Bilingual Latin–Gothic MSS have played a part in this, each side influencing the other. The version on the whole is extremely literal, especially in Matthew and John.

Text ed. W. Streitberg, *Die Gotische Bibel* (2 pts., Heidelberg, 1908–10). The Gospels were pub. from the 'Codex Argenteus' by A. Uppström (Uppsala, 1854); photographic facsimile edn. of this codex issued by order of the Senate of the University of Uppsala, with introd. by O. van Friesen, Uppsala [1928]. G. W. [S.] Friedrichsen, *The Gothic Version of the Gospels: A Study of its Style and Textual History* (1926); id., *The Gothic Version of the Epistles: A Study of its Style and Textual History* (Oxford, 1939); id., *Gothic Studies* (ibid., 1961). M. J. Hunter in G. W. H. Lampe (ed.), *The Cambridge History of the Bible*, 2 (1969), pp. 338–62. B. M. Metzger, *The Early Versions of the New Testament* (Oxford, 1977), pp. 375–93. J. N. Birdsall in *Anchor Bible Dictionary*, 6 (1992), pp. 803–5, s.v. 'Versions, Ancient (Gothic)'. See also bibl. to ULPHILAS.

Gothic vestments. The name popularly given to Eucharistic *vestments of medieval shape and pattern, the *stole and *maniple being long and narrow, and the *chasuble circular, or nearly so, when laid out flat. The name is applied by contrast with the (esp. post-*Tridentine) Roman pattern, in which the stole and maniple are broad and short, and the chasuble approximately rectangular. The older shape was that generally used, at any rate at first, when vestments were revived in the C of E in the 19th cent. In recent years Gothic vestments, which never became entirely obsolete, have become increasingly common in the RC Church, esp. in churches and religious communities influenced by the *Liturgical Movement.

Gottesfreunde (Ger. 'God's friends'). The adherents of an informal movement of mystical piety, centring upon the Rhineland and Switzerland in the 14th cent. The name reflects such passages as Jas. 2: 23 and Jn. 15: 14. They stressed inner transformation rather than the external forms of religion. Contemporary spiritual writers such as J. van *Ruysbroeck, J. *Tauler, *Eckhart, and the author of the '*Theologia Germanica' oppose the true friend of God to both those who pursue *antinomian ways and those who make a public show of religion.

Works by R. Merswin and others ed. P. Strauch, *Schriften aus der Gottesfreund-Literatur* (Altdeutsche Textbibliothek, 22, 23, and 27; 1927–9). Id. in *PRE* (3rd edn.), 17 (1906), pp. 203–27, s.v. 'Rulman Merswin und die Gottesfreunde', with bibl. to date. K. Rieder, *Der Gottesfreund vom Oberland: Eine Erfindung des Strassburger Johanniter Bruders Nikolaus von Löwen* (1905); important critique by P. Strauch in *Zeitschrift für deutsche Philologie*, 39 (1907), pp. 101–36. J. B. Schoemann, SJ, *Die Rede von den 15 Graden: Rheinische Gottesfreunde-Mystik* (Germanische Studien, Heft 80; 1930). R. M. Jones, *The Flowering of Mysticism: The Friends of God in the Fourteenth Century* (New York, 1939). On the name, E. Peterson, 'Der Gottesfreund. Beiträge zur Geschichte eines religiösen Terminus', *ZKG* 42 (1923), pp. 161–202. G. Steer in *Verfasserlexikon* (2nd edn.), 6 (1987), cols. 420–42, s.v. 'Merswin, Rulman', with extensive bibl.

Gotthard, St (960/61–1038), also **Godehard**, Bp. of Hildesheim. A native of Reichersdorf in Bavaria, he was educated mainly at Neideraltaich, where he made his monastic profession in 991, shortly after the house had adopted the Rule of St *Benedict. He was soon prior and in 996 made abbot. His success as a ruler attracted the attention of the Emp. Henry I (who when Duke of Bavaria had been present at Gotthard's installation), who later commissioned him to reform many of the monasteries in Upper Germany. In 1022 he became Bp. of Hildesheim, where he was a great builder and continued to promote reform. He was canonized in 1131. It is said that the famous St Gotthard Pass in the Alps takes its name from a former chapel dedicated to him on the summit. Feast day, 4 May.

Two Lives by his disciple, Wolfher, the one written shortly after his death, the other c.30 years later, ed. G. Pertz, in *MGH*, Scriptores, 11 (1854), pp. 167–218, with introd., pp. 162–5. Some letters addressed to him are ed. K. Strecker, ibid., Epistolae Selectae, 3 (1925), pp. 59–71 and 108–110. H. Goetting in *Germania Sacra*, NF 20 (Berlin and New York, 1984), pp. 230–56, and on his canonization, pp. 344–6. J. Fellenberg, *Die Verehrung der Heiligen Gotthard von Hildesheim in Kirche und Volk* (Rheinisches Archiv, 74; 1970 [mainly on the cult]). J. Fleckenstein in *Lexikon des Mittelalters*, 4 (1989), cols. 1531 f., s.v. 'Godehard'.

Gottschalk (c.804–c.869), heterodox monk and theologian. A son of the Saxon count Bern, he was entered by his parents as an *oblate in the Benedictine abbey of *Fulda. For part of his education he was sent to *Reichenau, where he became friendly with *Walafrid Strabo. When it was time for him to be ordained deacon, he sought to leave the monastic life; his abbot, *Rabanus Maurus, strongly opposed his wishes, and his case was discussed at the Synod of Mainz (829). The outcome is not clear. We next hear of him in France, first apparently at *Corbie, where he studied under *Ratramnus, and then at *Reims under the protection of Abp. Ebbo. Finally he moved to Orbais in the diocese of Soissons. Here he devoted himself to the study of theology and elaborated an extreme doctrine of Divine *predestination. Basing himself on the anti-Pelagian treatises of St *Augustine, he advocated a double predestination (the phrase came from *Isidore of Seville), acc. to which the chosen are predestined to blessedness and others to eternal fire, though not to sin; as a consequence of this view he restricted the universal saving will of God and the universality of Redemption. He obtained ordination at the hands of a *chorepiscopus, and after some years he set out with some companions to visit Rome. He propagated his views in Italy and the Balkans, where he preached to the Bulgars. Rabanus Maurus tried to stop his activities. In 848 Gottschalk returned to Germany to face his opponents, but at the Synod of Mainz his teaching was condemned. Rabanus sent him to *Hincmar, Abp. of Reims. In 849 at the Synod of *Quiercy he was again condemned, deprived of the orders he had received uncanonically, beaten, and sentenced to perpetual imprisonment. Hincmar sent him to the monastery of Hautvillers. Nevertheless, Gottschalk was able to continue his theological studies and to engage in controversy. Hincmar wrote a pastoral letter in which he warned the simple folk of his diocese against the errors of Gottschalk, who replied with a statement of his views known as the 'Confessio prolixior'. Hincmar consulted *Prudentius of Troyes; and Rabanus, Johannes Scottus *Erigena, and the Church of Lyons (in effect *Florus), Ratramnus, and Servatus *Lupus of Ferrières were drawn in, but these consultations only complicated the issue, and it was not until 860 at the Synod of Douzy that Hincmar was able to find a formula that satisfied those whom he

had consulted. Gottschalk remained obdurate, and hoped that Pope *Nicholas I would reopen the case, but Nicholas died (867) before it was heard, and Gottschalk himself died unreconciled about two years later. He also defended the use of the phrase 'trina deitas' against Hincmar and took part in the Eucharistic controversy raised by *Paschasius Radbertus. He was a religious poet of a high order. Apart from some of his poems, his works had little circulation, and it was not until 1631 that Abp. *Ussher printed his two 'Confessions', at a time when the doctrine of predestination was once more a live issue. They attracted the sympathetic notice of the *Jansenists. In 1930 G. *Morin discovered a collection of his theological writings, to which C. Lambot was able to add grammatical writings. These writings give a strong impression of unusual independence of mind, for example in criticizing not only classical authors like Priscian, but also Fathers, such as *Jerome and *Gregory the Great.

Gotteschalci et praedestinatianae controversiae ab eo motae historia, ed. J. Ussher (Dublin, 1631). G. Morin, OSB, 'Gottschalk retrouvé', *R. Bén.* 43 (1931), pp. 303–12. Crit. edn., with new texts, by C. Lambot, OSB (ed.), *Œuvres théologiques et grammaticales de Godescalc d'Orbais* (SSL 20; 1945). The projected vol. 2 on his life, writings, and doctrine did not appear, but see K. Vielhaber, *Gottschalk der Sachse* (Bonner historische Forschungen, 5; 1956). C. Lambot, OSB, 'Lettre inédite de Godescalc d'Orbais', *R. Bén.* 68 (1958), pp. 41–51. J. Jolivet, *Godescalc d'Orbais et la Trinité: La Méthode de la théologie à l'époque carolingienne* (Études de philosophie médiévale, 47; 1958). D. E. Nineham, 'Gottschalk of Orbais: Reactionary or Precursor of the Reformation?', *JEH* 40 (1989), pp. 1–18. Poems ed. L. Traube in *MGH*, Poetae, 3 (1896), pp. 707–38; K. Strecker, ibid. 4 (1923), pp. 934–6; and N. Fickermann, ibid. 6 (fasc. 1, 1951), pp. 86–106. Three of the poems are repr., with Eng. tr., in P. Godman, *Poetry of the Carolingian Renaissance* (1985), pp. 228–46. M.-L. Weber, *Die Gedichte des Gottschalk von Orbais* (Lateinische Sprache und Literatur des Mittelalters, 27; Frankfurt am Main, etc. [1992]). B. Bischoff, 'Gottschalks Lied für den Reichenauer Freund', in H. R. Jauss and D. Schaller (eds.), *Medium Aevum Vivum: Festschrift für Walter Bulst* (Heidelberg, 1960), pp. 61–8; repr. in his *Mittelalterliche Studien*, 2 (Stuttgart, 1967), pp. 26–34. J. Szövérffy, *Die Annalen der lateinischen Hymnendichtung*, 1 (1964), pp. 235–44, with bibl. refs. K. Schäferdiek in *TRE* 14 (1985), pp. 108–10, s.v. 'Gottschalk der Sachse'.

Grabe, Johannes Ernst (1666–1711), Anglican divine of German birth. Born and educated at Königsberg, where he was appointed Privatdozent in 1685, he was led to question the validity of Lutheran orders and contemplated becoming a RC. On the recommendation of P. J. *Spener, however, he made his way to England in 1697 in the belief that here he would find a Church possessing the *apostolic succession. He was ordained to the priesthood and entered into close relations with the *Nonjurors, but without losing his esteem for the Establishment. A royal pension having been soon settled on him, Grabe gave himself up to research into the texts of the Bible and the early Fathers. His published writings included *Spicilegium SS. Patrum, ut et haereticorum, seculi post Christum natum I, II, et III* (2 vols., 1698–9), editions of the *First Apology* of St *Justin (1700) and of St *Irenaeus (1702), and an edition of a considerable portion of the *Septuagint based on the *Codex Alexandrinus (1707–9).

G. Thomann, 'John Ernest Grabe (1666–1711): Lutheran Syncretist and Anglican Patristic Scholar', *JEH* 43 (1992), pp. 414–

27. R. Hooper in *DNB* 20 (1890), pp. 306 f., s.v. On his edn. of the Septuagint, H. B. *Swete, *An Introduction to the Old Testament in Greek* (1900), pp. 182–4.

Grabmann, Martin (1875–1949), historian of medieval philosophy and theology. He was born at Winterzhofen, ordained priest in 1898, and appointed professor of theology and philosophy at Eichstätt in 1906. In 1913 he became professor of Christian philosophy at Vienna University and in 1918 professor of theology at Munich. Inspired and encouraged by H. *Denifle and F. *Ehrle, by tireless research among manuscripts throughout Europe, he became the first to give a clear account of the development and ramifications of scholastic thought, and to seek in the works of *Thomas Aquinas the evolution and changes of thought rather than the outline of a fixed system. Through his own disciples, such as K. Baeumker and B. Geyer, and others such as É *Gilson who used his work, his influence lies behind almost all the advances made in this field of studies. His works include *Die Geschichte der scholastischen Methode* (1909–11), *Mittelalterliches Geistesleben* (3 vols., 1926–56), *Der lateinische Averroismus* (1931), *Die Werke des hl. Thomas von Aquin* (1931), *Die Geschichte der katholischen Theologie* (1933), and *Methoden und Hilfsmittel des Aristoteles-Studiums im Mittelalter* (1939). Accessible in English is *Thomas Aquinas* (1928), a brief compendious exposition.

Festschrift for Grabmann's 60th birthday, entitled *Aus der Geisteswelt des Mittelalters* (BGPM, Supplementband 3; 2 Hefte, 1935), with bibl. to date [1, pp. xxiii–xxxv]. Autobiog. introd. appended to Grabmann's *Mittelalterliches Geistesleben*, 3 (1956), pp. 1–9, and bibl. by L. Ott, pp. 10–35.

grace. In Christian theology, the supernatural assistance of God bestowed upon a rational being with a view to his sanctification. While the necessity of this aid is generally admitted, the manner of it has been a subject of discussion among Christians since the 4th cent.

In the Bible the word 'grace' is most common in the writings of St *Paul, but the idea is widespread. It is found in the OT, where the Prophets of the Exile taught that God would grant His people the ability to do His will (e.g. Jer. 31: 31–4; Ezek. 36: 26 f.). In the NT the sovereign divine favour is shown towards undeserving and ungrateful human beings simply on account of their need (Mt. 5: 45; Lk. 18: 9–14). Hence grace is not a matter of any legal claim on God but precedes faith in Him (Rom. 4, vv. 4 and 16; Eph. 2: 5–8). It is effectively displayed in particular divine activities—supremely in the redemptive death of Christ (Rom. 3: 21–5, 5: 6–8; Heb. 2: 9), then in the calling of believers (Gal. 1: 6; 2 Cor. 4: 15; 2 Tim. 1: 9) and in the gifts of ministry (Rom. 1: 5; 12: 6–8; Gal. 2: 9). Indeed the whole range of Christian life within the Church is derived from grace (as when the generous support of needy fellow-Christians is prompted by recalling 'the grace of our Lord Jesus Christ that though he was rich, yet for your sakes he became poor, so that by his poverty you might become rich', 2 Cor. 8: 9), and the most comprehensive blessing that can be invoked always includes 'the grace of our Lord Jesus Christ'.

The first attempt at formulating a doctrine of grace is found in *Tertullian, whose original contribution was the idea of grace as the Divine energy working in the soul.

Although at times he represented it as coercive, he elsewhere emphasized strongly man's responsibility (e.g. *Adv. Marc.* 2. 9). But the theology of grace first emerged clearly in the controversy between St *Augustine and *Pelagius, the complete divergence between whose doctrines was caused by their opposing views of human nature. To the former fallen man was 'one mass of sin' (*De div. quaest. ad Simplicianum*, 1. 2, 16); to the latter sin was only the following of an evil example. Logically, therefore, Augustine held that all deserved damnation (*De nat. et grat.* 5), from which, however, God's mercy reserved a fixed number of souls (*De corrept. et grat.* 39). A logical inference from this, though Augustine never taught it, was predestination to damnation. Grace was at all times necessary, since man by himself, in consequence of the Fall, could only sin (*De spir. et litt.* 5). In Baptism was received remission of sins and the grace of justification (*De pecc. mer. et remiss.* 3. 6, 9). Such grace was essential to the Christian for the performance of good works, and existed in an attenuated form in Jews and heretics. The apparent virtues of the heathen were only vices (*C. duas Epist. Pelag.* 3. 14). Against this teaching *Pelagianism held that grace was not needed for the performance of good actions, but was given in order that the commands of God might be more easily fulfilled (*De grat. Christi et de pecc. orig.* 1. 26). Augustine at times called such Divine grace the gift of the Spirit. At other times he equated it with the Spirit Himself. It was not indefectible since for salvation the gift of perseverance was needed (*De corrept. et grat.* 10), but it is not unfair to say it was irresistible; for he stated that it unfailingly attained its object (ibid. 38, 45).

Augustine endeavoured to preserve man's free will by distinguishing between prevenient grace (i.e. grace antecedent to conversion), which is the free gift of God, and subsequent grace, in which the Divine energy co-operates with man after his conversion, and also by distinguishing sufficient from efficacious grace. The former, though adequate, is not in fact followed by its proper result, while the latter is so followed. The effect depends on the congruity or appropriateness of the grace, and that is of God's choice. In practice, though controversy led him to emphasize the influence of God's grace at the expense of man's free will, he strongly emphasized man's responsibility (e.g. *De grat. et lib. arb.* 2, 5).

No such systematic development took place in the E. Church which continued to emphasize both the necessity of grace and the reality of human free will, and resisted the notion of predestination. Such ideas are reflected in the teaching of John *Cassian, whose doctrine of grace was seen in the W. as an attempt to mediate between Augustine and Pelagius, and hence has been dubbed '*Semipelagianism'. Cassian, while accepting Augustine's teaching on *original sin, rejected total depravity, irresistible grace, and unconditional predestination. Though grace was universally necessary, the will remained free at all stages.

The Second Council of *Orange (529) attempted to settle the question on an Augustinian basis, but with important modifications. Prevenient grace was taught, being rendered necessary by the Fall, but emphasis was laid on human co-operation after conversion. Reprobation (i.e. predestination to damnation) was anathematized. When in the 9th cent. *Gottschalk attempted to teach a sharpened Augustinianism, embodying double predestination and denying that Christ died for all, he was condemned by the Council of Mainz in 848.

Controversy revived in the 13th cent. St *Thomas Aquinas in general followed the teaching of St Augustine, though he differentiated more clearly between predestination to grace and that to glory and laid more stress on free will. He was the first to distinguish accurately between 'habitual' and 'actual' grace (v. inf.). The teaching of *Duns Scotus, *Alexander of Hales, and St *Bonaventure is of considerable interest. In general they are in sympathy with the teaching of Cassian, himself largely dependent on St John *Chrysostom. Original sin was reduced to a 'loss of original righteousness', owing to the 'deprivation of supernatural gifts' that Adam suffered at the Fall, so that even the unbaptized could, by initiating some movement towards virtue, merit '*congruous grace'. Other striking medieval doctrines are Alexander's identification of prevenient grace with the 'general assistance' (assistentia generalis) of God, and Scotus' teaching on the timelessness of God in relation to the theology of grace.

Later controversies are in essence contained in the above. The Reformers returned to Augustinianism. M. *Luther, at any rate in his earlier period, and the followers of J. *Calvin taught absolute predestination, to which the latter added the indefectibility of grace. In the Netherlands the followers of Jacobus Arminius (d. 1604) taught a doctrine (see ARMINIANISM) closely resembling that of Cassian, which had affinities with Caroline thought on the subject in England.

The Church of England in the *Thirty-Nine Articles and the Church of Rome at the Council of *Trent substantially followed the Council of Orange. An attempt to introduce Calvinist teaching in the *Lambeth Articles of 1595 was unsuccessful. In the RC Church there have been two serious controversies. The teaching of the later scholastics reappeared in the doctrines upheld by L. de *Molina, SJ, and the resultant controversy dragged on until 1607, when it was shelved by *Paul V. The *Jansenist controversy arose from the posthumous publication in 1640 of the Augustinus by C. O. *Jansen, Bp. of Ypres (d. 1638). Two propositions allegedly contained in it, and embodying an exaggerated Augustinianism, were condemned by *Innocent X in 1653. It is disputed how far they accurately represent Jansen's position.

The relation between grace and the Sacraments has produced similar difficulties. There are four main lines of approach. (1) The Sacraments are symbols, which produce feelings in the recipients which enable them to receive grace. This denies a unique status to the Sacraments. (2) They are God's instruments for the direct causation of grace. This needs to account for the difficulties that arise in the reception of, e.g., Baptism in bad faith. (3) The theory of moral causation, i.e. the Church impetrates for the recipient the particular grace implied. The Sacrament becomes an acted prayer of the Church, and therefore of Christ. (4) The Sacraments convey a title exigent of grace. The title can only be appropriated if a right disposition is attained.

In the 20th cent. various theologians have sought to cut through the complexities of the W. doctrine of grace. Among RCs there has been an attempt to assert the primacy of the notion of uncreated grace (the Holy Spirit Himself) over the various classifications of created grace (the effects of the Spirit's operation). This insight is used, e.g. by K. *Rahner, to emphasize the centrality of a personal encounter with God. A somewhat similar point is made more simply, though with less respect for tradition, by John *Oman.

In the theology of grace, the following distinctions have commonly been drawn:

(1) *Habitual or sanctifying grace.* The gift of God inhering in the soul, by which men are enabled to perform righteous acts. It is held to be normally conveyed in the Sacraments.

(2) *Actual grace.* A certain motion of the soul, bestowed by God ad hoc for the production of some good act. It may exist in the unbaptized.

(3) *Prevenient grace.* That form of actual grace which leads men to sanctification before the reception of the Sacraments. It is the free gift of God ('gratuitous'), and entirely unmerited.

See also EFFICACIOUS GRACE, SUFFICIENT GRACE.

The subject is treated at length in the standard textbooks of dogmatic theology. The Tridentine teaching is stated in full in D. *Soto, OP, Ad Sanctum Concilium Tridentinum de Natura et Gratia (Venice, 1547). The Jesuit doctrine had its classical exponent in various works of F. *Suárez, SJ (q.v.). Cf. also D. *Petavius, SJ, 'De Lege et Gratia', pr. in his Opus de Doctrina Temporum, 3 (new edn., Antwerp, 1703), pp. 212–55. J. [W.] Oman, Grace and Personality (Cambridge, 1917); N. P. *Williams, The Grace of God (1930); L. Hodgson, The Grace of God in Faith and Philosophy (Paddock Lectures, 1936; 1936); A. G. Hebert, SSM, Grace and Nature (1937); H. Rondet, SJ, Gratia Christi: Essai d'histoire du dogme et de théologie dogmatique (1948; Eng. tr., Westminster, Md., 1967); id., Essai sur la théologie de la grâce (1964); P. [F.] Fransen, SJ, De Genade: Werkelijkheid en Leven (Antwerp, 1969; Eng. tr., The New Life of Grace, 1969); H. Gross and others in J. Feiner and M. Löhrer (eds.), Mysterium Salutis, 4 (pt. 2, Einsiedeln [1973]), pp. 595–984; E. J. Yarnold, SJ, The Second Gift: A Study of Grace (Sarum Lectures, 1973; Slough, 1974); C. Ernst, OP, The Theology of Grace (Theology Today, 17; Notre Dame, Ind., and Cork [1974]). J. Moffatt, Grace in the New Testament (1931); T. F. Torrance, The Doctrine of Grace in the Apostolic Fathers (1948). K. Rahner, SJ, 'Zur scholastischen Begrifflichkeit der ungeschaffenen Gnade', in his Schriften zur Theologie, 1 (1954), pp. 347–75 (Eng. tr., 1961, pp. 319–46). B. J. F. Lonergan, SJ, Grace and Freedom: Operative Grace in the Thought of St Thomas Aquinas, ed. J. P. Burns, SJ (1971). H. de *Lubac, SJ, Augustinianisme et théologie moderne (Théologie, 63; 1965; Eng. tr., 1969). W. T. Whitley (ed.), The Doctrine of Grace (1932) [Essays prepared for the Theological Committee appointed by the Continuation Committee of the *Faith and Order Movement]; C. Mœller and G. Philips, The Theology of Grace and the Oecumenical Movement (Eng. tr., 1961). On the word, C. Moussy, Gratia et sa famille (Publications de la Faculté des Lettres et Sciences Humaines de l'Université de Clermont-Ferrand, 2nd ser. 25; 1966). H. R. *Mackintosh in HERE 6 (1913), pp. 364–7, s.v.; E. L. van Becelaere, ibid., pp. 367–72, s.v. 'Grace, Doctrine of (Roman Catholic)', with valuable bibl.; J. Van der Meersch in DTC 6 (1920), cols. 1554–687, s.v.; G. Baumgartner and P. Tihon in Dict. Sp. 6 (1967), cols. 701–50, s.v., with bibl.; H. G. Reventlow and others in TRE 13 (1984), pp. 459–511, s.v. 'Gnade', with extensive bibl.

Grace, Pilgrimage of. See PILGRIMAGE OF GRACE.

Grace at Meals (in earlier English, **Graces**). The custom of giving thanks before and after food is natural and not exclusively Christian. It was followed by Christ

(Jn. 6: 11) and the Apostles (e.g. Acts 27: 35). In religious houses, and later in schools and colleges, fixed forms were provided, and are recited audibly at the principal meals. The section of the *Rituale Romanum, *De Benedictionibus* (1984) provides four forms of Grace to be used before and after meals. These range from simple prayers to longer forms which include phrases from the Psalms, prayers of blessing and thanksgiving, and short biblical readings which vary according to the liturgical season. Many other forms of grace are traditional among both RCs and other Christians.

H. L. Dixon, *'Saying Grace' Historically Considered, and Numerous Forms of Grace, Taken from Ancient and Modern Sources* (1903). R. H. Adams, *The College Graces of Oxford and Cambridge* (Oxford, 1992 [Lat. texts with Eng. tr. and brief introd.]). E. von der Goltz, *Tischgebete und Abendmahlsgebete in der altchristlichen und in der griechischen Kirche* (TU 29 (2b); 1905). L. Gougaud, OSB, 'Notes sur les prières chrétiennes de la table', *Rassegna Gregoriana*, 8 (1909), cols. 524–7. W. E. Scudamore in *DAC* 1 (1875), pp. 745 f., s.v.; J. Baudot in *DACL* 1 (1910), cols. 713–16, s.v. 'Bénédiction de la table ou des aliments'; T. Barnes in *HERE* 6 (1913), pp. 372–4 (with many examples of liturgical graces).

gradine (a word of French origin). A ledge above and behind the altar upon which the cross, candlesticks, and other ornaments are sometimes placed. Such ledges became common from the 16th cent. Since the altar is properly a table, gradines are now very generally held to be the mark of a debased use, on the ground that the correct place for the ornaments is on the altar itself. See also RETABLE.

Gradual (Lat. *gradus*, 'step'). In the W. Church, the *responsory, usually from the Psalms, sung immediately after the first scriptural lesson. The name, which is found as far back as *Rabanus Maurus, derives from the practice of singing it either on the altar steps or while the deacon was ascending the steps of the *ambo. Originally it was chanted only by the cantors or choir, and not until later in the Middle Ages did the practice of its recitation also by the priest become established. The Gradual used to be omitted from the Sunday immediately after *Easter to the Saturday before *Whitsun. Since 1969 its place has usually been taken by a responsorial Psalm sung by the cantor or choir and the people, but the gradual texts may still be used. The word 'gradual' is also applied to the book containing the music for the *proper (and later also the *ordinary) of the Mass. The older English form of the word is 'Grail'.

Jungmann (1958 edn.), 1, pp. 543–57; Eng. tr. (New York, 1951), pp. 421–35, with refs. M. Huglo in *NCE* 6 (1967), pp. 685–7, s.v.

Gradual Psalms. The group of Psalms, Pss. 120–34, each of which bears a title in Hebrew rendered by St *Jerome 'canticum graduum', and in the AV 'A Song of Degrees' (RV, 'Ascents'). Various explanations of the title have been offered, referring it: (1) to the supposed literary character of the Psalms, as containing instances of a step-like progression; (2) to the 'lifting-up' of the heart in praise; (3) to the 'going up' of the Jews from Babylon to Jerusalem after the Exile; (4) to the 15 'ascents' or steps which led from the Women's Court to that of the men in the Temple area; or, most probably (5) to the 'going up' of pilgrims to Jerusalem for annual festivals.

In addition to comm. on Psalms (q.v.), see also C. C. Keet, *A Study of the Psalms of Ascents: A Critical and Exegetical Commentary upon Psalms CXX to CXXXIV* (1969). M. Mannati, 'Les Psaumes graduels constituent-ils un genre littéraire distinct à l'intérieur du Psautier biblique?', *Semitica*, 29 (1979), pp. 85–100.

graffiti (*Ital.*). The name given to ancient inscriptions which are merely roughly or casually scratched and not properly carved. Christian graffiti are numerous, esp. in the *catacombs of Rome and at other ancient holy places. They generally take the form of memorials of the dead and prayers to God or the saints commemorated there, scratched by mourners, worshippers, or visitors. Of particular interest are those under *St Peter's, Rome, and those under San Sebastiano by the Via Appia, which show a remarkable mixture of Latin and Greek and are in some cases quite illiterate.

G. B. *de Rossi, *La Roma sotterranea cristiana*, 2 (1867), pp. 13–20. G. F. Snyder, *Ante Pacem: Archaeological Evidence of Church Life Before Constantine* (Macon, Ga. [1985]), pp. 141–8. H. *Leclercq, OSB, in *DACL* 6 (pt. 2; 1925), cols. 1453–542, s.v. 'Graffites', with refs. J. [M. C.] Toynbee and J. [B.] Ward-Perkins, *The Shrine of St Peter* (1956), *passim* (see index); M. Guarducci, *I graffiti sotto la Confessione di San Pietro in Vaticano* (3 vols., 1958). See also works cited s.v. ST PETER'S, ROME.

Grafton, Richard (c.1507–73), printer of *Matthew's Bible and English Prayer Books. A London merchant, who had become an ardent supporter of the Reformation, he arranged c.1536 with a fellow-merchant, Edward *Whitchurch, for the printing at Antwerp of the modified form of M. *Coverdale's translation known as Matthew's Bible. A copy was dispatched to T. *Cranmer in July 1537 and six more to T. *Cromwell on 28 Aug. Their enthusiastic reception led Grafton to arrange for a large edition at Paris, then noted for its paper and founts, from the press of François Regnault, and in Nov. 1538 copies of the NT, with the Latin text against the English, were put on sale in London. The printing of the whole Bible (the '*Great Bible') was completed in 1539; but shortly afterwards it was suspended by the *Sorbonne. Grafton escaped to England and later the types were also rescued and brought over. Other works bearing his imprint (mostly in conjunction with Whitchurch) were *The Prymer* (1540; see PRIMER), the proclamation directing the Great Bible to be read in churches (6 May 1541), the English Gospels and Epistles (8 May 1546), the *First Book of *Homilies* (1547), and the First (1549) and Second (1552) *Books of Common Prayer*. Under *Mary he lost his position as King's Printer, and for a time he suffered imprisonment. In 1554 and again in 1558 he was elected MP for London and in 1563 for Coventry.

His Chronicle (2 vols., 1568) was repr. in 2 vols., London, 1809. J. A. Kingdon, *Incidents in the Lives of Thomas Poyntz and Richard Grafton* (privately pr., London, 1895); id., *Richard Grafton, Citizen and Grocer of London . . .* (privately pr., ibid., 1901). E. G. Hamann, 'The Clarification of Some Obscurities Surrounding the Imprisonment of Richard Grafton in 1541 and in 1543', *The Papers of the Bibliographical Society of America*, 52 (1958), pp. 262–82. E. J. Devereux, 'Empty Tuns and Unfruitful Grafts: Richard Grafton's Historical Publications', *Sixteenth Century Journal*, 21 (1990), pp. 33–56. H. Miller in S. T. Bindoff (ed.), *The History of Parliament: The House of Commons 1509–1558*, 2 (1982), pp. 240 f., s.v.; W. J. Jones in P. W. Hasler (ed.), *The History of*

Parliament: The House of Commons 1558–1603, 2 (1981), pp. 210 f., s.v.

Graham, 'Billy'

Graham, 'Billy' (William Franklin Graham, 1918–), American Evangelist. Born in Charlotte, North Carolina, he experienced conversion at the age of 16. He graduated from Wheaton College, Illinois, in 1943 and entered the Southern *Baptist ministry. When the American based 'Youth for Christ International' was founded in 1945, Graham became their first official field representative. In 1949 he began his first major evangelistic campaign in Los Angeles and in 1950 the Billy Graham Evangelistic Association was formed. Thereafter, he toured the world and became known for his 'stadium campaigns'; he visited Britain in 1954, 1966, 1984–5, and 1989. His friendships with various of the American Presidents, most notably Lyndon Johnson and Richard Nixon, received much publicity and he has been welcomed by leaders of denominations around the world, including Pope *John Paul II in 1978. In recent years his campaigns have made full use of modern technology, including *broadcasting. His 'Mission World' campaigns in 1989–90 were linked live by satellite to 33 countries in Africa and 26 countries in Asia.

The many studies include an 'authorised biography' by J. Pollock (London, 1966) and a substantial study by W. Martin, *The Billy Graham Story* (1992).

grail. An older form of the word '*Gradual' (q.v.), derived through the Old French *grael* from the same root.

Grail, the Holy

Grail, the Holy. In medieval romances, a vessel possessing spiritual powers and qualities, and affording, under certain conditions, mystical benefits to its beholders. The legend first appears in the *Perceval* of Chrestien de Troyes (?1180–90) and, in a Christianized version, in the *Estoire dou Graal* (or *Joseph d'Arimatie*) of Robert de Boron (c.1190). In the religiously inspired (possibly *Cistercian) *Queste del Saint Graal* and in the *Parzival* of Wolfram von Eschenbach (c.1200) the legend of the Grail is more fully integrated with the stories of Arthur and the Round Table, and made to bear an exalted moral interpretation. The origins of the legend, which appears to contain elements of the most diverse provenance, are obscure. In the extant versions, the Grail itself is sometimes identified with the cup used by Christ in the *Last Supper, which later belonged to *Joseph of Arimathaea, and its effects upon those who see it are made to correspond closely with the effects of Holy Communion upon communicants. The whole legend, however, remained within the field of secular literature, and was never recognized by any ecclesiastical authority.

Modern crit. edns. of *Perceval*, by F. Lecoy (Classiques Français du Moyen Age, 100, 103; 1972–5), of the *Estoire dou Graal*, by W. A. Nitze (ibid. 57; 1927), of *Queste del Saint Graal*, by A. Pauphilet (ibid. 33; 1923), and of *Parzival*, by G. Weber (Darmstadt, 1963; 4th edn., 1981). Eng. trs. of *Perceval*, by D. D. R. Owen (London, 1987), of *Queste*, by P. M. Matarasso (Harmondsworth, 1969), and of *Parzival*, by A. T. Hatto (ibid., 1980). There is a very wide lit. on the subject. Studies incl. D. Kempe, *The Legend of the Holy Grail, its Sources, Character and Development* (EETS, Extra Series, 95; 1905); R. S. Loomis, *Celtic Myth and Arthurian Legend* (New York, 1927), pp. 139–270; id., *Arthurian Tradition and Chrétien de Troyes* (ibid., 1949), pp. 335–459; id. in id. (ed.), *Arthurian Literature in the Middle Ages*

(Oxford, 1959), pp. 274–94 ('The Origin of the Grail Legends'); J. Marx, *La Légende arthurienne et le Graal* (1952); id., *Nouvelles Recherches sur la littérature arthurienne* (Bibliothèque Française et Romane, Série C: Études Littéraires, 9 [1965]); D. D. R. Owen, *The Evolution of the Grail Legend* (St Andrews University Publications, 58; 1968); H. Bayer, *Gral: Die hochmittelalterliche Glaubenskrise im Spiegel der Literatur* (Monographien zur Geschichte des Mittelalters, 28; 2 vols., Stuttgart, 1983). M. Cocheril, OCR, in *Dict. Sp.* 6 (1967), cols. 672–700, s.v. 'Graal (Le saint)'; E. Baumgartner and others in *Lexikon des Mittelalters*, 4 (1989), cols. 1616–21, s.v. 'Gra(a)l, -sdichtung', both with bibl.

Grande Chartreuse, La

Grande Chartreuse, La. The mother house of the *Carthusian Order, situated in the Dauphiné Alps, some 15 miles N. of Grenoble. A primitive monastery on the site was built by St *Bruno in 1084. It was many times destroyed by fire and rebuilt before the present monastery was begun in 1676. In 1904 the monks were forcibly ejected under the '*Associations Law' of 1901, and the building secularized. The famous liqueur was thereafter made by the expelled monks at Tarragona in Spain. In 1940 Carthusians were permitted to return to La Grande Chartreuse.

B. Bligny, *Recueil des plus anciens actes de la Grande-Chartreuse (1086–1196)* (Grenoble, 1958). [C. M. Boutrais, OSB,] *La Grande Chartreuse* (Grenoble, 1881, and numerous subsequent edns.; abridged Eng. tr., 1893). L. H. Cottineau, OSB, *Répertoire topo-bibliographique des abbayes et prieurés* (Mâcon, 1935), cols. 1322–4, s.v., for full refs. M. Laporte, OSB, in *DHGE* 21 (1986), cols. 1088–107, s.v.

Grandmont, Order of

Grandmont, Order of. French religious order, now extinct. It was founded by St Stephen of Muret (c.1054–1124/5). Its early history is uncertain, and its rule was drawn up only in the time of the fourth prior, Stephen of Liciac (1139–63). The order established its mother house, under a prior, at Grandmont, N. of Limoges. The discipline was severe and strict poverty was observed, although the rule was lenient about silence. Because of their generosity the Grandmontines were popularly known as 'Bonshommes'. From c.1184 disputes arose between monks and lay brothers, and though these were temporarily allayed, discipline began to relax more and more. In 1643 a Strict Observance branch was formed, but it was shortlived. The order came to an end before the French Revolution, Grandmont itself being suppressed in 1772. There had been three houses in England (c.1222–1464): Alderbury, Creswell, and Grosmont.

C. A. Hutchison, *The Hermit Monks of Grandmont* (Cistercian Studies Series, 118; Kalamazoo, Mich., 1989). *Scriptores Ordinis Grandimontensis*, ed. J. Becquet, OSB (CCCM 8; 1968). R. Graham and A. W. Clapham, 'The Order of Grandmont and its Houses in England', *Archaeologia*, 75 (1926), pp. 159–210. J. Becquet, OSB, in *Dict. Sp.* 4 (pt. 2; 1961), cols. 1504–14, s.v. 'Étienne (15) de Muret'; G.-M. Oury in *DIP* 4 (1977), cols. 1389–91, s.v.; J. Becquet, OSB, in *DHGE* 21 (1986), cols. 1129–40, s.v. 'Grandmont (Ordre et Abbaye de)', all with further bibl.

Gratian

Gratian (12th cent.: d. by c.1160), author of the 'Decretum Gratiani' and virtually the father of canon law. Practically nothing is known of his life. He prob. became a monk at some stage, but where is unknown, and he may have been a consultant to a Papal judge in 1143.

His 'Concordantia Discordantium Canonum', which later came to be known as the 'Decreta' or 'Decretum Gratiani', is a collection of nearly 4,000 patristic texts, conciliar decrees, and Papal pronouncements touching on all fields of Church discipline, which he presented in a framework of a treatise designed to resolve into harmony all the contradictions and inconsistencies of his sources. The date of the 'Decretum' is much disputed, but since it incorporates decisions of the Second *Lateran Council of 1139, it cannot have been completed earlier than that year. It quickly became the basic text on which masters of canon law lectured, first at Bologna, and before the end of the 12th cent. also at Oxford, Paris, and elsewhere. Although it never received formal approbation, it was used as an authority in the practice of the Papal curia and came to form the first part of the *Corpus Iuris Canonici. 'It has always been held one of Gratian's fundamental merits that he gave to Canon Law the shape of a legal system, approached it with juridical categories of thinking and separated it as an autonomous practical subject matter distinct from dogmatic theology' (S. Kuttner). *Dante (Paradiso, 10. 103–5) assigns to Gratian a place in paradise.

The standard edn. is that of A. Friedberg in his edn. of the Corpus Iuris Canonici, 1 (Leipzig, 1879). A. van Hove, Commentarium Lovaniense in Codicem Iuris Canonici, 1, tomus 1 (2nd edn., Mechlin and Rome, 1945), pp. 338–48, with refs. S. Kuttner, 'The Father of the Science of Canon Law', The Jurist, 1 (1948), pp. 2–19; various of Kuttner's other arts. on Gratian are repr. in his Gratian and the Schools of Law 1140–1234 (1983). P. Landau, 'Quellen und Bedeutung des Gratianischen Dekrets', Studia et Documenta Historiae et Iuris, 52 (Rome, 1986), pp. 218–35. S. Kuttner, 'Research on Gratian: Acta and Agenda', in P. Linehan (ed.), Proceedings of the Seventh International Congress of Medieval Canon Law (Monumenta Iuris Canonici, Series C: Subsidia, 8; Vatican, 1988), pp. 3–26. G. Le Bras, Histoire du droit et des institutions de l'Église en Occident, 7: L'Âge classique, by G. Le Bras, C. Lefebvre, and J. Rambaud (1965), pp. 47–129. A. Villien, SJ, and J. de Ghellinck, SJ, in DTC 6 (1920), cols. 1727–51, s.v.; J. Rambaud-Buhot in NCE 6 (1967), pp. 706–9, s.v. 'Gratian, Decretum of'; P. Landau in TRE 14 (1985), pp. 124–30, s.v., with full bibl. Studia Gratiana post Octava Decreti Saecularia (14 vols., Bonn, 1953–67; vol. 15 etc., Rome, 1972 ff.). See also bibl. to CANON LAW and CORPUS IURIS CANONICI.

Gratry, Auguste Joseph Alphonse (1805–72), French Catholic apologist. After a severe mental conflict, described in Souvenirs de ma jeunesse (published 1874 by A. Perraud), he was ordained priest in 1832. He was successively professor of the Petit Séminaire of Strasbourg (1828), director of the Collège Stanislas (1840), and chaplain of the École Normale Supérieure (1846). In 1861 he became Vicar General of Orléans and in 1867 was elected a member of the French Academy. He was deeply concerned for the revival of Church life in France and took a principal part in the restoration of the *Oratory (under the title of the Immaculate Conception). He was among the *Inopportunists in opposing the definition of Papal Infallibility, but, after the First *Vatican Council, submitted to the decrees. His many books, which sought to present the Christian faith to educated opinion and had a large circulation, include De la connaissance de Dieu (2 vols., 1853), La Logique (1855), Les Sources, conseils pour la direction de l'esprit (1861–2), La Morale et la loi de l'histoire (1868), and Lettres sur la religion (1869). His somewhat independent approach to theology, which included a proof of the existence of God by induction with the aid of the infinitesimal

calculus, brought him into conflict with some of the authorities during his lifetime. His teaching had some affinities with *Ontologism; but Gratry certainly rejected ontological doctrines in the form given them by N. *Malebranche.

A. Perraud, Le Père Gratry: Ses derniers jours, son testament spirituel (1872; Eng. tr., 1872); id., Le Père Gratry, sa vie et ses œuvres (1900); A. Chauvin, Le Père Gratry d'après des documents inédits (1901); J. Vaudon, Une L'Âme de lumière, le Père Gratry (1914). L. Foucher, La Philosophie catholique en France au XIXᵉ siècle (Bibliothèque de la Société d'Histoire Ecclésiastique de la France, 1955), pp. 197–236. A. Largent in DTC 6 (1920), cols. 1754–63, s.v.; M. Join-Lambert in Dict. Sp. 6 (1967), cols. 781–5, s.v., with bibl.

gravamen (med. Lat., a 'grievance'). A memorial sent from the Lower to the Upper House of *Convocation with a view to securing the remedy of disorders or grievances in the Church.

grave-diggers. See FOSSORS.

Gray, George Buchanan (1865–1922), OT and Semitic scholar. In 1893 he was ordained to the *Congregational ministry, and from 1900 until his death was professor of Hebrew and OT exegesis at Mansfield College, Oxford. He combined original and sound judgement with great knowledge of detail, and became one of the most respected OT scholars and teachers of his generation. Of outstanding merit were his volumes in the 'International Critical Commentary'—Numbers (1903), Isaiah I–XXVII (1912), and Job (with S. R. *Driver, 1921). In his Sacrifice in the Old Testament (1925, posthumous) he made a notable contribution to OT theology.

List of G. B. Gray's pub. writings in the last-named work, pp. ix–xi. G. R. *Driver in DNB, 1922–1930, pp. 356–8.

Gray, Robert (1809–72), Bp. of Cape Town and Metropolitan of the Anglican Province of *South Africa. He was the son of Robert Gray, Bp. of Bristol (1762–1834), who ordained him deacon in 1833. He was priested in 1834 and in 1845 became Vicar of Stockton-on-Tees. He soon afterwards reluctantly accepted the bishopric of Cape Town and was consecrated in 1847. He promoted the division of his diocese by establishing new bishoprics at Grahamstown and Natal, and resigned his see in 1853 in order to facilitate this division and the reconstitution of Cape Town as a metropolitan see. He was reappointed Bp. and Metropolitan by Letters Patent in the same year.

In 1861 he suspended from cure of souls, and in 1862 withdrew the licence of, Mr Long, a clergyman who had refused to attend synods on the grounds that Gray's Letters Patent gave him no authority to summon them. The colonial courts agreed that the Letters Patent of 1853, being issued after the establishment of constitutional rule in the colony, gave Gray no coercive jurisdiction, but held that Mr Long was bound by his oath of canonical obedience to submit to the decisions of the Bp. On appeal, however, the *Judicial Committee of the Privy Council in 1863 agreed that the Letters Patent were ineffectual to create any jurisdiction and held that the dispute must be treated as a suit between members of a religious body not established by law. It restored Mr Long to his property and income but admitted that it could give him no cure of souls. The judgement was of constitutional importance in that it demonstrated beyond doubt that the C of E was not automatically established by law in all the overseas dominions of the Crown.

Also in 1863, J. W. *Colenso, Bp. of Natal, was presented on a charge of heresy to Gray, who deposed and later excommunicated him. On appeal, Gray's decision was reversed by the Judicial Committee of the Privy Council who again in 1865 held that his Letters Patent could not grant him no coercive authority over Colenso, whose appointment antedated them. Gray gained some support from the *Convocation of Canterbury in 1866 and from the (Pan-Anglican) *Lambeth Conference in 1867 for his project of appointing another bishop for Natal with a different title. When W. K. Macrorie (1831–1905) accepted the post of Bp. of Maritzburg, there were legal difficulties about the consecration, which finally took place at Cape Town in 1869. By this time Gray's health was failing and he died in 1872. During his episcopate he added five new sees to the South African Church, namely, besides Grahamstown and Natal, St Helena (1859) and the missionary sees of Zambesi (1861) and the Orange Free State Territory (1863).

[H. L. Farrer,] *Life of Robert Gray, Bishop of Cape Town and Metropolitan of Africa*, ed. C. N. Gray (son; 2 vols., 1876). A. E. M. Anderson-Morshead, *A Pioneer and Founder: Reminiscences of some who knew Robert Gray* (1905). A. Brooke, *Robert Gray, First Bishop of Cape Town* (Cape Town, 1947). N. Pocock in *DNB* 33 (1890), pp. 17–19, s.v. See also works cited under COLENSO, J. W.

Great Awakening, the. A name applied to a widespread religious revival in USA. Beginnings of the movement may be traced among the Dutch Reformed Churches of New Jersey *c.*1726; it spread to the *Presbyterians and *Congregationalists in the following decade and reached its zenith in New England in the early 1740s. It was closely associated with the preaching of Jonathan *Edwards and George *Whitefield, though both preachers discouraged the excessive emotionalism which marked the revival. Stress was laid on the visible evidences of conversion and those who did not manifest such tokens of inward grace were openly denounced as unregenerate. Both the Presbyterians and the Congregationalists became deeply divided over the theological implications of the revival, esp. the relative importance of experiential faith and correct doctrine. J. Edwards's *Treatise concerning Religious Affections* (1746) was designed to discriminate between the healthy and the morbid elements in the revival. During the later 1740s and in the following decade the revival spread into Virginia and even further south. The movement may be regarded as parallel to Continental *Pietism and English *Evangelicalism.

A similar revival at the end of the 18th and beginning of the 19th cent. is sometimes known as the 'Second Great Awakening'. This began among the Congregational Churches of New England, but came to affect the Presbyterians, *Methodists, and *Baptists, and spread throughout the USA. The early leaders of this revival determined to restrain excessive emotionalism and laid stress on the need for active works of Christian benevolence. By analogy, a further revival in the period *c.*1875–1914 is some-

times called the 'Third Great Awakening'. Recent study tends to emphasize the social and political, as well as the religious, significance of these movements. See also REVIVALISM.

A. Heimert and P. Miller (eds.), *The Great Awakening: Documents Illustrating the Crisis and its Consequences* (Indianapolis and New York [1967]); R. L. Bushman (ed.), *The Great Awakening: Documents in the Revival of Religion, 1740–1745* (New York, 1970). J. Tracy, *The Great Awakening* (Boston, 1842); C. H. Maxson, *The Great Awakening in the Middle Colonies* (Chicago, 1920); W. M. Gewehr, *The Great Awakening in Virginia, 1740–90* (Durham, NC, 1930); M. W. Armstrong, *The Great Awakening in Nova Scotia, 1776–1809* (Studies in Church History, 7; Chicago, 1948); E. S. Gaustad, *The Great Awakening in New England* (New York, 1957); A. Heimert, *Religion and the American Mind from the Great Awakening to the Revolution* (Cambridge, Mass., 1966), pp. 1–236; D. R. Rutman (ed.), *The Great Awakening: Event and Exegesis* (New York and London, 1970); W. G. McLoughlin, *Revivals, Awakening, and Reform: An Essay on Religion and Social Change in America, 1607–1977* (Chicago History of American Religion, Chicago and London [1978]), with bibl.; S. A. Marini, *Radical Sects of Revolutionary New England* (Cambridge, Mass., and London, 1982).

Great Bible. The edition of the English Bible which Thomas *Cromwell ordered in Sept. 1538 to be set up in every parish church. It was not issued till the early summer of 1539 and was the work of M. *Coverdale, who had used as his basis *Matthew's Bible. The printing was begun in Paris, but owing to the hostility of the *Sorbonne, Coverdale was forced to transfer the type and such of the sheets as he could rescue to London. Its handsome title-page, which represents God blessing the King, who is handing out copies of the Bible to T. *Cranmer and T. Cromwell, is usually held to be the work of Hans Holbein. In Apr. 1540, after extensive revision by Coverdale, the 'Great Bible' was reissued with an important preface by Cranmer; in this version it is sometimes known as 'Cranmer's Bible'. From its rendering of Jer. 8: 22 the Great Bible was also popularly known as the *Treacle Bible. The 1539 edition was printed by R. *Grafton and E. *Whitchurch (qq.v.).

Darlow and Moule, 1 (ed. A. S. Herbert, 1968), pp. 25 f., later edns. pp. 28–35 and *passim*. A. W. Pollard, *Records of the English Bible* (1911), pp. 17–24, with docs., pp. 223–74, *passim*. J. Isaacs in H. Wheeler Robinson (ed.), *The Bible in its Ancient and English Versions* (1940), pp. 175–81. A. J. Slavin, 'The Rochepot Affair', *Sixteenth Century Journal*, 10 (1979), pp. 3–19. See also bibl. to BIBLE (ENGLISH VERSIONS) and GRAFTON, R.

Great Entrance (Gk. μεγάλη εἴσοδος). In the E. Church, the solemn procession in which the Eucharistic bread and wine are carried from the *prothesis to the *altar. See also LITTLE ENTRANCE.

Great Schism. The term is used in two senses:

(1) The breach between the East and West, traditionally dated 1054. Political and ecclesiastical differences, together with theological disputes, had long embittered relations before Pope *Leo IX and *Michael Cerularius inflamed matters by suppressing Greek and Latin usages in their respective domains. Leo sent *legates to Constantinople to refuse the title of *Oecumenical Patriarch to Cerularius and to demand acceptance to the Roman claim to be 'caput et mater ecclesiarum'. On the Greek refusal, the Latin

leader, Cardinal *Humbert, excommunicated Cerularius, while the latter excommunicated the Western legates. This event of 1054 is commonly taken as the beginning of the schism, but the Western act was of doubtful validity, since Leo was dead, and the Eastern was personal to the legates. Negotiations continued over a long period, but the cruelties inflicted during the *Crusades, the capture of *Constantinople in 1204 and the imposition of Latin Patriarchs rendered nugatory the work of the Councils of *Lyons (1274) and *Florence (1439) in endeavouring to restore unity. The formal repudiation of the Union of Florence by a Synod of Constantinople in 1484 marks the final breach. Though the division remains, in 1965 Pope *Paul VI and the Oecumenical Patriarch *Athenagoras simultaneously nullified the anathemas of 1054.

(2) The period 1378–1417, during which W. Christendom was divided by the creation of anti-popes. On the death of *Gregory XI, the last *Avignonese Pope, in 1378, the Abp. of Bari was elected as *Urban VI, the cardinals being subjected to considerable pressure by the local Roman populace. When, in attempting reforms, he showed signs of insanity, the cardinals withdrew to Anagni, where they elected Cardinal Robert of Geneva as Clement VII, on the ground that their previous action had been taken under duress. Clement VII set up court at Avignon, and the two leaders attracted support along strongly nationalist lines. The *Conciliar movement offered a means of resolving the schism, but the Council of *Pisa (1409) only produced another candidate for the papacy, *Alexander V. The Council of *Constance (1414–18) finally ended the schism by the election of *Martin V in 1417.

Popes and Antipopes:

Roman obedience: Urban VI (1378–89); Boniface IX (1389–1417); Innocent VII (1404–6); Gregory XII (1406–15).

Avignonese: Clement VII (1378–94); *Benedict XIII (1394–1417).

Pisan: Alexander V (1409–10); *John XXIII (1410–15).

(1) A. Michel, *Humbert und Kerullarios* (2 vols., Paderborn, 1924–30); id., *Die Kaisermacht in der Ostkirche (843–1204)* (Darmstadt, 1959). M. Jugie, AA, *Le Schisme byzantin, aperçu historique et doctrinal* (1941). [J. C.] S. Runciman, *The Eastern Schism* (Oxford, 1955). J. M. Hussey, *The Orthodox Church in the Byzantine Empire* (Oxford History of the Christian Church, 1986), pp. 129–36, with further refs. M. Jugie, AA, in *DTC* 14 (pt. 1; 1939), cols. 1312–468, s.v. 'Schisme byzantin', with older bibl.

(2) G. J. Jordan, *The Inner History of the Great Schism in the West* (1930); W. Ullmann, *The Origins of the Great Schism* (1948); J. H. Smith, *The Great Schism, 1378* (1970); R. N. Swanson, *Universities, Academics and the Great Schism* (Cambridge Studies in Medieval Life and Thought, 3rd ser. 12; 1979). J. Favier and others, *Genèse et débuts du Grand Schisme d'Occident: Avignon 25–28 septembre 1978* (Colloques internationaux du Centre National de la Recherche Scientifique, no. 586; 1980). M. Harvey, *Solutions to the Schism: A Study of some English Attitudes, 1378–1409* (Kirchengeschichtliche Quellen und Studien, 12; St Ottilien, 1983). E. Vansteenberghe in *DTC* 14 (pt. 1; 1939), cols. 1468–92, s.v. 'Schisme d'Occident', with extensive bibl. See also bibl. to CONCILIAR THEORY.

Greater Antiphons. See O-ANTIPHONS.

Greece, Christianity in. Christianity was first preached in Greece in the 1st cent., principally by St *Paul, whose main centre was *Corinth. Under the Christian Empire the Greek clergy won favour with their people by their general support of the popular cause, often against the Byzantine court and patriarchate. In the *Iconoclastic Controversy the Greeks always stood firm in the cause of the images against the iconoclastic emperors. Meanwhile, during the 8th to 10th cents., Slavonic invaders from the north were Hellenized and converted, chiefly by the exertions of the Greek clergy. During the Frankish occupation, from 1204 onwards, the Church, though subject to a RC archbishop, retained its E. character and its hold upon the affections of its people. When the Turks became masters of Greece during the 15th cent., the Greek clergy were somewhat favoured; they were given positions as minor officials and also acted as the representatives of their own nation in dealing with the Turks. In the War of Independence it was Abp. Germanos of Patras who raised the standard of revolt in Morea (Peloponnese) in 1821.

The Greek Church asserted its independence from *Constantinople in 1833, and was formally recognized as *autocephalous by the Oecumenical Patriarchate in 1850. It is governed by the 'Synod of the Hierarchy', which in principle meets once a year and is attended by all diocesan bishops; in the intervals between its meetings executive power is vested in the 12-member 'Permanent Holy Synod', on which the bishops serve annually in rotation. The Abp. of *Athens is president of both synods. The clergy are paid by the State, but Church–State links have been weakened since 1974. There are c.100,000–200,000 Orthodox following the 'Old' or Julian *Calendar, known as *Palaioimerologitai* or 'Old Calendarists', who have their own bishops, monasteries, and parishes. There is also an even smaller community (c.42,000) of RCs (mainly of the Latin Rite), with Abps. of Athens, Corfu, and Naxos, and there are a very few Protestants. See also ORTHODOX CHURCH.

Maximilian, Prince of Saxony, *Das christliche Hellas* (Leipzig, 1918). C. Papadopoulos, Ἱστορία τῆς Ἐκκλησίας τῆς Ἑλλάδος (Athens, 1920 [19th cent.]). G. J. Konidaris, Ἐκκλησιαστικὴ Ἱστορία τῆς Ἑλλάδος (2 vols., ibid., 1960–70). B. Atesis, Ἐπίτομος Ἐπισκοπικὴ Ἱστορία τῆς Ἐκκλησίας τῆς Ἑλλάδος ἀπὸ τοῦ 1833 μέχρι σήμερον (3 vols., ibid., 1948–69). P. Hammond, *The Waters of Marah: The Present State of the Greek Church* (1956). M. Rinvolucri, *Anatomy of a Church: Greek Orthodoxy Today* (1966). K. S. Latourette, *Christianity in a Revolutionary Age*, 2 (1960), pp. 479–84; 4 (1962), pp. 522–6. A. Fortescue in *CE* 6 (1909), pp. 737–44, s.v.; A. A. Angelopoulos in *TRE* 14 (1985), cols. 213–28, s.v. 'Griechenland'.

Greek (biblical and patristic). The basis of the Greek of both the *Septuagint and the NT is the Hellenistic Greek (known as the Κοινή or 'Common' dialect) which spread over the Near East as the result of the conquests of Alexander the Great (d. 323 BC). This was a simplified form of Attic Greek, with some contributions from other dialects, the more delicate refinements in the use of particles, prepositions, participial constructions, and use of moods being smoothed away. Hellenistic Greek in its literary form appears in such writers as Polybius (d. 122 BC), *Philo, and *Josephus. Until recently it was generally supposed that the differences between the common Hellenistic and biblical Greek were due to the influence on the latter of Hebrew and Aramaic; but the papyrus documents discovered in thousands in Egypt in the last hundred years or so have shown that very many of the usages and phrases supposed to be biblical are in fact part of the vernacular language of the time. Some Hebrew influence remains, esp. in the Septuagint (which in turn influenced the NT), but often this means no more than that, of two forms of phrase employed in the vernacular, that one is chosen which comes nearest to the Hebrew phraseology.

Subject to these general considerations, there are differences between different writers. In the Septuagint, the *Pentateuch and Is. are in literary Hellenistic Greek; the other Prophets, the Pss., Chron. and most of Sam. and Kgs. are nearer to the vernacular. On the other hand, some of the later books (Dan., 1 Esd., Est., Job, Prov., Wisd.) are deliberately artistic in style. In the NT, Luke is the most literary writer, then come St *Paul and the author of Heb. Paul's style is educated Hellenistic Greek, but without deliberate literary refinements, while Heb. shows some conscious rhetoric. At the other end of the scale, Rev. is in an uneducated vernacular Greek, being frequently quite ungrammatical, though not more so than some of the papyri (the want of grammar, of course, usually disappears in English translations).

Apart from the general loss of the finer shades of Attic idiom, Hellenistic Greek is marked by such changes as the disappearance of the dual, a diminished use of the dative, interchange of the prepositions ἐν and εἰς, a tendency to amalgamate the perfect and aorist (leading in patristic Greek to the gradual disuse of the perfect), an almost complete disuse of the optative, and many other modifications in the use of words. Just as in pronunciation the differentiation of vowels, and esp. of diphthongs, tends to become obliterated, so the whole system becomes that of a simple language for general utility, in place of the delicate sensitiveness of Attic Greek.

For the first three cents. Christian writers remained generally free from the influence of pagan literature. But when Christianity had become the religion of the Empire, Christians shared the education of the Greek world, and were moulded by the prevailing literary tendencies. These tendencies were pre-eminently a deliberate cultivation of Attic models, and a conscious elaboration of style fostered by the schools of rhetoric. *Patristic Greek is coloured by both these influences, found in varying degree in all the principal writers. Of the two most celebrated for their style, *Chrysostom, with his unselfconscious zeal for moral instruction, comes nearest to true Attic, while *Gregory of Nazianzus shows the elaborate rhetoric of the schools in all its intentional artistry. The Fathers in general—*Basil the Great, the *Cyrils, *Athanasius, and others of less note—show the current manner of Byzantine Greek on a lower plane of achievement. In all, however, the language is progressively affected by modifications in the meanings of words necessitated by the requirements of Christian theology and philosophy. These can be followed only in a detailed patristic lexicon. In general it may be said that biblical Greek is the common Hellenistic Greek of the people, somewhat modified by Hebrew or Aramaic influence, while patristic Greek is the Byzantine Greek of the rhetoricians and literary artists, somewhat modified to suit the needs of Christian thought and terminology.

The standard Greek–English Dictionary is that of H. G. *Liddell and *R. Scott (1st edn., Oxford, 1843), constantly revised and extended by the orig. editors until the last edn. of 1897 (often reissued); it was completely revised under the editor-

ship of H. S. Jones and R. Mackenzie and issued in 10 parts [2 vols., 1925–40] as the 'New Edition'. From this 'New Edition', however, words and usages found only in patristic and Byzantine authors were excluded, in view of work then in progress on *A Patristic Greek Lexicon*, pub. under the editorship of G. W. H. Lampe (5 fascs., Oxford, 1961–8). Of older lexicons, the most ambitious was that of H. *Stephanus (4 vols., Paris, 1572; new edn. in 10 vols., London, 1816–28; rev. in 8 vols., Paris, 1831–65). Of lexicons for the vocabulary of the NT only, the best of the older dictionaries was C. L. W. Grimm and J. H. Thayer (Edinburgh, 1886). More recent are the successive edns. of E. Preuschen (Giessen, 1910; 2nd edn. by W. Bauer, ibid., 1928; since 3rd edn., 1936, with Bauer's name only; 4th edn., 1952; 5th edn., 1958; 6th edn., by K. and B. Aland, 1988; adapted Eng. tr. of 4th edn. by W. F. Arndt and F. W. Gingrich, Cambridge, 1957; 2nd edn., taking account of 5th edn. of the Ger., by F. W. Gingrich and F. W. Danker, Chicago and London, 1979); this admirable work takes full account of the new knowledge of Hellenistic Greek and has full bibls. For words found in papyri, see also F. Preisigke, *Wörterbuch der griechischen Papyruskunden* (2 vols., 1925–7; suppl., 1931; with continuation by E. Kiessling, 1944 ff.). On the theological aspects of NT vocabulary, there is the important *Theologisches Wörterbuch zum Neuen Testament*, ed. G. *Kittel and G. Friedrich (10 vols. in 11; 1933–79; Eng. tr. by G. W. Bromiley, 10 vols., Grand Rapids, Mich., and London [1964–76]), and the more recent *Exegetisches Wörterbuch zum Neuen Testament*, ed. H. Balz and G. Schneider (3 vols., 1980–3). Good concise dictionary by A. *Souter, *A Pocket Lexicon to the Greek New Testament* (1916; often repr.).

Of NT Greek grammars, the most elaborate is F. [W.] *Blass, *Grammatik des Neutestamentlichen Griechisch* (1896; 4th edn. by A. Debrunner, 1913; 14th edn. by A. Debrunner and F. Rekhopf [1975]; Eng. tr. of 10th edn. (1959), with revisions by F. W. Funk, Cambridge, 1961). Different in approach is the illuminating work of J. H. *Moulton, *A Grammar of New Testament Greek* (1, Prolegomena, 1906; 2, Accidence and Word-Formation, ed. W. F. Howard, 1919–29; 3, Syntax, by N. Turner, 1963; 4, Style, by N. Turner, 1976; esp. notable is Moulton's introd. in vol. 1). C. F. D. Moule, *An Idiom Book of New Testament Greek* (1953).

For Patristic Greek, in addition to the above, E. A. Sophocles, *Greek Lexicon of the Roman and Byzantine Periods, B.C. 146–A.D. 1100* (Boston, 1870). Much useful material of a lexical and factual kind also in J. C. *Suicer (q.v.), *Thesaurus Ecclesiasticus e Patribus Graecis* (2 vols., Amsterdam, 1682). For OT Greek, H. St J. Thackeray, *A Grammar of the Old Testament in Greek*, vol. 1 (all pub., 1909) and R. Helbing, *Grammatik der Septuaginta* (2 vols., 1907–28). Cf. also F. M. Abel, OP, *Grammaire du grec biblique* (1927). E. Mayser, *Grammatik der griechischen Papyri aus der Ptolemäerzeit* (2 vols. in 4, 1906–1934).

Further important works incl. E. Hatch, *Essays in Biblical Greek* (1889); A. Thumb, *Die griechische Sprache im Zeitalter des Hellenismus* (1901); A. *Deissmann, *Licht vom Osten* (1908; 4th edn., 1923; Eng. tr. as *Light from the Ancient East*, 1910; rev. from the 4th Ger. edn., 1927); C. H. *Dodd, *The Bible and the Greeks* (1935); R. Devreesse, *Introduction à l'étude des manuscrits grecs* (1954); R. Browning, *Medieval and Modern Greek* (1969), pp. 11–58 (2nd edn., Cambridge, 1983, pp. 1–52).

J. Vergote in *Dict. Bibl.*, Suppl., 3 (1938), cols. 1320–69, s.v. 'Grec biblique', with good bibl. See also bibl. to PAPYROLOGY.

Green, Thomas Hill

Green, Thomas Hill (1836–82), philosopher. Educated at Rugby under E. M. Goulburn and at Balliol College, Oxford, under B. *Jowett, he was elected a Fellow of Balliol in 1860 and, after a period of unsettlement, eventually (1866) became a tutor at Balliol, where his unaffected sincerity exercised a deep and permanent influence over many of his pupils. From 1878 until his early death he was Whyte's Professor of moral philosophy at Oxford. In his later years he took an active part in projects for educational and social reform.

Green's main endeavour was to rethink and propagate in the English world the idealistic philosophical doctrines of I. *Kant and G. W. F. *Hegel. His position was largely worked out in polemic against the empirical views of D. *Hume and the then influential J. S. Mill. Theologically he owed much to F. D. *Maurice. He held that the analysis of consciousness proved that reality was an organic whole, a 'world of thought relations' and not a mere aggregate; that the evidence of art, morality, and religion all pointed to the spiritual nature of reality; that God, the eternal consciousness, was realized in each individual person; and that, since personality alone gave meaning to the evolutionary process, the permanence and immortality of the individual were assured. The basis of the State was not an externally imposed coercive authority, but a desire for the common good (a 'general will').

Green's teaching exercised a great influence on the *Lux Mundi school, which rejected, however, its extreme immanentism. His chief published works were his Introduction to an edition of Hume's *Treatise of Human Nature* (1875), *Prolegomena to Ethics* (ed. A. C. Bradley, 1883), and his *Lectures on the Principles of Political Obligation* (1895; ed. B. *Bosanquet).

Most of Green's writings were collected by R. L. Nettleship (3 vols., 1885–8). The 'Introduction to Hume' is in vol. 1; and a Memoir is prefaced to vol. 3. Selection of his writings on political philosophy, ed. P. Harris and J. Morrow (Cambridge, 1986). W. H. Fairbrother, *The Philosophy of T. H. Green* (1896); M. Richter, *The Politics of Conscience: T. H. Green and his Age* (1964); J. Pucelle, *La Nature et l'esprit dans la philosophie de T. H. Green* (2 vols. [1961]–1965); G. Thomas, *The Moral Philosophy of T. H. Green* (Oxford, 1987). L. Stephen in *DNB* 23 (1890), pp. 55 f.

Green Thursday (Lat. *dies viridium*; Ger. *Gründonnerstag*). The usual name in Germany, also occasionally found elsewhere, for *Maundy Thursday. Its origin is perhaps connected with a custom of providing penitents, who had made their confession on *Ash Wednesday, with green branches on that day as tokens that their *penance was completed and that they were thereby received back into full ecclesiastical communion.

Greenwood, John (*c*.1560–93), a leader among the early English *separatists. As a young man he was chaplain to Lord Rich, a *Puritan, and conducted unauthorized services in his house. When these were suppressed he moved to London, where he either found or created the 'Ancient Church' in a house in St Paul's Churchyard. For this he was imprisoned in 1587; and he remained in prison for seven years with a short interval in 1592. He was constantly examined before the *High Commission and other courts, but stood firm, and along with his fellow prisoner, H. *Barrow, wrote many pamphlets defending the separatist cause. Both Barrow and Greenwood were hanged in 1593.

The *Writings of John Greenwood 1587–1590, together with the joint writings of Henry Barrow and John Greenwood 1587–1590*, ed. L. H. Carlson (Elizabethan Nonconformist Texts, 4; 1962); *The Writings of John Greenwood and Henry Barrow 1591–1593*, ed. id. (ibid. 6; 1970). ('A Pastoral Letter from Prison', formerly ascribed to Greenwood, is now attributed to Barrow.) F. J. Powicke, *Henry Barrow, Separatist (1550?–1593), and the Exiled Church of Amster-*

dam (1593–1622) (1900), esp. pp. 31–79 *passim*; B. R. White, *The English Separatist Tradition from the Marian Martyrs to the Pilgrim Fathers* (Oxford Theological Monographs, 1971), esp. pp. 67–90.

Gregorian Calendar. The calendar as reformed in 1582 by *Gregory XIII, and now in use throughout most of the Christian world. As the Julian Calendar, devised by Julius Caesar (46 BC), did not correspond with sufficient accuracy to the period taken by the earth to go round the sun (just under $365\frac{1}{4}$ days), an error of ten days had accumulated by the 16th cent. Gregory in his bull 'Inter gravissimas' of 24 Feb. 1582 ordered that matters should be remedied by reckoning the day after 4 Oct. of that year as 15 Oct. To prevent a recurrence of the situation it was decided that the century years were only to be leap years when divisible by 400 (e.g. 1600, 2000). Protestant countries were reluctant to introduce it, and it was not adopted in England until 1752. In a few RC Churches of E. rites it had been accepted before the beginning of the 19th cent., but even now most of their individual members follow the Julian Calendar. The Orthodox Churches only began to accept it in 1924. In the Julian Calendar fixed feasts now fall thirteen days later than in the Gregorian. For differences in the date of observing Easter and the feasts dependent thereon, see PASCHAL CONTROVERSIES.

The classical early work on the subject is C. Clavius, SJ, *Romani Calendarii a Gregorio XIII P. M. Restituti Explicatio* (Rome, 1603). F. Kaltenbrunner, 'Die Vorgeschichte der gregorianischen Kalenderreform', *Sb.* (Wien), 82 (1876), pp. 289–414; id., 'Die Polemik über die gregorianische Kalenderreform', ibid. 87 (1877), pp. 485–586; id., 'Beiträge zur Geschichte der gregorianischen Kalenderreform', ibid. 97 (1881), pp. 7–54. G. V. Coyne, SJ, and others (eds.), *Gregorian Reform of the Calendar: Proceedings of the Vatican Conference to commemorate its 400th anniversary, 1582–1982* (Rome, 1983), pp. 137–297. C. Trasselli in *EC* 3 (1950), cols. 357 f., s.v. 'Calendario', with bibl., col. 364. See also works cited under CALENDAR.

Gregorian chant. See PLAINSONG.

Gregorian Sacramentary. The name given to a family of Sacramentaries traditionally ascribed to Pope *Gregory I (590–604). The most important of these is the book known to scholars as the 'Hadrianum'. In response to a request of *Charlemagne for the standard Roman Mass book, *c*.790 Pope *Hadrian I sent him a Sacramentary described both in the covering letter and in the earliest copy of the book itself as the work of Gregory. The original has not survived, but a copy made from it, dated 811 or 812, is preserved at Cambrai (MS 164). The ascription to St Gregory cannot be taken literally, since it contains a Mass for his feast, but it has been shown to include material composed by him. Charlemagne's purpose in sending for the book was to promote uniformity in liturgy as in creed and in canon law, but it is probable that the standard Mass book for which he asked did not exist. Certainly the book which Hadrian sent him was defective in that it made no provision for considerable parts of the year and was lacking in other respects. The deficiencies were made good from *Gelasian service books current in Gaul. From the fusion of these two sources, 'Gregorian' and 'Gelasian', the later Roman Missal is derived. The process by which this fusion came about is not completely documented. One important step was the formation of a supplement of

'Gelasian' material, known from the opening word of its preface as the '*Hucusque'. Originally it was kept distinct but later it was integrated with the 'Gregorian' text. An examination of the textual tradition of 9th-cent. Sacramentaries shows that there were other sources as well as this supplement, but they have not yet been clearly delimited. There is some evidence to show that *Alcuin played a part in this process.

The other important representative of the Gregorian family of Sacramentaries is a MS preserved in the Chapter Library of Padua (Cod. D. 47), which was written in the area of Lorraine. Although it dates from the 9th cent., it is thought to contain elements from the late 7th cent.

The text was first pub. by G. Pamelius (Cologne, 1571). Crit. edn. by H. A. Wilson (HBS, 1915). *Das Sacramentarium Gregorianum nach dem Aachener Urexemplar* ed. H. *Lietzmann (on the basis of Cambrai 164; Liturgiegeschichtliche Quellen, 3; 1921); Cod. Padua D. 47, ed. K. Mohlberg and A. *Baumstark (ibid. 11–12; 1927). J. Deshusses, OSB, *Le Sacramentaire grégorien: Ses principales formes d'après les plus anciens manuscrits* (Spicilegium Friburgense, 16, 24, 28; 1971–82). B. *Capelle, OSB, 'La Main de S. Grégoire dans le Sacramentaire grégorien', *R. Bén.* 49 (1937), pp. 13–28, repr. in his *Travaux liturgiques*, 2 (1962), pp. 161–75; H. Ashworth, OSB, 'The Influence of the Lombard Invasions on the Gregorian Sacramentary', *Bulletin of the John Rylands Library*, 36 (1954), pp. 305–27; id., 'The Liturgical Prayers of St. Gregory the Great', *Traditio*, 15 (1959), pp. 107–61. R. Amiet, 'Le Prologue *Hucusque* et la table de *Capitula* du Supplément d'Alcuin au Sacramentaire grégorien', *Scriptorium*, 7 (1953), pp. 177–209. E. Bourque, *Étude sur les sacramentaires romains*, 1 (Studi di Antichità Cristiana, 20; 1949), pp. 299–391, and 2. 2 (ibid. 25; 1958). K. Gamber, *Wege zum Urgregorianum: Erörterung der Grundfragen und Rekonstruktionsversuch des Sakramentars Gregors d. Gr. vom Jahre 592* (Texte und Arbeiten, 46; 1956). Vogel, *Sources*, pp. 79–102. F. *Cabrol, OSB, in *DACL* 6 (pt. 2, 1925), s.v. 'Grégorien (le Sacramentaire)', cols. 1766–96, with bibl.; H. Ashworth in *NCE* 12 (1967), pp. 795–8, s.v. 'Sacramentaries'.

Gregorian Water. In W. usage, solemnly blessed water formerly used in the consecration of churches and altars with which not only salt (as in ordinary *Holy Water), but also ashes and wine, had been mixed. The beginnings of its ceremonial use go back to the *Gelasian Sacramentary, and it has an established place in the 9th-cent. *Pontificals. It is so named from the formula used in blessing it being attributed to *Gregory the Great.

L. Eisenhofer, *Handbuch der katholischen Liturgik*, 2 (1933), pp. 455–68 passim. M. Kunzler in *L.Th.K.* (3rd edn.), 4 (1995), col. 1038, s.v. 'Gregoriuswasser', for further refs.

Gregorianum. The *Jesuit university (*Pontificia Università Gregoriana*) at Rome. It was founded in 1551 as the 'Collegium Romanum' by St *Ignatius Loyola, and in 1582–4 provided by Pope *Gregory XIII with adequate buildings and resources and constituted a university. Since 1920 it has published a quarterly periodical entitled *Gregorianum*.

R. G. Villoslada, SJ, *Storia del Collegio Romano dal suo inizio (1551) alla soppressione della Compagnia di Gesù (1773)* (Analecta Gregoriana, 66; 1954). P. [G.] Caraman, SJ, *University of the Nations: The Story of the Gregorian University . . . 1551–1962* (New York and Ramsey, NJ [1981]).

Gregorovius, Ferdinand (1821–91), German historian. After studying at Königsberg and some time spent as a schoolmaster, he went to Italy in 1852, where he stayed for more than 20 years. He afterwards took up residence at Munich. During his sojourn in Rome he wrote his *Geschichte der Stadt Rom im Mittelalter* (1859–1872; Eng. trs. as *History of Rome in the Middle Ages*, 13 vols., 1894–1900), covering the period from AD 400 to 1534. It was a monumental work and brilliantly written, though often somewhat subjective in its judgements. An English translation of his 'Roman Journals' (1892) was published in 1907.

J. Hönig, *Ferdinand Gregorovius als Dichter* (Breslauer Beiträge zur Literaturgeschichte, 39; 1914); id., *Ferdinand Gregorovius der Geschichtschreiber der Stadt Rom* (1921; with correspondence, pp. 183–528); enlarged edn., without the letters, as *Ferdinand Gregorovius: Eine Biographie* (1944). A. Forni, *La Questione di Roma Medievale: Una Polemica tra Gregorovius e Reumont* (Istituto Italiano per il Medio Evo, Studi Storici, 150–51; 1985).

Gregory I, St (*c*.540–604) (**Gregory the Great**), Pope from 590. He was the fourth and last of the traditional Latin '*Doctors of the Church'. The son of a senator, he became prefect of the city (Praefectus Urbi) in 573, but, like many of the finer men of the age, he sold his vast property and devoted the proceeds to the relief of the poor and monastic foundations. He founded seven monasteries, six in Sicily and one in *Rome, which last he himself entered as a monk *c*.574. After a few years of a very austere life, the Pope compelled him to leave the cloister, creating him 'regionarius', i.e. one of the seven deacons of Rome. Soon afterwards (*c*.578) he was made '*apocrisarius' at the Imperial court of *Constantinople. About 585 he returned to Rome and became abbot of his former monastery (St Andrew's). To this period may belong the famous story, related by *Bede, of his encounters with the fair Saxon slaves in the market ('Non Angli, sed angeli').

On his accession to the Papacy, accepted only after a severe interior struggle, Gregory found Italy in an alarming state. The land was devastated by inundations, famine, pestilence, and the invasion of the Lombards, and the position of the Church threatened by the claims of the Imperial power at Constantinople. It was owing to Gregory, in whom firmness and strength of character were tempered by gentleness and charity, that many of these evils were conquered. Of particular significance were his relations with the Lombards, with whom he concluded, in 592–3, what amounted to a separate peace. By this unprecedented step he set aside the authority of the exarch of *Ravenna, the Emperor's representative. Throughout this period of unrest, aggravated by financial and military weakness, Gregory took a number of initiatives in matters affecting the civil administration and the military defence of Italy. In his administration of the vast estates of the Church, in which he spent great sums on works of charity, he showed conspicuous ability. In his frequently strained relations with the E. he upheld the supremacy of the Roman see and refused to recognize the title of '*Oecumenical Patriarch', adopted by the Patr. of Constantinople. One of the greatest successes of his pontificate was the mission to England, for which task he selected St *Augustine, later of *Canterbury, with about 40 companions from his own monastery. He also intervened with some success to strengthen the Church in Spain, Gaul, and N. Italy.

Gregory was a very fertile author, of a practical rather than speculative bent of mind. His 'Liber Regulae Pastoralis' (c.591) sets out the directives for the pastoral life of a bishop, whom he regards first as a shepherd of souls. The book, which was translated by King *Alfred, was very widely read and influential in establishing a model for those exercising authority. The 'Dialogues' (c.593; traditionally and almost certainly correctly attributed to him) relate the lives and miracles of Italian saints, incl. St *Benedict; they provided models of holiness for Gregory's contemporaries taken from saints close to them in time and space. His 'Expositio in Librum Iob, sive Moralium Libri XXXV' is an exegesis of the Book of Job in the threefold literal, mystical, and moral sense, with special emphasis on the last. The 'Homilies on the Gospels' were sermons preached on texts from the Gospels; they were much drawn on as lessons for the third *Nocturn in the *Breviary of 1570. There is also a collection of 854 of Gregory's letters, which are of extreme interest for the information they supply on the Pope's character and multifarious activities.

Gregory was an ardent promoter of monasticism. By granting the monks 'privilegia', which partly restricted episcopal jurisdiction, he laid the foundations of the later *exemption of religious orders that brought them under direct Papal control. His theology was dominated by the ideal of the contemplative life. It did not aim at originality and owed much to the work of earlier writers, incl. St *Augustine and John *Cassian, whose writings helped him to formulate answers to the problems of his contemporaries. Some of his stories about the fate of souls after death played a part in the later development of the doctrine of *purgatory. He encouraged the veneration of relics if authentic. He made important changes in the liturgy, and some of the prayers in the *Gregorian Sacramentary (q.v.) are his, though the Sacramentary as a whole is a later compilation. He fostered the development of liturgical music, and his name has been so closely linked with *plainsong that it is commonly known as the 'Gregorian Chant' even though it continued to evolve long after his pontificate; he gave to the Roman '*Schola Cantorum' its definite form. His pontificate and personality did much to establish the idea in men's minds that the Papacy was the supreme authority in the Church, and his achievement was the more impressive in that (as is reflected in the title 'servus servorum Dei', which he applied to himself) he had great personal humility. He was canonized by popular acclamation immediately after his death. Feast day in the W., 3 Sept. (formerly 12 Mar., still observed in the E.).

The best edn. of his collected Works is that of the *Maurist, D. de Sainte-Marthe (4 vols., Paris, 1704), supplemented by J. B. Galliccioli (16 vols., Venice, 1768–76), repr. in J. P. Migne, PL 75–8. Crit. edns. of his 'Registrum Epistolarum' by D. Norberg (CCSL 140 and 140A; 1982), of his comm. on the Song of Songs and 1 Sam. by P. Verbraken, OSB (ibid. 144; 1963), of his comm. on Ezek. by M. Adriaen (ibid. 142; 1971), of his comm. on Job by id. (ibid. 143, 143A, and 143B; 1979–85), of his 'Dialogues' by A. de Vogüé, OSB (SC 251, 260, and 265; 1978–80), and of the Regula Pastoralis by F. Rommel, OSB (ibid. 381–2; 1992). The earliest Life is the brief one in LP (Duchesne), 1, p. 312, with notes, pp. 312–14. Other early Lives by an unnamed monk of Whitby (c.713), first edn. by F. A. *Gasquet (London, 1904), crit. edn., with Eng. tr., by B. Colgrave (Lawrence, Kan., 1968); by *Paul the Deacon, a late 8th-cent. *Cassinese monk, ed. in its

original form by H. Grisar, SJ, in ZKT 11 (1887), pp. 158–73, and in an expanded form in the older edns. of Gregory's Works (PL 75. 41–60); and by John the Deacon (9th cent.; PL 75. 59–242). There are important modern Lives by F. H. Dudden (2 vols., London, 1905), P. *Batiffol (Paris, 1928; Eng. tr., 1929), and J. Richards, Consul of God (1980). C. Dagens, Saint Grégoire le Grand: Culture et expérience chrétiennes (1977). J. Fontaine and others (eds.), Grégoire le Grand (Colloques internationaux du Centre National de la Recherche Scientifique [101]; 1986). R. A. Markus, Gregory the Great and his world (Cambridge, 1997). Gregory's life and work are also discussed in all histories of the Papacy and of the Middle Ages. E. Caspar, Geschichte des Papsttums, 2 (1933), pp. 306–514. [E.] C. Butler, OSB, Western Mysticism (1922), pp. 89–133 and 211–41. E. H. Fischer, 'Gregor der Grosse und Byzanz', Zeitschrift der Savigny-Stiftung für Rechtsgeschichte, 67, Kanonistische Abteilung, 36 (1950), pp. 15–144. K. Hallinger, OSB, 'Papst Gregor der Grosse und der hl. Benedikt', in B. Steidle, OSB (ed.), Commentationes in Regulam S. Benedicti (Studia Anselmiana, 42; 1957), pp. 231–319. R. A. Markus, 'The Chronology of the Gregorian Mission to England: Bede's Narrative and Gregory's Correspondence', JEH 14 (1963), pp. 16–30, repr. in id., From Augustine to Gregory the Great (1983), no. 10. P. Meyvaert, OSB, 'Diversity within Unity, a Gregorian Theme', Heythrop Journal, 4 (1963), pp. 141–62, repr. in id., Benedict, Gregory, Bede and Others (1977), no. 6; see also nos. 5 and 7. P. Boglioni, 'Miracle et nature chez Grégoire le Grand', Cahiers d'Études médiévales, 1 (1974), pp. 11–102. C. Straw, Gregory the Great: Perfection in Imperfection (Berkeley, Calif., and London [1988]). F. Clark, The Pseudo-Gregorian Dialogues (Studies in the History of Christian Thought, 37–8; Leiden, 1987 [challenging Gregory's authorship]; cf. P. Meyvaert in JEH 39 (1988), pp. 335–81). R. Godding, Bibliografia di Gregorio Magno, 1890–1990 (Opere di Gregorio Magno, Complementi, 1 [1990]). Bardenhewer, 5, pp. 284–302; Altaner and Stuiber (1978), pp. 466–72 and 649–51. R. Manselli in RAC 12 (1983), cols. 930–51, s.v. 'Gregor I (Gregor der Grosse)'; R. A. Markus in TRE 14 (1985), pp. 135–45, s.v. 'Gregor I', with bibl.; R. Gillet, OSB, in DHGE 21 (1986), cols. 1387–420, s.v. 'Grégoire (3)'.

Gregory II, St (669–731), Pope from 715. As a deacon in 710 he accompanied Pope Constantine I to *Constantinople, where he distinguished himself by his lucid answers in the discussions on the canons of the Council 'in *Trullo'. Having succeeded to the Papacy in 715, he was at once confronted with the Saracen danger, against which he had the walls of Rome repaired, and the paganism of the German tribes, esp. in Bavaria, Thuringia, and Hesse. In 719 he sent there St *Boniface, aided by British monks and nuns. In his instructions to the missionaries he advocated a lenient view in the question of marriage among the newly converted, authorizing separation in certain cases and exceptions in the matter of forbidden degrees. In 726 *Leo III, the Isaurian, inaugurated the *Iconoclastic Controversy, in the course of which Gregory severely rebuked the Emperor at the synod of Rome in 727 without, however, countenancing the planned revolt of Italy against Byzantium and the election of another Emperor. His relations with the Lombards who tried to conquer Italy under Liutprand were for the most part friendly, owing to his personal influence with their king. The *Benedictine Order enjoyed Gregory's special protection and during his reign King Ine of Wessex entered a Roman monastery. Feast day, 13 Feb.

The chief authorities are LP (Duchesne), 1, pp. 396–414 (Eng. tr. by R. Davis, Liverpool, 1992, pp. 1–16), *Bede, *Paul the Deacon, and Theophanes Confessor. A. Schäfer, Die Bedeutung *der Päpste Gregor II (715–731) und Gregor III (731–741) für die Gründung des Kirchenstaates* (Diss., Münster i.W.; 1913), esp. pp. 14–33. E. Caspar, 'Papst Gregor II. und der Bilderstreit', *ZKG*, Dritte Folge, 52 (1933), pp. 29–89. H. Grotz, 'Beobachtungen zu den zwei Briefen Papst Gregors II an Kaiser Leo III', *Archivum Historiae Pontificiae*, 18 (1980), pp. 9–40. J. T. Hallenbeck, 'The Roman-Byzantine reconciliation of 728: genesis and significance', *Byzantinische Zeitschrift*, 74 (1981), pp. 29–41. Mann, 1 (pt. 2; 1902), pp. 141–202. P. Moncelle in *DTC* 6 (1920), cols. 1781–5, s.v. 'Grégoire II', with suppl. by R Aubert in *DHGE* 21 (1986), cols. 1420 f.

Gregory VII (d. 1085), Pope from 1073. Born prob. at Sovana in Tuscany, he was given the name of Hildebrand. He is traditionally thought to have come from a poor family, but medical evidence has cast doubt on this view. The date of his birth is unknown; it cannot have been later than 1034 and was prob. *c.*1015. He went to Rome at an early age, was educated in the monastery of St Mary on the Aventine, and took monastic vows either then or in 1047/9. He was chosen by Pope Gregory VI as his chaplain, and went into exile with him to Germany in 1046. After the Pope's death in 1047, he remained there in reforming circles, and he was confirmed in his austere views of the obligations of clerical life. He returned to Rome in 1049 with the newly elected Pope *Leo IX, who appointed him administrator of the patrimony of St Peter. Under him and his successors, in whose elections he exercised great influence, Hildebrand was the virtual guide of the Papacy. Under Nicholas II he had a share in the decree which assigned the election of the Popes to the cardinals; in 1059 he became Archdeacon of the Roman Church.

After his election to the Papacy (1073), Gregory extended his work for the reform and moral revival of the Church by issuing decrees against the *simony and incontinence of the clergy in the Lenten synod of 1074. These measures, which were enforced by Papal legates who deposed simoniacal and immoral clerics, were violently opposed, esp. in Germany and France. In England *William I refused Gregory's request for fealty, but agreed to the payment of *Peter's Pence and was acknowledged by Gregory to be in many respects a worthy and reforming ruler. In France, too, Gregory's reforms made some progress, despite Philip I's opposition. In Germany *Henry IV, threatened with ban and deposition, held two synods at Worms and Piacenza (1076) which declared the Pope deposed. Gregory replied by deposing and banning Henry, and freeing his subjects from their oath of allegiance at the Lenten synod of 1076. Henry, whose situation soon became desperate, submitted to the Pope at *Canossa in 1077, did penance, and was absolved from his censures. In spite of this the German princes elected Rudolf of Rheinfelden as German king at Forchheim in the same year. The Pope did not recognize him until 1080, when he once more excommunicated Henry, who had not fulfilled the promises given at Canossa. The latter now planned to set up Wibert, the excommunicated Abp. of *Ravenna, as antipope and marched against Rome, which he took in 1084. Gregory was freed by Robert Guiscard, whose Norman troops, however, exasperated the Roman population, so that they turned against Gregory, who had called them in. The Pope had to flee first to *Monte Cassino and later to Salerno, where he died. His alleged last words, 'I have loved righteousness and hated iniquity, therefore I

died in exile', are now interpreted as an expression of confidence and hope, not of disillusion and bitterness.

Though Gregory was once regarded as an ambitious tyrant, most modern historians have revised this judgement and are agreed on his purity of intention and his desire for *iustitia* (righteousness). In his own lifetime the Church suffered division, and he himself incurred much criticism; but Gregory's example and the activities of his successors (esp. *Urban II) did much to regenerate the Church. He ultimately condemned the eucharistic theology of *Berengar of Tours, who had denied the real change of the Bread and Wine into the Body and Blood of Christ in the Mass. His efforts at reconciling the E. Church to the W. failed, and in 1074 he was not able to put into effect his plans for a campaign against the Turks. He was canonized in 1606. Feast day, 25 May.

His *Registrum*, ed. E. Caspar in *MGH*, Epistolae Selectae, 2 (pts. 1 and 2; 1920–3); Eng. tr. of selections by E. Emerton (Records of Civilisation, Sources and Studies, 14; New York, 1932); for letters not in *Registrum* see *Epistolae Vagantes* ed., with Eng. tr., by H. E. J. Cowdrey (Oxford, 1972); 'Privileges' ed. L. Santifaller (ST 190; 1957). A. Murray, 'Pope Gregory VII and his Letters', *Traditio*, 22 (1966), pp. 149–201. Life by Paul of Bernried, completed 1128, ed. J. M. Watterich, *Pontificum Romanorum . . . vitae*, 1 (Leipzig, 1862), pp. 474–546. A. Fliche, *La Réforme grégorienne* (SSL 6, 9, and 16; 1924–37), with full bibl. H. X. Arquillière, *Saint Grégoire VII: Essai sur sa conception du pouvoir pontifical* (1934). G. B. Borino and others (eds.), *Studi gregoriani per la storia di Gregorio VII e della riforma gregoriana* (1947 ff.), incl. H. E. J. Cowdrey, 'Pope Gregory VII and the Anglo-Norman Church and Kingdom', in vol. 9 (1972), pp. 79–114, repr. in id., *Popes, Monks and Crusades* (1984), no. 9; cf. also no. 10. A. Fliche, *Saint Grégoire VII* ('Les Saints'; 1920); A. J. Macdonald, *Hildebrand* (1932); J. P. Whitney, *Hildebrandine Essays* (1932), 1 and 2, pp. 1–94. L. F. J. Meulenberg, *Der Primat der römischen Kirche im Denken und Handeln Gregors VII* (The Hague, 1965). P. E. Hübinger, *Die letzten Worte Papst Gregor VII.* (Rheinisch-Westfälische Akademie der Wissenschaften, Vorträge G 185; 1973). W. Ullmann, *The Growth of Papal Power in the Middle Ages* (1955; 2nd edn., 1962), esp. pp. 262–309. C. Schneider, *Prophetisches Sacerdotium und heilsgeschichtliches Regnum im Dialog 1073–1077: Zur Geschichte Gregors VII. und Heinrich IV.* (Münstersche Mittelalter-Schriften, 9; 1972). J. Vogel, *Gregor VII. und Heinrich IV. nach Canossa: Zeugnisse ihres Selbstverständnisses* (Arbeiten zur Frühmittelalterforschung, 9; 1983). C. Morris, *The Papal Monarchy: The Western Church from 1050 to 1250* (Oxford History of the Christian Church, 1989), esp. pp. 109–21. A. Fliche in Fliche and Martin, 8 (1944), pp. 55–198, with bibl. Mann, 7 (1910), pp. 1–217. G. Miccoli in *Bibliotheca Sanctorum*, 7 (Rome, 1966), cols. 294–379, s.v., with extensive bibl.

Gregory IX (*c.*1148–1241), Pope from 1227. Count Ugolino of Segni, a near relation of *Innocent III, studied at *Paris and *Bologna. He was created Cardinal Deacon on the accession of Innocent in 1198, Cardinal Bp. of Ostia in 1206, and was employed as Papal legate on a series of diplomatic missions to Germany. In 1217 he was commissioned to preach a *Crusade in northern, and later in central, Italy; from him the Emp. *Frederick II took the Cross at his coronation (1220). Insisting on the immediate fulfilment of the vow as soon as he became Pope, he forced the Emperor to embark in 1227, excommunicated him (29 Sept.) when he returned a few days later, and refused his overtures for peace. When Frederick II sailed unreconciled (1228) he proclaimed an interdict over his lands and wherever he should go. After conducting an unsuccessful campaign against Sicily, he agreed in 1230 to the Treaty of San Germano with the Emperor, loosing him from the ban. In 1239, however, he again excommunicated Frederick for invading Lombardy and usurping the rights of the Church in Sicily, tried to secure the election of an antiking and in 1241 summoned a General Council to Rome which Frederick II, however, prevented from meeting. He died while the Emperor was besieging Rome (22 Aug. 1241).

A personal friend of St *Francis of Assisi, he was appointed Protector of the *Franciscan Order as early as 1220 and assisted in the development of the *Third Order. It was largely from the *Dominicans and Franciscans that he drew the full-time *Inquisitors appointed from c.1233. He canonized St Francis in 1228, St *Antony of Padua in 1232 and St *Dominic in 1234. In 1230 he commissioned *Raymond of Peñafort to collect the Papal decretals of the past hundred years in the so-called 'Liber Extra' (published in 1234) and in 1231 instructed William of Beauvais to examine the works of *Aristotle and prepare an orthodox edition to supersede the old Latin translation, the use of which had been forbidden in 1210 ('Physics') and 1215 ('Metaphysics'). Throughout his pontificate he laboured unsuccessfully to effect a union with the E. Church.

L. Auvray (ed.), *Les Registres de Grégoire IX* (Bibliothèque des Écoles Françaises d'Athènes et de Rome, 2nd ser. 9; 4 vols., 1896–1955). G. Levi (ed.), *Registri dei Cardinali Ugolino d'Ostia e Ottaviano degli Ubaldini* (Fonti per la storia d'Italia, 8; 1890), pp. 3–154. A contemporary Life, prob. by John of Ferentino, ed. P. Fabre and L. *Duchesne, *Liber Censuum*, 2 (Bibliothèque des Écoles Françaises d'Athènes et de Rome, 2nd ser. 6; 1910), pp. 18–36. P. Balan, *Storia di Gregorio IX e dei suoi tempi* (3 vols., Modena, 1872–3); J. Felten, *Papst Gregor IX* (1886); S. Sibilia, *Gregorio IX, 1227–1241* (Milan, 1961). C. Thouzellier, 'La Légation en Lombardie du Cardinal Hugolin (1221). Un épisode de la cinquième croisade', *RHE* 45 (1950), pp. 508–42, with refs. to earlier lit.; K. Esser, OFM, 'Die Briefe Gregor IX. an die hl. Klara von Assisi', *Franziskanische Studien*, 35 (1953), pp. 274–95. Mann, 13 (1925), pp. 165–441, with bibl. details. Fliche and Martin, 10 [1950], pp. 225–38. O. Bonmann, OFM, in *EC* 6 (1951), cols. 1134–40, s.v. 'Gregorio IX', with further bibl.; G. Mollat in *NCE* 6 (1967), pp. 775–7, s.v. See also bibl. to the Emperor FREDERICK II.

Gregory X (1210–76), Pope from 1271. Teobaldo Visconti was elected Pope at Viterbo after the Holy See had been vacant for three years, though he was neither cardinal nor even priest. He was forthwith summoned to Italy from Acre, whither he had accompanied Prince Edward of England on his pilgrimage to the Holy Land. The deliverance of *Jerusalem, the reform of the Church, reunion with the Greeks, and the pacification of the German Empire, were the leading ideas of his short pontificate. He solved the German question by recognizing Rudolf of Habsburg as Emperor and inducing Alfonso of Castile to resign his claims to the German throne. At the Council of *Lyons (1274–5), which Gregory had summoned immediately on his accession, the Greek Emp. Michael Paleologus made his submission to the Pope for purely political reasons, but the reunion was short-lived. The plan of a Crusade was discussed at the Council, but, though financial preparations were made, it came to nothing. One of the most important ecclesiastical innovations of Gregory's reign was

the introduction of the *conclave at the election of the Pope by the Constitution 'Ubi periculum' of 1274. After his death, which took place on his way back from the Council, he received a local cult in several dioceses, e.g. Arezzo and Piacenza; *Benedict XIV added his name to the *Roman Martyrology. Feast day, 10 Jan.; since 1963, 9 Jan.

Les Registres de Grégoire X, 1272–1276, ed. J. Guiraud, L. Cadier, and others (Bibliothèque des Écoles Françaises d'Athènes et de Rome, 2nd ser. 12; 1892–1960). For legislation at the Council of Lyons, see bibl. s.v. O. Joelson, *Die Papstwahlen des 13. Jahrhunderts bis zur Einführung der Conclaveordnung Gregors X* (Historische Studien, Heft 178; 1928). L. Gatto, *Il pontificato di Gregorio X (1271–1276)* (Istituto Storico Italiano per il Medio Evo. Studi Storici, 28–30; 1959). B. Roberg, *Das Zweite Konzil von Lyon [1274]* (Konziliengeschichte, Reihe A: Darstellungen, Paderborn, etc., 1990), pp. 17–31 ('Zur Biographie Gregors X.'). Mann, 15 (1929), pp. 347–501, with discussion of sources. A. Clerval in *DTC* 6 (1920), cols. 1806 f., s.v. 'Grégoire X', with further bibl.; F. Molinari in *Bibliotheca Sanctorum*, 7 (Rome, 1966), cols. 379–87, s.v. 'Gregorio X', with bibl.

Gregory XI (1329–78), Pope from 1370. Pierre Roger de Beaufort was the last French Pope. After being created cardinal-deacon by his uncle, *Clement VI, at the age of 18, he studied at Perugia. A skilled canonist, he was elected Pope at *Avignon in 1370. His chief efforts were directed towards pacifying the Papal states, which were then revolting against the foreign officials under the leadership of Florence. Gregory finally excommunicated the city and sent against it the ruthless cardinal, Robert of Geneva (Antipope Clement VII). The Florentines having thereupon persuaded St *Catherine of Siena to negotiate for them, the Pope yielded to the entreaties of the saint, and decided to return to Italy to restore order, despite the protests of the King of France and most of the cardinals. He solemnly entered Rome on 17 Jan. 1377. Unable to put an end to the disturbances, he contemplated returning to Avignon, but the plan was prevented by his death in the following year. While in Rome, Gregory condemned the teachings of J. *Wycliffe (May 1377). After his death began the '*Great Schism'.

Lettres secrètes et curiales du pape Grégoire XI (1370–1378) relatives à la France ed. L. Mirot, H. Jassemin, and others (Bibliothèque des Écoles Françaises d'Athènes et de Rome, 3rd ser. 7; 1935–57); *Lettres secrètes . . . intéressant les pays autres que la France* ed. G. Mollat (ibid., 1962–5); *Lettres communes* ed. A.-M. Hayez (ibid., 3rd ser., 6bis; 1992 ff.); *acta concerning Bohemia* ed. C. Stloukal (Monumenta Vaticana Res Gestas Bohemicas Illustrantia, 4; Prague, 1949–53); letters concerning Belgium ed. C. Tihon (Analecta Vaticano-Belgica, 11, 20, 25; Brussels and Rome, 1958–64); those on the E. Church ed. A. L. Tăutu (Pontificia Commissio ad redigendum Codicem Iuris Canonici Orientalis, Fontes, 3rd ser. 12; Rome, 1966). Five Lives in S. *Baluze, *Vitae Paparum Avenionensium* (ed. Mollat, 1, 1914, pp. 415–67; other material in vol. 4, 1922, *passim*). J. P. Kirsch, *Die Rückkehr der Päpste Urban V und Gregor XI von Avignon nach Rom* (Quellen und Forschungen aus dem Gebiete der Geschichte, 4; 1898), pp. 169–262. Pastor, 1 (1891), pp. 100–16, with refs.; G. Mollat, *Les Papes d'Avignon* (10th edn. [1965]), pp. 130–42 and *passim*; Eng. tr. of earlier edn. (1963), pp. 59–63 and *passim*. Id., 'Grégoire XI et sa légende', *RHE* 49 (1954), pp. 873–7. A. Pélissier, *Grégoire XI ramène la papauté à Rome [c.1962]*. A. Clerval in *DTC* 6 (1920), cols. 1807 f., s.v. 'Grégoire XI'.

Gregory XIII (1502–85), Pope from 1572. Ugo Buoncompagni was born in *Bologna, where he studied and later taught law. In 1539 he was summoned to Rome by *Paul III, where his appointment as judge of the Capitol opened a curial career. This included service as a Papal jurist at the Council of *Trent (in 1546–7 and again in 1561–3) and culminated in his appointment as Cardinal-Priest of San Sisto (1565) in order that he might become Papal legate to Spain. He was elected Pope in 1572 with the support of *Philip II, and his pontificate was notable for its pro-Spanish temporal policy and its vigorous promotion of the *Counter-Reformation. He was committed to implementing the decrees of the Council of Trent, esp. in the foundation of seminaries. At Rome he founded the German College in 1573, the Greek in 1577, the *English College and the Hungarian in 1579, and the Maronite in 1584. He entrusted several of them to the *Jesuits, who enjoyed his special favour, and who also received from him a monopoly over Catholic missions to *China and *Japan. He also favoured other orders, approving the Congregation of the *Oratory (1575) and the Discalced *Carmelites (1580). The vast sums he spent on rebuilding Rome contributed to the successful *Jubilee of 1575, but left the Papal finances badly depleted. He introduced some administrative reforms in the *Curia and issued an improved edition of the *Corpus Iuris Canonici in 1582. The same year also saw perhaps his most influential achievement, the promulgation of the *Gregorian Calendar.

M. A. Ciappi, *Compendio delle heroiche et gloriose attioni et santa vita di Papa Gregorio XIII* (1591); G. P. Maffei, SJ, *Degli annali di Gregorio XIII*, pub. by C. Cocquelines (2 vols., 1742). I. Bompiano, *Historia Pontificatus Gregorii XIII* (Rome, 1655). L. Karttunen, *Grégoire XIII comme politicien et souverain* (Annales Academiae Scientiae Fennicae, Ser. B, vol. 2; Helsinki, 1911). G. Levi della Vida, *Documenti intorno alle relazioni delle chiese orientali con la S. Sede durante il pontificato di Gregorio XIII* (ST 143; 1948). A. Fernández Collado, *Gregorio XIII y Felipe II en la nunciatura de Felipe Sega (1577–1581): Aspectos político, jurisdiccional y de reforma* (Toledo, 1991). Pastor, 19 and 20 (1930), with full bibl. P. Moncelle in *DTC* 6 (1920), cols. 1809–15, s.v. 'Grégoire XIII'; B. Roberg in *TRE* 14 (1985), pp. 155–8, s.v. 'Gregor XIII.', with bibl. See also bibl. to GREGORIAN CALENDAR.

Gregory XVI (1765–1846), Pope from 1831. Bartolomeo Cappellari entered the *Camaldolese monastery of San Michele di Murano in 1783. In 1799 he published *Il trionfo della Santa Sede*, in which he treated of the sovereignty of the Pope and developed the doctrine of Papal Infallibility. He was made Abbot of San Gregorio in 1805 and Procurator-General of his order in 1807, but had to leave Rome in the following year, owing to the Napoleonic suppression of the religious orders. He returned in 1814, was created Cardinal and Prefect of the *Propaganda in 1826, and elected Pope in 1831 by the party of the Zelanti after a conclave lasting over 50 days. Soon after, revolution broke out in the Papal states and was quelled only by the intervention of Austria, a fact which caused the five great powers—Austria, Russia, England, France, and Prussia—to demand reforms in their administration. As these were only partly carried out, the revolt began again, and in 1832 Austrian troops were recalled, whereupon the French occupied Ancona and did not withdraw till 1838. But the troubles continued, and on Gregory's death, in 1846, dissatisfaction was rife and the finances of the Holy See in disorder, owing to the heavy expenditure involved by the upkeep of a strong military force. Gregory's relations with

the foreign powers remained strained during the greater part of his reign. He condemned Liberalism in the person of F. R. de *Lamennais (encyclical *Singulari nos*, 1834) and also the semi-rationalist theology of G. *Hermes (brief *Dum acerbissimas*, 1835). Despite the political difficulties in which he was involved, Gregory XVI did much for the missions, erecting many new bishoprics and vicariates and encouraging the formation of a native clergy. His apostolic constitution *In supremo* (1839) denounced slavery and the slave-trade. He also founded the Etruscan and Egyptian museums at the Vatican and the Christian museum at the *Lateran.

Acta Gregorii Papae XVI, ed. A. M. Bernasconi (Rome, 1901–4) (defective); for the first five years of his pontificate, cf. A. Barberi (ed.), *Bullarii Romani Continuatio*, 19–20 (Rome, 1857–8). A. Bartoli and others, *Gregorio XVI: Miscellanea Commemorativa* (Miscellanea Historiae Pontificiae, 13–14; Rome, 1948). [N. P. S.] *Wiseman, *Recollections of the Last Four Popes and of Rome in their Times* (1858), pt. 4 (pp. 415–532). D. Demarco, *Il tramonto dello Stato pontificio: Il papato di Gregorio XVI* (Turin, 1949; repr. Naples [1992]). [W.] O. Chadwick, *A History of the Popes 1830–1914* (Oxford, 1998), esp. pp. 1–60. J. Leflon, 'La Crise révolutionnaire 1789–1846', in Fliche and Martin, 20 (1949), pp. 426–71.

Gregory, St (late 6th cent.), Bp. of Agrigentum (Girgenti) in Sicily. Born near Agrigentum, he made a pilgrimage to Palestine, where he was ordained deacon by the Patriarch of *Jerusalem. In Rome he was consecrated Bp. of Agrigentum and appears to have been the victim of a plot against his character. *Gregory the Great addressed several letters to him. He had either died or been deposed by 594. There is a long Greek Life of him by Leontius, apparently prior of the monastery of St Sabas in Rome (d. 688), which was revised by *Simeon Metaphrastes. A Greek commentary on Ecclesiastes was long attributed to him, but recently some scholars have maintained that this was the work of a different Gregory of Agrigentum, a contemporary of the Emp. Justinian II (reigned 685–711), who is venerated in the E. Church, where his feast is observed on 23 or 24 Nov.; it was prob. this Gregory of Agrigentum whose commemoration C. *Baronius introduced into the *Roman Martyrology on 23 Nov. It is possible that the Commentary may be considerably later still.

The Commentary on Eccles. was first pub. by S. A. Morcelli (Venice, 1791), repr. in J. P. Migne, *PG* 98. 741–1182. The Life by Leontius ibid. 549–716. Simeon Metaphrastes' Life ibid. 116. 189–270. Crit. edn. of the Life by Leontius, with Germ. tr. and comm., by A. Berger (Berliner Byzantinische Arbeiten, 60 [1995]). C. Mercurelli, *Agrigento paleocristiana: Memorie storiche e monumentali* (Atti della Pont. Accad. Romana di Archeologia. Serie III. Memorie, 8. 1; 1948), *passim*. I. Croce, 'Per la cronologia della vita di S. Gregorio Agrigentino', *Bollettino della Badia Greca di Grottaferrata*, NS 4 (1950), pp. 189–207; 5 (1951), pp. 77–91. S. Gennaro, 'Influssi di scrittori greci nel "Commento all'Ecclesiaste" di Gregorio di Agrigento', *Miscellanea di Studi di Letteratura Cristiana Antica*, 3 (1951), pp. 162–84; further art. by G. Mannelli, ibid., pp. 185–94. G. H. Ettlinger, SJ, 'The Form and Method of the Commentary on Ecclesiastes by Gregory of Agrigentum', in E. A. Livingstone (ed.), *Studia Patristica*, 18 (pt. 1; Kalamazoo, Mich., 1985), pp. 317–20. *CPG* 3 (1979), p. 493 (no. 7950). A. Amore in *Bibliotheca Sanctorum*, 7 (Rome, 1966), cols. 169–73; R. Aubert in *DHGE* 21 (1986), cols. 1464–7, s.v. 'Grégoire (27)', both s.v., with extensive bibl.

Gregory Dialogos, St. The title commonly given to St *Gregory the Great in the MSS and editions of the Greek 'Liturgy of the *Presanctified' which baselessly presuppose that he was its author.

Gregory of Elvira, St (d. after 392), Bp. of Elvira ('Illiberis'), near Granada. One of the most intransigent opponents of *Arianism, he supported the refusal of *Lucifer of Cagliari to pardon those who 'Arianized' at the Council of Ariminum (359), and after Lucifer's death became the leader of the 'Luciferians'. Acc. to St *Jerome (*De vir. ill.* 105), Gregory was the author of various writings, but these remained unknown until the 20th cent. Attributions by G. *Morin and A. *Wilmart have been confirmed by the discovery of MSS in Spanish libraries due to A. C. Vega; Gregory is revealed as an important theologian whose works are generally agreed to include the *Tractatus de libris sanctarum scripturarum* (published in 1900 as the '*Tractatus Origenis'), *De Arca Noe, In Cantica Canticorum* (Homilies on the Song of Songs), which all display a lively use of *allegory, and *De Fide*, a doctrinal work refuting Arianism.

Modern edns. of his works by A. C. Vega, OSA, *De la Santa Iglesia Apostólica de Eliberri (Granada)* (España Sagrada, 55–56; 1957), 1 and 2, pp. 1–116, and by V. Bulhart and J. Fraipont (CCLS 69, 1967, pp. 1–247, with 'Dubia et Spuria', pp. 251–83). *De Fide* also ed., with Ital. tr. and comm., by M. Simonetti (Corona Patrum, 3; Turin, 1975), and *Epithalamium sive Explanatio in Canticis Canticorum*, ed., with comm., by E. Schulz-Flügel (Vetus Latina. Aus der Geschichte der lateinischen Bibel, 26; 1994). A. Marazuela, 'El Salterio de Gregorio de Elvira y la Vetus Latina Hispana', *Biblica*, 40 (1959), pp. 135–59. F. J. Buckley, SJ, *Christ and the Church according to Gregory of Elvira* (Rome, 1964). M. Simonetti in Quasten (cont.), *Patrology*, 4 (1986), pp. 84–9.

Gregory the Illuminator, St (*c*.240–?332), the 'Apostle of *Armenia'. He appears to have been of noble descent and to have been brought up as a Christian while an exile in Cappadocia. After returning to Armenia, he eventually succeeded in converting the King, Tiridates (298–?330), to the Christian faith, which forthwith became the official religion of the country. He was consecrated Bishop (*Catholicos) by the Metropolitan of Caesarea in Cappadocia and the episcopate remained for some generations in his family. His son, Aristakes, whom Gregory had consecrated to succeed him, attended the Council of *Nicaea (325). The homilies and epistles ascribed to him are probably not genuine. The principal sources are a 'Life', which survives only in Greek and Arabic translations, and *Agathangelos' 'History of the Armenians', covering much the same material; the precise relationship between these is not clear. Feast day, 30 Sept.; in the American BCP (1979), 23 Mar.

G. Garitte, *Documents pour l'étude du livre d'Agathange* (ST 127; 1946), esp. ch. 10; id., 'La Vie grecque inédite de saint Grégoire d'Arménie (MS 4 d'Ochrida)', *Anal. Boll.* 83 (1965), pp. 233–90. H. Gelzer, 'Die Anfänge der armenischen Kirche', *Ber.* (Sächs.), 47 (1895), pp. 109–74. P. Ananian, 'La data e le circostanze della consacrazione di S. Gregorio Illuminatore', *Le Muséon*, 74 (1961), pp. 43–73, 317–60. P. Peeters, SJ, 'S. Grégoire l'Illuminateur dans le calendrier lapidaire de Naples', *Anal. Boll.* 60 (1942), pp. 91–130. Bardenhewer, 5, pp. 182–5. P. Ananian in *Bibliotheca Sanctorum*, 7 (Rome, 1966), cols. 180–90, s.v. 'Gregorio Illuminatore', with bibl. See also bibl. to ARMENIA and AGATHANGELOS.

Gregory of Nazianzus, St (329/30–389/90), 'the Theologian', one of the '*Cappadocian Fathers'. He was the son of the Bp. of Nazianzus in Cappadocia (also 'Gregory') and studied at the university of Athens, where he was a contemporary of St *Basil. Soon afterwards he adopted the monastic life. Under pressure and against his will he was ordained priest (?*c*.362), and *c*.372 was consecrated to the see of Sasima, a small village in Cappadocia (where, however, he never resided). Until his father's death in 374 he remained at Nazianzus to help his father as suffragan, and soon afterwards retired for some years to Seleucia in Isauria. In 379 he was summoned to Constantinople, where his eloquent preaching in the Church of the Anastasis was a great influence in restoring the *Nicene faith and leading to its final establishment at the Council of *Constantinople in 381. During the Council he was appointed Bp. of Constantinople, but he resigned the see before the end of the year, retiring first to Nazianzus and later to his own estate, where he died.

His more important writings include his 'Five Theological Orations', which date from his Constantinopolitan period and contain an elaborate treatment of the doctrine of the Holy Spirit; the '*Philocalia', a selection from the writings of *Origen which he compiled in conjunction with St Basil; several important letters against *Apollinarianism; and many poems. Feast day in the E., 25 Jan.; in the W., 2 Jan. (with St Basil) (formerly 9 May, as in the American BCP, 1979).

Early edns. of his Works were pub. at Basle (1550) and Paris (1609 and 1630). Much improved *Maurist edn. by C. Clémencet, OSB, and A. B. Caillau (Paris, vol. 1, 1778; vol. 2, 1840); repr. in J. P. Migne, *PG* 35–8. Crit. edns. of *Five Theological Orations* by A. J. Mason (Cambridge Patristic Texts, 1899), of his letters by P. Gallay (with Fr. tr., 2 vols., Collection des Universités de France, 1964–7, and text alone, GCS, 1969), of his theological letters (101–2 and 202) not incl. in the above, with Fr. tr., by id. (SC 208; 1974); and of *Orations*, with Fr. tr.: 1–3 by J. Bernardi (SC 247; 1978); 4–5 by id. (ibid. 309; 1983); 6–12 by M.-A. Calvet-Sebasti (ibid. 405; 1995); 20–3 by J. Mossay and G. Lafontaine (ibid. 270; 1980); 24–6 by idd. (ibid. 284; 1981); 27–31 by P. Gallay and M. Jourjon (ibid. 250; 1978); 32–7 by C. Moreschini and P. Gallay (ibid. 318; 1985); 38–41 by idd. (ibid. 358; 1990); 42–3 by J. Bernardi (ibid. 384; 1992). The nine Orations hastily tr. by *Rufinus into Lat. (nos. 2, 6, 16, 17, 26, 27, 38, 39, 41), ed. by A. Engelbrecht (CSEL 46; 1910). Eng. tr. of *Select Orations* and *Letters*, with introd., by C. G. Browne and J. E. Swallow in NPNCF, 2nd ser., vol. 7 (1894), pp. 185–498. Eng. tr. of the *Five Theological Orations* in F. W. Norris, cited below. The main sources for his Life are his own writings, esp. his poem 'De vita sua' (*PG* 37. 1029–1166; also ed., with Ger. tr., by C. Jungck, Heidelberg, 1974). Eng. tr. (with two other *carmina de se ipso*) by D. M. Meehan, OSB (Fathers of the Church, 75; Washington, DC, 1987). Biog. of ample dimensions by a 7th-cent. presbyter named Gregory (*PG* 35. 243–304). Modern Lives by C. Clémencet (*PG* 35. 147–242), C. Ullmann (Darmstadt, 1825; 2nd edn., Gotha, 1867; Eng. tr., 1851), and P. Gallay (Lyons, 1943). M. Pellegrino, *La poesia di S. Gregorio Nazianzeno* (1932). P. Gallay, *Langue et style de S. Grégoire de Nazianze dans sa correspondance* (1943). J. Plagnieux, *Saint Grégoire de Nazianze théologien* (Strasbourg thesis; Paris, 1952). M.-M. Hauser-Meury, *Prosopographie zu den Schriften Gregors von Nazianz* (Theophaneia, 13; 1960). J. Mossay, *La Mort et l'au-delà dans saint Grégoire de Nazianze* (Université de Louvain. Recueil de Travaux d'Histoire et de Philologie, 4th ser. 34; 1966). R. R. Ruether, *Gregory of Nazianzus: Rhetor and Philosopher* (Oxford, 1969). T. Špidlík, SJ, *Grégoire de Nazianze: Introduction à l'étude de sa doc-*

trine spirituelle (Orientalia Christiana Analecta, 189; 1971). D. F. Winslow, *The Dynamics of Salvation: A Study in Gregory of Nazianzus* (Patristic Monograph Series, 7; Philadelphia, 1979). *Forschungen zu Gregor von Nazianz*, ed. J. Mossay and others (Studien zur Geschichte und Kultur des Altertums, NF, 2. Reihe, 1981 ff.). B. Coulie, *Les Richesses dans l'Œuvre de Saint Grégoire de Nazianze* (Publications de l'Institut Orientaliste de Louvain, 32; 1985). F. W. Norris, *Faith Gives Fullness to Reasoning* (Supplements to *VC*, 13; Leiden, 1991), with Eng. tr. of the *Five Theological Orations* by L. Wickham and F. Williams. *CPG* 2 (1974), pp. 179–209 (nos. 3010–125). Bardenhewer, 3, pp. 162–88; Altaner and Stuiber (1978), pp. 298–303 and 609 f. J. Rousse, in *Dict. Sp.* 6 (1967), cols. 932–71, s.v. 'Grégoire (14) de Nazianze'; J. T. Cummings in *NCE* 6 (1967), pp. 791–4; B. Wyss in *RAC* 12 (1983), cols. 793–863, s.v. 'Gregor II (Gregor von Nazianz)'.

Gregory of Nyssa, St (*c.*330–*c.*395), Bp. of Nyssa, *Cappadocian Father. He was a younger brother of St *Basil. Though early destined for an ecclesiastical career he temporarily became a rhetorician, but returned to his first vocation and entered a monastery founded by his brother. He was consecrated Bp. of Nyssa, *c.*371. A supporter of the faith of *Nicaea, he was deposed by the *Arians in 376 and remained in exile until the death of the Emp. Valens in 378, when he regained his see. In 379 he attended the Council of Antioch, and in the next year he was elected Bp. of Sebaste, but protested and was soon replaced by his brother Peter. After the Council of *Constantinople in 381, the Emp. *Theodosius I charged him to promote orthodoxy in the civil diocese of Pontus. In his later life he was much in demand as a preacher. In 394 he took part in the Council of Constantinople convoked by the Patr. *Nectarius; he seems to have died soon afterwards.

St Gregory of Nyssa was a thinker and theologian of originality and learning, acquainted esp. with *Platonist speculation, as well as an outstanding exegete, orator, and ascetical author. His principal theological works are polemical treatises against *Eunomius, *Apollinarius, and the *Tritheistic teaching ascribed to a certain Ablabius. In his 'Catechetical Oration' he expounded the doctrines of the Trinity, Incarnation, and Redemption, and the Sacraments of Baptism and the Eucharist for those whose duty it was to instruct the catechumens. His exegetical works, which are influenced by *Origen and deal esp. with the mystical sense of Scripture, include a 'Life of Moses', 'Of the Pythonissa', and homilies on Ecclesiastes, the Song of Songs, the *Lord's Prayer, and the *Beatitudes. Among his ascetical works, his treatise 'On Virginity' links a Platonizing account of the Christian vocation to an Origenist understanding of the soul as the bride of Christ. *De Instituto Christiano* was almost certainly influenced by the *Great Letter* of *Macarius/Simeon, with its *Messalian undertones. He also wrote an attractive Life of his sister Macrina. Many of his sermons, funeral orations, and letters have also survived.

He was an ardent defender of the Nicene dogma of the Trinity, and distinguished carefully between the generation of the Son and the procession of the Holy Spirit. The Second Person of the Trinity was incarnate in the womb of Mary, who therefore is truly θεοτόκος, for Christ is one Person in two natures. In his eschatology he is influenced by Origen, with whom he holds that ultimately both the souls in hell and the devils will return to God. In his account of the Atonement he employs, prob. for the first time, the simile of the fish-hook by which the devil was baited. Feast day in the E., 10 Jan.; in the W., 9 Mar.

Works, ed. F. *Ducaeus, SJ, and J. Gretser, SJ (2 vols., Paris, 1615; rev. edn., 3 vols., ibid., 1638), repr. in J. P. Migne, *PG* 44–6. The text of this edn. remains unsatisfactory. Crit. text begun by W. Jaeger (Berlin, 1921–5) and cont. by W. Jaeger and H. Langerbeck (Leiden, 1960 ff.): vols. 1–2: *Contra Eunomium*, ed. W. Jaeger (1921; 2nd edn., 1960); 3: *Opera Dogmatica Minora*, part 1, ed. F. Mueller (1958); part 2, ed. J. K. Downing and others (1987); part 4, ed. E. Mühlenberg (1996); 5: *In Inscriptiones Psalmorum, In Sextum Psalmum, In Ecclesiasten Homiliae*, ed. J. McDonough, SJ, and P. Alexander (1962); 6: *In Canticum Canticorum*, ed. H. Langerbeck (1960); 7, part 1: *De Vita Moysis*, ed. H. Musurillo (1964); part 2: *De Oratione Dominica, De Beatitudinibus*, ed. J. F. Callahan (1992); 8, part 1: *Opera Ascetica*, ed. W. Jaeger and others (1952); 8, part 2: *Epistulae*, ed. G. Pasquali (1925; 2nd edn., 1959); 9 and 10, parts 1–2: *Sermones*, ed. G. Heil and others (1967–96). Separate crit. edns. of *De Anima et Resurrectione* by J. G. Krabinger (Leipzig, 1837), *De Oratione Dominica* by id. (Landshut, 1840); *Apologia in Hexaemeron*, etc., by G. H. *Forbes (2 pts., Burntisland, 1855–61), *Catechetical Oration* by J. H. Srawley (Cambridge Patristic Texts, 1903), *De Pauperibus Amandis Orationes duo* by A. van Heck (Leiden, 1964), *De Virginitate* by M. Aubineau (SC 119; 1966), *Encomium in Sanctum Stephanum Protomartyrem* by O. Lendle (Leiden, 1968), *Vita Macrinae* by P. Maraval (SC 178; 1971) and Letters by id. (ibid. 363; 1990). W. Jaeger, *Two Rediscovered Works of Ancient Christian Literature: Gregory of Nyssa and Macarius* (Leiden, 1954); on the relationship of the two works, cf. R. Staats, *Gregor von Nyssa und die Messalianer* (Patristische Texte und Studien, 8; 1968). Syr. version of Gregory's Commentary on Song of Songs ed. C. van den Eynde, OP (Bibliothèque du Muséon, 10; Louvain, 1939). Eng. tr. of 'Select Writings' in NPNCF, 2nd ser., vol. 5 (1890); of 'Life of St Macrina' ed. W. K. L. Clarke (London, 1916); of 'The Lord's Prayer' and 'The Beatitudes' by H. C. Graef (ACW 18; 1954), and of 'The Life of Moses' by A. J. Malherbe and E. Ferguson (Classics of Western Spirituality, 1978).

F. Diekamp, *Die Gotteslehre des hl. Gregor von Nyssa* (1896). H. F. Cherniss, 'The Platonism of Gregory of Nyssa', *University of California Publications in Classical Philology*, 11, for 1930–3 (1934), pp. 1–92. M. Pellegrino, 'Il platonismo di San Gregorio Nisseno nel dialogo "Intorno all'Anima e alla Risurrezione"', *Rivista di Filosofia Neo-Scolastica*, 30 (1938), pp. 437–74. G. González, *La fórmula μία οὐσία τρεῖς ὑποστάσεις en S. Gregorio de Nisa* (Analecta Gregoriana, 21; 1939). H. U. von *Balthasar, SJ, *Présence et pensée: Essai sur la philosophie religieuse de Grégoire de Nysse* (1942). J. *Daniélou, SJ, *Platonisme et théologie mystique: Essai sur la doctrine spirituelle de St Grégoire de Nysse* (1944); id., *L'Être et le temps chez Grégoire de Nysse* (Leiden, 1970). R. Leys, SJ, *L'Image de Dieu chez Saint Grégoire de Nyssa* (Museum Lessianum, 49; 1951). W. Völker, *Gregor von Nyssa als Mystiker* (Wiesbaden, 1955). W. Jaeger, *Gregor von Nyssa's Lehre vom heiligen Geist*, ed. H. Dörries (Leiden, 1966). E. Mühlenberg, *Die Unendlichkeit Gottes bei Gregor von Nyssa* (Forschungen zur Kirchen- und Dogmengeschichte, 16; 1966). M. Harl (ed.), *Écriture et culture philosophique dans la pensée de Grégoire de Nysse: Actes du Colloque de Chevetogne (22–26 septembre 1969)* (Leiden, 1971); Acts of subsequent *Colloquia* pub. ibid., 1976, and then in various places, 1981 ff. R. M. Hübner, *Die Einheit des Leibes Christi bei Gregor von Nyssa: Untersuchungen zum Ursprung der 'physischen' Erlösungslehre* (Philosophia Patrum, 2; Leiden, 1974). H. R. Drobner and C. Klock (eds.), *Studien zu Gregor von Nyssa und der christlichen Spätantike* (Supplements to *VC*, 12; Leiden, 1990). M. Altenburger and F. Mann, *Bibliographie zu Gregor von Nyssa* (Leiden, 1988). *CPG* 2 (1974), pp. 209–30 (nos. 3135–226). Bardenhewer, 3, pp. 188–220; Altaner and Stuiber (1978), pp. 303–8 and 610–12. M. Canévet in *Dict. Sp.* 6 (1967), cols. 971–1011, s.v. 'Grégoire (16) de Nysse'; H. Dörrie in *RAC* 12 (1983), cols. 863–95, s.v. 'Gregor III (Gregor von Nyssa)'.

Gregory Palamas, St (*c.*1296–1359), Greek theologian and chief exponent of *Hesychasm. He was born probably at *Constantinople of a noble Anatolian family. Attracted from his youth to the monastic ideal, he persuaded his brothers and sisters, as well as his widowed mother, to embrace the religious life. Around 1318 he went, with his two brothers, to Mt. *Athos, where he became familiar at first hand with the Hesychast tradition of mystical prayer. The advance of the Turks forced him to flee to *Thessalonica, where he was ordained priest in 1326; subsequently he retired as a hermit to a mountain near Beroea, whence he returned to Athos in 1331. In 1337 he became involved in controversy with Barlaam, a Greek monk from Calabria. Influenced by a one-sided interpretation of the writings of *Dionysius the Pseudo-Areopagite, Barlaam stated the doctrine of God's unknowability in an extreme form. When criticized by Gregory, he replied with a vigorous attack on the contemplative practices of the Hesychasts, and in answer Gregory composed his most important work, the *Triads in defence of the Holy Hesychasts* (*c.*1338). Gregory's teaching was approved by his fellow monks, who met in synod on Mt. Athos during 1340–1 and put out a statement known as the 'Hagioritic Tome' ('Αγιορειτικὸς Τόμος), supporting his views. A Council held at Constantinople in 1341 likewise took Palamas' side in the dispute and condemned Barlaam. Although in 1344 Palamas' opponents secured his conviction for heresy and his excommunication, the orthodoxy of his doctrines was reaffirmed by two further Councils at Constantinople in 1347 and 1351. Between these two Councils, Palamas produced a succinct exposition of his theology, the *One Hundred and Fifty Chapters*. In 1347 he was consecrated Abp. of Thessalonica, but political conditions made it impossible for him to take possession of his see until 1350. During a journey to Constantinople in 1354, he was captured by the Turks and remained in captivity for more than a year. He was canonized in 1368.

In his theological teaching Palamas stressed the biblical notion of man as a single and united whole, body and soul together; and in virtue of this he argued that the physical exercises used by the Hesychasts in prayer, as well as their claim to see the Divine Light with their bodily eyes, could be defended as legitimate. He distinguished between the essence and the energies of God: God's essence remains unknowable, but His uncreated energies—which are God Himself—permeate all things and can be directly experienced by man in the form of deifying grace. Like St *Simeon the New Theologian, Palamas laid great stress in his spiritual teaching upon the vision of Divine Light. Feast day in E., 14 Nov., and also the second Sunday in Lent.

The bulk of his work is still in MS. Various writings, in an inferior text, are repr. in J. P. Migne, *PG* 150. 771–1372, and 151. 9–678. Crit. edn. of his collected works by P. C. Chrestou (Thessalonica, 1962 ff.). The *Triads* (Περὶ τῶν ἱερῶς ἡσυχαζόντων) ed., with Fr. tr., by J. Meyendorff, *Défense des saints hésychastes* (SSL 30–1; 1959); partial Eng. tr. by [D. J.] N. Gendle (Classics of Western Spirituality, 1983). The *One Hundred and Fifty Chapters*, ed., with Eng. tr., by R. E. Sinkewicz, CSB (Pontifical Institute of Mediaeval Studies, Studies and Texts, 83; Toronto [1988]). Substantial passages of his works were included in the *Philocalia* (q.v.); Eng. tr. by G. E. H. Palmer and others, 4 (1955), pp. 287–425. J. Meyendorff, *Introduction à l'étude de Grégoire Palamas* (Patristica Sorbonensia, 3 [1959]; abbreviated Eng. tr., 1964); id., *St Grégoire Palamas et la mystique orthodoxe*

(Maîtres Spirituels [1959]; Eng. tr., New York, 1974); J. Lison, *L'Esprit répandu: La pneumatologie de Grégoire Palamas* (1994). G. Podskalsky, *Theologie und Philosophie in Byzanz* (Byzantinisches Archiv, 15; 1977), esp. pp. 150–7. M. Jugie, AA, in *DTC* 11 (pt. 2; 1932), cols. 1735–76; J. Meyendorff in *Dict. Sp.* 12 (pt. 1; 1984), cols. 81–107, s.v. 'Palamas Grégoire'.

Gregory of Rimini (d. 1358), 'Doctor authenticus', medieval philosopher. He joined the *Augustinian Hermits, studied in *Paris from 1323 to 1329, and subsequently taught at *Bologna, Padua, and Perugia. In 1341 he returned to Paris, where he lectured on the Sentences and in 1345 was made doctor of the *Sorbonne by *Clement VI. Elected *General of his order in 1357, he began at once to introduce reforms, but his work was cut short by his death in the following year. His philosophical doctrines carried further the *Nominalist teaching of *William of Ockham. His theology was thoroughly Augustinian. He taught that works done without grace are sinful and that unbaptized infants incur eternal damnation, an opinion which, though also held by St Augustine, earned him the title 'tortor infantium'. He also wrote a treatise on usury. Persistent attempts have been made to trace his influence on M. *Luther, perhaps not entirely convincingly.

His work on the Sentences was pub. Paris, 1482, and Venice, 1522; crit. edn. by A. D. Trapp, OSA, and others (Spätmittelalter und Reformation, Texte und Untersuchungen, 6–12; 1979–87); his *De usuris* was pub. Milan, 1508, and Rimini, 1622. J. Würsdörfer, *Erkennen und Wissen nach Gregor von Rimini: Ein Beitrag zur Geschichte der Erkenntnistheorie des Nominalismus* (BGPM 20, Heft 1; 1917); M. Schüler, *Prädestination, Sünde und Freiheit bei Gregor von Rimini* (Forschungen zur Kirchen- und Geistesgeschichte, 3; 1934); G. [A.] Leff, *Gregory of Rimini* (Manchester, 1961); W. Eckermann, OSA, *Wort und Wirklichkeit: Das Sprachverständnis in der Theologie Gregors von Rimini und sein Weiterwirken in der Augustinerschule* (Cassiciacum, 33; Würzburg, 1978); H. A. Oberman (ed.), *Gregor von Rimini: Werk und Wirkung bis zur Reformation* (Spätmittelalter und Reformation, Texte und Untersuchungen, 20; 1981). [A.] D. Trapp, OSA, in *TRE* 14 (1985), pp. 181–4, s.v.; R. Aubert in *DHGE* 22 (1988), cols. 28–31, s.v. 'Grégoire (107) de Rimini'.

Gregory Thaumaturgus, St (*c.*213–*c.*270). Greek Church Father. He came from a prosperous pagan family of Neocaesarea in Pontus, and studied law and rhetoric. About 233 he went to *Caesarea in Palestine, where he became a disciple of *Origen, who converted him to the Christian faith and with whom he remained for five, or perhaps eight, years. Soon after his return to his native city he was made its bishop, and during his episcopate converted its pagan population. The wealth of legends and miracles which were attributed to him in later times and to which he owes his surname of Thaumaturgus or wonder-worker, testify to his uncommon strength of character as well as to his popularity. In 253–4 he witnessed the Goths devastating Pontus, as described in his so-called 'Canonical Letter'. In 264–5 he took part in the first Synod of *Antioch against *Paul of Samosata; he also fought *Sabellianism and *Tritheism. Acc. to *Suidas he died in the reign of the Emp. Aurelian (270–5).

St Gregory was a practical Churchman rather than a speculative theologian. He based his teaching on Origen, but his terminology is still undeveloped and often equivocal. His name has been affixed to a number of treatises, only a few of which are authentic. His first extant work is his panegyric on Origen, Εἰς Ὠριγένην ... Προσφωνητικός, delivered when he took leave of his master. It contains much autobiographical material as well as an account of Origen's teaching methods. His Ἔκθεσις τῆς Πίστεως is a Trinitarian exposition of belief, the basis of his instructions to catechumens. Acc. to St *Gregory of Nyssa, whose grandmother St *Macrina had been instructed by Gregory Thaumaturgus, it was given to him in a vision by St *John the Apostle, at the command of the BVM, the first known instance of a record of a Marian apparition. His Ἐπιστολὴ Κανονική contains much information on the penitential discipline of the early Church. His Μετάφρασις εἰς τὸν Ἐκκλησιαστήν is a paraphrase of Ecclesiastes, and his letter to Theopompus, extant only in a Syriac translation, is a philosophical colloquy on the impassibility of God. Feast day, 17 Nov.

Life, by Gregory of Nyssa, in J. P. Migne, *PG* 46. 893–958. There also exist Syr., Armen., and Lat. Lives, all of little value. Works (incl. several *dubia* and *spuria*) pub. by G. Voss (Mainz, 1604) and others; repr. from A. *Gallandi in J. P. Migne, *PG* 10. 963–1232. Crit. text of Gregory's address to Origen ed. P. Koetschau (Sammlung ausgewählter Quellenschriften, 9; 1894), repr., with Fr. tr., introd. and notes by H. Crouzel, SJ (SC 148; 1969). Eng. tr. of his 'Canonical Letter' in P. [J.] Heather and J. [F.] Matthews, *The Goths in the Fourth Century* (Translated Texts for Historians, 11; Liverpool, 1991), pp. 5–11. V. Ryssel, *Gregorius Thaumaturgus: Sein Leben und seine Schriften* (1880). M. Jugie, AA, 'Les Homélies mariales attribuées à S. Grégoire le Thaumaturge', *Anal. Boll.* 43 (1925), pp. 86–95. On his Creed, cf. L. Froidevaux, 'Le Symbole de Saint Grégoire le Thaumaturge', *Rech. S.R.* 19 (1929), pp. 193–247. A. Poncelet, SJ, 'La Vie latine de Saint Grégoire le Thaumaturge', ibid. 1 (1910), pp. 132–60. W. Telfer, 'The Cultus of St Gregory Thaumaturgus', *HTR* 29 (1936), pp. 225–344. R. van Dam, 'Hagiography and History: The Life of Gregory Thaumaturgus', *Classical Antiquity*, 1 (1982), pp. 272–308. R. Lane Fox, *Pagans and Christians* (1986), pp. 516–42. *CPG* 1 (1983), pp. 238–47 (nos. 1763–94). Bardenhewer, 2, pp. 315–32; Altaner and Stuiber (1978), pp. 211 f. and 591. H. Crouzel in *Dict. Sp.* 6 (1967), cols. 1014–20, s.v. 'Grégoire (19), le Thaumaturge'; id. in *NCE* 6 (1967), pp. 797 f., s.v.; id. and H. Brakmann in *RAC* 12 (1983), cols. 779–93, s.v. 'Gregor I (Gregor der Wundertäter)'.

Gregory of Tours, St (538/9–94), Bp. of Tours and historian of the Franks. He came of a Gallo-Roman senatorial family which had already produced several bishops, and was elected Bp. of Tours in 573. Though he had at first to oppose King Chilperic, he readily supported the 'good king', Guntram, against the turbulent aristocracy, thus gaining royal favour for the Church. About 576 he began his *Historia Francorum*. Book 1 runs quickly from the Creation to 397; Books 2–4, based on valuable sources, relate early Frankish history to 575; and Books 5–9 cover the years 575 to 591 in detail. The important position Gregory filled in Church and State and the access he thus obtained to original documents made him a well-informed historian, without whose work the early history of France could hardly be written. But his History, though honest and vivid, was untidy and unreflective, and his knowledge of events outside France was slight. His chief hagiographical work is his eight *Miraculorum Libri*: (1) *In Gloriam Martyrum*, on the miracles of the Lord, the Apostles, and esp. Gallic martyrs; (2) *De Virtutibus S. Juliani*, on miracles at the tomb of St Julian, put to death at Clermont-Ferrand in 304; (3–6) *De Virtutibus S. Martini*,

on miracles at the tomb of St *Martin; (7) *De Vita Patrum*, lives of 23 Gallic saints; (8) *In Gloriam Confessorum*, miracles of (esp. Gallic) saints not martyrs. Here he often displays extreme credulity, so that the work is of altogether less historical value than his *Historia Francorum*. Feast day, 17 Nov.

Editio princeps of the *Historia Francorum*, with a few other works (Paris, 1522). Improved edn. of his works by T. *Ruinart, OSB (Paris, 1699), repr. in J. P. Migne, *PL* 71. Crit. edn. by W. Arndt and B. Krusch in *MGH*, Scriptores Rerum Merovingicarum, 1 (2 pts., 1884–5), which prints the author's orig. text with all its asperities before its 'revision' to conform it with the Carolingian standards of elegance; the *Historia Francorum* from this edn. was rev. by Krusch and W. Levison (ibid., 1951); Gregory's Lat. tr. of the 'Passio Septem Dormientium apud Ephesum' was ed. B. Krusch in *MGH*, loc. cit., 7 (pt. 2; 1920), pp. 757–69. Eng. trs. of *Historia Francorum*, with introd. and notes, by O. M. Dalton (2 vols., Oxford, 1927; vol. 1, introduction, vol. 2, tr.) and by L. Thorpe (Penguin Classics, 1974); of the *De Vita Patrum* by E. James (Translated Texts for Historians, Latin Series, 1; Liverpool, 1985); of *In Gloriam Martyrum* by R. van Dam (ibid. 3; 1988) and of *In Gloriam Confessorum* by id. (ibid. 4; 1988). *Gregorio di Tours, 10–13 Ottobre 1971* (Convegni del Centro di Studi sulla Spiritualità Medievale, 12; Todi, 1977). M. Weidemann, *Kulturgeschichte der Merowingerzeit nach den Werken Gregors von Tours* (Römisch-Germanisches Zentralmuseum, Forschungsinstitut für Vor- und Frühgeschichte, Monographien 3; 2 vols., Mainz, 1982), esp. 1, pp. 107–264; 2, pp. 157–237. L. Pietri, *La Ville de Tours du IVᵉ au VIᵉ siècle: naissance d'une cité chrétienne* (Collection de l'École française de Rome, 69; 1983), pp. 247–334. J. Verdon, *Grégoire de Tours, 'le père de l'Histoire de France'* (Le Coteau [1989]). J. M. Wallace-Hadrill, 'The Work of Gregory of Tours in the Light of Modern Research', *Transactions of the Royal Historical Society*, 5th ser. 1 (1951), pp. 25–45; rev. in *The Long Haired Kings and other Studies in Frankish History* (1962), pp. 49–70. W. Goffart, *The Narrators of Barbarian History (A.D. 500–800)* (Princeton, NJ, 1988), pp. 112–234. L. Pietri in *Dict. Sp.* 6 (1967), cols. 1020–5, s.v. 'Grégoire (20) de Tours'; B. K. Vollmann in *RAC* 12 (1983), cols. 895–930, s.v. 'Gregor IV (Gregor von Tours)'; L. Pietri in *TRE* 14 (1985), pp. 184–8, s.v. 'Gregor von Tours', all with bibl.

Gregory, Robert (1819–1911), Dean of *St Paul's. He came from a Nottingham *Methodist family. Influenced by the *Tractarian Movement, he studied at Corpus Christi College, Oxford, and was ordained priest in the C of E in 1844. He was vicar of St Mary-the-Less, Lambeth, from 1853 to 1873, interesting himself esp. in elementary education. In 1868 he was appointed Canon of St Paul's, where he collaborated with H. P. *Liddon and R. W. *Church in making the cathedral a centre of active religious life in London. The introduction of more elaborate ritual and decorations led to considerable hostility against him, esp. after he had been appointed Dean in 1890. He was succeeded as Dean by W. R. *Inge.

W. H. *Hutton (ed.), *Robert Gregory, 1819–1911, being the Autobiography of Robert Gregory, D.D., Dean of St Paul's* (1912). A. R. Buckland in *DNB, 1901–1911*, 2 (1912), pp. 163 f.

gremial. Acc. to W. liturgical usage, a cloth spread by the bishop upon his lap when he is seated during the singing of the *Kyries, *Gloria in Excelsis, and *Creed in the Mass, and on certain other occasions, to prevent the soiling of his vestments by his hands. Its use, originally not confined to bishops, first appears in the late 13th cent., though the name is not found until the 15th cent. In 1968 the Congregation of Sacred *Rites decreed that the use of silk gremials should cease; when required for practical purposes, e.g. at *anointings, they should be made of linen.

Braun, *LP*, pp. 231 f. J. Braun, SJ, in *CE* 7 (1910), p. 26.

Grey Friars. Friars of the *Franciscan Order (q.v.), so named from the colour of their habit (now generally brown), to distinguish them from the Black Friars (*Dominicans) and White Friars (*Carmelites). By analogy, some Franciscan nuns are called 'Grey Sisters'.

Grey Nuns. A name given to Sisters of Charity in various countries. The best known are the Grey Nuns of Charity in N. America. They were founded by Madame d'Youville (Ven. Marie-Marguerite Dufrost de Lajemmerais) at Montreal in 1737 as a small community of ladies who devoted themselves to the care of the sick. Eight years later they adopted a Rule which was sanctioned by episcopal authority in 1754 and approved by *Leo XIII in 1880. Besides the three religious vows, the Sisters promise to devote their lives to the relief of human suffering. From Montreal the Sisters spread to other parts of N. America, and separate congregations were formed in different cities, one of the most notable being the Grey Nuns of the Cross founded at Ottawa in 1845. Apart from the American Grey Nuns, the name is given to Sisters of Charity in France and in Germany ('Grey Sisters of St Elisabeth').

On the Grey Nuns of Charity in N. America, Sister Thomas Aquinas Keefe, *The Congregation of the Grey Nuns, 1737–1910* (Washington, DC, 1942); also Life of Mère d'Youville by A. Ferland-Angers (Montreal, 1945); M. E. Ward in *CE* 7 (1910), p. 31, s.v.; G. Pettinati, SSP, in *DIP* 2 (1975), cols. 348–52, s.v. 'Carità dell'Ospedale Generale'. On the Grey Nuns of the Cross, V. O'Leary in *CE*, loc. cit., pp. 31 f., and G. Pettinati, loc. cit., cols. 322 f., s.v. 'Carità, di Ottawa'. On the Grey Sisters of St Elisabeth, J. Schweter, *Geschichte der Kongregation der Grauen Schwestern von der heiligen Elisabeth* (2 vols., Breslau, 1937); Heimbucher, 2, pp. 481–3, and G. Rocca, SSP, in *DIP*, loc. cit., cols. 381 f., s.v. 'Carità di Santa Elisabetta'.

Griesbach, Johann Jakob (1745–1812), NT scholar. A pupil of J. S. *Semler, he was professor of the NT at Jena from 1775 until his death. The first critic to make a systematic application of literary analysis to the Gospels, he maintained that St *Mark was the latest of the three Synoptists and based his work on Mt. and Lk. (the 'dependence theory'). This view has been revived in the 20th cent. by W. R. Farmer and others, but it is accepted by only a minority of scholars (see SYNOPTIC PROBLEM). His most valuable work was in the field of *textual criticism. After travels in England and France to work at MSS, he published an edition of the Greek NT in which, for the first time in Germany, the '*Textus Receptus' was abandoned (2 vols., 1775–7), and thereby laid the foundations of all subsequent work on the Greek text. His other works include *Symbolae Criticae ad supplendas et corrigendas Variarum NT Lectionum Collectiones* (Halle, 2 vols., 1785–93) and *Commentarius Criticus in Textum Graecum Novi Testamenti* (Jena, 1793–1811).

A collection of his *Opuscula Academica* was issued by his pupil, J. P. Gabler (Jena, 2 vols., 1824–5). B. Orchard, OSB, and T. R. W. Longstaff (eds.), *J. J. Griesbach: Synoptic and Text-Critical Studies 1776–1976* (Society for New Testament Studies,

Monograph Series, 34; 1978), incl. Eng. tr. of an essay in which he defended the 'dependence theory'. C. M. Tuckett, *The Revival of the Griesbach Hypothesis* (ibid. 44; 1983); S. E. Johnson, *The Griesbach Hypothesis and Redaction Criticism* (Society of Biblical Literature, Monograph Series, 41; Atlanta [1991]).

Grignion de Montfort, Louis-Marie, St (1673–1716), popular missioner. Educated at the *Jesuit College at Rennes, he devoted himself early to a life of poverty and prayer, and was ordained priest in 1700. From 1701 to 1703 he was chaplain at a hospital at Poitiers, where he founded the 'Daughters of Wisdom', a congregation for nursing the sick and educating poor children. In 1704 he began to realize his true vocation, the giving of missions throughout W. France, where he suffered from persecutions from the *Jansenists, who grudged his influence. About 1712 he founded the 'Company of Mary', a congregation of missionaries. Both his foundations were almost extinct at his death, but they have subsequently revived. His *Traité de la vraie dévotion à la Sainte Vierge*, after having long been lost, was recovered in 1842 and has exercised a powerful influence on Catholic devotion. He was beatified in 1888, and canonized by *Pius XII on 20 July 1947. Feast day, 28 Apr.

Œuvres complètes, ed. M. Gendrot and others (Paris, 1966). There is an Eng. tr. of his *Traité de la vraie dévotion à la Sainte Vierge* by F. W. *Faber (London, 1863). There is much documentary material in the report of the inquiries leading up to his canonization, pub. by the Sacra Rituum Congregatio, Sectio Historica, nos. 66 and 67; Rome, 1947. Lives and studies incl. those of P. Grandet (Nantes, 1724), P. Picot de Clorivière, SJ (Paris, Saint-Malo, and Rennes, 1785), J. M. Quérard (4 vols., Rennes, 1887), 'A Secular Priest' ([Dr Cruikshank], *Blessed Louis Marie Grignon de Montfort and his Devotion*, 2 vols., London, 1892), A. Laveille, Cong. Orat. (Paris, 1907), E. Tisserant (Rome, 1943; incl. text of his Testament), G. Bernoville (Paris, 1946), P. Eyckeler (Maastricht, etc., 1947), and L. Pérouas, SMM (Paris, 1966, and Tours, 1973). P. Eyckeler, *Le Testament de S. Louis-Marie Grignion de Montfort: Étude historique* (Maastricht, etc., 1953). S. de Fiores, SMM, *Itinerario spirituale di S. Luigi Maria di Montfort (1673–1713) nel periodo fino al sacerdozio (5 guigno 1700)* (Marian Library Studies, NS 6; Dayton, Oh., 1974). L. Pérouas in *Dict. Sp.* 9 (1976), cols. 1073–81, s.v. 'Louis-Marie Grignion de Montfort'.

Grimshaw, William (1708–63), *perpetual curate of Haworth. Educated at Christ's College, Cambridge, he was ordained deacon in 1731 and for some years was chaplain at Todmorden, where he emerged from a long spiritual crisis a fervent missionary. Becoming perpetual curate of Haworth, W. Yorks, in 1742, by his devoted zeal and consistency he gained a remarkable influence in his own and the surrounding parishes. He welcomed to his pulpit *Methodists and *Evangelicals, among them J. *Wesley, G. *Whitefield, and H. *Venn, and later himself engaged in itinerant preaching, as well as assisting Wesley in supervising Methodist societies in the N. of England. When troubles arose from incumbents in the parishes where Grimshaw preached uninvited, his evident sincerity led his diocesan, the Abp. of *York (Matthew Hutton, 1747–57), to tolerate his behaviour. Grimshaw was himself a strong *Calvinist, though not intolerant of *Arminians and others with whom he disagreed.

F. Baker, *William Grimshaw 1708–1763* (1963). Older Lives by W. Myles (privately pr., Newcastle-upon-Tyne [1806]; 2nd edn.,

London, 1813), R. Spence Hardy (London, 1860), and G. C. Cragg (ibid., 1947). J. H. Overton in *DNB* 23 (1890), pp. 254 f.

Grindal, Edmund (?1519–83), Abp. of *Canterbury. The son of a Cumberland farmer, he was educated at Cambridge and became a fellow of Pembroke Hall in 1538, and later chaplain to *Edward VI and prebendary of *Westminster. He went into exile under *Mary to Frankfurt, where he sought to reconcile the party of J. *Knox and the defenders of the 1552 BCP. In 1559 he was made Bp. of London and one of the revisers of the BCP, in 1570 Abp. of *York, and in 1575 Abp. of Canterbury. On his refusal to suppress the Puritan 'prophesyings' he was suspended in 1577 from his jurisdictional, but not from his spiritual, functions; his resignation was under negotiation when he died. In theology he sympathized with moderate *Calvinism and even with some Puritan criticism of contemporary episcopacy. See also ELIZABETH I.

J. *Strype, *History of the Life and Acts of Edmund Grindal* (1710; new edn., 1821). W. Nicholson (ed.), *The Remains of Archbishop Grindal* (*Parker Society, 1843), with preface by the editor. H. Robinson (ed.), *The Zürich Letters* (2 vols., Parker Society, 1842–5), *passim*. P. Collinson, *Archbishop Grindal 1519–1583* (1979). M. *Creighton in *DNB* 23 (1890), pp. 261–4.

Grinfield, Edward William (1785–1864), biblical scholar. Educated at Lincoln College, Oxford, he was ordained in 1808, and wrote a large number of pamphlets and articles in defence of a rigid theological orthodoxy. He is remembered esp. by the lectureship at Oxford which he founded in 1859 to promote the study of the *Septuagint.

N. D. F. Pearce in *DNB* 23 (1890), p. 265.

Grocyn, William (?1449–1519), English Renaissance scholar. He was educated at Winchester and New College, Oxford, and was reader in theology at Magdalen College, 1483–8. He studied Greek and Latin in Florence from 1488 to 1490/1, when he returned to Oxford to give the first public lectures in Greek. His Greek learning was admired by such of his contemporaries as T. *Linacre, W. Latimer, J. *Colet, T. *More, and *Erasmus, the last of whom considered him first among classical scholars in England. For information about his opinions we depend upon a single letter published by Aldus, and upon Erasmus. He supported strongly the Aldine enterprise in publishing a humanistic edition of *Aristotle and of the Scriptures, while contrasting Aristotle and *Plato as dealing respectively with science and with myth. According to Erasmus, in the course of giving public lectures in London on the 'Ecclesiastical Hierarchy' Grocyn came to reject the traditional attribution to *Dionysius the Pseudo-Areopagite. His remarkable library of Greek manuscripts, the best evidence of his interests, became the foundation of that at Corpus Christi College, Oxford. While an earlier tradition held that Grocyn's religious views were more conservative than those of others who had come under similar influences, this inference was based on the slender evidence of his expressed preference for Aristotle over Plato and continued interest in the scholastics, which modern scholars regard as inconclusive.

Memoir by M. Burrows appended to his edn. of Linacre's catalogue of Grocyn's books, pr. in OHS *Collectanea*, 2 (OHS 16; 1890), pp. 332–80. N. R. Ker in *The History of the University of*

Oxford, 3, ed. J. [K.] McConica (Oxford, 1986), pp. 458 f. *BRUO* 2 (1958), pp. 827–30.

Groote (or **Grote**), **Geert** (1340–84), **Gerardus Magnus**, founder of the '*Brethren of the Common Life'. A native of Deventer, he was educated at *Paris, where he had a brilliantly successful career. For a time he taught at *Cologne and elsewhere, living (as his means easily allowed) in great luxury and self-indulgence. In 1374 he was converted and began to live a devout and simple life. After three years spent in the monastery of Munnikhuizen, he followed the advice of Jan van *Ruysbroeck and became (1379) missionary preacher in the diocese of Utrecht, though he was never ordained priest. Here his outspoken condemnation of the abuses of the time led his licence to be withdrawn in 1383; but his appeal against the sentence was never answered, as he died soon after. Groote gathered round him a few friends who lived a quasi-monastic life at Deventer and became the nucleus of the Brethren of the Common Life. Some years earlier he had started a community for women on similar lines in the town. His Life was written by *Thomas à Kempis.

Epistolae ed. W. Mulders, SJ (Tekstuitgaven van Ons Geestelijk Erf, 3; Antwerp, 1933). *Contra Turrim Traiectensem* ed. R. R. Post (The Hague, 1967). Life by Thomas à Kempis pr. among the latter's works (Nuremberg, 1494, fols. xxix–xxxviii); Eng. tr. by J. P. Arthur, *The Founders of the New Devotion* (1905), pp. 1–78. R. R. Post, *De Moderne Devotie: Geert Groote en zijn Stichtingen* (Amsterdam, 1940), esp. pp. 9–44; id., *The Modern Devotion: Confrontation with Reformation and Humanism* (Studies in Medieval and Reformation Thought, 3; Leiden, 1968), esp. pp. 51–196. T. P. van Zijl, *Gerard Groote Ascetic and Reformer 1340–1384* (Catholic University of America Studies in Mediaeval History, 18; 1963). G. Epiney-Burgard, *Gérard Grote (1360–1384) et les débuts de la dévotion moderne* (Veröffentlichungen des Instituts für europäische Geschichte Mainz, 54; Wiesbaden, 1970), with bibl.; J. Andriessen and others (eds.), 'Geert Grote & Moderne Devotie', *Ons Geestelijk Erf*, 59 (1985), pp. 112–505; also issued separately, Nijmegen, 1985. J. Tiecke, OCOS, in *Dict. Sp.* 6 (1967), cols. 265–74, s.v. 'Gérard (9) Groote'; C. C. de Bruin in *Verfasserlexikon* (2nd edn.), 3 (1981), cols. 263–72, s.v. See also bibl. to BRETHREN OF THE COMMON LIFE, DEVOTIO MODERNA, IMITATION OF CHRIST, and WINDESHEIM.

Gropper, Johann (1503–59), theologian. He studied jurisprudence and theology at *Cologne University, where he became known as 'Os cleri Coloniensis', and in 1532 he was appointed a Canon of Xanten. After attending a synod at Cologne (1536), called by the Abp. *Hermann to combat the teaching of the Reformers, he drew up an *Enchiridion* in which he included an exposition of the *Creed, the *Seven Sacraments, the *Lord's Prayer, and the *Decalogue, and put forward an early form of the doctrine of '*double justice'. This, though later (1596) placed on the *Index, was well received by the theologians of Cologne, and by Cardinals G. *Contarini, R. *Pole, and G. *Morone, who regarded it as a suitable basis for a reconciliation between the Protestants and Rome. In the cause of reunion Gropper negotiated with M. *Bucer in 1540, but, though some agreement was reached on grace and justification, none was attempted on authority and the Eucharist. He was one of the Catholic participants also at the Conference of *Ratisbon in 1541. When the Abp. of Cologne himself became a Protestant, Gropper secured his deposition, and restored the Catholic religion, for which services he was made Provost of Bonn in 1547, and in 1556 *Paul IV offered him a cardinal's hat.

Briefwechsel, ed. R. Braunisch (Corpus Catholicorum, 32 etc.; 1977 ff.). Lives by W. van Gulik (Freiburg i.B., 1906) and W. Lipgens (Münster i.W., 1951; with portrait and bibl.). H. Lutz, 'Reformatio Germaniae. Drei Denkschriften Johannes Groppers (1546, 1558)', *Quellen und Forschungen aus italienischen Archiven und Bibliotheken*, 37 (1957), pp. 222–310, incl. text. R. Braunisch, *Die Theologie der Rechtfertigung im 'Enchiridion' (1538) des Johannes Gropper* (Reformationsgeschichtliche Studien und Texte, 109; Münster, 1974); J. Meier, *Der priesterliche Dienst nach Johannes Gropper* (ibid. 113; 1977), with bibl. F. Zoepff in *Dict. Sp.* 6 (1967), cols. 1054–6; R. Braunisch in *TRE* 14 (1985), pp. 266–70, both with bibl.

Grosseteste, Robert (*c.*1170–1253), Bp. of *Lincoln. The child of a poor family in Suffolk, he seems to have been educated in Lincoln, perhaps by the charity of its leading citizen, Adam of Wigford. It has been generally said that he went to the schools of *Oxford and *Paris, but there is no early evidence for this. He was briefly a member of the household of St *Hugh, Bp. of Lincoln, in about 1191–2, and of that of William de Vere, Bp. of *Hereford, from *c.*1195 to 1198, but little else is certainly known of his early life. On 25 Apr. 1225 he received the benefice of Abbotsley. At about this date he is known to have been lecturing on theology in Oxford, and notes of his lectures and sermons of the period 1225–30 have survived. They are among the earliest theological records of the Oxford schools, and they brought him widespread recognition. At some point during these years the Masters of the University seem to have elected him as their Chancellor without the necessary approval of the Bp. of Lincoln; the whole incident is shrouded in obscurity. In 1229 he became archdeacon of Leicester, but he resigned in 1231, having already (*c.*1230) given up his position as university lecturer to become the first *lector* to the recently established community of *Franciscans outside the city walls of Oxford. These changes, together with his resignation of other emoluments, may have been the result of a spiritual conversion following the visit of Jordan of Saxony, the *Dominican Master General, to Oxford in 1229–30. Certainly after this date he and Jordan were close friends, and Grosseteste began his association with the work of both Orders of friars, which became even more important after his election as Bp. of Lincoln in 1235. Throughout his life he showed unbounding physical and intellectual energy.

Very broadly his intellectual interests can be traced chronologically as follows. Until 1225, he was mainly occupied with scientific studies. His writings during this period included a treatise on Computus (perhaps in three recensions which show increasing knowledge of recent translations from Arabic), as well as an outline of general astronomy, and short but pregnant works on Comets and Rainbows. But his most important and influential scientific work was a Commentary (the first that is known in the W.) on *Aristotle's *Posterior Analytics*.

After these early scientific works, he produced in Oxford from *c.*1225 to 1235 the main series of his theological works, notably the *Hexaemeron*, *De Decem Mandatis*, *De Cessatione Legalium*, and his commentaries on the Psalms and on Galatians, as well as several of his surviving sermons. During this period he also began to learn Greek,

and he acquired a competence scarcely paralleled by any W. scholar before his time. As bishop after 1235, his increased resources made it possible for him to plan and carry through some very large enterprises of translation from Greek into Latin. These included the works of *Dionysius the Pseudo-Areopagite and the commentaries on them; also the *Ethics* of Aristotle with commentaries. In addition, he translated several parts of the works of St *John of Damascus, St *Basil, the newly discovered *Testaments of the Twelve Patriarchs, and the Greek lexicon ascribed to '*Suidas'. He was able to carry out this vast programme of work by employing a group of scholars, supporting several of them by giving them benefices. In addition to these works, the problem of Light continued to exercise his mind for many years, and finally found expression in his *De Luce*.

Besides being responsible for this scholarly work, Grosseteste showed conspicuous energy and dedication in his work as a bishop. He was indefatigable in carrying out visitations of his diocese, organizing preaching by members of the Franciscan and Dominican Orders, drawing up regulations for both clergy and laity, and actively promoting political action against the intrusions of royal and finally—and most notoriously—of Papal officials into parochial benefices. In pursuit of this policy of episcopal independence he made his famous appeal to Pope *Innocent IV at Lyons in 1250. He went to the Papal court with a carefully prepared denunciation of the abuses of power in pursuit of family and personal gain by Papal officials, by the curia, and by the Pope himself. While giving an account of these abuses, their causes and development, he also made proposals for reform. These were ignored, and Grosseteste was perhaps lucky to escape the excommunication which Innocent was said to have been persuaded with difficulty to forgo. Whether he was officially suspended during his last years is not clear, but he died with a deep sense of failure and foreboding for the future, prob. on 8 Oct. 1253.

His death was followed by accounts of miracles at his tomb and elsewhere, and there were various unsuccessful attempts to secure his canonization in the century after his death. He left his books and literary remains to the Oxford Franciscans; this ensured their survival and growing influence in the 14th cent., culminating in the discovery by J. *Wycliffe that on several points (e.g. on the importance of pastoral work and of preaching, his sympathy with the Greek Church, and his criticism of the Papal curia), he had been anticipated by Grosseteste. He became a cherished name among the *Lollards and figures in J. *Foxe's *Book of Martyrs*. After the 16th cent. his reputation was eclipsed until it was revived by constitutional historians (esp. W. *Stubbs) in the 19th cent., and more recently by historians of science and theology who have brought to light the wide extent of Grosseteste's writings and the originality of his ideas in both fields. Feast day in the American BCP (1979), 9 Oct.

The principal edns. of his scientific and philosophical works are: L. Baur, *Die philosophischen Werke des Robert Grosseteste* (*BGPM* 9; 1912), which is valuable for the smaller treatises, but is largely occupied by a *Summa* falsely attributed to Grosseteste; *Commentarius in Posteriorum Analyticorum Libros*, ed. P. Rossi (Florence, 1981); *Commentarius in VIII Libros Physicorum Aristotelis*, ed. R. C. Dales (Boulder, Colo., 1963); and *Computus*, in R.

Steele (ed.), *Opera hactenus inedita Rogeri Baconi*, 6 (Oxford, 1926), pp. 212–67; of his theological works: *Hexaemeron*, ed. R. C. Dales and S. Gieben, OFM Cap. (Auctores Britannici Medii Aevii, 6; London, 1982); *De Cessatione Legalium*, ed. R. C. Dales and E. B. King (ibid. 7; 1986); *De Decem Mandatis*, ed. idd. (ibid. 10; 1987); Comm. on Gal., frags. of Glosses on Pauline Epp., and *Tabula*, ed. J. McEvoy and others (CCCM 130; 1995); selected sermons and *dicta*, ed. E. Brown, *Appendix ad Fasciculum rerum expetendarum & fugiendarum ab Orthuino Gratio*, 2 (London, 1690), pp. 244–307; *Le Chateau d'Amour*, ed. J. Murray (Paris, 1918); and S. Gieben, OFM Cap., 'Robert Grosseteste on Preaching, *Collectanea Franciscana*, 37 (1967), pp. 100–41, incl. text of sermon. His trs. of the works of Dionysius are contained in *Dionysiaca*, ed. P. Chevallier, OSB (2 vols., Paris and Bruges, 1937). Other trs. are incl. in *Aristoteles Latinus*, cited s.v. ARISTOTLE. The primary sources for his episcopal activity are his *Epistolae*, ed. H. R. Luard (RS, 1861); *Rotuli*, ed. F. N. Davis (*Canterbury and York Society, 10; 1913; Lincoln Record Society, 11; 1914); F. M. Powicke and C. R. Cheney (eds.), *Councils & Synods . . .*, 2, 1205–1313, 1 (Oxford, 1964), pp. 201–7, 261–78, and 467–72; and S. Gieben, OFM Cap., 'Robert Grosseteste at the Papal Curia, Lyons 1250. Edition of the documents', *Collectanea Franciscana*, 41 (1971), pp. 340–93. Studies by S. Harrison Thomson, *The Writings of Robert Grosseteste* (Cambridge, 1940); A. C. Crombie, *Robert Grosseteste and the Origins of Experimental Science* (Oxford, 1953); D. A. Callus, OP (ed.), *Robert Grosseteste, Scholar and Bishop* (ibid., 1955); J. [J.] McEvoy, *The Philosophy of Robert Grosseteste* (ibid., 1982); R. W. Southern, *Robert Grosseteste: The Growth of an English Mind in Medieval Europe* (ibid., 1986). J. [J.] McEvoy in *Dict. Sp.* 13 (1988), cols. 722–34, s.v. 'Robert (7) Grosseteste'.

Grote, Geert. See GROOTE, G.

Grotius, Hugo (1583–1645), Huig de Groot, Dutch jurist and theologian. He was the descendant of an influential family of Delft. A very precocious boy, at the age of 12 he went to *Leiden university, where he was deeply influenced by humanism (J. J. *Scaliger). At the age of 15 he accompanied J. van Oldenbarnevelt on a visit to France, and at 18 he was appointed Historian of the States General and in 1607 Advocate Fiscal of Holland, Zeeland, and W. Friesland. He now began to take a keen interest in theological questions, siding with the *Arminians. In 1613 he was sent on a diplomatic mission to England, where he acquainted *James I with the religious situation in the Netherlands, but without being able to gain him to his opinions. On his return (1613) he was made Pensionary of Rotterdam. By his support of moderation in his *Ordinum Pietas* (1613) he incurred the hostility of Prince Maurice of Nassau, the leader of the Calvinists. In 1614 he drafted a *Resolution for Peace in the Church*. His *Remonstrant sympathies, combined with his friendship for Oldenbarnevelt, led to a sentence of lifelong imprisonment in 1619. His wife having contrived to arrange his escape in a box of books, he settled at *Paris in 1621, where Louis XIII awarded him a pension. But though in sympathy with many Catholic doctrines, Grotius refused the advantages which conversion would have brought him and remained outside the RC Church. In 1622 he published in Dutch verse the earlier version of *De Veritate Religionis Christianae*, the first Latin edition of which was to appear in 1627 and to be subsequently further expanded. In 1623 he began the work that established his permanent fame as a jurist, *De Jure Belli ac Pacis* (Paris, 1625). Having returned to Holland in 1631, he was banished and went a little later

to Germany. In 1635 he returned to Paris as ambassador of Queen *Christina of Sweden. Moved by his ecumenical ideal, which he judged could be achieved only by interpreting the NT in terms of its original meaning in the early Church, Grotius discarded the current dogmatically based method of Scriptural commentary for that of philological criticism. His *Annotationes* on the NT (originally pub. in 3 parts, 1641–50) thus marked a new departure in the science of exegesis. Grotius' dedication to the cause of *reunion was also evident in his publication of *Via ad Pacem Ecclesiasticam* and *Votum pro Pace Ecclesiastica* (both 1642). He died at Rostock on his way back from Sweden to France from the consequences of a shipwreck and was buried in his native Delft.

As a poet, classicist, historian, jurist, and theologian, Grotius was prodigiously learned and accomplished, publishing extensively in all these spheres. His principal religious work was the *De Veritate Religionis Christianae*. Designed as a practical handbook for missionaries, it sought to uphold the evidences of natural theology and to establish the superiority of the Christian faith to all other creeds. It found the essentials of the Gospel in a perfect trust in Divine Providence and in the ordering of human life acc. to the principles laid down by Christ. The book contained much that was valued by Christians of all denominations and became a standard work. Appearing in numerous editions and translations until well into the 19th cent., it was especially popular in England. In his teaching on the *Atonement, Grotius anticipated some of the more liberal doctrines of the 19th and 20th cents.

His great work, *De Jure Belli ac Pacis*, also rests its theses to a large extent on tradition. Though it finally severed law from theology, fixing the principle of justice in the unalterable Law of Nature which has its source in man as a social being, it utilized medieval and modern theologians, and, by its comprehensive systematization, earned him the title of 'Father of International Law'.

Opera Omnia Theologica, 3 vols. in 4, fol., Amsterdam and London, 1679; also ed., with Eng. tr., by E. Rabbie, Assen, 1990 ff. Letters first ed. Leiden, 1648; fuller edn., Amsterdam, 1687. Modern crit. edn. by P. C. Molhuysen and others (Rijks Geschiedkundige Publicatiën, 64, 82, 105, 113, 119, 124, 130, 136, 142, 154, 179, 197, 213, 222, etc.; The Hague, 1928 ff.). Eng. tr. of *De Iure Belli* (abridged) by W. Whewell (3 vols., Cambridge, 1853). J. ter Meulen and P. J. J. Diermanse, *Bibliographie des écrits imprimés de Hugo Grotius* (The Hague, 1950); idd., *Bibliographie des écrits sur Hugo Grotius imprimés au XVIIᵉ siècle* (ibid., 1961). Lives by C. Brandt and A. van Cattenburgh (3 pts., Dordrecht and Amsterdam, 1727) and W. S. M. Knight (Grotius Society Publications, 4; London, 1925). J. Schlüter, *Die Theologie des Hugo Grotius* (Göttingen, 1919). F. [Pintacuda] de Michelis, *Le Origini Storiche e Culturali del Pensiero di Ugo Grozio* (Pubblicazione della Facoltà di Lettere e Filosofia dell'Università di Milano, 45; Florence, 1967); A. Droetto, *Studi Groziani* (Pubblicazioni dell'Istituto di Scienze Politiche dell'Università di Torino, 18; 1968); D. Wolf, *Die Irenik des Hugo Grotius* (Studia Irenica, 9; Marburg, 1969; 2nd edn., Hildesheim, 1972); *The World of Hugo Grotius (1583–1645): Proceedings of the International Colloquium . . . Rotterdam 6–9 April 1983* (Amsterdam, 1984); J. P. Heering, *Hugo de Groot als apologeet van de Christelijke Godsdienst* (The Hague, 1992), with Eng. summary. Introd. study by C. Gellinek, *Hugo Grotius* (Boston [1983]). R. S. Franks, *A History of the Doctrine of the Work of Christ in its Ecclesiastical Development*, 2 [1918], pp. 48–73. H. R. Guggisberg in *TRE* 14 (1985), pp. 277–80, s.v.

Grottaferrata (Lat. *Crypta ferrata*). The site of a
*Basilian monastery on the lower slopes of the Alban hills,
near Rome, founded in 1004 by St Nilus the Younger. It
has remained a centre of Greek learning in Italy, though
in the Middle Ages it came largely under Latinizing
influences. In the Renaissance period its (*commendatory)
abbots included many distinguished scholars, notably Cardinals *Bessarion, Giulio della Rovere (afterwards Pope
*Julius II), and E. *Consalvi. In 1881 *Leo XIII re-
established here a purely Byzantine Rite. The monastery
contains a fine collection of Greek MSS.

A. Rocchi, *Codices Cryptenses* (Rome, 1884); id., *La badia di S.
Maria di Grottaferrata* (ibid., 1884); id., *De Coenobio Cryptoferra-
tensi eiusque Bibliotheca et Codicibus praesertim Graecis Commentarii*
(Tusculum, 1893). P. *Batiffol, *L'Abbaye de Rossano* (Paris, 1891).
G. M. Croce, *La Badia Greca di Grottaferrata e la Rivista 'Roma
e l'Oriente': Cattolicesimo e Ortodossia fra Unionismo ed Ecumenismo
(1799–1923)* (2 vols., Vatican City, 1990). O. Marucchi, 'Grottaferrata. Scoperta di un antico cimitero cristiano', *Nuovo Bullettino di Archeologia Cristiana*, 19 (1913), pp. 230–7. M. Petta in
NCE 6 (1967), pp. 813 f.; P. Giannini in *DHGE* 22 (1988), cols.
388–96, both s.v.

Grou, Jean-Nicolas (1731–1803), French *Jesuit. From
1751 to 1755 he taught at the Jesuit college of La Flèche.
When the Society was expelled from France, he moved
to Lorraine; he taught for two years at the University of
Pont-à-Mousson and published various works on *Plato.
After Lorraine became part of France in 1766, Grou was
recalled by the Abp. of Paris and as a secular priest served
as chaplain to a convent of nuns. Here he began the spiritual writing for which he is chiefly remembered; he published the *Caractères de la vraie dévotion* (1788; Eng. tr.,
1791) and *Maximes spirituelles* (1789; Eng. tr. by J. M.
*Neale, 1874). In 1792 he came to England, spending the
rest of his life in the household of Thomas Weld at Lulworth Castle, near Weymouth. He continued his writings,
which include *Méditations en forme de retraite sur l'amour
de Dieu* (London, 1796; Eng. tr., 1928), and the posthumously published *Manuel des âmes intérieures* (1833; Eng. tr.,
1889) and *L'École de Jésus-Christ* (2 vols., 1885; Eng. tr.,
1932). A few months before his death he was able to renew
his vows when Papal approval was given to the restitution
of the Jesuits in England.

A. Cadrès, SJ, *Notice sur la vie et les œuvres du Père Jean-Nicolas
Grou* (1862; repr. in J. N. Grou, *L'Intérieur de Jésus et de Marie*,
posthumous, 1862, pp. xiii–cii). F. *von Hügel, 'The Spiritual
Writings of Father Grou, SJ', *The Tablet*, 74 (1889), pp. 990 f.,
1029–31, repr. in modern Eng. tr. of Grou's *Spiritual Maxims*
(1961), pp. 265–93. Sommervogel, 3 (1892), cols. 1868–82, and 9
(1900), 442 f.; Polgár, 2 (1990), pp. 103 f. P. Bernard in *DTC* 6
(1920), cols. 1888–90; A. Rayez, SJ, in *Dict. Sp.* 6 (1967), cols.
1059–83; H. Beylard in *Dictionnaire de Biographie Française*, 16
(1985), cols. 1345 f., all s.v.

group ministry. In the C of E, under the Pastoral Measure 1968, a number of neighbouring parishes may be
grouped together and the incumbent of each benefice, in
addition to attending to his own benefice, has the legal
authority to assist the incumbents of the other benefices in
the group. The incumbents meet as a chapter and it is
their duty to assist each other so as to make the best possible provision for the cure of souls throughout the area of
the group. After some amendments, the provisions for

group ministries were consolidated in the Pastoral Measure 1983.

Group Movement. See OXFORD GROUP.

Grundtvig, Nikolai Fredrik Severin (1783–1872),
Danish religious teacher. From 1839 till his death he was
preacher at the Vartov Hospital at Copenhagen, and in
1861 was given the title and rank of a 'Bishop'. In 1824,
after some deep religious experiences, he started a
reforming movement in Danish Lutheranism, attacking
the rationalism and state domination of religion, and seeking to restore dogmatic orthodoxy with the *Apostles'
Creed as the standard. With the movement thus begun
('Grundtvigianism') came a renewed understanding of the
Church and the Sacraments in Danish theology. He was
also active in founding the Folk High Schools in Denmark.
He was an authority on Anglo-Saxon and Norse literature.
He and S. *Kierkegaard together are the most notable
figures in Danish theology in the 19th cent.

Grundtvig's extensive MSS are housed in the Royal Library at
Copenhagen. No complete edn of his writings exists. The fullest
is that ed. H. Begtrup (10 vols., Copenhagen, 1904–9); selection
ed. G. Christensen and H. Koch, *Værker i Udvalg* (10 vols., ibid.,
1940–9). His poetry was ed. by Svend Grundtvig, C. J. Brandt,
and G. Christensen (9 vols., ibid., 1880–1930); correspondence,
ed. G. Christensen and Stener Grundtvig (2 vols., ibid., 1924–6);
hymns (*Sang-værk*) [ed. T. Balslev and others] (6 vols., ibid.,
1944–64); sermons dating from 1822–6 and 1832–9, ed. C. Thodberg (12 vols., ibid., 1983–6). Danish Life, setting Grundtvig in
relation to the history of Denmark in the 19th cent., by F. Rön-
ning (8 vols., ibid., 1907–14). Shorter Lives in Danish by H. Brun
(2 vols., Kolding, 1879–82) and H. Koch (Copenhagen, 1944;
Eng. tr., Yellow Springs, Oh., 1952). J. P. Bang, *Grundtvig og
England* (1932). H. Begtrup, *N. F. S. Grundtvigs danske Kristen-
dom: Historisk Fremstillet* (2 vols., 1936); also several other writings by the same author. P. G. Lindhardt, *Grundtvig: An Introduction* (1951); C. Thodberg and A. P. Thyssen (eds.), *N. F. S.
Grundtvig: Tradition and Renewal* (Eng. tr., Copenhagen, 1983);
A. M. Allchin, *N. F. S. Grundtvig: An Introduction to his Life
and Work* (1997). Id. and others (eds.), *Heritage and Prophecy:
Grundtvig and the English-Speaking World* (Norwich [1994]). S.
Johansen, *Bibliografi over N. F. S. Grundtvigs Skrifter* (4 pts.,
1948–54). C. Thodberg in *TRE* 14 (1985), pp. 284–9, s.v.

Grünewald, Matthias (c.1475–1528), German painter,
known in his lifetime as Mathis Gothart Nithart. Very
little is known of his life. The most famous work attributed
to him is the altar-piece of Isenheim, near Colmar, a
polyptych of 11 panels completed before 1516, and now in
the Colmar Museum. The Crucifixion is portrayed with
cruel realism, with St *John the Baptist directing an
exceptionally long index finger to the Cross, with the
inscription: 'He must increase and I must decrease' (Jn. 3:
30). K. *Barth saw in the Baptist the true type of the
Christian witness, pointing away from himself and his
experience to the objective Word of God.

Paintings and drawings ed. H. A. Schmid (2 parts and suppl.,
Strasbourg, 1908–11), also reproduced, with introd. by N.
Pevsner and M. Meier (London, etc., 1958). Collections of draw-
ings also ed. M. I. Friedländer (Berlin, 1927) and E. Ruhmer
(London [1970]). L. Behling, *Die Handzeichnungen des Mathis
Gothart Nithart genannt Grünewald* (Weimar, 1955). A. Burck-
hard, *Matthias Grünewald: Personality and Accomplishment*
(Cambridge, Mass., 1936), with detailed bibl. W. K. Zülch, *Der
historische Grünewald* (Munich, 1938). W. Fraenger, *Matthias*

Grünewald (Munich [1983]). R. Mellinkoff, *The Devil at Isenheim: Reflections of Popular Belief in Grünewald's Altarpiece* (California Studies in the History of Art, Discovery Series, 1; Berkeley, Calif., etc. [1988]).

Gualbert, St John. See JOHN GUALBERT, ST.

Guarantees, the Law of. The law passed on 13 May 1871 to regulate the relations between the first government of the new Kingdom of Italy and the Papacy. The Pope's person was declared sacred and inviolable; he was to receive an annual sum of 3,225,000 lire, free of taxation, for certain specified expenses; the *Vatican, the *Lateran Palace, and the Papal villa at *Castel Gandolfo were to remain in the Pope's possession; the freedom of *conclaves and of *General Councils was guaranteed; the diplomatic immunity of foreign envoys to the Holy See was recognized; and the seminaries in Rome and in the six *suburbicarian sees were to be under the sole authority of the Pope. Though the law was never recognized by the Vatican, in practice relations with the Italian government were regulated by it until the *Lateran Treaty of 1929.

Text conveniently pr. in A. C. Jemolo, *La Questione Romana* (Milan [1939]), pp. 108–14. Eng. tr., with introd., in S. Z. Ehler and J. B. Morrall, *Church and State through the Centuries* (1954), pp. 285–91. F. Olgiati, *La questione romana e la sua soluzione* (1929), pp. 75–91, with operative clauses of the text, pp. 77–81. A. C. Jemolo, *Chiesa e Stato in Italia negli ultimi cento anni* (1948), pp. 241–367 (2nd edn., Turin [1963], pp. 173–263), *passim*; Eng. tr. of abridged edn., *Church and State in Italy 1850–1950* (Oxford, 1960), pp. 28–52 *passim*, esp. pp. 48–52. G. Amabile, *La legge delle guarentigie: Studi giuridico-politico* (Cantania, 1897).

Guardia Nobile. See NOBLE GUARD.

Guardia Palatina d'Onore. See PALATINE GUARD.

guardian. The superior of a *Franciscan friary. He normally holds office for three years.

Guardian, The. A weekly Anglican religious newspaper, founded in 1846 by R. W. *Church, Frederic Rogers, and others, to uphold *Tractarian principles, and to show their relevance to the best secular thought of the day. The *Guardian* always claimed to be the offspring of the Tractarian movement, and to provide independent comment upon theological, political and social issues. It ceased publication in 1951.

guardian angels. The belief that God assigns to every man an angel to guard him in body and soul was common to the pagan (e.g. *Plato, *Phaedo*, 108 B) and the Jewish world, though it is not clearly formulated in the OT. It is expressed in 1 *Enoch (100: 5), where the author states that the just have protecting spirits. In the NT the popular belief is reflected in Acts 12: 15 and confirmed, in the case of children, by the Lord (Mt. 18: 10). Though the *Shepherd* of *Hermas (*c.*140–55) says that every man has an angel to guide him (Mand. 6. 2. 1–3), there is much variety of opinion among the Fathers in general. St *Ambrose (*In Ps.* 37. 43) believed that the righteous were deprived of guardian spirits in order that, having a harder struggle against evil, they might attain to greater glory, while St *Jerome (*In Jerem.* 30. 12) and St *Basil (*Hom. in Ps.* 33. 5)

state that sin drives them away. *Honorius 'of Autun' (early 12th cent.), who was followed by subsequent teachers, first defined the belief clearly. He held that each soul, at the moment that it was introduced into the body, was entrusted to an angel (*Unaquaeque etiam anima, dum in corpus mittitur, angelo committitur, Elucidarium*, 2. 31). St *Thomas Aquinas (*S. Theol.* 1, q. 113, a. 4) held that only angels of the lowest order fulfilled this function, whereas *Duns Scotus and others maintained that the mission might be committed to any member of the angelic host.

The function of the guardian angels is the protection of body and soul and the presentation of prayers to God (Rev. 8: 3 f.). They were originally commemorated with St *Michael, but an independent feast, first found in *Portugal in 1513, was extended to the whole RC Church by Clement X in 1670, and assigned to 2 Oct. See also ANGEL.

A. Wilmart, OSB, *Auteurs spirituels et textes dévots du moyen-âge latin* (1932), ch. 14, 'Prières à l'ange gardien', pp. 537–58. J. Duhr in *Dict. Sp.* 1 (1937), cols. 586–98, s.v. 'Anges gardiens', with refs.; further bibl., cols. 624 f. H. Pope in *CE* 7 (1910), pp. 49 f., s.v.

guardian of the spiritualities. In the C of E, when a diocesan bishopric is vacant, the archbishop of the province provides for the ecclesiastical administration of the diocese, usually by authorizing a *suffragan bishop in the diocese to act on his behalf. In this capacity the archbishop is described as 'the guardian of the spiritualities'. There are a few dioceses in which the Dean and Chapter of the cathedral claim, or have claimed, to be the guardians during the vacancy in the see. When an archbishopric becomes vacant, the Dean and Chapter of the cathedral of the metropolitan diocese are the guardians.

Gudule, St (d. *c.*710), patroness of Brussels. She is said to have belonged to a noble family of Brabant and to have devoted herself to prayer and charitable deeds. Acc. to the earliest Life (12th cent.), her remains were translated to the church of St Michael at Brussels in 1047; her cult is attested in the city from the late 11th cent. She is often depicted with a lantern, in reference to the legend that, when the devil had one morning blown out the taper by which she regularly discovered her way to church, it was miraculously rekindled. Feast day, 8 Jan.

AASS, Jan. 1 (1643), pp. 513–30, incl. (pp. 514–24) the Life by a certain Hubert (12th cent.; mainly apocryphal). J. *Bollandus and C. Smetius, 'De S. Gudila Virgine Commentarius Praevius', *Acta Sanctorum Belgii*, 5 (1789), pp. 667–89. R. Podevyn, OSB, 'Étude critique sur la *Vita Gudulae*', *Revue Belge de Philologie et d'Histoire*, 2 (1923), pp. 619–41. M. de Waha in *DHGE* 22 (1988), cols. 639–41, s.v.

Guéranger, Prosper Louis Pascal (1805–75), French *Benedictine monk. He was ordained to the priesthood in 1827. With a view to the re-establishment of the Benedictine Order in France, he bought the priory of *Solesmes in 1832, opened it in 1833, and in 1837 made his profession at Rome and was appointed by *Gregory XVI the first Abbot of Solesmes, where he spent the rest of his life. He was keenly interested in liturgical matters, and as a zealous *Ultramontane led the movement in France for replacing the existing local diocesan uses by the one rite of Rome.

He was a voluminous writer, whose popular style led some of his books to circulate very widely. Among the best known were his *Institutions liturgiques* (3 vols., 1840–51) and *L'Année liturgique* (a devotional commentary on the ecclesiastical year; 9 vols., 1841–66; Eng. tr., 1867–71).

For his writings (126 items) see F. *Cabrol, *Bibliographie des bénédictins de la congrégation de France* (Solesmes, 1889), pp. 3–33. [P. Delatte, OSB], *Dom Guéranger, abbé de Solesmes* (2 vols., 1909; repr., with additional material, no longer anonymous, Solesmes, 1984). E. Sevrin, *Dom Guéranger et Lamennais* (1933); L. Soltner, OSB, *Solesmes & Dom Guéranger (1805–1875)* (Solesmes, 1974). C. Johnson, OSB, *Prosper Guéranger (1805–1875): A Liturgical Theologian. An Introduction to his liturgical writings and work* (Studia Anselmiana, 89; 1984). J. Hourlier, OSB, in *Dict. Sp.* 6 (1967), cols. 1097–106, s.v., with extensive bibl.

Guest, Edmund

Guest, Edmund (1518–77), Bp. of *Salisbury. He was educated at Eton and King's College, Cambridge, of which he became a Fellow and vice-provost. In 1548 he published *A Treatise against the Privy Mass* in which he repudiated the Eucharistic Sacrifice and the adoration of the consecrated elements. In 1549 he spoke against the dogma of *transubstantiation in discussions held at Cambridge before the Commissioners. During the reign of *Mary he remained in hiding. On the accession of *Elizabeth I he became a domestic chaplain to M. *Parker (1559) and in the same year Archdeacon of *Canterbury. In 1560 he was appointed Bp. of *Rochester. He played a prominent part in the 1563 debate on the revision of the *Forty-Two Articles, and it was he who devised the statement (incorporated in Art. 28 of the *Thirty-Nine Articles) that the 'Body of Christ is given, taken, and eaten in the Supper, only after an heavenly and spiritual manner'. In 1571 he signed the Thirty-Nine Articles, despite some difficulties about Article 29 (that the wicked, in receiving communion, are not partakers of Christ). In the same year the Queen, one of whose favourites he was, appointed him to the see of Salisbury.

H. G. Dugdale, *The Life and Character of Edmund Geste* (1840). For his Eucharistic teaching, see also G. F. Hodges, *Bishop Guest: Articles Twenty-eight and Twenty-nine* (1894). W. P. Haugaard, *Elizabeth and the English Reformation* (Cambridge, 1968), esp. pp. 250–55. E. T. Bradley in *DNB* 23 (1890), pp. 316–18.

Gueux

Gueux (Fr., 'ragamuffins'). A title given (originally in contempt) to those who in 1566 petitioned Margaret of Parma, the regent of the Netherlands, against the *Inquisition. It was later adopted by other bodies of Protestants who opposed the Spaniards in the Low Countries.

Gui, Bernard

Gui, Bernard (c.1261–1331), *Dominican historian. Born at Royère, Haute-Vienne, he joined the Dominican Order at Limoges in 1279. After being lecturer and prior in various places, he was appointed *inquisitor of Toulouse in 1307. He undertook several, not very successful, diplomatic missions for Pope *John XXII; in 1323 he became Bp. of Tuy (Galicia), and was translated in 1324 to Lodève. He was a hard-working, cheerful man, but lacking in brilliance. He is remembered chiefly for his contributions to Church history, esp. the history of his own Order, for which his massive compilations are a major source. He was commissioned by Berengar of Landorra (Master of the Order 1312–17) to write a collection of saints' lives to replace the *Golden Legend, which Berengar regarded as suspect and unbalanced. In 1323–4 he wrote an important manual for inquisitors.

Selections from his manual for inquisitors conveniently ed., with Fr. tr., by G. Mollat and G. Drioux (Les Classiques de l'Histoire de France au moyen âge, 8–9; 1926–7). For details of other works, see Kaeppeli, 1 (1970), pp. 205–26. *Bernard Gui et son monde*, with introd. by M.-H. Vicaire [OP] (Cahiers de Fanjeaux, 16; Toulouse, 1981). W. A. Hinnebusch, OP, *The History of the Dominican Order*, 2 (Staten Island, NY, 1973), pp. 411–16. G. Mollat in *DHGE* 8 (1935), cols. 677–81, s.v. 'Bernard (145)'.

Guibert of Nogent

Guibert of Nogent (c.1053/65–c.1125), Abbot of Nogent, near Laon, from 1104. The youngest son of a noble Clermont family, he was dedicated to God by his widowed mother, and educated and later professed at the monastery of Saint-Germer-de-Fly (in the diocese of Beauvais). Visits there by *Anselm, then prior of Bec, encouraged him in his study both of the Latin classics (*Virgil and Ovid) and of St *Augustine and St *Gregory the Great. Gregory provided a model for Guibert's *Moralia* on Genesis, which is prefaced by an essay on biblical interpretation and preaching. Guibert opposed *Berengar's eucharistic doctrines. He wrote on the veneration of the BVM; a tract 'On the Incarnation against the Jews'; a history of the first *Crusade, touched with pride in the Franks' role; an astonishing onslaught on the abuse of *relics, *De pignoribus sanctorum*, criticizing the monks of Saint-Médard who claimed to have a tooth of the Lord; and an autobiography, partly modelled on Augustine, which is both a self-portrait of a complex character and a rich source for contemporary social history.

Works, ed. L. *d'Achery (Paris, 1651), repr. in J. P. Migne, *PL* 156. Crit. edns. of his autobiog. by G. Bourgin (Collection des Textes pour servir à l'étude et à l'enseignement de l'histoire, 40; 1907) and, with Fr. tr., by E.-R. Labande (Les Classiques de l'histoire de France au moyen âge, 34; 1981). Eng. tr., with notes and introd., by J. F. Benton, *Self and Society in Medieval France* (New York and Evanston, Ill. [1970]). K. Guth, *Guibert von Nogent und die hochmittelalterliche Kritik an der Reliquienverehrung* (Studien und Mitteilungen zur Geschichte der Benediktiner-Ordens und seiner Zweige, Ergänzungsband 21; Ottobeuren, 1970). F. Dolbeau, 'Deux nouveaux manuscrits des "Mémoires" de Guibert de Nogent', *Sacris Erudiri*, 26 (1983), pp. 155–76. C. D. Ferguson, 'Autobiography as Therapy: Guibert de Nogent, Peter Abelard, and the Making of Medieval Autobiography', *Journal of Medieval and Renaissance Studies*, 13 (1983), pp. 187–212; M. D. Coupe, 'The Personality of Guibert de Nogent Reconsidered', *Journal of Medieval History*, 9 (1983), pp. 317–29.

Guigo I

Guigo I (1083–1136), fifth prior of the *Grande Chartreuse. Born at the chateau of Saint-Romain-du-Val-Mordane, then in the diocese of Valence, he entered the Grande Chartreuse in 1106 and was prior from 1109 until he died. Soon after 1109, he began a collection of 'thoughts' (*Meditationes*) which has been compared to the *Pensées* of B. *Pascal. Under him the Grande Chartreuse began to have daughter-foundations, the first being Portes (1115); partly to meet their needs he compiled the *Carthusian *Customary between 1121 and 1128. Nine of his letters survive, as well as an edition he made of the letters of St *Jerome. He was friend of St *Bernard of Clairvaux and of *Peter the Venerable, both of whom held him in high esteem.

Crit. edns., with Fr. trs., of his *Meditationes* by A. *Wilmart, OSB (Études de Philosophie Médiévale, 22; 1936), and by Un Chartreux (SC 308; 1983); of the Carthusian Customary by id. (ibid. 313; 1984); and of his letters by id., *Lettres des premiers Chartreux*, 1 (ibid. 88; 1962; 2nd edn., 1988), pp. 95–225. Eng. tr. of the *Meditations* by J. J. Jolin, SJ (Milwaukee, Wis., 1951). A. Wilmart, OSB, 'Les écrits spirituels des deux Guigues', *Revue d'ascétique et de mystique*, 5 (1954), pp. 59–79 and 127–58, repr. in his *Auteurs Spirituels et Textes Dévots du Moyen Âge latin* (1932), pp. 217–60. G. Mursell, *The Theology of the Carthusian Life in the Writings of St Bruno and Guigo I* (Analecta Cartusiana, 127; Salzburg, 1988). M. Laporte, Ord. Cart., in *Dict. Sp.* 6 (1967), cols. 1169–75, s.v. See also bibl. to HUGH, ST, BP. OF GRENOBLE.

Guigo II (d. prob. 1188), ninth prior of the *Grande Chartreuse from some time after 1173 until 1180. His *Scala Claustralium* ('Ladder of Monks') influenced late medieval and early modern piety, though it was often ascribed to other writers, esp. St *Bernard. Guigo's fourfold 'spiritual exercise', consisting of reading, meditation, prayer, contemplation, was widely adopted, and it contributed to the development of later, more systematic, notions of the spiritual life. There is a lively and original adaptation of the *Scala* in Middle English.

Crit. edn. of the *Scala Claustralium* and Twelve Meditations, with introd., by E. Colledge, OSA, and J. Walsh, SJ, and Fr. tr. by Un Chartreux (SC 163; 1970). Modern Eng. tr. by E. Colledge, OSA, and J. Walsh, SJ (London and Oxford, 1978). Middle English version of the *Scala* ed. P. Hodgson, *Deonise Hid Diuinite and Other Treatises on Contemplative Prayer* (EETS [Original Series], 231; 1955), pp. 100–17, with refs. A. *Wilmart, OSB, 'Les écrits spirituels des deux Guigues', *Revue d'ascétique et de mystique*, 5 (1924), pp. 59–79 and 127–58, repr. in his *Auteurs Spirituels et Textes Dévots du Moyen Âge latin* (1932), pp. 217–60. S. [C. ff.] Tugwell, OP, *Ways of Imperfection* (1984), pp. 93–124. M. Laporte, Ord. Cart., in *Dict. Sp.* 6 (1967), cols. 1175 f.

Gunkel, Hermann (1862–1932), Protestant theologian. After holding teaching appointments at Göttingen (1888), Halle (1889), and Berlin (1894), he became Prof. of OT Theology at Giessen in 1907 and at Halle (succeeding C. H. *Cornill) in 1920. He was a leading member of the *Religionsgeschichtliche Schule and a pioneer of *Form Criticism. He worked out the method in his comm. on Genesis (1901) and then extended it to the Psalms. He concluded that Hebrew religious poetry had a long history and that its forms had taken shape in oral tradition at a comparatively early date and become fully developed before the Exile. His writings include *Die Wirkungen des heiligen Geistes nach der populären Anschauung der apostolischen Zeit* (1888), *Schöpfung und Chaos in Urzeit und Endzeit* (1895), *Zum religionsgeschichtlichen Verständnis des Neuen Testaments* (1903), his comm. on Psalms (1925–6) and *Einleitung in die Psalmen* (posthumously pub. 1933). He also contributed several important articles to *RGG*.

Eng. tr. of various short works by A. K. Dallas as *What Remains of the Old Testament and other Essays* (1928); also of the introd. to his comm. on Genesis as *The Legends of Genesis* (Chicago, 1901; repr., New York [1964]), of his art. on the Psalms in *RGG* (2nd edn.) as *The Psalms* (Facet Books, Biblical Series, 19; Philadelphia [1967], of extracts from *Schöpfung und Chaos* in B. W. Anderson (ed.), *Creation in the Old Testament* (Issues in Religion and Theology, 6; 1984), pp. 25–52, and of *Das Märchen im Alten Testament* (1917) as *The Folktale in the Old Testament* (Sheffield, 1987). On Gunkel's work on the Psalms, see A. R. Johnson in H. H. Rowley (ed.), *The Old Testament and Modern Study* (1951), pp. 162–81.

W. Klatt, *Hermann Gunkel: Zu seiner Theologie der Religionsgeschichte und zur Entstehung der formgeschichtlichen Methode* (Göttingen, 1969); P. Gibert, *Une théorie de la légende: Hermann Gunkel (1862–1932) et les légendes de la Bible* [1979]. J. C. O'Neill, *The Bible's Authority* (Edinburgh, 1991), pp. 230–47. R. Wonneberger in *TRE* 14 (1985), cols. 297–300, s.v.

Gunning, Peter (1614–84), Bp. of *Ely. He was a fellow of Clare Hall, Cambridge, from 1633 to 1644, when he migrated to Oxford. A staunch royalist and *High Churchman, opposed to both Romanism and Puritanism, he continued during the Commonwealth to minister to Anglican congregations and held the C of E service at Exeter House in the Strand. At the *Restoration he was rewarded with rapid promotion. In 1660 he became Lady Margaret professor, and in 1661 Regius professor, of divinity at Cambridge, in 1669 Bp. of *Chichester, and in 1675 Bp. of Ely. He took a leading part at the *Savoy Conference, where as 'the incomparable hammer of the schismatics' he argued against R. *Baxter.

Modern edn. of his treatise *The Paschal or Lent Fast* (1662) by C. P. Eden in LACT (1845). J. H. Overton in *DNB* 23 (1890), pp. 345–8.

Gunpowder Plot (1605). The attempt to blow up the Houses of Parliament and destroy the King, Lords, and Commons together, in the hope that the RCs would then be enabled to seize the government. A small band headed by R. *Catesby hired a cellar under the Houses of Parliament in 1604, stored it with gunpowder, and arranged for Guy *Fawkes to start the explosion. The plot was revealed to Lord Salisbury by Lord Monteagle, and the leading conspirators were executed. It resulted in the greater unpopularity of Popery and an increased severity in the Penal Code. A form of service in commemoration of the frustration of the Plot was added by Royal Proclamation to the BCP in 1605, and appointed to be used annually on 5 Nov. Its use was revoked in 1859.

The Trial of Guy Fawkes and Others (The Gunpowder Plot), ed. D. Carswell (London, 1934). D. Jardine (ed.), *Criminal Trials*, 2, The Gunpowder Plot (1835), with full introd. Id., *A Narrative of the Gunpowder Plot* (1857). J. Gerard, SJ, *What was the Gunpowder Plot? The Traditional Story Tested by the Original Evidence* (1897); S. R. Gardiner, *What the Gunpowder Plot was* (1897). P. Caraman, *Henry Garnet 1555–1606 and the Gunpowder Plot* (1964). A. J. Loomie, SJ, *Guy Fawkes in Spain: The 'Spanish Treason' in Spanish Documents* (Bulletin of the Institute of Historical Research, Special Supplement, 9; 1971); J. Wormald, 'Gunpowder, Treason, and Scots', *Journal of British Studies*, 24 (1985), pp. 141–68; M. Nicholls, *Investigating Gunpowder Plot* (Manchester and New York [1991]).

Günther, Anton (1783–1863), religious philosopher. He was ordained priest in 1820, spent two years in a *Jesuit novitiate, and settled down for the rest of his life at Vienna without official position; there he actively propagated in lectures and books a system of philosophy and speculative theology. He made it his aim to interpret Catholic sacramentalism in terms of modern pantheistic idealism, esp. that of F. W. J. von *Schelling and G. W. F. *Hegel. He held that the human reason could prove scientifically the mysteries of the Trinity and the Incarnation, and that there was no real cleavage between natural and supernatural truth. By a form of the *ontological argument, he maintained that the existence of God could be deduced from the analysis of self-consciousness. All the dogmas of the Church, he held, were liable to revision and improvement in the light of fuller knowledge. In spite of influential friends, all his works were condemned by the *Index in 1857, and Günther submitted to the decision. After the First *Vatican Council, most of those who still adhered to his philosophy joined the *Old Catholics.

Günther's writings include (titles abbreviated): *Vorschule zur spekulativen Theologie* (1828–9), *Peregrins Gastmahl* (1830), *Sü- dund Nordlichter* (1832), *Der letzte Symboliker* (1834; on the controversy between J. A. *Möhler and F. C. *Baur), *Thomas a Scrupulis* (1835; against Hegelianism), *Die Juste-Milieus in der deutschen Philosophie gegenwärtiger Zeit* (1838; against Baur), *Eurystheus und Herakles* (1843), and *Antisavarese* (posthumous, 1883). Collected works ed. in 9 vols., Vienna, 1882. P. Knoodt, *Anton Günther* (2 vols., Vienna, 1881). E. Winter, *Die geistige Entwicklung Anton Günthers und seiner Schule* (Geschichtliche Forschungen zur Philosophie der Neuzeit, 1; Paderborn, 1931). L. Orbán, *Theologia Güntheriana et Concilium Vaticanum: Inquisitio historico-dogmatica de re Güntheriana iuxta vota inedita consultoris J. Schwetz actaque Concilii Vaticani exarata* (Analecta Gregoriana, 28 and 50; 1942–9). P. Wenzel, *Das wissenschaftliche Anliegen des Güntherianismus* (Essen, 1961); id., *Der Freundeskreis um Anton Günther und die Gründung Beurons* (ibid., 1965). E. and M. Winter, *Domprediger Johann Emanuel Veith und Kardinal Friedrich Schwarzenberg: Der Guntherprozess in unveröffentlichen Briefen und Akten* (*Sb.* (Wien), 282, Abhandlungen 2; 1972). Other modern studies by J. Pritz (Wiener Beiträge zur Theologie, 4; 1963) and K. Beck (ibid. 17; 1967). H. Klinger, 'Sündenfall und Erbsünde bei A. Günther', in E. Mann (ed.), *Erbe als Auftrage . . . Joseph Pritz zum 60. Geburtstag* (ibid. 40; 1973), pp. 119–67. J. Pritz, 'Anthon Günther (1783–1863)', in H. Fries and G. Schwaiger (eds.), *Katholische Theologen Deutschlands im 19. Jahrhundert*, 1 [1975], pp. 348–75, with bibl. A. Bunnell, *Before Infallability: Liberal Catholicism in Biedermeier Vienna* (Rutherford, Madison, London, and Toronto [1990]), esp. pp. 51–94.F. Lauchert in *CE* 7 (1910), pp. 85–8; H. Thurston, SJ, in *HERE* 6 (1913), pp. 455 f., s.v. 'Güntherianism'; H. H. Schwedt in *L.Th.K.* (3rd edn.), 4 (1995), cols. 1105–7, s.v.

Gustav-Adolf-Verein,

Gustav-Adolf-Verein, since 1946 called the 'Gustav-Adolf-Werk'. A German Protestant society to aid the weaker sister Churches in the '*diaspora'. It was founded in 1832 by the Leipzig professor C. G. L. Grossmann, to commemorate the bicentenary of the death of King *Gustavus Adolphus of Sweden, but did not gain importance until, in 1842, the court preacher, Karl Zimmermann of Darmstadt, amalgamated it with a similar society of his own. Its activities extend to all Protestant Churches irrespective of denomination, and though mainly devoted to the needs of German Protestants, do not exclude members of other nations. The help it gives takes various forms, esp. the building of churches and schools and provision for pastors and teachers. As a consequence of the Second World War its contacts with E. Europe were sharply reduced and the demand for German literature gave way to requests, in the first instance from Latin America, for support of Protestant communities using the language of their own countries. In 1966, in addition to the Leipzig headquarters in the German Democratic Republic, a separate base was established at Kassel in the German Federal Republic. Since the 1970s, as a result of *détente*, relations with SE Europe have been renewed, and after the reunification of Germany in 1990 it was decided to revert to a single central headquarters in Leipzig from 1995.

K. Zimmermann, *Der Gustav-Adolf-Verein nach seiner Geschichte, seiner Verfassung und seiner Werken*, ed. W. Zimmermann

(son; Darmstadt, 1878), and other works of K. Zimmermann. H. W. Beyer, *Die Geschichte des Gustav Adolf-Vereins in ihren kirchen- und geistesgeschichtlichen Zusammenhängen* (Göttingen, 1932). P. W. Gennrich, 'Das Gustav-Adolf-Werk der evangelischen Kirche in Deutschland', *Kirchliches Jahrbuch für die Evangelische Kirche in Deutschland*, 82 (1955), pp. 310–56; K. Scholder, *Das Gustav-Adolf-Werk und die evangelische Kirche: Festvortrag zum 150jährigen Jubiläum* (Kassel, 1983). W. Zimmermann in *PRE* (3rd edn.), 7 (1899), pp. 252–7; P. Schellenberg in *TRE* 8 (1981), pp. 719–26, s.v. 'Diasporawerke'; II. Riess in *EKL* (2nd edn.), 2 (1988), cols. 360 f., s.v. all with bibl.

Gustavus II Adolphus (1594–1632), King of *Sweden. He was the son of Charles IX, received a careful Protestant upbringing, and succeeded his father in 1611, making Axel Oxenstjerna his chancellor. In 1613 he brought the war with Denmark to an end, and in 1617 successfully concluded that with Russia by the Peace of Stolbova. In 1621 he began a war against the Catholic Vasas in Poland, to uphold the Protestant cause and make Sweden the principal power in the Baltic. In 1626 he transferred the war to the Prussian provinces, occupying Pillau, Ermland, and the delta of the Vistula. After repeated defeats by the Poles in 1627 and 1628, he concluded the six years' truce of Altmark in 1629. In 1630 his fear of the increasing Imperial power in the Baltic led him to intervene in the *Thirty Years War. He landed a large army in Pomerania, and by the Treaty of Bärwalde obtained help from France for the promise of maintaining Catholic worship in the Catholic places he should conquer. The German Protestant princes at first opposed him, but the majority of them finally joined him after his victory over Tilly at Breitenfeld (1631). Acclaimed everywhere as the hero of Protestantism, he penetrated deeply into W. and S. Germany, wintered at Mainz, and in the spring of 1632 took the field against Tilly, whom he defeated in the battle of Rain on the Lech. After devastating Bavaria he turned against Wallenstein, whom he confronted for two months near Nuremberg. At last he offered battle at Lützen, where he was killed.

Though Gustavus Adolphus saved German Protestantism by his intervention, his premature death probably alone secured the survival of Germany. His powerful personality and his strategic gifts are generally praised; but the traditional notion that he took up arms in defence of the Gospel rather than for political reasons has been widely challenged in modern times.

Skrifter [ed. C. G. Styffe] (Stockholm, 1861). Studies by F. F. von Soden (3 vols., Erlangen, 1865–9), G. Droysen (2 vols., Leipzig, 1869–70), N. Ahnlund (Stockholm, 1918; Eng. tr., Princeton, NJ, 1940), G. Wittrock (Stockholm, 1927), G. MacMunn (London [1930]), J. Paul (3 vols., Leipzig, 1927–32), M. Roberts (2 vols., London, 1953–8), G. Barudio (Frankfurt am Main, 1982), and F. Berner (Stuttgart, 1982). *Gustaf II Adolf: Minnesskrift på 300-Årsdagen av Slaget vid Lützen utarbetad inom Generalstabens Krigshistoriska Avdelning* (Stockholm, 1932). Introductory account by M. Roberts, *Gustavus Adolphus and the Rise of Sweden* (1973; 2nd edn., 1992), with useful bibl. See also bibl. to THIRTY YEARS WAR.

Gutenberg, Johann (*c.*1396–1468), inventor of printing. Born at Mainz and trained as a goldsmith, Gutenberg went to Strasbourg *c.*1430. By *c.*1449, when he returned to Mainz, he seems already to have possessed movable metal type cast in separate letters and had invented a typecasting machine. At Mainz he received two loans from Johann Fust, a banker, to finance the printing of the 42-line (*Mazarin) Bible during the years 1453–55. But in 1455 the partners went to law and the partnership was dissolved. Peter Schoeffer, a scribe, who prob. designed the firm's types, became Fust's partner and the firm produced in 1457 the first dated book, a beautiful Psalter. Before 1461 a 36-line Bible was produced in a type previously used for smaller works. This Bible was prob. printed by Gutenberg, possibly in co-operation with others. It is also possible that he was involved with the production of Joannes Balbus de Janua's *Catholicon* (1460). From 1465 he was pensioned by the Abp. of Mainz. Schoeffer continued to print until 1502.

The best general study is the Life by A. Ruppel (Berlin, 1939; rev. edn., 1947; with bibl.). D. C. McMurtrie (ed.), *The Gutenberg Documents, with Translations of the Texts into English* (New York, 1941). H. Widmann (ed.), *Der gegenwärtige Stand der Gutenberg-Forschung* (Bibliothek des Buchwesens, 1; Stuttgart, 1972). Popular account of his work by J. Ing, *Johann Gutenberg and his Bible* (New York, 1988). Full bibl. in S. Corsten and F. W. Fuchs (eds.), *Der Buchdruck im 15. Jahrhundert: Eine Bibliographie*, 1 (Stuttgart, 1988), pp. 282–308.

Guthlac, St (?673–714), early English hermit. He was related by blood to the royal house of Mercia. Originally a monk at the *double monastery at Repton, he later migrated to an island in the marshes around the site of the present *Crowland Abbey, where for 15 to 20 years he lived a life of severe asceticism. Feast day, 11 Apr. (in some calendars, 12 Apr.).

The Guthlac Roll, now in the the British Library (Harley Roll Y 6), is a vellum roll consisting of 17½ drawings depicting the life of St Guthlac. It was probably executed in the later half of the 12th cent. for the Abbot of Crowland.

The primary authority is the Life (not later than 749) by one Felix, pr. in *AASS*, Apr. 2 (1675), pp. 38–50; crit. edn., with Eng. tr., by B. Colgrave (Cambridge, 1956). An Anglo-Saxon prose version of this Life ed., with Eng. tr., by C. W. Goodwin (London, 1848); also ed., with discussion by P. Gonser, *Das angelsächsische Prosa-Leben des hl. Guthlac* (Anglistische Forschungen, 27; 1909); and see B. P. Kurtz, 'From St. Antony to St. Guthlac. A Study in Biography', *University of California Publications in Modern Philology*, 12 (1925–6), pp. 133–46, with refs. The early English poem derived from the same source in the Codex Exoniensis (10th cent.) is ed. J. Roberts, *The Guthlac Poems of the Exeter Book* (Oxford, 1979). On the early Lives see Hardy, 1, pp. 404–10 (nos. 920–32), and *BHL* 1, pp. 555 f. (nos. 3723–32), and *Novum Supplementum* (1986), pp. 408 f. J. Roberts, 'An Inventory of Early Guthlac Materials', *Mediaeval Studies*, 32 (1970), pp. 193–233. Facsimile edn. of the Guthlac Roll, with useful introd. by G. F. Warner (Roxburghe Club, Oxford, 1928). C. Hole in *DCB* 2 (1880), pp. 823–6, s.v.

Guthrie, James (c.1612–61), Scottish *Presbyterian. He was educated at St Leonard's College, St Andrews. At first an Episcopalian, he became a Presbyterian under the influence of S. *Rutherford and was ordained a minister in 1642. From 1644 to 1651 he was a member of the *General Assembly. In 1650 he excommunicated General J. Middleton as an enemy of the *National Covenant and made him do public penance. In 1651 he became one of the 'Protesters' (or 'Remonstrants') against the ecclesiastical jurisdiction of the King and was deposed by the

Assembly, which favoured a less rigid policy. In 1654 the English Council of State appointed him one of the *Triers and a visitor for the universities. After the Restoration he attempted to prove his loyalty to the King, but his efforts were unsuccessful. In 1661 he was arraigned for high treason and tried by a commission presided over by Middleton, who had never forgiven the insult of compelling him to do public penance. He was hanged at the cross of Edinburgh after making a long speech from the scaffold.

T. McCrie and T. Thomson, *Lives of Alexander Henderson and James Guthrie* (1846), pp. 141–284 (by T. Thomson). J. D. Douglas, *Light in the North: The Story of the Scottish Covenanters* (Exeter, 1964), esp. pp. 70–5 and 86 f. A. Gordon in *DNB* 23 (1890), pp. 377–9.

Guthrie, Thomas (1803–73), Scottish divine and social reformer. He studied at Edinburgh University and the Sorbonne, was licensed as a preacher by the presbytery of Brechin in 1825, and inducted to the charge of Arbirlot in Angus in 1830. Revealing outstanding gifts as a preacher, he moved in 1837 to Edinburgh, where he became one of the ministers of Old Greyfriars. In 1840 he transferred to the newly created St John's nearby. A strong supporter of the Evangelical party during the *Ten Years' Conflict, he 'came out' at the *Disruption (1843), and soon gained recognition for his remarkable success in raising funds for manses for ministers of the Free Church. From 1847 he engaged in establishing his celebrated 'Ragged Schools', where poor children could be given a sound education on a Protestant basis. At the same time he was strongly opposed to educational segregation on denominational lines within Protestantism. He also identified himself with the cause of total abstinence and in his later years emerged as a strong advocate, with Hugh Miller, of a national rather than a denominational scheme of education for Scotland, realized in the Education (Scotland) Act 1872. He was the author of many popular tracts, his most substantial work being *The Gospel in Ezekiel* (1856).

Autobiog. [to 1843] ed. with a Memoir by D. K. and C. J. Guthrie, sons (2 vols., London, 1874–5). Shorter studies by T. Muller (Geneva, 1890) and O. Smeaton (Edinburgh and London, 1900); also by A. L. Drummond in R. S. Wright (ed.), *Fathers of the Kirk* (1960), pp. 167–81. C. J. Guthrie in *DNB* 23 (1890), pp. 380–2; I. Donnachie and G. Hewitt, *A Companion to Scottish History* (1989), pp. 84 f., s.v.

Guyard (or Guyart), Marie (1599–1672), Bl Marie de l'Incarnation, first Superior of the *Ursulines at Quebec. A native of Tours, she was early drawn to the religious life, but in 1617, in obedience to her parents, married Claude Joseph Martin (d. 1620), by whom she had a son, later Dom Claude *Martin. In 1631, parting from her young son, she entered the Ursuline convent at Tours, where she was appointed novice-mistress in 1633. Inspired by visions which she had received since her childhood, with the blessing of the Abp. of Tours, she joined Mme de la Peltrie (1603–71) and two other sisters in accepting an invitation of the *Jesuit mission to form a convent in Quebec in 1639. The community, of which she was appointed superior, settled first in Lower Quebec and in 1641 moved to its present site. It engaged in educational work among French and Indians, and despite hardships of climate, fire, and attacks by the natives, prospered, largely

owing to her leadership. She was the recipient of religious experiences which she recorded in obedience to her directors (1633 and 1654). Her works, published posthumously, include her letters (1681), *Retraites* (1682), and *L'École sainte, ou Explication familière des mystères de la foi* (1684). She was beatified in 1980.

Letters ed. C. Martin, OSB (Paris, 1681); fuller, more accurate edn. by G.[-M.] Oury, OSB (Solesmes, 1971). Eng. tr. of selected letters entitled *Word from New France* by J. Marshall (Toronto, 1967). *Écrits spirituels et historiques*, ed. A. Jamet, OSB (4 vols. only pub., Paris and Quebec, 1929–39), incl. her 'relations biographiques' of 1633 and 1654; the latter was repr. at Solesmes, 1976. C. Martin, OSB, *La Vie de la vénérable Mère de l'Incarnation* (Paris, 1677; repr., Solesmes, 1982). Other Lives by F. X. Charlevoix (Paris, 1724), H. R. Casgrain (Quebec, 1864), P. F. Richaudeau (Paris, 1874), and G.-M. Oury, OSB (*Mémoires de la Société Archéologique de Touraine*, 58–9; 1973), and other works of this author. P. Renaudin, *Une Grande Mystique française au XVIIᵉ siècle: Marie de l'Incarnation. . . . Essai de psychologie religieuse* (1935). Bremond, 6 (1922), pp. 3–176. G.-M. Oury, OSB, in *Dict. Sp.* 10 (1980), cols. 487–507, s.v. 'Marie de l'Incarnation'.

Guyon, Madame (1648–1717), French *Quietist writer. Jeanne Marie Bouvier de la Mothe was born at Montargis. After a disturbed childhood, in 1664 she married Jacques Guyon, an invalid and 22 years her senior. The unhappiness of her life with her husband and mother-in-law turned her increasingly to a life of intensive prayer and she began to have mystical experiences; she found encouragement and lifelong friendship in the Duchesse de Béthune. After her husband's death (1676), she met a *Barnabite priest, François Lacombe (1643–1715), who became her spiritual director. In his company she undertook a five years' journey through France, endeavouring to propagate her methods of prayer. Soon after their return to Paris (1686), and the condemnation of M. de *Molinos (1687), they were suspected of a similar heresy and of immorality and both imprisoned. Mme Guyon was released through the efforts of Mme de Maintenon, who invited her to lecture at her girls' school at St Cyr. F. *Fénelon, whom she met in 1688 and with whom she corresponded from that time, found her mystical experiences authentic; J. B. *Bossuet, however, distrusted her illuminism, though he judged her sincere and wrote her a doctrinal letter in 1694. In the following year she requested a theological commission to clear her of the suspicion of heresy. The Conference of *Issy (1695), in which Fénelon took part and defended her, condemned her writings and she was imprisoned in various convents and finally in the Bastille (1698). She was released in 1703 on making her submission and spent the rest of her life in Blois under the close supervision of her son. Her chief mystical writings include *Moyen court et très facile de faire oraison* (1685) and *Le Cantique des cantiques* (1688). She taught complete detachment from the world, indifference to suffering and misfortune, self-abasement, and submission to God's will in pure love. She also developed a devotion to the Child Jesus. Her prayer of quietude and simplicity found an echo among *Quakers, in J. *Wesley, and among German *Pietists.

Works ed. by her disciple, P. *Poiret (39 vols., 'Cologne', 1712–22 [completed by friends after his death]). Modern edns. by B. Sahler of her correspondence with Fénelon (Paris, 1982) and of her autobiog. (ibid., 1983). Part 4 of her autobiog., *Récits de captivité*, first ed. M.-L. Gondal (Grenoble [1992]). Eng. tr. of her autobiog. by T. T. Allen (2 vols., London, 1897); of her Poems by W. *Cowper (Newport Pagnell, 1801). M.-L. Gondal, *Madame Guyon (1648–1717): Un nouveau visage* (Textes, Dossiers, Documents, 12 [1989]). M. Masson, *Fénelon & Mme Guyon: Documents nouveaux et inédits* (1907). M. de la Bedoyere, *The Archbishop and the Lady: The Story of Fénelon and Madame Guyon* (1956). F. Mallet-Joris, *Jeanne Guyon* [1978]. H. *Bremond, *Apologie pour Fénelon* (1910), pp. 3–150. R. A. *Knox, *Enthusiasm* (1950), pp. 319–52. Pourra., 4, pp. 231–66. L. Cognet in *Dict. Sp.* 6 (1967), cols. 1306–36, s.v. See also bibl. to FÉNELON and QUIETISM.

H

Habakkuk, Book of. The eighth of the *Minor Prophets. It opens with Habakkuk's complaint at the reign of oppression and lawlessness and God's answer that punishment is imminent in the invasion by the Chaldeans. The Prophet, terrified lest God should abandon His people, is instructed that the Chaldeans, too, will eventually fall through pride and idolatry. Ch. 3, a poem (or psalm), describes a vision of the Holy God coming from Mount Paran to work the deliverance of His people and expresses the writer's unshakeable confidence in Him.

The date of the Book has been variously fixed between the last years of the reign of Manasseh (698–643) and the second cent. BC, but a date in the late 7th or early 6th cent. seems most probable. Scholars favouring an earlier date argue that the 'Chaldeans' mentioned in the Book in its present form have replaced an earlier 'Assyrians'; those who place it later maintain that the 'Chaldeans' (*Chasdim*) have either replaced or stand for an earlier 'Kittim', i.e. Cypriots or Greeks, a suggestion to some extent supported by a commentary on Habakkuk found among the *Dead Sea Scrolls which explains that Chaldeans 'refers to the Kittim'.

Most scholars are agreed that ch. 3 is an independent addition, and this hypothesis finds support in the fact that the Dead Sea commentary covers only chs. 1–2. It has long been recognized that this last chapter is a liturgical piece, but many now regard the first two chapters as the work of a cult prophet attached to the Jerusalem Temple, whether or not he was also the author of ch. 3.

Chs. 1–2 are written in the form of a dialogue of great power and beauty between Yahweh and His prophet. Their central message is that, while the Chaldean is filled with pride, 'the just shall live by his faith' (2: 4), which will sustain the innocent who is involved in the sufferings of the guilty. This passage has played an important part in Christian thought through its use in Rom. 1: 17 and in Gal. 3: 11, and also in Heb. 10: 38, as the starting-point of the theological concept of faith.

Comm. by W. H. Ward (ICC on Mic., Zeph., Nah., Hab., Obad., Joel, 1912; sep. pagination), J. H. Eaton (Torch Bib. Comm., on Obad., Nah., Hab., and Zeph., 1961, pp. 81–118), and J. D. Watts (Camb. Bib., NEB, on Joel, Obad., Jon., Nah., Hab., and Zeph., 1975, pp. 121–52). P. Humbert, *Problèmes du livre d'Habacuc* (Neuchâtel, 1944). W. H. Brownlee, *The Text of Habakkuk in the Ancient Commentary from Qumran* (Journal of Biblical Literature, Monograph Series, 11; 1959). P. Jöcken, *Das Buch Habakuk: Darstellung der Geschichte seiner kritischen Erforschung* (Bonner biblische Beiträge, 48 [1977]). R. D. Haak, *Habakkuk* (Supplements to *Vetus Testamentum*, 44; '1992' [1991]). W. F. Albright, 'The Psalm of Habakkuk', in *Studies in Old Testament Prophecy presented to ... Theodore H. Robinson*, ed. H. H. Rowley (1950), pp. 1–18; E. Nielsen, 'The Righteous and the Wicked in Habaqquq', *Studia Theologica*, 6 (1953), pp. 54–78; J. H. Eaton, 'The Origin and Meaning of Habakkuk 3', *ZATW* 76 (1964), pp. 144–71. E. Cothenet in *Dict. Bibl.*, Suppl. 8 (1972), cols. 791–811, s.v. 'Prophètes'; M. A. Sweeney in *Anchor Bible Dictionary*, 3 (1992), pp. 1–6, s.v.

habit (religious dress). The distinctive outward sign of the religious state. A habit is worn by all members of the old orders (monks, friars, and nuns), and normally consists of a tunic, belt or girdle, scapular, hood for men and veil for women, and a cloak for use in choir and out of doors. The colours are, as a rule, white, brown, or black. Some modern orders and congregations dispense with a habit in the case of men (e.g. the *Jesuits). In recent years drastic modifications have been made in the habits of some of the women's orders, esp. those engaged in teaching.

habitual grace. See GRACE.

haburah. See CHABURAH.

Hackney Phalanx. A rather loosely defined group of Anglican High Churchmen associated with Joshua Watson (1771–1855), his brother John James Watson (1767–1839), Rector of Hackney and later Archdeacon of St Albans, and Henry Handley Norris (1771–1850), Rector of South Hackney and one of the founders of the *National Society. They were sometimes referred to as the 'Clapton Sect' (from the nearby home of Joshua Watson), paralleling the Evangelical '*Clapham Sect'.

E. Churton (ed.), *Memoir of Joshua Watson* (2 vols., 1861), *passim*; A. B. Webster, *Joshua Watson* (1954), pp. 18–32. F. W. Cornish, *The English Church in the Nineteenth Century*, 1 (1910), pp. 62–76. C. Dewey, *The Passing of Barchester* (1991), pp. 125–41 and 149–68.

Hades (Gk. ᾅδης). The place or state of departed spirits. The word is used in the *Septuagint as a translation for the Hebrew '*Sheol' (e.g. Is. 38: 18). In later Judaism the term took on a more definite meaning, of a place of reward for the pious dead, or alternatively, and later, of a place of waiting before judgement. In English usage it first appears *c*.1600, as a term used to explain the article in the Creed, 'He descended into hell', where the place of waiting (the place of 'the souls in prison', 1 Pet. 3: 19) into which the Lord is there affirmed to have gone after the Crucifixion needed to be distinguished from that more usually called 'hell', i.e. the place or state of those finally damned. See also HELL and DESCENT OF CHRIST INTO HELL.

G. Beer, 'Der biblische Hades', in *Theologische Abhandlungen: Festgabe zum 17. Mai 1902 für H. J. Holtzmann*, ed. W. Nowack and others (1902), pp. 2–29. J. Jeremias in *TWNT* 1 (1933), pp. 146–50 (Eng. tr., 1 (1964), pp. 146–9), s.v. ᾅδης, with suppl. bibl. in 10 (pt. 2; 1979), p. 959; W. Bauer, *Griechisch-Deutsches Wörterbuch zum den Schriften des Neuen Testaments* (5th edn., 1958), cols. 32 f. (Eng. tr., 1979, pp. 16 f.), s.v. ᾅδης. See also bibl. to DESCENT INTO HELL.

Hadewijch (the Dutch equivalent of 'Hedwig'), 13th-cent. contemplative writer. She spoke the dialect of Brabant and a number of passages from her *Visions* and letters suggest that she belonged to a community of *Beguines. Nothing is known of her life except what can be deduced from her works, which show that she was well versed in the Latin Bible, in theology, and in secular French romantic literature. Her *Visions*, letter-treatises, *Poems in Stanzas*, and *Poems in Couplets* all treat of the union of the soul with a God who transcends all union. She reflected deeply on the poetic process. In Letter 17 she explains how she had been moved to compose seemingly artless couplets, alluding to the Trinitarian mysteries and to their reflection in human nature and in her love of the divine and of the human; she concludes that her work surpasses her own expository powers: 'The kingdom of this earth cannot understand heavenly things, for people can reason about everything on earth and find words enough for it, but I can find neither words nor reason for this'. Though her 'love-mysticism' (an unhappy rendering of *Brautmystik*) was in the tradition of St *Bernard, she was pre-eminent in assimilating this and adapting the concepts and terminology of courtly love for Christian ends. This begs the still-unanswered question whether the language and ideals of mystical theology are derived from earthly models or the other way round. In the 14th cent. her letters are quoted by J. van *Ruysbroeck and were translated into High German, but in modern times direct knowledge of her works was recovered only in 1838 when two 14th-cent. manuscripts in Brussels were studied and in 1857 positively identified as hers. A number of the *Poems in Couplets* (25–9), however, are now attributed to a follower, 'Hadewijch II', herself greatly gifted, and the authorship of others (17–24) is disputed.

Crit. edn. of Flemish texts by J. van Mierlo, SJ: *De Visioenen*, 2 vols., Louvain, 1924–5; *Strophische Gedichten* [*Poems in Stanzas*], 2 vols., Antwerp, 1942; *Brieven* [Letters], 2 vols., ibid., 1947; and *Mengeldichten* [*Poems in Couplets*] (incl. texts of Hadewijch II), ibid., 1952, and by R. Guarnieri: *Cinque lettere con testo brabantino*, Brescia, 1950. Eng. tr. of *Complete Works* [excl. works of Hadewijch II] by C. Hart, OSB (Classics of Western Spirituality, 1981). Letters 1–20 also tr. by E. Colledge, *Mediaeval Netherlands Religious Literature* (Leiden, etc., 1965), pp. 31–87. N. de Paepe, *Hadewijch, Strofische Gedichten: Een studie van de minne in het kader der 12ᵉ en 13ᵉ eeuwse mystiek en profane minnelyriek* (Koninklijke Vlaamse Academie voor Taal- en Letterkunde, 11.2; 1967) and other works of this author. J. van Mierlo, SJ, 'Hadewijch, une mystique flamande du treizième siècle', *Revue d'ascétique et de mystique*, 5 (1924), pp. 269–89 and 380–404. J. Reynaert, *De Beeldspraak van Hadewijch* (Amsterdam, 1981); P. Mommaers, *Hadewijch* [in Dutch] (Averbode and Kempen, 1989); S. M. M. Jansen, *The Measure of Mystic Thought: A Study of Hadewijch's Mengeldichten* (Göppinger Arbeiten zur Germanistik, 536; 1991); J. Reynaert, 'Hadewijch: mystic poetry and courtly love', in E. Kooper (ed.), *Medieval Dutch Literature in its European Context* (Cambridge, 1994), pp. 208–25. J.-B. M. Porion, O. Cart., in *Dict. Sp.* 7 (1969), cols. 13–23, s.v.

Hadrian I (d. 795), Pope from 772. He was a Roman of noble birth. During his long pontificate he continued the policy of *Stephen III of maintaining close relations with *Charlemagne. By persuading Charlemagne to conquer Lombardy (774) and depose its king, Desiderius, he freed the Papacy from a long-standing menace. But Charlemagne's increased power meant a corresponding limitation of the Church's freedom, though Hadrian's personal relations with Charlemagne continued for the most part amicable. Charlemagne occasionally intervened in purely ecclesiastical matters, e.g. in defending the claims of the Abp. of *Ravenna against the Pope. The Pope also enlisted

the King's help in suppressing *Adoptianism and supported him in his efforts for uniformity in liturgy and canon law. In the *Iconoclastic controversy, however, Hadrian and Charlemagne differed, and the latter, refusing to sanction the decisions of the Synod of *Nicaea of 787, formally condemned them at Frankfurt in 794. Hadrian was a notable administrator, restoring aqueducts, walls, and towers, and fortifying the city of Rome. See also GREGORIAN SACRAMENTARY.

His epp. are pr. in J. P. Migne, *PL* 96. 1203–44, and 98. 261–438. *LP* (Duchesne), 1 (1886), pp. 486–523 (Eng. tr., with introd., by R. Davis, Liverpool, 1992, pp. 107–72). L. *Duchesne, *Les Premiers Temps de l'état pontifical* (1911), pp. 134–48. E. Caspar, 'Das Papsttum unter fränkischer Herrschaft', *ZKG* 54 (1935), pp. 132–264, esp. pp. 150–214. M. Jugie, AA, in *DHGE* 1 (1912), cols. 614–19; O. Bertolini in *Dizionario Biografico degli Italiani*, 1 (1960), pp. 312–23, s.v. 'Adriano I'. On the collection of canons which goes under his name (the so-called 'Hadriana'), cf. F. *Maassen, *Geschichte der Quellen und der Literatur des canonischen Rechts im Abendlande*, 1 (1870), pp. 441–71.

Hadrian IV (*c.* 1100–59), Nicholas Breakspear, Pope from 1154. He is the only Englishman who has occupied the See of Peter. Prob. the son of a clerk attached to *St Albans, he studied in France, and having entered the *Augustinian monastery of St Rufus near *Avignon became Abbot in 1137. When on a mission to Rome he was retained by *Eugenius III (1145–53), who appointed him Cardinal Bp. of Albano at some date before 1150. Soon afterwards he was sent as Papal legate on a mission to Scandinavia, where he reorganized the Churches of *Sweden and *Norway, made Trondheim (Nidaros) an independent archbishopric (1152) and did much to reform abuses. In 1154 he was unanimously elected Pope. He forthwith forced the expulsion of *Arnold of Brescia (q.v.) and finally secured his execution (1155). In 1155 he exacted full homage from *Frederick I (Barbarossa) before consenting to crown him. He at first refused to recognize William I (d. 1166) as King of Sicily, but after a disastrous military campaign agreed to invest him with the territory he held in return for an oath of homage and annual tribute. His claim that the Emperor held his crown as a *beneficium* from the Pope precipitated a quarrel with Barbarossa which outlasted his pontificate and became acute under *Alexander III. Hadrian IV also intervened in France, where he confirmed a royal sentence against the Duke of Burgundy. Probably at the suggestion of *John of Salisbury, he granted to Henry II of England the overlordship of *Ireland; the authenticity of the bull 'Laudabiliter' by which he did so, was for long disputed, but is now generally accepted.

Surviving 'Epistolae et Privilegia' pr. in J. P. Migne, *PL* 188. 989–1088; further docs. calendared in P. Jaffé (ed.), *Regesta Pontificum Romanorum*, 2 (2nd edn. by G. Wattenbach, Leipzig, 1888), pp. 102–45. Life by Boso, his English disciple (d. *c.* 1178), in *LP* (Duchesne), 2 (1892), pp. 388–97. H. K. Mann, *Nicholas Breakspear (Hadrian IV)*, A.D. *1154–1159, the Only English Pope* (1914); E. M. Almedingen, *The English Pope: Adrian IV* (1925). H. Schroers, *Untersuchungen zu dem Streite Kaiser Friedrichs I mit Papst Hadrian IV*, *1157–1158* (1916); M. Maccarone, *Papato e impero dalla elezione di Federico I alla morte di Adriano IV (1152–1159)* (Lateranum, NS 25, 1–4; 1959). J. F. O'Doherty, 'Rome and the Anglo-Norman Invasion of Ireland', *Irish Ecclesiastical Record*, 5th ser. 42 (1933), pp. 131–45; M. P. Sheehy, 'The Bull *Laudabiliter*: A Problem in Medieval *Diplomatique* and History', *Journal of* the *Galway Archaeological and Historical Society*, 29 (1961), pp. 45–70. W. Ullmann, 'The Pontificate of Adrian IV', *Cambridge Historical Journal*, 11 (1953–5), pp. 233–52. R. W. Southern, *Medieval Humanism and Other Studies* (Oxford, 1970), pp. 234–52. Mann, 9 (1914), pp. 231–340. M. *Creighton in *DNB* 1 (1885), pp. 143–6; P. Lamma in *Dizionario Biografico degli Italiani*, 1 (1960), pp. 330–5, s.v. 'Adriano IV'; W. Ullmann in *NCE* 1 (1967), p. 146, s.v. 'Adrian IV'.

Hadrian VI (1459–1523), Pope from 1522. Adrian Dedel was a native of Utrecht. He studied under the *Brethren of the Common Life at Deventer or Zwolle, and later at Louvain, where he became a doctor of theology in 1492. In 1507 he was chosen as tutor to the future *Charles V, and from 1516 he was the virtual ruler of Spain. In the same year he became Bp. of Tortosa, and in 1517 he was made *Inquisitor of Aragon and Navarre and created cardinal. He was unanimously elected Pope in 1522 on the death of *Leo X. The principal aims of his pontificate were the reform of the Roman Curia, the reconciliation of the European princes, the check of the spread of Protestantism, and the deliverance of Europe from the menace of the Turks. But the times were against him, and Hadrian found himself compelled to struggle almost single-handed against the depravity, luxury, and restlessness of his age. His efforts after reform met with frustration on all sides. Nor was he more successful in arousing the princes of Christendom to defend Rhodes, which fell on 24 Oct. 1522. He died a premature death, worn out with the burdens of his office, after a pontificate of little over a year. He was the author of a number of theological writings, only two of which, the *Commentarii in IV libros Sententiarum* (1516) and the *Quaestiones Quodlibeticae* (1515), were published. Except Marcellus II, he is the only Pope of modern times who has retained his baptismal name.

M. Gachard (ed.), *Correspondance de Charles-Quint et d'Adrien VI* (1859). A. Mercati (ed.), *Diarii di Concistori del pontificato di Adriano VI* (ST 157, 1951, pp. 83–113). There are facsimile reprs. of parts of his two pub. works (listed above) from Italian edns. of 1522, Ridgewood, NJ, 1964. C. Burmann (ed.), *Hadrianus VI, sive Analecta Historica de Hadriano VI* (Utrecht, 1727). E. H. J. Reusens (ed.), *Anecdota Adriani Sexti . . . partim ex codice ipsius Adriani autographo, partim ex autographis* (Louvain, 1862). C. von Höfler, *Papst Adrian VI, 1522–3* (1880); E. Hocks, *Der letzte deutsche Papst* (1939), with further bibl. E. H. J. Reusens, *Syntagma Doctrinae Theologicae Adriani Sexti P.M. . . . una cum Apparatu de Vita et Scriptis Adriani* (Louvain, 1862). E. Rodocanachi, *Les Pontificats d'Adrien VI et de Clément VII* (1933), pp. 7–86 and 273–9, with bibl. pp. 281–4. Arts. by R. R. Post and others in *Ephemerides Theologicae Lovanienses*, 35 (1959), pp. 524–629 (issue commemorating the 5th centenary of his birth). K.-H. Ducke, *Handeln zum Heil: Eine Untersuchung zur Morallehre Hadrians VI*. (Erfurter Theologische Studien, 34; 1976). Pastor, 9 (1910), pp. 1–230. M. Rosa in *Dizionario Biografico degli Italiani*, 1 (1960), pp. 337–42, s.v. 'Adriano VI'.

Hadrian the African, St (d. 709/10), monk. An African by birth, he became head of a monastery near Naples and a great friend of Pope *Vitalian. Having declined the Pope's offer of the see of *Canterbury for himself, he was instrumental in securing the appointment for *Theodore of Tarsus, and set out with him for England in 668. He was detained in France on the way, but arrived at Canterbury two years later, where he became abbot of the monastery of Sts Peter and Paul (later St Augustine's) and

master of the school. For 40 years he furthered the movement for conforming the religious customs and practices of England to those of Rome. A man of great learning, he keenly furthered education, and established schools in different parts of England. Feast day, 9 Jan.

*Bede, *HE* 4. 1 f.; 5. 20, 23; notes to *Baedae Opera Historica*, ed. C. Plummer, 2 (1896), pp. 202–5, 233, and 329. The passages from Bede and the legend as given by J. Capgrave in *AASS*, Jan. 1 (1643), pp. 595–7. Hardy, 1, pt. 1 (1862), pp. 403 f. N. Brooks, *The Early History of the Church of Canterbury* (Leicester, 1984), pp. 94–7. B. Bischoff and M. Lapidge (eds.), *Biblical Commentaries from the Canterbury School of Theodore and Hadrian* (Cambridge, 1994), with introd., pp. 82 189.

Hadrianum. The name given by modern scholars to the book sent *c.* 790 by Pope *Hadrian I in response to *Charlemagne's request for a copy of the standard Roman Mass book. See GREGORIAN SACRAMENTARY.

Haeckel, Ernst Heinrich (1834–1919), German scientist. A native of Potsdam, he became director of the Zoological Institute of Jena in 1862 and professor of biology in 1865. He remained at Jena till his death. A keen naturalist, he popularized C. *Darwin's theory of evolution in a treatise on General Morphology (1866) and in *Natürliche Schöpfungsgeschichte* (1867; Eng. tr., 1892). In his most widely read book, *Die Welträtsel* (1899; Eng. tr., *The Riddle of the Universe*, 1901), he attempted to apply Darwin's theories to philosophical and religious questions. He upheld the essential unity of organic and inorganic nature and derived all the phenomena of life, physical, intellectual, and spiritual, from natural causes, denying all doctrines of a personal God, of human free will, and of the immortality of the soul. His theories are chiefly of historical interest.

Was wir Ernst Haeckel verdanken: Ein Buch der Verehrung und Dankbarkeit, ed. H. Schmidt (2 vols., 1914). Überweg, 4, pp. 321–5 (incl. list of Haeckel's writings) and 705–7 (long bibl.). D. Gasman, *The Scientific Origins of National Socialism: Social Darwinism in Ernst Haeckel and the German Monist League* (1971).

Haeretico Comburendo, De. See DE HAERETICO COMBURENDO.

Hagenau, Conference of. The gathering from 25 June to 28 July 1540 convened by the Emp. *Charles V to discuss the points of dispute between the Catholics and Protestants of Germany. Unable to agree on which points to discuss and how to proceed, the conference broke up without achieving any result. It was arranged that there should later be another gathering at Worms. See WORMS, CONFERENCE OF.

L. Cardauns, *Zur Geschichte der kirchlichen Unions- und Reformsbestrebungen von 1538 bis 1542* (Bibliothek des kgl. Preussischen historischen Instituts in Rom, 5; 1910), pp. 33–7, with various relevant docs., pp. 131–57; C. Augustijn, *De Godsdienstgesprekken tussen Rooms-Katholieken en Protestanten van 1538 to 1541* (Haarlem, 1967), pp. 36–45, with bibl., pp. 142–6. Pastor, 11 (1912), pp. 391–6, with refs. G. Kawerau in *PRE* (3rd edn.), 7 (1899), pp. 333–5, s.v. 'Hagenauer Religionsgespräch'. See also bibl. to CHARLES V and WORMS, CONFERENCE OF.

Haggadah (Heb. הַגָּדָה 'narrative'). In Judaism the term is used in two senses: (1) for the ritual of reading prayers that accompany the *Passover meal, consisting mainly of elaborations on the theme of the biblical narrative of the Exodus from Egypt; (2) (in this sense also 'Aggadah') for those parts of the traditional literature (*Midrash and *Talmud) not comprehended under the heading *Halachah, and in particular for tales and legends concerning biblical or rabbinic figures, prob. derived from ancient sources.

(1) C. Raphael, *A Feast of History: The drama of Passover through the ages, with a new translation of the Haggadah for use at the Seder* [1972]. (2) L. Ginzberg, *The Legends of the Jews*, tr. from Ger. by H. Szold and others (7 vols., Philadelphia, 1909–38). G. G. Porton in *Anchor Bible Dictionary*, 3 (1992), pp. 19 f., s.v.

Haggai, Book of. The tenth of the *Minor Prophets. The Book, dated in the second year of Darius, i.e. 520–519 BC, consists of four separate discourses concerned to promote the rebuilding of the *Temple. It is addressed esp. to the two leaders of the people, Zerubbabel, the governor of Judah, and Joshua, the son of Jehozadak, the high priest. Though the foundations of the Temple had been laid, the work had been interrupted. The first discourse (1: 4–11) attributes the prevalent drought and famine to the people's neglect of rebuilding the Temple; in the second (2: 2–9) the prophet consoles the Jews for the inferiority of the present building and prophesies a glorious future in the Messianic age, when all the nations will come to Jerusalem; the third prophecy (2: 11–19) predicts a return of fertility to the land; and the fourth (2: 21–24) promises Zerubbabel victory over his enemies. This last prophecy has traditionally been regarded as referring to the *Messiah. The Book has perhaps been edited in the light of the account in Ezra 3–6.

Comm. by H. G. Mitchell (ICC on Hag., Zech., Mal., and Jonah, 1912, pp. 3–79), R. [A.] Mason (Camb. Bib., NEB, on Hag., Zech., and Mal., 1977, pp. 12–26), D. L. Petersen (London, on Hag. and Zech. 1–8, 1985, pp. 17–127), and C. L. and E. M. Meyers (Anchor Bible, on Hag. and Zech. 1–8, 1987, pp. 1–84). P. R. Ackroyd, 'Studies in the Book of Haggai', *Journal of Jewish Studies*, 2 (1951), pp. 163–76; 3 (1952), pp. 1–13; F. S. North, 'Critical Analysis of the Book of Haggai', *ZATW* 68 (1956), pp. 25–46; K. Koch, 'Haggais unreines Volk', ibid. 79 (1967), pp. 52–66. H. W. Wolff in *TRE* 14 (1985), pp. 355–60, s.v. 'Haggai/ Haggaibuch', with extensive bibl.

Hagiographa (Gk. ἀγιόγραφα, 'sacred writings'; Heb. כְּתֻבִים, writings'). A title applied to the third division of the OT canonical Scriptures, i.e. all Books not belonging to the 'Law' or the 'Prophets'. The Books comprised are Pss., Prov., Job; the five *Megilloth, i.e. Ruth, Lam., Song of Songs, Eccles., and Esther; and Dan., 1 and 2 Chron., Ezra, Neh. They were the latest Books in the Hebrew OT to achieve canonicity.

hagiography. The writing of the lives of the saints. The lives vary widely in the importance their authors attach to historical accuracy, oral tradition (usually associated with the cult of a saint), and literary form. Recent scholarship has emphasized the influences possibly exerted by the ancient Greek novel, NT Apocrypha, collections of Lives of the philosophers and other literary works. The primary sources include *martyrologies, *passions, calendars, biographies, prose and verse compositions, and liturgical texts. The earliest collection of such material, now unhappily lost, was that compiled by *Eusebius (c.260–c.340).

The critical examination of these writings, which dates from the 17th cent., has been esp. fostered by the *Bollandists. See also ACTA SANCTORUM.

The principal collections of sources, besides the *Acta Sanctorum* (q.v.), are listed under the various countries and religious orders (qq.v.); many also in *EC* (see below). Socii Bollandiani, *Bibliotheca Hagiographica Graeca* (Brussels, 1895; 3rd edn. by F. Halkin, 1957; *Novum Auctarium*, by id., 1984); idd., *Bibliotheca Hagiographica Latina Antiquae et Mediae Aetatis* (2 vols., ibid., 1898–1901; new suppl., 1911; new suppl., by H. Fros, 1986); idd., *Bibliotheca Hagiographica Orientalis* (ibid., 1910). A. *Butler, *The Lives of the Fathers, Martyrs and other Principal Saints* (homiletic; 4 vols., 1756–9; rev. by H. Thurston and by D. Attwater, 12 vols., 1926–38, with suppl. vol. by D. Attwater, 1949; improved edn. in 4 vols., 1956); *Vies des saints et des bienheureux selon l'ordre du calendrier*, by the Benedictines of Paris (13 vols., 1935–59). F. G. Holweck, *A Biographical Dictionary of Saints* (1924). F. von S. Doyé, *Heilige und Selige der römischen Kirche* (2 vols., 1929). D. H. Farmer, *The Oxford Dictionary of Saints* (1978; 2nd edn., 1987). P. F. de' Cavalieri, *Note agiografiche* (ST, 8, 9, 22, 24, 27, 33, 49, 65, 176; 1902–53); id., *Hagiographica* (ibid. 19; 1908). H. *Delehaye, SJ, *Les Légendes hagiographiques* (1905; Eng. tr., 1907) and other works cited, s.v. J. Minischthaler, *Heiligenlegenden* (2 vols., 1911–13). A. Ehrhard, *Überlieferung und Bestand der hagiographischen und homiletischen Literatur der griechischen Kirche von den Anfängen bis zum Ende des 16. Jahrhunderts* (TU 50 and 52; 1937–52). F. Grossi-Gondi, *Principi e problemi di critica agiografica* (1919). P. Peeters, SJ, *Orient et Byzance: Le Tréfonds oriental de l'Hagiographie Byzantine* (Subsidia Hagiographica, 26; 1950). R. Aigrain, *L'Hagiographie, ses sources, ses méthodes, son histoire* (1953). B. de Gaiffier, SJ, 'Hagiographie et historiographie', in *La Storiografia altomedievale* (Settimane di Studi del Centro Italiano di Studi sull'Alto Medioevo, 17; Soleto, 1970), pp. 139–66. J. Gribomont, OSB, 'Panorama des influences orientales sur l'hagiographie latine', *Augustinianum*, 24 (1984), pp. 7–20; also other items in this number devoted to 'L'agiografia latina nei secoli IV–VII'. M. Van Uytfanghe, *Stylisation biblique et condition humaine dans l'hagiographie mérovingienne [600–750]* (Verhandelingen van de Koninklijke Academie voor Wetenschappen, Letteren en Schone Kunsten van België, Klasse der Letteren, Jaargang 49, nr. 120; 1987). R. Grégoire, *Manuale di Agiologia: Introduzione alla Letteratura agiografica* (Bibliotheca Montisfani, 12; Fabriano, 1987). *Analecta Bollandiana* (Brussels, 1882 ff.); *Hagiographica: Rivista di agiografia e biografia* (Turnhout, 1994 ff.). L. Oliger, OFM, in *EC* 1 (1948), cols. 449–54, s.v. 'Agiografia', for further bibl.; F. Halkin, SJ, in *NCE* 6 (1967), pp. 894–7, s.v.; M. Van Uytfanghe in *RAC* 14 (1988), cols. 150–83, s.v. 'Heiligenverehrung II (Hagiographie)'.

hagiology (from Gk. ἅγιος, 'holy', and λογία, 'discourse', i.e. the science of holiness). The literature dealing with the lives and legends of the saints and their cultus. See HAGIOGRAPHY.

Hagios o Theos. See AGIOS O THEOS.

hagioscope, also 'squint'. An opening in the chancel walls of ancient churches, to permit worshippers in the transepts, side aisles, or other parts of the church from which the altar is not otherwise visible to see the elevation of the *Host at Mass.

Hail, Holy Queen. See SALVE REGINA.

Hail Mary (Lat. *Ave Maria*; also known as the **Angelic Salutation**). The form of prayer to the BVM, based on the greetings of *Gabriel (Lk. 1: 28) and *Elizabeth (Lk.

1: 42). In its modern form it is as follows: (1) 'Hail Mary, full of grace, the Lord is with thee: Blessed art thou among women, and blessed is the fruit of thy womb, Jesus'. (2) 'Holy Mary, Mother of God, pray for us sinners now and in the hour of our death'. In the W. the devotional use of (1) is first attested in the 11th cent. and became common in the 12th, whereas the complete Hail Mary, with (2) added, did not come into general use until the 16th cent. In this later form it received official recognition from its inclusion by Pope *Pius V in the Roman *Breviary of 1568. It was dropped from the Office in 1955. The Orthodox form (an expanded version of (1), prefaced by 'Virgin, Mother of God' and concluding with 'for thou hast given birth to the Saviour of our souls', with the name Jesus omitted) is first attested in the 9th cent., though a very similar form is found in the Liturgies of St *James and St *Mark and may therefore have been in use much earlier. In the public liturgy it is said most frequently during Lent.

T. Esser, OP, 'Geschichte des englischen Grusses', *Hist. J.* 5 (1884), pp. 88–116. S. Beissel, SJ, *Geschichte der Verehrung Marias in Deutschland während des Mittelalters* (1909), ch. 13, 'Das "Gegrüsset seist du, Maria" und der Rosenkranz bis zum 15. Jahrhundert', pp. 228–50; id., *Geschichte der Verehrung Marias im 16. und 17. Jahrhundert* (1910), pp. 5–16 and *passim*; H. *Leclercq, OSB, 'Prière à la Vierge Marie sur un ostrakon de Louqsor', *Bulletin d'ancienne Littérature et d'Archéologie chrétiennes*, 2 (1912), pp. 3–32, repr. Hefele and Leclercq, OSB, 5 (pt. 2; 1913), App. 4, pp. 1734–59; E. Vacandard, 'L'Histoire de l'"Ave Maria" ', *Revue du Clergé français*, 71 (1912), pp. 315–19; H. Thurston, SJ, 'The Origins of the Hail Mary', *The Month*, 121 (1913), pp. 162–76 and 379–84; repr. in Thurston's *Familiar Prayers*, ed. P. Grosjean, SJ (1953), pp. 90–114. E. Campana, *Maria nel culto cattolico*, 1 (1933), pp. 519–64; G. M. Roschini, OSM, 'L'Ave Maria. Note storiche', *Marianum*, 5 (1943), pp. 177–85. H. Leclercq, OSB, in *DACL* 10 (pt. 2; 1932), cols. 2043–62, s.v. 'Marie (Je vous salue)'; A. A. De Marco in *NCE* 6 (1967), p. 898, s.v.

hair-shirt. A shirt made of cloth woven from hair, and from an early period to the present day worn as a means of discipline by penitents and ascetics.

Halachah (Heb. הֲלָכָה, 'that by which one walks'). In rabbinic Judaism, the body of teachings having a direct practical application, in contrast to *Haggadah. The main source of Halachah are the Bible (OT), *Talmud, medieval codifications (the last and most authoritative being the *Shulchan Aruch* or 'Prepared Table' of Joseph Caro, first published in 1565), and the vast body of *responsa*. In modern Judaism the status of the Halachah constitutes one of the principal points of disagreement between Orthodox Judaism on the one hand and Liberal or Reform Judaism on the other.

M. Elon (ed.), *The Principles of Jewish Law* (Jerusalem [1975]). S. B. Freehof, *The Responsa Literature* (Philadelphia, 1955). L. Jabobs and B. De-Vries in *Encyclopaedia Judaica*, 7 (Jerusalem, 1972), cols. 1156–66, s.v. 'Halakhah'.

Hales, Alexander of. See ALEXANDER OF HALES.

Hales, John (1584–1656), Anglican divine, known as the 'ever-memorable'. He was a native of Bath, and educated at Bath grammar school and at Corpus Christi College, *Oxford, where he took his degree in 1603. In 1605 he was elected Fellow of Merton, and in 1612 he became public lecturer in Greek at the university. He probably

had a large share in H. *Savile's edition of St *Chrysostom (1610–13). In 1613 he pronounced the funeral oration on Sir Thomas Bodley, and in the same year became Fellow of Eton. In 1616 he went to the Netherlands as chaplain to the English ambassador, Sir Dudley Carleton, in which capacity he was present at the Synod of *Dort (1618). In 1619 he returned to Eton. In 1639 he became chaplain to Abp. W. *Laud and canon of *Windsor. He was dispossessed of his canonry by the parliamentary committee in 1642, and of his Fellowship at Eton in 1649. He then became tutor to a nephew of the Bp. of *Salisbury. He died in retirement at Eton. Perhaps the best known of his works is his tract *Schism and Schismatics* (written 1636, first pub. 1642), which reflects his broadminded and eirenical position. The *Golden Remains* was published posthumously.

Collected Works [ed. David Dalrymple, Lord Hailes] (3 vols., Glasgow, 1765). Life by J. H. Elson (New York, 1948, with detailed bibl.). R. Peters, 'John Hales and the Synod of Dort', *Studies in Church History*, 7 (1971), pp. 277–88. A. Gordon in *DNB* 24 (1890), pp. 30–2.

Half-Way Covenant, the. A doctrine current in American *Congregationalism in the 17th and 18th cents. expressive of the relationship in which those (esp. baptized) members of the community who were devoid of describable religious experience were held to be bound to God. Its purpose was by giving such persons a definite status to prevent the Church from being reduced to an assemblage of individuals and Baptism from losing all significance for those who professed no change of heart. Its scriptural basis was found in Yahweh's Covenant with *Abraham (Gen. 17: 7). The doctrine has now been generally rejected as incompatible with the principles of Congregationalism, acc. to which the only true basis of relationship of man to God must be personal faith.

R. G. Pope, *The Half-Way Covenant: Church Membership in Puritan New England* (Princeton, NJ, 1969). See also bibl. to UNITED STATES OF AMERICA, CHRISTIANITY IN.

Halifax, Charles Lindley Wood (1839–1934), second Viscount Halifax. He was the son of Sir Charles Wood, first Viscount Halifax (1800–1885), and Mary, daughter of Earl Grey, and educated at Eton and at Christ Church, Oxford, where under the influence of E. B. *Pusey's sermons, J. M. *Neale's writings, H. P. *Liddon's friendship, and R. I. *Wilberforce's *Doctrine of the Incarnation* he became a strong and devoted High Churchman. In 1865 he was associated with the foundation of the *SSJE and himself had thoughts of joining the Society, but was dissuaded by R. M. *Benson. He continued, however, to take a keen interest in its work and made his annual retreat at Cowley until 1931. Acceptance in 1868 of the Presidency of the *English Church Union, vacant by Colin Lindsay's impending secession to Rome, brought him into most of the ecclesiastical controversies of his lifetime (*Athanasian Creed; *Public Worship Regulation Act; W. J. E. *Bennett and A. H. *Mackonochie cases; trial of Bp. E. *King; *Lambeth Opinions; *Deceased Wife's Sister bill; *Modernism; projects for revision of the BCP), in many of which he took a leading part. He held the office continuously until 1919 and again from 1927 until his death. A friendship with E. F. Portal which began at Madeira in

1890 led him to interest himself in promoting reunion between the C of E and the Holy See. With Portal he was responsible for initiating the conversations at Rome in 1894–6 and the publication of the *Revue Anglo-Romaine*; and their abortive termination by **Apostolicae Curae* (13 Sept. 1896), largely, as he thought, through the influence of the English RC hierarchy under Cardinal H. *Vaughan, caused him profound disappointment. He later published a fully documented account of the negotiations in *Leo XIII and Anglican Orders* (1912). After the *Lambeth Appeal of 1920 he reopened the matter with Cardinal D. J. *Mercier, with whom he arranged the *Malines Conversations (q.v.); but soon after Mercier's death in Jan. 1926 they were terminated. In Jan. 1928, impatient with the caution and delay of the Anglican authorities, he issued the Report himself and, soon after, his *Notes on the Conversations at Malines*. This was followed in 1930 by *The Conversations at Malines: Original Documents* (printed in France). In 1930 he also published *The Good Estate of the Catholic Church*, summing up many of his ecclesiastical ideals and expressing his long-held high regard for the BCP of 1549.

His son, **Edward Frederick Lindley Wood** (1881–1959), Baron Irwin (1925), 1st Earl of Halifax (1944), President of the Board of Education (1922–4 and 1932–5), Viceroy of India (1926–1931), Chancellor of Oxford University (from 1933 to his death), Foreign Secretary (1938–40), and British Ambassador in Washington (1941–6), was also a devoted High Churchman. He was the author of a *Life* of John Keble (1909) as well as an autobiography entitled *Fulness of Days* (1957).

J. G. Lockhart, *Charles Lindley Viscount Halifax*. Part 1, 1839–85 (1935); Part 2, 1885–1934 (1936). Id. in *DNB, 1931–1940*, pp. 919–21.
Life of Edward Frederick Lindley Wood by the Earl of Birkenhead (London, 1965). K. Rose in *DNB, 1950–1960*, pp. 1072–80.

Hall, Joseph (1574–1656), Bp. of *Norwich. He was educated at Emmanuel College, Cambridge, and soon became keenly interested in the Roman controversy. He won favour with *James I, who in 1616 made him Dean of *Worcester and in 1618 sent him as one of his representatives to the Synod of *Dort. In 1627 he became Bp. of *Exeter, but he was held suspect by W. *Laud as being too favourable to *Calvinism and *Puritanism, though he maintained conformity in his diocese. When the bishops were attacked by the Parliament of 1640, Hall came forward to defend his order, and pleaded for an unprelatical episcopacy in his *Episcopacy by Divine Right* (1640). His *Humble Remonstrance to the High Court of Parliament* (1640–1) evoked the reply of '*Smectymnuus'. In 1641 he was translated to Norwich, but before he could reach his see was sent to the Tower with the rest of the bishops. After release, his income was impounded by Parliament, and in 1647 he was ejected from his palace and lived in poverty until his death. Hall represented the moderating influence among the bishops. Of his voluminous writings the earlier ones were verse satires, the later ones controversial and devotional. His *Heaven upon Earth* (1606) was reprinted by J. *Wesley in his '*Christian Library'. His *Hard Measure* is autobiographical and narrates the persecution of the bishops by Parliament.

Collected edns. of his works by J. Pratt (10 vols., London, 1808), P. Hall (12 vols., Oxford, 1837–9), and P. Wynter (10 vols., ibid., 1863). Modern edns. of his poetry by A. Davenport (Liverpool, 1949), of *Heaven upon Earth* and *Characters of Virtues and Vices* by R. Kirk (New Brunswick, NJ, 1948), and of *Mundus Alter et Idem*, with Eng. tr. by J. M. Wands, with Eng. tr. (Yale Studies in English, 190 [1981]). Lives by T. F. Kinloch (London and New York, 1951) and F. L. Huntley (Cambridge, 1979). Id., *Bishop Joseph Hall and Protestant Meditation in Seventeenth-Century England: A Study with the texts of* The Art of Divine Meditation (1606) *and* Occasional Meditations (1633) (Medieval and Renaissance Texts and Studies, 1; Binghamton, NY, 1981). R. A. McCabe, *Joseph Hall: A Study in Satire and Meditation* (Oxford, 1982). G. G. Perry in *DNB* 24 (1890), pp. 75–80.

Hall, Robert (1764–1831), *Baptist preacher. Born at Arnesby, Leicestershire, he was trained at the Baptist Academy at Bristol and King's College, Aberdeen. Later he became an influential preacher in Bristol (1785–90 and 1826–31), Cambridge (1791–1806) and Leicester (1807–25). He was of commanding presence and eloquence; and his discourse on *Modern Infidelity* (1800), his sermon on the death of Princess Charlotte (1817), and his championship of the Leicestershire laceworkers brought him a wide following. His writings include *Christianity consistent with a Love of Freedom* (1791; defending J. *Priestley), *Reflections on War* (1802), *On Terms of Communion* (1815) and *Memoir of Thomas Toller* (1821).

Works, with Memoir by O. G. Gregory (6 vols., London, 1832). Brief modern study by G. W. Hughes (ibid., 1943). A. Gordon in *DNB* 24 (1890), pp. 85–7.

Hallel (Heb. הַלֵּל, 'praise'). A name given by Jews to Pss. 113–18. They are recited at most of the principal Jewish festivals and during the *Passover meal, and may have been the hymn sung by Christ and the Apostles after the *Last Supper (Mt. 26: 30). Ps. 136 is called the 'Great Hallel'.

Hallelujah. See ALLELUIA.

Haller, Berchtold (1492–1536), Reformer of Berne. After studying at *Cologne, he became chaplain of the bakers' guild at Berne in 1513 and in 1520 was given the canonry formerly held by T. *Wyttenbach. From 1521 onwards he was in contact with U. *Zwingli, whose doctrine he adopted, though he was acquitted on a charge of heresy in 1523. Together with Wyttenbach and the painter, Nicholas Manuel, he was at the centre of the 'Reformation Party' in Berne. He took part in the Disputations of Baden (1526) and *Berne (1528), collaborating with F. Kolb in the composition of a Protestant liturgy and the reformatory edict of 1528. In 1532 he took part, with W. *Capito, in the Synod which confirmed the Reformation in Berne and secured Haller's recognition as the city's religious leader. His attempts to establish Protestantism in Solothurn (1530) failed and his last years were filled with controversies against the *Anabaptist movement. He left no writings and his letters have not, so far, been collected.

M. Kirchhofer, *Bertold Haller oder die Reformation von Bern* (1828); C. Pestalozzi, *Bertold Haller* (Leben und ausgewählte Schriften der Väter und Begründer der reformirten Kirche; Elberfeld, 1861). G. [W.] Locher, *Der Berner Synodus von 1532*

(2 vols., Neukirchen, 1984–8, incl. edn. of proceedings in vol. 1). I. Backus, *The Disputations of Baden, 1526, and Berne, 1528* (Studies in Reformed Theology and History, 1, no. 1; Princeton, NJ, 1993), *passim*. F. Trechsel and E. Blösch in *PRE* (3rd edn.), 7 (1899), pp. 366–70, with bibl.

halo (or nimbus). A circle or disc of light round the head or, more rarely, round the whole body. It was used in the religious symbolism of the Hellenistic period as a distinguishing mark in the representation of gods and demigods, later also of the Roman Emperors. Christian art adopted it only gradually. In the 3rd and 4th cents. its use was restricted to Christ and the Lamb, from the 5th cent. it was extended to the BVM, the angels and the saints, and soon also to other important personages. In the Middle Ages the round halo was used only for angels and saints, in the case of Christ being usually distinguished by a cross or the monogram A and Ω (or, in the E., by the words ὁ ὤν [cf. Ex. 3: 14 LXX]), whereas at the same period a rectangular form was sometimes employed for the representation of living people, esp. Popes and bishops, as in the famous picture of St *Gregory the Great formerly in the monastery of Clivus Scauri at Rome. The colour of the halo seems originally to have been blue, but from the 5th and 6th cents. gold, yellow, or rainbow colours were preferred. In modern RC practice a halo is permitted only for persons canonized or beatified or whose cultus has been otherwise approved.

A. Krücke, *Der Nimbus und verwandte Attribute in der frühchristlichen Kunst* (Strasbourg, 1905); J. Wilpert, *Die römischen Mosaiken und Malereien der kirchlichen Bauten vom 4. bis 13. Jahrhundert*, 1 (2nd edn., 1917), pp. 97–113; 2 (2nd edn., 1917), pp. 1193–5; M. Collinet-Guérin, *Histoire du Nimbe des origines aux temps modernes* [1961]; K. Künstle, *Ikonographie der christlichen Kunst*, 1 (1928), pp. 25–9, with refs. H. *Leclercq, OSB, in *DACL* 12 (pt. 1; 1953), cols. 1272–312, s.v. 'Nimbe', and J. H. Emminghaus in *L.Th.K.* (2nd edn.), 7 (1962), cols. 1004 f., s.v. 'Nimbus'.

Hamann, Johann Georg (1730–88), German religious thinker. He was born at Königsberg. After having followed a rather irregular course of studies at the university from 1746, he became a private tutor in 1752. In 1756 he entered the service of a merchant of Riga, who in the following year sent him to London on a business enterprise which proved a failure. This disappointment was accompanied by an interior crisis, resulting in a conversion experience in March 1758. Having returned to Königsberg in 1759, he nursed his ailing father until his death in 1766. He then accepted a subaltern post at an excise office, which left him sufficient time for his literary pursuits.

Hamann was one of the fathers of the German 'Storm and Stress' movement. A prophet of religious 'immediacy', he proclaimed the rights of the individual personality and attacked the rationalism of the *Enlightenment. His works are written in an aphoristic and somewhat obscure style, which earned him the title of 'The Magus in the North'. The best known are *Sokratische Denkwürdigkeiten* (1759), *Aesthetica in nuce* (1761), and *Golgatha und Scheblimini!* (1784). In the last of these, his most important contribution to religious thought, he upholds Christianity as the historical revelation of the Triune God, of Atonement and of Redemption, against the rationalistic popular philosophy of Moses Mendelssohn. Though a personal friend

of I. *Kant, he opposed his philosophy and insisted on the importance of inner experience, esp. in matters of religion. He regarded himself as the rejuvenator of Lutheranism, and in this, as in other respects, was a precursor of S. A. *Kierkegaard.

Edns. of his Works by F. Roth and G. A. Wiener (8 Theile in 9 vols., Augsburg, 1821–43), C. H. Gildemeister (6 vols., Gotha, 1857–73), and J. Nadler (6 vols., Vienna, 1949–57); Correspondence ed. W. Ziesemer and A. Henkel (7 vols., Wiesbaden, 1955–79); *Hauptschriften erklärt* by F. Blanke and others (vols. 1, 2, 4, 5, and 7; Gütersloh, 1956–63), with bibl. in vol. 1; *Kreuz und Kritik: Johann Georg Hammans Letztes Blatt. Text und Interpretation*, ed. O. Bayr and C. Knudsen (Beiträge zur historischen Theologie, 66; Tübingen, 1983). Selections from his writings, in Eng. tr., in R. G. Smith, *J. G. Hamann . . . A Study in Christian Existence* (1960). Eng. tr. of his *Sokratische Denkwürdigkeiten*, with very full introd., by J. C. O'Flaherty (Baltimore, 1967). Studies by J. Nadler (Salzburg [1949]), H. A. Salmony (vol. 1 only; Zollikon, 1958), W. Koepp (Göttingen, 1965), W. M. Alexander (The Hague, 1966; in Eng.), T. J. German (Oxford Theological Monographs, 1981), and H. Corbin (Paris [1985]); also a collection of important arts. of various dates ed. R. Wild (Wege der Forschung, 511; Darmstadt, 1978). O. Bayer, *Zeitgenosse im Widerspruch: Johann Georg Hamann als radikaler Aufklärer* (Munich, 1988). I. Berlin, *The Magus of the North: J. G. Hamann and the Origins of Modern Irrationalism*, ed. H. Hardy (1993). O. Bayer in *TRE* 14 (1985), pp. 395–403, s.v.

Hamartolos, George. See GEORGE HAMARTOLOS.

Hamilton, John (1511–71), Abp. of St Andrews. The natural son of James Hamilton, first Earl of Arran, he entered the *Benedictine monastery of Kilwinning as a boy but probably never became a monk. In 1525 he was appointed Abbot of Paisley, and retained the office till his death. In 1540 he took a three-year course of studies at *Paris. On his return to Scotland he was appointed keeper of the privy seal and in 1544 Bp. of Dunkeld (consecrated 1546). After the assassination of D. *Beaton he was made Abp. of St Andrews and Primate of Scotland in 1547 (having effective tenure from 1549). From this time until his death he was one of the most influential opponents of Protestantism. He called a succession of synods (1548, 1549, 1552, and 1559) with the view to a reform of the morals of the clergy and the religious education of the laity, the chief result of which was the compilation of a valuable catechism in the vernacular, known as *Archbishop Hamilton's Catechism* (1552). In 1560 he protested against the acceptance by Parliament of J. *Knox's new confession of faith. Three years later he was imprisoned for saying Mass and hearing confessions, but was released at the intervention of Queen *Mary, whose son, later *James VI, he baptized in 1566. In her subsequent troubles he became her faithful supporter, advising her, though in vain, to remain in Scotland. After her flight he was pronounced a traitor and captured at Dumbarton Castle, where he had sought safety. Three days later he was hanged at Stirling in his pontifical vestments.

A man of political prudence and moderation and an intrepid defender of his religion, Hamilton was not blameless in his personal life. He had several illegitimate children, and his annulment of Bothwell's marriage which enabled him to marry the Queen was gravely irregular. On the other hand, his complicity in the assassinations of Darnley and Moray, of which he was accused, is doubtful.

His *Catechism* and *The Two-Penny Faith*, ed. together, with introd. by A. F. Mitchell (Edinburgh, 1882); the *Catechism* also ed. by T. G. Law (Oxford, 1884). J. Robertson, *Concilia Scotiae* (Bannatyne Club, 1866), 1, pp. 147–82. T. G. Law in *DNB* 24 (1890), pp. 190–2.

Hamilton, Patrick (c. 1504–28), Scottish Protestant proto-martyr. While still a boy, in 1517, he was made titular Abbot of Ferne. He studied at Paris, where M. *Luther's writings attracted his attention, and afterwards at St Andrews. From 1526 he began to show open sympathy with Lutheran ideas and in 1527 he visited both *Wittenberg, where he met Luther and P. *Melanchthon, and *Marburg with its newly founded Protestant university. Here he wrote his only work, a set of *Loci Communes* ('Patrick's Places'). Towards the end of 1527 he returned to Scotland. A. *Alesius, who was deputed to convince him of his errors, was himself converted to the Protestant creed. Early in the following year Hamilton was formally charged with heresy by Abp. James Beaton and burnt at the stake on 29 Feb.

A. Cameron (ed.), *Patrick Hamilton, First Scottish Martyr of the Reformation* (1929). W. A. Clebsch, *England's Earliest Protestants 1520–1535* (Yale Publications in Religion, 11; 1964), pp. 81–5; J. E. McGoldrick, 'Patrick Hamilton, Luther's Scottish Disciple', *Sixteenth Century Journal*, 18 (1987), pp. 81–8; id., *Luther's Scottish Connection* [Cranbury, NJ, etc., 1989], pp. 35–54, with tr. by J. *Frith of 'Patrick's Places', pp. 74–100. Æ. Mackay in *DNB* 24 (1890), pp. 201–3.

Hamilton, Walter Kerr (1808–69), Bp. of *Salisbury. He was the first of the *Tractarians to become a diocesan bishop in England. Educated at Christ Church, Oxford, he was for a time a Fellow and tutor of Merton College and from 1837 to 1841 Vicar of St Peter's-in-the-East, Oxford; and from c.1838 he came under the influence of the *Oxford Movement. In 1841 he became a canon of Salisbury and in 1854 Bishop. Here he did much to stimulate the spiritual life of his diocese, e.g. by instituting diocesan *retreats; and in 1860 he founded Salisbury Theological College. In 1861–4 he prosecuted Rowland *Williams (1817–70), one of the contributors to *Essays and Reviews*, whose benefice was in his diocese. In his Charge for 1867 he defended the Eucharistic Sacrifice, the Real Presence, and Sacramental Confession; and he was attacked by Lord Portman in the House of Lords. He was devoted to his work at Salisbury Cathedral and in 1853 issued *Cathedral Reform*.

H. P. *Liddon, *W. K. Hamilton. A Sketch*, repr. with Additions and Corrections, from the *Guardian* (1869); id., *Life in Death: A Sermon preached in Salisbury Cathedral on 8 Aug. 1869*. W. A. Greenhill in *DNB* 24 (1890), pp. 216 f.

Hammond, Henry (1605–60), Anglican divine. Born at Chertsey, Surrey, he was educated at Eton and Magdalen College, Oxford, where he became a Fellow in 1625. He was ordained in 1629. He belonged to the intellectual circle of Great Tew, Lord Falkland's house north of Oxford, along with Edward Hyde (the future Earl of Clarendon), G. *Sheldon, *W. Chillingworth, and others. In 1633 he was presented to the living of Penshurst, Kent, where he instituted daily services in church and monthly celebrations of the Holy Communion. In 1643 he was appointed Archdeacon of *Chichester and also nominated a member of the *Westminster Assembly, but never sat. Forced to leave Penshurst during the Civil War, he returned to Oxford and composed his *Practical Catechism* (pub. anon. 1645), which became very popular. As chaplain to the royal commissioners at the conference at Uxbridge in 1645, he defended *episcopacy. In the same year he was appointed a Canon of *Christ Church, Oxford, and Chaplain in Ordinary to *Charles I. He attended the King until his imprisonment at Carisbrooke in Dec. 1647. He was deprived of his canonry and confined first in Oxford and then under light restraint at Clapham, Bedfordshire. In 1649 or 1650 he moved to Westwood, Worcs. He suffered from the decree (1655) forbidding the clergy of the C of E to exercise their ministry and devoted himself to relieving the deprived clergy and to raising funds for the training of future ordinands. Throughout his life he maintained a discipline bordering on asceticism.

Besides publishing numerous pamphlets and pastoral treatises, Hammond compiled *A Paraphrase and Annotations upon all the Books of the New Testament* (1653), a pioneer work of English biblical criticism. He also assisted B. *Walton in the production of his *Polyglot Bible (1657) and wrote a prefatory letter for *The *Whole Duty of Man*.

Works ed. W. Fulman (4 vols., London, 1674–84); repr. by N. Pocock as *The Miscellaneous Theological Works of Henry Hammond* (LACT, 3 vols. in 4, 1847–50). Life by Bp. J. *Fell, orig. pub. London, 1661, is repr. among Hammond's works. Short Life by G. G. Perry (London [1862]). J. W. Packer, *The Transformation of Anglicanism 1643–1660, with special reference to Henry Hammond* (Manchester, 1969). P. Jansen, *De Blaise Pascal à Henry Hammond: Les Provinciales en Angleterre* (1954), esp. pp. 70–84. H. Trevor-Roper, *Catholics, Anglicans and Puritans: Seventeenth Century Essays* (1987), No. 4 ('The Great Tew Circle'), pp. 166–230, esp. pp. 215–27. R. Hooper in *DNB* 24 (1890), pp. 242–6.

Hampden, Renn Dickson (1793–1868), Bp. of *Hereford. After a brilliant university career he was elected a Fellow of Oriel College, Oxford, in 1814, and made friends with T. *Arnold and R. *Whately, both *Broad Churchmen like himself. In 1832 he expounded in his *Bampton Lectures on *The Scholastic Philosophy, considered in its relations to Christian Theology* a view of Christianity in which its dogmatic elements were greatly reduced. In 1833 he was appointed Principal of St Mary's Hall, Oxford. His name came into much prominence in 1836 when the *Tractarians, suspicious of his theology, unsuccessfully attempted to prevent his becoming Regius professor of divinity. In 1837, however, his suspension from the board which nominated Select Preachers was achieved. In 1847 Lord John Russell offered him the see of Hereford, and, despite violent High Church opposition, he was consecrated bishop in the following March. He administered his see conscientiously till his death, displaying tolerance and charity. His *Essay on the Philosophical Evidence of Christianity* (1827) and other writings illustrate a phase in liberal thought, but have little permanent value.

H. Hampden (daughter), *Some Memorials of Renn Dickson Hampden* (1871). H. F. G. Swanston, *Ideas of Order: Anglicans and the renewal of theological method in the middle years of the nineteenth century* (Assen, 1974), pp. 17–53, with bibl. pp. 225–9. G. C. Boase in *DNB* 24 (1890), pp. 264–6.

Hampton Court Conference. The conference held at Hampton Court in January 1604, between the English bishops and the *Puritan leaders and presided over by *James I. Its purpose was to consider the Puritan demands for reform in the Church, set out in the *Millenary Petition. The Puritans were led by John *Rainolds, Dean of Lincoln, and the bishops by R. *Bancroft and T. Bilson. When Rainolds demanded the modification of episcopacy, James declared that he had learnt in Scotland 'No bishop, no king', and so gave the bishops his support. All the Puritans won was a series of minor concessions, notably slight changes in the BCP and royal promises to restrict pluralism and enlarge the preaching ministry. The most substantial result of the conference was a new translation of the Bible issued as the *Authorized Version in 1611.

E. *Cardwell, *A History of the Conferences and other Proceedings Connected with the Revision of the Book of Common Prayer from 1558 to 1690* (1840), pp. 121–228. F. Shriver, 'Hampton Court Re-visited: James I and the Puritans', *JEH* 33 (1982) pp. 48–71. P. Collinson, 'The Jacobean Religious Settlement: The Hampton Court Conference', in H. Tomlinson (ed.), *Before the English Civil War* (1983), pp. 27–51. R. G. Usher in *DECH*, pp. 258 f., s.v.

Handel, George Frideric (1685–1759), musical composer. The original form of his name was Händel. He was born in Halle, Saxony, and spent the early years of his career in Hamburg and in Italy. In 1710 he visited London, which he made his home from 1712, becoming a naturalized British subject in 1727. He remained a *Lutheran, but worshipped regularly at his parish church, St George's, Hanover Square. He is rightly regarded as the originator of the English *oratorio, with its prominent role for the chorus. As Handel was essentially a man of the theatre, his oratorios are generally highly dramatic in style; they include *Esther* (1732), *Saul* (1738), *Israel in Egypt* (1738), *Judas Maccabeus* (1746), and *Solomon* (1748). For the most part they were originally performed in the theatre, but without scenery or theatrical dress. The most famous of all, *Messiah* (1741, first performed in 1742) is atypical in being non-dramatic. It has always enjoyed immense popularity. Handel himself inaugurated annual performances of it for the benefit of the Foundling Hospital, and over the years it has helped keep many an amateur choral society solvent. His other religious music includes 'Dixit Dominus' (1707), the set of extended anthems for the Duke of Chandos (1717–18), and four anthems for the coronation of George II (1727), of which 'Zadok the priest' has been sung at every subsequent coronation. Handel's genius may be said to lie in his ability to create the sublimest of effects with the simplest of means. He gave up composing after going blind in 1752, although he continued to play and direct performances of his works to the end of his life.

Collected Works ed. by [K. F. F. Chrysander for] the Händel-Gesellschaft (97 vols., pt. 49 never pub., Leipzig, 1858–1902); new edn. ('Hallische Händel-Ausgabe') by M. Schneider and others (Kassel, 1955 ff.). W. and M. Eisen (eds.), *Handel-Handbuch* (Gleichzeitig Supplement zu Hallische Händel-Ausgabe, 1978 ff.; incl. thematic catalogue and docs.). O. E. Deutsch, *Handel: A Documentary Biography* (1955). J. Mainwaring, *Memoirs of the Life of the late George Frideric Handel* (1760). P. H. Lange, *George Frideric Handel* (New York, 1966; London, 1967). C. Hogwood, *Handel* (London [1984]). H. Swanston, *Handel* (Outstanding Christian Thinkers, 1990). W. Dean, *Handel's Dramatic Oratorios and Masques* (1959). D. [J.] Burrows, *Handel and the English Chapel Royal* (lecture [1985]). K. Sasse,

Händel Bibliographie (Leipzig [1963]; 2nd edn., 1967); M. A. Parker-Hale, *G. F. Handel: A Guide to Research* (New York and London, 1988). W. Dean and A. Hicks in S. Sadie (ed.), *The New Grove Dictionary of Music and Musicians*, 8 (1980), pp. 83–140, s.v.

hands, imposition of. A ritual gesture which figures prominently in the Bible and in the life of the Church, and was also known in the classical world. Acc. to Num. 8, the Israelites were to lay their hands on the heads of the *Levites, and the Levites were to lay their hands on the heads of the bulls which were to be sacrificed. The predominant use of the gesture, however, is as a manner of blessing (e.g. Gen. 48), though in some cases an element of commission may be implied. The gesture was used by Christ in many of the healing miracles.

In the NT, and esp. in Acts, there are a number of references to the laying on of hands (χειροτονεῖν and its cognates) in the early Church; some of these have traditionally been taken as examples of *Confirmation (Acts 8 and 19) and *Ordination (Acts 13: 3). While the precise significance of these and other similar biblical texts is open to question, the placing of the bishop's hand on the head of each candidate has come to be the central action in both these sacraments. In the rite of *Unction the priest lays his hands upon the sick person, and a similar provision is made in various modern Anglican liturgies for the *Visitation of the Sick. Hands may be placed upon the head in the private blessing of individuals.

J. Behm, *Die Handauflegung im Urchristentum* (1911); J. Coppens, *L'Imposition des mains et les rites connexes dans le N.T. et dans l'Église primitive* (1925); id., 'L'Imposition des mains dans les Actes des Apôtres', in J. Kremer (ed.), *Les Actes des Apôtres* (Bibliotheca Ephemeridum Theologicarum Lovaniensium, 48 [1979]), pp. 405–38; P. A. Elderenbosch, *De Oplegging der Handen* (1953). C. H. *Turner 'Χειροτονία, χειροθεσία, ἐπίθεσις χειρῶν (and the accompanying verbs)', *JTS* 24 (1922–3), pp. 496–504. J.-T. Maertens, 'Un rite du pouvoir: L'imposition des mains', *Studies in Religion*, 6 (1976–7), pp. 637–49; 7 (1978), pp. 25–39. J. K. Coyle, OSA, 'The Laying on of Hands as Conferral of the Spirit: Some Problems and a Possible Solution', in E. A. Livingstone (ed.), *Studia Patristica*, 18 (pt. 2; Louvain, 1989), pp. 339–53. H. B. *Swete in *E.Bi.* 2 (1901), col. 1956, s.v. 'Laying on of Hands'; P. Galtier, SJ, in *DTC* 7 (pt. 2; 1923), cols. 1302–425; F. *Cabrol, OSB, in *DACL* 7 (pt. 1; 1926), cols. 391–413.

Hannington, James (1847–85), Bp. of Eastern Equatorial Africa. After offering himself to the *CMS, he landed in Zanzibar in June 1882 at the head of six missionaries, but fever and dysentery compelled him to return to England in the following May. On recovering, he again offered himself for the work, was consecrated the first Bp. of Eastern Equatorial Africa in June 1884, and was back in Mombasa in Jan. 1885. In Oct. 1885 he was murdered by the natives of *Uganda when leading a hazardous expedition to open up a shorter route to Lake Victoria Nyanza. Feast day in parts of the Anglican Communion, 29 Oct.

E. C. Dawson, *James Hannington* (1887); id., *The Last Journals of Bishop Hannington* (1888).

haplography. In the copying of manuscripts, the writing of any letter(s) or word(s) only once where it ought to be repeated. The opposite error is known as '*dittography'.

Hardenberg, Albert (*c.* 1510–74), Reformer. Educated by the *Brethren of the Common Life at Groningen, he entered the *Cistercian monastery of Aduard *c.*1527, and studied theology at the University of Louvain. In 1539 he took his doctor's degree at Mainz, where he came into contact with John *Laski. Under his influence he accepted Protestant teaching. Returning to Louvain, he was put on trial for heresy and left the city for Aduard. In 1542 he went to *Wittenberg, where he established close contact with P. *Melanchthon. At the Diet of *Speyer (1544) *Hermann of Wied asked him to help establish the Reformation in *Cologne. He travelled widely on Hermann's behalf, taking part in the Diet of *Worms (1545). After Hermann's resignation (1547), Hardenberg was appointed cathedral preacher at Bremen; but in 1561 he was expelled from this post for his denial of the *Lutheran doctrine of the Lord's Supper, and for the next four years he lived quietly under the protection of the Count of Oldenburg. In 1565 he became pastor at Sengwarden, and from 1567 to his death he was preacher at Emden.

Life by B. Spiegel (Bremen, 1869); lesser study by W. Schweckendieck (Emden, 1859). J. *Moltmann, *Christoph Pezel (1539-1604) und der Calvinismus in Bremen* (Hospitium Ecclesiae, Forschungen zur bremischen Kirchengeschichte, 2; Bremen, 1958), esp. pp. 16-29. Schottenloher, 1 (1933), p. 325 (nos. 7938-54). C. Bertheau in *PRE* (3rd edn.), 7 (1899), pp. 408-16; W. H. Neuser in *TRE* 14 (1985), pp. 442-4, both s.v., with bibl.

Hardenberg, Friedrich Leopold Freiherr von. See NOVALIS.

Harding, St Stephen. See STEPHEN HARDING, ST.

Hardouin, Jean (1646-1729), French scholar. A native of Brittany, he became a *Jesuit at about the age of 16 and for most of his life (from 1683) was Librarian of the Jesuit Collège de *Clermont at Paris. He published many excellent editions of the classics and other ancient writings. He took great delight in defending paradoxical and fantastic theories, maintaining, e.g. that the NT was originally written in Latin, that the great majority of the ancient classics were really the product of 13th-cent. monks, and that all the councils commonly supposed to have preceded that of *Trent (1546-63) were fabrications. The last of these theories did not prevent him from producing an edition of the texts of the ecclesiastical councils from NT times onwards (*Conciliorum Collectio Regia Maxima*, Paris, '1715', but for some years the French government withheld it from circulation owing to its *Ultramontane notes); it was largely drawn on by J. D. *Mansi and is still of some value. Hardouin was also a great authority on numismatics, his works in this field including *Chronologia Veteris Testamenti ad vulgatam versionem exacta et nummis antiquis illustrata* (1696).

H. *Quentin, OSB, *J. D. Mansi et les grandes collections conciliaires* (1900), pp. 38-54; E. Galletier, 'Un Breton du XVIIᵉ siècle à l'avant-garde de la critique. Le père Jean Hardouin de Quimper', *Annales de Bretagne*, 36 (1925), pp. 462-83, and 38 (1928), pp. 171-87. [W.] O. Chadwick, *From Bossuet to Newman: The Idea of Doctrinal Development* (Birkbeck Lectures, 1955-6; Cambridge, 1957), esp. pp. 49-51, 211-13. Sommervogel, 4 (1893), cols. 84-111; Polgár, 2 (1990), p. 123. P. Bernard in *DTC* 6 (1920), cols. 2042-6, s.v.

Hardwicke, Act of Lord. The Clandestine Marriages Act 1753 was passed 'for the Better Prevention of Clandes-

tine Marriages', and dealt with notorious abuses such as Fleet marriages and the prevalence of *bigamy. For the first time clandestine marriages, previously regulated by canon law, were made subject to statute. All marriages in England and Wales (except those of the Royal Family, Jews, and *Quakers) were required to be celebrated in the parish church of one of the parties and after banns, save that the Abp. of *Canterbury could grant a special licence for the marriage to be celebrated in some other church and without the delay entailed by *banns of marriage, and that the diocesan Bishop had the right to dispense from banns. All other unions, and the marriages of infants made without consent of parents or guardians, were declared invalid. The Act was the first step on the road to the transfer of jurisdiction in matrimonial causes from Church to State, completed by the introduction of judicial divorce on the passing of the Matrimonial Causes Act 1857. See also MATRIMONY.

Hare, Julius Charles (1795-1855), Archdeacon of Lewes. Having entered Trinity College, Cambridge, in 1812, he was elected a Fellow in 1818, and intended at first to enter the legal profession. In 1826, however, he was ordained, and in 1832 appointed Rector of Hurstmonceux. Through travel in Germany, he came much under the influence of German theologians and men of letters and introduced many German ideas to English theology. He was a *Broad Churchman. His writings, some of which secured great popularity, included *Guesses at Truth* (1827; it was written in conjunction with his brother Augustus), a collection of observations on philosophy, religion, literature, and other subjects; *The Victory of Faith* (1840; 3rd edn., 1874); and *Sermons preacht on Particular Occasions* (1858). He also issued, in conjunction with C. *Thirlwall, a translation of B. G. Niebuhr's *History of Rome* (2 vols., 1828-32). In 1840 he was appointed Archdeacon of Lewes.

Anon. introd. (by F. D. *Maurice) to *Charges to the Clergy of the Archdeaconry of Lewes, delivered at the Ordinary Visitations in the Years 1843, 1845, 1846* (1856), pp. i-lxiii, and anon. study (by A. P. *Stanley) in the *Quarterly Review*, 97 (1855), pp. 1-27, both repr. in Hare's *The Victory of Faith* (3rd edn., by E. H. Plumptre, 1874), pp. xvii-cxxxii. A. J. C. Hare (nephew), *Memorials of a Quiet Life* (2 vols., 1872). N. M. Distad, *Guessing at Truth: The Life of Julius Charles Hare (1795-1855)* (Shepherdstown, W. Va., 1979), with bibl. A. J. C. Hare in *DNB* 24 (1890), pp. 369-72.

Harklean Version. A revision of the *Philoxenian Syriac Version of the NT made by Thomas of Harkel ('Heraclea') in 616, on the basis of readings derived from Greek MSS in the library of the Enaton, near Alexandria. In the margin Thomas recorded many variants which are textually of great interest and value, mostly akin to those of *Codex Bezae. About 50 MSS of this version (mostly containing only the Gospels) have survived, the oldest dating from *c.* the 7th cent. It is this version of the text of Rev. which is printed in many current ('*Peshitta') Syriac New Testaments. The Harklean revision is the counterpart of the contemporary version of the OT made by Paul of Tella, known as the *Syro-Hexapla.

Only edn. is that of J. White with the inappropriate title 'Versio Philoxeniana': Gospels, Oxford, 1788; Acts and Epp., ibid., 1799-1803. Later (partial) edns. of Gospel of Jn. by G. H. Bernstein (Leipzig, 1853) and of Heb. 11: 28-13: 25 by R. L. Bensly (Cambridge, 1889). Facsimile of Rev. from MS Mardin Orth. 35

(prob. 13th cent.), with introd. by A. Vööbus, *The Apocalypse in the Harklean Version* (CSCO 400; Subsidia, 56; 1978). Peshitta and Harklean text of Jas., 1 Pet., and 1 Jn. ed. B. Aland, *Das Neue Testament in Syrischer Überlieferung*, 1 (Arbeiten zur neutestamentlichen Textforschungen, 7; 1986). List of MSS in J. D. Thomas, 'The Gospel Colophon of the Harclean Syriac Version', *Near East School of Theology*, 3, pt. 1 (Beirut, 1980), pp. 16–26. G. Zuntz, *The Ancestry of the Harklean New Testament* (British Academy Supplemental Papers, no. 7 [1945]). Id., 'Études harkléennes', *R. Bibl.* 57 (1950), pp. 550–82. B. M. Metzger, *The Early Versions of the New Testament* (Oxford, 1977), pp. 68–75. J. Gwynn in *DCB* 4 (1887), pp. 1014–21, s.v. 'Thomas (17) Harklensis'.

Harless, Gottlieb Christoph Adolph von (1806–79), German *Lutheran theologian. When a student at Halle University he was converted under the influence of F. A. G. *Tholuck to an ardent belief in the doctrine of justification by faith. From 1833 to 1845 he was Prof. of NT exegesis at Erlangen, where he considerably raised the standard of the theological faculty and founded the *Zeitschrift für Protestantismus und Kirche* (1838–76). From 1845 to 1850 he was professor at Leipzig. Appointed court preacher at Dresden in 1850, he was called to Munich two years later and made president of the supreme consistory of Bavaria. Here he reorganized the Lutheran State Church, to which he gave a new hymn-book and a new Order of Services. He was one of the most influential representatives of Lutheran orthodoxy of his generation.

W. Langsdorff, *Adolf von Harless: Ein kirchliches Charakterbild* (1898). T. Heckel, *Adolf von Harless: Theologie und Kirchenpolitik eines lutherischen Bischofs in Bayern* (Munich, 1933). A. von Stählin in *PRE* (3rd edn.), 7 (1899), pp. 421–32, s.v.; M. Hein in *TRE* 14 (1985), pp. 444–6, s.v.

Harmony, Pre-established. See PRE-ESTABLISHED HARMONY.

Harmony Society. A communist sect, also known as the 'Harmonists', founded by J. G. Rapp (1757–1847). Rapp first established his sect in Württemberg; but in 1803–4 he emigrated to the USA, and there settled his community on a site of some 5,000 acres in Butler County (Pa.), giving it the name of 'Harmony'. In 1814 his followers transferred themselves to a much larger estate in Posey County (Ind.), but in 1825 moved again to Economy (now called Ambridge), just north of Pittsburg. The Harmonists held many eccentric ideas. Rapp himself believed that Napoleon was God's ambassador, that attendance at school was wicked, and that Baptism and the Lord's Supper were the work of the devil. By the middle of the 19th cent. the Harmonists had largely died out; the Society was dissolved in 1905.

A. Williams, *The Harmony Society at Economy, Penn'a* (Pittsburgh, 1866); J. A. Bole, *The Harmony Society: A Chapter in German American Culture History* (Americana Germanica, NS, Philadelphia, 1904); C. F. Knoedler, *The Harmony Society* (New York [1954]); K. J. R. Arndt, *George Rapp's Harmony Society 1785–1847* (Philadelphia, 1965). W. E. Wilson, *The Angel and the Serpent: The Story of New Harmony* (Bloomington, Ind. [1964]). R. B. Taylor in *HERE* 3 (1910), pp. 780 f., s.v. 'Communistic Societies of America: I, The Harmony Society'.

Harms, Claus (1778–1855), German *Lutheran theologian. A native of Holstein, after helping his father in his

corn mill he went in 1799 to the University of Kiel, where the study of F. D. E. *Schleiermacher's writings made him a zealous Evangelical. In 1806 he was elected deacon at Lunden in Norder Ditmarschen (Holstein), where he became popular as a preacher. Ten years later he was appointed archdeacon at St Nicolai at Kiel, and in 1835 provost. In 1834 he had declined an offer to succeed Schleiermacher at the Dreifaltigkeitskirche in Berlin. He is chiefly remembered for his defence of *Lutheran theology at a time when its distinctive elements were threatened by the movement for reuniting the two Protestant confessions in Prussia. On the third centenary of the outbreak of the Reformation (1817) he published, together with M. *Luther's 95 theses, 95 theses of his own directed to the quickening of Lutheran piety. They stressed the necessity of the forgiveness of sins and the importance of the Sacraments, and won the approval of Schleiermacher. His other writings include a *Pastoraltheologie* (1830) and collections of sermons.

Lebensbeschreibung verfasset von ihm selber ('Zweite Auflage', Kiel, 1851). *Ausgewählte Schriften und Predigten*, ed. P. Meinhold (2 vols., Flensburg, 1955). F. Wintzer, *Claus Harms: Predigt und Theologie* (Schriften des Vereins für Schleswig-Holsteinische Kirchengeschichte, Reihe 1, 21; 1965), with extensive bibl. H.-F. Traulsen, *Schleiermacher und Claus Harms: Von den Reden, 'Über die Religion' zur Nachfolge an der Dreifaltigkeitskirche* (Schleiermacher-Archiv, 7; 1989). L. Hein in *TRE* 14 (1985), pp. 447–9, s.v., with bibl.

Harnack, Adolf (1851–1930), German Church historian and theologian. He was the son of Theodosius Harnack (1817–89), professor of pastoral theology at Dorpat and the author of *Luthers Theologie* (2 vols., 1862–86). He studied at Dorpat and then at Leipzig, where he became Privatdozent (1874) and Extraordinary Prof. (1876). He later held full professorships at Giessen (1879–86), Marburg (1886–8), and Berlin (1888–1921). From 1905 to 1921 he was also Director of the Prussian Staatsbibliothek and in 1910 he became President of the 'Kaiser Wilhelm Gesellschaft' for furthering learning and science. He was ennobled in 1914.

In the range of his achievements Harnack was prob. the most outstanding *patristic scholar of his generation. He made himself complete master of the early Christian literature, esp. of the pre-Nicene period, and published innumerable contributions to its history. In conjunction with O. von Gebhardt, he founded the important series *Texte und Untersuchungen zur Geschichte der altchristlichen Literatur* (1882 ff.), very many of its papers being his own compositions or owing their inspiration to his enthusiasm. These extended historical studies formed the basis of his *Lehrbuch der Dogmengeschichte* (3 vols., 1886–9; Eng. tr. as *History of Dogma*, 7 vols., 1894–9), which traced the history of Christian doctrine down to the Reformation, with esp. attention to the earlier period. The work reflected throughout Harnack's theological standpoint (a form of *Ritschlianism); he regarded the metaphysics which came into Christian theology as an alien intrusion from Greek sources ('Hellenization'). This critical attitude to traditional Christian dogma evoked strong opposition from conservative theologians, who resisted, but without success, his call to Berlin. Here he became involved in a long controversy on the *Apostles' Creed, embodying his views in *Das apostolische Glaubensbekenntnis* (1892). In the winter of 1899–1900 he delivered a celebrated course of lectures stressing the moral side of Christianity, esp. the claims of human brotherhood, to the exclusion of all that was doctrinal. They were subsequently published as *Das Wesen des Christentums* (1900; Eng. tr., *What is Christianity?*, 1901) and attracted very wide attention. Meanwhile, Harnack pursued his historical studies with sustained energy, issuing, *inter alia, Die Geschichte der altchristlichen Literatur bis Eusebius* (3 vols., 1893–1904). Later he published a series of notable studies on the *Synoptic Problem, in which (to the surprise of friends and foes alike) he upheld very early dates for the Synoptic Gospels and *Acts, holding e.g. that Acts was written by St *Luke when St *Paul was still in his (first) Roman Captivity and assigning a very early date to '*Q'. These studies were embodied in *Beiträge zur Einleitung in das Neue Testament* (4 parts, 1906–11; Eng. tr. under separate titles, e.g. *Luke the Physician*, 1907; *The Sayings of Jesus*, 1908; *The Acts of the Apostles*, 1909). His other writings included *Die Mission und Ausbreitung des Christentums in den ersten drei Jahrhunderten* (1902; 4th edn., much enlarged, 1924; Eng. tr. by J. *Moffatt, from 1st edn., 2 vols., 1904–5), *Entstehung und Entwickelung der Kirchenverfassung* (1910; Eng. tr., 1910), *Marcion* (1921; 2nd edn., 1924), and *Briefsammlung des Apostels Paulus* (1926). With E. *Schürer he also founded the *Theologische Literaturzeitung* (1876 ff.).

Correspondence with K. *Holl ed. H. Karpp (Tübingen, 1966). Eng. tr. of extracts from his works ed. M. Rumscheidt (Makers of Modern Theology, 1989). Life by A. von Zahn-Harnack (Berlin, 1936; 2nd edn., 1951). J. de Ghellinck, SJ, *Patristique et moyen-âge*, 3 (1948), Étude 3, pp. 1–102. G. W. Glick, *The Reality of Christianity: A Study of Adolf von Harnack as Historian and Theologian* (1967); W. Pauck, *Harnack and Troeltsch* (New York, 1968), pp. 3–42; K. H. Neufeld, *Adolf von Harnack: Theologie als Suche nach der Kirche* (Paderborn, 1977); id., *Adolf Harnacks Konflikt mit der Kirche: Weg-Stationen zum 'Wesen des Christentums'* (Innsbrucker theologische Studien, 4; 1979); E. P. Meijering, *Die Hellenisierung des Christentums im Urteil Adolf von Harnacks* (Amsterdam, etc., 1985). J. C. O'Neill, *The Bible's Authority* (Edinburgh, 1991), pp. 214–29. Bibl. by F. Schmend (Leipzig, 1927; 3rd edn. by J. Dummer, 1990).

Harris, Howel(l) (1714–73), one of the founders of Welsh *Calvinistic Methodism. Born at Trevecca, near Brecon, he was intended for ordination in the Anglican Church. In 1735 he was converted to a life of great religious seriousness, and later in the year went up to St Mary's Hall, Oxford. Unable to settle, he returned to Powys within a week to begin an itinerant lay ministry, organizing his converts into religious 'societies'. Owing to personal and doctrinal differences with others within the Welsh Methodist movement, most notably Daniel Rowland (1713–90), the curate of Llangeitho, Cards, he was driven to separation from it in 1750. Shortly afterwards he established a religious community at Trevecca, and during the 1760s was involved in the establishment of the Countess of *Huntingdon's college at a nearby farm. He remained an Anglican throughout his life.

A Brief Account of the Life of Howell Harris, Esq., Extracted from Papers written by himself, To which is added a concise Collection of his Letters from the Year 1738 to 1772 [ed. B. La Trobe and E. Moses] (Trevecca, 1791). Correspondence pub. as 'The Trevecka Letters' in suppls. to the *Journal of the Calvinistic Methodist Historical Society*; Calendar by M. H. Jones (Carnarvon, 1932); selections also ed. G. M. Roberts (ibid., 1956 and 1962). Lives in Eng. by H. J. Hughes (London, 1892), H. E. Lewis (ibid. [1912]), G. T. Roberts (Wesley Historical Lecture no. 17; London, 1951), G. F. Nuttall (Cardiff, 1965), and E. Evans (ibid., 1974). R. Bennett, *The Dawn of Welsh Calvinistic Methodism* ([in Welsh, 1909]; Eng. tr. *The Early Life of Howell Harris*, 1962; repub. with rev. bibl. as *Howell Harris and the Dawn of Revival*, Bridgend, 1987). R. J. Jones in *DNB* 25 (1891), pp. 6 f.

Harris, James Rendel (1852–1941), biblical scholar and orientalist. He was brought up as a *Congregationalist, but later became a *Quaker. Educated at Plymouth Grammar School and Clare College, Cambridge, he taught in the USA (1882–92), at Cambridge (1893–1903), and at Woodbrooke Settlement, Birmingham (1903–18), and from 1918 to 1925 was Curator of MSS at the John Rylands Library, Manchester. Harris was the author of many studies on biblical and early Christian texts and on the Mediterranean cults. In 1889 he discovered at the St Catherine's Monastery on Mount *Sinai the Syriac text of the 'Apology' of *Aristides (pub. 1891); and in 1909 he issued the *editio princeps* of the Syriac text of the 'Odes of *Solomon'. His numerous other works include *Biblical Fragments from Mount Sinai* (1890), *The *Diatessaron* (1890), *Lectures on the Western Text of the NT* (1894), *The Teaching of the Apostles and the *Sibylline Books* (1885), *Testimonies* (1917; 1920). In collaboration with R. L. Bensly and F. C. *Burkitt he edited *The Four Gospels from the Syriac Palimpsest* (1894), and, with A. Mingana, a definitive edition of the 'Odes of Solomon' (2 vols., 1916–20). His writings reflect his unconventional and speculative mind, and immense, if at times somewhat unbalanced, erudition.

C. A. Phillips, 'Rendel Harris', *Expository Times*, 52 (1941), pp. 349–52. H. G. Wood in *DNB, 1941–1950*, pp. 360–62.

Harris, William Wadé (c.1860–1929), West African evangelist known as 'Prophet Harris'; the best-known of the early 20th-cent. leaders of African mass movements towards the Christian faith. He belonged to the Glebo people of Liberia and had some knowledge of the outside world, partly acquired as a seaman. Coming from a *Methodist background, in which he underwent a conversion experience when he was about 20, he was confirmed in the (American) *Episcopal Church and trained as a *catechist and schoolmaster. In 1910, while in prison for anti-government, pro-British political activity, he became convinced of his calling as a prophet of the last times. In the course of 17 months in 1913–15 he preached across the Ivory Coast, through to Axim in the Gold Coast (now *Ghana), and back again, proclaiming the coming judgement of Christ, calling on all to abandon the traditional fetishes and worship God alone. In Ivory Coast, where Christianity had hitherto made little impact, he baptized not less than 100,000 people; perhaps twice that number were deeply affected as a result of his activity. The French colonial authorities, frightened at his success, imprisoned, mistreated, and expelled him. His ministry was thereafter restricted to Liberia, with visits to *Sierra Leone. He died paralysed and in poverty.

White-robed, bearing a cross and a Bible, and accompanied by women singers, engaging readily in trials of strength with traditional priests and diviners, Harris conveyed a sense of immense spiritual power. Independent of the missions, and often alarming them, he encouraged converts to attend churches where they existed and appointed local leaders where they did not. The Methodist Church and the indigenous 'Harrist' Church can claim to be his acknowledged heirs, but his preaching laid a foundation for all the Churches, RC and Protestant, of Ivory Coast, and for many beyond it. See also GHANA, CHRISTIANITY IN.

W. J. Platt, *An African Prophet* (1934); G. M. Haliburton, *The Prophet Harris* (1971); S. S. Walker, *The Religious Revolution in the Ivory Coast: The Prophet Harris and the Harrist Church* (Chapel Hill, NC, 1983). Study by D. A. Shank in preparation. D. A. Shank, 'The Prophet Harris: a Historiographical and Bibliographical Survey', *Journal of Religion in Africa*, 14 (1983), pp. 130–60; id., 'The Legacy of William Wadé Harris', *International Bulletin of Missionary Research*, 10 (1986), pp. 170–6.

Harrison, Frederic (1831–1923), English *Positivist. Educated at Wadham College, Oxford, where he was elected a Fellow in 1854, he began to practise as a barrister-at-law in 1858. In his earlier years he was a member of the C of E, influenced by the school of F. D. *Maurice and also by H. P. *Liddon, a school friend with whom he kept up a friendship till Liddon's death; but he came gradually under the influence of A. *Comte, and embraced Positivism in 1870. From 1880 to 1905 he was president of the 'English Positivist Committee', and the recognized leader in England of that school of thought. Among his writings were *The Creed of a Layman* (1907), *The Philosophy of Common Sense* (1907), and *The Positive Evolution of Religion* (1912).

Autobiographic Memoirs (2 vols., London, 1911); A. Harrison (son), *Frederic Harrison: Thoughts and Memories* (1926). M. S. Vogeler, *Frederic Harrison: The Vocations of a Positivist* (Oxford, 1984). A. Cochrane in *DNB, 1922–1930*, pp. 406–8.

Harrowing of Hell. The medieval English term for the defeat of the powers of evil at the *Descent of Christ into Hell after His death. It was a favourite theme of art and drama in the Middle Ages.

Hartmann, Eduard von (1842–1906), German philosopher. Born at Berlin, in 1858 he became an artillery officer in the Prussian Guards, but owing to an affliction of the knee he was forced to resign in 1865, and resided at Berlin for the rest of his life.

The main outlines of his system, which owed much to the influence of G. W. F. *Hegel, A. *Schopenhauer, and F. W. J. *Schelling, were already contained in his early treatise on the 'Philosophy of the Unconscious' (*Die Philosophie des Unbewussten*, '1869', really Nov. 1868; Eng. tr. by W. C. Coupland, 1884). He saw in the 'Unconscious' an all-pervasive monistic principle which was at once will (*Wille*) and presentation (*Vorstellung*), and the ground of evolutionary development. Rejecting mechanism in favour of a teleological vitalism, he became a robust champion of progress, enlightenment, and practical activity, uniting his disciples in the service of 'Concrete Monism'. Christianity, which was only a stage along the way to the religion of Absolute Spirit, was now at length dead and its gravedigger was modern Protestantism. He found an enthusiastic disciple in A. *Drews (q.v.).

Among von Hartmann's other writings those of specially religious import were *Die Selbstzersetzung des Christentums und die Religion der Zukunft* (1874) and *Die Krisis des Christentums und die moderne Theologie* (1880).

There is a large lit., mainly in German. Überweg, 5, pp. 331–9, also pp. 707 f. with list of his writings and full bibl. to date. In Eng. D. N. K. Darnoi, *The Unconscious and Eduard von Hartmann: A Historico-Critical Monograph* (The Hague, 1967), with bibl. L. E. Loemker in P. Edwards (ed.), *The Encyclopedia of Philosophy*, 3 (1967), pp. 419–21, with select bibl.

Harvest Thanksgiving. In Britain an unofficial religious festival of thanksgiving for the fruits of the earth, usually observed on a Sunday in Sept. or Oct. after the ingathering of the harvest. In the C of E and Free Churches, and of recent times in the RC Church also, it is customary to decorate the church with fruit, flowers, and vegetables which are later devoted to charity; special hymns are sung; and there is frequently a visiting preacher. In medieval England *Lammas Day (1 Aug.) was prob. recognized as a thanksgiving for the first fruits of the harvest, bread made with the new wheat being offered at Mass and solemnly blessed. This last custom was revived by R. S. Hawker (1804–75) at Morwenstow, Cornwall, in 1843. Although no provision is made for any such observance in the BCP, special forms of thanksgiving for abundant harvests were occasionally authorized from the end of the 18th cent. By the mid 19th cent. an annual festival was common and a parochial thanksgiving replaced the traditional Harvest Home. In 1862 the Convocation of Canterbury issued a form of service. The proposed Revised Prayer Book of 1927–8 provided a Collect, to follow that of the day, and an Epistle and Gospel, while the ASB has a complete set of Collect, Psalms, and biblical lections for use at all services. Various other modern Anglican liturgies make similar provision. The American Prayer Book of 1789 already contained a form of thanksgiving for the fruits of the earth which was used on 'Thanksgiving Day' (a general holiday, since 1941 observed on the fourth Thursday in November).

H. C. Batterbury in *PBD* (1912), pp. 377 f., s.v. 'Harvest Festival'.

Hase, Karl August von (1800–90), German Church historian. After teaching for a short time at Tübingen and Leipzig, he held a professorship at Jena from 1830 till 1883. In 1829 he published a Life of Christ in which the supernatural elements in the Gospels were rationalized. His *Kirchengeschichte* (1st edn., 1834) long remained a standard work.

Gesammelte Werke, ed. G. Krüger and others (12 vols., Leipzig, 1890–93). R. Bürkner, *Karl von Hase* (ibid., 1900). G. Krüger in *PRE* (3rd edn.), 7 (1899), pp. 453–61, s.v.

Hasidaeans. The Greek form ('Ασιδαῖοι) of the Heb. '*Chasidim' (q.v.), found e.g. in 1 Macc. 2: 42.

Hasmonaeans. The family name of the *Maccabees, apparently derived from one of their ancestors.

Hastings, James (1852–1922), *Presbyterian divine and editor of religious encyclopaedic works. Educated at the grammar school, the university, and the Free Church

Divinity College at Aberdeen, he was ordained a Presbyterian minister in 1884, and appointed pastor of Kinneff, Grampian, Free Church. From 1897 to 1901 he was pastor of Willison Church, Dundee, and from 1901 to 1911 of the United Free Church, St Cyrus, Grampian, after which he retired to Aberdeen. In 1889 he founded the monthly *Expository Times*, which he edited until his death. He is famous as the editor of the *Dictionary of the Bible* (5 vols., 1898–1904; 1-vol. edn., 1909; rev. by F. C. Grant and H. H. Rowley, 1963), the *Encyclopaedia of Religion and Ethics* (12 vols., 1908–21; Index vol., 1926), the *Dictionary of Christ and the Gospels* (2 vols., 1906–8), and the *Dictionary of the Apostolic Church* (2 vols., 1915–18).

Arts. by H. E. *Ryle, W. A. Curtis, and H. R. *Mackintosh in *Expository Times*, 34 (1922–3), pp. 102–6. E. R. Micklem in *DNB, 1922–1930*, pp. 409 f.

Hat, Cardinal's. See RED HAT.

Hatch, Edwin (1835–89), Anglican divine. Educated at Pembroke College, Oxford, he taught in Canada before becoming vice-principal of St Mary Hall, Oxford (1867), rector of Purleigh, Essex (1883), and reader in ecclesiastical history at Oxford (1884). In 1880 he preached a series of *Bampton Lectures on *The Organization of the Early Christian Churches* (1881) in which he maintained that the origin of the Christian episcopate lay in the ἐπίσκοποι or financial administrators of Greek religious associations. Of his other writings, the most important was his *Hibbert Lectures for 1888 on *The Influence of Greek Ideas and Usages on the Christian Church* (1890). At the time of his death he was engaged on a *Concordance to the *Septuagint* (subsequently completed by H. A. Redpath, 1897, with supplement, 1906).

S. C. Hatch (ed.), *Memorials of E. Hatch* (1890). W. *Sanday, 'In Memoriam Dr. Edwin Hatch', *The Expositor*, 4th ser. 1 (1890), pp. 93–111. N. F. Josaitis, *Edwin Hatch and Early Church Order* (Recherches et Synthèses, Section d'Histoire, 3; Gembloux [1971]). W. Sanday in *DNB* 25 (1891), pp. 149 f.

Hatfield, Council of (679). The Council arose out of the wish of Pope *Agatho to sound the English Church on the subject of *Monothelitism. As his intermediary the Pope chose John, Precentor of St Peter's, whom St *Benedict Biscop had brought back with him from Rome to instruct his monks at *Wearmouth in singing. The Council, which met under the presidency of Abp. *Theodore at Hatfield (or ? Heathfield), repudiated Monothelitism, accepted the decrees of the first five General Councils, and affirmed its belief in the *Double Procession of the Holy Spirit.

*Bede, *HE* 4. 17 f.; see comm. by J. M. Wallace-Hadrill (Oxford, 1988), pp. 157–9, with useful refs. A. W. Haddan and W. *Stubbs (eds.), *Councils and Ecclesiastical Documents Relating to Great Britain and Ireland*, 3 (1871), pp. 141–60. C. Cubitt, *Anglo-Saxon Church Councils c.630–c.850* (1995), esp. pp. 252–8. W. *Bright, *Chapters of Early English Church History* (1878), pp. 316–22. Hefele and Leclercq, 3 (pt. 1; 1909), pp. 475–84.

Hauck, Albert (1845–1918), German *Lutheran historian. He held professorships at Erlangen from 1878 to 1889 and at Leipzig from 1889. Of his writings, the most considerable was his *Kirchengeschichte Deutschlands* (5 vols., 1887–1920). He was at first joint editor (1880), and from

the death of J. J. *Herzog in 1882 sole editor, of the 2nd edition of the Herzog–Plitt *Realencyklopädie* (completed 1888); and he also edited the 3rd edition (1896–1913), cited as *PRE* in this dictionary.

Geschichtliche Studien A. Hauck zum 70. Geburtstage dargebracht (1916). List of his works by E. Hauck in *ZKG* 54 (1935), pp. 565–75, with further refs. K. Nowak in *TRE* 14 (1985), pp. 472–4, s v., with bibl.

Hauranne, Jean Duvergier de. See SAINT-CYRAN.

Havergal, Frances Ridley (1836–79), hymn-writer. She was the daughter of William Henry Havergal (1793–1870), the writer of much sacred music. Endowed with remarkable ability for composing verse, she contributed many poems and hymns to *Good Words* and other religious periodicals. Some of these have found their way into most hymnals, e.g. 'Take my life and let it be'.

Memorials of F.R.H., by her sister M. V. G. Havergal (1880). Other studies by T. H. Darlow (London, 1927, with substantial extracts of her work) and J. Grierson (Bromsgrove, 1979).

Hawkins, Edward (1789–1882), Provost of Oriel College, Oxford. Elected a Fellow of Oriel in 1813, he became Vicar of St Mary's, Oxford, in 1823, and Provost of Oriel in 1828. From 1847 to 1861 he was also (the first) Dean *Ireland Professor of the Interpretation of Holy Scripture. His sermon on Tradition (1818), urging that Scripture was intended to *prove* doctrine, not to *teach* it, had a profound influence on J. H. *Newman, then an undergraduate of Trinity. Later he developed the same subject in his *Bampton Lectures (1840). As a *High Churchman, he was influential in weaning Newman from his early *Evangelicalism and Newman supported Hawkins rather than J. *Keble for the Provostship of Oriel. Relations worsened, however, when Hawkins, suspicious of Newman's influence, in 1830 stopped him, R. H. *Froude, and R. I. *Wilberforce receiving tutorial pupils. In retrospect Newman saw this decision as paradoxically freeing him to give his energies to the *Tractarian cause. In 1841 Hawkins drew up the condemnation of Tract 90 by the Oxford Heads of Houses. In 1874 he withdrew to *Rochester, where he continued to hold the canonry until then attached to the provostship of Oriel.

J. W. *Burgon, *Lives of Twelve Good Men*, 1 (1888), 4, 'The Great Provost', pp. 374–465. W. A. Greenhill in *DNB* 25 (1891), pp. 208 f.

Haymo of Faversham (d. 1244), English *Franciscan friar. Born at Faversham in Kent, he became a Master of Divinity at Paris and, prob. in 1226, he entered the Order of Friars Minor. Soon afterwards he returned to England and lectured at *Oxford. In 1230 the General Chapter at *Assisi sent him as one of the deputies to *Gregory IX to seek an official explanation of the rule. In 1233 he was sent on a mission to *Constantinople to negotiate a reunion with the E. Church. He took a leading part in the deposition of Brother *Elias, which finally took place at the General Chapter of the Order at Rome in 1239. At that Chapter he became Provincial of the English Province; in 1240 he was elected General of the Order. At his request the 'Expositio Regulae Quatuor Magistorum' was written by the Four Masters of Paris (1241–2). He died at Anagni.

Among his surviving works are an order for private and conventual Mass on ferias ('Indutus planeta'), presented at the Chapter of *Bologna in 1243, and notes for a ceremonial ('Ordinationes Divini Officii'; 'Ad Omnes Horas'). At the behest of *Innocent IV, in 1243–4 he revised the *ordinals for the Roman Breviary, Missal, and *grace before and after meals.

Works ed. S. J. P. van Dijk, OFM, *The Sources of the Modern Roman Liturgy* (Studia et Documenta Franciscana, 1–2; Leiden, 1963), 2, pp. 1–331, with introd. 1, pp. 1–109 and 156–206. *Ordines* [also ed. id.] (HBS 85; 1959). R. B. Brooke, *Early Franciscan Government: Elias to Bonaventure* (Cambridge, 1959), esp. pp. 195–209. C. L. Kingsford in *DNB* 25 (1891), p. 299. Antoine de Sérent, OFM, in *DHGE* 1 (1912), cols. 1192–4, s.v. 'Aimon (14) de Faversham', with bibl.

Headlam, Arthur Cayley (1862–1947), Bp. of *Gloucester.

He was born at Whorlton, Durham, and educated at Winchester and New College, Oxford. Ordained priest in 1889, he was successively Fellow of All Souls (1885), Rector of Welwyn (1896), Professor of Dogmatic Theology at *King's College, London (1903), Regius Professor of Divinity at Oxford (1918), and Bp. of Gloucester (1923–45). A Central Churchman who disliked all ecclesiastical parties (*Anglo-Catholics, *Evangelicals, and *Modernists), he was one of the most influential of English prelates in the inter-war period. In his early years he devoted his attention esp. to NT problems, collaborating with W. *Sanday in his fine commentary on *Romans (1895) and contributing extensively to J. *Hastings's *Dictionary of the Bible* (4 vols., 1898–1902). His *Bampton Lectures, *The Doctrine of the Church and Christian Reunion* (1920), written with the forthcoming *Lambeth Conference in view, endeavoured to provide an ecclesiological basis for reunion between the C of E and other religious bodies. His other writings include *St Paul and Christianity* (1913), *The Life and Teaching of Jesus the Christ* (1923), *Christian Theology* (1934), and *The Fourth Gospel as History* (1948, posthumous; with biographical essay by Agnes Headlam-Morley).

Life and Letters by R. C. D. Jasper (London, 1960). A. T. P. Williams in *DNB, 1941–1950* (1959), pp. 369–71.

Hearne, Thomas (1678–1735), English antiquary.

The son of a parish clerk, he was born at Littlefield Green, Berks, and educated in *Nonjuring principles by Francis Cherry and H. *Dodwell. In 1695 he entered St Edmund Hall, Oxford. Here his close scholarly habits attracted the attention of the principal, John *Mills (d. 1707), and for some years Hearne collated MSS and held appointments in the *Bodleian Library. Refusing to take the oath to George I in 1716, he was deprived of his post in the Bodleian, and, though denied access to libraries, continued his medieval studies in Oxford, intransigent politically until his death. He produced over 40 learned volumes, including several editions of classical writers (Pliny, Eutropius, Livy, etc.) and esp. medieval authors (Chronicles, works on *Glastonbury, etc.). He also left 140 MS notebooks, now preserved in the Bodleian. Though at times uncritical, his meticulous accuracy in transcribing authorities makes his works valuable for reference. His diaries, published posthumously, contain intimate and often malicious comment on contemporary life in Oxford.

The Life of Mr. Thomas Hearne . . . from his own MS. Copy (Oxford, 1772). P. Bliss (ed.), *Reliquiae Hearnianae* (2 vols., 1867; abridged edn. by J. Buchanan-Brown, 1966). *Remains and Collections of Thomas Hearne*, ed. C. E. Doble, D. W. Rannie, H. E. Salter, and others (Oxford Historical Society, 2, 7, 13, 34, 42, 43, 48, 50, 65, 67, and 72; 1885–1921). P. Ouvry (ed.), *Letters Addressed to Thomas Hearne* (1874). *Impartial Memorials of the Life and Writings of Thomas Hearne . . . By Several Hands* (1736). W. D. Macray, *Annals of the Bodleian Library, Oxford* (1868; 2nd edn., 1890), *passim*; D. C. Douglas, *English Scholars* (1939), ch. 9, pp. 226–48; 2nd edn. (1951), pp. 178–94. H. R. Luard in *DNB* 25 (1891), pp. 335–8.

hearse. (1) Formerly **herse** (med. Lat. *hercia*). A triangular frame on a stand, holding 15 candles, formerly used at *Tenebrae in Holy Week, the candles being extinguished one by one during the service. There is also an obsolete use of the word for the triple candlestick formerly used in the *Holy Saturday rite.

(2) Various funeral furnishings. The current use of the word is for the carriage bearing the coffin, but it is also found for a *catafalque, or framework (permanent or temporary) bearing lighted tapers about a coffin.

heart (Heb. לֵבָב or לֵב, Gk. καρδία). In the Bible it usually designates the whole personality, though, in contrast to modern usage, the emphasis is on the activities of reason and will rather than the emotions. Both in the OT and NT it is the seat of wisdom (1 Kgs. 3: 12), and of thought and reflection (e.g. Jer. 24: 7, Lk. 2: 19), the instrument of belief (Rom. 10: 10) and of will, the principle of action (Ex. 35: 21) which may be hardened so that it resists God (Deut. 15: 7; Mk. 16: 14). It is the principle both of virtues and vices, of humility (Mt. 11: 29) and pride (Deut. 17: 20), of good thoughts (Lk. 6: 45) and of evil thoughts (Mt. 15: 19). Hence in Scripture the heart is the centre of the human person, in which the physical and the spiritual life are concentrated, and therefore in the NT the dwelling-place of Christ (Eph. 3: 17) in which reigns the peace of God (Col. 3: 15). In this sense it is used in the language of Christian spirituality, which regards the human heart as the special organ of the love of God; and it is here that is to be found the inspiration of the modern devotion to the *Sacred Heart of Jesus (q.v.).

H. W. Wolff, *Anthropologie des Alten Testaments* (Munich [1973]), pp. 68–95; Eng. tr. (1974), pp. 40–58. J. Baumgärtel and J. Behm in *TWNT* 3 (1938), pp. 609–16 (Eng. tr., 3, 1966, pp. 605–14), s.v. καρδία.

Heart of Jesus. See SACRED HEART.

Heaven. In Christian theology the dwelling-place of God and the angels, and ultimately of all the redeemed, wherein they receive their eternal reward.

In OT language the word 'heaven' or 'heavens' denotes the visible sky and also the abode of God, conceived as in or beyond the physical heavens, where, for example, Jacob saw Him in a dream (Gen. 28: 12 f.) and whence He could 'come down' upon the top of Mt. Sinai (Exod. 19: 18–20, cf. 20: 22); but it was also acknowledged that 'the heaven and heaven of heavens cannot contain' God (1 Kgs. 8: 27), who is omnipresent (Ps. 139: 8–10). In the NT heaven as God's dwelling-place is still conceived as high above the earth: thus Christ raised His eyes 'to heaven' in prayer

(Mk. 6: 41, Jn. 17: 1), and at His *Ascension seemed to the disciples to pass away from them upwards to heaven. The early Christians accepted the contemporary Jewish and Hellenistic conceptions of a series of heavens (cf. 2 Cor. 12: 2–4), together with that of angelic and demonic powers existing in the heavens (e.g. Eph. 6: 12, RV; cf. Rom. 8: 38 f.), over whom Christ since His Resurrection and Ascension reigns supreme with the Father 'far above all heavens' (Eph. 4: 10).

Whereas in Hebrew thought only exceptional human beings (esp. *Enoch and *Elijah) were conceived as being raised to heaven after this life, for Christians it was the distinctive Christian hope and belief that the faithful disciple, through Christ's victory over death, would eventually reign with Him in glory. On the one hand, this might be thought of as attained in the *Kingdom of God at the end of history, when Christ would descend from heaven and the dead would either be raised and caught up to meet Him (1 Thess. 4: 15–17) or enjoy a new life on earth (see MILLENARIANISM). On the other hand, as St Paul implies when he says that for him to die is to be with Christ (Phil. 1: 23), it was also believed that even before the general resurrection some at least of the redeemed would be with Christ, i.e. in heaven. Acc. to Catholic doctrine, these are the souls who, having died in a state of grace and been purged of their stains in *purgatory, have passed to heaven, where they enjoy perfect bliss; but, except for the Bl Virgin *Mary (see ASSUMPTION), these souls still await reunion with their bodies at the general *resurrection of the dead, after which both body and soul together will enjoy the life of heaven eternally. Some modern RC theologians, however, have suggested that this teaching involves an invalid extrapolation of the notion of time; they hold that, while it is not until the general resurrection that bodies and souls are reunited, it does not follow that there is a 'period' of bodiless existence in heaven corresponding with the interval between death and resurrection on the earthly time-scale. Catholic theology regards heaven as 'a place' but claims no knowledge of its spatial characteristics or its relation to the physical universe, stressing rather the essential quality of the life of heaven which consists in the enjoyment of the *Beatific Vision (q.v.). Virtually all Christians, while making greater or lesser reservations in regard to details, would agree that heaven is essentially the fulfilment, to a degree impossible on earth, of what is, acc. to the Shorter Catechism of the *Westminster Assembly, the 'chief end of man', that is, 'to glorify God, and to enjoy Him for ever'.

H. Bietenhard, *Die himmlische Welt im Urchristentum und Spätjudentum* (Wissenschaftliche Untersuchungen zum Neuen Testamentum, 2; 1951), U. Simon, *Heaven in the Christian Tradition* (1958); C. Rowland, *The Open Heaven: A Study of Apocalyptic in Judaism and Early Christianity* (1982); J. D. Tabor, *Things Unutterable: Paul's Ascent to Paradise in its Greco-Roman, Judaic, and Early Christian Contexts* (Lanham, Md., and London [1986]); C. McDannell and B. Lang, *Heaven: A History* (New Haven, Conn., and London, 1988).

hebdomadarian (Gk. ἑβδομάς, 'a period of seven days'). In cathedral churches and monasteries, the priest who presides at the Eucharist and Divine Office. He was so named because he held office for a week.

Heber, Reginald (1783–1826), Bp. of Calcutta. He was educated at Brasenose College, Oxford, and in 1805 elected a Fellow of All Souls. In 1807, on his return from a long tour in Europe, he was ordained and at once became vicar of Hodnet in Salop. In 1815 he delivered a course of *Bampton Lectures on *The Personality and Office of the Christian Comforter*. In 1823 he accepted the bishopric of Calcutta. In his short episcopate he laboured hard for the spread of Christianity in his large diocese and beyond. He is best remembered for his hymns, which include 'Brightest and best of the sons of the morning', 'Holy, holy, holy, Lord God Almighty', and 'From Greenland's icy mountains', while his prose works include a Life and edition of the writings of Jeremy *Taylor (1822).

His Journal of 1824–6, ed. by his widow, A. Heber (2 vols., 1828); Selections, with introd., ed. M. A. Laird, *Bishop Heber in Northern India* (Cambridge, 1971). A. Heber (widow), *The Life of Reginald Heber* (2 vols., 1830), incl. selections of correspondence and unpub. works. Some of his letters are also incl. in R. H. Cholmondeley (ed.), *The Heber Letters 1783–1832* (1950). Later Lives by G. Smith (London, 1895) and D. Hughes (Worthing, Sussex, 1986). J. H. Overton in *DNB* 25 (1891), pp. 355–7.

Hebrew (people). The Hebrews, the inhabitants of Palestine, who entered the land with the *Patriarchs and *Moses, generally spoke of themselves as the Israelites (בְּנֵי יִשְׂרָאֵל, *b'ne Yisrael*, 'the Sons of Israel', Gen. 32: 28, 35: 10). The term 'Hebrew' was largely used of them by other peoples, often with a shade of contempt (cf. esp. Gen. 43: 32, 1 Sam. 13: 19 f.). It disappeared with the rise of the monarchy.

The word 'Hebrew' (עִבְרִי, *'ibhrî*) was derived by popular Hebrew etymology from the root עבר, *'br*, 'to go over', 'to cross', with the meaning that *Abraham came from the other side of the Euphrates (cf. Josh. 24: 2 f.), but the real etymology of the word is uncertain. Similar words in the related languages seem to indicate at first an ethnic group and later a menial social class. It was only in Israel that the ethnic significance continued under the impulse of the new religious nationalism begun by Moses.

Hebrew (tongue). The language in which practically all the OT was written. It belongs to the NW division of the Semitic group of languages, so called by J. G. *Eichhorn because they were spoken by the races sprung from Noah's eldest son Shem (Gen. 9: 18, 26 f.; 10: 21–31). In the OT it is called the 'lip (i.e. speech) of Canaan' (Is. 19: 18) or the 'Jewish (language)' (2 Kgs. 18: 26); and in the NT 'Hebrew' may denote either classical Hebrew (e.g. Rev. 9: 11; 16: 16) or the colloquial Aramaic dialect of Palestine (e.g. Jn. 5: 2, 19: 13, 17).

The earliest attested forms of NW Semitic are preserved in cuneiform texts from Ebla (3rd millennium BC) and in Canaanite words which were incorporated in Egyptian texts (from the 2nd millennium BC onwards), while the Canaanite glosses in the letters from *Tell el-Amarna and the language of the *Ras Shamra tablets (both 14th cent. BC), are quite close to the archaic Hebrew in the early poems of the OT, such as Jgs. 5. Classical Hebrew first appears in a calendar engraved on a stone from Gezer (*c.*10th cent. BC). Hebrew continued to be used as a spoken and written language after the classical period, and is found in texts from *Qumran and in the *Mishnah; it survived as a written language to the present day, when it has also been revived as the official language of the state of Israel. In the NT period, spoken Hebrew had largely (but not entirely) been replaced by *Aramaic.

The surviving vocabulary of classical Hebrew is small, containing perhaps only some 7,000–8,000 words, many of them occurring only once or in set phrases of which the exact sense is not always clear. The absence of any surviving literature apart from the OT, except for a few brief inscriptions such as the Gezer calendar, often makes interpretation difficult. The student of the OT, therefore, unless the sense can be recovered from the ancient versions (themselves often incorrect or obscure) must often have recourse to the sister languages to discover the meaning of an otherwise unknown Hebrew word. Medieval Jewish commentators and European scholars from the 17th cent. onwards used Arabic for this purpose; modern scholars have also drawn on Aramaic, Syriac, Ethiopic, Assyrian, and Babylonian texts, and more recently on Ugaritic. Even so, the vocabulary of the classical language is preserved only in the OT, and countless words once in regular daily use have disappeared completely.

Hebrew style is simple and direct, and paratactic rather than syntactic—that is, dependent clauses are normally connected by 'and', as in 'keep my commandments and live', instead of 'if thou keepest my commandments, thou shalt live' (Prov. 7: 2). Poetry is distinguished from prose by the parallelism of ideas in the two halves of a verse, as was discovered by R. *Lowth, and by the number of units of sense (not of syllables) in each half of the verse, as was elucidated by K. *Budde. An illustration here is the so-called *qînah* or 'falling rhythm' characteristic of Lamentations, in which the verses consist of three beats followed by two.

The earliest Hebrew was written in a form of the ancient Phoenician script, running from right to left, which was also the ancestor of the Greek alphabet and ultimately of our own. During the *Babylonian captivity (c.586–c.538 BC), this gave way to an Aramaizing form of the same script, popularly ascribed to *Ezra, from which the modern so-called 'Assyrian' or 'square' script was developed. This is used in the Hebrew texts found near the *Dead Sea (prob. 3rd cent. BC–1st cent. AD), although the archaic script was revived as propaganda on *Maccabean coins and sporadically in the Scrolls. This alphabet consisted of 22 signs for the consonants, while the vowels were originally unrepresented. The absence of signs for vowels caused considerable confusion: e.g. the LXX misread *pehām* 'coals of fire' (at Ps. 11: 6) as *pahim* 'snares'. In early Hebrew inscriptions, certain consonants began to be used for vowels—e.g. *w* (ו) was inserted for *ū*, and *y* (י) for *ī* (especially at the end of words), and this system was later extended to cover other vowels such as *ō* or *ē*. As knowledge of the classical language died out, however, elaborate systems indicating the vowels by strokes and/or dots above or within or below the consonantal signs were developed and reached their highest point in the Tiberian and Babylonian systems in the 5th–8th centuries AD. The former, the more elaborate, has survived in modern Hebrew Bibles, while the latter, in which the signs are exclusively superlinear, is found in MSS of the Aramaic *Targums and in Yemenite Bibles.

In the Calendar from Gezer one or two clauses are separated by vertical strokes, but otherwise both clauses and words run on undivided. In the inscription from Siloam (c.700 BC) all the words are separated by dots. Thereafter dots are common but not universal. In the Scrolls from Qumran words are separated by short spaces, while paragraphs and chapters (though not always the same as in the *Massoretic text) are clearly defined by spaces of varying length.

The standard Eng. dict. is that of F. Brown, S. R. *Driver, and C. A. *Briggs (Oxford, 1906; corrected repr., 1952); this was based on the classic work of W. *Gesenius (q.v.), esp. the 12th edn. by F. Buhl (Leipzig, 1895). A more recent (Ger.) dict. is that of L. Koehler and W. Baumgartner (Leiden, 1953; suppl., 1958; 3rd edn., 4 vols., 1967–90; Eng. tr., Leiden, etc., 1994 ff.). New dict., including material from the Dead Sea Scrolls, ed. D. J. A. Clines (Sheffield, 1993 ff.). The basic work on Hebrew grammar is that of W. Gesenius (Halle, 1813; 22nd edn. by E. Kautzsch, 1878; Eng. tr. of 28th edn. by A. E. Cowley, 1910). Other grammars by P. Joüon, SJ (Rome, 1923; repr. with corrections, 1965) and G. Beer (2 vols., Berlin, 1915–16; ed. R. Meyer, 1952–5; 3rd edn., under the name of R. Meyer only, 4 vols., 1966–72). Introductory grammars by J. Weingreen (Oxford, 1939; 2nd edn., 1959) and T. O. Lambdin, *Introduction to Biblical Hebrew* (New York [1971]; London, 1973). On syntax: A. B. *Davidson, *Hebrew Syntax* (Edinburgh, 1894; 4th edn. by J. C. L. Gibson, 1994); C. Brockelmann, *Hebräische Syntax* (Neukirchen, 1956); and R. J. Williams, *Hebrew Syntax* (Toronto [1967]; 2nd edn. [1976]). On spelling: F. M. Cross and D. N. Freedman, *Early Hebrew Orthography* (American Oriental Series, 36; New Haven, Conn., 1952), and J. Barr, *The Variable Spellings of the Hebrew Bible* (Schweich Lectures, 1986; Oxford, 1989). On the comparative grammar of Heb. and other Semitic languages: G. Bergsträsser, *Einführung in die semitischen Sprachen* (Munich, 1928; Eng. tr. with notes and bibl. by P. T. Daniels, Winona Lake, Ind. [1983]); S. Moscati and others, *An Introduction to the Comparative Grammar of the Semitic Languages* (Porta Linguarum Orientalium, NS 6; Wiesbaden, 1964); and J. Barr, *Comparative Philology and the Text of the Old Testament* (Oxford, 1968). General surveys by C. Rabin, 'Hebrew', *Current Trends in Linguistics*, 6 (The Hague and Paris, 1970), pp. 304–46; J. Barr, 'Semitic Philology and the Interpretation of the Old Testament', in G. W. Anderson (ed.), *Tradition and Interpretation* (Oxford, 1979), pp. 31–64; E. Y. Kutscher, *A History of the Hebrew Language* (posthumous, ed. R. Kutscher, Jerusalem and Leiden, 1982); and A. Sáenz-Badillos, *Historia de la Lengua Hebrea* (Sadabell, 1988; Eng. tr., Cambridge, 1993).

Hebrews, Epistle to the.

Traditionally included among the letters of St *Paul, this Ep., unlike most others in the NT, does not contain the name of the writer or that of those addressed. In content it resembles a homily, though it has an epistolary close (13: 18–25). The traditional title (πρὸς Ἑβραίους), though found in the earliest MSS, is prob. an inference from its contents.

The Ep. asserts with emphasis the finality of the Christian dispensation and its superiority to that of the Old Covenant, as a dissuasive, apparently from any return to Judaism, but possibly from apostasy in general. Christ is God's Son, the 'effulgence of his glory' (1: 3, RV), the unique and supreme messenger from God to mankind (chs. 1, 2), and hence the Gospel demands unhesitating acceptance (3: 1–4: 13). Christ, moreover, is our High Priest, whose priesthood, unlike that of the Levitical (Aaronic) priests, is eternal (4: 14–6: 20). It is a priesthood 'after the order of *Melchizedek' (6: 20, cf. Ps. 110: 4), who was greater than *Abraham (Gen. 14: 18 ff.) and was thus *a fortiori* greater than the Levitical priests. In contrast to the repeated sacrifices of the Old Covenant, the Atonement in Christ is eternal. This New Covenant, which, as foretold by Jer. 31: 31–4, was to supersede the temporary covenant of the Old Dispensation, was made, acc. to Ps. 40: 6–8, by the perfect obedience offered by Christ to God (7: 1–10: 18). With these facts before them, the readers are encouraged to steadfastness, perseverance, watchfulness for the Coming of Christ, and to greater faith, of which a long roll of historic examples is cited (10. 19–11. 40). The Ep. concludes with particular ethical instructions and messages (chs. 12 f.).

From an early date the Ep. was received at *Alexandria as Pauline, whether considered as a translation by St *Luke from St Paul's Hebrew (*Clement of Alexandria, ap. *Eusebius, *HE* 6. 14), or as St Paul's in substance, but committed to writing by someone else (*Origen ap. Eusebius, *HE* 6. 24); while in the E. generally, e.g. by the Council of *Antioch (264) and the later E. Fathers, it was regularly quoted as St Paul's own composition. In the W. it was known to *Clement of Rome (*Ad Cor.* 36. 1–5; cf. Heb. 1: 1–13), but it was not quoted as Pauline or as certainly canonical before the 4th–5th cent. The Council of *Trent (sess. 4, 1546) affirmed its canonicity but not its Pauline authorship; but the RC *Biblical Commission ruled (1914) that it was in substance St Paul's. Modern scholars, however, almost unanimously consider that the internal evidence marks it as non-Pauline, while its style shows that it is unlikely to be a translation. The author and his intended readers were apparently thoroughly familiar with Jewish worship and the latter were perhaps converts from Judaism. But there are indications that this familiarity came through the biblical ordinances (e.g. those concerning the *Tabernacle) rather than through direct knowledge of the *Temple itself (destroyed AD 70), and it has been argued (on the basis of 6: 1 f.) that the recipients of the Ep. were Gentiles. We learn that the author was a contemporary of *Timothy (13: 23), temporarily absent from those whom he was addressing, and expecting to return to them (13: 19). His identification with *Barnabas (*Tertullian and certain modern scholars), *Apollos (M. *Luther, C. Spicq, and H. W. Montefiore), or others (e.g. *Priscilla by A. *Harnack) cannot be more than conjectural. The use of the Ep. by Clement of Rome and the delay in the W. (as compared with the E.) in accepting it into the *Canon (supposedly because there was here a genuine tradition of its non-Pauline authorship; so A. *Loisy, followed by A. H. McNeile), together with the ref. to Italy in 13: 24, have suggested to some scholars that the Ep. was originally connected with Rome. In that case 10: 32–4 might allude to the *Neronian persecution. On general grounds and because there is no unequivocal reference to the destruction of the Temple in AD 70, a date earlier than that has been supported by several scholars, e.g. B. F. *Westcott and J. A. T. *Robinson; the majority, however, argue for a date under *Domitian. Its theological teaching, notably on the Person of Christ (1: 1–14, etc.), His real Humanity and sinlessness (4: 14 f.), His heavenly Priesthood and the Sacrifice of Calvary (7: 24 ff., etc.), as well as its literary capacity and expository power, reach a level unsurpassed in the NT. But the circumstances of its composition and its authorship remain obscure.

Modern comm. incl. those by B. F. Westcott (London, 1889), C. Spicq, OP (Études Bibliques, 1952–3), J. Héring (Commentaire du Nouveau Testament, 12; 1954; Eng. tr., 1970), H. [W.] Montefiore (Black's NT Comm., 1964), F. F. Bruce (New London Comm. on the NT, 1964), J. H. Davies (Camb. Bib., NEB, 1967), G. Theissen (Studien zum Neuen Testaments, 2; Gütersloh [1969]), G. W. Buchanan (Anchor Bible, 1972), P. E. Hughes (Grand Rapids, Mich. [1977]), H. Braun (Hb. NT, 14; 1984), R. Mc. L. Wilson (New Cent. Bib., 1987), H. W. Attridge (Hermeneia; Philadelphia, [1989]), and H.-F. Weiss (KEK 13, 15th edn.; 1991). Studies on the theology of the Ep. by G. Milligan (Edinburgh, 1899), W. Manson (Baird Lecture for 1949; 1950), and M. Rissi (Wissenschaftliche Untersuchungen zum Neuen Testament, 41; Tübingen [1987]). A. Nairne, *The Epistle of Priesthood* (1913). A. Harnack, 'Probabilia über die Adresse und den Verfasser des Hebräerbriefs', *ZNTW* 1 (1900), pp. 16–41. E. Käsemann, *Das wandernde Gottesvolk: Eine Untersuchungen zum Hebräerbrief* (Forschungen zur Religion und Literatur des Alten und Neuen Testaments, 55; 1939; 2nd edn., 1957; Eng. tr., Minneapolis [1984]). A. Vanhoye, SJ, *La Structure littéraire de l'Épître aux Hébreux* (1963). R. A. Greer, *The Captain of our Salvation: A Study in the Patristic Exegesis of Hebrews* (Beiträge zur Geschichte der biblischen Exegese, 15; 1973). G. Hughes, *Hebrews and Hermeneutics: The Epistle to the Hebrews as a New Testament Example of Biblical Interpretation* (Society for New Testament Studies, Monograph Series, 36; Cambridge, 1979); D. Peterson, *Hebrews and Perfection* (ibid. 47; 1982). Kümmel, pp. 388–403. C. Spicq, OP, in *Dict. Bibl.*, Suppl. 7 (1966), cols. 226–79, s.v. 'Paul (Épîtres attribuées à saint), 5. Hébreux (Épître aux)', with bibl.

Hebrews, Gospel according to the. An *apocryphal Gospel in use among Jewish Christians, also called the 'Gospel of the Hebrews' and the 'Hebrew Gospel'. It is mentioned by *Clement of Alexandria and cited by *Origen. *Epiphanius seems to identify it with the 'Gospel according to the *Ebionites', *Jerome with the Aramaic Gospel used by the *Nazarenes, while *Eusebius seems to regard it as an independent work. Jerome, who claims that he himself translated it into Latin and Greek, also reports that it was composed in *Aramaic speech written in Hebrew letters and that some regarded it as the original version of St *Matthew's Gospel. The surviving fragments contain an account of the appearance of the Risen Christ to St *James ('the Lord's brother') and Dominical sayings not recorded in the canonical Gospels (e.g. 'Never be glad, except when you look upon your brother in love', 'He that wonders shall reign, and he that has reigned shall rest'). There is no agreement among scholars as to the relationship between the various Jewish Christian Gospels, or about their relationship to the heretical 'Gospel of the Twelve' mentioned by Origen. The 'Gospel of the Hebrews' seems to be independent of the canonical Gospels and may preserve traditions of historical value.

Clement of Alexandria, *Strom.* 2. 9. 45; Origen, *in Jn.* 2. 12; Eusebius, *HE* 3. 25. 5; 3. 27. 4; 3. 39. 17; 4. 22. 8; Epiphanius, *Haer.* 30; Jerome, *de vir. ill.* 2 f.; *Comm. in Eph.* 3 (on 5: 4); *in Mic.* 2 (on 7: 6); *in Isaiam*, 18 prol.; *Dial. adv. Pelag.* 3. 2. Frags. collected in M. J. *Lagrange, OP, 'L'Évangile selon les Hébreux', *R. Bibl.* 31 (1922), pp. 161–81 and 321–49, with crit. discussion. Eng. tr. in J. K. Elliott, *The Apocryphal New Testament* (Oxford, 1993), pp. 1–10. Ger. tr., with introd., by P. Vielhauer and G. Strecker in Schneemelcher, 1 (5th edn., 1987), pp. 142–7 (Eng. tr., 1 (1991), pp. 172–8), with discussion of the whole question of Jewish Christian Gospels (with bibl.), 1, pp. 114–28 (Eng. tr., pp. 134–53). R. Handmann, *Das Hebräer-Evangelium* (TU 5, Heft 3; 1888). A. Schmidtke, 'Zum Hebräerevangelium', *ZNTW* 35

(1936), pp. 24–44; H. Waitz, 'Neue Untersuchungen über die sogen. judenchristlichen Evangelien', ibid. 36 (1937), pp. 60–81; G. Bardy, 'Saint Jérôme et l'Évangile selon les Hébreux', *Mélanges de Science religieuse*, 3 (1946), pp. 5–36. A. F. J. Klijn, 'Das Hebräer- und das Nazoräerevangelium', in *Aufstieg und Niedergang der römischen Welt*, Teil 2, Band 25. 5, ed. W. Haase (1988), pp. 3997–4033.

Hebron, the modern *El-Ḥâlil*, some 23 miles SSW of *Jerusalem. It is believed to be one of the oldest cities in the world. It was chosen by *Abraham as his nomadic home when he arrived in Palestine (Gen. 13: 18), and he acquired here the Cave of Machpelah as the burying place for his family (Gen. 23). *Joshua made it one of the *Cities of Refuge (Josh. 20: 7). After the death of Saul, *David made it his headquarters (2 Sam. 2: 1–4) and ruled the kingdom from Hebron for seven years and six months (2 Sam. 2: 11) until he had secured possession of Jerusalem. Absalom in turn, on his revolt from David, made it his capital (2 Sam. 15: 7–11). It has sometimes been identified by Christian writers with the scene of the Visitation of the BVM.

L. H. Vincent, OP, E. J. H. Mackay, and F. M. Abel, OP, *Hébron: Le Ḥaram el-Khalîl, sépulture des patriarches* (1923, with sep. vol. of plates). F. M. Abel, OP, *Géographie de la Palestine*, 2 (1938), pp. 345–7, with further refs. S. Mowinckel, 'Die Gründung von Hebron', *Orientalia Suecana*, 4 (1955), pp. 67–76. Reports of excavations in *R. Bibl.* 72 (1965), pp. 267–70; 73 (1966), pp. 566–9; 75 (1968), pp. 253–8. P. W. Ferris in *Anchor Bible Dictionary*, 3 (1992), pp. 107 f., s.v.

Hecker, Isaac Thomas (1819–88), founder of the *Paulists. A native of New York, he was at first a keen *Methodist and as a youth took an active interest in the social conditions of the industrial classes. In 1844 he became a RC and, after spending some years in Europe, returned to New York in 1851. Meanwhile he had entered the novitiate of the *Redemptorists in Belgium in 1845 and been ordained priest by N. P. S. *Wiseman in 1849. In the early 1850s he devoted himself wholeheartedly to the many RC immigrants then entering the USA. Difficulties having arisen with his Redemptorist superiors in 1857 he was dispensed from his vows by *Pius IX, and founded a new congregation for missionary work in the States which was known as the 'Paulists'. After his death it was frequently suggested, but perhaps mistakenly, that the condemnation of *Americanism by *Leo XIII in his *Testem benevolentiae* (1899) had Hecker in mind.

The Correspondence between Hecker and O. A. Brownson (1803–76), a fellow convert to RCism, ed. J. F. Gower and R. M. Leliaert (Notre Dame Studies in American Catholicism, 1; Notre Dame and London, 1979). W. Elliott, *The Life of Father Hecker* (New York, 1891; Fr. tr., with preface by l'Abbé Félix Klein, 1897). C. Maignen, *Étude sur l'américanisme: Le Père Hecker, est-il un saint?* (1898). V. F. Holden, CSP, *The Yankee Paul: Isaac Thomas Hecker* (Milwaukee [1958]; deals with the period up to 1858). J. Farina (ed.), *Hecker Studies: Essays on the Thought of Isaac Hecker* (New York and Ramsey, NJ [1983]). V. F. Holden in *Dict. Sp.* 7 (pt. 1; 1969), cols. 126–31; id. in *NCE* 6 (1967), pp. 982 f., both s.v. See also bibl. to AMERICANISM.

hedonism. The ethical doctrine which maintains that the proper end of all moral action is pleasure (Gk. ἡδονή, 'pleasure'). It thus closely resembles *Utilitarianism (q.v.). It is also known, esp. by Continental moral philosophers,

as 'Eudaemonism' (Gk. εὐδαιμονία, 'true well-being'). The title 'psychological hedonism' is applied to the doctrine which holds that man is so constituted psychologically that he cannot avoid making 'pleasure' the end of his actions, i.e. that even though he may persuade himself that he is doing acts of great sacrifice, it is really his own pleasure that he is seeking all the time. See also EUDEMONISM.

Hefele, Karl Joseph (1809–93), Church historian. Appointed Privatdozent in Church history at Tübingen in 1836 and professor in 1840, he soon won fame both as teacher and scholar. In 1869 he was elected Bp. of Rottenburg. He spent the winter of 1868–9 at Rome, where he took a prominent part as consultor in the preparations for the *Vatican Council of 1870, and was entrusted, owing to his unrivalled historical knowledge in the field, with drawing up the procedure. At the Council itself he was among the most influential of those opposed to the definition of Papal *Infallibility; but after some initial hesitations, he decided (10 Apr. 1871) to publish the Vatican Decrees in his diocese. His most important work was his history of the ecclesiastical Councils (9 vols., 1855–90, the last two by J. *Hergenröther; the earlier vols. exist in an Eng. tr., and the whole is in a French translation with important additions by H. *Leclercq and others, bringing the whole up to 1949; 11 vols. in 22 parts; 1907–52).

Obituary notice by F. X. Funk in *Th.Q.* 76 (1894), pp. 1–14. R. Reinhardt, 'Karl Joseph Hefele', in H. Fries and G. Schwaiger (eds.), *Katholische Theologen Deutschlands im 19. Jahrhundert*, 2 [1975], pp. 163–211, with full bibl. V. Conzemius in *NCE* 6 (1967), pp. 985 f., s.v.; R. Reinhardt in *TRE* 14 (1985), pp. 526–9, s.v. See also works cited VATICAN COUNCIL, THE FIRST.

Hegel, Georg Wilhelm Friedrich (1770–1831), German Idealist philosopher. Born at Stuttgart, in 1788 he entered the Protestant seminary at Tübingen (known as the *Stift*), ostensibly with a view to the *Lutheran ministry. As a student he was undistinguished, his chief interest being in the classics rather than theology or philosophy. He first became concerned with Christian origins during a three-year private tutorship in Switzerland (1793–6), during which time he wrote a 'Life of Jesus', expounding the Gospel in terms of *Kantian ethics, and an essay on 'The Positivity of the Christian Religion', in which he criticized historic Christianity as a legalistic system at odds with Christ's own moral spontaneity. From 1797 to 1800 he held a similar post at Frankfurt, but by then his understanding of Christianity had changed considerably, as a new essay on 'The Spirit of Christianity and its Fate' clearly shows. The principle he now finds embodied in it is that of God's love for men as proclaimed by Christ, a love which, rekindled in man himself, overcomes humanity's alienation from God. It is thus the principle of ultimate unity.

The legacy which Hegel received on the death of his father enabled him to give up tutoring, and in 1800 he moved to Jena, where in the following year he was appointed a Privatdozent. Here he had F. W. J. *von Schelling as a colleague, with whom he collaborated on the *Kritisches Journal der Philosophie*. To the same year belongs his treatise on the difference between the systems of J. G. *Fichte and Schelling. His lecture-schedule covered logic and metaphysics, but he had also begun to develop his own system, having then come to view the rational understanding rather than love, philosophy rather than religion, as the key to the unity of truth and reality. Although at first under the influence of Schelling, Hegel soon revealed differences in his own thought, and after Schelling's departure for Würzburg (1803) he was plainly intent on going his own way. His break with Schelling was manifest with the publication of his first major and prob. most abidingly interesting work, *Die Phänomenologie des Geistes*, in 1807. Meanwhile Napoleon's victory at the Battle of Jena (1806) had abruptly ended his career at the university (he had become *professor extraordinarius* in 1805), and for the next 18 months he was editor of a newspaper, the *Bamberger Zeitung*. Then from 1808 to 1815 he was director of the Nuremberg *Gymnasium*, carrying out the duties of headmaster with signal competence and conscientiousness. He continued his philosophical studies, however, and in his *Wissenschaft der Logik* (1812–16) he set out the conceptual basis of his system in its final form. On the strength of it he was appointed to a professorship at Heidelberg in 1816. The *Logik* was followed in 1817 by the *Encyklopädie der philosophischen Wissenschaften im Grundrisse* (2nd edn., much enlarged, 1827; 3rd edn., 1830). In 1818 he was nominated as J. G. Fichte's successor in the chair of philosophy at Berlin. He took up his appointment at a time of considerable political unrest—Kotzebue was assassinated in 1819—and he saw it as his immediate task to lay the theoretical foundations of a stable political order. His *Naturrecht und Staatswissenschaft im Grundrisse*, which came out in 1821 (a 2nd edn., ed. by E. Gans as *Grundlinien des Philosophie des Rechts* was published in 1833), although standing above contemporary issues and in points of detail diverging from official policy, endorsed the aims of the Prussian government.

Hegel's system is of a scope to outdistance even *Aristotle's, its distinctive character lying in its attempt to present all philosophical problems and concepts in an essentially evolutionary or historical perspective. For him no idea has an unchanging and eternal validity, but discloses its meaning in the continuous process of its development; a process in which contrasts and oppositions, acute though they may be, become intelligible through an identity within which they are related, even if only as opposites. Moreover the antitheses which thought apprehends are also constitutive of reality, thought and reality being one. 'The real is the rational and the rational is the real.' Development is the outcome of a dialectical 'movement' in which a *thesis* is succeeded by an *antithesis*, the ensuing conflict resulting in the two being brought together on a higher plane (*aufgehoben*, 'sublated') as a *synthesis*. The ultimate resolution and sublation of all differences, alike in thought and reality, is attained in the Absolute. This evolutionary view of the universe comprehends not only the natural sciences but also the humanities, including history, law, ethics, aesthetics, and religion, since truth lies not in the individual disciplines—except as a merely partial disclosure—but in the whole ('Die Wahrheit ist die Ganze').

Hegel regarded himself as a Christian and a Lutheran, but in his philosophy of religion he sees religious ideas as figurative representations (*Vorstellungen*) of truths which philosophy restates in conceptual and fully rational terms (*Begriffe*). Although the notion of *Geist* (Spirit, Mind) is

the presiding concept of Hegel's thinking, he evidently did not understand by it a transcendent reality. In E. *Caird's words, it involves 'the complete rejection of ordinary supernaturalism'. Although some of Hegel's disciples, such as A. E. Biedermann (1819–85), found in his philosophy the true explanation and eventual justification of Christian doctrine, the general opinion has been to judge it pantheistic or even atheistic.

Although by the mid-19th cent. Hegel's system had passed under a cloud in his native Germany, it was to prove immensely influential on later thought in the realms of history, theology, politics, and sociology. After his death, his followers divided into two main camps, comprising on the one hand those who adhered more or less to Hegel's own system, and, on the other, those who developed his teaching along more 'naturalistic' or materialistic lines. The latter, often referred to as 'Young Hegelians', included B. *Bauer, L. *Feuerbach, and K. Marx, whose debt to Hegel is now fully recognized. Hegel's British disciples included T. H. *Green, E. Caird, F. H. *Bradley, and B. *Bosanquet, with whom may be associated Josiah Royce (1855–1916, from 1882 professor at Harvard) in America. Through Green especially, Idealism exercised a profound influence on English religious philosophy in the years between 1885 and 1920, but this was virtually eliminated by the subsequent vogue of empiricism and analysis. The last 30 years, however, have witnessed a widespread revival of interest in Hegel's own achievement as one of the highest points in the course of philosophical reflection.

The collected edn. of his *Werke* pub. in 19 vols., Berlin, 1832–87, was repr., with introd. by H. Glockner (26 vols., Stuttgart, 1927–40, incl. *Hegel-Lexikon* as vols. 23–6). The edn. begun by G. Lasson (Leipzig, 1905 ff.), rev. by id. and G. Hoffmeister (Hamburg, 1949 ff.), and ed. by various scholars, is incomplete. Crit. edn., sponsored by the Deutsche Forschungsgemeinschaft (Hamburg, 1968 ff.). Eng. versions of Hegel's works incl. *Phenomenology*, tr. J. B. Baillie (2 vols., 1910; rev. edn., 1931), and tr. A. V. Miller, with Analysis of the Text by J. N. Findlay (Oxford, 1977); *Hegel's Science of Logic*, tr. W. H. Johnson and L. G. Struthers (2 vols., 1929), and tr. A. V. Miller (1969); from the *Encyklopädie: The Logic of Hegel*, tr. W. Wallace (Oxford, 1874; 2nd edn., 1894; repr. 1975); *Hegel's Philosophy of Nature*, tr. A. V. Miller (ibid., 1970), and *Hegel's Philosophy of Mind*, tr. W. Wallace (ibid., 1894; repr., with additional matter tr. A. V. Miller, ibid., 1971); *Hegel's Philosophy of Right*, tr. T. M. Knox (from *Naturrecht*, ibid., 1942); also *Lectures on the Philosophy of History*, tr. J. Sibree (1888) and tr. H. B. Nisbet, with introd. by D. Forbes (Cambridge, 1975); *Lectures on the Philosophy of Religion*, tr. E. B. Speirs and J. B. Sanderson (3 vols., 1895) and tr. R. F. Brown and others, ed. P. C. Hodgson (Berkeley, Calif., and London [1984] ff.); and *Early Theological Writings*, tr. T. M. Knox (Chicago, 1948).

Works on Hegel's philosophy incl. E. Caird, *Hegel* (1883): K. Fischer, *Hegels Leben, Werken und Lehre* (2 vols., Heidelberg, 1901); W. T. Stace, *The Philosophy of Hegel* (1924); N. Hartmann, *Die Philosophie des deutschen Idealismus*, 2: *Hegel* (1929); T. L. Haering, *Hegel: Sein Wollen und sein Werk* (2 vols., 1929–38); J. Hyppolite, *Genèse et structure de la Phénoménologie de l'Esprit de Hegel* ([1946]; Eng. tr., Evanston, Ill., 1974); F. Grégoire, *Études hégéliennes: Les Points capitaux du système* (Bibliothèque philosophique de Louvain, 19; 1958); J. N. Findlay, *Hegel: A Reexamination* (1958); G. R. G. Mure, *The Philosophy of Hegel* (HUL, 1965); W. Kaufmann, *Hegel: Reinterpretation, Texts, and Commentary* (Garden City, NY, 1965; London, 1966); R. Plant, *Hegel* (London, 1973; 2nd edn., Oxford, 1983); C. Taylor, *Hegel*

(Cambridge, 1975); M. J. Inwood, *Hegel* (Arguments of the Philosophers, 1983); and H. Althaus, *Hegel und die heroischen Jahre der Philosophie* (Munich [1992]). On his religious philosophy, A. Chapelle, *Hegel et la religion* (3 vols. in 4 parts, 1964–71); E. L. Fackenheim, *The Religious Dimension in Hegel's Thought* (Bloomington, Ind., 1967; Chicago and London, 1982); B. M. G. Reardon, *Hegel's Philosophy of Religion* (1977); J. Yerkes, *The Christology of Hegel* (American Academy of Religion Dissertation Series, 23; Missoula, Mo. [1978]); Q. Lauer, SJ, *Hegel's Concept of God* (Albany, NY [1982]); R. K. Williamson, *Introduction to Hegel's Philosophy of Religion* (ibid. [1984]); L. Dickey, *Hegel: Religion, Economics, and the Politics of Spirit 1770–1807* (Cambridge, 1987); and A. Shanks, *Hegel's Political Theology* (ibid., 1991). K. Steinhauer, *Hegel Bibliography* (1980).

Hegesippus, St (2nd cent.), Church historian. He was prob. a native of Palestine, and acc. to *Eusebius, a converted Jew. He wrote five Books of 'Memoirs' (ὑπομνήματα) against the *Gnostics. Though they now survive, as far as is known, only in fragments (nearly all preserved in Eusebius' *HE*), the work is said to have existed entire in some libraries as late as the 16th–17th cents. The surviving portions deal for the most part with the early history of the Church at *Jerusalem. It appears (Eusebius, *HE* 4. 22. 1–3) that he drew up a 'succession-list' (διαδοχή) of the early bishops of the Church at Rome; and it has been argued that the list in *Epiphanius (*Haer.* 27. 6) is a reproduction of it. If so, it is the earliest witness to the names of the first Roman bishops. Feast day, 7 Apr.

Frags. collected in M. J. *Routh, *Reliquiae Sacrae*, 1 (2nd edn., 1846), pp. 207–19 (notes, pp. 220–84), and T. *Zahn, *Forschungen zur Geschichte des neutestamentlichen Kanons*, 6 (1900), pp. 228–73. N. Hyldahl, 'Hegesipps Hypomnemata', *Studia Theologica*, 14 (1960), pp. 70–113. W. Telfer, 'Was Hegesippus a Jew?', *HTR* 53 (1960), pp. 143–53. On his 'Papal List' see C. H. *Turner in H. B. *Swete, *Essays on the Early History of the Church and the Ministry* (1918), pp. 115–20 and 207; H. Kemler, 'Hegesipps römische Bischofsliste', *VC* 25 (1971), pp. 182–96, with refs. to earlier bibl. *CPG* 1 (1983), p. 109 (no. 1302). Further bibl. in Altaner and Stuiber (1978), pp. 109 f. and 570.

Hegira. See HIJRA.

hegumenos (Gk. ἡγούμενος, lit. 'leader'). A title in the E. for the ruler of a monastery. He is usually elected by the monks of the monastery, though confirmation is required from the patriarch, the diocesan bishop, or the patron (acc. to the status of the monastery).

Heidegger, Martin (1889–1976), German *existentialist philosopher. A native of Messkirch, Baden, and coming from a peasant background, Heidegger studied for a time at a Jesuit seminary before he went to Freiburg University. He was much influenced by the writings of F. *Brentano and the teaching of E. Husserl. After submitting a thesis on Pseudo-*Duns Scotus' *Grammatica Speculativa*, Heidegger became Privatdozent at Freiburg in 1915. In 1923 he was appointed Professor at Marburg, where his colleagues included R. *Bultmann and P. *Tillich. In 1929 he returned to Freiburg as Husserl's successor. At first he supported the Nazi regime and was Rector of the University from 1933 to 1934. In later years he spent much of his time in the Black Forest, though he did not resign his Professorship until 1951.

In an obscure language, consciously opposed to the intellectual vocabulary of the scientific Greek tradition,

Heidegger elaborated a metaphysic of the human person. Though trained in the neo-*Kantian school, he rejected Kant's 'self' as ignoring man's historical being in the world. He was indebted to Husserl's *Phenomenology for reflecting on the structure of consciousness, but felt that this was only a preliminary to philosophy's proper concern, that of the nature of being. Thus, his *Sein und Zeit* (1927; Eng. tr., 1962), with elaborate etymological excursuses, uncovers man's temporal being in order to focus on Being in its unity and totality. Man's personal existence (*Dasein*: literally 'there-ness') is a unique, transcendent possibility, which is rooted in immediate, temporal relationships. Authentic existence, facing nothingness, is lived out only in the full acceptance of death. The lectures which he gave in 1927, *Die Grundprobleme der Phänomenologie* (which he did not permit to be published until 1975), while intended as a continuation of *Sein und Zeit*, are in some ways an easier introduction to his early thought, since Heidegger is concerned to place himself in relation to the previous history of philosophy. In his later works (the extent of discontinuity with his earlier writings is much disputed) it seems that Being is intuitively grasped rather than philosophically explored. In *Hölderlin und das Wesen der Dichtung* (1936) he treats of language as the house of Being and of the poet as guardian of Being.

Heidegger's influence on theologians has been considerable. Bultmann, for instance, adopts his categories (of authentic and unauthentic existence), regarding them as a systematic and secularized version of NT anthropology; he maintains that Heidegger's analysis is correct, though it is only in Christian faith that the transition to authentic existence is realized. In Heidegger's later work some theologians have found suggestions for a 'non-objectifying' mode of theological discourse.

There is a massive *Gesamtausgabe* of his pub. and previously unpub. works (Frankfurt am Main, 1975 ff., incl., as vol. 24, *Die Grundprobleme der Phänomenologie*, ed. F.-W. von Herrmann, 1975; Eng. tr. by A. Hofstadter, Bloomington, Ind. [1982]). Several of his other works have been tr. into Eng., incl. 'Hölderlin und das Wesen der Dichtung', which is incl. in *Existence and Being* (1949), pp. 291–315, with useful introd. by W. Brock, pp. 20–248. *Basic Writings*, ed., in Eng. tr., by D. F. Krell (1978), with introd., pp. 3–35. J. M. Robinson and J. B. Cobb, Jun. (eds.), *The Later Heidegger and Theology* (1963); O. Pöggeler, *Der Denkweg Martin Heideggers* (1963; Eng. tr., Atlantic Highlands, NJ, 1987); id., *Neue Wege mit Heidegger* (Freiburg, etc. [1992]); M. King, *Heidegger's Philosophy: A Guide to his Basic Thought* (Oxford, 1964); G. Steiner, *Heidegger* (Modern Masters, 1978); M. Murray (ed.), *Heidegger and Modern Philosophy* (New Haven, Conn., and London, 1978); A. Jäger, *Gott: Nochmals Martin Heidegger* (Tübingen, 1978); T. Sheehan (ed.), *Heidegger the Man and the Thinker* (Chicago [1981]); H.-G. Gadamer, *Heideggers Wege* (Tübingen, 1983); M. Haar (ed.), *Martin Heidegger* (Cahiers de l'Herne, 45; 1983); F. A. Olafson, *Heidegger and the Philosophy of Mind* (New Haven, Conn., and London [1987]); H. Ott, *Martin Heidegger: Unterwegs zu seiner Biographie* (Frankfurt and New York [1988]); B. Martin (ed.), *Martin Heidegger und das 'Dritte Reich': Ein Kompendium* (Darmstadt, 1989); G. Kovacs, *The Question of God in Heidegger's Phenomenology* (Evanston, Ill. [1990]); D. Papenfuss and O. Pöggeler (eds.), *Zur philosophischen Aktualität Heideggers: Symposium der Alexander von Humbolt-Stiftung von 24.-28. April 1989* (3 vols., Frankfurt am Main [1991–2]). M. Wyschogrod, *Kierkegaard and Heidegger: The Ontology of Existence* (1954); J. Macquarrie, *An Existentialist Theology: A Comparison of Heidegger and Bultmann* (1955). H.-M. Sass, *Martin Heidegger: Bibliography and Glossary* (Bowling Green, Oh. [1982]).

Heidelberg Catechism. The Protestant confession of faith compiled in 1562 by Z. *Ursinus and K. Olevian, two Heidelberg theologians, at the instance of the Elector, *Frederick III, and accepted in the following year as the standard of doctrine in the Palatinate. In fundamentals its theology is *Calvinist, though the specific doctrines of J. *Calvin have sometimes been modified under the influence of H. *Bullinger and others of even stronger Lutheran sympathies. Translated into Dutch in 1563, and into English in 1572, it exercised influence in the Netherlands and in England.

A. Wolters, *Heidelberger Katechismus in seiner ursprünglichen Gestalt, herausgegeben nebst der Geschichte seines Textes im Jahre 1563* (1864). Text from 3rd edn. in H. A. Niemeyer, *Collectio Confessionum in Ecclesiis Reformatis Publicatarum* (Leipzig, 1840), pp. 390–461, with introd. pp. lvii–lxiii. Convenient Eng. trs. in T. F. Torrance, *The School of Faith: The Catechisms of the Reformed Church* (1959), pp. 67–96, and by A. O. Miller and M. E. Osterhaven (Philadelphia, 1962), repr. in A. C. Cochrane, *Reformed Confessions of the 16th Century* (1966), pp. 305–31, and, with introd., in M. A. Noll (ed.), *Confessions and Catechisms of the Reformation* (Leicester, 1991), pp. 133–64. P. *Schaff, *A History of the Creeds of Christendom*, 1 (1877), pp. 529–54. K. *Barth, *Die christliche Lehre nach dem Heidelberger Katechismus* (1948); id , *Einführung in den Heidelberger Katechismus* (1960; Eng. tr. of both as *The Heidelberg Catechism for Today*, 1964). W. Hollweg, *Neue Untersuchungen zur Geschichte und Lehre des Heidelberger Katechismus* (Beiträge zur Geschichte und Lehre der Reformierten Kirche, 13, 1961; 2nd ser., ibid. 28, 1968). D. Visser (ed.), *Controversy and Conciliation: The Reformation and the Palatinate 1559–1583* (Pittsburg Theological Monographs, NS 18; Allison Park, Pa., 1986), pp. 73–100 and 197–225. W. Heijting, *De Catechismi en Confessies in de Nederlandse Reformatie tot 1585*, 1 (Bibliotheca Bibliographica Neerlandica, 27; Nieuwkoop, 1989), pp. 232–79, on the Dutch trs. W. Metz and J. Fangmeier in *TRE* 14 (1985), pp. 582–90, s.v., with bibl. See also bibl. to URSINUS, Z.

Heiler, Friedrich (1892–1967), German religious writer. As a RC, he studied Catholic theology, philosophy, and oriental languages at Munich, but he soon came under the influence of Protestantism, especially of the Swedish theologian, N. *Söderblom. In 1919 he became a member of the Lutheran Church at *Uppsala. In 1922 he was appointed professor of the comparative history of religions at *Marburg. Influenced by the writings of F. *von Hügel, his later development took a more Catholic line. He became the organizer of a German High Church movement, and even founded an Evangelical order of Franciscan *Tertiaries. In his latter years he played an active part in the *Ecumenical Movement. His first and most important work is *Das Gebet* (1918; abridged Eng. tr., *Prayer*, 1932), a comprehensive historical analysis of the subject from its most primitive forms in the inarticulate shouts of the savage to the heights of mystic contemplation, the description of the latter being largely based on F. von Hügel, W. R. *Inge, and E. *Underhill. He later developed this comprehensive approach into a general phenomenology of religion in his *Erscheinungsformen und Wesen der Religion* (1961). His work on Catholicism, *Der Katholizismus* (1923), is remarkable for its appreciative understanding of it in its earlier expressions, but almost entirely negative on post-Tridentine developments. His profound interest in the Eastern *Orthodox Church bore fruit in *Die Ostkirchen* (pub. posthumously, 1971; a much-expanded version of his *Urkirche und Ostkirche*, 1937).

In Deo Omnia Unum: Eine Sammlung von Aufsätzen F. Heiler zum 50. Geburtstage dargebracht (ed. C. M. Schröder and others, Munich, 1942 [issue of periodical *Eine Heilige Kirche*]); *Interconfessiones . . . Friedrich Heiler zum Gedächtnis aus Anlass seines 80. Geburtstages*, ed. A. M. Heiler (widow) (Marburger Theologische Studien, 10; 1972), with bibl., pp. 154–96. G. Lanczkowski in *TRE* 14 (1985), pp. 638–41, s.v.

Heim, Karl (1874–1958), *Lutheran theologian. A native of Frauenzimmern in Württemberg, he studied at *Tübingen and was for some years a pastor and schoolmaster. In 1907 he became a Privatdozent at Halle, in 1914 Professor of Theology at Münster i.W., and in 1920 at Tübingen. For several years he was one of the leading opponents of the (pagan) German Faith Movement. His theology, which developed out of a *Pietistic background, stressed the *Ritschlian contrast of faith and reason and, while fully accepting the achievements of modern secular culture and science, emphasized the transcendence of faith. He was esp. concerned to analyse the conditions governing the valid apprehension of supernatural truth. In his personalism (the 'I–Thou' relationship; cf. M. *Buber) and his doctrine of 'perspectives', his teaching had affinities with certain *existentialist doctrines. Among his writings are *Das Weltbild der Zukunft* (1904), *Glaubensgewissheit* (1916; 2nd edn., 1923), *Das Wesen des evangelischen Christentums* (1926), *Glauben und Denken* (1931; 3rd edn., 1934; Eng. tr. as *God Transcendent*, 1935), *Glaube und Leben, Gesammelte Aufsätze und Vorträge* (1925; 3rd edn., 1928), and his autobiography, *Ich gedenke der vorigen Zeiten* (1957).

Many of Heim's works have been tr. into Eng. *Theologie als Glaubenswagnis: Festschrift für Karl Heim zum 80. Geburtstag dargebracht von der Evang.-theol. Fakultät in Tübingen* (Hamburg, 1954). Brief studies on various aspects of his theology by W. Ruttenbeck (Leipzig, 1925), H. E. Eisenhuth (Göttingen, 1928), F. Spemann (Tübingen, 1932), and A. Köberle (Hamburg, 1973, with substantial extracts of Heim's writings). H. Schwarz, *Das Verständnis des Wunders bei Heim und Bultmann* (1966), with bibl. In Eng., popular introd. by E. L. Allen, *Jesus Our Leader: A Guide to the Thought of Karl Heim* [1950]. Z. Kučera in *TRE* 14 (1985), pp. 774–7, s.v.

Heiric of Auxerre (841–876/7), teacher and hagiographer. When only about 7 years old he entered the monastery of St *Germanus at Auxerre as an oblate. There his teacher was Haymo of Auxerre. From 859 to 860 he studied under Servatus *Lupus at Ferrières, and from 862 to 865 he was at the abbey of St Médard at Soissons, where he came into contact with Johannes Scottus *Erigena. He then returned to his monastery at Auxerre and taught there until his death. His chief work was a metrical Life of St Germanus, one of the best hagiographical poems of the times, which he dedicated *c*.876 to Charles the Bald. He also wrote 'Miracula S. Germani' in prose, and put together 'Collectanea', partly classical from Valerius Maximus, *Suetonius and other sources, and partly theological; these were based on the teaching of Lupus and Haymo. He is important as a link between the Carolingian schools and the later Middle Ages, esp. as the teacher of *Remigius.

The best text of his metrical Life of St Germanus is that of L. Traube, with important introd., in *MGH*, Poetae, 3 (1896), pp. 421–517; it is also pr. in *AASS*, Jul. 7 (1731), pp. 221–55.

Miracula S. Germani, ibid., pp. 255–83. *Collectanea* ed. R. Quadri, OFM (Spicilegium Friburgense, 11; Fribourg, 1966); *Homiliae per circulum anni* [pieces intended for private reading rather than sermons preached], ed. id. and R. Demeulenaere (CCCM 116, 116A, 116B; 1992–4). G. Billanovich, 'Dall'antica Ravenna alle biblioteche umanistiche', *Aevum*, 30 (1956), pp. 319–53, rev. in *Annuario dell'Università Cattolica del Sacro Cuore*, Anni Accademici 1955–7 (Milan, 1958), pp. 71–107. É. Jeauneau, 'Dans le sillage de l'Érigène: une homélie d'Héric d'Auxerre sur le prologue de Jean', *Studi Medievali*, 3rd ser. 11 (1970), pp. 937–55, incl. text. P. Janin, 'Heiric d'Auxerre et les Gesta pontificum Autissiodorensium', *Francia*, 4 (for 1976; 1977), pp. 89–105, with further refs. J. J. O'Meara, *Eriugena* (Oxford, 1988), ch. 11, esp. pp. 205–9. R. Quadri and others in D. Iogna-Prat and others (eds.), *L'École Carolingienne d'Auxerre de Murethach à Remi 830–908: Entretiens d'Auxerre 1989* [1991], pp. 273–370. Manitius, 1, pp. 499–504. L. Barré in *Dict. Sp.* 7 (pt. 1; 1969), cols. 282–5, s.v.

heirmos (Gk. εἱρμός, 'chain'). The opening stanza in each ode of the *canon. All the remaining *troparia in the ode follow the same rhythm as the heirmos. In content it acts as a 'link' verse (hence its name), joining together: (1) the theme of the biblical canticle, which the ode of the canon was originally designed to accompany; and (2) the theme of the feast or commemoration of the day, which is developed in the troparia that follow.

Helena, St (*c*.255–*c*.330), also **Helen**, mother of the Emp. *Constantine. Born at Drepanum (later 'Helenopolis' after her) in Bithynia of humble parentage, she became the wife of the Emp. Constantius Chlorus, by whom she bore Constantine in 274. She was abandoned by her husband in 292 when political reasons led him to marry the stepdaughter of the Emp. Maximian. When Constantine became Emperor in 306, Helena was immediately raised to a position of great honour and zealously supported the Christian cause. In 326, at a great age, she made a visit to the Holy Land, where she founded the basilicas on the Mount of *Olives and at *Bethlehem, and (acc. to later tradition; *Sulpicius Severus, *Ambrose, *Rufinus, all *c*.395–400) discovered the Cross on which Christ was crucified.

The medieval belief that Helena was a native of England rests on confusion; its origins are complicated. A story in the Welsh *Mabinogion*, incorporating material from the late 7th cent., attributes the name of Helena to the wife of Magnus Maximus, Emp. in Britain, Gaul, and Spain from 383 to 388; in this story Constantine is given as the name of one of her sons, and Maximus is turned into the legendary figure of Macsen Wledig. *Geoffrey of Monmouth described Helena as the daughter of Coel ('Old King Cole') of Colchester. From the 9th cent. the abbey of Hautvillers, near *Reims, claimed to possess her body. Feast day in the W., formerly 18 Aug.; in the E., 21 May (with St Constantine, Emp.).

The chief early sources are *Eusebius, *Vita Constantini*, *Zosimus, *Historia*, 2. 8, and Eutropius, *Breviarium*, 10. 2. R. Couzard, *Sainte Hélène d'après l'histoire et la tradition* (1911). E. D. Hunt, *Holy Land Pilgrimage in the Later Roman Empire AD 312–460* (Oxford, 1982), esp. pp. 28–49 ('Helena—History and Legend'); J. W. Drijvers, *Helena Augusta: The Mother of Constantine the Great and the Legend of her Finding of the True Cross* (Brill's Studies in Intellectual History, 27; Leiden, 1992). For her church on the Mount of Olives, see L.-H. Vincent, OP, 'L'Éléona, sanctuaire primitif de l'Ascension', *R. Bibl.* 64 (1957), pp. 48–71; for that at Bethlehem, see bibl. s.v. H. *Leclercq,

OSB, in *DACL* 6 (pt. 2; 1925), cols. 2126–45, s.v. 'Hélène, Impératrice'; R. Klein in *RAC* 14 (1988), cols. 355–75, s.v. 'Helena II'.

For the legend, see *BHL* 1 (1899), nos. 3772–90. Life by Almannus of Hautvillers in *AASS*, Aug. 3 (1737), pp. 580–99. A. Linder, 'The Myth of Constantine in the West', *Studi Medievali*, 3rd ser. 16 (1975), pp. 43–95, esp. pp. 84–93; J. F. Matthews, 'Macsen, Maximus, and Constantine', *Welsh History Review*, 11 (1983), pp. 431–48, repr. in id., *Political Life and Culture in Late Roman Society* (1985), no. 12.

Heliand ('Saviour'; Old English *hælend*, Ger. *Heiland*). An Old Saxon biblical poem of the 9th cent. It owes its title to its first editor, A. Schmeller (1830), though the work had been discovered in the 17th cent. by F. Junius (d. 1671). It is based on *Tatian's harmony of the Gospels and is written in alliterative verse. The Latin 'Praefatio', now generally considered genuine, states that the *Heliand* was written by a well-known Saxon bard at the order of King *Louis I (the 'Pious') for the benefit of his Saxon subjects recently converted to Christianity; it is in any case a product of the 830s, possibly from *Fulda or, more probably, from Werden in Westphalia. The poem, which shows the influence of the contemporary Anglo-Saxon religious poetry, represents Christ as a liege-lord and the Apostles as His faithful vassals, and inculcates the virtues of humility and love of one's enemies.

The work survives complete in a 10th-cent. MS in the British Library (Cotton Caligula A. VII); a 9th-cent. MS at Munich has two lacunae; there are also 9th-cent. frags. at Prague and the Vatican, the latter also containing a fragment of a *Genesis* in the same style but by a later poet, and the 'Straubinger Fragment', of the mid-ninth cent., discovered in 1978. *Editio princeps* by J. A. Schmeller at Munich, 1830, with crit. apparatus as 'Lieferung 2', ibid., 1840. Other edns. by E. Sievers (Halle, 1878, with suppl. by E. Schröder, 1935) and O. Behaghel (ibid., 1882; 9th edn., rev. B. Taeger, Tübingen, 1984). Modern Eng. trr. of the text by M. Scott (University of North Carolina Studies in the Germanic Languages and Literatures, 52 [1966]) and, with comm., by G. R. Murphy, SJ (New York and Oxford, 1992). On MSS of the *Heliand*, see B. Bischoff, 'Die Schriftheimat der Münchener Heliand-Handschrift', *Beiträge zur Geschichte der deutschen Sprache und Literatur*, 101 (1979), pp. 161–70, repr. id., *Mittelalterliche Studien*, 3 (Stuttgart, 1981), pp. 112–19, and part of an earlier art., repr. ibid., pp. 103–5. R. Drögereit, *Werden und der Heliand* (Essen, 1950); B. Taeger, *Zahlensymbolik bei Hraban, bei Hincmar—und im 'Heliand'?* (Münchener Texte und Untersuchungen zur deutschen Literatur des Mittelalters, 30; 1970). J. Eichhoff and I. Rauch (eds.), *Der Heliand* (Wege der Forschung, 321; Darmstadt, 1973). G. R. Murphy, SJ, *The Saxon Savior: The German Transformation of the Gospel in the Ninth-Century Heliand* (New York and Oxford, 1989). J. K. Bostock, *A Handbook on Old High German Literature* (2nd edn., rev. K. C. King and D. R. McLintock, Oxford, 1976), pp. 168–83. J. Belkin and J. Meier, *Bibliographie zu Otfrid von Weissenburg und zur altsächsischen Bibeldichtung (Heliand und Genesis)* (Bibliographien zur deutschen Literatur des Mittelalters, 7; 1975) pp. 63–131.

Helkesaites. See ELKESAITES.

Hell. The word 'hell' is used in English translations of the Bible to represent both the Hebrew '*Sheol' (q.v.), meaning the place of the departed, and the Greek '*Gehenna' (q.v.), which came to denote the divinely ordained place of punishment for the wicked after death. In Christian theology it normally signifies the place or state to which unrepentant sinners are held to pass after this life, whereas the redeemed go either to *Purgatory (q.v.) or direct to *Heaven (q.v.). Its character is inferred from biblical teaching, esp. Christ's words in the Gospels about the fate of those who refuse the opportunity of entering the Kingdom of Heaven (cf. Matt. 13: 42; 25: 30 and 41). In Rev. the 'second death' (2: 11; 20: 14, etc.) is depicted symbolically as the fate of being cast into a 'lake which burneth with fire and brimstone' (21: 8; cf. 19: 20 and 20: 10). From such texts as this, often understood over-literally, the popular idea of hell was derived.

It is clear that in the NT hell in this sense is an ultimate state or destiny into which souls pass only by God's final and irrevocable judgement, whether that is conceived as the *Particular Judgement at death or the *General Judgement on the last day. Acc. to the traditional Scholastic theology, souls experience in hell both the *poena damni*, i.e. the exclusion from God's presence and loss of all contact with Him, and a certain *poena sensus*, denoted in the Bible by fire, which is usually interpreted as an external agent tormenting them. Modern theology tends rather to stress the fact that hell is but the logical consequence of ultimate adherence to the soul's own will and rejection of the will of God, which (since God cannot take away free will) necessarily separates the soul from God, and hence from all possibility of happiness. This exclusion from heaven (in which the unrepentant person would from his very character be both unable and unwilling to share) is held to be contrary neither to God's justice nor to His love, since He will not force response to the good from any creature against his will.

See also DESCENT OF CHRIST INTO HELL.

Helvetic Confessions, the. Two important Reformation Confessions of Faith.

(1) **First Helvetic Confession** (also known as the 'Second Confession of *Basle'). It was compiled at Basle in 1536 by H. *Bullinger of Zurich, *Myconius and Grynaeus of Basle, and others, after much dissension, esp. on the Eucharist, as a uniform confession of faith for the whole of German-speaking Switzerland. Its basis was *Zwinglian, but it contained a considerable *Lutheran element. It was accepted by all the Protestant Swiss cantons but rejected by Strasbourg and Constance.

(2) **Second Helvetic Confession.** This was the work of H. Bullinger, who made an early draft of it for himself in 1561. It was issued in 1566 in response to a request from the Elector-Palatine, *Frederick III ('the Pious'), who had announced his definite adhesion to *Calvinism. It is among the longest of the Reformation Confessions, in places taking on the character of a theological treatise. Its teaching is mainly Calvinist, with some Zwinglian elements. It soon won acceptance not only in all the Swiss Protestant Churches, but also among the 'Reformed' (i.e. Calvinists) outside Switzerland.

(1) Lat. and Ger. text in P. *Schaff, *Creeds of Christendom*, 3 (1877), pp. 211–31; Eng. tr. in A. C. Cochrane (ed.), *Reformed Confessions of the 16th Century* (1966), pp. 97–111.

(2) Latin text in P. Schaff, *Creeds of Christendom*, 3 (1877), pp. 233–306; Eng. tr. in A. C. Cochrane (ed.), *Reformed Confessions of the 16th Century* (1966), pp. 220–301. J. Staedtke (ed.), *Glauben und Bekennen: 400 Jahre* Confessio Helvetica Posterior. *Beiträge zu ihrer Geschichte und Theologie* (Zurich, 1966). E. Koch, *Die Theologie der Confessio Helvetica Posterior* (Beiträge zur Geschichte und Lehre der Reformierten Kirche, 27; 1968). E. Zsindeley in *TRE* 8 (1981), pp. 169–73, s.v. 'Confessio Helvetica Posterior'.

Helvidius (4th cent.). A Latin theologian who was attacked by St *Jerome for his denial of the perpetual virginity of the BVM. His underlying motive seems to have been the defence of marriage against the prevalent exaltation of virginity. Helvidius declared that the *brethren of the Lord were the natural sons of Joseph and Mary. Jerome replied in his *De perpetua virginitate B. Mariae adversus Helvidium* that they were the sons of another Mary, the wife of Alphaeus and the sister of the Virgin. Acc. to St *Augustine (*De haer.* 84), he won disciples who were known as 'Helvidians'.

Helvidius' tract has not survived. Jerome's reply is repr. in J. P. Migne, *PL* 23. 185–206. Bardenhewer, 3, p. 631. G. Jouassard, 'La Personnalité d'Helvidius', in *Mélanges J. Saunier* (Bibliothèque de la Faculté Catholique des Lettres de Lyon, 3; 1944), pp. 139–56. J. N. D. Kelly, *Jerome* (1975), pp. 104–7.

Helwys, Thomas (*c*.1550–*c*.1616), English *Baptist divine. Of a Nottinghamshire family, he studied at Gray's Inn. In 1608 he emigrated to Holland with J. *Smyth and became a member of the *Separatist Church at Amsterdam. Here, like Smyth, he became convinced that 'Infant Baptism' was not baptism at all, and accordingly received baptism at Smyth's hands. In consequence, when he and Smyth were excommunicated (1609), he joined Smyth's Separatist community at Amsterdam, the first Baptist Church to come into being. In 1612, feeling it his duty no longer to absent himself from the dangers of persecution, he returned to London, where he founded the first *General Baptist congregation in England at Pinners' Hall, London, and met with remarkable success as a preacher. Opposition was aroused, however, when he began to put into circulation his *Declaration of the Mystery of Iniquity*, which, written and printed in Holland (1611–12), contained the first sustained plea by an English divine for universal religious toleration and a denial of the right of the State to legislate on matters which concern a man's relation to God. There seems to be no record of the circumstances of Helwys's death.

A facsimile edn. of *The Mystery of Iniquity* was pub. for the Baptist Historical Society (London, 1935), with introd. by H. Wheeler *Robinson, pp. iii–xv. W. H. Burgess, *John Smith, the Se-Baptist, Thomas Helwys and the First Baptist Church in England* (1911), pp. 107–296 *passim*. E. A. Payne, *Thomas Helwys and the First Baptist Church in England* ([1962]; pamphlet). A. C. Bickley in *DNB* 25 (1891), pp. 375 f. See also works cited under BAPTISTS.

Hemerobaptists (Gk. ἡμέρα, 'day', and βαπτιστής 'baptist'), a Jewish sect for which daily ablution was an essential part of religion. Acc. to *Epiphanius (*Haer.* 1. 17) their doctrines were similar to those of the *Pharisees, except that they denied the resurrection. The sect is mentioned by *Hegesippus (Eus., *HE* 4. 22) and *Justin Martyr (*Dial. c. Tryph.* 80). The *Clementine Recognitions (2. 23) state that *John the Baptist was a Hemerobaptist. J. B. *Lightfoot (*Col.*, p. 402) identified them with the Hebrew sect of Toble-shacharith ('morning bathers').

Hemmerlin, Felix, also 'Hemerli' (*c*.1388–*c*.1460), also 'Malleolus', reformer. A native of Zurich, he studied canon law at Erfurt (1406–8 and 1413–18) and *Bologna (1408–12 and 1423–4) and states that he was present at the Council of *Constance (1415). In 1421 he became provost at St Ursus at Solothurn, where he revised the statutes of his collegiate clergy and defended their rights against the municipality. From now on he loudly advocated reforms of all kinds, e.g. suppression of concubinage and simony and reduction of feast-days; and he also attacked the *Mendicant Orders and the *Lollards. In 1428 he was made Cantor of the Stift at Zurich, and from 1429 onwards he appears as a canon of St Moritz at Zofingen. In his later years he took a prominent part in politics, supporting the alliance of Zurich with Austria against the Swiss Confederation, which he attacked violently in *Dialogus de Nobilitate et Rusticitate* (c.1452). On the reconciliation of Zurich with the Swiss in 1456 he was condemned to the loss of his ecclesiastical offices and perpetual imprisonment. He spent his last years in mild captivity with the *Franciscans at Lucerne. He was the author of over 30 polemical works.

A collection of his writings was pub. by S. Brant at Basle c.1497. Studies by B. Reber (Zurich, 1846) and H. Walser (ibid., 1940). A. Schneider in *PRE* (3rd edn.), 7 (1899), pp. 656–9, s.v. 'Hemerli'.

Henderson, Alexander (c.1583–1646), Scottish Covenanting leader.

As an Episcopalian he obtained a professorship at St Andrews, and in 1611 or 1612 was appointed to the parish of Leuchars in Fife. By 1618 he was sufficiently in sympathy with *Presbyterianism to oppose the Articles of *Perth, and later offered strong resistance to the Prayer Book of 1637. He was mainly responsible for drafting the *National Covenant of 1638, became Moderator of the Assembly which met at Glasgow in Nov. 1638, and in Jan. 1639 was inducted to Greyfriars, Edinburgh. During the *Bishops' Wars of 1639–40 he was the recognized leader of the Scottish Presbyterians, and even *Charles I, on his visit to Scotland in 1641, was forced to accept him as his chaplain and Dean of the Chapel Royal. In 1643 he went to Oxford in a vain attempt at mediation between King and Parliament, while in the following months he prepared the draft of the *Solemn League and Covenant for both Scotland and England (1643) and of the Directory for Public *Worship (1644). In 1646 he spent the last months of his life debating the presbyterian and episcopal systems of Church government with the King.

J. Aiton, *The Life and Times of Alexander Henderson* (1836); T. McCrie and T. Thomson, *Lives of Alexander Henderson and James Guthrie* (1846), pp. 1–140; G. W. Thomson, *Alexander Henderson: A Biography* (1883); R. L. Orr, *Alexander Henderson, Churchman and Statesman* (1919). There is also a short sketch by J. B. Salmond and G. H. Bushnell, *Henderson's Benefaction* (St Andrews, 1942), issued to mark the 3rd centenary of his donation of £1,000 to found the University Library at St Andrews.

Hengstenberg, Ernst Wilhelm (1802–69), biblical exegete.

From 1828 till his death he was Professor of Biblical Exegesis at Berlin. He was brought up in a rationalist atmosphere, then fell under *Pietist influences in 1824–6, and from c.1840 accounted himself an orthodox Lutheran. As editor from 1827 to 1869 of the *Evangelische Kirchenzeitung*, which he had himself founded, he possessed an influential organ in which he attacked the theology of F. D. E. *Schleiermacher and other unorthodox systems.

His works include many commentaries on OT and NT books, some of which were translated into English.

J. Bachmann and T. Schmalenbach, *Ernst Wilhelm Hengstenberg: Sein Leben und Wirken nach gedruckten und ungedruckten Quellen* (3 vols., 1876–92). J. [W.] Rogerson, *Old Testament Criticism in the Nineteenth Century: England and Germany* (1984), pp. 79–90. J. Mehlhausen in *TRE* 15 (1986), pp. 39–42, s.v.

Henotheism (Gk. ἑνός, 'one', and θεός 'god').

A term first employed by F. *Max Müller in 1860 for a primitive form of faith which, as distinct from *Monotheism (belief in the existence of a single god) and monolatry (restriction of worship to a single god), recognizes the existence of several gods, but regards one particular god as the deity of the family or tribe; makes him the centre of its worship; and in its relations with him neglects for practical purposes the existence of others. It thus stands mid-way between polytheism and monotheism. Modern scholars commonly hold that the early Hebrew faith in *Yahweh (down to the 8th cent. BC or later) took this form.

Henoticon (Gk. ἑνωτικόν).

The theological formula put forward in 482 to secure union between the *Monophysites and the Orthodox and sponsored by the Emp. *Zeno. It was apparently the work chiefly of Acacius, Patr. of *Constantinople, and *Peter Mongo, Patr. of *Alexandria. It reaffirmed the traditional faith of the Church epitomized in the *Nicene–Constantinopolitan Creed and accepted the Twelve Anathemas of St *Cyril of Alexandria, condemned both *Nestorius and *Eutyches, but it made no reference to the burning question of the number of 'natures' in Christ, issued an ambiguous disclaimer of the Council of *Chalcedon, and omitted all mention of the *Tome of Leo. Widely accepted in the E., but never countenanced at Rome, it provoked the *Acacian schism, the first division between E. and W. Christendom.

Text in *Evagrius, *HE* 3. 14 (*PG* 86. 2620–25). Crit. edn. by E. *Schwartz in *Codex Vaticanus gr. 1431: Eine antichalkedonische Sammlung aus der Zeit Kaiser Zenos* (Abh. (Bayr.), 32, Heft 6 [1927], pp. 52–4); Lat. tr. in Liberatus' *Breviarium*, pr. ibid., pp. 54–6. E. Schwartz, *Publizistische Sammlungen zum acacianischen Schisma* (Abh. (Bayr.), NF, Heft 10, 1934), esp. pp. 182–218. S. Salaville, AA, 'L'Affaire de l'hénotique ou le premier schisme byzantin au Vᵉ siècle', *ÉO* 18 (1918), pp. 255–66, 389–97; 19 (1920), pp. 49–68. A. Grillmeier, *Jesus der Christus im Glauben der Kirche* 2, pt. 1 [1986], pp. 279–358 (Eng. tr., 1987, pp. 247–317). 'L.' Salaville, AA, in *DTC* 6 (1920), cols. 2153–78, s.v. 'Hénotique', with bibl.

Henricians.

A medieval heretical sect which arose at Tours in the 12th cent. under the inspiration of *Henry of Lausanne (q.v.). They seem to have been closely connected with the followers of *Peter de Bruys (q.v.)

Henrietta Maria (1609–66), the Queen of *Charles I and daughter of *Henry IV of France.

She married Charles in 1625, on condition that the penal laws against RCs were suspended and that the Queen be allowed free exercise of her religion. After the assassination of Buckingham in 1628, the Queen acquired great influence over Charles. She never liked W. *Laud or the Earl of Strafford, and she formed a curious alliance with *Puritan courtiers in the 1630s to obstruct diplomatic rapprochement with

Spain; however, her Catholicism fuelled public fears about RC manipulation of Charles and his court. She has often been accused of encouraging Charles in his more despotic acts, e.g. his attempt to arrest the Five Members in 1642. During the Civil War she increased her unpopularity by attempting to raise money and forces for the King from France. She finally left Charles for France in Apr. 1644, where she remained until after the Restoration, when Somerset House was given her for a residence.

M. A. E. Green (ed.), *Letters of Queen Henrietta Maria* (1857); le Comte [C.] de Baillon, *Henriette-Marie de France, reine d'Angleterre: Étude historique . . . suivie de ses lettres inédites* (1877); H. Ferrero (ed.), *Lettres de Henriette-Marie de France, reine d'Angleterre, à sa sœur Christine, duchesse de Savoie* (Estratto dalla Miscellanea di Storia italiana, 2nd ser. 5; 1881). C. Cotolendi, *La Vie de très-haute et très-puissante Princesse Henriette-Marie de France, reine de la Grand'Bretagne* (1690). Modern Lives by I. A. Taylor (2 vols., London, 1905), Q. Bone (ibid., 1973), E. Hamilton (ibid., 1976), and R. K. Marshall (ibid., for the National Portrait Gallery, 1990). R. M. Smuts, 'The Puritan followers of Henrietta Maria in the 1630s', *EHR* 93 (1978), pp. 26–45. E. Veevers, *Images of Love and Religion: Queen Henrietta Maria and Court Entertainments* (Cambridge, 1989). S. R. Gardiner in *DNB* 25 (1891), pp. 429–36. See also bibl. to CHARLES I.

Henry II, St (972–1024), German King and Emperor.

The son of Henry, Duke of Bavaria ('the Quarrelsome'), he succeeded his cousin Otto III as King in 1002, intent on consolidating the political unity of Germany. In his earlier years he was involved in constant warfare first against attacks from the East and then in Lombardy, where he defeated Arduin of Ivrea. In 1007 he created and richly endowed the new see of Bamberg, largely to effect the Germanization of the Wends. He was crowned Emperor by Benedict VIII on 14 Feb. 1014 during an expedition to Rome. His frequent and often high-handed interference in Church affairs issued in many disputes with the ecclesiastical leaders in his domains, though he commonly had the political support of Rome. In his later years he gave his encouragement to the monastic reform movement centred on the abbey of *Gorze. In 1021, on a last journey to Rome, he assisted in preparations for ending the Greek supremacy in Italy. Later legends saw in him a monarch of outstanding piety and asceticism. He was canonized in 1146. Feast day, 13 (formerly 15) July. (His wife, Cunegund, was canonized in 1200; feast day, 3 Mar.)

H. Bresslau, H. Bloch, M. Meyer, and R. Holtzmann (eds.), *Die Urkunden Heinrichs II und Arduins* (MGH, Diplomata Regum et Imperatorum Germaniae, 3 (1900–3), with 'Nachträgen zu den Urkunden Heinrichs II' in 4 (1909), pp. 419–32 and 552). *AASS*, Jul. 3 (1723), pp. 711–93; crit. text of Life by Adalbold, Bp. of Utrecht, 1010–27, ed. G. Waitz, *MGH*, Scriptores, 4 (1841), pp. 679–95, and of mid-12th cent. Life by Adalbert, deacon of Bamberg, ibid., pp. 789–816, with 'Additamentum', pp. 816–820, and of 'Vita Sanctae Cunegundis', with miracles, pp. 821–8. Life by Adalbold also ed. H. van Rijn in *Nederlandse Historische Bronnen*, 3 (1983), pp. 7–95, with further refs. S. Hirsch, *Jahrbücher des deutschen Reiches unter Heinrich II* (Jahrbücher der deutschen Geschichte, 3 vols. in 2, 1862–75). H. L. Mikoletzky, *Kaiser Heinrich II und die Kirche* (Veröffentlichungen des Instituts für Österreichische Geschichtsforschung, 8; 1951). T. Schieffer, 'Heinrich II. and Konrad II. Die Umprägung des Geschichtsbildes durch die Kirchenreform des 11. Jahrhunderts', *Deutsches Archiv*, 8 (1951), pp. 384–437. S. Weinfurter, 'Die Zentralisierung der Herrschaftsgewalt im Reich durch Kaiser Heinrich II.', *Historisches Jahrbuch*, 106 (1986), pp. 241–97. H. Bloch, 'Die Urkunden Kaiser Hein-

richs II für Kloster Michelsberg zu Bamberg', *NA* 19 (1894), pp. 603–49. R. Klauser, *Der Heinrichs- und Kunigundenkult im mittelalterlichen Bistum Bamberg* (Bamberg, 1957). Further study of the development of his cult in Basle by C. Pfaff (Basle, 1963). R. Folz, *Les Saints Rois du moyen âge en occident* (Subsidia Hagiographica, 68; 1984), esp. pp. 84–91. Id. in *DHGE* 23 (1990), cols. 1047–50, s.v. 'Henri II'.

Henry IV (1050–1106), German King and Emperor.

The son of the Emp. Henry III (1039–56), he succeeded to the throne in 1056 and was declared of age in 1065. His reign was beset with difficulties owing to the rebellious Saxon princes on the one hand and the reforms of Pope *Gregory VII on the other. Gregory prohibited *simony and clerical marriage, and his energetic pursuit of reform provoked bitter resentment in some German Church circles. Henry, having conquered the Saxons in 1075, refused obedience to the Pope and answered the threat of excommunication by declaring Gregory deposed. Thereupon Gregory carried out his threat and released Henry's subjects from their oath of allegiance. The King's position having become desperate when the Saxons rose again and the princes refused obedience unless he was reconciled to the Pope, Henry submitted at *Canossa in 1077 and, having done penance, was freed from excommunication and returned to Germany. The peace between Pope and King was, however, short-lived. Three years later Henry was again excommunicated, but at the Council of Brixen selected an *antipope who in 1084 was enthroned at Rome as Clement III and crowned Henry Emperor. Gregory died the next year, but his successors Victor II and *Urban II carried on the struggle. The last years of Henry's reign were filled with revolts, two of his sons became rebels, and only his premature death saved Germany from civil war. Under his successor, Henry V (1106–25), the investiture conflict ended in the compromise of the Concordat of *Worms (1122).

Constitutiones ed. G. H. Pertz in *MHG*, Leges, 2 (1837), pp. 44–62; mostly repr. in J. P. Migne, *PL* 151. 1125–66; D. v. Gladiss and A. Gawlik (eds.), *Die Urkunden Heinrichs IV* (MGH, Diplomata Regum et Imperatorum Germaniae, 6; 3 parts, 1952–78). *Briefe*, ed. C. Erdmann (MGH, Deutsches Mittelalter, 1; 1937) and, with Germ. tr., by F.-J. Schmale, *Quellen zur Geschichte Kaiser Heinrich IV.* (Ausgewählte Quellen zur deutschen Geschichte des Mittelalters, 12; 1973), pp. 51–141. 'Vita Henrici IV. Imperatoris', ed. I. Schmale-Ott, ibid., pp. 407–67, with further docs., pp. 470–83. S. Hellmann, 'Die Vita Henrici IV. und die kaiserliche Kanzlei', *Historische Vierteljahrschrift*, 28 (1934), pp. 273–334. G. Meyer von Knonau, *Jahrbücher des deutschen Reiches unter Heinrich IV. und Heinrich V.*, vols. 1–5 (1890–1904). E. Boshof, *Heinrich IV.: Herrscher an einer Zeitenwende* (Göttingen, 1979). B. Schmeidler, *Kaiser Heinrich IV. und seine Helfer im Investiturstreit* (1927). H. F. Haefele, *Fortuna Heinrich IV. Imperatoris: Untersuchungen zur Lebenschreibung des dritten Saliers* (Graz and Cologne, 1954). K. Leyser, 'The crisis of medieval Germany', *Proceedings of the British Academy*, 69 for 1983 (1984), pp. 409–43. G. Tellenbach in *DHGE* 23 (1990), cols. 1050–5, s.v. 'Henri IV', with extensive bibl. See also bibl. to CANOSSA and GREGORY VII.

Henry IV (1553–1610), King of France.

Brought up as a Protestant, he became King of Navarre in 1572. He took part in the wars of religion on the Protestant side, and, on the assassination of Henry III in 1589, inherited the Crown of France. But his Protestantism made him unacceptable to the Catholic League, which was supported by *Philip II of Spain and the Pope; and though he defeated the

Guise party in the field he was not recognized as King until his conversion to Catholicism in 1593. Opinion is now against the popular legend that this was a merely political move ('Paris vaut bien une messe'). His lengthy discussions with theologians before his submission, together with his protestations that 'Religion is not changed as easily as a shirt', are considered sufficient proof of his sincerity. It was not until 1595, however, after many difficulties, esp. from Philip II, that the Pope solemnly absolved Henry from the crime of heresy. In 1598 the King promulgated the Edict of *Nantes, which gave freedom of worship to the Protestants in recognized places and permitted them to garrison certain towns as a security for its maintenance. By extending the powers of the Crown, and with the economic reforms undertaken by his minister, the Duc de Sully, Henry did much to restore prosperity to his country. The lines of his domestic and foreign policy were later continued by A. J. du P. *Richelieu. He was assassinated by the fanatic Ravaillac on 14 May 1610.

M. Berger de Xivrey and J. Guadet (eds.), *Recueil des lettres missives de Henri IV* (Collection de documents inédits sur l'histoire de France, publiés par ordre du Roi et par les soins du Ministre de l'Instruction Publique, 9 vols., 1843–76). Modern selection of *Les plus belles lettres de Henri IV*, ed. P. Erlanger (1962). B. Barbiche (ed.), *Lettres de Henri IV concernant les relations du Saint-Siège et de la France 1595–1609* (ST 250; 1968). N. Valois (ed.), *Inventaire des arrêts du Conseil d'État (règne de Henri IV)* (2 vols., 1886–93). Contemporary account of events in Pierre de L'Estoile's *Mémoires-Journaux*; his *Journal pour le règne de Henri IV*, ed. L.-R. Lefèvre and A. Martin (3 vols. [1948–60]); Eng. tr. of selections by N. L. Roelker, *The Paris of Henry of Navarre as seen by Pierre de l'Estoile* (Cambridge, Mass., 1958). There is a vast lit. on Henry IV. J. H. Mariéjol in E. Lavisse, *Histoire de France*, 6 (pt. 1; 1904), pp. 303–423 and (pt. 2; 1904), pp. 1–140, with full bibl. refs.; J.-P. Babelon, *Henri IV* (Paris [1982]), with full bibl.; D. [J.] Buisseret, *Henry IV* (London, 1984). Other modern studies include those of P. de Vaissière (Paris, 1925), M. Reinhard (ibid., 1943), R. Ritter (ibid., 1944), D. [E. C.] Seward, *The Last Bourbon* (London, 1971), and J. Garrison (Paris, 1984). R. Mousnier, *L'Assassinat d'Henri IV* (1964; Eng. tr., 1973). M. Greengrass, *France in the Age of Henri IV: The Struggle for Stability* (1984). See also bibl. to FRANCE, CHRISTIANITY IN, and NANTES, EDICT OF.

Henry VI (1421–71), King of England. He succeeded his father, Henry V, in 1422. During his minority England was ruled by a Council, the King's protector being John, Duke of Bedford, and his first spiritual guide the *Carmelite theologian, Thomas *Netter. He was crowned King of England in 1429 and King of France in 1431. Throughout his reign the difficulties in France increased, and the situation in England was unsettled, chiefly through differences between the Duke of Gloucester and Card. H. *Beaufort and popular opposition to the Duke of Suffolk's peace policy. After Suffolk's death (1450), Richard of York led opposition to the court and when Henry fell into a depressive stupor in August 1453 York became Protector. The birth of a son to Henry in 1453 had excluded York from the succession, and his rivalry with Edmund Beaufort, Duke of Somerset, led to a battle at St Albans in 1455 in which Somerset died. Relations between Henry and Richard of York deteriorated into civil war in 1459, and in 1460 Henry was taken prisoner and compelled to declare York his heir. After Richard's death (1460) he was freed, but Edward of York made himself King and Henry lived as an exile in Scotland. In 1465 he was captured and

imprisoned in the Tower, until in 1470 Warwick restored him to the throne. After six months, however, he was once more confined to the Tower, where he was murdered.

Henry VI was a deeply religious man, but too generous and trusting to be a successful ruler in his troubled age. He often sought refreshment in religious houses and gave much time to prayer and pious works. He was passionately devoted to the encouragement of learning, and was the founder of Eton and of King's College, Cambridge (1440 and 1441). The report of many miracles at his tomb at the *Benedictine monastery of Chertsey in Surrey soon made it a place of pilgrimage; and though Richard III had his body removed to St George's Chapel, *Windsor, he was unable to put a stop to the popular devotion. Henry VII petitioned Innocent VIII and *Alexander VI for his canonization, and in modern times renewed efforts have been made to this end.

J. Stevenson (ed.), *Letters and Papers Illustrative of the Wars of the English in France during the Reign of Henry the Sixth* (Rolls Series, 2 vols. bound in 3; 1861–4). Memoir of Henry VI by John Blacman, his confessor, orig. pub. London, 1510, repr. mainly from text of T. *Hearne, 1732, by M. R. James (Cambridge, 1919). The Lat. account of his miracles in Brit. Lib. Royal MS 13. C. VIII, written c.1500, ed. R. [A.] *Knox and S. Leslie, with introd. and Eng. tr. (Cambridge, 1923); crit. edn. by P. Grosjean, SJ (Subsidia Hagiographica, 22; 1935). R. A. Griffiths, *The Reign of King Henry VI* (1981); B. P. Wolffe, *Henry VI* (1981). R. Lovatt, 'John Blacman: Biographer of Henry VI', in R. H. C. Davis and J. M. Wallace-Hadrill (eds.), *The Writing of History in the Middle Ages: Essays Presented to Richard William Southern* (Oxford, 1981), pp. 415–44; id., 'A Collector of Apocryphal Anecdotes: Blacman Revisited', in T. Pollard (ed.), *Property and Politics: Essays in Later Medieval History* (Gloucester and New York), pp. 172–97. T. F. Tout in *DNB* 26 (1891), pp. 56–69.

Henry VIII (1491–1547), King of England from 1509. The second son of Henry VII and Elizabeth of York, Henry became heir apparent on the death of his brother Arthur in 1502. Although he learned Latin, French, Spanish, mathematics, and music, he was not given early responsibility or trained for kingship. He nevertheless became the symbol of an expected new age of military and cultural achievement, and there was great enthusiasm at his accession. While Henry planned war, the bishops, led by W. *Warham, attempted to recover the 'liberties' undermined by Henry VII and sought to stifle criticism and *Lollard heresy.

Henry disliked work and was willing to allow T. *Wolsey much freedom of action as chancellor and legate, but in 1515 the clergy's claim to exemption from trial in the royal courts drove Henry to defend his temporal jurisdiction. By 1521 M. *Luther's ideas had begun to influence the English universities, and Henry agreed to a demonstration of official orthodoxy. Although the drafting was assisted by theologians and T. *More, Henry took the responsibility—and credit—for the *Assertio Septem Sacramentorum* (1521). He was rewarded by *Leo X with the title '*Defender of the Faith' for his attack on heresy and defence of Papal authority.

By 1526 Henry was tired of his wife, Catherine of Aragon, restricted by the Spanish alliance which she represented, worried by the absence of a male heir—and in love with *Anne Boleyn. Anne was determined to be Queen, not another mistress; she insisted on marriage, and in 1527 Henry began his six-year quest for annulment of his marriage with Catherine. He argued that her brief marriage with his late brother Arthur invalidated his own union with her, despite the dispensation given by *Julius II. He tried many strategems: a collusive prosecution by Warham and Wolsey; a plan to have Papal authority delegated to Wolsey; a plea for dispensation for *bigamy; a demand for a *decretal commission which declared the law in Henry's favour; and threats that Papal authority and ecclesiastical jurisdiction were at risk if Rome was uncooperative.

Henry's conscience often followed where his wishes led. He became convinced that his marriage to Catherine contravened the law of God (as declared in Lev. 18: 16 and 20: 21), and that their failure to have a son proved as much. Annulment became an issue of principle as well as passion. But dominant canonical opinion held that the Levitical prohibition was not an immutable divine law, and *Clement VII was unlikely to agree that Julius II had infringed God's law. In June and July 1529 pleadings on the marriage were heard in London before the legates Wolsey and L. *Campeggio, but Clement revoked the suit to Rome. Henry's schemes and desires were frustrated by Clement's refusal to alienate the Emp. *Charles V, who was Catherine's nephew.

Henry summoned a Parliament for Nov. 1529, when criticism of Wolsey extended to criticism of ecclesiastical abuses associated with him, esp. pluralism and fees. Such attacks might frighten the Pope and prompt English churchmen to greater zeal in the royal cause. His team of divorce advisers organized the collection of opinions in support of his case from canon law and theology faculties in the universities of Europe and of evidence which might justify a unilateral solution in England. By Aug. 1530 the advisers had a dossier of precedents and texts which were said to prove that England had provincial independence and its King had sovereign authority; Henry now advanced these arguments with vigour. But a meeting of clergy and lawyers in Oct. 1530 refused to accept that the Pope's jurisdiction could be flouted.

After this rejection (and Clement's threat to excommunicate Henry if he remarried) the King adopted haphazard intimidatory measures designed to scare the Pope into recognizing England's jurisdictional independence and the English clergy into recognizing royal authority. In 1530–1 a charge of *praemunire against the whole clergy (for illegal exercise of ecclesiastical jurisdiction) was used to extract from *Convocation a heavy fine and a limited recognition of Henry's claims. In 1532 the Payment of *Annates Act 1531, which was conditional, threatened to cut off Papal revenues from England. A House of Commons petition against Church law and courts was used (prob. by T. *Cromwell rather than Henry) to secure the '*Submission of the Clergy' from a rump Convocation. In practice, however, these gains did little to advance the cause of Henry's marriage to Anne Boleyn.

The death of Warham in Aug. 1532 allowed Henry to appoint a more compliant Abp. of Canterbury: T. *Cranmer. In Dec. 1532 Anne became pregnant; in Jan. 1533 Henry secretly married her; in Apr. Parliament forbade appeals to Rome in temporal cases such as marriage; in May the Convocations declared marriage to a brother's widow contrary to God's law; Cranmer annulled Henry's

marriage to Catherine and pronounced that to Anne valid; and on 1 June Anne was crowned Queen. So far Henry had attempted to grasp just enough jurisdiction to gain a divorce, rather than to assert a true supremacy, but he was soon forced to go further. When the Pope threatened to excommunicate him unless he returned to Catherine, Henry sought to protect himself and the succession, even though Anne had disappointingly given birth to a daughter. In 1534 a Succession Act imposed a national oath recognizing his marriage to Anne and entailing the Crown on its children, a *Supremacy Act declared Henry 'supreme head' of the English Church, and a Treasons Act forbade denial of the supremacy.

Henry was now faced with the political consequences of the schism into which he had blundered. The most eminent of those who denied the royal supremacy (J. *Fisher, More, and some leading monks) were executed. The threat of a Catholic crusade against England forced Henry into defensive preparations; he paid for these by taking annates and tenths from ecclesiastical benefices, and began the *dissolution of the monasteries in 1536. His need for allies led to negotiations with Lutheran princes and the *Ten Articles and Royal *Injunctions of 1536. But in Oct. 1536 the *Pilgrimage of Grace showed that there was much hostility to change, at least in the northern counties. This outburst seems to have frightened Henry; he refused to give full official sanction in 1537 to the *Bishops' Book, and he began to draft his own more conservative revision, which eventually became the 1543 *King's Book.

Though further dealings with the Lutherans were necessary, and the 1538 Injunctions ordered the placing of an English Bible in every church, Henry would make no more concessions on crucial matters, esp. *transubstantiation, *celibacy of the clergy, and *Communion in one kind. These and other orthodox matters were prescribed by the 1539 Act of *Six Articles; H. *Latimer and N. *Shaxton felt obliged to resign their sees. In 1540 Cromwell tried to advance a Lutheran alliance by pressing Henry (now a widower) into marriage with Anne of Cleves, but as soon as it was diplomatically safe to do so Henry divorced her and Cromwell was executed. Henry now tried to maintain a balance in religion; it was symbolized in July 1540 by the simultaneous execution of three alleged Papalists and three Lutherans. In 1543 the reading of the English Bible was restricted by law, but in 1544 the English *Litany was issued. In 1545 a statute was passed permitting the King to seize the property of the *chantries, but little use had been made of this by the time of his death.

Though Henry allowed lesser fry to suffer, he protected Cranmer from attack by conservatives in 1543, and the conservative S. *Gardiner from attack by the reformers in 1544. In 1546, however, a reformist coup drove Gardiner and the Howard family into disfavour, and when Henry died in Jan. 1547, the reformers were left in effective control of the boy king *Edward VI. Henry was pious in his outward religious observances, his various drafts and revisions show that he had biblical and theological learning, and he formulated his own distinctive views, esp. on the position of priests. But his will was thoroughly Catholic in its emphases, and (despite the Dissolution of Colleges Act 1545) it endowed prayers for his soul.

Modern edn. of Henry's *Assertio septem sacramentorum adversus Martinum Lutherum* by P. Fraenkel (Corpus Catholicorum, 43; Münster [1992]). Documentary evidence of his reign in *Letters and Papers, Foreign and Domestic, of the Reign of Henry VIII*, vols. 1–4 ed. J. S. Brewer (1862–75); vols. 5–21 ed. J. *Gairdner and R. H. Brodie (1880–1907). Relevant section of Edward Hall's *Chronicle* (1548), ed. C. Whibley (2 vols., 1904). J. S. Brewer (ed. J. Gairdner), *The Reign of Henry VIII from his Accession to the Death of Wolsey* (2 vols., 1884). A. F. Pollard, *Henry VIII* (London, 1902); J. J. Scarisbrick, *Henry VIII* (ibid., 1968); L. B. Smith, *Henry VIII: The Mask of Royalty* (1971). N. S. Tjernagel, *Henry VIII and the Lutherans: A Study in Anglo-Lutheran Relations from 1521 to 1547* (St Louis, 1965). H. A. Kelly, *The Matrimonial Trials of Henry VIII* (Stanford, Calif., 1976); G. Bedouelle and P. Le Gal (eds.), *Le 'divorce' du roi Henry VIII: Études et documents* (Travaux d'Humanisme et Renaissance, 221; Geneva, 1987). S. E. Lehmberg, *The Reformation Parliament 1529–1536* (Cambridge, 1970); id., *The Later Parliaments of Henry VIII 1536–1547* (ibid., 1977). G. R. Elton, *Reform and Reformation: England 1509–1558* (1977), pp. 1–332. D. Starkey, *The Reign of Henry VIII: Personalities and Politics* [1985]. J. Guy, *Tudor England* (Oxford, 1988), pp. 80–199. Introductory essays on various aspects of the reign, ed. D. Starkey, *Henry VIII: A European Court in England* (1991). R. Rex, *Henry VIII and the English Reformation* (1993). Life of Catherine of Aragon by G. Mattingly (London, 1942). See also bibl. to REFORMATION.

Henry Beaufort. See BEAUFORT, HENRY.

Henry Bradshaw Society. The Society founded in 1890 in memory of Henry Bradshaw (1831–86), librarian of the University of Cambridge, 'for the purpose of printing liturgical MSS and rare editions of service books and illustrative documents, on an historical and scientific basis, preference being given to those which bear upon the history of the Book of Common Prayer or of the Church of England'. It has published a number of important texts, by no means all Anglican.

G. W. Prothero, *A Memoir of Henry Bradshaw* (1888). J. S. Crone, *Henry Bradshaw: His Life and Work* (Lecture; Dublin [1931]).

Henry of Blois (d. 1171), Bp. of *Winchester. The grandson of *William I ('the Conqueror') and brother of King Stephen, he was brought up at *Cluny, which imbued him with high ideals of religious discipline and of the rights of the Church. In 1126 Henry I made him Abbot of *Glastonbury, which he ruled impeccably for 45 years, and in 1129 Bp. of Winchester; by a Papal dispensation, he held both offices together. In 1135 he helped to make Stephen King. After the death of Abp. William of Corbeil (1136), he hoped for the see of *Canterbury; but it was granted to *Theobald (1139). In the same year, however, Innocent II granted Henry of Blois a legatine commission which made him in some matters the Archbishop's superior. In the Chronicles he is termed 'lord of England'. After Stephen's capture at the Battle of Lincoln (1141), Henry deserted Stephen's cause and declared for Matilda, accompanying her to London for the coronation (which never took place); but finding his assistance unwanted, he returned to Stephen's side and made formal profession of loyalty at a Council in London (Dec. 1141). Until his legatine powers terminated on Innocent's death (1143) he continued to oppose Abp. Theobald, one of his chief endeavours being the elevation of Winchester to an archiepiscopal see (with the seven suffragan sees of

*Salisbury, *Exeter, *Wells, *Chichester, *Hereford, and *Worcester and a newly created see of Hyde Abbey). After Stephen's death (Oct. 1154) his position under Henry II was insecure and in the *Becket controversy he did what he could for the Archbishop.

Henry was a great patron of the arts and builder. He much extended the fabric at Glastonbury; built several castles, including Farnham and Wolvesey; and founded the monastery of St Cross at Winchester (enlarged by Card. Henry *Beaufort). He was also a munificent benefactor to Cluny. His high character won the esteem of such men as *Peter the Venerable, Becket, and *John of Salisbury.

L. Voss, *Heinrich von Blois, Bischof von Winchester, 1129–71* (Historische Studien, Heft 210; 1932), with bibl. M. D. *Knowles, *The Episcopal Colleagues of Thomas Becket* (Ford Lectures for 1949; 1951), pp. 34–7 and *passim*. H. W. C. Davis in *DECH* (1912), pp. 264 f., s.v.

Henry of Ghent (d. 1293), 'De Gandavo', 'doctor solemnis', theologian. Archdeacon (1277) of Bruges and subsequently (1278 or 1279) of Tournai, he combined these offices with an active teaching career in the Theology Faculty of *Paris University, of which he was a master by 1276. In 1277 he was on the commission of theologians who enquired into the errors of the Arts Faculty. In 1282 he was one of several theologians who deliberated on the Papal privileges relating to confession granted to the Mendicant Orders; for the rest of his career he remained an outspoken opponent of these privileges, an attitude which earned him in 1290 a stiff rebuke from Bernard Gaetani, the future Pope *Boniface VIII. During the years 1276–92, he produced his extensive *Quodlibeta*, his *Summa*, *Quaestiones ordinariae*, at least two sermons, and probably also the questions on *Aristotle's *Physics* and the commentary on the *Hexaemeron* attributed to him. There is also a large body of work of which the attribution is more doubtful.

A critic of Greek and Arab necessitarianism, Henry was the chief representative among the secular clergy of neo-Augustinianism; he stressed God's omnipotence, God's free will in the act of creation, the existence of exemplar ideas or possible essences, man's need for divine illumination to attain true cognition, and the primacy of will over reason in human action. He denied that primary matter was pure potentiality; and on the question of essence and existence, he developed an 'intentional' distinction as a middle way between the real distinction favoured by *Giles of Rome and a distinction only of reason. His fusion of Aristotle, *Avicenna, and the *Neoplatonic tradition was much criticized both by his contemporaries and by the next generation of theologians, but it was destined to be influential, particularly on *Duns Scotus.

Opera Omnia, ed. R. Macken, OFM, and others (Ancient and Medieval Philosophy, 2nd ser.; Louvain and Leiden, 1979 ff.), with useful introd. on his life and works in vol. 5, pp. vii–xxiv. The *Quaestiones in Librum de Causis*, very doubtfully attributed to Henry, ed. J. P. Zwaenepoel, CICM (Philosophes médiévaux, 15; Louvain, 1974). J. Paulus, *Henri de Gand: Essai sur les tendances de sa métaphysique* (Études de Philosophie médiévale, 25; 1938); cf. A. Maurer, OSB, 'Henry of Ghent and the Unity of Man', *Mediaeval Studies*, 10 (1948), pp. 1–20. G. de Lagarde, 'La philosophie sociale d'Henri de Gand et Godefroid de Fontaines', *AHDLMA* 14 (1943), pp. 73–142; B. Smalley, 'A Commentary on the Hexaemeron by Henry of Ghent', *RTAM* 20 (1953), pp. 60–101; A. C. Pegis, 'Toward a New Way to God: Henry of Ghent', *Mediaeval Studies*, 30 (1968), pp. 226–47, and 31 (1969), pp. 93–116; R. Macken, 'La temporalité radicale de la créature selon Henri de Gand', *RTAM*, 38 (1971), pp. 211–72; id., 'La théorie d'illumination divine dans la philosophie d'Henri de Gand', ibid. 39 (1972), pp. 82–112; id, 'La volonté humaine, faculté plus élevée que l'intelligence selon Henri de Gand', ibid. 42 (1975), pp. 5–51; J. V. Brown, 'Divine illumination in Henry of Ghent', ibid. 41 (1974), pp. 177–99; S. P. Marrone, *Truth and Scientific Knowledge in the Thought of Henry of Ghent* (Speculum Anniversary Monographs, 11; Cambridge, Mass., 1985); A. J. Minnis, 'The *Accessus* Extended: Henry of Ghent on the Transmission and Reception of Theology', in M. D. Jordan and K. Emery (eds.), *Ad litteram: Authoritative Texts and Their Medieval Writers* (Notre Dame Conferences in Medieval Sudies, 3; Notre Dame and London [1992]), pp. 275–326. Bibl. by M. Laarmann in *Franziskanische Studien*, 73 (1991), pp. 324–68. J. Paulus in *NCE* 6 (1967), pp. 1035–7, s.v.; J. Ribaillier in *Dict. Sp.* 7 (pt. 1; 1969), cols. 197–210, s.v 'Henri (18) de Gand', with extensive bibl. See also art. by J. P. Wippel, cited under GILES OF ROME.

Henry of Lausanne (d. after 1145), medieval sectarian. Little is known of his life. He was probably a French monk who had left his monastery and may have been connected with *Cluny. He became an itinerant preacher and gave the Lenten sermons at Le Mans *c.* 1116 by permission of the bishop, *Hildebert of Lavardin. His invectives against the worldliness of the clergy and his insistence on the ideal of absolute poverty made him very popular. But he was expelled from the diocese because he carried anti-clericalism to the point of heresy; he continued his activities in the S. of France. Acc. to St *Bernard, he denied the objective efficacy of the Sacraments and made it dependent on the worthy character of the priest. In 1135 he was arrested and forced to recant at the Synod of Pisa, but soon resumed his anticlerical preaching, strongly opposed by St Bernard. He was arrested a second time *c.*1145 and probably died soon after. He was in some respects a precursor of the *Waldensians.

St Bernard, *Ep.* 241 (*Opera*, 8, Rome, 1977, pp. 125–7). Eng. tr. of primary material, with introd., in W. L. Wakefield and A. P. Evans, *Heresies of the High Middle Ages* (Records of Civilization, Sources and Studies, 81; 1969), pp. 107–17, with notes pp. 675 f. M. Esposito, 'Sur quelques écrits concernant les hérésies et les hérétiques aux XIIᵉ et XIIIᵉ siècles', 1, 'Traité contre Henri l'Hérésiarque', *RHE* 36 (1940), pp. 143 f. R. Manselli, 'Il monaco Enrico e la sua eresia', *Bullettino dell'Istituto storico italiano per il medio evo e Archivio Muratoriano*, 65 (1953), pp. 1–63. J. B. Russell, *Dissent and Reform in the Early Middle Ages* (Berkeley and Los Angeles, Calif., 1965), esp. pp. 68–78; see index. F. Vernet in *DTC* 6 (1920), cols. 2178–83, s.v. 'Henri, hérésiarque', with bibl.; R. Manselli in *Dict. Sp.* 7 (pt. 1; 1969), cols. 220 f., s.v. 'Henri (30) dit de Lausanne'.

Henry of Susa. See HOSTIENSIS.

Henry Suso, Bl (*c.*1295–1366), German spiritual writer. Prob. a native of Constance, he entered the *Dominican convent there at the age of 13. After five years of routine religious life, he experienced a conversion and adopted rigid standards focused on devotion to Holy Wisdom. About 1322 he was sent to study theology at Cologne, where he was profoundly influenced by *Eckhart. He returned to Constance as a lector *c.*1326 and shortly afterwards wrote *Das Büchlein der Wahrheit* ('The Little Book

of Truth'), a speculative elucidation of Eckhartian doctrines misunderstood by the *Brethren of the Free Spirit. In 1330 he fell victim to hostility to Eckhart's teaching and to the tension between the German Provincial and the Dominican reformers and was deprived of his teaching position. In the following years he preached widely, esp. in Switzerland and the Upper Rhine area; although he suffered persecution, his spiritual teaching was much valued, esp. in women's convents such as that of the Dominicans at Töss. He was prior of Constance *c.*1344–6, though at the time the community was dispersed and in exile. He was moved to Ulm *c.*1348, and spent the rest of his life there.

The chronology and extent of his writings is disputed. Two collections of letters survive, revealing the intimacy and tact of his spiritual direction. His main, undisputed, work, 'The Little Book of Eternal Wisdom' or 'Clock of Wisdom', was written in two versions, German (*Das Büchlein der ewigen Weisheit*), and Latin (*Horologium Sapientiae*). It is a practical, warmly devotional, though sometimes wryly humorous, book of meditation, and it was widely read in the 14th and 15th cents.; it was translated or adapted into several other European languages, incl. English.

His veneration began shortly after his death; his cult was approved by Pope *Gregory XVI in 1831. Feast day 23 Jan. (formerly 2 Mar., then 15 Feb.).

Collected edn. of orig. Ger. Works pub. Augsburg, 1482; crit. edn. by K. Bihlmeyer (Stuttgart, 1907; repr. Frankfurt, 1961). Crit. edn. of *Horologium Sapientiae* by P. Künzle, OP (Spicilegium Friburgense, 23; 1977). Modern Fr. tr. of his Works from the orig. Ger., by J. Ancelet-Hustache (Paris, 1943; 2nd edn., 1977). Eng. tr. made from modern Ger. version of N. Heller (Regensburg, 1926) by M. A. Edward, OP, *The Exemplar: Life and Writings of Blessed Henry Suso* (2 vols., Dubuque, Iowa, 1962). Separate Eng. trs. of his autobiog. by J. M. Clark (London, 1952), of the *Little Book of Eternal Wisdom and Little Book of Truth* by id. (ibid., 1953), and of the smaller collection of Letters by K. Goldman (ibid., 1955). C. Gröber, *Der Mystiker Heinrich Seuse: Die Geschichte seines Lebens. Die Entstehung und Echtheit seiner Werke* (1941). J. A. Bizet, *Henri Suso et le déclin de la scolastique* [1946]. E. M. Filthaut, OP (ed.), *Heinrich Seuse: Studien zum 600. Todestag 1366–1966* (Cologne, 1966). A.-M. Holenstein-Hasler, 'Studien zur Vita Heinrich Seuses', *Zeitschrift für Schweizerische Kirchengeschichte*, 62 (1968), pp. 185–332. E. Colledge, OSA, and J. C. Marler, ' "Mystical" Pictures in the Suso "Exemplar" MS Strasbourg 2929', *Archivum Fratrum Praedicatorum*, 44 (1984), pp. 293–354. J. M. Clark, *The Great German Mystics* (1949), pp. 54–74, with bibl. pp. 114–17. W. A. Hinnebusch, OP, *The History of the Dominican Order*, 2 (New York [1973]), pp. 312–23. A. Walz, OP, 'Bibliographiae susonianae conatus', *Angelicum*, 46 (1969), pp. 430–91. J. A. Bizet in *Dict. Sp.* 7 (pt. 1; 1969), cols. 234–57, s.v. 'Henri (43) Suso', with extensive bibl.

Henry, Matthew (1662–1714), Nonconformist biblical exegete. The son of Philip Henry, who was ejected in 1662 by the Act of *Uniformity, he began to study for the legal profession, but soon decided to devote himself to theology and resided at the Islington Academy under Thomas Doolittle from 1680 to 1682. From 1687 to 1712 he was Presbyterian Minister at *Chester, where a meeting-house was opened for him in Crook Lane (now Crook St.) in 1700. His *Exposition of the Old and New Testaments* (1708–10), a devotional commentary on the whole of the OT and the Gospels and Acts, is notable esp. for its good sense, pregnant thought, and felicitous expression. He was also the author of many devotional works and sermons.

Works, with a sermon preached at his funeral and Life by W. Tong (see below), pub. London, fol., 1726; additional matter incl. in *The Miscellaneous Works of Matthew Henry*, ed. S. Palmer (ibid., 1809); re-ed. with further additions, with preface by J. B. Williams (ibid., 1830). His Comm. on the Bible was ed. L. F. Church (Edinburgh, 1960), and a Topical Index compiled by W. T. Summers (Welwyn, 1982). Lives by W. Tong (London, 1716), J. B. Williams (ibid., 1828), and C. Chapman (ibid., 1859). A. Gordon in *DNB* 26 (1891), pp. 123 f.

Henson, Herbert Hensley (1863–1947), Bp. of *Durham. Educated at Oxford, he was elected a Fellow of All Souls in 1884. He was successively vicar of Barking (1888), Chaplain of St Mary's Hospital, Ilford (1895), rector of St Margaret's, Westminster (1900), Dean of Durham (1912), Bp. of *Hereford (1918), and Bp. of Durham (1920–39). Not long after ordination he abandoned his earlier *High Church sympathies for a *latitudinarian conception of the C of E, which he defended in several published collections of sermons and other writings, among them *Cross Bench Views of Current Church Questions* (1902), *Sincerity and Subscription* (1903), *The National Church* (1908), *The Liberty of Prophesying* (1909), *The Creed in the Pulpit* (1912), *Anglicanism* (1921), and *Quo Tendimus?* (1924). His doctrinal position, esp. his attitude to the Virgin Birth and the Gospel miracles, provoked strong protests when D. Lloyd George nominated him to Hereford late in 1917, and a serious crisis was averted only when the Abp. of Canterbury (R. T. *Davidson), who had had grave misgivings about consecrating him, and Henson issued a joint statement in which Henson appeared to retract his earlier views. Until his later years Henson was a strong advocate of the *Establishment, in which he saw the ideal of a nation-wide Church, which should ultimately include all Nonconformists, and a safeguard of theological freedom. But the rejection of the revised Prayer Books in Parliament (1927–8) convinced him that the Establishment was incompatible with the Church's freedom, and in his *Disestablishment* (1929) he pleaded for liberty for the Church from State control. His other writings include *Notes on Spiritual Healing* (1925); *The Oxford Groups* (1933), a pungent criticism; *Christian Morality* (1936), based on his *Gifford Lectures; and *The Church of England* (1939).

Henson pub. his autobiog., *Retrospect of an Unimportant Life* (3 vols., 1942–50); also a collection of papers repr. from *The Bishoprick* under the title *Bishoprick Papers* (1946). Collections of his *Letters* ed. E. F. Braley (1950); *More Letters* (1954). [W.] O. Chadwick, *Hensley Henson: A Study in the Friction between Church and State* (Oxford, 1983). A. T. P. Williams in *DNB*, 1941–1950, pp. 378 f.

heortology (Gk. ἑορτή, 'festival'). The study of the origin, history, and meaning of the festivals and seasons of the ecclesiastical *year, and thus a branch of *liturgiology.

Heptateuch (Gk. ἑπτά, 'seven' + τεῦχος, 'book'). A name sometimes used of the first seven books of the OT, i.e. the five Books of Moses together with Joshua and Judges, on account of their supposed unity. The word is formed on the analogy of '*Pentateuch'.

Heraclean Version. See HARKLEAN VERSION.

Heracleon (*fl. c.*145–80), *Gnostic teacher. He was a disciple of *Valentinus. He wrote a highly allegorizing commentary (Ὑπομνήματα) on St John's Gospel; but only fragments have survived, mainly in quotations in *Origen's commentary on that Gospel. He is sometimes credited with the authorship of the 'Tractate on the Three Natures' found at *Nag Hammadi (q.v.).

A. E. Brooke, *The Fragments of Heracleon* (Texts and Studies, 1, no. 4; Cambridge, 1891). Eng. tr. of frags. in W. Foerster (ed.), *Gnosis*, 1 (Eng. tr., Oxford, 1972), pp. 162–83. Y. Janssens, 'Héracléon. Commentaire sur l'Évangile selon saint Jean', *Muséon*, 72 (1959), pp. 101–51, 277–99. E. H. Pagels, *The Johannine Gospel in Gnostic Exegesis: Heracleon's Commentary on John* (Society of Biblical Literature, Monograph Series, 17 [1973]). H. C. Puech and G. Quispel, 'Le Quatrième Écrit gnostique du Codex Jung', *VC* 9 (1955), pp. 65–102. *CPG* 1 (1983), pp. 63 f. (no. 1138), with bibl. C. Gianotto in *DPAC* 1 (1983), cols. 1184 f., s.v. 'Eracleone'; Eng. tr. in *Encyclopedia of the Early Church*, 1 (1992), p. 374, s.v., with additional bibl.

Heraclius (575–641), Byzantine Emperor. A native of Cappadocia, he secured the throne in 610–11 in place of the usurper Phocas, and then founded a new dynasty which continued until 717. During his reign the Empire was repeatedly attacked. The Visigoths gained complete possession of Spain, and the Persians and later the Arabs invaded the E. On 21 Mar. 629 Heraclius solemnly brought back to *Golgotha the Cross which the Persians had removed from *Jerusalem in 614. In an attempt to secure doctrinal unity in his dominions he issued the *Ecthesis (q.v.) in 638. See also EXALTATION OF THE CROSS.

A. Pernice, *L'imperatore Eraclio* (1905). A. N. Stratos, Τὸ Βυζάντιον στὸν ζ' αἰῶνα, vol. 1 (1965), p. 226–vol. 3 (1969), p. 186 (Eng. tr., *Byzantium in the Seventh Century*, vol. 1 (Amsterdam, 1968), vol. 2 (ibid., 1972), p. 174). P. Speck, *Das geteilte Dossier: Beobachtungen zu den Nachrichten über die Regierung des Kaisers Herakleios und die seiner Söhne bei Theophanes und Nikephorus* (Ποικίλα Βυζαντῖνα, 9; Bonn, 1988). A. Frolow, 'La Vraie Croix et les expéditions d'Héraclius en Perse', *Revue des Études Byzantines*, 11 (1953), pp. 88–105. J. B. Bury, *The Later Roman Empire*, 2 (1889), pp. 197–398; N. H. Baynes in *C. Med. H.* 2 (1913), ch. 9, pp. 263–301 *passim*; Fliche and Martin, 5 (1947), pp. 79–150.

Herbert, Edward (1582–1648), first Lord Herbert of Cherbury; philosopher, deist, and poet. He was appointed ambassador at Paris in 1619, after a youth spent in study, much travel, and many duels. In 1624 he published at Paris his famous philosophical treatise, *De Veritate prout distinguitur a revelatione, a verisimili, a possibili, et a falso*, an original attack on empiricism. The first work of its kind to be written by an Englishman, it greatly influenced J. *Locke. His more specifically religious writings included *De Religione Laici* (1645) and *De Religione Gentilium* (1663). He maintained that common to all religions were five innate ideas: (1) that there is a God; (2) that He ought to be worshipped; (3) that virtue is the chief element in this worship; (4) that repentance for sin is a duty; and (5) that there is another life of rewards and punishments. His conviction that in these five innate ideas lay the essence of religion, combined with his denial of revelation, made him a forerunner of English *Deism.

His *Autobiography*, extending to 1624, survives in two forms: a contemporary MS, which is incomplete, and a prob. early 18th-cent. copy; the latter was ed. by H. Walpole (Strawberry Hill, 1764); text based on Walpole, ed. S. Lee (London, 1886; still valuable for its notes); crit. edn., based on the earlier text, augmented by the later, ed. J. M. Shuttleworth (London, etc., 1976). *Poems, English and Latin*, ed. G. C. W. Smith (1923). Modern edn. of his *De Religione Laici*, with Eng. tr. and crit. discussion of his life and philosophy, by H. R. Hutcheson (New Haven, Conn., and London, 1944), Eng. tr. of *De Veritate*, with introd., by M. H. Carré (Bristol, 1937). M. M. Rossi, *La vita, le opere, i tempi di Edoardo Herbert di Chirbury* (Biblioteca Storica Sansoni, NS 14; 3 vols., 1947). R. D. Bedford, *The Defence of Truth: Herbert of Cherbury and the Seventeenth Century* (Manchester, 1979). S. Lee in *DNB* 26 (1891), pp. 173–81.

Herbert, George (1593–1633), poet and divine. A younger brother of Edward, Lord *Herbert of Cherbury, he was educated at Westminster School and Trinity College, Cambridge, where his classical scholarship and musical ability (he played the lute and viol, and sang) secured him a Fellowship in 1614. He became Public Orator of the university in 1620, and his success seemed to mark him out for the career of a courtier. The death of *James I, however, and the influence of his friend, N. *Ferrar, led him to study divinity, and in 1626 he was presented to a prebend in Huntingdonshire. In 1630 he was ordained priest, and persuaded by W. *Laud to accept the rectory of Fugglestone with Bemerton, near *Salisbury, where in piety and humble devotion to duty he spent his last years.

Herbert's most famous prose work, *A Priest to the Temple; or the Country Parson* (1652), outlines a sober and well-balanced ideal of the English clergyman. In simple and homely language Herbert shows him as a well-read divine, temperate in all things, a man of duty and prayer, devoted to his flock, who has come to be the model of future generations. His collection of poems entitled *The Temple* was entrusted to N. Ferrar on his deathbed and first published in 1633. Herbert was a man of deep religious conviction and remarkable poetic gifts, masterly in handling both metre and metaphor. The 'conceits' in his verse are, with very few exceptions, still acceptable thanks to their genuine aptness and wit. The good sense of his didactic poems, and esp. the poignancy of the more personal lyrics, continue to ring true and have proved irresistible to many outside as well as within the Christian faith. His influence is acknowledged in the life and work of Henry *Vaughan, in the hymns of C. *Wesley, in the criticism of S. T. *Coleridge, and in G. M. *Hopkins's poetry. Among his compositions in current use as hymns are 'The God of love my Shepherd is' (Ps. 23), 'Teach me, my God and King' and 'Let all the world in every corner sing'. Feast day in parts of the Anglican Communion, 27 Feb.

Crit. edn. of his Works by F. E. Hutchinson (Oxford, 1941, repr., with corrections, 1945). I. *Walton, *The Life of Mr. George Herbert* (1670); A. M. Charles, *A Life of George Herbert* (Ithaca, NY, and London, 1977). R. Tuve, *A Reading of George Herbert* (1952); J. H. Summers, *George Herbert: His Religion and Art* (1954); C. Freer, *Music for a King: George Herbert's Style and the Metrical Psalms* (Baltimore and London [1972]); S. [E.] Fish, *The Living Temple: George Herbert and Catechizing* (Berkeley, Calif., and London [1978]); H. A. R. Asals, *Equivocal Prediction: George Herbert's Way to God* (Toronto and London [1981]); R. M. Van Wengen-Shute, *George Herbert and the Liturgy of the Church of England* (Leiden thesis, Oegstgeest, 1981); R. Steier, *Love Unknown: Theology and Experience in George Herbert's Poetry* (Chicago and London [1983]); C. [F.] Bloch, *Spelling the Word: George Herbert and the Bible* (Berkeley, Calif., and London [1985]); G. E. Veith, *Reformation Spirituality: The Religion of George Herbert* (Lewisburg, Pa., etc., 1985); T. G. Sherwood, *Herbert's Prayerful Art* (Toronto and London [1989]); J. Lull, *The Poem in Time: Reading George Herbert's Revisions of* The Church (Newark, Del., etc. [1990]); M. C. Schoenfeldt, *Prayer and Power: George Herbert and Renaissance Courtship* (Chicago and London, 1991). C. A. Patrides (ed.), *George Herbert: The Critical Heritage* (1983). J. R. Roberts, *George Herbert: An Annotated Bibliography of Modern Criticism 1905–1974* (University of Missouri Studies, 68; 1978); R. D. Dunn and J. Horden in *NCBEL* 1 (1974), cols. 1201–6. See also METAPHYSICAL POETS.

Herder, Johann Gottfried (1744–1803), German critic. With G. E. *Lessing he was a leader of the poetical movement which saved the *Enlightenment from a dry intellectualism. After various temporary posts, he became *General Superintendent and court preacher at Weimar (1776), where he spent the rest of his life. An early disciple of I. *Kant, he influenced J. W. Goethe in turn, and has been regarded as anticipating C. Darwin in treating human history as a natural science. His interests were as wide as the culture of his age, and his researches and writings dealt with poetry, art, language, and religion; but his most important contribution to the ideas of his time was in the philosophy of history. In his *Ideen zur Philosophie der Geschichte der Menschheit* (1784–91; Eng. tr., 1800) he discerned in the developments of the different nations the stages of an ascending process in the course of which the essence of 'Humanity' comes to progressively fuller expression. Of more exclusively religious interest was his book *Vom Geist der hebräischen Poesie* (1782–3), in which he urged the study of the Bible in a 'human' way. His mediating position in theology, in which he advocated critical principles and conservative findings, brought him the enmity of the orthodox and the suspicions of the rationalists.

Crit. edn. of Herder's Works by B. Suphan (33 vols., Berlin, 1877–99; 1913). Letters, ed. W. Dobbek and G. Arnold (9 vols., Weimar, 1977–88). Memoirs compiled by his widow, M. C. von Herder, ed. J. G. Müller (2 vols., Tübingen, 1820). Lives and general studies by R. Haym (2 vols., Leipzig, 1880–5), F. MacEachran (Oxford Studies in Modern Language and Literature, Oxford, 1939), A. Gillies (Oxford, 1945), R. T. Clark, Jun. (Berkeley and Los Angeles, 1955), and W. Koepke (Boston, [1987]); also collections of essays ed. id. (Bonn, 1982, and Columbia, SC [1990]) and ed. G. Sauder (Studien zum achtzehnten Jahrhundert, 9; Hamburg, 1987). F. M. Barnard, *Herder's Social and Political Thought* (Oxford, 1965); W. Dobbek, *J. G. Herders Weltbild* (Cologne and Vienna, 1969); R. E. Norton, *Herder's Aesthetics and the European Enlightenment* (Ithaca, NY, and London, 1991). W. L. Federlin, *Vom Nutzen des geistlichen Amtes: Ein Beitrag zur Interpretation und Rezeption Johann Gottfried Herders* (Forschungen zur Kirchen- und Dogmengeschichte, 33; 1982). I. Berlin, *Vico and Herder* (1976), pp. 143–216. P. Gardiner in P. Edwards (ed.), *Encyclopedia of Philosophy*, 3 (1967), pp. 486–9, s.v.

Hereford. The see was founded in 676 by Putta, Bp. of *Rochester from 669, who had fled from the heathen invaders of his diocese. St *Ethelbert, King of the East Angles (killed in 794), was buried in the cathedral, and with the BVM designated its joint patron soon afterwards. The original cathedral was damaged by the Welsh in 1055.

The main part of the present edifice dates from 1079–1110, though there are considerable later additions. The 'Use of Hereford', a variant of the Roman rite, with less individuality than that of *Sarum, was displaced by the latter only in the reign of *Henry VIII. The most famous medieval bishop was St Thomas of Hereford (Thomas de *Cantilupe), 1275–82, whose shrine, after his canonization in 1320, was a centre of pilgrimage from all over England. In 1786 the west end of the cathedral suddenly collapsed, carrying some of the nave with it, and the later restoration was poorly done, though the west front (early 20th cent.) is well in harmony with the building as a whole. The Cathedral has the largest surviving chained library in the world, the cases dating (now in the new Chained Library Mappa Mundi Building) from 1611. The Hereford *Mappa Mundi*, a late-13th cent. map of the world drawn on a single sheet of vellum, is the only complete survival of its kind. It shows the world as a circle with Jerusalem at its centre, the whole lying under a portrayal of the Last Judgement. The buildings of the College of Vicars-Choral remain intact, and the cathedral school, though its buildings are mostly of the 19th cent., has a continuous history from the 14th cent. The diocese includes Herefordshire, S. Salop, and a few parishes in other counties.

The Episcopal Registers are, exceptionally, nearly complete; the following have been pub. concurrently in the series of the Cantilupe Society [pub. dates in this series are added here] and of the *Canterbury and York Society: that of Thomas de Cantilupe (1275–82), ed. R. G. Griffiths and W. W. Capes (1906); of Richard de Swinfield (1283–1317), ed. W. W. Capes (1909); of Adam de Orleton (1317–27), ed. A. T. Bannister (1907); of Thomas de Charlton (1327–44), ed. W. W. Capes (1912); of John de Trillek (1344–61), ed. J. H. Parry (1910); of Lewis de Charlton (1361–9), ed. id. (1913); of William de Courtenay (1370–5), ed. W. W. Capes (1913); of John Gilbert (1375–89), ed. J. H. Parry (1913); of John Trefnant (1389–1404), ed. W. W. Capes (1914); Robert Mascall (1404–16), ed. J. H. Parry (1916); Edmund Lacy (1417–20), ed. id. and A. T. Bannister (1917); Thomas Poltone (1420–2), ed. W. W. Capes (1916); Thomas Stofford (1422–48), ed. A. T. Bannister (1917); Richard Beauchamp (1449–50), ed. id. (1917); Reginald Boulers (1451–3; register of first year only), ed. id. (1917); John Stanbury (1453–74), ed. J. H. Parry and A. T. Bannister (1918); Thomas Mylling (1474–92), ed. A. T. Bannister (1919); Richard Mayew (1504–16), ed. id. (1919); Charles Bothe (1516–35), with extracts from registers of Edmund Foxe and Edmund *Bonner, ed. id. (1921). J. Barrow (ed.), *English Episcopal Acta*, 7: *Hereford 1079–1234* (1993). W. W. Capes (ed.), *Charters and Records of Hereford Cathedral* (Cantilupe Society, 1908). Eng. tr. of *Extracts from the Cathedral Registers, A.D. 1275–1535*, by E. N. Dew (Hereford, 1932). The 'Missal according to the Use of Hereford' was repr. from the Rouen edn. of 1502 by W. G. Henderson (London, 1874); the 'Breviary', orig. pr. Rouen, 1505, was ed. by W. H. *Frere and L. E. G. Brown (HBS 26, 40, and 46; 1904–15). J. *Le Neve, *Fasti Ecclesiae Anglicanae 1300–1541*, Hereford Diocese, compiled by J. M. Horn (1962). H. W. Phillott, *Hereford* (Diocesan Histories, 1888). On the cathedral, W. *Dugdale, *Monasticon Anglicanum*, 6 (pt. 3; 1830 edn.), pp. 1210–17; B. Willis, *A Survey of the Cathedrals of York, Durham, Carlisle, Chester, Man, Lichfield, Hereford, Worcester, Gloucester and Bristol*, 2 (1727), pp. 499–622; A. H. Fisher, *The Cathedral Church of Hereford* (Bell's Cathedral Series, 1898); A. T. Bannister, *The Cathedral Church of Hereford: Its History and Constitution* (Studies in Church History, 1924); G. Marshall, *Hereford Cathedral: Its Evolution and Growth* (Worcester [1951]). Royal Commission on Historical Monuments, England, *An Inventory of Historical Monuments in Herefordshire*, 1, South-West (1931), pp. 90–120. R. A. B. Mynors and R. M. Thomson, *Cata-

logue of the Hereford Cathedral Manuscripts* (Cambridge, 1993). W. L. Bevan and W. J. Phillott, *Mediaeval Geography: An Essay in illustration of the Hereford Mappa Mundi* (1873); *The World Map by Richard of Haldingham in Hereford Cathedral*, with memoir by G. R. Crone (Royal Geographical Society, Reproductions of Early Manuscript Maps, 3; 1954); [E.] M. Jancey, *Mappa Mundi: The map of the world in Hereford Cathedral* (Hereford, 1987). B. H. *Streeter, *The Chained Library* (1931), pp. 77–119, 311–39.

Hereford, Nicholas. See NICHOLAS HEREFORD.

heresiarch (Gk. αἱρεσιάρχης; late Lat. *haeresiarcha*). The originator of a heresy, or founder of an heretical sect.

heresy. The formal denial or doubt of any defined doctrine of the Catholic faith. In antiquity the Greek word αἱρεσις, denoting 'choice' or 'thing chosen', from which the term is derived, was applied to the tenets of particular philosophical schools. In this sense it appears occasionally in Scripture (e.g. Acts 5: 17) and the early Fathers. But it was employed also in a disparaging sense (e.g. 1 Cor. 11: 19) and from St *Ignatius (*Trall.* 6, *Eph.* 6) onwards it came more and more to be used of theological error. From the earliest days the Church has claimed teaching authority and consequently condemned heresy, following Christ's command: 'If he refuse to hear the Church, let him be unto thee as the Gentile and the publican' (Mt. 18: 17). On the other hand the need to rebut heresy has sometimes stimulated the formation of orthodox Christian doctrine.

In the early centuries heresy was mainly a matter of erroneous attempts to understand the nature of the Person of Christ (e.g. *Docetism, *Apollinarianism, *Nestorianism, *Monophysitism, *Monothelitism), of the Trinity (e.g. *Monarchianism, *Tritheism, *Subordinationism), or both (e.g. *Arianism). These heresies were condemned at the *Oecumenical Councils. After the Church had become a highly structured and incidentally wealthy institution, many of the heretical movements were inspired by a desire to return to what was seen as the simplicity of the apostolic Church. They thus had much in common with the orthodox reform movements, such as the *mendicant orders, some of whose members (esp. among the *Franciscans) were charged with heresy. Many of the heretical bodies in the Middle Ages (e.g. the *Bogomils, *Cathari, *Waldensians, the followers of *Henry of Lausanne and *Peter de Bruys) came to reject the sacraments as well as other institutions of the Church. The *Inquisition was established to secure the conversion of heretics, and punished the obdurate. With the Reformation, the establishment of Protestant state Churches ended the power of the RC Church to coerce heretics in much of Europe, though in France the hierarchy long continued to regard the *Huguenots as heretics rather than granting them the toleration promised in the Edict of *Nantes; *Calvinists in Switzerland burnt those Protestants whom they regarded as heretics.

Acc. to RC canon law, heresy is defined as the obstinate denial or doubt, after Baptism, of a truth 'which must be believed with divine and catholic faith' (*CIC* (1983), can. 751). This 'formal' heresy is a grave sin involving *ipso facto* excommunication. Catholic theology distinguishes it from what is termed 'material heresy'. This means holding heretical doctrines through no fault of one's own, 'in good faith', as is the case, e.g., with most persons brought up in heretical surroundings. It constitutes neither crime nor sin, nor is such a person strictly speaking a heretic, since, having never accepted certain doctrines, he cannot reject or doubt them. Heresy is to be distinguished from *apostasy and *schism (qq.v.). See also BURNING, DE HAERETICO COMBURENDO, and individual heresies.

W. Bauer, *Rechtgläubigkeit und Ketzerei im ältesten Christentum* (Beiträge zur historischen Theologie, 10; 1934; 2nd edn. by G. Strecker, 1964; Eng. tr., Philadelphia, 1971; London, 1972). M. Simon, 'From Greek Hairesis to Christian Heresy', in W. R. Schoedel and R. L. Wilken (eds.), *Early Christian Literature and the Classical Intellectual Tradition in Honorem Robert M. Grant* (Théologie Historique, 53 [1979]), pp. 101–16. A. Le Boulluec, *La notion d'hérésie dans la littérature grecque, II*ᵉ*–III*ᵉ *siècles* (2 vols., Études Augustiniennes, 1985). W. L. Wakefield and A. P. Evans, *Heresies of the High Middle Ages: Selected Sources Translated and Annotated* (Records of Civilization, Sources and Studies, 81; 1969). [J. J.] I. von *Döllinger, *Beiträge zur Sektengeschichte des Mittelalters* (2 vols., Munich, 1890). G. [A.] Leff, *Heresy in the Later Middle Ages: The Relation of Heterodoxy to Dissent* c.*1250–c.1450* (2 vols., Manchester and New York, 1967). J. Le Goff (ed.), *Hérésies et sociétés dans l'Europe pré-industrielle 11*ᵉ*–18*ᵉ *siècles: Colloque de Royaumont, 27–30 Mai 1962* (Civilisations et sociétés, 10; 1968), with bibl. of post-1900 studies on medieval heresies, pp. 407–67. N. G. Garsoïn, 'Byzantine Heresy. A Reinterpretation', *Dumbarton Oaks Papers*, 25 (1971), pp. 85–113. W. Lourdaux and D. Verhelst (eds.), *The Concept of Heresy in the Middle Ages (11th–13th C.): Proceedings of the International Conference, Louvain May 13–16, 1973* (Mediaevalia Lovaniensia, 1st ser., vol. 4; 1976). M. D. Lambert, *Medieval Heresy: Popular Movements from Bogomil to Hus* (1977; 2nd edn. [1992]). G. G. Merlo, *Eretici e Inquisitori nella Società Piemontese del Trecento* (Turin [1977]). R. Kieckhefer, *Repression of Heresy in Medieval Germany* (Philadelphia and Liverpool, 1979). H. Schlier in *TWNT* 1 (1933), pp. 179–84 (Eng. tr., 1 (1964), pp. 180–5), s.v. αἱρέομαι. A. Michel in *DTC* 6 (1920), cols. 2208–57, s.v. 'Hérésie, Hérétique'; A. Patschovsky in *Lexikon des Mittelalters*, 4 (1989), cols. 1933–7, s.v. 'Häresie'. See also works cited under CATHARI and other heresies mentioned in the text.

Hergenröther, Joseph (1824–90), ecclesiastical historian. He was a native of Würzburg, where he taught from 1852 onwards. In 1857 he published *Photius 'Liber de Spiritus Sancti mystagogia', and in 1867–9 an elaborate work on Photius himself. He represented the more conservative element in German Catholicism, attacking J. J. I. von *Döllinger in 1861 with his *Der Zeitgeist und die Souveränität des Papstes*. Called to Rome in 1868 to act as a consultor for the forthcoming *Vatican Council, he defended the definition of Papal Infallibility, directing against Döllinger *Anti-Janus* (1869; see JANUS) and other pamphlets. His later writings include a treatise on Church history (*Handbuch der allgemeinen Kirchengeschichte*, 3 vols., 1876–80), which in its successive revisions long remained a standard work. In 1879 he was created a *cardinal. In his later years he devoted himself to continuing K. J. *Hefele's *Konziliengeschichte*.

M. Weitlauf, 'Joseph Hergenröther (1824–1890)', in H. Fries and G. Schwaiger (eds.), *Katholische Theologen Deutschlands im 19. Jahrhundert*, 2 [1975], pp. 471–551, with complete list of his works. J. P. Kirsch in *CE* 7 (1910), pp. 262–4, s.v.; V. Conzemius in *NCE* 6 (1967), p. 1070, s.v.

Heric of Auxerre. See HEIRIC OF AUXERRE.

Herimannus Contractus (1013–54), Hermann the

Lame, poet and chronicler. He was educated in the monastery at *Reichenau, where he later took his vows. Though suffering great physical infirmities, he possessed one of the most gifted minds of his age, and wrote extensively on a wide range of subjects including mathematics, music, astronomy, and chronography. His writings included a didactic poem 'De octo vitiis principalibus', based on classical models, and many hymns and antiphons. The widespread attribution to him of the '*Salve Regina' and the 'Alma Redemptoris Mater' rests in each case, however, on insufficient evidence. His 'Chronicon', which stretches from the beginning of the Christian era to 1054, is based, directly or indirectly, on a large variety of important sources and is of esp. value for its record of contemporary history.

His writings are pr. in J. P. Migne, *PL* 143. 9–458; crit. edn. of his 'Chronicon' by G. H. Pertz in *MGH*, Scriptores, 5 (1844), pp. 67–133, rev., with Ger. tr. and introd., by R. Buchner in W. Trillmich and R. Buchner (eds.), *Quellen des 9. und 11. Jahrhunderts zur Geschichte der Hamburgischen Kirche und des Reiches* (1961), pp. 617–707. H. Bresslau, 'Beiträge zur Kritik deutscher Geschichtsquellen des 11. Jahrhunderts. Neue Folge I, Hermann von Reichenau und das Chronicon Suevicum Universale', *NA* 27 (1902), pp. 127–69, with refs. to other arts. Good popular account by C. C. Martindale, SJ, *From Bye-Ways and Hedges* (1935), pp. 3–27. G. Michiels in *Dict. Sp.* 7 (pt. 1; 1969), cols. 293 f., s.v., with bibl. See also works cited under SALVE REGINA.

heritor. In *Scotland, heritors were the owners of heritable property in a parish to whom descended the ancient obligation to pay the *teinds or tithes to the minister and to keep the parish church and manse in repair. By an Act of Parliament, 1925, with a view to union between the Established and the *United Free Churches, provision was made for the termination of their rights and duties and the transfer of these responsibilities to the Church of Scotland itself.

Herman, Emma (1874–1923), writer on spiritual subjects. The wife of a *Presbyterian minister, she spent much of her early married life in *Constantinople and Sydney. In 1908 she began regular work as a journalist at Sydney, soon becoming widely known through her brilliant and penetrating writing. In 1913 she was appointed editor of the *Presbyterian* and later held posts in the *Challenge* and the *Church Times*. Towards the end of her life she joined the C of E, where she became warmly sympathetic to *Anglo-Catholicism. Her two chief books—*The Meaning and Value of Mysticism* (1915) and *Creative Prayer* (1921)—are notable for their understanding and interpretation of Christian spiritual values.

'An Appreciation of the Author' by D. C. Macgregor in her posthumously pub. *The Secret Garden of the Soul* [1924], pp. 11–26.

Hermann of Reichenau. See HERIMANNUS CONTRACTUS.

Hermann of Wied (1477–1552), German reformer. In 1515, while still a *subdeacon, he became Abp.-Elector of *Cologne. He governed his principality with marked efficiency, taking strong measures against the *Anabaptists and at a council at Cologne (1536) tightening up discipline and introducing some liturgical reforms. Throughout his earlier years he was hostile to the Protestant movement; but c.1539 he set out to create a parallel movement within the Catholic Church, making a start with his own arch-diocese and inviting the assistance of M. *Bucer and P. *Melanchthon. He embodied many proposals for a moder-ate reform of the Church in his *Einfaltigs Bedencken einer christlichen Reformation* (1543); a revised Latin translation by A. *Hardenberg was pub. at Bonn, 1545; this in turn was translated into English (*A Simple and Religious Consul-tation by us, Herman, by the grace of God, Archbishop of Cologne*, 1547) and was considerably drawn on by the com-pilers of the Anglican BCP. In 1544 J. *Gropper published an '*Antididagma' (q.v.) as a reply. Hermann's increasing adhesion to the Protestant cause was an important acces-sion to its strength, but his policy met with hostility from most of his own subjects, from the Emp. *Charles V, and from Pope *Paul III, who excommunicated and deposed him in 1546. He died a Lutheran.

C. Varrentrapp, *Hermann von Wied und sein Reformationsversuch* (1878). A. Franzen, *Bischof und Reformation: Erzbischof Hermann von Wied in Köln vor der Enstscheidung zwischen Reform und Reformation* (Katholisches Leben und Kirchenreform in Zeitalter der Glaubensspaltung, 31; Münster, 1971). C. Varrentrapp in *PRE* (3rd edn.), 7 (1899), pp. 712–14. For his influence on the BCP, see F. E. *Brightman, *The English Rite* (1915), Introd., *passim* (cf. index, p. 1063), and G. [J.] Cuming, *The Godly Order* (Alcuin Club Collections, 65; 1983), pp. 68–90.

Hermas (2nd cent.), author of 'The Shepherd'. He is accounted one of the '*Apostolic Fathers'. Of his life noth-ing certain is known except what he himself says in his work. We learn that he was a Christian slave, sold in Rome to a woman called Rhoda, who set him free. He married, became a merchant, and enriched himself by means that were not always lawful. In a persecution he lost all his property, was denounced by his own children, and finally he and his whole family did penance.

His book, 'The Shepherd' (ὁ Ποιμήν), purports to have been written in consequence of a series of visions. It is divided into three parts: five 'Visions', twelve 'Mandates', and ten 'Similitudes'. In the 'Visions' a matron appears to him who represents the Church, which is pictured as a tower. In the fifth Vision appears the Angel of Penance in the guise of a shepherd, whence the name of the treatise. In the following 'Mandates' Hermas gives us his teaching on Christian behaviour and virtues, such as faith in one God, truthfulness, chastity, etc. The third section, the 'Similitudes', represents various Christian principles under a series of sometimes very forceful images.

The person of the author of the work has given rise to much speculation. Hermas himself says that he is a con-temporary of St *Clement of Rome (*fl. c.*96; if he is the Clement mentioned at Vis. 2. 4. 3); but the *Muratorian Canon (*c.*180) attributes the work to a brother of Pope *Pius (d. *c.*154), while *Origen believes the Hermas men-tioned in Rom. 16: 14 to be its author. Many modern scholars accept the view of the Muratorian Canon, which would suggest a date between 140 and 155. This would also fit the internal evidence, which seems to suggest that the work was written after a considerable period of peace. In the Greek Church of the 2nd and 3rd cents. the work was widely regarded as Scripture, e.g. by St *Irenaeus, *Clement of Alexandria, also by *Tertullian in his pre-Montanist days, though there was no unanimity on the subject. It was, however, greatly esteemed for its moral

value and served as a textbook for catechumens, as is testi-fied by St *Athanasius. In the *Codex Sinaiticus it comes after the NT, together with the Pseudo-*Barnabas. In the Latin Church it was valued far less highly; the Muratorian Canon denies its inspiration and *Jerome asserts that it was almost unknown in the West (*De vir. illust.* 10). From the 4th cent. it came to be also more and more neglected in the East.

The principal aim of the book is the inculcation of the necessity of penance and of the possibility of the forgive-ness of sins at least once after Baptism, a doctrine which caused Tertullian, in his Montanist period, to call it the 'Shepherd of the adulterers'. The author seems to identify the Holy Spirit with the Son of God before the Incarna-tion, and to hold that the Trinity came into existence only after the humanity of Christ had been taken up into heaven.

The Gk. original of 'The Shepherd' is incomplete. In the Codex Sinaiticus the Gk. text is to be found up to Mand. 4, and in the MS of Mt. *Athos, ed. by C. *Tischendorf, Leipzig, 1856, as far as Sim. 9. The rest of the text is known from two Lat. versions, one of which, the 'Versio Vulgata', was first pub. by J. *Faber Stapulensis, Paris, 1513, the other, known as the 'Versio Palatina', by A. R. M. Dressel, Leipzig, 1857. Further additions to Gk. text from papyrus frags. ed. C. Wessely in *PO* 4 (1908), pp. 195–9, and 18 (1924), pp. 468–81. C. Bonner, *A Papyrus Codex of the Shepherd of Hermas (Simil. 2–9), with a Fragment of the Man-dates* (University of Michigan, Humanistic Series, 22; 1934). Crit. edns. by M. Whittaker (GCS, 1956; 2nd edn., 1967), and, with Fr. tr., by R. Joly (SC 53; 1958). The Gk. text is pr. in all edns. of the Apostolic Fathers (q.v.). J. A. *Robinson, *Barnabas, Hermas and the Didache* (Donnellan Lectures for 1920; 1920). M. *Dibe-lius, *Der Hirt des Hermas* (Hb. NT, Ergänzungsband, Die Aposto-lischen Väter, 4; 1923). E. Peterson, 'Beiträge zur Interpretation der Visionen im *Pastor Hermae*', *OCP* 13 (1947), pp. 625–35; S. Giet, *Hermas et les Pasteurs: Les trois auteurs du Pasteur d'Hermas* (1963); L. Pernveden, *The Concept of the Church in the Shepherd of Hermas* (Studia Theologica Lundensia, 27; Lund, 1966); J. Rei-ling, *Hermas and Christian Prophecy: A Study of the eleventh Man-date* (Supplements to *Novum Testamentum*, 37; 1973). N. Brox, *Der Hert des Hermas* (Ergänzungsreihe zum KEK, 7; 1991). R. Lane Fox, *Pagans and Christians* (1986), pp. 381–90. *CPG* 1 (1983), pp. 22 f (no. 1052). Altaner and Stuiber (1978), pp. 55–8 and 553. J. Paramelle and P. Adnès in *Dict. Sp.* 7 (pt. 1; 1969), cols. 316–34; A. Hilhorst in *RAC* 14 (1988), cols. 682–701, both s.v., with bibl.

hermeneutics (from Gk. ἑρμηνεύω, 'to interpret'). The science of the methods of *exegesis (q.v.). Whereas exegesis is usually the act of explaining a text, often in the case of sacred literature according to formally prescribed rules, hermeneutics is the science (or art) by which exeget-ical procedures are devised. In theology, hermeneutical theory arises out of awareness of the ambiguity of a sacred text and the consequent analysis of the act of understand-ing. There are traces of both these processes in St *Au-gustine, esp. in *De Doctrina Christiana*, though patristic and medieval exegesis was largely governed by formal rules of allegorical interpretation and the theory of scriptural infallibility. The Protestant emphasis on the importance of Scripture and belief in the possibility of comprehending it encouraged reflection on the act of understanding, as well as a return to more literal exegesis. Although the Latin term *hermeneutica* dates from the mid-17th cent. (the English form 'hermeneutics' is found only in the 18th cent.), it was F. D. E. *Schleiermacher who in modern times gave new prominence to the act of correctly understanding human utterance, thereby subsuming biblical hermeneutics into a general theory of interpretation. Building on Schleiermacher's work, W. *Dilthey and M. *Heidegger developed the philosophical analysis of understanding which sees interpretation, rather than perception, as the fundamental mode of man's relationship to the world. *Wahrheit und Methode* (1960; Eng. tr., *Truth and Method*, 1975), the work of Heidegger's pupil H.-G. Gadamer, represents a masterly and influential statement of this position. This emphasis has led some modern theologians (esp. R. *Bultmann and those influenced by him) to regard hermeneutics, rather than metaphysics, as the central intellectual task of Christian theology.

F. D. E. Schleiermacher, *Hermeneutik* (newly ed. from his MSS, with introd., by H. Kimmerle (*Abh.* (Heid.), 1959, Heft 2; Eng. tr., American Academy of Religion, Texts and Translation Series, 1; Missoula, Mont., 1977). R. Bultmann, 'Das Problem der Hermeneutik', *Zeitschrift für Theologie und Kirche*, 47 (1950), pp. 47–69, repr. in his *Glauben und Verstehen*, 2 (1952), pp. 211–35; Eng. tr., id., *New Testament and Mythology and other basic writings* (1985), pp. 69–93. G. Ebeling, 'Wort Gottes und Hermeneutik', *Zeitschrift für Theologie und Kirche*, 56 (1959), pp. 224–51; Eng. tr. in Ebeling's *Word and Faith* (1963), pp. 305–32. J. M. Robinson and J. B. Cobb (eds.), *The New Hermeneutic* (New York, 1964); R. E. Palmer, *Hermeneutics: Interpretation Theory in Schleiermacher, Dilthey, Heidegger, and Gadamer* (Evanston, Ill., 1969); A. C. Thiselton, *The Two Horizons: New Testament Hermeneutics and Philosophical Description with Special Reference to Heidegger, Bultmann, Gadamer, and Wittgenstein* (Exeter, 1980); id., *New Horizons in Hermeneutics* (1992). G. Ebeling in *RGG* (3rd edn.), 3 (1959), cols. 242–62, s.v.; C. v. Bormann and others in *TRE* 15 (1986), pp. 108–56, s.v.; B. C. Lategan in *Anchor Bible Dictionary*, 3 (1992), pp. 149–55, s.v.

Hermesianism. The system of philosophical and theological doctrines taught by Georg Hermes (1775–1831), Prof. of Theology at Münster i.W. It was an attempt to adjust the principles of RC theology to the supposed requirements of the philosophy of I. *Kant. Holding that our only certain knowledge was of ideas and notions actually present in the mind, it taught that the criterion of objective truth must be found in our subjective beliefs. Hermes believed that, starting from this principle, it was possible (as against the contentions of Kant) to prove the existence of God by the theoretical reason; and that when this fact had been established, the possibility of supernatural revelation could then be demonstrated. For a time Hermesian doctrines became very popular, esp. in the Rhineland, where many of the chief theological professorships were filled by Hermes' disciples. Soon after his death, Rome pronounced against them, however, and in 1835 *Gregory XVI put a number of Hermes' writings on the *Index.

Hermes' writings include *Untersuchung über die Wahrheit des Christentums* (1805), *Studirplan der Theologie* (1819), *Einleitung in die christkatholische Theologie* (1819–29), *Positive Einleitung* (1829), and *Christkatholische Dogmatik* (3 vols., 1834–5; posthumous, ed. J. H. Achterfeldt). His doctrines were condemned in the brief 'Dum Acerbissimas' (26 Sept. 1835); cf. Denzinger and Hünermann (37th edn., 1991), pp. 759 f. (nos. 2738–40). *Acta Romana*, ed. W. J. Braun and P. J. Elvenich (Hanover, 1838; pro-Hermesian). H. H. Schwedt, *Das römische Urteil über Georg Hermes (1775–1831): Ein Beitrag zur Geschichte der Inquisition im*

19. Jahrhundert (*RQ* Supplementheft 37 [1980]), with bibl. J. Schulte in *CE* 7 (1910), pp. 276–9; A. Thouvenin in *DTC* 6 (1920), cols. 2288–303; E. Hegel in *TRE* 15 (1986), pp. 156–8, all s.v. 'Hermes'.

Hermetic books. A collection of Greek and Latin religious and philosophical writings ascribed to Hermes Trismegistus ('Hermes the Thrice-Greatest'), a later designation of the Egyptian God, Thoth, who was believed to be the father and protector of all knowledge. Dating probably from between the middle of the 1st and the end of the 3rd cents. AD, these writings represent a fusion of *Platonic, *Stoic, Neo-Pythagorean, and eastern religious elements, in the form of the Platonic dialogues. The aim of their mystic teaching was the deification of man through 'Gnosis', i.e. the knowledge of God. The most important of the writings, '*Poimandres', contains much cosmological and astronomical teaching and describes the ascent of the soul to God through the seven spheres of the planets. Hermetic writings were among the works discovered at *Nag Hammadi.

Corpus Hermeticum, ed. A. D. Nock, with Fr. tr. by A.-J. Festugière, OP (Collection Budé, Paris, 4 vols., 1945–54). Elaborate edn. by W. Scott, *Hermetica* (4 vols., Oxford, 1924–36), with Eng. introd. and notes, suffers from the editor's over-drastic emendation of the text. The texts found at Nag Hammadi are ed., with Fr. tr. and full introd., by J.-P. Mahé, *Hermès en Haute-Égypte* (Bibliothèque copte de Nag Hammadi, Textes, 3 and 7; Quebec, 1978–82). A.-J. Festugière, OP, *La Révélation d'Hermès Trismégiste* (Études bibliques, 4 vols., 1944–54). G. Fowden, *The Egyptian Hermes: A historical approach to the later pagan mind* (Cambridge, 1986). C. H. *Dodd, *The Bible and the Greeks* (1935), pt. 2 (pp. 97–248, 'Hellenistic Judaism and the Hermetica'); id., *The Interpretation of the Fourth Gospel* (1953), pp. 10–53. G. van Moorsel, *The Mysteries of Hermes Trismegistus: A Phenomenological Study in the Process of Spiritualisation in the Corpus Hermeticum and Latin Asclepius* (Studia Theologica Rheno-Traiectina, 1; Utrecht, 1953); K.-W. Tröger, *Mysterienglaube und Gnosis in Corpus Hermeticum XIII* (TU 110; 1971); W. C. Grese, *Corpus Hermeticum XIII and Early Christian Literature* (Studia ad Corpus Hellenisticum Novi Testamenti, 5; Leiden, 1979). L. Delatte and others, *Index du Corpus Hermeticum* (Lessico Intellettuale Europeo, 13; Rome [1977]). See also bibl. to POIMANDRES.

Hermias (date uncertain), Christian philosophical writer. He is known only as the author of a small treatise, the 'Irrisio' or 'Mockery of the Heathen Philosophers' (Διασυρμὸς τῶν ἔξω Φιλοσόφων), which satirizes the conflicting opinions of pagan writers on the human soul (chs. 1–2) and the fundamental principles of the universe (chs. 3–10). The apology is clearly the work of a writer of very mediocre attainments. Some points of literary contact between the 'Irrisio' and the pseudo-*Justin's 'Cohortatio ad Gentiles' have been observed, but they are probably not sufficiently close to throw light on their relative dates, esp. in view of the possible use of common sources. Modern authors have assigned various dates to the 'Irrisio' from the 2nd to the 6th cents.

The *editio princeps* was issued by J. Oporinus (Basle, 1553). More recent editions are in J. C. T. de Otto, *Corpus Apologetarum Christianorum*, 9 (Jena, 1872), pp. 1–31, and H. Diels, *Doxographi Graeci* (Berlin, 1879), pp. 649–56. Crit edn., with introd., by R. P. C. Hanson and others, and Fr. tr. by Denise Joussot (SC 388; 1993). *CPG* 1 (1983), p. 56 (no. 1113).

hermit (Gk. ἐρημίτης, from ἐρημία, 'desert'). One who from religious motives has retired into a solitary life. Christian hermits first began to abound in Egypt and surrounding regions towards the close of the 3rd cent., and from that date the eremitical life quickly gained in popularity, being esp. cultivated in the cents. which witnessed the disintegration of the Roman Empire. In the W. hermits died out after the *Counter-Reformation, though much of their tradition is retained in certain monastic orders, notably the *Carthusians and *Carmelites. In the 20th cent. there has been a revival of the eremitical life in both the RC and Anglican Churches. In the E. it has continued to exist without interruption. Hermits observe no uniform rule of life. While some live in isolation, others are united in loosely organized communities which have sometimes formed the nucleus of a new monastery or order (e.g. the *Augustinian Hermits). See also ANCHORITES.

P. F. Anson, *The Call of the Desert* (1964).

Herod family. *Herod the Great* was appointed King of the Jews by the Romans in 40 BC, and ruled from 37 to 4 BC. He was of an Idumaean (Edomite) family, and married a number of wives, including Mariamme, a granddaughter of Hyrcanus, the last legal *Hasmonaean ruler. By ruthlessness and genuine ability he kept the peace for 37 years in a country very hard to rule. During his reign Christ was born, and the story of the Massacre of the Innocents (Mt. 2: 16) fits his reputation. On his death his territory was divided between his sons: *Archelaus*, as ethnarch of *Judaea, Idumaea, and Samaria; *Antipas*, as tetrarch of *Galilee and Peraea; and *Philip*, as tetrarch of the remaining territory to the NE (Lk. 3: 1). Archelaus was deposed in AD 6 and his territory put under Roman prefects, of whom Pontius *Pilate was the fifth. Antipas, the 'Herod the tetrarch' of the Gospels (4 BC–AD 39), who married Herodias and beheaded St *John the Baptist, and Philip (4 BC–AD 34) were ruling at the time of Christ's ministry. In 37–41 all these territories were successively conferred on *Agrippa I*, the son of Herod the Great's second son by Mariamme Aristobulus (d. 7 BC); he ruled till AD 44 with the title of King. It was he (called 'Herod' in Acts) who put St *James the Apostle to death and died 'eaten of worms' (Acts 12). *Agrippa II*, his son, was made king of various territories in N. Palestine *c*.50, and ruled until *c*.93 or 100. He was the 'King Agrippa' before whom St *Paul appeared (Acts 25: 13 ff.).

Much the most important authority is *Josephus (q.v.), who for the careers of Antipas and Herod the Great was mainly dependent on the 'Universal History' of Nicolaus of Damascus, Herod the Great's court historiographer. A. H. M. Jones, *The Herods of Judaea* (1938; by a first-class scholar, but without bibl. refs.). S. Perowne, *The Life and Times of Herod the Great* (1956); id., *The Later Herods: The Political Background of the New Testament* (1958). A. Schalit, *König Herodes: Der Mann und sein Werk* (Ger. tr. from Heb., Studia Judaica, 4; 1969), with bibl.; M. Grant, *Herod the Great* [1971]. H. W. Hoehner, *Herod Antipas* (Society for New Testament Studies, Monograph Series, 17; Cambridge, 1972). E. *Schürer, *The History of the Jewish People in the Age of Jesus Christ*, rev. Eng. tr. by G. Vermes and others, 1 (Edinburgh, 1973), pp. 234, n. 3, 287–357, 442–54, 471–83, and 571 f. H. Merkel and D. Karol in *RAC* 14 (1988), cols. 815–49, s.v. 'Herodes der Grosse'. A. C. *Headlam in *HBD* 2 (1899), pp. 353–62, with useful 'Index of Herod Family'. W. Otto in *PW*, Suppl. 2 (1913), cols. 1–200, s.v. 'Herodes'.

Herodians. A party twice mentioned in the Gospels (Mk. 3: 6, in Galilee; Mk. 12: 13, cf. Mt. 22: 16, at Jerusalem) as a group hostile to the Lord. They were presumably partisans or retainers of the *Herod family, which was ruling at the time of Christ's ministry in Galilee and Iturea, but no longer in Judaea. The view of Ps.-*Tertullian (*De praescr.* 45 fin.), *Philaster (*Haer.* 28), and others that they held Herod to be the Messiah was doubtless a mere (mistaken) conjecture.

H. H. Rowley, 'The Herodians in the Gospels', *JTS* 41 (1940), pp. 14–27. W. J. Bennett, 'The Herodians of Mark's Gospel', *Novum Testamentum*, 17 (1975), pp. 9–14. See also comm. on Mark, cited under MARK, GOSPEL OF ST.

Herring, Thomas (1693–1757), Abp. of *Canterbury. A native of Wisbech, he was educated at Jesus and Corpus Christi Colleges, Cambridge, where he early won fame as a preacher. After holding many ecclesiastical appointments he was promoted to the see of *Bangor in 1737. In 1743 he was translated to *York, where he was energetic in defence of the government during the 1745 revolt. In 1747 he became Abp. of Canterbury but did little of note there. In his religious outlook he was a *Latitudinarian without theological interests. His chief claim to fame is his episcopal Visitation Returns for 1743, which are an important document for the religious history of his times.

Seven Sermons (1763), with pref. Life [by W. Duncombe], pp. i–xli; *Letters* [1728–57] . . . *to William Duncombe* (1777). B. Garnett, 'Correspondence of Archbishop Herring and Lord Hardwicke during the Rebellion of 1745', *EHR* 19 (1904), pp. 528–50 and 719–42. *Visitation Returns* ed. S. L. Ollard and P. C. Walker (Yorkshire Archaeological Society, Record Series, 71, 72, 75, 77, and 79; 1928–31), with Life by S. L. Ollard as Appendix D, vol. 5, pp. 1–30. A. W. Rowden, *The Primates of the First Four Georges* (1916), pp. 167–229. R. Hooper in *DNB* 26 (1891), pp. 259 f.

Herrmann, Wilhelm (1846–1922), theologian. After an appointment at Halle in 1875, he became professor of systematic theology at *Marburg in 1879. He was a follower of I. *Kant in philosophy, of A. *Ritschl in theology. While, like the latter, he looked upon the Gospels as in some sense the record of a historical personality, he insisted that the Church should teach only those facts about Christ which will act upon man, e.g. His moral teaching as distinguished from His Virgin Birth or Resurrection. He held, too, that the aspects of Christ's Person which had value for the disciples are not necessarily those important for us. He went beyond Ritschl in excluding both mysticism (or personal religious experience) and metaphysics (or intellectual reasoning about ultimate reality) from religion, contending that religion is centred entirely in 'the historical Christ', whose life, however, is relevant to us only in so far as it possesses ethical value. The book in which these views are most fully expounded is *Der Verkehr des Christen mit Gott* (1886; Eng. tr., *The Communion of the Christian with God*, 1896). His other writings include *Die Religion im Verhältnis zum Welterkennen und zur Sittlichkeit* (1879), *Ethik* (1901), and *Christlich-protestantische Dogmatik* (in *Die Kultur der Gegenwart*, 4. 1 (2), 1906). He influenced both K. *Barth and R. *Bultmann.

Herrmann's 'Vorlesungsdiktate' on *Dogmatik* were ed. by M. Rade (1925; Eng. tr., *Systematic Theology*, by N. Micklem and K. A. Saunders, 1927). Several of his minor writings in

Gesammelte Aufsätze (ed. F. W. Schmidt, 1923), with bibl. of his works; *Schriften zur Grundlegung der Theologie*, ed. P. Fischer-Appelt (2 vols., Munich, 1966–7), with introd. The 1906 edn. of *The Communion of the Christian with God* was repr., with introd. by R. Voelkel (Philadelphia, 1971; London, 1972). P. Fischer-Appelt, *Metaphysik im Horizont der Theologie Wilhelm Herrmanns* (Forschungen zur Geschichte und Lehre des Protestantismus, 2. Reihe, 32; 1965), with list of his works, pp. 215–30, and bibl. pp. 233–42. W. Greive, *Der Grund des Glaubens: Die Christologie Wilhelm Herrmanns* (Forschungen zur systematischen und öku-menischen Theologie, 36 [1976]). M. Beintker, *Die Gottesfrage in der Theologie Wilhelm Herrmanns* (Theologische Arbeiten, 34; 1976). C. Welch, *Protestant Thought in the Nineteenth Century*, 2 (New Haven, Conn., and London [1985]), pp. 44–54 and 154–7, with bibl. p. 304. T. Mahlmann in *TRE* 15 (1986), pp. 165–72.

Herrnhut. The village in Saxony, some 40 miles E. of Dresden, built and settled in 1722 by a group of *Moravian Brethren (hence known on the Continent as 'Herrnhuter') under Christian David, an artisan, on a site presented by Count N. L. von *Zinzendorf. Institutions exist here for the brethren and sisters of the community, and from 1945 until 1992 the Directorate of the Moravian Church in the DDR (East Germany) was centred here. The Districts of the Church with headquarters at Herrnhut and Bad Boll were then united, though some work of the Provincial Board remains at Herrnhut. In 1738 J. *Wesley made a pilgrimage here and for some weeks actively took part in the life of the community.

hcrse. See HEARSE.

Hertford, Council of (672 or 673). A Council of bishops held on 24 Sept. 672 or 673, under *Theodore, Abp. of Canterbury, to promote the reorganization of the English Church. It issued 10 canons, concerned esp. with the rights and duties of clerics and monks. Bishops were not to intrude on the diocese ('parochia') of a neighbouring bishop (can. 2); precedence among bishops was to be determined by their dates of consecration (can. 8); and monks were not to leave their monasteries without their abbot's permission (can. 4). Synods were to be held twice annually, or, if that proved impossible, at least once a year on 1 Aug., at *Clovesho (can. 7). Divorce was forbidden except for fornication, and a man divorced from his wife was not to remarry (can. 10). The date for the keeping of Easter was settled (can. 1). The Council was the first occasion on which the English Church deliberated and acted as a unity.

*Bede, *HE* 4. 5; comm. by J. M. Wallace-Hadrill (Oxford, 1988), pp. 142–4. A. W. Haddan and W. *Stubbs (eds.), *Councils and Ecclesiastical Documents Relating to Great Britain and Ireland*, 3 (1871), pp. 118–22. W. *Bright, *Chapters of Early English Church History* (1878), pp. 240–9 and 441–4. Hefele and Leclercq, 3 (pt. 1; 1909), p. 310.

Hervetus, Gentian (1499–1584), French theologian, translator, and controversialist. He was a native of Olivet, nr. Orléans, where he studied. In 1519 he came to England, where he formed links with R. *Pole. In 1533 he dedicated an English translation of *Erasmus' *De immensa misericordia Dei* to Margaret, Countess of Salisbury, Pole's mother. For a short time, *c*.1534, he was professor of Greek at Orléans University. He translated several Greek writings into Latin, among them *Aristotle's *De Anima*

(1544) and Alexander of Aphrodisias' *De Fato* (1544). He then went to Rome, where he lived in the house of Cardinal Pole, whom he accompanied to *Trent in 1545. In his service he made more translations, esp. of the Greek Fathers, e.g. *Zacharias Scholasticus (1548). He also took an active part in the discussions preceding the decrees of the Council. In 1549 he entered the service of Card. M. Cervini, later Pope Marcellus II, for whom he translated works by *Theodoret (1549), St *Chrysostom (1549), and St *Clement of Alexandria (1551). In 1556 he was ordained priest, and shortly afterwards became Vicar General of Noyon. In 1561 he published a treatise *De Reparanda Ecclesiasticorum Disciplina*, in which he recommended the enforcing of episcopal residence as the chief means for the reform of the Church. In 1561 he joined the group of theologians formed by Card. Charles of Lorraine for fighting Protestantism and published a number of controversial pamphlets against it. From 1562 he was Canon of *Reims. In 1562 he again went to Trent, in the company of Charles of Lorraine. In 1564 he published a complete French translation of the decrees of the Council entitled *Le Saint, Sacré, Universel et Général Concile de Trente*. In his later years he wrote chiefly pamphlets, and in 1570 published a French translation of St *Augustine's *Civitas Dei*.

A. Humbert in *DTC* 6 (1920), cols. 2315–20, s.v. 'Hervet', with additional bibl. in *DHGE* 24 (1993), col. 246; A. Duval, OP, in *Catholicisme*, 5 [1963], cols. 693–7, also s.v. 'Hervet'.

Herzog, Johann Jakob (1805–82), Swiss Reformed theologian. A pupil of F. D. E. *Schleiermacher and J. A. W. *Neander, he began to teach at Lausanne in 1835, where he was professor of historical theology from 1838 to 1846. Later he held professorships at Halle (from 1847) and Erlangen (from 1854). His fame rests on his editing of the *Realencyklopädie für protestantische Theologie und Kirche* (22 vols., 1854–68), a standard work of reference which was adapted and condensed into an American version by P. *Schaff (3 vols., 1882–4). Both the German and American versions have been rewritten and expanded in more recent editions (see HAUCK, A.).

Herzog also issued a 2nd edn. of the *Realencyclopädie* (18 vols., 1877–88) in conjunction with G. L. Plitt. F. Sieffert in *PRE* (3rd edn.), 7 (1899), pp. 782–7.

Hesperinos. See VESPERS.

Hesychasm (from Gk. ἡσυχία, 'quietness'). In the E. Church, the tradition of inner, mystical prayer associated above all with the monks of Mt. *Athos. Its distant origins extend back to the 4th–5th cent., in particular to St *Gregory of Nyssa, *Evagrius Ponticus, the *Macarian Homilies, and *Diadochus of Photike. Other writers who exercised a formative influence on the growth of Hesychasm were St *John Climacus, St *Maximus the Confessor, and St *Simeon the New Theologian. Hesychasm in its developed form finds full expression in the works of St Gregory of Sinai, St Nicephorus of Mt. Athos, and esp. St *Gregory Palamas (q.v.), all of the 14th cent.

The Hesychasts attached particular importance to the unceasing repetition of the *Jesus Prayer (q.v.). To facilitate this continual recitation they recommended the aspirant to adopt a particular bodily posture—head bowed, eyes fixed on the place of the heart—and they taught that the breathing should be carefully controlled so as to keep time with the recitation of the prayer. This physical method was, of course, not regarded as the essential element in the practice of the Jesus Prayer, but simply as a useful accessory. The immediate aim of the Hesychasts was to secure what they termed 'the union of the mind with the heart', so that their prayer became 'prayer of the heart'. This prayer of the heart leads eventually, in those who are specially chosen by God, to the vision of the Divine Light, which, it was believed, can be seen—even in this present life—with the material eyes of the body, although it is first necessary for a man's physical faculties to be refined by God's grace and so rendered spiritual. The Hesychasts held this Light to be identical with the Light that surrounded the Lord at His *Transfiguration on Mt. Tabor, and to be none other than the uncreated energies of the Godhead. They considered this Light, and not (as in W. theology) God's essence, to be the object of the *Beatific Vision.

The Hesychast way of prayer, and above all the physical method, were fiercely attacked by the Calabrian Barlaam (esp. from 1337), who denounced the Athonite practices as gross superstition. He ridiculed the Hesychast claim to behold the Divine Light with bodily eyes, and he argued that the distinction which they drew between the essence and the energies of God impaired the Divine unity and simplicity. Barlaam's chief opponent, St Gregory Palamas, passionately defended Hesychasm, and was instrumental in securing its acceptance in the 'Hagioritic Tome' (1340-1) and also its formal adoption at the Councils of Constantinople in 1341, 1347, and 1351. Henceforward Hesychasm became an accepted part of the Orthodox tradition.

The chief texts embodying the Hesychast teaching on prayer are collected in the *Philocalia of St *Nicodemus of the Holy Mountain.

The fullest accounts are those of M. Jugie, AA, in DTC 11 (pt. 2; 1932), cols. 1777–818, s.v. 'Palamite (Controverse)', with bibl., based largely on unpub. MS material, and J. Meyendorff, Introduction à l'étude de Grégoire Palamas (Patristica Sorbonensia, 3 [1959]; abridged Eng. tr., 1964). V. *Lossky, Vision de Dieu (Neuchâtel, 1962; Eng. tr., 1963). I. Hausherr, SJ, La Méthode d'oraison hésychaste (Orientalia Christiana, 9, pt. 2; fasc. 36 of the series; 1927, paginated pp. 97–209); id., 'L'Hésychasme. Etude de spiritualité', OCP 22 (1956), pp. 5–40, 247–85, both repr., together with other arts. on the subject, in his Hésychasme et prière (Orientalia Christiana Analecta, 176; 1966). S. Guichardan, Le Problème de la simplicité divine en Orient et en Occident aux XIVᵉ et XVᵉ siècles: Grégoire Palamas, Duns Scot, Georges Scholarios (thesis; Lyons, 1933). P. Adnès in Dict. Sp. 7 (pt. 1; 1969), cols. 381–99, s.v.; F. v. Lilienfeld in TRE 15 (1986), pp. 282–9, s.v., with extensive bibl. See also bibl. to GREGORY PALAMAS.

Hesychius (fl. c.300), biblical textual critic. Acc. to St *Jerome (Praef. in lib. Paralipp.) he made a revision of the text of the *Septuagint at *Alexandria, which he corrected acc. to the Hebrew. He is perhaps to be identified with an Egyptian bishop, martyred in the *Diocletianic persecution (*Eusebius, HE 8. 13), who in conjunction with his colleagues, Pachomius, Theodore, and Phileas, sent a letter to Melitius of Lycopolis (see MELITIAN SCHISMS) which has survived in a Latin translation.

Lat. tr. of the letter sent to Melitius in J. P. Migne, PG 10. 1565–8. F. G. Kenyon, 'Hesychius and the Text of the New Testament', in Mémorial Lagrange (1940), pp. 245–50, with refs. to older lit. H. *Lietzmann in PW 8 (pt. 2; 1913), cols. 1327 f.

Hesychius of Alexandria (prob. 5th cent.), lexicographer. Nothing is known of his life. His elaborate lexicon (Συναγωγὴ πασῶν λέξεων κατὰ στοιχεῖον) is an important authority for the Greek dialects and the vocabulary of some of the Fathers. Based on the lexicon of Diogenianus of Heraclea (2nd cent. AD), it also drew on the compilations of Aristarchus, Heliodorus, Apion and others; and appears to have made extensive use of a glossary illustrating the vocabulary of St *Cyril of Alexandria. It survives in a single 15th-cent. MS (Venice 622), extensively interpolated and disfigured, from which the refs. to the sources of the words have been excised.

Edns. by J. Alberti (2 vols., Leiden, 1746–66), M. Schmidt (5 vols., Jena, 1858–68), and K. Latte (Copenhagen, 1953 ff.). A. von Blumenthal, Hesych-Studien: Untersuchungen zur Vorgeschichte der griechischen Sprache nebst lexicographischen Beiträgen (1930). H. Schultz in PW 8 (pt. 2; 1913), cols. 1317–22, s.v. 'Hesychios (9)'.

Hesychius of Jerusalem, St (5th cent.), Greek ecclesiastical writer and exegete. In early life he was a monk, and in 412, acc. to Theophanes Confessor, presbyter at *Jerusalem. Little, however, is known of him beyond the fact that he was held in high repute by his contemporaries. In his lost Church History, cited at the second Council of *Constantinople (553), he endorsed St *Cyril of Alexandria's position in the *Nestorian controversy and attacked both the exegetical method and the Christology of *Theodore of Mopsuestia. He was alive and strongly supporting the Alexandrians in the controversies that led up to the Council of *Chalcedon (451); as to whether he played any part in its aftermath, the evidence is scanty and unclear. He is said to have commented on the whole Bible. The surviving portions of his commentaries, glosses, and sermons make moderate use of *allegory, as would befit a supporter of the Alexandrian party. He defended orthodoxy against the *Manichees, *Arians, *Apollinarians, and other heretics. It seems probable that the bulk of the long commentary on the Psalms, ascribed by N. Antonelli, its first editor (1746), to St *Athanasius, is his work. The 'centuries' of ascetic maxims, printed among the works of Hesychius of Jerusalem, belong to an Abba Hesychius of Sinai (perhaps 6th–7th cent.). Feast day in the Greek Church, 28 Mar.

For his life, cf. *Cyril of Scythopolis, Vita S. Euthymii, 31 f. Works, incl. a 6th-cent. Lat. version of his Comm. on Lev. and other exegetical remains, in J. P. Migne, PG 93. 781–1560; Comm. on Pss., ibid. 27. 849–1344 (inter Opp. S. Athanasii). On this last see M. *Faulhaber, 'Eine wertvolle Oxforder Handschrift', Th.Q. 83 (1901), pp. 218–32. Parts of a different Comm. on Pss. (the 'Commentarius Magnus') are pr. in PG 93. 1180–340 and (among the spuria of J. *Chrysostom) in PG 55. 711–84; cf. R. Devreesse, Les Anciens Commentateurs grecs des Psaumes (ST 264; 1970), pp. 243–301, with further frags. Comm. on Is. ed. M. Faulhaber (Freiburg i.B., 1900). A. Vaccari, SJ, 'Esichio di Gerusalemme e il suo "Commentarius in Leviticum" ', Bessarione, 34 (1918), pp. 8–46, incl. frags. of Gk. text. Festal Homilies, ed. M. Aubineau (Subsidia Hagiographia, 59; 2 vols., 1978–80; index pub. separately, Hildesheim, 1983); Paschal Homilies, ed. id. (SC 187; 1972, pp. 35–166). Armenian version of Homilies on Job, ed. C. Renoux, with Fr. tr. by id. and C. Mercier, in PO 42 (1983), pp. 1–612. K. Jüssen, Die dogmatischen Anschauungen des Hesychius von Jerusalem (2 vols., 1931–4); id., 'Die Mariologie des Hesychius von Jerusalem', in J. Auer and H. Volk (eds.), *Theologie in Geschichte und Gegenwart: Michael Schmaus zum sechzigsten Geburtstag dargebracht* (Munich, 1957), pp. 651–70; A. Wenger, AA, 'Hésychius de Jérusalem. Notes sur les discours inédits et sur le texte grec du commentaire "In Leviticum" ', *Revue des Études Augustiniennes*, 2 (1956), pp. 457–70. *CPG* 3 (1979), pp. 257–69 (nos. 6550–96). M. Faulhaber in *CE* 7 (1910), pp. 303 f.; J. Kirchmeyer, SJ, in *Dict. Sp.* 7 (pt. 1; 1969), cols. 399–408, s.v. 'Hésychius (1) de Jérusalem'.

Hexaemeron (Gk. ἑξαήμερον, '[a work] of six days'). The account of the creation of the universe in six days, as set forth in Gen. 1. The name is also used of the *patristic commentaries on this narrative, notably those of St *Basil and St *Ambrose.

F. E. Robbins, *The Hexaemeral Literature* (thesis; Chicago, 1912); Y.-M.-J. *Congar, OP, 'Le thème de *Dieu-Créateur* et les explications de l'Hexaméron dans la tradition chrétienne', in *L'Homme devant Dieu: Mélanges offerts au Père Henri de Lubac*, 1 (Théologie, 56; 1963), pp. 189–222; *In Principio: Interprétations des premiers versets de la Genèse* (École pratique des Hautes Études, Section des Sciences religieuses, Centre d'Études des Religions du Livre, Laboratoire associé au C.N.R.S., 152; Études Augustiniennes, 1973); J. Zahlten, *Creatio mundi: Darstellungen der sechs Schöpfungstage und naturwissenschaftliches Weltbild im Mittelalter* (Stuttgarter Beiträge zur Geschichte und Politik, 13; 1979).

Hexapla (Gk. ἑξαπλᾶ 'sixfold'). The elaborate edition of the OT produced by *Origen, in which the Hebrew text, the Hebrew text transliterated into Greek characters, and the four Greek versions of *Aquila, *Symmachus, the *Septuagint (in a revised text with critical signs) and *Theodotion were arranged in parallel columns. For certain sections of the OT, up to three further Greek versions were added, making a total of nine columns. The work, begun before Origen left Alexandria for Caesarea in 231, was not finished until *c.*245. It was of such huge dimensions that it was probably never copied in its entirety, and St *Jerome expressly stated that he had used the original copy preserved in Origen's library at Caesarea. The text of the LXX in the fifth column, however, was widely copied and circulated on its own. Origen had adapted the LXX to the Hebrew, using asterisks and obeli to mark the differences, and though these signs tended to disappear when the LXX was copied on its own, this Hexaplaric recension was regarded as of great authority in the early Church. Fragments of the Hexapla have been identified at Milan and Cambridge, though in each case the first column (the Hebrew) is wanting. According to *Eusebius, Jerome, and other Fathers, the last four columns (Aquila, Symmachus, LXX, and Theodotion) also existed in a separate form known as the 'Tetrapla'. See also SYRO-HEXAPLA.

The most extensive collection of frags. is in F. *Field, *Origenis Hexaplorum quae Supersunt* (2 vols., Oxford, 1867–75); that at Cambridge was ed. by C. Taylor, *Hebrew-Greek Cairo Genizah Palimpsests* (Cambridge, 1900), pp. 1–50; those at Milan by G. *Mercati (*Codices ex Ecclesiasticis Italiae Bybliothecis delecti*, 8; with photographic reproduction and transcript of text, together with reconstruction of col. 1, Rome, 1958; vol. of 'Osservazioni', ibid., 1965). A. Schenker, OP, *Hexaplarische Psalmenbruchstücke: Die hexaplarischen Psalmenfragmente der Handschriften Vaticanus graecus 752 und Canonicianus graecus 62* (Orbis Biblicus et Orientalis, 8; 1975), incl. texts. *CPG* 1 (1983), pp. 174 f. (no. 1500). C. Taylor in *DCB* 3 (1882), pp. 14–23, s.v. See also works cited under SEPTUAGINT.

Hexateuch (Gk. ἕξ, 'six' + τεῦχος, 'book'). A name given by J. *Wellhausen (1876), and after him by many other modern biblical scholars, to the first six books of the Hebrew Bible (Genesis to Joshua), in the belief that all are compiled from a single set of literary sources. The word is formed on the analogy of *Pentateuch.

G. von *Rad, *Das formgeschichtliche Problem des Hexateuchs* (Beiträge zur Wissenschaft von Alten und Neuen Testament, Folge 4, Heft 26; 1938; Eng. tr., *The Problem of the Hexateuch and Other Essays* (Edinburgh, 1966), pp. 1–78).

Hexham, in Northumberland. The site of an abbey founded by St *Wilfrid of York in 674. In 678 the new see of Bernicia was set up here, which survived until 821, when it was united with the bishopric of *Lindisfarne. The abbey church of St Andrew is chiefly Early English and Transitional, and since the *Dissolution in 1536 has been used as the parish church. Only fragments of other parts of the monastery remain.

J. Raine (ed.), *The Priory of Hexham, its Chronicles, Endowments and Annals* (Surtees Society, 44 and 46; 1864–5). W. *Dugdale, *Monasticon Anglicanum*, 6 (pt. 1; 1830 edn.), pp. 179–85. C. C. Hodges, *The Abbey of St Andrew, Hexham* (1888). Id. and J. Gibson, *Hexham and its Abbey* (1919), pp. 24–122. *A History of Northumberland*, 3, by A. B. Hinds (1896), pp. 105–200. D. P. Kirby (ed.), *Saint Wilfrid at Hexham* (Newcastle-upon-Tyne, 1974).

Heylyn, Peter (1600–62), Anglican controversialist and historian. Educated at Burford and at Hart Hall and Magdalen College, *Oxford, he became a Fellow of Magdalen in 1618. In 1627 at a public disputation he defended against John Prideaux, the Regius professor of divinity, the visibility of the Church and soon attracted the attention of W. *Laud by his championship of *High Church views. In 1630 he was appointed by *Charles I a royal chaplain and also rector of Hemingford, Cambs. When J. *Williams, Bp. of Lincoln, declined to institute him at Hemingford, Charles made him a prebendary of *Westminster (1631), where he began a long feud with Williams which ended with Williams's suspension by the Star Chamber in 1637. Other preferments followed in the next years. In the 1630s he became the official apologist for the Laudian reforms: in *The History of the Sabbath* (1636) he defended anti-*sabbatarianism; in *A Coale from the Altar* (1636) and *Antidotum Lincolniense* (1637) he upheld the requirements that the *Communion table (or altar) be placed at the east end of the church and surrounded by a rail; and in *A Brief and Moderate Answer* (1637) he refuted charges of innovation. After 1640 his fortunes altered with the decline in the King's power. During the Civil War his issue of *Mercurius Aulicus*, a royalist news-sheet, caused his property at Alresford to be plundered and his library dispersed. Under the Commonwealth he lived quietly at first, but later renewed his controversial writings, one of which, *Ecclesia Vindicata, or the Church of England justified* (1657), again brought upon him the indignation of the government. This was followed in 1659 with an attack on T. *Fuller. At the Restoration (1660) he worked for the reinstatement of the C of E in all her traditional and legal rights and was particularly anxious for the revival of the *Convocations. As a writer, Heylyn was learned, trenchant, and critical, but he was above all a partisan. Among his other works are *Historia Quinquarticularis, or a Historical Declaration of the Five Controverted Points reproached in the Name of Arminianism* (1660); *Ecclesia Restaurata, or the History of the Reformation* (1661); *Cyprianus Anglicus* (1668), a defence of Laud; and *Aerius Redivivus: or, The History of Presbyterianism* (1670).

Photographic repr. of *The History of the Sabbath* (Amsterdam and New York, 1969). G. Vernon, *The Life of the Learned and Reverend Doctor Peter Heylyn* (1682) G. Barnard, *Theologico-Historicus, or True Life of the Most Reverend Divine and Excellent Historian, Peter Heylyn, D.D.* (1683), repr., with additional information from Vernon, in Heylyn's *Ecclesia Restaurata*, ed. J. C. Robertson (1849). M. *Creighton in *DNB* 26 (1891), pp. 319–23.

Hibbert, Robert (1770–1849), founder of the Hibbert Trust. He was born in Jamaica, was a pupil of Gilbert Wakefield at Nottingham, and studied at Emmanuel College, Cambridge, from 1788 to 1791. On his estate in Jamaica he kept slaves, for whose conversion he employed a *Unitarian minister. In 1847 he founded the Hibbert Trust for 'the spread of Christianity in its most simple and intelligible form' and also 'the unfettered exercise of the right of private judgement in matters of religion'. Its aims were anti-Trinitarian and its recipients must be 'heterodox'. Its best-known activities are the Hibbert Lectures (1878 onwards), and the publication of the *Hibbert Journal* (66 vols., 1902–68), which treated philosophical and religious subjects from a liberal point of view.

J. Murch, *Memoir of R. Hibbert, Esquire, Founder of the Hibbert Trust, with a Sketch of its History* (1874). A. R. Ruston, *The Hibbert Trust: A History* (1984). A. Gordon in *DNB* 26 (1891), p. 344.

Hickes, George (1642–1715), *Nonjuring bishop. Educated at Oxford, Hickes first served as Chaplain to the Duke of Lauderdale, *Charles II's Vice-regent in Scotland, where he greatly aided the episcopalian interest. In 1680 he became Vicar of All Hallows, Barking. In 1683 he published *Jovian*, a major work in defence of the *Divine Right of Kings, and in the same year he was appointed Dean of *Worcester. He opposed the pro-RC measures of *James II, but in 1689 he refused to take the oaths to William and Mary, and in 1690 he was deprived of his deanery. In his retirement, he remained firm in his principles. In 1694 he was consecrated titular Bp. of Thetford by the Nonjurors; and after the death in 1709 of W. Lloyd (formerly Bp. of *Norwich), he was their acknowledged head. Being anxious, in opposition to T. *Ken, to continue the Nonjuring succession, he consecrated three bishops in 1713, viz. J. *Collier, S. Hawes, and N. *Spinckes. Hickes was a man of great piety and wide scholarship. Besides his very learned *Linguarum veterum Septentrionalium Thesaurus* (1703–5), his writings included *The Case of Infant Baptism* (1683); *Speculum Beatae Virginis* (1686); *Institutiones Grammaticae Anglo-Saxonicae et Moeso-Gothicae* (1689); *Of the Christian Priesthood* (1707); and *Of the Dignity of the Episcopal Order* (1707). The posthumous publication of Hickes's *Constitution of the Catholic Church and the Nature and Consequences of Schism* (1716) was the immediate occasion of the *Bangorian Controversy.

His *Two Treatises on the Christian Priesthood and on the Dignity of the Episcopal Order* were ed. by I. B[arrow] in LACT (3 vols.,

1847–8). There are frequent refs. to him in T. *Hearne's *Remains and Collections*. J. H. Overton, *The Nonjurors* (1902), pp. 91–113 and *passim*; D. C. Douglas, *English Scholars, 1660–1730* (1939), ch. 4, pp. 93–119; 2nd edn. (1951), pp. 77–97. W. D. Macray in *DNB* 26 (1891), pp. 350–4.

Hicks, Elias (1748–1830), American *Quaker. He was born of Quaker parents at Hempstead, Long Island. After taking little interest in religion as a young man, he gradually came to feel a call to preaching and from 1779 onwards made evangelistic tours, becoming a commanding influence. He also took up the cause of the negroes, esp. in *Observations on the Slavery of the Africans and their Descendants* (1811). He strongly opposed the creation of any credal basis for Quakerism, notably in his *Doctrinal Epistle* (1824), where he protested against insistence on the orthodox doctrines of the Person of Christ and the Atonement. A schism ensued (1827–8) at Philadelphia and elsewhere between his followers (the 'Liberal Branch', called by their opponents 'Hicksites') and the orthodox, which had repercussions in England (see FRIENDS, SOCIETY OF).

Some of his discourses, taken down in shorthand by M. T. C. Gould, were pub. at Philadelphia in 1825. [V. Hicks and R. Seaman (eds.)], *Journal of the Life and Religious Labours of E. Hicks, written by himself* (3rd edn., New York, 1832). H. W. Wilbur, *The Life and Labours of Elias Hicks* (Philadelphia, 1910); E. Russell, *The Separation after a Century* (ibid., 1928); B. Forbush, *Elias Hicks, Quaker Liberal* (New York, 1956); R. W. Doherty, *The Hicksite Separation* (New Brunswick, 1967). R. M. *Jones in *Dict. Amer. Biog.* 9 (1932), pp. 6 f.

Hicks, George Dawes (1862–1941), philosopher. He was a *Unitarian minister at Islington from 1897 to 1903 and professor of philosophy at University College, London, from 1904 to 1928. From an intensive interest in I. *Kant, he became a lifelong student of the theory of knowledge. In his *Hibbert Lectures on *The Philosophical Bases of Theism* (1937) he defended the traditional Christian position, arguing that besides the strictly intellectual grounds of theistic belief there was a legitimate place for the argument from religious experience.

A. Dorward in *DNB, 1941–1950*, pp. 387–8.

Hicksites. See HICKS, ELIAS.

Hieracas of Leontopolis (late 2nd–early 3rd cent.), an ascetic and one of the leaders of the monastic movement in Egypt. Learned in both Greek and Coptic, he wrote works in both languages, incl. a commentary on the *Hexaemeron and several hymns, but nothing of his has survived. The main source is *Epiphanius' surprisingly genial account in his *Panarion* (*Haer.* 67). Hieracas was an *Origenist, upholding the pre-existence of souls and the spiritual nature of the resurrection body; *Peter of Alexandria's condemnation of Origenism may have been directed against him. He rejected marriage absolutely. *Arius (*Ep. ad Alex.* 3) mentions him as holding that the Son was derived from the Father as one flame from another, but Epiphanius says nothing of this.

P. Nautin, 'Hiérakas de Léontopolis', *École Pratique des Hautes Études, Ve Section, Annuaire*, 84 (1975–6), pp. 312–14. G. Salmon in *DCB* 3 (1882), pp. 24 f., s.v.

Hieracites. Followers of *Hieracas (q.v.).

hierarchy. The word has been in use for the ordained body of Christian clergy since patristic times. RC theologians used to distinguish the hierarchy of order from that of pastoral government. The former was subdivided into the three grades of divine institution (bishops, priests, and deacons) on the one hand, and the subdiaconate and minor orders, instituted by the Church, on the other. In the hierarchy of pastoral government, only the papacy and the episcopacy were held to be of divine institution. All the other grades were held to be of ecclesiastical origin. Since the Second *Vatican Council the hierarchical constitution of the Church has been conceived differently, and this understanding is reflected in the 1983 *Codex Iuris Canonici* (cans. 330–572). First there is the supreme Church authority, enjoyed by the Pope and college of bishops, with power over the universal Church. From this authority derives that of the synods of bishops, the cardinals, the Roman Curia, and pontifical legates. Secondly, there are particular Churches and their groupings; from these derive the authority of, e.g., diocesan synods, vicars general, etc. Only those in holy orders (bishops, priests, and deacons) are capable of the power of government or jurisdiction, but the laity can co-operate in the exercise of this power. The threefold hierarchical order of bishops, priests, and deacons has been retained in the C of E in common with the RC and E. Churches.

Hierome, Hieronymus. See JEROME.

Hieronymian Martyrology (Lat. *Hieronymianum*). A famous *martyrology (q.v.), based on an earlier Greek martyrology of Asia Minor, which was composed in Italy in the middle of the 5th cent. It gives, after the calendar date in the year, the names of the saints commemorated on that day, the places of their tombs (or alternatively where they were venerated), and other details connected with their cultus. It is so named from a statement in an apocryphal correspondence preceding the text that its compilation was the work of St *Jerome.

> Ed. princeps by F. Fiorentini (Lucca, 1668). Text also in D. *Vallarsi's edn. of Jerome, 11 (Verona, 1742), cols. 475–524; repr. in J. P. Migne, PL 30. 433–86. Crit. edn., with magisterial discussion, by G. B. *de Rossi and L. *Duchesne in AASS, Nov. 2 (pt. 1; 1894), pp. [1]–[195], with text of 'Bernensis', 'Epternacensis', and 'Wisseburgensis' in three columns, with the further text of the 'Laureshamensis' for 38 days, and with prolegomena, pp. [i]–[lxxxii]; 'Commentarius Perpetuus', by H. *Quentin, OSB, and H. *Delehaye, SJ, as Nov. 2 (pt. 2; 1931). J. Dubois, OSB, Les Martyrologes du Moyen Âge Latin (Typologie des Sources du Moyen Âge Occidental, 26; 1978), pp. 29–37, with further refs.

Hierusalem. A Latinized form of the word *Jerusalem (Gk. Ἱερουσαλήμ).

High Altar. The main altar of a church, traditionally standing in the centre of the east end. In ancient English Gothic churches the length was commonly the same as that of the splay of the east window, which formed the *reredos. Acc. to modern RC practice there should be only one altar in the principal part of the church, so placed as to form the focal point, and sufficiently separated from the wall to allow Mass to be celebrated facing the people. The altar is normally made of stone, though other solid material

may be used. It is normally fixed and consecrated. Either on or near the altar there is to be a cross (*crux*) and two, four, or six candlesticks.

High Churchmen. A term coined in the late 17th cent. to describe those members of the C of E who emphasized its historical continuity as a branch of the Catholic Church and upheld 'high' conceptions of the divine basis of authority in Church and State, of the rights of monarchy and episcopacy, and of the nature of the sacraments. The descent of the school can be traced from the Elizabethan age, when men such as R. *Bancroft and R. *Hooker resisted the attacks of radical *Puritans. In the 17th cent. the tradition was maintained by L. *Andrewes, W. *Laud, and many others. After the *Restoration of *Charles II, the High Church identification of Church and nation received legislative reinforcement, notably from the Act of *Uniformity of 1662 and the *Test Act (1673). The accession, first of William of Orange (1689) and then of the House of Hanover (1714) violated the principle of indefeasible hereditary succession (see DIVINE RIGHT OF KINGS) and precipitated the schism of the *Nonjurors, although men such as W. *Law and C. *Leslie continued to work closely with conforming High Churchmen to promote popular piety and to defend the C of E against spreading heterodoxy and toleration of Protestant dissenters. In the early 18th cent. there was strong support for the views of H. *Sacheverell and F. *Atterbury, and writers such as D. *Waterland and C. *Wheatly achieved lasting influence. High Churchmen were instrumental in securing episcopal consecration for S. *Seabury and in resisting the rationalist and democratic impulses of the French Revolution. Later High Churchmen of this school initially shared the concern of the *Oxford Movement at the erosion of the Church's privileges after 1828, but were soon alienated by what they regarded as its tendency to divisiveness and innovation. See also ANGLO-CATHOLICISM.

> J. Wickham Legg, English Church Life from the Restoration to the Tractarian Movement (1914); G. W. O. Addleshaw, The High Church Tradition (1941); G. Every, SSM, The High Church Party 1688–1718 (CHS, 1956); K. Hylson-Smith, High Churchmanship in the Church of England from the Sixteenth Century to the late Twentieth Century (Edinburgh, 1993); P. B. Nockles, The Oxford Movement in Context: Anglican High Churchmanship 1760–1857 (Cambridge, 1994). R. Sharp, 'New Perspectives on the High Church Tradition: Historical Background 1730–1780' in [D.] G. Rowell (ed.), Tradition Renewed: The Oxford Movement Conference Papers (1986), pp. 4–23; R. H. Fuller, 'The Classical High Church Reaction to the Tractarians', ibid., pp. 51–63. See also bibl. to Churchmen mentioned in the entry.

High Commission, Court of. From 1549 ecclesiastical commissions to check heresy and enforce the forms of worship prescribed by public authority were frequently appointed in England. From 1559 the power of the Crown to create such bodies was expressly recognized by the Elizabethan Act of *Supremacy. The actual term 'High Commission' begins to appear c.1570 and is employed normally after 1580, a development corresponding with the elevation of an *ad hoc* commission into a permanent court. At this stage the visitatorial function of the commission declined by comparison with the multiplication of suits between party and party, while professional lawyers played an increasing part and rigid procedure developed. The High Commission also became the normal court of appeal from the ancient ecclesiastical courts in doctrinal and disciplinary suits. Together with the other conciliar courts, it incurred the dislike and fear of the common lawyers, even Lord Burghley, Elizabeth's first minister, denouncing the procedure by the oath *ex officio* as savouring of the *Inquisition. In 1641 it was ended by the Abolition of High Commission Court Act 1640. In 1686 *James II instituted an Ecclesiastical Commission, which some authorities regard as a revival of the Court of High Commission. This in turn was discontinued in 1688 and condemned in the Bill of Rights. Besides the central High Commission, the Crown appointed diocesan ecclesiastical commissions, most of which ceased to be very active after 1600. There was also a High Commission for the Northern Province, which was closely associated with the Council in the North, and took a leading part in the repression of *recusancy.

The greater part of the Act Books and other papers belonging to the Registry of the Commission at London seems to have been lost, having probably been destroyed by order of Parliament during the Civil War; some records, however, survive among the State Papers. A large part of the papers of the Commission at Durham has survived; ed., in part, by W. H. D. Longstaffe, *The Acts of the High Commission Court within the Diocese of Durham* (Surtees Society, 34; 1858); F. D. Price (ed.), *The Commission for Ecclesiastical Causes within the Dioceses of Bristol and Gloucester, 1574* (Bristol and Gloucestershire Archaeological Society, Records Section, 10; 1972). R. G. Usher, *The Rise and Fall of the High Commission* (Oxford, 1913; repr., with introd. by P. Tyler, and further bibl., 1968). P. Tyler, 'The Significance of the Ecclesiastical Commission at York', *Northern History*, 2 (1967), pp. 27–44; R. B. Manning, 'The Making of a Protestant Aristocracy: the Ecclesiastical Commissioners of the Diocese of Chester, 1550–98', *Bulletin of the Institute of Historical Research*, 49 (1976), pp. 60–79; C. Cross, 'Sin and Society: The Northern High Commission and the Northern Gentry in the Reign of Elizabeth I', in id. and others (eds.), *Law and Government under the Tudors: Essays Presented to Sir Geoffrey Elton* (Cambridge, 1988), pp. 195–209. J. P. Kenyon, 'The Commission for Ecclesiastical Causes 1686–1688: A Reconsideration', *Historical Journal*, 34 (1991), pp. 727–36. R. G. Usher in *DECH*, pp. 275–8, s.v.

High Mass (Missa solemnis). In the W. Church for centuries the normal, though not the most usual, form of the Mass. Its essential feature was the presence of the *deacon and *subdeacon assisting the celebrant; they were accompanied by the choir, the *thurifer, and a number of servers or *acolytes. Their respective functions were carefully regulated, the chief office of the deacon being the chanting of the *Gospel and the *Ite, Missa Est, and that of the subdeacon the chanting of the *Epistle; whereas the choir and people sang the *proper and *common of saints respectively. Other distinctive features were the use of *incense and the giving of the *Kiss of Peace. Since the Second *Vatican Council the term 'High Mass' has disappeared from official documents and a more typical pattern of celebration is advocated; greater emphasis is placed on the part of the congregation and on the role of the deacon as their leader, as well as on his traditional functions of assisting the celebrant, while the celebrant is conceived as president of the liturgical assembly.

Jungmann (1958 edn.), 1, pp. 257–72; Eng. tr., pp. 195–207.

'High Places', the (Heb. הַבָּמוֹת). In the OT the local (usually hill-top) sanctuaries other than *Jerusalem at which Yahweh was worshipped with sacrifice in early times. Among the most renowned were *Bethel and Gibeon. Worship at these sites, which had Canaanite affinities and was often accompanied by sexual rites, was denounced by many of the Prophets (*Amos, *Hosea, etc.). The 'high places' were finally destroyed under Josiah in 621 BC (2 Kings 23: 5–20).

P. H. Vaughan, *The Meaning of 'bāmâ' in the Old Testament: A Study of Etymological, Textual and Archaeological Evidence* (Society for Old Testament Study Monograph Series, 3; Cambridge, 1974), with bibl. R. de Vaux, OP, *Les Institutions de l'Ancien Testament*, 2 (1960), pp. 107–13; Eng. tr. (2nd edn., 1965), pp. 284–8. W. B. Barrick in *Anchor Bible Dictionary*, 3 (1992), pp. 196–200, s.v., with bibl.

High Prayers. A title for service in certain college chapels in Oxford on great festivals.

High Priest. In the OT the head of the *Levitical priesthood whose institution and vestments are described in Exod. 28. Acc. to this account (usually assigned to *P), *Aaron, the brother of *Moses, was appointed the first high priest by Yahweh. The chief function of the high priest was the superintendence of the Temple worship, and his special prerogatives the offering of the Liturgy on the Day of *Atonement, when he alone was allowed to enter the Holy of Holies, and the consulting of '*Urim and Thummim'. His exalted office required an unusually high degree of ritual purity, which forbade him to 'defile himself' with the dead even in the case of his nearest relations. His vestments, more precious than those of the other priests, included a violet robe adorned with bells and tassels, a special mitre with a golden plate in front bearing the inscription 'Holy to the Lord', and a breastplate with the names of the twelve tribes of *Israel.

In post-exilic times, the high priest was the head of the Jewish state as well as the principal religious functionary. At first the office may have been for life and hereditary; but under *Antiochus Epiphanes and his successors the appointment and deposition of high priests passed more and more into the authority of the secular powers. In the time of the *Herods and the Roman occupation the high priests were usually taken from the most influential families; they seem to have adopted a worldly attitude, believing neither in an immortal soul nor in a future life, and, acc. to the *Talmud, they lived in luxury and self-indulgence.

Christian theology holds that the Saviour, by His death on the Cross, abolished for the redeemed the high-priestly office and sacrifices, perfecting them in His own Person. This teaching is developed in the NT in the Ep. to the Hebrews, which sets forth the Christ as the perfect high priest, unique and immortal, of whom the long series of imperfect high priests under the old dispensation had been but types and shadows.

W. W. Graf Baudissin, *Die Geschichte des alttestamentlichen Priesterthums* (1889), esp. pp. 26–8, 88 f., 127–30, 140–2, 251–3. F. Stummer, 'Gedanken über die Stellung des Hohenpriesters in der alttestamentlichen Gemeinde', in *Episcopus: Studien über das Bischofsamt seiner Eminenz Michael Kardinal von Faulhaber . . . zum 80. Geburtstag dargebracht* (Regensburg, 1949), pp. 19–48. R. de Vaux, OP, *Les Institutions de l'Ancien Testament*, 2 (1960), pp. 266–74, with bibl., p. 450; Eng. tr. (2nd edn., 1965), pp. 397–

403, with bibl., p. 546. E. *Schürer, *The History of the Jewish People in the Age of Jesus Christ*, Eng. tr. rev. by G. Vermes and others, 2 (1979), pp. 227–36, with bibl. On the high priest's vesture, see J. Gabriel, *Untersuchungen über das alttestamentliche Hohepriestertum, mit besonderer Berücksichtigung des hohepriesterlichen Ornates* (Theologische Studien der Österreichischen Leo-Gesellschaft, 33; 1933). W. [W.] Baudissin in *HDB* 4 (1902), pp. 67–97, s.v. 'Priests and Levites', esp. pp. 83 f.; G. Schrenk in *TWNT* 3 (1938), pp. 265–84 (Eng. tr., 1966, pp. 265–83), s.v. ἱερεύς [ἀρχιερεύς]; A. Cody, OSB, in *TRE* 1 (1977), pp. 2–5, s.v. 'Aaron, 2: Aaronitisches Priestertum'. For the conception of Christ as the high priest, see bibl. to HEBREWS, EP. TO THE.

Higher Criticism. The critical study of the literary methods and sources used by the authors of (esp.) the Books of the OT and NT, in distinction from *Textual ('Lower') Criticism, which is concerned solely with the recovery of the text of the Books as it left their authors' hands. The phrase, which is little used now, came into currency from its use by W. R. *Smith in *The Old Testament in the Jewish Church* (1881; p. 105).

Hijra (in older works often spelt **Hegira**). The emigration of Muhammad from Mecca to Medina, the traditional date for which is 16 July 622. From this event begins the Muslim era, though, as its (lunar) years (commonly AH) consist of only 354 or 355 days, it is not possible to relate it to the Christian era by simple addition or subtraction.

Tables for the conversion of Islamic and Christian dates incl. H. F. Wüstenfeld and E. Mahler, *Vergleichungs-Tabellen zur muslimischen und iranischen Zeitrechnung* (3rd edn. rev. by J. Mayr and B. Spuler, Wiesbaden, 1961), and G. S. P. Freeman-Grenville, *The Muslim and Christian Calendars* (1963). There is also a convenient handbook by [T.] W. Haig, *Comparative Tables of Muhammadan and Christian Dates* [1932].

Hilarion, St (*c*.291–371). The founder of the *anchoritic life in Palestine. A native of Palestine and the son of pagan parents, he was converted to Christianity at *Alexandria, and under the influence of St *Antony retired for a short time to the Egyptian desert as a hermit. In 306 he returned to his own land, where he settled in the wilderness S. of Maiuma, near Gaza, to live a life of extreme asceticism. As his fame and miraculous gifts became increasingly known, enormous crowds visited him, to escape from whom he returned *c*.353 to Egypt. Later he went to Libya, Sicily, and Cyprus, where he died. He was well known to St *Epiphanius, to whom St *Jerome, the chief authority for his life, was doubtless mainly indebted for his knowledge of him. Feast day, 21 Oct.

Jerome's *Vita* (*c*. AD 386–91) is repr. in J. P. Migne, *PL* 23. 29–54; cf. *Sozomen, *HE* 3. 14, 5. 10, and 6. 32. The letter of Epiphanius, mentioned by Jerome as his source, is lost. G. Grützmacher, *Hieronymus*, 2 (1906), pp. 87–91. E. Coleiro, 'St Jerome's Lives of the Hermits', *VC* 11 (1957), pp. 161–78. J. N. D. Kelly, *Jerome* (1975), pp. 172–4. J. P. Kirsch in *CE* 7 (1910), pp. 347 f.

Hilary of Arles, St (*c*.401–49), Bp. of Arles. He became a monk at *Lérins, under the influence of his kinsman, St *Honoratus, and in *c*.430 succeeded him as bishop of the *metropolitan see of Arles. In this capacity he presided over several councils, among them the First Council of *Orange (441) and that of *Vaison (442). In 444, by deposing a bishop, Chelidonius, Hilary appears to have exceeded his rights as metropolitan, and on the dethroned bishop's appeal to *Leo I, the Pope deprived Arles of its metropolitan jurisdiction and obtained from the Emp. Valentinian a decree granting Rome supreme authority over the Church in Gaul. Hilary wrote a Life of Honoratus which is still extant. A *Carmen de providentia divina*, ascribed to *Prosper of Aquitaine, has recently been attributed to Hilary, but the attribution is very doubtful. Feast day, 5 May.

Frags. of Hilary's works collected in edns. of Leo's *Opera* by P. *Quesnel (1675) and P. and H. *Ballerini (1753–7; qq.v.). Repr. from the latter in J. P. Migne, *PL* 50. 1213–92, with additions. Crit. text of Hilary's Life of Honoratus and a Life of Hilary, written *c*.475, ed. S. Cavallin (Skrifter utgivna av Vetenskaps-Societen i Lund, 40; 1952). Life of Honoratus also ed., with Fr. tr., by M.-D. Valentin, OP (SC 235; 1977); Eng. tr. in F. R. Hoare (ed.), *The Western Fathers* (1954), pp. 248–80. [W.] O. Chadwick, 'Euladius of Arles', *JTS* 46 (1945), pp. 200–5. É. Griffe, *La Gaule chrétienne à l'époque romaine*, 2 (1957), pp. 120–7 and 196–201; 2nd edn. (1966), pp. 154–62 and 244–50. G. Gallo, 'Uno scritto filo-pelagiano attribuibile a Ilario di Arles', *Aevum*, 51 (1977), pp. 333–48. S. Pricoco, *L'Isola dei Santi: Il cenobio di Lerino e le origini del monachesimo gallico* (Filologia e Critica, 23; 1978), *passim*. M. Jourjon in *Dict. Sp.* 7 (pt 1; 1969), cols. 463 f., s.v. 'Hilaire (1) d'Arles'; S. Pricoco in *DPAC* 2 (1984), cols. 1747 f., s.v. 'Ilario di Arles', with bibl.; Eng. tr., *Encyclopedia of the Early Church*, 1 (1992), p. 381, s.v.

Hilary of Poitiers, St (*c*.315–67/8), the 'Athanasius of the West'. An educated convert from paganism, he was elected Bp. of Poitiers *c*. 350 and subsequently became involved in the *Arian disputes. His condemnation at the Synod of Biterrae (356) is usually attributed to his defence of Catholic teaching, but some scholars have suggested that other factors may initially have been involved. It was followed by a four-year exile to Phrygia by the Emp. Constantius, whom Hilary later denounced as *Antichrist. In 359 he defended the cause of orthodoxy at the Council of *Seleucia, and he became the leading and most respected Latin theologian of his age. His chief works were a treatise 'De Trinitate' (against the Arians), in twelve books; 'De Synodis', very valuable for the doctrinal history of the period; and the so-called 'Opus Historicum'. His other writings include commentaries on Matthew and the Psalms, the latter of which clearly shows the influence of *Origen. His style is difficult and occasionally obscure. In matters of detail his doctrinal position deviated at points from later orthodoxy, e.g. he held an almost *Monophysite Christology. He is the earliest known writer of *hymns (q.v.) in the W. Church. In 1851 *Pius XI proclaimed him a '*Doctor of the Church'. His feast day (in the BCP, 13 Jan.; in the RC Calendar, 14 Jan.; from 1969, 13 Jan.) gives its name to the spring term at the Law Courts, and at Oxford and Durham universities.

Editio princeps, by *Erasmus (Basle, 1523). Greatly improved text by P. *Coustant, OSB (Paris, 1693), one of the best of the *Maurist edns.; further improved by F. S. *Maffei (2 vols., Verona, 1730). This last is repr. in J. P. Migne, *PL* 9 and 10; further texts in Suppl. to *PL* by A. Hamman, OFM, 4 (1958), cols. 241–86 (incl. 'Tractatus Mysteriorum'; see below). Crit. edns. of his Works in CSEL (vols. 22 and 65 by A. Zingerle and A. Feder, SJ, 1891 and 1916: all pub. to 1995) and in CCSL (62 etc.; 1979 ff. [incl. *De Trinitate*, ed. P. Smulders, 62 and 62A; 1979–80]). New edns., with Fr. tr., of his comm. on Mt. by J. Doignon (SC 254 and 258; 1978–9), of his comm. on Ps. 118 by M. Milhau (ibid. 344 and 347; 1988) and of *In Constantium* by

A. Rocher (ibid. 334; 1987). His *Tractatus Mysteriorum* (or 'De Mysteriis'), which treats of NT types in the OT, first pub. from frags. in the Arezzo MS, which contains the 'Peregrinatio *Egeriae*', by J. F. Gamurrini (Rome, 1887); new edn., with Fr. tr., by J.-P. Brisson (SC 19; 1947). Three certainly genuine hymns are also preserved in the Arezzo MS; modern edn., with Eng. tr. and notes, by W. N. Myers (Philadelphia, 1928). Eng. tr. of his Works with valuable introds., ed. W. *Sanday, in NPNCF, 2nd ser., vol. 9, 1899; also of his 'De Trinitate' by S. McKenna, CSSR (Fathers of the Church, 1954).

P. Smulders, SJ, *La Doctrine trinitaire de S. Hilaire de Poitiers* (Analecta Gregoriana, 32; Rome, 1944). C. F. A. Borchardt, *Hilary of Poitiers' Role in the Arian Struggle* (Kerkhistorische Studien, 12; The Hague, 1966). J. *Daniélou, SJ, H. I. Marrou, and others, *Hilaire de Poitiers, évêque et docteur: Cinq conférences données à Poitiers à l'occasion du XVIe centenaire de sa mort* (Études Augustiniennes, 1968); E. R. Labande (ed.), *Hilaire et son temps: Actes du colloque de Poitiers . . . à l'occasion du XVIe centenaire de la mort de saint Hilaire* (ibid., 1969). J. Doignon, *Hilaire de Poitiers avant l'exil* (ibid., 1971). L. F. Ladaria, *El Espíritu Santo en San Hilario de Poitiers* (Publicaciones de la Universidad Pontificia Comillas, Madrid, Estudios, 8; 1977); id., *La Cristología de Hilario de Poitiers* (Analecta Gregoriana, 255; 1989). M. Figura, *Das Kirchenverständnis des Hilarius von Poitiers* (Freiburger theologische Studien, 127; 1984). H. C. Brennecke, *Hilarius von Poitiers und die Bischofsopposition gegen Konstantius II* (Patristische Texte und Studien, 26; 1984). Modern Lives by P. Galtier, SJ (Paris, 1960), and others. M. Simonetti in Quasten (cont.), *Patrology*, 4 (1986), pp. 33–61. X. Le Bachelet in *DTC* 6 (1920), cols. 2388–462; C. Kannengiesser, SJ, in *Dict. Sp.* 7 (pt. 1; 1969), cols. 466–99, s.v. 'Hilaire (4) de Poitiers'; J. Doignon in *RAC* 15 (1991), cols. 139–67.

Hilda, St

Hilda, St (614–80), Abbess of Whitby. Descended from the Northumbrian royal line, she was baptized at Easter 627 by *Paulinus, Bp. of *York. When her sister, Hereswith, had been professed as a nun at Chelles, near Paris, Hilda sought to join her; but having reached East Anglia she was recalled by St *Aidan, who in 649 made her abbess of a religious house at Hartlepool. In 657 she founded a monastery for both men and women at 'Streanaeshalch', later named Whitby by the Danes, which rapidly grew in fame and influence. At the celebrated Synod of *Whitby (664), Hilda sided with St *Colman in his defence of the Celtic customs against St *Wilfrid, though after the decision had gone in favour of the Romanizing party, she loyally accepted it. Feast day, 17 Nov.; 18 Nov. in the American BCP (1979).

The principal authority is *Bede, *HE* 3. 24 f. and 4. 23; comm. by J. M. Wallace-Hadrill (Oxford, 1988), pp. 163–5 and 232. P. Hunter Blair, 'Whitby as a Centre of Learning in the Seventh Century', in M. Lapidge and H. Gneuss (eds.), *Learning and Literature in Anglo-Saxon England: Studies Presented to Peter Clemoes* (Cambridge, 1985), pp. 3–32, esp. pp. 3–14. E. Venables in *DCB* 26 (1891), pp. 381 f.

Hildebert of Lavardin

Hildebert of Lavardin (1056–1133), Abp. of Tours, poet and canonist. He was born at Lavardin near Montoire and came to be Master of the cathedral school of Le Mans, and Archdeacon in 1091. In 1096 he was elected Bp. of Le Mans. He had a powerful opponent in William Rufus, who, alleging that Hildebert had attacked the royal castle from the towers of his cathedral, forced him to follow him to England in 1099. On regaining his freedom (1100) he went to Rome, where *Paschal II confirmed him in his office. After his return to Le Mans he continued the building of his cathedral and made a reputation as a powerful

preacher. He was an ardent defender of the freedom of the Church and of sound doctrine; he expelled *Henry of Lausanne (q.v.) from his diocese, consecrated his cathedral on its completion in 1120, and probably took part in the First *Lateran Council of 1123. In 1125 he became Abp. of Tours. He was involved in a dispute with King Louis VI and presided over the important provincial Synod of Nantes (1127).

Hildebert is famous chiefly for his literary works. He had studied the best classical authors, and his Latin, superior to that of most of his contemporaries, was looked to as the model of elegant style in the Middle Ages. The original printed collection of his works contains much spurious material. Certainly genuine are most of the Letters, the 'Vitae' of St *Radegunde and St *Hugh of Cluny, the 'Liber de Querimonia', the longer poems, 'De Sacrificio Missae' and 'Vita Mariae Aegyptiacae', and over 50 other shorter poems on sacred and secular subjects.

Collected edn. of his Works by A. Beaugendre, OSB (Paris, 1708); repr. with certain alterations by J. J. Bourassé in J. P. Migne *PL* 171. 45–1458. Crit. edns. of *Carmina Minora* by A. B. Scott (Teub., 1969), and of 'The Biblical Epigrams' by id. and others in *Mediaeval Studies*, 47 (1985), pp. 272–316. A. Dieudonné, *Hildebert de Lavardin, évêque du Mans, archevêque de Tours (1056–1133), sa vie, ses lettres* (Paris, 1898; repr. from *Revue historique et archéologique du Maine*). F. X. Barth, *Hildebert von Lavardin (1056–1133) und das kirchliche Stellenbesetzungsrecht* (Kirchenrechtliche Abhandlungen, ed. U. Stutz, 34–6; 1906); P. von Moos, *Hildebert von Lavardin 1056–1133* (Pariser historische Studien, 3; 1965). W. von den Steinen, 'Les Sujets d'inspiration chez les poètes latins du XIIIe siècle, I: Hildebert et l'humanisme', *Cahiers de Civilisation médiévale*, 9 (1966), pp. 165–75. A. B. Scott, 'The poems of Hildebert of Le Mans: a new examination of the canon', *Mediaeval and Renaissance Studies*, 6 (1968), pp. 42–83; G. Orlandi, 'Doppia redazione nei "Carmina minora" di Ildeberto?', *Studio Medievali*, 3rd ser. 15 (1974), pp. 1019–49. A. *Wilmart, OSB, 'Les Sermons d'Hildebert', *R. Bén.* 47 (1935), pp. 12–51. Raby, pp. 265–73. Manitius, 3, pp. 853–65. P. von Moos in *Dict. Sp.* 7 (pt. 1; 1969), cols. 502–4, s.v., with additional bibl. in *DHGE* 24 (1993), cols. 483 f.; id. in *Lexikon des Mittelalters*, 5 (1991), cols. 11 f.

Hildebrand

Hildebrand. See GREGORY VII.

Hildefonsus, St, of Toledo

Hildefonsus, St, of Toledo. See ILDEFONSUS, ST.

Hildegard of Bingen, St

Hildegard of Bingen, St (1098–1179), Abbess of Rupertsberg, near Bingen. Born of a noble family in Bermersheim, near Alzey, she was apparently subject to supernatural religious experiences from early childhood. At the age of 8 she was entrusted to the care of Bl Jutta, a recluse attached to the *Benedictine monastery of Disibodenberg (near the convergence of the Rivers Glan and Nahe), and on Jutta's death in 1136 she succeeded her as Abbess of the community which had gathered round her. Under the direction of her confessor, in 1141 she began to record some of her visions. Having won the approval of the Abp. of Mainz, between 1141 and 1151 she dictated her *Scivias* (prob. intended as an abbreviation of 'scito vias [viventis luminis])'. Meanwhile *Eugenius III, under the influence of St *Bernard of Clairvaux, gave his guarded approbation of sections of that work and permission to continue writing (1147/8). Sometime between 1147 and 1152 she moved her community to Rupertsberg, near Bingen, where a large convent was built. Thence she undertook many journeys in the Rhineland and, prob. in 1165, founded a daughter house at Eibingen, near Rüdesheim. Towards the end of her life she had difficulty with the Chapter of Mainz, and for a short time the convent was placed under an interdict.

Hildegard seems to have exerted a wide influence, numbering the Emp. *Frederick Barbarossa and various kings, prelates, and saints among her correspondents. The basis of her writings was an awareness of her divinely appointed office as prophetess, in the conception of which she was indebted to *Dionysius the Pseudo-Areopagite and John Scottus *Erigena. Her *Scivias*, divided into three books containing 26 visions, combines insights into the nature of man and the world with her vision of salvation-history leading to the Last Judgement, a theme which is also taken up in her letters. It was followed by the *Liber vitae meritorum* in six books (1158–63), which is devoted to the disputation of the virtues and vices before the Divine Man and her visions of the joys and torments with which they are rewarded in the afterlife. Her third major work, the *Liber divinorum operum* in three books (1163–1173/4), contains visions of the cosmos, the earth, and created things. This work, like the *Scivias*, was provided with remarkable illustrations. An important element in the *Scivias* is a body of dramatic songs, also used in her musical play, the *Ordo virtutum*. Her remaining works include musical compositions (77 *carmina*), letters, theological treatises, and two important medical texts, the *Physica* and the *Causae et curae*, which reflect a degree of scientific observation unusual at the time. In later times various anticlerical prophecies came to be associated with her name. Miracles, already reported during her life, multiplied at her tomb after her death. Various efforts to secure her canonization during the 13th and 14th cents. were unsuccessful; but from the 15th cent. she is called a saint in the *Roman Martyrology. Feast day, 17 Sept. (observed in several German dioceses).

A number of her works are collected in J. P. Migne, *PL* 197 (incl. the *Scivias*, *Liber divinorum operum*, the *Physica*, and letters, but the text is very corrupt); further works (notably the *Liber vitae meritorum*, *Expositiones evangeliorum* and additional letters) ed. J. B. *Pitra, *Analecta sacra*, 8 (Paris, 1882; repr. Farnborough, 1966). *Scivias*, ed. J. *Faber Stapulensis, *Liber trium virorum et trium spiritualium virginum* (Paris, 1513), fols. 28–118v; crit. edn. by A. Führkötter, OSB, and A. Carlevaris (CCCM 43–43A; 1978); *Carmina*, ed., with Ger. tr., P. Barth and others (Salzburg [1969]); *Sequences and Hymns*, selected and ed., with Eng. tr., C. Page (Newton Abbot [1982]); *Symphonia armonie celestium revelationum*, ed., with Eng. tr. and comm. (but without the music), by B. Newman (1988); *Ordo virtutum*, ed. [E.] P. [M.] Dronke, *Poetic Individuality in the Middle Ages* (Oxford, 1970), pp. 180–92, 202–31; *Causae et curae* (*Liber compositae medicinae*), ed. P. Kaiser (Teub., 1903); *Epistolarium*, ed. L. Van Acker (CCCM 91, 91A, etc.; 1991 ff.). Further edns. are in preparation for CCCM. Eng. trs. of *Scivias* by C. Hart and J. Bishop (Classics of Western Spirituality [1990]); of *Liber divinorum operum* with letters and songs by M. Fox (Santa Fe, NM [1987]); of *Ordo virtutum* by [E.] P. [M.] Dronke, *Nine Medieval Latin Plays* (Cambridge, 1994), pp. 147–84 (incl. introd., notes, and Latin text); of *Liber vitae meritorum* (Garland Library of Medieval Literature, 89B; New York, etc., 1994); and of letters by J. L. Baird and R. K. Ehrman (New York and Oxford, 1994 ff.). Ger. trs. of *Liber vitae meritorum* by H. Schipperges (Salzburg [1972]); of *Causae et curae* by id. (ibid. [1957]; and of the letters by A. Führkötter, OSB (ibid. [1965]).

The contemporary Life by Godefridus, cont. by Theodericus, pr. in *AASS*, Sept. 5 (1755), pp. 629–701 (repr. J. P. Migne,

PL 197. 91–140); Ger. tr. by A. Führkötter, OSB (Düsseldorf, 1968). *Acta inquisitionis de virtutibus et miraculis S. Hildegardis*, ed. P. Bruder, *Anal. Boll.* 2 (1883), pp. 116–29. H. Liebeschütz, *Das allegorische Weltbild der heiligen Hildegard von Bingen* (Leipzig and Berlin, 1930; repr. Darmstadt 1964). C. Singer, 'The Scientific Views and Visions of Saint Hildegard', in id. (ed.), *Studies in the History and Method of Science*, 1 (Oxford, 1917), pp. 1–55. M. Schrader, OSB, and A. Führkötter, OSB, *Die Echtheit des Schrifttums der heiligen Hildegard von Bingen* (Beihefte zum Archiv für Kulturgeschichte, 6; Cologne, 1956). A. P. Brück (ed.), *Hildegard von Bingen 1179–1979: Festschrift zum 800. Todestag der Heiligen* (Quellen und Abhandlungen zur mittelrheinischen Kirchengeschichte, 33; Mainz, 1979). [E.] P. [M.] Dronke, *Women Writers of the Middle Ages* (Cambridge, 1984), pp. 144–201. A. Führkötter, OSB (ed.), *Kosmos und Mensch aus der Sicht Hildegards von Bingen* (Quellen und Abhandlungen zur mittelrheinischen Kirchengeschichte, 60; 1987). B. Newman, *Sister of Wisdom: St Hildegard's theology of the feminine* (1987). C. Meier, 'Hildegard von Bingen', in H. A. Glasser and others, *Deutsche Literatur: Eine Sozialgeschichte*, 1 (Rororo Handbuch, 6250; 1988), pp. 94–103; S. Flanagan, *Hildegard of Bingen, 1098–1179: A Visionary Life* (1989). G. J. Lewis, *Bibliographie zur deutschen Frauenmystik des Mittelalters* (Bibliographien zur deutschen Literatur des Mittelalters, 10; 1989), pp. 66–145. M. Schrader, OSB, in *Dict. Sp.* 7 (pt. 1; 1969), cols. 505–21; C. Meier in *Verfasserlexikon* (2nd edn.), 3 (1981), cols. 1257–80; U. Kern in *TRE* 15 (1986), pp. 322–6, all s.v.

Hilgenfeld, Adolf (1823–1907), German Protestant theologian. He taught in the University of Jena from 1847 till his death, and was editor of the *Zeitschrift für wissenschaftliche Theologie* which he founded in 1858. He adopted the principles of F. C. *Baur and the *Tübingen School, but gave them a somewhat less radical cast, e.g. he defended the genuineness of 1 Thess., Phil., Philem. He wrote extensively on later Judaism, biblical criticism, and patristics, and was the author of an important edition of the extra-canonical NT books, *Novum Testamentum extra Canonem receptum* (4 vols., 1866), as well as a notable work on Jewish *apocalyptic literature, *Die jüdische Apokalyptik in ihrer geschichtlichen Entwickelung* (1857).

List of his works, with brief Life by H. Hilgenfeld, son (Leipzig, 1906); additional material in *Zeitschrift für wissenschaftliche Theologie*, 50 (1908), pp. 14–24. Obituary notice by F. Nippold, ibid., pp. 154–75. [The *Zeitschrift* finally came to an end in 1914.]

Hillel, School of. The followers of Hillel, an influential Jewish teacher of the time of Christ. The rabbinic literature records many differences of opinion between this more liberal School and the rival School of *Shammai; indeed it would appear that these differences formed the basis for influential discussions of Jewish practice after the destruction of the *Temple in AD 70. The image of Hillel, seen as the ancestor of the patriarchal dynasty, is clearly romanticized; how much truth there may be in the legends about him it is impossible to say.

A. Schwarz, *Die Controversen der Schammaiten und Hilleliten*, 1 (1893). I. Sonne, 'The Schools of Shammai and Hillel seen from Within', in *Louis Ginzberg Jubilee Volume, on the Occasion of his Seventieth Birthday: English Section* (New York, 1945), pp. 275–91, with refs.; A. Guttmann, 'Hillelites and Shammaites—a clarification', *Hebrew Union College Annual*, 28 (1957), pp. 115–26. E. E. Urbach, *The Sages: Their Concepts and Beliefs*, 1 (Jerusalem, 1975; Eng. tr. from Heb. pub. 1969), pp. 576–93. J. Neusner, *The Rabbinic Traditions about Pharisees before 70* (3 vols., Leiden, 1971), esp. 1, pp. 212–340, and 3, pp. 255–72. E. *Schürer, *The

History of the Jewish People in the Age of Jesus Christ, rev. Eng. tr. by G. Vermes and others, 2 (Edinburgh, 1979), pp. 363–7. H. L. Strack, *Einleitung in Talmud und Midrasch* (5th edn., 1930), pp. 118–22 (Eng. tr., Philadelphia, 1931), pp. 108–10, with notes, pp. 301–6. P. Rieger, *Hillel und Jesus: Ein Wort zur Versöhnung* (1904). J. Klausner, *Jesus of Nazareth: His Life, Times and Teaching* (Eng. tr. from Heb. by H. Danby, 1925), esp. pp. 223–7.

Hilton, Walter (*c.* 1343–96), English contemplative writer. Of his life little is known. There is much circumstantial evidence that he studied canon law at *Cambridge, and he was one of a circle of clerks associated with T. *Arundel both when he was Bp. of *Ely and particularly in his campaign for spiritual and pastoral orthodoxy after he became Abp. of *York. After a period as a hermit, Hilton became an *Augustinian canon at Thurgarton Priory, Notts, *c.*1386.

His principal work is the *Scale of Perfection* or *Scala Perfectionis*, written in English. This describes the renewal of the defaced image of God in the soul. Book 1 contains practical ascetic and moral teaching; Book 2 develops the contrast between 'reforming in faith' and the experiential awareness of the life of grace, 'reforming in feeling' (an expression derived from Rom. 12: 2; *reformamini in novitate sensus vestri*). Between them is the 'luminous darkness' of mortification, the transition from disordered self-love to love of God. Associated with the *Scale of Perfection* is the practical booklet *Mixed Life* addressed to a devout man living in the world. Hilton also wrote in English *Angels' Song*, which is critical of some aspects of Richard *Rolle, and translated *Eight Chapters on Perfection* written by a Spanish *Franciscan studying at Cambridge. *The Pricking of Love*, an English version of the popular *Stimulus Amoris*, at one time wrongly ascribed to St *Bonaventure, may well be his, though this is not certain; so may the English exposition of the Psalm *Qui Habitat*. Various other works have at times been attributed to him. Four Latin letters of Hilton survive, together with his academic *quaestio* on the veneration of images.

Hilton stands in the tradition of St *Augustine, St *Gregory the Great, and St *Bernard, with influence also from St *Anselm and the *Victorines. There is evidence of mutual criticism between him and the author of the *Cloud of Unknowing*. His teaching on the 'luminous darkness', together with that of the *Cloud*, has been compared with that of St *John of the Cross on the 'dark night'.

Editio princeps of the *Scale of Perfection* and the *Mixed Life*, London, 1494. Crit. edns. of the *Scale of Perfection* in preparation for the EETS; of *Mixed Life* by S. J. Ogilvie-Thomson (Salzburg Studies in English Literature, Elizabethan & Renaissance Literature, 92: 15; 1986). Earlier edn. of the *Mixed Life* in C. Horstmann, *Yorkshire Writers: Richard Rolle of Hampole . . . and his Followers*, 1 (1895), pp. 264–92. *Angels' Song*, ibid., pp. 175–82; also ed. by T. Takamiya in *Studies in English Literature* (Tokyo), English Number 1977, pp. 3–31. *Eight Chapters on Perfection*, ed. F. Kuriyagawa (Keio Institute of Cultural and Linguistic Studies, Tokyo, 1967) and, from different MSS, by id. in *Studies in English Literature* (Tokyo), English Number 1971, pp. 7–34, and by T. Takamiya in *Poetica*, 12 (Tokyo, 1981), pp. 142–9. Crit. edns. of *Qui Habitat* (with the Psalm-commentary *Bonum Est*, which is unlikely to be Hilton's) by B. Wallner (Lund Studies in English, 23; 1954), and of *The Pricking of Love* by H. Kane (Salzburg Studies in English Literature, Elizabethan & Renaissance Studies, 92: 10; 2 vols., 1983). Latin Writings ed. J. P. H. Clark and C. Taylor (Analecta Cartusiana, 124; 2 vols., Salzburg, 1987).

Modernized version of the *Scale of Perfection*, based on MSS preferred by the EETS eds., by J. P. H. Clark and R. Dorward (Classics of Western Spirituality, New York, etc., 1991). Earlier modernized versions by E. *Underhill (London, 1923), G. Sitwell, OSB (ibid., 1953), and L. Sherley-Price ('Penguin Classics', 1957). Modernized versions of *The Minor Works of Walter Hilton* by D. Jones (London, 1929; incl. *dubia*); of *Eight Chapters* and *Angels' Song* by R. Dorward (Fairacres Publications, 85; Oxford [1983]); of the *Goad of Love* (the Eng. tr. of *Stimulus Amor*) by C. Kirchberger (London, 1929).

H. L. Gardner, 'Walter Hilton and the Mystical Tradition in England', *Essays and Studies*, 22 (1937), pp. 103–27; J. M. Russell-Smith, 'Walter Hilton and a Tract in defence of the Veneration of Images', *Dominican Studies*, 7 (1954), pp. 180–214; id., 'Walter Hilton', *The Month*, NS 22 (1959), pp. 133–48; repr. in J. Walsh, SJ (ed.), *Pre-Reformation English Spirituality* [1966], pp. 182–97; [M.] D. *Knowles, *The English Mystical Tradition* (1961), pp. 100–18; S. S. Hussey, 'The Text of the *Scale of Perfection*, Book II', *Neuphilologische Mitteilungen*, 65 (1964), pp. 75–92, and other works of this author; J. E. Milosh, *The Scale of Perfection and the English Mystical Tradition* (Madison, Wis., Milwaukee, and London, 1966); D. G. Kennedy, *Incarnational Element in Hilton's Spirituality* (Salzburg Studies in English Literature, Elizabethan & Renaissance Studies, 92: 3; 1982); also a series of arts. by J. P. H. Clark in *Downside Review*, 95 (1977), pp. 95–109; 96 (1978), pp. 61–78, 281–98; 97 (1979), pp. 69–80, 204–20, 258–74; 100 (1982), pp. 235–62; 101 (1983), pp. 15–29; 102 (1984), pp. 79–118; and 103 (1985), pp. 1–25; also id., 'Augustine, Anselm and Walter Hilton', in *The Medieval Mystical Tradition in England: Papers read at Dartington Hall, July 1982*, ed. M. Glasscoe (Exeter, 1982), pp. 102–26, and 'The Trinitarian Theology of Walter Hilton's *Scale of Perfection*. Book Two', in *Langland, the Mystics and the Medieval English Religious Tradition: Essays in Honour of S. S. Hussey*, ed. H. Phillips (Woodbridge, 1990), pp. 125–40. The introd. to the modernized version of the *Scale of Perfection* by Clark and Dorward, cited above, with useful bibl. pp. 329–35. *BRUC*, pp. 305–6. M. D. Knowles and J. Russell-Smith in *Dict. Sp.* 7 (pt. 1; 1969), cols. 525–30, s.v.

Hincmar (*c.* 806–82), Abp. of *Reims. He was educated at the abbey of *St-Denis, and in 822 accompanied his teacher, Abbot Hilduin, to the court of *Louis the Pious. In 834 he officially entered the King's service, and after Louis's death attached himself to Charles the Bald, whose loyal supporter he became. Through Charles's influence he was elected Abp. of Reims in 845 and at once began to reorganize his diocese. The Emp. Lothair I initially sought his deposition under the pretext of Hincmar's having unjustly nullified the ordinations of his predecessor. A synod at Soissons in 853, however, came out in his favour, and its decision was confirmed by Benedict III in 855. Hincmar strongly opposed Lothair, King of Lorraine (the second son of Lothair I), when he wished to divorce his wife, Teutberga. In 862 he deposed Rothad, Bp. of Soissons, who had attacked his privileges as metropolitan, but his action was not upheld by *Nicholas I. He succeeded, however, in procuring the condemnation of his own nephew, Hincmar, Bp. of Laon, who had refused to recognize his authority. After King Lothair's death (869) he advanced Charles the Bald's claims to Lorraine and crowned him at Metz, despite the objection of the Pope. In 876 he again opposed the Pope, whose appointment of a *Vicar Apostolic for Germany and Gaul he regarded as an interference with his metropolitan rights. He died at Épernay when fleeing from the Normans.

Though not a speculative theologian, Hincmar took a prominent part in the controversy with the monk

*Gottschalk on predestination. He wrote against him 'Ad Reclusos et Simplices', which elicited a sharp reply from *Ratramnus of *Corbie. Hincmar, after vainly seeking defenders among his friends, finally asked John Scottus *Erigena for help. The latter's work, 'De Divina Praedestinatione', roused a storm of indignation both against its author and against Hincmar. The controversy was continued at the Synods of *Quiercy (853), which gave a decision favourable to the archbishop, and *Valence (855), which was against him. Hincmar wrote in his defence 'De Praedestinatione Dei et Libero Arbitrio', a rather disorderly compilation of scriptural and patristic texts, in which he argued that, if God predestines the wicked to hell, He must be accounted the author of sin. A reconciliation of both parties, largely through weariness with the conflict, was reached at the Synod of Douzy in 860. Another dispute with Gottschalk and Ratramnus arose from Hincmar's changing the words 'Trina Deitas' from the *Vespers Hymn of the Common of Many Martyrs into 'Summa Deitas', because he suspected the former version of *Tritheism. He defended his view in the treatise 'De Una et Non Trina Deitate' (c.860), chiefly by quotations from authorities.

In his practical works, esp. 'De Divortio Lotharii et Teutbergae' (860), he displayed a vast knowledge of canon law, while in 'Opusculum LV Capitulorum', directed against Hincmar of Laon, he ably defended the rights of the metropolitan over his bishops. He was among the first writers to know of the *False Decretals, which were a product of the early years of his archiepiscopate. As a loyal and trusted supporter of successive Carolingian rulers he produced several works on kingship and the duties of the monarch, one of which (the 'De Ordine Palatii') contains important information on court administration. He was also the author of a Life of St *Remigius and of a number of poems, and the continuator of a chronicle (the so-called 'Annales Bertiniani') which is one of the chief sources for the political history of his time.

Opera, ed. J. *Sirmond, SJ (2 vols., Paris, 1645), repr. in J. P. Migne, PL 125 and 126. Crit. edns. of his Poems by L. Traube (MGH, Poetae, 3, 1896, pp. 406–20); Letters [ed. E. Perels] (ibid., Epistolae, 8, pars prior [up to Mar. 868] only, 1939); De Ordine Palatii, ed. T. Gross and R. Schieffer (ibid., Fontes Iuris Germanici Antiqui in usum scholarum, 3; 2nd edn., 1980); Eng. tr. by D. Herlihy, The History of Feudalism (1970), pp. 208–27; Collectio de Ecclesiis et Capellis, ed. M. Stratmann (MGH, Fontes Iuris Germanici Antiqui in usum scholarum, 14; 1990). Annales de Saint-Bertin, ed. F. Grat and others (Société de l'Histoire de France, 1964), pp. 84–251. Life by H. Schrörs (Freiburg i.B., 1884). Full study by J. Devisse, Hincmar, Archevêque de Reims (3 vols., Geneva, 1975–6), with extensive bibl. Id., Hincmar et la Loi (Université de Dakar, Faculté des Lettres et Sciences Humaines, Publications de la Section d'Histoire, 5; '1962' [1963]); M. Stratmann, Hinkmar von Reims als Verwalter von Bistum und Kirchenprovinz (Quellen und Forschungen zum Recht im Mittelalter, 6; Sigmaringen, 1991). H. H. Anton, Fürstenspiegel und Herrscherethos in der Karolingerzeit (Bonner Historische Forschungen, 32; 1968), pp. 281–355. J. L. Nelson, 'Kingship, Law and Liturgy in the Political Thought of Hincmar of Reims', EHR 92 (1977), pp. 241–79; J. M. Wallace-Hadrill, 'History in the Mind of Archbishop Hincmar', in The Writing of History in the Middle Ages: Essays Presented to Richard William Southern, ed. R. H. C. Davis and J. M. Wallace-Hadrill (Oxford, 1981), pp. 43–70; id., The Frankish Church (Oxford, 1983), pp. 292–303. E. S. Duckett, Carolingian Portraits (Ann Arbor, Mich. [1962]), pp. 202–83.

H. G. J. Beck in NCE 6 (1967), pp. 1122 f., s.v.; R. Schieffer in TRE 15 (1986), pp. 355–60, s.v. 'Hinkmar von Reims', with full bibl.

Hinnom, Valley of. See GEHENNA.

Hinsley, Arthur (1865–1943), Abp. of *Westminster and cardinal. He was educated at Ushaw and the *English College at Rome. After being headmaster of St Bede's grammar school at Bradford from 1899 to 1904, he was pastor of several parishes and from 1917 to 1928 rector of the English College. In 1930 he was made Titular Abp. of Sardis and *Apostolic Delegate in Africa, and in 1935 Abp. of Westminster. He was created cardinal in 1937. He became known to wide circles through his foundation, in 1940, of the '*Sword of the Spirit', and through the vigorous spiritual and national leadership he gave to English RCs during the first years of the Second World War.

J. C. Heenan, Cardinal Hinsley (1944). T. Moloney, Westminster, Whitehall and the Vatican: The Role of Cardinal Hinsley, 1935–43 (1985). D. Newton in DNB, 1941–1950, pp. 394 f.

Hippo, Council of. A council of the Catholic (i.e. non-*Donatist) Church in Latin Africa held on 8 Oct. 393. A breviarium of its canons was read at the Council of *Carthage (397) and their substance, then re-enacted, passed, via the *Hispana Collection and the *Quinisext Synod, into general canon law.

C. Munier (ed.), Concilia Africae A. 345–A. 525 (CCLS 149; 1974), pp. 20–53, incl. text of the breviarium and five canons. Hefele and Leclercq, 2 (pt. 1; 1908), pp. 82–91.

Hippolytus, St (c.170–c.236), ecclesiastical writer and Doctor. Though the most important 3rd-cent. theologian of the Roman Church, the facts of his life as well as his writings were soon forgotten in the W., perhaps by reason of his schismatic activities and of the fact that he wrote in Greek. Of his early life nothing is known. The assertion of *Photius that he was a disciple of St *Irenaeus is doubtful. During the first decades of the 3rd cent. he must have been an important personality among the Roman presbyters; when *Origen came to Rome (c.212) he attended one of his sermons. Soon afterwards Hippolytus took an active part in attacking the doctrines of *Sabellius. He refused to accept the teaching of Pope *Zephyrinus (198–217), and under his successor, *Callistus (217–22), whom he rejected as a heretic, he seems to have allowed himself to be elected as a rival Bp. of Rome. He continued to attack Callistus' successors, Urban (222–30) and Pontianus (230–5). In the *persecution of the Emp. Maximin (235–8), however, he and Pontianus were exiled together to Sardinia, and it is very probable that before his death he was reconciled to the other party at Rome; for under Pope *Fabian (236–50) his body with that of Pontianus was brought to Rome (236). The *Liberian Catalogue (q.v., in the part dated c.255) already considers him a Catholic martyr and gives him the rank of a priest, not of a bishop. When these facts had been forgotten in Rome, many legends grew up round his person. Pope *Damasus (366–84) makes him a priest of the *Novatianist Schism, a view later accepted by *Prudentius in his 'Passion of St Hippolytus'. In the Roman Passionals of the 7th and 8th cents. he is represented as a soldier converted by St *Laurence, a legend which long survived in the Roman *Breviary. He also has been confused with a martyr of the same name who was buried at Portus, of which city he was believed to have been a bishop. Feast day in the E. 30 Jan.; in the W. 13 Aug.

A list of several of Hippolytus' writings as well as his Easter tables were discovered on a statue, long thought to portray him, but now recognized as originally a female figure, perhaps personifying one of the sciences; it was found in Rome and heavily restored in 1551; it is now kept in the *Vatican Library. Many other works are listed by *Eusebius of Caesarea and St *Jerome. Hippolytus' principal work is his 'Refutation of all Heresies' (not listed on the statue). Books 4–10 of this were found in a MS on Mount *Athos and published (together with the already known Book 1) under the title 'Philosophumena' in 1851 at Oxford by E. Miller, who attributed it to *Origen; but J. J. I. von *Döllinger argued that its author was Hippolytus. Books 2–3 are lost. Its main aim is to show that the philosophical systems and mystery religions described in Books 1–4 are responsible for the heresies dealt with in the later Books. In the summary of 'true doctrine' at the end of the work, Hippolytus expresses his own trinitarian theology in a form of *Logos doctrine calculated to answer the charge of ditheism which Callistus had levelled against him. For this purpose he follows the Greek *Apologists, distinguishing between two states of the Word, the one immanent and eternal (ἐνδιάθετος λογισμός), the other external and temporal as the Father's voice. Containing in Himself all the Father's ideas, the Word is able to actualize them as the Father's creative agent. The absence of any explicit reference to the Holy Spirit in this system lends colour to Callistus' accusation; nevertheless Hippolytus frequently refers to the Holy Spirit at other points in the work. The 'Refutation' illustrates another important divergence between his teaching and that of the Roman bishops, namely his strenuous opposition to the mitigation of the penitential system necessitated by the influx of pagan converts in large numbers.

The other writings usually attributed to Hippolytus are: commentaries on Daniel and the Song of Songs as well as various other exegetical works, some of which survive only in translations or in fragments; a discourse against the followers of *Noetus; a historical work entitled the *Chronicon*; a treatise on the nature of the universe directed against *Plato, which survives only in fragments; and the *Syntagma*, an anti-heretical work, of which nothing remains. The statue also attributes to him the important treatise on the '*Apostolic Tradition' (q.v.), an attribution very generally accepted. Differences in style and theology, especially between the 'Refutation' and the *Contra Noetum*, led P. Nautin to attribute some of the works to a Hippolytus whom he identified as an E. bishop, and others to a virtually unknown Roman presbyter Josipus. Although the Josipus-theory won little support, Nautin's view that the works are to be divided between two authors has been more widely accepted. V. Loi ascribed some to Hippolytus of Rome and others to a second Hippolytus whom he believed to have been an E. bishop. Apart from these works, the '*Little Labyrinth' (q.v.) has sometimes been attributed to Hippolytus, as has a Paschal Homily, at one time ascribed to St John *Chrysostom; this is prob. of a later date.

The first collected edition was that of J. A. *Fabricius (2 vols., Hamburg, 1716–18; repr. with additions in J. P. Migne, *PG* 10. 261–962). P. A. de *Lagarde, *Hippolyti Romani quae feruntur omnia graece* (London, 1858). Crit. edn. by H. Achelis, G. Bonwetsch, and others in GCS (4 vols., 1897–1955). Separate edns. of *Refutatio omnium haeresium* by M. Marcovich (Patristische Texte und Studien, 25; 1986 [occasionally conjectural]); comm. on Dan., with Fr. tr., by M. Lefèvre and G. Bardy (SC 14; 1947); and *Contra Noetum* by P. Nautin (Paris, 1949); also, with Eng. tr., by R. Butterworth, SJ (Heythrop Monographs, 2; London, 1977). Paschal Homily ed., with Fr. tr., by P. Nautin, PSS, *Homélies Pascales*, 1 (SC 27; 1950); improved edn., with comm., by G. Visonà (Studia Patristica Mediolanensia, 15; Milan, 1988). Eng. tr. of many of his writings in ANCL (vols. 6 and 9, pt. 2); of the *Refutation of all Heresies* by F. Legge (2 vols., 1921). For edns. of the 'Apostolic Tradition', see bibl. s.v. J. J. I. von Döllinger, *Hippolytus und Kallistus* (1853; Eng. tr., 1876); C. *Wordsworth, *St Hippolytus and the Church of Rome* (1853); J. B. *Lightfoot, *The Apostolic Fathers*, 1 (2) (1890), pp. 317–477 ('Hippolytus of Portus'); G. Ficker, *Studien zur Hippolytfrage* (1893); H. Achelis, *Hippolytstudien* (TU 16, Heft 4, 1897; several other items in this series are devoted to Hippolytus); A. d'Alès, *La Théologie de Saint Hippolyte* (1906); G. Bovini, *Sant'Hippolito dottore e martire del III secolo* (1943); P. Nautin, *Hippolyte et Josipe* (1947); A. Hamel, *Kirche bei Hippolyt von Rom* (Beiträge zur Förderung christlicher Theologie, 2. Reihe, 49; 1951). R. Cantlamessa, OFM Cap., *L'omelia 'In S. Pascha' dello Pseudo-Ippolito di Roma* (Pubblicazioni dell'Università Cattolica del Sacro Cuore. Contributi, 3rd ser., Scienze Filologiche e Letteratura, 16; 1967), with refs. to earlier works. *Ricerche su Ippolito* (Studia Ephemeridis 'Augustinianum', 13; 1977), esp. M. Guarducci, 'La statua di "Sant'Ippolito" ' (pp. 17–30, with ref. to earlier art.), and V. Loi, 'L'identità letteraria di Ippolito di Roma' (pp. 67–88). A. Zani, *La Cristologia di Ippolito* (Pubblicazioni del Pontificio Seminario Lombardo in Roma, Ricerche di Scienze Teologiche, 22; Brescia [1984]). C. [J.] Osborne, *Rethinking Early Greek Philosophy: Hippolytus of Rome and the Presocratics* (1987). J. Frickel, *Das Dunkel um Hippolyt von Rom: Ein Lösungsversuch: Die Schriften Elenchos und contra Noëtum* (Grazer Theologische Studien, 13; 1988). J. Mansfeld, *Heresiology in Context: Hippolytus' Elenchos as a Source for Greek Philosophy* (Philosophia Antiqua, 56; Leiden, 1992). *CPG* 1 (1983), pp. 256–78 (nos. 1870–925). M. Richard in *Dict. Sp.* 7 (pt. 1; 1969), cols. 531–71, s.v. See also bibl. to APOSTOLIC TRADITION, esp. the work of J. M. Hanssens.

Hippolytus, Canons of St. A collection of canons, mainly on disciplinary and liturgical subjects, which were compiled in Greek, according to R. Coquin between 336 and 340. The Greek text is lost, but they survive in an Arabic version of a Coptic translation. They are dependent on the '*Apostolic Tradition' of St *Hippolytus, to whom they are wrongly attributed. The extant MSS are not earlier than the 13th cent. In the later 19th cent. they were generally held, notably by H. Achelis, to be prior to the 'Apostolic Tradition' (then dated in the 4th cent. or later) and St Hippolytus often held to be the real author, at least of most of the work; and hence they received disproportionate attention in liturgical studies. Since the researches of E. *Schwartz and R. H. *Connolly on the 'Apostolic Tradition', they have lost most of their importance.

Arab. text ed., with Lat. tr., by D. B. von Haneberg, Bp. of Speyer (Munich, 1870); improved tr. (but with many doubtful conjectures) by H. Achelis (TU 6, Heft 4; 1891); crit. edn., with Fr. tr., and valuable introd. with refs. to previous works, by R. G. Coquin (*PO* 31, fasc. 2; 1966); Eng. tr. by C. Bebawi in P. F. Bradshaw, *The Canons of Hippolytus* (Grove Liturgical Study, 50; 1987). See also bibl. to APOSTOLIC TRADITION.

Hispana Collection. A collection of canons and *decretals, so called because of its Spanish origin. Together with the collection made by *Dionysius Exiguus, it was the principal means by which the legislation of the early Church circulated in the W. In its earliest recorded form, which a persistent if disputed tradition associates with *Isidore of Seville, it consists of the canons of various councils arranged geographically, ending with the Fourth Council of *Toledo (633), followed by decretals of Popes from *Damasus to *Gregory I. In later revisions the Spanish councils up to the Seventeenth Council of Toledo (694) were added. The collection exists in a number of revised and rearranged forms, of which the 'Gallican' provided the basis for the '*False Decretals'.

The text as found in the False Decretals is pr. in all the principal edns. of the *Concilia* from J. Merlin (Paris, 1524 ['1523']) onwards. Only complete edn. based on early MSS is that of F. A. Gonzalez (Madrid, 1808), repr. in J. P. Migne, *PL* 84. Crit. edn., with substantial introd., by G. Martínez Díez, SJ, and F. Rodríguez, SJ (Monumenta Hispana Sacra, Serie Canónica, 1, 2, 3, 4, etc.; Madrid, 1966 ff.). F. Maassen, *Geschichte der Quellen und der Literatur des canonischen Rechts im Abendlande bis zum Ausgange des Mittelalters*, 1 (1870), pp. 667–716; J. Gaudemet, *Les Sources du Droit de l'Église en Occident du IIᵉ au VIIᵉ Siècle* (1985), pp. 149–61. Mordek, pp. 250–2, with bibl. G. Martínez Díez in *NCE* 7 (1967), p. 1, s.v.

Historical Jesus, Quest of the. W. Montgomery's English translation of A. *Schweitzer's *Von Reimarus zu Wrede* (1906) was published as *The Quest of the Historical Jesus* (1910), and this title has provided a label for the post-*Enlightenment attempts to reconstruct the life and teaching of Jesus of Nazareth by critical historical methods. The phrase implies a contrast to Christological definitions ('the dogmatic Christ') and other Christian accounts of Jesus ('the Christ of faith'), though Schweitzer showed that most 19th-cent. 'Lives of Jesus' were heavily influenced by their authors' beliefs.

The pioneer work of H. S. *Reimarus (1694–1768), *Apologie oder Schutzschrift für die vernünftigen Verehrer Gottes*, was not published in full until 1972, but its conclusions became known after G. E. *Lessing published the *Wolfenbüttel fragments in 1774–8. The subsequent challenges to the historicity of the Gospels by D. F. *Strauss in his *Leben Jesu* (1835) set Gospel criticism on its modern course. The floodgates of attempts to portray Jesus simply as a human person were opened by J. E. *Renan in 1863. Despite the reservations of A. *Ritschl, it became the central task of later liberal Protestantism in Germany and the *Social Gospel Movement in America. There were, however, some reactions. M. *Kähler issued a spirited protest against these liberal Lives in *Der sogennante historische Jesus und der geschichtliche, biblische Christus* (1892, 2nd edn., 1896; abridged Eng. tr., 1964), maintaining that the real Christ is the preached Christ of the whole Bible rather than any hypothesis of historical research. Soon afterwards W. *Wrede cast further doubts on the historicity of Mark by his history-of-traditions approach to the Gospels. K. *Barth and R. *Bultmann repudiated the whole quest for the historical Jesus and were largely successful in removing it from German Protestant theology for a generation. Some of Bultmann's pupils (E. Käsemann, G. Bornkamm, H. Conzelmann, E. Fuchs, and G. Ebeling) renewed it

in the 1950s, denying that *Form Criticism had made it impossible or kerygmatic theology unnecessary or irrelevant. This brief movement was dubbed by J. M. Robinson, *The New Quest of the Historical Jesus* (1959). Outside the Bultmann school, investigation of Jesus' life was continued without a break in many countries by Christian, Jewish, and independent writers. Today it is as strong as ever, stimulated and sustained by increased knowledge of 1st-cent. Judaism, reinforced by the renaissance of RC biblical scholarship and the international and interconfessional acceptance of critical historical methods, and enriched by sociological insights and modern literary analysis of Jesus' parables and aphorisms. The data remain fragmentary, and there is only limited consensus among historians, but the continuation of this investigation corresponds to both theological and wider cultural interests. See also JESUS CHRIST.

D. L. Pals, *The Victorian 'Lives' of Jesus* (Trinity University Monograph Series in Religion, 7; San Antonio [1982]). W. S. Kissinger, *The Lives of Jesus: A History and Bibliography* (New York and London, 1985); C. A. Evans, *Life of Jesus Research: An Annotated Bibliography* (New Testament Tools and Studies, 13; Leiden, 1989). Representative of the 'New Quest' is G. Bornkamm, *Jesus von Nazareth* (Stuttgart, 1956; Eng. tr., 1960). Bultmann responded in *Das Verhältnis der urchristlichen Christusbotshaft zum historischen Jesus* (Sb. (Heid.), 1960, Abh. 3; Eng. tr. in C. E. Braaten and R. A. Harrisville (eds.), *The Historical Jesus and the Kerygmatic Christ: Essays on the New Quest of the Historical Jesus* (New York and Nashville, 1964), pp. 15–42). N. T. Wright in *Anchor Bible Dictionary*, 3 (1992), pp. 796–802, 'Jesus Christ, Quest for the Historical Jesus', with bibl.

History of Religion School. See RELIGIONSGESCHICHTLICHE SCHULE.

Hoadly, Benjamin (1676–1761), Bp. in succession of *Bangor, *Hereford, *Salisbury and *Winchester. He was educated at Catharine Hall, Cambridge, where he was elected a Fellow in 1697 and was a tutor from 1699 to 1701. Ordained priest in 1701, he was lecturer at St Mildred's, Poultry, from 1701 to 1711, and rector of St Peter-le-Poor, London, from 1704 to 1724. At the beginning of his public life he advocated conformity for the sake of union; he soon won the leadership of the *Low Church divines favoured by the Whigs through his controversy with F. *Atterbury and O. Blackall, Bp. of *Exeter (1708–16), on passive obedience and non-resistance. Recommended to the Queen by the House of Commons in 1709, he became rector of Streatham in 1710 and chaplain to the Duke of Bedford. On the accession of George I he became chaplain to the King, and was consecrated Bp. of Bangor in 1716. His sermon of 31 Mar. 1717 on 'The Nature of the Kingdom or Church of Christ' provoked the *Bangorian Controversy (q.v.). Translated to Hereford in 1721 and to Salisbury in 1723, when he resigned the rectory of Streatham, he was translated to Winchester in 1734. He excited stiff opposition by maintaining that the Lord's Supper was purely commemorative and in upholding *Latitudinarian views generally.

He spent very little time in his dioceses, never visiting Bangor, but living mainly in London, where he engaged in political and theological controversy. His many publications include *A Defence of the Reasonableness of Conformity* (1707; against E. *Calamy the younger), *A Preservative against the Principles and Practices of Non-Jurors both in Church and State* (1716), *A Plain Account of the Nature and End of the Sacrament of the Lord's Supper* (1735), and *The Repeal of the Corporation and Test Acts* (1736; a plea for toleration).

J. Hoadly (son [1711–76], ed.), *The Works of Benjamin Hoadly* (3 vols., 1773), with account of author, 1, pp. v–xxv. N. Sykes, 'Benjamin Hoadly, Bishop of Bangor', in F. J. C. Hearnshaw (ed.), *The Social and Political Ideals of some English Thinkers of the Augustan Age* (1928), pp. 112–57; id., *Church and State in England in the XVIIIth Century* (1934), esp. pp. 332–62. G. G. Perry in *DNB* 28 (1891), pp. 16–21.

Hobbes, Thomas (1588–1679), philosopher. In early life he travelled much abroad as tutor to the Cavendish family, and met and was influenced by F. *Bacon, G. *Galileo, and M. *Mersenne, the philosopher friend of R. *Descartes. He displeased both Royalists and Parliamentarians by holding that, although sovereignty is ultimately derived from the people, it is transferred to the monarch by implicit contract, so that while the power of the sovereign is absolute, it is not of *Divine Right. From 1640 to 1651 Hobbes was in exile, for the most part in Paris, where from 1646 to 1648 he was tutor to the Prince of Wales (later *Charles II). In 1651 he returned and submitted to the Commonwealth, and in the same year published his greatest work, the *Leviathan*, which, though it has been called a reaction against the 'liberty' of the Renaissance and Reformation, is really a philosophical exposition of the system of political absolutism which replaced the supremacy of the medieval Church. In his *Questions Concerning Liberty, Necessity, and Chance* (1656) he expounded a doctrine of psychological *Determinism in opposition to Bp. J. *Bramhall's defence of free will. In 1666 the *Leviathan*, which from the first was considered to be atheistic, was censured by name by the House of Commons, and thereafter its author was not allowed to publish ethical writings in England. Hobbes was perhaps the first philosopher to attempt seriously to base a theory of human conduct upon natural science; he was a pioneer in psychology; and his early work *De Cive* (1642; Eng. tr., 1651) gives him some claim to be considered the founder of modern social science. His doctrine of political absolutism cut at the root of ethics, however, as it left no room for any genuine moral distinction between good and bad.

Collected edn. of Hobbes's *Opera Philosophica* (Amsterdam, 1668; suppl., London, 1675); of his *Moral and Political Works* (London, 1720), incl. his autobiog., pp. ix–xxviii. Complete edn. of his *English Works* (11 vols., London, 1839–45) and his *Opera Philosophica* (5 vols., ibid., 1839–45), both by Sir W. Molesworth. *Philosophical Works* also ed. by H. Warrender (Oxford, 1983 ff.). Repr. of the 1651 edn. of the *Leviathan*, with introd. by W. G. Pogson Smith (Oxford, 1909), and, with modernized spelling, by M. Oakeshott (ibid., 1955).

The vast literature on Hobbes includes studies by G. Croom Robertson (London, 1886), L. Stephen ('English Men of Letters', 1904), A. E. *Taylor (London, 1908), J. Laird (ibid., 1934), and T. Sorell (ibid., 1986). L. Strauss, *The Political Philosophy of Hobbes* (Oxford, 1936); H. Warrender, *The Political Philosophy of Hobbes* (ibid., 1957); S. I. Mintz, *The Hunting of Leviathan: Seventeenth-Century Reactions to the Materialism and Moral Philosophy of Thomas Hobbes* (Cambridge, 1962); F. C. Hood, *The Divine Politics of Thomas Hobbes: An Interpretation of Leviathan*

(Oxford, 1964); K. C. Brown (ed.), *Hobbes Studies* (ibid., 1965); J. W. N. Watkins, *Hobbes's System of Ideas* (1965; 2nd edn., 1973); D. P. Gauthier, *The Logic of Leviathan: The Moral and Political Theory of Thomas Hobbes* (Oxford, 1969); D. D. Raphael, *Hobbes, Morals and Politics* (1977); J. Hampton, *Hobbes and the Social Contract Tradition* (Cambridge, 1986); D. Baumgold, *Hobbes's Political Theory* (ibid., 1988); G. B. Herbert, *Thomas Hobbes: The Unity of Scientific and Moral Wisdom* (Vancouver, 1989); A. P. Martinich, *The Two Gods of Leviathan: Thomas Hobbes in Religion and Politics* (Cambridge, 1992). C. H. Hinnant, *Thomas Hobbes: A Reference Guide* (Boston [1980]).

Hocktide (also 'Hock Monday' and 'Hock Tuesday'). The second Monday and Tuesday after Easter, on which in medieval times money was collected for church and parish uses, and various sports and amusements took place. The merrymaking at this season survived in some places until the 19th cent. The origin of the name is unknown.

Hodge, Charles (1797–1878), American *Presbyterian theologian. He was ordained in 1821, and taught at Princeton for nearly his whole life. His most important works are his commentaries on Rom. (1835), Eph. (1856), 1 Cor. (1857), 2 Cor. (1859), as well as *Constitutional History of the Presbyterian Church in the United States* (2 vols., 1839–40), *Systematic Theology* (3 vols., 1871–3), and *What is Darwinism?* (1874). If less an original thinker than a systematizer and defender of traditional *Calvinism, Hodge has a real claim to be considered one of the greatest of American theologians, and he had a great influence and following. He took a broader and more tolerant view of other forms of Christianity than many of those in general sympathy with his position.

Selections from various works under the title *The Way of Faith*, ed. M. A. Noll (Sources of American Spirituality, New York [1987]). A. A. Hodge (son), *The Life of C. Hodge, D.D.* (1881); C. A. Salmond, *Princetoniana: Charles and A. A. Hodge* (1888); L. J. Trinterud in H. T. Kerr (ed.), *Sons of the Prophets* (Princeton, NJ, 1963), pp. 22–38. R. H. Nichols in *Dict. Amer. Biog.* 9 (1932), pp. 98 f.; J. W. Stewart in D. K. McKim (ed.), *Encyclopedia of the Reformed Faith* (1992), pp. 174–6.

Hody, Humphrey (1659–1707), Anglican divine. Having entered Wadham College, Oxford, in 1676, he was elected a Fellow in 1685. In his *Contra historiam Aristeae de LXX interpretibus Dissertatio* (1684) he proved that the 'Letter of *Aristeas' was a forgery. His support of the Established Church against the *Nonjurors brought him to the notice of Abp. J. *Tillotson, who made him his chaplain; and in 1698 he was made Regius professor of Greek at Oxford. His researches into the text of the *Septuagint are embodied in his *De Bibliorum Textis Originalibus* (4 vols., 1703). By his will a number of exhibitions for the study of Hebrew and Greek, which still bear his name, were established at Wadham College.

Study (in Latin) of his life and writings by S. Jebb prefixed to his edn. of Hody's *De Graecis Illustribus, Linguae Graecae, Literarumque Humaniorum Instauratoribus, eorum Vitis, Scriptis et Elogiis* (posthumous, 1742), pp. v–xxix. G. Goodwin in *DNB* 27 (1891), pp. 77 f.

Hofbauer, St Clement Mary (1751–1820), the 'Apostle of Vienna'. He was a native of Tasswitz in Moravia and the son of a grazier and butcher; and at the age of 15 he became a baker's apprentice. Led by his religious aspirations to become a hermit, and later a student for the priesthood (1780–4) in Vienna and Rome, he entered the congregation of the *Redemptorists at Rome in 1784 and was professed and ordained in 1785. In the same year he returned to Vienna, but, unable to found a house there because of the anti-religious *Josephinist legislation, he went on to Warsaw, where he laboured from 1787 to 1808, chiefly among the German-speaking population. Here he met with remarkable success, devoting himself esp. to the cure of souls and to educational and charitable activities. Appointed Vicar-General for the houses of his congregation N. of the Alps in 1793, he founded several establishments in Poland and one at Jestetten, nr. Schaffhausen (1802). In 1808 he was driven from Warsaw by Napoleon and went back to Vienna. At first he worked mainly at the Italian church, but from 1813 onwards he was confessor to the *Ursulines. His influence in the capital, which spread from the highest to the lowest, powerfully counteracted the effects of Josephinism and the *Aufklärung. The Redemptorists, however, could not be established in Austria till shortly after his death. He was canonized in 1909. Feast day, 15 Mar.

Monumenta Hofbaueriana (15 vols., Cracow, Thorn, Tournai, and Rome, 1915–51). Selection of his works, ed. J. Heinzmann, CSSR (Fribourg and Constance, 1986). Lives by S. Brunner (Vienna, 1858), A. Innerkofler (Ratisbon, 1910), J. Hofer (Freiburg i.B., 1920; Eng. tr., New York, 1926), G. Hünermann (Innsbruck, 1936; Fr. tr., 2nd edn., 1955), J. Carr, CSSR (London, 1939), E. Hosp, CSSR (Vienna, 1951), and K. Fleischmann (Graz, etc., 1988).

Høffding, Harald (1843–1931), Danish philosopher.

From 1883 to 1915 he was professor at Copenhagen. In his earlier years he was much under the influence of S. *Kierkegaard, but almost completely abandoned his teaching later. He sought at once to do full justice to the claims of the natural sciences and to show that all knowledge received meaning only in relation to the realm of value. But while he upheld a spiritual interpretation of the universe, he denied that there were sufficient theoretical grounds for applying the notions of 'cause' and 'personality' to the Absolute or for affirming (or denying) belief in personal immortality. He described his position as 'critical monism'. His many writings included a widely used history of philosophy, *Den nyere Filosofis Historie* (2 vols., 1894–5; Eng. tr., 1900) and a *Religionsfilosofi* (1901; Eng. tr., 1906).

His *Udvalgte Skrifter* (7 vols., Copenhagen, 1902–6); *Erindringer* [with portrait] (ibid., 1928). Correspondence with E. Meyerson, ed. F. Brandt and others (ibid., 1939); that with Ferdinand Tönnies, ed. C. Bickel and R. Flechner (Beiträge zur Sozialforschung, 4 [1989]). Complete list of his works by K. Sandelin in *Harald Høffding In Memoriam* (Copenhagen, 1932), pp. 43–76, with bibl. pp. 81–102. F. Brandt in *Encyclopedia of Philosophy*, ed. P. Edwards, 4 (1967), pp. 48 f., s.v.

Hoffmann or Hoffman, Melchior (c.1500–c.1543),

German *Anabaptist. A leather-dresser by profession, he joined the *Lutherans and became a lay preacher in Livonia in 1523. Having come into conflict with the authorities he left for Stockholm in 1526; there he became more and more imbued with eschatological ideas and prophesied the approaching end of the world. After a short stay in Holstein he had a disputation with J. *Bugenhagen at Flensburg in 1529 in which he denied the Lutheran doctrine of the Lord's Supper, holding it to be a mere sign. He was consequently banished from Denmark, and went to Strasbourg, where he joined the Anabaptists. Between 1530 and 1533 he preached there, in E. Friesland, and in Holland. In 1533 he returned to Strasbourg, which was to be the New Jerusalem, to await the Last Day. He was arrested and sentenced to imprisonment for life, but remained unshaken in his eschatological beliefs till his death. His influence on his contemporaries was considerable, and the 'Melchiorites' survived him as a distinct party among the Anabaptists.

Eng. tr. of his 'Ordinance of God' (first pub. in 1530), from the surviving Dutch tr., by G. H. Williams (ed.), *Spiritual and Anabaptist Writers* (Library of Christian Classics, 25; 1957), pp. 184–203. P. Kawerau, *Melchior Hoffman als religiöser Denker* (Haarlem, 1954); K. Deppermann, *Melchior Hoffman: Soziale Unruhen und apokalyptische Visionen im Zeitalter der Reformation* (Göttingen, 1979; Eng. tr., Edinburgh, 1987). G. H. Williams, *The Radical Reformation* (Philadelphia, 1957; London, 1962), esp. pp. 259–64, 292–5, 307–9, and 355–8; 3rd edn. (Sixteenth Century Essays & Studies, 15; Kirksville, Mo. [1992]), esp. pp. 387–93, 447–50, and 539–45. K. Deppermann in *TRE* 15 (1986), pp. 470–3, s.v.

Hoffmeister, Johannes (c.1509–47), *Augustinian Hermit.

He entered the Augustinian monastery at Colmar as a youth, studied at several German universities, and was made prior in 1533. His life was devoted to the defence of his order against *Lutheran teaching and to the inner reform of the Church by preaching and writing. In 1542 or 1543 he became provincial of the Rhenish-Swabian province, which had been severely affected by Protestantism. His powerful sermons soon made him widely known and he was frequently called upon to preach on important occasions, e.g. at the Diet of Worms (1545) and the (second) Colloquy of Ratisbon (1546). In 1546 he was made vicar-general of the Augustinian Hermits in Germany, but his work was cut short by his death in 1547. His writings, which are occasionally marred by their polemical extravagance, include two books of Dialogues (1538) and his *Loci Communes* (Mainz, 1547; often repr.), a collection of patristic extracts.

N. Paulus, *Der Augustinermönch J. Hoffmeister: Ein Lebensbild aus der Reformationszeit* (Freiburg i.B., 1891). A. von Druffel, 'Der Elsässer Augustinermönch Johannes Hoffmeister und seine Korrespondenz mit dem Ordensgeneral Hieronymus Seripando', *Abh.* (Bayr.), hist. Kl. 14, Abt. 1 (1879), pp. 135–96. R. Bäumer, 'Johannes Hoffmeister OESA', in E. Iserloh (ed.), *Katholische Theologen der Reformationszeit*, 4 (Katholisches Leben und Kirchenreform im Zeitalter der Glaubensspaltung, 47; 1987), pp. 43–57.

Hofmann, Johann Christian Konrad von (1810–77),

German *Lutheran theologian. A native of Nuremberg, he studied at Erlangen and Berlin, and became lecturer at Erlangen University in 1838. In 1842 he was called to Rostock as professor of theology, and in 1845 returned in the same capacity to Erlangen, where he remained till the end of his life. His most important works were *Weissagung und Erfüllung im Alten und Neuen Testament* (2 parts, 1841–4), a study of the theology of prophecy; *Der Schriftbeweis* (3 parts, 1852–6), a treatise in the course of which the vicarious Atonement was denied; *Schutzschriften für eine neue Weise, alte Wahrheit zu lehren* (1856–9), written in defence of the preceding; and *Die hl. Schriften des Neuen Testaments* (8 parts, 1862–78), an unfinished commentary on the NT. Hofmann aimed at being an uncompromising exponent of Lutheran doctrines. His disciples became known as the 'Erlangen School'.

Theologische Briefe der Professoren [F.] Delitzsch und von Hofmann (ed. W. Volck, 1891). Life by P. Wapler (Leipzig, 1914). P. Bachmann, *J. C. K. Hofmanns Versöhnungslehre und der über sie geführte Streit* (1910); M. Schellbach, *Theologie und Philosophie bei von Hofmann* (1935). E. W. Wendebourg, 'Die heilsgeschichtliche Theologie J. Chr. K. v. Hofmanns in ihrem Verhältnis zur romantischen Weltanschauung', *Zeitschrift für Theologie und Kirche*, 52 (1955), pp. 64–104. W. von Lowenich, 'Zur neueren Beurteilung der Theologie Johann Christian Konrad von Hofmanns', *Zeitschrift für bayerische Kirchengeschichte*, 32 (1963), pp. 315–31. A. Hauck in *PRE* (3rd edn.), 7 (1900), pp. 234–41; F. Mildenberger in *TRE* 15 (1986), pp. 477–9, s.v.

Hohenheim. See PARACELSUS.

Holcot, Robert (d. 1349), scholastic theologian and biblical commentator. A native of Northamptonshire, he entered the *Dominican Order and studied at Oxford. He lectured on the *Sentences* of *Peter Lombard probably during the two years 1331–3, and incepted in theology *c.*1335. He also wrote *quodlibets and biblical commentaries on the *Minor Prophets, Wisdom (possibly written at Cambridge), and Ecclesiasticus, as well as *Moralitates* and *Convertimini* (both aids to preaching) and sermons. By 1343 he was assigned to the Northampton house of his Order, where he is said to have died while nursing the sick during the plague. His commentary on the *Sentences* is extant in four redactions, and circulated widely outside England. Holcot was working in Oxford at a time when the impact of *William of Ockham's views was fresh, and when it had become difficult to maintain that a fully demonstrable proof could be found that God exists or that God is the creator of the world. Holcot was reduced to saying that God will communicate to men of goodwill sufficient knowledge of Himself for salvation. Views of this kind are found not only in the commentary on the *Sentences*, but also in the biblical commentaries. In his commentaries little attention is paid to the literal sense, and the main emphasis is on the application of the text for use in preaching, with many illustrations, and with an extensive use of classical and pseudo-classical quotations. Holcot also developed, but did not originate, the use of emblem-like 'pictures' of mythological and allegorical figures. He was among the scholars said to have been patronized by Richard de Bury (d. 1345), but the ascription of de Bury's 'Philobiblon seu de amore librorum' to Holcot in some MSS is not acceptable. He may have helped de Bury to collect material, but he was not the author of the book.

His comm. on Wisdom was pub. at Cologne, not later than 1474; that on the *Sentences* at Lyons in 1497; *Moralitates* at Venice, 1514. They were repr. in the 16th cent., but there are no modern edns. The comm. on Ecclesiasticus, pr. at Paris, 1515, is the work of Ralph Ringstead (d. 1366). Holcot's own comm. on Ecclus. is still unpub. 'Philobiblon' pub. Cologne, 1473; modern edn. by A. Altramura, Naples, 1954; Eng. tr. by J. B. Inglis (anon.), London, 1832. Holcot's 'Sermo finalis' ed. J. C. Wey, CSB, *Mediaeval Studies*, 11 (1949), pp. 219–24; Quodlibet 'Utrum

Theologia sit Scientia', ed. J. T. Muckle, CSB, ibid. 20 (1958), pp. 127–53; E. A. Moody, 'A Quodlibetal question of Robert Holkot, O.P., on the problem of the objects of knowledge and of belief', *Speculum*, 39 (1964), pp. 53–74, incl. text; W. J. Courtenay, 'A Revised Text of Robert Holcot's Quodlibetal Dispute on Whether God is Able to Know More than He Knows', *Archiv für Geschichte der Philosophie*, 53 (1971), pp. 1–21. P. Molteni, *Robert Holcot O.P.: Dottrina della grazia e della giustificazione, con due questioni quodlibetali inedite* (Pinerolo [*c.*1969]); two other *quodlibeta* and one *quaestio* from his comm. on the *Sentences* ed. H. Goodenough Gelber, *Exploring the Boundaries of Reason: Three Questions on the Nature of God* (Pontifical Institute of Mediaeval Studies, Studies and Texts, 62; Toronto [1983]). B. Smalley, 'Robert Holcot', *Archivum Fratrum Praedicatorum*, 26 (1956), pp. 5–97; id., *English Friars and Antiquity in the Early Fourteenth Century* (Oxford, 1960), pp. 133–202. A. Meissner, SAC, *Gotteserkenntnis und Gotteslehre nach dem englischen Dominikanertheologen Robert Holkot* (Limburg am Lahn [1953]), with bibl. H. Schepers, 'Holkot contra dicta Crathorn', *Philosophisches Jahrbuch*, 77 (1970), pp. 320–54; 79 (1972), pp. 106–36 and 361. F. Hoffmann, *Die theologische Methode des Oxforder Dominikanerlehrers Robert Holcot* (BGPM, NF 5; 1972). W. J. Courtenay, 'The Lost Matthew Commentary of Robert Holcot O.P.', *Archivum Fratrum Praedicatorum*, 50 (1980), pp. 103–112. Kaeppeli, 3 (1980), pp. 313–20, s.v. 'Robertus Holcot'.

Holgate, Robert (*c.*1481–1555), Abp. of *York. He was probably educated at the Gilbertine house of studies in Cambridge, where he was university preacher in 1524. He became Master of the Order of *Sempringham, and, on the eve of its dissolution (1537), Bp. of *Llandaff. He proved an active member of the King's Council in the North, and in 1538 he succeeded C. *Tunstall as Lord President. In 1545 he was translated to York. His marriage and strong support of the Edwardian reforming measures brought about his deprivation by the Marians in 1554. Holgate founded three grammar schools and an almshouse, all in Yorkshire.

A. G. Dickens, 'The Marriage and Character of Archbishop Holgate', *EHR* 52 (1937), pp. 428–42; id., *Robert Holgate, Archbishop of York and President of the King's Council in the North* (St Anthony's Hall Publications, 8; 1955), the last repr. in id. *Reformation Studies* (1982), no. 15. W. Hunt in *DNB* 27 (1891), pp. 128–30.

Holidays of Obligation. See FEASTS OF OBLIGATION.

Holiness Code, also 'Law of Holiness'. The collection of legal material in Lev. 17–26, so named by A. Klostermann in 1877, and designated 'H'. The subjects dealt with are animal sacrifice and the prohibition of eating blood (17), laws of marriage and chastity (18), miscellaneous religious and ethical precepts (19), penalties for violation of the ritual laws (20), the priesthood (21 f.), the sacred calendar, incl. *Sabbath, *Passover, *Weeks, and the Day of *Atonement (23), the sacred lamp and the *Shewbread (24: 1–9), punishment for blasphemy and the *Lex Talionis* (24: 10–25), the *Sabbatical Year and *Jubilee (25), with a final exhortation (26). The recurrence of certain phrases (in particular, 'for I, the Lord, am holy', e.g. 19: 2), supports the view that the section is a unity. There are internal indications that it is a product of the Exile in *Babylon (cf. 26: 34–45); moreover, it has a number of parallels with the exilic Book of Ezekiel. Scholars who follow the 'documentary hypothesis' of the origins of the *Pentateuch generally suppose the Holiness Code to have been incorporated into *P, after circulating independently for a period.

A. Klostermann, 'Beiträge zur Entstehungsgeschichte des Pentateuchs', *Zeitschrift für die gesammte lutherische Theologie und Kirche*, 38 (1877), pp. 401–45; id., *Der Pentateuch* (1893), pp. 386–418. B. Baentsch, *Das Heiligkeits-Gesetz* (1893). H. G. Reventlow, *Das Heiligkeitsgesetz formgeschichtlich untersucht* (Wissenschaftliche Monographien zum Alten und Neuen Testament, 6; 1961); R. Kilian, *Literarkritische und formgeschichtliche Untersuchung des Heiligkeitsgesetzes* (Bonner Biblischer Beiträge, 19; 1963). L. E. Elliott-Binns, 'Some Problems of the Holiness Code', *ZATW* 67 (1955; pub. 1956), pp. 26–40 [favours an earlier dating]. W. Thiel, 'Erwägungen zum Alter des Heiligkeitsgesetzes', ibid. 81 (1969), pp. 40–73; V. Wagner, 'Zur Existenz des sogenannten "Heiligkeitsgesetzes" ', ibid. 86 (1974), pp. 307–16 [questions the existence of 'H' as an independent collection]. Eissfeldt, pp. 233–9, with further refs. H. T. C. Sun in *Anchor Bible Dictionary*, 3 (1992), pp. 254–7, s.v. See also works cited under PENTATEUCH and comm. to LEVITICUS, cited s.v.

Holiness, His. A title which in the early Church was regularly used of all bishops. Since *c.*600 it has been restricted to *patriarchs, a use still followed in the E. Church. In the W., since the 14th cent., it has been used only of the Pope. The title was also occasionally given to the Byzantine Emperors, and there is an instance of its use by *John of Salisbury of Henry II of England.

Holiness Movement. A predominantly American religious movement which centres on the belief that entire sanctification takes place instantaneously in a crisis experience. It arose in the mid-19th cent., primarily in the *Methodist Church, in which some groups felt that J. *Wesley's teaching on *perfection was being eroded by declining standards. Their teaching came to be combined with *revivalist techniques. The movement was promoted from 1835 by Phoebe Palmer (1807–74), a Methodist lay leader, who taught that perfection in love was a second blessing distinct from regeneration and that it eliminated all sinful desires. It spread initially through meetings in private houses, and was fostered by the journal *Guide to Christian Perfection* (1839–45) which became the *Guide to Holiness* (1846–1901). Similar teaching was being adopted by the revivalist Charles G. *Finney (1792–1875) and his colleagues at the *Congregational Oberlin College in Oberlin, Ohio; this strand is often known as 'Oberlin Perfectionism'.

Aided by W. E. Boardman's *The Higher Christian Life* (1858) and Hannah Whitall Smith's *The Christian's Secret of a Happy Life* (1875), the movement reached a wider public through Holiness Camp Meetings, beginning in 1867 at Vineland, New Jersey, where an 'Association for the Promotion of Holiness' was formed. Though still predominantly Methodist, the movement was spreading to other Protestant Churches. During the last two decades of the 19th cent., tensions between the Holiness advocates and Methodist bishops led to seceding groups forming new Holiness denominations. Of these, the largest are the Church of the Nazarene, which emerged as a distinct denomination in the USA in 1908, and the Church of God (Anderson, Ind.), which traces its beginnings to 1881.

The movement modified Wesleyan teaching by emphasizing revivalistic techniques of invitation, decision, and testimony, and by an increasing insistence on visible evid-

ence. Holiness groups were among the first to admit women to ministry. By the late 19th cent. physical healing was commonly expected and the experience of sanctification was frequently called '*baptism with (or sometimes of) the Holy Spirit'. Greater emphasis came to be placed on external observance, esp. avoidance of all behaviour seen as worldly. Sharply divided in the early 20th cent. by the rise of *Pentecostalism, the surviving Holiness groups became less exuberant. Holiness Churches have about 2 million members in the USA, with strong missionary work in the Caribbean and E. Asia. The 19th-cent. perfectionist currents gave rise to related movements, incl. the *Keswick Conventions in Britain, but their emphasis on victory over the flesh is different from the teaching of the Holiness Churches on the eradication of sin.

The Holiness denominations in the UK are small. The largest is the Church of the Nazarene, with which three Holiness groupings of British origin have joined.

M. E. Dieter, *The Holiness Revival of the Nineteenth Century* (Metuchen, NJ, and London, 1980). A. C. Piepkorn, *Profiles in Belief: The Religious Bodies of the United States and Canada*, 3 (New York and London [1979]), pp. 3–85, with bibl. T. L. Smith, *Called unto Holiness: The Story of the Nazarenes: The Formative Years* (Kansas City, Mo., 1962). C. E. Brown, *When the Trumpet Sounded: A History of the Church of God Reformation Movement* (Anderson, Ind. [1951]). J. Ford, *In the Steps of John Wesley: The Church of the Nazarene in Britain* (Kansas City, Mo. [1968]). C. E. Jones, *A Guide to the Study of the Holiness Movement* (American Theological Library Association Bibliographical Series, 1; Metuchen, NJ, 1974).

Holl, Karl (1866–1926), German Protestant Church historian. After studying at Tübingen and Berlin, he became professor at Tübingen in 1900 and in 1906 at Berlin, where he was the colleague of A. *Harnack. He edited several patristic texts for the Prussian Academy, including the *Sacra Parallela* of St *John of Damascus (TU 16. 1; 1897) and the *Ancoratus* and *Panarion* of St *Epiphanius (GCS, 3 vols., 1915–33). Holl was an original and prolific scholar, dealing with a wide range of historical and theological subjects. His patristic work was noted for its sound philological basis (esp. *Amphilochius von Ikonium in seinem Verhältnis zu den grossen Kappadoziern*, 1904, and *Enthusiasmus und Bussgewalt beim griechischen Mönchtum*, 1898); his papers on M. *Luther inaugurated a new era in Luther studies.

Gesammelte Aufsätze zur Kirchengeschichte (3 vols., Tübingen, 1921–8), with list of his works by H. *Lietzmann in vol. 3, pp. 578–84. *Kleine Schriften*, ed. R. Stupperich (ibid., 1966). Correspondence with Harnack, ed. H. Karpp (ibid., 1966); with A. Schlatter, ed. R. Stupperich, *Zeitschrift für Theologie und Kirche*, 64 (1967), pp. 169–240. W. Bodenstein, *Die Theologie Karl Holls im Spiegel des antiken und reformatorischen Christentums* (Arbeiten zur Kirchengeschichte, 40; 1968). J. Wallmann in *TRE* 15 (1986), pp. 514–8, s.v., with further bibl.

Holland, Christianity in. See NETHERLANDS, CHRISTIANITY IN THE.

Holland, Henry Scott (1847–1918), theologian and preacher. Educated at Eton and at Balliol College, *Oxford, where he was influenced by T. H. *Green, he was a Senior Student at Christ Church from 1870 to 1884, canon of *St Paul's Cathedral from 1884 to 1910, and

Regius professor of divinity at Oxford from 1910 until his death. He shared the outlook of *Lux Mundi, to which he contributed the first essay (on 'Faith'). He was a robust and independent philosopher and theologian, keenly interested in relating Christian principles to the social and economic problems of human living. With C. *Gore, he established the Christian Social Union in 1889, under the presidency of Bp. B. F. *Westcott; he was himself its most brilliant spokesman. He was editor of the Commonwealth from 1895 to 1912. His writings, mainly collections of sermons, include Logic and Life (1882), Creed and Character (1887), and God's City (1894). He was also the author of the hymn 'Judge Eternal, throned in splendour' (EH 423).

S. Paget, Henry Scott Holland: Memoir and Letters (1921); E. Lyttelton, The Mind and Character of Henry Scott Holland (1926). D. M. MacKinnon, Borderlands of Theology and other Essays, ed. G. W. Roberts and D. E. Smucker (1966), pp. 105–20 ('Scott Holland and Contemporary Needs'; part 1 repr. from Theology, 55 (1952), pp. 407–12). T. B. Strong in DNB, 1912–1921, pp. 260–2.

Holocaust (Gk. ὁλόκαυστον, 'something entirely burnt up'). A sacrifice completely consumed by fire ('burnt-offering'), and thus a perfect sacrifice. Less accurately, the word is also used of a sacrifice with many victims. Since the 1950s it has come to be applied absolutely ('the Holocaust') to the Nazi persecution of European Jews between 1933 and 1945; this culminated in the attempt from 1942 onwards to exterminate them, esp. in the gas chambers of concentration camps in E. Europe.

Holste, Lucas (1596–1661) (**Holstenius**), *Vatican librarian. A native of Hamburg, he studied in *Leiden, where he was converted in 1625–6 to the RC Church. He became secretary, and later librarian (1636), to Cardinal Francesco *Barberini, and subsequently librarian of the Vatican. In 1655 he received Queen *Christina of Sweden's public abjuration of Protestantism at Innsbruck. He was a scholar of enormous erudition, whose writings included Codex Regularum Monasticarum et Canonicarum (3 vols., 1661), studies in many classical and ecclesiastical writings (*Porphyry; *Eusebius, Contra Hieroclem; the later Pythagoreans) and an edition of the Liber Diurnus (1660).

His correspondence (Epistolae ad Diversos) was ed. J. F. Boissonade (Paris, 1817). [N. Wilckens,] Leben des gelehrten Lucae Holstenii (Hamburg, 1723). L. G. Pélissier, 'Les Amis d'Holstenius', Mélanges d'Archéologie et d'Histoire de l'École française de Rome, 6 (1886), pp. 554–87; 7 (1887), pp. 62–128; and 8 (1888), pp. 323–402 and 521–608. R. Almagià, L'opera geografica di Luca Holstenio (ST 102; 1942). J. Bignami Odier, La Bibliothèque Vaticane de Sixte IV à Pie XI (ibid. 272; 1973), esp. pp. 138 f. and 148 f.

Holtzmann, Heinrich Julius (1832–1910), Protestant theologian and biblical critic. After study at Berlin University and a pastorate at Baden (1854–7), he taught at Heidelberg (1858–74) and Strasbourg (1874–1904). He was a moderate liberal in his beliefs. In Die synoptischen Evangelien (1863) he strongly defended the *Marcan hypothesis, at that date rarely accepted. In his later writings he argued for a psychological development in the Lord's self-consciousness, maintaining that there were two principal periods in His earthly life, that of 'success' which reached its climax at *Caesarea Philippi, and a subsequent period of 'failure', when the new conception of a suffering Mes-

siah supervened. His books include an Einleitung in das NT (1885); commentaries on the Synoptic Gospels (1889), the Johannine books (1890), and Acts (1901); a Lehrbuch der NT Theologie (2 vols., 1896–7); and Richard *Rothe's Speculatives System (1899).

Theologische Abhandlungen: Eine Festgabe zum 17. Mai 1902 für H. J. Holtzmann (1902). Brief Life by W. Bauer (Berlin, 1932). W. G. Kümmel, Das Neue Testament: Geschichte der Erforschung seiner Probleme ([1958]; 2nd edn., 1970), pp. 185–91 and 569; Eng. tr., Nashville [1972]; London, 1973), pp. 151–5 and 478 f. A. Faux in Dict. Bibl., Suppl. 4 (1949), cols. 112–16, s.v.; O. Merk in TRE 15 (1986), pp. 519–22, s.v.

Holy Alliance. The declaration signed by Alexander I of Russia, Francis I of Austria, and Friedrich Wilhelm III of Prussia on 26 Sept. 1815, and eventually by all the sovereigns of Europe except the Prince Regent of England, the Pope, and the Sultan. It laid down that the relations of the Powers would henceforth be based on 'the sublime truths which the Holy Religion of our Saviour teaches'; that the actions of princes would be guided by justice, charity, and peace; and that the signatories would regard each other as brothers and 'on all occasions and in all places lend each other aid and assistance'. The project originated with the Tsar, under the inspiration of Barbara J. von *Krüdener, and appears to have been conceived in sincerity, though Metternich called it a 'loud-sounding nothing', and Castlereagh 'a piece of sublime mysticism and nonsense'. It soon became synonymous, however, with the combined interests of the Great Powers by whom Europe was ruled after 1815 and their policy of reaction. As a diplomatic instrument it was never effective, though it inspired Nicholas II to summon the first international peace conference at The Hague in 1899.

Text in E. Reich (ed.), Select Documents Illustrating Mediaeval and Modern History (1905), pp. 119–21, with refs.; Eng. tr. in G. A. Kertesz (ed.), Documents in the Political History of the European Continent 1815–1939 (Oxford, 1968), pp. 7–9. J. H. Pirenne, La Sainte Alliance: Organisation européenne de la paix mondiale (2 vols. [1946–9]); M. Bourquin, Histoire de la Sainte Alliance (Geneva, 1954). H. A. Kissinger, A World Restored: Metternich, Castlereagh and the Problems of Peace 1812–22 (1957), esp. pp. 175–90. On the circumstances leading up to and following the making of the alliance, see also C. K. Webster, The Congress of Vienna, 1814–1815 ([1919] 2nd edn., 1934); id., The European Alliance 1813–1825 (Calcutta, 1929). H. G. Schenk, The Aftermath of the Napoleonic Wars (1947).

Holy City, the. *Jerusalem (Mt. 27: 53). Among the Arabs the city is now commonly known as el-Kuds, i.e. 'the Holy'.

Holy Club. The nickname given to the group of '*Methodists' which John *Wesley formed at Oxford in 1729 for the deepening of personal religion. This developed into a number of overlapping groups in various colleges. Beginning with classical and devotional reading, frequent Communion, and fasting on Wednesdays and Fridays, the groups soon added pastoral, charitable, and educational work, e.g. in Oxford gaol.

R. P. Heitzenrater, 'The Oxford Diaries and the First Rise of Methodism', Methodist History, 12 (1974), News Bulletin, pp. 111–35; id., Mirror and Memory: Reflections on Early Methodism (Nashville, 1989), pp. 63–77.

Holy Coat. Both the cathedral of Trier and the parish church at Argenteuil claim the possession of Christ's 'coat without seam' (Jn. 19: 23). Dating alike from about the 12th cent., the two traditions agree both in admitting the other's relic to be a genuine garment of Christ's, and in insisting that their own is that mentioned in Scripture. The Trier tradition would seem to hold the advantage in Papal utterances and popular devotion. Over two million pilgrims visited the Trier relic when it was exposed in 1933. At other places, e.g. Mantua, where an alleged garment of Christ is shown, there is a less-developed cultus.

O. Zöckler in *PRE* (3rd edn.), 17 (1906), pp. 58–61; E. Iserloh in *L.Th.K.* (2nd edn.), 8 (1963), cols. 1348–60, both s.v. 'Rock'; F. Lauchert in *CE* 7 (1910), pp. 400–2; all with bibl.

Holy Cross Day. The name given in the BCP calendar to 14 Sept., also known as the Feast of the '*Exaltation of the Cross' (q.v.).

Holy Days of Obligation. See FEASTS OF OBLIGATION.

Holy Door, the (*Porta Sancta*). The door in the façade of *St Peter's, Rome, which is nearest the *Vatican Palace. The Holy Door is normally sealed with brickwork, except during the *Holy Year, when it is opened for the passage of those wishing to gain the *Indulgence of the Holy Year. The opening and closing of the Holy Door at the beginning and end of the Holy Year are ceremonially performed by the Pope, assisted by the Cardinal Penitentiary. There are similar Holy Doors in each of the other Major *Basilicas in Rome; these are opened and closed by cardinal legates simultaneously with the one in St Peter's.

H. Thurston, SJ, *The Holy Year of Jubilee* (1900), ch. 2, 'The Porta Sancta', pp. 28–54, with refs.; Appendix C, 'The Porta Sancta and the Golden Gate of Jerusalem', pp. 405–11.

Holy Family, the. The Infant Jesus, His Mother (St *Mary, the Blessed Virgin), and His foster-father (St *Joseph). The cult of the Holy Family as such became widely popular in the RC Church in the 17th cent., and since that time several religious congregations have been founded under this title. A feast of the Holy Family was instituted by the Congregation of *Rites on 26 Oct. 1921, and was kept on the First Sunday after the *Epiphany until it was transferred to the First Sunday after Christmas in 1969. Of the innumerable paintings of the Holy Family one of the most celebrated is that by B. E. *Murillo (1670), now in the Louvre.

Institution of Feast in *AAS* 13 (1921), pp. 543 f. I. Noye, PSS, in *Dict. Sp.* 5 (1964), cols. 84–94, s.v. 'Famille (Dévotion à la Sainte Famille)'.

Holy Father, the Most (*Beatissimus Pater*). A title of the Pope (in common usage abbreviated to 'Holy Father'), which is first quoted in English *c*.1380.

Holy Ghost. An alternative title of the *Holy Spirit (q.v.), esp. in liturgical usage.

Holy Ghost Fathers (or Spiritans), a RC religious congregation of priests and lay brothers dedicated to missionary and social work. The Congregation of the Holy Ghost (Congregatio Sancti Spiritus, C.S.Sp.) was founded in Paris for the training of priests in 1703 by Claude-François Poullart des Places and survived his early death in 1707. After official approval in 1734, the congregation became interested in missionary work and assumed charge of territories in *Canada, French Guiana, and Senegal. It was nearly extinguished during the French Revolution, but it was revived through the efforts of Jacques Bertout (1753–1832), and recognized again for missionary work in the French colonies. In 1848, at the request of *Pius IX, François Marie Paul Libermann, a converted Jew from Alsace, merged the Congregation of the Holy Ghost with his own Congregation of the Immaculate Heart of Mary, founded in 1841 for the evangelization of Black ex-slaves. Libermann, who was an important spiritual writer, reorganized the Congregation before he died in 1852. The Holy Ghost Fathers were pioneers of RC missionary work in W. and E. Africa. They also work in N. and S. America, European countries (including Great Britain and Ireland), the West Indies and the islands of the Indian Ocean. Well-known members include Bl Jacques Desiré de Laval (1803–64), the Apostle of Mauritius, E. *Leen, and Bl Daniel Brottier (1876–1936), who transformed the orphanages of Autcuil.

H. J. Koren, C.S.Sp., *The Spiritans: A History of the Congregation of the Holy Ghost* (Pittsburgh, etc., 1958); id., *To the Ends of the Earth: A General History of the Congregation of the Holy Ghost* (ibid. [1983]). Poullart des Places's *Spiritual Writings*, ed., with Eng. tr., by H. J. Koren (ibid., 1959). J. Michel, C.S.Sp., *Claude-François Poullart des Places, fondateur de la Congrégation du Saint-Esprit 1679–1709* [1962]. A. [L.] Van Kaam, C.S.Sp., *A Light to the Gentiles: The Life of the Venerable Francis Libermann* (Milwaukee [1959]). H. J. Koren in *NCE* 7 (1967), pp. 70 f., s.v.

Holy Helpers. See AUXILIARY SAINTS.

Holy Innocents. The children of *Bethlehem, 'from 2 years old and under', according to the account in Mt. (2: 16–18) massacred by order of *Herod the Great, in a vain attempt to destroy the Infant Jesus. Their death is commemorated on 28 Dec. in the W. (29 Dec. in the E.). Until 1960, if it fell on a weekday it was celebrated in purple with a penitential rite, but in the Roman rite it is now kept with the full privileges of a martyrs' day (red vestments and the recital of the *Gloria in Excelsis).

H. *Leclercq, OSB, in *DACL* 7 (pt. 1; 1926), cols. 608–16, s.v. 'Innocents (Massacre des)'.

Holy Island. See LINDISFARNE.

Holy Lance. See LANCE, HOLY.

Holy Land. A name given to Palestine/Israel since the Middle Ages with reference both to its having been the scene of the Incarnation and also to the existing sacred sites there, esp. the Holy Sepulchre at Jerusalem.

Holy Mountain, the. A designation of Mount *Athos, called 'holy' because of the large collection of monasteries which covers it.

Holy Name of Jesus. See NAME OF JESUS.

Holy Office. The *Roman Congregation established in connection with the *Inquisition (q.v.) by *Paul III in

1542 to deal with heresy internationally. It came to be known as the 'Congregatio Romanae et Universalis Inquisitionis' or 'Congregatio Sancti Officii'. Originally composed of six cardinals, it was reorganized, and the number raised to 13, by *Sixtus V in 1588; soon afterwards the Pope became the Congregation's Prefect, though he was normally represented by a cardinal-secretary. In 1908 it was affected by *Pius X's general reorganization of the Roman Congregations (q.v.), and its title became definitively 'Congregatio Sancti Officii'. In 1965 *Paul VI reformed it under the title 'Congregatio pro Doctrina Fidei' and assigned it the more positive function of promoting as well as safeguarding sound doctrine on faith and morals. The following year he made the cardinal-secretary into a pro-prefect and in 1968 into a cardinal prefect, thus bringing its structure into line with that of other Congregations. The reforms of Paul VI were substantially preserved by the Apostolic Constitution 'Pastor Bonus' of 1988 reforming the Roman *Curia; the official title is now 'Congregatio de Doctrina Fidei'.

H. Bangen, *Die römische Curie, ihre gegenwärtige Zusammensetzung und ihr Geschäftsgang* (1854), pp. 91–124. J. Simor, 'De sacris Congregationibus Romanis S. Officii et Concilii. I: De sacra Congr. Officii', *Archiv für katholisches Kirchenrecht*, 15 (1866), pp. 133–6. For recent history, the fundamental work is the collection of *Documenta inde a Concilio Vaticano Secundo expleto edita (1966–1985)* issued by the Congregatio pro Doctrina Fidei (Rome, 1985). B. Ojetti, SJ, in *CE* 13 (1912), pp. 137–9, s.v. 'Roman Congregations'; U. Beste in *NCE* 4 (1967), pp. 944–6, s.v. 'Doctrine of the Faith, Congregation for the', both with bibl. See also works cited under INQUISITION and ROMAN CONGREGATIONS.

Holy Oils. See CHRISM.

Holy Orders. The higher grades (*sacri ordines*) of the Christian Ministry, i.e. those of *bishop, *priest, and *deacon (qq.v.). In the RC Church the *sub-diaconate (until suppressed) was also reckoned among the 'Major Orders' (q.v.).

Holy Places. The places in Palestine to which pilgrimage is made on account of their traditional association with many of the principal biblical events.

Holy Roman Empire. *Charlemagne was crowned as universal Roman Emperor by Pope *Leo III in Rome on Christmas Day 800, although Charlemagne himself claimed only to rule the W. section (*Europa*), thereby leaving the E. empire at *Constantinople to continue until 1453. After his son *Louis the Pious the imperial Roman title was held by W. rulers of diminishing territorial power until its temporary disappearance in 924. In 962 Otto I of Germany, who was already also King of Italy, was crowned Emperor in Rome by Pope *John XII; Otto's successors of the Saxon, Salian, and Hohenstaufen dynasties held the title until 1254. The expression 'holy empire' (*sacrum imperium*) was used from 1157 by *Frederick I as a counterpart to the spiritual jurisdiction of the Papacy (*sancta ecclesia*), and eventually the term 'Holy Roman Empire' came to be applied to the territories actually governed by the Emperor. Imperial power was, however, steadily diminishing in face of the claims of the Papacy (e.g. *Innocent III) and of the German princes, although the universal power of the Emperor continued to be

asserted in such works as *Dante's *Monarchia*, prob. written for Henry VII.

Of the German rulers after 1250 who claimed the imperial title only five actually achieved coronation in Italy, *Charles V (at Bologna in 1529) being the last; from 1440 the title was held by successive rulers of the Habsburg dynasty, the empire being known with justice as 'the Holy Roman Empire of the German nation'. *Ferdinand II sought to use the imperial position to further the *Counter-Reformation in Germany, but the Treaty of *Westphalia finally undermined the Habsburg position outside their hereditary lands. The dignity was abolished by Napoleon I in 1806.

J. Bryce, *The Holy Roman Empire* (1864; enlarged and rev. edn., 1904; classic but outdated). A. Dempf, *Sacrum Imperium: Geschichts- und Staatsphilosophie des Mittelalters und der politischen Renaissance* (1929). R. Folz, *L'Idée d'empire en Occident du Ve au XIVe siècle* (1953; Eng. tr., 1969). K. H. Schulze, *Hegemoniales Kaisertum: Ottonen und Salier* (Das Reich und die Deutschen [1991]). F. Heer, *Das Heilige Römische Reich* (Bern, 1967; abridged Eng. tr., 1968). J. W. Stieber, *Pope Eugenius IV, the Council of Basel and the Secular and Ecclesiastical Authorities in the Empire* (Studies in the History of Christian Thought, 13; Leiden, 1978), esp. pp. 114–31.

On the history of the empire in the Middle Ages, see also T. Reuter, *Germany in the Early Middle Ages c.800–1056* (1991); H. Fuhrmann, *Deutsche Geschichte im hohen Mittelalter* (1978; Eng. tr., *Germany in the High Middle Ages*, Cambridge, 1986); A. Haverkamp, *Aufbruch und Gestaltung: Deutschland 1056–1273* (Die Neue Deutsche Geschichte, 2; 1984; Eng. tr., *Medieval Germany*, Oxford, 1988; 2nd edn., 1992); F. R. H. Du Boulay, *Germany in the Later Middle Ages* (1983). B. Arnold, *Princes and Territories in Medieval Germany* (Cambridge, 1991), esp. pp. 17–19, with refs.

Holy Saturday. The day before *Easter Sunday, also known as Easter Even (as in the BCP). It commemorates the resting of Christ's body in the tomb. In early times there were no special services. The BCP provides a special Collect, Epistle, and Gospel for the day; these are commonly used at the *Ante-Communion service, without a Celebration. Some modern Anglican liturgies, while providing a special Collect, etc., specifically state (e.g. in the words of the American BCP (1979)), 'there is no celebration of the Eucharist on this day', though, as the South African Prayer Book of 1989 adds, 'the Easter Vigil may begin in the evening'. In the Middle Ages it became customary to anticipate the first Mass of Easter on the morning of Holy Saturday. This practice is still followed in the E. Orthodox Church, but in the RC Church it was abandoned after 1955, and the liturgy, with the traditional ceremonies, restored to the Saturday–Sunday night. See PASCHAL VIGIL SERVICE.

Holy See. The see of the Bishop of Rome. As commonly used, it denotes the Papacy, esp. in reference to the authority, jurisdiction, and functions of government which attach to it.

Holy Sepulchre. The rock cave in *Jerusalem where, acc. to an early tradition, Christ was buried and rose from the dead. The tomb is said to have been 'discovered' by St *Helena, mother of the Emperor *Constantine, and the first 'Church of the Holy Sepulchre' (more correctly, that of the 'Anastasis', or Resurrection) was dedicated *c.*335. In 626 a new church was completed, after the Persians had destroyed the first in 614, but this building was so much damaged in the 10th and 11th cents. that a third building was set up *c.*1050. In place of this church, the Crusaders built a much larger one (dedicated in 1149), to cover all the neighbouring holy places, including the site of *Calvary. This in turn, after having been rebuilt in 1310, was partly destroyed by fire in 1808. The present church largely dates from 1810, though some of the earlier bell tower (1160–80) remains, in a poor state of repair.

The main structure of the church consists of two halves: on the west the domed building which covers the Holy Sepulchre itself, and on the east the church proper. There are also several chapels and shrines in which many of the ancient Christian bodies have rights. The scene on Sunday mornings, when the various rites, all with music, are proceeding simultaneously, is unique in Christendom. Here also the Holy Week rites of the different Churches are carried out, each with its peculiar ceremonies and on the dates fixed by its own calendar. Anglicans, with the permission of the Orthodox authorities, have been allowed since the end of the 19th cent. to celebrate the *Eucharist in the 'Chapel of Abraham', which stands above the site of Calvary. The fact that the Holy Sepulchre lies within the city itself (contrast Heb. 13: 12) is attributed to the circumstance that the modern city occupies a slightly different position from that of NT times. See also GORDON'S CALVARY.

H. Vincent, OP, and F. M. Abel, OP, *Jérusalem*, 2 (1914–26), pp. 89–300, with plates 12–29. E. Wistrand, *Konstantins Kirche am heiligen Grab in Jerusalem nach den ältesten literarischen Zeugnissen* (Acta Universitatis Gotoburgensis, 58; 1952, 1). A. Parrot, *Golgotha et Saint-Sépulcre* (Cahiers d'Archéologie Biblique, 6; 1955; Eng. tr., 1957). C. Coüasnon, OP, *The Church of the Holy Sepulchre in Jerusalem* (1974). V. C. Corbo, OFM, *Il Santo Sepolcro di Gerusalemme* (3 parts, Studium Biblicum Franciscanum, Collectio Maior, 29; Jerusalem [1982]), with Eng. summary of pt. 1; pts. 2 and 3 (plans and photographs) with captions in Ital. and Eng. H. Busse and G. Kretschmar, *Jerusalemer Heiligtumstraditionen im altkirchlicher und frühislamischer Zeit* (Abhandlungen des Deutschen Palästinavereins [8]; Wiesbaden, 1987). W. Harvey, *Church of the Holy Sepulchre, Jerusalem: Structural Survey. Final Report* (1935). H. Cazelles, PSS, and others in *Dict. Bibl.*, Suppl. 11 (1991), cols. 399–431, s.v. 'Saint Sepulchre'.

Holy Shroud. A relic, preserved at Turin since 1578, and long venerated as the winding-sheet in which Christ's body was wrapped for burial (Mt. 27: 59, etc.). The shroud bears the imprint of the front and back of a human body marked with the traditional stigmata. Apart from attempts by I. Wilson and others to identify it with the Edessa Mandylion which was brought to Constantinople in 944, its history cannot be traced before the mid-14th cent., and carbon-dating tests carried out in 1988 indicated a date between 1260 and 1390 for the harvesting of the flax from which it is woven.

C. U. J. Chevalier, 'Le Saint Suaire de Turin est-il l'original ou une copie?', *Mémoires et Documents publiés par la Société savoisienne d'Histoire et d'Archéologie*, 38 (1899), pp. 105–33, also pub. separately; also later works of this author. Supporters of the genuineness of the relic, basing their conclusions on the photographic evidence obtained after the Exposition of 1898 and later, incl. P. Vignon, *Le Linceul du Christ: Étude scientifique* (1902; Eng. tr., 1902); id., *Le Saint Suaire de Turin devant la science, l'archéologie, l'histoire, l'iconographie, la logique* (1938); and P. M. Rinaldi, SDB, *It is the Lord: A Study of the Shroud of Christ* (New York,

1972; in Britain, *The Man in the Shroud*, 1972). I. Wilson, *The Shroud of Turin* (New York, 1978; in Britain, *The Turin Shroud*, 1978); A. Cameron, *The Sceptic and the Shroud* (Inaugural Lecture, London, 1980), repr. in *Continuity and Change in Sixth-Century Byzantium* (1981), no. 5. J. [E.] Walsh, *The Shroud* (New York, 1963; London, 1964). Works which take account of the carbon-dating incl. O. Celier, *Le signe du linceul: Le Saint Suaire de Turin. De la relique à l'image* (1992), and H. Kersten and E. R. Gruber, *Das Jesus Komplott* (Munich [1992]).

Holy Spirit. In Christian theology, the Third Person of the Holy *Trinity, distinct from, but consubstantial, coequal, and coeternal with, the Father and the Son, and in the fullest sense God. It is held that the mode of the Spirit's procession in the Godhead is by way of 'spiration' (not 'generation') and that this procession takes place as from a single principle.

Christian theologians point to a gradual unfolding of the doctrine in the OT, where the notion of the 'Spirit' (*ruach*) plays a large part as an instrument of Divine action, both in nature and in the human heart. The Spirit of God is already operative at the Creation, brooding on the face of the waters (Gen. 1: 2). In early times, the Hebrews saw evidence of the Spirit's action in deeds of valour and prowess. The Divine Spirit inspired the artistic skill of Bezaleel (Exod. 36: 1 f.), the successes of *Joshua (Deut. 34: 9), and the strength of *Samson (Jgs. 14: 6). In particular the Spirit was bestowed on those appointed to communicate Divine truth and esp. on the Prophets (Is. 61: 1 f.). He is also the chief power making for moral purity and holiness (Ps. 51: 11). Above all, the Spirit was to be the possession of the coming Davidic King (Is. 11: 2) and of the Servant of the Lord (Is. 42: 1); and in the future time of fulfilled hope there would be a large extension of the Spirit's activities and power (Ezek. 36: 26 f.; Joel 2: 28–32). In the later OT writings the Spirit was increasingly seen as the bestower of intellectual capacities. It is the Spirit of understanding which fills the devout man (Ecclus. 39: 6) and conveys to him wisdom and religious knowledge (Wisd. 7: 7 and 9: 17).

Although Jesus said little about the Spirit beyond promising that Christians on trial would be assisted by the Spirit (Mk. 13: 11; cf. Mt. 10: 20 and Lk. 12: 12), the Resurrection faith of His disciples was strongly marked by the experience of the Spirit and they interpreted this as God's gift at the dawn of the coming age. This central conviction is epitomized in the quotation of Joel 2: 28–32 in the Acts 2 account of St *Peter's speech on the day of *Pentecost following the dramatic outpouring of the Spirit on the disciples. The rest of Acts represents the early Christian mission as guided by the Spirit (e.g. 11: 12, 15: 28, and 16: 6 f.). On occasion the Apostles convey the Spirit by the laying on of hands (8: 15–17 and 19: 6). See HANDS, IMPOSITION OF.

The Gospels variously present Jesus as empowered by the Spirit at His baptism (Mk. 1: 10 and parallels), driven by the Spirit into the wilderness (Mk. 1: 12 and parallels), and performing *exorcism by the Spirit (Matt. 12: 28). Lk. sees this endowment as the fulfilment of prophecy (Is. 61: 1) and like Matt. 1: 18 and 20 claims the operation of the Spirit in the conception of Jesus (Lk. 1: 35). All agree with Jn. 7: 39 that the Spirit was not more generally available until after Jesus' death and resurrection.

The OT view of this intermittently active but impersonal power of God undergoes two developments in the NT. The Spirit is held to be given to all members at their *Baptism, and, understood in the light of Christ, by St *Paul and Jn. the concept is personalized and given ethical content. In the discourses of Jn. 14–16 the Spirit is 'another Comforter', distinct from Jesus, whom He succeeds, but performing similar works and making present what Jesus had said and done. Paul can call the Spirit 'the Spirit of Jesus' (Phil. 1: 19; cf. Rom. 8: 9 and Gal. 4: 6), and can associate this so closely with Jesus that they are almost identified (Rom. 8: 9–11; perhaps 2 Cor. 3: 17). The whole of Christian life is 'in Christ', or 'in the Spirit', 'being led by the Spirit'. Possessing the Spirit unites believers with the Lord (1 Cor. 6: 17) and has moral implications (1 Cor. 3: 16 and Gal. 5). The Spirit is active in Christian worship (Rom. 8: 26 f.; cf. 1 Cor. 14), proclamation and instruction (1 Cor. 2), and in moral discernment (1 Cor. 7: 40). The gift of the Spirit takes different forms (1 Cor. 12; cf. Rom. 12), implying different roles and responsibilities in the Church. Finally the 'first-fruits of the Spirit' (Rom. 8: 23; or 'earnest of the Spirit', 2 Cor. 1: 22 and 5: 5), possessed by and possessing believers, will be the means by which God raises them (Rom. 8: 11) as spiritual bodies (cf. 1 Cor. 15: 42–44).

The doctrine of the Spirit in a theologically elaborated form, though implicit in the NT, was not reached for some centuries. An important stage was reached in *Tertullian. The *Montanists (q.v.) showed the need to distinguish between true and false operations of the Holy Spirit; but despite the insistence of the Montanists on the Spirit's activities, their strange conceptions of the operation of the Spirit do not seem to have left any permanent mark on the development of the doctrine. *Origen emphasized that the characteristic sphere of the Spirit's operation was the Church, as contrasted with the whole of Creation which was that of the Word. From AD 360 onwards the doctrine of the Spirit became a matter of acute controversy. A group of theologians known as the '*Macedonians', while maintaining against the *Arians the full Divinity of the Son, denied that of the Spirit. The most considerable work which these discussions provoked was St *Basil's *De Spiritu Sancto*. At the Council of *Constantinople of 381 Macedonianism was finally repudiated and the full doctrine of the Spirit received authoritative acceptance in the Church. In the W. this doctrine was elaborated by St *Augustine in his *De Trinitate*, notably by his conception of the Spirit as the Bond of Union in the Holy Trinity.

On the difference between the E. and W. doctrines of the Spirit, see also DOUBLE PROCESSION; FILIOQUE.

See also CHARISMATIC RENEWAL MOVEMENT and PENTECOSTALISM.

Important Patristic discussions of the doctrine incl. St *Athanasius, *Epp. ad Serapionem*; St *Cyril of Jerusalem, *Catech. Lect.* 16; St Basil, *De Spiritu Sancto*; and St *Ambrose, *De Spiritu Sancto*. The doctrine also has a prominent place in St Augustine, *De Trinitate*. The subject is discussed in all systematic expositions of Christian doctrine, e.g. the works of St *John of Damascus and of St *Thomas Aquinas (*S. Theol.* 1, qq. 36–43), as well as in the modern treatises of D. *Petavius and K. *Barth. Modern works dealing expressly with the doctrine include: H. B. *Swete, *The Holy Spirit in the New Testament* (1909); id., *The Holy Spirit in the Ancient Church* (1912), and other works; H. Watkin-Jones, *The Holy Spirit in the Mediaeval Church* (1922); id., *The Holy Spirit from Arminius to Wesley* [1929]. B. H. *Streeter (ed.), *The Spirit: God and His Relation to Man considered from the standpoint of Philosophy, Psychology and Art* (1919). H. W. *Robinson, *The Christian Experience of the Holy Spirit* (1928). C. K. Barrett, *The Holy Spirit and the Gospel Tradition* (1947). M. H. Lavocat, OP, *L'Esprit d'amour: Essai de synthèse de la doctrine catholique sur le Saint-Esprit* (vol. 1 [1950: no more pub.]). G. S. Hendry, *The Holy Spirit in Christian Theology* (1957). H. Mühlen, *Der Heilige Geist als Person* (Münsterische Beiträge zur Theologie, 26 [1963]; 4th edn., 1980). H. Berkhof, *The Doctrine of the Holy Spirit* (Annie Kinkead Warfield Lectures, 1963–4; 1965). W.-D. Hauschild, *Gottes Geist und der Mensch: Studien zur frühchristlichen Pneumatologie* (Beiträge zur evanglischen Theologie, 63; 1972). J. V. Taylor, *The Go-Between God: The Holy Spirit and the Christian Mission* (1972). J. D. G. Dunn, *Jesus and the Spirit: A Study of the Religious and Charismatic Experience of Jesus and the First Christians as Reflected in the New Testament* (1975). G. W. H. Lampe, *God as Spirit* (Bampton Lectures, 1976; Oxford, 1977). C. F. D. Moule, *The Holy Spirit* (1978). E. Schweizer, *Heiliger Geist* (Stuttgart, 1978; Eng. tr., Philadelphia, 1980; London, 1981). Y. *Congar, OP, *Je crois en l'Esprit Saint* (3 vols., 1979–80; Eng. tr., 1983). A. I. C. Heron, *The Holy Spirit: The Holy Spirit in the Bible, in the History of Christian Thought and in Recent Theology* (1983). H. B. Swete in *DCB* 3 (1882), pp. 113–33, s.v.; E. Schweizer and others in *TWNT* 6 (1959), cols. 357–453, s.v. πνεῦμα; partial Eng. tr. as *Spirit of God* (1960); J. Guillet, SJ, J. Gribomont, OSB, and others in *Dict. Sp.* 4 (1960), cols. 1246–1333, s.v. 'Esprit Saint'.

Holy Synod.

From 1721 to 1917, the supreme organ of government in the *Russian Orthodox Church. It was not a real synod, but an ecclesiastical committee composed of bishops and clergy, established by Peter the Great to replace the earlier government of the Church by the Russian *Patriarch. The lay procurator attended as the Emperor's representative, but was not a member. In 1917, after the first Revolution, it was abolished and the patriarchate restored.

Holy Water.

Water which has been blessed for certain specific religious purposes. Acc. to W. usage, it is blessed by a priest acting in the name of the Church; he may add to it a small quantity of *salt, blessed with a separate prayer. In the E. water is blessed at the Great Blessing of the Waters on the feast of the *Epiphany, at Lesser Blessings of Water on the first day of each month, and on other occasions. By a natural symbolism holy water is used for blessings, dedications, and exorcisms, also at burials, and for ceremonial cleansing on entering a church, as well as in the W. in the *Asperges at the beginning of Mass. When the water is blessed during the Mass, the blessing of the water and the Asperges take the place of the normal penitential rite. The Christian use of water for religious purposes other than Baptism can be traced back to the 4th cent. in the E. and to the 5th in the W. The use of 'Holy Water stoups' at the entrance of churches had become general at any rate by Norman times. See also STOUPS.

A. Gastoué, *L'Eau bénite: Ses origines, son histoire, son usage* (1908); A. Franz, *Die kirchlichen Benediktionen im Mittelalter* (1909), pp. 43–220; A. A. King, *Holy Water: The Use of Water for Ceremonial and Purificatory Purposes in Pagan, Jewish and Christian Times* (1926).

Holy Week.

The week preceding *Easter, observed throughout Catholic Christendom both in E. and W. as a period of devotion to the Passion of Christ. The various traditional rites of the week, of which each day has its own, probably began to develop at *Jerusalem in the 4th cent., when pilgrimages became easily possible, and Christians could indulge a natural desire to re-enact the last scenes of the life of Christ in liturgical drama. The Pilgrimage of *Egeria, now generally thought to describe a visit in 381–4, gives a detailed account of the contemporary observance of Holy Week in Jerusalem. For the ceremonies proper to each day in more recent E. and W. liturgical practice, see PALM SUNDAY, MAUNDY THURSDAY, GOOD FRIDAY, HOLY SATURDAY, PASCHAL VIGIL SERVICE, EASTER.

H. A. P. Schmidt, SJ (ed.), *Hebdomada Sancta* (2 vols. in 3; Rome, 1956–7). J. W. Tyrer, *Historical Survey of Holy Week, its Services and Ceremonial* (*Alcuin Club Collections, no. 29; 1932). A. Löhr, *Die Heilige Woche* (Regensburg, 1957; Eng. tr., 1958). J. G. Davies, *Holy Week: A Short History* (Ecumenical Studies in Worship, 11; 1963). J. D. Crichton, *The Liturgy of Holy Week* (Dublin, 1983). T. J. Talley, *The Origins of the Liturgical Year* (New York [1986]), esp. pp. 42–54. R. Taft, SJ, 'A Tale of Two Cities: The Byzantine Holy Week Triduum as a Paradigm of Liturgical History', in J. N. Alexander (ed.), *Time and Community: In Honor of Thomas Julian Talley* (Washington, DC, 1990), pp. 21–41.

Holy Year. A year during which the Pope grants a special *indulgence, the so-called *Jubilee, to all those who visit Rome, on certain conditions. It was instituted in 1300 by *Boniface VIII, who had meant it to be celebrated every 100 years. *Clement VI, in 1343, however, changed the period to 50; *Urban VI, in 1389, to 33 in honour of the years of the Lord's earthly life; and Paul II, in 1470, settled on 25, the regular interval that has been kept ever since. The conditions and special benefits are laid down each time by a special bull, issued on the preceding Feast of the *Ascension. The chief conditions are normally worthy reception of the Sacraments and visits to the four *basilicas during a specified time. The benefits include 'plenary indulgence' and exceptional powers for the confessors, who may absolve from most sins ordinarily reserved to higher authority, and commute all vows except those reserved to the Pope. One of the most important ceremonies of the Holy Year is the opening of the *Holy Door (q.v.) by the Pope before the First Christmas Vespers, and its walling up again at the same time a year later. Originally the Jubilee Indulgence was to be gained only at Rome, but since 1500 it has been extended to all churches throughout the world, to which it is granted for the six months following the Roman year on similar conditions, among them visits to local shrines and works of penance and charity. A regular Holy Year was last celebrated in 1975.

In addition to the regular Holy Years, in the 20th cent. there have been special ones, which have taken two forms: Holy Years of Redemption and Marian Years. The former celebrate the *Crucifixion and *Resurrection of Christ (conventionally dated AD 33) and run from the Feast of the *Annunciation to Easter Sunday of the following year; they have taken place in 1933–4 and 1983–4. The Marian Years are in honour of the BVM. The first lasted from 8 Dec. 1953 to 8 Dec. 1954 and celebrated the centenary of the definition of the dogma of the *Immaculate Conception; the second lasted from *Whitsunday 1987 to the feast of the *Assumption 1988 and celebrated the presumed bimillenary of the birth of the BVM.

H. Thurston, SJ, *The Holy Year of Jubilee: An Account of the History and Ceremony of the Roman Jubilee* (1900). P. Bargellini, *L'Anno Santo: Nella storia, nella letteratura e nell'arte* (Florence, 1974). H. Smolinsky in *TRE* 17, pp. 282–5, s.v. 'Jubeljahr, II', with bibl.

Homberg, Synod of. A synod which *Philip, Landgraf of Hesse, convoked at Homberg, 20 miles S. of Cassel, on 21 Oct. 1526 to establish a constitution on Protestant principles for the Church of his domains. A set of 158 articles (*paradoxa*, pub. in Erfurt, 1527), prepared by F. *Lambert, was taken as the basis of the proceedings, while the opponent of the reforming doctrines was Nicolas Herborn (sometimes called Nicolas Ferber). The one important outcome of the Synod was the appointment of a committee to draw up a Church Order for Hesse, which issued the 'Reformatio Ecclesiarum Hassiae', a set of regulations on a Protestant basis covering the whole area of Church life. By insisting on the independence of each Christian community, responsible for the maintenance of its own discipline, the 'Reformatio' upheld a congregationalism which went far beyond M. *Luther's teachings. Largely through Luther's influence, Philip of Hesse refrained from allowing it to be promulgated, and in consequence it was never enforced, nor even published until 1748.

Crit. text of the 'Reformatio Ecclesiarum Hassiae' in E. Sehling (ed.), *Die evangelischen Kirchenordnungen des XVI. Jahrhunderts*, 8, I. Hälfte (Tübingen, 1965), pp. 43–65, with introd. material, pp. 9–42. More important clauses in Kidd, pp. 222–30 (no. 98). W. Schmitt, *Die Synode zu Homberg und ihre Vorgeschichte: Festschrift zur vierhundert-Jahrfeier der Homberger Synode* (Homberg, 1926). E. Kurten, OFM, *Franz Lambert von Avignon und Nikolaus Herborn in ihrer Stellung zum Ordensgedanken und zum Franziskanertum im Besonderen* (Reformationsgeschichtliche Studien und Texte, 72; 1950). G. Müller, 'Die Synode als Fundament der evangelischen Kirche in Hessen, Homberg 1526–1976', *Jahrbuch des hessischen Kirchengeschichtlichen Vereinigung*, 27 (1976), pp. 129–46; R. Haas, 'Lamberts "Paradoxa" und die hessischen Kirchenordnungen', in P. Fraenkel (ed.), *Pour retrouver François Lambert* (Bibliotheca Bibliographica Aureliana, 108; Baden Baden, 1987), pp. 257–72.

homiliary (Lat. *homiliarium*). A collection of homilies arranged acc. to the ecclesiastical calendar for reading at the office of *Mattins. Homiliaries were compiled esp. in the earlier Middle Ages, and among surviving examples are those of *Paul the Deacon (*c.* AD 790), made at the command of *Charlemagne, and of Alain of Farfa (d. 770).

H. Barré, C.S.Sp., *Les Homéliaires carolingiens de l'école d'Auxerre: Authenticité, inventaire, tableaux comparatifs, initia* (ST 225; 1962); R. Grégoire, OSB, *Les Homéliaires du Moyen Age: Inventaire et analyse des manuscrits* (Rerum Ecclesiasticarum Documenta, Series Maior, Fontes, 6; 1966); id., *Homéliaires liturgiques médiévaux: Analyse des manuscrits* (Biblioteca degli Studi Medievali, 12; Spoleto, 1980). Vogel, *Sources*, pp. 363–5, for further refs.

Homilies, the Books of. The plan of issuing prescribed homilies for the use of disaffected and unlearned clergy was agreed to in the Convocation which met on 20 Jan. 1542. A collection was duly produced 12 months later, but, prob. because *Henry VIII refused to authorize it, not formally issued until early in *Edward VI's reign, when it appeared with the authority of the Council on 31 July 1547. It reflected T. *Cranmer's pastoral concern for sound teaching in the vernacular. The subjects of its 12 homilies were: (1) A fruitful Exhortation to the Reading of Holy Scripture (Cranmer); (2) Of the Misery of all Mankind (Archdeacon John Harpsfield, 1516–78); (3) Of the Salvation of all Mankind (Cranmer); (4) Of the true and lively Faith (Cranmer); (5) Of Good Works (Cranmer); (6) Of Christian Love and Charity (E. *Bonner); (7) Against Swearing and Perjury; (8) Of the Declining from God; (9) An Exhortation against the Fear of Death (prob. Cranmer); (10) An Exhortation to Obedience; (11) Against Whoredom and Adultery; (12) Against Strife and Contention.

A 'Second Book', with 21 further homilies, was issued under *Elizabeth I. It was prob. completed by the beginning of 1563, but it was not published in its final form until 1571. Their titles are listed in Art. 35 of the *Thirty-Nine Articles. The majority are the work of J. *Jewel; but E. *Grindal wrote no. 5 and M. *Parker (prob.) no. 17. No. 21 ('Against Rebellion') was added in 1571 in view of the Northern Rebellion of 1569.

From Elizabethan times, the Homilies provided a considerable element in Anglican preaching, and acquired status alongside the BCP and Thirty-Nine Articles as a repository of Anglican doctrine. Bishops frequently enjoined that they should be read and inquired into practice during their triennial visitations. At the Restoration (1660) they were revived, and, though hopes of a revision were unfulfilled, they were frequently cited by R. *South, G. *Morley, G. *Hickes, and the later *Nonjurors. Though they are unsuitable for modern use, the Homilies retain a measure of authority in view of Art. 35, while Art. 11 refers to the 'Homily of Justification' (presumably no. 3 of the First Book) for a fuller account of the 'most wholesome doctrine' 'that we are justified by faith only'.

The Books of Homilies have frequently been repr. Crit. edn. of the 1547 Homilies, with Elizabethan Homily 'Against Rebellion', by R. B. Bond (Toronto, etc. [1987]), incl. introd., pp. 3–45. J. N. King, *English Reformation Literature* (Princeton, NJ [1982]), esp. pp. 123–7 and 131–4.

Homilies, Clementine. See CLEMENTINE LITERATURE.

Homoeans. The Arian party which came into existence *c*.355 under the leadership of *Acacius, Bp. of Caesarea. Repudiating both the *Homoousion and the Homoiousion, they sought to confine theological discussion about the Person of the Son to the assertion that He was like (Gk. ὅμοιος, 'like') the Father. For a brief interval they were closely associated with the more orthodox *Semiarians.

homoioteleuton (Gk. ὅμοιος, 'like', and τελευτή, 'ending'). In MSS, the repetition of the same sequence of letters or words in two neighbouring places, considered as a source of error in copying. Where the repeated sequence occurs at the beginning of a word or phrase, the alternative expression 'homoioarcton' is occasionally used.

Homoousion (Gk. ὁμοούσιον, 'of one substance'; rendered in Lat. *consubstantialis*). The term used in the *Nicene Creed to express the relations of the Father and the Son within the Godhead and originally designed to exclude *Arianism. Its earlier associations with the *Gnostics and *Paul of Samosata may have made it suspect at first, and many *Origenists, who had no sympathy

with Arianism, preferred the term 'Homoiousion' (ὁμοιούσιον, i.e. 'of like substance with the Father'), which was held to leave more room for distinctions in the Godhead.

J. F. Bethune-Baker, *The Meaning of Homoousios in the 'Constantinopolitan' Creed* (Texts and Studies, 7, no. 1; Cambridge, 1901). G. L. Prestige, *God in Patristic Thought* (1936), chs. 10 f., pp. 197–241. C. Hauret, *Comment le défenseur de Nicée a-t-il compris le dogme de Nicée?* (*Gregorian University thesis; Bruges, 1936). J. Lebon, 'Le Sort du "Consubstantiel" Nicéen', *RHE* 47 (1952), pp. 485–529, and 48 (1953), pp. 632–82. [G.] C. Stead, *Divine Substance* (Oxford, 1977), esp. pp. 190–266. See also works cited s.v. ARIANISM.

homosexuality. There are few biblical references to homosexual behaviour. In the OT the definite references are in the story of Sodom in Gen. 19: 4–11, the probably dependent incident recorded in Jgs. 19, and in Lev. 18: 22 and 20: 13. Both the infrequency of the references and their contexts encourage the view that this was not a subject of great concern to OT writers, and, although later Christian exegesis used the condemnation of Sodom as evidence of particular Divine displeasure at the homosexual assault intended by its inhabitants, the story itself does not emphasize this particular sin nor does subsequent OT reflection on it (Is. 1, Ezek. 16, and Jer. 23). In the NT homosexual behaviour is mentioned and condemned in 1 Cor. 6: 9–11, 1 Tim. 1: 10, and most influentially in Rom. 1: 27 which many moralists have seen as supporting the view that homosexuality is, with other sexual acts which are not procreative, contrary to *Natural Law.

Patristic, medieval, and later Christian moralists have not questioned this judgement, and it is only in recent times that some writers have argued that the quality of a relationship, be it homosexual or heterosexual, is what determines its moral value. Whether they have taken this view or have continued to regard homosexual behaviour as sinful, Christian Churches have usually favoured the reform of the civil law which has occurred in many countries, removing the harsh penalties previously imposed. In England the Churches played a significant part in supporting the appointment of the Committee responsible for the Wolfenden Report of 1957 and the enactment of its recommendations as the Sexual Offences Act 1967, which removed criminal sanctions from homosexual behaviour between consenting adults in private. These developments have been accompanied by changes in attitude among psychiatrists, who no longer tend to regard homosexual leaning as something to be cured. In 1991 the House of Bishops of the General Synod of the C of E, while emphasising that 'homophile [i.e. homosexual] orientation and its expression in sexual activity do not constitute a parallel and alternative form of human sexual activity as complete within the terms of the created order as the heterosexual', nevertheless did not reject homosexual activity in permanent relationships among the laity, but insisted that the clergy have a particular responsibility to maintain the Scriptural ideal; they 'cannot claim the liberty to enter into sexually active homophile relationships'. The 1998 *Lambeth Conference, however, expressed the belief that for all Christians 'abstinence is right for those not called to marriage'; while accepting that some experience themselves as having a homosexual orientation, the Conference rejected 'homosexual practices as incompatible with Scripture'.

D. S. Bailey, *Homosexuality and the Western Christian Tradition* (1955). The Report of a Working Party of the Board for Social Responsibility [of the C of E], *Homosexual Relationships: A Contribution to Discussion* (1979); *Issues in Human Sexuality: A Statement by the House of Bishops of the General Synod of the Church of England, December 1991* (1991). P. Coleman, *Christian Attitudes to Homosexuality* (1980; rev. as *Gay Christians: A Moral Dilemma*, 1989). J. Boswell, *Christianity, Social Tolerance, and Homosexuality: Gay People in Western Europe from the Beginning of the Christian Era to the Fourteenth Century* (Chicago and London, 1980). J. Dollimore, *Sexual Dissidence: Augustine to Wilde, Freud to Foucault* (Oxford, 1991).

Honoratus, St (d. 429/30), founder and first abbot of the monastery of *Lérins and later Bp. of Arles. Of consular family, he was converted to Christianity and set out with his brother Venantius on a pilgrimage to the holy places in Syria and Egypt; but on his brother's death in Achaia, he returned through *Rome and with the encouragement of Leontius, Bp. of Fréjus, settled in the island of Lérins, where he founded (*c*.410) the celebrated monastery. In 427 or early 428 he became Bp. of Arles. St *Hilary of Arles, his successor in the see and biographer, was probably a relative. His writings have been lost. Feast day, 16 Jan.

Crit. text of Hilary's Life of Honoratus by S. Cavallin, *Vitae Sanctorum Honorati et Hilarii* (Skrifter utgivna av Vetenskaps-Societeten i Lund, 40; 1952), pp. 47–78, with introd., pp. 13–34, and notes, pp. 111–13. It is also ed., with Fr. tr. and introd., by M.-D. Valentin, OP (SC 235; 1977). [W.] O. Chadwick, 'Euladius of Arles', *JTS* 46 (1945), pp. 200–5, esp. p. 205. S. Pricoco, *L'Isola dei santi: Il cenobio di Lerino e le origini del monachesimo gallico* (Filologia e Critica, 23 [1978]), *passim*.

Honorius I (d. 638), Pope from 625. He came from a noble family of the Campagna, but little is known of his life before his election to the Papacy. Like his predecessor, St *Gregory the Great (d. 604), he interested himself in the Christianization of the Anglo-Saxons, and sent his congratulations to King *Edwin of Northumbria on the occasion of his Baptism in 627. He also sent St *Birinus to preach in Britain, and gave the pallium to Honorius of Canterbury and *Paulinus of York. In 628 he granted the monastery of *Bobbio *exemption from episcopal jurisdiction other than that of the Pope. He gained considerable influence over the government of Italy by his wise administration of the patrimony of Peter, and despite heavy expenditure on churches and other buildings collected a considerable Papal treasure. One of his principal achievements was the ending of the schism of the patriarchs of *Aquileia-Grado, which had been renewed by Fortunatus, whom he deposed, probably with the help of the Exarch of *Ravenna. Gratitude for this assistance may have influenced his attitude towards the Emp. *Heraclius in the matter of the *Monothelite heresy, which has been among the chief historical arguments against Papal infallibility. About 634 *Sergius, the Patr. of *Constantinople, addressed a letter to the Pope interrogating him on the question of the 'one energy' (μία ἐνέργεια) of Christ. This formula, which, while confessing the two natures, attributed only one mode of activity—that of the Divine Word—to the Incarnate Christ, had been found useful in the E. for reconciling the Monophysites. It was strenuously opposed, however, by *Sophronius of Jerusalem, and Sergius, in his diplomatic letter to Honorius, stressed the unity of the Person of Christ safeguarded by the new formula, while disregarding the duality of natures. Without further inquiries, Honorius sent back a favourable reply in which he used the unfortunate expression 'one will' in Christ. When his injunction of silence on both parties was disobeyed, he wrote a second letter rejecting the expression 'two wills' as giving rise to contentions, though insisting strongly on the two natures. He died in 638, the year of the publication of the *Ecthesis, the charter of Monothelitism, which utilized Honorius' formula of the 'one will'.

His successors repeatedly condemned the heresy, and at the Council of *Constantinople (681) Honorius himself was formally anathematized. This condemnation, which was forgotten in the W. during the Middle Ages, was discussed in the 15th cent. at the negotiations for reunion between the Catholic and Orthodox Churches, and again in the *Gallican controversies of the 17th and 18th cents., and before the definition of Papal Infallibility in 1870. The authenticity of the letter of Honorius as well as of the Acts of the Council of Constantinople, once rejected by some RC scholars, e.g. C. *Baronius, is now generally admitted. The common argument in defence of Honorius is that the letters do not contain heretical teaching, but only gravely imprudent expressions, and that, in these circumstances, condemnation of a Pope's carelessness by a General Council was justified.

J. P. Migne, *PL* 80. 463–94. J. J. I. von *Döllinger, *Die Papstfabeln des Mittelalters* (1863), pp. 131–53; C. J. *Hefele, *Causa Honorii Papae* (Naples, 1870); J. *Chapman, OSB, 'The Condemnation of Pope Honorius', *Dublin Review*, 139 (1906), pp. 129–54; 140 (1907), pp. 42–72; P. Galtier, SJ, 'La Première Lettre du Pape Honorius', *Gregorianum*, 29 (1948), pp. 42–61. R. Bäumer, 'Die Wiederentdeckung der Honoriusfrage im Abendland', *RQ* 56 (1961), pp. 200–14. G. Kreuzer, *Die Honoriusfrage im Mittelalter und in der Neuzeit* (Päpste und Papsttum, 8; 1975). G. Schwaiger, 'Die Honoriusfrage', *ZKG* 88 (1977), pp. 85–97. Hefele and Leclercq, 3 (pt. 1; 1909), pp. 347–538. Mann, 1 (pt. 1; 1902), pp. 304–45. E. Amann in *DTC* 7 (pt. 1; 1922), cols. 93–131; G. Schwaiger in *TRE* 15 (1986), pp. 566–8, s.v.

Honorius III (d. 1227), Pope from 1216. Cencio Savelli was a native of Rome. He entered the household of Cardinal Giacinto Bobone (later *Celestine III) and became a canon of Sta Maria Maggiore and Papal subdeacon under Clement III (1187–91). His administrative career was associated at first with the Papal Chamber (Treasury). He became Papal chamberlain (1188) and from 1194 (when he was made a cardinal-deacon) until 1198 he held the office together with the chancellorship. He was promoted cardinal-priest in 1201. On 18 July 1216 he was elected to succeed *Innocent III and consecrated at Perugia on 24 July. In general he was concerned with the implementation of his predecessor's policies and of the decrees of the Fourth *Lateran Council. On 22 Nov. 1220 he crowned the Emp. *Frederick II in St Peter's on promises that he would uphold the rights of the Church and promote a crusade. He took a prominent part in political affairs throughout Europe, acting as arbitrator between Philip II of France and James of Aragon, supporting Henry III of England (which he virtually ruled during the King's minority), crowning Peter Altisodoreus Emp. of Byzantium (1217), and defending the privileges of the Church in Bohemia (1223). He also approved the *Dominican,

*Franciscan, and *Carmelite Orders and fostered the growth of their *Third Orders. The main sources for the pontificate are the Registers (the earliest complete set) and the original letters. In 1226 he approved the official collection of his decretals, the 'Compilatio Quinta'. He was the author of the *Liber Censuum (1192, q.v.), of the *Ordo Romanus XII (Mabillon), which included a coronation order, and of sermons. Also attributed to him are a Life of *Gregory VII and additions to the *Liber Pontificalis.

Opera Omnia, ed. C. A. Horoy, Medii Aevi Bibliotheca Patristica (5 vols., Paris, 1879–83); Selected Letters, ed. C. Rodenberg in MGH, Ep. Saec. XIII, 1 (1883), pp. 1–260; Calendar of his Register by P. Pressutti (2 vols., Rome, 1888–95). Docs. of his pontificate relating to Spain ed. D. Mansilla (Monumenta Hispaniae Vaticana. Sección: Registros, 2; Rome, 1965). J. E. Sayers, Papal Government and England during the Pontificate of Honorius III (1216–1227) (Cambridge Studies in Medieval Life and Thought, 3rd ser. 21; 1984), with bibl. F. Vernet, Études sur les sermons d'Honorius III (thesis, Lyons, 1888); A. Keutner, Papsttum und Krieg unter dem Pontificat des Papstes Honorius III (1935). W. Ullmann, 'Honorius III and the Prohibition of Legal Studies', Juridical Review, 60 (1948), pp. 177–86; S. [G.] Kuttner, 'Papst Honorius III. und das Studium des Zivilrechts', in Festschrift für Martin Wolff, ed. E. von Caemmerer and others (Tübingen, 1952), pp. 79–101. C. Thouzellier in Fliche and Martin, 10 (1950), pp. 291–304, with bibl. H. Schulz in PRE (3rd edn.), 8 (1900), pp. 318–33, s.v.; G. Mollat in EC 9 (1952), cols. 141–3, s.v. 'Onorio III'.

Honorius 'of Autun' (Augustodunensis) (early 12th cent.), popular theologian. In his De luminaribus ecclesiae he describes himself as 'Honorius Augustodunensis ecclesiae presbyter et scholasticus', and nothing more is certainly known of his life. The view of earlier scholars that 'Augustodunensis' refers to Autun has been abandoned, but no agreed alternative has been found. There are indications that he spent part of his life in England, but was not an Englishman, and that he had some connection with *Canterbury and came for a time under the influence of St *Anselm. It is also usually agreed that the later part of his life was spent in S. Germany as a monk, and probably a recluse. He was a very prolific writer. To his English period belong: the Elucidarium, one of the earliest surveys of Christian doctrine, in the form of a dialogue between pupil and master. It had a wide and lasting popularity, and was translated into several vernaculars, beginning with extracts in Anglo-Saxon in his own lifetime; the Sigillum sanctae Mariae, an exposition of the lessons for the feast of the *Assumption, including a short commentary on the Song of Songs, in which it is given a Marian interpretation; the Gemma animae, a work on the liturgy and liturgical practices with much allegory and symbolism. To his German period belong long commentaries on the Psalter and on the Song of Songs, which is here interpreted as applying to Christ and the Church; a Clavis physicae consisting of extracts from Johannes Scottus *Erigena; and the De luminaribus ecclesiae, a brief catalogue of Christian writers, ending with 21 works of his own, a list which is far from complete. Honorius also wrote Imago mundi, a compendium of cosmology and geography, which enjoyed very wide popularity throughout the Middle Ages and was translated into various vernaculars. Many of his shorter tracts are concerned with themes of topical interest in the period of the reforms associated with *Gregory VII, such

as the celibacy of the clergy. Honorius was not an original thinker or writer, but he wrote in simple language for those without access to many books, and he had the art of making interesting any subject on which he touched.

Of the works collected and pr. under the name of Honorius, with prolegomena, in J. P. Migne, PL 172. 9–1270, the De Philosophia (cols. 39–102) is the work of *William of Conches, the De Solis Effectibus (cols. 101–16) is of doubtful authorship, and the Quaestiones et ad easdem Responsiones in . . . Proverbia et Ecclesiasten (cols 311–48) is the work of Salonius of Geneva. His Cognitio Vitae is pr. among the works of St *Augustine in J. P. Migne, PL 40, 1005–32; further sections of his comm. on the Pss. are pr. among the works of *Gerhoh of Reichersberg in J. P. Migne, PL 193. 1315–72 (on Pss. 31–7), and 194. 485–730 (on Pss. 78–117); further 'Libelli' ed. I. Dieterich in MGH, Libelli de Lite Imperatorum et Pontificum Saeculis XI et XII, 3 (1897), pp. 29–80, with bibl. refs. The orig. text of the Inevitabile was pr. by J. Kelle (Sb. (Wien), 150, Heft 3; 1905). Modern edns. of the Elucidarium by Y. Lefèvre (Bibliothèque des Écoles françaises d'Athènes et de Rome, 170; 1954; ignores the early Eng. MSS); of the Clavis physicae by P. Lucentini (Temi e Testi, 21; Rome, 1974); and of the Imago mundi by V. I. J. Flint in AHDLMA 49 (1983), pp. 7–153.

J. A. Endres, Honorius Augustodunensis (Kempten and Munich, 1906). M.-T. d'Alverny, 'Le Cosmos symbolique du XIIᵉ siècle', AHDLMA, Année 28 (for 1953; 1954), pp. 31–81. H. Menhardt, 'Der Nachlass des Honorius Augustodunensis', Zeitschrift für deutsches Altertum und deutsche Literatur, 89 (1958/9), pp. 23–69. R. W. Southern, St Anselm and his biographer (Birkbeck Lectures, 1959; Cambridge, 1963), pp. 209–17. W. Beinert, Die Kirche— Gottes Heil in der Welt: Die Lehre von der Kirche nach den Schriften des Rupert von Deutz, Honorius Augustodunensis und Gerhoch von Reichersberg (BGPM, NF 13; 1973), with introd. on his life and work, pp. 38–50. M.-O. Garrigues, 'Quelques Recherches sur l'œuvre d'Honorius Augustodunensis', RHE 70 (1975), pp. 388–425, with refs. V. I. J. Flint, 'The Place and Purpose of the Works of Honorius Augustodunensis', R. Bén. 87 (1977), pp. 97–127, repr. in id., Ideas in the Medieval West: Texts and their Contexts (1988), no. 12, with other studies and recent bibl. W. Wattenbach and F. J. Schmale, Deutschlands Geschichtsquellen im Mittelalter von Tode Kaiser Heinrichs V. bis zum Ende des Interregnum, 1 (1976), pp. 27–38. Y. Lefèvre in Dict. Sp. 7 (pt. 1; 1969), cols. 730–7, s.v. 'Honorius (2) Augustodunensis'; R. Haacke and M. L. Arduini in TRE 15 (1986), pp. 571–8, s.v. 'Honorius Augustodunensis'.

Hontheim, Johann Nikolaus von (1701–90), founder of *Febronianism. He was a native of Trier, where he spent the greater part of his life. While a student at Louvain, he came under the influence of the *Gallican canonist, Z. B. *Van Espen. In 1728 he was ordained priest and in 1748 became suffragan Bp. of Trier. In 1742 he began an investigation, on behalf of the German Archbishop-Electors, of the historical position of the Papacy, and in 1763, under the pseudonym of 'Justinus Febronius', published his conclusions in his principal work, De statu ecclesiae et legitima potestate Romani Pontificis (see FEBRONIANISM). Owing to its Gallican doctrines the book was put on the *Index in 1764; but though for several years Hontheim was involved in controversy, he was not compelled to make a formal retractation until 1778. In 1781 he published Justini Febroni Commentarius in suam retractationem Pio VI, a work which, despite its conciliatory spirit, showed little real change of view. His other writings include two valuable historical works on the city of Trier, Historia Trevirensis Diplomatica (3 vols., 1750) and Prodromus Historiae Trevirensis (2 vols., 1757). His integrity, devotion to truth, and learning were admired even by his enemies.

See bibl. to FEBRONIANISM.

Hook, Walter Farquhar (1798–1875), Dean of *Chichester. Educated at Winchester and Oxford, he spent some years after his ordination in parochial work at Coventry and Leeds. As vicar of Leeds (1837–59), although sympathetic with the *Tractarian Movement, he became involved in a controversy with E. B. *Pusey over the alleged Romish practices at St Saviour's, Leeds. Differences in their interpretation of the effects of the Reformation on the Anglican Church led to an increasingly heated correspondence until finally their friendship was formally terminated by Hook, who declared himself an enemy of 'Romanism' and 'Puseyism'. In 1859 he became Dean of Chichester. He was the author of many historical and theological works, including a *Church Dictionary* (1842; often reprinted), a *Dictionary of Ecclesiastical Biography* (8 vols., 1845–52), and the *Lives of the Archbishops of Canterbury* (12 vols., 1860–76).

W. R. W. Stephens, *The Life and Letters of Walter Farquhar Hook* (2 vols., 1878). C. J. Stranks, *Dean Hook* (1954). H. W. Dalton, 'Walter Farquhar Hook, Vicar of Leeds: his Work for the Church and the Town, 1837–1848', *Publications of the Thoresby Society*, 63 (for 1988; 1990), pp. 27–79, with further refs. W. R. W. Stephens in *DNB* 27 (1891), pp. 276–9.

Hooker, Richard (*c.*1554–1600), Anglican divine. Born at Heavitree near Exeter, he was admitted through the influence of J. *Jewel at Corpus Christi College, Oxford, of which he became a Fellow in 1577. In 1579 he was appointed deputy professor of Hebrew. Vacating his fellowship on his marriage to Joan Churchman, who, acc. to I. *Walton, 'brought him neither beauty nor portion', in 1584 he was appointed rector of Drayton Beauchamp, and in 1585 Master of the Temple, where he controverted the *Calvinistic views of the Reader, W. *Travers. Later (1591) he became rector of Boscombe, Wilts, and finally (1595) of Bishopsbourne, near Canterbury, where he died.

Hooker was *par excellence* the apologist of the Elizabethan Settlement of 1559 and perhaps the most accomplished advocate that Anglicanism has ever had. He developed his doctrines in his treatise *Of the Laws of Ecclesiastical Polity*. Of the five Books which appeared in Hooker's lifetime 1–4 were published in 1593 and 5 in 1597. Books 6 (incomplete) and 8 did not appear until 1648 and Book 7 not until 1662. In conception the *Laws* was a *livre de circonstance*, designed to justify the constitutional structure of the Elizabethan Church, but it embodied a broadly conceived philosophical theology. His opposition to the *Puritans, who held to the literal following of the Scriptures as an absolute in the sense that whatever was not expressly commanded in Scripture was unlawful, led him to elaborate a whole theory of law, based on the 'absolute' fundamental of natural law, whose 'seat is the bosom of God, her voice the harmony of the world' (*LEP* 1. 16. 8). This natural law, which governs the universe and to which both ecclesiastical and civil polity are subservient, is the expression of God's supreme reason, and everything, including the Scriptures, must be interpreted in the light of it. 'Laws human must be made according to the general laws of nature, and without contradiction unto any positive law in Scripture. Otherwise they are ill made' (*LEP* 3. 9. 2).

The Puritans were wholly mistaken in regarding the Bible as a mechanical code of rules; for not everything that is rightful finds precise direction in the Scriptures. In a similar way the permanence of law does not preclude development of detail. The Church is an organic, not a static, institution, and the method of Church government and ecclesiastical administration will change acc. to circumstances. Hence the C of E, though reformed, possesses continuity with the medieval Church. Further, the visible organized Church is a political society, 'a court not temporal merely', yet able to control its own legislation in a way analogous to that in which the civil state through parliament makes its laws. Hooker developed an essentially contractual theory of political government which influenced future political writers, esp. J. *Locke.

In particular matters, Hooker has been less universally acceptable to Anglicans. In his unreadiness to condemn the orders of Continental Protestants, he denied the necessity of episcopal ordination. His doctrine of the Eucharist closely approximates in many places to *receptionism. His argument on points of detail is not infrequently difficult to grasp and not wholly clear. But Hooker remains one of the greatest theologians that the English Church has ever possessed; and he conveyed his beliefs in a masterly English prose. Feast day in parts of the Anglican Communion, 3 Nov.

Works ed. J. *Keble (3 vols., Oxford, 1836; 7th edn. rev. by R. W. *Church and F. *Paget, 1888); and, incl. autograph notes found in *Trinity College, Dublin, in 1971 among the papers of Abp. J. *Ussher, by W. S. Hill and others (vols 1–5, Cambridge, Mass., and London, 1977–90; vol. 6, in 2 parts, Binghamton, NY, 1993). Life by I. Walton (1665; repr. in Keble's edn. of *Works*). C. J. Sisson, *The Judicious Marriage of Mr Hooker and the Birth of the Laws of Ecclesiastical Polity* (1940). A. P. d'Entrèves, *The Medieval Contribution to Political Thought: Thomas Aquinas, Marsilius of Padua, Richard Hooker* (1939); P. Munz, *The Place of Hooker in the History of Thought* (1952); J. S. Marshall, *Hooker and the Anglican Tradition: An historical and theological Study of Hooker's Ecclesiastical Polity* (Sewanee, Tenn., and London, 1963); W. S. Hill (ed.), *Studies in Richard Hooker: Essays Preliminary to an Edition of Works* (Cleveland, Oh., and London, 1972); R. K. Faulkner, *Richard Hooker and the Politics of a Christian England* (1981). W. J. T. Kirby, *Richard Hooker's Doctrine of the Royal Supremacy* (Studies in the History of Christian Thought, 43; 1990). S. Lee in *DNB* 27 (1891), pp. 289–95.

Hooper, John (*c.*1495–1555), Bp. of *Gloucester and *Worcester, and Protestant martyr. A native of Somerset, he was educated at Oxford before entering the *Cistercian Priory of Cleeve. On the dissolution of the religious houses he went to London and began to interest himself in the Continental Reformers, esp. H. *Zwingli and H. *Bullinger, and returned to Oxford to propagate their views. After a disputation with S. *Gardiner, Bp. of Winchester, he was exiled for heresy and spent the next years travelling in Europe. From 1547 to 1549 he lived at Zurich, where he became friends with Bullinger and J. *Laski. In 1549 he came back to England and was made chaplain to the Protector *Somerset. In 1550 he was nominated to the see of Gloucester, which he accepted only after the reference to angels and saints had been omitted from the Oath of Supremacy and after further prolonged hesitation on the lawfulness of episcopal vestments, which led to a short term of imprisonment. In 1552, when Gloucester was temporarily reunited with the see of Worcester, Hooper was made bishop of the new diocese. He governed his diocese with exemplary zeal and vigour, introducing, however, many Continental customs. He was also very liberal to the poor. On the accession of *Mary he was imprisoned in the Fleet in 1553. In 1555 he was tried for heresy, and having refused to recant was excommunicated and burned at the stake (9 Feb. 1555). One of the chief English exponents of extreme Zwinglian Protestantism, he exercised a considerable influence on the later Puritans through his writings, which include *A Godly Confession and Protestation of the Christian Faith* (1551) and *A Brief and Clear Confession of the Christian Faith, containing an hundred Articles acc. to the Order of the Creed of the Apostles* (1581).

S. Carr (ed.), *The Early Writings of John Hooper* (*Parker Society, 1843); C. Nevinson (ed.), *Later Writings of Bishop Hooper* (ibid., 1852), with biog. sketch pp. vii–xxx. H. Robinson (ed.), *Original Letters Relating to the English Reformation, 1537–1558* (ibid., 2 vols., 1846–7). E. W. Hunt, *The Life and Times of John Hooper (c.1500–1555), Bishop of Gloucester* (Lewiston, Queenston, and Lampeter [1992]). F. D. Price, 'Gloucester Diocese under Bishop Hooper, 1551–3', *Transactions of the Bristol and Gloucester Archaeological Society*, 60 (1938), pp. 51–151. *BRUO, 1501–40*, pp. 296 f.

hope. One of the three *theological virtues. In its widest sense it may be defined as the desire and search for a future good, difficult but not impossible of attainment. In the course of OT history hope played an important part, often with a strong emphasis on material security and prosperity, as well as specifically religious desires. A particular focus of these hopes was the expectation of the *Messiah, which Christians believe to be fulfilled in Christ. By the *resurrection of Christ, mankind was 'begotten again unto a living hope' (1 Pet. 1: 3). As a Christian virtue its primary end, its motive, and its author is God Himself, and like faith it may continue even when charity has been lost by mortal sin. It is confined to this life and to purgatory, and has no place either in heaven (where its object, the *Beatific Vision, is already attained) or in hell. Hope, being confidence in God's goodness tempered by fear of His justice, is opposed to both despair and presumption.

J. *Moltmann, *Theologie der Hoffnung* (1964; Eng. tr., 1967). W. Zimmerli, *Der Mensch und seine Hoffnung im Alten Testament* (Kleine Vandenhoeck, Reihe 272 S; Göttingen [1968]; Eng. tr., *Man and his Hope in the Old Testament*, Studies in Biblical Theology, 2nd ser. 20; 1971). R. L. Ottley in *HERE* 4 (1913), pp. 779 f., s.v. 'Hope (Christian)'; R. *Bultmann and K. H. Rengstorf in *TWNT* 2 (1935), pp. 515–31 (Eng. tr., 1964, pp. 517–35), s.v. ἐλπίς, with refs.; J.-H. Nicolas, OP, in *Dict. Sp.* 4 (1960), cols. 1208–33, s.v. 'Espérance'.

Hopkins, Gerard Manley (1844–89), poet. He was educated at Balliol College, Oxford, where he was the pupil of B. *Jowett and W. Pater and the friend of R. *Bridges and D. M. Dolben. At this time he came under the religious influence of E. B. *Pusey and H. P. *Liddon. In 1866 Hopkins joined the RC Church, in 1868 he entered the *Jesuit novitiate, and in 1877 he was ordained priest. In 1884 he was appointed professor of Greek at the Royal University, Dublin, a position which he held till his death. He was unknown as a poet during his life, except to two or three friends, and the preservation of his MSS is due to R. Bridges, who first edited them in 1918. His poems,

the most ambitious of which is *The Wreck of the Deutschland* and perhaps the most representative *The Windhover: to Christ our Lord*, are marked by their great intensity of feeling, freedom in rhythm, and individual use of words, and have exerted much influence on more recent poets. They show a priest's pastoral care for souls, and conceive the fundamental personal relationship between the soul and its Redeemer as sacrificial. The opening words of *The Wreck of the Deutschland*, 'Thou mastering me God', were carved over the sculpture of the Re-creation of Man by E. *Gill at Geneva.

Crit. edn. of his *Poems* by N. H. Mackenzie (Oxford, 1990). *Editio princeps* with notes by R. Bridges (1918); 2nd edn., with an introduction by Charles *Williams (1930); 3rd edn., with notes and biog. introd. by W. H. Gardner (1948); 4th edn. by W. H. Gardner and N. H. Mackenzie (1967). C. C. Abbott, *The Letters of Gerard Manley Hopkins to Robert Bridges* (1935); id., *The Correspondence of Gerard Manley Hopkins and Richard Watson Dixon* (1935); id., *Further Letters of Gerard Manley Hopkins* (1938; 2nd edn. with additional letters, 1956); H. House, *Note-books and Papers of G. M. Hopkins* (1937); 2nd edn. by H. House and G. Storey, *The Journals and Papers of Gerard Manley Hopkins* (1959); C. Devlin, SJ, *The Sermons and Devotional Writings of Gerard Manley Hopkins* (1959). Poems with selections from his journals, sermons, and letters, ed. C. Phillips (Oxford Authors, 1986). W. H. Gardner, *Gerard Manley Hopkins (1844–1889): A Study of Poetic Idiosyncrasy in Relation to Poetic Tradition* (2 vols., 1944–9). J.-G. Ritz, *Le Poète Gérard Manley Hopkins* [1963]; R. B. Martin, *Gerard Manley Hopkins: A Very Private Life* (1991); N. White, *Hopkins: A Literary Biography* (Oxford, 1992). The numerous other studies incl. J. Pick, *Gerard Manley Hopkins: Priest and Poet* (1942); D. A. Downes, *Gerard Manley Hopkins: A Study of his Ignatian Spirit* (New York and London, 1960); and A. Thomas, SJ, *Hopkins the Jesuit* (1969). T. Dunne, *Gerard Manley Hopkins: A Comprehensive Bibliography* (Oxford, 1976). Polgár, 2 (1990), pp. 145–237.

Hormisdas, St (d. 523), Pope from 514. His chief importance lies in his success in healing the *Acacian schism which since 484 had divided the E. from the W. After attempts at union in 515 and again in 517 had come to grief through the obstinacy of the Emp. Anastasius I, Hormisdas secured in 519, under the new Emp. Justin I, the signature of John, the Patr. of Constantinople, and afterwards of some 250 E. bishops, to a dogmatic formula (the 'Formula Hormisdae') in which the *Chalcedonian Definition and Leo's *Tome were accepted, Acacius and other heretics were expressly condemned, and the authority of the Roman see (on the basis of Mt. 16: 18) was strongly emphasized. He also took a notable part in negotiating with the (*Arian) Goths matters of ecclesiastical concern to the W. Church, and maintained good relations with *Theodoric. It was under his direction that *Dionysius Exiguus made his second version of the Greek ecclesiastical canons. Feast day, 6 Aug.

Some 90 of Hormisdas' genuine letters survive; repr. in J. P. Migne, *PL* 63. 367–534; crit. texts in the so-called 'Collectio Avellana' ed. O. Guenther (CSEL 35, pt. 2; 1898). Life in *LP* (Duchesne), 1, pp. 269–74. L. *Duchesne, *L'Église au VIᵉ siècle* (1925), pp. 37–40 and 48–65. W. Haacke, *Die Glaubensformel des Papstes Hormisdas im Acacianischen Schisma* (Analecta Gregoriana, 20; 1939). J. S. Martin, 'La "Prima Salus" del Papa Hormisdas (514–523)', *Rivista Española de Teología*, 1 (1941), pp. 767–812. F. Dvornik, *The Idea of Apostolicity in Byzantium* (Cambridge, Mass., 1958), pp. 124–34. L. Magi, *La Sede Romana nella corrispondenza degli imperatori e patriarchi bizantini (VI–VII sec.)*

(Bibliothèque de la *RHE*, 57; 1972), esp. pp. 29–103. A. Grillmeier [SJ], *Jesus der Christus im Glauben der Kirche*, 2 (pt. 1; 1986), pp. 351–75; Eng. tr. (1987), pp. 310–33. É. Amann in *DTC* 7 (pt. 1; 1922), cols. 161–76, s.v.; J. Chapin in *NCE* 7 (1967), p. 148, s.v.

Horne, George (1730–92), Bp. of *Norwich. Born at Otham, nr. Maidstone, he was educated at University College, Oxford, where he became a friend of W. *Jones ('of Nayland'), his future biographer, and J. Moore, later Abp. of *Canterbury. In 1750 he was elected Fellow of Magdalen College, Oxford, of which he became president in 1768. He was appointed vice-chancellor of the University in 1776 and Dean of Canterbury in 1781. In 1790 he became Bp. of Norwich. Horne was a disciple of J. *Hutchinson, but rejected his more fanciful speculations on Hebrew etymology. Though an adherent of *High Church principles, he was in sympathy with the spiritual earnestness of the *Methodists and refused to forbid J. *Wesley to preach in his diocese. He also supported the Scottish bishops' petition to Parliament in 1789. Among his writings are many pamphlets directed in various ways against the views of I. *Newton, D. *Hume, W. *Law, and others, whose importance he seems not always to have understood. Horne was above all a preacher, and his sermons were frequently reprinted. His most important work is his *Commentary on the Psalms* (1771); in it he maintained that the greater number of the Psalms were Messianic.

Collected edn., 6 vols., London, 1809 (incomplete). W. Jones, *Memoirs of the Life, Studies and Writings of the Right Reverend George Horne* (1795; with list of Horne's writings, pp. 414–18). A. C. Bickley in *DNB* 27 (1891), pp. 356–8.

Horne, Thomas Hartwell (1780–1862), biblical commentator and bibliographer. He was the grandfather of T. K. *Cheyne. Educated at Christ's Hospital, where S. T. *Coleridge was his contemporary, he began as a barrister's clerk. To supplement his income he took up literary work and wrote on a great variety of subjects. For many years he was a Wesleyan *Methodist. In 1808 he was invited to catalogue the Harleian MSS in the British Library, and from then on was engaged in several bibliographical undertakings. In 1818 appeared the first edition of his *Introduction to the Critical Study and Knowledge of the Holy Scriptures* (3 vols.), which at once established itself by its completeness as a standard work, though it was without originality. A supplementary volume appeared in 1821, and it went through a large number of editions both in Great Britain and the USA down to 1860. Among those who helped in the revision of its later editions were S. Davidson and S. P. *Tregelles. In 1819 Horne was ordained by W. *Howley to the curacy of Christ Church, Newgate Street, and held various ecclesiastical offices in the London diocese till his death. His many other writings include an *Introduction to the Study of Bibliography* (2 vols., 1814), *Deism Refuted* (1819), *The Scripture Doctrine of the Trinity briefly stated and defended* (1820), and *A Compendious Introduction to the Study of the Bible* (1827).

Reminiscences Personal and Bibliographical of Thomas Hartwell Horne, with notes by his daughter, S. A. Cheyne (1862), incl. list of Horne's writings (pp. 199–208). T. Cooper in *DNB* 27 (1891), pp. 363 f.

Horneck, Anthony (1641–97), Anglican divine. He was a native of Bacharach on the Rhine, of Protestant parentage, who studied theology at Heidelberg and came to England *c*.1661. In 1663 he was made a member of Queen's College, Oxford, and vicar of All Saints, Oxford, in 1664. He became prebendary of *Exeter Cathedral in 1670, and in the following year preacher at the Savoy, where he enjoyed great popularity. In 1689 he was appointed chaplain to William III, and in 1693 prebendary of *Westminster. He wrote a number of devotional books which were widely used at the time, dealing esp. with Holy Communion. Among them are *The Happy Ascetic* (1681), *The Fire of the Altar* (1683), and *The Crucified Jesus* (1686).

Collected edn. of *Several Sermons upon the Fifth of St Matthew; Being Part of Christ's Sermon on the Mount* (2 vols., 1698), with Life by Richard Kidder, Bp. of Bath and Wells, vol. 1, pp. 3–58, and list of his works, pp. 61 f.; also pub. separately (London, 1698). *Four Tracts* by Horneck were ed. W. Edwards (London, 1697); *The Crucified Jesus* was also ed. W. F. *Hook (Leeds and London, 1848); extracts from *The Happy Ascetic* were ed. J. *Wesley, *The *Christian Library*, 16 (repr. 1823), pp. 291–432; short extract from *The Fire of the Altar* pr. in P. E. More and F. L. Cross (eds.), *Anglicanism* (1935), no. 359, p. 777. L. Stephen in *DNB* 27 (1891), pp. 367 f.

Horologion (Gk. ὡρολόγιον). In the E. Church, the liturgical book which contains the recurrent portions of the ecclesiastical *Office extending through the whole year.

Horsiesi, St. See ORSISIUS, ST.

Horsley, Samuel (1733–1806), Bp. of *St Asaph. He was born in London and educated at Trinity Hall, Cambridge. In 1759 he succeeded his father as rector of Newington (now part of London). His interests in science led him to become a Fellow of the Royal Society in 1767, and its Secretary from 1773 to 1784. In 1771 he was appointed domestic chaplain to the Bp. of London, who made him Archdeacon of *St Albans in 1781. In 1788 he was consecrated Bp. of *St Davids. He proved an energetic bishop, both in his diocese and in the House of Lords. In 1793 he was translated to *Rochester, and in 1802 once more translated to St Asaph. He is chiefly famous for his controversy with J. *Priestley over the doctrines of the Trinity and Christ's Divinity in which he defended the traditional view that the pre-Nicene Church was unanimous in its theology of the Lord's consubstantiality with the Father. His many writings, largely on scientific and philological subjects, include *Providence and Free Agency* (1778), *The Analogy between the Light of Inspiration and the Light of Learning* (1787), *Tracts in controversy with Dr. Priestley* (1789), *An Apology for the Liturgy and Clergy* (1790), *Hosea translated . . . with Notes* (1801), and *The Book of Psalms translated* (1815; posthumous). He also published many separate sermons.

Sermons [ed. H. Horsley] (2 vols., Dublin, 1810) and later edns.; *The Speeches in Parliament of Samuel Horsley* [ed. id.] (ibid., 1813); *The Charges of Samuel Horsley . . . delivered at his Several Visitations of the Dioceses of St David's, Rochester, and St Asaph* (ibid., 1813). H. H. Jebb [great-grandson], *A Great Bishop of One Hundred Years Ago, being a Sketch of the Life of Samuel Horsley* (1909). F. C. Mather, *High Church Prophet: Bishop Samuel Horsley (1733–1806) and the Caroline Tradition in the Later Georgian Church* (Oxford, 1992). A. Gordon in *DNB* 27 (1891), pp. 383–6.

Hort, Fenton John Anthony (1828–92), NT scholar. Educated at Rugby under T. *Arnold and A. C. *Tait, and at Trinity College, Cambridge, he was from 1852 to 1857 a Fellow of his college, from 1857 to 1872 incumbent of St Ippolyts, near Hitchin, and from 1872 till his death back at Cambridge, where he held various appointments, incl. the Hulsean (1878–87) and the Lady Margaret (1887–92) professorships. In his early years at Cambridge he became a lifelong friend and fellow-worker of E. W. *Benson, J. B. *Lightfoot, and B. F. *Westcott, and also came under the influence of F. D. *Maurice, C. *Kingsley, Tom Hughes, and others, with whose social endeavours he was in sympathy. His original intention was to publish large-scale commentaries on the Gospels, Acts, and some of the *Catholic Epistles; but most of his energies were in fact diverted to the Greek text of the NT, at which he worked, in conjunction with Westcott, almost continuously from 1852 till its publication in 1881. His work in this field, summarized in his fine 'Introduction' to the Westcott–Hort NT, was remarkable for the accuracy and sobriety of his judgements. Its somewhat difficult style, combined with a modesty which often conceals the range of its writer's learning, can still hide its distinction and erudition from those who handle it for the first time. From 1882 to 1890 he was engaged, with Westcott and W. F. *Moulton, in preparing the RV of Wisdom and 2 Macc. Of the first importance also were his *Two Dissertations* (1876) on Μονογενὴς Θεός and the *Nicene-Constantinopolitan Creed, and his (posthumous) *Judaistic Christianity* (1894) and *The Christian Ecclesia* (1897). He contributed a number of major articles to the first volume of *DCB*. Hort had also wide and constructive interests in theology, esp. in its relations with the natural sciences, but these found little expression in writing. His *Hulsean Lectures for 1871, *The Way, the Truth, and the Life* (pub. posthumously, 1893), were an impressive essay in philosophical theology.

Life and Letters, ed. A. F. Hort, son (2 vols., London and New York, 1896); full review of this work, with appreciation of Hort, by W. *Sanday in *American Journal of Theology*, 1 (1897), pp. 95–117; further appreciation of Hort by T. B. Strong in *JTS* 1 (1900), pp. 370–86. E. G. Rupp, *Hort and the Cambridge Tradition* (Inaugural lecture; Cambridge, 1970). G. A. Patrick, *F. J. A. Hort, Eminent Victorian* (Sheffield, 1988). H. E. *Ryle in *DNB*, Suppl. 2 (1901), pp. 443–7.

Hosanna (Gk. ὡσαννά). The Greek form of the Hebrew petition הוֹשַׁע נָא ('Save, we beseech Thee'). It was used by the multitude when they proclaimed Jesus to be the Messiah on His triumphal entry into Jerusalem on *Palm Sunday (Mt. 21: 9, 15, Mk. 11: 9 f., Jn. 12: 13); and was thence introduced into the Christian liturgies at a very early date (e.g. *Didache 10. 6). The words 'Glory be to thee, O Lord, most High' in the *Sanctus of the Anglican BCP are a rendering of the *Hosanna in excelsis* ('Hosanna in the highest') in the medieval and modern Latin rite.

Hosea, Book of. One of the *Minor Prophets. Its author, Hosea, son of Beeri, was apparently a near-contemporary of *Amos, prophesying in the northern kingdom of Israel in the years preceding its decline and eventual fall to the Assyrians in *c.*721 BC. Like Amos, Hosea condemns the injustice and exploitation prevalent in Israelite society, but

his oracles seem to reflect a slightly later date in that social injustices of a more subtle kind have now given way to outright violence and the beginnings of the political and social anarchy which hastened the fall of the kingdom (cf. 2 Kgs. 15). Central to Hosea's condemnation of Israel is his opposition to the syncretistic worship of the sanctuaries, where Canaanite religious traditions—esp. those centring on fertility—had overlaid or perhaps even replaced the more austere religion of Yahweh. Appropriately enough, in view of the sexual character of these syncretistic rites, Hosea describes the national apostasy as 'adultery' or 'prostitution'. The opening chapters (1–3) relate incidents from the Prophet's own domestic life and draw a parallel between Hosea's relationship with his wife and Yahweh's relationship with Israel. The details are open to more than one interpretation, but it appears that Hosea had married a prostitute (perhaps employed in the fertility cult) as a symbol of Yahweh's own love for his disobedient and 'adulterous' people. Hosea is among the earliest biblical writers to use close human relationships as an illustration of the relationship between God and man, and his realization of God's character of love paved the way for Jewish and Christian teaching on the Fatherhood of God. While sharing Amos's conviction that Yahweh would punish Israel, Hosea (perhaps because of his experience in his own marriage) believed that Yahweh's covenant love would not allow Him to cast off Israel for good. Oracles promising a glorious future thus appear interwoven with others whose ferocity fully matches those of Amos. The Book appears to be very loosely structured, and there is no scholarly consensus on its literary development. The Hebrew text is among the most corrupt of all the Prophetic Books.

Comm. by G. A. F. Knight (Torch Bible Commentaries, London, 1960), H. W. Wolff (*Dodekapropheton*, 1; Biblischer Kommentar, Altes Testament, 14/1; Neukirchen, 1961; 3rd edn., 1976; Eng. tr., Philadelphia [1974]), W. Rudolph (KAT 13/1; 1966), J. L. Mays (London, 1969), F. I. Andersen and D. N. Freedman (Anchor Bible, 1980), G. I. Davies (New Cent. Bib., 1992), and A. A. Macintosh (ICC, 1997). H. W. Wolff, *Die Hochzeit der Hure* (Munich, 1979). K. Koch, *Die Profeten*, 1 [1978], pp. 88–105; Eng. tr. (1982), pp. 76–93; J. Blenkinsopp, *A History of Prophecy in Israel* (1984), pp. 96–106. J. Jeremias in *TRE* 15 (1986), pp. 586–98, s.v. 'Hosea/Hoseabuch', with extensive bibl.

Hosius (or Ossius) (*c.*256–357/8), Bp. of Córdoba. He was consecrated Bp. of Córdoba *c.*295, and suffered in the persecution under Maximian. He took part in the Council of *Elvira and from 313 to the Council of *Nicaea seems to have acted as ecclesiastical adviser to the Emp. *Constantine. In the early stages of the Arian controversy he was sent to *Alexandria to investigate the dispute between *Alexander and *Arius, and it was apparently in consequence of his report that the Emperor summoned the Nicene Council. He prob. presided over the Council of *Antioch in 325, and played an important role at the Nicene Council. He also presided at the anti-Arian Council of *Sardica in 343. In 355 he was banished to Sirmium for his support of St *Athanasius, and from his exile addressed to Constantius a letter in which, on the basis of Mt: 22: 21, he affirmed the independence of ecclesiastical authority from political power. At the Synod of *Sirmium (357) he succumbed to pressure to the extent that he signed the 'Blasphemy' which involved communicating with the Arians and was allowed in consequence to return to his diocese. Acc. to Athanasius, he repudiated his action at Sirmium before his death, though W. writers provide no confirmation of this statement.

Primary sources (scattered) incl. Athanasius, *Hist. Ar.* 42–5; id., *Apol. c. Ar.* 89; id., *De Fuga*, 5; *Hilary, *Fragmenta*, 2 and 6; id., *De Synodis*, 10 f.; *Socrates, *HE* 2. 31. V. C. De Clercq, CICM, *Ossius of Cordova: A Contribution to the History of the Constantinian Period* (Catholic University of America Studies in Christian Antiquity, 13; 1954). U. Domínguez del Val, OSA, 'Osio de Córdoba', *Rivista Española de Teología*, 18 (1958), pp. 141–65 and 261–81. H. Chadwick, 'Ossius of Cordova and the Presidency of the Council of Antioch, 325', *JTS* NS 9 (1958), pp. 292–304, repr. in his *History and Thought of the Early Church* (1982), no. 10. M. Aubineau, SJ, 'La Vie grecque de "saint" Ossius de Cordoue', *Anal. Boll.* 78 (1960), pp. 356–61. For the spelling 'Ossius' see C. H. *Turner in *JTS* 12 (1910–11), pp. 275–7. *CPL* (3rd edn., 1995), pp. 188 f. (nos. 537–9a). M. Simonetti in Quasten (cont.), *Patrology*, 4 (1986), pp. 61 f., with bibl. T. D. C. Morse in *DCB* 3 (1882), pp. 162–74.

Hosius (or in Polish **Hozjusz**), **Stanislaus** (1504–79), Polish cardinal. He was a native of Cracow, of German origin, and studied law at Cracow, at *Bologna, where he came into touch with R. *Pole, and at Padua. Active at first as a royal secretary and *Erasmian Humanist, he was not ordained priest until 1543; after holding several benefices, in 1549 he was appointed Bp. of Kulm (in Polish Chetmno). In 1551 he was translated to the diocese of Ermland (in Polish Warmia), where one of his chief tasks was the fight against Protestantism. Here he preached extensively in Latin, Polish, and German. In 1552–3 he published his chief work, the *Confessio Catholicae Fidei Christiana*, in which he contrasted the Catholic dogmas with the opposing beliefs of the Reformers and endeavoured to prove from Scripture and tradition that Catholicism and Christianity were identical. The work had a great success, over 30 editions and many translations appearing in the author's lifetime. Among other controversial writings that followed were his *Confutatio Prolegomenorum Brentii* (1558) against the Württembergian *Lutheran theologian, J. *Brenz, which had a preface by St Peter *Canisius, and *De Expresso Dei Verbo* (1558), in which he claimed to demonstrate the necessity of an authoritative interpretation of Scripture. In 1558 *Paul IV called him to Rome as his adviser on the religious affairs of Poland and Prussia, and in 1560 *Pius IV appointed him nuncio to Ferdinand I. In this capacity he prepared the reopening of the Council of *Trent and brought back to the RC Church the Emperor's son, Maximilian, who had come under the influence of Protestant preachers. In 1561 he was created cardinal and appointed Papal legate at Trent, where he was entrusted esp. with the leadership in the doctrinal discussions. At the Council he vigorously upheld the primacy of the Pope. After returning to his diocese in 1564, he published the decrees of Trent at the Synod of Parczew (1564) and invited the *Jesuits to open a college, the later 'Lyceum Hosianum', at Braunsberg (in Polish Braniewo). In 1566 he was nominated legate *a latere* by *Pius V, and from 1569 resided in Rome as the permanent Polish representative. He upheld the use of violence against heretics, but in private life he was a man of a simple and unworldly faith.

Editio princeps of his collected works, Paris, 1562; the best edn. (still incomplete) is that pub. in 2 vols. fol., Cologne, 1584. Modern edns. of selections of his correspondence by F. Hipler and V. Zakrzewski [up to 1558] (Acta Historica Res Gestas Poloniae Illustrantia ab Anno 1507 ad Annum 1795, 4, 9, parts 1 and 2; Editionum Collegii Historici Academiae Litterarum Cracoviensis, 15, 34, 40; Cracow, 1879–88) and S. Steinherz (Nuntiaturberichte aus Deutschland, 1560–72, nebst ergänzenden Actenstücken, Zweite Abt., Bd 1; Vienna, 1897). Correspondence with Albert, Duke of Prussia, on the Council of Trent (1560–2), ed. E. M. Wermter (Reformationsgeschichtliche Studien und Texte, 82; 1957). Early Life (in Lat.) by S. Rescius (his secretary, Rome, 1587; repr. in edn. of his letters by F. Hipler and V. Zakrzewski, cited above, vol. 1, pp. ii–cxxiv). Modern studies by A. Eichhorn (2 vols., Kirchheim, 1854–5), B. Elsner (Königsberg, 1911), and J. Lortz (Braunsberg, 1931). S. Frankl, *Doctrina Hosii de Notis Ecclesiae, in luce s. XVI considerata* (Rome, 1934); L. Bernacki, *La Doctrine de l'Église chez le Cardinal Hosius* (1936). G. Grabka, 'Cardinal Hosius and the Council of Trent', *Theological Studies*, 7 (1946), pp. 558–76. F. J. Zdrodowski, *The Concept of Heresy according to Cardinal Hosius* (Catholic University of America, Studies in Sacred Theology, 2nd ser. 2; Washington, DC, 1947). G. H. Williams, 'Stanislaus Hosius', in J. Raitt (ed.), *Shapers of Religious Traditions in Germany, Switzerland, and Poland, 1560–1600* [1981], pp. 157–74. A. Humbert in *DTC* 7 (pt. 1; 1922), cols. 178–90, s.v.; W. Urban in *Polski Słownik Biograficzny*, 10 (Warsaw, 1962–4), pp. 42–6, s.v. 'Hozjusz'.

Hoskyns, Sir Edwyn Clement (1884–1937), Anglican biblical scholar. He was educated at Jesus College, Cambridge, and on the Continent, where he heard A. *Harnack and became a friend of A. *Schweitzer. From 1919 till his death he was Dean of Chapel of Corpus Christi College, Cambridge. He made a name by his essay 'The Christ of the Synoptic Gospels' in *Essays Catholic and Critical (1926), in which he argued that the so-called 'historical Jesus' of liberal Protestantism was unhistorical, and that the teaching behind the Synoptic Gospels was much more complex and 'Catholic' than was generally supposed by liberal NT critics. *The Riddle of the New Testament* (1931; 3rd edn., 1947), written in collaboration with F. N. Davey, deals with the principles underlying the critical and historical study of the NT. In these studies Hoskyns passed from a *Modernist position, influenced by A. Schweitzer and A. *Loisy, to an objective and dogmatic attitude. Later he took over much from K. *Barth, whose *Commentary on Romans* he translated (1933). In his posthumously published work, *The Fourth Gospel* (ed. F. N. Davey, 1940), he upheld the unity of St John's Gospel; he was concerned esp. to bring out the theological meaning of the whole, making full use both of patristic and modern exegetical works.

His sermons ed. with a memoir by C. H. Smyth, *Cambridge Sermons* (1938). *Crucifixion–Resurrection: The Pattern of the Theology and Ethics of the New Testament* by Hoskyns and F. N. Davey [orig. conceived as a sequel to the *Riddle of the New Testament*] was ed. after Davey's death by G. S. Wakefield (1981), with biog. introd., pp. 27–81. R. E. Parsons, *Sir Edwyn Hoskyns as a Biblical Theologian* [1985]. J. O. Cobham in *DNB*, *1931–1940*, pp. 448 f., s.v.

Hosmer, Frederick Lucian (1840–1929), American hymn writer. Born at Framingham, Mass., he was educated at Harvard. He was ordained in the *Unitarian ministry in 1869 and held charges at Quincy, Ill. (1872–7), Cleveland, Ohio (1878–92), St Louis (1894–9), and at

Berkeley, Calif. (1899–1904). In 1908 he delivered a series of lectures on Church hymnody at Harvard Divinity School, of which he was president for the year 1920–1. His hymns had a wide appeal, esp. among adherents of the emancipated liberal theology of the late 19th cent. They include 'Not always on the Mount may we', 'O beautiful my country', 'O Name all other names above', and 'Thy Kingdom come, On bended knee'. They were mainly published in three series of *The Thought of God in Hymns and Poems*, which he edited in conjunction with W. C. Gannett (1885, 1894, and 1918). He also issued *Way of Life* (1877) for use in Sunday schools and, with W. C. Gannett and J. V. Blake, edited *Unity Hymns and Carols* (1880, enlarged 1911).

H. E. Starr in *Dict. Amer. Biog.* 9 (1932), pp. 241 f.

hospice movement. See DYING, CARE OF THE.

Hospitallers (also **Knights Hospitaller**). At the end of the 11th cent. the headquarters of the order was a hospital at *Jerusalem which became dedicated to St *John the Baptist; hence its members were more fully described as 'Knights of the Order of the Hospital of St John of Jerusalem'. After 1310 they were also known as the **Knights of Rhodes**, and from 1530 as the **Knights of Malta**.

The origins of the order are to be found in the establishment c.1080 of a hospice for pilgrims by the old *Benedictine Abbey of S. Maria Latina in Jerusalem. Its first historical personage is Master Gerard, under whom, after the successes of the *Crusaders in 1099, the order greatly developed and obtained Papal sanction. Its original concern was the care of the sick poor, and its ideal of treating the poor as 'lords' and the medical practices in its hospitals were to have significant influence in medieval Europe, but under its second Master, Raymond du Puy (1120–1158/60) it developed a wing of brother knights, probably in imitation of the Knights *Templar (q.v.). All members of the order were bound by the three religious vows, together with a fourth: to be serfs and slaves of their lords the sick. They were divided into three classes: brother knights, from whom the Master was always drawn, at least from the 13th cent.; brother sergeants, -at arms and -at service, who did not need to have the qualifications, by birth and arms, of knights; and brother priests. The great officer in charge of the hospital, the Hospitaller, was always a knight. Nursing was performed by the sergeants-at-service. The order employed surgeons and physicians. There were also sisters of St John, who lived in enclosed communities as *canonesses regular. From the early 12th cent. the order was being granted properties in W. Europe. It developed a provincial structure of priories and subordinate commanderies to manage these and to transmit funds to the central convent in the East. The brothers shared both the successes and the defeats of the Crusaders; and after the fall of Acre (1291) they escaped to Cyprus and subsequently conquered Rhodes (1309), which became the centre of their activities for the next 200 years. Their power and wealth increased greatly after the suppression of the Templars (1312), whose possessions were assigned to the Hospitallers by the Pope. Their principal achievements during this period were their exploits against the Turks, notably the victorious defence of Rhodes by the Grand Master Pierre d'Aubusson in 1480 and that of

1522 against Suleiman II which ended in honourable defeat. After being without a home for seven years the order received the island of Malta from *Charles V in 1530. The knights continued fighting the Turks in many battles and in 1571 took part in the battle of *Lepanto. The 17th and 18th cents. saw the decline of the order in morals and discipline, culminating in the surrender of Malta to Napoleon in 1798. It now devotes itself to the maintenance of hospitals and still has knights under obedience to a Grand Master. Its distinctive sign is the eight-pointed *Maltese cross. Since the Malta period the order has been treated by many states and in international law as a sovereign entity.

There are four other recognized Orders of St John. Those in Germany, *Sweden, and the *Netherlands descend from a province in N. Germany which maintained its existence as a Protestant order after the Reformation. In England the property of the Grand Priory was sequestered in 1540. Apart from a brief revival under *Mary, the English Langue of the Hospitallers remained dormant with a series of non-resident titular priors, the last of whom held office from 1806 to 1815. In the 1820s, however, the French Knights of Malta, seeking money, men, and material for a scheme to reconquer an island in the E. Mediterranean in alliance with the Greeks who were in rebellion against their Turkish overlords, re-established an English branch on a mainly Anglican basis. A royal charter of 1888 constituted it an order of chivalry, with the sovereign as its head, and a charter of 1926 authorized the creation of priories and commanderies in other countries of the Commonwealth. The order was responsible for the foundation of the St John's Ambulance Association in 1877, the St John Ophthalmic Hospital in Jerusalem in 1882, and the St John Ambulance Brigade in 1888.

The term 'Hospitallers' is sometimes used in a wider sense, e.g. to include the *Brothers Hospitallers (q.v.) founded by St *John of God.

J. Delaville Le Roulx (ed.), *Cartulaire général de l'ordre de S. Jean de Jérusalem, 1100–1310* (4 vols., 1894–1906). Id., *Les Hospitaliers en Terre Sainte et à Chypre, 1100–1310* (1904); id., *Les Hospitaliers à Rhodes jusqu'à la mort de Philibert de Naillac, 1310–1421* (1913; repr., with introd. by A. T. Luttrell, London, 1974). Id., 'Les Statuts de l'ordre de l'hôpital de Saint-Jean de Jérusalem', *Bibliothèque de l'École des Chartes*, 48 (1887), pp. 342–56, and other works by the same author. E. J. King, *The Rule, Statutes, and Customs of the Hospitallers 1099–1319* [in Eng. tr.] (1934). R. Hiestand (ed.), *Papsturkunden für Templer und Johanniter* (Abh. (Gött.), Dritte Folge, 77 and 135; 1972–84). M. Gervers (ed.), *The Cartulary of the Knights of St John of Jerusalem in England: Secunda Camera, Essex* (Records of Social and Economic History, NS 6 [1982]), with refs. to earlier edns. of records of English Hospitallers. J. Riley-Smith, *The Knights of St John in Jerusalem and Cyprus c.1050–1310* (1967), with bibl. A. J. Forey, 'Constitutional Conflict and Change in the Hospital of St John during the Twelfth and Thirteenth Centuries', *JEH* 33 (1982), pp. 15–29; T. S. Miller, 'The Knights of Saint John and the Hospitals of the Latin West', *Speculum* 53 (1978), pp. 709–33. A. [T.] Luttrell, 'The Hospitallers at Rhodes, 1306–1421', in K. M. Setton (ed.), *A History of the Crusades*, 3 (Madison, Wis., 1975), pp. 278–313, repr. in Luttrell, *The Hospitallers in Cyprus, Rhodes, Greece and the West 1291–1400* (1978), no. 1; other relevant papers repr. in this volume and id., *Latin Greece, the Hospitallers and the Crusades 1291–1400* (1982), nos. 1–5. R. Cavaliero, *The Last of the Crusaders: The Knights of St John and Malta in the Eighteenth Century* (1960). [H. T.] M. de Pierredon, *Histoire politique de l'Ordre Sou-*

verain des Hospitaliers de Saint-Jean de Jérusalem, dit de Malte, depuis la chute de Malte jusqu'à nos jours (1926; much enlarged 2nd edn., *Histoire politique de l'Ordre Souverain de Saint-Jean de Jérusalem . . . de 1798 à 1955*, vols. 1–2 [to 1830], 1956–63). E. J. King, *The Grand Priory of the Order of the Hospital of St John of Jerusalem in England* (1924; 3rd edn., entitled *The Knights of St John in the British Realm*, by H. Luke, 1967).

hospitals. Christian hospitals were founded throughout E. Christendom from the 4th cent. onwards, and became exceedingly numerous in W. Europe during the earlier Middle Ages, when they were commonly associated with the monastic orders. From the earliest times different types were instituted to meet different problems, e.g. those of orphans, the sick, the aged, and the impotent poor. With some notable exceptions, e.g. St Bartholomew's Hospital, London (begun 1123), the medieval hospitals of England were for the most part almshouses for the aged. By the close of the 15th cent. a large proportion of these had been allowed to perish or to survive only in decadent forms. The secularization of the Reformation period interfered only temporarily with the hospitals of Europe, and numbers of important foundations by rulers, municipalities, and Christian societies took place in the 17th and 18th cents.

T. S. Miller, *The Birth of the Hospital in the Byzantine Empire* (Henry E. Sigerist Supplements to the Bulletin of History of Medicine, NS 10; Baltimore and London [1985]). R. M. Clay, *The Mediaeval Hospitals of England* (1909); W. H. Godfrey, *The English Almshouse, with some account of its predecessor, the Medieval Hospital* (1955); B. [J.] Bailey, *Almshouses* (1988); B. Howson, *Houses of Noble Poverty: A History of the English Almshouse* (Sunbury-on-Thames, 1993). J. Imbert, *Les Hôpitaux en droit canonique (du décret de Gratien à la sécularisation de l'administration de l'Hôtel-Dieu de Paris en 1505)* (L'Église et l'État au Moyen Age, 8; 1947). M. Mollat, *Les Pauvres au Moyen Age: Étude sociale* [1978], esp. pp. 165–91, with bibl. pp. 378–80. J. J. Walsh in *CE* 7 (1910), pp. 480–8, s.v.; E. Nasalli-Rocca and A. B. McPadden in *NCE* 7 (1967), pp. 159–66, s.v. 'Hospitals, History of'; U. Lindgren and E. Kislinger in *Lexikon des Mittelalters*, 5 (1991), cols. 133–7, s.v. 'Hospital', with bibl.

Host (Lat. *hostia*). A sacrificial victim, and so the consecrated bread in the *Eucharist, regarded as the Sacrifice of the Body of Christ.

Hostiensis (*c.*1200–71), canonist. Henry de Bartholomaeis, or Henry of Susa from his birthplace in NW Italy, was commonly known as Hostiensis because he was Cardinal-Bishop of Ostia. He ranks high among medieval canonists and was a prolific, even verbose, writer as well as being active internationally in diplomatic and government affairs, both secular and ecclesiastical. He is mentioned by *Dante in *Paradiso*, 12. 83. He studied law at *Bologna, lectured on the *Decretals at *Paris, and held benefices in England and Provence. He was Bp. of Sisteron (1244–50) and Abp. of Embrun (1250–62), both in Provence, before he was created Cardinal-Bishop of Ostia by Pope Urban IV in 1262. Outstanding among his works are his *Summa* and his *Apparatus* or *Lectura* on the Decretals of *Gregory IX. He began both works while teaching at Paris, completing the *Summa* by 1253 and the vast and intricate *Apparatus* only shortly before his death. Possibly less theological in tone than the *Apparatus*, the *Summa* provides a synthesis of canon and Roman law, designed to be of practical

use. It enjoyed great success, often being described as the *Summa Aurea* (the 'Golden *Summa*'), and was the *vade-mecum* of canonists until the 17th cent. His writings embody a wealth of personal experience and rest on a thorough grasp of sources; they contain a detailed analysis of Papal power.

There are no modern edns. of his works, though the 1581 Venice edn. of the *Apparatus* was repr. at Turin in 1965. For details of MSS and edns., see J. F. von Schulte, *Die Geschichte der Quellen und Literatur des Canonischen Rechts von Gratian bis auf die Gegenwart*, 2 (Stuttgart, 1875), pp. 123–9. C. Gallagher, SJ, *Canon Law and the Christian Community: The Role of Law in the Church according to the Summa Aurea of Cardinal Hostiensis* (Analecta Gregoriana, 208; Rome, 1978). C. Lefebvre, ' "Aequitas Canonica" et "Periculum Animae" dans la Doctrine de l'Hostiensis', *Ephemerides Iuris Canonici*, 8 (Rome, 1952), pp. 305–21. J. A. Watt, *The Theory of Papal Monarchy in the Thirteenth Century: The Contribution of the Canonists* [1965], pp. 107–33. C. Lefebvre in *DDC* 5 (1953), cols. 1211–27; id. in *NCE* 7 (1967), pp. 170 f., both s.v.

Hours, Canonical. The times of daily prayer laid down in the Divine *Office, and esp. the services appointed to be recited at these times. In the W. Church, the seven commonly recognized Hours have traditionally been *Mattins and *Lauds (reckoned as a single hour), *Prime, *Terce, *Sext, *None, *Vespers, and *Compline (qq.v.). The whole pattern of daily prayer, however, was much simplified in the 1971 Breviary. See OFFICE, DIVINE.

Housel. A medieval English name for the Eucharist, perhaps descended from a Teutonic stem meaning 'holy'. In *Ulphilas' rendering of Mt. 9: 13, a similar word (*hunsl*) is used for 'sacrifice'.

The 'houselling cloth' was the (late medieval) long white linen cloth spread before, or held by, the communicants at the time of receiving the Sacrament. It has survived continuously at St Mary the Virgin's, Oxford, at Wimborne Minister, and perhaps in a few other places. It has been restored in some other Anglican churches in modern times. In the RC Church the use of such a cloth was ordered by the '*Rituale Romanum' (4. 2. 1) but tended to become obsolete after 1929, when the Sacred Congregation for the Discipline of the Sacraments directed that a small metal plate should be held before communicants.

Arts. 'Housel' and 'Houseling' in *OED* (2nd edn.), 7 (1989), pp. 444 f.

Howard, John (*c.*1726–90), English philanthropist and prison reformer. A man of Evangelical piety, he was a moderate *Calvinist and though his second wife was a Churchwoman and he accompanied her to the local parish church, he remained a Dissenter (Independent) throughout his life. He maintained a wide religious acquaintance and his belief in the transforming power of religion motivated his reforming activity. In 1773 he became High Sheriff of Bedford, where what he saw of the terrible afflictions of both tried and untried in the county gaol inspired him to his work of prison reform. His first step (1774) was to secure official salaries for gaolers, who had hitherto depended on fees extorted from the prisoners. He then visited numerous prisons and lazarettos (quarantine hospitals) in England and throughout Europe, regardless of the dangers of entering infectious dwellings and noxious cells. His writings included *The State of the Prisons in England and Wales* (1777) and an *Account of the Principal Lazarettos in Europe* (1789).

The Howard League for Penal Reform, a small voluntary society, was founded in memory of John Howard in 1866. Its objectives include 'study and research into the treatment of offenders and the prevention of crime'. It championed the abolition of capital punishment and corporal punishment long before these subjects became popular issues, and it was largely instrumental in bringing about the provision of payment of prisoners for work done in prison and the institution of Legal Aid.

Howard's *State of the Prisons* and *Account of the Principal Lazarettos* were repr. as *Prisons and Lazarettos*, with introd. by R. W. England (2 vols., Montclair, NJ, 1973); *State of the Prisons*, also repr. in facsimile (Abingdon, 1977); and abridged, with some extracts from the vol. on lazarettos, by K. Ruck for Everyman's Library, no. 835 (1929). Principal biogs. by J. Aikin, *A View of the Character and Public Services of the late John Howard* (1792), and J. B. Brown, *Memoirs of the Public and Private Life of John Howard the Philanthropist* (1818). [W.] H. Dixon, *John Howard and the Prison-World of Europe* (1849), contrasts with J. Field, *The Life of John Howard* (1850), and id., *Correspondence of John Howard* (1855). Other studies by J. Stoughton (London, 1884), D. L. Howard (ibid., 1958), M. Southwood (ibid., 1958), and G. Pleuger (Bedford [1990]). R. Morgan, 'Divine Philanthropy: John Howard Reconsidered', *History*, 62 (1977), pp. 388–410; L. Radzinowicz, 'John Howard', in J. C. Freshman (ed.), *Prisons Past and Future* (Cambridge Studies in Criminology, 41; 1978), pp. 7–13, with other studies on Howard, pp. 15–51. Bibl. by L. Baumgartner in *Bulletin of the History of Medicine*, 7 (1939), pp. 486–534 and 595–626. G. F. R. Barker in *DNB* 28 (1891), pp. 44–8.

Howe, John (1630–1705), *Puritan divine and writer. In 1650 he became chaplain (though apparently unordained), and a little later Fellow, of Magdalen College, Oxford. In 1652 he was ordained by the Puritan rector of Winwick, whom he looked up to as a 'primitive bishop'. In 1654 he became incumbent of Great Torrington, Devon, and in 1657 O. *Cromwell made him his domestic chaplain, an office which he continued to hold under Richard Cromwell. On the latter's resignation he returned to Great Torrington, from which he was ejected in 1662 on the passing of the Act of *Uniformity. Unlike most of his contemporary fellow *Nonconformists, his standpoint inclined to *Latitudinarianism. After some years of wandering he published in 1668 *The Blessedness of the Righteous Discoursed from Psal. 17, 15*, which brought him to the notice of Lord Massereene, and in 1670 he became his chaplain at Antrim Castle with the approval of the bishop of the diocese. In 1676 he was appointed co-pastor of the Presbyterian congregation at Haberdashers' Hall in London, where he continued his publications and lived on friendly terms with eminent Anglicans. In 1685, owing to the increasing severity of measures against the Nonconformists, he went abroad, settling in 1686 at Utrecht, but in 1687 he returned to England to minister to his flock under the protection of *James II's first *Declaration of Indulgence. After the Revolution, he headed the deputation of Nonconformist ministers who congratulated William III in Jan. 1689. He continued to work for mutual forbearance among Christians of differing denominations, and unsuccessfully sought to unite the *Presbyterians and *Congregationalists.

Works (2 vols., London, 1724), with Memoir by E. *Calamy, vol. 1, pp. 1–88; new edn., 3 vols., ibid., 1848. Works also ed. J. Hunt (8 vols., ibid., 1810–22); Posthumous Works, ed. id. (4 vols., ibid., 1832); also pub., with general introd. by H. Rogers, by *Religious Tract Society (6 vols., 1862–3). H. Rogers, *The Life and Character of John Howe with an Analysis of his Writings* (1836); R. F. Horton, *John Howe* (1895). N. H. Keeble, *The Literary Culture of Nonconformity in Later Seventeenth-Century England* (Leicester, 1987), *passim*. A. Gordon in *DNB* 28 (1891), pp. 85–8.

Howells, Herbert Norman (1892–1983), English composer. He joined the staff of the Royal College of Music in London in 1920 and taught composition there for over 50 years. He was also Director of Music at St Paul's Girls' School in Hammersmith (1936–62) and King Edward VII Professor of Music at London University (1954–64). His masterpiece is the choral-orchestral *Hymnus Paradisi*, written in 1938 in memory of his son, and first performed at the Three Choirs Festival in *Gloucester in 1950. He is chiefly known for his choral and organ music that has provided English 20th-cent. Church music with one of its most distinctive sounds. Especially notable is the long series of service settings written for specific cathedral and collegiate choirs, beginning with the 'Collegium Regale' set for King's College, Cambridge, *c*.1944. His anthems include the well-known 'Like as the hart' and 'O pray for the peace of Jerusalem'. The hymn-tune *Michael* and his early Christmas *carol 'A spotless rose' achieved wide popularity.

R. Spearing, *H.H.: A Tribute to Herbert Howells on his Eightieth Birthday* (1972). C. Palmer, *Herbert Howells: A centenary celebration* (1992). K. R. Long, *The Music of the English Church* (1972), pp. 428–30. H. Ottaway in S. Sadie (ed.), *The New Grove Dictionary of Music and Musicians*, 8 (1980), pp. 746 f., s.v.

Howley, William (1766–1848), Abp. of *Canterbury. He was the last 'Prince-Archbishop', the revenues of the archiepiscopal see coming under the control of the *Ecclesiastical Commissioners at his death. Educated at Winchester and at New College, Oxford, he was appointed Regius Professor of Divinity at Oxford in 1809, Bp. of London in 1813, and Abp. of Canterbury in 1828. An 18th-cent. *High Churchman and an extreme Tory, he was opposed to political reform and relief for RCs and Jews, and it was largely his influence that secured the rejection of Lord John Russell's moderate education scheme in 1839. Though he at first supported the *Oxford Movement, he lost sympathy with it when it was perceived as encouraging 'Romish' tendencies, esp. after 1845. On the death of William IV (1837), whom he had attended on his sick-bed, it fell to him to announce to the Princess Victoria (whom he had baptized when he was Bp. of London) her accession to the Crown.

B. Harrison, *The Remembrance of a departed Guide and Ruler in the Church of God: A Charge delivered to the Clergy of the Archdeaconry of Maidstone* (1848). E. [F.] Carpenter, *Cantuar: The Archbishops and their Office* (1971; 2nd edn., Oxford, 1988), pp. 290–9. G. F. R. Barker in *DNB* 28 (1891), pp. 128 f.

Howson, John Saul (1816–85), Dean of *Chester. He was educated at Giggleswick School and Trinity College, Cambridge. After ordination he taught at Liverpool Collegiate Institute, where W. J. *Conybeare was headmaster, succeeding him in 1849. From 1867 till his death, he was Dean of Chester, where he laboured for the restoration of the fabric of the cathedral and for schools in the city. He is best known for his *Life and Epistles of St Paul* (2 vols., 1852), in which he collaborated with Conybeare. This book, based on extensive geographical, archaeological, and historical studies, was an impressive work of scholarship for its time, learned yet not beyond the general reader. Most of the descriptive passages were done by Howson. He also wrote other Pauline studies, as well as works on other NT subjects. An article on 'Deaconesses in the Church of England' in the *Quarterly Review* (1861), re-issued in 1862 as a pamphlet, did much to promote the systematized ministry of women in England.

E. Venables in *DNB* 28 (1891), pp. 130–2.

Hrabanus Maurus. See RABANUS MAURUS.

Hrosvit (10th cent.), German Christian poetess. Of a noble Saxon family, she became a *canoness of the abbey of Gandersheim in Saxony. She was very learned and well versed not only in Scripture and the Fathers but also in classical literature—Horace, Virgil, Ovid, Plautus, and esp. Terence, whom, acc. to her own admission, she took as her model. The MS of her writings, in Latin, was discovered by the humanist, Conrad Celtis, at Ratisbon and printed for the first time in 1501. Originally her works were divided into three parts containing 8 poems on saints, 6 plays, and a long panegyric on the Ottos which was left unfinished. Among the poems on saints the 'Passio Sancti Pelagii' is esp. interesting, since she claims to have derived her facts from an eye-witness of the martyrdom. It is printed in full by the *Bollandists in the '*Acta Sanctorum'. Other poems treat of the BVM, St *Basil, St *Dionysius of Paris (identified with *Dionysius the Areopagite), and St *Agnes. The main object of her plays was to oppose to Terence's representations of the frailty of women the chastity of Christian virgins and penitents. 'Gallicanus', 'Dulcitius', and 'Sapientia' describe the steadfastness of martyrs, whereas 'Calimachus', 'Abraham', and 'Paphnutius' deal with the struggle between the spirit and the flesh; and many of them reveal a remarkable sense of the dramatic. She was greatly encouraged by the scholars of her time, but soon after her death almost completely forgotten. In modern times she has once more aroused much interest.

Editio princeps by C. Celtis (Nuremberg, 1501); modern edns. by K. Strecker (Teub., 2nd edn., 1930) and H. Homeyer (Munich, 1970), and of her plays (with Ital. tr.) by F. Bertini (Milan, 1986), with introd. by P. Dronke. Eng. trs. of her plays by H. J. W. Tillyard (London, 1923) and K. [M.] Wilson (Saskatoon, 1986; rev. edn., New York and London, 1989), and of her non-dramatic works by Sister M. G. Wiegand (St Louis, 1936). A. L. Haight (ed.), *Hroswitha of Gandersheim* (New York, 1965), with extensive bibl. Other modern studies incl. those by B. Nagel (Stuttgart, 1965) and K. M. Wilson (Davis Medieval Texts and Studies, 7; Leiden, etc., 1988). Manitius, 1, pp. 619–32.

Hsi-an-Fu. See SIGAN-FU STONE.

Huber, Samuel (*c*.1547–1624), Protestant controversialist. A native of Burgdorf, near Berne, he took an active part in a series of religious disputes, generally defending *Lutheran doctrines against the *Calvinism of the Swiss Reformed Church. He caused special offence by his assertion of Christ's universal *atonement ('Christum Jesum esse mortuum pro peccatis totius generis humani'), and was banished from Switzerland on 28 June 1588. Shortly afterwards he signed the 'Formula of *Concord' (1580) and for a time held offices in the Lutheran Church in Germany until this too found his teaching on the atonement too extreme. The title 'Huberianism' was widely given to doctrines of the atonement identical with or similar to those which Huber advocated.

J. A. Schmid, *De Samuelis Huberi Vita Fatis et Doctrina* (Helmstedt, 1708), with full list of his works. G. Adam, *Der Streit um die Prädestination im ausgehenden 16. Jahrhundert: Eine Untersuchung zu den Entwürfen von Samuel Huber und Aegidius Hunnius* (Beiträge zur Geschichte und Lehre der Reformierten Kirche, 30; Neukirchen [1970]). K. R. Hagenbach and G. Müller in *PRE* (3rd edn.), 8 (1900), pp. 409–12, with bibl.

Hubert, St (*c*.657–727), 'Apostle of the Ardennes'. Perhaps of noble birth, he was a disciple of St *Lambert and active in missionary work in the middle Meuse region. He succeeded Lambert as Bp. of Tongeren/Maastricht in 705/6, and in 718 he had his relics moved from Maastricht to Liège and placed in a church dedicated to him (built four years earlier). The see was moved to Liège in 717/18. In 824 Hubert's bones were transferred from Liège to the monastery of *Andagium* (presumably St-Hubert in the Ardennes), which became a centre of pilgrimage; in the 9th cent. his cult spread to N. France and the Low Countries, and many religious houses were dedicated to him. The story (originally told of St *Eustace) that while hunting he saw a stag with a crucifix between its antlers, is not found before the 15th cent. He is the patron saint of huntsmen (with St Eustace), of furriers, metalworkers, and butchers, and is invoked against hydrophobia. Feast day, 3 Nov.

AASS, Nov. 1 (1887), pp. 759–930, with seven Lives; crit. edn. of the earliest, written soon after 744, by W. Levison in *MGH*, Scriptores Rerum Merovingicarum, 6 (1913), pp. 471–96. M. Coens, SJ, 'Notes sur la légende de S. Hubert', *Anal. Boll.* 45 (1927), pp. 345–62 (with review of recent lit.). T. Réjalot, OSB, *Le Culte et les reliques de saint Hubert* (Gembloux, 1928). F. Baix, 'Saint Hubert. Sa mort, sa canonisation, ses reliques', in *Mélanges Félix Rousseau: Études sur l'histoire du pays mosan au moyen âge* (Brussels, 1958), pp. 71–80, with refs. Modern studies by L. Huyghebaert (Antwerp, 1949) and A. Paffrath (Hamburg and Berlin, 1961). M. Werner, *Der Lütticher Raum in frühkarolingischer Zeit* (Göttingen, 1980), pp. 275–80.

Hubert Walter (d. 1205), Abp. of *Canterbury. A nephew and protégé of Ranulf Glanvill, justiciar of England under Henry II, Hubert was already a clerk experienced in the judicial and administrative business of Church and State when he became Dean of *York in 1186. Except for bishoprics, this was the highest office open to a secular clerk in the English Church. Three years later, when King Richard succeeded his father, Hubert became Bp. of *Salisbury. In 1190 he accompanied Abp. *Baldwin on the Third *Crusade; he was much praised for his capacity as a military leader, a diplomat, and a provident organizer of the Crusading army. After the Crusade, as the King's nominee he became Abp. of Canterbury in 1193. He negotiated Richard's release from captivity, and organized his ransom. In the King's absence overseas, Hubert was vicegerent of England, with the office of justiciar, from Dec. 1193 to July 1198. For part of this time he was also Papal legate for England and Wales, having been appointed by *Celestine III in March 1195. After Celestine's death in 1198, *Innocent III did not renew Hubert's legatine commission and Hubert resigned the justiciarship, thereafter held by a layman. But both in Church and State he continued to exert unequalled authority and influence. King *John made him chancellor in May 1199 and Innocent III relied on him greatly in major lawsuits and all other matters affecting the English Church. Many contemporaries noted his thirst for power and wealth, and his ruthless treatment of opponents was condemned by others besides *Giraldus Cambrensis. As leader of the English Church he did not neglect his ecclesiastical duties. His pontificate saw important advances in the practice of Church courts and in the conduct of various kinds of ecclesiastical business, such as canonical *visitations by bishops and legislation in Church councils. He was also instrumental in persuading Innocent III to canonize two English saints (*Gilbert of Sempringham and *Wulfstan of Worcester).

His official letters as Abp. ed. C. R. Cheney and E. John, *English Episcopal Acta*, 3 (1986). The correspondence over his foundation of a collegiate church at *Lambeth, which caused friction with the monks of Christ Church, Canterbury, is pr. in W. Stubbs (ed.), *Chronicles and Memorials of the Reign of Richard I*, 2: Epistolae Cantuarienses (RS, 1865), pp. 366–538. The constitutions of his legatine council at York in 1195 and his provincial council at Westminster in 1200 ed. D. Whitelock, M. Brett, and C. N. L. Brooke, *Councils & Synods* ... 1, A.D. 871–1204, 2 (Oxford, 1981), pp. 1042–52 and 1055–74. Modern accounts of Hubert's activities by C. R. Cheney, *Hubert Walter* (1967), and C. R. Young, *Hubert Walter, Lord of Canterbury and Lord of England* (Durham, NC, 1968). In a broader setting, see C. R. Cheney, *From Becket to Langton* (Manchester, 1956), pp. 31–41; id., *Pope Innocent III and England* (Päpste und Papsttum, 9; Stuttgart, 1976), pp. 27–286 *passim*. See also histories of the reign of John, cited s.v.

Hubmaier, Balthasar (?1485–1528), German *Anabaptist. He studied under J. *Eck at Freiburg (Breisgau) and Ingolstadt, at the latter place becoming professor and parish priest. In 1516 he was appointed preacher at Regensburg Cathedral, and in 1521 parish priest at Waldshut. Here he came into contact with the Swiss Reformers, allied himself with H. *Zwingli openly in 1523, and forthwith introduced the Reformation. Soon, however, he abandoned Zwinglian doctrines for those of the Anabaptists, and in his *Von dem Tauf der Gläubigen*, published in May 1525, asserted the necessity of personal faith for baptism and condemned infant baptism as idolatry. Soon afterwards he became entangled in the *Peasants' War and may have been the author of the *Twelve Articles. When in the night of 5–6 Dec. 1525 Waldshut was occupied by Austrian troops, Hubmaier fled to Zurich, where he was forced by Zwingli to abjure his Anabaptist views. But early in the next year he left Zurich, renounced his recantation, and in July 1526 settled at Nikolsburg (now called Mikulow) in Moravia, where he worked for the Anabaptist cause esp. by writing pamphlets on theological questions, e.g. on the Lord's Supper and in defence of free will. Of independent mind, he clashed with some of his fellow Anabaptists, esp. those who were absolute in their rejection of the civil power. In 1527 the Austrian authorities demanded his extradition, and he was taken to Vienna, where he was burnt on 10 Mar. 1528. A few days later his wife, with a stone tied round her neck, was thrown into the Danube and drowned.

Schriften ed. G. Westin and T. Bergsten (Quellen und Forschungen zur Reformationsgeschichte, 29; 1962). Eng. tr. of his Works by H. W. Pipkin and J. H. Yoder (Classics of the Radical Reformation, 5; Scottdale, Pa., etc., 1989). Life [in Ger.] by T. Bergsten (Acta Universitatis Upsaliensis. Studia Historico-Ecclesiastica Upsaliensia, 3; Kassel, 1961; abbreviated Eng. tr., Valley Forge, Pa., 1978). C. Windhorst, *Täuferisches Taufverständnis: Balthasar Hubmaiers Lehre zwischen traditioneller und reformatorischer Theologie* (Studies in Medieval and Reformation Thought, 16; Leiden, 1976). J. M. Stayer, *Anabaptists and the Sword* (Lawrence, Kan., 1972), pp. 104–7, 141–6, and 162–6. W. L. Moore, 'Catholic Teacher and Anabaptist Pupil: The Relationship between John Eck and Balthasar Hubmaier', *Archiv für Reformationsgeschichte*, 72 (1981), pp. 68–97. J. M. Stayer, 'Radikaler Frühzwinglianismus. Balthasar Hubmaier, Fabers "Ursach" und die Programme der Bauern', *Mennonitische Geschichtsblätter*, 42 (1985), pp. 43–59. C. Windhorst in *TRE* 15 (1986), pp. 611–13, s.v.

Huchyns, William, a pseudomyn used by W. *Tyndale.

Huck, Albert (1867–1942), NT scholar. He held pastoral appointments in several places in Germany. He compiled a very widely used 'Synopsis' of the first three Gospels, presenting their Greek text with the parallel passages in adjacent columns. The 1st edition appeared in 1892 and the 9th, much revised by H. *Lietzmann, in 1936. Its existence greatly assisted modern researches (esp. in the years 1895–1925) into the *Synoptic Problem.

Eng. adaptation of the 9th Ger. edn. by F. L. Cross (Tübingen, 1936; Oxford, 1949). Rev. edn., in Ger. and Eng., by H. Greeven (Tübingen, 1981).

Hucusque. The opening word of the preface to the supplement to the '*Gregorian' sacramentary composed at the end of the 8th, or beginning of the 9th, cent., and often applied to the supplement itself. The author explains the deficiencies of the sacramentary sent by *Hadrian I to *Charlemagne (known as the '*Hadrianum') and the means he has taken to remedy them. The supplement proper contains the Sunday masses, those of the *Common of the Saints, *votive masses and other pieces. There follows a series of 221 *prefaces, 52 episcopal blessings, and other texts. The authorship was formerly ascribed to *Alcuin, but it is now widely held that it was compiled by St *Benedict of Aniane.

Crit. edn. by J. Deshusses, OSB, *Le Sacramentaire grégorien: Ses principales formes d'après les plus anciens manuscrits* (Spicilegium Friburgense, 16; 1971), pp. 351–605, under the title 'Supplementum Anianense'. For earlier edns. see bibl. to GREGORIAN SACRAMENTARY. Eng. tr. of the preface in C. Vogel, *Medieval Liturgy: An Introduction to the Sources*, rev. Eng. tr., by W. G. Storey and N. K. Rasmussen, OP (Washington, DC [1986]), pp. 87 f. J. Deshusses, OSB, 'Le "Supplément" au sacramentaire grégorien: Alcuin ou saint Benoît d'Aniane?', *Archiv für Liturgiewissenschaft*, 9 (pt. 1; 1965), pp. 48–71. Vogel, op. cit., pp. 85–92, with further refs. p. 126, notes pp. 229 f.

Huddleston, Ernest Urban Trevor (1913–98), Abp. of the Province of the Indian Ocean. The son of Capt. Sir Ernest Huddleston, Royal Indian Navy, he was educated at Lancing College and Christ Church, Oxford. After training at *Wells Theological College, he was ordained deacon in 1936 (priest in 1937) to the title of St Mark's, Swindon. He joined the *Community of the Resurrection in 1941 and was sent to be in charge of the Community's work in the African townships of Sophiatown, Orlando, and Pimville (the area now known as Soweto). In 1956 he was recalled to become Novice Guardian of his Community at Mirfield. In 1960 he was elected Bp. of Masasi, Tanzania. In 1968 he again returned to England as Bp. of Stepney (in E. London) and in 1978 was elected Bp. of Mauritius and Abp. of the Province of the Indian Ocean. He resigned in 1983. He was closely involved in the struggle of the African people against apartheid; he became President of the Anti-Apartheid Movement in 1981 and was knighted in 1998. His writings include *Naught for Your Comfort* (1956), *The True and Living God* (1964), and *God's World* (1966).

D. D. Honoré (ed.), *Trevor Huddleston: Essays on his Life and Work* (Oxford, 1988).

Huet, Pierre Daniel (1630–1721), French scholar and bishop. In 1652 he accompanied S. *Bochart on a visit to the court of Queen *Christina of Sweden; in the Royal Library at Stockholm he discovered some fragments of *Origen's *Comm. in Matt*. He went on to produce an important edition of Origen's works (1668). He then edited, with Anne Lefèvre, the famous 'Delphin Classics' in some 60 volumes for the Dauphin, whose tutor (with J. B. *Bossuet) he was. He also wrote a *Traité de l'origine des romans* (1670; Eng. tr., 1672) and in 1674 was elected a member of the Académie française. His *Demonstratio evangelica* (1679) was an apology for Christianity. Having been at first sympathetic to the philosophy of R. *Descartes, he later criticized it in his *Censura philosophiae Cartesianae* (1689). He was nominated Bp. of Avranches in 1689, but was not consecrated until 1692; he resigned in 1699. He then lived with the *Jesuits in the rue St-Antoine in Paris; he bequeathed to them his books and valuable collection of MSS which, when the Society was suppressed, for the most part passed to the Royal Library, now incorporated into the Bibliothèque Nationale in Paris.

Huetiana, ou pensées diverses de M. Huet [ed. P. J. T. d'Olivet] ('1822' [1722]). *Memoirs of the Life of Peter Daniel Huet . . . written by himself*, tr. from the Lat. by J. Aikin (2 vols., 1810). Modern collection of extracts from various writings by D. Aubry, *Daniel Huet* (Paris [1943]). A. Dupront, *P. D. Huet et l'exégèse comparatiste du XVIIᵉ siècle* (1930); L. Tolmer, *Pierre-Daniel Huet (1630–1721), humaniste physicien* (Mémoire de l'Académie nationale des sciences, arts et belles-lettres de Caen, NS 11; 1949). C. Urbain, 'La Bibliothèque de P. D. Huet', *Bulletin du Bibliophile et du Bibliothécaire*, 1910, pp. 133–46. B. Heurtebize in *DTC* 7 (pt. 1; 1922), cols. 199–201.

Hügel, Baron Friedrich von. See VON HÜGEL, BARON FRIEDRICH.

Hugh, St (1024–1109), Abbot of *Cluny. Of a noble Burgundian family, he was brought up by his great-uncle, Hugh, Bp. of Auxerre. At the age of 14 he entered the monastery of Cluny under St *Odilo and owing to out-standing piety was allowed to take his vows only a year later. Before the age of 21 he was Prior and on Odilo's death (1 Jan. 1049) was unanimously chosen Abbot, being installed by the Abp. of Besançon on 22 Feb. 1049. *Leo IX took him into his confidence, and henceforward Hugh, as adviser to nine Popes, came to exercise a dominating influence in ecclesiastical and political affairs. He took part in securing the condemnation of *Berengar of Tours (1050) and upheld the privileges of the Cluniacs against the attacks of successive Abps. of Lyons and Bps. of Mâcon. He warmly encouraged *Gregory VII's efforts for reform and tried to mediate in the bitter feud between the Pope and Emp. *Henry IV. Despite his constant absence, the monastery suffered no relaxation in discipline and, indeed, reached under Hugh a position never surpassed. The Customs of Cluny compiled by Bernard and Ulrich illustrate the development of Cluniac monasticism during his reign, and they were influential both within and beyond the Cluniac family of monasteries. He induced Pope *Urban II (d. 1099) to consecrate in person the high altar of the new basilica at Cluny (25 Oct. 1095), then the largest church in Christendom. During his rule, the first Cluniac house in England, the priory of St Pancras at Lewes, was founded. At the Council of *Clermont (1095), he was present at the preaching of the First *Crusade. Among his liturgical reforms was the introduction of the singing of the *Veni Creator* at terce during Pentecost. He wrote a 'Life of the Blessed Virgin', but this, with most of his letters, has been lost. He was canonized by *Callistus II in 1120. Feast day, 29 April.

Early Lives by Gilo and Hugh the monk, letters, statutes, and other material, ed. H. E. J. Cowdrey in *Studi Gregoriani*, 11 (1978), pp. 9–175; Life by Rainaud, abbot of Vézelay, pr. in *AASS*, Apr. 3 (1675), pp. 648–53; that by *Hildebert of Lavardin, pr. ibid., pp. 634–48; other material, pp. 654–62, with introd. pp. 628–34; the whole entry in *AASS* is repr. in J. P. Migne, *PL* 159. 845–928. T. Schieffer, 'Notice sur les vies de Saint Hugues, abbé de Cluny', *Le Moyen-Âge*, 46 (3rd ser. 7; 1936), pp. 81–103. F. Barlow, 'William I's Relations with Cluny', *JEH* 32 (1981), pp. 131–41; id., 'The Canonization and Early Lives of Hugh I, Abbot of Cluny', *Anal. Boll.* 98 (1980), pp. 297–334, both repr. in id., *The Norman Conquest and Beyond* (1983), pp. 245–95. A. Kohnle, *Abt Hugo von Cluny (1049–1109)* (Beihefte der *Francia*, 32; Sigmaringen, 1993). On the development of Cluny under his rule, N. Hunt, *Cluny under Saint Hugh 1049–1109* (1967). G. de Valous in *DHGE* 13 (1956), cols. 49–56, s.v. 'Cluny'. See also other works cited under CLUNY.

Hugh, St (1052–1132), Bp. of Grenoble. Born at Châteauneuf, near Valence, he became (when still a layman) a Canon of Valence. In 1080 he was elected Bp. of Grenoble to reform the disorders in the diocese, where in a long episcopate he successfully redressed abuses and fostered devotion. He welcomed St *Bruno and his monks to his diocese, granting them the *Grande Chartreuse (1084). He was canonized by Innocent II in 1134, two years after his death. Feast day, 1 Apr.

The primary authority is the Lat. Life by his friend *Guigo I, Prior of the Grande Chartreuse, pr., with introd., in *AASS*, Apr. 1 (1675), pp. 36–46; repr. in J. P. Migne, *PL* 153. 759–84; also ed. C. Bellet (Montreuil, 1889); Fr. tr. by M.-A. Chomel, with introd. by B. Bligny (Analecta Cartusiana, 112: 3; Salzburg, 1986). Modern Life by A. Du Boys (Grenoble, 1837).

Hugh, St (*c.*1140–1200), Bp. of *Lincoln. He was the son of the Lord of Avalon in Burgundy. Brought up to be a member of an order of *canons regular near Grenoble, he was early attracted by the much more severe and secluded life of the newly founded *Carthusian Order, and took vows at the *Grande Chartreuse when he was about 25. His character and talents became known to Henry II, who was attempting to establish at Witham in Somerset the first Carthusian house in England, and *c.*1180 he secured the services of Hugh as its third prior. This was the beginning of a frequent intercourse between Hugh and the King. In 1186 he became, at Henry's earnest wish, Bp. of Lincoln, though he insisted that he should be freely elected before he accepted the office. As bishop he administered his huge diocese well and showed a courageous independence of the King, e.g. as champion of the people against the royal foresters. He later took the lead, with the Bp. of Salisbury, in refusing a demand of Richard I for money for the King's wars, an event of significance in constitutional history. But, despite his unwavering stand for the liberty of the Church, he always maintained good personal relations with the kings—Henry II, Richard I, and *John—under whom he lived. He never forgot that he was a monk, and every year retired for a time to the priory of Witham. Already in his own lifetime he was greatly revered for his holiness and devotion, e.g. his Christian love towards lepers, and in 1220 he was canonized. His tomb at Lincoln became second only to that of St Thomas *Becket at Canterbury as a place of popular devotion until it was spoiled by *Henry VIII. Feast day, 17 Nov.

Magna Vita, by Adam, monk of Eynsham and chaplain to St Hugh, ed. F. J. Dimock (Rolls Series, 1864) and, with Eng. tr. and full introd., by D. L. Douie and H. Farmer, OSB (2 vols., London, 1961–2; repr., with corrections and new introd., Oxford Medieval Texts, 1985); *Vita*, by *Giraldus Cambrensis in *Opera*, ed. F. J. Dimock, 7 (RS, 1877), pp. 83–147, with 'Legenda . . . to be Read . . . on the Day of his Obit' in Appendix D, pp. 172–92; metrical Life, written prob. shortly after his canonization (1220–35), ed. id. (London, 1860). H. Farmer, OSB, 'The Canonization of St Hugh of Lincoln', *Lincolnshire Architectural and Archaeological Society Reports and Papers*, NS 6, pt. 2 (1956), pp. 86–117. Modern Lives by 'Un Religieux de la Grande Chartreuse' (Montreuil, 1890; Eng. tr. with additions by H. Thurston, SJ, 'Quarterly Series', 99; 1898), R. M. Woolley (London, 1927), and D. H. Farmer (ibid., 1985). H. Mayr-Harting (ed.), *Saint Hugh of Lincoln Lectures . . .* (Oxford, 1987).

Hugh of St-Victor (d. 1142), *Victorine theologian. Little is known about his life. About 1115 he entered St-Victor, the house of *Augustinian Canons recently founded in Paris by *William of Champeaux. According to one account he was born in the region of Ypres, according to another he came from Saxony. His uncle is said to have been archdeacon of the church of Halberstadt, and Hugh dedicated his *De arrha animae* ('The Soul's Betrothal-gift') to the Augustinian Canons of Hamersleben near Halberstadt. The tradition that makes him a member of the family of the Counts of Blankenberg in Saxony is post-medieval. From the time of his arrival in Paris he does not seem to have left it except for a visit to the court of Pope Innocent II.

Hugh's works cover a very wide field. He wrote on grammar and geometry, an *Epitome in philosophiam*, a chronicle, the *Didascalion*, which is a guide to the study of

the *artes* and of theology, commentaries on the Octateuch and Lamentations, homilies on Ecclesiastes, a commentary on *Dionysius the Pseudo-Areopagite's *Celestial Hierarchy*, a large-scale *De sacramentis Christianae fidei*, and works of spirituality such as *De arca Noe* (*morali* and *mystica*), *De vanitate mundi*, *De laude caritatis*, and a number of shorter pieces. In all these fields Hugh made a distinctive contribution with no parade of learning or claims to originality. It has been said that his work is 'rich in new ideas and fresh presentations of old ones' (A. Squire). In his biblical commentaries he gave new emphasis to the historical study of Scripture and to the importance of studying the literal sense. The same feeling for history underlies the organization of the *De sacramentis* into the work of Creation and the work of Restoration. History was the foundation. From study (*lectio*) man must go on to meditation (*meditatio*) by which the soul tries to discover the Divine thoughts hidden under the veil of both creatures and the Scriptures and to achieve purity of life and strive after loving contemplation (*contemplatio*). For Hugh everything was ultimately to be subordinated to the contemplative life. Nevertheless, he was in close touch with the discussions and controversies of his day, and it is possible to see in his writings how he takes account of the views of e.g. Peter *Abelard, *William of Conches, and St *Bernard.

Collected edn. of his works first pub. at Paris, 1518; also ed. by the Canons of St-Victor, 3 vols., Rouen, 1648, virtually repr. in J. P. Migne, *PL* 175–7. Further works not incl. in these edns. are 'De Tribus Maximis Circumstantiis Gestorum' first pub. by W. M. Green in *Speculum*, 18 (1943), pp. 484–93, *Opera Propaedeutica* ['Practica geometriae', 'De Grammatica', and 'Epitome in philosophiam'] ed. R. Baron (University of Notre Dame Publications in Mediaeval Studies, 20; 1966), and 'Descriptio Mappe Mundi', ed., with Fr. tr., by P. G. Dalché (Études Augustiniennes, 1988). There are also modern edns. of 'De Arrha Animae' and 'De Vanitate Mundi', Books 1–2, by K. Müller (Kleine Texte für Vorlesungen und Übungen, 123; 1913); of 'Didascalion de Studio Legendi' by C. H. Buttimer (Catholic University of America Studies in Medieval and Renaissance Latin, 10; 1939), and of *Six Opuscules spirituels*, with Fr. tr., by R. Baron (SC 155; 1969). Further details of his works in R. Goy, see below. The 'De Contemplatione' pub. by [J.] B. Hauréau, *Hugues de Saint-Victor: Nouvel examen de l'édition de ses œuvres* (1859), pp. 177–210, is not genuine; there is a crit. edn. of this work by R. Baron (Monumenta Christiana Selecta, 2; Tournai, 1955). Eng. trs. of 'De Arrha Animae' by F. S. Taylor (London, 1945); of 'De Sacramentis' by R. J. Deferrari (Mediaeval Academy of America Publication, 58; 1951); of 'Didascalion' by J. Taylor (Records of Civilization. Sources and Studies, 64; 1961), with important introd. and comm.; and of *Selected Spiritual Writings* [incl. 'De arca Noe morali' and 'De vanitate mundi', Books 1–2] by Sr. [Penelope], CSMV (Classics of the Contemplative Life, 1962), with introd. by A. Squire, OP, pp. 13–42. The Explanation of the Rule of St *Augustine usually attributed to Hugh of St-Victor, but prob. the work of Lietbert of St-Ruf, tr. into Eng. by A. Smith, OSB (London, 1911). H. Ostler, *Die Psychologie des Hugo von St Viktor* (BGPM 6, Heft 1; 1906). H. Weisweiler, SJ, *Die Wirksamkeit der Sakramente nach Hugo von St-Viktor* (1932). R. Baron, *Science et sagesse chez Hugues de Saint-Victor* (1957). D. van den Eynde, OFM, *Essai sur la succession et la date des écrits de Hugues de Saint-Victor* (Spicilegium Pontificii Athenaei Antoniani, 13; 1960). J. Ehlers, *Hugo von St Viktor: Studien zum Geschichtsdenken und zur Geschichtsschreibung des 12. Jahrhunderts* (Frankfurter Historische Abhandlungen, 7; Wiesbaden, 1973.) R. Goy, *Die Überlieferung der Werke Hugos von St Viktor* (Monographien zur Geschichte des Mittelalters, 14; Stuttgart, 1976). S. Ernst, *Gewissheit des Glau-*

bens: Der Glaubenstraktat Hugos von St Viktor als Zugang zu seiner theologischen Systematik (BGPM, NF 30; 1987). G. A. Zinn, 'Mandala Symbolism and Use in the Mysticism of Hugh of St. Victor', *History of Religions*, 12 (1972–3), pp. 317–41. J. B. Schneyer, *Repertorium der lateinischen Sermones des Mittelalters für die Zeit von 1150–1350*, 2 (BGPM, NF 43, Heft 2, 1970) pp. 786–813. F. Vernet in *DTC* 7 (pt. 1; 1922), cols. 240–308, s.v. 'Hugues de Saint-Victor'; D. van den Eynde in *NCE* 7 (1967), pp. 194 f., s.v.; R. Baron in *Dict. Sp.* 7 (pt. 1; 1969), cols. 901–39, s.v. 'Hugues de Saint-Victor'; J. Châtillon in *TRE* 15 (1986), pp. 629–35, s.v 'Hugo von St. Viktor'.

Hughes, Hugh Price (1847–1902), *Methodist divine. A native of Carmarthen and son of a doctor, he began preaching at the age of 14 and, after entering the Wesleyan ministry, became a great preacher, who concerned himself especially with social problems such as the housing of the poor, conditions at work, and gambling. He was among the first of the Nonconformist leaders to espouse the platform of '*Christian Socialism'—hitherto largely an Anglican movement. Greatly influenced by Josephine *Butler, he came to see the need for moral reformation in society to receive legislative expression; he was thus a powerful spokesman for 'the Nonconformist Conscience', for demands that the State intervene to uphold a code of Christian practice. In 1885 he started the *Methodist Times*, a weekly which soon became one of the leading organs of Nonconformist opinion. He worked hard to secure co-operation among the various Nonconformist bodies, and in 1896 he became the first president of the National Council of the Evangelical Free Churches. He also took a prominent part in the Education Acts controversy, in which, though supporting the Nonconformist policy, he on one occasion expressed his willingness to accept the *Apostles' Creed as a basis of teaching in the schools.

[D. P. Hughes, daughter], *The Life of Hugh Price Hughes* (1904). J. [H. S.] Kent, 'Hugh Price Hughes and the Nonconformist Conscience', in G. V. Bennett and J. Walsh (eds.), *Essays in Modern English Church History in memory of Norman Sykes* (1966), pp. 181–205; N. McG. King, 'Hugh Price Hughes and the British "Social Gospel"', *Journal of Religious History*, 13 (1984–5), pp. 66–82. E. [R.] Norman, *The Victorian Christian Socialists* (Cambridge, 1987), pp. 144–61. P. S. Bagwell, *Outcast London: A Christian Response. The West London Mission of the Methodist Church 1887–1987* (1987), pp. 5–48, *passim*.

Huguenots, the *Calvinist French Protestants. The etymology of the name is controversial; Henri Estienne (*Stephanus) in 1566 explained it as a nickname based on a medieval romance about a King Hugo, but a derivation from *Eidgenossen* (Ger. 'confederates', i.e. those admitted to the Swiss Confederation, Gallicized in Geneva as *eigenotz*), is widely accepted. The beginnings of the movement have sometimes been traced back to the publication of J. Lefèvre d'Étaples's [J. *Faber's] *Sancti Pauli Epistolae XIV . . . cum commentariis* (1512), but any direct connection is unlikely. Its real originator was J. *Calvin, who, though he had to flee from France in 1534, dedicated his *Institutes* (1536) to Francis I. At its first Synod in Paris (1539) the French Protestant Church formally organized itself on a Calvinist basis. The movement was fiercely resisted by the family of the Guises who came into power with the accession of Francis II later in 1539. They later founded the Catholic League to fight against the Protestants, enlisting the help of Spain. By the time of their second Synod at Poitiers (1561), the Huguenots had grown into a sizeable national minority; after the Colloquy of *Poissy they obtained a measure of freedom to practise their religion. They came to be seen as a danger to the State and the ensuing religious wars (1562–94) were fought between Huguenots and Catholics, the most terrible event being the Massacre of St *Bartholomew's Day (1572). The increasing influence of the *Politiques and the tolerant attitude of *Henry IV led to their being granted extensive freedom of worship and other rights in the Edict of *Nantes (1598). The Huguenots built numerous churches (*temples*), including the one at Charenton (1606) to serve their adherents in Paris. They continued to be regarded as a disruptive element in an increasingly absolute State. After the fall of their fortress at La Rochelle (1628), by the Treaty of Alais (1629) they were deprived of their political rights and lost their fortified towns. Under Louis XIV their freedom continued to be curtailed until the Edict of Nantes was revoked by that of Fontainebleau (1685). Many were forced to accept Catholicism by the *Dragonnades and other pressures. Some 200,000 to 300,000 went into exile, seeking refuge in the Netherlands, Switzerland, England, Prussia, and America, but the majority remained. In 1702–3 Huguenot extremists raised the rebellion of the *Camisards. After its failure the influence of the Huguenots in the 18th cent. was negligible. Marriages before their ministers were not recognized until Louis XVI issued the Edict of Tolerance in 1787, and only in 1802 was the legal standing of their Church re-established. It then extended its activities in education and missions. A disagreement in 1852 between the liberal and more numerous traditionalist sections led to a split in 1872 and to a complete break in 1906. In 1907, however, the National Union of the Reformed [i.e. Calvinist] Churches of France was formed; in 1909 it combined with non-Calvinist bodies to form the Protestant Federation of France. In the 1970s they formed less than 2 per cent of the population of France. See also FRANCE, CHRISTIANITY IN, and DU PLESSIS-MORNAY, PHILIPPE.

A. J. Grant, *The Huguenots* (HUL, 1934); R. Stéphan [R. A. P Stoupan], *Histoire du Protestantisme français* [1961]; R. Mandrou and others, *Histoire des Protestants en France* (Toulouse [1977]). S. Mours, *Le Protestantisme en France au XVIe siècle* (1959); id., *Le Protestantisme en France au XVIIe siècle (1598–1685)* (1967); D. Ligou, *Le Protestantisme en France de 1598 à 1715* (1968); B. Dompnier, *Le Venin de l'hérésie: Image du protestantisme et combat catholique au XVIIe siècle* [1985]. A. Encrevé, *Les Protestants de France de 1800 à nos jours: Histoire d'une réintégration* [1985]; id., *Protestants français au milieu du XIXe siècle: Les Réformés de 1848 à 1870* (Geneva, 1986); J. Baubérot, *Le Retour des Huguenots: La vitalité protestante XIXe–XXe siècle* (1985). M. Yardeni, *Le Refuge protestant* [1985]; M. Magdelaine and R. von Thadden, *Le Refuge huguenot* [1985]; R. D. Gwynn, *Huguenot Heritage: The History and Contribution of the Huguenots in Britain* (1985); B. Cottret, *Terre d'exil: L'Angleterre et ses réfugiés français et wallons, de la Réforme à la Révocation de l'Édit de Nantes, 1500–1700* [1985]. J. G. Gray, 'The Origin of the word Huguenot', *Sixteenth Century Journal*, 14 (1983), pp. 349–59. Biogs. of individual Huguenots in E. and E. Haag, *La France protestante* (9 vols., 1846–59; 2nd edn. by H. Bordier, vols. 1–6 [to Gasparin], 1877–88). *Bulletin de la Société de l'Histoire du Protestantisme Français* (1853 ff.). See also works cited s.v. REFORMATION, esp. that of E. G. Léonard; also bibl. to FRANCE, CHRISTIANITY IN; CAMISARDS; HENRY IV OF FRANCE; NANTES, EDICT OF; and RICHELIEU.

Hulsean Lectures. The course of lectures delivered annually at Cambridge in acc. with the bequest of the Revd John Hulse (1708–90). The original distribution of the bequest provided: (1) two divinity scholarships at St John's College, (2) a prize for a dissertation, (3) a 'Christian Advocate', and (4) a preacher or lecturer. By a revision of the statutes in 1860, a divinity professorship was substituted for (3) and the status of (4) considerably altered. By a further revision in 1934, the Hulsean and Norrisian professorships were united to form the Norris–Hulse professorship, the first holder of the joint professorship being F. C. *Burkitt.

Hulst, Maurice d'. See D'HULST, MAURICE.

Humanae Vitae. The encyclical issued by Pope *Paul VI on 25 July 1968 condemning all forms of birth control except the 'rhythm method'. The majority of the Papal Commission appointed by *John XXIII in 1963 (during *Vatican II) and confirmed by Paul VI, appears to have favoured the legitimacy of contraception. The encyclical, however, taking its stand on the sanctity of *Natural Law, condemned abortion (even for therapeutic reasons), sterilization, or any action which, in connection with the conjugal act, purposes 'to render procreation impossible'. Although it merely reaffirmed the traditional doctrine of the Church, it appears to imply that, in view of the difficulty of its teaching, married couples unable to comply are not to be debarred from the Eucharist. See also CONTRACEPTION, PROCREATION, AND ABORTION, ETHICS OF.

Text in *AAS* 60 (1968), pp. 481–503; also pr., with Eng. tr. by R. Bogan, in P. Harris and others, *On Human Life* (1968), pp. 107–61. J. E. Smith, *Humanae Vitae a Generation Later* (Washington, DC [1991]).

Humani Generis. The encyclical of *Pius XII (12 Aug. 1950) aimed at correcting extreme opinions which had become prominent in the post-war theological revival. It rejected *Existentialism; excessive emphasis of the Word of God to the detraction of reason; distrust of theological dogmatism as incompatible with the language of Scripture and the Fathers; contempt for the authority of the Church and unwillingness to identify the Mystical Body of Christ with the Catholic Church in communion with the see of Rome; distrust of *Scholastic philosophy (esp. of St *Thomas Aquinas); the denial that *Adam existed as a historical person and that *original sin has reached us by direct descent from him; and undue freedom in the interpretation of the Books of the OT.

Text in *AAS* 42 (1950), pp. 561–78. Eng. tr. by R. A. *Knox in *The Tablet*, 2 Sept. 1950. J. M. Connolly in *NCE* 7 (1967), p. 214, s.v., with bibl.

Humbert of Romans (d. 1277), fifth Master of the *Dominican Order. Born at Romans, near Valence, in France, prob. in the last decade of the 12th cent., Humbert studied arts in Paris and then joined the Dominican Order there in 1224. After being prior of Lyons and, successively, provincial of the Roman and Paris provinces, he was elected Master of the Order in 1254. He resigned in 1263 and devoted his remaining years to writing.

Humbert's qualities as a shrewd Churchman were recognized early. In 1243 he received some votes in the Papal election, and at some stage he is said to have been offered the patriarchate of Jerusalem. As provincial and as Master of the Dominican Order, Humbert made definitive contributions to the final codification of the Dominican liturgy and to the organization of the Dominican nuns. He was responsible, as Master, for the incorporation of philosophical studies into the intellectual life of the Order and for the completion of its academic structure. He also clarified many other points of Dominican law and observance. Many of his decisions remained influential for centuries. It was he who, with considerable diplomatic skill, steered the Order through the worst of the anti-mendicant controversy.

His writings were mostly intended for the use of Dominicans and include a treatise (not all of which has survived) on how to be a preacher, complete with sermon material for 396 different occasions (*De Eruditione Praedicatorum*); an exposition of the Rule of St *Augustine; an unfinished commentary on the Constitutions and a very influential work on the officials of the Order. The chronology of these writings has not been securely established. Prob. in 1272 he was asked by Pope *Gregory X to write a preparatory document for the Second Council of *Lyons, and the resulting work, the *Opus Tripartitum*, exercised a real influence on the Council. Humbert's comments on the schism between Catholics and Greek Orthodox were a significant factor in medieval and even in modern attempts at ecumenism. After his death he was remembered above all as a man of sound judgement and reliable counsel.

There is no crit. edn. of his works. Most of those on the Dominican life are contained in his *Opera de Vita Regulari*, ed. J. J. Berthier, OP (2 vols., Rome, 1888–9; repr., Turin, 1956). A partial tr. of *De Eruditione Praedicatorum*, based on the MSS, by S. [C. ff.] Tugwell, OP (ed.), *Early Dominicans* (Classics of Western Spirituality, 1982), pp. 181–370. Other edns. of his works listed in Kaeppli, 2 (1975), pp. 283–95, with bibl. F. Heintke, *Humbert von Romans* (Historische Studien, 222; 1933); E. T. Brett, *Humbert of Romans: His Life and Views of Thirteenth-Century Society* (Studies and Texts, 67; Toronto, 1984). P. A. Throop, *Criticism of the Crusade: A Study of Public Opinion and Crusade Propaganda* (Amsterdam, 1940), esp. pp. 147–213; G. Every, 'The Empire and the Schism in the *Opusculum Tripartitum* of Humbert de Romanis', *Eastern Churches Review*, 5 (1973), pp. 136–42. M.-H. Vicaire, OP, in *Dict. Sp.* 7 (pt. 1; 1969), cols. 1108–16, s.v.

Humbert of Silva Candida (d. 1061), ecclesiastical reformer and statesman. Originally a monk of Moyenmoutier in Lotharingia, he came to Rome with *Leo IX in 1049; he had been made Cardinal-Bishop of Silva Candida by Feb. 1051 and became Papal Chancellor prob. in 1057. He was a learned man, who, apart from wide reading of the Latin Fathers, also knew some Greek, and he enjoyed a great deal of influence with the reforming Popes. He was deeply involved in negotiations with *Michael Cerularius, Patr. of *Constantinople. In the politics of reform he represented the rigorist party which refused to recognize the orders conferred by bishops guilty of *simony. There has been much discussion among historians about the body of writings which can be assigned to Humbert. Only one major work can be securely attributed to him, the *Adversus Simoniacos*, which he composed in 1058 as a reply to the *Liber Gratissimus* of *Peter Damian. Even this was little circulated, but it is a classic statement of the rigorist thesis and contains the first attack on the practice of lay *investiture. See also GREAT SCHISM (I).

Collection of his works in J. P. Migne, *PL* 143. 929–1218; crit. edn. of his *Adversus Simoniacos* by F. Thaner in *MGH*, Libelli de Lite Imperatorum et Pontificum Saeculis XI et XII, 1 (1891), pp. 95–253. A. Michel, 'Die folgenschweren Ideen des Kardinals Humbert und ihr Einfluss auf Gregor VII.', *Studi Gregoriani*, 1 (1947), pp. 65–92, takes a wide view of the range of his work and influence; see also H. Hoesch, *Die kanonischen Quellen im Werk Humberts von Moyenmoutier* (Forschungen zur Kirchlichen Rechtsgeschichte und zum Kirchenrecht, 10; 1970), and H.-G. Krause, 'Über den Verfasser der Vita Leonis IX papae', *Deutsches Archiv*, 32 (1976), pp. 49–85. Other modern studies include J. J. Ryan, 'Cardinal Humbert *De s. Romana ecclesia*: Relics of Roman-Byzantine Relations 1053–1054', *Mediaeval Studies*, 20 (1958), pp. 206–38; and J. T. Gilchrist, 'Humbert of Silva-Candida and the Political Concept of *ecclesia* in the Eleventh Century Reform Movement', *Journal of Religious History*, 2 (1962–3), pp. 13–28; id., 'Cardinal Humbert of Silva-Candida', *Annuale mediaevale*, 3 (1962), pp. 29–42; id., 'Cardinal Humbert of Silva-Candida, the Canon Law and Ecclesiastical Reform in the Eleventh Century', *Zeitschrift der Savigny-Stiftung für Rechtsgeschichte*, Kanonistische Abteilung, 58 (1972), pp. 338–49. U.-R. Blumenthal in *TRE* 15 (1986), pp. 682–5, s.v.

Humble Access, the Prayer of. The prayer in the BCP which opens with the words, 'We do not presume to come to this thy Table, O merciful Lord, trusting in our own righteousness'. Its name derives from the Scottish Liturgy of 1637, where it is entitled 'Collect of Humble Access to the Holy Communion'. It was composed for the new 'Order of the *Communion' of 1548 and thus stood between the Communion of the priest and that of the people. In the Book of 1549 it was moved with most of the items in the 'Order of the Communion' to a place immediately before the Communion of both priest and people. In the Book of 1552, however, it was separated from the other items of the 'Order of the Communion' and (with slight alterations in the wording) inserted immediately after the *Sanctus, and there it remained in the 1662 Book. In some modern Anglican liturgies it has been dropped. Where it is retained it is normally placed either before 'the Ministry of the Sacrament' (as in the ASB) or immediately before the Communion of the priest and people (e.g. in the American BCP (1979) and the BCP of the Church in Wales, 1984) and its use is often made optional. The clause 'that our sinful bodies may be made clean by his body, and our souls washed through his most precious blood' is sometimes omitted. Since about the 1960s in some places the prayer has been said aloud by the congregation as well as the celebrant.

J. Dowden, 'A Contribution towards the Study of the Prayer of Humble Access', *The Irish Church Quarterly*, 1 (1908), pp. 8–24, repr. in id., *Further Studies in the Prayer Book*, Appendix, pp. 317–43. W. W. S. March, *We do not presume: A Commentary on the Prayer of Humble Access* (Derby, 1965).

Hume, Basil. See HUME, GEORGE BASIL.

Hume, David (1711–76), Scottish philosopher and historian. He was a native of Edinburgh, where he was educated, and at an early age resolved to become a philosopher. From 1734 to 1737 he lived in France, where he elaborated his sceptical principles and wrote the *Treatise of Human Nature* (3 vols., 1739–40), the success of which

fell far short of his expectations. In 1741–2 appeared *Essays Moral and Political* (2 vols.), which was favourably received and much appreciated by Bp. J. *Butler. During the following years he held several secretarial and administrative posts in England and abroad. In 1748 he published *Philosophical Essays Concerning Human Understanding* which contained his famous 'Essay upon Miracles', followed, in 1751, by *An Enquiry Concerning the Principles of Morals*. By this time he had also completed his *Dialogues Concerning Natural Religion*, which was published only posthumously (1779). During the latter part of his life his interests turned to history; in 1752 he published his *Political Discourses*, the first of his works to attract general attention, and from 1754 to 1761 his famous *History of England* (6 vols.), written from the Tory standpoint, which long remained a standard work. In 1763 he accompanied Lord Hertford to France, where he was much admired and became the friend of J. Le R. *D'Alembert and A. R. J. Turgot. In 1766 he found for J.-J. *Rousseau a refuge in England. In his last years he almost ceased to write.

Hume's philosophy is based on the experimental method of J. *Locke and G. *Berkeley. By reducing reason to a product of experience he destroyed its claim to sole validity, which had been put forward by the thinkers of the *Enlightenment. All perceptions of the human mind are either impressions of experience or ideas, i.e. faded copies of these impressions. But whereas the relations between ideas can be known with certainty, the facts of reality cannot be established beyond an appearance of probability. Causality is not a concept of logic, but a result of habit and association, impressed on our imagination, and the human soul itself is but a sum of perceptions connected by association. Hence there is no such science as metaphysics; and belief in the existence of God and of the physical world, though a practical necessity, cannot be proved by reason. *Theism is neither the original nor the highest form of religion. The immortality of the soul is doubtful, and *suicide is permissible. Our moral life is dominated by the passions, which determine our will and our actions.

Hume was aware that, by reducing all cognition to single perceptions and by ruling out any purely intellectual faculty for recording and sifting them, he destroyed all real knowledge and taught pure scepticism. This scepticism is particularly evident in his 'Essay on Miracles', in which he argues that reports of miracles should always be doubted, since miracles are, by definition, highly unlikely. 'A miracle is a violation of the laws of nature; and as a firm and unalterable experience has established these laws, the proof against a miracle, from the very nature of the fact, is as entire as any argument from experience can possibly be imagined.'

Hume's influence has been widespread. Among the thinkers indebted to him are I. *Kant, J. Bentham, and A. *Comte; and he has received attention from modern philosophical empiricists.

Hume's autobiography appeared in 1777. His *Life and Correspondence* were ed. J. H. Burton in 1846. Modern edn. of his *Letters*, by J. Y. T. Greig (2 vols., Oxford, 1932); *New Letters*, ed. R. Klibansky and E. C. Mossner (ibid., 1954). J. Y. T. Greig, *David Hume* (London, 1931); E. C. Mossner, *The Life of David Hume* (1954; 2nd edn., 1980); A. [G. N.] Flew, *Hume's Philosophy of Belief: A Study of his first* Inquiry (1961); id., *David Hume, Philosopher of Moral Science* (Oxford, 1986); J. B. Stewart, *The Moral and Political Philosophy of David Hume* (New York and London, 1963); D. Forbes, *Hume's Philosophical Politics* (Cambridge, 1975); B. [G.] Stroud, *Hume* (London, 1977); J. C. A. Gaskin, *Hume's Philosophy of Religion* (1978; 2nd edn., 1988); J. L. Mackie, *Hume's Moral Theory* (1980); J. Harrison, *Hume's Theory of Justice* (Oxford, 1981). G. Strawson, *The Secret Connexion: Causation, Realism and David Hume* (ibid., 1989); D. Pears, *Hume's System: An Examination of the First Book of his* Treatise (ibid., 1990); K. E. Yandell, *Hume's 'Inexplicable Mystery': His Views on Religion* (Philadelphia, 1990). R. Hill, *Fifty Years of Hume Scholarship: A Bibliographical Guide* (Edinburgh [1978]). L. Stephen in *DNB* 28 (1891), pp. 215–26.

Hume, George Basil (1923–), Abp. of *Westminster. The son of Sir William Hume (1879–1960), a distinguished Scottish *Presbyterian physician, Hume was brought up as a RC by his mother. He was educated at *Ampleforth College and joined the *Benedictine Community there in 1941, being professed in 1942. He read Modern History at St Benet's Hall, Oxford, and went on to post-graduate study at Fribourg University in Switzerland. After his ordination as priest in 1950, he taught Modern Languages in the school at Ampleforth and then was a housemaster from 1955 until he was elected Abbot in 1963. In 1976 Pope *Paul VI nominated him Abp. of Westminster and made him a cardinal later in the same year. From 1978 to 1987 he was President of the Council of European Bishops' Conferences and since 1979 has also been President of the Bishops' Conference of England and Wales. In 1994 he was *relator* of the Synod of Bishops on the consecrated life and its mission in the Church and the world. He quickly became a national leader, widely respected both within and beyond his own communion; during his time at Westminster the RC Church in England came more fully into the mainstream of national life. His books, mainly based on lectures or addresses, are marked by spiritual insight. They include *Searching for God* (1977) and *To be a Pilgrim* (1984).

T. Castle (ed.), *Basil Hume: A Portrait* (1986).

humeral veil. In the W. Church, a silk shawl laid round the shoulders serving to cover the hands. At *High Mass the *subdeacon used to hold the *paten with it, from after the *Offertory till after the *Pater Noster. The humeral veil is already mentioned in the Roman '*Ordines' of the 8th and 9th cents., where it is worn by an *acolyte who then held the paten. When *c.* the 11th cent. the subdeacon became paten-bearer he used the *pall in place of the humeral veil and the latter did not come into use again for this purpose until the 15th cent. Its adoption became universal only in the 19th cent. It is still worn by the celebrant in processions of the Blessed Sacrament, at the service of *Benediction, and (in some countries) when the *Viaticum is taken to the sick.

Braun, *LP*, pp. 228–31. N. F. Robinson, SSJE, 'Concerning Three Eucharistic Veils of Western Use', *Transactions of the St Paul's Ecclesiological Society*, 6 (1906–10), pp. 129–60, esp. pp. 129 f. and 153–8. J. Braun, SJ, in *CE* 7 (1910), pp. 542 f., s.v.

Humiliati. An Italian penitential and apostolic movement, which later developed into a recognized institution in the Church. Its origins are obscure. Its adherents devoted themselves to mortification, the care of the sick and poor, and to preaching. In 1184, along with the *Waldenses and *Cathari, they were condemned for their disobedience to the hierarchy. Most of them, however, were reconciled to the Church and reorganized by *Innocent III in 1201 in the form of three orders, governed by a common general chapter: the first order consisted of double monasteries of canons and nuns, the second of houses of celibate lay men and women, the third of married people living at home. The first two orders shared a single rule and were progressively assimilated to the *mendicant orders, while the third came to be closer to the Order of Penance (see THIRD ORDERS). From *c.*1272 the third order detached itself from the other two and in 1291 held its own general chapter; it disappeared in the course of the 14th cent. The order as a whole was suppressed in 1571, after St *Charles Borromeo's endeavours to reform it led to an attempt on his life.

The principal authority is H. Tiraboschius, SJ, *Vetera Humiliatorum Monumenta* (3 vols., Milan, 1766–8). L. Zanoni, *Gli Umiliati nei loro rapporti con l'eresia, l'industria della lana ed i comuni nei secoli XII e XIII* (Milan, 1911). V. d'Alessandro (ed.), *Le Pergamene degli Umiliati di Cremona* (Università degli Studi di Palermo, Istituto di Storia, Testi e Documenti, 2; 1966). P. Guerrini, 'Gli Umiliati a Brescia', *Miscellanea Pio Paschini*, 1 (Lateranum, NS 14; 1948), pp. 187–214; G. *Mercati, 'Due ricerche per la storia degli Umiliati', *Rivista di Storia della Chiesa in Italia*, 11 (1957), pp. 167–94. F. Vernet in *DTC* 7 (pt. 1; 1922), cols. 312–21; A. Mens in *Dict. Sp.* 7 (pt. 1; 1969), cols. 1129–36, both s.v. 'Humiliés'.

humility (Lat. *humilitas*, from *humus*, ground). Originally denoting low estate and the cowed attitude likely to result from it, in Judaism and esp. in Christianity the word acquired more positive connotations. Humility, understood as submissiveness before God, came to be regarded as a virtue, modelled on the example of Christ 'who humbled himself and became obedient unto death' (Phil. 2: 8). In both pagan and Judaeo-Christian usage it could be applied to the voluntary adoption of a posture of self-degradation, usually intended to reinforce an appeal for God's mercy and help. In later Christian usage it came to mean primarily the virtue opposed to *pride, but for many centuries it could also be applied to outward gestures of self-abasement, such as bowing. Although humility has sometimes been seen as involving a refusal to regard oneself as superior to other people, St *Thomas Aquinas, for instance, thought of it as meaning essentially submission to God and a consequent moderation of ambition to keep it within the bounds appointed for each individual by God; this is compatible with recognizing that in certain ways one may be better endowed by God than someone else is (cf. *Summa Theologiae*, 2. 2. q. 161, a. 1 and a. 3). In this sense, humility has been seen as an aspect of truthfulness, neither exaggerating nor denigrating the truth of what one is. Humility has been variously defined by Protestant theologians: M. *Luther regarded it as the joyful acceptance of God's will, and modern Protestant moralists (e.g. A. *Ritschl) identify it as complete resignation to our unconditional dependence on God.

F. [A.] Pakenham, Earl of Longford, *Humility* (1969). R. L. Ottley in *HERE* 6 (1913), pp. 880–2, s.v., with useful refs.; P. Adnès, SJ, in *Dict. Sp.* 7 (pt. 1; 1969), cols. 1136–87, with bibl.

Hundred Chapters, Council of the. See RUSSIA, CHRISTIANITY IN.

Hungary, Christianity in. Christianity was first preached in what is now Hungary in the 4th cent., but made no permanent impression. In the 9th and 10th cents. more successful missionaries arrived, and Christianity spread in both its E. and W. forms; ultimately the W. Church prevailed. In 1001 a formal constitution was laid down for the Church by King (St) *Stephen I, who created 10 bishoprics and the archbishopric of Esztergom (Gran), which since 1279 has been the primatial see. There are now two other archbishoprics. State control of Church affairs has always been strong. In 1404 Sigismund (King of Hungary 1387–1437) introduced the *placetum regium*, which was acknowledged by the Council of *Constance in 1417. After Maria Theresa (1740–80) had obtained from Pope *Clement XIII the title of 'Apostolic King' (*sic*), she and Joseph II (1780–90) tried to consolidate their hold by means of their Church policy (see JOSEPHINISM); Joseph dissolved over a third of the monasteries, though some were restored soon after his death. The RC Church maintained great influence over political affairs until 1945, in spite of certain secular laws (esp. those providing for civil marriage) introduced in the last decade of the 19th cent. After the Communist takeover of the country in 1948–9, it was persecuted, with the primate, Cardinal József Mindszenty (1892–1975), imprisoned, and almost all religious orders dissolved. By the 1970s and 1980s the situation was much relaxed, even before the overthrow of the Communist regime in 1989.

In the 16th cent. most of Hungary was won over to the Reformation. Subsequently the RC Church reasserted itself, especially in the western part of the country. In the east and what is now Transylvania, Protestantism remained strong, despite intermittent persecution, particularly in its *Calvinist form (Debrecen, its ecclesiastical and cultural centre, became popularly known as the 'Calvinist Rome'). The territory of historic Hungary (embracing also parts of present-day Romania, Slovakia, Croatia, Slovenia, and Ukraine) still harbours the only significant Protestant populations in the E. half of Europe, including over 3 million Magyar Calvinists, over 1 million Slovak, Magyar, and German *Lutherans, and the lineal survivors of one of the original *Unitarian movements.

A. Theiner (ed.), *Vetera Monumenta Historica Hungariam Sacram Illustrantia* (2 vols., Rome, 1859–60). *Monumenta Vaticana Historiam Regni Hungariae Illustrantia* (Budapest; 1st ser. 6 vols., 1884–91; 2nd ser. 3 vols., 1884–1909). L. Lukács (ed.), *The Vatican and Hungary 1846–1878: Reports and Correspondence on Hungary of the Apostolic Nuncios in Vienna* (Budapest, 1981). P. Bod (1712–69), *Historia Hungarorum Ecclesiastica inde ab Exordio Novi Testamenti ad Nostra usque Tempora*, ed. L. W. E. Rauwenhoff and C. Szalay (3 vols., Leiden, 1888–90). C. Wolfsgruber, *Kirchengeschichte Österreich-Ungarns* (Vienna, 1909). E. Mályusz, *Das Konstanzer Konzil und das königliche Patronatsrecht in Ungarn* (Studia Historica, 18; Budapest, 1959); id., *Egyházi társadalom a Középkori Magyarországon* (Budapest, 1971). G. Klaniczay, 'Le culte des saints dans la Hongrie médiévale (Problèmes de recherche)', *Acta Historica Academiae Scientiarium Hungaricae*, 29 (1983), pp. 57–77. E. Hermann, *A katolikus egyház története Magyarországon 1914-ig* (Dissertationes Hungaricae ex Historia Ecclesia, 1; Munich, 1973), with summaries in Ger. and Fr. M. Bucsay, *Geschichte des Protestantismus in Ungarn* (Stuttgart, 1959;

much expanded 2nd edn., Studien und Texte zur Kirchengeschichte und Geschichte, I. Reihe, Bd. 3; 2 vols., Vienna, 1977–9). G. Gombos, *The Lean Years: A Study of Hungarian Calvinism in Crisis* (New York, 1960). R. J. W. Evans, 'Calvinism in East Central Europe: Hungary and her Neighbours, 1540–1700', in M. Prestwich (ed.), *International Calvinism 1541–1715* (Oxford, 1985), pp. 167–96. *Calvin et la Hongrie*, ed. Communauté Protestante Hongroise de Genève (Geneva, 1986). J. Zoványi, *Magyarországi protestáns egyháztörténeti lexikon* (Budapest, 1977). P. Walters (ed.), *World Christianity: Eastern Europe* (Keston Book, 29; Eastbourne, 1988), pp. 141–71. E. Horn in *DTC* 8 (pt. 1; 1922), cols. 41–61, s.v. 'Hongrie', and 9 (pt. 2; 1927), cols. 1566–71, s.v. 'Magyarie'; W. Juhász in *NCE* 7 (1967), pp. 255–66, s.v.; P. Radó and J. Félegyházy in *Dict. Sp.* 7 (pt. 1; 1969), cols. 675–704, s.v. 'Hongrie'.

Hunt, William Holman (1827–1910), Pre-Raphaelite painter. A native of London, he was destined by his father for a business career, but began to study art in 1843 and was admitted to the Royal Academy Schools in 1844. Here he began his lifelong friendship with J. E. Millais, and later he also formed a close connection with D. G. *Rossetti. In 1848 they founded the Pre-Raphaelite Brotherhood, in which Hunt was a leading light. In the following year he exhibited his first truly Pre-Raphaelite picture, *Rienzi*. Though much attacked by the press, he and the Brotherhood were warmly defended by J. *Ruskin. In 1852 he completed *The Hireling Shepherd*, and in 1854 the famous *Light of the World*, representing the Lord knocking at the door of the soul. From 1854 to 1856 he travelled, mostly in Palestine, which he revisited several times. Here he made studies for *The Scapegoat*, exhibited in 1856, *The Finding of the Saviour in the Temple*, completed in 1860, and *The Shadow of Death*, painted between 1869 and 1873. In 1875 he began *The Triumph of the Innocents*, which was finished in two versions in 1885. In 1899 he began a larger replica of *The Light of the World*, now in St *Paul's Cathedral, the original being in Keble College, Oxford. In 1905 he published a largely autobiographical work, *Pre-Raphaelitism and the Pre-Raphaelite Brotherhood* (2 vols.). Most of Hunt's works were executed very slowly, and with great love of detail, in which he excelled, though sometimes to the detriment of composition and colouring. His art is imbued throughout with strong religious feeling.

[F. G. Stephens,] *William Holman Hunt and his Works* (1860); A. *Meynell and F. W. *Farrar, *William Holman Hunt: His Life and Work* (1893). Lives by A. C. Gissing (London, 1936) and A. C. Amor (ibid., 1989). *William Holman Hunt: An Exhibition arranged by the Walker Art Gallery Liverpool, March–April 1969; Victoria and Albert Museum, May–June 1969* (Liverpool, 1969), with introd. by M. Bennett. G. P. Landow, *William Holman Hunt and Typological Symbolism* (New Haven, Conn., and London, 1979); id., 'Shadows Cast by *The Light of the World*: William Holman Hunt's Religious Paintings, 1893–1905', *Art Bulletin: A Quarterly published by the College Art Association of America*, 65 (1983), pp. 471–84. J. Maas, *Holman Hunt and The Light of the World* (1984). W. Armstrong in *DNB, 1901–1911*, 2, pp. 323–8.

hunting. Though this has been generally held to be lawful for the laity, it was forbidden to the clergy by a series of Gallic councils beginning with a canon (55) of the Council of *Agde (506) which reappears in the '*Corpus Iuris Canonici'. In the Scholastic period a distinction was made between 'quiet' and 'noisy' hunting (*quieta* and *clamorosa*), and there was a division of opinion whether both kinds or only the noisy were forbidden to the clergy. The common opinion was that only the noisy was illicit. By 'noisy' was meant the hunting of large or dangerous animals by a crowd of people accompanied by a numerous pack of hounds. 'Quiet hunting' meant the use of snares, nets, or small packs of hounds for the destruction of hares, foxes, and other small animals.

In modern times, hunting, for laity and clergy alike, has occasionally been condemned altogether by Christian moralists on humanitarian grounds. In the RC Church the stricter view forbidding hunting of either kind to the clergy was taken by *Benedict XIV. Current RC Canon Law makes no mention of the subject.

Huntingdon, Selina, Countess of (1707–91).

Selina Hastings, foundress of the body of *Calvinistic Methodists known as 'the Countess of Huntingdon's Connexion'. She joined the *Wesleys' Methodist society in 1739, and on her husband's death in 1746 gave herself wholly up to social and religious work, making herself the chief medium for introducing Methodism to the upper classes. In 1768 she opened Trevecca House, Talgarth, as a Methodist seminary. Her chief method of supporting Methodist ministers was by constituting them her *chaplains; but her opinion that she could, as a peeress, appoint to the rank of chaplain as many priests of the established C of E as she wished, and employ them publicly, was disallowed by the consistory court of London in 1779. In consequence of this decision she registered her chapels as dissenting places of worship under the *Toleration Act. In the disputes between J. Wesley and G. *Whitefield she took the side of the latter, at whose death she became trustee of his foundations in America. Before her own death she formed her chapels into an association (1790), but many of her followers were absorbed into *Congregationalism. There were 900 members left in 1992.

The Life and Times of Selina Countess of Huntingdon by a Member of the Houses of Shirley and Hastings [i.e. A. C. H. Seymour] (2 vols., 1839); index by F. M. Jackson in Proceedings of the Wesley Historical Society, 5 (1905), following page 256. J. B. Figgis, The Countess of Huntingdon and her Connexion [c.1892]. F. F. Bretherton, The Countess of Huntingdon (Wesley Historical Society Lecture, no. 6; 1940); K. M. Davies, 'Lady Huntingdon a Threfeca', Journal of the Historical Society of the Presbyterian Church of Wales, 27 (1942), pp. 66–75. The 1778–1811 minutes of the Spa Fields Chapel (the headquarters of Lady Huntingdon's Connexion), together with the Fifteen Articles and Plan of Association, are ed. E. Welch, Two Calvinistic Methodist Chapels 1743–1811 (London Record Society Publications, 11; 1975), pp. 46–95. Id., 'Lady Huntingdon and Spa Fields Chapel', Guildhall Miscellany, 4 (1971–3), pp. 175–83. J. H. Overton in DNB 25 (1891), pp. 133–5, s.v. 'Hastings, Selina'.

Hupfeld, Hermann (1796–1866),

German OT scholar. He was educated at *Marburg and (under W. *Gesenius) at Halle, and for most of his life taught in these two universities. In the history of *Pentateuchal Criticism he occupies an important place through having in his Die Quellen der Genesis und die Art ihrer Zusammensetzung (1853) distinguished for the first time between the two sources *P and *E, both of which in Gen. use the same word *Elohim as the Divine Name. He also wrote a commentary on the Pss. (4 vols., 1855–61) and works dealing with Semitic grammar and philology.

Life by E. Riehm (Halle, 1867). J. [W.] Rogerson, Old Testament Criticism in Nineteenth Century England and Germany (1984), esp. pp. 131–4.

Huss, John (c.1372–1415),

in Czech **Jan Hus**, Bohemian Reformer. Born of a peasant family at Husinec (whence 'Huss'), he entered Prague university c.1390 and took his Master's degree in 1396. In 1401 he was elected Dean of the Philosophical Faculty. Having been ordained priest in 1400, he soon became a well-known preacher in Czech at the 'Bethlehem Chapel' at Prague. This was at the time when knowledge of J. *Wycliffe's writings had become more widespread in Bohemia through the closer relations with England that followed the marriage (1382) of Anne, sister of King Wenceslaus IV (d. 1419), to Richard II; Huss was especially attracted to his political doctrines (rejection of the right to property and of the hierarchical organization of society), which had been independently advocated by *Jerome of Prague, and was also sympathetic to his teachings on *Predestination and the Church of the elect. At first he received considerable encouragement from the new Abp. of Prague, Sbinko von Hasenburg, who made him preacher of the synod in 1403, and supported his attack on the pilgrimage of *Wilsnack in 'De Omni Sanguine Christi Glorificato' (1404); and, despite the university's condemnation of 45 of Wycliffe's propositions in 1403, Huss translated Wycliffe's 'Trialogus' into Czech. But before long his violent sermons on the morals of the clergy provoked hostility. They were denounced at Rome in 1407 and Sbinko, at Innocent VII's orders, forbade Huss to preach. Huss replied by 'De Arguendo Clero pro Concione'. When the country became divided over the two claimants to the Papal see (*Alexander V and Gregory XII), Huss with Wenceslaus and the Czech 'nation' at the university upheld Alexander, while Sbinko and the other three 'nations' (Bavarians, Saxons, and Poles) supported Gregory. His influence was temporarily much increased by a royal decree (18 Jan. 1409) giving control of the university to the Czech nation, which became a stronghold of Wycliffite doctrines, with Huss as Rector. In his isolation Abp. Sbinko transferred his allegiance to Alexander V, who rewarded him with a bull (9 Mar. 1410) ordering the destruction of all Wycliffite books, the retraction of Wycliffite doctrines, and, to stop Huss's influence at the Bethlehem Chapel, the cessation of preaching in private chapels; and in Feb. 1411 Huss was excommunicated by Alexander's successor, *John XXIII. Opinion now moved against him and in 1412 John imposed on Huss the great excommunication and placed his followers under an interdict. To restore peace Wenceslaus forthwith removed Huss from Prague and he found refuge with his supporters among the Czech nobility. Two conferences in 1412 and 1413 having failed to achieve peace, Huss devoted himself to writing his chief work, 'De Ecclesia' (1413), the first ten chapters of which are taken over bodily from Wycliffe. Having appealed from the decision of the Papal curia to a general Council, he left Bohemia in 1414 for the Council of *Constance, with a safe-conduct of the Emp. Sigismund. Arriving on 3 November 1414, he soon found his liberty threatened. When the trial opened he was confined in the conventual prison of the *Dominicans, later in a castle of the Bp. of Constance, and in the end in the convent of the *Franciscans, the Emperor's endeavour to free him being of no avail. He suffered death at the stake with great fortitude on 6 July 1415.

By his death Huss became a national hero. The university of Prague declared him a martyr and fixed his feast on the day of his execution. Social and political grievance among the Czechs of Bohemia at the wealth and corruption of the Church and at the dominant position of Germans in the country, now overflowed into a violent movement of protest which assumed Huss' name. By the Four Articles of Prague (1420) the Hussites laid down a programme of secularization, *Utraquism, vernacular liturgy, and ecclesiastical reform which anticipated the *Reformation in important ways. During the Hussite Wars (1420–34) they were able to implement much of this in Bohemia, despite bitter opposition from Catholic Europe. Although international divisions gradually weakened the cause, it left a lasting legacy in Utraquism and the sect of the *Bohemian Brethren, and in a tradition of national Catholicism which revived in modern times as both a political and—to a lesser extent—a religious ideal (see CZECHOSLOVAK CHURCH).

Opera Omnia, ed. by V. Flajšhans (3 vols., Prague, 1903–8); also ed. under the auspices of the Academia Scientiarum Bohemoslovenica (Prague, 1959 ff.). Modern edn. of De Ecclesia by S. H. Thompson (Boulder, Col., and Cambridge, 1957). Eng. trs. of De Ecclesia by D. S. Schaff (New York, 1915), of his Letters by M. Spinka (Manchester [1972]), and of Peter of Mladoňovice's 'Relatio de Mag. Joannis Hus causa', with introd., notes, and other relevant docs., by M. Spinka, John Hus at the Council of Constance (Records of Civilization, Sources and Studies, 73; 1965). Much of the important lit. is in Czech, esp. the works of F. M. Bartoš, V. Novotný, and A. Molnár. J. Loserth, Hus und Wiclif: Zur Genesis der husitischen Lehre (1884; Eng. tr., 1884; 2nd edn. of Ger., 1925); M. Vischer, Jan Hus: Sein Leben und seine Zeit (2 vols., Frankfurt [1940]); M. Spinka, John Hus and the Czech Reform (Chicago, 1941); id., John Hus' Concept of the Church (Princeton, NJ, 1966); id., John Hus: A Biography (ibid., 1968); P. de Vooght, OSB, L'Hérésie de Jean Huss (Bibliothèque de la Revue d'Histoire ecclésiastique, 34; 1960); id., Hussiana (ibid., 35; 1960; 2nd edn. of both vols. under the title of the former, 1975); R. Kalivoda, Husitská Ideologie (Prague, 1961; Ger. tr., Revolution und Ideologie: Der Hussitismus, Cologne, 1976); id. and A. Kolesnyk, Das Hussitische Denken im Lichte seiner Quellen (Beiträge zur Geschichte des religiösen und wissenschaftlichen Denkens, 8; 1969); H. Kaminsky, A History of the Hussite Revolution (Berkeley and Los Angeles, Calif., 1967); J. Macek, Jean Hus et les traditions Hussites (XVᵉ–XIXᵉ siècles) [1973]; F. Šmahel, La révolution hussite, une anomalie historique (Collège de France, Essais et conférences [1985]); F. Seibt, Hussitenstudien (Veröffentlichung des Collegium Carolinum, 60; Munich, 1987). E. Werner, Jan Hus: Welt und Umwelt eines Prager Frühreformators (Forschungen zur mittelalterlichen Geschichte, 34; 1991). F. M. Bartoš, The Hussite Revolution 1424–1437 (East European Monographs, 203; New York, 1986 (Eng. tr. of Husitská revoluce, 2 vols., Prague, 1965–6)). M. Lambert, Medieval Heresy (2nd edn., 1992), esp. pp. 284–326. J. K. Zeman, The Hussite Movement and the Reformation in Bohemia, Moravia and Slovakia (1350–1650): A Bibliographical Study Guide (With Particular Reference to Resources in North America) (Ann Arbor, Mich., 1977). F. Machilek in TRE 15 (1986), pp. 710–35, s.v. 'Hus/Hussiten'.

Hutchinson, John (1674–1737), author. He was a native of Yorkshire, and, after being steward to the Earl of Scarborough and the Duke of Somerset, planned a work on the Mosaic account of the Flood. In his chief work, Moses's Principia (1724), he expounds a system of biblical philosophy, maintaining that Hebrew was the primitive language of mankind which, if rightly interpreted, gave the key to all knowledge whether secular or religious. The book was written in opposition to I. *Newton's Principia and had a considerable success. Its theories were developed by a circle of predominantly *High Church Anglicans called the 'Hutchinsonians', to which belonged, among others, G. *Horne and W. *Jones of Nayland. In their sacramental and mystical interpretation of orthodox Christianity, the 'Hutchinsonians' are often seen as precursors of the *Oxford Movement.

The Philosophical and Theological Works … of John Hutchinson, ed. R. Spearman and J. Bate (12 vols., London, 1748–9). An Abstract of the Works of J. Hutchinson (1753). J. P[arkhurst] (ed.), A Supplement to the Works of John Hutchinson … being an Index and Explanation of the Hebrew Words cited in the Second Part of his Moses's Principia, with additional Remarks, by R. Spearman (1765), and Life by R. Spearman, pp. i–xiv. G. Horne, An Apology for certain Gentlemen in the University of Oxford, Aspersed in a late Anonymous Pamphlet [B. *Kennicott, A Word to the Hutchinsonians] (Oxford, 1756). L. Stephen, History of English Thought in the Eighteenth Century, 1 (1876), pp. 389–91. Id. in DNB 28 (1891), pp. 342 f.

Hutten, Ulrich von (1488–1523), German Humanist and controversialist. He belonged to the lower nobility and was born at the castle of Steckelberg, nr. *Fulda. In 1499 he was placed in the monastery of Fulda by his parents, who designed him for the religious life, probably on account of his weak health. In 1505, however, he fled, and during the next years led an unsettled life, visiting many of the German universities, among them *Cologne, *Wittenberg, and Vienna. In 1512–13 he took part in the wars of Emp. Maximilian in Italy as a Landsknecht. In 1515 he began to write a series of attacks (pub. 1519) against Duke Ulrich of Württemberg, who had murdered a member of his family. About the same time he became a contributor to the famous Humanistic satire *Epistolae Obscurorum Virorum. In 1517 he received the laurel crown of the poet from the Emperor and entered the service of the Elector of Mainz, Abp. *Albert of Brandenburg. He edited L. *Valla's treatise on the '*Donation of Constantine' (pub. c.1520), with a sarcastic dedication to the Pope (dated 1 Dec. 1517). In 1518 he delivered an address to the Diet of Augsburg recommending rejection of the Roman taxation to finance a crusade against the Turks. From 1519 he dedicated his life to the propagation of M. *Luther's reformation, in which he saw the instrument for the deliverance of Germany from the power of Rome. His Latin dialogue Arminius (1520), depicts the hero as a symbol of German resistance to Roman tyranny throughout the ages. A series of Latin and German treatises, among them Febris Secunda, Vadiscus Dialogus (both 1520), and the famous Gesprächbüchlein (1521), served this purpose further. Having failed to gain the Archduke Ferdinand for the Reformation, he was dismissed from the service of the Abp. of Mainz, and being under an order of arrest from Rome, fled to Franz von *Sickingen. After the latter's defeat he was exiled from the Empire and sought the protection of *Erasmus (1522), who refused to receive him, and at last went to H. *Zwingli, who provided him, broken by disease and misfortune, with a refuge on the island of Ufenau in the Lake of Zurich.

Works ed. E. Böcking, 5 vols. and 2 suppl. vols., Leipzig, 1859–70. Ger. writings ed. S. Szamatólski, Strasbourg, 1891. Several modern Lives, among them those of D. F. *Strauss (3 vols., Leipzig, 1858–60; new edn. by O. Clemen, 1914; Eng. tr., 1874), H. Holborn (Leipzig, 1929; Eng. tr., Yale Historical Publications, no. 11, 1937), and C. Gräter (Stuttgart, 1988). P. Kalkoff, *Ulrich von Hutten und die Reformation* (1920), and other works; P. Held, *Ulrich von Hutten: Seine religiösgeistige Auseinandersetzung mit Katholizismus, Humanismus, Reformation* (Schriften des Vereins für Reformationsgeschichte, Jahrg. 46, Heft 1; 1928). F. Rueb, *Der hinkende Schmiedgott Vulkan: Ulrich von Hutten 1488–1523* (Zurich [1988]). J. Benzing, *Ulrich von Hutten und seine Drucker: Eine Bibliographie der Schriften Hutten im 16. Jahrhundert* (Beiträge zum Buch- und Bibliothekswesen, 6; Wiesbaden, 1956); W. Kreutz, *Die Deutschen und Ulrich von Hutten: Rezeption von Autor und Werk seit dem 16. Jahrhundert* (Munich, 1984). B. Könneker in P. G. Bietenholz and T. B. Deutscher (eds.), *Contemporaries of Erasmus*, 2 [1986], pp. 217–20, s.v. with further bibl.

Hutterites. See ANABAPTISTS.

Hutton, Richard Holt (1826–97), lay religious writer. The son of a *Unitarian minister, he was educated at University College, London, where he became a lifelong friend of Walter Bagehot (1827–77). In 1847 he entered Manchester New College to prepare for the Unitarian ministry and came under the influence of J. *Martineau; but failing to secure a permanent ministerial charge, in 1851 he became editor of the *Inquirer*, a Unitarian weekly. His tolerant outlook caused offence to conservative Unitarians and he was soon removed. From 1855 to 1864 he edited with Bagehot the *National Review*. Under the influence of F. W. *Robertson and F. D. *Maurice he was increasingly drawn to the C of E, of which he became a member. In 1861 he was offered by M. W. Townsend (1831–1911) the joint-editorship and proprietorship of the *Spectator*. He made the utmost of this opportunity, using the journal as a pulpit from which to challenge, on Christian principles, the prevailing agnosticism (J. S. Mill, T. H. *Huxley) and to present the case for many worthwhile causes; and he held his editorship until his death. He was one of the original members of the *Metaphysical Society (founded 1869) and in his later years became intimate with many leading *High Churchmen (R. W. *Church, H. P. *Liddon) and RCs (W. G. *Ward). In 1891 he wrote a Life of J. H. *Newman. His *Essays Theological and Literary* (2 vols., 1871) went through several editions.

J. Hogben, *Richard Holt Hutton of 'The Spectator': A Monograph* (1899); M. Woodfield, *R. H. Hutton: Critic and Theologian* (Oxford, 1986). *DNB*, Suppl. 3 (1901), pp. 19–22 [anon.].

Hutton, William Holden (1860–1930), Dean of *Winchester. Educated at Magdalen College, Oxford, he became in 1884 a Fellow of St John's, where he remained a history tutor for 25 years. From 1911 to 1919 he was Canon of *Peterborough, and from 1919 till his death Dean of Winchester. He was a devoted and influential sponsor of the conservative High Church tradition in *Anglicanism. His writings include Lives of *Sir Thomas *More* (1895), *William *Laud* (1895), and *Thomas *Becket* (1910), and a set of *Bampton Lectures on *The Lives of the English Saints* (1903).

C. W. C. Oman in *DNB, 1922–1930*, pp. 442 f., s.v.

Huvelin, Henri (1838–1910), priest and spiritual director. Born in Laon (and baptized Marie Joseph Philippe), he was brought up in Paris. After studying at the École Normale Supérieure, he trained for the priesthood in Rome. In 1875 he became curate at the church of St-Augustin in Paris, where he remained until his death. A noted spiritual director, sought out by Christian and non-Christian alike, he numbered Charles *de Foucauld and the Baron *von Hügel among his penitents.

He published almost nothing in his lifetime, but after his death two series of lectures were published: *Quelques directeurs d'âmes au XVIIᵉ siècle* (1911; Eng. tr., 1927), and *Bossuet, Fénelon et le quiétisme* (2 vols., 1912). M.-T. (L.-) Lefebvre, *Un Prêtre: L'abbé Huvelin* (1956; rev. edn., 1958; Eng. tr., 1967); L. Portier, *Un Précurseur: L'abbé Huvelin* (1979), with notes on sources, pub. and unpub., pp. 251–68. J.-F. Six in *Dict. Sp.* 7 (pt. 1; 1969), cols. 1200–4, s.v. See also bibl. to DE FOUCAULD, C.

Huxley, Thomas Henry (1825–95), biologist. A native of Ealing, after a precocious boyhood he studied medicine at Charing Cross Hospital from 1842 to 1845 and in 1846 secured an appointment in the Navy Medical Service, which soon enabled him to pursue scientific investigations in the *Rattlesnake* (1846–50) in southern tropical waters. Here he carried through some remarkable biological researches. Recognition quickly followed and in 1851 he was elected a FRS. In 1854 he left the Navy and accepted a post as lecturer at the Royal School of Mines. From the publication of *On the Educational Value of the Natural History Sciences* (1854) he became prominent as an advocate of scientific training as the surest remedy for man's intellectual, social, and moral needs. His campaign on behalf of science was greatly stimulated by the controversy aroused in 1859 by C. *Darwin's *Origin of Species*. At the meeting of the British Association at *Oxford in 1860 he had a memorable passage of words with the Bp. of Oxford (S. *Wilberforce) on the subject of evolution. In 1863 there appeared his *Evidence as to Man's Place in Nature*, a defence of man's descent from the lower animal world, and in 1868 he delivered a lecture on 'The Physical Basis of Life' in the course of which he discussed a form of '*agnosticism' (a term of his own coining a year or two later). Man, he argued, cannot know the nature of either spirit or matter; metaphysics is impossible; and man's primary duty in life is the relief of misery and ignorance. From c.1870 he filled several important administrative offices, in some of which he exercised great influence. As a member of the London School Board from 1870 to 1872 he laid stress on the merits of physical, moral, and esp. scientific education, but he held that such education should be supplemented by the study of the Bible as the only means by which religious feeling, the basis of moral conduct, could be sustained. In 1879 he published a study of D. *Hume with a special chapter on *miracles, which he declined to reject out of hand: 'Every event must be taken to be a part of nature, until proof to the contrary is supplied'.

Compelled in 1885 to retire from public work for reasons of health, he continued active in writing. His attacks on Christian orthodoxy became more persistent and he carried his agnosticism into the field of NT study, holding that certain knowledge as to the teaching and convictions of Christ was impossible. He summarized his final views in his Romanes Lecture on 'Evolution and Ethics', delivered at Oxford on 18 May 1893.

Collected Essays (9 vols., 1893–4); *Scientific Memoirs*, ed. M. Foster and E. R. Lankester (5 vols., 1898–1903). Selections from his writings, ed., with brief introd. essays, by C. Bibby (1967). *Evolution and Ethics*, ed. J. [G.] Paradis and G. C. Williams, with New Essays on its Victorian and Sociobiological Context (Princeton, NJ [1989]). L. Huxley, *The Life and Letters of Thomas Henry Huxley* (2 vols., 1900). His scientific achievements are treated in P. C. Mitchell, *Thomas Henry Huxley* (1900); C. Bibby, *T. H. Huxley: Scientist, Humanist and Educator* (1959). J. G. Paradis, *T. H. Huxley: Man's Place in Nature* (Lincoln, Neb., and London [1978]). M. A. di Gregorio, *T. H. Huxley's Place in Natural Science* (New Haven, Conn., and London [1984]). W. F. R. Weldon in *DNB*, Suppl. 3 (1901), pp. 22–31; W. C. Williams in *Dictionary of Scientific Biography*, 6 (1972), pp. 589–97.

Huysmans, Joris Karl (1848–1907), French Catholic novelist. Of Dutch descent, he was for 30 years a member of the French Ministry of the Interior, but his main claim to fame lay in his literary work. His early novels, *Marthe* (1876), *A rebours* (1884), and *Là-bas* (1891), reveal his association with the Goncourt–Zola school of literary realism, many of their characters being decadent types. He was converted to a living Christian faith by a visit to the *Trappist monastery of Igny. It found expression in *En route* (1895), *La Cathédrale* (1898), *Sainte Lydwine de Schiedam* (1901, a study in the value of suffering), *L'Oblat* (1903) and other books. His writings generally reflected his deep interest in religious art, ritual, and mysticism.

Œuvres complètes, ed. L. Descaves (18 vols., Paris, 1928–34). Life by R. Baldick (Oxford, 1955). K. Bosch, *J. K. Huysmans' religiöser Entwicklungsgang* (Constance, 1920); H. Bachelin, *J. K. Huysmans: Du naturalisme littéraire au naturalisme mystique* (1926). Other studies by L. Deffoux (Paris, 1927), E. Seillière (ibid., 1931), H. Trudgian (ibid., 1934), P. Cogny (Caen thesis; Paris, 1953), H. R. T. Brandreth, OGS (London, 1963), and M. M. Belval (Paris, 1968). *Huysmans*, ed. P. Brunel and A. Guyaux (Cahiers de l'Herne, 47; 1985), with bibl. covering 1949–84 by P. Rancœur, pp. 446–65.

Hyacinth, St (d. 1257), 'Apostle of *Poland'. It is difficult to disentangle the facts from the fanciful Life composed in the 14th cent. by Stanislaus, who also changed his name from Jacko (modern Polish Jacek) to Hyacinth. It is certain that he was born in Kamien, in the NE of Poland, that he went to Italy, perhaps as a student, and joined the *Dominican Order there *c*.1220. Probably in 1221 he was put in charge of a group of Dominicans sent to Poland. He was delayed by the urgent needs of the Dominicans in Friesach, and only in 1222 reached Cracow, where he founded a priory in 1223. He later established a priory in Gdansk (*c*.1225). From *c*.1229 he worked in Kiev for a few years and then returned to Poland and devoted himself to missionary work, particularly the campaign against the pagans in Prussia. He later retired to Cracow, where he died, having a reputation for sanctity and working miracles. The story of his extensive labours in Scandinavia lacks historical foundation. He was canonized in 1594. Feast day, 17 Aug. (formerly 16 Aug.).

L. Cwiklinski, 'De Vita et Miraculis S. Iacchonis (Hyacinthi) Ordinis Fratrum Praedicatorum, auctore Stanislao Lectore Cracoviensi eiusdem Ordinis' and other items in *Monumenta Poloniae Historica*, 4 (Lemberg, 1884), pp. 818–903. B. *Altaner, *Die Dominikanermissionen des 13. Jahrhunderts* (1924), pp. 196–214. R. J.

Loenertz, OP, 'La Vie de S. Hyacinthe du lecteur Stanislas envisagée comme source historique', *Archivum Fratrum Praedicatorum*, 27 (1957), pp. 5–38. J. Gottschalk, 'Zur Geschichte der Hyazinth-Verehrung', *Archiv für schlesische Kirchengeschichte*, 16 (1958), pp. 60–98, with other arts. by A. Seidel, pp. 99–110 and P. Birkner, pp. 111–36. V. J. Koudelka, OP, in *Bibliotheca Sanctorum*, 6 (1965), cols. 326–31, s.v. 'Giacinto'.

Hydroparastatae (Gk. Ὑδροπαράσταται, 'those who advocate water'). A name used from the 4th cent. of the *Aquarians.

hylomorphism. A metaphysical doctrine derived from *Aristotle, acc. to which the actual specific reality of a physical thing is the μορφή (*forma*), while the ὕλη (*materia*) contributes to its being only potentiality and limitation. It had a fundamental place in the systems of St *Albertus Magnus and St *Thomas Aquinas.

hylozoism. The doctrine that all matter is endowed with life. In a crude form it was taught by the ancient Greek philosophers (Thales, Anaximenes, Heraclitus) and the *Stoics ('world soul') and in a more spiritual form by many of the Renaissance thinkers (B. *Telesio, G. *Bruno), by some of the *Cambridge Platonists (H. *More, R. *Cudworth), and by G. T. *Fechner. A materialistic form of the doctrine was revived by E. H. *Haeckel.

Hymnary (Lat. *Hymnarium*). The medieval liturgical book of the W. rite which contained the metrical hymns of the Divine Office arranged acc. to the Liturgical Year. It was often appended to the *Psaltery and sometimes to the *Antiphonary. Its contents were later incorporated into the *Breviary.

J. Mearns, *Early Latin Hymnaries: An Index of Hymns in Hymnaries before 1100* (Cambridge, 1913). See also bibl. to following entry.

hymns (Gk. ὕμνος, 'song in praise of gods or heroes'). Sacred poetry set to music and sung in the course of the services of the Church has always formed part of Christian worship, whether to express doctrine or the devotion of individuals. At first the hymns of the Jewish Church, esp. the Psalms, were in use, and it is recorded that a hymn was sung at the *Last Supper (Mk. 14: 26); this was prob. the *Hallel. At an early date distinctively Christian compositions, e.g. *Magnificat, *Benedictus, and *Nunc Dimittis, appeared. What may to be quotations from early Christian hymns also occur in Eph. 5: 14, Phil. 2: 5–11, 1 Tim. 3: 16, 1 Tim. 6: 15 f., 2 Tim. 2: 11–13, Rev. 15: 3–4, and Rev. 22: 17, while hymns are differentiated from Psalms in Col. 3: 16 and Eph. 5: 19. *Pliny's famous letter (*Ad Traj.* 96) may refer to an antiphonal hymn or to a form of liturgy. The rhythmical prose in use in the early Church (1 *Clement 59–61, Ep. to *Diognetus, *Didache, *Melito's treatise *On the Passion*) furthered the development of hymnody. A 3rd-cent. writer (perhaps *Hippolytus) refers to 'psalms and odes such as from the beginning were written by believers, hymns to the Christ, the Word of God, calling Him God' (Eusebius, *HE* 5. 28. 5).

The earliest complete Christian hymn that survives, 'Bridle of colts untamed', is a hymn to Christ preserved by *Clement of Alexandria. Other hymns of pre-Nicene date are 'Up, Maidens', included by *Methodius of Olympus in his *Symposium*, and the Φῶς ἱλαρόν (*Phos Hilaron, 'Hail, gladdening Light', *AM* 18, *EH* 269), which is still part of the Evening Office of the E. Church. The *Gnostics (*Valentinus, *Bardesanes and his son Harmonius, *Marcion) made extensive use of hymns, but only traces of these remain. In Syriac there exists a collection of 42 'Odes of *Solomon' (q.v.), as well as two early hymns incorporated into the 'Acts of *Thomas' (q.v.; the 'Hymn on the Daughter of Light', 6–7, and the 'Hymn of the Pearl', 108–13).

From the 4th cent. the use of hymns became more general. A Greek form of the *Gloria in excelsis, which is of unknown authorship, is found in the *Apostolic Constitutions* (7. 47). In the Byzantine rite it forms part of *Orthros (the morning office) and of *Compline; in the W. it was introduced into the Mass, apparently under *Symmachus I (d. 514), though its use was long restricted. From this period hymns were also employed as a powerful means of promoting or refuting heresy. In the E. St *Ephraem Syrus (d. 373) wrote Syriac hymns to counter the heresy of Bardesanes and to celebrate the Christian mysteries. Early Greek hymn-writers include St *Gregory Nazianzen (d. 389/90) and *Synesius (d. *c*.413). Both used classical models, and the latter is notable for his introduction of *Neoplatonist ideas into Christian hymns. In both E. and W. hymnody played a part in the *Arian controversy. In Constantinople under the Emp. *Theodosius I (d. 395) the Arians sang hymns through the streets, while St John *Chrysostom (d. 407) organized orthodox hymn-singing. Similarly, St *Augustine (*Confessions*, 9. 7) records the introduction of the custom of singing psalms and hymns in the manner of the E. Church at Milan during the struggle of St *Ambrose with Justina.

From the 5th cent. the belief obtained in some quarters that no words other than those of Scripture should be allowed in the liturgy, and as late as 563 the Council of Braga forbade the singing of non-biblical poetical compositions in church (can. 12), a decision not reversed until the fourth Council of *Toledo in 633 (can. 13). From the 5th cent. *troparia (single-stanza hymns), of which the *Monogenes and the *Cherubicon are the most famous, are found in the E. service books. These were later joined together to form *contakia of 18 to 30 stanzas, and from the 7th cent. *canons. The classical Greek hymn-writers include *Romanos (6th cent.), to whom the authorship of the *Acathistos hymn is frequently attributed, *Sergius I, Patr. of Constantinople (d. 638), St *Andrew of Crete (d. 740), St *John of Damascus (d. *c*.750), St *Cosmas Melodus (d. *c*.751), and St *Joseph the Hymnographer (d. 886). Characteristic of Greek hymns are their dogmatic emphasis and faculty of sustained praise, often offset by monotony of thought and repetition of diction.

Latin hymns appear later than Greek. The most famous, the *Te Deum, is written not in verse but in rhythmical prose. The authorship of the first 21 verses has been assigned to *Niceta of Remesiana (d. *c*.414), but the whole may be derived from a *Paschal Vigil Baptismal Mass. St *Hilary (d. 367) wrote hymns, prob. under E. influence, when he was in exile, but the 'liber hymnorum' ascribed to him by St *Jerome is lost, except for a few fragments. The real impetus, however, came from St Ambrose. Though only three hymns can be ascribed to

him with certainty, they laid down the line of development of Latin hymnody as simple, devotional, and direct, and it was through his influence that hymns became a recognized and integral part of the public worship of the W. Church. Though hymns were not admitted to the Roman Office until the 12th cent. the development came to be towards an ordered sequence for use at different times and seasons. Other Latin hymn-writers include *Prudentius (d. *c*.410), *Sedulius (5th cent.), *Venantius Fortunatus (d. *c*.610) *Bede (d. 735), *Theodulph of Orleans (d. 821), *Notker of St Gall (d. 1022; the popularizer of *Sequences, the first hymns introduced into the Mass), P. *Abelard (d. *c*.1142), *Adam of St-Victor (d. between 1177 and 1192; 'the greatest of the sacred Latin poets of the Middle Ages', R. C. *Trench), Philip the Chancellor (d. 1236), and St *Thomas Aquinas (d. 1274). The *Counter-Reformation led to the remodelling of a number of the old *Office hymns and the composition of new ones in a more classical diction and metre, first in Italy under Pope *Urban VIII, and then in France. Among their authors were the brothers Claude and Jean Baptiste de Santeuil (d. 1684 and 1697) and Charles *Coffin (d. 1749). Some monastic orders, including the *Benedictines, did not adopt the new hymns. Two well-known hymns of the 17th or 18th cent. are '*Veni, veni, Emmanuel' (*AM* 49; *EH* 8) and '*Adeste Fideles' (*AM* 59, *EH* 28), both of obscure origin.

In England hymns first appear in the vernacular with *Caedmon (Bede, *HE* 4. 24), *Aldhelm (d. 709), and King *Alfred (d. 899). Towards the close of the Middle Ages hymns to Christ as Redeemer and to the BVM, together with translations of Latin hymns, became popular. Among the leading medieval English hymn-writers was Richard *Rolle of Hampole (d. 1349). Hymns in the vernacular were, with some individual exceptions, mainly the work of those outside the main religious stream. The most important, and essentially English, development of the period was the *carol. Its origin, and the derivation of the word itself, are both in dispute. The earliest printed collection of carols is that of Wynkyn de Worde of 1521. The carol flourished in England until the *Puritan ascendancy, and then survived in provincial broadsheet and oral tradition until the 19th cent., when interest rapidly revived; collections of carols were published by Davies Gilbert in 1822 and by W. Sandys in 1833. A fresh stimulus was provided by J. M. *Neale's discovery of the Swedish *Piae Cantiones* of 1582. Since then carols have been the subject of much serious study.

The Reformation had a deep and varied effect on the development of hymnody. *Lutheranism was marked by a wealth of new hymns written by M. *Luther himself (d. 1546), who was a skilled musician and imitated the pattern of medieval secular music, and by M. Weisse (d. 1534), P. Nicolai (d. 1609), and later by M. A. von Löwenstern (d. 1648) and P. *Gerhardt (d. 1676). Apart from J. S. *Bach (d. 1750), German hymnology has not since attained so high a standard. The first Protestant hymn-book was M. Weisse's *Ein New Geseng Buchlen* (1531). *Calvinism, on the other hand, would tolerate nothing but the words of Scripture in its services. Hence the Psalms were put into *metrical versions, first in French by C. *Marot (d. 1544) and T. *Beza (d. 1605), with L. Bourgeois (d. 1561) as musical editor; their work was collected in the 'Genevan Psalter' (1563). An attempt by M. *Coverdale to introduce

Lutheran chorales into England in his *Goostly Psalmes and Spirituall Songes* [undated] was unsuccessful, and hymns (with the exception of the two versions of the *Veni Creator in the *Ordinal) disappeared from the English service books, less, it would seem, on grounds of principle than because T. *Cranmer, on his own admission, lacked the 'grace and facility' to render Latin hymns well into English. Metrical versions of the Psalter were made and widely used in England from an early date, and continued in use until they were displaced by hymns in the 19th cent. The 'Old Version' of the Psalter of T. S. *Sternhold (q.v.) and J. Hopkins appeared in 1557, and was authorized by the Royal *Injunctions of 1559. In 1623 *Hymns and Songs of the Church* was published by George Wither (d. 1667). It gained considerable initial popularity, but was successfully opposed by the Company of Stationers, which had a monopoly of printing the metrical Psalter. The 'New Version' of N. *Tate and N. Brady, with a supplement, appeared in 1696, and was authorized as an alternative to the 'Old Version' by Order in Council. Hymns continued to be written for private and local use, e.g. by G. *Herbert (whose poems were edited and first used as hymns by J. *Wesley), H. *Vaughan, 'the Silurist' (d. 1695) and T. *Ken (d. 1711).

Modern hymn-writing and hymn-singing were mainly the creation of the 18th cent. A prominent place is filled by Isaac *Watts (d. 1748), the *Congregationalist, whose hymns were written to express the spiritual experience of the singer. In 1737 appeared John Wesley's *Collection of Psalms and Hymns*, the first hymn-book of modern type, followed in 1739 by *Hymns and Sacred Poems* by John and Charles *Wesley. The latter was the most prolific, and probably the most gifted, of all English hymn-writers. The practice of hymn-singing was much encouraged and developed by the *Methodists. It soon spread among the *Evangelical party of the C of E, though it was long frowned upon by authority. Other hymn-writers of this period were P. *Doddridge (d. 1751) and A. *Toplady (*Psalms and Hymns for Public and Private Worship*, 1776). In 1779 J. *Newton and W. *Cowper published *Olney Hymns*, a collection of hymns of the subjective and emotional type characteristic of the Evangelical school.

In America, social conditions in the 19th cent. found expression in the Negro *spiritual, which was a powerful factor in the Second *Great Awakening of 1797–1805. The most important collection of Negro spirituals is that of J. Ingall, *Christian Harmony* (1805). In the same tradition, the mission hymns of D. L. *Moody (d. 1899) and Ira D. Sankey (d. 1908) exerted considerable influence in both America and England.

By the beginning of the 19th cent., prejudice against the use of hymns in the C of E was dying, although the legality of hymns was challenged in the ecclesiastical courts by the parishioners of St Paul's, Sheffield, after the publication of a hymnal by the Vicar, T. Cotterill, in 1805. This dispute was settled in 1820 by a ruling of the Abp. of York, Vernon Harcourt, who sanctioned the use of a modified version of the hymnal. The time was now ripe for a hymn-book which could be integrated into the Prayer Book scheme of worship. R. *Heber (d. 1826), who both wrote and collected hymns, intended his (posthumous) *Hymns written and adapted to the Weekly Church Services of the Year* (1827) to be both 'literary' and 'liturgical'. Though

never widely used, it did much to break down the remaining hostility to hymns outside Evangelical circles. J. Montgomery (d. 1854) also wrote many hymns, including some still in use. A further important influence in fostering the use of hymns came from the *Oxford Movement. The hymns of the ancient and medieval Church were employed to emphasize the antiquity and catholicity of the Church. Translations were made by I. *Williams (d. 1865), J. M. *Neale (d. 1865), F. *Oakeley (d. 1880), E. *Caswall (d. 1878), and W. J. Copeland (d. 1885). Original compositions came from J. *Keble (d. 1866; *Christian Year*, 1827) and J. H. *Newman (d. 1890; *Dream of Gerontius*, 1865).

By the middle of the 19th cent., hymn-singing was firmly established in the C of E, and in 1890 Abp. E. W. *Benson in the '*Lincoln Judgement' allowed the use of hymns provided they did not interrupt the course of the service. Hymn-books were published which combined ancient hymns with those of recent composition. The *Sacred Hymns from the German* (1841) of Frances Cox (d. 1897) and the *Lyra Germanica* (1855) of Catherine Winkworth (d. 1878) introduced a knowledge of German hymnology into England. The *Hymnal Noted* (mainly the work of J. M. Neale) appeared in 1852 (Part 1) and 1854 (2). This was followed by *Hymns, Ancient and Modern* (1861), which set the pattern for Anglican hymn-books with hymns for the liturgical calendar as well as those of personal devotion. The publication of the *Yattendon Hymnal* (1895–9) of R. S. *Bridges (d. 1930) and the *Songs of Syon* (1904) edited by G. R. Woodward (d. 1934) set a new literary and musical standard which was followed by the widely used *English Hymnal* (1906). The 1980s saw a succession of new C of E hymn-books: *Hymns for Today's Church* (1982), *Hymns Ancient and Modern, New Standard* (1983), and *The New English Hymnal* (1986).

Among RCs there arose in the 19th cent. a demand for popular hymns, which was met by such writers as F. W. *Faber (d. 1863). In its time, a standard work was the *Westminster Hymnal* (1912; new edn., 1940). Pope *Pius XII's encyclical 'Musicae sacrae disciplina' (1955) and the Constitution on the Sacred Liturgy of the Second *Vatican Council (1963) encouraged the use of 'religious songs' by the people, while the new Missal of 1970 makes specific provision for hymns, which no longer have to be confined to those written by RC authors. In addition the Latin hymns in the 1971 Breviary have been extensively revised and many older hymns restored to their original form.

Apart from the *Quakers, other English-speaking Churches have all assigned an important place to hymns, as being an integral part of Christian worship rather than an addition to it. Over the years they have issued collections of hymns authorized for use in their own services; these have included the *Church Hymnary* of the Scottish and other Presbyterians (1898), the *Baptist Church Hymnal* (1900), and the *Methodist Hymn-Book* (1904). As in the C of E, recent years have seen the compilation of new hymn-books by the major Churches: a revision of the *Church Hymnary* (3rd edn., 1973), *Hymns and Psalms: A Methodist and Ecumenical Hymn Book* (1983; drawn up in consultation with representatives of a number of Churches), *Rejoice and Sing* for the *United Reformed Church (1991), and *Baptist Hymns and Worship* (1991).

In addition to the denominational hymn-books, there have been numerous hymnals for particular types of community. The first (successful) attempt to compile an ecumenical hymn book was *Songs of Praise (1925), which was widely adopted for use in schools. It was followed by the BBC Hymn Book (1951), the Cambridge Hymnal (1967), and by the Australian Hymn Book (1977), more widely known under the title With One Voice (1979).

All the new hymn-books draw in varying degrees upon the wide range of new and experimental hymnology which had appeared in supplements and smaller books during the 1970s and 1980s. Much of it is more akin to the carol than to the traditional hymn. These hymns and religious songs, often of charismatic inspiration, seek to express the theological and liturgical ideas of the time, and often make use of popular linguistic and musical idiom. But in spite of some attempts to alter hymns from the 'thou' to the 'you' form, most books have retained the traditional language of old and classical hymns.

W. Christ and M. Paranikas (eds.), Anthologia Graeca Carminum Christianorum (Leipzig, 1871). H. Follieri, Initia Hymnorum Ecclesiae Graecae (ST 211–215 bis; 1960–6). J. B. [F.] *Pitra, Hymnologie de l'Église grecque (1867). E. Wellesz, A History of Byzantine Music and Hymnography (Oxford, 1949; 2nd edn., 1961), with extensive bibl. H. A. Daniel (ed.), Thesaurus Hymnologicus (5 vols. bound in 2, Leipzig and Halle, 1841–56); F. J. *Mone, Lateinische Hymnen des Mittelalters (3 vols. bound in 2, 1853–5); G. M. Dreves, SJ, and C. Blume, SJ (eds.), Analecta Hymnica Medii Aevi (55 vols., Leipzig, 1886–1922; Register by M. Lütolf, 2 vols. in 3, Bern and Munich, 1978); A. S. Walpole and A. J. Mason, Early Latin Hymns (1922). W. Bulst, Hymni Latini Antiquissimi LXXV (Heidelberg, 1956). J. Connelly, Hymns of the Roman Liturgy (1957). H. Gneuss, Hymnar und Hymnen im englischen Mittelalter: Studien zur Überlieferung, Glossierung und Übersetzung lateinischer Hymnen in England (Buchreihe der Anglia, 12; Tübingen, 1968). F. J. E. Raby, A History of Christian-Latin Poetry from the Beginnings to the Close of the Middle Ages (Oxford, 1927; 2nd edn., 1953). J. Szövérffy, Die Annalen der lateinischen Hymnendichtung: Ein Handbuch (2 vols., 1964–5); id., Westliche Dichtungen des lateinischen Mittelalters: Ein Handbuch, 1: Von den Anfängen bis zum Ende der Karolingerzeit (1970); id., Latin Hymns (Typologie des sources du moyen âge occidental, 55; 1989). A. Michel, In hymnis et canticis: Culture et beauté dans l'hymnique chrétienne latine (Philosophes médiévaux, 20; 1976). U. Chevalier (ed.), Repertorium Hymnologicum: Catalogue des chants, hymnes, proses, séquences, tropes en usage dans l'Église latine depuis ses origines jusqu'à nos jours (6 vols., 1892–1921); C. Blume, Repertorium Repertorii: Kritische Wegweiser durch U. Chevalier's Repertorium Hymnologicum (Hymnologische Beiträge, 2; 1901); J. Szövérffy, Repertorium hymnologicum novum (Berlin, 1983 ff.). B. Stäblein (ed.), Die mittelalterlichen Hymnenmelodien des Abendlandes (Monumenta Monodica Medii Aevi, 1; Kassel, 1956).

B. L. Manning, The Hymns of Wesley and Watts (1942). E. [R.] Routley, Hymns and Human Life (1952), and other works of this author. [W.] C. Northcott, Hymns in Christian Worship (Ecumenical Studies in Worship, 13 [1964]). L. Adey, Hymns and the Christian 'Myth' (Vancouver, 1986), and other works of this author. W. Milgate (ed.), Songs of the People of God: A Companion to The Australian Hymn Book/With One Voice (1982). R. Watson and K. Trickett (eds.), Companion to Hymns and Psalms (Peterborough, 1988). A. [R.] Dunstan, The Use of Hymns: A Practical Exploration of the Place of Hymnody within the Liturgy [1990]. D. Davie, The Eighteenth-Century Hymn in England (Cambridge, 1993). J. R. Watson, The English Hymn: A Critical and Historical Study (Oxford, 1997). Bulletin of the Hymn Society of Great Britain and Ireland (Edinburgh, 1936 ff.); The Hymn: Journal of the Hymn Society of America (New York, 1949 ff.). J. Julian, A Dictionary of Hymnology (1892; rev. edn., 1907). A.

*Baumstark, A. J. Maclean, D. S. Margoliouth, G. M. Dreves, SJ, E. Hull, and T. G. Crippen in HERE 7 (1914), pp. 5–38, s.v.; H. *Leclercq, OSB, in DACL 6 (pt. 2; 1925), cols. 2826–928, s.v.; J. Szövérffy and others in NCE 7 (1967), pp. 287–304, s.v. 'Hymnology' and 'Hymns'; E. R. Routley in EB (1968 edn.), 11, pp. 986–91, s.v. See also works cited under entries on individual hymn-books.

Hymns, Ancient and Modern. This famous hymnal (pub. 1861), edited by H. W. *Baker (q.v.), was a product of the *Oxford Movement. It drew freely on ancient, medieval, and modern sources and also incorporated many of the traditional *Office hymns (often in the translation of J. M. *Neale). The music, expressive and tuneful, which greatly assisted its popularity, was edited by William Henry Monk (1823–89). In 1868 a supplement was added. In 1875 the whole work was completely revised; further supplements were added in 1889 and 1916; and from 1922 onwards these were issued as a single book ('Standard Edition'). A more drastic revision ('New Edition'), issued in 1904, never became popular.

In 1950 a completely new edition (Hymns Ancient and Modern: Revised, 1950) appeared, in which much new matter in both words and music was introduced, and many hymns were excised. In 1969, largely through the stimulus of J. A. T. *Robinson, Bp. of Woolwich, a new supplement entitled 100 Hymns for Today, was published, containing many examples from the 20th cent. Almost at once signs appeared of the so-called 'hymn explosion' which continued throughout the decade 1970–80 and beyond. This was reflected in the publication of a second hundred hymns entitled More Hymns for Today (1980). In 1983 an abridgement of the 1950 revised edition (333 hymns out of 626) was combined with the two modern supplements and issued under the title Hymns Ancient and Modern, New Standard.

In its various forms the book has familiarized many generations of Church people with the fundamentals of Anglican doctrine and practice. The Chairmen of the Proprietors, who control the hymnal, have included H. W. Baker, W. H. *Frere, S. H. Nicholson (1875–1947; from 1927 Director of the *Royal School of Church Music), W. K. Lowther Clarke (1879–1968), and H. Chadwick (b. 1920).

A 'Historical Edition', incl. notes on the words and tune of each hymn and the orig. texts in the case of translations, was pub. in 1909, with valuable introd. by W. H. Frere (pp. ix–cxi). W. K. L. Clarke, A Hundred Years of Hymns Ancient & Modern (1960). M. Frost (ed.), Historical Companion to Hymns Ancient & Modern (1962). S. Drain, The Anglican Church in Nineteenth Century Britain: Hymns Ancient and Modern (1860–1875) (Texts and Studies in Religion, 40; Lewiston, Lampeter, etc., 1989).

Hypapante (Gk. ὑπαπαντή, 'meeting'). The name used in the E. Church for the feast of *Candlemas, in reference to the meeting of *Simeon and Anna with the BVM and the Infant Christ at the *Presentation in the Temple. In the Middle Ages the title ('Occursus Domini') was also frequently used in the W.

Hypatia (c.375–415), *Neoplatonist philosopher. The daughter of Theon, the mathematician and philosopher, she was the glory of the Neoplatonic School of Alexandria, where *Synesius, Bp. of Ptolemais, was one of her pupils. On the suspicion that she had set the pagan prefect of Alexandria against the Christians, she was attacked by a

Christian mob under Peter the Reader and put to death. The archbishop, *Cyril, was suspected of complicity, but his responsibility was never proved. She was the authoress of works on philosophy and mathematics.

The chief sources are *Socrates, *HE* 7. 15 and *Suidas, s.v. W. A. Meyer, *Hypatia von Alexandria: Ein Beitrag zur Geschichte des Neuplatonismus* (1885). F. Schaefer, 'Cyril of Alexandria and the Murder of Hypatia', *Catholic University Bulletin* [Washington, DC], 8 (1902), pp. 441–53; J. Rougé, 'La politique de Cyrille d'Alexandrie et le meurtre d'Hypatie', *Cristianesimo nella Storia*, 11 (1990), pp. 485–504. K. Praechter in *PW* 9 (1916), cols. 242–9; C. Lacombrade in *RAC* 16 (1994), cols. 956–67. Her story was the basis of C. *Kingsley's novel, *Hypatia* (1853).

hyperdulia (Gk. ὑπέρ, 'more than'; δουλεία, 'servitude', 'veneration'). The special veneration paid to the BVM on account of her eminent dignity as Mother of God. It is of a more limited kind than '*latria', the worship due only to God, but higher than '*dulia', the honour paid to angels and saints.

hypocrisy (from Gk. ὑποκρίνομαι, 'to play a part', 'pretend'). The hiding of interior wickedness under the appearance of virtue. The Lord denounced it esp. in the case of the *Pharisees (Mt. 23. 1–36) as the vice of those who do their good deeds only in order to be seen by men and not for the glory of God. According to moral theologians hypocrisy is the fruit of pride. It is a sin against truthfulness, being a lie expressed by external actions with the intention of deceiving.

hypostasis (Gk. ὑπόστασις, lit. 'substance'). The Greek word has had a variety of meanings. In popular language it was used orig. for 'objective reality' as opposed to illusion (so also in *Aristotle and esp. the *Neoplatonists). In the NT this seems to be roughly its meaning at Heb. 1: 3. Allied to this was its use for 'basis' or 'foundation' and hence also 'confidence', e.g. in Heb. 3: 14 and 11: 1 and 2 Cor. 9: 4 and 11: 17. In early Christian writers it is used to denote 'being' or 'substantive reality' and is not distinguished in meaning from οὐσία; it was so used by *Tatian and *Origen, and also in the anathemas appended to the *Nicene Creed of 325.

From the middle of the 4th cent. onwards the word came to be contrasted with οὐσία and used to mean 'individual reality', esp. in Trinitarian and Christological contexts. It was mainly under the influence of the *Cappadocian Fathers that the terminology was clarified and standardized, so that the formula 'Three Hypostaseis in one Ousia' came to be everywhere accepted as an epitome of the orthodox doctrine of the Holy Trinity. But this consensus was not achieved without some confusion at first in the minds of W. theologians, who naturally translated ὑπόστασις by 'sub-stantia' ('substance') and understood the Easterns when speaking of three 'Hypostaseis' in the Godhead to mean three 'Substances', i.e. they suspected them of tritheism.

G. L. Prestige, *God in Patristic Thought* (1936), pp. 162–190. J. Tixeront, 'Des concepts de "Nature" et de "Personne" dans les pères et les écrivains ecclésiastiques des Vᵉ et VIᵉ siècles', *Revue d'Histoire et de Littérature religieuses*, 8 (1903), pp. 582–92; repr. in id., *Mélanges de patrologie et d'histoire des dogmes* (1921), pp. 210–27. M. Richard, 'L'Introduction du mot "Hypostase" dans la théologie de l'Incarnation', *Mélanges de Science religieuse*, 2 (1945), pp. 5–32, 243–70; repr. in id., *Opera Minora*, 2 (Turnhout, 1977), item 42. H. Dörrie, 'Ὑπόστασις. Wort- und Bedeutungsgeschichte', *Nachr.* (Gött.), 1955, pp. 35–92. A. de Halleux, '"Hypostase" et "Personne" dans la formation du dogme trinitaire (ca 375–381)', *RHE* 79 (1984), pp. 313–69 and 625–70. A. Michel in *DTC* 7 (pt. 1; 1922), cols. 369–437, s.v. 'Hypostase'; J. Hammerstaedt in *RAC* 16 (1994), cols. 986–1035, s.v., both with bibl.

Hypostatic Union. The union of the Divine and human natures in the One Person ('Hypostasis') of Jesus Christ. The doctrine was elaborated by St *Cyril of Alexandria and formally accepted by the Church in the Definition of *Chalcedon (451). See also preceding entry.

A. Michel in *DTC* 7 (pt. 1; 1922), cols. 437–568; P. Hünermann in *L.Th.K.* (3rd edn.), 5 (1996), cols. 371–7, s.v. See also bibl. to CHRISTOLOGY.

Hypsistarians (Gk. ὕψιστος, 'highest'). A 4th-cent. sect, probably confined to Cappadocia, which is mentioned by *Gregory of Nazianzus (*Orat.* 18. 5, where he says that his father had formerly belonged to it) and by *Gregory of Nyssa. It was so named because its members, refusing to worship God as 'Father' (πατήρ), revered Him only as the 'All Ruler and Highest' (παντοκράτωρ καὶ ὕψιστος). They incorporated into their system many oriental and Jewish elements.

C. Ullmann, *De Hypsistariis* (Heidelberg, 1825). G. T. Stokes in *DCB* 3 (1882), pp. 188 f.; G. Bareille in *DTC* 7 (pt. 1; 1922), col. 572; L. Spätling in *EC* 7 (1951), cols. 181 f.

I

Iamblichus (*c.*250–*c.*330). The chief *Neoplatonist of the Syrian school. Little is known of his life. He was a native of Chalcis in Coele-Syria; he may have studied under *Porphyry or perhaps only studied his works; he later taught in Syria, surrounded by many disciples. He held a very elaborate theory of mediation between the spiritual and physical worlds, radically modifying the doctrine of *Plotinus by duplicating the Plotinian One (ἕν) and distinguishing between its transcendental and creative aspects. This distinction lies at the basis of the negative (or *apophatic) and affirmative theologies which have differentiated E. and W. theology (see GOD).

Iamblichus incorporated in his system many Greek and Oriental pagan mythologies, whose deities he amalgamated with his orders of hypostases. He also carried a stage further the development of the number-symbolism cherished by the later Neoplatonists. His most substantial works were his commentaries on *Plato and *Aristotle, which we know only from quotations and allusions in later writers. He also wrote a commentary (now lost) on the Chaldean Oracles, which influenced *Proclus; a comprehensive exposition of the Pythagorean philosophy, entitled Συναγωγὴ τῶν Πυθαγορείων Δογμάτων (of this the only parts to survive are a treatise 'On the Pythagorean Life' (Περὶ τοῦ Πυθαγορικοῦ Βίου), an 'Exhortation to Philosophy' (Λόγος προτρεπτικὸς εἰς Φιλοσοφίαν), and various treatises of a speculative kind on mathematics); and, apparently, the 'Liber de Mysteriis', whose ascription has been doubted but is now generally accepted. This last work is of no philosophical importance, but is a curious guide to the superstitions of the age. There are apparently no direct references to Christianity in his writings, but it was from Iamblichus and his school that *Julian the Apostate learnt the Neoplatonism which he used as a weapon against Christianity.

Edns. of the treatise 'On the Pythagorean Life' by L. Deubner (Teub., 1937, rev. by U. Klein, 1975), of three mathematical treatises by N. Festa, H. Pistelli and V. de Falco (ibid., 1891, 1894, and 1922 respectively; all rev. by U. Klein, 1975), and of the 'Exhortation to Philosophy' by É. des Places, SJ, with Fr. tr. (Collection des Universités de France, 1989). 'Liber de Mysteriis', ed. id., with Fr. tr. and introd. (ibid., 1966; 2nd edn., 1989). B. D. Larsen, *Jamblique de Chalcis* (Aarhus diss., 2 vols., 1972), incl. edn. of testimonia and fragmenta exegetica. Frags. of the comm. on Plato's *Dialogues* ed., with Eng. tr., by J. M. Dillon (Philosophia Antiqua, 23; Leiden, 1973). Eng. trs. of 'Vita Pythagorica' by T. Taylor (London, 1818) and [E.] G. Clark (Translated Texts for Historians, 8; Liverpool, 1989); of 'De Mysteriis' by T. Taylor (Chiswick, 1821; 3rd edn., London, 1968). M. Sicherl, *Die Handschriften, Ausgaben und Übersetzungen von Iamblichos De Mysteriis* (TU 62; 1957). B. Nasemann, *Theurgie und Philosophie in Jamblichs de Mysteriis* (Beiträge zur Altertumskunde, 11; Stuttgart, 1991). H. J. Blumenthal and E. G. Clark (eds.), *The Divine Iamblichus: Philosopher and Man of Gods* (Bristol, 1993). A. C. Lloyd in A. H. Armstrong (ed.), *The Cambridge History of Later Greek and Early Medieval Philosophy* (Cambridge, 1967), pp. 294–301, with refs. Überweg, 1, pp. 612–17, with full bibl., pp. 191 f. G. Mau and W. Kroll in *PW* 17 (1914), cols. 645–51. See also bibl. to NEOPLATONISM.

Ibas, Bp. of *Edessa from 435 to 449 and from 451 to 457. In the contemporary Christological controversies, he took a mediating position between the dualistic teaching of the *Nestorians and the *Alexandrian position of St *Cyril, and was closely associated in doctrine and policy with *Theodoret. On account of his views, summarized in a famous letter addressed to one Mari in 433, he was deposed at the *Latrocinium at Ephesus in 449. Though he was vindicated at the Council of *Chalcedon (451), his epistle was condemned by *Justinian and anathematized by the Fifth General Council (553). None of his writings, apart from the Epistle to Mari in a Greek translation from the original Syriac, has survived. See also THREE CHAPTERS.

Text of Ep. to Mari in *acta* of Councils, e.g. *ACO* 2.1.3 (1935), pp. 32–4. A. d'Alès, SJ, 'La Lettre d'Ibas à Marès le Persan', *Rech. S.R.* 22 (1932), pp. 5–25. Bardenhewer, 4 (1924), pp. 410 f. E. Venables in *DCB* 3 (1882), pp. 192–6.

Iceland, Christianity in. Christianity reached Iceland from *Norway *c.*980 and was accepted by the Althing (the ruling council) in 999/1000. The medieval Church had two bishoprics, Skálholt and Hólar, and was at first under the administrative jurisdiction of Bremen, then of Lund, and finally of Trondheim (Nidaros). The breakdown of political stability in Iceland led to her subjection to Norway in 1262. *Benedictine and *Augustinian communities were established in the island for several centuries. At the Reformation Iceland followed *Denmark, to whose rule she had been subject since *c.*1380, in adopting *Lutheranism. In modern times there has been a revival of Church life, reflected, e.g., in the production of a new translation of the Bible (1981). The ecclesiastical government is in the hands of the Lutheran bishop, with deanery and parish councils; and the civil government has also some voice in ecclesiastical appointments.

F. Jónsson, *Historia Ecclesiastica Islandiae* (4 vols., Copenhagen, 1772–8; cont. by P. Pétursson, ibid., 1841). J. Helgason, *Islands Kirke fra dens Grundlæggsle til Reformationen* (ibid., 1925); id., *Islands Kirke fra Reformationen til vore Dage* (ibid., 1922). J. C. F. Hood, *Icelandic Church Saga* (1946). D. [A.] Strömbäck, *The Conversion of Iceland*, tr. and annotated by P. Foote (Viking Society for Northern Research of University College, London, Text Series, 6 [1975]). J. H. Adalsteinsson, *Under the Cloak: The Acceptance of Christianity in Iceland* (Studia Ethnologica Upsaliensia, 4; 1978). F. Siegmund-Schultze (ed.), *Ekklesia*, 2, Lieferung 7, pt. 2, 'Die Kirche in Island' (1937). L. S. Hunter (ed.), *Scandinavian Churches: A Picture of the Development of the Life of the Churches of Denmark, Finland, Iceland, Norway and Sweden* (1965), pp. 104–17. S. Einarsson in *TRE* 16 (1987), pp. 358–68, s.v. 'Island'.

ICF. See INDUSTRIAL CHRISTIAN FELLOWSHIP.

Ichabod, the son of Phinehas and grandson of the priest Eli, the tragic circumstances of whose birth are described in 1 Sam. 4: 19–22. The name, acc. to 1 Sam. 4: 21, means 'The glory has departed' (lit. 'no glory'); hence the use of 'Ichabod' as an exclamation.

ichthus. See FISH.

icon (Gk. εἰκών). Icons are flat pictures, usually painted in egg tempera on wood, but also wrought in mosaic, ivory, and other materials, to represent the Lord, the BVM, or another saint, which are used and venerated in the E. Church. The scenes depicted often relate to liturgical celebrations rather than directly to historical events. For protection, esp. in Russia, the figures are often covered with a metal shield on which the outlines of the clothes are carved, but which leave free the face and hands belonging to the painting underneath. Icons became numerous in the E. from the 5th cent., and the effect of the *Iconoclastic Controversy of the 8th and 9th cents. was to increase devotion to them among the people. Since then they have always played an essential part in the public as well as in the private worship of the Byzantine Church, and they are accorded all the external marks of veneration common in the E., such as kisses, prostrations, incense, etc. As it is believed that through them the saints exercise their beneficent powers, they preside at all important events of human life and are held to be effective remedies against illness, to drive away devils, to procure both spiritual and temporal blessings, and generally to be powerful channels of Divine grace. Many icons have been famous for their miracles, esp. that of Christ of *Edessa, believed 'not to have been made by hands' (ἀχειροποίητος), and that of the *Theotokos, also 'acheiropoietos', in the monastery of the Abramites at *Constantinople. Perhaps the best-known icon is that of the Trinity by St Andrey Rublev, now in the Tretiakov Gallery in Moscow. See also ICONOSTASIS and IMAGES.

O. Wullf and M. Alpatoff, *Denkmäler der Ikonenmalerei in kunstgeschichtlicher Folge* (1925). I. Dirks, OSB, *Les Saintes Icones* (2nd edn., Amay-sur-Meuse, 1939). W. P. Theunissen, *Ikonen: Historisch, Aesthetisch en Theologisch Belicht* (1948), with bibl. L. Ouspensky and V. *Lossky, *The Meaning of Icons* (Olten, 1952; repr., with additional material, Crestwood, NY, 1982). E. Kitzinger, 'The Cult of Images in the Age before Iconoclasm', *Dumbarton Oaks Papers*, 8 (1954), pp. 83–150. L. Ouspensky, *Essai sur la théologie de l'icone dans l'Église orthodoxe* (Recueil d'Études orthodoxes, 2; 1960; Eng. tr., Crestwood, NY, 1978; rev. tr., ibid., 1992); id., *La Théologie de l'icône dans l'Église orthodoxe* (1982; Eng. tr., Crestwood, NY, 1992). J. Stuart, *Ikons* (1975). C. von Schönborn, OP, *L'Icône du Christ: Fondements Théologiques* (Paradosis, 24; 1976). K. Weitzmann, *The Icon: Holy Image. Sixth to Fourteenth Century* (1978). Id. and others, *Le Icone* (Milan, 1981; Eng. tr., 1982). N. P. Kondakov (Eng. tr. by E. H. Minns from larger Russian work), *The Russian Icon* (Oxford, 1927). P. Muratov, *Les Icones russes* (1928). W. Felicetti-Liebenfels, *Geschichte der byzantinischen Ikonenmalerei* (Olten and Lausanne, 1956). K. Weitzmann and others, *Ikone sa Balkana* (1966; Eng. tr., 1968). *The 'Painter's Manual' of Dionysius of Fourna*, tr. P. Hetherington (1974: a notable source for the conventions of icon-painting). L. Ouspensky in *NCE* 7 (1967), pp. 324–6, s.v.

Iconoclastic Controversy (from εἰκονοκλάστης, 'iconoclast', 'image-breaker'). The controversy on the veneration of *icons (q.v.) agitated the Greek Church from *c.*725 to 842. At the end of the 7th and the beginning of the 8th cents. several influences hostile to the veneration of icons had made themselves felt in the E. Empire, notably the *Monophysite heresy, which minimized the human side of the Incarnation, the *Manichaean tendencies of the *Paulicians, who held that all matter was evil, and possibly also *Islam. The open outbreak of this hostility was due to the Emp. *Leo III, the Isaurian (717–41), who thought that the use of icons, which had admittedly become excessive, was the chief obstacle to the conversion of Jews and Muslims. In 726 he published an edict declaring all images idols and ordering their destruction. Very soon serious disturbances throughout the Empire followed. The patriarch *Germanus, who appealed to the Pope, was deposed in 730, and a systematic persecution unleashed, esp. against the monks, who were the most ardent defenders of the icons. At the same time St *John of Damascus wrote his famous apologies against the iconoclasts and Pope Gregory III held two synods at Rome condemning Leo's supporters (731).

In 741 Leo was succeeded by his son Constantine V (Copronymus), who, after a quickly suppressed revolt of his brother-in-law, Artabasdus, in favour of the icons, continued his father's policy. In 753 he called the Synod of Hieria, which neither the patriarchs of *Antioch, *Jerusalem, and *Alexandria nor the Pope attended. The synod alleged that, by representing only the humanity of Christ, the icon-worshippers either divided His unity as the *Nestorians or confounded the two Natures as the Monophysites; and it further declared that the icons of the BVM and of the saints were idols and decreed the destruction of all of them. The persecution now raged more fiercely than ever, many of the secular clergy giving way, but a great number of monks became martyrs in the cause of the icons.

Under Constantine's son, Leo IV (775–80), the persecution abated, and after his death his wife, the Empress Irene, regent for her young son Constantine, reversed the policy of her predecessors despite the iconoclastic leanings of the army. In 784 *Tarasius became Patr. of Constantinople and, in concert with Irene, opened negotiations with Pope *Hadrian I, who sent legates to the Seventh General Council which met at *Nicaea in 787. This Council completely undid the work of the Synod of Hieria, defined the degree of veneration to be paid to icons, and decreed their restoration throughout the country.

Though the decrees of the Council were officially received, Iconoclasm retained a strong following esp. in the army. In 814 the outbreak of the 'Second Iconoclastic Controversy' took place under Leo V the Armenian, a general elected Emperor by the army. Leo again began to remove icons from churches and public buildings; the Patr. *Nicephorus was deposed (815); St *Theodore of Studios, the foremost defender of images among the monks, sent into exile; and many others imprisoned and martyred. After Leo's assassination in 820 his successor, Michael II, continued his iconoclastic policy though in a milder form, whereas his son Theophilus, who succeeded him in 829, returned to the violence of Leo, esp. after the enthronization of the iconoclast patriarch John the Grammarian in 832. The persecution ended only with Theophilus' death in 842. His widow, Theodora, like Irene, regent for her son, caused the monk Methodius to be elected patriarch in 843, and on the first Sunday of Lent a great feast was celebrated in honour of the icons, since then solemnly kept in the E. Church as the 'Feast of *Orthodoxy'.

The few repercussions which the controversy had on theology in the W. were mainly caused by the misunderstanding of certain passages from the Acts of the Second Council of Nicaea. A faulty translation of the Acts, sent to *Charlemagne by Hadrian I, together with a general dislike of the Greeks and political friction, led to a manifesto against the Council by the Frankish bishops in 790, later expanded and issued as the 'Libri Carolini' (*Caroline Books). It was reiterated by the Synod of Frankfurt in 794 which formally condemned the Second Council of Nicaea, misunderstanding it to enjoin an adoration of images equal to that due to the Divine Trinity. A similar attitude was taken up by the bishops who met at Paris in 828, who would tolerate pictures only as ornaments. Owing to the authority of the Popes, however, and the influence of theologians such as *Walafrid Strabo and *Hincmar of Reims, the Frankish bishops gradually accepted the Nicene decrees, opposition to them having virtually ceased in the 10th cent.

The Iconoclastic Controversy, more important for its practical than for its theological results, is usually considered the last step towards the great schism between E. and W. before the actual breach. The Caesaro-Papism which showed itself during the struggle encountered in this period relatively little resistance in the Greek Church, esp. among the secular clergy, while it was viewed by the Popes with growing apprehension. The unity achieved by imperial decree in 787 and again in 843 proved artificial, and with the restoration of the Empire by the Franks and the development of the temporal power of the Papacy the ground was prepared for the final separation between the independent Church of the W. and the Church of the Byzantine Empire.

L. Bréhier, La Querelle des images: VIIIe–IXe siècles (1904). G. Ostrogorsky, Studien zur Geschichte des byzantinischen Bilderstreites (Historische Untersuchungen, 5; Breslau, 1929). Id., Geschichte des Byzantinischen Staates (Byzantinisches Handbuch, 12. 1. 2; 1940, pp. 97–146; 3rd edn., 1963), pp. 123–75 (Eng. tr., with additional material, Oxford, 1968, pp. 147–209). A. Grabar, L'Iconoclasme byzantin: dossier archéologique (1957). P. J. Alexander, The Patriarch Nicephorus of Constantinople (Oxford, 1958). P. Brown, 'A Dark-Age crisis: aspects of the Iconoclastic controversy', EHR 88 (1973), pp. 1–34. S. Gero, Byzantine Iconoclasm during the Reign of Leo III (CSCO, Subsidia, 41; 1973); id., Byzantine Iconoclasm during the Reign of Constantine V (ibid. 52; 1977). A. [A. M.] Bryer and J. Herrin (eds.), Iconoclasm: Papers given at the Ninth Spring Symposium of Byzantine Studies, University of Birmingham, March 1975 (Birmingham, 1977). D. Stein, Der Beginn des byzantinischen Bilderstreits und seine Entwicklung bis in die 40er Jahre des 8. Jahrhunderts (Miscellanea Byzantina Monascensia 25; 1980). H. G. Thümmel, Die Frühgeschichte der Ostkirchlichen Bilderlehre (TU 139; 1992), with primary docs. J. M. Hussey, The Orthodox Church in the Byzantine Empire (Oxford History of the Christian Church, 1986), pp. 30–68. H. *Leclercq, OSB, in DACL 6 (pt. 1; 1926), cols. 214–302, s.v. 'Images'.

iconography, Christian. The subject of Christian iconography is the pictorial or symbolical representation of Christian ideas, persons, and history. It is not a form of aesthetic criticism, but, like *archaeology, an auxiliary to historical and theological studies.

The earliest Christian art was mainly symbolical. Christ was represented by a *fish (Ichthus) or a young shepherd, a ship symbolized the Church, an anchor hope or salvation, a peacock immortality. Pictorial scenes, drawn from the Bible or the *Apocryphal literature, were also typical, not merely illustrative, e.g. Jonah's story symbolized death and resurrection.

From the time of *Constantine, Christian art could display Christianity triumphant. Under the influence of *Neoplatonic aesthetics, which saw art as disclosing a higher, spiritual realm, the conscious symbolism characteristic of *icons in the narrower sense developed. The chief descriptive monuments of the period are *catacomb painting, church mosaics, and *sarcophagi. Already there can be detected a difference of emphasis between E. and W., the E. stressing the liturgical function of art, whereas the W. regarded art as providing pictorial illustrations of biblical events and religious doctrines. Byzantine churches often exhibit a planned system of stylized and didactic decoration, covering the whole interior. After the *Iconoclastic Controversy this plan was adapted more precisely to the Liturgy and stereotyped for centuries.

In the W., partly under the influence of a growing devotion to Christ's sacred humanity, a more realistic, less symbolic style of art began to develop from the 12th cent. Gothic cathedrals, by their sculpture, glass, paintings, and textiles, were encyclopaedias of theology, history, hagiography, natural history (moralized, after the Bestiaries), learning (the seven arts), morality (following *Prudentius' 'Combat of Virtues and Vices'), and the trades and crafts. All activity, this indicated, is religious. While individualism had some play and not all art was didactic, art commonly conformed to a pattern determined by the Church. This was partly based on, partly explained by, the encyclopaedic writings of *Honorius 'of Autun', Bartholomaeus Anglicus (c.1250), and, above all, *Vincent of Beauvais, which developed the work of *Isidore of Seville and *Rabanus Maurus. Such a cathedral as *Chartres demonstrates a highly organized scheme of decoration. In the 14th cent. art grew less intellectual and more emotional or mystical. In the next century it became frankly realistic and picturesque. Didactic schemes were already dissolving when the Renaissance killed medieval methods. Since then there have been many experiments in both realism and symbolism, but, while religious art still abounds, it is impossible to discern any dominant tradition or system in Christian art and symbolism.

L. Bréhier, L'Art chrétien: Son développement iconographique des origines à nos jours (1918); K. Künstle, Ikonographie der christlichen Kunst (2 vols., 1926–8), with bibl. G. de Jerphanion, SJ, La Voix des monuments: Notes et études d'archéologie chrétienne (1930), esp. no. 2, 'Le Développement iconographique de l'art chrétien', pp. 30–54. D. T. Rice, The Beginnings of Christian Art (1957). F. van der Meer, Oudchristelijke Kunst (Zeist, 1959; Eng. tr., 1967). L. Réau, Iconographie de l'art chrétien (3 vols. in 6, 1955–8). A. Grabar, Christian Iconography: A Study of its Origins (1969). G. Schiller, Ikonographie der christlichen Kunst (3 vols., 1966–71; Eng. tr., 1971 ff.). G. Mathew [OP], Byzantine Aesthetics (1963). É. Mâle, L'Art religieux du XIIe siècle en France (1922); id., L'Art religieux du XIIIe siècle en France (1898; Eng. tr., 1913); id., L'Art religieux de la fin du moyen-âge en France (1908); id., L'Art religieux de la fin du XVIe siècle, du XVIIe siècle et du XVIIIe siècle (1932);

Eng. tr. of parts of these works issued as *Religious Art from the Twelfth to the Eighteenth Century* (1949). E. Kirschbaum, SJ, and others (eds.), *Lexikon der christlichen Ikonographie* (8 vols., 1968–76).

iconostasis. The screen which, in Byzantine churches, separates the sanctuary from the nave. Originally a low barrier, sometimes surmounted by columns joined by a decorated parapet and coping, since the 14th to 15th cents. the screen has presented the form of a wall of wood or stone, covered with *icons, from which it derives its name. It is pierced by three doors, the central or Holy Door admitting to the altar, and those on the right and left respectively to the *diaconicon and the *prothesis.

K. *Holl, 'Die Entstehung der Bilderwand in der griechischen Kirche', *Archiv für Religionswissenschaft*, 9 (1906), pp. 365–84; B. Pace, 'Nuova ipotesi sull' origine dell' iconostasio', *Byzantion*, 19 (1949), pp. 195–205; J. Walter, AA, 'The Origins of the Iconostasis', *Eastern Churches Review*, 3 (1971), pp. 251–67. A. W. Epstein, 'The Middle Byzantine Sanctuary Barrier: Templon or Iconostasis?', *Journal of the British Archaeological Association*, 134 (1981), pp. 1–28, with refs. M. Cheremeteff, 'The Transformation of the Russian Sanctuary Barrier and the role of Theophanes the Greek', in A. Leong (ed.), *The Millenium: Christianity and Russia (A.D. 988–1988)* (Crestwood, NY, 1990), pp. 107–40. H. *Leclercq, OSB, in *DACL* 7 (pt. 1; 1926), cols. 31–48, s.v. 'Iconostase'.

idiorrhythmic. A term applied to certain monasteries on Mount *Athos which, in contradistinction to the *coenobitic houses, used to allow considerable freedom to their monks, including the right to possess personal property.

Idiot, the (from the Gk. ἰδιώτης, a private person, one of no special skill), the pseudonym used by a medieval spiritual writer generally identified as Raymundus Jordanus, a French Canon Regular of St Augustine and Abbot of Selles-sur-Cher, who flourished *c*.1381. A collected edition of his devotional works in Latin, which were very popular in the Middle Ages, was published in 1654 by Théophile Raynaud, SJ, who first made the identification. The word 'idiot' long retained its original meaning in English; in 1657 some writings of Dame Gertrude *More, OSB (1606–33) were pub. at Paris under the title 'The Holy Practices of a Divine Lover, or, the Sainctly Idiots Devotions'.

Ignatius, Father. The Revd Joseph Leycester Lyne (1837–1908), mission preacher. In 1860 he was ordained deacon to the title of a curacy at St Peter's, Plymouth, under G. R. Prynne. Shortly afterwards he left Plymouth and worked for some months with the Revd C. F. *Lowder at St George's-in-the-East, London. He made it his chief aim to revive the *Benedictine Order in the Anglican Church, and after various abortive steps eventually acquired in 1869 a site for his monastery at Capel-y-ffin, some four miles from Llanthony. A striking preacher with great gifts of popular oratory, he carried out successful missions in many parts of England, mainly in secular buildings. He remained a deacon until 1898, when he was ordained priest by J. R. *Vilatte. On Ignatius's death, the buildings at Capel-y-ffin passed into the possession of the

Anglican Benedictines at *Caldey Island; in 1924 they were bought by Eric *Gill.

Baroness de Bertouch, *The Life of Father Ignatius, O.S.B.* (1904); D. Attwater, *Father Ignatius of Llanthony* (1931); A. Calder-Marshall, *The Enthusiast: An Enquiry into the Life, Beliefs and Character of the Rev. Joseph Leycester Lyne alias Fr. Ignatius, O.S.B.* (1962).

Ignatius, St (*c*.35–*c*.107), Bp. of *Antioch. Ignatius describes himself as also called 'Theophoros' (Θεοφόρος, 'bearer of God', or perhaps Θεόφορος, 'borne by God'). He was probably of Syrian origin, and J. B. *Lightfoot, basing himself on a passage from his *Ep. ad Romanos*, believed that he was a pagan and a persecutor of Christians before his conversion. Acc. to *Origen he was the second Bp. of Antioch, the successor of St *Peter; acc. to *Eusebius he was the third, following St Peter's successor, Euodius, *c*.69. Nothing is known of his life beyond his journey to martyrdom from Antioch to *Rome under a guard of ten soldiers. He was received *en route* at *Smyrna with great honour by St *Polycarp and visited by many members of neighbouring Christian communities, and wrote thence to the Churches of *Ephesus, Magnesia, and Tralles letters of encouragement, and a fourth to the Church at Rome, begging them not to deprive him of martyrdom by intervention with the pagan authorities. He was then taken to Troas, where he wrote three further letters to the Churches of *Philadelphia and Smyrna and to St Polycarp, and thence through Macedonia and Illyria to Dyrrhachium, where he was embarked for Italy. That the martyrdom to which Ignatius looked forward in his letters actually took place is already asserted by Polycarp and Origen, the latter of whom expressly mentions Rome as its place (traditionally the *Colosseum). The statement of *John Malalas (6th cent.) that Ignatius was martyred at Antioch is wholly without warrant. There survive five different accounts of his death (*Acta*), none of them meriting much credence.

The high esteem in which Ignatius's letters were held is proved both by patristic quotations, e.g. in Eusebius and *Theodoret, and also by interpolations and the circulation of spurious letters under his name. A Latin version of the seven genuine but interpolated letters, together with four spurious epistles, was first pub. by J. *Faber (Stapulensis) in 1498. The genuineness of this collection (the 'Long Recension') was a matter of prolonged dispute. It was accepted as authentic *in toto* by older RC scholars, but rejected equally *in toto* esp. by anti-episcopalian Protestant divines. The whole matter appeared in a new light when J. *Ussher, who observed that Ignatian quotations in medieval English authors differed from Faber's text but agreed with those in the Fathers, deduced both that the current text was interpolated and that the original text was probably to be found in England. He subsequently discovered a Latin translation which agreed with the old quotations. His *Polycarpi et Ignatii Epistolae* (1644) was a work of remarkable critical genius and erudition, its only serious error being the rejection of the letter to Polycarp. In 1646 Isaak *Voss edited the corresponding Greek text which Ussher had traced to a Florentine MS (Laur. Plut. lvii. 7). For a long time, however, many Protestant scholars continued to reject all the letters owing to their strong emphasis on episcopacy. The controversy was virtually settled in favour of the authenticity of the seven letters by J. *Pearson's *Vindiciae Epistolarum S. Ignatii* (1672).

In the 19th cent. the dispute arose afresh through W. *Cureton's publication (1845) of a *Syriac MS containing a recension of only the three genuine letters to the Ephesians, to the Romans, and to Polycarp. He maintained that this 'Short Recension' was the only authentic one. Lightfoot's learned defence of the authenticity of the seven letters in his monumental edition of the *Apostolic Fathers* (1885) has, however, won general acceptance. He maintained further that the six apocryphal letters and the interpolations of the 'Long Recension' are by the same 4th-cent. hand. It is very likely that the forger was the compiler of the *Apostolic Constitutions*, and if so, prob. an *Arian.

The authentic epistles, and esp. that to the Romans, reveal a man passionately devoted to Christ. His consuming desire for martyrdom comes out esp. in the Ep. to the Romans. In the other epistles he warns the recipients against a Judaizing heresy with *Docetic elements. He insists on the reality both of the Divinity and the Humanity of the Lord, whom he calls ὁ θεὸς ἡμῶν Ἰησοῦς Χριστός ('our God Jesus Christ'). His Birth, Passion, and Death were not appearances but realities. The life of Christ is continued in the Eucharist, which he calls 'the bread that is the flesh of Jesus Christ, this flesh which has suffered for our sins'. The best safeguard of the unity of the Christian faith is the bishop, who is pre-eminent because he is 'as the Lord', and without whose authority neither the Eucharist nor marriage may be celebrated. The Church of Rome is referred to with special reverence as 'presiding in the region of the Romans' (ἥτις προκάθηται ἐν τόπῳ χωρίου Ῥωμαίων). There is, however, no reference to the Bp. of Rome.

Feast day: 17 Oct. in the RC Calendar (formerly 1 Feb.), some Anglican Churches, and at Antioch; 20 Dec. in the Greek Church. (In the proposed BCP of 1928, 17 Dec., the commemoration of his translation in the *Roman Martyrology.)

The history of Ignatian criticism, with full survey of the MS material and discussions to date, is fully described in J. B. *Lightfoot, *The Apostolic Fathers*, pt. 2 (3 vols., 1885), with crit. text and Eng. tr. Gk. text and Eng. trs. also readily accessible in edns. of the '*Apostolic Fathers'. Convenient Eng. tr., with notes, by J. H. Srawley (Early English Church Classics, 2 vols., London, 1900); more recent edn., with Fr. tr. and comm., by P. T. Camelot (SC 10, 1944; 4th edn., 1969). Comm. by W. Bauer, rev. by H. Paulsen, *Die Apostolischen Väter*, 2 (Hb. NT 18; 1985), pp. 20–107, and by W. R. Schoedel (Hermeneia; Philadephia [1985]). H. Schlier, *Religionsgeschichtliche Untersuchungen zu den Ignatiusbriefen* (Beihefte zur ZNTW; 8; 1929). C. C. Richardson, *The Christianity of Ignatius of Antioch* (New York, 1935); H. W. Bartsch, *Gnostisches Gut und Gemeindetradition bei Ignatius von Antiochien* (1940). V. Corwin, *St Ignatius and Christianity in Antioch* (Yale Publications in Religion, 1; 1960). H. Rathke, *Ignatius von Antiochien und die Paulusbriefe* (TU 99; 1967). K. Bommes, *Weizen Gottes: Untersuchungen zur Theologie des Martyriums bei Ignatius von Antiochen* (Theophaneia, 27; 1976). H. Paulsen, *Studien zur Theologie des Ignatius von Antiochen* (Forschungen zur Kirchen- und Dogmengeschichte, 29; 1978). P. Meinhold, *Studien zu Ignatius von Antiochen* (Veröffentlichungen des Instituts für Europäische Geschichte Mainz, 97; 1979). C. Trevett, *A Study of Ignatius of Antioch in Syria and Asia* (Studies in the Bible and Early Christianity, 29; Lewiston, NY, and Lampeter [1992]). *CPG* 1 (1983), pp. 12–17 (nos. 1025–36). Altaner and Stuiber

(1978), pp. 47–50 and 551 f. G. Bareille in *DTC* 7 (pt. 1; 1922), cols. 685–713; P. T. Camelot, OP, in *Dict. Sp.* 7 (pt. 2; 1971), cols. 1250–66, s.v.

Ignatius Loyola, St (prob. 1491–1556), founder of the *Jesuits. Born of a noble family at the castle of Loyola, not far south of the Pyrenees, he spent his formative years (*c.*1506–17) in the household of Juan Velázquez de Cuéllar, the Royal Treasurer of Castile, and then embarked on a military career, taking service with the Duke of Nájera. A wound in the right leg which he received during the siege of Pamplona (1521) reduced him to a prolonged state of inactivity, during which the reading of *Ludolf of Saxony's *Vita Christi* and biographies of saints led him to change his life radically. After his recovery he went to *Montserrat, where he made a general confession, hung up his sword at the altar of the BVM, and exchanged clothes with a beggar. He then went to Manresa for a year (1522–3). Here he underwent a series of profound spiritual experiences, from which he derived many of the insights contained in the *Spiritual Exercises* (q.v.). Leaving Manresa, he travelled to *Jerusalem, subsisting on alms. Compelled to abandon his intention of remaining there permanently, he resolved during his return journey to study in order 'to help souls'. With short interruptions, he was a student for eleven years (1524–35), in Barcelona, Alcalá, Salamanca, and Paris.

In 1534 he and six companions, among them St *Francis Xavier and Bl Pierre Favre, made a vow of lifelong poverty and service to others, either in the Holy Land or, should that not be possible, wherever the Pope should send them. After Ignatius had returned briefly to Spain in 1535, they assembled in Venice early in 1537, planning to sail for Jerusalem. During that year Ignatius and six others from the group (which had already begun to expand) were ordained priests. Owing to Turkish attacks in the Mediterranean, no journey to the Holy Land was then possible, and the group dispersed over Italy, Ignatius himself going to Rome. At La Storta, just outside the city, he felt that God the Father had imprinted in his heart the words, 'I shall be favourable to you in Rome'; he also had a vision of himself being accepted as a servant, at the Father's request, by Christ, who was bearing the Cross. The following year the group finally abandoned the plan to go to Jerusalem, assembled in Rome, and in 1540 were definitively constituted as the Society of Jesus by the bull '*Regimini militantis Ecclesiae', Ignatius becoming its first *General. His remaining years were taken up with the organization of the rapidly spreading Society.

Ignatius's paramount aim was to rekindle religious fervour and practice in the Church through a more efficacious ministry. He also gave priority to pioneering mission work outside Europe and, after 1548, to the education of youth in schools. He was canonized in 1622. Feast day, 31 July.

Crit. edns. in *Monumenta Ignatiana*, 1st ser., S. Ignatii de Loyola . . . Epistolae et Instructiones (12 vols., Madrid, 1903–14); 2nd ser., Exercitia Spiritualia Sancti Ignatii de Loyola et eorum Directoria (Madrid, 1919; 2nd edn., 2 vols., Rome, 1955–69); 3rd ser., Constitutiones Societatis Jesu (4 vols., Rome, 1934–48); 4th ser., Scripta de Sancto Ignatio de Loyola (2 vols., Madrid, 1904–18; 2nd edn., 5 vols., Rome, 1943–77, incl. as vol. 4, crit. edn. of contemporary Life by P. Ribadeneira, SJ, first pub. Naples, 1572,

Eng. tr., 1616). Manual edn. of works by I. Iparraguirre, SJ, and C. de Dalmases, SJ (Madrid, 1952; 5th edn., rev. by M. Ruiz Jurado, SJ, 1991). Collected Eng. tr. of his *Spiritual Exercises* and of the account of his life during the years 1521–38 which Ignatius dictated, of some selections from his spiritual diary kept between 2 Feb. 1544 and 27 Feb. 1545 and from *The Constitutions of the Society of Jesus*, and of some letters, ed. G. E. Ganss, SJ (Classics of Western Spirituality, New York, etc., 1991). Full Eng. tr. of his spiritual diary by J. A. Munitiz, SJ (London, 1987), and of the *Constitutions* by G. E. Ganss, SJ (St Louis, 1970). Selection of letters in Eng. tr. by W. J. Young, SJ (Chicago, 1959), and convenient Eng. tr. of all his published *Letters to Women* (1960), with notes tr. from the German version of H. Rahner, SJ (orig. pub. Freiburg, 1956). Modern Lives by P. Dudon, SJ (Paris, 1934; Eng. tr., Milwaukee [1949]), C. de Dalmases, SJ (Madrid, 1979; 2nd edn., 1982; expanded Eng. tr., St Louis, 1985), R. García-Villoslada, SJ (Madrid, 1986), J. I. Tellechea Idígoras (Madrid, 1986), and P. [G.] Caraman, SJ (London, 1990). F. Wulf, SJ (ed.), *Ignatius von Loyola: Seine geistliche Gestalt und sein Vermächtnis 1556–1956* (Würzburg [1956]; partial Eng. tr., St Louis, 1977); P. de Leturia, SJ, *Estudios ignacianos* (Bibliotheca Instituti Historici S.I., 10–11; Rome, 1957). H. Rahner, SJ, *Ignatius von Loyola als Mensch und Theologe* (Freiburg, etc., 1964; Eng. tr. of chs. 11–16 as *Ignatius the Theologian*, London, 1968; of chs. 3, 7, 9, 17–19 as *Ignatius: The Man and the Priest*, Rome, 1977; 2nd edn., 1982; and of ch. 4 as *The Vision of St Ignatius in the Chapel of La Storta*, Rome, 1979). A. Ravier, SJ, *Ignace de Loyola fonde la Compagnie de Jésus* ([1974]; Eng. tr., San Francisco [1987]). D. Lonsdale, SJ, *Eyes to See, Ears to Hear: An Introduction to Ignatian Spirituality* (1990). W. W. Meissner, SJ, *Ignatius Loyola: The Psychology of a Saint* (New Haven and London [1992]). I. Iparraguirre, SJ, *Orientaciones bibliográficas sobre San Ignacio de Loyola* (Subsidia ad Historiam S.I., series minor, 1; Rome, 1957; 2nd edn., 1965); the material after 1965 is covered by M. Ruiz Jurado, SJ, *Orientaciones bibliográficas sobre San Ignacio de Loyola* (Subsidia ad Historiam S.I., 8, 10, etc.; Rome, 1977 ff.). L. Polgár, SJ, *Bibliographie sur l'histoire de la Compagnie de Jésus 1901–1980*, 1 (Rome, 1981), pp. 101–234.

ignorance, invincible. See INVINCIBLE IGNORANCE.

IHS. A monogram for the name Jesus, formed by abbreviating the corresponding Greek word which in *uncials is written ΙΗΣΟΥΣ. It is found, e.g., in the Latin text of Lk. 6: 3 in the *Codex Bezae. That the second symbol, H, was really a Greek η and not a Latin *h* was soon forgotten, and the abbreviation 'ihs' was thus often wrongly expanded to 'Ihesus'. Other attempts to explain the three letters as initials of separate words became very common. Thus they were held to denote *Iesus Hominum Salvator* (i.e. 'Jesus, Saviour of Men') or *In Hoc Signo* [*vinces*] (i.e. 'in this sign [thou shalt conquer]'). In the Middle Ages the IHS was widely used among the *Franciscans and later it became popular among the *Jesuits, who sometimes interpreted it as *Jesum Habemus Socium* (i.e. 'We have Jesus as our companion').

F. Victorius, *De Vetustate et Forma Monogrammatis . . . Nominis Jesu* (Rome, 1747). L. Traube, *Nomina Sacra* (1907), pp. 156–9; F. J. Dölger, ΙΧΘΥΣ: *Das Fischsymbol in frühchristlicher Zeit*, 1 (RQ, Suppl. 17; 1910), pp. 355–61.

Ildefonsus, St (*c*.607–67), Abp. of Toledo. He came from a noble family, and is traditionally believed to have been a pupil of St *Isidore of Seville. While still young, he entered the monastery of Agali, nr. Toledo, and later became its abbot. As such he attended the Councils of *Toledo in 653 and 655. He was appointed Abp. of Toledo

in 657. Acc. to St Julian of Toledo, he was the author of a long list of works, but only four have survived. His 'De Virginitate Beatae Mariae', in praise of the BVM, towards whom he showed great devotion, was a vigorous assertion of the privileges of the Mother of God. His 'Annotationes de Cognitione Baptismi' uses skilfully the works of older writers on the subject, esp. St *Augustine, St *Gregory the Great, and St Isidore of Seville, and contains much valuable information on the discipline of *catechumens. His 'De Progressu Spiritalis Deserti' (also known as the 'De Itinere Deserti quo Pergitur post Baptismum') completes the 'Annotationes' by a mystical application of the wanderings of the Israelites in the wilderness to the spiritual journey of the soul after Baptism. The fourth of his extant works, 'De Viris Illustribus', is an important document of the history of the Spanish Church during the first two-thirds of the 7th cent. St Ildefonsus was a favourite subject for medieval artists, esp. the legend of the apparition of the BVM presenting him with a chasuble. Feast day, 23 Jan.

Works ed. Card. F. de Lorenzana, Abp. of Toledo, in *Sanctorum Patrum Toletanorum quotquot extant Opera*, 1 (Madrid, 1782), pp. 94–290; repr. in J. P. Migne, *PL* 96. 9–330. Crit. text of 'De Virginitate Beatae Mariae', with discussion, by V. B. García (Textos latinos de la edad media española, Madrid, 1937) and of 'De Viris Illustribus' by C. Codoñer Merino (Acta Salmanticensia, Filosofia y Letras, 65; Salamanca, 1972). Spanish tr. of Life by A. Martínez de Toledo (Clásicos castellanos, no. 134; Madrid, 1952). Sister Athanasius Braegelmann, OSB, *The Life and Writings of Saint Ildefonsus of Toledo* (Catholic University of America Studies in Mediaeval History, NS 4; 1942). J. M. Cascante Dávila, *Doctrina Mariana de S. Ildefonso de Toledo* (Barcelona, 1958). J. Madoz, SJ, 'San Ildefonso de Toledo', *Estudios eclesiásticos*, 26 (1952), pp. 467–505. Mrs Humphry Ward in *DCB* 3 (1882), pp. 223–5; M. C. Díaz y Díaz in *Dict. Sp.* 7 (pt. 2; 1971), cols. 1323–5, s.v. 'Ildefonse (4)'; J. Fontaine in *DPAC* 2 (1984), cols. 1754 f., s.v. 'Ildefonso'; Eng. tr. in *Encyclopedia of the Early Church*, 1 (1992), p. 405, s.v.

Illingworth, John Richardson (1848–1915), English divine. From 1883 he was rector of Longworth, Oxon. A philosopher rather than a theologian, he applied some of the principles of Idealistic philosophy to the exposition of the Christian faith. His rectory became the centre of the '*Lux Mundi*' group, and Illingworth himself contributed two essays to the volume. His books include *Personality, Human and Divine* (*Bampton Lectures, 1894), *Divine Immanence* (1898), *Reason and Revelation* (1902), and *The Doctrine of the Trinity* (1907).

The Life and Work of J. R. Illingworth, by his wife (1917).

Illtyd or Illtud, St (5th–6th cent.), Welsh saint. All that is known is that he was abbot of a large monastery, which he is said to have founded. This community was later called after him 'Llanilltud Fawr'; it is mentioned in the early medieval Life of St *Samson and is prob. the modern Llantwit Major in Vale of Glamorgan. The 12th-cent. Life, which describes him as a native of Brittany who came to Britain and was converted to Christianity in 476, is of no historical value. Feast day, 6 Nov.

AASS, Nov. 3 (1910), pp. 219–36, incl. text of 12th-cent. Life, pp. 225–34; this is also pr., with Eng. tr., in A. W. Wade-Evans, *Vitae Sanctorum Britanniae et Genealogiae* (Cardiff, 1944), pp. 194–233. On this Life see J. S. P. Tatlock, 'The Dates of the

Arthurian Saints' Legends', *Speculum*, 14 (1939), pp. 345–65, esp. pp. 353–6. G. H. Doble, *Saint Iltud* (Cardiff, 1944); repr. in *Lives of the Welsh Saints*, ed. D. S. Evans (ibid., 1971), pp. 88–145. D. L. Thomas in *DNB* 28 (1891), pp. 416 f., s.v.

Illuminati. A name applied to several bodies of religious enthusiasts, among them:

(1) The Alumbrados (q.v.).

(2) The Rosicrucians (q.v.).

(3) A masonic sect founded in Bavaria in 1776 by Adam Weishaupt (1748–1830), who had been trained in a *Jesuit school and become a professor of *canon law at Ingolstadt. Its object was to diffuse knowledge and to stimulate humanistic ideals and brotherly fellowship among its members. Those who belonged to it took names of the ancients and called Munich 'Athens' and Vienna 'Rome'. They aimed at forming a classless society and at bringing about the 'restoration' of the patriarchal state. Repudiating the claims of all existing religious bodies, they professed themselves to be those in whom the 'illuminating' grace of Christ (hence their name; cf. Heb. 6: 4: τοὺς ἅπαξ φωτισθέντας) alone resided, and organized themselves on a new and very elaborate system, which required absolute obedience (largely modelled on Jesuit ideals) to the unknown superiors. In 1784 they were banished from Bavaria, but they continued to survive elsewhere, e.g. in France. They were also known as Perfectibilists. In modern times (1896, and again in 1925) they have been revived in Germany in a modified form.

(3) R. Le Forestier, *Les Illuminés de Bavière et la franc-maçonnerie allemande* (1914), esp. pp. 14–139 and 193–717. R. van Dülmen, *Der Geheimbund der Illuminaten: Darstellung, Analyse, Dokumentation* (Stuttgart [1975]). M. Agethen, *Geheimbund und Utopie: Illuminaten, Freimaurer und deutsche Spätaufklärung* (Ancien Régime, Aufklärung und Revolution, 11; 1984), esp. pp. 106–303. J. M. Roberts, *The Mythology of Secret Societies* (1972), pp. 118–45.

illuminative way. The intermediate stage of the spiritual life. See PURGATIVE, ILLUMINATIVE, AND UNITIVE WAYS.

Illyricus. See FLACIUS, MATTHIAS.

Image of God. Acc. to Gen. 1: 26 f. and elsewhere, man was created in the image of God. The term was fundamental to the patristic understanding of the human person. However, until St *Augustine, the primary significance of the expression 'Image of God' was the Son Himself, man being a derived image of God, created in accordance with (κατά) the Image, i.e. the Son. The two terms, 'image' and 'likeness' (Heb. צֶלֶם and דְּמוּת; Gk., εἰκών and ὁμοίωσις; Lat. *imago* and *similitudo*), used in Gen. 1: 26, were variously distinguished. Some (e.g. St *Irenaeus and *Origen) regarded 'image' as referring to man's original condition, and 'likeness' as referring to man's final state of glory (cf. 1 Jn. 3: 2); such a contrast fitted in conveniently with the *Platonic notion that man's goal is ὁμοίωσις θεῷ (*Theaet.* 176B) and also with the normal patristic understanding of salvation as *deification (q.v.). Other Fathers (e.g. St *Athanasius, St *Gregory of Nyssa) made no such distinction. The effect of the *Fall on the image received a similar variety of interpretation: for those who made the distinction the 'likeness' was lost, or its attainment rendered impossible apart from redemption; for others the image itself was damaged, or destroyed altogether. *Baptism was seen as an indispensable step in the restoration of the image-likeness. There have also been many theories to explain in what the image consists: most located it in human free will, but others found it in man's superiority to creation, or in a quality of his soul, such as simplicity or immortality, or in his reason. With St Augustine there was a new influential development in the doctrine of the image: the notion of the Son as the Image was dismissed as subordinationist and man's soul came to be regarded as a direct image of the Holy Trinity, manifesting a threefold structure in memory, understanding, and will (*memoria, intelligentia, voluntas*).

In the 16th cent. the Reformers expressed their doctrine of man's total depravity by asserting that the image was utterly lost as a result of the Fall. For those who opposed this view (not just RCs, but others such as the *Cambridge Platonists, and more recently some liberal Protestant theologians) the doctrine of the abiding image of God in man provided a convenient expression for their belief.

D. Cairns, *The Image of God in Man* (1953). T. Camelot, OP, 'La Théologie de l'Image de Dieu', *RSPT* 40 (1956), pp. 443–71. G. A. Jónsson, *The Image of God: Genesis 1: 26–28 in a Century of Old Testament Research* (Coniectanea Biblica, Old Testament Series, 26; Stockholm, 1988). H. Crouzel [SJ], *Théologie de l'Image de Dieu chez Origène* (Théologie, 34 [1956]); R. Leys, SJ, *L'Image de Dieu chez Saint Grégoire de Nysse* (Museum Lessianum, section théologique, 49; 1951); J. E. Sullivan, OP, *The Image of God: The Doctrine of St Augustine and its Influence* (Dubuque, Ia., 1963). W. Seibel in *Mysterium Salutis*, ed. J. Feiner and M. Löhrer, 2 (Einsiedeln [1967]), pp. 804–43.

images. The use of any representations of men, animals, and plants, whether carved or painted, was prohibited in the Mosaic Law (Exod. 20: 4), because of the danger of idolatry. In other parts of the OT, however, images are mentioned, such as the *brazen serpent made by *Moses himself (Num. 21: 9), the *Cherubim standing over the *Ark of the Covenant (Exod. 25: 18–22), and the carvings in *Solomon's Temple (1 Kgs. 6: 18–35). From the time of the *Maccabees, however, and prob. earlier, the Palestinian Jews observed the Second Commandment rigorously, at least as far as the Temple was concerned, though it appears that pictures were used to decorate *synagogues. There is no mention of imagery in the NT.

The earliest known Christian pictures are the paintings in the *catacombs, some of which date from the end of the 2nd cent. After the period of the *persecutions sacred images came to play an increasingly important part in the cultus, esp. in the E. This met with opposition from *Eusebius of Caesarea and *Epiphanius, among others, but it was justified by stressing the theological significance of the Incarnation in which God had become visible by taking human nature. After the *Iconoclastic Controversy (q.v.) of the 8th and 9th cents., and its final settlement in favour of icons, these have continued to be an integral element in Orthodox religion, whether public or private, in which they are given a much more important place than in the W. Church.

In the W. the veneration of images, which at an early age began to comprise also statues, made much slower progress. It was given a doctrinal basis by the Schoolmen, esp. St *Thomas Aquinas, who developed its theoretical justification on the lines laid down by the E. theologians, applying St *Basil's principle that the honour paid to the image passes on to its prototype, a principle which had already been accepted by the Second Council of *Nicaea (787).

In the 16th cent. the abuses which had grown up around the use of images in the later Middle Ages led the practice to be violently opposed by the majority of the Reformers, esp. U. *Zwingli and J. *Calvin, who were followed by the *Puritans. The *Lutherans were more tolerant of the practice, and to this day the crucifix is retained in the Lutheran churches. The Anglican Article XXII confines itself to condemning the 'Romish doctrine' on the subject. The Council of *Trent defined that due honour should be paid to images of the Lord, the BVM, and the other saints, on the ground not of any virtue inherent in the image, but because in it the person represented is venerated. This veneration is allowed only to images of actual human persons, not to such symbolical representations as that of God the Father as a venerable old man or the Holy Spirit as a dove, and similar devices.

St Thomas Aquinas, *In Sent.* lib. 3, dist. 9, a. 2, qu. 2; id., *S. Theol.* 3, 1, qu. 25, a. 3. The relevant clauses from the acts of the Second Council of Nicaea are conveniently repr. with Lat. and Eng. trs. in Tanner, *Decrees*, 1 (1990), pp. 135–7. The Tridentine ruling promulgated in sess. 25, sect. 'De Invocatione, Veneratione et Reliquis Sanctorum et Sacris Imaginibus', is repr., with Eng. tr., ibid., 2 (1990), pp. 774–6. E. [R.] Bevan, *Holy Images* (*Gifford Lectures for 1933; 1940). P. Evdokimov, *L'Art de l'Icône: Théologie de la beauté* [1970]. A. Nichols, OP, *The Art of God Incarnate: Theology and Image in Christian Tradition* (1980). A. *Fortescue in *CE* 7 (1910), pp. 664–72, s.v., with bibl.; V. Grumel, AA, in *DTC* 7 (pt. 1; 1922), cols. 766–84, s.v., with full refs. to classical lit.; A. D. Lee in *NCE* 7 (1967), pp. 370–2, s.v. 'Images, Veneration of'. See also bibl. to ICONOCLASTIC CONTROVERSY and to ICONOGRAPHY.

Imago Dei. Latin for *Image of God (q.v.).

Imitation of Christ, The. The purpose of this famous manual of spiritual devotion is to instruct the Christian how to seek perfection by following Christ as his model. The book is divided into four parts. The first two contain general counsel for the spiritual life, the third deals with the interior dispositions of the soul, and the fourth with the sacrament of the Holy Communion. It was first put into circulation (anon.) in 1418, and has traditionally been assigned to *Thomas à Kempis (c.1380–1471). Indeed a MS still exists at Brussels (Bibl. Roy., 5855–61) with his signature. Attempts have been made since the 17th cent. to assign it to an earlier writer, among those suggested being St *Bernard of Clairvaux, St *Bonaventure, G. *Groote, and J. *Gerson, none of whom are now considered likely. The attribution to a certain John Gersen of Canabaco, Abbot of Vercelli, suggested by the discovery by J. B. Rossignoli, SJ, in 1605 of a MS at Arona, describing it as the work of 'Abbatis Johannis Gersen', still finds supporters.

Facsimile reprod. of the *edito princeps*, which was pr. at Augsburg, 1471–2, ed. with introd. by W. J. Knox-Little (London, 1893). Crit. edns. by C. Hirsche (Berlin, 1874), by M. J. Pohl, among the works of Thomas à Kempis, vol. 2 (Freiburg i.B., 1904) and by T. Lupo, SDB (Vatican City, 1982). First Eng. tr. (mid 15th cent.) ed. J. K. Ingram (EETS, extra series, 63; 1892); modern edn. of Eng. tr. made by R. Whitford *c.*1530 by E. J. Klein with full introd. and notes prepared for EETS (New York and London, 1941). There have been a large number of Eng. trs., incl. that with introd. by J. *Wesley (London, 1735) and those by L. Sherley-Price (Penguin Classics, 1952) and R. A. *Knox and M. Oakley (London [1959]). Modern discussions on the authorship by J. Huijben and P. Debongnie, CSSR (Bibliothèque de la *RHE*, 30; 1957), L. M. J. Delaissé (Publications de Scriptorium, 2; 1956), R. R. Post, *The Modern Devotion* (Studies in Medieval and Reformation Thought, 3; Leiden, 1968), pp. 521–36, and A. Ampe, SJ (Sussidi eruditi, 25; 1973), all attributing it to Thomas à Kempis (as do most edns. of the work). J. van Ginneken, SJ (2 vols., Amsterdam, 1940–1), J. Tiecke (Nijmegen, 1941), and F. Kern (Olten, 1947) all attribute the work to G. Groote, mainly on the basis of certain 'pre-Kempistes' texts ed. by J. van Ginneken, op. cit. The attribution to John Gersen was accepted by J. *Mabillon and has been defended in modern times by P. E. Puyol (2 vols., Paris, 1889–1900) and P. Bonardi, CP, and T. Lupo, SDB (2 vols., Turin, 1964). The theory of the authorship of J. C. de Gerson has been championed by D. G. Barron, *Jean Charlier de Gerson: The author of the* De Imitatione Christi (1936), who gives a full discussion of the classic attempts at assigning the authorship. P. E. Puyol, *Descriptions bibliographiques des manuscrits et des principales éditiones du livre* De Imitatione Christi (1898). S. G. Axters, OP, *De Imitatione Christi: Een handschrifteninventaris bij het vijfhonderdste verjaren van Thomas Hemerken van Kempen †1471* (Kempen and Niederrhein, 1971). A. Ampe, SJ, and B. Spaapen, SJ, in *Dict. Sp.* 7 (pt. 2; 1971), cols. 2338–68, at end of vol. See also works cited under DEVOTIO MODERNA and THOMAS À KEMPIS.

Immaculate Conception of the BVM. The dogma that 'from the first moment of her conception the Blessed Virgin Mary was, by the singular grace and privilege of Almighty God, and in view of the merits of Jesus Christ, Saviour of mankind, kept free from all stain of original sin' (Bull '*Ineffabilis Deus' of *Pius IX, 8 Dec. 1854). The belief has had a long and varied history, largely bound up with the observance of a feast of the Conception of the BVM. Biblical support has been found for the doctrine in Gen. 3: 15 and Lk. 1: 28. The argument from tradition is taken from the teaching of the Fathers, who as early as *Justin Martyr and *Irenaeus regarded Mary as the 'new Eve' corresponding to Christ as the 'new Adam'. In the E., where *Andrew of Crete and *John of Damascus had extolled the perfect sinlessness of Mary as implicit in the title '*Theotokos', the feast of her Conception was known from the 7th cent. Nevertheless, the doctrine of the Immaculate Conception was never endorsed by E. Orthodox theologians, mainly because they did not share the W. understanding of *original sin. The observance of the feast spread to the W., where it is attested for Naples in the 9th, and for England in the first half of the 11th cent. On its introduction into France (c.1130–40) St *Bernard opposed it and a controversy went on for several centuries. Most of the great schoolmen, incl. St. *Albert, St *Bonaventure, and St *Thomas Aquinas, declared against the belief on the grounds that in every natural conception the stain of original sin is transmitted and that, as Mary was conceived in the natural way, she was not exempt from this law. In opposition to the Paris theologians the contrary opinion was defended by *Duns Scotus at Oxford and later in Paris, and in his wake the *Franciscans became its proponents as the *Dominicans, following St Thomas, its opponents. The 15th cent. brought decisive developments. The Council of *Basle affirmed (1439) the belief as a pious opinion in accordance with Catholic faith, reason, and Scripture; ten years later the *Sorbonne required an oath of all its candidates to defend it, and other universities followed. In 1476 Sixtus IV approved the feast with its own Mass and Office, and in 1708 *Clement XI extended it to the Universal Church and even imposed its observance as a *Feast of Obligation. The Council of *Trent had explicitly declared that its decree on original sin did not include the BVM, and from the 16th cent. belief in the Immaculate Conception became general and was defended not only by the Franciscans but also by the *Carmelites, by many Dominicans, and esp. by the *Jesuits. Of this development the definition of 1854 was the natural result. The Feast of the Immaculate Conception is kept on 8 Dec. (In the E. the Feast of the Conception of the BVM is kept on 9 Dec.)

C. Passaglia, SJ, *De Immaculato Deiparae Semper Virginis Conceptu Commentarius* (3 parts, Rome, 1854–5); A. Ballerini, SJ, *Sylloge Monumentorum ad Mysterium Conceptionis Immaculatae Virginis Deiparae Illustrandum* (2 vols., Rome, 1854–6). W. B. *Ullathorne, *The Immaculate Conception of the Mother of God* (1855). M. Jugie, AA, *L'Immaculée Conception dans l'Écriture sainte et dans la tradition orientale* (Rome, 1952). E. D. O'Connor (ed.), *The Dogma of the Immaculate Conception* (Notre Dame, Ind., 1958). E. *Bishop, *Liturgica Historica* (1918), ch. 10 ('On the Origins of the Feast of the Conception of the Blessed Virgin Mary'). A. W. Burridge, *White Father, 'L'Immaculée Conception dans la théologie de l'Angleterre médiévale', *RHE* 32 (1936), pp. 570–97; F. M. Mildner, OSM, 'The Oxford Theologians of the Thirteenth Century and the Immaculate Conception', *Marianum*, 2 (1940), pp. 284–306; I. Brady, OFM, 'The Development of the Doctrine on the Immaculate Conception in the Fourteenth Century after Aureoli', *Franciscan Studies*, 15 (1955), pp. 175–202. H. S. Box in E. L. Mascall and H. S. Box (eds.), *The Blessed Virgin Mary* (1963), pp. 77–88. X. Le Bachelet in *DTC* 7 (pt. 1; 1922), cols. 845–1218, s.v. 'Immaculée Conception', with bibl.; P. Bonnetain, PSS, in *Dict. Bibl.*, Suppl. 4 (1949), cols. 233–98, s.v. 'Immaculée Conception', with bibl.

Immaculate Heart of Mary. See SACRED HEART OF MARY.

Immanence, Divine. The omnipresence of God in His universe. The doctrine is a necessary constituent of the Christian conception of God, but, when held without the parallel doctrine of Divine transcendence, it is commonly indistinguishable from *pantheism (q.v.).

Immanuel or **Emmanuel** (Heb. עִמָּנוּאֵל, 'With us [is] God'). In the OT the word is used only in Is. 7: 14 and 8: 8. There are several interpretations. The prophet may here have meant by the expression (1) Hezekiah, the son of Ahaz; or (2) a son of his own; or (3) the *Messiah. It has also been suggested that no individual is referred to, but only future Divine deliverance. In Mt. 1: 23 the prophecy is interpreted with reference to the birth of Jesus Christ.

Besides comm. on Is. and Matt., see J. Lindblom, *A Study on the Immanuel Section in Isaiah* (Scripta Minora Regiae Societatis Humaniorum Litterarum Lundensis, 1957–8, no 4; 1958); W. McKane, 'The Interpretation of Isaiah VII 14–25', *Vetus Testamentum*, 17 (1967), pp. 208–19; R. Kilian, *Die Verheissung Immanuels: Jes. 7, 14* (Stuttgarter Bibelstudien, 35 [1968]). J. Jensen in *Anchor Bible Dictionary*, 3 (1992), pp. 392–5, s.v.

immersion. A method of *Baptism, employed at least from the 2nd cent., whereby part of the candidate's body was submerged in the baptismal water which was poured over the remainder. The rite is still found in the E. Church. In the W. it began to be replaced from *c.* the 8th cent. by the method of *affusion, though its use was still being encouraged in the 16th cent., as it still is in the Anglican and RC Churches. The term is occasionally loosely used to include *submersion, from which it is strictly to be distinguished.

immolation (Lat. *immolatio*, lit. 'the sprinkling of a sacrificial victim with meal' as required by the pagan ritual), an act of sacrificial offering. In early Christian usage the word was applied esp. to the actual slaughter of the victim, in the *Vulgate being often interchangeable with *mactatio* ('slaying'). In modern Eucharistic theology it has occupied an important place in view of the various doctrines held of the Immolation in the Mass, esp. since the publication of M. *de la Taille's *Mysterium Fidei* (1921).

immortality. Though in no sense a specifically Christian doctrine, the hope of immortality is an integral element in Christian belief, where it receives emphatic insistence and a characteristic shape. In pre-Christian times, the Greeks esp. developed a reasoned doctrine on the subject. The rationality of the human intellect seemed to imply an essential kinship of the soul with the principles of reason, so that it partook of their eternity. From this kinship *Plato inferred the existence of the soul before birth as well as its survival of death and saw in the process of learning the reminiscence (ἀνάμνησις) of knowledge possessed in a previous life. The striving of the virtuous man after the eternally valid principles of morality also pointed to the same belief. Plato and other Greeks insisted on the limitations which matter imposed on the soul. The body was an impediment, even a prison-house, from which death brought to the soul release into a fuller existence.

Such philosophical conceptions of immortality have commonly been confined to the few. In early times Hebrew thought about the next world hardly exceeded the conception of a very shadowy existence in *Sheol (q.v.). In later pre-Christian Judaism a greater sense of the reality of the future life developed, partly through reflection on the problem of suffering, partly from the ardent desire for abiding communion with God, partly through the recasting of the Messianic expectation. The Jewish hope became increasingly bound up with belief in the resurrection of the body, esp. in the *Apocalyptic writers. Esp. outside Palestine, Judaism borrowed extensively from Greek thought; in the Book of *Wisdom, e.g., the doctrine of immortality has a strong Platonic bent.

The essential shape which the doctrine assumed in Christianity arose from the fact of Christ's Resurrection. Man's highest destiny was more than the survival of an immortal soul. It was a life of abiding union with the risen Christ which reached its completion only by the reunion of body and soul. The teaching of St *Paul, embodied in 1 Cor. 15 and elsewhere, admirably expresses the essence of the Christian belief. Consequently, in Christian philosophy the defence of immortality after the manner of the Greek philosophers, i.e. apart from the resurrection, has always been an *argumentum ad hominem*.

The Fathers interpret the hope of immortality in close connection with the redemptive work of Christ. The *Fall of *Adam had brought death and it was through the *Second Adam that life was restored (*Irenaeus, *Athanasius, *Gregory of Nyssa). Most of the Fathers and the earlier Scholastics, however, were liable under Platonist influences to consider the relation of the soul to the body as extrinsic; and it was not until the 13th cent. that a fully elaborated defence of the specifically Christian doctrine appeared. Then the acceptance of the *Aristotelian tenet that the soul was the 'form' of the body gave philosophical justification for the beliefs that a disembodied soul was no true being and that the resurrection of the body was necessary for a full human life in the world to come.

The Scholastic arguments for the future life have been taken over since the later Middle Ages into popular apologetics. They were repeated, without substantial additions, by professional philosophers down to the end of the 18th cent. In R. *Descartes, with his sharp separation of mind and matter, they reappeared in a Platonic form. In G. W. *Leibniz they received a new emphasis through his belief that the human soul was the primary monad in man. The famous onslaught on the traditional arguments made by I. *Kant rested on his view of the limits of metaphysics. As the structure of the soul was outside the range of possible experience, it was beyond the competence of the 'theoretical reason' to establish its immortality or the contrary. Nevertheless Kant, who had no doubt about the fact of the future life, maintained that the soul's immortality could be established on the ground of moral experience, i.e. through the 'practical reason'. The abiding character of the moral law and the manifest injustices in this present life were a sure index that there was a purer and fuller life in which these injustices would be remedied. Since Kant's time philosophers have increasingly stressed the moral aspects of the problem of eternal life, and it has been esp. on these lines that immortality has been defended by such thinkers as W. R. Sorley, A. S. Pringle-*Pattison, and C. C. J. *Webb. See also CONDITIONAL IMMORTALITY; RESURRECTION OF THE DEAD.

D. R. Russell, *The Method and Message of Jewish Apocalyptic* (1964), pp. 353–90. F. *von Hügel, *Eternal Life: A Study of its Implications and Applications* (1912); A. S. Pringle-Pattison, *The Idea of Immortality* (1922); J. *Baillie, *And the Life Everlasting* (1934); A. E. *Taylor, *The Christian Hope of Immortality* (1938); F. Cumont, *Lux Perpetua* (Paris, 1949), *passim*; R. Aldwickle, *Death in the Secular City: A Study in the Notion of Life after Death in Contemporary Theology and Philosophy* (1972); H. D. Lewis, *The Self and Immortality* (1973); J. Hick, *Death and Eternal Life* (1976); H. *Küng, *Ewiges Leben?* (Munich, 1982; Eng. tr., 1984); S. [C. ff.] Tugwell, OP, *Human Immortality and the Redemption of Death* (1990). H. Grass in *RGG* (3rd edn.), 6 (1962), cols. 1174–8, s.v. 'Unsterblichkeit'; A. Solignac, SJ, in *Dict. Sp.* 7 (pt. 2; 1971), cols. 1601–14, s.v., with bibl.

Impanation. A term applied to certain doctrines of the *Eucharist. The first known occurrence of the word is in Guitmund of Aversa (d. *c*.1090), who says that while the followers of *Berengar all hold that in the Eucharist the Bread and the Wine are not essentially changed, some, poss. incl. Berengar himself, think that the Body and Blood of the Lord are 'truly present, but hidden, in such a way that they can in a certain manner be received, that is to say, that they are impanated' (*revera sed latenter conti-*

neri, et ut sumi possint quodammodo, ut ita dixerim, impanari, J. P. *Migne, *PL* 149. 1430 D). The reason why this word was used is indicated by a passage in Alger of Liège (d. *c*.1131) where certain unnamed heretics are stated to assert that 'Christ is in person impanated in the bread just as God was in person incarnate in human flesh' (*ita personaliter in pane impanatum Christum, sicut in carne humana personaliter incarnatum Deum,* id., *PL* 180. 754 B). In the later Middle Ages, and esp. during and after the Reformation, the term was applied to various Eucharistic doctrines which endeavoured to safeguard a belief in the *Real Presence while denying the destruction of the substance of the natural elements.

impassibility of God. There are three respects in which orthodox theology has traditionally denied God's subjection to 'passibility', namely (1) external passibility or the capacity to be acted upon from without, (2) internal passibility or the capacity for changing the emotions from within, and (3) sensational passibility or the liability to feelings of pleasure and pain caused by the action of another being. The doctrine was a regular tenet of philosophical theology among the Greeks, and its foundation in Christian sources is probably due to direct Greek influences. The human and Divine natures of Christ were often distinguished (e.g. at *Chalcedon, 451) as passible and impassible. On the other hand, Hebrew religion freely ascribed emotions to God (e.g. Hosea 11: 8).

In Christianity there is an acute tension between the Greek-philosophical and the Hebrew conceptions. On the one side there is the immutability, perfection, and all-sufficiency of God which would seem to exclude all passion, and this has been the basis of the traditional emphasis among theologians. But on the other side there is the central Christian conviction that God in His essence is love, that His nature is revealed in the Incarnate Christ and not least in His Passion, and that He 'sympathizes' with His creatures. Recognition of this second aspect has led some modern theologians to doubt whether it is legitimate to speak unreservedly of God's impassibility. Among the earliest writers to challenge the traditional view was James Hinton (*The Mystery of Pain*, 1866). In the 20th cent. Divine impassibility has been challenged by philosophers as incoherent, by *Process Theologians as a relic of an outmoded metaphysics, and by many other theologians as a blasphemous irrelevance in the light of the enormity of modern suffering, esp. under totalitarian regimes (e.g. J. *Moltmann and E. Jüngel). Nevertheless the traditional view has had its staunch defenders, e.g. F. *von Hügel (on the ground that God is 'Unmixed Joy, Entire Delectation'), J. K. Mozley, and E. L. Mascall.

F. von Hügel, *Essays and Addresses*, 2nd ser. (1926), ch. 7; J. K. Mozley, *The Impassibility of God* (1926); J. Moltmann, *Der gekreuzigte Gott* (1972; Eng. tr., 1974), *passim*; E. Jüngel, *Gott als Geheimnis der Welt* (Tübingen, 1977; Eng. tr., Grand Rapids, Mich., and Edinburgh, 1983), *passim*; E. L. Mascall, *Whatever Happened to the Human Mind? Essays in Christian Orthodoxy* (1980), pp. 64–96. R. E. Creel, *Divine Impassibility: An Essay in Philosophical Theology* (Cambridge, 1986). P. S. Fiddes, *The Creative Suffering of God* (Oxford, 1988).

impediment. In canon law, an obstacle, such as *consanguinity or *clandestinity, standing in the way of a properly constituted marriage. In RC canon law until 1983 impediments were either 'impedient' or 'diriment'. The former character, which prohibited a marriage but did not invalidate it, if contracted despite the impediment, no longer exists as such. A diriment impediment renders such a marriage null and void. Such impediments may be either 'irremovable' (e.g. close blood-relationship or the insanity of either party at the time of marriage) or 'removable' by *dispensation (e.g. the marriage of a RC to an unbaptized person). When a diriment impediment is removed by a *post factum* dispensation, the marriage is normally validated only from the moment when valid consent is exchanged. Canon law (but not English statutory law), however, provides for retrospective validation by the process termed *sanatio in radice*. See also DIRIMENT IMPEDIMENT.

imposition of hands. See HANDS, IMPOSITION OF.

imprecatory Psalms. A term apparently first used by W. Robertson *Smith (1881) for the Psalms which, in whole or in part, invoke the Divine vengeance (e.g. Pss. 58, 68: 21–3, 69: 23–9, 109: 5–19, 137: 7–9). The proposed revision of the BCP in 1928 provided for the omission from public recitation of such portions of the Psalter as were considered incompatible with the spirit of Christianity. In some modern Anglican Prayer Books such passages are printed in brackets and are commonly omitted.

imprimatur (Lat., 'let it be printed'). The certification that a book has been passed for publication by the appropriate authority.

(1) In England the origin of the licensing laws lies in the ordinances issued by the Star Chamber in 1586 and 1637; the latter provided an elaborate system of licensing which was in substance enacted after the Restoration. Acc. to the Licensing of the Press Act 1662 prohibiting the printing or importing of books contrary to the Christian faith or the doctrine and discipline of the C of E, or tending to the scandal of the government, all books were to be entered at the Stationers' Hall and licensed according to their subject by the Lord Chancellor, the Earl Marshal, one of the principal Secretaries of State, or the Abp. of Canterbury or the Bp. of London. Such licence was known as the *imprimatur*. The Act remained in force until 1679, was renewed in 1685 and expired in 1695.

(2) In the RC Church there is complex legislation relating to the means of public communication, and esp. the publication of books (*CIC* (1983), cans. 822–32). The approval of the local *Ordinary is needed before publication of certain kinds of books and other writings to certify that they are free from doctrinal or moral error. The Ordinary may appoint 'censors'. If the censor's verdict is favourable, the Ordinary may then give his permission for the work to be published, adding his own name and the place and date of permission. Canon law requires that the *imprimatur* be printed in the published book. Sometimes the name of the censor is given, with the words *nihil obstat* ('nothing prohibits'). In addition to this form of censorship, all members of religious orders or congregations (now technically known as *Institutes of Consecrated Life) require the permission of their major superiors, in accordance with their constitutions, to publish works on religion

or morals. This permission can be attested by the words *imprimi potest* ('it can be printed').

Improperia. See REPROACHES.

impropriation. The assignment or annexation of an ecclesiastical benefice, for the use of its property, into the hands of a lay proprietor or corporation. It has come to be distinguished from '*appropriation', which was used of benefices assigned to a religious house, Dean and Chapter, or other spiritual body. Many monastic benefices were impropriated by '*lay rectors' at the *Dissolution, and where the monastery was exempt from the requirement of endowing a *vicar (see APPROPRIATION), the lay rectors inherited this privilege. They would therefore appoint a *perpetual curate to discharge the spiritual duties of their benefices.

imputation (from Lat. *imputare*, Gk. λογίζεσθαι). A central aspect of classical *Protestant theologies of *justification, according to which the righteousness of Christ is imputed or reckoned to the believer, despite being extrinsic to his person, in order that he may be justified on its basis. This is contrasted with the teaching of the Council of *Trent, that the believer is justified on the basis of an imparted or infused righteousness, intrinsic to his person. Acc. to classical Protestant theology, the justification of the believer on account of the 'alien righteousness of Christ' is followed immediately by a process of renewal and growth in personal righteousness. Support for this doctrine is found in certain passages of St *Paul (notably Rom. 4; Gal. 3: 21 f).

For the concept in Anglican theology, see C. F. Allison, *The Rise of Moralism: The Proclamation of the Gospel from Hooker to Baxter* (1966), *passim*.

In Coena Domini (Lat., 'On the Lord's Supper'). A series of excommunications of specified offenders against faith and morals which was issued regularly in the form of a Papal bull at Rome. In later times publication was confined to *Maundy Thursday (hence its name), but originally it was read also on *Ascension Day and the feast of the Chair of St Peter (18 Jan.); and from the 15th cent. onwards it was also read outside Rome. The practice, which dates from at least the time of *Honorius III (1216–27), was constantly attacked by the civil authorities, who objected to its exalted claims for the Papacy, and in 1522 M. *Luther wrote a tirade against it (*Die Bulle vom Abendfressen des allerheiligsten Herrn*). The issue of the bull was suspended by *Clement XIV in 1773 and the practice finally abrogated by *Pius IX's bull 'Apostolicae Sedis' (12 Oct. 1869), which incorporated many of its censures. Some of these found their way into the 1917 *Codex Iuris Canonici* and, with further modifications, are in that of 1983.

The text of the bull issued by Pope Urban VIII 'in die Coenae Domini' 1627, after which its form remained practically unchanged until its abrogation, is pr. in *Bullarum, Diplomatum et Privilegiorum Sanctorum Romanorum Pontificum Taurinensis Editio*, 13 (Turin, 1868), pp. 530–7; principal clauses repr. in Mirbt, pp. 369–71 (no. 513), with refs. to other lit. The text of 'Apostolicae Sedis' is pr. in the *ASS*, 5 (1869), pp. 287–312, with notes and refs. J. F. Le Bret, *Pragmatische Geschichte der soberufenen Bulla Coena Domini* (Ulm, 1769). E. Göller, *Die päpstliche Pönitentiarie* von ihrem Ursprung bis zu ihrer Umgestaltung unter Pius V, 1 (pt. 1; Bibliothek des Kgl. Preussischen Historischen Instituts in Rom, 3; 1907), pp. 242–76, and 2 (pt. 1; ibid. 7; 1911), pp. 190–208. K. Pfaff, 'Beiträge zur Geschichte der Abendmahlsbulle vom 16. bis 18. Jahrhundert', *RQ* 38 (1930), pp. 23–76. J. Prior in *CE* 7 (1910), pp. 717 f., s.v.; F. C. Boúúaert in *DDC* 2 (1937), cols. 1132–6, s.v. 'Bulle In Coena Domini'.

in commendam. See COMMENDAM.

In Hoc Signo Vinces (Lat., 'by this sign thou shalt conquer'). Acc. to tradition, the words which the Emp. *Constantine saw inscribed across the sun (312). They are first mentioned in *Eusebius' *Life of Constantine* (1. 28), where they have the form 'by this, conquer' (τούτῳ νίκα).

incardination (Lat. *cardo*, 'hinge'; hence *incardinare*, 'to hang on a hinge'). In W. canon law, the permanent enlistment of a cleric under the jurisdiction of a new ordinary. From early times (cf. *Chalcedon, can. 6), all ordinands were ordered to be subject to an ecclesiastical superior; and the primitive rule (*Ap. Can. 15; *Nicaea, can. 16; *Antioch, can. 3; Chalcedon, can. 5) bound a cleric for life to the diocese in which he had been ordained. The process of incardination, with its correlative, *excardination (q.v.), was designed to avoid the inconveniences of the latter rule, while upholding its general principle. In the RC Church such transfers are permitted only for 'just causes' and always subject to the strict regulations of canon law. A cleric who has moved into another diocese, with due leave, is automatically incardinated into it if, after five years, he notifies its diocesan *bishop and his own that such is his desire and neither of them objects. The main regulations about incardination and excardination are set out in *CIC* (1983), cans. 265–72.

J. T. McBride, *Incardination and Excardination of Seculars: An Historical Synopsis and Commentary* (Catholic University of America, Canon Law Studies, 145; 1941). R. Naz in *DDC* 5 (1953), cols. 1293–6, s.v.

Incarnation. The Christian doctrine of the Incarnation affirms that the eternal Son of God took flesh from His human mother and that the historical Christ is at once both fully God and fully man. It is opposed to all theories of a mere theophany or transitory appearance of God in human form, frequently met with in other religions. By contrast, it asserts an abiding union in the Person of Christ of Godhead and manhood without the integrity or permanence of either being impaired. It also assigns the beginnings of this union to a definite and known date in human history.

The doctrine, which took classical shape under the influence of the controversies of the 4th–5th cents. (for history, see CHRISTOLOGY), was formally defined at the Council of *Chalcedon of 451 (q.v.). It was largely moulded by the diversity of traditions in the schools of *Antioch and *Alexandria, the one stressing the human aspects of the incarnate Christ, the other His Divinity. By its emphasis on the complete manhood of the incarnate Christ, the Antiochene theology sometimes tended to approximate Incarnation to inspiration. In Alexandrian circles, on the other hand, insistence on the full continuity between the Divinity of Christ and the Second Person of the Trinity could lead in careless hands to a view of the

Incarnation approximating to a theophany. It was these opposite tendencies which the Chalcedonian formula sought to hold in proper balance.

Yet the Definition was scarcely a solution; it only determined the limits to orthodoxy. Within these limits further refinements were added in the later patristic and medieval periods. Orthodox theologians held that the duality of natures entailed a duality of wills. They also emphasized that the Incarnation was an act of the whole Godhead, not of one Person acting independently. In the Middle Ages a much disputed (but never formally settled) question was whether the Incarnation would have taken place had the *Fall not occurred. While *Thomist theologians identified themselves with the belief that it was contingent on *Adam's transgression, *Scotists maintained the opposing doctrine. But in substance the Chalcedonian teaching was generally accepted by Christian theologians of all schools down to modern times. At the *Reformation both M. *Luther and J. *Calvin laid stress on the wonder of the Incarnation, God present in the child in the manger, God the Word incarnate in the teaching and actions of Jesus Christ. Reflection on the Incarnation has provided a dogmatic basis for the theology of *grace and of the *sacraments. Incarnation leads also to modern reflection on the theology of history, the involvement of God in contingency, *kenosis, and vulnerability.

The doctrine of the Incarnation raises questions of the relation of time and eternity, of finitude and infinity. Post-*Kantian Idealists saw in it the religious expression of the principle of immanence, i.e. the essential relatedness of man and God; and with this immanental reinterpretation the liberalizing movement in theology of the later 19th and early 20th cent. was in sympathy (*Foundations*). Among the more orthodox, the same tendency was reflected in a theological emphasis on the significance of culture and civilization in the purposes of God (*Christian Socialism). In both these schools stress was laid on the Incarnation rather than on the *Atonement as the fundamental Christian verity (*Lux Mundi*). Other theologians have sought to interpret the Incarnation in terms of moral values, and have seen the essence of Christ's Divinity in the complete conformity of His human will with that of God. Traditional theology has continued to emphasize the essential distinctness of the Lord's Divine and human natures, while some liberal theologians have questioned the appropriateness of the concept of Incarnation for expressing the true salvific significance of Jesus.

Useful collection of patristic passages ed. F. Diekamp, *Doctrina Patrum de Incarnatione Verbi: Ein griechisches Florilegium aus der Wende des siebenten und achten Jahrhunderts* (Münster, 1907). In addition to the items on the history and development of the doctrine cited under CHRISTOLOGY, the following works may be mentioned: H. P. *Liddon, *The Divinity of Our Lord and Saviour Jesus Christ* (*Bampton Lectures for 1866; 1867); A. B. *Bruce, *The Humiliation of Christ* (Cunningham Lectures for 1875; 1876); *Lux Mundi*, ed. C. *Gore (1889); C. Gore, *The Incarnation of the Son of God* (Bampton Lectures for 1891; 1891); A. M. *Fairbairn, *The Place of Christ in Modern Theology* (1893); C. Gore, *Dissertations on Subjects connected with the Incarnation* (1895); P. T. *Forsyth, *The Person and Place of Jesus Christ* (1909); W. *Sanday, *Christologies, Ancient and Modern* (1910); H. R. *Mackintosh, *The Doctrine of the Person of Jesus Christ* (1912); J. K. Mozley, *The Doctrine of the Incarnation* (1936); W. R. Matthews, *The Problem of Christ in the Twentieth Century: An Essay on the Incarnation* (Maurice

Lectures, 1949; 1950); G. S. Hendry, *The Gospel of the Incarnation* (Philadelphia, 1958; London, 1959); W. N. Pittenger, *The Word Incarnate: A Study of the Doctrine of the Person of Christ* (1959); T. F. Torrance, *Space, Time and Incarnation* (1969); W. [J.] Kasper, *Jesus der Christus* (Mainz, 1974; Eng. tr., 1976). J. [H.] Hick (ed.), *The Myth of God Incarnate* (1977); D. Cupitt, *The Debate about Christ* (1979); R. [C.] Morgan (ed.), *The Religion of the Incarnation: Anglican Essays in Commemoration of* Lux Mundi (Bristol, 1989). A. Michel in *DTC* 7 (pt. 2; 1923), cols. 1445–539, s.v. For studies on the historical Christ, see under JESUS CHRIST.

incense. Incense is used in many religious rites, the smoke being considered symbolical of prayer. It was used in the worship of the Jewish *Temple, at least in later times, while Rev. 8: 3–5 has been held to imply that it was used in sub-Apostolic Christian worship. There is, however, no clear evidence of its Christian use until the last quarter of the 4th cent.; *Egeria mentions its use in *Jerusalem and John *Chrysostom at *Antioch. Censers or *thuribles may at first have been fixed, both in the E. and W., and the portable thurible have originated, at least in the W., in imitation of that carried before Roman magistrates. The incensing of the altar, church, people, etc., is first recorded in the late 5th cent. in the E. (by *Dionysius the Pseudo-Areopagite) and in the W. in the 9th cent. (*Ordines Romani* and *Amalarius of Metz). Archaeological evidence, however, suggests that small portable thuribles were common in both E. and W. from the early 7th cent. In the W. incense was long used only at solemn services, though since 1969 it is more widely permitted, e.g. at any Eucharistic service. In the E. it is employed at all celebrations of the Liturgy, as well as at *Orthros, *Vespers, and most other services.

The use of incense appears occasionally in the C of E between the 16th and 19th cents., but it only became common in the ceremonial revival which followed the *Oxford Movement. It has been argued that it is required by the *Ornaments Rubric, though Abps. F. *Temple and W. D. Maclagan, in the Lambeth Opinion of 1899, gave it as their personal belief that it was not allowed.

The standard work on the subject is E. G. C. F. Atchley, *A History of the Use of Incense in Divine Worship* (*Alcuin Club Collections, 13; 1909). *The Case for Incense submitted to his Grace the Archbishop of Canterbury on behalf of the Rev. H. Westall on Monday, May 8, 1899, together with a legal argument and Appendices of the Experts* (London, 1899; incl. appendices by W. H. *Frere, W. J. Birkbeck, H. R. Percival, D. *Stone, E. Geldart, T. A. *Lacey, and W. H. St J. Hope). On the early Christian evidence, H. *Lietzmann, *Messe und Herrenmahl* (1926), pp. 86–93; Eng. tr. (Leiden, 1979), pp. 71–76. K. Nielsen, *Incense in Ancient Israel* (Suppl. to *Vetus Testamentum*, 38; 1986). E. Fehrenbach in *DACL* 5 (pt. 1; 1922), cols. 2–21, s.v. 'Encens'; M. F. Bond in *DECH* (3rd edn., 1948), pp. 302–4, s.v.; E. Pax in *L.Th.K.* 10 (1965), cols. 990–2, s.v. 'Weihrauch'.

Incorporated Church Building Society. See CHURCH BUILDING SOCIETY.

incubation. The term is used of the practice of sleeping in churches or their precincts in expectation of visions, revelations, and healing from disease. Of pagan origin, the custom was introduced into Christianity after the fall of paganism. Certain saints at definite places were believed in particular to perform the healing miracles formerly attributed to Asclepius, notably St *Michael in the church

of Anaplous near *Constantinople, Sts *Cosmas and Damian (who had been physicians in their lifetime) also at Constantinople, St *Andrew at Patras, and the BVM at Athens and in *Notre-Dame de Paris. The practice and the beliefs associated with it are not wholly extinct.

L. Deubner, *De Incubatione* (Teubner, 1900). M. Hamilton, *Incubation, or the Cure of Disease in Pagan Temples and Christian Churches* (St Andrews, 1906). R. Herzog, *Die Wunderheilungen von Epidauros* (Philologus, Supplementband 22, Heft 3; 1931). J. Gessler, 'Notes sur l'incubation et ses survivances', *Le Muséon*, 59 (1946), pp. 661–70; D. Mallardo, 'L'Incubazione nella Cristianità Medievale Napoletana', *Anal. Boll.* 67 (1949), pp. 465–98. G. G. Dawson, *Healing Pagan and Christian* (1935). H. *Leclercq, OSB, in *DACL* 7 (pt. 1; 1926), cols. 511–17, s.v.; C. Zintzen in *Der Kleine Pauly*, 5 (1975), cols. 583 f., s.v. 'Tempelschlaf'.

incumbent. In the C of E the holder of a parochial *benefice. An incumbent may therefore be a *rector, a *vicar, or (until 1968) a *perpetual curate. In Scotland the word is used only of those holding ecclesiastical office in the Episcopal Church. The term, which in this sense is peculiar to English, is apparently derived from the medieval Latin *incumbere* in the sense of obtaining possession (*obtinere, possidere*) of a benefice.

incunabula (Lat. *incunabula*, 'swaddling-clothes', hence 'cradle'). Books produced in the first stages of the art of printing, and esp. those printed before 1501, of which a very large proportion was religious. The earliest known book printed with movable type is the *Mazarin Bible (q.v.). The first known printed book with a date is the Mainz Psalter of 1457.

Gesamtkatalog ed. Kommission für den Gesamtkatalog der Wiegendrucke (Leipzig, 1925 ff.). K. Haebler, *Handbuch der Inkunabelkunde* (ibid., 1925; Eng. tr., New York, 1933). F. Geldner, *Inkunabelkunde* (Wiesbaden, 1978). S. Corsten and R. W. Fuchs (eds.), *Der Buchdruck im 15. Jahrhundert: Eine Bibliographie* (2 vols., Stuttgart, 1988–93).

Independents. Another name for the *Congregationalists (q.v.), as upholders of the independence or autonomy of each local congregation. It was in very general use in Britain (but not in the USA, where it was much disliked) down to the end of the 18th century.

Index, Congregation of the. See following entry.

Index Librorum Prohibitorum (Lat., 'List of prohibited books'), in short, just 'the Index', the official list of books issued by the RC Church which its members were forbidden, except in special circumstances, to read or possess. The first Index was issued by the Congregation of the *Inquisition under *Paul IV in 1557. In 1571 *Pius V established a special 'Congregation of the Index' to be in charge of the list and revise it as needed; and this Congregation survived until 1917, when *Benedict XV transferred its duties to the *Holy Office. In modern times the control of literature likely to be contrary to faith or morals rested much more than formerly with the diocesan bishops, whose duties were laid down by *Leo XIII in 'Officiorum ac Munerum' (25 Jan. 1897), whence they passed into the 1917 *Codex Iuris Canonici (cans. 1384–405). Hence the Index came to fill a less prominent place than formerly in the life of the RC Church and in fact many widely circulating books contrary to faith or morals never found their way to it. Besides the Index proper, the Holy Office also issued an 'Index Expurgatorius' of books which might be freely read after certain passages had been deleted from them. In 1966 the Index ceased to have the force of ecclesiastical law, with attached censures, but at the same time the Congregation for the Doctrine of the Faith stated that it retains its moral force. See also IMPRIMATUR.

J. Hilgers, SJ, *Der Index der verbotenen Bücher: In seiner neuen Fassung dargelegt und rechtlich-historisch gewürdigt* (1904); id., *Die Bücherverbote in Papstbriefen: Kanonistisch-bibliographische Studie* (1907). F. H. *Reusch, *Der Index der verbotenen Bücher* (2 vols., Bonn, 1883–5); id., *Die Indices Librorum Prohibitorum des sechzehnten Jahrhunderts* (Tübingen, 1886). A. Boudinhon, *La Nouvelle Législation de l'Index: Texte et commentaire de la constitution Officiorum ac Munerum du 25 janvier 1897* [1899]. In English, there is much information on the Index in P. F. Grendler, *The Roman Inquisition and the Venetian Press, 1540–1605* (Princeton, NJ, 1977). J. Hilgers in *CE* 7 (1910), pp. 721 f., s.v.; A. Thouvenin in *DTC* 7 (pt. 2; 1923), cols. 1570–80, s.v.; A. de Iorio in *EC* 6 (1951), cols. 1825–9, s.v. 'Indice dei libri proibiti'; H. Wagnon and R. Naz in *DDC* 5 (1953), cols. 1318–30, s.v.

India, Pakistan, and Bangladesh, Christianity in. There are some ambiguous references to Christianity in India (and conceivably Pakistan) in the 4th cent., but the earliest clear testimony is the assertion of *Cosmas Indicopleustes that there were Christians, believers and clergy, in India before 550. All sections of the Thomas Christians (see MALABAR CHRISTIANS) believe that their Church was founded by St *Thomas the Apostle, but this tradition can be regarded as no more than possible. The arrival of the Portuguese at the end of the 15th cent. led to the fragmentation of this Church. Originally it had belonged to the *Church of the East, but in 1599 one large section came under the jurisdiction of Rome. In the second half of the 17th cent. a group became attached to the *Syrian Orthodox patriarchate. In the 19th cent. a small group became Anglican; a larger group formed the 'Mar Thoma' Church. For centuries confined to their small territory in SW India, the 'Syrian' community has in modern times spread extensively in the East and developed strong missionary activity. In India they now number about 1.5 million.

Western Christianity came to India with the ships of Vasco da Gama in 1498. In their small territories of Goa, Cochin, etc., the Portuguese exercised strong pressure, though not actual coercion, on the inhabitants to become Christian, but they made no extensive attempts to convert the inhabitants of the country as a whole. Such general missionary activity was undertaken by the *Jesuits, who arrived in 1542. St *Francis Xavier organized the Church of the Fisher caste on the Coromandel coast. For many years a mission was maintained at the court of the Great Mogul at Lahore. Robert *de Nobili, who reached Madura, adopted the manner of life of a Hindu *guru* and thereby won a number of high-caste converts, though his methods were much criticized.

Under the *padroado* (or royal patronage) grants of the Pope, Portugal claimed the right to nominate all bishops and missionaries in the East. Goa, which became an archbishopric in 1557, was the centre of these missionary operations, and its Abp. still retains the honorary title of

Patriarch of the East Indies and Primate of the East. By the 17th cent., however, it was clear that Portugal could not fulfil all these obligations and in 1637 the *Propaganda in Rome consecrated a Brahman from Goa as *Vicar Apostolic for the non-Portuguese regions of India. Though the policy of choosing Indians for the office lapsed, Vicars Apostolic were appointed in increasing numbers, esp. after the suppression of the Jesuits in 1773. Portuguese hostility continued, and in the 19th cent. led to the Goa Schism, which lasted into the 20th cent. In 1886 *Leo XIII created a regular hierarchy for India and the future Pakistan and in 1896 he appointed bishops for the *Uniat section of the Thomas Christians.

From 1600 the English and later the Dutch were present in the Indian subcontinent. The greater part of their Church work consisted in the spiritual care of their own people through chaplains, but there are records of missionary work and a few conversions. Protestant missionary work began seriously in 1706, when King Frederick IV of Denmark founded a mission to work in his territory of Tranquebar in S. India. The pioneer, Bartholomäus Ziegenbalg (1683–1719), translated the NT and parts of the OT into Tamil. As the work spread beyond the limits of the Danish possession, the *SPCK took over the support of the missionaries, who served the Society in spite of the fact that they had not received Anglican ordination. The greatest of these *Lutheran missionaries, Christian Friedrich Schwartz (1726–98), who worked continuously in India from 1750 onwards, also served as a chaplain to the East India Company, and, at a time of hostility towards the missionaries, won the support of both the Indians and the British rulers. Another was John Zachary Kiernander (1714–98), who was invited to go to Calcutta by Lord Clive.

In 1793 the first English missionary, a *Baptist, W. *Carey, landed in Bengal. At that time the East India Company was opposed to missionary activity on the ground that it would influence opinion against Europeans. Carey, however, secured the protection of the Danish Crown and established a mission in the Danish territory of Serampore. He and his assistants translated the NT into Bengali and within 30 years had printed parts of the Bible in 37 Indian languages. At the revision of the East India Company's charter in 1813, *Evangelical opinion secured the insertion of provisions for a bishopric of Calcutta as well as freedom for missionary enterprise. T. F. *Middleton became the first bishop (1814–22); he had, however, clear jurisdiction only over chaplains and European congregations and was doubtful whether he had authority to ordain Indians to the ministry of the C of E. During his episcopate, in 1820, Bishop's College, Calcutta, was opened for the training of ordinands in India, but the work lapsed until it was resumed in 1917. R. *Heber, the second bishop (1823–6), licensed the missionaries, including some Lutherans supported by the SPCK, but laid down that for the future the missions should be solely Anglican. He also (re-)ordained a few Lutherans to make them acceptable in the East India Company's churches, including among those whom he (re-)ordained the first Indian Anglican priest (who had previously received Lutheran orders). From about this time the *CMS began to send missionaries, and Anglican clergy from England came in increasing numbers. Bishoprics were created for

Madras (1835) and Bombay (1837), and the Bp. of Calcutta was given the title of Metropolitan, though not Archbishop. Under D. *Wilson (Bp. of Calcutta 1835–58), the first Metropolitan, the provision of churches and chaplains for stations, regiments, and schools was much improved.

The removal of the restrictions on missionary enterprise when the East India Company's Charter was renewed in 1813 and 1834 was followed by a great increase in the number of non-British societies working in its territories. By the end of the 19th cent. American missionaries outnumbered British, and there were strong contingents from Switzerland, Germany, Sweden, Norway, and Denmark. In the same period the RC Church there became internationalized, receiving missionaries from the Netherlands, followed by Germans, Americans, and others. The British Government maintained an attitude of neutrality towards all religions that did not offend the law, though it did in 1829 abolish the Hindu custom of suttee (the burning of a widow on her husband's pyre), and it subsidized missionary schools prepared to accept a measure of government control. In the second half of the 19th cent. strenuous efforts were made to evangelize the aboriginal peoples, including the 'untouchables'. The Gossner Lutheran Church met with success among the Oraons and other peoples of Chota Nagpur. The Welsh Calvinists converted the Khasis in large numbers, and the Baptists worked among the tribes on the frontiers of Burma. From 1866 onwards there were widespread conversions among the most oppressed and poverty-stricken sections of the community, esp. in the Telugu-speaking areas of the Madras Presidency.

During the 19th cent. a native Indian village ministry was formed through the ordination of those trained in their own language and with no knowledge of English. The first ordination of such a candidate took place in 1850, and gradually the number of Indians ordained came to exceed the number of missionaries. Progress in this matter was slower in the RC Church than among other denominations, the demand for *celibacy posing difficulties. In S. India, Anglican training of candidates for the ministry in English began in 1883, and the United Theological College of Bangalore was founded in 1910. In 1912 the first Indian Anglican bishop in India was consecrated, to be followed by the first RC bishop of the Latin rite in 1923. In 1930 the Anglican Church in India, which had hitherto legally been a part of the C of E, acquired independence as the Church of India, Burma, and Ceylon (Pakistan was added to the title in 1947). This Church, while part of the Anglican Communion, had the right to draw up its own constitution, elect its own bishops, and settle its liturgical principles and practice.

Ecumenical relations developed early in India. Co-operation among non-RC missions began in 1855, and a long series of conferences (notably that of Bangalore in 1879) led to the formation in 1908 of the South India United Church (*Presbyterian and *Congregational), the first trans-confessional union in modern times. Out of this grew the movement which led in 1947 to the formation of the Church of *South India (q.v.), A parallel movement brought into being in 1970 the Churches of *North India and *Pakistan (qq.v.).

When the former British India became independent in 1947, the country was divided into the predominantly Hindu state of India and the mainly Muslim state of Pakistan, of which the eastern part became independent as Bangladesh in 1971. Religious liberty was written into the constitutions of all these states; Christians as well as others may practice and profess their faith. Conversions, however, are discouraged and in India restrictions were soon placed on foreign missionaries. Nevertheless, after Islam Christianity forms the second largest minority religion and the proportion of Christians in the population has remained at about 2.5 per cent. Of these the RC Church claims slightly over half (c.14.5 million in 1994), with 18 archdioceses and over a hundred dioceses. Christianity is strongest in the south of India and in the east (where minority tribes have been converted). In all denominations the increase in the proportion of Indians even among the most senior of the clergy accelerated after independence and in 1952 the first Indian was made a cardinal. The development of Christian ashram, both Catholic and Protestant, illustrates the way the Churches have adapted to local traditions. In the latter part of the 20th cent. there has been a shift in the emphasis of missionary work away from education of the upper classes to philanthropic activity among the very poor, exemplified in the dedication of Mother *Teresa and the Missionaries of Charity. In Pakistan there was originally less hostility towards missionaries from countries of the Commonwealth, and in 1950 a RC hierarchy was established. Though religious liberty was preserved when Pakistan became an Islamic republic in 1956, since 1969 the government has exercised increasing control over Christian institutions and the activities of foreign missionaries, and Christians have felt their position to be threatened. While the census figures provide no recent information, in 1972 Christians formed c.1.5 per cent of the population and it is unlikely that the proportion has increased. In Bangladesh in the 1980s they formed c.0.25 per cent of the population.

Introductory surveys by P. Thomas, *Christians and Christianity in India and Pakistan: A General Survey of the Progress of Christianity in India from Apostolic Times to the Present Day* (1954) and S. C. Neill, *The Story of the Christian Church in India and Pakistan* (Grand Rapids, 1970). Major work by id., *A History of Christianity in India*, 1: *The Beginnings to AD 1707* (Cambridge, 1984); 2: *1707–1858* (ibid., 1985: all pub.). *History of Christianity in India* (6 vols. planned): 1, *From the Beginning to the Middle of the Sixteenth Century*, by A. M. Mundadan, CMI (Bangalore, 1984); 2, *From the Middle of the Sixteenth to the End of the Seventeenth Century*, by J. Thekkedeth, SBB (ibid., 1982). J. Rooney, MHM, *Shadows in the Dark (A History of Christianity in Pakistan up to the 10th Century)* (Pakistan Christian History, Monograph 1; Rawalpindi, 1984); id., *The Hesitant Dawn (Christianity in Pakistan 1597–1760)* (ibid. 2; 1984). M. F. X. D'Sa, *History of the Catholic Church in India* (2 vols., Bombay, 1925). E. Maclagan, *The Jesuits and the Great Mogul* (1932). E. D. Potts, *British Baptist Missionaries in India 1793–1837* (Cambridge, 1967). E. Chatterton, *A History of the Church of England in India since the Early Days of the East India Company* (1924); C. J. Grimes, *Towards an Indian Church: The Growth of the Church of India in Constitution and Life* (1946); M. E. Gibbs, *The Anglican Church in India 1600–1970* (Delhi, 1972). A. Mayhew, *Christianity and the Government of India: An Examination of the Christian Forces at Work in the Administration of India and of the Mutual Relations of the British Government and Christian Missions, 1600–1900* (1929). J. C. B. Webster, *The Christian Community and Change in Nineteenth Century North India* (Delhi, etc., 1976). B. [G. M.] Sundkler, *Church of South India: The Movement towards Union, 1900–1947* (1954). A. V. Thomas, *Christians in Secular India* (Rutherford, NJ, etc.

[1974]). K. N. Sahay, *Christianity and Culture Change in India* (New Delhi, 1986). Bede Griffiths, *Christian Ashram: Essays towards a Hindu-Christian Dialogue* (1966); H. Ralston, *Christian Ashrams: A New Religious Movement in Contemporary India* (Studies in Religion and Society, 20; Lewiston and Queenston [1987]). G. A. Goodie (ed.), *Religion in South Asia: Religious Conversion and Revival Movements in South Asia in Medieval and Modern Times* (London, 1977), pp. 35–144; 2nd edn. (Monohar, 1991), pp. 39–174. There is also much information in the biographies of bishops and other leaders, and in the history of the various missionary societies. H. Grafe in *TRE* 16 (1987), pp. 102–16, s.v. 'Indien', with recent statistics. See also bibl. to MALABAR CHRISTIANS and SOUTH INDIA, CHURCH OF.

Indicopleustes. See COSMAS INDICOPLEUSTES.

Indonesia, Christianity in. Christianity was effectively brought to Indonesia through the Portuguese maritime trading empire in the early 16th cent. Its main religious rival was *Islam, which had been expanding through the region from Sumatra since the 13th cent. Apart from the *Church of the East (which may have established a small community in the 7th cent. and was certainly represented later), and visits by *Franciscans travelling to China in the 14th cent., the first Christian missionaries were Franciscans from *Portugal who established themselves in the Moluccas in 1534. They were followed by *Dominicans and *Jesuits; St *Francis Xavier spent 14 months in the region (1546–7). After the Dutch displaced the Portuguese in the Indonesian archipelago in the early 17th cent., the RC Church dwindled and Protestantism was introduced with the support of the Dutch East India Company. For the next 200 years the Dutch Reformed Church was the only officially recognized Church within the Company's sphere of influence. The Company brought clergy from the *Netherlands for its employees and some Indonesians were baptized. During the 19th and early 20th cents, under Dutch colonial rule, the extension of Christianity was largely undertaken by Dutch and German missionary societies. These included the Netherlands Missionary Society, the Netherlands Missionary Union, the Utrecht Missionary Union, the *Mennonites, the Rhenish Missionary Society, and the Basel Mission. RC missionary work was resumed in 1808 and an apostolic *vicariate was founded at Batavia in 1841. Both Protestant and RC missions received financial aid from the Dutch colonial government.

To avoid religious conflict, it was Dutch policy to assign different missionary bodies to separate areas. Christianity made little headway on the island of Java, where the majority of the population were Muslims, but in non-Muslim regions it was more successful. As a result of the work of the Rhenish Mission and the leadership of L. I. Nommensen (1834–1918), a large Protestant Church developed from the late 19th cent. among the Batak people of north Sumatra. Protestants became numerous also in Sulawesi (Celebes) and the Moluccas. Hendrik Kraemer (1888–1965), a notable missionary scholar, worked in Indonesia from 1922 to 1937, when he returned to *Leiden as Professor of the Phenomenology of Religion. In Indonesia he was invited to write his major work, *The Christian Message in a non-Christian World* (1938) for the *Tambaram Conference. In 1950 the Council (later Communion) of Churches in Indonesia was formed. The

RC missions expanded greatly in the 20th cent., esp. in the Lesser Sunda Islands. The first indigenous RC bishop was appointed in 1940 and an Indonesian hierarchy was established in 1961.

Dutch rule and European missionary activity were disrupted by Japanese occupation (1942–5) during the Second World War. In 1949 the new nation of Indonesia came into existence. One of the principles of the Indonesian state is belief in God, and Protestantism and RCism are officially recognized religions. Christians, who numbered 16 million in 1985, form 10 per cent of the population of Indonesia. About a quarter of the Christians are RC; the largest Protestant Churches are the Batak Protestant Christian Church, the Evangelical Christian Church in Minahasa, the Protestant Church in the Moluccas, and the Evangelical Christian Church in Timor.

F. L. Cooley, *Indonesia: Church & Society* (New York [1968]); id., *The Growing Seed: The Christian Church in Indonesia* (Jakarta, 1981). B. E. Colless, 'The Traders of the Pearl. The Mercantile and Missionary Activities of Persian and Armenian Christians in South-East Asia. 3. The Malay Archipelago', *Abr-Nahrain*, 11 (1971), pp. 1–21. M. P. M. Muskens, *Partner in Nation Building: The Catholic Church in Indonesia* (Aachen, 1979). T. Müller-Krüger, *Der Protestantismus in Indonesien: Geschichte und Gestalt* (Die Kirchen des Welt, Reihe B, Band 5; Stuttgart, 1968). H. Kraemer, *From Missionfield to Independent Church: Report on a Decisive Decade in the Growth of Indigenous Churches in Indonesia* (London, 1958). P. van Akkeren, *Sri and Christ: A Study of the Indigenous Church in East Java* (World Studies of Churches in Mission, 1970). P. B. Pedersen, *Batak Blood and Protestant Soul: The Development of National Batak Churches in North Sumatra* (Grand Rapids, Mich. [1970]); D. G. McKenzie, *The Mango Tree Church: The Story of the Protestant Christian Church in Bali* (Brisbane, 1988). R. A. F. P. Webb, *Palms and the Cross: Socioeconomic Development in Nusatenggara 1930–1975* (Townsville, Australia, 1986).

induction (in logic). The process of reasoning whereby a general law or principle is reached from the observance of particular instances. The word, which in its Lat. form (*inductio*) occurs in Cicero, is a rendering of *Aristotle's ἐπαγωγή. The opposite process is termed '*deduction'.

induction (to a benefice). The term used to denote the final stage, after nomination and *institution, in the appointment of a new *incumbent. The effect is to place the priest in legal possession of the temporalities of the *benefice, and in control of his parish. The bishop after institution issues a mandate to the *archdeacon or other person having the power to induct, who lays the hand of the person to be inducted on the key of the church door and causes him to toll the bell. The induction is also commonly accompanied by other ceremonial acts.

Indulgence, Declarations of. See DECLARATIONS OF INDULGENCE.

indulgences. The remission by the Church of the temporal penalty due to forgiven sin, in virtue of the merits of Christ and the saints. In the RC Church the granting of indulgences is now ordinarily confined to the Pope. The practice presupposes (1) a retributive basis for Divine justice, i.e. that sin must have a penalty either on earth or in purgatory, even after the sinner has been reconciled with God by penitence and absolution; (2) the doctrine of the

*Communion of Saints in the Body of Christ and the belief that through that communion all Christians can share both in the infinite merits of Christ's saving work and in the merits of the BVM and the saints (collectively referred to as the 'treasury of merits'); (3) the belief that the Church, by her power of jurisdiction, has the right of administering the benefit of these merits in consideration of prayers or other pious works undertaken by the faithful.

In the early Church, esp. from the 3rd cent., the intercession of confessors and those awaiting martyrdom was allowed by the ecclesiastical authorities to shorten the canonical discipline of those under penance; with the development of the doctrine of purgatory in the W., canonical penance came to be considered as a substitute for temporal punishment in purgatory, and from there the transition was easy to the belief that the prayers and merits of the saints availed to shorten such punishment itself, even for sins which did not require canonical penance. Later, with the relaxation of the penitential discipline, alternative works were permitted instead of the prescribed penances, and the merits of Christ and the saints applied to make up the deficiency. For general indulgences, there is no certain evidence datable before the 11th cent. In the 12th cent., however, the practice of granting indulgences became more common. *Plenary indulgences were offered to those who took part in the *Crusades, and bishops were authorized to give limited indulgences at the dedication of churches and their anniversaries, one of the most famous of these being the *Portiuncula Indulgence granted to St *Francis in 1221. The later Middle Ages saw the growth of considerable abuses, such as the unrestricted sale of indulgences by professional 'pardoners', whose false doctrine and scandalous conduct were an immediate occasion of the Reformation, and whose activities were finally prohibited by *Pius V in 1567.

Until recent times RC practice was to encourage piety and good works among the faithful by very liberal grants of indulgences, generally by the Pope himself, but also, within certain limits, by metropolitans and bishops. In response to suggestions made at the Second *Vatican Council, however, Pope *Paul VI in the constitution 'Indulgentiarum doctrina' (1 Jan. 1967) substantially revised the practical application of the traditional doctrine in order to make it clear that the Church's object was not merely to help the faithful to make due satisfaction for their sins, but chiefly to induce them to a greater fervour of charity. Under the new discipline, the number of plenary indulgences was greatly reduced, and it was emphasized that no plenary indulgence could be gained without a total conversion of heart from all sin. Partial indulgences are no longer reckoned in days and years; they simply supplement, and to the same degree, the remission which the person performing the indulgenced action has already gained by the charity and contrition with which he does it. At the same time, the former distinction between 'personal', 'real' and 'local' indulgences was abolished, in order to indicate that it is the personal actions of the faithful that are indulgenced, even when they are connected with some sacred office or place. Current RC canon law is to be found in *CIC* (1983), cans. 992–7. As well as the Pope, cardinals, patriarchs, metropolitans, and bishops can grant indulgences.

Indulgences can also be gained by the living for the souls in purgatory, but only *per modum suffragii*, i.e. by an act of intercession, since the Church on earth has no jurisdiction beyond the grave. See also MERIT; PLENARY INDULGENCE; and RACCOLTA.

Enchiridion Indulgentiarum: Normae et Concessiones (Rome, 1968; 3rd edn., 1986). E. Amort, *De Origine, Progressu, Valore ac Fructu Indulgentiarum* (2 pts., Augsburg, 1735; 2nd edn. with additions, Venice, 1738). F. Beringer, SJ, *Die Ablässe, ihr Wesen und Gebrauch* (1860; ed. P. A. Steiner, SJ, 2 vols., 1921–30; Fr. tr., 1890). A. H. M. Lépicier, *Indulgences: Their Origin, Nature and Development* (1895; rev. edn., 1928). H. C. Lea, *A History of Auricular Confession and Indulgences in the Latin Church*, 3 (Philadelphia, 1896; polemical and hostile). J. Hilgers, SJ, *Die katholische Lehre von den Ablässen und deren geschichtliche Entwicklung* (1914). N. Paulus, *Geschichte des Ablasses im Mittelalter, vom Ursprunge bis zur Mitte des 14. Jahrhunderts* (3 vols., 1922–3). B. Poschmann, *Der Ablass im Lichte der Bussegeschichte* (1948). J. E. Campbell, *Indulgences: The Ordinary Power of Prelates Inferior to the Pope to Grant Indulgences. An Historical Synopsis and a Canonical Commentary* (Ottawa thesis; Ottawa, 1953). K. *Rahner, SJ, 'Bemerkungen zur Theologie des Ablasses', *Schriften der Theologie*, 2 (1955), pp. 185–210; id., 'Zur heutigen kirchenamtlichen Ablasslehre', ibid. 8 (1967), pp. 488–518, with extensive bibl. (Eng. tr., 'Remarks on the Theology of Indulgences' and 'On the Official Teaching of the Church Today on the Subject of Indulgences', *Theological Investigations*, 2 (1963), pp. 175–201, and 10 (1973), pp. 166–98). W. E. Lunt, *Financial Relations of the Papacy with England 1327–1534* (Mediaeval Academy of America Publication, 74; 1962), pp. 447–620. E. Magnin in *DTC* 7 (1922), cols. 1594–636, s.v., with bibl.; G. Löw, CSSR, and S. De Angelis in *EC* 6 (1951), cols. 1901–10, s.v. 'Indulgenze', with bibl.; E. Jombart in *DDC* 5 (1953), cols. 1331–52, s.v.; G. L. Müller and others in *L.Th.K.* (3rd edn.), 1 (1993), cols. 51–8, s.v. 'Ablass'. See also works cited under PENANCE.

indult (Lat. *indultum*, 'a permission'). A faculty granted by the Pope or some other ecclesiastical authority to deviate from the common law of the Church. It is generally given for a specific case or for a specific period, and is commonly personal in reference, i.e. it cannot be communicated to others unless special permission is given.

Industrial Christian Fellowship (ICF). An Anglican organization which endeavours to present the Christian faith to the world of industry both by missions to industrial workers and by relating the theory and practice of Christianity to modern industry. It was formed in 1918 by the fusion of two earlier bodies, the Navvy Mission and the Christian Social Union, with the Revd P. T. R. Kirk as its first General Director. It was responsible for the convening of the *Malvern Conference in Jan. 1941, and for the meeting in the Albert Hall, London, on 26 Sept. 1942, when Abp. W. *Temple made a strong plea for the application of Christian principles to business and economics. The aims of the Fellowship have similarities with those of *Catholic Action in some RC countries.

[W.] G. Studdert-Kennedy, *Dog-Collar Democracy: The Industrial Christian Fellowship, 1919–1929* (1982).

Ineffabilis Deus. The constitution of *Pius IX, issued 8 Dec. 1854, defining the dogma of the *Immaculate Conception. It asserted that the BVM 'in the first instant of her conception was, by a singular privilege and grace granted by God, in view of the merits of Jesus Christ, the

Saviour of the human race, preserved exempt from all stain of original sin'. During the octave of the Feast (8–15 Dec.) it used to be read in the second *nocturn at *Mattins.

Text in *Acta et Decreta Sacrorum Conciliorum Recentiorum*. Collectio Lacensis. Auctoribus Presbyteris S. J. e Domo B. V. M. sine Labe Conceptae ad Lacum, 6 (Freiburg i.B., 1882), cols. 836–43. Extract in Denzinger and Hünermann (37th edn., 1991), pp. 774–6 (nos. 2800–4). See also bibl. to IMMACULATE CONCEPTION.

infallibility. Inability to err in teaching revealed truth. It is a negative condition, complementary to the positive quality of 'inspiration'. While many Christians maintain that the Church is infallible, upon the basis of such texts as Jn. 16: 13, Acts 15: 28, various beliefs have been held as to the seat where such infallibility resides. It has sometimes been sought in those doctrines and truths of revelation which have been accepted by all the historic branches of the Church; at other times in the definitions of such councils of the Church as have been generally accepted as *Oecumenical. At the First *Vatican Council (1870) the RC Church declared that the Pope was infallible when he defined that a doctrine concerning faith or morals was part of the deposit of divine revelation handed down from apostolic tradition and was therefore to be believed by the whole Church. In RC doctrine such a definition is infallible even antecedently to its acceptance by the Church. The RC Church also teaches that the same infallibility attaches to whatever is taught as part of the deposit of revelation by the entire body of RC bishops in union with the Pope, whether inside or outside an Oecumenical Council; this point, made in the First Vatican Council, was stressed at the Second Vatican Council.

Infancy Gospels. The apocryphal stories about the birth and childhood of Christ which were put into circulation in early Christian times. They are all of poor literary quality and devoid of historical value. The two most important are the 'Book of *James' (the '*Protevangelium') and the 'Infancy Gospel of *Thomas' (qq.v.).

Infant Baptism. Although from the first *Baptism was the universal means of entry into the Christian community, the NT contains no specific authority for its administration to infants. But by a tradition at least as old as the 3rd cent., and virtually universal until the *Reformation, children born to Christian parents have been baptized in infancy. In the 16th cent. this practice ('paedobaptism') was rejected by the *Anabaptists and since the early 17th cent. also by the *Baptists (and later by the *Disciples of Christ).

In the NT the children of Christian parents are themselves regarded as Christian (Col. 3: 20), while there is no suggestion that they will need to seek Baptism on reaching years of discretion. St *Paul speaks of Baptism as a spiritual counterpart to *circumcision, the rite whereby Jews were admitted as infants to the benefits of the Covenant and to membership of the religious community (cf. Col. 2: 11 f.). In households where Baptism is mentioned in Acts 16: 15 and 33 (cf. 18: 8) and 1 Cor. 1: 16, children may have been baptized along with adults. The absence of positive evidence has sometimes been explained by the fact that the NT documents are concerned mainly with the spread of Christianity in the non-Christian world and hardly at all with the recruitment of the Church from persons of Christian parentage and upbringing. On the other hand, it is claimed that the command to 'make disciples of (μαθητεύσατε) all nations, baptizing them . . .' (Mt. 28: 19) forbids Baptism without conscious discipleship. 1 Cor. 7: 14 has been used on both sides of the argument: the children of mixed marriages are said to be 'holy' and not 'unclean'; this description may perhaps suggest that they have been baptized, but explicitly the cleanness is ascribed to the faith of the believing partner.

In post-Apostolic times evidence for Infant Baptism has been seen in St *Justin Martyr's reference (*Apol.* 1. 15) to Christians then some 60 or 70 years old who had 'from childhood been made disciples' and in St *Polycarp's claim at the time of his martyrdom (prob. AD 155 or 156) to have been 'Christ's servant' for 86 years. St *Irenaeus (*Haer.* 2. 22) speaks of Christ as 'giving salvation to those of every age' who are 'regenerated' (*renascuntur*) through Him, and expressly includes 'infants and little children' among them. More explicitly, in its instructions for Baptism, the *Apostolic Tradition* (21) states that little children are to be baptized first, and that if they cannot answer for themselves, their parents or some other member of the family is to answer on their behalf. In the 3rd cent. *Origen (*Hom in Lev.* 8. 3, and *Comm. in Rom.* 5. 9) refers to the Baptism of infants as an established practice which the Church had received from the Apostles; he finds the practice justified by the need of infants, no less than of adults, for liberation from *original sin; *Cyprian (*Ep.* 64) takes a similar view. On the other hand, *Tertullian (*De Baptismo*, 18) opposed the practice (incidentally witnessing to its existence); he argued that the Baptism of children should be deferred until they can 'know Christ'. Even in the 4th cent. not all children of Christian parents were baptized in infancy: St *Basil and St *Gregory of Nazianzus, with both parents Christian, were baptized only in their twenties, and St *Augustine's deferment of Baptism is well known. But from about this time the Baptism of children became increasingly normal. Augustine's understanding of original sin entailed the corollary that children who died unbaptized were damned (cf. *Enchiridion* 23. 93); this teaching might have been expected to encourage the practice of baptizing infants at the earliest opportunity, but it was prob. not the principal factor at the time. Other changes fostered the custom of bringing infants to Baptism. With the toleration of Christianity under *Constantine, Baptism no longer entailed risks of persecution, and as the Church became identified with the State in the 5th cent., Baptism came to be regarded as a rite of passage associated with birth; Baptism of infants thus became the norm. In the Middle Ages the practice, by then virtually universal, was rejected only by a few small sects and movements which were heretical in other ways also.

In the E. Church, Infant Baptism is followed at once by the administration of *chrism and also of Holy Communion, while in the W., *Confirmation and Communion are deferred till the age of conscious participation, after instruction. Except in cases of emergency, sponsors (*godparents) are required for every baptized infant, whose duty it is to see that the child receives Christian instruction and is brought for Confirmation at the appropriate age. Acc. to Catholic doctrine (set forth, e.g., in the service of Infant Baptism in the BCP), the rite conveys the essential gift of regeneration, so that 'children which are baptized, dying before they commit sin, are undoubtedly saved'. The Baptists and other Protestants who reject Infant Baptism do so traditionally on the double ground that it is without warrant in the NT and that as a mere ceremony or ordinance (not a sacrament) it could convey no spiritual benefit to the unconscious recipient. Among those who retain it, e.g. *Lutheran, *Reformed (Presbyterian), *Methodist, and *Congregationalist bodies, many regard it as a dedication of the child and a declaration of the universal availability of the salvation wrought by Christ, which is prior to any individual response, holding that full Church membership is granted later in response to profession of faith.

In most Churches which practise Infant Baptism there has in modern times been much reconsideration of the traditional practice by individuals and unofficial groups, esp. in view of the fact that many who bring their children for Baptism are now only nominally Christian, and reasonable expectation of a Christian upbringing is lacking. In such cases the refusal of Baptism, or its deferment on condition of the parents' accepting instruction, has been advocated, and the 1969 RC Order for the Baptism of Infants envisages that in some circumstances Baptism should be delayed. On theological grounds this deferment had been defended by K. *Barth. Against this it is urged that such a rebuff to those who voluntarily, if ignorantly, seek Baptism for their children is inconsistent with the Church's duty to them and that a valuable pastoral opportunity is lost.

The classic Eng. defence of the practice is W. *Wall, *The History of Infant Baptism* (2 pts., London, 1705). D. *Stone, *Holy Baptism* (1899), pp. 96–109 and 254–8; N. P. *Williams, *The Ideas of the Fall and of Original Sin* (1927), esp. pp. 550–54; W. F. Flemington, *The New Testament Doctrine of Baptism* (1953), pp. 130–47; P. C. Marcel, *The Biblical Doctrine of Infant Baptism* (tr. from periodical arts. by P. E. Hughes), 1953). K. Barth, *Die kirchliche Lehre von der Taufe* (2nd edn., Theologische Studien, 14; Zurich, 1943; Eng. tr. 1948); id., *Kirchliche Dogmatik*, 4, Heft 4: *Die Taufe als Begründung des christlichen Lebens*, 1967; Eng. tr., 1969), both attacking the practice. A reply to the first by O. *Cullmann, *Die Tauflehre des Neuen Testaments* (Abhandlungen zur Theologie des Alten und Neuen Testaments, 12; Zurich, 1948; Eng. tr., Studies in Biblical Theology, 1; 1950); J. Jeremias, *Die Kindertaufe in den ersten vier Jahrhunderten* (1958; Eng. tr., 1960); K. Aland, *Die Säuglingstaufe im Neuen Testament und in der Alten Kirche: eine Antwort an Joachim Jeremias* (1961; Eng. tr., 1963); reply by J. Jeremias, *Nochmals: Die Anfänge der Kindertaufe* (Theologische Existenz heute, NF 101; 1962; Eng. tr., 1963); K. Aland, *Die Stellung der Kinder in den frühen christlichen Gemeinden—und ihre Taufe* (ibid. 138; 1967); id., *Taufe und Kindertaufe* [against Barth] (1971). A. S. Yates, *Why Baptize Infants? A Study of the Biblical, Traditional and Theological Evidence* (Norwich, 1993); C. Buchanan, *Infant Baptism and the Gospel: The Church of England's Dilemma* (1993). See also bibl. to BAPTISM.

infidel. A person who has a positive disbelief in every form of the Christian faith. In medieval times the word (Lat. *infidelis*) was employed esp. of the Muslims, and also, though less often, of Jews and pagans; but the distinction 'Jews, Turks, Infidels, and Hereticks' in the third *Good Friday *collect of the BCP points to its use in a narrower sense.

infirmarian. In a monastery or religious house, the person in charge of the sick-quarters.

Infralapsarianism. See SUBLAPSARIANISM.

infusion. See AFFUSION.

Inge, William Ralph (1860–1954), Dean of *St Paul's. He was born at Crayke, N. Yorks, educated at Eton and King's College, Cambridge, and successively Fellow of Hertford College, Oxford (1889–1905), Vicar of All Saints', Knightsbridge (1905–7), Lady Margaret Professor of Divinity at Cambridge (1907–11), and Dean of St Paul's (1911–34). His sympathies with *Platonic spirituality found their expression in a long series of theological and devotional writings, including *Christian Mysticism* (*Bampton Lectures, 1899) and *The Philosophy of Plotinus* (*Gifford Lectures, 2 vols., 1918). The latter was an attempt to assess the positive value of Plotinus' system for the modern world. There followed two widely read series of *Outspoken Essays* (1919; 1922); they included a notable 'Confessio Fidei', which upheld a philosophy of value in which God was the 'supreme value' and true faith 'belief in the reality of absolute value'. Inge's grasp of the tastes and prejudices of the English mind, his provocative and epigrammatic manner of writing and his pure English style made him one of the best-known Churchmen of his generation.

There is autobiographical material in Inge's *Vale* (1934) and *Diary of a Dean: St Paul's 1911–1934* [1950]. Life by A. Fox (London, 1960). R. M. Helm, *The Gloomy Dean: The Thought of William Ralph Inge* (Winston-Salem, 1962). W. R. Matthews in *DNB, 1951–1960*, pp. 529–32.

inhibition. An episcopal order suspending from the performance of his office an incumbent whose conduct makes such action advisable either for the avoidance of scandal or for some other reason in the interests of the parish. It is the duty of the inhibiting bishop to arrange and provide for the services during the suspension. Such orders are governed in the C of E by procedure under the *Ecclesiastical Jurisdiction Measure, 1963, and, except temporarily, can be made only after due judicial inquiry.

initiation. See BAPTISM.

Injunctions, Royal. A series of Tudor royal orders on ecclesiastical affairs, the most important of which are:

(1) By *Henry VIII, drawn up by T. *Cromwell, 1536. These required the clergy to observe the anti-papal laws and the abrogation of certain holy days and ceremonies, not to extol images, relics, or miracles, to discourage pilgrimages, and to teach their people the Pater Noster, the articles of the faith, and the Ten Commandments in English. The clergy were also ordered to teach and to administer the Sacraments more regularly and not to frequent taverns. Those with an income of £20 or more a year were to give a fortieth part of it to the poor; all incumbents were to devote a fifth part of their income to the repair of their own churches and parsonages.

(2) By Henry VIII, 1538, drawn up by Cromwell. This order, after confirming the previous injunctions, provided for the setting up of R. *Grafton's *Great Bible in all

churches, for the regular instruction of the people in the Scriptures, and for the checking of certain superstitions. Only duly licensed preachers were permitted to officiate. A register of all marriages, baptisms, and burials was to be kept and stored in the parish chest. The use of prayer addressed to the saints in processions was strongly discouraged.

(3) By *Edward VI, 1547. These Injunctions, issued from Grafton's press on 31 July, repeated most of the 1538 orders, but with important additions and modifications, e.g. all parishes were ordered to provide the *Paraphrases of Erasmus as well as a Bible, together with an alms-chest near the high altar and a pulpit; readings and responses in services were curtailed to make room for readings in English, processions were banned, and the Litany was to be said or sung in English kneeling. All *primers were banned apart from the last English and Latin versions provided by Henry VIII.

(4) By *Mary I, 1554. These Injunctions prohibited administration of the Oath of *Supremacy and required all canons not contrary to statute law to be enforced, married priests to be either removed or divorced, the neglect of Baptism and Confirmation to cease, heresy to be repressed, holy days and ceremonies to be restored as at the end of Henry VIII's reign, and clerics ordained 'after the new sort' to have 'that thing which wanted in them before' supplied.

(5) By *Elizabeth I, 1559. Thirty-two articles of this series are substantially re-enactments of various Edwardine orders, mostly from the Royal Injunctions of 1547, with their extreme anti-Romanism and hostility to images and pictures toned down, perhaps in the interests of comprehensiveness; 21 are new. Of these no. 29, without forbidding, sought to discourage the marriage of clergy, but from the first it proved a dead letter. No. 49 was designed to encourage music (apparently plainchant) in collegiate and parish churches, and permitted the use of hymns before or after service. No. 52 enjoined bowing at the Holy Name; no. 53 slow and distinct reading of the service. Others prescribed the proper habiting of the clergy (no. 30), the observance of holy days (46) and the saying of the litany and prayers on Wednesdays and Fridays (48).

Texts in Gee and Hardy: (1) pp. 269–74; (2) pp. 275–81; (4) pp. 380–3; and (5) pp. 417–42, with variants of (3) noted; full text of (3) in J. E. Cox (ed.), *Miscellaneous Writings and Letters of Thomas Cranmer* (*Parker Society, 1846), pp. 498–504.

Inner (or Inward) Light. The Divine light in every individual, which is held to guide, teach, and lead to salvation, and to bring those who accept it into unity with God and each other. This concept (deriving from Jn., esp. 1: 9) is characteristic of, but not exclusive to, the Society of *Friends.

Innere Mission. The term covers all voluntary religious, charitable, and social work organized within the Protestant Churches in Germany apart from the actual parish work. It was first employed by J. H. *Wichern (q.v.) in connection with his foundation at Hamburg, but he soon came to use it for all 'works of saving love'. The chief object of the Innere Mission is to reclaim those who have strayed, a task carried out by preaching, distributing of religious literature (Bible and Tract societies), and charitable works, such

as nursing the sick and assisting the poor. The years of its early enthusiasm (1848–c. 1860) produced a number of new associations and revived old ones for nursing, prison reform, care of the homeless and the mentally deficient, and the institution of deaconesses on the model of the early Church. From 1890 down to 1918 the social question played a paramount part and theoretical discussions on the attitude of the Protestant Churches to socialism, the emancipation of women, and other topical problems, were in the foreground. After 1918 the work was resumed with special stress on education and the winning back of the paganized youth of the cities to Christianity.

During the Second World War it made a notable and not completely unsuccessful stand against the Nazi policy of *euthanasia for the physically and mentally chronic sick. In 1957 it was united with the *Hilfswerk*, an organ of the *Evangelical Church in Germany established in 1945 to relieve distress and try to make contact with those alienated from the Church. It has spread to France, the Netherlands, Poland, and Scandinavia.

M. Gerhardt, *Ein Jahrhundert Innere Mission: Die Geschichte des Central-Ausschusses für die Innere Mission der Deutschen Evangelischen Kirche* (2 vols., 1948). J. M. Wischnath, *Kirche in Aktion: Das Evangelische Hilfswerk 1945–1957 und sein Verhältnis zu Kirche und Innerer Mission* (Arbeiten zur kirchlichen Zeitgeschichte, Reihe B, Band 14; 1986). J.-C. Kaiser, *Sozialer Protestantismus im 20. Jahrhundert: Beiträge zur Geschichte der Inneren Mission 1914–1945* (Munich, 1989). K. S. Latourette, *Christianity in a Revolutionary Age*, 2 (1960), esp. pp. 102–9; 4 (1962), pp. 251–3. W. Schütz in *RGG* (3rd edn.), 3 (1959), cols. 756–63; J. Albert in *TRE* 16 (1987), pp. 166–75, both s.v. with refs. See also bibl. to WICHERN, J. H.

Innocent I, St (d. 417), Pope from 402. A man of great ability, firm resolution, and high moral character, he made more substantial claims for the Papacy than any of his predecessors at *Rome. He insisted that major causes of dispute should be brought to the judgement of the Apostolic See. In the controversy with *Celestius, *Pelagius, and their supporters, Innocent took the side of St *Jerome against John, Bp. of Jerusalem, and endorsed the doctrines propounded by the African Councils. Through his Vicar, the Bp. of *Thessalonica, he exercised authority in a sphere which had recently come under the control of the E. Empire. He was, however, unable to save St John *Chrysostom from exile. His famous letter to Decentius, Bp. of Eugubium (19 Mar. 416), is important for the history of the *Canon of the Mass; it also speaks of *Confirmation as reserved for bishops and mentions the rites of *Unction and *Penance. Feast day, 28 July, dropped in 1969.

For his correspondence see J. P. Migne, *PL* 20. 457–636; also 'Collectio Avellana' (CSEL 35; 1895–8), pp. 92–8. Crit. edn. of his letter to Decentius, with Fr. tr. and comm., by R. Cabié (Bibliothèque de la *RHE*, 58; 1973); it is also conveniently pr. in G. A. Michell, *Landmarks in Liturgy* (1961), pp. 220–4. *LP* (Duchesne), 1, pp. 220–4. H. Gebhardt, *Die Bedeutung Innocenz I für die Entwickelung der päpstlichen Gewalt* (Diss., Leipzig, 1901). E. Demougeot, 'A propos des interventions du Pape Innocent Iᵉʳ dans la politique séculière', *RH* 212 (1954), pp. 23–38. B. *Capelle, OSB, 'Innocent Iᵉʳ et le Canon de la Messe', *RTAM* 19 (1952), pp. 5–16, repr. in his *Travaux liturgiques*, 2 (Louvain, 1962), pp. 236–47. E. Caspar, *Geschichte des Papsttums*, 1 (1930), pp. 296–343. C. Pietri, *Roma Christiana: Recherches sur l'Église de Rome . . . (311–440)* (Bibliothèque des Écoles françaises d'Athènes et de Rome, 224; 1976), esp. chs. 11–16 (see index). J. Barnaby in *DCB* 3 (1882), pp. 243–9, s.v.; É. Amann in *DTC* 7 (1922), cols. 1940–50, s.v.

Innocent III (1160/1–1216), Pope from 1198. Of a noble family, the Scotti, Lotario de' Conti di Segni was educated at *Paris, where he studied theology under Peter of Corbeil, and perhaps at *Bologna, where he may have learned canon law under Uguccio of Ferrara. Rising rapidly in the Papal service, he became cardinal in 1189 or 1190, and in 1198, when not yet in priest's orders, was elected Pope in succession to the aged *Celestine III (1191–8).

In method, Innocent was businesslike and legally minded. He was wholly sincere, diplomatic but opportunist, liable to fits of depression, and above all determined to enforce, extend, and define the 'plenitudo potestatis' of the Roman see. In making the right of the Papacy to interfere in secular affairs depend upon its duty to control the moral conduct of rulers and upon the theory of Papal feudal overlordship, Innocent was enabled by the circumstances of his age and his own will-power and personality to make theory and practice correspond to an extent without parallel, either before or afterwards.

With a view to establishing his authority in Rome and Italy, Innocent began by expelling the German mercenaries from Sicily and elsewhere. The Emp. Henry VI having died in 1197, Innocent used the opportunity for arbitrating between the rival claimants to the Imperial throne. In the bull 'Venerabilem' he laid down that, though the right of electing an emperor lay with the Imperial electors, the Pope must have 'the right and authority of examining the person elected' (*jus et auctoritas examinandi personam electam*), and that the appointment of an emperor came within the sphere of the Papal authority 'principaliter' and 'finaliter'—*principaliter* since the translation of the Empire from the Greeks to the Romans took place through the Pope, and *finaliter* because the blessing, coronation, and investiture of the Emperor lay with the Pope. He supported first Otto IV, then Philip of Swabia (Henry's brother), and then, after Philip's murder in 1208 (when Otto, who was left without a rival, became as anti-Papal as his predecessors), *Frederick II, the only son of Henry VI, who was elected on condition that he did homage to the Pope for Sicily.

Outside the Empire Innocent was equally successful in enforcing his authority. In France he compelled Philip Augustus to be reconciled to his wife, Ingeborg of Denmark; his consequent support of the French king issued in his victory over the discarded Emp. Otto at Bouvines in 1214. The quarrel over the appointment of Stephen *Langton to the see of *Canterbury led to the submission of King *John of England, who agreed to recognize Innocent as his feudal overlord. The Pope also made his authority felt in Scandinavia, the *Spanish peninsula, the Balkans, and even as far east as *Cyprus and *Armenia. His patronage of the new orders of Friars, the *Franciscans and *Dominicans, was further proof of his genius. Like most of the medieval Popes, he wished to preach a *crusade for the recovery of the Holy Land, but the Fourth Crusade, of 1204, was diverted from its true objective to operate against the Byzantine Empire; the

Greek patriarch of *Constantinople was then replaced by a Latin, Thomas Morosini, a Venetian.

The *Lateran Council of 1215 (q.v.) was the culminating event of his reign. Heresies, of which that of the *Albigensians, against whom Innocent had preached a crusade, was the most prominent, were condemned and doctrine clearly formulated. In addition reform decrees were passed, encouraging the foundation of schools and a higher standard of conduct for the clergy.

His pontificate may be considered as marking the climax of the medieval Papacy. He thought of his office in a semi-Divine light, 'set in the midst between God and man, below God but above man'. The vast extent of his ecclesiastical jurisdiction is seen in the number of cases which came up before him for decision from distant parts of the earth. He was the first regularly to employ the title 'Vicar of Christ'. 'No king can reign rightly unless he devoutly serve Christ's vicar.' 'Princes have power in earth, priests over the soul. As much as the soul is worthier than the body, so much worthier is the priesthood than the monarchy.' He was, so he affirmed, *Melchizedek, the priest-king, who would bring a centralized Christian society into being, and such was his genius that alone of all the Popes he was able to convert theory into short-lived but nevertheless active reality.

Innocent III was a considerable writer. Apart from his letters, sermons, and canonical rulings, his principal works were the *De Miseria Humanae Conditionis*, a widely read ascetical treatise written before he became Pope, and his *De Sacro Altaris Mysterio*, which is a valuable witness to the liturgy of his time.

Collected edn. of his *Opera* in J. P. Migne, *PL* 214–17; crit. eds. of his *Regestum super Negotio Romani Imperii* by W. Holtzmann (2 vols., Bonn, 1947–8) and F. Kempf, SJ (Miscellanea Historiae Pontificiae, 12; Rome, 1947) and of his annual Registers by O. Hageneder, A. Haidacher, and others (Publikationen des Österreichischen Kulturinstituts in Rom, II. Abteilung, Quellen. I. Reihe, 1964 ff.). C. R. Cheney and W. H. Semple (eds.), *Selected Letters of Pope Innocent III concerning England, 1198–1216* (Lat. text with Eng. tr., 1953). C. R. and M. G. Cheney (eds.), *The Letters of Pope Innocent III (1198–1216) concerning England and Wales: A Calendar with an Appendix of Texts* (Oxford, 1967). 'De Miseria Humanae Conditionis', ed. M. Maccarrone (Lugano, 1955); also ed., with Eng. tr., by R. E. Lewis (Athens, Ga., 1978; London, 1980). Studies by A. Luchaire (6 vols., Paris, 1904–6), H. Tillmann (Bonner historische Forschungen, 3; 1954; Eng. tr., 1980), and J. Sayers (Harlow, 1994). E. W. Meyer, *Staatstheorien Papst Innocenz' III.* (Jenaer historische Arbeiten, Heft 9; 1919); M. Maccarrone, *Chiesa e stato nella dottrina di Papa Innocenzo III* (Lateranum, NS 6, nos. 3–4; 1940); id., *Studi su Innocenzo III* (Italia Sacra, 17; 1972). F. Kempf, SJ, *Papsttum und Kaisertum bei Innocenz III.* (Miscellanea Historiae Pontificiae, 19; Rome, 1954). G. Barbéro, SSP, *La dottrina eucaristica negli scritti di Papa Innocenzo III* (1953). H. Roscher, *Papst Innocenz III. und die Kreuzzüge* (Forschungen zur Kirchen- und Dogmengeschichte, 21; 1969). C. R. Cheney, *Pope Innocent III and England* (Päpste und Papsttum, 9; Stuttgart, 1976); W. Imkamp, *Das Kirchenbild Innocenz' III.* (ibid. 22; 1983). M. Laufs, *Politik und Recht bei Innocenz III.: Kaiserprivilegien, Thronstreitregister und Egerer Goldbulle in der Reichs- und Rekuperationspolitik Papst Innozenz' III.* (Kölner historische Abhandlungen, 26; 1980). R. Foreville, *Le Pape Innocent III et la France* (Päpste und Papsttum, 26; 1992). J. Moore, 'Lotario dei Conti di Segni (Pope Innocent III) in the 1180s', *Archivum Historiae Pontificiae*, 29 (1991), pp. 255–8; C. Egger, 'Papst Innocenz III. als Theologe', ibid. 30 (1992), pp. 55–124. C. Morris, *The Papal Monarchy: The Western Church from*

1050 to 1250 (Oxford History of the Christian Church, 1989), esp. pp. 417–51, with bibl. pp. 636–9. R. W. and A. J. Carlyle, *A History of Mediæval Political Theory in the West*, 5 (1928), pp. 151–234. Mann, 11 and 12 (1915); Fliche and Martin, 10 (1950), pp. 11–213, with bibl. W. Ullmann in *NCE* 7 (1967), pp. 521–4, s.v.; G. Schwaiger in *TRE* 16 (1987), pp. 175–82, s.v. 'Innocenz III'.

Innocent IV (d. 1254), Pope from 1243. He was the most outstanding *canon lawyer ever to become Pope. Born as Sinibaldo Fieschi, a member of a Genoese noble family, he taught at *Bologna and was the author of a major commentary on the *Decretals, commonly known as the 'Apparatus'. He was elected Pope in the middle of a crisis in relations with the Emp. *Frederick II and after a vacancy of 18 months. An initially promising attempt at negotiation failed, and at the Council of *Lyons in 1245 he proclaimed the excommunication and deposition of Frederick, and waged war against him by all available means. After Frederick's death in 1250, he continued the struggle against his son Conrad IV. Although the propaganda that emerged from his curia made extreme claims for Papal authority (notably the letter 'Eger cui lenia', 1245), his own legal teachings were more measured. Under the pressure of the financial needs for the war with the Emperor, he hugely extended the system of *provisions, and many of his grants had to be revoked by his successor Alexander IV. He continued the activity of the *Inquisition against the threat of heresy, and in 'Ad extirpanda' in 1252 authorized the use of torture in the course of enquiries. For these reasons he has been harshly judged by historians, but he also co-ordinated the reaction of W. Europe to the threat of the Mongols, collecting information about them and sending friars as emissaries to the heart of Asia.

His *Apparatus* was pr. at Strasbourg in 1478 [not 1477]; there were various edns in the 16th cent., incl. that pub. at Venice, 1578. E. Berger (ed.), *Les Registres d'Innocent IV* (Bibliothèque des Écoles françaises d'Athènes et de Rome, 2nd ser.; 4 vols., 1884–1919; full text of docs. not given in all cases); F. Guerello, SJ, *Lettere di Innocenzo IV dai cartolari notarili genovesi* (Miscellanea Historiae Pontificiae, 23; Rome 1961); Acta concerning E. canon law ed. T. T. Haluščynskyj, OSBM, and M. M. Wojnar, OSBM (Pontificia Commissio ad Redigendum Codicem Iuris Canonici Orientalis, Fontes, 3rd ser., vol. 4, tom. 1; Rome, 1962); further important docs. are preserved by *Matthew Paris in his *Chronica Majora*. A. Potthast (ed.), *Regesta Pontificum Romanorum*, 2 (Berlin, 1875), pp. 943–1286. Contemporary Life by his chaplain, Nicolao de Carbio (or Calvi), ed., with introd. and other docs., by F. Pignotti in *Archivio della R. Società Romana di Storia Patria*, 21 (1898), pp. 7–120. E. Berger, *Saint Louis et Innocent IV* (1893). G. von Puttkamer, *Papst Innocenz IV: Versuch einer Gesamtcharakteristik aus seiner Wirkung* (1930). A. Melloni, *Innocenzo IV: La concezione e l'esperienza della cristianità come regimen unius personae* (Testi e ricerche di scienze religiose, NS 4; Genoa, 1990). L. Pisanu, OFM, *Innocenzo IV e i Francescani* (Studi e Testi Francescani, 41; 1968). M. Pacaut, 'L'Autorité pontificale selon Innocent IV', *Le Moyen Âge*, 66 (1960), pp. 85–119. J. A. Watt, *The Theory of Papal Monarchy in the Thirteenth Century: The Contribution of the Canonists* [1965], esp. pp. 58–73. J. M. Muldoon in *NCE* 7 (1967), pp. 524 f., s.v.; G. Schwaiger in *TRE* 16 (1987), pp. 182–6, s.v. 'Innocenz IV.', with bibl.

Innocent X (1574–1655), Pope from 1644. Giambattista Pamfili was a native of Rome. He became consistorial advocate in 1601, Auditor of the *Rota in 1604, *nuncio at Naples in 1621, and at Madrid in 1626. He was created

cardinal *in petto* in 1627, the appointment being published in 1629. On the death of *Urban VIII he was elected Pope despite the opposition of the French court, which resented his pro-Spanish views. He at once broke the power of the *Barberini, the hated relatives of his predecessor, who were supported by J. *Mazarin. In the bull 'Zelo domus Dei' (26 Nov. 1648) he confirmed the protest of the Papal legate, Fabio Chigi, against the Peace of *Westphalia (1648), on the ground that it violated the laws of the Church; but the protest was ignored. His most important doctrinal decision was the condemnation of the five propositions from the *Augustinus* of C. O. *Jansen by the bull '*Cum Occasione' (31 May 1653). A much-resented feature of his pontificate was the influence of Olimpia Maidalchini, the widow of his brother. He is the subject of the famous portrait by D. Velázquez in the Galleria Doria at Rome.

W. Friedensburg (ed.), 'Regesten zur deutschen Geschichte aus der Zeit des Pontifikats Innocenz' X', *Quellen und Forschungen aus italienischen Archiven und Bibliotheken* herausgegeben vom koenigl. preussischen historischen Institut in Rom, 5 (1903), pp. 60–124 and 207–22; 6 (1904), pp. 146–73; and 7 (1904), pp. 121–38. I. Ciampi, *Innocenzo X Pamfili e la sua corte: Storia di Roma dal 1644 al 1655, da nuovi documenti* (Imola, 1878). Pastor, 30 (1940). G. B. Picotti in *EC* 7 (1951), cols. 19–22, s.v. 'Innocenzo X'.

Innocent XI, Bl (1611–89), Pope from 1676. He became *cardinal in 1645, and Bp. of Novara in 1650, and in both offices was greatly loved for his piety and generosity. In 1669 his candidature for the Papacy was defeated through the influence of Louis XIV of France, but the latter's interference was unavailing in 1676. By careful economy he much improved the finances of the curia. He struggled continuously against the absolutism of Louis XIV in Church affairs, disapproving of Louis's revocation in 1685 of the Edict of *Nantes; and he also opposed *Gallicanism, which reached its climax in the *Gallican Articles of 1682. Similar motives led him to disapprove of the measures taken by *James II of England to restore RCism, and esp. of the *Declaration of Indulgence (1687). His piety and zeal inspired him to bring about several reforms within the Church, and he encouraged daily communion. In the bull 'Sanctissimus Dominus' (1679) he condemned 65 *Laxist propositions in moral theology; while in 1687 the bull 'Coelestis Pastor' condemned 68 *Quietist propositions. Innocent is thought, however, to have shown some favour to the *Jansenists, and for this reason his beatification, though begun in the next century, was long delayed. He was finally beatified in 1956. Feast day, 12 Aug.

I. I. Berthier, OP (ed.), *Innocentii P. P. XI Epistolae ad Principes* (2 vols., Rome, 1891–5); F. de Bojani (ed.), *Innocent XI: Sa correspondance avec ses nonces* (unfinished; up to 1684, 3 vols., 1910–12). G. B. P[ittoni], *Vita d'Innocenzo Undecimo* (Venice, 1691); F. Caccia, OFM, *Innocentia Apostolica* (1697). M. Immich, *Papst Innocenz XI, 1676–1689: Beiträge zur Geschichte seiner Politik und zur Charakteristik seiner Persönlichkeit* (1900). G. Papàsogli, *Innocenzo XI (1611–1689)* (1956); C. Miccinelli, *Il Beato Innocenzo XI* (1956). E. Michaud, *Louis XIV et Innocent XI* (4 vols., 1882–3). L. O'Brien, *Innocent XI and the Revocation of the Edict of Nantes* (thesis, Berkeley, Calif.; 1930); J. Orcibal, *Louis XIV contre Innocent XI: Les appels au futur concile de 1688 et l'opinion française* (Bibliothèque de la Société d'Histoire Ecclésiastique de la France; 1949). A. Latreille, 'Innocent XI, Pape "janséniste", Directeur de conscience de Louis XIV', *Cahiers d'Histoire publiés par les*

Universités de Clermont-Ferrand, Grenoble et Lyon, 1 (1956), pp. 9–39. Pastor, 32 (1940), pp. 1–524, with Appendix on the Biographies of Pope Innocent XI in vol. 30 (1940), pp. 449–51. S. Monti, *Bibliografia di Papa Innocenzo XI ... fino al 1927*, ed. M. Zecchinelli (Como, 1957). J. Paquier in *DTC* 7 (1922), cols. 2006–13, s.v., with bibl.; P. Gini in *Bibliotheca Sanctorum*, 7 (Rome, 1966), cols. 848–56, s.v. 'Innocenzo XI'.

Innocents, Holy. See HOLY INNOCENTS.

Inopportunists. Those at the *Vatican Council of 1869–70 who were opposed to defining Papal infallibility on the ground not that they positively disbelieved in it, but that they considered the moment for its promulgation 'not opportune'. This position was adopted by the great majority of the opponents of the dogma.

Inquisition, the. 'Inquisition' (Lat. *inquisitio*) means a legal inquiry, but in the later Middle Ages the term was used to describe a special ecclesiastical tribunal concerned with the detection and prosecution of heresy. In early times the usual punishment for heresy was *excommunication. The Fathers generally disapproved of physical penalties, though after Christianity had become the official religion of the Empire, secular rulers tended to regard heresy as a kind of *lèse-majesté* for which confiscation and even death could be inflicted, as in the case of *Donatism and *Priscillianism in the 4th and 5th cents. On the whole the Church kept to its original attitude as late as the 12th cent., when St *Bernard laid down the principle 'Fides suadenda, non imponenda'. This changed in 1184 when Pope Lucius III enacted in the bull 'Ad Abolendam' that bishops should make inquisition for heresy in their dioceses and hand over those who would not recant to the secular authorities for punishment. This episcopal inquisition proved ineffective, and in order to deal with the problem of *Catharism c.1233 Pope *Gregory IX appointed full-time Papal inquisitors drawn mainly from the *Dominican and *Franciscan Orders. They had jurisdiction over all Christians within a defined area, except for bishops and their officials, and were responsible to the Pope alone, but there was no central bureau to co-ordinate the work of inquisitors in different provinces. They had no coercive powers but relied on the co-operation of the secular authorities to enforce their decrees. Inquisitors were appointed only in areas where heresy was rife and where lay rulers were prepared to assist them; the Papal Inquisition was never established in the British Isles, Scandinavia, or the medieval kingdom of Castile. The inquisitors examined suspects *in camera* in the presence of sworn witnesses. The accused was not normally told the charges against him, or allowed to call witnesses in his defence, and lawyers were unwilling to defend such cases for fear of being accused of abetting heresy. In 1252 Pope *Innocent IV in the bull 'Ad Extirpanda' licensed the use of torture by the Inquisition against obdurate suspects, but there is no clear evidence that this power was widely used in the heresy trials of the 13th cent. The accused had the right to appeal to the Pope before sentence was pronounced. Inquisitors normally had no legal training and were advised by canon lawyers what sentences to impose; these were imposed at the *sermo generalis*. Heretics who recanted were given penances, most of which were of the same kind as those imposed in the

Sacrament of *Penance, such as fasting, pilgrimage, or the wearing of distinctive crosses on their clothes, but, unlike other penances, those imposed by the Inquisition were legally enforceable. Confinement in the Inquisition prisons was also technically a penance, and was reserved for serious offenders. Such sentences were terminable only by the Pope or at the discretion of the inquisitors. Unrepentant heretics were handed over to the secular authorities to be punished in accordance with the law of the state; this normally meant *burning at the stake. Yet such cases were exceptional; when the Inquisition was at the height of its powers in S. France in the mid-13th cent. only three people a year on average were burnt for heresy. Catharism disappeared throughout the W. by c.1325, although it is debatable whether the Inquisition did more than accelerate a decline produced by other factors, notably the pastoral work of the *Mendicant Orders and the intellectual challenge of 13th-cent. Catholicism. In the 14th cent. the Inquisition was used by Philip IV of France to initiate his prosecution of the *Templars in 1307 and by Pope *John XXII in his quarrel with the *Spiritual Franciscans.

After the medieval Inquisition had become moribund in the 15th cent., it was remodelled by *Paul III (see HOLY OFFICE). Despite the initial energy of G. P. Carafa (as cardinal and subsequently as Pope *Paul IV) in centralizing control of the Roman Inquisition, the effective power of the revived institution remained limited in the long term. The Roman Inquisition contributed to the eradication of incipient Protestantism in the Italian peninsula by the end of the 16th cent., but despite Papal efforts to assert its authority in the Netherlands, France, the Holy Roman Empire and the Austrian Habsburg lands, it was only in the Papal States that it exercised undisputed power, seen for example in the burning of G. *Bruno in 1600. Even in other Italian states the effective authority of inquisitors over accused persons and their property depended on the degree of co-operation of the secular authorities (esp. in *Venice).

In the Iberian peninsula the Inquisition took on a quite new form. In 1477 *Ferdinand V and *Isabella became concerned about the problem of only nominally Christianized Jews, and in 1478 they obtained permission from *Sixtus IV to set up a new Inquisition, backed by royal authority, in the territories subject to the Crown of Castile. Activated in 1480, the Spanish Inquisition soon became a highly centralized organization, especially after the appointment of Tomás de *Torquemada as Inquisitor General in 1483. In 1484, in spite of initial Papal opposition, its mandate was extended to the territory of the Crown of Aragon, and in due course it was established in all the lands subject to the Spanish monarchy, except Naples. Although the Inquisitor General was technically appointed by the Pope, the Spanish Inquisition operated largely as an instrument of Crown policy, in considerable independence of the Pope, though judgement was reserved to the Holy See in cases brought against senior ecclesiastics. In the 16th cent. the Inquisition turned its attention more particularly to the 'Moriscos' (nominally converted Muslims), the *Alumbrados and others suspected of purveying a false 'spiritual' version of Christianity, and Protestantism. To some extent different tribunals had different interests and responsibilities; for instance, sodomy was never subject to the Inquisition in Castile, but it was in

Aragon. *Witchcraft continued to concern the Inquisition in Navarre, although the Inquisition in general declined to believe that there was any such thing.

The methods of the Spanish Inquisition were essentially derived from those of its medieval precursor, including the anonymity of witnesses, which was considered controversial almost from the outset. Although the first decades of its operation were marked by considerable severity, the Spanish Inquisition seems to have been regarded by contemporaries as in some ways more benign than secular courts of the period. Its efficiency and thoroughness, however, induced widespread fear in certain quarters, and this fear was fostered by the staging of public *autos de fe. In some places in the early period 40 per cent. or more of those accused were handed over to the secular authorities and burnt, but from about the middle of the 16th cent. the percentage of cases resulting in capital punishment dropped to about 1 per cent. The tribunal was abolished by Joseph Bonaparte in 1808, restored by Ferdinand VII in 1814, abolished again under the liberal constitution of 1820–23, restored again in 1823, and finally suppressed in 1834.

In 1515 Manuel I of Portugal asked leave to establish an Inquisition in Portugal along the lines of the Spanish Inquisition, but Papal opposition thwarted his desire. Another attempt was made by John III in 1531 and eventually, in spite of continuing Papal resistance, the Portuguese Inquisition was set up in 1536. In 1561 it was extended to Goa. The Inquisitor General was appointed by the Pope, on the King's recommendation, and he in turn was to appoint other inquisitors. The Inquisition in Portugal was never as completely under royal control as it was in Spain, though it was closely identified with the traditional ruling class. After the restoration of the Portuguese monarchy in 1640 there was considerable tension between the Inquisition and the Crown. Under the Marquis of Pombal the Inquisition was brought almost entirely under secular control, and in 1821 it was abolished altogether.

The major concern of the Portuguese Inquisition throughout its history was the 'new Christians' (Christians of Jewish ancestry), of whom there were a great many, thanks to the forced conversions of 1496. It is unclear whether there was genuinely a serious problem of Judaizing or whether the Inquisition was more an expression of social tensions in the country, as has been suggested. The Inquisition also took complete control of the censorship of books.

H. C. Lea, *A History of the Inquisition of the Middle Ages* (3 vols., 1888; vol. 1, chs. 7–14, repr., with introd. by W. Ullmann, 1963). C. Douais, *L'Inquisition: Ses origines, sa procédure* (1906); J. [H.] Guiraud, *Histoire de l'Inquisition au moyen âge* (2 vols., 1935–8); H. Maisonneuve, *Études sur les origines de l'Inquisition* (1942; 2nd edn., 1960); Y. Dossat, *Les Crises de l'Inquisition toulousaine au XIIIᵉ siècle (1233–1273)* (Bordeaux, 1959). R. Kieckhefer, *Repression of Heresy in Medieval Germany* (Liverpool, 1979). B. [F.] Hamilton, *The Medieval Inquisition* (1981); L. Kolmer, *Ad Capiendas Vulpes: Die Ketzerbekämpfung in Südfrankreich in der ersten Hälfte des 13. Jahrhunderts und die Ausbildung des Inquisitionsverfahrens* (Pariser Historische Studien, 19; 1982); A. C. Shannon, *The Medieval Inquisition* (Washington, DC, 1983). R. Canosa, *Storia dell'Inquisizione in Italia dalla metà del Cinquecento alla fine del Settecento* (5 vols., 1986–1990). *L'Inquisizione Romana in Italia nell'Età Moderna: Archivi, Problemi di Metodo e Nuove*

Ricerche. Atti del seminario internazionale, Trieste, 18–20 maggio 1988 (Pubblicazioni degli Archivi di Stato, 19; 1991). E. van der Vekené, *Bibliotheca Bibliographica Historiae Sanctae Inquisitionis* (2 vols., Vaduz, Liechtenstein, 1982–3). E. Vacandard in *DTC* 7 (pt. 2; 1923), cols. 2016–68, s.v., with older bibl.; Y. Dossat in *NCE* 7 (1967), pp. 535–41, s.v., with further refs.

On the Spanish Inquisition, there is a useful collection of primary docs., ed. M. Jiménez Monteserín, *Introducción a la Inquisición Española* [1980]. H. C. Lea, *A History of the Inquisition in Spain* (4 vols., 1906–7). H. [A. F.] Kamen, *The Spanish Inquisition* (1965); id., *Inquisition and Society in Spain in the Sixteenth and Seventeenth Centuries* (1985). B. Bennassar and others, *L'Inquisition espagnole (xvᵉ-xixᵉ siècle)* [1979]. V. Pinto Crespo, *Inquisición y control ideolólogico en la España del siglo XVI* (La Otra Historia de España, 9 [1983]). J. Peréz Villanueva and B. Escandell Bonet (eds.), *Historia de la Inquisición en España y América* (Biblioteca de Autores Cristianos, 2nd edn., 1984 ff.). W. Monter, *Frontiers of Heresy: The Spanish Inquisition from the Basque Lands to Sicily* (Cambridge, 1990). L. Cardaillac (ed.), *Les Morisques et l'Inquisition* (1990). J. Lynch, *Spain under the Habsburgs* (2 vols., Oxford, 1964; 2nd edn., 1981); see index. Y. Dossat in *NCE*, loc. cit., pp. 540 f. See also bibl. to SPAIN.

On the Portuguese Inquisition, there are primary docs. in I. da Rosa Pereira (ed.), *Documentos para a História da Inquisição em Portugal* (Cartório Dominicano Português, Século XVI, fasc. 18; Oporto, 1984), and other vols. in this ser. A. J. Saraiva, *A Inquisição Portuguesa* (Lisbon, 1956); id., *Inquisição e Cristãos-Novos* (Oporto, 1969). L. M. E. Shaw, *Trade, Inquisition and the English Nation in Portugal, 1650–1690* (Manchester, 1989). F. Bethencourt, 'Les sources de l'Inquisition portugaise: évaluation critique et méthodes de recherche', in *L'Inquisizione Romana in Italia nell'Età Moderna*, op. cit., pp. 357–67.

INRI. The initial letters of the Latin words over the Cross of Christ, namely: 'Iesus Nazarenus Rex Iudaeorum' ('Jesus of Nazareth, the King of the Jews'). The superscription 'was written in Hebrew and in Latin and in Greek' (Jn. 19: 19 f.).

inscriptions, early Christian. Inscriptions on stone and other materials are a valuable supplement to other sources of Christian history. Though they abound at all periods, esp. in churches and cemeteries, Christian epigraphy is conventionally limited to texts of the first six cents. For practical purposes, inscriptions are 'Christian' if they bear evidence of Christianity, though others were doubtless set up by Christians.

Many Christian inscriptions are dated, by consular years, provincial eras, or indictions, but usually their date needs to be inferred from knowledge of either the site or building in which they are found or from the internal evidence of each inscription—its content, style of lettering, or accompanying symbols (e.g. the anchor is early and it is possible to date the forms of the Chi-Rho monogram (☧), which was used as a ligature in pre-Christian inscriptions and first appears in a Christian context, for the name of Christ, in the late-third cent.). If the well-known SATOR word-square is Christian, the examples of it found at Pompeii (destroyed in 79) must be the earliest extant Christian inscriptions. 3rd-cent. inscriptions are fairly common in the Roman catacombs; particularly interesting are those found under *St Peter's and under San Sebastiano by the Via Appia (see GRAFFITI). By the 4th cent. they are very common, esp. in *Rome, N. Africa, Syria, and Asia Minor. Some are heretical, *Montanist in Phrygia or *Donatist in Africa. Thousands of original inscriptions exist, mostly in Greek or Latin, and the text of others survives in copies.

In contrast to pagan custom, Christian inscriptions give little personal detail; epitaphs normally mention only the name, age, and date of death, occasionally adding the profession of the deceased. Prominent names occur, particularly in the memorials set up by Pope *Damasus in the catacombs, but the inscriptions are more valuable *en masse* as evidence of the texture of a community and the expansion of the Church; they bear witness to the beliefs of rank-and-file Christians of the period. Specially important are those which record the foundation of churches and witness to the cult of martyrs. Doctrine is illustrated vividly, but less fully and precisely than in the literary sources.

O. *Marucchi, *Epigrafia cristiana* (1910; Eng. tr., 1912); C. M. Kaufmann, *Handbuch der altchristlichen Epigraphik* (1917); P. Testini, *Archeologia Cristiana: Nozioni generali dalle origini alla fine del sec. VI* [1958], pp. 327–543 ('Epigrafia'). Selections in E. Diehl, *Lateinische altchristliche Inschriften* (2te Aufl., 1913, short); id., *Inscriptiones Latinae Christianae Veteres* (3 vols., 1925–31), with suppl. [vol. 4] by J. Moreau and H. I. Marrou (1967); corrections by A. Ferrua, SJ (Sussidi allo Studio delle Antichità Cristiane pubblicati a cura del Pontificio Istituto di Archeologia Cristiana, 7; 1981). General collections: *Corpus Inscriptionum Latinarum, passim; Corpus Inscriptionum Graecarum*, esp. vol. 4. There are many regional collections, notably G. B. *de Rossi, *Inscriptiones christianae urbis Romae*, 1861, cont. by I. Gatti, A. Silvagni, A. Ferrua, SJ, and D. Mazzoleni. J. Janssens, SJ, *Vita e morte del cristiano negli epitaffi di Roma anteriori al sec. VII* (Analecta Gregoriana, 223; 1981). H. *Leclercq, OSB, in *DACL* 7 (pt. 1; 1926), cols. 623–1089, s.v. 'Inscriptions'. This dictionary is rich throughout in discussion and illustration of inscriptions. The progress of Christian epigraphy may be followed in *L'Année épigraphique* (1888 ff.) and *Rivista di Archeologia cristiana* (1924 ff.). See also works cited under GRAFFITI.

installation. The formal induction by the Dean, Provost, or his representative of a canon or prebendary to a seat or stall in a cathedral or collegiate church, symbolizing his admission to the chapter and right to perform the duties and enjoy the privileges of his office. In the case of canons appointed by the Crown, it appears that installation is not strictly necessary. The term is also used of the ceremonies of admission in certain orders of chivalry, and incorrectly to include both the *enthronization of a bishop and *induction to a rectory or vicarage.

Instantius (late 4th cent.), a Spanish bishop of unknown see. He was one of the chief supporters of *Priscillian, whom he accompanied to Italy (381–2) in a fruitless endeavour to secure the favour of St *Ambrose and Pope *Damasus. In 384 he was deposed by the Council of Bordeaux. It has been suggested that he may be the author of one or more of the 11 treatises attributed by G. Schepss to Priscillian.

The 11 tractates discovered by G. Schepss were pub. by him under the name of Priscillian (CSEL 18; 1889). G. *Morin, OSB, 'Pro Instantio. Contre l'attribution à Priscillien des opuscules du manuscrit de Würzburg', *R. Bén.* 30 (1913), pp. 153–73. Critique of Morin by J. Martin, 'Priscillianus oder Instantius?', *Hist. J.* 47 (1927), pp. 237–51. H. Chadwick, *Priscillian of Avila: The Occult and the Charismatic in the Early Church* (Oxford, 1976), esp. pp. 31–40, 47–51, 62–9. B. Vollmann in *PW*, Suppl. 14 (1974), cols.

554–8, s.v. 'Priscillianus', with refs. to earlier discussions. See also bibl. to PRISCILLIANISM.

Institute of Charity. See ROSMINIANS.

Institute of Consecrated Life. See INSTITUTES OF CONSECRATED LIFE.

Institutes, The. The abbreviated English title of J. *Calvin's *Institutio Religionis Christianae*. The first edition was published in Latin at Basle in 1536. Deriving much of its form and substance from M. *Luther's *Kleiner Katechismus* (1529), in its six chapters it expounded the Decalogue, the Apostles' Creed, the Lord's Prayer, the sacraments, and Church government. Dedicated to Francis I, King of France, the work was intended as a defence of Reformation principles and a plea for religious toleration. During his exile in Strasbourg, Calvin revised and expanded the work to 17 chapters (1539), and issued a French translation (1541). The considerable interest in the work and the controversy which it generated heard Calvin to issue a much expanded edition of 80 chapters (Latin, 1559; French, 1560), possibly modelled on *Peter Lombard's *Sententiarum libri quattuor*. Its four sections set out Calvin's characteristic views on (1) God the creator, (2) God the redeemer, (3) the nature, means of appropriation, and effects of grace, and (4) the Church, ministry, and sacraments (see CALVINISM). Although the arrangement of topics was altered from the 1539 edition (largely in the interests of clarity of presentation), no significant doctrinal development is evident.

The highly systematic structure of the work, its clarity of presentation, its lucid prose and pithy style (esp. in the French editions), its constant appeal to Scripture, and its logical rigour led to its becoming the most important theological text of the Protestant Reformation. Lutheran theologians, who retained the clumsy *Loci communes* format developed by P. *Melanchthon, initially found themselves unable to meet the formidable challenge posed by Calvin's work. The 1559 edition was widely circulated in translation and abbreviated forms, rapidly achieving the status of a *Summa theologiae* of Protestantism.

Convenient variorum edition of the Latin text in Calvin's *Opera Selecta*, ed. P. Barth and W. Niesel, vols. 3–4 (Munich, 1928–31). Crit. edns. of the Fr. text of 1539 by J. Pannier (4 vols., Collection des Universités de France, 1936–9), and of that of 1560 by J.-D. Benoît (5 vols., Bibliothèque des Textes Philosophiques, 1957–63). The 1559 Lat. text was tr. into Eng. by T. Norton (London, 1561). Modern Eng. trs. of the 1556 text by F. L. Battles (Atlanta, Ga., 1975) and of the 1559 text by id., ed. J. T. McNeill (Library of Christian Classics, 20–1; 1961), with comprehensive list of edns., trs., and abridgements, pp. 1527–30. J. W. Marmelstein, *Étude comparative des textes latins et français de l'Institution de la religion chrestienne par Jean Calvin* (Paris thesis; Groningen, 1921). A. Autin, *L'Institution chrétienne de Calvin* (1929). A. Ganoczy, *Le Jeune Calvin* (Veroffentlichungen des Instituts für europäische Geschichte, Mainz, 40; Wiesbaden, 1966), pp. 136–269; Eng. tr. (Edinburgh, 1988), pp. 133–238. See also other works cited s.v. CALVIN, J.

Institutes of Consecrated Life. The technical term now used in official RC documents for ecclesiastical societies in which members make profession of the evangelical *counsels of perfection. They are established either by the *Holy See or a diocesan bishop. The main distinction, however, is between Religious Institutes (still popularly called 'religious orders') and Secular Institutes. The members of Religious Institutes take public *vows and live a common life. Religious Institutes are known as Orders (or regular Orders) if historically or by their nature some at least of their members take solemn vows. The rest, whose members take simple vows, are known as *Congregations. Members of Secular Institutes bind themselves to follow the evangelical counsels and dedicate themselves to the sanctification of the world while living in it. They live in ordinary conditions, either alone, in families, or in groups. The origins of Secular Institutes go back to the 16th cent., but they were only fully established legally by the Apostolic Constitution 'Provida Mater Ecclesia' of 2 Feb. 1947. The canon law governing Institutes of Consecrated Life is contained in *CIC* (1983), cans. 573–730.

J. Pathiyamoola, MCBS, *The Nature of the Religious State in the Latin and Oriental Codes* (Rome, 1992); V. Koluthara, CMI, *Rightful Autonomy of Religious Institutes in the Codes of Canons of the Oriental Churches (CCEO) and in the Code of Canon Law (CIC)* (ibid., 1994).

institution. The term used to denote the admission of a new *incumbent into the spiritual care of the parish. It is contrasted with the (subsequent) *induction, which admits him into the temporalities of the cure. The institution is performed by the bishop of the diocese and (unlike the induction) may take place anywhere.

Institution, the Words of. The words used by Christ in instituting the *Eucharist (cf. Mt. 26: 26–8, Mk. 14: 22–4, Lk. 22: 19–20, and 1 Cor. 11: 23–5). They appear in the central prayer of the Liturgy in all its forms, with one or two possible exceptions in very early times, and in the W. it has been commonly held that the words 'This is My Body' and 'This is My Blood' alone effect the consecration of the elements. This view clearly underlies the rubric in the BCP that if a second consecration of either *species is necessary during the communion of the people, only that section of the Prayer of Consecration which contains the relevant words for that species is to be repeated. See also EPICLESIS.

Jungmann (1958 edn.), 2, pp. 243–51; Eng. tr., 2, pp. 194–201. E. C. Ratcliff, 'The Institution Narrative of the Roman Canon Missae: its Beginnings and Early Background', in K. Aland and F. L. Cross (eds.), *Studia Patristica*, 2 (TU 64; 1957), pp. 64–82; repr. in Ratcliff's *Liturgical Studies*, ed. A. H. Couratin and D. H. Tripp (1976), pp. 49–65. R. F. Buxton, *Eucharist and Institution Narrative: A Study in the Roman and Anglican Traditions of the Consecration of the Eucharist from the Eighth to the Twentieth Centuries* (*Alcuin Club Collections, 58; 1976). E. J. Cutrone, 'The Liturgical Setting of the Institution Narrative in the Early Syrian Tradition', in J. N. Alexander (ed.), *Time and Community: In Honor of Thomas Julian Talley* (Washington, DC, 1990), pp. 105–14. See also works cited s.v. EUCHARIST.

Instituts Catholiques. The five 'free' Catholic institutions for higher studies at *Paris, Angers, Lille, Lyons, and Toulouse. These Institutes were founded on the basis of a French legal enactment of 1875 as Christian counterparts to the secularized state universities, though a later law of 1880 denied them the right of describing themselves as universities. In the concluding years of the 19th cent., the Institut Catholique at Paris was the chief centre of the

*Modernist Movement. Its professors have included M. *d'Hulst, L. *Duchesne, and A. F. *Loisy, and, more recently, L. Bouyer, Cong. Orat., J. *Daniélou, SJ, and P. Henry, SJ.

Instruments, Tradition of the (Lat. *Traditio* or *Porrectio Instrumentorum*). The solemn delivery to those being ordained of the instruments characteristic of their ministry. This ceremony, which now forms part of the Latin rites of Ordination, belonged originally to the *Minor Orders. At *Rome the ceremony was at first merely symbolical, as there was originally no formal ordination to these Orders, but in the *Gallican rites it was accompanied by a charge and formed part of a solemn Ordination. During the Middle Ages it was extended to the diaconate and priesthood. Deacons received the Gospel Book and priests the *paten with the bread and chalice, the delivery being accompanied in each case by an appropriate charge. In his 'Decretum de Unione Armeniorum' (1439) *Eugenius IV gave formal expression to the doctrine already asserted by St *Thomas Aquinas that this ceremony formed the essential 'matter' of the Sacrament, and this view was widely accepted by Latin theologians until the 17th cent., when J. *Morin, by his research into E. and early W. Ordination rites, showed it to be a comparatively late and entirely W. innovation and hence not an essential for Ordination. *Pius XII in his Apostolic Constitution 'Sacramentum Ordinis' of 30 Nov. 1947 laid down that the laying on of hands was the sole 'matter' of the Sacrament, and this view is now incorporated in the 1968 RC Ordination rite. In the first Anglican Ordinal (1550) the New Testament was delivered to deacons and the Bible and chalice with the bread to priests, each with a corresponding charge, but in the Ordinal attached to the Second BCP (1552) the chalice with the bread was omitted at the Ordination of priests, although the accompanying charge remained unchanged. In some modern rites the delivery of chalice and paten to priests has been restored (e.g. in the Book of Alternative Services of the Anglican Church in *Canada, 1985) or is allowed (e.g. by the Anglican Prayer Book of the Church of the Province of *Southern Africa, 1989).

St Thomas, *De Articulis Fidei et Ecclesiae Sacramentis*, 2 (in the Leonine edn. of his *Omnia Opera*, 42, 1979, p. 256, lines 348–52). Relevant section of Eugenius IV's decree is pr. in Denzinger and Hünermann (37th edn., 1991), p. 459 (no. 1326), with useful note, p. 453. 'Sacramentum Ordinis' is pr. in *AAS* 40 (1948), pp. 5–7. J. Morin, *Commentarius de Sacris Ecclesiae Ordinationibus* (Paris, 1655), esp. pt. 3, Exercitatio 7 (pp. 129–57, 'De Presbyteratus Materia et Forma'). F. Dalbus (pseud. of F. Portal), *Les Ordinations anglicanes* (Arras, 1894; orig. pr. in *La Science catholique* for 15 Dec. 1893, 15 Jan. 1894, and 15 April 1894) [by a *tour de force* argues that the suppression of the *porrectio instrumentorum* at the Reformation is the sole ground against the validity of Anglican Ordinations].

insufflation. The action of blowing or breathing upon a person or thing to symbolize the influence of the Holy Spirit. The *Vulgate uses the term of the Lord's breathing on the disciples (*haec cum dixisset insufflavit*, Jn. 20: 22). Its purpose is the expulsion of evil spirits. The RC Church still has a special rite of insufflation in connection with the consecration of chrism on *Maundy Thursday, and until recently also for that of the baptismal water. In the

*Orthodox rite and some other E. rites (e.g. the *Maronite) an insufflation is still found in all Baptisms, infant and adult.

intention. The word is used in religious contexts in several senses.

(1) In moral theology, for an act of free will directed to the attainment of an end. Such intention may be 'actual', if one wills with conscious attention; 'virtual', if one continues to will in virtue of an antecedent decision, though at the moment not consciously aware of it; 'habitual', if all voluntary action has ceased but without the original decision being revoked; and 'interpretative', if a certain intention is ascribed to a person who has no opportunity to confirm or deny the imputation. The intention influences the morality of an action. A good intention makes a morally indifferent action good and increases the worth of an action good in itself, but does not make a bad action good. A bad intention, on the other hand, whilst making an indifferent action bad and worsening an action bad in itself, ruins even a good action.

(2) In the administration of the Sacraments, the purpose of doing what the Church does (*quod facit ecclesia*). If the right *form and the right *matter were alone needed, apart from any intention, Sacraments might occasionally be conferred by accident, e.g. in religious drama or in demonstrations or rehearsals. The requirement of such intention was laid down by the Council of *Trent (Sess. 7, can. 11). In the 16th and 17th cents. it was held by some RC theologians, e.g. by A. *Catharinus in his *De Intentione Ministri* (Rome, 1552), that the required intention existed if the minister intended to perform the customary rites, though not to confer the Sacraments of the Church, i.e. if he possessed the so-called 'exterior intention'. This opinion has also been defended by some Anglican scholars. Most modern theologians, however, agree in requiring the 'interior intention' of the minister for the *validity of the Sacrament. It was esp. on the grounds of defect of intention that *Leo XIII condemned *Anglican Ordinations (q.v.) by the bull '*Apostolicae Curae' (1896). The nature of the intention required from the recipient (as opposed to the minister) varies with the particular Sacrament. In the case of children under the age of reason and mentally deficient persons, clearly no intention can be necessary for the validity of such Sacraments as they are capable of receiving. The sacramental theology of the E. Church on the whole avoids all use of the concept of intention.

(3) The special object, spiritual or material, for which a prayer of intercession is made. Thus a 'Mass intention' is the particular end to which the celebrant prays that the fruits of the sacrifice may be applied, e.g. the repose of the soul of one who has died.

(4) In the Scholastic theories of knowledge, the term was sometimes used of the objects of knowledge in so far as they are present to the knowing consciousness. Thus, as contrasted with the real tree, which is the object of external perception, there was held to be an 'intentional tree' in the mind of the knower, and the conceptual tree was thus said to have an 'intentional existence' (*ens* or *esse intentionale*). This doctrine, taken up in the 19th cent. by F. *Brentano, was developed by E. Husserl, who maintained that every mental act was directed towards some entity, and that thus intentionality was the characteristic mark of consciousness.

A. Thouvenin in *DTC* 7 (pt. 2; 1923), cols. 2267–80. S. da Romallo and G. Rambaldi in *EC* 7 (1951), cols. 66–73, s.v. 'Intenzione'. H. J. Fischer in *Dict. Sp.* 7 (pt. 2; 1971), cols. 1838–58, s.v., with bibl.

intercession. Petitionary prayer on behalf of others. Such prayer, implicit or explicit, forms part of almost all Christian worship, and in particular of all the traditional forms of the Liturgy of the *Eucharist. In an extended sense, acc. to Catholic theology, intercession can also be made by offering on behalf of others *meritorious deeds performed or *indulgences obtained for the sake of some specified intention.

Intercontinental Church Society or '**Intercon**'. See CCCS.

interdict. An ecclesiastical penalty in the RC Church, excluding the faithful from participation in spiritual things, but without loss of the Communion of the Church. In the past interdicts have been of various kinds: the 'personal' interdict was attached only to particular persons; the 'local' forbade sacred actions in particular places; the 'general' referred to a whole district and its population; and the 'partial' visualized only certain parts or inhabitants of a district. The chief effects of the 'general' and 'local' interdicts were the cessation of the administration of the Sacraments and all solemn services within the area concerned. Exceptions were, however, made for the Last Sacraments; for clerics not personally responsible for the interdict, who were allowed to perform all religious rites privately with doors locked and in a low voice; for one Mass in the cathedral or parish church; and for certain high feasts. In the 1983 *Codex Iuris Canonici* there is no mention of interdicts attached to places. An interdict now resembles *excommunication, but is less severe in its consequences; it forbids liturgical activities but does not affect governmental functions or personal income. A person placed under an interdict may not celebrate or receive the Sacraments or take any ministerial part in ceremonies of public worship (can. 1332).

Cases of interdicts are attested from the 6th cent. At first they were imposed only on the churches of a single city, but from the 9th cent. they were extended to dioceses, and from the 12th to whole countries. *Alexander III placed Scotland under an interdict for the expulsion of the Bp of St Andrews, and *Innocent III used this weapon in his struggles with Philip Augustus of France (1200) and *John of England (1208). With the decline of Papal influence in the later Middle Ages the interdict lost most of its force, and in modern times it is used very rarely. Modern examples are those imposed on the Convent of Marienthal near Strasbourg in 1921 and on the parish church of Barbentane in Provence in 1929.

A. Haas, *Das Interdikt nach geltendem Recht mit einem geschichtlichen Ueberblick* (1923). E. J. Coran, *The Interdict* (Washington, 1930). W. Richter, SJ, *De Origine et Evolutione Interdicti usque ad aetatem Ivonis Carnotensis et Paschalis II* (Textus et Documenta in usum Exercitationum et Praelectionum Academicarum, Series Theologica 12 and 13; Pontificia Universitas *Gregoriana, 1934). A. Auer, OSB, 'Eine verschollene Denkschrift über das grosse

Interdikt des 14. Jahrhunderts', *Hist. J.* 46 (1926), pp. 532–49; H. Maisonneuve, 'L'Interdit dans le droit classique de l'Eglise', *Mélanges d'histoire du moyen âge dédiés à la mémoire de Louis Halphen* (1951), pp. 465–81. A. Boudinhon in *CE* 8 (1910), pp. 73–5, s.v.; E. Jombart in *DDC* 5 (1953), cols. 1464–75, s.v. See also the works of C. R. Cheney and W. Imkamp cited s.v. INNOCENT III and arts. of C. R. Cheney listed under JOHN, KING OF ENGLAND.

Inter-Faith dialogue. See THEOLOGY OF RELIGIONS.

Interim of Augsburg. See AUGSBURG, INTERIM OF.

Interim rite. The Order of Holy Communion in the C of E proposed in 1931 by A. Chandler, formerly Bp. of Bloemfontein, after the rejection of the proposed BCP of 1927–8. Its distinctive feature was the placing of the Prayer of Oblation immediately after the Consecration, followed by the *Lord's Prayer, i.e. the use of the prayers of the 1662 BCP in the sequence of the 1549 Book. This order had been used by Bp. J. *Overall in the 17th cent. and recently urged by W. H. *Frere. In the post-1928 period it was thought in some circles to represent the probable direction of any future Prayer Book revision, and it was hoped that if a sufficient number of priests undertook to use it until a formal revision was authorized, it might receive episcopal approval; hence, it became known as the 'Interim' rite. In spite of the criticism of G. *Dix, it passed into frequent and widespread use. The *Alternative Services, Holy Communion Rite (Series 1), authorized a use closely akin to the Interim rite, and the ASB allows most of its elements.

J. M. M. Dalby, 'Alternative Services: The Canon of Series 1', *CQR* 168 (1967), pp. 442–51, with refs.

International Bible Students' Association. A corporation established by C. T. *Russell to deal with the affairs of his followers, called Bible Students, outside the USA. It is registered in London and shares responsibility for the affairs of British *Jehovah's Witnesses (q.v.) with the Watch Tower Bible and Tract Societies of New York and Pennsylvania.

interstices. The spaces of time which, by canon law, must elapse between the conferment of different *Orders in the Christian ministry upon the same person. In the RC Church there has to be an interval of at least six months between the time when a man is made *deacon and when he is made *priest. No one is to be made deacon until he has received and exercised 'for a suitable period of time' the ministries of *acolyte and *lector; at least six months is to elapse between the time when he became an acolyte (*CIC* (1983), cans. 1031 §1 and 1035). In the C of E the 1969 Canons reaffirm the prohibition against conferring the diaconate and priesthood upon the same man on the same day, 'unless they have a faculty from the Archbishop of Canterbury' (Can. C 3. 7) and add that a 'deacon shall not be ordained to the priesthood for at least one year, unless the bishop shall find good cause to the contrary' (Can. C 3. 8).

J. M. Gannon, *The Interstices Required for the Promotion to Orders* (Catholic University of America, Canon Law Studies, 196; 1944).

inthronization. See ENTHRONIZATION.

intinction. In liturgical usage, the practice of absorbing some consecrated or unconsecrated wine into the Eucharistic bread before Communion. There seem to be three distinct forms. (1) In Communion of the sick consecrated bread was moistened with unconsecrated wine to make consumption easier (cf. *Dionysius of Alexandria in *Eusebius, *HE* 6. 44); this may be called 'unsacramental intinction', as Communion is given in one kind. (2) It has been believed that the consecrated Host exercises a consecratory effect on the unconsecrated wine: a procedure based on this belief, is described in the *Ordines Romani*. (3) To avoid possible irreverence in the administration of the chalice to the laity, the Host may be immersed in the chalice and administered with a communion spoon (λαβίς), as is still the practice in the E. Church, or the Host may be marked with consecrated wine (by means of a Host dipped in the chalice, or with the *fistula, or with the λαβίς); this process can also be used in *reservation (q.v.). This third form of intinction was forbidden by the Council of *Braga in 675, but this decision may have been effective only locally and there is later attestation for this form, e.g. at *Cluny in the 10th cent. All forms of intinction had virtually disappeared in the W. by *c.*1200. The third form (dipping the Host into the consecrated wine) has been sporadically revived in modern times in the Anglican Communion as a method both of reservation and of giving Communion to the sick. In the 1980s, in response to fears about the spread of the virus that causes AIDS, Communion by intinction was made available in some Anglican churches and the practice was recognised in a statement on 'Hygiene and the Chalice' issued by the Abps. of *Canterbury and *York in June 1989. In the RC Church intinction was authorized in 1965 as one of the three ways of receiving Communion in both kinds; its use in some areas has increased in recent years.

W. H. Freestone, *The Sacrament Reserved* (Alcuin Club Collections, 21; 1917), pp. 144–75. M. Andrieu, 'Immixtio et Consecratio', *Rev.S.R.* 2 (1922), pp. 428–46; 3 (1923), pp. 24–61, 149–82, 281–304, 433–71; 4 (1924), pp. 65–96, 265–95, 454–84. J. M. Hanssens, SJ, 'Le Cérémonial de la communion eucharistique dans les rites orientaux', *Gregorianum*, 41 (1960), pp. 30–62.

Introit. In the W. Church, the opening act of worship in the Mass. Originally it consisted of a whole Psalm, sung with *antiphon and *Gloria Patri. It was sung as the celebrant entered the church. In the *Ordo Romanus Primus (early 8th cent.) it is prescribed that the celebrant should stop the singing when he reached the altar; by the time of (*Mabillon's) tenth *Ordo* (13th cent.) the practice of singing a single verse of the Psalm was established. Acc. to the present (1970) RC rite the Introit may be sung or said as the celebrant approaches the sanctuary; if it is said only the antiphon need be recited, but if sung the Psalm, or at least part of it, is required, unless some other chant is substituted. The 1549 BCP provided for an entire Psalm, with *Gloria Patri*, but without antiphon, to be sung as an Introit. In subsequent revisions of the English Prayer Book the Introits have been omitted, though their use has been widely revived unofficially in the C of E since the middle of the 19th cent. and the ASB specifically states that at the entry of the ministers a 'Sentence may be used; and a Hymn, a Canticle, or a Psalm may be sung'.

The Introit is thought to be of later origin than the *Gradual, from which it differs in not being an integral part of the service; it was introduced to accompany the entrance procession. In *Gallican rites the Introit was called 'Antiphona ad praelegendum'; in the *Ambrosian, 'Ingressa'; in the *Mozarabic and others, 'Officium'. The title 'antiphona ad introitum' was restored in the RC Holy Week liturgy of 1955 and remains in the 1970 Missal.

Eng. tr. of *Sarum Introits in *EH*, nos. 657–733. H. *Leclercq, OSB, in *DACL* 7 (pt. 1; 1926), cols. 1212–20. Jungmann (1958 edn.), 1, pp. 414–29; Eng. tr., 1, pp. 320–33.

Invention of the Cross. Acc. to legend the three crosses on *Cavalry (of Christ and the two robbers) were found (Lat. *inventae*) by St *Helena, the mother of *Constantine, that of Christ being identified by a miracle. St *Ambrose, whose 'Oratio de Obitu Theodosii' (395) is the first work to connect the event with St Helena, is followed by many other Fathers such as St John *Chrysostom and *Paulinus of Nola. St *Jerome, however, who lived quite near the place, is silent on the matter. St *Cyril of Jerusalem, without mentioning St Helena, states that the Cross was found at Jerusalem in the time of Constantine (d. 337), and it has been suggested that this occurred during the excavations for the Emperor's basilica of the *Holy Sepulchre. The relic was preserved in that church in a silver receptacle, after a large part of the wood had been distributed among the churches throughout the world. The veneration of the Cross at Jerusalem is first described in the Pilgrimage of *Egeria. The 'Doctrine of *Addai' attributes a similar miraculous finding of the Cross to Protonice, described as the wife of the future Emp. Claudius (d. AD 54), but this legend is clearly based on the story of St Helena. In the Greek Church the Feast of the Finding of the Cross was originally kept on 14 Sept., now the Feast of the *Exaltation of the Cross (q.v.), together with the consecration of Constantine's two Jerusalem basilicas. The commemoration on 3 May, which seems to go back to the apocryphal treatise 'De Inventione Crucis Dominicae', is not found in the *Gregorian Sacramentary. It was probably first observed on this day in Gaul in the 7th cent. and thence came to Rome c.800. It was suppressed in 1961.

J. Straubinger, *Die Kreuzauffindungslegende: Untersuchungen über ihre altchristlichen Fassungen mit besonderer Berücksichtigung der syrischen Texte* (Forschungen zur christlichen Literatur- und Dogmengeschichte, 11, Heft 3; 1912). A. Frolow, *La Relique de la Vraie Croix: Recherches sur le développement d'un culte* (Archives de l'Orient, 7; 1961); id., *Les Reliquaires de la Vraie Croix* (ibid. 8; 1965). S. Borgehammar, *How the Holy Cross was Found: From Event to Medieval Legend* (Stockholm, 1991). J. W. Drijvers, *Helena Augusta: The Mother of Constantine the Great and the Legend of her Finding of the True Cross* (Brill's Studies in Intellectual History, 27; Leiden, 1991), pp. 79–188. H. *Leclercq, OSB, in *DACL* 3 (pt. 2; 1914), cols. 3131–9, s.v. 'Croix (Invention et exaltation de la vraie)'. On the Feast, cf. A. Bugnini in *EC* 4 (1950), cols. 960–3, s.v. 'Croce, VII'. See also bibl. to EXALTATION OF THE CROSS and other works cited under HELENA, ST.

Investiture Controversy. A term which is often applied to the long series of disputes between popes and emperors from the time of the future Emp. *Henry IV's withdrawal of obedience from *Gregory VII at Worms in 1076 to the

Concordat of *Worms in 1122; it is also used of contemporary Papal disputes with the Anglo-Norman and French kings. The issue of investiture in the strict sense concerned the kings' right to confer upon bishops and abbots the *ring and *crosier that were their symbols of office. In the Empire the Investiture Controversy had three stages: the conflicts between Gregory and Henry between 1076 and Henry's establishing the antipope Clement III (Wibert of Ravenna) at Rome in 1084; the resulting Wibertine schism of 1084–1100; and the conflicts and disputes thereafter up to the Concordat of 1122. It is not clear when lay investiture was formally condemned by the Papacy. There is evidence that it was prohibited by Gregory VII in 1075, but the first clear prohibition which survives dates from 1078. In any event, it became the central issue only in the third stage of the controversy. *Urban II intensified the prohibition, and the effective ending of the schism in 1100 brought it decisively to the fore.

In England the matter became acute under St *Anselm, who tried to enforce Urban's decrees at the Council of Rome (1099) excommunicating all who gave or received lay investiture. He himself refused to do homage to Henry I (1100) or to consecrate bishops who had received lay investiture. In 1105 a compromise was reached at Bec and ratified in a Council at Westminster in 1107, acc. to which Henry was allowed to receive homage for temporalities before consecration in return for a complete renunciation of lay investiture.

In France a tacit understanding was apparently reached between Philip I and the Pope in the same year (1107). A formal settlement was at last reached in the Empire by the Concordat of Worms (1122; q.v.), the provisions of which were reasserted by the First *Lateran Council (1123; cans. 8 and 9), the Emperor relinquishing the right to invest with ring and staff but continuing to bestow the temporalities, and in Germany receiving homage before consecration and in other parts of the Empire after six months' delay. In Germany he was also allowed some influence in elections.

Although the Papacy won a complete victory over the issue of lay investiture itself, lay rulers retained a varying degree of control over elections.

For text of the official docs., see bibls. to Popes (Gregory VII, Urban II, *Paschal II, and *Callistus II), Emperor (Henry IV), and contemporary monarchs concerned. Contemporary information is pr. in *MGH*, Libelli de Lite Imperatorum et Pontificum Saeculis XI et XII (3 vols., 1891–7). Eng. tr. of a selection of the relevant docs. in B. Tierney, *The Crisis of Church and State 1050–1300* (Englewood Cliffs, NJ, 1964), pp. 33–95. E. Bernheim, *Quellen zur Geschichte des Investiturstreits* (Quellensammlung zur deutschen Geschichte; 2 Hefte, 1907); F.-J. Schmale (ed.), *Quellen zum Investiturstreit* (Ausgewählte Quellen zur deutschen Geschichte des Mittelalters, 12A–12B; 1978–84). A. Scharnagl, *Der Begriff der Investitur in den Quellen und der Literatur des Investiturstreits* (Kirchenrechtliche Abhandlungen, 56; 1908). P. Schmid, *Der Begriff der kanonischen Wahl in den Anfängen des Investiturstreits* (1926). G. Tellenbach, *Libertas, Kirche und Weltordnung im Zeitalter des Investiturstreites* (Forschungen zur Kirchen- und Geistesgeschichte, 7; 1936; Eng. tr., Oxford, 1940). R. Schieffer, *Die Entstehung des päpstlichen Investiturverbots für den deutschen König* (Schriften der MGH, 28; 1981). U.-R. Blumenthal, *Der Investiturstreit* (1982; Eng. tr., Philadelphia [1988]). I. S. Robinson, *The Papacy 1073–1198: Continuity and Innovation* (Cambridge, 1990). D. Whitelock, M. Brett, and C. N. L. Brooke (eds.), *Councils & Synods with other Documents relating to the*

English Church, 1: A.D. 871–1204, pt. 2: *1066–1204* (Oxford, 1981), pp. 634–94. F. Barlow, *The English Church 1066–1154* (1979), pp. 268–302. Z. N. Brooke, 'Lay Investiture and its Relation to the Conflict of Empire and Papacy', *Proceedings of the British Academy*, 25 (1939), pp. 217–47. A. Fliche in Fliche and Martin, 8 (1946), pp. 76–390 *passim*. C. Morris, *The Papal Monarchy: The Western Church from 1050 to 1250* (Oxford History of the Christian Church, 1989), pp. 109–33 and 154–81, with bibl. pp. 596–601. See also bibl. s.v. WORMS, CONCORDAT OF.

invincible ignorance. A term in *moral theology denoting ignorance of a kind that cannot be removed by serious moral effort. It totally excuses from sin because, being involuntary, it can involve no intention of breaking the law of God. It is to be distinguished from 'vincible ignorance', which, though partly excusing from sin, is culpable in itself, apart from the action to which it leads, as it involves neglect to acquire information necessary to avoid the transgression. The term 'invincible ignorance' is frequently used, esp. by RC theologians, with reference to those who, because of their upbringing and environment, are unable to accept the teachings of the Church.

K. E. *Kirk, *Ignorance, Faith and Conformity* (1925). E. Mangenot in *DTC* 7 (pt. 1; 1922), cols. 731–40, s.v. 'Ignorance'; L. Simeone in *EC* 6 (1951), cols. 1606–12, s.v. 'Ignoranza', both with bibl.

Invitatory. In liturgical usage, an invitation to pray. One of the most notable examples is that which precedes the *Lord's Prayer immediately after the *Eucharistic Prayer in the Roman Mass ('Praeceptis salutaribus moniti'), represented in many modern Anglican liturgies by such a phrase as 'As our Saviour taught us, let us pray' (ASB). The *Bidding Prayers (q.v.) are a form of Invitatory. The term is, however, used particularly of the *Venite* (AV Ps. 95; Vulg. Ps. 94), with its corresponding *antiphon, which in the *breviary stand at the beginning of the first *Office of the day. Before 1971 it invariably came at the beginning of *Mattins, but the breviary of that year orders that the Invitatory be said before *Lauds or before the *Office of Readings if either be the first Office of the day, and it provides Pss. 23, 66, or 99 (Vulg.) as alternatives. The antiphon (itself also sometimes termed the Invitatory) varies acc. to the season and is repeated several times in the course of the Psalm. The BCP retained the *Venite* at Morning Prayer, with the antiphon discarded ('without any Invitatory', 1549). See also VENITE.

J. Pascher, 'Das Invitatorium', *Liturgisches Jahrbuch*, 10 (1960), pp. 149–58. H. *Leclercq, OSB, in *CE* 8 (1910), pp. 89 f.; F. *Cabrol, OSB, in *DACL* 7 (pt. 1; 1926), cols. 1419–22, with bibl.

invocation of the saints. See SAINTS, DEVOTION TO THE.

IODG. See UIODG.

Iona. A small island of the Inner Hebrides, called in Gaelic *Í Chaluim Cille*, 'Í of St *Columba', variously spelt Hi, Hy or I; the modern form of the name derives from an error in copying *Adomnán's adjectival form 'Ioua Insula' in his Life of St Columba. The island was given to Columba by the local king soon after he came to Scotland in 563 and on it he founded a *Celtic monastery, which rapidly grew in importance. From here missionaries were sent to Scotland and N. England, and numerous dependent monasteries were founded in these lands and in Ireland. The monastery of Iona became famous for its learning and artistic achievement and was a popular centre for pilgrimage. From the 790s Iona was a frequent target of Viking attacks and in the mid-9th cent. Columba's relics were moved, partly to Kells in Ireland and partly to Dunkeld in central Scotland. Iona, however, was not abandoned, and there was still a flourishing Celtic religious community there in the 12th cent. In 1203 the monastery was reorganized under the *Benedictine rule, and at the same time an *Augustinian nunnery was founded. In 1499 the abbey was acquired by the Scottish Bishops of the Isles *in *commendam* and the church was used by them and their Protestant successors as *de facto* cathedral of the diocese until it fell into ruins in the 17th cent.

Excavations have revealed the probable site of St Columba's church and monastery in the vicinity of the present church, and also the monastic *vallum* and other earth and timber structures. The graveyard, known as Reilig Odhráin, was the burying place of the kings of Scotland from the 9th to the 11th cent. St Oran's chapel appears to be mostly 12th cent., but parts may be earlier. St Martin's cross exhibits 8th- or 9th-cent. carving, and there are fragments of other earlier crosses, of which one (St John's) has been reconstructed. Of the 13th-cent. abbey church (later used as the cathedral) only the N. transept and N. side of the choir remain; the greater part of the old building dates from the 15th-cent. rebuilding of the abbey. The ruined abbey church was restored and rerooved between 1902 and 1910. Rebuilding of the conventual buildings was carried out by the Iona Community between 1938 and 1966. The ruins of the nunnery are also preserved.

The Iona Community was founded in 1938 by G. F. *MacLeod for the general purpose of expressing in social terms the theology of the *Incarnation and using the co-operative rebuilding of the Benedictine abbey as the symbol of its purpose. It was officially recognized by the General Assembly of the Church of Scotland in 1951. Its members, laymen and ministers, were originally drawn mainly from the Church of Scotland; they lived together on Iona for three months in the year in preparation for work in Scottish industrial areas and in the mission field. Nowadays the lay members, men and women, come as much from the Anglican, RC, and Nonconformist Churches as from the Church of Scotland, and the period of residence on Iona is much more flexible. The Community lays special stress on the discipline of devotional and economic witness, on spiritual healing and political activity; it has taken a leading part in the peace movement.

E. C. Trenholme, SSJE, *The Story of Iona* (1909), with bibl.; T. Hannan, *Iona and Some of its Satellites* (1928). A. Macquarrie, *Iona through the Ages* (Breacachadl Castle, 1983). *Argyll: An Inventory of the Monuments*, 4, *Iona* (Royal Commission on the Ancient and Historical Monuments of Scotland, 1982). G. [F.] MacLeod, *We Shall Re-Build: The Work of the Iona Community on Mainland and Island* [1944]; T. R. Morton, *The Iona Community: Personal Impressions of the Early Years* (Edinburgh, 1977); R. Ferguson, *Chasing the Wild Geese* (1988). See also bibl. to ADOMNÁN, ST, and COLUMBA, ST.

iota. The Greek letter ι (corresponding to the Hebrew *yod* both in sound and as being the smallest letter of the alphabet), mentioned in Christ's saying that 'one jot or one tittle shall in no wise pass away from the law' (Mt. 5: 18). The English 'jot', a transliteration of this Greek word (ἰῶτα), derives its meaning from this text.

Ireland, Christianity in. Christianity began to spread to Ireland through trade with Roman Gaul and Britain in the 4th cent. Whether there were deliberate missions is unclear. The first firm date is the statement in the Chronicle of Prosper Tiro for AD 431 that Pope *Celestine I sent *Palladius 'as their first bishop to the Irish believing in Christ'. The second 5th-cent. source, the writings of St *Patrick, though informative about the character of Patrick himself, provides no clear picture of the Church in Ireland. Until the 7th cent. relations between Ireland and the other *Celtic Churches (q.v.) were close.

During the 7th cent. the Irish Church was riven by controversies between conservatives and innovators. The search for answers to the questions raised by these disputes led to the cultivation of Biblical, computistical, patristic, and legal scholarship, so that in this period Irish schools attracted students from Francia and the recently converted English. After three generations of division over the calculation of the date of *Easter, the innovators won the argument for the Roman date throughout Ireland. During the same period the advocates of institutional change gave way to conservative interests. Until the 12th cent. the Irish Church retained a structure that lacked metropolitan jurisdiction and remained unaffected by the developments which in the 9th and 10th cents. elsewhere established the boundaries between pastoral and monastic Churches.

Some of the monastic foundations of the 6th and 7th cents. grew into great self-governing communities whose numerous clergy included many for whom even *minor orders were largely notional. Places such as *Armagh, Kildare, Cork, and Clonmacnoise became towns under the jurisdiction of the head of the church, often a layman, known as the heir or *coarb of the founder, or as the erenagh (Old Irish *airchindech*, 'chief'; Lat. *princeps*). Many such churches and their estates were controlled by ecclesiastical dynasties, who acted like secular magnates, and in some cases these were cadet branches of the secular ruling dynasties. These churches, which in the 7th cent. had supported a flourishing Latin culture, later cultivated a unique learned literature in the vernacular and were patrons of art in manuscript, stone, and metal. Irish scholars also achieved fame in the Carolingian empire, among them *Sedulius Scottus and Iohannes Scottus *Erigena, but there was no corresponding flow of ideas from the Continent into Ireland.

During the 9th and 10th cents. major Churches, as centres of wealth and population, were natural targets for Viking attacks but they suffered no permanent damage. The establishment of Viking towns, however, particularly *Dublin, opened an avenue for change. In the 11th cent. the Norse settlers became Christian, and their Churches sought links with the English Church. This drew to Ireland the attention of the reforming Abps. of *Canterbury, *Lanfranc and *Anselm, and there were native reformers such as Gilbert, Bp. of Limerick 1106–40, and St *Malachy. The main problems were that the ecclesiastical rulers had too much power, bishops too little, and the Church was not organized in territorial dioceses. Three national synods, at Cashel (1101), Rath Breasail (1111), and Kells-

Mellifont (1152), established diocesan organization and absorbed Dublin into a national Church under the primacy of Armagh. Another aspect of reform was enthusiasm for the new religious orders; the *Cistercians in particular flourished in 12th-cent. Ireland. Many of the older churches had lost status, and though many adopted the Rule of St *Augustine, the 13th cent. saw a rapid decline, as hereditary coarbs and erenaghs now lived off estates that had once supported great churches. The new dioceses, inadequately endowed with assets taken from other churches, fared little better. The once great institutions of Clonmacnoise and Glendalough were too poor to survive as episcopal sees. The reforms were a disaster for Irish culture; nothing replaced the schools and learned cadres, no university emerged (though there was an attempt to establish one at Armagh), and learning became the preserve of secular families until the 17th cent. The reformers' moral programme, the imposition of clerical *celibacy and the enforcement of canonical marriage, largely failed.

The Anglo-Norman invasion of 1169, and the colonial occupation of much of eastern Ireland, gave rise to a divided Church. The second synod of Cashel (1172) marked the beginning of this division. The manorial settlement of the English colony produced arrangements for the support of a parish clergy different from those that continued to exist in Gaelic Ireland, and factional considerations influenced episcopal nominations. These divisions were deepened by the decline in royal power in Ireland in the 14th cent. In the 15th cent. the secular clergy were lax, secular control of churches was far advanced, pastoral care was poor, and the Cistercians were so reduced that only two houses observed the rule and wore the habit. An observer in 1515 noted that 'only the poor friars beggars'—mostly *Observants—preached the word of God.

Under *Henry VIII the majority of the clergy and laity in contact with the government gave nominal assent to the Irish Act of Supremacy 1537 and in 1560 the Church of Ireland was established by the Irish Parliament. The *Reformation, however, at first made little headway outside areas amenable to control from Dublin or recently settled from England or Scotland. As immigration increased in the early 17th cent., so did the strength of Protestantism, aided by the influx of English and Scottish clergy, the establishment in 1592 of *Trinity College, Dublin, and the promulgation in the first Irish Convocation of the Calvinist *Irish Articles of 1615. The moving spirit behind the Articles, J. *Ussher, successively Bp. of Meath and Abp. of Armagh, also elaborated a view of an independent Irish Church only lately corrupted by popery. At the same time, a revitalized Catholicism strengthened its hold on the indigenous population. By the later 16th cent. the religious orders had been suppressed, many dioceses were without bishops, or the bishops lived in exile. But colleges such as those in Paris (founded in 1578), Salamanca (1592), Bordeaux (1603), Louvain (1607), Prague (1620), and Rome (1625) trained novices from Ireland for service at home, while new orders, such as the *Jesuits, as well as the older orders (including the *Franciscans and *Dominicans) recruited from the Irish and were active among them. In 1618 a resident RC hierarchy again became a possibility, replacing for a time the *vicars apostolic who had been appointed since 1591. Thereafter, despite continuing dissensions between regular and secular clergy, between those of Gaelic and English origin, and over attitudes to the English sovereign, Catholicism has remained the religion of the majority in Ireland, increasingly linked with ethnicity and cultural identity.

The apparent links between Catholicism and rebellion in Ireland, demonstrated in the uprising of 1641, led to measures specifically directed against RCs. In 1653 the English law of 1585 was introduced in order to expel bishops and clergy; in 1657 the authority of the Pope was to be abjured. The Catholic revival under *James II, and his subsequent defeat in Ireland, prompted the renewal and extension of discriminatory measures, which after 1704 hit Protestant dissenters as well as RCs, and tried to confine political rights, office and ownership of land to members of the Church of Ireland. Except in the 1650s, 1673–4, and during the *Popish Plot and Jacobite panics, these inhibitions were enforced only intermittently; they caused irritation and inconvenience but neither prevented the practice nor arrested the growth of Catholicism. In 1731 there were perhaps 1,445 RC clergy in the country. After 1760 a Catholic Committee pressed for the removal of disabilities; some of these disappeared with the *Catholic Relief Acts in 1782, 1792, and 1793, but others survived until Catholic Emancipation in 1829.

Scottish settlers in east Ulster had spread *Presbyterianism during the 17th cent., and in 1690 they organized themselves under the Synod of Ulster as a Protestant Church alternative to the established Church of Ireland. In 1726 those who scrupled over subscription to the *Westminster Confession seceded into the Synod of Antrim and later split into *Burghers and *Anti-Burghers. The Presbyterians, like RCs, were subject to legal restrictions and could make common cause with the latter against the privileges of the Church of Ireland. Protestantism was further fragmented by groups of English Presbyterians, *Independents, *Baptists, and *Quakers, arriving from England during the 1650s and refusing to submit to the 1666 Act of Uniformity. Refugees from 17th-cent. France and in 1709 from the Rhineland introduced small but ethnically distinct communities of *Huguenots and Palatines, some of whom immediately conformed to the Church of Ireland.

Irish Protestants disagreed about whether evangelization should precede or follow conquest and anglicization. However, despite doubts as to whether the native Irish would respond to evangelism, by 1685 the Bible and the BCP were published in Irish. In the 18th cent. the Church of Ireland, with its 400–600 clergy, felt equally threatened by the RC majority and the Protestant dissenters concentrated mainly in Ulster and in the towns; little effort was made to convert either. Its leaders, aware that its position depended on legal privileges, formulated and defended the concept of a Protestant ascendancy over property and power just as it was weakened in the 1780s.

The end of the 18th cent. was overshadowed by the rebellion of 1798, which deepened religious distrust. The Act of Union of 1800 confirmed the position of the Church of Ireland as the established Church and an integral part of the united Church of England and Ireland. It disappointed RCs because it did not bring Catholic Emancipation which remained a divisive issue until D. *O'Connell forced the government to concede it in 1829. O'Connell's

success in mobilizing the RC masses was perceived as a threat by Protestants, both Anglicans and Dissenters, who closed ranks and supported the Union as a guarantee against RC supremacy. During the Great Famine of 1845–49, however, Protestant and RC clergy co-operated in providing relief. Emigration and other factors reduced the RC population from about 7 million in 1845 to 3.75 million in 1911, but Irish RC communities developed abroad, particularly in the *United States of America, and maintained links with home. Reforming bishops, such as James Warren Doyle (1786–1834, Bp. of Kildare and Leighlin from 1819) and Daniel Murray (1768–1852, Abp. of Dublin from 1823), revitalized Catholicism, the national Synod of Thurles in 1850 consolidated earlier reforms, and Paul Cullen (1803–78, Abp. of Dublin from 1850 and Cardinal from 1866) built a vigorous *Ultramontane Church on this basis. The increase in the number of priests and religious (both men and women), together with the sharp drop in population, favoured the emergence of a more disciplined and organized Church. Catherine Elizabeth McAuley (1778–1841) and Edmund Ignatius Rice (1762–1844) were among a number of charismatic people to found religious orders, which, together with religious orders from the Continent, provided RC schools, orphanages, hospitals, charitable works, and home missions. The foreign missionary enterprise of the religious orders and missionary societies constituted one of the most remarkable achievements of Irish RCs in the 19th and 20th cents.

The *Evangelical movement at the beginning of the 19th cent. renewed the spiritual life of the Church of Ireland and launched a campaign to convert RCs. Some success was achieved in the 1840s and 1850s but the 1861 census showed the relative numerical strength of the Churches almost unchanged. In 1869 W. E. *Gladstone's government disestablished the Church of Ireland, an action foreshadowed by the Church Temporalities Act 1833 which had reduced the number of Irish sees to ten. The General Synod then became the governing body of the Church. The BCP was revised in 1878, and again in 1924–6, and an Alternative Prayer Book was authorized in 1984.

The Presbyterian Church became theologically more conservative under the leadership of Henry Cooke (1788–1868) and after the formation of the General Assembly of the Presbyterian Church in 1840. Evangelicalism was strong within the Church as evidenced by the revival of 1859, known as 'the year of grace'. Its vigorous missionary thrust was not confined to Ireland but extended to *India and *China. Presbyterians worked with RCs for tenant rights, but on religious, economic, and political grounds remained, like Protestants generally, attached to the Union.

Despite examples of pastoral care and intellectual vitality in all denominations, the intractable problem of integrating popular beliefs and practices into organized religion was not undertaken systematically until the devotional 'revolution' of the latter part of the 19th cent. With the decline of Irish language and culture some native practices disappeared within Catholicism to be replaced by modern Continental devotions.

After the partition of Ireland in 1922, the legislation of the Free State (later the Republic) reflected the ethos of the RC majority but it avoided discrimination against its small Protestant minority. The Constitution of 1938 was specifically Christian. While (in an article removed in 1972) it recognized the special position of the RC Church as guardian of the faith of the majority, it accorded full recognition to the Protestant Churches and the Jewish community. In Northern Ireland the RCs, who composed over a third of the population, were never reconciled to the partition and their discontent at discrimination was one of the causes of the conflict that erupted in 1968/9. Despite underlying distrust between the Churches, the violence and length of that conflict pushed them to co-operate in seeking a solution. The Second *Vatican Council (1962–5) promoted a more open and *ecumenical spirit among RCs and in 1970 the Irish School of Ecumenics was founded. Regular meetings take place between Church leaders and theologians at a national and local level. Reaction against ecumenism has been a potent factor in the strength of the Free Presbyterian Church, founded by the Revd Ian Paisley in 1951.

According to the 1991 censuses, 91.6 per cent of the population in the Republic professed to be RC, 2.34 per cent Church of Ireland, and 0.37 per cent Presbyterian; in Northern Ireland 38.4 per cent to be RC, 21.4 per cent Presbyterian, and 17.7 per cent Church of Ireland, but it has been widely suggested that these figures do not give a true picture. All Churches have suffered lapses in membership in recent years and are being challenged by secularizing influences. In the Republic referenda on abortion and *divorce in 1983 and 1986 provoked public controversy. However, Christianity is still a vital force in Ireland which has the highest percentage of practising Christians in the European community.

J. F. Kenney, The Sources for the Early History of Ireland, 1: Ecclesiastical (Records of Civilization [11]; New York, 1929; repr. 1966). K. [W.] Hughes, The Church in Early Irish Society (1966); P. J. Corish (ed.), A History of Irish Catholicism, 1, 3: id., The Christian Mission (Dublin, 1972); R. Sharpe, 'Some problems concerning the organization of the Church in early medieval Ireland', Peritia, 3 (1984), pp. 230–70; H. Löwe (ed.), Die Iren und Europa im früheren Mittelalter (Veröffentlichungen des Europa Zentrums Tübingen, Kulturwissenschaftliche Reihe, 2 vols., Stuttgart, 1982); P. Ní Chatháin and M. Richter (eds.), Irland und Europa: Die Kirche im Frühmittelalter (ibid., 1984); idd. (eds.), Irland und die Christenheit: Bibelstudien und Mission (ibid., 1987); M. Sheehy, When the Normans came to Ireland (Cork, 1975); A. O. Gwynn, SJ, The Irish Church in the Eleventh and Twelfth Centuries, ed. G. O'Brien (Dublin [1992]); J. A. Watt, The Church and Two Nations in Medieval Ireland (Cambridge Studies in Medieval Life and Thought, 3rd ser. 3; 1970); id., The Church in Medieval Ireland (Dublin, 1972); A. Cosgrove (ed.), Medieval Ireland 1169–1534 (A New History of Ireland under the Auspices of the Royal Irish Academy, 2; Oxford, 1987); P. J. Corish (ed.), A History of Irish Catholicism, 2, 3–4: G. [J.] Hand, The Church in the English Lordship 1216–1307, and A. [O]. Gwynn, SJ, Anglo-Irish Church Life: Fourteenth and Fifteenth Centuries (Dublin, 1968), and 2, 5: C. Mooney, OFM, The Church in Gaelic Ireland: Thirteenth to Fifteenth Centuries (ibid., 1969).

T. W. Moody and others (eds.), Early Modern Ireland 1534–1691 (A New History of Ireland, op. cit., 3; Oxford, 1976); B. Bradshaw, The Dissolution of the Religious Orders in Ireland under Henry VIII (Cambridge, 1974); R. D. Edwards, Church and State in Tudor Ireland: A History of the Penal Laws against Irish Catholics 1534–1603 (1935); T. S. Flynn, OP, The Irish Dominicans 1536–1641 (Dublin [1993]); L. McRedmond, To the Greater Glory: A History of the Irish Jesuits (ibid., 1991). A. Ford, The Protestant Reformation in Ireland, 1590–1641 (Studien zur interkulturellen

Geschichte des Christentums, 34; Frankfurt am-Main [1985]). B. Mac Cuarta, SJ (ed.), Ulster 1641: Aspects of the Rising (Belfast, 1993). T. C. Barnard, Cromwellian Ireland: English Government and Reform in Ireland 1649–1660 (Oxford Historical Monographs, 1975), pp. 90–182. R. B. Knox, James Ussher, Archbishop of Armagh (Cardiff, 1967). T. W. Moody and W. E. Vaughan (eds.), Eighteenth-Century Ireland (A New History of Ireland, op. cit. 4; 1986). P. Kilroy, Protestant dissent and controversy in Ireland 1660–1714 (Cork, 1994); S. J. Connolly, Religion, Law and Power: The Making of Protestant Ireland 1660–1760 (Oxford, 1992). N. Williams, I bPrionta i Leabhar: Na Protastúin agus Prós na Gaeilge 1567–1724 (Dublin, 1986). T. P. Power and K. Whelan (eds.), Endurance and Emergence: Catholics in Ireland in the Eighteenth Century (Dublin [1990]). T. Bartlett, The Fall and Rise of the Irish Nation: The Catholic Question 1690–1830 (ibid. [1992]). C. D. A. Leighton, Catholicism in a Protestant Kingdom: A Study of the Irish Ancien Régime (1994). D. Keogh, The French Disease: The Catholic Church and Irish Radicalism, 1790–1800 (Dublin [1993]). S. J. Connolly, Priests and People in Pre-Famine Ireland 1780–1845 (ibid., 1982). I. d'Alton, Protestant Society and Politics in Cork 1812–1824 (Cork, 1980). D. A. Kerr, Peel, Priests, and Politics: Sir Robert Peel's Administration and the Roman Catholic Church in Ireland, 1841–1846 (Oxford Historical Monographs, 1982); id., 'A Nation of Beggars'? Priests, People and Politics in Famine Ireland (Oxford, 1994). E. Larkin, The Making of the Roman Catholic Church in Ireland, 1850–1860 (Chapel Hill, NC [1980]); id., The Consolidation of the Roman Catholic Church in Ireland, 1860–1870 (Dublin [1987]); id., 'The Devotional Revolution in Ireland, 1850–75', American Historical Review, 77 (1972), pp. 625–52; id., The Roman Catholic Church and the Creation of the Modern Irish State 1878–1886 (Memoirs of the American Philosophical Society, 108; Philadelphia, 1975). D. Keogh, The Vatican, the Bishops, and Irish Politics 1918–1939 (Cambridge, 1986). J. H. Whyte, Church and State in Modern Ireland [from 1923] (Dublin, 1971; 2nd edn., 1980). M. Harris, The Catholic Church and the Foundation of the Northern Irish State (Cork, 1993); O. P. Rafferty, SJ, Northern Catholicism (Dublin, 1994). J. Fulton, The Tragedy of Belief: Division, Politics, and Religion in Ireland (Oxford, 1991). J. S. Reid, History of the Presbyterian Church in Ireland (3 vols., Edinburgh, 1834–53; rev. D. W. Killen, 3 vols., Belfast, 1867); R. F. G. Holmes, Our Irish Presbyterian Heritage (Belfast, 1985). J. I. McGuire and others (eds.), Towards a new history of the Church of Ireland (Dublin, 1994). A. Ford and others (eds.), As by Law Established: The Church of Ireland since the Reformation (ibid., 1995). R. B. McDowell, The Church of Ireland 1869–1969 (1975). J. Murray and others, 'The Church of Ireland: a critical bibliography, 1536–1992', Irish Historical Studies, 28 (1993), pp. 345–84. W. J. Sheils and D. Wood (eds.), The Churches, Ireland and the Irish: Papers read at the 1987 Summer Meeting and the 1988 Winter Meeting of the Ecclesiastical History Society (Studies in Church History, 25; 1989).

Ireland, John (1761–1842), Dean of *Westminster. Having entered Oriel College, Oxford, as a Bible clerk in 1779, he became Vicar of Croydon in 1793, and Dean of Westminster in 1816. He gave large sums to the University of Oxford for classical scholarships, and in his will he founded the chair of Exegesis of Holy Scripture (since 1947 confined to the NT) which goes by his name, and some exhibitions at Oriel College.

E. *Hawkins, An Inaugural Lecture upon the Foundation of Dean Ireland's Professorship, read before the University of Oxford, Nov. 2, 1847, with brief notices of the Founder (1848), esp. pp. 9–12, and Appendix, pp. 45–59, with refs. to obituary notices.

Irenaeus, St (c.130–c.200), Bp. of Lyons. Relatively little is known of his life, but as he heard *Polycarp as a boy, it is generally supposed that he was a native of Smyrna. He studied at *Rome, and later became a presbyter of Lyons, in which capacity he was commissioned to take letters to Pope Eleutherius at Rome, requesting toleration for the *Montanists of Asia Minor. There is no evidence, however, to show that Irenaeus himself sympathized with the sect. During his absence fierce persecution took place at Lyons (c.177), in which *Pothinus, the bishop, was among the martyrs; and on his return (c.178) Irenaeus succeeded to the see. In 190 he wrote to Pope *Victor on behalf of the *Quartodecimans of Asia Minor. Whether or not he met a martyr's death is uncertain. Feast day in the W., 28 June; in the E., 23 Aug.

Both in his life and in his thought, Irenaeus forms a link between the E. and W. His theological writing grew out of his work as a missionary and pastoral bishop in an era when *Gnosticism was a serious threat to the Church. His principal treatise, the 'Adversus omnes Haereses' (Ἔλεγχος καὶ Ἀνατροπὴ τῆς Ψευδωνύμου Γνώσεως), is a detailed attack on Gnosticism, and esp. on the system of *Valentinus. Part of it is preserved in Greek, but the whole text survives in a literal Latin version and sections of it are also extant in *Syriac and *Armenian. As sources Irenaeus appears to have drawn upon *Justin and *Theophilus of Antioch, and he was himself drawn upon regularly by subsequent heresiologists. In modern times a second work, 'The Demonstration of the Apostolic Preaching' (Εἰς Ἐπίδειξιν τοῦ Ἀποστολικοῦ Κηρύγματος), has been discovered in an Armenian translation. It is an apologetic work, notable for its lavish use of the OT.

Irenaeus is the first great Catholic theologian. Unlike *Clement of Alexandria, he opposed Gnosticism, not by setting up a rival Christian Gnosis, but by emphasizing the traditional elements in the Church, esp. the Episcopate, Scripture (in which he included not only the OT but also most of the Books now known as the NT), and the religious and theological tradition. His opposition to Gnosticism also led to an emphasis on Christian Monotheism, on the unity of Father and Son in the work of Revelation and Redemption, and on the reality of the Incarnation of Christ. He developed a doctrine of the 'recapitulation' (ἀνακεφαλαίωσις; Lat. recapitulatio), or summary, of human evolution in the Incarnate Christ, and thereby gave a positive value of its own to the manhood of Christ. He also laid great stress on the co-ordinate authority of all four Gospels. See also PFAFF FRAGMENTS.

The Adv. Haer. was ed. by *Erasmus (Basle, 1526). Later edns. by A. Stieren (Leipzig, 1848–53) and W. W. Harvey (Cambridge, 1857). Crit. text by A. Rousseau, OSB, and L. Doutreleau, SJ, and others (SC 100, 152 f., 210 f., 263 f., and 293 f.; 1965–82). The 'Demonstration' was first pub. by K. Ter-Mekerttschian and E. Ter-Minassiantz (TU 31, Heft 1; 1907); also, with Eng. tr. by K. Ter-Mekerttschian and S. G. Wilson in PO 12 (1919), pp. 653–731. Further Armenian frags. of the Adv. Haer. and the 'Demonstration', ed. C. Renoux, with Lat. tr., ibid. 39 (1978–9), pp. 1–164. Eng. tr. of Adv. Haer. by J. *Keble in LF (posthumous, 1872) and by A. Roberts and W. H. Rambaut in ANCL (2 vols., 1868–9); of chief passages in Adv. Haer. by F. R. M. Hitchcock in SPCK 'Early Christian Classics' (2 vols., 1916); of 'Demonstration' by J. A. *Robinson, with good notes, in SPCK 'Translations of Christian Literature' (1920) and J. P. Smith (ACW 16; 1953).

There is an immense modern lit. Studies in Eng. incl. F. R. M. Hitchcock, Irenaeus of Lugdunum (1914); J. Lawson, The Biblical Theology of St Irenaeus (1948); and D. Minns, OP, Irenaeus (1994; introductory). On Irenaeus' biblical text, W. *Sanday and C. H.

*Turner, Novum Testamentum Sancti Irenaei (Oxford, 1923). On the Lat. vers. of Adv. Haer., S. Lundström, Studien zur lateinischen Irenäusübersetzung (Lund, 1943); id., Neue Studien zur lateinischen Irenäusübersetzung (ibid., 1948). F.-M.-M. Sagnard, OP, La Gnose valentinienne et le témoignage de Saint Irénée (1947). G. Wingren, Människan och Inkarnationen enligt Irenaeus (Lund, 1947; Eng. tr., Man and the Incarnation, 1959). A. Houssiau, La Christologie de Saint Irénée (Louvain, 1955). A. Benoît, Saint Irénée: Introduction à l'étude de sa théologie (1960). N. Brox, Offenbarung, Gnosis und gnostischer Mythos bei Irenäus von Lyon (Salzburger Patristische Studien, 1; 1966). A. Orbe, SJ, Antropología de San Ireneo (Biblioteca de Autores Cristianos, 1969); id., Parábolas evangélicas en San Ireneo (2 vols., ibid., 1972); id., Teología de San Ireneo: Comentario al Libro V del 'Adversus haereses' (3 vols., ibid., 1985–88); id., Espiritualidad de San Irenaeo (Analecta Gregoriana, 256; 1989). R. Tremblay, La Manifestation et la Vision de Dieu selon saint Irénée de Lyon (Münsterische Beiträge zur Theologie, 41; 1978). Y. de Andia, Homo vivens: Incorruptibilité et divinisation de l'homme chez Irénée de Lyon (Études Augustiniennes, 1986). J. Fantino, Le théologie d'Irénée: Lecture des Écritures en réponse à l'exégèse gnostique. Un approche trinitaire (1994). CPG 1 (1983), pp. 110–18 (nos. 1306–21), incl. details of various frags. J. Quasten, Patrology, 1 (Utrecht, 1950), pp. 287–313; Altaner and Stuiber (1978), pp. 110–17 and 570–72. F. Vernet in DTC 7 (1923), cols. 2394–533, s.v., with full bibls. to date (esp. cols. 2407–10); L. Doutreleau, SJ, and L. Regnault, OSB, in Dict. Sp. 7 (pt. 2; 1971), cols. 1923–69, s.v.; A. Orbe in DPAC 2 (1984), cols. 1804–16; Eng. tr., Encyclopedia of the Early Church, 1 (1992), pp. 413–6, s.v.

Irish Articles. The 104 articles of faith adopted by the Irish Episcopal Church in 1615 at its first Convocation. More definitely *Calvinistic than the *Thirty-Nine Articles of the C of E (1562), which had never been accepted in Ireland, they were apparently compiled by J. *Ussher, then head of the faculty of theology at Dublin. They teach absolute predestination and perseverance, affirm that the Pope is antichrist, and make no mention of the threefold ministry or of the necessity of Episcopal Ordination. They remained the official statement of faith in the Church of Ireland down to 1635, when at a Convocation held under Strafford and his chaplain, J. *Bramhall, the Anglican Thirty-Nine Articles were adopted, apparently with the intention that they should replace those of 1615. Ussher, however, continued for a time to require subscription to both series, though ultimately the earlier ones became a dead letter. They seem to have exercised considerable influence on the text of the *Westminster Confession.

The text is in P. *Schaff, The Creeds of Christendom, 3 (1877), pp. 526–44. Cf. also ibid. 1, § 85, pp. 662–5.

irmos. See HEIRMOS.

Iron Crown, of Lombardy. A crown made for Theodelinda, widow of Authoris, King of Lombardy, and presented in 594 to the Duke of Turin, from whom it passed eventually to the recent royal house of Italy. It is of gold with an inner circlet of iron which is said to have been made from a nail of the true Cross. It is preserved in the cathedral church of Monza.

Irving, Edward (1792–1834), Scottish minister associated with the origins of the '*Catholic Apostolic Church' (q.v.). He was a native of Annan, Dumfriesshire, and educated at Edinburgh University. He was appointed master of a school at Haddington in 1810 and at Kirkcaldy in 1812. Having been licensed to preach in the Church of

Scotland in 1815, in 1819 he became the assistant of T. *Chalmers at Glasgow, where he had a great influence among the poorer population. In 1822 he was appointed minister of the Caledonian chapel in Hatton Garden, London, where his magnetic personality soon drew large congregations. But his merciless criticism of society and personalities later lost its attraction, and Irving then turned to *millenarian ideas. He was greatly impressed by a work of the Spanish *Jesuit, Lacunza (1816), which he translated under the title *The Coming of the Messiah in Glory and Majesty* (1827). This work brought Irving into contact with the circle of H. *Drummond, who was devoted to eschatological speculations. In 1828 he lectured at Edinburgh on the Book of Revelation. In 1830 he was excommunicated by the London presbytery for his tract on *The Orthodox and Catholic Doctrine of our Lord's Human Nature*, in which he declared Christ's human nature to be sinful; but he rejected their decision and continued to minister. In 1831 disturbances of a revivalist character began to occur at the services in his church at Regent Square, from which he was finally removed in 1832. His followers now constituted themselves the 'Catholic Apostolic Church'. In 1833 he was expelled from the ministry of the Church of Scotland. After travelling for some time in Dumfriesshire he returned to London, but, surprisingly, was accorded only an inferior rank in the sect which he had helped to found, and he died soon afterwards.

His *Collected Writings* appeared in 5 vols. in 1864–5. Life by M. O. W. Oliphant (2 vols., 1862). A. L. Drummond, *Edward Irving and his Circle* (1938). C. G. Strachan, *The Pentecostal Theology of Edward Irving* (1973). A. Dallimore, *The Life of Edward Irving, Fore-runner of the Charismatic Movement* (Edinburgh and Carlisle, Pa., 1983). See also works cited under CATHOLIC APOSTOLIC CHURCH.

Isaac, OT *Patriarch. His story is told in Gen. 21–35. The divinely promised son of *Abraham and Sarah after a long childless marriage, he became the heir of the covenanted blessings (cf. Gen. 17: 19 and 21). To try Abraham's faith Yahweh demanded Isaac in sacrifice, but, satisfied with Abraham's perfect obedience, accepted at the last moment a ram instead (Gen. 22). After Sarah's death, Abraham procured a wife for Isaac from his own family, Rebecca, who became the mother of Esau and *Jacob (Gen. 24 and 25). On the likely dating of these traditions, see ABRAHAM.

In the NT Isaac is referred to in Gal. 4: 22–31, prefiguring Christians as children of promise. He is perhaps alluded to as a type of Christ in Rom. 8: 32. In Heb. the sacrifice of Isaac is seen as an example of faith and a type of the death and resurrection of Christ (11: 17–19). This theme was developed in the Fathers, who regard his intended sacrifice as a type of that of *Golgotha. Thus *Tertullian sees in Isaac carrying the wood the type of Christ carrying His Cross, and both St *Cyril of Alexandria and St *Augustine elaborate the similarities of the two sacrifices. In the Middle Ages the sacrifice of Isaac as a prefiguration of the Passion was a favourite topic of theologians. The important part which this conception has played in Christian art is shown by the paintings in the *catacombs, where the representation of the scene is used as a figure of the Eucharist.

See comm. on Gen., cited s.v. H. J. Schoeps, 'The Sacrifice of Isaac in Paul's Theology', *Journal of Biblical Literature*, 65 (1946), pp. 385–92; J. *Daniélou, SJ, 'La Typologie d'Isaac dans le christianisme primitif', *Biblica*, 28 (1947), pp. 363–93; D. Lerch, *Isaaks Opferung christlich gedeutet* (Beiträge zur historischen Theologie, 12; 1950). N. A. Dahl, 'The Atonement—An Adequate Reward for the Akedah? (Ro 8: 32)', in E. E. Ellis and M. Wilcox (eds.), *Neotestamentica et Semitica: Studies in Honour of Matthew Black* (Edinburgh, 1969), pp. 15–29. J. Gribomont, OSB, in *Dict. Sp.* 7 (pt. 2; 1971), cols. 1987–2005; R. Martin-Achard in *Anchor Bible Dictionary*, 3 (1992), pp. 461–70, both s.v.

Isaac the Great, St (*c.*350–438), 10th *Catholicos of the *Armenian Church. He was the son of St *Nerses and a lineal descendant of St *Gregory the Illuminator. After studying at *Constantinople, he married, and then, after the early death of his wife, became a monk. He was appointed Catholicos of Armenia *c.*389. By gaining from Constantinople the recognition of the metropolitical rights of the Armenian Church, he terminated its long dependence on Caesarea in Cappadocia. He was also very active in fostering a national Armenian literature, translating in conjunction with St *Mesrob much of the Bible and many other Greek works. Tradition also ascribes to him the authorship of many Armenian hymns, as well as (apparently erroneously) the Armenian Liturgy. In 425 he was deposed from his office by the Persians, but allowed later, in view of strong popular support, to regain his see. Feast days ('St Sahak') in the Armenian Church, 9 Sept. and 25 Nov.

Three of Isaac's letters are preserved by *Moses of Chorene in his 'History of Armenia Major' (3. 57); further letters ed. J. Izmiveantz in his 'Book of Letters' (Tiflis, 1901; in Armenian). K. Sarkissian, *The Council of Chalcedon and the Armenian Church* (1965), pp. 88–147 *passim*. Bardenhewer, 5, pp. 195–7; Altaner and Stuiber (1966), pp. 350 f. S. Vailhé in *CE* 8 (1910), pp. 175 f., s.v.; I. Ortiz de Urbina, SJ, in *EC* 10 (1953), col. 1616, s.v. 'Sahak (Isaac) I'; A. Renoux, OSB, in *Dict. Sp.* 7 (pt. 2; 1971), cols. 2007–10, s.v. 'Isaac (3) le Grand'.

Isaac of Nineveh (d. *c.*700), also 'Isaac the Syrian', monastic writer. Little is known of his life: he came originally from Qatar, where he became a monk; *c.*676, in the monastery of Beth 'Abe (in Kurdistan) he was made Bp. of Nineveh by the *Catholicos of the *Church of the East, but shortly afterwards he retired from his see to live a life of solitude in Khuzistan, moving in old age to the monastery of Rabban Shabur. His writings, on ascetic subjects, belong to the end of his life; they were translated at an early date into Greek, Arabic, Georgian, and Ethiopic. A selection of 25 homilies was translated into Latin in the 15th cent. The Greek version of the 'First Part' of his collected writings (82 homilies), the work of two monks of St Saba, Patrikios and Abramios, was first published by Nicephorus Theotokes (Leipzig, 1770) under the title Τοῦ ὁσίου πατρὸς ἡμῶν Ἰσαὰκ . . . τὰ εὑρεθέντα ἀσκητικά (this edition includes some texts by two other Syriac authors, *Philoxenus and *John of Dalyatha, wrongly attributed to Isaac). Extracts are included in the Russian *Philocalia. In modern times Isaac continues to exert an influence on both *Athonite and *Coptic monasticism. Feast day in the E., 28 Jan.

Isaac of Nineveh is to be distinguished from Isaac the Great (previous entry) and from three other Syriac writers of the 5th/6th cent. who often go under the name of Isaac of Antioch, extracts of whose writings have been published by G. Bickell (2 vols., 1873–7) and P. Bedjan (1903).

The whole of the 'First Part' of Isaac's collected works was ed. by P. Bedjan, *De Perfectione Religiosa* (Paris, 1909). Eng. tr. by A. J. Wensinck (Amsterdam, 1923). Eng. tr. of the Gk. version, with many refs. to the Syriac, by 'The Holy Transfiguration Monastery' [D. Miller], *The Ascetical Homilies of Saint Isaac the Syrian* (1984). Lat. versions in J. P. Migne, *PG* 86 (1). 811–86 ('De Contemptu Mundi'). A complete MS of the 'Second Part' was discovered in the Bodleian Library by S. P. Brock in 1983; chapters 4–41, ed., with Eng. tr., by id. (CSCO 554–5, Scriptores Syri, 224–5; 1995); Ital. tr. of the rest by P. Bettiolo (1985; 2nd edn., 1990). I. B. Chabot, *De S. Isaaci Ninivitae Vita, Scriptis et Doctrina* (Paris, 1892). A. *Baumstark, *Geschichte der syrischen Literatur* (1922), pp. 223–5. E. Khalifé-Hachem in *Dict. Sp.* 7 (pt. 2; 1971), cols. 2041–54, s.v. (On the other Syriac Isaacs, R. Graffin, SJ, ibid., cols. 2010 f., s.v. 'Isaac d'Amid et Isaac d'Antioche'.)

Isaac of Stella (*c*.1100–*c*.1178). *Cistercian monk. Little is known for certain about his life. He was of English origin and by 1147 was abbot of Stella (some 12 miles NE of Poitiers), which had been founded in 1124 and recently become Cistercian. It seems likely that he studied in France before joining the Cistercians. Prob. in 1167, and perhaps because of his support for Thomas *Becket, who had fallen out of favour with the Cistercian authorities, Isaac left Stella to set up a monastery (Notre Dame des Châteliers) on the Île de Ré, a few miles off the French coast near La Rochelle. Fifty-five of his sermons survive and two treatises in the form of letters: *De Anima*, addressed to Alcher of *Clairvaux, and *De Officio Missae*, addressed to John, Bp. of Poitiers. He stands somewhat apart from other Cistercians of the 12th cent. in his positive attitude to the *Platonic tradition. Influenced by the so-called 'School of *Chartres' and the *Victorines, and still more deeply by St *Augustine, he developed, on the basis of his analysis of the human soul, an understanding of the soul's ascent to God whereby, through a purification of love, the *intelligentia* or *mens* attains union with God in an act of intuitive knowledge.

Works repr. in J. P. Migne, *PL* 194. 1689–896. Crit. edn. of his Sermons, with Fr. tr., by A. Hoste, OSB, and others (SC 130, 207, and 339; 1967–87). L. Bouyer [Cong. Orat.], *La Spiritualité de Cîteaux* (1955), pp. 195–232 (Eng. tr., 1958, pp. 161–89). B. McGinn, *The Golden Chain: A Study in the Theological Anthropology of Isaac of Stella* (Cistercian Studies Series, 15; Washington, DC, 1972). G. Raciti, OCR, in *Dict. Sp.* 7 (pt. 2; 1971), cols. 2011–38, s.v. 'Isaac de l'Étoile'.

Isabella I of Castile (1451–1504), 'the Catholic', Queen of Castile, León, and Aragon. The daughter of John II, King of Castile and León, in 1469 she married *Ferdinand, heir to the Crown of Aragon. On the death of Henry IV, her half-brother, in 1474, she successfully challenged the claims of Juana, Henry's daughter, to the throne. With Ferdinand she fought Portuguese support for Juana, who was backed by many important noble families in Extremadura and Andalusia. Once established on the throne, she and her husband initiated a series of reforms which strengthened royal jurisdiction, reorganized governmental and ecclesiastical institutions, gaining a number of concessions from the Papacy over royal patronage and the appointment of bishops, and they launched campaigns which restored the Kingdom of Granada and Lower Navarre to Castile. She also laid the basis for overseas expansion by annexing the Canary Islands and funding Christopher Columbus's explorations of a new route to the Far East, during which he landed on various islands in the Caribbean. A woman of strong religious principles and personal piety, she exercised a bracing influence at the Castilian court. She and Ferdinand, who were named the '*Catholic Kings' by *Alexander VI (an Aragonese Pope), are best known for their insistence on religious unity within their kingdoms at home and abroad. To this end they established the Spanish *Inquisition, expelled those subjects who professed *Judaism or *Islam (even converted Moors were to be expelled in 1609), and organized the evangelization of the American Indians.

W. H. Prescott, *History of the Reign of Ferdinand and Isabella* (3 vols., '1838' [1837] and many later edns.). Modern Lives by M. Ballesteros Gaibrois (Segovia, 1953), Tarsicio de Azcona, OFM Cap. (Madrid, 1964), and P. K. Liss (Oxford, 1992). O. Ferrara, *L'Avènement d'Isabelle la Catholique* (Fr. tr., 1958). Tarsicio de Azcona, OFM Cap., *La elección y reforma del episcopado español en tiempo de los reyes católicos* (1960). R. García y García de Castro, *Virtudes de la Reina Católica* (1961); M. I. del Val, *Isabel la Católica, Princesa (1468–1474)* (Instituto 'Isabel la Catolica' de Historia Ecclesiastica, Documentos, 9; Valladolid, 1974). See also bibl. to FERDINAND V.

Isaiah. The Hebrew prophet of the 8th cent. BC. He exercised influence at the court of the kings of Judah, and took a prominent part esp. in foreign politics. Called to the prophetic office in the year of King Uzziah's death (*c*.740; Is. 6: 1), he continued his prophetic work till the Assyrian invasion of Judah in 701 BC. Tradition relates his death by martyrdom in the reign of Manasseh (*c*.690–*c*.640).

In his teaching Isaiah followed *Amos and *Hosea in asserting the supremacy of *Yahweh, the God of Israel, and in emphasizing His moral demands on His worshippers. He laid special stress on the Divine holiness (ch. 6), giving to this conception a strong ethical content. From these beliefs much of his teaching on particular matters followed, e.g. his political counsels, urging Judah to keep out of foreign alliances and trust only in God; his confidence in the inviolability of *Jerusalem; and his insistence that sacrificial worship must be accompanied by spiritual effort in the participants. The names of his sons were symbolic (7: 3; 8: 3), indicating his conviction that a 'remnant' (or, perhaps, no more than a remnant) of Judah would be saved from the downfall which was awaiting those who relied on human assistance. His expectations for the future were chiefly centred on his belief in the permanence of God's choice of Jerusalem as His sanctuary on earth, and around these expectations gathered the fervent hopes of successive generations of Jews. From NT times onwards the so-called Messianic passages in the prophecies ascribed to Isaiah (esp. 9: 2–7 and 11: 1–9) have very frequently been referred by Christian writers to the historic Christ, but it is a matter of dispute how far these can be attributed to the prophet himself. See also the following entries.

Isaiah, Ascension of. An apocryphal work well known in the early Church. It divides naturally into two parts. The first part (chs. 1–5) describes the circumstances of Isaiah's martyrdom by being 'sawn asunder' (though the thread of the narrative is awkwardly interrupted in chs. 3 and 4 by the detailed description of a vision); the second part (chs. 6–11) describes Isaiah's ascent in ecstasy through the heavens and the revelations made to him there. The work is extant complete only in Ethiopic; but a series of fragments makes it certain that there were at one time complete *Coptic and Latin texts as well. There are also both Latin and Slavonic versions of chs. 6–11 only.

It used to be held that the basis was a document describing Isaiah's martyrdom, probably Jewish in origin and perhaps originally in *Hebrew or *Aramaic, into which a Christian editor had inserted a Christian apocalypse (3. 13–4. 22) and also made other minor additions and adaptations. The existence of a separate martyrdom is now disputed; it is held rather that the whole work is Christian in origin, though Jewish traditions have been used. E. Norelli argues that ch. 6–11 date from the end of the 1st cent., and chs. 1–5 from the beginning of the 2nd. The original language was almost certainly Greek. There are striking parallels with the Acts of *Peter.

Ethiopic, Greek, Coptic, Latin and Slavonic texts ed. P. Bettiolo and others (CCSA, 7; 1995), with comm. by E. Norelli (ibid., 8; 1995). Eng. tr. by R. H. Charles (London, 1900) rev. by J. M. T. Barton in H. F. D. Sparks (ed.), *The Apocryphal Old Testament* (Oxford, 1984), pp. 775–812; Eng. tr. by M. A. Knibb in J. H. Charlesworth (ed.), *The Old Testament Pseudepigrapha*, 2 (1985), pp. 143–76. A. K. Helmbold, 'Gnostic Elements in the "Ascension of Isaiah"', *New Testament Studies*, 18 (1972), pp. 222–7. M. Pesce (ed.), *Isaia, il Diletto e la Chiesa: Visione ed esegesi profetica cristiano-primitiva nell'Ascensione di Isaia. Atti del Convegno di Roma, 9–10 aprile 1981* (Brescia, 1983); A. Acerbi, *Serra Lignea: Studi sulla Fortuna della* Ascensione di Isaia [1984]; id., *L'Ascensione di Isaia: Cristologia e profetismo in Siria nei primi decenni del II Secolo* (Milan, 1989); J. [M.] Knight, *Disciples of the Beloved One: The Christology, Social Setting and Theological Context of the Ascension of Isaiah* (Journal for the Study of the Pseudepigrapha, Supplement Series, 18; Sheffield [1996]). E. *Schürer, *The History of the Jewish People in the Age of Jesus Christ*, rev. Eng. tr. by G. Vermes and others, 3 (part 1; Edinburgh, 1986), pp. 335–41. J. [M.] Knight, *The Ascension of Isaiah* (Guides to Apocrypha and Pseudepigrapha: Sheffield [1995]).

Isaiah, Book of. Traditionally the whole Book is ascribed to *Isaiah (q.v.), but critics are now generally agreed that everything after ch. 36, as well as considerable portions of the earlier chapters, have no real claim to be his.

The Book falls naturally into three divisions.

(1) Chs. 1–35. The sections which can be ascribed to Isaiah with most plausibility are the greater part of chs. 1–12, 16–22, and 28–32. Apart from the Prophet's inaugural vision (6) these prophecies are concerned chiefly with the political situation in Judah under Syrian pressure in the years 740–700 BC. The so-called Syro-Ephraimite War (735 BC) was the occasion of the famous *Immanuel Prophecy (cf. Matt. 1: 22 f.), and most scholars hold that 1: 2–9 reflects the circumstances of the invasion of Judah by Sennacherib of Assyria in 701 BC (cf. 2 Kgs. 18: 13–19: 34). The definitely non-Isaianic items in this part of the Book include the Ode against Babylon (13: 1–14: 23), the Pronouncement of World Judgement or so-called 'Isaiah Apocalypse' (24–7), and the Prophecies on the Downfall of Edom and the Blessedness of God's People (34 f.), all of which would seem to be of considerably later date than the age of Isaiah.

(2) Chs. 36–9. A section taken over from 2 Kgs. 18: 13–20: 19, with the addition of the 'Song of Hezekiah' (Is. 38: 10–20).

(3) Chs. 40–66. These chapters appear to be of a later date than the two previous sections and were known collectively to 19th-cent. critics as '*Deutero-Isaiah'. More recently scholars have subdivided the section, applying the title 'Deutero-Isaiah' to chs. 40–55 and attributing chs. 56–66, which seem to presuppose that the *Temple had been rebuilt, to a later author or authors dubbed '*Trito-Isaiah'.

The main theme of chs. 40–66 is Israel's redemption and her mission to the world. The purpose of chs. 40–55 is to encourage the Jewish exiles in Babylon; they are usually dated shortly before the release of the Jews by Cyrus in 537 BC. Chs. 56–66 are dated after 520 BC. They form less of a unity than 40–55, containing some oracles (e.g. 60–2) which continue Deutero-Isaiah's promises of a renewed Jerusalem but others (e.g. 58–9) which are strongly critical of post-exilic practices. 66: 1–2 even seems to be opposed to the rebuilding of the Temple. See also SERVANT SONGS.

The chief patristic comm. on Isaiah come from *Origen, St *Basil, St *Cyril of Alexandria, and St *Jerome. Of the older Eng. works the principal is that of R. *Lowth (London, 1778). More modern comm. incl. those of G. B. *Gray (on chs. 1–27; ICC, 1912), O. Procksch (KAT 9; 1930), O. Kaiser (on chs. 1–12; Das Alte Testament Deutsch, 17; 1960; 2nd edn., 1963; Eng. tr., 1972; on chs. 13–39, ibid. 18; 1973; Eng. tr., 1974), C. R. North (on chs. 40–55; Oxford, 1964), C. Westermann (on chs. 40–66; Das Alte Testament Deutsch, 19; 1966; Eng. tr., 1969), A. S. Herbert (Camb. Bib., NEB, 2 vols.; 1973–5), H. Windberger (on chs. 1–39, Biblischer Kommentar, Altes Testament, 10; 3 vols., Neukirchen, 1972–80; 2nd edn. of vol. 1 (on chs. 1–12), 1980), R. N. Whybray (on chs. 40–66; New Cent. Bib., 1975), K. Elliger and H.-J. Hermisson (on chs. 40–55, Biblischer Kommentar, Altes Testament, 11; 2 vols., 1978 ff.), and R. E. Clements (on chs. 1–39; New Cent. Bib., 1980). J. Lindblom, *Die Jesaja Apokalypse, Jes. 24–7* (Lunds Universitats Årsskrift, NF, Avd. I, Bd. 34, no. 3; 1938). C. R. North, *The Suffering Servant in Deutero-Isaiah: An Historical and Critical Study* (Oxford, 1948; 2nd edn., 1956). J. Vermeylen, *Du Prophète Isaïe à l'apocalyptique* (Études Bibliques, 2 vols., 1977–8). R. E. Clements, *Isaiah and the Deliverance of Jerusalem* (Journal for the Study of the Old Testament, Supplement Series, 13; Sheffield, 1980). H. G. M. Williamson, *The Book Called Isaiah: Deutero-Isaiah's Role in Composition and Redaction* (Oxford, 1994). A. Neubauer and S. R. *Driver, *The Fifty-Third Chapter of Isaiah according to the Jewish Interpreters* (2 vols., 1876–7; text and Eng. tr.). G. von *Rad, *Theologie des Alten Testament*, 2 (1960), pp. 158–85; 7th edn. (1980), pp. 155–81; Eng. tr. (1965), pp. 147–75. A. Feuillet in *Dict. Bibl.*, Suppl. 4 (1949), cols. 647–729, s.v. 'Isaie', with bibl.; C. R. Seitz, W. R. Millar, and R. J. Clifford in *Anchor Bible Dictionary*, 3 (1992), pp. 472–507, s.v. See also bibl. to SERVANT SONGS.

Iscariot. See JUDAS ISCARIOT.

Isho'dad of Merv (9th cent.), Bp. of Hedatta in the *Church of the East. He wrote commentaries on the whole of both the OT and the NT, packed with quotations from earlier exegetes, e.g. *Theodore of Mopsuestia, *Ephraem Syrus ('Commentary on the *Diatessaron'), and many little-known Syriac authors. His works (all in Syriac) throw valuable light on the history of biblical interpretation.

OT Comm. ed. J. M. Vosté and C. van den Eynde (CSCO, Scriptores Syriaci, 67 [Gen.], 80 [Exod.–Deut.], 96 [Jos., Jgs., Sam., Kgs., Prov., Eccles., Ecclus., Song of Songs, Ruth and Job], 128 [Is. and Minor Prophets], 146 [Jer., Ezek., and Dan.] and 185 [Pss.], with Fr. tr., ibid. 75, 81, 97, 129, 147, and 186; 1950–81). NT Comm., ed., with Eng. tr., by M. D. Gibson, and introd. by J. R. *Harris (Horae Semiticae, 5–7, Cambridge, 1911 [Gospels]; and 10 and 11, 1913–16 [Acts and three Catholic Epistles, and Epistles of St Paul, respectively]). J. M. Vosté, OP, 'Mar Išo'dad de Merw sur les Psaumes', Biblica, 25 (1944), pp. 261–96. A. *Baumstark, Geschichte der syrischen Literatur (1922), p. 234.

Isidore, St (d. *c*.440), of Pelusium, ascetic and exegete. He was prob. a teacher in the Church of Pelusium before he retired to a monastery not far from the city on a hill on the eastern estuary of the Nile. He corresponded with *Cyril of Alexandria during the Third Council of *Ephesus (431). An admirer of the *Cappadocian Fathers and St John *Chrysostom, he led a life of rigorous asceticism, while still staying close to those in the world. Of his large correspondence, which contains much of doctrinal, exegetical, and moral interest, some 2,000 items have survived. Feast day in E., 4 Feb.

Editio princeps by J. Billius (Paris, 1585). Later edns. by C. Rittershaus (Heidelberg, 1605) and A. Schott (Antwerp, 1623); a combination of these two edns. was issued by A. Morel (Paris, 1638); repr., with notes from a work by J. Possinus (Rome, 1670), in J. P. Migne, PG 78. 103–1674. Crit. edn., with Fr. tr., by P. Évieux (SC, 422, etc.; 1997 ff.). R. Aigrain (ed.), *Quarante-neuf Lettres de St Isidore de Péluse: Édition critique de l'ancienne version latine contenue dans deux manuscrits du Concile d'Éphèse* (1911). H. A. Niemeyer, *De Isidori Pelusiotae Vita, Scriptis et Doctrina Commentatio Historico-theologica* (Halle, 1825; repr. in PG 78. 9–102). A. Schmid, OSB, *Die Christologie Isidors von Pelusium* (Paradosis, 2; Fribourg, 1948). P. Évieux, *Isidore de Péluse* (Théologie Historique, 99; 1995). Id., 'Isidore de Péluse. La numérotation des lettres dans la tradition manuscrite', *Revue d'Histoire des Textes*, 5 (1975), pp. 45–72. CPG 3 (1979), pp. 82–4 (nos. 5557 f.). Bardenhewer, 4, pp. 100–7; Altaner and Stuiber (1978), pp. 267 f. and 602. J. Quasten, *Patrology*, 3 (Utrecht and Westminster, Md., 1960), pp. 180–5. G. Bareille in DTC 8 (pt. 1; 1924), cols. 84–98; A. M. Ritter in Dict. Sp. 7 (pt. 2; 1971), cols. 2097–103, both s.v.

Isidore, St (*c*.560–636), 'Hispalensis', Bp. of Seville and Metropolitan of Baetica. His earlier life is obscure. His family, of the nobility of Cartagena, fled to Seville in the face of fighting between the Visigoths and the troops of the Byzantine Empire. He was educated either in a monastery or in the episcopal school in the city, under the supervision of his brother, St *Leander, who was a monk before becoming Bp. of Seville *c*.580. Isidore succeeded him as bishop *c*.600. As such he was much concerned with monastic discipline, clerical education, liturgical uniformity, and the conversion of the Jews. He enjoyed close relations with the devout and cultured King Sisebut (612–21) and his successors, and he used his ecclesiastical position to strengthen the unstable Visigothic monarchy with religious sanctions. It may be argued that he evolved the concept of a Spanish Church and united Hispano-Gothic State independent of external authority. He presided over the Second Council of Seville (619) and the important Fourth Council of *Toledo (633), and he is traditionally associated with the development of the *Hispana Collection of conciliar acts. His influence did much to secure the general acceptance of the *Filioque clause in the W. Acc. to his pupil, Braulio, Bp. of Saragossa, he restored tradi-

tions of learning in an increasingly ignorant Spain. He founded a line of clerical scholars in Spain and had a profound impact upon the culture and educational practice of W. medieval Europe. He was canonized in 1598 and in 1722 formally declared a '*Doctor of the Church'. Feast day, 4 April.

His works became a storehouse of knowledge freely utilized by innumerable medieval authors. The most important is the extremely popular 'Etymologiae' or 'Origines', an encyclopedia in 20 books, containing information on the *seven liberal arts and such subjects as medicine, agriculture, geography, architecture, the books and offices of the Church, and other theological matters. It is organized partly on the principle that etymologies usually give information on the things to which the words refer. Derivative and often fanciful, it is impressive overall, and a valuable source for the learning and thought of the time. The 'De Natura Rerum' expounds classical cosmology with Christian allegorical interpretations. The 'Sententiae' is a manual of Christian doctrine and practice which draws freely on St *Augustine and St *Gregory the Great; it is important for its emphasis on the duties of secular authorities. The 'De Ecclesiasticis Officiis' is a useful source for the *Mozarabic liturgy as well as for the duties and rights of the various orders in the Church, both clerical and lay. The 'Synonyma' combines material for spiritual meditation and exhortation with instruction in eloquence. The 'Chronica Maiora', extending from the Creation to AD 615, is largely derivative, but it has original information on the history of Spain. The otherwise jejune 'Historia Gothorum, Vandalorum et Suevorum' is also a primary source for Spanish history, and of interest for its political attitudes. The 'De Viris Illustribus' is a continuation of similar works by St *Jerome and *Gennadius, with special attention to authors of the Spanish and African Churches. Isidore also wrote the 'Differentiae' (on words); 'Proemia', 'De Ortu et Obitu Patrum', 'Liber Numerorum', 'De Nominibus Legis et Evangeliarum', 'De Variis Quaestionibus', all on biblical topics; the 'De Haeresibus', 'Contra Iudaeos', 'Regula Monastica', and some verse. Of the 14 letters attributed to him, only those to Braulio are certainly genuine. Many other works ascribed to him are forgeries or of doubtful authenticity. See also the following entry.

The best, and nearly complete, edn. of his works is that of F. Arevalo [SJ] (7 vols., Rome, 1797–1803), repr. in J. P. Migne, PL 81–4. Further material from other sources in Suppl. 4 (1967), cols. 1801–66. Crit. edns. of his 'Etymologiae' by W. M. Lindsay (2 vols., Oxford, 1911); with Fr. tr., by J. André and others (Auteurs Latins du Moyen Âge, 1981 ff.); and, with Sp. tr., by J. Oroz Reta and M.-A. Marcos Casquero, with important introd. by M. C. Díaz y Díaz (Biblioteca de Autores Cristianos, 433–4; 1982–3); of 'Historia Gothorum' and 'Chronica Maiora' by T. *Mommsen in MGH, Auctores Antiquissimi, 11 (1894), pp. 241–506; of 'De Haeresibus' by A. C. Vega, OSA (Scriptores Ecclesiastici Hispano-Latini Veteris et Medii Aevi, fasc. 5; The Escurial, 1940); of 'De Variis Quaestionibus' by id. and A. E. Anspach (ibid. 6–9; 1940); of 'De Natura Rerum', with Fr. tr., by J. Fontaine (Bibliothèque de l'École des Hautes Études Hispaniques, 28; 1960); of 'De Viris Illustribus' by C. Codoñer Merino (Theses et Studia Philologica Salmanticensia, 12; 1964); of 'Regula Monastica' and 'Sententiae', with Sp. tr., by J. Campos Ruiz and I. Roca Meliá, *Reglas monásticas de la España visigoda* (Biblioteca de Autores Cristianos: Santos Padres Españoles, 2; 1971), pp. 77–125 and 213–525, respectively; of 'De Ortu et Obitu Patrum' by C. Chaparro Gómez (Auteurs Latins du Moyen Âge, 1985); of

'De Ecclesiasticis Officiis' by C. M. Lawson (CCSL 93; 1989); and of 'De Differentiis', I, with Sp. tr., by C. Codoñer [Merino] (Auteurs Latins du Moyen Âge, 1992). Eng. trs. of his 'Historia Gothorum' by G. Donini and G. B. Ford (Leiden, 1966) and by K. B. Wolf, *Conquerors and Chronicles of Early Medieval Spain* (Translated Texts for Historians, 9; Liverpool, 1990), pp. 81–110, and of his Letters by G. B. Ford (Catania, 1966; 2nd edn., Amsterdam, 1970).

E. Brehaut, *An Encyclopedist of the Dark Ages, Isidore of Seville* (Columbia University Studies in History, Economics and Public Law, 48, no. 1; New York, 1912), incl. Eng. tr. of extensive extracts of the 'Etymologiae'; C. H. Beeson, *Isidor-Studien* (Quellen und Untersuchungen zur lateinischen Philologie des Mittelalters, 4, Heft 2; 1913), incl. text of his Poems, pp. 135–66; *Miscellanea Isidoriana: Homenaje a S. Isidoro de Sevilla en el XIII centenario de su muerte* . . . Lo edita la provincia de Andalucia S.I. (Rome, 1936); J. Fontaine, *Isidore de Séville et la Culture Classique dans l'Espagne Wisigothique* (2 vols., 1959 + suppl., 1983); id., 'Théorie et Pratique du Style chez Isidore de Séville', *VC* 14 (1960), pp. 65–101; J. Madoz, 'San Isidoro de Sevilla. Semblanza de su personalidad literaria', *Archivos Leoneses*, 14 (1960), pp. 1–188; M. C. Díaz y Díaz (ed.), *Isidoriana: Estudios sobre San Isidoro de Sevilla en el XIV centenario de su nacimiento* (1961); H.-J. Diesner, *Isidor von Sevilla und das westgotische Spanien* (*Abh.* (Sächs.), 67, Heft 3; 1977); P. Cazier, *Isidore de Séville et la naissance de l'Espagne Catholique* (Théologie Historique, 96 [1994]). M. Reydellet, *La Royauté dans la Littérature Latine de Sidoine Apollinaire à Isidore de Séville* (Bibliothèque des Écoles Françaises d'Athènes et de Rome, 243; 1981), pp. 505–97; J. Herrin, *The Formation of Christendom* (1987), esp. pp. 233–49. *CPL* (3rd edn., 1995), pp. 398–413 (nos. 1186–229a). Manitius, I, pp. 52–70. J. Fontaine in *Dict. Sp.* 7 (pt. 2; 1971), cols. 2104–2116, s.v., with bibl.

Isidore Mercator. The pseudonym adopted by the author of the *False Decretals (q.v.), doubtless to suggest a connection (if not an identity) with St *Isidore of Seville.

Islam (i.e. 'submission', usually understood as submission to the will of God), the religion preached by Muhammad (prob. *c.*570–632), the adherent of which is called a Muslim. Islam is the religion of the majority of the population of the northern half of Africa, the Middle East, Pakistan, Bangladesh, Malaysia, *Indonesia, and Papua-New Guinea. There are substantial Muslim minorities in several European countries, Russia and the successor states of the former USSR in the Caucasus and Central Asia, *India, and *China.

Muslim doctrine is derived from the interpretation of the *Koran (or Qur'ān) and the 'Sunna', i.e. 'established practice', a body of tradition which records the actions and sayings of the Prophet and the first four 'Rightly Guided' caliphs. Muslim law or 'Sharia' derives from the reform by early jurists of existing legal practice in line with the Koran and Sunna. Islam contains Arabian, Jewish, Christian, Gnostic, and other elements, and the extent to which these were incorporated during the lifetime of the Prophet in Arabia or during the subsequent three centuries in the lands of the Arab conquests is a matter of scholarly debate. The central dogmas of Islam are the absolute unity of God (*Allah) and the prophethood of Muhammad. The chief Islamic practices are confession of the unity of God and the mission of Muhammad, ritual prayer practised five times a day, alms-giving, fasting during the month of Ramadan, and pilgrimage to Mecca. Among a wide variety of sects, two main branches stand out. Both the Sunnites

and the Shiites accept the authority of the Sunna, but the Sunnites also recognize the possibility of appeal to the 'Ijma' (i.e. the consensus of believers) and an interpretative tradition which is regarded as having been closed since the 9th cent. and can no longer be added to. The Ijma is represented and interpreted by the 'Ulama' or religious scholars. The Shiites originally comprised those who recognized the sole right to the caliphate of Ali, the nephew and son-in-law of Muhammad (Shiite from Ar. 'Shia Ali', the party of Ali), and they came to believe that the Sunna was not sufficient but must be constantly reinterpreted by an authoritative spokesman of divine will, i.e. Ali and his descendants, the true 'Imam,' or by his representatives or 'Mujtahids'. The number of Imams may be reckoned as seven or twelve according to the sect, and some, including the followers of the Aga Khan, hold that the succession of Imams is perpetual and still operative today. Mysticism plays a large part in Islam, and the 'Sufis' aim, by spiritual and bodily ascesis, at achieving direct apprehension of God and ultimately total submerging of self in the Divine. Since the demise of the Abbasid caliphate in 1258, the Ulama and the Sufis have constituted the main sources of religious authority in Islam.

Islam is seen as the aboriginal religion, from which both Judaism and Christianity are deviations. At several periods of history God has sent prophets, the first of whom was *Adam, and the last Muhammad: *Abraham, *Moses and Jesus are all recognized. God made a covenant with Abraham, awarding his descendants through Hagar's son Ishmael (i.e. the Arabs) the status of a chosen people. Muhammad's mission was to lead the Arabs and, perhaps, all mankind, back to the aboriginal 'religion of Abraham'. In Muslim belief, Jesus, though born of a virgin, is created and not begotten; his crucifixion was only apparent (cf. *Docetism). In the E., Christian writers, e.g. St *John of Damascus, reacted promptly to the rise of Islam with anti-Muslim polemic, but others were conciliatory, e.g. Timothy I (780–823), Patriarch of the *Church of the East, author of so-called *Parable of the Pearl*, a Syriac apology for Christianity in the form of a debate with the Abbasid caliph al-Mahdi (775–85). W. scholars first took an interest in Islam and Arabic learning in 10th-cent. Spain, e.g. Gerbert of Aurillac (*Sylvester II), and in 11th- to 13th-cent. Spain and S. Italy, mathematical, astronomical, and medical texts were translated from Arabic. But it was not until the *Crusades that W. scholars took an interest in Islam itself. The translations of Islamic texts, sponsored by *Peter the Venerable and others, and the commentaries that they provoked constituted the principal source of informed knowledge of Islam. From the 12th cent., Islamic logic and metaphysics, e.g. the writings of *Avempace, *Averroes, and *Avicenna, exercised a profound influence on W. philosophers and theologians, e.g. R. *Bacon and St *Thomas Aquinas, and the universities of *Bologna, *Oxford, *Paris, Rome, and Salamanca all had chairs of Arabic. During the Renaissance, with the rise of the Ottoman empire and its expansion into Europe, this peaceable interest waned.

The Arab conquests of the 7th–8th cent. subjected large communities of Christians (and Jews) to Muslim rule. Unlike pagans, they were recognized as 'people of the book' and incorporated into the Muslim State as 'dhimmis', who in return for payment of the 'jizya', part tribute and part penal tax, were awarded protected status and permitted to retain their own religion and laws. The dhimmis have usually suffered a varying degree of fiscal, legal, and social oppression, and more rarely violent persecution. The survival of the E. Churches under Muslim rule attests to the success of this regime, and contrasts with the failure of medieval Christian Spain and Sicily to incorporate their subject communities of Muslims. Modern Arab states have usually treated Christian minorities with a tolerance predicated on the equality of all religions, but this is threatened by the recent upsurge of revivalist Islam and the return of sharia law, e.g. in Iran and *Sudan.

Christian missions have never had a significant impact upon Islam. In the 13th cent., the *Mendicant Orders organized missions to Islam, and St *Francis preached to the Ayyubid sultan al-Kamil in 1219. In modern times missionary activity has been resumed by both Protestant and RC bodies. See also THEOLOGY OF RELIGIONS.

M. G. S. Hodgson, *The Venture of Islam* (3 vols., Chicago and London [1974]); P. M. Holt and others (eds.), *The Cambridge History of Islam* (2 vols, Cambridge, 1970); A. Hourani, *A History of the Arab Peoples* (1991); I. M. Lapidus, *A History of Islamic Societies* (Cambridge, 1988). *The Encyclopaedia of Islam* (ed. M. T. Houtsma and others, 4 vols and suppl., Leiden, 1913–38; 2nd edn., ed. H. A. R. Gibb and others, 1960 ff.). R. Roolvink, *Historical Atlas of the Muslim Peoples* (Amsterdam, 1957); F. [C. R.] Robinson, *Atlas of the Islamic World since 1500* (Oxford [1982]). M. Ruthven, *Islam in the World* (Harmondsworth, 1984); F. Rahman, *Islam* (1966; 2nd edn., Chicago, 1979); L. Gardet, *L'Islam: Religion et communauté* (1967). I. Goldziher, *Muhammedanische Studien* (2 vols., 1889–90; Eng. tr., 1967–71); J. Schacht, *An Introduction to Islamic Law* (Oxford, 1964); H. Laoust, *Les Schismes dans l'Islam* (Bibliothèque historique, 1965). A. Schimmel, *The Mystical Dimensions of Islam* (Chapel Hill, NC, 1975); G.-C. Anawati and L. Gardet, *Mystique musulmane* (Études musulmanes, 8; 1961); J. S. Trimingham, *The Sufi Orders in Islam* (Oxford, 1971). M. Cook, *Muhammad* (Past Masters; Oxford, 1983); W. M. Watt, *Muhammad, Prophet and Statesman* (1961). The Patr. Timothy's 'Parable of the Pearl' is pr. (facsimile of the Syriac text), with Eng. tr. and introd., by A. Mingana and J. R. *Harris in *Bulletin of the John Rylands Library*, 12 (1928), pp. 137–298. T. Andrae, *Les Origines de l'Islam et le Christianisme*, tr. J. Roche, from a series of arts. which appeared 1923–5 (Initiation à l'Islam, 8; 1955); R. Bell, *The Origin of Islam in its Christian Environment* (1926); H. Speyer, *Die biblischen Erzählungen im Qoran* (Gräfenhainichen, 1931; repr. Hildesheim, 1961). N. Daniel, *Islam and the West: The Making of an Image* (Edinburgh, 1960); id., *The Arabs and Mediaeval Europe* (1975; 2nd edn., 1979); R. W. Southern, *Western Views of Islam in the Middle Ages* (Cambridge, Mass., 1962). B. Z. Kedar, *Crusade and Mission: European Approaches toward the Muslims* (Princeton, NJ [1984]); A. Hourani, *Islam in European Thought* (Cambridge, 1991). A. S. Tritton, *The Caliphs and their Non-Muslim Subjects* (1930); B. Ye'or, *Le Dhimmi: Profil de l'opprimé en Orient et en Afrique du Nord depuis la conquête arabe* (1980: rev. Eng. tr. [1985]).

Israel. The Hebrew nation, thought of as descending from the Patriarch Israel (*Jacob). Acc. to Gen. 32: 28, the name Israel was bestowed upon Jacob by the mysterious divine stranger with whom he wrestled at Peniel; and it is frequently used of Jacob from this point in the narrative. The twelve tribes of Israel bore the names of the twelve sons of Jacob/Israel (cf. Gen. 49). In their history of the period of the Monarchy the biblical writers normally applied the word Israel (esp. in contrast to '*Judah') to the *ten northern tribes, i.e. to those which attached themselves to Jeroboam I on the death of *Solomon (c. 930 BC) and were carried away to Assyria two cents. later (c.721 BC). (The name is already found on the *Moabite Stone, c.850 BC). In a theological sense, the word Israel was used of the people of Yahweh as a whole (including the South as well as the North), esp. in their covenant-relation to their God. In the NT it was transferred to the Christian Church, considered as the 'Israel of God' (Gal. 6: 16) and spoken of as inheriting the privileges of the ancient Israel.

The modern Jewish State established in the Holy Land in 1948 bears the name Israel.

M. *Noth, *Geschichte Israels* (Göttingen, 1950; 2nd edn., 1954; Eng. tr., 2nd edn., 1960); J. Bright, *A History of Israel* (1960; 3rd edn., 1981); R. de Vaux, OP, *Histoire ancienne d'Israel* (Études Bibliques, 2 vols. only, out of 3 projected, 1971–3; Eng. tr., 2 vols., 1978); S. Herrmann, *Geschichte Israels in alttestamentlicher Zeit* (Munich, 1973; 2nd edn., 1980; Eng. tr., 1975; 2nd edn., 1981). E. P. Sanders, *Paul and Palestinian Judaism: A Comparison of Patterns of Religion* (1977). N. P. Lemche and others in *Anchor Bible Dictionary*, 3 (1992), pp. 526–76, s.v. 'Israel, History of', with bibl.

Issy, Articles of (1695). The 34 articles drawn up at Issy (the summer residence of the Society of *Saint-Sulpice), near Paris, which condemned certain *Quietist teachings. The commission was assembled by J. B. *Bossuet in response to a request from Mme *Guyon (who wanted to be cleared of suspicion of heresy), supported by F. *Fénelon. Mme Guyon and Fénelon both submitted works which were examined by the commission. Thirty articles were drawn up, to which four others were added, with some minor concessions to Fénelon, by then nominated Abp. of Cambrai. The first articles stated undisputed points of doctrine. The crucial ones dealt with the Quietist conception of pure love, without concern for one's own salvation, with the nature of contemplation, and with passive, non-discursive prayer, directly inspired without recourse to reasoning. The articles were signed by Bossuet, Fénelon and Mme Guyon, but a prolonged literary feud between Bossuet and Fénelon culminated in the condemnation in 1699 of 23 propositions from Fénelon's *Explication des Maximes des Saints sur la Vie Intérieure*.

Text pr. among J. B. Bossuet's *Œuvres*, 27 (Versailles, 1817), pp. 12–22. E. Levesque, 'Les Conférences d'Issy sur les États d'Oraison. Bossuet et Fénelon', *Revue Bossuet*, 6 (1905), pp. 176–203, with 'Premières explications donneés par Fénelon de son dissentiment avec Bossuet', pp. 204–20. L. Cognet, *Crépuscule des Mystiques* (Tournai [1958]), pp. 221–302, esp. pp. 278–302. R. A. *Knox, *Enthusiasm* (1950), pp. 341 f. A. Largent in *DTC* 6 (1913), cols. 2146–50, s.v. 'Fénelon', with text of articles repr., cols. 2146–9. See also bibl. to BOSSUET, FÉNELON, GUYON, and QUIETISM.

Istanbul. See CONSTANTINOPLE.

Itala (Lat., 'Italian (version)'). A name sometimes given in the past, esp. by German scholars, to the *Old Latin (pre-*Vulgate) text of the Bible (q.v.). The term derives from a passage in St *Augustine (*Doctr. Christ.* 2. 22), where he commends the 'Itala' as the best 'interpretation' (i.e. version or recension) among those current in his day. In this its original context it probably refers to a European form of the Old Latin, though a variety of other explanations have been given (e.g. by F. C. *Burkitt, who equated it with the Vulgate).

F. C. Burkitt, *The Old Latin and the Itala* (Texts and Studies, ed. J. A. *Robinson, 4, no. 3; 1896), pp. 55–78; id., 'St Augustine's Bible and the *Itala*', *JTS* 11 (1910), pp. 258–68 and 447–58. L. Ziegler, *Die lateinischen Bibelübersetzungen vor Hieronymus und die Itala des Augustinus* (1879). B. M. Metzger, *The Early Versions of the New Testament* (Oxford, 1977), pp. 290–93. B. Botte, OSB, in *Dict. Bibl.*, Suppl. 4 (1949), cols. 777–82, s.v.

Italo-Greeks. The extant Greek communities descended from (1) Greek settlements in Sicily and S. Italy in Byzantine times, (2) later Greek colonies established in Italian seaports, and (3) Greek and Albanian refugees from the Muslim invasion. Their ecclesiastical status is *Uniat, their rite and usages being Byzantine with some Roman modifications. The abbey of *Grottaferrata is an Italo-Greek monastery, which, however, has its own rite.

M. Petta in *NCE* 7 (1967), pp. 747–51, s.v. 'Italo-Albanian Rite', with bibl.

Ite, missa est. The concluding formula of the Roman Mass. The word *missa* is the Low Latin form of *missio*, 'dismissal', and the meaning of the formula is 'Go, you are dismissed'. During the Middle Ages it became customary to add a blessing and to restrict the use of the *Ite, missa est* to Masses at which the *Gloria in excelsis* was recited. In 1967 its use was restored at all Masses except those for the dead when the commendation followed immediately; since 1969 it has been omitted when any other liturgical function follows. Where used, it now follows the blessing.

T. Michels, OSB, *Ite Missa Est. Deo Gratias* (Per Hanc Lucis Viam, 8; Salzburg, 1929). F. Dölger, 'Zu den Zeremonien der Messliturgie. III. *Ite missa est* in kultur- und sprachgeschichtlicher Beleuchtung', *Antike und Christentum*, 6 (1940), pp. 81–132. B. Botte, OSB, 'Ite Missa Est', in id. and C. Mohrmann, *L'Ordinaire de la Messe* (Études liturgiques, 2; 1953), pp. 145–9; C. Mohrmann, 'Missa', *VC* 12 (1958), pp. 67–92. Jungmann (1958 edn.), 2, pp. 535–41 and 595–7; Eng. tr., 2, pp. 432–7.

Itinerarium. A brief office formerly included in the *Breviary and prescribed for recitation by clerics about to set out on a journey. The prayers and the use of the *Benedictus (Lk. 1: 68–79) suggest that it originated in a blessing of pilgrims setting out for the Holy Places in Palestine.

Ives, St (? 7th cent.). Ostensibly, a British bishop of Persian birth. Acc. to the account written by *Goscelin between 1087 and 1091, Ives came to Great Britain from Persia via Rome, and with three companions preached Christianity in Cambridgeshire. His cult began when his alleged bones were discovered at St Ives in that county in 1001. His tomb was reopened at the beginning of the 12th cent. He is commemorated on 24 Apr. and 10 June. The town of St Ives in Cornwall seems to be named after another saint (a maiden, also known as St Ia, Hia, or Iva) of whom the extant legends seem equally unhistorical. Her feast day is 1 Feb.

Goscelin's *vita* is pr. in *AASS*, Jun. 2 (1698), pp. 288–92, repr. in *PL* 155. 79–90, but the text is defective; his *miracula*, augmented in the reign of Henry I, are pr. by W. D. Macray, *Chronicon abbatiae Rameseiensis* (RS 83; 1886), pp. lix–lxxxiv. The MSS are Bodley 285, fols. 99–111, and Dublin, Trinity College MS 171 (B. 1. 16), pp. 230–50. G. H. Doble, 'Saint Ivo, Bishop and Confessor, Patron of the Town of St. Ives', *Laudate*, 12 (1934), pp. 149–56. C. Hole in *DCB* 3 (1882), pp. 324 f., s.v. 'Ivo, St'. On the Saint after whom St Ives in Cornwall is named, see *AASS*, Oct. 12 (1867), pp. 293–6, with refs.; G. H. Doble, *Saint Euny . . . with St Ya and St Erc* (Cornish Saints Series, 2; c.1924), pp. 18–23; L. Gougaud, OSB, *Les Saints irlandais hors d'Irlande* (Bibliothèque de la *Revue d'Histoire ecclésiastique*, 16; 1934), pp. 83 f. C. W. Boase in *DCB* 3 (1882), p. 23, s.v. 'Hia'.

Ivo, St (*c.*1040–1115), Bp. of *Chartres (hence **Carnotensis**). Educated at Paris and (under *Lanfranc) at *Bec, he became prior of the *canons regular of St-Quentin at Beauvais by 1079 and Bp. of Chartres in 1090. His courageous opposition to the adulterous intentions of King Philip I led to his imprisonment in 1092. The most learned canonist of his age, his three treatises, the *Collectio Tripartita*, the *Decretum* (in 17 books), and esp. the *Panormia* (in 8 books), exercised a determining influence on the development of canon law. Special importance attaches to the principles of the interpretation of canon law, laid down in the 'Prologus' attached to the *Decretum*, and to his teaching on dispensation. A large collection of his letters has survived which throws much light on the ecclesiastical and religious issues of his age, as well as 25 of his sermons. In the *Investiture struggle, in which he took a prominent part, he advocated moderation. Feast day, 20 or 23 May.

The *Panormia* was first pr. [ed. S. Brant] at Basle, 1499; the *Decretum*, ed. J. Molin, at Louvain, 1561; the *Collectio Tripartita* has not been pub.; cf. A. Theiner, repr. in J. P. Migne, *PL* 161, cols. li–lxxxviii. Collected edn. of his other works by J. Fronteau, with brief Life (no pagination), Paris, 1647; repr., with further notes, in J. P. Migne, *PL* 161 and 162. Crit. edn. of his correspondence with Fr. tr., by J. Leclercq, OSB, 1 (1090–8; Les Classiques de l'histoire de France au moyen âge, 1949 [no more pub.]). P. Fournier, 'Les Collections canoniques attribuées à Yves de Chartres', *Bibliothèque de l'École des Chartes*, 57 (1896), pp. 645–98; 58 (1897), pp. 26–77, 410–44, 624–76; P. Fournier and G. Le Bras, *Histoire des collections canoniques en occident*, 2 (1932), pp. 55–114. H. Hoffman, 'Ivo von Chartres und die Lösung des Investiturproblems', *Deutsches Archiv*, 15 (1959), pp. 393–440. R. Sprandel, *Ivo von Chartres und seine Stellung in der Kirchengeschichte* (Pariser Historische Studien, 1; Stuttgart, 1962), with full bibl. P. Landau, 'Die Rubriken und Inskriptionen von Ivos Panormie', *Bulletin of Medieval Canon Law*, NS 12 (1982), pp. 31–49; id., 'Das Dekret des Ivo von Chartres', *Zeitschrift der Savigny-Stiftung für Rechtsgeschichte*, Kanonistische Abteilung, 70 (1984), pp. 1–44. E. Amann and L. Guizard in *DTC* 15 (pt. 2; 1950), cols. 3625–40, s.v. 'Yves de Chartres', with full refs. (but confuse him with the later Master Ivo of Chartres, the author of the gloss on the Psalms; cf. B. Smalley in *EHR* 50 (1935), pp. 680–6); C. Munier in *Dict. Sp.* 16 (1994), cols. 1551–64, s.v. 'Yves (1) de Chartres'.

Iznik. The modern name of the ancient *Nicaea, now little more than a village.

J

'J'. A symbol widely used by scholars who follow the 'documentary hypothesis' of the origins of the *Pentateuch; it denotes the Jahvistic (Yahwistic or Jehovistic) source. This consists largely of narrative, beginning with the story of *Adam and *Eve (Gen. 2: 4b ff.) and including, in conjunction with 'E' (q.v.), most of the famous stories of the Patriarchs and the Exodus. It is distinguished from the later sources, 'D' and 'P' (qq.v.), by its simple narrative style and *anthropomorphism (e.g. Gen. 3: 8), and from 'E' (and also from 'P') by its use of the divine name *Yahweh (*Jehovah; 'the LORD' in AV and RV) from the first, even before its revelation to Moses in Ex. 3: 14 f. Where this criterion is absent, 'J' cannot always be certainly distinguished from 'E', with which it may have been combined in one cycle of stories before the date of 'D' (7th cent. BC). It is commonly thought to embody the traditions current in the Southern Kingdom of Judah; it is usually dated under the early monarchy (perhaps 9th cent. BC).

For bibl. see PENTATEUCH.

Jabneh. See JAMNIA.

Jackson, Thomas (1579–1640), *Anglican theologian. He was educated at Queen's and Corpus Christi Colleges, Oxford, and resided at Oxford for several years studying and teaching theology. Presentation to the living of St Nicholas, Newcastle-upon-Tyne, in 1623 did not seriously interrupt his work at Oxford. In 1630 he became president of Corpus and in 1639 Dean of *Peterborough. Although originally of *Puritan sympathies, he soon became identified with the *High Church party of Richard Neile, Bp. of *Durham (later Abp. of *York) and of W. *Laud; his great learning and theological ability made him one of the most widely esteemed of Caroline divines down to the middle of the 19th cent. His principal work, *Commentaries upon the Apostles' Creed*, was arranged in twelve Books, of which nine had appeared before his death (1613–38). The first complete edition of all 12 books was in his *Collected Works* (3 vols., 1672–3). Jackson was also the author of several volumes of sermons and of a tract against the Puritans.

The last collected edn. of Jackson's works was issued at Oxford (12 vols., 1844). N. Tyacke, *Anti-Calvinists: The Rise of English Arminianism c.1590–1640* (Oxford, 1987), esp. pp. 7, 65–7, 83 f., 120 f., 142–4, and 159 f.; S. Hutton, 'Thomas Jackson, Oxford Platonist, and William Twisse, Aristotelian', *Journal of the History of Ideas*, 39 (1978), pp. 635–52. E. T. Bradley in *DNB* 29 (1892), pp. 107 f.

Jacob, OT *Patriarch. The story of Jacob, the son of *Isaac and grandson of *Abraham, is told in Gen. 25–50. After depriving his brother Esau of his birthright by an elaborate ruse, he fled to his mother's brother, Laban, who lived at Haran in Mesopotamia. On the journey, at *Bethel, he received a vision of angels of God ascending and descending on a ladder reaching up to heaven, in which God promised him blessing and posterity (Gen. 28: 10–22). In Mesopotamia, Jacob served Laban for 20 years, married his two daughters, Leah and Rachel, and prospered greatly. On his way back to Canaan, at Peniel, by the brook Jabbok, he wrestled with a mysterious Divine stranger, who gave him the name of '*Israel' (Gen. 32). Towards the end of his life, during a period of famine, he received news that his favourite son, Joseph, whom he had supposed killed by wild beasts, had become a great man in Egypt, and at his invitation Jacob and all his family 'went down into Egypt' (Gen. 46; cf. Deut 26: 5). Jacob died in Egypt, but had made Joseph promise to take his body back to the burying-place of his ancestors (Gen. 50). The twelve tribes of Israel bore the names of the twelve sons of Jacob.

Acc. to legend, the stone of *Scone beneath the sovereign's coronation chair in *Westminster Abbey is that which served as Jacob's pillow at Bethel (Gen. 28: 11 and 18).

See comm. to GENESIS, cited s.v.

Jacob Baradaeus (*c*.500–78), after whom the nickname 'Jacobite' was given to the *Syrian Orthodox Church. He was born in Tella and educated at the monastery of Phesilta, near Nisibis. He spent 15 years in *Constantinople, where he was welcomed by the Emp. *Theodora. In about 542, when the *Monophysite king of the Ghassanids asked for a bishop, Jacob was secretly consecrated Bp. of *Edessa. He spent the rest of his life travelling around, clandestinely ordaining clergy and helping to establish a separate hierarchy; his disguise as a beggar gave rise to the epithet 'Baradaios' (from Syriac *burdʿānā*, 'of the saddle-cloth', *sc.* cloak). Several of his letters survive. An anaphora and a profession of faith are ascribed to him, prob. incorrectly. Feast day in the Syrian Orthodox Church, 31 July. See also SYRIAN ORTHODOX CHURCH.

Syriac Life in *John of Ephesus, 'Lives of the Eastern Saints', chs. 49–50, ed., with Eng. tr., by E. W. Brooks in *PO* 18 (1924), pp. 690–7, and 19 (1926), pp. 153–8 [the text in *PO* 19 (1926), pp. 228–68, is not authentic]. E. Honigmann, *Évêques et évêchés monophysites d'Asie antérieure au VIᵉ siècle* (CSCO 127; 1951), pp. 157–77. A. *Baumstark, *Geschichte der syrischen Literatur* (1922), pp. 174 f. D. D. Bundy, 'Jacob Baradaeus. The state of research, a review of sources and a new approach', *Le Muséon*, 91 (1978), pp. 45–86. E. Venables in *DCB* 3 (1882), pp. 328–32, s.v. 'Jacobus (15)'.

Jacob of Edessa (*c*.640–708), *Syrian Orthodox scholar and exegete. In 684 he became Bp. of *Edessa, but after less than five years he withdrew from his see owing to the refusal of his flock to accept certain reforms. Subsequently he lived in monasteries at Kaisum and Tell 'Ada. He was one of the most learned men of his time, and knew some Hebrew as well as Greek. He produced a revision of some books of the *Peshitta OT, using both the LXX and the

*Syro-Hexapla. His own writings include a treatise on grammar, a continuation of *Eusebius' Chronicle down to AD 692, a 'Hexaemeron' (completed by *George, Bp. of the Arabians), and many *scholia on the Bible. He also translated and annotated some of the works of *Severus of Antioch, including his hymns and his Ὁμιλίαι ἐπιθρόνιοι. Of his many letters on liturgical and other subjects, only a small proportion have survived. Feast day in the Syrian Orthodox Church, 31 May.

His principal writings (many still unpub.) are listed in A. *Baumstark, Geschichte der syrischen Literatur (1922), pp. 248–56, with notes of edns. to date. Crit. edn. of his 'Hexaemeron' by I. B. Chabot and A. Vaschalde (CSCO, Scriptores Syri, Series Secunda, 56; 1928; with Lat. tr. by A. Vaschalde, ibid., 1932); also of his tr. of hymns by Severus of Antioch and others, with Eng. tr., by E. W. Brooks in PO 6 (1911), pp. 5–179 (fasc. 1); 7 (1911), pp. 592–805 (fasc. 5); for edns. of his tr. of Severus' Ὁμιλίαι ἐπιθρόνιοι, see s.v. SEVERUS OF ANTIOCH. C. Kayser, Die Canones Jacob's von Edessa (Leipzig, 1886) [Ger. tr. and comm.], with introd. on his life and works, pp. 48–78. 'Discourse on the Myron' [or *Chrism], ed., with Eng. tr., by S. [P.] Brock in OC 63 (1979), pp. 20–36. I. Ortiz de Urbina, SJ, Patrologia Syriaca (2nd edn., Rome, 1965), pp. 177–83. E. Tisserant in DTC 8 (pt. 1; 1924), cols. 286–91, s.v.; F. Graffin, SJ, in Dict. Sp. 8 (1974), cols. 33–5, both s.v. 'Jacques d'Édesse'.

Jacob of Nisibis, St (d. 338), the 'Moses of Mesopotamia', Bp. of Nisibis. He was always a prominent figure in Syriac Church tradition, and in later times acquired a reputation for great learning, ability, and holiness; but beyond his presence at the Council of *Nicaea (325), where acc. to *Theodoret he took a leading part in opposing *Arius, little about him is beyond dispute, and Theodoret's account contains many anachronisms. He is still honoured, esp. as a theological doctor, by both *Syrians and *Armenians. His relics, saved from the oncoming Persians, finally reached Constantinople c.970. The Armenian translation of *Aphrahat's Demonstrations was wrongly ascribed to Jacob. Feast day, 15 July.

*Gennadius, De Viris Illustribus, 1 [PL 58, 1060 f.; ascribing to Jacob certain works of Aphrahat]. P. Peeters, SJ, 'La Légende de saint Jacques de Nisibe', Anal. Boll. 38 (1920), pp. 285–373. P. Krüger, 'Jakob von Nisibis in syrischer und armenischer Überlieferung', Muséon, 81 (1968), pp. 161–79. A. Vööbus, History of Asceticism in the Syrian Orient, 1 (CSCO 184; 1958), esp. pp. 141–3. D. Bundy, 'Jacob of Nisibis as a model for the episcopacy', Muséon, 104 (1991), pp. 235–49. E. Tisserant in DTC 8 (pt. 1; 1924), pp. 292–5, s.v. 'Jacques de Nisibe'; J.-M. Sauget in Bibliotheca Sanctorum, 6 (1965), cols. 411 f., s.v. 'Giacomo, vescovo di Nisibi'.

Jacob of Sarug (or more properly **Serugh**) (c.451–521), Syriac ecclesiastical writer. After education at *Edessa, he was ordained to the priesthood, and during the severe sufferings of his countrymen at the hands of the Persians, did much to encourage his people. In 519 he became Bp. of Batnae, the chief town of Sarug in Osrhoene, but died shortly afterwards. His principal writing was a long series of metrical homilies, most of them on biblical themes and written in a dodecasyllabic metre, which earned him the title of 'The Flute of the Holy Spirit'. He was also the author of some prose homilies and several letters; some hymns and three anaphoras are ascribed to him. His doctrinal position has been a subject of dispute in modern times. Older scholars, such as J. S. *Assemani, considered

him to be orthodox, but since the publication of his letters to the monks of the monastery of Mar-Bassus, near Apamea, most scholars (though not P. Peeters) have seen him as disapproving of all *Dyophysite Christology. Many of his homilies remain unpublished and only a few of his works have been translated. Feast day in the Syrian Orthodox Church, 29 Nov.

Homiliae Selectae, ed. P. Bedjan (5 vols., Paris, 1905–10; Syr. text only). Epp. ed. G. Olinder (CSCO, Scriptores Syri, 57; 1937). Verse homilies against the Jews ed., with Fr. tr., by M. Albert in PO 38 (1976–77), pp. 3–242; six prose homilies ed., with Fr. tr., by F. Rilliet, ibid. 43 (1986), pp. 513–663. S. Euringer, Die äthiopischen Anaphoren . . . des hl. Jacobus von Sarug (Orientalia Christiana, 33, no. 1 (1934), pp. 79–122). 'Anaphora Syriaca Iacobi Sarugensis, prima, secunda, tertia' ed., with Eng. tr., by H. W. Codrington, in Anaphorae Syriacae, 2, fasc. 1 (Rome, 1951), pp. 1–83. Ital. tr. of his Mariological sermons, with introd. and comm., by C. Vona (Lateranum, NS 19, nos. 1–4; 1953). Fr. tr. of several of his homilies and other material in L'Orient Syrien, 2–12 (1957–67), passim. P. Peeters, SJ, 'Jacques de Saroug, appartient-il à la secte monophysite? [No!]', Anal. Boll. 66 (1948), pp. 134–98. T. Jansma, 'Die Christologie Jakobs von Serugh und ihre Abhängigkeit von der alexandrinischen Theologie und der Frömmigkeit Ephraems des Syrers', Muséon, 78 (1965), pp. 5–46. A. Vööbus, Handschriftliche Überlieferung der Mēmrē-Dichtung der Ja'qōb von Serūg (CSCO, Subsidia, 39, 40, 60, and 61; 1973–80). A. *Baumstark, Geschichte der syrischen Literatur (1922), pp. 148–58; I. Ortiz de Urbina, SJ, Patrologia Syriaca (2nd edn., Rome, 1965), pp. 104–9. E. Tisserant in DTC 8 (pt. 1; 1924), cols. 300–5; F. Graffin, SJ, in Dict. Sp. 8 (1974), cols. 56–60, both s.v. 'Jacques de Saroug'.

Jacob of Voragine. See JAMES OF VORAGINE.

Jacobins. A name given originally to the *Dominican friars in France, from the fact that their first house in the north of France was established at Paris in 1218 in the rue St-Jacques. In 1789 this house was acquired by the revolutionary political club which thence assumed the name Jacobins.

Jacobites. An alternative name for the *Syrian Orthodox (q.v.). It derives from *Jacob Baradaeus, who in the mid-6th cent. was instrumental in building up a separate (*Monophysite) hierarchy in Syria, alongside that of the official Church which accepted the *Chalcedonian teaching on the Person of Christ. The term first appears c.600 and remains in popular use in some quarters.

Jacobson, William (1803–84) Bp. of *Chester. After being brought up a Nonconformist, he was elected a scholar of Lincoln College, Oxford, in 1825 and held various other appointments in Oxford, until he became Regius Professor of Divinity in 1848. In 1865 he was appointed Bp. of Chester. One of the more learned patristic scholars of his day, he issued a scholarly edition of the *Apostolic Fathers (2 vols., 1838, and later edns.) based on a study of the MSS, in which against W. *Cureton he upheld the genuineness of the now generally acknowledged seven Epistles of St *Ignatius. He also published an edition of the writings of R. *Sanderson, Bp. of *Lincoln (6 vols., 1854). Theologically, from his undergraduate days onwards, he was an old-fashioned *High Churchman.

For a good sketch of him as 'The Single-Minded Bishop' see J. W. *Burgon, *Lives of Twelve Good Men* (1888), 2, pp. 238–303. W. Hunt in *DNB* 29 (1892), pp. 124 f.

Jacobus. See JACOB, and also JAMES.

Jacopone da Todi (Jacopo Benedetti) (*c.*1230–1306), *Franciscan poet. The relatively late date of the records raises some uncertainty about the facts of his life, but the following account seems probable. After studying law, perhaps at *Bologna, and living for some years a worldly life, he was converted on the death of his wife in 1268 and scandalized his friends by becoming a 'Christian Diogenes'. About 1278 he became a Franciscan lay-brother and in 1294 he and some of his brethren were granted permission by *Celestine V to live in a separate community, in order to observe the rule of the order in its original strictness. This decision, however, was reversed by *Boniface VIII on his accession in 1298, and Jacopone as one of the *Spirituals was imprisoned till 1303. He wrote many exquisite and deeply devotional poems (*Laude*) in Latin and in the Umbrian dialect. These have traditionally, but prob. mistakenly, been thought to include the *Stabat Mater*. His outstanding austerities and the fame of his mystical poems would probably have induced his canonization but for his satirical attacks upon Boniface VIII. There is a local cultus at Todi. Feast day, 25 Dec.

Editio princeps of the 'Laude' by F. Bonaccorsi (Florence, 1490), repr., with introd., by G. Ferri (Rome, 1910). Improved edn., together with his short Latin treatise and a number of sayings taken down by his admirers, ed. F. Ageno (Florence, 1953). Crit. edn. of 'Laude' by F. Mancini (Scrittori d'Italia, 257; Bari, 1974). Eng. tr. by S. and E. Hughes (Classics of Western Spirituality, 1982). Italian text with an earlier Eng. tr. of a selection of the 'Laude' by Mrs T. Beck appended to E. *Underhill, *Jacopone da Todi, Poet and Mystic* (1919), pp. 249–501. R. Bettarini, *Jacopone e il Laudario Urbinate* (Florence [1969]). G. T. Peck, *The Fool of God: Jacopone da Todi* (University, Ala., 1980). The many other studies include A. d'Ancona, *Jacopone da Todi, il Giullare di Dio del secolo XIII* (Todi, 1914); M. Casella, 'Jacopone da Todi', *Archivum Romanicum*, 4 (1920), pp. 281–339, 429–85; N. Sapegno, *Frate Jacopone* (Turin, 1926); *Iacopone e il suo tempo: Convegni del Centro di Studi sulla spiritualità medievale*, 1, *13–15 ottobre 1957* (Todi, 1959); and E. Menstò (ed.), *Atti del Convegno Storico Iacoponico in occasione del 750° anniversario della nascita di Iacopone da Todi, Todi, 29–30 novembre 1980* (Florence, 1981). Raby, pp. 429–39 and 484 (bibl.).

Jahweh. See TETRAGRAMMATON.

Jairus. A Galilaean 'ruler of the synagogue' (ἀρχισυνάγωγος) whose young daughter Christ restored to life (Mk. 5: 21–43).

James. The normal English form of Lat. *Jacobus*, Gk. Ἰάκωβος, representing the declinable form of the Hebrew name which is transliterated directly into English as 'Jacob'. In English versions of the Bible the form 'Jacob' is retained in the OT and in those passages of the NT which refer to the OT patriarch (Gk. Ἰακώβ; Lat. *Jacob*, indeclinable). See also following entries.

James, St, 'the Lord's brother' (Mk. 6: 3 and parallels). The natural interpretation of the NT evidence would imply that he was the son of the BVM and St *Joseph, but for other possibilities see BRETHREN OF THE LORD. From 1 Cor. 15: 7 it appears that he was granted a special appearance of the Lord after the Resurrection. From an early date he was, with St *Peter, a leader of the Church at Jerusalem (e.g. Gal. 1: 19), and from the time when Peter left Jerusalem after Herod's attempt to kill him (Acts 12), James appears as the principal authority, who presided at the council of Jerusalem recorded in Acts 15. Acc. to *Clement of Alexandria, as reported by *Eusebius (*HE* 2. 1), he was chosen 'bishop of Jerusalem'. On the basis of Gal. 1: 19 it has been argued that he was an Apostle, and he has been identified with the son of Alphaeus (see JAMES THE LESS); both Clement and *Hegesippus describe him as 'James the Just'. Acc. to Hegesippus (ap. Eusebius, *HE* 2. 23) he was put to death by the Sanhedrin in AD 62. Among Jewish Christians he was held in high repute, and elaborate stories of his sanctity are reported by Hegesippus. The (fictitious) 'Clementine Homilies' and 'Recognitions', prob. 3rd-cent. Judaistic writings, purport to be addressed to him, while the apocryphal Infancy Gospel known as the 'Book of James' is ascribed to him, as is also the Gnostic 'Apocryphal Epistle of James' (qq.v.). Feast day in E., 23 Oct.; also in the American BCP (1979). See also JAMES, APOCALYPSES OF; JAMES, BOOK OF; JAMES, EPISTLE OF ST; JAMES, LITURGY OF ST.

W. Patrick, *James, the Lord's Brother* (1906). W. Pratscher, *Der Herrenbruder Jakobus und die Jakobustradition* (Forschungen zur Religion und Literatur des Alten und Neuen Testaments, 139; 1987). See also bibl. to BRETHREN OF THE LORD.

James, St, 'the Great', Apostle. He was a son of Zebedee, elder brother of St *John, and with St *Peter and John he belonged to the privileged group of disciples who were present at the raising of Jairus' daughter (Mk. 5: 37), the *Transfiguration, and the Agony in *Gethsemane. James and John, acc. to Mk. 3: 17, were named '*Boanerges, that is Sons of Thunder' by the Lord, perhaps because of their ardent zeal (cf. Lk. 9: 54 and Mk. 10: 37). James was the first of the Twelve to suffer martyrdom, being beheaded by *Herod Agrippa I in AD 44 (Acts 12: 2).

Since the 7th cent. it has been alleged that before his martyrdom he preached in *Spain, but the tradition of the early Church, acc. to which the Apostles did not leave Jerusalem till after his death, as well as Rom. 15: 20 and 24, are against the authenticity of this story, which is now almost universally abandoned. Acc. to a Spanish tradition (not older than the 9th cent.), the body of St James was translated to Santiago de *Compostela (q.v.). In the Middle Ages St James was one of the most popular Spanish saints, whose patronage was invoked esp. against the Muslims. Feast day in E., 30 Apr.; in W., 25 July.

AASS, Jul. 6 (1729), pp. 5–124. Gk. text of his *acta* (prob. 8th cent.) ed. J. Ebersolt (Paris, 1902). On the origins of the Spanish cult of St James, R. A. Fletcher, *Saint James's Catapult* (Oxford, 1984), pp. 53–77.

James, St, 'the Less'. The title derives from the description of 'James the less' (Gk. ὁ μικρός) in Mk. 15: 40, but is commonly applied to James, the son of Alphaeus (Mk. 3: 18 etc.), one of the Twelve Apostles, who is thus identified with the James of Mk. 15: 40. There is, however, no sufficient reason for the identification, and the epithet is prob. attached to the Apostle only as a convenient way of distinguishing him from James 'the Great' (see previous entry). Unless (as is unlikely) the tradition which identifies the Apostle with *James, 'the Lord's brother' is correct, nothing further is known of him. Feast day of the Apostle in the E., 9 Oct.; in the W., with the Apostle St *Philip, formerly 1 May and still so in the BCP; in RC Church transferred to 11 May in 1955 and then to 3 May in 1969.

James, Apocalypses of. Two short *Gnostic works contained in Codex V of the *Nag Hammadi Library. They embody dialogues between Jesus and James, who is called 'the Just' and the Lord's 'brother'. The theme of the first is redemption, in the sense of the liberation of the Gnostic from the pains of earthly existence and his reunion with the primal ground of being; the second is largely concerned with a speech delivered by James in the context of his martyrdom.

Coptic text ed., with Ger. tr., by A. Böhlig and P. Lahib, *Koptisch-gnostische Apokalypsen aus Codex V von Nag Hammadi* (Wissenschaftliche Zeitschrift der Martin-Luther Universität Halle-Wittenberg, Sonderband; 1963), pp. 27–85. Texts also ed., with Eng. trs. by W. R. Schoedel and C. W. Hedrick in D. M. Parrott (ed.), *Nag Hammadi Codices V, 2–5 and VI* (Nag Hammadi Studies, 11; Leiden, 1979), pp. 65–103 and 105–49 respectively. Eng. trs. also in J. M. Robinson (ed.), *The Nag Hammadi Library in English* (3rd edn., Leiden, 1988), pp. 260–76. Ger. tr. and introd. by W.-P. Funk in Schneemelcher, 1 (5th edn., 1987), pp. 253–75; Eng. tr., 1 (1991), pp. 313–41. W. Pratscher, *Der Herrenbruder Jakobus und die Jakobustradition* (Forschungen zur Religion und Literatur des Alten und Neuen Testaments, 139; 1987), pp. 162–72; C. Scholten, *Martyrium und Sophiamythos im Gnostizismus nach den Texten von Nag Hammadi* (Jahrbuch für Antike und Christentum, Ergänzungsband, 14; 1987), pp. 47–61 and 68–80.

James, Apocryphal Epistle of. A previously unknown work contained in Codex I of the *Nag Hammadi Library. It begins in the form of a letter, but soon passes over into a description of a final discourse delivered by Jesus to *Peter and *James (ostensibly the writer) '550 days after He had risen'. One of its major themes is the attitude to be adopted in the face of suffering (regarded as inevitable). The prominence of Peter and James and the sayings-traditions it contains suggest an origin in Jewish-Christian circles, and it was probably written about the middle of the 2nd cent., since it shows no dependence on canonical texts; some scholars, however, suggest an Egyptian origin and a later date. It has some affinities with *Gnostic writings, but cannot be attributed to any known Gnostic sect; some critics have denied that it is Gnostic at all.

Text ed., with Fr., Ger., and Eng. trs., and introd. by M. Malinine and others (Zurich and Stuttgart, 1968); also ed., with Eng. tr., by F. E. Williams in H. W. Attridge (ed.), *Nag Hammadi Codex I* (Nag Hammadi Studies, 22–23; Leiden, 1985), 1, pp. 13–53, with notes, 2, pp. 7–37; and with Ger. tr. and comm. by D. Kirchner (TU 136; 1989); Eng. tr. also in J. M. Robinson (ed.), *The Nag Hammadi Library in English* (3rd edn., Leiden, 1988), pp. 29–37. Ger. tr., with introd., by D. Kirchner in Schneemelcher, 1 (5th edn., 1987), pp. 234–44; Eng. tr., 1 (1991), pp. 285–99. C. Scholten, *Martyrium und Sophiamythos im Gnostizismus nach den Texten von Nag Hammadi* (Jahrbuch für Antike und Christentum, Ergänzungsband, 14; 1987), pp. 35–47.

James, Book of. An apocryphal *Infancy Gospel, apparently compiled by a Jewish Christian from a variety of sources, including the canonical Gospels of Mt. and Lk. Since the 16th cent. it has also been known as the '*Protevangelium'. It consists in the main of a highly embellished account of the events connected with Christ's birth, as related in Lk. 1 f. The Book, which professes to be by *James, the Lord's brother, was possibly known to *Justin Martyr, probably to *Clement of Alexandria, and certainly to *Origen; and seems to date from the 2nd cent. The oldest Greek MS is *Bodmer Papyrus V, and there are also versions in Latin, Syriac, Armenian, Slavonic, and other languages. Much of its contents were incorporated into later Infancy Gospels. In the Middle Ages its legends about the BVM became popular subjects with artists. It is here that the names of her parents, *Joachim and *Anne, occur for the first time.

Gk. text in C. *Tischendorf, *Evangelia Apocrypha* (2nd edn., 1876), pp. 1–50; also ed., with Fr. tr., by É Amann, *Le Protévangile de Jacques et ses remaniements latins* (1910), and by É. de Strycker, SJ, *La Forme la plus ancienne du Protévangile de Jacques* (Subsidia Hagiographica, 33; 1961). Eng. tr. in J. K. Elliott, *The Apocryphal New Testament* (Oxford, 1993), pp. 48–67. H. R. Smid, *Protevangelium Jacobi: A Commentary* (Eng. tr., Apocrypha Novi Testamenti, 1; Assen, 1965). On the Lat. workings-over of the text, see also M. R. James, *Latin Infancy Gospels* (1927), who prints those found in MSS Hereford O.III.9 and Brit. Lib., Arundel 404. O. *Cullmann in Schneemelcher, 1 (5th edn., 1987), pp. 334–49; Eng. tr., 1 (1991), pp. 421–39 (incl. Eng. tr. of text). J. H. Charlesworth, *The New Testament Apocrypha and Pseudepigrapha: A Guide to Publications, with Excursuses on Apocalypses* (Metuchen, NJ, and London, 1987), pp. 218–28.

James, Epistle of St. This NT Book, in the form of an Ep. of 'James, a servant of God and of the Lord Jesus Christ, to the twelve tribes of the Diaspora' (1: 1), stands first among the '*Catholic Epistles'. The writer opens by insisting on the joy which temptation brings, since by enduring it with prayer a man 'shall receive the crown of life' (1: 2–12); the sins into which he falls, however, are not to be imputed to God (1: 13–15). As the first-fruits of God's creatures (1: 18), we are to avoid wrath and meekly receive the Word (1: 19–21), not being mere hearers (1: 22 f.); the test of religion is its practical manifestations (1: 27). Subservience to the rich and despising the poor are fundamentally opposed to the Christian ethic (2: 1–13). To make profession of faith which does not issue in works is valueless (2: 14–26). Wisdom requires strict control of the tongue, which, though of Divine origin, may issue in great evil (3: 1–12); when wisdom comes from God it manifests itself in peaceableness (3: 13–18). The lustful, the proud, those who do not resist the devil, the censorious, and the presumptuous are never close to God (4: 1–17). The rich are warned of their fate (5: 1–6); patience is commended (5: 7–11); oaths are disallowed (5: 12); and *Unction is recommended for the sick (5: 13–15), together with mutual confession of sins (5: 16) and prayer (5: 17 f.). Finally, to convert a man from error is to save one's own soul (5: 19 f.).

The Epistle is written in a clear forceful style, using good Greek, and is almost entirely moral in content. Apart from two verses (1: 1 and 2: 1) there is nothing incontestably Christian in it and it has been argued by F. *Spitta that the work is a revision of a Jewish writing; but the similarities to the *Sermon on the Mount and other of the Lord's teachings suggest rather a Jewish-Christian writing.

The traditional view that the author was St *James the Lord's brother has to face the difficulty that the Epistle presupposes a good Greek culture; the suggestion that it is a translation from an original Aramaic is unlikely on stylistic grounds. Other arguments urged against the traditional authorship are the absence of reference in the *Muratorian fragment or any other 2nd-cent. writing, the doubts of *Origen and *Eusebius, and the extent to which it stands apart from the Judaizing controversy in the 1st cent. in which James is a central figure. None of these objections, however, is quite conclusive. There remain the close parallels with the speech of James recorded in Acts 15; and the most natural interpretation of 'James' (alone) in the opening verse is that it refers to the Lord's brother, though it is possible that the ascription to James may not be original. Even if the Epistle is not the work of St James, it seems likely that it was composed before AD 95. Some scholars, impressed by its primitive nature, argue for a very early date, c. AD 50. It is first mentioned by Origen and seems to have been widely known in the E. soon afterwards. In the W. it is not quoted before the middle of the 4th cent., but it was recognized as canonical at the Council of *Hippo of 393. It was translated into Syriac as part of the *Peshitta in the early 5th cent. In modern times the Epistle was disliked by M. *Luther ('a right strawy epistle') and has been little valued by orthodox *Protestants.

Modern comm. by J. B. Mayor (London, 1892; 3rd edn., with additions, 1913; with full bibl.), H. Windisch (Hb. NT, 4, Heft 2, 1911; on the Catholic Epistles, 3rd edn., with H. Preisker, 15, 1951, pp. 1–36), J. H. Ropes (ICC, 1916), M. *Dibelius (KEK 15, 7th edn., 1921; 11th edn. by H. Greeven, 1964; Eng. tr., Hermeneia, Philadelphia [1976]), F. Mussner (Herders Theologischer Kommentar zum Neuen Testament, 13, Fasz. 1; 1964), C. L. Mitton (London [1967]), E. M. Sidebottom (New Cent. Bib., Jas., Jude, and 2 Pet., 1967, pp. 1–64), J. Cantinat, CM, *Les Épîtres de Saint Jacques et de Saint Jude* (Sources Bibliques, 1973), pp. 9–263, S. [S. S. C.] Laws (Black's NT Comm., 1980), and R. P. Martin (Word Biblical Commentary, 48; Waco, Tex. [1988]); also F. J. A. *Hort (as far as Jas. 4: 7; posthumously pub., London, 1909). A. Meyer, *Das Rätsel des Jacobusbriefes* (Beihefte zur ZNTW, 10; 1930). S. [S. S. C.] Laws in *Anchor Bible Dictionary*, 3 (1992), pp. 621–8, s.v.

James, Liturgy of St. This ancient liturgy, extant in a Greek and a Syriac form, is traditionally ascribed to St *James, the Lord's brother and the first Bp. of *Jerusalem. It has many points of contact with the liturgy known to St *Cyril, Bp. of Jerusalem (d. 387), and contains an apparent reference to the discovery of the true cross at Jerusalem in AD 326. It came to be much used in the *Syriac-, *Armenian-, and *Georgian-speaking parts of the Church, as well as in Egypt and Ethiopia. Its use by the *Syrian Orthodox Church (which became a separate body after the Council of *Chalcedon in 451), as well as by the main Orthodox Churches, shows that it cannot be later than the middle of the 5th cent. By the latter it is now celebrated at Zante (and sometimes elsewhere) on 23 Oct. (acc. to the E. Church, the day of St James's death) and at Jerusalem on the Sunday after Christmas.

Text in Brightman, *LEW*, pp. 31–68 [Gk. text]; 69–110 [Syr. text]. Crit. text, with Lat. tr., ed. B. C. Mercier, OSB, in *PO* 26 (1950), pp. 119–256. Cf. also O. Heiming, OSB, 'Palimpsestbruchstücke der syrischen Version der Jakobusanaphora aus dem 8. Jahrhundert', *OCP* 16 (1950), pp. 190–200; A. Rücker, *Die syrische Jakobusanaphora nach der Rezension des Je'qob(h) von Edessa* (Liturgiegeschichtliche Quellen, 4; 1923). Eng. tr. in J. M. *Neale, *The Liturgies of S. Mark, S. James, S. Clement, S. Chrysostom and the Church of Malabar* (1859), pp. 31–65. Classic comm. by (1) Moses bar Kēphā (813–903), ed., with Eng. tr., by R. H. *Connolly and H. W. Codrington, *Two Commentaries on the Jacobite Liturgy* (1913), pp. 16–66 (in Syriac script); Eng. tr., pp. 24–90, and (2) Dionysius bar Salibi (d. 1171), ed., with Lat. tr., by H. Labourt (CSCO, Scriptores Syrici, 93; 1903). L. *Allatius, Σύμμικτα ('Coloniae Agrippinae' [Amsterdam?] 1653), 1, pp. 176–203 ('Ep. i ad Bartodum Nihusium de Liturgia S. Iacobi'), an attempt to prove the Liturgy to be the work of St James the Apostle. A. Tarby, *La Prière Eucharistique de l'Église de Jérusalem* (Théologie historique, 17 [1972]), with bibl. L. Ligier, SJ, 'Célébration divine et Anamnèse dans la première partie de l'Anaphore ou Canon de la Messe Orientale', *Gregorianum*, 48 (1967), pp. 225–52, repr. in B. Botte and others, *Eucharisties d'Orient et d'Occident: Semaine liturgique de l'Institut Saint-Serge*, 2 (Lex Orandi, 47; 1970), pp. 139–78. J. R. K. Fenwick, *The Anaphoras of St Basil and St James: An Investigation into their Common Origin* (Orientalia Christiana Analecta, 240; 1992). A. *Fortescue in *CE* 1 (1907), pp. 571–4, s.v. 'Antiochene Liturgy'; H. *Leclercq, OSB, in *DACL* 7 (pt. 2; 1927), cols. 2116–21.

James I (1566–1625), King of England and VI of Scotland. The only son of Henry Stuart, Lord Darnley, and *Mary, Queen of Scots, on the abdication of his mother he became King of Scotland in 1567. He was educated mainly by George *Buchanan, who endeavoured to inculcate doctrines of constitutional monarchy. Undertaking the direction of government in 1578, he tried to build up the royal power amid strong rival factions of the Scottish nobility. In 1586 he entered an alliance with England, raising few objections to the execution of his mother. In 1589 he married Anne of Denmark (1574–1619). He generally supported the clergy against the nobility, but he resented the political influence of the Kirk. From 1598 he sought the restoration of episcopacy, in 1600 appointing three representatives of the Church in Parliament under the title of Bishops.

On the death of *Elizabeth I (1603), he succeeded to the English throne by right of his mother's descent from Henry VII, under the new style of King of Great Britain. Travelling immediately to London, he was met by the *Puritans, who presented the *Millenary Petition. James heard their case at the *Hampton Court Conference (1604), at which he offered a series of concessions in return, he hoped, for conformity and subscription. He also took the opportunity to express his complete opposition to *Presbyterianism, and upheld the connection between the *Divine Right of Kings and *Apostolic Succession. At the same time he authorized a new translation of the Bible (the *Authorized Version of 1611). He favoured lenient treatment of RCs and made peace with Spain in 1604, though the *Gunpowder Plot of 1605 inevitably provoked stricter laws against the *Recusants. During his reign the influence of the clergy at court increased dramatically; James appointed seven bishops to the Privy Council; in 1621 he chose John *Williams, Bp. of Lincoln, as Lord Keeper, the first cleric to hold the office since 1558; and he allowed the bishops to resume their traditional role as counsellors or intimates of the Crown. In Scotland, in

1610 he persuaded the Assembly of the Church to agree to the introduction of episcopacy. Three bishops were consecrated in England and he prob. hoped to extend the English rite to Scotland. In 1614 and 1615 he ordered that all persons in Scotland should receive the Holy Communion on Easter Day, and in 1616 called upon the Assembly of Aberdeen to pass the Five Articles, which (after James's visit to Scotland in 1617) were finally accepted at *Perth in 1618. He issued the 'Book of *Sports' (1618) approving lawful sport on Sundays.

James's attempts to negotiate a marriage treaty with Spain were frustrated by Parliament's refusal to repeal the laws against RCs, while he was equally unsuccessful in his attempts to mediate in Bohemia. He negotiated an alliance with France in 1624, but he was unable to disclose the terms of a treaty which promised relief to Catholics. Throughout his reign he quarrelled with his Parliaments over foreign policy and never saw that parliamentary control over finance made compromise necessary. Although renowned for his erudition, he failed to win sympathy because of his pedantry and high opinion of his own ability. His published works include *Essays of a Prentice in the Divine Art of Poetry* (1584), *Poetical Exercises* [1591], *Daemonology* (1597), *Basilikon Doron* (1599), *The True Law of Free Monarchies* (anon. 1598; 1603), *A Counter Blast to Tobacco* (anon. 1604), *Triplici Nodo, Triplex Cuneus; or an Apology for the Oath of Allegiance* (anon. 1607), *Declaratio pro Iure Regio* (1615), *The Peacemaker* (anon. 1618) and *Meditations on the Lord's Prayer* (1619) and on Mt. 27: 27–9 (1620).

Collected edn. of his prose works to date pub. by James [Montague], Bp. of Winchester, in 1616. Repr. of his political works by C. H. MacIlwain, 1918. Poems ed. J. Craigie (Scottish Text Society, 3rd ser. 22 and 26; 1955–8). R. Ashton (ed.), *James I by his Contemporaries: An Account of his Career and Character as Seen by Some of his Contemporaries* (1969). S. R. Gardiner, *History of England from the Accession of James I to the Outbreak of the Civil War*, vols. 1–5 (1883–4). D. H. Willson, *King James VI and I* (1956); W. McElwee, *The Wisest Fool in Christendom: The Reign of King James I and VI* (1958). D. Mathew, *James I* (1967). J. Wormald, 'James VI and I: Two Kings or One?', *History*, 68 (1983), pp. 187–209. K. Fincham, *Prelate as Pastor: The Episcopate of James I* (Oxford, 1990). S. R. Gardiner in *DNB* 29 (1892), pp. 161–81, s.v. 'James VI'.

James II (1633–1701), King of England and VII of Scotland, 1685–8. The second son of *Charles I, James fought in the Civil War as Duke of York, but after being captured escaped abroad, where he served with the French army. At the Restoration (1660), he was made Lord High Admiral and in 1662 issued 'Instructions' to the Navy which remained in force until the 19th cent. He married twice: first in 1660 Anne Hyde, who died a RC; by her he had two daughters, Mary and *Anne; and secondly in 1673 the RC Princess Mary Beatrice of Modena. About 1670 he was received into the RC Church. This step involved him in trouble both at Court and in Parliament, which tried to exclude him from the succession. The *Exclusion Bill was, however, rejected in 1680 by the Lords, many of whom believed in the hereditary *Divine Right. As High Commissioner in Scotland, James was careful to countenance the Episcopal Church of Scotland, and so encouraged Anglican loyalty in England. In 1685 he ascended the throne and openly professed his Roman allegiance. At the beginning of his reign he continued to support the C of E, but after quelling the Duke of Monmouth's Rebellion, he increasingly sought to improve the position of his co-religionists. In order to check Anglican criticism, he created the Court of Ecclesiastical Commission (see HIGH COMMISSION), which suspended H. *Compton, Bp. of London. He claimed the power to dispense from the provisions of the *Test Act of 1673 and appointed RCs to office in the state and armed forces. He also intruded RC dons into the Universities of Oxford and Cambridge. A collision with the hierarchy of the C of E was occasioned by his issuing two *Declarations of Indulgence in 1687 and 1688. In the second case he ordered the clergy to publish his *Declaration of Liberty of Conscience* from the pulpit. When W. *Sancroft, Abp. of *Canterbury, and six other bishops refused to carry out the order and presented a petition to the King, they were committed to the Tower and charged with publishing a seditious libel (see SEVEN BISHOPS, TRIAL OF). Their acquittal was marked by general rejoicing. Alarmed by the approaching invasion by William, Prince of Orange, James reversed most of his measures and promised once more to uphold the established rights of the C of E. But this did not stop William and the Whigs from deposing him. He fled to France. He later attempted to recover Ireland, but was eventually defeated at the Boyne in 1690. He returned to France. His exclusion gave rise to the *Nonjuring Schism and the longer-lived Jacobite movement. He died in 1701 after spending the last four years of his life in religious observance.

The principal authority, apart from the State Papers (of which the Calendar of the Domestic Series was ed. by E. K. Timings and others, 3 vols., 1970–2), is *The Life of James the Second . . . Collected out of Memoirs Writ with his own Hand* [compiled at his son's command shortly after his death], ed. J. S. Clarke (2 vols., London, 1816). On this Life cf. L. von *Ranke, *Englische Geschichte vornehmlich im sechszehnten und siebzehnten Jahrhundert*, 7 (1868), pp. 137–54; Eng. tr., 6 (1875), pp. 29–45. Modern works include F. C. Turner, *James II* (1948) and J. [L.] Miller, *James II: A Study in Kingship* (Hove, 1978; London, 1989). W. A. Speck, *Reluctant Revolutionaries: Englishmen and the Revolution of 1688* (Oxford, 1988). R. [A.] Beddard, *A Kingdom without a King: The Journal of the Provisional Government in the Revolution of 1688* (ibid. [1988]); id. (ed.), *The Revolutions of 1688* (ibid., 1991).

James Baradaeus. See JACOB BARADAEUS.

James the Deacon (7th cent.), companion of St *Paulinus, Bp. of *York. When Paulinus returned to Kent in 633, James was apparently the sole member of the mission to the N. left behind. Acc. of *Bede (*HE* 2. 16 and 20), he resided chiefly at a village near Catterick. On the restoration of Christianity in Northumbria, James took an active and successful part in spreading the Gospel and, skilful in music, he taught his converts the Gregorian chant. In 664 he was present, on St *Wilfrid's side, at the Synod of *Whitby. He survived until Bede's time.

James of Edessa. See JACOB OF EDESSA.

James of Nisibis, St. See JACOB OF NISIBIS, ST.

James of Sarug. See JACOB OF SARUG.

James of Voragine, more correctly called **James of Varagine** (*c.*1230–98), author of the '*Golden Legend'. Born in Genoa, he entered the *Dominican Order in 1244. He was twice Provincial of Lombardy (1267–77 and 1281–6) and in 1283, on the death of the Master, he became Vicar of the Order until the election of Munio of Zamora in 1285. In 1285 and 1288 he undertook diplomatic missions for the Pope. In 1290 he appears to have had some involvement in the Papal deposition of Munio of Zamara, but the story that he was threatened with assassination by some of the brethren is prob. apocryphal. In 1292 he reluctantly became Abp. of Genoa. His cult was ratified in 1816. Feast day, 13 July.

Besides the 'Golden Legend', he wrote a chronicle of Genoa, part of which is of value for local history, and a series of sermons, incl. the *Mariale*, in which the material is arranged alphabetically under the various attributes and titles of the BVM.

Early pr. edns. of his Sermons include 'Sermones de Tempore', Strasburg, not later than 1473; 'Sermones de Sanctis', Cologne, *c.*1478; 'Sermones Quadragesimales', Brixen, 1483; and 'Mariale', Hamburg, 1491; frequent later edns. 'Chronicon Genuense', pr. by L. A. *Muratori, *Rerum Italicarum Scriptores*, 9 (Milan, 1726), cols. 2–56; modern edn. by G. Monleone (R. Istituto Storico Italiano per il Medio Evo. Fonti per la storia d'Italia [84–6]; 1941). E. C. Richardson, *Materials for a Life of Jacopo da Varagine* (New York, 1935). G. Airaldi, *Jacopo da Varagine, tra santi e mercanti* (Milan [1988]). A. Boureau, 'Le prêcheur et les marchands. Ordre divin et désordres du siècle dans la Chronique de Gênes de Jacques de Voragine (1297)', *Médiévales*, 4 (1983), pp. 102–22. E. Colledge, OSA, 'James of Voragine's "Legenda sancti Augustini" and its Sources', *Augustiniana*, 35 (1985), pp. 281–314. Kaeppeli, 2 (1975), pp. 348–69. P. Raffin in *Dict. Sp.* 8 (1974), cols. 62–4, s.v. 'Jacques de Voragine'. See also bibl. to GOLDEN LEGEND.

James, William (1842–1910), American *Pragmatist philosopher. The son of a *Swedenborgian theologian and brother of the novelist Henry James, he was Professor successively of Psychology (1887–97) and Philosophy (1897–1907) at Harvard University. He held that we have a 'right to believe in' the existence of God (because it makes us 'better off'), but no scientific certainty of the validity of that belief. In his *Gifford Lectures, *The Varieties of Religious Experience* (1902), he drew the now familiar distinction between 'once-born' and 'twice-born' religious types, and made a scientific analysis of conversion. The cases he quotes have been widely criticized on the ground that they are too predominantly morbid, irrational, and Protestant, but the book remains a classic, and has stimulated much fruitful study of the psychology of religion. His other writings include his *Principles of Psychology* (2 vols., 1890), an epoch-making contribution to its subject; *The Will to Believe and Other Essays* (1897); and *Pragmatism* (1907).

Collected Essays and Reviews ed. R. B. Perry (1920); *Letters* ed. H. James, son (1920); *Selected Unpublished Correspondence 1885–1910* ed. F. J. D. Scott (Columbus, Oh. [1986]). *Works* ed. F. H. Burkhardt and others (19 vols. Cambridge, Mass., and London, 1975–88). R. B. Perry, *The Thought and Character of William James* (2 vols. [1936]). Other studies by G. W. Allen (London, 1967; a biography), G. E. Myers (New Haven, Conn., and London, 1986), G. Bird (London, 1986), and D. W. Bjork (New York, 1988). A. J. Ayer, *The Origins of Pragmatism* (1968), pp. 183–336. R. B. Perry in *Dict. Amer. Biog.* 9 (1932), pp. 590–600.

Jamnia (or **Jabneh**). A city *c.*13 miles S. of Joppa. After the fall of *Jerusalem (AD 70), an assembly of religious teachers was established at Jamnia; this body was regarded as to some extent replacing the *Sanhedrin, though it did not possess the same representative character or national authority. It appears that one of the subjects discussed among the rabbis was the status of certain biblical books (e.g. Eccles. and Song of Songs) which some said did not 'defile the hands'—a phrase taken by many scholars to refer to their canonicity (cf. *Mishnah, Yadaim, 3.5). The suggestion that a particular synod of Jamnia, held *c.*100 AD, finally settled the limits of the OT Canon, was made by H. E. *Ryle; though it has had a wide currency, there is no evidence to substantiate it.

F. M. Abel, OP, *Géographie de la Palestine*, 2 (1938), pp. 352 f., with refs. H. E. Ryle, *The Canon of the Old Testament* (1892), pp. 171 f. J. P. Lewis, 'What do we mean by Jabneh?', *Journal of Bible and Religion*, 32 (1964), pp. 125–32; S. Z. Leiman, *The Canonization of Hebrew Scripture: The Talmudic and Midrashic Evidence* (Transactions of the Connecticut Academy of Arts and Sciences, 47; 1976), pp. 120–4. J. P. Lewis in *Anchor Bible Dictionary*, 3 (1992), pp. 634–7, with bibl.

Jane Frances de Chantal, St (1572–1641), foundress of the Order of the *Visitation. Her father, Bénigne Frémyot, held a legal position in Dijon. In 1592 she married the Baron Christophe de Chantal, and on his death in 1601 she took a vow of chastity. St *Francis de Sales became her spiritual director in 1604 and with his help she founded the first house of the Visitation in Annecy in 1610; it was intended for women unable to endure the severe ascetic life of other religious orders. On leaving her family she had to overcome the protests of her 14-year-old son and was often criticized on this account. She spent the remainder of her life organizing the new order and founding houses in various parts of France. She cared for the poor and sick (esp. in the plague epidemic of 1628–9). At her death there were 86 houses in existence. She was beatified in 1751 and canonized in 1767. Feast day 12 Dec. (formerly 21 Aug.).

Sainte J. F. Frémyot de Chantal: Sa vie et ses œuvres. Mémoires sur la vie et les vertus de sainte Jeanne-Françoise Frémyot de Chantal . . . par la mère Françoise-Madeleine de Chaugy (8 vols., 1874–9), with Life forming vol. 1; Eng. tr. of vol. 2 as *Exhortations, Conferences, Instructions and Retreat* (Clifton, 1888). Modern edn. of the deposition which she made in 1627 for the beatification of St Francis de Sales by I. van Houtryve, OSB (Namur [1960]); Eng. tr. by E. [C. V.] Stopp (London, 1986). Crit. edn. of her correspondence by M.-P. Burns, VSM (6 vols., Paris, 1986–96). [L. V.] E. Bougaud, *Histoire de Sainte Chantal et des origines de la Visitation* (2 vols., 1861; Eng. tr., *St Chantal and the Foundation of the Visitation*, 2 vols., New York, 1895). A Gazier, *Jeanne de Chantal et Angélique Arnauld d'après leur correspondance, 1620–1641* (1915). Other Lives by H. *Bremond ('Les Saints', 1912) and E. [C. V.] Stopp (London, 1962). R. Devos in *Dict. Sp.* 8 (1974), cols. 859–69, s.v. 'Jeanne-François de Chantal', with extensive bibl.

Jannes and Jambres. Two reputed Egyptian magicians who imitated the miracles performed by *Moses before Pharaoh (Ex. 7 ff.). Though their names do not occur in the OT, they are mentioned in the NT at 2 Tim. 3: 8. There are many references to them in other literature of the early Christian period, Jewish as well as Christian, while *Origen (*Comm. in Mt.* 27. 9) refers to an apocryphal

'Book of Jannes and Jambres', of which, however, only small fragments survive.

J. A. *Fabricius, *Codex Pseudepigraphus Veteris Testamenti*, 1 (Hamburg and Leipzig, 1713), pp. 813–25, and 2 (Hamburg, 1723), pp. 105–11. M. R. James, 'A Fragment of the "Penitence of Jannes and Jambres" ', *JTS* 2 (1901), pp. 572–7, with text, pp. 573 f. A. Pietersma and R. T. Lutz in J. H. Charlesworth (ed.), *The Old Testament Pseudepigrapha*, 2 (1985), pp. 427–42, incl. Eng. tr. of fragments of the 'Book of Jannes and Jambres'. E. *Schürer, *The History of the Jewish People in the Age of Jesus Christ*, rev. Eng. tr. by G. Vermes and others, 3 (pt. 2; Edinburgh, 1987), pp. 781–3.

Jansen, Cornelius Otto (1585–1638) (**Jansenius**), the author of the *Augustinus* (q.v.). He is to be distinguished from his uncle, Cornelius Jansen the Elder (1510–76), who was Bp. of Ghent from 1564 (confirmed by *Pius V, 1568). After two years in the Collège du Faucon at Louvain, he migrated in 1604 to Paris. Here he met *Saint-Cyran, with whom, at Bayonne and Champré, he spent the years 1612–17 in unremitting study. In these years, as his later correspondence with Saint-Cyran reveals, he conceived an elaborate plan of concerted action against the theologians of the *Counter-Reformation. In 1617 he became the director of a newly founded college at Louvain, and in 1626–7 defended at Madrid the cause of the University of Louvain against the aspersions of the *Jesuits. In 1628 he began to write the *Augustinus*, for which purpose he read the whole of St *Augustine's writings ten times and the anti-Pelagian writings thirty; but it was not published till 1640, after his death. In 1636 he was consecrated Bp. of Ypres. See also following entry.

J. Orcibal, *Correspondance de Jansénius* ('Les Origines du jansénisme', 1; Bibliothèque de la *RHE* 25; 1947). Id., *Jansénius d'Ypres (1585–1638)* (Études Augustiniennes, 1989). E. J. M. van Eijl (ed.), *L'Image de C. Jansénius jusqu'à la fin du XVIIIe siècle: Actes du Colloque, Louvain, 7–9 novembre 1985* (Bibliotheca Ephemeridum Theologicarum Lovaniensium, 79; 1987). H. de *Lubac, SJ, *Augustinisme et théologie moderne* (Théologie, 63; 1965), pp. 49–112; Eng. tr. (1969), pp. 34–96. J. Carreyre in *DTC* 8 (pt. 1; 1924), cols. 319–30 (Life, with bibl.) and 330–448 (full analysis of the *Augustinus*). See also bibls. to AUGUSTINUS and JANSENISM.

Jansenism. Dogmatically, Jansenism is summed up in five propositions, derived in substance from the *Augustinus* (1640) of C. O. *Jansen, and condemned as heretical by the *Sorbonne (1649) and Innocent X (1653). The sense of these propositions is (1) that without a special *grace from God the performance of His commandments is impossible to men, and (2) that the operation of grace is irresistible; and hence, that man is the victim of either a natural or a supernatural determinism, limited only by not being violently coercive. This theological pessimism was expressed in the general harshness and moral rigorism of the movement.

The first generation of French Jansenists were all disciples of *Saint-Cyran (Duvergier), Jansen's friend and collaborator. This party of 'Cyranists', which included the convent of *Port-Royal, was already in existence in 1638. After Saint-Cyran's death in 1643, Antoine *Arnauld succeeded him as its leader, and in *De la fréquente communion* (1643), *La Théologie morale des Jésuites* (1643), and two *Apologies pour M. Jansénius* (1644–5) defined the directions of the movement. These were (1) the defence of St *Au-

gustine's theology of grace, as interpreted by Jansen, against *Molinism; (2) a rigorist tendency in all matters of ecclesiastical discipline; (3) hostility to *Probabilism. The unifying characteristic of the movement was antagonism to the *Jesuits. (2) and (3) remained unchanged throughout the whole history of Jansenism, and were exhibited in all its principal monuments, from the *Lettres provinciales* (1656–7) of *Pascal onwards.

In 1653 five propositions were condemned by Innocent X in the bull '*Cum Occasione' as summarizing the Jansenist position. The supporters of the movement sought to evade the condemnation by their distinction of 'fact' (*fait*) and 'law' (*droit*). The five propositions were admitted to be heretical, but in 'fact' they were declared unrepresentative of Jansen's doctrine, which the Jansenists held to be a fair presentation of the teaching of St Augustine. After this distinction had been disallowed by *Alexander VII (1656), attempts were made to compel the Jansenists to sign a formulary embodying the Papal anathema. In 1668 they were persuaded into a qualified submission, but the movement continued to gain sympathizers, particularly among the *Oratorians and *Maurists. P. *Quesnel's *Réflexions morales* (1693), in which some tenets of Jansenism were reaffirmed, was condemned in the bull '*Unigenitus' (1713). The bull was not accepted by the Jansenists, who consequently had to face sporadic persecution in France during much of the 18th cent. In their opposition to the Jesuits, however, they found support among the *Gallican members of the *Parlements* who in 1762 took steps to have the Jesuits expelled from France. In the Netherlands, where many prominent Jansenist clerics took refuge, Jansenism was tolerated or encouraged by successive *Vicars Apostolic, and in 1723 the Dutch Jansenists nominated for themselves a schismatic Bishop of Utrecht (see OLD CATHOLICS). In Tuscany, chiefly owing to the anti-Papal policy of the Grand Duke Leopold, Jansenism became so strong that the local Synod of *Pistoia (1786) promulgated one of the most comprehensive statements of Jansenist positions that exist. After Napoleon's *Concordat of 1801, French Jansenism survived only as the secret conviction of a few Catholics and as the guiding spirit of a few pious institutions.

The principal primary docs. concerning Jansenism and the opposition to it are ed. by L. Ceyssens, OFM, lately in conjunction with S. de Munter, OFM: those covering the period 1640–3 (Bibliothèque de la *RHE* 31; 1957); 1644–53 (Bibliothèque de l'Institut historique Belge de Rome, 9–10; 1961–2); 1654–60 (ibid. 12–13; 1963–5); 1661–72 (Bibliothèque de la *RHE* 45; 1968); 1673–6 (Bibliothèque de l'Institut historique Belge de Rome, 17; 1968); 1677–9 (Bibliothèque de la *RHE*, 59; 1974); and 1680–82 (Bibliothèque de l'Institut historique Belge de Rome, 19; 1974). The 'Five Propositions' are conveniently pr. in Denzinger and Hünermann (37th edn., 1991), pp. 614 f. (nos. 2001–5); Eng. tr. in Bettenson (2nd edn., 1963), pp. 379 f.

There has been an immense lit. from the outbreak of the controversy onwards. Modern studies incl. A. Gazier, *Histoire générale du mouvement janséniste* (2 vols., 1922); E. Préclin, *Les Jansénistes du XVIIIe siècle et la constitution civile du clergé* (1928); L. Ceyssens, OFM, *Jansenistica: Studien in verband met Geschiedenis van het Jansenisme* (4 vols., Malines, 1950–62); id., *Jansenistica Minora* (1–10, Malines, 1951–68; 11–12, Amsterdam, 1973–5); cf., for details of arts. by Ceyssens, bibl. in *Antonianum*, 53 (1978), pp. 194–266 and in J. van Bavel and M. Schrama (eds.), *Jansénius et le Jansénisme dans les Pay-Bas: Mélanges Lucien Ceyssens* (Bibliotheca Ephemeridum Theologicarum Lovaniensium, 56;

1982), pp. 9 f., incl. his important art. 'L'Authenticité des cinq propositions condamnées de Jansenius', *Antonianum*, 55 (1980), pp. 368–424; P. de Leturia, SJ, and others, *Nuove ricerche storiche sul giansenismo* (Analecta Gregoriana, 71; 1954); L. Cognet, *Le Jansénisme* (1961). J. Orcibal and A. Barnes, *Les Origines du jansénisme* (6 vols., 1947 ff.). J. Orcibal, 'Qu'est-ce le Jansénisme?', *Cahiers de l'Association Internationale des Études françaises*, nos. 3–5 (1953), pp. 39–53. A. Adam, *Du mysticisme à la révolte: Les Jansénistes du XVIIᵉ siècle* (1968). A. Sedgwick, *Jansenism in Seventeenth-Century France* (Charlottesville, Va., 1977). J. Carreyre, *Le Jansénisme durant la régence, 1715–23* (Bibliothèque de la *RHE*, 2–4; 1929–33). D. [K.] Van Kley, *The Jansenists and the Expulsion of the Jesuits from France 1757–1765* (New Haven, Conn., and London, 1975); id., *The Damiens Affairs and the Unravelling of the Ancien Régime 1750–1770* (Princeton, NJ [1984]), passim. A. C. Jemolo, *Il giansenismo in Italia prima della rivoluzione* (Bari, 1928). E. Appolis, *Les Jansénistes espagnols* (Bordeaux [1966]). B. Neveu, *L'Erreur et son Juge: Remarques sur les censures doctrinales à l'époque moderne* (Istituto Italiano per gli Studi Filosofici, Serie Studi, 19: Naples, 1993), esp. 505–746. Bremond, 4. List of Jansenist works in L. Patouillet (ed.), *Dictionnaire des livres jansénistes* (4 vols., Antwerp, 1752). L. Willaert, SJ, *Bibliotheca Janseniana Belgica: Répertoire des imprimés concernant les controverses théologiques en relation avec le jansénisme dans les Pays-Bas catholiques et le Pays de Liège aux XVIIᵉ et XVIIIᵉ siècles* (Bibliothèque de la Faculté de Philosophie et Lettres de Namur, 4, 5, 12; 1949–51). J. Carreyre in *DTC* 8 (pt. 1; 1924), cols. 318–529, s.v.; J. Gres-Gayer in *NCE* 18 (1989), pp. 207–10, s.v. See also bibl. to PORT-ROYAL.

Januarius, St, Bp. of Benevento, patron saint of Naples. Several late and mainly legendary accounts of his martyrdom survive, but beyond the fact of his death in the neighbourhood of Naples, perhaps at Pozzuoli in the *Diocletianic persecution, nothing is known of him. His fame rests on the alleged 'liquefaction' of his blood, preserved in a small glass phial, which is believed to take place on some eighteen occasions every year. A vast crowd gathers in the cathedral at Naples to witness the ceremony. Formerly a body of poor and aged women, the *zie di San Gennaro* ('aunts of St Januarius'), played a semi-official part in the event. Feast day in E., 21 Apr.; in W., 19 Sept.

List of 'Acta' in *BHL* 1 (1898–9), nos. 4115–40. P. Franchi de' Cavalieri, 'San Gennaro, vescovo e martire', *Note agiografiche*, fasc. 4 (ST 24; 1912), pp. 79–102 (with edn. of Gk. text, pp. 105–14). A further Gk. text ed., with Fr. tr., by F. van Ommeslaeghe, SJ, in *Anal. Boll.* 102 (1984), pp. 135–55. G. B. Alfano and A. Amitrano, *Il miracolo di S. Gennaro: Documentazione storica e scientifica* (2nd edn., Naples [1950]). H. Thurston, SJ, 'The Blood-Miracles of Naples', *The Month*, 149 (1927), pp. 44–55, 123–35, 236–47, and id., 'The "Miracle" of St Januarius', ibid. 155 (1930), pp. 119–29. H. *Delehaye, SJ, 'Hagiographie napolitaine', *Anal. Boll.* 59 (1941), pp. 1–33, esp. pp. 1–13. H. Thurston, SJ, in *CE* 8 (1910), pp. 295–7, s.v.; E. Josi, C. Testore, and P. Toschi in *EC* 6 (1951), cols. 9–16, s.v. 'Gennaro', with bibl.

Janus. The pseudonym over which J. J. I. von *Döllinger, with J. N. Huber and J. *Friedrich, issued a series of letters in the Augsburg *Allgemeine Zeitung* early in 1869, attacking the Papal *Syllabus Errorum* of 1864 as tending to obscurantism and tyranny. The purpose of the letters was to promote anti-*Ultramontane tendencies in view of the forthcoming *Vatican Council. See also QUIRINUS.

The letters were issued in book form in the same year, both in the original and in an Eng. tr.

Japan, Christianity in. St *Francis Xavier first brought Christianity to Japan in 1549, and he and his successors gained many converts. In 1587, under the suspicion that the missions were merely preparing the way for a coming conquest of the country, Christianity was proscribed, but still made progress down to 1596. From 1596 to 1598 persecution raged and in 1597 claimed 26 Japanese converts, who suffered martyrdom by crucifixion at Nagasaki (canonized in 1862; feast day, 6 Feb.). It broke out again in 1613, and by 1640 many thousands, both Japanese and foreigners, had suffered for their faith. Then all foreigners were excluded from Japan under pain of death. Their exclusion continued in force, together with the proscription of Christianity, down to 1859, when a treaty between the Japanese Government and France partially removed the former restriction, allowing also liberty of worship to foreigners, though complete toleration for all was not conceded till 1890. In 1859 RC missions re-entered the country and shortly afterwards (1865) discovered that thousands of Christians, in small local communities, had, though without priests or education, secretly kept and handed on their faith through the two centuries of persecution.

In 1859 some American (Anglican) missionaries arrived, and in 1861–3 the Presbyterians. In 1861 came a mission, sent by the Russian Orthodox Church, under Fr. (later Abp.) Nicolai Kassatkin (canonized by the Orthodox in 1977 and second only to Xavier as the apostle of Japan), who founded a communion whose numbers were exceeded only by that of the Roman obedience. Missions of other denominations followed. Though temporarily hindered by the persecution of 1867–73, in which many thousands of Christians were exiled, work went steadily forward in the later years of the 19th cent. The RCs set up a Vicariate-Apostolic in 1866 and a hierarchy in 1891. In 1877 the various Presbyterian bodies at work in Japan began an amalgamation which was completed in 1891, while the American Episcopalian missions united with missions from the Churches of England and Canada to form the 'Nippon Sei Ko Kwai' (Holy Catholic Church of Japan) (1887). At first conversions were aided not only by the thirst of younger Japanese for W. education, but through desire to enter the civilization of the W. By 1890, however, a reaction towards national self-reliance had set in. This was symbolized by the Imperial Rescript on Education (1890) and confirmed by the defeat of Russia in the Russo-Japanese War (1905). Events from 1931 onwards intensified the nationalist spirit, reinforcing the State religion of Shinto. Christianity was often attacked as incompatible with the loyalty of Japanese subjects. During this period the writings of T. *Kagawa on the social implications of Christianity became well known in the W.

The outbreak of war with the USA and Great Britain in Dec. 1941 led to the removal of all European bishops (some of whom suffered harsh imprisonment) and clergy, and the government endeavoured to force all non-RC Christians into a single Protestant Church, the United Church of Christ in Japan (the 'Kyodan'). Some Anglicans joined under duress, while others refused. After the defeat of Japan in 1945, State-Shintoism was disestablished and freedom of religion was granted. In this new atmosphere, Christianity enjoyed a brief resurgence of popularity, assisted by financial and relief aid from Churches in N.

America. The Anglicans, *Lutherans, and several other groups withdrew from the 'Kyodan', but it remained the largest Protestant body in Japan. The 'Nippon Sei Ko Kwai' was reconstituted under a Japanese episcopate.

Indigenous expressions of Christianity in Japan include the 'Mukyokai' or Non-Church Movement, founded by K. Uchimura (1861–1930). In 1990 Christians numbered about 1 per cent of the total Japanese population, but the influence of Christianity on that section of society which is educated and well-informed is wider than this figure might suggest. S. Endo (1923–96), a RC novelist, was a prominent literary figure.

O. Cary, *A History of Christianity in Japan* (2 vols. [1909]); R. H. Drummond, *A History of Christianity in Japan* (Grand Rapids, Mich. [1971]). C. R. Boxer, *The Christian Century in Japan, 1549–1650* (1951). J. F. Schütte, SJ, *Introductio ad historiam Societatis Jesu in Japonia 1549–1650* (Rome, 1968). A. C. Ross, *A Vision Bretrayed: The Jesuits in Japan and China 1542–1742* (Edinburgh [1994]), pp. 1–117. G. Elison, *Deus Destroyed: The Image of Christianity in Early Modern Japan* (Cambridge, Mass., 1973). N. S. Fujita, *Japan's Encounter with Christianity: The Catholic Mission in pre-modern Japan* (New York [1991]). H. St G. Tucker, *The History of the Episcopal Church in Japan* (Hale Lectures, 1937; 1938 [Anglican]). C. W. Iglehart, *A Century of Protestant Christianity in Japan* (Rutland, Va., and Tokyo, 1959). A. Lande, *Meiji Protestantism in History and Historiography: A Comparative Study of Japanese and Western Interpretation of Early Protestantism in Japan* (Studien zur interkulturellen Geschichte des Christentums, 58; 1989). J. M. Oe, 'The Conflict of Church Views in Japan during Wartime 1940–1945: The Church Unification Problem of the Anglican Church in Japan (The Nippon Sei Ko Kwai)', *Anglican and Episcopal History*, 58 (1989), pp. 448–97. R. Lee, *Stranger in the Land: A Study of the Church in Japan* (World Studies of Churches in Mission, 1967). J. M. Phillips, *From the Rising of the Sun: Christians and Society in Contemporary Japan* (New York [1981]). R. A. Moore (ed.), *Culture and Religion in Japanese-American Relations: Essays on Uchimura Kanzō, 1861–1930* (Ann Arbor, Mich., 1981). Latourette, 3, pp. 322–35; 6, pp. 370–411; and 7, pp. 379–400, with bibl. refs.; K. S. Latourette, *Christianity in a Revolutionary Age*, 3 (1961), pp. 450–7; 5 (1963), pp. 424–42.

Jarrow. See WEARMOUTH AND JARROW.

Jaspers, Karl (1883–1969), German philosopher. His early interests were in medicine and psychiatry. In 1913 he became Privatdozent, and in 1921 Professor of Philosophy, at Heidelberg, where he remained until forced for political reasons to resign in 1937. He was reinstated in 1945, but moved to Basle, where he was Professor of Philosophy from 1948 to 1961.

Under the influence of S. *Kierkegaard, F. W. *Nietzsche and Protestant theology he developed a Christian *Existentialism, akin to (but not directly influenced by) the teaching of G. Marcel, in an endeavour to interpret the crisis in post-1918 Germany in secular philosophy and culture. Jaspers put religion and philosophy in contrast, and stressed the limits of science, notably in its ability to reach the self. This self is the ground of all existence and esp. characterized by the need for self-communication. Later Jaspers criticized R. *Bultmann on the grounds that his attempts at *demythologization presupposed that science had a total world-view, while he himself held that myths are rather particular signs or ciphers by which alone finite being can be brought into

relationship with Transcendence. He repudiated the exclusive claims of Christ, whom he regarded as one cipher among many, though in his last works he seems to have accorded Him a special position. His writings include *Die geistige Situation der Zeit* (1931; Eng. tr. as *Man in the Modern Age*, 1933), *Philosophie* (3 vols., 1932; Eng. tr., 3 vols., Chicago, 1969–71), *Der philosophische Glaube* (1948; Eng. tr. as *The Perennial Scope of Philosophy*, 1950), *Vom Ursprung und Ziel der Geschichte* (1949; Eng. tr. as *The Origin and Goal of History*, 1953), and *Der philosophische Glaube angesichts der Offenbarung* (1962; Eng. tr. as *Philosophical Faith and Revelation*, 1967).

Festschriften for his 70th birthday, K. Piper (ed.), *Offener Horizont* (Munich, 1953), with bibl. to date, pp. 449–59, and for his 80th birthday, id. (ed.), *Karl Jaspers Werk und Wirkung* (ibid., 1963), with bibl. pp. 173–216. P. A. Schilpp (ed.), *The Philosophy of Karl Jaspers* (New York, 1957; 2nd edn., La Salle, Ill., 1981), incl. a 'Philosophical Autobiography' by Jaspers, tr. into Eng., pp. 5–94. M. Dufrenne and P. Ricœur, *Karl Jaspers et la philosophie de l'existence* (1947); X. Tilliette, *Karl Jaspers: Théorie de la vérité métaphysique des chiffres, foi philosophique* (Théologie, 44 [1960]); W. Schneiders, *Karl Jaspers in der Kritik* (1965); G. Simon, *Die Achse der Weltgeschichte nach Jaspers* (Analecta Gregoriana, 147; 1965); L. H. Ehrlich, *Karl Jaspers: Philosophy as Faith* (Amherst, Mass., 1975) (2nd edn. has additional section on M. *Heidegger interpolated between pp. 75 and 76); A. M. Olson, *Transcendence and Hermeneutics: An Interpretation of the Philosophy of Karl Jaspers* (Studies in Philosophy and Religion, 2; 1979); E. Young-Bruehl, *Freedom and Karl Jasper's Philosophy* (New Haven, Conn., and London [1981]). J. Salaquarda in *TRE* 16 (1987), pp. 539–45, with bibl.

Jassy, Synod of (1642). Next to the Synod of *Jerusalem (1672), that of Jassy (in Moldavia: i.e. the modern *Romania) is the most important Council in the history of the Orthodox Church since the fall of Constantinople. Meeting as it did in the border country between the Ottoman Empire and Russia, it included representatives of both the Greek and the Slav Orthodox Churches. Its chief work, besides condemning the Calvinist teachings of Cyril *Lucar, was to ratify the *Orthodox Confession* of Peter *Mogila, Metropolitan of Kiev, who was present at the Synod. Before approval was secured, however, Meletius Syrigos, one of the two delegates of the Patriarchate of *Constantinople, made extensive alterations in Mogila's original text, aimed at lessening its markedly Latin and Scholastic character; but even in its revised form the *Confession* remains strongly influenced by RC theology.

Acts of the Synod in I. N. Karmires, Τὰ δογματικὰ καὶ συμβολικὰ Μνημεῖα τῆς Ὀρθοδόξου Καθολικῆς Ἐκκλησίας, 2 (1953), pp. 575–82. [J. C.] S. Runciman, *The Great Church in Captivity* (Cambridge, 1968), pp. 342–7. See also bibl. to MOGILA, PETER.

Jean-Baptiste Marie Vianney, St. See CURÉ D'ARS, THE.

Jeanne d'Arc, St. See JOAN OF ARC, ST.

Jeanne Françoise Frémyot de Chantal. See JANE FRANCES DE CHANTAL, ST.

Jebb, John (1775–1833), Bp. of Limerick. A native of Drogheda, he entered *Trinity College, Dublin, in 1791. After ordination as deacon in 1799 he held curacies in *Ireland and became Rector of Abington, Co. Limerick, in 1809. In 1820 he published his *Essay on Sacred Literat-*

ure, which made his name as an author. In 1822 he was appointed Bp. of Limerick.

A lifelong friend of Alexander *Knox, he anticipated certain of the leading doctrinal emphases of the *Oxford Movement, e.g. he laid stress on the unbroken continuity of the Church and on the *via media* of the C of E. His tract on the 'Peculiar Character of the Church of England' provided the starting-point for the exchange of letters between J. H. *Newman and the Abbé J. N. Jager which shaped Newman's *Lectures on the Prophetical Office of the Church* (1837). Jebb's concern for spirituality is seen in his *Piety without Asceticism* (1830).

He is to be distinguished from **John Jebb** (1736–86), a Fellow of Peterhouse, Cambridge, who in 1771 advocated the abolition of clerical subscription to the *Thirty-Nine Articles at graduation and in his later life gave up his ecclesiastical preferments and practised as a physician.

Jebb's tract on the 'Peculiar Character of the Church of England' was first pub. (with no title) as an appendix to his *Sermons* (1815), pp. 357–98, and subsequently issued separately. C. Forster (ed.), *Thirty Years' Correspondence, between John Jebb ... and Alexander Knox* (2 vols., 1834). Life by id., incl. selection of his letters (2 vols., London, 1836). L. Allen (ed.), *John Henry Newman and the Abbé Jager: A controversy on Scripture and Tradition (1834–1836)* (1975), *passim* (see index). A. Gordon in *DNB* 29 (1892), pp. 259–61.

Jehoshaphat, the Valley of. On the basis of Joel 3: 2 and 12 (the only OT refs.), the traditional scene of the Lord's Coming Judgement. The name is perhaps to be connected with King Jehoshaphat (1 Kgs. 15: 24, 22: 41–50) or some other historic person, but is prob. artificial, since 'Jehoshaphat' means 'Yahweh has judged'. Since the 4th cent. AD (*Eusebius, *Bordeaux Pilgrim, *Jerome) the name has been in current use among Jews, Christians, and Muslims for the valley separating *Jerusalem on the E. from the Mount of *Olives and traversed by the brook *Cedron, though the valley is not so described in the NT or by *Josephus.

H. Vincent, OP, and F. M. Abel, OP, *Jérusalem: Recherches de topographie, d'archéologie et d'histoire*, 2, Jérusalem nouvelle (1926), pp. 849–52. G. M. Perrella, CM, 'La valle di Giosafat e il giudizio universale', *Divus Thomas* (Piacenza), 36 (1933), pp. 45–50.

Jehovah. A form of the Hebrew Divine Name (more properly '*Yahweh', q.v.), which was popularized at the Renaissance. See TETRAGRAMMATON.

Jehovah's Witnesses. The popular name given since 1931 to the Watch Tower Bible and Tract Society which traces its origins in the 1870s to the *Adventist doctrines of the American lay preacher C. T. *Russell (q.v.). His main claim was that Jesus Christ, a perfect man, had returned invisibly to earth in 1878 in order to prepare for the Kingdom of God which was expected to materialize after the Battle of Armageddon in 1914. The overriding responsibility of believers was to study the Bible and to warn as many people as possible about the impending 'end time' so that they might survive on earth, in turn, a First Judgement, Christ's millennial reign on earth, and a Second Judgement. Only a 'small flock' of 144,000 people drawn from the whole of human history were to expect eternal life in heaven.

Schisms and reinterpretations of prophecy were frequent among Russell's followers until his successor, J. F. *Rutherford (q.v.), turned them, after the First World War, into a '*theocratic' organization demanding from its members exclusive commitment, rigid adherence to 'the Truth', and strict indifference to the world. Rutherford's uncompromising criticism of all political ideologies gave rise to frequent clashes with governments in many countries; it may also have helped to bring about more liberal legislation in regard to conscientious objection and the free exercise of religion. Nathan H. Knorr, who succeeded him in 1942, directed Jehovah's Witnesses progressively away from confrontation with the world and towards missionary activity at home and abroad. Their governance became less oligarchic and more bureaucratic under the presidency of Frederick W. Franz (1977–92).

The most visible hallmarks of Jehovah's Witnesses are their Kingdom Halls, their door-to-door ministry, the public sale of their magazines *The Watchtower* (1879 ff.) and *Awake!* (1946 ff.), and their vast assemblies held in public stadia. They are also distinctive in their taboo against blood transfusions, their practice of Baptism by complete *immersion, their own translations of the Bible, their refusal to honour symbols of nationhood, and their reluctance to mix with non-members. They have *c*.4 million members in more than 200 countries. Growth in membership is now higher in developing countries than in the advanced industrial societies, but they retain an American ethos and are still governed from the USA. The organization had about 129,000 active members in the UK in 1994.

T. White, *A People for His Name: A History of Jehovah's Witnesses and an Evaluation* (New York, etc. [1967]); A. Rogerson, *Millions now Living will Never Die: A Study of Jehovah's Witnesses* (1969); J. A. Beckford, *The Trumpet of Prophecy: A Sociological Study of Jehovah's Witnesses* (Oxford [1975]); J. M. Penton, *Apocalypse Delayed: The Story of Jehovah's Witnesses* (Toronto and London [1985]). J. Bergman, *Jehovah's Witnesses and Kindred Groups: A Historical Compendium and Bibliography* (New York and London, 1984).

Jeremiah (7th cent. BC), prophet of Judah. He was a native of Anathoth, nr. *Jerusalem, and probably belonged to the family of Abiathar, the high priest whom King *Solomon had deprived of his priestly functions. He was born *c*.650, and received his vocation to the prophetic office *c*.626 (Jer. 1: 1–19). Although he seems to have played no prominent role in public affairs during the first years of his ministry, he probably approved Josiah's reform (2 Kgs. 22: 1–23: 30), but without taking part in it. The death of Josiah at Megiddo (*c*.608) caused a change in the people and its rulers, under Jehoiakim (*c*.607–*c*.597), who reversed the religious reforms of Josiah, and from now on Jeremiah proclaimed the destruction of Jerusalem and the *Temple. After the battle of Carchemish (*c*.606) the prophet counselled submission to the Babylonians, but the king resisted, and Judah did not give in until after Jehoiakim's death *c*.597. Under the new king, Zedekiah, however, Judah continued to side with Egypt against Babylon, despising the warnings of the prophet, who, during the siege of Jerusalem, was first imprisoned and then thrown into a pit from which he was rescued by the Ethiopian eunuch Ebed-melech (38: 7–13). After the final destruction of the city (c.586) Jeremiah was left free to live in Judah, but after the assassination of the governor, Gedaliah, the Jews forced him to flee with them into Egypt, where he continued to reproach his countrymen for their idolatry (ch. 44). There is no record of his death in Scripture; acc. to a tradition mentioned by *Tertullian he was stoned to death by the Jews (cf. Heb. 11: 37). The same tradition is found, together with many colourful details, in the 'Rest of the Words of Baruch' (see BARUCH, III AND IV).

The Book of Jeremiah presents him as the most personal and sensitive of the OT prophets, conscious throughout of a close union with God. His prophetic office, which entailed the denunciation of the sins of Judah and the proclamation of their punishment, was in tragic conflict with his love for his people, which led him to intercede repeatedly on his nation's behalf.

Jeremiah's sufferings, caused by the ingratitude and misunderstanding of his people, his prophecy of the destruction of Jerusalem and his weeping over the doomed city, have traditionally been interpreted as figures of the life of Christ, and the W. Church has used the Book, together with the Book of *Lamentations ascribed to him, in her Offices for Passiontide.

For bibl., see foll. entry.

Jeremiah, Book of. The Jewish tradition, which ascribes it to *Jeremiah (q.v.), is ancient and unanimous, and is supported by frequent NT quotations. Many modern critics ascribe a great part of the Book to editors. The promises of restitution and the giving of a New Covenant (chs. 30 and 31) so closely resemble *Deutero-Isaiah that they are frequently attributed to ('deuteronomistic') scribes of the exilic or early post-exilic age; such scribes may also be responsible for the extensive narrative material, which is close to (in some places excerpted from) *Kings, though some scholars ascribe this to Jeremiah's amanuensis *Baruch. The so-called Oracles to the Nations are also often denied to Jeremiah, esp. the prophecy against Babylon (chs. 50 and 51), which contradicts the policy of submission consistently advocated by the prophet in other parts of the Book. The greatest critical problem raised by the Book, however, is the striking difference between the *Septuagint and the *Massoretic texts. The former is about one-eighth shorter than the latter, and in the Septuagint the Oracles against the Nations do not come at the end, but follow 25: 14. This divergence has been explained in many different ways; but most modern critics believe that the order of the Greek is original. The different order of the two texts may, however, arise from the amalgamation of two collections of prophecies, which were combined in two different ways, a theory which would also explain the chronological confusion noticeable throughout the Book. In ch. 36 the prophet himself tells us something of its origin. The prophecies, he says, were written down in the fourth year of Jehoiakim by Baruch, read to the king and burned by him, and then written again with additional material. These prophecies are usually believed to form the kernel of the Book, to which other material was added later, either by Jeremiah himself or by his disciples.

The prophecies generally held to be authentic relate to the ruin of Judah and Jerusalem, to the victories of Nebu-

chadnezzar, and to the captivity; and the prophet's chief object was the preparation of the Judaean people for receiving the lesson of the Exile. Emphatic in his scorn of idols (e.g. 2: 27 f.; 10: 1–5; 11: 10–13), he extols the transcendence of Yahweh, the ruler of the nations (10: 10; 25: 15 ff.), who are to Him as clay to the potter (18: 5–10). He is the God of justice and goodness, who condemns His people because they have abandoned righteousness (e.g. 7: 4–15). This sense of Divine justice causes Jeremiah's astonishment at seeing the wicked prosper (12: 1 f.), and here is raised for the first time in the OT the problem of the good fortune of sinners and the sufferings of the just. In face of the hostility of the official representatives of the religion of Judah, Jeremiah emphasizes the interior cult of the righteousness of the heart and of the observance of the moral law (22: 3), and has hard words for a purely external cult (6: 20; 7: 21 f.), though he assigns a place to a true ritual worship in Messianic times (17: 26; 31: 14) and insists on the importance of the Sabbath (17: 19–27). He denounces the universality of sin, which reigns in Judah from the highest to the lowest, among young and old, men and women (2: 29–37; 5: 1), and destroys almost all hope of salvation (5: 20–9). But (according to the present form of the Book) in the midst of this world of despair the prophet proclaims hope for the future (chs. 30 and 31). The most striking characteristic of Jer. is the New Covenant (31: 31–4) which God will make with His people, writing His Law in their hearts, and in which the Gentiles, too, will participate (16: 19–21) under the rule of the Messianic King, of the seed of David (23: 5–8; 33: 14–26). The Book of Jeremiah has had a great influence on the formation of exilic and post-exilic Jewish piety, and is one of the most striking adumbrations of the religion of the NT.

Modern comm. incl. B. *Duhm (KHC 11; 1901), W. Rudolph (HAT, I. 12; 1947), J. Steinmann (Lectio Divina, 9; Paris, 1952), A. Weiser (Das Alte Testament Deutsch, 20/21; 1952; 6th edn., 1969), J. Bright (Anchor Bible [1965]), E. W. Nicholson (Camb. Bib., NEB, 2 vols., 1973–5), R. P. Carroll (London, 1986), W. McKane (ICC, 2 vols., 1986–96) and D. R. Jones (New Cent. Bib., 1992). J. Skinner, *Prophecy and Religion: Studies in the Life of Jeremiah* (1922). G. A. *Smith, *Jeremiah* (Baird Lecture for 1922 [1923]). W. F. Lofthouse, *Jeremiah and the New Covenant* (1925). A. C. Welch, *Jeremiah: His Time and his Work* (1928). V. Herntrich, *Jeremia der Prophet und sein Volk* (1938). S. [O. P.] *Mowinckel, *Zur Komposition des Buches Jeremia* (Skrifter utgit av Videnskapsselskapet i Kristiania, 2, historisk-filosofisk Klasse, 1913, no. 5). P. Volz, *Studien zum Text des Jeremia* (Beiträge zur Wissenschaft vom Alten Testament, 25; 1920). H. H. Rowley, 'The Book of Jeremiah and the Book of Deuteronomy', in *Studies in Old Testament Prophecy Presented to Professor Theodore H. Robinson* (1950), pp. 157–74, repr. in *From Moses to Qumran* (1963), pp. 187–208; id., 'The Early Prophecies of Jeremiah in their Setting', *Bulletin of the John Rylands Library*, 45 (1963), pp. 198–234, repr. in *Men of God* (1963), pp. 133–68, with extensive refs. E. W. Nicholson, *Preaching to the Exiles: A Study in the Prose Tradition of the Book of Jeremiah* (1970). R. P. Carroll, *From Chaos to Covenant: Uses of Prophecy in the Book of Jeremiah* (1981). S. Herrmann in *TRE* 16 (1987), pp. 568–86, s.v. 'Jeremia/Jeremiahbuch', with extensive bibl.; J. R. Lundbom in *Anchor Bible Dictionary*, 3 (1992), pp. 706–21, s.v.

Jeremiah, Lamentations of. See LAMENTATIONS OF JEREMIAH.

Jeremy, Epistle of, or **Letter of Jeremiah.** A short item in the OT *Apocrypha. In what purports to be a letter (cf. Jer. 29: 1–23), the Prophet *Jeremiah (q.v.) declaims to the exiles whom Nebuchadnezzar transported to Babylon (c.597 and c.586 BC) against the folly of idol-worship. The traditional view that it was written in Hebrew has had its modern defenders; but most scholars hold that the Book was composed in Greek, in which alone it survives. It prob. dates from the 3rd or 2nd cent. BC. In most Greek MSS it is a separate item, and so appears in some modern English Bibles; but in a few MSS, as well as in the *Vulgate (and in the AV and RV), it appears at the conclusion of the Book of *Baruch (Bar. 6).

C. J. Ball in R. H. *Charles (ed.), *The Apocrypha and Pseud-epigrapha of the Old Testament*, 1 (Oxford, 1913), pp. 596–611; J. C. Dancy, *The Shorter Books of the Apocrypha* (Camb. Bib., NEB, 1972), pp. 197–209; C. A. Moore, *Daniel, Esther and Jeremiah: The Additions* (Anchor Bible, 44; 1977), pp. 317–58. W. Naumann, *Untersuchungen über den apokryphen Jeremiasbrief* (Beihefte zur ZATW, 25; 1913). H. St J. Thackeray, *Some Aspects of the Greek Old Testament* (Arthur Davis Memorial Lecture, 1927), pp. 54–64. Eissfeldt, pp. 594 f. E. *Schürer, *The History of the Jewish People in the Age of Jesus Christ*, rev. Eng. tr. by G. Vermes and others, 3 (pt. 2; Edinburgh, 1987), pp. 743–5, with bibl. See also bibl. to BARUCH, BOOK OF.

Jericho. A town of Palestine, near the Jordan, NE of *Jerusalem. Its miraculous capture by Joshua is narrated in Josh. 6. A later city on the site, in a very fertile valley, was favoured by *Herod the Great and visited by Christ (Mk. 10: 46, Lk. 19: 1, etc.).

K. M. Kenyon and T. A. Holland, *Excavations at Jericho* (5 vols., 1960–83). Popular account by K. M. Kenyon, *Digging up Jericho* (1957). J. R. Bartlett, *Jericho* (Cities of the Biblical World; Guildford, 1982). K. M. Kenyon and others in E. Stern and others (eds.), *The New Encyclopedia of Archaeology in the Holy Land*, 2 (Jerusalem and New York [1993]), pp. 674–97, s.v.

Jerome. Eng. form of Lat. 'Hieronymus'. The form 'Hierome' is sometimes found in older (e.g. 17th-cent.) English.

Jerome, St (c.345–420), Eusebius Hieronymus, biblical scholar. (The date of Jerome's birth at Strido, near *Aquileia, has been the subject of dispute: *Prosper of Aquitaine says that he was 90 when he died, implying that he was born in 330; though a chronology based on Prosper's statement has recently found some support (P. Hamblenne and J. N. D. Kelly), most scholars argue for a later date.) Jerome studied at *Rome, where he was baptized, and then travelled in Gaul before devoting himself to an ascetic life with friends at Aquileia. About 374 he set out for Palestine. He delayed in *Antioch, where he heard the lectures of *Apollinarius of Laodicea until self-accused in a dream of preferring pagan literature to religious ('Ciceronianus es, non Christianus'). He then settled as a hermit at Chalcis in the Syrian desert for four or five years, and while there learnt Hebrew. On his return to Antioch he was ordained priest by *Paulinus, next spent some time in *Constantinople, and from 382 to 385 was back in Rome, where he acted as secretary to Pope *Damasus and successfully preached asceticism (see MELANIA; PAULA). After Damasus' death he visited Antioch, Egypt, and Palestine, and in 386 finally settled at *Bethlehem, where he ruled a newly founded men's monastery and devoted the rest of his life to study.

Jerome's writings issued from a scholarship unsurpassed in the early Church. His greatest achievement was his translation of most of the Bible into Latin from the original tongues, to which he had been orig. prompted by Damasus (see VULGATE). He also wrote many biblical commentaries, in which he brought a wide range of linguistic and topographical material to bear on the interpretation of the sacred text. Further, he anticipated the Reformers in advocating the acceptance by the Church of the Hebrew *Canon of Scripture, thereby excluding those Books which came to be called the *Apocrypha. In addition to his biblical work, he translated and continued *Eusebius' 'Chronicle'; compiled a 'De Viris Illustribus', a bibliography of ecclesiastical writers; and translated into Latin works by *Origen and *Didymus. His correspondence is of great interest and historical importance. His passionate nature also led him to throw himself into many controversies and to attack *Arianism, *Pelagianism, and *Origenism (the last of which had led to a bitter quarrel with his friend *Rufinus of Aquileia who had remained faithful to Origen). In some of his letters to friends and in his tracts against *Helvidius and *Jovinian, he advocated extreme asceticism.

Since the 13th cent. he has often been depicted in art with a red hat, on the supposition that Damasus created him a cardinal. He is also often represented with a lion at his feet. Feast day, 30 Sept. See also PSALTER.

Jerome himself gives a list of his writings prior to AD 392 in his *De Viris Illustribus*, 135. Earliest collected edn. by *Erasmus (9 vols., Basle, 1516). The best collected edn. is that of D. *Vallarsi (11 vols., Verona, 1734–42), repr. in J. P. Migne, *PL* 22–30. A modern edn. in CCSL 72–80 etc., 1958 ff., is in progress. Separate works include Letters, ed. J. Hilberg (CSEL 54–6; 1910–18) and, with Fr. tr., by J. Labourt (Collection des Universités de France; 8 vols., 1949–63); and Comm. on Mt. ed., with Fr. tr., by É. Bonnard (SC 242 and 259; 1977–9). Eng. trs. of *Liber Quaestionum Hebraicarum in Genesim* by C. T. R. Haward (Oxford Early Christian Studies, 1995), of *De Viris Illustribus* by E. C. Richardson (NPNCF, 2nd ser. 3, 1892, pp. 359–84), and of Letters and other select works by W. H. Fremantle and others (ibid. 6, 1893). 'Select Letters' ed., with Eng. tr., by F. A. Wright (Loeb, 1933). Further Eng. tr. of Letters, by C. C. Mierow, with notes by T. C. Lawler (ACW 33, etc.; 1963 ff.). B. Lambert, OSB, *Bibliotheca Hieronymiana Manuscripta: La Tradition manuscrite des œuvres de saint Jérôme* (4 vols., Instrumenta Patristica, 4; 1969–72). Extended studies by G. Grützmacher (3 vols., Leipzig, 1901–8) and F. Cavallera, SJ (SSL 1 and 2; 1922; all pub.). Other studies by O. Zöckler (Gotha, 1865), P. Monceaux (Paris, 1932; Eng. tr. of pt. 1, 1933), A. Penna (Turin and Rome [1949]), P. Antin, OSB (Paris, 1951), J. Steinmann (ibid., 1958; Eng. tr., 1959), M. Testard (ibid., 1969), and J. N. D. Kelly (London, 1975). *Miscellanea Geronimiana: Scritti varii pubblicati nel XV centenario dalla morte di San Girolamo* (Rome, 1930). F. X. Murphy, CSSR (ed.), *A Monument to Saint Jerome: Essays on some Aspects of his Life, Works and Influence* (1952). Y. Bodin, *Saint Jérôme et l'Église* (Théologie historique, 6; 1966). P. Antin, OSB, *Recueil sur saint Jérôme* (Collection Latomus, 95; 1968). Y.-M. Duval, *Le Livre de Jonas dans la Littérature Chrétienne grecque et latine: Sources et influences du Commentaire sur Jonas de saint Jérôme* (2 vols., Études Augustiniennes, 1973); P. Jay, *L'Exégèse de saint Jérôme d'après son 'Commentaire sur Isaïe'* (ibid., 1985). Y.-M. Duval (ed.), *Jérôme entre l'Occident et l'Orient . . .: Actes du Colloque de Chantilly* (ibid., 1988). S. Rebenich, *Hieronymus und sein Kreis* (Historia, Einzelschriften, 72; 1992). P. Hamblenne, 'La longévité de Jérôme: Prosper avait-il raison?', *Latomus*, 28 (1969), pp. 1081–119; P. Jay, 'Sur la date de naissance de Saint Jérôme', *Revue des Études latines*, 51 (1973), pp. 262–80. H. F. D. Sparks, 'Jerome as Biblical

Scholar', in P. R. Ackroyd and C. F. Evans (eds.), *The Cambridge History of the Bible*, 1 (Cambridge, 1970), pp. 510–41. Bardenhewer, 3, pp. 605–54; Altaner and Stuiber (1978), pp. 394–404 and 632–4. W. H. Fremantle in *DCB* 3 (1882), pp. 29–50, s.v. 'Hieronymus (4)'; J. Forget in *DTC* 8 (pt. 1; 1924), cols. 894–983; F. Cavallera, SJ, in *Dict. Bibl.*, Suppl. 4 (1949), cols. 889–97, s.v.; J. Gribomont, OSB, in *Dict. Sp.* 8 (1974), cols. 901–18, s.v.; H. Hagendahl and J. H. Waszink in *RAC* 15 (1991), cols. 117–39, s.v. 'Hieronymus'. See also bibl. to VULGATE.

Jerome Emiliani, St (1481–1537), the founder of the *Somaschi. A native of *Venice, after service in the army he was ordained priest in 1518, and devoted himself for the rest of his life to work among the poor and afflicted, establishing orphanages, hospitals, and houses for fallen women. To foster this work he founded in 1532 a society, with its mother-house at the village of Somasca, between Milan and Bergamo. He was canonized in 1767 and made the patron saint of orphans and abandoned children by *Pius XI in 1928. Feast day, 8 Feb. (formerly 20 July).

Life by A. Tortora (Milan, 1620), repr. in *AASS*, Feb. 2 (1658), pp. 220–74. G. Landini, *S. Girolamo Miani dalle testimonianze processuali, dai biografi, dai documenti editi e inediti fino ad oggi* (1947). S. Raviolo, *San Girolamo Emiliani* (1947). S. Raiteri in *Dict. Sp.* 8 (1974), cols. 929–35, s.v. 'Jérôme (9) Miani', with bibl. col. 932. See also bibl. to SOMASCHI.

Jerome of Prague (*c.*1370–1416), Bohemian Reformer and friend of J. *Huss. Very little is known of his early life. He was prob. a native of Prague, where he studied and came under the influence of Huss and of the *Wycliffite philosophy. Encouraged by Huss to visit the European centres of learning, after taking his degree at Prague he made his way (1398) to *Oxford. Here he studied the theological writings of Wycliffe, esp. his 'Dialogus' and 'Trialogus', and brought them back to *Paris and Prague (*c.*1402). Acc. to his own testimony he was in *Jerusalem in 1403; he was in Paris again in 1404, at Heidelberg in 1405 and Cologne in 1406. In all these universities his exaggerated *Realism aroused much opposition. On his return to Prague in 1407 he took an active part in the religious controversies and became a leader of the nationalist university students. Wishing to gain also the neighbouring countries to Wycliffe's ideas, he had a discussion with King Sigismund of Hungary at Ofen in 1410 on the vices of the clergy. Being declared suspect of heresy, he fled to Moravia, but in 1412 he was back at Prague, where he violently attacked the bull of *John XXIII proclaiming an Indulgence for the crusade against Ladislaus of Naples. In 1413 he accompanied Grand Duke Witold of Cracow to Russia and Lithuania, and aroused suspicion by showing himself favourable to heterodox rites. In 1415 he followed Huss to *Constance. He escaped when he realized his danger, but was brought back to the Council in chains. After Huss's death (6 July), which led to a schism in Bohemia, the Council wished to avoid a second execution and applied pressure to obtain a retractation from Jerome. On 11 Sept. 1415 he consented to read a document anathematizing the teaching of Wycliffe and Huss and accepting the authority of the Papacy and the Council. The sincerity of this abjuration, however, soon became suspect, and the trial was resumed in May 1416. Jerome defended himself with great eloquence, but in the last part of his speech he took back his abjuration, proclaimed the

innocence and sanctity of Huss, and his own adherence to the teaching of Wycliffe on all points except *transubstantiation, which he accepted. After a last attempt to obtain his submission he was condemned to the stake, where he died with great courage, reciting hymns to the BVM.

The principal sources are the acts of the Council of Constance, and works dealing with Huss (q.v.). *Processus Iudiciarius contra Jeronimum de Praga habitus Viennae A. 1410–1412*, ed. L. Klicman (Česká Akademie Císaře Františka Josefa pro Vědy, Slovesnost a Umění v Praze, Historický Archiv, 12; Prague, 1898). F. Šmahel, *Jeroným Pražský* (Prague, 1966), summarized [in Germ.] in *Historica*, 13 (Prague, 1966), pp. 81–111. R. R. Betts, 'Jerome of Prague', *University of Birmingham Historical Journal*, 1 (1947), pp. 51–91; P. P. Bernard, 'Jerome of Prague, Austria and the Hussites', *Church History*, 27 (1958), pp. 3–22. *BRUO* 3 (1959), pp. 1512 f., s.v. 'Prague, Jerome of'.

Jerusalem. Referred to in the Egyptian Execration Texts (mid-19th cent. BC) as 'Rushalimum' and again in the *Tell el-Amarna Tablets (14th cent. BC) as 'Urusalim' (then subject to Egypt), the city became the capital of Judah, the site of its religious sanctuary (the *Temple, q.v.), and as such the 'Holy City'. The town, with its highest point *c.*2,680 ft. above sea-level, controls the north–south route along the hilly backbone of the country, though it stands apart from the coastal route connecting Egypt with Syria and Mesopotamia. The earliest Jerusalem lies to the south of the present Old City, on the eastern of the two ridges running south from the present walls. To the east, the *Cedron valley bounds both the Old City and the original site. The latter is separated from the western ridge by the Tyropoeon valley, now largely silted up. The Hinnom Valley (see GEHENNA) bounds the Old City and the western ridge on the west and curves round to the east to join the Cedron.

Archaeological evidence indicates the existence of habitation on the eastern portion of the site (Ophel) as early as *c.*3000 BC. In pre-Israelite times the inhabitants of the township seem to have been of mixed race. Ezek. 16: 3 appears to imply that they included Amorites and Hittites, while elsewhere (e.g. Josh. 15: 63) they are called 'Jebusites'. About 1000 BC the Jebusite stronghold known as 'Zion' was captured by *David, who refortified it as his own city (the 'City of David') and made Jerusalem, which had previously belonged to the territory of neither the northern nor the southern tribes, the capital of the United Monarchy. *Solomon, his successor, built the Temple some 950 ft. to the north of the original north wall, and enlarged the city by fortifying the intervening space. Settlement gradually extended on to the western ridge and by the 7th cent. BC, if not earlier, a substantial area there was walled. About 700 BC Jerusalem was threatened by attack from the Assyrians (2 Kgs. 18 f.). Among the measures taken by Hezekiah to counter this attack was the cutting of the 'Siloam Tunnel' through solid rock a distance of some 1,700 ft. to carry the water of the spring Gihon from the exposed east flank of the town to a rock-cut cistern on the west side. About 597 BC, and again *c.*586 BC, it was captured and devastated by Nebuchadnezzar, and many of its inhabitants were deported to Babylon (2 Kgs. 24 f.).

The return from exile was followed, after some years, by the rebuilding of the Temple, in 520–515 BC (the 'Second

Temple'). The walls of the city were not restored until the time of *Nehemiah (*c.*444 BC). After the Exile the Jews were an ecclesiastically governed state under the suzerainty first of Persia and then of the Greeks, the Ptolemies, and the Seleucids. This period ended with the *Maccabaean wars of the 2nd cent. BC, during which the Temple was profaned under *Antiochus Epiphanes (167 BC). After the rededication of the Temple in 164 BC, there followed a revival of Jewish national glory under a short dynasty of priest-kings. During this period the city was extended on to the northern end of the western ridge. The Maccabaean period ended with the Roman conquest by Pompey (63 BC), after which the country was ruled directly or indirectly from Rome. The Temple was extensively renovated by *Herod the Great, who ruled as a vassal of Rome from 37 to 4 BC. The turbulence of the people and the misgovernment of Roman procurators and local rulers combined to produce the rebellion of AD 66, which was followed by a four-year siege, and, on the fall of Jerusalem in 70, the extermination or removal of most of the population and the destruction of the city, incl. the Temple. A small and scattered population survived, however, until Hadrian, after the Jewish revolt in his reign, refounded the place as a Gentile city under the name of *Aelia Capitolina (AD 135).

The Christian history of the city begins with the short ministry of the Lord, culminating in His Crucifixion and Resurrection. There the Apostles lived and taught for some time after *Pentecost, and after they had scattered farther afield they met in Jerusalem with the 'elders' of the Church for the first Christian council (Acts 15; *c.* AD 49). St *James, 'the Lord's brother', presided over the local Church after the dispersion of the Twelve, and it seems likely that the kinsmen of the Lord exercised some measure of leadership among the neighbouring Christian community until the foundation of Aelia Capitolina and the banishment at that time of all Jews from the region. From that date the local Church was purely Gentile in composition.

It was not until the visit of St *Helena (*c.* AD 326), the mother of *Constantine, and the beginning of the fashion of venerating the holy places set by her visit, that the Christian see became of any importance. Until the 5th cent. the see was suffragan to *Caesarea. But at the Council of *Chalcedon (451) the bishopric (see JUVENAL) was granted patriarchal dignity. The see never attained, however, to the prestige of the other patriarchates, and when the Crusaders held the city in the 12th cent. the (E.) patriarch lived in *Constantinople. Though for some periods afterwards the patriarchs came back to Jerusalem, they have been permanently settled there only since 1845; since the first half of the 16th cent. the patriarch has always been a Greek, although the great majority of the faithful were and are Arabs. A Latin patriarchate was in existence from 1099 till 1291, and nominally till 1374, and was again constituted in 1847. There is also a (Gregorian) *Armenian patriarchate, and the *Melchite Patr. of Antioch adds the title of Jerusalem to his others.

The Christian centre of Jerusalem is the Church of the Resurrection, commonly known outside the country as the Church of the *Holy Sepulchre. The site of the Temple was long in Muslim hands, and is occupied mostly by the *Dome of the Rock. There are numerous other holy places within and outside the city. Where both Orthodox and Latins claim that their particular site is the genuine scene of the mystery commemorated, the Easterns have usually the more ancient tradition, the Latin sites generally having been established at earliest in Crusading times.

The present city covers only part of that of NT times. During the reign of Herod Agrippa (AD 40–4) the whole of the western ridge was enclosed, with a wall joining the southern tip of the original city on the eastern ridge, and to the north by *c.* half a mile. When Aelia Capitolina was built on the ruins of Jerusalem, the whole of the area to the south, including the entire original city, was left outside the walls, while the north wall of Aelia followed that of Herod the Great. The walls of the Old City now follow approximately those of Aelia Capitolina. The traditional sites of *Calvary and the Holy Sepulchre lie in the area outside the walls of the town of Herod the Great, but inside those of Herod Agrippa built some 14 years after the date of the Crucifixion, and are therefore within the present Old City. The alternative site to the north of the present wall (see GORDON'S CALVARY) can no longer be accepted. The walls of the present city date from the 16th cent., though much of the work done in the Frankish rebuilding (*c.*1230) still remains.

L. H. Vincent, OP, and F. M. Abel, OP, *Jérusalem: Recherches de topographie, d'archéologie et d'histoire* (2 vols. bound in 4, 1912–26); J. Simons, SJ, *Jerusalem in the Old Testament: Researches and Theories* (Leiden, 1952); L. H. Vincent, OP, and A. M. Steve, OP, *Jérusalem de l'Ancien Testament: Recherches d'archéologie et d'histoire* (3 parts in 2 vols. + 2 vols. of plates, 1954–6). K. M. Kenyon, *Digging up Jerusalem* (1974); Y. Yadin (ed.), *Jerusalem Revealed: Archaeology in the Holy City 1968–1974* (Jerusalem, 1975); N. Avigad, *Discovering Jerusalem* (Oxford, 1984; tr. from Heb. pub. at Jerusalem, 1980). F. E. Peters, *Jerusalem: The Holy City in the Eyes of Chroniclers, Visitors, Pilgrims, and Prophets from the Days of Abraham to the Beginnings of Modern Times* (Princeton, NJ [1985]), with Eng. tr. of texts. G. A. *Smith, *Jerusalem: The Topography, Economics and History from the Earliest Times to A.D. 70* (2 vols., 1907–8). J. Jeremias, *Jerusalem zur Zeit Jesu* (4 parts, 1923–37; 3rd edn., 1962; Eng. tr., 1969). J. [D.] Wilkinson, *Jerusalem as Jesus knew it: Archaeology as Evidence* ([1978; popular]); id., *Jerusalem Pilgrims before the Crusades* (Warminster [1977]), with convenient Eng. tr. of texts. E. D. Hunt, *Holy Land Pilgrimages in the Later Roman Empire, A.D. 312–460* (Oxford, 1982). H. Busse and G. Kretschmar, *Jerusalemer Heiligtumstraditionen im altkirchlicher und frühislamischer Zeit* (Abhandlungen des Deutschen Palästinavereins [8]; Wiesbaden, 1987). P. W. L. Walker, *Holy City, Holy Places? Christian Attitudes to Jerusalem and the Holy Land in the Fourth Century* (Oxford Early Christian Studies, 1990). On modern Jerusalem, K. Prag, *Jerusalem* (Blue Guide, 1989). On the Greek Patriarchate, M. *Le Quien, OP, *Oriens Christianus*, 3 (1740), pp. 101–528; C. Papadopoulos, Ἱστορία τῆς Ἐκκλησίας Ἱεροσολύμων (1910); T. Dowling, *The Orthodox Greek Patriarchate of Jerusalem* (1913). J. D. Purvis, *Jerusalem, the Holy City: A Bibliography* (2 vols., Metuchen, NJ, and London, 1988–91). L. H. Vincent in *Dict. Bibl.*, Suppl. 4 (1949), cols. 898–966, s.v.; P. J. King in *Anchor Bible Dictionary*, 3 (1992), pp. 747–66, s.v.; B. Mazar and others in E. Stern and others (eds.), *The New Encyclopedia of Archaeological Excavations in the Holy Land*, 2 (Jerusalem and New York [1993]), pp. 698–804, s.v. There are also continuing series of technical reports on excavations undertaken since 1960.

Jerusalem, Anglican Bishopric in. In 1841 a bishopric was set up in *Jerusalem by the joint efforts of England and Prussia to serve the Anglicans and Protestants of

Syria, Chaldaea, Egypt, and *Ethiopia. The scheme, which provided that the bishop was to be nominated by England and Prussia alternately, excited opposition both among *Lutherans, who disliked any semblance of episcopal order, and *High Church Anglicans, who objected to a virtual union with a Protestant body, without guarantees for the preservation of Church order or doctrine. The first holder of the see was M. S. *Alexander (q.v.), a Christian convert from orthodox Judaism. Estrangement between the two communities increased as the numbers of Germans living in Palestine grew, and the scheme finally collapsed in 1886, when the Anglicans required that the bishop should always be consecrated acc. to the Anglican rite and should assent to the *Thirty-Nine Articles. Since then the see has been maintained by the Anglicans alone. It was an archbishopric from 1957 to 1976, when the Episcopal Church of Jerusalem and the Middle East was established. Besides serving the spiritual needs of Anglicans in the area, it does missionary work and is a valued point of contact for Anglicanism with the E. Churches and, to a lesser degree, with the Latin Churches in the E.

[H. Abeken, anon.], *Das evangelische Bisthum in Jerusalem: Geschichtliche Darlegung mit Urkunden* (Berlin, 1842). Eng. tr. of this work, with additions, in W. H. Hechler (ed.), *The Jerusalem Bishopric* (1883). K. Schmidt-Clausen, *Vorweggenommene Einheit: Die Gründung des Bistums Jerusalem im Jahre 1841* (Arbeiten zur Geschichte und Theologie des Luthertums, 15; 1965). P. J. Welch, 'Anglican Churchmen and the Establishment of the Jerusalem Bishopric', *JEH* 8 (1957), pp. 193–204, with refs. S. L. Ollard in *DECH*, pp. 298 f., s.v.

Jerusalem, Knights of St John in. See HOSPITALLERS.

Jerusalem, Synod of (1672). The most important modern Council in the *Orthodox Church, held in the Basilica of the Nativity at *Bethlehem (hence sometimes known as the 'Synod of Bethlehem'). It was convened by *Dositheus (q.v.), Patr. of Jerusalem, and sought to repudiate the movement fostered by Cyril *Lucar towards accommodation with *Calvinism. Along with the Synod of *Jassy (1642) it marked the closest approximation of E. Orthodoxy, of which it desired to be fully representative, to *Tridentine Catholicism. It decreed, *inter alia*, that the Church is equally infallible with Scripture; that predestination depends on foreknowledge and takes account of works; that God cannot be the cause of evil; that the Church has a part in the mediatorial office of Christ; that justification is through faith working by love; that natural virtue is to be distinguished from that of the regenerate; that souls which have fallen from grace may be purified in Hades after death, so as to be fit for the final vision of God; that there are seven sacraments; that *receptionism, or the doctrine that the beneficial operation of the sacrament depends upon the faith of the recipient, is to be condemned; that Baptism is an effectual sign of grace; that in the Eucharist the elements are transubstantiated (though doubt has been sometimes expressed as to whether the philosophical implications of μετουσιοῦσθαι are the same as those of *transubstantiari*); and that 2 Esdras, Tobit, Judith, Wisdom, Ecclus., the Song of the Three Children, Susanna, Bel and the Dragon, and 1–3 Maccabees are all to be regarded as canonical.

Acta first pr. by the *Maurist, M. Foucqueret, OSB, *Synodus Bethleemitica adversus Calvinistas Haereticos* (Paris, 1676); repr. in Hardouin, 9, cols. 179–274; also in E. J. Kimmel (ed.), *Monumenta Fidei Ecclesiae Orientalis* (Jena, 1850), 1, pp. 325–487, and in I. N. Karmires, Τὰ δογματικὰ καὶ συμβολικὰ Μνημεῖα τῆς Ὀρθοδόξου Καθολικῆς Ἐκκλησίας, 2 (Athens, 1953), pp. 694–773. Eng. tr., with tr. of Cyril Lucar's Confession of 1631 in an appendix, by J. N. W. B. Robertson, *The Acts and Decrees of the Synod of Jerusalem* (1899). [J. C.] S. Runciman, *The Great Church in Captivity* (Cambridge, 1968), bk. 2, ch. 9, esp. pp. 351 f. See also further works cited s.v. DOSITHEUS.

Jesse window. A window whose design is based on the descent of Jesus from the royal line of *David, in most cases taking the form of a tree springing from Jesse, the father of David, and ending in Jesus or the Virgin and Holy Child, with the intermediary descendants placed on scrolls of foliage branching out of each other. Examples of the window are to be seen at the cathedrals of *Wells and *Chartres, St George's, Hanover Square (a 16th-cent. window from Antwerp), and in *Dorchester Abbey, near Oxford, where the tree forms the mullions.

A. Watson, *The Early Iconography of the Tree of Jesse* (1934); C. Woodforde, 'A Group of Fourteenth Century Windows showing the Tree of Jesse', *Journal of the British Society of Master Glass Painters*, 6 (1937), pp. 184–90; H. T. Kirby, 'The "Jesse Tree" motif in Stained Glass. A comparative study of some English examples', *The Connoisseur*, 141 (1958), pp. 77–82; id., 'The "Jesse Tree" motif in stained glass: a comparative study of some English examples—Part 2', *The Connoisseur Year Book*, 1959 [1958], pp. 85–90.

Jesu, Dulcis Memoria. The celebrated late 12th-cent. poem, very familiar through the translations of sections of it in the English hymns 'Jesu, the very thought of Thee With sweetness fills my breast' (by E. *Caswall) and 'Jesu! the very thought is sweet! In that dear name all heart-joys meet' (by J. M. *Neale). The intense mysticism and honeyed beauty of its language are unsurpassed in medieval devotional literature, though the complete poem (168 lines) suffers from a certain monotony in ideas. It has traditionally (but certainly wrongly) been ascribed to St *Bernard of Clairvaux. A. *Wilmart has shown that it is prob. the work of an English Cistercian. Sections of it have been used as a *Sequence and an *Office Hymn for the Feast of the Holy *Name. It is sometimes known as the 'Rosy Sequence' or as the 'Joyful' (or 'Jubilee') 'Rhythm'.

The best edn. of the Lat. text is that in A. Wilmart, OSB, *Le 'Jubilus' dit de Saint Bernard* (Storia e Letteratura, 2; Rome, 1944), pp. 183–97. Convenient text also in *Oxford Book of Medieval Latin Verse* (new edn. by F. J. E. Raby, 1959), no. 233, pp. 347–53. H. Lausberg, *Der Hymnus 'Jesu dulcis memoria'* (Hymnologische und hagiographische Studien, 1; Munich, 1967 [an exhaustive study]). E. *Gilson, 'Sur le *Iesu Dulcis Memoria*', *Speculum*, 3 (1928), pp. 322–34. J. Szövérffy, *Die Annalen der lateinischen Hymnendichtung*, 2 (1965), pp. 79–83.

Jesuits. The Society of Jesus, founded by St *Ignatius Loyola (q.v.) with nine companions, was approved by *Paul III in the bull '*Regimini militantis ecclesiae' in 1540. The constitutions of the Society, constructed by Ignatius and his secretary, Juan de Polanco, were officially approved by the membership in 1558. Beyond securing the spiritual benefit of its members, the more immediate aim of the Society was through its various ministries to labour 'for the propagation of the faith' and the promotion of Christian piety, esp. through the '*Spiritual Exercises' written by Ignatius. The most characteristic institutions of the Society, however, were the humanist schools, not foreseen at the beginning but founded in great numbers everywhere in the world after the first opened in Messina in 1548. Among the most important schools of the first generation were the Roman College (*Gregorianum) and the German College in Rome, where several decades later the Jesuits undertook the direction of the *English College. Contrary to what is often said, the Society was not founded to oppose the *Reformation, but by 1550 it began under St Peter *Canisius to be intensely engaged with the situation in Germany, and then with similar situations elsewhere. None the less, the Society flourished during its first century esp. in the Iberian and Italian peninsulas.

Peculiar to the Jesuits is a special vow to travel for ministry anywhere in the world that the Pope may order, an indication of the missionary aim that motivated Ignatius and his companions from the beginning. Hardly had the Society been approved when St *Francis Xavier established it in *India and *Japan and Manuel de Nóbrega in *Brazil. Several other features pointing to a missionary and strongly ministerial character also distinguish Jesuits from other religious orders: they are bound by vows not to accept any position in the hierarchy except under direct constraint by the Pope; they have no distinctive habit; are exempt from the obligation to chant or recite the *Office in choir. At an early stage careful provision was made for the spiritual and intellectual formation of those entering the Order and for their extended probation after admission. Superiors hold office for limited periods, usually six years. Supreme authority is vested in a General Congregation representative of the members; this body has to be summoned on the death of a General to elect his successor and if a lesser Congregation, drawn from the delegates of the provinces sent at intervals to report to the General, requires him to summon it. For routine administration authority is concentrated in the General, who is elected for life.

Often with their schools as their basis of operation, the Jesuits engaged extensively in preaching, adult education through series of lectures on Scripture, giving the 'Spiritual Exercises', the hearing of confessions, and in 'missions' (an early form of religious 'revival') to remote parts of the countryside that might last several weeks. They were esp. noted for promoting more frequent reception of the Eucharist. They taught catechism, which they often set to tunes, and used children to teach other children. Jesuits also founded orphanages, half-way houses for reformed prostitutes, and other 'works of mercy', which they then turned over to confraternities under autonomous lay management. At Ignatius's death the Society had about a thousand members. During the first hundred years it included, besides those already mentioned, D. *Laínez (the second General), St Francis *Borgia, St *Aloysius Gonzaga, St Robert *Bellarmine, C. *Aquaviva, F. *Suárez, and M. *Ricci. By 1600 the Order numbered over 8,500 members in 23 provinces, grouped in four assistancies, whose heads resided with the General. Under Aquaviva (General, 1581–1615) the Order achieved an organization of high efficiency, with an elaborate code, the *Ratio Studiorum, to govern its work in education. At the beginning of the 17th cent. the Society appeared secure both in Europe and the mission field. In 1623 a province was formed in England, where St Edmund *Campion and R. *Parsons had been sent in 1580 to work alongside the seminary priests among the *recusants. In the prevailing situation they could readily be represented as especially obnoxious, not least because they had an effective organization behind them, and there was some hostility towards them even among a few English RCs. In France they made little progress because of the Wars of Religion and the influence of *Gallicanism, but they were protected by *Henry IV, who chose a Jesuit as his confessor, starting a tradition which lasted for nearly two centuries in France and spread to other courts. In Flanders the Jesuits made a large contribution to the establishment of Catholic reform, and the Jesuit J. *Bollandus inaugurated the publication of critical editions of lives of the saints (see ACTA SANCTORUM).

In the later 17th cent. the Jesuits met with serious opposition within the RC Church. The debate on the question of free will and grace which *Paul V tried to close by ending the 'Congregatio *De Auxiliis' was reopened on a new foundation by C. O. *Jansen in a work so learned that few immediately grasped its full implications. His followers attacked the Jesuits for their lax casuistry, and not long afterwards the Jesuits also came under attack on the question of *accommodation in the Chinese Rites controversy. A combination of the opponents of the Jesuits, led by the *Parlement* of Paris, compelled Louis XV to withdraw his protection and expel them from France in 1764. In 1759, under the influence of the Marquis de Pombal, the Society was banished from *Portugal, and in 1767, by order of the Count of Aranda, chief minister of Charles III, 5,000 Jesuits were deported from Spain and its Empire. In 1773 Pope *Clement XIV gave way to the demands of France, Spain, Portugal, and many of the Italian states, and issued the brief '*Dominus ac Redemptor' suppressing the Society.

The suppression did not mean that the Society was extinguished. In Austria and Germany Jesuits were allowed to teach, and they were protected by both Frederick II of Prussia and the Empress Catherine of Russia. In White Russia, indeed, a noviciate was opened in 1780. They also survived and were able to retain their possessions in England, where the government took no action and the local RC bishops were deterred from enforcing the brief by fears of the penalties of *praemunire. In 1794 they established their school at *Stonyhurst (q.v.). The mission in Maryland, USA (founded in 1634), continued almost unaffected. Elsewhere they gradually managed to re-establish themselves, and in 1814 the Society was formally restored by *Pius VII in the bull 'Sollicitudo omnium ecclesiarum'.

At present the Society is to be found in most countries of the world, and in 1990 had some 24,500 members. Jesuits are responsible for numerous institutions in Rome (including the Vatican Radio Station) and for schools and academic centres in many parts of the world, as well as for supplying priests in hundreds of parishes. They also edit a number of periodicals, incl. *Gregorianum, Analecta Bollandiana, Biblica, Études, Civiltà Cattolica, The Heythrop Journal, Theological Studies*, and *The Month*.

D. Bartoli, SJ, *Dell'istoria della Compagnia de Giesu* (5 vols., Genoa and Rome, 1656–73). J. Cretineau-Joly, SJ, *Histoire religieuse, politique et littéraire de la Compagnie de Jésus* (6 vols., 1844–6). W. V. Bangert, SJ, *A History of the Society of Jesus* (St Louis, 1972; 2nd edn., 1986). J. Brodrick, SJ, *The Origin of the Jesuits* (1940); id., *The Progress of the Jesuits, 1556–79* (1946). W. V. Bangert, SJ, and T. M. McCoog, SJ, *Jerome Nadal, SJ, 1507–1580: Tracking the First Generation of Jesuits* (Chicago [1992]); J. W. O'Malley, *The First Jesuits* (Cambridge, Mass., and London, 1993). Convenient Eng. tr. of *The Constitutions of the Society of Jesus*, with comm. and introd., by G. E. Ganss, SJ (St Louis, 1970). Further comm. on them by A. M. de Aldama, SJ (6 vols., Rome, 1973–89; Eng. tr., St Louis, Mo., 1989 ff.). M. Sievernich, SJ, and G. Switek, SJ (eds.), *Ignatianisch: Eigenart und Methode der Gesellschaft Jesu* (Freiburg, etc., 1990). J. de Guibert, SJ, *La Spiritualité de la Compagnie de Jésus* (posthumous; Bibliotheca Instituti Historici S.I., 4; Rome, 1953; Eng. tr., Chicago, 1964). J.-F. Gilmont, SJ, *Les écrits spirituels des premiers Jésuites: Inventaire commenté* (Subsidia ad historiam S.I., 3; Rome, 1961). G. Codina Mir, SJ, *Aux Sources de la Pédagogie des Jésuites: Le 'Modus Parisiensis'* (Bibliotheca Instituti Historici S.I., 28; Rome, 1968). A. Scaglione, *The Liberal Arts and the Jesuit College System* (Amsterdam and Philadelphia, 1986). A. L. Martin, *The Jesuit Mind: The Mentality of an Elite in Early Modern France* (Ithaca, NY, and London, 1988). Valuable account of the suppression of the Society in Pastor, 38 ('1951' [1952]), based on unpub. sources placed at the author's disposal by the Society. Augustin de Backer, SJ, Aloys de Backer, SJ, and A. Carayon, SJ, *Bibliothèque de la Compagnie de Jésus* (ed. C. Sommervogel, SJ, 10 vols., 1890–9, with 2 suppl. vols. by E. M. Rivière, SJ, 1911–13); L. Polgár, SJ, *Bibliographie sur l'histoire de la Compagnie de Jésus 1901–1980* (6 vols., Rome, 1981–90). L. Koch, SJ, *Jesuiten-Lexikon: Die Gesellschaft Jesu einst und jetzt* (1934). *Monumenta Historica Societatis Jesu* (Madrid, 1894 ff., and Rome, 1925 ff.); *Archivum Historicum Societatis Jesu* (Rome, 1932 ff.).

H. Foley, SJ, *Records of the English Province of the Society of Jesus* (7 vols. bound in 8, 1877–83). M. V. Hay, *The Jesuits and the Popish Plot* (1934). E. F. Sutcliffe, SJ, *Bibliography of the English Province of the Society of Jesus, 1773–1953* (1957). T. Hughes, SJ, *The History of the Society of Jesus in North America* (3 vols. bound in 4, 1907–17). H. Fouqueray, SJ, *Histoire de la Compagnie de Jésus en France des origines à la suppression, 1528–1762* (5 vols., 1910–25). A. Astráin, SJ, *Historia de la Compañía de Jesús en la Asistencia de España* (7 vols., 1902–25). L. Frías, SJ, *Historia de la Compañía de Jesús en su Asistencia moderna de España* (2 vols., 1923–44). F. Rodrigues, SJ, *História da Companhia de Jesus na Assistência de Portugal* (4 vols. in 7 parts, 1931–50). P. Tacchi Venturi, SJ, *Storia della Compagnia di Gesù in Italia* [1534–1556] (2 vols. in 4, 1910–51), cont. as vols. 3 and 4 by M. Scaduto, SJ, *L'epoca di Giacomo Laínez* (2 vols., 1964–74). B. Duhr, SJ, *Geschichte der Jesuiten in den Ländern deutscher Zunge* (4 vols. bound in 5, 1907–28). J. A. Otto, *Gründung der neuen Jesuitenmission durch General Pater Johann Philipp Roothaan* (1939). See also bibls. under separate countries. Heimbucher, 2, pp. 130–340 and 666 f. X. Le Bachelet and others in *DTC* 8 (pt. 1; 1924), cols. 1012–1108; J. F. Broderick in *NCE* 7 (1967), pp. 898–909, s.v.; A. Derville, SJ, and others, in *Dict. Sp.* 8 (1974), cols. 958–1065, s.v.; also pub. separately, with introd. by A. Guillermou, as *Les Jésuites: Spiritualité et activités. Jalons d'une histoire* (1974). See also works cited under IGNATIUS LOYOLA, ST.

Jesus. The Gk. form ('Ιησοῦς) of the Heb. Joshua (יְשׁוּעַ; lit. 'Yahweh saves'), who is thus referred to in the NT at Heb. 4: 8 (AV). By Divine command (Lk. 1: 31, Mt. 1: 21) the name was bestowed on the Infant Christ, the Saviour of mankind.

Jesus, Name of. See NAME OF JESUS.

Jesus, Sayings of. See SAYINGS OF JESUS.

Jesus Christ. Jesus of *Nazareth is called by His followers '*Christ', χριστός, translating the Hebrew מָשִׁיחַ, i.e. (God's) *Messiah or anointed one (Mt. 1: 16). His historical existence was not doubted by early Roman sources (*Pliny, *Tacitus, *Suetonius), by *Josephus, or later by the *Talmud, and the modern so-called 'Christ-myth' theory (that Jesus never lived) has convinced few. Jesus was apparently born shortly before the death in 4 BC of *Herod the Great and was executed in or around AD 30 after condemnation by Pontius *Pilate (for discussion of dates, see CHRONOLOGY, BIBLICAL).

The Gospel of St *Mark (c. AD 70) reports His *Baptism by *John the Baptist in the river *Jordan, His *Temptation in the desert, and a ministry of preaching, teaching, and healing in *Galilee and *Judaea. The narrative centres on a *Transfiguration. Jesus chose twelve disciples (*Apostles) and attracted other supporters, including women. Crowds gathered, but the religious leadership was hostile and finally handed Him over to Pilate for trial and *crucifixion. He was buried but the tomb was found empty, and a 'young man' in white (Mk. 16: 5) told the women that He had been raised. Mark's narrative is generally followed in the Gospels of St *Matthew and St *Luke but substantially expanded, notably by their birth and infancy stories, a considerable body of teaching from Jesus and a little from the Baptist, a few new incidents, and their varying accounts of *Resurrection appearances, including in Matthew a command to 'disciple all nations', baptizing them into the three-fold name, and in Luke–Acts the *Ascension.

The author of St *John's Gospel evidently had access to an alternative narrative tradition which gave greater prominence to Jesus' activity in Judaea and probably included a collection of 'signs'. He omits the *Synoptists' accounts of the institution of the *Eucharist at the Last Supper, but includes a Eucharistic section in his discourse on the bread of life (6: 51–8). He makes no mention of a Transfiguration, presumably because his whole story reveals the glory of Jesus. Similarly, the Synoptic accounts of the temptations, *exorcisms, and agony in *Gethsemane, all highly important in Mark's portrayal of Jesus' struggle against evil, find no place in John's representation of Jesus as the man from heaven who is barely touched by human weakness and pain. However, even John is clear that Jesus was a human being, whose mother *Mary and *brethren (7: 3) were known (Mk. 6: 3 and Mt. 13: 56 include sisters), and who suffered an ignominious death on a cross outside *Jerusalem. He tells of other disciples unknown to the Synoptics, including the mysterious '*beloved disciple' for whom he claims eye-witness testimony (19: 35; 21: 24).

Little is known of Jesus' early life. His 'presumed father' (Lk. 3: 23) *Joseph does not appear during the ministry and was perhaps dead by that time. Jesus was brought up in Nazareth, a builder or carpenter by trade (τέκτων, Mk. 6: 3), perhaps like his father (Mt. 13: 55). The birth narratives are partly modelled on Scripture, but Matthew and Luke are in both artistry and theology far superior to the later apocryphal *Infancy Gospels. Matthew uses scriptural quotations, typology, symbol, and in his *genealogy a numerical pattern, to establish the messianic identity of Jesus as son of David and son of God. Jesus is also called son of Abraham (Mt. 1: 1). *Moses typology in Mt. 2 and 4 prepares the reader for Jesus declaring God's will to His people. Luke's much longer prelude roots God's saving intervention on behalf of both *Gentiles and His people Israel in biblical tradition, and so affirms the Church's legitimacy and reinforces its identity as God's multiracial people (Acts 2: 9–11) in the long-awaited age of the *Holy Spirit. Its story about the birth of John underlines his theological relationship to Jesus.

Most scholars accept the arguments of *Form Criticism that the traditions from and about Jesus reached the evangelists already soaked in theological reflection about His meaning and significance. All four presentations of the Baptist reflect his importance for the Churches, but they show his importance for Jesus too. It is widely agreed that He acknowledged John's calling (cf. Mt. 11: 7–14; Mk. 11: 30) and was baptized by Him. Their ministries perhaps overlapped (Jn. 3: 22–6; 4: 1), and some of Jesus' first followers apparently came from John (Jn. 1: 35; Acts 18: 25). But He saw differences between His own and John's message and activity. Both included the note of Divine judgement in their *eschatological proclamation (cf. Mt. 10: 15; 11: 20–4), but in His certainty of the nearness of God's rule, Jesus stressed the positive side of what this meant for the poor, hungry, and suffering, and the lost sheep of the house of Israel.

The forms of this preaching and teaching can be analysed by the historian more easily than its content, and widely different accounts are to be found in the writings of equally skilled and responsible scholars. Jesus' remembered words consist largely of *parables and aphorisms. He used this-worldly realities to confront His hearers with the moral and religious challenge of God. He proclaimed and exemplified the will of God with prophetic and more than prophetic authority. Unlike the scribes this charismatic teacher and healer did not derive His authority from the law of Moses. While taking its validity for granted He acted and spoke with an immediacy grounded in His consciousness of an intimate relationship with God. This relationship is reflected in His addressing God as Father, *Abba, an intimacy He communicated in teaching His disciples how to pray.

Debates about the interpretation of the *Sabbath laws were not unusual among Jewish religious teachers of the day, but Jesus' extraordinary powers provoked controversy when He healed someone on the sabbath. His clear sense of God's will and the intention of the law led Him to criticize the traditions of scribal interpretation and perhaps to sit lightly to the laws on purity. Conversely, His prohibition of *divorce, based on the dictum that the end-time would be like the primal time of creation, was stricter than *Deuteronomy (24: 1–4). In both areas Jesus' teaching was later appealed to in support of divergent Christian practice, but it seems that He was less concerned to legislate for the contemporary or future covenant people than to confront individuals most urgently and directly with the challenge and opportunity of the present moment. As the record of God's revealed will and promise, the law of Moses provided a natural point of reference for any religious proclamation in the culture, but Jesus' teaching was not based on this, as was that of the scribes.

The most important symbol by which He expressed His religious meaning was God's rule or kingship, מלכות, translated ἡ βασιλεία τοῦ θεοῦ and in English often 'the *Kingdom of God'. It is scarcely possible to define this. It was and still is best spoken of in parables, i.e. open-ended metaphors, stories, and riddles, which engage their hearers and draw them into thought, contemplation, and action. Jesus spoke of the 'coming' of God's rule, and assumed it could and should be 'entered', perhaps already here and now, as it made its presence felt in Jesus' powerful activity in liberating those subject to demons (Mt. 12: 22–9). Modern historical study has elucidated the background of this phrase and in doing so has perhaps been unduly influenced by *apocalyptic literature where it seldom appears. Jesus did not write an apocalypse, and the apocalyptic strand in the Gospels, esp. the echo of Dan. 7: 13 in a few of the '*Son of Man' passages, may have been developed by disciples 'searching the scriptures' in order to understand what they believed had begun to happen. There is also a possibility that early Christian *prophets speaking in Jesus' name (cf. Rev. 22: 16) may have attributed this material to Him. It is unsafe to make it the key to any reconstruction. The limited, fragmentary, and indirect nature of the evidence, and the symbolic nature of any talk of God, combine to subvert attempts to say exactly how Jesus understood the coming of God's rule, or precisely what kind of eschatological transformation He envisaged, and even whether He thought such precision necessary or appropriate. There is no reason to doubt that we have in the Gospel tradition several authentic fragments of His teaching (albeit in Greek translation), but their original context and meaning can be reconstructed only in quite general terms.

Jesus' deeds and words expressed God's providence, universal and unbounded love, judgement, and forgiveness. The symbol of sovereignty is accordingly qualified by that of fatherhood in Jesus' speaking of God. Both are prominent in the *Lord's Prayer. His healings and exorcisms expressed a compassion that corresponded to what His stories and illustrations implied about the character of God. Attempts to represent the inner unity of this theological, moral, and utopian vision must take account of the disciples' fuller knowledge of the outcome of Jesus' ministry. Their hopes of its future consummation and their present needs may have influenced their memories and structured their accounts of what happened. Thus many critical historians have assumed a symbolic heightening of the *miraculous, and have supposed that such details as Jesus' Divine status and foreknowledge, the sacrificial interpretations of His death, and the fulfilment of Scripture, may at least partly reflect subsequent convictions (cf. 1 Cor. 15: 3–5).

Some historians begin their reconstructions with the well-attested details which are unlikely to stem from Christian experience. Other material may then be found to cohere with this critically assured minimum, or (if apparently incompatible with it) may provisionally be assigned to the developing post-resurrection faith of the disciples. This approach highlights Jesus' Baptism, betrayal, and execution, which caused embarrassment to His followers, and also looks for what might help explain but does not quite correspond to their post-resurrection belief. It is also appropriate to look for correlations between Jesus' activity and its outcome in His execution on a political charge as 'the king of the Jews'. Thus the potentially political implications of 'the Kingdom of God' have since the 18th cent. occasionally been taken to suggest that He was a political national messiah, but the evidence that Jesus Himself intended His phrase in an anti-Roman sense is negligible. References to the redemption of Israel (Lk. 24: 21) and the restoration of the kingdom to Israel (Acts 1: 6) are probably later formulations. The request of *James and John at Mk. 10: 25–40 is evidence of a misunderstanding which Jesus repudiated. If Jn. 6: 15 is right that the crowd wished to make Him king, it is also clear that Jesus rejected the idea.

The crucifixion is not easily connected with religious hostility to Jesus' healing and teaching, but a political motivation can accommodate the strongly attested claim that the *Sadducean high-priestly leaders and their associates in Jerusalem (not the *Pharisees or the Jewish people in general) were responsible for handing Jesus over to the Roman authorities for trial and execution on 14 or 15 Nisan, i.e. around the time of *Passover. Jesus attracted crowds, and fears that enthusiasm might lead to Roman intervention (Jn. 11: 48) could explain His arrest regardless of His preaching. He was perhaps considered a destabilizing factor and removed as a precautionary measure. His arrest was facilitated by 'one of the twelve', *Judas Iscariot, whose motives remain unclear. It seems that Jesus' arrival in Jerusalem for the feast of the Passover was heralded by other pilgrims, and it is possible that the decision to arrest Him was precipitated by the disturbance in the *Temple precincts even though this did not lead to His immediate arrest by the Roman soldiers stationed in the nearby Antonia (cf. Acts 21). The fact that His followers were not captured and executed with Him (contrast the uprising of Judas the Galilean in AD 6) suggests that the movement was not perceived as a serious political threat. This view corresponds to the general tenor of Jesus' teaching. It had social and political implications, but Jesus expected God to inaugurate His rule and so is unlikely to have mobilized any latent opposition to Rome.

The overturning of the tables in the Temple perhaps symbolized its destruction (cf. Mk. 13: 2), but there is insufficient evidence to justify interpreting this in terms of Jewish hopes for restoration. Neither that nor the notion that Jesus was a *Zealot does justice to the different kinds of material found in the earliest strata of the Synoptic tradition. The utopian vision of the *Beatitudes (Lk. 6: 20 f.) and other sayings is complemented by the moral dimensions of Jesus' parables and aphorisms. Conclusions about what Jesus meant by the coming of God's rule should not be drawn directly from very different contemporary literature but depend on sifting the Gospel tradition as a whole and considering the phrase in the light of all that is known of 1st-cent. Palestine, its languages, politics, economics, and religion. The history of the Gospel tradition is uncertain and can be construed in various ways to support different possible understandings of Jesus' ministry and passion. Any theory must make sense of what followed, or at least be compatible with it. Here the religious character of the source material is itself part of the evidence, as it reflects the continuing history of Jesus' influence. If the disciples totally misunderstood or misrepresented Him, then historical research has little to work on. If not, even

their religious interpretations may be expected to throw light on the historical reality. When due allowance has been made for the evangelists' post-resurrection perspective, their theological portraits probably take us closer to the historical reality of Jesus than speculative reconstructions which have little textual basis.

The relationship between the evangelists' portraits, accepted as normative by the Christian Church, and the traditions available to the evangelists, have been clarified by *Redaction Criticism and can be illustrated at many points. Mark highlights the reality of the cross and the certainty of vindication to show his contemporaries that their sufferings are meaningful. Luke transmits Jesus' teaching about wealth and possessions, mission and persecution, to communicate the grace of His challenge in fresh circumstances. Matthew both preserves and refocuses the close relationship which Jesus maintained between eschatology and ethics: the Son of Man will declare God's judgement on workers of lawlessness. The dawning of God's rule and its righteousness in Jesus makes doing God's will both urgent and possible, command and gift. Matthew schematizes Jesus' uncompromising statements on anger, lust, divorce, *oaths, retaliation, and hatred of enemies (5: 21–48). He is teaching his contemporaries to 'observe all that Jesus commanded' (28: 20). John's conviction that in handing on and interpreting the memory of Jesus believers may be guided by the *Paraclete (16: 13; 14: 26) has allowed him to exercize an astonishing freedom to recast in christological discourses the tradition of what Jesus taught. He has made explicit what Christians find implied in the historical mission and message, life, and death of Jesus: that He is the decisive and saving revelation of God (1: 18; 14: 9, and *passim*).

How exactly Jesus understood what the evangelists have interpreted in these ways is uncertain but His powerful works placed the one who proclaimed the coming of God's rule at the centre of what was already beginning to happen (Mt. 12: 28; Lk. 11: 20). He evidently understood Himself to be playing a decisive role in God's saving work, and it became clear that this would involve suffering. His consciousness of mission or status did not need to be made explicit. The ambiguous phrase 'the Son of Man' was apparently sufficient self-reference for one whose actions and passion finally revealed His significance. *Christological claims followed at once. His execution on a political charge and the inscription over His cross may have helped crystallize the disciples' growing conviction that He was, or was designated to become, the Christ. But the decisive factor was what they believed had followed His death. They described it as exaltation (cf. Ps. 110: 1; Is. 52: 13) and resurrection (cf. Dan. 12: 2), and understood it to signify His vindication by God (cf. Phil. 2: 9). Their experience of the Spirit convinced even doubters that the new age had indeed dawned, and that Jesus was living Lord and Messiah (cf. Acts 2: 36).

The messianic claim gives unity to the NT witness. All the canonical writers presuppose that their exalted Lord is the One who was crucified under Pontius Pilate (cf. 1 Tim. 6: 13). Denials of His real humanity were met with a conviction that the Son sent by God and vindicated by God was the crucified man from Nazareth (1 Jn. 4: 2), and that He is central for humanity's relationship to God. The later *credal affirmations refer to a man in history. However little they can be confirmed by historical scrutiny, the man himself is a proper subject for historical inquiry. It is a sound instinct which makes believers reluctant to distinguish too sharply between the historical and religious claims that the Gospels have fused. But theology cannot avoid the risks of an enquiry which may erode its claims. The commitment of modern theology to the search for historical as well as religious truths by whatever methods are currently available has enabled it to meet on their own ground attacks on Christian faith disguised as objective enquiry. It has also made possible a clearer perception of the real humanity of Jesus Christ, whom Christians acknowledge as their Lord and their God.

There is a huge literature, both critical and devotional, from all periods. Modern scholarly works include G. Bornkamm, *Jesus von Nazareth* (1956; 3rd edn., 1959; Eng. tr. 1960); P. Winter, *On the Trial of Jesus* (Studia Judaica, 1; Berlin, 1961; 2nd edn., 1974); F. Hahn, *Christologische Hoheitstitel* (Forschungen zur Religion und Literatur des Alten und Neuen Testaments, 83; Göttingen, 1963; Eng. tr., *The Titles of Jesus in Christology*, 1969); C. K. Barrett, *Jesus and the Gospel Tradition* (1967); M. Hengel, *Nachfolge und Charisma: Eine exegetisch-religionsgeschichtliche Studie zu Mt. 8, 21 f. und Jesu Ruf in die Nachfolge* (Beiheft zur *ZNTW*, 34; 1968; Eng. tr., *The Charismatic Leader and His Followers*, Edinburgh, 1981); id., *Der Sohn Gottes* (Tubingen, 1975; Eng. tr., 1976); J. Jeremias, *Neutestamentliche Theologie*, 1: *Die Verkündigung Jesu* (Gütersloh, 1971; Eng. tr., 1971); G. Vermes, *Jesus the Jew* (1973); E. [C. F. A.] *Schillebeeckx, OP, Jezus, het verhaal van een levende* (1974; Eng. tr., *Jesus*, 1979); B. F. Meyer, *The Aims of Jesus* (1979); A. E. Harvey, *Jesus and the Constraints of History* (Bampton Lectures, 1980; 1982); E. P. Sanders, *Jesus and Judaism* (1985); id., *The Historical figure of Jesus* (1993); P. Fredriksen, *From Jesus to Christ: The Origins of the New Testament Images of Jesus* (New Haven, Conn., and London, 1988); J. D. Crossan, *The Historical Jesus: The Life of a Mediterranean Jewish Peasant* (San Francisco [1991]; Edinburgh, 1993); R. Schnackenburg, *Die Person Jesu Christi im Spiegel der vier Evangelien* (Herders Theologischer Kommentar zum Neuen Testament, Supplementband 4; 1993; Eng. tr., *Jesus in the Gospels*, Louisville, Ky. [1995]). See also HISTORICAL JESUS, QUEST OF THE, and MESSIANIC SECRET; also bibl. to CHRISTOLOGY, LAST SUPPER, MESSIAH, MIRACLE, PARABLE, RESURRECTION OF CHRIST, SON OF MAN, and VIRGIN BIRTH; and to the individual Gospels.

Jesus Movement (or Jesus Revolution). A popular term of the late 1960s and early 1970s for the amorphous movement of relatively spontaneous groupings, normally fervent, *evangelical, and *fundamentalist, which emerged in the youth culture of the period, beginning in California. The 'Jesus people', who combined much of the unconventional life-style of that culture with ethical rigorism and often *millenarian expectations, widely distrusted the established Churches; many adopted *Pentecostal practices and teaching. The 'Children of God' (later called the 'Family of Love'), a sect which emerged from the movement, has won adherents in Europe as well as in the USA.

R. M. Enroth, E. E. Ericson, and C. B. Peters, *The Story of the Jesus People* (Grand Rapids and Exeter, 1972). On the 'Children of God', R. Wallis, *Salvation and Protest* (1979), pp. 53–90.

Jesus Prayer. The prayer 'Lord Jesus Christ, Son of God, have mercy upon me' (sometimes 'a sinner' is added at the end, or the prayer may be said in the plural, 'us' instead of 'me'). The continual repetition of this prayer is specially recommended in Byzantine *Hesychasm, and its recitation is sometimes associated with a certain 'physical

method': head bowed, eyes fixed on the place of the heart, careful control of the breathing. To assist the repetition, a rosary or *komvoschinion is frequently employed. The full text of the Jesus Prayer is first found in a work of the 6th–7th cent., the Life of the Abba Philemon; Greek spiritual writers of earlier date, such as *Diadochus of Photike and *Nilus the Ascetic, speak of the invocation or 'remembrance' of the Name of Jesus, without specifying exactly what form this invocation took. The 'physical method' seems to be considerably later than the Prayer as such; it is first described in a text attributed to St *Simeon the New Theologian, 'The Method of Sacred Prayer and Attention' (perhaps by Nicephorus of Mount Athos, 14th cent.). The Jesus Prayer is widely practised in the Orthodox Church today; but the use of the 'physical method' is now generally discouraged and it is very little followed.

'Un Moine de l'Église d'Orient' [L. Gillet], 'La Prière de Jésus', *Irénikon*, 20 (1947), pp. 249–73, 381–421; id., 'Sur l'usage de la Prière de Jésus', ibid. 25 (1952), pp. 371–82; also issued separately as *La Prière de Jésus* (3rd edn., Chevetogne, 1959; Eng. tr., New York etc. [1967]; rev. edn., 1987). I. Hausherr, SJ, *Noms du Christ et voies d'oraison* (Orientalia Christiana Analecta, 157; Rome, 1960; Eng. tr., Cistercian Studies Series, 44; Kalamazoo, Mich., 1978). Id., *La Méthode d'oraison hésychaste* (Orientalia Christiana, 9, pt. 2; fasc. 36 of the series; Rome, 1927). B. Krivocheine, 'Date du texte traditionnel de la "Prière de Jésus"', *Messager de l'Exarchat du Patriarche russe en Europe occidentale*, 7–8 (1951), pp. 55–9. K. [T. R.] Ware, 'The Jesus Prayer in St Diadochus of Photice', in *Aksum-Thyateira: A Festschrift for Archbishop Methodios of Thyateira and Great Britain*, ed. G. D. Dragas (1985), pp. 557–68. P. Adnès in *Dict. Sp.* 8 (1974), cols. 1126–50, s.v.

Jeu, Books of. The title of two *Gnostic treatises mentioned in the *Pistis Sophia* which are ascribed to *Enoch. They have been identified with the first two treatises in the Bruce codex (see GNOSTICISM).

Text ed. by C. Schmidt, *Gnostische Schriften in Koptischer Sprache aus dem Codex Brucianus* (TU 8, Hefte 1–2; 1892), pp. 38–141, with Ger. tr. pp. 142–225. Coptic text repr., with Eng. tr. and notes by V. MacDermot, *The Books of Jeu and the Untitled Text in the Bruce Codex* (Nag Hammadi Studies, 13; Leiden, 1978), pp. 1–211. See also bibl. to GNOSTICISM.

Jeunesse Ouvrière Chrétienne. See JOCISTS.

Jew, the Wandering. See WANDERING JEW, THE.

Jewel, John (1522–71), Bp. of *Salisbury. Educated at Merton and Corpus Christi Colleges, Oxford, he was elected in 1542 a Fellow of Corpus. After 1547, largely through the influence of *Peter Martyr, he became one of the intellectual leaders of the Reforming party. Under *Mary, Jewel signed a set of anti-Protestant articles (1554), but notwithstanding he was forced to flee to Frankfurt (1555), where he opposed J. *Knox and the advanced *Calvinists. A little later he joined Martyr at Strasbourg and travelled with him to Zurich. On the accession of *Elizabeth I he returned to England, and in 1560 was consecrated Bp. of Salisbury. From now onwards he became a strong supporter of the Anglican settlement, opposing both RCs and Puritans, and taking his stand on the Fathers of the first six centuries. In 1562 he published his celebrated treatise in defence of the C of E, the *Apologia Ecclesiae Anglicanae*, which established itself at once as the best defence of the Anglican claims. It endeavoured to prove that a general Reformation had been necessary, that reform by such a body as the Council of *Trent was impossible, and that local Churches had the right to legislate through provincial synods. In the prolonged and bitter controversy that followed with Thomas Harding (1516–72), who defended the Papacy, the lines which the Roman controversy was to take in the 17th cent. were mainly determined; and under *James I, Abp. R. *Bancroft gave official approval to Jewel's teaching. Jewel, who administered his diocese with a vigour unusual in the Elizabethan Church, made several visitations, preached frequently, and built the library of Salisbury Cathedral. Among a number of poor boys whom Jewel maintained and prepared for the university was R. *Hooker, whose *Ecclesiastical Polity* owed much to his patron's teaching.

Collected Works ed. under the direction of R. Bancroft, London, fol., 1609, with memoir [by D. Featly] (no pagination; 2nd edn., 1611). Modern edns. by J. Ayre (*Parker Society, 4 vols., 1845–50), with memoir in vol. 4, pp. v–xxx; and R. W. Jelf (8 vols., Oxford, 1848). The principal authority is the official Life, sponsored by Abp. M. *Parker, by Jewel's friend Laurence Humphrey (in Latin; London, 1573); it is the basis of all subsequent memoirs. More modern Life by C. W. Le Bas (London, 1835). W. M. Southgate, *John Jewel and the Problem of Doctrinal Authority* (Cambridge, Mass., 1962); J. E. Booty, *John Jewel as Apologist of the Church of England* (CHS, 1963). *BRUO, 1501–1540*, pp. 317 f. M. *Creighton in *DNB* 29 (1892), pp. 378–82.

Jewish People. See JUDAISM.

Jews, Christian attitudes to. Christianity shares much common ground with Judaism. Jesus Christ was Himself a Jew, as were the earliest members of the Church. St *Paul's practice of not requiring Gentile converts to Christianity to be circumcised and observe the whole Jewish law, and his argument that their new covenant relationship with God was based on faith in Christ, not on works of the law, laid the foundation for the separation of Gentile Christianity from Judaism. For himself, however, the Jews were still God's chosen people; some of them had rejected Christ, but, he trusted, they would not finally be rejected (Rom. 9–11). The persecution of Jewish Christians and their expulsion from the synagogue caused much bitterness, which is reflected in Mt. 23 and Jn. 5–8. All four Gospels show a tendency to exonerate the Roman power that crucified Jesus by shifting more blame on to the Jewish authorities (e.g. Mk. 15: 11, Jn. 11: 49–53) and even the crowd (Mt. 27: 25). Isolated texts such as these and 1 Thess. 2: 14–6 can be explained by the polemical situation, but when they became a part of Christian Scripture they fuelled anti-Judaism over many centuries. The supercessionist theology found in discussions of the two covenants (Gal. 3–4, 2 Cor. 3, Heb. 8), and the assumption that the Church is the true Israel (Mt. 21: 43) have also contributed to the history of denigration. From the early 2nd cent. onwards Christian writers and preachers put forward an aggressively negative image of the Jews, calling them God-killers, children of the Devil, and enemies of mankind. At the same time a positive appreciation of Judaism, which existed in various parts of the Church, whether under the influence of Jewish ancestry, devotion to the OT, or direct influence of Jews, was vigorously suppressed. The surviving homilies attacking Judaism or Judaizing include several by *Origen and a famous series

delivered by St John *Chrysostom in *Antioch in 387. Polemical treatises *Adversus Judaeos* became virtually a distinct genre of Christian literature. Successive ecclesiastical councils legislated to end social and religious contacts with Jews, except for the purpose of converting them. The political triumph of the Church in the Roman Empire led to the introduction of a similar tendency in imperial legislation, and although at first the laws protected the ancient rights and dignities of the Jews, these were gradually undermined: the Jewish Patriarchate was abolished, no new synagogues were to be built, Jews were excluded from government service and the army, and they were not to make converts or own Christian slaves. The legislation of the Church and State seems to have been intended to isolate Jews and prevent them from enjoying any power or influence over Christians. Nevertheless, while the use of vitriolic language becomes increasingly pronounced, and local acts of violence by Christians against Jews become more common, measures aimed at the forcible extinction of Judaism are rare in the first six centuries. This contrasts with the treatment of pagan cults and indeed of Christian heresy, and may be connected in part with the concept of a 'witnessing people' first enunciated by St *Augustine: the Jews are to be preserved, albeit in a state of subjection, so as to testify to their own wickedness and to the Christian truth, until they finally accept Christ at the Second Coming.

In the early 7th cent. the baptism of all Jews was decreed in several countries (Spain in 613, the Byzantine Empire and France, 632), and although these decrees did not lead to the permanent elimination of Judaism in these lands, the position of Jews under Christian rule became increasingly circumscribed. From the time of the first *Crusade onwards, there were violent attacks on Jews, often under the influence of Christian preachers, and in some places entire communities were massacred. There were some, including St *Bernard of Clairvaux, who protested against this attitude, but they were lone voices. The Fourth *Lateran Council (1215) imposed the wearing of distinctive clothing so that Jews could be distinguished from Christians. Excluded from society and demonified, the Jews became the victims of false accusations, e.g. of desecrating the Host, murdering children for ritual purposes, or poisoning the water supply. These charges often led to violence, despite the repeated protests of Popes and other leading Churchmen. Massacres were succeeded by expulsions, notably from England (1290), France (1394, after a series of temporary banishments), Spain (1492), and Portugal (1496). By 1500 most of Europe was free of Jews, and those who remained lived under severe restrictions, which were reinforced and extended during the *Counter-Reformation. (The physical segregation of Jews in a *ghetto was first instituted in Rome by Pope *Paul IV in 1556.) Nor were conditions much better in Protestant lands. M. *Luther, after professing sympathy for the Jews at first, turned against them when he found that his conciliatory stance did not win widespread conversions, and he influenced Protestant rulers to expel them or implement the medieval restrictions.

The subjugation of the Jews was accompanied by efforts to convert them. In many places they were compelled to listen to sermons in church and were subject to various pressures to change their faith, including in some instances the threat of death. Coercion made insincere converts, and the forcible baptism of whole populations, as happened, for example, in Spain in 1391 and again in 1492, and in Portugal five years later, gave rise to well-founded fears of crypto-Judaism. Converts and their descendants were subjected to discriminatory measures and the scrutiny of the *Inquisition, in 1478 established in Spain in a new form more directly focused against Jews and extended subsequently to Portugal and their overseas possessions. Many were publicly *burnt.

From the 18th cent., under the influence of the *Enlightenment, efforts were made to improve the condition of the Jews and to reintegrate them into European society. While some Christian voices were heard on the side of reform, Churchmen on the whole were more vocal on the side of reaction. In 1775 Pope *Pius VI renewed and extended the restrictive legislation: Jews were even forbidden to ride in carriages or erect tombstones. Meanwhile new missions arose directed specifically at Jews, and sometimes promoted by converts from Judaism. The most notable among these missionary bodies was the 'London Society for Promoting Christianity among the Jews' (founded in 1809), later known as the '*Church's Ministry among the Jews'. Antisemitism, an anti-Jewish political movement originating in the last quarter of the 19th cent., exploited many of the traditional Christian arguments and counted on Christian support (both RC and Protestant). The Berlin court chaplain, Adolph Stöcker (1835–1909), was among its leading proponents, and it was favoured, in various forms, by Christian movements in Austria, Germany (see GERMAN-CHRISTIANS), France, and elsewhere; many prominent Christians, however, opposed it.

After the *Holocaust a new era began. In 1947 a conference was convened at Seelisberg in Switzerland under the auspices of the newly formed International Conference of Christians and Jews. It issued a list of 'ten points' aimed at eradicating anti-Judaism from Christian teaching. The *World Council of Churches at its inaugural meeting in 1948 acknowledged a connection between Christian anti-Judaism and antisemitism, which it declared to be 'irreconcilable with the practice of the Christian faith and a sin against God and man'. In 1965 the Second *Vatican Council promulgated a declaration on the Jewish people (§ 4 in the Declaration on the Relationship of the Church to Non-Christian Religions, *Nostra Aetate*) which, while it reasserts some of the traditional rebukes, firmly states that 'the Church, mindful of the patrimony she shares with the Jews, ... decries hatred, persecutions, displays of antisemitism, directed against Jews at any time and by anyone'. In most of the main Churches serious attention is now being paid to fostering contacts and co-operation, and even religious dialogue, between Christians and Jews, to healing the wounds of the past, to revising those teachings which are recognized to have been harmful, and to facing up to the theological questions raised by this new approach.

R. R. Ruether, *Faith and Fratricide: The Theological Roots of Anti-Semitism* (New York [1974]); J. G. Gager, *The Origins of Anti-Semitism: Attitudes Toward Judaism in Pagan and Christian Antiquity* (New York and Oxford, 1983). M. Simon, *Verus Israel: Étude sur les relations entre Chrétiens et Juifs dans l'Empire Romain (135–425)* (Bibliothèque des Écoles françaises d'Athènes et de Rome, 166; 1948; 2nd edn., 1964; Eng. tr., Oxford, 1986). R. L.

Wilken, *Judaism and the Early Christian Mind: A Study of Cyril of Alexandria's Exegesis and Theology* (Yale Publications in Religion, 15; New Haven, Conn., and London, 1971); id., *John Chrysostom and the Jews* (Berkeley and Los Angeles, Calif., and London [1983]). A. Linder, *The Jews in Roman Imperial Legislation* (Detroit and Jerusalem, 1987 [primary texts, in Eng. tr., with comm.]). B. Blumenkranz, *Juifs et Chrétiens dans le monde occidental 430–1096* (École Pratique des Hautes Études-Sorbonne, Section 6ᵉ· Études Juives, 2; Paris and The Hague, 1960) id., *Les auteurs chrétiens latin du moyen âge sur les juifs et le judaïsme* (ibid. 4; 1963). J. [W.] Parkes, *The Conflict of the Church and the Synagogue* (1934); H. Schreckenberg, *Die christlichen Adversus-Judaeos-Texte und ihr literarisches und historisches Umfeld (1.–11. Jh.)* (Europäische Hochschulschriften, Reihe 23, Bd. 172; Frankfurt-am-Main, 1982; 2nd edn., 1990); id., *Die christlichen Adversus-Judaeos-Texte (11.–13. Jh.)* (ibid. 335; 1988; 2nd edn., 1991); A. Lukyn Williams, *Adversus Judaeos: A Bird's-Eye View of Christian Apologiae until the Renaissance* (Cambridge, 1935). S. Grayzel, *The Church and the Jews in the XIIIth Century: A Study of their Relations during the Years 1198-1254, based on the Papal Letters and Conciliar Decrees of the Period* (Philadelphia, 1933; rev. edn., New York, 1966). H. A. Oberman, *Wurzeln des Antisemitismus: Christenangst und Judenplage im Zeitalter von Humanismus und Reformation* (1981; Eng. tr., Philadelphia [1984]).

M. Hay, *The Foot of Pride: The Pressure of Christendom on the People of Israel for 1900 Years* (Boston, 1950). L. Poliakov, *Histoire de l'antisémitisme* (4 vols. [1955–1977]; Eng. tr., Oxford, 1974–85). J. Isaac, *L'Enseignement du mépris: Verité historique et mythes théologiques* (1962; Eng. tr., *The Teaching of Contempt*, New York [1964]). F. Heer, *Gottes Erste Liebe. 2000 Jahre Judentum und Christentum* (Munich [1967]; Eng. tr., *God's First Love: Christians and Jews over two thousand years* [1970]). S. Rappaport, *Jew and Gentile: The Philo-Semitic Aspect* (New York [1980]). A. R. Eckardt, *Christianity and The Children of Israel* (Morningside Heights, NY, 1948). A. Gilbert, *The Vatican Council and the Jews* (Cleveland and New York [1968]). H. Croner (ed.), *Stepping Stones to Further Jewish–Christian Relations ...: Christian documents* (New Malden, Surrey, 1977). *The Theology of the Churches and the Jewish People: Statements by the World Council of Churches and its Member Churches*, with commentary by A. Brockway and others (Geneva [1988]). C. Klein, *Theologie und Anti-Judaismus* (Munich, 1975; Eng. tr., 1978); C. Thoma, *Christliche Theologie des Judentums* (Aschaffenburg, 1978; Eng. tr., New York [1980]). P. van Buren, *A Theology of Jewish Christian Reality* (New York, 1980 ff.). E. Fleischner, *Judaism in German Christian Theology since 1956* (Metuchen, NJ, 1975).

Jiménez de Cisneros, Francisco. See XIMÉNEZ DE CISNEROS, FRANCISCO.

Joachim, St. The husband of St *Anne and the father of the BVM. He is first mentioned in the '*Protevangelium of James' (2nd cent.), where the birth of the Virgin, promised by an angel to her aged and childless parents, is recorded. Apart from this passage, he is rarely referred to in Christian tradition till much later times—in the E. seldom before the 7th cent., and in the W. not till the Middle Ages. In later medieval times he became a frequent subject for the religious artist. He has been commemorated on many different dates: from 1913 to 1969 his feast day in the RC Church was assigned to 16 Aug.; it was then joined with St Anne on 26 July; in E., 9 Sept. (with St Anne).

É. Amann, *Le Protévangile de Jacques et ses remaniements latins* (1910), pp. 45–51. On his reputed tomb at Jerusalem, see L. Cré, 'Tombeau de St Joachim et de Ste Anne', *R. Bibl.* 2 (1893), pp. 245–74, and H. Vincent, OP, 'La Crypte de sainte Anne à Jérusalem', ibid. 13 (1904), pp. 228–41. J. B. Bauer and others in

Marienlexikon, ed. R. Bäumer and L. Scheffczyk, 3 (1991), pp. 378–82, s.v. See also other works cited under JAMES, BOOK OF.

Joachim of Fiore (*c.*1135–1202), biblical exegete and *mystic. Two contemporary biographical fragments were expanded and embellished with legends in the two 17th-cent. Lives upon which the account in the *Acta Sanctorum* was based. Born in Celico, Calabria, as a young man he went on a pilgrimage to the Holy Land, where he may have had the first of three experiences of spiritual illumination, the latter two, at Easter and Pentecost, being recorded in his own writings. He became a monk in the *Benedictine, later *Cistercian, monastery of Corazzo. Elected abbot against his will in 1177, he later relinquished this office to lead a more contemplative life, finally receiving Papal permission in 1196 to establish his own congregation in the Sila mountains. Three Popes encouraged his writing and in a testamentary letter he required his successors to submit his works to the Holy See. When the Fourth *Lateran Council (1215) condemned his Trinitarian doctrine, his reputation for sanctity was safeguarded. *Dante placed him in Paradise—*di spirito prophetico dotato*.

The central doctrine of his three chief works, 'Liber de Concordia Novi ac Veteris Testamenti', 'Expositio in Apocalypsim', and 'Psalterium decem Chordarum', is a Trinitarian conception of the whole of history, viewed in three great periods ('status'). The first, characterized by the 'Ordo conjugatorum', was the Age of the Father in which mankind lived under the Law until the end of the OT dispensation; the second, characterized by the 'Ordo clericorum', is that of the Son, lived under Grace and covering the NT dispensation which Joachim calculated as forty-two generations of about thirty years each; the third, that of the 'Ordo monachorum' or 'contemplantium', is the Age of the Spirit, to be lived in the liberty of the 'Spiritualis Intellectus' proceeding from the Old and New Testaments. This age would see the rise of new religious orders to convert the whole world and usher in the 'Ecclesia Spiritualis'. Joachim never advanced his doctrine of the third age to a point of danger to ecclesiastical authority, but his expectations concerning history had a far-reaching influence in the following centuries among groups who carried his ideas to revolutionary conclusions, notably certain *Franciscans and *Fraticelli. The Franciscan Gerard of Borgo San Donnino in 1254 claimed to complete Joachim's pattern of threes by proclaiming the *Eternal Gospel* (excerpts from Joachim's works) which superseded the OT and NT. His views received Papal condemnation in 1255 and in 1263 the provincial Council of Arles condemned the doctrine of Joachim himself. But Joachim's vision continued to captivate the imagination of many throughout the later medieval and Renaissance period.

His three chief works, mentioned above, pub. Venice 1519 and 1527, are available in photographic repr.; the first four books of the *Liber de Concordia Novi ac Veteris Testamenti* also ed. E. R. Daniel (Transactions of the American Philosophical Society, 73, pt. 8; 1983). There are modern edns. of his *Tractatus super Quatuor Evangelia* by E. Buonaiuti (Fonti per la Storia d'Italia, 67; 1930); of his *Expositio de Articulis Fidei* by id. (ibid. 78; 1936); of *Adversus Iudaeos* by A. Frugoni (ibid. 95; 1957); of his *Liber Figurarum* by L. Tondelli (2 vols., Turin [1940]; 2nd edn., ibid., 1953, vol. 1, ed. L. Tondelli, vol. 2, ed. L. Tondelli, M. [E.] Reeves, and B. [M.] Hirsch-Reich); and of his *De Vita Sancti Benedicti* by C. Baraut, OSB, *Analecta Sacra Tarraconensia*, 24 (1951), pp. 33–122.

AASS, Mai. 7 (1688), pp. 89–143. H. Grundmann, *Studien über Joachim von Floris* (Beiträge zur Kulturgeschichte des Mittelalters und der Renaissance, 32; 1927); id., *Neue Forschungen über Joachim von Fiore* (Münstersche Forschungen, 1; 1950). E. Buonaiuti, *Gioacchino da Fiore: I tempi, la vita, il messaggio* (1931). A. Crocco, *Gioacchino da Fiore* (Naples, 1960). M. [E.] Reeves, *The Influence of Prophecy in the Later Middle Ages: A Study in Joachimism* (Oxford, 1969; repr., with additional bibl., Notre Dame, Ind., and London, 1993). Id. and B. [M.] Hirsch-Reich, *The Figurae of Joachim of Fiore* (Oxford, 1972). D. C. West (ed.), *Joachim of Fiore in Christian Thought* (2 vols., New York [1975]). H. Mottu, *La Manifestation de l'Esprit selon Joachim de Fiore* (Université de Genève thesis; Neuchâtel and Paris, 1977). H. de *Lubac, SJ, *La Postérité spirituelle de Joachim de Flore* (2 vols. [1979–81]). *Storia e Messaggio in Gioacchino da Fiore: Atti del I Congresso Internazionale di Studi Gioachimiti . . . 19–23 settembre 1979* (Fiore, 1980); A. Crocco (ed.), *L'Età dello spirito e la fine dei tempi in Gioacchino da Fiore e nel Gioachimismo medievale: Atti del II Congresso Internazionale di Studi Gioachimiti . . . 6–9 settembre 1984* (2 vols., ibid., 1986); G. L. Potestà (ed.), *Il Profetismo gioachimita tra Quattrocento et Cinquecento: Atti del III Congresso Internazionale di Studi Gioachimiti . . . 17–21 settembre 1989* (Genoa, 1991). B. McGinn, *The Calabrian Abbot: Joachim of Fiore in the History of Western Thought* (1985); M. [E.] Reeves and W. Gould, *Joachim of Fiore and the Myth of the Eternal Evangel in the Nineteenth Century* (Oxford, 1987). M. W. Bloomfield, 'Recent Scholarship on Joachim of Fiore and his Influence', in *Prophecy and Millenarianism: Essays in Honour of Marjorie Reeves*, ed. A. Williams (1980), pp. 21–52.

Joan, Pope. The legend of a female Pope first appears in the (13th-cent.) *Dominican chronicler Jean de Mailly, and was repeated in various versions by historical writers of the following centuries. The gist of the story is that about the year 1100 (later forms say after St *Leo IV, d. 855) a woman in male disguise, after a distinguished career as a scholar, succeeded to the chair of St Peter. After reigning more than two years she gave birth to a child during a procession to the *Lateran and died immediately afterwards. There is no evidence whatever to substantiate the tale, but it was widely believed in the Middle Ages. Today it is rejected as an invention by all serious scholars. J. J. I. von *Döllinger explained it as an ancient Roman folk-tale.

J. J. I. von Döllinger, *Die Papst-Fabeln des Mittelalters* (1863), pp. 1–45 (Eng. tr., 1871, pp. 1–67); E. Vacandard, *Études de critique et d'histoire religieuse*, 4th ser. (1923), pp. 15–39 (La Papesse Jeanne); C. A. Patrides, *Premises and Motifs in Renaissance Thought and Literature* (Princeton, NJ [1982]), pp. 152–81 ('A palpable hieroglyphick': The Fable of Pope Joan), with refs. See also BLONDEL, DAVID.

Joan of Arc, St (1412–31), called 'La Pucelle', the 'Maid of Orléans'. The setting of her life was the Hundred Years War and the civil war within France between the great houses of Orléans and Burgundy. The daughter of a peasant, she was born and brought up in Domrémy, Champagne. A pious child, she experienced in 1425 the first of her supernatural visitations, which she described as a voice accompanied by a blaze of light. Gradually her 'voices' increased and she was able to identify St *Michael, St *Catherine, St *Margaret, and others, who revealed to Joan her mission to save France. She was unsuccessful in a first attempt in 1428 to persuade the French commander at Vaucouleurs of the genuineness of her visions; but after a second attempt in 1429 she was sent to the as yet unconsecrated King (Charles VII), who was convinced when she apparently recognized him in disguise. Joan then gave the King a secret sign, which she never revealed. After close examination of her case by a body of Charles's theologians at Poitiers, it was decided to allow her to lead an expedition to Orléans. Clad in a suit of white armour and bearing a banner with a symbol of the Trinity and the words 'Jesus, Maria', she inspired Charles's troops and the city was relieved. After a short campaign in the Loire valley, she persuaded Charles VII to proceed to *Reims for his coronation, which took place on 17 July 1429, with Joan at his side. The relief of Orléans and the crowning of the Dauphin were notable victories for the Valois cause. After six months of military inactivity fresh campaigns took place in the spring of 1430 in which she was less successful. She was taken prisoner by Burgundian troops near Compiègne on 24 May 1430, sold to the English by the Duke of Burgundy on 21 Nov. 1430, and appeared before the court of the Bp. of Beauvais (Pierre Cauchon) at Rouen on 21 Feb. 1431 on charges of witchcraft and heresy. After further examination in her cell, a summary of her statements was compiled. The judges of the *inquisitorial court declared her visions 'false and diabolical' and the summary was also denounced by the University of *Paris. After some form of recantation on 23 May, she resumed male attire, which she had agreed to abandon, and on 29 May was condemned as a relapsed heretic and on 30 May burnt at Rouen. Her death did not bring about the end of the Hundred Years War, and her personal heroism, rather than her political and military achievement, has been a source of inspiration to later generations. A revision of her trial by an appellate court appointed by Pope *Callistus III in 1456 declared her to have been unjustly condemned. Canonized on 9 May 1920 by *Benedict XV as a holy maiden, she is the second patron of France. Feast day, 30 May.

J. Quicherat (ed.), *Procès de condamnation et de réhabilitation de Jeanne d'Arc* (Société de l'histoire de France; 5 vols., 1841–9); P. Champion (ed.), *Procès de condamnation de Jeanne d'Arc* (2 vols., 1920–1), with introd., Fr. tr., and notes; P. Tisset and Y. Lanhers (eds.), *Procès de Jeanne d'Arc* (Société de l'histoire de France; 3 vols., 1960–71); P. Duparc (ed.), *Procès en nullité de la condamnation de Jeanne d'Arc* (ibid. 5 vols., 1977–88). Eng. tr. of docs. of the trial by W. P. Barrett, *The Trial of Joan of Arc* (1931). P. Doncœur, SJ, and Y. Lanhers (eds.), *Documents et recherches relatives à Jeanne la Pucelle* (5 vols., 1952–61). Studies incl. those by A. Lang (London, 1908), G. Hanotaux (Paris, 1911), A. Fabre (ibid., 1912), V. Sackville-West (London, 1936), J. Calmette (Paris, 1946), R. Pernoud (ibid., 1954; Eng. tr., 1961), and other works of this author, [J.] E. [M.] Lucie-Smith (London, 1976), M. [S.] Warner (ibid., 1981), and A. L. Barstow (Studies in Women and Religion, 17; Lewiston, NY, etc. [1986]).

Joasaph, St. See JOSAPHAT, ST.

Job, Book of. The main portion of the Book, which is in poetical form, is preceded by a prose Prologue (1 and 2) and is followed by a prose Epilogue (42: 7–17). Discussions between Job and his three 'friends', Eliphaz, Bildad, and Zophar, appear in three cycles (3–14, 15–21, 22–31), culminating in an appeal to the Almighty. There follow the speeches of Elihu (32–7), which are sometimes regarded as an intrusion since they add nothing to the arguments of the friends and interrupt the connection of

chs. 31 and 38. The Divine reply and Job's acceptance of it are recorded in chs. 38–42: 6.

The Book stands in the *Wisdom tradition of ancient *Israel. Its main subject is the perennial problem of innocent suffering. Job rejects the traditional view that suffering is the result of sin, for he has no doubt of his innocence. Although no final solution to the problem is offered, apart from the emphasis on the omnipotence of God in 38–42: 6, the Book none the less offers the most thorough treatment of the subject in the OT. Already in the NT (Jas. 5: 11) the patience of Job has become proverbial. Owing to the universal nature of its subject-matter, the Book has enjoyed wide appeal in almost every period. While there is no scholarly consensus about the date of its composition, many critics favour a date in the region of 400 BC.

Modern comm. incl. those of S. R. *Driver and G. B. *Gray (ICC, 1921), E. P. Dhorme, OP (Études Bibliques, 1926; Eng. tr., 1967), G. Hölscher (HAT, Reihe 1, Bd. 17; 1937; 2nd edn., 1952), A. Weiser (Das Alte Testament Deutsch, 13; 1951; 4th edn., 1963), N. H. Tur-Sinai ([in English] Jerusalem, 1957), G. Fohrer (KAT 16; 1963), F. Horst (Biblischer Kommentar, Altes Testament, 16 [on 1–19]; 1968), M. H. Pope (Anchor Bible, 15 [1965]; 3rd edn. [1973]), H. H. Rowley (New Cent. Bibl., 1970), R. Gordis (Maresheth Series, 2; New York, 1978), N. C. Habel (Old Testament Library, 1985), and D. J. A. Clines (Word Biblical Comm. 17 [on 1–20]; Dallas [1989]), with full bibl. G. Richter, *Textstudien zum Buche Hiob* (Beiträge zur Wissenschaft vom Alten und Neuen Testament, Folge 3, 7; 1927). Id., *Studien zu Hiob: Der Aufbau des Hiobbuches, dargestellt an den Gattungen des Rechtslebens* (Theologische Arbeiten, 11 [1959]). W. B. Stevenson, *The Poem of Job: A Literary Study with a New Translation* (Schweich Lectures, 1943; 1947). Id., *Critical Notes on the Hebrew Text of the Poem of Job* (Aberdeen, 1951). C. Westermann, *Der Aufbau der Buches Hiob* (Beiträge zur historischen Theologie, 23; Tübingen, 1956; 2nd edn., Stuttgart, 1977; Eng. tr., Philadelphia [1981]). N. H. Snaith, *The Book of Job: Its Origin and Purpose* (Studies in Biblical Theology, 2nd ser. 11; 1968). R. Polzin and D. Robertson (eds.), *Studies in the Book of Job* (Semeia, 7; Missoula, Mont., 1977). R. Girard, *La Route antique des hommes pervers* (1985; Eng. tr., *Job, the Victim of his People*, 1987). J. H. Eaton, *Job* (Old Testament Guides, Sheffield [1985]). H. W. *Robinson, *The Cross of Job* (1916), repr. in id., *The Cross in the Old Testament* (1955), pp. 10–54. J. Barr, 'The Book of Job and its Modern Interpreters', *Bulletin of the John Rylands Library*, 54 (1971–2), pp. 28–46. Soggin, pp. 449–57. J. L. Crenshaw in *Anchor Bible Dictionary*, 3 (1992), pp. 858–68, s.v.

Jocists. The organized association of factory workers in the RC Church known as the **Jeunesse Ouvrière Chrétienne (JOC)**, or in English-speaking countries as 'Young Christian Workers'. Building on the ideals of *Leo XIII's *Rerum Novarum*, the movement grew out of the groups gathered by J.-L. *Cardijn in and around Brussels after the 1914–18 war and received Papal approbation in 1925. It spread to France in 1926 and gradually expanded worldwide. It encourages young factory workers to develop their self-awareness and to take responsibility for the evangelization of their fellow workers. Corresponding associations have been created for agricultural workers (**JAC: Jeunesse Agricole Chrétienne**) and sailors (**JMC: Jeunesse Maritime Chrétienne**). Recently tensions have developed within the movement due to conflicting analyses of contemporary society.

M. A. Walckiers, *Sources inédites relatives aux débuts de la J.O.C. 1919–1925* (Centre Interuniversitaire d'Histoire Contemporaine,

Cahiers 61; Louvain, 1970); M. Launay and others in G. Cholvy (ed.), *Mouvements de Jeunesse Chrétiens et Juifs* (1985), pp. 223–99; J. Debès and É. Poulat, *L'appel de la JOC (1926–1928)* (1986). Useful pamphlet by G. W. O. Addleshaw, *Jocism: An Account of the Continental Youth Movement, La Jeunesse Ouvrière Chrétienne* (1939). See also bibl. to CARDIJN, J. L.

Joel, Book of. One of the twelve *Minor Prophets of the OT. Wide differences exist among scholars about the origin, purpose, and date of the Book, and about 'Joel, the son of Pethuel', nothing is known at all. The prophecy, for the most part written in poetic form, has two sections. The first (1: 1–2: 17) tells of a plague of locusts and its results, and draws against this background a picture of the approaching Day of the Lord with its call to repentance. The rest of the Book (2: 18–3: 21) foretells the future outpouring of the Spirit on all flesh, the final salvation of Judah, and the destruction of foreign nations, all subjects of the kind more fully developed in the Apocalyptic literature. The passage predicting the outpouring of the Spirit of God and its effects (2: 28–32) is cited in Acts 2: 17–21 as foreshadowing the gift of the Holy Spirit at Pentecost.

Comm. by J. A. Bewer (ICC on Mic., Zeph., Nah., Hab., Obad., and Joel, 1912; sep. pagination), H. W. Wolff (on Joel and Amos, *Dodekapropheton*, 2, Biblischer Kommentar, Altes Testament, 14/2; Neukirchen, 1969, pp. 1–104; Eng. tr., Philadelphia [1977], pp. 1–86), W. Rudolph (KAT 13/2 on Joel, Amos, Obad., and Jon., 1971, pp. 35–92), and J. D. Watts (Camb. Bib., NEB, on Joel, Obad., Jon., Nah., Hab., and Zeph., 1975, pp. 12–50). A. S. Kapelrud, *Joel Studies* (Uppsala Universitets Årsskrift, 1948, no. 4; 1948). J. M. Myers, 'Some Considerations bearing on the Date of Joel', *ZATW* 74 (1962), pp. 177–95. W. Prinsloo, *The Theology of Joel* (Beihefte zur ZATW, 163; 1985). Eissfeldt, pp. 391–5, with additions, p. 760. J. Jeremias in *TRE* 17 (1988), pp. 91–7, s.v. 'Joel/Joelbuch', with extensive bibl.

Johannine Comma, also known as the 'Three Witnesses'. An interpolation in the text of 1 Jn. 5: 7 f., that is, the words in italics in the following passage from the AV: 'For there are three that bear record *in heaven, the Father, the Word, and the Holy Ghost, and these Three are One. And there are three that bear witness in earth*, the Spirit, and the Water, and the Blood, and these three agree in one.' They occur in Latin MSS from about AD 800 onwards and so became established in the official Latin text of the Bible, but they are found in no Greek MS before the 12th cent., are certainly not part of the original Epistle, and are omitted from the RV and other scholarly modern translations. The origin of the interpolation is obscure. Traces of a mystical interpretation of the phrase about the Spirit, the Water, and the Blood, applying it to the Trinity, are to be found in *Cyprian and *Augustine; but the earliest evidence for the insertion of a gloss in the text of the Epistle comes from a MS of *Priscillianist provenance discovered by G. Schepss at Würzburg in 1885. Later the insertion is found in quotations in African authors. It would thus seem to have originated in N. Africa or Spain and to have found its way into the Latin Bibles used in those districts (both *Old Latin and *Vulgate), possibly under the stress of *Arian persecution.

K. Künstle, *Das* Comma Ioanneum *auf seine Herkunft untersucht* (1905); E. Riggenbach, *Das* Comma Johanneum (Beiträge zur Förderung christlicher Theologie, 31, Heft 4; 1928; posthumous). T. A. Marazuela, 'Nuevo estudio sobre el "Comma Ioanneum" ', *Biblica*, 28 (1947), pp. 83–112, 216–35; 29 (1948), pp. 52–76. W.

Thiele, 'Beobachtungen zum Comma Iohanneum (1 Joh 5 7 f.)', *ZNTW* 50 (1959), pp. 61–73. B. M. Metzger, *The Text of the New Testament* (Oxford, 1964; 3rd edn., 1992), pp. 101 f. See also commentaries on 1 Jn., esp. A. E. Brooke, *The Johannine Epistles* (ICC, 1912), pp. 154–65.

John, St, Apostle. Acc. to tradition, the author of the Fourth Gospel, the Book of Revelation, and three of the Catholic Epistles. He was the son of Zebedee (Mt. 4: 21), and, together with his brother St *James and St *Peter, he belonged to the inner group of disciples who were present at the raising of Jairus's daughter (Mk. 5: 37), the *Transfiguration (Mt. 17: 1), and the Agony in the Garden (Mt. 26: 37). The Lord designated him and his brother Boanerges, which acc. to Mk (3: 17) means 'sons of thunder'. This would fit the impetuous character apparent at Mk. 9: 38 and Lk. 9: 54; but the etymology is obsure. In any case, they were also generous, willing to drink with Christ the cup of suffering (Mt. 20: 22). In Acts John is several times mentioned with Peter (3: 1 and 11), with whom he is imprisoned and appears before the Sanhedrin (4: 1–21). Later he is sent to Samaria with Peter, to transmit the Holy Spirit to the new converts (8: 14 f.). He was present also at the Apostles' council at *Jerusalem (Gal. 2: 9).

In the Fourth Gospel John is never mentioned by name, but tradition identifies him with the anonymous disciple to whom St *John the Baptist shows the Lamb of God (1: 35–40) and with the disciple 'whom Jesus loved', who reclined on His bosom at the Last Supper (13: 23), to whom He entrusted His Mother at the foot of the Cross (19: 26), who ran with Peter to the tomb on the morning of the Resurrection (20: 2–8), and who recognized the Risen Lord at the Sea of Tiberias (21: 7). The words of the Lord recorded on this last occasion were interpreted as meaning that he would not die. This traditional identification of the '*beloved disciple' with John, the son of Zebedee, has been contested in modern times; and the idea has been put forward, notably by H. Delff, W. *Bousset, and H. B. *Swete, that he was not one of the Twelve, but a Jerusalem disciple. Defenders of the traditional view have argued: (1) that, just as the John of the Synoptics and Acts is always shown in close association with Peter, so also is the 'beloved disciple' of the Fourth Gospel; and (2) that the consistent omission in the Fourth Gospel of so important a disciple as John is inexplicable except on the assumption that he is referred to under some other designation.

Acc. to tradition, John later went to Asia Minor and settled at *Ephesus. Under *Domitian he was exiled to *Patmos, where he wrote the Book of Revelation (Rev. 1: 9), and under Nerva returned to Ephesus and there wrote the Gospel and Epistles in his old age. Against this Mk. 10: 39 has sometimes been urged by critics as a 'vaticinium ex eventu', implying that John suffered martyrdom with James (cf. Acts 12: 2). Support for this theory is claimed in an alleged passage from *Papias, referred to by writers of the 5th and the 9th cents., mentioning the death of John and James at the hands of the Jews, and also in a notice of their death in several *martyrologies. But the evidence is both flimsy and imprecise, and is wholly inconclusive.

Both the question of the identity of the 'beloved disciple' and that of the date of St John's death have played a considerable part in the controversy over the authorship of the Gospel according to St John. Feast day in E., 26 Sept. (also 8 May); in W., 27 Dec. Acc. to later Latin legend, St John was ordered by Domitian to be thrown into a cauldron of boiling oil 'before the Latin Gate', i.e. the gate leading southwards from Rome to Latium, and came out unharmed. This event was long commemorated in his feast 'ante portam Latinam' on 6 May.

The principal discussions occur in comm. and studies on the Gospel acc. to St John (q.v.), though Bousset's speculations are included in his comm. on Rev. Modern discussion of the various problems by F.-M. Braun, OP, *Jean le théologien et son évangile dans l'Église ancienne* (Études Bibliques, 1959), pp. 301–92 and 407–11, with extensive refs. R. A. Culpepper, *John, the Son of Zebedee: The Life of a Legend* (Studies on Personalities of the New Testament; Columba, SC [1994]). H. B. Swete, 'The Disciple whom Jesus Loved', *JTS* 17 (1916), pp. 371–4; id., 'John of Ephesus', ibid., pp. 375–8; J. N. Sanders, 'Who was the Disciple whom Jesus Loved?', in F. L. Cross (ed.), *Studies in the Fourth Gospel* (1957), pp. 72–82; id., 'St John on Patmos', *New Testament Studies*, 9 (1963), pp. 75–85. H. D. Saffrey, 'Le témoignage des Pères sur le martyre de S. Jean Évangéliste', *RSPT* 69 (1985), pp. 265–72. On the church dedicated to St John at Ephesus, *Die Johanneskirche* (Forschungen in Ephesos, Band 4, Heft 3; Vienna, 1951). D. Mollat, SJ, in *Dict. Sp.* 8 (1974), cols. 192–247, s.v. 'Jean l'Évangéliste (saint)'. See also comm. to JOHN, EPISTLES OF ST., and REVELATION, BOOK OF, cited s.vv.

John, Acts of. A Greek apocryphal treatise, not later than the early 3rd cent., describing events in the life of the Apostle St *John. Large parts of it have come down to us in a number of scattered MSS, all incomplete. A fragment, discovered by M. R. James in 1886, contains an extended account of Christ's passion in highly *Docetic language, and a hymn which at a much later date was used by the *Priscillianists; it is commonly known in modern times as the 'Hymn of Jesus' and was set to music by Gustav Holst (d. 1934). A long account of the death of St John has also survived. As the events described are mainly connected with *Ephesus, it is likely that the treatise is of Ephesian provenance. It was known to *Clement of Alexandria, and apparently also to the author of *Monarchian Prologues to the Gospels. It was ascribed, esp. in later times, to a certain *Leucius.

Refs. in *Eusebius, *HE* 3. 25. 6, *Epiphanius, *Haer.* 47. 1, and *Philaster, *Haer.* 88. Crit. edn., with full introd. and comm., by E. Junod and J.-D.Kaestli (CC, Series Apocrypha, 1–2; 1983). Eng. tr. by J. K. Elliott, *The Apocryphal New Testament* (Oxford, 1993), pp. 303–49; Ger. tr. and introd. by K. Schäferdiek in Schneemelcher (5th edn.), 2 (1989), pp. 138–93; Eng. tr., 2 [1992], pp. 152–212. The *Acta Ioannis*, attributed to a certain Prochorus and pub. by T. *Zahn (Erlangen, 1880), are a later (5th-cent.) orthodox revision of the orig. Gnostic Acts; on this work see E. Junod and J.-D. Kaestli, op. cit., pp. 718–49, and A. de Santos Otero in Schneemelcher, 2 (5th edn.), pp. 385–91; Eng. tr., 2 [1992], pp. 429–35.

John, Apocryphon of. A Coptic document known from a Berlin MS since 1896, but first pub. in 1955. It was at first claimed as the source of *Irenaeus' account of the 'Barbelognostics' (*Adv. Haer.* 1. 29), with which it has parallels; but there are also differences. Three further copies were found at *Nag Hammadi, one of them closely parallel to the Berlin text, the others presenting a longer version. It takes the form of a dialogue between Christ and St

*John, the son of Zebedee, but there are indications that the dialogue form is part of a secondary Christianization. The text was clearly popular in some circles, and is important (1) as a document of early *Gnosticism, (2) for the insights which it may afford into the development of Gnostic literature, and (3) as a possible source for some *Valentinian ideas (unless, as Simone Pétrement argues, it is dependent on Valentinianism).

Berlin text, with Ger. tr., ed. W. C. Till, *Die gnostischen Schriften des koptischen Papyrus Berolinensis 8502* (TU 60; 1955), pp. 78–193, with introd., pp. 33–51; 2nd edn. by H.-M. Schenke (1972), with additional material, pp. 325, 327–9. Eng. tr. of the Berlin text in W. Foerster (ed.), *Gnosis*, 1 (Oxford, 1972), pp. 105–20. The Nag Hammadi texts were ed., with Ger. tr., by M. Krause and P. Labib, *Die Drei Versionen des Apokryphon des Johannes im Koptischen Museum zu Alt-Kairo* (Abhandlungen des Deutschen Archäologischen Instituts Kairo, Koptische Reihe, 1; Wiesbaden, 1962). Eng. tr. of long recension by F. Wisse in J. M. Robinson (ed.), *The Nag Hammadi Library in English* (3rd edn., Leiden, 1988), pp. 104–23. H.-C. Puech in Schneemelcher, 1 (1959), pp. 229–43; Eng. tr. (1963), pp. 314–31. S. Pétrement, *Le Dieu séparé: Les origines du gnosticisme* (1984), pp. 529–72; Eng. tr. (1991), pp. 387–419. *CPG* 1 (1983), pp. 75 f (no. 1180).

John, Epistles of St. There are three '*Catholic Epistles' which tradition ascribes to St *John, the Apostle and author of the Fourth Gospel. The longest and most important of them is the First. It is reckoned by *Eusebius among the 'homologoumena' and is attested by *Papias, *Polycarp, the *Muratorian Canon, and *Irenaeus. Modern scholars who defend the Apostolic authorship of the Gospel commonly also admit that of this Epistle. Among the great majority who reject the Apostolic authorship of the Gospel, opinion is divided. Some, e.g. A. *Harnack, attribute both the Gospel and the First Epistle to the same author; others, e.g. C. H. *Dodd, distinguish their authors. The other two Epistles are intimately connected with each other. They were, however, not generally admitted as authentic in antiquity. Eusebius placed them among the 'antilegomena' and St *Jerome reports that many attributed them to one 'John the Elder' because of their opening words (see JOHN THE PRESBYTER). They are not contained in the Syriac (*Peshitta) Version, and not a few modern critics assign them to a different author from that of the First Epistle. The Second Epistle is addressed to 'the elect lady and her children', which words are generally believed to refer not to a person but to a church; the Third to a Christian named Gaius.

The First Epistle reflects many of the themes of the Fourth Gospel: God is light, life, and love, manifested in the sending of Jesus, the Son of God, the *Messiah. Jesus Christ is the Saviour of the world (4: 14), through whom we possess eternal life (5: 12 f.), receive expiation and cleansing from our sins (1: 7) and become children of God (3: 1 f. and 5: 1). The writer stresses the continuity of Christian tradition and experience from the beginning (1: 1 ff.), and at some points is closer to the emphases of the earlier tradition than the Fourth Gospel, esp. in some eschatological statements. There is strong polemic against 'false brethren' who have broken away from the writer's community (2: 19); they are denounced for denying that Jesus Christ 'has come in the flesh', i.e. is truly incarnate (4: 2), for flouting the demands of righteousness and love, and belonging to 'the world' and the devil (4: 5 and

3: 8 f.). Their claim to inspiration is false; they are seen as embodying the *antichrist (2: 18). In making this sharp distinction between the children of God and the children of the devil or the godless world, the writer uses language suggesting not just a moral *dualism but an ultimate dualism incompatible with the biblical doctrine of *creation by one God; but it is unlikely that he intends to go so far. Similarly he urges the ideal of sinless perfection in language suggesting that Christians cannot, and presumably therefore do not, sin (3: 7–10). This is balanced by equally emphatic statements that we do sin, and need and receive forgiveness. Both points are important, although the writer fails to harmonize them. Some scholars therefore infer that there must be two sources or even writers; a third has been suggested for the passage which distinguishes mortal and unforgivable sins from less serious ones (5: 16 f.). Others ascribe the awkwardness to the necessity of attacking contradictory positions of the heretics themselves, who, like some later *Gnostics, combined an arrogant claim to spiritual perfection with a practical disregard of moral standards.

The Second Epistle insists esp. on the necessity of professing the right doctrine (2 Jn. 9) and of avoiding communion with the teachers of error (vv. 10, 11), and the Third on hospitality, reprimanding one Diotrephes for evading the practice of this virtue. The teaching of all three Epistles centres in the love of one's neighbour, for our love of God is best proved by the practice of fraternal charity.

On 1 Jn. 5: 7 f. see JOHANNINE COMMA.

Patristic comm. incl. the 'Adumbrationes' of *Clement of Alexandria (i.e. Lat. tr. of part of Clement's 'Hypotyposeis' made by *Cassiodorus c.540) and the 'Decem Tractatus' of St *Augustine. The more important modern comm. on the Epp. are those of B. F. *Westcott (London, 1883), A. E. Brooke (ICC, 1912), H. Windisch (Hb. NT 4, Heft 2; 1911, on the Catholic Epistles; 3rd edn. by H. Preisker, 15, 1951, pp. 106–44 and 166–72), J. Chaine (Études bibliques, 1939, on the Catholic Epistles, pp. 97–260), C. H. Dodd (Moff. Comm., 1946), R. Schnackenburg (Herders Theologischer Kommentar zum Neuen Testament, 13, Fasz. 3; 1953; 3rd edn., 1965), R. R. Williams (on 1–3 John and James, Cambridge, 1965, pp. 3–72), R. *Bultmann (KEK 14; 1967; Eng. tr., Hermeneia; Philadelphia [1973]), J. L. Houlden (Black's NT Comm., 1973), R. E. Brown, SS (Anchor Bible, 30; 1982), S. S. Smalley (Word Biblical Comm. 51; Waco, Tex. [1984]), G. Strecker (KEK 14; 1989; Eng. tr., Hermeneia; Minneapolis [1996]) and F. Vouga (Hb. NT 15, Heft 3; 1990). M. Hengel, The Johannine Question (1989), esp. pp. 24–73. R. Law, The Tests of Life: A Study of the First Epistle of St John (Edinburgh, 1909). C. H. Dodd, 'The First Epistle of St John and the Fourth Gospel', Bulletin of the John Rylands Library, 21 (1937), pp. 129–56. J. C. O'Neill, The Puzzle of 1 John: A New Examination of Origins (1966). A. Harnack, Über den dritten Johannesbrief (TU 15, Heft 3; 1897). J. Lieu, The Second and Third Epistles of John: History and Background (Edinburgh, 1986). R. Leconte in Dict. Bibl., Suppl. 4 (1949), cols. 797–815, s.v. 'Jean (Épîtres de saint)'; R. Kysar in Anchor Bible Dictionary, 3 (1992), pp. 900–12, s.v.

John, Gospel of St. The tradition that the Fourth Gospel was written by St *John the Apostle goes back to at least the end of the 2nd cent., when it is attested by St *Irenaeus (Adv. Haer. 3. 1. 1.). Irenaeus was acquainted with, and perhaps derived his information from St *Polycarp. Polycarp (quoted in *Eusebius, HE 5. 20. 6), may, however, have been referring to another John, sc. *John the Presbyter, whom many, esp. in the first half of the

20th cent., have supposed to be the true author. The Gospel was already in existence early in the 2nd cent., as is indicated by the reflection of its ideals in Polycarp and St *Ignatius of Antioch and has been confirmed by the discovery of the '*Rylands St John' papyrus. Apostolic authorship would account for the close acquaintance with Palestine and esp. *Jerusalem shown in some passages and for the precise details often given of time and place (e.g. 1: 29, 35, 39; 4: 6 etc.). But it has been recognized since *Clement of Alexandria that the Gospel as a whole is not a plain account of the Lord's *miracles and popular teaching, but a deeply meditated representation of His Person and doctrine. To most modern scholars direct apostolic authorship has therefore seemed unlikely; and only a few (e.g. J. A. T. *Robinson) would favour a date before c. AD 80 or 90. Good sources or historical traditions at many points are probable, and in any case the author emphatically claims to be witnessing to what 'we' have seen (1: 14; cf. 19: 35, 21: 24, and see JOHN, ST, for the relationship of 'the *beloved disciple' to the author).

Questions arise from a comparison of the Fourth Gospel with the 'Synoptics' from which it differs widely in content, style, and outlook. For example, the Lord's ministry extends over three *Passovers, and alternates between Jerusalem and *Galilee; the expulsion of the moneychangers from the *Temple is placed not at the close but at the beginning of His ministry; the Crucifixion is evidently dated on Nisan 14, not 15; and the *Last Supper is not the Passover Meal. Further, there is no mention of certain important events, e.g. the *Transfiguration and the institution of the *Eucharist, nor yet (unless by implication) of the *Baptism of Christ. There are no exorcisms, no *parables of the familiar kind, and only two occurrences of the phrase '*Kingdom of God'. On the other hand, John includes some events—most conspicuously the Raising of *Lazarus—about which the Synoptists say nothing; and there are extended discourses and dialogues on clearly defined themes with a characteristic style and vocabulary. Above all, Jesus speaks openly and frequently of His unique Sonship to God and His saving mission, whereas in the Synoptics such explicit claims are comparatively rare, and even then are sometimes accompanied by injunctions to secrecy. But there are also many points of similarity, and the main outline of the story is the same. Jesus is preceded by St *John (not here called 'the Baptist'), although their ministries overlap and his witness to the Lord is given unambiguously; Jesus has a ministry of teaching and miracles, at least part of which is in Galilee. He visits Jerusalem and is rejected by its leaders, who plot and encompass His Crucifixion; He is buried, and the tomb is found empty on the first day of the week, and the Risen Christ reveals Himself alive to His disciples.

What liberties the author of the Fourth Gospel has taken in rewriting the traditions he received is disputed, but there is general agreement that he is largely responsible for their shape and wording. For him the significance of the events is paramount, but 19: 35 indicates that the historicity of the death of Jesus is fundamental. There are a few similarities with the Synoptics (esp. Mark) in wording as well as substance, but it is uncertain whether he was familiar with one or more of them. He perhaps drew not on the Synoptic Gospels themselves, but on parallel traditions and sources. In either case, he supplemented and corrected his material, but was concerned chiefly to interpret it. For all its theological profundity, the Gospel has simplicity and directness; narratives and characters are often vivid.

The structure is clear: (1) the Prologue (1: 1–18), in which Jesus is presented as the eternal Word (*Logos, q.v.) of God; (2) the public ministry (1: 19–12: 50); (3) private teaching and prayer to the Father at the Last Supper (13–17); and (4) narrative of the Crucifixion and Resurrection (18–21). Although John has often been described as a 'seamless robe' (though with 'loose threads'), there are indications of dislocation (e.g. 14: 31 looks like an end to the Farewell Discourses) and some scholars have argued that the Gospel was composed in a number of stages, with one or more redactors; that the Prologue was taken over from an existing hymn and perhaps added at a later stage in the composition; and that a collection of 'signs' existed earlier. Ch. 21 (in which the 'beloved disciple' is claimed to be the author, 21: 24) is commonly assumed to be an appendix, probably added to allay anxiety after the death of the beloved disciple. 20: 31 seems to be the original ending of the Gospel, stating its purpose ('that ye may believe [or go on believing] that Jesus is the Christ, the Son of God; and that believing ye may have life in his name'). The aim is probably to strengthen the faith of Christians rather than to win belief from outsiders. The so-called '*pericope adulterae' (7: 53–8: 11; q.v.) cannot have been part of the original text.

The central teaching of the Gospel is Christological. Jesus is the eternal Son of God, pre-existent before *Abraham (8: 58), and indeed before the world (17: 5). The Son has been given everything that the Father has, including authority to give life and to execute judgement (5: 21–7); no one comes to the Father except through Him (14: 6), and He can say 'whoever has seen me has seen the Father' (14: 9). The 'Word' was made flesh, and His Divine nature is unequivocally affirmed (1: 1; 1: 14). The Jews accuse Him of blasphemy (5: 18), but Jesus stresses His total dependence on the Father and obedience in all that He says and does (5: 19; 5: 30). His deeds and words are regularly rejected or misunderstood by His opponents, or 'the world', but to those who accept and believe they are the revelation of God. Although the chief stress is on Jesus' Divine origin and status, His humanity is presupposed and affirmed, perhaps in conscious opposition to *Docetists (e.g. 4: 6). Many scholars have nevertheless detected docetic tendencies in the evangelist's own apparent reluctance to concede that Jesus could ever be ignorant (6: 6; 11: 42) or subject to temptation (12: 27, esp. if punctuated as in modern translations).

The Lord's message and mission for the salvation of all humanity (3: 16) are expounded in terms of 'light' and 'life'. Light is related to knowing, in contrast with darkness, ignorance, and sin (3: 19). In view of this moral dualism, it is not surprising that the Gospel had early popularity among the *Gnostics, esp. the 2nd-cent. Valentinians. But it also stresses 'life', i.e. eternal life, as promised in the Jewish and Christian traditions to whose who will be raised 'at the last day' (6: 39–40), in John most characteristically depicted as life that begins immediately through believing in Jesus (5: 24). The Christian teaching that salvation is dependent on the death (and resurrection) of Christ is spelt out clearly (e.g. 10: 15). Special emphasis is

put on the gift of the *Holy Spirit, consequent upon these events (16: 7 ff.).

The response required from disciples is threefold: to believe in Jesus as the Son of God sent by the Father in order to bring them into God's family and fellowship as His children; to practise in that fellowship the same love that Christ has shown them; and to witness to this faith and love that others may be brought in. If they do this, they will be sound branches of the 'vine' that is Christ (15: 1; 15: 5), and sheep of the flock of which Christ is the 'good shepherd' (10: 14); and they will enjoy the same unity which the Son enjoys with the Father (17: 22).

Ancient Gk. comm. incl. those of the Gnostic *Heracleon (fragmentary), *Origen (only 8 out of 32 books survive), *Chrysostom, *Theodore of Mopsuestia (many Gk. frags. and complete in Syr.), *Cyril of Alexandria, *Theophylact and *Euthymius Zigabenus; the most important Lat. work is St *Augustine's collection of Tractates on the Gospel. *Rupert of Deutz and *Nicholas of Lyre were notable among medieval commentators. Several of the Reformers wrote comm., notably J. *Calvin. RC commentators include T. de V. *Cajetan and J. *Maldonatus. Later comm. incl. those by B. F. *Westcott (Speaker's Commentary, 1881; Gk. text, 2 vols., London, 1908), A. F. *Loisy (Paris, 1903), T. *Zahn (in his own Kommentar zum Neuen Testament, 4; 1908), J. *Wellhausen (Berlin, 1908), W. Bauer (Hb. NT, 1912; 3rd edn., 1933), M. J. *Lagrange, OP (Études Bibliques, 1924), J. H. *Bernard (2 vols., ICC, 1928), A. *Schlatter (Tübingen, 1930), E. C. *Hoskyns (ed. F. N. Davey, 2 vols., London, 1940), R. *Bultmann (KEK, Abt. 2, 11th edn.; 1941; Eng. tr. of 1964 edn., with additions, Oxford, 1971), H. Strathmann (Das Neue Testament Deutsch, 4, 1951; 2nd edn., 1955), C. K. Barrett (London, 1955; 2nd edn., 1978), R. Schnackenburg (Herders theologischer Kommentar zum Neuen Testament, 4; 3 vols., 1965–75, with additional vol., 1984; Eng. tr., 3 vols., 1968–82), R. E. Brown, SS (2 vols., New York, 1966–70; London, 1971), J. N. Sanders (ed. B. A. Mastin, Black's NT Comm., 1968), J. C. Fenton (New Clar. Bib., 1970), B. Lindars, SSF (New Cent. Bib., 1972), E. Haenchen, posthumously ed. U. Busse (Tübingen, 1980; Eng. tr., Hermeneia, 2 vols., Philadelphia [1984]), J. Becker (2 vols., Göttingen, 1979–81), G. R. Beasley-Murray (Word Biblical Comm. 36; Waco, Tex. [1987]), and D. A. Carson (Leicester and Grand Rapids, Mich., 1991).

Modern research begins with K. G. Bretschneider, Probabilia de Evangelii et Epistolarum Joannis, Apostoli, Indole et Origine (Leipzig, 1820), which questioned the historicity of John. Turning-points have been marked by the work of F. C. *Baur, 'Ueber die Composition und der Charakter des johanneischen Evangeliums', Theologische Jahrbücher, 3 (1844), pp. 1–191, 397–475, 615–700, of which the substance was incorporated in his Kritische Untersuchungen über die kanonischen Evangelien (1847), pp. 79–389, and the comm. of Bultmann cited above. Later works incl. J. N. Sanders, The Fourth Gospel in the Early Church (1943); C. H. Dodd, The Interpretation of the Fourth Gospel (Cambridge, 1953); id., Historical Tradition in the Fourth Gospel (ibid., 1963); F. M. Braun, OP, Jean le théologien et son évangile dans l'Église ancienne (3 vols., Études Bibliques, 1959–66); M. F. Wiles, The Spiritual Gospel: The Interpretation of the Fourth Gospel in the Early Church (Cambridge, 1960); E. Käsemann, Jesu letzter Wille nach Johannes 17 (Tübingen, 1966; Eng. tr., The Testament of Jesus, 1968); J. L. Martyn, History and Theology in the Fourth Gospel (New York, etc. [1968]); R. A. Culpepper, Anatomy of the Fourth Gospel: A Study in Literary Design (Philadelphia [1983]); M. Hengel, The Johannine Question (1989), pp. 1–23 and 74–135; D. Rensberger, Johannine Faith and Liberating Community (Philadelphia, 1988; in UK, Overcoming the World: Politics and Community in the Gospel of John, 1989 [from a 'Liberationist angle']). A collection of papers, tr. into Eng. where necessary, ed. J. Ashton, The Interpretation of John (Issues in Religion and Theology, 9; 1986). Id., *Understanding the Fourth Gospel* (Oxford, 1991), with admirable survey of modern research, pp. 9–111, revising the earlier perspective of W. F. Howard, *The Fourth Gospel in Recent Criticism and Interpretation* (1931; rev. C. K. Barrett, 1955). E. Malatesta, SJ, *St John's Gospel 1920–1965: A Cumulative and Classified Bibliography of Books and Periodical Literature on the Fourth Gospel* (Analecta Biblica, 32; Rome, 1967); H. Thyen, 'Aus der Literatur zum Johannesevangelium', *Theologische Rundschau*, 39 (1974), pp. 1–69, 222–52, and 289–330. R. Kysar, 'The Fourth Gospel. A Report on Recent Research', *Aufstieg und Niedergang der römischen Welt*, 2. 25. 3, ed. W. Haase (1985), pp. 2389–480. Id. in *Anchor Bible Dictionary*, 3 (1992), pp. 912–31.

John XII (d. 964), Pope from 955. Octavian was the son of the Roman patrician, Alberic the younger, who, after the death of his mother, Marozia, had become the absolute ruler of Rome and obliged the noblemen of the city to make his son Pope on the death of Agapetus II. Octavian, who took the name of John XII, thus became Pope at the early age of 18. The main cause of the troubles of his pontificate was his decision to call in Otto I from Germany to help him against the rulers of N. Italy, King Berengar II and his son Adalbert. Otto arrived in Rome in 962 and on 2 Feb. was crowned Roman Emperor by John, who also sanctioned the erection of the archbishopric of Magdeburg and of the bishopric of Merseburg. The Emperor, who had been given an ornamental copy of the '*Donation of Constantine', on 13 Feb. issued the 'Privilegium Ottonis' or 'Ottonianum' recognizing the Papal territories (including the Carolingian donations) in central Italy. He then left Rome, ostensibly to conquer and defend them, but in fact demanded allegiance to himself. John then engineered a revolt against the imperial troops in Rome and sought assistance both from Berengar and the Byzantines. Amid mutual accusations of betrayal, Otto returned to Rome and on 6 Dec. 963 presided over a synod which deposed the Pope for immoral life and elected in his place a layman (Leo VIII), who received all the orders within two days. Otto also issued a revised form of the 'Ottonianum' with additional clauses (based on a forged version of the concessions made to Lothar I in 824) requiring, among other things, that a newly elected pope should take an oath of fealty to the emperor before consecration. After Otto's departure, John returned to Rome and in Feb. 964 deprived Leo VIII in a synod of his own, but was killed soon afterwards. His successor, Benedict V, was in turn expelled by Otto the following June and Leo VIII reinstated.

'Epistolae et Privilegia' in J. P. Migne, *PL* 133. 1013–41. P. Jaffé, *Regesta Pontificum Romanorum*, 1 (2nd edn. by W. Wattenbach, Leipzig, 1885), pp. 463–7. *LP* (Duchesne), 2, pp. 246–9. W. Ullmann, 'The Origin of the *Ottonianum*', *Cambridge Historical Journal*, 11 (1953–5), pp. 114–28. H. Zimmermann, 'Prozess und Abstzung Papst Johannes XII. im Jahre 963. Quellen und Urteile', *Österreichisches Archiv für Kirchenrecht*, 12 (1961), pp. 207–30. Id., *Das dunkle Jahrhundert* [1971], pp. 134–56. H. Wolter, *Die Synoden im Reichsgebiet und in Reichsitalien von 916 bis 1056* (1988), pp. 69–86. L. *Duchesne, *Les Premiers Temps de l'état pontifical* (2nd edn., 1904), pp. 337–51. Mann, 4 (1910), pp. 241–72. Fliche and Martin, 7 (1940), pp. 44–55, with refs. E. Amann in *DTC* 8 (pt. 1; 1924), cols. 619–26, s.v. 'Jean XII', with further refs. to sources.

John XXI (d. 1277), Pope from 1276. Peter of Spain (Petrus Hispanus) was born at Lisbon, prob. not later than *c*.1205, studied arts and theology at *Paris, and taught medicine at Siena. By 1250 he was Dean of Lisbon and Archdeacon of Vermoin in the diocese of Braga; in 1272 he became court-physician to Pope *Gregory X at Viterbo. In 1273 he was elected Abp. of Braga and created Cardinal Bp. of Frascati; in this capacity he attended the Second Council of *Lyons (1274). After the death of Hadrian V he was elected Pope on 15 Sept. 1276, taking the title 'John XXI', although no John XX had existed. During his brief pontificate he was active to preserve the union with the Greek Church achieved at Lyons. His bull 'Relatio nimis implacida' of 18 Jan. 1277 required the Bp. of Paris to report to him those who were teaching errors prejudicial to the faith. On 7 Mar. 1277 Bp. Stephen Tempier condemned 219 errors, some associated with the teachings of St *Thomas Aquinas, others with the supposed influence of *Averroism on masters of arts at Paris, such as *Siger of Brabant and Boethius of Dacia (*fl.* 1270–80). On 28 Apr. 1277 the bull 'Flumen aquae vivae' called for a further report on the errors of the Parisian masters. On 20 May 1277 the Pope died from injuries sustained when the roof collapsed in an apartment constructed for his use at Viterbo. It is unlikely that he had any responsibility for the details of the 1277 condemnations; his intellectual achievements were considerable and the influence of his writings enduring.

Peter of Spain's *Tractatus*, or *Summulae logicales*, was prob. composed in N. Spain in the early 1230s. It survives in more than 300 manuscripts and *c*.200 editions printed between 1474 and 1639, being the most influential of all medieval manuals of logic. He also composed other logical works and was among the first to comment on *Aristotle's *De anima*, *De sensu et sensato*, *De morte et vita*, *De longitudine et brevitate vitae*, and *Historia animalium*. His *Thesaurus pauperum*, a manual of medicine, enjoyed a large circulation with other medical writings. His chief theological work was an *Expositio librorum beati Dionysii*.

Crit. edn. of his *Tractatus* by L. M. de Rijk (Philosophical Texts and Studies, 22; Assen, 1972), with introd. and bibl. Part also ed., with Eng. tr., by J. P. Mullally (Publications in Mediaeval Studies, 8; Notre Dame, Ind., 1945). Eng. tr. of other logical works from *Copulata omnium tractatuum Petri Hispani* (Cologne, 1489) and *Textus et Copulata . . .* (ibid., 1494) by id., *Tractatus syncategorematum and selected anonymous Treatises* (Mediaeval Philosophical Texts in Translation, 13; Milwaukee, Wis., 1964). Further Eng. tr. of his *De Compositione* and *De Negatione*, with 'semi-critical' edn. of text, by J. Spruyt (Aristarium, Supplementa, 5; Nijmegen, 1989). *Obras filosóficas*, ed. M. [A.] Alonso, SJ (Consejo Superior de Investigaciones Científicas, Serie A, 1, 3, and 4; 1941–52; 2nd edn. of vol. 1, 1961). *Expositio librorum beati Dionysii*, ed. id. (Lisbon, 1957). *Obras Médicas*, ed. M. H. da Rocha Pereira (Acta Universitatis Conimbrigensis, 1973). *Le Registre de Jean XXI*, ed. E. Cadier [appended to the Register of Gregory X] (Bibliothèque des Écoles Françaises d'Athènes et de Rome, 2nd ser. 12, fasc. 3; 1898; with tables, 1960). The bull 'Relatio nimis implacida' is pr. in the *Chartularium Universitatis Parisiensis*, ed. H. Denifle, OP, and E. Chatelain, 1 (Paris, 1899), pp. 541 f. (no. 471); condemned propositions, ibid., pp. 543–58 (no. 473); 'Flumen aquae vivae' pr. in A. Callebaut, OFM, 'Jean Pecham, O.F.M., et l'Augustinisme', *Archivum Franciscanum Historicum*, 18 (1925), pp. 459 f. R. Stapper, *Papst Johannes XXI*. (Münster, 1898). M. *Grabmann, *Handschriftliche Forschungen und Funde zu den philosophischen Schriften des Petrus Hispanus, des späteren Papstes Johannes XXI*. (†1277) (*Sb*. (Bayr.), 1936, Heft 9; repr. id., *Gesammelte Akademieabhandlungen*, 2 (Veröffentlichungen des Grabmann-Institutes, NF 25, Heft 2; 1979), pp. 1123–254). R. Hissette, *Enquête sur les 219 articles condamnés à Paris le 7 mars 1277* (Philosophes médiévaux, 22; 1977). P. Glorieux in *Catholicisme*, 6 (1967), cols. 488 f., s.v. 'Jean XXI'.

John XXII (1249–1334), Pope from 1316. Jacques Duèse, a native of Cahors, after studying law at Paris and other French universities, was appointed Bp. of Fréjus by *Boniface VIII in 1300, Bp. of *Avignon in 1310, and Card. Bp. of Porto in 1312. Elected Pope in 1316 as the candidate of Robert of Anjou, he set out deliberately to transfer the Papacy to Avignon, on the quasi-imperial principle of 'ubi papa, ibi Roma'. Since the current Bp. of Avignon was his nephew (Jacques de Via), John was able easily to promote him cardinal and take over the episcopal palace himself. He worked hard to make Avignon a centre of culture, gathering artists and craftsmen as well as scholars such as the canonist Johannes Andreae (c.1270–1348), *Marsiglio of Padua, and *Petrarch. His reign was filled with theological and political conflicts. Almost at once he became involved in the difficulties threatening to split the *Franciscan Order (q.v.) and in 1317 dissolved the party of the *Spirituals, whose doctrines he denounced as heretical. He soon afterwards condemned the thesis, held by the bulk of the Franciscans, that the poverty of Christ and His Apostles was absolute. His decision won the assent of the majority of the order, but several of the more fanatical Franciscans fled to Louis of Bavaria, who gave them his support. In 1324 the Pope declared Louis a heretic and the quarrel became the occasion of a violent literary feud in which *William of Ockham and John of Jandun (d. 1328) took part. The literary conflict culminated in Marsiglio of Padua's 'Defensor Pacis' (anathematized by John in 1327), which upheld the absolute supremacy of the Emperor over the Pope, as one who may be elected, censured, and deposed at the Imperial pleasure. In 1328 Louis seized Rome and had himself crowned Roman Emperor, appointing a Spiritual Franciscan as Antipope under the name of Nicholas V on the ground that John had deposed himself by his absence from the Roman Church. Nicholas submitted to John two years later, but Louis was never reconciled.

John was an expert canonist, but at best an amateur theologian. In 1317 he promulgated the *Clementines, the last official book of the *Corpus Iuris Canonici, but a collection of his own decrees later achieved similar status as the *Extravagantes Johannis XXII. He insisted that as sovereign he could not be held to the ruling of previous Popes, notably Nicholas III (1277–80) in the controversy over apostolic poverty, but he became confused by his own declarations that he must adhere to scriptural authority in matters of faith and by his opponents' arguments that Papal infallibility reduced the competence of subsequent Popes. The charges of heresy levelled against him were strengthened by his involvement in the theological dispute on the *Beatific Vision. He opposed the general opinion and denied its enjoyment to the souls of the blessed before the Last Judgement, a doctrine which met with strong resistance from the Masters of the University of Paris, and one which he renounced on his deathbed as a personal opinion. His successor, *Benedict XII, adopted the more generally accepted view, which he defined in 1336.

John was a very capable administrator. He reorganized the Curia, establishing the *Rota Romana in 1331 as the tribunal of the Papal court, put Papal finances on a sound footing by some unpopular taxation, exerted firm supervision of the French clergy to counteract its '*Gallican' tendencies, although his numerous *provisions and nominations were as unpopular as his taxation, and he redefined many dioceses, esp. in Asia, where he established a new province at Sultaniyah with six Armenian suffragan bishops. He also introduced the universal observance of *Trinity Sunday in 1334. The authorship of the famous prayer *Anima Christi, used and popularized by St *Ignatius Loyola, has been assigned to him.

S. Riezler (ed.), *Vatikanische Akten zur deutschen Geschichte in der Zeit Kaiser Ludwigs des Bayern* (1891), pp. 1–577. G. Mollat (ed.), *Jean XXII (1316–1334): Lettres communes* (Bibliothèque des Écoles Françaises d'Athènes et de Rome, 3rd ser. 1 bis, 16 vols. bound in 13; 1904–47). A. Coulon (ed.), *Lettres secrètes et curiales du Pape Jean XXII ... relatives à la France* (ibid. 1; 5 fascs. [to 1324]; 1906–13). A. Fayen (ed.), *Lettres de Jean XXII* [concerning the Low Countries] (Analecta Vaticano-Belgica publiés par l'Institut historique Belge de Rome, 2–3; 1908–12). A. L. Tàutu (ed.), *Acta Ioannis XXII* (Pontificia Commissio ad redigendum Codicem Iuris Canonici Orientalis, Fontes, 3rd ser. vol. 6, tom. 2; Rome, 1952). J. Tarrant (ed.), *Extrauagentes Iohannis XXII* (Monumenta Iuris Canonici, Series B, vol. 6; Vatican City, 1983). M. Dykmans, SJ (ed.), *Les Sermons de Jean XXII sur la Vision Béatifique* (Miscellanea Historiae Pontificiae, 34; Rome, 1973). É. *Baluze, *Vitae Paparum Avenionensium*, ed. G. Mollat, 1 (1916), pp. 107–94. V. Verlaque, *Jean XXII, sa vie et ses œuvres d'après des documents inédits* (1883). N. Valois, 'Jean Duèse, pape sous le nom de Jean XXII', *Histoire littéraire de la France*, 34 (1914), pp. 391–630. H. Otto, 'Zur italienischen Politik Johanns XXII', *Quellen und Forschungen aus italienischen Archiven und Bibliotheken*, 14 (1911), pp. 140–265, with texts. A. Esch, *Die Ehedispense Johanns XXII und ihre Beziehung zur Politik* (Historische Studien, 183; 1929). G. Tabacco, *La Casa di Francia nell'azione politica di Papa Giovanni XXII* (Istituto Storico Italiano per il Medio Evo. Studi Storici, fascs. 1–4; 1953). H. O. Schwöbel, *Die diplomatische Kampf zwischen Ludwig dem Bayern und der römischen Kurie im Rahmen des kanonischen Absolutionsprozesses 1330–1346* (Quellen und Studien zur Verfassungsgeschichte des Deutschen Reiches im Mittelalter und Neuzeit, 10; Weimar, 1968). L. Caillet, *La Papauté d'Avignon et l'Église de France: La politique bénéficiale du Pape Jean XXII en France (1316–1334)* [1975]. B. Tierney, *Origins of Papal Infallibility 1150–1350* (Studies in the History of the Christian Church, 6; Leiden, 1972), pp. 171–204 ('John XXII and the Franciscans'); J. L. Heft, SM, 'Nicholas III (1277–1280) and John XXII (1316–1334): Popes in Contradiction?', *Archivum Historiae Pontificiae*, 21 (1983), pp. 245–57; id., *John XXII and Papal Teaching Authority* (Texts and Studies in Religion, 27; Lewiston, NY, etc. [1986]); T. Turley, 'John XXII and the Franciscans: A Reappraisal' in J. R. Sweeney and S. Chodorow (eds.), *Popes, Teachers and Canon Law in the Middle Ages* (Ithaca, NY, and London, 1989), pp. 74–88. G. Mollat, *Les Papes d'Avignon* (10th edn. [1965]), pp. 39–71, with detailed bibl.; Eng. tr. of earlier edn. (1963), pp. 9–25. D. L. Douie in *NCE* 7 (1967), pp. 1014 f., s.v.; C. A. Lückerath in *TRE* 17 (1988), pp. 109–12, s.v. 'Johannes XXII', with bibl.

John XXIII (d. 1419), Antipope to both *Benedict XIII and Gregory XII from 1410 to 1415. Baldassare Cossa was the descendant of a noble but impoverished Neapolitan family. After a military career during which he is said to have engaged in piracy, he studied law at *Bologna and entered the service of the *Curia. Boniface IX, who appreciated his administrative and military talents, created him cardinal in 1402, and made him legate of Romandiola in 1403 and of Bologna in 1409. He was crowned Pope in

1410, but the validity of his election has been contested as being simoniacal. Of the three Popes then existing he had the largest number of supporters, esp. after Ladislaus of Naples, defeated at Roccasecca on 19 May 1411, transferred his allegiance from Gregory XII to John. In 1412 he called a synod at Rome which was very poorly attended and soon dissolved. In 1413, at the persuasion of King Sigismund, he convoked a General Council to end the W. Schism, which met at *Constance in 1414. Though he promised to cede his claims to the Papacy if Gregory XII and Benedict XIII would do the same, his sincerity was suspected, and he actually fled soon afterwards, so as to deprive the Council of its authority, under the pretext that he enjoyed no liberty. After being brought back by force he was imprisoned and deposed (1415), accepting his fate with unexpected meekness. He was held a prisoner in Germany for three years, but was set free in 1419, when he recognized *Martin V, who made him Card. Bp. of Tusculum. He died soon afterwards.

J. Schwerdfeger, *Papst Johann XXIII und die Wahl Sigismunds zum römischen König, 1410* (1895). E. J. Kitts, *Pope John the Twenty-Third and Master John Hus of Bohemia* (1910). H. Finke, 'Zur Charakteristik des Hauptanklägers Johanns XXIII auf dem Konstanzer Konzil', *Miscellanea Francesco Ehrle*, 3 (ST 39; 1924), pp. 157–63. H. G. Peter, *Die Informationen Papst Johanns XXIII. und dessen Flucht von Konstanz bis Schaffhausen* (Freiburg, 1926). H. Diener, 'Rubrizellen zu Kanzleiregistern Johanns XXIII. und Martins V.', *Quellen und Forschungen aus italienischen Archiven und Bibliotheken*, 39 (1959), pp. 117–72. L. Waldmüller, 'Materialien zur Geschichte Johannes' XXIII. (1410–1414)', *Annuarium Historiae Conciliorum*, 7 (1975), pp. 229–37. W. Brandmüller, '*Infeliciter electus fuit in Papam.* Zur Wahl Johannes' XXIII', in D. Berg and H.-W. Goetz (eds.), *Ecclesia et Regnum: Beiträge zur Geschichte von Kirche, Recht und Staat im Mittelalter. Festschrift für Franz-Joseph Schmale zu seinem 65. Geburtstag* (1989), pp. 309–22, repr. in Brandmüller, *Papst und Konzil im Grossen Schisma* (1990), pp. 71–84. G. Mollat in *DTC* 8 (pt. 1; 1924), cols. 641–4, s.v. 'Jean XXIII', with refs. to sources; id. in *NCE* 7 (1967), pp. 1020 f. See also bibl. to CONSTANCE, COUNCIL OF.

John XXIII (1881–1963), Pope from 1958. Angelo Giuseppe Roncalli was the third of thirteen children born to a peasant family at Sotto il Monte near Bergamo. From the seminary at Bergamo he won a scholarship to the San Apollinare college in Rome, where he was ordained priest in 1904. At this time he began the spiritual diary which he kept throughout his life (pub. in 1964; Eng. tr., *The Journal of a Soul*, 1965). He was secretary to Count Giacomo Radini-Tedeschi from the time of the latter's appointment as Bp. of Bergamo in 1905 until his death in 1914. In his spare time he engaged in study of the history of the diocese and in 1909 embarked on his main scholarly work, *Gli atti della visita apostolica di S. Carlo Borromeo a Bergamo (1575)* (5 vols., 1936–58). His research in the *Ambrosian Library brought him into touch with A. Ratti (later Pope *Pius XI).

During the First World War he served as a hospital orderly and then as an army chaplain. In 1921 he was summoned to Rome as director of the Society for the Propagation of the Faith in Italy; under him the Society was reorganized and brought by Pius XI under the Congregation of the *Propaganda. In 1925 Roncalli was consecrated titular Bp. of Areopolis and sent as *Vicar Apostolic to *Bulgaria. In 1934 he was translated to the titular see of Mesembria and appointed Apostolic Delegate to Turkey and Greece. During his time in the Balkans he established good relations with the Orthodox, visiting the *Oecumenical Patriarch of Constantinople in 1939. In the Second World War he organized relief supplies to German-occupied Greece, as well as assisting Jews in Istanbul. At the end of 1944, after the German retreat from France, he was sent as Papal Nuncio to Paris. Here he dealt tactfully with the problem of the numerous French bishops accused of having collaborated with the Vichy regime; in the face of delays he pressed for the speedy return of German prisoners-of-war (meanwhile arranging study for the ordinands among them); and he won some concessions from the French goverment over the financing of Church schools. He showed sympathy with the motives (if not all the actions) of the worker priests (who were restricted after his departure). In 1953 he was created a cardinal. When he left France, he expected to have to work in the *Curia, but on the death of the Patr. of *Venice later in 1953, Roncalli succeeded him, glad to be returning to pastoral work.

In 1958, on the death of *Pius XII, he was elected Pope at the age of 77. He caused surprise by taking the name of John, long discredited because of the antipope *John XXIII. Among his first acts was the creation on 15 Dec. 1958 of 23 new cardinals, including G. B. Montini (later Pope *Paul VI), and the number of cardinals soon exceeded the level of 70 laid down by *Sixtus V. In 1959 he proposed to the cardinals three undertakings: a diocesan synod for Rome, an oecumenical council for the Church, and a revision of the code of *canon law. The synod was held in Rome in 1960 and dealt with local problems of Rome. The council, soon to be known as the Second *Vatican Council, is the most important event of his pontificate. He attributed the calling of it to the inspiration of the Holy Spirit and gave it the task of renewing (*aggiornamento*) the religious life of the Church; it was to express the substance of its faith in new language and bring up to date its discipline and organization, with the ultimate goal of the unity of all Christians. To realize his ecumenical aim he set up the Secretariat for Promoting Christian Unity in 1960 and invited to the Council observers from other Churches. He opened and closed the first session of the Council, once intervening to give encouragement to those in favour of change. (For details of the legislation and significance of the Council, see VATICAN COUNCIL, SECOND). Other reforms of his pontificate included permission for the use of the vernacular in the Byzantine liturgy of the *Melchites (5 April 1960), approval of a new code of rubrics for the *Missal and *Breviary (25 July 1960), the insertion of the name of St *Joseph in the Canon of the Mass (13 Nov. 1962), and the creation of a pontifical commission to revise the code of canon law (28 Mar. 1963). He renewed the social teaching of the Church in '*Mater and Magistra' (1961) and in '*Pacem in Terris' (1963) he encouraged the end of colonialism and improvements in the position of women, as well as pleading for abandonment of the arms race. In the Cuban missile crisis of 1962 he publicly urged caution on the leaders of the United States and the Soviet Union. In 1960 he welcomed G. F. *Fisher, the first Abp. of Canterbury to be received at the Vatican since the Reformation, and in 1961 the RC Church was for the first time represented at an assembly of the *World Council of Churches. Throughout his pontificate there was a feeling that there was a desire in the RC Church to soften the obstacles to reunion with other Christian bodies, while he also sought to improve relations with Judaism by removing from the Good Friday liturgy the passages which caused most offence. He was mourned by those within and beyond the RC Church, and proceedings for his beatification were initiated by Paul VI.

The official acts of his pontificate are pr. in *AAS*. *Acta* also ed. D. Bertetto, SDB (Bibliotheca Theologica Salesiana, 2nd ser.; Zurich, 1964). John XXIII's *Souvenirs d'un nonce: Cahiers de France (1944–1953)* ed. L. Capovilla (Rome, 1963; Eng. tr., 1966); *Il giornale dell'anima e altri scritti di pietà* ed. id. (ibid., 1964; Eng. tr., 1965); *Lettere ai familiari* ed. id. (ibid., 1968; Eng. tr., 1970). *Quindici letture* also ed. id. (3rd edn., 1970), with detailed chronology of his life and other material in appendices. Correspondence with the future Pope Paul VI, 1925–1962, ed. id. (Brescia, 1982). His Life of Radini-Tedeschi, orig. pub. at Bergamo in 1916, was tr. into Eng. from 3rd edn., Rome, 1963, in 1970. The many studies include those of E. Balducci (Florence, 1964; Eng. tr., 1965), E. E. Y. Hales (London, 1965), M. Trevor (ibid., 1967), B. R. Bonnot (New York [1979]), and P. Hebblethwaite (London, 1984), with bibl. and refs. F. Della Salda, *Obbedienza e Pace: Il vescovo A. G. Roncalli tra Sofia e Roma 1925–1934* (Genoa, 1989); V. Branca and S. Rosso Mazzinghi (eds.), *Angelo Giuseppe Roncalli dal Patriarcato di Venezia alla Cattedra di San Pietro* (Florence, 1984); M. Manzo, *Papa Giovanni vescovo a Roma* [1991]. R. Trisco in *NCE* 7 (1967), pp. 1015–20, s.v.

John of Antioch (d. 441), Bp. of *Antioch from 429. The leader of the moderate Easterns in the *Nestorian controversy, he gave active support to his friend, Nestorius, in his dispute with *Cyril of Alexandria. In 431 he failed to arrive at the Council of *Ephesus in time for its opening meeting (22 June); and Cyril, suspecting him (probably wrongly) of employing Fabian tactics to aid his friend, refused to wait and proceeded to condemn Nestorius forthwith. When John eventually reached Ephesus a few days later, he held a counter-council which condemned Cyril and vindicated Nestorius. In 433 he became reconciled with Cyril on the basis of a theological formula devised as a compromise; but John thereby lost many supporters in his own patriarchate. Some of his letters are extant.

His letters are mostly pr. in *ACO* 1; for details see *CPG* 3 (1979), pp. 219–31 (nos. 6301–60). D. Stiernon in *DPAC* 2 (1984), cols. 1541–3, s.v. 'Giovanni di Antiochia'; Eng. tr. in *Encyclopedia of the Early Church*, 1 (1992), p. 444, s.v. See also bibl. to CYRIL OF ALEXANDRIA and to EPHESUS, COUNCIL OF (431).

John of Apamea (flourished early 5th cent.), Syriac spiritual writer, also known as John the Solitary. His writings include a 'Dialogue on the Soul' and a number of letters and tractates. There is some uncertainty about his identity and date; some of his works have been wrongly attributed to John of Lycopolis (d. 394).

Dialogue on the Soul, ed., under the name of John of Lycopolis, by S. Dedering (Leipzig, etc., 1936); Fr. tr. by I. Hausherr, SJ (Orientalia Christiana Analecta, 120; Rome, 1939). L. G. Rignell (ed.), *Briefe von Johannes dem Einsiedler* (Lund, 1941); id. (ed.), *Drei Traktate von Johannes dem Einsiedler* (Lunds Universitets Årsskrift, NF, Avd. I, Bd. 54, no. 4; 1960), both with Ger. tr. Further texts ed. W. Strothmann, *Johannes von Apamea* (Patristische Texte und Studien, 11; 1972); Fr. tr. by R. Lavenant, SJ (SC 311; 1984). S. [P.] Brock, 'John the Solitary, On Prayer',

JTS NS 30 (1979), pp. 84–101, incl. text and Eng. tr. A. de Halleux, 'La Christologie de Jean le Solitaire', *Le Muséon*, 94 (1981), pp. 5–36. B. Bradley in *Dict. Sp.* 8 (1974), cols. 764–72, s.v. 'Jean le Solitaire (d'Apamée)'.

John of Ávila, St (1499/1500–69), 'Apostle of Andalusia'. Born at Almodóvar del Campo (Ciudad Real), he first studied law at Salamanca (1513–17) and then, from 1520 to 1526, arts at Alcalá and the biblically based theology fostered there. Ordained in 1526, his plan to go to *Mexico as a missionary failed, partly prob. because of difficulties arising from his Jewish paternal ancestry, and partly because Alonso de Manrique (Abp. of Seville and Inquisitor General) wanted to keep him in Spain. His apostolate of preaching throughout Andalusia soon began and continued until prolonged ill-health obliged him to remain at Montilla (from 1554). In 1531 he was denounced to the Seville *Inquisition on various charges, including illuminism and undue religious partisanship on behalf of the poor. A prisoner for a year (1532–3), he was released with a warning to 'moderate his language' in his future preaching.

His concern with the need to improve the quality of the parish clergy and the pastoral care they gave, and to instruct lay people in the Christian faith, led him to establish at least 15 colleges or schools for the laity and two for the clergy. His preoccupation with the pastoral and spiritual shortcomings of the clergy later found expression in the two *Memoriales* (1551 and 1561) written for Pedro Guerrero, Abp. of Granada, a participant in the Council of *Trent; also in his *Advertencias* for the provincial synod of Toledo (1565). His many disciples and admirers included St *Peter of Alcántara, St Francis *Borgia, and *Luis of Granada. He conducted a wide correspondence with those seeking spiritual guidance: St *Teresa of Ávila obtained his judgement on her *Life* in his last months. He had high hopes of the *Jesuits, encouraging several of his followers to enter the Society, though he never did so himself (partly because of the prejudice against those with Jewish backgrounds which he believed to exist in the Society).

His one major spiritual treatise ('*Audi, filia*'), though originally written, in the mid-1530s, for a young aristocratic nun, in its developed form expounds the way of perfection for all Christian people. As also in his spiritual letters, he here urges confident trust in God and meditation on the sufferings and merits of Christ, through which man finds pardon. The centrality of this theme helps to explain why, even after making revisions, he more than once delayed publication. An unauthorized version (Alcalá, 1556) was one of the many spiritual works banned by the Valdés *Index* of 1559. It was prob. at this point that, reportedly, he destroyed much other MS material. The definitive version of his treatise appeared posthumously in 1574 and was printed several times until 1604, though little thereafter. His works were appreciated in different quarters, including the English *recusants of the early 17th cent. and at *Port-Royal, where Robert Arnauld d'Andilly translated them into French (1673). Attempts to secure his beatification in the 1730s were unsuccessful; he was beatified in 1894 and canonized in 1970. Feast day, 10 May.

Crit. edn. of his works by L. Sala Balust, rev. by F. Martín Hermández (Biblioteca de Autores Cristianos, 6 vols., 1970–1), with biographical introd., 1, pp. 3–389. *Escritos sacerdotales* (incl. *Memoriales* for the Council of Trent), ed. J. Esquerda Bifet (ibid., 1969); and *Audi, filia*, ed. L. Sala Balust (Espirituales Españoles, Series A, Textos, 10; 1963). Eng. tr. of selected letters by the *Benedictines of Stanbrook Abbey (1904); Fr. tr. of letters of direction, with introd., by J. M. de Buck (Museum Lessianum, Section Ascétique et Mystique, 25; 1927). Early Life by his disciple, Luis of Granada (1588); also ed. L. Sala Balust (Espirituales Españoles, Series A, Textos, 14; 1964). C. M. Abad, SJ, 'El proceso de la Inquisición contra el Beato Juan de Ávila', *Miscelánea Comillas*, 6 (1946), pp. 95–167; M. Ruiz Jurado, SJ, 'San Juan de Ávila y la Compañía de Jesús', *Archivum Historicum Societatis Iesu*, 40 (1971), pp. 153–72. There is a specialist review *Maestro Avila* (Montilla, 1946 ff.).

John the Baptist, St, the 'Forerunner of Christ'. Acc.

to Lk. (1: 5–25), he was the son of *Zachariah, a priest of the *Temple, and of *Elizabeth, a kinswoman of the BVM, to whom he was born in old age. His birth had been foretold by an angel (1: 13–20), who had instructed Zachariah that he should be called John. On the fulfilment of this injunction his father uttered the *Benedictus (q.v.). All the Gospels record his appearance *c.* AD 27 as a mission preacher on the banks of the *Jordan demanding repentance and baptism from his hearers in view of the approach of the *Kingdom of God. His dress and diet (locusts and wild honey) were reminiscent of the OT prophets, though some of his preaching foreshadowed that of Christ. Large crowds were attracted to him and among those who submitted to his baptism was the Lord Himself. Later his denunciation of *Herod Antipas for his marriage led to his imprisonment and subsequent beheading (Mt. 14: 1–12). His influence 20 years later is attested in Acts (18: 25, 19: 1–7). He is highly revered by the *Mandaeans (q.v.), who may possibly have some remote connection with his original disciples.

Outside the NT, John is also mentioned by *Josephus (*Antiq.* 18. 5. 2) in a passage of which there is no good reason to doubt the authenticity. Though there are differences in detail, his account and that in the NT are not incompatible. The place of his imprisonment and death are given as the fortress of Machaerus by the Dead Sea. He was believed to have been buried at Sebaste (Samaria), where his tomb was honoured in the 4th cent. On its desecration under *Julian the Apostate (*c.*362) his relics appear to have been scattered, numerous churches claiming to possess them.

Acc. to tradition (*Origen, *Ambrose, *Jerome, and *Leo the Great), John the Baptist was endowed with prenatal grace at the time of the *Visitation of the BVM (Lk. 1: 41). Consequently the Feast of his Nativity, originally celebrated in connection with the *Epiphany but from *c.* the late 4th cent. fixed on 24 June (six months before *Christmas), is regarded as of greater solemnity than that of his death ('Decollation'), observed on 29 Aug. from *c.* the 5th cent. The liturgy for the feast of his Nativity has retained certain affinities with that of Christmas, but because of its date the feast has become linked with certain customs connected with the summer solstice. The early importance of his cult is testified by his place in the *Canon of the Mass and formerly in the *Confiteor.

In art, at first depicted only in connection with the Baptism of the Lord, he is later represented as an ascetic preacher wearing camel hair and carrying a staff and scroll saying 'Ecce Agnus Dei' (cf. Jn. 1: 29); he often bears a book or dish with a lamb on it. In Orthodox *icons he often appears with the wings of an angel (Mk. 1: 2 describes him as ἄγγελος, i.e. messenger).

C. H. Kraeling, *John the Baptist* (New York, 1951). C. H. H. Scobie, *John the Baptist* (1964). J. *Daniélou, SJ, *Jean-Baptiste témoin de l'Agneau* (1964). W. Wink, *John the Baptist in the Gospel Tradition* (Society for New Testament Studies. Monographs Series, 7; 1968). J. Ernst, *Johannes der Täufer: Interpretation—Geschichte—Wirkungsgeschichte* (Beihefte zur *ZNTW*, 53; 1989) E. Malatesta, SJ, and R. Marichal, SJ, in *Dict. Sp.* 8 (1974), cols. 175–92, s.v. 'Jean le Baptiste'; P. W. Hollenbach in *Anchor Bible Dictionary*, 3 (1992), pp. 887–99, s.v.

John Baptist de La Salle, St (1651–1719), founder of

the Institute of the Brothers of Christian Schools. Born at *Reims of noble family, he received the tonsure in 1662 and was installed as Canon of Reims in 1667. After studying at the seminary of *Saint-Sulpice from 1670 to 1672, he was ordained priest in 1678. In 1679 he assisted in the opening of two free schools in Reims, where he soon became interested in fostering religious principles in the teachers. The original group, which he had taken into his own house in 1681, having resisted his attempt to enforce a semi-monastic discipline, soon left him; but in 1682 others came forward. Resigning his canonry in 1683, he distributed his fortune to the poor (1684) and devoted himself to the training of his new community. In 1688 he took charge of the free school in the parish of Saint-Sulpice, founded by J.-J. *Olier. In 1699 he opened in Paris the first Sunday Schools giving technical and religious instruction to the sons of artisans; and he was also asked by *James II to educate the Irish boys at his court in exile. In subsequent years schools were started in other parts of France and beyond. In 1690 he finally decided against including priests in the Institute and in 1694 he drew up the first rule. Although as a result of local disagreements, the Bps. of Paris (in 1702) and Rouen (in 1712) imposed superiors from outside the Institute on houses in their dioceses, de La Salle in fact retained personal control until 1717.

Apart from his spiritual importance, de La Salle is significant as a pioneer in educational practice. First in the field for training colleges for teachers, as distinct from ecclesiastical seminaries, he popularized the teaching of the vernacular in French schools and the use of the simultaneous method. His boarding school at Saint-Yon (est. 1705) has been considered the prototype of modern secondary educational institutions. His works include *Conduite des écoles chrétiennes* (1720; Eng. tr., 1935) and three sets of meditations for Sundays, the principal feasts and for use in *retreats (*c.*1729; Eng. tr. of all three, 1953). He was canonized in 1900. Feast day, 7 Apr. (formerly 15 May).

Crit. edn. of his *Lettres* by Félix-Paul [P. Vandamme], FSC (Paris [1954]). His other works are repr. in *Cahiers Lasalliens*, 12–25 (Rome [1962–5]). Crit. edn. of his *Explication de la méthode d'oraison* by M. Campos, FSC, and M. Sauvage, FSC (ibid. 50; 1989). Eng. tr. of *Letters and Documents* by W. J. Battersby (London, 1952) and of *Letters* by C. Malloy, FSC, ed. A. Loes, FSC (Romeoville, Ill., 1988). Lives by J.-B. Blain (2 vols., Rouen, 1733; Eng. tr., 3 vols., Romeoville, Ill. [1982–6]), W. J. Battersby (London, 1957), and S. Gallego (2 vols., Biblioteca de Autores Cristianos, 1986, with Sp. tr. of selected works in vol. 2). W. J.

Battersby, *De La Salle: A Pioneer of Modern Education* (1949); id., *De La Salle: Saint and Spiritual Writer* (1950); Y. Poutet, *Le XVIIe siècle et les origines lasalliennes* (2 vols., Rennes, 1970); O. Würth, FSC, *La pédagogie de Jean-Baptiste de La Salle* (Lasallianum, 15; Rome, 1972; adapted Eng. tr., Romeoville, Ill., 1988); M. A. Campos, FSC, *L'Itinéraire évangélique de saint Jean-Baptiste de La Salle et le recours à l'Écriture dans ses Méditations pour le Temps de la Retraite* (Cahiers Lasalliens, 45–6; 1974); based on vol. 1 of this work is E. Bannon, FSC, *De La Salle: A Founder as Pilgrim* (1988); M. Sauvage and M. Campos, *Jean Baptiste de La Salle: Annoncer l'Évangile aux pauvres* (Bibliothèque de Spiritualité, 11 [1977]; Eng. tr., Romeoville, Ill. [1981]). G. Rigault, *Histoire générale de l'Institut des Frères des Écoles chrétiennes* (9 vols., 1937–53); W. J. Battersby, *History of the Institute of the Brothers of the Christian Schools* (2 vols. in 3 [1960–3]). A. Hermans, FSC, and M. Sauvage, FSC, in *Dict. Sp.* 8 (1974), cols. 802–21, s.v. 'Jean-Baptiste (5) de La Salle'.

John Baptist Mary Vianney, St. See CURÉ D'ARS, THE.

John of Beverley, St (d. 721), Bp. of *York. A monk of St *Hilda's double-abbey at Whitby and a diligent scholar and teacher, he was consecrated Bp. of *Hexham *c*.687. In 705 he was translated to the see of York, then being claimed by *Wilfrid. Before his death he retired to the abbey at Inderawood, afterwards *Beverley, of which he had himself been the founder. The reputation he acquired for sanctity during his lifetime increased after his death, and in the Middle Ages he enjoyed a widespread cultus in England, and many miracles were attributed to his prayers. Henry V ascribed the victory of Agincourt (1415) to his intercession and in 1416 ordered his feast to be kept throughout England. Feast days, 7 May (death) and 25 Oct. (translation of relics).

The chief authority for his life is *Bede, *HE* 4 and 5. A Life by Folcard, based on Bede, in J. Raine, *The Historians of the Church of York and its Archbishops*, 1 (Rolls Series, 1879), pp. 239–91. W. Hunt in *DNB* 29 (1892), pp. 435 f.

John Bosco, St. See BOSCO, ST JOHN.

John Capistran, St. See GIOVANNI CAPISTRANO, ST.

John Capreolus. See CAPREOLUS, JOHN.

John Chrysostom, St. See CHRYSOSTOM, ST JOHN.

John Climacus, St (*c*.570–*c*.649), ascetic and writer on the spiritual life, so called after his famous 'Ladder' (Κλῖμαξ). He was also known as σχολαστικός, but is not to be confused with *John Scholasticus, Patr. of Constantinople (q.v.). He arrived at Mt *Sinai as a novice when he was 16; after his profession he spent some years as an *anchorite and was later Abbot of Sinai. His celebrated 'Ladder of Paradise' or 'Ladder of Divine Ascent' treats of the monastic virtues and vices, the anchoritic and coenobitic life, and the nature of complete dispassionateness (ἀπάθεια), which is upheld as the ideal of Christian perfection. There are 30 'steps of the ladder' (i.e. 30 chapters) to correspond with the age of Christ at His Baptism. Feast day, in W., 30 Mar.; in E., 4th Sunday in Lent (also 30 Mar.).

There is no critical text. Ed. M. Rader, SJ (Paris, 1633); repr., with additional material, in J. P. Migne, *PG* 88, 585–1248; another edn. from MS on Mt *Athos by the hermit Sophronios

(Constantinople, 1883); text based on Migne, with Ital. tr., by P. Trevisan (Corona Patrum Salesiana, Series Graeca, 8–9; Turin, 1941); further edn., based mainly on a 14th-cent. MS from Stavronikita (Cod. 895.30), with modern Gk. tr., by Archimandrite Ignatios (Oropos, 1978). Medieval Lat. trs. by Ambrogio *Traversari and others; a Sp. tr. of one of these Lat. texts of John Climacus was destined to be the first book to be pr. in the New World (Mexico, 1532). Eng. trs. by L. Moore (London, 1959) and by C. Luibheid and N. Russell (Classics of Western Spirituality, 1982), with important introd. by K. [T. R.] Ware, pp. 1–70. W. Völker, *Scala Paradisi: Eine Studie zu Johannes Climacus und zugleich eine Vorstudie zu Symeon dem neuen Theologen* (Wiesbaden, 1968), with refs. J. R. Martin, *The Illustration of the Heavenly Ladder of John Climacus* (Studies in Manuscript Illumination, 5; Princeton, NJ, 1954). L. Petit in *DTC* 8 (pt. 1; 1924), cols. 690–3, s.v. 'Jean 30. Jean Climaque'; G. Couilleau in *Dict. Sp.* 8 (1974), cols. 369–89, s.v. 'Jean 60. Jean Climaque (saint)'.

John of the Cross (1), St (1542–91), mystical Doctor and joint founder of the Discalced *Carmelites. The son of a poor family, he entered the Carmelite monastery of Medina del Campo in 1563, studied theology at Salamanca (1564–8), and was ordained priest in 1567. Dissatisfied with the prevalent laxity in his order, he considered becoming a *Carthusian, but was dissuaded by St *Teresa. Then with her aid he brought her Reform to include friars. He was Master of the Discalced Carmelite College at Alcalá de Henares (1571–2) and from 1572 to 1577 confessor of the Convent of the Incarnation at Ávila, where St Teresa had returned as prioress in 1571. After the anti-Reformist General Chapter of the Calced Carmelites (i.e. of the Mitigated Observance) held in Italy at Piacenza in 1575, he was seized at the order of the Visitor General, taken to Toledo, and imprisoned in their monastery there (Dec. 1577). After nine months of great hardships he escaped to a convent in Toledo and thence to the monastery of El Calvario, in Andalusia. The separation between the Calced and Discalced Carmelites was soon to be effected (1579–80). From 1579 to 1582 John was rector of the college which he established at Baeza; in 1582 he went to Granada as prior. From 1588 he was prior at Segovia. Having incurred the hostility of Nicolás Doria, Vicar General of the Discalced Carmelites, *inter alia* by resisting his wish to impose the observance of additional detailed rules on the Discalced Nuns, he was banished to the province of Andalusia, in mid-1591, and after severe illness and great suffering died at Úbeda at the end of the year. He was beatified in 1675, canonized in 1726, and declared a '*Doctor of the Church' in 1926. Feast day, 14 Dec. (formerly, 24 Nov.).

The writings of John of the Cross possess the paradoxical character of works in which the imagination and sensitivity of a poet are combined with the intellectual activity of a theologian trained in *Thomist philosophy. They seek to capture and communicate the mystic's apprehension of a living and loving Being which is found essentially beyond the reach of feeling, imagination, and understanding; it can ultimately be known in itself only as these modes give way to the response of pure love. His extensive treatises on the mystical life consist of commentaries which he gradually built up on three of his poems, which are among the greatest in Spanish. His longest poem ('¿Adónde te escondiste, Amado?') was largely composed during his imprisonment (1578); the *Spiritual Canticle* treatise, which he began soon after his escape, expounds its rich imagery in terms of the *purgative, illuminative, and unitive ways. Deeply influenced by the mystical exegesis of the Song of Solomon, it is less systematic than the *Ascent of Mount Carmel* and the *Dark Night of the Soul* (a single, unfinished treatise based on the poem 'En una noche oscura'), written soon afterwards. This deals with the purgation of the soul through the 'night of the senses' and the 'night of the spirit'. These nights have an active and passive aspect: actively the soul detaches itself from dependence on things of the senses (incl. all sensible devotion) and adheres in pure faith to God alone; passively, God acts to fit it for the transforming Union with Himself, described in the *Living Flame* (written c.1583–4), which expounds the poem '¡Oh llama de amor viva!'. Both nights, esp. in their passive aspects, are often accompanied by intense suffering. Though presented in schematic form, they are best thought of not as consecutive phases but as complementary parts of one single process, the purifying of the soul for transformation and participation in God. John's general debt to the N. European mystical tradition of the preceding centuries is suggested by the important similarities that exist between the *Cloud of Unknowing* (which he almost certainly did not know) and the more developed analyses of John himself. Together with Teresa, to whose spiritual experience he seems to have owed more than a little of his own understanding of the spiritual life, John of the Cross brought into being a uniquely comprehensive and analytical account of the successive stages of purgation, illumination and union through which the soul passes in the course of its approach to God. The accounts of this progress given by these two Carmelites are commonly regarded as possessing unique authority.

Crit. edns. of his collected works are those of Silverio de Santa Teresa, OCD (Biblioteca Mistica Carmelitana, vols. 10–14, Burgos, 1929–31) and Lucinio del SS. Sacramento, OCD (Biblioteca de Autores Cristianos, 1946, with Life by Crisógono de Jesús, OCD, pp. 3–488; 4th edn., with Life rev. by Matías del Niño Jesús, OCD, 1960; 11th edn. rev., but without Life, 1982). Eng. trs. of his works by E. A. Peers (3 vols., London, 1934–5; 2nd edn. with additional material, 3 vols., 1953) and K. Kavanaugh, OCD, and O. Rodríguez, OCD (ibid., 1966). Lives by Bruno de Jésus-Marie, OCD, *Saint Jean de la Croix* (1929; rev., 1961; Eng. tr., 1932), and Crisógono de Jesús, OCD (see above; Eng. tr. of 3rd edn., 1958). E. A. Peers, *Handbook to the Life and Times of St Teresa and St John of the Cross* (1954). Crisógono de Jesús, OCD, *San Juan de la Cruz: su obra científica y su obra literaria* (2 vols., 1929). J. Baruzi, *Saint Jean de la Croix et le problème de l'expérience mystique* (1924; 2nd edn., 1931), with bibl. D. Alonso, *La poesía de San Juan de la Cruz* (1942; 4th edn., 1966). Efrén de la Madre de Dios, OCD, *San Juan de la Cruz y el misterio de la Santísima Trinidad en la vida espiritual* (1947), with bibl. J. Vilnet, *Bible et mystique chez saint Jean de la Croix* (1949). M. Milner, *Poésie et vie mystique chez saint Jean de la Croix* (1951). H. Sanson, *L'Esprit humain selon saint Jean de la Croix* (1953). *The Mediaeval Mystical Tradition and St John of the Cross* by a Benedictine of Stanbrook Abbey (1954). G. Morel, *Le Sens de l'existence selon saint Jean de la Croix* (3 vols., 1960–1). E. W. T. Dicken, *The Crucible of Love: A Study of the Mysticism of St Teresa of Jesus and St John of the Cross* (1963). J. Orcibal, *Saint Jean de la Croix et les mystiques rhéno-flamands* (Bruges, 1966). F. Ruiz Salvador, OCD, *Introducción a San Juan de la Cruz: El escritor, los escritos, el sistema* (Biblioteca de Autores Cristianos, 1968). G. Brenan, *St John of the Cross: His Life and Poetry* (Cambridge, 1973). C. P. Thompson, *The Poet and the Mystic: A Study of the Cántico Espiritual de San Juan de la Cruz* (Oxford,

1977; Sp. tr., with additional material, 1985). A. Cugno, *Saint Jean de la Croix* (1979; Eng. tr., 1982). D. B. Tillyer, *Union with God: The Teaching of St John of the Cross* (1984). L. López Baralt, *San Juan de la Cruz y el Islam* (Mexico City, 1985). O. Steggink, O. Carm. (ed.), *Juan de la Cruz, Espíritu de Llama: Estudios con ocasión del cuarto centenario de su muerte (1591–1991)* (Vacare Deo 10, Studies in Spirituality, Suppl. 1; Kampen, 1991). Other studies include those of B. Frost (London, 1937) and E. A. Peers (ibid., 1943). Id., *Studies of the Spanish Mystics*, 1 (1927; 2nd edn., 1951), pp. 227–88. R. [D.] Williams, *The Wound of Knowledge: Christian Spirituality from the New Testament to St John of the Cross* (1979), pp. 159–79. J. L. Astigarraga and others, *Concordancias de los escritos de San Juan de la Cruz* (Rome, 1990). Pourrat, 3, pp. 269–308. B. Zimmerman, OCD, in *CE* 8 (1910), pp. 480 f., s.v.; Lucien-Marie de Saint-Joseph in *Dict. Sp.* 8 (1974), cols. 408–47, s.v. 'Jean de la Croix'. 'Bibliographia carmelitana annualis', *Carmelus* (Rome, 1954 ff.). *Archivum bibliographicum carmelitanum* (Rome, 1956 ff.).

John of the Cross (2) (c.1505–c.1560), *Dominican spiritual writer. Born at Talavera in Spain, he became acquainted with the work of the Dominican reformer, J. Hurtado de Mendoza, and entered the recently founded Dominican priory at Atocha, in Madrid, making his profession in 1525. He studied at Salamanca and in 1538 he was sent with a group of other Spanish friars to help reform the Dominican Order in *Portugal; he spent the rest of his life there, and became known for his educational work. He was closely associated with *Luis of Granada. His main work was a 'Dialogue on the Necessity of Vocal Prayer' (*Dialogo sobre la Necesidad de la Oracion Vocal*, 1555). Against the prevalent spirituality of *recollection, he argues that the spiritual life consists in the serious, deliberate practice of the virtues and not in interior devotional fervour. He was much influenced by G. *Savonarola. He also published some Spanish translations of Latin works and wrote a Chronicle of the Dominican Order, published posthumously in 1567.

He is sometimes confused with a Dominican namesake, also from Talavera, who studied in Valladolid (1583) and published an *Epitome de Statu Religionis* (1613) and *Directorium Conscientiae* (1620).

Modern edn. of the 'Dialogue' in M. Cano, D. de Soto, and Juan de la Cruz, OP, *Tratados Espirituales*, ed. V. Beltrán de Heredia, OP (Biblioteca de Autores Cristianos, 221; Madrid, 1962), pp. 187–512. M. Andrés Martín, *Los Recogidos: Nueva visión de la mística española (1500–1700)* (Publicaciones de la Fundacion Universitaria Española, Monografías, 13; 1975 [1976]), pp. 419–27. Quétif and Echard, 2, pp. 174 f. R. Hernandez, OP, in *Dict. Sp.* 8 (1974), cols. 407 f., s.v. 'Jean 68, Jean de la Croix'.

John of Dalyatha (8th cent), writer on the spiritual life. He is almost certainly to be identified with John of Saba, i.e. 'John the Elder'. A member of the *Church of the East, he was born in N. Iraq and lived as a monk in various monasteries in the Qardu mountains (NW Iraq); for a time he was a hermit in the nearby mountains of Dalyatha, living off vine branches (dalyāthā). He belonged to monastic circles misguidedly accused of *Messalianism and *Sabellianism; owing to this circumstance his writings were condemned by the Catholicos Timothy I in 786. Some 25 Discourses, 50 letters, and a set of 'Kephalaia on Knowledge' survive. Several of his works were translated from Syriac into Arabic and Greek (in the latter four of his Discourses have been published among the works of

*Isaac of Nineveh, and his Letter 15 is attributed to *Dorotheus of Gaza).

Letters ed., with Fr. tr., by R. Beulay, OCD, in *PO* 39 (1978–9), pp. 253–538; an edn. of the Discourses by B. Colless is in preparation. R. Beulay, *L'Enseignement Spirituel de Jean de Dalyatha* (Théologie Historique, 83 [1990]). B. Colless, 'The Mysticism of John Saba', *OCP* 39 (1973), pp. 83–102. R. Beulay in *Dict. Sp.* 8 (1974), cols. 449–52, s.v. 'Jean 71: Jean de Dalyatha'.

John of Damascus, St (*c*.655–*c*.750), Greek theologian and '*Doctor of the Church'. Little is known of his life, and such sources as exist are in considerable conflict. Born of a rich Christian family of *Damascus, like his father, he held a position of importance at the court of the Caliph. He resigned his office *c*.725 and became a monk at the monastery of St *Sabas near *Jerusalem, where he became a priest. He was a strong defender of *images in the *Iconoclastic Controversy, writing three discourses on the subject between 726 and 730.

His most important work, the 'Fount of Wisdom' (Πηγὴ γνώσεως), was written at the suggestion of his former fellow-monk, *Cosmas Melodus, Bp. of Maïuma. It is divided into three parts, dealing with philosophy ('Dialectica'), heresies, and the Orthodox faith ('De Fide Orthodoxa'), the most important of the three. For his philosophical doctrines he is indebted to *Aristotle, though he also borrowed from *Plato through *Maximus the Confessor, whereas the book of heresies is for the most part a reproduction of the 'Anakephalaiosis', attributed to St *Epiphanius. The 'De Fide Orthodoxa' is a comprehensive presentation of the teaching of the Greek Fathers on the main Christian doctrines, esp. the Trinity, Creation, and the Incarnation; the Sacraments, Mariology, images, and other subjects are also treated, but less systematically. In his demonstration of the existence and unity of God he adduces the metaphysical arguments from the contingency of creatures and the order of the universe. His Trinitarian theology sums up the doctrine esp. of the *Cappadocian Fathers and develops the conception of περιχώρησις ('*circumincession') in order to express the inner-Trinitarian relations. His angelology reproduces that of St *Gregory of Nazianzus, his favourite Father, and of *Dionysius the Pseudo-Areopagite. His treatment of the Incarnation is a representative synthesis of Greek theological thought, finding its end in the restoration of fallen man to his former state. He teaches that in the *Hypostatic Union the Word served as 'hypostasis' ('Person') to the humanity which He took; hence he adopted the *Enhypostasia of *Leontius of Byzantium, which he interprets along the lines of the '*communicatio idiomatum'. He saw in the interpenetration of the two natures in Christ the formation of '*theandric activities', a term he takes over from Dionysius, interpreting it in an orthodox sense. A corollary of his Christological doctrine was his fully developed Mariology. He teaches the Divine maternity of Mary, her exemption from all stain of sin, and her assumption into heaven. In the doctrine of the Eucharist he insists that the bread and wine are really changed into the Body and Blood of Christ, regarding the physical appearance of the elements after the consecration as a mere concession to human weakness.

His other great work, the 'Sacra Parallela', preserved only in fragments, is a vast compilation of scriptural and patristic texts on the Christian moral and ascetical life. It received its name from the parallel treatment of virtues and vices in its third part. He also wrote a comprehensive commentary on the Pauline Epp. and several homilies of a strongly dogmatic bent, e.g. on the Transfiguration, on Holy Saturday, and on the death of the BVM. Besides his prose works he composed a number of poems which form part of the Greek Liturgy, though not all of those attributed to him are authentic. Some of these have found their way into modern English hymnbooks, e.g. 'Come, ye faithful, raise the strain' and 'The Day of Resurrection! Earth, tell it out abroad' (both in J. M. *Neale's renderings). The Life of *Barlaam and Joasaph (q.v.), traditionally ascribed to the Damascene, is prob. not his work.

John of Damascus exercised a considerable influence on later theology. 'De Fide Orthodoxa', in the inadequate translation of *Burgundio of Pisa, was known to *Peter Lombard and St *Thomas Aquinas, and his authority was invoked in favour of the Latin doctrine of the *Double Procession of the Holy Spirit by the Unionist Greek theologians of the later 13th cent. and by Card. *Bessarion at the Council of *Florence. All through the Middle Ages his works were used by the Greeks and esp. by the Slavs, though they were never commented on nor did they lead to the formation of a school as did those of Peter Lombard and St *Thomas Aquinas in the W. In modern times they have retained their influence in the formation of E. theologians, though supplemented by later W. writers (RC and Protestant). John of Damascus, whose cult developed soon after his death, was declared a Doctor of the Church by *Leo XIII in 1890. Feast day, in the Greek Church, 4 Dec.; in the W., 4 Dec. (formerly, 27 Mar.).

Earliest collected edn. by M. *Le Quien, OP (2 vols. fol., Paris, 1712, with important prolegomena and dissertations); repr. in J. P. Migne, *PG* 94–6, with additions from A. *Gallandi, A. *Mai, and others. Crit. text ed., under the auspices of the Byzantinisches Institut der Abtei Scheyern, by B. Kotter, OSB (Patristische Texte und Studien, 7, 12, 17, 22, 29; 1969–88). Homilies on the Nativity and Dormition of the BVM ed., with Fr. tr., by P. Voulet, SJ (SC 80; 1961). B. Kotter, OSB, *Die Überlieferung der Pege Gnoseos des hl. Johannes von Damaskos* (Studia Patristica et Byzantina, 5; 1959). The Latin tr. of the 'Dialectica' by R. *Grosseteste ed. O. A. Colligan, OFM (Franciscan Institute Publications, Text Series, 6; 1953) and that of the 'De Fide Orthodoxa' by Burgundio of Pisa, together with the slightly earlier, partial, tr. made in Hungary by Cerbanus, ed. E. M. Buytaert, OFM (ibid. 8; 1955). Eng. tr. of 'De Fide Orthodoxa' by S. D. F. Salmond (NPNCF, 2nd ser. 9, 1899); also of the 'Fount of Wisdom' by F. H. Chase (Fathers of the Church, 37; 1958), and of 'De Imaginibus' by D. Anderson (Crestwood, NY, 1980). Arabic Life by Michael of Antioch (1085; ed. by C. Bacha, Harisa (Lebanon), 1912; Ger. tr. by G. Graf in *Der Katholik*, 93 (1913), pp. 164–190, 320–31); this Arabic Life was tr. into Gk. by Patr. John VIII of Jerusalem. On the details of John's life see M. Jugie, AA, 'La Vie de saint Jean Damascène', *ÉO* 23 (1924), pp. 137–61; id., 'Une Nouvelle Vie et un nouvel écrit de saint Jean Damascène', ibid. 28 (1929), pp. 35–41. J. Nasrallah, *Saint Jean de Damas: Son Époque, sa vie, son œuvre* ('Les Souvenirs chrétiens de Damas', 2; Paris, 1950). On the *Sacra Parallela*, F. *Loofs, *Studien über die dem Johannes von Damaskus zugeschriebenen Parallelen* (1892); K. *Holl, *Die Sacra Parallela des Johannes Damascenus* (TU 16, Heft 1; 1896); id., *Fragmenta vornicänischer Kirchenväter aus den Sacra Parallela* (ibid. 20, Heft 2; 1899). J. Bilz, *Die Trinitätslehre des hl. Johannes von Damaskus* (Forschungen zur christlichen Literatur- und Dogmengeschichte 9, Heft 3; 1909). B. Studer, OSB, *Die theologische Arbeitsweise des Johannes von Damaskus* (Studia

Patristica et Byzantina, 2; 1956); K. Rozemond, *La Christologie de Saint Jean Damascène* (ibid. 8; 1959); G. Richter, *Die Dialektik des Johannes von Damaskos* (ibid. 10; 1964). D. J. Sahas, *John of Damascus on Islam: The 'Heresy of the Ishmaelites'* (Leiden, 1972). *CPG* 3 (1979), pp. 511–36 (nos. 8040–127). Beck, pp. 476–86; Altaner and Stuiber (1978), pp. 526–32 and 661 f. M. Jugie, AA, in *DTC* 8 (pt. 1; 1924), cols. 693–751, s.v. 'Jean 31: Jean Damascène (Saint)'; B. Kotter in *NCE* 7 (1967), pp. 1047–9, s.v.; B. Stuber, OSB, in *Dict. Sp.* 8 (1974), cols. 452–66, s.v. 'Jean 72: Jean Damascène'. See also bibl. to ICONOCLASTIC CONTROVERSY.

John, King of England

John, King of England (1167–1216), King from 1199. He was the youngest son of Henry II and Eleanor of Aquitaine. He was early nicknamed Lackland because he had not been provided like his brothers with an apanage of land by his father, though he was Henry's favourite and richly endowed with castles and rents. In 1177 he was made 'King of Ireland', which he was sent to govern in 1185. Alienating the Irish by his insolence and misrule, he was recalled after a few months. In 1189 he took part in the conspiracy of his brother Richard and the King of France against his father, whose death was hastened by this treachery. After his accession (1189) Richard I confirmed him in his possessions, which were increased by his marriage to Isabella of Gloucester. During Richard's absence on the Third *Crusade John expelled his chancellor, William Longchamp, and intrigued with the King of France against Richard. After Richard's return (1194) the brothers were reconciled; John assisted the King against Philip of France; and Richard named John as his successor. On his accession (1199) John was recognized by England and Normandy, and in 1202 defeated Anjou and Brittany, who urged the claims of his nephew Arthur (whom John murdered in 1203). During the following years he lost most of his possessions in France, and with the death of Abp. *Hubert of Canterbury in 1205 he was deprived of the only counsellor able to exercise on his acts a measure of restraint. The election of a new archbishop involved him in a quarrel with the chapter of *Canterbury, and when *Innocent III appointed Stephen *Langton (1207) John refused to recognize him. In 1208 England was placed under an *interdict and in 1209 John was excommunicated. Unsure of his barons, threatened with deposition by the Pope and with invasion from France, in 1213 John made his submission to the Pope, promised full reconciliation and restitution, and placed England and Ireland under the suzerainty of Innocent and his successors. The last years of his reign were troubled by renewed war with France in which he was defeated in 1214. In 1215 the barons obtained the famous grant of Magna Carta, but soon afterwards John regretted his action and civil war broke out, France intervening on the side of the barons. John died during the struggle, leaving his kingdom in confusion.

Recent historians have taken a less critical view of John than some 19th-cent. writers or some chroniclers of his own time. He was profligate and could be ruthless, violent, treacherous, grasping, and arbitrary; but he was not wholly unsympathetic towards the Church and possessed considerable skill as a strategist, politician, administrator, and judge. However, he failed to manage his magnates, was an indifferent military tactician, and above all lacked judgement in a crisis.

The principal modern studies are S. Painter, *The Reign of King John* (Baltimore, 1949), and W. L. Warren, *King John* (1961; 2nd edn., 1978). See also [F.] M. Powicke, *The Loss of Normandy, 1189–1204* (2nd edn., Manchester, 1961); J. C. Holt, *The Northerners: A Study in the Reign of King John* (Oxford, 1961); id., *King John* (Historical Association Pamphlet G 53; 1963), repr. in id., *Magna Carta and Medieval Government* (1985), pp. 85–109, with other relevant material; id., *Magna Carta* (Cambridge, 1965); and C. R. Cheney, *Innocent III and England* (Päpste und Papsttum, 9; Stuttgart, 1976). On the interdict, see also id., 'King John and the Papal Interdict', *Bulletin of the John Rylands Library*, 31 (1948), pp. 295–317; id., 'King John's Reaction to the Interdict on England', *Transactions of the Royal Historical Society*, 4th ser. 31 (1949), pp. 129–50; id., 'A Recent View of the General Interdict on England, 1208–1214', in G. J. Cuming (ed.), *Studies in Church History*, 3 (1966), pp. 159–68; all repr. in id., *The Papacy and England 12th–14th Centuries* (1982), nos. 9–11. A. L. Poole, *From Domesday Book to Magna Carta* (Oxford History of England, 3; 1951; 2nd edn. 1955), esp. pp. 425–86.

John of Ephesus

John of Ephesus (*c.*507–86), *Syrian Orthodox historian. Born near Amid in Mesopotamia, he was sent by *Justinian I in 542 to convert the pagans in the region of Ephesus, of which he was later consecrated bishop by *Jacob Baradaeus. His *Ecclesiastical History*, of which only the third part survives complete, covers the period 571–85. His *Lives of Eastern Saints* consists of 58 short accounts of contemporary hermits and others. Both works are in Syriac.

The Third Part of his *Ecclesiastical History*, ed. E. W. Brooks (CSCO 105; 1935, with Lat. tr., ibid. 106; 1936); frags. of First and Second Part, ed. id. in *Incerti Auctoris Chronicon Pseudo-Dionysianum vulgo dictum*, ed. I. B. Chabot, 2 (CSCO 104; 1933), pp. 402–20. Eng. tr. of Third Part by R. Payne Smith (Oxford, 1860). *Lives of Eastern Saints*, ed., with Eng. tr., by E. W. Brooks in *PO* 17 (1923), pp. 1–307; 18 (1924), pp. 513–698; and 20 (1926), pp. 153–285. S. A. Harvey, *Asceticism and Society in Crisis: John of Ephesus and the* Lives of the Eastern Saints (Berkeley, Calif., etc. [1990]). I. Ortiz de Urbina, SJ, *Patrologia Syriaca* (2nd edn., Rome, 1965), pp. 166 f. D. Stiernon, AA, in *Dict. Sp.* 8 (1974), cols. 484–6, s.v. 'Jean 85: Jean d'Ephèse'.

John Eudes, St.

John Eudes, St. See EUDES, ST JOHN.

John the Faster, St

John the Faster, St (d. 595), John IV, Patriarch of *Constantinople from 582. His renown as an ascetic won him the title of 'Faster' (ὁ νηστευτής, 'jejunator'). Though personally unambitious, he had great influence at court, and was jealous of the (by then) traditional claims of the patriarchate of Constantinople to be second in honour after Rome. When in 588 he assumed the challenging title of 'Oecumenical [οἰκουμενικός, "Universal"] Patriarch' (a style which had earlier been applied to his predecessors by *Justinian), Pope Pelagius II, and later St *Gregory the Great, protested, the latter interpreting the description as a claim to be sole bishop and source of the episcopate. Their objections, however, did not prevent John from bequeathing the description to his successors. Attributed to him is a manual for confessors, commonly known as his 'Penitential' ('Ακολουθία καὶ τάξις ἐπὶ ἐξομολογουμένων), but it is of much later date, and not earlier than the 9th cent. The only surviving work with any claim to be genuine appears to be a sermon on 'Repentance, Self-control and Virginity', largely based on St *Chrysostom. Feast day in E., 2 Sept.

V. Grumel, AA (ed.), *Les Regestes des Actes du Patriarcat de Constantinople*, 1, fasc. 1 (2nd edn., 1972), pp. 193–201 (nos. 264–72). J. P. Migne, *PG* 88. 1887–978. E. Herman, SJ, 'Il più antico penitenziale greco', *OCP* 19 (1953), pp. 71–127. Beck, pp. 423–5. R. Janin, AA, in *DTC* 8 (pt. 1; 1924), cols. 828 f., s.v. 'Jean IV le Jeûneur'; D. Stiernon, AA, in *Dict. Sp.* 8 (1974), cols. 586–9, s.v. 'Jean 129: Jean le Jeûneur'.

John of Fidanza. See BONAVENTURE, ST.

John Fisher, St. See FISHER, ST JOHN.

John of Gaza. See BARSANUPHIUS, ST.

John of God, St (1495–1550), founder of the 'Order of Charity for the Service of the Sick', or '*Brothers Hospitallers' (q.v.). He was born in *Portugal and, after a pious upbringing, joined a company of foot soldiers and forsook the practice of religion. At the age of about 40 he changed his mode of life in an attempt to atone for his past waywardness. He hoped for martyrdom in Morocco; but, this being denied him, he returned to the south of *Spain and spread the faith by hawking tracts and pictures until in 1538 he was converted to a life of great sanctity by St *John of Ávila. At first his excesses of penitence and devotion caused him to be treated as a lunatic, but a further interview with John of Ávila directed his energies to the care of the sick and poor. After his death his order gradually took shape. He was canonized in 1690 and in 1886 declared by *Leo XIII the heavenly patron of all hospitals and sick folk. He is also often regarded as the patron of printers and booksellers. Feast day, 8 Mar.

Life, written within 20 years of his death, by Francis de Castro, Rector of the Hospital of St John at Granada, pub. at Granada, 1585; Lat. tr., 1623; excerpts (Lat.) in *AASS*, Mar. 1 (1668), pp. 814–35; excerpts from early 17th-cent. Life, ibid., pp. 835–58. M. Gomez-Moreno, *Primicias históricas de San Juan de Dios* (1950). Modern studies incl. those of I. M. Magnin (Lille, 1887; Eng. tr., 1936), N. McMahon, OSJD (Dublin, 1952), J. Cruset (Barcelona, 1958), and J. C. Cousson, OH (Paris, 1973). G. Russotto, FBF, *San Giovanni di Dio e il suo Ordine Ospedaliero*, 1 (1969), pp. 11–99. Id. in *Bibliotheca Sanctorum*, 6 (Rome, 1965), cols. 740–8, s.v. 'Giovanni di Dio'; T. J. Munn in *NCE* 7 (1967), p. 1052, s.v.

John the Grammarian (*fl. c.*515), theologian. Little is known of his life, except that he came from Caesarea (either in Palestine or Cappadocia) and was a grammarian, i.e., a schoolmaster. He is one of the earliest representatives of *Neo-Chalcedonianism. Of his works there survive fragments of a defence of the *Chalcedonian Definition in *Severus of Antioch's spirited response to it, several works against the *Monophysites and against the *Manichees, and a few other fragments.

Works ed. M. Richard and M. Aubineau (CCSG 1; 1977), with introd.

John Gualbert, St (d. 1073), founder of the *Vallumbrosan Order (q.v.). After generously pardoning on a *Good Friday the murderer of one of his relatives, he entered the *Benedictine monastery of San Miniato, near Florence. Disturbed by a *simoniacal election there, he withdrew *c.*1036 and finally settled *c.*1040 at Vallombrosa, where he collected around him a body of monks who followed a strict observance of the Benedictine Rule

under the conditions of a semi-eremetical existence. He made provision for *conversi, whose labours freed the monks from manual labour. In the later part of his life, John Gualbert took a prominent part in assisting the Papacy in its struggles against simony; he was a particularly strong opponent of the simoniacal Bp. of Florence, Peter Mezzabarba (1061–8). Feast day, 12 July.

The earliest authority is the Life by Andrew of Strumi, who became Abbot of Vallombrosa in 1085 (d. 1097), pr. in *AASS*, Jul. 3 (1723), pp. 343–65; also ed. F. Baethgen in *MGH*, Scriptores, 30 (pt. 2; 1934), pp. 1080–104, with introd. pp. 1076–8. Life by St Atto, later Bp. of Pistoia (d. 22 May 1153), also pr. in *AASS*, loc. cit., pp. 365–82. Third Life (12th cent.) first pr. by R. Davidsohn, *Forschungen zur älteren Geschichte von Florenz*, 1 (Berlin, 1896), pp. 55–60, with introd. pp. 50–4; also ed. F. Baethgen, op. cit., pp. 1104–10, with introd. pp. 1078 f. Further sources in *BHL*, pp. 651 f. (nos. 4397–406), and *Novum Supplementum* (1986), pp. 488 f. D. de Franchi, *Historia del Patriarcha S. Giovan Gualberto* (Florence, 1640). Modern Lives (in Italian) by A. Salvini (Alba, 1943; 3rd edn., Bari, 1961), and E. Lucchesi (Florence, 1959). B. Quilici, 'Giovanni Gualberto e la sua riforma monastica', *Archivio Storico Italiano*, 99, Disp. 1–2 (1941), pp. 113–32, Disp. 3–4 (for 1941; 1942), pp. 27–62; 100, Disp. 1–2 (for 1942; 1943), pp. 45–99. G. Spinelli and G. Rossi, *Alle origini di Vallombrosa: Giovanni Gualberto nella società dell'XI secolo* (Milan, 1984), incl. Ital. tr. of 1st and 3rd of primary lives mentioned above. A. *Wilmart, OSB, 'Le Manuel des prières de saint Jean Gualbert', *R. Bén.* 48 (1936), pp. 259–99. R. Volpini in *Bibliotheca Sanctorum*, 6 (Rome, 1966), cols. 1012–29, with extensive bibl.; N. R. Vasaturo in *DIP* 4 (1977), cols. 1273–6, both s.v. 'Giovanni Gualberto'.

John Lateran, Church of St. See LATERAN BASILICA.

John Malalas (*c.*490–*c.*575), i.e. 'John Rhetor', Byzantine chronicler. He has sometimes been identified with *John Scholasticus, Patr. of *Constantinople (d. 577; q.v.), but it is more likely that he was a civil servant, based first in Antioch and later in Constantinople. His 'Chronography' (Χρονογραφία) in 18 Books covers the period from Creation, Book 10 beginning with the birth of Christ; it survives to 563, but originally extended to 565 or perhaps 574. It is possible that all or part of Book 18, on *Justinian I, may be by a different author. Written in the 'vulgar' Greek of the time, it preserves valuable information, both secular and ecclesiastical; it was widely used by later Greek and Syriac writers and was translated into Slavonic.

'Chronicle' (Gk. text preserved only in Bod. Barocc. gr. 182 and a few frags.), ed. L. Dindorf, in C.S.H. Byz., 1831; repr. J. P. Migne, *PG* 97. 9–790. Crit. text of Bks. 9–12, ed. A. Schenk Graf von Stauffenberg, *Die römische Kaisergeschichte bei Malalas* (1931), with important comm. Eng. tr. by E. Jeffreys and others (Byzantina Australiensia, 4; Melbourne, 1986). Idd. (eds.), *Studies in John Malalas* (ibid. 6; Sydney, 1990). *CPG* 3 (1979), pp. 400 f. (no. 7511). H. Hunger, *Die hochsprachliche profane Literatur der Byzantiner*, 1 (Byzantinisches Handbuch, Teil 5; Munich, 1978), pp. 319–26.

John Mark, St. See MARK, ST.

John of Matha, St (d. 1213), founder of the *Trinitarian Order. Practically all that is known of him is that he was a native of Provence, founded his Order for the redemption of captives, and died at Rome on 17 Dec. 1213. The abundant details in the older biographies are based on spurious records fabricated in the 15th and 16th cents. Feast day, 8 Feb.

Uncritical Lives include those of G. Gonzales de Ávila (Madrid, 1630), J. M. Prat, SJ (Paris, 1846), and le Père Calixte de la Providence, Trinitarian (ibid., 1867). Much early material is also pr. in Antoninus ab Assumptione, Trinitarian, *Monumenta Ordinis Excalceatorum SS. Trinitatis Redemptionis Captivorum ad Provinciam S.P.N. Ioannis de Matha Spectantia* (Rome, 1915). G. Antignani, *Vita di Giovanni de Matha e repercussioni della sua opera nei tempi* (Sienna, 1982). J. Pujana, OST, in *Dict. Sp.* 15 (1991), cols. 1261–7, s.v. 'Trinitaires'. See also other works under TRINIT-ARIANS.

John Moschus. See MOSCHUS, JOHN.

John of Nepomuk, St (c.1340–93), Bohemian martyr.

As Vicar General of the Archdiocese of Prague, John resisted the attempts of Wenceslas IV to suppress an abbey in order to create a see for one of his favourites and to interfere with clerical prerogatives. By the King's orders he was drowned in the Vltava (Moldau) in consequence; but his recovered body became the centre of a widespread cultus during the *Counter-Reformation and this spread throughout Central Europe after he was canonized in 1729. Tradition credits him with having incensed the monarch by refusing to betray the Queen by breaking the *seal of the confessional. The details of his life are shrouded in obscurity, and some have held that two Johns suffered martyrdom in similar circumstances at the hands of Wenceslas. Feast day, 16 May.

Life by B. Balbín, SJ (written in 1670), in *AASS*, Mai. 3 (1680), pp. 668–80. Acts of the Process of his Canonization, pub. Verona, 1725. J. T. A. Berghauer, *Proto-martyr Poenitentiae eiusque Sigilli Custos semper Fidelis Divus Joannes Nepomucenus* (Augsburg, 1736). A. H. Wratislaw, *The Life, Legend, and Canonization of St John Nepomucen* (1873). J. Pekař, *Z duchovních dějin českých* (Prague, 1941), pp. 141–77; J. V. Polc and V. Ryneš, *Svatý Jan Nepomucký* (2 vols., Rome, 1972). P. de Vooght, 'Jean de Pomuk', *RHE* 48 (1953), pp. 777–95.

John of Parma, Bl (1209–89), *Franciscan Minister General. He taught logic for several years at Parma, where he took the Franciscan habit, probably in 1233, and was later sent to *Paris to continue his studies. A popular teacher and preacher, he was elected Minister General of his order in 1247, and as such he endeavoured to restore its asceticism and discipline to the original standards of St *Francis, while realizing the need to adapt to the times. In pursuit of this aim he carried out visitations throughout Europe, journeying to France, England, Spain, and Greece, and working, but without success, for the reunion of East and West. Although he himself lived very simply, he did not impose his austerity on others, and it seems that it was his *Joachimist sympathies, rather than his views on poverty, that made him enemies and led to accusations of heresy in Rome. Under pressure from the Pope, he resigned his office in 1257, but his nomination of St *Bonaventure as his successor shows that the gap between the two wings of the order was not yet unbridgeable. On the examination of his doctrine he narrowly escaped condemnation and retired into the hermitage of Greccio, where for 32 years he led a solitary life of penance and contemplation. In 1289 he was sent once more on an embassy to Greece on matters of reunion, but died on his

way at Camerino. He left no substantial body of writings. Many miracles were reported at his tomb, but owing to his Joachimite views his cultus was not confirmed until 1777. Feast day, 20 Mar.

A contemporary account is provided by Salimbene of Parma, *Chronica* (ed. F. Bernini, 1, Bari, 1942, pp. 429–67). Lives by F. Camerini (Ravenna, 1730) and I. Affo (Parma, 1777). René de Nantes, 'Quelques pages d'histoire franciscaine', *Études franciscaines*, 15 (1906): 6, 'Le Bienheureux Jean de Parme', pp. 148–67, and 7, 'Le B. Jean de Parme et le joachimisme', pp. 277–300. R. B. Brooke, *Early Franciscan Government: Elias to Bonaventure* (Cambridge, 1959), pp. 255–72. D. Burr, *Olivi and Franciscan Poverty: The Origins of the* Usus Pauper *Controversy* (Philadelphia [1989]), pp. 8, 17 f., 23 f., 26 f., 30, 149 f. E. d'Alençon, OFM, in *DTC* 8 (pt. 1; 1924), cols. 794–6, s.v. 'Jean de Parme'.

John and Paul, Sts. Two Roman martyrs of the 4th cent. of whom virtually nothing further is known. Their 'Acta', whose trustworthiness, however, is doubtful, testify to their having served Constantia, daughter of the Emp. *Constantine, and been instrumental in the conversion to Christianity of one of his generals, and having been finally martyred by the Emp. *Julian for their firm adherence to the Christian faith. A cult of these saints existed from the latter half of the 4th cent. and their names stand in the Roman *Canon of the Mass. A Council at *Oxford in 1222 made the hearing of Mass by all the faithful of England obligatory on their feast day, 26 June.

V. L. Kennedy, CSB, *The Saints of the Canon of the Mass* (Rome, 1938), pp. 131–7. P. F. de' Cavalieri, *Note Agiografiche*, 2 (ST 9; 1902), pp. 53–65, and 5 (ibid. 27; 1915), pp. 41–62. On the Acts, H. Grégoire and P. Orgels, 'S. Gallicanus, consul et martyr dans la passion des SS. Jean et Paul, et sa vision "constantinienne" du Crucifié', *Académie Royale de Belgique, Bulletin de la Classe des Lettres et des Sciences Morales et Politiques*, 5th ser. 42 (1956), pp. 125–46. G. De Sanctis, CP, *I santi Giovanni e Paolo: Martiri celimontani* (1962; much criticized). For their reputed house on the Celian Hill, see also P. Germano di S. Stanislao, *La casa celimontana dei SS. Martiri Giovanni e Paolo* (1894); A. Prandi, *Il complesso monumentale della Basilica Celimontana dei SS. Giovanni e Paolo nuovamente restaurato per la munificenza del Cardinale Titolare Francesco Spellman* (1953; Eng. tr., Rome, 1958); C. Pietri, *Roma Christiana: Recherches sur l'Église de Rome . . . (311–440)* (Bibliothèque des Écoles françaises d'Athènes et de Rome, 224; 1976), 1, pp. 481–90; and bibl. to ROME, CHURCHES OF.

John Paul I (1912–78), Pope from 26 Aug. to 28 Sept. 1978. Albino Luciani was born at Forno di Canali, near Belluno, SW of *Venice, the son of a labourer who did seasonal work in Switzerland and Germany. Ordained priest in 1935, he taught at the seminary in Belluno at the same time as doing pastoral work; in 1947 he became pro-chancellor of the diocese and later chancellor. Meanwhile he continued his studies at the *Gregorianum with a thesis on *L'origine dell'anima umana secondo Antonio *Rosmini* (1950). In 1958 *John XXIII ordained him Bp. of Vittorio Veneto. He took part in the Second *Vatican Council, but was not conspicuous. In 1969 *Paul VI nominated him Patriarch of Venice and in 1973 created him a cardinal. At Venice he acted as host to five ecumenical conferences, including the *Anglican–Roman Catholic International Commission which produced an Agreed Statement on *Authority in 1976.

He was elected Pope with surprising swiftness; the *conclave lasted only one day. Though he was little known outside Italy, it appears that the majority of cardinals were anxious for a new style of Pope, without curial connections but with pastoral experience, and his election was welcomed as that of 'God's candidate'. His choice of name reflects his devotion to his two immediate predecessors and his intention to carry on their work. His desire for simplicity was reflected in the ceremony marking the beginning of his Papacy. Instead of the traditional coronation with the *tiara, he inaugurated his 'pastoral ministry as supreme pastor' by receiving the pallium. After 33 days as Pope, he died of a heart attack while reading personal papers in bed. Vatican ineptitude allowed the spread of rumours of foul play, though the evidence adduced was totally unconvincing. His death was a profound disappointment to the millions of people who had been drawn to him by the warmth of his personality.

The official docs. of his pontificate are pr. in *AAS* 70 (1978), pp. 677–776 and 797–903. Letters addressed to various individuals, some fictional and some historical, originally pub. in the newspaper *Messaggero di Sant'Antonio*, were collected as *Illustrissimi* (1976; Eng. tr., 1978). Other *Scritti e Discorsi*, ed. A. Cattabiani (Padua [1979]). D. A. Yallop, *In God's Name* (1984); J. Cornwell, *A Thief in the Night: The Death of Pope John Paul I* (1989). J. N. D. Kelly, *The Oxford Dictionary of Popes* (1986), pp. 325 f.

John Paul II (1920–   ), Pope from 1978. Karol Wojtyla, the son of a Polish soldier, was born in the industrial town of Wadowice, not far from Cracow. His family was poor. In 1938 he entered the Jagiellonian University at Cracow. During the German occupation of *Poland he worked in a quarry and then in a chemical factory. Recognizing a vocation to the priesthood in 1942, he began studying theology; he completed his studies at the seminary in Cracow after the end of the Second World War and was ordained in 1946. He then went to the Angelicum (the *Dominican University) in Rome. On his return to Cracow he served as a parish priest and university chaplain, and lectured on ethics and moral theology. Under a pseudonym he published plays and poetry. In 1958 *Pius XII nominated him titular Bp. of Ombi and auxiliary to the Administrator Apostolic of Cracow; in 1964 *Paul VI appointed him Abp. of Cracow and in 1967 made him a cardinal. When the Second *Vatican Council was announced, he became a member of the Preparatory Commission and he attended all four Sessions of the Council. He also served on various post-Conciliar Commissions and from 1971 was a permanent member of the Council of the Roman Synod of Bishops. He became known in the W. through his lectures in America and elsewhere, assisted by his outstanding linguistic skill. Together with Cardinal Wyszinski, the Primate, he was a leading figure in the Church's struggle against the Communist Government in Poland.

When he was elected Pope on the death of *John Paul I in 1978, he was the first Slav to hold that office and the first non-Italian since *Hadrian VI (1522–3). He began his pontificate with a simple ceremony of inauguration. Early in 1979 he went to *Mexico to open the Latin American Bishops' Conference at Puebla. On that occasion he set the pattern for his later foreign visits, kissing the ground of the country and celebrating Mass in front of vast crowds. Later in 1979 he visited Poland (where dramatic scenes of

welcome were tolerated by the Government), *Ireland, the *United States of America, and Turkey. An attempt to assassinate him in Rome on 13 May 1981 did not for long delay further travel. In 1982 he was the first Pope to visit Britain and he subsequently visited over 100 countries in Europe, Africa, N. and S. America, and Asia.

In Mexico at the beginning of his pontificate John Paul II appeared cautious in his approach to *Liberation Theology and insisted that politics was the business of the laity. While he continued to condemn the use of violence, his commitment to the pursuit of human rights and human dignity was made clear in his first encyclical, *Redemptor hominis* (1979), which called for a reordering of social and economic structures; it was reiterated in *Dives in misericordia* (1980), *Laborem exercens* (1981), and *Sollicitudo rei socialis* (1987), the first encyclical addressed to non-RCs. His encyclical *Slavorum apostoli* (1985) appealed to a religion and culture common to both E. and W. Europe as a source for ending divisions in that continent. He is credited with a crucial role in the collapse of Communism which spread from Poland. On 1 Dec. 1989 he received Mikhail Gorbachev, President of the USSR, at the Vatican, and later in that month the *Uniat Church was restored in the Soviet Union. The Pope warned the E. not to capitulate to the materialism of the W. and was again critical of Capitalism as well as Communism in *Centesimus Annus* (1991), the encyclical marking the centenary of *Rerum Novarum*. At Epiphany 1991 he launched a 'Decade of Evangelization', adopted in other Churches as a 'Decade of Evangelism'.

The pontificate has been marked by a concern for orthodoxy. John Paul II consistently declined to make any concessions in the Church's attitude to such issues as *contraception, abortion, and *homosexuality. The traditional teaching on these matters, as well as on the dangers of admitting relativist interpretations of doctrine, was notably upheld in the encyclical *Veritatis Splendor* (1993). In 1982 he designated the conservative *Opus Dei as the first *personal prelature. In the Church's spiritual life he stressed the importance of traditional discipline, the Eucharist, and the place of the BVM. He performed an unprecedentedly large number of *beatifications and *canonizations, including the beatification of *Duns Scotus (1993). In 1985 he convened a second Extraordinary Synod of Bishops to assess the impact of the Second Vatican Council and to prevent divergent interpretations of it. The Synod suggested a universal *Catechism of the Catholic Church which was issued in 1992. During his pontificate the teaching of various theologians was held suspect and in 1979 H. *Küng had his licence to teach as a Catholic theologian withdrawn. Ten years later a new profession of faith and oath of fidelity was introduced for Church officials and the Congregation of the Doctrine of the Faith issued an Instruction on the vocation of theologians dealing with the relationship of the theologian to the teaching authority of the Church. At the other end of the spectrum the traditionalist Abp. M. Lefebvre, who refused to accept the changes brought about by the Second Vatican Council, in June 1988 led his followers into schism when he consecrated four bishops without the Pope's approval.

Visiting the *World Council of Churches in June 1984, John Paul II spoke of the *ecumenical movement as irreversible, though he rejected intercommunion as a means for attaining unity of faith. He especially promoted good relations with the *Orthodox. For the first time in modern history the Pope and the *Oecumenical Patriarch attended each other's liturgies in Istanbul in 1979 and issued a call for dialogue leading to full communion. The re-emergence of Catholicism in E. Europe in the late 1980s led, however, to new disputes concerning Church property and RC proselytization in traditionally Orthodox regions. Despite the Pope's prayer with Abp. R. Runcie at *Canterbury in 1982, relations with the C of E also suffered setbacks. While the 1991 Vatican response to the Final Report of the *Anglican–Roman Catholic International Commission called for further clarification on various issues, the Pope had written to the Abp. of Canterbury in 1986 warning of the danger to reunion of the ordination of *women to the priesthood in the Anglican Communion. A 'Directory for the Application of Principles and Norms on Ecumenism', issued in 1993, encouraged, but defined current limits to, RC participation in ecumenical activity. John Paul II also sought good relations with other world religions, esp. *Islam and *Judaism. On 13 Apr. 1986 he joined the Chief Rabbi at prayer in a Roman synagogue, and on 16 Oct. 1986 he led the representatives of 12 world religions in a day of prayer for peace at *Assisi. In 1993 the Vatican formally recognized the State of Israel.

John Paul II reorganized the *Curia by his Apostolic Constitution *Pastor Bonus* (1988), confirming new regulations in 1992, and he continued to internationalize both the Curia and the Cardinals. He promulgated the new *Codex Iuris Canonici* in 1983 and the first ever Codex for the Uniat Churches in 1990. In 1984 he concluded a revision of the *Lateran Treaty, conceding separation of Church and State in Italy and allowing that Rome should no longer be regarded as a 'sacred city'. Full diplomatic relations were established with Britain in 1982, with the USA in 1984, and with Mexico in 1992.

There are Eng. trs. of his *Collected Poems* (1982) and of his best-known play, *The Jeweller's Shop* (1980). Official docs. are pr. in the *AAS* for the years of his pontificate. The many studies incl. G. H. Williams, *The Mind of John Paul II: Origins of his Thought and Action* (New York, 1981); C. de Montclos, *Les Voyages de Jean-Paul II: Dimensions sociales et politiques* [1990]); M. Walsh, *John Paul II* (1994); and T. Szulc, *Pope John Paul II: The Biography* (New York and London [1995]). G. H. Williams in *NCE* 18 (1989), pp. 221–33, with bibl.

John Philoponus (*c*.490–*c*.570), philosopher and *Monophysite theologian. Philoponus means literally 'lover of work', but it is not certain whether the nickname directly reflected his personal character or whether he belonged to a group of lay workers so designated. A Christian from childhood, Philoponus lived in *Alexandria and was a pupil there of the *Neoplatonist philosopher Ammonius. As a philosopher he is remembered chiefly for his rejection of Aristotelian science, though in other respects he was deeply indebted to *Aristotle. His philosophical works include many commentaries on Aristotle and the *De Aeternitate Mundi*, an attack on the pagan Neoplatonist *Proclus. His most important theological works (which belong to his latter years) include the *De Opificio Mundi*, a commentary on the *Hexaemeron (much influenced by St *Basil the Great), and the Διαιτητής ('The Arbiter'). His Christology was close to that of *Severus of

Antioch, and his trinitarian theology was condemned as *tritheist at the Sixth Oecumenical Council of *Constantinople (680–1).

Various theological works (incl. the Διαιτητής) preserved in Syriac, ed., with Lat. tr., by A. Sanda (Beirut, 1930). 'Les fragments trithéites de Jean Philopon', ed. A. Van Roey in *Orientalia Lovaniensia Periodica*, 11 (1980), pp. 135–63, with further refs. *De Opificio Mundi*, ed. G. Reichardt (Teub., 1897); *De Aeternitate Mundi*, ed. H. Rabe (ibid., 1899). Comm. on Aristotle are pr. in *Commentaria in Aristotelum Graeca*, vols. 13–17 (Berlin, 1887–1909). Ger. tr of selected works by W. Böhm (Munich, etc., 1967). R. [R. K.] Sorabji (ed.), *Philoponus and the Rejection of Aristotelian Science* (Ithaca, NY, 1987), with bibl. H.-D. Saffrey [OP], 'Le chrétien Jean Philopon et la survivance de l'école d'Alexandrie au VIᵉ siècle', *Revue des Études grecques*, 67 (1954), pp. 396–410. K. Verrycken, 'The Development of Philiponus' Thought and its Chronology', in R. [R. K.] Sorabji (ed.), *Aristotle Transformed* (1990), pp. 233–74. *CPG* 3 (1979), pp. 366–70 (nos. 7260–82). T. Hainthaler in A. Grillmeier, *Jesus der Christus im Glauben der kirche*, 2/4 (1990), pp. 109–49; Eng. tr. (1996), pp. 107–46. G. Bardy in *DTC* 8 (pt. 1; 1924), cols. 831–9, s.v. 'Jean Philopon'; R. R. K. Sorabji in *TRE* 17 (1988), pp. 144–50, s.v. 'Johannes Philoponus'.

John the Presbyter. The term 'the Presbyter' ('elder', Gr. πρεσβύτερος) is applied to himself by the author of 2 and 3 Jn., while a 'John the Presbyter' is referred to by *Papias (*Eusebius, *HE* 3. 39. 4); but the inference to be drawn from these data is disputed. (1) Some think that Papias's evidence points to the existence at *Ephesus of a second John besides the Apostle (the son of Zebedee), and ascribe to him the Canonical Gospel of Jn. and the three Johannine Epistles; this was the view of B. H. *Streeter, for whom 2 and 3 Jn. were 'the author's signature' to the Gospel and First Epistle. Among those who have held this view, some (J. H. *Bernard) identify the '*beloved disciple' of the Gospel (Jn. 13: 23, 20: 2, 21: 15–23) with the Apostle; others (W. *Sanday, H. B. *Swete) equate him with the Presbyter. (2) Acc. to others, e.g. J. *Moffatt, merely the last two Epistles and possibly the Apocalypse (Rev.) are to be attributed to 'John the Presbyter'; the ascription of 2 and 3 Jn. to him was a view already known to *Jerome (*De vir. illustr.* 9. 18). (3) But the common view of Christian tradition, i.e. that 'the Presbyter' was a local designation for the Apostle himself (cf. e.g. 1 Pet. 5: 1, where St *Peter is apparently termed a presbyter), still has its advocates.

See bibl. to JOHN, GOSPEL OF ST.

John the Prophet. See BARSANUPHIUS, ST.

John of Ragusa (*c*.1395–1443), *Dominican theologian. John Stojković was a native of Ragusa who entered the Dominican Order at an early age, and in 1420 became master of theology at Paris. In 1422 he was appointed one of the university's representatives at the Council of Pavia and in 1431 *Martin V sent him to the Council of *Basle as Papal theologian, where he preached the opening sermon. From 1435 to 1437 he acted as legate of the Council to Constantinople in order to gain the Greeks for union with Rome, and the sending of an embassy by John Palaeologus was largely due to his influence. In 1438 he seems to have been made Bp. of Ardijsek and in 1440 cardinal by Felix V, though some authors have asserted that he remained faithful to the allegiance of *Eugenius IV, from whom he received the bishopric of Argos. Several of his writings have been printed, among them a treatise 'De Communione sub utraque Specie' against the *Hussites, a history of the Council of Basle and an unfinished history of the negotiations for union with the Greeks. While he was in Constantinople he assembled an important collection of Greek MSS, which were bequeathed to the Dominican house at Basle; MSS from this collection were used as printer's copy by *Erasmus for the first edition of the NT, as well as providing readings for editions of various Fathers.

He is not to be confounded with Cardinal Giovanni Dominici (c.1356–1419), another Dominican, also known as 'John of Ragusa', who was appointed Abp. of Ragusa before 26 Mar. 1408 and took a prominent part at the Council of *Constance (q.v.).

Several of his writings are contained in the Conciliar collections of Basle. A. Krchňák, De Vita et operibus Ioannis de Ragusio (Lateranum, NS 26, 3–4; 1960). B. Duda, OFM, Joannis Stojković de Ragusio, O.P. (†1443) Doctrina de Cognoscibilitate Ecclesiae (Studia Antoniana, 9; 1958). R. W. Hunt, 'Greek Manuscripts in the Bodleian Library from the Collection of John Stojković of Ragusa', in F. L. Cross (ed.), Studia Patristica, 7 (TU 92; 1966), pp. 75–82, with refs.

On Giovanni Dominici, Kaeppeli, 2 (1975), pp. 406–13, with bibl.

John of Ruysbroeck. See RUYSBROECK, JAN VAN.

John of Saba. See JOHN OF DALYATHA.

John of St Thomas (1589–1644), Spanish *Dominican theologian. John Poinsot was born in Lisbon, and acquired his BA at Coimbra in 1605. He then began his theological studies, moving, prob. in 1606, to Louvain, where he came under the influence of the Dominican Thomas de Torres. In 1609 he entered the Dominican order in Madrid, taking the name 'John of St Thomas', to express his devotion to the teaching of St *Thomas Aquinas. In 1625 he was sent to teach in Alcalá, where he remained until 1643, when he became confessor to Philip IV. He became a Master of Theology in 1633. His major works are the Cursus Philosophicus (1631–5) and the Cursus Theologicus, a commentary on the 'Summa Theologiae' of St Thomas (1637–67), of which only the first three volumes were published during his lifetime. As against the modified Thomism of the *Jesuit theologians, F. *Suárez and G. *Vázquez, John's system claimed to follow exactly the principles of St Thomas, in that it paid heed not only to Aquinas' conclusions, but also to his arguments; however, there is also a perceptible influence from contemporary, more spiritual interests in some of his writing.

Modern edns. of his Cursus Philosophicus by B. Reiser, OSB (3 vols., Turin, 1930–7); of his Cursus Theologicus (10 vols., Paris, 1883–6) and by the Benedictines of *Solesmes (Paris, etc., 5 vols. only pub., 1931–62), with major biographical material in vol. 1, pp. i–cviii. Material on Semiotics (from the Cursus Philosophicus), repr., with Eng. tr., ed. J. N. Deely (Berkeley, Calif., etc., 1985). Separate Eng. trs. of parts of his Cursus Philosophicus by Y. R. Simon and others, The Material Logic of John of St Thomas (Chicago, 1955), and of parts of his Cursus Theologicus by D. Hughes, OP, The Gifts of the Holy Spirit (London and New York, '1950' [1951]). T. Trapiello, OP, Juan de Santo Tomás y sus obras (Oviedo, 1889). V. Beltrán de Heredia, 'La enseñanza de S.

Tomás en la Universidad de Alcalá', La Ciencia tomista, 14 (1916, 2), pp. 267–97. M. B. Lavaud, OP, 'Jean de Saint Thomas', Vie Spirituelle, 14 (1926), pp. 387–415. La Ciencia tomista, 69 (1945), is devoted to John of St Thomas. J. Paquin, 'La Lumière de gloire selon Jean de Saint-Thomas', Sciences Ecclésiastiques, 3 (1950), pp. 5–66. J. M. Ramírez in DTC 8 (1924), cols. 803–8; D. Hughes, OP, in NCE 7 (1967), pp. 1070 f.

John of Salisbury (c.1115–80), medieval humanist. A native of *Salisbury, he studied at *Paris under *Abelard, *William of Conches, and *Gilbert de la Porrée. From 1147 he was a member of the household of *Theobald, Abp. of Canterbury, serving him especially in his relations with the Papal curia, which he frequently visited. On Theobald's death, he entered the service of his successor, Thomas *Becket. He supported Becket in his quarrel with Henry II; he was present at Canterbury on the fatal 29 Dec. 1170. In 1176 he became Bp. of Chartres, where he remained for the rest of his life.

His chief writings are the 'Policraticus, sive nugis curialium et vestigiis philosophorum', a survey of the courtly life of his time with a discussion of political problems, and the 'Metalogicon', a defence of the study of grammar, rhetoric, and especially logic. Both these works were composed mainly during a period in which he fell into disfavour with Henry II and were finished in 1159. Many of his letters, most related to the affairs of the Abps. whom he served, survive and are an important historical source for the contest between Henry and Becket. He also wrote (c.1164–7) a historical work known as the 'Historia Pontificalis' covering the years 1148–51, which deals chiefly with the affairs of the Papal court. John was an accomplished Latinist and man of letters, and one of the leaders of the literary renaissance of the 12th cent. He had an extensive knowledge of Latin classical writers on which he drew freely in his writings. One of the earliest medieval writers to be acquainted with the whole of *Aristotle's 'Organon', he was well versed in the logical questions which formed the staple of the discussion of philosophical problems in his day, but he cannot be termed an original philosopher.

Works ed. J. A. Giles (5 vols., Oxford, 1848); repr. in J. P. Migne, PL 199. 1–1040. Crit. edns. of his Policraticus by C. C. J. *Webb (2 vols., Oxford, 1909) and by K. S. B. Keats-Rohan (CCCM 118 etc.; 1993 ff); of his Metalogicon by C. C. J. Webb (Oxford, 1929) and by J. B. Hall (CCCM 98; 1991); of his Historia Pontificalis by R. L. Poole (Oxford, 1927) and, with Eng. tr., by M. Chibnall (London, 1956; repr., with corrections, Oxford, 1986); and of his Letters, with Eng. tr., by W. J. Millor, SJ, H. E. Butler, and C. N. L. Brooke (2 vols., London and Oxford, 1955–79; vol. 1, repr., with corrections, 1986). Eng. tr. of Policraticus, 4–6, with selections from 7 and 8, by J. Dickinson (New York, 1927), of 1–3, with selections from 7 and 8, by J. B. Pike (Minneapolis, 1938); and of Metalogicon by D. D. McGarry (Berkeley and Los Angeles, Calif., 1955). C. C. J. Webb, John of Salisbury ('Great Medieval Churchmen', 1932); H. Liebeschütz, Mediaeval Humanism in the Life and Writings of John of Salisbury (Studies of the Warburg Institute, 17; 1950); G. Miczka, Das Bild der Kirche bei Johannes von Salisbury (Bonner Historische Forschungen, 34; 1970); M. Kerner, Johannes von Salisbury und die logische Struktur seines Policraticus (1977); K. Guth, Johannes von Salisbury (Münchener Theologische Studien, I. Historische Abteilung, 20; 1978); M. Wilks (ed.), The World of John of Salisbury (Studies in Church History, Subsidia, 3; 1984). B. Smalley, The Becket Conflict and the Schools (Oxford, 1973), pp. 87–108. R. L.

Poole in *DNB* 29 (1892), pp. 439–46; N. M. Haring in *NCE* 7 (1967), pp. 1071 f., s.v.

John Scholasticus (d. 577), John III, Patriarch of *Constantinople from 565. In his early years he was a lawyer (σχολαστικός) at *Antioch, where he made a famous collection ('Synagoge') of canons. Later, after he had become patriarch, he re-edited and enriched it from the 'Novellae' of *Justinian, and the work became one of the primary sources for subsequent E. canon law (see NOMOCANON). He is also said to have written a 'Catechetical Oration' on the Trinity. He is not to be confounded with *John Climacus, also known as 'John Scholasticus', and is prob. distinct from *John Malalas (q.v.).

'Synagoge', ed., with Lat. tr., by G. E. Heimbach, Ἀνέκδοτα, 2 (Leipzig, 1840), pp. 202–34. Crit. edn. by V. N. Beneševič (*Abh.* (Bayr.), NF 14; 1937). E. *Schwartz, *Die Kanonessammlung von Johannes Scholastikos* (*Sb.* (Bayr.), 1933, Heft 6). P. van den Ven, 'L'Accession de Jean le Scolastique au siège patriarcal de Constantinople en 565', *Byzantion*, 35 (1965), pp. 320–52. *CPG* 3 (1979), pp. 410 f. (nos. 7550 f.). L. Petit in *DTC* 8 (pt. 1; 1924), cols. 829–31, s.v. 'Jean 77: Jean le Scolastique'; E. Herman in *DDC* 6 (1957), cols. 118–20, s.v. 'Jean III le Scolastique'.

John the Scot. See ERIGENA.

John the Solitary. See JOHN OF APAMEA.

John of Wesel (**John Rucherat or Ruchrat**) (*c.*1400–81), ecclesiastical reformer. A native of Oberwesel am Rhein, he was educated at Erfurt University, where he was rector in 1456–7. Later he became canon at Worms (1460), professor at Basle (1461), and cathedral-preacher (*Dompediger*) at Worms (1463). Charged with preaching *Hussite doctrines on the Church and Sacraments, he was deposed by Reinhard, Bp. of Worms, from his preaching office in 1477 and in 1479 tried by the *Inquisition. After a public recantation at Worms on 21 Feb. 1479, he was sentenced to lifelong confinement in the *Augustinian monastery at Mainz, where he died some two years later. Several of his writings, many of them still unpublished, survive, among them a 'Commentary on the Sentences' (from his Erfurt period), a treatise against *indulgences (1475), and a work on the *Immaculate Conception. He rejected *Original Sin, *transubstantiation, compulsory fasting, indulgences, and Extreme *Unction, and held that Scripture alone was the final authority in faith.

Modern edn. of his 'De Indulgentiis' in G. A. Benrath (ed.), *Reformtheologen des 15. Jahrhunderts* (Texte zur Kirchen- und Theologiegeschichte, 7; Gütersloh, 1968), pp. 39–60. C. Ullmann, *Johann Wesel, ein Vorgänger Luthers* (1834). N. Paulus, 'Johann von Wesel über Busssacrament und Ablass', *ZKT* 24 (1900), pp. 644–56; id., 'Die verloren geglaubten philosophischen Schriften des Johann von Wesel', ibid. 27 (1903), pp. 601 f. G. Ritter, *Studien zur Spätscholastik*, 3, 'Neue Quellenstücke zur Theologie des Johann von Wesel' (*Sb.* (Heid.), Jahr. 1926/7, Abhandlung 5). G. A. Benrath in *TRE* 17 (1988), pp. 150–3, s.v. 'Johann Rucherat von Wessel'.

Johnson, John (1662–1725), English theologian. Educated at Magdalene and Corpus Christi Colleges, Cambridge, he became Vicar of Boughton-under-Blean in 1687, of St John's, Margate, in 1697, and of Cranbrook, Kent, in 1710. He wrote several works, the theology of

which has considerable affinities with that of the *Nonjurors, among whom he had close personal friends. His best-known treatise is his *Unbloody Sacrifice and Altar, Unvailed and Supported, in which the Nature of the Eucharist is explained according to the Sentiments of the Christian Church in the Four First Centuries* (1714–18), in which he affirmed that the sacrifice is 'proper', 'expiatory', and 'propitiatory', and described the elements after the Consecration as the 'Sacramental' or 'Eucharistical body and blood' of the Lord. He held, however, that Christ was present in the elements in power and effect rather than in actuality. He also wrote *The Clergy-Man's Vade Mecum: or, an Account of the Antient and Present Church of England* (1706) and *The Propitiatory Oblation in the Holy Eucharist* (1710).

The Unbloody Sacrifice was repr. in LACT, 1847. Posthumous Life by T. *Brett prefixed (pp. i–lvi) to three posthumous tracts by Johnson, namely (1) 'The Primitive Communicant', (2) 'A Sermon . . . on Numb. xi. 29', and (3) 'An Explanation of Daniel's Prophecy of the LXX Weeks' (1748). W. J. Grisbrooke, *Anglican Liturgies of the Seventeenth and Eighteenth Centuries* (Alcuin Club Collections, 40; 1958), pp. 71–88. J. H. Overton in *DNB* 30 (1892), p. 906.

Johnson, Samuel (1709–84), author, lexicographer, and conversationalist. A serious Anglican, he ascribes his conversion as a young man to reading W. *Law's *Serious Call*, and, although unlike Law he was never a *Nonjuror, he was a strong *High Churchman, regular and sincere in his religious duties, and very generous to his friends and to the poor. He sometimes caused surprise by his marked tolerance of RCism, but, though he was on friendly terms with individuals, he was at no pains to conceal his dislike of Presbyterianism and Nonconformity.

Besides his famous *Dictionary of the English Language* (2 vols., 1755), his works include *The Vanity of Human Wishes* (1749); *The Prince of Abissinia* [*Rasselas*] (1759); *A Journey to the Western Islands of Scotland* (1775), *The Lives of the English Poets* (3 vols., 1779–81), and the twice-weekly essays entitled the *Rambler*, which appeared from 1750 to 1752 and earned him the title of 'the Great Moralist'. He also wrote many sermons for friends.

The American preacher and author, **Samuel Johnson** (1822–82), author of 'City of God, how broad and far' (*EH* 375) and other hymns, is not to be confused with the lexicographer.

Collected Works ed. by his friend and executor, Sir John Hawkins and others (13 vols., London, 1787–9), with Life as vol. 1. Crit. edn. of his Works by E. L. McAdam, Jun., D. and M. Hyde, and others (New Haven, Conn., and London, 1958 ff.: 'The Yale Edition'). *Letters*, ed. B. Redford (6 vols., Princeton, NJ, 1992–4). His prayers and private devotions were first pub. as *Prayers and Meditations* ed. G. Strahan (1785); they are incl. in vol. 1 of the Yale edn. of Johnson's Works. A collection of his Sermons was pub. under the name of John Taylor (2 vols., 1788–9). The classic biography is that of James Boswell (2 vols., London, 1791; standard edn. by G. B. Hill (6 vols., London, 1887; rev. by L. F. Powell, 6 vols., Oxford, 1934–50, with revisions to vols. 5 and 6, 1964). Biographical sources in A. L. Reade, *Johnsonian Gleanings* (11 vols., privately pr., 1909–52). Modern Lives by W. J. Bate (London, 1978) and R. DeMaria (Oxford, 1993). J. L. Clifford, *Young Samuel Johnson* (1955). J. Gray, *Johnson's Sermons: A Study* (Oxford, 1972). Other works on his religious or moral thought by R. Voitle (Cambridge, Mass., 1961), M. J. Quinlan (Madison, Wis., 1964), C. F. Chapin (Ann Arbor, Mich., 1968), P. K. Alkon (Evanston, Ill., 1967), R. B. Schwartz (Madison, Wis., 1975),

C. E. Pierce (London, 1983), and J. C. D. Clark (Cambridge, 1994). G. M. Ditchfield, 'Dr. Johnson and the Dissenters', *Bulletin of the John Rylands University Library of Manchester*, 68 (1986), pp. 373–409. Introd. by P. Rogers, *Johnson* (Past Masters, Oxford, 1993). J. L. Clifford, *Johnsonian Studies, 1887–1950: A Survey and Bibliography* (1951).

Joinville, Jean de (*c*.1224–1319), French historian. Seneschal of Champagne from 1233, Joinville accompanied St *Louis IX to Egypt and Palestine on the Sixth *Crusade in 1248. In this disastrous venture both he and the King were taken prisoner. In 1254 they returned to France, and Joinville spent most of the rest of his life on his estates, except when in attendance at court. He declined to accompany the King on the Crusade of 1270. In 1282 he was one of the chief witnesses for Louis's canonization and was present at the exhumation of his body in 1298. During the next ten years he wrote his famous Life of the King, *Le Livre des saintes paroles et des bonnes actions de St Louis*, at the request of Queen Jeanne. It is the work of an old man, garrulous and discursive, but it gives a charming account of its hero, contains an illuminating picture of the Crusade of 1248, and is full of accurate observations. A 'Credo' which he drew up at Acre in 1252 while on the Crusade epitomizes his religious faith.

His History of St Louis was first pub. at Poitiers in 1547. Crit. edn. of his Works by N. de Wailly (Paris, 1867; rev. 1874); Eng. tr. by R. Hague (London, 1955). History of St Louis also ed. N. L. Corbett (Sherbrooke, Quebec, 1977); Eng. trs. of the History by J. Evans (Newtown, 1937; London, 1938), with good introd., and by M. R. B. Shaw (*Joinville & Villehardouin: Chronicles of the Crusades*, Penguin Classics, 1963, pp. 163–353). L. J. Friedman, *Text and Iconography for Joinville's* Credo (Mediaeval Academy of America, Publication 68; 1958), incl. text. A. Firmin-Didot, *Études sur la vie et les travaux de Jean Sire de Joinville* (2 pts., Paris, 1870); H. F. Delaborde, *Jean de Joinville et les seigneurs de Joinville* (1894). G. P[aris], 'Jean, Sire de Joinville', *Histoire littéraire de la France*, 32 (1898), pp. 291–459.

Jonah, Book of. This Book, which is included among the twelve *Minor Prophets, is unlike the other prophetical books in being almost entirely in narrative form. It describes Yahweh's call to Jonah to go to Nineveh, the Assyrian capital, to preach repentance, his disobedience, his attempted escape by sea to Tarshish, his punishment of being thrown overboard and swallowed by a great fish, his deliverance after three days and nights, and the final success of his mission (chs. 1, 3, 4). The psalm in ch. 2 is widely held by modern critics to be independent of the rest of the Book. If the aim of the Book is primarily didactic, seeking to stress God's care for Gentiles and Jews alike, then this fact, together with considerations of language, style, and theology suggest that it was written in the post-exilic period, at a time when *Judaism was in danger of becoming narrowly exclusive. In the Gospels Christ refers more than once to the 'sign of Jonah' (Mt. 12: 39, 16: 4, Lk. 11: 29), which is interpreted in Mt. 12: 40 as a prophecy of his resurrection.

Comm. by J. A. Bewer (ICC on Hag., Zech., Mal., and Jon., 1912; sep. pagination), W. Rudolf (KAT 13/2 on Joel, Amos, Obad., and Jon., 1971, pp. 321–71), and J. Limburg (Old Testament Library, 1993). H. Schmidt, *Jona: Eine Untersuchung zur vergleichenden Religionsgeschichte* (Forschungen zur Religion und Literatur des Alten und Neuen Testaments, 9; 1907). A. R. Johnson, 'Jonah II. 3–10: A Study in Cultic Phantasy', in H. H.

Rowley (ed.), *Studies in Old Testament Prophecy presented to Professor Theodore H. Robinson* (1950), pp. 82–102. U. Steffen, *Das Mysterium von Tod und Auferstehung: Formen und Wandlungen des Jona-Motivs* (Göttingen [1963]). R. E. Clements, 'The Purpose of the Book of Jonah', in *Congress Volume, Edinburgh 1974* (Supplements to *Vetus Testamentum*, 28; 1975), pp. 16–28. T. E. Fretheim, *The Message of Jonah: A Theological Commentary* (Minneapolis [1977]). J. Blenkinsopp, *A History of Prophecy in Israel* (1984), pp. 268–73. R. A. Edwards, *The Sign of Jonah in the Theology of the Evangelists and Q* (Studies in Biblical Theology, 2nd ser. 18; 1971). J. Jeremias in *TWNT* 3 (1938), pp. 410–13 (Eng. tr., 1965, pp. 406–10), s.v. 'Ἰωνᾶς; H.-J. Zobel in *TRE* 17 (1988), pp. 229–34, s.v. 'Jona/Jonabuch', with extensive bibl.

Jonas, Justus (1493–1555), orig. 'Jodocus Koch', German reformer. Educated at the universities of Erfurt and *Wittenberg, in 1518 he was appointed professor of law at Erfurt and canon of the church of St Severus. In 1519 he was elected rector of the university, where he introduced Greek and Hebrew into the curriculum. A great admirer of *Erasmus and M. *Luther, he accompanied the latter to *Worms in 1521. From 1523 until 1533 he was dean of the theology faculty at Wittenberg and he took a prominent part in the Protestant cause, notably at the *Marburg Conference (1529), the Diet of *Augsburg (1530), and in reform at Halle (1541). His greatest service to the Reformation movement was his translation of the writings of Luther and *Melanchthon from German into Latin and the other way round. He also left an extensive correspondence and several Church Orders (including one for Halle, 1543). In 1546 he preached Luther's funeral sermon. After the outbreak of the Schmalkaldic war he was for a time a fugitive, but in 1553 was appointed superintendent at Eisfeld, where he remained till his death.

Briefwechsel, ed. G. Kawerau (2 vols., Halle, 1884–5, photographically repr., Hildesheim, 1964); suppl. by W. Delius in *Archiv für Reformationsgeschichte*, 42 (1951), pp. 136–45. Id., *Justus Jonas* (Gütersloh, 1952). M. E. Lehmann, *Justus Jonas, loyal reformer* (Minneapolis, 1963). P. Kalkoff, *Humanismus und Reformation in Erfurt* (1926). E. Kleineidam in P. G. Bietenholz and T. B. Deutscher (eds.), *Contemporaries of Erasmus*, 2 [1986], pp. 244–6, s.v.; H.-G. Leder in *TRE* 17 (1988), pp. 234–6, s.v.

Jones, Griffith (1683–1761), the founder of the Welsh circulating schools. Of Nonconformist parentage, he was received into the C of E, ordained in 1708, and became rector of Llanddowror in 1716. He set himself to further social and religious reforms and to this end made successful preaching tours. In 1730 he began to found his 'circulating schools' for adults and children, with travelling teachers who instructed their pupils in reading the Welsh Bible. Largely through help from England, e.g. from the *SPCK, the scheme rapidly developed, so that at his death over 3,000 of these greatly valued institutions were in existence. Jones published annually *Welsh Piety*, an account of the work and progress of his schools. He was also the author of a large number of writings in Welsh.

Lives by D. Jones (London and Bangor, 1902), F. A. Cavenagh (Cardiff, 1930), and T. Kelly (ibid., 1950). J. McLeish, *Evangelical Religion and Popular Education: A Modern Interpretation* (1969), esp. pp. 5–40. R. Williams in *DNB* 30 (1892), pp. 102 f., s.v.

Jones, Inigo (1573–1652), the first British classical architect. He was born in London, the son of a Welsh cloth-maker. Little is known of his early life, but *c.*1600 and again in 1613–14 he visited Italy. Here he studied the work of the great Italian classical architect Andrea Palladio (d. 1580) in his native Vicenza and elsewhere; Jones's annotated copy of Palladio's seminal book, *I Quattro Libri . . .* (1570), is in Worcester College, Oxford. He began work as a general impresario and designer of masques, often in collaboration with Ben Jonson, with whom he had a famous quarrel. By *c.*1608 he knew enough about architecture to make a design for the W. front of *St Paul's cathedral which is close to the engravings for a projected façade of the Gesù in Rome, the mother church of the *Jesuits. In 1613 he was granted the reversion of the Royal Surveyorship and his architectural career assumed a new importance. The first classical buildings in England were his Banqueting House, Whitehall (1619–22), and the Queen's House, Greenwich (1616–35). His importance as a designer of churches lies in his use of classical forms based on the ancient temple, in contrast to the contemporary Gothic style. His ecclesiastical work included the Queen's Chapel at St James's Palace, built for *Charles I's Catholic Queen *Henrietta Maria (begun in 1623), St Paul's, Covent Garden (begun in 1631, rebuilt to his design in 1795), and the huge classical portico added to the W. front of Old St Paul's (1634–42), destroyed in the Great Fire of 1666. The Civil War effectively ended his career. As with C. *Wren, there are many doubtful attributions, including the porch of St Mary the Virgin, Oxford, which was probably designed by Nicholas Stone (1637). Many of Jones's books and drawings are in Worcester College, Oxford, and other drawings are in the Royal Institute of British Architects, London.

J. Summerson, *Inigo Jones* (Harmondsworth, 1966). S. Orgel and R. Strong, *Inigo Jones: The Theatre of the Stuart Court, including the Complete Designs for Productions at Court* (2 vols., 1973); J. [F.] Harris and G. Higgott, *Inigo Jones: Complete Architectural Drawings* (New York, 1989). J. [F.] Harris and A. A. Tait, *Catalogue of the Drawings by Inigo Jones . . . at Worcester College, Oxford* (Oxford, 1979), pp. 1–29. *DNB* 30 (1892), pp. 111–19; H. Colvin, *A Biographical Dictionary of British Architects 1600–1840* (1978), pp. 467–74, s.v.

Jones, Rufus Matthew (1863–1948), American *Quaker. Educated at Haverford College and in Europe, he was principal of Oak Grove Seminary from 1889 to 1893 and professor of philosophy at Haverford College from 1904 to 1934. Among his many works are: *A Dynamic Faith* (1901), *Social Law in the Spiritual World* (1904), *Studies in Mystical Religion* (1909), *Spiritual Reformers in the 16th and 17th Centuries* (1914), *The Later Periods of Quakerism* (1921), *The Faith and Practice of the Quakers* (1927), *New Studies in Mystical Religion* (1927), and *George Fox, Seeker and Friend* (1930).

H. E. *Fosdick (ed.), *Rufus Jones Speaks to Our Times: An Anthology* (New York, 1951; London, 1953). H. H. Brinton (ed.), *Children of Light: In Honor of Rufus M. Jones* (New York, 1938), with introd. by H. H. Brinton, pp. ix–xii, and list of Jones's Works, pp. 407–11. E. G. Vining, *Friend of Life: The Biography of Rufus M. Jones* (Philadelphia, 1958; London, 1959).

Jones, William, 'of Nayland' (1726–1800), Anglican divine. A native of Lowick in Northants, he was educated at Charterhouse and at University College, Oxford, where with his friend G. *Horne he studied the writings of J.

*Hutchinson. Having been ordained in 1751 he held several curacies, and became rector of Pluckley, Kent, in 1765. In 1777 he accepted the perpetual curacy of Nayland, Suffolk, whence his traditional epithet. He endeavoured to keep alive the High Church traditions of the *Nonjurors. His best-known work, *The Catholic Doctrine of the Trinity* (1756), sought to prove from scriptural texts that the Trinitarian dogma is contained in the Bible. In his later work on the same subject, *A Short Way to Truth* (1792), he attempts to find arguments for the doctrine of the Trinity in nature, e.g. in the three primary colours, the three dimensions, and other groups of three. In 1792 he assisted in the formation of a 'Society for the Reformation of Principles', designed to counteract the influence of the French Revolution. His sound and solid piety finds expression in *The Scholar armed against the Errors of the Time* (1792).

The Theological, Philosophical and Miscellaneous Works of the Rev. William Jones [ed. W. *Stevens] (12 vols., London, 1801), with short account of his life and writings by the editor, 1, pp. l–lv. Further Sermons (*Sermons on Various Subjects and Occasions*), ed. W. H. Walker [grandson] (2 vols., London, 1830). W. H. Teale, *Lives of English Divines* (1866), pp. 345–419. J. H. Overton in *DNB* 30 (1892), pp. 177 f.; S. L. Ollard in *DECH*, p. 303.

Jordan, River. Formed from the waters of four streams which converge in the upper part of the plain of Lake Huleh, the Jordan expands into the now much-reduced Lake Huleh (poss. the 'Waters of Merom' of Josh. 11: 5), flows through a narrow gorge and then forms a delta at the head of the Sea of *Galilee (q.v.). Emerging from the south of the lake, it meanders for some 200 miles before it eventually enters the *Dead Sea (65 miles distant). The fault which contains it extends from northern Syria to Ezion-geber on the eastern arm of the *Red Sea.

Flowing through a steep infertile valley in the centre of biblical Palestine, the Jordan was a natural barrier between the settled and the nomadic populations of the area. By their passage of the Jordan, when its waters were miraculously divided, the *Hebrews first entered the Promised Land (Josh. 3: 16; cf. the crossing of the Red Sea, Exod. 14); it was the scene of Elijah's ascent to Heaven (2 Kgs. 2: 11); in its waters Naaman the Syrian was cleansed (2 Kgs. 5: 14) after he had contrasted it unfavourably with the rivers of his own land. In NT times St *John the Baptist preached on its banks and the Lord Himself was among those baptized in its waters (Mt. 3: 13). From these associations it became an emblem of the achievement of purity (esp. in Baptism) and of the last hindrance to final blessedness, and as such features in numerous *hymns and *spirituals.

W. Libbey and F. E. Hoskins, *The Jordan Valley and Petra* (2 vols., 1905); N. Glueck, *The River Jordan* (Philadelphia and London, 1946; rev. edn., New York and London, 1968). M. *Noth, 'Der Jordan in der alten Geschichte Palästinas', *Zeitschrift des Deutschen Palästina-Vereins*, 72 (1956), pp. 123–48. G. A. *Smith, *The Historical Geography of the Holy Land* (25th edn., 1931), pp. 405–96. [A.] D. Baly, *The Geography of the Bible* (2nd edn. [1974]), esp. pp. 191–202.

Josaphat, St, also **Joasaph.** In medieval legend, the son of an Indian king, Abenner, who was converted to Christianity by the hermit Barlaam. The name 'Josaphat' appears to be a corruption of 'Bodisatva' (Bodhisattva), a title of the Buddha. He is commemorated in the *Roman Martyrology on 27 Nov. See also BARLAAM AND JOASAPH, STS.

Josaphat, St (1580 or 1584–1623), Abp. of Polotsk, the first saint of the E. Church to be formally canonized after process in the Congregation of *Rites, in 1867. John Kunsevich became a monk at Vilna in 1604. In 1617 he was consecrated Bp. of Vitebsk with right of succession to Polotsk, to which he succeeded a few months later. He did much to restore the ecclesiastical life of the eparchy, in which there was still much unrest following the Union of *Brest-Litovsk. He was killed by a rival faction. Feast day, now 12 Nov.

Docs. of his beatification and canonization ed. A. G. Welykij, OSBM (Analecta Ordinis S. Basili Magni, 2nd ser., sectio 3, vols. 1–3; Rome, 1952–67). *Miscellanea in honorem S. Josaphat* (ibid., 2nd ser., sectio 2, vol. 6; 1967). Life by A. Guépin, OSB (2 vols., Paris, 1874). Further study by E. Unger-Dreiling (Vienna [1960]).

Joseph, St, the spouse of the BVM. He figures prominently in the two Infancy narratives of the Gospels—in Mt. 1–2 and to a less extent in Lk. 1–2. Both state that Mary was 'betrothed' to him at the time of the Lord's birth, but both emphasize her virginity. He was a pious Jew of Davidic descent (Mt. 1: 19 f., Lk. 2: 4) but of humble situation, and acc. to Mt. 13: 55 a carpenter (τέκτων). Christ grew up in his household at Nazareth for at least 12 years (Lk. 2: 42, 51). Afterwards Joseph is mentioned only once by name in the NT (Lk. 4: 22; cf. Mt. 13: 55, Mk. 6: 3), but he is often referred to in later traditions. In the 'Book of *James' he is said to have been very old at the time of his marriage to Mary; and as a pattern of holiness he is the subject of various legends. The special veneration of St Joseph seems to have originated in the E., where the apocryphal 'History of Joseph the Carpenter' (4th–7th cents.) enjoyed considerable popularity. It developed comparatively late in the W. Church, though a commemoration is mentioned in the Irish *Félire* of St *Oengus, dated to the 9th cent. Among the earliest promoters of his cult are St *Bernardino of Siena and John *Gerson in the 15th cent., who laid its theological foundations by drawing out the implications of his office as foster-father of Jesus, and whose teaching found liturgical expression in the introduction of his feast (19 Mar.) into the Roman Calendar in 1479. The devotion was popularized esp. by St *Teresa of Ávila and St *Francis de Sales. In 1714 *Clement XI composed a special office for his feast, and in 1729 *Benedict XIII inserted his name in the Litany of the Saints. He was declared 'Patron of the Universal Church' by *Pius IX in 1870, when his principal feast (apart from 19 Mar.) became his 'Patronage', since 1914 celebrated on the 3rd Wednesday after Easter. This feast was suppressed in 1955, when the feast of St Joseph the Worker on 1 May was promulgated by *Pius XII. In 1969 this latter observance ceased to be obligatory. His pre-eminent sanctity, which places him next to the BVM among the saints, was confirmed by *Leo XIII in his encyclical 'Quanquam pluries' of 1889. In 1962 the name of St Joseph was added to the list of saints in the *Communicantes in the *Canon of the Roman Mass (now the First Eucharistic Prayer). St Joseph is invoked as the patron of a good death; the month of March and each Wednesday used to be dedicated to

him. He is usually represented with the Child Jesus and a lily or staff. Feast day in E., the first Sunday after Christmas.

A. H. Lépicier, *Tractatus de S. Joseph* (Paris [1908]). 'C.A.', 'Le Développement historique du culte de S. Joseph', *R. Bén.* 14 (1897), pp. 104–14, 145–55, and 203–9. J. Seitz, *Die Verehrung des hl. Joseph in ihrer geschichtlichen Entwickelung bis zum Konzil von Trient* (1908). U. Holzmeister, SJ, *De Sancto Ioseph Quaestiones Biblicae* (Scripta Pontificii Instituti Biblici; Rome, 1945). F. L. Filas, SJ, *The Man nearest to Christ: Nature and Historic Development of the Devotion to St Joseph* (Milwaukee, 1944; London, 1947), with Eng. tr. of principal Papal docs. to date. The proceedings of a series of symposia on St Joseph are pr. in the *Cahiers de Joséphologie*, pub. by the Centre de Recherches et de Documentation, Oratoire Saint-Joseph, Montreal, 1953 ff.: *Saint Joseph durant les quinze premiers siècles de l'Église* (Cahiers, 19; 1971); *Saint Joseph à l'Époque de la Renaissance (1450–1600)* (Cahiers, 25; 1977); *Saint Joseph au XVIIᵉ siècle* (Cahiers, 29; 1981); and *Présence de Saint Joseph au XVIIᵉ siècle* (Cahiers, 35; 1987). Bibl. by A. Trottier, CSB, in *Cahiers de Joséphologie*, 1 (1953), pp. 55–117, 247–95; 2 (1954), pp. 77–140, 227–64; and 3 (1955), pp. 51–117. P. Grelot and others in *Dict. Sp.* 8 (1974), cols. 1289–323, s.v. 'Joseph (2)'.

Joseph of Arimathaea, St. The 'councillor' (βουλευτής, Lk. 23: 50) who after the Crucifixion requested from Pilate the body of Christ and gave it burial the same day (Mt. 27: 60, Mk. 15: 46, Lk. 23: 53; cf. Jn. 19: 42, etc.). He is described as a 'good and a just man' (ἀνὴρ ἀγαθὸς καὶ δίκαιος; Lk. 23: 50) and as a disciple, 'but secretly for fear of the Jews' (Jn. 19: 38). Acc. to the apocryphal 'Gospel of *Nicodemus' he played an important part in the foundation of the first Christian community at Lydda. In the 'De Antiquitate Glastoniensis Ecclesie', written by *William of Malmesbury between 1129 and 1139, occurs the earliest mention of the story that St Joseph came to England with the Holy Grail and built the first church in the country at *Glastonbury, but the passage relating this incident was added to the book at least a century later. Feast day in E., and the American BCP (1979), 31 July; in W., 17 Mar.

E. von Dobschütz, 'Joseph von Arimathia', *ZKG* 23 (1902), pp. 1–17; T. Kluge, 'Die apokryphe Erzählung des Joseph von Aramathäa über den Bau der ersten christlichen Kirche in Lydda', *Oriens Christianus*, NS 4 (1914), pp. 24–38. See also comm. to Gospels, ad locc. For works on the legend connecting St Joseph with Glastonbury, see bibl. to GLASTONBURY.

Joseph Calasanctius, St (1557–1648), founder of the *Piarists. José de Calasanz was born in Peralta de la Sal in NW Spain. He studied law and theology in the universities of Lérida, Valencia, and Alcalá, was ordained priest in 1583, and held various administrative and pastoral positions in Spain. In 1592 he went to Rome, where he lived for some years in the *Colonna Palazzo. Though he had originally intended to seek a well-endowed benefice in Spain, he was deeply moved by the terrible conditions of the children in the poorer parts of Rome and decided to devote the rest of his life to their Christian education. In 1597 he opened in Rome what L. von *Pastor claims was the first free public school in Europe. To give permanence to the work, which grew rapidly, he established a religious order, the Piarists, whose members took a fourth vow dedicating themselves to the education of children; it was recognized by Pope *Paul V in 1617 and approved by Gregory XV in 1621. In Calasanctius's schools, which were known as 'Pious Schools', children were taught reading, writing, arithmetic, and grammar, as well as Christian doctrine, and Catholic, Protestant, and Jewish children were admitted on equal terms. He was especially concerned about scientific education and sent some of the masters to study in the schools of *Galileo and T. *Campanella. He set out his pedagogical principles in his voluminous correspondence and in the Constitutions of his order, which during his lifetime spread through Italy, Moravia, and Poland. In 1643, however, he was arraigned before the *Holy Office and deposed from his office. He was canonized in 1767 and declared Patron of Christian Schools in 1948. Feast day, 25 (formerly 27) Aug.

Letters, ed. L. Picanyol, Sch. P., and C. Vilá-Palá, Sch. P. (10 vols., Rome, 1950–88), with introd., vol. 1, pp. ix–xliv. *Obra [pedagógica]*, ed. G. Sántha, Sch. P. (Biblioteca de Autores Cristianos, 159; Madrid, 1956; 2nd edn., 1984); anthology ed. V. Faubell (Salamanca, 1988). C. Bau, *Biografía crítica de S. José de Calasanzio* (Madrid, 1949); S. Giner Guerri, Sch. P., *San José de Calasanz: Maestro y Fundador* (Biblioteca de Autores Cristianos, maior 41; 1992). G. Giovannozzi, *Il Calasanzio e l'opera sua* (Florence, 1930); C. Vilá Palá, *Fuentes immediatas de la pedagogiá calasancia* (Madrid, 1960); J. Santha, *Ensayos críticos sobre S. José de Calasanz y las Escuelas Pías* (Salamanca, 1976). G. Cianfrocca and G. Ausenda in *DIP* 4 (1977), cols. 1343–51, s.v. 'Giuseppe Calasanzio', with extensive bibl.

Joseph of Cupertino, St (1603–63), *Franciscan friar. Joseph Desa was the son of a poor carpenter in Cupertino in the Kingdom of Naples. In his youth he became a *Capuchin lay brother. When the Capuchins dismissed him on account of his awkwardness, the *Conventual Franciscans at La Grotella, nr. Cupertino, accepted him as a tertiary. He became a cleric in 1625 and was ordained priest in 1628, despite doing poorly in his studies. During the rest of his life he experienced *ecstasies which were remarkable for the phenomena of levitation which accompanied them. Since these caused wonder and curiosity among the people, his superiors tried to keep him from public view, especially after he was denounced to the *Inquisition. He spent the last ten years of his life in seclusion in out-of-the way Capuchin convents and at the Conventual friary at Osimo where he died. A meeting with him is said to have been decisive in converting the Lutheran Duke John Frederick of Brunswick to Catholicism. He was canonized in 1767. Feast day, 18 Sept., suppressed in 1969.

[A. Pastrovicchi, OFMC], *Compendio della Vita, Virtù, e Miracoli del B. Giuseppe da Copertino* (1753; adapted Eng. tr., 1918); Lat. tr., with introd. and other material, in *AASS*, Sept. 5 (1755), pp. 992–1060. G. Parisciani, OMFC, *San Giuseppe da Copertino (1603–1663) alla luce dei nuovi documenti* (Osimo, Ancona [1964]), with extensive refs. Id. and G. Galleazi (eds.), *S. Giuseppe da Copertino tra storia ed attualità* (Ricerche Francescane, Padua, 1984). A. *Butler, *Lives of the Saints*, ed. H. Thurston, SJ, and D. Attwater, 3 (1956), pp. 587–91.

Joseph the Hymnographer, St (*c*.810–86), one of the most voluminous of the Greek hymn-writers. Around 830 he left his native Sicily when it was invaded by the Arabs for the monastic life at Thessalonica. Some time later he went on to *Constantinople, which he left for *Rome during the *Iconoclastic persecution (841). Captured by pirates, he was for several years a slave in Crete, but even-

tually escaped and *c*.850 established a monastery at Constantinople. He suffered a further exile in the Chersonese for his defence of the icons and yet another in the company of *Photius. He is reputed to have composed 1,000 canons, over 200 being contained in the **Menaion* under the acrostic of his name. A large part of the **Octoechos* has also been attributed to him, but this is more probably the work of Joseph of Thessalonica (also 'Joseph of the Studium'), the brother of *Theodore Studites. Feast day in the E. Church, 3 Apr.

Text of canons in J. P. Migne, *PG* 105. 983–1426, with introds. and Gk. Life by John the Deacon, cols. 925–82; cf. also *Anal. Boll.* 65 (1947), pp. 134–8. *AASS*, Apr. 1 (1675), pp. 266–76, and *Bollettino della Badia greca di Grottaferrata*, 11 (1948), pp. 87–98, 177–92. C. van de Vorst, 'Note sur S. Joseph l'Hymnographe', *Anal. Boll.* 38 (1920), pp. 148–54. M. E. Colonna, 'Biografie di Giuseppe Innografo', *Università di Napoli, Annali della Facoltà di Lettere e Filosofia*, 3 (for 1953; 1954), pp. 105–12. E. I. Tomadakes, Ἰωσὴφ ὁ Ὑμνογράφος. Βίος καὶ ἔργον (1971, with summary in Ital.). D. Stiernon, AA, in *Dict. Sp.* 8 (1974), cols. 1349–54, s.v. 'Joseph (10)'.

Joseph of Volokolamsk, St (1439/40–1515), Russian saint and monastic founder. After some years of monastic life he instituted a strict reform and founded the celebrated monastery of Volokolamsk, not far from Moscow. Unlike *Nil Sorsky, he welcomed gifts of money and land, and created a large community with a rigorous life of obedience, work and lengthy liturgical services. He aimed at educating 'learned monks' for high office in the Church, and his followers collaborated in the 16th-cent. expansion of the Muscovite state, founding urban monasteries and making possible the later subservience of monks to government. His activist, rigorous teaching won the day for a time against the contemplative ideal of Sorsky. Feast day, 9 Sept.

Eng. tr. of his monastic rule by D. M. Goldfrank (Cistercian Studies Series, 36; 1983). T. Špidlík, SJ, *Joseph de Volokolamsk: Un Chapitre de la Spiritualité Russe* (Orientalia Christiana Analecta, 146; 1956). M. Szeftel, 'Joseph Volotsky's Political Ideas in a New Historical Perspective', *Jahrbucher für Geschichte Osteuropas*, NF 13 (1965), pp. 19–29. H.-D. Döpmann, *Die Einfluss der Kirche und moskowitische Staatsidee: Staats- und Gesellschaftsdenken bei Josif Volockij, Nil Sorskij und Vassian Patrikeev* (1967). T. Špidlík, SJ, in *Dict. Sp.* 8 (1974), cols. 1408–11, s.v. 'Joseph (30)'.

Josephinism. The principles which actuated the ecclesiastical reforms of Joseph II, Holy Roman Emperor from 1765 to 1790. They included religious toleration, the right of the State to regulate ecclesiastical affairs and to reform ecclesiastical abuses, irrespective of Rome, and the restriction of the rights and powers of the Pope within spiritual limits, as laid down by *Febronius. They issued in the Toleration Edict of 1781, which granted all religious bodies the right to practise their beliefs unhindered, the suppression of certain religious orders, the transference of monasteries from the jurisdiction of the Pope to that of the diocesan bishops, and the requirement of civil consent for the publication of any Papal bull, brief, or other document. A similar policy was introduced into Tuscany, under the direction of his brother Leopold, the Grand Duke, who was assisted by Scipione de' *Ricci, Bp. of Pistoia. Josephinism completely collapsed with the Emperor's death.

Docs. in F. Maass, *Der Josephinismus* (Fontes rerum Austriacarum, Abt. 2, 71–5; 1951–61). There is an immense lit. Modern works incl. F. Valjavec, *Der Josephinismus: Zur geistigen Entwicklung Österreichs im achtzehnten und neunzehnten Jahrhundert* (2nd edn., Munich, 1945); E. Winter, *Der Josefinismus: Die Geschichte des österreichischen Reformkatholizismus, 1740–1848* (1962); F. Maass, *Der Frühjosephinismus* (Vienna, etc., 1969). Studies in Eng. incl. S. K. Padover, *The Revolutionary Emperor Joseph II* (1934; 2nd edn., 1967), and Sr. Mary C. Goodwin, *The Papal Conflict with Josephinism* (New York, 1938). G. Mollat in *DTC* 8 (pt. 2; 1925), cols. 1543–7; F. Maass in *NCE* 7 (1967), pp. 1118 f.; R. Zinnhobler in *L.Th.K.* (3rd edn.), 5 (1996), cols. 1008–10, all with bibl. See also bibl. to FEBRONIANISM.

Josephus, Flavius (*c*.37–*c*.100), Jewish historian. He was a native of Palestine of priestly descent who received a thorough education based on study of the Jewish Law. Having lived for three years in the desert as the disciple of the hermit Bannos, he became a *Pharisee. In 64 he went to Rome to plead for the release of some of his fellow-Jews, and after enlisting the sympathies of the Emp. *Nero's wife, Poppea, returned to Palestine. In 66 he took a leading part in the Jewish war. In 67 he was besieged in Jotopata, but escaped death and was taken prisoner by Vespasian, whose favour he won by prophesying that he would become emperor. On the fulfilment of the prophecy in 69 Josephus was set at liberty and took the name of 'Flavius'. During the siege of *Jerusalem (70) he acted as interpreter to Titus, with whom he returned to Rome, as his surrender had earned him the hostility of the Jews. In Rome he was highly honoured by Vespasian as well as by his successors, Titus and *Domitian, and received the Roman citizenship and a pension which enabled him to devote himself entirely to literary work. In 77–8 he published his 'Jewish War' (Περὶ τοῦ Ἰουδαϊκοῦ πολέμου), probably written originally in Aramaic. It opens with a historical summary of the events from the time of *Antiochus Epiphanes to the outbreak of the war. The latter part is largely an eye-witness account, though supplemented by borrowings from other authors. Though the introduction promises an impartial treatment of the subject, the work is written from the standpoint of a Jew trying to gain the sympathy of the Roman public and therefore omits or minimizes all that might offend Roman susceptibilities, such as the activities of the *Zealots and the importance of the Messianic hope. He brought out *c*.94 his second great work, the 'Antiquities of the Jews' (Ἰουδαϊκὴ Ἀρχαιολογία), the 20 books of which trace the history of the Jews from the creation of the world to the beginning of the Jewish war. Down to *c*.400 BC Josephus mainly reproduces the Bible narratives; later he uses many other sources, among them Dionysius of Halicarnassus and Nicolaus of Damascus, as well as apocryphal books. The famous reference to Christ in 18. 3. 3, calling Him 'a wise man, if indeed one should call him a man', is in its present form not authentic. The most generally accepted opinion is that Josephus mentioned the Lord, as he refers to Him later on in a passage on St James, but that the original 'Testimonium Flavianum' was recast by a Christian writer at an early date, certainly before the time of *Eusebius, who already knew it in its present form (*HE* 1. 11. 7 f.). There are also two further works extant, an autobiography and 'Contra Apionem', in the latter of which he presents a skilfully planned, well written, and clever apology for Judaism.

The works of Josephus were highly appreciated by the Fathers, e.g. *Jerome, whom they furnished with a wealth of material for their apologetics.

Editio princeps of the Gk. text of his works, with Lat. tr. [ed. A. P. Arlenius], Basle, 1544. Best crit. edn. is that of B. Niese (6 vols. and index, Berlin, 1887–95); also ed. S. A. Naber (Teub., 6 vols., 1888–96). Edn. based on Niese and Naber, with modern Eng. tr., by H. St J. Thackeray and others (Loeb, 9 vols., 1926–65). Older Eng. tr. by W. *Whiston (2 vols., London, 1737) frequently repr.; rev. by A. R. Shilleto, with topographical notes by C. W. Wilson (Bohn's Standard Library, 5 vols., 1889–90). Eng. tr. of *Jewish War* by G. A. Williamson (Penguin Classics, 1959). N. Bentwich, *Josephus* (Philadelphia, 1914). R. Laqueur, *Der jüdische Historiker Flavius Josephus* (1920). H. St J. Thackeray, *Josephus, the Man and the Historian* (Hilda Stich Stoock Lectures; New York, 1929). R. J. H. Shutt, *Studies in Josephus* (1961). G. A. Williamson, *The World of Josephus* (1964). T. Rajak, *Josephus: The Historian and his Society* (1983). S. Zeitlin, *Josephus on Jesus* (Philadelphia, 1931). A. *Schlatter, *Die Theologie des Judentums nach dem Bericht des Josephus* (Beiträge zur Förderung christlicher Theologie, 2. Reihe, 26; 1932). E. *Schürer, *The History of the Jewish People in the Age of Jesus Christ*, rev. Eng. tr. by G. Vermes and others, 1 (Edinburgh, 1973), pp. 43–63 and 428–41, with refs. to earlier discussions of the 'Testimonium Flavianum'. *Aufstieg und Niedergang der römischen Welt*, 2. 21, ed. W. Haase (pt. 2; 1984), pp. 763–1217. L. H. Feldman and G. Hata (eds.), *Josephus, Judaism, and Christianity* (Leiden, 1987). K. H. Rengstorf (ed.), *A Complete Concordance to Flavius Josephus* (4 vols. + Suppl., Leiden, 1968–83). L. H. Feldman, *Josephus and Modern Scholarship (1937–1980)* (Berlin and New York, 1984); id., *Josephus: A Supplementary Bibliography* (New York and London, 1986). H. St J. Thackeray in *HDB*, Extra Vol. (1904), pp. 461–73; L. H. Feldman in *Anchor Bible Dictionary*, 3 (1992), pp. 981–98, s.v.

Joshua, Book of. The first of the 'historical books' in the OT and, acc. to the Hebrew division, the first of the 'Former Prophets'. It traces the history of the Israelites from the death of *Moses to the death of his successor, Joshua, and gives an account of the entry into and conquest of Palestine, its partition among the twelve tribes, and Joshua's last speeches. Among the better-known incidents in the Book are the hiding of the spies in *Jericho by Rahab the harlot (2), the miraculous crossing of the *Jordan commemorated by the twelve stones representing the twelve tribes of Israel (3 f.), the Fall of Jericho (6), and the standing still of the sun on Gibeon (10). Chs. 12–21 record in detail the divison of Palestine among the twelve tribes.

Though some of the sources of Joshua may date from the 9th cent. BC or even earlier, the Book prob. did not reach its present form before the 6th cent. or later. Many scholars have held that its compilers made use of the same set of literary sources which have been recognized in the *Pentateuch, and in consequence have classed Joshua with the five Books of the Law in what is termed the '*Hexateuch'. Other critics reckon Joshua as the second Book in the series Deuteronomy–2 Kings known as the '*Deuteronomistic History'. The Book affords an interesting example of the way in which the compilers' religious beliefs have influenced the historical record, e.g. in the description of the speedy and complete conquest of Canaan in the post-Exodus period which is at variance with the account at the beginning of the Book of *Judges.

Comm. by M. *Noth (HAT, Reihe 1, Bd. 7, 1938; 2nd edn., 1953), H. W. Hertzberg (Das Alte Testament Deutsch, 9, on Jos.,

Jgs. and Ruth, 1953; 2nd edn., 1959, pp. 7–140), J. Gray (New Cent. Bib. on Jos., Jgs., and Ruth, 1967, pp. 1–200; 2nd edn., 1986, pp. 1–183), J. A. Soggin (Neuchâtel, 1970; Eng. tr., 1972), J. M. Miller and G. M. Tucker (Cam. Bib., NEB, 1974), R. G. Boling (Anchor Bible, 1982), and T. C. Butler (Word Biblical Comm., 7; Waco, Tex. [1983]). J. Garstang, *Joshua–Judges* (1931), pp. 3–260. M. Weippert, *Die Landnahme der israelitischen Stämme* (Forschungen zur Religion und Literatur des Alten und Neuen Testaments, 92; 1967; Eng. tr., *The Settlement of the Israelite Tribes in Palestine*, Studies in Biblical Theology, 2nd ser. 21; 1971). N. K. Gottwald, *The Tribes of Yahweh: A Sociology of the Religion of Liberated Israel, 1250–1050 B.C.E.* (Maryknoll, NY, 1979; London, 1980), *passim*. Soggin, pp. 187–97, with further bibl. R. G. Boling in *Anchor Bible Dictionary*, 3 (1992), pp. 1002–15, s.v.

Jovian (*c.*332–64), Roman Emperor from June 363 to Feb. 364. He was born at Singidunum in Moesia. On the Emp. *Julian's fatal expedition against the Persians he was captain of his bodyguard; and when, after Julian's death (26 June 363), Sallust, the Prefect of the East, had declined to receive the purple at the hands of the army, Jovian was chosen. He was forced to conclude a humiliating peace with Sapor II, King of the Persians, abandoning Nisibis and the other territories conquered under *Diocletian in 298, and the Christian kingdom of *Armenia. In the theological disputes he supported orthodoxy and on his way back to the W. he received St *Athanasius, who presented a Confession of Faith at *Edessa and prob. accompanied the Emperor to *Antioch. Before reaching *Constantinople, Jovian died suddenly one night (17 Feb. 364) at Dadastana, apparently through overeating or suffocation. His support of orthodoxy made him for Catholics a welcome successor to Julian; and in *Syriac literature he even became the subject of a Christian romance.

The chief source is Ammianus Marcellinus, 25. 5–10. Further information will be found in the Church historians, *Socrates (*HE* 3. 22–6), *Sozomen (*HE* 6. 3–6), and *Theodoret (*HE* 4. 1–4). J. *Wordsworth in *DCB* 3 (1882), pp. 461–5; O. Seeck in *PW* 9 (pt. 2; 1916), cols. 2006–11; s.v. 'Jovianus'.

Jovinian (d. *c.*405), an unorthodox monk, condemned by synods at Rome (under *Siricius) and at Milan (under St *Ambrose in 393). He denied that virginity as such was a higher state than marriage, and that abstinence as such was better than thankful eating. He also attacked the tendency to associate differences of reward in heaven with different earthly states (virgins, widows, wives; monks, priests, laymen), and shared the disbelief of *Helvidius in the perpetual virginity of *Mary. *Jerome (*Adversus Jovinianum*, 1–2, AD 393) and *Augustine (in *De bono conjugali* and *De sancta virginitate*, AD 401) both wrote against him.

Jovinian's own writings are lost. W. Haller, *Jovinianus* (TU 17, no. 2; 1897; a comprehensive study). F. Valli, *Gioviniano: Esame delle fonti e dei frammenti* (Pubblicazioni dell'Università di Urbino. Serie di Lettere e Filosofia, 2; 1953). J. N. D. Kelly, *Jerome* (1975), pp. 180–7. A. Rayez, SJ, in *Dict. Sp.* 8 (1974), cols. 1469 f., s.v.

Jowett, Benjamin (1817–93), Master of Balliol College, Oxford. Educated at St Paul's School London, in 1836 Jowett entered Balliol, where he was elected a Fellow while still an undergraduate. He held a succession of college offices, finally becoming Master (1870). He was ordained

priest in 1845. In 1855 he succeeded T. *Gaisford as Regius Professor of Greek.

In strong contrast with his early colleague, W. G. *Ward, Jowett distrusted logic and, under the influence of Greek studies and German philosophy (esp. G. W. F. *Hegel), became a keen theological liberal. His theological views were first elaborated in his *Commentaries on the Epp. of St Paul* (Thess., Gal., and Rom.; 2 vols., 1855). The work contained a personal and subjective exposition of the *Atonement which he redrafted in a 2nd edition (1859) to meet objections, but without modifying it. His essay on 'The Interpretation of Scripture' in *Essays and Reviews* (1860, q.v.) was one of the most debated items in the book; and henceforth Jowett's orthodoxy remained under grave suspicion and he ceased to write on theological subjects. His most important work was his translation of *Plato (4 vols., 1871; 3rd edn., 5 vols., 1892); this, together with his translation of *Aristotle's *Politics* (2 vols., 1885), made these works widely available to non-classical students. To the end of his life he continued to take an active part in academic affairs, instituting reforms in the interests of poorer students, and he secured for his college a unique place in the University.

E. Abbott and L. Campbell, *The Life and Letters of Benjamin Jowett* (2 vols., 1897); L. A. Tollemache, *Benjamin Jowett* (1895); G. Faber, *Jowett* (1957; 2nd edn., 1958). A Selection of Jowett's Letters to Florence *Nightingale, 1860–93, was ed. [E.] V. Quinn and J. [M.] Prest, *Dear Miss Nightingale* (Oxford, 1987). P. [B.] Hinchliff, *Benjamin Jowett and the Christian Religion* (ibid., 1987); id., *God and History: Aspects of British Theology 1875–1914* (ibid., 1992), pp. 50–72. E. Abbott in *DNB*, Suppl. 3 (1901), pp. 49–56.

Joyful Mysteries, the five. The first chaplet of the *rosary (q.v.), consisting of (1) the *Annunciation, (2) the *Visitation, (3) the Nativity of Christ, (4) the *Presentation of Christ in the Temple, and (5) the Finding of the Child Jesus in the Temple.

jube (pron. as two syllables). The rood loft dividing the nave of a church from the choir. The name is said to derive from the words 'Jube, domine, benedicere' ('Pray, sir, a blessing'), pronounced by the *deacon before the reading of the Gospel, which took place on the rood loft in medieval times.

Jubilate (Lat., 'O be joyful'). The first word of Ps. 100, to which it thus gives the name. It is provided as an alternative to the *Benedictus at Morning Prayer in the BCP. The rubric requires its use only when the Benedictus occurs elsewhere in the service, though it is apparently permitted on other days. It was first inserted in 1552, probably owing to the dislike of the extreme Reformers for the traditional *canticles (so also Pss. 98 and 67 at Evening Prayer). The ASB provides it as an alternative to the *Venite.

Jubilee, Year of. (1) Acc. to the *Mosaic legislation (Lev. 25), a year occurring once every fifty years, when Jewish slaves regained their freedom and land reverted to its former owners. Just as the *sabbatical year occurred every seven years, the jubilee year occurred after seven sabbatical years. It is questionable how far the law was actually observed in OT times. (2) In the RC Church, a 'year of remission' or '*Holy Year' (q.v.) in which a special *indulgence is granted to Catholics who visit *Rome and fulfil certain conditions.

(1) R. North, SJ, *Sociology of the Biblical Jubilee* (Analecta Biblica, 4; Rome, 1954). R. de Vaux, OP, *Les Institutions de l'Ancien Testament*, 1 (1958), pp. 267–70; Eng. tr., 2nd edn., (1965), pp. 175–7. A. van Selms in *The Interpreter's Dictionary of the Bible*, ed. K. Crim and others, Suppl. vol. (Nashville [1976]), pp. 496–8, s.v.; C. J. H. Wright in *Anchor Bible Dictionary*, 3 (1992), pp. 1025–30.

Jubilees, Book of. An apocryphal Jewish work, also called 'The Little Genesis'. It purports to have been delivered by God to *Moses on Mt. *Sinai. It reinterprets the contents of Gen. 1–Exod. 12 (or, acc. to some scholars, Gen. 1–Exod. 15: 22 or Exod. 16), which are here arranged in 49 periods, each of 49 years' length, the whole forming a Jubilee of Jubilees (cf. Lev. 25: 8–13). Its purpose appears to be to show that the Law, with its prescriptions about feasts, the Sabbath, offerings, abstinence from blood and fornication (which for the writer includes intermarriage with the Gentiles), dated from patriarchal times. The original Hebrew text survives only in fragments found at *Qumran; until their discovery the work was known only from an Ethiopic translation of the whole and incomplete versions in Latin and Syriac. The fact that the surviving Hebrew fragments are from at least 12 different MSS and that they were found in three different caves indicates that the Book enjoyed considerable popularity among the Qumran community; some scholars indeed have argued that it is the work of a member of that sect. The Book, which certainly appears to stem from priestly circles, is generally dated to the 2nd cent. BC.

Ethiopic text first pub. by A. *Dillmann (Kiel, 1859); Lat. frags. ed. A. M. Ceriani, *Monumenta Sacra et Profana*, 1, part 1 (Milan, 1861), pp. 15–54; Syriac frag., 2 (ibid., 1863), pp. ix f. Crit. edn. of Ethiopic text by J. C. VanderKam (CSCO 510, Scriptores Aethiopici, 87, with Eng. tr., CSCO 511, Scriptores Aethiopici, 88; 1989). Further Syriac frags. ed., with comm., by E. Tisserant, in *R. Bibl.* 30 (1921), pp. 55–86 and 206–32. Eng. trs., with introd., by R. H. *Charles in id. (ed.), *The Apocrypha and Pseudepigrapha of the Old Testament*, 2 (Oxford, 1913), pp. 1–82; rev. by C. Rabin in H. F. D. Sparks (ed.), *The Apocryphal Old Testament* (1984), pp. 1–139, and by O. S. Wintermute in J. H. Charlesworth (ed.), *The Old Testament Pseudepigrapha*, 2 (1985), pp. 35–142. Ger. and Fr. trs., with comm., by K. Berger (Jüdische Schriften aus hellenistisch-römischer Zeit, Band 2, Lieferung 3; 1981) and by A. Caquot in A. Dupont-Sommer and M. Philonenko (eds.), *La Bible: Écrits intertestamentaires* [1987], pp. 627–810. M. Testuz, *Les Idées religieuses du Livre des Jubilés* (1960), with bibl.; G. L. Davenport, *The Eschatology of the Book of Jubilees* (Studia Post-Biblica, 20; Leiden, 1971); J. C. VanderKam, *Textual and Historical Studies in the Book of Jubilees* (Harvard Semitic Monographs, 14; Missoula, Mont., 1977); E. Schwarz, *Identität durch Abgrenzung: Abgrenzungsprozesse in Israel im 2. vorchristlichen Jahrhundert und ihre traditionsgeschichtlichen Voraussetzungen. Zugleich ein Beitrag zur Erforschung des Jubiläenbuches* (Europäische Hochschulschriften, Reihe 23, Band 162; Frankfurt, 1982); J. C. Endres, SJ, *Biblical Interpretation in the Book of Jubilees* (Catholic Biblical Quarterly Monograph Series, 18; Washington, DC, 1987). E. *Schürer, *The History of the Jewish People in the Age of Jesus Christ*, rev. Eng. tr. by G. Vermes and others, 3 (pt. 1; Edinburgh, 1986), pp. 308–18. J. C. VanderKam in *Anchor Bible Dictionary*, 3 (1992), pp. 1030–2, s.v.

Judaea. The term used in Christ's time to describe the territory corresponding broadly to that covered by the kingdom of *Judah before the *Babylonian captivity. It designated the most southern of the three districts, Galilee, Samaria, and Judaea, into which Palestine, west of the *Jordan, was divided; but in a wider sense it could be used to include the whole of Palestine (e.g. Lk. 23: 5, RV; 'Jewry' AV).

Judah. The tribe of Judah was the most powerful of the twelve tribes of *Israel. Possibly its earliest history is represented in the story of Judah, the fourth son of *Jacob (Gen. 29: 35 and ch. 38). Already in the reigns of *David and *Solomon (c.1000 BC) it was the predominant tribe. After Solomon's death (c.930 BC), Judah, with Benjamin, formed a separate kingdom (known as the kingdom of Judah) which outlasted that of the northern tribes, and in general maintained a purer religious faith. It came to an end with the *Babylonian captivity (c.586 BC). In NT times the area was known as *Judaea.

Judaism. The faith and practice of the Jewish people. The word, Greek in origin ('Ιουδαϊσμός), and familiar from the NT (Gal. 1: 13 f., AV: 'the Jews' religion'), first occurs in 2 Macc. (2: 21, 8: 1, and 14: 38). It is ultimately derived from the name of *Judah, the biblical Southern Kingdom which came to an end with the *Babylonian captivity. In modern scholarship the term is used for the faith and practice of the Jews from that time to the present day. In a wider sense, however, Judaism may be said to go back to the *Patriarchs many centuries earlier (see also ISRAEL).

An accurate assessment of the number of Jews in the world today is impossible to achieve, both for want of reliable statistics and because of serious problems of definition. According to widely accepted estimates (which include many people having little if any attachment to traditional beliefs and practices), there are about 13 million Jews, half of whom live in N. and S. America and about a quarter each in Europe and Asia (mainly in Israel). Israel, established in 1948 as a Jewish state (although without any official State religion), is the only country in the world where Jews constitute more than a small element in the population (here well over 80 per cent).

The history of Judaism may be divided into three main phases:

(1) Until AD 70 Jewish religious life and thought were focused on the *Temple in Jerusalem, with its hereditary priesthood and its daily rituals and annual celebrations involving animal and vegetable offerings. By the end of this period various sects had arisen (e.g. the *Sadducees, *Pharisees, and *Essenes), some of them profoundly critical of the Temple and its priestly establishment, and the ever-spreading *diaspora meant that pilgrimage to Jerusalem was beyond the aspirations of many Jews. The local *synagogue became the place for public gatherings for purposes of scriptural study and religious teaching, and possibly also (particularly in the diaspora) for worship. The Judaism of this period betrays some influence of the Persian and Hellenistic environment. It is the period in which the later books of the Hebrew Bible were written and the whole was edited. It was also translated into Greek (see SEPTUAGINT). The large surviving literature also includes the *Pseudepigrapha, the *Dead Sea Scrolls, and the writings of *Philo.

(2) After the destruction of the Temple by the Romans in AD 70, we lose sight of the sects, and the sacrificial form of worship ceased. Gradually, religious—and to a large extent secular—authority was concentrated in the hands of *rabbis, a new style of leadership with distinct but interrelated centres in the Holy Land and Babylonia. Rabbinic Judaism gradually spread to most parts of the Jewish world, and it remained the most characteristic form of Judaism until the 19th cent. Its classical written text is the *Talmud, but the rabbinic literature includes also the *Midrashim, various medieval biblical commentaries (e.g. the writings of *Rashi), and works of *Halachah (of which the last and most authoritative was the *Shulhan Arukh* or 'Spread Table' of Joseph Caro, first pub. in 1565). Rabbinic Judaism, as a form of Jewish 'orthodoxy', was largely shaped by its reaction to successive challenges from (among others) *Gnosticism, early Christianity, *Karaism, mystical theosophy or *Kabbala, and *Aristotelian rationalism (of which the outstanding Jewish exponent was *Maimonides).

(3) From the beginning of the *Enlightenment in 17th-cent. Europe, with the accompanying social and political changes, rabbinic orthodoxy found it increasingly difficult to resist challenges emanating from the contemporary situation, whether these took the form of religious enthusiasm (as in the case of the Messianic movement led by Shabbetai Zvi, which was halted only by his conversion to *Islam in 1667) or of rationalism and critical scholarship. The medieval political structures which had supported the rabbis and upheld their power were weakened, and very gradually the way was opened to religious pluralism, which has now again become characteristic of Judaism, at least in W. Europe and America. The first dramatic breakthrough was the success of Hasidism, a revivalist movement which swept through E. European Jewry in the period 1730–1830, subverting the authority of the rabbis in every region except Lithuania. In W. Europe various modernist movements emerged in the course of the 19th cent., laying the foundations for the best-known religious denominations in W. Judaism today: Liberalism, Reform, Conservatism, and Orthodoxy (sometimes termed 'neo-Orthodoxy' or 'moderate Orthodoxy' to distinguish it from the various forms of traditional Judaism which are still strong in Israel and elsewhere). All these modernist movements share a strong attachment to biblical and rabbinic tradition (and in the case of Conservatism and Orthodoxy a particular loyalty to rabbinic Halachah), but in many ways they have made crucial compromises with the modern world, notably in the areas of rabbinic jurisdiction, liturgical reform, and general lifestyle.

Contemporary Judaism is strongly marked by the events of the past 100 years or so, and most notably the rise of political antisemitism in Europe, the Russian pogroms and subsequent mass emigration of Jews from the Russian Empire, the emergence of various forms of Jewish nationalism, the racial persecution of the Jews in Nazi Germany, the *Holocaust, the creation of the State of Israel in 1948, and the protracted conflict between Israel and the countries of the Arab League.

Theology is less central to Judaism than to Christianity, but there is a broad acceptance (seriously challenged only in recent times) of the idea of a single, unique, incorporeal God, who created the world, acts in it, and will eventually redeem it, and who revealed His will in the *Torah and elsewhere. The form and authority of revelation constitute a major problem in contemporary Judaism, broadly dividing the 'progressive' trends (Liberalism, Reform, Conservatism) from Orthodoxy and the traditionalist camp. A non-personal conception of God was advanced by M. M. Kaplan (1881–1983), the founder of the American movement known as Reconstructionism. Other outstanding theologians in the modern period include L. Baeck (1873–1956), M. *Buber, F. Rosenzweig (1886–1929), I. Maybaum (1897–1976), and A. J. Heschel (1907–72).

Jewish worship traditionally consists of readings from the Torah, Prophets, Psalms, hymns, and set prayers. Of the many liturgical rites current in the Middle Ages, two are dominant today: the Sephardic (or Spanish and Portuguese) and Ashkenazic (or German and Polish). Movements for liturgical reform originating in the 19th cent. have resulted (particularly in the 'progressive' movements) in considerable revision, and in the introduction of vernacular languages into the synagogue.

The influence of Judaism upon Christianity has been considerable, particularly in the early Church. The Jewish tradition of Hebrew language study and biblical commentary has been exploited freely by Christian scholars of all ages. Jewish religious thinkers (such as Philo, *Avicebron, Maimonides, B. *Spinoza, and Buber) have also influenced the Christian intellectual tradition.

See also JEWS, CHRISTIAN ATTITUDES TO.

General surveys incl. L. Baeck, *Das Wesen des Judentums* (1905; Eng. tr., *The Essence of Judaism*, 1936); L. Finkelstein (ed.), *The Jews: Their History, Culture and Religion* (2 vols., New York [1949]; 3rd edn., ibid., 1960; London, 1961); I. Epstein, *Judaism: A Historical Presentation* (Harmondsworth, 1959); L. Jacobs, *Principles of the Jewish Faith* (1964); id., *A Jewish Theology* (1973); P. R. Mendes-Flohr and J. Reinharz (eds.), *The Jew in the Modern World: A Documentary History* (New York and Oxford, 1980); N. [R. M.] de Lange, *Atlas of the Jewish World* (Oxford [1984]); id., *Judaism* (ibid., 1986). Works on Jewish history and particular aspects of Judaism incl. C. Roth, *A Short History of the Jewish People 1600 B.C.–A.D. 1935* (1936; enlarged edn., 1969), and other works of this author; S. W. Baron, *A Social and Religious History of the Jews* (3 vols., New York, 1937; 2nd edn., on a larger scale, 1952 ff. [18 vols., covering the period to 1650, by 1983]); *The Cambridge History of Judaism*, ed. W. D. Davies and L. Finkelstein (1984 ff.). G. F. Moore, *Judaism in the First Centuries of the Christian Era: The Age of the Tannaim* (3 vols., Cambridge, Mass., 1927–30). E. *Schürer, *The History of the Jewish People in the Age of Jesus Christ* (rev. Eng. tr. by G. Vermes and others, 3 vols. in 4 parts, Edinburgh, 1973–87). S. Safrai and M. Stern (eds.), *The Jewish People in the First Century* (Compendia Rerum Iudaicarum ad Novum Testamentum, 1; 2 vols., Assen, 1974–6). E. P. Sanders, *Judaism: Practice and Belief 63 BCE–66 CE* (1992). M. Hadas-Lebel, *Jérusalem contre Rome* [1990]. F. Rosenzweig, *Der Stern der Erlösung* (Frankfurt, 1921; 2nd edn., 1930; Eng. tr., *The Star of Redemption*, 1971). J. Guttmann, *Die Philosophie des Judentums* (Munich, 1933; rev. Eng. tr. [1964]). C. G. Montefiore and H. Loewe (eds.), *A Rabbinic Anthology* (1938; repr., with introd. by R. Loewe, New York, 1974). S. T. Katz (ed.), *Jewish Philosophers* (Jerusalem and New York [1975]). M. M. Kaplan, *The Religion of Ethical Nationhood: Judaism's Contribution to World Peace* (New York [1970]). G. G. Scholem, *Major Trends in Jewish Mysticism* (Hilda Stich Stroock Lectures, 1938; Jerusalem, 1941; 2nd edn., New York, 1946; 3rd edn., London, 1955); id., *Sabbatai Sevi: The Mystical Messiah 1626–1676* (1973; rev. Eng. tr. of work pub. in Hebrew at Tel Aviv in 1957). A. Z. Idelsohn, *Jewish Liturgy and* *its Development* (New York [1932]); S. C. Reif, *Judaism and Hebrew Prayer: New perspectives on Jewish liturgical history* (Cambridge, 1993). Representative forms of worship incl. the *Authorized Daily Service Book of the United Hebrew Congregations of the British Empire*, ed. S. Singer (1890; 3rd edn., rev. by E. Cashdan, ed. I. Jacobovits, 1990), also ed., with comm. by J. H. Hertz (2 vols., 1946), and *Forms of Prayer for Jewish Worship*, ed. by the Assembly of Rabbis of the Reform Synagogues of Great Britain, 7th edn., vol. 1: *Daily, Sabbath, and Occasional Prayers* (1977).

Periodical Jewish publications incl. *Jewish Quarterly Review* (Philadelphia, 1888 ff.), *Revue des Études juives* (Paris, 1880 ff.), *Hebrew Union College Annual* (Cincinnati, 1924 ff.), *Jewish Social Studies* (New York, 1939 ff.), and *Journal of Jewish Studies* (London, 1948–74; Oxford, 1975 ff.); and for bibl., *Kirjath Sepher* (Jerusalem, 1924 ff.). The chief reference works are *The Jewish Encyclopedia*, ed. I. Singer (12 vols., New York and London, 1901–6), the *Encyclopædia Judaica*, ed. J. Klatzkin and others (10 vols., Berlin, 1928–34; incomplete), and C. Roth (ed.) *Encyclopaedia Judaica* (16 vols., Jerusalem [1972]).

Judaizers. In the early Church a section of Jewish Christians who regarded the OT Levitical laws as still binding on all Christians. They tried to enforce on the faithful such practices as *circumcision and the distinction between clean and unclean meats. Their initial success brought upon them the strong opposition of St *Paul, much of whose writing was concerned with refuting their errors.

Judas Iscariot. The Apostle who betrayed Christ to the Jewish authorities (Mk. 14: 10 f. and 43 f., etc.). The Gospels leave his motive uncertain, as the hint given in Jn. 12: 6 is not supported by the other three. His death is recorded in three places—in Mt. 27: 3–5, in Acts 1: 16–20, and in *Papias—but only the account in Mt. is unequivocal in seeing it as *suicide. He has been regarded with universal abhorrence in the Christian Church, though he was venerated in the *Gnostic sect of the *Cainites. If, as is usually thought, the epithet 'Iscariot' signifies 'man of Kerioth' (a place in S. Palestine), it would seem likely that Judas came from *Judaea, whereas nearly all the other Apostles were Galilaeans.

There is a vast literature; besides comm. on the Gospels and Acts, see A. Spiteri, *Die Frage der Judaskommunion neu untersucht* (Theologische Studien der Oesterr. Leo-Gesellschaft, 23; 1918); D. Haugg, *Judas Iskarioth in den neutestamentlichen Berichten* (1930); and H.-J. Klauck, *Judas—ein Jünger des Herrn* (Quaestiones Disputatae, 111 [1987]), with bibl. P. F. Baum, 'The Mediaeval Legend of Judas Iscariot', *Publications of the Modern Language Association of America*, NS 24 (1916), pp. 481–632, with extensive refs. W. Klassen in *Anchor Bible Dictionary*, 3 (1992), pp. 1091–6, s.v.

Judas Maccabaeus (d. 161 BC), leader of the Jews in the revolt against the Seleucid king of Syria. The third son of the priest, Mattathias (d. 166), who nominated him to succeed him as captain of the hosts, he won a series of spectacular victories against the Syrians in the years 166–164. In 164 he purified the *Temple and restored its worship, and in 163, partly because of dynastic troubles of the Syrians, was able to obtain full religious liberty from Antiochus V Eupator (164–162). After defeating the Idumaeans and the Ammonites, he eventually overcame the opposition of the Hellenizing party among the Jews in a battle near Beth-horon in 161. He asserted political independence by entering into negotiations with Rome to aid him against the Seleucid kings of Syria. Although his mission was diplomatically successful, before the results were known he was defeated by the Syrian general, Bacchides, and killed in a battle near Eleasa. His career is recounted in the Books of *Maccabees (q.v.).

B. Bar-Kochva, *Judas Maccabaeus: The Jewish Struggle against the Seleucids* (Cambridge, 1989). [O.] Wolff in *PW* 9 (pt. 2; 1916), cols. 2461–4, s.v. 'Judas Makkabaios'. See also works cited under MACCABEES (family) and MACCABEES, BOOKS OF.

Jude, St, *Apostle. In the lists of the Apostles at Lk. 6: 16 and Acts 1: 13 he is referred to as 'Judas of James' and in Jn. 14: 22 as 'Judas not Iscariot'. (Many identify him with *Thaddaeus or Lebbaeus who is mentioned in the lists of Apostles at Mt. 10: 3 and Mk. 3: 18.) The description 'of James' in Lk. 6: 16 and Acts 1: 13 is most naturally interpreted as 'son of James' (RV), but the Apostle has generally been identified, at least in the W., with Jude the 'brother of *James' (Jude 1), one of the '*brethren of the Lord', and the author of the Ep. of Jude (q.v.). The apocryphal 'Passion of *Simon and Jude' describes the preaching and martyrdom of the two Apostles in Persia, and in the W. Church the two saints are commemorated together. In modern times St Jude has become a popular saint in the RC Church and is much invoked in circumstances of special difficulty. Feast day in E., 19 June; in W., with St Simon, 28 Oct.

Jude's descendants are mentioned by *Eusebius, *HE* 3. 19 f. and 3. 32, citing *Hegesippus. O. *Cullmann, 'Le Douzième Apôtre', *RHPR* 42 (1962), pp. 133–40. R. [J.] Bauckham, *Jude and the Relatives of Jesus in the Early Church* (Edinburgh, 1990), pp. 1–133 *passim*. On the 'Passion of St Simon and St Jude' see R. A. *Lipsius, *Die apokryphen Apostelgeschichten und Apostellegenden*, 2 (pt. 2; 1884), pp. 142–200. J. van Hecke, SJ, in *AASS*, Oct. 12 (1867), pp. 437–49. R. Sinker in *DCA* 1 (1875), pp. 891–3, s.v. 'Jude the Apostle, St., Legend and Festival of'. See also introd. to comm. on JUDE, EPISTLE OF ST, cited s.v., and bibl. to BRETHREN OF THE LORD.

Jude, Epistle of St. One of the '*Catholic Epistles' of the NT. It purports to be written by 'Jude . . . brother of James', who is identified by *Origen, St *Jerome, and others as the *Apostle, 'Judas of James', of Lk. 6: 16 and Acts 1: 13. The aim of the Epistle was to combat the spread of dangerous doctrines through false teachers 'having not the Spirit', whose immoral life it denounces. It was recognized as canonical by the *Muratorian Canon, *Clement of Alexandria, and *Tertullian, though *Eusebius puts it among the 'Antilegomena'. The doubts were due chiefly to vv. 9 and 14; the former seems to reproduce a passage from the apocryphal 'Assumption of *Moses', while the latter definitely quotes *Enoch (1 Enoch 1.9). The date is uncertain, perhaps before the destruction of *Jerusalem, which is not mentioned among the calamities enumerated in vv. 5–7. The striking similarities between the Ep. of Jude and 2 Peter are most probably due to the use made of it by the latter.

Modern comm. by C. *Bigg (ICC, with 1–2 Pet., 1901, pp. 305–44), J. B. Mayor (London, 1907), J. N. D. Kelly (Black's NT Comm. on 1 and 2 Pet. and Jude, 1969, pp. 223–94), R. J. Bauckham (Word Biblical Comm. 50, with 1 Pet., Waco, Tex. [1983], pp. 1–127), H. Paulsen (KEK 12/2, with 2 Pet., 1992, pp. 41–87), and J. H. Neyrey (Anchor Bible, 37 C on Jud. and 2 Pet.,

1993, pp. 21–105). A. Albin, *Judasbrevet: Traditionen, Texten, Tolkningen* (Stockholm, 1962), with extensive bibl. R. [J.] Bauckham, *Jude and the Relatives of Jesus in the Early Church* (Edinburgh, 1990), pp. 134–314. J. D. Charles, *Literary Strategy in the Epistle of Jude* (Scranton, Pa., London, and Toronto [1993]). R. J. Bauckham in *Anchor Bible Dictionary*, 3 (1992), pp. 1098–103, s.v.

Judgement, General (Particular). See GENERAL (PARTICULAR) JUDGEMENT.

Judges, Book of. The Book traces the history of the Israelites from Joshua's death to the beginning of the monarchy, describing incidents connected with the conquest of Palestine, and woven round the names of several leaders ('judges') who ruled the country before the time of Saul. It professes at the outset (1: 1) to be a sequel to the Book of Joshua (q.v.), but in fact covers the same period. Its account of the entry of the Israelites into *Canaan, which depicts the settlement as gradual and spread over many years, is prob. more accurate than that in Joshua, which claims for Israel the credit of a swift and thorough victory.

After an introductory section describing the attempts of the Israelites to secure a footing at *Hebron, Debir, and *Bethel (1: 2–2: 5), the exploits of the judges are described in turn. Of these the most notable are Ehud (3: 12–30); Deborah, the prophetess (4, 5); Gideon, also called Jerubbaal (6–8); Abimelech (9); Jephthah (11, 12); and *Samson (13–16). Less prominent figures (sometimes the 'minor judges') are listed in 10: 1–5 and 12: 8–15. The compiler of the Book has supplied a framework which enabled a continuous historical narrative to be constructed out of what were probably really separate and unrelated histories of the individual judges, and has used it to illustrate his philosophy of history (2: 11–19), which saw a regular sequence of sin, punishment, penitence, and deliverance. The concluding chapters of the Book (17–21) contain incidents relating to the period, but outside this framework.

Some scholars maintain that some of the *Pentateuchal sources are identifiable in Judges and consequently have classed it as the last Book in the '*Heptateuch'. But most reckon Judges as the third Book in the series Deuteronomy–2 Kings known as the '*Deuteronomistic History'. In either case the Book throws valuable light on the pre-monarchical period, esp. on the beliefs of the early Israelites and the relation of their faith to the already existing religion in Canaan. There has been much debate about the social organization of Israel in the period portrayed in the Book, notably whether it was a tightly structured confederacy or merely a loose association of tribes.

Comm. by G. F. Moore (ICC, 1895), H. W. Hertzberg (Das Alte Testament Deutsch, 9, on Jos., Jgs., and Ruth, 1953; 2nd edn., 1959, pp. 141–256), J. Gray (New Cent. Bib., on Jos., Jgs., and Ruth, 1967, pp. 1–13 and 202–396; 2nd edn., 1986, pp. 1–38 and 185–364), R. G. Boling (Anchor Bible [1975]), and J. A. Soggin (Eng. tr. by J. S. Bowden, Old Testament Library, 1981; 2nd edn., 1987). J. Garstang, *Joshua–Judges* (1931), pp. 3–115, 263–343. W. Richter, *Traditionsgeschichtliche Untersuchungen zum Richterbuch* (Bonner biblische Beiträge, 18; 1963); id., *Die Bearbeitungen des 'Retterbuches' in der deuteronomischen Epoche* (ibid. 21; 1964). B. G. Webb, *The Book of Judges: An Integrated Reading* (Journal for the Study of the Old Testament, Suppl. Series, 46 [1987]). A. Malamat, 'The Period of the Judges', in B. Mazar (ed.), *The World History of the Jewish People*, 3 (Tel Aviv, 1971),
pp. 129–63. Brief introd. by A. D. H. Mayes, *Judges* (Old Testament Guides, Sheffield, 1985). R. G. Boling in *Anchor Bible Dictionary*, 3 (1992), pp. 1107–17.

Judicial Committee of the Privy Council. A Court of Appeal constituted in 1833 to regularize the extensive jurisdiction of the King in Council. Until the Reformation the final appeal in English ecclesiastical causes was to Rome. Under *Henry VIII, in 1533 the Ecclesiastical Appeals Act 1532 abolished appeals to Rome, and in 1534 the final appeal was transferred by the *Submission of the Clergy Act 1533 to the King in Chancery, although the jurisdiction was actually exercised by a Commission of Delegates, later known as the Court of *Delegates. By the Privy Council Appeals Act 1832 this jurisdiction was transferred to the Privy Council, and then the Judicial Committee Act 1833 constituted a Judicial Committee to hear these and other appeals. It consists of at least three senior serving or retired English or Commonwealth judges, who sit unrobed. Initially it determined appeals from both the Court of the Arches (now the *Arches Court of Canterbury) and the Chancery Court of *York, and gained much notoriety through a series of ritual and doctrinal cases brought before it in the 19th cent., of which the *Gorham case was the most celebrated. Under the *Ecclesiastical Jurisdiction Measure 1963 it ceased to have any jurisdiction in cases of discipline, but it continues to hear faculty appeals not involving doctrine, ritual, or ceremonial. It also hears appeals against schemes proposed under the Cathedrals Measure 1976 and the Pastoral Measure 1983. See also LINCOLN JUDGEMENT.

Judith, Book of. OT Apocryphal Book. The Book relates how Nebuchadnezzar, 'who reigned over the Assyrians in Nineveh' (1: 1), failed to gain the support of certain nations, including the Jews, in his conflict with Arphaxad, King of the Medes, and determined to punish them by his general Holofernes (1: 1–2: 13). At first the Jews decide to resist (2: 14–4: 15). But when their city Bethulia is besieged and deprived of its water supply, they weaken through the persuasions of Ozias (5–7). Judith, a young and beautiful widow of great piety, upbraids Ozias and promises to deliver her people. (The name 'Judith' means 'Jewess', and she appears to personify faithful and resistant Israel.) She makes her way to the camp of Holofernes, who is captivated by her charms (10–12), and, having enticed him into a state of drunkenness, seizes a sword, cuts off his head and carries it back in a bag to Bethulia (13). The head is publicly displayed (14), the Israelites are encouraged to advance, and the Assyrians flee in panic (15). The narrative concludes with Judith's hymn of thanksgiving (16), perhaps the oldest part of the Book.

The whole Book is wildly unhistorical and was prob. never intended to be read as history. Its orig. language was Heb., but it now exists only in Gk. and other versions dependent upon Gk. texts. It prob. dates from the Maccabaean period, though some modern scholars have connected it with the time of Artaxerxes Ochus (359–338), chiefly because a Cappadocian named Holofernes fought in his armies. In the Christian Church it was known to *Clement of Rome, *Clement of Alexandria, and *Origen. In the Roman Breviary, part of the 'Hymn of Judith' (16:

2–3, 15–19) is now recited at *Lauds on Wednesdays in the first week of the monthly cycle.

Crit. edn. of the Gk. text by R. Hanhart (Septuaginta. Vetus Testamentum Graecum auctoritate Academiae Scientiarium Gottingensis editum, 8.4; Göttingen, 1979). Gk. text, with Eng. tr. and comm. by M. S. Enslin, ed. S. Zeitlin (Dropsie University Jewish Apocryphal Literature, 7; Leiden, 1972). Eng. tr., with comm., by A. E. Cowley in R. H. *Charles (ed.), *The Apocrypha and Pseudepigrapha of the Old Testament*, 1 (Oxford, 1913), pp 242–67, and J. C. Dancy, *The Shorter Books of the Apocrypha* (Camb. Bib., NEB, 1972), pp. 67–131. E. Haag, *Studien zum Buche Judith: Seine theologische Bedeutung und literarische Eigenart* (Trierer theologische Studien, 16; 1963). A. M. Dubarle, OP, *Judith: Formes et sens des diverses traditions* (Analecta Biblica, 24; 2 vols., Rome, 1966). G. Brunner, *Der Nabuchodonosor des Buches Judith* (1940; 2nd edn., 1959). G. W. E. Nickelsburg, *Jewish Literature Between the Bible and the Mishnah* (Philadelphia [1981]), pp. 105–9, with bibl. p. 158. E. *Schürer, *A History of the Jewish People in the Age of Jesus Christ*, rev. Eng. tr. by G. Vermes and others, 3 (pt. 1; 1986), pp. 216–22. Eissfeldt, pp. 585–7. See also bibl. to APOCRYPHA.

Judson, Adoniram (1788–1850), American *Baptist missionary to *Burma. He was born at Malden, Mass., and educated at Brown University (1804–7). In 1808 he entered the Andover Theological Seminary, and in 1810 went to England to confer with the *LMS and to seek for co-operation with the American Board of Foreign Missions in the East. Having been ordained a *Congregational minister in 1812, he sailed for Calcutta. On reaching Serampore, Judson became a Baptist. After permission to continue in the territories of the East India Company was refused, he went to Mauritius, and in 1813 to Rangoon, where he began to translate the Bible into Burmese. During the war with England in 1824–5 he was imprisoned. In 1829 he transferred the seat of the mission to Moulmein, but travelled also among the Karens, a tribe living farther north, where he met with great success. In 1842 he began work on a Burmese dictionary, which was eventually completed in 1849. He died soon afterwards on a voyage undertaken to recover his broken health. His first wife, Ann Hasseltine (d. 1826), and his second wife, Sarah Boardman, gave him notable assistance in his work and are remembered on their own account.

Lives by F. Wayland (London, 2 vols., 1853), L. Bonar (ibid., 1871) and Edward Judson (son; ibid., 1883). Modern sketch by B. R. Pearn (ibid., 1962). W. H. Allison in *Dict. Amer. Biog.* 10 (1933), pp. 234 f.

Julian (c.386–454), *Pelagian theologian, briefly Bp. of Eclanum, in Apulia. Born in Apulia of Christian parents, he married before he was ordained. In 416 he became Bp. of Eclanum. On his refusal to subscribe, in 417, the condemnation of Pelagianism published by *Zosimus, he was deprived of his see and banished. He travelled widely in search of protection or toleration, appealing in turn to *Theodore of Mopsuestia, *Nestorius, Sixtus III, and others; but was repeatedly condemned in various local councils, and repeatedly exiled by the civil powers. He is believed to have died in Sicily. His only uncontested works, besides three letters, are four books 'Ad Turbantium' and eight 'Ad Florum'; considerable portions of these are preserved in St *Augustine's replies. They belong to the period 418–26. In them Julian appears to

have possessed keen dialectical ability, as well as philosophical insight. His account of the worth and powers of human nature is coherent, and his indictment of Augustine's doctrine of the total depravity of fallen man (which he held to be a consequence of the *Manichaean errors of Augustine's youth), although couched in rather scurrilous terms, is powerful; but his conception of human self-sufficiency is not easily reconciled with the Christian doctrine of man's sinfulness. During the 20th century various exegetical works have been ascribed to him, as well as a Latin translation of Theodore of Mopsuestia's commentary on the Psalms.

Works, incl. those recently ascribed to him, ed. L. de Coninck (CCSL 88 and 88 A; 1977). A. Bruckner, *Julian von Eclanum, sein Leben und seine Lehre* (TU 15. 3; 1897); id., *Die vier Bücher Julians von Aeclanum an Turbantius* (1910). G. Morin, 'Un Ouvrage restitué à Julien d'Éclane', *R. Bén.* 30 (1913), pp. 1–24; A. Vaccari, SJ, *Un commento a Giobbe di Giuliano di Eclano* (1915). G. Bouwman, SVD, *Des Julian von Aeculanum Kommentar zu den Propheten Osee, Joel und Amos: Ein Beitrag zur Geschichte der Exegese* (Analecta Biblica, 9; 1958). H. I. Marrou, 'La Canonisation de Julien d'Éclane', *Hist. J.* 77 (1958), pp. 434–7, repr. in id., *Patristique et Humanisme* (Patristica Sorbonensia, 9 [1976]), pp. 373–7. F. Refoulé, OP, 'Julien d'Éclane, théologien et philosophe', *Rech. S.R.* 52 (1964), pp. 42–84, 233–47. Y.-M. Duval, 'Julien d'Éclane et Rufin d'Aquilée. Du Concile de Rimini à la répression pélagienne. L'intervention impériale en matière religieuse', *Revue des Études Augustiniennes*, 24 (1978), pp. 243–71. CPL (3rd edn., 1955), pp. 262–4 (nos. 773–7a). V. Grossi in Quasten (cont.), *Patrology*, 4 (1986), pp. 487–92.

Julian (d. after 518), Bp. of Halicarnassus in Caria. On the accession of the Emp. Justin I (518), he was deposed from his see because of his refusal to accept the Christological teaching of the Council of *Chalcedon (see MONOPHYSITISM) and took refuge in *Alexandria. His friendship with *Severus of Antioch was brought to an end by the *Aphthartodocetic controversy in which Julian upheld the incorruptibility of the body of Christ. Fragments of his works can be recovered from Severus' polemic against him. The Commentary on Job formerly ascribed to him appears to be the work of an unknown *Arian author of the 4th cent., dubbed *Julian the 'Arian'.

The standard work is R. Draguet, *Julien d'Halicarnasse et sa controverse avec Sévère d'Antioche sur l'incorruptibilité du corps du Christ* (Louvain, 1924; with frags. in Syr. and Gk. retranslated, also full bibl.). Id., 'Pièces de polémique antijulianiste', *Muséon*, 44 (1931), pp. 255–317 (text and Lat. tr.), and 54 (1941), pp. 59–89 (text and Fr. tr.). Severus' works against Julian ed., with Fr. tr., R. Hespel (CSCO 244–5, 295–6, 301–2, and 318–19; 1964–71). M. Jugie, AA, 'Julien d'Halicarnasse et Sévère d'Antioche', *ÉO* 24 (1925), pp. 129–62, 257–85. Altaner and Stuiber (1978), p. 507. R. Draguet in *DTC* 8 (pt. 2; 1925), cols. 1931–40; M. Simonetti in *DPAC* 2 (1984), cols. 1603 f., s.v. 'Giuliano di Alicarnasso'; Eng. tr. in *Encyclopedia of the Early Church*, 1 (1992), p. 458, s.v.

Julian, St (c.644–90), Abp. of Toledo. Born into a converted Jewish family, he was educated at the episcopal school of Toledo. Though initially attracted to the monastic life, he was ordained as a secular priest and in 680 consecrated Bp. of Toledo. During his episcopate he consolidated the position of Toledo as the most important metropolitan see in Spain; he revived the tradition of holding national councils in the Visigothic capital, presiding over four Councils of *Toledo between 681 and 688, and asserted the right of Spanish bishops to independent judgement on matters of theological debate. His insistence on choosing his own terms for the rejection of *Monothelitism after the Third Council of *Constantinople (680–81) earned him a reproof from Pope Benedict II and placed a temporary strain on relations between Spain and Rome. As a bishop he was renowned for his alms-giving, sense of justice, and concern for the liturgy. His extant theological works include the *Apologeticum de tribus capitulis*, a defence of his Christology (in particular his use of the phrases *voluntas genuit voluntatem* of the relation of the Father to the Son and 'three substances in Christ' of the body, soul, and divinity of Christ) against the criticism of Pope Benedict; the *De comprobatione sextae aetatis*, a refutation of the Jewish belief that Christ has not yet come; the *Antikeimena*, a series of solutions to apparent contradictions in the Bible; and the *Prognosticum futuri saeculi*, a treatment of the *Last Things which was to prove popular during the Middle Ages. In all these he displays a vigorous and economical style, combined with impressive mastery of patristic sources. His other works include an account of a military expedition undertaken by the Visigothic king Wamba (*Historia Wambae regis*) and a eulogy of his predecessor, St *Ildefonsus. Feast day, 8 Mar.

Works ed. Card. F. de Lorenzana, Abp. of Toledo, in *Sanctorum Patrum Toletanorum quotquot extant Opera*, 2 (Madrid, 1785), pp. 1–384; repr. in J. P. Migne, *PL* 96. 453–808. Crit. edns. of major writings apart from the *Antikeimena*, by J. N. Hillgarth and others (CCSL 115; 1976), with valuable introd.; of *Elogium Ildefonsi* by J. Madoz, SJ, in *Estudios Eclesiásticos*, 26 (1952), pp. 468–71; and of an *Ars grammatica* traditionally ascribed to Julian by M. A. H. Maestre Yenes (Toledo, 1973). Analysis of possible 'Julianic' recension of the *Hispana Collection by G. Martínez Díez, SJ, *La Colección Canónica Hispana*, 1 (Monumenta Hispaniae Sacra, serie canónica, 1; 1966), pp. 218–38. The main source for his biography is a 7th-cent. Life by his successor, Felix of Toledo, pr. in J. P. Migne, *PL* 96. 445–52. J. Madoz, SJ, 'San Julián de Toledo', *Estudios Eclesiásticos*, 26 (1952), pp. 39–69. F. X. Murphy, CSSR, 'Julian of Toledo and the Condemnation of Monothelitism in Spain', *Mélanges Joseph de Ghellinck*, 1 (Gembloux, 1951), pp. 361–73; id., 'Julian of Toledo and the Fall of the Visigothic Kingdom in Spain', *Speculum*, 27 (1952), pp. 1–27. J. N. Hillgarth, 'St. Julian of Toledo in the Middle Ages', *Journal of the Warburg and Courtauld Institutes*, 21 (1958), pp. 7–26 (repr. in id., *Visigothic Spain, Byzantium and the Irish* (1988), no. 4); id., 'Las fuentes de San Julián de Toledo', *Anales Toledanos*, 3 (1971), pp. 97–118. J. Campos, 'El "De comprobatione sextae aetatis libri tres" de Julián de Toledo', *Helmantica*, 18 (1967), pp. 297–340. U. Dominguez del Val, *Estudios sobre literatura latina hispano-cristiana*, 1: 1955–1971 (Corpus Patristicum Hispanum, 2; Madrid, 1986), pp. 362–9. A. Robles Sierra in *Dict. Sp.* 8 (1974), cols. 1600–2, s.v., with further bibl.

Julian the Apostate (332–63), 'Flavius Claudius Julianus', Roman Emperor from 361. He was born at *Constantinople, the nephew of *Constantine the Great (Emp. 311–37) and cousin of Constantius II (Emp. 337–61). In 337, after the murder of all his near male relations except his half-brother Gallus, Julian, a very precocious child, was entrusted to the care of a eunuch, Mardonius, and *Eusebius of Nicomedia. Already possessing strong pagan leanings, he was banished with Gallus in 345 to the remote fortress of Macellum in Cappadocia, where efforts were made to bring him under Christian influences. In

351, when Gallus was made Caesar, Julian became free to leave Cappadocia. He went first to Constantinople and then to Nicomedia, where before long he was won to *Neoplatonism, mainly through the influence of the Sophist, Maximus of Ephesus. After Gallus' execution (end of 354), Julian was held captive at Milan; but in 355 he gained permission to visit the schools at Athens, where he was initiated into the Eleusinian mysteries. Among his fellow-students at Athens was St *Gregory of Nazianzus. On 6 Nov. 355 he was presented to the army as Caesar. He soon justified his nomination by his successes in a difficult military situation, in Aug. 357 inflicting a decisive defeat on the Alamanni at Strasbourg. He also carried through some drastic administrative reforms in Gaul. When Constantius, jealous of Julian's popularity, sought to take over the flower of Julian's army for his Persian campaigns, the soldiers resisted and proclaimed Julian Emperor (360). Civil war was prevented only by Constantius' death in Nov. 361.

Now that he was sole Emperor, Julian embarked on an ambitious programme for reform. With regard to the Church, his policy was to degrade Christianity and promote paganism by every means short of open persecution. He sought to re-establish the heathen worship throughout the empire; ordered all instruction in the Imperial schools to be completely paganized; retracted the legal and financial privileges accorded to the Christians by his predecessors; published polemical treatises against Christian doctrine; and even inflicted barbarous sentences on persons guilty only of Christian faith and practice. He also attempted to weaken the Church internally by allowing all exiled Bishops to return to their sees with a view to creating dissensions. At the same time he attempted to reform the morals and elevate the theology of paganism, himself giving (it must be allowed) a conspicuous example of austerity and purpose.

Having spent the winter of 361–2 at Constantinople, in May 362 he set out for *Antioch in preparation for a campaign against the Persians. In Asia Minor and Syria his strict discipline and strong anti-Christian policy made him very unpopular. In March 363 he set out for Mesopotamia. On 26 June 363 he was struck by an arrow and died the same night. The well-known story that he died with the words 'Vicisti Galilaee' ('Thou hast conquered, Galilean!') is a late embellishment of a passage in Theodoret (*HE* 3. 25).

Julian was an extensive author. His chief writings are (1) a set of eight Orations, including two panegyrics on Constantius, two on true and false cynicism, and theosophical orations on King Helios and on the Mother of the Gods; (2) a set of letters, more than 80 of which have come down under Julian's name (some perhaps spurious); (3) 'Symposium' or 'Caesares', a satire on the vices of past Emperors; (4) 'Misopogon' (the 'Beard Hater'), a satire written at Antioch on the licentiousness of the inhabitants; (5) some epigrams. Unique interest attaches to (6) his 'Adversus Christianos', written during the Persian campaign. Though no MS of this last survives, nearly the whole text can be recovered from *Cyril of Alexandria's refutation of the work.

Collected edns. by E. Spanheim (Leipzig, 1696), F. C. Hertlein (2 vols., Teub., 1875–6), W. C. Wright (with Eng. tr., 3 vols., Loeb, 1913–23), and crit. edn., incorporating six new letters discovered by A. Papadopoulos-Kerameus at Halki in 1884, by J.

Bidez, G. Rochefort, and C. Lacombrade (Collection Guillaume Budé, 2 vols. in 4, 1924–64, with Fr. tr.). His work against the Christians, reconstructed from Cyril of Alexandria (not included in edns. of Hertlein or Bidez, etc.), ed. C. J. Neumann (Scriptorum Graecorum qui Christianam impugnaverunt religionem quae supersunt, fasc. 3; Leipzig, 1880).

The chief ancient authority for his life is Ammianus Marcellinus (*Hist.* 15. 8–25). Other pagan sources are Libanius, Eunapius, and Claudius Mamertinus. Christian writers (naturally all very hostile) incl., besides the Church Historians and Chroniclers, some poems of St *Ephraem Syrus, two invectives of St Gregory of Nazianzus, and St Cyril of Alexandria's reply already mentioned. Convenient Eng. tr. of a panegyric by Claudius Mamertinus and a homily and hymns against Julian by St John *Chrysostom and Ephraem Syrus respectively, ed., with introd. and bibl., by S. N. C. Lieu (Translated Texts for Historians, 2; Liverpool, 1986; 2nd edn., 1989).

The study of J. Bidez, *La Vie de l'empereur Julien* (Collection des Études anciennes publiée sous le patronage de l'Association Guillaume Budé, 1930), supersedes all earlier works. Other studies by P. Allard (3 vols., Paris, 1900–3), G. Ricciotti (Milan, 1946; Eng. tr., Milwaukee [1960]), R. Browning (London, 1975), and G. W. Bowersock (ibid., 1978). P. Athanassiadi-Fowden, *Julian and Hellenism: An Intellectual Biography* (Oxford, 1981). R. Braun and J. Richer (eds.), *L'Empereur Julien: De l'histoire à la légende* (2 vols., 1978). W. J. Malley, SJ, *Hellenism and Christianity: The Conflict between Hellenic and Christian Wisdom in the* Contra Galilaeos *of Julian the Apostate and the* Contra Julianum *of St Cyril of Alexandria* (Analecta Gregoriana, 210; Rome, 1978). B. de Gaiffier, SJ, ' "Sub Iuliano Apostata" dans le Martyrologe Romain', *Anal. Boll.* 74 (1956), pp. 5–49. There are also full accounts by J. *Wordsworth in *DCB* 3 (1882), pp. 483–525; A. *Harnack in *PRE* (3rd edn.), 9 (1900), pp. 609–19; and E. von Borries in *PW* 10 (pt. 1; 1917), cols. 26–91, all s.v.

Julian the 'Arian' (4th cent.), theologian. Many passages in the *catenae ascribed to 'Julian', and attributed by an older generation of scholars to *Julian, Bp. of Halicarnassus, are now thought to come from the 4th cent. and betray a loosely *Arian provenance. In 1973 D. Hagedorn published a reconstructed text of a commentary on Job which he ascribed to Julian the 'Arian'. Hagedorn also argued that this Julian may be the compiler of the *Apostolic Constitutions and be responsible for the long recension of the letters of St *Ignatius of Antioch.

D. Hagedorn, *Der Hiobkommentar des Arianers Julian* (Patristische Texte und Studien, 14; 1973). *CPG* 2 (1974), p. 10 (no. 2075), with refs. to earlier lit.

Julian of Norwich (*c.*1342–after 1416), English spiritual writer. Little is known of her life, except that by 1394 she was an *anchoress, prob. at St Julian's church, *Norwich. Acc. to her own account, in May 1373 she received a revelation, consisting of 15 'showings' (and one more 'showing' the day after). Her book, commonly known in modern times as *Showings* or *Revelation(s) of Divine Love*, survives in two recensions. The first draft (the Short Text) was prob. written soon after 1373, but it was not until 1393 at the earliest that she completed the Long Text, in which she expounds an original and competent theological vision of life, on the basis of the revelation and her reflections upon it. She freed herself from conventional 'contemplative' notions and came to see that the content of the revelation was identical with that of the faith, and must therefore contain doctrine applicable to all Christians. The kernel of her message is God's love, but she does not shrink from the speculative problems posed by sin and evil. She develops a twofold understanding of human life in terms of 'substance', which is inseparably united with God, and 'sensuality', which is the life we perceive ourselves to be living in this world, and which is characterized in varying degrees by an inability to see God's love clearly. 'Substance' and 'sensuality' are united in Christ by the Incarnation, and esp. by the Passion and Resurrection. Julian finds in the Passion the key to the understanding of all that is wrong with this world, as somehow part of God's purpose in creating human beings in whom 'sensuality' can become capable of union with God. Her doctrine is essentially one of the coherence of creation and redemption in the *predestination of the elect in Christ; it is exemplified, for instance, in her uniquely unsentimental use of the fairly common medieval idea of Christ as mother, which she sees at work in human motherhood and in the way in which Divine providence allows people to get hurt, while protecting them from ultimate harm. No literary sources have been certainly identified, but it is clear that Julian was theologically well informed. Feast day in parts of the Anglican Communion, 8 May.

Crit. edn. of both texts by E. Colledge, OSA, and J. Walsh, SJ (Pontifical Institute of Mediaeval Studies, Studies and Texts, 35; Toronto, 1978). The Long Text is also conveniently ed., on the basis of one MS, for the use of students, by M. Glasscoe (Exeter Medieval English Texts, 1976). Modern trs. by C. Wolters (Penguin Classics, 1966) and E. Colledge, OSA, and J. Walsh, SJ (Classics of Western Spirituality, 1978). P. Molinari, SJ, *Julian of Norwich* (1958). W. Riehle, *Studien zur englischen Mystik des Mittelalters* (Anglistische Forschungen, 120; 1977; Eng. tr., 1981). J. P. H. Clark, '*Fiducia* in Julian of Norwich', *Downside Review*, 99 (1981), pp. 97–108, 214–29; id., 'Predestination in Christ according to Julian of Norwich', ibid. 100 (1982), pp. 79–91; id., 'Nature, Grace and the Trinity in Julian of Norwich', ibid., pp. 203–20; R. Bradley, 'Christ the Teacher in Julian's *Showings*. The Biblical and Patristic Traditions', in M. Glasscoe (ed.) *The Medieval Mystical Tradition in England: Papers Read at Dartington Hall, July 1982* (Exeter, 1982), pp. 127–42. B. Pelphrey, *Love was his Meaning: The Theology and Mysticism of Julian of Norwich* (Salzburg Studies in English Literature, Elizabethan & Renaissance Studies, 92: 4; Salzburg, 1982). M. A. Palliser, OP, *Christ, our Mother of Mercy: Divine Mercy and Compassion in the Theology of the* Shewings *of Julian of Norwich* (Berlin and New York, 1992). S. [C. ff.] Tugwell, OP, *Ways of Imperfection* (1984), pp. 187–207. V. M. Lagorio and R. Bradley, *The 14th-Century English Mystics: A Comprehensive Annotated Bibliography* (New York and London, 1981), pp. 105–26. E. Colledge, OSA, and J. Walsh, SJ, in *Dict. Sp.* 8 (1974), cols. 1605–11, s.v. 'Julienne de Norwich'.

Juliana of Liège, Bl (*c.*1192–1258), champion of the Feast of *Corpus Christi. Born at Retinnes, near Liège, and bereft of her parents, she was placed in the *Augustinian convent of Mont Cornillon, near Liège, where she made rapid spiritual progress and experienced visions. Once professed (1206), she devoted all her energies to securing the establishment of a Feast of Corpus Christi. In 1230 she became superior; but meeting with great opposition in the convent, she was forced to leave and took refuge in the city of Liège. Here, through the intervention of a recluse at St Martin's church, she won to her cause John of Lausanne, one of the canons, who secured in turn the warm interest of James Pantaléon, then Archdeacon of Liège and later Pope Urban IV. The Bp. of Liège having obtained her restoration for a brief space, the feast was formally proclaimed in 1246, to be observed in the diocese of Liège for the next year. But the Bishop died (16 Oct. 1246) before the year was up; the feast was not repeated in Juliana's lifetime; and she herself was again exiled and passed the last years of her life first in a monastery near Namur and later as a recluse at Fosses. The real reward of her efforts was the institution of the Feast of Corpus Christi after her death by Urban IV in 1264. Her cultus was confirmed in 1869. Feast day, 5 Apr.

Latin tr. of contemporary Fr. Life (1258–62) in *AASS*, Apr. 1 (1675), pp. 443–75. Later Lives by U. Berlière, OSB (anon., Namur, 1884), G. Simenon (Brussels, 1946), and J. Coenen ('Heiligen van onzen Stam', Bruges, 1946). E. Denis, *La Vraie Histoire de sainte Julienne de Liége et l'institution de la Fête-Dieu* (Tournai, 1935). F. Baix and C. Lambot, OSB, *La Dévotion à l'eucharistie et VIIe centenaire de la Fête-Dieu* (Namur, 1946), *passim*. E. W. McDonnell, *The Beguines and Beghards in Medieval Culture* (New Brunswick, NJ, 1954), esp. pp. 299–309. A. Piolanti in *EC* 6 (1951), cols. 736–8, with bibl. See also other works cited s.v. CORPUS CHRISTI.

Jülicher, Adolf (1857–1938), NT scholar. Born at Falkenberg, he received a pastoral appointment at Rummelsburg near Berlin in 1882. From 1889 to 1923 he was professor of theology at Marburg. His two principal writings were *Die Gleichnisreden Jesu* (2 vols., 1888–9), in which he insisted that the Lord's *Parables must be understood as real similes and not as allegories, and *Die Einleitung in das Neue Testament* (1894; Eng. tr., 1904), a careful critical introduction to the NT writings. He also made extensive studies in the *Old Latin versions of the NT (*Itala*. 1: 'Matthäus-Evangelium', 1938). His other writings included *Paulus und Jesus* (1907), *Hat Jesus gelebt?* (1910), and an edition of St *Vincent of Lérins' *Commonitorium* (1895).

Autobiography in E. Stange (ed.), *Die Religionswissenschaft der Gegenwart*, 4 (1928), pp. 159–200. *Festgabe für A. Jülicher*, hrsg. von R. *Bultmann und H. von Soden (1927). H.-J. Klauck, 'Adolf Jülicher—Leben, Werk und Wirkung', in G. Schwaiger (ed.), *Historische Kritik in der Theologie* (Studien zur Theologie und Geistesgeschichte des Neunzehnten Jahrhunderts, 32; 1980), pp. 99–150. N. van Bohemen, OFM, in *Dict. Bibl.*, Suppl. 4 (1949), cols. 1414–17, s.v.

Julius I, St (d. 352), Pope from 337. In the *Arian struggle he was a strong supporter of orthodoxy and one of the chief influences leading to its ultimate triumph. He gave shelter to *Marcellus of Ancyra at Rome after his condemnation at the Council of *Constantinople (336), and later to *Athanasius after his escape from *Alexandria in 339. In 342–3 he convoked the Council of *Sardica, which consolidated the W. against Arianism and pronounced Athanasius the rightful occupant of his see. Through the appellate jurisdiction allowed by can. 3 (Gk.) of the Council to Julius as Bp. of Rome, his name has secured notoriety in connection with the rise of the Papal claims. Two of Julius' letters, which survive in Greek, are evidence of his remarkable statesmanship. His pontificate was marked by the building of two new churches in Rome, S. Maria in Trastevere and the Basilica Julia (now the Church of the Twelve Apostles). Feast day, 12 Apr.

The two letters mentioned are preserved in Athanasius, *Apologia c. Arianos*, 21–35 and 52 f. Other (spurious) Epp. attributed to him are by *Apollinarian writers; texts in H. *Lietzmann, *Apol-*

linarius von Laodicea und seine Schule, 1 (1904), pp. 185–93, 193–203, 256–62, 283–6, 292 f., 307–10, 310–18, 318. Material on Julius collected in J. P. Migne, *PL* 8. 857–944, and Suppl. by A. Hamman, OFM, 1 (1958), cols. 191 f. C. Pietri, *Roma Christiana: Recherches sur l'Église de Rome . . . de Miltiades à Sixte III* (Bibliothèque des Écoles Françaises d'Athènes et de Rome, 224; 1976), pp. 187–237. J. Barmby in *DCB* 3 (1882), pp. 526–32; J. P. Kirsch in *CE* 8 (1910), p. 561; J. Chapin in *NCE* 8 (1967), pp. 51 f.

Julius II (1443–1513), Pope from 1503. Giuliano della Rovere was the descendant of an impoverished noble family of Albissola, nr. Savona. He lived for some time at a house of Conventual *Franciscans under the supervision of his uncle, Francesco della Rovere. On the latter's accession to the Papacy as *Sixtus IV in 1471 he was created cardinal and loaded with benefices, holding several bishoprics and abbacies *in *commendam*. He took part in many political missions, and under Innocent VIII, whose election he had secured by means of bribery, continued to play a leading role in Papal affairs. When in 1492 his personal enemy, Rodrigo Borgia, was elected as *Alexander VI he fled to Charles VIII of France, and even after a formal reconciliation with the Pope in 1498 continued to live in hiding, mostly in N. Italy. After Alexander's death in 1503 he returned to Rome, and after the short reign of Pius III was himself elected Pope in the same year, having promised the cardinals to continue the war against the Turks, to call a General Council within two years, and to follow their advice in all matters of importance. These undertakings, however, which would have seriously limited the Papal power, he did not carry into effect. The principal achievement of his pontificate was the restoration and enlargement of the temporal power, which was to safeguard Papal independence in times to come. To assist in this aim he drove Cesare *Borgia from Italy in 1504. In 1506 he conducted an expedition against Perugia and *Bologna, both of which submitted to his sovereignty, and in 1509 he joined the League of Cambrai against *Venice, which had frequently resisted Papal claims. After the city had been defeated with the help of France he turned against the latter and, in 1511, founded the Holy League, including England, Spain, Venice, and Switzerland, for the purpose of defeating it. Louis XII replied by calling a Council to depose the Pope at Pisa in 1511. After Julius had deprived the rebellious cardinals who attended the Council of their dignity it retired to Milan, where Julius was declared suspended in 1512. At the same time the Pope called a Council at the Lateran and won the Emp. Maximilian over to his side. The *Pragmatic Sanction was condemned and France thus remained isolated. The death of Julius on 20–21 Feb. 1513, however, ended the conflict.

Though Julius II was chiefly a statesman and a military leader, he initiated certain important ecclesiastical reforms. His constitution 'De fratrum nostrorum' (1503) declared null and void every pontifical election brought about by simony. He was a patron of Renaissance art and recognized the genius of *Raphael, *Michelangelo, and Bramante. In 1506 he laid the cornerstone of the Basilica of *St Peter. Among the many immortal works inspired by his generosity are Michelangelo's statue of Moses in San Pietro in Vincoli, the paintings in the *Sistine Chapel, and Raphael's frescoes in the Vatican. His indulgence for the rebuilding of St Peter's was the occasion later of M.

*Luther's 95 Theses. His warlike character was scathingly attacked by *Erasmus in his *Moriae Encomium* ('Praise of Folly').

E. Rodocanachi, *Le Pontificat de Jules II* (1928); I. Cloulas, *Jules II: Le Pape Terrible* [1990]; C. Shaw, *Julius II: The Warrior Pope* (Oxford, 1993). F. Seneca, *Venezia e Papa Giulio II* (Padua, 1962). W. Ullmann, 'Julius II and the Schismatic Cardinals', in D. Baker (ed.), *Schism, Heresy and Religious Protest* (Studies in Church History, 9; 1972), pp. 177–93. L. Partridge and R. Starn, *A Renaissance Likeness: Art and Culture in Raphael's* Julius II (Berkeley, Calif., and London, 1980). Pastor, 6 (1923), pp. 185–607. G. Mollat in *DTC* 7 (pt. 2; 1925), cols. 1918–20, s.v. 'Jules II'; G. B. Picotti in *EC* 6 (1951), cols. 750–8, s.v. 'Giulio II'; D. R. Campbell in *NCE* 8 (1967), pp. 52–4, s.v.

Julius III (1487–1555), Pope from 1550. Giovanni Maria Ciocchi del Monte studied jurisprudence at Perugia and Siena, was made Abp. of Siponto in 1511, and under *Clement VII and *Paul III held administrative posts in Rome and the Papal states. He was taken as a hostage by the Imperial forces after the sack of Rome in 1527. In 1545 he opened the Council of *Trent as its first president and Papal legate, and had an important share in its transference to Bologna in 1547. Elected Pope in 1550 after a long and stormy conclave, in 1551 he commanded the Council to resume its sessions, but had to suspend it in the next year owing to political difficulties. During his pontificate he did much for the *Jesuits, confirming the order and endowing it with new privileges. On the death of *Edward VI in 1553, he sent Cardinal R. *Pole to England with far-reaching faculties. During the last three years of his life, however, Julius III more and more lost interest in the reform of the Church. His love of the arts—he was a protector of *Michelangelo—and of pomp, as well as his nepotism, range him with the typical Renaissance Popes.

The principal source is A. Massarelli, *Diaria*, 5–7 (ed. S. Merkle, *Concilii Tridentini Diariorum*, 2, Freiburg i.B., 1911, pp. 1–249). V. Schweitzer, *Zur Geschichte der Reform unter Julius III* (Görres-Gesellschaft, 3; 1907). C. Erdmann, 'Die Wiedereröffnung des Trienter Konzils durch Julius III', *Quellen und Forschungen aus italienischen Archiven und Bibliotheken*, 20 (1928–9), pp. 238–317. H. Jedin, 'Analekten zur Reformtätigkeit der Päpste Julius' III. und Pauls IV.', *RQ* 42 (1934), pp. 305–32; 43 (1935), pp. 87–156. G. De Leva, 'La elezione di Papa Giulio III', *Rivista Storica Italiana*, 1 (1884), pp. 22–38. Pastor, 13 (1924). Fliche and Martin, 18 (1948), pp. 105–45, with refs. G. Mollat in *DTC* 8 (pt. 2; 1925), cols. 1920 f., s.v.; G. B. Picotti in *EC* 6 (1951), cols. 758–605, s.v. 'Giulio III'. See also works cited under TRENT, COUNCIL OF.

Julius Africanus, Sextus (c.180–c.250), Christian writer. Acc. to *Suidas, he was born in Libya, but the facts of his life are unclear. He may originally have been a Jew. He enjoyed close relations with the royal house of *Edessa. He went on a successful embassy from *Emmaus to the Emp. Heliogabalus (218–22) which led to the township being rebuilt as Nicopolis. Under the Emp. Alexander Severus (222–35) he played a significant part in planning the new public library at the Pantheon at Rome. He also had connections with *Origen. Despite a later tradition (Dionysius bar-Salibi) that he was ordained, it is likely that he remained a layman.

His chief work was a 'History of the World' (Χρονογραφίαι) to AD 217 in five Books, of which fragments are preserved in *Eusebius' 'Chronicle', *George

Syncellus, and other writers. He held that the world would last for 6,000 years from the Creation and that the Birth of Christ, which he antedated in relation to his own times by three years, took place in the year 5500. His 'Embroidered Girdles' (Κεστοί) is an encyclopaedic work in 24 Books, dedicated to Alexander Severus, on natural history, medicine, military science, magic, and miscellaneous subjects. This, too, survives only in fragments. He was also the author of two letters, one to Origen contesting the genuineness of the story of *Susanna and the other to a certain Aristides on the *genealogies of Christ in Matthew and Luke, both epistles showing good critical powers.

Frags. collected by M. J. *Routh, *Reliquiae Sacrae* (2nd edn., 1844), 2, pp. 238–309; repr. in J. P. Migne, *PG* 10. 63–94. New edn. of *Epp.* by W. Reichardt in *TU* 34. 3 (1909); of frags. of Κεστοί, with Fr. tr., by J.-R. Vieillefond (Publications de l'Institut Français de Florence, 1ʳᵉ Série, no. 20; 1970). His 'Ep. to Origen' will be found in all edns. of Origen. Both it, and Origen's reply, are ed., with Fr. tr. and introd., by N. de Lange (SC 302, 1983, pp. 469–578). H. Gelzer, *Sextus Iulius Africanus und die byzantinische Chronographie* (2 vols., 1880–98); F. Granger, 'Julius Africanus and the Library of the Pantheon', *JTS* 34 (1933), pp. 157–66. H. Chantraine, 'Der metrologische Traktat des Sextus Iulius Africanus, seine Zugehörigkeit zu den Κεστοί und seine Authentizität', *Hermes*, 105 (1977), pp. 422–41. F. C. R. Thee, *Julius Africanus and the Early Christian View of Magic* (Hermeneutische Untersuchungen zur Theologie, 19; 1984), incl. Eng. tr. of frags. of Κεστοί. E Amann in *DTC* 8 (1924), cols. 1921–5, s.v. with bibl.; and W. Kroll and J. Sickenberger in *PW* 10 (1919), cols. 116–25. See also bibl. to GEORGE SYNCELLUS.

Jumièges (Lat. *Gemeticum*), *Benedictine abbey on the Lower Seine 17 miles W. of Rouen. Founded c.654 by St *Philibert (q.v.), it rapidly developed in size and influence, sending missionaries to England and Ireland. In 841 it was plundered by the Normans and ten years later almost completely destroyed. After restoration and a second destruction, it rose to become one of the chief cultural centres in N. Europe, and through the patronage of *William the Conqueror, under whom the partly surviving abbey church was built (1040–67), it became the richest monastery in Normandy, continuing to prosper through most of the Middle Ages. Despoiled in 1562 by the *Huguenots, it was restored in 1573, and in the 17th cent. became linked to the *Maurist reform. Benedictine life finally came to an end in 1790, after which the buildings were largely destroyed. Since 1918 its imposing ruins have been under State protection.

J. Loth (ed.), *Histoire de l'abbaye royale de Saint-Pierre de Jumièges par un religieux bénédictin de la congrégation de Saint-Maur* (3 vols., Rouen, 1882–5). R. Martin du Gard, *L'Abbaye de Jumièges: Étude archéologique des ruines* (Montdidier, 1909). J. J. Vernier (ed.), *Chartes de l'abbaye de Jumièges (v. 825 à 1204), conservées aux archives de la Seine-Inférieure* (2 vols., Rouen, 1916). *Jumièges: Congrès Scientifique du XIIIᵉ Centenaire* (2 vols., ibid., 1955). L. Musset, *Normandie romane*, 2 (La Pierre-qui-Vire, 1974; 2nd edn., 1985), pp. 59–126, with summary in Eng., pp. 296–8. H. *Leclercq, OSB, in *DACL* 8 (pt. 1; 1928), cols. 412–20, s.v., with bibl. L. M. Cottineau, OSB, *Répertoire topo-bibliographique des abbayes et prieurés* (Mâcon, 1935), cols. 1496–9, s.v., for detailed refs.

Jumpers. A nickname of the Welsh *Calvinistic Methodists, from their former custom of 'leaping for joy' at their meetings.

Jung Codex. The title given to Codex I of the *Nag Hammadi papyri which was acquired in 1952 by the Jung Institute for Analytical Psychology at Zurich. It is now with the other codices in Cairo.

Jurieu, Pierre (1637–1713), French *Calvinist controversialist. A grandson of the Reformed theologian Pierre *du Moulin, he was born at Mer, in the diocese of Blois, where his father was minister. He studied at Saumur, then at Sedan, where he obtained his doctorate in theology in 1658. He then travelled, possibly to Holland, certainly to England. He is said to have received Anglican orders, but this is uncertain. He was ordained minister at Mer, prob. in 1661. In 1674 he was appointed professor of theology and Hebrew at Sedan. His *Traité de la dévotion* (1675; Eng. tr., 1692) had a huge circulation. His many works of controversy are energetic and not always orthodox. The important *Traité de la puissance de l'Église* (1677) uses juridical arguments to vindicate the Calvinist view of authority in the Church. From this date he also espouses a pluralist ecclesiology. His anonymous *Politique du clergé* (1681; Eng. tr., 1681), suggesting that the primary loyalty of the French Catholic clergy was to Rome not France, put him in danger. On the suppression of the Academy at Sedan in 1681 he became minister in the Walloon church at Rotterdam, where he remained for the rest of his life. He continued to publish works against his French Catholic adversaries, notably J.-B. *Bossuet, A. *Arnauld, and P. *Nicole. A tireless worker for all aspects of the Calvinist cause, and confidant of William of Orange, he dominated the growing French refugee community in the Netherlands. The revocation of the Edict of *Nantes (1685) led him to write *L'Accomplissement des prophéties* (1686; Eng. tr., 1687) predicting the Divine reinstatement of the Calvinist Church in France for 1689. His famous *Lettres pastorales*, published fortnightly from 1686 to 1689, record the sufferings and constancy of the oppressed Protestants in France, urging them to witness publicly to their faith. The work also includes an important theory of political authority, to justify the 1689 revolution in England. From the later 1680s he was increasingly involved in internecine quarrels, opposing toleration and 'liberal theology'. His critics included P. *Bayle.

There is much primary material in J. G. de Chaufepié, *Nouveau Dictionnaire historique et critique*, 3 (Amsterdam, 1753), 1/J, pp. 57–82, s.v. F. R. J. Knetsch, *Pierre Jurieu: Theoloog en Politikus der Refuge* (Kampen, 1967); R. J. Howells, *Pierre Jurieu: Antinomian Radical* (Durham Modern Language Series, FM 2; Durham, 1983). E. Labrousse, 'Note sur Pierre Jurieu', *RHPR* 58 (1978), pp. 277–97. R. Struman, 'La Perpétuité de la foi dans la controverse Bossuet–Jurieu, 1686–1691', *RHE* 37 (1941), pp. 145–89. G. H. Dodge, *The Political Theory of the Huguenots of the Dispersion, with special Reference to the Thought and Influence of Pierre Jurieu* (New York and London, 1947). E. Kaeppler, 'Bibliographie chronologique des œuvres de Pierre Jurieu (1637–1713)', *Bulletin de la Société de l'Histoire du Protestantisme Français*, 84, 6th ser. 8 (1935), pp. 391–440; F. R. J. Knetsch, 'Un contributo alla bibliografia di Pierre Jurieu (1637–1713)', *Rivista di Storia e Letteratura Religiosa*, 9 (1973), pp. 457–76.

jus devolutum. In the Church of *Scotland, the right devolving on a *Presbytery to elect a minister to a vacant charge when the congregation, after nine months, has failed to make an appointment. It is only rarely exercised,

as an extension of time, if requested, can be granted to the congregation concerned.

justification. In dogmatic theology, the event or process by which man is made or declared to be righteous in the sight of God. Despite the suggestion of the etymological form of the Latin verb *justificare* (*justum facere*, 'to make righteous'), it is widely held that in the NT (and esp. in St *Paul) the Greek δικαίωσις and its cognates reflect Hebrew usage, and are thus to be understood as legal metaphors signifying 'vindication' or 'declaring to be righteous'. St *Augustine, however, interpreted the Latin term *iustificatio* to mean 'making righteous', thus establishing a tradition which remained unchallenged until the end of the Middle Ages. At the time of the *Reformation, controversy surrounded both the meaning of the term, as well as the means by which justification comes about. In classical *Protestant theology, 'justification' was interpreted as God 'declaring man to be righteous' (thus recovering the sense of the original Hebrew term), to be distinguished from sanctification, in which man is 'made righteous'. The Council of Trent defined justification in strongly transformational terms, rejecting the Protestant understanding of the concept. In both *Lutheranism and *Calvinism, justification is an act of God, effected without man's co-operation (an idea expressed in formulae such as *sola fide* ('by faith alone') and *sola gratia* ('by grace alone')). According to the Council of Trent, justification requires man's co-operation with God. A further difference of importance concerns the formal cause of justification, which Protestants held to be the imputed righteousness of Christ, and Trent defined as the inherent or imparted righteousness of Christ. Much Anglican theology has followed the Calvinist tradition on this point, though classical High Anglicanism of the 17th and 18th cents., while affirming that man is justified by grace through faith, insisted that he must also labour for salvation, doing the good works prepared by God for him to walk in. Recent ecumenical discussions have suggested that many of these distinctions are verbal rather than substantial, with the result that a degree of consensus on the doctrine has emerged, for instance in the Agreed Statement of the Second *Anglican–Roman Catholic International Commission (1987). However, the biblical roots of the doctrine have been challenged by some NT scholars whose interpretation of Pauline theology, and the function of justification language within it, have cast doubts upon traditional (esp. Lutheran) accounts.

The subject is treated in all major works of dogmatic theology and in comm. on the Pauline Epp. (esp. Rom. and Gal.). The classic study of the Protestant doctrine is A. *Ritschl, *Die christliche Lehre von der Rechtfertigung und Versöhnung*, 1 (Bonn, 1870; Eng. tr., Edinburgh, 1872). J. H. *Newman, *Lectures on Justification* (1838; 3rd edn., 1874). J. Buchanan, *The Doctrine of Justification* (Edinburgh, 1867). H. Rückert, *Die Rechtfertigungslehre auf dem Tridentinischen Konzil* (Arbeiten zur Kirchengeschichte, 3; 1925). H. *Küng, *Rechtfertigung: Die Lehre Karl Barths und eine katholische Besinnung* (Einsiedeln, 1957; Eng. tr. of 4th edn., 1964, repr. with additional material, 1981). J. Baur, *Salus Christiana: Die Rechtfertigungslehre in der Geschichte des christlichen Heilsverständnisses*, 1 (Gütersloh, 1968; all pub.). J. A. Ziesler, *The Meaning of Righteousness in Paul* (Society for New Testament Studies, Monograph Series, 20; Cambridge, 1972). J. [H. P.] Reumann, *'Righteousness' in the New Testament: 'Justi-*

fication' in the United States Lutheran–Roman Catholic Dialogue, with responses by J. A. Fitzmyer, SJ, and J. D. Quinn (Philadelphia, 1982). P. Toon, *Justification and Sanctification* (1983). A. E. McGrath, *Iustitia Dei: A History of the Christian Doctrine of Justification* (2 vols., Cambridge, 1986). *Salvation and the Church: An Agreed Statement by the Second Anglican–Roman Catholic International Commission* (1987). J. D. G. Dunn, 'The Justice of God. A renewed perspective on justification by faith', *JTS* NS 43 (1992), pp. 1–22. J. Rivière in *DTC* 8 (pt. 2; 1925), cols. 2042–227, s.v.; G. Quell and G. Schrenk in *TWNT* 2 (1935), pp. 176–229 (Eng. tr., 2 (1964), pp. 174–225), s.v. δίκη; G. Klein and others in *RGG* (3rd edn.), 5 (1961), cols. 825–46, s.v. 'Rechtfertigung'; M. D. Crossan and P. de Letter, SJ, in *NCE* 8 (1967), pp. 77–92, s.v.

Justin Martyr, St (*c.*100–*c.*165), early Christian *Apologist. He was born of pagan parents at Flavia Neapolis ('Nablus'), the ancient Shechem in *Samaria. He was converted from pagan philosophy to Christianity *c.*130, though whether the account of his search through various philosophies (*Dial.* 2) is historically accurate, is disputed. He continued as a philosopher (wearing the *pallium*), now teaching Christianity, first at *Ephesus, where he engaged in his Disputation with Trypho the Jew (*c.*135), and later at *Rome, where he opened a Christian school, having *Tatian (q.v.) as one of his pupils. Here he wrote his 'First Apology' (*c.*155), addressed to the Emp. Antoninus Pius and his adopted sons (*Marcus Aurelius and Lucius Verus), and soon afterwards issued his 'Dialogue with Trypho'. His 'Second Apology', addressed to the Roman Senate, was apparently written shortly after the accession of Marcus Aurelius (161). He and some of his disciples were denounced as Christians *c.*165 (acc. to Tatian, by the Cynic philosopher Crescens); and on refusing to sacrifice they were scourged and beheaded. The authentic record of their martyrdom ('Martyrium S. Iustini et Sociorum'), based on an official court report, survives. Feast day in the E., 1 June; in the W., formerly 14 April; since 1969, 1 June.

Justin is the most outstanding of the 'Apologists', i.e. of those writers (mainly in the 2nd cent.) who, in the face of persecution by the Roman authorities, wrote defences (ἀπολογίαι) of Christianity. Their first concern was to rebut charges of *atheism and immorality ('Thyestian feasts, Oedipodean intercourse') and the underlying charge of sedition. But they went further and argued that Christianity was a true philosophy, in comparison with which other philosophies were either false, or (as Justin himself argued) shadows of the truth fulfilled in Christ. In support of this argument Justin developed his doctrine of the 'generative' or 'germinative' Word (λόγος σπερματικός), who had sown the seed of truth in all men and who had become incarnate in Christ, to teach men the whole truth and to redeem them from the power of the demons. Justin also used his doctrine of the Logos to explain why Christians, while remaining *monotheists, worshipped Jesus Christ, regarding Him as an incarnation of the Logos, 'in second place' to God.

This teaching is expounded in his two 'Apologies' and in the 'Dialogue with Trypho'. The later chapters of the 'First Apology' give a brief account of the ceremonies of *Baptism and the *Eucharist. The 'Dialogue' argues that the fulfilment of the prophecies in Christ proves the transitoriness of the Old Covenant and the vocation of the Gentiles to take the place of Israel, and uses Middle Platonic ideas to interpret OT theophanies as manifestations of the Logos. Justin also taught a form of *Millenarianism.

A large number of other works have circulated from early times under Justin's name, all of them spurious. One group belongs to the late 2nd and 3rd cents. and consists of an 'Address to the Greeks', an 'Exhortation to the Greeks,' and a work 'On the Monarchy of God'. Another group is probably all the work of a single author of the Aristotelian school (4th–5th cent.). Yet another pseudo-Justinian work—the 'Expositio Rectae Fidei'—is by *Theodoret.

Of the earlier edns. of Justin, the best is that of P. *Maran, OSB (Paris, 1742). The only complete modern crit. edn. is that of J. C. T. Otto (2 vols., Jena, 1842–3; 3rd edn. in 5 vols., 1876–81). J. P. Migne, *PG* 6 (1857). *Apologies*, ed. with notes by A. W. F. Blunt (1911), by M. Marcovich (Patristische Texte und Studien, 38; 1994), and, with Fr. tr., by C. Munier (Paradosis, 38; 1994). Eng. tr. in *ANCL* (1867); also of 'Dialogue with Trypho', by A. L. Williams (Translations of Christian Literature, 1930), with useful introd. Comm. on 'Dialogue with Trypho', 1–9, by J. C. M. van Winden, *An Early Christian Philosopher* (Philosophia Patrum, 1; Leiden, 1971). Modern edn. of Pseudo-Justin's 'Address to Greeks', 'Exhortation to the Greeks' and 'On the Monarchy of God' by M. Marcovich (Patristische Texte und Studien, 32; 1990).

E. R. Goodenough, *The Theology of Justin Martyr* (1923); P. Prigent, *Justin et l'Ancien Testament* (Études Bibliques, 1964); N. Hyldahl, *Philosophie und Christentum: Eine Interpretation der Einleitung zum Dialog Justins* (Acta Theologica Danica, 9; Copenhagen, 1966); A. J. Bellinzoni, *The Sayings of Jesus in the Writings of Justin Martyr* (Supplements to *Novum Testamentum*, 17; Leiden, 1967); L. W. Barnard, *Justin Martyr: His Life and Thought* (Cambridge, 1967); E. F. Osborn, *Justin Martyr* (Beiträge zur historischen Theologie, 47; 1973); R. Joly, *Christianisme et Philosophie: Études sur Justin et les Apologistes grecs du deuxième siècle* (Université Libre de Bruxelles, Faculté de Philosophie et Lettres, 52; 1973). O. Skarsaune, *The Proof from Prophecy: A Study in Justin Martyr's Proof-Text Tradition: Text-Type, Provenance, Theological Profile* (Supplements to *Novum Testamentum*, 56; 1987). B. *Capelle, 'Le Rescrit d'Hadrien et S. Justin', *R. Bén.* 39 (1927), pp. 365–8. W. Schmid, 'Die Textüberlieferung der Apologie des Justin', *ZNTW* 40 (1941), pp. 87–138. C. Andresen, 'Justin und der mittlere Platonismus', ibid. 44 (1952–3), pp. 157–95; R. Holte, 'Logos Spermatikos. Christianity and Ancient Philosophy according to St. Justin's Apologies', *Studia Theologica*, 12 (1958), pp. 109–68; J. H. Waszink, 'Bemerkungen zu Justins Lehre vom Logos Spermatikos', in *Mullus: Festschrift Theodore Klauser* (Jahrbuch für Antike und Christentum, Ergänzungsband 1; 1964), pp. 380–90. H. Chadwick, 'Justin Martyr's Defence of Christianity', *Bulletin of the John Rylands Library*, 47 (1965), pp. 275–97. *CPG* 1 (1983), pp. 29–35 (nos. 1073–89). J. Quasten, *Patrology*, 1 (Utrecht, 1950), pp. 196–219. Altaner and Stuiber (1978), pp. 65–71 and 554 f. H. S. *Holland in *DCB* 3 (1882), pp. 560–87, s.v. 'Justinus (2) Martyr, St.'; G. Bardy in *DTC* 8 (pt. 2; 1925), cols. 2228–77, s.v. 'Justin'; C. Kannengiesser, SJ, and A. Solignac, SJ, in *Dict. Sp.* 8 (1974), cols. 1640–7, s.v., with extensive bibl.

Justina, St. See CYPRIAN, ST, OF ANTIOCH.

Justinian I (*c.*483–565), Roman Emperor from 527. He was the most energetic of the early Byzantine Emperors, making it his aim to restore the political and religious unity of the empire in E. and W. He reconquered N. Africa from the Vandals and Italy from the Goths. A great builder, he erected many *basilicas at *Constantinople (including

*Sancta Sophia), *Ravenna, and elsewhere; and a sound juridical basis for the empire was established by his new legal Code (see following entry). As the champion of orthodoxy he persecuted the *Montanists, whom he almost exterminated, closed the celebrated ancient philosophical schools at Athens in 529, and forced many pagans to accept Baptism. His unsuccessful efforts to reconcile the *Monophysites issued not only in his condemnation of the memory, as well as some alleged doctrines, of *Origen (see ORIGENISM), but also in the *Three Chapters controversy (which led to the Second Council of *Constantinople, 533), in the humiliation of Pope *Vigilius, and in a schism in the W.

C. Diehl, *Justinian et la civilisation byzantine au VI⁰ siècle* (1901); J. B. Bury, *History of the Later Roman Empire*, 2 (1923); P. N. Ure, *Justinian and his Age* (Pelican Book, A 217; 1951); A. H. M. Jones, *The Later Roman Empire*, 1 (Oxford, 1964), pp. 269–302; J. W. Barker, *Justinian and the Later Roman Empire* (Madison, Wis., and London, 1966). W. Schubart, *Justinian und Theodora* [1943]; R. Browning, *Justinian and Theodora* (1971; rev. edn., 1987). G. G. Archi (ed.), *L'Imperatore Giustiniano: Storia e Mito. Giornate di Studi a Ravenna, 14–16 ottobre 1976* (Circolo Toscano di Diritto Romano e Storia del Diretto, 5; Milan, 1978). A. Cameron, *Procopius and the Sixth Century* (1985), *passim.* A. Knecht, *Die Religionspolitik Kaiser Justinians I* (1896). E. K. Chrysos, Ἡ Ἐκκλησιαστικὴ Πολιτικὴ τοῦ Ἰουστινιανοῦ (Analecta Vlatadon, 3; 1969), with summary in Ger. A. Grillmeier, SJ, *Jesus der Christus im Glauben der Kirche*, 2 (pt. 2; Freiburg etc, 1989), pp. 331–498; Eng. tr. (1995), pp. 315–475. Krumbacher (2nd edn.), pp. 57 f., 928–41; Bardenhewer, 5, pp. 20–4. J. Bryce in *DCB* 3 (1882), pp. 538–59; M. Jugie, AA, in *DTC* 8 (pt. 2; 1925), cols. 2277–90, s.v.; H. *Leclercq, OSB, in *DACL* 8 (pt. 1; 1928), cols. 507–604, s.v.; P. Gray in *TRE* 17 (1988), pp. 478–86, s.v., with full bibl.

Justinian, Code of. This revision, enlargement, and rearrangement of the *Theodosian Code (q.v.) was published by *Justinian (q.v.) in 529. It survives only in a revised edition embodying later constitutions which dates from 534. It was supplemented by further constitutions known as 'Novellae' and also by the 'Digest' (533), a comprehensive set of passages from juristic textbooks and commentaries of the classical period, and the 'Institutes of Justinian' (533), a revised and modified edition of those of Gaius with extracts from similar works. Together the Code, Novellae, Digest, and Institutes constituted the so-called *Corpus Juris Civilis*; this became the authoritative and ordered statement of Roman law which was gradually accepted, subject to local variations, throughout W. Europe (to a lesser extent than elsewhere in England), until it was superseded by modern codes which are still partly based on it. The sixth 'Novella' provides the classic formulation of the Byzantine theory concerning the relationship between Church and State. A distinction is drawn between the imperial authority (*imperium*) and the priesthood (*sacerdotium*), the former being concerned with human affairs and the latter with things divine; the two are regarded as closely interdependent, but, at least in theory, neither is subordinated to the other. The Code much influenced the development of *canon law in the W., esp. in the later Middle Ages.

Standard edns. of the Code by P. Krueger (Berlin, 1877); of the Digest by T. *Mommsen (2 vols., ibid., 1870); of the Institutes by P. Krueger (ibid., 1869); and of the Novellae by R. Schoell and G. Kroll (ibid., 1895). The text of the Institutes was repr., with

Eng. tr., by J. B. Moyle (2 vols., Oxford, 1883); that of the Digest with Eng. tr. ed. A. Watson (4 vols., Philadelphia [1985]). R Mayr, *Vocabularium Codicis Justiniani* (2 vols., Prague, 1923–5 P. Collinet, *Études historiques sur le droit de Justinien* (5 vols., 1912 53); H. S. Alivisatos, *Die kirchliche Gesetzgebung des Kaisers Justin ian I* (Neue Studien zur Geschichte der Theologie und de Kirche, 17; 1913). A. A. Schiller, *Roman Law: Mechanisms Development* (The Hague, Paris, and New York [1978]), pp. 37– W. Ullmann, *Law and Politics in the Middle Ages* (1975), pp 53–69. G. Mollat in *DDC* 4 (1949), cols. 644–81, s.v. 'Corpu Juris Civilis', with bibl.

Justus, St (d. *c.*627), Abp. of *Canterbury. He was sen to England in 601 in Pope *Gregory's second band of mis sionaries. When *Ethelbert created a second Kentish se at *Rochester in 604, St *Augustine appointed Justus it first bishop. In the pagan reaction under Eadbald he fled with *Mellitus, Bp. of London, to Gaul, but came bac when the Kentish Church again received royal protection On the death of Mellitus (624), Justus succeeded him a Canterbury, where he consecrated St *Paulinus for mis sion work in Northumbria. He was buried at St Au gustine's Abbey, Canterbury. Feast day, 10 Nov.

The main source is *Bede, *HE* 1. 29, 2. 3–9 and 2. 18; comm by J. M. Wallace-Hadrill (Oxford, 1988), pp. 43, 64 f., and 8: There is an 11th-cent. Life by *Goscelin, mainly based on Bede pr. by H. *Delehaye, SJ, in *AASS*, Nov. 4 (1925), pp. 535– with comm., pp. 532–5. W. *Stubbs in *DCB* 3 (1882), pp. 592 f s.v. 'Justus (22)'.

Juvenal (d. 458), Bp. of *Jerusalem from *c.*422. Nothin is known of his early life. His chief ambition seems to hav been to make Jerusalem into a *'Patriarchal see' at th expense of the metropolitical see of *Caesarea and th 'Patriarchal see' of *Antioch. For this purpose he side with *Cyril, Bp. of Alexandria, against *Nestorius at th Council of *Ephesus in 431, asserting that the Bp. Antioch (John) 'ought to have obeyed the apostolic see Jerusalem, by which the throne of Antioch should be cor rected and judged'. But Cyril, though glad of his support refused to further his claims. In the *Eutychian contro versy he figured as the chief supporter of *Dioscorus, th successor of Cyril, in his violent proceedings at th *Latrocinium of Ephesus (449). But when two years late Dioscorus was tried at the Council of *Chalcedon, Juvena went over to the winning side and voted for his condemna tion. As a reward, perhaps, he secured the Council's recog nition of Jerusalem as a Patriarchal see with jurisdictio over the whole of Palestine. On his return he was faced b a revolt organized by the monks who favoured Dioscorus and only the action of the Imperial government enable him to regain his see. In parts of the E. he is revered as saint; feast day, 2 July.

S. Vaillé, AA, 'Formation du patriarcat de Jérusalem', *ÉO* 1 (1910), pp. 325–36. F. M. Abel, OP, 'Saint Cyrille d'Alexandri dans ses rapports avec la Palestine', in *Kyrilliana, 444–194 (Cairo, 1947), pp. 214–20. E. Honigmann, 'Juvenal of Jerusalem *Dumbarton Oaks Papers*, 5 (1950), pp. 209–79. E. Venables in *DC. 3 (1882), pp. 595–8, s.v. 'Juvenalis (2)'; G. Fedalto in *L.Th.K (3rd edn.), 5 (1996), col. 1116.

Juvencus, Caius Vettius Aquilinus (early 4th cent. Christian Latin poet. He was a Spanish presbyter of nobl descent, who wrote *c.*330 a Life of Christ in some 3,20 lines of hexameter verse, based mainly on Matthew supplemented by the infancy narratives from Luke an some of the early chapters of John; it emphasized the transitoriness of the created universe and contrasted it with the glory and eternity of the Christian hope. The author's purpose was evidently to provide Christian readers with religious poetry to take the place of the popular pagan works. In its execution his work shows at every turn the influence of the study of *Virgil.

Works in J. P. Migne, *PL* 19. 9–388; crit. edns. of his *Libri Evangeliorum IIII* by C. Marold (Teub., 1886) and J. Huemer (CSEL 24; 1891). K. Marold, 'Ueber das Evangelienbuch des Juvencus in seinem Verhältniss zum Bibeltext', *Zeitschrift für wissenschaftliche Theologie*, 33 (1890), pp. 329–41. N. Hansson, *Textkritisches zu Juvencus* (Lund, 1950). J.-M. Poinsotte, *Juvencus et Israël: La représentation des Juifs dans le premier poème latin chrétien* (Publications de l'Université de Rouen [1979]). A. di Berardino in Quasten (cont.), *Patrology*, 4 (1986), pp. 265–9.

Juxon, William (1582–1663), Abp. of *Canterbury. He was educated at St John's College, Oxford, where he studied law, and in 1609 became Vicar of St Giles, Oxford. In 1621 he succeeded his friend, W. *Laud, as president of St John's College, and actively assisted him in his revision of the university statutes. In 1633 he succeeded him as Bp. of London. Though known to be a *High Churchman, he had a reputation for tolerance, and this fact, combined with his integrity and generosity, led him to be trusted by Churchmen of all types. After Laud's imprisonment, he became the regular adviser of *Charles I, whom he attended at his execution (1649). A little later he was deprived of his bishopric; but otherwise he was practically unmolested under the Commonwealth. At the Restoration he was the obvious choice for the see of Canterbury, but survived for only three years.

T. A. Mason, *Serving God and Mammon: William Juxon, 1582–1663* (Newark, Del., and London [1985]). W. H. *Hutton in *DNB* 30 (1892), pp. 233–7.

K

Kabbala (Rabbinic Heb. קַבָּלָה, *qabbālāh*, 'tradition'). A system of Jewish *theosophy which, by the use of an esoteric method of interpretation of the OT, including cyphers, was believed to reveal to its initiates hidden doctrines, e.g. the creation of the world by means of emanations from the Divine Being. It was a development of tendencies akin to *Gnosticism, and reached the height of its influence in the later Middle Ages and at the Renaissance. A Christian form of it also had considerable vogue in the 15th–16th cents., its Christian exponents such as J. *Reuchlin and *Paracelsus professing to deduce by its means such doctrines as the Trinity, the Atonement, and the Divinity of Christ.

The *Zohar* tr. into Eng. by H. Sperling, M. Simon, and P. P. Levertoff (5 vols., 1931–4). Extensive extracts ed. F. Lachower and I. Tishby, tr. D. Goldstein, *The Wisdom of the Zohar* (3 vols., Oxford, 1989), with introd. by I. Tishby, 1, pp. 1–126. Shorter selection tr. by D. C. Matt (Classics of Western Spirituality, 1983). Other material tr. by R. C. Keiner, *The Early Kabbalah*, ed. with introd., by J. Dan (ibid. [1986]). G. G. Scholem, *Major Trends in Jewish Mysticism* (Jerusalem, 1941; 2nd edn., New York, 1946; 3rd edn., London, 1955); id., *Zur Kabbala und ihre Symbolik* (Zurich, 1960; Eng. tr., 1965); id., *Ursprung und Anfänge der Kabbala* (Studia Judaica, 3; 1962; Eng. tr., Princeton, NJ [1987]); id., *Kabbalah* (Jerusalem [1974]); M. Idel, *Kabbalah: New Perspectives* (New Haven, Conn., and London [1988]). J. L. Blau, *The Christian Interpretation of the Cabala in the Renaissance* (New York, 1944); F. Secret, *Les Kabbalistes chrétiens de la Renaissance* (1964). G. G. Scholem, *Bibliographia Kabbalistica* (Berlin, 1933; additions in *Kirjath Sepher*, Jerusalem, 1933 ff.). Id. in *Encyclopaedia Judaica*, 10 (Jerusalem, 1971), cols. 489–653, s.v. 'Kabbalah'; R. Goetschel and O. Betz in *TRE* 17 (1988), cols. 487–509, s.v., both with bibl.

Kaftan, Julius Wilhelm Martin (1848–1926), Protestant theologian. A native of Schleswig, he became professor of systematic theology at Basle in 1881 and of apologetics and the philosophy of religion at Berlin in 1883. He sought to reinterpret the *Ritschlian soteriology so as to allow an adequate place for personal experience in religion. Believing that St Paul's system of theology was the outcome of reflection on his vision of Christ on the Damascus road, he held that the Atonement must be understood by mystical and ethical categories, and that there was no place in the doctrine of Christ's work for any notion of satisfaction or of the reconciliation of God with man (as contrasted with that of man with God). His writings include *Das Wesen der christlichen Religion* (1881), *Die Wahrheit der christlichen Religion* (1888), and a *Dogmatik* (1897 and many later editions). Among his later works were *Kant, der Philosoph des Protestantismus* (1905) and *Jesus und Paulus* (1907).

His elder brother, **Theodor Kaftan** (1847–1932), who was General Superintendent for Schleswig from 1886 to 1917, was also a theologian of some influence, who held similar beliefs.

J. W. M. Kaftan, *Neutestamentliche Theologie* (1927; from his remains). Short autobiog. in E. Stange (ed.), *Die Religionswissen-schaft der Gegenwart in Selbstdarstellungen*, 4 (1928), pp. 201–31. Notice by A. Titius in *Zeitschrift für Theologie und Kirche*, NF 8 (1927), pp. 1–20. W. Göbell in *TRE* 17 (1988), pp. 518–21, s.v.

On Theodor Kaftan, *Erlebnisse und Beobachtungen . . . von ihm selbst erzählt* (Kiel, 1924; 2nd edn., Gütersloh, 1931). W. Göbell, loc. cit., pp. 521–3, s.v.

Kagawa, Toyohiko (1888–1960), Japanese Christian social reformer. He came of a wealthy family and received his early education in a Buddhist monastery. After conversion to Christianity and disinheritance by his family, he studied at the *Presbyterian seminary at Kobe from 1905 to 1908. Here he became acutely conscious of Christian responsibility in the face of existing social evils and spent several years among the poor in the bad slums of Shinkawa. In 1914 he went to Princeton, USA, to study modern social techniques, and after returning to Japan in 1917 devoted himself entirely to the improvement of social conditions. In 1921 he founded the first Labour Union and the first Peasant Union in the country; in 1923 he organized relief work after the Yokohama earthquake; in 1928 he founded the National Anti-War League; and in 1930 he established the Kingdom of God Movement to promote conversions to Christianity. In 1940 he was imprisoned for a time as a pacifist. After the War he became a leader in the movement for democracy in Japan. He expounded his ideals in innumerable writings, incl. *The Religion of Jesus* (Eng. tr., 1931), *New Life through God* (Eng. tr., 1932), and *Brotherhood Economics* (Rauschenbusch Lectures, 1937).

There is a biog. introd. by E. M. Hinder and H. F. Topping in J. F. Gressitt's tr. into Eng. of Kagawa's *Love the Law of Life* (1930), pp. 1–37. W. Axling, *Kagawa* (1932; 8th edn. rev., 1946). C. J. Davey, *Kagawa of Japan* (1960). G. B. Bikle, *The New Jerusalem: Aspects of Utopianism in the Thought of Kagawa Toyohiko* (Association for Asian Studies, Monograph, 20; Tucson, Ariz. [1976]).

Kähler, Martin (1835–1912), *Lutheran theologian. He was born at Neuhausen in E. Prussia, the son of a pastor. Apart from three years teaching at the University of Bonn (1864–7), his professional academic life was spent at Halle, where he became professor of systematic theology and NT in 1879. His principal work was a major book on dogmatics, *Die Wissenschaft der christlichen Lehre* (1883), which took the doctrine of *justification as its central theme. He is, however, chiefly remembered for a pamphlet entitled *Der sogenannte historische Jesus und der geschichtliche, biblische Christus* (1892; extended 1896), in which he attacked the 19th cent. attempts to reconstruct the Jesus of history. Such attempts were, he claimed, just as much exercises in human speculation as the dogmatic Christological theories against which their authors were reacting. The real Christ is the Christ of the Bible, and He is the Christ of the *kerygma, rather than of doctrine or of historical research. However, Kähler was not indifferent to the historical question. He claimed that the impression of the Lord in the NT is realistic, and that poetic imagination could not have produced a convincing picture of a unique sinless person. His negative view of the '*historical Jesus' was taken up by K. *Barth and R. *Bultmann in their *dialectical theology. He also contributed a number of important articles to *PRE* (3rd edn.).

The orig. 1892 *Der sogenannte historische Jesus und der geschichtliche, biblische Christus* consisted of a single lecture in 2 parts given to a clergy conference. This was incorporated, as the 2nd of 4 chs., in the much enlarged 2nd edn. (1896). The 1st edn., with some extracts from the 2nd edn., ed. E. Wolf (Munich, 1953); 2nd edn. ed. id. (ibid., 1956). The *So-Called Historical Jesus and the Historic, Biblical Christ*, ed. C. E. Braaten (Philadelphia, 1964) comprises an Eng. tr. of the 1892 edn. (pp. 42–97) and of the 1st ch. of the 1896 edn. (pp. 100–148), with a useful introd. by the ed. (pp. 1–38). Further works of Kähler ed. by his son, E. Kähler: *Geschichte der protestantischen Dogmatik im 19. Jahrhundert* (Munich, 1962), with list of his works, pp. 292–307, and *Aufsätze zur Bibelfrage* (ibid., 1967). A. Kähler (daughter, ed.), *Theologe und Christ: Erinnerungen und Bekenntnisse von Martin Kähler* (1926), incl. text of Kähler's autobiog. for the years 1835–67, pp. 1–234. H.-G. Link, *Geschichte Jesu und Bild Christi: Die Entwicklung der Christologie Martin Kählers in Auseinandersetzung mit der Leben-Jesu-Theologie und der Ritschl-Schule* (Neukirchen, 1975). D. L. Deegan, 'Martin Kähler: Kerygma and Gospel History', *Scottish Journal of Theology*, 16 (1963), pp. 50–67. C. E. Braaten, 'Martin Kähler on the Historic, Biblical Christ', in id. and R. A. Harrisville (eds.), *The Historical Jesus and the Kerygmatic Christ* (Nashville, 1964), pp. 79–105. H.-J. Kraus in *TRE* 17 (1988), pp. 511–15, s.v.

Kaiserswerth. The band of Protestant *deaconesses in this Rhineland town was begun by T. Fliedner in 1836 to meet the need of the reformed Churches for an organization of women devoted to the care of the sick and the education of neglected children, on the same lines as the corresponding institutes in the RC Church. The house at Kaiserswerth trains three kinds of deaconesses, who devote themselves either to the care of the sick and the poor, or to teaching, or to parish work. Candidates must be unmarried or widows and undertake to remain in the institute for five years, and are governed by a clergyman who is assisted by a woman superior. The Kaiserswerth deaconesses not only supply numerous charitable institutions in Germany with workers, but also have branches in other places, e.g. at *Jerusalem, *Alexandria, and Cairo. See also DEACONESS.

J. Disselhoff, *Das Diakonissen-Mutterhaus zu Kaiserswerth a. Rhein und seine Töchterhäuser* (rev. edn., 1903; Eng. tr., 1883).

kamelavchion (Gk. καμηλαύχιον, καλυμμαύχιον). The black cylindrical hat worn by monks and clergy in the E. Church. In the Greek Church, secular clergy in major orders have a projecting brim round the top of the kamelavchion. In the Russian Church there is no brim, but the diameter at the top is slightly greater than at the bottom. See also CAMELAUCUM and EPANOKAMELAVCHION.

Kant, Immanuel (1724–1804), German philosopher. He was born and died at Königsberg in E. Prussia and never went beyond the confines of the province. In early life he was attracted to the study of mathematics and physics, and retained interest in the natural sciences throughout his life. After some years as a private tutor, he became a Privatdozent at Königsberg University in 1755, and in 1770

Professor of Logic, holding the post until his death. His dissertation *De Mundi Sensibilis et Intelligibilis Forma et Principiis* (1770) marks an important stage in his development, but it was not until after another eleven years (during which Kant wrote practically nothing) that he expounded his epoch-making 'Critical Philosophy' in *Der Kritik der reinen Vernunft* (1781). Its treatment of the problems of speculative philosophy was carried further in his *Prolegomena zu einer jeden künftigen Metaphysik* (1783), and esp. in the second (and in essentials final) edition of the *Kritik der reinen Vernunft* (1787). The *Kritik der praktischen Vernunft* (1788) and the *Kritik der Urtheilskraft* (1790) applied the principles of the earlier *Kritiken* to the problems of morals and to those of teleology and aesthetics respectively. In 1792 the divergence of Kant's teaching from orthodox *Lutheranism brought him into difficulties with the Prussian government. He was not prevented, however, from completing the publication of his *Religion innerhalb der Grenzen der blossen Vernunft* in 1793, the last of his large-scale works. His later writings include a monograph, *Zum ewigen Frieden* (1795). In his last years, as shown by his MSS (pub. in their fullest form by E. Adickes as *Kant's Opus Postumum*, 1920), Kant moved towards a position more akin to that of B. *Spinoza.

It would seem that Kant's main object was to discover a definitive rationale for the admitted validity of mathematics and natural science (esp. the *Newtonian physics). This meant finding a way out of the deadlock arising from the co-existence, on the one hand, of Continental 'rationalism' (R. *Descartes, B. Spinoza, G. W. *Leibniz, and C. *Wolff), and, on the other, of British empiricism (J. *Locke, G. *Berkeley, D. *Hume). He felt that there could be only one solution, namely that it was the understanding (*Verstand*) which prescribed to nature her laws. The validity of the causal law ('every event has a cause') rests not on some constraining principle in the external world of nature, but in the fact that consciousness is so constituted that it cannot but so interpret the empirical *data* which it receives. Knowledge is thus the result of a synthesis between an intellectual act (through the twelve 'categories') and what is presented to the mind from without. The latter is received by the understanding under the two 'forms of perception' (*Anschauungsformen*) of space and time.

In holding that all knowledge required an ingredient derived from nature, Kant cut at the root of traditional metaphysics, with its claim to provide knowledge of subjects which wholly transcended nature. For being thus constituted the human mind could have no knowledge of the three central 'Ideas' (*Ideen*) of Metaphysics: God, Freedom, and Immortality. The three traditional proofs of God's existence (*Ontological, *Cosmological, and *Teleological) were all invalidated.

But while insisting that Natural Theology was an illusion, Kant believed that the validity of the Ideas could be established in another way. The stern voice of conscience in man assures him of truths which reason is impotent to establish. Kant summarized this belief in his dictum: 'I had to remove knowledge to make room for faith.' The sense of duty assures us of Freedom. And correlative with this belief in Freedom are those in Immortality and in a Divine Being, since the maladjustment of virtue and happiness in the present world requires a righteous God who will vindicate the claims of justice, and another world for His operation.

In his treatise on *Religion* (1793) Kant elaborated his ethical doctrines in relation to the traditional theology of Lutheranism. Its four sections treat of: (1) the existence of radical evil in human nature; (2) the conflict of the good and evil principles; (3) the victory of the good principle and the foundation of a Kingdom of God on earth; and (4) religion and priestcraft. Despite his constant use of accustomed theological terminology, his presentation of religion did not transcend the limits of morality, and he expressly defined religion as the recognition of all our duties as Divine commands. The moral law had no purpose beyond itself. There was no place for mystical experience, no need for a personal redeemer and no place (as in traditional Christianity) for the historical as such. Kant once expressed the view that as a man advanced in moral perception he found the practice of prayer increasingly unprofitable. *Miracles, if they ever happened, could have no religious significance.

Kant made no attempt to round off his beliefs into a system. This task was soon undertaken by others, who constructed on a Kantian basis a series of grandly conceived systems. J. G. *Fichte, F. W. J. von *Schelling, and G. W. F. *Hegel (*Absolute Idealism) were all directly inspired by and looked back to Kant. In the latter part of the 19th cent. there arose in Germany a widespread and diversified philosophical movement seeking inspiration in a more literal interpretation of Kant. In Great Britain a similar, but independent, movement drew its inspiration from Kant and Hegel conjointly, its leading members being T. H. *Green, F. H. *Bradley, and B. *Bosanquet, and this in turn had a marked influence on Anglican theology (C. C. J. *Webb, W. *Temple, A. E. *Taylor). The moralism of Kant and his critique of metaphysics have made him congenial to some Protestant theologians. RC philosophical theologians tend to see in Kant esp. the critic of the (scholastic) proofs of God's existence and hence to be very critical of him.

Collected edn. of Kant's *Werke* by G. Hartenstein (1867-9). The best crit. edn. is that of the Berlin Academy (1910 ff.; still unfinished). Most of the individual writings are obtainable in convenient form, with introds. and notes, in the *Philosophische Bibliothek* (pub. F. Meiner, Leipzig). His more important writings exist in Eng. tr. The best version of the *Critique of Pure Reason* is by N. K. Smith (1929). From the vast lit., the following is a small selection: E. *Caird, *The Critical Philosophy of Immanuel Kant* (2 vols., 1889); H. A. Prichard, *Kant's Theory of Knowledge* (1909); E. Cassirer, *Kants Leben und Lehre* (1918; Eng. tr., New Haven, Conn., and London [1981]); N. K. Smith, *A Commentary to Kant's 'Critique of Pure Reason'* (1918); A. C. Ewing, *Kant's Treatment of Causality* (1924); C. C. J. Webb, *Kant's Philosophy of Religion* (1926); F. E. England, *Kant's Conception of God, with a translation of the 'Nova Dilucidatio'* (1929); A. D. *Lindsay, *Kant* (1934); H. J. Paton, *Kant's Metaphysic of Experience* (2 vols., 1936); H. J. de Vleeschauer, *La Déduction transcendentale dans l'œuvre de Kant* (3 vols., 1934-7); id., *L'Évolution de la pensée kantienne* (1939; Eng. tr., 1962); A. C. Ewing, *A Short Commentary on Kant's Critique of Pure Reason* (1938); H. J. Paton, *The Categorical Imperative: A Study in Kant's Moral Philosophy* [1947]; S. Körner, *Kant* (Harmondsworth, 1955); L. W. Beck, *A Commentary on Kant's Critique of Practical Reason* (Chicago, 1960); G. Rabel, *Kant* (Oxford, 1963); J. [F.] Bennett, *Kant's Analytic* (Cambridge, 1966); id., *Kant's Dialectic* (ibid., 1974); K. Ward, *The Development of Kant's View of Ethics* (Oxford, 1972); R. S. C.

Walker, *Kant* (The Arguments of the Philosophers, 1978); B. M. G. Reardon, *Kant as Philosophical Theologian* (1988); G. Buchdahl, *Kant and the Dynamics of Reason: Essays on the Structure of Kant's Philosophy* (Oxford, 1992). Überweg, 3, pp. 488-620, with bibl. pp. 709-58; F. Copleston, SJ, *A History of Philosophy*, 6 (1960), pp. 180-439, with bibl., pp. 466-71. E. *Troeltsch in HERE 7 (1914), pp. 653-9, s.v.; P. Charles, SJ, in DTC 8 (pt. 2; 1925), cols. 2297-331, s.v. 'Kant et le kantisme' (on theological aspects of Kant's writings); W. H. Walsh in P. Edwards (ed.), *The Encyclopedia of Philosophy*, 4 (1967), pp. 305-24, s.v.

Karaites (Heb. קְרָא, 'to read'). A Jewish sect, dating from the 8th cent. AD, which rejects rabbinical tradition and the *Talmud, and bases its teaching solely on the Scriptures. It survives mainly in Russia and Israel, and probably numbers c.13,000 members.

The leading authority is S. A. Poznański (1864-1921), whose works are listed in the *Livre d'hommage à la mémoire du Dr Samuel Poznański* (1927), pp. xxix-xxxix. Z. Ankori, *Karaites in Byzantium* (New York, 1959). S. Hofman in *Encyclopaedia Judaica*, 10 (Jerusalem, 1972), cols. 761-85, with bibl.

Karlstadt. See CARLSTADT.

katavasia (Gk. καταβασία, from καταβαίνω, 'go down'). In the E. Church, the concluding stanza of an ode of the *canon, so called because originally the two choirs of singers at this point came down from their stalls and joined in the middle of the church (a custom maintained by some monasteries in Lent). On feast days there is a katavasia at the end of each ode; on ordinary weekdays, after the 3rd, 6th, 8th, and 9th odes only.

kathisma (Gk. κάθισμα, from καθῆσθαι, 'to be seated'). A term in the E. Church applied to (1) each of the twenty sections into which the Byzantine Psalter is divided; (2) a brief liturgical hymn sung during *Orthros at the end of each kathisma of the Psalter.

Kattenbusch, Ferdinand (1851-1935), historian of the Creeds and theologian. A pupil of A. *Ritschl, he became professor of systematic theology at Giessen (1878), Göttingen (1904), and Halle (1906). His principal work, *Das apostolische Symbol* (1, 1894; 2, 1900), was an erudite treatise built on the researches of C. P. *Caspari, which brought together a vast body of literary material on the history of the *Apostles' Creed. He also contributed to the history of the Reformation confessions and, in his later years, concerned himself with systematic theology.

Autobiog. in E. Stange (ed.), *Die Religionswissenschaft der Gegenwart*, 5 (1929), pp. 85-121. O. Ritschl, 'Ferdinand Kattenbusch als Persönlichkeit, Forscher und Denker', *Theologische Studien und Kritiken*, 107 (1936), pp. 289-311.

Keble, John (1792-1866), *Tractarian leader and author of *The *Christian Year* (q.v.). He was the son of John Keble, Vicar of Coln St Aldwyn, a priest of the High Church school. Born at Fairford, after a brilliant career at Corpus Christi College, Oxford, he was elected in 1811 at the age of 19 to one of the much-coveted Fellowships of Oriel. In 1815 he was ordained deacon and in 1816 priest. In 1817 he became a tutor at Oriel, but resigned in 1823 to assist his father in his country cure in the Cotswolds.

There he composed the poems which, at the insistence of close friends, he published in 1827 as *The Christian Year*. In 1831 he was elected professor of poetry at Oxford in succession to H. H. *Milman. With many of his friends there and elsewhere (J. H. *Newman, I. *Williams, R. H. *Froude, E. B. *Pusey, W. *Palmer of Worcester College, J. B. *Mozley, H. J. *Rose), he became increasingly conscious of the dangers threatening the C of E from the reforming and liberal movements, and on 14 July 1833 preached before the University an assize sermon on *National Apostasy (q.v.), directed esp. against the proposed suppression of ten Irish bishoprics. From now on he took a leading part in the *Oxford Movement. He co-operated with Newman in the issue of the *Tracts for the Times*, to which he himself contributed nos. 4, 13, 40, 52, 54, 57, 60, and 89. No. 4, which bore the title 'Adherence to the Apostolical Succession the Safest Course', was a brief but forceful appeal to the clergy to take a high view of their privileges and duties. In 1836 he issued a learned edition of R. *Hooker's *Works* and in 1838, with Newman and Pusey, he became one of the editors of the '*Library of the Fathers', to which he himself contributed the translation of St *Irenaeus (pub. posthumously, 1872). His publication, with Newman, of the *Remains* (1838–9) of their close friend R. H. Froude (q.v.) provoked a storm. His tract no. 89, 'On the Mysticism attributed to the Early Fathers of the Church' (1840–1), a defence of Alexandrian theology and religious 'reserve', also met with a very hostile reception. After the cessation of the *Tracts*, he continued the close friend and adviser of Newman until Newman's secession in 1845.

After 1845 Keble remained the firm associate of Pusey and co-operated with him in keeping the High Church movement steadily attached to the C of E. In 1857 he published two pamphlets against the Divorce Act, as well as a treatise *On Eucharistical Adoration*, defending the doctrine of the *Real Presence from its attack in the G. A. *Denison case. In 1863 he issued a *Life* of T. *Wilson, Bp. of Sodor and Man (d. 1755). His later poetry included contributions to the *Lyra Apostolica* (1836), an English rendering of the *Psalter* (1839) and *Lyra Innocentium* (1846).

Meanwhile, since 1836, Keble had been Vicar of Hursley, near Winchester. He was never offered (and never wished for) preferment, remaining at Hursley, a devoted parish priest, for the rest of his life. He died at Bournemouth on 29 Mar. 1866. His beauty of character impressed all who came into contact with him, and his advice on spiritual matters, always given with great diffidence, was widely sought after. In 1870 Keble College, Oxford, was founded in his memory, with E. S. *Talbot as the first warden. Feast day in parts of the Anglican Communion, 29 Mar.

A set of *Letters of Spiritual Counsel and Guidance* (Oxford, 1870) was ed. by R. J. Wilson. *Memoir*, with many extracts from letters, by Sir J. T. Coleridge (ibid., 1869). C. M. *Yonge, *Musings over the 'Christian Year' and 'Lyra Innocentium'*, together with a few Gleanings of Recollections of the Rev. John Keble, gathered by several friends (1871). Lives by W. Lock (London, 1893); E. F. L. Wood, later Lord Halifax (ibid., 1909); K. Ingram (ibid., 1933); and G. Battiscombe (ibid., 1963). B. W. Martin, *John Keble: Priest, Professor and Poet* [1976]. W. J. A. M. Beek, *John Keble's Literary and Religious Contribution to the Oxford Movement* (Nijmegen,

1959). R. W. *Church, *The Oxford Movement* (1890), ch. 2. S. L. Ollard in *DECH* (3rd edn.), pp. 314–16.

Kedron. See CEDRON.

Keith, George (*c*.1638–1716), 'Christian *Quaker'. Born in Aberdeenshire, he was educated for the *Presbyterian ministry at Marischal College, but in 1663 became a Quaker, and apparently exercised considerable influence on R. *Barclay. After several imprisonments for preaching, in 1684 he emigrated to America, having secured appointment as Surveyor General of the colony of E. Jersey. He was censorious of much that he considered lax in the discipline and teaching of the American Quakers and their belief in the 'sufficiency of the light within'. When disowned by them, he gathered around him followers whom he called 'Christian Quakers'. He returned to England late in 1693 and engaged in much controversy. In 1700 he conformed to the C of E; and, after ordination, he conducted from 1702 to 1704 a successful mission in America as one of the first missionaries sent out by the *SPG. In 1705 he became rector of Edburton in W. Sussex. His many writings include *The Benefit, Advantage and Glory of Silent Meetings* (1670), *The Deism of William Penn and his Brethren* (1699), and *The Standard of the Quakers examined* (1702), the last directed against Barclay.

E. W. Kirby, *George Keith, 1638–1716* (The American Historical Association, New York and London, 1942), with full bibl. A. Gordon in *DNB* 30 (1892), pp. 318–21, s.v., with further refs.

Kells, Book of. A finely ornamented Latin MS of the Gospels, so named from the monastery of Kells (Ceanannus Mór) in Co. Meath, where it was long thought to have been written; it was certainly at Kells from the 12th (and very probably from the early 11th) to the mid-17th cent., when it was given to *Trinity College, Dublin (A. 1.6(58)). Acc. to tradition, it belonged to St *Columba (d. 597), but it really dates from *c*.800. It is now a matter of debate whether it was written at Kells or brought there (complete or incomplete) from *Iona or elsewhere. Some scholars hold that it may have been written and decorated in the North of England (perhaps at *Lindisfarne) or even in east Scotland.

Facsimile, partly in colour, with introds. by E. H. Alton and P. Meyer (3 vols., Berne, 1950–1). Sir Edward Sullivan, *The Book of Kells* (1914; with 24 coloured plates). Partial reproduction in colour, with study of the MS by F. Henry (London, 1974). T. J. Brown, 'Northumbria and the Book of Kells', *Anglo-Saxon England*, 1 (1972), pp. 219–46. J. J. G. Alexander, *Insular Manuscripts, 6th to the 9th Century* (A Survey of Manuscripts Illuminated in the British Isles, 1; 1978), pp. 71–6 (no. 52, ills. 231–60).

Kempe, John (*c*.1380–1454), Abp. of *Canterbury. He first became prominent in the ecclesiastical courts and by 1414 he was *Dean of the Arches. He filled in turn the sees of *Rochester (1419), *Chichester (1421), London (1421), *York (1425), and Canterbury (1452). He was a prominent member of the Council of Regency for *Henry VI, in which he was a supporter of H. *Beaufort. During the years following 1430 he was a strong but ineffectual advocate of a policy of peace with France. In 1439 he was made a cardinal. In his later years he espoused the Lancastrian cause, and checked the Kentish rebellion of 1450; but he died before the struggle was far advanced. He was far more a politician than a Churchman, and took little interest in the care of his dioceses.

W. F. *Hook, *Lives of the Archbishops of Canterbury*, 5 (1867), pp. 188–267. W. Ullmann, 'Eugenius IV, Cardinal Kemp, and Archbishop Chichele', in J. A. Watt and others (eds.), *Medieval Studies Presented to Aubrey Gwynn, S.J.* (Dublin, 1961), pp. 359–83. T. F. Tout in *DNB* 30 (1892), pp. 384–8, s.v. 'Kemp, John' [date of death erroneously given as 1447]; *BRUO* 2 (1958), pp. 1031–2.

Kempe, Margery (c.1373–after 1438), author of the *Book of Margery Kempe*. Born at Lynn, Norfolk, the daughter of John Burnham (d. 1413), who was several times Mayor of Lynn, c.1393 she married John Kempe (d. prob. 1431), burgess of Lynn, by whom she had 14 children. After she had received several visions following a period of madness, she and her husband went on a pilgrimage to *Canterbury. Her fervent denunciation of all pleasure aroused stiff opposition and the first taunts of *Lollardy, which later developed into formal accusations. In 1413 Margery and John took vows of chastity before Philip *Repington, Bp. of *Lincoln. She publicly rebuked Abp. *Arundel for the behaviour of his followers. In 1413 she went on a pilgrimage to the Holy Land. On her return she was prob. encouraged by *Julian of Norwich. She visited *Compostela in 1417 and *Norway and Danzig in 1433.

The *Book of Margery Kempe*, which is almost the sole source of information about the author, describes her travels and mystical experiences. She was endowed with the gift of tears and seems to have been favoured with singular signs of Christ's love, whereby for long periods she enjoyed consciousness of close communion with Him and developed a strong compassion for the sins of the world. Only one MS of the Book is known to exist. It was at one time in the possession of the *Carthusian house at Mount Grace, and from at least 1754 in the Butler-Bowden family; in 1980 it was acquired by the British Library and is now Add. MS 61823. Unrepresentative selections, prob. from another MS, were published by W. de Worde (prob. 1501).

Crit. edn. by S. B. Meech and H. E. Allen (EETS, orig. ser. 212; 1940. The projected 2nd vol. of introd. and other material was never pub.). Modern versions by W. Butler-Bowdon (London, 1936) and B. A. Windeatt (Penguin Classics, 1985), with bibl. K. Cholmeley, *Margery Kempe: Genius and Mystic* (1947); M. [S. F.] Thornton, *Margery Kempe: An Example in the English Pastoral Tradition* (1960); L. Collis, *The Apprentice Saint* (1964); C. W. Atkinson, *Mystic and Pilgrim: The* Book *and the World of Margery Kempe* (1983); J. C. Hirsh, *The Revelations of Margery Kempe: Paramystical Practices in Late Medieval England* (Leiden, etc., 1989). [M.] D. *Knowles, *The English Mystical Tradition* (1961), pp. 138–50. Id. in *Dict. Sp.* 8 (1974), cols. 1696–8, s.v.

Kempis, Thomas à. See THOMAS À KEMPIS.

Ken, Thomas (1637–1711), Bp. of *Bath and Wells. He was educated at Winchester and Hart Hall, Oxford, and in 1657 became a Fellow of New College, Oxford. After several pastoral cures he taught at Winchester College from 1672. Here he wrote a manual of devotion for boys and possibly his two famous morning and evening hymns, 'Awake, my soul, and with the sun' and 'Glory to Thee, my God, this night' (*EH* 257 and 267). In 1679 *Charles

II appointed him chaplain to Princess Mary at The Hague, where he braved the anger of William of Orange in a matrimonial case. In 1683 as chaplain to Charles II he refused the use of his house to the royal mistress, Nell Gwyn. The King respected his boldness and, in 1684, conferred on him the bishopric of Bath and Wells, and it was Ken who gave the King absolution on his deathbed. Ken was one of the *Seven Bishops who refused to read the *Declaration of Indulgence at the command of *James II, but he declined to take the oath to William. Deposition from his see followed, and Ken then allied himself with the *Nonjurors. For the rest of his life he lived in retirement, refusing the offer of reinstatement on the death of Kidder (1703), who had held the see since his deposition. He opposed, however, the consecration of further nonjuring bishops. He lived an ascetic life as a celibate, and, true to the Laudian tradition, he wrote in his will: 'I die in the Holy Catholic and Apostolic Faith, professed by the whole Church, before the disunion of East and West: more particularly I die in the Communion of the Church of England, as it stand distinguished from all Papal and Puritan Innovations.' His *Exposition on the Church Catechism; or, The Practice of Divine Love* (1685) is a classic expression of Laudian doctrine. Feast day in ASB, 20 Mar.; in American BCP (1979), 21 Mar.

[Poetical] Works ed. W. Hawkins (4 vols., London, 1721); Prose Works ed. J. T. Round (ibid., 1838), with Life by W. Hawkins (orig. pub., London, 1713), repr., pp. 1–23. Other Lives by W. L. Bowles (2 vols. bound in 1, London, 1830), J. L. Anderson (anon., London, 1851), E. H. Plumptre (2 vols., ibid., 1888; 2nd edn. 1890), F. A. Clarke ('Leaders of Religion', London, 1896), and H. A. L. Rice (London, 1958). E. Marston, *Thomas Ken and Izaak Walton* (1908), pp. 3–78. [F.] J. Hoyles, *The Edges of Augustanism: The Aesthetics of Spirituality in Thomas Ken, John Byrom and William Law* (International Archives of the History of Ideas, 53; The Hague, 1972), pp. 9–77 and 151–3. W. Hunt in *DNB* 30 (1892), pp. 399–404.

Kenites. An obscure Semitic clan which belonged to the S. of Palestine and is listed among the pre-Israelite inhabitants of the land in Gen. 15: 19. It had several associations with the Hebrews, esp. with the tribe of *Judah: *Moses' father-in-law was a Kenite (Jgs. 1: 16), Jael the Kenite is responsible for the death of Sisera, the enemy of Israel (Jgs. 4–5), and the *Rechabites were apparently of Kenite origin. It has sometimes been held that the Kenites exercised an important influence on the shaping of Hebrew religion (the 'Kenite hypothesis' of the origins of Yahwism). Num. 24: 21 f. associates them with the name 'Cain'.

Kennett, White (1660–1728), Bp. of *Peterborough. Educated at *Westminster and at St Edmund Hall, Oxford, he was successively vicar of Ambrosden, Oxon (1685), tutor and vice-principal of St Edmund Hall (c.1690), Archdeacon of Huntingdon (1701), and Dean (1707) and Bp. (1718) of Peterborough. He was an active supporter of the Revolution of 1689, became a leading Low Churchman, and in the *Bangorian Controversy opposed the proceedings against B. *Hoadly. He was, however, a close friend of G. *Hickes, the *Nonjuror, whom he encouraged in the preparation of his *Thesaurus*. A keen antiquary, he was the author of a long list of works, including sermons. Among them were *Parochial Antiquities*

(1695; a history of Ambrosden, etc.), *Ecclesiastical Synods and Parliamentary Convocations* (1701), *Compleat History of England* (1706), and *Register and Chronicle, Ecclesiastical and Civil* (1728). Kennett urged that in every collegiate church a dignity should be reserved for a student of its antiquities, and founded an Antiquarian and Historical Library for the use of his cathedral.

Many of Kennett's valuable unpub. collections are preserved in the British Library. Anonymous Life [by W. Newton] (London, 1730). Modern Life by G. V. Bennett (Thirlwall Prize Essay for 1955; CHS, 1957). T. Cooper in *DNB* 31 (1892), pp. 2–6.

Kennicott, Benjamin

Kennicott, Benjamin (1718–83), biblical scholar and Hebraist. By the generosity of friends he was enabled to enter Wadham College, Oxford, in 1744, where, while still an undergraduate, he published two dissertations. From 1747 to 1771 he was a Fellow of Exeter College, from 1767 to 1783 Radcliffe Librarian, and from 1770 till his death Canon of Christ Church. His life-work was the critical study of the Hebrew text of the OT, in which he was assisted by collations of MSS from many parts of Europe. His wife, whom he married in 1771, gave him considerable help in his researches. Their fruits were collected in his *Vetus Testamentum Hebraicum cum variis lectionibus* (2 vols., 1776–80), a work which established the important negative conclusion that the variants in the Heb. MSS of the OT are so slight as to be of minimal importance for establishing the correct text.

W. McKane, 'Benjamin Kennicott: An Eighteenth-Century Researcher', *JTS* NS 28 (1977), pp. 445–64. W. Michels in *Dict. Bibl.* 3 (1903), cols. 1887–9, s.v.

kenotic theories

kenotic theories. Certain theories which are concerned to explain the condescension involved in the Incarnation. The title comes from the Greek verb (κενόω) in Phil. 2: 7, translated in the RV 'emptied himself'. A number of 19th-cent. *Lutheran theologians held that the Divine Son abandoned His attributes of deity, such as omnipotence, omniscience, and cosmic sovereignty, in order to become man. A more moderate theory, defended by C. *Gore, maintained that, within the sphere of the Incarnation, the deity so restrained its activity as to allow the existence in the Lord of a limited and genuinely human consciousness. The term κένωσις was used in patristic theology to describe the action of the Son in the Incarnation, but implied no special theory. Traditional orthodoxy has generally admitted a self-emptying of the Lord's deity only in the sense that, while remaining unimpaired, it accepted union with a physically and emotionally limited humanity.

The early exponents of the modern theory were G. Thomasius (*Beiträge zur kirchlichen Christologie*, 1845, and *Christi Person und Werke*, 1853) and W. F. Gess (*Die Lehre von der Person Christi*, 1854). Gore's modified form of this appears in his *Bampton Lectures and, more fully, in his essay 'The Consciousness of Our Lord in His Mortal Life', in *Dissertations on Subjects connected with the Incarnation* (1895), pp. 69–226. D. G. Dawe, 'A Fresh Look at the Kenotic Christologies', *Scottish Journal of Theology*, 15 (1962), pp. 337–49, with further refs. Imp. arts. by F. *Loofs in *PRE* (3rd edn.), 10 (1901), pp. 246–63 and in *HERE* 7 (1914), pp. 680–7; and esp. the valuable study by P. Henry, SJ, in *Dict. Bibl.*, Suppl. 5 (1957), cols. 7–161, s.v. 'Kenose', with bibl. G. W. H. Lampe (ed.), *Patristic Greek Lexicon* (1961), pp. 744–6, s.v. 'κένωσις'. See also works cited under CHRISTOLOGY and comm. on PHILIPPIANS, cited s.v.

Kensit, John

Kensit, John (1853–1902), Protestant propagandist. An early supporter of the more extreme type of Protestantism, he started the City Protestant bookshop in Paternoster Row in 1885 and later used the *Churchman's Magazine* for the propagation of his opinions. In 1890 he became secretary of the newly-founded 'Protestant Truth Society' and from that date took an increasingly violent and individualist stand against what he believed to be Romanizing tendencies in the C of E. From 1898 to 1902 he organized resistance to the growth of 'ritualism' in the dioceses of London (e.g. at St Ethelburga's, Bishopsgate) and Liverpool, causing considerable friction and disturbance wherever he went. At the general election of 1900 he unsuccessfully contested Brighton as an Independent Conservative.

J. C. Wilcox, *John Kensit: Reformer and Martyr* [*c*.1903]. M. Wellings, 'The First Protestant Martyr of the Twentieth Century: the Life and Significance of John Kensit (1853–1902)', in D. Wood (ed.), *Martyrs and Martyrologies* (Studies in Church History, 30; Oxford, 1993), pp. 347–58.

Kent, Maid of

Kent, Maid of. See BARTON, ELIZABETH.

Kentigern, St

Kentigern, St (d. *c*.612), also known as **St Mungo**, missionary in Scotland. A 12th-cent. Life, only partly reliable, states that he was a grandson of a British prince in S. Scotland and brought up by St Serf in a monastic school at Culross on the Firth of Forth; later he became bishop of the Britons of Strathclyde and founded the Church of Glasgow; after being driven out by persecution he preached in Wales (where he is credited with the foundation of *St Asaph) and later in Cumbria, but eventually returned to Strathclyde and was buried in Glasgow, where his reputed tomb stands in the cathedral. The only known facts are his connection with Strathclyde and the approximate date of his death. Feast day, 13 Jan.

Life by Jocelin, monk of Furness (*c*.1180) and a fragment of an anonymous Life (*c*.1150), ed. A. P. *Forbes, *Lives of S. Ninian and S. Kentigern* (Historians of Scotland, 5; 1874), pp. 159–252, with Eng. tr. pp. 27–133. J. MacQueen, 'Yvain, Ewen and Owein ap Urien', *Transactions of the Dumfriesshire and Galloway Natural History and Antiquarian Society*, 3rd ser. 33 (for 1954–5; 1956), pp. 107–31; K. H. Jackson, 'The Sources for the Life of St Kentigern', in N. K. Chadwick and others, *Studies in the Early British Church* (Cambridge, 1958), pp. 273–357; D. McRoberts, 'The Death of St Kentigern of Glasgow', *Innes Review*, 24 (1973), pp. 43–50; A. Macquarrie, 'The Career of Saint Kentigern of Glasgow: *Vitae, Lectiones,* and Glimpses of Fact', ibid., 37 (1986), pp. 3–24.

Kenya, Christianity in

Kenya, Christianity in. A few African converts were made during the two centuries of Portuguese domination of the E. African coast, but no lasting Church was established, although a number of both Portuguese and African Christians died for their faith in a Muslim uprising in Mombasa in 1631. Modern Christianity dates from 1844, when Johann Ludwig Krapf of the *CMS settled at Rabai, near Mombasa, but little progress was made by missionaries in this predominantly Muslim area until the 1870s, when attention was drawn to the E. African slave trade and a settlement for freed slaves was established at Freretown, Mombasa. This eventually prospered and the first Kenyans were ordained in 1885. The Uganda Railway, begun in 1896, gave access to the cool, densely populated central highland and RC and Protestant missionaries quickly increased in number. In 1902 work began in W. Kenya. The principal RC missionary societies were the *Holy Ghost Fathers, *Consolata Fathers, and *Mill Hill Fathers; the principal Protestant ones were the CMS, the Church of *Scotland Mission, and the American African Inland Mission.

The Kikuyu of Central Kenya were deeply suspicious of the missions which they saw as allies of the White settlers who were taking their land. Missionaries found themselves caught between the settlers who disparaged them for being 'pro-native' and African politicians who judged them weak in defence of African rights. J. H. *Oldham of the International Missionary Council helped to defeat attempts of the settlers to introduce forced labour, and W. E. Owen, Archdeacon of Kavirondo, fought civil rights cases on behalf of Africans. Bitter controversy broke out in 1929 over the attempt by some Protestant missions, led by J. W. Arthur of the Church of Scotland Mission, to get the practice of clitoridectomy among the Kikuyu outlawed. Many Kikuyu left the mission churches and schools on this account and started their own free of missionary control. When anger over land alienation erupted into the Mau Mau uprising in 1952, some Christians, esp. those influenced by the East African Revival Movement, refused to take the secret Mau Mau oath. A number died for this refusal and are commemorated in the Anglican Cathedral at Murang'a.

The years following political independence in 1964 saw a huge influx into the Churches. The RC and Anglican are by far the largest, but the African Inland Church and the *Seventh-day Adventists are also strong, while independent Church movements have continued to grow and multiply. They include the Mario Legio, the largest breakaway Church from RCism in Africa. By 1980 over 70 per cent of the population claimed to be Christian.

D. B. Barrett and others (eds.), *Kenya Churches Handbook: The Development of Kenyan Christianity, 1498–1973* (Kisumu, Kenya [1973]), with extensive bibl. Other general works include H. R. A. Philp, *A New Day in Kenya* (1936 [surveys position of various Churches]); R. Oliver, *The Missionary Factor in East Africa* (1952), *passim*; G. S. P. Freeman-Grenville, 'The Coast, 1498–1840', in R. Oliver and G. Mathew (eds.), *History of East Africa*, 1 (Oxford, 1963), pp. 129–68, *passim*; A. J. Temu, *British Protestant Missions* (1972); R. W. Strayer, *The Making of Mission Communities in East Africa: Anglicans and Africans in Colonial Kenya, 1875–1935* (1978); D. Sandgren, *Christianity and the Kikuyu* (New York [1989]). G. S. P. Freeman-Grenville, *The Mombasa Rising against the Portuguese, 1631, from sworn evidence* (Fontes Historiae Africanae, 1980), incl. text and Eng. tr. of the *processus* of the martyrs of Mombasa. E. Stock, *The History of the Church Missionary Society*, 1 (1899), pp. 458–62; 2 (1899), pp. 124–36, 427–34; 3 (1899), pp. 82–93, 406–9, 731–5; 4 (1916), pp. 75–82, and 409–24; G. Hewitt, *The Problems of Success: A History of the Church Missionary Society 1910–1942*, 1 (1971), pp. 121–73. R. Macpherson, *The Presbyterian Church in Kenya* (Nairobi, 1970). F. B. Welbourn and B. A. Ogot, *A Place to Feel at Home: A Study of Two Independent Churches in Western Kenya* (1966 [on the Church of Christ in Africa and the African Israel Church Nineveh]). E. N. Wanyoike [grandson], *An African Pastor: The Life and Work of the Rev. Wanyoike Kamawe 1888–1970* (Nairobi, 1974). Scattered references in A. Hastings, *The Church in Africa 1450–1950* (Oxford History of the Christian Church, 1994) (see index).

Kepler, Johann (1571–1630), German astronomer. He was educated at *Tübingen, where he received instruction

in *Copernican principles, and in 1594 was appointed professor of mathematics at Graz. In 1600 he went to Prague, to Tycho Brahe, and there he became court astronomer in 1601. In 1613 he took part in the Diet of Ratisbon, where he defended the Gregorian reform of the calendar against the many attacks of his fellow-Protestants. He was led to his discovery of the three laws of planetary motion, to which his fame is chiefly due, in part by *Neoplatonist mystical doctrines and also by the observations of Tycho Brahe (1545–1601). His understanding of nature was in many respects pantheistic, though he accepted the traditional authority of the Bible. He held the world to be an order expressing the being of God Himself, particularly in the relations between the sun, the image of God the Father, and the planets. The appearance of a new star in 1604–5 caused him to propose in his *De Jesu Christi Servatoris Nostri Vero Anno Natalitio* (1606) and later writings a new theory concerning the star of the *Magi, which he tried to explain by the unusual conjunction of Mars, Saturn, and Jupiter in the sign of the Taurus, calculated by him for the beginning of the year 6 BC.

Works ed. C. Frisch (8 vols., Frankfurt, 1858–71), also ed. W. von Dyck, M. Caspar, and others (22 vols., Munich. 1937 ff.). M. Caspar, *Johann Kepler* (Stuttgart, 1948; Eng. tr., 1959); C. Baumgardt, *Johannes Kepler: Life and Letters* (1952). *Johann Kepler, 1571–1630: A Tercentenary Commemoration of his Life and Work. A Series of Papers prepared under the Auspices of the History of Science Society* (Baltimore, 1931); A. and P. Beer (eds.), *Kepler: Four Hundred Years. Proceedings of Conferences held in honour of Johannes Kepler* (Vistas in Astronomy, 18; Oxford, etc., 1975), with papers on his religious and philosophical beliefs, pp. 317–96. J. Hübner, *Die Theologie Johannes Keplers zwischen Orthodoxie und Naturwissenschaft* (Beiträge zur historischen Theologie, 50; 1975). J. V. Field, *Kepler's Geometric Cosmology* (1988). Popular presentation by A. Koestler, *The Sleepwalkers* (1959), pp. 225–422, pub. separately as *The Watershed: A Biography of Johannes Kepler* (1961). M. Caspar (ed.), *Bibliographia Kepleriana* (Munich, 1936; 2nd edn., 1968), with continuation by M. List in A. and P. Beer, op. cit., pp. 955–1010.

kerygma (Gk. κήρυγμα, 'preaching'). The element of proclamation in Christian apologetic, as contrasted with '*didache' or its instructional aspects.

Kerygma Petri. See PETER, PREACHING OF.

Keswick Convention. An annual gathering of Evangelical Christians for prayer, Bible study, and addresses. It began at Keswick in 1875 with the aim of 'the promotion of Practical Holiness'. Its motto is 'All One in Christ Jesus'. The meeting is for a week every year, and it attracts visitors from many countries.

C. F. Harford (ed.), *The Keswick Convention* [1907]; S. Barabas, *So Great Salvation: The History and Message of the Keswick Convention* (1952); J. C. Pollock, *The Keswick Story: The Authorized History of the Keswick Convention* (1964). The Convention also publishes an annual report, *Keswick Week*.

Kethubim (Heb. כְּתוּבִים, 'writings'). The Jewish name for the third and last division of the OT, more commonly known to Christian scholars as the '*Hagiographa' (q.v.).

Ketteler, Wilhelm Emmanuel von (1811–77), Bp. of Mainz from 1850 and a pioneering figure in modern Catholic social thought. His interest in social questions is reflected in his *Die Arbeiterfrage und das Christenthum* (1864), though his most important pronouncement was made in a sermon preached at the episcopal conference at Fulda in 1869, in which he drew out the contradictions between economic liberalism and Christian principles. At the First *Vatican Council (1869–70) he opposed the definition of Papal infallibility on the ground that its promulgation was 'inopportune'; he returned to Germany before the voting took place, but subsequently accepted the Council's decrees (Aug. 1870). He also opposed the *Kulturkampf, championing the freedom of the RC Church in Germany from state control.

Sämtliche Werke und Briefe, ed. E. Iserloh and others (Mainz, 1977 ff.). Eng. tr. by R. J. Ederer of six sermons, *Die grossen socialen Fragen der Gegenwart* (pub. Mainz, 1849; ed. E. Deuerlein, 1948), as *The Social Teaching of Wilhelm Emmanuel von Ketteler* (Washington, DC [1981]). Lives by O. Pfülf (3 vols., Mainz, 1899), F. Vigener (Munich, 1924), and L. Lenhart (3 vols., Mainz [1966–8]). E. Fastenrath, *Bischof Ketteler und die Kirche* (Beiträge zur neueren Geschichte der katholischen Theologie, 13; Essen [1971]). A. M. Birke, *Bischof Ketteler und der deutsche Liberalismus* (Veröffentlichungen der Kommission für Zeitgeschichte bei der Katholischen Akademie in Bayern, Reihe B, Bd. 9; 1971). K. J. Rivinus, *Bischof Wilhelm Emmanuel von Ketteler und die Infallibilität des Papstes* (Europäische Hochschulschriften, Reihe 23, Bd. 48; 1976). Series of studies by E. Iserloh (Abhandlungen der Geistes- und Sozialwissenschaftlichen Klasse der Akademie der Wissenschaften und der Literatur, Mainz, 1975, no. 3; 1978, no. 7; and 1987, no. 8). L. Lenhart in *NCE* 8 (1967), pp. 170 f.; E. Iserloh in *TRE* 18 (1989), pp. 109–13, both s.v.

Kettlewell, John (1653–95), devotional writer and

*Nonjuror. He was educated at St Edmund Hall, Oxford, and in 1675 became a Fellow of Lincoln College, where he was tutor from 1677 to 1684. He was ordained in 1678 and about the same time wrote his first book, *The Measures of Christian Obedience*, which, however, was not published till 1681. It had a great success and led to his appointment as vicar of Coleshill, Warwickshire, in 1682. In 1687 he wrote a popular devotional work, *The Practical Believer*, which was widely read. During the revolution of 1689 he preached against rebellion under any pretext, an attitude which resulted in his being deprived of his living in 1690. He spent his remaining years in retirement in London, writing devotional books and controversial tracts. His *Companion for the Persecuted* (1693) was esteemed as a book of comfort among his Nonjuring fellow-sufferers. His advocacy of a relief fund for the deprived clergy came to nothing owing to the opposition of the government.

Complete Works (2 vols., 1719). [F. Lee,] *Memoirs of the Life of Mr. John Kettlewell* (1718; repr. in his works); T. T. *Carter (ed.), *The Life and Times of John Kettlewell* (1895). W. D. Macray in *DNB* 31 (1892), pp. 80–2.

Kevin, St (d. 618), also named 'Coemgen', Abbot of

Glendalough, Co. Wicklow. The sources for his life are late and untrustworthy. Acc. to these, he was born in Leinster of royal descent, given the name of Kevin (i.e. 'fair-begotten') at his baptism, and educated by St *Petrock during the latter's stay in Ireland. For a time he later established his permanent foundation at Glendalough, the parent of several other monasteries and destined to become, with its seven churches, one of the chief centres of pilgrimage in Ireland. Feast day, 3 June.

Three Irish Lives pr. by C. Plummer in *Bethada Naem nÉrenn* (1922), i, pp. 125–67; Eng. tr., 2, pp. 121–61. One of the Latin Lives is contained in C. Plummer, *Vitae Sanctorum Hiberniae*, i (1910), pp. 234–57, the other in W. K. Heist (ed.), *Vitae Sanctorum Hiberniae ex Codice olim Salmanticensi* (Subsidia Hagiographica, 28; 1965), pp. 361–5. L. Price, 'Glendalough: St Kevin's road', in J. Ryan, SJ (ed.), *Essays and Studies presented to Professor Eoin MacNeill* (Dublin, 1940), pp. 244–71. P Grosjean, SJ, 'Notes d'hagiographie celtique', 13: 'Relations mutuelles des Vies latines de S. Cáemgen de Glenn Dá Locha', *Anal. Boll.* 63 (1945), pp. 122–9; and 20: 'Les Vies latines de S. Cáemgen et de S. Patrice du manuscrit 121 des Bollandistes', ibid. 70 (1952), pp. 313–15.

Khomiakov, Alexis Stepanovich (1804–60), Russian

philosophical theologian. He was born at Moscow into a family which fled with him from the city in 1812, when their house was burnt by the French. Later he studied literature and mathematics at the University of Moscow. After two attempts at a military career (1822 and 1828), he abandoned it for the study of art. After marriage in 1836 he found his vocation in the service of 'true Russia' and became with Ivan Kireevsky one of the founders of the Slavophile movement, which he sought to build up on Orthodox Christianity. He attacked the scholastic rationalism ('Aristotelianism') of W. philosophy and was esp. critical of German Idealism (F. W. J. von *Schelling and G. W. F. *Hegel), then influential in Russia. Over against the RC ('unity without freedom') and Protestant ('freedom without unity') conceptions of the Church, Khomiakov saw in the Orthodox Church an organic society of which Christ was the Head and the Holy Spirit the Soul and whose essence was 'freedom in the spirit at one with itself'. Of this Church the essential quality was inward holiness, and those who partook of it could be saved even though not in external communion with it. Here, as in other dogmatic matters, Khomiakov's liberal and independent attitude came under ecclesiastical suspicion during his own lifetime; but since his death, and in particular during the 20th cent., his conception of the Church (often summed up in the term '*sobornost') has exercised considerable influence on Orthodox ecclesiology, Greek as well as Russian. His writings were largely occasional. From 1856 until his death he collaborated in the *Russkaia Beseda*, a review newly founded to further Slavophile ideals. A number of essays and polemical writings which originally appeared in French were reissued by his son Dmitri Alexeevich Khomiakov, as *L'Église latine et le protestantisme au point de vue de l'Église d'Orient* (Lausanne, 1872). Khomiakov also cultivated close relations with some English theologians, notably (from 1844) W. *Palmer ('of Magdalen'), with whom he stayed on a visit to Oxford in 1847.

Collected edn. of his works by his son, D. A. Khomiakov (8 vols., Moscow, 1900). His correspondence with Palmer, and an Eng. tr. of his essay, 'The Church is One', are pr. in W. J. Birkbeck (ed.), *Russia and the English Church during the Last Fifty Years*, i (1895). Eng. tr. of another of his essays in A. Schmemann (ed.), *Ultimate Questions: An Anthology of Modern Russian Religious Thought* (New York, 1965), pp. 29–69. Life by V. Z. Zavitnevitch (2 vols., Kiev, 1902–13); study by N. *Berdyaev (Moscow, 1912). G. Samarine, *Préface aux œuvres théologiques de A. S. Khomiakov* (Unam Sanctam, 7; 1939). A. Gratieux, *A. S. Khomiakov et le mouvement slavophile* (2 vols., ibid., 5 and 6; 1939). P. Baron, *Un Théologien laïc orthodoxe russe au XIXᵉ siècle, Alexis Stépanovitch Khomiakov (1804–1860)* (Orientalia Christiana

Analecta, 127; 1940). E. C. Suttner, *Offenbarung, Gnade und Kirche bei A. S. Chomjakov* (Das östliche Christentum, NF 20; 1967). A. Walicki, *The Slavophile Controversy* (Oxford, 1975; Eng. tr. of a work pub. Warsaw, 1964), pp. 179–237.

Kiddush (Heb. קדוש, 'sanctification'). The Jewish ceremony of the sanctification of the *Sabbath or other holy day. The rite is thought to go back to pre-Christian times. On Friday afternoon the household assembles for the evening meal and, at the beginning of the Sabbath, the head fills a cup of wine and water and says over it the Kiddush or 'Blessing' of the day. The same custom is observed on the eves of festivals, when the Kiddush makes reference to the festival as well as to the Sabbath. It has been argued that the custom was observed also by *chaburoth, and that Christ's blessing of the cup at the *Last Supper was the Kiddush of the *Passover. This theory is defended by alleged reminiscences of the idea and phraseology of the Kiddush in Eucharistic prayers, quoted or described in early Christian writings, e.g. the *Didache, *Ignatius, and *Justin. This theory presupposes the *Synoptic synchronism of the Last Supper with the Passover meal. Other scholars, preferring the Johannine dating of the Last Supper 24 hours before the Passover, hold that the blessing over the cup was the ordinary Jewish *berakah at the end of a chaburah meal.

J. Elbogen, 'Eingang und Ausgang des Sabbats nach Talmudischen Quellen', in *Festschrift zu Israel Lewy's siebzigstem Geburtstag* (Breslau, 1911), pp. 173–87. Text and Eng. tr. of Kiddush rite in *The Authorised Daily Prayer Book of the United Hebrew Congregations of the Commonwealth*, tr. by S. Singer, 3rd edn., rev. E. Cashdan, ed. I. Jakobovits (1990), pp. 275–6 (Sabbath evening), 427–8 (Sabbath morning), 633–6 (festival evenings), 695–6 (festival mornings). A. Rothkoff in *Encyclopaedia Judaica*, 10 (Jerusalem, 1972), pp. 974–7, s.v.

The identification of the Last Supper with the Kiddush ceremony, orig. suggested by F. *Spitta, was first defended by G. H. Box, 'The Jewish Antecedents of the Eucharist', *JTS* 3 (1901–2), pp. 357–69. W. O. E. Oesterley, *The Jewish Background of the Christian Liturgy* (1925), esp. pp. 79–81 and 167–77; H. *Lietzmann, *Messe und Herrenmahl* (1926), pp. 202–10; Eng. tr. (Leiden, 1979), pp. 165–71; F. Gavin, *The Jewish Antecedents of the Christian Sacraments* (1928), esp. pp. 64–9; cf., however, J. Jeremias, *Die Abendmahlsworte Jesu* (1935), pp. 18–21; 3rd edn. (1960), pp. 20–3; Eng. tr. (1966), pp. 26–9.

Kidron. See CEDRON.

Kierkegaard, Søren Aabye (1813–55), Danish philosopher. The son of a wealthy hosier who was a devout *Lutheran, he spent practically his whole life at Copenhagen. After a secluded and unhappy childhood his university years were given over partly to idleness and amusements, partly to an inborn melancholy. He passed his theological examination in 1840, and in the following year became engaged to Regina Olsen; but, feeling marriage to be impossible, he broke off the engagement shortly afterwards. In the twelve years from 1843, the year of the publication of his first book, *Enten-Eller* ('Either-Or'), till his death, he produced the series of works which were to place him in the first rank of modern philosophical writers, though his influence was hampered for a long time by the fact of his writing in Danish. In 1846 he was subjected to a long and cruel attack by the comic Copenhagen paper, *Den Corsaren*, and in 1854 he launched his great assault on

the Established Church, criticizing it because it had sought to accommodate the Christian revelation to human desires.

He was one of the most personal of thinkers, and his successive publications mark the development of his thought from the aesthetic to the religious and soon to the definitely Christian point of view. He was reared in the atmosphere of *Hegelian dialectics—the only philosophy then taught in Denmark; he attacked this interpretation of Christianity as 'the system', esp. in the *Philosophiske Smuler* (1844; Eng. tr., 'Philosophical Fragments') and *Afsluttende uvidenskabelig Efterskrift* (1846; 'Concluding Unscientific Postscript'). He opposed to it his own powerful '*Existential' dialectics, pointing out with uncompromising vigour, though often in abstruse terminology, the dialectics involved in the position of man 'existing before God'. The whole complex of sin and redemption was described with profound psychological insight in *Begrebet Angest* (1844; Eng. tr., 'The Concept of Dread') and *Sygdommen til Döden* (1849; Eng. tr., 'Sickness unto Death'). His thought, though deeply original and in its ascetic tendencies showing a marked leaning to Catholic ideals, reflects at many points its Lutheran ancestry, e.g. in its opposition of faith to reason and the stress laid on the relation of the individual soul with God almost to the exclusion of the idea of a Christian community. His often-repeated statement, 'truth is subjectivity', though it should not be understood in the sense of a shallow individualism, links up truth with the existing subject instead of with its object, and so, in the last resort, makes its communication to other subjects impossible. Kierkegaard draws the theological consequences from this position by denying the possibility of an objective system of doctrinal truths.

As contrasted with his philosophical writings, his properly religious books, e.g. the *Christelige Taler* (1850; Eng. tr., 'Christian Discourses') and *Indøvelse i Christendom* (1850; Eng. tr., 'Training in Christianity'), have aroused less interest, but they are in many respects of great devotional value and show a profound understanding of the redemptive work of Christ and the meaning of the Cross. His total influence on contemporary thought is very considerable. Both the *Dialectical Theology of K. *Barth and his followers and the Existential philosophy, esp. as expounded by M. *Heidegger, owe their inspiration to him.

Collected edn. of *Samlede Værker* by A. B. Drachmann, J. L. Heiberg, and H. O. Lange (15 vols., Copenhagen, 1901–36; ed. P. P. Rohde, 20 vols., ibid., 1962–4); of his 'Papirer' by P. A. Heiberg, V. Kuhr, and E. Torsting (11 vols. in 19 parts, ibid., 1909–48, repr., with additional material ed. N. Thulstrup, 16 vols., ibid., 1968–78). *Breve og Aktstykker vedrørende Søren Kierkegaard*, ed. N. Thulstrup (2 vols., Copenhagen, 1953–4). Eng. tr. of *Kierkegaard's Writings*, ed. H. V. Hong (Princeton, NJ, 1978 ff.). Earlier trs. of many individual works by W. Lowrie, A. Dru, D. F. Swenson, and L. Swenson; details of those pub. before 1955 in bibl. by J. Himmelstrup, listed below, pp. 38–43 (nos. 1286–516a). Selection from his *Journals* tr. and ed. A. Dru (London and Princeton, NJ, 1938); *Journals* for 1853–5 ed. and tr. R. G. Smith (1965). Life by W. Lowrie (Princeton, NJ, and London, 1938); shorter Life by id. (ibid., 1942); biog. study by J. Thompson (London, 1974). Modern studies include E. Hirsch, *Kierkegaard Studien* (2 vols., 1933); J. Wahl, *Études kierkegaardiennes* (1938; with bibl.); J. Hohlenberg, *Søren Kierkegaard* (Copenhagen, 1940; Eng. tr., 1954); R. Thomte, *Kierkegaard's Philosophy of Religion* (Princeton, NJ, and London, 1948); H. Diem, *Die Existenzdialektik von Sören Kierkegaard* (Zollikon,

1950; Eng. tr., 1959); J. Collins, *The Mind of Kierkegaard* (Chicago, 1953; London, 1954); T. H. Croxall, *Kierkegaard Commentary* (1956); L. Dupré, *Kierkegaards Theologie* (Theologische Bibliotheek, 1958; Eng. tr., 1963); P. Rohde, *Søren Kierkegaard* (Hamburg, 1959; Eng. tr., 1963); N. Thulstrup, *Kierkegaards Forhold til Hegel* (1967; Eng. tr., Princeton, NJ, 1980); P. Sponheim, *Kierkegaard on Christ and Christian Coherence* (1968); N. Viallaneix, *Écoute, Kierkegaard: Essai sur la communication de la parole* (2 vols., 1979); J. W. Elrod, *Kierkegaard and Christendom* (Princeton, NJ [1981]); A. Hannay, *Kierkegaard* (Arguments of the Philosophers, 1982); B. H. Kirmmse, *Kierkegaard in Golden Age Denmark* (Indiana Series in the Philosophy of Religion, Bloomington and Indianapolis [1990]); M. J. Ferreira, *Transforming Vision: Imagination and Will in Kierkegaardian Faith* (Oxford, 1991); G. Pattison, *Kierkegaard: The Aesthetic and the Religious* (1992); D. R. Law, *Kierkegaard as Negative Theologian* (Oxford Theological Monographs, 1993). Good introd. by P. Gardiner, *Kierkegaard* (Past Masters, Oxford and New York, 1988). Series of studies [largely in Eng.] in *Bibliotheca Kierkegaardiana*, ed. N. and M. M. Thulstrup (16 vols., Copenhagen, 1978–88). J. Himmelstrup, *Søren Kierkegaard International Bibliography* (Copenhagen, 1962); A. Jørgensen, *Søren Kierkegaard-litteratur 1961–1970* (Aarhus, 1971); id., *Søren Kierkegaard-litteratur 1971–1980* (ibid., 1983). H. Schröer in *TRE* 18 (1989), pp. 138–55, s.v.

Kikuyu. The village in *Kenya where a Missionary Conference of Anglicans, Presbyterians, and other Protestants was held in June 1913, under the leadership of the Bps. of Mombasa (W. G. Peel) and Uganda (J. J. Willis). A federation of the constituent Churches was proposed, on the basis of common acceptance of the *Apostles' and *Nicene Creeds and the recognition of common membership between the Churches in the federation, carrying with it the right of receiving Communion in any of them. Strong opposition was raised by F. *Weston, Bp. of Zanzibar, who appealed to the Abp. of *Canterbury. The latter gave his 'opinion' that Nonconformists in these areas might be admitted to Communion in Anglican churches, but that Anglicans should not seek Communion at the hands of Nonconformist ministers.

J. J. Willis, *The Kikuyu Conference* (1914); [R. T. *Davidson,] Abp. of Canterbury, *Kikuyu* (1915); H. M. Smith, *Frank* [Weston], *Bp. of Zanzibar* (1926), ch. 8.

Kilham, Alexander (1762–98), founder of the '*Methodist New Connexion'. The son of *Methodist parents, he was admitted a preacher in 1785. After J. *Wesley's death in 1791, he became leader of the radical wing of the movement and advocated complete separation from the Established Church and lay representation in all Church courts. In several pamphlets, of which the most notorious was *The Progress of Liberty* (1795), he expounded his views with vigour, and even violence, and in 1797 was in consequence expelled by the Methodist Conference. In 1798 he founded the New Connexion, but died later in the same year.

Autobiog., ed. J. Grundell and R. Hall (Nottingham [*c.*1799]). Anon. Life [by J. Blackwell], based on materials supplied by his widow and daughter (London, 1838). Shorter Life by W. J. Townsend (ibid. [1890]). A. Gordon in *DNB* 31 (1892), pp. 102 f.

Kilian, St (d. *c.*689), 'Apostle of Franconia'. A native of *Ireland, Kilian was probably already a bishop when he went as a missionary to the Franks and established his headquarters at Würzburg. Acc. to the most ancient account, he converted the local ruler, Duke Gozbert, and much of the population of E. Franconia and Thuringia, before he was put to death in the duke's absence through the enmity of his wife. His feast day, 8 July, is that of the solemn translation of his remains in 752 to the cathedral of Würzburg, of which he is the patron saint. Despite the fame of the early medieval library of Würzburg in Kilian's day, no books from his lifetime are extant.

His *Acta* and *Passio*, pr. in *AASS*, Jul. 2 (1721), pp. 612–18. Modern crit. edn. of *Passio Kiliani Martyris* by W. Levison in *MGH*, Scriptores Rerum Merovingicarum, 5 (1910), pp. 711–28 (text, pp. 722–8). A. Bigelmair, 'Die Passio des heiligen Kilian und seine Gefährten', in *Herbipolis Jubilans: 1200 Jahre Bistum Würzburg. Festschrift zur Säkularfeier der Erhebung der Kiliansreliquien* (Würzburg, 1952), pp. 1–25. B. Bischoff and J. Hofmann, *Libri Sancti Kyliani: Die Würzburger Schreibschule und die Dombibliothek im VIII. und IX. Jahrhundert* (Quellen und Forschungen zur Geschichte des Bistums und Hochstifts Würzburg, 6; 1952). J. Dienemann, *Der Kunst des heiligen Kilian im 8. und 9. Jahrhundert* (ibid. 10, 1955); cf. A. Gwynn, SJ, 'New Light on St Kilian', *Irish Ecclesiastical Record*, 6th ser. 83 (1957), pp. 1–16. A. Wendehorst, 'Die Iren und die Christianisierung Mainfrankens', in H. Löwe (ed.), *Die Iren und Europa im früheren Mittelalter*, 1 (Stuttgart, 1982), pp. 319–29, with bibl.

Kilwardby, Robert (d. 1279), Abp. of *Canterbury. A master of arts in the University of Paris, he made his reputation by commentaries on the grammatical works of Priscian and Donatus and the logic and ethics of *Aristotle. Returning to England, he entered the *Dominican Order and studied theology at Oxford. He was elected provincial prior for England in 1261. He was consecrated Abp. of Canterbury in 1273, on the nomination of Pope *Gregory X, and was assiduous in visitations and in works of charity. In 1277 he visited Oxford and in conjunction with the masters of the University he issued a condemnation of 30 propositions in grammar, logic, and natural philosophy. The condemnations concerning natural philosophy were chiefly directed against certain views maintained by *Thomas Aquinas, notably those connected with the doctrine of the unity of form, a view which seemed to Kilwardby irreconcilable with the Christian faith. In 1278 he was made a cardinal and translated to the see of Porto in Italy. He died at Viterbo.

Kilwardby wrote the 'De ortu scientiarum', a classification of knowledge, largely based on Aristotle. He also wrote an important commentary on the 'Sentences' of *Peter Lombard, and treatises on relation, time, imagination, and conscience. He was responsible for organizing large-scale indexes of patristic writings, mainly of St *Augustine. For this purpose the texts were divided into sections and provided with summaries, an arrangement which has left traces in modern editions.

Kilwardby's *In Donati Artem Maiorem III*, ed. L. Schmücker (Brixen, 1984). *De ortu scientiarum*, ed. A. G. Judy, OP (Auctores Britannici Medii Aevi, 4; London and Toronto, 1976), with extensive bibl. F. Stegmüller, 'Les Questions du Commentaire des Sentences de Robert Kilwardby', *RTAM* 6 (1934), pp. 55–79, 215–28, with text of the questions; the *quaestio De natura theologiae* [the prologue of the Commentary], ed. id. (Opuscula et Textus, series scholastica, 17; Münster, 1935); *Quaestiones* on the Sentences, ed. E. Gössmann and others (Bayerische Akademie der Wissenschaften Veröffentlichungen der Kommission für die Herausgabe ungedruckter Texte aus der mittelalterlichen Geisteswelt, 10, 12, 13, 16, 17, and 19; Munich, 1982–95). *De natura* relationis, ed. L. Schmücker (Lenggries and Schloss Hohenburg, 1980). *De tempore* and *De spiritu fantastico*, ed. P. O. Lewry, OP (Auctores Britannici Medii Aevi, 9; 1987; Eng. tr. and introd. by A. Broadie, ibid. 9 (2) [1993]). M.-D. Chenu, OP, 'Le "De Conscientia" de R. Kilwardby, O.P., † 1279', *RSPT* 16 (1927), pp. 318–26, with text of questions. D. A. Callus, OP, 'The "Tabulae Super Originalia Patrum" of Robert Kilwardby, O.P.', in *Studia Mediaevalia in Honorem Admodum Reverendi Patris Raymundi Josephi Martin ... LXXum Natalem Diem Agentis* (Bruges [1949]), pp. 243–70. The *Injunctions of Archbishop Kilwardby 1276* [on his Visitation of the University of Oxford], ed. H. W. G[arrod], privately pr. (Oxford, 1929). H.-F. Dondaine, OP, 'Le "De 43 Quaestionibus" de Robert Kilwardby', *Archivum Fratrum Praedicatorum*, 47 (1977), pp. 5–50, incl. text. F. *Ehrle, SJ, 'Ein Schreiben des Erzbischofs von Canterbury Robert Kilwardby zur Rechtfertigung seiner Lehrverurtheilung von 18. März 1277', *Archiv für Literatur- und Kirchengeschichte des Mittelalters*, 5 (1889), pp. 607–32, with text. E. M. F. Sommer-Seckendorff, *Studies in the Life of Robert Kilwardby, O.P.* (Dissertationes Historicae, 8; Rome, 1937), with bibl. Kaeppeli, 3 (1980), pp. 320–5, s.v. 'Robertus Kilwardby'; *BRUO* 2 (1958), pp. 1051–2. M. D. Chenu, OP, in *DTC* 8 (pt. 2; 1925), cols. 2354–6, s.v.; J. A. Weisheipl, OP, in *NCE* 12 (1967), p. 533, s.v. 'Robert Kilwardby'.

Kimbangu, Simon (c.1889–1951), Church founder. A member of the *Baptist Church of Lower *Zaire, he was baptized in 1915. After temporary employment as a catechist, he experienced a visionary calling while in Kinshasa and returned to his village home at Nkamba; here his healing ministry soon drew vast crowds. The British Baptist missionaries were unsupportive; RC missionaries and Belgian colonial officials wholly opposed. Kimbangu was arrested six months after beginning his ministry, was tried on a charge of sedition and sentenced to death but, on the appeal of the Baptist authorities to the King of the Belgians, the sentence was commuted to life imprisonment. He died, in prison, in Oct. 1951. Many of his followers, including a number of Baptist deacons, were arrested and deported to other parts of the Congo. This dispersal contributed to the spread of the movement which continued underground in various forms until the 1950s when a legal Church (Église de Jésus-Christ sur la Terre par le prophète Simon Kimbangu) was established, led by Kimbangu's son, Joseph Diangienda. Its ritual centre remains in Nkamba to which Kimbangu's body was translated in 1960, the year of political independence of the Belgian Congo (now Zaire). It claims some millions of members and was admitted to the *World Council of Churches in 1969.

M.-L. Martin, *Kirche ohne Weisse* (Basle [1971]; Eng. tr., *Kimbangu: An African Prophet and his Church*, Oxford [1975]); W. Ustorf, *Afrikanische Initiative: Das aktive Leiden des Propheten Simon Kimbangu* (Studien zur interkulturellen Geschichte des Christentums, 5; Berne, 1975). J. Chomé, *La Passion de Simon Kimbangu* (Brussels [1959]). P. Raymaekers, 'Histoire de Simon Kimbangu, prophète, d'après les écrivains Nfinangani et Nzungu (1921)', *Archives de Sociologie des Religions*, 31 (1971), pp. 15–42; C. Irvine, 'The Birth of the Kimbanguist Movement in the Bas-Zaire 1921', *Journal of Religion in Africa*, 6 (1974), pp. 23–76, with docs.; H. Desroche and P. Raymaekers, 'Départ d'une prophète, arrivée d'une église. Textes et recherches sur la mort de Simon Kimbangu et sur sa survivance', *Archives de Sciences Sociales des Religions*, 42 (1976), pp. 117–62. D. J. Mackay, 'Simon Kimbangu and the B.M.S. tradition', *Journal of Religion in Africa*, 17 (1987), pp. 113–71. See also bibl. to ZAIRE, CHRISTIANITY IN.

Kindred and Affinity, Table of. This Table, published by Abp. M. *Parker in 1563 and printed by custom at the end of the BCP, is based on the degrees of intermarriage prohibited in Lev. 18. It follows J. *Calvin's interpretation, namely that marriage is forbidden between any two persons related more nearly than, or as nearly as, any pair mentioned in Lev. 18, in contrast with M. *Luther's view, favoured by *Henry VIII, that only those marriages are forbidden by God's law which are expresssly named in Lev. 18. The intention of the Table was to set out clearly the marriages forbidden by Divine law and therefore incapable of being allowed by dispensation. Can. 99 of 1604 gave the 1563 Table canonical authority in the C of E, and although it judged such marriages to be 'incestuous and unlawful, and consequently ... dissolved as void from the beginning', at law they were voidable only, until the Marriage Act 1835 ('Lord *Lyndhurst's Act') brought the State law more nearly into line with that of the Church. In 1946 Can. 99 was amended by canon to allow marriage with a deceased wife's sister (on the ground that Calvin's interpretation of Lev. 18 was no longer upheld by modern scholarship), and also with an aunt by marriage or a niece by marriage, thus incidentally bringing the law of the Church into conformity with that of the State (see DECEASED WIFE'S SISTER'S MARRIAGE ACT 1907). Canon B31 of 1969 added an adopted son or daughter to the Table, and specified that the terms 'brother' and 'sister' included brothers and sisters of the half-blood.

Kindred and Affinity as Impediments to Marriage, being the Report of a Commission appointed by his Grace the Archbishop of Canterbury (1940).

King, Edward (1829–1910), Bp. of *Lincoln. He was successively assistant curate of Wheatley, Oxon (1855), chaplain of Cuddesdon Theological College (1858), principal of Cuddesdon (1863), Regius professor of pastoral theology at Oxford (1873), and Bp. of Lincoln (1885). A man of personal holiness, he is most remembered for his teaching on the pastoral duties and spiritual life of the clergy exemplified in his fatherly care for individuals, both as priest and bishop. In his moral and pastoral theology he was much influenced by the work of the German *Jesuit theologian Johann Michael Sailer (d. 1832). He was a Tractarian *High Churchman, and a friend of E. B. *Pusey and H. P. *Liddon. In 1888 a 'ritual prosecution' was brought against him by the *Church Association, and in 1890 decided in the court of the Abp. of Canterbury (E. W. *Benson) substantially in his favour (see LINCOLN JUDGEMENT). Feast day in ASB, 8 Mar.

Collections of his devotional works include his *Spiritual Letters*, ed. B. W. Randolph (1910), *The Love and Wisdom of God: ... Sermons*, ed. id. (1910); *Sermons and Addresses*, ed. id. (1911), and *Pastoral Lectures* [delivered in 1874], ed. E. Graham (1932). Life by G. W. E. Russell (London, 1912). B. W. Randolph and J. W. Townroe, *The Mind and Work of Bishop King* (1918); Lord Elton, *Edward King and our Times* (1958); J. A. Newton, *Search for a Saint: Edward King* (1977); [D.] G. Rowell, *The Vision Glorious: Themes and Personalities of the Catholic Revival in Anglicanism* (Oxford, 1983), pp. 141–57. [W.] O. Chadwick, *The Spirit of the Oxford Movement* (Cambridge, 1990), pp. 256–306. G. W. E. Russell in *DNB, 1901–1911*, pp. 397–400.

King, Martin Luther (1929–68), Black *Baptist minister and champion of civil rights in the USA. The son of a

Baptist pastor, he was born in Atlanta and educated at Morehouse College and Boston University. In 1954 he became pastor of a church in Montgomery, Alabama. Here he became involved in the struggle over segregation and in 1955 he organized a boycott of buses by Blacks which lasted more than a year; it inspired opposition to discrimination which resulted in an order of the Supreme Court imposing desegregation on Alabama buses. In 1959 he resigned from his pastorship in Montgomery and, though co-pastor with his father of a church in Atlanta from 1960 until his death, he devoted himself mainly to the civil rights movement. In 1963 he was arrested in the course of a major confrontation between his supporters and the police in Birmingham, Alabama, but in the following year a Civil Rights Bill was passed. Also in 1964 King was awarded a Nobel Peace Prize. He organized further demonstrations in Florida, Alabama, Mississippi, and elsewhere; throughout he adhered to principles of non-violence. He was much influenced by the thinking of Gandhi, but he went further in believing that the reconciliation of the Black to the White population was as important as that of the Whites to the Blacks. He aroused the opposition of both races and was assassinated in 1968. In 1986 the third Monday in January was made a federal holiday in the USA in commemoration of his birthday (actually 15 Jan.). His writings include *Stride toward Freedom* (1958), *Why We Can't Wait* (1964) and *Where Do We Go From Here: Chaos or Community?* (1967).

His books and various other writings collected as *A Testament of Hope*, ed. J. M. Washington (San Francisco, etc. [1986]). D. L. Lewis, *Martin Luther King: A Critical Biography* (New York and London, 1970; 2nd edn., with rev. title, Urbana, Ill., 1979); S. B. Oates, *Let the Trumpet Sound: The Life of Martin Luther King Jr.* (New York and London, 1982). W. R. Witherspoon, *Martin Luther King, Jr. ...: To the Mountaintop* (New York, 1985). R. D. Abernathy, *And the Walls Came Tumbling Down* (San Francisco, 1989). D. J. Garrow, *Protest at Selma: Martin Luther King, Jr., and the Voting Rights Act of 1965* (New Haven, Conn., and London, 1978); id., *Bearing the Cross: Martin Luther King, Jr., and the Southern Leadership Conference* (New York [1986]). C. Carson and others, *A Guide to Research on Martin Luther King, Jr., and the Modern Black Freedom Stuggle* (Stanford University Libraries, Occasional Publications in Bibliography Series, 1; Stanford, Calif., 1989).

King, William (1650–1729), Abp. of *Dublin. Born in Antrim of Scottish parents, he was educated at *Trinity College, Dublin. He was ordained in 1674 and became Chancellor (1679–89) and Dean (1689–91) of St Patrick's Cathedral in Dublin. During this time he conducted extensive controversies with both RCs and *Presbyterians. As a supporter of William III, he was imprisoned by the Jacobites, but in 1691 he was appointed Bp. of Derry and in 1703 Abp. of Dublin. In these offices, while continuing to oppose Presbyterianism, he energetically promoted the spiritual and temporal welfare of the Church of Ireland. He was passed over for the primacy on account of his Whig sympathies. He showed himself a convinced patriot, resisting all attempts to introduce Englishmen into high office. He was hampered in later years by ill health and, to some extent, by his duties as Lord Justice.

His writings include controversial pieces, a large correspondence which is of value for our knowledge of Ireland in his time, and his most important work, *De Origine Mali*

(1702; Eng. tr., 1731), which attempts to reconcile the existence of evil, and esp. moral evil, with the conception of an omnipotent and beneficent deity; P. *Bayle and G. W. *Leibniz issued rejoinders.

C. S. King (ed.), *A Great Archbishop of Dublin* (1906), incl. text of his autobiog. and correspondence. Diary kept during his imprisonment in 1689 ed. H. J. Lawlor in the *Journal of the Royal Society of Antiquaries of Ireland*, 33 for 1903 (1904), pp. 119–52, 255–83, 389–411. Royal Commission on Historical Manuscripts Report on the Lyons Collection of his Correspondence (3 vols., London, 1987). Study by H. J. Lawlor in *Peploographia Dublinensis* (London, 1902), pp. 101–42. R. Dunlop in *DNB* 31 (1892), pp. 163–7.

King James Version. A title used, esp. in America, for the English translation of the Bible commonly known in England as the *Authorized Version (1611).

King's Book. The name commonly given to *A Necessary Doctrine and Erudition for any Christian Man*, put forth by *Henry VIII in the summer of 1543 after it had been presented to *Convocation earlier in the year. It was based upon the *Bishops' Book of 1537, but except for the facts that the King's supremacy was more strongly asserted and the statements on *purgatory further weakened, its theology was a reaction in a Catholic direction. *Transubstantiation was more clearly defined, some additional articles on Free Will, Good Works, etc., were added, and fuller treatment was given to such subjects as Justification. It was provided with a preface, apparently written by Henry VIII himself, and a preliminary article on Faith, probably the work of T. *Cranmer. In 1544 a free translation into Latin appeared, entitled *Pia et Catholica Christiani Hominis Institutio*.

The King's Book, ed. T. A. *Lacey (1932). Earlier edn. by C. *Lloyd (Oxford, 1825 and 1856).

King's Books. See VALOR ECCLESIASTICUS.

King's College, London. The College was incorporated in 1829 to provide an education on Anglican principles. It was designed as a counterweight to the undenominational University College, London, established by charter in 1827 (then the only English college of University status for Nonconformists, who were still excluded from Oxford and Cambridge). In 1836 a charter established the 'University of London' as a body empowered to grant degrees, for which members of King's College could apply. The opening of the theological department in 1846 was soon followed by a fierce controversy involving the removal of F. D. *Maurice from his position as professor in 1853. By the King's College, London (Transfer) Act, 1908, the greater part of the College was placed within the legal framework of the reconstituted (teaching) University of London, while the theological department gained a separate identity. In 1980 under a new royal charter the College as a whole recovered a legal existence separate from the University and the theological department was reintegrated into the new College structure as its Faculty of Theology and Religious Studies. Until the late 1970s the 'Associateship of King's College' (AKC) was an academic qualification often taken by non-graduate ordinands of the C of E.

F. J. C. Hearnshaw, *History of King's College, London, 1828–1928* (1929); G. Huelin, *King's College London 1828–1978* (1978). Much historical information is to be found in the Calendar of King's College, pub. annually.

King's Confession. The very Protestant statement of belief drawn up by John Craig (*c.*1512–1600) in 1581 when it was feared that Popery might be revived in Scotland through the recent arrival of the Duke of Lennox from France. Its formal title was 'A Short and General Confession of the True Christian Faith and Religion according to God's Word and Acts of our Parliaments', but as it was signed by the King (*James [VI of Scotland]) and his household, it was commonly known as the 'King's Confession'. All parish clergy (and from 1585 also all graduates) were required to sign it. It was reaffirmed in 1590 and 1595, and was the basis of the '*National Covenant' of 1638. It was also known as the 'Negative Confession', since it denied all religion and doctrine not in accord with the *Scottish Confession of 1560. See also COVENANTERS.

Text (Latin and Scots) in P. *Schaff, *A History of the Creeds of Christendom*, 3 (1877), pp. 480–5; also in G. D. Henderson (ed.), *Scots Confession, 1560 (Confessio Scoticana) and Negative Confession, 1581 (Confessio Negativa)* (Edinburgh, 1937), pp. 101–11. See further bibl. s.v. COVENANTERS.

King's evil, touching for the. The tradition that there existed some virtue in the royal touch for healing the 'King's evil', or scrofula, can be traced back to the 11th cent. In France general curative powers were attributed to Robert II (996–1031) and there is evidence that touching for scrofula was regarded as hereditary in the Capetians from the time of Philip I (1060–1108). In England his early biographer records various healings by *Edward the Confessor (1042–66) and *Goscelin in his Life of St Edith (written in 1080) uses the term 'morbus regis'. The custom of touching for the King's evil was practised under Henry I (1100–35) and Henry II (1154–89) and is found again during the reign of Henry VII (1485–1509). *James I encouraged it as proof of his *Divine Right, and it has been estimated that *Charles II touched in all as many as 100,000 persons. Queen *Anne was the last sovereign to perform it, among those whom she touched being the infant Samuel *Johnson. There was often printed a form of service for the touching in editions of the BCP between the reign of *Charles I and 1719.

M. Bloch, *Les Rois thaumaturges* (1924; Eng. tr., 1973 [requires revision on the early period]). K. [V.] Thomas, *Religion and the Decline of Magic* (1971), esp. pp. 192–8, 200–4. F. Barlow, 'The King's Evil', *EHR* 95 (1980), pp. 3–27.

Kingdom of God. The conception of the Kingdom of God (or in Mt. the 'Kingdom of Heaven') is a central element in the teaching of Jesus Christ and has formed the core of attempts to reconstruct what He taught. Its origins lie in the OT, where the kingship of God is acknowledged (Pss. 97, 99, etc.). God's reign was expected to bring with it order and justice, thereby manifesting God's purpose for creation. When political reality conflicted with such convictions, and particularly when the Jews lacked political autonomy, the Kingdom became linked with ideas about the future manifestation of Divine sovereignty in history. Though references to the phrase are not frequent in the inter-testamental period (e.g. *Testaments of the Twelve

Patriarchs, Dan. 5: 10–13, and the Assumption of *Moses, 7–10), the coming of God's reign was seen as one of the events which would herald the end of the present world order; this, it was thought, would involve the overthrow of powers opposed to God and the transfer of power to Israel or to God's agent, the *Messiah. In some later rabbinic texts the coming of the Kingdom of God was identified with obedience to the commands of God (Sifra on Lev. 20: 26).

Acc. to Mk. (1: 15), the ministry of Jesus began with the proclamation of the imminence of the Kingdom. Occasionally the Gospels suggest that it may be already present, e.g. Lk. 17: 21. This is particularly the case in the accounts of the *exorcisms which the Lord performed (Lk. 11: 20; Mt. 12: 28). Entry into the Kingdom is a present possibility, but it demands patterns of behaviour which contrast with the current perceptions of the nature of human dominion (Mk. 10: 13–27). There is, however, little explicit teaching on the nature of the Kingdom. Throughout the Synoptic Gospels, Jesus uses *parables to illustrate the meaning of God's Kingdom, its novelty, and its demands. There are hints that He may have expected its arrival within a generation (Mk. 9: 1). According to the Synoptic Gospels, the rejection of the message of the Kingdom by the religio-political establishment in Jerusalem is linked with judgement on the city and its *Temple (Mk. 13; Mt. 24–5, and Lk. 21). The journey to Jerusalem, the triumphal entry and the incident in the Temple have sometimes been taken to suggest that there may have been a political component in Jesus' understanding of the Kingdom of God as well as in the reasons for His arrest and execution. See JESUS CHRIST.

There has been much discussion about the nature of Jesus' expectation of the Kingdom of God. Some, such as J. *Weiss and A. *Schweitzer, rejected the liberal or *Ritschlian view that the coming of the Kingdom would evolve gradually in history; instead they argued that Jesus expected a cataclysmic irruption into the present world order. Others (notably C. H. *Dodd) argued that He thought the Kingdom of God was a present reality which He had already inaugurated. The eschatological view has exercised a profound influence on NT scholarship, but the practical ethics of the *Sermon on the Mount suggest that an exclusively eschatological focus fails to do justice to the teaching of Jesus on the Kingdom. The evidence of the Gospels does not allow certainty about whether Jesus thought of Himself as the Messiah, but the early Christian conviction about His messianic dignity has roots in His preaching of the Kingdom.

In Jn. the Kingdom is replaced by references to '*eternal life' (the close link between the concepts is evident in 3: 3–5), and elsewhere in the NT there are few references to the Kingdom (Rom. 14: 17; 1 Cor. 4: 20; and Col. 1: 13). Nevertheless, anticipation of the future coming of the Kingdom was an important element in early Christian thought, and throughout the NT and early patristic period it was expected to take place in this world. By the 3rd cent. belief in the imminence of the *Parousia had begun to fade, and St *Augustine was articulating earlier trends when he argued that the Kingdom of God was a supernatural entity whose presence could be only dimly perceived in the time between the first and second comings of Christ. His interpretation set the pattern of discussion of eschatology in the W. Church in the following centuries. *Joachim of Fiore's interpretation of Rev. opened again the possibility of a visible establishment of the Kingdom of God in this world and his writings exercised great influence on radical religious groups in the Middle Ages. Much modern political theology has also refused to accept the view that the Kingdom is utterly transcendent and has sought to find a place for human endeavour in its establishment. Though it is indebted to G. W. F. *Hegel and Karl Marx, it has echoes in the early eschatological tradition of Christianity. See also ESCHATOLOGY, LIBERATION THEOLOGY, MILLENARIANISM, and PAROUSIA.

There are discussions of the passages in biblical Books in the various comm. listed s.vv. The works of Weiss, Schweitzer, and Dodd are listed in the entries, s.vv. G. Lundström, *Gude Rike i Jesu Förkunnelse* (Lund, 1947; Eng. tr., with continuation, *The Kingdom of God in the Teaching of Jesus: A History of Interpretation from the Last Decades of the Nineteenth Century to the Present Day*, 1963); N. Perrin, *The Kingdom of God in the Teaching of Jesus* (1963); W. Willis (ed.), *The Kingdom of God in 20th-century Interpretation* (Peabody, Mass. [1987]); C. Rowland, *Radical Christianity* (Cambridge, 1988); B. E. Daley, SJ, *The Hope of the Early Church: A Handbook of Patristic Eschatology* (ibid., 1991), *passim*; R. S. Barbour (ed.), *The Kingdom of God and Human Society* (Edinburgh, 1993). See also other works cited under ESCHATOLOGY.

Kings, Books of. These two Books, which record the history of the Hebrew monarchy from the accession of *Solomon (c.970 BC) to the Fall of *Jerusalem (c.586 BC), are structurally a continuation of the Books of *Samuel. The division into two books is not original, but comes from the Greek translators, who also grouped them with the Books of Samuel and designated all four as the 'Books of the Reigns'. In the MS tradition of the *Vulgate there are two Books, namely Samuel and Kings. In some quarters, however, the division into four persisted and this method of designation (*1–4 Regum*) came to be printed in the headlines of the Clementine edition of the Vulgate (and survives in some RC translations); hence, in the AV, the headings 'The First (Second) Book of the Kings, commonly called The Third (Fourth) Book of the Kings'.

The narrative opens with an account of the events leading up to the accession of Solomon (1 Kgs. 1–2). The reign of Solomon, esp. the building of the Temple, is described with great fullness (3–11). The history of the two separate kingdoms of Judah and Israel, formed from the partition of Solomon's domains at his death, then follows on a carefully arranged plan, the events of each reign being fitted into a standard framework which allowed the events of the two kingdoms to be treated alternately. This plan is adopted down to the fall of the kingdom of Israel to Assyria c.721 BC (2 Kgs. 17), after which the narrative is concerned solely with Judah (2 Kgs. 18–25). Of the later kings, the writer paid special attention to Josiah, whose reforming work he commended.

The author's main interest is religious throughout. This is seen from the way in which events and reigns of religious significance are described in great detail, whereas those of the highest political importance are often passed over very cursorily. Modern critics have come to see close affinities between the theological outlook of the author and that reflected in the Book of *Deuteronomy, and many of them regard Kings as the last two Books in the so-called '*Deuteronomistic History' (q.v.). The author of the Books evidently had access to several sound historical sources. Some of these are cited in the text, e.g. the 'Acts of Solomon' (1 Kgs. 11: 41), the 'Chronicles of the Kings of Israel' (1 Kgs. 14: 19 etc.) and 'of Judah' (1 Kgs. 15: 7 etc.), and the probability is that there were others not named, such as official court records and collections of stories centred on the activities of the Prophets *Elijah and Elisha.

Comm. by J. A. Montgomery (posthumous, ed. H. S. Gehman, ICC, 1951), J. Gray (London, 1964; 2nd edn., 1970). M. *Noth ([to 1 Kgs. 16] Biblischer Kommentar, *Altes Testament*, 9; 1964–8), M. Rehm (2 vols., Würzburg [1979–82]), G. H. Jones (New Cent. Bib., 2 vols., 1984), S. J. De Vries (on 1 Kgs., Word Biblical Comm. 12; Waco, Tex. [1985]), T. R. Hobbs (on 2 Kgs., ibid. 13 [1985]), and M. Cogan and H. Tadmor (on 2 Kgs., Anchor Bible, 1988). C. F. *Burney, *Notes on the Hebrew Text of the Books of Kings* (1903). G. von *Rad, 'Die deuteronomistische Geschichtstheologie in den Königsbüchern', *Forschungen zur Religion und Literatur des Alten und Neuen Testaments*, NF 40 (1947), pp. 52–64, repr. in *Gesammelte Studien zum Alten Testament* (1958), pp. 189–204; Eng. tr., *The Problem of the Hexateuch and Other Essays* (1966), pp. 205–21. A. Jepsen, *Die Quellen des Königsbuches* (Halle/Saale, 1953). J. Begrich, *Die Chronologie der Könige von Israel und Juda und die Quellen des Rahmens der Königsbücher* (Beiträge zur historischen Theologie, 3; 1929); E. R. Thiele, *The Mysterious Numbers of the Hebrew Kings* (Chicago, 1951; Exeter, 1966); K. T. Andersen, 'Die Chronologie der Könige von Israel und Juda', *Studia Theologica*, 23 (1969), pp. 69–112, with refs. B. Halpern, *The First Historians: The Hebrew Bible and History* (San Francisco and London [1988]), esp. pp. 144–80 and 207–65.

Kingship of Christ, Feast of the. See CHRIST THE KING, FEAST OF.

Kingsley, Charles (1819–75), Anglican divine, social reformer, and novelist. Born at Holne in Devonshire, he was educated locally, at *King's College, London (1836–8), and at Magdalene College, Cambridge (1838–42). In 1842 he was ordained to the curacy of Eversley, Hants, where he became vicar in 1844 and spent most of the rest of his life. From 1860 to 1869 he was Regius Professor of Modern History at Cambridge (a post for which he came to recognize that he was ill-qualified; it required only a short period of residence each year). Later he held canonries at *Chester (1869–73) and *Westminster (1873–5).

Kingsley, who fell under the influence of F. D. *Maurice and T. *Carlyle, became keenly interested in the movement for social reform. He was a leading spirit in the *Christian Socialist Movement (q.v.), but he looked to the extension of the co-operative principle and educational and sanitary reform rather than radical political change for the amelioration of the condition of the people. He was at first the principal pamphleteer and spokesman of the group and under the pseudonym 'Parson Lot' contributed to *Politics for the People* (1848) and *The Christian Socialist* (1850–1). He was strongly averse to all forms of asceticism (monasticism; clerical celibacy; non-smoking) and as such was a critic of *Tractarian ideals. He soon came to be regarded as a leading exponent of 'muscular Christianity'.

The Saint's Tragedy (1848; preface by F. D. Maurice), written in dramatic form, developed out of a Life of St *Elizabeth of Hungary, begun in 1842 as a critique of asceticism. His principal novels were *Yeast* (1850; orig. pub. by 'Parson Lot' in *Fraser's Magazine*, 1848), *Alton*

Locke (1850), *Hypatia* (1853; on the factions in the Church of *Alexandria in the early 5th cent.), *Westward Ho!* (1855), *The Heroes* (1856), *Two Years Ago* (1857), and *Hereward the Wake* (1866). An ill-considered jibe at J. H. *Newman in 1863 ('Truth for its own sake has never been a virtue of the Roman clergy. Father Newman informs us that it need not and on the whole ought not to be') led to the publication of the latter's **Apologia* (q.v.) in 1864. To this period his popular children's book, *The Water-Babies* (1863), also belongs.

The novelist **Henry Kingsley** (1830–76), the author of *Ravenshoe* (1862), was a younger brother.

Collected Works (28 vols., 1880–5; 19 vols., 1901–3). Life by his widow (2 vols., 1877; abridgements, 1879, 1883). Other studies by M. F. Thorp (Princeton, NJ, 1937), U. C. Pope-Hennessy (London, 1948), R. B. Martin (ibid., 1959), S. Chitty, *The Beast and the Monk* (ibid., 1974), and B. Colloms (ibid., 1975). S. Harris, *Charles Kingsley: A Reference Guide* (Boston [1981]). L. Stephen in *DNB* 31 (1892), pp. 175–81.

Kirk. The Scottish equivalent of 'Church'. Although the Church of Scotland has ceased to be officially designated 'The Kirk' since the *Westminster Assembly (1645–8), the term is retained in the name of its lowest court, the *Kirk session, and popularly the old Presbyterian Establishment is still occasionally called 'the Auld Kirk'.

Kirk, Kenneth Escott (1886–1954), Bp. of *Oxford. Educated at St John's College, Oxford, he was ordained deacon in 1912 and priest in 1913. He was Chaplain to the Forces (1914–19), Fellow and chaplain of Trinity College, Oxford (1922–33), and Regius professor of moral and pastoral theology (1932–7). In 1937 he became Bp. of Oxford. He was widely recognized as the most outstanding of Anglican writers on moral theology in his day. His principal writings include *Some Principles of Moral Theology* (1920), *Ignorance, Faith, and Conformity* (1925), *Conscience and its Problems* (1927), and *The Vision of God* (1931; the *Bampton Lectures for 1928). Kirk also published a commentary on Romans (Clarendon Bible, 1937) and edited *Personal Ethics* (1934), *The Study of Theology* (1939), and *The Apostolic Ministry* (1946).

Collected addresses and papers, *Beauty and Bands*, ed. E. W. Kemp (1955). E. W. Kemp, *The Life and Letters of Kenneth Escott Kirk* (1959). Id. in *DNB, 1951–1960*, pp. 589–91.

Kirk session (also known simply as the **session**). The lowest court in the Church of *Scotland and other Presbyterian Churches. It consists of the minister and elders of a local congregation. Its main duties are to supervise and control the congregation and to keep the Communion roll up to date.

Kiss of Peace (also **Pax**). The mutual greeting of the faithful in the Eucharistic Liturgy, as a sign of their love and union. It is first mentioned by St *Justin Martyr (2nd cent.) and is probably a usage of the Apostolic period (cf. Rom. 16: 16, 1 Pet. 5: 14, etc.). In the *Byzantine, *Gallican, and *Mozarabic rites the Peace is given before or after the offering of the Oblations, a position suggested by Mt. 5: 23 f.; in the Roman rite it is given later in the service, namely, shortly before the Communion. Traces of the former position are also found in the *Ambrosian rite.

Originally an actual kiss, the form of the Peace has been modified in all rites. In the W. the traditional practice was for the person giving the Peace to place his hands on the shoulders of the recipient, who in turn placed his hands on the elbows of the giver, each bowing their heads towards each other, but in recent years hand-shaking has become more common outside monastic houses. In 1969 the official English RC rendering of 'osculum pacis' was given as the 'sign of peace', but no special manner of giving it was laid down. It was, however, no longer to be passed from the celebrant to the deacon, the deacon to the subdeacon and finally to the people, but the celebrant now gives the sign of peace to any ministers present and the people give it among themselves independently. The Peace was formerly omitted on *Maundy Thursday, *Good Friday, *Holy Saturday, and in Masses for the Dead, but is now permitted on these occasions and indeed prescribed in the *Paschal Vigil Service. Its use was confined to *High Mass but prescribed for all Masses in 1969. Modern Anglican liturgies provide for an (optional) exchange of 'a sign of peace' (ASB) or mutual greetings, normally before the offertory. In E. Orthodox practice a Kiss of Peace is exchanged by the whole congregation at the end of Easter Mattins (which forms part of the midnight vigil; see PASCHAL VIGIL SERVICE). In the *Church of the East it is given at the end of the evening office. See also PAX BREDE.

Jungmann (1958 edn.), 2, pp. 399–413; Eng. tr., pp. 321–32, with refs. H. Thurston, SJ, in *CE* 8 (1910), pp. 663–5, s.v.; F. *Cabrol, OSB, in *DACL* 2 (1910), cols. 117–30, s.v. 'Baiser'.

Kittel, Gerhard (1888–1948), German Protestant theologian. The younger son of the OT scholar Rudolf Kittel, he studied at Leipzig, *Tübingen, Berlin, and Kiel. After an appointment at Leipzig in 1917, he became professor at Greifswald in 1922, at Tübingen in 1926, at Vienna in 1939, and again at Tübingen in 1943. His most important scholarly work was the *Theologisches Wörterbuch zum Neuen Testament* (9 vols., 1933–73 + register and supplement, 1978–9; Eng. tr., 10 vols., 1964–76), on which he worked from 1928 until his death, editing the first four volumes and contributing a number of articles. The purpose of this massive dictionary was to show the meanings which Greek words took on in the language of the NT. Most of the contributors belonged to the '*Biblical Theology' movement and the work was influential in popularizing this outlook, but subsequent work by J. Barr and others suggests that the articles, though assembling valuable material, were often tendentious, and their linguistic conclusions untenable. Kittel's early work on the relationship of primitive Christianity to Palestinian Judaism led on to consideration of the status of the Jews in contemporary Germany. His writings on this subject (notably *Die Judenfrage*, 1933, and *Die historischen Voraussetzungen der jüdischen Rassenmischung*, 1939) lent scholarly support to Nazi anti-Semitism and in 1945 he was arrested and dismissed from his university post by the French authorities. He remains a controversial figure.

List of his works by G. Friedrich and G. Reyher in *TLZ* 74 (1949), pp. 171–5. J. Barr, *The Semantics of Biblical Language* (Oxford, 1961), pp. 206–62. L. Siegele-Wenschkewitz, *Neutestamentliche Wissenschaft vor der Judenfrage: Gerhard Kittels theologische Arbeit im Wandel deutscher Geschichte* (Munich, 1980).

R. P. Ericksen, *Theologians under Hitler* (New Haven, Conn., and London, 1985), pp. 28–78. J. S. Vos, 'Antijudaismus/Antisemitismus im Theologischen Wörterbuch zum Neuen Testament', *Nederlandse Theologisch Tijdschrift*, 38 (1984), pp. 89–110. G. and J. Friedrich in *TRE* 19 (1990), pp. 221–5, s.v., with bibl.

Klopstock, Friedrich Gottlieb (1724–1803), German poet. The son of a lawyer, he was born at Quedlinburg and studied at Schulpforta (1739–45), at Jena (1745–6), and Leipzig (1746–8). He completed *c.*1746 the first section of an epic in prose inspired by a translation (1732) by J. Bodmer (1698–1783) of J. *Milton's *Paradise Lost*. At Leipzig he began to transpose it into hexameters and in 1748 issued part of it in the *Bremer Beiträge* as the first three cantos of *Der Messias* (completed 1773); though published anonymously, its authorship was soon known. In 1751 he was offered a pension by King Frederick V of Denmark to enable him to complete *Der Messias*. He resided at Copenhagen until 1770, when he retired to Hamburg. In 1789 he was visited by S. T. *Coleridge and W. *Wordsworth.

Der Messias, a poem of nearly 20,000 lines distributed in 20 cantos, is concerned with the Passion and 40 days after the Resurrection. It not only describes events on earth, but introduces hosts of angels and devils, even the Trinity itself appearing, giving to every event and action its deeper significance. In the opening portions its bold suggestion of intensity and infinity raised reflective German poetry to a new level, but later the theme became wearisome. From a literary point of view the work is important as the first modern German epic. His other poetry included two volumes of *Geistliche Lieder* (1758 and 1769), as well as religious drama, some of it in verse. He devoted the last years of his life to philology.

Crit. edn. of his *Werke und Briefe* by H. Gronemeyer and others ('Hamburger Ausgabe', Berlin and New York, 1974 ff., with bibl. and further subsidiary material in Abteilung Addenda, 1975 ff.), Eng. tr. of *Der Messias* [by J. Collyer], 2 vols., London, 1763. Classic Life by F. Muncker (Stuttgart, 1888). E. Bailly, *Étude sur la vie et les œuvres de Frédéric Gottlieb Klopstock* (Lyons thesis; Paris, 1888); K. Kindt, *Klopstock* (Berlin, 1941). K. Hilliard, *Philosophy, Letters, and the Fine Arts in Klopstock's Thought* (Bithell Series of Dissertations, 12; 1987). M. Freivogel, *Klopstock der heilige Dichter* (Basler Studien zur deutschen Sprache und Literatur, 15; 1954); G. Kaiser, *Klopstock: Religion und Dichtung* (Gütersloh, 1963); A. Bogaert, *Klopstock: La Religion dans la Messiade* (Germanica, 6; Paris, 1965). K. Hurlebusch in *TRE* 19 (1990), pp. 271–5, s.v.

Klosterneuburg, a celebrated monastery of *canons regular of St Augustine, nr. Vienna. It was founded not later than 1108 by Margrave Leopold III and his consort, Agnes, for secular canons, and was given to the *Augustinian Canons in 1133. As it became very rich, it was frequently raided in times of war and civil strife, e.g. during the *Hussite wars, in the Reformation period, and in the wars against the Turks. It possesses great art treasures, e.g. the famous 'Verdun Altar' and precious stained glass dating from the 13th to the 15th cents., as well as a large library with important MSS and *incunabula. Its present buildings date from the finest period of the Austrian Baroque. In modern times Klosterneuburg has become noted for its active support of the *Liturgical Movement, fostered esp. by Pius Parsch, the editor of several liturgical periodicals.

There is a considerable lit., of which the chief items to date are listed by F. Röhrig in *L.Th.K.* (3rd edn.), 6 (1997), cols. 148 f., s.v. Id., *Klosterneuburg* (Wiener Geschichtsbücher, 11 [1972]). Catalogue of MSS ed. H. Pfeiffer and B. Černík (1, Vienna, 1922; 2, Klosterneuburg, 1931); also by A. Haidinger (Österreichische Akademie der Wissenschaften, philosophisch-historische Klasse, Denkschriften, 168, 225, etc.; 1983 ff.). Useful introd. by O. L. Kapsner, OSB, *Monastic Manuscript Microfilm Project: Progress Report*, 4 (Saint John's University, Collegeville, Minn., 1968), pp. 1–4. Catalogue of the 'Kunst-Sammlungen', ed. by the Director of the Kunst-historisches Museum at Vienna (1937 ff.; pt. 1 at Klosterneuburg; pts. 3 ff. at Vienna). *Jahrbuch des Stiftes Klosterneuburg* (9 vols., Klosterneuburg, 1908–20; NF, 1961 ff.).

kneelers. See GENUFLECTENTES.

Kneeling, Declaration on. See BLACK RUBRIC.

Knights Hospitaller; Knights of Malta; and Knights of Rhodes. See HOSPITALLERS.

Knights Templar. See TEMPLARS.

Knowles, David (1896–1974), monastic historian. Michael Clive Knowles was educated at *Downside and became a monk there in 1914, taking the name David. He read classics at *Cambridge (1919–22) and studied theology in Rome (1922–3). It was only in 1929 that he began research into monastic history. He planned a new monastic community which would return to a more primitive, contemplative observance, abandoning the school-teaching functions of *Benedictine houses in England; the project was forbidden by Rome (1934) and in 1939 Knowles left the community; though formally reconciled in 1952 he lived apart from it for the rest of his life. From 1944 he was a Fellow of Peterhouse, Cambridge; he was Professor of Medieval History (1947–54) and then Regius Professor of Modern History (1954–63). His principal work was *The Monastic Order in England, 943–1216* (1940; 2nd edn., 940–1210, 1963), with its sequel, *The Religious Orders in England* (3 vols., 1948–59); these volumes provide a magisterial survey of the subject up to the *dissolution of the monasteries, combining insight with critical judgement, and deep scholarship with superb English style. His other works include *The Episcopal Colleagues of Archbishop Thomas Becket* (Ford Lectures, 1949; 1951), *The English Mystical Tradition* (1961), *The Evolution of Medieval Thought* (1962; rev. edn., 1988) which was based on lectures which inspired a group of younger scholars, and *From Pachomius to Ignatius: A Study in the Constitutional History of the Religious Orders* (1966). In his last years he was known as a conservative RC theologian.

Some of his essays were collected and presented to him in *The Historian and Character and other Essays* (Cambridge, 1963), with bibl. to 1962, pp. 363–73; bibl. from 1963 by A. Stacpoole, OSB, in *Ampleforth Journal*, 80, pt. 3 (1975), pp. 48–55; 81, pt. 1 (1976), p. 40. Memoir by A. Morey, OSB (London, 1979). C. [N. L.] Brooke and others, *David Knowles Remembered* (Cambridge, 1991). C. N. L. Brooke, 'David Knowles', *Proceedings of the British Academy*, 61 (1975), pp. 439–77; id. in *DNB, 1971–1980*, pp. 474 f.

Knox, Alexander (1757–1831), Irish Anglican theological writer. He was a descendant of J. *Knox. In much of his teaching he anticipated the *Oxford Movement. Thus he affirmed that the C of E was not a 'protestant' Church, but a reformed branch of the Church Catholic, and he stressed the need for adherence to the *Apostolic Succession, the BCP, and the *Thirty-Nine Articles. He stressed the importance of the mystical tradition in Christianity and saw the liturgy as encouraging inward religion. From his friend, J. *Wesley, he learnt the value of frequent communion and for many years worked in harmony with Bp. J. *Jebb, whose *Thirty Years' Correspondence* gives a valuable picture of him.

His writings were collected as *The Remains of Alexander Knox*, by J. J. Hornby (4 vols., 1834–7). Y. Brilioth, *The Anglican Revival: Studies in the Oxford Movement* (1925), pp. 45–55 and 331–3. J. H. Overton in *DNB* 31 (1892), pp. 304 f., with further refs.

Knox, Edmund Arbuthnott (1847–1937), Bp. of Manchester. Educated at Corpus Christi College, Oxford, he held a Fellowship at Merton from 1869 to 1884, and after various parochial charges became (suffragan) Bp. of *Coventry in 1894. From 1903 to 1921 he was Bp. of Manchester. He was one of the most prominent *Evangelicals of his generation, a great preacher (esp. famed were his missions on the Blackpool sands), and a strong advocate of Church schools. His writings include *Sacrifice or Sacrament?* (1914), a defence of the Protestant doctrine of the Lord's Supper, and *On What Authority?* (1922), attacking the liberal school of Biblical critics. After his retirement he continued to take an active part in ecclesiastical affairs and vigorously opposed the Revised Prayer Book (rejected 1927 and 1928). He was also the author of an interesting study, *The Tractarian Movement, 1833–1845* (1933).

E. A. Knox, *Reminiscences of an Octogenarian, 1847–1934* (1935). L. W. Grensted in *DNB, 1931–1940*, pp. 516 f.

Knox, John (*c*.1513–72), Scottish Reformer. He was born at Haddington, educated at Glasgow and possibly St Andrews, received minor orders, perhaps even the priesthood, and set up as a notary in his native town. Having given up his profession he became a private tutor *c*.1544, and soon afterwards, under the influence of the reforming G. *Wishart, embraced the principles of the Reformation. In 1547 he became preacher at St Andrews; at the capture of the castle by the French galleys he was taken prisoner and sent to France, but released in 1549, when he came to England. In 1551 he was made chaplain to *Edward VI and as such assisted in the final stages of the revision of the Second Prayer Book; he appears to have been chiefly responsible for the *Black Rubric. In 1553 he went as a preacher to Bucks, but on *Mary's accession fled to the Continent. He met J. *Calvin at Geneva, and in 1554 was for a short time pastor of the English refugees at Frankfurt, but was expelled after a dispute over ceremonial in community worship. In 1555 he returned to Scotland. Here his preaching and writing met with great success, but the continuing persecution of Protestants led him in 1556 to accept a call to the English church at Geneva, where he published several tracts concerning the situation in Scotland, among them *The First Blast of the Trumpet against the Monstrous Regiment of Women* (1558), a violent diatribe against Mary of Guise and Mary Tudor, asserting that government by a woman is contrary to the law of nature and to Divine ordinance. This pamphlet, which appeared shortly before the accession of *Elizabeth, earned him the hostility of the English Queen, who refused to let him pass through England on his way back to Scotland in 1559.

Becoming leader of the Reforming party, he devoted himself to preaching and to procuring money and troops from England. After the death of Mary of Guise (1560), he drew up the *Scottish Confession (q.v.) and brought into being a commission which abolished the authority of the Pope, 'idolatry', and the Mass, the celebration of and attendance at which was forbidden under pain of death. The *First Book of *Discipline (q.v.) was largely his work. Also in 1560, his only theological work was published at Geneva: *An Answer to a great number of blasphemous cavillations written by an Anabaptist, and adversary to God's eternal Predestination*, in which he defended the *supralapsarian form of *predestination. After *Mary Stuart's return to Scotland (1561), Knox came into repeated conflicts with the Queen over the question of having Mass celebrated for her as well as over the worldliness of her court, on both of which subjects he preached violent sermons. The 'Book of *Common Order' (1556–64), the Scottish service book, was largely his work. In 1567 he preached daily against the Queen, and after her abdication preached the sermon at the coronation of *James and became closely connected with the regent, the earl of Moray. After the murder of Moray in 1570 Knox's political power diminished, and it was only after his death that his cause finally triumphed. Outspoken in his hatred of Catholicism, Knox easily made enemies; yet, fearless and straightforward, he wielded an enormous influence. His principal work is the *History of the Reformation of Religion within the Realm of Scotland*. An early (unfinished) edition was issued by T. Vautrollier in 1587 and immediately seized and suppressed. The first complete edition appeared in 1644.

His works were ed. by D. Laing (6 vols., Edinburgh, 1846–64). Modern edns. of his *History of the Reformation in Scotland* by W. C. Dickinson (2 vols., London, 1949), and of *The First Blast of the Trumpet* and some other political writings by M. A. Breslow (Washington, DC, London, and Toronto [1985]). Lives by T. McCrie (Edinburgh, 1812), P. Hume Brown (2 vols., London, 1895), E. Muir (ibid., 1929), G. MacGregor (ibid., 1958), and J. Ridley (Oxford, 1968). J. S. McEwen, *The Faith of John Knox* (Croal Lectures for 1960; 1961). R. G. Kyle, *The Mind of John Knox* (Lawrence, Kan., 1984). Id., 'John Knox's Concept of Divine Providence and its Influence on his Thought', *Albion*, 18 (1986), pp. 395–410. I. Hazlett, 'A Working Bibliography of Writings by John Knox', in R. V. Schnucker (ed.), *Calviniana: Ideas and Influence of John Calvin* (Sixteenth Century Essays and Studies, 10; Kirksville, Mo. [1988]), pp. 185–93. Æ. Mackay in *DNB* 31 (1892), pp. 308–28.

Knox, Ronald Arbuthnott (1888–1957), Catholic apologist and translator of the Bible. The son of E. A. *Knox, he had a brilliant career at Eton and Balliol College, Oxford, and was soon a leading personality in the extreme *Anglo-Catholic movement. In 1912 he became Fellow and Chaplain of Trinity College, Oxford. He became widely known in ecclesiastical circles through his attack on *Foundations* in a satirical poem in the style of J. *Dryden, 'Absolute and Abitofhell', originally pub. in the *Oxford*

Magazine, 28 Nov. 1912. In 1917 he was received into the RC Church at Farnborough Abbey; in 1918 he published *A Spiritual Aeneid* (autobiographical); and in 1919 he was ordained to the RC priesthood. After teaching for some years at St Edmund's College, Ware, he became chaplain to the RC undergraduates at Oxford in 1926. In 1939 he resigned this appointment to devote himself to a translation of the Bible. Working from the Latin *Vulgate text, he sought to put the Bible into timeless English, and his version has considerable literary merit. The NT was completed in 1945 and the OT in 1949; the whole Bible in one volume was issued in 1955. After some hesitations, the edition was authorized by the RC hierarchy for public use in church. Knox's other writings include *Some Loose Stones* (1913), *On Englishing the Bible* (1949), *Enthusiasm* (1950), and many books of popular apologetic and fiction, esp. detective stories.

Life by E. Waugh (London, 1959). T. Corbishley, SJ, *Ronald Knox the Priest* (1964); R. Speaight, *Ronald Knox the Writer* (1966). C. Hollis in *DNB, 1951–1960*, pp. 595–7.

Koch, Johann. See COCCEIUS, JOHANNES.

Kohler, Christian and Hieronymus. See BRÜGGLERS.

Kolbe, St Maximilian (1894–1941), martyr. Raymond Kolbe was born at Zduńska Wola, near Łódź, studied at Lvov and later Cracow, and in 1910 joined the *Franciscans, taking the name of Maximilian. He continued his studies in Rome, and there in 1917 founded his Marian *Militia Immaculatae* to oppose the encroachment of secularism in modern society. In poor health, he returned to Cracow in 1919 to teach Church history in a seminary. In 1922 he set up a magazine, *Rycerz Niepokalanej* (Knights of the Immaculate) to promote Christian teaching, and also a friary at Grodno to assist in the enterprise; in 1927 this community moved to a site near Teresin (W. of Warsaw), and the new friary was called Niepokalanów ('City of the Immaculate'). Another community was established in Japan, but Kolbe was recalled to Niepokalanów in 1936. His publishing continued after the German occupation of Poland in 1939 and Kolbe was arrested and sent to Auschwitz in 1941. Soon he volunteered to take the place of a young man chosen for death by starvation in reprisal for an attempted escape. After surviving a fortnight, Kolbe was killed by a lethal injection. He was beatified in 1971 and canonized in 1982. Feast day, 14 August.

Most of the literature is in Polish. D. Dewar, *Saint of Auschwitz: The story of Maksymilian Kolbe* (1982). E. Piacenti, OFM Conv, in *DIP* 5 (1978), cols. 362–7, s.v., with extensive bibl.; D. H. Farmer, *The Oxford Dictionary of Saints* (3rd edn., 1992), pp. 283 f.

kollyva (Gk. κόλλυβα). In the E. Church, a cake made of grains of wheat or rice, spices, dried fruit, and pomegranate seeds, and usually covered with sugar; this is blessed during memorial services for the departed and distributed to those present.

Komenský, Jan Amos. See COMENIUS, J. A.

komvoschinion (Gk. κομβοσχοίνιον; Slavonic, *vervitsa* or *tchotki*). In the E. Church, a knotted cord of wool or other material (less commonly, a string of beads), corresponding to the W. *rosary, although differing in structure. It is often used when reciting the *Jesus Prayer.

Konkordienformel. See CONCORD, FORMULA AND BOOK OF.

kontakion. See CONTAKION.

Koran (Arab. *Qur'ān*, 'recitation'). The sacred book of *Islam, which Muhammad claimed had been revealed to him as the very Word of God, through the mediation of the archangel *Gabriel. It is made up of short passages revealed at intervals throughout Muhammad's prophetic career; although committed to writing during his life, the present text dates from the recension of the Caliph Uthman (643–56), as does also its arrangement in 114 sections (*sūras*), placed roughly in decreasing order of length, irrespective of date of revelation. It lays strong stress on God's unity and omnipotence, and on the rewards and punishments of the life to come, but it also embodies the basic principles of Islamic law, ethics, and institutions, and some homiletic material based on Jewish and Christian sources, esp. the *Haggadah and the NT apocrypha.

The first Eng. tr. direct from the Arabic was that of G. Sale (London, 1734). That of R. Bell (2 vols., Edinburgh, 1937–9; rev. edn. by W. M. Watt, 1970) and the Fr. tr. of R. Blachère (2 vols., Paris, 1949–51) are representative of the European scholarly approach; that of N. J. Dawood (Penguin Classics, 1956) is based on traditional Muslim scholarship; A. J. Arberry, *The Koran Interpreted* (2 vols., 1955), seeks rather to give an impression of the literary form. R. Bell, *Introduction to the Qur'ān* (1953). R. Blachère, *Introduction au Coran* (1947; 2nd edn., 1959). J. Burton, *The Collection of the Qur'ān* (Cambridge, 1977). A. Rippin (ed.), *Approaches to the History of the Interpretation of the Qur'ān* (Oxford, 1988). T. Noeldcke, *Geschichte des Qorāns* (1860; 2nd edn. by F. Schwally and others, 3 vols., 1909–38).

Korea, Christianity in. The first Korean Christians were converted in *Japan at the end of the 16th cent.; they were prisoners captured during the Japanese invasions of Korea in 1592–98. The second introduction of Christianity was from *China. Korean envoys to Beijing (Peking) had contact with the *Jesuit missionaries there and Korean scholars obtained books on Christianity translated into Chinese. A Korean was baptized in Beijing in 1784. Although the Confucian rulers of the Korean kingdom opposed the spread of a foreign religion, by the end of the 18th cent. the Christian community numbered several thousand. In 1831 the Congregation of *Propaganda created an apostolic *vicariate in Korea. The first European missionaries, of the Société des Missions Étrangères de Paris, arrived in 1835. Korean Christians were subjected to waves of persecution, the most severe being in 1866–9, when more than 2,000 were killed; 103 of those martyred in 1839–46 and 1866–7 were canonized by Pope *John Paul II on his visit to South Korea in 1984. In 1876 the first Korean Protestant converts were baptized in Manchuria by Scottish missionaries. In the 1880s, following treaties between Korea and the W. powers, freedom of religion was granted. From 1884 a large number of Protestant missionaries began work in Korea, mainly American *Presbyterians and *Methodists. An Anglican bishop arrived from England in 1890. Protestant missionaries founded many educational and medical institutions. Presbyterians, who adopted the principles of self-support advocated by the Chinese missionary John L. Nevius, became the largest Christian body. The National Christian Council (later the National Council of Churches in Korea) was founded in 1924. In the RC Church the first Korean bishop was appointed in 1942 and a hierarchy established in 1962.

After the annexation of Korea by Japan in 1910, many Protestants supported the Korean nationalist movement. In the 1930s there was conflict with the government when some Christians refused to participate in Shinto ceremonies. After the defeat of Japan in the Second World War, Korea was divided at the 38th degree of latitude. In 1948 the Republic of Korea was inaugurated in the South and the (Communist) Democratic People's Republic of Korea in the North. In N. Korea the state attempted to eradicate religious institutions and many Christians migrated south. During the Korean War (1950–53) many Christians in N. Korea were killed; little is known about those who remain there.

In S. Korea Christianity is vigorous but fragmented. As a result of extensive evangelistic work, Church membership has grown rapidly since the 1950s. Among Protestants many schisms have occurred, and there are now more than a hundred indigenous sects and denominations. The Holy Spirit Association for the Unification of World Christianity (the 'Moonies'), founded in 1954 by Sun Myung Moon, has spread to many other countries. The Full Gospel Central Church in Seoul claims to be the largest single Christian congregation in the world. Christians, who numbered 12.7 million in 1989, comprise about 30 per cent of the population of S. Korea. More than half of them belong to indigenous denominations not connected with the National Council of Churches. The largest Protestant bodies are the Presbyterians and Methodist Churches; a fifth of the Christians are RC.

A. D. Clark, *A History of the Church in Korea* (Seoul, 1961; rev. edn., 1971); S. H. Moffett, *The Christians of Korea* (New York [1962]). J. H. Grayson, *Early Buddhism and Christianity in Korea: A Study of the Emplantation of Religion* (Studies in the History of Religion, 47; Leiden, 1985), pp. 70–129 and 133–43; id., *Korea: A Religious History* (Oxford, 1989), esp. pp. 176–84 and 194–212, with bibl., pp. 299–301. C. Dallet, *Histoire de l'Église de Corée* (2 vols., 1874; on the RC Church). W. E. Biernatzki, SJ, and others, *Korean Catholicism in the 1970s* (Maryknoll, NY [1975]). L. G. Paik, *The History of Protestant Missions in Korea 1832–1910* (P'yongyang, Korea, 1927; 4th edn., Seoul, 1987). E. N. Hunt, *Protestant Pioneers in Korea* (American Society of Missiology Series, 1; Maryknoll, NY [1980]). R. E. Shearer, *Wildfire: Church Growth in Korea* (Grand Rapids, Mich. [1966]; mainly Presbyterian, but covers other non-RC denominations). D. N. Clark, *Christianity in Modern Korea* (Asia Agenda Report, 5; Lanham, Md. [1986]).

Koridethi Codex. A MS of the Gospels, dating prob. from the 9th cent.; it is written in rough *uncials and is known to textual critics as Θ. It is now at Tiflis, but it formerly belonged to the monastery of Koridethi, near the Caspian Sea. Its text of Mk., which differs widely from that of this Gospel in the other uncial MSS and is akin to that of two groups of *minuscules (those designated by the numbers 1–118–131–209 and 13–69–124–346), was named by B. H. *Streeter the '*Caesarean Text' (q.v.), in

the belief that it represented the text of the Gospel current at *Caesarea in Palestine in the 3rd cent.

The MS, found in the church of Sts Kerykos and Julitta at Koridethi, was first pub. (in facsimiles) by the Imperial Moscow Archaeological Society at Moscow, 1907; later ed. by G. Beermann and C. R. Gregory, Leipzig, 1913, with a study of the history of the MS based on its many marginal notes in Gk. and Georgian. K. *Lake and R. P. Blake, 'The Text of the Gospels and the Koridethi Codex', *HTR* 16 (1923), pp. 267–86; B. H. Streeter, *The Four Gospels* (1924), esp. ch. 4. B. M. Metzger, *Manuscripts of the Greek Bible* (New York and Oxford, 1981), pp. 100 f.

Kornthal, NW. of Stuttgart, *Pietist settlement. It was founded in 1819 as a centre of Pietist life in opposition to the increasing rationalism of the contemporary *Lutheran state Church. Its members accepted the *Augsburg Confession with a few alterations, but their teaching was coloured by belief in the speedy coming of the *Millennium. Inspired by *Moravian influence, their daily life was strictly regulated down to matters of food and clothing, and they were exempted by the civil power from taking the oath and from military service. Their principal achievements were educational institutions for boys, girls, and neglected children, and missionary work on the lines of the '*Innere Mission'. At the beginning of 1988 the membership of the community was 1,166.

J. Hesse, *Korntal einst und jetzt* (Stuttgart, 1910). F. Grünzweig, *Die evangelische Brüdergemeinde Korntal: Weg, Wesen und Werk* (Metzingen, Württemberg, 1958). J. Trautwein in *TRE* 19 (1990), pp. 640–5, s.v. See also bibl. to PIETISM.

Kraus, Franz Xaver (1840–1901), ecclesiastical historian. After studying at several German universities, he was ordained priest in 1864, and in 1872 became professor-extraordinary of the history of Christian art at the university of Strasbourg. In 1878 he was appointed professor of Church history at Freiburg, where he filled a number of important civil offices and came into repute as a scholar of great learning. His political theories, which upheld the rights of the State against interference from the Church, led the government to support his candidature for the episcopate, but opposition from the ecclesiastical authorities prevented the appointment being made. Some of his books also gave offence to his religious superiors through their political teaching. He remained in communion with the RC Church, however, till his death. The most considerable of his numerous works was his *Geschichte der christlichen Kunst* (2 vols., 1896–1900; the last section of the work was completed after his death by Joseph Sauer in 1908). His other writings include *Roma sotterranea* (1873), *Real-Encyklopædie der christlichen Altertümer* (2 vols., 1882–6), and *Die christlichen Inschriften der Rheinlande* (2 vols., 1890–4). In 1904 a 'Krausgesellschaft' was formed to further his supposed ecclesiastico-political doctrines.

Two collections of *Essays* were pub. (Berlin, 1896–1901). A selection of *Essays*, ed., with comm., by C. Weber (Bibliothek des deutschen historischen Instituts in Rom, 57; Tübingen, 1983). Diaries ed. H. Schiel (Cologne, 1957), with extensive bibl. Correspondence with Anton Stöck ed. id. (Quellen und Abhandlungen zur Mittelrheinischen Kirchengeschichte, 21; Mainz, 1974). Lives by K. Braig (Freiburg i.B., 1902) and E. Hauviller (Colmar, 1904). Notice by K. Künstle in *RHE* 3 (1902), pp. 431–41. O. Köhler, 'Franz Xaver Kraus (1840–1901)', in H. Fries and G. Schwaiger (eds.), *Katholische Theologen Deutschlands im 19. Jahrhundert*, 3

(Munich [1975]), pp. 241–75. H. *Leclercq, OSB, in *DACL* 8 (pt. 1; 1928), cols. 854–73 (with full bibl. of Kraus's works, but scornful of him as a scholar). K. Maier in *L.Th.K.* (3rd edn.), 6 (1997), cols. 431 f.

Krüdener, Barbara Juliana Freifrau von (1764–1824), *Pietist. After deserting her Russian husband and forming a liaison with a young French officer at Paris—during which period of her life she wrote a novel, *Valérie* (2 vols., 1803)—she was suddenly converted during a sojourn at Riga in the summer of 1804. She became an ardent devotee of the German Pietistic Movement, and in 1815 exercised great influence on the Tsar Alexander I, proclaiming that Napoleon was the Apollyon of Rev. 9: 11 and thus winning the Tsar's support for the idea of the *Holy Alliance.

C. Eynard, *Vie de Madame de Krudener* (2 vols., 1849). H. von Redern, *Zwei Welten: Das Leben von Juliane von Krüdener* (1927); A. Hermant, *Madame de Krüdener, l'amie du Tsar Alexandre* (1934). E. J. Knapton, *The Lady of the Holy Alliance: The Life of Julie de Krüdener* (New York, 1939), with full bibl. F. Ley, *Madame de Krüdener et son temps, 1764–1824* [1961], also with bibl.

Kuenen, Abraham (1828–91), Dutch OT scholar. Appointed professor at Leiden in 1855, he became one of the most prominent advocates of liberal theological thought in the Netherlands. At first he was a follower of H. G. A. *Ewald, under whose influence he wrote his *Historisch-Kritisch Onderzoek* (3 vols., 1861–5; 2nd edn., 1885–93; tr. in part into Eng. by J. W. *Colenso [1865], by whom Kuenen was much influenced); but he later came to hold the current opinion that the priestly code (P) was the latest element in the Pentateuch. His later views were embodied in his book *De Godsdienst van Israel* (1869–70; Eng. tr., *The Religion of Israel*, 1874–5) and in *De Profeten en de Profetie onder Israel* (1875; Eng. tr., *The Prophets and Prophecy in Israel*, 1877). He delivered the *Hibbert Lectures in 1882 on *National Religion and Universal Religion*.

K. Budde (ed. and tr.), *Gesammelte Abhandlungen zur biblischen Wissenschaft* (1894; with full bibl. of Kuenen's writings, compiled by W. C. van Manen). P. B. Dirksen and A. van der Kooij (eds.), *Abraham Kuenen (1828–1891): His Major Contributions to the Study of the Old Testament* (Oudtestamentische Studiën, 29; Leiden etc., 1993). J. Hahn in *TRE* 20 (1990), pp. 129–31, s.v.

Kulturkampf. The repressive political movement in Germany in the 1870s against the RC Church. It was mainly inspired by Bismarck, who feared that the influence of Catholicism would endanger the unity of the German Empire.

In its earlier years the conflict was very bitter, provoked chiefly by the anti-Catholic legislation. In 1871 Bismarck suppressed the Catholic department of the Prussian Ministry of Public Worship, and in 1872 appointed P. L. A. *Falk Minister of Public Worship, under whose aegis the *Jesuits were expelled, education was brought under the control of the state, and the famous '*May Laws' (1873) were passed. The opposition to this legislation was very strong, and several Catholic bishops, including Cardinal M. H. von Ledóchowski of Gnesen-Posen and K. Martin of Paderborn, were imprisoned. The German embassy at the Vatican was also recalled, and owing to the condemnatory tenor of the encyclical 'Quod nunquam' (7 Feb. 1875)

the RC Church was deprived of all financial assistance from the state. Further, the religious orders were ordered to leave the country.

Bismarck, however, had misunderstood the extent and strength of the opposition, and gradually became convinced that a *concordat with the Vatican was the better solution. He also hoped by a change of tactics to gain the aid of the Catholic Church in the fight against Social Democracy. Hence at the end of the '70s the previous policy was reversed and peace was made with the new Pope, *Leo XIII. By 1887 most of the anti-Catholic laws, with the exception of that expelling the Jesuits, had been nullified. The Kulturkampf had the undesigned effect of creating in some measure a religious revival inside Germany. It certainly strengthened the hold of Roman Catholicism on the German people in the latter years of the 19th cent. See also CENTRE PARTY.

A. Constabel (ed.), *Die Vorgeschichte des Kulturkampfes: Quellenveröffentlichung aus dem Deutschen Zentralarchiv* (1956). Substantial works incl. J. B. Kissling, *Geschichte des Kulturkampfs im Deutschen Reich* (3 vols., 1911–16); G. Goyau, *Bismarck et l'Église: Le Culturkampf, 1870–1878* (4 vols., 1911–13); G. Franz, *Kulturkampf: Staat und katholische Kirche in Mitteleuropa von der Säkularisation bis zum Abschluss des Preussischen Kulturkampfes* (Munich [1954]); and E. Schmidt-Volkmar, *Der Kulturkampf in Deutschland 1871–1890* (Göttingen, 1962). M. L. Anderson, *Windhorst* (Oxford, 1981), pp. 130–200 *passim*; and id., 'The Kulturkampf and the Course of German History', *Central Church History*, 19 (1986), pp. 82–115, with further refs. L. Gall, *Bismarck: Der weisse Revolutionär* (Frankfurt am Main, 1980), esp. pp. 459–502; Eng. tr., 2 (1986), pp. 1–39. H. W. L. Freudenthal in *NCE* 7 (1967), pp. 267–9; G. Besier in *TRE* 20 (1990), cols. 209–30, both, s.v., with bibl. See also works cited under FALK, P. L. A.

Küng, Hans (1928–), RC theologian. Born in Switzerland, he studied in Rome and Paris. In 1957 he published his doctoral dissertation on *justification, *Rechtfertigung: die Lehre Karl Barths und eine katholische Besinnung* (Eng. tr., 1964), and in 1960 he was appointed Professor of Fundamental Theology at Tübingen. His active involvement in the preparations for the Second *Vatican Council and his presence there as a *peritus* appointed by Pope *John XXIII brought him to the centre of the conflict between reformers and traditionalists in the RC Church. In 1963 he became the first Professor of Dogmatic and Fundamental Theology at Tübingen and director of the newly-established Institute for Ecumenical Research. Disappointed with the progress of the Vatican Council, he became increasingly critical of the Church and outspoken in his protests against Papal encyclicals (notably those on priestly *celibacy in 1967 and on *contraception in 1968). This criticism found expression in his books *Die Kirche* (1967; Eng. tr., *The Church*, 1967) and *Unfehlbar?* (1970; Eng. tr., *Infallible?*, 1971), a trenchant criticism of modern Papal claims and the Papacy's exercise of authority, which precipitated wide controversy. *Christus sein* (1974; Eng. tr., *On Being a Christian*, 1977) and *Existiert Gott?* (1978; Eng. tr., *Does God Exist?*, 1980), which are less concerned with ecclesiastical structure, though no less controversial, won an unusually wide readership in Germany and beyond. In 1979 his *missio canonica* (authority to teach as a Catholic theologian) was withdrawn, but he retained his post in the University of Tübingen until his retirement in 1996. Latterly he turned his attention to the relationship between

Christianity and other faiths, and produced a stream of books, often in dialogue with representatives of these religions. They include *Christentum und Weltreligionen* (1984; Eng. tr., *Christianity and the World Religions*, 1987), *Christentum und Chinesische Religionen*, with Julia Ching (1988; Eng. tr., *Christianity and Chinese Religions*, New York, 1989; London, 1993), and *Das Judentum* (1991; Eng. tr., *Judaism*, 1992).

N. Greinacher and H. Haag (eds.), *Der Fall Küng: Eine Dokumentation* (Munich and Zurich [1980]). H. Häring and K.-J. Kuschel (eds.), *Hans Küng: Weg und Werk* (Munich [1978]; Eng. tr., 1979), with list of his works to date. R. [A.] Nowell, *A Passion for Truth. Hans Küng: A Biography* (1981). E. Huovinen, *Idea Christi: Idealistinen ajattelumuoto ja kristologia Hans Küngin teologiassa* (Suomalaisen teologisen kirjallisuusseuran julkaisuja, 111; Helsinki, 1978; Ger. tr., Arbeiten zur Geschichte und Theologie des Luthertums, NF 6 [1985]). K.-J. Kuschel and H. Häring (eds.), *Hans Küng: Neue Horizonte des Glaubens und Denkens* (Munich and Zurich [1993]; Eng. tr., 1993), with select bibl.

Kuyper, Abraham

(1837–1920), Dutch *Calvinist theologian and politician. Having studied theology at *Leiden, where he was influenced by the rationalistic modernism of his professors, J. H. Scholten and L. W. E. Rawenhof, he became a minister at Beesd. The example of the simple piety of his parishioners here was largely responsible for his conversion to traditional orthodox Calvinism. After further ministries in Utrecht and Amsterdam, he moved into politics. A member of the Second Chamber of Parliament (1874–8), in 1879 he founded the Anti-Revolutionary Party with the intention of transforming the orthodox Calvinist sector of the population into a political force, and to this end he also founded the Free University in Amsterdam (1880), where he held a chair until 1901. In 1886 he led a secession from the Dutch Reformed Church (*Hervormde Kerk*), uniting his followers with Churches which had already seceded in 1834, to form the Reformed Churches (*Gereformeerde Gemeente*). In 1898 he was invited to the USA where he gave the Stone Lectures, published in England in 1932 under the title *Calvinism*. These set out his view of Calvinism as a way of life satisfying all contemporary needs and emphasized the notion of 'common grace'. He reached the height of his political influence during his period as Minister-President (1901–5) but encountered problems both at home by his use of parliamentary legislation to crush a national rail strike and abroad by his fervent support of the Boers in their struggle against the British in South Africa. Following the defeat of his government in 1905 he spent his last years leading his party, from 1913 as a member of the Upper Chamber, and continuing his editorship of *De Standaard*, the anti-revolutionary newspaper he had founded in 1872.

Kuyper was the author of a large number of writings. J. C. Rullmann, *Kuyper-Bibliografie* (vol. 1, The Hague, vols. 2–3, Kampen, 1923–40). Lives by P. Kasteel (Kampen, 1938) and F. Vandenberg, *He called my name* (Grand Rapids, 1960). S. J. Ridderbos, *De theologische cultuurbeschouwing van Abraham Kuyper* (Kampen, 1947); C. Augustijn and others (eds.), *Abraham Kuyper: zijn volksdeel, zijn invloed* (Delft [1987]). S. van der Linde in *RGG* (3rd edn.), 4 (1960), cols. 191 f, s.v.

Kyriale.

The Latin liturgical book containing the musical chant for the *Ordinary of the Mass. It is so named from its opening part, the *Kyrie. As a separate book it seems to owe its existence to printers who sought to satisfy the convenience of choirs wanting the fixed parts of the Mass in a different book from that containing the variable parts such as the *Gradual. *Pius X issued an authoritative revision known as the *Kyriale Vaticanum*, with the music for 18 different plain-chant Masses. The name 'Graduale' is occasionally used to cover the Kyriale as well as the Gradual in its proper sense.

Kyrie Eleison

(Gk. Κύριε ἐλέησον, 'Lord, have mercy'). A brief prayer for Divine mercy which from an early date has been used in the liturgical worship of the Church. The use of the words in non-Christian cultus is also attested (cf. *Epictetus, *Diss*. 2. 7). In Christian worship their use in the latter part of the 4th cent. is recorded in the *Apostolic Constitutions* (8. 6), where they appear as the response of the people to the petitions made by the deacon; *Egeria (*Peregrinatio*, 24. 5) also reports that at Jerusalem they were used as a response in a litany at Vespers. In the W., it was long thought that the litany which replaced the general intercession in the Mass towards the end of the 5th cent. contained the response 'Kyrie eleison', but it has been questioned whether the so-called '*Deprecatio Gelasii' in fact included these words. The Council of *Vaison in 529, however, ordered that the Kyrie should be said in France as it was in the Holy See and throughout Italy and the provinces of the East (can. 3). Soon afterwards the Rule of St *Benedict (chs. 9 and 17) records the use of the Kyrie in the Office. Under *Gregory the Great (590–604) various changes in the Mass were made: on many days in the year the customary invocations were to be omitted and only the response 'Kyrie eleison' was to be sung; in a letter of 598 Gregory mentions that at Rome the 'Kyrie eleison' is supplemented by a similar prayer, 'Christe eleison' ('Christ, have mercy'), not found in the East; and the whole seems soon to have been placed in what became its traditional position near the beginning of the Mass. What is commonly known as the ninefold Kyrie (that is, 'Kyrie eleison' recited three times, followed by 'Christe eleison' recited three times, and 'Kyrie eleison' three times) occurs in the *Ordo Romanus of St Amand (*Ordo Romanus* IV; 8th–9th cent.); it became the traditional pattern in the Roman Mass. The three groups were sometimes later conceived as directed to the Father, Son, and Holy Spirit respectively. Elaborate musical settings were devised, and these led to the development of 'farced' Kyries, in which additional words were inserted.

In the Eucharistic Rite of the BCP of 1549, the ninefold Kyrie survived in an English translation ('Lord have mercy upon us'), but in 1552 the Ten *Commandments were substituted. From the middle of the 19th cent. use of the Kyrie both in Greek and English came to be adopted unofficially in many quarters and it is permitted in the ASB and other modern Anglican liturgies. The use of the Kyrie in an English form at *Mattins, *Evensong and in the *Litany has been continuous since 1549.

In the present RC Eucharistic Rite a sixfold Kyrie, usually in the vernacular (each of the three petitions, 'Lord have mercy', 'Christ have mercy', and 'Lord have mercy', being said by the celebrant or sung by the choir and repeated by the people as a response) forms one of the penitential acts at the beginning of Mass, and the Kyrie may also be used as the people's response in the Prayer of the Faithful.

E. *Bishop, *Liturgica Historica* (1918), ch. 6, pp. 116–36. B. *Capelle, 'Le Kyrie de la messe et le pape Gélase', *R. Bén.* 46 (1934), pp. 126–44; repr. in *Travaux Liturgiques*, 2 (Louvain, 1962), pp. 116–34. C. Callewaert, 'Les Étapes de l'histoire du Kyrie', *RHE* 38 (1942), pp. 20–45. A. Chavasse, 'L'Oraison "super sindonem" dans la liturgie romaine', *R. Bén.* 70 (1960), pp. 313–23. P. De Clerck, *La 'Prière Universelle' dans les liturgies latines anciennes* (Liturgiewissenschaftliche Quellen und Forschungen, 62; 1977), pp. 166–87 and 282–95. Texts of 'farced' Kyries, ed. C. Blume, SJ, and H. M. Bannister, *Tropen des Missales im Mittelalter*, 1 (AHMA 47; 1905). M. Landwehr-Melnicki, *Das einstimmige Kyrie des Lateinischen Mittelalters* (Forschungsbeiträge zur Musikwissenschaft, 1; 1955). Jungmann (1958 edn.), 1, pp. 429–46; Eng. tr., 1, pp. 333–46.

L

Labadists. A Protestant sect named after Jean de Labadie (1610–74), its founder, who had been a *Jesuit from 1625 to 1639, had joined the Reformed Church at Montauban in 1650, and after preaching at various places on the Continent, esp. in the Netherlands, settled temporarily in 1670 at Herford in Westphalia with about 55 followers. On being forced to leave Herford in 1672, he moved first to Bremen and later to Altona, where he died. His followers held extreme *Pietist views. They believed that the Bible could be understood only by the immediate inspiration of the Holy Spirit, rarely celebrated the Eucharist, and held that marriage with an unregenerate person was not binding; and they were organized on a communistic basis. They survived de Labadie's death by some 50 years.

H. van Berkum, *De Labadie en de Labadisten* (2 pts., Sneek, 1851). T. J. Saxby, *The Quest for the New Jerusalem, Jean de Labadie and the Labadists, 1610–1744* (International Archives of the History of Ideas, 115; 1987). A. *Ritschl, *Geschichte des Pietismus*, 1 (1880), pp. 194–268. Entry 'd'après une étude de Michel de Certeau' in *Dict. Sp.* 9 (1976), cols. 1–7; D. Nauta in *Biografisch Lexicon voor de Geschiedenis van het Nederlandse Protestantisme*, 2 (Kampen, 1983), pp. 293–7, with bibl. by F. H. Danner, ibid., pp. 297–302, both s.v. 'Labadie, Jean de'.

labarum. The military standard adopted by the Emp. *Constantine after his vision. In form it seems to have been an adaptation of the Roman cavalry standard, with the pagan emblems replaced by a Christian monogram, i.e. the two Greek letters *X* and *P* (the first two of *ΧΡΙΣΤΟΣ*, 'Christ') intersecting. It was at first the banner of only the W. Empire, but after Licinius' defeat at the battle of Chrysopolis (324) it was adopted by the E. as well. The name is probably an incorrect form of *laureum*, a Latin word used by the Roman soldiery for a standard (*vexillum*).

For the extensive modern literature, with discussion, see N. H. Baynes, *Constantine the Great and the Christian Church* (1929), pp. 60–5. H. Grégoire, 'L'Étymologie du "Labarum" ', *Byzantion*, 4 (1929), pp. 477–82. J. J. Hatt, 'La Vision de Constantin au sanctuaire de Grand et l'origine celtique du labarum', *Latomus*, 9 (1950), pp. 427–36. R. Egger, *Das Labarum, die Kaiserstandarte der Spätantike* (*Sb.* (Wien), 234, Heft 1; 1960; repr. in id., *Römische Antike und frühes Christentum*, ed. A. Betz and G. Moro, 2 (Klagenfurt, 1963), pp. 325–44).

Labbe, Philippe (1607–67), Church historian. In 1623 he joined the *Jesuits. A prolific writer and compiler, he published over 80 works, of which the most important was his collection of the Church Councils under the title *Sacrosancta Concilia ad Regiam Editionem exacta*. Before his death vols. 1–8 and 12–15 had been printed, but they were not published until 1671–3. The outstanding volumes were completed by his fellow-Jesuit, G. Cossart. This collection, the most extensive of its age, was later incorporated into the *Concilia* of J. D. *Mansi.

H. *Quentin, OSB, *J. D. Mansi et les grandes collections conciliaires* (1900), pp. 29–33 and 182 f. Sommervogel, 4 (1893), cols. 1295–328; 9 (1900), cols. 561–3.

Laberthonnière, Lucien (1860–1932), RC *Modernist theologian. In 1886 he was ordained priest as an *Oratorian. He taught at the Collège at Juilly (1887) and at the École Massillon at Paris (1896), and in 1900 became rector of the Collège at Juilly. From 1905 to 1913 he edited the *Annales de philosophie chrétienne*. He joined with M. *Blondel in a vigorous attack on C. Maurras and the *Action Française. In theology he developed a pragmatic view of religious truth, called moral dogmatism, which he expounded in *Essais de philosophie religieuse* (1903) and *Le Réalisme chrétien et l'idéalisme grec* (1904). Both works were put on the *Index in 1906, and in 1913 he was prohibited from all further publication. His writings exercised considerable influence on G. *Tyrrell.

There is a list of his pub. work in P. Beillevert, Cong. Orat. (ed.), *Laberthonnière: L'homme et l'œuvre . . . Textes et communications* [1972], pp. 243–73. Several works were pub. after his death by L. Canet, his literary executor (8 vols., 1935–55); the first three vols. were put on the Index. Other posthumously pub. works incl. *Correspondance philosophique* of Blondel and Laberthonnière, ed. C. Tresmontant [1961]; two further vols. of correspondence and other material ed. M.-T. Perrin: *Laberthonnière et ses amis* (Théologie Historique, 33 [1975]) and *Dossier Laberthonnière* (Textes, Dossiers, Documents, 8 [1983]); also a series of articles from *Annales de philosophie chrétienne* was repr., with other material, ed. M.-M. d'Hendecourt, as *Dogme et Théologie* (Recherches et Synthèses, Section de Dogme, 6 [1977]). Id., *Essai sur la philosophie du Père Laberthonnière* (1947); A. Ngindu Mushete, *Le Problème de la connaissance religieuse d'après Lucien Laberthonnière* (Recherches Africaines de Théologie, 7; Kinshasa [1978]); M.-T. Perrin, *La Jeunesse de Laberthonnière* (Le Point Théologique, 34 [1980]). A. R. Vidler, *A Variety of Catholic Modernists* (Sarum Lectures 1968–9; Cambridge, 1970), pp. 82–90. P. Beillevert in *Dict. Sp.* 9 (1976), cols. 9–16, with bibl.

Labre, St Benedict Joseph (1748–83), pilgrim and mendicant saint. Born at Amettes near Béthune, he showed pious dispositions from childhood and was strongly drawn to one of the religious orders. After vain attempts to be received by the *Trappists and the *Carthusians, he was rejected by all as unsuitable to community life and found his vocation in a life of solitude and pilgrimage. He visited most of the leading sanctuaries of Europe (some many times), among them *Loreto, *Assisi, and *Einsiedeln. Everywhere he begged his food, giving away the alms offered him and spending much of his time in churches. For his last few years he lived at Rome, except for an annual pilgrimage to Loreto. Here he became a familiar figure in the city, known from his devotion to the *Quarant' Ore* as the 'Saint of the *Forty Hours'. Exhausted by his austerities, he died outside his favourite church, Sta Maria dei Monti, in Holy Week 1783. A local cultus soon developed; and he was pronounced Venerable by *Pius IX in 1859 and canonized by *Leo XIII in 1881. Feast day, 16 Apr.

G. L. Marconi (his confessor), *Ragguaglio della vita del servo di Dio, Benedetto Labre Francese* (1783; abridged Eng. version, 1786).

F. Gaguère, *Le Saint Pauvre de Jésus-Christ, Benoît-Joseph Labre* (Avignon, 1936). Other modern Lives by A. de La Gorce (Paris, 1933; Eng. tr., 1952), J. Riverain (ibid., 1948), and P. Doyère, OSB (ibid., 1964). Y.-M. Hilaire (ed.), *Benoît Labre: Errance et sainteté, Histoire d'un culte 1783–1983* (1984), with bibl.

Lacey, Thomas Alexander (1853–1931), Anglican divine. Educated at Balliol College, Oxford, he was ordained in 1876 and after holding various scholastic and parochial appointments became Canon of *Worcester in 1918. Imbued with a sympathetic understanding of modern problems, he became known as an effective apologist for the *Anglo-Catholic presentation of the Christian faith. Throughout his life he was devoted to the cause of reunion. He took an active part at Rome in 1896, when a Papal commission was examining the validity of *Anglican Ordinations, supplying, in conjunction with his friend Fr. F. W. Puller, SSJE, much of the material from the Anglican side. His most important writings were *De Hierarchia Anglicana Dissertatio Apologetica* (1895; in conjunction with E. Denny); *A Roman Diary and other Documents relating to the Papal Enquiry into English Ordinations, MDCCCXCVI* (1910); *Marriage in Church and State* (1912; revised by R. C. Mortimer, 1947); and *Unity and Schism* (1917). He was joint editor of the *English Hymnal* and translated for it many Latin hymns.

Wayfarer's Essays [collection of Lacey's papers ed., with short memoir (pp. v–xi) and list of his books (pp. xiii f.), by A. Wilson] (1934). C. B. Mortlock in *DNB, 1931–1940*, pp. 519 f., s.v.

Lachmann, Karl (1793–1851), philologist and textual critic. From 1825 to 1827 he was extraordinary, and from 1827 until his death ordinary, professor of classical and German philology at Berlin. Besides editions of classical authors, he issued two editions of the Greek NT, the smaller in 1831 and a fuller one in 2 vols., 1842–50. He applied to the biblical text the same methods of textual criticism in evaluating variant readings which he had previously used on works of Lucretius. Using the oldest Greek manuscripts and the testimony of the Fathers, he aimed at presenting the text, not as it was originally composed—this he thought an impossible task—but as it circulated in E. Christendom at the end of the 4th cent.; though his *modus operandi*, partly conditioned by this limited aim, suffered from being over-mechanical, he gave the impetus to the later work of C. *Tischendorf and B. F. *Westcott and F. J. A. *Hort. Lachmann was also the first scholar to put the *Marcan hypothesis on a sound footing; he did this in an article in the *Theologische Studien und Kritiken* for 1835.

K. Lachmann, 'Rechenschaft über seine Ausgabe des Neuen Testaments', *Theologische Studien und Kritiken*, 3 (1830), pp. 817–45; id., 'De Ordine Narrationum in Evangeliis Synopticis', ibid. 8 (1835), pp. 570–90. A. Leitzmann, *Briefe Karl Lachmanns (Abh.* (Berl.), 1942, no. 8). Life by M. Hertz (Berlin, 1851). A. Rüegg, *Die neutestamentliche Textkritik seit Lachmann* (Zurich, 1892). S. Timpanaro, Jun., 'La genesi del "Metodo del Lachmann" ', *Studi Italiani di Filologia Classica*, NS 31 (1959), pp. 182–228; 32 (1960), pp. 38–63. N. H. Palmer, 'Lachmann's Argument', *New Testament Studies*, 13 (1967), pp. 368–78. B. M. Metzger, *The Text of the New Testament* (3rd edn., Oxford, 1992), pp. 124–6.

Lacordaire, Henri-Dominique (1802–61), French *Dominican preacher. He was born at Recey-sur-Ource and, after losing his faith at an early age, became a disciple of J.-J. *Rousseau. He studied law at Dijon and *Paris and speedily made a reputation as an orator at the Paris bar. In 1824 he was converted, entered the seminary at Issy, and was ordained priest at *Saint Sulpice in 1827. In the next year he was appointed chaplain to the Convent of the *Visitation in Paris. In 1830 he became a contributor to F. de *Lamennais's periodical *L'Avenir*, but severed connection with it on its condemnation by *Gregory XVI in 1832. He replied to Lamennais's *Paroles d'un croyant* (1834) with *Considérations sur le système philosophique de M. de La Mennais* (1834). In 1835–6 he gave the first two series of his famous Conferences at *Notre-Dame which drew a vast concourse, largely from the intelligentsia. His political liberalism and *ultramontane theology aroused distrust, however, and at the height of his influence he retired to Rome. Here in 1839, with the encouragement of P. *Guéranger, then engaged in restoring the *Benedictine Order in France, Lacordaire entered the Dominican Order with the intention of re-establishing it in France, having earlier in the year published his *Mémoire pour le rétablissement en France de l'Ordre des Frères Prêcheurs*. After his return to Paris in 1841 he resumed his Conferences, and preached also in other cities (Bordeaux, Nancy, etc.). In 1843 he established at Nancy the first Dominican House in France since the suppression of the Order in 1790. He maintained his political interests and in 1848 was elected deputy for Marseilles in the National Assembly; in the same year, with A. F. *Ozanam he founded the journal *L'Ère nouvelle*. From 1850 to 1854 and again from 1858 to 1861 he was Provincial of the newly-founded French Dominican province. In 1852 he founded the teaching *Third Order, of which he became Vicar General in 1854, at the same time taking charge of the college at Sorèze in the S. of France. In 1860 he was elected a member of the Academy. If hardly a profound theologian or philosopher, he was fully conversant with the religious needs of his time. His most influential work was his *Conférences de Notre-Dame de Paris* (4 vols., 1844–51), directed esp. to unbelievers. His other writings include *Vie de Saint Dominique* (1841), which may have some historical value, *Sainte Marie-Madeleine* (1860), which has none (both books have inspired passages), and his *Notice sur le rétablissement en France de l'Ordre des Frères Prêcheurs* (an autobiographical work, posthumously ed. by C. R. F. *Montalembert as *Le Testament*, 1870).

Edns. of his works incl. those in 6 vols., Paris, 1857–61; 9 vols., ibid., 1872; and 4 vols., ibid., 1912. Among the numerous collections of his correspondence, listed in detail by H. D. Noble, OP, cited below, those of most general interest are his *Lettres à jeunes gens*, ed. H. Perreyve [1862]; (Eng. tr., 1902), and his correspondence with Montalembert, 1830–1861, ed. L. Le Guillou and A. Duval [OP] (Paris, 1989). Modern edns., with introds. by A. Duval, of his *Lettres à un jeune homme sur la vie chrétienne* (1988), and of his *Vie de Saint Dominique* (1989). Eng. tr. of his *Mémoire pour le rétablissement en France de l'Ordre des Frères Prêcheurs*, ed. S. [C. ff.] Tugwell, OP (Dominican Sources, 2; Oak Park, Ill., and Dublin, 1983). G. Ledos, *Morceaux choisis et bibliographie de Lacordaire* [1923]. Primary Lives by C. R. F. Montalembert (Paris, 1862; Eng. tr., 1863), B. Chocarne, OP (Paris, 1866; Eng. tr., Dublin [1868]), and [J. T.] Foisset (2 vols., Paris, 1870). P. Fesch, *Lacordaire Journaliste (1830–1848)* (1897); J. Favre, *Lacordaire orateur: Sa formation et la chronologie de ses œuvres* (1906); P. Baron, OP, *La Jeunesse de Lacordaire* (1961); J. Cabanis, *Lacor-*

daire et quelques autres: Politique et religion [1982], passim; B. Bonvin [OP], Lacordaire, Jandel: La restauration de l'Ordre dominicain en France après la Révolution écartelée entre deux visions du monde (1989), with text of Mémoire Jandel. G. Bedouelle [OP] (ed.), Lacordaire, son pays, ses amis et la liberté des ordres religieux en France (1991). A. Duval, OP, 'Lacordaire et Buchez. Idéalisme révolutionnaire et réveil religieux en 1839', RSPT 45 (1961), pp. 422–55; id., 'Le rapport du P. Lacordaire au Chapitre de la Province de France (septembre 1854)', Archivum Fratrum Praedicatorum, 31 (1961), pp. 326–64; id., 'Les premiers entretiens du Père Lacordaire et de l'abbé Jandel sur la restauration dominicaine en France (31 oct. 1839)', ibid. 36 (1966), pp. 493–542; id., 'Lacordaire et Monseigneur de Quelen 1836–1838', ibid. 56 (1986), pp. 381–428; 57 (1987), pp. 291–340; id., 'Lacordaire: La Vie de Saint Dominique', ibid. 59 (1989), pp. 267–96. In Eng. there is a popular Life by L. C. Sheppard (London and New York, 1964). P. Spencer, Politics of Belief in Nineteenth Century France (1954), pp. 17–115. H. D. Noble in DTC 8 (pt. 2; 1925), cols. 2394–424, s.v., with detailed bibl.

Lactantius (c.250–c.325), Christian apologist. A pupil of *Arnobius, Lucius Caelius Firmianus Lactantius was appointed by *Diocletian as a teacher of rhetoric at Nicomedia. He is generally thought to have been a convert to Christianity, but the date of his conversion is disputed; he had certainly lost his post at the time when persecution broke out in 303. Later the Emp. *Constantine made him tutor to his son Crispus. His main surviving works are 'Divinae Institutiones' (first version 305–11), a treatise which sought to commend the truth of Christianity to men of letters and thereby for the first time set out in Latin a systematic account of the Christian attitude to life; 'De Opificio Dei', an attempt to prove the existence of God from the marvels of the human body; 'De Ira Dei', which deals with God's punishment of human crime; and 'De Mortibus Persecutorum', which describes with a wealth of lurid detail the horrible deaths of the persecutors of the Church. The authenticity of the last-mentioned treatise, though formerly contested, is now generally admitted. A charming poem 'De Ave *Phoenice', ascribed to him by St *Gregory of Tours, may well be his work. In his prose style Lactantius was deliberately Ciceronian; in his theology he was concerned to maintain the unity of God in the face of contemporary polytheism.

*Jerome, De Viris Illustribus, 80. Lactantius' theological writings have been constantly reissued since the 15th cent. Editio princeps of 'Divinae Institutiones', 'De Ira Dei' and 'De Opificio Dei' pub. Subiaco, 1465 (the second dated printed book issued in Italy). The text of J. B. le Brun and N. Lenglet du Fresnoy (2 vols., Paris, 1748) is repr. in J. P. Migne, PL 6 and 7. Crit. text ed. S. Brandt and G. Laubmann (CSEL 19 and 27; 1890–7); also, of 'Divinae Institutiones', by P. Monat (Book 1, SC 326; 1986), 2 (SC 337; 1987), 4 (SC 377; 1992), 5 (SC 204–5; 1973); of 'Epitome' by M. Perrin (SC 335; 1987); of 'De Opificio Dei' by id. (SC 213–4; 1974); of 'De Ira Dei' by C. Ingremeau (SC 289; 1982); and of 'De Mortibus Persecutorum' by J. Moreau (SC 39, 2 vols., 1954; rev. by J. Rougé, 39bis, forthcoming, and by J. L. Creed (with Eng. tr., Oxford Early Christian Texts, 1984). Eng. trs. of his works by W. Fletcher (ANCL 21–2; 1871) and M. F. McDonald, OP (Fathers of the Church, 49 and 54; 1964–5).

R. Pichon, Lactance: Études sur le mouvement philosophique et religieux sous le règne de Constantin (1901). J. Stevenson, 'The Life and Literary Activity of Lactantius', in K. Aland and F. L. Cross (eds.), Studia Patristica, 1 (TU 63; 1957), pp. 661–77. A. Wlosok, Laktanz und die philosophische Gnosis (Abh. (Heid.), 1960, Abh. 2). J. Speigl, 'Zum Kirchenbegriff des Laktanz', RQ 65 (1970), pp. 15–28. E. Heck, Die dualistischen Zusätze und die Kaiseranreden bei Lactantius: Untersuchungen zur Textgeschichte der Divinae institutiones und der Schrift De opificio dei (Abh. (Heid.), 1972, Abh. 2). E. Messmer, Laktanz und die Dichtung (Diss., Munich, 1974). J. Fontaine and M. Perrin (eds.), Lactance et son temps (1978); M. Perrin, L'Homme antique et Chrétien: L'Anthropologie de Lactance, 250–325 (Théologie historique, 59 [1981]). P. Monat, Lactance et la Bible: Une propédeutique latine à la lecture de la Bible dans l'Occident constantinien (2 vols., Études Augustiniennes, 1982). J. Quasten, Patrology, 2 (Utrecht, 1953), pp. 392–410. É. Amann in DTC 8 (pt. 2; 1925), cols. 2425–44, s.v. 'Lactance'.

On 'De Ave Phoenice', see bibl. to PHOENIX.

lacticinia. Milk and foods such as cheese or butter, made from milk, which (as well as meat and eggs) were often forbidden on fast days in the early and medieval Church, and this is still the rule for all fast days in the E. Church.

Ladislaus (in Hungarian, László), St (1040–95), King of Hungary. He was elected by the nobles in 1077; but the first years of his reign were troubled by the conspiracies of Solomon, son of a former king and rival claimant to the throne, who was finally defeated in 1089. In the *Investiture struggle between the German Emperor and the Pope he took the side of *Gregory VII and Victor III, and he laboured incessantly to spread the Christian faith among his subjects, esp. in Croatia and Dalmatia, which he annexed in 1091. He built many churches, obtained the canonization of *Stephen I and his son Emeric, and promulgated a series of laws on religious and civil matters at the Synod of Szabolcs (1092). However, when *Urban II refused to acknowledge his suzerainty over Croatia, his relations with the Papacy came under strain. He died amid plans to participate in the First *Crusade, and was buried at his new episcopal foundation of Nagyvárad (today Oradea in Romania). Venerated as a saint by his people, he was canonized in 1192. Feast day, 27 June.

Vita from 15th cent. MS ed. E. Bartoniek in E. Szentpétery (ed.), Scriptores Rerum Hungaricarum, 2 (Budapest, 1938), pp. 509–27; Ger. tr., with introd., by J. M. Bak in T. von Bogyay and others, Die heiligen Könige (Graz and Vienna, 1976), pp. 147–65. J. Karácsonyi, Szent László király élete (Budapest, 1926); L. Mezey (ed.), Athleta Patriae: Tanulmányok Szent László történetéhez (ibid., 1980). G. Györffy, 'A "lovagszent" uralkodása (1077–1095)', Történelmi Szemle, 20 (1977), pp. 533–64. Z. J. Kosztolnyik, Five Eleventh Century Hungarian Kings: Their Politics and their Relations with Rome (East European Monographs, 79; New York, etc., 1981), pp. 92–109.

Lady, Our. A common designation in use among Catholics for the Blessed Virgin *Mary (BVM). It is derived from the Latin 'Domina nostra'. Since 1559 the feast of the *Annunciation has been described in the Table of Lessons in the BCP as the 'Annunciation of our Lady'. In earlier times, the Annunciation (25 Mar.) was known as 'Our Lady in Lent' or 'in March'; the *Assumption (15 Aug.) as 'Our Lady in Harvest'; and the *Conception (8 Dec.) as 'Our Lady in December'.

Lady Chapel. A chapel dedicated to the BVM ('Our *Lady') when it forms part of a larger church. From the 13th cent. onwards the practice of constructing such chapels, often as later additions and to the east of the High Altar, became common in England, e.g. Henry VII's Chapel at *Westminster Abbey.

Lady Day. The feast of the *Annunciation of the BVM, 25 Mar. The name was used in earlier times of any feast of Our *Lady. In the Middle Ages and later 25 Mar. was reckoned the first day of the civil year. It is still a quarter day and Old Lady Day (6 April) still starts the fiscal year in Britain, e.g. for income-tax purposes.

Laetare Sunday. The Fourth Sunday in *Lent ('Mid-Lent Sunday', *Mi-carême*), so named from the opening words of the *Introit at the Mass (Is. 66: 10, 'Rejoice ye with Jerusalem'). In W. Christendom certain relaxations of the penitential observances of Lent are allowed, e.g. the wearing of rose-pink instead of purple vestments. The Sunday is also known as *Mothering Sunday and *Refreshment Sunday.

Laetentur Coeli (Lat., 'Let the heavens rejoice'). Two important theological documents, so named from their opening words. (They are otherwise quite unrelated.)

(1) The Greek Formulary of Union, sent on 23 Apr. 433 by *Cyril, Patr. of *Alexandria, to *John, Bp. of *Antioch, embodying the terms of reunion agreed upon by both parties, after John had previously given qualified support to the teaching of Cyril's adversary, *Nestorius. Inasmuch as the document was formally approved by the Council of *Chalcedon (451), it possesses *oecumenical authority. It expounds the Antiochene doctrine of the Person of Christ in terms acceptable to the Alexandrians, insisting on the *Theotokos and both the unity of person and the distinction of the natures.

(2) The bull issued by Pope *Eugenius IV on 6 July 1439 decreeing the union settled at the Council of *Florence between the Orthodox E. Church and the W. It laid down that the Orthodox should accept, *inter alia*, the doctrine of the *Double Procession of the Holy Spirit and the primacy of the see of Rome. It had been signed by Latins and Greeks alike on the previous day. See also FLORENCE, COUNCIL OF.

(1) The formulary (Gk. opening, Εὐφραινέσθωσαν οἱ οὐρανοί) is *Ep.* 39 of the correspondence of Cyril of Alexandria (J. P. Migne, *PG* 77. 173–82). It has often been repr. in collections of 'Oecumenical Documents', e.g. T. H. Bindley, *Oecumenical Documents of the Faith* (4th edn. by F. W. Green, 1950), pp. 138–48. The only critical text is in E. *Schwartz, *ACO* 1. 1. 4, pp. 15–20.

(2) Text in G. Hoffmann, SJ (ed.), *Concilium Florentinum: Documenta et Scriptores*, Series A. *Epistolae Pontificiae ad Concilium Florentinum Spectantes*, pt. 2 (Rome, 1944), pp. 68–79. Lat. text of the principal clauses repr. in Denzinger and Hünermann (37th edn., 1991), pp. 449–52 (nos. 1300–8). See also bibl. to FLORENCE, COUNCIL OF.

Lagarde, Paul Anton de (1827–91), Protestant theologian and critic. In 1854 he exchanged his earlier name of Bötticher for de Lagarde. From 1854 to 1866 he was a schoolmaster at Berlin, and from 1869 till his death professor at Göttingen. His opposition to all forms of liberalism and economic materialism, his hatred of the Jews, and his intensely national feeling anticipated many subsequent developments in German thought. On the other hand he was a keen upholder of the rights of individual personality and deprecated any attempt to set up the state as an absolute norm. Possessed of untiring industry and an extraordinary range of knowledge, he produced a number of erudite works, covering an unusually wide range of subjects. Among those of importance to the ecclesiastical historian are *Didascalia Apostolorum Syriace* (1854), *Onomastica Sacra* (1870), *Psalterium iuxta Hebraeos Hieronymi* (1874), *Aegyptiaca* (1883), *Septuaginta-Studien* (1891; 1892), as well as an edition of part of the *Lucianic Recension of the *Septuagint (1883).

A. de Lagarde (widow), *Paul de Lagarde: Erinnerungen aus seiner Leben zusammengestellt* (Göttingen, 1894). Other studies by L. Schemann (Leipzig, 1919; 3rd edn., 1943), A. Rahlfs (Mitteilungen des Septuaginta-Unternehmens der Wissenschaften zu Göttingen, 4, Heft 1; 1928), R. W. Lougee (Cambridge, Mass., and London, 1962), and a thesis by A. Favrat (Université de Paris IV, 1979), with bibl. pp. 613–41. F. [R.] Stern, *The Politics of Cultural Despair: A Study in the Rise of Germanic Ideology* (Berkeley and Los Angeles, Calif., 1961), pp. 3–94. R. Hanhart, 'Paul Anton de Lagarde und seine Kritik an der Theologie', in B. Moeller (ed.), *Theologie in Göttingen* (Göttingen [1987]), pp. 271–305. R. Heiligenthal in *TRE* 20 (1990), pp. 375–8, s.v.

Lagrange, Marie-Joseph (1855–1938), biblical scholar. He entered the *Dominican Order in 1879. In 1890 he founded at *Jerusalem the 'École Pratique d'Études Bibliques', and in 1892 the *Revue Biblique [Internationale]*. He gave his warm support to *Leo XIII's efforts to encourage the critical study of the Bible in the RC Church, and in Jan. 1903 he was appointed a member of the *Biblical Commission. In matters of OT criticism, which was the chief field of his earlier labours, perhaps his position approached as nearly to that of the *Higher Critics as was then compatible with Catholic orthodoxy. His sympathies with the critical position became manifest in a memorandum which he presented in 1897 to the International Congress of Catholics at Fribourg (Switzerland) and later published in the *Revue Biblique* (Jan. 1898). His original interest was in the OT, but in 1907 the *Holy See forbade him to continue this work and he turned his attention to the NT. His monumental commentaries on the four Gospels (*Marc*, 1911; *Luc*, 1920; *Matthieu*, 1923; *Jean*, 1925) at once established themselves as standard works.

Le Père Lagrange au service de la Bible: Souvenirs personnels, ed. P. Benoit, OP (Chrétiens de tous les temps, 22; 1967; Eng. tr., New York [1985]), incl. text of unpub. memoirs. Lagrange's correspondence with H.-M. Cormier, Master General of the Dominicans (1904–16), ed. B. Montagnes, OP, *Exégèse et Obéissance* (Études Bibliques, NS 11; 1989). L. H. Vincent, OP (ed.), *Mémorial Lagrange* (Paris, 1940), with an 'Essai d'une bibliographie sommaire du Père Lagrange' by id., pp. 1–11. F. M. Braun, *L'Œuvre du Père Lagrange* (1943; Eng. adaptation, Milwaukee [1963]). J. T. Burtchaell, CSR, *Catholic Theories of Biblical Inspiration since 1810* (Cambridge, 1969), esp. pp. 132–46.

Laínez, Diego (1512–65), second *General of the *Jesuits. After studying at the University of Alcalá, he joined St *Ignatius Loyola in Paris and with him helped to found the Society of Jesus. He was appointed professor of scholastic theology at the Sapienza at Rome, and was largely responsible for crushing incipient Protestant opinion at Piacenza and other cities in N. Italy. He took a very prominent part in the Council of *Trent, where he represented the more irreconcilable elements (e.g. on *justification) and supported stronger views on Papal jurisdiction than many others. On Ignatius' death (1556)

Laínez succeeded him first as 'General-Vicar' and (from 1558) as General. His term of office was notable for the continued success and expansion of the order.

Lainii Monumenta: Epistolae et Acta Patris Jacobi Lainii (8 vols., Monumenta Historica Societatis Jesu, Madrid, 1912–17); his *Disputationes Tridentinae*, ed. H. Grisar, SJ (2 vols., Innsbruck, 1886). Lives by P. de Ribadeneira, SJ (Madrid, 1594; modern edn. by E. Rey, SJ, under the title *Historias de la Contrarreforma* (1945), pp. 429–581), and F. Dilarino (pseudonym of C. M. Rinaldi, SJ, Rome, 1672). Modern studies by A. Martínez de Azagra y Beladiez (Madrid, 1933), H. Flichter, SJ (St Louis, 1944), and F. Cereceda, SJ (2 vols., Madrid, 1945–6). M. Scaduto, SJ, *L'epoca di Giacomo Lainez* (Storia della Compagnia di Gesù in Italia, 3 and 4; 1964–74). J. Brodrick, SJ, *The Progress of the Jesuits, 1556–79* (1946), pp. 66–111. Polgár, 2 (1990), pp. 359–62. M. Scaduto, SJ, in *Dict. Sp.* 9 (1976), cols. 110–15, s.v. 'Laínez (Laynez; Jacques)'.

laity. The term is derived from the phrase λαὸς θεοῦ, the 'people of God', contrasted with those who had not been called by God to be His people (originally the 'Gentiles', but already in 1st-cent. Christian usage sometimes the Jews as well). In early Christian literature a lay person is a member of the Church not otherwise distinguished as being in *major or *minor orders (cf. I Clem. 40). Gradually, but unevenly, the laity came to be defined negatively as 'not the clergy'. Another traditional division is into clergy, religious, and laity. The distinction between clergy and laity has always been most marked in the RC Church, less so in the C of E, while some sects such as the *Quakers admit no distinction at all. In the RC Church the emphasis has been modified by the Second *Vatican Council: this Council stressed the role of the laity as part of the 'people of God' in the 'Constitution on the Church' (1964); in the 'Constitution on the Liturgy' (1963) the laity were said to have a share in the 'priestly, prophetic and royal office of Christ' and were assigned various duties in public worship; while the 'Decree on the Apostolate of the Laity' (1965) recognized their special gifts (*charismata*) for building up the body of Christ and stressed their vocation to ameliorate the social order as well as their part in the Gospel. A similar change of emphasis in the C of E is reflected in the enhanced position assigned to the laity in the government of the Church by the *Synodical Government Measure 1969. The laity, however, owe allegiance to the clergy in spiritual matters and in most Churches are bound to contribute to the support of their ministers.

Lake, Kirsopp (1872–1946), biblical and patristic scholar. Educated at Lincoln College, Oxford, he was ordained in 1895, and after holding two curacies in England, was professor of NT exegesis at *Leiden from 1904 to 1914. Later he held professorships at Harvard University, USA. Esp. in his earlier years he was a provocative NT critic. In his *Historical Evidence for the Resurrection of Jesus Christ* (1907) he challenged the sufficiency of the evidence for the empty tomb, and in his *Earlier Epistles of St Paul* (1911) maintained that the course of primitive Christianity was profoundly affected by the influence of the mystery religions. These books were followed by *The Beginnings of Christianity: The Acts of the Apostles* (5 vols., 1920–33), a co-operative work in the editing of which he was associated with F. J. Foakes Jackson. Throughout his life he was a devoted student of the palaeography of Greek MSS. *The Early Days of Monasticism on Mount *Athos*

(1909) was the fruit of an early visit to Greece for the study of MSS, and from 1934 onwards he edited with his wife *Monumenta Palaeographica Vetera, First Series*, a fine set of facsimiles of 'Dated Greek Minuscule Manuscripts to the Year 1200'. From 1934 until his death he and his wife also edited the series *Studies and Documents*.

R. P. Casey, S. Lake, and A. K. Lake (eds.), *Quantulacumque: Studies presented to Kirsopp Lake by Pupils, Colleagues and Friends* 2[1937], with biog. note by G. K. Lake (son), pp. vii f. F. C. Grant in *DNB, 1941–1950*, pp. 466 f.

lamb. The use of a lamb as a symbol of Christ is based on such passages as Jn. 1: 29, Rev. 5: 12. Occasionally in early times a lamb with or near a cross was used to represent the sacrifice of Christ, e.g. in a 3rd-cent. inscription in the *Catacomb of San Callisto. Another common type of symbolism represents the lamb as standing on Mt. *Zion (cf. Rev. 14: 1), from which flow the four rivers of Paradise, while other passages in the NT (e.g. Jn. 10: 14) suggest the representation of the Christian believers as sheep, and where this symbolism is used the Good Shepherd carries His lambs or, alternatively, stands among them. After the *Trullan Synod in 692 (can. 82) forbade the representation of Christ under the form of a lamb, such imagery was confined to the W. In the E. Church, however, the portion of bread that is consecrated in the Liturgy is called the 'lamb' (see PROSPHORA). See also AGNUS DEI and PASCHAL LAMB.

F. Gerke, 'Der Ursprung der Lämmerallegorien in der altchristlichen Plastik', *ZNTW* 33 (1934), pp. 160–96. F. [G. L.] van der Meer, *Maiestas Domini: Théophanies de l'apocalypse dans l'art chrétien* (Studi di antichità cristiana, 13; 1938), pp. 27–174. F. Nikolasch, *Das Lamm als Christussymbol in den Schriften der Väter* (Wiener Beiträge zur Theologie, 3; 1963). H. *Leclercq, OSB, in *DACL* 1 (pt. 1; 1907), cols. 877–905, s.v. 'Agneau'; A. Romeo and A. Ferrua, SJ, in *EC* 1 (1948), cols. 459–64, s.v. 'Agnello'; *Lexikon der Christlichen Ikonographie*, 3 (1971), cols. 7–14, s.v. 'Lamm, Lamm Gottes'; J. R. Miles in *Anchor Bible Dictionary*, 4 (1992), pp. 132–4, s.v.

Lambert, St (*c.*635–before 705/6), also 'Landebertus', martyr. A member of a noble family of Austrasia, he was Bp. of Tongeren/Maastricht from *c.*670 until his death, though from *c.*675 to 682 he was, for political causes, exiled from his see to the monastery of Stavelot. In his later life he worked zealously as a missionary in what is now Brabant. It seems indisputable that he suffered a violent death, but the circumstances are differently recorded. Acc. to some authorities it occurred in a blood feud, while there is another story (insufficiently attested) that it was the result of his outspoken reproof of Pepin II, Mayor of the Palace, for adultery. He was succeeded by St *Hubert, who transferred the see to Liège. Feast day, 17 Sept.; of the 'Translation' (of Lambert's remains to Liège in 718), 31 May.

Life (*c.* AD 730) by Godescalcus, deacon of Liège, and three other medieval Lives, pr. in *AASS*, Sept. 5 (1755), pp. 574–617; J. Demarteau, *Vie la plus ancienne de S. Lambert* (Liège, 1890), incl. text of first, pp. 39–64; crit. edn. of the four Lives by B. Krusch in *MGH*, Scriptores Rerum Merovingicarum, 6 (1913), pp. 299–429; cf. H. Moretus in *Anal. Boll.* 33 (1914), pp. 247–9. M. Zender, *Räume und Schichten mittelalterlicher Heiligenverehrung in ihrer Bedeutung für die Volkskunde* (Düsseldorf, 1959), pp. 27–60. M. Werner, *Der Lütticher Raum in frühkarolingischer Zeit*

(Göttingen, 1980), pp. 241–74. J.-L. Kupper, 'Saint Lambert: de l'histoire à la légende', *RHE* 79 (1984), pp. 5–49.

Lambert, François (1486/7–1530), Reformer of Hesse. At the age of 15 he entered the *Franciscan Order at *Avignon and in 1517 was appointed *praedicator apostolicus*. While travelling through Switzerland in 1522, he met U. *Zwingli; he left his order and continued his journey under a false name to *Wittenberg (1523), where M. *Luther obtained a pension for him from the Elector, and where he married. In 1524 he went to Metz, but after eight days fled to Strasbourg, where he wrote several treatises and commentaries on the *Minor Prophets. In 1526 he was called to Hesse by the Landgraf *Philip. Here he took a prominent part in the *Homberg Synod, was charged with the preparation of a new Protestant 'Church Order' for Hesse, and in 1527 became professor of theology at the newly-founded *Marburg University. After the *Marburg Colloquy of 1529, he adopted the *Zwinglian doctrine of the Eucharist. He was the author of commentaries on the Song of Songs (1524) and the Apocalypse (1528) as well as several polemical writings, including an attack (in an excursus to his commentary on Hosea, 1525), on *Erasmus' doctrine on free will.

Studies by J. W. Baum (Strasbourg, 1840 [Ger.]; repr. Geneva, 1971) and R. L. Winters (Philadelphia, 1938). G. Müller, *Franz Lambert von Avignon und die Reformation in Hessen* (Veröffentlichungen der Historischen Kommission für Hessen und Waldeck, 24, 4; Marburg, 1958). P. Fraenkel (ed.), *Pour retrouver François Lambert: Bio-bibliographie et études* (Bibliotheca Bibliographica Aureliana, 108; Baden-Baden, 1987). R. Haas in *Dict. Sp.* 9 (1976), cols. 143–5; G. Müller in *TRE* 20 (1990), pp. 415–18, both s.v. See also works cited under HOMBERG, SYNOD OF.

Lambert of Hersfeld. See LAMPERT OF HERSFELD.

Lambeth. For over 700 years Lambeth has been the London residence of the Abps. of *Canterbury. Abp. *Baldwin (1185–90) acquired from the possessions of the see of *Rochester the manor of Lambeth and the manor-house, which was called 'Lambeth House' until about 1658, when, owing to the decay of the palace at Canterbury, the title of palace was transferred to Lambeth. Both Baldwin and his successor *Hubert Walter were prevented by the opposition of the monks at Christ Church, Canterbury, from establishing a collegiate church at Lambeth. The chapel, built in 1245 by Abp. *Boniface in the Early English style, is the oldest part of the building. The South Gateway with its two towers was erected by Cardinal John Morton (Abp., 1486–1501). The Water Tower, known in recent times as the 'Lollards' Tower' (on the supposition that *Lollards were imprisoned in it), is a massive square keep, erected by Abp. H. *Chichele in 1434. Abp. M. *Parker was consecrated at Lambeth in 1559 and is the only archbishop buried in the palace. The Great Hall, built by Abp. W. *Juxon in 1663, contains part of the Library (founded by Abp. R. *Bancroft in 1610), which has some 2,500 MSS, including the Registers of the archbishops from 1279 to 1928. The part of the palace occupied by modern archbishops dates from 1829–34. It was seriously damaged in 1940 in an air raid; restorations were completed *c*.1956. See also LAMBETH CONFERENCES.

[A.C.] Ducarel, *The History and Antiquities of the Archiepiscopal Palace of Lambeth* (1785; incl. in J. Nichols, Bibliotheca Topo-graphica Britannica, 2, 1790, no. 4). J. C. Browne, *Lambeth Palace and its Associations* (1882). H. Roberts and W. H. Godfrey (eds.), *The London County Council Survey of London*, 23 (1951), pp. 81–103. C. R. Dodwell, *Lambeth Palace* (1958). Catalogues of the MSS in the archiepiscopal library by H. J. Todd (London, 1812; cont. by E. G. W. Bill [MSS 1222–1860], Oxford, 1972; [1907–2340], ibid., 1976; and [2341–3119 (excluding 2690–2750)], ibid., 1983) and M. R. James and C. Jenkins (5 parts, Cambridge, 1930–2); of some early pr. books by S. R. Maitland (London, 1843); index of Eng. pr. books up to 1550 by id. (ibid., 1845). There are also a number of more recent works on the Archives in the library, incl. calendars of the American Colonial Section of the Fulham Papers, by W. W. Manross (Oxford, 1965), of the Original Papal Documents, by J. E. Sayers (London, 1967), and of SPG Papers by W. W. Manross (Oxford, 1974).

Lambeth Appeal. See LAMBETH CONFERENCES.

Lambeth Articles. Nine theological propositions compiled at Lambeth in 1595 by a committee that met under Abp. J. *Whitgift. Drawn up in the interests of a pronounced *Calvinism, they maintained the *Supralapsarian doctrine that God from all eternity had predestined by an unchangeable decree a definite number of persons to salvation, and that the elect were saved not because God had foreseen their merits but through His good pleasure alone. Although they represented a considerable body of theological opinion at the time, they were never formally authorized and they were strongly disapproved of by *Elizabeth I.

The text is in E. *Cardwell, *Documentary Annals of the Reformed Church of England* (1839), 2, pp. 30–4. Eng. tr. in H. C. Porter, *Reformation and Reaction in Tudor Cambridge* (Cambridge, 1958), p. 371, with discussion, pp. 364–75. P. [G.] Lake, *Moderate Puritans and the Elizabethan Church* (ibid., 1982), pp. 201–42, *passim*.

Lambeth Conferences. Assemblies of the bishops of the Anglican Communion held about every ten years under the presidency of the Abp. of *Canterbury. From 1867 to 1958 they were held in *Lambeth Palace; in 1968 in *Church House, Westminster; and in 1978 and 1988 in the University of Kent at Canterbury. Though a council of bishops was mentioned in a letter of Bp. J. H. Hopkins of Vermont to Abp. J. B. *Sumner in 1851, it was a request for such a meeting from the Synod of the Anglican Church in *Canada, held in 1865, to Abp. C. T. *Longley, which led to the first Conference. The Canadian bishops and others were concerned about the unsettling effects of the case of Bp. J. W. *Colenso and the publication of *Essays and Reviews*. After the original idea of a council authorized to define doctrine had been abandoned, owing to strenuous opposition, the first Conference, attended by 76 bishops, met in 1867; it issued an 'Address to the Faithful'. Subsequent Conferences have been attended by an increasing number of bishops: from *c*.100 in 1878 to 518 in 1988. The Conference of 1888 accepted the *Lambeth Quadrilateral as a foundation in the search for the reunion of Christians; it was also the first to issue a specific list of resolutions. That of 1908 was preceded by a large Pan-Anglican Congress, composed of some 7,000 clerical and lay delegates. The Conference of 1920 (delayed because of the First World War) was important for its 'Appeal to All Christian People' for reunion, which was sent to the heads of Christian communities throughout the world. That of 1930 returned to the subject of unity, as have all later Conferences. Its leading theme was the doctrine of God. It also gave guarded approval to the *South India scheme, and radically condemned racism. The chief subjects of the seventh Conference, postponed until 1948 because of the Second World War, were the doctrine of man, the Church in the modern world, and marriage discipline. One result was the issue of rules of churchmanship. The Conference of 1958 dealt with the authority of the Bible, peace, and the family in contemporary society, giving approval, with reservations, to family planning. This marked a change from the resolutions of the 1908 and 1920 Conferences, which had condemned *contraception. The Conference of 1968 devoted itself largely to considerations of the renewal of the Church in faith, ministry, and unity. One of its resolutions led to the establishment of the Anglican Consultative Council (see ANGLICAN COMMUNION). For the first time a number of observers were present, as well as Anglican consultants who were not bishops. The 1978 Conference accepted the de facto ordination of *women in some Provinces, and at the same time called for the preservation of communion and mutual respect between those Provinces which ordained women and those which did not. The 1988 Conference dealt with a wide range of issues, including world peace, polygamy, *homosexuality, and AIDS, but most of the time was devoted to ecumenism and the ordination of women to the priesthood and episcopate. The Conference endorsed the Final Report of the first *Anglican–Roman Catholic International Commission and asked the Abp. of Canterbury to establish a Commission to report to the Archbishops and Primates on women in the episcopate. (The Commission, under the chairmanship of Abp. R. Eames of Armagh, presented its findings in 1989.) The 1998 Conference passed an important resolution on homosexuality and called upon the Provinces to affirm that 'those who dissent from, as well as those who assent to, the ordination of women . . . are both loyal Anglicans'. Resolutions of Lambeth Conferences, though not binding, are regarded by member Churches as significant.

The Reports of the first five Conferences were ed. [by H. Thomas] under the direction of R. T. *Davidson (1920; rev. as *The Six Lambeth Conferences 1867–1920*, 1929). Reports of the Conferences 1930–68 were issued by the SPCK; those of 1978 and 1988 by the Church Information Office. R. Coleman (ed.), *Resolutions of the Twelve Lambeth Conferences 1867–1988* (Toronto, 1992). W. R. Curtis, *The Lambeth Conferences: The Solution for Pan-Anglican Organization* (New York, 1942). A. M. G. Stephenson, *The First Lambeth Conference 1867* (CHS, 1967); id., *Anglicanism and the Lambeth Conferences* (1978). A special issue of *Anglican and Episcopal History*, 58 (1989), pp. 251–408, was devoted to a series of arts. on 'Lambeth Conferences, Past and Present'.

Lambeth degrees. The degrees in Divinity, Arts, Law, Medicine, and Music, which the Abp. of *Canterbury confers from time to time in virtue of the Ecclesiastical Licences Act 1533 (passed in 1534), which committed to his immediate possession many rights previously enjoyed by the Primate as '*legatus natus' of the Pope. Their recipients usually wear the academic dress of the university to which the Archbishop belongs. Since 1906 Lambeth diplomas in theology have also been awarded; these are frequently supplemented by the Abp. of Canterbury's 'Licence and Authority to teach Sacred Theology'.

Lambeth Opinions. The first 'Lambeth Opinion' was

delivered on 31 July 1899, by the Abps. of Canterbury (F. *Temple) and York (W. D. Maclagan), at *Lambeth Palace, in response to questions raised by some of the English bishops. It stated that the liturgical use of *incense and the carrying of lights in procession were 'neither enjoined nor permitted' in the C of E. In the matter of incense, however, the archbishops added that there was nothing to prevent its use for sweetening the atmosphere of a church and that it was not in itself an undesirable accompaniment to Divine service. A year later (1 May 1900) the two archbishops issued further opinions (on this occasion that of Canterbury was separate from that of York, though they agreed in substance) denying the legality of *Reservation of the Sacrament. These opinions are sometimes described as the 'Lambeth Judgements', but less correctly, as the two archbishops did not sit as an ecclesiastical court.

The official texts were pub. by Macmillan under the titles *The Archbishops on the Lawfulness of the Liturgical Use of Incense and the Carrying of Lights in Procession* (1899); *The Archbishop of Canterbury on Reservation of the Sacrament* (1900, signed F. Cantuar.); *Archbishop of York on Reservation of Sacrament* (1900).

Lambeth Quadrilateral (1888), sometimes called the 'Chicago–Lambeth Quadrilateral'. A slightly revised edition of the four Articles agreed upon at the General Convention of the *Episcopal Church in the United States of America in Chicago 1886. These were initially inspired by the work of William Reed Huntington. In the revised form the Articles were approved by the *Lambeth Conference of 1888 as stating from the Anglican standpoint the essentials for a reunited Christian Church. The text of the Articles is as follows:

'A. The Holy Scriptures of the Old and New Testaments, as "containing all things necessary to salvation", and as being the rule and ultimate standard of faith.

'B. The Apostles' Creed, as the Baptismal Symbol; and the Nicene Creed, as the sufficient statement of the Christian Faith.

'C. The two Sacraments ordained by Christ Himself— Baptism and the Supper of the Lord—ministered with unfailing use of Christ's Words of Institution, and of the elements ordained by Him.

'D. The Historic Episcopate, locally adapted in the methods of its administration to the varying needs of the nations and peoples called of God into the Unity of His Church'.

The full text of the Chicago Quadrilateral is pr. in G. R. Evans and J. R. Wright (eds.), *The Anglican Tradition* (1991), pp. 345 f. (no. 343). W. R. Huntington, *The Church-Idea* (New York, 1870); id., *The Peace of the Church* (ibid., 1891); id., *A National Church* (ibid., 1898). J. R. Wright (ed.), *Quadrilateral at One Hundred: Essays on the Centenary of the Chicago–Lambeth Quadrilateral 1886/88–1986/88* (Cincinnati, Oh., and London, 1988); J. Draper (ed.), *Communion and Episcopacy: Essays to Mark the Centenary of the Chicago–Lambeth Quadrilateral* (Ripon College, Cuddesdon, Oxford, 1988).

Lamennais, Félicité Robert de (1782–1854), French religious and political author. He was a member of a well-to-do family of St-Malo. While still a child he read widely, esp. J.-J. *Rousseau, whose influence contributed to his loss of religious faith at an early age. But under the guidance of his brother Jean Marie (c.1780–1860), who had become a priest, he was converted and made his first communion at the age of 22. He was appointed professor of mathematics at the episcopal college of St-Malo in 1804; later he retired to the country house of his grandfather, La Chênaie, which became the centre of his circle of like-minded friends. In 1808 he published his *Réflexions sur l'état de l'Église*, written in collaboration with his brother. The book aimed at showing the futility of trust in individual reason, which led to rationalism, atheism, and intellectual anarchy, and called for systematic clerical organization. This demand brought him into conflict with Napoleon's policy and caused him to flee to London during the Hundred Days in 1815. After his return, against his own inclinations, he became a priest in 1816.

In 1818 he published the first volume of his chief work, the *Essai sur l'indifférence en matière de religion*. Lamennais here developed the principle of authority, which he equated with the 'raison générale' or 'sens commun'. He maintained that the individual is dependent on the community for his knowledge of the truth; to isolate oneself is to doubt; and toleration is an evil. His eloquence gained him fervent disciples, esp. among the *Ultramontanists and Royalists, and effected many conversions; but its ideas were suspect esp. to the *Sulpicians and *Jesuits and opposed by the *Gallicans. The later volumes of the work (1820, 1823) were still more opposed to the traditional doctrines. They equated Catholic Christianity with the religion of all mankind, denied the supernatural, and proclaimed subjects freed from loyalty to their temporal sovereigns when rulers refused to conform their conduct to Christian ideals. In order to counteract the evils of the time he desired a theocracy, with the Pope as supreme leader of kings and peoples. The work received the approval of Pope Leo XII, who possibly intended to make him a cardinal. In *Des progrès de la Révolution* (1829) he prophesied an impending revolution and demanded the separation both of the Church and of the entire educational system from the State, as well as the freedom of the press. In order to carry out these ideas he founded a religious congregation, the short-lived Congrégation de St Pierre (1828), an Agence Générale pour la Défense de la Liberté Religieuse (1830), and the paper *L'Avenir* (1830–1), and won the co-operation of a number of brilliant younger religious thinkers, among them C. de *Montalembert and H. *Lacordaire. He asserted that the essence of Christianity was freedom, but freedom understood in a political sense and guaranteed by the Papacy. In the last number of *L'Avenir* he launched the 'Acte d'Union', in which he called for the union of all freedom-loving men. Convinced that the Pope would put himself at the head of this crusade for freedom, he went to Rome in 1832 to defend his ideas before *Gregory XVI; they were, however, condemned in the encyclical '*Mirari vos' of 15 Aug. 1832. Lamennais, though submitting externally, retired to La Chênaie, where he wrote his reply, the famous *Paroles d'un croyant* (1834). Though admitting the authority of the Church in questions of faith, he denied it in the sphere of politics. In apocalyptic language he presented a picture of the ideal community in which production and consumption were to be harmoniously balanced. The book aroused tremendous excitement throughout Europe; it was condemned in the encyclical 'Singulari nos' of 25 June 1834.

Lamennais's friends submitted, but he himself left the Church.

From this time Lamennais's interests became more and more exclusively political. He gave his views on the social needs of the times in *Le Livre du peuple* (1837; Eng. tr., 1838) and *L'Esclavage moderne* (1839; Eng. tr., 1840). The *Discussions critiques* (1841) marked the final end of his Christian faith. He denied the whole supernatural order together with the doctrinal beliefs of Catholicism and tended more and more to a vague pantheism, expressed also in *Esquisse d'une philosophie* (4 vols., 1841–6). In 1846 he published a translation of the Gospels with commentary, *Les Évangiles*, which was placed on the *Index. In the Revolution of 1848 he became a member of Parliament, but the political reaction of 1852 completely disillusioned him. All efforts, even those of the new Pope *Pius IX, to reconcile him to the Church were in vain. An extraordinarily gifted writer, Lamennais was one of the greatest inspirers of the new social and political ideas of the 19th and 20th cents. as well as a forerunner of *Modernism.

Œuvres complètes (12 vols. bound in 6, Paris, 1836–7); *Œuvres posthumes*, ed. E. D. Forgues (2 vols., ibid., 1856–9); *Œuvres inédites*, ed. A. Blaize (2 vols., ibid., 1866); *Correspondance générale*, ed. L. Le Guillou (9 vols., ibid., 1971–81). Also posthumously pub. was his *Essai d'un système de philosophie catholique*, ed. Y. Le Hir (Rennes, 1954). M. J. Le Guillou [OP] and L. Le Guillou (eds.), *La Condamnation de Lamennais* (Textes, Dossiers, Documents, 5; 1982). There is a considerable lit. about the various aspects of Lamennais's life, thought, and influence, esp. in Fr., but no fully documented biog. The two best general studies are C. Boutard, *Lamennais: Sa vie et ses doctrines* (3 vols., 1905–13); F. Duine, *La Mennais: Sa vie, ses idées, ses ouvrages, d'après les sources imprimées et les documents inédits* (1922). Further items listed in F. Duine, *Essai de bibliographie de Félicité Robert de La Mennais* (1923). L. Le Guillou, *L'Évolution de la pensée religieuse de Félicité Lamennais* (1966); G. Hourdin, *Lamennais: Prophète et combattant de la liberté* (1982). In Eng. the main items incl. W. Gibson, *The Abbé de Lamennais and the Liberal Catholic Movement in France* (1896); A. R. Vidler, *Prophecy and Papacy: A Study of Lamennais, the Church, and the Revolution* (Birkbeck Lectures, 1952–1953; 1954); W. G. Roe, *Lamennais and England: The Reception of Lamennais's Religious Ideas in England in the Nineteenth Century* (Oxford, 1966), with bibl. A. Fonck in *DTC* 8 (pt. 2; 1925), cols. 2473–526, s.v., with detailed bibl.

Lamentabili. The decree of the *Holy Office issued on 3 July 1907 in which 65 propositions believed to be derived from the teaching of the contemporary *Modernists on the subjects of the Church, of Revelation, of Christ, and of the Sacraments, were condemned. It was shortly afterwards followed by the encyclical *Pascendi* (8 Sept. 1907).

Text in *ASS* 40 (1907), pp. 470–8; operative clauses in Denzinger and Hünermann (37th edn., 1991), pp. 932–9 (nos. 3401–66). F. Heiner, *Der Neue Syllabus Pius X* (1907). J. Rivière, *Le Modernisme dans l'Église* (1929), pp. 331–48. G. Thils, 'Le Décret "Lamentabili sane Exitu" et la convergence de probabilité', *Ephemerides Theologicae Lovanienses*, 32 (1956), pp. 65–72, with further refs.

Lamentations of Jeremiah. In the Hebrew Bible, as one of the five *Megilloth, this Book is placed in the third main division of the OT, called the 'Writings' (*Kethubim). In the English Bible, as in the *Septuagint and *Vulgate, it follows Jer. The Book consists of five chapters, all dealing with the desolation of Judah after the destruction of Jerusalem c.586 BC. They show considerable literary art, extensive use being made of acrostic arrangement and the greater part of the Book being composed in the metre used in Hebrew dirges (the 'Qinah'; see HEBREW (TONGUE)). Traditionally the Book has been ascribed to the prophet *Jeremiah, but the tradition may not be more than a misinterpretation of 2 Chr. 35: 25, and the tendency of modern biblical scholarship is against this attribution, though the Book prob. derives from a time not long after the destruction of the city, and so during Jeremiah's lifetime. In Jewish worship it was appointed to be read at the annual commemoration of the destruction of Jerusalem, and in the Christian Church it has been commonly interpreted in reference to Christ's Passion and in the W. used in the liturgy of *Holy Week.

Comm. by W. Rudolph (KAT 16. 3; 1939; 2nd edn. 17. 1–3, on Ruth, Song of Songs, Lam., 1962, pp. 187–263), A. Weiser (Das Alte Testament Deutsch, 16. 2, by H. Ringgren and A. Weiser, on Song of Songs, Lam., and Esther, 1958, pp. 39–112; 2nd edn., 1969, pp. 295–370), H.-J. Kraus (Biblischer Kommentar, Altes Testament, 20; 3rd edn., 1968), O. Plöger (HAT, Reihe I, Bd. 18, 2nd edn., by E. Würthwein, K. Galling, and O. Plöger, on Ruth, Song of Songs, Eccles., Lam., Esther, 1969, pp. 127–64), D. R. Hillers (Anchor Bible, 1972), and H. Gross (Neue Echter Bibel, 14, 1986, on Lam. and Bar., pp. 3–42). H. Jahnow, Das hebräische Leichenlied im Rahmen der Völkerdichtung (Beihefte zur ZATW, 36; 1923). N. K. Gottwald, Studies in the Book of Lamentations (Studies in Biblical Theology, 14; 1954); B. Albrektson, Studies in the Text and Theology of the Book of Lamentations, with a critical edn. of the Peshitta text (Studia Theologica Lundensia, 21; 1963); G. Brunet, Les Lamentations contre Jérémie: Réinterprétation des quatre premières Lamentations (Bibliothèque de l'École des Hautes Études, Section des sciences religieuses, 75; 1968). D. R. Hillers in Anchor Bible Dictionary, 4 (1992), pp. 137–41, s.v.

Lammas Day. The term 'Lammas', denoting 1 August, is found in the work of King *Alfred and was common throughout the Middle Ages; though now archaic, it occurs in the BCP. By etymology it derives from 'loaf' and 'mass', and in the early English Church it was customary to bless bread made from the first-ripe corn at Mass on this day, prob. in thanksgiving for the harvest. A later explanation (dating from the 15th cent.) suggested that it derived from 'lamb' and 'Mass', denoting the time at which a feudal tribute of lambs was paid (at *York). The day, to which some chronological significance always seems to have attached, is observed as a quarter-day in Scotland. It used also to be the feast of St *Peter ad Vincula ('St Peter's Chains'; cf. Acts 12: 3, 6 f.).

Lampert of Hersfeld (c.1024–after 1081), medieval chronicler. Little is known of his life, except that he became a monk at the *Benedictine abbey of Hersfeld in 1058, and after 1077 he became the first abbot of Hasungen (Hesse). Of his writings, much the most important is his Annals; these begin with the creation of the world and from 708 to 1039 are brief; from 1040 to 1068 they become fuller, increasing in scope from 1069 to 1072; from 1072 to 1077 they provide a very detailed account of events. Lampert wrote with great skill, using classical models extensively but unobtrusively, and giving an impression of objectivity and fairness. From the time of the first edition (1525) until the middle of the 19th cent. he was regarded as the main source for the history of the

struggle between *Henry IV of Germany and Pope *Gregory VII, but from the time of L. von *Ranke (1854), who showed that many of his statements were motivated by strong prejudices against Henry, 19th-cent. historians became severely critical of his reliability. Recent research has done much to rehabilitate his value as a source.

The best edn. of his Opera by O. Holder-Egger (MGH, Scriptores Rerum Germanicarum in usum Scholarum; 1894). E. E. Stengel, 'Lambert von Hersfeld der erste Abt von Hasungen', in Aus Verfassungs- und Landesgeschichte: Festschrift zum 70. Geburtstag von Theodor Mayer dargebracht von seinen Freunden und Schülern, 2 (Constance, 1955), pp. 245–58; J. Semmler, 'Lambert von Hersfeld und Giselbert von Hasungen', Studien und Mitteilungen zur Geschichte des Benediktiner-Ordens, 67 (1956), pp. 261–76. T. Struve, 'Lampert von Hersfeld. Persönlichkeit und Weltbild eines Geschichtsschreibers am Beginn des Investiturstreits', Hessisches Jahrbuch für Landesgeschichte, 19 (1969), pp. 1–123; 20 (1970), pp. 32–142. Full bibl. in W. Wattenbach and R. Holtzmann, Deutschlands Geschichtsquellen im Mittelalter: Die Zeit der Sachsen und Salier, new edn. by F.-J. Schmale, 2 (Cologne, etc., 1967), pp. 456–71, and 3 (1971), pp. 141* f.

lamps. These were probably used in Christian worship from the first, as it usually took place at night. The ceremonial lighting of the evening lamp that accompanied the singing of the '*Phos Hilaron' is attested by St. *Basil as already an ancient custom in his time. From the time of *Constantine lamps were burnt in large chandeliers during the Liturgy, and this custom has continued in E. worship. It became customary to burn lights—lamps and later candles—before shrines and relics (and in the E. before *icons) at least as early as the 6th cent. The burning of lights before the *altar is prob. very ancient; the burning of a perpetual light before the reserved Sacrament came into general use in the 13th cent. in connection with the contemporary development of Eucharistic devotion, but was not to become obligatory until the 16th cent. See also CANDLE.

Rohault, 6 (1888), pp. 1–58. D. R. Dendy, The Use of Lights in Christian Worship (Alcuin Club Collections, 41; 1959). C. Babington, 'Lamps' in DCA 2 (1880), pp. 919–23; H. *Leclercq, OSB, in DACL 8 (pt. 2; 1928), cols. 1086–221, s.v. 'Lampes', with full refs.

lance (liturgical). In the Byzantine rites, a small knife (Gk. λόγχη), shaped like a lance, with a handle ending in a small cross, which is used to cut the Eucharistic bread at the *Proskomide.

Lance, Holy. A relic, believed to be the lance mentioned in Jn. 19: 34 as having been used by a Roman soldier for piercing the Lord's dead body. The first record of its existence occurs in the 6th cent., when the Piacenza pilgrim states that he had seen it at *Jerusalem in the basilica of Mount Sion. Its presence there is also attested by *Cassiodorus and St *Gregory of Tours. At the capture of Jerusalem by the Persians in 615, it fell into the hands of the pagans, together with the other relics of the Passion; but its point, which had been broken off, was saved and given to Nicetas, who brought it to *Constantinople, where it was kept in *Sancta Sophia, set in an icon. In 1241 it was given to St *Louis and preserved in the *Sainte-Chapelle together with the *Crown of Thorns. It disappeared during the French Revolution. The other part of the Lance was stated to have been seen in Jerusalem by the Frankish pilgrim, Arculf (c.670), but after that nothing is heard of it until it reappears in Constantinople before the 10th cent. In 1492 it fell into the hands of the Turks, who sent it to the Pope as a present. Since then it has been kept at Rome in St *Peter's, but its authenticity has always been doubted.

There have been several other relics, claimed to be the Holy Lance. One of them was found by the Crusaders at Antioch in 1098 in consequence of a vision. Another was kept among the Imperial insignia of the Holy Roman Empire, having been taken to Prague by Charles IV in 1350, to Nuremberg in 1424, and finally to Vienna in 1800. A special feast of the Holy Lance was kept in Germany, on the Friday after the Octave of Easter.

F. de Mély, *Exuviae Sacrae Constantinopolitanae* (Paris, 1904), pp. 22–163. C. Rohault de Fleury, *Mémoire sur les instruments de la Passion de N.-S. J.-C.* (1870), pp. 272–5. S. Runciman, 'The Holy Lance found at Antioch', *Anal. Boll.* 68 (1950), pp. 197–209. A. Hofmeister, *Die heilige Lanze, ein Abzeichen des alten Reiches* (Untersuchungen zur Deutschen Staats- und Rechtsgeschichte, 96; 1908); P. E. Schramm, *Herrschaftszeichen und Statussymbolik* (Schriften der Monumenta Germaniae historica, 13), 2 (1955), pp. 492–537 ('Die "Heilige Lanze" ') with additional material in 3 (1956), pp. 1101 f., and *Nachträge* (1978), pp. 28–31. H. Thurston, SJ, in *CE* 8 (1910), pp. 773 f., s.v.; J. A. Brundage in *NCE* 7 (1967), pp. 75 f., s.v. 'Holy Lance'.

Lanfranc (c.1010–89), scholar and Abp. of *Canterbury. Born in Pavia and educated there and elsewhere in N. Italy, Lanfranc came to N. France as a young man and built up a reputation as an itinerant scholar. In 1042 he entered the recently-founded abbey of *Bec, where he became prior (1045). In 1063 he became abbot of *William I's prestigious new foundation of St Stephen's, Caen, and in 1070 the first Norman Abp. of Canterbury.

As a scholar, Lanfranc initially worked on the *trivium; none of this material survives. At Bec he commented on the Psalms and the Pauline Epistles, and made linguistic notes on certain works of the Fathers. His biblical commentary was used by *Anselm of Laon and thus passed into the '*Glossa Ordinaria'. Lanfranc's pupils at Bec included *Anselm of Canterbury and possibly *Ivo of Chartres. His *De Corpore et Sanguine Domini* (written in the 1060s) was the first widely-known criticism of the Eucharistic teaching of *Berengar of Tours. It consists essentially of patristic and Carolingian proof-texts, with a brief excursion into the terminology of logic (chs. 7–9). Lanfranc maintained that the Sacred Species in the Eucharist contained the invisible Body of Christ, identical with the body born of the BVM, but hidden under the species of bread and wine; here he approached the doctrine of *transubstantiation.

Lanfranc was a brilliant administrator. He raised Bec from poverty to a substantial monastery. He became William the Conqueror's most trusted counsellor. As archbishop, he restored the demoralized monastic community of Christ Church, Canterbury, rebuilding the cathedral church, recovering lands and rights lost at the Conquest, and providing a set of constitutions (the 'Decreta Lanfranci') for the improved observance of the monastic life. At least for his own lifetime, he enforced the juridical supremacy of Canterbury over *York. His practical authority within the English Church was well demon-

strated in the synod of 1075, which transferred the sees of Selsey to *Chichester, *Lichfield to *Chester, and Ramsbury to Old Sarum (near *Salisbury). Lanfranc's canon law book was the '*False Decretals', a Carolingian collection that was still widely used; his view of clerical reform was correspondingly traditional. Opposing clerical marriage and concubinage and (like everyone else) condemning *simony, he still regarded lay *investiture as normal practice. Lanfranc was thus out of sympathy with *Gregory VII, though not disloyal to him. He sent Gregory *Peter's Pence (1080) and even in the later 1080s, when the imperial cause seemed to be triumphing, he withheld recognition from the antipope Clement III.

Collected edn. of his works by L. *d'Achery, OSB (Paris, 1648); this *Maurist edn. is largely repr. in J. P. Migne, *PL* 150. 9–782. Crit. edns. of 'Acta Lanfranci' (a memorandum of the circumstances of his taking up office in Canterbury) by C. Plummer and J. Earle, *Two of the Saxon Chronicles Parallel*, 1 (Oxford, 1892), pp. 287–92; of his monastic Constitutions by [M.] D. *Knowles, OSB, with Eng. tr. (Nelson's Medieval Classics, 1951; rev. [text only] in Corpus Consuetudinum Monasticarum, 3; Siegburg, 1967); and of his Letters and Acts of the 1075 Council (item 11), with Eng. tr., by [V.] H. Clover and M. [T.] Gibson (Oxford Medieval Texts, 1979). The main source for Lanfranc's early life is Gilbert Crispin's 'Vita Herluini' (first abbot of Bec); crit. edn. by A. S. Abulafia and G. R. Evans, *The Works of Gilbert Crispin* (Auctores Britannici Medii Aevi, 8; Oxford [1986]), pp. 183–212. M. [T.] Gibson, *Lanfranc of Bec* (Oxford, 1978). R. W. Southern, 'Lanfranc of Bec and Berengar of Tours' in R. W. Hunt, W. A. Pantin, and R. W. Southern (eds.), *Studies in Medieval History Presented to Frederick Maurice Powicke* (Oxford, 1948), pp. 27–48; id., 'The Canterbury Forgeries', *EHR* 73 (1958), pp. 193–226. J. de Montclos, *Lanfranc et Bérenger: La controverse eucharistique du XIᵉ siècle* (SSL 37; 1971), esp. pp. 249–482. G. D'Onofrio (ed.), *Lanfranco di Pavia e l'Europa del Secolo XI nel IX Centenario della Morte (1089–1989): Atti del Convegno Internazionale di Studi (Pavia . . ., 12–24 settembre 1989)* (Italia Sacra, 51; 1993). R. Gem, 'The Significance of the 11th-century Rebuilding of Christ Church and St Augustine's, Canterbury, in the Development of Romanesque Architecture', in *Medieval Art and Architecture at Canterbury before 1220* (British Archaeological Association Conference Transactions for the Year 1979, 5; 1982), pp. 1–19; H. J. A. Strik, 'Remains of the Lanfranc Building in the Great Central Tower and the North-West Choir/Transept Area', ibid., pp. 20–6, with plans. F. Barlow, *The English Church 1066–1154* (1979), *passim* (see index).

Lang, Cosmo Gordon (1864–1945), Abp. of *Canterbury. A Scotsman by birth and of *Presbyterian upbringing, he was educated at Glasgow University and at Balliol College, Oxford, and then studied for the Bar. In 1888 he was elected to a fellowship at All Souls College, Oxford. In 1890 he was ordained in the C of E, and after working as a curate of Leeds Parish Church from 1890 to 1893 under E. S. *Talbot, he returned to Oxford to become Dean of Divinity at Magdalen, and from 1894 to 1896 was vicar of St Mary's, the university church. From 1896 to 1901 he was vicar of Portsea. In 1901 he became (suffragan) Bp. of Stepney and in 1908 Abp. of *York. He was translated to Canterbury in 1928 and resigned in 1942. A committed ecumenist, he was chairman of the Reunion Committee of the *Lambeth Conference of 1920, which issued the influential 'Appeal to All Christian People'. He presided over the Lambeth Conference of 1930, to which he significantly invited a delegation of the *Old Catholics; full communion between the Old Catholics and the

C of E was established in 1932. In 1933 he set up the Council on Foreign Relations, called for by the *Church Assembly; he had originally opposed its establishment, but came to welcome it. His many journeys abroad included the first visit of an Archbishop of Canterbury to the *Oecumenical Patriarch in the Phanar in 1939. In Dec. 1936 he played an important part in public affairs in connection with the abdication of Edward VIII.

J. G. Lockhart, *Cosmo Gordon Lang* (1949). A. C. Don in *DNB, 1941–1950* (1959), pp. 474–8.

Langton, Stephen (*c.*1150/55–1228), Abp. of *Canterbury. He came of a family of Lincolnshire gentry. From *c.*1170 he studied in *Paris, where he was a pupil of *Peter the Chanter and gained a high reputation as a biblical commentator, preacher, and theologian. He made a permanent mark on biblical studies. By 1206 he was a canon of *York and Paris and in that year *Innocent III made him cardinal priest of St Chrysognus; Langton left Paris for Rome. In 1207, when irregular elections at Canterbury followed the death of *Hubert Walter, the Pope nominated and consecrated Langton Abp. of Canterbury. The appointment showed little awareness of or regard for English opinion. King *John's refusal to admit Langton as archbishop excluded him from his see until June 1213. He spent much of this time at Pontigny. Meanwhile, from May 1208 until July 1214, England and Wales were placed under *interdict by the Pope. The English clergy were exposed to great hardships and could not carry on their normal ecclesiastical and spiritual guidance of the laity. When Langton returned, he prob. disliked the terms of John's submission, by which the realm came under Papal suzerainty. During the next two years he showed sympathy with baronial grievances against the King. Although his influence in the framing of Magna Carta has perhaps been exaggerated, he certainly approved the principles of government which it asserted, gave the support of his office to the rebels, and thereby forfeited the Pope's favour. In 1215 he was suspended. After the deaths of Innocent III and John in 1216, in 1218 Langton resumed his place as metropolitan with the favour of *Honorius III. He returned to the tasks of ecclesiastical government, notably seeking to secure better clerical discipline and improved pastoral care. He gave a foretaste of this concern in diocesan statutes of 1213–14 which have affinities with the constitutions which his English colleague, Cardinal Robert Courçon, published as legate in France. This impulse, intensified by the canons of the Fourth *Lateran Council (1215), caused Langton to promulgate in his provincial council of Oxford (1222) constitutions which set patterns for the future and stimulated several English bishops to similar activity before his death. Under him, standards of clerical conduct and rudimentary religious education were raised. One initiative with both devotional and political aspects was his translation in 1220 of the remains of his predecessor Thomas *Becket and the celebration of the jubilee of his martyrdom. Little is known of his character, but he certainly had a profound influence on the Church in England. He was the first Abp. of Canterbury appointed since the Norman Conquest who had not been either a monk or a minister of the Crown, and in this office he began a tradition exemplifying the new learning of the nascent universities in arts, theology, and law.

Langton's writings (apart from his official acts) grew out of his teaching at Paris. They consist mainly of theological *quaestiones* and commentaries (*glosae*) on Books of the Old and New Testaments, on the 'Historia Scholastica' of *Peter Comestor, and the 'Sentences' of *Peter Lombard, all with a pronounced moral purpose. He is credited with the division of the Books of the Bible into chapters which, with small modification, is still in use. He also prob. wrote the '*Veni Sancte Spiritus'.

Comm. on the 'Sentences' of Peter Lombard (known also as Langton's 'Summa'), ed. A. M. Landgraf (BGPM 37, Heft 1; 1952); comm. on 1–2 Chron., ed. A. Saltman (Ramat-Gan, Israel, 1978); *Selected Sermons*, ed. P. B. Roberts (Toronto Medieval Latin Texts, 10; 1980). His *Acta* as Abp., ed. K. Major (Canterbury and York Society, 50; 1950). His diocesan statutes of Canterbury and the Constitutions of the Council of Oxford, ed. F. M. Powicke and C. R. Cheney, *Councils & Synods . . .* 2: A.D. 1205–1313, 1 (Oxford, 1964), pp. 23–36 and 100–25. F. M. Powicke, *Stephen Langton* (Ford Lectures for 1927; Oxford, 1928). K. Major, 'The "Familia" of Archbishop Stephen Langton', *EHR* 48 (1933), pp. 529–53. G. Lacombe, B. Smalley, and A. L. Gregory, 'Studies on the Commentaries of Cardinal Stephen Langton', *AHDLMA* 5 ('1930' [1931]), pp. 5–266. B. Smalley, *The Study of the Bible in the Middle Ages* (2nd edn., Oxford, 1952), esp. ch. 5. J. W. Baldwin, *Masters, Princes, and Merchants* (2 vols., Princeton, NJ, 1970), esp. 1, pp. 25–31. P. B. Roberts, *Stephanus de Lingua-Tonante: Studies in the Sermons of Stephen Langton* (Pontifical Institute of Mediaeval Studies, Studies and Texts, 16; Toronto, 1968); J. B. Schneyer, *Repertorium der lateinischen Sermones des Mittelalters für die Zeit von 1150–1350*, 5 (1974), pp. 466–507. R. Quinto, '*Doctor Nominatissimus*'. *Stefano Langton (†1228) e la tradizione delle sue opere* (BGPM, NF 39; 1994). R. Foreville in *Dict. Sp.* 4 (1961), cols. 1495–1502, s.v. 'Étienne Langton'. See also bibl. to JOHN, KING OF ENGLAND, and esp. arts. on the interdict by C. R. Cheney.

Laodicea. A Hellenistic city of the Roman province of Asia. It was the seat of an early Christian Church to which St *Paul wrote an epistle (Col. 4: 16), perhaps the same as the extant Eph. The city was reproved at a somewhat later date by the writer of *Rev. (3: 14 ff.) for being 'neither cold nor hot'. It was materially very prosperous in Apostolic times, and a bishopric of some importance for several centuries. It is not to be confounded with the town of Laodicea on the Syrian coast, the home of *Apollinarius.

W. M. *Ramsay, *Cities and Bishoprics of Phrygia*, 1 (1895), pp. 32–83. C. J. Hemer, *The Letters to the Seven Churches of Asia in their Local Setting* (Journal for the Study of the New Testament, Supplement Series, 11; Sheffield [1986]), pp. 178–209. F. F. Bruce in *Anchor Bible Dictionary*, 4 (1992), pp. 229–31, s.v., with bibl.

Laodicea, Canons of. A set of 59 4th-cent. canons which were embodied in the early collections of ecclesiastical law. They fall into two groups, acc. to their opening words (1–19: περὶ τοῦ and 20–59: ὅτι οὐ δεῖ). Among the subjects dealt with are the treatment of heretics (*Quartodecimans, *Novatianists, *Montanists, etc.), liturgy, penance, Church order, and the observance of *Lent. Nothing definite is known of the 'Council of Laodicea', though a mention of the *Photinians in can. 7 points to a date not before *c.*345, and prob. the Council took place at least 20 years later. Acc. to A. Boudinhon, the 'canons' are really subject-headings of canons issued by earlier 4th-cent. councils, among them that of *Nicaea (325) and an otherwise unknown Council of Laodicea. In some texts there is appended a list of the Canonical Scriptural Books closely akin to that of *Apostolic Canons, can. 85 (84), e.g. it omits the OT Apocrypha and Rev.; this list is sometimes called can. 60. Acc. to T. *Zahn and others (against C. J. *Hefele), it is prob. a later addition.

Hardouin, 1 (1715), cols. 777–92; Mansi, 2 (1759), cols. 563–600. Crit. edn. of Lat. canons in *EOMIA* 2. 3 (1939), pp. 321–400; Lat. and Gk. text also pr., with Fr. tr. and introd., in Joannou, 1, pt. 2 (1962), pp. 127–55. Eng. tr. in H. R. Percival, *The Seven Ecumenical Councils of the Undivided Church* (NPNCF 14; 1900), pp. 123–60. Hefele and Leclercq, 1 (pt. 2; 1907), pp. 989–1028. A. Boudinhon, 'Note sur le concile de Laodicée', in *Congrès scientifique international des Catholiques tenu à Paris, 1888* (1889), 2, pp. 420–47 (resumed in Hefele and Leclercq, loc. cit., pp. 992–4, n.). On the appended list, see B. F. *Westcott, *A General Survey of the History of the Canon of the New Testament* (1855), pp. 498–508; T. Zahn, *Geschichte des Neutestamentlichen Kanons*, 2 (pt. 1; 1890), pp. 193–202. *CPG* 4 (1980), p. 29 (no. 8607). G. Bardy in *DDC* 6 (1957), cols. 338–43.

Laodiceans, Epistle to the. A letter of St *Paul to Laodicea is mentioned at Col. 4: 16, but has not survived. Acc. to *Tertullian (*Adv. Marc.* 5, 11 and 17), *Marcion and his followers gave this name to the Epistle to the *Ephesians. The *Muratorian Canon mentions a letter to Laodicea 'forged for the sect of Marcion'. The Latin apocryphal Ep. of this name, found in many 6th–15th-cent. Latin MSS of the NT and in some early printed editions of the Bible, is an artless collection of St Paul's own words (esp. from Phil.), which was doubtless produced to supply the missing letter. It appears to date from the 2nd–4th cent., and was perhaps originally composed in Greek. It is mentioned in the *Liber de divinis scripturis* (ch. 50), attributed to St *Augustine, and seems to have been known to St *Gregory the Great (*Moralia*, 35. 20). A. *Harnack sought, without success, to prove that it was a 2nd-cent. Marcionite forgery.

Crit. edn. of Lat. text, with discussion, in J. B. *Lightfoot, *St Paul's Epistles to the Colossians and to Philemon* (1879 edn.), pp. 274–300 (actual text, pp. 287–9). Eng. tr. in J. K. Elliott, *The Apocryphal New Testament* (Oxford, 1993), pp. 543–6. B. Carra de Caux, 'L'Épître aux Laodicéens en arabe', *R. Bibl.* 5 (1896), pp. 221–6, with Arabic text, pp. 223 f. Ger. tr., with introd. by W. Schneemelcher in Schneemelcher, 2 (5th edn., 1989), pp. 41–44; Eng. tr., 2 [1992], pp. 42–6. A. von Harnack, 'Der apokryphe Brief des Apostels Paulus an die Laodicener, eine marcionitische Fälschung aus der 2. Hälfte des 2. Jahrhunderts' in *Sb.* (Berl.), 1923, pp. 235–45. C. P. Anderson in *Anchor Bible Dictionary*, 4 (1992), pp. 231–3, s.v., with bibl.

lapcloth. See GREMIAL.

Lapide, Cornelius a. See CORNELIUS A LAPIDE.

lapsi (Lat., 'the fallen'). Those who in varying degrees denied the Christian faith under persecution. *Apostasy was regarded as the most serious sin a Christian could commit; although there is some conflicting evidence, it is widely thought that at least in some parts of the Church it was at first regarded as unforgivable. However, when the problem became serious during the Decian *persecution of 250–251, the Church, guided by such leaders as Pope *Cornelius, *Dionysius of Alexandria, and St *Cyprian of Carthage, decided to readmit such persons as showed repentance after *penance and a period of probation. This decision led the *Novatianist rigorists to make open schism. The Councils of *Elvira (*c.*306), *Arles (314), *Ancyra (314), and *Nicaea (325) also legislated on the subject. See also TRADITORS.

H. J. Vogt in *DPAC* 2 (1984), cols. 1899–901, s.v.; Eng. tr. in *Encyclopedia of the Early Church*, 1 (1992), p. 473. See also works cited under PERSECUTIONS, EARLY CHRISTIAN.

Lardner, Nathaniel (1684–1768), Nonconformist apologist. He was a native of Hawkhurst in Kent, studied at Utrecht and *Leiden (1699–1703), and became an Independent minister in 1709. After being a private chaplain and tutor from 1713 to 1721, he began to give lectures in 1723. These developed into his famous work on *The Credibility of the Gospel History* (14 vols., 1727–57), in which he set himself the task of reconciling the discrepancies in the biblical narratives. Its collection of materials on the date and authorship of the NT books, together with a large apparatus of footnotes, made the work a mine of information for scholars, for whom it was of greater service than for the ordinary reader for whom it was originally intended. Lardner's interpretation is based on patristic texts as well as on the commentaries of H. *Grotius. He also published sermons and a *Letter concerning the Logos* (1759), expounding his Christological doctrine.

Works [ed. B. Cole], 11 vols., London, 1788, with Life by A. Kippis in vol. 1, pp. i–cviii. A more important authority for his life is the anonymous *Memoirs of the Life and Writings of the late Reverend Nathaniel Lardner, . . . with a Catalogue of his Works* [by J. Jennings], pub. along with eight of Lardner's Sermons (London, 1769), memoir, pp. 1–134. A. Gordon in *DNB* 32 (1892), pp. 147–51.

La Salette. The village in the Alps near Grenoble, where on 19 Sept. 1846 a peasant boy and girl saw a vision of the BVM, who through them gave 'to all her people' a promise of the Divine Mercy after repentance. A special secret, communicated by the Virgin to each child, was afterwards sent to *Pius IX. At first doubts were thrown on the vision; but a commission appointed by the Bp. of Grenoble convinced itself of its reality, and miraculous cures were soon alleged to occur. Pilgrimages quickly followed, and in 1852 the first stone of the present church was laid on the scene of the vision. The church has been served from the first by religious known as the 'Missionaries of La Salette'. Many thousands annually make pilgrimages to the 'Virgin of the Alps'.

There is a vast lit., mostly of little critical value. More substantial works include I. Bertrand, *La Salette* (1888); id., *La Salette: Documents et bibliographie pour servir de pièces justificatives à l'ouvrage portant le même titre* (1889); J. Giray, *Les Miracles de La Salette* (2 vols., Grenoble, 1921); J. Jaouen, *La Grâce de La Salette* (1946; rev. edn., 1964); id., *Les Missionnaires de Notre-Dame de La Salette* (Les Grands Ordres monastiques et Instituts religieux, 63 [1953]); J. Stern, *La Salette: Documents authentiques* (1980 ff.). In Eng. there is a popular account by J. S. Kennedy, *Light on the Mountains: The Story of La Salette* (Dublin, 1954). J. Stern, MS, 'La Salette. Bibliographie', *Marian Library Studies*, NS 7 (Dayton, Oh., 1975), pp. 3–302.

Las Casas, Bartolomé de (1484–1566), Spanish missionary to the New World, sometimes known as 'The Apostle of the Indies'. Originally a lawyer, he accompanied the Spanish governor, Ovando, to Hispaniola (Haiti) in 1502. Having been ordained, prob. on a visit to Rome in 1507, he delayed his 'first Mass' until he could celebrate it in Hispaniola in 1510, the first time any priest said his 'first Mass' in the New World. From 1514 he devoted himself to the interests of the Indians by opposing, both in America and at the court of Spain, the cruel methods of exploitation of the Spanish settlers. These activities were strongly resented by his countrymen, and in 1515 he went back to Spain, where he successfully presented the cause of the Indians to *Ferdinand V and *Charles V. He returned to America with far-reaching powers; but though supported by his fellow-clergy and many settlers, his projects of colonization miscarried owing to a revolt of the Indians in 1522. In the same year (1522) Las Casas joined the *Dominicans. He continued to labour for the Indians and put together many lurid reports on the abuses of the settlers, notably his famous *Destrucción des las Indias* (pub. 1552), in which he roundly condemned the horrors perpetrated by the colonists. He was the instigator of famous 'New Laws of the Indies'. In 1543 he became Bp. of Chiapa in Mexico, but he left his diocese in 1547 to return to Spain, where he spent the rest of his life championing the rights of the Indians at court and in numerous publications. He was in favour of limited importation of negro slaves into America to help the enfeebled Indians, but he was completely opposed to the 'slave-trade' and mass importation which benefited merchants. At the time of his death he was mainly occupied in trying to resolve the problems of the Peruvian natives with *Philip II.

Selected works ed. J. Pérez de Tudela Buesca (Biblioteca de Autores Españoles, 95, 96, 105, 106 and 110; 1957–8). Crit. edn. of his complete works, ed. P. Castañeda Delgado (Madrid, 1988 ff.). Eng. tr. of *De Unico Vocationis* (a treatise first pub. in 1942 but incl. in later edns. of his works) by P. F. Sullivan, SJ, *The Only Way* (New York and Mahwah, NJ [1992]), with introd. by H. R. Parish. There is much biog. material in A. Dávila Padilla, *Historia de la fundación y discurso de la provincia de Santiago de México de la Orden de Predicadores* (Madrid, 1596) and in A. de Remesal, OP, *Historia de la Provincia de S. Vicente de Chýapa ý Guatemala de la Orden de . . . Sancto Domingo* (ibid., 1619). The basic modern work is I. Pérez Fernández, OP, *Inventario documentado de los ecritos de Fray Bartolomé de las Casas* (Bayamón, Puerto Rico, 1981); id., *Cronología documentada de los viajes, estancias y actuaciones de Fray Bartolomé de las Casas* (ibid., 1984). L. U. Hanke, *Bartolomé de Las Casas: Bookman, Scholar and Propagandist* (Rosenbach Lectures; Philadelphia, 1952), and other works of this author. M. Bataillon, *Études sur Bartolomé de las Casas* (1965). *Estudios lascasianos: IV Centenario de la Muerte de Fray Bartolomé de las Casas (1566–1966)* (Publicaciones de la Escuela de Estudios Hispano-Americanos de Sevilla, 175; 1966). H. R. Wagner, *The Life and Writings of Bartolomé de las Casas* (posthumously ed. H. R. Parish, Albuquerque, NM, 1967). J. Friede and B. Keen (eds.), *Bartolomé de las Casas in History: Toward an Understanding of the Man and his Work* (Dekalb, Ill. [1971]). P. I. André-Vincent, *Bartolomé de la Casas, Prophète du Nouveau Monde* (1980); M. Mahn-Lot, *Bartolomé de las Casas et le droit des Indiens* (1982), with list of modern edns. and trs. G. Gutiérrez, *En Busca de los Pobres de Jesucristo* (Lima, 1992; Eng. tr., *Las Casas: In search of the poor of Jesus Christ*, Maryknoll, NY [1993]). There is also an important introd. by I. Pérez Fernández to his edn. of Las Casas' *Brevísima relación de la destruccion de Africa* (part of his *Historia de las Indias*, Salamanca, 1989), pp. 11–190. L. Hanke and M. Giménez Fernández, *Bartolomé de las Casas 1474–1566: Bibliografía crítica y cuerpo de materiales para el estudio de su vida, escritos, actuación y polémicas que suscitaron durante cuarto siglos* (Santiago, 1954).

Laski or **à Lasco, John** (1499–1560), Protestant Reformer. He was a Polish nobleman by birth, who, after studying at *Bologna from 1514 to 1518, visited Basle in 1524; here he met *Erasmus and later lived in his house for nearly a year (1525). From 1526 he showed an increasing interest in reforming the Church, while disapproving of M. *Luther as too extreme. In 1529 he was nominated Bp. of Veszprem and in 1538 made Archdeacon of Warsaw. He was stripped of all his ecclesiastical offices on his marriage in 1540. Two years later he openly broke with the RC Church and was appointed *Calvinist minister at Emden. Having made friends with J. *Hooper, he came to England in 1548 at the invitation of T. *Cranmer to advise on the projected reforms and returned in 1550 to become superintendent of the Foreign Protestants in London. He is generally held to have influenced the BCP of 1552. Between 1553 and 1556 he lived in several places on the Continent before returning to direct the Calvinist Church in Southern Poland.

Works ed. by A. Kuyper (2 vols., Amsterdam, 1866). H. Dalton, *Johannes a Lasco* (Gotha, 1881; earlier part tr. into Eng. by M. J. Evans, 1886); G. Pascal, *Jean de Lasco, baron de Pologne, évêque catholique, réformateur protestant, 1499–1560: Son temps, sa vie, ses œuvres* (1894); *Lasciana* (1898). Further Lives by P. Bartels (*Leben und ausgewählte Schriften der Väter und Begründer der reformirten Kirche*, 9; 1860), and O. Bartel (vol. 1, covering the period up to 1556; Warsaw, 1955), with Eng. summary. [K. A. R.] Kruske, *Johannes a Lasco und der Sacramentsstreit* (Studien zur Geschichte der Theologie und der Kirche, 7, Heft 1; 1901). A. Jobert, *De Luther à Mohila: La Pologne dans la crise de la Chrétienté 1517–1648* (Collection historique de l'Institut d'Études Slaves, 21; 1974), pp. 95–120. B. Hall, *John à Lasco, 1499–1560: A Pole in Reformation England* (Friends of Dr Williams' Library Lecture, 1971). M. Cytowska in P. G. Bietenholz and T. B. Deutscher (eds.), *Contemporaries of Erasmus*, 2 (Toronto, etc., 1986), pp. 297–301, s.v., with bibl.

Lassus, Orlande de (Flemish form, or **Orlando di Lasso**, Italian) (c.1532–94), composer. Born at Mons (in modern Belgium), he received most of his musical education in Italy, and was briefly (1553–4) 'Maestro di Capella' of St John *Lateran in Rome, preceding G. P. da *Palestrina in this office. In 1556 he went to Munich as a tenor at the court of Duke Albrecht V of Bavaria, and in 1563 became 'Maestro di Capella', remaining in this post for the rest of his life. Enormously prolific in all the forms of vocal music of his day, sacred and secular, his technique was equal to that of Palestrina, while his style and range of expression were far more varied. Much of his output was printed (starting in his Italian days), and widely known throughout Europe. Less affected by the *Counter-Reformation than Palestrina, his sacred music included over 60 Masses, 80 settings for the *Magnificat, and some 500 *motets.

Collected edn. of his works ed. F. X. Haberl and A. Sandeberger (21 vols., Leipzig, 1894–1926; not complete); new edn. by S. Hemelinck and others (Kassel, 1956 ff.). W. Boetticher, *Orlando di Lasso und seine Zeit*, 1: *Monographie* (1958 [all pub.]); H. Leuchtmann, *Orlando di Lasso* (2 vols., Wiesbaden [1976–7], incl. vol. of letters); F. Messmer, *Orlando di Lasso* (Munich, 1982).

J. Roche, *Lassus* (Oxford Studies in Composers, 19; London, 1982). J. Erb, *Orlando di Lasso: A Guide to Research* (New York and London, 1990). J. Haar in S. Sadie (ed.), *The New Grove Dictionary of Music and Musicians*, 10 (1980), pp. 480–502, s.v.

Last Gospel. A second reading from the Gospels which used to take place at the very end of Mass in the W. rite. In medieval times it was said as a private devotion by the celebrant as he went back to the sacristy, but it was later read by the priest at the altar aloud. The usual Last Gospel was Jn. 1: 1–14; but on a small number of days different passages were appointed. The reading of the Last Gospel was suppressed on 26 Sept. 1964.

Jungmann (1958 edn.), 2, pp. 554–9; Eng. tr., 2 (1953), pp. 447–51.

Last Judgement. See GENERAL JUDGEMENT.

Last Supper. The final meal of Christ with His Apostles on the night before the Crucifixion. The institution of the *Eucharist is seen in the symbolic acts which He performed with the bread and wine at this meal. There is no mention of these in St *John's Gospel; it alone records the washing of the Apostles' feet (13: 1–11). Traditionally it has been held that the meal was the *Passover, in agreement with the *Synoptic Gospels, which appear to put it on the evening when the Passover celebrations began and the paschal lamb was consumed. Jn., however, asserts that the Crucifixion itself took place on the 'preparation' (Παρασκευή) of the Passover, i.e. a few hours before the Passover meal. If the latter assertion is correct, we may regard the Last Supper as an anticipation of the Passover meal or, perhaps less probably, as either a *Kiddush or some other form of religious meal, such as was celebrated by families or groups of friends. See also EUCHARIST, CHABURAH, KIDDUSH, and PASSOVER.

The principal lit. on the Last Supper is found in works on the Eucharist (q.v.) and in comm. on the Gospels. A. Jaubert, *La Date de la Cène: Calendrier biblique et liturgie chrétienne* (Études Bibliques, 1957), suggested a new chronology for the week of the Passion, according to which the Last Supper was a Passover meal on the Tuesday evening, the time of the Passover meal in the ancient sacerdotal calendar found at *Qumran. Though support for this view may be found in the *Didascalia, 21, in the work of *Victorinus of Pettau, and in a letter of *Epiphanius of Salamis, the theory has not been generally accepted. Cf. J. Jeremias, *Die Abendmahlsworte Jesu* (3rd edn., 1960; Eng. tr., 1966).

Last Things. See ESCHATOLOGY.

Lateran Basilica (S. Giovanni in Laterano). The present basilica stands on the site of an ancient palace on the Celian Hill at Rome which formerly belonged to the family of the Laterani. This palace, part of the dowry of Fausta, the wife of the Emp. *Constantine, who gave it to the Church, was the official residence (*patriarchium*) of the Popes from the 4th cent. until their departure for *Avignon (1309); it covered a much larger area than the present buildings. In 1308 it was nearly all destroyed by fire; only the 'Sancta Sanctorum' chapel now survives (see SCALA SANCTA). In 1586 *Sixtus V entrusted Domenico Fontana (1543–1607) with the erection of a new palace. This building remained unoccupied until 1693, when it was converted by Innocent XII into an asylum for

orphans; in 1843 it was transformed into a museum for antiquities; it now houses the offices of the diocese of Rome. For the *Lateran Councils, see following entry.

The Lateran Basilica, which remains the cathedral church of Rome ('omnium urbis et orbis ecclesiarum mater et caput'), is one of the four 'Major *Basilicas'. The original dedication was to the Redeemer (S. Salvator); but after destruction by an earthquake in 896 the church was rebuilt by Sergius III (904–11), who dedicated it to St *John the Baptist (with whom has since been associated St *John the Apostle). After the fire of 1308 it was restored by *Clement V (1305–14); but it was again burnt down in 1361. The present church was built under the direction of a succession of Popes beginning with *Urban V, among the architects being D. Fontana (1543–1604) and F. Borromini (1599–1667). The façade to the E. (1730–32) is by Alessandro Galilei (1691–1737). On the NW is an octagonal *baptistery (S. Giovanni in Fonte), the traditional site of Constantine's baptism by Pope *Sylvester in 324 (in fact Constantine was baptized on his deathbed near Nicomedia in 337); the outer building belongs to the first half of the 4th cent., but the interior was remodelled and embellished by Sixtus III (432–40). Feast of dedication of the Lateran Basilica, 9 Nov.

A. Valentini, *La Patriarcale Basilica Lateranense* (2 vols., fol., 1836). P. Lauer, *Le Palais de Latran* (1911). A. M. Colini, *Storia e topografia del Celio nell'antichità* (Atti della Pontificia Accademia Romana di Archeologia, Serie 3, Memorie, 7; 1944); G. Pelliccioni, *Le nuove scoperte sulle origini del Battistero Lateranense* (ibid. 12/1; 1973); R. Krautheimer and others, *Corpus Basilicarum Christianarum Romae*, 5 (Rome, 1977), pp. 1–92 [Eng.], with full bibl. J. Freiberg, *The Lateran in 1600* (Cambridge, 1995). H. *Leclercq, OSB, in *DACL* 8 (pt. 2; 1929), cols. 1529–887, s.v. 'Latran', with extensive bibl.; E. Josi in *EC* 10 (1953), cols. 1213–20, s.v. 'Roma. V. Topografia, ii. San Giovanni in Laterano e il Patriarchium'.

Lateran Councils. A series of councils were held in the Lateran Palace at Rome from the 7th to the 18th cents. Five of these rank as *oecumenical in the W. Church and are thus of special interest:

(1) First (1123). Convoked by *Callistus II for the solemn confirmation of the Concordat of *Worms which ended the *Investiture contest. Twenty-two disciplinary canons were also promulgated, most of them repeating and emphasizing previous decrees.

(2) Second (1139). Convoked by Innocent II for the reformation of the Church after the schism which had taken place at his election. It issued 30 canons, and condemned the followers of *Arnold of Brescia.

(3) Third (1179). Convoked by *Alexander III to remove the traces of the schism of the antipope Callistus III. The most important decree of the Council concerned Papal elections. The right to elect the Pope was restricted to the college of cardinals, and a two-thirds majority was declared necessary. Another important canon (can. 18) provided for the establishment at every cathedral of a school for clerics.

(4) Fourth (1215). Convoked by *Innocent III, it was much the most important of the Lateran Councils. In the course of it an official statement of the doctrine of the *Eucharist (in which the word 'transubstantiate' is used officially for the first time) was given, and annual confession for all Christian people was prescribed. Rules were

made concerning preaching in cathedral churches; bishops were reminded of their duties as teachers; and steps were taken to withdraw ecclesiastical countenance from judicial *ordeals. The foundation of new religious orders was also forbidden, one consequence of which was that St *Dominic was compelled to take an already existing rule as the basis of his Friars Preachers.

(5) Fifth (1512–17). Convened by Pope *Julius II, the Council's immediate purpose was to invalidate the decrees of the antipapal Council of Pisa convoked by Louis XII of France. It promulgated a few minor reforms, but left the main causes of the *Reformation untouched.

(1) Hardouin, 6 (pt. 2), cols. 1109–18; Mansi, 21 (1776), cols. 277–304. Canons, with Eng. tr. and introd., in Tanner, *Decrees* (1990), pp. 187–94. Hefele and Leclercq, 5 (pt. 1; 1912), pp. 630–44. A. Fliche in Fliche and Martin, 8 (1946), pp. 391–5. See also bibl. to CALLISTUS II and below.

(2) Hardouin, 6 (pt. 2), cols. 1207–18; Mansi, 21 (1776), cols. 525–46. Canons, with Eng. tr. and introd., in Tanner, *Decrees* (1990), pp. 195–203. Hefele and Leclercq, 5 (pt. 1; 1912), pp. 721–46. See also bibl. to ARNOLD OF BRESCIA and below.

(3) Hardouin, 6 (pt. 2), cols. 1671–876; Mansi, 22 (1778), cols. 209–468. Canons, with Eng. tr. and introd., in Tanner, *Decrees* (1990), pp. 205–25. Hefele and Leclercq, 5 (pt. 2; 1913), pp. 1086–112. J. Longère (ed.), *Le troisième concile de Latran (1179): Sa place dans l'histoire. Communications présentées à la Table Ronde du C.N.R.S., le 26 avril 1980* (1982). See also below.

(4) Hardouin, 8, cols. 1–86; Mansi, 22 (1778), cols. 953–1086. A. García y García (ed.), *Constitutiones Concilii quarti Lateranensis una cum Commentariis glossatorum* (Monumenta Iuris Canonici, Series A: Corpus Glossatorum, 2; Vatican City, 1981). Constitutions, with Eng. tr. and introd., in Tanner, *Decrees* (1990), pp. 227–71. Hefele and Leclercq, 5 (pt. 2; 1913), pp. 1316–98. S. Kuttner and A. García y García, 'A New Eyewitness Account of the Fourth Lateran Council', *Traditio*, 20 (1964), pp. 115–78, incl. text. A. Luchaire, *Innocent III* (6 vols., 1904–8), esp. vol. 6, 'Le Concile de Latran et la réforme de l'Église'. A. Fliche in Fliche and Martin, 10 (1950), pp. 194–211. See also other works cited under INNOCENT III and below.

(5) Hardouin, 8, cols. 1561–856. Decisions, with Eng. tr. and introd., in Tanner, *Decrees* (1990), pp. 593–655. Hefele and Leclercq, 8 (pt. 1; 1917), pp. 339–558. O. de la Brosse, OP, in id. and others, *Latran V et Trente* (Histoire des Conciles Œcuméniques, 10; 1975), pp. 13–114. The sections of the diary of Paride de Grassi dealing with the preparation and events of the Council, ed. M. Dykmans in *Annuarium Historiae Conciliorum*, 14 (1982), pp. 271–369; cf. art. by N. H. Minnich, ibid., pp. 370–460. See also bibl. to LEO X.

V. Tizzani, *I concili lateranesi* (1878). R. Foreville, *Latran I, II, III et Latran IV* (Histoire des Conciles Œcuméniques, 6; 1965), with full bibl. F. Vernet in *DTC* 8 (pt. 2; 1925), cols. 2628–67, s.v. 'Latran (Iᵉʳ, IIᵉ, IIIᵉ et IVᵉ Concile[s] œcuménique[s] de)'; R. Naz in *DDC* 6 (1957), cols. 344–53, s.v. 'Latran (Conciles de)'; C. Duggan in *NCE* 4 (1967), pp. 406–10, s.v.

Lateran Treaty. This treaty, signed on 11 Feb. 1929, 'finally and irrevocably' settled the Roman question, and established the *Vatican City as a sovereign state. The Holy See recognized the Italian state with Rome as capital. The Italian state recognized 'the Catholic, Apostolic and Roman Religion as the sole religion of the State', 'the sovereign independence of the Holy See in the international field', and the Holy See's 'sovereign jurisdiction' in the Vatican City. Attached to the Treaty was a *Concordat which provided for Catholic religious instruction in the schools, the civil recognition of marriage performed in accordance with canon law, the freedom of *Catholic

Action on condition of its being non-politically conducted, and the swearing of an oath of allegiance to the King by bishops before taking possession of their dioceses. The 1929 Concordat was substantially modified by an agreement signed on 18 Feb. 1984, which came into force in 1985. In particular, the Catholic religion is no longer the sole religion of the Italian state, but 'the State and the Catholic Church are, each in its proper sphere, sovereign and independent'.

Text in *AAS* 21 (1929), pp. 209–74, followed by text of Concordat, pp. 274–94, with 'Processo-Verbale' p. 295; that of the 1984 Concordat and appended docs., ibid. 77 (1985), pp. 521–78. J. F. Pollard, *The Vatican and Italian Fascism, 1929–32* (Cambridge, 1985), with Eng. tr. of 1929 texts, pp. 197–215, and extensive bibl. L. Mistò (ed.), *Il 'Nuovo' Concordato* (Turin [1986]). R. Danielo in *EC* 9 (1953), cols. 990–5, s.v. 'Patti lateranensi'.

Latimer, Hugh (c.1485–1555), Bp. of *Worcester and Reformer. He was the son of a yeoman farmer of Thurcaston in Leicestershire, educated at Cambridge, and in 1510 elected Fellow of Clare Hall. In his earlier years he was an ardent opponent of the New Learning. He was ordained priest, and in 1522 his eloquence and zeal in reforming abuses and defending social justice led the University to license him as one of the 12 preachers commissioned to preach anywhere in England. From c.1523 his opinions began to become suspect to the ecclesiastical authorities; according to his own account, he was dramatically converted to the doctrines of the Reformers by T. *Bilney in 1524, and when in 1525 he declined the request of his bishop, N. West of *Ely, to preach a sermon against M. *Luther, he was forbidden to preach in the diocese. After skilfully defending himself before T. *Wolsey, he was again allowed to preach throughout England. The directness of his method, his understanding of human character, his homely style, and his ready wit won his sermons increasing influence. A sermon before *Henry VIII in Lent 1530, though it attacked the use of temporal weapons for the defence of God's Word, won him the royal favour, and in 1531 he was given the living of West Kington, Wilts. But his preaching, which now openly challenged ecclesiastical authority and spread Protestant doctrines, was censured by Convocation in Mar. 1532. Later in the year he submitted and signed a set of articles required by the bishops.

After T. *Cranmer's appointment to *Canterbury (1533), Latimer's position improved, and when, in 1534, Henry formally broke with the Pope, Latimer became a royal chaplain. In 1535 he was appointed Bp. of Worcester. In his sermons he continued to denounce social injustices and other contemporary corruptions, attacking also Catholic teaching on purgatory, images, etc. He also supported the King in the *Dissolution of the Monasteries. In 1538 he preached at the execution of John Forest, and in the same year approved the putting to death of the family of R. *Pole. But his career was cut short in 1539, when, in acc. with his Protestant beliefs, he opposed the Act of the *Six Articles, and resigned his see on hearing from T. *Cromwell that this was the King's wish. Taken into custody, he was freed in 1540, but ordered to leave London and forbidden to preach. Very little is known of the next few years of his life. In 1546 he was confined to the Tower, but was released on *Edward VI's accession in the following year. On New Year's Day 1548 he preached his famous sermon 'Of the Plough' at Paul's Cross, and became very popular as a court preacher, continuing to denounce social and ecclesiastical abuses and supporting the government of Somerset. On the accession of *Mary he was arrested and committed to the Tower (1553). In 1554, together with T. Cranmer and N. *Ridley, he was taken to Oxford to dispute with Catholic theologians of both universities esp. on *transubstantiation and the sacrifice of the Mass. Having refused to accept the medieval doctrine, he was excommunicated. He was examined again in 1555 and, after a renewed refusal to recant, was burnt with Ridley at Oxford on 16 Oct. 1555. In the American BCP (1979), feast day (with Cranmer and Ridley), 16 Oct.

Collected edn. of his *Sermons* (2 vols., London, 1758), with Life in vol. 1, pp. ix–lxxxvii; *Sermons and Remains*, ed. G. E. Corrie (2 vols., *Parker Society, 1844–5, with extract from J. *Foxe, *Acts and Monuments*, repr. in vol. 2, pp. ix–xxxi). Lives by R. Demaus (Religious Tract Society, London, 1869; many subsequent edns.), R. M. and A. J. Carlyle (London, 1899), H. S. Darby (ibid., 1953), and A. G. Chester (Philadelphia, 1954, with detailed bibl.). J. *Gairdner in *DNB* 32 (1892), pp. 171–9.

Latin. The language of government and the courts, Latin was also the ordinary spoken language for many people throughout the W. provinces of the Roman empire. It was naturally used as one of the languages of the early Christians, though it was only in the 4th cent. that it came to supersede Greek. The earliest evidence for a Latin translation of the Bible comes from N. Africa and S. Gaul before the end of the 2nd cent. From N. Africa too came the first Latin-speaking Bp. of Rome, *Victor I (189–98), and the first of the Latin Fathers, *Tertullian (c.160–c.225). The beginnings of Christian Latin thus coincided with the period when Classical Latin gave way to Late Latin; the changes at one level involved the decay of a Classical literary standard and the adoption into literary use of the more popular spoken language. The vulgar tongue was by its nature more productive of linguistic change than was literary Latin. The linguistic differences affect the accidence only in the replacement of rarer inflexions with common ones; syntactical constructions show much more variation as rules are less rigidly observed; but the most conspicuous difference is in vocabulary, in that words are allowed to extend their range of meaning and many new words are admitted to written use. Fixed standards of pronunciation also begin to yield to diversity.

In the late 4th cent. a series of major figures writing in Latin established it as the language of the W. Church. St *Hilary and St *Ambrose from Gaul, St *Augustine from Africa and St *Jerome from Italy were the authors who most gave the Latin Church its independent catholic tradition. *Jerome's *Vulgate translation, intended to replace the wide variety of *Old Latin versions of the Bible, quickly spread through the W. Church; already in the 5th cent. St *Patrick in Ireland was using it for the Old Testament, though for the New he continued to quote from the Old Latin. In the same period Jerome's friend *Rufinus prepared Latin translations of older Greek theological authors, including *Origen and *Eusebius, while some of the contemporary writings of St John *Chrysostom were put into Latin by Anianus. The 4th and 5th cent. also saw

the beginnings of Christian literature in Latin, in the works of writers such as *Prudentius, St *Paulinus of Nola, and John *Cassian. From this period until the *Reformation Latin held a dominant position in the W.; it was for centuries not only the language of biblical study, theology, and the liturgy, it was the only language of literacy in much of W. Europe.

The fragmentation of the W. empire and the establishment of barbarian kingdoms in Italy, Gaul, and Spain led to a decline in the grammatical and rhetorical schools of the empire and a corresponding increase in the importance of the Church in education. *Boethius and *Cassiodorus are among the last representatives of an older secular-trained élite. Instead of a rhetorical training the Latin Bible became during the 5th and 6th cent. the text which most influenced the style of the written language. Spoken Latin increasingly diversified from the written standard as the many Romance dialects of Italian, French, and Spanish began to emerge. The writings of many Late Latin authors, such as St *Gregory of Tours, show a marked indifference to the grammatical structure of the language. Case-endings, probably no longer pronounced, are written indiscriminately; certain tenses and moods of verbs are confused; concord is not observed: this is the work of someone who still thought of himself as speaking Latin but who was not in control of the differences between the written and the spoken language. Others, better schooled, continued to write grammatical Latin whether in a simple practical style like that of Pope *Gregory I or in the more complex style of St *Ennodius.

The pronunciation of the language, dropping the endings of cases and reducing the inflexion of verbs, meant that the liturgy, though formally spoken and sung in Latin, was tending to follow the lines of divergence into the Romance languages during the 6th–8th cent. Latin might have gone the way of Greek with a separation between the formal written language and the spoken demotic language. The spread of Christianity beyond the area of Romance speech, however, meant that Latin was also being studied to be written and spoken as the learned language of the Church. Writers from the British Isles, both Celtic and English, exemplify this, among them St *Gildas, St *Adomnán, St *Aldhelm, and, supremely, the Ven. *Bede. In the Carolingian period strenuous efforts were made under the patronage of *Charlemagne and guided by *Alcuin, a Northumbrian like Bede, to establish a common core to the liturgy and an established pronunciation for Latin for the whole Carolingian empire. From c.800 Medieval Latin was for most of its users a learned language, no longer confused with the Romance vernaculars. Only in the lowest forms of written texts, for example in the private deeds of Italy and Spain, do we find grammatical disorder continuing until the 9th and 10th cent.

From the 8th to the 13th cent. Latin was used for almost all literate activity in the W. Church. In the late 11th and 12th cent. a deepening study of the Fathers and the Classics led to the cultivation of Latin as a spoken language in Church courts, schools, and universities, and by the higher clergy in general. Medieval Latin may be thought to have reached a high point in the works of such Churchmen as St *Anselm, St *Bernard, and *John of Salisbury.

Preaching to the laity was the only area in which the Church, of necessity, used the vernacular throughout the period. Increasing literacy in N. Europe in the 13th cent. gave rise to a literature of entertainment in the vernacular; biblical translations and literature of devotion followed. The reforming spirit, first recognizable among the *Lollards and the *Hussites, gave a further impetus to the translation of the Bible and led to a new interest in presenting theological debate in the vernacular, which had already found a role as the language of devotional reading for lay men, religious women, and an increasing proportion of the lower clergy. The cultivation of Humanist Latin was a scholarly pursuit, and in the 15th and 16th cent. the use of Latin became increasingly academic. With the Reformation it was all but abandoned for liturgical purposes in the Reformed Churches. The ever increasing restriction in its use to academic or formal purposes is just as apparent in RC Italy or Spain as in Protestant Germany or England.

Latin has continued to be used into the modern period as an occasional language of international scholarly communication, but increasingly since the 17th cent. it has been ousted by vernacular languages except in the official documents of the RC Church, for which the Latin text serves as the authority for vernacular translations worldwide. Even its use in this Church has declined dramatically since the Second *Vatican Council. In spite of a rearguard action by Pope *John XXIII in his Apostolic Constitution *Veterum sapientia* (22 Feb. 1962), the use of Latin in seminaries and pontifical universities has now dwindled probably to the point of extinction. In the same Constitution John XXIII called for the setting up of a Latin academy in the Vatican to adapt Latin vocabulary to the needs of the Church in the modern world. Since then several small dictionaries and lists of place-names in Latin have been issued. The Second Vatican Council declared that the use of Latin was to be maintained in the liturgy, though permission was granted for some use of the vernacular; in the outcome, the use of the vernacular has almost entirely triumphed, although the official books continue to be published in Latin. In the C of E the Latin versions of the Book of *Common Prayer have never been widely used, though, for instance, John *Wesley used the Latin text in doctrinal writings. The option of using traditional Latin texts in sung worship has been retained by choirs in both the Anglican and Lutheran Churches.

The standard Latin–English dictionary was long that of C. T. Lewis and C. Short (Oxford, 1879; frequently reissued); it has now been superseded for the classical period by P. G. W. Glare (ed.), *Oxford Latin Dictionary* (ibid., 1982). The *Thesaurus linguae Latinae*, orig. pub. under the auspices of the Academies of Berlin, Göttingen, Leipzig, Munich, and Vienna (Leipzig, 1900 ff.) provides the fullest dictionary of classical and patristic Latin. Medieval Latin is covered by C. Du Fresne *Du Cange, *Glossarium ad scriptores mediae et infimae latinitatis* (3 vols., Paris, 1678; ed. G. A. L. Henschel and L. Favre, 10 vols., Niort, 1883–7). Also useful are A. *Souter, *A Glossary of Later Latin to 600 A.D.* (Oxford, 1949); J. H. Baxter and C. Johnson, *Medieval Latin Word-List from British and Irish Sources* (1934; rev. by R. E. Latham, 1965); F. Blatt and others, *Novum glossarium mediae Latinitatis* (Copenhagen, 1957 ff.); R. E. Latham and others, *Dictionary of Medieval Latin from British Sources* (Oxford, 1975 ff.); F. Blaise, *Lexicon Latinitatis Medii Aevi* (CCCM, 1975 [Lat.–Fr.]); J. F. Niermeyer and others, *Mediae Latinitatis Lexicon Minus* (2 vols., Leiden, 1976–84).

On the specifically ecclesiastical use of Latin: C. Mohrmann, *Études sur le Latin des Chrétiens* (Storia e Letteratura, 65, 87, 103, and 143; Rome, 1958–77); id., *Liturgical Latin: Its Origin and Character* (Washington, DC, 1957); J. E. Collins, *A Primer of Ecclesiastical Latin* (Washington, DC [1985]); G. Sanders and M. Van Uytfanghe, *Bibliographie signalétique du Latin des Chrétiens* (CC, Lingua Patrum, 1; 1989). More general works on Latin in the Middle Ages include E. Auerbach, *Literatursprache und Publikum in der lateinischen Spätantike und im Mittelalter* (Bern, 1958; Eng. tr. 1965); E. Löfstedt, *Late Latin* (Instituttet for Sammenlignende Kulturforskning, Serie A, 25; Oslo, etc., 1959), and other works of this author; J. IJsewijn, *Companion to Neo-Latin Studies* (Amsterdam, etc., 1977; 2nd edn., rewritten, 2 vols., Louvain, 1990–98 [introduces Humanist and academic Latin]); F. A. C. Mantello and A. G. Rigg (eds.), *An Introduction to Medieval Latin Studies* (forthcoming, Washington, DC).

The standard history of medieval Latin literature is still M. Manitius, *Geschichte der lateinischen Literatur des Mittelalters* (Handbuch der klassischen Altertumswissenschaft, 9, Abt. 2; 3 vols., 1911–31).

Latitudinarianism. A term opprobriously applied in the 17th cent. to the outlook of a group of Anglican divines who, while continuing to conform with the C of E, attached relatively little importance to matters of dogmatic truth, ecclesiastical organization, and liturgical practice. It found characteristic representatives in the '*Cambridge Platonists'. In general the sympathies of Latitudinarian divines lay with the *Arminian theology. Their views did much to prepare the way for the religious temper of England in the 18th cent.

la Trappe. Abbey near Soligny (Orne), from which the *Trappists take their name. (The form la Grande Trappe, dating from 1843, was discarded in the 1930s.) Founded in 1122 as a house of the *Savigny Order, like other Savigny houses la Trappe joined the *Cistercian Order, in the filiation of *Clairvaux, in 1148. Material and spiritual decline set in with the introduction of *commendatory abbots in the early 16th cent.; it continued until A. J. de *Rancé, the last of them, introduced the Strict Observance in 1662 and then, on becoming regular abbot in 1664, initiated his own, much stricter, reform (only much later known as Trappist). The community continued to flourish until at the time of the French Revolution it numbered 100 monks, more than any other Cistercian house in France. In 1791 about a third of the monks chose exile rather than secularization, and after wandering as far as Russia to avoid the French armies, returned to build the ruins of their abbey in 1815, having survived continuously, under the same superior, throughout. La Trappe ranks second after *Cîteaux in the Cistercian Order of the Strict Observance.

H. de Charencey (ed.), *Cartulaire de l'abbaye de Notre-Dame de la Trappe* [Alençon, 1889]. Id., *Histoire de l'abbaye de la Grande-Trappe* (2 vols., Mortagne, 1896–1911). H. Tournoüer, *Bibliographie et iconographie de la Maison-Dieu Notre-Dame de la Trappe* (2 pts., ibid., 1894–6). G. Guérout, CSCO, 'La Communauté de la Trappe face à la Révolution', *Cîteaux*, 40 (1989), pp. 376–478. L. H. Cottineau, OSB, *Répertoire topo-bibliographique des abbayes et prieurés* (Mâcon, 1935), cols. 3201 f., for further bibl.

latria (λατρεία), as contrasted with 'dulia' (δουλεία; q.v.), that fullness of Divine worship which may be paid to God alone.

Latrocinium (i.e. 'Robber Council'). The Council held at *Ephesus in Aug. 449. Summoned by *Theodosius II, to deal with difficulties arising out of the condemnation of *Eutyches for unorthodoxy at a synod at *Constantinople (the σύνοδος ἐνδημοῦσα) in Nov. 448 (see MONOPHYSITES), it was under the domination of *Dioscorus, Patr. of Alexandria, a strong upholder of Monophysitism. Eutyches was acquitted of heresy and reinstated in his monastery, Flavian and other bishops were deposed, and the Roman legates, who had brought with them St Leo's *Tome, were insulted. Its decisions were reversed by the Council of *Chalcedon in 451. The name 'Latrocinium' was derived from Leo's letter (Ep. 95) to the Empress Pulcheria, where he describes the synod as 'non iudicium, sed latrocinium'.

ACO 2. 1. 1 (1933), pp. 68–101; 2. 3. 1 (1935), pp. 42–92. Crit. text of Syriac Acts, with Ger. tr., by J. Flemming (*Abh*. (Gött.), 15, Heft 1; 1917); Eng. tr. by S. G. F. Perry, *The Second Synod of Ephesus* (Dartford, 1881). W. de Vries, SJ, 'Das Konzil von Ephesus 449, eine "Räubersynode"?', *OCP* 41 (1975), pp. 357–98. *DHGE* 15 (1963), cols. 574–9, s.v. 'Ephèse (3), Concile dit Brigandage d''.

Latter-day Saints. See MORMONS.

Laud, William (1573–1645), Abp. of *Canterbury. The son of a master tailor, he was born at Reading and educated at St John's College, *Oxford, of which he became a Fellow in 1593. In 1601 he received holy orders, and in 1611 he was made President of St John's. From a very early date he opposed the prevailing *Calvinist theology, and sought to restore something of the pre-Reformation liturgical practice to the C of E. In 1616 he was made Dean of *Gloucester, where he moved the communion table to the east end of the choir, an action that brought him into violent conflict with the local *Puritans. On being appointed Bp. of *St Davids in 1621, he resigned the presidency of St John's College. In 1622 he conducted a controversy with the Jesuit, J. Percy, commonly known as '*Fisher the Jesuit' (q.v.), in which he maintained that the RC Church and the C of E are both parts of the same Church Catholic. Under *Charles I his influence increased. In 1626 he was translated to *Bath and Wells, and in 1628 to London. In 1630 he became chancellor of the university of Oxford, where he carried through many necessary and enduring reforms, codifying the statutes, enforcing discipline, instituting the ('Laudian') professorship in Arabic, and presenting a large collection of MSS to the *Bodleian Library, including the so-called 'Codex Laudianus' of Acts. He did much to encourage individual scholars, and among those who enjoyed his patronage were J. *Hales and W. *Chillingworth. In 1633 he was again translated to become Abp. of Canterbury.

For some years past Laud had been taking a leading part in the administration of the country, and now his work on the *High Commission and his attempts to impose liturgical uniformity by force increasingly aroused the intense hostility of the Puritans. Among the chief grievances were that he made the communion table rather than the pulpit the centre of the church, that he suppressed Puritan *lecturers, and that he punished all opposition to his designs with heavy penalties. His attempts to enforce a new liturgy in Scotland (1637) proved the turning-point of his career. At the sitting of Convocation in 1640 he introduced new canons, proclaiming the *Divine Right of Kings, and compelling whole classes of men to swear never to 'consent to alter the government of this Church by archbishops, deans, and archdeacons, etc.'. This formula, known as the 'etcetera oath', exposed him to general ridicule and had to be suspended at the order of the King. Soon afterwards he was impeached by the Long Parliament. In 1641 he was imprisoned in the Tower, but his trial did not begin until 1644. It is generally held to have been conducted without regard for the demands of justice, the Commons imposing their will on the Lords by force. He was executed on Tower Hill, London, on 10 Jan. 1645, after repudiating the accusation of 'Popery' and declaring his adherence to the Protestant Church of England.

Laud's apparent failure arose from his inability to understand the popular leaning towards Puritanism and the hatred aroused by his violent measures against all who did not share his own views on ritual. In doctrinal matters he showed himself broad-minded and conciliatory. He sought to improve the economic condition of the national Church, but thereby he promoted its identification with a political party. He left a remarkable private diary recording esp. the events of his last years. In the American BCP (1979), feast day, 10 Jan.

Works ed. W. Scott and J. Bliss (LACT, 7 vols., 1847–60). Apart from the records among the State Papers, the principal authority is the Life by his disciple P. *Heylyn, *Cyprianus Anglicus* (London, 1668). Modern Lives by W. H. *Hutton (London, 1895), A. S. Duncan-Jones (ibid., 1927), and H. R. Trevor-Roper (ibid., 1940; 3rd edn., 1988). E. C. E. Bourne, *The Anglicanism of William Laud* (1947). [J. E.] C. Hill, *Economic Problems of the Church from Archbishop Whitgift to the Long Parliament* (Oxford, 1956). N. [R. N.] Tyacke, *Anti-Calvinists: The Rise of English Arminianism c.1590–1640* (ibid., 1987), *passim* (see index). Id., 'Archbishop Laud' in K. Fincham (ed.), *The Early Stuart Church, 1603–1642* (1993), pp. 51–70. J. Davies, *The Caroline Captivity of the Church* (Oxford, 1992), esp. pp. 46–86. Catalogue of the MSS which he presented to the Bodleian Library by H. O. Coxe, *Catalogi Codicum Manuscriptorum Bibliothecae Bodleianae pars prima* (Oxford, 1853), cols. 491–582, and *pars secunda* (1858–85). S. R. Gardiner in *DNB* 32 (1892), pp. 185–94; W. H. Hutton in *DECH*, pp. 316–20.

Lauda Sion. The opening words, and hence the name, of the *sequence (now optional) for the feast of *Corpus Christi, composed for the occasion by St *Thomas Aquinas (c.1264). Summoning the Church (here addressed as Sion) to the adoration of the Eucharist, it contains a doctrinal exposition of the Presence, closely following that in the *Summa Theologiae*. The hymn combines with close philosophical reasoning a severity of form and economy of expression which give it a grandeur and austerity lost in most English translations. These include versions by R. *Crashaw, E. B. *Pusey, F. *Oakeley, and E. *Caswall; the most familiar, 'Laud, O Sion, thy Salvation', is the work of several authors.

Crit. edn. of text in G. M. Dreves (ed.), *Lateinische Hymnendichter des Mittelalters* (AHMA 50; 1907), pp. 584 f. Raby, pp. 405–8, with refs. and bibl., p. 483; J. Szövérffy, *Die Annalen der lateinischen Hymnendichtung*, 2 (1965), pp. 246–251, with refs.

Lauds. The morning *office of the W. Church, from primitive times centred around Pss. 148–50, with their frequent use of *Laudate* ('Praise ye . . .'); hence the name.

The widespread conception of the rising sun symbolizing the Risen Christ was reflected in the custom of offering Him praise at dawn and was prob. connected with the origins of this office. Pss. 148–50 came to be prefaced by elements connected with the development of *Vigils: the *Benedicite and Cantemus (Exod. 15: 1–18) which were part of the *Paschal Vigil, and psalms expressive of waiting (Ps. 63; see MATTINS) or waiting for mercy (Ps. 51). The service was closely linked with Mattins which immediately preceded it from an early date. From late antiquity until 1911 the Roman form of Lauds comprised four largely unchanging psalms, with *antiphons (to each psalm or group of psalms), an OT canticle with antiphon (e.g. the Benedicite on Sundays), Pss. 148–50 under one antiphon, a short reading from the Bible, a hymn (from the Middle Ages), *versicle, and the *Benedictus with its antiphon, followed by concluding prayer(s). It was simplified by *Pius X in 1911, when the psalms, including Pss. 148–50, were redistributed; they were, however, retained at Lauds in the *Monastic Breviary until recent times. In the 1971 Roman Breviary, in which it is entitled Laudes Matutinae, it begins with Ps. 95 (if it is the first office of the day), followed by a hymn; then a psalm, an OT canticle, another psalm (each of these having an antiphon); a short reading from the Bible, a short *responsory, the Benedictus with antiphon, intercessions, the *Lord's Prayer, *collect for the day, blessing, and dismissal. Before 1960 Lauds was joined to Mattins and said on the previous day by anticipation, but it may not now be anticipated. Parts of Lauds were used by T. *Cranmer for the BCP order of Morning Prayer or Mattins.

C. Callewaert, 'De Laudibus Matutinis', Collationes Brugenses, 27 (1927), pp. 383–9, 448–51; 28 (1928), pp. 63–72, 152–66, 245–50, and 328–38; repr. in his Sacris Erudiri (Steenbrugge, 1940), pp. 53–89. I. M. Hanssens, SJ, Aux origines de la prière liturgique: Nature et genèse de l'office des matines (Analecta Gregoriana, 57; 1952), passim. H. *Leclercq, OSB, in DACL 8 (pt. 2; 1929), cols. 1887–98. See also OFFICE, DIVINE.

laura. See LAVRA.

Laurence, St (d. 258), deacon and martyr. He was one of the seven deacons at Rome during the pontificate of Sixtus II (257–8), and suffered martyrdom in the *persecution under Valerian. Acc. to a tradition handed down by St *Ambrose, *Prudentius, and others, on being asked by the prefect of Rome to deliver up the treasure of the Church, he assembled the poor among whom he had distributed the ecclesiastical possessions and presented them to the prefect, saying, 'These are the treasure of the Church', an action for which he was punished by being slowly roasted to death on a gridiron. This story has been widely rejected by modern scholars, who maintain that he was beheaded like Sixtus II and other contemporary martyrs. He was one of the most famous saints of the Roman Church. During the reign of *Constantine a chapel was built over his tomb in a *catacomb (Cyriaca) on the Via Tiburtina, and this was later linked with a basilica built by Pelagius II (579–90), the present San Lorenzo fuori le Mura. His feast occurs in the Roman 'Depositio Martyrum' of the 4th cent. and his name is also found in the *Canon of the Mass and in the Litanies. Feast day, 10 Aug. See also ROME, CHURCHES OF (6).

AASS, Aug. 2 (1735), pp. 485–532. BHL, pp. 708–12 (nos. 4751–89), and novum suppl. (1986), pp. 518–21. P. F. de' Cavalieri, 'S. Lorenzo e il supplizio della graticola', RQ 14 (1900), pp. 159–76; id., Note agiografiche, 5 (ST 27; 1915), no. 3, 'Assum est, versa et manduca', pp. 65–82. H. Grisar, SJ, 'Zum ältesten Kultus des Märtyrers Laurentius', ZKT 27 (1903), pp. 133–8. V. L. Kennedy, CSB, The Saints of the Canon of the Mass (Studi di Antichità Cristiana, 14; 1938), esp. pp. 124–8, with refs. R. Krautheimer and others, Corpus Basilicarum Christianarum Romae, 2 (Rome, 1959), pp. 1–144 [Eng.], with bibl. H. *Leclercq, OSB, in DACL 8 (pt. 2; 1929), cols. 1917–61, s.v. 'Laurent'. See also bibl. to SIXTUS II.

Laurence of Brindisi, St (1559–1619), *Capuchin friar. Giulio Cesare de' Rossi, who was born at Brindisi, near Naples, joined the Capuchins at Verona, in 1575, taking the name of Laurence. He studied at the University of Padua, where he developed his remarkable gifts for learning languages, incl. Hebrew. He soon became a noted preacher and held various offices in his Order. As chaplain of the Imperial troops, holding a crucifix aloft, he rode before them against the Turks at the battle of Székesfehérvár in Hungary in 1601. In 1602 he was elected Vicar General of the Capuchins, but three years later he refused a further period of office. He took part in much diplomatic activity and died at Lisbon on a mission to Philip III. Between 1599 and 1602 and again from 1606 to 1613 he worked to combat *Lutheranism in Bohemia, Austria, and Germany. Apart from an extensive treatise Lutheranismi Hypotyposis (first pub. in his collected works, vol. 2), his writings comprise commentaries on Gen. and Ez. and sermons. He was canonized in 1881 and in 1959 Pope *John XXIII declared him a '*Doctor of the Church'. Feast day 21 (23 until 1959) July.

Opera Omnia, ed. by the Capuchins of the Province of Venice (10 vols. in 15 parts, Padua, 1928–56 + appendices, 1959 ff.). Miscellanea Laurentiana (8 vols. in 9 parts, ibid., 1951–63, incl. substantial study by Arturo da Carmignana di Brenta, OFM Cap. as vols. 4–7 (2), 1960–3). Commentarii Laurentiani Historici Quarto Revoluto Saeculo ab ortu Sancti Laurentii Brundusini novi Ecclesiae Doctoris (Bibliotheca Seraphico-Capuccina, Sectio Historica, 18; Rome, 1959). Other Lives incl. those of A. Brennan, OFM Cap. (London, 1911) and Arturo da Carmignana di Brenta, OFM Cap. (Rome, 1959; Eng. tr., Westminster, Md., 1963). Felix a Mareto, OFM Cap., Bibliographia Laurentiana (Subsidia Scientifica Franciscalia, 1; Rome, 1962). T. Mac Vicar, OFM Cap., in NCE 8 (1967), pp. 566 f., s.v. 'Lawrence of Brindisi, St'.

'Lausanne'. The first Conference of the *Ecumenical Movement of '*Faith and Order' held at Lausanne under Bp. C. H. *Brent in 1927. It aimed at promoting doctrinal unity among the diverse branches of Christianity, about 90 different Churches being represented. Among those not represented were the RC Church, the Russian Orthodox, and several *Baptist Churches. The subjects discussed were the call to unity, the message of the Church to the world, the essence of the Church, Episcopacy and Apostolic succession, the Sacraments, and the Unity of Christendom in general. Great differences became apparent esp. as regards the doctrine of the Sacraments, of which the Orthodox recognized seven and the *Quakers none. The difficulties were emphasized by the Greek Abp. Germanos, who declared a union impossible without the acceptance of the Seven *Oecumenical Councils. None the less, the Conference did much to stimulate interest in reunion and to encourage theological co-operation.

Faith and Order: Proceedings of the World Conference, Lausanne, August 3–21, 1927, ed. H. N. Bate (1928). *Convictions: A Selection from the Responses of the Churches to the Report of the World Conference on Faith and Order, held at Lausanne in 1927*, ed. L. Hodgson, with the assistance of H. N. Bate and R. W. Brown (1934).

lavabo (Lat., 'I will wash'). The washing of the celebrant's fingers after the offering of the oblations in the Mass, so called from the initial Latin word of Ps. 26: 6-end (Vulg., Ps. 25: 6-end) with the recitation of which the celebrant formerly accompanied the action. In 1969 the traditional text was replaced by Ps. 51 (Vulg. 50), verse 4.

Jungmann (1958 edn.), 2, pp. 95–103; Eng. tr., 2, pp. 76–82.

Lavigerie, Charles-Martial Allemand- (1825–92), cardinal, founder of the *White Fathers and *White Sisters, and anti-*slavery campaigner. Born near Bayonne, Lavigerie studied theology at *Saint-Sulpice in Paris. After ordination and further study, he was appointed professor of Church history at the *Sorbonne in 1854. As director of the Oriental Schools, he travelled to Syria in 1860 to administer relief to Christians after the massacre by the Druses, and met the exiled Algerian leader, Abd-el Kader. In 1863 he was appointed Bp. of Nancy and four years later accepted appointment as Abp. of Algiers, with the ultimate purpose of evangelizing the African continent. To this end he founded the Society of Missionaries of Africa (White Fathers) in 1868 and the Missionary Sisters of Our Lady of Africa (White Sisters) in 1869. In 1878 *Leo XIII entrusted him with the organization of RC missions in Central Africa, in 1882 created him a cardinal, and in 1884 revived for him the see of Carthage with the title of primate of Africa. Throughout 1888 Lavigerie conducted a campaign in European capitals which resulted in the anti-slavery conferences of Brussels and Paris (both 1890). At the request of Leo XIII he proclaimed before a large gathering of officials in Algiers on 12 Nov. 1890 the obligation of French RCs to adhere to the republican government (the famous 'toast of Algiers'). He was a passionate and far-sighted man who believed in the effective evangelization of Africa by Africans themselves.

Modern selections from his writings, *Écrits d'Afrique*, ed. A. Hamman (Paris, 1966) and *La Mission Universelle de l'Église*, ed. X. de Montclos (ibid. [1968]). Docs. on *Le Toast d'Alger*, ed. id. (1966). Official biog. by L. Baunard (2 vols., Paris, 1896). R. F. Clarke, SJ (ed.), *Cardinal Lavigerie and the African Slave Trade* (1889); J. Tournier, *Le Cardinal Lavigerie et son action politique (1863–1892)* (1913); J. de Arteche, *Lavigerie, el Cardenal de África* (1963; Eng. tr., 1964); W. Burridge, WF, *Destiny Africa: Cardinal Lavigerie and the Making of the White Fathers* (1966); X. de Montclos, *Lavigerie, le Saint-Siège et l'Église, 1846–1878* (1965); F. Renault, *Lavigerie, l'esclavage africain et l'Europe 1868–1892* (2 vols., 1971); id., *Le Cardinal Lavigerie* ([1992]; Eng. tr. 1994). J. D. O'Donnell, *Lavigerie in Tunisia: The Interplay of Imperialist and Missionary* (Athens, Ga. [1979]). R. X. Lamey, WF, *Cardinal Lavigerie* (Rome, 1990).

lavra (Gk. λαύρα, literally, 'street' or 'alley'). In the early Church a colony of *anchorites who, while living in separate huts, were subject to a single abbot. The oldest lavras were founded in Palestine in the early 4th cent., where for some centuries they continued to flourish. Esp. famous were those under the direction of St Euthymius the Great (d. 473) and his pupil, St *Sabas (d. 532), the founder of the lavra, Mar Saba (μεγίστη λαύρα), SE of Jerusalem. In more recent times the term 'lavra' has also come to be applied to *coenobitic communities of particular importance.

law, canon. See CANON LAW.

Law, Natural. See NATURAL LAW.

Law, William (1686–1761), *Nonjuror and spiritual writer. He was born at Kings Cliffe, Northants, and educated at Emmanuel College, Cambridge, of which he became a Fellow in 1711. On the accession of George I Law refused the Oath of Allegiance, was deprived of his fellowship, and became a Nonjuror. From 1727 to 1737 he lived in the household of the *Gibbons at Putney as tutor to the father of the historian. In 1740 he retired to Kings Cliffe, where he was joined later by a Mrs Hutcheson and Miss Hester Gibbon, with whom he organized schools and almshouses, and, until his death, led a life of great simplicity, devotion, and pursuits of charity.

Among his earlier writings are *Three Letters to the Bishop of Bangor* (1717–19) which were welcomed as a convincing reply to B. *Hoadly's attack on *High Church principles, and in 1726 appeared his *Absolute Unlawfulness of the Stage Entertainment*, a strong but somewhat one-sided attack on the evils of the contemporary theatre. In the same year he published the first of his treatises, *On Christian Perfection*, which was followed, in 1728, by the most famous of his works, *A Serious Call to a Devout and Holy Life*. Inspired by the teaching of J. *Tauler, J. *Ruysbroeck, *Thomas à Kempis, and other orthodox spiritual writers, the book is a forceful exhortation to embrace the Christian life in its moral and ascetical fullness. The author insists on the exercise of those virtues practised in everyday life, temperance, humility, and self-denial, all animated by the intention to glorify God, to which every human activity should be directed. The simplicity of its teaching and its vigorous style soon established the work as a classic, which has probably had more influence than any other post-Reformation spiritual book except The *Pilgrim's Progress, and was greatly appreciated e.g. by J. *Wesley, S. *Johnson, the elder H. *Venn, and J. *Keble. In 1732 he published his *Case of Reason* against M. *Tindal and the *Latitudinarian position generally; and his attitude towards Rome is to be found in his *Letters to a Lady inclined to enter the Church of Rome* (1779). He became acquainted c.1734 with the writings of the German Protestant mystic, J. *Boehme, whose influence is noticeable in his later works, esp. *The Spirit of Prayer* (2 parts, 1749–50) and *The Spirit of Love* (2 parts, 1752–4), which emphasize the indwelling of Christ in the soul. This development of his spirituality estranged many of his former disciples, e.g. Wesley, and led him, though he always remained faithful to the C of E, to a doctrine resembling the *Quaker conception of the '*Inner Light'. Feast day in parts of the Anglican Communion, 9 Apr.

Collected edn. of his works, 9 vols., London, each with a general title-page, 1762 (sets being made up from various edns.). Works also ed. 'G. Moreton', 9 vols., privately pr., London, 1892–3. *Selected Mystical Writings of William Law*, ed. with notes and studies by S. [H.] Hobhouse (London, 1938). There has been a steady flow of edns. of *A Serious Call to a Devout Life*. J. H. Overton, *William Law, Non-Juror and Mystic* (1881). S. [H.] Hobhouse, *William Law and Eighteenth Century Quakerism*, with some unpub. Letters and Fragments (1927). A. W. Hopkinson, *About William Law: A Running Commentary on his Works* (1948). E. W. Baker, *A Herald of the Evangelical Revival: A Critical Inquiry into the Relation of William Law to John Wesley and the Beginnings of Methodism* (1948). H. Tallon, *William Law: A Study in Literary Craftsmanship* [1948]. A. K. Walker, *William Law: His Life and Thought* (1973). [E.] G. Rupp, *Religion in England 1688–1791* (Oxford History of the Christian Church, 1986), pp. 218–42. L. Stephen in *DNB* 32 (1892), pp. 236–40.

Lawrence, Brother. See BROTHER LAWRENCE.

Lawrence, St. See LAURENCE, ST.

Laws, Robert (1851–1934), missionary in *Malawi. The son of an Aberdeen cabinet-maker, he was trained in his father's trade, but was determined to be a missionary. He studied arts and medicine at Aberdeen University and completed his theological training at the College of the *United Presbyterian Church in Edinburgh. Ordained in 1875, he was in the same year seconded by his Church to the pioneer party of *Free Church of Scotland 'Livingstonia' mission to the Lake Malawi area. From 1878 he was head of that mission until his retirement in 1927. After a brief stay at Cape Maclear at the south end of the lake, Laws moved the mission to Bandawe, 200 miles north on the lakeshore where the indigenous Tonga and Tumbuka people could be reached, as well as the Ngoni/Zulu conquering incomers. After the establishment of the British Protectorate in 1891, in 1894 he founded the Overtoun Institute, an educational institute modelled on *Lovedale which trained men and women from central and N. Malawi and E. Zambia both as pastors and in secular trades. President H. Kamuzu Banda of Malawi was one of its pupils. In 1888 Laws had arranged for the Cape Synod of the Dutch Reformed Church to send a mission to fill the gap in the south of Malawi between the Free Church Mission and the Church of Scotland Mission. He played a leading role in the union of the Churches produced by these missions in 1924 to form the Church of Central Africa Presbyterian. He was its first Moderator.

Laws published his autobiog., *Reminiscences of Livingstonia* (1934). W. P. Livingstone, *Laws of Livingstonia* [1921]; H. McIntosh, *Robert Laws, Servant of Africa* (Edinburgh, 1993). J. McCracken, *Politics and Christianity in Malawi 1875–1940: The impact of the Livingstonia Mission in the Northern Province* (Cambridge, 1977).

Laxism. A system in *moral theology which relaxed the obligations of natural and positive law on grounds deemed by its critics to be insufficient. It developed in the 17th cent., when modern conditions, e.g. the growing practice of taking interest on money loans, hitherto forbidden by the Church as *usury, raised several difficult cases of conscience. Its formulation is connected with the appearance of *Probabilism (q.v.), of which it may be considered a perversion. First attacked in France, esp. in B. *Pascal's *Lettres provinciales* (1657), it was rather clumsily defended by the *Jesuit G. Pirot in *L'Apologie pour les casuistes* (1657), which provoked great scandal. In 1658 certain propositions in Pirot's book which asserted that even the

slightest degree of probability, derived either from reason or from authority, suffices to excuse from sin were condemned by the *Sorbonne, and in 1659 the *Holy Office censured the book itself. In 1665 and 1666 *Alexander VII condemned Laxism, and in 1679 *Innocent XI condemned 65 propositions drawn from Laxist casuists.

M. Petrocchi, *Il problema del lassismo nel secolo XVII* (1953), with refs. A. Degert, 'Réaction des "Provinciales" sur la théologie morale en France', *Bulletin de Littérature ecclésiastique publié par l'Institut Catholique de Toulouse*, 5th ser. 5 (1913), pp. 400–20 and 442–51. A. Molien and E. Amann in *DTC* 9 (pt. 1; 1926), cols. 37–86, s.v. 'Laxisme'. See also works cited under PROBABILISM.

lay brother, lay sister. A member of a religious order who is not bound to the recitation of the Divine Office and is occupied in manual work. The institution, which originated in the 11th cent., developed as a result of the general literacy of the monks and their abandonment of manual labour, and of the increasingly general custom of monks proceeding to holy orders if admitted to the monastery in youth. A similar development took place in the orders of women, where lay sisters were employed to leave the 'choir nuns' free for the Office, mental prayer, and intellectual pursuits. Lay brothers and sisters assist daily at Mass and recite a short Office. The Second *Vatican Council's 'Decree on the Appropriate Renewal of the Religious Life' (1965), however, now requires that lay brothers be drawn into the heart of the community's life and activities, and, in the case of women's communities, that there should, if possible, be only one category of nun.

K. Hallinger, OSB, 'Woher kommen die Laienbrüder?', *Analecta Sacri Ordinis Cisterciensis*, 12 (1956), pp. 1–104. J. Dubois, 'L'Institution des convers au XIIe siècle. Forme de vie monastique propre aux laïcs', in *I laici nella 'Societas Christiana' dei secoli XI e XII*. Miscellanea del Centro di Studi Medioevali, 5 (Pubblicazioni dell'Università Cattolica del Sacro Cuore. Contributi, 3rd ser. 5 [1968]), pp. 183–261; G. Constable, ' "Famuli" and "Conversi" at Cluny. A Note on Statute 24 of Peter the Venerable', *R. Bén.* 83 (1973), pp. 326–50, esp. pp. 334–50; W. Teske, 'Laien, Laienmönche und Laienbrüder in der Abtei Cluny', *Frühmittelalterliche Studien*, 10 (1976), pp. 248–322; 11 (1977), pp. 288–339. M. Toepfer, *Die Konversen der Zisterzienser* (Berliner Historische Studien, 10; 1983). J. S. Donnelly, *The Decline of the Medieval Cistercian Laybrotherhood* (Fordham University Studies, History Series, 3; New York, 1949). J. Dubois, OSB, in *DIP* 3 (1973), cols. 110–20, s.v. 'Converso'. See also bibl. to FRATERNITIES and OBLATE.

lay reader. See READER.

lay rector. In the C of E, a lay person who was formerly entitled to receive the rectorial tithes of a benefice. By custom he or she enjoys the right to the chief seat in the chancel of the parish church for self and family, and the freehold of the whole church, but this gives no right of possession or of entering it when not open for divine service. Lay rectors also have the duty of repairing the chancel, for the neglect of which duty they may be sued by the *Parochial Church Council in the county court. They may compound for this liability, however, with the Diocesan Board of Finance subject to the approval of the Parsonages Board, in default of agreement the amount to be decided by the *Church Commissioners.

laying on of hands. See HANDS, IMPOSITION OF.

laymen. See LAITY.

Laynez, James. See LAÍNEZ, DIEGO.

Lazarists. The name popularly given to the 'Congregation of the Mission' (CM), a congregation of secular priests living under religious vows, founded by St *Vincent de Paul in 1625. The name comes from the priory of St-Lazare, which was Vincent's headquarters in Paris. At first they were confined to France and territories under French influence, but have now spread all over the world. The original work of the congregation was the preaching of missions in the various parishes of France, and conducting *retreats. Later they established seminaries. Only with great reluctance, however, did they accept the charge of parishes. Outside France the work of the Lazarists lay for many years chiefly in Tunis and Algiers, where they brought succour to the Christian captives of the Barbary pirates, and in Madagascar.

P. Coste, *La Congrégation de la mission dite de Saint-Lazare* (1927). A. Haas, *Die Lazaristen in der Kurpfalz* (privately pr., Speyer, 1960). L. Chierotti, CM, in *DIP* 2 (1975), cols. 1543–51, s.v. 'Congregazione della Missione'.

Lazarus. The name given to two apparently separate figures in NT. (1) The poor man in the parable of *Dives and Lazarus (Lk. 16: 19–31); he was venerated as the patron of lepers in the middle ages. (2) The brother of *Martha and Mary, and intimate friend of Jesus. Acc. to Jn., the Lord raised him from the dead (11: 1–44), the chief priests then tried to kill him (12: 10–11), and these events led on directly to the crucifixion of Jesus. It is surprising that there is no mention of them in the Synoptic Gospels, and some critics have speculated that the story was constructed out of the parable mentioned above in which the poor man is quite exceptionally assigned a name (Lazarus) and the suggestion is made that he (or someone else) might rise from the dead. Another possibility is that the parable has been influenced by the story.

Acc. to E. tradition Lazarus, with Martha and Mary and some friends, was put into a leaking boat by the Jews and, being miraculously preserved, landed on Cyprus, where he was made Bp. at Kition. In 890 his supposed relics were translated to *Constantinople, where a church was built in his honour by *Leo VI ('the Philosopher'). In the 11th cent. the legend spread in the W. that he had been Bp. of Marseilles and martyred under *Domitian, a story probably due to confusion with a 5th-cent. Bp. Lazarus of Aix whose epitaph is preserved in the crypt of St Victor's at Marseilles, or, alternatively, with St Nazarius, Bp. of Autun. Devotion to Lazarus appears to have been widespread in the early Church. The 'Peregrinatio *Egeriae' describes a procession to *Bethany on the Saturday before *Palm Sunday to the church erected over his tomb. On this day ('Lazarus Saturday') his feast is still observed in the E.; in the W. Church he is commemorated in the *Roman Martyrology on 17 Dec.

For (1) see comm. to Lk, cited s.v.; (2) comm. to Jn, cited s.v. A. Marchadour, *Lazare: Histoire d'un récit. Récits d'une histoire* (Lectio Divina, 132; 1988). On the post-biblical legend see also G. *Morin, OSB, 'Saint Lazare et saint Maximin', *Mémoires de la Société des Antiquaires de France*, 56 (1897), pp. 27–51; and L. *Duchesne, *Fastes épiscopaux de l'ancienne Gaule*, 1 (2nd edn.,

1907), pp. 321–59. On the iconography, G. Schiller, *Ikonographie der christlicher Kunst*, 1 (Gütersloh [1966]), pp. 189–94 (Eng. tr., 1971, pp. 181–6), and plates 559–85. H. *Leclercq, OSB, in *DACL* 8 (pt. 2; 1929), cols. 2009–86, s.v., and E. Josi in *EC* 7 (1951), cols. 996–8. See also bibl. to MARY MAGDALENE and MARTHA.

Leander, St (*c*.540–*c*.600), Bp. of Seville, prob. from 577/8. He was the brother of St *Isidore. Between 580 and 585 he made one, or perhaps two, visits to *Constantinople, where he met *Gregory the Great. He influenced Gregory's *Moralia in Iob*, and prob. helped to disseminate his writings in Spain. A leading champion of Catholic orthodoxy in Spain against the *Arianism of the Visigoths, he converted Prince Hermenegild, perhaps in 579, and in 589 he presided over the celebrated Third Council of *Toledo. A rule for nuns ('De Institutione Virginum') and a homily delivered at the Council of Toledo are his only certain works to survive. Feast day, 27 Feb.

The Rule for Nuns and homily are repr. in J. P. Migne, *PL* 72. 869–98; both ed., with full introd., by A. C. Vega, OSA (Scriptores Ecclesiastici Hispano-Latini Veteris et Medii Aevi, 16–17; Madrid, 1948); Rule also ed., with Sp. tr., by J. Velázquez (Corpus Patristicum Hispanum, 1; Madrid, 1979). Eng. tr. of Rule and homily by C. W. Barlow, *Iberian Fathers*, 1 (Fathers of the Church, 62; Washington, DC [1969]), pp. 175–235. The principal source is Isidore of Seville, *De Viris Illustribus*, 41 [28 in edn. of C. Codoñer Merino]. U. Domínguez del Val, *Leandro de Sevilla y la Lucha contra el Arianismo* (Biblioteca de Visionarios, Heterodoxos y Marginados, 2nd ser. 12; 1981). L. Navarra, *Leandro di Siviglia: Profilo Storico-Letterario* (Collana di Testi Storici, 17 [1987]). J. Madoz, SJ, 'San Leandro de Sevilla', *Estudios Eclesiásticos*, 56 (1981), pp. 415–53. Mrs Humphry Ward in *DCB* 3 (1882), pp. 637–40, s.v.; L. Ladaria, SJ, in *Dict. Sp.* 9 (1976), cols. 444–6, s.v.

leavened bread. See BREAD, LEAVENED AND UNLEAVENED.

Lebbaeus. An alternative name for *Thaddaeus, found in many MSS of Mt. 10: 3 and also in a few at Mk. 3: 18. In the AV and NEB it occurs only at the former place, and in the RV not at all.

Le Brun, Pierre (1661–1729), French liturgical scholar. A native of Brignoles, he entered the *Oratory *c*.1682. Having studied theology at Marseilles and Toulouse, he taught philosophy at Toulon and theology at Grenoble. In 1690 he was called to the seminary of Saint-Magloire, where he lectured on the Scriptures, the Councils, and Church history. His principal liturgical work, *Explication littérale, historique et dogmatique des prières et des cérémonies de la sainte messe* (4 vols., 1716–26), embodied many extended studies. In its important preface he takes up an intermediary position between the excessive symbolism of the Middle Ages and an exaggerated naturalism. In the later volumes, which contain much curious information about usages in the French churches, he gives detailed studies of the various rites, stressing their unanimity in regard to liturgical essentials. In his *Défense de l'ancien sentiment sur la forme de la consécration* (1727) he maintained that the *Epiclesis was an integral element in Eucharistic consecration. He also advocated a more understanding participation in the Liturgy by the laity, for whom he compiled a liturgical prayer book, *Heures ou manuel pour assister à la messe* (1716).

New edn. of *L'Explication de la messe* (Lex Orandi, 9; 1949) by E. Bonnardet, Cong. Orat., with biog., full acct. of Le Brun's works, earlier edns., and bibl., pp. xi–xxxiii. Fascimile repr. of the 1726 edn. of *L'Explication de la messe* and the 1729 edn. of the *Défense* (4 vols., Farnborough, 1970). A Lat. text of the *Explication de la messe*, pub. by J. A. Dalmasius (Venice, 4 vols., 1770). A. Molien in *DTC* 9 (1926), cols. 101–3, s.v., and H. *Leclercq, OSB, in *DACL* 8 (pt. 2; 1929), cols. 2218–29.

Le Clerc, Jean (1657–1736), 'Clericus', *Arminian theologian and biblical scholar. Born at Geneva, he studied at Grenoble and Saumur, and later gave up strict *Calvinism, in which he had been brought up, and became an Arminian. In 1684 he was appointed professor of philosophy, afterwards of Church history, at the *Remonstrant College at Amsterdam, where he met J. *Locke. In his first work, *Liberii de Sancto Amore Epistolae Theologicae* (1679), he stated his theological convictions, explaining the mysteries of the *Trinity, the *Incarnation and *Original Sin on rationalistic lines. In *Sentiments de quelques théologiens de Hollande* (1685) he attacked R. *Simon, esp. his plan of a *polyglot Bible, and he denied the Mosaic authorship of the *Pentateuch. In 1696 he published an *Ars Critica*, and in 1699 a harmony of the Gospels, *Harmonia Evangelica*, in Greek and Latin. He brought out a Commentary on the Pentateuch in 1699, an annotated translation of the NT in 1703, and Commentaries on the historical books of the OT in 1708 and on the Psalms, the writings of Solomon, and the prophets in 1731. He made a new edition of the 'Apostolic Fathers' of J. B. *Cotelier and revised writings of D. *Petavius, H. *Grotius, and others; he also edited three influential periodical works, *Bibliothèque universelle et historique* (26 vols., 1686–93), *Bibliothèque choisie* (28 vols., 1703–13), and *Bibliothèque ancienne et moderne* (29 vols., 1714–30). A champion of freedom of thought and an enemy of all dogmatism, he defended the unlimited rights of reason in the domain of faith. He held very advanced critical views on the inspiration of Scripture, which he denied altogether for Job, Proverbs, Ecclesiastes, and the Song of Songs. The historic portions of the Pentateuch he assigned to King Josiah (637–608).

Vita et Opera ad annum 1711, pub. Amsterdam, 1711. His letters to Locke are included in the latter's Correspondence, cited s.v.; Correspondence with P. van Limborch, ed. L. Simonutti, *Arminianesimo e Tolleranza nel Seicento Olandese* (Accademia Toscana di Scienze e Lettere 'La Colombaria', Studi, 70; Florence, 1984). A. Barnes, *Jean Le Clerc (1657–1736) et la République des lettres* (1938). Other studies by A. des Amorie van der Hoeven (Amsterdam, 1843) and J. Collen (thesis, Geneva, 1884). J. Carreyre in *DTC* 9 (pt. 1; 1926), cols. 105–7.

Leclercq, Henri (1869–1945), *Benedictine scholar. A native of Tournai (Belgium), he became a naturalized French subject and after profession at *Solesmes was sent to Farnborough Abbey in 1896. He was ordained priest in 1898. From 1914 till his death he lived in London, where he became a very familiar reader at the British Museum. He was a prolific and voluminous editor and writer, esp. concerned with the history of Latin Christianity. His numerous publications include *L'Afrique chrétienne* (2 vols., 1904); *L'Espagne chrétienne* (1906); *Manuel d'archéologie chrétienne depuis les origines jusqu'au VIIIᵉ siècle* (2

vols., 1907); *Monumenta Ecclesiae Liturgica* (4 vols., 1900–13), in conjunction with F. *Cabrol, a collection of early liturgical documents; *Histoire des conciles* (10 vols., 1907–38), a completely recast French edition of K. J. *Hefele's *Conciliengeschichte*; and a large number of articles in the *Dictionnaire d'archéologie chrétienne et de liturgie* (ed. by F. Cabrol and himself, 1903–53), the later volumes being almost wholly Leclercq's work. His major work on J. *Mabillon (2 vols., 1953–7) was virtually complete at the time of his death. The range of his writing led it to suffer seriously in accuracy and to compel him to borrow extensively from other writers, so that his work can seldom be used without checking. It is, however, always readable, and often clothed in a lively and controversial style.

T. Klauser, *Henri Leclercq 1869–1945: Vom Autodidakten zum Kompilator grossen Stils* (Jahrbuch für Antike und Christentum, Ergänzungsband 5; 1977).

lectern (Lat. *legere*, 'to read'). A bookstand used to support the liturgical books, usually of wood or metal and movable, often taking the form of an eagle or pelican with outstretched wings.

J. C. Cox, *Pulpits, Lecterns and Organs in English Churches* (1915), pp. 163–203. C. C. Oman, 'Medieval Brass Lecterns in England', *Archaeological Journal*, 87 (1930), pp. 117–49; id., 'English Brass Lecterns of the Seventeenth and Eighteenth Centuries', ibid. 88 (1931), pp. 218–27.

lectionary. A book containing the extracts ('pericopes') from Scripture appointed to be read at public worship. The apportionment of particular extracts to particular days began in the 4th cent. Originally the beginning (*incipit*) and ending (*explicit*) of each pericope was noted in the margin of the church Bible, and a 'capitulary', or table of *incipits* and *explicits*, was made for reference. Later the pericopes were collected into lectionaries, those for the Mass being further separated into *Epistolaries and *Evangeliaries. With the appearance of the Missal in the 10th cent. all the passages used in the Mass were incorporated in it. In the 1970 RC Missal, however, the biblical readings were omitted. They were issued in the form of a separate lectionary (1969, revised 1981), which provides for a three-year cycle of three readings for Masses on Sundays, and a two-year cycle of two readings for weekday Masses.

The lessons read at *Mattins and *Evensong in the C of E were long regulated by a lectionary ('Table of Lessons') issued in 1871, or, alternatively, by a revised Table of 1922. Since 1944 there has been a series of revisions, culminating in the 1961 Lectionary. This provides for continuous reading of the OT at Mattins and Evensong, with readings from the NT generally in separate sequences in each Office. The Alternative Calendar and Lectionary, introduced in 1979 and incorporated in the ASB, provides separate sequences for both Lessons at each Office. It also provides for the Psalms to be spread over a period of about ten weeks. The ASB has, in addition, a 'Daily Eucharistic Lectionary' of Psalms and Lessons.

S. Beissel, SJ, *Entstehung der Perikopen des Römischen Messbuches* (Ergänzungsheft zu den *Stimmen aus Maria-Laach*, 96; 1907). A. Chavasse, *Les lectionnaires romains de la messe au VIIᵉ et au VIIIᵉ siècle: Sources et dérivés* (2 vols., Spicilegii Friburgensis Subsidia, 22; 1993). G. G. Willis, *St Augustine's Lectionary* (Alcuin Club

Collections, 44; 1962). R. Cabié in A. G. Martimort, *L'Église en Prière* (new edn.), 2: *L'Eucharistie* [1983], pp. 77–84, 213–18; Eng. tr. (1986), pp. 61–6 and 197–202, with bibl. A. A. McArthur, *The Christian Year and Lectionary Reform* (1958). On early Christian lectionaries, F. H. Scrivener in *DCA* 2 (1893), pp. 953–67, s.v., and K. Junack in *Anchor Bible Dictionary*, 4 (1992), pp. 271–3, s.v. See also bibl. to EVANGELIARY.

lector (also **reader**). In the E. and RC Churches, one of the *Minor Orders of the ministry. In early times his main function was to read the OT Prophecies, the Epistle, and in some places (e.g. Africa, Spain) the Gospel. The first traces of the order may be seen in Col. 4: 16 and Rev. 1: 3, and express mention of a liturgical reader is found in St *Justin (*Apol.* 1. 67. 3 f.). From the end of the 2nd cent. there is plentiful but widely scattered evidence, e.g. St *Cyprian (*Epp.* 29; 38. 2; 39. 4). Can. 10 of *Antioch (330 or 341) sanctioned their ordination by *chorepiscopi. In Syria (*Ap. Const.* 8. 2) and elsewhere they were appointed by the laying on of hands, accompanied in the W. ('Conc. Carth. 4', can. 8) by the delivery of a codex. From the Middle Ages the office ranked as the second of the Minor Orders. In 1972 it was constituted the lower of the two remaining *ministeria* and allotted various duties, incl. that of reading the Scriptures (except the Gospel) and, when there is no deacon or cantor present, of announcing the petitions in the General Intercession at Mass. Only laymen are eligible for the office (*CIC* (1983), can. 230), but the duties of the lector may be assigned to laymen or women. In the E. Church it is common for the lector to be ordained also subdeacon and deacon at the same service. For the office in the Anglican Communion, see READER.

A. *Harnack, *Die Quellen der sogenannten Apostolischen Kirchenordnung* (TU 2, Heft 5; 1886), pp. 57–100, 'Über den Ursprung des Lectorats und den anderen niederen Weihen'. F. Wieland, *Die genetische Entwicklung der sog. Ordines Minores in den drei ersten Jahrhunderten* (RQ, Supplementheft 7; 1897), pp. 67–114 and 165–72. J. G. Davies, 'Deacons, Deaconesses and the Minor Orders in the Patristic Period', *JEH* 14 (1963), pp. 1–15, esp. pp. 10–14. H. *Leclercq, OSB, in *DACL* 8 (pt. 2; 1929), cols. 2241–69, s.v. 'Lecteur'.

lecturers. Rare before the *Reformation, lecturers were originally ordained stipendiary ministers (often deacons), appointed during the century after 1559 by town corporations, by many parishes (esp. in London), and in a few cases by individual laymen, to provide for regular frequent preaching. By 1600 about 100 sermons a week were preached by lecturers in London. Most lecturers (e.g. J. *Field) were appointed by parishes, and the most influential by corporations. Lectureships were not benefices. Some stipendiary lecturers were themselves incumbents of the same or another parish, and some held more than one lectureship; they were supported by endowments, voluntary contributions, or levies on parishioners. A parallel and equally important feature were the 'lectures by combination', whereby groups of beneficed clergy qualified to preach would combine to provide a regular rota of sermons in some central church, usually on market days.

Many stipendiary lectureships became a *Puritan device to secure preachers with views of which Puritans could approve; they were used in cathedrals in aid of the establishment, but were otherwise bitterly resisted by many bishops, e.g. by J. Aylmer and R. *Bancroft and esp. by

W. *Laud. The Long Parliament encouraged lectureships; but in the 1650s Anglicans contrived to use them in London. The system was dealt its death-blow by the Act of Uniformity in 1662; a few lectureships still remain as archaic survivals.

P. S. Seaver, *The Puritan Lectureships: The Politics of Religious Dissent 1560–1662* (Stanford, Calif., 1970). P. Collinson, 'Lectures by Combination: Structures and Characteristics of Church Life in 17th-Century England', *Bulletin of the Institute of Historical Research*, 48 (1975), pp. 182–213, repr. in id., *Godly People* (1983), pp. 467–98. See also bibl. to PURITANS.

Ledger, St. See LEODEGAR, ST.

Lee, Frederick George (1832–1902), theological writer. From 1867 to 1899 he was vicar of All Saints', Lambeth. He actively promoted reunion between the C of E and the RC Church, and to this end helped to found the *APUC in 1857, started the *Union Review* in 1863, and was one of the founders of the Order of Corporate Reunion in 1877. It appears that *c*.1877 he was secretly consecrated Bp. at or near *Venice by some prelate in communion with the see of Rome and took the title of 'Bp. of *Dorchester (Oxon)' (see EPISCOPI VAGANTES). He also took a prominent part in furthering the ceremonial revival in the C of E. His voluminous writings, the historical ones mostly very partisan, include *The Validity of the Holy Orders of the Church of England* (1869), *Historical Sketches of the Reformation* (1879) and a *Glossary of Liturgical and Ecclesiastical Terms* (1877). His widely used *Directorium Anglicanum* (1865; a much revised edn. of an earlier book issued by J. *Purchas in 1858) was a manual of directions for clergy at the altar. In 1901 he became a RC.

H. R. T. Brandreth, *Dr Lee of Lambeth: A Chapter in Parenthesis in the History of the Oxford Movement* (1951). W. G. D. Fletcher in *DNB, 1901–1911*, 2, pp. 440–2.

Leen, Edward (1885–1944), Irish spiritual writer. A native of Co. Limerick, he entered the Congregation of the *Holy Ghost and studied at Rockwell College and Rome. He was ordained priest in 1914, became dean of studies at Blackrock College in 1922, and its president in 1925. From 1939 he was superior of the house of his congregation at Kimmage. Leen was among the most popular RC spiritual authors. Among his best-known works are *Progress through Mental Prayer* (1935), containing practical instructions on the lower stages of mental prayer up to the Prayer of Quiet; *The Holy Ghost* (1936), considered esp. in His workings in souls; *Why the Cross?* (1938), meditations on the problem of pain; and *The Church before Pilate* (1939). He also wrote numerous pamphlets and articles on Catholic education.

His *The Voice of A Priest* posthumously ed. B. J. Keily, C.S.Sp. (1947); 14 talks on the BVM were also posthumously pub., *Our Blessed Mother: Talks on Our Lady by Edward Leen . . . and John Kearney*, ed. id. (Dublin, 1947), pp. 1–106, and notes taken on his *Last Retreat* ed. R. F. Walker, C.S.Sp. (Cork, 1959). Life by M. O'Carroll (Dun Laoghaire [1952]).

Lefèvre d'Étaples, Jacques. See FABER, JACOBUS.

legate, Papal. A personal representative of the *Holy See who has been entrusted with a mission. The sending of envoys by the Pope dates from early times, but they grew in importance from the 11th cent. There came to be three kinds of legates: *legati missi*, legates *a latere*, and *legati nati*. *Legati missi* are legates sent to carry out particular tasks; those appointed for more exalted occasions came to be known as legates *a latere*, i.e. from the side of the Pope. In practice legates *a latere* are still invariably *cardinals, and such cardinals represent the Pope as his *alter ego* at solemn celebrations or gatherings. *Legati nati* were the holders of certain important residential archbishoprics to whom legatine status was conferred on a stable basis; to some extent their powers survive in the office of certain primates. Before the Reformation the Abp. of *Canterbury was such a *legatus natus*. The system of legates has been reorganized at various times, and from the 16th cent. permanent *nunciatures to secular governments have been established. Though a modern legate is usually fortified with various powers, his principal task is to make effective the bonds of unity between the *Holy See and particular Churches. He is to assist the local bishops, while leaving intact the exercise of their lawful powers, and he is to act with them in relations with the civil authorities. The position of legates is governed mainly by the *motu proprio* 'Sollicitudo Omnium Ecclesiarum' issued by *Paul VI on 24 June 1969 (*AAS* 61 (1969), pp. 473–84) and *CIC* (1983), cans. 358 and 362–7. See also APOSTOLIC DELEGATE and NUNCIO.

V. E. Hrabar (ed.), *De Legatis et Legationibus Tractatus Varii* (Dorpat, 1905). M. Oliveri, *The Representatives: The Real Nature and Function of Papal Legates* (Gerrards Cross, 1980); P. Blet, SJ, *Histoire de la Répresentation Diplomatique du Saint Siège des origines à l'aube du XIX* siècle (Collectanea Archivi Vaticani, 9; Vatican City, 1982). J. A. Abbo in *NCE* 8 (1967), pp. 607–9, s.v.

Leger, St. See LEODEGAR, ST.

Leibniz, Gottfried Wilhelm (1646–1716), philosopher. He was a native of Leipzig, where after a precocious boyhood he entered the university in 1661 as a student of law. Here philosophy and mathematics soon became his chief interests, and in 1663 he wrote a dissertation on the Principle of Individuation, a subject which remained of permanent interest to him. A tract, *De Arte Combinatoria*, which elaborated a new system of symbolic logic, followed in 1666. In 1667 he declined a chair at Altdorf, the university town attached to Nuremberg. Shortly afterwards his friendship with J. C. von Boyneburg (1622–72) introduced him to the Elector of Mainz, who employed him on several political projects, including a plan to persuade Louis XIV to divert his attention from Germany to an attack on Egypt. Contacts with French *savants* while in Paris on this mission much widened his outlook; and it was at about this date that he made his celebrated discovery of the infinitesimal calculus. In 1673 he changed to the service of the Duke of Brunswick-Lüneburg, in the employ of whose family he remained for the rest of his life, residing from 1676 at Hanover. Here his main official task was the assembly of a vast body of material relating to the history of the House of Brunswick. But he developed and maintained a great number of other interests. A Protestant by upbringing, he engaged in correspondence with J.-B. *Bossuet on Christian reunion, and to this end published his *Systema Theologicum* (1686). The Prussian Academy, founded in 1700, was virtually Leibniz's creation, and he

also exerted himself to promote the erection of similar institutions in other European states. Most of his philosophical writings date from the last 16 years of his life in which he conducted a large correspondence with A. *Arnauld, S. *Clarke, and others. He also contributed to learned journals, and wrote an extensive critique of J. *Locke's *Essay* which, owing to Locke's death in 1704, he withheld from publication. (It was first issued by R. E. Raspe in 1765.) In 1710 appeared his *Essais de Théodicée sur la bonté de Dieu, la liberté de l'homme et l'origine du mal*, his one considerable theological work. In 1714 he wrote the *Monadologie* (pub. 1720) and *Principes de la nature et de la grâce* (pub. 1718), which though brief contain the only systematic account of his metaphysical doctrines. Throughout his life Leibniz was ardently devoted to the cause of international peace.

Acc. to the *Monadology*, the universe consisted of an infinite number of 'monads', i.e. simple substances, and nothing else. These monads are indivisible, yet, unlike the atoms of Democritus, ever-active. As every monad contains within itself the whole infinity of substance, each is a living mirror of all existence. Each is, however, limited and different from all the rest, as it mirrors the universe in its own way. All difference is relative and gradual, not absolute, and the universe is governed by a law of continuity. The monads form a continuously ascending series from the lowest, which is next to nothing, to the highest, which is God. Yet though Leibniz sometimes described God as the highest of the monads, he could not avoid the difficulties in the way of reconciling the inclusion of God in the monadic series with the Christian doctrine of the Divine transcendence. In some places he speaks as though God were outside the series and the cause of the monads' existence, or as though they proceeded from Him by 'fulgurations'. A radical optimism pervaded his whole system, expressed in his belief that this world is 'the best of all possible worlds'.

Leibniz defended the validity of the traditional proofs of God's existence, though he thought that they needed modification in detail, notably the *Ontological Argument. In general he was much more favourably disposed towards Scholastic principles than most philosophers who had come under the influence of F. *Bacon and R. *Descartes, and he firmly believed in final causes. He believed that one of the merits of his doctrine of substance was that it was in harmony with *transubstantiation and *consubstantiation alike.

A complete edn. of his works is being pub. under the auspices of the Berlin Academy (Darmstadt, Leipzig, Berlin, 1923 ff.). Details of earlier edns. in E. Ravier, *Bibliographie des œuvres de Leibniz* (1937). R. Latta, *The Monadology and other Writings* (Eng. tr. with introds. and notes, 1898). Eng. tr. of selected *Philosophical Papers and Letters*, with introd., by L. E. Loemker (Chicago, 1956; 2nd edn., Dordrecht, 1969). There are also Eng. trs. of *The Leibniz–Clarke Correspondence* by H. G. Alexander (Manchester, 1956) and *The Leibniz–Arnauld Correspondence* by H. T. Mason (ibid. and New York, 1967). Lives by G. E. Guhrauer (2 vols., Breslau, 1846) and E. J. Aiton (Bristol and Boston [1985]). Collection of mainly biog. essays ed. W. Totok and C. Haase, *Leibniz* (Hanover [1966]). B. Russell, *A Critical Exposition of the Philosophy of Leibniz* (1900). L. Couturat, *La Logique de Leibniz d'après des documents inédits* (1901). H. W. B. Joseph, *Lectures on the Philosophy of Leibniz* (posthumously pub., Oxford, 1949). G. Martin, *Leibniz: Logik und Metaphysik* (Cologne, 1960; Eng. tr., Manchester,

1964). Y. Belaval, *Leibniz: Initiation à sa philosophie* (1962). B. Mates, *The Philosophy of Leibniz* (New York and Oxford, 1986). C. Wilson, *Leibniz's Metaphysics: A Historical and Comparative Study* (Princeton, NJ [1989]). Short studies by C. B. Broad, ed. C. Lewy (London, 1975), N. Rescher (Oxford, 1979), and S. Brown (Brighton, 1984). G. J. Jordan, *The Reunion of the Churches: A Study of G. W. Leibnitz and his Great Attempt* (1927). É. Naert, *Leibniz et la querelle du pur amour* (1959). J. Jalabert, *Le Dieu de Leibniz* (1960). Bibl. by K. Müller (Frankfurt am Main [1967]) Überweg, 3, pp. 299–340, with bibl., pp. 673–81. L. J. Russell in P. Edwards (ed.), *Encyclopedia of Philosophy*, 4 (1967), pp. 422–34, s.v.; W. R. Sorley and M. Kneale in *EB* (1968 edn.), 13, pp. 913–17, s.v., with bibl.

Leiden. To mark its heroic defence against the Spanish (1574), William of Orange, in 1575, gave the city a university. Although this was formally free from Church control, *Calvinist influence was powerful and, strengthened by the foundation of a College for training theological students (1592), Leiden soon became a stronghold of Calvinist orthodoxy and a refuge of the English *Puritans; from 1609 to 1620 it gave hospitality to the *Pilgrim Fathers. About the same time the *Arminians engaged in religious disputes with the *Gomarists; other great 17th-cent. controversies connected with the name of the city concerned the theology of J. *Cocceius and the *Cartesian philosophy, which had been defended by A. van der Heyden. The *Elzevir family of printers had their headquarters here; but, despite the imprint 'Lugdunum Batavorum' on books issued from Leiden, the modern city has no connection with this Roman town. Famous scholars of the university during its golden era include H. *Saravia, J. Lipsius (1547–1606), C. *Salmasius, G. J. *Voss, H. *Grotius, D. Heinsius (1580–1655), and J. J. *Scaliger. The 18th cent. saw both a decline in prestige and a move towards a more liberal theology; a trend which continued in the 19th cent. under such professors as J. H. Scholten (1811–85) and A. *Kuenen. Today Leiden is a major university with the full range of faculties, amongst which that of oriental studies has a particular reputation.

P. J. Blok, *Geschiedenis eener Hollandsche Stad* (4 vols., The Hague, 1910–18). P. C. Molhuysen (ed.), *Bronnen tot de Geschiedenis der Leidsche Universiteit* (7 vols., ibid., 1913–24). C. A. Siegenbeek van Heukelon-Lamme, *Album Scholasticum Academiae Lugduno-Batavae MDLXXV–MCMXL* (Leiden, 1941). T. H. Lunsingh Scheurleer and G. H. M. P. Meyjes (eds.), *Leiden University in the Seventeenth Century* (ibid., 1975).

Leighton, Robert (1611–84), Abp. of Glasgow. After spending some time in France, he was ordained in 1641, became principal of Edinburgh University in 1653, Bp. of Dunblane in 1661, and Abp. of Glasgow in 1670. His acceptance of a bishopric was not due to abandonment of *Presbyterian principles, or to mere compromise, but to his belief that he had been chosen to help bring peace in the conflict between Presbyterianism and Episcopalianism. He laboured hard for the restoration of Church unity in Scotland, but failed in his hopes of accommodating the two systems. He purposed to retire from his bishopric of Dunblane when the Government continued persecuting the *Covenanters (1665), but on being reassured by *Charles II, relented. He finally resigned his archbishopric in 1674, after vainly redoubling his efforts towards conciliation. Learned in Latin, Greek, and Hebrew, he combined a deep-seated Calvinist belief with a quality of devotion which he learnt in part from the writings of St *Bernard and *Thomas à Kempis.

His writings have never been satisfactorily ed. Early edns. by J. Fall (1692–1708) and P. *Doddridge (2 vols., 1748). More recent edn. by W. West (vols. 2–7, 1869–75; vol. 1 never pub.). Selections ed. by W. Blair (1883). D. Butler, *Life and Letters of Robert Leighton* (1903), E. A. *Knox, *Robert Leighton, Archbishop of Glasgow* [1931]. W. O. Chadwick, 'Robert Leighton after three hundred years', *Journal of the Society of Friends of Dunblane Cathedral*, 14 (1985), pp. 116–26. G. W. Sprott in *DNB* 33 (1893), pp. 4–7.

Leipzig, Disputation of. The disputation held at Leipzig from 27 June to 16 July 1519, under the orders of George, Duke of Saxony (1500–39), was provoked by J. *Eck's challenge of *Carlstadt, in which M. *Luther felt himself included. It began with a rather academic discussion between Eck and Carlstadt on the relations of grace and free will, but the appearance of Luther on 4 July turned the disputation to the question of the doctrinal authority of the Church. Under the pressure of Eck, Luther was led to the decisive statement that Councils not only may err, but actually have erred, holding that among the doctrines of J. *Huss condemned at *Constance some were very Christian and evangelical, and that the same Council had been wrong in affirming the primacy of the Pope. The disputation resulted in the clearing of the issues on both sides and furnished Rome with new material for the process against Luther.

The standard edn. of the text is that of O. Seitz (Berlin, 1903). Extracts of some docs. are conveniently pr. in Kidd, pp. 44–51. J. C. Seidemann, *Die Leipziger Disputation im Jahre 1519* (1843). K.-V. Selge, 'Der Weg zur Leipziger Disputation zwischen Luther und Eck im Jahre 1519', in B. Moeller and G. Ruhbach (eds.), *Bleibendes im Wandel der Kirchengeschichte* (Tübingen, 1973), pp. 169–210.

Leipzig Interim. See AUGSBURG, INTERIM OF.

Le Neve, John (1679–1741), English antiquary. He was educated at Eton and at Trinity College, Cambridge. His *Fasti Ecclesiae Anglicanae, or an Essay towards deducing a regular Succession of all principal Dignitaries in every Cathedral in those parts of Great Britain called England and Wales* (fol., 1716), based on the collections of White *Kennett, was a work of immense industry and has remained a standard treatise on matters of ecclesiastical chronology, etc. His other publications include a Life of R. *Field, Dean of Gloucester (1717; but perhaps only the preface is Le Neve's own work), and *The Lives and Characters . . . of all the Protestant Bishops in the Church of England since the Reformation* (1720).

His *Fasti Ecclesiae Anglicanae* was 'corrected and continued from the Year M.DCC.XV. to the present time' by T. D. Hardy (3 vols., Oxford, 1854), with biog. note of Le Neve in vol. 1, pp. xiii–xx. Modern edn. of the section covering the period 1300–1541 by H. P. F. King, J. M. Horn, and B. Jones (12 vols., 1962–7); of that covering 1066–1300 by D. E. Greenway and others (1968 ff.); and of that covering 1541–1857 by J. M. Horn and others (1969 ff.). W. Rye in *DNB* 33 (1893), pp. 35 f.

Le Nourry, Denis Nicolas (1647–1724), *Maurist historian. Educated by the *Oratorians, in 1655 he joined the

*Benedictine Order at *Jumièges. From c.1685 till his death he lived at *Paris. He took part in preparing some of the standard editions of the Fathers, notably of *Cassiodorus (with J. Garet) and St *Ambrose (with J. Du Friche). His own principal work was his *Apparatus ad Bibliothecam Maximam Veterum Patrum et Antiquorum Scriptorum* (2 vols., 1703 and 1715), a very learned set of dissertations on several of the leading early Fathers and their writings, issued as an Appendix to the Lyons *Bibliotheca*. His *Liber ad Donatum Confessorem de Mortibus Persecutorum* (1710) is notable as the first modern attempt to prove that *Lactantius did not write the treatise 'On the Deaths of Persecutors'.

J. Baudot in *DTC* 9 (pt. 1; 1926), cols. 217 f., s.v. with bibl.

Lent. The fast of 40 days before *Easter. In the first three centuries the period of fasting in preparation for Easter did not, as a rule, exceed two or three days, as is evident from a statement of *Irenaeus recorded by *Eusebius (*Hist. Eccl.* 5. 24. 12). The first mention of a period of 40 days (τεσσαρακοστή), prob. of Lent, occurs in the Canons of *Nicaea (AD 325; can. 5). The custom may have originated in the prescribed fast of candidates for baptism, and the number 40 was evidently suggested by the 40 days' fasts of *Moses, *Elijah, and esp. the Lord Himself, though till a much later date the period was reckoned differently in the different Churches. In the E. Churches the Lenten Fast was observed during seven weeks, but as Saturdays and Sundays (except *Holy Saturday) were exempt there were only 36 actual fast days. The W. Church, on the other hand, fasted during six weeks but also counted 36 days, as they normally left out only the Sundays. Apparently only in *Jerusalem were the actual 40 days observed as early as the 4th cent. by fasting on five days for eight weeks, but local customs long varied and acc. to *Socrates (*Hist. Eccl.* 5. 22) even a fast of three weeks or a fortnight was called τεσσαρακοστή. C. Callewaert argued that in Rome the original fast was of 40 days from the First Sunday in Lent to *Maundy Thursday, the fasts of Good Friday and Holy Saturday being independent. It is, however, generally held that the number of 40 was not made up in the Latin Church until the 7th cent., when the four days from *Ash Wednesday to the First Sunday in Lent were added, a practice first attested by the *Gelasian Sacramentary and spreading from Rome throughout the W.

During the early centuries the observance of the fast was very strict. Only one meal a day, taken towards evening, was allowed, and flesh-meat and fish, and in most places also eggs and *lacticinia*, were absolutely forbidden. From the 9th cent. onwards in the W. the practice began to be considerably relaxed. The hour for breaking the fast was gradually anticipated to three o'clock in the afternoon, and by the 15th cent. it had become the general custom even for religious to eat at noon. These relaxations entailed not only the anticipation of the evening office of *Vespers to before midday (in order to keep the rule of not eating before Vespers), but also the concession of a 'collation' in the evening. This consisted originally only of a drink, but from the 13th cent. included some light food. Fish was allowed throughout the Middle Ages, and from the 15th cent. abstinence from *lacticinia* came to be more and more

generally dispensed. By the Apostolic Constitution *Paenitemini* (1966) in the RC Church the obligation to fast was restricted to the first day of Lent and *Good Friday. In the E. Church, however, abstinence from meat, fish, eggs, and *lacticinia* is still widely practised.

In the W. Church the penitential character of Lent is reflected in various features in the liturgy, such as the use of purple vestments and the omission of the *Alleluia and (except on great feasts) of the *Gloria in excelsis* at Mass. There has long been a proper Mass for each day in Lent; despite some recent rearrangement of the lections, the Lenten Masses (except those for the Thursdays which are later than the rest) are among the earliest in the Missal. Since the time of *Pius X the ferial Masses of Lent have been gradually restored to prominence and now take precedence over all but the most important feasts. In the E. Church in Lent the celebration of the Eucharist is confined to Saturdays and Sundays; on Wednesdays and Fridays the Liturgy of the *Presanctified is used.

Lent is generally observed as a time of penance by abstaining from festivities, by almsgiving, and by devoting more than the usual time to religious exercises. Of recent years in the W. Church more emphasis has been placed on these aspects than on physical fasting.

The observance of Lent continued in the C of E after the Reformation. It was expressly prescribed by the BCP, and sometimes enforced even by the secular authorities. Dispensations allowing the use of meat were issued in special cases, e.g. by Abp. W. *Juxon. Falling into comparative disuse in the 18th cent., it was revived by the Tractarians in the 19th and is now widely kept. See also REFRESHMENT SUNDAY; HOLY WEEK.

H. Thurston, SJ, *Lent and Holy Week* (1904). J. Pascher, *Das liturgische Jahr* (Munich, 1963), pp. 47–156. F. X. Funk, *Kirchengeschichtliche Abhandlungen und Untersuchungen*, 1 (1897), 'Die Entwickelung des Osterfastens', no. 9, pp. 241–78. C. Callewaert, *Sacris Erudiri* (Steenbrugge, 1940), pp. 449–671. A. Chavasse, 'La Structure du Carême et les lectures des messes quadragésimales dans la liturgie romaine', *Maison-Dieu*, 31 (1952, no. 3), pp. 76–119, and other specialized arts. by this author; cf. J. A. Jungmann, SJ, 'Die Quadragesima in den Forschungen von Antoine Chavasse', *Archiv für Liturgiewissenschaft*, 5 (pt. 1; 1957), pp. 84–95. V. Peri, 'La Durata e la Struttura della Quaresima nell'antico uso ecclesiastico Gerosolimitano', *Aevum*, 37 (1963), pp. 31–62. P. Radó, OSB, *Enchiridion Liturgicum*, 2 (2nd edn., Rome, 1966), pp. 1145–218, with bibl. and suppl. 2/8° f. P. Jounel in A. G. Martimort (ed.), *L'Église en Prière* (new edn.), 4 (1983), pp. 78–90; Eng. tr. [1985], pp. 65–76. R. Sinker in *DCA* 2 (1880), pp. 972–7; H. Thurston in *CE* 9 (1910), pp. 152–4; E. Vacandard in *DTC* 2 (1905), cols. 1724–50, and in *DACL* 2 (pt. 2; 1910), cols. 2139–58, both s.v. 'Carême'; R. Pierret, OSB, and E. Flicoteaux, OSB, in *Dict. Sp.* 2 (1953), cols. 136–52, also s.v. 'Carême'.

Leo I, St (d. 461), 'Leo the Great', Pope from 440. Little is known of his early life beyond the fact that as a Roman deacon he opposed *Pelagianism. His Papacy is remarkable chiefly through the enormous extent to which he advanced and consolidated the influence of the Roman see. At a time of general disorder he sought to strengthen the Church by energetic central government, based on a firm belief that the supremacy of his see was of Divine and Scriptural authority, and he pressed his claims to jurisdiction in Africa, Spain, and Gaul. He also secured from Valentinian III a rescript which recognized his jurisdiction over all the W. provinces. Though his jurisdiction was not recognized in the E., he was drawn into E. affairs by the *Eutychian controversy, and his support was coveted by all parties. His legates spoke first at the Council of *Chalcedon (451), where his *Tome (449) was accepted as a standard of Christological orthodoxy. In the political sphere he also much increased Papal prestige by persuading the Huns to withdraw beyond the Danube (452) and securing concessions when the Vandals took Rome (455). Doctrinally Leo was clear and forcible, but not profound. He knew no Greek. 143 genuine letters and some 97 sermons have survived. The latter cover the whole ecclesiastical year; they provide important evidence of contemporary liturgical practices (e.g. the observance of four sets of fast days, later known as *Ember Days) and reveal a remarkable grasp of liturgical principles. Both his letters and his sermons are distinguished by clarity of thought and purity of language. Mainly on grounds of style, many scholars have claimed to detect his hand in some of the prayers in the so-called *Leonine and *Gelasian Sacramentaries. He was declared a '*Doctor of the Church' by *Benedict XIV. Feast day, in the E., 18 Feb.; in the W., 10 Nov. (formerly 11 Apr.). See also TOME OF I.EO.

Works ed. P. *Quesnel (2 vols., Paris, 1675; strongly *Gallicanist) and by P. and H. *Ballerini (3 vols., Venice, 1753–7, with replies to Quesnel's Disquisitions from the *Ultramontane standpoint); both deservedly famous patristic edns. The latter is repr. in J. P. Migne, PL 54–6. Modern crit. edn. of Leo's Epistles in E. *Schwartz, ACO 2. 4 (1932). Eng. tr. of Letters by C. L. Feltoe (1896). Migne text of sermons repr., with two further sermons, Fr. tr. and notes by R. Dolle, OSB (SC 22, 49, 74, 200; [1947]–1973); crit. edn. of sermons by A. Chavasse (CCSL 138 and 138A; 1973). Eng. tr. of selected sermons by W. *Bright (1862; 2nd edn., 1886). T. [G.] Jalland, The Life and Times of St Leo the Great (1941). A. P. Lang, Leo der Grosse und die Texte des Altgelasianums (1957). M. B. de Soos, OSB, Le Mystère liturgique d'après saint Léon le Grand (Liturgiewissenschaftliche Quellen und Forschungen, 34; 1958). G. Hudon, OMI, La Perfection chrétienne d'après les sermons de saint Léon (Lex Orandi, 26; 1959). P. Stockmeier, Leo I des Grossen Beurteilung der kaiserlichen Religionspolitik (Münchener Theologische Studien, 1. Historische Abteilung, 14; 1959). P. A. McShane, La Romanitas et le pape Léon le Grand: L'apport culturel des institutions impériales à la formation des structures ecclésiastiques (1979). S. O. Horn, Petrou Kathedra: Der Bischof von Rom und die Synoden von Ephesus (449) und Chalcedon (Konfessionskundliche und Kontroverstheologische Studien, 45; Paderborn, 1982). W. Ullmann, 'Leo I and the Theme of Papal Primacy', JTS NS 11 (1960), pp. 25–51. B. Studer in J. Quasten (cont.), Patrology, 4 (1986), pp. 589–612, with bibl. H. *Lietzmann in PW 12 (pt. 2; 1925), cols. 1962–73; P. *Batiffol in DTC 9 (pt. 1; 1926), cols. 218–301; F. X. Murphy in NCE 8 (1967), pp. 637–9, s.v.; B. Studer [OSB] in TRE 20 (1990), pp. 737–41, s.v. See also works cited under LEONINE SACRAMENTARY.

Leo III (c.675–741), Byzantine Emperor, usually 'the Isaurian', but more correctly the Syrian. Born at Germanicia in Commagene, he won distinction as a soldier and became commander of the eastern army under Anastasius II. In 717 he was elected Emperor in place of the usurper Theodosius III. In the same year began the siege of *Constantinople by the Saracens, ending with Leo's victory in 718, which saved Europe from Islam. He then effected many administrative reforms, and in 726 issued a new code of law, the 'Ecloge'. He also introduced reforms in the religious sphere. From 726 to 729 he published a

number of edicts against image worship and thus initiated the *Iconoclastic Controversy. In 730 he replaced the Patr. *Germanus I, an upholder of images, by Anastasius, against popular opinion, which was supported by the monks and the majority of Byzantine theologians. The defence of the veneration of images by the Popes, *Gregory II and Gregory III, in letters and synodal decrees caused the Emperor to annex the Papal Patrimonies in S. Italy and the province of Illyria; he failed, however, to abolish image worship. In 740 he won another decisive victory over the Arabs, and thus at his death left the Empire well consolidated.

Crit. edn. of the Ecloge, with Ger. tr. and introd., by L. Burgmann (Forschungen zur Byzantinischen Rechtsgeschichte, 10 [1983]). Eng. tr. by E. H. Freshfield, with full introd. (Cambridge, 1926). K. Schenk, Kaiser Leon III: Ein Beitrag zur Geschichte des Bilderstreits (Inaugural Diss., Halle, 1880); id., 'Kaiser Leons III Walten im Innern', BZ 5 (1896), pp. 257–310. A. A. Vasiliev, History of the Byzantine Empire, 324–1453 (Eng. tr. from Russ., 2nd edn., Oxford, 1952), pp. 234–59. M. V. Anastos in C.Med.H. 4 (pt. 1; 1966), pp. 61–72. See also bibl. to ICONOCLASTIC CONTROVERSY.

Leo III, St (d. 816), Pope. A Roman priest of humble birth and blameless character, he was unanimously elected Pope in 795. From the beginning of his reign he had to contend with the opposition of the ambitious relatives of his predecessor, *Hadrian I, who, during the procession of St Mark's Day in 799, set on him and tried to mutilate him. After recovering from his wounds he fled to *Charlemagne, to whom he had sent the keys of the confessio of St Peter in 795, and who now provided him with an escort back to Rome. In 800, when Charles had himself come to investigate the charges brought against the Pope, Leo cleared himself by an oath of compurgation. On Christmas Day, two days later, he crowned Charles Roman Emperor. At Charlemagne's instigation the Pope took severe measures against the *Adoptianist heresy, but refused to accede to the Emperor's request to include the *Filioque in the *Nicene Creed, in order not to alienate the Greeks. Several times he intervened in the differences between the Archbishops of *Canterbury and the Anglo-Saxon kings, excommunicating the usurper of the throne of Kent, Eadbert Praen, and withdrawing the *pallium from *Lichfield. In the E. he encouraged the monks in their opposition to the Emp. Constantine VI, who had divorced his wife. After Charlemagne's death in 814, trouble began again for the Pope, who had to crush another conspiracy against himself and, shortly afterwards, revolts of nobles and peasants of the Campagna by the help of the Duke of Spoleto. Assisted by Charlemagne's rich gifts, Leo III did much to adorn the churches in Rome and other cities of Italy, and was an efficient and charitable ruler of the *Patrimony. He was canonized in 1673. Feast day, 12 June.

Some of his Correspondence and Privilegia are repr., mainly from J. D. *Mansi, in J. P. Migne, PL 102. 1023–72; 10 letters also ed. P. Jaffé, Bibliotheca Rerum Germanicarum, 4, Monumenta Carolina (Berlin, 1867), pp. 307–34. Id., Regesta Pontificum Romanorum, 1 (2nd edn. by W. Wattenbach, Leipzig, 1885), pp. 307–16. LP (Duchesne), 2, pp. 1–48 (Eng. tr., with introd., by R. Davis, Liverpool, 1992, pp. 173–230). E. Caspar, 'Das Papsttum unter frankischer Herrschaft', ZKG 54 (1935), pp. 132–264, esp. pp. 214–64; L. Wallach, 'The Genuine and Forged Oath of Pope

Leo III', *Traditio*, 11 (1955), pp. 37–63; id., 'The Roman Synod of December 800 and the Alleged Trial of Leo III', *HTR* 49 (1956), pp. 123–42; W. Mohr, 'Karl der Grosse, Leo III. und der römische Aufstand von 799', *Bulletin Du Cange*, 30 (1960), pp. 39–98. T. F. X. Noble, *The Republic of St Peter: The Birth of the Papal State, 680–825* (Philadelphia, 1984), pp. 184–324 *passim*. Mann, 2 (1906), pp. 1–110. Fliche and Martin, 6 (1937), pp. 148–203. É. Amann in *DTC* 9 (pt. 1; 1926), cols. 304–12, s.v. 'Léon III'. See also bibl. to CHARLEMAGNE.

Leo IV, St (d. 855), Pope. A native of Rome, he became cardinal-priest of the *titulus* of the *Quattro Coronati and in 847 was elected to succeed Sergius II. He at once set about repairing the damage done by the Saracens (846), putting a wall, 40 ft. high, round the part of Rome on the right of the Tiber (henceforward the '*Leonine City'); he restored many churches (*Vatican, *Lateran, St Martin's, Quattro Coronati); and he rebuilt and fortified ravaged cities (Porto, Subiaco). In 850 he crowned Louis, the son of Lothair, as co-Emperor. In 853 he is said to have 'hallowed' the young *Alfred as future King of England. Among those whom he sought to bring under his authority were *Anastasius Bibliothecarius (later antipope), John, Abp. of Ravenna, *Hincmar of Reims, and Nomenoe, Duke of Brittany. He was keenly interested in the liturgical chant and the *Asperges is ascribed to him. A terrible conflagration in the Borgo, said to have been extinguished in answer to Leo's prayers, is the subject of *Raphael's celebrated fresco in the Stanza dell'Incendio in the Vatican. Feast day, 17 July.

Various 'Epistolae et Decreta et Homilia' in J. P. Migne, *PL* 115. 629–84; frags. of his Register ed. P. Ewald in *NA* 5 (1879), pp. 375–98, and ed. A. de Hirsch-Gereuth in *MGH*, Epistolae, 5 (1899), pp. 585–612. *LP* (Duchesne), 2, pp. 106–39 (Eng. tr., with introd., by R. Davis, Liverpool, 1995, pp. 99–159). L. *Duchesne, *Les Premiers Temps de l'état pontifical* (2nd edn., 1904), pp. 217–29. Mann, 2 (1906), pp. 258–307. É. Amann in Fliche and Martin, 6 (1931), pp. 281–8. Id. in *DTC* 9 (pt. 1; 1926), cols. 312–16, s.v. 'Léon IV' with further bibl. J. N. D. Kelly, *The Oxford Dictionary of Popes* (1986) pp. 104 f.

Leo VI (866–912), generally known as **Leo the Philosopher** or **Leo Sapiens**, Byzantine Emperor. Succeeding Basil I in 886, he opened his reign by banishing the Patr. of Constantinople, *Photius, to a monastery and installing his own brother Stephen in his place, thus restoring normal relations with the W. In the disputes that followed his fourth marriage he appealed from the Patriarch, now Nicolas Mysticus, to the Pope, who recognized the validity of the marriage against the Patriarch, whom Leo then deposed in favour of Euthymius I. The extensive writings of the Emperor contain many *novellae* and other items of ecclesiastical legislation, two homilies attacking the *Double Procession of the Holy Spirit, and hymns and treatises in honour of the BVM.

Collection of his works in J. P. Migne, *PG* 107; further panegyrics ed. Akakios, monk of Mt *Athos (Athens, 1868); funeral oration of his father ed. A. Vogt and I. Hausherr, SJ (Orientalia Christiana, vol. 26, no. 1 (fasc. 77); 1932]; 'Problemata' ed. A. Dain (Paris, 1935). Standard edn. of his *Novellae*, with Fr. tr., by P. Noailles and A. Dain (ibid., 1944). H. J. W. Tillyard, 'The Morning Hymns of the Emperor Leo', *Annual of the British School at Athens*, 30 (1932), pp. 86–108; 31 (1933), pp. 115–47, incl. text. J. M. Hussey, *The Orthodox Church in the Byzantine Empire* (Oxford History of the Christian Church, 1986), pp. 102–8. L.

Petit, 'Notes sur les homélies de Léon le Sage', *ÉO* 2 (1899–1900), pp. 245–9; D. Serruys, 'Les Homélies de Léon le Sage', *BZ* 12 (1903), pp. 167–70. S. Salaville, AA, in *DTC* 9 (1926), cols. 365–94, s.v. 'Léon VI le Sage'.

Leo IX, St (1002–54), Pope from 1048. His original name was Bruno. A native of Alsace of noble birth, he was educated at Toul, where he was later successively canon and, from 1026, bishop. Through the influence of the Emp. Henry III, whose favour he had secured, he was elected Pope in 1048, and at once began to reform the Church from its decadence of a century and a half. In his pastoral zeal and personal humility, he did much to foster a wholly new ideal of the Papacy. At the Easter Synod of 1049 *celibacy was enforced on all clergy from the rank of *subdeacon upwards and shortly afterwards Councils were held at Pavia, *Reims, and Mainz, at which decrees were promulgated against *simony and other abuses. In carrying out his programme Leo travelled extensively and was assisted by several able advisers, among them Hildebrand (*Gregory VII), *Humbert, and St *Peter Damian. At the Easter Synod at Rome in 1050, *Berengar of Tours was condemned for his Eucharistic doctrine. The latter years of his pontificate were marred by defeat at the hands of the Normans at Civitate (18 June 1053) and the breach with the E. Church. He has a place in the *Roman Martyrology for 19 Apr.

Contemporary biog. ed. A. Poncelet, 'Vie et miracles du Pape S. Léon IX', *Anal. Boll.* 25 (1906), pp. 258–97, with further notes ibid. 26 (1907), pp. 302–4. L. Sittler and P. Stintzi, *Saint Léon IX: Le Pape alsacien* (Colmar [1950]). J. Drehmann, *Leo IX und die Simonie* (Beiträge zur Kulturgeschichte des Mittelalters, 2; 1908); P. P. Brucker, *L'Alsace et l'Église au temps du Pape Saint Léon IX* (2 vols., 1889). H. Tritz, CSSR, 'Die hagiographischen Quellen zur Geschichte Papst Leos IX.', *Studi Gregoriani*, 4 (1952), pp. 191–364. A. Fliche, *La Réforme grégorienne*, 1 (SSL 6; 1924), pp. 129–59. Mann, 4 (1910), pp. 18–182, with refs. to sources. J. Choux in *Bibliotheca Sanctorum*, 7 (1966), cols. 1292–301, s.v. 'Leone IX'.

Leo X (1475–1521), Pope from 1513. Giovanni de' Medici was the second son of Lorenzo 'the Magnificent'. He was destined early for an ecclesiastical career and created a cardinal in 1489, but not invested with the insignia of office until he had completed three years' study of theology and canon law at Pisa. After the expulsion of his family from Florence in 1494 he led a wandering and almost Bohemian life in Germany, the Netherlands, and France, returning to Rome in 1500. Towards the end of the pontificate of *Julius II, the affairs of the young cardinal began to improve. In 1511 he became legate in *Bologna and the Romagna, and in 1513, at the age of 38, he was elected Pope.

The high hopes which had been placed upon him were soon disappointed. Leo was, indeed, a person of moral life and sincerely religious, but he was pleasure-loving, easygoing, and far too liberal with money and offices. Within two years he had squandered the fortune left by Julius II and was in serious financial embarrassment. In politics, concern for the independence of the Papal states led him to pursue a shifting course. Eventually he concluded a concordat with Francis I of France (in place of the *Pragmatic Sanction of Bourges) which firmly established royal influence over the French Church (1516). He was completely blind to what was involved in the revolt of M. *Luther, whom he excommunicated in 1520. He did, however, continue the Fifth *Lateran Council.

Regesta ed. J. *Hergenröther (2 vols. only, to 16 Oct. 1515; Freiburg i.B., 1884–91). Life by Paolo Giovio, Bp. of Nocera (Florence, 1548). W. Roscoe, *The Life and Pontificate of Leo the Tenth* (4 vols., 1805). E. Rodocanachi, *Le Pontificat de Léon X* (1931). F. S. Nitti, *Leone X e la sua politica* (1892). G. B. Picotti, *La giovinezza di Leone X* [1928]. G. Truc, *Léon X et son siècle* (1941). C. L. Mee, Jun., *White Robe, Black Pope* (1973 [popular]). H. M. Vaughan, *The Medici Popes* (1908), pp. 1–284. Pastor, 7 and 8 (1908), with full bibl. G. Mollat in *DTC* 9 (pt. 1; 1926), cols. 329–32, s.v. 'Léon X', with bibl.; G. B. Picotti in *EC* 7 (1951), cols. 1150–5, s.v. 'Leone X'; J. G. Gallaher in *NCE* 8 (1967), pp. 643–5, s.v.; G. Simon in *TRE* 20 (1990), pp. 744–8, s.v. See also bibl. to REFORMATION.

Leo XIII (1810–1903), Pope from 1878. Vincenzo Gioacchino Pecci was a native of Carpineto. He was educated by the *Jesuits of Viterbo and later studied at the 'Academy of Noble Ecclesiastics' in Rome. Ordained priest in 1837, he was sent on a mission to Benevento in the next year. In 1843 he was appointed nuncio to Brussels, where he gained considerable diplomatic experience. On missions to London, *Paris, *Cologne, and many other European cities he became acquainted with modern social questions which were to play an important part in his pontificate. In 1846 *Gregory XVI made him Bp. of Perugia, and in 1853 he was created cardinal by *Pius IX. When, in 1860, Perugia passed under the secular power of Piedmont, the Cardinal opposed the new laws, esp. the suppression of ecclesiastical jurisdiction, the institution of civil marriage, and the spoliation of the religious orders.

After his election to the Papacy in 1878, Leo continued many of the policies of *Pius IX, while attempting to bring the Church to terms with modern civilization. This aim, reflected in the programme he outlined in his first encyclical, 'Inscrutabili Dei Concilio' (21 Apr. 1878), determined his attitude towards the great powers. He restored good relations with Germany after the *Kulturkampf by procuring the gradual abolition of the *May Laws in 1886 and 1887, and with Belgium after the victory of the Catholic party in 1884. In 1892 he established an Apostolic Delegation in Washington, and he renewed contacts with Russia and Japan. The improvement of relations with Great Britain found expression in King Edward VII's visit to the *Vatican in 1903. His policy failed, however, in the Italian question; the Pope remained the 'Prisoner of the Vatican', and the prohibition of the participation of Catholics in Italian politics was retained. In France, too, relations between Church and State deteriorated, and the Pope's last years were darkened by the increasingly anti-Catholic French legislation, esp. the *Associations Law of 1901.

Leo XIII's pontificate was esp. important for the lead he gave on the burning political and social questions of his time. In some notable encyclicals he developed the Christian doctrine of the State on the basis of St *Thomas Aquinas. In 'Immortale Dei' (1 Nov. 1885) he defined the respective spheres of spiritual and temporal power; 'Libertas Praestantissimum' (20 June 1888) deals with the freedom of citizens, and 'Graves de Communi' (18 Jan. 1901) with Christian democracy. He upheld the dignity and rights of the State, whether monarchy or republic, and

emphasized the compatibility of Catholic teaching with a moderate democracy. His most important pronouncement on social questions was the famous '*Rerum Novarum' (q.v.) of 15 May 1891. Among his activities in the doctrinal sphere his injunction of the study of St Thomas Aquinas by '*Aeterni Patris' (q.v.) of 4 Aug. 1879 had far-reaching consequences, leading to a great revival of Thomist studies. In 1883 he opened the Vatican archives to historical research; he encouraged the study of the Bible in the encyclical '*Providentissimus Deus' (18 Nov. 1893) and instituted the *Biblical Commission in 1902. He gave a limited measure of encouragement to the new methods of biblical criticism, which ceased in the pontificate of his successor. His attitude to other Christian Churches is marked by the letter 'Praeclara' of 1894, in which he invited Greeks and Protestants of all shades to unite with Rome; but he rejected the conception of union as a federation of Churches in the encyclical '*Satis Cognitum' of 1896. In his Apostolic Letter 'Ad Anglos' (1895) he encouraged Anglican aspirations to union as promoted by Lord *Halifax and the *English Church Union, and in the same year appointed a commission for the investigation of *Anglican Ordinations. They were rejected as invalid in '*Apostolicae Curae' (1896). Leo XIII promoted the spiritual life of the Church in many encyclicals dealing with the redemptive work of Christ, the Eucharist, and devotion to the BVM and the *Rosary; and he sought to renew the spirit of St *Francis by modifying the rules of the *Third Order in accordance with the requirements of the times. Following a revelation received by Mary von Droste-Vischering, religious of the Good Shepherd of Angers, he consecrated the whole human race to the *Sacred Heart of Jesus in the jubilee year 1900. He also encouraged the work of the missions, esp. the formation of a native clergy. In 1887 he condemned 40 propositions from the works of A. *Rosmini contradicting the doctrine of St Thomas, and in 1899 he censured in 'Testem Benevolentiae' the teaching known as '*Americanism'.

Acta (22 vols., index and appendix, Rome, 1881–1905); *Allocutiones, Epistolae, Constitutiones, aliaque Acta Praecipua* (8 vols., Bruges, 1887–1910). *Carmina, Inscriptiones, Numismata*, ed. J. Bach (Cologne, 1903). The basic Life is that of C. de t'Serclaes (3 vols., Bruges, 1894–1906). The many others incl. those by M. Spahn (Munich, 1905), F. Hayward (Paris, 1937), and L. P. Wallace (Durham, NC, 1966). E. Soderini, *Il pontificato di Leone XIII* (3 vols., Milan [1932–3]; Eng. tr. of vols. 1 and 2, 1934–5). E. Lecanuet, *La Vie de l'Église sous Léon XIII* (1930). G. Rossini (ed.), *Aspetti della cultura cattolica nell'età di Leone XIII: Atti del convegno tenuto a Bologna il 27, 28, 29 dicembre 1960* (1961). E. T. Gargan (ed.), *Leo XIII and the Modern World* (New York [1961]). G. Jarlot, SJ, *Doctrine pontificale et histoire: L'Enseignement social de Léon XIII, Pie X et Benoît XV vu dans son ambiance historique* (Studia Socialia, 9; 1964), pp. 17–257. [W.] O. Chadwick, *A History of the Popes 1830–1914* (Oxford, 1998), esp. pp. 273–331. R. F. Esposito, SSP, *Leone XIII et l'oriente cristiano* [1960]. V. C. Orti, *Leon XIII y los Catolicos Españoles: Informes vaticanos sobre la Iglesia en España* (Pamplona, 1988). G. Goyau in *DTC* 9 (pt. 1; 1926), cols. 334–59, s.v. 'Léon XIII'; R. Aubert in *TRE* 20 (1990), pp. 748–53, s.v., both with bibl. See also bibl. to ANGLICAN ORDINATIONS.

Leodegar, Ledger, or Leger, St (*c.*616–678/9), Bp. of Autun. Of noble Neustrian family (his brother was Count of Paris), he was trained at the royal court and at the age of 20 made an archdeacon by his uncle, Bp. Dido of Poitiers; in 653 he became Abbot of St Maxentius. Through the patronage of Queen Balthild, he was raised to the bishopric of Autun in 663 after rival factions of aristocrats had quarrelled over it. As bishop he presided over a Council of Autun (the date is not known) which recommended the use of the Rule of St *Benedict in all monasteries of his diocese (which had previously followed a wide variety of rules) and insisted that his clergy should know by heart the *Quicumque Vult* (*Athanasian Creed); the *canones Augustodunenses* are thought to have been produced under his aegis. After the death of Clothar III in 673 Leodegar, a champion of royal power, was bitterly opposed by the Neustrian Mayor of the Palace Ebroin. Ebroin defeated Leodegar, who was tortured and killed on 3 Oct. 678 or 679. Though killed in a political cause he was soon regarded as a saint and martyr, and his cultus became popular throughout France. Feast day, 2 (occasionally 3) Oct.

The earliest Life, written *c*.690 by a monk of St Symphorian of Autun, was reconstructed by B. Krusch in *MGH*, Scriptores Rerum Merovingicarum, 5 (1910), pp. 282–322. Two later Lives, of the 8th and 11th cents., pr. in *AASS*, Oct. 1 (1765), pp. 355–491 and by B. Krusch, op. cit., pp. 323–62. All three Lives are repr. from Krusch's edn. in CCSL 117 (1957), pp. 519–644. The *Passio Praeiecti*, ed. B. Krusch in *MGH*, loc. cit, pp. 226–48, also contains valuable information on Leodegar as one of Praejectus' chief opponents. J.-C. Poulin, 'Saint Léger d'Autun et ses premiers biographes', *Bulletin de la Société des Antiquaires de l'Ouest et des Musées de Poitiers*, 4th ser. 14 (1977–8), pp. 167–200, with refs R. A. Gerberding, *The Rise of the Carolingians and the* Liber Historiae Francorum (Oxford Historical Monographs, 1987), pp. 69–78. H. *Leclercq, OSB, in *DACL* 8 (pt. 2; 1929), cols. 2460–92, s.v. 'Léger'.

León, Luis de (1527/8–91), Spanish theologian and poet. Of prosperous Castilian family, he made his profession as an *Augustinian Hermit at Salamanca in 1544. He studied there and at Alcalá before becoming a professor at Salamanca in 1561. Here both St *John of the Cross and F. *Suárez were among his pupils. In 1572 he was denounced to the *Inquisition and imprisoned, accused of undermining the authority of the *Vulgate by preferring the Hebrew OT. He encountered strong *Dominican antagonism, led by Bartolomé *Medina. He was, however, vindicated of all charges, released late in 1576, and returned to his teaching in Salamanca. In 1579 he was elected to the professorship of biblical studies there.

Luis de León is one of the greatest lyric poets of Spain, and his harmonious polished prose style brought a new richness and beauty to the language. He wrote Latin commentaries on the Song of Solomon (the most important, the *Triplex Explanatio* was pub. in 1589) and on other Books of the Bible; his Spanish exposition of Job was not published until 1779. His treatise on the duties of a Christian wife, *La Perfecta Casada* (1583) has remained a classic, but his devotional masterpiece is *De los Nombres de Cristo* (1583–95), a dialogue on some of the Scriptural names of Christ in which he expounds the Lord's universal ministry of reconciliation. In 1588 he edited the works of St *Teresa of Ávila.

His poetry was first pub. posthumously by F. de Quevedo (Madrid, 1631), Modern edns. of his Lat. *Opera*, ed. M. Gutiérrez, OSA (7 vols., Salamanca, 1891–5) and of his Span. *Obras completas castellanas*, ed. F. García, OSA (Biblioteca de Autores

Cristianos, 4–5; 1944). Eng. tr. of his Poems by W. Barnstone (Albany, NY, 1979) and of the *Nombres* by M. Durán and W. Kluback (Classics of Western Spirituality, 1984). A. F. G. Bell, *Luis de Leon* (Oxford, 1925); M. Durán, *Luis de León* (New York, 1971). A. Guy, *La Pensée de Fray Luis de León* (Limoges, 1943); S. Muñoz Iglesias, *Fray Luis de León, Teólogo* (1950); R. J. Welch, OSA, *Introduction to the Spiritual Doctrine of Fray Luis de León* (Washington, DC, 1951); K. A. Kottman, *Law and Apocalypse: The Moral Thought of Luis de Leon* (International Archives of the History of Ideas, 44; 1972), with useful bibl. C. P. Thompson, *The Strife of Tongues: Fray Luis de León and the Golden Age of Spain* (Cambridge, 1988). R. Lazcano González, 'Fray Luis de León Bibliografía', *Revista Agustiniana*, 31 (1990), pp. 3–278 (also issued separately, Madrid, 1990). D. Gutiérrez, ESA, in *Dict. Sp.* 9 (1976), cols. 634–43, s.v.

Leonard, St (6th cent.), hermit. Despite his great popularity in the Middle Ages, nothing was heard of him before the 11th cent. Acc. to the *Vita* (*c*.1050), he was a Frankish nobleman of the court of King *Clovis, whom St *Remigius converted to Christianity. He lived in a cell at Noblac, nr. Limoges, and later founded a monastery. His cult spread in the 12th cent. to England, France, Italy, and Germany, and many churches were dedicated to him. He is the special patron of prisoners and also of peasants, the sick, and horses. Feast day, 6 Nov.

Excerpts of the *Vita* ed. B. Krusch in *MGH*, Scriptores Rerum Merovingicarum, 3 (1896), pp. 394–9; full text in *AASS*, Nov. 3 (1910), pp. 149–55, with comm. by A. Poncelet, SJ, pp. 139–49, and other material pp. 155–209. [F.] Arbellot, *Vie de saint Léonard, solitaire en Limousin, ses miracles et son culte* (1883). J. A. Aich, *Leonard, der grosse Patron des Volkes* (Vienna, 1928). G. Kapfhammer, *St Leonhard zu Ehren: Vom Patron der Pferde. Von Wundern und Verehrung. Von Leonhardifahrten und Kettenkirchen* (Rosenheim, 1977). B. Cignitti and C. Colafrancheschi in *Bibliotheca Sanctorum*, 7 (1966), cols. 1198–208, s.v. 'Leonardo', with bibl.

Leonardo da Vinci (1452–1519), Italian painter and scholar. The natural son of a Florentine notary and a peasant woman, he became a pupil of A. del Verrocchio at Florence, where he stayed till 1482. From 1483 to 1499 he lived at Milan, and during this period executed some of his best-known works, among them the *Virgin of the Rocks* and the *Last Supper* (1495–8), the latter done on the refectory wall of the *Dominican convent of Sta Maria delle Grazie. The originality of the *Last Supper* lay in that it depicted not the institution of the Eucharist but the moment of the announcement of the betrayal, the quiet superiority of the sublime figure of Christ dominating a scene filled with human emotions and agitation. When the French invaded Milan (1499), Leonardo left and began to lead a nomadic life mainly devoted to scientific and scholarly work. In this he covered an enormous field of knowledge, and made creative contributions to such different branches as geological research and the construction of guns and even air-machines. To this period belong his *St Anne, Mona Lisa*, and *St John the Baptist*. In 1517 he went to France, where he died. With his complete mastery of technique, Leonardo introduced the style of the High Renaissance.

Reproductions of his pictures (in black and white) ed. H. Bodmer (Klassiker der Kunst in Gesamtausgaben, 37 [1931]); smaller collection of reproductions (incl. some colour plates) ed. L. Goldscheider (London, 1943; 7th edn., 1964). Drawings ed., with introd. and notes, by A. E. Popham (ibid., 1946). K. [M.] Clark, *A Catalogue of the Drawings of Leonardo da Vinci in the Collection of his Majesty the King at Windsor Castle* (2 vols., with reproductions, 1935; 2nd edn., with the assistance of C. Pedretti, 3 vols., 1969). *Leonardo da Vinci on the Human Body: The Anatomical, physiological, and embryological drawings*, with Eng. tr. and biog. introd. by C. D. O'Malley and J. B. de C. M. Saunders (New York [1952]). K. D. Keele and C. Pedretti, *Leonardo da Vinci: Corpus of the Anatomical Studies in the Collection of Her Majesty the Queen at Windsor Castle* (2 vols. + box of plates, 1978–80). Literary Works, with Eng. tr., ed. J. P. Richter (London, 1883; 3rd edn., 2 vols., 1970); comm. by C. Pedretti (2 vols., Oxford, 1977). Facsimile reproduction of his MSS, with transcription and Fr. tr., by C. Ravaisson-Mollien (6 vols., Paris, 1881–91). Eng. tr. of Selections from his Notebooks, ed. I. A. Richter (World's Classics, 530; 1952; repr., Oxford, 1977). Eng. tr. of his *Treatise on Painting*, with facsimile of MS, by A. P. McMahon (2 vols., Princeton, NJ, 1956). General studies incl. E. McCurdy (London, 1928), K. [M.] Clark (Ryerson Lectures for 1936; Cambridge, 1939; 2nd edn., 1952; rev. by M. [J.] Kemp, 1988), L. H. Heydenreich (Berlin, 1943; rev. edn., 2 vols., Basle [1953]; Eng. tr., 1954), M. [J.] Kemp (London, etc., 1981), with useful bibl., and S. Bramly (Paris, 1988; Eng. tr., New York, 1991; London, 1992). E. Solmi, *Scritti vinciani* (1924). I. B. Hart, *The Mechanical Investigations of Leonardo da Vinci* (1925; 2nd edn., Berkeley and Los Angeles, Calif., 1963). C. D. O'Malley (ed.), *Leonardo's Legacy: An International Symposium* (ibid., 1969). C. Pedretti, *Leonardo: A Study in Chronology and Style* (ibid., 1973); id., *Leonardo architetto* ([1978]; Eng. tr., 1986). L. H. Heydenreich, *Leonardo: The Last Supper* (1974). C. [H. M.] Gould, *Leonardo the Artist and the Non-Artist* (1975). E. Winternitz, *Leonardo da Vinci as a Musician* [1982]. M. Guerrini, *Bibliotheca Leonardiana 1493–1989* (3 vols., Milan [1990]).

Leonine City (Lat. *Civitas Leonina*; Ital. *Città Leonina*). The part of Rome on the right bank of the Tiber, fortified with a wall by Pope *Leo IV in 848–52. Besides the *Vatican, it contains the Castello S. Angelo.

Leonine Prayers. In the Roman rite, the prayers which, until 1964, were recited in the vernacular by priest and people at the end of Mass. Their ultimate form (three '*Hail Mary*'s, the *Salve Regina*, a collect *Deus refugium nostrum*, an invocation of St *Michael) went back to *Leo XIII. In 1859 *Pius IX had introduced for local use similar prayers for the preservation of the Papal States, which continued to be said even after the end of the temporal power in 1870; in 1884 Leo XIII extended their use to the whole world, with special reference to the last stages of the *Kulturkampf; and in 1886 he reissued them in a revised form, adding the invocation of St Michael. A final optional petition ('Most Sacred Heart of Jesus, have mercy on us', three times) was added by *Pius X in 1904. After the signing of the *Lateran Treaty (1929), *Pius XI directed that they should be said on behalf of the Church in Russia, but when they had come to be omitted on an increasing number of occasions, they were suppressed on 26 Sept. 1964.

Jungmann (1958 edn.), 2, pp. 565–70; Eng. tr., 2, pp. 455–9.

Leonine Sacramentary. The earliest surviving book of *Mass prayers acc. to the Roman rite. It exists in a single MS of the early 7th cent., preserved in the Chapter Library at *Verona (cod. lxxxv), and was first published in 1735 by J. Bianchini. Its attribution to Pope *Leo I (d. 461) is quite arbitrary, though certain of its prayers may well be Leo's compositions. It is not a *sacramentary in the proper sense, but a private collection of *libelli; it drew on Roman material of the 5th or 6th cent., but was put together outside Rome. It possesses no *Ordinary or *Canon of the Mass, and contains only the variable parts of the liturgy. It is arranged according to the civil year, but three quires at the beginning (covering 1 Jan.–14 Apr.) are lost.

J. Bianchini, *Vitae Romanorum Pontificum*, 4 (1735), pp. xii–lvii. Text also ed. P. and H. *Ballerini, *S. Leonis Opera*, 2 (Venice, 1756, cols. 1–160, repr. J. P. Migne, *PL* 55. 21–156); C. L. Feltoe (Cambridge, 1896); and L. C. Mohlberg, OSB, and others, *Sacramentarium Veronense* (Rerum Ecclesiasticarum Documenta, Series Maior, Fontes, 1; Rome, 1955). P. Bruylants, 'Concordance verbale du sacramentaire léonien', *Archivum Latinitatis Medii Aevi*, nos. 18–19 (Brussels, 1945–8). Fundamental is A. Stuiber, *Libelli Sacramentorum Romani* (Theophaneia, 6; Bonn, 1950). D. M. Hope, *The Leonine Sacramentary: A Reassessment of its Nature and Purpose* (Oxford Theological Monographs, 1971). B. *Capelle, OSB, 'Messes du pape S. Gélase dans le sacramentaire léonien', *R. Bén.* 56 (1945–6), pp. 12–41; id., 'Retouches gélasiennes dans le sacramentaire léonien', ibid. 61 (1951), pp. 3–14; C. Callewaert, 'Saint Léon le Grand et les textes du Léonien', *Sacris Erudiri*, 1 (1948), pp. 35–132; C. Coebergh, OSB, 'S. Gélase Iᵉʳ, auteur principal du soi-disant sacramentaire léonien', *EL* 64 (1950), pp. 214–37, and 65 (1951), pp. 171–81; E. Dekkers, OSB, 'Autour de l'œuvre liturgique de S. Léon le Grand', *Sacris Erudiri*, 10 (1958), pp. 363–98; A. Chavasse, 'Le Sacramentaire, dit léonien, conservé par le Véronensis LXXXV (80)', ibid. 27 (1984), pp. 151–90. Vogel, *Sources*, pp. 38–46, with notes pp. 55–9. F. *Cabrol, OSB, in *DACL* 8 (pt. 2; 1929), cols. 2549–73.

Leontius of Byzantium (6th cent.), anti-*Monophysite theologian. He is prob. to be distinguished from the Scythian monk of the same name who took a prominent part in the *Theopaschite controversy and with whom he was formerly identified; on the other hand he seems to be the same person as the *Origenist Leontius mentioned in *Cyril of Scythopolis' 'Vita S. Sabae', though what his Origenism amounted to is much disputed. Despite his theological importance, virtually nothing is known of his life. He was a staunch upholder of the *Chalcedonian Christology, introducing the notion of the *Enhypostasia (q.v.). In his polemic he made full use of contemporary philosophy (*Aristotelianism in logic, *Neoplatonism in psychology). His chief theological work is his 'Libri III contra Nestorianos et Eutychianos' (c.543–4), of which Book 2 took the form of a dialogue between an Orthodox and an *Aphthartodocetist, and Book 3 is directed esp. against *Theodore of Mopsuestia. He also wrote two works against *Severus of Antioch ('Solutio Argumentorum Severi' and 'Triginta Capita adversus Nestorium'). There is much dispute as to whether he is the author of 'Adversus Fraudes Apollinistarum', a work of considerable critical acumen on the forgeries of the *Apollinarians (q.v.). Of other works traditionally ascribed to him the 'De Sectis' (also attributed to *Theodore of Raïthu) is prob. not his, while the 'Contra Nestorianos' and 'Contra Monophysitas' are now assigned to *Leontius of Jerusalem (q.v.).

Works in J. P. Migne, *PG* 86. 1185–2016. F. *Loofs, *Leontius von Byzanz und die gleichnamigen Schriftsteller der griechischen Kirche* (TU 3, Hefte 1–2; 1887); J. P. Junglas, *Leontius von Byzanz* (Paderborn, 1908). M. Richard, 'Léonce de Byzance était-il Origéniste?', *Revue des Études Byzantines*, 5 (1947), pp. 31–66, repr.

in his *Opera Minora*, 2 (Turnhout and Louvain, 1977), no. 57; B. *Altaner, 'Der griechische Theologe Leontius und Leontius der skythische Mönch', *Th.Q.* 127 (1947), pp. 147–65, repr. in his *Kleine Patristische Schriften* (TU 83; 1967), pp. 375–91. S. Rees, 'The Literary Activity of Leontius of Byzantium', *JTS* NS 19 (1968), pp. 229–42. S. Otto, *Person und Subsistenz: Die philosophische Anthropologie des Leontios von Byzanz. Ein Beitrag zur spätantiken Geistesgeschichte* (Munich, 1968). D. B. Evans, *Leontius of Byzantium: An Origenist Christology* (Dumbarton Oaks Studies, 13; 1970). B. Daley, 'The Origenism of Leontius of Byzantium', *JTS* NS 27 (1976), pp. 333–69; id., ' "A Richer Union": Leontius of Byzantium and the Relationship of the Human and Divine in Christ', in E. A. Livingstone (ed.), *Studia Patristica*, 24 (1993), pp. 239–65. A. Grillmeier, SJ, *Jesus der Christus im Glauben der Kirche*, 2 (pt. 2; Freiburg, etc., 1989), pp. 190–241; Eng. tr. (1995), pp. 181–229. *CPG* 3 (1979), pp. 293–5 (nos. 6813–23). Beck (1959), pp. 373 f. V. Grumel, AA, in *DTC* 9 (pt. 1; 1926), cols. 400–26 [excellent for its period, but superseded in detail]; L. Perrone in *DPAC* 2 (1984), cols. 1928–30, s.v. 'Leonzio di Bisanzio'; Eng. tr., *Encyclopedia of the Early Church*, 1 (1992), pp. 480 f.

On the 'De Sectis', M. Richard, 'Le Traité "De Sectis" et Léonce de Byzance', *RHE* 35 (1939), pp. 695–723, repr. in his *Opera Minora*, 2 (Turnhout and Louvain, 1977), no. 55; J. Speigl, 'Der Autor der Schrift De Sectis über die Konzilien und die Religionspolitik Justinians', *Annuarium Historiae Conciliorum*, 2 (1970), pp. 207–30; M. van Esbroeck, SJ, 'La Date et l'Auteur du De Sectis attribuée à Léonce de Byzance', in *After Chalcedon: Studies in Theology and Church History offered to Professor Albert van Roey*, ed. C. Laga and others (Orientalia Lovaniensia Analecta, 18; Louvain, 1985), pp. 415–24.

Leontius of Jerusalem

Leontius of Jerusalem (6th cent.). The name given by modern scholars to the author of the treatises *Contra Monophysitas* and *Contra Nestorianos*, formerly ascribed to *Leontius of Byzantium. He may have been the monk Leontius who took part in the discussions with the supporters of *Severus of Antioch in 532 and in a Council of Constantinople in 536. His Christology was 'neo-Chalcedonian', i.e. he interpreted the teaching of that Council in the light of the doctrine and language of St *Cyril of Alexandria.

The *Contra Monophysitas* and *Contra Nestorianos* are repr. in J. P. Migne, *PL* 86. 1399–902. M. Richard, 'Léonce de Jérusalem et Léonce de Byzance', *Mélanges de Science Religieuse*, 1 (1944), pp. 35–88, repr. in his *Opera Minora*, 3 (Turnhout and Louvain, 1977), no. 59; C. Moeller, 'Textes "Monophysites" de Léonce de Jérusalem', *Ephemerides Theologicae Lovanienses*, 27 (1951), pp. 467–82; P. T. R. Gray, *The Defence of Chalcedon in the East (451–553)* (Studies in the History of Christian Thought, 20; Leiden, 1979), pp. 122–41. A. Grillmeier, SJ, *Jesus der Christus im Glauben der Kirche*, 2 (pt. 2; Freiburg, etc., 1989), pp. 286–328; Eng. tr. (1995), pp. 271–312. *CPG* 3 (1979), p. 309 (nos. 6917 f.). Beck (1959), p. 379. L. Perrone in *DPAC* 2 (1984), cols. 1931–3, s.v. 'Leonzio di Gerusalemme'; Eng. tr., *Encyclopedia of the Early Church*, 1 (1992), p. 481, s.v.

Lepanto, Battle of

Lepanto, Battle of. The naval battle, fought on 7 Oct. 1571, in which the 'Christian League' created chiefly by the efforts of *Pius V between Venice and Spain, with help from the Papal states and Genoa, decisively beat the Turks, who were threatening W. Christendom. Lepanto, on the N. entrance to the Gulf of Corinth, is the ancient Naupactos. In thanksgiving for the victory, the Pope instituted a special feast of the BVM on 7 Oct., which since 1573 has been kept as the feast of the *Rosary (q.v.).

Leporius

Leporius (early 5th cent.), monk and then (by 430) priest. Perhaps a native of Trier, he issued a letter (no longer extant) in which he emphasized the distinction of the two natures in Christ at the expense of the unity of His person. Rebuked by his superiors in S. Gaul, he went to Africa, where he came into contact with St *Augustine (Aug., *Ep*. 219) and in 418 publicly confessed his error at Carthage in a 'Libellus Emendationis' subscribed by *Aurelius, Bp. of Carthage, and by Augustine. John *Cassian presented him as a doctrinal forerunner of *Nestorius and, less justifiably, as a sympathizer of *Pelagius. His 'Libellus' was frequently cited by later theologians for its Christological formulae.

'Libellus' first pub. by J. *Sirmond, SJ, *Opuscula Dogmatica Veterum Quinque Scriptorum* (Paris, 1630), pp. 1–34; repr. in J. P. Migne, *PL* 31. 1221–30. Crit. edn. by R. Demeulenaere (CCSL 64; 1985, pp. 95–123), with introd. [in Fr.] and bibl. A. Grillmeier [SJ], *Jesus der Christus im Glauben der Kirche*, 1 (1979), pp. 661–5; Eng. tr. of an earlier recension of this work, *Christ in Christian Tradition*, 1 (2nd edn., 1975), pp. 464–7. A. Mandouze, *Prosopographie Chrétienne du Bas-Empire*, 1: *Prosopographie de l'Afrique Chrétienne (303–533)* (1982), pp. 634 f. A. Hamman in Quasten (cont), *Patrology*, 4 (1986), pp. 524 f. É. Amann in *DTC* 9 (pt. 1; 1926), cols. 434–40.

Le Quien, Michel

Le Quien, Michel (1661–1733), patristic scholar. In 1681 he entered the *Dominican Order at Paris, where he spent most of his life. His two principal works were (1) *Oriens Christianus* (published posthumously [1740] in 3 vols.), in which he collected a vast amount of material on the history of the E. Churches, and (2) his edition of the works of St *John of Damascus (1712). His other writings included *La Nullité des ordinations anglicanes* (2 vols., 1725) and *La Nullité des ordinations anglicanes démontrée de nouveau* (2 vols., 1730), both in answer to P. *Courayer's book on the subject.

Quétif and Échard, 2 (1721), pp. 808–10. S. Salaville, AA, 'IIᵉ Centenaire de Michel Le Quien', *ÉO* 32 (1933), pp. 257–66. J. Carreyre in *DTC* 9 (pt. 1; 1926), cols. 441–3, s.v., with bibl.

Lérins

Lérins. The ancient name of two islands off Cannes in the Mediterranean, on the smaller of which (formerly 'Lerinum', now 'St-Honorat') a celebrated abbey was founded by St *Honoratus *c.*410. It was the nursery of a long line of scholars and bishops, among them St *Hilary of Arles, St *Vincent (author of the *Commonitorium*), St *Lupus (Bp. of Troyes), St *Eucherius (Bp. of Lyons), St *Faustus of Riez, and St *Caesarius of Arles. Its religious history continued unbroken down to 1788, when it was secularized. Since 1871 a *Cistercian convent has been re-established on the island.

H. Moris, *L'Abbaye de Lérins: Histoire et monuments* (1909); A. C. Cooper-Marsdin, *The History of the Islands of the Lerins* (Cambridge, 1913; uncritical); L. Cristiani, *Lérins et ses fondateurs* (Abbaye S. Wandrille, 1946). S. Pricoco, *L'Isola dei Santi: Il Cenobio di Lerins e le origini del monachesimo gallico* (Filologia e Critica, 23; 1978). V. Barralis, *Chronologia Sanctorum et aliorum Virorum illustrium ac Abbatum Sacrae Insulae Lerinensis* (Lyons, 1613). 'Cartulary' of Lérins, ed. H. Moris and E. Blanc (2 vols., Paris, 1883–1905); reconstructed 'Bullarium', ed. L. H. Labande in *Annales de la Société des Lettres, Sciences et Arts des Alpes Maritimes*, 24 (1922–3), pp. 117–98. H. *Leclercq, OSB, in *DACL* 8 (pt. 2, 1929), cols. 2596–627, with full bibl.; F. Prinz in *DIP* 5 (1978), cols. 609–23, s.v.

Leslie, Charles (1650–1722), *Nonjuring divine and controversialist. After studying law at *Trinity College, Dublin, he was ordained in 1680 and presented to the chancellorship of Connor. Refusal to take the oaths after the Revolution of 1688 deprived him of his benefice, and in 1689 he withdrew to London. His most celebrated production was an attack on the *Deist philosophy, *A Short and Easy Method with the Deists* (1698; many later editions and translations). His other works included *Gallienus Redivivus* (1695), an important historical authority for the Glencoe massacre; *The Snake in the Grass* (1696), against the *Quakers; and *The Case of the Regale and of the Pontificat* (1700), an assertion of the divine and inherent rights of the Church. He was also an influential proponent of the patriarchal theories of government derived from Sir Robert Filmer, and developed similar views in his periodical *The Rehearsal* (1704–9). In 1710 a warrant for his arrest was issued on the grounds of his Jacobitism, and in 1711 he escaped to join the Stuart Court in exile at St Germains. He followed the Pretender to Bar-le-Duc, Avignon, and Rome, while maintaining his loyalty to the C of E, which found expression in *The Case Stated between the Church of Rome and the Church of England* (1713). He returned to Ireland in 1721.

Collected edn. of his *Theological Works* (2 vols., London, 1721); fuller edn. (7 vols., Oxford, 1832), with Life from *Biographia Britannica* and list of other works, vol. 1, pp. i–xii. R. J. Leslie, *Life and Writings of Charles Leslie* (1885). J. A. W. Gunn, *Beyond Liberty and Property: The Process of Self-Recognition in Eighteenth Century Political Thought* (Kingston, Ont., and Montreal, 1983), pp. 132–6. J. M. Rigg in *DNB* 33 (1893), pp. 77–83.

Leslie, John (1527–96), Bp. of Ross. Born at Kingussie, south of Inverness, he studied at Aberdeen, *Paris, and Poitiers. Returning to Scotland in 1554, he strongly opposed the introduction of the Reformation and in 1561 he took part in a disputation at Edinburgh with J. *Knox and John Willock (d. 1585). In 1562 he was appointed professor of canon law at Aberdeen and in 1566 Bp. of Ross. A strong supporter of *Mary, Queen of Scots, he became her ambassador to *Elizabeth I in 1569. In 1571 he was imprisoned for assisting Mary in her projected marriage to the Duke of Norfolk, but was set free in 1573 on condition that he left the country. Proceeding to Paris and Rome he tried to arrange the capture and Catholic education of the young James VI (later *James I of England) and to further other plans in the Catholic interest. In 1578 he published at Rome his *De Origine, Moribus, et Rebus Gestis Scotorum*, which had been partly written originally in Scots and intended for Queen Mary. The latter part is an important authority for contemporary history. In 1579 he was appointed suffragan bishop and Vicar General of Rouen, and in 1593 Bp. of Coutances; but unable to reach his diocese he spent his last years with the *Augustinian Canons at Guirtenburg, near Brussels.

Contemporary Eng. version of the latter part of his *De Origine, Moribus et Rebus Gestis Scotorum*, from the reign of James II (1436), ed. for the Bannatyne Club, 39 (1830); a Scots version of the history made by Fr. James Dalrymple in 1596, ed. E. G. Cody, OSB, for the Scottish Text Society (2 vols., 1888–95). His 'Narrative of the Progress of Events in Scotland, 1562–1571', is also pr. in W. Forbes-Leith, SJ (ed.), *Narratives of Scottish Catholics under Mary Stuart and James VI* (1885), pp. 85–126; a letter from him to Cardinal de Cosmo (June 1579), ibid., pp. 134–40. His

Diary from 11 Apr. to 16 Oct. 1571 in *The Bannatyne Miscellany*, 3 (1855), pp. 111–56. Short Life pr. Brussels, 1596, repr. in J. Anderson (ed.), *Collections Relating to the History of Mary Queen of Scotland*, 1 (1727), pp. 1–19; Eng. tr. in vol. 3 (1727), pp. vii–xx. Pre-1641 edns. of his works listed in A. F. Allison and D. M. Rogers, 'A Catalogue of Catholic Books in English . . .', *Biographical Studies*, 3 (1956), pp. 214 f. (nos. 451–5), and idd., *The Contemporary Printed Literature of the English Counter-Reformation*, 1 (Aldershot, 1989), pp. 99–101 (nos. 719–35). T. F. Henderson in *DNB* 33 (1893), pp. 93–9.

Lesser Entrance. See LITTLE ENTRANCE.

Lesser Ministries. See MINOR ORDERS.

Lessing, Gotthold Ephraim (1729–81), one of the principal figures of the *Enlightenment. As the eldest son of a *Lutheran pastor he was intended to study theology, but soon took up a literary career and made himself a name as a drama and art critic and as a playwright. In his later years he was chiefly concerned with theological and philosophical problems, his interest receiving a strong stimulus from the fragments of H. S. *Reimarus which Lessing edited (1774–8). He saw the essence of religion in a purely humanitarian morality independent of all historical revelation, and embodied his views in the principal figure of the play *Nathan der Weise* (1779), an ideal Jew of serene tolerance, benevolence, and generosity, conceived on the lines of enlightened rationalism. His chief theoretical writings on the same subject are *Ernst und Falk* (1778–80) and *Die Erziehung des Menschengeschlechts* (1780), in which he laid the foundations of the Protestant Liberalism that was to hold sway in Germany throughout the 19th cent. He rejected Christianity as an historical religion on the ground that 'the accidental truths of history can never become the proof of necessary truths of reason', and that the disinterested search for truth was intrinsically preferable to its possession.

Besides publishing the remains of Reimarus, the so-called *Wolfenbüttel Fragments* (7 parts, 1774–8, q.v.), Lessing himself made original studies in Gospel origins. In his *Neue Hypothese über die Evangelisten als blosse menschliche Geschichtsschreiber betrachtet* (1788) he argued that an Aramaic original underlay St *Matthew's Gospel, and that this was known to, and supplemented by, Mk. and Lk. He also discovered, in 1770, an incomplete MS of *Berengar's famous treatise on the *Eucharist, the text of which was first published by A. F. and F. T. Vischer in 1834.

Collected edns. of Lessing's works incl. those by K. *Lachmann (13 vols., Berlin, 1838–40), F. Muncker (23 vols., Stuttgart, 1886–1924), J. Petersen and W. von Olshausen (25 vols., Berlin, 1925–9, incl., as vols. 20–3, the 2nd edn. of his 'Theological Writings' ed. L. Zscharnack, 4 vols., ibid., 1929), and H. G. Göpfert and others (8 vols., Darmstadt, 1970–79). Eng. tr. of selected Theological Writings by H. Chadwick (1956), with introd. pp. 9–49. Lives by C. G. Lessing (3 vols., Berlin, 1793–5) and E. Schmidt (2 vols., ibid., 1884–92). Lives in Eng. by J. Sime (2 vols., London, 1877), H. Zimmern (ibid., 1878), and T. W. Rolleston (ibid., 1889; repr., 1972). W. Oehlke, *Lessing und seine Zeit* (2 vols., 1919). H. B. Garland, *Lessing: The Founder of Modern German Literature* (Cambridge, 1937; 2nd edn., London, 1962). E. H. Gombrich, 'Lessing', *Proceedings of the British Academy*, 43 (1957), pp. 133–56. H. E. Allison, *Lessing and the Enlightenment: His Philosophy of History and its Relation to Eighteenth-Century*

Thought (Ann Arbor, Mich., 1966). F. J. Lamport, *Lessing and the Drama* (Oxford, 1981). E. M. Batley, *Catalyst of Englightenment: Gotthold Ephraem Lessing* (Berne, etc. [1990]). F. *Loofs, *Lessings Stellung zum Christentum* (Lecture before Univ. of Halle, 1910, with bibl.). E. Zeller, 'Lessing als Theolog', *HZ* 23 (1870), pp. 342–83; repr. in Zeller's *Vorträge und Abhandlungen*, 2 (1877), pp. 283–327. K. Aner, *Die Theologie der Lessingzeit* (Halle, 1929). A. Cozzi, *Lessing teologo* (Naples, 1960). A. Schilson, *Geschichte im Horizont der Vorsehung: G. E. Lessings Beitrag zu einer Theologie der Geschichte* (Tübinger theologische Studien, 3; 1974). L. P. Wessell, *G. E. Lessing's Theology: A Reinterpretation* (The Hague and Paris [1977]). J. von Lüpke, *Wege der Weisheit: Studien zu Lessings Theologiekritik* (Göttinger theologische Arbeiten, 41, 1989). S. Seifert, *Lessing-Bibliographie* (1973); D. Kuhles, *Lessing-Bibliographie 1971–1985* (1988). H. Chadwick in P. Edwards (ed.), *Encyclopedia of Philosophy*, 4 (1967), pp. 443–6, s.v.

Lessius, Leonhard (1554–1623), *Jesuit theologian. A native of Brecht, near Antwerp, he taught philosophy at *Douai from 1574 to 1581 and at Louvain from 1585 to 1600, and studied for a time under F. *Suárez at Rome. Among his pupils was *Cornelius a Lapide. He took a prominent part in the controversies then raging on the nature of grace (see DE AUXILIIS), defending a position closely akin to that of L. *Molina, with the result that in 1587 M. *Baius secured the censure by the Louvain Theological Faculty of 34 theses taken from his writings. His principal work on the subject of grace was his *De gratia efficaci* (Antwerp, 1610). He also wrote extensively on moral theology, his *De justitia et jure* (1605) being one of the earliest treatises to investigate the ethics of economics.

Opuscula Varia (Paris, 1626). Texts on Holy Scripture from various sources collected and ed. by A. M. Artola, CP (Biblica Victoriensia, 1; 1974). Works listed in Sommervogel, 4 (1893), cols. 1726–51, and 9 (1900), cols. 588 f.; Polgár, 2 (1990), pp. 406–11. L. Scotts, *De Vita et Moribus R. P. Leonardi Lessii Liber* (Paris, 1644). K. van Sull, SJ, *Leonardus Lessius, 1554–1623* (Wetteren, 1923; French edn., Museum Lessianum, Section théologique, 21; 1930). A. Ampe, SJ, 'Marginalia Lessiana', *Ons Geestelijk Erf*, 28 (1954), pp. 329–73; 29 (1955), pp. 5–29, with summary in Lat.; L. Ceyssens, OFM, 'Marginalia Lessio-Janseniana', *Bijdragen tot de Geschiedenis*, 3ᵉ Reeks, 10 (1958), pp. 95–142 [in Fr.]. J. de Ghellinck, SJ, in *CE* 9 (1910), pp. 192 f.

Letters Commendatory. The document issued by an ecclesiastical superior to one of his clerical subjects when travelling, testifying that he is of irreproachable morals and doctrine.

Letters Dimissory. In the C of E the licence which the bishop of a diocese where a candidate for Holy Orders has his title issues to the bishop of another diocese to perform the ministerial act of ordination when the former bishop finds it inconvenient or impossible to ordain the candidate. By Canon C 5 of the 1969 Canons, the bishop who ordains must require the production of such letters from the candidate. They are to be distinguished from 'Letters of Request', which ask the ordaining bishop to examine as well as to ordain the candidate. The practice of providing a candidate with such Letters directed to 'any bishop' (*literae dimissoriae ad omnes*) was formerly common, despite the abuse to which it was open; and, though now obsolete, it still appears to be legal. During the vacancy of a see the issue of such Letters is vested in the *guardian of the spiritualities.

Letters of Business. The document issued by the Crown from time to time since the reign of *Anne to the English *Convocations permitting them to prepare canons on a prescribed subject. Without these Letters any such action was of doubtful legality. The Letters did not dispense the Convocations from the necessity of obtaining a further licence before any canons so prepared might be enacted. Canons are now made by the General *Synod and Letters of Business are no longer required.

Letters of Orders. A certificate issued to those who have been ordained, bearing the seal and signature of the officiating bishop. The C of E Canon C 10 of the 1969 Canons requires that 'Letters of Orders or other sufficient evidence' of ordination be shown to the bishop before *institution to a benefice, except when the presentee was ordained by the instituting bishop. Formerly Letters of Orders were the normal means of proving a claim to *Benefit of Clergy.

Letters Testimonial. The certificate of 'good life and conversation from three priests, of whom one at least must be beneficed' and from 'any college or hall in any university, or . . . any theological college' in which he may have resided, which a candidate for ordination in the C of E was until 1977 required to present to the ordaining bishop by Canon C 6 of the 1969 Canons. Candidates are now required to present to the bishop of the diocese 'testimony of . . . former good life and behaviour from persons specified by the bishop'.

Leucius. The name of a (real or fictitious) companion of St *John the Apostle, to whom *inter alia* the apocryphal 'Acts of *John' is attributed. From the time of *Photius (Bibl. cod. 114), he was generally known as Leucius Charinus.

Leuenberg Concord. A statement of concord between the *Lutheran and *Reformed Churches of both E. and W. Europe adopted at Leuenberg in Switzerland on 16 Mar. 1973. It affirms that their common understanding of the Gospel enables them to declare and realize Church fellowship; 16th cent. disagreements on the Lord's Supper, Christology, and *predestination are revoked, and diversity in worship and Church order are accepted. The Concord was signed by more than 60 Churches. It pledged the signatories to continuing discussions; these have taken place both on a regional basis and in full assemblies at Sigtuna in Sweden in 1976 and at Driebergen in the Netherlands in 1981. While the Concord was criticized by some conservative Lutherans, it brought intercommunion and provided a framework for further growing together between the Churches.

Text and introd. by W. Lohff, *Die Konkordie reformatorischer Kirchen in Europa: Leuenberger Konkordie* (Frankfurt, 1985). Eng. tr. of the text in *Ecumenical Review*, 25 (1973), pp. 355–9; also, of the Concord and certain preliminary documents in *Lutheran World*, 20 (1973), pp. 347–53. The *Lutheran World* material, with introd, repr. in J. A. Andrews and J. A. Burgess (eds.), *An Invitation to Action: The Lutheran–Reformed Dialogue, Series III, 1981–1983* (Philadelphia, 1984), pp. 61–73.

Leutholf, Hiob. See LUDOLF, HIOB.

Levellers, 17th-cent. English political and religious party. They were opposed to kingship and advocated complete freedom in religion and a wide extension of the suffrage. The name, to which they themselves objected, first occurs in 1647. Mainly supported by the Army, they found their chief leader in J. Lilburne, who, in *The Case of the Army Truly Stated* (1647), urged the dissolution of Parliament and its re-establishment on democratic lines. In 1648 Lilburne was temporarily imprisoned and his party was treated by O. *Cromwell with marked suspicion. After the execution of *Charles I (1649), they resumed their agitation, demanding the dissolution of the Council of State and a reformed Parliament; and Lilburne and other leaders were again arrested. Mutinies in the Army were suppressed, and the Levellers faded out after making contact with *Charles II in exile. By the *Restoration (1660) they had almost completely disappeared.

W. Haller and G. Davies (eds.), *The Leveller Tracts* (New York, 1944); D. M. Wolfe (ed.), *Leveller Manifestoes of the Puritan Revolution* (1944); G. E. Aylmer (ed.), *The Levellers in the English Revolution* (1975). W. Haller (ed.), *Tracts on Liberty in the Puritan Revolution* (Records of Civilization, Sources and Studies, 18; 3 vols., New York, 1934–7); A. S. P. Woodhouse (ed.), *Puritanism and Liberty: Being the Army Debates (1646–9) from the Clarke Manuscripts with Supplementary Documents* (1939); J. R. McMichael and B. Taft (eds.), *The Writings of William Walwyn* (Athens, Ga., and London [1989]). J. Frank, *The Levellers: A History of the Writings of Three Seventeenth-Century Social Democrats: John Lilburne, Richard Overton, William Walwyn* (Cambridge, Mass., 1955); H. N. Brailsford, *The Levellers and the English Revolution*, ed. [J. E.] C. Hill (1961); C. B. Macpherson, *The Political Theory of Possessive Individualism: Hobbes to Locke* (Oxford, 1962), pp. 107–59; [J. E.] C. Hill, *The World Turned Upside Down* (1972), esp. chs. 4 and 7; J. C. Davis, 'The Levellers and Christianity', in B. Manning (ed.), *Politics, Religion and the English Civil War* (1973), pp. 225–50; A. [H.] Woolrych, *Soldiers and Statesmen: The General Council of the Army and its Debates, 1647–1648* (Oxford, 1987). M. [P.] Ashley, *John Wildman: Plotter and Postmaster* (1947); P. [E.] Gregg, *Free-born John: A Biography of John Lilburne* (1961); M. Gimelfarb-Brack, *Liberté, Égalité, Fraternité, Justice! La vie et l'œuvre de Richard Overton, Niveleur* (Berne, 1979).

Levi, son of Alphaeus. The tax-gatherer whom the Lord called to be one of His disciples (Mk. 2: 14). He is apparently to be identified with St *Matthew (Mt. 9: 9; 10: 3).

Leviathan. A mythological sea-serpent or dragon, mentioned several times in the Ugaritic texts, the OT, and later Jewish literature. The leviathan of Ps. 104: 26 has sometimes been identified with a whale, that of Job. 41: 1 (AV, RV, RSV, and NRSV) with a crocodile. The name was transferred to the devil (e.g. Is. 27: 1). T. *Hobbes gave his famous treatise (1651) on 'the matter, form and power of a Commonwealth, ecclesiastical and civil' this title on the ground that the commonwealth was 'that great Leviathan, or rather, to speak more reverently ... that mortal god, to which we owe under the immortal God, our peace and defence'.

J. Day, *God's Conflict with the Dragon and the Sea* (Cambridge, 1985), pp. 62–75; id. in *Anchor Bible Dictionary*, 4 (1992), pp. 295 f.

levirate marriage (Lat. *levir*, 'husband's brother'), the marriage of a man with his brother's widow. The Mosaic legislation (Deut. 25: 5–10) required that if a man died, leaving his widow without offspring, his surviving brother should marry the widow so that he might not be without descendants. Reference is made to the practice in the question on the *resurrection of the dead put by the *Sadducees (Mk. 12: 19, etc); but it seems probable that by NT times the requirement was already a dead letter. In the *Talmud, the subject is dealt with in the tractate 'Jebamoth'. For canonical legislation, see AFFINITY.

Levites. Members of one of the twelve tribes, descended from Levi, one of the sons of *Jacob, and acc. to the biblical account specially set apart as ministers of the sanctuary. Some modern scholars, however, have doubted the existence of such a tribe and have held that the term 'Levite' designated primarily a priestly functionary and that only when the function became hereditary was the idea of a tribe developed, with Levi as a quasi-fictional eponymous ancestor. In the *Deuteronomic legislation, the terms 'priest' and 'Levite' are virtually interchangeable and are sometimes used in apposition. In the 7th and 8th cents. BC, the Levites came to be distinguished from the priests, the latter term being restricted to those of Levitical descent who could trace their ancestry through Zadok. Acc. to Ezek. 44: 10–4, the Levites were now allotted only the inferior duties in the *Temple: they provided the officers and judges, the porters and players of musical instruments, and they were to slay the burnt offerings and sacrifice for the people. After the Exile their status improved. Acc. to 1 Chron. 15: 15, they had had the prerogative of carrying the *Ark, and their role as musicians was seen as having been so important that two groups of Psalms are attributed to them (the 'Psalms of the sons of Korah', Pss. 42–9, and the 'Psalms of the sons of Asaph', Pss. 50 and 70–83). Their status in NT times is confirmed by Lk. 10: 32. In the Middle Ages, the term *levitae* was applied to *deacons.

The subject is regularly discussed in works on the Pentateuch and in histories of the OT sacrificial system. G. E. Wright, 'The Levites in Deuteronomy', *Vetus Testamentum*, 4 (1954), pp. 325–30; J. A. Emerton, 'Priests and Levites in Deuteronomy', ibid. 12 (1962), pp. 129–38. E. Nielsen, 'The Levites in Ancient Israel', *Annual of the Swedish Theological Institute*, 3 (1964), pp. 16–27. R. de Vaux, OP, *Les Institutions de l'Ancien Testament*, 2 (1960), pp. 213–31, 254–63, with bibl. pp. 447 f.; Eng. tr. (2nd edn., 1965), pp. 358–71, 388–94, with bibl. pp. 544 f.; E. *Schürer, *The History of the Jewish People in the Age of Jesus Christ*, rev. Eng. tr. by G. Vermes and others, 2 (Edinburgh, 1979), pp. 250–6. G. Hölscher in *PW* 12 (pt. 2; 1925), cols. 2155–208, s.v. 'Levi'. See also works cited under PRIEST.

Leviticus, Book of. The third Book of the *Pentateuch. The English title follows the Gk. and Lat. versions, the Hebrew title (וַיִּקְרָא, 'And he called') being the first word of the text. The Book consists almost wholly of legislation, the general subjects of which are sacrifice (1–10), ritual purification and holiness (11–26), and vows and tithes (27). Acc. to modern critical theories, the bulk of the Book, except chs. 17–26, is derived from the Priestly document ('P') and is thus not earlier than the 6th cent. BC, while 17–26, which form a clearly defined unity and are generally known as 'The *Holiness Code' (q.v.), seem to be older than the rest. The language and theology of Lev. are reflected in the terminology and conceptions of certain NT writers, notably the author of Heb., where the priesthood of Christ is contrasted with the Levitical priesthood, and the ritual and aim of the Jewish Day of *Atonement (Lev. 16, 23: 26 ff.) are explained as receiving their full significance and final realization in Christ's atoning death (Heb. 9 and 10).

Comm. by M. *Noth (Das Alte Testament Deutsch, 6; 1962; Eng. tr., 1965), K. Elliger (HAT, Reihe 1. 4; 1966), N. H. Snaith (Cent. Bib., new edn., on Lev. and Num., 1967, pp. 28–178), J. R. Porter (Camb. Bib, NEB, 1976), G. J. Wenham (New International Comm. on the OT, 1979), and J. E. Hartley (Word Biblical Comm., 4; Dallas [1992]). R. de Vaux, OP, Les Sacrifices de l'Ancien Testament (Cahiers de la Revue Biblique, 1; 1964), pp. 28–96 passim; Eng. tr. (Cardiff, 1966), pp. 27–108 passim. [M.] M. Douglas, Purity and Danger: An Analysis of Concepts of Pollution and Taboo (1966), pp. 41–57. J. Milgrom, Cult and Conscience: The Asham and Priestly Doctrine of Repentance (Studies in Judaism in Late Antiquity, 18; Leiden, 1976), passim. L. L. Grabbe, Leviticus (Old Testament Guides; Sheffield, 1993). B. A. Levine in Anchor Bible Dictionary, 4 (1992), pp. 311–21, s.v.

Lewis, Clive Staples (1893–1963), scholar and Christian apologist. Born in Belfast, he was educated mainly privately until he entered University College, Oxford, in 1917. He was Tutor and Fellow of Magdalen College, Oxford, from 1925 to 1956, when he was appointed Professor of Medieval and Renaissance Literature in the University of Cambridge. His critical works include The Allegory of Love (1936), A Preface to Paradise Lost (1942), and English Literature in the Sixteenth Century (vol. 3 of the Oxford History of English Literature, 1954). At Magdalen Lewis underwent a gradual conversion experience described in his spiritual autobiography, Surprised by Joy (pub. 1955). He became widely known as a Christian apologist through a series of broadcast talks given between 1941 and 1944 and later published in book form, and through a number of other popular religious works which had a very wide circulation; these included The Problem of Pain (1940), The Screwtape Letters (1942; ostensibly from a senior devil to his nephew, a junior devil), and Miracles (1947). His clarity, wit, and skill as a communicator meant that he, like D. L. *Sayers and Charles *Williams, carried considerable weight; many Christians had their faith confirmed and a number of agnostics were brought closer to the Christian faith through reading his works. Lewis also published three science fiction novels with a strong Christian flavour: Out of the Silent Planet (1938), Perelandra (1943), and That Hideous Strength (1945). A series of seven 'Narnia' stories for children began in 1950 with The Lion, the Witch and the Wardrobe. In 1956 he married Joy Gresham (née Davidman); A Grief Observed (originally pub. under a pseudonym in 1961) is a profound treatment of bereavement written after her death. A group of his friends, including Charles Williams, was known as 'The Inklings'; they met regularly for many years in his rooms to talk and read aloud their works.

Letters of C. S. Lewis, ed., with a memoir, by W. H. Lewis [brother] (1966); They Stand Together: The Letters of C. S. Lewis to Arthur Greeves (1914–1963), ed. W. Hooper (1979). R. L. Green and W. Hooper, C. S. Lewis: A Biography (1974); A. N. Wilson, C. S. Lewis: A Biography (1990). P. L. Holmer, C. S. Lewis: The Shape of his Faith and Thought (1976). H. Carpenter,

The Inklings (1978). J. A. W. Bennett in DNB, 1961–1970 (1981), pp. 651–3.

libellatici. The name given to those who during the *Decian persecution (249–51) had procured certificates ('libelli pacis') by purchase from the civil authorities stating that they had sacrificed to the pagan idols when, in fact, no such sacrifice had been offered. The practice was condemned by the Church authorities, but those guilty of the circumvention were treated more leniently than those who had actually sacrificed (the 'sacrificati').

The chief authority is the correspondence of St *Cyprian and the same writer's De Lapsis. Several actual libelli, from among the Egyptian papyri, have been pub. since 1897 by U. Wilcken, C. Wessely, P. M. Mayer, and others; cf. summary report in J. R. Knipfing, 'Libelli of the Decian Persecution', HTR 16 (1923), pp. 345–90. A. Bludau, Die ägyptischen Libelli und die Christenverfolgung des Kaisers Decius (RQ, Suppl. 27; 1931). R. Andreotti, 'Religione ufficiale e culto dell'imperatore nei "Libelli" di Decio', in Studi in onore di Aristide Calderini e Roberto Paribeni, 1 (Milan, 1956), pp. 369–76. P. Keresztes, Imperial Rome and the Christians, 2 (New York and London [1989]), pp. 43–65. See also works cited under PERSECUTIONS, EARLY CHRISTIAN.

Libelli Missarum. The name given to the precursors of the *Sacramentary. They were booklets containing the formularies for one or more Masses for a given period for the use of a particular church. They did not include the *Canon, which was fixed, the readings from Scripture or the parts which were sung. They formed the link between the period of free composition and the organization of fixed formularies in a Sacramentary. No examples have survived, but there are literary references to them and the so-called *Leonine Sacramentary contains a series of them.

The fundamental work is A. Stuiber, Libelli Sacramentorum Romani (Theophaneia, 6; Bonn, 1950). F. L. Cross, 'Early Western Liturgical Manuscripts', JTS NS 16 (1965), pp. 61–7. Vogel, Sources, pp. 37–43.

Liber Antiphonarius. See ANTIPHONAL.

Liber Censuum. The official register of the Roman Church, which recorded the dues (census) payable by various institutions, esp. monasteries, churches, cities, dominions, and kingdoms, to the Holy See. It was drawn up by Cencio Savelli (later Pope *Honorius III), the 'chamberlain' of Clement III (Pope, 1187–91) and *Celestine III (Pope, 1191–8). It drew extensively on the Liber Canonum of the younger *Anselm of Lucca, the Collectio Canonum attributed to Deusdedit (Pope, 616–18), the Liber Politicus of Canon Benedict (fl. c.1140), and other sources. The original MS is preserved in the *Vatican (lat. 8486). Besides the list of census, it contains a list of the bishoprics and monasteries directly dependent on the Holy See, a treatise Mirabilia Urbis Romae, and other documents.

Crit. edn. by P. Fabre (d. 1899) and L. *Duchesne, completed by G. Mollat (3 vols., Bibliothèque des Écoles Françaises d'Athènes et de Rome, 2nd ser.; '1910'–52). V. Pfaff, 'Der Liber Censuum von 1192', Vierteljahrschrift für Sozial- und Wirtschaftsgeschichte, 44 (1957), pp. 78–96, 105–20, 220–42, 325–51. P. Fabre, Étude sur le Liber Censuum de l'Église de Rome (1892). R. Elze, 'Der Liber Censuum des Cencius (Cod. Vat. lat. 8486) von 1192 bis 1228. Zur Überlieferung des Kaiserkrönungsordo Censius II', Bullettino dell' 'Archivio Paleografico Italiano', NS 2–3 (pt. 1; 1956–7), pp. 251–70. H. *Leclercq, OSB, in DACL 9 (pt. 1;

1929), cols. 180–220, s.v. 'Liber Censuum Romanae Ecclesiae', with further bibl.; M. Michaud in *DDC* 3 (1942), cols. 233–53, s.v. 'Censuum (Liber)'.

Liber Comicus. See COMES.

Liber de Causis. A treatise, consisting for the most part of extracts from *Proclus' 'Elements of Theology', which was put together in Arabic by an unknown Muslim philosopher, prob. in Baghdad, *c*.850. It exercised an important influence on medieval philosophy through Gerard of Cremona, who translated it into Latin at Toledo between 1167 and 1187. Following its title in Arabic, he announced it as a work of *Aristotle, with the result that many *Neoplatonist doctrines were mistakenly held to be Aristotelian. *William of Moerbeke's translation of Proclus' 'Elements of Theology' into Latin (completed on 18 May 1268) revealed to St *Thomas Aquinas and medieval philosophers generally the true character of the *Liber de Causis*.

Arab. text, with Ger. tr. and version of Gerard of Cremona, in O. *Bardenhewer, *Die pseudo-aristotelische Schrift Ueber das reine Gute, bekannt unter dem Namen Liber de Causis* (Freiburg, 1882). Crit. edn. of Lat. text, with introd. and notes by A. Pattin in *Tijdschrift voor Filosofie*, 28 (1966), pp. 90–203. It is also conveniently pr. in R. Steele (ed.), *Opera hactenus inedita Rogeri Baconi*, 12 (Oxford, 1935), pp. 161–87. H. D. Saffrey, OP, *Sancti Thomae de Aquino Super Librum de Causis Expositio* (Textus Philosophici Friburgenses, 4–5; 1954). R. C. Taylor, 'The *Kalām fī Maḥd al-khair* (*Liber de causis*) in the Islamic Philosophical Milieu', in J. Kraye and others (eds.), *Pseudo-Aristotle in the Middle Ages: The Theology and Other Texts* (Warburg Institute Surveys and Texts, 11; 1986), pp. 37–52; see also C. H. Lohr, ibid., pp. 53–62. L. Sweeney in *NCE* 8 (1967), pp. 693 f., s.v.

Liber Gradualis. See GRADUAL.

Liber Pontificalis (Lat., 'the Papal Book'). A collection of early Papal biographies. The account of each Pope is written acc. to a regular plan, with stereotyped formulae and exact chronological data. The biographies of the earliest Popes are quite short, but from the 4th cent. onwards they tend gradually to increase in size until those of the 8th–9th cents. have the dimensions of a small book. The whole is prefaced by an apocryphal letter of Pope *Damasus to St *Jerome, begging him to provide a history of the Popes from St Peter down to his own times. The work was issued in a series of 'editions', which were brought up to date by the addition of later Lives. The earliest form of it, which was dependent on the *Liberian Catalogue (354), appears to have been the work of a Roman presbyter at the time of Boniface II (530–2). Subsequent redactions carry the history down to the death of *Martin V (1431), and even later.

Important crit. edns. by L. *Duchesne (2 vols., Bibliothèque des Écoles Françaises d'Athènes et de Rome, 2nd ser. 3; 1886–92 + further vol. of additions and corrections by C. Vogel, ibid., 1957) and T. *Mommsen (*MGH*, Gesta Pontificum Romanorum, 1, vol. 1, to AD 715, all pub., 1898). Eng. tr. of section to 715, with introd. by R. Davis, *The Book of Pontiffs* (Translated Texts for Historians, Latin Series, 5; Liverpool, 1989); of section 715–817 by id., *The Lives of the Eighth-Century Popes* (Translated Texts for Historians, 13; ibid., 1992); of section 817–91 by id., *The Lives of the Ninth-Century Popes* (ibid. 20; 1995). L. Duchesne, *Étude sur le* Liber Pontificalis (Bibliothèque des Écoles

Françaises d'Athènes et de Rome, 1st ser. 1; 1877; esp. on MSS). J. B. *Lightfoot, *Apostolic Fathers*, 1. 1 (S. Clement of Rome; 2nd edn., 1890), pp. 303–25. O. Bertolini, 'Il "Liber Pontificalis" ', *Settimane di Studio del Centro Italiano di Studi sull'Alto Medioevo*, 17 (1970), pp. 387–455. C. Vogel, 'Le "Liber Pontificalis" dans l'Édition de Louis Duchesne', in *Monseigneur Duchesne et son temps: Actes du Colloque organisé par l'École Française de Rome (Palais Farnèse, 23–25 mai 1973)* (Collection de l'École Française de Rome, 23; 1975), pp. 99–127; cf. also pp. 129–40. J. P. Kirsch in *CE* 9 (1910), pp. 224–6; H. *Leclercq, OSB, in *DACL* 9 (pt. 1; 1930), cols. 354–460; E. Josi in *EC* 7 (1951), cols. 1278–82; all s.v. and with further bibl.

Liber Praedestinatus. See PRAEDESTINATUS.

Liber Regalis. The book containing the English *Coronation Service introduced for the crowning of Edward II in 1308. The rubrics were extended for Richard II (1377). The book was translated into English for *James I (1603), and continued in use until discarded by *James II in 1685. Its unknown compiler possessed considerable competence and knowledge. Among its many new features were the introduction of the *seven Penitential Psalms, of the *Veni Creator Spiritus*, and the homage of the peers after the enthronement. Several 14th- and 15th-cent. MSS survive.

Text ed., with Eng. tr., by L. G. Wickham Legg, *English Coronation Records* (1901), pp. 81–130. E. C. Ratcliff, *The English Coronation Service* (1936). See also other works cited under CORONATION RITE IN ENGLAND.

Liber Sacramentorum. See SACRAMENTARY.

liber vitae (Lat., 'book of life'). A name occasionally given in the early Church to the *diptychs, i.e. the lists of those who were recognized members of the Christian community. It was doubtless derived from the references in Scripture to the '*book of life' (e.g. Rev. 3: 5).

liberal arts, seven. See SEVEN LIBERAL ARTS.

Liberal Evangelicalism. The outlook of those within the C of E who, while maintaining their spiritual kinship with the *Evangelical Revival, have been concerned to restate old truths, e.g. concerning the Atonement and the authority of the Bible, in terms thought to be more consonant with modern thought with its stress on historical method and the philosophy of personality. See also ANGLICAN EVANGELICAL GROUP MOVEMENT.

T. G. Rogers (ed.), *Liberal Evangelicalism. By Members of the Church of England* (1923).

liberalism. The word, which came into use early in the 19th cent., has been defined as 'the holding of liberal opinions in politics or theology'. In theology it has been used with many different shades of meaning. If taken to mean freedom from bigotry and readiness to welcome new ideas or proposals for reform, it is a characteristic which many people will readily profess, but in itself it gives no indication of their beliefs or aspirations. There have been 'Liberal Catholics', 'Liberal Protestants', and 'Liberal Evangelicals'; but all that they have had in common is a general tendency to favour freedom and progress. Such a tendency may lead to many different results. The 'Liberal Catholics' who formed a distinguished group in the RC Church in

the 19th cent. were for the most part theologically orthodox, but they favoured political democracy and ecclesiastical reform. Père H. D. *Lacordaire (1802–61), the famous
French Dominican, said: 'I die a penitent Catholic, but an
impenitent Liberal.' 'Liberal Protestantism', on the other
hand, developed into an anti-dogmatic and humanitarian
reconstruction of the Christian faith which at one time
appeared to be gaining ground in nearly all the Protestant
Churches.

The word is sometimes also used of the belief in secular
or anthropocentric humanism which has its origins in the
Renaissance and which is quite inconsistent with biblical
and dogmatic orthodoxy. It was in this sense that the
*Tractarians were fiercely opposed to liberalism. On the
other hand, by many orthodox Christians the word 'liberal'
is felt to have positive associations of great value. Hence
the confusion which surrounds its use.

Liberation Theology. A theological movement that
came to prominence in the second Conference of Latin
American bishops (CELAM) held at Medellín in Columbia in 1968 at the request of Pope *Paul VI. A third Conference under *John Paul II was held at Puebla (in
*Mexico) in 1979. In the interval the Medellín meeting
had given impetus to a great flowering of theological
reflection, as well as to numerous practical measures. The
term 'liberation' stems from dislike of 'development',
which is understood to imply an imposed solution to
South America's problems, determined by the industrialized nations and involving no real initiative on the part of
the people.

Of the theological writings of the movement, the Peruvian Gustavo Gutierrez's *Teología de la liberación*, published
at Lima in 1971 (Eng. tr., *A Theology of Liberation*, 1974),
has attained the status of a minor classic. He has been
followed by a large number of other writers, most of whose
works have been translated into English and so in turn
influenced related movements such as *Black and
*Feminist Theology. Other important figures include two
Brazilians, Hugo Assmann and Leonardo Boff, until
recently OFM, the Argentinians José Míguez Bonino (a
Protestant) and Jan Luis Segundo, José P. Miranda of
Mexico, and Jan Sobrino, SJ, in San Salvador. All have
been influenced in varying degrees by Karl Marx and
20th-cent. Marxist philosophers such as Louis Althusser
and Ernst Bloch, but they would insist that this is so only
with regard to Marx's sociological analysis and not to his
ideological commitments on religion and materialism. The
salient features of their thought are: (1) a preferential
option for the poor, that is the idea that the Church's
primary duty in a situation of oppression is to support the
poor; (2) liberation is regarded as an essential element in
salvation, since salvation is concerned with the whole man
and not just his spiritual needs; (3) the *Exodus is taken
as the biblical paradigm, since individual salvation can
come only through social transformation; (4) Christ's
apparent lack of involvement in politics is countered by
saying that His teaching was in fact highly political (e.g.
by Miranda), or by maintaining that His confrontation was
really with social structures (e.g. by Sobrino and
Segundo); (5) the priority of praxis, the view that right
belief (orthodoxy) can issue only from right action
(orthopraxis); and (6) structural or institutional violence,

the view that structures that coerce are no less violent than
the actual physical use of force. In 1984 the Sacred Congregation for the Doctrine of the Faith (formerly the
*Holy Office), under the aegis of Cardinal Ratzinger,
issued 'Libertatis Nuntius'. While endorsing 'a preferential option for the poor', it was severely critical of the use
of Marxist analyses in Liberation Theology, arguing that
it is impossible to separate analysis and ideology, and it
rejected any suggestion that orthopraxis takes precedence
over orthodoxy. In the same year Leonardo Boff was summoned to Rome to answer charges made on the basis of his
Igreja: Carisma e poder (Petropolis, 1981; Eng. tr., *Church,
Charism and Power*, 1985). Despite the support of two cardinals who accompanied him, Boff was required to submit
to an indefinite period of 'obedient silence'; in 1992 he was
secularized. His writings are in fact more moderate than
those of many others, and the main source of concern
seems to have been the way in which he applied the principles of Liberation Theology to the structures of ecclesiastical authority. In 1986 the Sacred Congregation issued
a further Instruction, 'Libertatis Conscientia', which many
have read as offering a more favourable assessment of the
contribution of Liberation Theology. Certainly some of its
concerns and terminology figure prominently in John Paul
II's encyclical 'Sollicitudo Rei Socialis' (1987), but against
this must be set his continuing promotion of leading critics
of the movement, most notably perhaps in the appointment of Alfonso López Trujillo as Abp. of Medellín in
1979 (made a cardinal in 1983) and José Cardoso Sobrinho
in succession to Helder *Câmara as Abp. of Recife in 1985.

The most obvious practical expression of Liberation
Theology has been in the growth of *comunidades eclesiales
de base*, small communities of 15–20 families that are led
by laymen and try to integrate spiritual and social issues.
There are over 70,000 of these in *Brazil alone, and in El
Salvador they were consulted by Abp. O. A. *Romero
both over decisions and in the composition of some of his
pastoral letters. Under the influence of the educationalist
Paulo Freire one aim all such base communities share is
concientización, making people more aware of their situation and rights. On occasion this has led to the endorsement of a specific political party, as in the case of the poet
and priest, Ernesto Cardenal, in Solentiname in Nicara-
gua, where active support for the Sandinista guerillas was
encouraged, Cardenal himself along with several other
priests eventually joining the Revolutionary Government
after the overthrow of the Somoza dictatorship in 1979.
Of the religious orders the *Jesuits have been prominent
as has the Catholic Foreign Mission Society of America at
Maryknoll, NY. In their attitudes to the use of force, positions have ranged from, at the one end, the pacifism of
Abp. H. Câmara in Brazil that was combined with fearless
denunciation of the abuse of rights under General Branco,
to open resort to arms at the other, as with the minority
who followed the example of Fr. Camilo Torres who was
killed while resisting the government in Colombia in 1966.

Exponents of Liberation Theology include: J. P. Miranda,
Marx y la biblia (Salamanca, 1971; Eng. tr., *Marx and the Bible*,
Maryknoll, NY, 1974; London, 1977); E. [D.] Dussel, *Caminos de
liberación latinoamericana* (Buenos Aires, 1972; Eng. tr., *History
and the Theology of Liberation*, Maryknoll, NY, 1976); H.
Assmann, *Teología desde la praxis de la liberación* (Salamanca, 1973;
Eng. tr., *Practical Theology of Liberation*, 1975); J. L. Segundo,

Liberación de la teología (Buenos Aires, 1975; Eng. tr., *The Liberation of Theology*, New York, 1976); J. Míguez Bonino, *Revolutionary Theology comes of Age* (1975; in USA entitled, *Doing Theology in a Revolutionary Situation*, Philadelpha, 1975); E. Cardenal, *El Evangelio en Solentiname* (2 vols, Salamanca, 1975–7; Eng. tr., *The Gospel in Solentiname*, 4 vols, Maryknoll, NY, 1976–82); J. Sobrino, SJ, *Cristología desde américa latina* (Mexico, 1976; rev. Eng. tr., *Christology at the Crossroads*, 1978); id., *Resurreción de la verdadera Iglesia: Los pobres, lugar teológico de la eclesiología* (Santander, 1981; Eng. tr., *The True Church of the Poor*, 1984); L. Boff, OFM, *A Graça liberadora* (Petropolis, 1977; Eng. tr., *Liberating Grace*, Maryknoll, NY, 1981); P. Berryman, *The Religious Roots of Rebellion* (1984). Useful collection of works, by L. Boff and others, in Eng. tr., in the series 'Liberation and Theology' (Maryknoll, NY, and Tunbridge Wells, 1987 ff.). A. T. Hennelly (ed.), *Liberation Theology: A Documentary History* (Maryknoll, NY, 1990). P. E. Sigmund, *Liberation Theology at the Crossroads: Democracy or Revolution?* (New York and Oxford, 1990).

The text of 'Libertatis Nuntius' pub. in *AAS* 76 (1984), pp. 876–909; 'Libertatis Conscientia', ibid. 79 (1987), pp. 554–99. Eng. trs. were pub. by the *Catholic Truth Society, *Instruction on Certain Aspects of the Theology of Liberation* (CTS pamphlet Do 560; 1984) and *Instruction on Christian Freedom and Liberation* (pamphlet Do 570; 1986). Other critics incl. R. Vekemans, SJ, *Iglesia y mundo político; sacerdocio y política* (Lima, 1970; Eng. tr., *Caesar and God*, Maryknoll, NY, 1972); A. Fierro, *El evangelio beligerante* (Estella, Navarra, 1975; Eng. tr., *The Militant Gospel*, 1977); E. [R.] Norman, *Christianity and the World Order* (Reith Lectures, 1978; Oxford, 1979); D. P. McCann, *Christian Realism and Liberation Theology* (Maryknoll, NY [1981]); J. V. Schall, *Liberation Theology in Latin America* (San Francisco, 1982). M. Novak, *The Spirit of Democratic Capitalism* (New York [1982]), chs. 17–18.

Liberian Catalogue. An early list of the Popes down to *Liberius (352–66). It is one of the items in a collection of documents made by a compiler known (since T. *Mommsen's studies) as the '*Chronographer of 354' (q.v.). Its earlier section, which goes down to Pope Pontianus (230–5) and appears to be dependent on a list in the 'Chronicle' of St *Hippolytus, is less reliable than its latter half. First edited by the Jesuit, A. Bucherius, at Antwerp in 1636, it used sometimes to be called the 'Bucherian Catalogue'.

For edns., see art. CHRONOGRAPHER OF AD 354. Text also pr. in *LP* (Duchesne), 1 (1886), pp. 1–12. Eng. tr. in R. Davis, *The Book of Pontiffs* (Translated Texts for Historians, Latin Series, 5; Liverpool, 1989), pp. 93–6. Critical discussions in H. *Lietzmann, *Petrus und Paulus in Rom* (2nd edn., 1927), esp. pp. 1–28, and E. Caspar, *Die älteste römische Bischofsliste* (Schriften der Königsberger gelehrten Gesellschaft, 2, Geisteswissenschaftliche Klasse, Heft 4; 1926), pp. [170–8] (pp. 384–92 of vol. 2 of the Schriften). C. Pietri, *Roma Christiana: Recherches sur l'Église de Rome . . . (311–440)* (Bibliothèque des Écoles françaises d'Athènes et de Rome, 224; 2 vols., 1976), 1, pp. 389–97.

Liberius, Pope from 352 to 366. Ordered by the *Arian Emperor, Constantius, to assent to the condemnation of St *Athanasius as a rebel, Liberius refused and was banished from Rome in 355. In 357 he submitted to Constantius, after a collapse of his morale which can be traced in four letters ('Studens pace', 'Pro deifico', 'Quia scio', and 'Non doceo') preserved by *Hilary of Poitiers. In 358 he was permitted to reoccupy his see, having agreed to the deposition of Athanasius and having signed a confession of faith passed at a council of Sirmium (prob. that of 351, not the 'Blasphemy of *Sirmium') which, while not mentioning the *homoousion, is otherwise orthodox. St

*Jerome and Athanasius agree that his subscription was forced. He built a celebrated church on the Esquiline Hill (the 'Basilica Liberiana') which was the ancestor of the present *Santa Maria Maggiore. Though his name does not appear in modern calendars, his feast occurs on 23 Sept. in the *Hieronymian Martyrology.

Letters and other writings mainly repr. from P. *Coustant in J. P. Migne, *PL* 8. 1349–1410; crit. text of the nine Epp. found in Hilary by A. L. Feder (CSEL 65; 1916). A Sermon of Liberius survives in a modified form in *Ambrose, *De Virginibus*, 3. 1–3 (text in *PL* 8. 1345–50). A. L. Feder, *Studien zu Hilarius von Poitiers*, 1 (Vienna, 1910), pp. 153–83; cf. also *LP* (Duchesne), 1, pp. 207–10. E. Caspar, *Geschichte des Papsttums*, 1 (1930), pp. 166–95. M. Simonetti, *La crisi ariana nel IV secolo* (Studia Ephemerides 'Augustinianum', 11; 1975), esp. pp. 216–43, 395–7. C. Pietri, *Roma Christiana: Recherches sur l'Église de Rome . . . (311–440)* (Bibliothèque des Écoles françaises d'Athènes et de Rome, 224; 2 vols., 1976), 1, pp. 237–68. C. Dagens, 'Autour du pape Libère. L'Iconographie de Suzanne et des martyrs romains sur l'Arcosolium de Celerina', *Mélanges d'Archéologie et d'Histoire*, 88 (1966), pp. 327–81. H. *Leclercq, OSB, in *DACL* 9 (pt. 1; 1930), cols. 497–530; É Amann in *DTC* 9 (pt. 1; 1926), cols. 631–59; P. T. Camelot, OP, in *NCE* 8 (1967), pp. 714–16, s.v.

Library of the Fathers. The series of English translations of selected writings of the early Christian Fathers, published under the inspiration of the *Oxford Movement. The first volume to appear was the *Confessions* of St *Augustine (1838; edited by E. B. *Pusey).

H. P. *Liddon, *Life of Edward Bouverie Pusey*, 1 (1893), pp. 409–47. R. W. Pfaff, 'The Library of the Fathers: The Tractarians as Patristic Translators', *Studies in Philology*, 70 (1973), pp. 329–44.

Libri Carolini. See CAROLINE BOOKS.

licences, marriage. See MARRIAGE LICENCES.

Lichfield. The seat of the Mercian diocese under St *Chad, it was constituted an archbishopric in 787. Though the Abp. retained his title at least until 799, he gradually lost control over his suffragans and in 803 the see was again formally subjected to the authority of *Canterbury. Despite the nominal removal of the see to *Chester in 1075 and to *Coventry in 1095, Lichfield remained throughout the Middle Ages a centre of episcopal administration in the diocese. The formation of the Chester diocese in 1541, and various 19th-cent. changes, greatly reduced its importance. The present cathedral dates mainly from the 13th cent. An Anglican theological college in the city was founded in 1857; closed in 1972.

E. Hobhouse, 'The Register of Roger of Norbury, Bishop of Lichfield and Coventry, from A.D. 1322 to A.D. 1358. An Abstract of Contents and Remarks', in *Collections for a History of Staffordshire edited by the William Salt Archaeological Society*, 1 (1880), pp. 241–88; Registers of Bishop Robert de Stretton, 1358–1385, abstracted into Eng. by R. A. Wilson (ibid., NS 8 and 10, pt. 2; 1905–7); Register of John Catterick, 1415–9, ed. R. N. Swanson (Canterbury and York Society, 150; 1990). H. E. Savage (ed.), *The Great Register of Lichfield Cathedral known as* Magnum Registrum Album (William Salt Archaeological Society, for 1924; 1926). 'The Muniments of the Dean and Chapter of Lichfield', in *Fourteenth Report of the Historical Manuscripts Commission*, Appendix 8 (1895), pp. 205–36. J. W. Lamb, *The Archbishopric of Lichfield (787–803)* (1964). C. J. Godfrey, 'The Archbishopric of Lichfield', in C. W. Dugmore and C. Duggan (eds.), *Studies in Church*

History, 1 (1964), pp. 145–53. N. Brooks, *The Early History of the Church of Canterbury* (Leicester, 1984), pp. 118–27. T. Harwood, *The History and Antiquities of the Church and City of Lichfield* (Gloucester, 1806). There is much information on the cathedral and diocese in the 26 lectures given on St Chad's Day by H. E. Savage (Lichfield, 1913–37). On the glass in Lichfield Cathedral, Y. Vanden Bemden and J. Kerr, 'The Glass of Herkenrode Abbey', *Archaeologia*, 108 (1986), pp. 189–226. A. J. Kettle and D. A. Johnson in *VCH*, Stafford, 3, ed. M. W. Greenslade (1970), pp. 140–99. T. Barns in *DECH* (1912), pp. 322–6, s.v.

lich-gate. See LYCH-GATE.

Liddell, Henry George (1811–98), Greek lexicographer. He was educated at Charterhouse and *Christ Church, Oxford, where he became tutor (1836) and censor (1845). He was later headmaster of Westminster (1846–55) and Dean of Christ Church (1855–91). In 1852 he was appointed to sit on the commission for University Reform. Later he was a decisive influence in the radical plan of internal reconstruction embodied in the Christ Church, Oxford, Act of 1867. The famous Greek Lexicon, in which Liddell had the collaboration of R. *Scott (q.v.), appeared in a modest form in 1843, the original edition being based on the Greek–German lexicon of F. Passow, professor at Breslau. It was constantly revised and extended during Liddell's lifetime, the last (8th) edition being issued in 1897. It was later completely recast by H. Stuart Jones (1867–1939) and R. McKenzie (1887–1937), who greatly enlarged it by full attention to recent archaeological and papyrological discoveries, but with the exclusion of *patristic usages (issued in 10 parts, 1925–40, + supplement, 1968).

Memoir by H. L. Thompson (London, 1899). F. *Max Muller, 'Dean Liddell: as I knew him', *Fortnightly Review*, 71 (1899), pp. 10–24, repr. in Max Muller's *Last Essays*, First Series (*Collected Works*, 17; 1901), pp. 314–32. H. L. Thomson in *DNB*, Suppl. 3 (1901), pp. 94–6.

Liddon, Henry Parry (1829–90), Canon of *St Paul's. He was educated at King's College School, London, and *Christ Church, Oxford, where he held a Studentship until his death. He was successively one of W. J. *Butler's curates at Wantage (1852–4), first vice-principal of Cuddesdon Theological College (1854–9), and vice-principal of St Edmund Hall, Oxford (1859–62). At Cuddesdon he developed a ministry of spiritual direction which continued throughout his life. In the 1860s he began to exercise great influence in face of the post-Tractarian Oxford liberalism. In 1864 Bp. W. K. *Hamilton appointed him a prebendary of *Salisbury Cathedral and in 1870 he was installed as a Canon of St Paul's, where his powerful preaching attracted large audiences. In 1870 he was also appointed Dean Ireland's professor of exegesis at Oxford; this combination of offices strengthened his influence in the C of E, which he used chiefly for extending Catholic principles. He also stood firmly against the attempts made in the 1870s to lessen or abandon the use of the *Athanasian Creed in the C of E services. After resigning his professorship in 1882 he travelled extensively, esp. in Russia, Palestine, and Egypt. He was much interested in the *Old Catholics, and at the invitation of J. J. I. von *Döllinger, whom he visited in Munich many times, he attended the *Bonn Reunion Conferences. In 1886 he was

made chancellor of St Paul's. In his last years he watched with growing apprehension the spread of critical doctrines of the OT among the younger generation even of his own party, and the publication of *Lux Mundi* (1889) was a great grief to him. He was also a considerable, if hardly an original, theologian, whose *Bampton Lectures for 1866, on *The Divinity of Our Lord and Saviour Jesus Christ* (1867), were deservedly held in high repute as a well-argued defence of Christian orthodoxy. His intense admiration for E. B. *Pusey led him to devote himself assiduously in his later years to writing Pusey's life (4 vols., posthumously pub., 1893–7), and it was for this purpose that he resigned his professorship. Liddon House, in South Audley Street, was founded in his memory as a religious centre in London for educated Anglican Churchmen.

J. O. Johnston, *Life and Letters of Henry Parry Liddon* (London, 1904). Shorter Life by G. W. E. Russell (ibid., 1905). Centenary memoir with contributions by W. M. Whitley, T. B. Strong, D. *Stone, E. S. *Talbot, and A. B. Emden (ibid., 1929). [W.] O. Chadwick, *The Spirit of the Oxford Movement* (Cambridge, 1990), pp. 214–46 ('The Young Liddon'). H. Scott *Holland in *DNB* 33 (1893), pp. 223–8.

Lieber, Thomas. See ERASTIANISM.

Lietzmann, Hans (1875–1942), Church historian. He studied philosophy and theology at Jena and Bonn from 1893 to 1898. After being lecturer at Bonn from 1900 he was appointed professor at Jena in 1905. In 1924 he succeeded A. *Harnack at Berlin. His early studies were largely in the little-worked Greek patristic *catenae*, which bore fruit in a Catalogue (1902; in conjunction with G. Karo) and a series of *Catenenstudien* under his editorship. In 1904 there followed *Apollinaris von Laodicea und seine Schule*, which by a fresh attempt to distinguish the genuine and spurious works completely transformed Apollinarian studies. *Petrus und Paulus in Rom* (1915; 2nd edn., 1927) was the outcome of long archaeological and chronological researches. In the field of liturgy, he published an edition of the *Gregorian Sacramentary which derived from the ancient Aachen MS (1921), and *Messe und Herrenmahl* (1926; Eng. tr., Leiden, 1953–79), in which he sought to trace the Eucharistic rite back to two distinct primitive types. In his later years he issued a manual of Church history, *Geschichte der alten Kirche* (4 vols., 1932–44; Eng. tr., 1937–51). From 1902 onwards he edited *Kleine Texte für Vorlesungen und Übungen*, from 1906 the *Handbuch zum Neuen Testament* (to which he himself contributed the commentaries on Rom., Cor., and Gal.), and from 1920 the *Zeitschrift für die neutestamentliche Wissenschaft*.

Gedächtnisrede by H. Bornkamm and bibl. by K. Aland (490 items) in *ZNTW* 41 (1942), pp. 1–33. Three vols. of Lietzmann's *Kleine Schriften* ed. K. Aland in TU 67 (1958), 68 (1958), and 74 (1962; with reissue of items by H. Bornkamm and K. Aland just mentioned). K. Aland (ed.), *Glanz und Niedergang der deutschen Universität: 50 Jahre deutscher Wissenschaftsgeschichte in Briefen an und von Hans Lietzmann, 1892–1942* (1979).

Life and Work. The branch of the *Ecumenical Movement concerned with the relation of the Christian faith to society, politics, and economics. It held notable conferences at *Stockholm (1925) and *Oxford (1937). It owed its existence esp. to N. *Söderblom. See also FAITH AND ORDER, REUNION, and WORLD COUNCIL OF CHURCHES.

N. Karlström and N. Ehrenström in R. Rouse and S. C. Neill (eds.), *A History of the Ecumenical Movement 1517–1948* (1954), pp. 509–96.

Light of the World, the (Lat. *Lux Mundi*). A title of Christ, derived from Jn. 8: 12. It is the subject of Holman *Hunt's famous picture (of which the artist painted two copies, the one at Keble College, *Oxford, and the other at *St Paul's Cathedral).

J. Maas, *Holman Hunt and The Light of the World* (1984). See also other works cited s.v. HUNT, W. H.

Lightfoot, John (1602–75), biblical and *rabbinic scholar. Educated at Christ's College, Cambridge, he was from 1630 to 1642 rector of Ashley, Staffs. In 1643 he became one of the original and more influential members of the *Westminster Assembly, opposing the extreme *Presbyterians. In 1643 he became master of Catharine Hall, Cambridge, and rector of Much Munden, Herts, and held both offices for the rest of his life. He early developed an interest in Hebrew and Talmudic studies and in 1629 published *Erubhin; or Miscellanies, Christian and Judaical*, followed later by a book on *Genesis* (1642) and many further learned writings. He also materially assisted B. *Walton with the *Polyglot Bible which appeared in 1657. His best-known work, his series of *Horae Hebraicae et Talmudicae* (6 vols., 1658–78), was designed to show the bearing of Jewish studies on the interpretation of the NT. It is a mine of information and has never been wholly superseded.

Works in Eng. ed. G. Bright (2 vols., London, 1684); in Lat. [ed. J. Texelius] (2 vols., Rotterdam, 1686), also ed. J. Leusden (2 vols., Utrecht, 1699). Complete works ed. J. R. Pitman (13 vols., London, 1822–5). J. Hamilton in *DNB* 33 (1893), pp. 229–31.

Lightfoot, Joseph Barber (1828–89), Bp. of *Durham. He was educated at King Edward's School, Birmingham, where he made a lifelong friendship with E. W. *Benson (q.v.), and at Trinity College, Cambridge, where he was a private pupil of B. F. *Westcott (q.v.). He was ordained deacon in 1854 and priest in 1858. Becoming a tutor at Trinity College in 1857, he made classical and biblical subjects his main interest. In 1861 he succeeded C. J. *Ellicott as Hulsean professor of divinity, his lectures on the NT being the basis of his later commentaries. In 1871 he was appointed a Canon of *St Paul's and in 1875 Lady Margaret professor of divinity at Cambridge. From 1870 to 1880 he was also one of the leading members of the Company of Revisers of the NT. Having accepted the see of Durham with great reluctance (1879), he here proved himself a remarkably successful administrator, did much for the adornment of Auckland Castle, and personally trained many promising men for the priesthood.

The excellence of Lightfoot's critical work on the NT and the Fathers, which from the first won the highest recognition in Britain and beyond, has stood the test of time. His famous commentaries on St Paul's Epistles— *Galatians* (1865), *Philippians* (1868), and *Colossians with Philemon* (1875)—were marked by a wide and original patristic and classical erudition, lucid presentation, free-

dom from technicalities, and avoidance of sectional controversies; esp. notable were their long dissertations, e.g. the well-known essay on 'The Christian Ministry' in *Philippians*. The same qualities marked his work on the Apostolic Fathers, which perhaps showed an even greater mastery of learning and technique. His first edition of *Clement of Rome* appeared in 1869 (Appendix, 1877), a second and much extended recasting, revised in the light of the newly recovered full text, in 1890. In 1885 there followed his famous *Ignatius* (2 vols. in 3, 1885; 2nd edn., 1889), which finally disposed of W. *Cureton's contention that only the three Epp. in the Syriac recension were genuine. His other writings included *A Fresh Revision of the New Testament* (1871), the valuable art. 'Eusebius of Caesarea' in the *Dictionary of Christian Biography* (vol. 2, 1880), and several volumes of Sermons.

Brief account (attributed to H. W. Watkins) in *Quarterly Review*, 176 (1893), pp. 73–105, repr. separately, with prefatory note by B. F. Westcott (London, 1894). G. R. Eden and F. C. Macdonald (eds.), *Lightfoot of Durham: Memoirs and Appreciations* (1932). A. C. Benson, *The Leaves of the Tree* (1911), pp. 187–211. J. A. T. *Robinson, *Joseph Barber Lightfoot* (Durham Cathedral Lecture, 1981). F. J. A. *Hort in *DNB* 33 (1893), pp. 232–40.

Lightfoot, Robert Henry (1883–1953), NT scholar. Educated at Eton and at Worcester College, Oxford, after ordination he taught at Wells Theological College and at Oxford, where he was a Fellow of Lincoln College (1919–21) and of New College (1921–50) and Dean Ireland's professor of the exegesis of holy scripture (1934–49). His chief publications were *History and Interpretation in the Gospels* (*Bampton Lectures for 1934; 1935), *Locality and Doctrine in the Gospels* (1938), *The Gospel Message of St Mark* (1950), and *St John's Gospel* (1956; ed. C. F. Evans). From 1941 until his death he edited the *Journal of Theological Studies*. Influenced by German *Form Criticism, and by contemporary American scholarship, he was a pioneer of *Redaction Criticism. His work was marked by accuracy and caution, combined with scepticism regarding the historicity of the Gospel narratives. Of deep, if reticent, Christian faith, Lightfoot exercised a considerable influence, esp. on a group of younger Oxford NT students.

D. E. Nineham (ed.), *Studies in the Gospels: Essays in Memory of R. H. Lightfoot* (1955), with memoir, pp. vi–xvi. Obituary notice by R. L. P. Milburn in *Proceedings of the British Academy*, 40 (1954), pp. 253–61.

Lights, Feast of. See DEDICATION, THE JEWISH FEAST OF THE.

Ligugé, Defensor of. See DEFENSOR.

Liguori, St Alphonsus. See ALPHONSUS LIGUORI, ST.

Lima Document. See BAPTISM, EUCHARIST AND MINISTRY.

limbo. In Latin theology the abode of souls excluded from the full blessedness of the Beatific Vision, but not condemned to any other punishment. There are distinguished (1) the *limbus patrum*, in which the saints of the Old Covenant remained until Christ's coming and redemption of the world; and (2) the *limbus infantium*, the everlasting state of those who die unregenerate, e.g. unbaptized infants, and hence in *original sin, but innocent of personal guilt. Those in limbo are held to be excluded from supernatural beatitude, but, acc. to St *Thomas Aquinas, enjoy full natural happiness. St *Augustine, however, esp. in combating the *Pelagians, taught that all who die unbaptized, being in original sin, suffer some degree of positive punishment. The existence of limbo is a matter of theological opinion on which the Church has never pronounced definitively either way.

Limina Apostolorum. See AD LIMINA APOSTOLORUM.

Linacre, Thomas (c.1460–1524), humanist and founder of the Royal College of Physicians. He was among the first to cultivate Greek letters in England. He was educated at *Canterbury Cathedral School and at Oxford and in 1484 became a Fellow of All Souls. In 1487 he made his way to Italy, where he studied medicine and the classics, spending two years in Florence (c.1488–90) as the pupil of Angelo Poliziano and Demetrius Chalcondylas; he then went on to Rome and Padua. By 1499 he had returned to London and was at once recognized as one of the foremost humanist scholars of England. He was physician to Henry VII and *Henry VIII, and many great statesmen (e.g. T. *Wolsey, W. *Warham) were his patients. He was also the intimate friend of J. *Colet, *Erasmus, and T. *More. In 1520 he was ordained deacon, having already acquired various ecclesiastical preferments. The College for which he secured the royal charter (23 Sept. 1518) was designed to regulate the practice of medicine and to discourage the quacks who flourished at the time in London. He also founded chairs of medicine at Oxford and Cambridge. Among his writings are a treatise on Latin composition and Latin translations from Galen.

Linacre College, founded in 1962 (until 1965 Linacre House), in Oxford is named after him.

J. N. Johnson, *Life of Thomas Linacre* (1835). F. Maddison and others (eds.), *Linacre Studies: Essays on the Life and Work of Thomas Linacre c.1460–1524* (Oxford, 1977). J. F. Payne in *DNB* 33 (1893), pp. 266–71 [cf. P. S. Allen in *EHR* 18 (1903), pp. 514–17, and R. J. Mitchell, ibid. 50 (1935), pp. 696–8]. *BRUO* 2 (1958), pp. 1147–9.

Lincoln. A see was established here by Bp. Remigius (d. 1092), who transferred it from *Dorchester, Oxon. The diocese became the largest in England, extending from the Thames to the Humber, and including the present dioceses of *Oxford, *Peterborough, and Leicester, as well as the present Lincoln. The cathedral, begun in 1086 and largely completed before 1300, contains fine Early English and Decorated architecture. Among celebrated Bps. of Lincoln are St *Hugh (1186–1200), R. *Grosseteste (1235–53), Richard *Fleming (1420–31), Thomas *Barlow (1675–91), W. *Wake (1705–16), E. *Gibson (1716–23), and E. *King (1885–1910).

W. P. W. Phillimore (ed.), *Rotuli Hugonis de Welles, Episcopi Lincolniensis* A.D. *MCCIX–MCCXXXV* (Cant. and York Society, 1, 3, and 4; 1907–9, and in The Lincoln Record Society, 3, 6, and 9; 1912–14); F. N. Davis (ed.), *Rotuli Roberti Grosseteste, Episcopi Lincolniensis* A.D. *MCCXXXV–MCCLIII* (Cant. and York Society, 10; 1913, and, with the *Rotulus Henrici de Lixington, Episcopi Lincolniensis* A.D. *MCCLIV–MCCLIX*, in The Lincoln Record Society, 11; 1914); id., C. W. Foster and A. H. Thompson (eds.),

Rotuli Ricardi Gravesend [Bp., 1258–79] (Cant. and York Society, 31; 1925, and Linc. Record Society, 20; 1925); R. M. T. Hill (ed.), *The Rolls and Register of Bishop Oliver Sutton, 1280–1299* (Linc. Record Society, 39, 43, 48, 52, 60, 64, 69, 76; 1948–86). A. H. Thompson, 'Registers of John Gynewell, Bishop of Lincoln, for the Years 1347–1350', *Archaeological Journal*, 68 (1911), pp. 301–60, with extracts. *The Register of Bishop Philip Repingdon 1405–1419*, ed. M. Archer (Linc. Record Society, 57, 58, 74; 1963–82). *The Register of Richard Fleming, Bishop of Lincoln, 1420–31*, ed. N. H. Bennett (Cant. and York Society, 146, etc.; 1984 ff.). C. W. Foster (ed.), *Lincoln Episcopal Records in the Time of Thomas Cooper . . . Bishop of Lincoln* A.D. *1571 to* A.D. *1584* (Linc. Record Society 2; 1912). A. H. Thompson (ed.), *Visitations of Religious Houses in the diocese of Lincoln* [1420–49] (ibid. 7, 14, and 21; 1914–29). R. E. G. Cole (ed.), *Chapter Acts of the Cathedral Church of St Mary of Lincoln* A.D. *1520–1559* (ibid. 12, 13, and 15; 1915–20). C. W. Foster and K. Major (eds.), *The Registrum Antiquissimum of the Cathedral Church of Lincoln* (ibid. 27, 28, 29, 32, 34, 41, 46, 51, 62, 67, 68; 1931–73). A. H. Thompson (ed.), *Visitations in the Diocese of Lincoln 1517–1531* (ibid. 33, 35, and 37; 1940–7). C. W. Foster, *The State of the Church in the Reigns of Elizabeth and James I as Illustrated by Documents Relating to the Diocese of Lincoln*, vol. 1 (ibid. 23; 1926). M. Bowker, *The Secular Clergy in the Diocese of Lincoln 1495–1520* (Cambridge, 1968); id., *The Henrician Reformation: The Diocese of Lincoln under John Longland 1521–1547* (ibid., 1981). H. Bradshaw and C. *Wordsworth (eds.), *Statutes of Lincoln Cathedral* (2 vols., 1892–7). K. Major, *A Handlist of the Records of the Bishops of Lincoln and of the Archdeacons of Lincoln and Stow* (1953). G. F. Apthorp, *A Catalogue of the Books and Manuscripts in the Library of Lincoln Cathedral* (Lincoln, 1859). W. *Dugdale, *Monasticon Anglicanum*, 6 (pt. 3; 1830), pp. 1266–92. B. Willis, *A Survey of the Cathedrals of Lincoln, Ely, Oxford and Peterborough* (1730), pp. 1–330. J. H. Srawley, *The Story of Lincoln Minster* (1933). D. [M.] Owen (ed.), *A History of Lincoln Minster* (Cambridge, 1994). J. W. F. Hill, *Medieval Lincoln* (ibid., 1948); id., *Tudor & Stuart Lincoln* (ibid., 1956); id., *Georgian Lincoln* (ibid., 1966). P. Wragge, 'Lincoln Cathedral' in *VCH*, Lincoln, 2 (1906), pp. 80–96. W. Hunt in *DECH*, pp. 328–32, s.v.

Lincoln, Use of. The liturgical usage adopted in the vast pre-Reformation diocese of Lincoln and referred to by T. *Cranmer in the preface to the 1549 BCP (see *CONCERNING THE SERVICE OF THE CHURCH). Among the few traces of it which have survived are three leaves of a 15th cent. MS Missal *secundum usum Lincoln.*, now among the Tanner MSS in the *Bodleian Library (MS 9824).

Lincoln Judgement. The Judgement, given in 1890 by E. W. *Benson, Abp. of Canterbury, upon the complaints made two years before by the *Church Association against Edward *King, Bp. of Lincoln, for consecrating the Eucharist in the eastward position, having lighted candles on the altar, mixing water and wine in the chalice, allowing the *Agnus Dei to be sung after the Consecration, absolving and blessing with the *sign of the Cross, and taking the ablutions of the sacred vessels. The Judgement upheld the Bishop in the main, but ordered that the chalice must be mixed, if at all, before the service, that the *manual acts of consecration must be visible to the people, and that the sign of the Cross may not be used. The Judgement was notable in that it ignored previous decisions of the secular courts and the *Judicial Committee of the Privy Council.

E. S. Roscoe, *The Bishop of Lincoln's Case: A Report of the Proceedings in the Court of the Archbishop of Canterbury . . .* (1889). *Read and Others v. the Lord Bishop of Lincoln*: Judgment, Nov. 21, 1890. A. C. Benson, *The Life of Edward White Benson*, 2 (1899), pp. 319–81; G. W. E. Russell, *Edward King, Sixtieth Bishop of Lincoln* (1912), pp. 143–210.

Lindisfarne. From the 11th cent. it has also been called 'Holy Island'. Its history begins with St *Aidan's arrival from *Iona in 635, when it became a missionary centre and episcopal see, and a large number of churches were founded by its efforts from Edinburgh to the Humber and beyond. Among those educated in the monastery were St *Chad, St *Cedd, St *Egbert, and St *Wilfrid. The church was rebuilt by Aidan's successor, St *Finan (d. 661). In the latter part of the 7th cent. the Scoto-Irish monks, with some of their English brethren, withdrew to Iona, as they disliked the Roman discipline agreed upon at the Synod of *Whitby (664), and from that time the monastery looked towards Rome. St *Cuthbert's association with it added to its celebrity. In 793 and again in 875 the monastery and church were pillaged by the Danes and the monks fled. Eardulf (d. 900), the last of the 16 bishops, fixed his see in 875 at Chester-le-Street, but it was transferred to *Durham in 995. From 1082 to the Dissolution there was continuous monastic life on the island. The abbey church was a small copy of Durham cathedral, and dedicated to St Cuthbert.

The MS known as the 'Lindisfarne Gospels', now in the British Library (Cotton MS Nero D. iv), was written and decorated *c*.696–8 by Eadfrith (afterwards Bp. of Lindisfarne) 'in honour of St *Cuthbert'. Its script is of a formal insular style, and its decoration one of the finest surviving monuments of early Hiberno-Saxon art. Its text is closely related to that of the *Codex Amiatinus. An interlinear gloss in Anglo-Saxon was added by Aldred, who was provost of Lindisfarne in 970.

The *Liber Vitae Ecclesiae Dunelmensis* (also in the Brit. Lib., Cotton MS Domitian A. vii) contains the names of the benefactors of the Church of St Cuthbert, Lindisfarne, and others entitled to commemoration. Begun in the 9th cent. (prob. *c*.840) and written in silver and gold, it was later removed to Durham.

'Annales Lindisfarnenses et Cantuarienses a. 618–690', ed. G. H. Pertz in *MGH*, Scriptores, 4 (1841), pp. 1 f.; 'Annales Lindisfarnenses' [AD 532–993], ed. id., ibid. 19 (1866), pp. 502–7. W. *Dugdale, *Monasticon Anglicanum*, 1, (1846 edn.), pp. 220–52. J. Raine, *The History and Antiquities of North Durham* (1852), pp. 73–188. H. *Leclercq, OSB, in *DACL* 9 (pt. 1; 1930), cols. 1186–92, s.v. Fine facsimile of the Lindisfarne Gospels (Olten and Berne, 1956, with important vol. of comm. by T. J. Brown, R. L. Bruce-Mitford and others, ibid., 1960). Text ed. J. Stevenson and G. Waring (Surtees Society, 28, 39, 43, and 48; 1854–65). Lat. text collated in the edn. of the *Vulgate by J. *Wordsworth and H. J. White (Oxford, 1889). Plates, with introd. by E. G. Millar (British Museum, 1923). J. Backhouse, *The Lindisfarne Gospels* (Oxford, 1981). J. J. G. Alexander, *Insular Manuscripts, 6th to the 9th century* (*A Survey of Manuscripts illuminated in the British Isles*, 1; 1978), pp. 35–40 (no. 9, ills. 28–46). *Liber Vitae*, ed. J. Stevenson (Surtees Society, 13, 1841); facsimile edn. by A. H. Thompson (ibid., 136; 1923).

Lindsay, Thomas Martin (1843–1914), Church historian. He was educated at Glasgow and Edinburgh, and was for a time assistant at the latter to A. C. *Fraser in philosophy. He decided, however, to become a minister in the *Free Church of Scotland, and in 1873 he became professor of church history at the theological college at Glas-

gow. His main interest was the history of the Protestant Reformation on the Continent, his two principal books being *Luther and the German Reformation* (1900) and *A History of the Reformation in Europe* (2 vols., 1906–7). His other writings include *The Church and the Ministry in the Early Centuries* (Cunningham Lectures, 1903).

His son Alexander Dunlop, first **Lord Lindsay of Birker** (1879–1952), Master of Balliol College, Oxford (1924–49), took a prominent and effective part in furthering Christian principles in their bearing on social and ethical problems. In addition to philosophical works, notably studies of H. *Bergson (1911) and I. *Kant (1934), he wrote on personal, social, and political ethics.

A Collection of *College Addresses: and Sermons preached on Various Occasions by the late Thomas Martin Lindsay*, ed. A. D. Lindsay, son (Glasgow, 1915). *Letters of Principal T. M. Lindsay to Janet Ross* (1923), with introd. by J. [A.] Ross, pp. v–x. R. S. Rait in *DNB, 1912–1921*, pp. 338 f., s.v.
Life of Alexander D. Lindsay by [A.] D. Scott (daughter) (Oxford, 1971); [J. E.] C. Hill in *DNB, 1951–1960*, pp. 641–4.

Lindsey, Theophilus (1723–1808), English *Unitarian. Educated at Leeds and at St John's College, Cambridge, of which he was later elected a Fellow (1747), he held two other livings before becoming vicar of Catterick in 1763. In 1760 he married the stepdaughter of his friend Archdeacon Francis Blackburne (1705–87), with whose *Latitudinarian ideas he was much in sympathy. Having become doubtful about the doctrine of the Trinity, he supported Blackburne in the controversy arising out of the latter's *Confessional* (1766) and, stimulated in his unorthodoxy by friendship with J. *Priestley, he joined in the *Feathers Tavern Petition to Parliament against subscription to the *Thirty-Nine Articles. The failure of the petition and a change in his own intellectual position led him to adopt Unitarianism. He went to London, where, from 1774, he conducted services in Essex Street. His writings include *Apology on Resigning the Vicarage of Catterick* (1774), *A Sequel to the Apology* (1776), *Historical View of the State of the Unitarian Doctrine and Worship from the Reformation to our own Time* (1783), *Vindiciae Priestleianae* (1788), and *Conversations on the Divine Government* (1802).

Collected edn. of his *Sermons* (2 vols., London, 1810). T. Belsham, *Memoirs of . . . Theophilus Lindsey . . . including a Brief Analysis of his Works* (1812). H. McLachlan, *Letters of Theophilus Lindsey* (Publications of the University of Manchester, 134; 1920), with introductory 'Sketch of the Life of Theophilus Lindsey', pp. ix–xii. A. Nicholson in *DNB* 33 (1893), pp. 317 f.

Lingard, John (1771–1851), English historian. He came from an old Lincolnshire RC family which had migrated to *Winchester, where he was born. He entered the English College at *Douai in 1782, but had to leave in 1793 on account of the French war. Having finished his theological studies at Crook Hall, nr. *Durham, he was ordained priest in 1795, made prefect of studies, and taught natural and moral philosophy. In 1806 he published his *Antiquities of the Anglo-Saxon Church* (3rd edn., much enlarged, 1845), and in 1808 he went to Ushaw, where he helped with the foundation of the College and became its vice-president. In 1811 he moved to Hornby, nr. Lancaster, a small country mission, where he spent most of the rest of his life writing. In 1817 he paid a visit to Rome, where he negotiated the reopening of the *English College. In 1819 appeared the first three volumes of his *History of England*, the great work on which his fame rests. The eighth and last volume was published in 1830, carrying the history down to 1688. The work had a great success, which it owed esp. to its objectivity, its extensive use of contemporary documents, and the new light in which it viewed esp. such controversial periods as the *Reformation. It was translated into many European languages and earned its author the triple doctorate of theology, canon, and civil law from *Pius VII in 1821. There is some evidence that Leo XII created him cardinal *in petto* in 1826. Among his many other writings are a *New Version of the Four Gospels* (1836) and manuals of prayer and instruction, as well as some controversial treatises.

J. Hughes, *John Lingard* (1907); M. Haile and E. Bonney, *Life and Letters of John Lingard* (1911). J. P. Chinnici, OFM, *The English Catholic Enlightenment: John Lingard and the Cisalpine Movement, 1780–1850* (Shepherdstown, W.Va., 1980). G. Culkin, 'The Making of Lingard's History', *The Month*, 192 (1951), pp. 7–18. T. Cooper in *DNB* 33 (1893), pp. 320–3.

Linus, St. Acc. to all the early episcopal lists, Linus was the first Bp. of Rome after the Apostles Peter and Paul, but nothing else is known with certainty about him. A Christian of this name sends greetings, perhaps from Rome, in 2 Tim. 4: 21; and *Irenaeus and *Eusebius of Caesarea identify him with the Bishop. Feast day, 23 Sept., suppressed in 1969.

St Linus is mentioned by Irenaeus, *Adv. Haer.* 3. 3. 3, and Eusebius, *HE* 3. 2 and 5. 6. *LP* (Duchesne), 1. 121. *AASS*, Sept. 6 (1757), pp. 539–45. J. B. *Lightfoot, *The Apostolic Fathers*, 1 (pt. 1; 2nd edn., 1890), pp. 76–9. V. L. Kennedy, CSB, *The Saints of the Canon of the Mass* (Studi di Antichità Cristiana, 14; 1938), esp. pp. 111–13. É. Amann in *DTC* 9 (pt. 1; 1926), col. 772, s.v. 'Lin', with further refs.

lion. The lion appears in early Christian art esp. in two connections. (1) In representations of the story of *Daniel, conceived as a 'type' of God's redemption of His chosen people. This occurs among the earliest *catacomb paintings. (2) As the symbol of St *Mark. This symbolism, based on Ezek. 1 and Rev. 4, was discussed by St *Jerome and St *Augustine. In art its use dates from the 5th cent.

H. *Leclercq, OSB, in *DACL* 9 (pt. 1; 1930), cols. 1198–207, s.v.

Lippi, Fra Filippo (*c.*1406–69), Italian painter. Brought up as an orphan by *Carmelites in Florence, he took the habit in 1420. The earliest reference to him as a painter dates from 1431. He led an immoral life and *c.*1461 he was released from his vows by *Pius II and allowed to marry. He was much patronized by the Medici in Florence and also worked in Padua, Prato, and Spoleto, where he died. His style of painting was influenced by contemporary developments in sculpture. Among his principal pictures are the *Barbadori Altarpiece* (1437), the *Coronation of the Virgin* (1441), and his great fresco cycles in Prato of *St *John the Baptist* and *St *Stephen* (1452–65). Though he belonged to the second generation of Renaissance artists and his work did not reach the spiritual heights of a Fra *Angelico (except perhaps in his representations of the *Adoration of the Child* and the *Annunciation*), he none the less exercised a considerable influence on the subsequent

development of devotional art. He was the father of the painter Filippino Lippi (*c.*1457–1504).

Studies, with reproductions, by H. Mendelsohn (Berlin, 1909), R. Oertel (Vienna, 1942), M. Pittaluga (Florence, 1949), G. Marchini (Florence, 1975), and J. Ruda (Oxford, 1987).

Lipsius, Richard Adelbert (1830–92), German Protestant theologian. He studied at Leipzig, and after holding other academic appointments became professor of systematic theology at Jena in 1871. In his *Pilatus-Acten* (1871; new edn., 1886) and his *Die Apokryphen Apostelgeschichten und Apostellegenden* (4 vols., 1883–90) he did much towards unravelling problems connected with early Christian apocryphal literature, and in 1891 he edited, in association with M. Bonnet, the still standard collection of Apocryphal Acts. He also made researches into the early history of the Popes, arguing that St Peter was never in Rome, and into the literary relationships of the early antiheretical Christian writings. A pronounced liberal in dogmatic theology, he set out his systematic doctrines in a *Lehrbuch der evangelisch-protestantischen Dogmatik* (1876) and in *Philosophie und Religion* (1885); but he differed from A. *Ritschl and his disciples in a greater readiness to draw on the theoretical aspects of I. *Kant's idealism.

A. Neumann, *Grundlagen und Grundzüge der Weltanschauung von R. A. Lipsius* (1896). Short study by H. Weinel (Tübingen, 1930). F. R. Lipsius in *PRE* (3rd edn.), 11 (1902), pp. 520–4; M. Scheibe in *Allegemeine Deutsche Biographie*, 52 (1906), pp. 7–27.

Lisle, Ambrose Lisle March Phillipps de. See DE LISLE, AMBROSE LISLE MARCH PHILLIPPS.

Lismore, Book of. A 15th-cent. MS found in 1814 at Lismore Castle, the Irish seat of the dukes of Devonshire, and now at Chatsworth House. It contains a miscellaneous collection of medieval Irish literature, secular and ecclesiastical, including Lives of saints in Middle Irish.

Facsimile, with introd. by R. A. S. Macalister (Facsimiles in Collotype of Irish Manuscripts, 5; Dublin, 1950). *Lives of Saints from the Book of Lismore*, ed., with Eng. tr. and notes, by W. Stokes (Anecdota Oxoniensia, Mediaeval and Modern Series, 5; 1890). B. Ó Cuív, 'Observations on the Book of Lismore', *Proceedings of the Royal Irish Academy*, 83 C (1983), pp. 269–92.

litany (Gk. λιτανεία, 'a supplication'). A form of prayer consisting of a series of petitions or biddings which are sung or said by a deacon, a priest, or cantors, and to which the people make fixed responses, e.g. *Kyrie eleison, 'Grant, Lord', 'We beseech thee, hear us', etc. The litany apparently originated at *Antioch in the 4th cent., and thence by way of Asia Minor passed to *Constantinople, whence it spread to the rest of the E. Litanies said by the deacon (ἐκτεναί) figure largely in the Greek liturgies, being the principal element of the devotion of the congregation, from whom the main parts of the service which take place in the sanctuary are concealed by the *iconostasis. From Constantinople the litany spread also to Rome and the W. Pope *Gelasius I (492–6) introduced a litanic intercession (the *Deprecatio Gelasii*) into the Mass of which the *Kyrie* may be a relic. The litany became also a favourite form of private prayer. Invocations of saints were a feature in many litanies (see LITANY OF THE SAINTS). The procession of St *Mark's Day, instituted at

Rome in the 5th cent. or earlier to replace a similar pagan observance, acquired the name of *litaniae majores*, while the *Rogations were by contrast known as the *litaniae minores*.

N. Serarius, SJ, *Litaneutici seu de Litaniis* (Cologne, 1609; repr. in his *Opuscula Theologica*, 3 (Mainz, 1611), pp. 60–94). *Irish Litanies*, ed., with Eng. tr., by C. Plummer (HBS 62; 1925). L. Eisenhofer, *Handbuch der katholischen Liturgik*, 1 (1932), pp. 193–202. A. *Baumstark, *Liturgie comparée* (3rd edn. by B. Botte, OSB, 1953), pp. 80–90; Eng. tr. (1958), pp. 74–80. P. De Clerck, *La 'Prière Universelle' dans les liturgies latines anciennes* (Liturgiewissenschaftliche Quellen und Forschungen, 62; 1977), esp. pp. 114–314. D. E. Moeller, 'Litanies majeures et rogations', *Questions Liturgiques et Paroissiales*, 23 (1938), pp. 75–91. H. J. Hotham in *DCA* 2 (1880), pp. 999–1005, s.v.; F. *Cabrol, OSB, in *DACL* 9 (pt. 2; 1930), cols. 1540–71, s.v. 'Litanies', with bibl. See also bibl. to KYRIE ELEISON, LITANY OF THE SAINTS, and ROGATION DAYS.

Litany, the BCP. The form of 'general supplication' appointed to be sung or said after *Morning Prayer on *Sundays, *Wednesdays, and *Fridays. It is also included, with the addition of special suffrages, in the rites of *Ordination. It falls into two parts: (1) the invocation of the Persons of the Trinity, the deprecations, the obsecrations, the intercessions, and a final section consisting of invocations, *Kyrie eleison* and the Lord's Prayer; and (2) versicles and responses, followed by collects, which are an adaptation of a special intercession in time of war. The Litany was first issued by T. *Cranmer in 1544 for use in the processions ordered by *Henry VIII at a time when England was at war with Scotland and France. Cranmer drew mostly on the Latin litanies then in use in England, esp. the *Sarum *Rogationtide Litany, but also on M. *Luther's 'Latin Litany' of 1529 and the Deacon's Litany in the 'Liturgy of St John *Chrysostom'. Though he added little or nothing of his own, he made a notable change in the rhythm by grouping several suffrages under one response. In 1544 the invocations of the Trinity were followed by three invocations of saints; these were omitted when the Litany was included in the First BCP (1549). Minor changes were made in later versions of the BCP and the collects at the end have been altered several times. The appointment of Wednesday and Friday as Litany days coincides with Lutheran usage.

Text of the Litanies of 1544, 1552, and 1661, with indication of sources, in F. E. *Brightman, *The English Rite*, 1 (1915), pp. 174–91. W. H. Karslake, *The Litany of the English Church Considered in its History, its Plan, and the Manner in which it is Intended to be Used* (1876). E. G. C. F. Atchley, *The People's Prayers: Being some Considerations on the Use of the Litany in Public Worship* (*Alcuin Club Tracts, 6; 1906). Cf. also Brightman, op. cit., pp. lviii–lxviii, and see bibl. to COMMON PRAYER, THE BOOK OF.

litany desk. In the C of E, a low movable desk placed in the midst of the church, within or without the chancel, at which the minister kneels to recite the Litany in acc. with *Injunctions 24 of 1547 and 18 of 1559.

Litany of Loreto. A litany in honour of the BVM, consisting of a series of invocations of our Lady under various honorific titles, such as 'Mother of Divine grace', 'Virgin most prudent', 'Queen of Angels', etc., each followed by the request: 'Pray for us'. It derives its name from the famous Italian shrine, where its use is attested for the year 1558; but it is doubtful whether it was first sung at *Loreto and did not rather arise under *Dominican influence in the confraternities of the Rosary and thence make its way to the shrine. It is a simplified version of older Litanies of our Lady, which first appeared in the 12th cent. It was approved and indulgenced by *Sixtus V in 1587, and again by *Clement VIII in 1601. In the course of time more titles were added to the original series, e.g. 'Queen of the Most Holy Rosary', 'Queen conceived without Original Sin', and 'Mother of Good Counsel' by *Leo XIII, 'Queen of Peace' by *Benedict XV in 1917, and 'Queen assumed into Heaven' by *Pius XII after the definition of the doctrine of the *Assumption of the BVM. It is often recited in RC churches after the service of *Benediction, and has been used in many religious orders, e.g. by the *Carmelites, every day after Vespers, and by the Dominicans on Saturdays after *Compline.

A. De Santi, SJ, *Le Litanie lauretane* (1897; Fr. tr., 1900). J. Sauren, *Die lauretanische Litanei nach Ursprung, Geschichte und Inhalt dargestellt* (Kempten, 1895). K. Kammer, *Die lauretanische Litanei* (Innsbruck, 1960). A. De Santi in *CE* 9 (1910), pp. 286–90, s.v.

Litany of the Saints. In the W. Church this litany is in regular use. It consists of invocations for mercy and deliverance addressed to the three Persons of the Trinity and for intercession to the BVM and a list of prophets, patriarchs, angels, apostles, saints, confessors, and virgins individually and in classes. Early forms of such a litany are found in the E. from the end of the 3rd cent. and in the W. from the late 5th cent. A later stage is represented in the 'Athelstan Psalter' (9th cent.), the *Stowe Missal and the 'Book of *Cerne'. The list of saints invoked varied locally and increased in length through the Middle Ages until in 1570 it became necessary to obtain Papal licence to differ from the use of Rome. It was revised in 1969, when some modern saints were introduced. Acc. to current RC practice, the longer form may be used for solemn intercessions at any time; a shortened form is used for *Ordinations, dedications of churches and during the *Paschal Vigil Service; and a further form exists in the Commendation of the Dying. The practice of reciting the Greater Litanies on St *Mark's day was suppressed in 1969 and it is no longer obligatory on the *Rogation Days (q.v.). Other litanies, e.g. the *Litany of Loreto and that of St *Joseph, are used in private devotion. See also DEPRECATIO GELASII.

C. Kammer, *Die Litanei von Allen Heiligen, die Namen-Jesu-Litanei, die Josefs-Litanei* (Innsbruck, 1962). E. *Bishop, 'The Litany of the Saints in the Stowe Missal', *JTS* 7 (1906), pp. 122–36; repr., with additional note, in *Liturgica Historica* (Oxford, 1918), pp. 137–64. M. Coens, SJ, 'Anciennes Litanies des saints', *Anal. Boll.* 54 (1936), pp. 5–37; 55 (1937), pp. 49–69; 59 (1941), pp. 272–98; 62 (1944), pp. 126–68, rev. and repr. in id., *Recueil d'études bollandiennes* (Subsidia Hagiographica, 37; 1963), pp. 131–322. P. De Clerck, *La 'Prière Universelle' dans les liturgies latines anciennes* (Liturgiewissenschaftliche Quellen und Forschungen, 62; 1977), pp. 275–81. S. A. van Dijk, OFM, 'The Litany of the Saints on Holy Saturday', *JEH* 1 (1950), pp. 51–62. M. Lapidge (ed.), *Anglo-Saxon Litanies of the Saints* (HBS 106; 1991), with general introd., pp. 1–61, and bibl. pp. 86–8.

Literary Criticism. See HIGHER CRITICISM.

literate. In the C of E a cleric who has been admitted to holy orders without a university degree. Canon 58 of 1604 permitted such ministers 'to wear upon their surplices, instead of hoods, some decent *tippet of black, so it be not silk'.

Little Brothers of Jesus. See DE FOUCAULD, CHARLES EUGÈNE.

Little Entrance (Gk. μικρὰ εἴσοδος). In the E. Church, the procession at the *Liturgy with the *Gospel Book. In origin it was the procession of the bishop and clergy into the church, thus marking the beginning of the Liturgy proper; it is thus the first intervention in the service of the bishop, who at this point is fetched from the nave. The procession now takes place whether or not the bishop is present in person. See also GREAT ENTRANCE.

Little Flower of Jesus. A popular designation of St *Teresa of Lisieux (q.v.), who frequently so describes herself in her autobiography.

Little Flowers of St Francis (the 'Fioretti'). A classic collection of stories and traditions about St *Francis of Assisi (d. 1226) and his companions. It is apparently an anonymous Tuscan translation of 53 chapters of the 'Actus Beati Francisci et Sociorum Eius' which was written by Fra Ugolini Boniscambi of Montegiorgio c.1335, to which the translator added 'Five Considerations of the Holy Stigmata' derived from other sources as well as from the 'Actus'. The translation dates from c.1375. It gives an exquisite picture of the religious life and spirit of the early Franciscans. In some 15th-cent. MSS and modern editions other material has been added.

Editio princeps, Vicenza, 1476. Modern edns. by G. Pagnani, OFM (Rome, 1959), and incl. the later additions, by R. Pratesi, OFM, with note by B. Bughetti, OFM (Florence, 1960), and among the writings of St Francis ed. A. Vicinelli (Verona, 1955), pp. 255–397. The numerous Eng. trs. incl. those of R. Brown (Garden City, NY [1958]) and L. Sherley-Price (Penguin Classics, 1959). 'Actus Beati Francisci et Sociorum Eius' ed. P. *Sabatier (Collection d'Études et de Documents sur l'Histoire religieuse et littéraire du Moyen Âge, 4; 1902) and J. Cambell, M. Bignori, OFM, and G. Boccoli, OFM (Pubblicazione della Bibliotheca Francescana Chiesa Nuova—Assisi, 5; Assisi, 1988). Eng. tr. by E. M. Blaiklock and A. C. Keys (London, 1985). R. Brown in NCE 5 (1967), pp. 932 f., s.v. 'Fioretti, The'.

Little Gidding. A manor, 11 miles NW of Huntingdon, where the Ferrar family lived under a definite religious rule in the C of E from 1625 to 1646. The household, some 40 persons in all, consisted of N. *Ferrar, in deacon's orders, his mother Mary, and the families of his brother and sister. A systematic rule of devotion and work was followed. At the beginning of every hour, from 6 a.m. to 8 p.m., there was an Office of a quarter of an hour, in which several groups of the community took their turn. It consisted of a hymn and portions from the Psalms and the Gospels, the whole of the Psalter being thus recited every day and the Gospels once a month. In addition to this two or more members watched every night from 9 p.m. to 1 a.m., once more reciting the whole of the Psalter. Ferrar himself kept this watch two, and later three, times a week. Besides prayer, the community engaged in charitable

works for the whole neighbourhood. Its members visited and relieved the poor and sick, and ran a dispensary and a school for the village children. They were also skilled in the art of bookbinding, and the famous 'Harmonies', now in the British Library, were arranged, illustrated, and bound by them under Ferrar's direction. For recreation they had a study circle called the Little Academy, which met frequently to tell and discuss stories illustrating events in the Church's year and Christian virtues.

The house was visited by *Charles I and G. *Herbert. After Nicholas Ferrar's death in 1637 the community continued until it was raided by O. *Cromwell's soldiers in 1646, when its members were dispersed. The house has disappeared, but the church still stands. Interest in Ferrar and his community was reawakened by the publication of J. H. *Shorthouse's famous novel, *John Inglesant* (1881), with its vivid and, except for the romance of Mary Collett, historically accurate picture of life at Little Gidding; it received further impetus from the poem 'Little Gidding' included in T. S. *Eliot's *Four Quartets* (1944).

In 1977 a new (ecumenical) community was founded at Little Gidding. It is named 'The Community of Christ the Sower', and, with a membership of about 35 people, including some resident families, it has houses also at Leighton Bromswold and Great Gidding. A simple daily Office is recited in common, and the community receives guests, publishes in the field of Christian spirituality, and tends a small farm.

The Arminian Nunnery; or a Brief Description and Relation of the late erected Monastical Place, called the Arminian Nunnery, at Little Gidding in Huntingdonshire (1641). H. Collett, Little Gidding and its Founder (1925). A. [L.] Maycock, Chronicles of Little Gidding (1954; on the history of Little Gidding from 1637 to 1748, when the estate passed out of the Ferrar family). J. E. Acland, Little Gidding and its Inmates in the Time of Charles I (1903). Appendix on 'Little Gidding' by W. Page in The Victoria History of the County of Huntingdon, 1 (1926), pp. 399–406. E. C. Sharland (ed.), The Story Books of Little Gidding (1899); A. M. Williams (ed.), Conversations at Little Gidding: 'On the Retirement of Charles V', 'On the Austere Life'. Dialogues by Members of the Ferrar Family (Cambridge, 1970). See also bibl. s.v. FERRAR, NICHOLAS.

Little Labyrinth, The. A lost 3rd-cent. treatise which, acc. to *Eusebius, was directed against the *Adoptionist heretics, *Theodotus and *Artemon. It is referred to under this title (ὁ σμικρὸς λαβύρινθος) by *Theodoret (Haer. Fab. Comp. 2. 5), who says that some ascribe it to *Origen. Two passages are quoted by Eusebius (HE 5. 28). In modern times, its authorship has been assigned to St *Hippolytus by J. B. *Lightfoot (followed by A. *Harnack and O. *Bardenhewer), though G. Salmon wished to ascribe it to *Gaius. Its attribution is still disputed. It is to be distinguished from another writing, the 'Labyrinth', mentioned by *Photius (Cod. 48), which is very probably to be identified with St Hippolytus' Refutatio.

J. B. Lightfoot, St Clement of Rome, 2 (1890 edn.), pp. 377–80. R. H. *Connolly, OSB, 'Eusebius H.E. v. 28', JTS 49 (1948), pp. 73–9. P. Nautin, Le Dossier d'Hippolyte et de Méliton (Patristica, 1; 1953), pp. 115–20. CPG 1 (1983), p. 275 (no. 1915). Bardenhewer, 2, pp. 567 f. G. Salmon in DCB 1 (1877), pp. 384–6, s.v. 'Caius (2)'.

Little Office of Our Lady (Officium Parvum Beatae Mariae Virginis). A brief office in honour of the BVM, modelled on the Divine *Office; it was thus divided into the traditional seven hours, but Mattins had only one *Nocturn with three Psalms and three Lessons, and the Psalms of the other hours did not vary acc. to the days of the week. It was first known in the 10th cent. It originated in the religious orders, being early adopted by the *Cistercians and *Camaldolese, and was later taken over by the secular clergy. In the Middle Ages the Little Office of Our Lady was widely reproduced in 'Books of Hours', many of which were richly illuminated. It was retained at the *Breviary reform of *Pius V in 1568, though the obligation of its recitation was no longer binding under sin; *Pius X removed the obligation altogether, though recommending it as a private devotion. It became the ordinary form of vocal prayer of a number of new congregations of women and its recitation was frequently enjoined upon *Tertiaries. In 1953 a revision was approved. This affords greater variety by dividing the year into six seasons (instead of two), with special lessons, collects, etc., and provides for the observance of 28 feasts (of which 12 are Marian). See also PRIMER.

Facsimile edn. of two 11th-cent. MSS ed., with introd., by E. S. Dewick (HBS 21; 1902), with refs.; a 15th-cent. MS ed. H. Littlehales, *The Prymer or Lay Folks' Prayer Book* (EETS, Orig. Series, 105, 109; 1895–7), with important essay by E. *Bishop, 'The Origin of the Prymer', pp. xi–xxxviii, repr. in Bishop's *Liturgica Historica* (1918), pp. 211–27. E. Taunton, *The Little Office of Our Lady: A Treatise Theoretical, Practical, and Exegetical* (1903). E. Hoskins, *Horae Beatae Mariae Virginis or Sarum and York Primers with Kindred Books and Primers of the Reformed Roman Use* (1901). J. Leclercq, OSB, 'Fragmenta Mariana', pt. 2, 'Formes successives de l'office votif de la Vierge', *EL* 72 (1958), pp. 294–301; id., 'Formes anciennes de l'office mariale', ibid. 74 (1960), pp. 89–102. H. Bohatta, *Bibliographie des Livres d'heures* (Vienna, 1909). L. A. St L. Toke in *CE* 9 (1910), pp. 294 f.

Little Offices. Originally, very short offices modelled on the *Little Office of Our Lady, intended for devotional recitation. Recently the term has been more commonly used of forms of prayer, based on the Divine *Office, usually with a reduced content of Psalms and a modern lectionary. While it had long been customary for devout laity and religious not bound to recite the choir offices acc. to the Roman or monastic *Breviary to use the *Day Hours alone (omitting *Mattins) or the Little Office of Our Lady, in modern times a number of other 'Little Offices' have been compiled, mainly in the vernacular, to meet the needs of those not completely satisfied with the existing books and to provide some liturgical content for their common prayer. Among those most widely used were the *Officium Divinum Parvum* compiled by H. Fleischmann, OSB (Freiburg, 1933; rev. 1950), used esp. in German-speaking countries; *A Short Breviary for Religious and the Laity*, edited by the Monks of St John's Abbey, Collegeville (Collegeville, Minn., 1940; new edn. by W. G. Heidt, OSB, ibid., 1954), which circulated widely esp. in USA; *Klein Brevier* by T. Stallaert, CSSR (Haarlem and Antwerp, 1950; Eng. tr., 1957; also tr. into Fr. and Ital.); *Bréviaire des fidèles* by A. M. Henry, OP (1951); and the *Livre d'heures* compiled by the Benedictines of En-Calcat (1952), which has predominated in French-speaking countries. Although these shortened offices were given a certain status by the 'Constitution on the Liturgy' of the Second *Vatican Council (1963), they were virtually superseded

when the Office was reordered by *Paul VI's *Liturgia Horarum* (1971); those not bound to recite the whole Office normally use Morning and Evening Prayer (*Lauds and *Vespers).

H. A. P. Schmidt, SJ, *Introductio in Liturgiam Occidentalem* (Freiburg, 1960), pp. 472–83; L. J. Doyle in *NCE* 2 (1967), p. 793, s.v. 'Breviary, Short'.

Little Sisters. See DE FOUCAULD, CHARLES EUGÈNE.

Littledale, Richard Frederick (1833–90), liturgical writer and Anglo-Catholic apologist. He came of an Irish family but lived in England from c.1855, holding curacies from 1856 to 1861, when ill-health forced him to abandon parochial work. In an essay in *The Church and the World*, ed. O. Shipley (1866), he argued that Ritualism had an important missionary dimension. His *Plain Reasons against joining the Church of Rome* (1880) enjoyed a wide circulation. He also completed J. M. *Neale's *Commentary on the Psalms from Primitive and Medieval Writers* (4 vols., 1860–74). With J. E. Vaux, he was the first editor of *The Priest's Prayer Book* (1864).

G. C. Boase in *DNB* 33 (1893), pp. 364 f., s.v.

liturgical colours. See COLOURS, LITURGICAL.

Liturgical Movement. A movement of which the object is the restoration of the active participation of the people in the official worship of the Church. In the RC Church the revival may be traced to P. L. P. *Guéranger (q.v.), but it received its chief impetus from the directions of *Pius X relating to Church music (1903) and to the promotion of Eucharistic piety and frequent communion. It was fostered esp. by the *Benedictines, e.g. the abbeys of *Solesmes in France, *Maredsous and Mont-César in Belgium, and *Maria Laach in Germany. From c.1910 the movement spread to the Netherlands, Italy, and England, and later to the USA and elsewhere. In England there had been some restoration of traditional liturgical worship under Cardinal N. P. S. *Wiseman in the 19th cent., but a later stage of the Continental movement was popularized largely through the writings of F. *Cabrol on the liturgy and esp. his English–Latin Missal (1921). In 1929 the Society of St Gregory was founded to encourage the active participation of the laity in worship through the propagation of *plainsong. At about the time of the Second World War in France, and soon afterwards in Germany, the impetus of the movement spread outside the monastic centres into the parochial and missionary spheres, and from then on the movement took a more pastoral direction. The attempt to restore the scrupulous observance of the rite in the form in which it had developed in the Middle Ages and later was joined by pressure for a reform of the rite itself in order to bring it into line with much earlier liturgical understanding and practice and with the pastoral and evangelistic needs of the day. These aspirations lay behind the development of the 'dialogue mass' in which the people joined in the responses, and the custom of reading a vernacular version of the liturgy in the body of the church at the same time as the priest celebrated in Latin. In his encyclical *Mediator Dei* (20 Nov. 1947) *Pius XII gave considerable encouragement to the liturgical movement by his insistence on the importance of the liturgy and the need for the participation of the people, though at the same time he stressed the need for proper order. From this time permission was given for the use of the vernacular in the administration of all sacraments except the Eucharist; and the reform of the rites began with the revision of the Holy Week liturgy in 1951 and 1955 (see GOOD FRIDAY, MAUNDY THURSDAY and PASCHAL VIGIL SERVICE). The Second *Vatican Council in its 'Constitution on the Sacred Liturgy' (1963) endorsed the aims of the liturgical movement, encouraging the active participation of the people in the liturgy, and legislated for the use of the vernacular and the reform of the rites (a new *Ordo Missae*, lectionary, and calendar appeared in 1969 and a definitive Roman Missal in 1970; for details of new rites of Baptism, Confirmation, Dedication of Churches, etc., see s.vv.). More recently consideration has been given to the possibility of adapting liturgies for use in different parts of the world where different cultures prevail.

The renewed interest in the liturgy has not been confined to the RC Church. The Ritualist Movement, inaugurated by the *Tractarians to give sacramental worship a central place in the C of E, grew steadily in the early part of the 20th cent. More recently there has been a tendency to change the traditional pattern of Sunday worship from a plain celebration of the Eucharist at an early hour, followed by either Morning Prayer or a Solemn Eucharist at which only the celebrant communicated; the tendency has been to replace these services by one 'Parish Communion' at which there is some singing and often a short sermon and at which nearly all present communicate. This has often been accompanied by ceremonial developments (mainly taken over from the RC Church) which are intended to stress the corporate aspects of the liturgy, such as the adoption of a '*westward position' by the celebrant and an 'offertory procession' in which members of the congregation bring the bread and wine up to the altar. The same influences which have been felt at work in the RC Church have also played some part in the revisions of the liturgy authorized by the Prayer Book (*Alternative and Other Services) Measure (1965). Similar tendencies have been at work in most other Churches, possibly partly at least in reaction against the individualism by which nearly all Churches have been affected since the 16th cent.

O. Rousseau, OSB, *Histoire du mouvement liturgique: Esquisse historique depuis le début du XIXe siècle jusqu'au pontificat de Pie X* (Lex Orandi, 3; 1945; Eng. tr., Westminster, Md., 1951), with bibl.; J. H. Srawley, *The Liturgical Movement: Its Origin and Growth* (*Alcuin Club Tracts, 27; 1954). E. B. Koenker, *The Liturgical Renaissance in the Roman Catholic Church* (Chicago, 1954). J. D. Benoit, *Liturgical Renewal: Studies in Catholic and Protestant Developments on the Continent* (Studies in Ministry and Worship, 5; 1958). *What is the Liturgical Movement?* by Priests of St Séverin (Paris) and St Joseph (Nice), adapted into Eng. by L. C. Sheppard [1964]. [D.] H. [M.] Davies, *Worship and Theology in England: The Ecumenical Century, 1900–1965* (1965), esp. pp. 13–49.

L. *Beauduin, OSB, *La Piété de l'Église* (1914; Eng. tr., *Liturgy, the Life of the Church*, Collegeville, Minn., 1926). *La Participation active des fidèles au culte* (Cours et conférences des Semaines Liturgiques, 11; Louvain, 1933). A. G. Hebert (ed.), *The Parish Communion* (1937). A. R. Shands, *The Liturgical Movement and the Local Church* (1959; rev. edn., 1965). M. H. Shepherd, Jun. (ed.), *The Liturgical Renewal of the Church: Addresses of the Liturgical Conference held in Grace Church, Madison, May 19–21, 1958* (New York, 1960). Id., *The Reform of Liturgical Worship: Perspectives*

and Prospects (Bohlen Lectures, 1959; New York, 1961). J. D. Crichton, *The Church's Worship: Considerations on the Liturgical Constitution of the Second Vatican Council* (1964), incl. Eng. tr. of the Constitution. Id., H. E. Winstone, and J. R. Ainslee (eds.), *English Catholic Worship: Liturgical Renewal in England since 1900* (1979). H. E. Chandlee in *A New Dictionary of Liturgy & Worship*, ed. J. G. Davies (1986), pp. 307–14, s.v.

liturgiology. A cumbersome term for the scientific study of liturgies and related subjects. Its first appearance is in the title of J. M. *Neale's *Essays on Liturgiology and Church History* (1863).

Liturgy (Gk. λειτουργία from λεώς 'people' and ἔργον 'work'). The original Gk. word was used of a public work of any kind, not only religious, but in the *Septuagint it is applied particularly to the services of the *Temple. The word in English is used in two senses: (1) of all the prescribed services of the Church, e.g. incl. the canonical hours, as contrasted with private devotion; and (2) specifically as a title of the *Eucharist (as the chief act of public worship). It is commonly so used among the E. Churches. In derived senses the word is further used: (1) of the written texts which order such services (e.g. the 'Liturgy of St John Chrysostom'), and (2) as a general name for the branch of study (more cumbrously 'liturgiology') which concerns itself with these liturgies.

Among the classic collections of liturgical docs. and texts are those of J. *Mabillon, E. *Martène, B. *Gavanti, G. M. *Tommasi, E. *Renaudot (qq.v.). Cf. also F. *Cabrol, OSB and H. *Leclercq, OSB, *Monumenta Ecclesiae Liturgica*, 1: *Reliquiae Liturgicae Vetustissimae* (Paris, 1900–2), F. E. *Brightman, *Liturgies Eastern and Western*, 1 (Eastern Liturgies, 1895; all pub.), and J. Quasten (ed.), *Monumenta Eucharistica et Liturgica Vetustissima* (Florilegium Patristicum, 7; Bonn, 1935). Imp. modern studies incl. P. *Guéranger, OSB, *Institutiones Liturgicae* (4 vols., Paris, 1878–85); L. *Duchesne, *Origines du culte chrétien* (1889); L. Eisenhofer, *Grundriss der Liturgik des römischen Ritus* (1924; 5th edn., J. Lechner, 1950); id., *Handbuch der Katholischen Liturgik* (2 vols., 1932–3); C. Harris and W. K. Lowther Clarke (eds.), *Liturgy and Worship: A Companion to the Prayer Books of the Anglican Communion* (1932); C. Callewaert, *Liturgicae Institutiones: De Sacra Liturgia universim* (Bruges, 1933); A. *Baumstark, *Liturgie comparée* (Chevetogne, 1939; 3rd edn. by B. Botte, OSB, 1953; Eng. tr., 1958); M. Righetti, UJD, *Manuale di storia liturgica* (4 vols., Milan, 1944–53; 2nd edn., 1950–59; 3rd edn., 1964 ff.); A. G. Martimort and others, *L'Église en prière: Introduction à la liturgie* ([1962]; new edn., 4 vols. [1983–4]; Eng. tr., 1986); C. [P. M.] Jones and others (eds.), *The Study of Liturgy* (1978; 2nd edn., 1992). On the whole subject, A. Baumstark, *Vom geschichtlichen Werden der Liturgie* (Ecclesia Orans, 10; 1923), and K. Mohlberg, OSB, *Ziele und Aufgaben der liturgiegeschichtlichen Forschungen* (Münster i.W., 1919). Among periodicals devoted mainly or exclusively to the furtherance of liturgical studies are *Ephemerides Liturgicae* (Rome, 1887 ff.), *Les Questions liturgiques et paroissiales* (Louvain, 1911 ff.), *Jahrbuch für Liturgiewissenschaft* (1921 ff.), contd. since 1951 as *Archiv für Liturgiewissenschaft*, *Ambrosius* (Milan, 1925 ff.), *Sacris Erudiri* (Bruges, 1948 ff.), and *Liturgisches Jahrbuch* (Münster, 1951 ff.); also the series *Liturgiegeschichtliche Quellen und Forschungen* (Münster, 1918 ff.), *Rerum Ecclesiasticarum Documenta cura Pontificii Athenaei Sancti Anselmi de Urbe edita* (Rome, 1956 ff.), and the *DACL* (unhappily its interesting and often sparkling arts. suffer from innumerable inaccuracies). P. Radó, OSB, *Enchiridion Liturgicum* (2 vols., Rome, 1961; 2nd edn., 1966); L. Brinkhoff, OFM, and others, *Liturgisch Woordenboek* (2 vols., 1958–68).

Liudhard, St (d. *c.*602), chaplain of Queen Bertha, who brought him from Gaul to England, as was arranged by the terms of her marriage to *Ethelbert, King of Kent (*Bede, *HE* 1. 25). He probably ministered in St Martin's Church at *Canterbury. *William of Malmesbury (untrustworthy) represents him as having been prominent in preparing for the evangelization of Kent by the Roman mission of St *Augustine. Feast day, 4 Feb.

The principal authority is Bede, *HE* 1. 25; notes in edn. by C. Plummer, 2 (Oxford, 1896), p. 42; comm. by J. M. Wallace-Hadrill (ibid., 1988), pp. 33, 36 f., 39. Later Lives listed in Hardy, 1 (pt. 1; 1862), pp. 175 f. William of Malmesbury, *Gesta Regum*, 1. 9 (ed. W. *Stubbs, 1, Rolls Series, 1887, p. 13).

Liudprand (*c.* 922–*c.*972), or 'Liutprand', Bp. of Cremona. A member of a Lombard family prominent in Pavia, he entered the service of Berengar, ruler of northern Italy, who sent him in 949 on an embassy to the Byzantine court. He subsequently transferred his allegiance to the Emp. Otto I, who nominated him Bp. of Cremona in 961. In 963 he was sent as an ambassador to Rome, where he took part in the assembly which deposed *John XII, and in 968 he undertook a mission to Constantinople, after Otto's invasion of Byzantine territory in SE Italy. His unsuccessful negotiations with the Byzantine Emp. Nicephorus Phocas II are described in his entertaining 'Relatio de Legatione Constantinopolitana'. It is possible, though not probable, that he may have taken part in the embassy to Constantinople in 971 which negotiated the marriage between Otto's son (later Otto II) and the Byzantine princess Theophano. His most important work is the 'Antapodosis', which relates events from 888 to 949; while the 'Historia Ottonis' covers the years 960–4. Liudprand is the chief authority for the Italian history of the period, but he allowed rhetoric and prejudice to obscure accuracy and objectivity. The ascription of the '*Liber Pontificalis' to him is erroneous.

Collected edn. of his works by H. de la Higuera and L. Ramirez de Prado (Antwerp, 1640); crit. edn. by J. Becker (*MGH*, Scriptores Rerum Germanicarum in Usum Scholarum; 1915). Eng. tr. by F. A. Wright (Broadway Medieval Library, 1930), with introd., pp. 1–24. 'Relatio de Legatione Constantinopolitana' also ed., with Eng. tr. and useful introd., by [A.] B. Scott (London, 1993). M. Lintzel, *Studien über Liutprand von Cremona* (Historische Studien, Heft 233; 1933), with further refs., repr. in his *Ausgewählte Schriften*, 2 (1961), pp. 351–98. M. Rentschler, *Liudprand von Cremona* (Frankfurter wissenschaftliche Beiträge, Kulturwissenschaftliche Reihe, 14; 1981). J. N. Sutherland, *Liudprand of Cremona, Bishop, Diplomat, Historian* [posthumously pub.] (Biblioteca degli *Studi Medievali*, 14; Spoleto, 1988). K. [J.] Leyser, 'Liudprand of Cremona, Preacher and Homilist', in K. Walsh and D. Wood (eds.), *The Bible in the Medieval World: Essays in Memory of Beryl Smalley* (Studies in Church History, Subsidia, 4; 1985), pp. 43–60.

Liverpool Cathedrals. (1) THE ANGLICAN CATHEDRAL was designed in the Romantic Gothic style by G. G. *Scott (RC; 1880–1960), the winner of an architectural competition in 1903. Built of local sandstone, on a massive scale, high on St James's Mount, it dominates Merseyside. The foundation stone was laid in 1904. The Lady Chapel was consecrated in 1910 and the chancel in 1924. After his death, Scott's partner shortened and simplified the plans

for the west end, consolidating the building symmetrically about the central tower. It was completed in 1978.

(2) THE RC CATHEDRAL. A large Gothic revival building was originally designed by A. W. *Pugin in 1853, on a site at Everton, but only the Lady Chapel was built. In 1930 Sir Edwin Lutyens (1869–1944) designed a massive domed building for a new site in the centre of the city; the foundation stone was laid in 1934, but the Second World War and rises in building costs caused it to be abandoned on completion of the crypt. The design of Sir Frederick Gibberd (1908–84), the winner of an architectural competition in 1959, is a circular and completely modern building, incorporating the crypt. A congregation of 2,000 people can encircle the central altar, which is surmounted by a tower of coloured glass. The Cathedral is dedicated to Christ the King and was consecrated in May 1967.

(1) V. E. Cotton, *The Book of Liverpool Cathedral* (1928; rev., 1964). J. Riley, *Today's Cathedral: The Cathedral Church of Christ, Liverpool* (1978).

(2) F. Gibberd, *Metropolitan Cathedral of Christ the King Liverpool* (1968). A. S. G. Butler and others, *The Architecture of Sir Edwin Lutyens*, 3 (1950), pp. 47–51.

J. N. Tarn, 'Liverpool's Two Cathedrals', in D. Wood (ed.), *The Church and the Arts* (Studies in Church History, 28; Oxford, 1992), pp. 537–69.

Livingstone, David (1813–73), missionary and explorer. A native of Blantyre in Strathclyde, he educated himself by omnivorous reading while employed in a cotton factory. The study of Thomas Dick's *Philosophy of a Future State* determined him to devote his life to missionary work and the alleviation of suffering; and after attending medical classes in Glasgow, in 1838 he went to London, where he joined the *LMS, at first contemplating work in *China. In 1840, inspired by R. *Moffat, he embarked for the Cape of Good Hope and for some years worked as a missionary in the Bechuana country. Here he became passionately interested in Africa and worked for several years among her people, winning their confidence by his medical work and schools. Reports of his explorations and experiences aroused wide interest in England and he was greeted with enthusiasm on his return in 1856. In 1858 he resumed his travels in Africa, no longer under the auspices of the LMS, as he had ceased to be a missionary in the technical sense. In 1861, however, he gave pioneer help to the *UMCA (q.v.). In 1859 he discovered the lakes of Shirwa and Nyasa; he later explored the basin of the Upper Nile and discovered Lake Bangweulu in 1868. In 1871 he was found in a state of exhaustion by H. M. *Stanley of the *New York Herald*. He died in 1873 in the village of Ilala and was buried in *Westminster Abbey. His principal works were his *Missionary Travels and Researches in South Africa* (1857) and *The Zambesi and its Tributaries* (1865), which both had a wide circulation.

Livingstone's Private Journals, 1851–1853, ed. I. Schapera (London, 1960); *African Journal, 1853–1856*, ed. id. (2 vols., ibid., 1963); *The Zambesi Expedition . . ., 1858–1863*. Journals with letters and dispatches, ed. J. P. R. Wallis (2 vols., ibid., 1956); *Last Journals in Central Africa from 1865 to his Death*, ed. H. Waller (2 vols., ibid., 1874). *Some Letters from Livingstone, 1840–1872*, ed. D. Chamberlin (ibid., 1940); *Family Letters, 1841–1856*, ed. I. Schapera (2 vols., ibid., 1959). *The Zambesi Doctors: David Livingstone's Letters to John Kirk 1858–1872*, ed. R. Foskett (Edinburgh, 1964). Lives incl. those of W. G. Blaikie (London,

1880; the official biography), R. J. Campbell (ibid., 1929), G. Seaver (ibid., 1957), and O. Ransford (ibid., 1978). R. Coupland, *Livingstone's Last Journey* (1945). D. O. Helly, *Livingstone's Legacy: Horace Waller and Victorian Mythmaking* (Athens, Oh., and London [1987]). J. A. Casada, *Dr David Livingstone and Sir Henry Morton Stanley: An Annotated Bibliography* (1976), pp. 15–102, 192–4. R. H. Vetch in *DNB* 33 (1893), pp. 384–96.

Llandaff. Welsh episcopal see, two miles north of the centre of Cardiff. The diocese used to cover most of SE Wales, but in 1921 the diocese of Monmouth was formed out of it. Its early history, to the first part of the 12th cent., is told in the 'Book of Llandaff', which is not a trustworthy source. Written mainly in Latin, with some pieces in Welsh, it was largely inspired by Bp. Urban (1107–33) and produced to assert the rights of the see over territory claimed by *Hereford and *St Davids; it includes fictitious Lives of St *Dubricius, St *Teilo, and Oudoceus, who, though associated with St *Peter in the dedication of the cathedral, prob. had nothing to do with Llandaff. It has none the less been argued that the charters in the Book are based on original records and show something of the ecclesiastical life of SE Wales before fixed dioceses were established. When, under the Norman kings, diocesan organization of the Church spread to Wales, the see (originally of Glamorgan) emerged, with the head of the monastic community as its bishop. In 1107 Bp. Urban formally recognised the jurisdiction of *Canterbury. In 1120 he began to build the cathedral. Bp. Anthony Kitchin (d. 1563) was the only Marian bishop to take the Oath of Supremacy in 1559. In the early years of the Elizabethan Reformation the diocese was a centre of *recusancy, but in the later 17th cent. it became a stronghold of *Puritanism. During the 18th and the first half of the 19th cent. Llandaff was unfortunate in its bishops, who were mostly Englishmen with little interest in their diocese; but from the middle of the 19th cent. Church life revived. Between 1844 and 1869 the medieval cathedral, much of which was in a ruinous condition, was restored. Many new churches and mission halls were built, and in 1907 St Michael's Theological College (originally founded at Aberdare in 1892) was moved to Llandaff. The cathedral was badly damaged in an air raid in 1941; when it was restored in 1957 an impressive figure of 'Christ in Majesty' by Sir Jacob Epstein (d. 1959) was placed high at the east end of the nave.

The 'Book of Llandaff', ed., with Eng. tr., by W. J. Rees (Welsh Manuscript Society, 1; 1840); suppl. notes by T. Wakeman appended (sep. pagination) to W. J. Rees, *Lives of the Cambro-British Saints* (ibid. 4; 1853). Text reproduced from the Gwysaney MS, with transcription, by J. G. Evans and J. Rhys (Series of Old Welsh Texts, 4; Oxford, 1893; repr. Aberystwyth, 1979). W. Davies, *The Llandaff Charters* (ibid., 1979). Id., *An Early Welsh Microcosm: Studies in the Llandaff Charters* (Royal Historical Society Studies in History Series, 9; 1978). J. C. Davies (ed.), *Episcopal Acts and Cognate Documents relating to Welsh Dioceses 1066–1272*, 2 (Historical Society of the Church in Wales, 3–4; 1948), pp. 607–753. D. Crouch (ed.), *Llandaff Episcopal Acta 1140–1287* (Publications of the South Wales Record Society, 5; 1988). J. A. Bradney (ed.), *Acts of the Bishops of Llandaff* [1660–1724] (4 books in 3 vols., Llandaff Records, 2–4; 1908–12). C. [N. L.] Brooke, 'The Archbishops of St David's, Llandaff and Caerleon-on-Usk', in N. K. Chadwick and others, *Studies in the Early British Church* (Cambridge, 1958), pp. 201–42, rev. in id., *The Church and the Welsh Border in the Central Middle Ages*

(Studies in Celtic History, 8; Woodbridge, Suffolk, 1986), pp. 16–46. W. de G. Birch, *Memorials of the See and Cathedral of Llandaff* (Neath, 1912). B. Willis, *A Survey of the Cathedral Church of Llandaff* (1719). E. J. Newell, *Llandaff* (Diocesan Histories; 1902); E. [A.] Foord, *St David's, Llandaff and Brecon* (Cathedrals, Abbeys, and Famous Churches; 1925), pp. 97–124. J. Fisher in *DECH*, pp. 333–5, s.v. See also works cited s.v. WALES, CHRISTIANITY IN.

Lloyd, Charles (1784–1829), Bp. of Oxford from 1827. After a brilliant career at Christ Church, Oxford, where he was in turn lecturer, tutor, and censor, he was appointed Regius professor of divinity in 1822, an office which he retained until his death. He was a *High Churchman, and by his teaching influenced J. H. *Newman, E. B. *Pusey, and R. H. *Froude. He emphasized, as *Tract 90 did later, the importance of distinguishing between the decrees of the Council of *Trent and popular RC practice, and he insisted upon the primitive and medieval elements in the BCP. He was the tutor, friend, and counsellor of the statesman Sir Robert Peel.

W. J. Baker, *Beyond Port and Prejudice: Charles Lloyd of Oxford 1784–1829* (Orono, Me., 1981). R. Garnett in *DNB* 33 (1893), pp. 411–14.

Llull, Ramon (*c.*1233–*c.*1315) (also **Lull**) lay missionary and philosopher. Of well-to-do parents, Llull was born in Majorca, which had recently been recovered after three cents. under *Islamic rule. He was educated as a knight and became seneschal to the son of James I of Aragon, later James II of Majorca. He married and had two children. At the age of 30 he had a vision of Christ crucified, which led him to devote himself wholly to His service. His chief mission was the conversion of Islam. On the advice of St *Raymond of Peñafort he remained in Majorca studying Arabic and Christian thought for nine years. During this time he composed his first work, the 'Book of Contemplation'; it was written in Arabic and translated into Catalan. This period of his life culminated in a vision on Mt. Randa (*c.*1274), in which the form in which he was to set out his ideas was revealed to him; he worked this out in his 'Art of Finding Truth'. In 1276 he persuaded James II to set up a place of study at Miramar in Majorca where 13 *Franciscans could study oriental languages. The next decade of his life is obscure. From 1287 onwards, when he made his first visit to Paris, he was engaged in constant travel, visiting the courts of France, Aragon, and the Pope, trying to win support for his plans for converting Islam, elaborating his ideas, and writing a large number of books and tracts. On three occasions he went on missions in N. Africa. His one practical success was the decree of the Council of *Vienne (1311–12) establishing *studia* of oriental languages in five universities. The often repeated statement that he died a martyr's death at Bougie in N. Africa, stoned by the populace, does not rest on any contemporary evidence.

Llull's basic aim in his writings was the conversion of Islam and of the Jews, 'that in the whole world there may not be more than one language, one belief, one faith' (*Blanquerna*, c. 94). With this aim he elaborated an approach by which he hoped to convince them by rational argument, without recourse to the authority of Scripture. In his *Art* (in its final elaboration, *Ars generalis ultima*, finished in 1308), he attempted to relate 'all forms of knowledge (including religious belief) to the manifestations of God's "Dignities" [i.e. Divine Attributes] in the universe, taking for its point of departure the monotheistic vision common to Judaism, Islam and Christianity, and their acceptance of a broadly Neoplatonic exemplarist world-picture, and arguing ... analogically up and down "the ladder of being" ' (R. D. F. Pring-Mill). In his exposition Llull made extensive use of diagrams and of the representation of philosophical terms by letters of the alphabet, which, rightly combined, could, he held, provide the solution to any problem. He had no training in the scholastic theology of the universities and his works seemed difficult and strange to many, but for a few they had a strong attraction, and his writings were widely diffused. Among those whom he influenced was *Nicholas of Cusa.

As a mystic Llull has been considered the forerunner of St *Teresa and St *John of the Cross. His conception of the mystic life centres in the contemplation of the Divine perfections, which is achieved by the purification of memory, understanding, and will, and results in action for the greater glory of God. He was one of the most ardent defenders of the *Immaculate Conception in the Middle Ages. His cult, which developed soon after his death, was hindered by the ecclesiastical authorities owing to the difficulties in his teaching, but it was approved by *Pius IX in 1847. Interest in him has been steadily growing in recent times.

Opera Latina, ed. F. Stegmüller (1–5, Majorca, 1959–67); cont. by H. Harada, OFM, and others (CCCM 32–9; 1975–85; and 75, 76, 78, 79, 80, 111, etc., 1986 ff.). *Obres*, ed. M. Obrador y Bennásar and others (Majorca, 1906 ff.). *Obres essencials*, ed. M. Batllori, SJ (2 vols., Barcelona, 1957–[60]), incl. Life. *Liber Predicationis Contra Judaeos*, ed. J. M. Millás Vallicrosa (Madrid and Barcelona, 1957). Eng. trs. from the Catalan by E. A. Peers of his *Blanquerna: A Thirteenth-Century Romance* (London [1926]), *The Book of the Lover and the Beloved* (ibid., 1923), *The Art of Contemplation* (ibid., 1925), *The Tree of Life* (ibid., 1926) and *The Book of the Beasts* (ibid., 1927). Eng. tr. of *Selected Works*, with valuable introds., by A. Bonner (2 vols., Princeton, NJ [1985]). The principal authority for his life is a contemporary Life surviving in Lat. and Catalan. Lat. text ed. B. de Gaiffier, SJ, in *Anal. Boll.* 48 (1930), pp. 130–78, with refs. E. A. Peers, *Ramón Lull: A Biography* (1929). E. W. Platzeck, *Raimund Lull: Sein Leben, seine Werke, die Grundlagen seines Denkens* (Bibliotheca Franciscana, 5–6; Düsseldorf, 1962–4). J. N. Hillgarth, *Ramón Lull and Lullism in Fourteenth-Century France* (Oxford Warburg Studies, 1971). M. D. Johnston, *The Spiritual Logic of Ramon Llull* (Oxford, 1987); id., *The Evangelical Rhetoric of Ramon Llull* (New York and Oxford, 1996). *Raymond Lulle et le Pays d'Oc*, with introd. by M.-H. Vicaire (Cahiers de Fanjeaux, 22 [1987]). E. Longpré, OFM, in *DTC* 9 (pt. 1; 1926), cols. 1072–141, s.v., with full bibl. R. D. F. Pring-Mill in *EB* (1968 edn.), 13, pp. 173 f., s.v. 'Llull, Ramon'; A. Bonner and C. Lohr in *Dict. Sp.* 13 (1988), cols. 171–87, s.v. 'Raymond Lulle'.

LMS. The 'London Missionary Society' was founded in 1795 by a body of *Congregationalists, *Anglicans, *Presbyterians, and *Wesleyans who combined to promote Christian missions to the heathen. The first 29 missionaries under its auspices sailed to Tahiti in 1796. It was one of its principles that no form of denominationalism should be preached by its members, but that decisions about the form of Church government be left to those whom they should convert. In recent times the Society, which carried on extensive work in *China, *India, SE Asia, S. and E. Africa and the *South Pacific was maintained almost exclusively by Congregationalists, and in 1966 responsibility for its work passed to the (then Congregational) *Council for World Mission.

R. Lovett, *The History of the London Missionary Society, 1795–1895* (2 vols., 1899); N. Goodall, *A History of the London Missionary Society, 1895–1945* (1954). A. J. Hanna, 'The Role of the London Missionary Society in the Opening Up of East Central Africa', *Transactions of the Royal Historical Society*, 5th ser. 5 (1955), pp. 41–59.

Locke, John (1632–1704), English philosopher. A native of Wrington, Avon, he was educated at Westminster School and *Christ Church, Oxford, where he was deeply influenced by the works of R. *Descartes, whose emphasis on reason made a lasting impression on him. In 1666 he became acquainted with Lord Ashley, later first Earl of Shaftesbury, who made him his secretary, and with whom he moved to London. In 1675 he went to France, returning to England in 1679, but after the fall of Shaftesbury escaped to the Netherlands in 1683, where he remained till 1689. After the accession of William and Mary he once more returned to London. After the *Exclusion Controversy, he had been expelled from his Studentship at Christ Church (1684); from 1691 till his death he lived in the manor house of Oates, in Essex.

Locke was the foremost defender of free inquiry and toleration in the later 17th cent. His system is a combination of Christian rationalism and empiricism. In the *Letters concerning Toleration* (1689, 1690, and 1692) he pleaded for religious liberty for all except atheists and RCs, who were excluded because he held them to be a danger to the state. His ideal was a national Church with an all-embracing creed that made ample allowance for individual opinion, on the ground that human understanding was too limited for one man to impose his beliefs on another. In 1690 he published his *Two Treatises of Government*, expounding the principles of the Whig Revolution of 1688. They were hardly profound, but their historical importance was great through their influence in the following century. The substance of his philosophical thought is contained in the famous *Essay concerning Human Understanding* (1690 [in fact pub. in 1689]). In it he attacks the Platonist conception of 'innate ideas'. The human mind is a *tabula rasa* and all our ideas come from experience, i.e. from sensation or reflection, knowledge through reason being, acc. to him, a 'natural revelation'. Pure reality cannot be grasped by the human mind; consequently there is no sure basis for metaphysics, and substance is 'an uncertain supposition of we know not what'. The spirituality of the soul, though not certain, is at least probable; the existence of God, on the other hand, can be discovered with certainty by reason, and His law gives men their rule of conduct.

Locke's religious ideas were further developed in *The Reasonableness of Christianity as Delivered in the Scriptures* (1695). Here he maintains that the only secure basis of Christianity is its reasonableness, though he accepts the miracles recorded in Scripture as proofs of its Divine origin. Reason, however, has the last word in the acceptance of the supernatural and the interpretation of Scripture. The essence of Christianity is the acknowledgement of Christ as the Messiah, who was sent into the world chiefly to spread the true knowledge of God and of our duties. All other doctrines are secondary and incapable of conclusive proof. The book roused much controversy, among its critics being John Edwards (1637–1716), J. *Sergeant and Thomas Burnet (1635–1715). In his last years Locke devoted himself to the study of Scripture; the outcome was two posthumous works, *A Paraphrase and Notes on the Epistles of St Paul* (1705–7) and *A Discourse on Miracles* (1706).

The many collected edns. of his Works incl. 3 vols., fol., London, 1714; ed. E. Law, Bp. of Carlisle, 4 vols., London, 1777; and the Clarendon Edition, ed. successively P. H. Nidditch and J. W. Yolton (Oxford, 1975 ff.). This last incl. his *Essay concerning Human Understanding*, ed. P. H. Nidditch (1975; text repr., without introd., 1979); *Correspondence*, ed. E. S. de Beer (9 vols., 1976 ff.); and *A Paraphrase and Notes on the Epistles of St Paul*, ed. A. W. Wainwright (2 vols., 1987). Three sets of early writings pub. for the first time by W. von Leyden, *Essays on the Law of Nature: The Latin text with a translation, introduction and notes, together with transcripts of Locke's shorthand in his Journal for 1676* (Oxford, 1954). *Two Tracts on Government*, ed., with Eng. tr., by P. Abrams (Cambridge, 1967). Crit. edns. of his *Two Treatises of Government* by P. Laslett (ibid., 1960; 2nd edn., 1967) and of the orig. Lat. text of his *Epistola de Tolerantia* (orig. pub. anonymously in 1689) by R. Klibansky, with Eng. tr. by J. W. Gough (Oxford, 1968). *The Reasonableness of Christianity*, with *A Discourse of Miracles* and part of *A Third Letter concerning Toleration*, abridged, with introd., by I. T. Ramsey (1958). The standard Life of Locke is that of H. R. Fox Bourne (2 vols., London, 1876). The best modern Life, with material from the Lovelace Collection, is that of M. Cranston (ibid., 1957). Other general studies by R. I. Aaron ('Leaders of Philosophy', Oxford, 1937; 3rd edn., 1971), D. J. O'Connor (Harmondsworth, 1952; repr., New York, 1967), R. S. Woolhouse (Brighton, 1983), J. W. Yolton (1985), and M. Ayers ('The Arguments of the Philosophers', 2 vols., London, 1991). H. McLauchlan, *The Religious Opinions of Milton, Locke and Newton* (Publications of the University of Manchester, 276, Theological Series, 6; 1941), pp. 67–114. J. W. Gough, *John Locke's Political Philosophy* (1950). J. W. Yolton (ed.), *John Locke: Problems and Perspectives* (Cambridge, 1969); id., *John Locke and the Compass of Human Understanding: A Selective Commentary on the 'Essay'* (ibid., 1970). J. Dunn, *The Political Thought of John Locke: An Historical Account of the Argument of the 'Two Treatises of Government'* (ibid., 1969). J. L. Mackie, *Problems from Locke* (Oxford, 1976). I. C. Tipton (ed.), *Locke on Human Understanding* (ibid., 1977). W. M. Spellman, *John Locke and the Problem of Depravity* (ibid., 1988). R. Ashcraft, *Revolutionary Politics & Locke's* Two Treatises of Government (Princeton, NJ [1986]). Id. (ed.), *Locke: Critical Assessments* (4 vols., 1991). A. J. Simmons, *The Lockean Theory of Rights* (Princeton, NJ [1992]). J. Harrison and P. Laslett, *The Library of John Locke* (Oxford Bibliographical Society Publications, NS 13; 1965; 2nd edn., 1971). R. Hall and R. [S.] Woolhouse, *80 Years of Locke Scholarship* (Edinburgh [1983]); J. S. and J. W. Yolton, *John Locke: A Reference Guide* (Boston [1985]).

loculus. (1) The commonest type of tomb in the *catacombs, in the form of a horizontal rectangular niche. The *loculi* are cut, one above another, in the sides of the corridors. Each is closed at the front by a tile or marble slab which bears the epitaph. (2) A name sometimes given to the hole ('sepulchre') in a fixed *altar in which relics were placed before 1977.

On (1) H. Leclercq, OSB, in *DACL* 9 (pt. 2; 1930), cols. 1934–43, s.v., with refs. E. Diehl, *Inscriptiones Latinae Christianae Veteres* (3 vols., Berlin, 1925–31), esp. vol. 2, pp. 222–32 and 279–86.

logia (Gk. λόγια, 'sayings'). In NT criticism the term is applied to a supposed collection of the sayings of Christ which circulated in the early Church. The use of the word in this connection derives from the statement of *Papias that 'Matthew compiled the logia (τὰ λόγια) in the Hebrew language, and each person interpreted them as he was able'. As many scholars have held that the reference here is to the lost document '*Q' (q.v.) which was drawn upon by Mt. and Lk., the term has often been used as a synonym for 'Q'. The word is also used of the '*Sayings of Jesus' (q.v.) discovered at *Oxyrhynchus in 1897 and 1904.

Logos (Gk. Λόγος, 'Word' or 'Reason'), used esp. in Christian theology with reference to the Second Person of the Trinity. The term was known both in pagan and in Jewish antiquity. Heraclitus (*c.*500 BC) conceived of the Logos in a pantheistic way as the universal reason governing and permeating the world, and the Stoics took over the idea and popularized it. In the OT God's word was not only the medium of his communication with men: what God said had creative power (Gen. 1, vv. 3, 6, 9, etc., Ps. 33: 6), and by the time of the Prophets the Word of the Lord was presented as having an almost independent existence (1 Sam. 15: 10; Is. 55: 11; Jer. 23: 29). In the *Targums the Word was used as a means of speaking of God without using his name (see MEMRA). In Hellenistic Judaism the concept of the Logos as an independent *hypostasis was further developed, and the Logos also came to be associated with the figure of Wisdom (Wisd. Sol. 9: 1–2; 18: 15). *Philo to some extent combined the Greek and the biblical concepts: for him the Logos is the Divine pattern from which the material world is copied, the Divine power in the cosmos, the Divine purpose or agent in creation and an intermediary between God and man.

In the NT the term in its technical sense is confined to the Johannine writings (Jn. 1: 1 and 14; 1 Jn. 1: 1; and Rev. 19: 13). In the Prologue of the Gospel the Logos is described as God from eternity, the Creative Word, who became incarnate in the man, Jesus Christ of Nazareth. Though various antecedents for the Evangelist's ideas have been suggested, his identification of the Logos with the Messiah was entirely new.

In patristic times teaching about the Logos was developed by St *Ignatius and by the *Apologists of the 2nd cent., who saw in it a welcome means of making the Christian teaching compatible with Hellenistic philosophy. *Justin Martyr, e.g., held that the Logos was generated by an act of will of the Father with a view to creation, and *Theophilus, following the Stoics, distinguished the λόγος ἐνδιάθετος, i.e. the Logos immanent in God before creation, from the λόγος προφορικός, i.e. the Logos externalized as the instrument of creation. Speculation about the Logos is also found among the *Gnostics. *Clement of Alexandria made the Logos doctrine a chief part of his teaching, whilst *Irenaeus pointed out the dangers of going into too detailed speculations. St *Athanasius is among the first to give a comprehensive and completely satisfactory presentation of the Christian Logos conception by linking it up with the whole doctrine of Redemption. St *Augustine connected it with the image of the Trinity in the human soul. The whole complex of earlier teaching was eventually systematized in the teaching of the

Schoolmen, esp. in the *Summa Theologiae* of St *Thomas Aquinas.

A. Aall, *Der Logos: Geschichte seiner Entwickelung in der griechischen Philosophie und der christlichen Literatur* (2 vols., 1896–9). J. Réville, *La Doctrine du Logos dans le quatrième évangile et dans les œuvres de Philon* (1881). J. Lebreton, *Histoire du dogme de la Trinité des origines au concile de Nicée*, 1 (1910), pp. 41–73; Eng. tr., 1 (1939), pp. 40–60. G. L. Prestige, *God in Patristic Thought* (1936), esp. ch. 6. W. Kelber, *Die Logoslehre von Heraklit bis Origenes* (Stuttgart, 1958). B. L. Mack, *Logos und Sophia: Untersuchungen zur Weisheitstheologie im hellenistischen Judentum* (Studien zur Unwelt des Neuen Testaments, 10 [1973]). J. D. G. Dunn, *Christology in the Making: A New Testament Inquiry into the Origins of the Doctrine of the Incarnation* (1980), pp. 213–50. T. F. Glasson, 'Heraclitus' alleged Logos Doctrine', *JTS* NS 3 (1952), pp. 231–8, with refs. W. R. *Inge in *HERE* 8 (1915), pp. 133–8, s.v.; H. Leisegang in *PW* 13 (1926), cols. 1035–81, s.v.; H. Kleinknecht and others in *TWNT* 4 (1942), pp. 76–140 (Eng. tr., 4, 1967, pp. 76–136), s.v. λέγω etc., with further bibl., 10/2 (1979), pp. 1157–60; A. Michel in *DTC* 15 (pt. 2; 1950), cols. 2639–72, s.v. 'Verbe'; R. J. Tournay, OP, and others in *Dict. Bibl.*, Suppl. 5 (1957), cols. 425–97, s.v.

Loisy, Alfred Firmin (1857–1940), French *Modernist biblical scholar. A native of Ambrièrcs (Marne), he came of farming stock. Educated at the diocesan seminary at Châlons-sur-Marne and at the *Institut Catholique in Paris, he was ordained priest in 1879. After a short time as a country curé, he returned to Paris at the instigation of L. *Duchesne, who inspired him with zeal for historico-critical study. It was to the critical study of the Bible that Loisy devoted himself, and in this sphere he came to feel the need for a radical renewal of conventional ecclesiastical teaching. Although by 1886 his own faith in traditional Catholicism had been severely strained he remained in the RC Church in the hope of modernizing its teaching. In 1890, when he was appointed Professor of Sacred Scripture at the Institut Catholique, he was already publishing the results of his critical studies, which were arousing both enthusiasm and suspicion. In 1893 he was dismissed from his professorship and urged to confine himself to oriental languages. From this time he received encouragement from his friends E. I. Mignot (1842–1918), Abp. of Albi, and F. *von Hügel. From 1894 to 1896 he was chaplain to the *Dominican nuns and their school at Neuilly; here he had ample time to work out a new apologetic for Catholicism. From 1900 he taught at the École Pratique des Hautes Études.

In 1902 Loisy published *L'Évangile et l'Église*; it took the form of a reply to A. *Harnack's *Wesen des Christentums* (1900), but it was in effect a sensationally novel defence of Catholicism. As against Harnack, who sought to base Christianity on the teaching of the historic Jesus apart from later dogmatic accretions, Loisy maintained that its essence was to be sought in the faith of the developed Church as expanded under the guidance of the Spirit. The fact that Christ did not found a Church or institute Sacraments did not detract from their central place in the Christian life. The book was welcomed in some quarters, but also violently attacked. It was condemned by the Abp. of Paris and by a few other French bishops, but the Papacy refrained from intervening. When, however, in the following year Loisy published not only *Autour d'un petit livre*, which dealt with the controversy

that had arisen, but also *Le Quatrième Évangile*, Pope *Pius X, who had just succeeded *Leo XIII, placed both these books and other works of his on the *Index. In 1904 Loisy reluctantly made a formal act of submission, resigned his lectureship at the École Pratique des Hautes Études, and retired to the country. In 1906 he abandoned his priestly functions. A final breach with the Church came after the Papal acts of 1907 which condemned Modernism. Loisy published *Simples Réflexions sur le décret du Saint-Office Lamentabili sane Exitu et sur l'encyclique* Pascendi Dominici gregis (1908), as well as his great work *Les Évangiles synoptiques* (2 vols., 1907–8). On 7 Mar. 1908 he was excommunicated.

From 1909 to 1930 Loisy was professor of the history of religions at the Collège de France. He was a prolific writer and during this period he published major works on Christian origins and on the comparative history of religions, such as *Les Actes des Apôtres* (1920) and *Essai historique sur le sacrifice* (1920), and smaller books in which he foreshadowed his own religious and moral philosophy, notably *La Religion* (1917; 2nd edn., 1924). In his autobiographical writings, *Choses passées* (1913) and *Mémoires pour servir à l'histoire religieuse de notre temps* (3 vols., 1930–1), he sought to justify his part in the Modernist movement and to interpret its history. After his break with the Church, his work as a biblical critic, despite the brilliance of style and learning which characterized it, was generally regarded as erratic and recklessly conjectural. His final views on the NT are summed up in *La Naissance du christianisme* (1933), in which he treated the Gospels not as historical documents but as catechetical and cultural literature with but slight historical basis. The works of his last years, however, attacked the proponents of the Christ-myth theories and appear more in line with his earlier Christian faith. Since 1968 many volumes of his private papers have been accessible in the Bibliothèque Nationale at Paris. They emphasize that he was a mystic, with a pastoral sense, as well as a savant, and reveal the complexity of his character as well as the range of his interests and friendships.

R. Marlé, SJ, *Au cœur de la crise moderniste: Le dossier inédit d'une controverse. Lettres de Maurice Blondel, H. Bremond, Fr. von Hügel, Alfred Loisy, Fernand Mourret, J. Wehrlé* (1960). Contemporary accounts by [H. *Bremond], *Un Clerc qui n'a pas trahi*, pub. under the pseudonym Sylvain Leblanc (1931); M. J. *Lagrange, OP, *M. Loisy et le modernisme* (1932); and A. Houtin (d. 1926) and F. Sartiaux (d. 1944), *Alfred Loisy: Sa Vie, son œuvre*, ed. E. Poulat (1960). M. D. Petre, *Alfred Loisy: His Religious Significance* (1944); F. *Heiler, *Der Vater der katholischen Modernismus, Alfred Loisy* (Munich, 1947); R. de Boyer de Sainte Suzanne, *Alfred Loisy entre la foi et l'incroyance* [1968], with some unpub. letters; M. Guasco, *Alfred Loisy in Italia* (Pubblicazioni dell'Istituto di Scienze Politiche dell'Università di Torino, 33; 1975), also with unpub. letters. F. Turvasi, *The Condemnation of Alfred Loisy and the Historical Method* (Uomini e Dottrine, 24; 1979). A. R. Vidler, *The Modernist Movement in the Roman Catholic Church* (1934), pp. 67–139; id., *A Variety of Catholic Modernists* (Sarum Lectures for 1968–9; Cambridge, 1970), esp. pp. 20–56. J. Ratté, *Three Modernists* (1968), pp. 43–141, with bibl. pp. 353 f. A. H. Jones, *Independence and Exegesis: The Study of Early Christianity in the Work of Alfred Loisy ... Charles Guignebert ... and Maurice Goguel ...* (Beiträge zur Geschichte der Biblischen Exegese, 26; 1983), pp. 60–127. J. Bonsirven in *Dict. Bibl.*, Suppl. 5 (1957), cols. 530–44. See also other works cited s.v. MODERNISM.

Lollardy. A 'Lollard' was originally a follower of J. *Wycliffe; later, the name was applied somewhat vaguely to anyone seriously critical of the Church—knights who hankered after Church property, dissatisfied tenants of an oppressive abbey, parishioners who refused to pay tithes, and apocalyptic visionaries. The original meaning of the term would appear to be a 'chanter' and so a 'mumbler of prayers' (cf. Middle Dutch *lollen* or *lullen*, 'to sing'); but it was associated with the Latin *lolia* ('tares'). Its first use occurs in 1382 (as a term of contempt) and its first official use in 1387.

The Lollards, following Wycliffe, based their teaching on personal faith, Divine election, and, above all, the Bible. The Scriptures were the sole authority in religion and every man had the right to read and interpret them for himself. The Lollards commonly attacked clerical *celibacy, *transubstantiation, obligatory oral *confession, *indulgences, and *pilgrimages; and they held that the validity of priestly acts was determined by the priest's moral character and that endowments, the Pope, the hierarchy, and 'private religions' (of monks, friars, and canons) were all unscriptural. They propagated their teaching by various unlicensed preachers and by books.

The movement went through several phases. For about 20 years it enjoyed some academic support, though in 1382 Abp. W. *Courtenay condemned Wycliffe's teachings and started to deprive Lollardy of a base at Oxford. (see NICHOLAS HEREFORD and REPINGTON, P.) The chroniclers' allegations that some knights of Richard II's court supported Lollardy have been shown to have some justification. Following the accession of Henry IV and the return of Abp. T. *Arundel, rigorous persecution, esp. the passing of the statute *De Haeretico Comburendo* (1401) and the introduction of his Constitutions (1408), seriously diminished the number of the movement's adherents. After Sir J. *Oldcastle's rising in 1414, and another attempted rising in 1431, the movement went underground. Recent research into heresy cases suggests that (despite the attention given to it by Bp. R. *Pecock) Lollardy may have declined after the middle of the 15th cent., but revived after c.1490; early Tudor heresy trials reveal significant pockets of Lollardy composed mostly of craftsmen and town workers, esp. in the Chilterns, London, Kent, Essex, Coventry, and parts of the North.

Lollardy, while powerful enough to inhibit Catholic reforms in the 15th cent., at no time won over the governing classes in strength, and thus could not achieve a reformation unaided; but it contributed to the English Reformation by providing areas and minds receptive to *Lutheranism, and its influence continued in the movement now seen as its direct heir, the congregational dissent of the 17th cent. Lollardy was also powerful in Scotland and exercised an important influence on the development of the *Hussite rising in Bohemia.

A. Hudson (ed.), *Selections from English Wycliffite Writings* (Cambridge, 1978); *English Wycliffite Sermons*, ed. A. Hudson and P. Gradon (5 vols., Oxford, 1983–96). H. B. Workman, *John Wyclif: A Study of the English Medieval Church* (2 vols., 1926). K. B. McFarlane, *John Wycliffe and the Beginnings of English Nonconformity* (1952); id., *Lancastrian Kings and Lollard Knights* (posthumous; Oxford, 1972), esp. pp. 139–232. A. G. Dickens, *Lollards and Protestants in the Diocese of York 1509–1558* (1959). J. A. F. Thomson, *The Later Lollards 1414–1520* (Oxford, 1965).

M. E. Aston, 'Lollardy and Sedition 1381–1431', *Past and Present*, no. 17 (1960), pp. 1–44; id., 'Lollardy and the Reformation: Survival or Revival?', *History*, 49 (1964), pp. 149–70; id., 'John Wycliffe's Reformation Reputation', *Past and Present*, no. 30 (1965), pp. 23–51; repr., with other papers, in *Lollards and Reformers* (1984). A. Hudson, 'A Lollard Compilation and the Dissemination of Wycliffite Thought' *JTS* NS 23 (1972), pp. 65–81; id., 'The Examination of Lollards', *Bulletin of the Institute of Historical Research*, 46 (1973), pp. 145–59; id., 'The Debate on Bible Translation, Oxford 1401', *EHR* 90 (1975), pp. 1–18; repr., with other papers, in *Lollards and their Books* (1985). Id., *The Premature Reformation: Wycliffite Texts and Lollard History* (Oxford, 1988), with further bibl. M. Lambert, *Medieval Heresy* (2nd edn., 1992), pp. 243–83.

Lombard, Peter. See PETER LOMBARD.

London. See BOW CHURCH, BROMPTON ORATORY, ST PAUL'S CATHEDRAL, WESTMINSTER ABBEY and WESTMINSTER CATHEDRAL.

London Missionary Society. See LMS.

Longinus, St (prob. from Gk. λόγχη, 'lance'). The name traditionally given to the soldier who pierced the side of Christ with his spear. It can be traced back to the apocryphal 'Acts of *Pilate', one version of which also gives it to the centurion who, standing by the Cross, confessed Christ as the Son of God. In the later forms of the legend the two persons are often confused. *Bede, who is followed by many medieval authors, among them the author of the *Golden Legend, reports that he was martyred for his faith at Caesarea in Cappadocia in AD 58 and gives as his feast, which occurs in several old martyrologies, 15 Mar. In the E. his feast is observed on 16 Oct.

'Acta' of Longinus the soldier and of Longinus the centurion pr. in *AASS*, Mar. 2 (1668), pp. 376–90. 'Martyrium Sancti Longini Centurionis' attributed to *Hesychius of Jerusalem pr. in J. P. Migne, *PG* 93. 1546–60; Gk. text of 'Martyrium . . . Sancti Longini Centurionis' in *Simeon Metaphrastes, ibid. 115. 32–41. Though he does not accept its attribution to Hesychius, the 'Martyrium' and another 'Passio' are ed., with Fr. tr. and full introd., by M. Aubineau [SJ], *Les Homélies Festales d'Hésychius de Jérusalem*, 2 (Subsidia Hagiographica, 59; 1980), pp. 778–901. The cultus of the centurion (unnamed) in Cappadocia is attested by *Gregory of Nyssa, *Ep.* 17 (*PG* 46. 1061). F. J. Dölger, *Antike und Christentum*, 4 (1934), pp. 81–94 ('Die Blutsalbung des Soldaten mit der Lanze im Passionsspiel *Christus Patiens*'). R. J. Peebles, *The Legend of Longinus in Ecclesiastical Tradition and in English Literature and its Connection with the Grail* (Diss., Bryn Mawr College Monographs, Monograph Series, 9; 1911).

Longland, John (1473–1547), Bp. of *Lincoln. After a long period of study at Oxford, where he became Fellow of Magdalen, Longland was made Dean of *Salisbury in 1514 and Bp. of Lincoln in 1521. He was a staunch upholder of the royal supremacy, and as *Henry VIII's confessor took a prominent part in furthering the divorce proceedings with Catherine of Aragon. A preacher and a humanist of considerable repute, he enjoyed the warm friendship of *Erasmus.

A. H. Thompson (ed.), *Visitations in the Diocese of Lincoln, 1517–1531* (Lincoln Record Society, 33, 35, 37; 1940–7; discussion of injunctions and docs. relating to monasteries issued by Longland, ibid., vol. 2, pp. 201–22. Further extracts in A. Clark (ed.), *Lincoln Diocese Documents, 1450–1544* (EETS, Original

Series, 149; 1914), pp. 133–244, 245–54, incl. text of Longland's directions for publication in his diocese of Henry VIII's repudiation of the Pope's Supremacy, pp. 188–91. His Benedictional, ed. R. M. Woolley (HBS 64; 1927). M. Bowker, *The Henrician Reformation: The Diocese of Lincoln under John Longland 1521–1547* (Cambridge, 1981). *BRUO* 2 (1958), pp. 1160–2. M. Feingold in P. G. Beitenholz and T. B. Deutscher (eds.), *Contemporaries of Erasmus*, 2 [1986], pp. 341 f.

Longley, Charles Thomas (1794–1868), Abp. of *Canterbury. He was educated at Christ Church, Oxford, where he taught for some years before becoming headmaster of Harrow in 1829. In 1836 he brought to the school as a master J. W. *Colenso. In the same year he became Bp. of the newly-created diocese of *Ripon. A moderate *High Churchman, he opposed the ritualism of some *Tractarians and held that as a bishop he had the authority and duty to suppress such practices; he did so, amid much controversy, at E. B. *Pusey's newly-built church of St Saviour's, Leeds. He became Bp. of *Durham in 1856 and subsequently Abp. of *York (1860) and then of Canterbury (1862). At Canterbury he supported R. *Gray, Bp. of Cape Town, against Colenso and proceeded as far as he could in the case without provoking a conflict with the law. He disapproved of *Essays and Reviews* and was among those who urged its condemnation in *Convocation in 1864. The most significant event of his primacy was the first *Lambeth Conference in 1867. His cautious handling of requests and questions before the Conference and his judicious chairmanship of it contributed to the desire for a second such meeting of bishops in 1878 and did much to establish the ethos of successive Lambeth Conferences.

J. E. Sayers and E. G. W. Bill, *Calendar of the Papers of Charles Thomas Longley . . . in Lambeth Palace Library* (1976). E. [F.] Carpenter, *Cantuar: The Archbishops in their Office* (1971; 2nd edn., 1988), pp. 312–33. A. M. G. Stephenson, *The First Lambeth Conference 1867* (CHS, 1967). G. C. Boase in *DNB* 34 (1893), pp. 121 f.

Loofs, Friedrich (1858–1928), historian of doctrine. He studied at Leipzig, where under A. *Harnack he became a keen student of the history of dogma, and at Göttingen, where A. *Ritschl stimulated his interest in systematic theology. From 1882 to 1887 he taught at Leipzig. In 1887 he became extraordinary, and in 1888 full, professor at Halle, where he remained till his death. He took a prominent part in *Lutheran ecclesiastical affairs, becoming a member of the Saxon Consistory in 1910. Among many important essays in patristic subjects are a monograph on *Leontius of Byzantium (1887), his significant *Leitfaden zur Dogmengeschichte* (1890), works on the 'Sacra Parallela' of St *John of Damascus (1892) and *Eustathius of Sebaste (1898), a collection of the then-known *Nestoriana* (1905), and a comprehensive study of *Paul of Samosata (1924). He also took an active part in opposing E. *Haeckel's materialism in his *Anti-Haeckel* (1900; Eng. tr., 1903). An original interpretation of *Nestorian teaching was presented in *Nestorius and his Place in the History of Christian Doctrine* (1914), the substance of four lectures delivered at London in 1913.

Autobiog. notice in *Die Religionswissenschaft der Gegenwart in Selbstdarstellungen* (ed. E. Stange), 2 (1926), pp. 119–60, with bibl. S. Bitter in *TRE* 21 (1991), pp. 464–6, s.v.

Lopez, Gregory (1615/6–91), first native Chinese bishop. His native name was Lo Wên-tsao. Born of pagan parents in the province of Fukien, he embraced Christianity when he grew up, and was baptized by the *Franciscans. After studying at Manila, he joined the *Dominican Order; he was professed in 1651. In 1654 he was ordained the first Chinese priest. His success and zeal led the French bishops in Tonkin and Siam in 1674 to induce Clement X to offer him the titular bishopric of Basilopolis in Bithynia and the office of Vicar Apostolic of Nanking. Lopez, however, modestly declined the promotion. In 1679 *Innocent XI overruled his objections and ordered him to accept consecration. Now, however, the Dominican Master wanted him to have a European associate to advise him, and the Dominicans in Manila, where Lopez went for consecration, were apparently unwilling to proceed because of his attitude to the Rites Controversy (see CHINA, CHRISTIANITY IN). He was eventually consecrated in 1685 at Canton at the hands of Italian Franciscans. Later he was promoted to the new see of Nanking, but did not live to employ the title. There was no further native RC bishop in China until 1918.

B. [M.] Biermann, OP, 'Briefe des ersten chinesischen Priesters und Bischofs Fray Gregorio López, O.P. aus dem Indias-Archiv zu Sevilla (Fil. 305)', in J. Beckmann, SMB (ed.), *Der Einheimische Klerus in Geschichte und Gegenwart: Festschrift P. Dr Laurenz Kilger OSB zum 60. Geburtstag dargeboten von Freunden und Schülern* (Neue Zeitschrift für Missionswissenschaft, Supplementa 2; 1950), pp. 99–117, incl. text. J. M. González, OP, *Biografía del primer obispo Chino, Excmo. Sr. D. Fr. Gregorio Lo o López O.P.* (Manila 1946; enlarged edn., Pamplona, 1971). J. Hao Sy, OP, 'The Chinese indigenous clergy: the case of the Dominican Gregorio Lo Wen Tsao (1615–1691)', *Philippiniana Sacra*, 27 (Manila, 1992), pp. 313–25. Quétif and Échard, 2, pp. 708 f.; Eng. tr. by A. C. Moule in *New China Review*, 1 (Hong Kong, 1919), pp. 480–7; suppl. note by id., ibid. 3 (1921), pp. 138 f. A. Duval, OP, in *Catholicisme*, 7 (1975), cols. 1074 f., s.v. See also works cited s.v. CHINA, CHRISTIANITY IN.

Lord of Hosts (Heb. יְהוָה צְבָאוֹת). This Divine title occurs in the OT 282 times, all except 36 of them in the Prophetic writings. In its earliest usage among the Hebrews, it was probably based on the belief that it was their God *Yahweh who led and defended their armies against their enemies (cf., e.g., Ex. 7: 4, where the forces of Israel are described as 'the hosts of the Lord'), but in later times its reference was to God's dominion in majesty and power over the angels and other celestial beings and, *a fortiori*, His supremacy over the destinies of men. In the LXX the term is variously rendered as κύριος σαβαώθ (e.g. Is. 1: 9, which is quoted in the NT at Rom. 9: 29 and there traditionally rendered in English as 'Lord of Sabaoth', leaving the word 'Sabaoth' untranslated), κύριος τῶν δυνάμεων (e.g. Ps. 23: 10; Eng. versions 24: 10), and κύριος παντοκράτωρ (e.g. Hag. 1: 2). This last was rendered in Latin as *Deus omnipotens*, hence the English 'Almighty God'.

S. R. *Driver in *HDB* 3 (1900), pp. 137 f.; E. Kautzsch in *PRE* (3rd edn.), 21 (1908), pp. 620–7, s.v. 'Zebaoth'; M. Rose in *TRE* 16 (1987), pp. 438–41, s.v. 'Jahwe'; C. L. Seow in *Anchor Bible Dictionary*, 3 (1992), pp. 304–7, s.v. 'Hosts, Lord of'.

Lord of Misrule. See MISRULE, LORD OF.

Lord's Day, the. A Christian appellation of *Sunday, based on Rev. 1: 10 (ἡ κυριακὴ ἡμέρα). In recent times it has been used (esp. by Protestants) when special stress is laid on the sacred character of the day. In the 17th–18th cents., however, the title 'Lord's Day' (without the article) was fairly widely used as an ordinary name for the day, and not only among *Puritans. The Lord's Day Observance Society, founded in 1831 by D. *Wilson, later Bp. of Calcutta, has as its two principal objects the diffusion of information about the blessings of Sunday and the promotion of its observance as a weekly day of rest and worship.

Lord's Prayer (Lat. *Oratio Dominica* or *Pater Noster*), the prayer, 'Our Father', taught by the Lord to His disciples. In the NT it is given in two slightly different forms: in Mt. 6: 9–13, in the teaching on prayer in the *Sermon on the Mount, and in Lk. 11: 2–4, where Christ gives it in answer to the request 'Lord, teach us to pray'. The form in Mt. is that universally used by Christians; that in Lk. is shorter. In Lk. 11: 2 some MSS replace 'Thy kingdom come' with 'May thy Holy Spirit come upon us and cleanse us'. A concluding doxology was probably added in early times, for it occurs in the *Didache; a longer form of the doxology, based on 1 Chron. 29: 11, and corresponding to the formula in the BCP, is found in some later Gospel MSS. E. liturgies expand this with a reference to Father, Son, and Holy Spirit.

The Lord's Prayer is usually divided into the address and seven petitions, the first three asking for the glorification of God, the latter four being requests for the chief physical and spiritual needs of man. The meaning of ἐπιούσιος used to describe the bread which is sought (translated 'daily') is, however, uncertain. As a prayer given to the Church by the Lord Himself, it has always been regarded by Christians as uniquely sacred.

From early times the Lord's Prayer was taught to the *catechumens at *Baptism and used in the Liturgy. St *Cyprian already calls it 'the public and common prayer'. It has also regularly found a place in the celebration of the Eucharist. The first witness to it in this connection is St *Cyril of Jerusalem (c.350). Acc. to St *Augustine and to the *Ambrosian and *Mozarabic Liturgies, it was said after the Breaking of the Bread, immediately before the *Kiss of Peace and the Communion. St *Gregory the Great (d. 604), however, following the Greek Liturgies, placed it at the end of the Canon, before the Breaking of the Bread. He also appears to have held the opinion that the Apostles used the Lord's Prayer to consecrate the Eucharist. In the BCP, since 1552, it has followed the Communion. The ASB provides for its use either here or before or after the Breaking of the Bread. In the Divine *Office the Prayer has also occupied a prominent place. It is mentioned as part of *Lauds and *Vespers by the Synod of Gerona of 517, and St *Benedict prescribed it in his rule for all the Canonical Hours.

The *Breviary of 1568 laid down that it should be said before every Office except *Compline and before the ferial prayers. In *Paul VI's Breviary of 1971 it is said after the NT *Canticles and the intercessions, before the collect at Morning and Evening Prayer.

The Lord's Prayer has played a prominent part in Christian devotion. *Tertullian called it the 'epitome of the whole Gospel' (*breviarium totius evangelii*) and St Augustine the source of all other prayers. It has been frequently expounded either in commentaries on the Gospels or in separate treatises, notably by St *Maximus the Confessor, St *Thomas Aquinas, and St *Teresa of Ávila.

The version of the Lord's Prayer traditionally used by English-speaking Catholics and Protestants alike owed its general acceptance to an ordinance of *Henry VIII in 1541. It follows closely the form of the Prayer in W. *Tyndale's version of the NT. The concluding Doxology, however, which was not traditional in the liturgical tradition of W. Christendom, is first found in the Scottish BCP of 1637, whence it was taken over in many places in the revision of 1662.

Patristic comm. incl. Tertullian, *De Oratione*, 1–10, *Origen, *De Oratione*, esp. 22–30, Cyprian, *De Dominica Oratione*, and Augustine, *De Sermone Domini in Monte*, 2. 15–39. F. H. Chase, *The Lord's Prayer in the Early Church* (Texts and Studies, 1. 3; Cambridge, 1891); O. *Dibelius, *Das Vaterunser: Umrisse zu einer Geschichte des Gebets in der alten und mittleren Kirche* (Giessen, 1903); G. Walter, *Untersuchungen zur Geschichte der griechischen Vaterunser-Exegese* (1914); P. Fiebig, *Das Vaterunser: Ursprung, Sinn, und Bedeutung des christlichen Hauptgebetes* (Gütersloh, 1927); E. Lohmeyer, *Das Vater-unser* (1946; 3rd edn., 1952; Eng. tr., 1965); J. Lowe, *The Interpretation of the Lord's Prayer* (Evanston, Ill., 1955; expanded and rev. by C. S. C. Williams, Oxford, 1962); J. Jeremias, *Das Vater-Unser im Lichte der neueren Forschung* (Calwer Hefte zur Förderung biblischen Glaubens und christlichen Lebens, 50; Stuttgart, 1962; Eng. tr. in *The Prayers of Jesus* (Studies in Biblical Theology, 2nd ser. 6; 1967), pp. 82–107); C. F. Evans, *The Lord's Prayer* (1963); J. Carmignac, *Recherches sur le 'Notre Père'* (1969), with extensive bibl. Works of spirituality often take the form of comm. on the Lord's Prayer; these include L. Boff, *O pai-nosso: a oração de libertação integral* ([1979]; Eng. tr., Maryknoll, NY [1983]). E. *Nestle and J. C. Lambert in *DCG* 2 (1908), pp. 57–63, s.v., with full bibl. p. 60; H. *Leclercq, OSB, in *DACL* 12 (pt. 2; 1936), cols. 2244–55, s.v. 'Oraison dominicale'; J. L. Houlden in *Anchor Bible Dictionary*, 4 (1992), pp. 356–62, s.v.

Lord's Supper. A title for the Holy Communion, now used esp. among Protestants. It is taken from 1 Cor. 11: 20 (τὸ κυριακὸν δεῖπνον), where the rendering 'Lord's Supper' is found in the English *Lollard version of 1382. Its occurrence in the title of N. *Ridley's *Brief Declaration of the Lord's Supper*, written in 1554 while its author was in prison, helped to popularize the name. See also EUCHARIST.

Loreto, near Ancona in Italy, is the site of the Holy House, alleged to have been inhabited by the BVM at the time of the *Annunciation and to have been miraculously transported by angels from *Nazareth to Tersatz in Dalmatia in 1291 and thence by the same agency to Loreto in 1295. The earliest attestation of the legend is an account of the sanctuary written c.1470. The whole story is now commonly regarded as unhistorical, not least by RC writers of unquestioned orthodoxy. See also LITANY OF LORETO.

The traditional account in H. Tursellinus, *Lauretanae Historiae Libri V* (1597), and P. V. Martorelli, *Teatro Historico della S. Casa Nazarena* (3 vols., fol., 1732–5). Somewhat more critical, J. A. Vogel, *De Ecclesiis Recanatensi et Lauretana* (1859; but written in 1806), and Mgr Leopardi, *La Santa Casa di Loreto* (Lugano, 1841). The attack on the tradition, led by H. Grisar, SJ, at the Munich Congress in 1900, was brought to a conclusion by C. U. J. Chevalier, *Notre-Dame de Lorette: Étude historique sur l'authenticité de la Santa Casa* (1906). G. Hueffer, *Loreto: Eine geschichts-*

kritische Untersuchung der Frage des heiligen Hauses (2 vols., 1913–21). N. Alfieri and others, 'Contributi archeologici per la storia S. Casa di Loreto', *Studia Picena*, 35 (1967), pp. 64–128; idd., 'Nuovi contributi archeologici per la storia della S. Casa di Loreto', ibid. 36 (1968), pp. 1–112 [after excavations in 1962]. K. Weil-Garris, *The Santa Casa di Loreto: Problems in Cinquecento Sculpture* (2 vols., New York, 1977). F. [Grimaldi] da Morrovalle, OFM Cap., *L'archivio storico della Santa Casa di Loreto: Inventario* (Vatican City, 1965), H. Thurston in *CE* 13 (1912), pp. 454–6, s.v. 'Santa Casa di Loreto'.

Loric of St Patrick. See BREASTPLATE OF ST PATRICK.

Lorsch, *Benedictine Abbey near Worms. Founded in 764 with monks sent by *Chrodegang of Metz from *Gorze, it enjoyed the special favour of *Charlemagne and became one of the largest and best-endowed abbeys in Germany. Under St *Bruno (brother of the Emp. Otto I), in the middle of the 10th cent. it was a centre of the Gorze reform movement. Later it declined in importance. It became *Cistercian in 1232 and *Premonstratensian in 1248. In the Carolingian age there was built up one of the largest libraries in Europe, which is of great importance for the transmission of patristic texts. Considerable remains survive among the Palatine MSS in the *Vatican Library and among the Laudian MSS in the *Bodleian Library in Oxford.

Codex Laureshamensis, ed. K. Glöckner (Arbeiten der historischen Kommission für den Volksstaat Hessen; 3 vols., Darmstadt, 1929–36, repr., 1963); Ger. tr. by K. J. Minst (6 vols., Lorsch, 1966–72). *Laurissa Jubilans: Festschrift zur 1200-Jahrfeier von Lorsch* (Darmstadt, 1964); *Die Reichsabtei Lorsch: Festschrift zum Gedenken an ihre Stiftung 764*, ed. F. Knöpp (2 vols., ibid., 1973–7), incl. repr. in vol. 2, pp. 7–128, of B. Bischoff, *Lorsch im Spiegel seiner Handschriften* (Münchener Beiträge zur Mediävistik und Renaissance-Forschung, Beiheft, 1974). A number of important older arts. are repr. in *Beiträge zur Geschichte des Klosters Lorsch* (Geschichtsblätter für den Kreis Bergstrasse, Sonderband 4; Lorsch, 1978). Medieval library catalogue pr. in G. Becker, *Catalogi bibliothecarum antiqui* (Bonn, 1885), pp. 82–125. H. Hoffmann, *Buchkunst und Königtum im ottonischen und frühsalischen Reich* (Schriften der MGH, 30/1; 1986), pp. 203–26.

Lossky, Vladimir (1903–58), Russian lay theologian. The son of the philosopher Nicolas Lossky, he studied first at the University of St Petersburg and then, after expulsion from Russia by the Soviet government in 1922, at Prague and the *Sorbonne. He lived for the rest of his life in France. He became one of the leading exponents of Orthodox thought to the western world and a vigorous opponent of the sophiological doctrines of S. *Bulgakov. He devoted his concluding years to the study of *Eckhart, but his work on this subject was unfinished at the time of his death. His published writings include *Essai sur la théologie mystique de l'Église d'Orient* (1944; rev. Eng. tr., 1957); *Théologie négative et connaissance de Dieu chez Maître Eckhart* (1960); *Vision de Dieu* (Neuchâtel, 1962; Eng. tr., 1963); *À l'Image et à la ressemblance de Dieu* (1967; Eng. tr., 1974); and, with L. Ouspensky, *The Meaning of Icons* (Bern and Olten, 1952).

O. Clément, 'Vladimir Lossky, un théologien de la personne et du Saint-Esprit', *Messager de l'Exarchat du Patriarche russe en Europe occidentale*, 30–1 (1959), pp. 137–206.

Los von Rom (Ger., 'free from Rome'). A vigorous anti-Roman Movement begun in Austria in 1897 and fostered by the Pan-German party, who aimed at the incorporation of an Austria, freed from the Pope, into Germany under the protection of the Protestant Hohenzollern Emperors. The Movement, which owed its name to the shout of a student at the Deutscher Volkstag at Vienna (1897), came to have its centre at Innsbruck. Its chief organization was the 'Ulrich-Hutten-Bund', and among its principal leaders were G. von Schönerer, V. Eisenkolb, and Superintendent F. Meyer. Its influence was increased by the unsatisfactory situation of the Church in Austria, e.g. the unwieldy size of the dioceses, the lack of German priests, and esp. the anticlerical spirit of the secondary schools. Though most of those who left the RC Church (up to 1914 *c*.75,000) became nominal Protestants, the Movement was essentially anti-Christian, as the Pan-Germans favoured a neo-pagan 'German' religion, an aim later realized on a much greater scale by the National Socialists. From Austria parallel Los von Rom movements spread to other countries, e.g. *Poland (see MARIAVITES), *France, *Belgium, *Sri Lanka, and *Mexico, but with comparatively little success.

P. Braunlich, *Berichte über den Fortgang der 'Los von Rom-Bewegung'* (1. Reihe, Hefte 1–10, 2. Reihe, Hefte 1–10; 1899–1910). On the background, J. W. Boyer, *Political Radicalism in late Imperial Vienna: Origins of the Christian Social Movement 1848–1897* (Chicago and London [1981]), pp. 122–83. F. Lau in *RGG* (3rd edn.), 4 (1960), cols. 451–5, s.v.; H. Grote in *TRE* 21 (1991), pp. 469–71, s.v.

Lotze, Hermann (1817–81), logician and metaphysician. A native of Bautzen, he studied medicine and philosophy at Leipzig. After teaching for a short time at Leipzig (1839–42), he became professor of philosophy at Göttingen (1842; full professor 1844), where he remained until called to Berlin (1881) shortly before his death. He combined a firm belief in the reign of scientific law with conviction of the need for metaphysics, and opposed alike the theory of a specific *Lebenskraft* in nature ('vitalism') and the *a priori* constructions of the German Idealists (F. W. J. von *Schelling, G. W. F. *Hegel). He was insistent that philosophy must be rooted in the natural sciences, in which he retained his interest until his death. He had a firm faith in *Theism; and, believing in the validity of moral judgements, he became an early exponent of 'value philosophy'. His doctrines, first formulated in his *Metaphysik* (1841) and *Logik* (1843), were elaborated in a semi-popular form in his *Mikrokosmus* (3 vols., 1856–64; Eng. tr., 2 vols., 1885). He devoted his later years to the elaboration of a *System der Philosophie*, of which only two volumes were published, the *Logik* (1874; Eng. tr. by B. *Bosanquet, 1884) and *Metaphysik* (1879; Eng. tr. by id., 1884).

Lotze's main Works have been reissued, with introds., in the *Philosophische Bibliothek. Kleine Schriften*, ed. D. Peipers, 3 vols., 1885–91. T. M. *Lindsay, 'Hermann Lotze', *Mind*, 1 (1876), pp. 363–82. E. Pfleiderer, *Lotzes philosophische Weltanschauung nach ihren Grundzügen* (1882); E. von *Hartmann, *Lotzes Philosophie* (1888); H. Jones, *A Critical Account of the Philosophy of Lotze* (1895); R. Falckenberg, *Hermann Lotze* (1901); M. Wentscher, *Hermann Lotze* (vol. 1, 1913), and other works; P. Gese, *Lotzes Religionsphilosophie* (1916); E. E. Thomas, *Lotze's Theory of Reality* (1921). R. Gotesky in P. Edwards (ed.), *The Encyclopedia of Philosophy*, 5 (1967), pp. 87–9, s.v.

Lou, Tseng-tsiang. See LU, CHENG-HSIANG.

Louis I (778–840) (**the Pious** or **le Débonnaire**). The third son of *Charlemagne (d. 814), by whom he was appointed King of Aquitaine in 781 and joint Emperor in 813. He married Ermengard, daughter of Count Ingrawn c.794. As King in Aquitaine he exerted himself with considerable success in military campaigns into Spain, and promoted monastic reform. On his accession to the Empire in 814 (on Charlemagne's death) he extended the monastic reforms, under the direction of St *Benedict of Aniane, to embrace the entire Frankish kingdom, and promulgated major legislation concerning monasticism in 816–17. In 817, with the *Ordinatio Imperii*, he associated his eldest son Lothar with him as Emperor and gave subkingdoms to his other sons, Louis (Bavaria) and Pepin (Aquitaine). The birth of a fourth son, Charles, by his second wife, Judith, in 823, eventually upset this arrangement, and the latter years of his reign were marred by disputes with his sons and their supporting aristocratic factions, culminating in his temporary deposition in 833 and his performance of public *penance. Despite the political difficulties of his reign, Louis was an efficient and innovative administrator, as well as zealous in the promotion of monasticism and missionary work, and enjoying considerable success in his relations with the Papacy, the Danes, and the Slavs. The royal library remained important during Louis's reign, and the work of *Carolingian scholars and artists is notable in this period.

J. F. Böhmer, *Die Regesten des Kaiserreichs unter den Karolingern* (2nd edn. by E. Mühlbacher, 1908), pp. 234–412. Life by Theganus, written in 835, ed. G. H. Pertz in *MGH*, Scriptores, 2 (1829), pp. 589–603; further early Life by an anonymous writer known as the 'Astronomer', ibid., pp. 604–48; Eng. tr. of the latter, with introd. and notes, by A. Cabannis (Syracuse, NY, 1961). B. Simson, *Jahrbücher des fränkischen Reiches unter Ludwig dem Frommen* (Jahrbücher der deutschen Geschichte, 2 vols. in one, 1874–6). R. McKitterick, *The Frankish Kingdoms under the Carolingians, 751–987* (1983), pp. 106–39. F. L. Ganshof, 'Louis the Pious Reconsidered', *History*, 42 (1957), pp. 171–80. P. Godman and R. Collins (eds.), *Charlemagne's Heir: New Perspectives on the Reign of Louis the Pious (814–840)* (Oxford, 1990). T. Schieffer, 'Die Krise des karolingischen Imperiums', in J. Engel and H. M. Klinkenberg (eds.), *Aus Mittelalter und Neuzeit: Gerhard Kallen zum 70 Geburtstag* (Bonn, 1957), pp. 1–15; B. Bischoff, 'Die Hofbibliothek unter Ludwig dem Frommen', in J. J. G. Alexander and M. T. Gibson (eds.) *Medieval Learning and Literature: Essays Presented to Richard William Hunt* (Oxford, 1976), pp. 3–22. T. F. X. Noble, *The Republic of St Peter: The Birth of the Papal State, 680–825* (Philadelphia [1984]), esp. pp. 299–323. J. M. Wallace-Hadrill, *The Frankish Church* (Oxford History of the Christian Church, 1983), pp. 226–41.

Louis IX, St (1214–70), King of France. Born at Poissy, he was the son of Louis VIII (d. 1226) and Blanche of Castile (d. 1252), who acted as regent during his minority. In 1226 he was crowned at *Reims and in 1234 he married Margaret of Provence. In 1242 he defeated an attempt by Henry III of England to recover the lost Angevin territories in western France. Having resolved during an illness in 1244 to take the cross, he sailed in 1248 and captured the Egyptian port of Damietta in 1249; but owing to floods and lack of co-operation the crusaders were routed in 1250 and Louis IX taken prisoner. Securing his own release by the surrender of Damietta and that of his men by the pay-

ment of their ransoms, he proceeded to Syria in 1250 to fortify the strongholds still in Christian hands. He returned to France in 1254, imposed peace on Flanders in 1256 and signed the Treaties of Corbeil with Aragon in 1258 and of Paris with Henry III in 1259, the terms of both illustrating his desire for equity and a lasting settlement. Between 1258 and 1265 he several times arbitrated between Henry III and his barons. Having planned a further crusade in 1267, he embarked on 1 July 1270 and landed at Tunis, where he died of dysentery on 25 Aug.

In his austere and prayerful private life, with its close links with the *Franciscan and *Dominican Orders, his energy, his determination that every man should have his due, and the paramount consideration which he gave to the defence of the Holy Land, Louis embodied the highest ideals of medieval kingship. He reformed the administration of France, frequently meting out justice himself. He built the *Sainte-Chapelle in Paris (c. 1245–8) for the *Crown of Thorns which he had acquired from the Latin Emp. of Constantinople, Baldwin II, in 1239; he endowed various religious houses and supported the theological college founded by Robert de *Sorbon in 1257. He was canonized by *Boniface VIII in 1297. Feast day, 25 Aug.

Crit. edn. of the instructions which Louis compiled for his son Philippe by D. O'Connell as *The Teachings of Saint Louis* (University of North Carolina Studies in the Romance Languages and Literatures, 116; Chapel Hill, NC, 1972); those which he compiled for his daughter Isabelle, ed. id. as *The Instructions of Saint Louis* (ibid. 216; 1979). The principal authority is the Life by J. de *Joinville (q.v. for edns. and trs.). Life by William of Saint-Pathus, written some time between 1302 and 1307, ed. H. F. Delaborde (Collection de textes pour servir à l'étude et à l'enseignement de l'histoire; 1899); *Miracles* by the same author ed. P. B. Fay in Les Classiques français du moyen âge, 70; 1931. Lives by Geoffrey de Beaulieu, OP, and William of Chartres, OP, his confessors and chaplains, pr., with other material, in *AASS*, Aug. 5 (1741), pp. 275–672. *BHL*, pp. 747–50 (nos. 5034–52), and *Suppl. Novum* (1986), pp. 549 f. Classic Lives by L. S. Le N. de *Tillemont, *Vie de saint Louis*, first ed. in full, J. de Gaulle (6 vols.; Société de l'Histoire de France; 1847–51) and H. Wallon (2 vols., Paris, 1875). J. Richard, *Saint Louis, roi d'une France féodale, soutien de la Terre sainte* (1983; abridged Eng. tr., Cambridge and Paris, 1992). W. C. Jordan, *Louis IX and the Challenge of the Crusade* (Princeton, NJ [1979]). L. Carolus-Barré and others (eds.), *Septième Centenaire de la Mort de Saint Louis: Actes des Colloques de Royaumont et de Paris (21–27 Mai 1970)* (Paris, 1976). L. Buisson, *König Ludwig IX., der Heilige, and das Recht* (Freiburg, 1954). L. Carolus-Barré, 'Les Enquêtes pour la Canonisation de Saint Louis—de Grégoire X à Boniface VIII—et la Bulle *Gloria Laus*, du 11 août 1297', *Revue d'Histoire de l'Église de France*, 57 (1971), pp. 19–29; R. Folz, 'La Sainteté de Saint Louis d'après les Textes liturgiques de sa Fête', ibid., pp. 31–45. J. Le Goff in *TRE* 21 (1991), pp. 487–90, s.v. 'Ludwig IX'.

Louis of Granada. See LUIS OF GRANADA.

Lourdes, a famous French place of pilgrimage in the Department of Hautes-Pyrénées. In 1858 the 14-year-old peasant girl, *Bernadette Soubirous, had visions of the BVM in the grotto of a rock at Lourdes in which the Virgin told her that she was the Immaculate Conception. At the same time a spring appeared; miraculous healings were soon reported to have taken place; and the faithful began to flock to Lourdes. In 1862 the pilgrimage received official ecclesiastical recognition, a church was built above the grotto, and beside it from 1883 to 1901 the magnificent church of the Rosary. The crypt of the Basilica of the Immaculate Conception (above the grotto) and a vast underground church dedicated to Pope *Pius X were consecrated by the future Pope *John XXIII in 1958. Millions of pilgrims have visited the shrine, a medical bureau has been established to investigate the character of the cures, and an enormous literature, much of it controversial, has sprung up around it. In 1891 a local feast of the apparition of Our Lady of Lourdes (11 Feb.) was sanctioned, and extended to the universal Church by Pius X in 1907; since 1969 its observance has been optional.

L.-J.-M. Cros, SJ, *Histoire de Notre-Dame de Lourdes d'après les documents et les témoins* (3 vols., 1925–6); id., *Lourdes 1858*, ed. P. M. Olphe-Galliard, SJ [1957]. R. Laurentin, *Lourdes: Histoire authentique des apparitions* (6 vols., 1961–4). There is also a very large number of popular studies such as J. Jørgensen, *Lourdes* (Copenhagen, 1910; Eng. tr., 1914), and R. Laurentin, *Sens de Lourdes* (2nd edn., 1958; Eng. tr., 1959). T. F. Casey in *NCE* 8 (1967), pp. 1031–3, s.v. See also bibl. to BERNADETTE, ST.

love. In Christian theology, the principle of God's action and man's response. In the OT the loving character of God was recognized, notably by *Hosea, but it was only in the NT that the doctrine that love constitutes the essential nature of God was developed (e.g. 1 Jn. 4: 8). Love, as the bond between the Father and the Son, is particularly associated with the Holy Spirit by St *Augustine and other writers. The OT commandments that man should love God (e.g. Deut. 6: 5) and his neighbour (Lev. 19: 18) are joined together by Christ (Mk. 12: 29–31), but the peculiarly Christian character of the love required is emphasized by the Lord's description of the demand for love as a 'new commandment' (Jn. 13: 34). One special characteristic of this commandment is that love must be extended even to one's enemies (Mt. 5: 43–8). This Christian love (called ἀγάπη in the NT, traditionally rendered 'charity' in English) is the greatest of the *theological virtues (1 Cor. 13: 13; Col. 3: 14). In 1 Cor. 13: 1–8 its manifestations are described; it is a matter of the will rather than the emotions, and it appears (1 Jn. 5: 3) to consist in keeping God's commandments. St *Augustine developed a theology of the Christian life as consisting essentially in charity, understood as a supernatural gift obtained only by means of divine *grace; without the motivation supplied by charity, mere outward observance of God's Law is insufficient for salvation. In the Augustinian tradition some theologians (e.g. *Peter Lombard) identified our charity with the Holy Spirit, but this was rejected by St *Thomas Aquinas and others, who regard charity as a created effect of grace in us. In the late Middle Ages some devotional writers interpreted love of God in primarily emotional terms, which sometimes made it difficult to leave room for love of neighbour, whether affective or practical, but theologians insisted on an 'ordered love', in which we love God for himself and creatures in God and for God. Some, like St *Catherine of Siena, resolved the tension between the two precepts of love by insisting that in each case it is God's own love which draws the believer into itself, making him love God and creatures supernaturally. See also AGAPE.

C. E. Raven, *Jesus and the Gospel of Love* (Albert Robertson Lectures for 1931; 1931). J. Burnaby, *Amor Dei: A Study of the Religion of St Augustine* (Hulsean Lectures for 1938; 1938).

H. Riesenfeld, 'Étude bibliographique sur la notion biblique d' 'ΑΓΑΠΗ', *Coniectanea Neotestamentica*, 5 (Uppsala, 1941), pp. 1–32. M. C. *D'Arcy, SJ, *The Mind and Heart of Love* (1945). H. Pétré, *Caritas: Étude sur le vocabulaire latin de la charité chrétienne* (SSL 22; 1948). V. Warnack, *Agape: Die Liebe als Grundmotiv der neutestamentlichen Theologie* (1951). P. Gilleman, SJ, *Le Primat de la charité en théologie morale: Essai méthodologique* (Museum Lessianum, Section théologique, 50; 1952; Eng. tr. [1959]). C. S. *Lewis, *The Four Loves* (1960). C. Spicq, OP, *Agapè dans le Nouveau Testament: Analyse des textes* (3 vols., Études Bibliques, 1958–9; Eng. tr., 2 vols., 1963–5). D. D. Williams, *The Spirit and the Forms of Love* (1968). G. [H.] Outka, *Agape: An Ethical Analysis* (Yale Publications in Religion, 17; 1972). W. H. Vanstone, *Love's Endeavour, Love's Expense: The Response of Being to the Love of God* (1977). G. Quell and E. Stauffer in *TWNT* 1 (1933), cols. 20–55, s.v. ἀγαπάω; Eng. tr. of this art., with bibl., by J. R. Coates (London, 1949). F. Prat and others in *Dict. Sp.* 2 (1953), cols. 508–691, s.v. 'Charité'; K. D. Sakenfeld and W. Klassen in *Anchor Bible Dictionary*, 4 (1992), pp. 375–96, s.v. See also works cited under AGAPE (1).

Lovedale. Missionary educational centre in the Eastern Cape, *South Africa. In 1824 missionaries of the Glasgow Missionary Society, an offshoot of the *LMS, founded a mission station in the Tyume valley. In 1841 the Lovedale Institution was inaugurated there; until its effective abolition as a result of the Bantu Education Act of 1952, it was the leading educational institution for Africans, not only in South Africa but in the whole of Southern Africa. Under its first two principals, William Govan and James Stewart (1870–1905), a primary school, a high school, a teacher-training college, a theological school, and a technical college were developed. Later Dr Neil MacVicar (1902–37) created the first school to train African nurses to SRN standard. Southern Africa's first university college for Africans, Fort Hare, also developed out of Lovedale, again led by a Scottish missionary, Alexander Kerr, its first principal (1918–48). From the beginning Lovedale was multiracial as well as coeducational, until this arrangement was terminated by Government action. It was also a publishing house of some importance and produced *The Christian Express* (1871–1921; from 1922 *The South African Outlook*), long one of the few journals of liberal Christian opinion in South Africa.

R. H. W. Shepherd, *Lovedale, South Africa: The Story of a Century 1841–1941* (Lovedale [1940]). Various papers which had previously appeared in *The South African Outlook*, some shortened, ed. F. Wilson and D. Perrot, *Outlook on a Century: South Africa 1870–1970* (Lovedale, 1973).

Low Churchmen. The group in the C of E which gives a relatively unimportant or 'low' place to the claims of the episcopate, priesthood, and sacraments, and generally approximates in its beliefs to those of Protestant Nonconformists. The term 'Low Churchman', which dates from the early 18th cent., was coined in contrast to '*High Churchman', but orig. used of the *Latitudinarian (liberal) group. It went out of use; when revived in the mid-19th cent. it was applied to the *Evangelicals, whereas the liberal group then came to be dubbed '*Broad Churchmen'. See also EVANGELICALISM.

Low Mass. In the W. Church, the simplified form of Mass, until modern times the form in most frequent use. It grew up in the Middle Ages, when the practice of each priest saying a Mass daily became common and the elaborate ceremonial and considerable number of assistants traditionally required for the Liturgy were no longer practicable. In a Low Mass, where the celebrating priest had no ministers to assist him except a single server, he read both the *Epistle and *Gospel himself, and no part of the service was sung. Except in cathedral and capitular churches, Low Mass was the usual form of celebration except on Sundays and greater feast days; and even on these days all except one of the Masses in any church was usually a Low Mass. The current RC *Ordo Missae*, however, no longer uses the term; it requires that all Masses celebrated with the people shall be community Masses with full participation; if there is no deacon or *lector some other lay person may read the first two lessons, and it is urged that there should be singing at all Masses. In the E. Low Masses have never been known, though some *Uniat bodies adopted a somewhat similar form of celebration. See also HIGH MASS.

Jungmann (1958 edn.), 1, pp. 279–306; Eng tr. (1951), pp. 212–33.

Low Sunday. The first Sunday after *Easter, probably so called in contrast to the 'high' feast of Easter Sunday itself. In Latin it used to be termed *Dominica in albis*. In the RC Church it is now officially designated the second Sunday in Eastertide.

Lowder, Charles Fuge (1820–80), vicar of St Peter's, London Docks. Educated at Exeter College, Oxford, he was ordained priest in 1844, and in 1851 became curate at the *Anglo-Catholic parish of St Barnabas, Pimlico. With others he founded the *Society of the Holy Cross in 1855 and stressed the importance of groups of *celibate clergy living under a simple rule for mission work in the slums. In 1856 he joined the staff of St George's in the East, where he took a leading part in the first regular mission work in E. London, with A. H. *Mackonochie as his colleague from 1858. The advanced ceremonial led to fierce riots. His mission work expanded, however, and he built the church of St Peter's, London Docks (1860–6). Known always as 'Father Lowder', he was the means of bringing many thousands of E. Londoners to the Christian faith.

Anonymous Life by M. Trench (London, 1881). L. E. Ellsworth, *Charles Lowder and the Ritualist Movement* (1982). S. L. Ollard in *DECH*, pp. 342 f.

Lowth, Robert (1710–87), Bp. of London. He was educated at Winchester and at New College, Oxford. From 1741 to 1750 he was professor of poetry at Oxford, and later Bp. successively of *St David's (1776), of Oxford (also 1766), and of London (1777). His chief contributions to biblical learning arose from his study of the forms of Hebrew poetry. In his *De sacra poesi Hebraeorum Praelectiones Academicae* (1753; J. D. *Michaelis added notes in 1775; Eng. tr. of this expanded revision, 1793) he recognized the existence of '*parallelism' as a regular device of Hebrew poetry. In a controversy with W. *Warburton, Lowth defended the extreme antiquity of the Book of *Job. His commentary on *Isaiah (1778) pointed the way to later criticism of that Book.

Sermons and Other Remains of Robert Lowth, ed. P. Hall (London, 1834), with introd. Memoir, pp. 1–42. Extracts from

the 1787 Eng. tr. of his *De sacra poesi Hebraeorum* repr., with introd., in J. Drury (ed.), *Critics of the Bible 1724–1873* (Cambridge, 1989), pp. 69–102. Short *Memoirs of the Life and Writings of . . . Robert Lowth* (London, 1787). B. Hepworth, *Robert Lowth* (Boston [1978]). W. Hunt in *DNB* 34 (1893), pp. 214–16.

Loyola, St Ignatius. See IGNATIUS LOYOLA, ST.

Lu, Cheng-hsiang (1871–1949), Chinese statesman and Benedictine monk and abbot. The son of a Protestant catechist, he was born at Shanghai and educated at Shanghai and Peking. He was interpreter and secretary to the Chinese Legation at St Petersburg (1893–1906), Minister at The Hague (1907–11) and St Petersburg (1911–12) and Foreign Minister (1912–20; with brief interruptions). In 1912 and 1915 he was also Prime Minister and from 1922 to 1927 Chinese Minister at Berne. In Oct. 1911 he was received into the RC Church. After the death of his wife (a Belgian whom he had married in 1899) in 1926, he entered the *Benedictine Abbey of St-André, near Bruges (1927), where he was later professed as Dom Pierre Célestin Lou. In 1946 he was appointed Titular Abbot of St-Pierre-de-Gand by *Pius XII. His intention of returning to the East to establish a Benedictine Congregation in China was prevented by ill health. As a Christian statesman he had been a reformer not a revolutionary. In the sphere of religion he saw in Christianity the fulfilment of Confucianism, finding St *John's doctrine of the *Logos paralleled by Lao-Tse's teaching of the Tao. He believed Classical Chinese to be the appropriate liturgical language for the worship of his countrymen. His writings include *Souvenirs et pensées* (1945; Eng. tr. as *Ways of Confucius and of Christ*, 1948) and *La Rencontre des humanités* (1949; posthumous).

Wu Ching-Hioung, *Dom Lou: Sa vie spirituelle* [1949]; E. Neut, OSB, *Jean-Jacques Lou, Dom Lou* (Suppl. to nos. 192–3 of *Synthèses*, Brussels, 1962). H. L. Boorman (ed.), *Biographical Dictionary of Republican China*, 2 (1968), pp. 441–4, s.v. 'Lu Cheng-hsiang'.

Lubac, Henri de (1896–1991), French *Jesuit theologian. Born in Cambrai, he became a Jesuit in 1913. He fought in the French Army in the First World War and was severely wounded. After studying in England, the Channel Islands, and France, he was ordained priest in 1927 and taught theology at Lyons from 1929 (as professor from 1934); here he had many distinguished pupils, incl. J. *Daniélou and H. U. von *Balthasar. A *peritus* at the Second *Vatican Council, he was made a cardinal in 1983.

His *Mémoire sur l'occasion de mes écrits* (1989) recounts a vast literary output, covering a wide range of subjects. He wrote on the doctrine of the Church in *Catholicisme* (1938; Eng. tr., 1950) and *Corpus Mysticum* (1944) and on grace and the supernatural in *Surnaturel* (1946), *Augustinisme et théologie moderne* (1965; Eng. tr., 1969) and *Le Mystère de surnaturel* (1965; Eng. tr., 1967). He produced two important works on the history of *exegesis and the value of *allegory: *Histoire et esprit* (1950), in which he supported the position of *Origen, and *Exégèse médiévale* (1959–64), which contains an appreciation of Renaissance humanism as well as discussion of the apocalyptic views of *Joachim of Fiore. These interests were developed in his study of *Pico della Mirandola (1974) and in *La Posterité *spirituelle de Joachim de Flore* (1979–81). He was appreciative, but not uncritical, of the work of P. *Teilhard de Chardin; he edited a number of volumes of his correspondence and devoted three books to his thought: *La Pensée religieuse de Père Teilhard de Chardin* (1962; Eng. tr., 1967), *La Prière du Père Teilhard de Chardin* (1964; Eng. tr., 1965), and *L'Éternel féminin* (1968; Eng. tr., 1971). His other works include *Le Drame de l'humanisme athée* (1944; Eng. tr., 1949), *Aspects du bouddhisme* (1951–5; Eng. tr. of vol. 1, 1953), *La Rencontre du bouddhisme et de l'occident* (1952), and *Athéisme et sens de l'homme* (1968). De Lubac was one of the thinkers who created the intellectual climate that made possible the Second *Vatican Council, largely by opening up the vast spiritual resources of the Catholic tradition which had been cramped by post-Tridentine 'baroque' theology. He was also one of the founders of the collection 'Sources Chrétiennes', an important series of patristic and medieval texts, with French translation, now involving scholars from all over the world.

L'Homme devant Dieu: Mélanges offerts au Père Henri de Lubac (Théologie, 56–8 [1964]), with bibl. of his works, 3, pp. 347–56. K. H. Neufeld and M. Sales, *Bibliographie Henri de Lubac S.J.* (Einsiedeln, 1971; 2nd edn., 1974). H. U. von Balthasar, *Henri de Lubac: Sein organisches Lebenswerk* (ibid. [1976]). Polgár, 2 (1990), pp. 449–52.

Lubbertus, Sibrandus (*c.* 1555–1625), Dutch *Calvinist theologian. Born at Langwarden in Oldenburg and educated first at the Latin School at Bremen, he studied theology at *Wittenberg, *Geneva (under T. *Beza), *Marburg, and Neustadt (under Z. *Ursinus). In 1585 he became professor of theology at the newly-founded University of Franeker where he remained till his death, combining his duties in the faculty with a ministry in the local church. Lubbertus' prime concern was to counter RC teaching and esp. that of R. *Bellarmine, against whom he directed *De Principiis Christianorum Dogmatum* (1591; 2nd edn., 1595), *De Papa Romano* (1594), *De Conciliis* (1601), and *De Ecclesia* (1607). His role as defender of orthodox Calvinism was also exercised in response to *Socinianism, esp. in *De Jesu Christo Servatore contra Faustum Socinum* (1611) and in his opposition to *Arminianism. In the latter controversy, he took a prominent part in The Hague Conference of 1607, and corresponded extensively with foreign theologians (among them A. *Melville and G. *Abbot) to warn them against Arminius' teaching. He further attacked the Arminianism of P. Bertius in *Epistolica Disceptatio de Fide Justificante* (1612), C. *Vorstius in two works (1611 and 1613), and the *Ordinum Hollandiae ac Westfrisiae Pietas* of H. *Grotius (1613) in his *Responsio ad Pietatem Grotii* (1614). At the Synod of *Dort (1618–19), at which he was a prominent defender of the Calvinist position, albeit an opponent of F. *Gomar's *Supralapsarianism, he was appointed to the Commission preparing a new Dutch version of the OT. His last published work was a commentary on the *Heidelberg Catechism.

More than 700 items of his correspondence are preserved in the British Library, MSS Add. 22960–2. C. Van der Woude, *Sibrandus Lubbertus: Leven en Werken in het bijzonder naar zijn correspondentie* (Kampen, 1963). Id. in *Biografisch Lexicon voor de Geschiedenis van het Nederlandse Protestantisme*, 1 (1978), pp. 143–5.

Lüber, Thomas. See ERASTIANISM.

Lucar, Cyril (1570–1638), Patriarch of *Constantinople. He was a Cretan by birth. After studying at *Venice and Padua, where he came into contact with Latin thought, he became *syncellus to Meletios Pegas, Patr. of *Alexandria, whom he succeeded in 1601. His presence at the Synod of *Brest-Litovsk in 1596 had already turned him against Rome and the *Jesuits, and he now became more and more friendly disposed towards the Reformed Churches. His sympathies towards the C of E were expressed in his dispatch of *Metrophanes Critopoulos to study at Oxford in 1617. In 1620 he was appointed Patr. of Constantinople, an appointment as welcome to the Protestants, esp. the Dutch, as disagreeable to the Jesuits. In 1623, 1633 (twice), and 1634 he was removed from the patriarchal throne, but later restored, partly through the help of the English and Dutch ambassadors, particularly Sir Thomas Roe (1621–8) and Cornelius van Haga. Through the former he presented the famous '*Codex Alexandrinus' to King *Charles I in 1628. With the support and encouragement of the *Calvinist theologian Antoine Léger, a translation of the Bible into the vernacular for the use of his flock was begun and eventually published in Geneva in 1638; and in 1629 there was published at the same place a *Confessio Fidei*, to which Cyril had appended his signature. This reinterprets the traditional E. Orthodox faith in thoroughly Calvinistic terms. Eight years later his enemies accused him of inciting the Cossacks against the Turkish government, and he was put to death on the orders of the Sultan Murad. He was the first important theologian of the E. Church since the fall of Constantinople in 1453; but his sympathies with Calvinism, in which he saw a legitimate way of clarifying and purifying Orthodox faith and life, led to the condemnation of his teaching by synods held at Constantinople (1638, 1642), *Jassy (1642), and *Jerusalem (1672). He remains, however, the most brilliant and politically outstanding Greek Patriarch and national leader ('ethnarch') of the 17th century.

For his 'Confession', see E. Kimmel, *Libri Symbolici Ecclesiae Orientalis* (Jena, 1843), pp. 24–44; Eng. tr. in J. N. W. B. Robertson, *The Acts and Decrees of the Synod of Jerusalem* (1899), pp. 185–215; Eng. tr. of the main part also in G. A. Hadjiantoniou, op. cit. infra, pp. 141–5. *Sermons 1598–1602*, ed. K. Rozemond (Leiden, 1974). E. Legrand, *Bibliographie hellénique ou description raisonnée des ouvrages publiés par des Grecs au dix-septième siècle*, 4 (1896), pp. 161–521. G. A. Hadjiantoniou, *Protestant Patriarch: The Life of Cyril Lucaris (1572–1638), Patriarch of Constantinople* (1961). S. Runciman, *The Great Church in Captivity* (Cambridge, 1968), pp. 259–88. G. Podskalsky, *Griechische Theologie in der Zeit der Türkenherrschaft (1453–1821)* (Munich, 1988), pp. 162–80. P. Meyer in *PRE* (3rd edn.), 11 (1902), pp. 682–90, with full bibl., and C. Emereau in *DTC* 9 (pt. 1; 1926), cols. 1003–19, s.v., with bibl.

Lucian of Antioch, St (d. 312), theologian and martyr. A presbyter of *Antioch, he was an influential teacher, counting both *Arius and *Eusebius of Nicomedia among his pupils; indeed his *subordinationist teaching seems to have been the immediate source of the Arian heresy. Only a few fragments of his writings have survived; but acc. to *Sozomen (*HE* 3. 5), the second of the four Creeds put forward by the Council of *Antioch in 341 was said to be his composition. He was a keen biblical student, who revised the Greek text (see LUCIANIC TEXT). His reputation for sanctity was not less than his fame as a scholar; and after enduring many tortures he was martyred at Nicomedia in 312. The long-prevalent view that he was a pupil of *Paul of Samosata has been disputed by F. *Loofs and G. Bardy. Feast day in E, 15 Oct.; in W., 7 Jan.

Frags. collected in M. J. *Routh, *Reliquiae Sacrae* (2nd edn., 4, 1846), pp. 3–10 (texts), 11–17 (notes). Eusebius, *HE* 8. 13. 2 and 9. 6. 3; Jerome, *De Vir. Illustr.* 77. *Vita* in *Philostorgius, *HE* (ed. J. Bidez in GCS, pp. 184–201). G. Bardy, *Recherches sur Lucien d'Antioche et son école* (1936). A. d'Alès, 'Autour de Lucien d'Antioche', *Mélanges de l'Université Saint-Joseph, Beyrouth,* 21 (1938), pp. 185–99. E. Boularand, 'Aux Sources de la doctrine d'Arius. La théologie antiochienne', *Bulletin de Littérature Ecclésiastique,* 68 (1967), pp. 241–72, esp. pp. 241–58. *CPG* 1 (1981), pp. 218 f. (nos. 1720–23). Bardenhewer, 2, pp. 279–85; Altaner and Stuiber (1978), pp. 214 f. J. Quasten, *Patrology,* 2 (Utrecht, 1953), pp. 142–4. G. Bardy in *DTC* 9 (pt. 1; 1926), cols. 1024–31; J. Liébaert in *Catholicisme,* 7 (1975), cols. 1245 f. See also bibl. to LUCIANIC TEXT.

Lucian of Samosata (*c.*115–*c.*200), pagan satirist. His interest to the student of early Christianity lies chiefly in some references in his 'Alexander of Abonuteichos' and esp. in 'De Morte Peregrini'. The former confirms the testimony of *Pliny that Christianity had made much progress in Bithynia-Pontus. The latter treats of the philosopher Peregrinus, a historical person who exchanged paganism for Christianity and was even imprisoned for his faith; but later he apostatized and became a cynic. Being expelled from Rome he made his way to Athens, where he burned himself at a stake during the Olympic Games, in order, as he said, to crown an exemplary life by an exemplary death. Lucian describes the generosity with which the Christians looked after their fellow-believer, Peregrinus, when imprisoned; but, believing that the philosopher was an impostor, he scoffs at their simplicity.

The '*Philopatris' (q.v.), which purports to be a work of Lucian and directly attacks Christianity, is of much later date, prob. 10th century.

Editio princeps of his collected works, Florence, 1496; modern edns. by C. Jacobitz (4 vols., Leipzig, 1836–41; 3 vols., Teub., 1852–3, and subsequent edns.) and M. D. Macleod (Oxford Classical Texts, 4 vols., 1972–87). Selection repr., with introd., Eng. tr., and comm. by id. (Warminster [1991]). Eng. tr. of *Works* by A. M. Harmon and others (8 vols., Loeb, 1913–67). J. Bompaire, *Lucien écrivain* (Bibliothèque des Écoles françaises d'Athènes et de Rome, 190; 1958); J. Schwartz, *Biographie de Lucien de Samosate* (Collection Latomus, 85; 1965). C. P. Jones, *Culture and Society in Lucian* (Cambridge, Mass., and London, 1986). M. Caster, *Lucien et la pensée religieuse de son temps* (1937; with bibl.). H. D. Betz, *Lukian von Samosata und das Neue Testament: Religionsgeschichtliche und paränetische Parallelen* (TU 76; 1961), with bibl. on Lucian, pp. 218–51. A.*Harnack in *PRE* (3rd edn.), 11 (1902), pp. 659–66, s.v.

Lucianic text. The text of the Gk. Bible, as revised by *Lucian of Antioch (q.v.). Its marks are the elimination of barbarisms and obscurities, the conflation of variant readings, intelligibility, and smoothness. Quotations in the Fathers indicate that it very soon became the accepted standard text in Syria, Asia Minor, and *Constantinople. The researches of F. J. A. *Hort and H. von Soden in the NT indicate that Lucian's text is now represented by the great body of the surviving Gk. MSS. and is thus embod-

ied in the 'Textus Receptus' (q.v.) and the AV. See also BYZANTINE TEXT and SYRIAN TEXT OF THE NT.

B. M. Metzger, *Chapters in the History of New Testament Textual Criticism* (New Testament Tools and Studies, 4; Leiden, 1963), pp. 1–41 ('The Lucianic Recension of the Greek Bible'), with bibl. S. Jellicoe, *The Septuagint and Modern Study* (Oxford, 1968), pp. 157–71. G. Mercati, 'Di alcune testimonianze antiche sulle cure bibliche di S. Luciano', *Biblica,* 24 (1943), pp. 1–17. M. Spanneut, 'La Bible d'Eustathe d'Antioche—contribution à l'histoire de la "version lucianique" ', in F. L. Cross (ed.), *Studia Patristica,* 4 (TU 79; 1961), pp. 171–90. E. Tov, 'Lucian and Proto-Lucian. Toward a new solution of the problem', *Revue Biblique,* 79 (1972), pp. 101–13.

Lucifer (Lat., 'light-bearer'), in Is. 14: 12 (Vulgate, followed by AV), an epithet of the King of Babylon. Taken in conjunction with Lk. 10: 18 it was used as a synonym for the devil by St *Jerome and other Fathers. With the use of the word in classical mythology for the planet Venus may be compared the RV rendering 'day star' in Is. 14: 12. The imagery is applied to Christ in 2 Pet. 1: 19 (φωσφόρος, 'day star'), Rev. 22: 16 (ὁ ἀστὴρ ὁ πρωϊνός, 'the morning star'), and in the *Exultet.

Lucifer (d. 370 or 371), Bp. of Cagliari. A fiercely anti-Arian theologian, at the first session of the Council of Milan (354) he resisted the proposal to condemn *Athanasius with such vehemence that the Arians prevailed on the Emp. Constantius to confine him for three days in the Imperial Palace. His personal altercations with the Emperor which followed led to his banishment first to Palestine and later to the Thebaid (Egypt). During his exile he addressed several violent writings to Constantius with the evident, but unsuccessful, intent of courting martyrdom. They include 'De non conveniendo cum haereticis', 'De regibus apostaticis', and 'De S. Athanasio'. Soon after the accession of *Julian, in common with the exiled bishops generally, he was released (362). He then made his way to Antioch, where he vigorously resisted all conciliatory action towards repentant Arians, and by consecrating Paulinus, an Antiochene presbyter, bishop, created an unfortunate schism. A little later, it appears, he went back to his see. Whether or not he was ever formally excommunicated is uncertain, though this is suggested by passages in St *Ambrose and St *Augustine, and St *Jerome refers to his followers as 'Luciferians'.

His writings survive in the single MS Cod. Vat. 133 (9th–10th cent.). J. P. Migne, *PL* 13. 767–1038. Modern edns. by W. Hartel (CSEL 14; 1886) and by G. F. Diercks (CCSL 8; 1978). G. Krüger, *Lucifer Bischof von Cagliari und das Schisma der Luciferianer* (1886); F. Piva, *Lucifero di Cagliari contro l'imperatore Costanzo* (Trent, 1928); G. Thörnell, *Studia Luciferiana* (Uppsala, 1934). C. Zedda, 'La teologia trinitaria di Lucifero di Cagliari', *Divus Thomas,* 52 (Piacenza, 1949), pp. 276–329. A. Figus, *L'Enigma de Lucifero di Cagliari* (Cagliari, 1973), with bibl. Bardenhewer, 3, pp. 469–77; Altaner and Stuiber (1978), pp. 367 and 626. É. Amann in *DTC* 9 (pt. 1; 1926), cols. 1032–44.

Lucina. Several pious women of this name figure in the early traditions and legends of the Roman Church. Acc. to the *Liber Pontificalis* (s.v. *Cornelius, AD 251–3), a certain Lucina had the bodies of Sts *Peter and *Paul removed from their resting-place at the *catacombs ('ad Catacumbas') and laid that of St Paul in her own property on the *Ostian Way. It appears that she or another Lucina was buried in another property, the 'Crypt of Lucina', on the *Appian Way, which also contains the tomb of Cornelius. G. B. *de Rossi sought to identify the Lucina who gives her name to the crypt with *Pomponia Graecina (1st cent.; q.v.).

H. *Lietzmann, *Petrus und Paulus in Rom* (2nd edn., 1927), pp. 179–89. L. Reekmans, *La tombe du pape Corneille et sa région cémétériale* (Roma Sotterranea Cristiana, 4; Vatican City, 1964). H. *Leclercq, OSB, in *DACL* 9 (pt. 2; 1930), cols. 2636–61, s.v. 'Lucine (Crypte de)'; H. Grieser in *L.Th.K.* (3rd edn.), 6 (1997), cols. 1084 f. See also bibl. to POMPONIA GRAECINA.

Lucius. In legend, the first Christian King of Britain. Acc. to an early form of the story (based apparently on a statement in the *Liber Pontificalis* that a British king, Lucius, sent a request to the Pope that he might become a Christian), Lucius successfully appealed to Pope Eleutherius (174–89) for Christian teachers to be sent to Britain, and together with large numbers of his subjects received Baptism at their hands; the heathen temples were converted into Christian churches; the heathen priesthood abandoned their pagan functions for the Christian ministry; and Lucius is said to have died at *Gloucester in 156. In later times (9th–16th cents.) the legend was considerably embellished. King Lucius becomes the son of *Simon of Cyrene, is converted by St *Timothy, and goes as a missionary to Rhaetia, where he establishes himself as the first Bp. of Chur and is martyred by stoning. The details of the later story are apparently due to the conflation of legends about the King of Britain with independent traditions about a Lucius of Chur, who was possibly a historical person. A. *Harnack suggested that the statement in the *Liber Pontificalis* is due to a confusion between 'Britain' and 'Britis', a name for *Edessa, and that the king mentioned was really *Abgar IX [VIII] of that city.

The story is related by *Bede, *HE* 1. 4 and 5. 24 (cf. notes to edn. by C. Plummer, 2, Oxford, 1896, p. 14, and comm. by J. M. Wallace-Hadrill, ibid., 1988, p. 11); *William of Malmesbury, *De Antiquitate Glastoniensis Ecclesiae*, 2, and *Geoffrey of Monmouth, *Historia Regum Britanniae*, 4. 19 and 5. 1. A. Harnack, 'Der Brief des britischen Königs Lucius an den Papst Eleutherus', *Sb.* (Berl.), 1904, 1, pp. 909–16. A. W. Haddan and W. *Stubbs, *Councils and Ecclesiastical Documents Relating to Great Britain and Ireland*, 1 (1869), pp. 25 f. V. Berther, 'Der hl. Lucius', *Zeitschrift der Schweizerischen Kirchengeschichte*, 32 (1938), pp. 20–38, 103–24; I. Müller, 'Die Verehrung des hl. Lucius im 9.–12. Jh.', ibid. 48 (1954), pp. 96–126; id., 'Zur karolingischen Hagiographie. Kritik der Luciusvita', *Schweizer Beiträge zur allgemeinen Geschichte*, 14 (1956), pp. 5–28. A. Smith, 'Lucius of Britain: Alleged King and Church Founder', *Folklore*, 90 (1979), pp. 29–36.

Lucy, St. Acc. to tradition, she was a native of Syracuse who openly proclaimed her Christian faith by distributing her goods to the poor at the height of the *Diocletianic persecution. For this act she was denounced to the authorities by the young man to whom she had been betrothed by her parents, and suffered martyrdom in 303. She was much venerated in the early Church, as is shown by her inclusion in the *Canon of the Roman and *Ambrosian Mass. Her *acta* were utilized by St *Aldhelm in *Tractatus de Laudibus Virginitatis*, 42, and in his poem *De Laudibus Virginum*. There is also a long poem by *Sigebert of Gembloux in her honour. Feast day, 13 Dec.

The details of the *acta* (prob. 5th–6th cent., surviving in various Gk. and Lat. recensions) from which the story derives are untrustworthy. The Gk. *passio* ed. G. di Giovanni (Palermo, 1758), C. Barreca (Rome, 1902), and G. R. Taibbi (Istituto Siciliano di Studi Bizantini e Neogreci. Testi e Monumenti, Testi 6; 1959); the Lat. *passio* frequently ed., e.g. in A. Beaugrand, *Sainte Lucie* (1882). The most reliable authority for her early cult appears to be an inscription described by P. Orsi, 'Insigne epigrafe del cimitero di S. Giovanni in Siracusa', *RQ* 9 (1895), pp. 299–308. S. L. Agnello, 'Recenti esplorazioni nelle catacombe siracusane di S. Lucia', *Riv. A.C.* 30 (1954), pp. 7–60; 31 (1955), pp. 7–50. G. Goyau, *Sainte Lucie* (1921); O. Garana, *S. Lucia nella tradizione, nella storia, nell'arte* (Syracuse, 1958). Collection of pictures ed. M. Capdevila, *Iconografía de Santa Lucía* (Barcelona, 1949). H. *Leclercq, OSB, in *DACL* 9 (pt. 2; 1930), cols. 2616–18, s.v. 'Lucie (Sainte)'.

Ludlow, John Malcolm Forbes (1821–1911), the founder of *Christian Socialism. Educated in France, where he got to know Charles Fourier and other Socialist pioneers, he came to London in 1838, and in 1843 he was called to the bar at Lincoln's Inn. In a letter to F. D. *Maurice from *Paris after the Revolution of 1848, he insisted that 'the new Socialism must be Christianized'. Many of the English leaders of Christian Socialism were not really Socialist in any political sense, but Ludlow was a convinced Socialist, and it was he who acquainted the English movement with European political ideas. He soon became active in literary propaganda, helped to form some co-operative associations for production, which, however, were short-lived, and was largely responsible for promoting the Industrial and Provident Societies Act of 1852. Later he co-operated with Maurice in the founding of the Working Men's College, where he taught for many years. Although overshadowed in public estimation by Maurice and C. *Kingsley, Ludlow was the real founder of the movement and remained its organizer and co-ordinator. He was never quite at home in the C of E, and, although he adhered to Anglicanism, he often worshipped at the French Protestant church in London. He believed in Socialism as the truest expression of democracy, but was also convinced that Christian Socialism was possible only if political and industrial emancipation were accompanied by an education spiritual and moral as well as intellectual. Ludlow was well versed in law, politics, and economics, and an accomplished linguist. His influence did much to prevent in England the antagonism between the Church and Socialism that existed in many other countries.

Life by N. C. Masterman (Cambridge, 1963). Sir Norman Moore in *DNB, 1901–1911* (1912), pp. 487 f., s.v. See also works cited under CHRISTIAN SOCIALISM.

Ludolf, Hiob (1624–1704), also spelt 'Leutholf', German orientalist. A native of Erfurt, after studying there and at *Leiden he travelled extensively to increase his linguistic knowledge. In 1649 in Italy he met an Ethiopian scholar, Abba Gregorius, who taught him Amharic and served as a valuable informant. From 1652 to 1678 he was in the employment of the Duke of Saxe-Gotha. In 1683 he visited England to try to establish trade with Ethiopia, but, owing to obstacles raised by the *Ethiopian Church, met with no success. For the rest of his life he devoted himself to study. His many publications did much to introduce to the W. a knowledge of Ethiopic sources and history, which did not advance appreciably till the work of A. *Dillmann. They include a *Grammatica Aethiopica* (1661; 2nd edn., much enlarged and improved, 1702; photographically repr., Halle, 1986), a *Historia Aethiopica* (1681), and a *Commentarius ad suam Historiam Aethiopicam* (1691). In the last-named the '*Apostolic Tradition' of St *Hippolytus was first made accessible to W. scholars. He also published an edition of the Psalter in Ethiopic and Latin (1701).

His correspondence with Leibniz (mainly on linguistic subjects) was ed. by A. B. Michaelis (Göttingen, 1755); Eng. tr. of excerpts by J. T. Waterman (University of California Publications in Linguistics, 88 [1978]). His 'Theologia Aethiopica' was first pub. by S. Uhlig (Äthiopische Forschungen, 14A–B; 1983). Eng. tr. of his 'New History of Ethiopia' by 'J. P., Gent.' (London, 1682). J. Fleming, 'Hiob Ludolf. Ein Beitrag zur Geschichte der orientalischen Philologie', *Beiträge zur Assyriologie*, 1 (1890), pp. 537–58, 2 (1894), pp. 63–110. C. F. Bauer, *Hiob Ludolf: Der Begründer der äthiopischen Sprachwissenschaft und des äthiopischen Buchdrucks* (1937; brief, with specimens of his Ethiopic type and bibl.). E. Ullendorff, *The Ethiopians* (1960; 2nd edn., 1965), pp. 9–11.

Ludolf of Saxony (*c*.1300–78), also 'Ludolf the *Carthusian', spiritual writer. Little is known of his early life, except that he entered the *Dominican Order and became a Master of Theology before he joined the Carthusians at Strasbourg in 1340. From 1343 until 1348 he was Prior of the Charterhouse at Koblenz, but he then resumed his status as an ordinary monk and spent the rest of his life at Mainz and Strasbourg. His two principal works are a 'Commentary on the Psalms' and his celebrated 'Vita Christi'. The latter is not a biography but a meditation on the life of Christ, with doctrinal, spiritual, and moral instructions as well as prayers and extensive patristic citations; it became very popular.

His 'Vita Christi' was pr. at Cologne, 1474. It has frequently been reissued in many languages. The fullest modern edn. is that of A.-C. Bolard and others (Paris and Rome, 1865); also ed. L. M. Rigollot (Paris, 1878). His Comm. on the Psalms was pr. at Speyer, *c*.1491. Eng. tr. of the prayers at the end of the *Vita Christi* by M. I. Bodenstedt, SNB (Analecta Cartusiana, 15; Salzburg, 1973). Id., *The Vita Christi of Ludolphus the Carthusian* (Catholic University of America, Studies in Medieval and Renaissance Latin Language and Literature, 16; Washington, DC, 1955), with bibl. A. Passmann, OFM Cap., 'Probleme um Ludolf von Sachsen', *Archives de l'Église d'Alsace*, NS 3 (1949–50), pp. 13–34. W. Baier, *Untersuchungen zu den Passionsbetrachtungen in der Vita Christi des Ludolf von Sachsen* (Analecta Cartusiana, 44; 3 vols., Salzburg, 1977). Id. in *Dict. Sp.* 9 (1976) cols. 1130–8, s.v. 'Ludolphe de Saxe'.

Lugo, John de (1583–1660), Spanish *Jesuit. After studying law at Salamanca till 1603, he entered the Society in that year. From 1611 he taught philosophy at several Spanish colleges, and from 1616 theology at Valladolid. Called to the Jesuit College at Rome in 1621, he soon achieved international fame as a theologian, and was made cardinal by *Urban VIII in 1643. During these years were published his chief works, *De Incarnatione* (1633), *De Sacramentis in Genere* (1636), *De Virtute Fidei Divinae* (1646), *Responsa Moralia* (1651). An independent thinker, Lugo is chiefly important for his teaching on faith and on the sacrifice of the Mass. He held that God gives light sufficient for salvation to every soul, so that all men of good will can find among the errors of their human religious or philo-

sophical systems the elements of Divine truth which will enable them to be saved. In his Eucharistic teaching he emphasized the element of destruction as the distinctive characteristic of sacrificial worship. He held that in the act of Consecration, Christ's human nature is in some manner 'destroyed' by being changed into a lower state from which the normal human activities are excluded and the primary object of its existence is henceforward to be consumed as food. His contributions to dogmatic theology, combined with his luminous exposition of many problems of moral theology, caused St *Alphonsus Liguori to regard Lugo as 'the most important theologian after St *Thomas Aquinas'.

Works listed in Sommervogel, 5 (1894), cols. 176–80, and 9 (1900), cols. 619 f., with details of pr. edns. More recent bibl. in Polgár, 2 (1990), pp. 454 f. L. Gómez Hellin, SJ, *Praedestinatio apud Ioannem Cardinalem de Lugo* (Analecta Gregoriana, 12; 1938). G. Brinkman, OFM, *The Social Thought of John de Lugo* (Catholic University of America Studies in Sociology, 41; Washington, DC, 1957). D. *Stone, *A History of the Doctrine of the Holy Eucharist*, 2 (1909), pp. 373–7. P. Bernard in *DTC* 9 (pt. 1; 1926), cols. 1071 f.

Luis de León. See LEÓN, LUIS DE.

Luis of Granada (1504–88), Spanish spiritual author. Luis de Sarria, who was born at Granada, was professed there as a *Dominican in 1525. He studied at the college of San Gregorio in Valladolid, where he became a close friend of Bartolomé de Carranza, later Primate of Spain and a victim of the Spanish *Inquisition. Back in Andalusia, he spent 11 years (1534–45) at the Dominican convent of Escalaceli, near Córdoba, restoring the house and studying works of spirituality. He read the *Imitation of Christ* and was long thought, probably wrongly, to have translated it into Spanish. He became the foremost disciple of *John of Ávila and himself one of the most widely admired preachers of his day. In 1550/1, after some time in Extremadura, he was invited to go to Portugal by the Cardinal Infante Henry and scarcely ever returned to Spain. Provincial of the Portuguese Dominicans from 1556 to 1560, he acted as confessor to the great of the land and later included the Duke of Alba among his penitents. He refused the archbishopric of Braga, recommending instead his fellow-Dominican *Bartholomew of the Martyrs; his own life he gave to prayer, writing, and preaching. His fame and importance rest on his books of spiritual guidance, esp. the *Libro de la oración y meditación* ('Book on Prayer and Meditation', 1554) and the *Guía de pecadores* ('Guide for Sinners', 1556–7). He sought to give spiritual guidance to laymen as well as religious. He urged the practice of Christian virtues, which he saw as bringing a sense of confidence, Christian wisdom, liberation from sin, illumination, and transformation by the Holy Spirit. He attributed great importance to the interior life, to mental as distinct from vocal prayer, and saw outward ceremonies as relatively unimportant in comparison with the inner religious life, which was the life of grace. He drew his ideas from many sources, but was particularly indebted to G. *Savonarola and the *Erasmus of the *Enchiridion*, and stood in the tradition that linked them. His concern with interiority led to both his most celebrated works being placed on the Spanish *Index in 1559, but his ideas largely survived in the revised versions of 1566–7. He much admired, and was admired by, the *Jesuits. In his eighties he wrote an account of John of Ávila as a preacher and began a life of Bartholomew of the Martyrs. Among Spanish religious writers his works enjoyed a uniquely abundant circulation in Spanish and in translation, Italian, French, and English, esp. in his own and the following century. He wrote exceptionally fine Spanish prose, and his writings include superb renderings of biblical passages.

Collected edn. of his works by J. Cuervo, OP (14 vols., Madrid, 1906–8); also by A. Huerga [OP] and others (Madrid, 1994 ff.). Letters also ed. A. Huerga, OP (Córdoba, 1989). Fr.tr. of his works by J.-F. Bareille and others (22 vols., Paris, 1862–8). *Sermones* tr. from Lat. into Sp. by P. Duarte (14 vols., Madrid, 1790–93). A. Huerga, OP, *Fray Luis de Granada: una vida al servicio de la Iglesia* (Biblioteca de autores cristianos, 496; 1988), with bibl. E. A. Peers, *Studies of the Spanish Mystics*, 1 (1927), pp. 31–76. M. Bataillon, 'De Savonarole à Louis de Grenade', *Revue de Littérature Comparée*, 16 (1936), pp. 23–39. Id., *Érasme et l'Espagne* (Bibliothèque de l'École des Hautes Études Hispaniques, 21; 1937; new edn. by D. Devoto, ed. C. Amiel, Travaux d'Humanisme et Renaissance, 250; 3 vols., Geneva, 1991: see index s.v. Grenade (Louis de)). Fidel de Ros, OFM Cap., 'Los místicos del Norte y Fray Luis de Granada', *Archivo Ibero-Americano*, 7 (1947), pp. 5–30, 145–65. R. L. Oechslin, OP, *Louis de Grenade ou la rencontre avec Dieu* (1954; Eng. tr., 1962). M. I. R. Rodrigues, *Fray Luis de Granada y la Literatura de Espiritualidad en Portugal (1554–1632)* (1988). M. Llaneza, *Bibliografía del V.P.M. Fr. Luis de Granada, O.P.* (4 vols., Salamanca, 1926–8). Quétif and Échard, 2, pp. 285–91. Pourrat, 3 (1925), pp. 143–53; Eng. tr., 3 (1927), pp. 95–101. A. Huerga, OP, in *Dict. Sp.* 9 (1976), cols. 1043–54, s.v. 'Louis (9) de Grenade', with bibl.

Luke, St, Evangelist; acc. to tradition the author of the Third Gospel and of *Acts. Several facts of his life can be gathered from the Pauline Epp. and from Acts, if the 'we-sections' (Acts 16: 10–17; 20: 5–21: 18; 27: 1–28: 16) are parts of his travel journal. Acc. to Col. 4: 14 he was a physician, and it has been inferred from Col. 4: 11 that he was a Gentile (an inference corroborated by his idiomatic Greek). He accompanied St Paul on his Second Missionary Journey from Troas to Philippi (Acts 16: 10–17) and on the Third from Philippi to *Jerusalem (Acts 20: 5–21: 18), and he went with him to Rome, where he stayed during his captivity (Col. 4: 14, 2 Tim. 4: 11, Philem. 24). A variant in *Codex Bezae at Acts 11: 28 implies that he was one of the early members of the Christian community at *Antioch, a hypothesis made plausible by his other references to the Church in Antioch, and supported by statements in *Eusebius, St *Jerome, and others. Acc. to a tradition recorded in the *Anti-Marcionite Prologues, St Luke was unmarried, wrote his Gospel in Greece, and died at the age of 84. *Origen is the first to identify him with 'the brother' of 2 Cor. 8: 18, a view followed by the BCP collect for his feast. In 356–7 Constantius II had his relics translated from Thebes in Boeotia to *Constantinople, where they were preserved at the Church of the Apostles, built soon afterwards. The *Acta* of his alleged martyrdom are legendary.

St Luke is the patron of doctors. Acc. to later legends he was one of the Seventy of Lk. 10: 1, the unnamed disciple of *Emmaus (Lk. 24: 13–35), and a painter, and in the Middle Ages a picture of the BVM in *Santa Maria Maggiore, Rome, was ascribed to him. He is therefore also the patron of artists. Feast day, 18 Oct.

For bibl., see works cited under foll. entry.

Luke, Gospel of St. The third of the Synoptic Gospels. From the end of the 2nd cent. its authorship has been attributed to St *Luke (q.v.), the companion of St *Paul. The tradition has been widely accepted on the ground that there is no reason why a Gospel should have been falsely assigned to a comparatively unimportant person. It forms a single work with the *Acts of the Apostles (q.v.). Luke's probable dependence on Mark and the prediction of the fall of *Jerusalem (19: 43 f. and 21, verses 20 and 24) in more precise terms than in Matthew and Mark, have seemed to require a date after AD 70, but this inference has been contested.

According to most modern scholars, the author drew on two main sources, Mark and the so-called '*Q'. Some, however, think that his second source was Matthew. (On these questions, see SYNOPTIC PROBLEM.) The similarities with Matthew and Mark indicate that the author could follow sources closely, but his work is more than a compilation; it has the broad characteristics of literature, history, and theology.

The author can write in idiomatic and elegant Greek, but he sometimes uses the style of the Greek OT. The prologue (1: 1–4), addressed to His Excellency Theophilus, might suggest that he is writing for readers outside the Christian circle, and claims that he is giving an authentic account based on material supplied by eye-witnesses. He presents his material in the most favourable light from the point of view of the Roman authorities. Thus Pilate is recorded three times as saying that he finds no fault in Jesus (23, verses 4, 14, and 22) and responsibility for the Crucifixion is placed on the Jews. There are also a number of other specific references to persons and events in contemporary history (e.g. in 3: 1), though the accuracy of details (e.g. the date of the census in 2: 1–2) has been disputed.

The narrative opens with an account of the birth of *John the Baptist and of Christ, and then follows the same course as in Mark (and Matthew) from John's preaching, through the Galilean ministry, to *Jerusalem and the account of the Passion and Resurrection, though it differs at a number of points. For instance, it has no parallel to Mk. 6: 45–8: 26 (= Mt 14: 22–16: 12), and the section setting Christ's journey to Jerusalem by way of *Samaria (9: 51–18: 14) and the account of His hearing before *Herod Antipas (23: 8–12) are peculiar to Luke. Other passages which occur only in this Gospel stress the Lord's kindness and human understanding, e.g. the Parable of the Prodigal (15: 11–32) and the promise to the good thief (23: 43); His care for outcasts, e.g. the woman who was a sinner (7: 37–50), and for the poor, in the first *Beatitude (6: 20) and the Parable of Dives and Lazarus (16: 19–31). There are numerous references to women not found in the other Gospels, e.g. *Elizabeth (1: 5–66) and the widow of Nain (7: 11–17), while it is Mary, not *Joseph, who plays the principal part in the Birth stories. Luke assigns a more prominent place to prayer in the picture of Christ than do the other Gospels (e.g. 3: 21) and constantly stresses the activity of the Holy Spirit in the Incarnation (1: 35), in the events of the Lord's life (4, verses 1, 14, 18), and as the guide and inspiration of the Christian community (11: 13, 12: 12).

An important feature in Luke–Acts is the insistence that the salvation offered by Christ's life, death, and teaching is addressed to all, and not to the Jews only. This teaching is brought out in the scene at the synagogue in *Nazareth; Christ's message is welcomed, but when He makes clear that it will have a better welcome from the Gentiles the reception turns hostile (4: 16–30). It can be seen also in other passages in Luke (e.g. 2: 32, 3: 6, 24: 47), though it is only in the events recorded in Acts that it is fully realized. The growth and activity of the Church, regarded as the inheritor of the promises of the OT, is seen as an integral stage in the history of salvation. Some scholars have credited Luke with expressing this in a scheme of three distinct ages: the age of expectation, the teaching and ministry of Christ, and its proclamation in the Church. Although belief in the Lord's return is retained, the expectation of the end of the world is minimized. Salvation through Christ is proclaimed, but the significance of the Cross is not spelt out in detail.

Patristic works on the Gospel include the Homilies of *Origen on chs. 1–4 and comm. in Greek by *Cyril of Alexandria, *Theophylact, and *Euthymius Zigabenus, and in Lat. by *Ambrose, *Bede, and *Walafrid Strabo. Modern comm. by A. Plummer (ICC, 1896), E. Klostermann (Hb. NT 2. 1; 1919), M. J. *Lagrange (Études Bibliques, 1921), W. Manson (Moff. Comm., 1930), J. M. Creed (London, 1930), A. R. C. Leaney (Black's NT Comm., 1958; 2nd edn., 1966), E. E. Ellis (New Cent. Bib., 1966; 2nd edn., 1974), H. Schürmann (Herders Theologischer Kommentar zum Neuen Testament, 3; 1969 ff.), G. H. P. Thompson (New Clar. Bib., 1972), I. H. Marshall (New International Greek Testament Commentary, 1978), E. Schweizer (Das Neue Testament Deutsch, 3; 1982; Eng. tr., 1984), J. A. Fitzmyer, SJ (Anchor Bible, 2 vols.; 1981–5), J. Nolland (Word Biblical Comm., 35; 3 vols., Dallas [1989–93]), C. F. Evans (London and Philadelphia, 1990), and L. T. Johnson (Sacra Pagina, 3; Collegeville, Minn. [1991]).

H. J. *Cadbury, The Style and Literary Method of Luke (1920); B. H. *Streeter, The Four Gospels (1924), pp. 199–270; V. Taylor, Behind the Third Gospel: A Study of the Proto-Luke Hypothesis (1926); H. J. Cadbury, The Making of Luke–Acts (1927); H. Conzelmann, Die Mitte der Zeit: Studien zur Theologie des Lukas (Beiträge zur historischen Theologie, 17; 1954; Eng. tr., 1960); H. Flender, Heil und Geschichte in der Theologie des Lukas (Beiträge zur Evangelischen Theologie, 41; 1965; Eng. tr., 1967); I. H. Marshall, Luke: Historian and Theologian [1970]; J. Drury, Tradition and Design in Luke's Gospel (1976); D. L. Tiede, Prophecy and History in Luke and Acts (Philadelphia [1980]); J. Jeremias, Die Sprache des Lukasevangeliums: Redaktion und Tradition im Nicht-Markusstoff des dritten Evangeliums (KEK, Sonderband, 1980); R. Maddox, The Purpose of Luke–Acts (Forschungen zur Religion und Literatur des Alten und Neuen Testaments, 126; 1982; also Edinburgh, 1982); R. C. Tannehill, The Narrative Unity of Luke–Acts: A Literary Interpretation, 1: The Gospel according to Luke (Philadelphia, 1986); P. F. Esler, Community and Gospel in Luke–Acts: The Social and Political Motivation of Lucan Theology (Society for New Testament Studies, Monograph Series; Cambridge, 1987); J. T. Sanders, The Jews in Luke–Acts (1987); M. D. Goulder, Luke: A New Paradigm (2 vols., Journal for the Study of the New Testament, Supplement Series, 20; Sheffield [1989]). See also bibl. to ACTS.

Lull, St (d. 786), Bp. of Mainz. Like St *Boniface an Anglo-Saxon, he was educated and ordained priest at *Malmesbury. Proceeding to Rome and then to Germany, he became closely associated with Boniface who appointed Lull his successor in the see of Mainz; by a special concession from Pope *Zacharius Lull was consecrated bishop c.752 and took over Mainz after Boniface's death (754). He did not, however, receive the *pallium until c.781, after a petition had been sent to Pope *Hadrian I, who ordered an examination of Lull by three Frankish bishops; in the course of this Lull made a Profession of Faith. A long dispute between Lull and Sturm, the Abbot of *Fulda, began when Lull attempted to end the exemption of Fulda from the jurisdiction of Mainz and its direct dependence on Rome, which Sturm's predecessor had secured; the consequence was that Fulda was taken under the protection of *Pepin III, to whom both Lull and the monks had appealed, and it became a royal monastery, coming within the sphere of Frankish influence. Lull founded the monastery at Hersfeld, where he was afterwards buried. His interest in learning is reflected in his correspondence with some of the most notable clerics of his time, esp. in England. Feast day, 16 Oct.

Letters of Boniface and Lull ed. M. Tangl (MGH, Epistolae Selectae, 1; 1916). J. F. Böhmer and C. Will (eds.), Regesten zur Geschichte der Mainzer Erzbischöfe, 1 (Innsbruck, 1887), pp. 34–45. Life by *Lampert of Hersfeld pr. among the latter's works (ed. O. Holder-Egger, Hanover, etc, 1894), pp. 305–40; cf. also Eigil's Life of Sturm, ed. G. H. Pertz in MGH, Scriptores, 2 (1829), pp. 366–77. T. Schieffer, 'Angelsachsen und Franken', Akademie der Wissenschaften und der Literatur [in Mainz]. Abhandlungen der Geistes- und Sozialwissenschaftlichen Klasse, Jahrg. 1950, no. 20, pt. 2: 'Erzbischof Lul und die Anfänge des Mainzer Sprengels', pp. 1471–529. J. Hörle, 'Breviarium Sancti Lulli—Gestalt und Gehalt', Archiv für Mittelrheinische Kirchengeschichte, 12 (1960), pp. 18–52. For Lull's Profession of Faith see W. Levison, England and the Continent in the Eighth Century (Ford Lectures for 1943; 1946), Appendix 2, pp. 233–40; text repr. in T. Schieffer, op. cit., pp. 1535–9. W. *Stubbs in DCB 3 (1882), pp. 757–61.

Lull, Raymond. See LLULL, RAMON.

Luna, Pedro de. See BENEDICT XIII, ANTIPOPE.

Lund. Constituted a bishopric suffragan to Hamburg-Bremen in the middle of the 10th cent., it was established as an independent archbishopric in 1104. Apart from a brief period from 1133 onwards, it continued to possess its archiepiscopal status till the see was suppressed in 1536. The university dates from 1668. In the 19th cent. its theological faculty stood for a conservative and 'High Church' tradition in contrast to the liberalizing theology of *Uppsala. From 15 to 28 Aug. 1952 it was the scene of a Conference of the *Faith and Order Commission of the *World Council of Churches on 'The Church, Ways of Worship and Intercommunion'. This Conference's 'Word to the Churches' enunciated what came to be known as the 'Lund Principle': 'Should not our Churches ask themselves ... whether they should not act together in all matters, except those in which deep differences of conviction compel them to act separately?'

L. Weibull (ed.). Diplomatarium Diocesis Lundensis: Lunds Ärkestifts Urkundsbok, vols. 3–6 ([covering 1421–1502], Lund, 1900–39 [vols. 1 and 2 not pub.]). Studies on the Cathedral by O. Rydbeck (Lund, 1915), E. H. G. Wrangel (ibid., 1923), and E. Newman (2 vols., Stockholm, 1946). J. Rosén and others, Lunds Universitets Historia (4 vols., 1968–82). C. Fehrman, Lärdomens Lund (1984; abridged Eng. tr., Lund and Learning: An Informal History of Lund University, Lund, 1987). A. Radler in TRE 21 (1991), cols. 506–13, s.v. 'Lund, Universität'. The Transactions of the Third World Conference on Faith and Order held at Lund, Aug. 1952, ed. O. S. Tomkins (London, 1953).

Lupercalia. A pagan festival which continued to be observed in Christian Rome at least until the 5th cent. *Gelasius I (or his predecessor Felix III) made strenuous efforts to suppress it.

Survey in introd. by G. Pomarès to his edn. of the letter 'Adversus Adromachum contra Lupercalia' attributed to Gelasius (SC 65; 1959), pp. 21–34.

Lupus, St (c.395–479), Bp. of Troyes. A native of Toul (in modern Lorraine), he married Pimeniola, the sister of St *Hilary of Arles. After seven years of wedlock, he and his wife agreed to adopt an ascetic life and moved to *Lérins (426). Shortly afterwards (427), however, he accepted the bishopric of Troyes, and held the see for some 50 years. Acc. to his Life (now dated in the 6th cent.), he accompanied St *Germanus of Auxerre on his mission to Britain against the *Pelagians in 429, and by his entreaties preserved his country from the ravages of *Attila. Feast day, 29 July.

A letter, pr. in J. P. Migne, PL 58. 66–8, survives; crit. edn. by C. Munier, Concilia Galliae A. 314–A. 506 (CCSL 148, 1963), pp. 140 f. His Life, ed. by B. Krusch in MGH, Scriptores Rerum Merovingicarum, 7 (pt. 1; 1919), pp. 284–302; Krusch doubted its value, but it has been upheld by L. *Duchesne, Fastes épiscopaux de l'ancienne Gaule, 2 (1899), p. 449, and by E. Ewig, 'Bemerkungen zur Vita des Bischofs Lupus von Troyes', in K. Hauck and H. Mordek (eds.), Geschichtsschreibung und Geistiges Leben im Mittelalter: Festschrift für Heinz Löwe zum 65. Geburtstag (Cologne, 1978), pp. 14–26. CPL (3rd edn., 1995), p. 320 (nos. 988 f.).

Lupus, Servatus (c.805–62), Abbot of Ferrières, classical scholar. Born into a Bavarian family with extensive interests in W. Francia, he spent his youth in the abbey of Ferrières (NE of Orleans) before going on to study under *Rabanus Maurus at *Fulda (c.829–36). His uncle and brother were successively bishops of Auxerre; another brother was abbot of St Germanus, Auxerre; in 840 Lupus himself received from Charles the Bald the abbey of Ferrières. He supported Charles throughout the turbulent years preceding the division of the Empire in 843, and took an active part in ecclesiastical affairs. He attended at least six synods, for one of which (that at Vers, south of Senlis; 844) he wrote the official report.

Lupus' principal literary monument is a collection of over 100 letters. These are both a primary source for the history of his time and evidence of his remarkable knowledge of classical and patristic authors, his determination in searching out rare texts, and his zeal to improve corrupt readings. A number of MSS written, corrected, and annotated in his hand have survived. His pupils included *Heiric of Auxerre. Lupus' strictly ecclesiastical writings range from a prose Life of St Wigbert of Fritzlar (836, arising out of his years at Fulda) and the revision of a Life of St Maximinus of Trier (839) to a treatise on *predestination, the Liber de tribus questionibus (c.850). With its supporting series of proof-texts (the Collectaneum de tribus questionibus) this treatise is a measured, but not unsympathetic, response to the doctrine of double predestination proposed by *Gottschalk, whom Lupus had known since their student days at Fulda. It affirmed that

in fallen man free will left to its own powers was capable only of evil, that there was a predestination to hell as well as to eternal life, and that the biblical assertion that it is God's will that all men should be saved (1 Tim. 2: 4) is to be interpreted as applying only to the elect.

Collected edn. of his works by É. *Baluze (Paris, 1664; 2nd edn., Antwerp, 1710; repr. in J. P. Migne, PL 119. 427–700). Crit. edns. of his Vita Wigberti by O. Holder-Egger in MGH, Scriptores, 15 (pt. 1; 1887), pp. 36–43, and of his letters by E. Dümmler in MGH, Epistolae, 6 (1925), pp. 1–126, and by P. K. Marshall (Teub., 1984, with good bibl.). Eng. tr. of his letters by G. W. Regenos (The Hague, 1966). E. von Severus, OSB, Lupus von Ferrières: Gestalt und Werk eines Vermittlers antiken Geistesgutes an das Mittelalter im 9. Jahrhundert (Beiträge zur Geschichte des alten Mönchtums und des Benediktinerordens, 21; Münster, 1940). W. Levison, 'Eine Predigt des Lupus von Ferrières', in Kultur- und Universalgeschichte Walter Goetz zu seinem 60. Geburtstage dargebracht (1927), pp. 3–14; repr. in id., Aus Rheinischer und Fränkischer Frühzeit (Düsseldorf, 1948), pp. 557–66; C. H. Beeson, Lupus of Ferrières as Scribe and Text Critic (Mediaeval Academy of America Publication, 4; Cambridge, Mass.), 1930); É. Pellegrin, 'Les Manuscrits de Loup de Ferrières. À propos du MS. Orléans 162 (139) corrigé de sa main', Bibliothèque de l'École des Chartes, 115 (for 1957; 1958), pp. 5 31; W. Edelstein, Eruditio und Sapientia: Weltbild und Erziehung in der Karolingerzeit (Freiburg i.B., 1965), pp. 169–218; R. J. Gariépy, 'Lupus of Ferrières: Carolingian Scribe and Text Critic', Mediaeval Studies, 30 (1968), pp. 90–105; P. von Moos, Consolatio: Studien zur mittellateinischen Trostliteratur über den Tod und zum Problem der christlichen Trauer (Münsterische Mittelalter-Schriften, 3; 4 vols., 1971–2), 1, pp. 111–31; 2, pp. 78–94; V. Brown, 'Lupus of Ferrières on the metres of Boethius', in J. J. O'Meara and B. Naumann (eds.), Latin Script and Letters A.D. 400–900. Festschrift presented to Ludwig Bieler (Leiden, 1976), pp. 63–79. E. S. Duckett, Carolingian Portraits (Ann Arbor, Mich.), 1962), pp. 161–201. J. M. Wallace-Hadrill, The Frankish Church (Oxford History of the Christian Church, 1983), pp. 304–14, with bibl. pp. 435 f. Manitius, 1 (1911), pp. 483–90. R. B. Palmer in NCE 8 (1967), p. 1078, s.v.

Luther, Martin (1483–1546), founder of the German *Reformation. The son of a miner at Mansfeld in Saxony, he was educated at Magdeburg and Eisenbach, and then at Erfurt University (1501–5). His studies in the faculty of arts brought him under the influence of leading *Nominalists such as Jodocus Trutvetter and Bartholomäus Arnoldi of Usingen. In 1505 he entered the monastery of the *Augustinian Hermits at Erfurt, and was ordained priest in 1507. In the following year he was sent to be professor of moral philosophy in the faculty of arts at the recently-founded University of *Wittenberg, in the aftermath of university reforms which appear to have established the presence of a Nominalist faction within that faculty. In 1510 he went to Rome on affairs of his order. Soon after his return to Wittenberg in 1511, with the support of his superior, Johannes von Staupitz, he became a doctor of theology and professor of biblical exegesis in the university faculty of theology, retaining this position until his death. In 1515 he was made vicar of his order, an office entailing the charge of 11 Augustinian monasteries.

Initially Luther appears to have adopted a form of biblical exegesis and theology of *justification similar to that of Nominalism, allowing man a definite, if limited, role in his own justification. During the years 1512–19, however, he developed insights concerning man's incapacity to justify himself which led him initially to modify, and then to reject, this position. He came to believe that man is unable to respond to God without divine grace, and that man can be justified only through faith (*per solam fidem*), by the merits of Christ imputed to him: works or religious observance are irrelevant. In an autobiographical fragment of 1545, Luther indicated that this theological breakthrough was linked with the discovery of a new understanding of 'the righteousness of God' (Rom. 1: 17). On the basis of internal evidence within his writings of the period, this discovery is generally regarded as having taken place in the period 1514–15. It is often, though perhaps unwarrantably, referred to as the 'Turmerlebnis' ('Tower Experience'). During the period 1515–19, Luther consolidated his doctrine of man's justification before God (*coram Deo*), emphasizing that justification was a work of God within man. Although in many respects Luther's theology of justification at this stage parallels that found in St *Augustine's anti-*Pelagian writings, important differences emerged, esp. in relation to the nature of justifying righteousness. Parallels have also been noted with the writings of J. *Tauler and the *Theologia Germanica* (which Luther edited in 1516 and 1518). In April 1517 *Carlstadt (then dean of the faculty of theology at Wittenberg) lent his support to Luther, after a close reading of Augustine's *De Spiritu et Littera*, with the result that by March 1518 the Wittenberg faculty of theology was committed to a programme of theological reform based on 'the Bible and St Augustine'.

On 31 Oct. 1517 Luther's 95 theses on *indulgences were posted on the door of the castle church at Wittenberg. They were written largely in response to the preaching of J. *Tetzel on the indulgences granted by *Leo X for contributions towards the renovation of *St Peter's in Rome. Although possessing the status of a purely academic disputation, and stating little that was exceptionable or radical, given the variety of opinions on the subject at the time, the theses came to be viewed as a manifesto of reform, and attracted considerable attention throughout Germany within weeks of their publication. In April 1518 Luther defended his position in the Heidelberg Disputation, held during a meeting of the chapter of his order; he won over several of his brethren and the Dominican M. *Bucer. In the same year he was tried (in his absence) in Rome on charges of heresy, and was summoned before Card. *Cajetan at Augsburg. Refusing to recant, he fled to Wittenberg under the protection of the Elector *Frederick III of Saxony. Negotiations with the Papal camerarius, C. von *Miltitz, elicited from Luther nothing more than a promise that he would remain silent if his opponents did likewise. In 1519 Luther and J. *Eck confronted each other at the *Leipzig Disputation, at which Luther denied both the primacy of the Pope and the infallibility of General Councils. By this time Luther was the object of considerable admiration in humanist circles, being 'productively misunderstood' as sharing the humanist concern for the institutional and moral reform of the Church. Acc. to Bucer and others, Luther and *Erasmus differed only in the extent to which they voiced their views. Recent scholarship has drawn attention to the way in which the humanist movement expanded what was initially little more than an academic debate into an international *cause célèbre*.

In 1520 Luther's programme of reform was further consolidated by a direct appeal to the German people to take the initiative in reforming the Church. Three major reforming treatises were published. The first, *An den christlichen Adel deutscher Nation*, addressed to the German princes, laid the foundations for a programme of lay reform by rejecting the distinction between the 'spiritual' and 'temporal' orders, by insisting on the right to challenge the Pope on the interpretation of Scripture, and the right of the laity to summon a reforming General Council. It encouraged the princes to abolish tributes to Rome, the celibacy of the clergy, Masses for the dead, and many other Catholic practices and institutions. This was followed by *De Captivitate Babylonica Ecclesiae* (pub. in Latin and German, *Von der babylonischen Gefangenschaft der Kirche*); here Luther criticized the subjection of the laity to the institution of the Church which he particularly identified with the denial to the laity of Communion in both kinds, the doctrine of *transubstantiation, and the Sacrifice of the Mass, and only Baptism and the Eucharist were recognized as possessing sacramental character. In the final work of the trilogy, *Von der Freiheit eines Christenmenschen*, the liberation of the Christian from a 'bondage of works' through his justification was enthusiastically proclaimed. The cumulative effect of these treatises was considerable. Even before they were published, however, Luther was condemned in the bull '*Exsurge Domine' of 12 June 1520, which censured 41 theses drawn from his works to date. Luther replied by burning the bull, along with many Catholic books; this action led to his excommunication by the bull 'Decet Romanum Pontificem' of 3 Jan. 1521.

In the aftermath of this excommunication, Luther was summoned before the Diet of *Worms, where he refused to recant (acc. to an early but unreliable tradition, in the famous words 'Hier stehe ich. Ich kan nicht anders', 'Here I stand, I can do no other'). On 26 May 1521 his teachings were formally condemned in the Edict of Worms and Luther was put under the ban of the Empire. Fearing for his safety, the Elector of Saxony arranged for Luther to be abducted in June to the *Wartburg, near Eisenach, where he spent the next eight months under the pseudonym 'Junker Georg'. In many respects, this was one of the most constructive periods of Luther's career, witnessing the beginning of his translation of the Bible into German, of which the NT was published in Sept. 1522. His important attack on Jacobus Latomus, in which Luther's views on the relation of grace and faith are explained with some brilliance, also dates from this period.

In his absence, however, the situation at Wittenberg had deteriorated, with radical elements (such as the '*Zwickau Prophets'), recently joined by Carlstadt, causing religious anarchy. Luther was obliged to return to Wittenberg on 7 May 1522, and to restore order with the assistance of the secular authorities. In this period of liturgical reform and consolidation Luther issued the *Forma Missae et Communionis* (1523), an important pamphlet explaining the new Protestant rite and clarifying his attitude to the Eucharist; in the following year the first Wittenberg hymnal (incl. four of Luther's own compositions) appeared. Having already abandoned many Catholic practices, incl. private Masses and fasts, since leaving the *Wartburg, Luther finally discarded his Augustinian habit in 1524. After the death of the Elector, who had remained hostile to the marriage of priests and religious, he married the former *Cistercian nun, Katharina von Bora, on 13 June 1525. In the same year Luther's pamphlet advising the German princes to wage war against the peasants who had risen in arms appeared; this cost him the sympathies of a section of the population (see PEASANTS' WAR). His open attack on Erasmus in De Servo Arbitrio (1525) exposed the tension between them, causing some embarrassment to the more humanist of the Wittenberg Reformers, such as P. *Melanchthon (even though U. *Zwingli had independently set out what were to be the main elements of Luther's attack in a work published earlier the same year, but not known to the German Reformer).

The religious and political situation, however, continued to favour the spread of Luther's views. The use of the vernacular in the liturgy (the Deutsche Messe was published in 1526), in the public reading of the Bible, and in the singing of hymns, all served to further Luther's end. His work was considerably facilitated by the Diet of *Speyer (1526), which established the right of the princes to organize national Churches. Although Luther was unable to be present at the Diet of Augsburg (1530) on account of the ban of the Empire, he lent his approval to the comparatively conciliatory '*Augsburg Confession (Confessio Augustana)', drawn up by Melanchthon, which established the doctrinal basis of the Lutheran Church.

At this time, however, the differences between the Lutheran and Reformed wings of the Reformation became increasingly evident, esp. in relation to sacramental theology. At the Colloquy of *Marburg (1529) the deep division between Luther and Zwingli over the nature of the Presence of Christ in the Eucharist proved unbridgeable: Luther argued that after consecration the substances both of the Body and Blood of Christ and of the bread and wine coexist in union with each other ('*consubstantiation'), Zwingli that the Presence of Christ was purely symbolic. The renewal of the Eucharistic controversy within Lutheranism itself in the 1540s, in addition to the continued tension between the Lutheran and Reformed wings of the Reformation, illustrates how serious this division would prove to be. The final years of Luther's life were marked by controversy, arising over such matters as his covert approval of the bigamous marriage of *Philip of Hesse and the appointment of Nikolaus von *Amsdorf as Bp. of Naumburg in 1541. Luther died on 18 Feb. 1546 and was buried in the castle church at Wittenberg. The rumour that his body had been disinterred and reburied in a field during the Schmalkaldic War was finally silenced through its recovery during the restoration of the castle church on 14 Feb. 1892.

Apart from his three treatises of 1520, Luther published a considerable number of works, mostly small occasional pamphlets, with no attempt at a systematic elaboration of his doctrine, and prone to frequent lapses into personal abuse of his opponents. His passionate reply to *Henry VIII's Defence of the Seven Sacraments, entitled Contra Henricum Regem Anglicanum (1522) lost him the sympathies of England. But several such works are of importance. In De Servo Arbitrio (1525) Luther defended his radical views on the impotence of the human free will against the criticisms of Erasmus in De Libero Arbitrio. His pedagogical works, Kleiner Katechismus and Grosser Katechismus

(both 1529) heightened the attraction of the Reformation for humanists, allowing them to regard the movement as fundamentally educational. His abilities as a biblical commentator are perhaps best seen from the 1535 Galatians commentary. A more informal, and perhaps rather inaccurate, view of the Reformer may be gained from the Tischreden (records of conversations over Luther's dinnertable in the period 1529–45). Many of his German hymns, an important means of disseminating the ideas of the Reformation among the people, are still in general use, the most celebrated being 'Ein feste burg ist unser Gott' (Eng. tr., 'A safe stronghold our God is still', EH 362), prob. written in 1528.

Luther's distinctive ideas were considerably modified by the Lutheran Church after his death (see LUTHERANISM), with the Formula of *Concord (1577) explicitly rejecting some of the ideas defended by Luther in De Servo Arbitrio (e.g. the doctrine of double *predestination, and of God as auctor peccati). In the 20th cent., however, Luther's '*theologia crucis' has been reappropriated, esp. by theologians such as Jürgen *Moltmann and Eberhard Jüngel, as a fruitful way of exploring the nature of God's presence in and dealings with the world.

The standard critical edn. of Luther's works is the 'Weimarer Ausgabe' in some 100 vols. (Weimar, 1883 ff.; text completed 1983, though since 1963 some works in the edition have been re-edited; indexes, 1986 ff.). Its four sections contain his writings and lectures, the Tischreden, his correspondence, and material on his tr. of the Bible. Selected docs. on his intellectual development to 1519 in O. Scheel, Dokumente zu Luthers Entwicklung (2nd edn., Sammlung ausgewählter kirchen- und dogmengeschichtlicher Quellenschriften, NF 2; Tübingen, 1929). Standard Eng. tr. of Luther's Works [not exhaustive], ed. J. Pelikan and H. T. Lehmann (54 vols. + introd., St Louis and Philadelphia, 1955–76).

Modern historical and biographical studies incl. G. [G. B.] Ritter, Luther: Gestalt und Tod (1925; 6th edn., 1959; Eng. tr., 1963); J. Mackinnon, Luther and the Reformation (4 vols., 1925–30); E. G. Schwiebert, Luther and his Times (St Louis [1950]); R. H. Bainton, Here I Stand: A Life of Martin Luther (1951); A. G. Dickens, The German Nation and Martin Luther (1974); H. Bornkamm, Martin Luther in der Mittes seines Leben (posthumously ed. K. Bornkamm, Göttingen, 1979; Eng. tr., 1983); H. G. Haile, Luther: A Biography (New York, 1980; London, 1981); M. Lienhard, Martin Luther: Un temps, une vie, un message (1983); H. Junghans (ed.), Leben und Werk Martin Luthers von 1526 bis 1546: Festgabe zu seinem 500. Geburtstag (2 vols., 1983).

On his theology, there is a classic work by K. *Holl, Gesammelte Aufsätze, Bd. 1: Luther (1921); Bd. 3: Der Westen (1928), pp. 130–243. More recent studies incl. P. S. Watson, Let God be God! An Interpretation of the Theology of Martin Luther (1947); [E.] G. Rupp, The Righteousness of God: Luther Studies (Birkbeck Lectures, 1947; 1953); G. Ebeling, Luther: Einführung in sein Denken (Tübingen, 1964; Eng. tr., 1970). Seminal essays on specific doctrines by W. von Loewenich, Luthers Theologia Crucis (Munich, 1929; 4th edn., 1954; Eng. tr., Belfast, 1976); R. Prenter, Spiritus Creator: Studier i Luthers Teologi (Copenhagen, 1944; 2nd edn., 1946; Eng. tr., Philadelphia, 1953); H. Sasse, This is my Body: Luther's Contention for the Real Presence in the Sacrament of the Altar (Minneapolis [1959]; rev. edn., Adelaide, 1977); E. Bizer, Fides ex auditu: Eine Untersuchungen über die Entdeckung der Gerechtigkeit Gottes durch Martin Luther (Neukirchen, 1958; 3rd edn., 1966); I. D. K. Siggins, Martin Luther's Doctrine of Christ (1970); G. Ebeling, Lutherstudien (3 vols. in 4, Tübingen, 1971–85); M. Lienhard, Luther, témoin de Jésus-Christ (1973; Eng. tr., Minneapolis, 1982); M. Brecht, Martin Luther: Sein Weg zur

Reformation 1483–1521 (Stuttgart, 1981; Eng. tr., Philadelphia, 1985); A. E. McGrath, *Luther's Theology of the Cross: Martin Luther's Theological Breakthrough* (Oxford, 1985); H.-M. Gutmann, *Über Liebe und Herrschaft: Luthers Verständnis von Intimität und Autorität im Kontext des Zivilisationsprozesses* (Göttinger theologische Arbeiten, 47 [1991]).

Full bibl. of the vast lit. is provided in the authoritative *Jahrbuch der Luther-Gesellschaft* (1919; from 1920 *Luther-Jahrbuch*) and a shorter account in the annual *Literaturberichte* of the *Archiv für Reformationsgeschichte* (1903 ff.).

M. Brecht and others in *TRE* 21 (1991), pp. 514–94, s.v., with extensive bibl. E. G. Rupp in *EB* (1985 edn.), 23, pp. 364–72, both s.v., with bibl. See also bibl. to REFORMATION.

Lutheranism. A confessional movement within the W. Church tracing its origins to the theology of M. *Luther and various formulae collected in the *Book of *Concord (1580, q.v.). These writings, which claim to 'introduce nothing . . . that is either contrary to Holy Scripture or the universal Christian church' (*Augsburg Confession, 1530), promote *justification by faith alone as the 'first and chief article' on which rests 'all that we teach and practise' (*Schmalkaldic Articles, 1537). After Luther's death (1546), Lutherans divided over issues such as *original sin, free will, good works, the Lord's Supper, the Person of Christ, indifferent matters (*adiaphora), and divine foreknowledge and election (*predestination). Appealing to Scripture as the 'only rule and norm' of doctrine, accommodation was reached in the *Formula of Concord* (1577), drafted by J. *Andreae and M. *Chemnitz. Lutherans modified, though generally retained, traditional liturgical forms, placing equal emphasis on preaching and sacraments. The Eucharist was celebrated 'every Sunday and on other festivals' (Apology of the Augsburg Confession, 1531).

P. *Melanchthon formulated the first systematic presentation of Lutheran theology. His *Loci communes* (1521) became the foundation of Lutheran dogmatics. The need for consolidation in the face of challenges from Rome, the *Calvinists, and rationalists, spurred the development of Lutheran 'orthodoxy', which dominated the 17th cent. It was elaborated in a Scholastic mould which gave it a somewhat intellectual cast. The publication of P. J. *Spener's *Pia Desideria* (1675) and the emergence of *Pietism was a reaction against this orthodoxy, as well as against confessional strife and the consolidation of state Churches after the *Thirty Years War. The Pietists proposed a less intellectualized, more irenic form of Christianity, appealing to Luther's ideas on the sufficiency of Scripture and the personal nature of faith. However, by developing subjective trends in late orthodoxy, e.g., the 'order of salvation' (*ordo salutis*), which delineated various stages in the process of conversion, Pietism stressed religious experience to the detriment of the original Lutheran insistence on the objectivity of the means of grace in word and sacraments.

In the 16th cent. Lutheranism spread through much of Germany, *Denmark, *Norway, *Sweden, *Finland, and E. Europe (e.g. in *Poland, *Hungary and Latvia), though in E. Europe and in Germany RCism and Calvinism later reversed or modified this situation. In the 19th cent. Frederick William III promoted a union of Reformed (Calvinist) and Lutheran Churches in Prussia (1817). Such political pressures, combined with the reductionist tendencies inherent in both the *Enlightenment and in a resur-

gent Pietism, and the challenge of biblical and historical criticism, stimulated a romantic rediscovery of Luther and a renewed confessionalism, e.g., by W. Löhe (1808–72) and the Erlangen school led by J. K. von Hofmann (1810–77). Early in the 20th cent. a Luther renaissance was promoted by K. *Holl, N. *Söderblom, and L. Ihmels (1858–1933). The First World War, National Socialism and Communism, however, decisively challenged any romantic views, provoking an intense critique of Luther's distinctive 'two kingdoms' ethic. This teaching distinguishes, without separating, two ways, spiritual and secular, in which God effects His will in the world. It is an interim ethic in which Christians are powerless themselves to bring about God's kingdom. Thus Lutherans in Germany were accused of uncritical accommodation and of 'quietism', esp. by the influential Swiss Reformed theologian K. *Barth, though many Lutherans such as H. Asmussen (1898–1968) and M. *Niemöller actively offered resistance, joining with the *Confessing Church.

In Germany after 1918, with the separation of Church and state (though the Church still retained its right to receive taxes), new structures were developed based upon a combination of synodical and episcopal forms. Thus the autonomous territorial Churches (*Landeskirchen*) continued to receive support from the regional governments. Lutheranism struggled to retain its identity as it participated in efforts to establish a combined Protestant Church. After 1945 attempts were made to unite all Lutheran Churches in the *Vereinigte Evangelisch-Lutherische Kirche Deutschlands* (VELKD), formed in 1948, though Württemberg and Oldenburg declined membership. The VELKD became part of the *Evangelical Church in Germany embracing Lutherans, Reformed, and 'United' Churches. Churches in the former German Democratic Republic were fully integrated into this body in 1991. In Scandinavia Lutheranism is the officially recognized religion. In the Church of Sweden debate continues over the question of membership, whether it should be by baptism, or by birthright, as is customary, through one baptized parent. Lutheranism in Sweden and Finland has retained the historic episcopal succession.

Lutheranism came to N. America in the 17th cent., but remained very small until after 1730 when German emigration surged. Many of the Lutherans who went to America were influenced by Pietism. In 1742 H. M. *Muhlenberg was sent from Halle to Pennsylvania to organize the Lutheran Church; he established the first Lutheran synod, the Ministerium of Pennsylvania, in 1748. Successive waves of immigrants from varied backgrounds settling in different regions led to a proliferation of Lutheran Church bodies. The history of Lutheranism in N. America is marked by struggles for confessional identity and increasingly for visible unity. By 1988 there were three major Lutheran Churches in N. America: (1) the Evangelical Lutheran Church in America, formed in 1988 by merging the Lutheran Church in America (itself the result of a merger in 1962 of the United Lutheran Church in America (formed 1918), the Augustana Evangelical Lutheran Church (formed 1948), and others) with the American Lutheran Church (the result of a merger in 1960 of the old American Lutheran Church (formed 1930), and others), and the Association of Evangelical Lutheran Churches (which separated from the Lutheran Church-

Missouri Synod in 1976); (2) the Lutheran Church-Missouri Synod, stemming from a group of Saxon immigrants to Perry County and St Louis, Missouri, in 1839, joined in 1947 by a merger of the Evangelical Lutheran Synod of Missouri, Ohio, and Other States (formed 1847), and in 1971 by the Synod of Evangelical Lutheran Churches (formed 1959); and (3) the Evangelical Lutheran Church in Canada, a merger in 1986 of the Evangelical Lutheran Church of Canada (formed 1967; formerly the Canada District of the American Lutheran Church), and the Lutheran Church in America–Canada Section (formed 1962). Inter-church co-operation was furthered by the National Lutheran Council (formed 1918) and the Lutheran Council in the USA (1967–88).

European missionary efforts, dating from the 18th cent., joined in the 19th cent. by Lutherans from America, established Lutheranism in *India, the *South Pacific and other parts of Asia, in Africa, Latin America, and *Australia. In 1923 many Lutherans joined to form the Lutheran World Convention, which in 1947 developed into the Lutheran World Federation. In 1984 at its 7th assembly, member Churches declared themselves to be in 'altar and pulpit' fellowship; at its 8th assembly in 1990, the Lutheran World Federation officially proclaimed itself a worldwide 'communion' of Churches. By the 1990s it included most but not all of the world's Lutherans (the Lutheran Church-Missouri Synod, e.g., is not a member). Notable ecumenical developments include the *Leuenberg Concord between European Lutheran and Reformed Churches (1973), the Lutheran–Episcopal Agreement in the USA (1982), the Meissen Common Statement between the Evangelical Church of Germany and the C of E (1988) and the Porvoo Agreement between the Nordic and Baltic Lutheran Churches and the C of E (1992) and, since 1965, a productive series of dialogues with RCs in Europe and N. America.

Die Bekenntnisschriften der evangelisch-lutherischen Kirche, ed. by the Deutscher Evangelischer Kirchenausschuss (Göttingen, 1930; 10th edn., 1986). Convenient Eng. tr. by T. G. Tappert, *The Book of Concord: The Confessions of the Evangelical Lutheran Church* (Philadelphia [1959]). 16th-cent. 'Kirchenordnung', ed. E. Sehling and others (Leipzig, and later Tübingen, 1902 ff.). H. [F. F.] Schmid, *Die Dogmatik der Evangelisch-Lutherischen Kirche* (Erlangen, 1843; Eng. tr., *The Doctrinal Theology of the Evangelical Lutheran Church*, Philadelphia, 1876; 3rd edn., 1899; repr., Minneapolis [1961]). W. Elert, *Morphologie des Luthertums* (2 vols., 1931–2; Eng. tr. of vol. 1, Saint Louis, 1962); id., *Der christliche Glaube: Grundlinien der lutherischen Dogmatik* (1940; 3rd edn. by E. Kinder, 1956); id., *Das christliche Ethos: Grundlinien der lutherischen Ethik* (1949). E. Schlink, *Theologie der lutherischen Bekenntnisschriften* (1940; 3rd edn., 1948; Eng. tr., Philadelphia, 1961); P. Althaus, *Die christliche Wahrheit: Lehrbuch der Dogmatik* (2 vols., 1947–8). E. Kinder, *Der evangelische Glaube und die Kirche: Grundzüge des evangelisch-lutherischen Kirchenverständnisses* (1958; 2nd edn., 1960). E. W. Gritsch and R. W. Jenson, *Lutheranism: The Theological Movement and its Confessional Writings* (Philadelphia [1976]). T. G. A. Hardt, *Venerabilis et adorabilis Eucharistia: Eine Studie über die lutherische Abendmahlslehre im 16. Jahrhundert* (Forschungen zur Kirchen- und Dogmengeschichte, 24; 1988). H.-C. Rublack (ed.), *Die lutherische Konfessionalisierung in Deutschland: Wissenschaftliches Symposion des Vereins für Reformationsgeschichte 1988* (Schriften des Vereins für Reformationsgeschichte, 197; 1992). H. Leube, *Kalvinismus und Luthertum im Zeitalter der Orthodoxie* (vol. 1 only pub., 1928); H. E. Weber, *Reformation, Orthodoxie und Rationalismus* (Beiträge zur Förderung christlicher Theologie, Reihe 2, Bde. 35, 51, pts.

1 and 2 only pub., 1935–51); H. Stephan, *Geschichte der evangelischen Theologie seit dem Idealismus* (Sammlung Töpelmann, Reihe 1, 9; 1938). E. Fischer, *Zur Geschichte der evangelischen Beichte* (Studien zur Geschichte der Theologie und der Kirche, 8, Heft 2, and 9, Heft 4; 1902–3); E. *Troeltsch, *Die Soziallehren der christlichen Kirchen und Gruppen* (1912), pp. 427–605 (Eng. tr., 1931, 2, pp. 461–576). A. Jundt, *Histoire résumée de l'Église luthérienne en France* (1935). A. R. Wentz, *A Basic History of Lutheranism in America* (Philadelphia, 1955). V. Ferm, *The Crisis in American Lutheran Theology: A Study of the Issue between American Lutheranism and Old Lutheranism* (New York, 1927). T. G. Tappert (ed.), *Lutheran Confessional Theology in America 1840–1880* (Library of Protestant Thought, New York, 1972). E. C. Nelson (ed.), *The Lutherans in North America* (Philadelphia [1974]; 2nd edn. [1980]). Id., *The Rise of World Lutheranism: An American Perspective* (Philadelphia [1982]). R. C. Wolf (ed.), *Documents of Lutheran Unity in America* (Philadelphia, 1966). A. R. Wentz (ed.), *The Lutheran Churches of the World, 1952* (Geneva, 1952). V. Vajta and H. Wiessgerber (eds.), *Das Bekenntnis im Leben der Kirche: Studien zur Lehrgrundlage und Bekenntnisbildung in der lutherischen Kirchen* (Berlin and Hamburg, 1963). V. Vajta, *From Generation to Generation: The Lutheran World Federation 1947–1982* (Lutheran World Federation Report, 16; Geneva, 1983). E. T. and M. B. Bachmann, *Lutheran Churches in the World: A Handbook* (Augsburg, 1989). J. Bodensieck (ed.), *The Encyclopedia of the Lutheran Church* (3 vols., Minneapolis, 1965). G. Gassmann in *TRE* 21 (1991), pp. 599–616, s.v. 'Lutherische Kirchen', and pp. 616–20, s.v. 'Lutherischer Weltbild', with bibl. See also bibl. to preceding entry, to REFORMATION and to individual countries where Lutherans are the main religious body.

Lux Mundi. A 'Series of Studies in the Religion of the Incarnation' published in 1889 by a group of Oxford Anglican teachers under the editorship of C. *Gore, then Principal of Pusey House. The other contributors included H. S. *Holland, E. S. *Talbot, R. C. *Moberly, and F. *Paget. Its purpose was 'to put the Catholic faith into its right relation to modern intellectual and moral problems'. At the time interest in the book was directed esp. to a few pages in Gore's own essay on 'The Holy Spirit and Inspiration', in which by accepting in principle the new critical views of the OT, he definitely broke with the conservative position of E. B. *Pusey and the *Tractarians. For this reason the book caused grave distress to many of the older school of High Churchmen, e.g. H. P. *Liddon.

[D.] G. Rowell, 'Historical Retrospect: Lux Mundi 1889', in R. [C.] Morgan (ed.), *The Religion of the Incarnation* (Bristol, 1989), pp. 205–17. P. [B.] Hinchliff, *God and History* (Oxford, 1992), pp. 99–121.

Luxeuil. The abbey, established *c.*590 by St *Columbanus on the site of the Roman Luxovium (about 20 miles NE of Vesoul), soon became the most important in France. The abbey of *Corbie was founded *c.*660 by some of its monks. Destroyed in 732 by the *Saracens, under *Charlemagne it was re-established, henceforward under the *Benedictine Rule. The abbey ceased to exist in 1790, though the abbey church is still in use as a parish church.

'Chronicon Luxoviense Breve' (from origins to 1039), ed. G. H. Pertz in *MGH*, Scriptores, 3 (1839), pp. 219–21. H. Baumont, *Étude historique sur l'abbaye de Luxeuil, 590–1790* (Luxeuil, 1895); E. de Beauséjour, *L'Église abbatiale de Luxeuil* (Besançon, 1891). Lectionary of Luxeuil [Par. lat. 9427], ed. P. Salmon, OSB (Collectanea Biblica Latina, 7 and 9; Rome, 1944–53). *Mélanges colombaniens: Congrès International d'Études Colombaniennes. Luxeuil, 20–23 juil. 1950* (Paris, 1951). F. Prinz, *Frühes Mönchtum im Frankreich* (Munich, 1965; repr. with additional material as 2nd edn., Darmstadt, 1988), *passim.* H. *Leclercq, OSB, in *DACL* 9 (pt. 2; 1930), cols., 2722–87; G. Oury in *DIP* 5 (1978), cols. 790 f., both s.v.

LXX. An abbreviation in common use for the *Septuagint (q.v.).

lych-gate (Old Eng. *lic* [cf. Ger. *Leiche*], 'corpse'). The roofed gateway to a churchyard beneath which the coffin is set down to await the arrival of the officiating minister.

lying. A lie is a statement not in accordance with the mind of the speaker, made with the intention of deceiving. In the OT the practice of lying is denounced as an attribute of sinners (Lev. 19: 11, Ps. 5: 6, Prov. 6: 17), though it is sometimes recorded of otherwise righteous people, e.g. of *Abraham (Gen. 20: 2), *Jacob (Gen. 27: 32), and *David (1 Sam. 21: 2). These lies, however, are usually regarded as excusable because they were told in cases of necessity without the intention to hurt. In the NT the standard is higher, and lying is so abhorrent that for the disciple a simple affirmation of the truth is to take the place of an oath (Mt. 5: 37). St *Paul, too, exhorts Christians to put away falsehood (Col. 3: 9; cf. Eph. 4: 25), and in the Bk. of Rev. the virgins who follow the Lamb are praised because 'in their mouth was found no lie' (14: 5). The NT teaching is followed by the Fathers, though with slight divergences. Some of them, e.g. *Origen, St *Hilary of Poitiers, St *Jerome, and St *Chrysostom, held that a lie may be lawful, e.g. in order to save an innocent man from death. St *Augustine, however, and following him St *Thomas Aquinas, hold that lying is always sinful, because it perverts the nature of human speech, which is meant to express man's thought, not to disguise it. Acc. to St Thomas lies are never lawful, and even 'officious' lies, i.e. those told for the benefit of someone without the intention of deceiving, and 'jocose' lies, told for amusement, are reprehensible. St Thomas admits, however, that in certain cases it may be prudent to hide the truth under some 'dissimulation'. In modern times the problem of the lawfulness of lying in these cases, when, e.g., human life would be endangered or a secret violated not only by speaking the truth but also by preserving silence, has given rise to several theories attempting a solution. They either permit *mental reservation (q.v.) or assert that not everyone has the right to the truth (so, e.g., H. *Grotius and S. *Pufendorf), or, what seems most in agreement with common sense, that there may arise conflicts of duty in which the choice of a lie is a lesser evil. These, however, are exceptional cases which do not prejudice the general obligation of speaking the truth, without which an ordered human society which is built on mutual trust would become impossible.

Lyndhurst, Act of Lord. The Marriage Act 1835 made all future marriages within the *prohibited degrees (e.g. marriage with a deceased wife's sister) *ipso facto* null and void, and not voidable (as had been the previous rule) only by an explicit pronouncement of the ecclesiastical courts.

Lyndwood, William (*c.*1375–1446), English canonist and Bp. of *St Davids. Educated at Gonville and Caius College, Cambridge, he became a Fellow of Pembroke

Hall; later he migrated to Oxford, where he took his doctorate in canon and civil law. In 1414 he was commissioned by Abp. H. *Chichele as both his Chancellor and Auditor of Causes in the Court of *Audience, and in 1417 he was appointed *Official Principal of the Provincial Court of *Canterbury. In 1432 he became Keeper of the Privy Seal. He held a considerable number of benefices, in 1442 becoming Bp. of St Davids. He was closely associated with Chichele's administration and in his proceedings against the *Lollards. His celebrated *Provinciale* (completed in 1430) is the most substantial work on English canon law surviving from the later Middle Ages. It is a collection in five books of the provincial constitutions of the Abps. of Canterbury from S. *Langton (1222) to Chichele (1416), with an extensive gloss and detailed index (completed in 1433). It remains a standard authority on English ecclesiastical law and his text of the constitutions is that generally used for official purposes. As F. W. *Maitland pointed out in his discussion with W. *Stubbs over the authority of Papal law in pre-Reformation England, Lyndwood regarded the law of the Church in England as dependent on the Papal codes and held that local constitutions must be interpreted in accordance with Papal law. Similarly the Archbishop's legislative and jurisdictional authority is superior to that of the provincial councils, but the Archbishop himself is bound by the legatine constitutions.

The latest and best edn. of Lyndwood's *Provinciale* is that pub. at Oxford, 1679; repr. Farnborough, 1968. Text of Canons (only) repr. from Eng. tr. made in 1534, ed. J. V. Bullard and H. Chalmer Bell, London, 1929. A. C. Reeves, 'The Careers of William Lynwood', in J. S. Hamilton and P. J. Bradley (eds.), *Documenting the Past: Essays in Medieval History Presented to George Peddy Cuttino* (Woodbridge, Suffolk, 1989), pp. 197–216. F. W. Maitland, *Roman Canon Law in the Church of England* (1896), pp. 1–50. C. R. Cheney, 'William Lyndwood's Provinciale', *The Jurist*, 21 (1961), pp. 405–34, repr. in id., *Medieval Texts and Studies* (Oxford, 1973), pp. 158–84. B. E. Ferme, *Canon Law in Late Medieval England: A Study of William Lyndwood's* Provinciale *with particular reference to Testamentary Law* (Pontificia Studiorum Universitas Salesiana, Facultas Iuris Canonici. Studia et Textus Historiae Iuris Canonici, 8; Rome [1996]). *BRUO* 2 (1958), pp. 1191–3; *BRUC*, pp. 379–81 and 679.

Lyne, Joseph Leycester. See IGNATIUS, FATHER.

Lyons, First Council of (1245). Acc. to RC numbering the 13th *Oecumenical Council. The Council was convoked by *Innocent IV to deal with what, in his opening sermon, he called the five wounds of the Church, the bad lives of the clergy and faithful, the danger of the Saracens, the Greek Schism, the invasion of Hungary by the Tatars, and the rupture between the Church and the Emp. *Frederick II. The bishops present, who did not greatly exceed 150, came chiefly from France, Italy, and Spain. The principal achievement of the Council was the formal deposition of the Emperor, who had been repeatedly excommunicated for having imprisoned cardinals and bishops on their way to a Council convoked by *Gregory IX, for being suspect of heresy through his association with the Saracens, and for pursuing a violently anti-ecclesiastical policy in Sicily. The objections of Thaddaeus of Suessa, Frederick's ambassador, that the accused had not been cited to the Council, that it was wholly irregular for the Pope to be plaintiff and judge at once, and that the

Council was not truly oecumenical, were over-ruled. At the last session the *Dominicans and *Franciscans were charged with the publication of the decree throughout Christendom. The Council also enjoined the preaching of a Crusade for the liberation of the Holy Land from the Saracens, which, however, came to nothing.

Hardouin, 7, cols. 375–406; Mansi, 23 (1779), cols. 605–86. Bull deposing Frederick II and Constitutions also pr., with Eng. tr., introd., and bibl., in Tanner, *Decrees* (1990), pp. 273–301. Hefele and Leclercq, 5 (pt. 2; 1913), pp. 1633–79. J. B. Martin, *Conciles et bullaires du diocèse de Lyon* (Lyons thesis; 1905), pp. 252–83, 624–9. H. Wolter, SJ, and H. Holstein, SJ, *Lyon I et Lyon II* (Histoire des conciles œcuméniques, 7; 1966), pp. 11–128, 245–67. Contemporary accounts of the Council in the 'Brevis nota eorum quae in primo Concilio Lugdunensi Generali gesta sunt' (repr. in Mansi, loc. cit., cols. 610–13), and by *Matthew Paris, *Chronica Majora*, under the year 1245 (ed. H. R. Luard, 4, RS, 1877, pp. 430–79). M. Tangl, 'Die sogenannte *Brevis Nota* über das Lyoner Concil von 1245', *Mittheilungen des Instituts für Oesterreichische Geschichtsforschung*, 12 (1891), pp. 246–53. T. G. von Karajan, 'Zur Geschichte des Concils von Lyon 1245', *Denkschriften der kaiserlichen Akademie der Wissenschaften*, Phil.-hist. Kl. 2 (Vienna, 1851), pp. 67–100, with texts, pp. 103–17. S. Kuttner, 'Die Konstitutionen des ersten allgemeinen Konzils von Lyon', *Studia et Documenta Historiae et Iuris*, 6 (Rome, 1940), pp. 70–131. F. Vernet in *DTC* 9 (pt. 1; 1926), cols. 1361–74, s.v. 'Lyon (Iᵉʳ Concile œcuménique de)', with detailed bibl. See further bibl. to GREGORY IX and INNOCENT IV.

Lyons, Second Council of (1274). Acc. to RC numbering the 14th *Oecumenical Council. It was convoked by *Gregory X to bring about the union with the Greek Church, the liberation of the Holy Land, and the reform of morals. It was attended by about 500 bishops, 60 abbots, and 1,000 other prelates. Among its better-known members were St *Albert the Great, St *Bonaventure, St Philip Benizi, General of the *Servites, *Humbert of Romans, and Peter of Tarentaise, the future Pope Innocent V. St *Thomas Aquinas died on the way to the Council. The desire of the Greeks for reunion with Rome arose chiefly from their fear of Charles of Anjou, who sought to become Latin Emp. of Constantinople. The legates of the Greek Emperor, Michael VIII Paleologus, presented letters declaring their adherence to the obedience of the RC Church and to the articles of faith which the Apostolic nuncios had asked them to subscribe, and at the High Mass, at which St Bonaventure preached the sermon, they repeated three times the *Filioque of the Creed. Besides defining in detail the *Double Procession of the Holy Spirit, the Council gave rulings about the election of the Pope in *conclave, suppressed some of the newly founded mendicant orders while approving esp. the *Dominicans and *Franciscans, and deposed several prelates. Its principal achievement, the union of the Churches, proved ephemeral; it came to an end in 1289.

Hardouin, 7, cols. 669–722; Mansi, 24 (1780), cols. 38–136. Constitutions also pr., with Eng. tr., introd., and bibl., in Tanner, *Decrees* (1990), pp. 303–31. Hefele and Leclercq, 6 (pt. 1; 1914), pp. 153–209. J. B. Martin, *Conciles et bullaires du diocèse de Lyon* (Lyons thesis, 1905), pp. 403–61, 651–6. H. Wolter, SJ, and H. Holstein, SJ, *Lyon I et Lyon II* (Histoire des conciles œcuméniques, 7; 1966), pp. 129–241, 268–87. B. Roberg, *Das Zweite Konzil von Lyon [1274]* (Konziliengeschichte, Reihe A: Darstellungen, Paderborn, etc., 1990). A. Franchi, OFM (ed.), *Il Concilio II di Lione (1274) secondo la Ordinatio Concilii Generalis Lugdunensis* (Studi e testi francesani, 3; 1965). V. Laurent and J. Darrouzès, *Dossier Grec de l'Union de Lyon (1273–1277)* (Archives de l'Orient Chrétien, 16; 1976 [Gk. text with Fr. tr. and introd.]). S. Kuttner, 'Conciliar Law in the Making. The Lyonese Constitutions (1274) of Gregory X in a MS. at Washington', in *Miscellanea Pio Paschini*, 2 (Lateranum, NS 15; 1949), pp. 39–81, with useful refs. L. Gatto, *Il pontificato di Gregorio X (1271–1276)* (Istituto Storico Italiano per il Medio Evo. Studi Storici, 28–30; 1959), pp. 82–98 and 107–62. J. M. Hussey, *The Orthodox Church in the Byzantine Empire* (Oxford History of the Christian Church, 1986), pp. 223–42. A. Fliche in Fliche and Martin, 10 (1950), pp. 487–503, with bibl. F. Vernet and V. Grumel, AA, in *DTC* 9 (pt. 1; 1926), cols. 1374–410, s.v. 'Lyon (IIᵉ Concile œcuménique de)', with detailed bibl.; M. Jugie, AA, in *EC* 7 (1951), cols. 1398–401, s.v. 'Lione, Secundo Concilio'.

Lyons, rite of. The minor local variations to the fused *Gregorian Sacramentary which developed in the course of the Middle Ages and are peculiar to Lyons. They were swept away in the 18th cent. but some of them were restored by *Pius IX in 1863. In 1904 the Congregation of *Rites approved a *Missale Romanum in quo antiqui ritus Lugdunenses servantur*. The Pontifical High Mass is characterized by great splendour, the bishop being assisted by six priests (in *chasubles), seven deacons (in *dalmatics), seven subdeacons (until their suppression, in *tunicles), seven acolytes (in *albs), and seven clerics (in capes).

D. Buenner, OSB, *L'Ancienne Liturgie romaine: Le rite lyonnais* (1933). A. A. King, *Liturgies of the Primatial Sees* (1957), pp. 1–154. R. X. Redmond in *NCE* 8 (1967), pp. 1112–14, s.v. 'Lyonese Rite'.

Lyre. See NICHOLAS OF LYRE.

M

Maassen, Friedrich (1823–1900), historian of early canon law. He began life as an advocate in N. Germany; but, finding himself debarred from public office through his conversion to the RC faith in 1851, he decided to devote himself to academic teaching, and later held professorships at Innsbruck (1857), Graz (1860), and Vienna (1871). He was at first a strong opponent of the decrees of the First *Vatican Council on Papal Infallibility, but in the *Kulturkampf he strenuously defended the claims of the RC Church. Of the first importance were his studies in the history of the ecclesiastical canons, embodied in his *Geschichte der Quellen und der Literatur des canonischen Rechts im Abendlande bis zum Ausgange des Mittelalters* (Bd. 1, 1870 [all published]), which were the basis of the later researches of E. *Schwartz, C. H. *Turner, and others. Among his other writings were his *Pseudoisidorstudien* (1885).

Obituary notice by R. von Scherer in *Hist. J.* 21 (1900), pp. 640–2. N. Grass, 'Österreichische Kanonistenschulen aus drei Jahrhunderten', *Zeitschrift der Savigny-Stiftung für Rechtsgeschichte*, 72. Kanonistische Abteilung, 41 (1955), pp. 290–411, esp. pp. 300–48. R. Naz in *DDC* 6 (1957), cols. 687–9, s.v.

Mabillon, Jean (1632–1707), *Maurist scholar. He entered the *Benedictine abbey of Saint-Rémy at Reims in 1653, but in 1664 he was sent to *Saint-Germain-des-Prés, at the request of J. L. *d'Achery, to help edit texts. Prob. the most erudite of all the Maurists, Mabillon rendered immense services to historical research. He produced some 20 folio works, including an edition of the writings of St *Bernard (1667); the *Acta Sanctorum Ordinis Sancti Benedicti* (with d'Achery, 9 vols., 1668–1701); the first four volumes of the Benedictine *Annales* (to AD 1066; 1703–7); and several collections of documents, notably the *Museum Italicum* (2 vols., 1687–9), which included a set of *Ordines Romani. His collections incorporated the fruits of his journeys in quest of manuscripts and rare books, of which the most famous was that to Italy in 1685–6 undertaken at the expense of the King of France. In his *De Re Diplomatica* (1681), conceived as a reply to attacks on the authenticity of early charters by the *Bollandist D. *Papebroch, he put the study of palaeography and diplomatic on a scientific footing. The attacks made by A.-J. le B. de *Rancé on the engagement of religious in scholarly pursuits provoked his *Traité des études monastiques* (1691; repr. Farnborough, 1967).

Ouvrages Posthumes de D. Jean Mabillon et de D. Thierri Ruinart, ed. V. Thuillier, OSB (1724; repr. Farnborough, 1967), 1 and 2, pp. 1–396. T. *Ruinart, OSB, *Abrégé de la vie de Dom Jean Mabillon* (1709; modern edn. in 'Collection Pax', 35; 1933). *Mélanges et documents publiés à l'occasion du 2ᵉ centenaire de la mort de Mabillon* (Archives de la France Monastique, 5; 1908). H. *Leclercq, OSB, *Dom Mabillon* (2 vols., Paris, 1953–7). B. Barret-Kriegel, *Les Historiens et la Monarchie*, 1: *Jean Mabillon* [1988], pp. 7–159; 2: *La défaite de l'érudition* [1988], esp. pp. 145–75. M. D. *Knowles, OSB, 'Jean Mabillon', *JEH* 10 (1959), pp. 153–73, repr. in *The Historian and Character and Other Essays* (Cambridge, 1963), pp.

213–39. H. Leclercq, OSB, in *DACL* 10 (pt. 1; 1931), cols. 427–724, s.v.; G.-M. Oury OSB, in *Dict. Sp.* 10 (1980), cols. 1–4, s.v. See also works cited under MAURISTS.

Macarius, St (d. c.334), Bp. of Jerusalem from c.311. He is mentioned in *Arius' letter to *Eusebius of Nicomedia (c.320) as one of the few 'bishops of the East' who denied him support. At the Council of *Nicaea (325) he was resolutely opposed to *Arianism. Soon after the Council he was commissioned by *Constantine to build the Church of the *Holy Sepulchre at Jerusalem after St *Helena's celebrated '*invention of the Cross' (326). Later he and his fellow-bishops of Palestine received a further letter from Constantine providing for the erection of a church at Mamre. Feast day, 10 Mar.

Arius' letter mentioning Macarius is preserved by *Theodoret, *HE* 1. 5 [*PG* 1. 4]; Constantine's letters to Macarius in *Eusebius of Caesarea, *Vita Constantini*, 3. 30–2 and 52 f. E. Venables in *DCB* 3 (1882), p. 765, s.v.

Macarius, St (1481/2–1563), Metropolitan of Moscow and All Russia. Born in Moscow and christened Michael, he became a monk with the name of Macarius. In 1526 he became Archbishop of Novgorod, and in 1542 Metropolitan of Moscow. He embarked on a reform of the Russian Church, both in its canon law and in its liturgical practice, and had the newly-compiled liturgical books made available in printed form. He was canonized by the 1988 Synod of the Russian Church; feast day, 30 Dec.

Detailed account, in Russian, by E. E. Golubinsky, *Istoriya Russkoy Tserkvi*, 2 (Moscow, 1911), pt. 2. M. Veretennikov, 'Makarij, Metropolit von ganz Russland', in K. C. Felmy and others (eds.), *Tausend Jahre Christentum in Russland* (Göttingen, 1988), pp. 687–716.

Macarius, St, of Alexandria (d. c.394), Egyptian hermit. (He is often confused with St *Macarius of Egypt, q.v.) He retired into the desert at the age of 40 and seems to have lived near St *Antony. He was ordained priest c.355, when he was in his 60s, to serve the monks at Kellia. He was persecuted by the Arian Patr. of Alexandria and, like Macarius of Egypt, was a miracle-worker of repute. A monastic rule has been ascribed to him, probably erroneously. Feast day, 2 Jan. in the W., 19 Jan. or 1 May in the E.

On the various Macarii see C. Butler, *The Lausiac History of Palladius*, 2 (1904), pp. 193 f. and A. Guillaumont, 'Le problème des deux Macaire dans les *Apophthegmata Patrum*', *Irénikon*, 48 (1975), pp. 41–59. The early authorities for Macarius the Alexandrian are *Palladius, *Hist. Laus.* 18, and *Rufinus, *Hist. Mon.* 29, and *HE* 2. 4. Coptic Life, ed. by E. Amélineau in *Annales du Musée Guimet*, 25 (1894), pp. 235–61. Writings ascribed to him in J. P. Migne, *PG* 34 ('Rule', cols. 967–70 [Lat.], 'Sermo de Exitu Statuque Animarum post hanc Vitam', 385–92). A. Guillaumont in *Dict. Sp.* 10 (1980), cols. 4 f., s.v.

Macarius, St, of Egypt (*c*.300–*c*.390), also known as **Macarius the Great**. He was a native of Upper Egypt who, at about the age of 30, founded a colony of monks in the desert of Scetis (Wadi-el-Natrun), which became one of the chief centres of Egyptian monasticism. Renowned for his sanctity and miracles, he was ordained priest *c*.340. He certainly knew, and seems to have been much influenced by, the great St *Antony; and, as a staunch supporter of St *Athanasius, he suffered a brief period of exile under Athanasius' Arian successor, Lucius. For the homilies ascribed to him in some MSS, see MACARIUS/SIMEON. Feast day, 15 Jan. in the W.; 19 Jan. or 9 Mar. in the E.

Our knowledge of him derives chiefly from the *Apophthegmata Patrum*, s.v. '*Μακάριος*'; *Rufinus' tr. of the *Historia Monachorum*, 28; and *Palladius, *Historia Lausiaca*, 17. A. Guillaumont in *Dict. Sp.* 10 (1980), cols. 11–13, s.v. 'Macaire l'Égyptien', with further refs.

Macarius Magnes (4th–5th cent.), Christian apologist. Nothing is known of his life, unless he is to be identified with the Bp. of Magnesia who was the accuser of Heraclides of Ephesus at the Synod of the *Oak (403). He was the author of an apology in five books known as the 'Apocriticus', *Μονογενὴς ἢ Ἀποκριτικὸς πρὸς Ἕλληνας περὶ τῶν ἀπορουμένων ἐν τῇ Καινῇ Διαθήκῃ ζητημάτων καὶ λύσεων*, in which the objections which a learned and clever Neoplatonist (perhaps *Porphyry) had raised against the Christian faith were (not altogether effectively) attacked. In the 9th cent. the treatise was used by the *Iconoclasts in defence of their doctrines, and in the 16th cent. it was quoted by F. *Torres from a copy in the *Marciana. Later the MS was lost and the text not recovered till 1867, when a defective MS was found at Athens; but this appears now to have also been lost. There also survive fragments of an almost entirely spurious series of 'Homilies on Genesis' ascribed to Macarius.

Text of 'Apocriticus' ed. C. Blondel [and P. Foucart] (Paris, 1876). L. *Duchesne, *De Macario Magnete et Scriptis ejus* (Paris, 1877, with text of the spurious Gen. frags., pp. 39–43). Eng. tr. of extracts of 'Apocriticus' by T. W. Crafer (1919). On the MS tradition G. Schalkhausser, *Zu den Schriften des Makarios von Magnesia* (TU 31, Heft 4; 1907). A. *Harnack, *Kritik des Neuen Testaments von einem griechischen Philosophen des 3. Jahrhunderts: Die im Apocriticus des Macarius Magnes enthaltene Streitschrift* (ibid. 37. 4; 1911). G. *Mercati, *Nuove note di letteratura biblica e cristiana antica* (ST 95; 1941), pp. 49–84 ('Per l'Apocritico di Macario Magnete. Una tavola dei capi libri I, II e III'). J. W. J. Palm, *Textkritisches zum Apokritikos des Makarios Magnes* (Scripta minora Regiae Societatis Humaniorum Litterarum Lundensis, 1959/60, no. 4; 1961). R. Waelkens, *L'Économie, thème apologétique et principe herméneutique dans l'*Apocriticos *de Macarius Magnès* (Université de Louvain, Recueil de Travaux d'Histoire et de Philologie, 6th ser. 4; 1974). R. Goulet, 'La Théologie de Makarios Magnès', *Mélanges de Science Religieuse*, 34 (1977), pp. 45–69 and 145–80. G. *Salmon in *DCB* 3 (1882), pp. 766–71; R. Waelkens in *Dict. Sp.* 10 (1980), cols. 13–17.

Macarius of Moscow (1816–82), Metropolitan of Moscow. Michael Bulgakov, son of a country priest, was educated at the seminary of Kursk and at the ecclesiastical academy of Kiev. After finishing his studies he became a monk, taking the name of Macarius, and later was appointed assistant lecturer in ecclesiastical and civil history at Kiev. From 1842 to 1857 he was professor of dogmatic theology at the academy of St Petersburg. In 1857

he was appointed Bp. of Tambov, in 1859 transferred to Kharkov, and in 1868 to Vilna. He became Metrop. of Moscow in 1879. He is the best representative of 19th-cent. Russian theologians. His two most important works, which were translated into several languages, were the *Introduction à la théologie dogmatique orthodoxe* (1847) and *Théologie dogmatique orthodoxe* (5 vols., 1845–53). They reflect the official orthodoxy which was imposed on the Russian Church by A. S. Protasov (lay procurator of the Holy Synod) to counteract Protestant influences, and are based on the Scriptures, the tradition as recognized by the Orthodox Church, and on arguments from reason. He also wrote a comprehensive *History of the Russian Church* (12 vols., 1857–82), which he traces from its beginnings to the Council of Moscow of 1667.

Life by T. Titov (2 vols., Kiev, 1895–8, in Russian). M. Jugie, AA, in *DTC* 9 (pt. 2; 1927), cols. 1443 f., s.v. 'Macaire Bulgakov'; P. Mailleux in *NCE* 2 (1967), pp. 861 f., s.v. 'Bulgakov, Macarius'.

Macarius/Simeon (4th–5th cent.), author of the so-called homilies ascribed in most MSS to St *Macarius of Egypt, though in some MSS (incl. all the Arabic versions) to a certain Simeon. The homilies survive in Greek in four collections: Collection I, the most extensive, which begins with the 'Great Letter' and contains 63 other homilies; Collection II, the most popular, the *Fifty Spiritual Homilies*, of which two MSS contain seven additional homilies; Collection III, of 43 homilies, which largely overlap with I and II; and Collection IV, of 26 homilies, all of which are to be found in I, for which it seems to have been a source. There are versions in many languages, the Arabic being particularly important, since it preserves homilies lost in Greek. In form some 'homilies' are homilies proper, others ἐρωταποκρίσεις (Questions and answers), recalling the Short Rules of St *Basil, and others are letters. The ascription to Macarius of Egypt is impossible, for the geography and climate envisaged, as well as various historical allusions, point to Syria. Syrian provenance is further supported by the parallels between the homilies and the tenets of *Messalianism. The relation of the homilies to Messalianism is disputed, but it seems clear that many of the passages from the Messalians' *Asceticon* (condemned at the Council of *Ephesus in 431) were taken from the homilies, and the conclusion is often drawn that the 'Simeon' whom some MSS claim as the author is Simeon of Mesopotamia, a leader of the Messalians mentioned by *Theodoret. There are, however, also differences. There are parallels between the homilies and at least two of the *Cappadocian Fathers, St Basil and St *Gregory of Nyssa. The links with Messalianism suggest a date for the homilies between 380/90 and 430.

The teaching of the homilies is that, as a result of the *Fall of *Adam, the devil has gained control over man's heart so that sin has become natural to him. The only remedy is prayer, prayer for the gift of the Holy Spirit who alone can overcome the power of the devil. Grace, or the presence of the Holy Spirit, is something that can be felt; it is an experience that brings assurance, an experience which often takes the form of a vision of the light of the Godhead. In this teaching the homilies foreshadowed a characteristic doctrine of the *Hesychasts. The homilies have proved very influential, treasured esp. by the monastic spirituality of E. Orthodoxy. In modern times they have found favour, notably among the German *Pietists and the English *Methodists; the first volume of J. *Wesley's '*Christian Library' included a translation of 22 Macarian homilies.

There are modern edns. of Collections I–III: Collection I (apart from the 'Great Letter'), ed. H. Berthold (2 vols., GCS, 1973); the 'Great Letter', ed. R. Staats (*Abh.* (Gött.), Folge 3, 134; 1984). Collection II: The 'Fifty Spiritual Homilies', first pr. by J. Picus (Paris, 1559), repr. in J. P. Migne, *PG* 34. 449–822; crit. edn. H. Dörries, E. Klostermann, and M. Kroeger (Patristische Texte und Studien, 4; 1964). Eng. tr. by A. J. Mason (London, 1921). The seven additional homilies, ed. G. L. Marriott (Harvard Theological Studies, 5; 1918). Collection III (except for homilies also in Collection II), ed. E. Klostermann and H. Berthold (TU 72; 1961); repr. (but omitting homilies also in Collections I and II), with Fr. tr. and introd. by V. Desprez, OSB (SC 275; 1980). Eng. tr. of the 'Fifty Spiritual Homilies' and the 'Great Letter' by G. A. Maloney, SJ (Classics of Western Spirituality [1992]). The homilies found only in Arabic are tr. into Ger. by W. Strothmann (Göttinger Orientforschungen, I Reihe: Syriaca, 11; 1975).

J. Stiglmayr, SJ, *Sachliches und Sprachliches bei Makarius* (Innsbruck, 1912). L. Villecourt, OSB, 'La Date et l'origine des "Homélies spirituelles" attribuées à Macaire', in *Comptes Rendus des séances de l'Académie des Inscriptions et des Belles-Lettres* (Paris, 1920), pp. 250–8; G. L. Marriott, 'The Messalians; and the Discovery of their Ascetic Book', *HTR* 19 (1926), pp. 191–8; H. Dörries, *Symeon von Mesopotamien: Die Überlieferung der messalianischen 'Makarius'-Schriften* (TU 55, Heft 1; 1941); W. Jaeger, *Two Rediscovered Works of Ancient Christian Literature: Gregory of Nyssa and Macarius* (Leiden, 1954), incl. text of the 'Great Letter', pp. 233–301; G. Quispel, *Makarius, das Thomasevangelium und das Lied von der Perle* (Supplements to *Novum Testamentum*, 15; 1967); R. Staats, *Gregor von Nyssa und die Messalianer* (Patristische Texte und Studien, 8; 1968); E. A. Davids, *Das Bild vom neuen Menschen: Ein Beitrag zum Verständnis des Corpus Macarianum* (Salzburg, 1968); J. Gribomont, OSB, 'Le Dossier des origines du messalianisme', in *Epektasis: Mélanges patristiques offerts au Cardinal Jean Daniélou*, ed. J. Fontaine and C. Kannengiesser (1972), pp. 611–25. H. Dörries, *Die Theologie des Makarios/Symeon* (*Abh.* (Gött.), Folge 3, 103; 1978). H. Berthold, 'Die Ursprünglichkeit literarischer Einheiten im Corpus Macarianum', in F. Paschke (ed.), *Überlieferungsgeschichtliche Untersuchungen* (TU 125; 1981), pp. 61–76. C. Stewart, OSB, '*Working the Earth of the Heart*': *The Messalian Controversy in History, Texts, and Language to A.D. 431* (Oxford Theological Monographs, 1991). *CPG* 2 (1974), pp. 73–7 (nos. 2410–27). V. Desprez, OSB, and M. Canévet in *Dict. Sp.* 10 (1980), cols. 20–43, s.v. 'Macaire (Pseudo-Macaire)'.

Macaulay, Zachary (1768–1838), Anglican *Evangelical and philanthropist and father of Thomas Babington Macaulay (1800–59), the historian. At the age of 16 he went to Jamaica, where he became manager of an estate which used slave labour. Disgust at the conditions under which the slaves worked determined him to wage war on the practice of slavery, and on returning to England in 1792 he made the cause of abolition his main concern. In 1793 he became governor of the colony of Sierra Leone, where he remained intermittently until 1799. A member of the '*Clapham Sect', he became deeply interested in the work of the *BFBS and of the *CMS. From 1802 to 1816 he edited the *Christian Observer*, the organ of the Clapham Sect. He was also one of the founders of London University.

Viscountess Knutsford [M. J. Holland, granddaughter], *Life and Letters of Zachary Macaulay* (1900). C. Z. Booth, *Zachary*

Macaulay: His Part in the Movement for the Abolition of the Slave Trade and of Slavery (1934). L. Stephen in *DNB* 34 (1893), pp. 418–20. See also bibl. to CLAPHAM SECT.

Maccabees. The celebrated Jewish family, which played a major role in arousing armed opposition by Judaean Jews to the introduction of pagan cult into the *Temple at Jerusalem by *Antiochus Epiphanes, and thus at a very critical period of its history stemmed the threatened destruction of Judaism. The revolt was begun in 168 BC at Modin, where Mattathias, then an aged priest, killed an apostate Jew who was about to offer a pagan sacrifice. The struggle was carried on by his five sons, three of whom in turn, *Judas (who alone in the *Apocrypha is given the epithet 'Maccabaeus', Gk. Μακκαβαῖος, meaning perhaps 'hammerer'), Jonathan, and Simon, led the Jews in their struggle. Acc. to *Josephus (*Antiq.* 12. 6. 1), Mattathias was the great-great-grandson of Hasmon, and they are thus often known as the 'Hasmonaeans'.

The principal authority for the history of the family, besides Josephus, is 1 and 2 Macc. (see following entry). A. Momigliano, *Prime linee di storia della tradizione maccabaica* (1930). E. Bickermann, *Der Gott der Makkabäer* (1937; Eng. tr., Studies in Judaism in Late Antiquity, 32; Leiden, 1979). W. R. Farmer, *Maccabees, Zealots, and Josephus: An Inquiry into Jewish Nationalism in the Greco-Roman Period* (New York, 1956). M. Hengel, *Judentum und Hellenismus* (Wissenschaftliche Untersuchungen zum Neuen Testament, 10; 1969), pp. 464–564; Eng. tr., *Judaism and Hellenism* (2 vols., 1974), I, pp. 255–309, with notes, 2, pp. 169–205; cf. F. Millar, 'The Background to the Maccabean Revolution', *Journal of Jewish Studies*, 29 (1978), pp. 1–21. B. Bar-Kochva, *Judas Maccabaeus* (Cambridge, 1989). E. *Schürer, *The History of the Jewish People in the Age of Jesus Christ*, rev. Eng. tr. by G. Vermes and others, 1 (Edinburgh, 1973), pp. 125–242. T. Rajak in *Anchor Bible Dictionary*, 3 (1992), pp. 67–76, s.v. 'Hasmonean Dynasty'.

Maccabees, Books of. Four Books, so called after the hero of the first two, *Judas Maccabaeus, are found in certain MSS of the *Septuagint, of which the first three are included in the *Canon of the E. Church and the first two in that of the RC Church and the *Apocrypha of (non-RC) English Bibles. (A fifth Book, contained in the Ambrosian *Peshitta (B. 21 Inf.) and thus designated by Henry Cotton (1789–1879), is merely a Syriac version of *Josephus, *Jewish War*, book 6.)

The First Book consists of a history of the Jews from the accession of *Antiochus Epiphanes (175 BC) to the death of Simon Maccabaeus in 135 BC. After a brief note on the reign of Alexander, it describes the desecration of the *Temple and the resistance of Mattathias the priest, continued by his sons, Judas, Jonathan, and Simon Maccabaeus. It closes with the escape of Simon's son, John Hyrcanus, on a note of reassurance for the future. Extant only in Greek, though written in Hebrew (known to St *Jerome, *Prol. Gal. ad Lib. Reg.*), it appears to have been the work of a Palestinian Jew of nationalist sympathies, prob. *c.*100 BC. It is the primary historical source for the period.

The Second Book describes the history of the Maccabean wars from the close of the reign of the Syrian king Seleucus IV (176 BC) to the victory of Judas Maccabaeus over Nicanor and the death of the latter (161 BC). It is an epitome of a larger work by Jason of Cyrene (otherwise unknown; 2: 23) and appears to have been written in

Greek by a Jew some time before 63 BC. It has a marked devotional note, emphasizing the care of God for His people in all things.

The Third Book describes the attempt of Ptolemy IV to enter the Sanctuary of the Temple (217 BC), his frustration, and his unsuccessful attempt to take vengeance on the Jews of Egypt. It appears to have been written in Greek, prob. by an Alexandrian Jew between 100 BC and AD 70, and is prob. thus named on the analogy of the events described with those of the Maccabaean period. Listed in the biblical catalogue in the *Apostolic Canons (can. 85), the Book appears to have been held in high esteem in the early Church, but its canonicity is now admitted only by the E. Church.

The Fourth Book is a Greek philosophical treatise addressed to Jews on the supremacy of devout reason over the passions, illustrated by examples from the history of the Maccabees. The work was erroneously attributed to Josephus by *Eusebius, ('*Suidas', and others. It was prob. written by a Hellenistic Jew at some time later than Book 2 and before AD 70.

The Books of the Maccabees contain important doctrinal teaching on immortality (2 Macc. 7: 9, 23, 37 and 4 Macc.), the value of suffering as a means of expiation (2 Macc. 7: 37 f.), and prayers for the dead (2 Macc. 12: 43–5). This last passage has played an important part in the defence of the doctrine of *purgatory.

The Gk. text of 1–4 Macc. is pr. in H. B. *Swete, *The Old Testament in Greek*, 3 (1894), pp. 586–762, and other edns. of the LXX, the most scholarly text of 1–3 Macc. being that in the edn. of the LXX under the auspices of the Göttingen Academy, vol. 9: 1 Macc. ed. W. Kappler (1936; 2nd edn., 1967); 2 Macc. ed. W. Kappler and R. Hanhart (1959; 2nd edn., 1976); 3 Macc. by R. Hanhart (1960; 2nd edn., 1980). Crit. edn. of Syriac text of 4 Macc. by R. L. Bensly (Cambridge, 1895). H. Cotton, *The Five Books of Maccabees in English, with notes* (Oxford, 1832). Modern comm. on 1 and 2 Macc. by W. O. E. Oesterley in R. H. *Charles (ed.), *The Apocrypha and Pseudepigrapha of the Old Testament*, 1 (1913), pp. 59–124 (on 1 Macc.), and J. Moffatt, ibid., pp. 125–54 (on 2 Macc.), H. Bévenot, OSB (Das Heilige Schrift des Alten Testaments, 1931), F.-M. Abel, OP (Études bibliques, 1949), S. Zeitlin (Jewish Apocryphal Literature, 1950, on 1 Macc.; 1954, on 2 Macc.), F.-M. Abel, OP and J. Starcky (La Sainte Bible, traduite en français sous la direction de l'École Biblique de Jérusalem, 3rd edn.; Paris, 1961), and J. A. Goldstein (Anchor Bible, 1976, on 1 Macc.; 1983 on 2 Macc.); also on 1 Macc. by J. C. Dancy (Oxford, 1954); on 3 Macc. by C. Emmet in R. H. Charles (ed.), op. cit., pp. 155–73; and on 4 Macc. by R. B. Townshend, ibid. 2, pp. 653–85, and A. Dupont-Sommer (Bibliothèque de l'École des Hautes Études, 274; 1939); and on 3 and 4 Macc. by M. Hadas (Jewish Apocryphal Literature, New York, 1953). D. de Bruyne, OSB, 'Le Texte grec des deux premiers Livres des Machabées', *R. Bibl.* 31 (1922), pp. 31–54. Id. and B. Sodar, OSB (eds.), *Les Anciennes Traductions latines des [1 and 2] Machabées* (Anecdota Maredsolana, 4; 1932). B. Niese, *Kritik der beiden Makkabäerbücher* (1900). E. J. B. Bickerman, 'The Date of Fourth Maccabees', in *Louis Ginzberg Jubilee Volume on the Occasion of his Seventieth Birthday. English Section* (New York, 1945), pp. 105–12. E. *Schürer, *The History of the Jewish People in the Age of Jesus Christ*, rev. Eng. tr. by G. Vermes and others, 3 (pt. 1; Edinburgh, 1986), pp. 180–5, 531–42, and 588–93, with bibl. T. Fischer in *Anchor Bible Dictionary*, 4 (1992), pp. 439–50 (on 1–2 Macc.); A. Anderson, ibid., pp. 450–54 (on 3–4 Macc.). See also bibl. to APOCRYPHA.

Maccabees, Feast of the Holy. The feast formerly kept in the W. Church (and still observed in the E.) on 1 Aug.

to commemorate the seven Jewish brethren whose sufferings and deaths are described in 2 Macc. 7. The incident, which is doubtless referred to in Heb. 11: 35, struck the imagination of the early Christians and was celebrated by many of the Church fathers, notably St *Gregory of Nazianzus (*Serm.* 15) and St *Augustine (*Serm.* 300–2). The reputed relics of the martyrs were honoured at Antioch, the scene of their deaths, and later at S. Pietro in Vincoli in Rome (see LAMMAS DAY, also observed on 1 Aug.).

M. Maas, 'Die Maccabäer als christliche Heilige', *Monatsschrift für Geschichte und Wissenschaft des Judenthums*, 44 (1900), pp. 145–56; H. Bévenot, OSB, 'The Holy Machabees', *The Month*, 150 (1927), pp. 107–14. On the early veneration of the Maccabees at Antioch, where the cultus prob. originated, see also H. *Leclercq, OSB, in *DACL* 1 (pt. 2; 1907), cols. 2375–9, s.v. 'Antioche (archéologie), IV: La Basilique et le culte des Macchabées'; cf. ibid. 10 (pt. 1; 1931), cols. 724–7. F. Spadafora and M. C. Celletti in *Bibliotheca Sanctorum*, 8 (1967), cols. 434–9, s.v. 'Maccabei'.

MacDonald, George (1824–1905), Scottish novelist and poet. Educated at the University of Aberdeen and at Highbury College, London, he became a *Congregational minister, but in 1853 left the ministry to devote himself to literature. His writings, largely based on the life and customs of NE Scotland, include the novels *David Elginbrod* (1863), *Alec Forbes of Howglen* (1865), *Malcolm* (1875), and *Donal Grant* (3 vols., 1883). MacDonald's books, which were highly valued by C. S. *Lewis, reveal firm religious faith, moral enthusiasm, and Christian optimism. He was also the author of several religious works, including *Unspoken Sermons* (1867, 1885, 1889) and *The Miracles of our Lord* (1886).

The Poetical Works of George MacDonald (2 vols., 1893). His romance, *Lilith* (1895), was ed. by G. MacDonald (son) (1924), with introd., pp. ix–xx. C. S. Lewis (ed.), *George MacDonald: An Anthology* (1946). J. M. Bulloch, 'A Bibliography of George MacDonald', *Aberdeen University Library Bulletin*, 5 (1925), pp. 679–747, also issued separately (1925). G. MacDonald (son), *George MacDonald and his Wife* (1924). R. MacDonald (son), 'George MacDonald: A Personal Note', in F. Watson (ed.), *From a Northern Window: Papers, Critical, Historical and Imaginative* (1911), pp. 55–113. R. L. Wolff, *The Golden Key: A Study in the Fiction of George MacDonald* (New Haven, Conn., 1961). K. Triggs, *The Stars and the Stillness: A Portrait of George MacDonald* (Cambridge, 1986). D. S. Robb, *George MacDonald* (Scottish Writers, 11; Edinburgh, 1987). A. Matheson in *DNB, 1901–1911*, pp. 513–15.

Mace, Daniel (d. c.1753), NT textual critic. Little is known of his life beyond the fact that he was a *Presbyterian minister at Newbury from 1727 till his death. He anticipated conclusions which only met with general acceptance among textual critics over a century later, e.g. he disproved the authenticity of the text known as the *Johannine Comma (1 Jn. 5: 7). His results were incorporated in *The New Testament in Greek and English* (2 vols., 1729), to which a reply in defence of the *Textus Receptus was issued shortly afterwards by L. Twells (d. 1742).

H. McLachlan, 'An Almost Forgotten Pioneer in New Testament Criticism', *Hibbert Journal*, 37 (1939), pp. 617–25. A. Gordon in *DNB* 35 (1893), pp. 68 f.

Macedonius (d. *c*.362), Bp. of *Constantinople. In the divisions which followed the death of *Eusebius of Nicomedia (*c*.341) he was one of the rival claimants to the see, and seems to have gained possession of it *c*.342. He strongly supported the *Semiarian cause and defended his position at the Council of *Seleucia in 359. In 360 he was deposed by the Arian Council of Constantinople. From the end of the 4th cent. onwards he has been regarded as the founder of the '*Pneumatomachi' (q.v.) and thus caused the sect to be known as the 'Macedonians'; but it is doubtful how far this association is correct, as it seems clear that disputes about the Divinity of the Holy Spirit did not arise until after Macedonius' deposition. It is not known whether he left any writings.

J. M. Fuller in *DCB* 3 (1882), pp. 775–7, s.v. F. *Loofs in *PRE* (3rd edn.), 12 (1903), pp. 41–8, s.v.; G. Bardy in *DTC* 9 (1926), cols. 1464–78, s.v., both with bibl. See also bibl. to PNEUMATOMACHI.

Machutus (otherwise Malo, Maclovius, Maclou), St (d. *c*.640), early Breton saint. Acc. to tradition, he was of either Welsh or Breton descent, and trained in the monastic life by St *Brendan. He settled at Aleth, opposite the present town of St-Malo, and is said to have lived an ascetic life, preached with great success, and founded several monasteries in the surrounding districts. One tradition asserts that he accompanied St Brendan on his journey to *Iona. Feast day, 15 Nov.

Two Lives (both *c*. AD 850–900) exist, the one by the deacon Bili of Aleth, ed. by F. Plaine, OSB, in *Bulletins et Mémoires de la Société archéologique du département d'Ille-et-Vilaine*, 16 (1883), pp. 167–256; the other by an Anon. of Saintes, ed. by A. de La Borderie, ibid., pp. 267–93. For texts cf. also F. Lot, *Mélanges d'histoire bretonne* (1907), pp. 294–329 and 331–430; and id., 'Les Diverses Rédactions de la vie de saint Malo', ibid., pp. 97–206. The Life by Bili, together with an Old English tr., also ed. G. Le Duc (St-Malo, 1979). More satisfactory edn. of the Old English tr., with Lat. text opposite, by D. Yerkes (Toronto Old English Series, 9 [1984]). L. *Duchesne, 'La Vie de saint Malo. Étude critique', *Revue celtique*, 11 (1890), pp. 1–22. A. Poncelet, 'Une Source de la vie de S. Malo par Bili', *Anal. Boll.* 24 (1905), pp. 483–6. P. Riché, 'Translation de reliques à l'époque carolingienne. Histoire des reliques de Saint-Malo', *Le Moyen Âge*, 82 (1976), pp. 201–18. H. *Leclercq, OSB, in *DACL* 10 (pt. 1; 1931), cols. 1293–318, s.v. 'Malo (Saint)'.

Mackay, Alexander Murdoch (1849–90), *C.M.S. Missionary in *Uganda. The son of a Free Church minister, he was educated at Edinburgh, and in 1873 he obtained a post as a draftsman in Berlin. His thoughts had long turned to missionary work, however, and in 1876 he was accepted by the CMS for work in Africa. Having embarked for Victoria Nyanza, he finally reached Uganda in 1878 after constructing 230 miles of road. His printing of part of the Scriptures in Swahili interested King Mtesa, and he was granted permission to carry on missionary work. Soon, however, he met with opposition both from RCs and from Muslims. In 1884, when King Mtesa was succeeded on the throne of Uganda by Mwanga, Mackay was threatened with expulsion, but allowed to remain by reason of his engineering skill. The Christians meanwhile had to face fierce persecution, and many were slain. In 1887 Mackay was expelled, and settled at Usambiro on the southern end of Lake Victoria, where he reduced the vernacular of Uganda to writing, and then translated the Scriptures into it.

A. M. Mackay, Pioneer Missionary of the C.M.S. Uganda, by his sister [Mrs J. W. Harrison] (1890). A. H. Millar in *DNB* 35 (1893), p. 118.

Mackintosh, Hugh Ross (1870–1936), Scottish theologian. After a distinguished undergraduate career at Edinburgh, he studied at *Marburg, specializing in philosophy. He was ordained in 1897, and after some years of pastoral work at Tayport and at Beechgrove Church, Aberdeen, he was appointed professor of systematic theology at New College, Edinburgh, in 1904. Here he exercised great influence as a teacher. He showed marked sympathy with the Liberal Movement in German Protestant theology and made it one of his chief objects to make German doctrines better known in Britain. In 1932 he was elected Moderator of the General Assembly of the Church of Scotland. Among his written works the more important are *The Doctrine of the Person of Christ* (1912), in which he showed himself critical of the *Chalcedonian Christology and defended a modified *kenotic doctrine, *The Christian Experience of Forgiveness* (1927), and *Types of Modern Theology* (1937, posthumous).

Sermons (1938), with Memoir by A. B. Macaulay, pp. 1–33, and list of his chief pubs., p. ix. J. W. Leitch, *A Theology of Transition: H. R. Mackintosh as an approach to Barth* (1952). D. M. Baillie in *DNB, 1931–1940*, pp. 581 f.

Mackonochie, Alexander Heriot (1825–87), *Anglo-Catholic leader. Educated at Wadham College, Oxford, he was ordained in 1849, and served in turn under W. J. *Butler at Wantage (1852–8) and C. F. *Lowder at St George's in the East (1858–62). By 1862, when he was put in charge of the newly built church of St Alban's, Holborn, he was recognized as an advanced 'ritualist', and from 1867 onwards was constantly prosecuted by the *Church Association for his ceremonial practices (e.g. the *mixed chalice and *altar lights). He eventually resigned in 1882, though he worked unofficially in the parish from 1883 until his sudden death in the Highlands in Dec. 1887.

E. A. Towle, *A. H. Mackonochie* (1890); H. Reynolds, *Martyr of Ritualism: Father Mackonochie of St Alban's, Holborn* (1965). W. A. J. Archbold in *DNB* 35 (1893), pp. 185 f.

Maclaren, Alexander (1826–1910), *Baptist preacher and expositor. Trained at Glasgow University and Stepney College, after twelve years as minister in Southampton (1846–58) he moved to Manchester and from the pulpit of Union Chapel (1858–1903) achieved a world-wide reputation by his sermons and writings. Twice President of the Baptist Union (1875; 1901), he also presided at the first Congress of the Baptist World Alliance in 1905.

G. G. Atkins (ed.), *The Best of Alexander Maclaren* (New York, 1949), with introd. pp. vii–xix (London, 1950, with introd. pp. 7–22). G. Eayrs, *An Index to Expositions of Holy Scripture by Alexander Maclaren* [1912], with an Appreciation of Dr Maclaren by W. R. *Nicoll (repr. from the *British Weekly*), pp. v–xviii. D. Williamson and J. H. Shakespeare, *The Life of Alexander Maclaren* [1910]; E. T. McLaren (cousin and sister-in-law), *Dr. McLaren of Manchester: A Sketch* (1911). A. Gordon in *DNB, 1901–1911*, p. 534, with list of pubs.

MacLeod, George Fielden (1895–1991), Lord MacLeod of Fuinary, founder of the *Iona Community. Born of a notable Scottish ecclesiastical dynasty, MacLeod went to Winchester College and began reading law at Oriel College, Oxford, but in 1914 enlisted for service in the First World War, in which he was decorated for bravery. He then trained for ministry in the Church of Scotland at Edinburgh University, worked for *Toc H in Scotland, and in 1926 was appointed minister of the fashionable St Cuthbert's Church in Edinburgh. Despite his popularity here, in 1930 he accepted an invitation to become minister of Govan Old Parish Church in the slums of Glasgow. During the 1930s he became a pacifist and a socialist, and an outstanding radio preacher. In 1938 he founded the Iona Community, which was intended to express in social terms the theology of the Incarnation, and he began the rebuilding of the living quarters of the ruined medieval abbey on the island. He exercised a wide influence and received many honours both in Britain and the USA. In 1956 he was appointed a chaplain to the Queen and in the following year he became *Moderator of the General Assembly of the Church of Scotland. He was elevated to the House of Lords in 1967, resigning as Leader of the Iona Community; he became president of the International Fellowship of Reconciliation the same year. An international youth and reconciliation centre on Iona, opened in 1988, was named in his honour. His works include *Gowan Calling: Sermons and Addresses* (1934); *We Shall Re-Build: The Work of the Iona Community on Mainland and Island* [1944]; and *Only One Way Left* (1956).

Life by R. Ferguson (London, 1990).

Macleod, Norman (1812–72), Scottish divine. Educated at Glasgow and Edinburgh (under T. *Chalmers), he travelled on the Continent before his ordination in 1838. After holding appointments at Loudoun, Ayrshire, and Dalkeith, he became minister of the Barony Church, Glasgow, in 1851, and in 1857 chaplain to Queen Victoria, with whom he was a great favourite. In 1869 he was elected *Moderator of the General Assembly of the Church of Scotland. He was one of the most prominent and respected parochial ministers in Scotland in the 19th cent. Besides being the editor of the successful periodical *Good Words* (from 1860), he was the author of several books, among the best-known being his *Reminiscences of a Highland Parish* (1867).

Memoir by his brother, D. Macleod (2 vols., London, 1876). Shorter study by J. Wellwood ('Famous Scots Series', Edinburgh and London [1897]). T. Hamilton in *DNB* 35 (1893), pp. 217 f.

Macrina, St (*c.*327–80), the elder sister of St *Basil the Great and St *Gregory of Nyssa. She is sometimes known as 'Macrina the Younger' to distinguish her from 'Macrina the Elder', her paternal grandmother. By her strength of character she exercised a deep influence upon her brothers, esp. in winning Basil from a promising secular career for the Christian priesthood. She also established a flourishing community on the family estate in Pontus. The chief source for knowledge of her life is Gregory of Nyssa's *Vita Macrinae Junioris*, which also preserves a vivid account of their meeting at her deathbed. Her competence as a theologian is attested by the same writer's *De Anima et Resurrectione*. Feast day, 19 July [of Macrina the Elder, 14 Jan.].

For the *Vita* see J. P. Migne, *PG* 46. 959–1000. Crit. edns. by V. W. Callahan in *Gregorii Nysseni Opera*, ed. W. Jaeger and others, 8, pt. 1 (Leiden 1952), pp. 347–414, and, with Fr. tr., by P. Maraval (SC 178; 1971). There is an Eng. tr., with introd., by W. K. L. Clarke (1916). R. Albrecht, *Das Leben der heiligen Makrina auf dem Hintergrund der Thekla-Traditionen* (Forschungen zur Kirchen- und Dogmengeschichte, 38; 1986).

Madauran Martyrs (2nd cent.), the first reputed Christian martyrs in Africa. The four martyrs, all of whom had Punic names (Namphamo, Miggin, Lucitas, Samae), supposedly suffered at Madaura in 180. Our knowledge of them comes from Maximus of Madaura, a pagan grammarian of the late 4th cent., who inveighs against the populace for deserting the pagan cults and visiting the tombs of such uncultured barbarians. But J. H. Baxter has argued that the evidence is very insecure, and that the martyrs were in fact 4th-cent. *Circumcellions from a wider area.

Maximus' letter and St Augustine's reply are pr. among the latter's Epp., nos. 16 f. (CSEL 34, pt. 1, 1895, pp. 37–44). J. B. *Lightfoot, *The Apostolic Fathers*, pt. 2, vol. 1 (1885), pp. 506 f.; 2nd edn. (1889), pp. 522 f. (Note ζ). J. H. Baxter, 'The Martyrs of Madaura, A.D. 180', *JTS* 26 (1924–5), pp. 21–37.

Madeba Map. A map of Palestine and the Near East in coloured mosaics, uncovered in 1896 in the church at Madeba to the east of the Dead Sea. It almost certainly dates from the 6th cent. and it throws important light on the history of Palestinian topography.

M. J. *Lagrange, 'La Mosaïque géographique de Mâdaba', *R. Bibl.* 6 (1897), pp. 165–84. M. Avi-Yonah, *The Madaba Map* (Jerusalem, 1954). H. Donner and H. Cüppers, *Die Mosaikkarte von Madeba* (Abhandlungen des Deutschen Palästinavereins, 1977 ff.). R. T. O'Callaghan, SJ, in *Dict. Bibl.*, Suppl. 5 (1957), cols. 627–704, s.v. 'Madaba (Carte de)', with bibl.

Madonna, Ital. for 'My Lady'. A designation of the BVM, used esp. with reference to statues and pictures of her, e.g. 'The *Sistine Madonna'. The Madonna lily is the White Lily (*Lilium candidum*), which on account of its pure whiteness is a frequent emblem of Mary in art.

Madras Conference (1938). See TAMBARAM CONFERENCE.

Maffei, Francesco Scipio (1675–1755), polyhistorian. A native of *Verona, he studied under the *Jesuits at Parma, fought in the Spanish Succession War, and became the friend of *Benedict XIV. He took a lively and practical interest in a variety of problems, attacking duelling (1710) and magic (1754) and defending the theatre (1713), which he actively fostered. His historical work centred on his native city, and he published *Verona illustrata* (4 vols., Verona, 1731–2). In the contemporary controversies on grace, he attacked the *Jansenists in *De Haeresi Semipelagiana* (Rovereto, 1743) and other writings. His defence of usury in *Dell'impiego del danaro* (Verona, 1744) provoked Benedict XIV's encyclical of 1 Nov. 1745; but Maffei's work was not actually condemned and a 2nd edition appeared in 1746. In 1712 he rediscovered the ancient manuscripts in the Chapter Library of Verona. An examination of them led Maffei to a much clearer understanding of the development of Latin script than had been reached by J. *Mabillon, which he set out in *Istoria Diplomatica* (Mantua, 1727). He used these MSS for his edition of *Hilary of Poitiers (2 vols., Verona, 1730, a revision of the text of P. *Coustant) and other treatises. He also edited for the first time the 'Historia Acephala', a primary source for the Life of St *Athanasius, from Cod. Ver. LX (58) (*Osservazioni letterarie*, 3 (1738), pp. 60–83).

Opere (ed. A. Rubbi), 21 vols., Venice, 1790. *Opuscoli letterarii di Scipione Maffei con alcune sue lettere edite e inedite* (Venice, 1829), Modern edn. of *Opere drammatiche e poesie* by A. Avena (Bari, 1928) and of his *Epistolario* (1700–55) by C. Garibotto (2 vols., Milan, 1955). L. Traube, *Vorlesungen und Abhandlungen* (ed. F. Boll), 1 (1909), pp. 43–8; cf. also W. Telfer, 'The Codex Verona LX (58)', *HTR* 36 (1943), pp. 169–246, esp. pp. 228–31. G. Silvestri, *Un Europeo del settecento, Scipione Maffei* (Treviso, 1954; 2nd edn., Verona, 1968 [popular]); A. Momigliano, 'Gli studi classici di Scipione Maffei', *Giornale Storico della Letteratura Italiana*, 133 (1956), pp. 363–83, repr. with further bibl. in *Secondo contributo alla storia degli studi classici* (1960), pp. 255–71.

Magdalene, St Mary. See MARY MAGDALENE, ST.

Magdalens. In reference to St *Mary Magdalene, the word has often been applied to reformed prostitutes. As a title it was widely adopted in the Middle Ages by religious communities consisting of penitent women ('*White Ladies'), to whom others of blameless lives often joined themselves. These communities, widely established in the 13th cent. in Germany, France, Belgium, Italy, Spain, and Portugal, often followed the Rule of St *Augustine, though many German houses were affiliated to *Dominicans and *Franciscans. They are now reduced to one convent, at Vilsbiburg. The 'Magdalonettes', an order of Magdalens founded for the reformation of women in 1618 by Père Athanase Molé, a *Capuchin, is extinct.

Magdeburg, Centuriators of. See CENTURIATORS OF MAGDEBURG.

Magi. The first Gentiles to worship Christ, acc. to Mt. 2: 1–12. Guided by a mysterious star, they came from the East to *Bethlehem with gifts of gold, frankincense, and myrrh for the Christ Child. They are called in the NT μάγοι (sages). The idea that they were kings first appears in Christian tradition in *Tertullian, who calls them *fere reges* ('almost kings'; *Adv. Jud.* 9 and *Adv. Marc.* 3. 13), and it became general from the 6th cent., on the basis of the implied reference in Ps. 72 (71): 10. The NT account says nothing of their number. *Origen is the first to give it as three, probably on account of their three gifts, and this has become the general tradition. Their names, Gaspar, Melchior, and Balthasar, are first mentioned in the 6th cent. *Excerpta Latina Barbari* and later in a work of pseudo-*Bede known as the *Collectanea*. In the Middle Ages they were venerated as saints, and the Milanese claimed to possess their relics, brought from *Constantinople in the 5th cent. These were taken to Germany by *Frederick Barbarossa in 1162, and are now enshrined in *Cologne Cathedral. The Adoration of the Magi early became one of the most popular subjects of representation in art, the first extant painting being in the 'Cappella greca' of the Priscilla Catacomb dating from the 2nd cent. See also EPIPHANY.

H. Kehrer, *Die hl. drei Könige in Literatur und Kunst* (2 vols., 1908–9). R. E. McNally, 'The Three Holy Kings in Early Irish Latin Writing', in P. Granfield and J. A. Jungmann (eds.), *Kyri-*

akon: Festschrift Johannes Quasten, 1 (Münster, 1970), pp. 667–90. H. Hofmann, *Die heiligen drei Könige: Zur Heiligenverehrung im kirchlichen, gesellschaftlichen und politischen Leben des Mittelalters* (Rheinisches Archiv, 94; 1975). F. H. Dudden in *DCG* 2 (1908), pp. 97–101, s.v., with bibl.; W. Schulten in *TRE* 9 (1982), pp. 166–9, s.v. 'Drei Könige' with bibl. For iconography, H. *Leclercq, OSB, in *DACL* 10 (1931), cols. 980–1067, s.v. 'Mages'.

Magnificat. The song of praise (Lk. 1: 46–55) sung by the BVM when her cousin *Elizabeth had greeted her as the mother of the Lord. It is so named from the opening word of the Latin text, 'Magnificat anima mea Dominum' ('My soul doth magnify the Lord'). From a very early date, probably since St *Benedict, it has been the canticle of *Vespers of the W. Church, and its importance is emphasized by its special antiphons and the censing of the altar at solemn Vespers. It was adopted at Evensong in the BCP and in modern Anglican liturgies retains its place, though sometimes not on every day of the week. In the E. Church it is sung daily in the morning office (the *Orthros), except on certain great feasts, and it is followed by the *Benedictus (but in practice this last is usually omitted). Its language, which is steeped in the poetic tradition of the OT, shows notable resemblances to that of the 'Song of Hannah' (1 Sam. 2: 1 ff.); this fact, among others (notably that at Lk. 1: 46 a few Latin MSS read *et ait Elisabeth*, instead of *et ait Maria*) has led some scholars to argue that Luke attributed it originally to Elizabeth and not to Mary.

H. P. *Liddon, *The Magnificat: Sermons in St Paul's* (1889). S. Farris, *The Hymns of Luke's Infancy Narrative* (Journal for the Study of the New Testament, Supplement Series, 9; Sheffield, 1985), with refs. The ruling of the *Biblical Commission in 1912 defending the attribution of the Magnificat to the BVM is discussed by L. Pirot in *Dict. Bibl.*, Suppl. 2 (1934), cols. 1269–72, s.v. 'Évangile et commission biblique', with bibl. See also comm. to LUKE, GOSPEL OF ST, cited s.v.

Magnus, St. (1) Martyr. The supposed existence of the saint of this name occurring in the Roman martyrology for 19 Aug., where he is asserted to have suffered in the Decian *persecution, seems to have arisen from a blunder. In Latin lists 'St Andrew the Tribune', who in Greek calendars is described as the 'Megalomartyr' (μεγαλομάρτυς, i.e. the Great Martyr), became *Andreas Tribunus Magnus Martyr*; and this description was later erroneously understood to refer to two saints, Andrew the Tribune and Magnus the Martyr.

(2) of Füssen (d. *c.*770), Apostle of the Allgäu, Bavaria. Practically the only source is the Life dating from 1065–70, rewritten by Otloh of Saint-Emmeran from an earlier document. The first part, depicting Magnus as a companion of St *Gall and St *Columbanus in Ireland and then in Gaul, is clearly unhistorical. The second part, which is more reliable, describes his mission to the Allgäu, supported by Wichpert, Bp. of Augsburg. The mission was centred on Füssen, where Magnus began to exploit the deposits of iron. Feast day, 6 Sept.

(3) (d. 1116), son of Earl Erlin, ruler of the Orkneys. Having been captured by the Norwegian king, Magnus Barefoot, he escaped to Malcolm III of Scotland (d. 1093), and later lived in the house of a British bishop. During the latter part of his life he devoted himself to prayer and penance. After Magnus Barefoot's death he returned to

the Orkneys, where he shared the government with his cousin Hakon, who treacherously killed him. Because of his saintly life he was soon venerated as a martyr though he did not die for the faith. He is supposed to have appeared to Robert Bruce before the battle of Bannockburn (1314) and promised him victory. Feast day, 16 Apr.

(1) On the cult, AASS, Aug. 3 (1737), pp. 717–9; for the blunder over the name of Andrew, ibid., p. 720.

(2) Text of Life by Otloh, ed. M. Coens, SJ, in Anal. Boll. 81 (1963), pp. 159–227, incl. discussion of its relation to the earlier tradition. A shorter version, for liturgical use, ed. id., ibid., pp. 321–32.

(3) The principal sources are the Orkneyinga Saga and Magnus Saga (longer and shorter forms), both ed., with Eng. tr., by G. Vigfusson and G. W. Dasent, Icelandic Sagas, 1 and 3 (RS, 1887–94); Eng. tr. of Orkneyinga Saga by H. Pálsson and P. Edwards (London, 1978). J. Mooney, St Magnus—Earl of Orkney (Kirkwall, 1935).

Mahometanism. See ISLAM.

Mai, Angelo (1782–1854), Italian philologist and palaeographer. Born of poor parents, he was educated at the Collegium Romanum and for a time belonged to the Society of Jesus (*Jesuits). In 1813 he was appointed custodian of the *Ambrosiana at Milan, and in 1819 prefect of the *Vatican library. In 1838 he became cardinal. He was renowned esp. as a reader of *palimpsests. He published four large collections of classical and theological texts, chiefly based on unpublished MSS in the Vatican and Ambrosian libraries: Classici Auctores (10 vols., 1828–38), Scriptorum Veterum Nova Collectio (10 vols., 1830–8), Spicilegium Romanum (10 vols., 1839–44), and Nova Patrum Bibliotheca (8 vols., 1844–71; vols. 9 (1888) and 10 (1905) added later by J. Cozza-Luzi).

Letters ed. G. Cozza Luzi (Bergamo, 1883) and G. Gervasoni (Florence, 1954 ff.). Lives by B. Prina (Bergamo, 1882) and G. Poletto (ibid., 1882; 2nd edn., Siena, 1886). A. Bonnetty, Table alphabétique analytique et raisonnée de tous les auteurs sacrés et profanes qui ont été découverts et édités récemment dans les 43 vol. publiés par le cardinal Mai (1850). G. Cozza-Luzi, 'I grandi lavori del cardinale Mai', Bessarione, 2nd ser. 7 (1904), pp. 103–33; 8 (1905), pp. 59–74; 9 (1905), pp. 308–17; 10 (1906), pp. 169–82. G. Gervasoni, L'ambiente letterario milanese nel secondo decennio dell'ottocento: Angelo Mai alla Bibliotheca Ambrosiana (Fontes ambrosiani, 11; Florence, 1936), with full bibl. S. Timpanaro, 'Angelo Mai', Atene e Roma, NS 1 (1956), pp. 3–34. Bergomum (Bollettino della civica biblioteca, vol. 28, no. 4. Numero speciale dedicato alle celebrazioni in onore del Card. Angelo Mai nel centenario della morte; 1954). Polgár, 2 (1990), pp. 469–73. H. *Leclercq, OSB, in DACL 10 (pt. 1; 1931), cols. 1196–202, s.v.

Maid of Kent. See BARTON, ELIZABETH.

Maid of Orléans. See JOAN OF ARC, ST.

Maier, Johannes. See ECK, JOHANN.

Maimonides, Moses (1138–1204), Jewish philosopher. He is known to Jewish writers as 'Rambam' (the consonants being the initial letters of 'Rabbi Moses ben Maimon'). Born at Córdoba, he lived for a time in Fez, and eventually, after a brief stay in Palestine, settled at Fostat (Old Cairo), where he became head of the Jewish

community (c.1171). In 1168 he completed his commentary on the *Mishnah, known as the Siraj or 'Luminary'; it was a notable contribution to exegesis and scholarship. He brought out c.1180 his 'Mishneh Torah' in Hebrew, a Talmudic code in 14 parts arranged by subject matter. His reputation as one of the leading *halachists (legal authorities) rests mainly on this masterly distillation of traditional sources and in part on his many responsa. His other works were written in Arabic. In 1190 appeared his principal treatise, the 'Guide for the Perplexed' (Dux Neutrorum sive Dubiorum). Its purpose was to achieve a working harmony between reason and faith. Its three parts treat of: (1) the idea of God; (2) the arguments for the existence of God, His manifestations, the world of spirits, the creation of the world in time, and prophecy; and (3) the interpretation of *Ezekiel's vision, the problem of evil, the end of creation, Divine Providence, and Divine knowledge. Maimonides' aim was to achieve a synthesis of the data of the Jewish revelation and the findings of human reason proposed by *Aristotle. His 'Guide' had a profound influence on the Christian thought of the Middle Ages, esp. on St *Albert the Great and St *Thomas Aquinas.

Maimonides' works have been repeatedly repr. from the 15th cent. onwards, but there is no collected edn. The principal edns. of his 'Guide' (Arab. text) are those of S. Munk, with Fr. tr. (3 vols., Paris, 1856–66) and J. Kafih, with modern Hebrew tr. (3 vols., Jerusalem, 1972); Eng. trs. by M. Friedländer (3 vols., London, 1881–5) and S. Pines (Chicago, 1963). Eng. tr. (in progress) of the Mishneh Torah by J. J. Rabinowitz, H. Danby, H. Klein, and others (Yale Judaica Series, New Haven, Conn., 1949 ff.). I. Twersky, Introduction to the Code of Maimonides (Mishneh Torah) (ibid. 22; 1980). Eng. tr. from various works by A. Cohen as The Teachings of Maimonides (1927). Studies by D. Yellin and I. Abrahams (London, 1903; rev. edn., New York [1972]), J. Müntz (Frankfurt am Main, 1912; Eng. tr., Boston, 1935), A. Heschel (Berlin, 1935; Eng. tr., New York, 1982), S. Zeitlin (New York, 1935), H. Sérouya (Paris, 1964), and O. Leaman (London and New York, 1990). I. Epstein (ed.), Moses Maimonides, 1135–1204: Anglo-Jewish Papers in connexion with the eighth centenary of his birth (1935), with bibl. of Eng. works, pp. 231–48. S. W. Baron (ed.), Essays on Maimonides: An Octocentennial Volume (New York, 1941). N. Roth, Maimonides: Essays and Texts. 850th Anniversary (Madison, Wis., 1985). J. L. Kraemer (ed.), Perspectives on Maimonides (Oxford, 1991). S.-D. Goitein, 'Moses Maimonides, Man of Action. A revision of the master's biography in the light of the Geniza documents', in G. Nahon and C. Touati (eds.), Hommage à Georges Vajda: Études d'histoire et de pensée juives (Louvain, 1980), pp. 155–67. L. Roth, The Guide for the Perplexed: Moses Maimonides (1948). D. B. Burrell, CSC, Knowing the Unknowable God: Ibn-Sina, Maimonides, Aquinas (Notre Dame, Ind. [1986]). L. I. Rabinowitz and others in Encyclopaedia Judaica, 11 (Jerusalem, 1972), pp. 754–81, s.v.

Maistre, J. Comte de. See DE MAISTRE, J.

Maitland, Frederic William (1850–1906), historian. The grandson of the ecclesiastical historian, Samuel Roffey Maitland (1792–1866), he was educated at Eton and at Trinity College, Cambridge, and called to the bar at Lincoln's Inn in 1876. In 1884 he was appointed reader in, and in 1888 Downing professor of, English law at Cambridge. In his Roman Canon Law in the C of E (1898) he maintained against nearly all previous writers, including W. *Stubbs (who was convinced by Maitland's arguments), that in the Middle Ages the English secular courts recognized the Roman canon law as binding on the

English clergy apart from its re-enactment in the English synods. His crucial instance was the legitimation of natural-born children by subsequent matrimony. He also contributed the chapter on 'The Anglican Settlement and the Scottish Reformation' to the *Cambridge Modern History* (vol. 2, ch. 16) and was the author of a large number of other historical writings.

Collected Papers, ed. H. A. L. Fisher (3 vols., Cambridge, 1911); some of these, with additions, ed. H. D. Hazeltine, G. Lapsley, and P. H. Winfield, as *Selected Essays* (ibid., 1936); *Selected Historical Essays*, chosen and with introd. by H. M. Cam (ibid., 1957); *Letters*, ed. C. H. S. Fifoot (ibid., 1965). A. L. Smith, *Frederic William Maitland: Two Lectures and a Bibliography* (Oxford, 1908). Fuller Lives by H. A. L. Fisher (Cambridge, 1910) and C. H. S. Fifoot (Cambridge, Mass., 1971). H. E. Bell, *Maitland: A Critical Examination and Assessment* (1965). J. R. Cameron, *Frederick William Maitland and the History of English Law* (Norman, Okla. [1961]). G. R. Elton, *F. W. Maitland* (Historians on Historians, 1985). B. F. Lock in *DNB, 1901–1911*, pp. 552–5.

Major (or Maier), Georg

(1502–74), *Lutheran theologian. He studied at *Wittenberg under M. *Luther and P. *Melanchthon. After eight years as a schoolmaster in Magdeburg, he returned to Wittenberg in 1537, first as court preacher and then (from 1545) as a member of the theological faculty. He enjoyed the favour of John Frederick, Elector of Saxony, and supported his resistance to the Emp. *Charles V in the Schmalkaldic Wars. After his defeat, Major fled briefly to Magdeburg before making peace with the new ruler, Duke Maurice. Apart from brief periods elsewhere, he spent the rest of his life at Wittenberg, involved in producing the Wittenberg edition of Luther's works and serving as dean of the theology faculty from J. *Bugenhagen's death (1558) until his own. He is famous chiefly as the protagonist of the 'Majoristic Controversy'. This broke out in the wake of the *Leipzig Interim, which Major, like his mentor Melanchthon, supported. In defending his role in the Interim against harsh criticism from N. von *Amsdorf, Major asserted in his *Auff des Ehrenwirdigen Herren Niclas von Ambdsorff ... Antwort* (1552) that good works were necessary for salvation. This statement was denounced by Amsdorf, M. *Flacius, and other *Gnesio-Lutherans as incompatible with the doctrine of *justification by faith alone. In the ensuing controversy Major, without fully retracting his views, qualified them to the extent of claiming that good works were only a token of justification and that his teaching was never intended in the sense that his opponents attached to it.

Werke were ed. in 3 vols., Wittenberg (1569–70; many works omitted). R. Kolb, 'Georg Major as Controversialist: Polemics in the Late Reformation', *Church History*, 45 (1976), pp. 455–68. H. Scheible in *TRE* 21 (1991), pp. 725–30, with bibl.

Majoristic Controversy.

See previous entry.

Major Orders.

The higher grades of the Christian ministry in contradistinction from the *Minor Orders (q.v.). In the early Church these were generally held to be *bishop, *priest, and *deacon. From the time of *Innocent III, the *subdiaconate was accounted a major order and the diaconate and priesthood (in which the episcopate was included) reckoned as the other two to preserve the original number of three in all. In modern times the Second

*Vatican Council implied a restoration of the primitive conception of a ministry consisting of episcopate, priesthood, and diaconate, and in 1972 the subdiaconate was suppressed. Acc. to RC canon law no one can receive major orders who has not previously received the lesser ministries; within the Latin rite, but not in the *Uniat Churches, those on whom they are conferred (except permanent deacons) are bound to *celibacy and the recitation of the Divine *Office. The obligations and rights of clerics are listed in *CIC* (1983), cans. 273–89.

majuscule script.

See UNCIAL SCRIPT.

Malabar Christians.

A title applied in a wider sense to all the Christian communities of the Syriac rite living in Kerala in SW *India (also known as 'Thomas Christians'), and in a narrower sense to the community of the E. Syrian rite in communion with Rome (the 'Syro-Malabar Church'). All claim that their Church was founded by St *Thomas the Apostle, who is held to have been martyred near Madras; a shrine of St Thomas near Madras is marked by a cross bearing a 7th-cent. Pahlavi inscription. Though the tradition is not impossible, there is no certain evidence earlier than the assertion of *Cosmas Indicopleustes that there were Christians in India before 550. These early Christians were probably originally from E. Syria, with which India conducted considerable trade; their bishops came from the Patriarch of the *Church of the East in Baghdad, and Syriac was used exclusively in liturgical worship. When the Portuguese arrived at the end of the 15th cent. they were originally friendly towards the 'Syrians'. At the Synod of *Diamper in 1599 the Malabar Christians renounced *Nestorius and allied themselves with Rome. Interference with their customs, esp. by the *Jesuits, caused a breach with the W. in 1653; but, largely as a result of the ministrations of the *Carmelites, about two-thirds of them returned to communion with Rome in 1662. They use the Liturgy of *Addai and Mari and still form the largest body of Malabar Christians. In recent years there have been various moves to restore the Syro-Malabar liturgy which had undergone considerable Latinization as a result of the Synod of Diamper.

Those who did not return to Rome in 1662 joined themselves to the *Syrian Orthodox and adopted the W. Syrian Antiochene liturgy. They were prevented by the Portuguese from receiving a bishop from Mesopotamia, but eventually they obtained a bishop from the Patriarch in Homs. From 1816 to 1836 they were in close touch with the Anglican Church and received missionaries from the *CMS. Until recently, they have been constantly disturbed by internal dissensions, and at the end of the 19th cent. there was a further split, the reforming party constituting themselves the 'Mar Thoma' Church, which has maintained close links with the C of E and later the Church of *South India. There were also various attempts to obtain union with Rome; after the secession of Mar Ivanios in 1925 more serious negotiations were opened and in 1930 the *Malankarese Uniat Church (q.v.) came into being. As a result of a recent schism in the Syrian Orthodox Church in India there are now two Catholicoi, one recognizing the Patriarch as the supreme head, the other independent. Since 1907 there has been a small community once again subject to the Patriarch of the Church of the East. The Syrian Orthodox Church in India is one of the most literate communities in the country and is active in missionary work in Africa and in most parts of Asia.

The best account is that of L. W. Brown, *The Indian Christians of St Thomas* (Cambridge, 1956; reissued with additional ch., 1982). Earlier works include M. Geddes, *The History of the Church of Malabar from the Time of its first being discovered by the Portuguese in the Year 1501* (tr. from the Portuguese into Eng., London, 1694). J. F. Raulin, *Historia Ecclesiae Malabaricae cum Diamperitana Synodo* (Rome, 1745). T. Whitehouse, *Lingerings of Light in a Dark Land: being researches into the past history and present condition of the Syrian Church of Malabar* (1873); N. J. Thomas, *Die Syrisch-Orthodoxe Kirche der Südindischen Thomas-Christen* (Das östliche Christentum, NF 19; 1967). J. Vellian (ed.), *The Malabar Church: Symposium in honour of Rev. Placid Podipara, C.M.I.* (Orientalia Christiana Analecta, 186; 1970). P. J. Podipara, CMI, *The Thomas Christians* (1970). P. Verghese (ed.), *Die Syrischen Kirchen in Indien* (Die Kirchen der Welt, 13; Stuttgart, 1974). P. Cheriyan, *The Malabar Syrians and the Church Missionary Society 1816–1840* (Kottayam, 1935); J. F. Coakley, 'The Archbishop of Canterbury's Assyrian Mission and the Consecration of Mar Abimalek Timotheus of Malabar' [in 1907], in R. Lavenant, SJ (ed.), *IIIe Symposium Syriacum 1980* (Orientalia Christiana Analecta, 221; 1983), pp. 203–12. R. H. *Connolly, 'The Work of Menezes on the Malabar Liturgy', *JTS* 15 (1914), pp. 396–425, 569–89, with addition by E. *Bishop, pp. 589–93. L. K. Ananthakrishna Ayyar, *Anthropology of the Syrian Christians* (Ernakulam, 1926). G. B. Howard, *The Christians of St Thomas and their Liturgies* (1864; with trs. of several liturgies). J. P. M. van der Ploeg, OP, *The Christians of St Thomas in South India and their Syriac Manuscripts* (Bangalore, 1983). G. Menachery (ed.), *The St Thomas Christian Encyclopaedia of India* (Trichur, 1973 ff.). M. Mundadan, *History of Christianity in India*, 1: *From the Beginnings up to the Middle of the Sixteenth Century* (Bangalore, 1984). A. J. Maclean in *HERE* 12 (1921), pp. 178–80, s.v. 'Syrian Christians, 9'. É. Amann in *DTC* 9, (pt. 2; 1927), cols. 1704–45, s.v. 'Malabres (Rites)'; E. Tisserant, ibid. 14 (pt. 2; 1941), cols. 3089–162, s.v. 'Syro-Malabare (Église)'; adapted into Eng. as *Eastern Christianity in India* (1957). See also bibl. to INDIA, CHRISTIANITY IN, and THOMAS, ACTS OF.

Malachi, Book of. The last of the 12 *Minor Prophets and the last Book of the OT, acc. to the English order. The Heb. 'Malachi' מַלְאָכִי means 'my messenger', and the word is probably not to be considered the actual name of the prophet, although a few scholars hold that one of *Ezra's assistants was so called. The writer, whoever he was, begins by emphasizing the love of God for His people (1: 2–5), which is reciprocated only by insincere worship and empty, corrupt, and unworthy practices by the priests (1: 6–2: 9); he then condemns the practice of mixed marriages and divorce (2: 10–16); he announces that a day of judgement will surely come (2: 17–3: 6) and that happiness and prosperity can be restored only by the regular payment of tithes and other dues (3: 7–12); he touches on the age-long problem of innocent suffering and the ultimate reward of the righteous (3: 13–4: 3); and in conclusion he exhorts his readers to keep the law of *Moses (4: 4–6).

The language and thought of the Book are those of the age following the Exile (i.e. after 538), and the Jewish *Temple has evidently been rebuilt. Contemporary Jewish expectations for the future may be seen in the role given to *Elijah (4: 5; cf. Lk. 1: 17). The prophecy about the messenger who shall prepare the way of the Lord in 3: 1 is applied in the Gospels to *John the Baptist (Mk. 1: 2), while the reference to the 'pure offering' in 1: 11 is often

taken in Christian tradition as a prophecy of the *Eucharist.

Comm. by J. M. P. Smith (ICC on Hag., Zech., Mal., Jon., 1912; separate pagination), W. Rudolph (KAT 13/4, on Hag., Zech., Mal., 1976, pp. 245–99), and R. [A.] Mason (Camb. Bib., NEB, on Hag., Zech., Mal., 1977, pp. 135–62). K. Elliger, 'Maleachi und die kirchliche Tradition', in E. Würthwein and O. Kaiser (eds.), *Tradition und Situation: Studien zur alttestamentlichen Prophetie Artur Weiser zum 70. Geburtstag ... dargebracht* (Göttingen, 1963), pp. 43–48. B. Glazier-McDonald, *Malachi: The Divine Messenger* (Society of Biblical Literature, Dissertation Series, 98; Atlanta, Ga. [1987]).

Malachy, St (1094–1148), Abp. of *Armagh. After restoring monastic life at the ancient site of *Bangor (in Co. Down), Malachy was made Bp. of Connor in 1124. He was a strong advocate for reform in the Irish Church. When he was appointed Abp. of Armagh in 1129, he was opposed by a rival chosen by the hereditary clerical families; he was not installed until 1134, and resigned within three years, preferring an inspirational role. He became Bp. of Down, but prob. lived at Bangor. In 1139 he set out for Rome to seek the *pallium for the two Irish metropolitans from Innocent II, and on the way at *Clairvaux met St *Bernard, who became his close friend and biographer. Though the Pope received him favourably, he refused to grant the pallia until the request was made by an Irish synod. On the return journey, Malachy again visited Clairvaux, and taking thence four of its monks, introduced the *Cistercian Order into Ireland. In 1148 he was dispatched to Rome with the same request as before, but died at Clairvaux on the way in the arms of St Bernard. (The pallia were brought to Ireland by a Papal legate in 1152.) Feast day, 3 Nov.

Best edn. of Life by St Bernard is that in *S. Bernardi Opera*, 3, ed. J. Leclercq, OSB, and H. M. Rochais, OSB (Rome, 1963), pp. 297–378; Epitaph and hymn, ibid., pp. 517–26. Eng. tr. of Life, with notes, by R. T. Meyer (Cistercian Fathers Series, 10; Kalamazoo, Mich., 1978). E. Vacandard, 'Un Évêque d'Irlande, au XIIe siècle. Saint Malachie O'Margair', *RQH* 52 (1892), pp. 5–72. A. Gwynn, SJ, 'St. Malachy of Armagh', *Irish Ecclesiastical Record*, 70 (1948), pp. 961–78; 71 (1949), pp. 134–48, 317–31. J. Leclercq, OSB, 'Documents on the Cult of St. Malachy', *Seanchas Ardmhacha: Journal of the Armagh Diocesan Historical Society*, 3 (1959), pp. 318–32. Study by A. B. Scott (Dublin, 1976). J. F. Kenney, *Sources of the Early History of Ireland*, 1 (New York, 1929), pp. 764–7, with further bibl.

Malachy, Prophecies of. The so-called Prophecies of Malachy, which are contained in a document apparently composed in 1590, have no connection with St *Malachy except their erroneous attribution to him. They purport to give a concise motto for every Pope from Celestine II (1143–4) to 'Peter II' at the end of the world (*In persecutione extrema S.R. Ecclesiae sedebit Petrus II Romanus*). *Pius IX, e.g., corresponded with *crux de cruce*; *Pius X with *ignis ardens*; *Pius XII was *pastor angelicus*; *John XXIII, *pastor et nauta*; and *John Paul II is *de labore solis*. Esp. inappropriate was the description of *Benedict XIV as a 'rustic animal' (*animal rurale*).

Text first pr. by A. Wion, OSB, *Lignum Vitae, Ornamentum et Decus Ecclesiae*, 1 (Venice, 1595), pp. 307–11. M. J. O'Brien, *An Historical and Critical Account of the So-Called Prophecy of St Malachy* (Dublin, 1880), incl. text. Also ed., with introd. and comm., by P. Bander (Gerrards Cross, 1969). A. *Harnack, 'Über den Verfasser und den Zweck der Prophetia Malachie de Summis Pontificibus (1590)', *ZKG* 3 (1879), pp. 315–24. H. Thurston, SJ, *The War and the Prophets* (1915), pp. 120–41 ('The So-Called Prophecy of St. Malachy'). R. Thibaut, SJ, *La Mystérieuse Prophétie des Papes* (Bibliothèque de la Faculté de Philosophie et Lettres de Namur, 10; 1951).

Malalas, John. See JOHN MALALAS.

Malankarese Church. The group of *Malabar Christians (q.v.) of the W. Syrian rite who entered into communion with Rome in 1930. Several earlier unsuccessful attempts to achieve union with Rome had been made. The group, which became *Uniat in 1930, consisted of Mar Ivanios (who had shortly before been raised to the rank of metropolitan) and his suffragan, Mar Theophilus, with some 10,000 followers. By the Papal constitution *Christo pastorum principi* of 11 June 1932, Trivandrum was made the metropolitan see. They retain their ancient Antiochene rite.

C. Malancharuvil, OIC, *The Syro Malankara Church* (The Syrian Churches Series, 7; Ernakulam, 1974). D. Attwater, *The Catholic Eastern Churches* (Milwaukee, Wis. [1935]), pp. 196–9, rev. as *The Christian Churches of the East*, 1 ([Leominster] 1961; London, 1963), pp. 169–71. M. Ivanios, 'The Malabar Reunion', *Pax* 21 (1931), pp. 1–4. See also bibl. to MALABAR CHRISTIANS.

Malawi, Christianity in. It is possible that in the 17th cent. *Jesuit missionaries visited Nyasaland, as the country was called before it became independent in 1964, but there is no sure evidence for their presence. D. *Livingstone reached Lake Malawi in 1859. With his encouragement the first expedition of the *UMCA arrived in 1861; after the death of Bp. C. F. Mackenzie in 1862, the UMCA withdrew to Zanzibar, but returned in 1879. In a national movement commemorating Livingstone's death, the *Free Church of Scotland and Established Church of *Scotland sent out co-operating missions in 1875 and 1876; the first resulted in the establishment of Livingstonia in the north of the country, the second in Blantyre in the south. They were joined by the Cape Synod of the Dutch Reformed Church in 1888. These missions united to establish the Church of Central Africa Presbyterian in 1924, its first Moderator being R. *Laws. The *White Fathers arrived in 1889 to be aided later by the *Marists in building up the RC Church in Malawi. After Nyasaland became a British Protectorate in 1891, a number of small Protestant evangelical missions arrived, to be joined later by American-based *Pentecostal and Adventist missions. The most significant of the African Independent Churches is the Providence Industrial Mission founded by the nationalist leader John Chilembwe, who was killed in the Nyasaland Rising of 1915. Of the total population of 10 million in 1994, *c.* 7 million are Christian. The RC Church is the largest denomination, with a membership of 2.5 million, while the Church of Central Africa Presbyterian has 2.25 million members. The Anglican dioceses belong to the Church of the Province of Central Africa.

J. McCracken, *Politics and Christianity in Malawi 1875–1940: The Impact of the Livingstonia Mission in the Northern Province* (Cambridge, 1977). K. N. Mufuka, *Mission and Politics in Malawi* (Modern Africa Series, 1; Kingston, Ont. [1977]). I. and J. Linden, *Catholics, Peasants, and Chewa Resistance in Nyasaland 1889–1939* (1974). J. Weller and J. Linden, *Mainstream Christian-ity to 1980 in Malawi, Zambia and Zimbabwe* (Gweru, 1984), *passim*. G. Shepperson and T. Price, *Independent Africa: John Chilembwe and the Origins, Setting and Significance of the Nyasaland Rising of 1915* (Edinburgh, 1958). [W.] O. Chadwick, *Mackenzie's Grave* [1959].

Malchion (3rd cent.), *Antiochene presbyter. He was head of the Hellenic rhetorical school at Antioch and chosen for his orthodoxy and great learning to interrogate *Paul of Samosata at the Council of Antioch (*c.*270). He successfully forced Paul to reveal his heretical doctrines and, acc. to St *Jerome, himself composed the synodical letter which condemned them.

The chief early authorities are *Eusebius, *HE* 7. 29 f., and Jerome, *De vir. ill.* 71. The (scattered) frags. of Malchion's Dialogue with Paul, taken down in shorthand, have been collected by F. *Loofs, *Paulus von Samosata* (TU 44, no. 5; 1924), pp. 334–7. Cf. also G. Bardy, *Paul de Samosate* (1923), and H. de Riedmatten, OP, *Les Actes du procès de Paul de Samosate* (Paradosis, 6; Fribourg, 1952). Brief art. by G. Bardy in *DTC* 9 (pt. 2; 1927), cols. 1765 f., s.v.

Maldonado, Juan (1533–83), 'Maldonatus', Spanish theologian and exegete. After being educated at the university of Salamanca, he entered the Society of Jesus in 1562. In 1564 he became professor at the *Jesuit Collège de Clermont at Paris, where his theological lectures attracted enormous audiences. In 1574 the *Sorbonne attacked his teaching as heretical; and, though vindicated by the Bp. of Paris in 1576, he withdrew from Paris. His work went far towards rescuing Catholic theology from the barbarous language and barrenness of ideas then prevalent, and his commentaries on the Gospels (2 vols., 1596–7) are held in deservedly high repute. All his writings were published posthumously, and some of those attributed to him are to be treated with caution, as they appear to be inaccurate reproductions of notes taken down at his lectures.

Opera Varia Theologica, pub. in 3 vols. (Paris, 1677), with short Life in vol. 3. R. Galdos, SJ (ed.), *Miscellanea de Maldonato anno ab eius nativitate quater centenario, 1534?–1934* (Madrid, 1947), with Life, pp. 11–16, and bibl., pp. 17–21, and certain of his Orations. J. M. Prat, SJ, *Maldonat et l'université de Paris au XVIᵉ siècle* (Paris, 1856); J. I. Tellechea Idigoras, *La Inmaculada Concepción en la controversia del P. Maldonado, S.J., con la Sorbona* (Victoriensia, 7; Vitoria, 1958), with docs. and bibl. A. Astrain, SJ, *Historia de la Compañía de Jesús en la asistencia de España*, 2 (1905), pp. 357–65. J. Iturrioz, 'Maldonado en Salamanca', *Estudios eclesiásticos*, 16 (1942), pp. 221–34. Sommervogel, 5 (1894), cols. 403–14; 9 (1900), col. 631; and 12 (1911–30), cols. 1144–6; Polgár, 2 (1990), pp. 477 f. E. Amann in *DTC* 9 (pt. 2; 1927), cols. 1772–6, s.v. 'Maldonat'.

Malebranche, Nicolas (1638–1715), French philosopher. He became an *Oratorian in 1660. His most important works are *Recherche de la vérité* (1674) and *Traité de la nature et de la grâce* (1680). Some of his positions derive from *Augustine and *Descartes, but his system is profoundly original. He denied that any action of matter upon mind was possible, and explained sensation as the effect of a new creative act in the mental order to correspond with things in the physical creation ('*Occasionalism'). His principle of *simplicité des moyens* (that God exhibits His omnipotence by acting always in the simplest possible way) led him into a form of

*Ontologism, in which God was the immediate cause of all human knowledge, and the 'place of our ideas'; consequently, he taught that our first and simplest idea is that of the infinite. Again, the complexity of the natural creation as a whole was justified in his system solely by the fact of its being eternally ordained (as the simplest possible means) towards the Incarnation of the Word and the reign of grace. A. *Arnauld, J.-B. *Bossuet, and F. *Fénelon wrote against various aspects of his doctrine during his lifetime.

Crit. edns. of Malebranche's works by A. Robinet (Bibliothèque des Textes Philosophiques; 20 vols. + index, Paris, 1958–1970) and by G. Rodis-Lewis (Bibliothèque de la Pléiade, 2 vols., ibid., 1979–92). Besides various older trs. of Malebranche's writings, there is a good Eng. tr. of the *Dialogues on Metaphysics and on Religion* by M. Ginsberg ('Library of Philosophy', 1923); also of *The Search for Truth* by T. M. Lennon and P. J. Olscamp (Columbus, Oh., 1980) and of the *Treatise on Nature and Grace* by P. Riley (Oxford, 1992). E. A. Blampignon, *Études sur Malebranche d'après des documents manuscrits, suivie d'une correspondance inédite* (1862). Studies by L. *Ollé-Laprune (2 vols., Paris, 1870), H. Joly ('Les Grands Philosophes', 1901), R. W. Church (London, 1931), M. Guéroult ('Philosophie de l'Esprit', 3 vols., 1955–9), P. Blanchard (Paris, 1956), G. Rodis-Lewis ('Les Grands Penseurs', 1963), B. K. Rome (Chicago, 1963), A. Robinet (Bibliothèque d'Histoire de la Philosophie, 1965), F. Alquié (ibid., 1974), and D. Radner (Assen, 1978). *Malebranche nel terzo centenario della nascita*. Pubblicazione a cura della Facoltà di Filosofia dell'Università Cattolica del Sacro Cuore (Rivista di Filosofia Neo-Scolastica, Supplemento speciale al volume 30; Milan, 1938). *Malebranche: L'Homme et l'œuvre, 1638–1715*, by A. Robinet and others (Centre International de Synthèse, 1967). H. Gouhier, *La Philosophie de Malebranche et son expérience religieuse* (1926); Y. de Montcheuil, *Malebranche et le quiétisme* (Théologie, 10; 1946); D. Connell, *The Vision in God: Malebranche's Scholastic Sources* (Louvain and Paris, 1967); M. E. Hobart, *Science and Religion in the Thought of Nicolas Malebranche* (Chapel Hill, NC [1982]). C. J. McCracken, *Malebranche and British Philosophy* (Oxford, 1983). J. Wehrlé in *DTC* 9 (pt. 2; 1927), cols. 1776–804, s.v.; G. Rodis-Lewis in *NCE* 9 (1967), pp. 110–12, s.v.; W. Doney in P. Edwards (ed.), *The Encyclopedia of Philosophy*, 5 (1967), pp. 140–4, s.v.

Malines Conversations. The meetings of a group of Anglican and RC theologians held at Malines between 1921 and 1925 under the presidency of Cardinal D. J. *Mercier. The initiative came from Lord *Halifax. The others who took part were, on the Anglican side, J. A. *Robinson, W. H. *Frere, C. *Gore, and Dr B. J. Kidd (the Warden of Keble College, Oxford), and on the Roman side Mgr. J. E. van Roey, the Abbé F. Portal, P. *Batiffol, and the Abbé H. Hemmer; and all the meetings except the first took place with the cognizance of the Holy See and the Abp. of *Canterbury. It was agreed that the Pope should be given primacy of honour; that the Body and Blood of Christ are indeed taken in the Eucharist; that the Sacrifice of the Eucharist is a true sacrifice, but after a mystical manner; that Episcopacy is by Divine law; and that Communion in both kinds is a matter of discipline not of dogma. The more Protestant sections of the C of E viewed the Conversations with great suspicion, and the publication of the Report was long delayed for fear that it might fan the opposition to the Revised Prayer Book. Lord Halifax, however, published it early in 1928. Though the Conversations issued in no tangible result and further progress was hindered by *Pius XI's encyclical '*Mortalium

Animos' (1928), they indirectly stimulated the movement for co-operation between the C of E and the RC Church.

Lord Halifax, *The Conversations at Malines, 1921–5* (1930); W. H. Frere, *Recollections of Malines* (1935); G. K. A. *Bell, *Randall Davidson* (1935), ch. 79; J. G. Lockhart, *Viscount Halifax*, vol. 2 (1936), chs. 18–22. J. de Bivort de la Saudée, *Anglicans et Catholiques* (2 vols., Brussels, 1949), with docs. in vol. 2. H. Hemmer, *Monsieur Portal, prêtre de la mission (1855–1926)* (posthumously pub., 1947; Eng. tr. and edn. by A. T. Macmillan, 1961), pp. 121–68. J. A. Dick, *The Malines Conversations Revisited* (Bibliotheca Ephemeridum Theologicarum Lovaniensium, 85; 1989), with bibl.

Malleolus (or Malleus) Haereticorum (Lat., 'Hammer of the Heretics'). A title applied to various persons who contended vigorously with heretics, among them St *Antony of Padua, St Peter *Canisius, and Johann *Faber (1478–1541).

Malmesbury. The town, formerly the seat of a *Benedictine abbey, traces its origin to the Scottish or Irish monk Meldum (also written Meildulf), who founded a school there *c*.635. It developed into a monastery under his pupil, St *Aldhelm, who became its first abbot and later Bp. of *Sherborne. The house flourished under him and his successors, and enjoyed the favour of many English kings, *Athelstan, *William I, and later Richard II and Henry V, among them. Throughout the Middle Ages it remained one of the principal English monasteries and sent its mitred abbots to Parliament; its most famous member was the historian, *William of Malmesbury. The monastery was dissolved in 1539. The principal portions of the abbey that remain now form the parish church of St Mary and St Aldhelm.

J. S. Brewer and C. T. Martin (eds.), *Registrum Malmesburiense* (RS, 2 vols., 1879–80). R. H. Luce, *Pages from the History of the Benedictine Monastery of Malmesbury* (Devizes, 1929). H. Breakspear, 'Malmesbury Abbey', *Archaeologia*, 64 (1913), pp. 399–436. W. *Dugdale, *Monasticon Anglicanum*, 1 (1817 edn.), pp. 253–64. A. Watkin, OSB, in *VCH*, Wilts, 3, ed. R. B. Pugh and E. Crittall (1956), pp. 210–31.

Malo, St. See MACHUTUS, ST.

Malta, Knights of. See HOSPITALLERS.

Maltese Cross. A black cross of eight points on a white ground, so named because it was adopted by the Knights of Malta, i.e. the *Hospitallers of St John of Jerusalem.

Malvern Conference. The Anglican Conference which met at Malvern, 7–10 Jan. 1941, under the presidency of Abp. W. *Temple, to consider in the light of the Christian faith the crisis confronting civilization. In its 'findings', which were esp. concerned with the relation of the Church to economic life, the Conference asserted its belief that the continued private ownership of the industrial resources of the country imperilled the Christian doctrine of man, and it urged that the C of E should radically reform its own economic and administrative system.

The Resolutions were issued as a leaflet entitled *The Life of the Church and the Order of Society* by the *Industrial Christian Fellowship. Most of the papers read were pr. in *Malvern 1941* (1941).

Mamertine Prison. A building in the centre of Rome consisting of two cells, one above the other, in which, acc. to tradition, St *Peter was imprisoned and converted his two gaolers, Processus and Martinianus. It was certainly in use as a prison from Republican times. The small church of San Giuseppe dei Falegnami now stands above the site.

H. Grisar, SJ, 'Der mamertinische Kerker und die römischen Traditionen vom Gefängnisse und den Ketten Petri', *ZKT* 20 (1896), pp. 102–20. L. *Duchesne, 'Le Forum Chrétien', *Mélanges de littérature et d'histoire religieuses publiés à l'occasion du jubilé épiscopal de Mgr de Cabrières*, 1 (1899), II, 'La Prison mamertine', pp. 128–31. H. *Leclercq, OSB, in *DACL* 10 (pt. 1; 1931), cols. 1356–60, s.v.

Mamertus, St (d. *c.*475), Bp. of Vienne. The brother of *Claudianus Mamertus (q.v.), he was Bp. of the metropolitan see of Vienne in Gaul by 463. For consecrating a Bishop of Die and overriding the attempted settlement of the conflicting claims of the sees of Arles and Vienne (450), he received a rebuke from Pope Hilary (464). He is esp. remembered for having introduced (*c.*470) the 'litanies' on the days immediately preceding *Ascension Day as an act of intercession against earthquakes and other perils, a practice which led later to the institution of the *Rogation Days. Feast day, 11 May.

*Avitus, *Homilia de Rogationibus* (*PL* 59. 289–94). *AASS*, Mai. 2 (1680), pp. 629–31. É. Griffe, *La Gaule Chrétienne*, 2 (1957), pp. 215 f.; 2nd edn. (1966), pp. 268 f. J. P. Kirsch in *CE* 9 (1910), p. 580. See also bibl. to ROGATION DAYS.

Man, Isle of. See SODOR AND MAN.

Manasses, Prayer of. This short book in the OT *Apocrypha consists of a penitential prayer put into the mouth of Manasseh, King of Judah (2 Kgs. 21: 1–18). Though the prayer contains no reference to Manasseh by name (apart from the heading) and in content resembles some of the *Penitential Psalms, there are some indications that it was composed with Manasseh's situation, as described in 2 Chron. 33: 12 f., in view. In some early Greek Bibles it is found among the biblical *canticles appended to the Psalter, and its use in the early Christian Church is attested by its embodiment in the *Didascalia and the *Apostolic Constitutions. All that can be said with certainty about its date is that it must be earlier than that of the Didascalia (early 3rd cent.). It is a matter of dispute whether it was originally written in a Semitic language (Hebrew, Aramaic, or Syriac) or in Greek. In printed *Vulgates, since the time of *Clement VIII (1592–1605) it has formed an appendix. In the E. Church it is recited in Great *Compline during Lent and on the eves of certain great feasts.

The numerous edns. of the LXX text incl. H. B. *Swete, *The Old Testament in Greek*, 3 (1894), pp. 802–4. Syriac texts ed. W. Baars and H. Schneider, *The Old Testament in Syriac according to the Peshitta Version*, pt. 4, fasc. 6 (Leiden, 1972), separate pagination. H. E. *Ryle in R. H. *Charles (ed.), *The Apocrypha and Pseudepigrapha of the Old Testament*, 1 (1913), pp. 612–19; J. H. Charlesworth in id. (ed.), *The Old Testament Pseudepigrapha*, 2 (1985), pp. 625–37, both with Eng. tr. H. Volz, 'Zur Überlieferung des Gebetes Manasse', *ZKG* 70 (1959), pp. 293–307, with refs. H. Schneider, 'Der Vulgata-Text der Oratio Manasse', *Biblische Zeitschrift*, NF 4 (1960), pp. 277–82. A.-M. Denis, *Introduc-*

tion aux pseudépigraphes grecs d'Ancien Testament (Studia in Veteris Testamenti Pseudepigrapha, 1; Leiden, 1970), pp. 177–81. E. *Schürer, *The History of the Jewish People in the Age of Jesus Christ*, rev. Eng. tr. by G. Vermes and others, 3 (pt. 2; Edinburgh, 1987), pp. 730–3. F. Prat, SJ, in *Dict. Bibl.* 4 (1908), cols. 654–83, s.v. 'Manassé (Prière de)'; J. B. Frey, ibid., Suppl. 3 (1928), cols. 442–5, s.v. 'Apocryphes de l'Ancien Testament 13'. See also bibl. to APOCRYPHA.

Mandaeans (also known as **Nasoreans**). A *Gnostic sect which survives as a small community in S. Iraq and SW Iran. Their origins may go back to a group practising repeated baptisms, living to the east of the R. *Jordan in the 1st and 2nd cent. AD. Their extant writings, the chief of which is the *Ginza* or 'Treasure', mostly date from the 7th or 8th cent. or later, though some of their hymns must be considerably older, since the *Manichaean Psalm Book (3rd–4th cent.) in places makes use of them. Their doctrines are based on a dualistic opposition between the World of Light and the World of Darkness. They teach that man's soul, unwillingly imprisoned in the body and persecuted by demons, will finally be freed by the redeemer, *Manda de Hayyê*, the personified 'Knowledge of Life' (sometimes also called *Hibel*, or *Enoš Uthra*), who was himself once on earth and defeated the powers of darkness, and hence can guide souls through the heavenly spheres. Their most important rituals are various kinds of baptismal rites (one initiatory, the others repeated regularly), and the *masiqta*, a rite to assist the souls of the departed to ascend to the World of Light. Although Mandaean texts are hostile to Judaism and Christianity, many elements appear to have been derived from these sources. As St *John the Baptist plays a large part in some Mandaean writings (esp. those dating from the Islamic period), the Christian missionaries who first came across them in the 16th cent. mistakenly called them 'Christians of St John'.

Modern crit. edns. of several Mandaean texts by M. Lidzbarski, incl. *Das Johannesbuch der Mandäer* (2 parts, Giessen, 1905–15), *Mandäische Liturgien* (Abh. (Gött.), 17, Heft 1; 1920), and *Ginza, der Schatz oder das grosse Buch der Mandäer* (Quellen der Religionsgeschichte, 13; 1925 [Ger. tr.]). Collection of extracts in Eng. tr., with useful introd. by K. Rudolf, in W. Foerster, *Gnosis*, Eng. tr. ed. R. McL. Wilson, 2 (Oxford, 1974), pp. 123–319. Eng. tr., with notes, of *The Canonical Prayerbook of the Mandaeans* by E. S. Drower (Leiden, 1959). Id., *The Mandaeans of Iraq and Iran: Their Cults, Customs, Magic, Legends, and Folklore* (1937); id., *The Secret of Adam: A Study of Nasoraean Gnosis* (Oxford, 1960). K. Rudolph, *Die Mandäer* (Forschungen zur Religion und Literatur des Alten und Neuen Testaments, NF 56–7; Göttingen, 1960–1). G. Widengren (ed.), *Der Mandäismus* (Weg der Forschung, 167; 1982). E. Segelberg, *Maṣbūtā: Studies in the Ritual of the Mandaean Baptism* (Uppsala, 1958). On the language, T. Nöldeke, *Mandäische Grammatik* (1875); E. S. Drower and R. Macuch, *A Mandaic Dictionary* (Oxford, 1963); R. Macuch, *Handbook of Classical and Modern Mandaic* (Berlin, 1965); id., *Zur Sprache und Literatur der Mandäer* (1976). S. A. Pallis, *Essay on Mandaean Bibliography, 1560–1930* (London and Copenhagen, 1933). J. Schmitt in *Dict. Bibl.*, Suppl. 5 (1957), cols. 758–88, s.v. 'Mandéisme', with bibl.

Mande, Hendrik (*c.*1360–1431), one of the *Brethren of the Common Life. He came under the influence of G. *Groote and *Florentius Radewijns and in 1395 entered the monastery at *Windesheim, where he was subject to visionary experiences. Here he wrote in Flemish 11 or 12 mystical tracts which embodied and developed many of J. van *Ruysbroeck's ideas.

Modern edn. of three of his tracts by T. Mertens: *Een minnent-like claege* (Veröffentlichungen des Instituts für Niederländische Philologie der Universität zu Köln, 6; 1984); *Een spiegel der waerheit* (ibid. 7; 1984); *Vanden licht der waerheit* (ibid. 8; 1984). The chief source is Jan *Busch, *Chronicon Windeshemense* (ed. K. Grube, Halle, 1886), pp. 122–35. G. Visser, *Hendrik Mande: Bijdrage tot de Kennis der Noord-Nederlandsche Mystiek* (The Hague, 1899; with repr. of 5 of Mande's writings). T. F. C. Mertens, *Hendrik Mande (?–1431): Tekshistorische en literairhistorische studies* (Nijmegen thesis, 1986), with summaries in Fr. G. de Baere, SJ, 'Hendrik Mandes *Liber de sapida sapientia* teruggevonden?', *Ons Geestelijk Erf*, 63 (1989), pp. 288–95. T. Mertens, 'Hendrik Mande (± 1360–1431). Een geannoteerde bibliografie van de werken over hem en van de uitgaven van zijn geschriften', ibid. 52 (1978), pp. 363–96. B. Spaapen in *Dict. Sp.* 7 (pt. 1; 1969), cols. 222–5, s.v. 'Henri (32) Mande'.

mandyas (Gk. μανδύας). A form of cloak worn by monks and bishops in the E. Church. The ordinary monastic mandyas is black; bishops and abbots wear a larger mandyas, usually of purple, with a train extending behind.

Mani (or **Manes**) and **Manichaeism**. It is impossible to state in brief compass the facts relating to the life of Mani (or, acc. to the usual W. form of his name, 'Manichaeus'), the founder of Manichaeism, as the relatively late sources of his life are mutually contradictory in their details. The chief sources are: (1) the writings of certain of the Church Fathers, notably St *Ephraem Syrus, *Titus of Bostra, *Serapion of Thmuis, and esp. St *Augustine of Hippo (who was himself a Manichee for nine years before his conversion); (2) a report of a reputed dialogue between Mani and a bishop, Archelaus, the so-called 'Acta Archelai', which was issued by one Hegemonius; (3) references in various medieval Muslim historians who came across Manichaeism in Babylonia, notably Al-Biruni; (4) a collection of Manichaean documents, discovered in 1904–5 at Turfan and elsewhere in Chinese Turkestan, and published by F. W. K. Müller and others; (5) another collection of Manichaean documents of the 3rd and 4th cents. found in Egypt in 1930 and published by C. Schmidt, H. J. Polotsky, and others, which, if not from Mani himself, embody the teaching of his earliest disciples; and (6) a biography of Mani, prob. translated from a Syriac original, more recently discovered in Egypt. This casts a new light on his evolution as a young man, in the environment of a Judaeo-Christian sect, the *Elkesaites.

From our extant sources it would seem that Mani (c.216–276) was born near Seleucia-Ctesiphon, the capital of the Persian Empire; that he began his own special teaching in 240; that opposition from the *Zoroastrians forced him into exile in India, and that he propagated his teaching rapidly by preaching far and wide in the E.; that in 242 he returned to the capital and may have approached Sapor I, who first gave him active support and then attacked him; and that under his second successor, Bahram I, he was put to death by being flayed alive, and his disciples banished.

Mani's system was a radical offshoot of the *Gnostic traditions of E. Persia. Deeply influenced by St *Paul (Manichaeism struck Christians as a 'Pauline heresy'), Mani transformed the cramped, ritualist views of the Judaeo-Christian sect in which he had been brought up

into a coherent body of Gnostic dogma, uncompromisingly dualistic, consequential, and deeply conscious of having 'unveiled' truths of universal validity. It was based on a supposed primeval conflict between light and darkness. It taught that the object of the practice of religion was to release the particles of light which Satan had stolen from the world of Light and imprisoned in man's brain and that Jesus, Buddha, the Prophets, and Mani had been sent to help in this task. For the Manichaean believer, the whole physical universe was mobilized to create this release. The Gnostic myth of salvation has seldom been presented on so grandiose a cosmic scale, worked out in rigorous detail; every phase of the movements of the sun, moon, and stars was a stage in the deliverance of the believer's soul, and every ritual act of the individual had resonance among the heavenly bodies.

To achieve this release, severe asceticism, including vegetarianism, was practised. There existed in the sect a hierarchy of grades professing different standards of austerity; the 'Elect' were supported by the 'Hearers' in their determined missionary endeavours and in an otherworldly state of perfection. The Manichaeans' enemies attributed to them many abominable practices, but St Augustine, with his exceptional opportunities for being well informed, nowhere criticized their morals.

The sect spread rapidly. It appears to have been established in Egypt before the end of the 3rd cent., and at Rome early in the 4th. In the later 4th cent. Manichaeans were numerous in Africa. How far the sect directly influenced such heretics as the *Albigensians, *Bogomils, and *Paulicians is disputed; for some similarities of practice would account for the charges of 'Manichaeism' laid against them. On the other hand, the Turfan fragments attest its survival in Chinese Turkestan down to the 10th cent.; and, as the 'Doctrine of Light', it still flourished in 13th-cent. Fukien.

Convenient collection of texts ed. A. Adam, *Texte zum Manichäismus* (Kleine Texte für Vorlesungen und Übungen, 175; 1954; enlarged edn., 1969); fuller collection of texts, in Ger. tr., by J. P. Asmussen and A. Böhlig, *Die Gnosis* [ed. W. Förster], 3: *Der Manichäismus* (Zurich, 1980). The texts discovered in Egypt in 1930, which were reported in 1933, were shared mainly between the *Chester Beatty Collection and the Berlin Academy; those in the former collection have been ed. by H. J. Polotsky, *Manichäische Homilien* (Stuttgart, 1934) and C. R. C. Allberry, *A Manichaean Psalm-Book*, pt. 2 (ibid., 1938), and those in the latter by C. Schmidt and others, *Kephalaia*, 1. Hälfte (ibid., 1940), all with introds. by H. Ibscher. On the recently recovered Life of Mani, see A. Henrichs and L. Koenen, 'Ein griechischer Mani-Codex (P. Colon. inv. nr. 4780)', *Zeitschrift für Papyrologie und Epigraphik*, 5 (1970), pp. 97–216 (the first report). It is now ed., with comm., by idd., ibid. 19 (1975), pp. 1–85 (pp. 1–72.7 of the codex); 32 (1978), pp. 87–199 (pp. 72. 8–99. 9 of the codex); 44 (1981), pp. 201–318 (pp. 99. 10–120 of the codex); and 48 (1982), pp. 1–59 (pp. 121–92 of the codex). Pages 1–99.8 of the codex is repr., with Eng. tr., by R. Cameron and A. J. Dewey, *The Cologne Mani Codex* (Society of Biblical Literature, Texts and Translations, 15; Missoula, Mont., 1979). Crit. edn., with Ger. tr., by L. Koenen and C. Römer (Papyrologica Coloniensia, 14; Opladen, 1988). The first crit. study of Manichaeism was I. de Beausobre, *Histoire critique de Manichée et du manichéisme* (2 vols., Amsterdam, 1734–9). Important later works include F. C. *Baur, *Das manichäische Religionssystem* (1831); G. Flügel, *Mani, seine Lehre, seine Schriften* (1862); F. Cumont and M. A. Kugener, *Recherches sur le manichéisme* (2 vols., 1908–12); P. Alfaric, *Les Écritures manichéennes* (2 vols., 1918–19). F. C. *Burkitt, *The Religion of* the Manichees (Donnellan Lectures for 1924; 1925); H. C. Puech, *Le Manichéisme* (1949); G. Widengren, *Mani und der Manichäismus* (Urban-Bücher, 57; Stuttgart [1961]; Eng. tr. 1965); F. Decret, *Aspects du manichéisme dans l'Afrique romaine: Les controverses de Fortunatus, Faustus et Felix avec Saint Augustin* (Études Augustiniennes, 1970); id., *L'Afrique Manichéenne (IVᵉ–Vᵉ siècles): Étude historique et doctrinale* (2 vols., ibid., 1978). There is also a more popular study by id., *Mani et la tradition manichéenne* (Maîtres spirituels, 1974). E. Rose, *Die manichäische Christologie* (Studies in Oriental Religions, 5; Wiesbaden, 1979). S. N. C. Lieu, *Manichaeism in the Later Roman Empire and Medieval China* (Manchester [1985]). P. Brown, 'The Diffusion of Manichaeism in the Roman Empire', *Journal of Roman Studies*, 59 (1969), pp. 92–103.

maniple. A strip of silk, two to four inches wide and a little over a yard in length, sometimes worn over the left arm by the ministers at Mass. In origin it was a handkerchief carried, as pagan and Christian monuments attest, in the left hand. It was first used liturgically in Rome, but in the 6th cent. is found in *Ravenna, and by the 9th cent. was in use all over Europe. In the Middle Ages it was sometimes worn by all clerks, but in post-Tridentine times it came to be confined to those who had attained at least the rank of *subdeacon. Its colour accords with that of the liturgical season and until recently it usually carried three crosses. The use of the maniple was made optional on 3 May 1967, and it is not mentioned in the 1969 *Ordo Missae*.

Braun, *LG*, pp. 515–61. J. H. Crehan, SJ, 'The Bishop's Maniple', *Downside Review*, 84 (1966), pp. 280–4. J. Braun, SJ, in *CE* 9 (1910), pp. 601 f.

manna. The food miraculously provided for the *Israelites on their pilgrimage through the wilderness from Egypt to the *Holy Land (Exod. 16). In Exod. 16: 15 the word 'manna' is explained as deriving from the Israelites' question 'What is it?' (Heb. מָן הוּא, *man hu*). It was a white substance which fell along with the dew, and was collected every morning except on the *Sabbath, for which an additional portion was gathered on the previous day. In Jn. 6 Christ speaks of Himself as the True Bread of life, apparently in contrast to the manna given in the wilderness, but in 1 Cor. 10: 3 and elsewhere the manna is regarded as a type of the Christian Eucharist.

P. Borgen, *Bread from Heaven: An Exegetical Study of the Concept of Manna in the Gospel of John and the Writings of Philo* (Supplement to *Novum Testamentum*, 10; 1965). See also comm. on EXODUS and JOHN, GOSPEL OF ST, cited s.v.

Manners-Sutton, Charles (1755–1828), Abp. of *Canterbury. A grandson of the third Duke of Rutland, he was educated at Emmanuel College, Cambridge. In 1791 he became Dean of *Peterborough and in 1792 Bp. of *Norwich. In 1794 he was appointed Dean of *Windsor *in *commendam* and lived on intimate terms with the family of George III. In 1805 he became Abp. of Canterbury. A *High Churchman of the old school, he was dignified, gracious, and highly respected. He was opposed to RC emancipation, but favoured concessions to dissenters. He gave active support to many initiatives of the '*Hackney Phalanx', presiding over the formation of the *National Society (for the education of the poor) in 1811,

and using his influence in securing the foundation of an Anglican episcopate in *India.

A. W. Rowden, *The Primates of the First Four Georges* (1916), pp. 380–426. J. H. Overton in *DNB* 36 (1893), pp. 57 f.

Manning, Henry Edward (1808–92), Abp. of *Westminster. The youngest son of William Manning, MP, he was educated at Harrow and Balliol College, Oxford. His early ambition was for a parliamentary career, but his father's bankruptcy compelled him to accept a clerkship in the Colonial Office. In 1832 he was elected to a fellowship at Merton College, and in the same year he returned to Oxford and was ordained deacon. In Jan. 1833 he went as curate to John Sargent, rector of Lavington, whom he succeeded in May, and whose daughter Caroline (d. 1837) he married in Nov. In 1841 he became Archdeacon of *Chichester. Manning, who had begun life as an Evangelical, now gradually swung round to the *Tractarian side. He contributed no. 78 to the *Tracts for the Times*, and after J. H. *Newman's secession (1845) he was looked on as one of the leaders of the *Oxford Movement. He had disapproved, however, of the contents of Tract 90, and on 5 Nov. 1843 preached a strongly anti-Papal sermon before the University. The *Gorham Judgement destroyed his faith in Anglicanism and in 1851 he was received into the RC Church. Two months later he was (re-)ordained priest by N. *Wiseman, and after studying for two years at Rome, he founded the Congregation of the Oblates of St *Charles Borromeo, based in Bayswater, primarily to undertake mission work for the poor of London. He was made Provost of the Westminster Metropolitan Chapter in 1857. In 1865 he succeeded Wiseman as Abp. of Westminster, on the personal appointment of *Pius IX. At the First *Vatican Council (1869–70) he was a staunch supporter of Papal *Infallibility, taking a vow to do his utmost to secure its promulgation. His bitter hostility to the admission of RCs to the universities and other differences completely alienated him from Newman after 1866. After 1875, when he was made a cardinal, he was prominent in social work of all kinds, and in 1889 mediated successfully in the London Dock Strike. His body was buried in Kensal Green Cemetery, but was later brought back to Westminster Cathedral, which he had founded.

Official Life by E. S. Purcell (2 vols., London, 1896; cynical, also inaccurate). In a similar vein L. Strachey, *Eminent Victorians* (1918), pp. 3–115 ('Cardinal Manning'). Other Lives by A. W. Hutton (London, 1892, with list of Manning's works; rev. edn., 'English Leaders of Religion', 1894) S. Leslie (ibid., 1921), and R. Gray (London, 1985). J. Fitzsimons (ed.), *Manning: Anglican and Catholic* (1951). V. A. McClelland, *Cardinal Manning: His Public Life and Influence 1865–1892* (1962). J. E. C. Bodley, *Cardinal Manning [and other Essays]* (1912), pp. 1–65. D. [H.] Newsome, *The Parting of Friends: A Study of the Wilberforces and Henry Manning* (1966); id., *The Convert Cardinals: John Henry Newman and Henry Edward Manning* (1993). J. M. Rigg in *DNB* 36 (1893), pp. 62–8; A. W. Hutton in *EB* (11th edn.), 17 (1911), pp. 589–91.

manse. There are three principal meanings:

(1) The dwelling-house of a nonconformist minister.

(2) In *Scotland, also the dwelling-house of a minister of the Church of Scotland, he having right to occupy the house during his incumbency. The manse is available for

the minister for use in the fulfilment of his ministerial functions and duties and for the accommodation of his family. It is the obligation of the Financial Board of the Congregation concerned to meet the costs of maintenance and taxes payable in connection with the manse. In the old Church of Scotland, prior to 1925, it was usually the legal obligation of the *heritors of the Parish to provide the manse in country areas but, in consequence of the Church of Scotland (Property and Endowment) Act 1925, the rights of property in such manses have been transferred to the Church of Scotland General Trustees.

(3) In English ecclesiastical law, the parsonage house and *glebe belonging to a *benefice, taken together.

Mansel, Henry Longueville (1820–71), Anglican divine. He was successively scholar (1839) and tutor (1844) of St John's College, Oxford. In 1859 he became the first Waynflete professor of moral and metaphysical philosophy at Oxford, in 1866 (somewhat incongruously) Regius professor of ecclesiastical history, and in 1868 Dean of *St Paul's. He delivered a course of *Bampton Lectures in 1858 on *The Limits of Religious Thought*, in which he argued that the limitations of the human intellect meant that the truths of religion are not speculative but regulative. God is in Himself unknowable and human knowledge of the nature of God is acquired from supernatural revelation alone. His contentions, which had been reached esp. from study of the doctrines of Sir William Hamilton, provoked much hostile criticism, notably from F. D. *Maurice and J. S. Mill. Mansel's other writings include *Artis Logicae Rudimenta* (1849), a widely used compendium of logic based on H. *Aldrich's manual; *The Limits of Demonstrative Science* (1853); the article 'Metaphysics' in the 8th edition of the *Encyclopaedia Britannica* (1857); and a set of lectures on the *Gnostic Heresies* (1875; issued by J. B. *Lightfoot). His witty pen was often employed in matters of domestic controversy in the university, e.g. *Phrontisterion, or, Oxford in the 19th Century* (1852), a satire on the University Commission of 1850.

A collection of Mansel's *Letters, Lectures and Reviews, including the* Phrontisterion, ed. H. W. Chandler (London, 1873). The *Phrontisterion* was repr. in *Three Oxford Ironies*, ed. G. Gordon (London, 1927), pp. 77–102, with introd., pp. 17–23. J. W. *Burgon, *The Lives of Twelve Good Men*, 2 (1888), pp. 149–237. W. R. Matthews, *The Religious Philosophy of Dean Mansel* (Friends of Dr Williams's Library, 10th Lecture; 1956). K. D. Freeman, *The Role of Reason in Religion: A Study of Henry Mansel* (The Hague, 1969). D. Cupitt, 'What was Mansel trying to do?', *JTS* NS 22 (1971), pp. 544–7, with refs. to other recent works; D. W. Dockrill, 'The Doctrine of Regulative Truth and Mansel's Intentions', ibid. 25 (1974), pp. 453–65. L. Stephen in *DNB* 36 (1893), pp. 81–3.

Mansi, Giovanni Domenico (1692–1769), canonist and Abp. of Lucca. A native of Lucca, where he spent most of his life, he was professed a Clerk Regular of the Mother of God in 1710 and in 1765 was elected Abp. of Lucca. In 1724 he published *Tractatus de Casibus et Censuris Reservatis*, his only considerable original work. But he issued a vast series of publications in which his own part usually did not go beyond annotations (some 90 folio vols. have Mansi's name on their title-pages). The most celebrated was his edition of the Councils. In its original shape it was designed as a supplement to N. Coleti's collection (1728–

33) and issued in 6 vols. (1748–52). Its success encouraged Mansi to produce his well-known 'Amplissima', the *Sacrorum Conciliorum Nova et Amplissima Collectio* (31 vols., 1759–98). It goes down to the Council of *Florence, but Mansi himself supervised only the first 14 vols. Its only real merit is its completeness. The editing is poor and uncritical and the older editions are often to be preferred. A continuation under the editorship of L. Petit, AA, and J. B. Martin (26 vols., 1901–27) takes the collection to the First *Vatican Council. Among earlier scholars whose writings (in whole or part) Mansi re-edited were C. *Baronius (1738–56), J. A. *Fabricius (1754), *Pius II (Aeneas Silvius Piccolomini, 1755), and É. *Baluze (1761).

H. *Quentin, OSB, *J. D. Mansi et les grandes collections conciliaires* (1900). Hefele and Leclercq, 1 (pt. 1; 1907), pp. 111–14. H. Chadwick in J. Cannon and others (eds.), *The Blackwell Dictionary of Historians* (1988), pp. 267 f.

Mant, Richard (1776–1848), Bp. of Down, Connor, and Dromore. Educated at Winchester and Trinity College, Oxford, he was elected a Fellow of Oriel College in 1798 and ordained deacon in 1802. After holding several livings, he was appointed Bp. of Killaloe and Kilfenoragh in 1820 and of Down and Connor in 1823 (with Dromore from 1842). His best-known work, which he prepared with G. D'Oyly (d. 1846), was an edition of the Bible with notes selected from Anglican divines (1814). His other writings include an annotated *Book of Common Prayer* (1820) and, the fruit of wide research, a *History of the Church of Ireland* (1840). He was also the author of 'Bright the vision that delighted' and other well-known hymns, as well as of much indifferent poetry.

Memoirs by [E.] Berens (London, 1849) and Walter Bishop Mant (Dublin, 1857). Detailed list of his pub. works in H. Cotton (ed.), *Fasti Ecclesiae Hibernicae*, 3 (Dublin, 1849), pp. 213–17. A. Gordon in *DNB* 36 (1893), pp. 96–8.

Mantegna, Andrea (1431–1506), Italian painter. Adopted as a child by the painter Francesco Squarcione, he received an artistic education from his early youth, and in 1452 he married the daughter of Jacopono Bellini. His series of fresco paintings representing the *Histories of St James and St Christopher* (1448–57) in the church of the Eremitani at Padua (almost completely destroyed by bombing in March 1944) established his reputation. A second series of frescoes painted in the Palazzo Ducale (Camera degli Sposi), Mantua, finished in 1474, treats of scenes from the *Life of Marquess Lodovico Gonzaga*, and a third sequence, painted in tempera on canvas, now at Hampton Court, depicts the *Triumphs of Caesar* (1484–92). Towards the end of his life he executed paintings (*Parnassus*, *Pallas expelling the Vices*, and *Comus*, all now in the Louvre) for the Studiolo of Isabella d'Este at Mantua. A distinct line of development is noticeable in his altar-pieces. His earliest works follow the traditional side-by-side grouping of saints' figures, e.g. *St Luke's Altar* (1453–5) of St Giustina's at Padua, now in the Brera at Milan; but his later altar-pieces, e.g. that of San Zeno at Venice (1457–9), the triptych of the *Adoration of the Magi* (c.1465), the *Madonna della Vittoria* (1495–6, Louvre), and the *Madonna and Child in Glory with SS John the Baptist, Gregory the Great, Benedict, and Jerome* (1496–7, Milan, Museo del Castello Sforzesco), show considerable originality in composition. He also used in his compositions half-length figures (e.g. *The Adoration of the Magi*, in the J. Paul Getty Museum, Malibu). One of his last works, the famous *Dead Christ* in the Brera at Milan, is remarkable for its virtuosity in foreshortening the body. Mantegna's copper engravings, which are among the earliest Italian specimens of this technique, are remarkable for the austerity of their style.

E. Tietze-Conrat, *Mantegna. Paintings: Drawings: Engravings* (1955); R. Lightbown, *Mantegna* (Oxford, 1986), with a complete catalogue of his paintings, drawings, and prints, and select bibl.; J. Martineau (ed.), *Andrea Mantegna* (London, 1992). P. Kristeller, *Andrea Mantegna* (Berlin and Leipzig, 1902; Eng. tr., 1901), with plates and orig. docs. G. Fiocco, *L'arte di Andrea Mantegna* (Bologna, 1927). G. Paccagnini, *Andrea Mantegna: Catalogo della Mostra* (Venice, 1961). E. Camesasca, *Mantegna* (Milan, 1964). A. Martindale, *The Triumphs of Caesar by Andrea Mantegna . . . at Hampton Court* [1979].

mantelletta. In the W. Church a short cloak open in front and reaching to the knees which, since 1969, has been reserved to prelates of the Roman *Curia and Protonotaries *supra numerum*.

The principal legislation governing the dress of senior members of the RC hierarchy is contained in the Instruction 'Ut sive sollicite' issued by the Papal Secretariate of State, 31 Mar. 1969, printed in *AAS* 61 (1969), pp. 334–40. J. Braun, SJ, in *CE* 9 (1910), p. 611, s.v.; P. Siffrin, OSB, in *EC* 7 (1951), cols. 1985 f., s.v.

mantellone. A purple-coloured cloak of silk or wool, until 1969 worn by certain lesser prelates of the Papal court. It was fastened at the neck, reached to the ground, and had slits for the arms.

G. Felici in *EC* 7 (1951), cols. 1986 f., s.v. T. Ortolan in *DTC* 3 (1908), col. 1972, s.v. 'Cour romaine'. See also bibl. to previous entry.

mantum. A red cloak of the Pope which from the 11th to the 14th cents. played an important part in the Papal elections, since the investiture with it (the so-called *immantatio*) expressed the transference to the Pope of his right to govern the Church.

Manual Acts. The rubrics in the 1662 BCP require the celebrant of Holy Communion at the consecration to take the paten into his hands, to break the bread, lay his hand upon it, and to perform corresponding acts at the consecration of the wine. In 1549 the rubrics were less detailed, while from 1552 to 1662 they were omitted altogether, though some of the traditional ceremonies at the consecration no doubt continued. In the *Ridsdale case (1875–7) the Privy Council held that the rubric at the head of the Prayer of Consecration requiring the priest to break the bread 'before the people' meant that he must not intentionally so stand at the consecration as to prevent the congregation from seeing the manual acts. This decision was reaffirmed in substance in the *Lincoln Judgement (q.v.). It is now rarely observed except among extreme Evangelicals. The problem no longer arises where the *westward position has been adopted. See also 'NORTH END'.

V. Staley, *The Manual Acts* (*Alcuin Club Prayer Book Revision Pamphlets, 4; 1913).

Manuale (Lat., 'a book of handy size'). In the Middle Ages the usual name for the book containing the forms prescribed to the parish priest for the administration of the sacraments. It now commonly goes by the name of the *'Rituale' (q.v.).

manuscripts of the Bible. Writing in the ancient world was usually either on papyrus (made from the stems of the papyrus plant which once flourished in the marshes of the Nile; see PAPYROLOGY) or on specially prepared skins of animals ('parchment' or 'vellum'). For short communications, such as a letter or a business contract, a single sheet would be sufficient; but for longer items, such as a philosophical treatise or most Books of the Bible, a number of sheets would be joined together to form either a roll or a 'codex' (in which the sheets were first folded in quires and then sewn together as in a modern book).

The earliest part of the OT about the writing of which we have any definite information is the Book of *Jeremiah; this is clearly stated to have been written on a roll both in its first edition (Jer. 36: 2, 4, 6, etc.) and its second (Jer. 36: 32), though whether a papyrus or a parchment roll is not stated. It seems that the roll was the normal form of book used among the Jews at the time (cf. Ezek. 2: 9, 3: 3) and it continued so until well into the Christian era. The 'book' handed to the Lord in the synagogue at Nazareth will have been a roll because he is said to have 'opened' (lit. 'unrolled') it, and, after reading, rolled it up again before giving it back to the attendant (Lk. 4: 17–20). The evidence of the *Dead Sea Scrolls proves that both parchment and papyrus were used, but that parchment was preferred, particularly for biblical Books; especially noteworthy here is the celebrated Isaiah roll (DS. Isa^A) found in Qumran Cave 1, which, apart from a few small *lacunae*, has been preserved complete, and is dated in either the 1st or the 2nd cent. BC. Some time later the Jews adopted the codex for private use, the earliest surviving examples being the British Library Pentateuch (*c.* AD 850), the Cairo Prophets (AD 895), and the Leningrad Codex of the whole OT (AD 1008), though for reading in synagogue they have remained faithful to the parchment roll to the present day.

The first Greek translations of the OT Books are likely to have been written on papyrus, since they seem to have been made in Egypt, the home of papyrus. The only certain survivals from the pre-Christian period are fragments from two papyrus rolls (Pap. Rylands Gr. 458 and Pap. Fouad 266), both containing portions of Deuteronomy and both dated 2nd–1st cent. BC. From *c.* AD 100 come the fragments of Genesis now at Yale (Pap. Yale 1); these are thought to be Christian in origin and to have been part of a codex, not a roll. In any case, the many Christian biblical fragments datable in the 2nd and 3rd cents. AD, whether of OT or NT Books, are without exception all from codices: outstanding in this group are those in the *Chester Beatty collection. During the 4th cent. there was a tendency for parchment to replace papyrus, at least for MSS written for public reading in church. Acc. to *Eusebius (*Vit. Const.* 4. 36), the Emp. *Constantine gave instructions *c.* AD 330 for the preparation of 'fifty copies of the sacred scriptures . . . to be written on fine parchment . . . by professional scribes' for the new churches which he was building in *Constantinople. There is no reason to suppose that any of these 50 copies has survived, but a very good idea of what they must have been like can be gained from the appearance of the *Codex Sinaiticus or the *Codex Vaticanus, both of the 4th cent. Such MSS might contain the whole Bible or only a part of it; their text is arranged in columns (two, three, or even four, to a page); and they were called 'uncials' because written in the formal *uncial script, roughly equivalent to our 'capitals'. About the beginning of the 9th cent. a new style of script was introduced (known as 'minuscule'; see CURSIVE SCRIPT); the use of this script made it possible to accommodate the whole of the NT in one convenient volume. There are altogether some six or seven thousand Greek MSS of different parts of the Bible accessible today (some as late as the 17th cent. and written on paper); the great majority of them are minuscules.

The oldest known Latin biblical MS is the 4th-cent. Codex Vercellensis; this is a sumptuous volume, written in uncial with silver ink on purple parchment, and contains an almost complete *Old Latin text of the Gospels. Even more substantial is the Old Latin 'Lyons Heptateuch' (Codex Lugdunensis, 5th–6th cent.), which contains about a third of Genesis, half of Exodus, three-quarters of Leviticus, and the whole of Numbers, Deuteronomy, Joshua and Judges, except the last chapter and a half of Judges. Of St Jerome's *Vulgate, the most ancient relic is the fragmentary 5th-cent. Codex Sangallensis of the Gospels; the most ancient complete Bible is the *Codex Amiatinus, written in Northumberland at the very end of the 7th cent. All these are parchment codices, and the script of all of them is uncial. As in the East, minuscule types of script were developed, the most influential being that associated with the ecclesiastical reforms of *Charlemagne and known as 'Carolingian minuscule' (see CAROLINGIAN SCHOOLS); this in turn provided the basis for yet further developments until the invention of printing. The extant Latin MSS are even more numerous than their Greek counterparts (well over 8,000). One of them is said to be the largest book in the world, Codex Gigas, written in Bohemia in the 13th cent. and now at Stockholm, which is c.20 inches wide and over 36 inches high and contains not only the Bible but a variety of other works as well. Also in the 13th cent. the use of very thin parchment and small writing made it possible to accommodate the text of the whole Bible within single conveniently sized volumes which are termed 'pocket Bibles'.

Of the *Old Syriac version only two MSS are known (the 'Curetonian' and the 'Sinaitic'), both of the Gospels and both incomplete; but of the *Peshitta and the later *Syriac versions there are many, dating from the 5th cent. onwards. Among the MSS and fragments in the various *Coptic dialects several have been dated as early as the 4th cent. (e.g. the sub-Akhmimic papyrus of St John). Of the *Armenian version(s) well over a thousand MSS are known to exist; of the *Gothic, only the remains of some half a dozen of the Gospels and Pauline Epistles in the NT and in the OT only fragments of Gen. 5, Ps. 52: 2–3, and Neh. 5–7. A mid-10th-cent. translation of the Gospels into West Saxon is preserved in four MSS of the 11th and two of the 12th cents.

Finally, there are 'bilingual' MSS: these are of three kinds. Either the secondary text is written immediately above the primary text, or the two texts are copied in two parallel columns on the same page, or they are arranged to face one another on opposite pages. The first ('interlinear') arrangement is found, e.g., in the Codex Bœrnerianus of the Pauline Epistles, where the Latin is a more or less word-for-word equivalent of the Greek underneath; in the Codex Claromontanus (also of the Paulines) the Greek and Latin are in parallel columns; and in the *Codex Bezae they are on opposite pages.

For the use of biblical MSS in preparing a text, see TEXTUAL CRITICISM.

F. G. Kenyon, *Our Bible and the Ancient Manuscripts* (1895; rev. by A. W. Adams, 1958). B. J. Roberts, *The Old Testament Text and Manuscripts* (Cardiff, 1951); E. Würthwein, *Der Text des Alten Testaments: Ein Einführung in die Biblia Hebraica* (1952; 4th edn., 1973; Eng. tr., *The Text of the Old Testament*, Grand Rapids, Mich., 1979, London, 1980). B. M. Metzger, *The Early Versions of the New Testament* (Oxford, 1977); id., *Manuscripts of the Greek Bible* (New York, 1981). W. L. Petersen (ed.), *Gospel Traditions in the Second Century: Origins, Recensions, Text, and Transmission* (Notre Dame, Ind., and London [1989]). T. C. Skeat, 'Early Christian Book Production: Papyri and Manuscripts', in G. W. H. Lampe (ed.), *The Cambridge History of the Bible*, 2 (Cambridge, 1969), pp. 54–79; C. H. Roberts and T. C. Skeat, *The Birth of the Codex* (1987). M. Haran, 'Book-Scrolls in Israel in Pre-Exilic Times', *Journal of Jewish Studies*, 33 (1982), pp. 161–73. K. Aland, *Kurzgefasste Liste der griechischen Handschriften des Neuen Testaments* (Arbeiten zur Neutestamentlichen Textforschung, 1; 1963); id., *Repertorium der griechischen christlichen Papyri*, 1: *Biblische Papyri* (Patristische Texte und Studien, 18; 1976); J. van Haelst, *Catalogue des Papyrus littéraires juifs et chrétiens* (Paris, 1976), pp. 1–198. C. Van Puyvelde, OSB, and B. Botte, OSB, in *Dict. Bibl.*, Suppl. 5 (1957), cols. 793–835, s.v. 'Manuscrits bibliques'. See also bibl. to MASSORETES and individual MSS and subjects referred to above.

maphrian (Syriac *mafriano*, 'one who bears fruit', i.e. 'a consecrator'). The title of the bishop of the *Syrian Orthodox who holds rank immediately after the Patriarch.

Maran, Prudentius (1683–1762), *Maurist scholar. Born at Sézanne, he entered the *Benedictine Order at Saint-Faron in Meaux, in 1703. Later he went to *Saint-Germain-des-Prés, where he co-operated with A. A. Touttée (1677–1718) and completed his edition of St *Cyril of Jerusalem (1720). In 1734 he was exiled from Saint-Germain-des-Prés on account of his refusal to accept the anti-*Jansenist Bull *Unigenitus. In 1737 he returned to Paris and spent the rest of his life at the abbey of Blancs-Manteaux. Of his patristic editions his masterpiece was his edition of St *Justin Martyr and the other *Apologists (1742), with learned prolegomena. He also completed the editions of St *Cyprian, begun by É. *Baluze (1726), and of St *Basil, begun by Julien Garnier (1730). His other writings (anon.) include a *Dissertation sur les Semi-ariens* (1722; in defence of Touttée's edition of St Cyril) and *La Divinité de Jésus Christ prouvée contre les Hérétiques et les Déistes* (3 vols., 1751).

[R. P. Tassin, OSB,] *Histoire littéraire de la congrégation de Saint-Maur* (Brussels, 1770), pp. 741–9. J. Daoust in *Dictionnaire des Lettres Françaises. Le dix-huitième siècle*, 2 (1960), pp. 160 f.; G.-M. Oury, OSB, in *Dict. Sp.* 10 (1980), cols. 238 f., both s.v. See also bibl. to MAURISTS.

maranatha. This Aramaic word, which occurs at 1 Cor. 16: 22, was understood by the Christian Fathers as 'The Lord has come', but it is probably more correctly rendered by the imperative 'O Lord, come' (cf. Rev. 22: 20). Its use by St *Paul reflects the strong eschatological hopes of the early Church.

See comm. to 1 Cor. 16: 22 and *Didache, 10. 6 (the only other literary occurrence of the word). J. A. T. *Robinson, 'Traces of a Liturgical Sequence in 1 Cor. 16. 20–24', *JTS* NS 4 (1953), pp. 38–41; C. F. D. Moule, 'A Reconsideration of the Context of *Maranatha*', *New Testament Studies*, 6 (1960), pp. 307–10; B. Botte, OSB, 'Maranatha', in A. M. Dubarle, B. Botte, and others, *Noël-Épiphanie: Retour du Christ* (Semaine Liturgique de l'Institut Saint-Serge; Lex Orandi, 40; 1967), pp. 25–42; J. A. Emerton, 'Maranatha and Ephphatha', *JTS*, NS 18 (1967), pp. 427–31, esp. p. 427. K. G. Kuhn in *TWNT* 4 (1942), pp. 470–5; Eng. tr., 4 (1967), pp. 466–72. G. Schneider in H. Balz and G. Schneider (eds.), *Exegetisches Wörterbuch zum Neuen Testament*, 2 (1981), cols. 947 f. s.v., with further refs.

Marburg, Colloquy of (1529).

The meeting convened by *Philip of Hesse with a view to achieving unity between the *Lutherans and Zwinglians. It met in the castle at Marburg-on-the-Lahn on 1–4 Oct. 1529, with M. *Luther and P. *Melanchthon on the one side, and U. *Zwingli, J. *Oecolampadius, and M. *Bucer on the other. It is usually thought that complete accord was reached on 14 of the 15 'Marburg Articles' drawn up by Luther and that the conference failed solely because of Zwingli's refusal to accept the Lutheran doctrine of the Eucharist (*consubstantiation) contained in the remaining article. Some historians, however, consider that the agreement on the 14 articles was only apparent. Luther revised the Marburg articles shortly after the conference; in this form, as the 'Articles of *Schwabach', they were the first Lutheran credal statement and a precursor of the *Augsburg Confession of 1530.

Text in H. Heppe (ed.), *Die fünfzehn Marburger Artikel vom 3. Oktober 1529 nach dem wieder aufgefundenen Autographen der Reformatoren als Facsimile veröffentlicht* (Cassel, 1847; 2nd edn., 1854). 'Relatio Rodolphi Collini de Colloquio Marburgensi', in U. Zwingli's *Opera*, ed. M. Schuler and J. Schulthess, 4 (Zurich, 1841), pp. 173–82, mostly repr. in Kidd, no. 109, pp. 247–54. An account of the proceedings by the Strasbourg theologian Caspar Hedio, with a different text of the Marburg Articles, is pr. in M. Bucer's *Opera Omnia*, 1st ser., *Deutsche Schriften*, 4, ed. R. Stupperich (Gütersloh, 1975), pp. 323–64. G. May (ed.), *Das Marburger Religionsgespräch 1529* (Texte zur Kirchen- und Theologiegeschichte, 13; Gütersloh [1970]). They are also pr. in a way which shows their relationship to the Augsburg Confession in *Die Bekenntnisschriften der evangelisch-lutherischen Kirche* herausgegeben im Gedenkjahr der Augsburgischen Konfession 1930 (10th edn., Göttingen, 1986), pp. 52–83d. W. Köhler, *Das Marburger Religionsgespräch 1529: Versuch einer Rekonstruktion* (Schriften des Vereins für Reformationsgeschichte, no. 148; 1929). S. Haussmann, 'Die Marburger Artikel—eine echte Konkordie?', *ZKG* 77 (1966), pp. 288–321. Schottenloher, 4 (1938), pp. 533 f. (nos. 41337a–62), and 7 (1966), p. 463 (nos. 63967 f.). G. May in *TRE* 22 (1992), pp. 75–9, s.v. 'Marburger Religionsgespräch'.

Marburg, University of.

Founded by *Philip, Landgraf of Hesse, in 1527, it was the first Protestant university established in Europe. Its theological faculty, esp. since the middle of the 19th cent., has been famous through its long line of distinguished professors (including W. *Herrmann, K. *Budde, A. *Harnack, J. *Weiss, C. Mirbt, R. *Otto, F. *Heiler, R. *Bultmann). The university was also the centre of an influential philosophical school (the 'Marburg School'), which on Neo-Kantian principles conceived of religion as purely immanental. The chief representatives of this school were H. Cohen, P. Natorp, E. Cassirer, and (in his first phase) N. Hartmann.

Die Philipps-Universität zu Marburg, 1527–1927: Fünf Kapitel aus der Geschichte der Universität Marburg, 1527–1866, von H. Hermelink und S. A. Kaehler; *Die Universität Marburg seit 1866—in Einzeldarstellungen* (Marburg, 1927). F. Gundlach (ed.), *Die akademischen Lehrer der Philipps-Universität in Marburg von 1527 bis 1910* (Veröffentlichungen der Historischen Kommission für Hessen und Waldeck, no. 15; Marburg, 1927). I. Schnack (ed.), *Marburger Gelehrte in der ersten Hälfte des 20. Jahrhundert* (Veröffentlichungen der Historischen Kommission für Hessen, 35; Marburg, 1977). H. Schneider in *TRE* 22 (1992), pp. 68–75, s.v.

Marca, Pierre de (1594–1662),

French canonist. After filling several important civil offices, he was commissioned by the King to publish his dissertations *De Concordia Sacerdotii et Imperii* (1641). A defence of *Gallican doctrines, it was put on the *Index in the following year. In 1642 he was ordained priest (having been widowed in 1631); but though nominated by the King in 1643 to the bishopric of Conserans, he did not obtain Papal confirmation until 1647. In 1652 he became Abp. of Toulouse and in 1662, shortly before his death, he was appointed Abp. of Paris. A much enlarged edition of the *De Concordia* was issued in 1663 by É. *Baluze, but this too was put on the Index in 1664.

Early Lives by É. Baluze, in the form of 'Epistola ad Clarissimum et Eruditissimum Virum Samuelem Sorberium', prefixed to his edn. of Marca's *Dissertationes de Concordia Sacerdotii et Imperii* (Paris, 1663), pp. 1–32; and P. de Forget, prefixed to his collection of Marca's *Dissertationes Posthumae* (Paris, 1669). F. Gaquère, *Pierre de Marca, 1594–1662: Sa vie, ses œuvres, son gallicanisme* (1932). J. Carreyre in *DTC* 9 (pt. 2; 1927), cols. 1987–91; G. Mollat in *DDC* 6 (1957), cols. 726–9, s.v.

Marcan Hypothesis, the.

The theory that St Mark's is the earliest of the four Gospels and that in its presentation of the life of Christ the facts of history are set down with a minimum of disarrangement, interpretation, and embellishment. The hypothesis was first put on a seemingly secure footing in 1835 by K. *Lachmann, who based his case on an analysis of the literary relationship between the three *Synoptic Gospels. It was adopted almost at once by C. H. Weisse (1801–66) and C. G. Wilke (1788–1854) and in the latter part of the 19th cent. became very widely accepted. Later study, though leaving the literary priority of Mark generally unchallenged, has tended to discover a much greater element of theological interpetation in the Gospel. It has also generally discounted the possibility that the author had access to an independent historical framework.

Marcella, St (c.325–411),

Christian ascetic. Of a noble Roman family, she determined to devote herself, after the early death of her husband, to a life of charitable works, study, and asceticism. Her palace on the Aventine Hill became a centre of Christian influence and St *Jerome once referred to her as 'the glory of the ladies of Rome'. She suffered bodily ill-treatment at the hands of the Goths when they captured Rome in 410 and died from its effects. Feast day, 31 Jan.

Practically all our information is derived from the Epp. of St Jerome, esp. *Ep.* 127 (J. P. Migne, *PL* 22. 1087–95). F. Cavallera, *St Jérôme: Sa vie et son œuvre*, 1. 1 (SSL 1; 1922), pp. 85–9 and 114–19. A. Solignac, SJ, in *Dict. Sp.* 10 (1980), cols. 293–5, s.v.

Marcellina, St (*c*.330–*c*.398), the sister of St *Ambrose. After the death of her father, she assisted her mother in the education of her brother, and was consecrated a virgin by Pope *Liberius in 353. Later she lived at Milan with her brother, who tried to dissuade her from her excessive austerities. St Ambrose dedicated to her his three sermons 'De Virginibus'. Feast day, 17 July.

For Ambrose's three sermons, *De Virginibus*, see J. P. Migne, *PL* 16. 187–232. Marcellina was also the recipient of Ambrose's three *Epp.* 20, 22, and 41 (ibid. 994–1002, 1019–26, and 1115–21), and she is mentioned in his *De Excessu Satyri*, 33 and 76. A Lat. panegyric, pr. by B. Mombritius, is repr. in *AASS*, Jul. 4 (1725), pp. 234–8. A. Rimoldi in *Bibliotheca Sanctorum*, 8 (1967), cols. 646–8, s.v.

Marcellus (d. *c*.374), Bp. of Ancyra and a strong supporter of the *Homoousion at the Council of *Nicaea. In 336 he was deposed from his see on the ground of certain statements in his work against the Arian *Asterius. He was restored on the death of *Constantine (337), but *c*.339 again expelled. The W. accepted his orthodoxy at Councils held at Rome *c*.340 and at *Sardica in 343, on the ground that the offending passages were merely conjectures. The E. was more critical of his orthodoxy and here the Nicene party found his support embarrassing. Marcellus taught that in the Unity of the Godhead the Son and the Spirit only emerged as independent entities for the purposes of Creation and Redemption. After the redemptive work is achieved they will be resumed again into the Divine Unity and 'God will be all in all'. The clause in the *Nicene Creed, 'whose Kingdom shall have no end', was inserted to combat his teaching. The Creed which Marcellus embodied in his Ep. to Pope *Julius (in *Epiphanius, *Haer.* 72) is generally considered a primary witness for the history of the *Old Roman Creed.

Frags. coll. by C. H. G. Rettberg (Göttingen, 1794); crit. edn. by E. Klostermann in *Eusebius' Werke*, vol. 4 (GCS, 1906; rev. by G. C. Hansen, 1972), pp. 183–215 (129 items). F. *Loofs, 'Die Trinitätslehre von Marcellus von Ancyra', *Sb.* (Berl.), 1902, pp. 764–81; W. Gericke, *Marcell von Ancyra* (1940); M. Tetz, 'Zur Theologie des Markell von Ankyra', *ZKG* 75 (1964), pp. 217–70; 79 (1968), pp. 3–42; 83 (1972), pp. 145–94. G. Feige, *Die Lehre Markells von Ankyra in der Darstellung seiner Gegner* (Erfurter Theologische Studien, 58; 1991). A. H. B. Logan, 'Marcellus of Ancyra and the Councils of AD 325: Antioch, Ancyra, and Nicaea', *JTS* NS 43 (1992), pp. 428–46. K. Seibt, *Die Theologie des Markell von Ankyra* (Arbeiten zur Kirchengeschichte, 59; 1994). *CPG* 2 (1974), pp. 135–7 (nos. 2800–6). J. Quasten, *Patrology*, 3 (Utrecht and Westminster, Md., 1960), pp. 197–201; Altaner and Stuiber (1978), pp. 289 and 606. M.-D. Chenu, OP, in *DTC* 9 (pt. 2; 1927), cols. 1993–8, s.v. 'Marcel d'Ancyre'; C. Kannengiesser, SJ, in *DPAC* 2 (1984), cols. 2089–91, s.v. 'Marcello di Ancira'; Eng. tr. in *Encyclopedia of the Early Church*, 1 (Cambridge, 1992), p. 552, s.v., with extensive bibl.

Marcian (396–457), the soldier who by his marriage with *Pulcheria, the sister of the Emp. *Theodosius II, became the E. Emperor in 450. His financial reforms made his reign one of considerable prosperity. Theologically his rule was marked by his successful repression of *Monophysitism, Marcian himself attending personally at the sixth session of the Council of *Chalcedon (451) and even resorting to arms to enforce its theological decrees. He stood in good relations with Pope *Leo I (440–61), his correspondence with whom has survived.

E. Stein and J. R. Palanque, *Histoire du Bas-Empire*, 1 (1959), pp. 311–15 and 351–3; A. H. M. Jones, *The Later Roman Empire*, 1 (Oxford, 1964), pp. 217–21. F. H. B. Daniell in *DCB* 3 (1882), pp. 815 f., s.v. 'Marcianus (8)'; W. Ensslin in *PW* 14 (pt. 2; 1930), cols. 1514–29, s.v. 'Marcianus (34)'; H. Chirat in *NCE* 9 (1967), pp. 192 f., s.v.

Marcian the Monk (prob. late 4th cent.), ascetical writer. Marcian has long been known as the author of three short extracts found in the *Florilegium Edessenum*, but in modern times J. Lebon attributed to him nine other works, two of them doctrinal in character, one ascetical. Though for the most part surviving only in Syriac, they were clearly written in Greek. Lebon sought to identify the author with the Marcian mentioned by *Theodoret (*Religious History*, 3); he lived in the desert of Chalcis towards the end of the 4th cent. (d. *c*.385). Other scholars have attributed the works, or some of them, to Marcian of Bethlehem, mentioned by *Cyril of Scythopolis; he died in 492.

J. Lebon, *Le Moine Saint Marcien: Étude critique des sources, Édition de ses écrits*, posthumously ed. A. van Roey (SSL 36; 1968). J. Kirchmeyer, SJ, 'Le moine Marcien (de Bethléem?)', in F. L. Cross (ed.), *Studia Patristica*, 5 (TU 80; 1962), pp. 341–59. *CPG* 2 (1974), pp. 362–6 (nos. 3885–900).

Marciana. The famous library at Venice, named after St *Mark, the patron saint of the city. The nucleus of the library was the valuable collection of (largely Greek) MSS made in the 15th cent. by Cardinal *Bessarion. Besides a very large number of important classical, biblical, and patristic MSS, the library contains the autographs of Bessarion's 'Encomium on Trebizond' and of P. *Sarpi's *History of the Council of Trent*, as well as many early printed works. Since 1904 the library has been housed in the Palazzo della Zecca (the Mint).

J. Valentinelli (ed.), *Bibliotheca Manuscripta ad S. Marci Venetiarum: Codices Latini* (6 vols., Venice, 1868–73); P. Zorzanello, *Catalogo dei Codici Latini della Biblioteca Nazionale Marciana di Venezia non compresi nel Catalogo di G. Valentinelli* (3 vols., Trezzano, 1980–5); E. Mioni (ed.), *Bibliothecae Divi Marci Venetiarum Codices Graeci Manuscripti* (5 vols. in 6 parts, Rome, 1960–85). *Miscellanea Marciana di Studi Bessarionei* (Medioevo e Umanesimo, 24; 1976). M. Zorzi (ed.), *Biblioteca Marciana, Venezia* (Florence [1988]), with fine illustrations. See also bibl. to BESSARION.

Marcion (d. *c*.160), heretic. He was a native of Sinope in Pontus and a wealthy shipowner. Acc. to *Hippolytus (*Syntagma* ap. *Epiphanius, *Haer.* 42) he was the son of a Bishop who excommunicated him on grounds of immorality. Making his way to Rome, *c*.140, he attached himself to the local orthodox Church. In the next few years he worked out his system and began to organize his followers as a separate community; and in 144 he was formally excommunicated. From now on, apparently from Rome as a centre, he devoted his gifts as an organizer to the propagation of his views and established compact communities over a large part of the Empire which admitted converts of every age, rank, and background. His many and widely scattered opponents (among them *Dionysius of Corinth, *Irenaeus of Lyons, *Theophilus of Antioch, Philip of Gortyna, *Tertullian at Carthage, Hippolytus and *Rhodo at Rome, *Clement and *Origen at Alexandria, *Bardesanes at Edessa) sufficiently attest Marcion's success. His followers were certainly the chief danger to the Church from dogmatic unorthodoxy in the latter half of the 2nd cent. By the end of the 3rd cent. most of the Marcionite communities had been absorbed in *Manichaeism, but they continued to exist in small numbers down to a much later date.

Marcion's central thesis was that the Christian Gospel was wholly a Gospel of Love to the absolute exclusion of Law. This doctrine, which he expounded esp. in his 'Antitheses', led him to reject the OT completely. The Creator God or *Demiurge, revealed in the OT from Gen. 1 onwards as wholly a God of Law, had nothing in common with the God of Jesus Christ. Study of the OT indicated that this Jewish God constantly involved himself in contradictory courses of action, that he was fickle, capricious, ignorant, despotic, cruel. Utterly different was the Supreme God of Love whom Jesus came to reveal. It was His purpose to overthrow the Demiurge.

Acc. to Marcion, this contrast of law and grace was fully understood by St *Paul alone, the Twelve Apostles and Evangelists being largely blinded to the truth by the remnants of Jewish influence. Hence for Marcion the only Canonical Scriptures were ten of the Epp. of St Paul (he either rejected or did not know the *Pastorals) and an edited recension of the Gospel of St *Luke. He seems to have encouraged in his disciples a close study of the Bible and to have rejected all *allegorical methods of exegesis. He even exercised a certain influence on the history of the Catholic Bible. The so-called *Marcionite Prologues to the Pauline Epp. found their way into Latin biblical MSS of orthodox *provenance*, while his rejection of three of the Gospels was an important factor in compelling the Church to differentiate between true and spurious works and construct its own *Canon. His Christology was *Docetic. Christ, who was an emissary of the Father, suddenly appeared preaching and teaching in the Synagogue at *Capernaum. His Passion and Death were the work of the Creator God.

Marcion's writings have all been lost; but it is possible to deduce a good deal about them and to reconstruct much of his biblical text, esp. from Tertullian. He has often been reckoned among the *Gnostics, but it is clear that he would have had little sympathy with their mythological speculations. He inculcated a severe morality and some of his followers suffered in the persecutions.

The standard modern work, with full analysis of sources and attempted reconstruction of Marcion's biblical text, is A. *Harnack, *Marcion: Das Evangelium vom fremden Gott* (TU 45; 1921; 2nd edn., 1924); its value as a history is not seriously affected by its attempt to see in Marcion a precursor of classical Protestantism. Id., *Neue Studien zu Marcion* (ibid. 44, Heft 4; 1923). E. C. Blackman, *Marcion and his Influence* (1948). U. Bianchi, 'Marcion: théologien biblique ou docteur gnostique?', *VC* 21 (1967), pp. 141–9. H. von Campenhausen, *Die Entstehung der christlichen Bibel* (Beiträge zur historischen Theologie, 39; 1968), pp. 173–94 (Eng. tr., 1972, pp. 147–65). B. Aland, 'Marcion. Versuch einer neuen Interpretation', *Zeitschrift für Theologie und Kirche*, 70 (1973), pp. 420–47. R. J. Hoffmann, *Marcion: On*

the Restitution of Christianity (American Academy of Religion, Academy Series, 46; Chico, Calif., 1984), with bibl. Altaner and Stuiber (1978), pp. 106 f., and 570. G. *Salmon in *DCB* 3 (1882), pp. 816–24; É. Amann in *DTC* 9 (pt. 2; 1927), cols. 2009–32; G. Bardy in *Dict. Bibl.*, Suppl. 5 (1957), cols. 862–77; G. Pelland, SJ, in *Dict. Sp.* 10 (1980), cols. 311–21, all s.v. See also bibl. to GNOSTICISM and following entry.

Marcionite Prologues. A set of short introductory prologues to each of the Pauline Epistles which are to be found in a majority of the best MSS of the *Vulgate. D. de Bruyne argued that the prologues to Gal., 1 Cor., Rom., 1 Thess., Col., Phil., and Philem. originated in Marcionite circles. The theory that *all* the prologues were of Marcionite origin received the support of A. *Harnack, while the Marcionite origin of any of them was rejected by M.-J. *Lagrange and others. De Bruyne's position is now generally accepted (if not the extended claim).

Text pr. in J. *Wordsworth and H. J. White, *Novum Testamentum Latine*, 2 (1913–41), at the head of each Epistle, and in A. Harnack, *Marcion* (TU 45; 1921), pp. 136*–8*. D. de Bruyne, OSB, 'Prologues bibliques d'origine marcionite', *R. Bén.* 14 (1907), pp. 1–16; A. Harnack, 'Der marcionitische Ursprung der ältesten Vulgata-Prologe zu den Paulusbriefen', *ZNTW* 24 (1925), pp. 204–18. M.-J. Lagrange, 'Les Prologues prétendus marcionites', *R. Bibl.* 35 (1926), pp. 161–73; H. J. Frede, *Altlateinische Paulus-Handschriften* (Vetus Latina. Aus der Geschichte der lateinischen Bibel, 4; Freiburg, 1964), pp. 171–8; K. T. Schäfer, 'Marius Victorinus und die marcionitischen Prologe zu den Paulusbriefen', *R. Bén.* 80 (1970), pp. 7–16.

Marcosians, the followers of the *Gnostic Marcus, a disciple of *Valentinus. Acc. to *Irenaeus, from whom our knowledge of the sect is derived, they flourished in the Rhône valley in the middle of the 2nd cent. Irenaeus represents Marcus as a charlatan, who made use of magical devices esp. to deceive women to be his prophetesses, and his followers as indulging in elaborate sacramental rites and fantastic speculations about numbers. As Scriptures they used the 'Acts of *Thomas' and other apocryphal books. They represent Gnosticism in its later and most decadent phase.

Irenaeus, *Adv. Haer.* 1. 12–21, is the sole source; both *Hippolytus, *Haer.* 6. 39–55, and *Epiphanius, *Haer.* 34, refer explicitly to Irenaeus. F.-M.-M. Sagnard, OP, *La Gnose valentinienne et le témoignage de St Irénée* (1947), pp. 358–86. G. *Salmon in *DCB* 3 (1882), pp. 827–9, s.v., and É. Amann in *DTC* 9 (1926), cols. 1960–2, s.v.

Marcus, *Gnostic heretic. See preceding entry.

Marcus Aurelius (121–80), Roman Emperor from 161. The adopted son of his predecessor, Antoninus Pius (138–61), whose daughter he married, he was a professed *Stoic, though influenced by other philosophical teaching. His extant *Meditations* are best interpreted as a work of spiritual reflection intended only for his own eyes and designed to fortify himself in fidelity to his own convictions. Very little in it bears directly on what he saw as his providential role as Emperor, though parts at least were written during the campaigns which occupied much of his reign; the Empire was afflicted with plague and foreign invasions; Marcus ultimately restored the imperial defences. As a professed disciple of Antoninus Pius, not a Stoic, whom he depicts as having conformed to the principles which the ruling classes had always desired in an Emperor, he followed traditional policies. Hence the Christians still suffered sporadic persecutions, perhaps aggravated by the misfortunes of his reign, if these were ascribed to divine retribution for Christian 'impiety'. He himself denied that the gods were ever responsible for evil, but he adhered to Trajan's attitude to the Christians (see PERSECUTIONS, EARLY CHRISTIAN). Some scholars see dark allusions to them in the *Meditations*, and one text (11. 3) explicitly imputes to them a spirit of refractory opposition; it may be a gloss, and no clear view of Marcus' opinions on the Christians (if he had any) can be extracted from the *Meditations*. A number of Christian writers addressed 'Apologies' to him, including *Athenagoras and perhaps *Theophilus of Antioch, whose works survive, and *Miltiades, Claudius *Apollinarius, and *Melito, whose Apologies are lost, but there is no reason to think that he read them. See also THUNDERING LEGION.

The *editio princeps* of his *Meditations* was pub. at Zurich, 1558–9. Crit. edn., with Eng. tr. and comm., by A. S. L. Farquharson (posthumously pub. by J. Sparrow, 2 vols., Oxford, 1944); useful text, Eng. tr., and notes, by C. R. Haines (Loeb, 1916); Teubner edn., with *index verborum*, by J. Dalfen (1979). R. B. Rutherford, *The Meditations of Marcus Aurelius: A Study* (Oxford Classical Monographs, 1989). Marcus' philosophical views were close to those of *Epictetus; see also works cited s.v. For his reign, A. Garzetti, *From Tiberius to the Antonines* (rev. Eng. tr., 1974), pp. 472–527, with bibl. pp. 708–25 and 768–73. A. [R.] Birley, *Marcus Aurelius* (London, 1966). P. A. Brunt, 'Marcus Aurelius in his *Meditations*', *Journal of Roman Studies*, 64 (1974), pp. 1–20; id., 'Marcus Aurelius and the Christians' in C. Deroux (ed.), *Studies in Latin Literature and Roman History*, 1 (Collection Latomus, 164; 1979), pp. 483–520.

Marcus Diadochus. The reputed author of a 4th-cent. sermon against the *Arians. It has been suggested that the name 'Marcus' arose out of a MS confusion for 'Blessed Diadochus' (μακάριος Διάδοχος). He is not to be identified, however, with *Diadochus of Photice.

The sermon is pr. in J. P. Migne, *PG* 65. 1149–66. *CPG* 3 (1979), p. 189 (no. 6105).

Marcus Eremita. See MARK THE HERMIT.

Maredsous. The seat of a Belgian *Benedictine abbey, founded in 1872 as a daughter house of *Beuron in Germany. It is a noted centre of scholarship and publishes the *Revue Bénédictine* (from 1890; originally, from 1884, the *Messager des fidèles*) and the collection *Anecdota Maredsolana* (from 1893). Dom Columba *Marmion was Abbot from 1909 to 1923. After the war of 1914–18, Maredsous separated from Beuron and became one of the constituent abbeys in the newly constituted 'Belgian Congregation' of the order.

G. Ghysens, OSB, 'Fondation et essor de Maredsous 1872–1923', *R. Bén.* 83 (1973), pp. 229–75. L. H. Cottineau, OSB, *Répertoire topo-bibliographique des abbayes et prieurés* (Mâcon, 1939), col. 1744, with good bibl. H. Ledoyen, OSB, in *DIP* 5 (1978), cols. 904–6, s.v.

Margaret, St, of Antioch (in Pisidia). She is also known as St Marina. A reputed martyr of the *Diocletianic persecution, of whom, however, nothing certain is known. From an early date she was honoured in the E. Church, and

from the 7th cent. also in the W., though devotion to her did not become popular in the W. till the 12th. In more recent times she has been included among the 14 *Auxiliary Saints, and is invoked esp. by women in travail. In art she is often depicted with a dragon (representing the devil). Many of the numerous legends which have gathered round her have also attached themselves to St *Pelagia (q.v.). Feast day in the W., 20 July; in the E., 17 July.

AASS, Jul. 5 (1727), pp. 22–44. *BHL*, pp. 787 f. (nos. 5303–13). H. *Delehaye, SJ, *Les Légendes hagiographiques* (1905), pp. 222–34. J. M. Sauget in *Bibliotheca Sanctorum*, 8 (Rome, 1967), cols. 1150–60, s.v. 'Marina'. See also bibl. to PELAGIA, ST.

Margaret, 'The Lady' (1443–1509), Margaret Beaufort, Countess of Richmond and Derby. She was the daughter of the 1st Duke of Somerset and was married to *Henry VI's half-brother, Edmund Tudor, the Earl of Richmond, in 1455. He died in 1456 before the birth of his son, the later Henry VII. Before 1464 she married a distant cousin, Lord Henry Stafford, and after his death Lord Stanley, later Earl of Derby (?1473). She had a considerable part in the insurrection which ended in the decisive victory of Bosworth (1485) and in the accession of her son as Henry VII, for whom she had arranged a marriage with Elizabeth of York to reconcile the rival houses. She used her important position as the King's mother mostly for religious and educational interests. In 1494 or 1495 she became acquainted with J. *Fisher, whom she later chose as her spiritual director. Under his guidance she took religious vows and gave herself up to a life of prayer and good works, reciting the Divine Office as well as the Office of Our Lady and hearing several Masses every day. She also was a 'Sister' of many religious houses, among them *Charterhouse, *Durham, and *Westminster. Fisher also encouraged the foundations by which her name still survives in the older universities. She established the Lady Margaret professorships (originally readerships) at Oxford (1502) and Cambridge (1503) as well as a preachership at Cambridge (1504), and she refounded God's House as Christ's College, Cambridge, in 1505. Her other foundation, St John's College, Cambridge, was completed only after her death.

Her translation from the Fr. of the *Imitation of Christ*, bk 4, was orig. pub. by R. Pynson at London, 1503; reissued by W. de Worde, ibid. ?1519, repr., ibid., 1904; also ed. J. K. Ingram (EETS, Extra Series, 63, 1893, pp. 259–83). C. H. Cooper, *Memoir of Margaret Countess of Richmond and Derby* (posthumously pub. by J. E. B. Mayor, Cambridge, 1874), with orig. docs. M. K. Jones and M. G. Underwood, *The King's Mother: Lady Margaret Beaufort, Countess of Richmond and Derby* (ibid., 1992). H. A. Tipping in *DNB* 4 (1885), pp. 48 f., s.v. 'Beaufort, Margaret'.

Margaret Clitherow, St. See CLITHEROW, ST MARGARET.

Margaret Mary Alacoque, St (1647–90), *Visitandine, chief founder of devotion to the *Sacred Heart (q.v.). After an unhappy childhood—she was for years unable to leave her bed, and later had to suffer much from unsympathetic relatives—she entered the Convent of the Visitation at Paray-le-Monial in central France in 1671, where she subsequently became Novice Mistress and Assistant Superior. Here she received several revelations of the Sacred Heart, the first in Dec. 1673, and the final one 18 months later. The visions revealed to her the form of the devotion, the chief features being Holy Communion on the *First Friday of each month, the Holy Hour on Thursdays, and the Feast of the Sacred Heart. Her visions were at first treated with contempt by her superiors, who regarded them as delusions, but under the influence of her temporary confessor, Bl Claude de la Colombière, SJ (d. 1682), the opposition softened and eventually ceased. The devotion, however, was not officially recognized till 75 years after her death. She was beatified in 1864 and canonized in 1920. Feast day, 16 (formerly 17) Oct.

Crit. edn. of *Vie et œuvres de la bienheureuse Marguerite-Marie Alacoque* by L. Gauthey (3rd edn., 3 vols., Paris, 1915; incl. the best text of her autobiog., also pub. separately, 1920). Eng. tr. of her autobiog. by V. Kerns (1961). The standard Lives are those by J. J. Languet (Paris, 1729; ed. L. Gauthey, 1890; Eng. tr. in the series 'The Saints and Servants of God', ed. F. W. *Faber, 1850), E. Bougaud (Paris, 1874; Eng. tr., New York, 1920), and A. Hamon, SJ (Paris, 1907; vol. 1 of his *Histoire de la dévotion au sacré-cœur*; frequently pub. separately). Among the better-known popular Lives is that of Mgr. M. Deminuid ('Les Saints', 1912); in Eng. there is a Life by G. Tickell, SJ (London, 1869). P. Blanchard, *Ste Marguerite-Marie: Expérience et doctrine* (1962). Pourrat, 4, pp. 402–19. J. Le Brun in *Dict. Sp.* 10 (1980), cols. 349–55, s.v. 'Marguerite-Marie Alacoque'. See also bibl. to SACRED HEART.

Margaret of Scotland, St (*c.*1046–93), wife of Malcolm III of Scotland, and granddaughter of the English king, Edmund Ironside. She was probably born in Hungary. In 1067, after the battle of Hastings, she left England with her mother and sister and found refuge at the court of Malcolm, to whom she was married in 1070, despite a leaning to the religious life. At her instigation many abuses were reformed, and synods held to regulate the Lenten fast and Easter Communion and the observance of the prohibited degrees in marriage. Her great personal piety found expression in her practice of prayer and fasting, in her charity to the poor, and in the royal benefactions to religion in her lifetime, which included the foundation of the Church of the Holy Trinity at Dunfermline. She was canonized by Innocent IV in 1250. She died on 16 Nov., in some places observed as her feast day. There seems no satisfactory explanation of the date of her feast day in the *Roman Martyrology of 1584, namely 10 June, to which, after being transferred to 8 July, it was restored by Innocent XII in 1693 (at the request of the deposed *James II to mark the birthday of his son). In 1969 it was transferred to 16 Nov.

Life, prob. by Turgot, her confessor and later Bp. of St Andrews, pr. in *AASS*, Jun. 2 (1698), pp. 328–35, also in [J.] Pinkerton's *Lives of the Scottish Saints*, rev. and enlarged by W. M. Metcalfe, 2 (Paisley, 1889), pp. 159–182; Eng. tr. by W. M. Metcalfe, *Ancient Lives of Scottish Saints* (ibid., 1895), pp. 298–321. The numerous modern studies include those by L. Menzies (London, 1925) and T. R. Barnett (Edinburgh and London, 1926). D. Baker, ' "A nursery of saints": St Margaret of Scotland reconsidered', in id. (ed.), *Medieval Women: Dedicated and Presented to Professor Rosalind M. T. Hill* (Studies in Church History, Subsidia, 1; 1978), pp. 119–41. W. M. Bryce, 'Saint Margaret of Scotland and her Chapel in the Castle of Edinburgh', *The Book of the Old Edinburgh Club*, 5 (Edinburgh, 1912), pp. 1–66.

Marheineke, Philipp Konrad (1780–1846), Protestant theologian. From 1811 till his death he was professor at Berlin, and from 1820 in charge also of the important Drei-

faltigkeitskirche. A warm admirer of the philosophy of G. W. F. *Hegel, then exercising a dominating influence on all aspects of German culture, Marheineke sought to invoke its support for the Christian faith, though not without radically transforming it. He professed to be, in Hegelian language, a 'theologian of the concept' (*Begriffstheologe*), as opposed to a 'theologian of faith' (the standpoint of traditional historic Christianity) or 'of feeling' (F. D. E. *Schleiermacher). Characteristic of his theological method and attitude was his thesis that 'the Church is the truth (*Wahrheit*) of the State, the State the reality (*Wirklichkeit*) of the Church'. The Protestant and Catholic Confessions were to be united in a higher Hegelian synthesis. His writings include a *Symbolik* (3 vols., 1810–14, which brought him into conflict with J. A. *Möhler), a history of the German Reformation (2 vols., 1816), and *Die Bedeutung der Hegelschen Philosophie in der christlichen Theologie* (1842). Much of his most characteristic teaching was formulated in his lectures, many of which were published by his pupils soon after his death.

His theological lectures were ed. by S. Matthies and W. Vatke (4 vols., Berlin, 1847–9). [M.] E. Ihle, *P. K. Marheineke: Der Einfluss der Philosophie auf sein theologisches System* (Diss., Leipzig, 1938). K. *Barth, *Die protestantische Theologie im 19. Jahrhundert* (Zurich, 1947), pp. 442–9; Eng. tr. (1972), pp. 491–8. V. Drehsen in *TRE* 22 (1992), pp. 109–15.

Maria Laach ('Maria ad lacum'), *Benedictine abbey near Andernach, some 15 miles NW of Koblenz. Founded in 1093, it flourished under the customary of *Cluny. The fine Romanesque church, with five towers and a dome, was consecrated in 1156. In 1474 the community joined the Bursfeld Union, taking a leading role after the Reformation. In the aftermath of the French Revolution, the abbey was suppressed in 1802; the buildings were secularized, the church taken into Prussian government possession (in 1815), and the property granted to individuals. The *Jesuits acquired Maria Laach in 1862/3 and in 1864 established a *collegium maximum*. They produced various learned works with titles associated with Maria Laach, including the periodical *Stimmen aus Maria Laach* (1871–1915, thereafter called *Stimmen der Zeit*). They were expelled in 1872 during the *Kulturkampf*, and sold the property to the Benedictines of *Beuron in 1892. Under Ildefons Herwegen (abbot 1913–46; commemorated in the Abt Herwegen Institut established in 1948), Maria Laach became a centre of liturgical study and played an influential part in the *Liturgical Movement. Herwegen himself edited *Ecclesia Orans* (1918 ff.), a popular series of source material and studies of liturgical subjects, while monks of Maria Laach, including O. *Casel, undertook academic work in the field of liturgy, publishing the *Jahrbuch für Liturgiewissenschaft* (1921–38; revived as *Archiv für Liturgiewissenschaft*, 1950 ff.), as well as series of texts and studies. From 1921 a 'missa recitata' or 'dialogue mass' was celebrated from a *westward position in the crypt of the abbey church; this so-called 'crypt mass' was a major contribution to the Liturgical Movement, and a spiritual source of resistance to the Nazis.

A. Schippers, OSB, *Das Laacher Münster* (1927), and other works by this author. H. Emonds, OSB (ed.), *Enkainia: Gesammelte Arbeiten zum 800jährigen Weihegedächtnis der Abteikirche Maria Laach am 24. August 1956* (Düsseldorf [1956]). T. Bogler,

OSB (ed.), *Benedikt und Ignatius: Maria Laach als Collegium maximum der Gesellschaft Jesu 1863–1872–1892* (Liturgie und Mönchtum, Laacher Heft 32; 1963). B. Neunheuser, OSB, ' "Das Krypta-Messe" in Maria Laach', in T. Bogler, OSB (ed.), *Beten und Arbeiten* (ibid. 28, 1961), pp. 70–82; id., 'Towards a history of Maria Laach between the Wars, 1918–1939', *Monastic Studies*, 13 (1982), pp. 217–26. I. Herwegen, OSB, in *CE* 9 (1910), p. 658.

Mariana, Juan (1536–1624), Spanish *Jesuit. He joined the order in 1554, and held teaching appointments at Rome (1561–5), Loreto (1565–7), Messina (1567–9), Paris (1569–74), and Toledo (from 1574). He became famous through his book *De Rege et Regis Institutione* (1559), justifying tyrannicide. The book encouraged the belief that the Jesuits were responsible for the assassination of *Henry IV of France and the *Gunpowder Plot in England, and in 1610 the Jesuit General, C. *Aquaviva, expressly forbade members of the order to teach this doctrine. Mariana is also one of the foremost historians of Spain (the 'Spanish Livy'). In 1592 he issued his *Historia de rebus Hispaniae*, translated into Spanish as *Historia general de España* (2 vols., 1601).

An Eng. tr. of his *History of Spain* was pub. at London, 1699. G. Cirot, *Études sur l'historiographie espagnole: Mariana historien* (Bibliothèque de la Fondation Thiers, 8; 1905). M. Ballesteros-Gaibrois, *Juan de Mariana* (2 vols., Santander, 1938–9). J. Laures, SJ, *The Political Economy of Juan de Mariana* (New York, 1928); M. B. Amzalak, *As teorias monetários do Padre João de Mariana* (1944). G. Lewy, *Constitutionalism and Statecraft during the Golden Age of Spain: A Study of the political philosophy of Juan de Mariana, S.J.* (Geneva, 1960). D. Ferraro, *Tradizione e Ragione in Juan de Mariana* [1989]. F. Asensio, 'El profesorado de Juan de Mariana y su influjo en la vida del escritor', *Hispana*, 53 (1953), pp. 581–639. Sommervogel, 5 (1894), cols. 547–67; Polgár, 2 (1990), pp. 488–92. A. Lehmkuhl in *CE* 9 (1910), pp. 659 f., s.v.; E. Rey in Q. Alden Vaquero and others (eds.), *Diccionario de historia eclesiástica de España*, 3 (1973), pp. 1417 f., s.v., with bibl.

Marianists. The 'Society of Mary', of Bordeaux (to be distinguished from the *Marists, q.v.). The congregation, which consists of priests and laymen, was founded at Bordeaux in 1817 by the theologian Guillaume-Joseph Chaminade (1761–1850); it received first approval by decree of praise from Rome in 1839 and definitive approval of its constitutions in 1891. It was instituted to fight religious indifference, and its members, who devote themselves esp. to educational work, add to the three vows of poverty, chastity, and obedience a fourth, promising stability in the service of the BVM, originally expressed in the daily recitation of the *Rosary and of the *Little Office of Our Lady. The congregation spread rapidly in many European countries as well as in America, Africa, and Asia. The members of the female Institute, the 'Daughters of Mary', founded in 1816, also devote themselves to education; their constitutions were finally confirmed in 1888.

Lives of the founder by J. Simler (Paris, 1901), H. Rousseau, SM (ibid., 1913), G. Goyau (ibid., 1914), and K. Burton (Milwaukee, 1949). G. J. Ruppel, SM, in *NCE* 9 (1967), pp. 214–16, s.v., with bibl.; V. Vasey, SM, and A. Albano, SM, in *DIP* 8 (1988), cols. 1616–24, s.v. 'Società di Maria'.

Mariavites. A Polish sect, founded in 1906 by J. Kowalski, a priest of Warsaw, and Felicia Kozlowska, a *Tertiary sister (d. 1922), on their excommunication from the RC Church. Many years earlier the latter had laid claim to

private revelations and these formed the doctrinal basis of the new communities. Their name is derived from their profession of great devotion to the BVM ('qui Mariae vitam imitantur'). They acknowledged the first seven *Oecumenical Councils, accepted the '*Filioque' as a 'theological opinion', and incorporated into their practice many ascetic elements, combined with some unconventional arrangements about the marriage of the clergy. Relations having been established with the *Old Catholics, in 1909 Kowalski was consecrated a bishop by the Abp. of Utrecht; and in 1911 they were officially recognized by the Duma. But after a few brief years of prosperity their numbers and influence declined, their discipline deteriorated, and in 1924 the Old Catholics severed communion with them.

K. Gajowski, *Mariavitensekte: Einige Blätter aus der neuesten Kirchengeschichte Russisch-Polens* (Cracow, 1911); A. Rhode, *Bei den Mariaviten: Eindrücke von einer neuen romfreien katholischen Kirche* (1911). J. Peterkiewicz, *The Third Adam* (1975). R. Janin, 'Les Mariavites et l'orthodoxie', *ÉO* 30 (1927), pp. 216–20; M. Niwinski, 'Les Mariavites de Pologne', *Revue apologétique*, 54 (1932), pp. 570–80. E. Appolis, 'Une Église des derniers temps. L'Eglise Mariavite', *Archives de Sociologie des Religions*, 19 (1965), pp. 51–67. I. Rhode in *RGG* (3rd edn.), 4 (1960), cols. 752–4, s.v. 'Mariaviten'.

Mariolatry. A term derived from 'Maria' and '*latria*' (Gk. λατρεία, worship), denoting erroneous attribution of Divine honours to the BVM. An early instance of it is found in the 4th cent., when the sect of the *Collyridians was condemned by St *Epiphanius for offering sacrificial worship to Mary. A more recent example is the cult of the BVM in the Eucharist, advocated by the Franciscan *Recollect, Z. de Someire, and condemned by *Benedict XIV. By Protestants the word is often employed in an abusive sense of what they consider the excessive devotion to the BVM in the RC Church.

Mariology. The systematic study of the person of the Blessed Virgin *Mary and of her place in the economy of the *Incarnation.

Marisco, Adama de. See ADAM OF MARSH.

Marists. The 'Society of Mary' was founded at Lyons in 1816 by the Ven. Jean Claude Marie Colin (1790–1875), though the original idea seems to have come from his fellow seminarian, Jean Claude Courveille (1787–1866), who left the Marists in 1826. The Society was approved by *Gregory XVI in 1836, when the first 20 Marists took simple perpetual vows and the W. Pacific was allotted to them as their special mission field, and finally sanctioned in 1873. It spread rapidly in many European countries, in N. America, and esp. in *Australia and *New Zealand, and was introduced into England by N. *Wiseman in 1850. The congregation comprises priests and lay brothers whose main activities are educational and missionary work. Their rule, which is based on that of the *Jesuits, aims esp. at fostering devotion to the BVM. Several other institutes are connected with the Marists, among them the Marist School-brothers founded in 1817 by the Ven. Marcellin Joseph Benedict Champagnat and approved by the Holy See in 1863 and 1903, the Marist Sisters (Sisters of the Holy Name of Mary), founded by Colin in 1823 for the education of young girls, and the Third Order of the Society of Mary, founded in 1850 for persons living in the world, with its seat in Rome.

J. Coste, SM, and G. Lessard, SM (eds.), *Origines Maristes (1786–1836)* (Fontes historici Societatis Mariae, 3; 4 vols, Rome, 1960–7). H. [M.] Laracy, *Marists and Melanesians* (Honolulu, 1976). S. W. Hosie, *Anonymous Apostle: The Life of Jean-Claude Colin* (New York, 1967). J. L. White, SM, in *NCE* 9 (1967), pp. 229 f., s.v. 'Marist Fathers'; J. Coste, SM, in *DIP* 8 (1988), cols. 1624–7, s.v. 'Società di Maria'; A. G. di Pietro, ibid. 4 (1977), cols. 653–65, s.v. 'Fratelli Maristi delle Scuole'.

Maritain, Jacques (1882–1973), French *Thomist philosopher. A native of Paris, he studied at the *Sorbonne, where he came under the influence of H. *Bergson. He was converted to Roman Catholicism in 1906. After a short period devoted to biology at Heidelberg (1907–8), he turned to the study of St *Thomas Aquinas, whose philosophy he sought to relate to modern culture. He held professorial chairs successively at the *Institut Catholique in Paris (1914–33), at the Institute for Mediaeval Studies in Toronto (1933–45) and at Princeton (1948–52). From 1945 to 1948 he was French ambassador to the Holy See. In 1961 (after the death of his wife in the previous year) he went to live with the *Little Brothers of Jesus in Toulouse and in 1970 he became a Little Brother himself.

In his numerous books Maritain endeavoured to apply the classical doctrines of Thomist philosophy in turn to metaphysics and theoretical philosophy, moral, social, and political philosophy, the philosophy of education, history, and culture, as well as to art and poetry. He also wrote on the relations of philosophy to religious experience and mysticism. His principal works include *La Philosophie bergsonienne* (1914; Eng. tr., New York, 1955; a critique of his former master); *Distinguer pour unir, ou Les degrés du savoir* (1932; Eng. tr., 1959); *Humanisme intégral* (1936; Eng. tr., 1938); *La Philosophie morale* (1960; Eng. tr., 1964), and *Le Paysan de la Garonne* (1966; Eng. tr., 1968), in which he sought to present a synthesis of his views on life.

Complete edn. of his works (together with those of his wife, Raïssa) by J.-M. Allion and others (15 vols., Fribourg and Paris, 1982–95). Selected works, ed. H. Bars (Bibliothèque Européenne, 2 vols. [1975–9]). Festschrift for his Sixtieth Birthday (New York, 1943); *Jacques Maritain: Son œuvre philosophique* (Bibliothèque de la *Revue Thomiste* [1949]), both with lists of works. Studies by G. B. Phelan (London, 1937), J. Croteau, OMI (Ottawa, 1955), H. Bars (Paris, 1959), L. F. de A. Sampaio, CR (Paris, 1963), G. Forni (Bologna [1965]), J. W. Hanke (The Hague, 1973), B. E. Doering (Notre Dame, Ind., and London, 1983), ed. D. W. Hudson and M. J. Mancini (Mercer, Ga. [1987]) and by R. McInerny (Notre Dame, Ind. [1988]). His 90th birthday was marked by a special issue of *New Scholasticism*, 46 (1972), pp. 1–128, incl. list of his works, pp. 118–28.

Marius Mercator (early 5th cent.), a Latin Christian writer, formerly regarded as of African origin, but more prob. born in Italy. A friend and disciple of St *Augustine, *c*.418 in Rome he wrote against *Pelagius two works which have not survived. Some ten years later, when in Constantinople, he again wrote in defence of orthodoxy, this time attacking both *Nestorians and Pelagians. A collec-

tion of his writings, compiled about 100 years after his time, has survived in a Vatican MS (Cod. Vat. Pal. 234). It consists largely of Mercator's translations of and replies to Nestorius' writings, made (acc. to E. *Schwartz) for the Latin-speaking monks of Thrace, and is one of the more important sources for our knowledge of Nestorius' doctrines.

Writings ed. J. *Garnier, SJ (Paris, 1673; repr. in J. P. Migne, *PL* 48), on the basis of a Beauvais MS, since lost. Another edn. by É. *Baluze (Paris, 1684) from Vat. Pal. 234. Crit. text, with discussion, by E. Schwartz in *ACO* 1. 5 (1), pp. 5–70 (acc. to Schwartz, the Counter-Anathematisms of Nestorius, ibid., pp. 71–84, although commonly ascribed to Marius Mercator, are not his work). E. Amann, 'L'affaire Nestorius vue de Rome', *Rev. S.R.* 23 (1949), pp. 5–37, esp. pp. 5–17 (against the view that Mercator acted as an agent of Pope *Celestine in Constantinople); S. Prete, *Mario Mercatore, polemista antipelagiano* (Scrinium Theologicum, 11; Turin, 1958). V. Grossi in Quasten (cont.), *Patrology*, 4 (1986), pp. 499–501. W. Eltester in *PW* 14 (1930), cols. 1831–5; O. Wermelinger in *Dict. Sp.* 10 (1980), cols. 610–15, s.v.

Marius Victorinus. See VICTORINUS AFER.

Mark, St, Evangelist. *Papias asserts that Mark, having become the interpreter of St *Peter, set down accurately everything that he remembered of the words and actions of the Lord, and Mark is associated with Peter in 1 Pet. 5: 13. He has traditionally been identified with John Mark, the cousin of St *Barnabas (Col. 4: 10), a Jew, who set out with Barnabas and St *Paul on their first missionary journey, but for reasons which failed to satisfy Paul turned back (Acts 12: 25; 13: 5 and 13; 15: 37 f.); afterwards he accompanied Barnabas on a mission to *Cyprus (Acts 15: 39), and he was in Rome with St Paul (Col. 4: 10, Philem. 24, 2 Tim. 4: 11). The identification may not be justified. Acc. to *Eusebius (*HE* 2. 16. 1 and 2. 24. 1), who was perhaps relying on early sources, Mark went to *Alexandria and was its first bishop, while in later tradition he is also associated with *Venice. The tradition that Mark was κολοβοδάκτυλος (prob. 'stump-fingered', i.e. Mark himself, and not an allusion to the brevity of his Gospel) is found in the *Anti-Marcionite Prologues and in St *Hippolytus, *Haer.* 7. 30. Feast day, 25 Apr.

The processional Major Litanies (*Litaniae Majores*) traditionally observed at Rome on 25 Apr. (but abolished in 1969) appear to have arisen quite independently of the feast. They go back to the time of St *Gregory the Great (d. 604), when they were introduced as a Christian substitute for the pagan *robigalia* on that day.

AASS, Apr. 3 (1675), pp. 344–58, and Sept. 7 (1760), pp. 379–90. C. N. Jefford in *Anchor Bible Dictionary*, 4 (1992), pp. 557 f., s.v. 'Mark, John', with further refs. On the Major Litanies, see bibl. s.v. LITANY.

Mark, Gospel of St. The earliest reference to the Gospel comes through *Papias, who states, on the authority of *John the Presbyter, that St *Mark was 'the interpreter (ἑρμηνευτής)' of St *Peter, adding that he wrote down accurately what he heard and remembered. Later tradition amplifies Papias' statement and connects the Gospel with *Rome.

The Gospel may have been written by John Mark (see the preceding entry); there is no obvious reason why tradition should have wrongly assigned it to so unimportant a character. 'Mark', however, is a common name. Speculation has sometimes identified the young man in *Gethsemane (14: 51 f.) with the author.

The Gospel is written in 'Koine *Greek', i.e. the popular language that was the *lingua franca* of the E. Mediterranean. It is the least polished of the Gospels, though the narratives are extremely vivid and full of circumstantial detail. Mark has some knowledge of Palestine and Jewish partics and officials, and his Aramaic quotations are striking. He nevertheless presents Jesus as not bound by Jewish laws on food (7: 19) or the *sabbath (2: 27 f.). A date soon after the death of Peter (commonly put in AD 64) and during the siege of *Jerusalem has been accepted by many scholars; others prefer a date soon after AD 70.

Many attempts have been made to detect sources underlying Mark, whether some continuous primitive Gospel or briefer collections (e.g. Petrine material, parables, or controversy stories, etc.), but no theories have been firmly established. With the rise of *Form Criticism it came to be held that in oral tradition the material was used and preserved in small units, and that Mark, or someone before him, put them together 'like beads on a string'. Whether he had access to a firm historical framework has been a matter of dispute. Interest later shifted to Mark's own contribution as author or editor (see REDACTION CRITICISM), but no consensus emerged and more recently wider literary approaches to the Gospel have become common.

Mark makes it clear that Jesus is *Messiah (q.v.) and Son of God (1: 1). In the narrative this truth, though known to demons, and implicit in the miracles and in the Lord's authority as teacher, is disclosed only by degrees (8: 29; 14: 62; 15: 39), and the disciples are slow to comprehend. At least until the entry into Jerusalem, Christ maintains an element of secrecy (8: 30, 9: 9), preferring to refer to Himself in the enigmatic phrase '*Son of Man'. See MESSIANIC SECRET.

The narrative opens with the preaching of St *John the Baptist. After the Baptism and Temptation of Christ, the Messianic ministry at once begins: disciples are called, miracles are performed, and teaching is given, chiefly in the form of *parables. The whole emphasizes the idea of fulfilment; the *Kingdom of God, though still the object of hope, is already active in Christ. A turning point is reached at 8: 27 ff., with Peter's confession that Jesus is the Messiah. From that point the burden of the Lord's teaching is that the Son of Man must suffer, die, and rise from the dead. The story of the Passion (which many have held to have existed as a continuous narrative at an earlier date) includes the account of the Last Supper and describes the death of Christ as a fulfilment of OT prophecy and as a sacrifice inaugurating the new covenant. The Crucifixion is followed by the Resurrection; but Mark's Gospel concludes abruptly at 16: 8, perhaps because Mark intended it to end there, possibly because the end has been lost. 16: 9–20 is one of two supplements, not in the oldest MSS, which were added to the Gospel at an early date. See ARISTION; also MARCAN HYPOTHESIS and SYNOPTIC PROBLEM.

The patristic and medieval commentators paid scant attention to St Mark's Gospel, probably because of its brevity and the inclusion of nearly all its matter in the other Synoptics. Those who commented on it include *Victor of Antioch, *Theophylact, and *Euthymius Zigabenus among the Greeks and *Bede among the Latins. In modern times, on the other hand, it has attracted close attention from all students of the Gospels. Comm. incl. those of E. P. Gould (ICC, 1896), H. B. *Swete (London, 1898), M. J. *Lagrange (Études bibliques, 1911), A. E. J. Rawlinson (West. Comm., 1925), E. Lohmeyer (KEK, 10th edn.; 1937), V. Taylor (London, 1952; 2nd edn., 1966), P. Carrington (Cambridge, 1960), D. E. Nineham (Pelican Gospel Commentaries, 1963; rev. edn., 1968), E. Schweizer (Das Neue Testament Deutsch, 1967; Eng. tr., 1971), W. L. Lane (New London Commentary on the New Testament, 1974), H. Anderson (New Cent. Bib., 1976), J. Gnilka (Evangelisch-Katholischer Kommentar zum Neuen Testament, 2 vols., 1978–9), C. S. Mann (Anchor Bible, 1986), D. Lührmann (Hb. NT, 1987), R. A. Guelich (Word Biblical Comm., 34; Dallas, Tex. [1986 ff.]), and M. D. Hooker (Black's NT Comm., 1991).

Other studies include R. H. *Lightfoot, *The Gospel Message of St Mark* (1950); A. M. Farrer, *A Study in St Mark* (1951; 2nd edn., 1966); W. Marxsen, *Der Evangelist Markus: Studien zur Redaktionsgeschichte des Evangeliums* (Forschungen zur Religion und Literatur des Alten und Neuen Testaments, NF 49; 1956; 2nd edn., 1959; Eng. tr., 1969); T. A. Burkill, *Mysterious Revelation: An Examination of the Philosophy of St Mark's Gospel* (Ithaca, NY, 1963); id., *New Light on the Earliest Gospel* (ibid., 1972); E. Trocmé, *La Formation de l'Évangile selon Marc* (1963; Eng. tr., 1975); C. F. Evans, *The Beginning of the Gospel* (1968); R. P. Martin, *Mark: Evangelist and Theologian* (Exeter [1972]); W. H. Kelber (ed.), *The Passion in Mark: Studies on Mark 14–16* (Philadelphia [1976]); W. R. Farmer, *The Last Twelve Verses of Mark* (Cambridge, 1974); H. C. Kee, *Community of the New Age: Studies in Mark's Gospel* (1977); E. Best, *Mark: The Gospel as Story* (Edinburgh, 1983); id., *Disciples and Discipleship: Studies in the Gospel according to Mark* (ibid., 1986), and other works of this author; M. Hengel, *Studies in the Gospel of Mark* [Eng. tr. of various papers pub. 1982–4] (1985); W. Telford (ed.), *The Interpretation of Mark* (Issues in Religion and Theology, 7; 1985); B. van Iersal, *Belichting van het Bijbelboek: Marcus* (1986; Eng. tr., *Reading Mark*, Edinburgh, 1989); C. Myers, *Binding the Strong Man: A Political Reading of Mark's Story of Jesus* (Maryknoll, NY [1988]); M. A. Tolbert, *Sowing the Gospel: Mark's World in Literary-Historical Perspective* (Minneapolis [1989]); R. M. Fowler, *Let the Reader Understand: Reader-Response Criticism and the Gospel of Mark* (Minneapolis [1991]). See also bibl. to SYNOPTIC PROBLEM.

Mark, Liturgy of St. The traditional Greek Eucharistic Liturgy of the Church of *Alexandria, formerly used by the Egyptian *Melchites. It survives in various forms in three late MSS, the Cod. Rossanensis (Vat. gr. 1970; 13th cent.; the source of the *textus receptus*), the Rotulus Vaticanus (Vat. gr. 2281; 13th cent.), and the Rotulus Messanensis (Cod. Messin. gr. 177; 12th cent.). Behind these texts, all much altered by foreign influences (*Constantinople and/or *Jerusalem), lies a primitive local Egyptian text, in which the great intercessory prayer stood before the *Sanctus and there was no *Benedictus at the end of the Sanctus. In 1928 a fragment of the authentic text of the Liturgy was recovered on a Strasbourg papyrus (4th–5th cent.), and in 1966 a further papyrus fragment (4th cent.) at Barcelona was identified. Other Egyptian fragments have been discovered which show a close affinity to the text, esp. the *Der Balyzeh Papyrus. A modified form of the rite in Coptic (known alternatively as 'The Coptic Liturgy of St Mark' or 'of St Cyril') is still in use in the *Coptic Church; another form of it, in Ethiopic, in the *Ethiopian Church.

Text in E. *Renaudot, *Liturgiarum Orientalium Collectio*, 1 (Paris, 1716), pp. 131–65; in C. A. Swainson, *The Greek Liturgies*

(1884), pp. 2–73; and in Brightman, *LEW*, pp. 115–88. Crit. edn., incl. readings from the frags. and complete text of some of them, with conjectural reconstruction (in Eng.) of the anaphora of St Mark *c.*350 and *c.*450, comm., and full bibl., by G. J. Cuming, *The Liturgy of St Mark* (Orientalia Christiana Analecta, 234; Rome, 1990). The Strasbourg papyrus was orig. ed. by M. Andrieu and P. Collomp, *Rev. S.R.* 8 (1928), pp. 489–515; that at Barcelona by L. Roca-Puig, *Aegyptus*, 46 (1966), pp. 91 f.

Mark, Secret Gospel of. In 1958, at the monastery of Mar Saba near Jerusalem, Morton Smith found a letter ascribed to *Clement of Alexandria written on the blank pages at the back of a 17th-cent. edition of the works of *Ignatius. It gave warning of a 'secret Gospel of Mark' falsified by the *Carpocratians, and quoted from it. Even if the letter is authentic, Smith's contention that the quotations go back to an original Aramaic version of Mark, which served as a source both for the canonical Mark and John, has not found favour among scholars.

M. Smith, *Clement of Alexandria and a Secret Gospel of Mark* (Cambridge, Mass., 1973), with text and Eng. tr. of the letter, pp. 446–52. Id., *The Secret Gospel: The Discovery and Interpretation of the Secret Gospel according to Mark* (New York, 1973; London, 1974). H. Merkel in Schneemelcher, 1 (5th edn., 1987), pp. 89–92, with bibl; Eng. tr., 1 (1991), pp. 106–9.

Mark the Hermit (date disputed; prob. early 5th or possibly 6th cent.), ascetical writer. Very little is known of his life. He is said to have been a disciple of St *Chrysostom (like his contemporary, *Nilus the Ascetic), but this is not certain. He may at one period of his life have been abbot of a community near Ancyra; later he was a hermit, possibly in Palestine or in Egypt. H. Chadwick has argued that he is to be identified with Mark, priest and hegumen of a monastery near Tarsus, mentioned by *Severus of Antioch in two letters written between 515 and 518. His writings, for the most part of a practical character, include treatises 'On Repentance', 'On the Spiritual Law', and 'On Those who suppose Justification is from Works'. His vigorous attack on human merit in the last-named writing commended him to older Protestant theologians. A work 'On Temperance' (Κεφάλαια νηπτικά), which is ascribed to him, is certainly spurious; and another 'On Fasting' (Περὶ νηστείας) is now attributed to *Marcian the Monk.

Works in J. P. Migne, *PL* 65. 893–1140. His 'Adversus Nestorianos', pub. from a 13th-cent. Jerusalem MS by A. Papadopoulos-Kerameus at St Petersburg in 1891, was issued in an improved text by J. Kunze, *Marcus Eremita* (Leipzig, 1895; important study, esp. on Mark's Baptismal Creed), pp. 6–30; further ed. by A. Rocchi in Mai, *NPB* 10, pt. 1 (1905), pp. 201–47. Fr. tr. of his works by C.-A. Zirnheld, OSCO (Spiritualité Orientale, 41; Bellafontaine [1985]); Ger. tr., with valuable introd., by O. Hesse (Bibliothek der griechischen Literatur, 19; 1985). K. T. Ware, 'The Sacrament of Baptism and the Ascetic Life in the Teaching of Mark the Monk', in F. L. Cross (ed.), *Studia Patristica*, 10 (TU 107; 1970), pp. 441–52. H. Chadwick, 'The Identity and Date of Mark the Hermit', *Eastern Churches Review*, 4 (1972), pp. 125–30 (repr. in his *History and Thought of the Early Church* (1982), no. 15); O. Hesse, 'Was Mark the Monk a Sixth-Century Hegumen near Tarsus?' [No!], ibid. 8 (1976), pp. 174–8. *CPG* 3 (1979), pp. 184–8 (nos. 6090–102). J. Gribomont, OSB, in *Dict. Sp.* 10 (1980), cols. 274–83, s.v. 'Marc le Moine'; O. Hesse in *TRE* 22 (1992), pp. 101–4, s.v. 'Marcus Eremita'.

Marks of the Church. See NOTES OF THE CHURCH.

Marmion, Columba (1858–1923), Abbot of *Maredsous. He was an Irishman by birth, who, though he lived mainly surrounded by French culture, retained his Irish characteristics and sympathies till his death. In 1886 he entered the Benedictine house at Maredsous; in 1899 he became prior of the Abbey of Mont-César at Louvain; and from 1909 till his death was Abbot of Maredsous. Basing his teaching on the Christocentric teaching of St *Paul, he drew largely on the patristic and liturgical traditions of *Benedictine monasticism, without at the same time failing to appreciate *Thomist theology. He was an unusually gifted spiritual writer and director, whose main works, the fruit of series of spiritual addresses, are *Le Christ, vie de l'âme* (1918, over 100,000 copies issued; Eng. tr., 1922), *Le Christ dans ses mystères* (1919; Eng. tr., 1924), and *Le Christ, idéal du moine* (1922; Eng. tr., 1926).

Life by R. Thibaut (Maredsous, 1929; Eng. tr., 1932). M. M. Philipon, OP, *La Doctrine spirituelle de Dom Marmion* (1954; Eng. tr., 1956). T. Delforge, OSB, in *Dict. Sp.* 10 (1980), cols. 627–30, s.v.

Marnix, Philipp van (1540–98), Baron de Sainte-Aldegonde, Dutch *Calvinist theologian and statesman. Having studied at *Geneva under J. *Calvin and T. *Beza, he became a lifelong upholder of rigid Calvinist theology. Between 1562 and 1569 he won fame by his Protestant and nationalist writings, of which the most celebrated was the bitterly satirical *De biënkorf der heilige roomsche kerche* (1569; Eng. tr. by G. Gilpin, 1579). About 1566–7 he took up arms as an anti-Spanish leader, and formed a close friendship with William the Silent, for whose conversion to Calvinism he was partly responsible. A constant adviser to the Prince of Orange, he became a member of the Council of State in 1577 and burgomaster of Antwerp in 1583, but lost his political influence in 1585 by his surrender of the town to the Duke of Parma. Devoting himself for the rest of his life to literary activity, most notably to his Dutch version of the Psalms, he was charged by the States of Holland with the translation of the Bible, a task which he did not fulfil.

Œuvres de P. de Marnix de Sainte-Aldegonde, with introd. by E. Quinet (8 vols., Brussels, 1857–60); *Godsdienstige en Kerkelijke Geschriften*, ed. J. J. van Toorenenbergen (3 vols., The Hague, 1871–91); *Epistulae*, ed. A. Gerlo and R. de Smet (Brussels, 1990 ff.). A. A. van Schelven, *Marnix van Sint Aldegonde* (Utrecht, 1939). W. A. Nolet, *Marnix als Theoloog: Historische Inleiding* (Amsterdam, 1948), with bibl. F. van Kalken and T. Jonckheere, *Marnix de Sainte Aldegonde* (Neuchâtel [1952]). Facsimile of the *Catalogue of the Library of Philips van Marnix van Sint-Aldegonde sold by auction (July 6th), Leiden, Christophorus Guyot, 1599* (Nieuwkoop, 1964), with introd. in Eng. T. Schott and S. D. van Veen in *PRE* (3rd edn.), 12 (1903), pp. 347–55, s.v.

Maronites. A Christian community of Syrian origin, the greater part of whom still live in their native land of Lebanon, though some are to be found elsewhere in Syria, Israel, and Cyprus. Many have also emigrated to N. and S. America and to Australia. Since 1182 they have been in formal communion with the RC Church.

By their own theologians it is claimed that their existence can be traced back to St Maro, a friend of St *Chrysostom (d. 407), whose disciples shortly after his death founded the monastery on the Orontes that now goes by his name, and that the modern Maronites derive directly from this foundation. Their origin as a separate community, however, goes back only to the *Monothelite controversy of the 7th and 8th cents., when they rejected the teaching of the Third Council of *Constantinople that in the Person of Christ there are two wills, the one human and the other Divine. Their monastery on Mt. Lebanon was destroyed by the Arab invasion at the beginning of the 10th cent. Since their union with Rome in the 12th cent. relations with the W. have been continuously maintained. In 1584 *Gregory XIII founded a Maronite college in Rome, which was later the home of the *Assemani and several other notable scholars. In the 19th cent. they suffered severe treatment at the hands of the Turks and the Druses. Today they constitute the largest single religious body in the Lebanon.

As a *Uniat body they possess their own liturgy, which is in essence an Antiochene rite in the Syriac language, in parts modified by Latin influences. They employ several (Syriac) anaphoras, of which the oldest, known from its opening word as the 'Sharrar', has links with the anaphora of '*Addai and Mari'. Their hierarchy consists of a *patriarch (whose see is Bkerké in Lebanon), 10 bishops (Aleppo, Baalbek, Beirut, Cairo, Cyprus, Damascus, Sarba, Sidon, Tripoli, Tyre), an Apostolic Exarch in USA, an auxiliary bishop in Brazil and three titular bishops.

T. Anaissi (ed.), *Bullarium Maronitarum* (Rome, 1911). P. Dib (ed.), *Quelques Documents pour servir à l'histoire des Maronites* (1945). J. Gribomont [OSB], 'Documents sur les origines de l'Église maronite', *Parole de l'Orient*, 5 (1974), pp. 95–132. M. *Lequien, OP, *Oriens Christianus*, 3 (Rome, 1740), cols. 1–100. P. Dib, *Histoire de l'Église maronite* (2 vols., Beirut, 1962; Eng. tr., Detroit, 1971). Id. in *Codificazione Canonica Orientale*, Fonti, fasc. 8 (Rome, 1932), pp. 90–116; P. Sfair, ibid., fasc. 12, *Ius Particolare Maronitarum* (ibid., 1933). G. J. Mahfoud, *L'Organisation monastique dans l'Église maronite* (Bibliothèque de l'Université Saint-Esprit, Kaslik, Jounieh, Liban, 1; Beirut, 1967). M. Hayek, *Liturgie maronite: Histoire et textes eucharistiques* (1964). J. Feghali, *Histoire du droit canonique de l'Église maronite*, 1 (Bibliothèque de la faculté de droit canonique de Paris; 1962; no more pub.). P. Raphael, *Le Rôle du Collège maronite romain dans l'orientalisme aux XVIIᵉ et XVIIIᵉ siècles* (Beirut, 1950). A. S. Atiya, *A History of Eastern Christianity* (1968), pp. 389–423. J. Raymond, *Essai de bibliographie maronite* (Bibliothèque de l'Université Saint-Esprit, 9; Kaslik, Lebanon, 1980). P. Dib in *DTC* 10 (pt. 1; 1928), cols. 1–142, s.v., with full bibl.; P. Sfair and A. Raes, SJ, in *EC* 8 (1952), cols. 177–84, s.v. 'Maroniti'; E. El-Hayek in *NCE* 9 (1967), pp. 245–53, s.v. 'Maronite Rite'; M. Hayek in *Dict. Sp.* 10 (1980), cols. 631–44, s.v. 'Maronite (Église)'. On canon law in force before 1990, C. de Clercq in *DDC* 6 (1957), cols. 811–29, s.v. 'Maronite (Droit canonique)'.

Marot, Clément (*c.*1497–1544), French poet and translator. Some controversy surrounds his exact religious affiliations, but his association with the circle of Marguerite de Navarre would clearly ally him with *évangélisme*, a biblical and humanist, though in other respects essentially orthodox, tendency. He none the less went into exile to Ferrara and Venice in 1535, in the intolerant climate following the Protestant manifestations known as the *affaire des placards*; and again, to *Geneva, in 1542. His French verse paraphrase of 49 selected Psalms appeared between 1538 and 1542. It was received with great acclaim by the Protestant community. T. *Beza admired his work and in 1562 completed a verse translation of the Psalms based on it, thereby bringing into being the first vernacular Psalter in French.

Crit. edn. of all his works by C. A. Mayer: *Épîtres* (London, 1958), *Œuvres satiriques* (ibid., 1962), *Œuvres lyriques* (ibid., 1964), *Œuvres diverses* (ibid., 1966), *Epigrammes* (ibid., 1970), and *Traductions* (Geneva, 1980). O. Douen, *Clément Marot et le psautier huguenot* (2 vols., 1878–9); P. A. Becker, *Clément Marots Psalmenübersetzungen* (Ber. (Sächs.), 72, Heft 1, for 1920; 1921); P. Leblanc, *La poésie religieuse de Clément Marot* (1955); C. A. Mayer, *La religion de Marot* (Travaux d'Humanisme et de Renaissance, 39; 1960); M. Jeanneret, 'Marot traducteur des Psaumes entre le néoplatonisme et la Réforme', *Bibliothèque d'Humanisme et Renaissance*, 27 (1965), pp. 629–43; id., *Poésie et tradition biblique au XVIᵉ siècle: Recherches stylistiques sur les paraphrases des psaumes de Marot à Malherbe* (1969), pp. 51–87. M. A. Screech, *Marot évangélique* (Geneva, 1967; Eng. adaptation, *Clément Marot: A Renaissance Poet Discovers his Gospel*, Studies in Medieval and Reformation Thought, 54; Leiden, 1994). H. P. Clive, *Clément Marot: An Annotated Bibliography* (1983).

Marprelate Tracts. A series of violent and frequently scurrilous *Puritan tracts attacking *episcopacy, issued under the pseudonym of Martin Marprelate in 1588 and 1589. They reflect the heightened atmosphere of confrontation between Puritanism and the Church establishment which resulted from Abp. J. *Whitgift's drive for conformity from 1583. The titles (abbreviated) of the seven which survive are *The Epistle, The Epitome, Mineral and Metaphysical School-points, Hay any Work for Cooper, Theses Martinianae, The Just Censure and Reproof,* and *The Protestation.* They appear to have been published successively at East Moseley (Surrey), Fawsley House (nr. Daventry), Coventry, Wolston, and prob. Haseley (both Warwicks). Among those accused of writing them were Job Throckmorton (1545–1601; prob. the principal author) and J. *Udall, who both denied the charges, and J. *Penry, who was executed. Replies were published by T. *Cooper, Bp. of Winchester, R. *Bancroft, J. Lyly, and T. Nash. The tracts themselves, though prob. the most brilliant prose satire of the period, by their violence aroused hostility rather than sympathy for the Puritan party.

Modern edn. of Tracts with historical notes by W. Pierce (London, 1911). Facsimile of original edn., Leeds, 1967. There is a useful account of the Marprelate Controversy in *The Works of Thomas Nashe*, ed. R. B. McKerrow and F. P. Wilson, 5 (Oxford, 1958), pp. 34–65. D. J. McGinn, *John Penry and the Marprelate Controversy* (New Brunswick, NJ, 1966). L. H. Carlson, *Martin Marprelate, Gentleman: Master Job Throkmorton Laid Open in his Colors* (San Marino, Calif. [1981]). P. G. Stanwood in *NCBEL* 1 (1974), cols. 1957–64.

Marriage. See MATRIMONY.

marriage licences. Licences to dispense with the necessity of *banns have been granted by bishops since the early 14th cent. The power to issue such licences was confirmed to them in 1534 by the Ecclesiastical Licences Act 1533 (commonly known as the *Peter's Pence Act). The Clandestine Marriages Act 1753 (Lord *Hardwicke's Marriage Act) provided that marriages solemnized without banns or licence should be void according to the secular law, although acc. to Anglican Church law they were irregular but valid. It was repealed by the Marriage Act 1823, which declared clandestine marriages valid, but the officiating minister a felon.

Acc. to Canon B 34 of the 1969 Canons, marriage licences may be issued by those having episcopal authority or the commissary for faculties, Vicars General of the Archbishops and Bishops *sede plena* or *sede vacante*, the *guardian of the spiritualities, or *Ordinaries exercising the right of episcopal jurisdiction in the several jurisdictions respectively, but in practice they are generally granted by *surrogates appointed by the *chancellor. They are entirely a matter of grace. The Marriage Act 1949 requires that before a licence is granted one of the parties shall swear before the surrogate that he knows of no impediment or suit pending in any court to bar the marriage and that one of the parties has for the past 15 days had his or her abode in the parish or chapelry in which the marriage is to be solemnized, or that the church or chapel in which the marriage is to be solemnized is the usual place of worship of one of the parties.

The power to grant special licences to marry at any time and in any church, chapel, or other suitable or convenient place was exercised in both provinces by the Abps. of *Canterbury as *legati nati*. It was confirmed to them by the Peter's Pence Act, and specifically reserved in the Marriage Act 1823. In 1995 the fee was £90.

By the Marriage Act 1836, superintendent registrars were authorized to issue licences for marriages in the office of a registrar or a nonconformist place of worship. The Marriage Act 1949 extended this provision to C of E churches and chapels in which banns may be called, provided that the consent of the minister of the church or chapel is obtained and the marriage is solemnized by a clergyman. The law is now contained in the Marriage Act 1949 as amended by the Registration Service Act 1953 and the Marriage Act 1983.

The rulings mentioned do not apply to Scotland, where the law is completely different.

R. Phillimore, *The Ecclesiastical Law of the Church of England* (2nd edn., 1895), pp. 607–17; R. D. H. Bursell, *Liturgy, Order and Law* (Oxford, 1996), pp. 87–91. C. C. A. Pearce, 'The Roles of the Vicar-General and Surrogate in the Granting of Marriage-Licences', *Ecclesiastical Law Journal*, 2 (1990), pp. 28–36.

Marriott, Charles (1811–58), English divine. He was educated at Exeter and Balliol Colleges, Oxford, and in 1833 was elected a Fellow of Oriel, where he became closely associated with several of the *Tractarian leaders and a devoted disciple of J. H. *Newman. After Newman seceded to the RC Church Marriott remained with E. B. *Pusey a leader in Oxford of the High Church Movement. As a religious counsellor he exercised a wide influence, esp. on young men, notably E. *King. From 1839 to 1841 he was the first principal of Chichester Theological College, and from 1850 to 1855 vicar of the University Church at Oxford. A meticulous scholar, from 1841 onwards he collaborated with Pusey and J. *Keble in producing the '*Library of the Fathers', and bore the chief burden of the work of direction.

J. W. *Burgon, *Lives of Twelve Good Men* (1888), i, pp. 296–373 (no. 3: 'The Man of Saintly Life'); R. W. *Church, *The Oxford Movement* (1891), ch. 5. J. H. Overton in *DNB* 36 (1893), pp. 196–8.

Marrow Controversy. A protracted controversy in the Church of *Scotland arising out of the condemnation by the *General Assembly in 1720 of *The Marrow of Modern Divinity*, a book written in 1645 by 'E.F.' (Edward Fisher, d. 1650, a London barber-surgeon, not, as sometimes thought, by the Oxford-educated Edward Fisher, *fl.* 1627–55). The book had been reissued, with a preface by James Hog of Carnock, in 1718. It advocated strongly *Calvinistic doctrines and was held to favour *antinomianism.

D. C. Lachman, *The Marrow Controversy, 1718–1723* (Edinburgh [1988]).

Marsh, Herbert (1757–1839), Bp. of *Peterborough. Educated at King's School, *Canterbury, and St John's College, Cambridge, of which he was elected a Fellow in 1779, he studied in Germany under J. D. *Michaelis. Here he became conversant with the prevalent critical methods, esp. as applied to the Gospels, and after his return translated into English Michaelis's *Introduction to the New Testament* (4 vols., 1793–1801), adding a 'hypothesis' of his own on the mutual relations of the Gospels. In 1805 he preached a series of sermons against the *Calvinist doctrines of *justification and the inamissibility of grace which provoked a violent controversy with C. *Simeon and other *Evangelicals. In 1807 he was elected Lady Margaret professor of divinity at Cambridge, holding the post until his death. His lectures on biblical criticism (1809–16), among the first to popularize German critical methods in England, were enthusiastically listened to by the University and *The History of Sacred Criticism* (1809) was based on the first of his courses. In 1814 he issued *A Comparative View of the Churches of England and Rome*, and in 1815 *Horae Pelasgicae* (pt. 1, all pub.), a learned study of the origin and language of the Pelasgi. In 1816 he was appointed Bp. of *Llandaff and three years later translated to Peterborough. The early years of his episcopate were marked by controversy arising from his anti-Evangelical measures and his refusal to license clergy of Calvinist beliefs. His profound and extensive erudition, his clear and active mind, his belief in the *Establishment, his ideal of rigid uniformity in matters of doctrine and liturgical practice, and his capacity for business made him the foremost English bishop of his age.

E. Venables in *DNB* 36 (1893), pp. 211–15.

Marsiglio (or Marsilius) of Padua (*c.*1275–1342), Italian scholar and author of the 'Defensor Pacis'. After studying at Padua, he went to Paris *c.*1311 to devote himself to medicine, was made rector of the university in 1313, and, after a period in N. Italy and Avignon, practised medicine and possibly studied theology in Paris from 1320. In 1324 he completed the 'Defensor Pacis', his principal work. When, in 1326, his authorship became known he fled to the Emperor, Louis of Bavaria, who had just been excommunicated. In 1327 *John XXII condemned five propositions of the 'Defensor' and excommunicated its author. From 1327 to 1329 Marsiglio accompanied the Emperor to Rome, where he was made Imperial Vicar. After the failure of Louis's policy he spent the remainder of his life at the court of Munich.

The 'Defensor Pacis' is one of the most challenging works produced in the Middle Ages. Acc. to Marsiglio, the State is the great unifying power of society to which the Church must be completely subordinated. It derives its authority from the people, who retain the right to censure and depose the Ruler. The Church, on the other hand, has no inherent jurisdiction whether spiritual or temporal. All her rights in this regard are given her by the State, which may withdraw them at will. She may own no property, but only use what the State lends her; her hierarchy is not of Divine but purely human institution; St *Peter was never given the primacy, and the Papacy owes its prerogatives chiefly to the *Donation of the Emp. *Constantine (a document the authenticity of which Marsiglio did not doubt). The principal authority in all ecclesiastical matters is the *General Council, which should be composed of priests and laymen. These ideas, which ran counter to the whole medieval conception of society, have led to Marsiglio of Padua's being claimed as a forerunner of the Reformers, modern democracy, and even totalitarianism.

The *Defensor Pacis* was first pr. at Basle in 1522, and was put on the *Index in 1559. *De Translatione Imperii* and *De Iurisdictione Imperatoris in causis matrimonialibus*, ed. M. Goldast, *Monarchia S. Romani Imperii*, 2 (Frankfurt, 1614), pp. 147–53 and 1383–91 respectively. Crit. edns. of the *Defensor Pacis* by C. W. Previté-Orton (Cambridge, 1928), with introd. and notes, and by R. Scholz (Fontes Iuris Germanici Antiqui in Usum Scholarum; Hanover, 1933). The *Defensor Minor* was ed. by C. K. Brampton (Birmingham, 1922); *Defensor Minor* and *De Translatione Imperii*, ed., with Fr. tr., by C. Jeudy and J. Quillet as *Œuvres mineures* (Paris, 1979). A. Gewirth, *Marsilius of Padua, the Defender of Peace* (2 vols., Records of Civilization. Sources and Studies, 46; New York, 1951–6, with Eng. tr. of *Defensor Pacis* in vol. 2). Fr. tr. of *Defensor Pacis*, with comm., by J. Quillet (Paris, 1908). G. de Lagarde, *La Naissance de l'esprit laïque au déclin du moyen-âge*, 2 (Saint-Paul-Trois-Châteaux, 1934); rev. edn., 3 (Louvain, 1970). C. Pincin, *Marsilio* (Pubblicazioni dell'Istituto di Scienze Politiche dell'Università di Torino, 17; 1967). J. Quillet, *La Philosophie politique de Marsile de Padoue* (L'Église et l'État au Moyen Âge, 14; 1970). *Marsilio da Padova: Convegno Internazionale (Padova, 18–20 settembre 1980)* (Medioevo. Rivista di Storia della Filosofia Medievale, 5 (for 1979) and 6 (for 1980); [1982]). D. Sternberger, *Die Stadt und das Reich in der Verfassungslehre des Marsilius von Padua* (Sitzungsberichte der wissenschaftlichen Gesellschaft an der Johann Wolfgang Goethe-Universität Frankfurt am Main, 18, no. 3; Wiesbaden, 1981). J. Haller, 'Zur Lebensgeschichte des Marsilius von Padua', *ZKG* 48 (1929), pp. 166–97. A. P. d'Entrèves, *The Medieval Contribution to Political Thought* (1939), chs. 3 and 4, pp. 44–87. A. Gewirth, 'John of Jandun and the *Defensor Pacis*', *Speculum*, 23 (1948), pp. 267–72, establishing that Marsiglio was the sole author. N. Rubinstein, 'Marsilius of Padua and Italian Political Thought of his Time', in J. R. Hale and others (eds.), *Europe in the Late Middle Ages* (1965), pp. 44–75. M. [J.] Wilks, 'Corporation and representation in the Defensor Pacis', *Studia Gratiana*, 15 (1972), pp. 251–92. J. Rivière in *DTC* 12 (pt. 1; 1928), cols. 153–77, s.v. 'Marsile de Padoue', with bibl.

Martène, Edmond (1654–1739), liturgist. In 1672 Martène made his profession as a *Benedictine at the *Maurist house at *Reims and was later sent to *St-Germain-des-Prés to be trained under J. L. *d'Achery and J. *Mabillon. Of his many writings the chief is his *De antiquis ecclesiae ritibus* (3 vols., Rouen, 1700–2), a large collection of liturgical texts, with disquisitions on their historical significance. This he supplemented in 1706 by a *Tractatus de antiqua ecclesiae disciplina*. From 1708 till 1715 he worked on the *Gallia Christiana*, travelling extensively with Ursin Durand (d. 1773) through France and Belgium

in search of MSS and other materials. Later the two scholars visited many religious houses of the Netherlands and Germany for documents, which were embodied in their *Veterum scriptorum et monumentorum ecclesiasticorum et dogmaticorum amplissima collectio* (9 vols. fol., 1724–33). Their journeys are described in the two volumes, *Voyage littéraire de deux religieux bénédictins* (1717 and 1724; both repr. Farnborough, 1969). Martène was a disciple of Claude *Martin, the son of Marie *Guyard, and the author of his biography (1697). He was also the sole compiler of the *Annales Ordinis S. Benedicti*, vol. 6 (1739), begun by Mabillon.

[R. P. Tassin,] *Histoire littéraire de la congrégation de Saint-Maur* (1770), pp. 542–71. H. Wilhelm and U. Berlière, *Nouveau Supplément à l'histoire littéraire de la congrégation de Saint-Maur*, 2 (Maredsous, 1931), pp. 48–57. J. Daoust, *Dom Martène: Un géant de l'érudition bénédictine* (Abbaye S. Wandrille, 1947). A.-G. Martimort, *La Documentation liturgique de Dom Edmond Martène: Étude codicologique* (ST 279; 1978). Bremond, 6 (1922), ch. 6: 'Dom Martin et Dom Martène', pp. 177–266. H. *Leclercq, OSB, in *DACL* 10 (pt. 2; 1932), cols. 2297–322. G.-M. Oury, OSB, in *Dict. Sp.* 10 (1980), cols. 662–4.

Martensen, Hans Lassen (1808–84), Danish Protestant theologian. He was a native of Flensburg. After studying theology at Copenhagen (1827–32), and further studies in Germany and at Paris, he became a lecturer in Copenhagen in 1838 and professor of systematic theology in 1840. In 1854 he succeeded J. P. Mynster as Bp. of Seeland. As a theologian he was greatly influenced by G. W. F. *Hegel and German Idealism. His principal work, *Den Christelige Dogmatik* (1849; Eng. tr., 1866) rests on the principle of the harmony between faith and knowledge, in the light of which he interpreted the *Lutheran system of doctrine. His search for harmony led to an interest in *theosophical speculation, manifest in his *Den Christelige Ethik* (3 vols., 1871–8; Eng. tr., 1873–82), and in the German theosophical writer J. *Boehme, on whom he published an influential study (1881; Eng. tr., 1885). He was popular in English theological circles in his day, but is now chiefly remembered as S. *Kierkegaard's principal opponent in his attack upon the Established Church, in the course of which Kierkegaard died.

Coll. of his lesser works ed. Julius Martensen, Copenhagen, 1885, with detailed bibl. Eng. tr. of his *Jacob Boehme* (London, 1885); new edn., with notes by S. Hobhouse (ibid., 1949). Correspondence with I. A. *Dorner, ed. posthumously, 2 vols., Berlin, 1888. Martensen wrote some autobiog. reflections, pub. Copenhagen, 1882–3 (Ger. tr., 3 vols., 1883–4). The material that constituted Kierkegaard's attack was tr. by W. Lowrie, *Kierkegaard's Attack upon 'Christendom' 1854–1855* (1944; repr., with new introd. by H. A. Johnson, Princeton, NJ, 1968). Lives of Martensen by V. Nannestad (Copenhagen, 1897) and S. Arildsen (vol. 1, all pub., ibid., 1932). P. Madsen in *PRE* (3rd edn.), 12 (1903), pp. 373–9; P. G. Lindhardt in *Dansk Biografisk Leksikon*, 9 (1981), pp. 445–50.

Martha, St. The sister of Mary and *Lazarus, who received Christ in her house during His ministry. From the incident related in Lk. 10: 38–42, she is commonly regarded as typifying the 'active' Christian life as contrasted with Mary, who typifies the 'contemplative'. Acc. to a medieval legend, Martha, Mary, and Lazarus came to the S. of France and founded churches at Marseilles, Aix, *Avignon, and other places. Feast day in E., 4 June; in W., 29 July.

On the legend, besides the collections of docs. listed under MARY MAGDALENE, L. *Duchesne, *Fastes épiscopaux de l'ancien Gaule*, 1 (1894), pp. 310–44 ('La Légende de sainte Marie-Madeleine', esp. sect. 3, pp. 325–9, 'La Légende de sainte Marthe'); G. *Morin, OSB, 'La Formation des légendes provençales. Faits et aperçus nouveaux', *R. Bén.* 26 (1909), pp. 24–33, with refs. to earlier lit.; E. Vacandard, 'La Venue de Lazare et Marie-Madeleine en Provence', *RQH* 100 (1924), pp. 257–305. G. Constable, *Three Studies in Medieval Religious and Social Thought* (Cambridge, 1995), pp. 1–141 ('The Interpretation of Mary and Martha'). H. *Leclercq, OSB, in *DACL* 8 (pt. 1; 1929), cols. 2044–86, s.v. 'Lazare', with detailed bibl.; A. Solignac, SJ, and L. Donnat, OSB, in *Dict. Sp.* 10 (1980), cols. 664–73, s.v. 'Marthe et Marie'. See also bibl. to LAZARUS.

Mar Thoma Church. See MALABAR CHRISTIANS.

Martin, St (d. 397), Bp. of Tours and a patron saint of France. He was born to pagan parents at Sabaria (now Szombathely, Hungary) either *c*.315 (as implied by *Dialogues*, 2. 7. 4), or *c*.336 (as implied by *Vita*, 3–4). Forced to adopt his father's profession of soldiering, Martin was already behaving exemplarily, giving half his cloak—his only garment—to a naked beggar at Amiens. A subsequent vision of Christ inspired him to seek baptism at the age of 18, though he remained a soldier until 356. Various travels and adventures ensued, including a spell as a hermit. In 360 Martin joined *Hilary at Poitiers and founded the nearby monastery of Ligugé, the first known north of the Alps. His growing fame as a holy man and healer led to his being popularly elected Bp. of Tours *c*.371. As bishop, Martin continued to practise and promote monasticism; he was active in evangelizing the countryside, replacing pagan shrines with churches; he healed the sick and championed the oppressed; and *Priscillian's condemnation by a secular court led him to denounce secular interference in Church matters. His younger contemporary and disciple *Sulpicius Severus wrote a Life and other hagiographical works about him, and his cult reached its zenith under the Merovingians. *Gregory of Tours preserves some independent information, as well as detailing miracles at his shrine. Feast day in W., 11 Nov.; in E., 12 Nov.

Sulpicius Severus, *Vita Martini*, to which are appended three letters, and *Dialogi*; also *Chronica*, 2. 50; Gregory of Tours, *Historia Francorum*, 10. 31. 3; for details of edns. see under SULPICIUS and GREGORY. The edn. of Sulpicius' *Vita* by J. Fontaine (SC 133–5; 1967–9), with Fr. tr., includes valuable introd. and extensive notes. E.–C. Babut, *Saint Martin de Tours* [1912], though highly tendentious, opened a new era of Martinian scholarship; cf. crit review art. by H. *Delehaye, SJ, 'Saint Martin et Sulpice Sévère', *Anal. Boll.* 38 (1920), pp. 5–136. *Saint Martin et son temps: Mémorial du XVIᵉ centenaire des débuts du monasticisme en Gaule 361–1961* (Studia Anselmiana, 46; Rome, 1961). C. [E.] Stancliffe, *St Martin and his Hagiographer* (Oxford Historical Monographs, 1983). L. Pietri, *La ville de Tours du IVᵉ au VIᵉ siècle* (Collection de l'École française de Rome, 69; Rome 1983), pp. 36–87; D. von der Nahmer, 'Martin von Tours: sein Mönchtum—seine Wirkung', *Francia*, 15 (for 1986; 1988), pp. 1–41 (with summary in Fr.). J. Fontaine in *Dict. Sp.* 10 (1980), cols. 687–94, s.v. 'Martin (8)'.

On the cult, *Mémorial de l'année martinienne M.DCCCC.LX–M.DCCCC.LXI*, with preface by G. Le Bras (Bibliothèque de la Société d'Histoire ecclésiastique de la France, 1962); E. Ewig, 'Der Martinskult im Frühmittelalter', *Archiv für mittelrheinische Kirchengeschichte*, 14 (1962), pp. 11–30. L. Pietri, op. cit., *passim*; R. Van Dam, 'Images of Saint Martin in Late Roman and Early Merovingian Gaul', *Viator*, 19 (1988), pp. 1–27; S. [A.] Farmer,

Communities of Saint Martin: Legend and Ritual in Medieval Tours (Ithaca, NY, and London, 1991).

Martin, St (*c*.520–79), Bp. of Braga. He was a Pannonian by birth. After visiting the Holy Land, he travelled to Spain (*c*.550) and founded a monastery at Dumio, becoming its first abbot and later bishop for the community. In *c*.570 he was made bishop of the metropolitan see of Braga and presided at the Second Council of Braga (572). He was active in furthering the conversion of the Sueves of Galicia, formerly *Arians, to Catholicism, and in promoting the cult of St *Martin of Tours in the Spanish peninsula. He wrote a letter to a bishop, Boniface, 'De Trina Mersione', opposing the Spanish practice of using one immersion only at baptism, which, adopted probably through fear of Arianism, he considered to smack of *Sabellianism. He also wrote several moral treatises, among them the 'Formula Vitae Honestae' and the 'De Ira' (both based on *Seneca), translated a collection of the sayings of the Desert Fathers into Latin ('Sententiae Patrum Aegyptiorum'), and compiled an important collection of canons relating to the duties and status of clergy and laity (the so-called 'Capitula Martini'). A sermon 'De Correctione Rusticorum' has considerable interest for the light it throws on the older pagan beliefs of the country population. Feast day, 20 Mar.

J. P. Migne, *PL* 72. 17–52 (from A. *Gallandi), and 84. 574–86 ('Capitula Martini'). Mod. crit. edn. of Works by C. W. Barlow (New Haven, Conn., 1950); Eng. tr., with introd., by id. (Fathers of the Church, 62, 1969, pp. 3–109). C. P. *Caspari, *Martin von Braccaras Schrift De Correctione Rusticorum* (Christiania, 1883), with imp. introd. The chief authorities for his life are St *Gregory of Tours and *Venantius Fortunatus; also St *Isidore of Seville, *De Vir. Ill.* 35 [22 in edn. of Carmen Codoñer Merino]. J. Madoz, SJ, 'Martín de Braga. En el XIV centenario de su advenimiento a la Península (550–1950)', *Estudios eclesiásticos*, 25 (1951), pp. 219–42. U. Domínguez del Val, *Estudios sobre literatura latina hispano-cristiano*, 1: 1955–1971 (Corpus Patristicum Hispanum, 2; Madrid, 1986), pp. 201–14. Bardenhewer, 5, pp. 379–88; Altaner and Stuiber (1978), pp. 492 f. and 656. M. C. Díaz y Díaz in *Dict. Sp.* 10 (1980), cols. 678–80, s.v., with bibl.

Martin I, St (d. 655), Pope from 649. He was a vigorous opponent of the *Monothelites. Before his election as Pope had been confirmed from Constantinople by the Emp. Constans II, Martin had condemned Monothelitism at a Synod at the *Lateran in 649. When Constans found Martin unwilling to sign the *Typos, he tried to induce his exarch, Olympius, to seize the Pope's person, but in vain. Olympius' successor, Theodore Calliopas, did so, however, and after a year in captivity at Naxos on the way, Martin arrived at Constantinople in Dec. 653. Here he was condemned to exile, though the sentence was commuted to banishment to the Chersonesus (Crimea), where he died soon afterwards. He is the last of the Popes who is venerated as a martyr, and is actually mentioned by name in the *Canon of the Mass in the *Bobbio Missal. Feast day, 13 Apr.; in E., also 20 Sept.; in W., formerly 12 Nov.

A few of his letters and privilegia repr. from G. D. *Mansi in J. P. Migne, *PL* 87. 119–211; others calendared in P. Jaffé (ed.), *Regesta Pontificum Romanorum*, 1 (ed. G. Wattenbach, Leipzig, 1885), pp. 230–4. Crit. edn. of the docs. relating to the 649 Lateran Council by R. Riedinger (ACO, 2nd ser. 1; Berlin, 1984). *LP* (Duchesne), 1, pp. 336–40. *Anastasius Bibliothecarius in J. P. Migne, *PL* 129. 586–604. P. Peeters, SJ, 'Une Vie grecque du pape S. Martin I', *Anal. Boll.* 51 (1933), pp. 225–62, with text. W. M. Peitz, SJ, 'Martin I und Maximus Confessor. Beiträge zur Geschichte des Monotheletenstreites in den Jahren 645–68', *Hist. J.* 38 (1917), pp. 213–36 and 429–58; O. Bertolini, 'Riflessi politici delle controversie religiose con Bisanzio nelle vicende del sec. vii in Italia', *Settimane di Studi del Centro Italiano di Studi sull' Alto Medievo*, 5 (Spoleto, 1958), pp. 733–89. E. Caspar, 'Die Lateransynode von 649', *ZKG* 51 (1932), pp. 75–137. Hefele and Leclercq, 3 (pt. 1; 1909), pp. 435–61. E. Michael, SJ, 'Wann ist Papst Martin I bei seiner Exilierung nach Constantinopel gekommen?', *ZKT* 16 (1892), pp. 375–80. *Martino I Papa (649–653) e il suo tempo: Atti del XXVIII Convegno storico internazionale Todi, 13–16 ottobre 1991* (Spoleto, 1992). L. *Duchesne, *L'Église au VIe siècle* (1925), pp. 441–53. Mann, 1 (pt. 1; 1902), pp. 385–405. É. Amann in *DTC* 10 (pt. 1; 1928), cols. 182–94; C. M. Aherne in *NCE* 9 (1967), pp. 300 f., both s.v.

Martin IV (*c.*1210–85), Pope from 1281. Simon de Brie (or Brion) was a native of Touraine. After being canon and treasurer at St Martin's at Tours, he was appointed Chancellor of France by *Louis IX in 1260. In 1261 Urban IV created him Cardinal-priest of St Cecilia. As Papal legate he conducted the negotiations for the crown of Sicily with Charles of Anjou and presided over several French synods, including that held at Bourges in 1276. In 1281 he was elected Pope at Viterbo against his will through the influence of Charles of Anjou, on whom he remained dependent throughout his pontificate. He restored Charles to the influential position of Roman Senator of which Nicholas III had deprived him, and with a view to assisting the planned attack on the Greek Empire he excommunicated in 1281 its Emperor, Michael Palaeologus, thus destroying the union between the Latin and Greek Churches achieved at the Second Council of *Lyons in 1274. His unpopularity with the Roman people led to his expulsion from the city, and he died at Perugia. He was a supporter of the *Franciscan Order, whose privileges he extended by the bull 'Ad fructus uberes' in 1281.

Les Registres de Martin IV, 1281–1285 (Bibliothèque des Écoles Françaises d'Athènes et de Rome, 2nd ser. 16; 1935). Two contemporary biogs. repr. in *LP* (Duchesne), 2, pp. 459–65. N. Backes, *Kardinal Simon de Brion (Papst Martin IV)* (Breslau Diss., Berlin, 1910), with bibl. pp. 10 f. Mann, 16 (1932), pp. 171–356. R. Sternfeld, 'Das Konklave von 1280 und die Wahl Martins IV. (1281)', *Mitteilungen des Instituts für Österreichische Geschichtsforschung*, 31 (1910), pp. 1–53. R. Kay, 'Martin IV and the Fugitive Bishop of Bayeux', *Speculum*, 40 (1965), pp. 460–83. É. Amann in *DTC* 10 (pt. 1; 1928), cols. 194–7, s.v.

Martin V (1368–1431), Pope. Oddo (Otto) *Colonna, a man of simple tastes and free from intrigue, was unanimously elected Pope at the Council of *Constance in 1417. His reign marked the end of the *Great Schism, the Antipope Clement VIII submitting to him in 1429. Three years after his election Martin entered Rome, then in a ruinous condition, and restored its churches and other public buildings. In the Papal States he also re-established order with the help of his relatives, among whom he distributed honours and offices. He strengthened the Papal power by dissolving the Council of Constance in 1418, and that of Pavia and Siena in 1424. In the following years he curtailed the liberties of the Church of France and increased the influence of the Papacy in England, though he failed to secure the repeal of the Statutes of *Provisors and *Praemunire. His attempts at suppressing the *Hussites

and at restoring union with the Greek Church were also unsuccessful.

E. v. Ottenthal, 'Die Bullenregister Martin V. und Eugen IV.', *Mittheilungen des Instituts für Österreichische Geschichtsforschung*, Ergänzungsband, 1 (1885), pp. 401–589, esp. pp. 401–568. K. A. Fink, *Verzeichnis der in den päpstlichen Registern und Kameralakten Martins V. vorkommenden Personen, Kirchen und Orte des Deutschen Reiches* (Repertorium Germanicum, 4; 3 parts, 1943–58). F. Baix (ed.), *La Chambre apostolique et les 'Libri Annatarum' de Martin V (1417–1431)* (Analecta Vaticano-Belgica, 14; 2 vols. in 3 parts, '1942' [1947]–60). P. Partner, *The Papal State under Martin V: The administration and government of the temporal power in the early fifteenth century* (1958). K. A. Finke, *Martin V. und Aragon* (Historische Studien, 340; 1938). J. Haller, 'England und Rom unter Martin V.', *Quellen und Forschungen aus italienischen Archiven und Bibliotheken*, 8 (1905), pp. 249–304; K. A. Finke, 'Martin V. und Bologna (1428–1429)', ibid. 23 (1931–2), pp. 182–217. M. Dykmans, SJ, 'D'Avignon à Rome. Martin V et le cortège apostolique', *Bulletin de l'Institut Historique Belge de Rome*, 39 (1968), pp. 203–310, with texts. R. G. Davies, 'Martin V and the English episcopate, with particular reference to his campaign for the repeal of the Statute of Provisors', *EHR* 92 (1977), pp. 309–44. Pastor, 1, pp. 208–82. G. Mollat in *DTC* 10 (pt. 1; 1928), cols. 197–202, s.v.; K. A. Fink in *NCE* 9 (1967), pp. 301 f., s.v.

Martin, Claude (1619–96), *Maurist. The son of Marie *Guyard, he deeply resented being parted from his widowed mother when she joined the *Ursulines in 1631 and went to Canada in 1639. In 1641 he entered the Maurist abbey at Vendôme and came to hold various offices in houses of the Congregation, being assistant general in 1668–75 and 1681–90. He encouraged and supported work on the Maurist editions of St *Augustine and later of the Greek Fathers. He was particularly concerned, however, with the development of the spiritual training of monks, and it is in this sphere that his importance has been recognized in modern times. His *Pratique de la Règle de Saint Benoît* (1680) had a considerable influence in the Maurist Congregation and in other parts of the *Benedictine Order. It emphasized the place of contemplation and withdrawal from the world, rather than of activity, however laudable. Martin himself would have preferred a solitary life and was attracted to contemplative or passive forms of prayer. He was influenced by his mother's spirituality, edited her letters (infelicitously changing her style), and wrote her Life. His own disciples include E. *Martène.

For details of edns. of works on his mother see GUYARD, M. His *Conférences ascétiques* were ed. by R.-J. Hesbert, OSB (2 vols. [1956–7]). Life of Martin by E. Martène, OSB (Tours, 1697). Modern study by G.-M. Oury, OSB (Solesmes, 1983). Bremond, 6 (1922), pp. 177–226. G.-M. Oury, OSB, in *Dict. Sp.* 10 (1980), cols. 695–701, s.v., with bibl.

Martin, Gregory (d. 1582), biblical translator. One of the original scholars of St John's College, Oxford, he became a tutor in the household of Thomas Howard, Duke of Norfolk. On the Duke's imprisonment for Catholicism, Martin escaped to *Douai, where he joined W. *Allen. In 1573 he was ordained priest. After some time in Rome he returned to Douai in 1578, where he spent most of the rest of his life translating the *Vulgate into English. He described the religious life and organized charities of Rome in a work written in 1580–1, entitled 'Roma Sancta', which remained unpublished until 1969. He died on 28 Oct.

1582, the year in which the NT appeared at Reims. See also DOUAI–REIMS BIBLE.

The MS of his *Roma Sancta* (now in the National Library of Australia), ed. by G. B. Parks (Rome, 1969), with introd. on 'The Life and Works of Gregory Martin', pp. xi–xxxii. W. McKane, *Selected Christian Hebraists* (Cambridge, 1989), pp. 76–110, with notes pp. 226–31 and bibl. p. 250.

Martineau, James (1805–1900), *Unitarian divine. He was the brother of Harriet Martineau (1802–76). Educated at Norwich Grammar School, he was converted in 1822 and in the same year entered Manchester College at York. After work as a Unitarian minister at Dublin and Liverpool, during which he became increasingly interested in problems of philosophy, he became professor of philosophy (1840) at, and afterwards principal of, Manchester New College (1869), but continued his pastoral activities. He was a strong and ardent upholder of the theist position against the negations of physical science and elaborated the 'Design argument' with the modifications made necessary by the Darwinian theory of evolution; and did much to convince many of his contemporaries of all shades of theological belief that the Monism of H. *Spencer and the Materialism of John Tyndall (1820–93) did not cover all the facts. In *Types of Ethical Theory* (2 vols., 1885) and in *A Study of Religion* (2 vols., 1888) he found powerful arguments for theism in the facts of the moral consciousness and the existence of the laws of nature. He also did much for the organization of the Unitarian body in England and Ireland.

Martineau's other writings include *A Study of Spinoza* (1882), *The Seat of Authority in Religion* (1890), and some collections of Hymns and 'Home Prayers'.

Essays, Reviews and Addresses. Selected and revised by the Author (4 vols., 1890–1). *Life and Letters*, ed. J. *Drummond and C. B. Upton (London, 1902). A. H. G. Craufurd, *Recollections of James Martineau* (1903). Other Lives by A. W. Jackson (London, 1900) and J. E. *Carpenter (ibid., 1905). H. *Sidgwick, *Lectures on the Ethics of T. H. Green, Mr. Herbert Spencer, and J. Martineau* (1902; posthumous), pp. 313–74. A. Gordon in *DNB*, Suppl. 3 (1901), pp. 146–51. A. M. *Fairbairn in *EB* (11th edn.), 17 (1911), pp. 797–800, s.v.

Martínez de Ripalda, Juan. See RIPALDA, JUAN MARTÍNEZ DE.

Martyn, Henry (1781–1812), Anglican missionary. He was born at Truro and studied at St John's College, Cambridge (1797–1801), of which he became a Fellow in 1802. His acquaintance with C. *Simeon awakened his interest in missionary work, and having been ordained deacon in 1803, he became a chaplain of the East India Company at Calcutta in 1805. Besides doing missionary work among the natives he translated the NT into Hindustani and Persian, the Psalms into Persian, and the BCP into Hindustani. He also prepared a translation of the NT into Arabic. On his way back from Persia he died at Tokat, where he was given Christian burial by the *Armenian clergy. His life of devotion to the cause of the missions made a great impression in Britain and he became the hero of several literary publications. In the American BCP (1979), feast day, 19 Oct.

Journals and Letters of the Rev. Henry Martyn, ed. S. *Wilberforce (2 vols., London, 1837). Lives by J. Sargent (London, 1819;

repr., Edinburgh, 1985) and G. Smith (London, 1892); more popular account by C. E. Padwick (ibid., 1922). M. L. Loane, *They were Pilgrims* (Sydney, 1970), pp. 45–98; rev. in id., *Three Faithful Servants* (Blackwood, SA, 1991), pp. 21–88. Unsigned art. in *DNB* 36 (1893), pp. 315–17.

martyr (Gk. μάρτυς, 'witness'). The term was originally used of the Apostles as witnesses of Christ's life and resurrection (e.g. Acts 1: 8, 1: 22), but with the spread of *persecution it was reserved to those who had undergone hardships for the faith, and finally it was restricted to those who had suffered death. The age before *Constantine was the classic period of martyrs, esp. the era of *Diocletian. As those who had followed Christ's example literally, they quickly became the focus of veneration in the Church. They were also regarded as specially inspired by the Holy Spirit, and their utterances greatly treasured; some scholars see in this belief a reference to Mk. 13: 11. From the earliest time martyrdom, the 'baptism of blood', was considered an equivalent of normal Baptism where this had not been received. Since the end of the 2nd cent. the anniversary of the martyr's death (*natalis*, i.e. his [heavenly] birthday) was kept as a feast with a liturgical celebration at his tomb; and later churches were frequently built on the site. The fame of the martyrs often spread beyond their city and country. They were venerated as powerful intercessors, their relics were sought after, and their Lives widely read and often embellished by numerous legends.

In the Roman liturgy, after the BVM and the Apostles, martyrs rank before all other saints. The liturgical colour is red, to signify that they shed their blood for the faith, and acc. to RC practice until 1969 relics of martyrs had to be contained in every consecrated altar. This is still the law in the E. Church.

H. *Delehaye, SJ, *Les Origines du culte des martyrs* (Subsidia Hagiographica, 20; 1912); id., *Les Passions des martyrs et les genres littéraires* (1921). O. Michel, *Prophet und Märtyrer* (Beiträge zur Förderung christlicher Theologie, 37, Heft 2; 1932); H. von Campenhausen, *Die Idee des Martyriums in der alten Kirche* (1935); E. Günther, *Μάρτυς: Die Geschichte eines Wortes* (1941); M. Lods, *Confesseurs et martyrs: Successeurs des prophètes dans l'Église des trois premiers siècles* (Cahiers théologiques, 41 [1958]); J. Jeremias, *Heiligengräber in Jesu Umwelt (Mt. 23, 29; Lk. 11, 47): Eine Untersuchungen zur Volksreligion der Zeit Jesu* (Göttingen, 1958); N. Brox, *Zeuge und Märtyrer: Untersuchungen zur frühchristlichen Zeugnis-Terminologie* (Studien zum Alten und Neuen Testament, 5; Munich, 1961). T. Klauser, *Christlicher Märtyrerkult, heidnischer Heroenkult und spätjüdische Heiligenverehrung* (Arbeitsgemeinschaft für Forschung des Landes Nordrhein-Westfalen, 91 [1960]). W. H. C. Frend, *Martyrdom and Persecution in the Early Church* (Oxford, 1965). T. Baumeister, *Die Anfänge der Theologie des Martyriums* (Münsterische Beiträge zur Theologie, 45; 1980). R. Lane Fox, *Pagans and Christians* (1986), pp. 434–50. D. Wood (ed.), *Martyrs and Martyrologies* (Studies in Church History, 30; Oxford, 1993). H. *Leclercq, OSB, in *DACL* 10 (pt. 2; 1932), cols. 2359–512; W. Rordorf and A. Solignac, SJ, in *Dict. Sp.* 10 (1980), cols. 718–37, both s.v. H. Strathmann in *TWB* 4 (1942), pp. 477–520; Eng. tr., 4 (1967), pp. 474–514, s.v. μάρτυς.

Martyr, Peter. See PETER MARTYR.

martyrium (Gk. μαρτύριον). A church built over the tomb or relics of a *martyr or occasionally a church built just in honour of a martyr. The cleric in charge of such a church was sometimes known as the 'martyrarius'.

A. Grabar, *Martyrium: Recherches sur le culte des reliques et l'art chrétien antique* (Collège de France. Fondation Schlumberger pour les Études byzantines, 2 vols., 1946; Album, 1943). H. *Leclercq, OSB, in *DACL* 10 (pt. 2; 1932), cols. 2512–23, s.v.

martyrology. An official register of Christian martyrs. As distinct from individual 'Passions' describing the martyrdoms of those who have suffered for the Christian faith, martyrologies are collective in structure. The earliest are calendars, merely naming the martyr and the place of martyrdom under the day of the festival. They may be local, like the calendars of Rome (354) and Carthage (*c*.505), or general, like the '*Hieronymian Martyrology' (q.v.) and the 'Breviarium Syriacum' (411). The later 'historical' martyrologies, notably those of *Bede (*c*.730), *Florus of Lyons, *Rabanus, *Ado, and *Usuard (all 9th cent.), add stories of martyrs from sources of varying value. The '*Roman Martyrology' (q.v.; 1584) is a revision of Usuard's. The practice of reading in choir at *Prime the martyrology for the day is already laid down by *Chrodegang of Metz and in the Aachen Capitula of 817, and until recently was preceptive in religious houses.

The standard source is the magisterial edn. and discussion of the 'Hieronymian Martyrology' in *AASS*, Nov. 2, 1 (1894); new edn. by H. *Quentin, OSB, with important notes by H. *Delehaye, SJ, in *AASS*, Nov. 2, 2 (1931). H. Achelis, *Die Martyrologien: Ihre Geschichte und ihr Wert* (*Abh.* (Gött.), NF 3, Heft 3; 1900); H. Quentin, OSB, *Les Martyrologes historiques du moyen âge* (1908); J. Dubois, *Les Martyrologes du Moyen Âge Latin* (Typologie des Sources du Moyen Âge Occidental, fasc. 26; 1978). R. Aigrain, *L'Hagiographie* (1953), pp. 11–106. B. de Gaiffier, 'De l'usage et de la lecture du martyrologe. Témoignages antérieurs au XIᵉ siècle', *Anal. Boll.* 79 (1961), pp. 40–59. H. Delehaye, SJ, in *CE* 9 (1910), pp. 741 f., s.v.; H. Leclercq, OSB, in *DACL* 10 (pt. 2; 1932), cols. 2523–619, s.v.; J. Dubois, OSB, in *Catholicisme*, 8 (1979), cols. 776–83, s.v., repr. in id., *Martyrologes d'Usuard au Martyrologe Romain* (Abbeville, 1990), pp. 3–15. See also bibl. to separate martyrologies and authors mentioned above.

Martyrs, Acts of the. See ACTS OF THE MARTYRS.

Martyrs, Era of the. See DIOCLETIANIC ERA.

Martyrs, Four Crowned. See QUATTRO CORONATI.

Marucchi, Orazio (1852–1931), Italian archaeologist. Under the influence of G. B. *de Rossi, the *catacombs of Rome became the chief object of his research. In 1879 he founded the 'Collegium Cultorum Martyrum' and in quick succession became Scriptor of the *Vatican Library, director of the *Lateran Museum, lecturer on Christian archaeology at several institutes, and, after de Rossi's death (1894), editor of the *Nuovo Bullettino di Archeologia Cristiana*. As secretary of the pontifical 'Commissione di Archeologia Sacra', he conducted the excavations of many famous tombs, such as the 'Coemeterium Valentini' (1876 ff.) and parts of the Catacomb of *Priscilla. Owing to the considerable diversity of his interests, his work was sometimes wanting in precision in its details. Among his principal writings are *Éléments d'archéologie chrétienne* (1900–3) and *Le catacombe romane* (1903; 2nd edn., 1933), besides a great number of contributions to learned periodicals.

The 2nd edn. of Marucchi's *Le catacombe romane* was pub. posthumously by E. Josi [1933], with biog. introd., pp. xix–xxxi.

C. Cecchelli, 'Scrittori contemporanei di cose romane. Orazio Marucchi', *Archivio della R. Società Romana di Storia Patria*, 52 (1929; stampato nel 1931), pp. 381–406, with list of his works, pp. 407–52. H. *Leclercq, OSB, in *DACL* 10 (pt. 2; 1932), cols. 2619–38, s.v.

Mary, the Blessed Virgin, the Mother of Christ. The place accorded to her in Catholic and Orthodox theology and devotion issues from her position as Mother of the Redeemer. She is accounted pre-eminent among the *saints (q.v.).

In the NT the Blessed Virgin figures prominently in the birth stories of Mt. (1–2) and esp. Lk. (1–2). Though mentioned several times during Christ's public ministry, she remains mainly in the background; acc. to the Fourth Gospel she reappears at the foot of the Cross (Jn. 19: 25). In the Upper Room at Jerusalem she witnessed the growth of the early Church (Acts 1: 14). Both her maternity and her virginity are stated in the Gospels; she conceived and gave birth to Jesus (Lk. 1: 31–3) without losing her virginity (Mt. 1: 20 and 23; Lk. 1: 34 f.). See VIRGIN BIRTH.

In the earliest patristic writings Mary is mentioned only rarely, and then usually in conjunction with *Eve. *Justin Martyr (d. *c*.165) contrasts her obedience with the disobedience of Eve, and the same theme is developed by *Irenaeus (d. *c*.202). Her perpetual virginity was first asserted in the apocryphal Book of *James; it may have been taught by Irenaeus and *Clement of Alexandria, but was certainly held by *Athanasius, who used the term 'ever virgin' (ἀειπάρθενος); and, though contested by *Jovinian, it was accepted by orthodox Fathers of the E. and W. from the 5th cent. onwards. The development of Marian doctrine received considerable impetus at the Council of *Ephesus (431), which upheld the title *Theotokos (θεοτόκος). This expression was prob. in use among Alexandrian theologians perhaps from as early as *Origen; it became common in the 4th cent.; and, though it was contested by *Nestorius as being Christologically incorrect, it was defended by *Cyril of Alexandria and became generally accepted after 431. In the W., where at this time Mary played a lesser role than in the E., she was esp. associated with the Church; St *Ambrose held her to be a type of the Church, in that in giving birth to Christ she also brought forth Christians who were formed in her womb with Him. In the 6th cent. the doctrine of the corporeal *Assumption of Mary was formulated in orthodox circles by *Gregory of Tours (d. 594); it had previously been found in apocryphal documents dating from the late 4th cent. onwards. Also in the 6th cent. the feast of the Assumption of the BVM became more widely observed, and sermons preached on the occasion, e.g. by Theoteknos of Livias (between 550 and 650) and by *Germanus of Constantinople, emphasized her power in heaven. Belief in the Assumption seems to have spread in both E. and W. without arousing opposition in the pre-Reformation period; it was defined for RCs in 1950. The doctrine of the *Immaculate Conception of the BVM, on the other hand, was a matter of dispute throughout the Middle Ages. In England *Eadmer wrote a treatise in defence of the doctrine, which had been denied by his master, *Anselm of Canterbury; Eadmer sought to solve the problem of the universal transmission of *original sin in the sexual act by teaching the 'passive' conception, that is, that only Mary herself, without reference to the parental act, was without stain of original sin from the moment of her conception; he argued that because God could do it and because it was fitting, He also did do it. This teaching was developed in more stringently scholastic terms by *Duns Scotus and led to a long-drawn-out controversy. The doctrine of the Immaculate Conception was defended by the *Franciscans and later the *Jesuits against the *Dominicans; it was defined for RCs in 1854.

In modern times, esp. in the 19th and 20th cents., efforts have been made to secure a Papal definition of Mary as 'Mediatrix of All Graces' and 'Co-Redemptrix'. The former description was widely popularized by St *Alphonsus Liguori, and Pope *Benedict XV sanctioned a Mass and Office of the BVM under this title. At the Second *Vatican Council, however, a chapter on Mary was added to the Constitution on the Church, against the wishes of those who sought a separate document on her. The chapter is remarkable for its restraint, its insistence on Scripture and the Fathers, and its stress on Mary's complete dependence on her Son.

The Marian doctrine of the Orthodox Church is very similar to that of the RC Church, though the corporeal Assumption of the BVM has not been made a dogma and the Immaculate Conception is denied. The Reformers, esp. M. *Luther, stressed the humility of Mary and attacked her glorification by the RC Church. Among all Protestant bodies there was a strong reaction against excessive devotion to her. In the C of E the *Thirty-Nine Articles forbade the invocation of saints, incl. the BVM, but the *Caroline Divines insisted on her holiness, and A. *Stafford could call her 'fountain of grace'. Since the *Oxford Movement certain Anglican theologians have accorded the BVM an increasingly important place which has come to differ little from the RC position. On the Continent also there has been a tendency among German Protestant theologians to restore an element of Marian doctrine.

Belief in the efficacy of Mary's intercession and hence direct prayers to her is prob. very old. It is attested in a Greek form of the well-known prayer 'Sub tuum praesidium' found in a papyrus dating from the late 3rd to early 4th cent. After the Council of Ephesus devotion to the Theotokos became so strong that her name was even substituted in the official service books in place of that of the Lord at the end of some of the liturgical prayers. In the W. St *Thomas Aquinas formulated the doctrine of the '*hyperdulia' proper to her, which, though infinitely inferior to the 'latria' (worship of adoration) due to her Son, surpasses that befitting angels and saints.

Liturgical devotions in the W. came to include the '*Little Office of Our Lady' as well as the Saturday Mass and Office. Popular piety found expression in the *Hail Mary, *Rosary, *Angelus, May and October devotions, and pilgrimages, esp. to *Lourdes and *Fatima. Since the Second Vatican Council, however, these practices have come to occupy a less prominent place in the RC Church. In the Orthodox Church Marian devotion is expressed in the *Acathistus hymn and the Theotokia or short prayers to the Theotokos following the invocation of the Trinity which came into use in the 8th century.

The first Marian feast was called the Commemoration ($\mu\nu\acute{\eta}\mu\eta$) of St Mary and was kept in many places on the Sunday before Christmas; this developed into the feast of the Assumption (15 Aug.). The other major feasts of the BVM are the (Immaculate) Conception (8 Dec.), the *Nativity (8 Sept.), traditionally the *Annunciation (25 March; now in the RC Church called the Annunciation of the Lord and accounted a feast of Christ), the *Purification (2 Feb.; since 1960 called the Presentation of Christ), and the *Visitation (2 July; in the RC Church and some modern Anglican calendars, now 31 May). The calendar of the BCP retains all of these except the Assumption (which is retained in the Oxford University Calendar), but only the Annunciation and the Purification have a proper Collect, Epistle, and Gospel. A major general feast of the BVM is included in some modern Anglican calendars, e.g. in the ASB on 8 Sept., and in the American BCP (1979) on 15 Aug. Since 1969 the RC Church has observed 1 Jan. as the 'Solemnity of Holy Mary, the Mother of God' (in place of the *Circumcision), thus reverting to a practice attested at Rome in the *Gregorian Sacramentary. A number of minor feasts have also been observed in the RC Church; they include the (*Seven) Sorrows of the BVM (15 Sept.), the Presentation of St Mary in the Temple (21 Nov.), Our Lady of the Snows (5 Aug.; now renamed the 'Dedication of the Basilica of St Mary'), Our Lady of Mt. *Carmel (16 July; now reduced to an optional memorial) and the Holy Name of Mary (12 Sept.; now suppressed).

The earliest recorded vision of the BVM is supposed to be that of *Gregory Thaumaturgus (d. c.270), recorded in a panegyric almost certainly by *Gregory of Nyssa. The most famous modern apparitions are those of Lourdes and Fatima; lesser ones are those of *La Salette, Knock in Ireland (1879), Beauraing (1932–3) and Banneux (1933) in Belgium, and Medjugorje (1981) in what was then Yugoslavia; in all these (except Knock) the recipients were children. The apparition which resulted in the striking of the popular 'miraculous medal' took place in 1830; the visionary was Catherine Labouré, a 'Daughter of Charity' of St *Vincent de Paul. See also ECUMENICAL SOCIETY OF THE BLESSED VIRGIN MARY, LORETO, and WALSINGHAM.

There is an extensive collection of patristic texts ed. S. A. Campos, OFM, Corpus Marianum Patristicum (Facultas Theologica Hispaniae Septentionalis, Sedes Burgensis; 6 vols. in 7, Burgos, 1970–81). Classical discussions include St Thomas Aquinas, ST 3, qq. 27–30, and P. *Canisius, De Beata Maria Virgine (Ingoldstadt, 1577). Modern general studies from the RC position include P. Sträter, SJ, Katholische Marienkunde (3 vols., Paderborn, 1948–51); H. du Manoir, SJ, Maria: Études sur la Sainte Vierge (8 vols., 1949–71); E. *Schillebeeckx, OP, Maria, Moeder van de verlossing (Antwerp, 1954; Eng. tr., 1964); K. McNamara (ed.), Mother of the Redeemer: Aspects of Doctrine and Devotion (Dublin, 1959); H. [C.] Graef, Mary: A History of Doctrine and Devotion (2 vols., 1963–5); A. Müller in Mysterium Salutis, ed. J. Feiner and M. Löhrer, 3 (pt. 2; Einsiedeln [1969]), pp. 393–510; R. Laurentin, ibid. 4 (pt. 2 [1973]), pp. 316–37; J. McHugh, The Mother of Jesus in the New Testament (1975); G. Söll, Mariologie (Handbuch der Dogmengeschichte, 3, Heft 4; 1978), with extensive bibl. C. Miegge, La Vergine Maria (Torre Pellice, 1950; Eng. tr., 1955; a Protestant critique of the RC position). M. Thurian, Marie: Mère du Seigneur, Figure de l'Église (Taizé, 1962; Eng. tr., 1963). R. E. Brown and others, Mary in the New Testament: A Collaborative Assessment by Protestant and Roman Catholic Scholars (Philadelphia and London, 1978). A. M. Allchin, The Joy of All Creation: An Anglican Meditation on the Place of Mary (1984; 2nd edn., 1993). M. P. Carroll, The Cult of *the Virgin Mary: Psychological Origins* (Princeton, 1986). R. Schimmelpfennig, *Die Geschichte der Marienverehrung im deutschen Protestantismus* (Paderborn, 1952). R. Caro, SJ, *La Homiletica Mariana Griega en el Siglo V* (Marian Library Studies, NS 3–5; Dayton, Oh., 1971–3). J. Ledit, *Marie dans la Liturgie de Byzance* (Théologie Historique, 39 [1976]). Periodicals include *Marianist* (Dayton, Oh., 1905 ff. [suspended 1922–6]), *Marianum* (Rome, 1939 ff.), *Marian Studies* (Paterson, NJ, 1950 ff.), *Ephemerides Mariologicae* (Madrid, 1951 ff.). C. P. Ceroke and others in *NCE* 9 (1967), pp. 335–86, s.v. 'Mary, Blessed Virgin'; P. Grelot and others in *Dict. Sp.* 10 (1980), cols. 408–82, s.v. 'Marie (Vierge)'. See also works cited under ASSUMPTION, IMMACULATE CONCEPTION, and other feasts.

Mary, Gospel of. An apocryphal Gnostic Gospel. Two pages of the original Greek survive in a 3rd-cent. *Oxyrhynchus papyrus, now in the John Rylands Library, Manchester (Pap. Ryl. III, 463), and a further fragment (Oxyrhynchus 3525) from a different 3rd-cent. papyrus. An incomplete 5th-cent. papyrus MS in Berlin (Pap. 8502) contains some eight pages (out of a total of 18) of a Coptic (Sahidic) version, including the passages extant in Greek, with some variations. In this Gospel *Mary [Magdalene] describes a vision in which the progress of the Gnostic through the seven planetary spheres is explained.

The Manchester text is ed. by C. H. Roberts in his *Catalogue of the Greek and Latin Papyri in the John Rylands Library, Manchester*, 3 (Manchester, 1938), pp. 18–23, incl. Eng. tr. and notes. P. Oxy. 3525, ed. P. J. Parsons, *Oxyrhynchus Papyri*, 50 (1983), pp. 12–14. Coptic text ed., with Ger. tr. and introd., by W. C. Till, *Die gnostischen Schriften des koptischen Papyrus Berolinensis 8502* (TU 60; 1955), pp. 24–32 and 62–79; 2nd edn. by H.-M. Schenke (ibid., 1972), with additional material, pp. 336 and 338 f.; also, with Eng. tr. by R. McL. Wilson and G. W. MacRae in D. M. Parrott (ed.), *Nag Hammadi Codices V, 2–5 and VI with Papyrus Berolinensis 8502, 1 and 4* (Nag Hammadi Studies, 11; Leiden, 1979), pp. 453–71; and, with Fr. tr., by A. Pasquier (Bibliothèque Copte de Nag Hammadi, Section 'Textes', 10; 1983). H. C. Puech in Schneemelcher, 1 (5th edn., 1987), pp. 313–15; Eng. tr., 1 (1991), pp. 391–5.

Mary, Gospel of the Birth of. An apocryphal book containing a narrative of the birth of the BVM to St *Joachim and St *Anne, her life in the Temple from the age of 3 to 12 years, her betrothal to St *Joseph, the *Annunciation, and the *Virgin Birth of Christ. It is a Latin work of the Middle Ages, though in a preface sometimes attached to it is attributed to St *Jerome, who is stated to have composed it after a Hebrew original. Its compiler drew largely on the canonical Gospels and other sources, esp. the Book of *James (the 'Protevangelium').

The text is taken over almost bodily in the '*Golden Legend' (q.v.). Crit. edn. by C. *Tischendorf (ed.), *Evangelia Apocrypha* (2nd edn., Leipzig, 1876), pp. 113–21. Brief summary of contents in M. R. James, *The Apocryphal New Testament* (1924), pp. 79 f. Bardenhewer, 1, pp. 536 f.

Mary of Egypt, St (5th cent.), penitent. After a career of infamy at Alexandria as an actress and courtesan, she is said to have been converted on the threshold of the Holy Sepulchre at *Jerusalem and fled to the desert E. of Palestine to expiate her sins. Here she is recorded to have lived a life of complete isolation for 47 years, and then made the acquaintance of a priest, Zosimas, who gave her communion and prepared her for death. Her story became very popular and she was the subject of many elaborate legends. Her 'Life' was translated into a number of languages; it found a place in the '*Golden Legend' and forms part of the liturgy for the 5th Sunday of Lent in the Orthodox Churches. Feast day in the E., 5th Sunday in Lent (also 1 Apr.); in the W., 2 (also 3 and 9) Apr.

The earliest account of St Mary of Egypt is in *Cyril of Scythopolis' 'Life of St Cyriacus'. This material was developed in legendary fashion by *Sophronius of Jerusalem (7th cent.). *AASS*, Apr. 1 (1675), pp. 67–90, with Gk. text, pp. xiii–xxi (of which Lat. tr., pp. 76–82). Eng. tr. (of Slavonic version) by Sisters Katherine and Thecla in their translation of St *Andrew of Crete, *The Great Canon ...* (Newport Pagnell, 1974), pp. 65–84. F. Delmas, 'Remarques sur la vie de Sainte Marie l'Égyptienne', *ÉO* 4 (1900–1), pp. 35–42; id., 'Encore Sainte Marie l'Égyptienne', ibid. 5 (1901–2), pp. 15–17. A. T. Baker, 'Vie de Sainte Marie l'Égyptienne', *Revue des langues romanes*, 59 (1916–17), pp. 145–401. 13th-cent. Life by Rutebeuf ed., with introd. on the legend, by B. A. Bujila (University of Michigan Contributions in Modern Philology, 12; Ann Arbor, 1949). K. Kunze (ed.), *Die Legende der heiligen Maria Aegyptiaca: Ein Beispiel hagiographischer Überlieferung in 16 unveröffentlichen deutschen niederländischen und lateinischen Fassungen* (Texte des späten Mittelalters und der frühen Neuzeit, 28; 1978). M. Schiavone de Cruz-Sáenz, *The Life of Saint Mary of Egypt: An Edition and Study of the Medieval French and Spanish Verse Redactions* (Biblioteca Universitaria Puvill, Estudios, 1; Barcelona [1979]). K. Kunze, *Studien zur Legende der heiligen Maria Aegyptiaca im deutschen Sprachgebiet* (Philologische Studien und Quellen, 49; 1969), esp. ch. 1. H. *Leclercq, OSB, in *DACL* 10 (pt. 2; 1932), cols. 2128–36, s.v. 'Marie l'Égyptienne', with bibl.

Mary of the Incarnation, Bl (1566–1618). See ACARIE, MADAME.

Mary of the Incarnation, Bl (1599–1672). See GUYARD, MARIE.

Mary Magdalene, St. A follower of Christ out of whom He is said to have cast 'seven devils' and who ministered to Him in Galilee (Lk. 8: 2). Later she stood by His cross at the Crucifixion (Mk. 15: 40), with two other women discovered the empty tomb and heard the angelic announcement of His *Resurrection (Mk. 16: 1 ff., etc.), and was granted an appearance of the Risen Christ early on the same day (Mt. 28: 9, Jn. 20: 11 ff.). At least since the time of St *Gregory the Great, W. tradition has identified her with the 'woman which was a sinner' who anointed Christ's feet in Simon's house (Lk. 7: 37), and with Mary the sister of *Martha, who also anointed Him (Jn. 12: 3); but the Gospels give no real support to either identification and they have now been abandoned by the RC Church. In several *Gnostic texts (e.g. the Gospel of *Mary and *Pistis Sophia) Mary Magdalene plays a prominent role as a mediator of revelation or in conversation between the risen Christ and His disciples. Acc. to an early legend in the E. Church, she went to *Ephesus with St *John and died there, whence her body was later taken to *Constantinople. In the W. a very popular but late and quite unfounded legend had arisen by the 9th cent. that she, with Martha and *Lazarus, came to the S. of France by sea, and in the Middle Ages her supposed relics were venerated at various places in Provence, and also at Vézelay. Feast day, 22 July.

Classic studies by J. *Faber Stapulensis (Paris, 1517 and 1519). *AASS*, Jul. 5 (1727), pp. 187–225. M. J. *Lagrange, OP, 'Jésus a-t-il été oint plusieurs fois et par plusieurs femmes?', *R. Bibl.* NS

9 (1912), pp. 504–32; R. E. Brown, SS, *The Gospel according to John*, 1 (Anchor Bible, 1966), pp. 449–52; A. Feuillet, 'Les deux onctions faites sur Jésus, et Marie-Madeleine', *Revue Thomiste*, 75 (1975), pp. 357–95. U. Holzmeister, SJ, 'Die Magdalenfrage in der kirchlichen Überlieferung', *ZKT* 46 (1922), pp. 402–22 and 556–84. F. Bovon, 'Le Privilège pascal de Marie-Madeleine', *New Testament Studies*, 30 (1984), pp. 50–62. On the NT material, see also other comm. to the Gospels. [E. M. Faillon (ed.)], *Monuments inédits sur l'apostolat de sainte Marie-Madeleine en Provence et les autres apôtres de cette contrée* (pub. by J. P. *Migne, 2 vols., 1848); C. Chabaneau (ed.), *Sainte Marie-Madeleine dans la littérature provençale: Recueil des textes provençaux en prose et en vers relatifs à cette sainte* (1887). H. M. Garth, *Saint Mary Magdalen in Mediaeval Literature* (Johns Hopkins University Studies in Historical and Political Science, 47th ser., no. 3; 1950). N. Hansel, *Die Maria-Magdalena-Legende* (Greifswalder Beiträge zur Literatur- und Stilforschung, 16, Heft 1; 1937). V. Saxer, 'Les Saintes Marie Madeleine et Marie de Béthanie dans la tradition liturgique et homilétique orientale', *Rev. S.R.* 32 (1958), pp. 1–37; id., *Le Culte de Marie Madeleine en occident des origines à la fin du moyen âge* (Cahiers d'archéologie et d'histoire, 3; 1959); cf. B. de Gaffier, SJ, in *Anal. Boll.* 78 (1960), pp. 161–8; V. Saxer, *Le Dossier vézelien de Marie Madeleine* (Subsidia Hagiographica, 57; 1975). E. Duperray (ed.), *Marie-Madeleine dans la mystique, les arts et les lettres: Actes du Colloque international, Avignon, juillet 1988* (1989). S. Haskins, *Mary Magdalene: Myth and Metaphor* (1993). V. Saxer in *Bibliotheca Sanctorum*, 8 (Rome, 1967), cols. 1078–1104, s.v. 'Maria Maddalena', with extensive bibl.; P.-M. Guillaume in *Dict. Sp.* 10 (1980), cols. 559–75, s.v. 'Marie-Madeleine (sainte)'. For other works on the legend of her connection with S. France, see bibl. to MARTHA, ST.

Mary Magdalene de' Pazzi, St (1566–1607),

*Carmelite mystic. Born of a noble family of Florence, she entered the Carmelite convent in her native town in 1582 and was professed during a grave illness two years later. In 1598 she was made novice-mistress and later subprioress. During the first years after her profession she was severely tried by spiritual desolation, temptations, and physical sufferings, but from 1590 her life became a series of ecstasies during which she often gave spiritual counsels which were taken down by her fellow-nuns and published after her death. She was an ardent believer in the value of suffering for the spiritual life and the salvation of souls, and the last three years of her life were spent bedridden in constant pain and often in great spiritual aridity. She was canonized in 1669. Feast day, 25 (formerly 29) May.

Works ed. L. M. Brancaccius, Florence, 1609; modern edn. under the direction of F. Nardoni (7 vols., Florence, 1960–6; Eng. tr. by G. M. Pausback, O. Carm., 5 vols., Fatima, 1969–75; also distributed by the Carmelites at Aylesford, Kent, and Aylesford, Ill.). Early Lives in Italian by V. Puccini, Carmelite, her last confessor (1st draft written in 1609; final version pub. Florence, 1621), and V. Cepari, SJ, also her confessor (written *c.*1626; first pub., Rome, 1669); both tr. into Lat. and pr., with introd. and other material, in *AASS*, Mai. 6 (1688), pp. 177–351; Eng. tr. of Life by V. Cepari in the series 'The Saints and Servants of God' (ed. F. W. *Faber, 1849). Modern studies by Sister Maria Minima di Gesù Sacramentato, O. Carm. (Florence, 1941; Eng. tr., Chicago, 1958), E. Ancilli, OCD (Rome, 1967), and B. Secondin, O. Carm. (ibid., 1974). A. E. Verbrugghe, O. Carm., *The Image of the Trinity in the Works of St Mary Magdalene de' Pazzi* (Rome, 1984). E. Ancelli, OCD, in *Dict. Sp.* 10 (1980), cols. 576–88, s.v. 'Marie-Madeleine de Pazzi'.

Mary Major, Church of St. See SANTA MARIA MAGGIORE, ROME.

Mary, Queen of Scots (1542–87). She was the only child of James V, who died when she was a few days old, leaving her heiress to the throne of Scotland, of which she was crowned Queen in 1543. Her mother was Mary of Lorraine (or 'Mary of Guise', 1515–60). In 1548 she was sent to France for her education, and in 1558 married to the Dauphin Francis, becoming Queen Consort in 1559. After the early death of Francis (1560) she returned to Scotland (1561), where nationalist hatred of the pro-French Guise regime had combined with Protestant agitation led by J. *Knox to establish a Protestant-led government. Mary had a series of stormy interviews with Knox, who remained impervious to her charm. During her reign she displayed no understanding of her native kingdom, showed little inclination to defend Catholicism, and dissipated the considerable reserves of loyalty among her subjects. In 1565 she married her cousin, Henry Stewart, Lord Darnley. The match was approved both by the Pope and *Philip II of Spain, and by Darnley she became the mother of the future James VI of Scotland (*James I of England) in 1566. In 1566 Darnley collaborated in the murder of Mary's secretary, David Rizzio, of whom he had become jealous. This murder caused her complete estrangement from Darnley, who, in 1567, was assassinated by James Hepburn, Earl of Bothwell, who had become her favourite. In the same year Bothwell obtained a divorce from his wife and married Mary, after he had been tried for the murder of Darnley but found not guilty by judges who are generally held not to have been impartial. This marriage, which was concluded acc. to the Protestant rite, was denounced by the Pope and opposed by most European courts. How far she was implicated in the murder of Darnley is still disputed; the verdict depends chiefly on the contested authenticity of the so-called *Casket Letters*, purporting to have been written by Mary to Bothwell. Soon after this third marriage the Protestant lords rose against her, defeated her army at Carberry Hill, and imprisoned her in Lochleven Castle. Bothwell, whom she refused to give up, fled to Scandinavia; the rebellious lords confirmed the position of Protestantism as the established Church and suppressed Catholicism. In 1567 Mary signed her abdication and James VI was crowned king. In 1568 she escaped from Lochleven and raised an army, but was once more defeated at Langside. She fled to England, where she was imprisoned and tried by a commission, which produced the *Casket Letters* against her with a series of the most humiliating accusations against which she refused to defend herself. The commission of peers gave an open verdict, stating that nothing derogatory to her had been proved. This verdict technically restored her reputation, which had been gravely injured by the Bothwell marriage, and *Pius V wrote her a conciliatory letter. *Elizabeth I, however, who, on account of the legally ambiguous circumstances of her own birth, feared for the security of her throne as long as Mary was at liberty, continued to hold her in close captivity. There was a proposal, supported by the Catholic powers, to have her marriage with Bothwell annulled, to enable her to marry the Duke of Norfolk; but when a Catholic uprising in the north failed, the scheme came to nothing and Norfolk was executed (1572). For the next 14 years Mary was held a prisoner, at first in honourable house arrest guarded by the Earl of Shrewsbury, and later by Sir Amias Paulet.

Her secret correspondence was watched by spies, and an unguarded letter, written in 1586, which implicated her in the Babington Plot to murder Elizabeth, brought about her condemnation. She met her death at Fotheringay on 8 Feb. 1587 with great courage.

A. Labanoff, *Lettres, instructions, et mémoires de Marie Stuart* (7 vols., 1844); A. Teulet, *Lettres de Marie Stuart* (1859); *Calendar of State Papers, Scotland*. Modern rendering of the contemporary hostile account of the reign by George Buchanan (1506–82) by W. A. Gatherer (Edinburgh, 1958). J. H. Pollen, SJ, *Papal Negotiations with Mary, Queen of Scots, etc.* (Scot. Hist. Soc. 37; 1901); id., *A Letter from Mary, Queen of Scots, to the Duke of Guise* (ibid. 43; 1904); id., *Mary, Queen of Scots, and the Babington Plot* (ibid., 3rd ser. 3; 1922). Modern studies by D. Hay Fleming (London, 1897), A. Fraser (ibid., 1969), J. Wormald (ibid. [1988]) and ed. M. Lynch (Oxford, 1988). G. Donaldson, *All the Queen's Men: Power and Politics in Mary Stewart's Scotland* (1983). On the *Casket Letters* controversy, W. Goodall, *Examination of the Letters said to be written by Mary, Queen of Scots, to Bothwell* (2 vols., 1754); T. F. Henderson, *The Casket Letters* (1890); M. H. Armstrong Davison, *The Casket Letters: A Solution to the Mystery of Mary Queen of Scots and the Murder of Lord Darnley* (1965); G. Donaldson, *The First Trial of Mary, Queen of Scots* (1969). S. A. and D. R. Tannenbaum, *Marie Stuart, Queen of Scots (A Concise Bibliography)* (Elizabethan Bibliographies, 30–2; New York, 1944–6). T. F. Henderson in *DNB* 36 (1893), pp. 373–90.

Mary Tudor (1516–58), Queen of England from 1553. The daughter of *Henry VIII and Catherine of Aragon, she was betrothed to the Dauphin of France in 1518, and in 1522 by the Treaty of Windsor to the Emp. *Charles V, who, however, married a Portuguese princess in 1526. The disgrace and unhappiness of her mother and the subsequent separation made a deep impression on her. During *Anne Boleyn's ascendancy (1527–36) she was in disfavour; she was excluded from the succession at the birth of *Elizabeth (1533), regarded as the King's bastard, and placed in the humiliating position of lady-in-waiting to Anne Boleyn's daughter. In 1536 she signed a document acknowledging Henry's religious supremacy and the illegitimacy of her mother's marriage, and so was received back into favour, under the influence of Jane Seymour. In 1537 she was godmother to the future *Edward VI, and during the next years lived quietly in retirement. After Henry's last marriage she was on affectionate terms with Catherine Parr, and in 1544 was given the second place in the succession, after Edward, during whose reign she continued to live away from Court on her extensive estates. She made a courageous stand against the demands of the Protector *Somerset and his successors in government that she should abandon her maintenance of the traditional Catholic liturgy, particularly the *Mass, in her household.

On Edward's death (1553) Mary became Queen, despite the attempt by the dying King and his leading Protestant advisers to put Lady Jane Grey in her place. Her accession was welcomed with enthusiasm by the supporters of the old religion, and, acting on the advice of the Emperor, she at first showed leniency to her Protestant opponents though proscribing their religion. She was crowned by Stephen *Gardiner, Bp. of Winchester, and soon afterwards betrothed to *Philip II of Spain despite the opposition of Parliament. In 1554 she displayed great courage in quelling Thomas Wyatt's plot, and resolved to rule henceforth with greater sternness. Among the many victims of the persecution following the plot were Jane Grey and her husband; and Elizabeth, who had possibly been implicated, was committed to the Tower. In July 1554 Philip landed in England, but the marriage proved a failure and was disliked by the people. Early in 1555 R. *Pole, who had arrived in England at the end of 1554, reconciled the country to the Papacy. In the same year the heresy laws were restored, and the trials for heresy began, the steadfastness of the condemned greatly serving the cause of Protestantism. This persecution and her inability to have children lost her the affection of her people; Philip returned to the Continent; and in 1555 Mary also lost Gardiner, her trusted Chancellor. In 1555–6 T. *Cranmer, H. *Latimer, N. *Ridley, J. *Hooper, and others were burned as heretics; and new conspiracies, with Elizabeth at their centre, were discovered and severely quelled. In 1557 Philip, needing English aid against France, temporarily returned to the Queen; and war was declared on France in June, the French being defeated at St-Quentin. But in 1558 Calais fell, a blow which severely damaged Mary's remaining prestige. From this time her health began to fail, and she died at St James's Palace on 17 Nov. 1558.

P. F. Tytler, *England under the Reigns of Edward VI and Mary*, 2 (1839), pp. 186–500. *The Chronicle of Queen Jane, and of the two years of Queen Mary*, ed. J. Gough Nichols (Camden 1st ser. 48; 1850), and 'The *Vita Mariae Angliae Reginae* of Robert Wingfield of Brantham', ed. D. MacCulloch, *Camden Miscellany*, 28 (Camden 4th ser. 29; 1984), pp. 181–301, are contemporary accounts of the early days of Mary's reign. Modern Lives by H. F. M. Prescott (London, 1940; 2nd edn., 1952) and D. [M.] Loades (Oxford, 1989), with bibl. D. M. Loades, *The Reign of Mary Tudor* (1979; 2nd edn., 1991). J. Loach and R. Tittler (eds.), *The Mid-Tudor Polity c.1540–1560* (1980). S. Lee in *DNB* 36 (1893), pp. 333–54.

Marys in the NT. Besides (1) the Virgin *Mary and (2) St *Mary Magdalene, there are four (or perhaps three) others. These are: (3) 'The wife of Cleopas' (Jn. 19: 25), who stood by the Cross. Some have identified her with '[Christ's] mother's sister', who is mentioned immediately before, but different women are probably meant. (4) 'The mother of James and Joses' (Mk. 15: 40), who stood by the Cross and was a witness of the Empty Tomb (Mk. 16: 1). She may well be the same as (3); and if this is so, her sons *James and Joses may be identified with the *Brethren of the Lord of those names. (5) Mary of Bethany, the sister of *Martha and *Lazarus (Jn. 11: 1 ff.), who sat at Christ's feet when he visited their village (Lk. 10: 38 ff.). Acc. to Jn. 12: 1–3, during the last week of the Lord's life she 'anointed the feet of Jesus, and wiped his feet with the hair of her head'. She has, particularly in the liturgy, been identified with Mary Magdalene (q.v.). (6) 'The mother of John *Mark' (Acts 12: 12).

Maskell, William (1814–90), ecclesiastical antiquary. Educated at University College, Oxford, he became an extreme *High Churchman and took holy orders in 1837. His two books, *The Ancient Liturgy of the Church of England* (1844) and *Monumenta Ritualia Ecclesiae Anglicanae* (1846), were important contributions to the revival of liturgical studies in the C of E. As chaplain to H. *Phillpotts, Bp. of Exeter, Maskell conducted the examination of G. C. *Gorham when the latter was presented to the vicarage of Brampford Speke; and the issue of the case led Maskell to secede to the RC Church in 1850. He never received RC ordination, but devoted himself to antiquarian studies and public service in Cornwall.

J. M. Rigg in *DNB* 36 (1893), pp. 413 f., s.v.

Mason, Francis (1566–1621), Archdeacon of Norfolk. He was educated at Oriel College, Oxford, and later had connections with Merton and Brasenose Colleges. His best-known writing was *Of the Consecration of the Bishops in the Church of England* (1613), written with the encouragement of Abp. G. *Abbot in refutation of the recently fabricated *Nag's Head Story. Composed in dialogue form and in an entertaining style and drawing on the records of *Lambeth Palace, it sought to establish the validity of the consecration esp. of M. *Parker. In reply to several attacks by RC writers, Mason revised and enlarged the work, and in this form it was reissued posthumously in a Latin translation by N. Brent in 1625. Its spirited defence of the C of E against Rome procured for him the title 'Vindex Ecclesiae Anglicanae'.

Extract from *Of the Consecration of the Bishops* in P. E. More and F. L. Cross (eds.), *Anglicanism* (1935), pp. 378–89 (no. 163). A. Wood, *Athenae Oxonienses* (ed. P. Bliss), 2 (1815), cols. 305–8. B. Porter in *DNB* 36 (1893), pp. 417–19.

Mass (Lat. *missa*). A title of the *Eucharist (q.v.). The word is a late form of *missio* (cf. late Lat. *ascensa* for *ascensio*, *collecta* for *collectio*), itself derived from *mittere*, 'to send'. (The older attempts to trace it back to a Heb. root may safely be ignored.) St *Avitus of Vienne (*c.*500) refers to its use, in churches and in the law courts, for the dismissal of the people (*ep.* 1 to Gundobald, *PL* 59. 199). The same use is attested by St *Isidore of Seville (*Etymol.* 6. 19. 4). But the word had long been current also for the service from which the people were dismissed. St *Ambrose (*ep.* 20; *PL* 16. 995) already applies to the Eucharist the expression 'missam facere' ('to perform the Mass'). The term was also used (less commonly) of other services, e.g., in the Rule of St *Benedict, of the Divine Office. In the present Roman Rite, '*Ite, missa est' remains the regular form of dismissal at the end of Mass. The word was retained by T. *Cranmer in the 1549 BCP ('The Supper of the Lord and the Holy Communion, commonly called the Mass'), but disappeared from later editions. In modern times it has come to be associated with the doctrine of the Eucharistic Sacrifice and in the C of E its use as a title of the Eucharist was revived by *High Churchmen.

J. A. Jungmann, SJ, 'Zur Bedeutungsgeschichte des Wortes *Missa*', *ZKT* 64 (1940), pp. 26–37. A. Pagliaro, 'Da *missa est a missa* "messa" ', *Atti della Accademia Nazionale dei Lincei*, 8th ser., Rendiconti. Classe di Scienze morale, storiche e filologiche, 10 (1955), pp. 104–35. C. Mohrmann, 'Missa', *VC* 12 (1958), pp. 67–92, repr. in her *Études sur le latin des Chrétiens*, 3 (1965), pp. 351–76. Jungmann (1958 edn.), 1, pp. 230–3 (Eng. tr., 1, 1951, pp. 173–5). A. *Fortescue in *CE* 9 (1910), pp. 790–2, s.v. 'Mass, Liturgy of the. A. Name and Definition'.

Mass, music for the. Those parts of the service sung by the choir or congregation (known as the *concentus*) may be divided into music for (1) the *Ordinary of the Mass (the *Kyrie, *Gloria in Excelsis, *Creed, *Sanctus and *Benedictus qui venit, *Agnus Dei and *Ite, missa est) in

which the words are always the same; and (2) the *Propers, in which the words vary acc. to the occasion. These have traditionally comprised the *Introit, *Gradual (replaced in the 1970 Missal by a *responsorial Psalm), *Offertory (dropped in 1970), and *Communion anthem. The Gradual used to be followed by *Alleluia and a verse, replaced on Sundays in Lent and certain penitential days by a *tract (verses of a Psalm); since 1970 the Alleluia has been sung after the second biblical reading, i.e. immediately before the Gospel. *Sequences were common in the Middle Ages but their number was drastically reduced at the Council of *Trent and has been still further curtailed in recent years.

The oldest chant for the Ordinary is little more than an inflective recitative corresponding to that used in the *accentus (or parts of the Mass sung by the officiant), and the *Ite, missa est* usually repeated the melody of the *Kyrie*. With the growth of polyphony from the 11th cent. onwards compositions for two or more voices began to appear. In the early 15th cent. the *Sanctus* and *Agnus* occur with a common musical arrangement, to be followed shortly by *Gloria–Credo* pairs, and later in the 15th cent. a complete series (or 'Mass-cycle') became common. England and France seem to have been in the van of this development, except that in England the *Kyrie* was not usually included. In the earliest examples the Gregorian chant forms a substratum of the composition, occurring as a *cantus firmus* for one of the voices. The full development of polyphony in the 16th cent. led to the composition of very elaborate settings, such as those of G. P. da *Palestrina and W. *Byrd. In the 18th cent. orchestral settings became popular on the Continent and eventually led to the introduction of music ostensibly designed for the Mass into the concerthall. After the Reformation some of the choral parts of the Mass were preserved in Latin in the *Lutheran Church and it was for liturgical use that J. S. *Bach originally composed parts of his Mass settings. At about this time it became customary to divide the liturgical texts (esp. the *Gloria in Excelsis* and the Creed) into a series of separate musical numbers, in order to provide a variety of movement; this practice continued in the RC Church until it was forbidden by *Pius X in 1903. As the music was elaborated it became increasingly divorced from the words of the liturgical texts and the *Sanctus* grew so long that it was often not completed by the time the celebrant reached the consecration; it then became usual to postpone the *Benedictus* until after the consecration. Against this background, the proponents of the *Liturgical Movement encouraged the revival of plainchant. In recent years, and esp. since the Second *Vatican Council, there has been increased emphasis on the need for music in which the congregation can take part.

The translation of the liturgy into the vernacular in England in the 16th cent. created a need for new musical settings to fit the new text, and these were provided by a succession of English composers from J. *Merbecke to C. V. *Stanford and H. Darke (1883–1976). Until the 19th cent. the use of musical settings for the Eucharist in the C of E, however, was largely confined to cathedral and *collegiate churches, and even there usually only the *Kyrie* and Creed were set to music. When the *Oxford Movement led to the introduction of *High Mass into parish churches, new settings of the full texts became common, while those of Merbecke enjoyed a widespread revival. The recent modern-language liturgies have led to the composition of new musical settings, mostly designed for congregational singing and often employing the idioms of 20th-cent. popular music.

P. Wagner, *Geschichte der Messe*, 1: *Bis 1600* (Leipzig, 1913 [all pub.]). O. Ursprung, *Die katholische Kirchenmusik* (Potsdam, 1931). W. Apel, *Gregorian Chant* [1958]. A. Hughes, OSB, 'The Enrichment of the Gregorian Cycle. Notes on the Music of the *Ordinarium Missae*', *Laudate*, 21 (1943), pp. 78–85; 22 (1944), pp. 41–7. E. H. Fellowes, *English Cathedral Music from Edward VI to Edward VII* (1941; 5th edn. by J. A. Westrup, 1969). B. Stäbelin and others in *Die Musik in Geschichte und Gegenwart*, 9 (1961), cols. 147–218, s.v. 'Messe'; R. Steiner and others in S Sadie (ed.), *The New Grove Dictionary of Music and Musicians*, 11 (1980), pp. 769–97, s.v., both with further bibl.

Mass of the Catechumens. See CATECHUMENS, MASS OF THE.

Mass of the Faithful. See FAITHFUL, MASS OF THE.

'Massa Candida' ('White Lump'). See UTICA, THE MARTYRS OF.

Massillon, Jean-Baptiste (1663–1742), French *Oratorian preacher. A native of Hyères in Provence, he joined the Oratory in 1681 was ordained priest in 1691, and in 1696 L. A. *de Noailles appointed him Director of the Seminary of St-Magloire at Paris. From 1699 he often preached before Louis XIV (who voiced the *mot* that whereas hitherto he had been very well satisfied with his preachers, after hearing Massillon he was very ill-satisfied with himself). In 1717 he was nominated Bp. of Clermont (consecrated 1718) and in 1719 became a Member of the Academy. He was one of the foremost preachers of a great generation, much respected even by leaders of the *Enlightenment (*Voltaire, J. Le R. *D'Alembert). If his classical style fell short of the sublimity of J.-B. *Bossuet, his sermons were marked by unsurpassed brilliance, colour, and vehemence and he was unrivalled as a preacher of moral seriousness. Among his most celebrated sermons were the discourse 'On the Fewness of the Elect' (1704) and his series of *Lent sermons ('Le Petit Carême') delivered before Louis XV in 1718. He preached the funeral orations of C. de N. de Villeroy, Abp. of Lyons (1693), of Louis XIV 'le Grand' (1715; which began *Dieu seul est grand*) and of Liselotte of the Palatinate, Duchess of Orléans (1723). He spent his last 20 years in the devoted service of his diocese.

Sermons ed. J. Massillon, Cong. Orat. (nephew), in 15 vols. (Paris, 1745–9); later edn. of his *Œuvres complètes* by E. A. Blampignon (Bar-le-Duc, 3 vols., 1865–7). M. A. Bayle, *Massillon, étude historique et littéraire* (1867). E. A. Blampignon, *Vie de Massillon d'après des documents inédits* (1879); id., *L'Épiscopat de Massillon* (1884); id., *Massillon: Supplément à son histoire et à sa correspondance* (1891); J. Janin, *Massillon et l'éloquence de la chaire* (1882); A. A. L. Pauthe, *Massillon* (1908). J. Ehrard and A. Poitrineau (eds.), *Études sur Massillon* (*Actes de la "Journée Massillon", Clermont-Ferrand, ... 25 mai 1974*) (Publications de l'Institut d'Études Massif Central, 13; Clermont-Ferrand [1975]); J. Ehrard and J. Renwick (eds.), *Catalogue de la Bibliothèque de Jean-Baptiste Massillon* (ibid. 15 [1977]). A. M. P. Ingold, *L'Oratoire et le jansénisme au temps de Massillon* (1880). S. J. Washington in *NCE* 9

(1967), pp. 435 f., s.v.; P. Auvray in *Dict. Sp.* 10 (1980), cols. 753–6, s.v.

Massoretes (from Heb. מסרת, *Mas(s)oreth*, prob. 'tradition'), Jewish grammarians who worked on the Hebrew text of the OT between about the 6th and 10th cents. AD. There were three main centres of Massoretic activity, Palestinian, Babylonian, and Tiberian, of which the last (based in Tiberias in N. Palestine) eventually gained the supremacy; the text of the Tiberian Massoretes thus finally became the recognized text form (although the Babylonian system continued to be used by Yemenite communities). In their endeavours to preserve a biblical text free from accretion, alteration, or corruption, the Massoretes provided marginal notes, which sometimes preserve careful reproductions of irregularities, and detailed instructions for copyists. There are two main types of Massoretic note: abbreviated notes which were written in the left- or right-hand margins of the text (the *massorah parva*), and more detailed explanations written in the upper or lower margins (the *massorah magna*). The latter includes detailed lists, which were sometimes copied at the end of the text if they could not be fitted into the margins (*massorah finalis*). These were subsequently collected in alphabetical order and printed at the end of Rabbinic Bibles. Among the best known aspects of the work of the Massoretes was their introduction into the text of the OT of *vowel points and accents, which were intended to show how words should be pronounced at a time when Hebrew had ceased to be a living language. The system was based on the pronunciation of the Synagogues and Schools. The text which derives from the work of the Massoretes is known as the 'Massoretic text'.

C. D. Ginsburg (ed.), *The Massorah compiled from MSS* (4 vols. in 3, 1880–1905). Modern scholars now hold that the Massorah is not and never existed as an independent corpus, but that it was essentially associated with a given text form. Thus the Leningrad MS B. 19a had its own Massorah; this has been ed. by G. Weil in the new edn. of the *Biblia Hebraica Stuttgartensia* by K. Elliger and W. Rudolph (Stuttgart [1978]), and the Hebrew University Bible Project, based on the Aleppo codex, contains the Massorah, magna and parva, as well as the text; pub. began with *The Book of Isaiah*, ed. M. H. Goshen-Gottstein (Jerusalem, 1975 ff.). The classic study is J. Buxtorf (the elder), *Tiberias sive Commentarius Masorethicus Triplex* (Basle, 1620). C. D. Ginsburg, *Introduction to the Massoretico-Critical Edition of the Hebrew Bible* (1897; repr. with prolegomenon by H. M. Orlinsky, New York, 1966). C. D. Ginsburg (ed.), *Jacob ben Chajim's Introduction to the Rabbinic Bible* (1865); id. (ed.), *The Massoreth ha-Massoreth of Elias Levita* (1867); these two works are repr. with prolegomenon by N. H. Snaith (New York, 1968); R. Butin (ed.), *The Ten Nequdoth of the Torah* (Baltimore, 1906; repr. with prolegomenon by S. Talmon, New York, 1969). S. Frensdorff, *Die Massora Magna*, 1. *Massoretisches Wörterbuch* (Hanover and Leipzig, 1876; repr. with prolegomenon by G. E. Weil, New York, 1968). W. Wickes, *A Treatise on the Accentuation of the Three so-called Poetical Books of the Old Testament, Psalms, Proverbs, and Job* (Oxford, 1881); id., *A Treatise on the Accentuation of the Twenty-One so-called Prose Books of the Old Testament* (ibid., 1887); these last two works were repr. with prolegomenon by A. Dotan (New York, 1970). P. Kahle, *Der masoretische Text des Alten Testaments nach der Überlieferung der babylonischen Juden* (1902); id., *Masoreten des Ostens* (1913); id., *Masoreten des Westens* (2 vols., 1927–30). G. E. Weil, *Élie Lévita, humaniste et massorète* (Studia Post-Biblica, 7; Leiden, 1963); id., *Initiation à la Massorah: L'Introduction au Sépher Zikhronot d'Élie Lévita* (Leiden, 1964). I. Yeivin, *Introduction to the Tiberian*

Masorah, Eng. tr. of Heb. (orig. pub., Jerusalem, 1971/2), tr. and ed. E. J. Revell (Society of Biblical Literature, Masoretic Studies, 5; Missoula, Mont. [1980]). *Textus: Annual of the Hebrew University Bible Project* (Jerusalem, 1965 ff.). A. Dotan in *Encyclopedia Judaica*, 16 (Jerusalem, 1972), cols. 1401–82, with detailed bibl.

Master of Misrule. See MISRULE, LORD OF.

Master of the Sentences (Lat. *Magister Sententiarum*). A title in use from the 12th cent. onwards for *Peter Lombard (d. *c.*1160) on account of the central place which his 'Libri Sententiarum' occupied as a textbook in the medieval schools.

Mater et Magistra. The encyclical letter issued by Pope *John XXIII 'On Recent Developments of the Social Question in the Light of Christian Teaching'. It was dated 15 May 1961 to commemorate the 70th anniversary of *Rerum Novarum*, but it was not published until 15 July of that year.

Text in *AAS* 53 (1961), pp. 401–64. Convenient Eng. tr. in D. J. O'Brien and T. A. Shannon (eds.), *Catholic Social Thought* (Maryknoll, NY [1992]), pp. 84–128, with introd. pp. 82 f. J. N. Moody and J. G. Lawler, *The Challenge of* Mater et Magistra (New York [1963]); J.-Y. Calvez, SJ, *Église et société économique* (1963; Eng. tr. [1964]); J. F. Cronin, PSS, *Christianity and Social Progress: A Commentary on* Mater et Magistra (Baltimore and Dublin [1965]).

material sin. An action which though in itself ('materially') contrary to the Divine law is not culpable, because the agent acted either in ignorance (e.g. when someone takes another's property, believing it to be his own) or under external constraint. It is contrasted with '*formal sin' (q.v.).

Mathew, Arnold Harris (1853–1919), *Old Catholic bishop. Educated for the Anglican ministry, he was ordained priest in the RC Church in 1878; but in 1892 he lost his status by a marriage and later was allowed to officiate in the C of E with the sanction of Abp. F. *Temple. On 28 Apr. 1908 he received episcopal consecration at Utrecht from the Dutch Old Catholic Church as their Archbishop in Great Britain. In 1910, however, he was repudiated by the Dutch Old Catholics on the ground that his consecration had been obtained under a misconception of the extent of his following in England (which appears to have been virtually non-existent). He continued to describe himself as 'Archbishop of the London Area' and (later) as 'Archbishop and Metropolitan of the English Catholic Church', and left irregular episcopal successions (see EPISCOPI VAGANTES) which were repudiated by the *Lambeth Conference of 1920. See also OLD CATHOLICS.

A. H. Mathew, *An Episcopal Odyssey: An Open Letter to His Grace the Right Hon. and Most Rev. Randall Thomas Davidson, D.D.* . . . (privately pr., Kingsdown, Kent, 1915), with docs. H. R. T. Brandreth, OGS, *Episcopi Vagantes and the Anglican Church* (1947), pp. 12–30, with bibl. pp. 71 f.

Mathurins. Another name for members of the *Trinitarian Order (q.v.), founded for the redemption of Christian captives in 1198 by St *John of Matha.

Matilda of Magdeburg. See MECHTHILD OF MAGDEBURG.

Matins. See MATTINS.

Matrimony. Christian marriage, though it claims to be based on the natural law, differs from earlier practice, whether Jewish or pagan, and also from modern secular usage, notably in the dignity it has sought for the woman and the life-long nature it ascribes to the marriage bond.

Early Hebrew law, which was founded on marriage by purchase, assigned a low status to the woman, who became in effect the property of her husband, though he could not sell her (Deut. 21: 14; cf. Ex. 21: 7 f.). The woman could neither own nor inherit property and had no rights of divorce, while the man might divorce her for some 'indecency' (Deut. 24: 1 RSV). Polygamy was practised, sometimes with the consent of the wife, as in the case of Sarah (Gen. 16: 2), that the bond might be preserved, but in later Judaism there was a growing realization that monogamy represented the ideal.

In His teaching about matrimony Jesus was concerned to restore it to its original place in God's plan of creation (Mk. 10: 6–9; Mt. 19: 4–6), and insisted therefore that divorce (allowed to the husband by Mosaic law) was contrary to God's will. This negative attitude to divorce, found also in the Damascus Document from *Qumran (*CD* 4. 20–5. 6), is based on a positive ideal of the marriage relationship as God's gift in creation (cf. Gen. 2: 18). It is expressed in different ways in the Synoptic Gospels. Acc. to Mk. 10: 12 Christ directs His teaching to the Greek and Roman setting in which, contrary to Jewish law, a woman was allowed to divorce her husband. Mt. 5: 31 f. (unlike Lk. 16: 18) and Mt. 19: 9 (unlike Mk. 10: 11) assume that the Lord intended an exception in cases of unchastity, implying His agreement with Deut. 24: 1. Remarriage is excluded to underline the Divine intention that the union should be for life. Unlike other Jewish thinkers, Christ also saw a place for celibacy for the sake of the *Kingdom of God (Mt. 19: 10–12), and Lk. 18: 29 includes 'a wife' among the list of what might be renounced for the sake of the Kingdom of God. In 1 Cor. 7: 25–40 Paul recommends celibacy in view of the imminence of the end (*Parousia), but recognises that this special gift is not granted to all (v. 7). His remark in v. 9 that it is better to be married than to burn (with desire) has often been taken out of its context of advice on *asceticism to suggest wrongly a low view of marriage. His position is that marriage is good, but in this time of crisis celibacy is better (vv. 38, 40), This religiously motivated enthusiasm for celibacy later found expression in *monasticism.

While acknowledging the Lord's opposition to divorce (1 Cor. 7: 10), Paul's pastoral practice permitted separation (1 Cor. 7: 11) and in some circumstance apparently freedom to remarry (v. 15). This became the basis of the so-called *Pauline Privilege developed (and widened) in RC moral theology (*CIC* (1983), cans. 1143–9). Paul teaches the equality of men and women in Christ (Gal. 3: 28), which some hold makes Christian marriage a partnership of equals, but at 1 Cor. 11. 3–12 he also echoed the patriarchal assumptions of his Jewish background and Greco-Roman context. The 'household codes' of the later NT Epistles assimilate those cultural norms without, however, losing the Christian principle of reciprocity in marriage (Eph. 5: 22–33, Col. 3: 18–19; 1 Pet. 3: 1–7). The importance of love and tenderness in marriage is christologically motivated and an elevated view of marriage expressed in Eph. 5: 25–33, where the union of man and woman is compared to that of Christ and the Church.

Roman matrimonial practice was in many ways also influential in the formation of Christian doctrine. Though under the Empire divorce was readily available to both parties, the jurist Modestinus could define marriage as 'a lifelong partnership, and a sharing of civil and religious rights' (consortium omnis vitae, divini et humani iuris communicatio, L. I, Dig. 23. 2), while the legal commonplace that it was not consummation but consent that made a marriage was equally agreeable to Christian belief. One part of Roman law, however, that there could be no marriage between bond and free, was repugnant to Christian sentiment and set aside in the 3rd cent.

The purpose of matrimony has traditionally been understood as threefold: fidelity, the procreation of children, and union of the parties in the marriage (fides, proles, sacramentum). The procreative, often understood as the primary end, demands that the good of children (bonum prolis) be put before all other considerations. This has led many Christian moralists to repudiate all artificial methods of family limitation (see CONTRACEPTION, PROCREATION, AND ABORTION, ETHICS OF). The unitive end has often been understood in a limited way, as no more than a means of avoiding sexual sin. This negative view has been influential in the W., owing esp.to St *Augustine's belief in the inextricable link between sexual intercourse and the transmission of *original sin. A more positive appreciation of the unitive aspect is seen in the Lord's teaching (Mt. 19: 5, Mk. 10: 8) and developed in Eph. 5: 31 f. Marriage came to be regarded as a *Sacrament. In the W. it was reckoned such by *Hincmar of Reims (d. 882), and from St *Thomas Aquinas onwards it was taught that it conferred grace (ST 3, Suppl. 49. 3). In the W. it is accounted peculiar among the Sacraments in that the parties themselves are the ministers, the priest being only the appointed witness. This view is not shared by the E. Church, where marriage was not usually included in the lists of Sacraments until the W. concept of seven Sacraments was adopted in the 17th cent.

Traditionally the rite of marriage consists of two parts: the betrothal and the marriage proper. This distinction goes back to Roman practice and is still present in the Christian ceremony, though obscured in modern W. rites. The betrothal (which originally took place some time before the marriage, and at the church door or in the *narthex, not in the church itself) consists of the giving of gifts, representing the marriage settlement, the exchange of a kiss (both of these usually omitted now), the giving of a *ring (or exchanging of rings), and the joining of hands. The making of vows (explicitly or implicitly) is part of the betrothal rite. The marriage service, essentially a service of blessing, from the time of *Tertullian included the celebration of the Eucharist (*Nuptial Mass), replacing the sacrificial rites (the confarreatio) of the Romans. The Nuptial Mass was frequently replaced by a service of blessing even in the medieval Church, but it still took place in church, in front of the altar, and this arrangement is preserved among Protestant Churches. In the E., the marriage service proper is rarely a Nuptial Mass, but it is more elaborate than a simple service of blessing: it preserves an epistle and gospel, the couple are given crowns (representing the crowns of the martyrs) and then share a cup of wine.

It was only in the 11th cent. that the claim of the Church to exclusive jurisdiction over matrimonial cases was conceded. The Reformation in England did not affect this, and the first breach with Canon Law was effected by the Clandestine Marriages Act 1753 (Lord *Hardwicke's Marriage Act), and more notably by the Marriage Act 1836 which established civil marriage. The Matrimonial Causes Act 1857 abolished the jurisdiction of the ecclesiastical courts, and also allowed divorce a vinculo for adultery when allied to cruelty or desertion (hitherto it had been available only by private Act of Parliament). A series of subsequent acts widened the grounds for divorce until the Divorce Reform Act 1969 made the 'irretrievable breakdown' of marriage the sole ground of divorce. This criterion was preserved in the Matrimonial Causes Act 1973. Similar developments have taken place in most W. countries.

Civil legislation has not affected the belief of the Church, both RCs and many Anglicans holding that indissolubility is of Divine institution. In modern times, however, in the RC Church there has been an increase in the number of petitions for *nullity (i.e. to obtain a declaration that there has been no true marriage) which are allowed on various grounds by the Church courts. In some parts of the Anglican Communion after a civil divorce another Church marriage is often allowed; in other Provinces (e.g. the C of E), where a second Church marriage is not normally permitted during the lifetime of the first spouse, a blessing is sometimes given after a civil marriage, and the parties are subsequently admitted to Communion. In the Orthodox Church divorce was already formally tolerated in Byzantine times and is still recognized, though a different form of ceremony is used for second and third marriages.

The principle that any Christian man or woman may marry has naturally been subjected to limitation (see AFFINITY). The lifelong character of Christian marriage prohibits bigamy, which was made a felony in England in 1604 (it is now classed as an arrestable offence). The minimum age for marriage, which has varied, was fixed by the Age of Marriage Act 1929 at 16 for both parties, marriage below this age being void. The various restrictions were divided by RC canon law into impedient and *diriment impediments (q.v.), but the 1983 *Codex Iuris Canonici mentions only the latter.

As the Church took over the Roman view of marriage as the consent of the parties a certain publicity has always been required. Apart from the period 1753–1823 English civil law has accepted the teaching of the canonists that clandestine marriages are valid but irregular (for RC Canon Law on this subject, see NE TEMERE). The necessary publicity is secured by the publishing of *banns on three Sundays in the parishes of residence of both parties, and the celebration of marriage in one or the other (by the Marriage Act 1949 marriage may be celebrated in the usual place of worship of one party whose name is entered on the church electoral roll of that parish). Marriage may also be celebrated by licence, obtainable from *surrogates, or by special licence (normally only for weddings in nonparochial churches), obtainable from the Abp. of Canterbury, in virtue of his original legatine authority. Similar publicity is required for a civil marriage. Canon 62 of 1604 fixed the hours when marriages might be solemnized as between 8 a.m. and noon, but the latter was extended in 1886 to 3 p.m., and in 1934 to 6 p.m., and Convocation amended the Canon accordingly. The requirement that marriages should be solemnized only between 8 a.m. and 6 p.m. was retained in the 1969 Canons (B 35). See also MARRIAGE LICENCES.

Practice varies among the Christian bodies concerning clerical marriage. While the Orthodox Church preserves the primitive practice, that ordinands must either be already married or elect to remain celibate, the RC church (at least for all who follow the Latin rite) has generally enforced celibacy, while the Anglican Church (Art. 32 of the *Thirty-Nine Articles) and Nonconformist bodies allow a free choice.

See also DIVORCE.

G. Farnedi, OSB (ed.), *La Celebrazione Cristiana del Matrimonio: Atti del II Congresso Internazionale di Liturgia, Roma, 27–31 maggio 1985* (Studia Anselmiana, 93; 1986). On the comparative study of the institution, E. Westermarck, *The History of Human Marriage* (1891 [partly issued, Helsingsfors, 1889]; 5th edn., rewritten, 3 vols., 1921); F. Meyrick in *DCA* 2 (1880), pp. 1092–1114, s.v. 'Marriage'; L. Godefroy, G. Le Bras, and M. Jugie, AA, in *DTC* 9 (pt. 2; 1927), cols. 2044–335, s.v. 'Mariage'; R. Naz and C. de Clercq in *DDC* 6 (1957), cols. 731–802, s.v. 'Mariage'; J. C. Davies and others in id. (ed.), *A New Dictionary of Liturgy and Worship* (1986), pp. 349–64, s.v. 'Marriage', all with bibl. Studies free from technicalities by Anglican writers include O. D. Watkins, *Holy Matrimony* (1895); T. A. *Lacey, *Marriage in Church and State* (1912; rev. edn. by R. C. Mortimer, 1947); K. E. *Kirk, *Marriage and Divorce* (1933; rev. edn., 1948); by RC writers, G. H. Joyce, SJ, *Christian Marriage* (1933; 2nd edn., 1948); H. Rondet, SJ, *Introduction à l'étude de la théologie du mariage* [1960]; E. [C. F. A.] *Schillebeeckx, OP, *Het Huwelijk, aardse werkelijkheid en heilsmysterie* (Bilthoven, 1963; Eng. tr., *Marriage: Secular Reality and Saving Mystery*, 2 vols., 1965); and W. Kasper, *Zur Theologie der christlichen Ehe* (Mainz, 1977; Eng. tr., 1980). Official RC teaching in the Second *Vatican Council's Constitution 'Gaudium et Spes', nos. 47–52, *Paul VI's encyclicals '*Humanae Vitae' (25 Jul. 1968) and 'Matrimonia Mixta' (31 Mar. 1970), and *CIC* (1983), cans. 1055–165. D. Palmieri, *De Matrimonio Christiano* (Paris, 1880). A. Esmein, *Le Mariage en droit canonique* (1891; 2nd edn. by R. Génestal and J. Dauvillier, 2 vols., 1929–35). P. Gasparri, *Tractatus Canonicus de Matrimonio* (2 vols., Paris, 1891; rev. edn., Vatican City, 1932); L. Örsy, SJ, *Marriage in Canon Law: Texts and Comments. Reflections and Questions* (Wilmington, Del., 1986; Dublin and Leominster, 1988) [on *CIC* (1983), cans. 1055–165]. Useful Guide to the law for Clergy of the C of E and the Church in Wales, *Anglican Marriage in England and Wales*, issued by the Faculty Office of the Archbishop of Canterbury [1992]. J. A. Brundage, *Law, Sex, and Christian Society in Medieval Europe* (Chicago and London, 1987). C. N. L. Brooke, *The Medieval Idea of Marriage* (Oxford, 1989). J. Zhishman, *Das Eherecht der orientalischen Kirche* (1863–5); A. Raes, SJ, *Le Mariage: Sa célébration et sa spiritualité dans l'Église d'Orient* (Collection Irénikon [1959]); J. Meyendorff, *Marriage: An Orthodox Perspective* (New York, 1971; 2nd edn., 1975). K. Ritzer, OSB, *Formen, Riten und religiöses Brauchtum der Eheschliessung in den christlichen Kirchen des ersten Jahrtausends* (Liturgiewissenschaftliche Quellen und Forschungen, 38 [1962]; Fr. tr., *Le mariage dans les Églises chrétiennes du Iᵉ au XIᵉ siècle*, Lex orandi, 45 [1970]). K. [W.] Stevenson, *Nuptial Blessing: A Study of Christian Marriage Rites* (*Alcuin Club Collections, 64; 1982); id., *To Join Together: The Rite of Marriage* (Studies in the Reformed Rite of the Catholic Church, 5; New York [1987]; L. Stone, *The Family, Sex and Marriage in England 1500–1800* [1977].

matter. In medieval philosophy, the stuff underlying all material existence before it is determined and actualized by *form (q.v.). The conception is derived from *Aristotle, where it is used to explain the fact of change in the physical world. Since one substance passes into another, originates, and decays, but never springs from nothing or turns into nothing, Aristotle postulated 'matter' (ὕλη) as a common substratum. It is the mere potentiality of physical being and becoming, and hence no immediate object for the intellect, but something that can be known only through the body in which it is actualized by the form.

The conception (called '*hylomorphism') was developed and applied by the Schoolmen of the 13th cent. to the Sacraments. They substituted the terms 'matter' and 'form' for the older expressions 'things' and 'words'. The matter was the sensible element in the Sacraments, e.g. the water of *Baptism and the bread and wine of the *Eucharist. Though possessing a certain significance (cleansing and nourishing) in itself, the Sacramental matter or action needed for its perfection a more decisive determination, which it receives through the form, i.e. the accompanying words. The Scholastic terminology was accepted by Pope *Eugenius IV in his instruction to the Armenians and by the Council of *Trent; but it is not easily adapted to certain Sacraments, e.g. matrimony.

Matthew, St, Apostle and Evangelist. His name occurs in all four lists of the 12 Apostles (Mt. 10: 3, Mk. 3: 18, Lk. 6: 15, and Acts 1: 13). In Mt. 10: 3 he is described as a *publican. The call of Matthew by Christ is recorded in Mt. 9: 9 (in the parallel passages in Mk. 2: 14 and Lk. 5: 27 the name of the person called is given as 'Levi'). Acc. to *Papias he made a collection of Christ's sayings in Hebrew, and he is traditionally held to be the author of the First Gospel (see following entry).

Acc. to *Eusebius (*HE* 3. 24) Matthew preached to the Hebrews. Other traditions about his later life conflict and merit little credence. The *Roman Martyrology states that he was martyred 'in Ethiopia', the *Hieronymianum puts his death 'in Persia in the town of Tarrium' (perhaps Tarsuana east of the Persian Gulf, so A. von Gutschmid), while some apocryphal Greek Acts (prob. *Gnostic) state that he suffered in Pontus. In later times Salerno and other places laid claim to his relics. He is credited with a 6th-cent. apocryphal Latin work on the Lord's Infancy (*De Ortu Beatae Mariae et Infantia Salvatoris*), an adaptation of the *Protevangelium of St James. In Christian symbolism he has commonly (*Irenaeus, *Jerome, *Augustine) been allotted the figure of a man (cf. Rev. 4: 7) on the ground that his *Genealogy (1: 1–17) emphasizes the Lord's human origin. In art he is depicted with a sword, a money-bag, or a carpenter's square. Feast day in the E., 16 Nov.; in the W., 21 Sept.

'Passio' in R. A. *Lipsius and M. Bonnet (eds.), *Acta Apostolorum Apocrypha*, 2 (pt. 1; Leipzig, 1898), pp. 217–62. *AASS*, Sept. 6 (1757), pp. 194–227. B. de Gaiffier, SJ, 'Hagiographie salernitaine. La translation de S. Matthieu', *Anal. Boll.* 80 (1962), pp. 82–110, with refs. to other works on the post-biblical material. F. Spadafora and P. Cannata in *Bibliotheca Sanctorum*, 9 (1967), cols. 110–45, s.v. 'Matteo', incl. section on iconography.

Matthew, Gospel acc. to St. Traditionally held to be the oldest of the four, this Gospel stands first in the

*Canon. It was prob. known to the author of the *Didache* (perh. *c*. AD 100) and St *Ignatius of Antioch (*c*. AD 110); and from the time of St *Irenaeus onwards it was regularly ascribed to the Apostle *Matthew by name. *Papias (*c*. AD 130) records that Matthew wrote the 'Logia' (τὰ λόγια) 'in the Hebrew tongue'; if the reference be to our Gospel (which, however, was written in Greek), this is still earlier evidence for its ascription to him. The Gospel is probably to be dated *c*. AD 80–90, and unlikely to have been written by an eye-witness.

Most scholars hold that the author drew extensively on Mark, which he expanded with other sources, esp. '*Q', whether this be regarded as a single source or a collection of material which circulated for teaching purposes. In addition to the (mainly discourse) material which is paralleled in Luke, however, there is much that is peculiar to Matthew. This last is often described as 'M'.

The Gospel begins with a *Genealogy of Christ (1: 1–17) and 'Infancy Narrative' (1: 18–2 end). It records the mission of St *John the Baptist (3: 1–12), the Baptism and Temptation of Christ (3: 13–4: 17), His Mission in Galilee (4: 18–15: 20), His work further afield including the revelation of His Messiahship to St *Peter at *Caesarea Philippi (15: 21–18 end), His Last Journey to Jerusalem (19 f.), concluding with the account of His last week, Passion and Resurrection (21–8). Matthew interpolates long sections of 'discourse' into the Marcan framework, and rearranges the narrative so as to bring 10 miracles together in chs. 8–9. His record of the teaching of Christ groups similar material, notably in the '*Sermon on the Mount' (5–7), whereas many of the parallel passages in Luke are widely scattered. This ordered presentation of the teaching is intended to guide Christian observance (28: 20), and the moral claim of the Gospel is underlined by references to God's judgement exercised by the *Son of Man. Christ is also presented as the fulfilment of prophecy and the true interpreter of the Jewish law. He is '*Immanuel', 'God with us' (1: 23) and remains with His disciples from the Resurrection to the end of time (28: 20).

The special commission given to Peter (16: 17–20) has been highly influential (see PETER, ST). It has contributed to the impression of an 'ecclesiastical' Gospel, the only occurrences of ἐκκλησία in the Gospels being here at 16: 18 and at 18: 17.

The Greek of the Gospel is 'correct, if rather colourless' (J. H. Moulton). Matthew avoids some of Mark's undignified words and is more concise, but much of Mark's subtlety and artistry is lost. Of the three Synoptic Gospels it is the most suitable for public reading; and it has probably always been the best-known of them.

Patristic comm. in Gk. incl. those of *Origen, St John *Chrysostom, and *Peter of Laodicea; in Lat., those of *Hilary of Poitiers and St *Jerome. Modern comm. incl. those by E. Klostermann (Hb. NT 5, 1909, pp. 121–52; 2nd edn., 3, 1927), A. H. McNeile (London, 1915), M. J. *Lagrange, OP (Études Bibliques, 1923; 7th edn., 1948), E. Lohmeyer and W. Schmauch (KEK, 1956), F. V. Filson (Black's NT Comm., 1960), J. C. Fenton (Pelican Gospel Commentaries, 1963), E. Schweizer (Das Neue Testament Deutsch, 1973; Eng. tr., 1976), H. B. Green, CR (New Clar. Bib., 1975), F. W. Beare (Oxford, 1981), D. A. Carson (*The Expositor's Bible Commentary*, ed. F. E. Gaebelein and others, 8, Grand Rapids, Mich. [1984], pp. 1–599), U. Luz (Evangelisch-Katholischer Kommentar zum Neuen Testament, 1; 3 vols., Neukirchen, 1985 ff.; Eng. tr., Minneapolis, 1989 ff., and Edin-

burgh, 1990 ff.), and W. D. Davies and D. C. Allison (ICC, 3 vols., 1988–97).

G. D. Kilpatrick, *The Origins of the Gospel according to St Matthew* (1946). E. Massaux, *Influence de l'évangile de saint Matthieu sur la littérature chrétienne avant saint Irénée* (Louvain, 1950; ed. F. Neirynck, with bibl. by B. Dehandschutter, 1986). A. M. Farrer, *St Matthew and St Mark* (The Edward Cadbury Lectures, 1953–4; 1954; 2nd edn., 1966). K. Stendahl, *The School of Matthew* (Acta Seminarii Neotestamentici Upsaliensis, 20; 1954). G. Bornkamm, G. Barth, and H. J. Held, *Überlieferung und Auslegung im Matthäusevangelium* (Wissenschaftliche Monographien zum Alten und Neuen Testament, 1; 1960; Eng. tr., *Tradition and Interpretation in Matthew*, 1963; enlarged edn., 1982). M. J. Suggs, *Wisdom, Christology, and Law in Matthew's Gospel* (Cambridge, Mass., 1970). M. D. Goulder, *Midrash and Lection in Matthew* (1974). G. Stanton (ed.), *The Interpretation of Matthew* (Issues in Religion and Theology, 3; 1983); id., *The Gospel for a New People: Studies on Matthew* (Edinburgh, 1992). See also SYNOPTIC PROBLEM.

Matthew of Aquasparta (*c*.1240–1302), *Franciscan theologian. A native of Aquasparta near Todi in Umbria, he became a Franciscan *c*.1254. By 1268 he was studying theology in Paris, and in due course he occupied one of the Franciscan chairs. He is also known to have taught in Bologna. In 1279 he succeeded John *Pecham, under whom he had studied in Paris, as *lector sacri palatii* in Rome. In 1287 he became General of his Order, in 1288 Cardinal, and in 1291 Cardinal Bp. of Porto and Rufina. He stood high in the confidence of *Boniface VIII, whose views on Papal power he endorsed, and who entrusted him with political missions. His writings include sermons and biblical commentaries, and a commentary on the Sentences as well as *quodlibets* and *Quaestiones disputatae*. These last, which, like his other works, had little circulation, are perhaps the most important. They are notable for their clarity. They show him as a disciple of St *Bonaventure in following the *Augustinian doctrine on divine illumination and innate ideas, and on the direct knowledge which the soul has of its essence. Matthew was not content to be a slavish follower, and in more than one respect, as in his view of our direct knowledge of the singular and posterior knowledge of the universal, he looks forward to *Duns Scotus.

His *Quaestiones Disputatae* have now all been pub. at Quaracchi in the Bibliotheca Franciscana Scholastica Medii Aevi, 1 (1903; 2nd edn., 1957); 2 (1914; 2nd edn., 1957); 11 (1935), incl. important introd. on his life and works by V. Doucet, OFM, pp. xi–clxiii; 17 (1956); and 18 (1959); except for the *Quaestiones de Anima VI*, ed. A. J. Gondras in *AHDLMA* 32, for 1957 (1958), pp. 203–352, and the *Quaestiones Disputatae de Anima XIII*, ed. id. (Études de Philosophie Médiévale, 1; 1961). Various sermons ed. C. Piana, OFM, and G. Gál, OFM (Bibliotheca Franciscana Ascetica Medii Aevi, 9 and 10; Quaracchi, 1962). M *Grabmann, *Die philosophische und theologische Erkenntnislehre des Kardinals Matthaeus ab Aquasparta* (Theologische Studien der Leo-Gesellschaft, 14; 1906). H. M. Beha, OSF, 'Matthew of Aquasparta's Theory of Cognition', *Franciscan Studies*, 20 (1960), pp. 161–204; 21 (1961), pp. 1–79, 383–465. Z. Hayes, OFM, *The General Doctrine of Creation in the Thirteenth Century, with special emphasis on Matthew of Aquasparta* (Munich, 1964). E. Brocchieri, *La legge naturale nel pensiero di Matteo d'Acquasparta* (Rovigo, 1967). P. Weber, 'La Liberté dans la théologie de Matthieu d'Aquasparta', *RTAM* 34 (1967), pp. 238–54, with bibl. P. Mazzarella, *La dottrina dell'anima e della conoscenza in Matteo d'Acquasparta* (Padua [1969]). *Matteo d'Acquasparta, Francescano, Filosofo, Politico: Atti del XXIX Convegno storico internazionale, Todi, 11–14 ottobre 1992* (Spoleto, 1993). E. Longpré, OSB, in *DTC* 10 (pt.

1; 1928), cols. 375–89, s.v.; G. Gál, OFM, in *NCE* 9 (1967), p. 491, s.v.

Matthew Paris (*c.*1200–59), medieval chronicler. He became a member of the Benedictine monastery of *St Albans in 1217 and, as an expert scribe and illuminator, annalist of the monastery in 1236. His chief claim to fame lies in his *Chronica Majora*, a history of the world from the Creation to 1259. Its earlier sections are almost entirely a transcription of Roger of Wendover's *Flores Historiarum*, but its later pages are his own narration of contemporary events. The work is characterized by trenchant criticism of ecclesiastical abuses (in particular, Papal venality) and of Henry III's employment of foreigners in England, and was the fruit of his own experiences at St Albans and his wide travels, both at home and abroad. Matthew was also the author of a *Historia Anglorum sive Historia Minor*, an abridgement of his longer history.

His *Chronica Majora*, ed. H. R. Luard (7 vols., RS, 1872–83); his *Historia Anglorum*, ed. F. Madden (3 vols., ibid., 1866–9), with biog. preface in vol. 3, pp. vii–liv; the part of the 'Gesta Monasterii Sancti Albani' which is prob. mainly his work, ed. H. T. Riley in *Gesta Abbatum Monasterii Sancti Albani a Thoma Walsingham*, 1 (ibid., 1867), pp. 3–324. The section of his *Chronica Majora* and its continuation dealing with the period 1235–73 is tr. into Eng. by J. A. Giles, *Matthew Paris's English History* (Bohn's Antiquarian Library, 3 vols., 1852–4). The section of the *Chronica Majora* covering the period 1247–50 and the part of the 'Gesta Monasterii Sancti Albani' 1195–1255 also tr. into Eng. by R. Vaughan, *The Chronicles of Matthew Paris* (Gloucester and New York, 1984). Id., *Matthew Paris* (Cambridge Studies in Medieval Life and Thought, NS 6; 1958). S. Lewis, *The Art of Matthew Paris in the Chronica Majora* (California Studies in the History of Art, 21; Berkeley, Calif., and London [1987]). V. H. Galbraith, *Roger Wendover and Matthew Paris* (lecture; 1944). W. Hunt in *DNB* 43 (1895), pp. 207–13, s.v. 'Paris, Matthew'.

Matthew's Bible. This edition of the English Bible was issued in 1537. It was a revision of the work of W. *Tyndale, pieced out with Tyndale's unpublished MSS and portions of M. *Coverdale's OT, with expository notes drawn from Conrad Pellican (1478–1556). Printed at Antwerp in 1537, it was dedicated to *Henry VIII, who licensed it for general reading. 'Thomas Matthew', the name of the supposed editor, was a mere *alias* for John *Rogers (q.v.).

S. L. Greenslade in id. (ed.), *The Cambridge History of the Bible: The West from the Reformation to the Present Day* (Cambridge, 1963), pp. 150–2. W. T. Whitley, 'Thomas Matthew's Bible', *CQR* 125 (1937), pp. 48–69. Whitley's attempt to defend the existence of Thomas Matthew as a real person has been disposed of by J. F. Mozley, *William Tyndale* (1937), Appendix E. Darlow and Moule, ed. A. S. Herbert, 1 (1968), pp. 18 f. (no. 34).

Matthias, St, Apostle. According to the tradition preserved in Acts 1: 15–26, he was chosen by lot after the Ascension to fill the vacancy in the Twelve left by the treachery of *Judas Iscariot, and it is implied that he had been a follower of Christ from the beginning of His ministry, but he is not mentioned elsewhere in the NT. Acc. to apocryphal traditions, he (or, acc. to some versions, *Matthew) preached the Gospel in Ethiopia, or among the 'Anthropophagi', while the *Gnostic *Basilides claimed that his own doctrines derived from a private tradition going back to St Matthias. *Eusebius (*HE* 1. 12. 3, 2. 1. 1) and St *Epiphanius (*Haer.* 1. 22) believed that he was

one of the Lord's 'Seventy Disciples' (Lk. 10: 1). Feast day in the W., 14 May (formerly 24, or, in leap years, 25 Feb.; 24 Feb. still observed in some Anglican Churches); in the Greek Church, 9 Aug.

AASS, Feb. 3 (1658), pp. 431–54. J. Renié, SM, 'L'Élection de Mathias (Act. 1, 15–26). Authenticité du récit', *R. Bibl.* 55 (1948), pp. 43–53; P. Gaechter, SJ, 'Die Wahl des Matthias (Apg. 1, 15–26)', *ZKT* 71 (1949), pp. 318–46; K. H. Rengstorf, 'Die Zuwahl des Matthias (Apg. 1. 15 ff.)', *Studia Theologica*, 15 (1961), pp. 35–67. See also comm. on Acts (s.v.), esp. that of E. Jacquier (2nd edn., Paris, 1926), pp. 30–41.

Matthias, Gospel of St. A lost apocryphal Gospel, mentioned by *Origen, *Hom. I in Lc.* and other early Christian writers. Perhaps it is to be identified with the treatise referred to by *Clement of Alexandria as 'the Traditions of Matthias' (*Strom.* 2. 9. 45, etc.).

H. C. Puech in Schneemelcher, 1 (5th edn.; 1987), pp. 306–9; Eng. tr., 1 (1991), pp. 382–6.

Mattins (from Lat. *matutinus*, 'of the morning', 'early in the morning'). Originally, the morning service in the primitive round of daily prayer. As the name implies, it was an early morning office, initially held at dawn or in the period between dawn and sunrise. Later, when it was more closely associated with dawn, it was preceded by an early morning *Vigil kept by the more devout. Ps. 63 was frequently a component because of a Latin rendering of v. 1: 'Deus, Deus meus es tu; ad te de luce vigilo', which passed into traditional English versions as 'O God, thou art my God: early will I seek thee'. In the W. the name was eventually attached to the Vigil or night part of the office, the older morning part becoming known as *Lauds. A real distinction of the two separate offices was apparent only from the later Middle Ages. Mattins itself, which remained basically unchanged until 1912, was composed as follows: some prayers said silently and opening *versicles led to Ps. 95 (the *Invitatory), a hymn suited to the hour, feast, or season, and then on Sundays and feasts, three divisions called *Nocturns (q.v.), the first of 12 and the other two of three psalms on Sundays and three psalms each on feasts; on weekdays there was a single nocturn of 12 psalms. The *Te Deum concluded the office on Sundays (except in Advent and the period from *Septuagesima to *Palm Sunday), feasts, and the weekdays of Eastertide. The number of psalms was reduced to nine in both Sunday and weekday offices by Pope *Pius X in 1912. Mattins was completely replaced by the *Office of Readings in 1971. From the Middle Ages until the 20th cent. Mattins and Lauds were often together anticipated on the previous evening. In modern Byzantine use, the office of *Orthros, which corresponds to Mattins and Lauds, is similarly anticipated on certain occasions.

In the C of E Thomas *Cranmer retained the name Mattins as a secondary designation for his 1549 order of Morning Prayer, but after 1552 it was dropped. The name seems to have come back into popular use in the 19th cent. The structure of the office is identical with that of *Evensong (q.v.), except that Ps. 95 is sung before the psalms for the day (except on the 19th day of the month, when it is in the ordinary course of the psalms, and on *Easter Day, when a special anthem is ordered). Also on 13 feast days in the year the *Athanasian Creed is ordered to be said in substitution for the Apostles' Creed, but in modern times this rubric has been widely disregarded. After the First (OT) Lesson, the Te Deum or, as an alternative, mainly in penitential seasons, the *Benedicite, is said or sung, and after the Second (NT) Lesson, the *Benedictus or *Jubilate. The Te Deum comes from the medieval office of Mattins, the Benedicite and Benedictus from Lauds, but the Apostles' Creed and Lord's Prayer with *Preces and Responses seem to owe more to forms found in *Prime, which also supplied one of the two fixed collects that follows that of the day. The ASB provides a wide choice of Canticles, and in the Shorter Form only one Canticle is used. If the Eucharist follows immediately, most of the latter part of the office may be omitted. Other modern Anglican liturgies provide similar flexibility.

J. A. Jungmann, SJ, 'Beiträge zur Geschichte der Gebetsliturgie I. Die Entstehung der Matutin', *ZKT* 72 (1950), pp. 66–79; repr. in id., *Liturgisches Erbe und Pastorale Gegenwart* (1960), pp. 139–62; Eng. tr., *Pastoral Liturgy* (1962), pp. 105–22. J. M. Hanssens, SJ, *Aux origines de la prière liturgique: Nature et genèse de l'office des matines* (Analecta Gregoriana, 57; 1952). See also works cited under VIGIL and OFFICE, DIVINE.
F. Procter and W. H. *Frere, *A New History of the Book of Common Prayer* (1901), esp. pp. 368–401. F. E. *Brightman, *The English Rite*, 1 (1915), esp. pp. lxxxv xcii. R. C. D. Jasper and P. F. Bradshaw, *A Companion to the Alternative Service Book* (1986), pp. 75–125.

Mattins of Bruges. The massacre of the French lodged in Bruges by the Flemish inhabitants at daybreak on 18 May 1302. Those who fell had been marked by their inability to pronounce a prearranged Flemish shibboleth.

The principal authority is the contemporary author of the *Annales Gandenses* (ed. with Eng. tr. by H. Johnstone, London, 1951, pp. 23–5). E. Vanden Bussche, 'Les Matines de Bruges. Note pour l'histoire de Jean Breidel et Pierre de Coninc', *La Flandre: Revue des Monuments d'Histoire et d'Antiquités*, 12 (1881), pp. 319–28. J. Frederichs, 'Note sur le cri de guerre des Matines brugeoises', *Compte Rendu des séances de la Commission royale d'Histoire*, 5th ser. 3 (1893), pp. 263–74. F. Funck-Brentano, *Philippe le Bel en Flandre* (1896), pp. 388–94. H. Pirenne, *Histoire de Belgique*, 1 (1900), p. 382, with note on sources; id. in *C. Med. H.* 8 (1936), pp. 339 f.

Maundy Thursday. The traditional English name for the Thursday preceding *Easter, derived from the first antiphon of the ceremony of the washing of the feet, '*mandatum novum*' (Jn. 13: 34). Its special celebration in commemoration of the Lord's Institution of the Eucharist on that day is attested already for the 4th cent. by the Council of *Hippo (393). Two other traditional liturgical features are the Blessing of the Holy Oils and the Reconciliation of Penitents, though the latter has long been obsolete. Two or even three Masses were celebrated on the day in the early centuries, but the *Gregorian Sacramentary and the oldest *Ordines Romani* allow only one. In the W. Church since 1955 the Maundy Thursday Mass has been celebrated in the evening. White vestments are worn and the altar is adorned in festive manner. Before the Mass the tabernacle is emptied (any Hosts required for sick communion are taken to some other place of reservation without ceremony) because all are expected to receive Holy Communion from Hosts consecrated at this Mass. The Mass is marked by the solemn ringing at the *Gloria in Excelsis* of all bells, which are henceforth silent until the *Paschal

Vigil, and a special formula for the Consecration. A sermon is recommended and also the ceremony of foot-washing (see PEDILAVIUM). After the Mass the Hosts needed for the Liturgy of *Good Friday (which are consecrated at the Maundy Thursday Mass; see PRESANCTIFIED, MASS OF THE) are taken in solemn procession to the Altar of *Repose, where a watch is kept for some hours. The altars are stripped and holy water stoups emptied. In cathedral churches the Holy Oils are blessed during a special *Chrism Mass in the morning. The royal 'Maundy Ceremony' in England is an abbreviated survival of the *Pedilavium*. See also GREEN THURSDAY and SHEER THURSDAY.

H. A. P. Schmidt, SJ, *Hebdomada Sancta*, 1 (Rome, 1956), pp. 64–91; 2, pt. 1 (1957), *passim*; 2, pt. 2 (1957), pp. 710–77. J. W. Tyrer, *Historical Survey of Holy Week, its Services and Ceremonial* (*Alcuin Club Collections, 29; 1932), pp. 79–115. H. Thurston, SJ, *Lent and Holy Week* (1904), pp. 274–325. K. [W.] Stevenson, *Jerusalem Revisted: The Liturgical Meaning of Holy Week* (Washington, DC [1986]), pp. 29–50 [in origin devotional]. A. *Wilmart, OSB, *Auteurs spirituels et textes dévots du moyen-âge latin* (1932), no. 2, 'L'Hymne de la charité pour le Jeudi-Saint', pp. 26–36. W. J. O'Shea in *NCE* 7 (1967), pp. 105–7, s.v. 'Holy Thursday'.

Maurice, St, Primicerius ('leader') of the *Theban Legion. Acc. to the 5th-cent. 'Passio Agaunensium Martyrum', a composition of *Eucherius of Lyons, the Emp. Maximian (Caesar from 286 to 305) took an army to Gaul during *Diocletian's persecution, which included a wholly Christian 'Theban legion' (from the Thebaïd, Egypt) commanded by Mauricius. As it refused to sacrifice, it was massacred by Maximian at Agaunum (now St-Maurice-en-Valais; not to be confounded with other places of the same name, e.g. St-Moritz in the Engadine). The story, though unhistorical in this form, may spring from some action of Christian soldiers during Maximian's campaign against the Bagaudae (286). Feast day, 22 Sept.

The best text of the 'Passio Acaunensium Martyrum' is that ed. B. Krusch in *MGH*, Scriptores Rerum Merovingicarum, 3 (1896), pp. 20–41. Further details of edns. and other sources in *BHL*, pp. 841–4 (nos. 5737–64), and novum suppl. (1986), pp. 630 f. *AASS*, Sept. 6 (1757), pp. 308–403 and 895–926. Of the considerable literature the fullest account is that of J. Bernard de Montmélian, *Saint Maurice et la légion thébéenne* (2 vols., 1888; detailed but not entirely accurate); among the more reliable discussions is that of M. Besson, *Monasticon Acaunense* (Fribourg, 1913). L. Dupraz, *Les Passions de S. Maurice d'Agaune: Essai sur l'historicité de la tradition et contribution à l'étude de l'armée pré-dioclétienne (260–286) et des canonisations tardives de la fin du IVe siècle* (Studia Friburgensia, NS 27; Fribourg, 1961). H. *Leclercq, OSB, in *DACL* 10 (pt. 2; 1932), cols. 2699–729, s.v.; R. Henggeler and M. C. Celletti in *Bibliotheca Sanctorum*, 9 (1967), cols. 193–205, s.v. 'Maurizio'.

Maurice, Frederick Denison (1805–72), Anglican divine. He was born at Normanstone, near Lowestoft, the son of a *Unitarian minister. After a boyhood spent among long and painful religious disputes in his family he entered Trinity College, Cambridge, in 1823 (where F. *Field was his tutor) with a view to becoming a barrister. In 1825 he migrated with his close friend, John Sterling, to Trinity Hall. Refusal to subscribe the *Thirty-Nine Articles excluded him from a degree and fellowship and he moved to London, where he wrote in defence of social reforms, criticizing the Benthamite materialism.

Having gradually accepted the Anglican faith, in 1830 Maurice went up to Exeter College, Oxford, and in 1834 was ordained to the curacy of Bubbenhall, Warwickshire. Here he wrote *Eustace Conway* (1834), an autobiographical novel, and *Subscription No Bondage* (1835), a pamphlet defending the imposition of religious tests at the universities. In 1836 he became chaplain of Guy's Hospital, where he lectured regularly on moral philosophy and wrote his most enduring book, *The Kingdom of Christ; or Hints to a Quaker concerning the Principle, Constitution and Ordinances of the Catholic Church* (1838). Its philosophical, yet fundamentally orthodox, presentation of theology was misunderstood and subjected to attacks from all ecclesiastical points of view. In 1840 he was elected Professor of English Literature and History at *King's College, London; in 1845 Warburtonian Lecturer (his lectures, *The Epistle to the Hebrews*, 1846, contained a reply to J. H. *Newman's *Essay on the Development of Christian Doctrine* [described as his *Theory of Development*]); in 1846 Chaplain at Lincoln's Inn; and in 1846 Professor of Theology in the newly created Theological School at King's College.

Maurice, who had been deeply moved by the political events of 1848, now became actively interested again in the application of Christian principles to social reform. Acquaintance with J. M. F. *Ludlow led to the formation of the *Christian Socialists (q.v.), which brought him into close contact with C. *Kingsley and others. But his orthodoxy was constantly under suspicion and in 1853 his *Theological Essays*, in which he attacked the popular view of the endlessness of future punishment and maintained that in the NT 'eternity' had nothing to do with time, provoked a crisis which resulted in his dismissal from King's College. In 1854 he started a 'Working Men's College' in London to promote his socialistic ideals. In *What is Revelation?* (1859) he made a fierce attack on the *Bampton Lectures of H. L. *Mansel (1858), who had defended Theism on the basis of the limitations of human reason and by implication repudiated philosophical theology. In 1860 he was appointed to the chapel of St Peter's, Vere Street, and in 1866 Knightsbridge Professor of Moral Philosophy at Cambridge. In 1870 he became incumbent of St Edward's, Cambridge. Among his other writings were *Three Letters to the Rev. W. *Palmer* (1842; defending the *Jerusalem Bishopric), *The Lord's Prayer* (1848), *The Old Testament* (1851), *The Unity of the New Testament* (1854), *The Epistles of St John* (1857), *The Gospel of St John* (1857), *The Gospel of the Kingdom of Heaven* (1864) and *The Conscience: Lectures on Casuistry* (1868). He also wrote a long article, 'Moral and Metaphysical Philosophy', originally published in the *Encyclopaedia Metropolitana* and later expanded and reissued in various forms. Many of his other writings were considerably revised in later editions.

In the American BCP (1979), feast day, 1 Apr.

Life and Letters, ed. by his son, F. Maurice (2 vols., 1884); C. F. G. Masterman, *F. D. Maurice* (1907); C. Jenkins, *F. D. Maurice and the New Reformation* (1938); M. B. Reckitt, *Maurice to Temple* (Scott Holland Memorial Lectures, 1946; 1947); F. Higham, *F. D. Maurice* (1947); A. R. Vidler, *The Theology of F. D. Maurice* (1948; pub. in New York as *Witness to the Light*); id., *F. D. Maurice and Company* (1966), pp. 13–202; A. M. *Ramsey, *F. D. Maurice and the Conflict of Modern Theology* (1951); W. M. Davies, *An Introduction to F. D. Maurice's Theology*

based on the first edition of The Kingdom of Christ (1838) and The Faith of the Liturgy and the Doctrine of the Thirty-Nine Articles (1860) (1964); F. M. McClain, *Maurice: Man and Moralist* (1972); T. Christensen, *The Divine Order: A Study in F. D. Maurice's Theology* (Acta theologica Danica, 11; Leiden, 1973); D. Young, *F. D. Maurice and Unitarianism* (Oxford, 1992). L. Stephen in *DNB* 37 (1894), pp. 77–104.

Maurists. The *Benedictine monks of the *Congregation of St-Maur. The Congregation, which takes its name from St *Maurus (6th cent., q.v.), was founded in 1618 to represent in France the reform initiated in the Abbey of St-Vanne in 1600; it received Papal approval in 1621. The historical and literary work, for which the Congregation is famous, was largely centered at *St-Germain-des-Prés. The Maurists numbered among their members a succession of remarkable scholars, incl. J. L. *d'Achery, J. *Mabillon, E. *Martène, T. *Ruinart, and B. de *Montfaucon; they were able to undertake monumental works, since they trained younger monks to take over when older ones died. Their editions were based on a wide range of MSS, many of which have since perished. Some of the monks had *Jansenist sympathies and appealed against the Bull *Unigenitus; the subsequent internal divisions and relaxation of discipline led to the disintegration of the Congregation. Suppressed in 1790 by the Revolutionary government, it was finally dissolved by *Pius VII in 1818.

E. Martène, OSB, cont. by J. Fortet, OSB, *Histoire de la congrégation de Saint-Maur*, ed. G. Charvin, OSB (Archives de la France Monastique, 31–5, 42–3, 46–7; 1928–43); id., *Les Vies des Justes*, ed. B. Heurtebize, OSB (ibid. 27–8, 30; 1924–6). [R. P. Tassin, OSB], *Histoire littéraire de la congrégation de Saint-Maur, ordre de S. Benoît* (Brussels, 1770); suppl. by U. Robert (Paris, 1881); further suppl. by H. Wilhelm and U. Berlière, OSB (ibid., 1908). *Mémorial du XIVᵉ centenaire de l'abbaye de Saint-Germain-des-Prés: Recueil de travaux sur le monastère et la congrégation de Saint-Maur* (Bibliothèque de la Société d'histoire ecclésiastique de la France, 1959). Y. Chaussy, OSB, *Les Bénédictins de Saint-Maur* (2 vols., Études Augustiniennes, 1989–'91'[92]). R. Lemoine, OSB, 'Histoire des Constitutions de la Congrégation de Saint-Maur', in *Études d'histoire du droit canonique dediées à Gabriel Le Bras*, 1 (1965), pp. 215–48. E. de Broglie, *Mabillon et la société de l'abbaye de Saint-Germain-des-Prés à la fin du XVIIᵉ siècle, 1664–1707* (2 vols., 1888); id., *La Société de l'abbaye de S.-Germain-des-Prés au XVIIIᵉ siècle: Bernard de Montfaucon et les Bernardins 1715–1750* (2 vols., 1891). [M.] D. *Knowles, *Great Historical Enterprises* (1963), pp. 33–62. B. Barret-Kriegel, *Les Historiens et la Monarchie*, 3: *Les Académies de l'Histoire* (1988), pp. 19–167. On the Maurist edn. of the works of St *Augustine, J. de Ghellinck, SJ, *Patristique et Moyen Âge*, 3 (Museum Lessianum, Section Historique, 9; 1948), pp. 412–84. L. A. St L. Toke in *CE* 10 (1911), pp. 69–72, s.v.; J. Baudot in *DTC* 10 (1928), cols. 405–43, s.v.; J. Hourlier, OSB, in *DIP* 5 (1978), cols. 1082–9, s.v. 'Maurini'.

Maurus, St (6th cent.), disciple of St *Benedict of Nursia. There are references to him in St *Gregory the Great's *Dialogues*, but practically nothing is certainly known of his career. Acc. to a biography ascribed to his companion, Faustus of *Monte Cassino (but apparently a 9th-cent. forgery by Abbot Odo of Glanfeuil), he made his way to France in 543, where he founded the abbey of Glanfeuil, afterwards St-Maur-sur-Loire; and, after resigning the abbacy to Bertulf in 581, spent the rest of his life in solitude and contemplation. He is the patron of charcoal-burners, and is invoked against gout and other diseases. Feast day, 15 Jan.

Life ascribed to Faustus of Monte Cassino pr. in *Acta Sanctorum Ordinis S. Benedicti*, 1 (Paris, 1668), pp. 275–98; also, with other material, in *AASS*, Jun. 1 (1643), pp. 1038–62. A. Giry, 'La Vie de saint Maur du Pseudo-Faustus', *Bibliothèque de l'École des Chartes*, 57 (1898), pp. 149–52. B. F. Adloch, OSB, 'Die Benedictiner-Tradition über den hl. Maurus und Abt Odo von Glanfeuil', *Studien und Mitteilungen aus dem Benedictiner- und dem Cistercienser-Orden*, 19 (1898), pp. 310–26; id., 'Zur Vita S. Mauri', ibid. 26 (1905), pp. 3–22 and 202 26; id., ' "Les Légendes hagiographiques" und die "Vita Sancti Mauri" per Faustum', ibid. 28 (1907), p. 101, all with refs. to other lit. H. *Leclercq, OSB, in *DACL* 6 (pt. 1; 1924), cols. 1285–319, s.v. 'Glanfeuil', with full discussion of authenticity of Life, and bibl.

Maximilian, St (d. 295), also Marmilian, martyr.
It is recorded that he was executed at Theveste in Numidia, his native town, because he refused to serve in the Roman army. Feast day, 12 Mar.

'Acta' pr. in T. *Ruinart (ed.), *Acta Primorum Martyrum Sincera et Selecta* (Paris, 1689), pp. 309–11, repr., with Eng. tr., in H. Musurillo, *The Acts of the Christian Martyrs* (Oxford, 1972), pp. 242–9; and A. *Harnack, *Militia Christi: Die christliche Religion und der Soldatenstand in den ersten Jahrhunderten* (1905), pp. 114–17. H. *Delehaye, SJ, *Les Passions des martyrs et les genres littéraires* (1921), pp. 104–10. L. J. Swift, *The Early Fathers on War and Military Service* (Message of the Fathers of the Church, 19; Delaware, 1983), pp. 71–4. H. *Leclercq, OSB, in *DACL* 11 (pt. 1; 1933), cols. 1133–7, s.v. 'Militarisme. XIII, le martyre du conscrit Maximilien', with bibl.

Maximus, St (d. 408/23).
Nothing is known of his life, except that he was bishop of Turin, and that he died in the reign of Honorius and Theodosius the Younger (408–23). Confusion about the dates of his life has been caused by an arbitrary conjecture of C. *Baronius, who identified him with a Bp. Maximus who was present at synods in Milan in 451 and Rome in 465. Over 100 of his sermons survive, chiefly in a collection found in three early MSS. Some of them had a wide circulation in medieval homiliaries. They are for the most part short, pithily expressed, sometimes over-rhetorical, and marked by a strong popular appeal. They throw much light on the history of the liturgy and the survival of paganism in N. Italy. Feast day, 25 June.

Editio princeps (only 74 sermons), by J. Gymnicus (Cologne, 1535). The edn. of B. Bruni (Rome, 1784), repr. in J. P. Migne, *PL* 57, contains much spurious material; cf. *CPL* (3rd edn., 1995), pp. 84–7 (nos. 220–6b). First crit. edn. by A. Mutzenbecher (CCSL 23; 1962). Eng. tr. by P. Ramsey, OP (ACW 50 [1989]). A. Merkt, *Maximus I. von Turin* (Supplements to *VC*, 40; 1997). B. Studer in Quasten (cont.), *Patrology*, 4 (1986), p. 574. M. R. P. McGuire in *NCE* 9 (1967), p. 516; M. Pellegrino in *DPAC* 2 (1984), cols. 2176–9, s.v. 'Massimo di Torino (1)'; Eng. tr. in *Encyclopedia of the Early Church*, 1 (Cambridge, 1992), pp. 548 f.

Maximus the Confessor, St (c.580–662),
Greek theologian and ascetic writer. A member of the old Byzantine aristocracy, after holding the post of Imperial Secretary under the Emp. *Heraclius, c.614 he became a monk (later abbot) of the monastery of Chrysopolis. During the Persian invasion (626) he fled to Africa. From c.640 onwards he was a determined opponent of *Monothelitism. After Pyrrhus, the temporarily deposed Monothelite Patriarch

of *Constantinople, had declared his defeat in a dispute at Carthage (645), Maximus procured the condemnation of the heresy by several African Synods, and also had a share in its condemnation by the *Lateran Council of 649. In 653 he was brought to Constantinople, where pressure was put upon him to obtain his adherence to the '*Typos' of Constans II. On his refusal he was exiled to Thrace. In 661 he was again brought to the capital and severely questioned; a probably true tradition says that on this occasion his tongue and his right hand were cut off. He was then exiled to the Caucasus, but died soon afterwards.

Maximus the Confessor was a prolific writer on doctrinal, ascetical, exegetical, and liturgical subjects. His works include the 'Quaestiones ad Thalassium', 65 questions and answers on difficult passages of Scripture, the 'Ambigua', an exegetical work on *Gregory of Nazianzus, Paraphrases on the works of *Dionysius, the Pseudo-Areopagite (though many of the Paraphrases which have come down under Maximus' name are the work of John of Scythopolis, who wrote in the first half of the 6th cent.), several dogmatic treatises against the *Monophysites and Monothelites, the 'Liber Asceticus' and 'Capita de Caritate', and the 'Mystagogia', a mystical interpretation of the Liturgy. He maintained that the purpose of history was the Incarnation of the Son of God and the *deification (θέωσις) of man, which consisted in the restoration of the Image impaired by Original Sin. Man, created in an incorruptible nature devoid of passion, caused evil to come into the world by his desire for pleasure, which destroyed the dominion of reason over the senses; hence Christ had to redeem the race by pain to restore the equilibrium. It was through the Incarnate Word, the centre of Maximus' speculative as of his mystical doctrine, that man is not only freed from ignorance but given the power to practise virtue. The goal of the human life, attained through abnegation, is union with God by charity. Feast day in the W., 13 Aug.; in the E., 21 Jan. (also 13 Aug.).

Works ed. F. *Combefis, 2 vols., Paris, 1675 (the projected 3rd vol. never appeared). The Scholia to St Gregory of Nazianzus and the Ps.-Dionysius were first pr. in F. Oehler, *Anecdota Graeca*, 1 (Halle, 1857). All these repr. in J. P. Migne, *PG* 90 and 91, and (Scholia to Ps.-Dionysius), ibid. 4. 15–432 and 527–76. His 'Computus Ecclesiasticus' is in J. P. Migne, *PG* 19. 1217–80 (among the works of *Eusebius of Caesarea). Crit. edn. of 'Capita de Caritate' by A. Ceresa-Gastaldo, with Ital. tr. (Verba Seniorum, NS 3; Rome, 1963); of 'Quaestiones ad Thalassium' by C. Laga and C. Steel (CCSG 7 and 22; 1980–90); of 'Quaestiones et Dubia' by J. H. Declerck (ibid. 10; 1982); and of 'Opuscula Exegetica Duo' (incl. his Comm. on the *Lord's Prayer) by P. Van Deun (ibid. 23; 1991). Eng. tr. of *Selected Writings* by G. C. Berthold (Classics of Western Spirituality, 1985), with refs. to earlier trs. of individual works. On the Life of Maximus, repr. from Combefis in *PG* 90. 68–109, cf. R. Devreesse, 'La Vie de saint Maxime le Confesseur et ses Recensions', *Anal. Boll.* 46 (1928), pp. 5–49. W. Lackner, 'Zu Quellen und Datierung der Maximos-vita (BHG³ 1234)', ibid. 85 (1967), pp. 285–316. S. [P.]. Brock, 'An Early Syriac Life of Maximus the Confessor', ibid. 91 (1973), pp. 299–346, incl. text and Eng. tr. H. U. von *Balthasar, *Kosmische Liturgie: Maximus der Bekenner. Höhe und Krise des griechischen Weltbildes* (1941; 2nd edn., 1961; Fr. tr., 1947); I. Hausherr, SJ, *Philautie: De la tendresse pour soi à la charité selon Saint-Maxime le Confesseur* (Orientalia Christiana Analecta, 137; 1952). P. Sherwood, OSB, *An Annotated Date-List of the Works of Maximus the Confessor* (Studia Anselmiana, 30; 1952); id., *The Earlier Ambigua of Saint Maximus the Confessor and his Refutation of Origenism* (ibid. 36; 1955). L. Thunberg, *Microcosm and Mediator: The Theological Anthropology of Maximus the Confessor* (Acta Seminarii Neotestamentici Upsaliensis, 25; Lund, 1965; 2nd edn., Chicago, 1995). W. Völker, *Maximus Confessor als Meister des geistlichen Lebens* (Wiesbaden, 1965). A. Riou, *Le Monde et l'Église selon Maxime Confesseur* (Théologie historique, 22; 1973); J. M. Garrigues, *Maxime le Confesseur: La charité avenir divin de l'homme* (ibid. 38; 1976); F.-M. Léthel, *Théologie de l'Agonie du Christ: La Liberté humaine du Fils de Dieu et son importance sotériologique mises en lumière par saint Maxime Confesseur* (ibid. 52; 1979); P. Piret, *Le Christ et la Trinité selon Maxime le Confesseur* (ibid. 69; 1983); F. Heinzer, *Gottes Sohn als Mensch: Die Struktur des Menschseins Christi bei Maximus Confessor* (Paradosis, 26; 1980); Id. and C. Schönborn (eds.), *Maximus Confessor: Actes du Symposium sur Maxime le Confesseur Fribourg, 2–5 Septembre 1980* (ibid. 27; 1982); A. Louth, *Maximus the Confessor* (1996). B. R. Suchla, *Die sogennanten Maximus-Scholien des Corpus Dionysiacum Areopagiticum* (*Nachr.* (Gött.), 1980, no. 3). Bibliography, with discussion of works listed, by M. L. Gatti (Metafisica del Platonismo nel suo sviluppo storico e nella filosofia patristica, 2; Milan, 1987). Beck, pp. 356–9 and 436–42. *CPG* 3 (1979), pp. 431–50 (nos. 7688–721). Altaner and Stuiber (1978), pp. 521–4 and 660 f. V. Grumel, AA, in *DTC* 10 (pt. 1; 1928), cols. 448–59; C. De Vocht in *TRE* 22 (1992), pp. 298–304, s.v.

Maximus the Cynic (4th cent.), intruded Bp. of Constantinople. After a disreputable life at *Alexandria, he conceived the idea of supplanting St *Gregory Nazianzen, and with the support of Peter II, Bp. of Alexandria, he went to Constantinople in 379. He ingratiated himself with Gregory, who even pronounced a panegyric on him (calling him 'Hero' acc. to St *Jerome). One night in 380, when Gregory was ill, Maximus was consecrated to the see. He then set out immediately for Thessalonica to secure the recognition of the Emp. *Theodosius, but in this he was unsuccessful. The Council of *Constantinople of 381 (can. 4) declared that Maximus 'neither is nor was a bishop'. Meanwhile, Peter recognized what Maximus was worth and withdrew his support. However, Maximus convinced St *Ambrose and others in the W., where only his version of events was known, of his claims, and some W. synods threatened to break off relations with the E. Church if Maximus was not restored to his see; but at the Council of Rome in 382 they were undeceived and abandoned him. Acc. to Jerome, he wrote a treatise *De Fide adversus Arianos*, now lost. He professed to combine belief in the Cynic philosophy with profession of the Nicene faith.

The chief sources are Gregory Nazianzen, *Orat.* 25–6; id., *De Vita Sua (Poema de Seipso)*, ll. 728–1112; Ambrose, *Ep.* 13; Jerome, *De Vir. Ill.* 117 and 127; *Sozomen, *HE* 7. 9; *Theodoret, *HE* 5. 8. J. Mossay, introd. to his edn. of Gregory's *Discours 24–26* (SC 284; 1981), pp. 120–41; id., 'Note sur Héron-Maxime, écrivain ecclésiastique', *Anal. Boll.* 100 (1982), pp. 229–36. E. Venables in *DCB* 3 (1882), pp. 878–80, s.v.

Maximus the Greek, St (*c.*1470–1556), monk. Michael Trivolis was a member of a Byzantine family who in his childhood moved from Arta in Epirus to Corfu. In 1492 he went to Florence, where he came under the influence of the Platonist M. *Ficino and of G. *Savonarola. After further travels in Italy, he entered the *Dominican Order in 1502. By 1504, however, he had left the Order and by 1505/6 he was a monk on Mt *Athos. In response to a request in 1516 from the Muscovite ruler for a competent scholar to translate works from Greek into Slavonic,

Maximus was sent to Moscow, where he arrived in 1518. His first task was to prepare a translation of Greek commentaries on the Psalter. Besides a large number of translations from Greek, he produced works on theology, philosophy, statecraft, and social problems. He became involved in disputes over the ownership of monastic property (see RUSSIA, CHRISTIANITY IN) and seems to have been indiscreet in his comments on public affairs; in particular he held that the Russian Church should return to the obedience of its mother-church of *Constantinople. After trials in 1525 and 1531, he was sentenced to long terms of imprisonment and solitary confinement; prob. in 1548 he was released and allowed to spend the rest of his life in the monastery of the Holy Trinity near Moscow. He was canonized by the 1988 Synod of the Russian Orthodox Church; feast day, 21 Jan.

É Denissoff, *Maxime le Grec et l'Occident* (Université de Louvain, Recueil de Travaux d'Histoire et de Philologie, 3rd ser., fasc. 14; 1943). J. V. Haney, *From Italy to Muscovy: The Life and Works of Maxim the Greek* (Humanistische Bibliothek, Abh. I, Bd. 19; Munich, 1973). D. Obolensky, 'Italy, Mount Athos, and Muscovy: The Three Worlds of Maximos the Greek (*c.*1470–1556)', *Proceedings of the British Academy*, 67, for 1981 (1982), pp. 143–61, repr. in *Six Byzantine Portraits* (Oxford, 1988), pp. 201–19.

Max Müller, Friedrich (1823–1900), comparative philologist and religious writer. A native of Dessau in Germany, he was educated at the universities of Leipzig (1841–3) and Berlin (1844–5), and in 1845 went to Paris, where he began to work on an *editio princeps* of the Rig-Veda. In 1846 he came to England, and in 1848 went to Oxford to supervise its printing (6 vols., 1849–75). In 1850 he was appointed deputy, and in 1854 full, Taylorian professor of modern European languages. He was elected a Fellow of All Souls in 1858. In 1859 he published his *History of Ancient Sanskrit Literature*, important esp. for its studies in chronology. Having failed to secure the Sanskrit professorship at Oxford in 1860, he devoted himself largely to other studies, esp. to comparative philology, on which he lectured at the Royal Institution in 1861 and 1863. In 1868 he was appointed to the chair of comparative philology at Oxford, founded esp. for him. In 1875 he undertook the edition of *The Sacred Books of the East*, a series of translations of E. religious classics in 51 vols., over 30 of which are devoted to the religions of India. Much of his work on the comparative study of religions is embodied in *The Origin and Growth of Religion* (*Hibbert Lectures (1878) and the *Gifford Lectures from 1888 to 1892, on *Natural Religion* (1889), *Physical Religion* (1891), *Anthropological Religion* (1892), and *Theosophy or Psychological Religion* (1893)). He also interested himself in comparative mythology, on which he wrote a large work, *Contributions to the Science of Mythology* (1897).

Max Müller was among the most learned and popular figures in post-*Tractarian Oxford. Through the influence of C. C. J. von *Bunsen, his work also attracted the attention of the Queen and the Prince Consort. His wide range of interests, his facility of expression, and his readiness to put forward highly speculative (and often inadequately tested) theories made his writings congenial to the religious liberals of his age. Though mostly without permanent theological importance, they exercised a great influence on the ideas of the later 19th century.

A collected edn. of his works appeared in 1898–1903. *My Autobiography: A Fragment*, ed. W. G. Max Müller (son) (1901) covers his life up to his early days in Oxford. His *Life and Letters* (2 vols., London, 1902) were ed. by his widow. N. C. Chaudhuri, *Scholar Extraordinary: The Life of Professor the Rt. Hon. Friedrich Max Müller, P.C.* (1974). A. A. Macdonell in *DNB*, Suppl. 3 (1901), pp. 151–7.

May Laws. The legislation associated with Bismarck's *Kulturkampf and directed against the RC Church in Germany. These laws, passed in May 1873 under the direction of P. L. A. *Falk, were based on the theory of the absolute supremacy of the state. They limited the extent of the disciplinary powers of the Church, instituted a Supreme Ecclesiastical Court whose members were appointed by the Emperor and directly under state control, ordered all ordinands to pass through a state Gymnasium and to take a state examination (the '*Kultur-Examen*'), and brought all ecclesiastical seminaries under state control. The laws, with others of a similar nature, were condemned by *Pius IX in the encyclical 'Quod nunquam' (1875) as subversive of the constitution and rights of the Church, and also strongly opposed by many German Protestants.

P. Hinschius, *Die preussischen Kirchengesetze des Jahres 1873* (1873), with full text. Eng. tr. of the most important clauses in R. G. D. Laffan (ed.), *Select Documents of European History*, 3, ed. H. Butterfield (1931), pp. 167 f. The encyclical 'Quod Nunquam' is pr. in Mirbt, no. 613, pp. 471–3, with further refs. See also bibl. to KULTURKAMPF.

Mayne, St Cuthbert (1544–77), the first RC seminary priest executed in England. Born in Devon, he was ordained at the age of 18. At St John's College, Oxford, he came under the influence of E. *Campion, and secretly became a RC. He then entered the English College at *Douai, where he was ordained to the RC priesthood. In 1576 he was sent on the English Mission and became chaplain to a landowner in Cornwall, passing as his steward. In 1577, however, a search was made, and Mayne was found concealed. On being tried at Launceston, he was sentenced to death. It was difficult to find grounds for a capital charge, as the Act of Parliament making it high treason to receive orders abroad had not yet been passed, and he was therefore condemned on the alleged grounds of denying the Queen's spiritual supremacy, saying Mass, possessing a printed copy of a bull for a jubilee, and wearing an *Agnus Dei. He was executed at Launceston on 29 Nov. 1577. He was beatified in 1888 and was among the *Forty Martyrs of England and Wales canonized on 25 Oct. 1970. The engraved portrait frequently reproduced as his likeness is prob. not authentic. Feast day, formerly 29 Nov.

R. A. McElroy, CRL, *Blessed Cuthbert Mayne: Protomartyr of the English Seminaries* (1929); H. Whelan, *Snow on the Hedges: A Life of Cuthbert Mayne* (posthumous, Leominster, 1984). E. S. Knox, Cong. Orat., in B. Camm, OSB (ed.), *Lives of the English Martyrs Declared Blessed by Pope Leo XIII in 1886 and 1895*, 2 (1905), pp. 204–22 and 656. T. Cooper in *DNB* 37 (1894), pp. 161 f., s.v., for further refs.

Maynooth College. The 'Royal Catholic College' at Maynooth, Co. Kildare, 15 miles NW of Dublin, established in 1795 by the Irish Parliament for the education of RC clergy for Ireland. The present building was erected by A. W. N. *Pugin from funds supplied by Parliament in 1846. Until the disestablishment of the (Anglican) Church of Ireland in 1869, when the payment was commuted, the College was supported by an annual grant, originally of £8,000 but in 1845 raised by Sir Robert Peel from £9,500 to £26,000. Since 1896, as well as being the National Seminary for Ireland, Maynooth College has been a Pontifical University, and since 1910 also a College of the National University of Ireland.

P. J. Corish, *Maynooth College 1795–1995* (Dublin, 1995). D. A. Kerr, *Peel, Priests, and Politics* (Oxford, 1982), esp. pp. 224–89.

Mazarin, Jules (1602–61), French statesman and cardinal. A native of Piscina in the Abruzzi, he was educated by the *Jesuits in Rome and accompanied Jerome *Colonna to the university of Alcalá, where he studied law. On his return to Rome *c.*1622, he became a captain in the army of the Colonna. His diplomatic skill attracted the attention of *Urban VIII, who in 1629 gave him the difficult task of ending the war of the Mantuan succession. From 1632 to 1634, and again from 1636 to 1640, he was vice-legate at *Avignon, where he promoted French interests. In 1639 he became a naturalized Frenchman and in 1640 entered the service of Louis XIII. At the king's instigation he was created a cardinal in 1641 and in 1642 he succeeded A. J. du P. *Richelieu as prime minister. He continued Richelieu's domestic and foreign policy and from now on virtually ruled France until his death. As Louis XIV's godfather he undertook his political education and had the complete confidence of Anne of Austria, the Queen Regent. At the Peace of *Westphalia (1648) he succeeded in enlarging French territory, but he could not prevent the economic crisis of the country or the civil wars of the Fronde (1648–53). He antagonized leaders of the nobility and *parlementaires* alike, and in a series of venomous *Mazarinades* he was attacked for his policies and as a foreigner. In 1651–3 he was temporarily banished, but he continued to handle the affairs of the country. His refusal to allow de *Retz to occupy the see of *Paris led to a long dispute with the Papacy. Towards the *Huguenots he pursued a conciliatory policy, maintaining the edicts in their favour and employing them in the service of France. In the *Jansenist controversy he furthered the acceptance of *Innocent X's constitution '*Cum Occasione' (1653). He concluded a trade treaty with Oliver *Cromwell, continued the war against Spain with success, and secured the marriage of Louis XIV to the Infanta Maria Theresa and the victorious Treaty of the Pyrenees (1659). Though he never received Major Orders, he held the see of Metz and a great number of abbeys; from these and other sources he amassed a large fortune. A great art and book collector, he founded the *Collège des quatre nations* (known as the 'Collège Mazarin') for students from the provinces added to France under his government and bequeathed to it his library, which he intended should be open to all scholars; it became the Bibliothèque Mazarine. Part of his own palace in the rue de Richelieu in Paris was incorporated into the Bibliothèque Nationale. See also following entry.

Lettres du cardinal Mazarin pendant son ministère, ed. [P.] A. Chéruel and G. d'Avenel (9 vols., Collection de documents inédits sur l'histoire de France publiés par les soins du Ministère de l'Instruction Publique, 1st ser., Histoire politique; 1872–1906). C. Moreau (ed.), *Choix de Mazarinades* (2 vols., Société de l'Histoire de France, 1853); id., *Bibliographie des Mazarinades* (3 vols., ibid., 1850–51). [P.] A. Chéruel, *Histoire de France pendant la minorité de Louis XIV* (4 vols., 1879–80); id., *Histoire de France sous le ministère de Mazarin*: (3 vols., 1882). Studies of Mazarin by A. Hassall ('Foreign Statesmen', London, 1903), ed. G. Mongrédien (Paris, 1959), and by G. Dethan (ibid., 1981). This last incorporates much of Dethan's earlier work, *Mazarin et ses amis* (1968), with unpub. letters; Eng. tr., without the letters, *The Young Mazarin* [1977]. P. Jansen, *Le Cardinal Mazarin et le mouvement janséniste français 1653–1659 d'après les documents inédits conservés dans les Archives du Ministère des Affaires Étrangères* (Bibliothèque de la Société d'histoire ecclésiastique de la France, 1967); V. Tornetta, 'La politica del Mazzarino verso il Papato (1644–1646)', *Archivio storico italiano*, 99, Disp. 3–4 for 1941 (1942), pp. 86–116; and 100, Disp. 3–4 for 1942 (1943), pp. 95–134. M.-N. Grand-Mesnil, *Mazarin, la Fronde et la Presse 1647–1649* [1967]. J. Serroy (ed.), *La France et l'Italie au temps de Mazarin. 15ᵉ Colloque du C.M.R. 17 . . . (Grenoble, 25–27 janvier 1985)* (Grenoble, 1986), pp. 9–65. *Mazarin: Homme d'état et collectionneur 1602–1661* (Bibliothèque Nationale. Exposition organisée pour le troisième centenaire de sa mort; 1961). G. Dethan in *EB* (1977 edn.), Macropaedia, 11, pp. 725 f., s.v.

Mazarin Bible. So called from a copy in the library of Card. *Mazarin which first attracted the attention of scholars to this magnificent work, it is also known as the 'Gutenberg Bible', after J. *Gutenberg, its printer, or again as the '42-line Bible', from having that number of lines to each column. It is both the first full-length book ever printed, and the first printed edition of the Bible. Gutenberg contributed to it the technical inventions of making matrices and casting movable type from them; his experiments were financed by Johann Fust, a Mainz banker, and the design of the type-face was the work of Peter Schoeffer, a professional scribe. In 1455 this triple partnership was dissolved after a lawsuit; it is probable that the printing of the Bible occupied the years 1453–5 (Enea Silvio de' Piccolomini, later *Pius II, reports that he saw the Bible in sheets, prob. visiting Mainz from Frankfurt am Main between 5 and 31 Oct. 1454, and one surviving copy bears notes that its 2 vols. had been rubricated and bound by 15 and 24 Aug. 1456). Following experiments with an earlier type (afterwards used to print the '36-line Bible'), the text of the Latin *Vulgate began to be set up at Mainz on no less than six presses at once. During production, the number of copies to be printed was increased and parts therefore had to be reset; also the number of lines per column was altered from 40 to 42 by filing down the body of the type, thus enabling more matter to be set in the same space.

Darlow and Moule, 2 (1911), pp. 905 f. See also works cited under GUTENBERG, J.

Mazzolini, Sylvester. See PRIERIAS, SYLVESTER.

Mechitarists. A community of *Uniat *Armenian monks, founded at *Constantinople in 1701. They live under a modified form of the *Benedictine Rule. Founded by Mechitar of Sebaste (1676–1749), an Armenian priest who had submitted to Rome and been ordained in the RC Church in 1696, the community was driven from Constantinople in 1703 and took refuge in Modon in the Morea, then Venetian territory. Upon the conquest of the Morea by the Turks, the Venetian senate gave the community the island of San Lazzaro, Venice, where it settled in 1717. Another section of the community later established itself at Vienna. The Mechitarists devote themselves to study, education, and missionary work, and have issued many important Armenian publications from their printing-houses in Venice and Vienna. Both communities have important collections of Armenian MSS. They use the Armenian liturgy.

V. Langlois, *Notice sur le couvent arménien de l' île de S. Lazare* (Venice, 1869; Eng. tr., Venice, 1874). V. Inglisian, *Der Diener Gottes Mechitar von Sebaste: Stifter der Mechitaristen (der armenischen Benediktiner) und Kulturapostel der armenischen Volkes* (Vienna, 1929) and other works of this author. P. Krüger, 'Die armenischen Mechitharisten und ihre Bedeutung', *Ostkirchliche Studien*, 16 (1967), pp. 3–14, with bibl. R. Janin, AA, in *DTC* 10 (pt. 1; 1928), cols. 497–502, s.v. 'Mékhitaristes'; E. El-Hayek in *NCE* 9 (1967), p. 545, s.v.; G. Amadouni and others in *DIP* 5 (1978), cols. 1112–23, s.v.

Mechlin, Conversations of. See MALINES CONVERSATIONS.

Mechthild of Magdeburg (*c.*1207–1282 or somewhat later), author of a book of mystical Revelations. Descended from a noble family in Saxony, she experienced visions from the age of 12 and left her family home *c.*1230 to become a *Beguine at Magdeburg under the spiritual guidance of the *Dominicans. Books 1–5 of her visions, entitled 'Das fliessende Licht der Gottheit' and containing dialogues with the Lord, bridal mysticism, as well as trinitarian theology and eschatology, were written down *c.*1250–9, a sixth book *c.*1260–70 (books 1–6 were posthumously rendered into Latin by the Dominicans at Halle, before 1298), and a final book *c.*1271–82. From the Revelations, which are the only document of her life, it emerges that in addition to the tribulations of illness she suffered personal threats and much disapproval from official sources, including the threat to burn her writings. During the 1260s, when opposition to the Beguines became intense, she returned for a time to her family, and around 1270 she became a nun at the *Cistercian-inspired convent at Helfta, where she had contact with younger visionary women, St Mechthild of Hackeborn (with whom she has sometimes been confused) and St *Gertrude the Great. The Revelations, which number among the most forceful and poetic examples of women's writing to have survived from the Middle Ages, are no longer extant in the original Low German, but only in a High German translation made towards the middle of the 14th cent. in the circle of Henry of Nördlingen and the *Friends of God at Basle.

Her work, discovered in 1860, was first ed. by G. Morel (Regensburg, 1869); crit. edn. by H. Neumann and G. Vollmann-Profe (Münchener Texte und Untersuchungen zur deutschen Literatur des Mittelalters, 100–101; 1990–93); the Lat. tr. ed. by the monks of *Solesmes, *Revelationes Gertrudianae ac Mechtildianae*, 2 (Poitiers and Paris, 1877), pp. 435–643; Eng. tr. by S. L. Clark and C. M. Galvani (New York, 1991). H. Neumann, 'Beiträge zur Textgeschichte des "Fliessenden Lichts der Gottheit" und zur Lebensgeschichte Mechthilds von Magdeburg', *Nachr.* (Gött.), 1954, pp. 27–80, repr. in K. Ruh (ed.), *Altdeutsche und altniederländische Mystik* (Wege der Forschung, 23; Darmstadt, 1964), pp. 175–239. A. M. Haas, *Sermo mysticus* (Fribourg, 1979), pp. 67–135. Id. in H. De Boor and R. Newald, *Geschichte der deutschen Literatur*, 3. 2, ed. I. Glier (Munich, 1987), pp. 242–54.

W. Haug, 'Das Gespräch mit dem unvergleichlichen Partner', in K. Stierle and R. Warning (eds.), *Das Gespräch* (Munich, 1984), pp. 251–79. N. F. Palmer, 'Das Buch als Bedeutungsträger bei Mechtild von Magdeburg', in W. Harms and others (eds.), *Bildhafte Rede in Mittelalter und früher Neuzeit* (Tübingen, 1992), pp. 217–35. J. Howard, 'The German Mystic Mechthild of Magdeburg', in K. M. Wilson (ed.), *Medieval Women Writers* (Athens, Ga. [1984]), pp. 153–85. G. J. Lewis, *Bibliographie zur deutschen Frauenmystik des Mittelalters* (Bibliographien zur deutschen Literatur des Mittelalters, 10; 1989), pp. 164–83 (nos. 1339–502/1). M. Schmidt in *Dict. Sp.* 10 (1980), cols. 877–85; II. Neumann, in *Verfasserlexikon* (2nd edn.), 6 (1987), cols. 260–70, s.v.

Mede, Joseph (1586–1638), also 'Mead', biblical scholar. He was a native of Berden in Essex and educated at Christ's College, Cambridge, of which he was elected a Fellow in 1613, and where he remained for the rest of his life. He was a scholar of encyclopaedic knowledge. Though regarding the Pope as the antichrist, he admitted that the RC Church taught the principal doctrines of Christianity, and defended the sacrificial aspect of the Eucharist. Mede's best-known work, *Clavis Apocalyptica* (1627), is an interpretation of the Book of Rev. on the principle that its visions form an organic and related whole in chronological order; the Day of Judgement is a period of a thousand years of peace for the Church on earth. His *millenarian doctrines were partly influenced by the astrological studies of his youth. Among his other writings are treatises *Of the Name Altar* (1637) and on *The Apostasy of the Latter Times* (1641).

Collected Works, 2 vols., London, 1648; enlarged edn. [by J. Worthington], 2 vols., ibid., 1663–4; further extension, 2 vols., ibid., 1672. Brief Life appended to his posthumously pub. *Diatribae: Discourses on Divers Texts of Scripture* (4 parts, 1643–52); Life, pt. 4, pp. 675 ff. [no pagination]. K. R. Firth, *The Apocalyptic Tradition in Reformation Britain 1530–1645* (Oxford, 1979), pp. 213–28 and 242–6. A. Gordon in *DNB* 37 (1894), pp 178 80, s.v. 'Mead'.

Medina, Bartolomé (1527–80), Spanish *Dominican theologian. He taught theology first at the college of Alcalá, and from 1576 to his death as principal professor at the University of Salamanca; his main interest was centred upon commenting on St *Thomas Aquinas. He has been given the title of 'Father of *Probabilism', though whether he was the real author of this doctrine is still a matter of controversy. His opinions on the subject are laid down in an essay inserted in his Commentary on the 'Prima Secundae' of St Thomas, where he defends the view that of two opinions both of which are probable, though in an unequal degree, the less probable may be followed. This thesis was immediately taken up and defended by other Dominicans, esp. D. *Báñez, though in the subsequent development of the doctrine, in which the notion of the 'probable' was more and more enlarged, the *Jesuits had the main share in upholding it, whilst Dominican moralists came to reject it. See also SALMANTICENSES.

His Comm. on *Summa Theol.* II (1) was issued at Salamanca, 1572; on III, qq. 1–59, ibid., 1578; and *Breve Instrucción de como se ha de administrar el sacramento de la penitencia* (Huesca, 1579). Two sets of Lectures on *Summa Theol.* I (1) and his 1569 lectures on II (2) survive in Vatican MSS. I. G. Menéndez Reigada, 'El pseudo-probabilismo de Fray Bartolomé de Medina', *La Ciencia Tomista*, 20 (1928), pp. 35–57; M.-M. Gorce, 'Le Sens du mot "Probable" et les origines du probabilisme', *Rev. S.R.* 10 (1930),

pp. 460–4; cf. J. de Blic, 'Barthélemy de Medina et les origines du probabilisme', *Ephemerides theologicae Lovanienses*, 7 (1930), pp. 46–83. C. Pozo, SJ, *La Teoría del Progreso Dogmático en los Teólogos de la Escuela de Salamanca* (Biblioteca Theologica Hispana, 1st ser. 1; 1959), pp. 181–92. M.-M. Gorce in *DTC* 10 (pt. 1; 1928), cols. 481–5, s.v., with bibl.; T. Deman, ibid. 13 (pt. 1; 1936), cols. 463–70, s.v. 'Probabilisme'.

meditation (μελετή, *meditatio*) has been used in a variety of different senses in the Christian tradition: (1) the recitation or memorizing of Scriptural texts (this is the predominant sense in early monastic literature, but later fell into disuse); (2) keeping various religious truths or inspirational thoughts in mind during the day (sometimes with different thoughts being recommended for different periods of the day); (3) thinking about things, whether the emphasis is on intellectual rigour, acuteness of perception, or devotional fervour (the object of such meditation might be Scripture, doctrine, life, the world, or almost anything); (4) the application of the mind and often the imagination to the truths of the faith and esp. to episodes in the life of Christ, with a view to stirring an intense affective response (this tends to become a more or less formal exercise). Meditation in all these senses is easily associated with *prayer, because some of the favourite biblical texts are themselves prayers, and thinking about Christian truth sharpens a desire for God's gifts, and thinking about life reveals man's need of God; in sense (4) meditation came in due course to be regarded as part of prayer and so it could be integrated into various methods of prayer. Following St *Teresa of Ávila and St *John of the Cross, many writers have posited a sharp distinction between meditation (in sense (4)) and *contemplation. In modern times various forms of meditation have been adopted or adapted from Eastern non-Christian religions, often involving the abandonment of deliberate thought rather than its focusing on a specific religious object.

See works cited under PRAYER.

Megilloth (Heb. מְגִלּוֹת, 'rolls'). The name given to five Books in the OT, all of them in the third and latest section of the OT *canon known as the 'Writings' ('*Hagiographa'), which are read by the Jews on certain holy days. They are the Song of *Solomon (read at the *Passover), *Ruth (at the Feast of *Weeks), the *Lamentations of Jeremiah (at the anniversary of the Babylonian destruction of *Jerusalem), *Ecclesiastes (at the Feast of *Tabernacles), and *Esther (at the Feast of *Purim).

Meinrad, St (d. 861), Patron of *Einsiedeln (q.v.). Born near Tübingen, he became a monk at *Reichenau and for several years was active in teaching and pastoral work. In middle life he felt called to greater austerity, left his monastery and eventually settled at the spot in the Swiss forests where Einsiedeln ('hermitage') now stands, and here lived the life of a hermit for 25 years. A statue of the Virgin, given to him by a Benedictine abbess and placed in his chapel, is still venerated at Einsiedeln. He was put to death by two ruffians to whom he had given hospitality. His body was taken back to Reichenau and he became venerated as a martyr. Feast day, 21 Jan. His symbol is two ravens.

The late 9th-cent. Life by a monk of Reichenau was orig. ed. by S. Brandt (Basle, 1496); modern edns. by O. Holder-Egger in *MGH*, Scriptores, 15 (pt. 1; 1887), pp. 444–8, and O. Ringholz, OSB, *Geschichte des fürstlichen Benediktinerstiftes U.L.F. Einsiedeln*, 1 (Einsiedeln, etc., 1904), pp. 648–51; Life written in 1378 by Gergius de Gengenbach, pr. ibid., pp. 653–7. The Einsiedeln 'Blockbuch' of 1450, with legends of St Meinrad, ed. G. Morell (ibid., 1861); facsimile, with introd. by L. Helbling, OSB (ibid., 1961). O. Ringholz, OSB, *Meinrads-Büchlein: Das Leben und Verehrung des Märtyrs von Einsiedeln* (Einsiedeln, etc., 1905), pp. 1–80. *Sankt Meinrad zum elften Zentenarium seines Todes 861–1961*, ed. by the Benedictines of Einsiedeln, with preface by L. Helbling, OSB (ibid., 1961). T. Klüppel, *Reichenauer Hagiographie zwischen Walahfrid und Berno* (Sigmaringen, 1980), pp. 45–56. See also works cited under EINSIEDELN.

Meissen Agreement. See REUNION.

Mekitarists. See MECHITARISTS.

Melanchthon, Philipp (1497–1560), German Reformer. The name 'Melanchthon' (the Greek version of his German surname Schwartzerdt, 'Black earth') was given to him in 1509 by J. *Reuchlin, his mother's uncle and his patron. He studied at Heidelberg (from 1509) and Tübingen (from 1512). In 1518 he became professor of Greek at *Wittenberg, where he both influenced M. *Luther and was influenced by him. He took part in the *Leipzig Disputation (1519) and in the ensuing controversy with *Carlstadt. In 1521 he found himself at the head of the Reformation Movement while Luther was confined in the *Wartburg. Lecturing on Rom. at this time, he divided the Epistle into sections dealing with key doctrines: sin, Law, grace, etc. This work was the basis of the first of the many versions of his most influential book, *Loci communes* (1521). During 1521–7 he corrected Luther's translation of the NT and wrote several biblical commentaries.

One of the most erudite and intellectually powerful figures of his age, Melanchthon was closer than Luther to RC teaching on the Law, free will, and questions of *adiaphora. On the other hand, his concern to prevent further divisions in the Church (although it did not extend to embracing the *Anabaptists and other radical sects) made him more open to *Zwinglian and *Calvinist doctrines of the Eucharist. Unlike Luther, he considered philosophy and other 'profane disciplines' to be of great value to theology.

His distancing from Luther's doctrine dates from 1527–8 and the publication of the Thüringen Visitation Articles in which Melanchthon emphasizes that *penance (in a modified form) is dictated by Divine Law. There was, however, no question of a break, at least before Luther's death in 1546, and Melanchthon sided with him firmly against the Zwinglians in the controversy on Eucharistic doctrine in 1525–36. He took part in the Diet of *Speyer (1529), the *Marburg Colloquy (1529), and the Diet of Augsburg (1530), where he was the chief architect of the *Augsburg Confession. In 1537, however, he alone among the Protestant theologians objected to the overt condemnation of the Papacy in the *Schmalkaldic Articles. He was present at the Catholic-Protestant colloquies of *Worms (1540–1) and *Ratisbon (1541) and, together with M. *Bucer, he went to great lengths to unite the Reformed and the RC Church. In his later years he was largely concerned with the organization of the Church in Saxony on a semi-episcopal basis. At the same time, his apparently

favourable attitude to the *Augsburg Interim (1548) made him many opponents among the Lutherans, who also objected increasingly to his *Crypto-Calvinism and his views on free will and to his acceptance of RC rituals as matters of no importance—questions which remained controversial until they were settled by the Formula of *Concord in 1577.

Melanchthon's characteristic teaching on free will, known as *synergism (q.v), received its definitive formulation in the 1535 edition of the *Loci communes*. In this he also stresses that Christians are bound by the Law of God contained in the Bible: they are not to rely on their *predestination to salvation, but must act justly. Besides the *Loci* and many biblical commentaries, he wrote a commentary on *Aristotle, works on logic, rhetoric, philosophy, and science, and edited historical documents such as the *Chronicon Carionis*. He was also responsible for innovations in the German educational system.

Collected Works and Letters ed. K. G. Bretschneider and E. Bindseil (Corpus Reformatorum, 1–28; Brunswick, 1834–60), works omitted from this collection pub. as *Supplementa Melanchthoniana* (Leipzig, 1910 ff. [5 vols. to 1929]). Selected Works ed. R. Stupperich (7 vols., Gütersloh, 1951–75). Separate modern edns. of *Loci Communes* by G. L. Plitt (Erlangen, 1864; rev. T. Kolder, ibid., 1890; 4th edn., ibid., 1925; Eng. tr. by C. L. Hill, Boston, 1944) and of Correspondence by H. Scheible (Stuttgart and Bad Cannstatt, 1977 ff.). Further Eng. trs. of *Loci communes* by C. L. Manschreck (Library of Protestant Thought, New York, 1965) and in W. Pauck (ed.), *Melanchthon and Bucer* (Library of Christian Classics, 19 [1969]), pp. 3–152 (incl. introd.). Lives by C. Schmidt (Elberfeld, 1861), G. Ellinger (Berlin, 1902), C. L. Manschreck (New York [1958]), and R. Stupperich (Berlin, 1960; Eng. tr., 1966). C. Hartfelder, *Melanchthon als praeceptor Germaniae* (1889). O. Clemen, *Studien zu Melanchthons Reden und Gedichten* (1913). F. Hildebrandt, *Melanchthon, Alien or Ally?* (1946). A. Agnoletto, *La Filosofia di Melantone* (Milan, 1959). P. Fraenkel, *Testimonia Patrum: The Function of Patristic Argument in the Theology of Philip Melanchthon* (Geneva, 1961). W. Maurer, *Der junge Melanchthon zwischen Humanismus und Reformation* (2 vols., Göttingen [1967–9]). H. Pfister, *Die Entwicklung der Theologie Melanchthons unter dem Einfluss der Auseinandersetzung mit Schwarmgeistern und Wiedertäufern* (Freiburg i.B. Diss., 1968). S. Wiedenhofer, *Formalstrukturen humanistischer und reformatorischer Theologie bei Philipp Melanchthon* (Regensburger Studien zur Theologie, 2; 2 vols., 1976). R. W. Quere, *Melanchthon's Christum Cognoscere: Christ's Efficacious Presence in the Eucharistic Theology of Melanchthon* (Bibliotheca Humanistica & Reformatorica, 22; Nieuwkoop, 1977). C. E. Maxcey, *Bona Opera: A Study in the Development of the Doctrine in Philip Melanchthon* (ibid. 31; 1980). T. Wengert, *Philip Melanchthon's 'Annotationes in Johannem' in Relation to its Predecessors and Contemporaries* (Travaux d'Humanisme et Renaissance, 220; Geneva, 1987). W. Hammer, *Die Melanchthonforschung im Wandel der Jahrhunderte* (Quellen und Forschungen zur Reformationsgeschichte, 35, 36, and 49; 1967–81). Survey of works pub. 1945–65 by P. Fraenkel and M. Greschat (Geneva, 1967). J. Paquier in *DTC* 10 (pt. 1; 1928), cols. 502–13; W. Maurer in *RGG* (3rd edn.), 4 (1960), cols. 834–41; H. Scheible in *TRE* 22 (1992), pp. 371–410, all s.v., with further bibl.

Melanesian Brotherhood. An Anglican religious order of evangelists who take the traditional vows of poverty, chastity, and obedience, but normally for a limited period only. It was founded in 1925 by a Solomon Islander, Ini Kopuria, with the encouragement of the Bp. of Melanesia. It works in the Solomon Islands, Vanuatu, Fiji, Papua New Guinea, and *Australia, and is prob. the largest community for men in the Anglican Communion. The parallel Community of the Sisters of Melanesia was founded by Solomon Island women in the 1970s.

M. Lycett, *Brothers: The Story of the Native Brotherhood of Melanesia* (1935); C. E. Fox, *Kakamora* (1962). History by B. J. Macdonald-Milne in preparation.

Melania (*c*.342–*c*.410), 'the Elder'. A Roman lady of aristocratic descent and great wealth, on the early death of her husband she adopted the ascetic life, in 372 or 374 left Rome for Egypt and Palestine, and founded a double monastery with *Rufinus of Aquileia on the Mount of *Olives. In 399 or 400 she returned to Italy. Some time before 408 she fled before the Goths by way of Sicily and Africa to *Jerusalem, where she died.

The chief sources are the Life of St Melania the Younger (see below), and scattered refs. in *Palladius' *Lausiac History* and in the *Epp.* of *Jerome and *Paulinus of Nola. F. X. Murphy, CSSR, 'Melania the Elder: a Biographical Note', *Traditio*, 5 (1947), pp. 59–77; N. Moine, 'Melaniana', *Recherches Augustiniennes*, 15 (1980), pp. 3–79. W. H. Fremantle in *DCB* 3 (1882), pp. 888 f.; N. Moine in *Dict. Sp.* 10 (1980), cols. 955–60, s.v. 'Mélanie (1)'. See also bibl. to foll. entry.

Melania, St (*c*.385–438/9), 'the Younger', granddaughter of the preceding. She fled with her husband Pinian to Africa, where they founded two monasteries at Tagaste. Later they joined St *Jerome and entered monasteries at *Bethlehem. After Pinian's death (431/2), Melania founded another monastery on the Mount of *Olives. She also visited Constantinople, but returned to *Jerusalem to die. Feast day, 31 Dec.

Lat. Life ed. [prob. H. *Delehaye, SJ] in *Anal. Boll.* 8 (1889), pp. 16–63 (incomplete); Gk. Life ed. H. D[elehaye, SJ], ibid. 22 (1903), pp. 5–50, and, with Fr. tr., by D. Gorce (SC 90; 1962). Complete Lat. text, with Gk. text, ed. Card. M. Rampolla del Tindaro (Rome, fol., 1905). Eng. tr., with introd. and comm., by E. A. Clark (New York and Toronto [1984]). It is disputed whether the Gk. or Lat. text is the original; cf. A. d'Alès, 'Les Deux Vies de sainte Mélanie la Jeune', *Anal. Boll.* 25 (1906), pp. 401–50. N. Moine, 'Melaniana', *Recherches Augustiniennes*, 15 (1980), pp. 3–79. W. H. Fremantle in *DCB* 3 (1882), p. 889, s.v.; N. Moine in *Dict. Sp.* 10 (1980), cols. 960–5, s.v. 'Mélanie (2)'.

Melchiades, St. See MILTIADES, ST.

Melchiorites. See HOFFMANN, MELCHIOR.

Melchisedech. An alternative spelling of *Melchizedek (q.v.).

Melchites (or **Melkites**). This term, derived from the Gk. form of the Syriac adjective *mālkāyā*, 'imperial', is used of those Christians of Syria and Egypt who, refusing *Monophysitism and accepting the Definition of Faith of the Council of *Chalcedon (451), remained in communion with the Imperial see of Constantinople as 'Emperor's men'. Today the term is applied to Christians of the Byzantine rite (particularly the *Uniats, but to a lesser degree the Orthodox also) belonging to the Patriarchates of Antioch, Jerusalem, and Alexandria. The Orthodox, most of whom are under the jurisdiction of the Patriarch of Antioch (resident in Damascus), number *c*.750,000, while the Uniats (for whom there has been a separate hier-

archy since 1684) number *c*.400,000. Since the 8th cent. the Melchites have produced a large literature in Arabic.

K. P. Karalevsky, *Histoire des patriarcats melkites (Alexandrie, Antioch, Jérusalem) depuis le schisme monophysite du sixième siècle jusqu'à nos jours* (tom. 2, fasc. 1; tom. 3, fascs. 1–2; all pub., Rome, 1909–11). C. Descy, *Introduction à l'histoire et l'ecclésiologie de l'Église melkite* (Jounieh, Lebanon, 1986; Eng. tr., *The Melkite Church*, Newton, Mass., 1993). A. *Fortescue, *The Uniate Eastern Churches* (1923), pp. 185–233. J. Hajjar, *Les Chrétiens Uniates du Proche-Orient* [1982]. C. H. Malik in A. J. Arberry (ed.), *Religion in the Middle East*, 1 (Cambridge, 1969), pp. 297–346, and G. C. Anawati, ibid., pp. 366–8. J. Nasrallah, *Histoire du mouvement littéraire dans l'Église Melchite du Ve au XXe Siècle* (1979 ff.). C. Karalevskij in *DHGE* 3 (1924), cols. 563–703, s.v. 'Antioche'; R. Janin, AA, in *DTC* 10 (pt. 1; 1928), cols. 516–20, s.v.

Melchizedek. Acc. to Gen. 14: 18, the 'King of Salem' and 'Priest of the Most High God (El Elyon)' who offered *Abraham bread and wine as he was returning from his defeat of the four kings. The only other mention of him in the OT occurs in Ps. 110: 4, where the King addressed is styled 'a priest for ever after the order of Melchizedek'. Both these passages were used by the author of the Ep. to the Hebrews (6: 20; 7: 1 ff.) to prove the superiority of the priesthood of Christ, prefigured by Melchizedek, over that of Aaron and the Levites. In the *Dead Sea Scrolls there are speculative traditions about Melchizedek as a heavenly being who will judge the world. From the time of *Clement of Alexandria (*c*.200) onwards his offering of bread and wine has been regarded as a type of the Eucharist, esp. in the W., and *Cyprian argued from it the necessity of using wine, and not merely water, for the celebration of the Christian sacrifice. In the same connection the name of Melchizedek was introduced into the Roman *Canon of the Mass, where his offering is mentioned together with those of Abel and Abraham as an acceptable sacrifice typifying that of Christ on the Cross. Another liturgical mention occurs in the first antiphon of the Second *Vespers of *Corpus Christi, where Christ is called in the words of Ps. 110 'Sacerdos in aeternum . . . secundum ordinem Melchisedech'. In the first Christian centuries several heretical interpretations of his person were condemned by the Fathers, e.g. the belief that he was a power of God superior to Christ (by St *Epiphanius), that he was the Holy Spirit (by St *Ambrose), and that he was an incarnation of the Logos (by *Mark the Hermit).

See comm. *ad locc.* F. L. Horton, *The Melchizedek Tradition: A Critical Examination of the Sources to the Fifth Century A.D. and in the Epistle to the Hebrews* (Society for New Testament Studies, Monograph Series, 30; Cambridge, 1976), with bibl. M. de Jonge and A. S. van der Woude, '11Q Melchizedek and the New Testament', *New Testament Studies*, 12 (1966), pp. 301–26. On the 'Melchisedekians', described by Epiphanius (*Haer.* 55), see also G. Bardy in *DTC* 10 (pt. 1; 1928), cols. 513–16, s.v. 'Melchisédéciens'.

Melitian Schisms. Two 4th-cent. schisms go under this name:

(1) That due to Melitius (often, but wrongly, spelled 'Meletius'), Bp. of Lycopolis in Egypt. It arose out of Melitius' objections to the terms laid down by *Peter, Bp. of Alexandria, during a lull in the Diocletianic persecution *c*.306, for the return of the lapsed to the Church. Thinking the conditions too lax, Melitius created disturbances, and

ordained some of his supporters, whereupon he was excommunicated by Peter. After a further period of persecution, during which Peter was martyred and Melitius himself banished to the mines, he returned to Egypt and founded a schismatic Church with clergy of his own ordination.

The schism continued to flourish for several decades. At the *Council of Nicaea (325), where the matter was raised, it was determined that Melitian clergy should be allowed to continue their functions, but to be subordinate to *Alexander (who had meanwhile succeeded Peter). Their bishops, if legally elected, might take the places of the Catholic bishops when the latter died. Melitius himself was to retain the title of bishop, but to have no see. On the accession of St *Athanasius (328), however, this arrangement broke down, as the Melitians, encouraged by *Eusebius of Nicomedia, again went into schism. Melitius was succeeded by John Arkaph of Memphis. The sect continued, and evidence for the life of Melitian monastic communities has come to light in a number of British Library papyri. It seems to have survived as a small body down to the 8th cent.

(2) The 4th-cent. schism at Antioch which followed the leadership of Melitius. See the next entry.

The chief authorities for the Egyptian Schism are the Melitian docs. in the *Theodosian Codex (Ver. lx [58]); the papyri, ed., with introd., in H. I. Bell, *Jews and Christians in Egypt* (1924), pp. 38–99; scattered refs. in Athanasius; and *Epiphanius, *Haer.* 68. E. *Schwartz, 'Zur Geschichte des Athanasius', *Nachr.* (Gött.), 1905, pp. 164–87, repr. in his *Gesammelte Schriften*, 3 (1959), pp. 87–116; F. H. Kettler, 'Der melitianische Streit in Ägypten', *ZNTW* 35 (1936), pp. 155–93; R. [D.] Williams, 'Arius and the Melitian Schism', *JTS* NS 37 (1986), pp. 35–52. F. J. Foakes-Jackson in *HERE* 8 (1915), p. 538, s.v. 'Meletianism'; É. Amann in *DTC* 10 (pt. 1; 1928), cols. 531–6; C. Vagaggini, OSB, in *EC* 8 (1952), cols. 640 f., s.v. 'Melezio (Melizio) di Licipoli'.

Melitius, St (d. 381), Bp. of *Antioch. He was translated from the see of Sebaste to Antioch in 360, and both *Arians and Nicenes looked for his support. An orthodox inaugural sermon on Prov. 8: 22 led to his immediate exile by the Emp. Constantius; but when he returned in 362 under *Julian, he failed to secure the support of *Athanasius for his claim to the see. He was twice banished under Valens, from 365 to 366 and from 371 to 378, St *Basil being unswerving in support for his claims, but Alexandria wavering and Rome hostile. He was finally restored in 378 and presided at the Council of *Constantinople of 381, during which he died. The schism at Antioch called by his name (not to be confused with the *Melitian Schism in Egypt half a century earlier) arose from the presence of two rival orthodox parties at Antioch which failed to co-operate. The supporters of *Eustathius (Bp. of Antioch *c*.324–*c*.327) suspected the theology of Melitius and created the schism by securing the consecration of one Paulinus in 362. Though it lasted until after the death of Melitius, canonical right was on his side. Feast day, 12 Feb.

F. Cavallera, *Le Schisme d'Antioche* (1905), *passim*. G. Bardy, 'Le Concile d'Antioche (379)', *R. Bén.* 45 (1933), pp. 196–213. E. *Schwartz, 'Zur Kirchengeschichte des vierten Jahrhunderts', *ZNTW* 34 (1935), pp. 129–213; repr. in his *Gesammelte Schriften*, 4 (1960), pp. 1–110. W. A. Jurgens, 'A Letter of Meletius of Antioch', *HTR* 53 (1960), pp. 251–60. CPG 2 (1974), pp. 254–6

(nos. 3415–25). F. *Loofs in *PRE* (3rd edn.), 12 (1903), pp. 552–8, s.v., and É. Amann in *DTC* 10 (1930), cols. 520–31, s.v., both with bibls.

Melito, St (d. *c*.190), Bp. of Sardis. Apart from the fact that he made a visit to Palestine to visit the Holy Places, practically nothing is known of his life. He was described by *Polycrates (ap. *Eusebius, *HE* 5. 24. 5) as one of the great lights of Asia and an upholder of *Quartodeciman practice, and the author of the '*Little Labyrinth' applauded him as an upholder of orthodox Christology. He was a prolific writer, but only fragments of his works were known until 1940, when C. Bonner published a work preserved in a papyrus shared between the *Chester Beatty collection and the University of Michigan. The work bore no title in this papyrus, but a further text found among the *Bodmer papyri (pub. 1960) and also the Coptic and Georgian versions provide the title 'On the Pasch' (Περὶ Πάσχα, *Peri Pascha*). A Latin epitome survives among the sermons of both *Augustine and *Leo I. Its main theme is the new *Pasch inaugurated by Christ. The liturgical context appears to be the Quartodeciman Pasch, and there are interesting parallels with the Jewish Passover haggadah. There is much polemic against the Jews who crucified the Lord. The Christology of the work bears out Melito's reputation: he describes Christ as 'by nature God and Man' (φύσει θεὸς ὢν καὶ ἄνθρωπος). There is an anti-Gnostic insistence on the true humanity of Christ and on the unity of the Old and New Covenants. Man was created a harmonious unity of body and soul, and Redemption consists in the restoration of this unity, which has been dissolved by sin and death. The surviving fragments of his other works include parts of an 'apology' addressed to the Emp. *Marcus Aurelius and a treatise on Baptism, which seems to owe something to Stoic sources. Melito's theology prob. influenced *Irenaeus and *Tertullian. Feast day, 1 Apr.

Crit. edn. with Fr. tr. of *Peri Pascha* and frags. of other works by O. Perler (SC 123; 1966); and with Eng. tr. by S. G. Hall (Oxford Early Christian Texts, 1979). Chester Beatty–Michigan papyrus of the *Peri Pascha* ed. C. Bonner (Studies and Documents, 12; Philadelphia and London, 1940); the Bodmer text by M. Testuz (Papyrus Bodmer, 13; Cologny and Geneva, 1960); and the Georgian version, with Eng. tr., by J. N. Birdsall in *Muséon*, 130 (1967), pp. 121–38. H. Chadwick, 'A Latin Epitome of Melito's Homily on the Pascha', *JTS* NS 11 (1960), pp. 76–82. F. L. Cross, *The Early Christian Fathers* (1960), pp. 103–9. CPG 1 (1983), pp. 35–43 (nos. 1092–8). O. Perler in *Dict. Sp.* 10 (1980), cols. 979–90, s.v., with bibl.

Mellitus, St (d. 624), Abp. of *Canterbury. Sent to England by St *Gregory I in 601, he was consecrated by St *Augustine missionary bishop for the East Saxons in 604, with London (where *Ethelbert built the church of St Paul for him) as his headquarters. After some years, evangelization was arrested by the accession of kings of the East Saxons and of Kent who were hostile to Christianity, and Mellitus was forced to take refuge for a time in Gaul. In 619, soon after his return to England, he succeeded Lawrence as the third Abp. of Canterbury. Feast day, 24 Apr.

The main source is *Bede, *HE* 1. 29 f. and 2. 3–7; cf. comm. by J. M. Wallace-Hadrill (Oxford, 1988), pp. 39, 42 f., 62, 64. W. *Stubbs in *DCB* 3 (1882), pp. 90 f.

Melville, Andrew (1545–1622), Scottish *Presbyterian Reformer and theologian. He was born at Baldovie, nr. Montrose, and educated at St Andrews, where he was the only member of the university who knew Greek. In 1564 he went to Paris to study oriental languages, and thence to Poitiers (1566), where he read civil law. The political troubles in France led him to retire to *Geneva in 1569, where T. *Beza procured him the professorship of humanity at the Academy. On his return to Scotland in 1574 he became principal of Glasgow university. His educational reforms, which included a new plan of studies and the establishment of chairs in languages, science, philosophy, and theology, met with great success. He also took an active part in attacking what was left of the Scottish episcopal system. In 1575 he was entrusted with the drawing up of the 'Second Book of *Discipline' (q.v.), which was largely inspired by the Genevan model and sought to discard the remnants of prelacy. In 1578 he was appointed commissioner for the visitation of St Andrews, and in 1580 he became principal of St Mary's College, St Andrews. When Moderator of the General Assembly of 1582, he prosecuted R. Montgomery, one of the '*tulchan' bishops, who had accepted the see of Glasgow from *James VI [I] and the Duke of Lennox on condition that the bulk of the revenues should revert to the Duke. Thereby brought into opposition to the King, he was charged at Edinburgh in 1584 with treason, and fled to England to escape imprisonment and possible death. In 1585 he returned to Scotland, was again Moderator of the General Assembly in 1587, and became rector of St Andrews in 1590. His attacks on the King's interference in religious matters led to the loss of his rectorship in 1597, but he was made Dean of the Theological Faculty at St Andrews in 1599. After the accession of James to the English throne he again incurred the royal displeasure by insisting on the right of a free Assembly and was summoned to London in 1606. A sarcastic Latin poem on Anglican worship caused him to be charged before the Privy Council and confined to the Tower in 1607, whence he was released in 1611 on being offered the chair of biblical theology at Sedan university. Here he spent the remaining years of his life. Though his bitter invective frequently marred the success of his work, his reform of the Scottish universities and of Scottish Presbyterianism are lasting achievements. Among his writings are Latin poems on biblical subjects, the finest of which is the *Carmen Mosis* (1573); a treatise on free will (1597); and a commentary on Romans (pub. 1850).

The standard modern work is the Life by T. McCrie (2 vols. bound in 1; Edinburgh, 1819; 2nd edn., 1823). Study by S. Mechie in R. S. Wright (ed.), *Fathers of the Kirk* (1960), pp. 37–48. A. Gordon in *DNB* 37 (1894), pp. 230–7, with further refs.

Memling (or **Memlinc**), Hans (*c*.1440–94), painter. A native of Seligenstadt on the Main, he was registered as a citizen of Bruges by 1465, and was among its wealthiest inhabitants. The legend that he became an inmate of St John's Hospital is an 18th-cent. fabrication, though the Hospital possesses a fine collection of his works. Despite his German origins, the main influences on his style were Netherlandish, esp. Roger van der Weyden. His paintings, which are notable for their colour and harmony, include the Shrine of St *Ursula, the Donne Triptych in the National Gallery, London, as well as several Madonnas

and other altarpieces. His precise drawing and high finish are most apparent in his portraits.

Reproductions of his pictures, with introd. by K. Voll (Klassiker der Kunst in Gesamtausgaben, 14; 1909). Details of his 'Passionsaltar' at Lübeck ed. C. G. Heise (Hamburg, 1950). Studies by L. von Baldass (Vienna, 1942) and [K.] B. McFarlane (posthumously ed. E. Wind and G. Harriss; Oxford Studies in the History of Art and Architecture, 1971). M. J. Friedländer, *Die altniederländische Malerei*, 6 (1928), pp. 9–70, with plates i–lxvi and suppl., 14 (1937), pp. 102 f.; Eng. tr., 6 (pt. 1; Leiden, 1971).

Memorare (Lat., 'Remember'). A widely used intercessory prayer addressed to the BVM. It is commonly ascribed to St *Bernard of Clairvaux, prob. owing to a confusion with Claude Bernard ('The Poor Priest'; 1588–1641), who popularized the prayer; but its real author is unknown. The earliest known texts date from the late 15th cent. when they are embodied in a much longer prayer to the BVM. In 1846 Pope *Pius IX attached considerable indulgences to its recitation, and it is included in the 1849 edn. of the *Raccolta. The most popular Eng. version begins, 'Remember, O most loving Virgin Mary'.

N. Paulus, 'Das Alter des Gebetes *Memorare*', *ZKT* 26 (1902), pp. 604–6. H. Thurston, SJ, 'The *Memorare*', *The Month*, 132 (1918), pp. 269–78, repr. in his *Familiar Prayers*, ed. P. Grosjean, SJ (1953), no. 9, pp. 152–63, with refs.

memoria (Lat., commonly rendered in English 'memorial'). The name given in current RC liturgical documents to the least important of the three categories of *feast. The class is divided into obligatory and optional *memoriae*. See also FEASTS, ECCLESIASTICAL, and SOLEMNITAS.

Memoriale Rituum (also known as **Rituale parvum**). A Latin liturgical book containing the forms traditionally used in the blessing of candles (for *Candlemas), ashes (for *Ash Wednesday), and palms (for *Palm Sunday), as well as the services for the last three days in *Holy Week in the shortened form usual in smaller RC parish churches. The book was first issued in 1725 by *Benedict XIII for use at Rome, and nearly 100 years later (1821) approved by *Pius VII for the whole Church of the Roman rite. It has been rendered obsolete by *Pius XII's reordering of the Holy Week liturgy and subsequent changes.

P. Siffrin in *EC* 8 (1952), cols. 666 f., s.v.

Memphitic. See BOHAIRIC.

Memra (Aram. מֵימְרָא 'word'). The word was used in a specifically theological sense in Jewish literature, esp. for the Divine creative Word (see LOGOS), manifesting God's power in the material world and in the human mind, and acting as His agent and as the mediator between God and men. In the *Targums 'Memra' is sometimes used where the OT has '*Yahweh', to avoid anthropomorphism. The Memra concept possibly underlies the 'Logos' or 'Word' of Jn. 1: 1–14.

[C. T.] R. Hayward, *Divine Name and Presence: The Memra* (Oxford Centre for Postgraduate Hebrew Studies Publications; Totowa, NJ [1981]).

Menaion (Gk. μηναῖον, from μήν, 'month'). In the E. Church, the name given to each of the 12 liturgical books (one for each month) which contain the variable parts of the Divine *Office for the immovable feasts. They correspond with the *proprium sanctorum* in the W. The series begins with the Greek ecclesiastical year, in September. An appendix contains the rite for the saints which have no *proper office, corresponding to the *commune sanctorum* of the Latin *Breviary. See also MENOLOGION.

Partial Eng. tr. by Mother Mary and K. [T. R.] Ware, *The Festal Menaion* (The Service Books of the Orthodox Church, 1969).

Menas, St (*c*.3rd–4th cent.), Egyptian martyr. He was probably born and martyred in Egypt, but his story was apparently fused with that of a soldier executed in Phrygia under the Emp. *Diocletian, possibly another Menas, possibly St Gordian. His reputed birthplace, to the SW of Lake Mareotis, became an important pilgrimage centre, associated with miraculous cures by water. The church and town were excavated in 1905–8, and many further *ampullae bearing a figure of Menas between camels were found. He was a popular saint and there are many other representations of him, incl. a 6th-cent. ivory *pyx in the British Museum. He is the patron saint of merchants. Feast day, 11 Nov.

'Acta S. Menae' (Gk. text, with Lat. tr.) in *Anal. Boll.* 3 (1884), pp. 258–70. Selection of Coptic texts relating to St Menas ed., with Fr. tr., by J. Drescher (Publications de la Société d'Archéologie Copte; Cairo, 1946). P. Devos, 'Un Récit des miracles de S. Ménas en copte et en éthiopien', *Anal. Boll.* 77 (1959), pp. 451–63; 78 (1960), pp. 154–60; id., 'Le Juif et le Chrétien. Un miracle de saint Ménas', ibid. 78 (1960), pp. 275–308, both with text and Fr. tr. The primary sources are the Reports of C. M. Kaufmann (3 vols., Cairo, 1906–8), who directed the Frankfurt expedition to the site. C. M. Kaufmann, *Die Menasstadt und das Nationalheiligtum der altchristlichen Ägypter in der westalexandrinischen Wüste* (1910). M. A. Murray, 'St Menas of Alexandria', *Proceedings of the Society of Biblical Archaeology*, 29 (1907), pp. 25–30, 51–60, and 112–22 (with plates). H. *Delehaye, SJ, 'L'Invention des reliques de St Ménas à Constantinople', *Anal. Boll.* 29 (1910), pp. 117–50. H. *Leclercq, OSB, in *DACL* 11 (pt. 1; 1933), cols. 324–97, s.v., with bibl.

Menas, St (also **Mennas**) (d. 552), Patr. of Constantinople from 536. He was consecrated by Pope *Agapetus (535–6) to succeed the *Monophysite, Anthimus. In 543 he presided over an anti-Origenist Council. At the beginning of the *Three Chapters' controversy (543) he subscribed with some hesitation to the Imperial Edict and forced his suffragans to do the same. But on their complaining to the vacillating Pope, *Vigilius (537–55), Menas was excommunicated, first in 547, and again in 551. In neither instance did the sentence last for long and he died in full communion with the Papacy. His patriarchate was a high-water mark of Papal influence at Constantinople. Feast day, 25 Aug.

AASS, Aug. 5 (1741), pp. 164 f. The chief docs. of Menas' patriarchate are calendared in V. Grumel, AA, *Les Regestes des actes du patriarcat de Constantinople*, 1: *Les Actes des patriarches*, fasc. 1 (2nd edn., 1972), pp. 169–76 (nos. 232–43). L. Magi, *La Sede Romana nella corrispondenza degli imperatori e patriarchi bizantini (VI–VII sec.)* (Bibliothèque de la RHE, 57; 1972), pp. 124–48 and *passim*. CPG 3 (1979), pp. 310–12 (nos. 6923–34). W. M. Sinclair in *DCB* 3 (1882), pp. 902 f.; A. Stiernon, AA, in

DPAC 2 (1984), cols. 2217–18, s.v. 'Mena'; Eng. tr. in *Encyclopedia of the Early Church*, 1 (Cambridge, 1992), p. 553.

Mendicant Friars. Members of those orders which were forbidden to own property in common. Unlike the monks, they work or beg for their living and are not bound to one convent by a vow of 'stability'. In the Middle Ages their activities were carried on chiefly in towns, and their privileges, esp. exemption from episcopal jurisdiction and extensive faculties for preaching and hearing confessions, aroused much hostility among the bishops and the secular clergy as well as in the universities. Opposition was particularly strong at *Paris, where it was led by William of St Amour and where St *Thomas Aquinas and St *Bonaventure wrote in their defence. In 1256 the dispute was settled in their favour by Alexander IV.

Originally restricted to the *Franciscans and *Dominicans, the name and privileges of Mendicant Friars were given to the *Carmelites by *Innocent IV in 1245, to the Hermits of St *Augustine by Alexander IV in 1256, and to the *Servites by *Martin V in 1424, several other orders following later. Acc. to RC canon law Mendicant Friars may seek funds whilst others are forbidden to do so without the written permission of their own *Ordinary and that of the local Ordinary. However, National Conferences of Bishops can determine norms on seeking alms which are binding even on mendicants (*CIC* (1983), can. 1265).

The Mendicant Orders are listed in the *Annuario Pontificio*. F. Vernet, *Les Ordres mendiants* (Bibliothèque Catholique des Sciences Religieuses, 1933). L. Gillet, *Histoire artistique des ordres mendiants: Étude sur l'art religieux en Europe du XIIIᵉ au XVIᵉ siècle* (1912). Y. J.-M. *Congar [OP], 'Aspects ecclésiologiques de la querelle entre mendiants et séculiers dans la seconde moitié du XIIIᵉ siècle et le début du XIVᵉ', *AHDLMA* 28, for 1961 (1962), pp. 35–151, with further refs. F. Dal Pino and others in *DIP* 5 (1978), cols. 1163–89, s.v. 'Mendicanti, Ordini'; A. Carpaneto, OFM Cap., and E. Piacenti, OFM Conv., ibid. 7 (1983), cols. 1154–60, s.v. 'Questua'. See further bibl. under separate Mendicant Orders.

Mennonites, the followers of Menno Simons (1496–1561), from whom they take their name. At one time parish priest in Dutch Friesland, he renounced his connections with the RC Church in 1536 and joined the *Anabaptists, then suffering severe persecution and obloquy after the attempted Kingdom of the Saints at Münster. For 25 years he shepherded and reorganized the stricken companies in the Netherlands and neighbouring territories. His views, which were similar to those of the *Swiss Brethren, included stress on believers' Baptism, a connectional type of Church organization with an emphasis on the responsibilities and rights of the local congregation, a rejection of Christian participation in the magistracy, and non-resistance. John *Smyth and other English Separatist exiles in the Netherlands were in friendly touch with Mennonites. In the 17th and 18th cents. the Mennonites became a numerous and influential community in the Netherlands; certain branches adopted *Socinian views. The number of Mennonites in 1990 was said to be over 856,500. In Europe the largest numbers were in Germany (*c*.18,500) and the Netherlands (*c*.18,000), with perhaps some 26,000 in all the territories of the former Soviet Union. There were *c*.226,000 in the

*United States of America (where there has been much internal division), *c*.114,000 in *Canada, perhaps nearly 113,000 in *Zaire, *c*.76,000 in *India, *c*.65,000 in *Indonesia, and *c*.19,500 in *Mexico.

Common ground of the different Mennonite communities is the practice of believers' Baptism and a symbolic interpretation of the Lord's Supper. Each congregation is independent. Preaching occupies a central place in worship, and both men and women may preach. Most communities stipulate that their members should undertake some sort of social work, either at home or abroad, in place of military service. Some groups are full members of the *World Council of Churches; others have observer status. The Mennonite World Conference comprises all groups.

C. H. Smith, *The Story of the Mennonites* (Berne, Ind., 1941; 5th edn. by C. Krahn, Newton, Kan., 1981); C. J. Dyck (ed.), *An Introduction to Mennonite History* (Scottdale, Pa., 1967; rev. 1981). R. Friedmann, *Mennonite Piety Through the Centuries: Its Genius and its Literature* (Studies in Anabaptist and Mennonite History, 7; Goshen, Ind., 1949). J. Horsch, *Mennonites in Europe* (Scottdale, Pa., 1942; 2nd edn., 1950); J. C. Wenger, *The Mennonite Church in America* (ibid., 1966); F. H. Epp, *Mennonites in Canada, 1786–1920* (Toronto, 1974); id., *Mennonites in Canada, 1920–1940* (ibid., 1982). B. S. Hostetler, *American Mennonites and Protestant Movements* (Studies in Anabaptist and Mennonite History, 28; Scottdale, Pa., etc., 1987). C. [W.] Redekop, *Mennonite Society* (Baltimore and London [1989]). H. S. Bender and others (eds.), *The Mennonite Encyclopedia* (4 vols., Scottdale, Pa., 1955–9). N. P. Springer and A. J. Klassen, *Mennonite Bibliography 1631–1961* (2 vols., ibid. and Kitchener, Ont., 1977).

The Complete Writings of Menno Simons c.1496–1561, tr. from the Dutch by L. Verduin, ed. J. C. Wenger, with biog. by H. S. Bender (Scottdale, Pa., 1956). Further studies of Menno Simons by J. Horsch (ibid., 1916), C. Krahn (Karlsruhe, 1936), and C. Bornhäuser (Beiträge zur Geschichte und Lehre der Reformierten Kirche, 35; Neukirchen, 1973). I. B. Horst, *A Bibliography of Menno Simons* (Nieuwkoop, 1962). Id. in *Biografisch Lexicon voor de Geschiedenis van het Nederlandse Protestantisme*, 2 (1983), pp. 318–22, s.v. 'Menno Simons'; H.-J. Goertz in *TRE* 22 (1992), pp. 444–57, s.v. 'Menno Simons/Mennoniten', both with bibl.

Menologion (Gk. μηνολόγιον, from μήν, 'month'). In the E. Church, a liturgical book containing the Lives of the saints, arranged by months throughout the ecclesiastical year (which begins with September). The word is used in a variety of senses, being applied to several distinct books current in the E. Church corresponding to the description just given, e.g. counterparts of the W. '*Proper of the Saints' (the 'Menaion', q.v.), '*martyrology' and 'Acta Sanctorum'. One of the most celebrated Menologia is that compiled by *Simeon Metaphrastes. The term has also been applied (in the W.) to private non-liturgical collections of the Lives of saintly persons, and esp. to books of the Lives of members of religious orders arranged according to their date of death. See also SYNAXARION.

[H. *Delehaye, SJ,] *Le Synaxaire de Sirmond', *Anal. Boll.* 14 (1895), pp. 149–434; [id.,] 'Les Ménologes grecs', ibid. 16 (1897), pp. 311–29; [id.,] 'Le Ménologe de Métaphraste', ibid. 17 (1898), pp. 448–52. Id., *AASS*, Propylaeum ad Nov. (1902), pp. iv–lxxvi. H. Thurston, SJ, in *CE* 10 (1911), pp. 191 f.; H. *Leclercq, OSB, in *DACL* 11 (pt. 1; 1933), cols. 419–30, both s.v.; G. Bottereau, SJ, in *Dict. Sp.* 10 (1980), cols. 1024–7, s.v. [mainly on the private biog. collections of religious orders]. See also bibl. to SIMEON METAPHRASTES.

mensa (Lat., 'table'). In early Christian times the word was applied esp. to the large tablets of stone set over or near a grave, and used apparently for receiving food for meals in memory of the deceased. A large number of such *mensae* have been recovered from N. Africa, and in recent times also from N. Germany (Bonn, Xanten). In Africa their use was widespread among the pagans, and the superstitious and unbecoming nature of the associated rites led St *Augustine and other Christian theologians to denounce them.

The word is also in common use among liturgists for the flat stone which forms the top of an altar. Acc. to modern RC requirements, it should normally be of stone, but may be of other solid material (*Ordo Missae*, General Instruction, 263).

H. *Leclercq, OSB, in *DACL* 11 (pt. 1; 1933), cols. 440–53, s.v. On the use of the word in the second sense, see Braun, *CA* 1 (1924), pp. 245–316, with pls. 41–5.

mental prayer. Since prayer should come from the heart, not just from the lips, all prayer needs to be attended by an interior sincerity. In this sense some medieval writers say that all prayer is 'mental', whether or not it is spoken aloud. St *Thomas Aquinas argues that it is 'intention' rather than 'attention' that is required, but other writers put more stress on 'attention' and fervour. In the 16th cent. 'mental prayer' comes to be used in a confusing variety of new senses: (1) prayer of love, as opposed to discursive meditation, (2) meditation or contemplation, (3) discursive meditation as opposed to contemplation (q.v.). The third sense prevailed and remained normative until the modern period.

See works cited under PRAYER.

mental reservation. The conflict which may arise between the duty of telling the truth and that of keeping a secret has caused the development of the doctrine of mental reservation. RC moral theology distinguishes between *restrictio pure mentalis* ('strict mental reservation') and *restrictio late mentalis* ('wide mental reservation'). In the former a qualification is added mentally which completely alters the statement pronounced, so that the hearer is necessarily deceived; it has been thought that it was this form that was condemned by *Innocent XI in 1679. In the 'wide mental reservation', on the other hand, words are used which, acc. to the circumstances, are susceptible of more than one interpretation, without the speaker giving an indication as to the sense in which he uses them. The wide mental reservation may be used when the person who puts a question has no right to the truth, or else only where a professional secret is involved, as, e.g., in the case of a priest denying knowledge of a fact with the mental reservation 'apart from confession'. In instances such as these the deception of the hearer is allowable for a good reason and involves no sin on the part of the speaker. In an extreme form, the teaching was developed by the *Jesuit theologian J. Caramuel, in his *Haplotes de restrictionibus mentalibus* (Leiden, 1672).

Merbecke (or **Marbeck**), **John** (d. *c*.1585), English divine and musician. Appointed organist at St George's Chapel, *Windsor, in 1541, he was condemned to the stake for heresy in 1543, because he had written the first *concordance in English of the Bible. He was pardoned, however, through the influence of Bp. Stephen *Gardiner, and the concordance was published in 1550 with a dedication to *Edward VI. In 1550 he produced his *Book of Common Prayer Noted*, in which he composed plainchant-style music for Edward VI's first (1549) liturgy. Although its use did not survive the appearance of the 1552 liturgy, it underwent a notable revival with the *Oxford Movement in the 19th cent. He continued his musical and theological studies for some years and apparently died about 1585.

Extracts from his works, ed., with introd., by R. A. Leaver (Courtenay Library of Reformation Classics, 9; Sutton Courtenay [1978]). E. H. Fellowes, *The Office of the Holy Communion as set by John Merbecke* (1949). J. Blezzard in *New Grove Dictionary of Music and Musicians*, ed. S. Sadie, 12 (1980), pp. 168–70, s.v. 'Merbecke, John'.

Mercati, Giovanni (1866–1957), Prefect of the *Vatican Library. Born in 1866 at Villa Gaida in the province of Reggio Emilia, he was ordained priest in 1889, and from 1893 until 1919 was on the staff of the 'Bibliotheca *Ambrosiana' at Milan. In 1898 he was nominated Scriptor of the Greek Language at the Vatican Library, pro-Prefect in 1918, and Prefect in 1919. In 1936 he was created cardinal. Mercati wrote innumerable studies, esp. on matters of patristic and palaeographical interest; and he was one of the editors of the Catalogue of the Vatican Greek MSS (1923 ff.).

His brothers, **Angelo Mercati** (1870–1955) and **Silvio Giuseppe Mercati** (1877–1963), were also distinguished scholars.

Mercati's chief papers to date assembled in *Opere minori raccolte in occasione del settantesimo natalizio sotto gli auspicii de S.S. Pio XI*, ed. A. M. Albareda, OSB (ST 76–80; 5 vols., 1937–41), with biog. notice and bibl. [for years 1890–1941] in vol. 80. *Miscellanea Giovanni Mercati* (ibid. 121–6; 6 vols., 1946). Further list of his works in *Nel novantesimo anno del cardinale Mercati 1866–1956* (Vatican, 1956), pp. 57–130. P. Simonelli, *Il Card. Giovanni Mercati: Profilo biografico* (Reggio Emilia, 1956). There was also a commem. vol. ed. L. Donati in *La Bibliofilia*, 60 (1958; issued separately, Florence, 1959).

Angelo Mercati's *Saggi di storia e letteratura* collected at Rome, vol. 1, 1951. Vols. in his honour in ST 165, 1952, and *Fontes Ambrosiani*, 30 (Milan, 1956), with list of his works, pp. 7–25. Vols. in honour of S. G. Mercati in *Studi Bizantini e Neoellenici*, 9 (1957), with list of his works, pp. ix–xxiii, and 11 (1964), and *Byzantion*, 34 (1964).

Mercator, Marius. See MARIUS MERCATOR.

Mercedarians. A religious order of men, dedicated to Our Lady of Ransom (Nuestra Señora de la Merced), which was founded in the 13th cent. by St *Peter Nolasco to assist in the ransoming of Christians captured by the Moors. The exact date of its foundation is uncertain, but it was confirmed by *Gregory IX in 1235. Its first base was in Barcelona, but it spread fairly rapidly throughout most of the Iberian peninsula and then into Italy. Later it was also very strong in Latin America. At first it was almost entirely lay, but it soon began attracting clerics, and early in the 14th cent. the clerics took control. Its main work was collecting alms and raising money from its own properties for the ransoming of captives, but its members also travelled regularly into Muslim lands to negotiate the freeing of Christians. Later, some of its members devoted themselves to academic work and theology, and in the 19th cent. its apostolate was defined in broader educational, charitable, and missionary terms. There is also a second order, of nuns, whose roots go back to the 13th cent. In 1603 an order of Discalced Mercedarians was founded.

Tirso de Molina (Gabriel Téllez) [d. 1648], Mercedarian, *Historia general de la Orden de Nuestra Señora de las Mercedes*, ed. M. Penedo Rey, Mercedarian (2 vols., Madrid, 1973–4). G. Vásquez Núñez, Mercedarian, *Manual de Historia de la Orden de Nuestra Señora de la Merced*, 1 *(1218–1574)* (Toledo, 1931); 2 *(1574–1935)* (posthumously pub., Madrid, 1936). F. D. Gazulla Galve, Mercedarian, *La orden de Nuestra Señora de la Merced: Estudios histórico-críticos, 1218–1317* (1934). J. W. Brodman, *Ransoming Captives in Crusader Spain: The Order of Merced on the Christian–Islamic Frontier* (Philadelphia, 1986). P. N. Pérez, Mercedarian, *Religiosos de la Merced que pasaron a la América Española, 1514–1777* (Seville, 1924). V. M. Barriga, Mercedarian, *Los Mercedarios en el Perú en el Siglo XVI: Documentos inéditos del Archivo General de Indias*, 1 (Rome, 1933), 2–5 (Arequipa, 1939–54); id., *Mercedarios ilustres en el Perú* (2 vols., ibid., 1943–9). Y. Dossat, 'Les Ordres de Rachat. Les Mercédaires', *Cahiers de Fanjeaux*, 13 (1978), pp. 365–87, with bibl. G. Placer López, Mercedarian, *Bibliografía Mercedaria* (3 vols., Madrid, 1963–83; detailing works by Mercedarians). A. Morales, Mercedarian, in *NCE* 9 (1967), pp. 669 f., s.v.; A. Rubino, Mercedarian, in *DIP* 5 (1978), cols. 1219–34, s.v. 'Mercedari', 'Mercedari Scalzi', 'Mercedarie'.

Mercersburg Theology. A school of thought originating in one of the smaller *Reformed Churches in America (the 'German Reformed Church'). It opposed both the emotionalism and the rationalism of the mid-19th cent. by emphasizing the importance of doctrine, with special stress on Christology and sacramental theology; while upholding the teaching of the Reformers, it saw this in relation to patristic and subsequent thought. The name derives from the small town of Mercersburg in the Appalachian foothills in Pennsylvania, in which Marshall College and the Theological Seminary of the German Reformed Church were situated. The intellectual roots of the movement were in the organic philosophy of Frederick A. Rausch (1806–41), who sought to combine the insights of German and Scottish systems of philosophy in what he called an 'Anglo-German philosophy'. His method appealed both to J. W. *Nevin and his colleague, P. *Schaff. The movement came into prominence with the publication of Nevin's work, *The Anxious Bench* (1843), which attacked the current methods of revivalist preaching. The stress which Nevin and his colleagues laid on the need for liturgical renewal and their teaching about the 'Mystical Presence' of Christ in the Eucharist have led to comparisons with the *Oxford Movement in England, but it seems that the Mercersburg theologians drew their inspiration from contemporary thought in Germany. Indeed Nevin was critical of some aspects of *Anglo-Catholicism, and Schaff was favourably impressed by the views of F. D. *Maurice. See also NEVIN, J. W.

Extracts, mainly from the works of Nevin and Schaff, ed., with introd., by J. H. Nichols, *The Mercersburg Theology* (New York, 1966). L. J. Binkley, *The Mercersburg Theology* (Lancaster, Pa., 1953); J. H. Nichols, *Romanticism in American Theology: Nevin and Schaff at Mercersburg* (Chicago, 1961); J. M. Maxwell, *Worship and Reformed Theology: The Liturgical Lessons of Mercersburg* (Pittsburgh Theological Monographs, NS 10; Pittsburgh, 1976). *New Mercersburg Review* (Reading, Pa., 1985 ff.).

Mercier, Désiré Joseph (1851–1926), Belgian philosopher and prelate. Educated at Malines and Louvain and ordained to the priesthood in 1874, in 1877 he became Professor of Philosophy at the Petit Séminaire at Malines and in 1882 first Professor of Thomist Philosophy at Louvain. From the first he was an ardent promoter of the Thomist revival heralded by *Aeterni Patris* (1879), esp. interesting himself in the application of Thomist principles to modern science. The new school ('Neo-Scholasticism') developed in conscious opposition both to the Scientific *Positivism of J. S. Mill and H. *Spencer and to the Neo-Kantian Idealism. Under Mercier's inspiration an Institute of Philosophy was founded at Louvain which gave a prominent place to experimental methods. Mercier expounded his own philosophical position in a tetralogy—*Psychologie* (1892), *Logique* (1894), *Métaphysique* (1894), and *Critériologie* (1899). He was also mainly responsible for the *Revue Néoscolastique de Philosophie* (1894 ff.).

In 1906 Mercier was made Abp. of Malines and in 1907 created a cardinal. He was in many ways a model prelate, ever concerned for the spiritual life of his clergy and people. He naturally had little interest in the activist philosophy of the *Modernist school; and in his Lenten Pastoral for 1908 he denounced G. *Tyrrell, who replied in his *Medievalism* (1908). During the World War of 1914–18 he strenuously upheld Belgian interests against the German invaders, and encouraged resistance by his own example. Prompted by his desire for the promotion of Christian unity, he was the leading spirit on the RC side in the Conversations at *Malines (1921, 1923, 1925, q.v.), which were cut short by his death.

Mercier's correspondence with the German Government during the occupation, 1914–18, ed. F. Mayence (Brussels, 1919; Eng. tr. as *Cardinal Mercier's Own Story*, 1920). His *Œuvres pastorales* were pub. in 7 vols., Brussels and Louvain, 1911–29. Commemorative vol. under the title *Le Cardinal Mercier (1851–1926)*, pub. Brussels, 1927, with list of his works, pp. 341–72. Other Lives incl. those by G. Ramaekers (Brussels, 1926), H. L. Dubly (Paris, 1927; Eng. tr., 1928), and A. Simon (Brussels, 1960). The centenary of his birth was marked by celebrations at Louvain; a commemorative vol. was prepared by L. de Raeymaeker and others, *Le Cardinal Mercier: Fondateur de l'Institut Supérieur de Philosophie à l'Université de Louvain* [1952]. A. Simon, *Position philosophique du cardinal Mercier: Esquisse psychologique* (Académie Royale de Belgique. Classe de Lettres. Mémoires. Collection in-8°, 2nd ser. 56, fasc. 1; 1962). I. Meseberg-Haubold, *Der Widerstand Kardinal Merciers gegen die deutsche Besetzung Belgiens 1914–1918* (Europäische Hochschulschriften, Reihe 3, Bd. 176; 1982).

mercy, corporal works of. See CORPORAL WORKS OF MERCY.

Mercy, Sisters of. See SISTERS OF MERCY.

mercy, spiritual works of. See SPIRITUAL WORKS OF MERCY.

mercy-seat. In the Jewish Temple, the covering of solid gold laid on the '*Ark of the Covenant' which was conceived to be God's resting-place. The Hebrew כַּפֹּרֶת, Greek (LXX, ἱλαστήριον), and Latin (Vulgate, *propitiatorium*) words are all connected with the idea of 'propitiation'. The AV rendering 'mercy seat' goes back to

W. *Tyndale's version, following M. *Luther's *Gnadenstuhl*.

G. A. *Deissmann in *E.Bi.* 3 (1902), cols. 3027–35, s.v.; J. Herrmann and F. Büchsel in *TWNT* 3 (1938), pp. 319–24 (Eng. tr., 1966, pp. 318–23), s.v. ἱλαστήριον. H. Reventlow in *TRE* 13 (1984), pp. 459–64, s.v. 'Gnade I'; B. Lang in *Theologisches Wörterbuch zum Alten Testament*, ed. G. J. Botterweck and others, 4 (Stuttgart, 1984), pp. 303–18, s.v. 'Kippaer'. See also bibl. to ARK (2).

merit. In the theological sense of the term, 'merit' designates man's right to be rewarded for a work done for God. The conception has its foundation in the Bible, where in both the OT and the NT rewards are promised to the just for their good works (e.g. Exod. 23: 20–2, Deut. 5: 28–33 and *passim*, Mt. 5: 3–12, 6: 4, 19 f., 7: 21). The term appears to have been first employed by *Tertullian, who already recognizes diversity of merit followed by diversity of reward, 'Quomodo multae mansiones apud Patrem si non pro varietate meritorum?' (*Scorp.* 6). This doctrine was endorsed by *Cyprian, *Augustine (partly), and the later Fathers, until the theology of merit was fully developed by the Schoolmen. These last distinguish two kinds of merit, *meritum de condigno* and *meritum de congruo*. *Condign merit confers a claim to reward due in justice to services rendered, whilst *congruous merit may only claim the reward on grounds of fitness. In the relation between God and man, condignity of merit in the strict sense is impossible owing to the creature's absolute dependence on the Creator. It is, however, admitted in the sense that God, by His free promise, has bound Himself to confer rewards on certain works. The following are the conditions to be fulfilled in order to obtain merit *de condigno*. The work must be morally good, be done freely, be assisted by actual grace, performed with a supernatural motive (whether with charity or whether faith alone is sufficient is contested by theologians) in the sphere of this life (*in statu viae*), be done in the state of grace, and, lastly, God must have promised to reward it. Merit *de congruo* is held to be conferred on similar conditions except for the state of grace, as it may be possessed by those not yet justified in so far as they cooperate with actual grace.

The traditional doctrine of merit was repudiated by the Reformers, esp. by M. *Luther, who taught the sinfulness of all human works whether done before or after justification. Most subsequent Protestant theology has denied that merit is a valid Christian category. The medieval doctrine was reformulated by the Council of *Trent, which, while maintaining the impossibility of meriting the initial grace of justification, emphasized the reality of human merit, based on the supernatural life communicated by Christ as the Head to the members of His Mystical Body.

K. H. Wirth, *Der 'Verdienst'-Begriff in der christlichen Kirche* (2 vols., 1892–1901; on Tertullian and Cyprian). C. S. Sullivan, FSC, *The Formulation of the Tridentine Doctrine of Merit* (Catholic University of America, Studies in Sacred Theology, 116; Washington, DC, 1959). R. S. Franks in *HERE* 8 (1915), pp. 561–5, s.v. 'Merit (Christian)'; J. Rivière in *DTC* 10 (pt. 1; 1928), cols. 574–785, s.v. 'Mérite'; N. J. Hein and others in *RGG* (3rd edn.), 6 (1962), cols. 1261–70, s.v. 'Verdienst'; C. S. Sullivan in *NCE* 9 (1967), pp. 683–6, s.vv.; A. Solignac, SJ, in *Dict. Sp.* 10 (1980), cols. 1040–51, s.v. 'Mérite et Vie spirituelle', with extensive bibl.

Merle d'Aubigné, Jean Henri (1794–1872), Swiss historian of the *Reformation. The son of French Protestant refugee parents, he studied at Berlin under J. A. W. *Neander and W. M. L. *de Wette. After taking charge of the French Protestant church in Hamburg from 1819 to 1823, he became pastor to a congregation and court preacher at Brussels. In 1831 he returned to *Geneva as professor of Church history in the new theological faculty. Here he wrote his popular, but unreliable, *Histoire de la Réformation du XVIᵉ siècle* (5 vols., 1835–53). His *Histoire de la Réformation en Europe au temps de Calvin* (8 vols., 1863–78) was a more finished work.

J. Winkler, *Der Kirchenhistoriker Jean Henri Merle d'Aubigné* (Basler Studien zur historischen und systematischen Theologie, 12; 1968), with extensive bibl. —. Duchemin in *PRE* (3rd edn.), 12 (1903), pp. 637–43.

Merry del Val, Rafael

Merry del Val, Rafael (1865–1930), Cardinal. The son of Don Rafael Merry del Val, secretary to the Spanish Legation in London, he was educated by the *Jesuits at Namur and Brussels, at Ushaw College, Durham (1883–5), and at the Roman Accademia dei Nobili (1885–1891). He was ordained priest in 1888. Singled out by *Leo XIII for the Papal service, he became secretary to the commission which pronounced against *Anglican Ordinations (1896). In 1897 he was entrusted with important negotiations in *Canada on the schools question which arose out of the Manitoba Laws of 1890. In 1900 he became titular Abp. of *Nicaea. In 1903 he was created Cardinal and also Secretary of State by *Pius X, with whose intransigent policy (*Loi de Séparation* in France, anti-*Modernism) he became closely identified. After he had ceased to be Secretary of State, in acc. with custom, on the Pope's death, he became Secretary of the *Holy Office, where he unobtrusively exercised great influence. He had a strong pastoral sense; and he often regretted that his career gave him only limited scope (e.g. through spiritual correspondence) for its exercise. His tomb in the crypt of St Peter's, Rome, near that of Pius X, is inscribed 'Da mihi animas. Caetera tolle.'

Life by P. Cenci (Rome, 1933, with preface by E. Pacelli, afterwards *Pius XII); popular Life based on Cenci by V. Dalpiaz, *Attraverso una porpora* (1935; Eng. tr., 1937). Other studies by F. A. Forbes (London, 1932), I. Flores de Lemus (Madrid, 1956), M. C. Buehrule (London, 1957), H. Mitchell (Paris, 1957), and J. M. Javierre (Barcelona, 1961; 2nd edn., 1965).

Mersch, Émile

Mersch, Émile (1890–1940), *Jesuit theologian. He was ordained priest at Louvain in 1917 and taught philosophy at Namur from 1920 to 1935. Throughout his life his aim was to construct a theological synthesis in terms of the 'Mystical Body of Christ'. In *Le Corps mystique du Christ: Études de théologie historique* (2 vols., Louvain, 1933; Eng. tr., *The Whole Christ*, Milwaukee, 1938; London, 1949), he traced the development of the doctrine of the Church, so understood, through history; in *La Théologie du corps mystique* (ed. J. Levie, SJ; 2 vols., Louvain, 1946; posthumous; Eng. tr., 1951) he expounded the doctrine from a more systematic standpoint. He was killed at Lens in an air attack on 23 May 1940.

Memoir by J. Levie, SJ, prefixed to Mersch's *La Théologie du corps mystique*, 1, pp. vii–xxxiii, with full list of Mersch's writings, pp. xxxi–xxxiii. Full edn. of his introd. to *La Théologie du corps mystique*, which was abridged in the 1946 edn., issued as *Le Christ, l'homme et l'univers* (Museum Lessianum, Section théologique, 57; 1962). G. Dejaifve, SJ, ' "La Théologie du corps mystique" du P.

Ém. Mersch', *Nouvelle Revue Théologique*, 67 (1945), pp. 408–16.

Mersenne, Marin

Mersenne, Marin (1588–1648), French philosopher, scientist, and theologian. He was educated at the *Jesuit College at La Flèche, where he formed a lifelong friendship with his younger fellow-pupil, R. *Descartes. In 1611 he joined the *Minims and finally settled in 1620 at the convent of L'Annonciade at Paris. Though himself the author of several works, among them *Quaestiones celeberrimae in Genesim* (1623), *L'Impiété des déistes* (1624), and *La Vérité des sciences* (1624), 'Père Mersenne' (as he was universally known) fills a place in the history of modern philosophy which rests on the links that he forged by his friendship and correspondence between many of the leading French philosophers and scientists of his day. In this way he did much to foster the new scientific movement and also to prevent it from developing in an anti-religious direction.

Correspondance de Mersenne, crit. edn. by Mme P. Tannery, C. de Waard and others (17 vols., Paris, 1932–88), with substantial introd. by A. Beaulieu in vol. 17; 2nd edn. of vol. 3, 1969. Contemporary Life by Hilarion de Coste (Paris, 1649; new edn. by B. T. de Sarroque, with unpub. letters, ibid., 1932). R. Lenoble, *Mersenne ou la naissance du mécanisme* (1943). H. Ludwig, *Marin Mersenne und seine Musiklehre* (1935). P. Dear, *Mersenne and the Learning of the Schools* (Ithaca, NY, and London, 1988). Series of arts. on Mersenne in *Revue d'histoire des Sciences et de leurs applications*, 2 (1948), pp. 5–89. E. Dumoutet in *DTC* 10 (pt. 1; 1928), cols. 788 f.; A. C. Crombie in *Dictionary of Scientific Biography*, 9 (1974), pp. 316–22.

Merton, Thomas

Merton, Thomas (1915–68), *Trappist monk and writer. Born in Prades, in the French Pyrenees, he was educated in England at Oakham School and Clare College, Cambridge (which he left without taking a degree), before he went on to Columbia University in New York. In the USA he became a RC and in 1941 he joined the Trappists at Gethsemani Abbey in Kentucky, taking the name of Louis. His autobiography, *The Seven Storey Mountain* (1948; pub. in a slightly abridged form in England in 1949 as *Elected Silence*) portrayed a traditional conversion to Catholicism, but at the same time it presented monastic spirituality to the public, and it had a very wide appeal. Merton's development, recorded in his immense literary output, echoes the changes in modern RCism, leading to a greater openness to other traditions (both Christian and non-Christian), and to a deep concern for the moral dilemmas of modern man. His understanding of monasticism also developed, leading him eventually to seek the life of a *hermit. He died, electrocuted by a faulty shower, while attending a world conference of contemplatives in Bangkok.

M. Mott, *The Seven Mountains of Thomas Merton* (Boston, 1984; London, 1986). D. Grayston, *Thomas Merton: The Development of a Spiritual Theologian* (Toronto Studies in Theology, 20 [1985]). Popular Life by M. Furlong (London, 1980).

Mesha, inscription of

Mesha, inscription of. See MOABITE STONE.

Mesonyktikon

Mesonyktikon (Gk. μεσονυκτικόν). In the E. Church, the Midnight Office. There is no exactly corresponding service in the Roman rite.

Mesrob, St

Mesrob, St (*c*.361–439), *Armenian ecclesiastic and translator. Over a long period he was coadjutor-bishop to the Catholicos *Isaac, and on Isaac's death acted as *locum tenens*, but died himself within less than six months. Zealous for a Christian national culture in Armenia, he made it one of his main objects to eliminate from Armenian life all traces of Syriac institutions. His ardent love of learning induced him to compose for the Armenians an alphabet which was adopted in 406; and, gathering round him a band of keen scholars (among them, acc. to a doubtful tradition, *Moses of Chorene), he sent some of his disciples as far as Rome in search of MSS of the Scriptures and of ecclesiastical and profane writers. In the Armenian Bible, based on the Syriac and issued *c*.410, Mesrob was himself the translator of the NT and Prov.; and later (*c*.433) he assisted in its revision with the use of Gk. MSS. He also did much to encourage the development of monastic institutions. Feast days in the Armenian *menologion, 19 Feb. and 25 Nov. (the latter also in W. calendars).

Armenian Lives, of uncertain trustworthiness, by Koriun, his pupil (ed. Venice, 1833; modern edn. by M. Abelyan, Erevan, 1941; Ger. tr. and comm. by G. Winkler, Orientalia Christiana Analecta, 245; 1994), and by Lazarus Pharbetzi. Many sermons, theological discourses, hymns, and other writings which pass under the name of *Gregory the Illuminator are prob. the work of Mesrob. Bardenhewer, 5, pp. 197–201. J. Marquart, *Über den Ursprung des armenischen Alphabets in Verbindung mit der Biographie des heiligen Mast'oc'* (Vienna, 1917). F. Feydit, *Considérations sur l'alphabet de saint Mesrop* (Studien zur armenischen Geschichte, 11; 1964). J. Karst in *DTC* 10 (pt. 1; 1928), cols. 789–92; P. Ananian in *Bibliotheca Sanctorum*, 9 (Rome, 1967), cols. 374–9; B. L. Zekiyan in *Dict. Sp.* 10 (1980), cols. 1070–4, all s.v. 'Mesrop', with bibl.

Messalians, also known as **Euchites** (Εὐχῖται), a pietistic mendicant sect. Their name is derived from a Syriac word which, like the corresponding Greek, means 'praying people'. They appear to have originated in Mesopotamia soon after the middle of the 4th cent. and to have spread to Syria, Asia Minor, Thrace, etc., and later to Egypt. They were attacked by *Amphilochius of Iconium, Flavian of Antioch, and St *Epiphanius, and condemned at the Council of *Ephesus of 431. They survived, however, down to the 7th cent. They held that in consequence of Adam's sin everyone had a demon substantially united with his soul, and that this demon, which was not expelled by Baptism, was completely liberated only by concentrated and ceaseless prayer, the aim of which was to eliminate all passion and desire. Those who had in this way become spiritual and perfect received an immediate vision of the Holy Trinity. In recent years there has been much debate about the connections with Messalianism of the writings of *Diadochus, *Gregory of Nyssa, and *Macarius/Simeon.

The earliest mention of the sect is in *Ephraem Syrus, *Contra Haereses*, 22. 4; fuller details (but unreliable) in Epiphanius, *Haer.* 80 ('Contra Messalianos'). The main sources are conveniently collected by M. Kmosko in the preface to his edn. of the 'Liber Graduum', in *Patrologia Syriaca* (ed. R. Graffin), 3 (Paris, 1926), cols. clxxi–ccxciii. I. Hausherr, SJ, 'L'Erreur fondamentale et la logique du messalianisme', *OCP* 1 (1935), pp. 328–60; H. Dörries, *Symeon von Mesopotamien: Die Überlieferung der messalianischen 'Makarios' Schriften* (TU 55, Heft 1; 1941); R. Staats, *Gregor von Nyssa und die Messaliander* (Patristische Texte und Studien, 8; 1968); H. Dörries, 'Die Messalianer im Zeugnis ihrer Bestreiter', *Saeculum*, 21 (1970), pp. 213–27; J. Gribomont, OSB, 'Le dossier des origines du Messalianisme', in J. Fontaine and C. Kannen-giesser (eds.), *Epektasis: Mélanges patristiques offerts au Cardinal Jean Daniélou*, (1972), pp. 611–25. C. Stewart, OSB, 'Working the Earth of the Heart': The Messalian Controversy in History, Texts, and Language to AD 431 (Oxford Theological Monographs, 1991). E. Peterson in *EC* 8 (1952), cols. 841 f., s.v.; A. Guillaumont in *Dict. Sp.* 10 (1980), cols. 1074–83, s.v. See also works cited under DIADOCHUS and MACARIUS/SIMEON.

Messiah (מָשִׁיחַ, lit. 'anointed'). The term denotes a person invested by God with special powers and functions. It was rendered into Greek by χριστός (from χρίω, 'anoint'), from which the title '*Christ' derives.

In the OT the term could be applied to anyone set apart for any special function, such as the priest in Lev. 4: 3, 5, who is described as 'the priest that is anointed'. It was however used more particularly of the king, who was conceived as anointed by Divine command (cf. 1 Sam. 10: 1); and his person, as 'the Lord's anointed', was held to be sacrosanct (1 Sam. 24: 6). After the promise made to *David through the prophet Nathan that the throne of his 'seed' should be established 'for ever' (2 Sam. 7: 12–13), the whole Davidic dynasty came to be regarded as especially chosen by God (2 Sam. 22: 51; Ps. 89: 35 f.). Nevertheless, the term could still be used of other people, such as the patriarchs (1 Chron. 16: 22) or even a pagan like Cyrus (Is. 45: 1). Under the later monarchy, when the kingdom was threatened by Assyria and Babylon, the appearance of a future king of the house of David, whose rule would be glorious, wise, and secure, was foretold by *Isaiah and *Jeremiah; and after Jerusalem had fallen *Ezekiel, in exile, had no doubt that the restored Israel in Palestine would be shepherded by 'my servant David' (Ezek. 34: 23 f.; 37: 24 f.). Immediately after the return from exile it seemed possible that the kingship might be restored in the person of the Davidic prince Zerubbabel (cf. Zech. 4: 6–10) in association with Joshua the *High Priest, but in the event it was the High Priests alone who became the secular rulers down to the time of the *Maccabees, from whom (and not from the Davidic line) the *Hasmonaeans, who ruled Palestine from the middle of the 2nd cent. until the middle of the 1st cent. BC, were descended. But the hope of a king who should be both 'the Lord's anointed' and 'the son of David' never died and is reflected e.g. in the Psalms of *Solomon (17: 23–38). The *Qumran community may have looked for *two* 'Messiahs', one royal and the other priestly (e.g. 1QS 9. 11, CD 8)—the 'Messiah of Aaron' and the 'Messiah of Israel'.

In the NT, Jewish expectations of a deliverer are echoed at Lk. 24: 21 and Acts 1: 6, and at Mt. 2: 2–4 where, using the absolute form not found in early Judaism, he is called 'the Christ' (AV) or 'the Messiah' (modern translations commonly render the word thus where the Greek has a definite article, and leave it as 'Christ' where there is no such article). The expectation that this deliverer would be descended from David is present in the Bethlehem tradition (cf. Lk. 2) and more directly in the Christological titles 'Son of David' (Mk. 10: 47 f., more frequently in Mt., and cf. Lk. 1: 32, Acts 2: 30–6, Rom. 1: 3, Rev. 5: 5, 22: 16), 'King of Israel' (Mk. 15: 32, Mt. 27: 42, Jn. 1: 49, 12: 13), and the non-Christian title 'King of the Jews' (Mt. 2: 2 and all Passion narratives). Even if Mk. 12: 35–7 indicates some earlier dispute or unease about the Davidic title, the Christian belief was subsequently secured by the genealogies. Jesus was executed as a Messianic figure, as the inscription on the Cross confirms, but the traditions leave room for debate whether He Himself defined His unique eschatological role in these terms. Some 500 occurrences of χριστός (Christos) in the NT testify to the general conviction about Jesus which can be traced back behind St *Paul (1 Cor. 15: 3). As early as the epistles the title 'Christ' (or 'Messiah') was on the way to becoming simply a name. Though much rarer in the Gospels, it usually retains its full significance. Throughout the NT it is interpreted in the light of Jesus' death and exaltation, and equated not only with 'Son of David' but more importantly with the title 'Son of God' (Mk. 1: 1–11, 14: 61, Jn. 20: 31, an identification with roots in 2 Sam. 7 and Ps. 2: 7). At the central point of Mark's narrative, St *Peter confesses Jesus as Messiah (8: 29), but the disciples are silenced and Jesus begins to teach that the *Son of Man must suffer and be vindicated. This Gospel thus insists that the Messiah is a Crucified Messiah. Jesus' true identity is revealed only at His Passion (14: 61 f.) and in His death (15: 39). The other Gospels use the title 'Christ' rather more frequently than Mk., and Jn. 1: 41 and 4. 25 explain the Hebrew word, but as 'Christ' becomes a proper name, it is the synonym 'Son of God' which is commonly used by Mt. and Jn., opening a way for subsequent Christology. See also CHRISTOLOGY, JESUS CHRIST, and MESSIANIC SECRET.

Modern works incl. W. *Wrede, *Das Messiasgeheimnis in den Evangelien* (1901; Eng. tr., 1971); A. *Schweitzer, *Von Reimarus zu Wrede* (1906; 2nd edn., 1913; Eng. tr., *The Quest of the Historical Jesus*, 1910); W. *Bousset, *Kyrios Christos* (1913; 2nd edn., 1921; Eng. tr., Nashville, 1970); W. Manson, *Jesus the Messiah* (1943); A. Bentzen, *Messias, Moses Redivivus, Menschensohn* (Abhandlungen zur Theologie des Alten und Neuen Testaments, 17; 1948; Eng. tr., 1955); S. [O. P.] *Mowinckel, *Han som Kommer: Messiasforventningen i det Gamle Testament og på Jesu tid* (Copenhagen, 1951; Eng. tr., *He that Cometh*, Oxford, 1956); H. Ringgren, *The Messiah in the Old Testament* (Studies in Biblical Theology, 18; 1956); J. Klausner, *The Messianic Idea in Israel from its Beginning to the Completion of the Mishnah* (Eng. tr. from Heb., 1956); F. Hahn, *Christologische Hoheitstitel: Ihre Geschichte im frühen Christentum* (Forschungen zur Religion und Literatur des Alten und Neuen Testaments, 83; 1963; Eng. tr., *The Titles of Christ in Christology*, 1969); W. Kramer, *Christos Kyrios Gottessohn* (Abhandlungen zur Theologie des Alten und Neuen Testaments, 44; 1963; Eng. tr., Studies in Biblical Theology, 50; 1966); J. Coppens, *Le Messianisme royal: Ses origines. Son développement. Son accomplissement* (Lectio divina, 54; 1968); id., *Le Messianisme et sa relève prophetique* (Bibliotheca Ephemeridum Theologicarum Lovaniensium, 38; 1974); id., *La Relève apocalyptique du messianisme royal* (ibid. 50, 55, and 61; 1979–83); D. Lauenstein, *Der Messias: Eine biblische Untersuchung* (Stuttgart [1971]. G. [G.] Scholem, *The Messianic Idea in Judaism and Other Essays on Jewish Spirituality* (1971), pp. 1–77. E. *Schürer, *The History of the Jewish People in the Age of Jesus Christ*, rev. Eng. tr. by G. Vermes and others, 2 (Edinburgh, 1979), pp. 488–554. V. H. Stanton in *HDB* 3 (1900), pp. 352–7, s.v.; W. Fairweather, ibid., Extra Vol. (1904), pp. 295–302, s.v. 'Development of Doctrine in the Apocryphal Period. V: The Messianic Hope'; L. Dennefeld in *DTC* 10 (pt. 2; 1929), cols. 1404–568, s.v. 'Messianisme'; A. Gelin in *Dict. Bibl.*, Suppl. 5 (1957), cols. 1165–212, s.v. 'Messianisme'; H. L. Ginsberg and others in *Encyclopaedia Judaica*, 11 (Jerusalem, 1972), cols. 1407–17. K. Seybold in *Theologisches Wörterbuch zum Alten Testament*, ed. G. J. Botterweck and others, 5 (1986), pp. 46–59, s.v. 'māšaḥ'.

Messianic Secret. The phrase was given currency by W.

*Wrede, *Der Messiasgeheimnis in den Evangelien* (1901; Eng. tr., 1971) and designates a central issue in Gospel criticism. Wrede argued that Jesus' silencing of the demoniacs and the secrecy about His *messianic identity in St *Mark's Gospel, together with the obtuseness of the disciples and the theory that the *parables were intended to conceal, were not historical reminiscences but arose out of a tension between the early Church's post-resurrection messianic belief and the historical reality of Jesus's ministry and self-understanding. Opinion remains divided over how far this motif can be credited to Mark, how far to the tradition available to him, and how far, if at all, it represents the self-consciousness and practice of Jesus Himself. The reasons for it are also a matter of continuing debate.

A selection of critical opinion is available in Eng. tr. in C. [M.] Tuckett (ed.), *The Messianic Secret* (Issues in Religion and Theology, 1; 1983).

Metaphrast, the. A traditional name for the Byzantine hagiographer, *Simeon (q.v.; fl. *c*.960), derived from his translation (Gk. *metaphrasis*, μετάφρασις) of older versions of the saints' Lives.

Metaphysical Poets. The term was first adapted by Dr S. *Johnson for a group of 17th-cent. poets in a pejorative sense implying a pretentious display of learning, strained images, and wit leading to wilful obscurity. Their contemporaries, however, had hailed the style as 'strong lines', accepting the difficulty as a challenge to the prevailing facile convention. Critics from the end of the 19th cent. have effected a remarkable revaluation. The skill shown in conducting a lyric along the lines of an argument; the wit in deploying philosophical or theological concepts; the concentration of statement; the daring use of unconventional imagery, and the occasional prosodic ingenuity now command admiration for many, if not all, whose work exhibits these features in varying degrees. The Metaphysical Poets specially concerned with religious insights and sentiments are J. *Donne, G. *Herbert, R. *Crashaw, Henry *Vaughan, Sir Fulke Greville (1554–1628), St Robert *Southwell, Henry King (1592–1669, Bp. of *Chichester), William Alabaster (1567–1640), F. *Quarles, T. *Traherne, Andrew Marvell (1621–78), and Abraham Cowley (1618–67).

Metaphysical Lyrics and Poems of the Seventeenth Century, Donne to Butler, selected and ed. H. J. C. Grierson (1921), with introd. pp. xiii–lviii; *The Metaphysical Poets*, selected and ed. H. [L.] Gardner (1957; 2nd edn., Oxford, 1967). *European Metaphysical Poetry*, ed. F. Warnke (New Haven, Conn., and London, 1961). S. Johnson, *The Lives of the English Poets*, 1 (1779), pp. 19–42 (in his 'Life of Cowley'). J. B. Leishman, *The Metaphysical Poets: Donne, Herbert, Vaughan, Traherne* (Oxford, 1934); L. L. Martz, *The Poetry of Meditation: A Study in English Religious Literature of the Seventeenth Century* (Yale Studies in English, 125; 1954; rev. edn., 1962); id., *The Paradise Within: Studies in Vaughan, Traherne, and Milton* (New Haven, Conn., and London, 1964); W. H. Halewood, *The Poetry of Grace: Reformation Themes and Structures in English Seventeenth-Century Poetry* (ibid., 1970); [J.] P. Grant, *The Transformation of Sin: Studies in Donne, Herbert, Vaughan, and Traherne* (Montreal and London, 1974); A. Low, *Love's Architecture: Devotional Modes in Seventeenth-Century English Poetry* (New York, 1978); B. K. Lewalski, *Protestant Poetics and the Seventeenth-Century Religious Lyric* (Princeton, NJ [1979]); S. C. Seelig, *The Shadow of Eternity: Belief and Structure in Herbert, Vaughan and Traherne* (Lexington, Ky. [1981]); I.

Clark, *Christ Revealed: The History of the Neotypological Lyric in the English Renaissance* (Gainesville, Fla., 1982); D. R. Dickson, *The Fountain of Living Waters: The Typology of the Waters of Life in Herbert, Vaughan, and Traherne* (Columbia, Mo., 1987); J. N. Wall, *Transformations of the Word: Spenser, Herbert, Vaughan* (Athens, Ga., and London [1988]). R. D. Dunn and J. Horden in *NCBEL* 1 (1974), cols. 1161–70.

Metaphysical Society. A society founded in 1869 by Sir James Knowles (1831–1908) to foster constructive debate between leading exponents of science and religion. Its last meeting was held on 16 May 1880. Many of its members were later prominent in the 'Synthetic Society' (1869–1908), founded with similar but rather more definitely religious interests.

A. W. Brown, *The Metaphysical Society* (New York, 1947).

metaphysics. The name given by the Greek editors of *Aristotle to his 'First Philosophy', and by analogy to all philosophical treatises concerning cognate topics. The title was merely intended to indicate the position of the books on this subject in the Aristotelian *corpus*—τὰ μετὰ τὰ φυσικά, 'the [books] that succeed the *Physics*'. The precise scope of metaphysical inquiry is very hard to define. To Aristotelians, it is the study of being *qua* being; to idealists, that of the ultimate implication of experience, cognitional, volitional, and aesthetic; to modern realists, that of the most pervasive features of reality (self-consistency, spatial and temporal relatedness, causality, substantiality, etc.). Several currents in modern philosophy have cast doubts on the validity of metaphysics. I. *Kant's *Critique of Pure Reason* attacked the current metaphysical proofs of God, freedom, and immortality, yet he insisted that God, freedom, and immortality were all necessary postulates of practical reason, thus 'destroying reason to make room for faith'. Other trends, e.g. Marxism and Freudianism, seek to undermine traditional metaphysics by demonstrating that the real determinants of philosophical belief are unconscious. Overall these doubts have tended to modify and deepen the enterprise of metaphysics rather than to overthrow it altogether. Christian theology has tended to take a realist metaphysics more or less for granted (see ANALOGY; THOMAS AQUINAS), but modern theology has not been immune from the influence of contemporary philosophical preoccupations.

Since nearly the whole range of philosophical speculation has at different times been comprised under the term 'metaphysics', the literature is virtually limitless. Works in Eng. incl. A. E. *Taylor, *Elements of Metaphysics* (1903); J. S. Mackenzie, *Elements of Constructive Philosophy* (1917); R. G. Collingwood, *Philosophical Essays* (2 vols., 1933–40); S. E. Toulmin and others, *Metaphysical Beliefs* (1957); D. F. Pears (ed.), *The Nature of Metaphysics* (1957); G. Martin, *Einleitung in die allgemeine Metaphysik* (1957; Eng. tr. 1961); P. F. Strawson, *Individuals: An Essay in Descriptive Metaphysics* (1959); W. H. Walsh, *Metaphysics* (1963); M. Lazerowitz, *Studies in Metaphilosophy* (1964); E. E. Harris, *The Foundations of Metaphysics in Science* (1965); J. W. Yolton, *Metaphysical Analysis* (Toronto, 1967; London, 1968); E. L. Mascall, *The Openness of Being: Natural Theology Today* (Gifford Lectures, 1970–1; 1971); D. M. Mackinnon, *The Problem of Metaphysics* (Cambridge 1974); G. E. M. Anscombe, *Collected Philosophical Papers*, 2: *Metaphysics and the Philosophy of Mind* (Oxford, 1981); S. Körner, *Metaphysics: Its Structure and Function* (Cambridge, 1984). W. *Pannenberg, *Metaphysik und Gottesgedanke* (Göttingen, 1988; Eng. tr., with additional material, 1990). See also bibls. to such

entries as PLATO; ARISTOTLE; NEOPLATONISM; SCHOLASTICISM; DESCARTES, R.; SPINOZA, B.; LEIBNIZ, G. W.; WOLFF, C.; KANT, I.; FICHTE, J. G.; SCHELLING, F. W. J. VON; HEGEL, G. W. F.; LOTZE, H.; DILTHEY, W.; BRADLEY, F. H.; BOSANQUET, B.; CROCE, B.; PATTISON, A. S. PRINGLE-; HEIDEGGER, M.; WITTGENSTEIN, L.; PHENOMENOLOGY; EXISTENTIALISM.

metempsychosis. The doctrine that souls migrate from one body into another until complete purification has been achieved. The belief is widespread, esp. in India, where it forms an integral part of Hinduism and Buddhism; but it is also found in the later Jewish teaching of the *Kabbala and among many savage races. In pre-Christian Europe its most outstanding advocates were *Plato and Pythagoras, both of whom were probably influenced by Orphism, and the doctrine was generally accepted among the later Platonists, by whom the word μετεμψύχωσις was in current use. In the Christian era *Origen's doctrine of the pre-existence of souls often approached actual metempsychosis. It was frequently attacked, e.g. by St *Augustine and by *Aeneas of Gaza, and it was implicitly condemned by the Councils of *Lyons (1274) and *Florence (1439), which affirmed that souls go immediately to heaven, purgatory, or hell. In modern times belief in metempsychosis was revived by Giordano *Bruno, G. E. *Lessing, Charles Fourier, and others, and recently it has come to the fore through the spread of *Spiritualism and *Theosophy. Its attraction lies partly in its claim to provide a morally satisfying explanation of the inequalities of fortune and character among mankind, which it ascribes to deeds done in former lives. Belief in metempsychosis is fundamentally at variance with the Christian doctrine of the resurrection of the body.

Methodism. The system of religious faith and practice promoted, orig. at Oxford in 1729, by John and Charles *Wesley and their followers in the *Holy Club. The term was then applied to the evangelical movement led by the Wesleys and George *Whitefield from the late 1730s. In the 18th cent. it was often used loosely of evangelicals of all sorts. Since the organization of the movement as a separate denomination, the designation has been confined to members of this Church and the other Churches derived from it. The circumstances of the original application of the word 'Methodist' to the followers of the Wesleys (first recorded instance, 1732) have never been satisfactorily explained. Various religious groups were so designated in the 17th cent.

Most of the Methodist Churches, including the influential Methodist Episcopal Church of the USA, are *Arminian in their theological sympathies. The '*Calvinistic Methodists' (q.v.) of Wales, however, are *predestinarian and federated with the Presbyterian Churches. See also WESLEY, JOHN and CHARLES; WHITEFIELD, GEORGE; BIBLE CHRISTIANS; METHODIST CHURCHES; METHODIST NEW CONNEXION; PRIMITIVE METHODIST CHURCH; UNITED METHODIST CHURCH; and UNITED METHODIST FREE CHURCHES.

R. P. Heitzenrater, *Mirror and Memory: Reflections on Early Methodism* (Nashville, 1989), pp. 13–32.

Methodist Churches. In 1784 J. Wesley (q.v.) made provision for the continuance as a corporate body of the

'Yearly Conference of the People called Methodists' by nominating under a deed poll 100 persons whom he declared to be its members and laying down the method by which their successors were to be appointed. The Conference had power to appoint preachers to the various 'Preaching Houses' (later 'chapels'), the ownership of which was vested in boards of trustees acc. to a model trust deed, which since 1763 had already specified Wesley's *Notes on the New Testament* (1754) and his four volumes of sermons as a doctrinal standard. Provision was made for the case of preachers who should be, like J. and C. *Wesley, clergy of the C of E, but in fact there were few such. On Wesley's death in 1791 the future relations of Methodism with the C of E were a matter of dispute, but the 'Plan of Pacification' adopted by the Conference of 1795 eventually led to the administration of the sacraments (i.e. Baptism and esp. Holy Communion) in all Methodist chapels and the declaration that the admission of a preacher to 'full connexion with the Conference' conferred ministerial rights without any form of ordination. Ordination by the imposition of the hands of ministers was again adopted by the Conference in 1836.

The secession of the *Methodist New Connexion (q.v.) in 1797 was relatively small, the great majority of Methodists remaining in connexion with the Conference thus constituted by Wesley, and organized according to his principles in local societies and circuits. There were further small secessions in 1805, of a body mainly in the N. of England who later became the 'Independent Methodists'; in 1810 of the followers of H. Bourne and W. Clowes who became the *Primitive Methodist Church (q.v.); and in 1815 of those of W. O'Bryan, known as the *Bible Christians (q.v.). The causes were in each case disputes over revivalism, discipline, and polity, not on doctrine. Economic, social, and political tensions, however, helped to aggravate these conflicts. Similar disagreements with the official policy arising out of such matters as the installation of an organ in a chapel at Leeds (1827) and the foundation of a theological college for the training of ministers (1834) led to the formation of the Wesleyan Methodist Association. A more serious controversy over the expulsion of three ministers in 1849 led to the formation of the Wesleyan Reformers. Some of the Reformers united with the Association in 1857 to form the *United Methodist Free Churches (q.v.). The original body of Methodists continued, considerably weakened by these latter secessions. In course of time more friendly relations between all branches of Methodism were re-established and all took part, with Methodist Churches abroad, in a decennial Ecumenical Conference (first held 1881). In 1907 the Methodist New Connexion, the Bible Christians, and the United Methodist Free Churches came together in a union as the *United Methodist Church (q.v.), and this itself reunited in 1932 with the original or 'Wesleyan' Methodist Church and the Primitive Methodist Church to form the Methodist Church in Great Britain as it now exists. The United Methodists and Wesley Reform Union remain separate bodies. The *Calvinistic Methodists in England, who were followers of G. *Whitefield, were eventually absorbed into *Congregationalism; those in Wales, whose origins had nothing to do with Wesley, are also known as the Presbyterian Church of Wales.

The Methodist Church considers itself part of the Church Universal but claims no rights for its particular form of Church order *iure divino*, believing in the priesthood of all believers and following in organization the principles laid down by Wesley for the pastoral oversight of the societies of Methodists which had grown up as a result of his preaching. Though not usually so called, the resulting organization is in principle, in the judgement of at least one Methodist scholar (H. B. Workman), presbyterian. The supreme authority is the Conference, the legal successor of that originally constituted by Wesley, and now regulated in Statute law by the Methodist Church Union Act 1929, and the Methodist Church Act 1976. It consists of 288 ministers and 288 laymen for the most part elected by the District Synods; the ministers sit separately in 'Ministerial Session' to decide affairs concerning ministers, but decisions affecting the whole Church are taken by the full Conference ('Representative Session'). A minister as President and, for the Representative Session, a layman as Vice-President are elected annually by the Conference. The Conference delegates certain duties to the Synods, held twice-yearly in each District, of which there are 33 in Great Britain, containing mostly about 20 or 30 Circuits in each; it also appoints ministers as Chairmen of each District and Superintendents of each circuit, the latter consisting normally of a number of local 'societies' (Wesley's term for the local bodies of Methodists), which form the several churches of the denomination. A distinction is made between those on the 'Community Roll' who may be in fact regular members of a congregation, and 'full members' who have been formally admitted to the Church. 'All those who confess Jesus Christ as Lord and Saviour and accept the obligation to serve Him in the life of the Church and the world are welcome as full members of the Methodist Church.' Those who apply on this basis are admitted first for a probationary period and then (after Baptism, if previously unbaptized) by a public service of reception into membership at which the Holy Communion is celebrated. Acc. to Wesley's system, which is peculiar to Methodism, 'All members shall have their names entered on a Class Book, shall be placed under the pastoral care of a Class Leader, and shall receive a Quarterly Ticket of Membership'. The weekly class-meeting for 'fellowship in Christian experience' has from the beginning been a valuable institution. On removing to another place a member receives a recommendation which entitles him to membership in another local society.

In each circuit there is a Circuit Meeting consisting of ministers and lay office-holders, including Class Leaders, and in each Society there is a Church Council on the same basis. A meeting of all Church members is held annually in each Society to appoint representatives to the Church Council and for fellowship and consultation, but it has few of the powers of a Church Meeting in the Congregational or Independent Churches. Ministers are not 'called' to particular churches, but may be invited, the appointment being made by authority of the Conference, which also regulates the whole organization of Districts and Circuits, sets up special enterprises (e.g. the *Anglican-Methodist Conversations, revision of the liturgy), and controls other central organizations and committees, which are responsible to it. It also governs the selection, training, and ordination of ministers. The ordained ministry is open to women on virtually the same terms as men.

By tradition Methodism has an active concern with both evangelism and social welfare and by means of its centralized organization it is able to make co-ordinated efforts in these directions. Under the leadership of Hugh Price *Hughes (q.v.) the Methodist Forward Movement was active from 1885 in founding Missions in various parts of London, beginning with the East London Mission in Stepney, and in Manchester. Hughes's preaching at the West London Mission (from 1887) was a notable force in presenting Christianity as intimately concerned with social betterment and public morals: it was through his influence that the phrase 'the Nonconformist conscience' gained currency in connection with the divorce suit involving C. S. Parnell (1846–91), and Hughes willingly accepted the phrase as a description of his standpoint. J. Scott Lidgett (1854–1953), founder in 1891 of the Bermondsey Mission and its Warden till 1949, was another outstanding figure.

Methodism outside Great Britain dates from the lifetime of Wesley, who in 1784 'set apart' T. *Coke and others for N. America, where by 1791 there were already 42,265 members of Methodist Societies, compared with 71,688 in Great Britain. With the growth of the USA Methodist numbers increased and now greatly exceed those in Britain. After the Civil War there were two main Churches, in North and South respectively, which were reunited in 1939. In 1968 the Methodist Church of the United States was joined by the Evangelical United Brethren to form the United Methodist Church; there are still also a number of smaller Methodist bodies. Wesley had 'set apart' Coke as 'Superintendent'; Coke, with others, ordained F. *Asbury to the same office, and himself, against Wesley's opinion, took the title of 'bishop', and American Methodism is largely 'episcopal' in possessing superintendents who are called bishops, though claiming no Episcopal Orders in the Catholic sense. There are also Methodist Churches under separate Conferences in *Ireland, *New Zealand, Southern Africa, *Nigeria, Ghana, *Sri Lanka, Upper *Burma, Samoa, Fiji, the Caribbean and the Americas (incl. the *West Indies), *Kenya, *Sierra Leone, Hong Kong, *Zimbabwe, Italy, the Ivory Coast, and Tonga. In continental Europe there are several small Methodist Churches, some of British and some of American origin. In Germany the union of the Methodist Church of the United States with the Evangelical United Brethren in 1968 entailed a parallel union of German Methodists with the Evangelische Gemeinschaft. Methodists have also united with other Protestant Churches in *Belgium, *Spain, and *France (though some congregations in France have remained independent). They entered the United Church of *Canada (1925), the Church of *South India (1947), the United Church of Papua and the Solomon Islands (1968), and the Uniting Church of *Australia (1977), while the Methodist Districts formerly related to the British and Australian Conferences entered the Church of *North India (1977). This world-wide extension of Methodism has been largely due to the vigorous work of the (British) Methodist Missionary Society which was formally organized on a national basis in 1818, though the British Conference had sent out missionaries as early as 1786. In other parts of the world, notably in South America, SE Asia, and N. *India, there are Churches resulting from the work of American Methodists. The world total of Methodist members in 1990 was over 20 millions, of whom 12.5 millions were in the USA and c.500,000 in Britain. The total world Methodist community was estimated at over 49 millions. See also ANGLICAN–METHODIST CONVERSATIONS.

W. J. Townsend, H. B. Workman, and G. Eayrs (eds.), *A New History of Methodism* (2 vols., 1909); R. [E.] Davies, [E.] G. Rupp, and A. R. George (eds.), *A History of the Methodist Church in Great Britain* (4 vols., 1965–88). R. E. Davies, *Methodism* (1963; rev. 1976). F. Baker, *A Charge to Keep: An Introduction to the People Called Methodists* (1947). R. F. Wearmouth, *Methodism and the Common People of the Eighteenth Century* (1945); id., *Methodism and the Working Class Movements in England, 1800–1850* (1937); id., *The Social and Political Influence of Methodism in the Twentieth Century* (1957). W. J. Warner, *The Wesleyan Movement in the Industrial Revolution* (1930). M. [L.] Edwards, *After Wesley: A Study of the Social and Political Influence of Methodism in the Middle Period (1791–1849)* (1935); id., *Methodism and England: A Study of Methodism in its Social and Political Aspects during the Period 1850–1932* (1943). D. Hempton, *Methodism and Politics in British Society 1750–1850* (1984). J. C. Bowmer, *The Sacrament of the Lord's Supper in Early Methodism* (1951); id., *The Lord's Supper in Methodism 1791–1960* (1961). G. S. Wakefield, *Methodist Devotion: The Spiritual Life in the Methodist Tradition 1791–1945* (1966). T. B. Shepherd, *Methodism and the Literature of the Eighteenth Century* (1940). W. W. Sweet (ed.), *Religion on the American Frontier, 1783–1840, 4: The Methodists: A Collection of Source Material* (Chicago, 1946). Id., *Methodism in American History* (New York, 1933); E. S. Bucke (ed.), *The History of American Methodism* (3 vols., New York, 1964); F. A. Norwood, *The Story of American Methodism: A History of the United Methodists and their Relations* (Nashville and New York, 1974). F. Baker, *From Wesley to Asbury: Studies in Early American Methodism* (Durham, NC, 1976). G. G. Findlay and W. W. Holdsworth, *The History of the Wesleyan Methodist Missionary Society* (5 vols., 1921–4). W. C. Barclay, *History of Methodist Missions* (6 vols. planned; 1–3, New York, 1949–57; 4, by J. T. Copplestone, 1973). J. Kent, *The Age of Disunity* (1966). R. Currie, *Methodism Divided: A Study in the Sociology of Ecumenicalism* (1968). H. Spencer and E. Finch, *The Constitutional Practice and Discipline of the Methodist Church* (1951; 4th edn., 1964), with text of historical docs. K. E. Rowe, *Methodist Union Catalog* (Methuen, NJ, 1975 ff.). N. B. Harmon (ed.), *The Encyclopedia of World Methodism* (2 vols., Nashville [1974]). See also bibl. to PRIMITIVE METHODIST CHURCH; WESLEY, J.

Methodist New Connexion. The group of Methodists which in 1797 seceded from the Wesleyan *Methodist Church and in the union of 1907 was incorporated in the *United Methodist Church.

This, the first of the Methodist secessions, originated six years after the death of *J. Wesley (1791). The leader of the 'reforming' movement which led to the disruption, Alexander *Kilham (q.v.), was ordained a minister in the Methodist Church in 1792. In the controversy on the relationship of Methodism to the C of E he strongly supported complete separation, contending that Methodists should have the right to receive Communion from their own preachers. He also desired the lay members of the Church to take a much greater part in its administration than government through Wesley's Conference of preachers allowed. Kilham embodied his proposals for reform in a series of polemical pamphlets in which he also exposed what seemed to him abuses of the existing system. His writings and agitation led to his trial by the Wesleyan Conference of 1796 and expulsion.

In 1797 Kilham and his supporters summoned a Convention to negotiate with the Conference; but as the Conference's concessions did not affect the central issue, namely the representation of the laity in the ruling courts of the Church, Kilham at once founded the 'New Itinerancy' or 'Methodist New Connexion'. When its second Conference was held, a year later, the denomination had 19 ministers. On Kilham's death in 1798 he was succeeded by William Thom. The Connexion achieved only slow and limited growth, reaching 37,017 members at its maximum in 1906. It differed from Wesleyan Methodism chiefly in the matter of Church government and the exclusion of any use of Anglican worship; it made no doctrinal changes.

In 1907 the Methodist New Connexion united with the *Bible Christians and the *United Methodist Free Churches to form the United Methodist Church.

For bibl. see previous entry; also *The Jubilee of the Methodist New Connexion* [by T. R. Allin and others] (1848). O. A. Beckerlegge and E. A. Rose, *A Bibliography of the Methodist New Connexion* (Westcliff-on-Sea, 1988).

Methodius and Cyril, Sts. See CYRIL, ST, AND METHODIUS, ST.

Methodius of Olympus, St (d. *c*.311), bishop in Lycia. Very few biographical details are known. St *Jerome's assertion (*De Vir. Illus.* 83) that he was also Bp. of Tyre, and probably, too, that of '*Leontius of Byzantium' (*De Sectis*, 3. 1) that he was Bp. of Patara, seem mistaken. He was apparently put to death in the concluding years of the *Diocletianic persecution. Feast day in W., 18 Sept.; in E., 20 June.

One of the first assailants of *Origen—perhaps the reason for the absence of mention of him by *Eusebius—Methodius wrote extensively, though only a small portion of his works has been preserved. The 'Symposium [Banquet], or On Chastity' (Συμπόσιον, ἢ Περὶ ἁγνείας) also known as the 'Banquet of the Ten Virgins' alone remains entire. Written in dialogue form after the manner of *Plato, it extols the excellence of virginity. At the end is a hymn to Christ as the Bridegroom of the Church. In a treatise on the Resurrection (Ἀγλαοφῶν, ἢ Περὶ τῆς ἀναστάσεως) he upheld against Origen the identity of the resurrection body with that worn in this life. His work on Free Will (Περὶ τοῦ Αὐτεξουσίου) is a defence of human liberty against the fatalism of the *Gnostics. Considerable portions of the Greek text of these two writings have come down. His other works, surviving only in Slavonic, include writings on the food laws of the OT, on the mystical interpretation of the references to leprosy in Lev. 13, and on the leech in Prov. 30: 15. His lost writings include an extensive work against *Porphyry, commentaries on Genesis and the Song of Songs, and a treatise on the Witch of Endor (1 Sam. 28) directed against Origen.

Earliest collection of Methodius' writings ed. (with those of other Fathers) by F. *Combefis, OP, Paris, 1644; the 'Symposium', however, was first pub. by L. *Allatius, Rome, 1656. Crit. edn. by G. N. Bonwetsch (GCS 27; 1917). Slavonic version of 'De Autexousio', with Gk. texts, ed. A. Vaillant in *PO* 22. 5 (1930). Collected works also in J. P. Migne, *PG* 18. 9–408. Eng. tr. by W. R. Clark in ANCL 14 (1869), pp. 1–230. Modern edn. of 'Symposium' by H. Musurillo, SJ, with Fr. tr. by V. H. Debidour (SC 95; 1963); Eng. tr. by H. Musurillo (ACW 27; 1958). G. N. Bonwetsch, *Die Theologie des Methodius von Olympus* (1903);

J. Farges, *Les Idées morales et religieuses de Méthode d'Olympe* (1929); M. Pellegrino, *L'Inno del Simposio de S. Metodio Martire: Introduzione, testo critico e commento* (Università di Torino. Pubblicazioni della Facoltà di Lettere e Filosofia, 10, fasc. 1; 1958). V. Buchheit, *Studien zu Methodios von Olympos* (TU 69; 1958). A. Vítores, OFM, *Identidad entre el Cuerpo Muerto y Resucitado en Origenes según el 'De Resurrectione' de Metodio de Olimpo* (Studium Biblicum Franciscanum, Analecta, 18; Jerusalem, 1981). L. G. Patterson, *Methodius of Olympus* (Washington, DC, 1997). CPG 1 (1983), pp. 248–53 (nos. 1810–30). Bardenhewer, 2, pp. 334–51; Altaner and Stuiber (1978), pp. 215 f., and 591. G. *Salmon in *DCB* 3 (1882), pp. 909–11; H. A. Musurillo, SJ, in *Dict. Sp.* 10 (1980), cols. 1109–17, s.v. 'Méthode (3)'; R. [D.] Williams in *TRE* 22 (1992), pp. 680–4.

Methuselah. The eighth in the list of antediluvian patriarchs in Gen. 5 and the longest lived (969 years; Gen. 5: 27). He appears in the parallel list in Gen. 4 as 'Methusael' (RV 'Methushael') (v. 18).

metrical psalters. At the Reformation metrical psalmody was introduced in the Low Countries and in the French and Swiss Reformed Churches as a more biblical form of musical worship than the German *Lutheran hymns. M. *Coverdale published adaptations of German hymns and tunes for England [?1535], but these were suppressed by *Henry VIII; under *Edward VI metrical versions of the Psalms were published by T. *Sternhold (d. 1549) and others. In 1556 the Marian exiles in Geneva, doubtless inspired by the work of C. *Marot (q.v.) and L. Bourgeois (*c*.1510/15–*c*.1560), published along with their *Book of Common Order* 51 metrical psalms composed by Sternhold, J. Hopkins (d. ?1570), and W. *Whittingham (d. 1579). In 1562 the first complete Anglo-Genevan edition was printed in England. Until the middle of the 19th cent., when the use of metrical psalmody waned, many English versions were produced. The most widely used of these was the *New Version of the Psalms* (1696) of N. *Tate and N. Brady.

In Scotland the use of a metrical psalter became a permanent and characteristic feature of national worship. The Anglo-Genevan version was printed with additions in 1564 (with 105 tunes). An important harmonized edition followed in 1635. In 1650 in place of this Old Version the Scottish General Assembly adopted, in a much revised form, the simple, rugged and dignified version of Francis Rous, which had earlier been commended by the *Westminster Assembly and approved by the English House of Commons. The Assembly made no provision, however, for music for the new book and gradually many of the old tunes were forgotten. *The Scottish Psalter* (1929) revived the old tradition, and has much influenced subsequent hymnals such as the Church of Scotland's *Church Hymnary* (3rd edn., 1973).

R. R. Terry (ed.), *Calvin's First Psalter* (1932). N. Livingston (ed.), *The Scottish Metrical Psalter of A.D. 1635 reprinted in full from the original work . . . and . . . illustrated by Dissertations, Notes, and Facsimiles* (Glasgow, 1864). P. Pidoux (ed.), *Le Psautier huguenot du XVI*e *siècle*, 1 and 2 (Basle, 1962). R. Zim, *English Metrical Psalms: Poetry as Praise and Prayer 1535–1601* (Cambridge, 1987). R. A. Leaver, '*Goostly psalmes and spirituall songes*': *English and Dutch Metrical Psalms from Coverdale to Utenhove 1535–1566* (Oxford, 1991). N. Temperley, *The Music of the English Parish Church* (Cambridge Studies in Music, 2 vols., 1979), 1, pp. 13–243 *passim*; 2, pp. 30 f., 37–53. Id. and others in S. Sadie (ed.),

New Grove Dictionary of Music and Musicians, 15 (1980), pp. 347–82, s.v. 'Psalms, metrical'.

Metrophanes Critopoulos (1589–1639). A Greek monk of Mt. *Athos who was sent by Cyril *Lucar to study theology in England at the invitation of G. *Abbot. From 1617 to 1622 he was at Balliol College, Oxford, and then in London, partly with Abbot, until 1624. After visiting universities and Protestant churches in Germany (1624–7) and Switzerland (1627), he returned via Venice (1627–30) to Egypt in 1631. In 1633 he became Metropolitan of Memphis in Egypt, and in 1636 Patriarch of Alexandria. In 1638 he signed the anathemas pronounced against Cyril Lucar for Calvinism. His works include a Ὁμολογία τῆς ἀνατολικῆς ἐκκλησίας (ed. J. Horne, Helmstedt, 1661).

His Ὁμολογία τῆς ἀνατολικῆς ἐκκλησίας (Wolfenbüttel MS 1048) has also been ed. by H. Weissenborn in E. J. Kimmel, *Monumenta Fidei Ecclesiae Orientalis*, 2 (Jena, 1850), pp. 1–213, and in I. N. Karmires, Τὰ δογματικὰ καὶ συμβολικὰ Μνημεῖα τῆς Ὀρθοδόξου Καθολικῆς Ἐκκλησίας, 2 (Athens, 1953), pp. 489–561. Modern studies by I. N. Karmires (Athens, 1937 and 1948). C. Davey, *Pioneer for Unity: Metrophanes Kritopoulos (1589–1639) and Relations between the Orthodox, Roman Catholic and Reformed Churches* (1987; repr. of earlier arts.), with bibl. G. Podskalsky, *Griechische Theologie in der Zeit der Türkenherrschaft (1453–1821)* (Munich, 1988), pp. 219–29. E. Legrand, *Bibliographie hellénique ... au XVIIᵉ siècle*, 5 (1903), pp. 192–218. V. Grumel, AA, in *DTC* 10 (pt. 2; 1929), cols. 1622–7; D. Stiernon, AA, in *Dict. Sp.* 10 (1980), cols. 1125 f., both s.v.

metropolitan. The title of a bishop exercising provincial, and not merely diocesan, powers. The organization of the early Church broadly followed that of the Roman Empire. Each city, with its territory, was governed by a bishop, and in each province the bishop of the civil metropolis (normally) came to possess rights over his comprovincial bishops, later called suffragans. These rights were determined by local custom before the Council of *Nicaea (325), whose 4th canon, in which the title metropolitan first appears, began the gradual process of legal definition. The duties and rights of a metropolitan have varied in time and place. Chief among them are the summoning and presidency of provincial synods, the visitation of dioceses, the care of vacant sees, some share in the appointment and consecration of suffragans and some disciplinary powers over them. Owing to *Diocletian's grouping of civil provinces into civil dioceses, metropolitans were in time subordinated to synods of the civil diocese or to a superior bishop (*exarch, *patriarch). The W. Church saw many conflicts between metropolitans and Popes, the latter being generally victorious (see PALLIUM). Provincial organization continues in episcopal Churches (*Canterbury, *York), though the metropolitical see is not always the civil capital. In the early Church, the metropolitan of some African provinces was the bishop senior by consecration. Metropolitans have commonly the titles of *archbishop and *primate.

At the present time, in the Church of Greece all diocesan bishops have the title Metropolitan, but in the Russian Church the title retains more or less its original meaning.

Mexico, Christianity in. The pre-Spanish Aztec empire of Mexico appears to have had vague traditions of biblical and Christian ideas, but their source cannot be traced. But within five years of the first Spanish invasion (1519) *Franciscan and other missionaries arrived. Conversions were numerous, though not always entirely voluntary, and Mexican Christians have, from the first, kept much of the old paganism under an outward profession of Christianity. Throughout Mexican history from the 16th cent. onwards, hardly any Christians of other denominations have entered the country to challenge the prevailing RCism.

Mexican independence was won in 1821 after a decade of war with Spain but, despite the many fundamental changes which then occurred, the Church's influence in political, social, and esp. financial affairs remained exceptionally strong. For more than 30 years liberals struggled to reduce clerical power, but it was not until the mid-19th-cent. Reform, led by President Benito Juárez, that Church and State were separated, all ecclesiastical property nationalized, and the process of secularization of the clerical colonial society really began. After the 1910 Mexican Revolution, the 1917 Constitution, which still prevails, incorporated much of the Juárez anticlerical legislation. The Church was again banned from owning land or mortgages, Church schools were closed, the number of priests was strictly regulated, and the Juárez suppression of all religious orders was reaffirmed. These measures were not strictly enforced until 1926 when the so-called Cristero rebellion began and the last major conflict between Church and State took place. The intransigence of both sides resulted in the closing of churches, the deportation of bishops, and considerable bloodshed among both clergy and laity. By 1929 a compromise was reached; although from time to time there were serious disagreements between Church and State, by and large a *modus vivendi* was achieved whereby, provided the Church accepted the supremacy of the State and did not intervene in politics, the restrictive measures in the constitution were not all rigidly enforced. The accession to power of Carlos Salinas de Gortari in 1988 marked the beginning of a *rapprochement* between the Church and State. In 1992 amendments to the constitution recognized Churches of all denominations as legal entities, with the right to hold property, and legalized the presence of foreign clergy, removing a number of restrictions. In the same year diplomatic relations between Mexico and the Vatican were restored.

M. Cuevas, *Historia de la Iglesia en México* (5 vols., Tlalpam, 1921–8). C. Alvear Acevedo, *La iglesia en la historia de México* (Mexico, 1975). C. S. Braden, *Religious Aspects of the Conquest of Mexico* (Durham, NC, 1930). P. Ricard, *La 'Conquête spirituelle' du Mexique: Essai sur l'apostolat et les méthodes missionnaires des ordres mendiants en Nouvelle-Espagne de 1523 à 1572* (thesis, Paris, 1933; Eng. tr., Berkeley, Calif., 1966). N. Farriss, *Crown and Clergy in Colonial Mexico, 1759–1821: The Crisis of Ecclesiastical Privilege* (1968). W. H. Callcott, *Church and State in Mexico, 1822–1857* (Durham, NC [1926]). M. P. Costeloe, *Church Wealth in Mexico: A Study of the 'Juzgado de Capellanias' in the Archbishopric of Mexico, 1800–1856* (Cambridge, 1967); id., *Church and State in Independent Mexico: A Study of the Patronage Debate 1821–1857* (Royal Historical Society Studies in History, 1978). R. E. Quirk, *The Mexican Revolution and the Catholic Church 1910–1929* (Bloomington, Ill., and London, 1973). J. A. Meyer, *La Cristiada* (3 vols., Mexico, 1973–4; Eng. tr., *The Cristero Rebellion: The Mexican People between Church and State 1926–1929*, 1976). J. L. Mecham, *Church and State in Latin America* (rev. edn., Chapel Hill, NC, 1966), pp. 340–415. G. W. Grayson, *The*

Church in Contemporary Mexico (Significant Issues Series, 14, no. 5; Washington, DC [1992]). J. Bravo Ugarte, SJ, Bio-Bibliografía Eclesiástica Mexicana (1821–1943) (3 vols., Mexico, 1949). On the Evangelical Church, D. McGavran and others, Church Growth in Mexico (Grand Rapids, Mich. [1963]). Latourette, 3, pp. 108–23; 6, pp. 72–7 passim and 113–15; and 7, pp. 176–81, with further refs.; K. S. Latourette, Christianity in a Revolutionary Age, 3 (1961), pp. 303–10; 5 (1963), pp. 170–80.

Meyer, Heinrich August Wilhelm (1800–73), German NT scholar. Born at Gotha, he studied theology at the University of Jena and held various ecclesiastical offices at Hanover. The chief work of his life was his editorship of the well-known Kritisch-exegetischer Kommentar zum Neuen Testament (16 vols., 1832–52; Eng. tr., 20 vols., 1873–95), to which he himself contributed the Gospels, Acts, and most of the Pauline epistles. It was highly praised for its completeness and philological exactness, and has been constantly revised and rewritten by a long series of distinguished scholars down to the present time.

F. Düsterdieck in PRE (3rd edn.), 13 (1903), pp. 39–42.

Meynell, Alice Christiana Gertrude (1847–1922), née Thompson, poet and essayist. Having become a RC c.1872, in 1877 she married Wilfrid Meynell, to whom she gave much help in his literary work. A great part of her writing both in prose and verse has religion as its subject or background. Her verse, collections of which appeared at intervals from Preludes (1875) to the posthumously edited Last Poems in 1923, developed from the more emotional poetry of her earlier period to the subtle thought and restrained language of her riper years. In 1912 she published Mary, the Mother of Jesus, a collection of essays.

Centenary edn. of her Poems by F. Meynell (son) (1947) and of selected Prose and Poetry (1947), with introd. by V. [M.] Sackville-West, pp. 7–26. V. Meynell (daughter), Alice Meynell: A Memoir (1929). J. [Countess] Badeni, The Slender Tree: A Life of Alice Meynell (Padstow, 1981). A. K. Tuell, Mrs. Meynell and her Literary Generation (New York, 1925). F. Page in DNB, 1922–1930, pp. 584–6.

Micah, Book of. The sixth of the *Minor Prophets. From Mic. 1: 1 it appears that the author after whom the book is named lived in the 8th cent. BC and began to prophesy (Mic. 1: 5–7) before the fall of *Samaria (c.721). The first three chapters are generally accepted as the genuine work of this author, who is mentioned by *Jeremiah (Jer. 26: 17–19) as preaching with some success. They foretell the destruction of Samaria and of *Jerusalem. The rest of the book is regarded by most critics as of later date. Chs. 4–5 predict the regeneration of the people and the advent of a *Messiah. Chs. 6–7 are mainly occupied with a dispute between Yahweh and his people; they are usually recognized as a collection of material from miscellaneous sources, the last section (7: 7–20) being identified as a prophetic liturgy.

The Book foretells the destruction of the *Temple (Mic. 3: 12) as a punishment for presumption on the trust in Divine protection. Mic. 6: 8 sums up true religion as justice, mercy, and humble communion with God, and the complaints of Yahweh in Mic. 6: 3–5 are the model on which have been formed the *Reproaches in the liturgy used in the W. Church on *Good Friday.

Comm. by J. M. P. Smith (ICC on Mic., Zeph., Nah., Hab., Obad., Joel, 1912, pp. 5–156), J. L. Mays (London, 1976), H. W. Wolff (Dodekapropheton, 4; Biblischer Kommentar, Altes Testament, 14/4; Neukirchen, 1982), and D. R. Hillers (Philadelphia [1984]). J. Lindblom, Micha literarisch untersucht (Acta Academiae Aboensis, Humaniora, 6. 2; 1929). W. Beyerlin, Die Kulttradition Israels in der Verkündigung des Propheten Micha (Göttingen, 1959). B. Renaud, Structure et attaches littéraires de Michée iv–v (Cahiers de la Revue Biblique, 2; 1964). T. Lescow, Micha 6, 6–8: Studien zu Sprache, Form und Auslegung (Arbeiten zur Theologie, 1, Heft 25; 1966). H. W. Wolff, Mit Micha reden: Prophetie einst und jetzt (Munich, 1978; Eng. tr., Micah the Prophet, Philadelphia [1981]). K. Jeppesen, 'New Aspects of Micah Research', Journal for the Study of the Old Testament, 8 (1978), pp. 3–32. E. Otto in TRE, 22 (1992), pp. 695–704, s.v. 'Micha/Michabuch'.

Mi-Carême. See LAETARE SUNDAY.

Michael the Archangel, St. He is mentioned four times in Scripture: twice in Dan. (10: 13 ff. and 12: 1), where he is represented as the helper of the Chosen People, once in Jude (5: 9), disputing with the devil over the body of *Moses, and once in Rev. (12: 7–9), fighting the dragon. He also plays an important part in the apocryphal literature, e.g. in the 'Assumption of *Moses', in '*Enoch', and in the 'Ascension of *Isaiah' (qq.v.), where he appears as 'the great captain' 'who is set over the best part of mankind'. In connection with the scriptural and apocryphal passages he was early regarded in the Church as the helper of Christian armies against the heathen, and as a protector of individual Christians against the devil, esp. at the hour of death, when he conducts the souls to God, a belief echoed in the Offertory of the Roman Mass for the Dead until 1970: 'Signifer S. Michael repraesentet eas in lucem sanctam'.

His cult originated in Phrygia, where he was chiefly venerated as a healer, and many hot springs were dedicated to him both in Greece and Asia. The cult soon spread to the W., and in the *Leonine Sacramentary St Michael is named in four of the five Masses for 30 Sept. of a dedication festival of a basilica erected in his honour on the Via Salaria. This feast, which is kept throughout the W. Church on 29 Sept., is identical with that of the BCP of St Michael and All Angels. (In the RC Church the day now commemorates St *Gabriel and St *Raphael, with St Michael.) The cult of St Michael in the W. Church received a strong impetus from the famous apparition on Mt. Garganus in the time of Pope *Gelasius (492–6), in commemoration of which a feast was kept in the RC Church on 8 May until 1960. Throughout the Middle Ages St Michael enjoyed general veneration. His feast, 'Michaelmas Day', is connected with many popular usages and numerous churches are dedicated to him. He is usually represented with a sword, standing over, or fighting with, a dragon. Feast day in E., 8 Nov. See also MONT-ST-MICHEL.

AASS, Sept. 8 (1762), pp. 4–123. W. Lueken, Michael: Eine Darstellung und Vergleichung der jüdischen und der morgenländisch-christlichen Tradition vom Erzengel Michael (Göttingen, 1898). O. Rojdestvensky, Le Culte de Saint Michel et le moyen âge latin (1922); Millénaire Monastique du Mont Saint-Michel, 3: Culte de Saint Michel et Pèlerinages au Mont, sous la direction de M. Baudot (1971), pp. 7–234 and 297–520. J. P. Rohland, Der Erzengel Michael: Arzt und Feldherr. Zwei Aspekte des vor- und frühbyzantinischen Michaelskultes (Beihefte der Zeitschrift für

Religions- und Geistesgeschichte, 19; Leiden, 1977). J. Lemarié, OSB, 'Textes liturgiques concernant le culte de S. Michel', *Sacris Erudiri*, 14 (1963), pp. 277–85. R. H. *Charles in *HDB* 3 (1900), pp. 362 f.; F. Spadafora and M. G. Mara in *Bibliotheca Sanctorum*, 9 (Rome, 1967), cols. 410–46.

Michael Cerularius

Michael Cerularius (d. 1058), Patr. of *Constantinople from 1043, to whose period of office the beginning of the schism between the E. and W. Churches is conventionally dated. Destined for a political career, he was implicated in a conspiracy against the Emp. Michael IV, and became a monk *c.*1040, perhaps to escape the consequences. In outlook he was violently anti-Latin, fiercely attacking the *Filioque and unleavened *bread in the Eucharist. The attempted mediation at Constantinople between a Roman legation, led by Cardinal *Humbert of Silva Candida, and the E. Emp., Constantine IX (Monomachus), failed; the Latins laid a bull of excommunication against the Easterns on the altar of *Sancta Sophia; and Cerularius replied by anathemas (21 and 24 June 1054) and an encyclical embodying the Byzantine case. Later he took part in the political plot to put Isaac Comnenus (Emp. 1057–9) on the throne in place of Michael VI, but then came into conflict with Isaac, was exiled, and would have been deposed if he had not died.

Collection of his works in J. P. Migne, *PG* 120. 719–820, with refs., but incl. also material of an anterior date. Some of his correspondence also pr. in C. Will (ed.), *Acta et Scripta quae de Controversiis Ecclesiae Graecae et Latinae Saeculo Undecimo Composita Exstant* (Leipzig and Marburg, 1861), pp. 65–85, 89–92, 153 f., and 172–204. V. Grumel, AA (ed.), *Les Regestes des actes du patriarcat de Constantinople*, 1, 2nd edn. of fascs. 2–3 by J. Darrouzès (1989), pp. 358–73 (nos. 855a–86). A. Michel, *Humbert und Kerullarios* (Quellen und Forschungen aus dem Gebiete der Geschichte herausg. von der Görres-Gesellschaft, 21 and 23; 1925–30). Id., 'Verstreute Kerullarios- und Humbert-Texte', *RQ* 39 (1931), pp. 355–76. M. Jugie, AA, *Le Schisme byzantin* (1941), pp. 187–246. M. H. Smith, *And Taking Bread . . .: Cerularius and the Azyme Controversy of 1054* (Théologie Historique, 47 [1978]). F. Tinnefeld, 'Michael I. Kerullarios, Patriachen von Konstantinopel (1043–58)', *Jahrbuch der Österreichischen Byzantinistik*, 39 (1989), pp. 95–127. J. M. Hussey, *The Orthodox Church in the Byzantine Empire* (Oxford History of the Christian Church, 1986), pp. 129–38. É. Amann in *DTC* 10 (pt. 2; 1929), cols. 1677–703, s.v. 'Michel (4) Cérulaire', with detailed refs.; M. J. Higgins in *NCE* 9 (1967), pp. 796 f.

Michael Psellus

Michael Psellus. See PSELLUS, MICHAEL.

Michael the Syrian

Michael the Syrian (1126–99), *Syrian Orthodox Patr. of *Antioch. He was a monk and later archimandrite of the monastery of Barsauma; when he became Patriarch of Antioch in 1166 he had for some time to struggle against a rival supported by the Armenians. He compiled a chronicle covering the period from the creation to 1194/5. This work preserves many Syriac sources now lost and affords important evidence for the history of the Syrian Orthodox Church and for the *Crusades. The original Syriac was discovered in 1888; previously the Chronicle had been known only in a shortened Armenian version.

Syriac text of the Chronicle ed., with Fr. tr., by J. B. Chabot (4 vols., Paris, 1899–1910). Fr. tr. of Armenian version by V. Langlois (Venice, 1868). A. *Baumstark, *Geschichte der syrischen Literatur* (1922), pp. 298–300. E. Tisserant in *DTC* 10 (pt. 2; 1929), cols. 1711–19, s.v. 'Michel (9) le Syrien'.

Michaelis, Johann David

Michaelis, Johann David (1717–91), German Protestant theologian. He was professor of oriental languages and theology at Göttingen from 1746 to his death, and is important chiefly for his studies in Hebrew and Arabic and his research work on the early versions of the Bible, esp. the *Peshitta. In 1750 he published his critical *Einleitung in das NT*, and from 1769 to 1791 his influential annotated translation of the OT in 13 volumes. In his famous *Mosäisches Recht* (6 vols., 1770–5; Eng. tr., 4 vols., 1840) he treated the legislation of the Pentateuch as a human achievement, and thus appeared to deny its character as Divine Revelation. His rationalist methods as well as his comprehensive linguistic studies had a far-reaching influence on the development of German biblical criticism.

Michaelis's correspondence ed. J. G. Buhle (3 vols., Leipzig, 1794–6). J. M. Hassencamp, *Leben des Herrn Johann David Michaelis, von ihm selbst beschrieben* (Rinteln, 1793). R. Smend in B. Moeller (ed.), *Theologie in Göttingen* (Göttingen, 1987), pp. 59–71. J. C. O'Neill, *The Bible's Authority* (Edinburgh, 1991), pp. 28–38.

Michelangelo

Michelangelo (1475–1564), Italian Renaissance artist. Michelangelo Buonarroti was the son of the Podestà of the village of Caprese. In 1488 he became the pupil of the Florentine painters Domenico and Davide Ghirlandaio, but, following his attraction for sculpture, went the next year to Bertoldo, a disciple of *Donatello, who introduced him into the circle of Lorenzo the Magnificent (de' Medici). Here he learnt to appreciate the classic ideal of sensuous beauty, which was for a long time to struggle in him with the ideal of religious asceticism represented by his older contemporary *Savonarola. In 1496 he went to Rome, where he did a *Pietà* (finished in 1500) in which Christian austerity and classic beauty are admirably harmonized. During a temporary stay at Florence he carved his famous *David* (1501–4). In 1505 *Julius II called him back to Rome to execute the Papal tomb. His design, which was on so grand a scale that it would have been almost impossible to carry it through in a lifetime, seems to have been meant to represent the three orders of Nature, Law, and Grace in their relation to the Papacy. Its most important finished part is the great figure of *Moses* (1513–6) representing to perfection the majestic wrath of the Law-Giver of the Old Dispensation.

Between 1508 and 1512, under pressure from Julius II, Michelangelo painted the celebrated frescoes on the ceiling of the *Sistine Chapel. Their subject is the *praeparatio evangelica*, leading from the Creation of the world through temptation and sin to the Prophets of the OT and the Sibyls of the Gentiles. The two frescoes representing the 'Creation of Light' and the 'Creation of Man' are among the most grandiose paintings of all time, combining in the Creator human tenderness with stupendous force. The artist continued in Papal employment under *Leo X and his successors, executing for them (*c.*1524/5) parts of his plan for a mortuary chapel of the Medici in San Lorenzo with its famous figures of Night and Day, Morning and Evening, representing the frailty of human greatness. From 1534 to 1541 he was engaged on the *Last Judgement* in the Sistine Chapel. After the death of his friend Vittoria Colonna (1547), to whom he addressed many sonnets full of devotion and religious feeling, he was entrusted with the direction of the building of *St Peter's, and he was engaged on this work till his death.

Letters, ed. G. Milanesi (Florence, 1875) and in Eng. tr. by E. H. Ramsden (2 vols., London, 1963). Complete correspondence ed. G. Poggi, P. Barrochi, and R. Ristori (5 vols., Florence, 1965–83). Notebooks (*Ricordi*), ed. L. Bardeschi Ciulich and P. Barocchi (Florence [1970]). Poems, ed. C. Frey (Berlin, 1897; 2nd edn., 1964) and by E. N. Girardi (Scrittori d'Italia, 217; Bari, 1960). Edn., based on that of Girardi, with Eng. tr., by C. Ryan (London, 1996). Further Eng. tr. of Poems and Selected Letters, by C. Gilbert (New York [1963]). Collection of reproductions (in black and white), ed. F. Knapp (Klassiker der Kunst in Gesamtausgaben, 7; 1906); of his paintings, ed. L. Goldscheider (London [1939]); of his sculpture, by id. (ibid. [1940]; 2nd edn., 1950) and by F. Hartt (ibid., 1969); of his drawings by K. Frey (3 vols., Berlin, 1909–11), L. Goldscheider (London [1951]; 2nd edn., 1966), F. Hartt (New York, 1970; London, 1971), and C. de Tolnay (4 vols., Novara [1975–80]). Selection of his paintings, sculpture, and architecture (some in colour) by L. Goldscheider (London, 1953; 5th edn., 1975).

Lives by G. Vasari (Florence, 1550), ed. K. Frey (Munich, 1911) and P. Barocchi (5 vols., Milan and Naples, 1962); by A. Condivi (Rome, 1553), ed. E. Spina Barelli (Milan, 1964); Eng. tr. of the latter by A. S. Wohl, ed. H. Wohl (London, 1976). Modern studies by J. [A.] Symonds (2 vols., London, 1892), C. Justi (Leipzig, 1900), H. Thode (6 vols. bound in 7, Berlin, 1902–13), K. Frey (vol. 1 only pub., ibid., 1907), C. de Tolnay (5 vols., Princeton, NJ, 1943–60, also, ibid., 1975), H. von Einem (Stuttgart, 1957; rev. Eng. tr., 1973), F. Hartt (New York and London, 1965), H. Hibbard (London, 1975), J. Wilde (Oxford, 1978), and L. Murray (London, 1984). J. Wilde, *Italian Drawings in the Department of Prints and Drawings in the British Museum: Michelangelo and his Studio* (1953); *Drawings by Michelangelo in the Collection of Her Majesty the Queen . . . and other English Collections: An Exhibition held . . . in the British Museum . . . 1975* [1975]; L. Steinberg, *Michelangelo's Last Paintings* [1975]; L. Berti, *Michelangelo: I Disegni di Casa Buonarroti* (Florence [1985]); M. Hirst, *Michelangelo and his Drawings* (New Haven, Conn., and London [1988]). J. S. Ackerman, *The Architecture of Michelangelo* (2 vols., 1961); P. Portoghesi and B. Zevi (eds.), *Michelangelo architetto* (Turin, 1964). M. Weinberger, *Michelangelo the Sculptor* (2 vols., 1967); U. Baldini, *Michelangelo scultore* (Florence, 1981; Eng. tr. 1982). D. Summers, *Michelangelo and the Language of Art* (Princeton, NJ [1981]). E. Steinmann and R. Wittkower, *Michelangelo Bibliographie 1510–1927* (Leipzig, 1927); L. Dussler, *Michelangelo-Bibliographie 1927–1970* (Wiesbaden, 1974).

Micrologus. An 11th-cent. Roman *Mass book, attesting several practices, e.g. the omission of **Gloria in Excelsis* in *Advent and *Septuagesima and the use of *Placeat tibi* after the dismissal, which later became universal in the Latin West. There is still never more than one *collect, the *Creed has not yet been introduced, *incense at the *Offertory is discouraged, as are Offertory prayers. The author was prob. Bernhold of Constance (c.1054–1100), a monk of Schaffhausen and a supporter of *Gregory VII; he was trying to restore a purely Roman use but had to tolerate certain local additions. The work was formerly attributed to St *Ivo of Chartres.

Editio princeps (incomplete), Paris, 1510. First complete edn. by J. Pamelius, Antwerp, 1560 (repr. in J. P. Migne, *PL* 151. 973–1022). S. B[äumer], OSB, 'L'Auteur du Micrologue', *R. Bén.* 8 (1891), pp. 193–201, incl. text of two additional chs., pp. 200 f. G. *M[orin], OSB, 'Que "L'Auteur du Micrologue" est Bernold de Constance', ibid., pp. 385–95; S. Bäumer, OSB, 'Der Micrologus ein Werk Bernold's von Konstanz', *NA* 18 (1892–3), pp. 429–46. V. L. Kennedy, CSB, 'For a new edition of the Micrologus of Bernold of Constance', in *Mélanges en l'honneur de Mon-*

seigneur Michel Andrieu (Revue des Sciences Religieuses, volume hors série; Strasbourg, 1956), pp. 229–41. F. *Cabrol, OSB, in *DACL* 2 (pt. 1; 1910), cols. 817–20, s.v. 'Bernold (de Constance) et le Micrologue', and H. *Leclercq, OSB, ibid. 11 (pt. 1; 1933), cols. 908–12, s.v. 'Micrologue'.

Middle Ages, the. The era preceding the Renaissance, formerly taken to date from the fall of the W. Roman Empire in 476, but in more recent writers from c.1100, and extending down to the end of the 15th cent. The conception of the 'medium aevum' is to be found in the writings of Flavio Biondo (1388–1463), and was in established use by 1467. Once viewed as a sterile period, it has come to be regarded as one of the most creative and fruitful periods in the world's history. For the historian of Christianity it has special interest as the age which approached most nearly the realization of Christendom as a cultural unity.

G. Gordon, *Medium Aevum and the Middle Age* (Society for Pure English, Tract 19; 1925).

Middleton, Thomas Fanshawe (1769–1822), first Bp. of Calcutta. After graduating at Pembroke College, Cambridge, he was ordained in 1792 and held a number of livings before being appointed vicar of St Pancras in 1811. Three years later he was consecrated first Bishop of Calcutta, constituted as a vast diocese covering all the territories of the East India Company. His episcopate witnessed a great advance in Church life, including the foundation at Calcutta of the Bishop's College, a training college for missionaries in Asia, in 1820. Possessed of a somewhat chill exterior, Middleton was a man of great ability as well as a scholar of note, his chief work being *The Doctrine of the Greek Article applied to the Criticism and Illustration of the New Testament* (1808; rev. edn. by H. J. *Rose, 1833).

C. W. Le Bas, *Life of T. F. Middleton* (2 vols., 1831). W. Wroth in *DNB* 37 (1894), pp. 363–5.

Mid-Lent. See LAETARE SUNDAY.

Midrash (Heb., 'investigation/study [sc. of Scripture]'). The term, which occurs as early as 2 Chron. 24: 27 ('midrash of the Book of Kings', commonly rendered in English Bibles as 'commentary' or 'discourse of the book of the kings') and in the *Dead Sea Scrolls in the Manual of Discipline, 8. 15 ('midrash of the *Torah'), is commonly applied to the whole tradition of Jewish biblical exegesis (incl. the Book of *Jubilees, *Philo, and the *Liber Antiquitatum Biblicarum*). However, it primarily denotes Rabbinic interpretation of the Bible as it flourished in Palestine, and to a lesser extent in Babylonia, in the Tannaitic and Amoraic periods (2nd–8th cent. AD). The extensive corpus of midrashic texts is classified in a number of ways. The Halachic Midrashim (i.e. the Mechilta on Exod., Sifra on Lev., and Sifrei on Num. and Deut.) concentrate on the *halachic (or legal) portions of the Pentateuch, as opposed to the *haggadic (narrative, non-legal) portions. They are also known as the Tannaitic Midrashim, because they largely cite authorities from the time of the *Mishnah (i.e. before c. AD 200). The Homiletic Midrashim (e.g. Tanḥuma and Pesiqta de Rab Kahana) expound only the opening verse(s) of the Sabbath or Festival lection used in synagogue, in contrast to the

Exegetical Midrashim (e.g. Genesis Rabba), which give a running commentary on each biblical verse. The largest collection of classic Midrashim is Midrash Rabba. First published in Constantinople in 1512, it contains texts ranging in date from the 5th cent. AD (Genesis Rabba and Lamentations Rabba) to the 13th (Numbers Rabba, in its present form).

All the Midrashim exhibit a similar hermeneutical approach to Scripture, the spirit of which is summarized in the maxim, 'Turn it [Torah] over and over again, for everything is in it. Reflect upon it. Grow old and worn in it, and do not stir from it, for you have no better rule than it' (*Pirqe Aboth, 5. 22). Scripture is the primary source of all wisdom and truth. It originated in the mind of God and so is inerrant and totally coherent. The aims of the expositor (the *darshan*) are to explain apparent errors, to harmonize contradictions and demonstrate the unity of Scripture, and to draw out the teachings of the Torah and apply them to Jewish life. To this end he may resort even to extreme techniques of text-manipulation, such as *notariqon* (treating the words of Scripture as acronyms), *gematria* (computing the numerical values of the words of Scripture), and *al tiqrei* (revocalizing words). Though they make some use of a tradition of popular Bible exegesis in synagogue (the *Petiḥah* [Proem] and *Yelammedenu* forms appear to represent preaching styles), the Midrashim as they stand are scholastic commentaries which reflect learned discussions on Scripture in the Rabbinic academies. They sometimes incorporate much earlier material, but broadly they appear to be post-Mishnaic in origin, an attempt to read Scripture in the light of the Mishnah and to justify the distinctive Rabbinic view of the world.

The classic phase of midrash ended around the 8th cent. AD. Though Midrashim were composed later, in the 10th cent. a new style of biblical commentary (known as *parshanut*) emerges, which, though sometimes citing Midrash (notably in the case of *Rashi, 1040–1105), is distinct from it. Despite the chronological problems the Rabbinic Midrashim have been used to elucidate the methods, content, and form of NT exegesis of the OT. They also shed light on the writings of *Origen and *Jerome, both of whom drew extensively on Jewish tradition. In recent years literary critics have seen in midrash anticipations of modern ways of reading texts.

Trs. of major Midrashim (into Eng., unless otherwise specified) include: Mechilta by J. Z. Lauterbach (3 vols., Philadelphia, 1933–5); Sifra by J. Neusner (Brown Judaic Studies, 138–40 and 142; Atlanta, Ga. [1988]) and J. Winter (Schriften der Gesellschaft zur Förderung der Wissenschaft des Judentums, 42; Breslau, 1938; Ger.); Sifrei Numbers by J. Neusner (Brown Judaic Studies, 118–19 [1986]); Sifrei Deuteronomy by R. Hammer (Yale Judaica Series, 24; New Haven, Conn., and London [1986]); Midrash Rabba by H. Freedman, M. Simon, and others (10 vols., London, 1939); Pesiqta Rabbati by W. G. Braude (Yale Judaica Series, 18; 2 vols., 1968); Pesiqta de Rab Kahana by W. G. Braude and I. J. Kapstein (Philadelphia and London, 1975) and J. Neusner (Brown Judaic Studies, 122–3 [1987]); Tanhuma by J. T. Townsend (Hoboken, NJ, 1989 ff. [Gen. only to date]) and H. Bietenhard (2 vols., Judaica et Christiana, 5–6; Bern and Frankfurt, 1980–2; Ger.); Midrash Psalms by W. G. Braude (Yale Judaica Series, 13; 2 vols., 1959). The best general introd. is H. L. Strack, *Einleitung in Talmud und Midrash* (1887; 7th edn. by G. Stemberger, 1982; Eng. tr., Edinburgh, 1991), with bibl., incl. details of major edns. of the

texts. Other works incl. G. Vermes, *Scripture and Tradition in Judaism: Haggadic Studies* (Studia Post-Biblica, 4; Leiden, 1961, 2nd edn., 1973); id., 'Bible and Midrash: Early Old Testament Exegesis', in P. R. Ackroyd and C. F. Evans (eds.), *The Cambridge History of the Bible*, 1 (1970), pp. 199–231, repr. in Vermes, *Post-Biblical Jewish Studies* (Studies in Judaism in Late Antiquity, 8; Leiden, 1975), pp. 59–91; J. Neusner, *Midrash in Context: Exegesis in Formative Judaism* (Philadelphia [1983]); P. S. Alexander, 'The Rabbinic Hermeneutical Rules and the Problem of the Definition of Midrash', *Proceedings of the Irish Biblical Association*, 8 (1984), pp. 97–120; id., 'Quid Athenis et Hierosolymis? Rabbinic Midrash and Hermeneutics in the Graeco-Roman World', in P. R. Davies and R. T. White (eds.), *A Tribute to Geza Vermes* (Journal for the Study of the Old Testament, Supplement Series, 100; Sheffield [1990]), pp. 101–24; G. G. Porton, *Understanding Rabbinic Midrash: Texts and Commentary* (Hoboken, NJ, 1985); M. Fishbane, *Biblical Interpretation in Ancient Israel* (Oxford, 1985); A. Goldberg, 'Form-Analysis of Rabbinic Literature as a Method of Description', *Journal of Jewish Studies*, 36 (1985), pp. 159–74; id., 'The Rabbinic View of Scripture', in *A Tribute to Geza Vermes*, op. cit., pp. 153–66; G. H. Hartman and S. Budick (eds.), *Midrash and Literature* (New Haven, Conn. [1986]); D. Boyarin, *Intertextuality and the Reading of Midrash* (Bloomington, Ill., and Indianapolis [1990]); A. Samely, 'Between Scripture and its Rewording: Towards a Classification of Rabbinic Exegesis', *Journal of Jewish Studies*, 42 (1991), pp. 39–67.

Migetius (8th cent.), Spanish heretic. The little that is known of him comes from the letters of his opponents, esp. *Elipandus. He seems to have taught the curious doctrine that God was revealed successively in David (as Father), in Jesus (as Son), and in St Paul (as Holy Spirit). He was condemned at synods held at Seville in 782 and 785.

É. Amann in *DTC* 10 (pt. 2; 1929), cols. 1720–2, s.v. See also bibls. to ADOPTIANISM and ELIPANDUS.

Migne, Jacques Paul (1800–75), editor and publisher of theological literature. A parish priest near Orléans from 1824 to 1833, he then went to Paris, where he founded a printing-house and published an immense collection of religious texts and dictionaries, notably the *Patrologia Latina*, a corpus of Latin ecclesiastical writers up to *Innocent III (221 vols., 1844–64), and the *Patrologia Graeca*, of Greek writers to 1439 (162 vols., Greek text with Latin tr., 1857–66). He used many editions since superseded and printers' errors abound, but for most of the authors the collections remain the standard means of reference and citation. Migne's commercial activities were disliked by H. L. Quelen, Abp. of Paris (1817–39), but subsequent archbishops were more favourable. In 1868 his workshops and stereotype moulds were destroyed by fire.

A series of suppl. to *PL* ed. A. [G.] Hamman, OFM (5 vols., Paris, 1958–74). Useful index to *PG* by F. Cavallera (Paris, 1912); to the same series there is also a more elaborate *Index Locupletissimus* by T. Hopfner (2 vols., ibid., 1928–45). P. Glorieux, *Pour revaloriser Migne: Tables rectificatives* (Mélanges de Science religieuse, IXᵉ Année, 1952. Cahier Supplémentaire). A. G. Hamman [OFM], *Jacques-Paul Migne: Le Retour aux Pères de l'Église* (Le Point Théologique, 16 [1975]). A. Mandouze and J. Fouilheron (eds.), *Migne et le Renouveau des Études Patristiques: Actes du Colloque de Saint-Flour, 7–8 juillet 1975* (Théologie historique, 66 [1985]), esp. pp. 93–317. R. H. Bloch, *God's Plagiarist: Being an Account of the Fabulous Industry and Irregular Commerce of the Abbé Migne* (Chicago and London, 1994). L. Marchal in *DTC* 10 (pt. 2; 1929), cols. 1722–40, s.v.; H. *Leclercq, OSB, in *DACL* 11 (pt. 1; 1933), cols. 941–57, s.v.

Milan, Edict of. The document so called is in fact a circular of 313 to provincial governors issued in Bithynia by the Emp. Licinius. In accordance with an agreement made with *Constantine at Milan, he extended to the E. provinces freedom of worship for all, including Christians, and the restitution of possessions lost by the Churches since the persecution of 303, concessions previously made in the W. by Constantine and Maxentius. It is preserved in divergent forms by *Lactantius (*De Mortibus Persecutorum*, 48) and *Eusebius (*Hist. Eccl.* 10. 5). See also PERSECUTIONS, EARLY CHRISTIAN.

Comm. by J. Moreau in his edn. of Lactantius, *De Mortibus Persecutorum* (SC 39), 2 (1955), pp. 456–64. N. H. Baynes, *Constantine the Great and the Christian Church* (Raleigh Lecture for 1929; 1930), pp. 69–74 (full and valuable bibl.).

Milanese rite. See AMBROSIAN RITE.

Mildred, St (*c.*700), Abbess of Minster-in-Thanet. Acc. to late and not wholly reliable sources (among them, *Goscelin, Thorn, *William of Malmesbury), she was the granddaughter of Penda, King of Mercia, and daughter of St Ermenburga, the foundress and abbess of the nunnery at Minster. She was sent for education to the convent of Chelles near Paris, whence, after resisting strong inducements to marriage, she returned to Minster, and became a nun at her mother's house, later succeeding her as abbess. After the destruction of Minster by the Danes in 1011, two of the monasteries at *Canterbury (St Augustine's and St Gregory's) laid claim to the possession of her relics; the resulting dispute provoked Goscelin's 'Libellus contra usurpatores S. Mildrithae'. Later her remains found their way to Deventer in the Netherlands. Feast day, 13 July (more recently, 20 Feb.).

Life repr. from J. Capgrave, with introd. and other late material, in *AASS*, Jul. 3 (1723), pp. 512–23. Earlier material described in Hardy, 1 (pt. 1; 1862), pp. 376–84. *BHL* 2, p. 870 (nos. 5960–94). D. W. Rollason, *The Mildrith Legend: A Study in Early Medieval Hagiography in England* (Leicester, 1982); id., 'Goscelin of Canterbury's Account of the Translation and Miracles of St Mildrith . . . An Edition with notes', *Mediaeval Studies*, 48 (1986), pp. 139–210. W. *Stubbs in *DCB* 3 (1882), pp. 914 f., s.v.

Milíč, Jan (*c.*1325–74), the most important of the pre-*Hussite reformers in Bohemia and Moravia. A native of Kroměříž (Kremsier), he held offices in the Imperial chancery of Charles IV, but abandoned all his temporal interests before the end of 1363 and vigorously preached against the vices of the clergy at Prague and elsewhere. During the later 1360s he was for a time imprisoned by the *Inquisition at Rome, and he died at *Avignon while still under suspicion of heresy. His writings include a *Libellus de Antichristo* and many Latin sermons, but his significance lies in his handling of the spoken word. His moral and eschatological vision, which drew on the teaching of Konrad Waldhauser and was passed on to Matthias of Janov and Tomáš Štítný in the next generation, laid the ideological ground for the Hussite revolt.

Tres Sermones Synodales, ed. V. Herold and M. Mráz (Prague, 1974). Idd., 'Johann Milíč von Kremsier—ein ideologischer Wegbereiter des Hussitentums und des deutschen Bauernkrieges', *Deutsche Zeitschrift für Philosophie*, 23 (1975), pp. 570–82. M. Kaňák, *Milíč z Kroměříže* (Prague, 1975). E. [J.] Winter, *Früh-*

humanismus: Seine Entwicklung in Böhmen und deren europäische Bedeutung für die Kirchenreformbestrebungen im 14. Jahrhundert (Beiträge zur Geschichte des Religiösen und Wissenschaftlichen Denkens, 3; 1964), esp. pp. 86–103; id., *Ketzerschicksale: Christliche Denker aus neun Jahrhunderten* (1979), pp. 48–63.

militant, the Church. The body of Christians still on earth, as distinct from those in *Purgatory (*expectant) and those in *Heaven (*triumphant) (see COMMUNION OF SAINTS). Cf. the 'Prayer for the Church Militant' in the BCP.

Mill, John. See MILLS, JOHN.

Mill, William Hodge (1792–1853), English orientalist and *High Church divine. Educated at Trinity College, Cambridge, where he was elected Fellow in 1814, he was from 1820 to 1838 the first principal of Bishop's College, Calcutta. Here he became keenly interested in Arabic and Sanskrit studies and assisted with the publication of works in the Indian vernaculars for spreading the Christian faith. Forced through ill-health to return to England in 1838, he became chaplain to Abp. W. *Howley and *Hulsean advocate (1839) and later Regius professor of Hebrew at Cambridge (1848). His support of the 'Cambridge *Camden Society' did much to further the interests of *Tractarian principles at the university.

His *Lectures on the Catechism*, delivered in the Parish Church of Brasted, Kent, were posthumously ed. by his son-in-law B. *Webb, (1856), who also ed., with notes, a 2nd edn. of his *Five Sermons on the Temptation of Christ Our Lord in the Wilderness: preached before the University of Cambridge, in Lent 1844* (1873). C. Bendall in *DNB* 37 (1894), p. 400, s.v.

Millenarianism. The belief in a future 'millennium', i.e. a thousand-year period of blessedness. The Christian concept may owe something to the Book of Daniel and to ideas popular in late pre-Christian Jewish apocalyptic literature, esp. 2 Esd., and the non-canonical Books of Enoch. The main source of the teaching is, however, the Book of Rev., ch. 20.

Its advocates fall into two groups, pre- and post-millennialists. The former maintain that the millennium will follow the Second Coming of Christ, but are divided as to whether it will be spent by the saints in heaven or upon earth; the latter believe that it precedes the Advent and, indeed, prepares the way for it by the spread of righteousness over the earth, a view which, in its modern form, owes much to D. *Whitby (1638–1726).

In the early Church, Millenarianism was found among the *Gnostics and *Montanists, but was also accepted by more orthodox writers such as St *Justin Martyr, St *Irenaeus, and St *Hippolytus of Rome, all of whom were pre-millennialists. Millenarianism came, however, increasingly to stress the carnal pleasures to be enjoyed during the thousand years of the saints' earthly reign and eventually a revulsion against the whole concept set in, initiated by *Origen and completed by St *Augustine. During the medieval period the principal exponent of millenarian themes was *Joachim of Fiore, whose doctrines aroused much excitement in the W. Church but were treated with suspicion by the ecclesiastical authorities.

At the Reformation many *Anabaptists, as well as the *Bohemian Brethren, were millenarians, and millenarian beliefs were widely held in 16th- and 17th-cent. English Protestantism, finding particular expression in the writings of Joseph *Mede. In Germany the millenarian view gained its widest currency in the *Pietist Movement of the 17th and 18th cents. In 18th-cent. England also there were millenarian groups, some inspired by *Huguenot piety, but also later in reaction to the upheavals of the French Revolution. In the 19th cent. new advocates of apocalyptic and millenarian ideas arose in the USA and in Britain, among them the *Irvingites, *Plymouth Brethren, and *Adventists, the last-named reviving the concept of a heavenly millennium after the Second Advent. In the 20th cent. the indigenous Churches of Asia, Africa, and South America have produced a rich variety of millenarian beliefs. In the RC Church the *Holy Office gave a ruling against post-millenarianism in 1944, and all the larger Christian bodies have treated the subject with the greatest reserve.

L. Gry, Le Millénarisme dans ses origines et son développement [1904]; C. E. Hill, Regnum Caelorum: Patterns of Future Hope in Early Christianity (Oxford Early Christian Studies, 1992). M. Simonetti, 'Il millenarismo in Oriente da Origene a Metodio', in Corona Gratiarum: Miscellanea patristica, historica et liturgica Eligio Dekkers, O.S.B. . . . oblata, 1 (Instrumenta Patristica, 10; Brugge, 1975), pp. 37–58. N. Cohn, The Pursuit of the Millenium (1957; rev. edn., 1970). M. [E.] Reeves, Joachim of Fiore and the Prophetic Future (1976). R. B. Barnes, Prophecy and Gnosis: Apocalypticism in the Wake of the Lutheran Revolution (Stanford, Calif., 1988). B. S. Capp, The Fifth Monarchy Men: A Study in Seventeenth-century English Millenarianism (1972); K. R. Firth, The Apocalyptic Tradition in Reformation Britain 1530–1645 (Oxford, 1979), esp. pp. 204–54. J. S. Erwin, The Millennialism of Cotton Mather (Studies in American Religion, 45; Lewiston, NY [1990]). H. Schwartz, The French Prophets: The History of a Millenarian Group in Eighteenth-Century England (Berkeley, Calif., and London [1980]). C. Garrett, Respectable Folly: Millenarians and the French Revolution in France and England (Baltimore and London, 1975). E. R. Sandeen, The Roots of Fundamentalism: British and American Millenarianism 1880–1930 (Chicago and London, 1970); J. F. C. Harrison, The Second Coming: Popular Millenarianism 1780–1850 (1979). W. H. Oliver, Prophets and Millennialists: The Uses of Biblical Prophecy in England from the 1790s to the 1840s (Auckland and Oxford, 1978). A. Taylor, Visions of Harmony: A Study in Nineteenth-Century Millenarianism (Oxford, 1987). T. P. Weber, Living in the Shadow of the Second Coming: American Premillenialism 1875–1925 (New York and Oxford, 1979; enlarged edn., covering 1875–1982, Grand Rapids, Mich., 1983; Chicago and London, 1987). M. [E.] Reeves and W. Gould, Joachim of Fiore and the Myth of the Eternal Evangel in the Nineteenth Century (Oxford, 1987). M. Adas, Prophets of Rebellion: Millenarian Protest Movements against the European Colonial Order (Chapel Hill, NC [1979]; Cambridge, 1987); K. E. Fields, Revival and Rebellion in Colonial Central Africa (Princeton, NJ [1985]). The 1944 ruling of the Holy Office is conveniently pr. in Denzinger and Hünermann (37th edn., 1991), pp. 1066 f. (no. 3839). W. Bauer in RAC 2 (1954), cols. 1073–8, s.v. 'Chiliasmus'; B. E. Daley [SJ] in E. Ferguson (ed.), Encyclopedia of Early Christianity (New York and London, 1990), pp. 193–7, s.v. 'Chiliasm'. See also bibl. to ESCHATOLOGY, ADVENTISTS, JEHOVAH'S WITNESSES, JOACHIM OF FIORE, PLYMOUTH BRETHREN, SEVENTH-DAY ADVENTISTS, etc.

Millenary Petition. The petition presented in Apr. 1603 by the Puritans to *James I on his way from Scotland to London, in which they prayed to be relieved from their 'common burden of human rites and ceremonies'. It was so called from the thousand ministers whose wishes it professed to embody. The practices objected to included the cross in Baptism, *Confirmation, the surplice, the ring in marriage, the length of the service, the profanation of the Lord's Day, bowing at the name of Jesus, and the reading of the *Apocrypha in the lessons; but to avoid giving offence nothing was said against episcopacy as such. It was the immediate occasion of the *Hampton Court Conference (q.v.).

Text in T. *Fuller, The Church History of Britain from the Birth of Jesus Christ to the Year M.DC.XLVIII (1655), bk. 10, pp. 21–3 [Fuller's comments (p. 7; cf. also pp. 23 f.) have very frequently been repeated]. Text repr. in Bettenson (2nd edn., 1963), pp. 397–400, and J. P. Kenyon, The Stuart Constitution 1603–1688 (Cambridge, 1966), pp. 132–4 (no. 37). Useful note in S. R. Gardiner, History of England from the Accession of James I to the Disgrace of Chief Justice Coke, 1 (1863), p. 163, n. 1. See also bibl. to HAMPTON COURT CONFERENCE, JAMES I, and PURITANS.

Mill Hill Missionaries, officially 'St Joseph's Society for Foreign Missions', a RC missionary society of secular priests and lay brothers, devoted to the propagation of the Gospel among unevangelized peoples. It was founded in 1866 at Mill Hill, in NW London, by H. *Vaughan (q.v.). The foundation was one of the first foreign missionary initiatives by English RCs after emancipation; it was given final approval by the Holy See in 1908. Although an English society, using English as its common language, it recruited members from many different countries, esp. the *Netherlands and the Tyrol. In the *United States of America, it developed an independent community, the Josephite Fathers, but since 1951 members have again been recruited there. More recently non-western students are being enrolled. As a society of English origin, the Mill Hill Missionaries played an important role in *Uganda when a British Protectorate was established in 1894, after bitter conflict between RC and Anglican factions. In Africa they also work in *Kenya, *Sudan, *Zaire, and Cameroon; elsewhere in *India, Pakistan, Malaysia, the *Philippines, *New Zealand, *Chile, *Brazil, and the Falklands.

Accounts of their work in different parts of the world by J. Dempsey, Mission on the Nile (1955); H. P. Gale, Uganda and the Mill Hill Fathers (1959), pp. 88–318; H. Burgman, The Way the Catholic Church Started in Western Kenya (1990). See also works cited under VAUGHAN, H.

Mills, John (1645–1707), NT textual critic. From 1670 to 1682 he was a fellow of Queen's College, Oxford, and from 1685 till his death principal of St Edmund Hall. His edition of the Greek text of the NT, published in 1707, was a great advance on any of its predecessors, as Mills added to it a critical apparatus containing the readings of nearly 100 MSS. His correct name appears to have been 'Mills', not (as commonly given) 'Mill'.

D. *Whitby, Examen Variantium Lectionum J. Millii . . . in Novum Testamentum (Leiden, 1724; hostile). A. Fox, John Mill and Richard Bentley: A Study of the Textual Criticism of the New Testament 1675–1729 (1954), pp. 3–102. B. Porter in DNB 37 (1894), pp. 388–90.

Milman, Henry Hart (1791–1868), Dean of *St Paul's. After a brilliant career at Oxford, Milman was ordained in 1816 and in 1818 appointed rector of St Mary's, Reading. In early life he was known esp. as a poet and writer of plays, and held from 1821 to 1831 the professorship of poetry at Oxford, where he was the immediate predecessor of J. *Keble. His *History of the Jews* (1829; anon.) first brought his name prominently before the theological world. The way in which it handled the OT narratives, treating the Jews as an oriental tribe and attaching relatively little weight to the influence of the miraculous, met with much criticism. In 1835 Peel made him rector of St Margaret's, Westminster, and in 1849 he became Dean of St Paul's. While in the latter office he published his well-known treatise on the *History of Latin Christianity* (1855), a work which, despite many blemishes in matters of detail, treated a vast subject with balance, candour, and sympathy, and did much to foster the study of medieval life and institutions. Among his other writings were editions of E. *Gibbon's *Decline and Fall* (1838) and of his Life and Correspondence (1839), a *History of Christianity to the Abolition of Paganism in the Roman Empire* (1840) and *Annals of St Paul's Cathedral* (1868; posthumous).

The standard Life is by his son, A. Milman (London, 1900; not entirely satisfactory). C. [H. E.] Smyth, *Dean Milman* (1949). R. Garnett in *DNB* 38 (1894), pp. 1–4.

Milner, Isaac. See MILNER, JOSEPH.

Milner, John (1752–1826), RC apologist. Educated at the English College at *Douai, he was ordained priest in 1777. He soon returned to England as a zealous propagandist for his creed, where, however, his extreme claims in the matter of Catholic Emancipation alienated many of his co-religionists. In 1803 he was appointed titular Bp. of Castabala and *Vicar Apostolic of the Midland District. As an enthusiastic *Ultramontane, he eagerly pressed the case for Papal Infallibility. His chief work, *The End of Religious Controversy* (written 1801–2; published 1818; new edition by L. Rivington, 1896), forcefully presented the RC case in a series of letters, and has gone through many editions.

F. C. Husenbeth, *Life of John Milner* (1862). M. N. L. Couve de Murville, *John Milner* (Archdiocese of Birmingham Historical Commission, Publication 2; 1986). T. Cooper in *DNB* 38 (1894), pp. 14–16.

Milner, Joseph (1744–97), *Evangelical divine. He was educated at Leeds grammar school and Catharine Hall, Cambridge. After ordination he was curate at Thorp Arch, W. Yorks (near Tadcaster), until 1768, when he moved to Hull. In 1770 he became an ardent Evangelical, and for the rest of his life was successively curate and vicar of North Ferriby on the Humber. Shortly before his death he was presented to the living of Holy Trinity, Hull, mainly through the efforts of W. *Wilberforce. His *History of the Church of Christ*, largely put into shape and extended by his brother, Isaac Milner (1750–1820, from 1791 Dean of *Carlisle), was brought out in stages between 1794 and 1809. Though inaccurate and uncritical, it won great popularity. It was one of the few Evangelical works to quote extensively from the Fathers, and it had an influence on the young J. H. *Newman. Among Joseph Milner's other writings were *Gibbon's Account of Christianity Considered* (1781) and *Essays on Several Religious Subjects* (1789). After his death many of his sermons (*Practical Sermons*, 4 vols., 1800–30) were published.

Life by I. Milner, prefixed to Joseph Milner's *Practical Sermons* (London, 1800). J. D. Walsh, 'Joseph Milner's Evangelical

Church History', *JEH* 9 (1959), pp. 174–87. J. H. Overton in *DNB* 38 (1894), pp. 17 f.

Miltiades (2nd cent.), early Christian *Apologist. *Tertullian (*Adv. Valent.* 5) and *Eusebius (*HE* 5. 17. 1 and 5) mention him as having written against the pagans and the Jews, as well as against the *Montanists and *Valentinians; but all his works are lost. He wrote in Asia Minor.

Testimonia on Miltiades assembled in J. C. T. Otto (ed.), *Corpus Apologetarum Christianorum Saeculi Secundi*, 9 (Jena, 1872), pp. 364–73. Bardenhewer, 1 (1913), pp. 284–6. G. *Salmon in *DCB* 3 (1882), pp. 916 f., s.v.; É. Amann in *DTC* 10 (pt. 2; 1929), col. 1765, s.v.

Miltiades, St (d. 314), less correctly, Melchiades, Pope from 310 (or perhaps 311). Acc. to the *Liber Pontificalis*, he was an African by birth. His pontificate was remarkable for *Constantine's victory over Maxentius and the issue of the so-called 'Edict of *Milan'. In Oct. 313 he held a Council at the *Lateran at which *Donatism was condemned. G. B. *de Rossi believed, but on evidence now generally thought insufficient, that he had discovered his tomb in the Catacomb of St Callistus. Feast day, 10 Dec.

LP (Duchesne), 1, pp. 8 f., 74 f., 168 f. C. Pietri, *Roma Christiana: Recherches sur l'Église de Rome . . . (311–440)* (Bibliothèque des Écoles Françaises d'Athènes et de Rome, 224; 2 vols., 1976), esp. 1, pp. 154 f., 159–67; see index in vol. 2. G. B. de Rossi, *Roma sotterranea cristiana*, 2 (1867), pp. 188–90 and pl. xxiii. H. U. Instinsky, 'Zwei Bischofsnamen konstantinischer Zeit. I. Miltiades von Rom', *RQ* 55 (1960), pp. 203–6, with refs. H. *Leclercq, OSB, in *DACL* 11 (pt. 1; 1933), cols. 1199–203, s.v., and 13 (pt. 1; 1937), cols. 1194–6, s.v. 'Pape'; J. N. D. Kelly, *Oxford Dictionary of Popes* (1986), pp. 26 f., s.v.

Miltitz, Carl von (c.1480–1529), Papal nuncio. Born near Meissen of a noble Saxon family, after studying at Mainz, Trier, and *Cologne, he made his way to Rome, where he was appointed Papal chamberlain (c.1514) and acted as agent of *Frederick III ('the Wise'), Elector of Saxony. After Card. T. de V. *Cajetan's attempts to silence M. *Luther had failed, Miltitz, by now a respected German curialist, was chosen late in 1518 to take the *Golden Rose to Frederick and to try to win his support against Luther. He took it upon himself to negotiate a compromise, and at a meeting in Altenburg (4–6 Jan. 1519), Luther agreed to cease from further action pending reference of the matter to a German bishop, but made no offer of recantation. Miltitz then proceeded to Leipzig, where, in the hope of restraining the movement, he disavowed J. *Tetzel. He soon discovered that nothing could be achieved by conciliation and two further meetings with Luther, at Liebenwerda (5 Oct. 1519) and Lichtenberg, near *Wittenberg (12 Oct. 1520), were fruitless. After a further visit to Rome, he returned to Germany, where he spent his last years at Mainz and Meissen. He was accidentally drowned in the Main on 20 Nov. 1529 and was buried in Mainz Cathedral.

H. A. Creutzberg, *Karl von Miltitz, 1490–1529: Sein Leben und seine geschichtliche Bedeutung* (Studien und Darstellungen aus dem Gebiete der Geschichte, 6, Heft 1; 1907). P. Kalkoff, *Die Miltitziade: Eine kritische Nachlese zur Geschichte des Ablassstreites* (1911).

Milton, John (1608–74), poet and controversialist. The son of a scrivener, he was educated at St Paul's School, London, and at Christ's College, Cambridge (1625–32), where he won a high reputation for his scholarship and literary gifts; his famous *Ode on the Morning of Christ's Nativity* (1629) belongs to this period. From 1632 to 1638 he lived on his father's estate at Horton in Buckinghamshire. Having abandoned his original intention of taking orders because of the 'tyranny' that had invaded the Church under Abp. W. *Laud, he devoted himself entirely to scholarship and literature. Among his finest poems of this period are *L'Allegro* and *Il Penseroso*, which are sometimes taken as expressing the two sides of his nature, torn between the desire for pleasure and the love of meditation and silence. In 'A Maske Presented at Ludlow Castle, 1634' [*Comus*] (pr. 1637), he sings the praises of chastity in a dramatic poem. In 1637 he wrote the monody *Lycidas* on the death of a friend, containing a sharp satiric allusion to the clergy, one of his main themes in later years. Next year he travelled in Italy, and after his return moved to London, where he spent many years in political and religious controversy. In 1641 he joined the *Presbyterians and took part in the famous '*Smectymnuus' affair, and about the same time wrote *The Reason of Church Government Urged against Prelacy*, a fierce attack on episcopacy in which he saw only an instrument of tyranny. In 1643 he married Mary Powell, a member of a strongly royalist family. She left him shortly afterwards, and he returned once more to the question of the reform of the divorce laws, writing *The Doctrine and Discipline of Divorce* (1643), in which he made a passionate appeal for the solubility of marriage on the grounds of incompatibility of character and declared the sanctity and sacramental character of marriage to be a clerical invention. The treatise, which roused a heated discussion, caused his break with the Presbyterians. Its publication without a licence from the censor led the case to be submitted to Parliament and drew from Milton his celebrated *Areopagitica* (1644) in defence of the freedom of the press. Parliament dropped the case, but the real success of Milton's pleading came only many years later. From this time his religious views tended more and more towards the *Independents, and he came to regard sects and schisms as a sign of health in the body politic. In 1645 he was reconciled to his wife, and in the same year published the first collection of his *Poems*. From 1649 Milton supported the new government. He defended the execution of the King in his *Tenure of Kings and Magistrates* (1649) and accepted a government post as secretary for foreign tongues, which involved chiefly the drafting of letters in Latin to foreign governments. In the same year he published *Eikonoklastes*, his reply to the royalist pamphlet *Eikon Basilike*. In 1651 he wrote his *Pro Populo Anglicano Defensio*, an answer to the accusations of regicide levelled (esp. by *Salmasius) against the English people. It was followed by the *Defensio Secunda* (1654). In 1651 he became totally blind, and in 1652 he lost his wife. Despite his admiration for O. *Cromwell he disagreed with the ecclesiastical policy of his later years, which ran counter to Milton's main idea of a complete disestablishment of Churches everywhere. After Cromwell's death his chief preoccupation was to prevent the re-establishment of the monarchy, and after the Restoration he was for a short

time imprisoned. With the fall of his religious and political hopes he turned once more to poetry, and from 1658 to 1665 wrote his greatest work, *Paradise Lost* (q.v., pub. 1667), in which he undertook to 'justify the ways of God to men' and to show the cause of evil and injustice in the world. In 1671 appeared its sequel, *Paradise Regained*, which dealt with the temptation of Christ in the wilderness, and *Samson Agonistes* (which is now thought to have been written before *Paradise Lost*). In the latter, which described in dramatic form the last hours of Samson 'before the prison in Gaza', the blind hero partly represented Milton himself, a trait that added poignancy to the masterly representation of the tragic death of the OT hero. Milton's theological testament is contained in the treatise *De Doctrina Christiana*, which was published posthumously. It contains much unorthodox doctrine, denying the coeternity and coequality of the Divine Persons as well as the dogma of creation *ex nihilo*, and asserting that matter is inherent in God. Despite his attachment to the Puritan party, his independent outlook can hardly be forced under a party label. His theological as well as his political opinions were highly individualistic and a strange blend of love of order and hierarchical values with the revolutionary ideas of a mind wishing to be a law to itself.

Collected edn. of his works in prose and verse by F. A. Patterson and others (18 vols. in 21 parts, New York, 1931–8, with index, 2 vols., ibid., 1940). First edn. of his collected verse, 5 parts, fol., London, 1695; modern edns. incl. those by H. Darbishire (2 vols., Oxford, 1952–5; London, 1958 and 1961) and J. Carey and A. Fowler (London, 1968); prose writings ed. J. *Toland (3 vols., fol., 'Amsterdam' [London], 1698); also ed. J. A. St John (5 vols., London, 1848–53) and D. M. Wolfe and others (8 vols., New Haven, Conn., and London, 1953–82). *Private Correspondence and Academic Exercises* tr. into Eng. by P. B. Tillyard, ed., with introd., by E. M. W. Tillyard (Cambridge, 1932). S. *Johnson, *The Lives of the English Poets*, 1 (Dublin, 1779), pp. 137–230 (often repr.). H. Darbishire (ed.), *The Early Lives of Milton* (1932) with useful introd. J. M. French (ed.), *The Life Records of John Milton* (5 vols., New Brunswick, NJ, 1949–58). Standard Life by D. Masson (6 vols., London, 1859–80; index, 1894); modern biog. by W. R. Parker (2 vols., Oxford, 1968; rev. ed. by G. Campbell, 2 vols., 1996). D. Saurat, *La Pensée de Milton* (Paris thesis, 1920), expanded and tr. as *Milton, Man and Thinker* (1925). R. D. Havens, *The Influence of Milton on English Poetry* (Cambridge, Mass., 1922). H. F. Fletcher, *The Use of the Bible in Milton's Prose* (University of Illinois Studies in Language and Literature, 14, no. 3; 1929); id., *The Intellectual Development of John Milton* (2 vols., Urbana, Ill., 1956–61). E. M. W. Tillyard, *The Miltonic Setting, Past and Present* (1938); id., *Studies in Milton* (1951). A. Sewell, *A Study in Milton's Christian Doctrine* (1939). D. M. Wolfe, *Milton in the Puritan Revolution* (1941). A. Barker, *Milton and the Puritan Dilemma, 1641–1660* (University of Toronto, Department of English, Studies and Texts, 1; 1942). J. H. Sims, *The Bible in Milton's Epics* (Gainesville, Fla., 1962). F. M. Krouse, *Milton's Samson and the Christian Tradition* (Princeton, NJ, 1963). C. A. Patrides, *Milton and the Christian Tradition* (Oxford, 1966). B. K. Lewalski, *Milton's Brief Epic: The Genre, Meaning, and Art of Paradise Regained* (Providence, RI, and London, 1966). [J. E.] C. Hill, *Milton and the English Revolution* (1977). G. Grose, *Milton and the Sense of Tradition* (New Haven, Conn., and London [1988]). J. Bradshaw, *A Concordance to the Poetical Works of John Milton* (1894); I. Sterne and H. H. Kollmeier, *A Concordance to the English Prose of John Milton* (Medieval and Renaissance Texts and Studies, 35; Binghamton, NY, 1985). D. H. Stevens, *Reference Guide to Milton from 1800 to the Present Day* (Chicago, 1930); addenda by H. F. Fletcher (University of Illinois Studies in

Language and Literature, 16, no. 1; 1931); C. Huckaby, *John Milton: A Bibliographical Supplement 1929–1957* (Duquesne Studies. Philological Series, 1; Pittsburgh and Louvain, 1960; rev. to cover period 1929–1968; 1969); P. J. Klemp, *The Essential Milton: An Annotated Bibliography of Major Modern Studies* (Boston [1989]). L. Stephen in *DNB* 38 (1894), pp. 24–41.

Milvian Bridge, Battle of the. The battle on 28 Oct. 312 between the Emps. *Constantine and Maxentius (Emperor in Italy and Africa). Maxentius, who had made a sortie from Rome, met his rival advancing from the north, and after being outmanœuvred was defeated at the 'Saxa Rubra' on the Flaminian Way. On taking flight he was drowned in the Tiber some five miles nearer Rome at the Ponte Milvio (whence the battle is named, somewhat inaccurately). The battle was decisive for the history of Christianity, for it enabled Constantine to establish himself with Licinius as joint Emperor and thus prepared the way for the 'Edict of *Milan'.

N. H. Baynes, *Constantine the Great and the Christian Church* (Raleigh Lecture for 1929; 1930), pp. 65 f. (full and valuable bibl.).

Minims (Ordo Fratrum Minimorum). The order of friars founded by St *Francis of Paola; the traditional date of the foundation is 1435. As their name indicates, they meant to practise humility as their chief virtue, regarding themselves as the least (*minimi*) of all religious. Their first rule, confirmed by *Alexander VI in 1493, was based on that of St *Francis of Assisi, whereas the second one, sanctioned by the same Pope in 1501, was more or less independent. Its chief characteristic was the fourth vow of perpetual abstinence not only from fresh meat and fish, but also from eggs, cheese, butter, and milk. The penitential aspects of the rule were, however, somewhat mitigated in 1973. Members of the order wear a black habit, and the superiors have traditionally been called 'correctors'. The order spread quickly, and by the time of the death of the founder (1507) had over 30 houses in Italy, France, Spain, Germany, and Bohemia. It reached its zenith in the 16th–17th cents., suffered severely in the secularization of the late 18th and 19th cents., but has experienced some revival in the 20th cent., expanding into the United States of America and Brazil. There is also a Second Order of enclosed nuns (of which the community at Andujar in Spain was addressed in a letter of 1489, though the date of the foundation is commonly given as 1495) and a Third Order for people living in world; its rule was approved in 1501 and confirmed in 1506.

G. Moretti, *Acta Capitulorum Generalium Ordinis Minimorum* (2 vols., Rome, 1916). G. M. Roberti, *Disegno storico dell'ordine dei Minimi* (3 vols., 1902–22). A. [M.] Galuzzi, OM, *Origini dell'Ordine dei Minimi* (Corona Lateranesis, 11; 1967). P. J. S. Whitmore, *The Order of Minims in Seventeenth-Century France* (Archives Internationales d'Histoire des Idées, 20; 1967). A. Bellantonio, OM, in *NCE* 9 (1967), pp. 869 f., s.v.; A. M. Galuzzi, OM, in *DIP* 5 (1978), cols. 1356–61, s.v. 'Minimi'; id., ibid., cols. 1346–8, s.v. 'Minime'; id. and R. Darricau in *Dict. Sp.* 10 (1980), cols. 1239–55, s.v. 'Minimes'.

minister (Lat., 'servant'). A person officially charged to perform spiritual functions in the Christian Church. As a general designation for any clergyman, it is used esp. in non-episcopal bodies. In the BCP it usually means the conductor of a service who may or may not be a priest. A minister is also one who assists the higher orders in discharging their functions, and in this sense the *deacon and *subdeacon at *High Mass were known as the 'Sacred Ministers'. In yet another sense, the word is used semi-technically of one who 'administers' the outward and visible signs of a Sacrament. Thus, should a layman baptize in a case of necessity, he would in that case be the 'minister' of the Sacrament.

minor canon. A cleric attached to a cathedral or collegiate church to assist in the rendering of the daily service. He holds a position analogous to that of a *canon, but is not a member of the *chapter. In cathedrals of the Old Foundation the Minor Canons are often known as Vicars Choral.

Minor Orders. The inferior degrees of the ministry, below the three *Major Orders of *bishops, *priests, and *deacons, to which, in the past, the W. Church added *subdeacons. These last were formally placed among the major orders by Pope *Innocent III in 1207; until then they were commonly reckoned as minor orders, as they still are in the E. Church. In the W. until 1972 there were four minor orders, namely *doorkeepers, *lectors, *exorcists, and *acolytes. They are first mentioned in a letter of Pope *Cornelius to Fabian of Antioch in 251. By the *motu proprio* 'Ministeria quaedam' of 1972 the minor orders, henceforth to be called 'ministeria', were reduced to two, lectors and acolytes alone surviving. In the E., since the *Trullan Council of 692, lectors and cantors have survived, whereas the other three—doorkeepers, exorcists, and acolytes—have been merged in the subdiaconate.

The rite by which minor orders are conferred differs essentially from ordination to major orders. In the W. it has remained in essentials as laid down in the '*Statuta Ecclesiae Antiqua' (*c*.450–500). It consists chiefly of a commission to exercise their office and the handing over of the *Instruments. According to present RC usage they are conferred by a bishop (or his delegate), but an abbot who has received episcopal benediction or a major religious superior may confer them on his own subjects. Before 1972 the minor orders had become no more than transitory stages to the priesthood, but the ministry of acolyte and lector may now be conferred on laymen. To these offices have been assigned the former duties of the subdeacon (suppressed in 1972).

F. Wieland, *Die genetische Entwicklung der sog.* Ordines Minores *in den drei ersten Jahhunderten* (*RQ* Suppl. 7; 1897). M. Andrieu, 'Les Ordres mineurs dans l'ancien rite romain', *Rev. S.R.* 5 (1925), pp. 232–74. For post-1972 practice in the RC Church, see P. Jounel in G. A. Martimort (ed.), *L'Église en Prière* (new edn.), 3 (1984), pp. 197–200; Eng. tr. (1988), pp. 181–184.

Minor Prophets, the. In the OT the authors of the 12 shorter Prophetic Books, as contrasted with the three Major Prophets—*Isaiah, *Jeremiah, and *Ezekiel. They are *Hosea, *Joel, *Amos, *Obadiah, *Jonah, *Micah, *Nahum, *Habakkuk, *Zephaniah, *Haggai, *Zechariah, and *Malachi. This, the usual order, is apparently based on chronological considerations. In the Greek Bible they were termed collectively the 'Twelve' (δωδεκαπρόφητον). (*Daniel, although placed in English Bibles between

Ezekiel and Hosea, is assigned in the Hebrew Bible to the *Hagiographa and thus not included among the Prophetic Books at all.)

See bibl. to individual Books.

Minorites. An older name for the *Franciscan 'Friars Minor'. The street in the city of London called the 'Minories' takes its name from a convent of the 'Minoresses' (Minorite nuns).

minster (Lat. *monasterium*, 'monastery'; cf. Ger. *Münster*). A name applied to certain cathedrals and other large churches in England, esp. the cathedrals of *York, *Lincoln, *Ripon, *Southwell, and *Lichfield, and the churches at *Beverley, Wimborne, etc. As a common noun it originally meant any monastic establishment or its church, whether strictly a monastery (e.g. the abbey at *Westminster) or a house or college of secular canons (which was also often called 'monasterium' in the Middle Ages), such as were all those mentioned above. In Anglo-Saxon England 'old minsters' founded by kings and bishops on their estates and staffed by groups of clergy living in community, were the centres of vast parishes, within which new churches, each served by a single priest, were created to serve smaller areas. One such minster is still recalled by Minster Street in Reading; Lambourn, Aylesbury, Bampton, and Sonning were others in the same region.

Minucius Felix (2nd or 3rd cent.), author of the 'Octavius'. Apparently an African, he wrote in Latin an elegant defence of Christianity in the form of a conversation between Octavius, a Christian, and Caecilius, a pagan, who was converted by the argument. The book refutes the common charges against Christians (see PERSECUTIONS, EARLY CHRISTIAN), argues the case for monotheism and providence, and attacks pagan mythology, but says little of specifically Christian doctrines. It is probably a 3rd-cent. work, dependent on *Tertullian's 'Apology' (*c*.197), though some scholars believe it to be Tertullian's source.

The 'Octavius' survives in a poor text in Cod. Par. 1661 (9th cent.), where it appears as Bk. 8 of *Arnobius, *Adversus Nationes*. *Editio princeps* in Works of Arnobius, ed. Rome, 1543. Crit. edns. by M. Pellegrino (Turin, 1950; with introd. and comm.), J. Beaujeu (Collection des Universités de France, 1964), and B. Kytzler (Teub., Leipzig, 1982). J. P. Migne, *PL* 3. 193–652. Eng. trs. by G. H. Rendall (Loeb edn., 1931, with Tertullian, *Apology* and *De Spectaculis*, pp. 303–437) and by G. W. Clarke (ACW 39; New York [1974]). J. P. Waltzing, *Lexicon Minucianum*, with edn. of text (Bibliothèque de la Faculté de Philosophie et Lettres de l'Université de Liège, 3; 1909). P. Monceaux, *Histoire littéraire de l'Afrique chrétienne*, 1 (1901), pp. 463–508. H. J. Baylis, *Minucius Felix and his Place among the Early Fathers of the Latin Church* (1928). C. Becker, *Der 'Octavius' des Minucius Felix: Heidnische Philosophie und frühchristliche Apologetik* (Sb. (Bayr.), Jahrgang 1967, Heft 2). Altaner and Stuiber (1978), pp. 146–8 and 577, with bibl. H. von Geisau in *PW*, Suppl. 11 (1968), cols. 952–1002 and 1365–78, s.v. with bibl.

minuscule script. See CURSIVE SCRIPT.

miracle. Acc. to the traditional view, a miracle is a sensible fact (*opus sensibile*) produced by the special intervention of God for a religious end, transcending the normal order of things usually termed the Law of Nature. The possibility of miracles began to be questioned with the rise of modern science in the 17th and 18th cents., with its ever-growing tendency to regard the world in which we live as a closed system, subject to the laws of nature, and to exclude all interference from a higher power. Neither *pantheism (B. *Spinoza, G. W. F. *Hegel), which identifies God with the Law of Nature, nor *Deism (J. *Toland, M. *Tindal), which separates God from the world, nor 18th-cent. thought as represented by the scepticism of D. *Hume, accorded a place to supernatural intervention. Thus the miracles of Scripture and Church history were normally regarded as facts within the sphere of natural explanation, misrepresented by credulous contemporaries, and the term 'miracle' came to be treated as a cover for human ignorance. Such views were widely held by rationalistic exponents of Christianity in the 19th cent., e.g. E. *Renan, D. F. *Strauss, T. H. *Huxley, and M. *Arnold.

In support of the traditional belief it has been argued that on a genuinely theistic view miracles are not only possible but even probable, for if God is held to be the supreme First Cause responsible for, but not subject to, the Laws of Nature, it would be likely that He should, from time to time, act directly without the intervention of secondary causes. The latest developments in the field of science, which move further and further away from a hard-and-fast determinism, may indicate an approaching reconciliation between the Christian tradition and modern scientific research.

Whereas Protestant orthodoxy normally confines itself to belief in the miracles recorded in Scripture, Catholic orthodoxy claims that miracles have at all times occurred within the pale of the Church. The reputed cures at *Lourdes are among the best known, and acc. to current RC practice a reputation for successfully interceding in requests for graces and favours (*fama signorum*) and proof of one miracle are required for *beatification, and proof of another miracle since beatification is needed for *canonization; the procedure is, however, under review.

F. R. Tennant, *Miracle and its Philosophical Presuppositions: Three Lectures* (1925); I. T. Ramsey, *Miracles: An Exercise in Logical Mapwork* (Inaugural Lecture, Oxford, 1952); J. S. Lawton, *Miracles and Revelation* (1959); C. F. D. Moule (ed.), *Miracles: Cambridge Studies in their Philosophy and History* (1965). E. and M.-L. Keller, *Der Streit um die Wunder* (Gütersloh, 1968; enlarged Eng. tr., *Miracles in Dispute*, 1969); G. Theissen, *Urchristliche Wundergeschichten: Ein Beitrag zur formgeschichtlichen Erforschung der synoptischen Evangelien* (Studien zum Neuen Testament, 8; Gütersloh, 1974; Eng. tr., *The Miracle Stories of the Early Christian Tradition*, Edinburgh, 1983); H. C. Kee, *Miracle in the Early Christian World: A Study in Sociohistorical Method* (New Haven, Conn., and London [1983]); H. Hendrickx, *The Miracle Stories of the Synoptic Gospels* (1987); R. A. Greer, *The Fear of Freedom: A Study of Miracles in the Roman Imperial Church* (University Park, Pa., and London [1989]).

Miracle Plays. See MYSTERY PLAYS.

Mirari Vos. *Gregory XVI's encyclical (15 Aug. 1832) condemning the social and political doctrines of F. R. de *Lamennais and his circle. Without naming Lamennais it censured his writings in defence of social liberty as inciting to sedition and as contrary to the spirit of obedience inculcated by the Gospel, as well as his teaching on the liberty of worship and of the press as opposed to the maxims of the Church. Its reactionary standpoint foreshadowed the *Syllabus Errorum of 1864. After Lamennais's reply in Paroles d'un croyant the Pope reiterated the condemnations in the encyclical 'Singulari Nos' of 25 June 1834.

Text of 'Mirari Vos' is pr. among the Acta Gregorii Papae XVI, ed. A. M. Bernasconius, 1 (Rome, 1901), pp. 169–74; text of 'Singulari Nos', ibid. 3 (Rome, 1902), pp. 356–8; the principal clauses are repr. in Denz.-Bann. (1952 edn.), pp. 447 f. (nos. 1613–16) and pp. 448 f. (no. 1617) respectively, with refs. to other edns. of texts. See also bibl. to LAMENNAIS, F. R. DE.

Mirfield. See COMMUNITY OF THE RESURRECTION.

Mirk, John. See MYRC, JOHN.

Miserere. A common designation of Ps. 51 (Vulg. 50) derived from the initial word of the Latin version, 'Miserere mei, Deus'. The term is sometimes inaccurately applied to the '*misericord'.

misericord (Lat. misericordia, 'mercy'). The projection on the underside of a hinged seat of a choir-stall, designed to provide support to those incapable of standing for long periods during Divine worship. The term is also sometimes used of a room set apart in a monastery for the use of those monks whose health or age requires some relaxation of the observance of the rule.

F. Bond, Wood Carvings in English Churches, 1, 'Misericords' (1910), with bibl. M. D. Anderson, Misericords (King Penguin Books, 72; 1954). G. L. Remnant, A Catalogue of the Misericords in Great Britain, with an essay on their iconography by M. D. Anderson (Oxford, 1969). M. Laird, English Misericords (1986).

Mishnah (Heb., מִשְׁנָה, 'repetition', hence 'instruction'). One of the earliest and most authoritative documents of rabbinic Judaism, it is attributed to Rabbi Judah ha-Nasi (d. c.AD 229). In slightly different recensions, it forms the basis of both the Palestinian and the Babylonian *Talmuds. The Mishnah is a redaction and collection of earlier material; apart from *Pirqe Aboth, it consists almost entirely of *Halachic material; and it is written in the Hebrew characteristic of Jewish scholars of the time. Each of the six divisions—Seeds (laws on agriculture), Festivals, Women (marriage laws), Injuries (civil and criminal law), Holy Things (ritual law), Purifications—is divided into parts ('Tractates'), the parts further subdivided into chapters, and the chapters into paragraphs. Among the Tractates are the well-known 'Yoma' (on the Day of *Atonement) and the 'Pirqe Aboth' (q.v.).

The Mishnah and the Talmud have had an influence on the life of Judaism second only to that of the Scriptures. Its authority rests on the view that the Oral Law was given to Moses on *Sinai at the same time as the Written Law and so is of Divine origin. In a wider sense the word 'Mishnah' was used of the teaching and learning of the tradition and then of the tradition itself, the study of which goes back to at least the 2nd cent. BC. See also TOSEFTA.

Editio princeps of the entire Mishnah pub. at Naples, 1492. There is no crit. edn. of the Heb. text; the edn. with most comprehensive comm. is that pub. by Widow Romm and Brothers, Vilna, 50th edn., 6 vols., 1922. Mod. edn., with Eng. tr., by P. Blackman, 7 vols., London, 1951–6. There are many trs. of the Mishnah into W. languages; good Eng. version by H. Danby, Oxford, 1933,

with introd. and notes; also by J. Neusner (New Haven, Conn., and London [1988]). Concordance to Heb. text by H. J. Kassowski (2 vols., Frankfurt a.M., 1927). C. Albeck, Untersuchungen über die Redaktion der Mischna (Veröffentlichungen der Akademie für die Wissenschaft des Judentums, Talmudische Sektion, 2; 1923). S. Rosenblatt, The Interpretation of the Bible in the Mishnah (Baltimore, 1935). H. Strack, Einleitung in Talmud und Midras (7th edn. by G. Stemberger, 1982), pp. 111–49; Eng. tr. (Edinburgh, 1991), pp. 119–66. The best general study is that by J. N. Epstein (Heb.; 2 vols., Jerusalem, 1948; rev. edn., 1964). J. [W.] Bowker, The Targums and Rabbinic Literature (Cambridge, 1969), pp. 40–61. A. Goldberg in S. Safrai (ed.), The Literature of the Sages, 1 (Compendia Rerum Iudaicarum ad Novum Testamentum, section 2, vol. 3, pt. 1; Assen and Philadelphia, 1987), pp. 211–62. E. E. Urbach in Encyclopaedia Judaica, 12 (Jerusalem, 1972), cols. 93–109, s.v.

Misrule, Lord of (also known as the **Abbot** or **Master of Misrule**). In medieval times, a person selected to preside over the Christmas revels and games. The custom was closely connected with the 'Feast of *Fools' kept at this season, it being the practice to nominate at the celebration a 'precentor of the fools' (praecentor stultorum). In a secularized form the institution survived till the 17th cent. See also BOY BISHOP; ASSES, FEAST OF.

E. K. Chambers, The Medieval Stage (1903), 1, pp. 390–419 ('Masks and Misrule').

Missa Cantata (Lat., 'Sung Mass'). In the W. Church the form of celebrating Mass in which the celebrant and congregation sang the liturgical parts of the rite set to music for *High Mass, but without *deacon and *subdeacon. It was in essence a simplification of High Mass, esp. used in places where there were insufficient ministers for the full ceremonial. Since the Second *Vatican Council the RC Church has encouraged singing at all Masses and the term has been rendered obsolete.

Jungmann (ed. 1958), 1, pp. 273–9; Eng. tr. (1951), 1, pp. 207–12.

Missa Catechumenorum. See CATECHUMENS, MASS OF THE.

Missa Fidelium. See FAITHFUL, MASS OF THE.

Missa Illyrica. A Mass ordo published by M. *Flacius 'Illyricus' at Strasbourg in 1557. Acc. to J. Braun, it was composed at Minden for the use of Bp. Sigebert (c.1030). (F. *Cabrol's contention that it came from the Court of *Charlemagne rests on a confusion between *Alcuin and the Ps.-Alcuin of the 10th cent.) It is characterized by the unusually large number of 'apologiae' (i.e. avowals of personal unworthiness interpolated into the Liturgy by the celebrant) at various points of the rite. Flacius, who argued that the rite was free from the corruptions of medieval Eucharistic doctrine, wrongly dated the Mass at c.700. The stir which its publication created among 16th-cent. theologians and liturgists was hardly justified by its contents.

The text is repr. in E. *Martène, De antiquis Ecclesiae Ritibus (Rouen, 1700), lib. 1, cap. 4, ordo 4 (vol. 1, pp. 481–513); also in J. P. Migne, PL 138. 1305–36. J. Braun, 'Alter und Herkunft der sog. Missa Illyrica', Stimmen aus Maria Laach, 69 (1905, 2), pp. 143–55. F. Cabrol, OSB, 'La Messe de Flacius Illyricus', R. Bén.

22 (1905), pp. 151–64. O. K. Olson, 'Flacius Illyricus als Liturgiker', *Jahrbuch für Liturgie und Hymnologie*, 12 (for 1967; 1968), pp. 45–69. F. Cabrol in *DACL* 5 (pt. 2; 1923), cols. 1625–35, s.v. 'Flacius Illyricus (La Messe latine de)'.

Missal (Lat. *Liber missalis*, also *Missale*), the book usually containing everything to be sung or said at, with ceremonial directions for, the celebration of the *Mass throughout the year. As a liturgical book, the Missal began to make its appearance in the 10th cent. as a combination of the *Antiphonal, the *Gradual, the *Epistolary and *Evangeliary, and the *Ordo with the *Sacramentary. Its development was fostered by the custom of saying private Masses. The 1970 *Missale Romanum* does not, however, contain the biblical readings; these were issued separately in an independent *lectionary in 1969.

A. Ebner, *Quellen und Forschungen zur Geschichte und Kunstgeschichte des* Missale Romanum *im Mittelalter: Iter Italicum* (1896). J. Baudot, OSB, *Le Missel romain: Ses origines, son histoire* (2 vols., 1912). A. *Baumstark, *Missale Romanum* (Eindhoven, 1930). H. Grisar, SJ, *Das Missale im Lichte der römischen Stadtgeschichte* (1925). J. B. Ferreres, *Historia del misal romano* (Barcelona, 1929). S. J. P. van Dijk, OFM, and J. Hazelden Walker, *The Origin of the Modern Roman Liturgy: The Liturgy of the Papal Court and the Franciscan Order in the Thirteenth Century* (1960), esp. pp. 57–66. O. Nussbaum, *Kloster, Priestermönch und Privatmesse: Ihr Verhältnis im Westen, von Anfängen bis zum hohen Mittelalter* (Theophaneia, 14; 1961). W. H. I. Weale, *Bibliographia Liturgica: Catalogus Missalium Ritus Latini . . . Impressorum* (London, 1886; ed. H. Bohatta, 1948). F. *Cabrol, OSB, in *DACL* 11 (pt. 2; 1934), cols. 1431–68 and 1468–94, s.v. 'Missel' and 'Missel romain'; A. P. Frutaz and G. Ronci in *EC* 8 (1952), cols. 831–41, s.v. 'Messale'.

Missale Francorum. An incomplete Sacramentary, formerly thought to be of Gallican *provenance*, but now generally recognized to be closely related to the (Roman) *Gelasian Sacramentary. It contains rites of Ordination, of the blessing of virgins and widows, and of the consecration of altars, and 11 Masses, concluding with the *Canon of the Roman Mass as far as **Nobis quoque peccatoribus*. The MS, which is in *uncials, was written in France *c*.700. In the 13th cent. it was in the possession of the abbey of *St-Denis and is now in the *Vatican Library (Reg. lat. 257).

Text ed. by G. M. *Tommasi (Rome, 1680), J. *Mabillon (Paris, 1685; repr. in J. P. Migne, *PL* 72. 317–40), and L. A. *Muratori (Venice, 1748). Crit. edn. by L. C. Mohlberg, OSB (Rerum Ecclesiasticarum Documenta, Series Maior, Fontes, 2; Rome, 1957).

Missale Gallicanum Vetus. This is the name given to a MS now in the *Vatican Library (Pal. lat. 493). It consists of fragments of two *Gallican *Sacramentaries written in the 8th cent. The first contains a Mass for the feast of St *Germanus, formularies for the consecration of virgins and widows, together with a Mass and homily for use 'in symboli *traditione'. The second contains Masses for Advent, Lent, Easter, and the Rogation days. The parts were bound with other material which came to be preserved at *Lorsch.

The text has been pr. by G. M. *Tommasi (Rome, 1680), J. *Mabillon (Paris, 1685; repr. in J. P. Migne, *PL* 72. 339–82), L. A. *Muratori (Venice, 1748), and J. M. *Neale and G. H. *Forbes (Burntisland, 1855). Crit. edn. by L. C. Mohlberg, OSB

(Rerum Ecclesiasticarum Documenta, Series Maior, Fontes, 3; Rome, 1958).

Missale Gothicum. A *Gallican *Sacramentary, now in the *Vatican (Reg. lat. 317). It contains Masses of the season from Christmas Eve to Whitsunday interspersed with some for saints' days, and followed by Masses for the *Common of Saints, six Sunday Masses, and a fragment of a Mass for use on ferias described as 'romensis'. Some of its formularies are Roman, but the arrangement throughout is acc. to the order of the Gallican Mass. It was written in the scriptorium of *Luxeuil *c*.700. The misleading title, 'Missale Gothicum', which was added to the MS in the 15th cent., wrongly suggested to G. M. *Tommasi, its first editor, that it was from the province of Narbonne when under Visigothic rule. It was prob. drawn up for the Church of Autun.

Earlier edns. by G. M. Tommasi (Rome, 1680), J. *Mabillon (Paris, 1685; repr. in J. P. Migne, *PL* 72. 225–318), L. A. *Muratori (Venice, 1748), A. F. Vezzozi (Rome, 1747), and J. M. *Neale and G. H. *Forbes (Burntisland, 1855). Modern edns., with introd. and notes, by H. M. Bannister, HBS 52 (1917 for 1916) and 54 (1919 for 1917), and L. C. Mohlberg, OSB (Rerum Ecclesiasticarum Documenta, Series Maior, Fontes, 5; Rome, 1961). Facsimile ed. L. C. Mohlberg, OSB, 2 vols. (Tafelband and Textband), Augsburg, 1929.

Missale speciale. A smaller version, containing selections from the complete *missal, drawn up for special needs. The best known is that which came to be called the *Missale Speciale Constantiense* (of Constance), though liturgical evidence now indicates only a general affinity with Upper Rhineland uses. This edition is unsigned and undated, but printed with an imperfect state of the smaller of the two types cast for the 1457 Mainz Psalter, the first printed book with a date. Hence the discoverer of the first known copy of the *Missale speciale*, Otto Hupp, claimed the missal as the earliest book ever printed. But in 1967 Allan Stevenson showed from watermark evidence that batches of the same Basle-made papers used for the *Missale speciale* were being used for other books dating from 1472–4. Stevenson's work demonstrates that the missal was printed during 1473 and suggests Johannes Meister (Hans Koch; d. 1487), a little-known journeyman at Basle, as the actual printer. Only four copies are known, plus some fragments, and a single copy of a shortened version, the *Missale abbreviatum*, which was completed first.

O. Hupp, *Ein Missale Speciale, Vorläufer des Psalteriums von 1457* (1898); id., *Zum Streit um das Missale Speciale Constantiense* (1917). A. [H.] Stevenson, *The Problem of the* Missale Speciale (1967). S. Corsten, 'Das Missale speciale', in H. Widmann (ed.), *Der gegenwärtige Stand der Gutenberg-Forschung* (Bibliothek des Buchwesens, 1; 1972), pp. 185–99.

Missionary Sisters of Our Lady of Africa. See WHITE SISTERS.

missions. Missionary enterprise, i.e. the propagation of the Christian faith, was one of the main tasks of the Christian Church from its beginning. To the Risen Christ Himself was attributed the command to 'make πάντα τὰ ἔθνη (all nations, or all the Gentiles) my disciples' (Mt. 28: 19) and the prediction 'ye shall be witnesses unto me, both in Jerusalem, and in all Judaea, and in Samaria, and unto the ends of the earth' (Acts 1: 8). Apart from the labours of St *Paul and the missionary journeys attributed rightly or wrongly to the Apostles (notably St *Thomas), unknown Christians soon carried the Gospel to the far corners of the Roman world (including Britain) and beyond it. In the early period *Pantaenus (d. c.190) is said to have preached in 'India'; St *Gregory the Illuminator (c.240–332) took Christianity to *Armenia; the (*Arian) *Ulphilas (c.311–83) converted Goths; St *Frumentius (c.300–c.380) preached in *Ethiopia, and missionaries of the *Church of the East went to *Sri Lanka, *Malabar, *Indonesia, and *China (where the Church was esp. active in the 7th and 8th cents.). In the W., St *Patrick's work in *Ireland (5th cent.) was followed by intensive *Celtic missionary enterprise embracing *Scotland (where St *Columba established the monastery of *Iona and further advance was made during the 5th to 7th cent. by St *Ninian, St *Kentigern, and St Maol Rubh), Gaul (where St *Columbanus worked), and England, where St *Aidan's work in the North was supplemented in the South by the Roman mission of St *Augustine. Pope *Gregory I's instruction to him (601) not to destroy pagan shrines but to convert them into Christian churches was important in the development of missionary thought. The evangelization of Britain was so successful that in the 8th cent. British missionaries took a prominent part in the conversion of northern and central Europe. Most notable was the work of St *Willibrord (in Frisia) and St *Boniface (in Thuringia and Hesse). The conversion of Scandinavia (where the task was long and difficult) also owed much to English missionary enterprise. Of the missionaries to *Sweden in the 9th cent. St *Anskar is the most notable. The conquests of *Charlemagne (d. 814) were accompanied by the forcible Baptism of the vanquished to the Christian faith. In Slavonic lands the chief missionaries were St *Cyril and St Methodius (9th cent.), *Bulgaria witnessing a struggle between the rival 'missionary' interests of Rome and Constantinople. This early stage of missionary enterprise culminated in the conversion of the *Poles, the Magyars (esp. through St *Stephen at the end of the 10th cent.), and the *Russians (esp. through St *Vladimir, d. 1015).

The first half of the second millennium witnessed three aspects of missionary work:

(1) Efforts were made to convert the remaining heathen tribes in Europe. The task was gradually completed through the labours of St Adalbert (the martyr-apostle of Prussia), *Vicelin (among the Wends), Meinhard and Albert of Apeldern (in Livonia), the *Teutonic Knights and others.

(2) Missions among the Muslims were initiated. Though St *Francis of Assisi may well claim to have begun this branch of missionary activity, the missions were overshadowed by the *Crusades until the end of the medieval period. The need for more specific missionary work was urged, however, by the Spanish mystic, Ramon *Llull, who emphasized the need to study oriental languages.

(3) Work was carried on further afield among Tartars, Chinese, and, to a lesser extent, Indians (e.g. Bishop Jordanus in the 14th cent.). In 1245 *Innocent IV sent two embassies, whilst a few years later St *Louis IX sent a Franciscan, William of Rubruck, to the Mongols. The Emperor Kublai, whose court the Polo brothers visited at

the end of the 13th cent., apparently asked for more information about Christianity, and, although his request went for the moment unanswered, missionaries very soon penetrated his dominions. The Franciscan, John de Monte Corvino, who worked for over thirty years in China until his death in 1328, made many converts, and even hoped to convert the Emperor himself. His work included a translation of the NT and Pss. The success of such missionary enterprise was impeded by the nationalist and isolationist policy pursued by the Ming dynasty, whilst in the Nearer East, for which *John XXII had appointed an archbishop with his seat at the Ilkhan's capital, Sultaniyah, in 1318, further advance was stayed by the invasions of Timur (1380–1405).

With the Reformation missionary enterprise slackened, particularly in the Reformed Churches which were busily engaged in establishing themselves against the attacks of the *Counter-Reformation, while the seas were chiefly the preserve of RC *Spain and *Portugal. In addition, the call to evangelize the non-Christian world was blunted by the *predestinarianism held in some *Calvinist Churches and the perception in *Lutheran orthodoxy of missionary enterprise as human interference in God's work, as well as by the individualism sponsored by the Reformation. In the RC Church, the Counter-Reformation and colonialism brought about a rebirth of missionary work. New gains were sought to counteract the 'losses' in north-western Europe, and the *Dominicans, *Franciscans, Augustinians, and the newly founded *Capuchins and *Jesuits worked unstintingly in the Americas, in *India, *Japan, China (where the RC Church flourished in the 17th cent.), and in *Africa. In Paraguay the Jesuits not only sought to make converts but experimented with 'reductions', safe havens for the American Indian populations. In 1622 Gregory XV formed the Congregatio de propaganda fide (popularly, the *Propaganda) which struggled to liberate missionary work from Spanish and Portuguese secular interests; its establishment was an indirect result of the protests from the Christian kingdom of the *Congo against colonialism and the slave trade. It subsequently had general supervision of missionary work in the RC Church. Early in the 19th cent. RC foreign missions experienced a powerful revival. It was supported by such societies as the 'Associations for the Propagation of the Faith' (founded at Lyons in 1822) and a number of modern religious orders devoted themselves specifically to missionary work, including the *Marists, the *Holy Ghost Fathers, the 'Congregatio Immaculati Cordis Mariae' or Scheut Fathers (founded in 1862), the *Mill Hill Missionaries, the Society of the *Divine Word, and the *White Fathers. Notable in this period was the prominence given to charitable and educational works, and also the important part taken by women religious, who had hitherto been practically excluded from work abroad. It has been estimated that the number of converts to RCism in mission centres in the 19th cent. was over 8 million. In the early 20th cent. a different approach was foreshadowed by *Benedict XV in his encyclical Maximum illud (1919); this was directed to the firm establishment of the Church locally, with clergy and hierarchy of its own, aiming ultimately at self-sufficiency. The Second *Vatican Council's decree on the missionary activity of the Church ('Ad Gentes', 7 Dec. 1965) not only emphasized the missionary nature of the

Church but also stressed the need to understand peoples and cultures as a precondition for adapting liturgy and theology. These concerns were reinforced by *John Paul II in his encyclical *Redemptoris Missio* (7 Dec. 1990).

In the Reformed Churches there was at first little missionary activity, for the reasons outlined above. Gradually, however, missionary societies were established throughout the Protestant world. In England a Corporation for the Propagation of the Gospel in New England was founded in 1649, but more important was the establishment of the *SPCK (1698) and the *SPG (1701), both largely inspired by Dr Thomas *Bray. None the less, the main success and burden of missionary work rested with the *Moravians, who under the inspiration of Count N. L. *Zinzendorf regarded themselves as a missionary community, and the Danish-Halle missions in India. Through the influence of the *Evangelical Revival, fostered in England by the work of the *Wesleys and G. *Whitefield, a new impetus was given to evangelization on a world-wide scale, which caused K. S. Latourette to speak of the 19th cent. as the 'Great Century' in this respect. (Nevertheless, there were more W. missionaries (esp. from N. America) working in non-Western countries in 1990 than there were in 1890.) The Methodist Missionary Society dates its origin from 1786 and the *Baptist Missionary Society from 1792, the Baptist, W. *Carey, sailing for India in 1793. They were followed by the founding of the London Missionary Society (*LMS, 1795), the Church Missionary Society (*CMS, 1799), the *British and Foreign Bible Society (1804), and the London Society for Promoting Christianity amongst the Jews (1809). In the meantime, similar organizations were springing up in Scotland, America, Germany, France, Scandinavia, and the Netherlands. The phenomenal expansion of the work saw the rise of innumerable Societies, most being specialized in their sphere of activity. Among the larger of these in England were the South American Missionary Society (1844), the Melanesian Mission (1846), and the *Universities' Mission to Central Africa (1859), the last-named being the outcome of the challenge sent out by D. *Livingstone. In 1965 it joined with the SPG to become the *United Society for the Propagation of the Gospel.

The evangelistic missions held by D. L. *Moody in America and England were largely responsible for the rise of a distinctive feature in more modern missionary effort— the interdenominational Missionary Society. Of such Societies the largest was the *China Inland Mission (1865), founded by J. Hudson *Taylor, but many have in the 20th cent. reached large proportions, with work in most parts of the world.

In the 20th cent. the nature of missionary enterprise has changed. Medicine and education have increasingly become the responsibility of the state, and, though expatriate advice and financial assistance are still sought, the social elements in missionary work are largely channelled through such specialist bodies as *Christian Aid. Native ministries have taken over responsibility in most areas and indigenous Churches have been established. At the same time, Christian missionaries from the non-western world are playing an increasingly important role, including attempts to reintroduce the Gospel to W. culture and to overcome the gulf between the established Churches and secularized people. The so-called 'inculturation' of the Gospel (interpreting it in terms of a particular culture) and the tasks of freeing the Church and theology from the restrictions of W. thought patterns are part of the present missionary enterprise. Within the Anglican Communion, the importance of missionary work and the changed nature of it were emphasized at the *Lambeth Conference of 1988, which envisaged the remaining years of the 20th cent. as a 'Decade of Evangelism', esp. in Britain.

A feature of missionary activity in the modern period has been the growth of ecumenism. Though the (*Orthodox) Holy Synod of the Church of Constantinople had in 1919 sought to propagate the idea of a 'league of Churches', missionary co-operation was until recently confined to Protestant denominations, with the Anglican Communion taking a part which usually stopped short of regional unions. A series of conferences, beginning in New York in 1854, culminated in the World Missionary Conference at *Edinburgh in 1910; this aimed at world-evangelism on an ecumenical basis. The International Missionary Council was founded in 1921 to further the same purpose; in 1961 it joined the *World Council of Churches and became its Division of World Mission and Evangelism (now its Mission, Education and Witness unit). Since 1963 this has enjoyed the co-operation of the Orthodox Church, which in the 20th cent. has expanded from Europe and America to parts of Africa and the Far East. A considerable amount of missionary work, however, is carried out by those who see themselves as non-denominational. The RC Church remains formally outside the World Council of Churches' mission structures, but for the most part the old hostilities have disappeared and there is increasing co-operation in many fields, e.g. in the International Association for Mission Studies. Another element in the missionary scene is the activity of the various 'independent' Churches which are often not affiliated to the World Council of Churches. This has to some extent balanced the decline in missionary activity in the mainstream Churches.

K. S. Latourette, *History of the Expansion of Christianity* (7 vols., 1939–45); id., *Christianity in a Revolutionary Age* (5 vols., 1959–63). S. [C.] Neill, *Christian Missions* (Pelican History of the Church, 6; 1964; rev. by [W.] O. Chadwick, 1986). M. [D.] Goodman, *Mission and Conversion: Proselytizing in the Religious History of the Roman Empire* (Oxford, 1994). R. E. Sullivan, 'The Carolingian Missionary and the Pagan', *Speculum*, 28 (1953), pp. 705–40, repr., with other relevant material, in his *Christian Missionary Activity in the Early Middle Ages* (Aldershot [1994]). B. Z. Kedar, *Crusade and Mission: European Approaches toward the Muslims* (Princeton, NJ [1984]). C. H. Robinson, *History of Christian Missions* (1915 [mainly post-Reformation]). G. Warneck, *Geschichte der protestantischen Missionen* (10th edn., 1913; Eng. tr., 7th edn., 1901). S. Bolshakoff, *The Foreign Missions of the Russian Orthodox Church* (1943). S. Delacroix (ed.), *Histoire universelle des missions catholiques* (4 vols., 1956–9). M. [A. C.] Warren, *The Missionary Movement from Britain in Modern History* (1965); id., *Social History and Christian Mission* (1967). T. Yates, *Christian Mission in the Twentieth Century* (Cambridge, 1994).

H. Kraemer, *The Christian Mission in a Non-Christian World* (1938). G. E. Phillips, *The Gospel in the World: A Re-Statement of Missionary Principles* (1939). M. Jarrett-Kerr, CR, *Patterns of Christian Acceptance: Individual Response to Missionary Impact 1550–1950* (1972). A. Camps and others, *Oecumenische Inleiding in de Missiologie* (Kampen, 1988). R. Gray, *Black Christians and White Missionaries* (New Haven, Conn., and London, 1990). C. P. Williams, *The Ideal of the Self-Governing Church: A Study in Victorian Missionary Strategy* (Studies in Christian Mission, 1;

Leiden, 1990). D. J. Bosch, *Transforming Mission: Paradigm Shifts in Theology of Mission* (American Society of Missiology Series, 16; Maryknoll, NY [1991]). J. A. Schere and S. B. Bevans (eds.), *New Directions in Mission and Evangelization: Basic Statements 1974–1991* (ibid. [1992]). S. [C.] Neill and others (eds.), *Concise Dictionary of the Christian World Mission* (1970); H. Rzepkowski, *Lexikon der Mission: Geschichte, Theologie, Ethnologie* (Graz, 1992). Also reports of the International Missionary Conferences at Edinburgh (1910), Jerusalem (1928), and *Tambaram (1938), and histories of individual missionary societies, missionary orders, and individual countries; also THEOLOGY OF RELIGIONS.

Mit brennender Sorge (Ger., 'with burning anxiety'). The German encyclical of *Pius XI ordered to be read from all Roman Catholic pulpits in Germany on *Palm Sunday, 21 Mar. 1937. In it the Pope, whose fear of Communism had induced him to make a Concordat with Hitler in 1933, gave unequivocal expression to his belief that Nazism is fundamentally unchristian. It denounced Nazi breaches of the Concordat and attacked the idea of a German National Church, the abolition of the OT from the schools, and other views typical of the '*German-Christians' which the Nazis were imposing on the Church.

Text in *AAS* 29 (1937), Ger. pp. 145–67; Ital. pp. 168–88. Eng. tr. of main clauses in P. Matheson, *The Third Reich and the Christian Churches* (Edinburgh, 1981), pp. 67–71. H.-A. Raem, *Pius XI und der Nationalsozialismus: Die Enzyklika 'Mit brennender Sorge' vom 14. März 1937* (1979).

Mithraism. Mithras was a god associated with light and the sanctity of oaths in India and Iran; he became the object of a distinctive cult in the Roman Empire prob. *c.*AD 100. The mysteries of Mithras were celebrated by small groups of male initiates in underground temples, lined on either side by benches used for ritual meals, and dominated by a representation of the god slaying the primal bull. Over 100 Mithraic caves, as the temples were called, have been found in the W. Roman Empire, esp. near the frontiers, where they were frequented by soldiers, but also at *Rome (e.g. under the churches of San Clemente and Santa Prisca), Ostia, and elsewhere. There were seven ascending grades of initiation, corresponding to the seven planetary spheres; neophytes passed through tests of endurance and took an oath before admission to each level. Modern knowledge of the significance of the rites is heavily dependent upon the philosopher *Porphyry and on the hostile accounts of Christians. *Tertullian (*de praescriptione haereticorum*, 40) denounced the mysteries as a parody of the Christian sacraments, but generally the Fathers directed less polemic against the private cult of Mithras than against the traditional public cults of the pagan world. Mithraism appears to have died out in the 4th cent.; some Mithraea, e.g. at Rome (*Jerome, *ep.* 107. 2) and three on Hadrian's Wall seem to have been closed by Christian action. Earlier scholarship emphasized the affinities of Mithraism with *Zoroastrianism; some recent work (R. L. Gordon) has presented it as a product of its Roman context.

F. Cumont, *Textes et monuments figurés relatifs aux mystères de Mithra* (2 vols., Brussels, 1896–9); M. J. Vermaseren (ed.), *Corpus Inscriptionum et Monumentorum Religionis Mithriacae* (2 vols., The Hague, 1956–60). F. Cumont, *Les Mystères de Mithra* (Brussels, 1900; 3rd edn., 1913; Eng. tr., 1903); an abridgement of Cumont's earlier work with additional bibl. A. Dieterich, *Eine Mithrasliturgie* (1903; 2nd edn., 1910). R.[-A.] Turcan, *Mithras Platonicus: Recherches sur l'Hellénisation philosophique de Mithra* (Études Préliminaires aux Religions Orientales dans l'Empire Romain, 47; Leiden, 1975); id., *Mithra et le Mithriacisme* (1981); R. Merkelbach, *Mithras* (Königstein i. Ts., 1984). A. D. Nock, 'The Genius of Mithraism', *Journal of Roman Studies*, 27 (1937), pp. 108–13, repr. in Nock's *Essays on Religion and the Ancient World*, ed. Z. Stewart, 1 (Oxford, 1972), pp. 452–8; R. L. Gordon, 'Mithraism and Roman Society', *Religion*, 2 (1972), pp. 92–121. J. P. Gillam, I. MacIvor, and E. Birley, 'The Temple of Mithras at Rudchester', *Archaeologia Aeliana*, 4th ser. 32 (1954), pp. 176–219; M. J. Vermaseren and C. C. van Essen, *The Excavations in the Mithraeum of the Church of Santa Prisca in Rome* (Leiden, 1965). There have also been international conferences on Mithraic Studies: the Proceedings of the first were ed. by J. R. Hinnells (2 vols., Manchester, 1975); a second ed. by J. Duchesne-Guillemin (Acta Iranica, 17; 1978); and of that held in Rome, 1978, ed. U. Bianchi (Études Préliminaires aux Religions Orientales dans l'Empire Romain, 80; 1979). E. Wüst in *PW* 15 (pt. 2; 1932), cols. 2131–55; K. Prümm, SJ, in *Dict. Bibl.*, Suppl. 6 (1960), cols. 136–51, s.v. 'Mystères, VIII. Le Culte de Mithra'.

mitre (Gk. μίτρα, 'turban'). The liturgical head-dress and part of the insignia of a bishop. In the E. Church it takes the form of a crown, decorated with medallions in enamel or embroidery; it is apparently derived from the crown of the Byzantine Emperors, and was not worn by bishops until after the fall of Constantinople (1453). In the Russian Church *archimandrites and certain *archpriests have the privilege of wearing a mitre, but in the Greek Church its use is restricted to bishops.

In the W. Church the mitre is shield-shaped and was originally always of white linen, but later the common material was embroidered satin, which was often jewelled. Two fringed lappets (*infulae* or *fanones*) hang down at the back. The mitre is not found before the 11th cent. and apparently took its origin in the '*camelaucum' of the Pope, an unofficial hat worn chiefly in procession. In certain cases permission to wear it has been granted to prelates other than bishops, notably to many *abbots and formerly to members of certain cathedral chapters, e.g. *Ravenna. It is worn in the W. Church at all solemn functions, but is removed during the prayers (cf. 1 Cor. 11: 4) and the *Canon of the Mass. In modern practice, three types of mitre have been distinguished, namely: (1) the Precious Mitre, adorned with gold and precious stones, worn on feasts and ordinary Sundays; (2) the Golden Mitre, of cloth-of-gold, worn in penitential seasons and when the Bishop has to remain seated during a sacred function; and (3) the Simple Mitre, of plain white silk or linen, worn at funerals, on Good Friday, at the blessing of the candles at *Candlemas, and on certain other occasions. Since 1968, however, only one mitre at any one celebration has been required in the RC Church.

Though the frontispiece of T. *Cranmer's 'Catechism' depicts bishops wearing mitres, this attire was rarely, if ever, used in the C of E from the Reformation to the 19th cent., except at *coronations (down to that of George III). Mitres were, however, regularly borne at the funerals of bishops.

J. Braun, *LG* (1907), pp. 424–98; P. Hofmeister, OSB, *Mitra und Stab der wirklichen Prälaten ohne bischöflichen Charakter* (Kirchenrechtliche Abhandlungen, Heft 104; 1928), *passim*; T. Klauser, *Der Ursprung der bischöflichen Insignien und Ehrenrechte*

(Bonner Akademische Reden, 1 [1949]), pp. 17–22. J. Braun, SJ, in *CE* 10 (1911), pp. 404–6, with illustrations; O. J. Blum in *NCE* 9 (1967), pp. 981 f., s.v. 'Miter', with further refs.

Mixed Chalice. The practice of mixing water with wine for drinking was general in the ancient world. From allusions in the writings of *Justin Martyr, *Irenaeus, *Clement of Alexandria, and *Cyprian, it would appear that the ancient Church continued at the *Eucharist what had probably been the practice of the Lord at the *Last Supper; and, with the exception of the *Armenian, the historic Liturgies all enjoin or presuppose the mixture of water with the wine in the Eucharistic chalice. The First BCP of 1549 directed the continuance of this traditional usage; but the direction disappeared in the Book of 1552 and was not restored in 1662. The usage was not wholly abandoned, however, and its widespread revival during the 19th cent. was the subject of controversy between the adherents of the *Anglo-Catholic Revival and their opponents. The usage was declared to be not contrary to the law of the C of E by Abp. E. W. *Benson's *Lincoln Judgement (1890). See also SIX POINTS.

mixed marriage. A marriage between Christians of different denominations or of a Christian and an unbaptized person. A marriage is so described esp. when one of the parties is a RC. Such marriages, which used to be tolerated only in exceptional cases, still require the express permission of the diocesan bishop or other competent ecclesiastical authority. The *motu proprio* 'Matrimonia Mixta' (31 Mar. 1970) permitted more liberal arrangements than had formerly been allowed. The marriage may now be conducted before a minister of another denomination using the liturgical rite of that denomination. The basic law is contained in *CIC* (1983), canons 1124–9. National conferences of bishops decide on such local variations as are allowed. See also NE TEMERE.

Moabite Stone (*c.*850 BC). An inscription in Moabite (a dialect very closely related to Hebrew) discovered in 1868 by F. Klein at Dîbân, E. of the Dead Sea (the biblical Dibon, Num. 21: 30, etc.; the Moabite capital), and commemorating the successes gained by Mesha, King of Moab, against *Israel. The text, which has several points of contact with the Bible (particularly 2 Kgs. 3: 4–27, which gives an account of the same events from the Hebrew side), indicates a close kinship between the Moabite religion of Chemosh and the contemporary conception of *Yahweh in Israel. The stone was broken up by the local Bedouin during its removal; but a squeeze had already been taken and this, together with many fragments of the stone, is preserved in the Louvre at *Paris.

Crit. edn. of the text by J. C. L. Gibson, *Textbook of Syrian Semitic Inscriptions*, 1 (Oxford, 1971), pp. 71–83, with Eng. tr. and comm. Eng. tr. and comm. also by E. Ullendorff in D. W. Thomas (ed.), *Documents from Old Testament Times* (1958), pp. 195–9, with bibl. [J.] M. Miller, 'The Moabite Stone as a Memorial Stela', *Palestine Exploration Quarterly*, 106 (1974), pp. 9–18.

Moberly, Robert Campbell (1845–1903), *Anglican theologian. He was the son of George Moberly, Bp. of *Salisbury, 1869–85. Educated at New College, Oxford, he was Regius Professor of Pastoral Theology and Canon of Christ Church, Oxford (1892–1903). He belonged to the school of *High Churchmen which produced *Lux Mundi (1889), to which he contributed 'The Incarnation as the Basis of Dogma'. His two principal works were *Ministerial Priesthood* (1897), a theological study of the Christian ministry, with a notable appendix on the validity of *Anglican Ordinations, and *Atonement and Personality* (1901), an original and profound study of the doctrine of the *Atonement.

His son, Sir **Walter Hamilton Moberly** (1881–1974), who held several distinguished academic and civil appointments, contributed the essays on 'The Atonement' and 'God and the Absolute' to *Foundations* (1912).

Appreciations of R. C. Moberly by W. *Sanday in *JTS* 5 (1903), pp. 481–99, and by W. H. Moberly [son], ibid. 6 (1905), pp. 1–19. H. S. *Holland, *Personal Studies* (1905), pp. 272–9. A. Clark in *DNB, 1901–1911*, pp. 624–6.
On W. H. Moberly, P. R. Clifford in *DNB, 1971–1980* (1986), pp. 572 f.

Modalism. In the early Church a form of unorthodox teaching on the Trinity which denied the permanence of the three Persons and maintained that the distinctions in the Godhead were only transitory. Among its leading exponents were *Praxeas, *Noetus, and Sabellius (see SABELLIANISM). It was a form of *Monarchianism (q.v.) and also known as *Patripassianism.

For bibl. see s.v. MONARCHIANISM.

Moderates. In the Church of *Scotland, the party in the ascendant in the second half of the 18th cent. which held a more moderate conception of doctrine and discipline than their opponents (the 'Evangelicals'). Under the leadership of W. *Robertson, they sought to be friends of learning, culture, and order and emphasized morality rather than dogma. They were opposed to the abolition of lay patronage, insisting that presbyteries should induct patrons' presentees acc. to the law of the land, whether the people called them or not. The *Disruption of 1843 (q.v.) under T. *Chalmers was largely inspired by hostility to the principles of the Moderates.

I. D. L. Clark, 'From Protest to Reaction: The Moderate Regime in the Church of Scotland, 1752–1805', in N. T. Phillipson and R. Mitchison (eds.), *Scotland in the Age of Improvement* (Edinburgh, 1970), pp. 200–24. R. B. Sher, *Church and University in the Scottish Enlightenment: The Moderate Literati of Edinburgh* (Princeton, NJ [1985]). See also works cited under SCOTLAND, CHRISTIANITY IN.

Moderator. In *Presbyterian church courts the Moderator is the presbyter appointed *primus inter pares* to constitute the court and to preside over its proceedings. He has only a casting vote. In the lowest court, the *Kirk session, the minister is Moderator *ex officio*. In *presbyteries and synods one of the members, as a rule a minister, is appointed Moderator for a term, generally six months. The Moderator of the *General Assembly is elected for a year. In the Church of Scotland, the Moderator of the General Assembly is given the courtesy title 'Right Reverend' during his period of office and afterwards is styled 'Very Reverend'. Although it is inaccurate to speak of him as the Moderator of the Church, he serves as its representative, wears distinctive dress, and in court precedence in Scotland he comes before the peers.

Modern Church People's Union. An Anglican society, for the advancement of liberal religious thought, esp. in the C of E. Founded in 1898 as the 'Churchmen's Union', from 1928 to 1987 it was called the 'Modern Churchmen's Union'. Among its aims are to uphold the comprehensiveness of the C of E and to maintain the legitimacy of doctrinal re-statement and the adjustment of the forms of worship in acc. with the believed requirements of modern discovery. Its policy has been marked by hostility to *Anglo-Catholic and RC ideals and (esp. latterly) to socialistic programmes of reform in Church or State. Among those who have taken a prominent part in the movement are H. *Rashdall, W. R. *Inge, E. W. Barnes (Bp. of Birmingham, 1924–53), K. *Lake, and W. R. Matthews (Dean of *St Paul's, 1934–67). *The Modern Churchman* (1911–93; *Modern Believing*, 1994 ff.), founded by H. D. A. Major (1871–1961; principal of Ripon Hall, Oxford, 1919–48), serves as its organ.

A. M. G. Stephenson, *The Rise and Decline of English Modernism* (Hulsean Lectures, 1979–80; 1984).

Modern Devotion. See DEVOTIO MODERNA.

Modernism. A movement within the RC Church which aimed at bringing the tradition of Catholic belief into closer relation with the modern outlook in philosophy, the historical and other sciences and social ideas. It arose spontaneously and independently in several different countries in the later years of the 19th cent. In France, where it was most vigorous, it was fostered in its earlier years esp. by a number of professors at the *Institut Catholique at Paris, notably L. *Duchesne (who himself, however, stood apart from the Movement when it had developed) and his pupils. It reached the height of its influence in the first years of the 20th century. It was formally condemned by *Pius X in 1907.

The Modernists, having no common programme, differed widely among themselves. The leading ideas and tendencies to be found in the Movement were:

(1) The whole-hearted adoption of the critical view of the Bible, by this date generally accepted outside the RC Church. The Bible was to be understood as the record of a real unfolding of Divine truth in history. Abandoning artificial attempts at harmonizing inconsistencies, the Modernists recognized that the biblical writers were subject to many of the limitations of other historians. They approached the scriptural record with considerable independence, indeed often with much greater scepticism than the Protestant scholars. In the 1890s they found encouragement in *Leo XIII's two-edged *'Providentissimus Deus' (1893).

(2) A strong inclination to reject the 'intellectualism' of the Scholastic theology and correspondingly to subordinate doctrine to practice. Many of the Modernists accepted a philosophy of 'action' (M. *Blondel) and welcomed the *Pragmatism of W. *James and the Intuitionism of H. *Bergson. They sought the essence of Christianity in life rather than in an intellectual system or creed.

(3) A teleological attitude to history, finding the meaning of the historic process in its issue rather than in its origins. Since the Church's growth took place under the guidance of the Spirit, the essence of the Gospel will lie in its full expansion rather than in its primitive historic kernel. This belief was sometimes reflected in an extreme historical scepticism about Christian origins. Thus, whether or not the historic Jesus founded a Church was a question of small importance and one to which we should never know the answer: the significant fact was that the seed then sown had developed into the worldwide institution for bringing men into touch with supernatural reality and saving their souls; the Mass was to be understood in its developed glory, and this would remain whether or not the historic Christ instituted it.

Among the leaders in the Modernist Movement were, in France, A. F. *Loisy, M. Blondel, E. I. Mignot (1842–1918; Abp. of Albi from 1899), L. *Laberthonnière, and Édouard Le Roy (1870–1954); in Italy, Romolo Murri (1870–1944) and A. Fogazzaro (1842–1911); and in the British Isles, F. *von Hügel and G. *Tyrrell. In some ways von Hügel filled a special position in the Movement as the chief link between the Modernists in the different countries.

The accession of Leo XIII (Pope, 1878–1903) gave those who held liberal views considerable encouragement, for Leo had a real respect for learning and sought to abandon the isolationism of his predecessor. But his tolerance of Modernism prob. rested rather on grounds of expediency than on any personal sympathy with its ideals; and in his later years he became increasingly critical of the Movement. His successor, St Pius X (Pope, 1903–14), wholly distrusted the Movement from the first. Officially described as the 'synthesis of all the heresies', Modernism was finally condemned in 1907 by the decree '*Lamentabili' and the encyclical 'Pascendi'. These decrees were carried into effect by the *motu proprio* 'Sacrorum Antistitum' (1910), imposing an Anti-Modernist oath on all clerics at their ordination and on taking up various offices. While the clergy who had been identified with the Movement were for the most part excommunicated, the laymen, such as von Hügel and Blondel, were generally left untouched.

With regard to the word 'Modernism', it should be noted that it was apparently not applied to the Movement until after the turn of the 20th century. In a wider sense the term 'Modernist' has been used more recently of radical critics of traditional theology in the non-RC Churches, esp. of the thought of those associated with the *Modern Church People's Union (q.v.).

For the official condemnation of Modernism, see bibl. to the decree, LAMENTABILI. Other primary sources for the history of the Movement are the works of A. Loisy (esp. *Mémoires*, 3 vols., 1930–1), G. Tyrrell and F. von Hügel (esp. *Selected Letters*, 1927). R. Marlé, SJ (ed.), *Au cœur de la crise moderniste: Le dossier inédit d'une controverse. Lettres de Maurice Blondel, H. Bremond, Fr. von Hügel, Alfred Loisy, Fernand Mourret, J. Wehrlé ...* (1960). Collection of extracts from the writings of the chief modernists tr. into Eng., with introd., by B. M. G. Reardon, *Roman Catholic Modernists* (1970). The most comprehensive single study is J. Rivière, *Le Modernisme dans l'Église: Étude d'histoire religieuse contemporaine* (1929). É Poulat, *Histoire, dogme et critique dans la crise moderniste* (1962; 2nd edn., 1979); id., *Modernistica: Horizons, physionomies, débats* (1982 [collected papers repr. from various sources]). Good summary also in A. R. Vidler, *The Modernist Movement in the Roman Church* (Cambridge, 1934); id., *A Variety of Catholic Modernists* (Sarum Lectures, 1968–9; ibid., 1970). A. L. Lilley, *Modernism: A Record and a Review* (1908); A. Houtin, *Histoire du modernisme catholique* ('1913' [pub. 1912]); M. D. Petre, *Modernism: Its Failure and its Fruits* (1918). L. da

Veiga Coutinho, *Tradition et histoire dans la controverse moderniste (1898–1910)* (Analecta Gregoriana, 73; 1954). P. Scoppola, *Crisi modernista e rinnovamento cattolico in Italia* [Bologna, 1961], with unpub. 'Petite Consultation sur les difficultés concernant Dieu' by F. von Hügel, pp. 365–92. T. M. Loome, *Liberal Catholicism, Reform Catholicism, Modernism: A Contribution to a New Orientation in Modernist Research* (Tübinger Theologische Studien, 14; 1979). G. Daly, OSA, *Transcendence and Immanence: A Study of Catholic Modernism and Integralism* (Oxford, 1980). B. M. G. Reardon in N. Smart and others (eds.), *Nineteenth Century Religious Thought in the West*, 2 (Cambridge, 1985), pp. 141–77. A. L. Lilley in *HERE* 8 (1915), pp. 763–8, s.v.; J. Rivière in *DTC* 10 (pt. 2; 1935), cols. 2009–47, s.v. 'Modernisme'.

Moffat, Robert (1795–1883), pioneer missionary in *South Africa. Born at Ormiston, in Lothian, he was apprenticed as a gardener. Under *Wesleyan influence he was drawn to missionary work. In 1815 he became engaged to Mary Smith (1795–1870), his employer's daughter, who was to be a constant assistant in his work. Becoming a *Congregationalist he was accepted in 1816 as a candidate by the *London Missionary Society and sent to South Africa. He arrived at Cape Town in 1817 and proceeded NE to Namaqualand, where he stayed over a year. Here he succeeded in converting the Hottentot chief known as Africaner, and by reconciling him to the British Government gained official support. From 1821 to 1830 he worked among the Bechuanas. In 1825 they began to lay out for him a new station at Kuruman, where a native convert organized the erection of a school-house. Moffat then began a translation of the Gospel of Luke into Sechwana and in 1830 the printing started at Cape Town. This was the first of a series of translations which extended to hymns and other literature and which laid the foundations for subsequent missionary enterprise. Meanwhile he had established his first contact with the Matabele tribe (1829–30), to which other visits followed in 1835, 1854, 1857, and 1859–60. In 1839 he returned to England and in 1840 persuaded D. *Livingstone, his future son-in-law, to go out to Africa. In 1843 he returned to S. Africa, where he remained until 1870. In 1857 he completed his translation of the Bible. His publications include *Missionary Labours and Scenes in Southern Africa* (1842), *Rivers of Water in a Dry Place* (1863), and *The Bible translated into Sechwana* (1872).

J. P. R. Wallis (ed.), *The Matabele Journals of Robert Moffat, 1829–60* (Government Archives of Southern Rhodesia, Oppenheimer Series, 1; 2 vols., 1945); I. Schapera (ed.), *Apprenticeship at Kuruman, being the Journals and Letters of Robert and Mary Moffat, 1820–28* (Central African Archives, Oppenheimer Series, 5; 1951). J. S. Moffat (son), *The Lives of Robert and Mary Moffat* (1885). Other Lives by W. Walters (London, 1881), E. W. Smith (ibid., 1925), and [W.] C. Northcott (ibid., 1961), with bibl. R. H. Vetch in *DNB* 38 (1894), pp. 97–101.

Moffatt, James (1870–1944), NT scholar. A native of Glasgow, where he was educated at the University and the Free Church College, he was ordained in 1896, and after some years in the ministry of the Free Church of Scotland taught at Mansfield College, Oxford, from 1911 to 1915 and at Glasgow from 1915 to 1927. From 1927 to 1939 he was professor of Church history in the *Union Theological Seminary, New York. Encyclopaedic and versatile, he became well known as a writer in many fields. His *Introduction to the Literature of the NT* (1911) is a comprehensive survey of contemporary NT scholarship. Of his translation of the Bible, which is written in a colloquial style, the NT appeared in 1913, the OT in 1924, and the whole was revised in 1935. Moffatt also edited a complete commentary on the NT (17 vols., 1928–49), for which his version is taken as the textual basis and to which he himself contributed the volumes on 1 Cor. and the 'General Epistles' (Jas., 1 and 2 Pet., and Jude). Besides many other writings on biblical matters and Church history, he also produced works on general English literature, among them a book on the novels of G. Meredith.

E. F. Scott in *DNB, 1941–1950*, pp. 602 f., s.v.

Mogila, Peter (1596–1646), Orthodox theologian. A Wallachian of noble birth, he studied at the University of Paris, and became abbot of a monastery at Kiev in 1627 and Metropolitan of Kiev in 1632. The most important of his writings was the 'Confession', the first draft of which he prepared at the behest of Abbot Kozlovsky of Kiev with the aid of three bishops in 1638. A comprehensive survey of the faith of the Greek Orthodox Church, it was formally approved by the Synod of *Jassy (1642) and by the four E. Patriarchs (1643), was first published in 1645 as Ὀρθόδοξος ὁμολογία τῆς πίστεως τῆς καθολικῆς καὶ ἀποστολικῆς ἐκκλησίας τῆς ἀνατολικῆς, and again approved by the Synod of *Jerusalem in 1672. It remains one of the primary witnesses to Orthodox doctrine. Mogila also issued in 1645 his very widely circulated 'Catechism'.

The Gk. text of his Confession is pr., with modern Lat. tr., in E. J. Kimmel, *Monumenta Fidei Ecclesiae Orientalis*, 1 (Jena, 1850), pp. 56–324; also by I. N. Karmires, Τὰ δογματικὰ καὶ συμβολικὰ Μνημεῖα τῆς Ὀρθοδόξου Καθολικῆς Ἐκκλησίας, 2 (Athens, 1953), pp. 582–686. Early Lat. tr. in the MS Par. gr. 1265, ed., with notes and introd., by A. Malvy and M. Viller (Orientalia Christiana, 10, fasc. 39; 1927; an important study of Mogila and his Confession). Eng. tr. of Gk. text by Philip Lodvel (orig. pub. 1762), ed. J. J. Overbeck (London, 1898). The classic study on Mogila is the work (in Russian) of S. Golubev (2 vols., Kiev, 1883–98). E. Picot in E. Legrand, *Bibliographie hellénique . . . au XVIIᵉ siècle*, 4 (1896), pp. 104–59. T. Ionesco, *La Vie et l'œuvre de Pierre Movila, métropolite de Kiev* (1944); O. Barlea, *De Confessione Orthodoxa Petri Mohilae* (Frankfurt a.M., 1948). I. Ševčenko, 'The Many Worlds of Peter Mohyla', *Harvard Ukrainian Studies*, 8 (1984), pp. 9–40, with other arts. on him by F. E. Sysyn, pp. 155–87, and M. Cazacu, pp. 188–221. [C. J.] S. Runciman, *The Great Church in Captivity* (Cambridge, 1968), pp. 340–7. G. Podskalsky, *Griechische Theologie in der Zeit der Türkenherrschaft (1453–1821)* (Munich, 1988), pp. 229–36. M. Jugie, AA, in *DTC* 10 (pt. 2; 1929), cols. 2063–81, s.v. 'Moghila', with full bibl.

Mohammedanism. See ISLAM.

Möhler, Johann Adam (1796–1838), RC historian and theologian. He was educated at Ellwangen and the University of Tübingen, and in 1819 ordained priest. In 1828 he became professor of Church history at Tübingen, later (1835) moving to Munich. Shortly before his death he was appointed Dean of Würzburg Cathedral. One of the principal representatives of the Catholic 'Tübingen School', he sought to revive RC theology by emphasizing the nature of the Church as a living community filled with the Holy Spirit, rather than seeing it as an institution. In developing this approach he was influenced by German *Romanticism and the Idealism of F. W. J. von *Schelling and G. W. F. *Hegel. He has been both accused of foreshadowing *Modernism and hailed as a precursor of the theology of the Second *Vatican Council. His works include *Die Einheit in der Kirche oder das Prinzip des Katholizismus* (1825; Fr. tr., 1939), the controversial *Symbolik, oder Darstellung der dogmatischen Gegensätze der Katholiken und Protestanten nach ihren öffentlichen Bekenntnisschriften* (1832; Eng. tr., 1843), a Life of *Athanasius (2 vols., 1827), and, among posthumous writings, a commentary on Romans (1845) and a Church History (3 vols., ed. P. B. *Gams, 1867–70).

Collected essays ed. J. J. I. *Döllinger, 2 vols., Ratisbon, 1839–40. *Die Einheit in der Kirche*, ed., with comm. by J. R. Geiselmann (Cologne and Olten, 1957); *Symbolik*, ed., with comm. by id. (2 vols., ibid., 1960–1). *Nachgelassene Schriften*, from shorthand notes taken by S. Lösch (1881–1966), ed. R. Reinhardt (Konfessionskundliche und Kontroverstheologische Studien, 52–3 [1989–90]). Studies by J. *Friedrich (Munich, 1894; with unpub. docs.), E. Vermeil (Paris, 1913), K. Eschweiler (Braunsberg, 1930). J. R. Geiselmann (Mainz, 1942; 2nd edn., 1966, and Freiburg, 1955), P. W. Scheele (Munich, 1964), H. Savon (Théologiens et Spirituels Contemporains, 1 [1965; Eng. tr., Glen Rock, NJ 1966]), and H. Geisser (Kirche und Konfession, 18 [1971]). P. Chaillet, SJ (ed.), *L'Église est une: Hommage à Möhler* (1939). S. Bolshakoff, *The Doctrine of the Unity of the Church in the Works of Khomyakov and Moehler* (1946), pp. 217–62. H. Wagner, *Die eine Kirche und die vielen Kirchen: Ekklesiologie und Symbolik beim jungen Möhler* (Beiträge zur ökumenischen Theologie, 16; 1977). J. T. Burtchaell, CSC, in N. Smart and others (eds.), *Nineteenth Century Religious Thought in the West*, 2 (Cambridge, 1985), pp. 125–35, with bibl., p. 138 f. J. R. Geiselmann in *L.Th.K.* (2nd edn.), 7 (1962), cols. 521 f.; H. Holstein in *Dict. Sp.* 10 (1980), cols. 1446–8, s.v. with bibl.

Molina, Luis de (1535–1600), Spanish *Jesuit theologian. In 1553 he entered the Society of Jesus, and later taught at Coimbra (1563–7) and Evora (1568–83). He then spent several years at Lisbon writing, and in 1588 published his *Concordia liberi arbitrii cum gratiae donis*. In 1590 he retired to Cuenca, where he remained until, in the year of his death, he was appointed professor of moral theology at Madrid. His major work on political theory, *De Justitia et Jure* (1593–1609), was completed by other Jesuits and partly published after his death.

The term 'Molinism' is used loosely by theologians to describe doctrines of grace of the kind elaborated in de Molina's *Concordia* (1588) and unified (in spite of divergences of detail) by the central tenet that the efficacy of grace has its ultimate foundation, not within the substance of the Divine gift of grace itself (*ab intrinseco*), but in the Divinely foreknown fact of free human co-operation with this gift. It is claimed that human free will is not adequately safeguarded by any other system. The Divine foreknowledge of free human actions is held to imply a knowledge, peculiar to God Himself, of hypothetical future contingents; and it is maintained that this *scientia conditionata* or *media* is therefore fundamental.

The system, which was widely adopted by the Jesuits, was soon attacked by conservative theologians, esp. the *Dominicans, and the ensuing controversies '*De Auxiliis' were the subject of a special Congregation in Rome (1598–1607). The points at issue, however, were left undecided.

F. Stegmüller (ed.), *Geschichte des Molinismus*, 1, Neue Molinaschriften [all pub.] (BGPM 32; 1935). E. Vansteenberghe in *DTC* 10 (pt. 2; 1929), cols. 2094–187, s.v. 'Molinisme', with detailed bibl. On de Molina, J. Rabeneck, SJ, 'De Ludovici de Molina Studiorum Philosophiae Curriculo', *Archivum Historicum Societ-*

atis Iesu, 6 (1937), pp. 291–302; id., 'De Vita et Scriptis Loudovici Molina', ibid. 19 (for 1950; 1951), pp. 75–145; id., 'Antiqua Legenda de Molina narrata examinatur', ibid. 24 (1955), pp. 295–326. Eng. tr. of pt. 4 of the *Concordia* ('*On Divine Foreknowledge*'), with introd. and notes, by A. J. Fredosso (Ithaca, NY, and London, 1988). V. Muñoz, Mercedarian, *Zumel y el molinismo: Informe del P. Francisco Zumel, Mercedario, sobre las doctrinas del P. Luis Molina, S.J., presentado en julio de 1595* (1953). B. Hamilton, *Political Thought in Sixteenth-Century Spain: A Study of the Political Ideas of Vitoria, De Soto, Suárez, and Molina* (Oxford, 1963); F. B. Costello, SJ, *The Political Philosophy of Luis de Molina, S.J. (1535–1600)* (Bibliotheca Instituti Historici S.I., 38; 1974). Sommervogel, 5 (1894), cols. 1167–79; Polgár, 2 (1990), pp. 544–9. J. Pohle in *CE* 10 (1911), pp. 437–41, s.v.; F. Stegmüller in *L.Th.K.* (2nd edn.), 7 (1962), cols. 527–30, s.v. 'Molinismus', and col. 526, s.v. 'Molina', the latter with list of specialized arts.

Molinaeus, Petrus. See DU MOULIN, PIERRE.

Molinos, Miguel de (1628–96), Spanish *Quietist. Born at Muniesa in Aragon, he trained for the priesthood in Valencia and was ordained in 1652; he styled himself doctor, without justification. He was sent to Rome in 1663, and soon became a much-sought-after confessor and spiritual director, and had friends in the *Curia. He founded a branch in Rome of the Valencian *Escuela de Cristo* (confraternity). In 1675 he published both an Italian translation of his *Breve tractado de la comunión frecuente* (the Spanish appeared only in 1677) and the *Guía espiritual que desembaraza al alma y la conduce por el interior camino para alcanzar la perfecta contemplación y la conduce al rico tesoro de la interior paz*. In one he advocated daily communion, and in the other, a didactic, but impersonal work, he recommended the prayer of acquired or active *contemplation. Unlike discursive *meditation, the prayer of quietude requires no help from reason or imagination, but a total submission to the will of God and, once all obstacles have been overcome, temptations can be disregarded (Book I). This imperfect contemplation is open to all under the guidance of an expert spiritual director (Book II). Infused or passive (perfect) contemplation, which is entirely God's gift, is described in a somewhat confused way in Book III. Molinos quotes mystical writers, notably St *Teresa of Ávila, and draws upon the works of St *John of the Cross.

In spite of his reputation and connections Molinos was arrested by the *Holy Office in 1686, tried and condemned on propositions culled from his letters and from witnesses rather than from the *Guide*, and on perhaps doubtful accusations of immorality. He submitted in 1687, but remained in prison until his death.

Many of his followers gave up the usual practice of vocal prayer and the Sacraments and took disregard of temptations to immoral lengths. His teaching became influential in the Quietist movement in France (F. de S. de la M. *Fénelon and Mme *Guyon) and among the *Pietists.

Crit. edn. of the *Guía espiritual* (the 'Guide') by J. I. Tellechea Idígoras (Madrid, 1976), with concordance (ibid., 1991). An Eng. tr. of both his works, made from an Ital. version, was pub., London, 1688; repr. Glasgow, 1885, and (*Guide* only), London, 1928. An extract from the 1688 tr. of the *Guide*, somewhat adapted, was incl. by J. *Wesley in the *Christian Library*, 38 (Bristol, 1754), pp. 247–93. Molinos' letters and papers concerning his trial disappeared from the archives of the Holy Office during the French occupation of Rome in 1810–14; only a summary of the case and unreliable accounts, such as that of Card. C. d'Estrées, remain. The basis of the charges was a set of 263 'Theses Damnandae', pr. in *Analecta Juris Pontificii*, 10 (1869), cols. 574–94; the 68 errors condemned on 28 Aug. 1687 and inserted by Innocent XI on 19 Nov. 1687 in the bull *Coelestis Pastor*, are repr. in Denzinger and Hünermann (37th edn., 1991), pp. 645–56 (nos. 2201–69). Molinos' *Defensa de la Contemplación*, ed. F. Trinidad Solano (Biblioteca de Visionarios Heterdoxos y Marginados [1983]). J. Fernandez Alonso, 'Una Bibliografia inédita de Miguel de Molinos', *Anthologica Annua*, 12 (1964), pp. 293–321 [despite title, an early Life]. G. *Burnet, *Three Letters concerning the Present State of Italy* (1688), pp. 1–95 (no. 1: 'Relating to the Affair of Molinos and the Quietists'). Modern Life by P. Dubon, SJ (hostile; Paris, 1921). J. Ellacura Beascoechea, *Reacción española contra las ideas de Miguel de Molinos (Procesos de la Inquisición y refutación de los teólogos)* (1956). F. Sánchez-Castañer, *Miguel de Molinos en Valencia y Roma (Nuevos Datos Biográficos)* (Valencia, 1965). L. Kolakowski, *Chrétiens sans Église* (Fr. tr. from Polish, 1969), pp. 494–566 *passim*. R. Robres Lluch, 'En torno a Miguel de Molinos y los orígenes de su doctrina. Aspectos de la piedad barroca en Valencia (1578–1691)', *Anthologica Annua*, 18 (1971), pp. 353–465; J. I. Tellechea Idígoras, 'Molinos e el Quietismo Español', in R. García-Villoslada (ed.), *Historia de la Iglesia en España* (1979), pp. 475–521, repr. in id., *Molinosiana: Investigaciones históricas sobre Miguel Molinos* (1987), pp. 17–63. R. A. *Knox, *Enthusiasm* (Oxford, 1950), pp. 295–318. E. Pacho in *Dict. Sp.* 10 (1980), cols. 1486–514, s.v.

Moltmann, Jürgen (b. 1926), German Reformed theologian. A native of Hamburg, he saw his home town destroyed in an air-raid in 1943. Both his Christian faith and the roots of his particular theological perspective date from his experience as a prisoner-of-war; he was captured by the British in 1945 and not repatriated until 1948. On his return to Germany, he studied theology at Göttingen and served a pastorate in Bremen-Wasserhorst. He held chairs in the universities of Wuppertal (1958–63) and Bonn (1963–67), was visiting professor at Duke University, North Carolina (1967–8), and in 1967 was appointed Professor of Systematic Theology at *Tübingen. He is best known for a trilogy of writings comprising complementary perspectives on theology: *Theologie der Hoffnung* (1964; Eng. tr., *Theology of Hope*, 1967); *Der gekreuzigte Gott* (1972; Eng. tr., *The Crucified God*, 1974), and *Kirche in der Kraft des Geistes* (1975; Eng. tr., *The Church in the Power of the Spirit*, 1977). A second series of six major works on *messianic theology is planned: *Trinität und Reich Gottes* (1980; Eng. tr., *The Trinity and the Kingdom of God*, 1981), *God in Creation* (*Gifford Lectures for 1984–5; 1985; translated from *Gott in der Schöpfung*, 1985), *Der Weg Jesu Christi* (1989; Eng. tr., *The Way of Jesus Christ*, 1990), *Der Geist des Lebens* (1991; Eng. tr., *The Spirit of Life*, 1992), and *Das Kommen Gottes: Christliches Eschatologie* (1995; *The Coming of God*, 1996) have appeared to date. His earlier work was characterized by a strong eschatological orientation towards the coming kingdom of God. *Theology of Hope* was influential in rehabilitating and reinvigorating futurist *eschatology. As one of the pioneers of the German political theology of the late 1960s, Moltmann also developed the political implications of Christian hope. *The Crucified God* sets the cross in the context of the theological problem of suffering, presenting it as God's act of loving solidarity with the suffering. In his later work the christological, eschatological, and political perspectives are retained, while Moltmann's understanding of God and the relationship between God and the world is further developed. This is characterized especially by Divine passibility (in contrast with the traditional notion of *impassibility) and social trinitarianism. The three Divine Persons are seen as deeply involved in a history of mutual relationships with the world and the world is seen as moved by God's suffering love towards His eschalotogical glory. Moltmann has also written in collaboration with his wife, the feminist theologian Elisabeth Moltmann-Wendel.

H. Deuser and others (eds.), *Gottes Zukunft, Zukunft der Welt: Festschrift für Jürgen Moltmann zum 60. Geburtstag* (1986). M. D. Meeks, *Origins of the Theology of Hope* (Philadelphia [1974]); R. Gibellini, *La Teologia di Jürgen Moltmann* (Brescia, 1975); R. J. Bauckham, *Moltmann: Messianic Theology in the Making* (Basingstoke, 1987); id., *The Theology of Jürgen Moltmann* (Edinburgh, 1995). D. Ising and others, *Bibliographie Jürgen Moltmann* (Munich, 1987).

Mommsen, Theodor (1817–1903), Roman historian and jurist. The eldest son of a Lutheran pastor in Schleswig, he studied law at Kiel. He was involved in the political upheaval of 1848, but when the liberal cause failed he became Professor Extraordinarius at Leipzig. He was subsequently appointed to professorial chairs at Zurich (1852) and Breslau (1854) and elected to the Berlin Academy (1854). In 1858 he moved to Berlin to edit the *Corpus Inscriptionum Latinarum* (vol. 1, 1863), on which he worked until 1883. In 1861 he became Professor of Ancient History at Berlin. His reputation had been established with the publication of the first three volumes of his *Römische Geschichte* (1854–6; Eng. tr., 1862–6), the first complete survey of Roman Republican history; the fifth volume, on the Roman provinces from Caesar to *Diocletian, followed in 1885 (Eng. tr., 1886). In *Römisches Staatsrecht* (3 vols., 1871–88) Mommsen provided the first systematic treatment of Roman constitutional law. He also wrote the standard text on Roman criminal law, *Römisches Strafrecht* (1899). As Secretary of the Berlin Academy (1874–95), Mommsen sponsored work in prosopography, *archaeology, and *papyrology. He touched on NT studies in his work on Roman Law, and on Church History in his study of the relations between Church and State during the *persecutions; and he produced fine editions of the *Liber Pontificalis* (1898) and the *Variae* of *Cassiodorus (1894).

Gesammelte Schriften (8 vols. only pub., Berlin, 1905–13). E. *Schwartz (ed.), *Mommsen und Wilamowitz, Briefwechsel: 1872–1903* (1935); L. Wickert (ed.), *Theodor Mommsen–Otto Jahn: Briefwechsel, 1842–1868* (Frankfurt [1962]). *Theodor Mommsen als Schriftsteller: Ein Verzeichnis seiner Schriften* von Karl Zangemeister, ed. E. Jacobs (1905). L. Wickert, *Theodor Mommsen: Eine Biographie* (4 vols., Frankfurt [1959–80]). A. Wucher, *Theodor Mommsen: Geschichtschreibung und Politik* (Göttinger Bausteine zur Geschichtswissenschaft, 26 [1956]). A. Heuss, *Theodor Mommsen und das 19. Jahrhundert* (Veröffentlichungen der Schleswig-Holsteinischen Universitätsgesellschaft, NF 19; Kiel, 1956). G. P. Gooch, *History and Historians in the Nineteenth Century* (1913), pp. 454–65; K. Christ, *Von Gibbon zu Rostovtzeff* (Darmstadt, 1972), pp. 84–118. A. Demandt in W. W. Briggs and W. M. Calder (eds.), *Classical Scholarship: A Biographical Encyclopedia* (New York and London, 1990), pp. 285–309, s.v.

Mommsen Catalogue. Also known as the **Cheltenham List.** The early list of biblical Books and of the works of St *Cyprian discovered in 1885 by T. *Mommsen in the *Phillipps MS 12266 at Cheltenham (10th cent.) and first published in *Hermes*, 21 (1886), pp. 142–56. The list dates from the year 359. Notable points about it are the number of the Psalms (151, not 150), the order of the Gospels (Mt., Mk., Jn., Lk.), the omission of Heb., the inclusion of Rev., and an abridged list of the *Catholic Epp. (Jas. and Jude wanting). It is generally agreed that the list is of W. origin. The MS is now in the Biblioteca Nazionale at Rome, Fondo Vittorio Emanuele 1235.

W. *Sanday, 'The Cheltenham List of the Canonical Books of the OT and NT and of the Writings of Cyprian', *Studia Biblica et Ecclesiastica*, 3, § 6 (1891), pp. 217–325.

monachism. See MONASTICISM.

Monarchianism. A theological movement in the 2nd and 3rd cents. In its attempt to safeguard *Monotheism and the Unity ('Monarchy') of the Godhead, the movement became heretical, as it failed to do justice to the independent subsistence of the Son. There were two distinct groups of Monarchian theologians. (1) The '*Adoptionist' or 'Dynamic' Monarchians, who included *Artemon, two persons named *Theodotus, and perhaps also *Paul of Samosata. They maintained that Jesus was God only in the sense that a power or influence from the Father rested upon His human person. (2) The 'Modalist' Monarchians or *Sabellians, of whom the most notable were *Noetus, *Praxeas, and Sabellius. They held that in the Godhead the only differentiation was a mere succession of modes or operations. They were also called '*Patripassians', as it was a corollary of their doctrine that the Father suffered as the Son. The term *monarchia*, in itself susceptible of a perfectly orthodox meaning, was used as a slogan by *Tertullian's opponents (*Adv. Praxean*, 3 and 9) who thus came to be known as 'Monarchians'.

A. *Harnack, *History of Dogma* (Eng. tr.), 3 (1897), ch. 1, pp. 1–118. E. Evans in introd. to Tertullian, *Adversus Praxean* (London, 1948), pp. 6–31. J. N. D. Kelly, *Early Christian Doctrines* (1958; 5th edn., 1977), pp. 115–23. M. Simonetti, 'Sabellio e il Sabellianismo', *Studi storico-religiosi*, 4 (1980), pp. 7–28. A. Harnack in *PRE* (3rd edn.), 13 (1903), pp. 303–36, s.v.; G. Bardy in *DTC* 10 (pt. 2; 1929), cols. 2193–209.

Monarchian Prologues. The short introductory narrative passages prefixed in many MSS of the *Vulgate to each of the four Gospels. They contain brief accounts of the respective evangelists and of their supposed objects in writing the Gospels. Their Latin is very involved and their meaning uncommonly obscure; but it was obviously one of their purposes to inculcate a particular dogmatic position. Until the 20th cent. it was widely held that they were of 2nd–3rd cent. date and came from *Monarchian sources; hence their name. Most recent critics, however, following J. *Chapman, hold that they are *Priscillianist in inspiration and date from the late 4th or early 5th cent. Their undoubtedly close literary relationship with the *Anti-Marcionite Prologues (q.v.) has been variously explained.

Text conveniently pr. by H. *Lietzmann in Kleine Texte, no. 1 (1902), pp. 12–16; also in Regul (see below). P. Corssen, *Monarchianische Prologe zu den vier Evangelien* (TU 15, Heft 1; 1896);

J. Chapman, OSB, *Notes on the Early History of the Vulgate Gospels* (1908), pp. 217–88. J. Regul, *Die antimarcionitischen Evangelienprologe* (Vetus Latina. Ergänzende Schriftenreihe aus der Geschichte der Lateinischen Bibel, 6; 1969), esp. pp. 40–74 (incl. text) and 207–67. H. Chadwick, *Priscillian of Avila* (Oxford, 1976), pp. 102–9.

monastery. The house of a monastic community of *monks or *nuns. The modern custom of using the word to describe all religious houses of men and of calling houses of nuns '*convents' has no authority behind it. The Lat. *monasterium*, with its English form '*minster', was formerly applied vaguely to large churches, whether served by religious or secular priests.

Monastic Breviary. The *Breviary formerly used by monks and nuns following the Rule of St *Benedict. It developed out of the directions given by St Benedict in chs. 8–19 of his rule, and was revised by *Paul V (1608–11) on the lines of the Roman Breviary. Among its distinctive features were a different distribution of the Psalms, the omission of the *Nunc Dimittis at *Compline, and differences in the text of some of the hymns. It has been replaced by the four alternative forms of the *Office provided in the *Thesaurus Liturgiae Monasticae Horarum* (1977).

monasticism. Christian monasticism is motivated by a desire to seek God through a life of *asceticism and *prayer. It is the oldest form of Christian *religious life which exists today. It is generally considered to be fundamentally different from non-Christian monasticism because the Christian monk seeks God through following Christ, and believes himself to have received a personal call from God to lead the monastic life on a permanent basis. The two main forms of the monastic life are the eremitical or *hermit life, and the *cenobitical or common life. Men leading the monastic life are called *monks; women are called *nuns.

Monasticism involves a celibate life and a certain amount of seclusion from the world, normally including the renunciation of private property. Prayer, reading, and work form the framework of the monk's daily life, which is so structured as to facilitate his progress towards his spiritual goal. Unlike some later forms of the religious life, monasticism does not have the pursuit of some specific work of charity as its secondary purpose. The principal duty of the monk is to offer praise to God within the confines of the monastery; in cenobitic monasticism the liturgy, and particularly the Divine *Office, came to play a central part in monastic prayer. Monastic work may take any form. Traditionally it includes agriculture, teaching, art, and all kinds of scholarly research. In the Middle Ages copying MSS was a work often associated with monks. In both E. and W., the practice of appointing monks as bishops has meant that monasticism has had a considerable impact on the life of the Church as a whole, and in the Middle Ages monks and nuns were among the chief teachers of Europe and an influential civilizing force.

The roots of monasticism should probably be seen in the ascetical movements of the early Church. Its development in Egypt in the 4th cent. was of particular importance; St *Antony and St *Pachomius are generally seen as the forerunners of the eremitical and cenobitical life respectively. Syria, Palestine, and Asia Minor also saw a rapid development of monasticism.

In the W., although there were independent ascetical movements, E. monastic tradition became increasingly important as the monastic literature of the E. became known in the 5th cent., through the translations of *Rufinus and St *Jerome, and the writings of John *Cassian and others. Cassian, together with the anonymous *Regula Magistri*, had a strong influence on St *Benedict, who wrote his Rule for cenobitical monasteries in the early 6th cent. (SEE BENEDICT, RULE OF ST). The E. monastic tradition, as interpreted in the W., was also influential in the development of monasticism in *Ireland, with its more vigorous ascetical traditions. Irish monasticism was in turn brought to Europe, and the Rule of St *Columbanus was widely used in the 7th cent.; however by the 9th cent. the Rule of St Benedict had obtained dominance in W. Europe (see BENEDICTINE ORDER). The new forms of religious life which began in the W. in the Middle Ages, the *canons regular and the *mendicant friars, borrowed many of their institutions from monasticism. The 11th to 14th cents. saw the institution of many new monastic orders following the Rule of St Benedict (notably the *Cistercian Order), and also the *Carthusian Order (the only monastic order in the W. which does not follow the Rule of St Benedict) which practises a more eremitical form of life. In the 16th cent. monastic life disappeared in the Reformed Churches, but it continued (often in a flourishing condition) in RC countries until the French Revolution and Napoleonic conquests, when it came close to extinction. A revival took place in the mid-19th cent. in many European countries, and monasticism spread to N. America and *Australia. In the 20th cent. monasticism has begun to take root in Africa, Asia, and S. America.

Monasticism also flourished in the Byzantine empire, esp. in *Constantinople and its environs. Here it enjoyed great influence within society and monks took part in the theological and ecclesiastical controversies of the time. Although monasticism in the E. never divided into different vocations and orders, as it did in the W., there are several forms of the tradition. The main distinction is between the ancient *lavra* or *skete* on the one hand, and monasteries on the other. The former groups together monks living an eremitical life, while monasteries may be either cenobitic (with a strict common life) or *idiorrhythmic, in which the monks are relatively free to choose their own way of life. The doctrine and practice of the Desert Fathers, of St *Basil the Great and St *Theodore of Studios, are of great importance, but there is no single rule in the E. with the same authority as that held by the Rule of St Benedict in the W. Monasticism spread with Christianity to the Slav countries; St Antony of Pechersk (983–1073) founded monasteries in Kiev, and in the 14th cent. the influence of St *Sergius of Radonezh prompted the establishment of a flourishing monastic life round Moscow. The 19th cent. saw a strong revival in Russian monasticism, which continued until 1917. In Orthodox monasticism a special place is held by Mount *Athos in Greece, which is inhabited by monks from all the Orthodox Churches, and which continues today, albeit with diminished numbers.

See also under the various monastic orders mentioned above; also RELIGIOUS ORDERS IN ANGLICANISM.

There is an immense literature; many of the principal items are listed under the separate orders. Useful survey of existing orders and congregations in M. Heimbucher, *Die Orden und Kongregationen der katholischen Kirche* (3rd edn., 2 vols., 1933–4). [M.] D. *Knowles, *From Pachomius to Ignatius: A Study in the Constitutional History of the Religious Orders* (Sarum Lectures, 1964–5; Oxford, 1966); id., *Christian Monasticism* (1969). C. J. Peifer, OSB, *Monastic Spirituality* (New York [1966]). P. Levi, *The Frontiers of Paradise: A Study of Monks and Monasticism* (1987). Good introd. on early monasticism by T. Fry, OSB (ed.), *RB 1980: The Rule of St Benedict* (Collegeville, Minn. [1981]), pp. 3–64. K. Heussi, *Der Ursprung des Mönchtums* (Tübingen, 1936). D. J. Chitty, *The Desert a City: An Introduction to the History of Egyptian and Palestinian Monasticism under the Christian Empire* (Birkbeck Lectures for 1958–9; Oxford, 1966). A. Vööbus, *History of Asceticism in the Syrian Orient* (CSCO 184 and 197; 1958–60). A. J. Festugière, OP (ed.), *Les Moines d'Orient* (4 vols. in 5, 1961–5; primary texts tr. into Fr., with introd.). B. Lohse, *Askese und Mönchtum in der Antike und in der alten Kirche* (Religion und Kultur der alten Mittelmeerwelt in Parallelforschungen, 1; 1969). H. Bacht, *Die Vermächtnis des Ursprungs: Studien zum frühen Mönchtum* (Studien zur Theologie des geistlichen Lebens, 5 and 8; 1972–83). G. M. Colombás, OSB, *El monacato primitivo* (Biblioteca de Autores Cristianos, 2 vols., 1974–5). F. Prinz, *Askese und Kultur: Vor- und frühbenediktinisches Mönchtum an der Wiege Europas* (Munich [1980]). Id., *Frühes Mönchtum im Frankenreich: Kultur und Gesellschaft in Gallien, den Rheinlanden und Bayern am Beispiel der monastischen Entwicklung (4. bis 8. Jahrhundert)* (Munich, 1965; 2nd edn., repr. with additional material, Darmstadt, 1988).

J. Ryan, SJ, *Irish Monasticism: Origins and Early Development* (1931). M. Pacaut, *Les ordres monastiques et religieux au moyen âge* (1970), pp. 3–115 and 147–69. Useful collections of essays ed. K. S. Frank, *Askese und Mönchtum in der alten Kirche* (Wege der Forschungen, 409; 1975); F. Prinz (ed.), *Mönchtum und Gesellschaft im Frühmittelalter* (ibid. 312; 1976). [M.] D. Knowles, *The Monastic Order in England, 943–1216* (Cambridge, 1940; 2nd edn., 1963); id., *The Religious Orders in England* (3 vols., ibid., 1948–59). Id. and R. N. Hadcock, *Medieval Religious Houses, England and Wales* (1953; rev. edn., 1971); D. E. Easson, *Medieval Religious Houses, Scotland* (1957); A. [O.] Gwynn and R. N. Hadcock, *Medieval Religious Houses, Ireland* (1970). On Orthodox monasticism, see also I. Smolitsch, *Russisches Mönchtum: Entstehung, Entwicklung und Wesen 988–1917* (Das östliche Christentum, NF 10–11; 1953). J. M. Hussey, 'Byzantine Monasticism' in id. (ed.), *C.Med.H.* (2nd edn.), 4 (pt. 2; 1967), pp. 161–84, with bibl. pp. 439–43. G. Barone Adesi, *Monachesimo Ortodosso d'Oriente e Diritto Romano nel Tardo Antico* (Università di Roma Pubblicazioni dell'Istituto di Diritto Romano e dei Diritti dell'Oriente Mediterraneo, 65; 1990). G. Constable, *Medieval Monasticism: A Select Bibliography* (Toronto Medieval Bibliographies, 6; 1976). J. Leclercq, OSB, J. Gribomont, OSB, and others in *DIP* 5 (1978), cols. 1672–742, s.v. 'Monachesimo'; A. Solignac, SJ, and others in *Dict. Sp.* 10 (1980), cols. 1524–617, s.v. 'Monachisme', both with bibl. See also works cited under individual orders, esp. the BENEDICTINE ORDER.

Monasticon Anglicanum. The title under which Sir William *Dugdale published a vast collection of monastic charters and other sources relating to the history of English monasteries and collegiate churches in the Middle Ages. It was a co-operative work based in the main on the collections of Roger Dodsworth, and issued in three vols. in 1655, 1661, and 1673 respectively.

The best edn. is that of J. Caley, H. Ellis, and B. Bandinel (6 vols., London, 1817–30; new edn., 8 vols., 1846).

Mone, Franz Joseph (1796–1871), German historian and liturgical scholar. He was a native of Baden and studied at Heidelberg University, where he was professor from 1819 to 1827. From 1827 to 1831 he taught at Louvain, returned to Heidelberg in 1831, and in 1835 was appointed Director of the Baden Archives, a post he held till 1868. He did important research work on Latin medieval literature and early German history. His chief liturgical publication was his *Lateinische und griechische Messen aus dem zweiten bis sechsten Jahrhundert* (1850), which contains the text of eleven (properly, seven) Masses of the pure Gallican type, notable for the absence of all reference to the cycle of liturgical feasts. He also published a collection of medieval hymns, *Lateinische Hymnen des Mittelalters* (1853–5).

The 'Masses of Mone' are repr. in J. P. Migne, *PL* 138. 863–82; crit. edn. by L. C. Mohlberg, OSB, *Missale Gallicanum Vetus* (Rerum Ecclesiasticarum Documenta, Series Maior, Fontes, 3; Rome, 1958), pp. 74–91. A. *Wilmart, OSB, 'L'Âge et l'ordre des messes de Mone', *R. Bén.* 28 (1911), pp. 377–90. L. Eizenhöfer, 'Arator in einer Contestio der Mone-Messen und in einer Mailändischen Praefation', ibid. 63 (1953), pp. 329–33, with further refs.

Monica, St (*c*.331–87), mother of St *Augustine of Hippo (q.v.). (In the oldest MSS the spelling is 'Monnica'.) Presumably a native of Tagaste, she was of Christian upbringing. Her husband, Patricius, a *vir curialis*, was a pagan of apparently dissolute habits and violent temper, whom she eventually won over to the faith; he became a *catechumen when Augustine was about 15. At the age of 40 Monica was left a widow. Of her three children (Augustine, Navigius, Perpetua), Augustine was the eldest; and, in acc. with a common custom of the time, Monica had him enrolled as a catechumen without having him baptized. Apprehensive at her son's waywardness she earnestly prayed for his conversion, and after Augustine had set out for Italy (383) she resolved to follow him. From *Rome she pursued him to Milan, where she came under the influence of St *Ambrose, took a devout part in public worship and witnessed her son's conversion. She and Augustine then retired to Cassiciacum, where she appears as an interlocutor in the dialogues 'De Ordine' and 'De Beata Vita'. Having set out with Augustine on his return to Africa, she died at Ostia on the way.

A cult of St Monica began to develop in the later Middle Ages and in 1430 *Martin V transferred her supposed relics from Ostia to Rome, where they rest in the church of S. Agostino. She has often been chosen as the patron of associations of Christian mothers. Feast day, 27 Aug. (formerly, 4 May, as in the American BCP, 1979).

The main source is St Augustine, *Confessions*, bk. 9. *AASS*, Mai. 1 (1680), pp. 473–92. Modern Lives by L. V. É. Bougaud (Paris, 1865; Eng. trs. by Lady Herbert of Lea, 1894, and by Mrs Edward Hazeland, 1886, repr. Chumleigh, Devon, 1983) and L. Cristiani (Paris, 1959). P. Henry, SJ, *La Vision d'Ostie: Sa place dans la vie et l'œuvre de St Augustin* (1938). A. Mandouze, *Prosopographie Chrétienne du Bas-Empire*, 1: *Prosopographie de l'Afrique Chrétienne (303–533)* (1982), pp. 758–62. H. C. G. *Moule in *DCB* 3 (1882), pp. 932–4, s.v.; H. *Leclercq, OSB, in *DACL* 11 (pt. 2; 1934), cols. 2232–56, s.v.

Monism. The philosophy which seeks to explain all that is in terms of a single reality. The term was first used by C. *Wolff. Typical exponents of different varieties of Monism are the earliest Greek philosophers, e.g. Thales of Miletus (who held that everything was a form of water), B. *Spinoza, and G. W. F. *Hegel. Modern forms of Monism (E. H. *Haeckel) are often esp. concerned to eliminate the dualism of the physical and the psychical by postulating a reality transcending these, of which both are modes. Materialism is another form of Monism. All forms of Monism are in conflict with the Christian belief in a radical distinction between the uncreated God and the created order.

monk (Gk. μοναχός, from μόνος, 'single' or 'one alone'). The original meaning of the word is uncertain. In popular use it is applied to any member of a *religious community of men, living under vows of chastity, poverty, and obedience. Its use is properly confined to *hermits or members of a monastic community, whose principal duty is to offer praise to God within the confines of the *monastery. The term is therefore not properly used of other religious (such as *canons regular, *mendicant friars, *clerks regular). See also MONASTERY, MONASTICISM.

J. Leclercq, OSB, *Études sur le vocabulaire monastique du moyen âge* (Studia Anselmiana, 48; 1961), pp. 7–38; F.-E. Morard, 'Monachos, Moine. Histoire du terme grec jusqu'au 4ᵉ siècle', *Freiburger Zeitschrift für Philosophie und Theologie*, 20 (1973), pp. 332–411; E. A. Judge, 'The Earliest Use of Monachos for "Monk" (P. Coll. Youtie 77) and the Origins of Monasticism', *Jahrbuch für Antike und Christentum*, 20 (1977), pp. 72–89.

Monnica, St. See MONICA, ST.

Monogenes, The (Gk. μονογενής, 'only-begotten'). The hymn beginning Ὁ Μονογενὴς Υἱὸς καὶ Λόγος τοῦ Θεοῦ addressed to the Triumphant Redeemer which forms the conclusion of the second *antiphon in the *Enarxis of the Byzantine Liturgies. It also occurs in the Liturgies of St *James and St *Mark, where it is found at the *Little Entrance, probably its original position. It is traditionally ascribed to the Emp. *Justinian (527–65).

Gk. text in Brightman, *LEW*, pp. 365 f. J. Puyade, OSB, 'Le Tropaire Ὁ Μονογενής', *Revue de l'Orient chrétien*, 17 (1912), pp. 253–67, with Syriac and Gk. text; V. Grumel, AA, 'L'Auteur et la date de composition du tropaire Ὁ Μονογενής', *ÉO* 22 (1923), pp. 398–418. J. Breck, 'The Troparion Monogenes: An Orthodox Symbol of Faith', *St Vladimir's Theological Quarterly*, 26 (1982), pp. 203–28.

monolatry (Gk. μόνος, 'single' and λατρεία, 'worship'). Restriction of worship to one god, when other gods may be held to exist. The term was introduced *c*.1880 by J. *Wellhausen and taken up by W. R. *Smith. It has been held by some OT historians to be a necessary stage in the transition from polytheism to monotheism, and to have marked Israel's religious condition from the time of the *Sinai Covenant (Exod. 24) to that of the prophets.

Monophysitism (Gk. μόνος, 'only one', and φύσις, 'nature'). The doctrine that in the Incarnate Christ there is only one nature, not two. Monophysitism which represents a strict form of *Alexandrian Christology, covers a variety of positions, some capable of orthodox interpretation, others not. The term 'Monophysite' was first used in the aftermath of the Council of *Chalcedon (451) to describe all those who rejected the Council's Definition that the Incarnate Christ is one Person 'in two Natures', and upheld, as their key formula the phrase of St *Cyril of Alexandria, 'one Incarnate Nature of the Word'. It is still sometimes used to refer to the *Oriental Orthodox Churches.

*Eutyches taught a heretical form of Monophysitism, namely that after the Incarnation there was only one nature in Christ, and that nature was not 'consubstantial with us'. The Eutychian position was condemned at the Council of Chalcedon and seems never to have been widely held; it has likewise been explicitly condemned at the outset by most other Monophysites (and all the Oriental Orthodox Churches).

Moderate Monophysitism, on the other hand, teaches that in the Incarnate Christ there was 'one Nature out of two' (i.e. Divine and Human), a phrase which was prob. once in the draft of the Chalcedonian Definition. Owing to their different understandings of the meaning of the term 'nature', the Monophysites rejected the final form of the Definition ('One Person in Two Natures') on the grounds that it obscured the full reality of the Incarnation and appeared to them to verge on *Nestorianism. Among the early leaders of moderate Monophysitism (which remained implacably opposed to the Chalcedonian Definition and to the *Tome of Leo) were *Timothy Aelurus and *Peter the Fuller; the most important theologian was *Severus of Antioch.

Many variant forms of Monophysitism soon developed. An extreme type was that held by the followers of *Julian, Bp. of Halicarnassus ('Julianists'), who taught the incorruptibility and immortality of the Body of the Human Christ from the first moment of the Incarnation; this group was dubbed by their opponents '*Aphthartodocetae', or 'Phantasiastae'. Opposed to them were the followers of Severus, Patr. of Antioch, who held a doctrine much closer to Catholic teaching and whose only divergence from orthodoxy may have been terminological; they in turn were termed by the Julianists 'Corrupticolae'.

During the later 5th and the 6th cents. many attempts were made at reconciling the Monophysites to the Catholics. The Emp. *Zeno (474–91) drew up the *Henoticon (q.v.) to replace the Chalcedonian definition; but his formula was rejected by the Pope as well as by the extremist Egyptian Monophysites and resulted in the *Acacian schism. *Justinian I (527–65) sought to win them over on several occasions, but his attempts failed, perhaps more for political than theological reasons. Some further attempts were made by later emperors, in particular Justin II (565–78) and *Heraclius (610/11–61), but by then positions had hardened and separate hierarchies had emerged to constitute the *Armenian, *Coptic, *Ethiopian, and *Syrian Orthodox Churches; the political separation of Armenia, Syria, and Egypt from the Byzantine Empire, brought about by the Arab invasions of the 7th cent., then removed these Churches from the sphere of Byzantine influence and control. In modern times, however, there have been renewed contacts both between the Oriental Orthodox and the Orthodox Churches and the RC Church, and a large measure of agreement on Christology is reflected in the Common Declarations of Pope *Paul VI and the Coptic Orthodox Pope Shenouda III in 1973 and that of Pope

*John Paul II and the Syrian Orthodox Patriarch Ignatius Zakka II in 1984.

In modern times the subject has attracted much attention. Important new work in A. Grillmeier, SJ, and H. Bacht, SJ (eds.), *Das Konzil von Chalcedon: Geschichte und Gegenwart* (3 vols., 1951–4), notably the essays in vol. 1 by J. Lebon, C. Moeller, and M. Richard; this treatise has full bibl. refs. W. H. C. Frend, *The Rise of the Monophysite Movement* (Cambridge, 1972). The radical differences between the Eutychian and Severian doctrines were first emphasized in J. Lebon, *Le Monophysisme sévérien* (Louvain, 1909). R. Draguet, *Julien d'Halicarnasse et sa controverse avec Sévère d'Antioche sur l'incorruptibilité du corps du Christ* (ibid., 1924). A. A. Luce, *Monophysitism Past and Present: A Study in Christology* (1920). W. A. Wigram, *The Separation of the Monophysites* (1923). R. G. Roberson, CSP, 'The Modern Roman Catholic-Oriental Orthodox Dialogue', *One in Christ*, 21 (1985), pp. 238–54. G. Krüger in *HERE* 8 (1915), pp. 811–17, s.v.; M. Jugie, AA, in *DTC* 10 (pt. 2; 1929), cols. 2216–51, s.v. 'Monophysisme', with bibl.; id. in *EC* 8 (1952), cols. 1299–302, s.v. 'Monofisiti'.

Monotheism. Belief in one personal and transcendent God, as opposed to polytheism on the one hand and *pantheism on the other. Acc. to traditional Christian teaching it was the original religion of man revealed to our first parents, but subsequently lost by most men as a consequence of the Fall. In the 19th cent., under the influence of the newly aroused interest in comparative religion and natural science, this account of the beginnings of Monotheism was largely abandoned in favour of the evolutionary theory. Acc. to this view, defended by E. B. Tylor and many others, the religious beliefs of mankind have progressed from *animism by way of polytheism to Monotheism as the last link in a long chain of development. Today this theory is less widely held. It is pointed out that on the one hand neither *Judaism nor Christianity nor *Islam, the three great monotheistic religions properly so called, have grown up as developments of polytheism but rather in opposition to it, and the same may be said of the Monotheism of Greek philosophy. On the other hand, known polytheistic religions do not show signs of issuing in Monotheism, whereas, acc. to some scholars, there is evidence among primitive peoples for a residue of Monotheism, belief in the 'High God', inherited from a forgotten past. See also HENOTHEISM.

It is sometimes alleged against Christianity that it does not profess pure Monotheism because of its dogma of the Holy *Trinity (q.v.). Christian orthodoxy, however, has consistently denied this charge, maintaining that though there are Three Persons in the One Godhead, yet, as the *Athanasian Creed affirms, there are 'not three Gods, but One God'.

The subject is regularly discussed in works on the philosophy of religion and Christian doctrine. W. Schmidt, *Der Ursprung der Gottesidee* (12 vols., 1912–55). E. Peterson, *Der Monotheismus als politisches Problem: Ein Beitrag zur Geschichte der politischen Theologie im Imperium Romanum* (1935). W. F. Albright, *From the Stone Age to Christianity: Monotheism and the Historical Process* (Baltimore, 1942; 2nd edn., 1946). P. Hartill, *The Unity of God: A Study in Christian Monotheism* (1952). O. Keel (ed.), *Monotheismus im Alten Israel und seiner Umwelt* (Biblische Beiträge, 14; 1980). J. Royce in *HERE* 8 (1915), pp. 817–21, s.v. [philosophical]; P. Palazzini and L. Vannicelli in *EC* 8 (1952), cols. 1311–19, s.v. 'Monoteismo'; W. Holsten and F. Baumgärtel in *RGG* (3rd edn.), 4 (1960), cols. 1109–15, s.v. 'Monotheismus und Polytheismus'. See also bibl. s.v. GOD.

Monothelitism (Gk. μονοθελῆται, from μόνος 'one', and θέλειν, 'to will'; the more correct, but less usual, spelling of the word is 'Monotheletism'). A 7th-cent. heresy confessing only one will in the God-man. The heresy was of political rather than of religious origin, being designed to rally the *Monophysites to their orthodox (*Chalcedonian) fellow-Christians when division endangered the Empire, faced with Persian and later with Islamic invasions. In 624 conferences of the Monophysite leaders with the Emp. *Heraclius resulted in producing a formula seemingly acceptable to both, which asserted two natures in Christ but only one mode of activity (μία ἐνέργεια)—a solution often termed 'monenergism'. It was referred to *Sergius, the Patr. of *Constantinople, who, having found a similar formula in the writings of St *Cyril of Alexandria, approved the Imperial expedient. When, by its means, Cyrus of Alexandria had reconciled a large number of Monophysites to the Church, its success seemed to prove its truth. It was vigorously rejected, however, by *Sophronius of *Jerusalem, whose opposition caused Sergius *c.*634 to write to Pope *Honorius (q.v.). In two unguarded letters the Pope approved the Patriarch's conduct and himself used the unfortunate expression of 'one will' in Christ, which henceforth replaced the 'one energy'. Honorius' term was taken up in the '*Ecthesis' ("Ἔκθεσις), probably drawn up by Sergius and issued by Heraclius in 638. This Ecthesis, the chief document of the Monothelites properly so called, forbids the mention of one or two energies and admits only one will (ἕν θέλημα) in Christ. In two Councils held at Constantinople in 638 and 639 the E. Church accepted the Ecthesis. But the successors of Honorius, Severinus, John IV, and Theodore I all condemned Monothelitism, so that the Emp. Constans II, in order to obtain religious peace, withdrew the Ecthesis in 648, replacing it by another document, the so-called *Typos. In it he rejected both the monothelitic and the dyothelitic formulas and forbade their use. This, however, did not solve the problem, and the Typos was condemned at the *Lateran Council of 649. The controversy was finally settled by the Council of Constantinople in 681, which confirmed the decisions of a synod held at *Rome in 680. The Council condemned the Monothelitic formulas and their adherents, and proclaimed the existence of two wills in Christ, Divine and human, to be the orthodox faith.

Theologically, the issues at stake in the controversy were closely similar to those raised by Monophysitism (q.v.).

The main sources are preserved in the Acta of the 7th-cent. Councils, pr. in the standard collections of J. *Hardouin and J. D. *Mansi; much material also in the writings of St *Maximus the Confessor and St *Anastasius of Sinai (q.v.). Primary docs. are listed, with refs., in *CPG* 4 (1980), pp. 167–72 (nos. 9369–97). L. J. Tixeront, *Histoire des dogmes*, 3 (1912), pp. 160–92. V. Grumel, AA, 'Recherches sur l'histoire du monothélisme', *EO* 27 (1928), pp. 6–16, 257–77; 28 (1929), pp. 19–34, 272–82; and 29 (1930), pp. 16–28. G. Krüger in *HERE* 8 (1915), pp. 821–5, s.v.; M. Jugie, AA, in *DTC* 10 (pt. 2; 1929), cols. 2307–23, s.v. 'Monothélisme'; A. Mayer, OSB, in *EC* 8 (1952), cols. 1319–24, s.v. 'Monotelismo'; F. Winkelmann in *TRE*, 23 (1994), pp. 205–9, s.v. 'Monenergetisch-monotheletischer Streit', with bibl.

Monsignor, usually abbreviated Mgr. In the RC Church, an ecclesiastical title attached to an office or distinction ordinarily bestowed by the Pope. It is also used in some countries, e.g. France (in the form Monseigneur), as a regular style for archbishops and bishops.

monstrance. The vessel, also known as an 'ostensorium', used for exposing relics or, more usually, the Eucharistic Host for veneration. In its modern form it normally consists of a disc-shaped receptacle, framed by gold or silver rays, with a glass window through which the Host may be seen by the people. When the cultus of the Blessed Sacrament began to spread in the later Middle Ages, the Host was at first venerated in a closed *ciborium, but later a transparent cylindrical container became customary, and by the late 15th cent. the monstrance had assumed its present shape.

Braun, *AG* (1932), pp. 348–411, with pls. 62–78. M. Andrieu, 'Aux origines du culte du Saint-Sacrement. Reliquaires et monstrances eucharistiques', *Anal. Boll.* 68 (1950), pp. 397–418. L. Perpeet-Frech, *Die gotischen Monstranzen im Rheinland* (Bonner Beiträge zur Kunstwissenschaft, 7; Düsseldorf, 1964). C. C. Kovacs, 'Monstrances', in *Eucharistic Vessels of the Middle Ages: Exhibition Catalogue, Busch-Reisinger Museum* (Cambridge, Mass., 1975), pp. 97–109.

Montagu, or **Montague, Richard** (1577–1641), successively Bp. of *Chichester and *Norwich. Educated at Eton and King's College, Cambridge, he held two country benefices before he was appointed Dean of *Hereford in 1616, and in the following year Canon of *Windsor. An eloquent but somewhat intemperate champion of the C of E, he claimed 'to stand in the gap against puritanism and popery, the Scylla and Charybdis of Ancient Piety'. His *Appello Caesarem*, a defence against charges of Popery and *Arminianism, was condemned by Parliament (1626), but this did not prevent its bringing Montagu into favour with *Charles I, who appointed him to the see of Chichester in 1628. At both Chichester and Norwich, whither he was translated in 1638, he showed himself a stern opponent of Puritanism, a faithful shepherd of his dioceses, and a follower of Abp. W. *Laud. An erudite if somewhat cumbrous scholar, his best-known books, apart from his controversial writings, are *Eusebii De Demonstratione Evangelica* (1628) and *De Originibus Ecclesiasticis* (1636).

Extracts in P. E. More and F. L. Cross, *Anglicanism* (1935), nos. 3, 137, 160, 237. N. [R. N.] Tyacke, *Anti-Calvinists: The Rise of English Arminianism c.1590–1640* (Oxford, 1987), esp. pp. 125–67. W. H. *Hutton in *DNB* 38 (1894), pp. 266–70.

Montaigne, Michel de (1533–92), French essayist. Of recently ennobled family, he was born at Montaigne, near Bordeaux, the son of Pierre Eyquem, a merchant. He was brought up to speak Latin as his first language, and at the age of 6 was sent to the Collège de Guyenne in Bordeaux, where George Buchanan was one of the masters. Later he studied law, prob. at Toulouse. When he was 21 he became a counsellor in the *Cours des Aides* at Périgueux; from 1557 he served in the *Parlement* of Bordeaux, with which the Périgueux *Cours* had merged. In 1559 and again in 1561 he visited the Court at Paris, partly in connection with the religious strife in Guyenne. He married Françoise de La Chassaigne in 1565. On succeeding to the family estates (1568), he sold his office as counsellor in 1570, and in 1571 he retired to the Chateau de Montaigne, planning for a life of studious leisure. He edited the works of his friend Étienne La Boëtie (1530–63), including the *Discours de la Servitude Volontaire* or *Contr'un* (1576), and defended his memory against charges of sedition. In the 1570s he also wrote most of the *Essais* for the first two books, pub. in 1580. He travelled in Italy in 1580–1, and was twice elected Mayor of Bordeaux (in 1581 and 1583). In 1588 he published a new edition of his *Essais*, adding a third book written after he had ceased to be Mayor in 1585.

For his father, Montaigne translated the *Theologia Naturalis* of *Raymond of Sebonde (pub. 1569), and the longest of his *Essais* is his 'Apologia' for Raymond. In this he demonstrates the fallibility of the human mind and its inability to know anything with certainty; he concludes that judgement must be suspended and adopts the famous motto '*Que sais je?*'. At the same time, scepticism is used to humble man's pride and defend the Faith, revealed exclusively to the RC Church, by destroying all philosophical and religious certainty based on unaided human reason, and by emphasizing each man's need for grace. The design of the *Essais* arose from an acute attack of melancholy. Man is body wedded to soul; he should enjoy his being, joyfully grateful for both bodily necessities and spiritual delights, but only a handful of saints privileged by special grace should practise separating body and soul in ecstasy: for most of humanity this leads to madness. Montaigne lived and died a Catholic. He fought for the Catholics in the Wars of Religion; he nevertheless believed toleration to be unavoidable, though it could weaken Christianity. The main impact of his thought came from his scepticism, which in later generations caused his works to be favoured by free-thinkers who ignored his total submission to the Church. After his death, owing to its excessive trust in reason the preface to the *Théologie Naturelle* was placed on the *Index in 1595, as were the whole of the *Essais* in 1676. Modern editions of the *Essais* are normally based less on the posthumous edition of 1595, prepared by his widow and his admirer or *fille d'alliance*, Marie de Gournay, than on the copy prepared by Montaigne for the printers and covered with numerous additions (known as the *exemplaire de Bordeaux*).

The best edn. of his complete works is that of A. Armaingaud (12 vols., Paris, 1924–41). Works also ed. A. Thibaudet and M. Rat (ibid., 1962). Eng. tr. his works by D. M. Frame (Stanford, Calif. [1957]; London [1958]). Among the many modern edns. of his *Essais*, the standard text is that of F. Strowski and others (5 vols., Bordeaux, 1906–33); convenient edn. by P. Villey (3 vols., Paris, 1922–3; ed. V.-L. Saulnier, ibid., 1965). Eng. trs. by J. Florio (London, 1603) and C. Cotton (3 vols., ibid., 1685–6); both frequently republished. Modern Eng. trs. by E. J. Trechmann (2 vols., London, 1927) and by M. A. Screech (ibid., 1991).

Biog. by D. M. Frame (New York and London, 1965); R. Trinquet, *La Jeunesse de Montaigne* (1972). P. Villey, *Les Sources et l'Évolution des Essais de Montaigne* (2 vols., 1908; 2nd edn., 1933). The many other studies incl. works by H. Friedrich (Bern, 1949; 2nd edn., 1967), D. M. Frame (Englewood Cliffs, NJ, 1969), R. A. Sayce (London, 1972), P. Burke (Oxford, 1981 [brief]), J. Starobinski (Paris, 1982), M. A. Screech (London, 1983), Y. Bellenger (Paris [1987]), and M. Lazard (ibid. [1992]). H. Janssen, CSSR, *Montaigne fidéiste* (Nijmegen and Utrecht, 1930). R. H. Popkin, *The History of Scepticism from Erasmus to Descartes* (Assen, 1960), esp. pp. 44–56. D. L. Schaefer, *The Political Philosophy of Montaigne* (Ithaca, NY, and London, 1990). P. Bonnet, *Bibliographie méthodique et analytique des ouvrages et documents relatifs à Montaigne* [to 1975] (1983); H. P. Clive, *Bibliographie annotée des*

ouvrages relatifs à Montaigne publiés entre 1976 et 1985 (Études montaignistes, 4; 1990); R. A. Sayce and D. Maskell, *A Descriptive Bibliography of Montaigne's Essais 1580–1700* (1983).

Montalembert, Charles René Forbes (1810–70), French RC historian. He was the son of a French *émigré* and born in London. An ardent religious *liberal who desired to see the Church freed of State control, he soon associated himself with the movement sponsored by F. R. de *Lamennais and H.-D. *Lacordaire, and enthusiastically supported Lamennais's newspaper, *L'Avenir*. A journey to Rome to win Papal support, however, proved fruitless, and when in 1832 *Gregory XVI condemned liberalism in his '*Mirari Vos', Montalembert submitted and ceased to propagate his views, though he did not altogether abandon them. From 1848 to 1857 he sat in the French Chamber of Deputies, where he became a vehement champion of Catholic principles. His revived advocacy of liberal views, notably in *Des intérêts catholiques au XIXᵉ siècle* (1852), in *Le Correspondant*, and at the Congress of Malines in 1863, made him an object of dislike to more reactionary Catholics. His historical writings were composed under the influence of the *Romantic Movement. Their style was polished and eloquent, and their purpose edifying, but as works of history they were uncritical. The best known is his *Moines d'occident* (5 vols., 1860–7; Eng. tr., 1896), which developed out of a study of the life of St *Bernard of Clairvaux.

Collected Works in 9 vols. (Paris, 1860–8). His addresses ed. by C. de Meaux (son-in-law; 3 vols., ibid., 2nd edn., 1892). *Lettres à un ami de collège* [L. Cornudet] (ibid., 1873); much enlarged edn., 1905. Letters to F. R. de Lamennais, ed. by G. Goyau and P. de Lallemand (ibid. [1932]); Correspondence with C. Cantù, ed. F. Kaucisvili Melzi d'Eril (Milan, 1969); *Catholicisme et Liberté: Correspondance inédite avec le P. Lacordaire, Mgr. de Mérode et A. de Falloux*, ed. P. Baron, OP, and others (1970); *Lacordaire–Montalembert: Correspondance inédite 1830–1861*, ed. L. Le Guillou and A. Duval [OP] (1989). E. Lecanuet, *Montalembert d'après son journal et sa correspondance* (3 vols., 1895–1902). Shorter Lives by Mrs M. O. Oliphant (2 vols., London, 1873), V. Bucaille (Paris, 1927), and A. Trannoy (ibid., 1947). P. de Lallemand, *Montalembert et ses amis dans le romantisme (1830–40)* (1927); id., *Montalembert et ses relations littéraires avec l'étranger jusqu'en 1840* (1927); A. Trannoy, *Le Romantisme politique de Montalembert avant 1843* (1942). A. Latreille, 'Les Dernières Années de Montalembert', *Revue d'Histoire de l'Église de France*, 54 (1968), pp. 281–314; series of arts. by B. Aspinwall, V. Conzemius, and others, ibid. 56 (1970), pp. 1–137. G. Goyau in *CE* 10 (1911), pp. 513–16; Y. Marchasson in *Dict. Sp.* 10 (1980), cols. 1662–6, both s.v.

Montanism. An apocalyptic movement in the latter half of the 2nd cent. which is to be traced back to one Montanus in Phrygia. It lived in expectation of the speedy outpouring of the Holy Spirit (the Paraclete) on the Church, of which it saw the first manifestation in its own prophets and prophetesses. Montanus himself, who began to prophesy either in 172 (*Eusebius' *Chronicle*) or 156–7 (*Epiphanius, *Haer.* 48. 1), proclaimed that the Heavenly Jerusalem would soon descend near Pepuza in Phrygia. Closely associated with him were two women, Prisca and Maximilla.

The movement soon developed ascetic traits which became esp. prominent in an offshoot of Montanism in Roman Africa. Here, where *c.*206 it won the allegiance of

*Tertullian (q.v.), it disallowed second marriages, condemned the existing regulations on fasting as too lax, imposing a discipline of its own, and forbade flight in persecution. Tertullian also condemned the current penitential discipline for its leniency and termed the Catholics 'Psychics' (*psychici*), or 'animal men', as opposed to their own members, who were the 'Pneumatics' (*pneumatici*) or 'Spirit-filled'.

Certain elements in the movement (enthusiasm, ecstatic prophecy) had their parallels in primitive Christianity, and in modern times it has sometimes been regarded (e.g. by A. *Harnack) as an attempt to revert to primitive fervour in the face of a growing institutionalism and secularization of the Church. More probably the movement is to be understood as an early instance of the apocalyptic groups which have constantly sprung up in Christian history. It was attacked by a large number of orthodox writings most of which have unhappily been lost, among them those of Claudius *Apollinarius, *Miltiades, and *Rhodo. It was formally condemned by Asiatic Synods before AD 200 and also, after some hesitation, by Pope *Zephyrinus.

The chief sources are to be found in P. de Labriolle, *Les Sources de l'histoire du montanisme* (1913); more selective collection ed. R. E. Heine, *The Montanist Oracles and Testimonies* (North American Patristic Society Patristic Monograph Series, 14; Macon, Ga., 1989). Among patristic writers they incl. *Hippolytus' *Syntagma* (lost in its orig. form; but in substance in later writers), Eusebius, *HE* 5. 16 f., and Epiphanius, *Haer.* 48; and the later writings of Tertullian. P. de Labriolle, *La Crise montaniste* (1913), with full bibl.; W. Schepelern, *Montanismen og de Phrygiske Kulter* (1920; Ger. tr., Tübingen, 1929). B. Poschmann, *Paenitentia Secunda: Die kirchliche Busse im ältesten Christentum bis Cyprian und Origenes* (1940), pp. 261–348. K. Aland, *Kirchengeschichtliche Entwürfe* (Gütersloh, 1960), esp. pp. 105–48 ('Bemerkungen zum Montanismus und zur frühchristlichen Eschatologie'); J. M. Ford, 'Was Montanism a Jewish-Christian heresy?', *JEH* 17 (1966), pp. 145–58; T. D. Barnes, 'The Chronology of Montanism', *JTS* NS 21 (1970), pp. 403–8; F. Blanchetière, 'Le Montanisme originel', *Rev. S.R.* 52 (1978), pp. 118–34, and 53 (1979), pp. 1–22. H. Kraft, 'Die Lyoner Martyrer und der Montanismus', in E. Dassmann and K. S. Frank (eds.), *Pietas: Festschrift für Bernhard Kötting* (Jahrbuch für Antike und Christentum, Ergänzungsband, 8; 1980), pp. 250–66. A. Strobel, *Das heilige Land der Montanisten: Eine religionsgeographische Untersuchung* (Religionsgeschichtliche Versuche und Vorarbeiten, 37; 1980). C. Trevett, *Montanism: Gender, Authority and the New Prophecy* (Cambridge, 1996). G. *Salmon in *DCB* 3 (1882), pp. 935–45, s.v. 'Montanus'; G. Bardy in *DTC* 10 (pt. 2; 1929), cols. 2355–70, s.v.; H. Bacht, SJ, in *Dict. Sp.* 10 (1980), cols. 1670–6, s.v. See also works cited under TERTULLIAN.

Montboissier, Peter of. See PETER THE VENERABLE.

Monte Cassino. The principal monastery of the *Benedictine Order, founded by St *Benedict *c.*529 when he migrated from *Subiaco; it lies midway between Rome and Naples. He and his sister St *Scholastica were buried there. The buildings were destroyed by the Lombards *c.*585, and the monks fled to the *Lateran basilica. The monastery was rebuilt by Abbot Petronax *c.*717, but was destroyed yet again by the Saracens in 884 and by earthquake in 1347. The house reached the peak of its prosperity under Desiderius (Abbot, 1058–87, later Pope Victor III) and Oderisius I (1087–1105), when the church was consecrated (1071) and the fame of the scriptorium established. With varying prosperity it has remained the chief

house of the order. In 1866 it was declared a national monument by the Italian government, with the monks as guardians. The buildings were almost totally destroyed in 1944, but have been restored. The rebuilt abbey was reconsecrated by *Paul VI on 24 October 1964. See also CASSINESE CONGREGATION.

Chronica Monsterii Casinensis, ed. H. Hoffmann (*MGH*, Scriptores, 34; 1980). E. Gattula, OSB, *Historia Abbatiae Cassinensis* (2 pts., Venice, 1733); id., *Ad Historiam Abbatiae Cassinensis Accessiones* (2 pts., ibid., 1734), with orig. sources. L. Tosti, OSB, *Storia della badia di Monte-Cassino* (3 vols., Naples, 1842–3). Series of specialized studies in *Miscellanea Cassinese, ossia Nuovi contributi alla storia, alle scienze e arti religiose* (Monte Cassino, 1897 ff.). *Casinensia: Miscellanea di studi cassinesi pubblicati in occasione del XIV centenario della fondazione della badia di Monte-Cassino* (ibid., 1929). T. Leccisotti, OSB, *Montecassino: La vita. L'irradiazione* (Florence, 1946; 10th edn., 1983; Eng. tr., Monte Cassino, 1987), and other works of this author. H. Bloch, *Monte Cassino in the Middle Ages* (3 vols., Rome, 1986). Further bibl. in L. H. Cottineau, OSB, *Répertoire topo-bibliographique des abbayes et prieurés* (Mâcon, 1935), cols. 1913–16. H. *Leclercq, OSB, in *DACL* 11 (pt. 2; 1934), cols. 2451–84, s.v. 'Mont-Cassin'; H. Bloch in *NCE* 9 (1967), pp. 1080–2, s.v.; A. Pantoni, OSB, in *DIP* 6 (1980), cols. 80–9, s.v.

Montefiore, Claude Joseph Goldsmid (1858–1938), biblical student and prominent advocate of 'Liberal Judaism'. A Jew by religion, he was educated at Balliol College, Oxford, under B. *Jowett, with T. H. *Green as his tutor, who imbued him with an idealist outlook on life. His writings, based on a wide, rather than deep, learning, include a set of *Hibbert Lectures on *The Origin and Development of the Religion of the Ancient Hebrews* (1892); *The Synoptic Gospels* (2 vols., 1909; 2nd edn., much rev., 1927); *Liberal Judaism and Hellenism* (1918); and *Rabbinic Literature and Gospel Teachings* (1930). In his insistence on the importance of the Rabbinic writings for the understanding of the NT, he was at one with his friend Israel *Abrahams, with whom he worked in close conjunction.

Extracts of his writings, with introd., ed. E. Kessler, *An English Jew* (1989). Appreciation by F. C. Burkitt in *Speculum Religionis: Being Essays . . . presented . . . to . . . Montefiore* (Oxford, 1929), pp. 1–17, incl. list of his works. L. Cohen, *Some Recollections of Claude Goldsmid Montefiore* (1940), with bibl. M. G. Bowler, *Claude Montefiore and Christianity* (Brown Judaic Studies, 157; Atlanta, Ga. [1988]). H. Danby in *DNB, 1931–1940*, pp. 624 f.

Montes Pietatis. In the later Middle Ages, charitable institutions for lending money in cases of necessity. The first was started by Michael Northburgh (d. 1361), Bp. of London, but failed because it charged no interest. From the middle of the 15th cent., Italian *Franciscans established many successful *montes* which charged a low contribution towards expenses. They were opposed esp. by the *Dominicans on the ground that they offended against the canonical prohibition of *usury, but were approved by *Leo X at the Fifth *Lateran Council in 1515. They then spread to the Low Countries, France, Spain, and Germany, but failed in England. In modern times they have been superseded in some countries by secular institutions with similar objects.

H. Holzapfel, OFM, *Die Anfänge der Montes Pietatis (1462–1515)* (Veröffentlichungen aus dem kirchenhistorischen Seminar München, 11; 1903). V. Meneghin, *Bernardino da Feltre e i Monti di Pietà* (Vicenza, 1974), with refs. and docs. A. McPadden in

NCE 9 (1967), pp. 1086 f., s.v.; J. Heers in *Lexikon des Mittelalters*, 6 (1993), cols. 794 f., s.v. 'Montes', with bibl.

Montesquieu, Charles Louis Joseph de Secondat, Baron de la Brède et de (1689–1755), French historian and philosopher. He was educated by the *Oratorians at Juilly and studied law at Bordeaux, where he became counsellor of the *Parlement* of Guyenne in 1714, but soon embraced a literary career. In 1721 he published anonymously his *Lettres persanes*, a witty satire on European society which had a resounding success. The *Lettres* criticized Louis XIV's government and the Catholic Church, ridiculing esp. the dogmas of the *Trinity and of *transubstantiation, and accusing Christianity of the worst crimes. In 1728 he was elected a member of the French Academy, and, after travelling for several years in Europe and England, he wrote his *Considérations sur les causes de la grandeur et de la décadence des Romains* (also anonymous; 1734). Its thesis was that the history of empires was governed by moral and physical causes, and, apart from the writings of G. B. *Vico, it may be considered the first important work on the philosophy of history. In 1748 Montesquieu published at Geneva his most important work, the *Esprit des lois* (2 vols.), strongly influenced by J. *Locke and Viscount Bolingbroke, and defending the English principle of the division of powers as the safeguard of liberty and the way to an ideal form of government. In *L'Esprit des lois* he takes a more positive view of religion than in *Lettres persanes*, regarding Christianity as a powerful moral force in society which, though directly occupied only with the next life, makes for order and happiness in this; but he strongly attacked clerical celibacy and doctrinal intolerance, and the book was placed on the *Index in 1752. Montesquieu's ideas were later taken up and developed by A. de Tocqueville (1805–59).

The classic edn. of his works is that by E. Laboulaye (7 vols., Paris, 1875–9); more recent edns. by R. Callois (2 vols., ibid., 1949–51) and by A. Masson and others (3 vols., ibid., 1950–5). Eng. tr. of works so far pub., 4 vols., London, 1777. The best biog. is that of R. Shackleton (Oxford, 1961). Other studies incl. those by J. Dedieu ('Les Grands Philosophes', 1913; also shorter study, 'Le Livre de l'étudiant', 12 [1941]), G. Lanson ('Réformateurs sociaux', 1932), and P. Gascar (Paris [1989]). Introd. by J. N. Shklar (Past Masters, Oxford, 1987). E. Carcassonne, *Montesquieu et le problème de la Constitution Française au XVIII* siècle* [1927]. F. T. H. Fletcher, *Montesquieu and English Politics, 1750–1800* (1939). E. Vidal, *Saggio sul Montesquieu* (Pubblicazioni dell'Istituto di Filosofia del Diritto dell'Università di Roma, 17; 1950); G. C. Vlachos, *La Politique de Montesquieu* (1974); C. Dédéyan, *Montesquieu ou les lumières d'Albion* (1990). C. Rosso, *Montesquieu moralista* (Pisa, 1965). P. Kra, *Religion in Montesquieu's Lettres persanes* (Studies on Voltaire and the Eighteenth Century, 72; Geneva, 1970). D. C. Cabeen, *Montesquieu: A Bibliography* (New York, 1947), with suppl. in *Revue Internationale de Philosophie*, 9 (1955), pp. 409–34; C. Rosso, 'Montesquieu présent: études et travaux depuis 1960', *Le XVIII* Siècle*, 8 (1976), pp. 373–404. C. Constantin in *DTC* 10 (pt. 2; 1929), cols. 2377–88, s.v.; R. Shackleton (rev.) in *EB* (1985 edn.), micropaedia, 8, pp. 283–5, s.v.

Montfaucon, Bernard de (1655–1741), one of the foremost *Maurist patristic scholars. After embarking on a military career he joined the Maurist Benedictine congregation in 1676. He produced splendid editions of St *Athanasius (3 vols., 1698), of the '*Hexapla' of *Origen

(2 vols., 1713), and of St *Chrysostom (13 vols., 1718–38), this last using MSS which he found during his searches in Italy in 1698–1701. In his *Collectio nova patrum et scriptorum graecorum* (2 vols., 1706), he printed for the first time many previously unedited texts. His *Palaeographia graeca* (1708; repr. Farnborough, 1970) virtually created the science of Greek palaeography. His other writings include his survey of MSS in his *Bibliotheca Bibliothecarum* (2 vols., 1739), the work by which he is prob. best known, treatises incorporating masses of material on French historical antiquities, and a defence (1699) of the Benedictine edition of the works of St *Augustine against continued *Jesuit attacks.

E. de Broglie, *La Société de l'abbaye de Saint-Germain-des-Prés au XVIII* siècle: Bernard de Montfaucon et les Bernardins* (2 vols., 1891). M. Valéry, *Correspondance inédite de Mabillon et de Montfaucon avec l'Italie* (3 vols., 1846). List of Montfaucon's works with short Life in [R. P. Tassin,] *Histoire littéraire de la congrégation de Saint-Maur*, 2 (Brussels, 1770), pp. 585–616. H. *Leclercq, OSB, in *DACL* 11 (pt. 2; 1934), cols. 2608–72; E. Peterson in *EC* 8 (1952), cols. 1374–6, for further bibl.

Month's Mind. The *Requiem Mass until 1970 celebrated on the 30th day after death or burial. The custom of observing this day as the conclusion of a thirty-days mourning was known already to the Jews (cf. Num. 20: 29; Deut. 34: 8) and the Greeks. For the W. Church it is attested in the 'Dialogues' of St *Gregory the Great (4. 55) and the *Gelasian Sacramentary, which has a special Mass for it.

Montini, Giovanni Battista. See PAUL VI.

Mont-St-Michel. The abbey and fortress of this name lie on a rocky island a mile or so off the north coast of France, near St-Malo. An oratory is said to have been established there by St Aubert, Bp. of Avranches (early 8th cent.), in obedience to the commands of an apparition of St *Michael. In 966 a *Benedictine monastery was founded on the mount, to which a fortress was added later; and the sanctuary gradually became the most famous of all shrines dedicated to St Michael. The monastery is now secularized, but the buildings remain, surmounted by a Gothic spire on which is a statue of St Michael. St Michael's Mount, Cornwall, is an English counterpart on a smaller scale and of less fame.

Millénaire monastique du Mont-Saint-Michel, ed. J. Laporte, OSB, and others (6 vols., 1967 ff.), with full bibl. refs. P. Gout, *Le Mont-Saint-Michel: Histoire de l'abbaye et de la ville. Étude archéologique et architecturale des monuments* (2 vols., 1910; rev. edn., 1978); G. Bazin, *Le Mont Saint-Michel* (1933). H. J. L. J. Massé, *A Short History and Description of the Church and Abbey of Mont S. Michel* (Bell's Handbooks to Continental Churches, 1902). J. J. G. Alexander, *Norman Illumination at Mont St Michel 966–1100* (Oxford, 1970), with 'History of Abbey to c. 1100', pp. 1–21, incl. detailed bibl. refs. J. Hourlier, OSB, in *DIP* 6 (1980), cols. 127–9, s.v.

Montserrat (Lat. *Mons Serratus*). This celebrated mountain near Barcelona is surrounded by legends which locate there the Castle of the Holy Grail. The *Benedictine monastery, whose church enshrines the famous image of 'Our Lady of Montserrat', was founded between 1025 and 1035 by Abbot Oliba of Ripoll (d. 1046) and raised to the rank of an abbey in 1409. In 1493 it joined the congregation of Valladolid, and soon became a popular place of pilgrimage. One of its most distinguished visitors was St *Ignatius Loyola, who hung up his sword there after his conversion. Partly destroyed in the Napoleonic wars of 1811–12, and sacked by Spanish militia in 1820 and 1834, the abbey was abolished in 1835. It was restored, however, in 1844 and in 1862 affiliated to the congregation of *Subiaco, of which it is now the principal monastery in the Spanish province. Its monks are famous for their researches into Catalonian culture, ecclesiastical history and Scripture, their interest in sacred music, and their extensive library. They also care for the numerous pilgrims who visit the shrine.

G. de Argais, *La perla de Cataluña: Historia de Nuestra Señora de Montserrate* (Madrid, 1677). M. Muntadas, OSB, *Montserrat: Su pasado, su presente y su porvenir, ó lo que fué hasta su destrucción el año 1811, lo que es desde su destrucción y lo que será en adelante* (Barcelona, 1867). A. M. Albareda, OSB, *Història de Montserrat* (Montserrat, 1931; rev. by J. Massot i Muntaner, 1972); Id., *L'Abat Oliva, fundador de Montserrat (971[?]–1046)* (ibid., 1931; repr. 1972). *Analecta Montserratensia* (Montserrat, 1918 ff.). A. Mundó, OSB, in *EC* 8 (1952), cols. 1327–30, s.v. 'Monserrato', with bibl.

Moody, Dwight Lyman (1837–99), evangelist. The son of a bricklayer, he left his home at Northfield, Mass., in 1854 for work in Boston. After reception into the *Congregational Church in 1856, he moved to Chicago, where he prospered in business (which he abandoned in 1860) and entered on successful evangelical work in connection with his Sunday School. During the Civil and Spanish wars (1861–5) he worked under the *YMCA, labouring particularly to evangelize the wounded. Returning to Chicago in 1865, he organized several state and international Sunday School teachers' Conventions, during which he met Ira David Sankey (1840–1908), who joined him in 1870 and regularly accompanied his preaching with singing and organ-playing. After a first visit to England in 1867, he returned with Sankey on a preaching tour from 1872 to 1875, in the course of which the 'Sankey and Moody Hymn Book' was published (1873) with many of the songs used by Sankey and other revivalists who found the hymns in use in England unsuited to their type of appeal. The tour through England, Scotland, and Ireland, which was supported by clergy of many denominations, met a wide and enthusiastic response. After conducting similar missions to Brooklyn, Philadelphia, New York, and Boston, Moody founded the Northfield Seminary for Young Women in 1879 and the Mount Hermon School for Young Men in 1881. After a second tour in Great Britain from 1881 to 1884, during which he made his first appeal to the academic world, he began organizing annual student conferences for Bible study. In 1893 he organized a mission in connection with the World Fair at Chicago, out of which grew the Bible Institute Colportage Association, for the production of cheap religious literature (founded 1895).

Moody's success as an evangelistic preacher was the fruit of his undaunted courage in pursuing converts in spite of all opposition, the frankness, vigour, and urgency of his appeal, and the use of the inquiry-room and other revivalist methods.

W. R. Moody (son), *The Life of Dwight L. Moody* [1900]. Modern studies by J. C. Pollock (London, 1963) and J. F. Find-

lay, Jun. (Chicago and London, 1969). J. [H. S.] Kent, *Holding the Fort: Studies in Victorian Revivalism* (1978), pp. 132–214. L. A. Weigle in *Dict. Amer. Biog.* 13 (1934), pp. 103–6.

Moore, Aubrey Lackington (1848–90), Anglican theologian. Educated at St Paul's School and Exeter College, Oxford, he was successively Fellow of St John's College, Oxford (1872–6), rector of Frenchay, Avon (1876–81), and tutor at Keble College (1881–90). His keen intellect, equally at home in philosophy and the natural sciences, and a rare depth of spiritual power made him one of the chief religious influences in Oxford. His publications included the essay on 'The Christian Doctrine of God' in *Lux Mundi* (1889), a collection of papers on *Science and the Faith* (1889), and *Lectures on the History of the Reformation* (1890; posthumous); but these books in no sense reflect his real abilities.

R. D. Middleton, 'Aubrey Moore', *Theology*, 51 (1948), pp. 85–9. H. E. D. Blakiston in *DNB* 38 (1894), p. 342.

moral philosophy. In current usage, the branch of philosophy which explores questions of what is good and right apart from any considerations derived from a supernatural revelation; in particular, it examines the nature, meaning, and justification of moral concepts. The word is thus another name for what philosophers also term 'ethics'.

Moral Re-Armament (MRA). The name by which the work of the *Oxford Group came to be generally known after 1938, when F. N. D. *Buchman called for 'moral and spiritual re-armament'. The idea was suggested to him by the Swedish socialist author Harry Blomberg (1893–1950) who, as the armaments race intensified, spoke of the need to 'rearm morally'. For the history and bibl. see OXFORD GROUP.

moral theology. A term used since the late 16th cent. to denote the study of moral questions and the foundations of morality in the light of Christian belief. From the earliest times Christian thinkers were concerned with questions of morality; they developed the ideas of pre-Christian philosophers on the nature of true happiness and built on the teaching of the Bible (esp. the Ten *Commandments and the *Sermon on the Mount) and Jewish writers. Moral theology, however, began to emerge as a discipline independent of dogmatic theology only at the end of the 16th cent. Since then, in the RC and Anglican Churches the term has become associated with the attempts of *casuistry to relate the tradition of moral teaching derived from St *Augustine and St *Thomas Aquinas more closely to individual cases and circumstances. By contrast, Protestants since the early 19th cent. have generally preferred the title 'Christian ethics' for the discipline of Christian moral enquiry.

The '*Didache' contains perhaps the earliest Christian treatise of moral theology in its teaching of the Two Ways, and the 'Shepherd' of *Hermas gives a compendium of Christian moral teaching in the twelve 'Mandates'. *Clement of Alexandria produced guides to the Christian life in the 'Protrepticus' and 'Paedagogus', which give a detailed description of the morality of the true Christian. *Tertullian taught that the will of God was the first principle of the moral life, and he and St *Cyprian wrote several practical treatises on patience, almsgiving, and virginity. With the conversion of large numbers of pagans in the 4th cent. strict moral teaching became particularly urgent. It was given in the E. by, among others, all three *Cappadocian Fathers, and by St *Cyril of Jerusalem, esp. in his 'Catecheses'. In the W. St *Ambrose produced a Christian counterpart to Cicero's 'De Officiis' in his 'De Officiis Ministrorum'. St Augustine's adaptation of classical and *Neoplatonist thought to Christian theological purposes was the dominant patristic influence on W. medieval ethical thought. He established *charity (or love) as the fundamental principle of Christian morality from which flow all other virtues (esp. in his 'Enchiridion' and 'De Moribus'), and he wrote smaller treatises on marriage, continence, and similar subjects. The moral teaching of antiquity was summed up by St *Gregory I in his 'Moralium Libri XXV' and 'Liber Regulae Pastoralis', in which also were laid the foundations of medieval developments.

New needs were reflected in the appearance of the '*Penitential Books', dating from the 5th–7th cents. These deal with the practical moral requirements of the newly-converted barbarians and reflect the resulting weakening of the penitential practice of the Church. Most medieval thought followed St Augustine in his orientation towards the *summum bonum* of mankind, identified objectively with God, and subjectively with ultimate happiness (which was sited by some in the volitional act of love, and by others in the intellectual act of *contemplation). The criterion of moral action was conformity to the Divine law known through Scripture and reflection on natural experience. *Platonism was the dominant philosophical inspiration until the revival of *Aristotelianism in the 13th cent., largely under the influence of St Thomas Aquinas. Building on St Augustine and Aristotle, Aquinas devoted the whole of the second part of his 'Summa Theologiae' to moral theology, treating it from the point of view of the speculative theologian, and linking it closely to *natural law, the natural and supernatural virtues, and the gifts of the Holy Spirit. At the same time precursors of the modern casuistry made their appearance with *Raymond of Peñafort's famous 'Summa de Poenitentia' (c.1225), a compilation of relevant passages from the Fathers, Councils, and Papal decisions, and a century later, with the even more practical so-called 'Summa Astensis' of an unknown *Franciscan of Asti, in Italy (c.1317). In the 14th and 15th cents. a large number of similar 'Summae' were produced, usually arranged in alphabetical order, one of the most celebrated being the 'Summa Theologica Moralis' of St *Antoninus of Florence, which proved an important source of information for all subsequent manuals of casuistry.

At the time of the *Counter-Reformation, the RC Church was much influenced by the need to respond to the Protestant emphasis on grace. The period was marked esp. by the many commentaries on the 'Summa Theologiae', by the growth of and controversies over different systems of casuistry, esp. *Probabilism, and by the numerous manuals and treatises on moral theology, produced largely by members of the *Dominican and *Jesuit Orders. This development was greatly fostered by the increased frequency of sacramental confession. Among the commentaries on the second part of the 'Summa', those by B. *Medina, G. *Vázquez, F. *Suárez, and D. *Báñez are held in great esteem by RC moralists, as is also the comprehensive work of the *Salmanticenses 'Cursus Theologiae Moralis' (1665 ff.). Of the casuists M. de *Sá's *Aphorismi Confessariorum* (1595) was widely used, and J. de *Lugo's *Disputationes scholasticae et morales* (1644) is still frequently regarded as the classic textbook of casuistry. Perhaps the most renowned moral theologian of modern times, whose work received the special approval of the RC Church, is St *Alphonsus Liguori. Against the harsher *Probabiliorist method, which was common at that time in France and Italy after the attacks of e.g. B. *Pascal on the laxist tendency of casuistry, Liguori's *Theologia Moralis* (1753–5) finally established the milder *Equiprobabilism. Most subsequent RC handbooks on moral theology have been strongly influenced by his teaching.

In response to widespread criticism of the prevailing casuistical approach, in the 20th cent. RC moral theology has developed significantly, esp. since the Second *Vatican Council. Attempts are being made to give greater prominence to Biblical authority, the role of moral theology in providing positive guidance in Christian living rather than simply instructions to confessors about minimum standards of obligation, the social dimensions of human existence, contemporary philosophical discussion, the place of moral theology within theology as a whole, and *ecumenical and interdisciplinary dialogue.

Protestants have tended to dissociate themselves from attempts to produce detailed systems of duties binding on all Christians, on the ground that good works are a free and grateful response to the completed work of *justification in Christ. Thus for M. *Luther Christians are freed from the self-concern implicit in 'works–righteousness' to serve their neighbours in love. J. *Calvin, while admitting the liberty of the Christian, gives a greater weight to the directive use of the moral law. Many English Protestants in the 17th cent. were attracted by the claims of the casuistical approach to govern in detail every aspect of human existence, and important contributions to moral theology were made by *Puritans (e.g. W. *Perkins and R. *Baxter) as well as by *High Churchmen (e.g. R. *Sanderson and Jeremy *Taylor). During the 18th cent. Protestant thinkers (including divines, esp. Joseph *Butler) looked increasingly to *moral philosophy for guidance. Throughout the 19th cent. moral theologians were greatly influenced by I. *Kant's ethics, attempting either to incorporate his doctrine of ethical autonomy into a theological framework or to qualify it by developing specifically Christian ethics in response to it.

In the 20th cent. K. *Barth's revolt against liberal theology helped to reinstate in Europe a distinctively theological conception of ethics (cf. E. *Brunner and D. *Bonhoeffer), while in the *United States of America R. *Niebuhr's attack on the '*Social Gospel' movement employed an Augustinian awareness of sin to criticize the dominant optimism. The diverse and conflicting trends in recent Protestant ethics include: attempts wholly to subordinate norms to particular situations; by contrast, a stress on order and the principled analysis of recurrent moral problems; a recovered awareness of the importance of hope; and the reassertion of non-violence as an approach to social and political reform. At the same time distinctions between RC and Protestant moral theology have become less sharp and in all the Churches rapid cultural and technological change has set the agenda for many current debates in moral theology, e.g. concerning *bioethics, social and economic justice, and the morality of modern *war; business and professional ethics and comparative religious ethics are also receiving attention, while *liberation and *feminist theologies are introducing new factors into the task of providing Christian guidance for living in and evaluating the contemporary world.

Modern works on RC moral theology include B. Häring, CSSR, *Das Gesetz Christi* (Freiburg i.B., 1954; 8th edn., 1967; Eng. tr., 3 vols., Cork [1963–7]); id., *Free and Faithful in Christ* (3 vols., New York and Slough, 1978–81 [the latter book written after the Second Vatican Council]); and G. [G.] Grisez, *The Way of the Lord Jesus*, 1: *Christian Moral Principles* (Chicago [1983]). There is a useful introd. from a largely Catholic point of view by an Anglican, R. C. Mortimer, *Elements of Moral Theology* (1947). Other Anglican works include several writings of K. E. *Kirk, esp. *The Vision of God* (1931), and O. [M. T.] O'Donovan, *Resurrection and Moral Order: An Outline for Evangelical Ethics* (Leicester and Grand Rapids, 1986). On the development of moral theology, see G. W. Forell, *History of Christian Ethics* (Minneapolis, 1979 ff.); J. Mahoney, *The Making of Moral Theology: A Study of the Roman Catholic Tradition* (Oxford, 1987); J. Liébaert, *Les enseignements moraux des pères apostoliques* (Gembloux, 1970); E. F. Osborn, *Ethical Patterns in Early Christian Thought* (Cambridge, 1976); T. Wood, *English Casuistical Divinity during the Seventeenth Century* (1952); E. Rose, *Cases of Conscience: Alternatives open to Recusants and Puritans under Elizabeth I and James I* (Cambridge, 1975). Modern Protestant works incl. K. Barth, *Die kirchliche Dogmatik*, 3, part 4 (Zurich, 1951; Eng. tr., Edinburgh, 1961); D. Bonhoeffer, *Ethik*, ed. E. Bethge (Munich, 1949; Eng. tr., 1955); R. Niebuhr, *An Interpretation of Christian Ethics* (New York, 1935; London, 1936); H. R. *Niebuhr, *Christ and Culture* (New York [1951]; London, 1952); H. Thielicke, *Theologische Ethik* (3 vols. in 4, Tübingen, 1951–64; abridged Eng. tr. of vol. 1, Philadelphia, 1966, London, 1968; vol. 2, Philadelphia and London, 1969; vol. 3, entitled *The Ethics of Sex*, New York and London, 1964); [R.] P. Ramsey, *Deeds and Rules in Christian Ethics* (Scottish Journal of Theology Occasional Papers, 11, 1965; repr. with important additional material, New York [1967]); I. T. Ramsey (ed.), *Christian Ethics and Contemporary Philosophy* (1966); and G. H. Outka and [R.] P. Ramsey, *Norm and Context in Christian Ethics* (New York [1968]; London, 1969). For comparative work in contemporary moral theology, see J. M. Gustafson, *Protestant and Roman Catholic Ethics* (Chicago and London, 1978). Questions of recent concern are considered by T. Rendtorff, *Ethik* (2 vols., 1980–81); S. Hauerwas, *The Peaceable Kingdom: A Primer in Christian Ethics* (Notre Dame, Ind., 1983; London, 1984); and C. E. Curran, *Critical Concerns in Moral Theology* (Notre Dame, Ind. [1984]). J. Macquarrie and J. Childress (eds.), *A New Dictionary of Christian Ethics* (1986). B. Häring and W. Trillhaas in *Sacramentum Mundi*, ed. K. *Rahner, SJ, and others, 4 (1969), pp. 122–33, s.v., with bibl. Surveys of recent work on moral theology are pub. annually in *Theological Studies*.

Morality Play, or **Morality.** A form of drama, popular in the 15th and 16th cents., in which a moral truth or lesson was inculcated by the chief characters personifying various abstract qualities. It developed independently of the *Mystery Plays, but at the same time. Originally the interest of these plays was mainly religious, but from the end of the 15th cent. onwards they became more secular in character, though in their later form they were sometimes used, e.g., for defending Protestantism against Cath-

olicism. 'Everyman', the best known of them, is a translation from a Dutch original. The name 'Morality', which is derived from the French, was not applied to them till the late 18th cent.

Anthology of texts in D. Bevington, *Medieval Drama* (Boston [1975]), pp. 789–963. R. Potter, *The English Morality Play* (1975). See also bibl. to MYSTERY PLAYS; also to DRAMA.

Moravian Brethren, now more usually known as the **Moravian Church.** The remnant of the *Bohemian Brethren (Unitas Fratrum) who from 1722 onwards settled at *Herrnhut under the patronage of N. L. von *Zinzendorf, became known as the Moravian or United Brethren. As a consequence of Zinzendorf's influence, there was a strong *pietistic element in the community, and in the early years they were closely linked to the *Lutheran Church. They came to feel that they had a particular calling to witness to Christ among people who did not know Him rather than to establish a new Church in places where Christianity was already established, and in 1732 Moravian missionaries began work in the *West Indies, soon going also to Greenland (1733), *South Africa (1736), Labrador (1752), and elsewhere. Other groups settled in N. America. In 1738 the Moravian Peter Boehler, who exercised a deep influence on J. *Wesley, established a 'religious society' at Fetter Lane, London. This became the first Moravian Church in Britain.

Moravians have always emphasized fellowship and service rather than credal statements. They accept the *Apostles', *Athanasian, and *Nicene Creeds and the main Reformation statements of faith (including the *Augsburg Confession, the shorter Catechism of M. *Luther and the *Thirty-Nine Articles of the C of E) as helpful in formulating Christian truth, but they do not make adherence to any of them a requirement for membership. The Liturgy, esp. the Easter Liturgy, conveys the essence of Moravian belief. In their worship hymns, from many sources, play an important part. A 'Text Book' with OT and NT passages for daily meditation is issued annually. Moravians have retained the offices of *bishop, *presbyter, and *deacon, but they do not wholly correspond with their Catholic counterparts. The oversight of each Province is the responsibility of the Provincial Board, elected by its Synod. The Moravian Church is now made up of 19 self-governing Provinces, closely linked through the international Unity Synod and Unity Board. It has a total membership of c.600,000, of whom over a quarter are in Tanzania, where missionary work started in 1890.

H.-C. Hahn and H. Reichel (eds.), *Zinzendorf und die Herrnhuter Brüder: Quellen zur Geschichte der Brüder-Unität von 1722 bis 1760* (1977). D. Cranz, *Alte und neue Brüder-Historie oder Kurzgefasste Geschichte der Evangelischen Brüder-Unität in den altern Zeiten und insonderheit in dem gegenwärtigen Jahrhundert* (Barby, 1771; Eng. tr., 1780). E. [A.] De Schweinitz, *The History of the Church known as the Unitas Fratrum* (Bethlehem, Pa., 1885); J. E. Hutton, *A Short History of the Moravian Church* (1895; enlarged edn. as *A History of the Moravian Church*, 1909); J. T. Hamilton, *A History of the Church known as the Moravian Church . . . during the Eighteenth and Nineteenth Centuries* (Bethlehem, Pa., 1900; rev. by K. G. Hamilton as *History of the Moravian Church . . . 1722–1957*, ibid., 1967); W. G. Addison, *The Renewed Church of the United Brethren, 1722–1930* (1930); E. Langton, *History of the Moravian Church* (1956); A. W. Schattschneider, *Through Five Hundred Years: A Popular History of the Moravian*

Church (Bethlehem, Pa. [1956]; rev. edn., 1990). M. P. van Buijtenen and others (eds.), *Unitas Fratrum: Herrnhuter Studien* (Utrecht, 1975). W. R. Ward, 'The Renewed Unity of the Brethren: Ancient Church, New Sect or Interconfessional Movement?', *Bulletin of the John Rylands University Library*, 70 no. 3 (1988), pp. 77–92. J. E. Hutton, *A History of Moravian Missions* [1922]; H. Beck, *Brüder in vielen Völkern: 250 Jahre Mission der Brüdergemeine* (Erlanger Taschenbücher, 58; 1981). *Transactions of the Moravian Historical Society* (Nazareth, Pa., 1876 ff.). On the early history see also bibl. to ZINZENDORF, N. L. VON, and BOHEMIAN BRETHREN.

More, Dame Gertrude (1606–33), *Benedictine nun and spiritual writer. A direct descendant of St Thomas *More, she entered the house of the English Benedictine congregation at Cambrai in 1623 as one of its first postulants. During her novitiate she was much troubled by scruples and temptations, which continued after she had made her vows, until she came under the direction of Dom Augustine *Baker. On account of her repute for sanctity she was nearly made abbess at the age of 23. She died four years later of smallpox. Her writings, which were published after her death as *The Holy Practices of a Deuine Lover, or, the Sainctly Ideot's Deuotions* (Paris, 1657) and *Confessiones Amantis* (ibid., 1658), contain affective meditations of considerable beauty and an apology for her way of prayer. See also IDIOT, THE.

Her Life, written by her director, A. Baker, was lost to sight until comparatively recent times. The first half of Baker's MS, recovered in Germany *c*.1850, is in the possession of Stanbrook Abbey, Worcs.; the whole Life, somewhat abbreviated by a copyist, has since been identified in another MS now at *Ampleforth Abbey. The Life was first pr. by Dom B. Weld-Blundell in a vol. entitled *The Inner Life of Dame Gertrude More* (London, 1911; the ed. appears to have dealt rather freely with the text and, somewhat misleadingly, omitted to print Baker's name on the title-page). Modern edns. of her 'Devotions' by H. Collins (London, 1873), of the *Holy Practices* by H. Lane Fox, OSB, (ibid., 1909), and of her 'Writings' by B. Weld-Blundell, OSB (ibid., 1910). Life by H. Collins (London, 1875). M. Norman, IBVM, 'Dame Gertrude More and the English Mystical Tradition', *Recusant History*, 13 (1976), pp. 196–211.

More, Hannah (1745–1833), religious writer and philanthropist. Born at Stapleton, Avon, from *c*.1757 she attended a school established by her sisters in Bristol. About 1773 she came into contact with the literary circle of David Garrick (1717–79) and S. *Johnson, who encouraged her to publish plays and poems. After Garrick's death she devoted herself more to religious activities, though she distrusted the more emotional aspects of *Evangelicalism. She published a series of *Sacred Dramas* for the instruction of young persons in 1782 and *Thoughts on the Importance of the Manners of the Great to General Society* (anon.) in 1788; this last had a very wide circulation. In 1787 she became closely acquainted with W. *Wilberforce and also with J. *Newton, who became her spiritual adviser. Under Wilberforce's influence she established schools at Cheddar and in the neighbouring villages at a time when schemes of popular education were almost unprecedented; religious education was combined with a training in spinning, designed to relieve poverty. She also established friendly societies and other philanthropic organizations for the relief and education of adults. In spite of initial opposition her system of schools was finally commended by R.

Beadon, Bp. of *Bath and Wells from 1802 to 1824. Four of the schools which she founded survived. Between 1793 and 1799 she wrote a large number of Tracts designed to counteract the influence of the French Revolution (collected under the title *Cheap Repository Tracts*). Moving to Barley Wood in 1802, she came into closer contact with the *Clapham Sect and in 1809 anonymously published *Coelebs in Search of a Wife* (2 vols.), the most popular of her books. Although suffering from ill-health during the last years of her life, she continued to write religious and moral treatises.

Collected edn. of her Works in 8 vols., London, 1801; rev. edn., 11 vols., ibid., 1830. W. Roberts, *Memoirs of the Life and Correspondence of Mrs Hannah More* (4 vols., 1834); A. Roberts (ed.), *Letters of Hannah More to Zachary Macaulay* (1860); selected letters ed. R. Brimley Johnson (London, 1925). Further contemporary Life by H. Thompson (ibid., 1838); modern Lives by C. M. *Yonge ('Eminent Women Series', 1888) and M. G. Jones (Cambridge, 1952, with list of 'Cheap Repository Tracts' ascribed to Mrs More, pp. 272 f.). F. K. Brown, *Fathers of the Victorians* (Cambridge, 1961), *passim*. J. McLeish, *Evangelical Religion and Popular Education: A modern interpretation* (1969), *passim*. S. Pedersen, 'Hannah More Meets Simple Simon: Tracts, Chapbooks, and Popular Culture in Late Eighteenth-Century England', *Journal of British Studies*, 25 (1986), pp. 84–113. L. Stephen in *DNB* 38 (1894), pp. 414–20.

More, Henry (1614–87), *Cambridge Platonist. Educated at Christ's College, of which he became a Fellow in 1639, he remained in Cambridge all his life, despite the fact that he was offered several rich preferments. His chief interests were theological, philosophical, and ethical. Among his principal works were *Antidote against Atheism* (1653), *The Immortality of the Soul* (1659), and *Divine Dialogues* (1668). In these discursive writings he sought to vindicate theism and immortality against the materialism represented by T. *Hobbes. He emphasized in particular the instinctive reasonableness of Divine truth and affirmed the existence of a higher principle, 'more noble and inward than reason itself', which he termed the 'Divine Sagacity'. He held that it was possible to apprehend this higher truth only through the cultivation of a righteous disposition and a free intellect, though afterwards this intuitive instinct might be confirmed by the methods of reason. He also defended innate ideas and notions, and postulated the existence of a Spirit of Nature or 'anima mundi'. Despite his curiously superstitious leanings, he had a high reputation for learning and saintliness.

Works collected in 3 vols., fol., London, 1675–9. Modern edn. of selection of his philosophical works, with introd. and notes, by F. I. Mackinnon (New York, 1925); philosophical poems ed. G. Bulloch (Publications of the University of Manchester, 209; English Series, 20; 1931). The 1662 edn. of *The Immortality of the Soul* was repr., with introd. by A. Jacob (International Archives of the History of Ideas, 122; Dordrecht, etc., 1987). Life by R. Ward, rector of Belton (London, 1710; ed. M. F. Howard, ibid., 1911). Modern studies by A. Lichtenstein (Cambridge, Mass., 1962), S. Hutin (Studien und Materialien zur Geschichte der Philosophie, 2; 1966), and P. Cristofolini (Urbino [1974]). [F.] J. Hoyles, *The Waning of the Renaissance 1640-1740* (International Archives of the History of Ideas, 39; The Hague, 1971), pp. 3–72. J. Henry, 'A Cambridge Platonist's Materialism. Henry More and the Concept of Soul', *Journal of the Warburg and Courtauld Institutes*, 49 (1986), pp. 172–95. J. H. Overton in *DNB* 38 (1894), pp. 421–3. See also works cited s.v. CAMBRIDGE PLATONISTS.

More, St Thomas (1478–1535), Lord Chancellor of England. The son of Sir John More (a judge of the King's Bench), he embarked on the study of law in 1494, after spending some years in the household of Abp. J. Morton and at Oxford. Called to the bar in 1501, he had a distinguished career at Lincoln's Inn. After testing his vocation to the religious life at the London *Charterhouse, he decided against celibacy, and married Jane Colt in 1505. Upon her death in 1511, he took a second wife, Alice Middleton. His household in Chelsea became a centre of learning and piety, frequented by such humanist scholars as J. *Colet, *Erasmus, and W. *Grocyn. His public career began with his appointment as Under-Sheriff of London in 1510, and his abilities won him a place on an embassy to Flanders in 1515. There he wrote his most famous work, *Utopia* (Louvain, 1516). This description of an ideal community living by natural law, religion, and reason aimed many satirical barbs at contemporary abuses. More joined the Privy Council in 1517, and soon afterwards became Master of Requests, to be knighted three years later. Speaker of the House of Commons in 1523, he was made Chancellor of the Duchy of Lancaster in 1525, and finally replaced T. *Wolsey as Lord Chancellor in 1529.

During the 1520s, when the *Lutheran controversy raged throughout Europe, More emerged as a zealous defender of Catholicism. He had a hand in *Henry VIII's attack on M. *Luther, the *Assertio Septem Sacramentorum* (1521), and under the pseudonym of Gulielmus Rosseus he vilified Luther's reply to Henry in his *Responsio ad Lutherum* (1523). From 1528 he produced a succession of polemical writings against, among others, W. *Tyndale and the anticlerical propagandist Christopher St German. However, his reluctance to support Henry VIII in his pursuit of a divorce was rendering his political position difficult. Henry's attack on the liberties of the Church in England rendered it untenable, and More resigned the Chancellorship—ostensibly on grounds of ill-health—on 16 May 1532, within hours of the *Convocation's acceptance of Henry's demands (see SUBMISSION OF THE CLERGY). In his retirement he held aloof from all political engagements, even refusing to attend the coronation of *Anne Boleyn in 1533—to Henry's annoyance. This strategy served him well, for he was able to persuade the House of Lords to delete his name from the bill of Attainder against Elizabeth *Barton and her followers in 1534. However, it could not protect him from the Act of Succession. On his refusal to take an oath to this Act in April 1534, he was confined to the Tower of London, where he spent the rest of his life in prayer and penance, composing several devotional treatises, including the fine *Dialogue of Comfort against Tribulation*. On 1 July 1535 he was tried for high treason on the charge of having denied the Royal *Supremacy. Convicted on the probably perjured evidence of Richard Rich, he was sentenced to death, and was executed on 6 July 1535. He was beatified by *Leo XIII in 1886 and canonized by *Pius XI in 1935. Feast day, formerly 9 July; now, with St. John *Fisher, 22 June. He is commemorated in the ASB on 6 July.

Eng. works ed. by his nephew William Rastell (London, 1557); Lat. works pub. at Louvain, 1565, and at Frankfurt a.M., 1689. Yale Edition of Complete Works, under the auspices of R. G. L. Carroll and J. B. Murray (New Haven, Conn., and London, 1963 ff.). Eng. works also ed. W. E. Campbell (London, 1931 ff.

[only 2 vols. pub.]). *The Correspondence of Sir Thomas More*, ed. E. F. Rogers (Princeton, NJ, 1947); further letters ed. H. S. Herbrüggen (Münster, 1966). The earliest Life, based on orig. docs., is that by William Roper, More's son-in-law (first pr., Paris, 1626; crit. text by E. V. Hitchcock, EETS, Original Series, 197; 1935); other early Lives by Thomas Stapleton (*Tres Thomae*, Douai, 1588; Eng. tr. by P. E. Hallett, 1928), Nicholas Harpsfield (d. 1575; Harleian MS 6253; ed. E. V. Hitchcock, EETS, Original Series, 186; 1932), Cresacre More, his great-grandson [Antwerp, c.1630], and 'Ro. Ba.', ed. E. V. Hitchcock and P. E. Hallett (EETS, Original Series, 222; 1950). Modern Lives by R. W. Chambers (London, 1935), L. Paul (ibid., 1953), E. E. Reynolds (ibid., 1953 and 1968), A. Prévost ([Paris,] 1969), and R. Marius (New York and London, 1984). G. Marc'Hadour, *L'Univers de Thomas More: Chronologie critique de More, Érasme et leur époque (1477–1536)* (De Pétrarque à Descartes, 5; 1963). J. A. Guy, *The Public Career of Sir Thomas More* (Brighton, Sussex, 1980); A. Fox, *Thomas More: History and Providence* (Oxford, 1982). R. W. Gibson, *St Thomas More: A Preliminary Bibliography of his Works and of Moreana to the Year 1750* (1961). S. Lee in *DNB* 38 (1894), pp. 429–49.

Morgan, William (1545–1604), translator of the *Welsh Bible. Born in the Conway valley, the son of a tenant farmer, he was educated in the free school maintained by his father's landlord, and, through his patronage, at St John's College, Cambridge. Though ordained in 1568, it was only on his induction to the living of Llanrhaedr-ym-Mochnant, ten years later, that he undertook full-time parish duties. He was appointed Bp. of *Llandaff in 1595 and in 1601 translated to *St Asaph, where he died in penury.

It was during his time as a parish priest that Morgan translated the Bible into Welsh, a task completed with its publication in 1588. He based his version of the NT on a translation made by William Salesbury and Richard Davies (1567), but he rendered the OT and Apocrypha from the original languages single-handed. As a work of scholarship his translation stands on a par with the English AV. It is clear that he was well-versed in the biblical languages and consulted the standard versions of his day. His Bible was epoch-making in that it not only gave the people of Wales the Scriptures in their mother-tongue, but it also saved the Welsh language from extinction.

Life by W. Hughes (London, 1891). P. Morgan, *A Bible for Wales* (Aberystwyth, 1988); I. Thomas, *William Morgan and his Bible* (Cardiff, 1988). G. [R.] Gruffydd, 'The Translating of the Bible into the Welsh Tongue' by William Morgan in 1588 (1988); G. Williams and T. M. Bassett, *William Morgan's Bible 1588–1988* (1988). J. E. Lloyd in *DNB* 39 (1894), pp. 38 f.; M. Stephens (ed.), *The Oxford Companion to the Literature of Wales* (Oxford and New York, 1986), pp. 409–11, both s.v. See also works cited s.v. WELSH BIBLE AND PRAYER BOOK.

Morin, Germain (1861–1946), *patristic scholar. A native of Caen, in 1881 he became a Benedictine monk at *Maredsous in Belgium. From 1907 to 1916, and again in his later years, he resided chiefly at Munich. He made many important original contributions to Latin patristics and liturgy, mostly in the *Revue Bénédictine*, and published an outstanding edition of the works of St *Caesarius of Arles (1937–42). He also issued collections of previously unpublished sermons of St *Jerome (1897, 1903) and of St *Augustine (1917, 1930).

G. Ghysens and P.-P. Verbraken, *La Carrière Scientifique de Dom Germain Morin (1861–1946)* (Instrumenta Patristica, 15; 1986).

Morin, Jean (1591–1659), *Oratorian theologian. The son of *Calvinist parents, he was converted to Catholicism in 1617 under the influence of P. de *Bérulle, became an Oratorian in the following year, and devoted his life almost wholly to studies in patristics and the text of the Bible. At the invitation of Pope *Urban VIII he spent nine months in Rome in 1639–40 as theological adviser in the matter of *Orders during the attempts to reunite the E. and W. Churches. His works included *De patriarcharum et primatum origine . . . atque antiqua et primigenia censurarum in clericos praxi* (1626), *Vetus Testamentum secundum LXX* (3 vols., 1628), *Exercitationes ecclesiasticae in utrumque Samaritanorum Pentateuchum* (1631) and *De Sacris Ecclesiae Ordinationibus* (1655). A notable feature of the last-named work was its rejection of the view formerly widely held among Latin theologians that the Tradition of the *Instruments constituted the *matter of the Sacrament of Orders.

R. *Simon in *Antiquitates Ecclesiae Orientalis cum Notis et Vita I. Morini* (London, 1682), pp. 1–117 (hostile, Simon having then left the Oratory). P. Auvray, Cong. Orat., 'Jean Morin (1591–1659)', *R. Bibl.* 66 (1959), pp. 397–414. A. Molien in *DTC* 10 (pt. 2; 1929), cols. 2486–9. See also works cited under ORATORIANS (2).

Morison, James (1816–93), founder of the '*Evangelical Union'. Educated at Edinburgh University, he was trained for the ministry of the *United Secession Church. In 1839 he was appointed to the charge of Cabrach and in 1840 to a church at Kilmarnock. His preaching of the universal atonement of Christ and the publication of his beliefs in a short tract, *The Question 'What must I do to be saved?' Answered* (1840), led his teachings to be challenged as incompatible with the *Westminster Confession, and in 1841 he was expelled from the United Secession Church. In 1843, with three other ministers and nine laymen, he founded at Kilmarnock the 'Evangelical Union', and later was joined by others. In 1851 he left for Glasgow. He retired from active work in 1884.

Memorial Volume, ed. G. G[ladstone] (on occasion of Morison's ministerial jubilee; 1889). Lives by W. Adamson (London, 1898) and [W. H.] O. Smeaton (Edinburgh, 1901). R. Small, *History of the Congregations of the United Presbyterian Church from 1733 to 1900*, 2 (1904), pp. 288–91; [T. E.] H. Escott, *A History of Scottish Congregationalism* (Glasgow, 1960), pp. 116–34. A. Gordon in *DNB* 39 (1894), pp. 57 f.

Moritz, St. See MAURICE, ST.

Morley, George (1597–1684), Bp. of *Winchester. Educated at Westminster and at Christ Church, Oxford, he became rector of Mildenhall, Wilts, in 1641. He was ejected as a royalist in 1648 and was abroad until the Restoration, conducting services in many places for the Anglican exiles. Soon after his return (1660) he became Dean of Christ Church and later in the year Bp. of *Worcester. On 23 Apr. 1661 he preached the Coronation Sermon and in May took a prominent part at the *Savoy Conference. He was translated to Winchester in 1662. Despite his close associations with the *High Church party, his theology was *Calvinistic. His writings, however, were short and

mostly occasional. He was a great benefactor, notably to the diocese of Winchester, and rebuilt Wolvesey Palace. He was also the patron of T. *Ken, whom he made his chaplain in 1665.

A. Wood, *Athenae Oxonienses* (ed. P. Bliss), 4 (1820), cols. 149–58. F. Bussby, 'An Anglican in Exile', *CQR* 156 (1965), pp. 426–38; id., 'George Morley, Bishop of Worcester 1660–62', *Transactions of the Worcester Archaeological Society*, NS 37 (1961), pp. 11–23; id., 'George Morley; Bishop of Winchester, 1662–1684', *CQR* 158 (1967), pp. 432–42. W. Hunt in *DNB* 39 (1894), pp. 74–8.

Mormons. The popular name for the 'Church of Jesus Christ of Latter-day Saints'. They were founded in Manchester, New York, in 1830 by Joseph Smith (1805–44), who claimed to have been given, through a revelation, *The Book of Mormon*. This, together with the Bible and two other works, *Doctrine and Covenants* and *The Pearl of Great Price*, comprise the Mormon canon of Scripture. In 1843 Smith had another revelation sanctioning polygamy. In 1844 he was killed by a mob in Carthage, Ill., near the Mormon establishment at Nauvoo. Brigham Young (1801–77), an able leader and administrator, succeeded him as President of the Mormons and in 1847 moved their headquarters to Salt Lake Valley in Utah. The practice of polygamy brought them into conflict with the Federal Government until 1890, when Wilford Woodruff, then their President, advised his followers to conform to the law. In 1978 the priesthood was opened to 'all worthy male members . . . without regard for race or color', thus ending a ban on Blacks from full membership. In the 1936 US census Mormons numbered just under 775,000; by 1993 they claimed over 8 million members, of whom just under half were in the *United States of America.

The Mormons accept a modified form of the doctrine of the *Trinity, in which Father, Son, and Holy Spirit are believed to be three separate Gods united in a common godhead of purpose and perfection. Their teaching has a strong *Adventist element; they hold that Israel will literally be gathered together and the ten tribes restored and that Christ will personally reign over a new earth. They maintain that after His resurrection Christ ministered briefly in America and that Zion will be built in the W. hemisphere. They lay great stress on missionary activity, both in the USA and elsewhere, and each male is expected to devote two years to this work at his own expense. They control considerable resources, since members are expected to devote one tenth of their gross income to the Church. In addition to local churches (called 'wards'), Mormons build temples (45 by 1993), in which alone various ceremonies can be performed; these include marriages and baptisms for the dead. Mainstream Mormonism continues to condemn the practice of polygamy, but some breakaway groups engage in it, and it is official doctrine that the custom of plural marriage will be restored at the Second Coming. The largest offshoot is the 'Reorganized Church of Jesus Christ of Latter Day Saints', which has its headquarters in Independence, Missouri.

The Mormons use the AV of the Bible, with certain retranslations by Smith. *The Book of Mormon* first pub. at Palmyra, NY, 1830; *A Book of Commandments*, comprising revelations to Smith and others, pub. at Independence, Mo., 1833; it was enlarged as *Doctrine and Covenants* (Kirtland, Oh., 1835); *The Pearl of Great Price*, which comprises selections from Smith's writings, was first pub. in Liverpool, 1851; all these works are available in many edns. The large lit. on the Mormons incl. B. R. McConckie, *Mormon Doctrine* (Salt Lake City, 1958; 2nd edn., 1966); W. Mulder and A. R. Mortensen (eds.), *Among the Mormons: Historic Accounts by Contemporary Observers* (New York, 1958); N. F. Furniss, *The Mormon Conflict 1850–1859* (New Haven, Conn., 1960); J. B. Allen and G. M. Leonard, *The Story of the Latter-day Saints* (Salt Lake City, 1976; 2nd edn. [1992]); L. J. Arrington and D. Bitton, *The Mormon Experience: A History of the Latter-day Saints* (New York and London, 1979); K J. Hansen, *Mormonism and the American Experience* (Chicago [1981]); R. Gottlieb and P. Wiley, *America's Saints: The Rise of Mormon Power* (New York [1984]; repr. San Diego, New York, and London [1986]). J. Shipps, *Mormonism: The Story of a New Religious Tradition* (Urbana, Ill., and Chicago [1985]); P. L. Barlow, *Mormons and the Bible: The Place of Latter-day Saints in American Religion* (New York and Oxford, 1991).

On Joseph Smith, see Lucy Smith (mother), *Biographical Sketches of Joseph Smith the Prophet and his Progenitors for many Generations* (Liverpool, 1853); F. McK. Brodie, *No Man Knows my History* (New York, 1945; 2nd edn., 1971; London, 1963); R. L. Bushman, *Joseph Smith and the Beginnings of Mormonism* (Urbana, Ill., and Chicago [1984]), with bibl.

Morning Prayer. See MATTINS.

Morone, Giovanni (1509–80), Bp. of Modena. He came of an old and distinguished family of Milan, where his father, Ieronimo Morone (d. 1529), was chancellor. In 1529 he was nominated Bp. of Modena by *Clement VII, but was prevented by the opposition of Cardinal Ippolito d'Este from taking possession of his see. After various diplomatic missions on behalf of the Pope, he became nuncio to Germany in 1536 and was present at the Diets of *Hagenau (1540), *Ratisbon (1541), and Speyer (1542). Like J. *Sadoleto, he showed considerable sympathy with the Reformers' grievances and tried to establish less embittered relations. In 1542 he was created cardinal and nominated with Paul Parisio and R. *Pole to preside over the forthcoming Council at *Trent, but though his reforming zeal did much to keep the prospect of the Council alive he did not eventually take part at the opening group of sessions. In 1557 he was incarcerated by *Paul IV in the Castel Sant'Angelo for supposed heresy on justification, the invocation of saints, and the veneration of relics. He was completely cleared of these charges under the more liberal *Pius IV, who employed him during the concluding sessions of the Council of Trent to win the goodwill of the secular powers needed to ensure the Council's success. In his later years he was employed on diplomatic missions to Genoa (1575) and Augsburg (1576), and in 1578–9, as Cardinal Protector of England, he took an active part in administering the *English College at Rome.

F. Dittrich (ed.), *Nuntiaturberichte Giovanni Morones vom deutschen Königshofe, 1539, 1540* (Quellen und Forschungen aus dem Gebiete der Geschichte. In Verbindung mit ihrem historischen Institut in Rom herausgegeben von der Görres-Gesellschaft, 1, Teil 1; 1892); W. Friedensburg (ed.), *Nuntiatur des Morone, 1536–1538* (Nuntiaturberichte aus Deutschland, Abt. 1, Bd. 2; 1892); id. (ed.), *Nuntiaturen Fabio Mignanelli's 1538–1539 und Giovanni Morone's Bischofs von Modena 1539* (ibid. 3; 1893); id. (ed.), *Nuntiatur Giovanni Morone's Bischofs von Modena, 1539 Juli–Oktober* (ibid. 4; 1893); L. Cardauns (ed.), *Nuntiaturen Morones und Poggios, Legationen Farneses und Cervinis, 1539–1540* (ibid. 5; 1909); id. (ed.), *Gesandtschaft Campegios, Nuntiaturen Morones und Poggios, 1540–1541* (ibid. 6; 1910). M. Firpo and D. Marcatto (eds.), *Il Processo inquisitoriale del Cardinal Giovanni Morone* (5 vols., 1981–9). Modern Life by N. Bernabei (Modena, 1885). G. Constant, *La Légation du Cardinal Morone près l'empereur et le concile de Trent, avril–décembre, 1563* (Bibliothèque de l'École des Hautes Études, 233; 1922). J. Grisar, 'Die Sendung des Kardinals Morone als Legat zum Reichstag von Augsburg 1555', *Zeitschrift des Historischen Vereins für Schwaben*, 61 (1955), pp. 341–87. H. Thurston, SJ, in *CE* 10 (1911), pp. 575 f.; P. Paschini in *EC* 8 (1952), cols. 1420–4; H. Lutz in *NCE* 9 (1967), p. 1150, all s.v. See also bibl. to TRENT, COUNCIL OF.

Morris, William (1834–96), English artist and author. He was educated at Marlborough and Exeter College, Oxford, where contact with the *Oxford Movement stimulated his interest in the Middle Ages. He studied Anglican theology, but, abandoning his plan to take Orders, he embraced the intellectual and social movement associated with the names of T. *Carlyle, J. *Ruskin, and C. *Kingsley. D. G. *Rossetti persuaded him to give up architecture and devote his energies to painting. In 1861 Morris took part in the foundation of a firm established to give artistic form to objects of everyday life. A series of romances, modelled on G. *Chaucer, and published under the single title, *The Earthly Paradise* (3 vols., 1868–70), established his literary fame. They were followed by poems and a free translation of the *Aeneid* (1875). In the following years he became increasingly convinced that the prerequisite of healthy art was a sound social life, and that this could be achieved only by the regeneration of society. In 1883 he became a member of the Democratic Federation and in 1884 the leader of the Socialist League, which sought to promote a social revolution and issued the periodical *Commonweal*. His *Dream of John *Ball* (1888) gives a philosophy of history. When his socialist ideas seemed destined to remain unfulfilled, he turned again to romances, dealing either with the remote past or the distant future. In 1890 he founded the Kelmscott Press. Morris's main ideal, to which all his various activities were devoted, was the reintegration of life and art, the unity of which he held had been broken up by the specialization and mechanization which had begun at the end of the Middle Ages.

Collected edn. of his works, 24 vols., London, 1910–15, with introd. by his daughter, M. Morris, in vol. 1, pp. ix–xxxi. Extracts from his writings also ed., with introd., by M. Morris (2 vols., Oxford, 1936). Letters, ed. N. Kelvin (4 vols. in 5, Princeton, NJ, [1984–96]). The primary authority is the Life by J. W. Mackail (2 vols., London, 1899). Modern studies by E. P. Thompson (ibid., 1955), P. Thompson (ibid., 1967; 3rd edn., Oxford, 1991), P. Henderson (London, 1967), J. Lindsay (ibid., 1975), and P. Faulkner (ibid., 1980). R. Watkinson, *William Morris as designer* (1967). C. Harvey and J. Press, *William Morris: Design and Enterprise in Victorian Britain* (Manchester and New York [1991]). W. S. Peterson, *The Kelmscott Press: A History of William Morris's Typographical Adventure* (Oxford, 1991). T. Scott, *A Bibliography of the Works of William Morris* (1897). J. W. Mackail in *DNB*, Suppl. 3 (1901), pp. 197–203.

Morrison, Robert (1782–1834), first Protestant missionary in *China. A native of Morpeth in Northumberland, he was apprenticed to a last-maker. He studied theology in his spare time. In 1798 he joined the *Presbyterian Church. He became a member of the *LMS in 1804, went to the Missionary Academy at Gosport, and, after studying medicine and astronomy, as well as some Chinese, was ordained and sent to Canton in 1807. Here with great difficulty he secured lessons in Chinese, which could not then be taught to foreigners. In 1809 he became translator to the East India Company. In 1814 he published a Chinese grammar and a translation of the NT, based partly on an old *Jesuit version. In 1818 he finished a translation of the OT, and in 1818 he founded the Anglo-Chinese College at Malacca (charter, 1820). His chief work, the Chinese Dictionary, appeared in 6 vols. in 1821 and remained a standard work for a long time. It was followed, in 1823, by the publication of the whole Chinese Bible in 21 vols. He also translated the BCP and a large number of hymns and tracts.

Memoirs of the Life and Labours of Robert Morrison, compiled by his widow, with critical notes on his Chinese works by S. Kidd (2 vols., 1839). M. Broomhall, *Robert Morrison* (1924). R. K. Douglas in *DNB* 39 (1894), pp. 111 f.

mortal sin. The traditional designation of the most serious category of sin (called in 1 Jn. 5: 16 'sin unto death'); in the RC Church it is now also officially described as 'grave sin'. Acc. to Catholic teaching such sin consists in a deliberate act of turning away from God as man's last end by seeking satisfaction in a creature. This frustration of God's purpose is held to involve the loss of sanctifying grace and eternal damnation, unless it is followed by adequate repentance. To fall into this category a sin must be committed with a clear knowledge of its guilt and with full consent of the will, and must concern a 'grave matter'. It is required that where circumstances allow every such sin committed after Baptism must be confessed to a priest; but if such confession is impossible, the desire to do so and an act of *contrition are sufficient for obtaining God's pardon. See also VENIAL SIN.

Mortalium Animos. The Papal encyclical, issued on 6 Jan. 1928, 'On Fostering True Religious Unity', which forbade RCs to take part in such reunion movements as *Faith and Order.

Text in *AAS* 20 (1928), pp. 5–16.

mortification. An ecclesiastical term used to describe the action of 'killing' or 'deadening' the lusts of the flesh through spiritual self-denial and the infliction of bodily discomfort. Fasting and abstention from pleasure are among the many means of mortification. It is because Christians have died with Christ in Baptism that they are bidden to mortify the works of the flesh (Rom. 8: 13, Col. 3: 3–5). Though M. *Luther protested that works were of no avail in putting the old nature to death, both he and other 16th-cent. Reformers insisted on a discipline of mortification as a consequence of the righteousness that comes through faith. See also ASCETICISM.

Mortmain. A term used for the condition of land that could not be alienated because it was held by an ecclesiastical or other corporation. Statutes of Mortmain, having as their purpose the setting of limitations on the Church's power of acquiring property, date from an early period. In England, ch. 43 of Magna Carta as revised in 1217 attempted to deal with the problem. The drastic Mortmain Act 1279 forbade anyone under pain of forfeiture to buy, sell, or receive lands or tenements and thereby cause them to come into mortmain (*per quod ad manum mortuam terrae*

et tenementa hujusmodi deveniant quoquo modo). The laws, which met with indifferent success and were constantly evaded, were often re-enacted and altered. Of more recent statutes the most famous is the Charitable Uses Act 1735 (commonly known as the 'Mortmain Act'), which in 1736 imposed restrictions on the devising of property to ecclesiastical uses. Much of the law of mortmain was repealed by the Mortmain and Charitable Uses Act 1888, and the concept was finally laid to rest by the Charities Act 1960.

Text of the third issue of Magna Carta (1217), ch. 43, is repr. in W. *Stubbs (ed.), *Select Charters and other Illustrations of English Constitutional History* (9th edn. by H. W. C. Davis, 1913), p. 343; that of the Mortmain Act 1279, with introd., ibid., pp. 450–2; Eng. tr. of the latter in Gee and Hardy, pp. 81 f. (no. 28). L. Shelford, *A Practical Treatise on the Law of Mortmain and Charitable Uses and Trusts* (1836), esp. pp. 1–266, with Eng. tr. of the relevant statutes in appendix. S. [G.] Raban, *Mortmain Legislation and the English Church 1279–1500* (Cambridge Studies in Medieval Life and Thought, 3rd ser. 17; 1982). On more recent legislation, O. D. Tudor, *On Charities* (5th edn., by H. G. Carter and F. M. Crashaw, 1929), pp. 413–72, with texts of the 1888, 1891, and 1892 Acts. W. Kahl, *Die deutschen Amortisationsgesetze* (1879). On mortmain in France, E. Magnin in *DDC* 1 (1935), cols. 468–71, s.v. 'Amortissement', with bibl.

Morton, Thomas (1564–1659), Bp. of *Durham. He was educated at York and Halifax and at St John's College, Cambridge, where he was elected Fellow in 1586 and taught logic for several years. In 1598 he became rector of Long Marston, near York, and later Dean of *Gloucester (1606), Dean of *Winchester (1609), Canon of York (1610), Bp. of *Chester (1616), of *Lichfield and Coventry (1618), and of Durham (1632). As a resident diocesan, he preached regularly and patronized preaching ministers. On the abolition of episcopacy in 1646 he was deprived and lived for the rest of his life in retirement. He was a well-known anti-Roman controversialist, among his numerous writings being *Apologia Catholica* (1605), prob. written with the assistance of J. *Donne; *A Catholic Appeal* (1609); *Of the Institution of the Sacrament of the Blessed Body and Blood of Christ* (1631); and *De Eucharistia Controversiae Decisio* (1640).

Funeral Sermon by J. Barwick, Dean of St Paul's, with Life of Morton appended (London, 1660). Another Life 'begun by R. B., Secretary to his Lordship [i.e. Richard Baddeley] . . . and finished by J. N., D.D., his Lordship's Chaplain [Joseph Naylor]' (York, 1669). P. E. More and F. L. Cross, *Anglicanism* (1935), no. 206. K. [C.] Fincham, *Prelate as Pastor: The Episcopate of James I* (Oxford, 1990), pp. 88, 253–63, and 312. R. B. Prosser in *DNB* 39 (1894), pp. 160–6.

Moschus, John (b. *c*.550; d. 619 or 634), 'Eukratas', spiritual writer. In *c*.575 he retired from the world to the monastery of St Theodosius, near *Jerusalem. Later he journeyed widely, with his friend *Sophronius, the future Patr. of Jerusalem, visiting or settling at many notable centres of monasticism, among them Egypt, Mt. *Sinai, *Antioch, *Cyprus, and Rome. His 'Pratum Spirituale' (Λειμών, i.e. 'The Meadow') contains a large collection of anecdotes on the monastic life, derived from his personal experience and from communications of others. The book became extremely popular as a devotional manual and its text was continually added to and revised.

Gk. text, ed. F. *Ducaeus, in *Bibliotheca Veterum Patrum*, 2 (1624), pp. 1057–169, and J. B. *Cotelerius, *Ecclesiae Graecae Monumenta*, 2 (Paris, 1681), pp. 341–456; suppl. chs. from MS Par. Reg. 2464, pr. in J. P. Migne, *PG* 87. 2851–3112; Lat. tr. by A. *Traversari, orig. pub. Venice, 1475, repr. in *PL* 74. 119–240. Crit. text, with Eng. tr. and comm., by P. Pattenden in preparation; id., 'The Text of the *Pratum Spirituale*', *JTS* NS 26 (1975), pp. 38–54. Fr. tr. of the *Pratum*, with introd. and notes, by M. J. Rouët de Journel, SJ (SC 12; 1946). N. H. Baynes, 'The *Pratum Spirituale*', *OCP* 13 (1937), pp. 404–14, repr. in id., *Byzantine Studies and Other Essays* (1955), pp. 261–70; E. Mihevc-Gabrovec, *Études sur la Syntaxe de Ioannes Moschos* (Ljubljana, 1960); H. Chadwick, 'John Moschus and his friend Sophronius the Sophist', *JTS* NS 25 (1974), pp. 41–74, repr. in id., *History and Thought of the Early Church* (1982), no. 18. J. S. Palmer, *El Monacato oriental en El Pratum Spirituale de Juan Mosco* (1993). *CPG* 3 (1979), pp. 379–81 (no. 7376). E. Mioni in *Dict. Sp.* 8 (1974), cols. 632–40, s.v. 'Jean (160) Moschus'; P. Pattenden in *TRE* 17 (1988), pp. 140–4, s.v. 'Johannes Moschus', with further refs.

Moses, the Founder and Lawgiver of Israel. Acc. to the *Pentateuchal narrative, he was born in Egypt at a time when Hebrew male children were under sentence of drowning and owed his life to being hidden in a basket and rescued by Pharaoh's daughter (Exod. 2: 1–10). After living the life of a shepherd in the desert for 40 years, he received a Divine commission to rescue the Hebrews from the bondage of Egypt (Exod. 3). After much opposition from Pharaoh, which was met by the infliction of the ten plagues on the Egyptians, on the night of the *Passover Moses led the people out of Egypt (Exod. 7–12). During the journey across the desert they frequently rebelled against Moses, but by his mediation they were given *manna for food and the Ten *Commandments to guide their common life. On reaching the Desert of Paran, Moses dispatched spies to the Promised Land. When exaggerated reports of the strength of the inhabitants were brought back, the Israelites again turned against Moses and incurred the Divine sentence that they should wander in the desert for 40 years. Later Moses and *Aaron, because of their unbelief, were told that they would not enter the Promised Land (Num. 20: 12). Moses, however, was granted a sight of it from Mt. *Pisgah. Shortly afterwards he blessed the tribes of Israel (Deut. 33) and died on Mt. Nebo in Moab.

Opinions on the reliability of this account range widely from those who would regard the narrative about Moses as substantially true to those who would deny his historical existence altogether (see PENTATEUCH). The great majority of biblical scholars would at least agree that some such commanding figure as Moses is presupposed by the unity of the Israelite tribes and that it is highly unlikely that the Hebrew people would have sought their beginnings in bondage unless such had been the fact. The dates assigned to Moses vary widely (see EXODUS).

In Christian tradition Moses takes a prominent place. In the Gospels he appears at the Transfiguration Scene as the Representative of the Law (Matt. 17: 3 and parallels). In Heb. 3: 1–6 his mission is compared on a lower plane with that of Christ. A Jewish tradition preserved in the 'Assumption of *Moses', acc. to which St *Michael and the Devil contested for the body of Moses, is alluded to in Ep. of Jude (v. 9). In later tradition he became the subject of many, often extravagant, legends.

Besides comm. on the Books of the Pentateuch and histories of Israel, E. Sellin, *Mose und seine Bedeutung für die israelitisch-jüdische Religionsgeschichte* (1922). M. *Buber, *Moses* (Oxford, 1946); E. Auerbach, *Moses* (Amsterdam, 1953 [Ger.]; Eng. tr., Detroit, 1975). H. Cazelles and others, *Moïse, l'homme de l'alliance* (special issue of Cahiers Sioniens, 1955). H. Schmid, *Mose: Überlieferung und Geschichte* (Beiheft zur ZATW, 110; 1968). R. Martin-Achard and others, *La Figure de Moïse* (Publications de la Faculté de Théologie de l'Université de Genève, 1 [1978]). H. Cazelles, *A la recherche de Moïse* (1979). G. W. Coats, *Moses, Heroic Man, Man of God* (Journal for the Study of the Old Testament, Supplement Series, 57, Sheffield [1988]). I. Abrahams and others in *Encyclopaedia Judaica*, 12 (Jerusalem, 1972), cols. 371–411, s.v.

Moses, The Assumption of ('Ἀνάληψις or Διαθήκη Μωυσέως). A composite Jewish work, written in Hebrew or Aramaic during the first half of the 1st cent. AD. It contained a speech of *Moses to *Joshua, prophesying the history of the Israelite nation, and probably also an account of Moses' death and taking up into heaven. It appears to have been the work of a *Pharisee who wished to protest against the rapid secularization of his party and recall it to the Law and the old ideals. It was soon translated into Greek, and a few phrases of this edition are probably preserved in Acts 7: 36 and Jude 9, 16, 18. Part of a Latin version, made from the Greek, survives; but for the rest, apart from one or two brief fragments, the work has been lost.

Lat. text discovered and pub. by A. M. Ceriani (ed.), *Monumenta Sacra et Profana*, 1, pt. 1 (Milan, 1861), pp. 55–64. Crit. edn. by R. H. *Charles, *The Assumption of Moses translated from the Latin Sixth Century MS.* (1897). Facsimile of Ceriani's text, with Fr. tr., notes and full introd., by E. M. Laperrousaz (Semitica, 19; 1970). R. H. Charles (ed.), *The Apocrypha and Pseudepigrapha of the Old Testament*, 2 (Oxford, 1913), pp. 407–24; H. F. D. Sparks (ed.), *The Apocryphal Old Testament* (ibid., 1984), pp. 601–16. J. Priest in J. H. Charlesworth (ed.), *The Old Testament Pseudepigrapha*, 1 (1983), pp. 919–34. E. *Schürer, *The History of the Jewish People in the Age of Jesus Christ*, rev. Eng. tr. by G. Vermes and others, 3 (pt. 1; Edinburgh, 1986), pp. 278–88, with bibl. J. B. Frey in *Dict. Bibl.*, Suppl. 1 (1928), cols. 403–9, s.v. 'Apocryphes de l'Ancien Testament, 6', with bibl.

Moses bar Kepha (c.815–903), *Syrian Orthodox bishop. A native of Balad in Mesopotamia, he was educated at a nearby monastery. He was elected Bp. of Mosul c.863, and held office for about 40 years, taking the episcopal name of Severus. He is said to have written commentaries on most Books of the Bible; parts of those on Gen., the Gospels and the Pauline Epistles survive. He also wrote a number of homilies and treatises on liturgical subjects which are largely still unpublished.

Lat. tr. of *De Paradiso*, by A. Masius (Antwerp, 1569), repr. in J. P. Migne, *PG* 91. 481–608; Exposition on the Liturgy ed. R. H. *Connolly and H. W. Codrington, *Two Commentaries on the Jacobite Liturgy* (1913), with Eng. tr. pp. 24–90; part of his *Hexaemeron* ed., with Ger. tr., by J. Bakoš, *Archiv Orientální*, 2 (1930), pp. 327–61, 460–91; Ger. tr. of complete text by L. Schlimme (Göttinger Orientforschungen, I. Reihe, 14; 2 vols., 1977). Comm. on Jn. ed., with Ger. tr., by id. (ibid. 18; 4 vols., 1978–81). Discourse on the Myron (Chrism), ed., with Ger. tr., by W. Strothmann (ibid. 7; 1973). Ger. tr. of *De Anima* by O. Braun, *Moses bar Kepha und sein Buch von der Seele* (Freiburg i.B., 1891). R. A. Aytoun, 'The Mysteries of Baptism by Moses bar Kepha compared with the Odes of Solomon', *Expositor*, 8th ser. 2 (1911), pp. 338–58, incl. Eng. tr. of text. J.-M. Vosté, OP, 'L'Introduction de Mose bar Kepa aux Psaumes de David', *R. Bibl.* 38 (1929), pp. 214–28. A. *Baumstark, *Geschichte der syrischen Literatur* (1922), pp. 281 f. F. Graffin, SJ, in *Dict. Sp.* 10 (1980), cols. 1471–3, s.v. 'Moïse bar Képha'.

Moses ben Maimon. See MAIMONIDES.

Moses of Chorene, author of an influential 'History of the Armenians'. Moses purports to be a pupil of St *Mesrob; if this were the case he would have lived in the early 5th cent. This traditional dating, though still accepted by scholars in Armenia, seems hardly credible, and the work, which is highly patriotic in character, is best dated in the late 8th cent. Other writings were later wrongly attributed to Moses, including the 'Book of Rhetoric' and the 'Geography'.

The 'History' was first pub. at Amsterdam, 1695; crit edn., Tiflis, 1913, repr. (with introd. by R. W. Thomson), Delmar, NY, 1981. Lat. tr. by W. and G. *Whiston (London, 1736); Eng. tr. by R. W. Thomson (Cambridge, Mass. and London, 1978), with introd. (pp. 1–61) and bibl. (pp. 371–86). The collected works (Armenian text) attributed to Moses were pub. by the *Mechitarists of Venice in 1843 and 1865. On the 'Geography', R. W. Hewsen, 'On the date and authorship of the Ašxarhac'oyc' ', *Revue des études arméniennes*, NS 4 (1967), pp. 409–32.

Moses Maimonides. See MAIMONIDES.

Mosheim, Johann Lorenz von (1694–1755), ecclesiastical historian and divine. Educated at the University of Kiel, in 1723 he became professor of theology at Helmstedt and in 1747 at Göttingen, in the founding of which university he himself had taken an important part. His historical work was marked by a hitherto unprecedented objectivity and penetration and he may be considered the first of modern ecclesiastical historians. His *Institutiones historiae ecclesiasticae* (1726; Eng. tr. by J. Murdock, 1841) went through many editions and revisions. He was also an excellent preacher. His numerous writings include *Sittenlehre der heiligen Schrift* (5 vols., 1735–53), a *Ketzer-Geschichte* (2 vols., 1746–8), and *De rebus Christianorum ante Constantinum Magnum Commentarii* (1753).

K. Heussi, *Die Kirchengeschichtsschreibung J. L. von Mosheims* (1904); id., *J. L. Mosheim* (1906). B. Moeller, 'Johann Lorenz von Mosheim und die Gründung der Göttinger Universität', in id. (ed.), *Theologie in Göttingen* (Göttingen [1987]), pp. 9–40. J. S. Oyer in *TRE* 23 (1994). pp. 365–7, with bibl.

Moslems. See ISLAM.

Mosque of Omar. See DOME OF THE ROCK.

motet. A term, derived from the French *mot* ('word'), denoting, in church use, a type of polyphonic musical composition, occupying an important interpolative place in the liturgy. Although originating in French liturgical practice of the early 13th cent., the motet soon spread throughout Europe and flourished mainly in a secular form until the 15th cent., when its liturgical links were firmly re-established. The precise liturgical role of the motet has varied with time and place, although its predominant use has been at the *Offertory and *Elevation of the Mass. The medieval motet was designed for performance by a group of solo voices, and used a *plainsong melody as its constructional basis, but this became less in evidence as the form developed and other techniques were introduced. From the 15th cent. it became choral in style, and reached its peak with Josquin des Prés (*c.*1440–1521), O. de *Lassus, G. P. da *Palestrina, and others. In the 17th cent. new developments included once again the use of solo voices and instrumental accompaniment. The motet declined in importance from the 18th cent., and by a *motu proprio* of Pope *Pius X (1903) attempts were made to encourage a return to the older unaccompanied practice. In the *Lutheran Church in Germany a vernacular form of the motet often used the chorale as its foundation, as in the examples of J. S. *Bach; in the post-Reformation C of E the motet's traditions were continued in the *anthem.

H. Leichtentritt, *Geschichte der Motette* (Leipzig, 1908). E. H. Sanders and others in S. Sadie (ed.), *The New Grove Dictionary of Music and Musicians*, 12 (1980), pp. 617–47, s.v.

Mother of God. See THEOTOKOS.

Mothering Sunday. The Fourth Sunday in Lent, also known as *Laetare Sunday. The name has been referred (1) to the custom in some parts of England of paying a visit to one's mother on this day; or (2) to the practice of visiting the cathedral or mother church on this day; or (3) to the words occurring in the traditional *Epistle for the day, 'Jerusalem . . . which is the mother of us all' (Gal. 4: 26).

Mothers' Union, the. An organization of women in the C of E, which aims at upholding 'the sanctity of marriage' and developing in mothers a sense of responsibility in the training of their children. The Mothers' Union was founded in 1876, originally as a parochial organization, by Mary Elizabeth Sumner (née Heywood, 1828–1921), wife of George Henry Sumner (son of C. R. *Sumner), then rector of Old Alresford, Hants. In 1885, after a speech by Mary Sumner at the Portsmouth Church Congress, the Bp. of *Winchester (Harold Browne) and the Bp. of Newcastle (Ernest Wilberforce) launched the Mothers' Union as a diocesan organization. The movement spread rapidly, the first branch overseas being founded in 1897. In 1882 the first number of the *Mothers' Union Journal* was issued (superseded in 1954 by *Home and Family*), to be followed in 1891 by *Mothers in Council* (edited until 1901 by C. M. *Yonge), which continued until 1951. In 1895 a Central Council was formed; this body framed a constitution and formulated the Union's objectives, which include the organization in every place of a band of mothers to unite in prayer and 'seek by their own example to lead their families in purity and holiness of life'. In 1909, after the Gorell Commission on Marriage, the Mothers' Union added to their object of upholding the sanctity of marriage an affirmation of 'the Christian principle of the permanence of the relationship between husband and wife'. The Union was incorporated in 1910 and granted a royal charter in 1926. In 1930 the first Overseas Conference was held, with 38 diocesan Presidents and 400 members from overseas. The Mother's Union now operates in 150 dioceses of the Anglican Communion, has over 750,000 members, and maintains some 250 workers overseas. It is growing rapidly in Africa. It has long been customary to admit spinsters to associate membership, and in provinces where the Canons on Marriage have been revised, the original membership rule about divorce has been waived. Since 1925 the headquarters of the Mothers' Union has been at Mary Sumner House in Tufton Street, Westminster.

Mrs H. Porter, *Mary Sumner: Her Life and Work* (Winchester, 1921; 2nd edn., London, 1928). J. Coombs, *George and Mary Sumner: Their Life and Times* (1965), esp. pp. 81–106; [W.] O. Chadwick, *The Victorian Church*, 2 (1970), pp. 192 f.

Mott, John Raleigh (1865–1955), American *Methodist. After studying at Upper Iowa and Cornell universities, he became student secretary of the International Committee of the *YMCA (1888), chairman of the executive committee of the Student Volunteer Movement, and then in 1895 general secretary of the World Student Christian Federation, for whose formation he was largely responsible. In 1901 he was appointed assistant general secretary of the YMCA. He is chiefly known for his zealous propaganda on behalf of missions, based upon the watchword 'The Evangelization of the World in our Generation', and he acted as chairman of the committee which called the first International Missionary Conference at *Edinburgh in 1910. His interest in the *Ecumenical Movement may be dated from this time; he took part in the '*Faith and Order' Conference at Lausanne in 1927 and was Vice-President of the Edinburgh Conference in 1937. In the same year he was chairman of the '*Life and Work' Conference at Oxford. He played a considerable part in the foundation of the *World Council of Churches and was elected Honorary President at its first meeting in 1948. His numerous books, relating to missionary work, include *The Evangelization of the World in this Generation* (1900), *The Present-Day Summons to the World Mission of Christianity* (1932) and his collected *Addresses and Papers* (6 vols., New York, 1946–7).

B. [J.] Mathews, *John R. Mott: World Citizen* (1934); C. H. Hopkins, *John R. Mott 1865–1955* (Geneva and Grand Rapids, Mich., 1979).

motu proprio (Lat. 'on his own impulse'). A letter, addressed by the Pope either to the Church at large or to some part of it or to some particular persons, which has been written on his personal initiative and bears his personal signature.

F. Grat, *Étude sur le motu proprio des origines au début du XVIe siècle* (Melun, 1945).

Moule, Handley Carr Glyn (1841–1920), Bp. of *Durham. He had a brilliant career at Trinity College, Cambridge, where he was elected a Fellow in 1865. After a period as a master at Marlborough College (1865–7) he was ordained at Ely and acted for some years as his father's curate at Fordington, Dorset, returning temporarily to Cambridge from 1873 to 1877. On the establishment of Ridley Hall, Cambridge, in 1881 as a theological college on *Evangelical principles, Moule became its first Principal and was soon a leading influence for Evangelicalism at Cambridge. In 1899 he was elected Norrisian Professor of Divinity and in 1901 he succeeded B. F. *Westcott as Bp. of Durham, where he continued to promote Evangelical ideals. His writings include *Outlines of Christian Doc-*

trine (1889), *Veni Creator* (1890), *Charles Simeon* (1892), *Philippian Studies* (1897), *Colossian Studies* (1898), *Ephesian Studies* (1900), and *Christus Consolator* (1915).

J. B. Harford (ed.), *Letters and Poems of Bishop Moule* [1922]. Life by J. B. Harford and F. C. Macdonald (London [1922]). J. Baird, *The Spiritual Unfolding of Bishop H. C. G. Moule* [1926]. W. Lock in *DNB, 1912–1921*, pp. 390 f.

Moulton, James Hope (1863–1917), classical, Iranian, and NT scholar. The eldest son of W. F. *Moulton, he was appointed tutor at the Wesleyan College at Didsbury, Manchester, in 1902 and Greenwood Professor of Hellenistic Greek and Indo-European Philology at Manchester University in 1908. In 1915 he went to India to lecture on and pursue his studies of *Zoroastrianism. He lost his life through submarine action on the return journey in 1917.

In the field of the NT he did important work, esp. in bringing to bear on NT Greek the new evidence from nonliterary papyri (the significance of which he had come to understand through the writings of A. *Deissmann). His brilliant 'Prolegomena' (vol. 1, 1906) to his *Grammar of New Testament Greek* embodied many of his conclusions. In conjunction with G. Milligan he began in 1914 the issue of his important *Vocabulary of the Greek Testament, illustrated from the Papyri and other non-literary Sources* (completed in 1930). His other works included *Early Zoroastrianism* (*Hibbert Lectures for 1912; 1913). The second vol. of his *Grammar of New Testament Greek* (vol. 2: Morphology) was posthumously ed. by W. F. Howard (1929); the work was completed by two further vols. on Syntax and Style respectively by N. Turner (1963–76).

Life by his brother [W. F. Moulton] (London, 1919). Short sketch by H. K. Moulton (son) and others (ibid., 1963). A. S. *Peake in *DNB, 1912–1921*, pp. 391 f.

Moulton, William Fiddian (1835–98), biblical student. Having entered the *Wesleyan ministry in 1858, he was at once appointed to a teaching post at Richmond College, which he held till 1874. In the latter year he became the first headmaster of the Leys School, Cambridge. He was one of the foremost authorities on NT Greek in his day. In 1870 he became secretary of one of the NT committees occupied on the RV, and work in connection with the RV filled a great part of his life. His published writings include a fresh Eng. tr. of J. G. B. *Winer's *Grammar of NT Greek* (1870) and, in conjunction with A. S. Geden, a *Concordance* (1897) to the Greek NT.

Memoir by W. F. Moulton (son), with ch. on his biblical work and opinions by J. H. *Moulton (London, 1899). Shorter sketch by G. G. Findlay (ibid., 1910). G. Le G. Norgate in *DNB*, Suppl. 3 (1901), pp. 204 f.

Mount Carmel. See CARMEL, MOUNT.

Mount of Olives. See OLIVES, MOUNT OF.

movable feasts. Annual ecclesiastical feasts which do not fall on a fixed date in the secular calendar, but vary acc. to certain determined rules. Thus *Easter Day is the first Sunday after the ('ecclesiastical') full moon between 21 Mar. and 18 Apr., and a number of other feasts fall at a fixed number of days or weeks from Easter. *Advent Sunday is the Sunday falling on or nearest to 30 November.

Mowinckel, Sigmund Olaf Plytt (1884–1965), OT scholar. He was born at Kjerringøy and educated at the Cathedral School in Bergen and at the Universities of Oslo, Copenhagen, Marburg, and Giessen. His entire teaching career was spent in the University of Oslo, where he was successively *dosent* (1917–22), *professor extraordinarius* (1922–33), and *professor ordinarius* (1933–54). Of his many contributions to OT study, the most noteworthy are related to the Psalms. In his *Psalmenstudien* (6 parts, 1921–4) the influence of H. *Gunkel's literary classification of the Psalms, and of V. Grønbech's interpretation of the thought and worship of 'primitive' peoples, is evident. The most influential of Mowinckel's hypotheses is that the Psalms which celebrate *Yahweh's kingship are parts of the liturgies of a pre-exilic festival in which the enthronement of Yahweh was annually celebrated, and that its themes provided the pattern of the later eschatological hope. He reiterated his views on the Psalter, with some modifications, in *Offersang og sangoffer* (1951; Eng. tr., *The Psalms in Israel's Worship*, 2 vols., 1962). In *Han som kommer* (1951; Eng. tr., *He That Cometh*, 1956) some of the results of his work on the Psalms are combined with those of his studies of prophecy (notably the problem of the Servant of Yahweh) and of the Son of Man to form a comprehensive survey of the *Messianic hope. He also made important contributions to the study of Ezra-Nehemiah—*Statholderen Nehemia* (1916), *Ezra den skriftlærde* (1916), *Studien zu dem Buche Ezra-Nehemia* (3 vols.; 1964–5), and to the problem of the *Hexateuch—*Zur Frage nach dokumentarischen Quellen in Josua 13–19* (1946), *Tetrateuch–Pentateuch–Hexateuch* (1964), *Erwägungen zur Pentateuch Quellenfrage* (1964). Two posthumously published works are devoted to the early history of Palestine and of Israel—*Palestina før Israel* (1965) and *Israels opphav og eldste historie* (1967). He was responsible for the greater part of a translation (with commentary) of the Old Testament into Norwegian. His great academic achievement was combined with much practical service.

D. R. Ap-Thomas, 'An Appreciation of Sigmund Mowinckel's Contribution to Biblical Studies', *Journal of Biblical Literature*, 85 (1966), pp. 315–25; A. S. Kapelrud, 'Sigmund Mowinckel and Old Testament Study', *Annual of the Swedish Theological Institute*, 5 (1966–7), pp. 4–29; J. Barr, 'Mowinckel, the Old Testament, and the Question of Natural Theology', *Studia Theologica*, 42 (1988), pp. 21–38; H. M. Barstad and M. Ottosson (eds.), 'The Life and Work of Sigmund Mowinckel', *Scandinavian Journal of the Old Testament*, 2 (1988), pp. 1–168, with bibl. pp. 95–168.

Mozambique, Christianity in. Portuguese occupation of the coast of Mozambique began in 1505 and spread up the Zambesi valley. From 1577 there were *Dominican missionaries, who were joined in 1610 by *Jesuits—at most, *c*.1630, some 25 of each. They included João dos Santos, OP, author of *Ethiopia Oriental* (Evora, 1609), a major account of Portuguese expansion in Africa in the 16th cent. The old Mozambique mission never had a bishop of its own but became a 'Perpetual Vicariate' in 1612. After the suppression of the Jesuits in Portugal (1759), followed by that of other religious orders (1834), Christianity almost died out. Missionaries began to return towards the end of the 19th cent., most notably the *Franciscans (1898), but no diocese was established until after the 1940 Vatican–Portugal Concordat. All bishops

were Portuguese until after political independence (1975), but extreme tension developed between many missionaries and the colonial government in the previous ten years over repression of the nationalist movement. The *White Fathers took the unusual step of publicly withdrawing from the country in 1971 and a considerable number of priests (including one bishop) were imprisoned or expelled in 1972–4. After Independence the Marxist government at first took up a strongly anti-religious position and much Church property was confiscated, but relations were subsequently normalized. About half the population is Christian, of whom about three quarters are RC. A small *Presbyterian Church developed in the S. of the country as a result of the work from 1880 of the Mission Suisse, whose members included the outstanding ethnographer Henri-Alexandre Junod (1863–1934), author of the *Life of a South African Tribe* (1912–13; 2nd edn., 1927). In the N. the Anglican Church was built up by the *UMCA on the eastern shores of Lake Malawi. The Pentecostal *Assemblies of God now form the largest Protestant group.

Primary sources, with Eng. tr., in *Documentos sobre os Portugueses em Moçambique e na África Central 1497–1840* (Lisbon, 1962 ff. [9 vols., covering period to 1615 by 1989]). W. F. Rea, SJ, *The Economics of the Zambesi Missions 1580–1759* (Bibliotheca Instituti Historici S.I., 39; Rome, 1976). A. Hastings, *Wiriyamu* (1974); id., *A History of African Christianity 1950–1975* (Cambridge, 1979), pp. 202–4 and 210–14. J. Van Butselaar, *Africains, Missionaires et Colonialistes: Les origines de l'Église Presbytérienne du Mozambique (Mission Suisse) 1880–1896* (Studies on Religion in Africa, 5; Leiden, 1984).

Mozarabic chant. The music of the Mozarabic rite has been preserved in many MSS from the 9th–11th cents., which enshrine chant possibly dating back to the early 8th cent. The neumes in which it is written, however, cannot now be read, because the Mozarabic chant had been ousted by the *Gregorian before the four-line staff came into use; hence the neumes are legible only to the extent of the number of their notes, but there is no means of determining the relations of tonal height within the notes of a neume, nor its melodic connection with the preceding or following neumes. A MS of San Millán de la Cogolla (printed by C. Rojo and G. Prado), however, has preserved some 21 melodies in legible notation of the Aquitanian type. At least two early chant traditions have been distinguished, those of Toledo and León, the latter exemplified esp. in the 10th cent. Antiphoner of León. Both the Mass and Office were provided with melodies varying greatly in style from the syllabic to the highly melismatic, resembling in this respect the *Ambrosian as much as the Gregorian chant. There exists at Toledo an extensive collection of melodies in a small collection of MSS dating from *c*.1500; these are written in staff notation with some rhythmic indications. There are blank staves for the priest's music and some of the congregational responses in the Ordinary and Canon of the Mass in the *Missale mixtum* published by Card. F. *Ximénez de Cisneros in 1500, and in some copies the chant has been added by hand. (This is reproduced, in a somewhat debased form, in the editions of 1757 and 1804.) The relationship between all this material and the earlier medieval traditions is a question that has not yet been satisfactorily resolved, though the 'Pater Noster' in the Missal looks ancient.

C. Rojo, OSB, and G. Prado, OSB (eds.), *El canto mozárabe: Estudio histórico-crítico de su antigüedad y estado actual* (Barcelona, 1929). The León Antiphoner was first pub. by the Benedictines of Silos at León in 1928; also ed. by L. Brou, OSB, and J. Vives (Monumenta Hispaniae Sacra, Serie Liturgica, 5. 1; Barcelona and Madrid, 1959); facsimile (ibid. 5. 2; 1953). G. Prado, OSB, 'Mozarabic Melodics', *Speculum*, 3 (1928), pp. 218–38. L. Brou, OSB, 'L'Antiphonaire wisigothique et l'antiphonaire grégorien au début du viiiᵉ siècle. Essai de musicologie comparée', *Annuario Musical*, 5 (1950), pp. 3–10; id., 'L'Alleluia dans la liturgie mozarabe. Étude liturgico-musicale d'après les manuscrits de chant', ibid. 6 (1951), pp. 3–90; id., 'Notes de paléographie musicale mozarabe', ibid. 7 (1952), pp. 51–76; id., 'Le Joyau des antiphonaires latins. Le Manuscrit 8 des archives de la cathédrale de León', *Archivos Leoneses*, 8 (1954), pp. 7–114, and other arts. in this issue. C. W. Brockett, Jun., *Antiphons, Responsories and other Chants of the Mozarabic Rite* (Musicological Studies, 15; New York [1968]). D. M. Randel, *The Responsorial Psalm Tones for the Mozarabic Office* (Princeton Studies in Music, 3; 1969); id., *An Index to the Chant of the Mozarabic Rite* (ibid. 6 [1973]). I. Wortman in *NCE* 10 (1967), p. 60, s.v. 'Mozarabic Rite, Chants of'; D. M. Randel in S. Sadie (ed.), *The New Grove Dictionary of Music and Musicians*, 12 (1980), pp. 667–75, s.v. 'Mozarabic rite, music for the'.

Mozarabic rite. The conventional name given to the liturgical forms which were in use in the Iberian Peninsula from the earliest times until the 11th cent. It is, however, a misnomer, for the term 'Mozarabic' is correctly applied only to that part of Spain which fell under Moorish rule after 711; but alternative names, such as Visigothic or Old Spanish, have not won general acceptance.

The early history of the rite is very obscure. From the conversion of the Visigothic King *Recared (589) until the Moorish invasion (711) we have the evidence of frequent national councils and of the writings of the Spanish fathers *Isidore (esp. his *De ecclesiasticis officiis*), *Leander, *Ildefonsus, and others. Much attention was then paid to the establishment and promulgation of a uniform rite for the Mass and for the Offices. The Fourth Council of *Toledo, for instance, in 633 decreed that there should be *unus . . . ordo orandi atque psallendi . . ., unus modus in missarum solemnitatibus, unus in vespertinis matutinisque officiis* (can. 2). The practice of composing Masses, notably by three bishops of Toledo, Eugenius II (646–57), Ildefonsus (657–67) and Julian (680–90), led to increasing elaboration and prolixity in accordance with the literary taste of the day. The only extant service-book dating from the period before the Moorish invasion is the Verona *Liber orationalis*, but it is probable that the MSS of the 10th and 11th cents. faithfully preserve, for the most part, the essential features of the 7th-cent. liturgy.

The replacement of the Mozarabic by the Roman rite was a consequence of the Christian reconquest of Spain. The Cluniac monks brought the Roman rite with them into Catalonia. In Navarre it was introduced into the abbey of San Salvador at Leyre in 1067, in Aragon into the abbey of San Juan de la Peña in 1071. At the Council of Burgos in 1080 it was prescribed for the kingdoms of Castile and León. On the reconquest of Toledo (1085) there was resistance to the abolition of the Mozarabic rite and it was allowed to remain in use in the six old parishes of the city. Its preservation in modern times is due to Francisco *Ximénez de Cisneros, who became Abp. of Toledo in 1495. He founded the Corpus Christi chapel in the Cathedral and endowed chaplains to use the Mozarabic

rite. He also caused a Missal and a Breviary to be printed (1500 and 1502). In modern times there have been various attempts to introduce the rite more widely. In 1989 approval was given by the *Roman Congregation for Divine worship for the general use in the region of Toledo (and with the permission of the *Ordinary, throughout Spain) of a new *Missale Hispano-Mozarabicum*, revised on the basis of the oldest MSS and with regard to the reforms of the Second *Vatican Council.

The Mozarabic rite has close affinities with the *Gallican, though influences from North Africa and possibly Byzantium have also been detected. Distinctive features in the Mass include the use of the *Trisagion in Greek; a chant known as the 'Sacrificium' (corresponding to the *Offertory), followed by two prayers, of which the first, the 'Missa' or 'Oratio Admonitionis' is addressed to the people that 'they may be stirred to pray earnestly before God'; a long and elaborate 'Illatio' (corresponding to the *Preface), varying each day; the recitation of the (*Nicene) Creed immediately before (or, in one tradition, after) the *Lord's Prayer; and the *Fraction of the Host into seven (or according to the Missal of Ximénez, nine) pieces, representing the mysteries of the life of Christ, a practice found also in the *Celtic rites of the 10th and 11th cent. In the Office a distinction between the secular (*ordo cathedralis*) and monastic Office survived in Spain when it disappeared in the Roman rite. The secular Office consisted only of *Vespers and *Mattins, with selected Psalms or portions of Psalms, which were sung, with refrains, as responds and antiphons. The monastic Office in its developed form appears to have had twelve Offices by day and twelve by night.

The principal service-books were the Psalter; *Liber canticorum*; *Liber hymnorum*; *Antiphonarium*, comprising antiphons and responds both for the Mass and for the Offices; *Liber orationum*, containing collects for the Offices; *Liber missarum*, corresponding to the *Sacramentary; and *Liber ordinum*, containing occasional Offices, Ordination rites and Votive Masses. These books are of an earlier type than the combination or mixture of elements found in the Roman Missal and Breviary. The process by which the printed *Missale mixtum* and *Breviarium* of Ximénez were compiled is still obscure, but these printed books preserve ancient texts not otherwise known, and also show the infiltration of the Roman rite.

The early Irish service books contain borrowings from the Mozarabic rite ('Spanish symptoms'), which most scholars believe to have been imported direct from Spain to Ireland. The Roman books include Mozarabic material in the prayers of the *Rituale* for the dying and dead, which came in by way of the supplement *Hucusque to the Gregorian Sacramentary. At a later date the Mozarabic 'benedictio fontis' was used in compiling the *Baptismal Office of the 1549 BCP.

The *editio princeps* of the Missal was the *Missale Mixtum secundum Regulam Beati Isidori, dictum Mozarabes* (Toledo, 1500). Later edn. by A. Lesley, SJ, Rome, 1755; repr. in J. P. Migne, *PL* 85. *Editio princeps* of the Breviary was the *Breviarium secundum Regulam Beati Isidori* (Toledo, 1502); also ed. F. A. Lorenzana, Madrid, 1775; repr., Rome, 1804; also in J. P. Migne, *PL* 86. M. Férotin, OSB (ed.), *Le Liber Ordinum en usage dans l'Église wisigothique et mozarabe de l'Espagne du cinquième au onzième siècle* (Monumenta Ecclesiae Liturgica, 5; Paris, 1904); id. (ed.), *Le*

Liber Mozarabicus Sacramentorum et les manuscrits mozarabes (ibid. 6; 1912); J. P. Gilson (ed.), *The Mozarabic Psalter (MS. British Museum, Add. 30,851)* (HBS 30; 1905); J. Vives and J. Claveras (eds.), *Oracional Visigótico* (Monumenta Hispaniae Sacra, Serie Liturgica, 1; 1941); J. Pérez de Urbel, OSB, and A. Gonzalez y Ruiz-Zorrilla (eds.), *Liber Commicus* (ibid. 2–3; 1950–5). W. C. Bishop, *The Mozarabic and Ambrosian Rites* (*Alcuin Club Tracts, 15; 1924), pp. 1–97. W. S. Porter, *The Gallican Rite*, ed. F. L. Cross (1958). M. Ramos, SJ, *Oratio Admonitionis: Contribución al estudio de la Antigua Misa Española* (Biblioteca Teológica Granadina, 8; 1964). J. F. Rivera Recio (ed.), *Estudios sobre la liturgia mozarabe* (Toledo, 1965), incl. list of primary sources, with places of pub., by J. M. Pinell, OSB, pp. 109–64, and general bibl. by J. M. Mora Ontalba, pp. 165–87. T. C. Akeley, OGS, *Christian Initiation in Spain c.300–1100* (1967). On the 1988 *Missale Hispano-Mozarabicum*, see J. Pinell, OSB, in *Notitiae*, 24 (1988), pp. 670–727. Vogel, *Sources*, pp. 35 f., 109, 277–80, 333–5, and 361. F. *Cabrol, OSB, in *DACL* 12 (pt. 1; 1935), cols. 390–491, s.v.; J. Pinell, OSB, in *LW* 2 (1968), cols. 1796–1825, s.v., with extensive bibl. See also works cited under MOZARABIC CHANT.

mozetta. A short cape-like garment to which until 1969 a small hood was attached, worn by the Pope, cardinals, exempt abbots, abbots-general, and other privileged dignitaries. It came into use in the later Middle Ages. Its colour depends on the office of the wearer and the occasion on which it is worn.

Braun, *LG*, pp. 357 f.

Mozley, James Bowling (1813–78), post-*Tractarian theologian. Educated at Oriel College, Oxford, where his brother, Thomas (q.v.), became a Fellow, he was elected to a fellowship at Magdalen in 1840. From the first he had taken a keen interest in the *Oxford Movement, and after the secession of J. H. *Newman in 1845 was for a time one of its foremost representatives in Oxford. Largely under the influence of the *Gorham Case, he was led to modify his Tractarian beliefs in a more moderate direction, though he continued a strong Churchman. His books include *On the Augustinian Doctrine of Predestination* (1855) and *The Primitive Doctrine of Baptismal Regeneration* (1856); but much of his most brilliant writing is to be found in his essays and articles, collected as *Essays Historical and Theological* (2 vols., 1878). His *Bampton Lectures on 'Miracles' (1865) were acclaimed a masterly contribution to a then very pressing issue. From 1871 till his death he was Regius professor of divinity at Oxford. From 1856 he also held the living of Old Shoreham in W. Sussex, where he died on 4 Jan. 1878.

Collected edn. of *University and other Sermons* (1876). Mozley's *Essays Historical and Theological* (2 vols., 1878; with biog. introd., 1, pp. xi–xlviii), and *Letters* (1885; also with biog. introd. pp. 1–30), both ed. by his sister, A. Mozley (1809–91). His fine sermon on 'The Reversal of Human Judgment', repr. in H. H. *Henson (ed.), *Selected English Sermons* (World's Classics, 1939), pp. 279–304. W. A. Greenhill in *DNB* 39 (1894), pp. 249–51.

Mozley, Thomas (1806–93), divine and journalist. The brother of J. B. *Mozley, he was educated at Oriel College, Oxford (where J. H. *Newman was his tutor), and elected a Fellow of the College in 1829. A staunch supporter of the *Tractarian Movement, he edited the *British Critic* (1841–3), wrote extensively for *The Times* newspaper, and held a succession of parochial appointments. He is remem-

bered particularly for his *Reminiscences, chiefly of Oriel College and the Oxford Movement* (2 vols., 1882), which is valuable for the light it throws on many aspects of the *Oxford Movement, and *Letters from Rome on the Occasion of the* [First *Vatican] *Council, 1869–1870* (2 vols., 1891). Though a gifted writer, Mozley was apt to be inaccurate in his record of facts.

There is no Life, but much is to be gleaned from scattered refs. to him in the lit. of the Oxford Movement. A. F. Pollard in *DNB* 39 (1894), pp. 251 f., s.v.

Muggletonians. A sect founded in 1652 by John Reeve (1608–58) and his cousin, Ludowicke Muggleton (1609–98), who claimed to be the 'two witnesses' of Rev. 11: 3–6. They denied the doctrine of the Holy Trinity, and held that during the period of the Incarnation the government of heaven was left to *Elijah. Believing that God would never again interfere with the world after His revelation to Reeve, they condemned prayer and preaching. They also taught that matter was eternal and reason the creation of the devil. The Muggletonians long survived as a very small sect; the last member died in 1979.

[J. E.] C. Hill, B. Reay, and W. Lamont, *The World of the Muggletonians* (1983). W. Lamont, 'The Muggletonians 1652–1979: a "vertical" approach', *Past and Present*, 99 (1983), pp. 22–40; cf. [J. E.] C. Hill and W. Lamont, 'Debate: The Muggletonians', ibid. 104 (1984), pp. 152–63.

Muhlenberg, Henry Melchior (1711–87), 'Patriarch' of the *Lutheran Church in America. He was born in Einbeck, Hanover, and educated at Göttingen, where he was imbued with a broad form of *Pietism. He soon expressed interest in missionary work first to the Jews and then in India (in the Danish-Halle mission), but in 1742 he was sent to America by the mission centre in Halle which had been established by the Pietist leader A. H. *Francke. He was sent in response to an appeal made by three Lutheran congregations in Pennsylvania in 1733; he was to instruct them in confessional Lutheranism, recover disaffected members, and to see to the organization and extension of the Lutheran Church. He founded numerous congregations and schools and strengthened existing ones, mostly in the area of Philadelphia, but he also visited, encouraged and corresponded with many settlements along the eastern seaboard. He recruited European Lutheran pastors for service in America, continually and successfully solicited assistance from Germany, and trained an American clergy. In 1748 he organized the Ministerium of Pennsylvania, the first permanent Lutheran Synod in America.

His autobiog., covering his life to 1743, ed. W. Germann (Allentown, Pa., and Halle/Salle, 1881). Correspondence, ed. K. Aland (Texte zur Geschichte des Pietismus, Abt. 3. Bd. 2, 5, etc.; 1986 ff.). Eng. tr. of his Journals, ed. T. G. Tappert and J. W. Doberstein (3 vols., Philadelphia, 1942–58). M. L. Stoever, *Memoir of the Life and Times of Henry Melchior Muhlenberg* (ibid., 1856); W. J. Mann, *Life and Times of Henry Melchior Muhlenberg* (ibid., 1887). P. A. W. Wallace, *The Muhlenbergs of Pennsylvania* (ibid., 1950), pp. 1–273. G. H. Genzmer in *Dict. Amer. Biog.* 13 (1934), pp. 310 f., s.v.

Müller, F. Max. See MAX MÜLLER, FRIEDRICH.

Müller, George (1805–98), philanthropist and preacher. He was born near Halberstadt in Germany, but later became a British subject. Though intended for the ministry Müller was profligate as a youth until in 1825, while a student at Halle, he came into contact with a group of earnest Christians and experienced a religious conversion. In 1829 he came to London to take up an appointment with the Society for Promoting Christianity among the Jews. Forced by ill-health to leave London, in 1830 he moved to Teignmouth, where he associated himself with the *Plymouth Brethren, resigned from his previous appointment, and became a preacher to the local community. Believing that temporal as well as spiritual needs could be supplied through faith and prayer, he abolished pew rents and refused a salary, supporting himself and his charitable work with offerings from his followers. Two years later he moved to Bristol, where he devoted his life to the care of orphan children, relying on voluntary contributions which flowed in through the deep impression made by his *Narrative of the Lord's Dealings with George Müller* (pt. 1, 1837; 2, 1841). Starting with only a few children, he eventually had 2,000 under his care, accommodated in large houses at Ashley Down, near Bristol. At the age of 70, leaving this work in the hands of his daughter and her husband, James Wright, Müller set out with his second wife on a preaching mission to Europe, America, India, Australia, and China extending over 17 years. He died at Bristol.

Autobiography of George Müller compiled by G. F. Bergin, with preface and concluding ch. by A. T. Pierson (London, 1905). Mrs [S. G.] Müller, *Preaching Tours and Missionary Labours of George Müller* (1883), with introd. by G. Müller, pp. iii–xiv. E. K. Groves (nephew), *George Müller and his Successors* (1906). Lives by F. G. Warne (London [1898]; enlarged [1935]); A. T. Pierson (ibid., 1899; with additions [1949]); N. Garton (ibid., 1963); and R. Steer (ibid., 1975; rev. edn., 1990). T. B. Johnstone in *DNB*, Suppl. 3 (1901), pp. 208 f.

Müller, Julius (1801–78), German Protestant theologian. He studied law at Breslau and Göttingen universities, but finding his spiritual aspirations unsatisfied, under the influence of F. A. G. *Tholuck, who urged him to come to Berlin (1823), he studied theology. In 1825 he was ordained pastor at Breslau. In 1831 he was appointed university preacher at Göttingen, and in 1835 professor of dogmatics at *Marburg. Here he upheld a conservative Protestant theology against the *Hegelianism of the *Tübingen School, esp. F. C. *Baur, and the *Leben Jesu* of D. F. *Strauss. In 1839 he was appointed to the chair of theology at Halle. In his principal work, *Die christliche Lehre von der Sünde* (vol. 1, 1839; 2, 1844), he sought to interpret the fact of sin on the assumption of an extra-temporal fall occasioned by a free and intelligible act of decision on the part of each individual. As one of the most prominent theologians of his time he took a leading part in the negotiations for the Prussian Evangelical Union. In 1850 he founded, with J. A. W. *Neander and K. I. *Nitzsch, the *Deutsche Zeitschrift für christliche Wissenschaft und christliches Leben*; most of his contributions to it were collected in the *Dogmatische Abhandlungen* (1870).

Life by his son-in-law, L. Schultze (Bremen, 1879); also L. Schultze, *D. Julius Müller als Ethiker und die Glaubensfrage mit Bezug auf das Apostolicum* (1895). K. *Barth, *Die protestantische Theologie im 19. Jahrhundert* (Zurich, 1947), pp. 535–43; Eng. tr. (1972), pp. 588–96.

Müller, Ludwig (1883–1945), German *Reichsbischof. He was born at Gütersloh and educated at Münster i.W. When an army chaplain at Königsberg, he met Hitler (1926), who in 1933 made him his confidential adviser in Church matters; and, under strong Nazi pressure, he was elected Bp. of Prussia and also Reichsbischof. Resistance from the embryonic *Confessing Church to his Aryanizing policy led to his virtual supersession in 1935 by the appointment of H. Kerrl as Minister for Church Affairs, though Müller nominally remained in office. In 1936 he published a Germanized version of the Sermon on the Mount.

J. C. R. Wright, '*Above Parties': The Political Attitudes of the German Protestant Church Leadership 1918–1933* (Oxford Historical Monographs, 1974), pp. 118–60 *passim*; rev. Ger. tr. (1977), pp. 183–6 and 196–234 *passim*.

Mungo, St. See KENTIGERN, ST.

Munificentissimus Deus. The opening words and hence the name of the Apostolic Constitution issued by *Pius XII on 1 Nov. 1950 defining the doctrine of the *Assumption of the BVM (q.v.). The Pope declared it as a matter of divinely revealed dogma that the BVM 'having completed her earthly course was in body and soul assumed into heavenly glory', to deny which would incur the wrath of Almighty God and the Holy Apostles. The definition of the dogma aroused considerable opposition among members of the E. Churches and among some Anglicans who feared that it would impede any plans for union, though the statement of the doctrine was very moderate.

Text in *AAS* 42 (1950), pp. 753–73. B. *Capelle, OSB, 'Théologie de l'Assomption d'après la bulle "Munificentissimus Deus"', *Nouvelle Revue théologique*, 72 (1950), pp. 1009–27.

Münster, Sebastian (1488–1552), Hebrew scholar. He studied at Heidelberg, *Tübingen, and Vienna and later entered the *Franciscan Order, which he abandoned for Protestantism. From 1529 until his death he taught at Basle. He produced the first German edition of the Hebrew Bible (2 vols., Basle, 1534–5; with a literal Latin version and notes), extensive use of which was made by M. *Coverdale for the OT of the *Great Bible (1539). His most widely read work, his *Cosmographia Universalis* (Basle, 1544), was a geographical description of the world after the manner of Strabo, written in German. He also published an Aramaic (1527, 'Chaldaica') and several Hebrew grammars (notably those of 1536 and 1542, the latter much influenced by E. Levita).

Letters ed. K. H. Burmeister (Ingelheim am Rhein, 1964). Facsimile reprod. of his edn. of Ptolemy's *Geographia* (orig. pub. Basle, 1540) with introd. by R. A. Skelton (Amsterdam, 1966). V. Hantzsch, *Sebastian Münster: Leben, Werke, wissenschaftliche Bedeutung* (*Abh.* (Sächs.), 23, Heft 3; 1898). K. H. Burmeister, *Sebastian Münster: Versuch eines biographischen Gesamtbildes* (Basler Beiträge zur Geschichtswissenschaft, 91; 1963). A. Wolkenhauer, *Sebastian Münsters handschriftliches Kollegienbuch aus den Jahren 1515–1518 und seine Karten* (*Abh.* (Gött.), NF 11, Heft 3; 1909). J. Friedman, *The Most Ancient Testimony: Sixteenth-Century Christian-Hebraica in the Age of Renaissance Nostalgia* (Athens, Oh. [1983]), pp. 44–8, 165–8, and 212–44. K. H. Burmeister, *Sebastian Münster: Eine Bibliographie* (Wiesbaden, 1964).

Müntzer (sometimes **Münzer**), **Thomas** (*c.*1489–1525), German radical reformer. A native of Stolberg in the Harz mountains, he may have studied at Leipzig and he certainly gained a degree at Frankfurt an der Oder. After serving as a chantry-priest in Brunswick from 1514, in 1517/18 he attended lectures at *Wittenberg on classical authors and the Church Fathers. He studied medieval spiritual writers, esp. J. *Tauler and *Henry Suso, while he was confessor to a *Cistercian nunnery in Thuringia in 1519/20. Probably on M. *Luther's recommendation, he became preacher in Zwickau in May 1520; here he developed a spiritual and mystical theology increasingly at odds with the literal biblical interpretation of Wittenberg. After expulsion for an alleged breach of the public peace, in 1521 he went to Prague, where, convinced that the Apocalypse was at hand, he tried to revive a true apostolic Church, building on the legacy of the *Hussites. Again expelled, he spent 1522 without a permanent post, sustained by a belief in the need for the soul to be purified by suffering and tribulation before it could receive the Holy Spirit. In 1523 he became pastor in Allstedt, where he composed the first liturgies in German and also several tracts, in which he attacked 'counterfeit' faith and expressed reservations about *Infant Baptism. Faced with Catholic persecution in the area, Müntzer formed a defensive 'Christian League' as a new covenant with God (on the analogy of 2 Kgs. 23), which he later revived as an active clarion to rebellion in the *Peasants' War. Luther's warning to the Protestant Saxon princes about his 'fanaticism' led to Müntzer's expulsion from Allstedt in late 1524. After a brief stay in Mühlhausen, occasioning civil unrest, in Sept. 1524 he went to the heartland of the gathering peasant rebellion in SW Germany. Returning to Mühlhausen in the spring of 1525, he recast the city government as an eternal council, pledged to the Word of God, and completed the establishment of reformed worship. As the peasants' rebellion approached, he placed himself at the head of the local troops, convinced that the struggle of the saints in the Last Days had begun. After the defeat of the rebels at the battle of Frankenhausen (15 May 1525), Müntzer was tortured and executed, without recanting his fundamental beliefs. Several subsequent *Anabaptist leaders, notably Hans Hut, invoked his name and theology in their cause.

Schriften und Briefe, ed. P. Kirn and G. Franz (Quellen und Forschungen zur Reformationsgeschichte, 33; Gütersloh, 1968). *Schriften* also ed. G. Seebass and E. Wolgast (in preparation) and *Briefe*, ed. S. Bräuer and M. Kobuch (in preparation). Eng. tr. of *Collected Works*, ed. and tr. by P. Matheson (Edinburgh, 1988). W. Elliger, *Thomas Müntzer: Leben und Werk* (Göttingen, 1975); H.-J. Goertz, *Thomas Müntzer: Mystiker-Apokalyptiker-Revolutionär* (Munich, 1989; Eng. tr., 1993); M. Bensing, *Thomas Müntzer und der Thüringer Aufstand 1525* (Leipziger Übersetzungen und Abhandlungen zum Mittelalter, Reihe B, 3; Berlin, 1966); H.-J. Goertz, *Innere und äussere Ordnung in der Theologie Thomas Müntzers* (Studies in the History of Christian Thought, 2; Leiden, 1967); [E.] G. Rupp, *Patterns of Reformation* (1969), pp. 157–353; R. Schwarz, *Die apokalyptische Theologie Thomas Müntzers und der Taboriten* (Beiträge zur historischen Theologie, 55; Tübingen, 1977); T. Scott, *Thomas Müntzer: Theology and Revolution in the German Reformation* (1989); E. W. Gritsch, *Thomas Müntzer: A Tragedy of Errors* (Minneapolis [1989]); S. Bräuer and H. Junghans (eds.), *Der Theologe Thomas Müntzer: Untersuchungen zu seiner Entwicklung und Lehre* (Berlin and Göttingen, 1989); U. Bubenheimer, *Thomas Müntzer: Herkunft und Bildung* (Studies in Medieval and Reformation Thought, 46; Leiden, etc., 1989); A. Friesen, *Thomas Muentzer, a Destroyer of the Godless* (Berkeley, Calif., etc., 1990).

Muratori, Lodovico Antonio (1672–1750), Italian historian and theological scholar. Born at Vignola, near Modena, he was educated by the *Jesuits at Modena and, after becoming *doctor utriusque juris* (1694), was ordained priest in 1695. In the same year he became attached to the *Ambrosiana in Milan, where he remained until 1700, when the Duke of Modena offered him the post of archivist and librarian of his library. In 1716 he combined with his librarianship the position of Provost of Santa Maria della Pomposa, living in Modena until his death.

Muratori became involved in the diplomatic controversy between the Emperor and the Pope about the fief of Comacchio. It was in this connection that he wrote his *Piena esposizione de i diritti imperiali ed estensi sopra la città di Comacchio* (Modena, 1712), a work of some judicial importance. He collaborated with G. W. *Leibniz on a projected history of the houses of Brunswick and da Este, which was never completed; his research on the subject, however, issued in the publication of a vast corpus of medieval sources of Italian history, *Rerum Italicarum Scriptores* (25 vols., Milan, 1723–51), which was followed by *Antiquitates Italicae Medii Aevi* (6 vols., 1738–48). He also published an important collection of liturgical documents under the title *Liturgia Romana Vetus* (2 vols., Venice, 1748; repr. Naples, 1760, and largely reproduced in various volumes of J. P. *Migne, *Patrologia Latina*); he printed the texts of the *Leonine, *Gelasian, and *Gregorian Sacramentaries, followed by the '*Missale Gothicum', the '*Missale Francorum', the '*Missale Gallicanum Vetus', the 'Sacramentarium Gallicanum' (i.e. the *Bobbio Missal) and the First and Second '*Ordines Romani'. He was influenced by the historical method of the *Maurists and corresponded with J. *Mabillon and B. de *Montfaucon. His numerous theological works, often pseudonymous, provoked attacks on his orthodoxy: in 1748 the Spanish *Inquisition initiated proceedings against him, but he was protected by Pope *Benedict XIV. See also the following entry.

Collected Works ed. at Arezzo (13 vols., 1767–73) and at Venice (48 vols., 1790–1800). [Selected] *Opere* ed. G. Falco and F. Forti (La Letteratura Italiana, Storia e Testi, 44; 2 vols. [1964]), with full introd. *Epistolario*, ed. M. Campori (14 vols., Modena, 1901–22). *Trattato della carità cristiana e altri scritti sulla carità* ed. P. G. Nonis [1961]. Life by his nephew, Gian Francesco Soli Muratori (Modena, 1756). G. Cavazzuti, *Lodovico Antonio Muratori, 1672–1750* (1950). M. Monaco, *La Vita, le opere, il pensiero di L. A. Muratori e la sua concezione della pubblica felicità* (Lecce, 1977). *Miscellanea di Studi Muratoriani* (Atti e Memorie della R. Deputazione di Storia Patria per le Provincie Modenesi, 7th ser. 8; 1933); *Miscellanea di Studi Muratoriani* (Modena, 1951). A. C. Jemolo, 'Il pensiero religioso di Ludovico Antonio Muratori', *Rivista trimestrale di studi filosofici e religiosi*, 4 (1923), pp. 23–78. A. Vecchi, *L'opera religiosa del Muratori* (Accademia di Scienze, Lettere e Arti di Modena, 1955). S. Bertelli, *Erudizione e storia in Ludovico Antonio Muratori* (Istituto Italiano per gli Studi Storici in Napoli, 1960). E. Raimondi, 'I padri maurini e l'opera del Muratori', *Giornale storico della Letteratura italiana*, 128 (1951), pp. 429–71, and 129 (1952), pp. 145–78; repr. in id., *I Lumi dell'Erudizione* (Arti e Scritture, 2; Milan, 1989), pp. 3–77, with other work on Muratori repr., pp. 79–124. E. Cochrane, 'Muratori: The Vocation of a Historian', *Catholic Historical Review*, 51 (1965), pp. 153–72, with refs. L. Brandolini, CM, 'La Pastorale dell'Eucharistia di Ludovico A. Muratori', *EL* 81 (1967), pp. 333–75; 82 (1968), pp. 81–118. T. Sorbelli, *Bibliografia muratoriana* (2 vols., Modena, 1943–4). H. *Leclercq, OSB, in *DACL* 12 (pt. 1; 1935), cols. 536–43; and F. Cognasso in *EC* 8 (1952), cols. 1523–7, with bibl.

Muratorian Canon. The oldest extant list of NT writings, discovered by L. A. *Muratori in an 8th-cent. *Ambrosiana MS (J. 101 sup.). It is generally held to date from the (later) 2nd cent., because *Pius I, *Hermas, *Marcion, *Basilides, and *Montanus are mentioned as contemporaries of the author, though it has been argued that it dates from the 4th cent. The list comprises 85 lines; the beginning and probably also the end are missing, for it starts with what must be the conclusion of a notice on St Mark and continues with accounts of Luke and John, enumerated as the third and fourth Gospels respectively. It mentions all the NT books except Heb., Jas., and 1 and 2 Pet., and also the *Apocalypse of Peter and the Wisdom of *Solomon, though with a *caveat*. It rejects the 'Shepherd' of Hermas, the Marcionite Epistles of St *Paul to *Laodicea and *Alexandria, and a series of other *Gnostic and Montanist writings. The Canon is written in very bad Latin, full of orthographical and grammatical errors. Some scholars believe it to be a translation from the Greek.

The Muratorian Canon was first pub. by Muratori in *Antiquitates Italicae Medii Aevi*, 3 (Milan, 1740), pp. 851–4. Facsimile edn. by S. P. *Tregelles, *Canon Muratorianus* (1867). Rev. text by E. S. Buchanan in *JTS* 8 (1906–7), pp. 537–45. Comm., with text, in NT handbooks, e.g. B. F. *Westcott, *A General Survey of the History of the Canon of the New Testament* (1st edn., 1855), Appendix C. H. von Campenhausen, *Die Entstehung der christlichen Bibel* (Beiträge zur historischen Theologie, 39; 1968), pp. 282–303 (Eng. tr., 1972, pp. 243–62). A. C. Sundberg, Jun., 'Canon Muratori: a Fourth-Century List', *HTR* 66 (1973), pp. 1–41. G. M. Hahneman, *The Muratorian Fragment and the Development of the Canon* (Oxford Theological Monographs, 1992). *CPG* 1 (1983), p. 256 (no. 1862). Altaner and Stuiber (1978), pp. 94 f. and 560 f. H. *Leclercq OSB, in *DACL* 12 (pt. 1; 1935), cols. 543–60, s.v. 'Muratorianum', with good photographic reprods. G. A. Robbins in *Anchor Bible Dictionary*, 4 (1992), pp. 928 f., s.v. 'Muratorian Fragment'.

Murillo, Bartolomé Esteban (1617–82), Spanish painter. Except for short visits to Madrid, Murillo spent all his life in Seville. He is esp. known as the painter of the 'Immaculate Conception', which he executed more than 20 times, and he was the foremost Spanish artist of the theme of the 'Virgin and Child'. A supreme painter of children, his interest ranged from the infancy of Christ and of St *John the Baptist into the secular sphere. His treatment of religious themes was often combined with a fascination for genre anticipating the 18th cent. He was a prolific artist; his work is well represented in the Prado Museum, Madrid.

Reprods. of his paintings (in black and white), ed. A. L. Mayer (Klassiker der Kunst in Gesamtausgaben, 22; 1913). D. A. Iñiguez, *Murillo* (3 vols., Madrid, 1981), with full bibl. and reprods. of his painting, many in colour. J. Brown, *Murillo and his Drawings* (Princeton, NJ [1976]). *Bartolomé Esteban Murillo 1617–1682.* Catalogue of an Exhibition at the Museo del Prado, Madrid, 1983, and the Royal Academy of Arts, London, 1983 (1982), with select bibl. C. B. Curtis, *Velázquez and Murillo: A Descriptive and Historical Catalogue of the Works of . . . Velázquez and Bartolomé Esteban Murillo* (1888), pp. 109–352.

Myconius, Friedrich (1490–1546), *Lutheran reformer of Thuringia. Born at Lichtenfels on the Main, he studied at Annaberg. After entering the *Franciscan Order (14 July 1510) he was transferred to Leipzig, and in 1512 to Weimar. In 1516 he was ordained priest and soon became known as a persuasive preacher. Although he was an ardent student of Scholastic theology, he found that it did not meet all his needs and he sympathized with M. *Luther's attack on *indulgences in 1517. Consequently he was confined in various houses of the Order in the following years. In 1524 he finally fled and in the same year was appointed by Duke Johann preacher at Gotha, where he married, reformed the schools, and exercised a powerful moral influence. In correspondence with Luther from 1525 and with P. *Melanchthon from 1527, he played a leading part in the Reform Movement. He was present at the Conferences at *Marburg (1529), *Wittenberg (1536), *Schmalkalden (1537), Frankfurt and Nuremberg (1539), and *Hagenau (1540). In 1538 he visited England on the embassy which hoped to win *Henry VIII over to the *Schmalkaldic League. He returned to Gotha in 1540.

Although known in his lifetime mainly as a preacher and educational reformer, Myconius also wrote extensively. His main work, *Historia Reformationis*, written in conjunction with J. Heller (ed. by E. S. Cyprian, 1715; modern edn. by O. Clemen, 1914), is a valuable contemporary source esp. for the movement in Thuringia. He also wrote tracts in the vernacular, among them *Wie man die Einfältigen, und sonderlich die Kranken, im Christenthum unterrichten soll* (1539).

H. U. Delius (ed.), *Der Briefwechsel des Friedrich Mykonius (1524–1546)* (Schriften zur Kirchen- und Rechtsgeschichte, 18/19; 1960); H. Ulbrich, *Friedrich Mykonius 1490–1546: Lebensbild und neue Funde zum Briefwechsel des Reformators* (ibid. 20; 1962). P. Scherffig, *Friedrich Mekum von Lichtenfels* (Quellen und Darstellungen aus der Geschichte des Reformationsjahrhunderts, 12; 1909). O. Schmidt and G. Kawerau in *PRE* (3rd edn.), 13 (1903), pp. 603–7, and 24 (1913), p. 191. Schottenloher, 2 (1935), pp. 83 f. (nos. 16188–211).

Myconius, Oswald (1488–1552), originally Geisshäusler, Swiss Reformer and humanist. It appears that the name 'Myconius' was given him by *Erasmus. A native of Lucerne, he studied at Basle from 1510 to 1514. In 1516 he went to Zurich, where he became the cathedral schoolmaster and induced the chapter to elect his friend, U. *Zwingli, as people's priest. From 1520 to 1522 he taught at Lucerne; but soon becoming an upholder of the Reformed cause, he was compelled, on account of his Protestant sympathies, to leave the city. In 1523 he was back in Zurich, where he collaborated closely with Zwingli. In 1532 he became the successor of J. *Oecolampadius at Basle, remaining here for the rest of his life. His undogmatic temper, which found expression in a desire to reach a compromise with the Lutheran theologians on the matter of *consubstantiation, and his distrust of the increasing part of the secular authorities in such matters as *excommunication, aroused suspicion among the stricter Zwinglians. Among his works are a Life of Zwingli (1536), the *Basle Confession of 1534, and commentaries on several biblical books.

K. R. Hagenbach, *Johann Oekolampad und Oswald Myconius* (Leben und ausgewählte Schriften der Väter und Begründer der reformierten Kirche, 2; 1859), pp. 309–462; P. Wernle, *Calvin und Basel bis zum Tode des Myconius, 1535–52* (Programm zur Rektoratsfeier der Universität Basel, 1910). W. Brändly, 'Oswald Myconius in Basel', *Zwingliana*, 11 (1959–63), pp. 183–92. B. Riggenbach and E. Egli in *PRE* (3rd edn.), 13 (1903), pp. 607 f.

Myrc, John, also spelt **Mirc** (*fl. c.*1400), religious writer. Beyond the fact that he was the prior of the *canons regular of Lilleshall in Salop, nothing is known of his life. His surviving writings are his *Liber Festialis*, a collection of sermons for the more important festivals of the Christian year, beginning with the first Sunday in *Advent; a *Manuale Sacerdotum*; and *Instructions for Parish Priests*, an English poem written in rhyming couplets for the instruction of the clergy in their various duties. His works are important sources for the Church life of his age.

The works mentioned survive in several MSS (Brit. Lib., Bod., Camb. Univ. Lib.). Early pr. edns. of the 'Liber Festialis' by W. *Caxton (1483) and Wynkyn de Worde (1493). His 'Instructions for Parish Priests' were ed. by E. Peacock, with introd. note by H. Bradshaw, for the EETS (Orig. Ser. 31, 1868; rev. edn., F. J. Furnivall, 1902) and by G. Kristensson (Lund Studies in English, 49; 1974). D. B. Foss, 'John Mirk's *Instructions for Parish Priests*', in W. J. Sheils and D. Wood (eds.), *The Ministry: Clerical and Lay* (Studies in Church History, 26; Oxford, 1989), pp. 131–40. M. Bateson in *DNB* 38 (1893), pp. 50 f., s.v. 'Mirk'.

Mysteries of the Rosary. The 15 subjects of meditation connected with the 15 *decades of the *Rosary. They are divided into three groups of five, corresponding to the three *chaplets of which the devotion is composed, and known as the *Joyful, *Sorrowful, and *Glorious Mysteries (qq.v.). The whole in order forms an epitome of the lives of Christ and His Mother.

Mystery (or Miracle) Plays. The terms 'mystery' and 'miracle' have long been loosely applied to the vernacular religious drama of the later Middle Ages, notably the English *Corpus Christi plays and the French Passion Plays. Much is uncertain about the precise origins of this type of drama, though the shaping influence of the Liturgy, esp. the offices of *Holy Week and *Easter, is clear. More immediate sources used by the dramatists were early vernacular paraphrases of the Bible and Gospel harmonies. Apocryphal and legendary subjects such as the *Harrowing of Hell, the life of the BVM, *Antichrist, and the Last Judgement were commonly introduced. Plays dramatizing the lives of the saints could also be described as 'miracles', and surviving English examples deal with St *Paul and St *Mary Magdalene. Performance usually took place out of doors. In the N. of England (notably at *York and *Chester) the Corpus Christi cycles were given processionally on wagons used as movable stages. In East Anglia, Cornwall, London, and on the Continent of Europe, fixed stages in a variety of configurations were employed. In the later 14th cent. mystery and miracle plays in England were opposed by the *Lollard movement. They were eventually suppressed in the latter half of the 16th cent. under the impact of Protestant reform. Texts of the plays began to appear in editions by antiquaries and others in the 18th and 19th cents., and in recent years the plays have been revived before large and appreciative audiences in productions resembling the *Oberammergau Passion Play. See also DRAMA, CHRISTIAN.

Anthology of texts in D. Bevington, *Medieval Drama* (Boston [1975]), pp. 225–788; P. Meredith and J. E. Tailby (eds.), *The Staging of Religious Drama in Europe in the Later Middle Ages: Texts and Documents in English Translation* (Kalamazoo, Mich., 1983). V. A. Kolve, *The Play called Corpus Christi* (1966); R. [E.] Woolf, *The English Mystery Plays* (1972); B.-D. Berger, *Le Drame liturgique de Pâques du Xe au XIIIe siècle: Liturgie et Théâtre* (Théologie historique, 37 [1976]); W. Tydeman, *The Theatre in the Middle Ages* (Cambridge, 1978).

mysticism, mystical theology. In modern usage 'mysticism' generally refers to claims of immediate knowledge of Ultimate Reality (whether or not this is called 'God') by direct personal experience; 'mystical theology' is used to mean the study of mystical phenomena or the science of the mystical life. It has sometimes been suggested that such experience is the goal of all religion, and that there are certain experiences or patterns of experience which are common to believers in different religions or even in none, but this suggestion has been challenged on both philosophical and theological grounds. Paranormal phenomena, such as trances, visions and locutions, are often regarded as 'mystical', though their value and significance is assessed differently by different thinkers; they are usually not regarded as essential. Protestant theologians, from M. *Luther onwards, have tended to regard mysticism with suspicion. E. *Brunner and R. *Niebuhr held it to be anti-Christian because of its close link with *Neoplatonism, which seemed to bring it closer to pagan gnosis than to the Gospel's offer of salvation; others feared dangers of pantheism. In recent years there has been a marked increase in interest in mysticism.

Language connected with 'mystery' ($\mu\nu\sigma\tau\eta\rho\iota\upsilon$) was widely used in the early Church, often in a fairly routine way; the use of such language depends on the conviction that Christian doctrine and liturgy involve matters known only by revelation, which are incomprehensible to, or which need to be shielded from profanation by, outsiders and those insufficiently purified by faith and moral conversion. The sacred words of Scripture and the deeds of God recorded in Scripture and enacted in the Eucharist contain a 'mystic' significance, into which believers can be progressively initiated by Christ through the working of the Holy Spirit. The mystery of God remains mysterious even in its revelation, so that we need to 'hear the quietness' of Jesus as well as receiving His word (*Ignatius, *Eph.* 15).

The phrase 'mystical theology' is first used by *Dionysius the Pseudo-Areopagite, for whom our approach to God must be entirely governed by His self-disclosure in Christ and in the Bible. In addition to 'philosophical theology', which uses clear concepts and arguments, there is a 'mystical theology' which has to do with symbols and ritual ($\sigma\upsilon\mu\beta\omega\lambda\iota\kappa\eta\nu$ $\kappa\alpha\grave{\iota}$ $\tau\epsilon\lambda\epsilon\sigma\tau\iota\kappa\eta\nu$, *Letters*, 9. 1), leading us beyond intellectual notions of God to a real union with Him in the 'truly mystic darkness of unknowing' (*Mystical Theology*, 1. 3); here the height of the 'mystic words' of Scripture is apprehended and the 'mysteries of theology' are revealed in silence (ibid. 1. 1). 'Mystical theology' does not just persuade us, it acts on us (*Letters*, 9. 1); in submitting to the effects of the Church's rites, we 'undergo divine things' ($\pi\alpha\theta\grave{\omega}\nu$ $\tau\grave{\alpha}$ $\theta\epsilon\hat{\iota}\alpha$, *Divine Names*, 2. 9).

In some later Byzantine writers, the third phase of spiritual progress, which Dionysius called *unitive, is named 'mystical' (e.g. *Nicetas Stethatos, *Capita Gnostica*, 3. 41 (*PG* 120. 972)), and this is taken to mean that one is now in a position to 'initiate' others into the mysteries of God (ibid. 3. 44). The *Hesychasts defended the possibility and importance of an 'experience of the mystery of God or of the working of the Spirit' (*Gregory Palamas, *Triads*, 3. 3. 3).

Medieval W. interpreters of Dionysius tended to see 'mystical theology' as leading, through the *purgative and illuminative ways, to a loving union with God at the peak of our affectivity (*apex affectivae*), in which all intellectual operations are left behind. Thus some writers locate 'mystical theology' entirely in the will and the affections. Others combine this doctrine with the *Augustinian tradition that 'love itself is knowledge' (cf. *Gregory the Great, *PL* 76. 1207A), and maintain that 'mystical theology' imparts a special kind of knowledge of God not attainable by ordinary intellectual operations. Both views find supporters among the *Franciscans. Other theologians, esp. *Dominicans, held that 'mystical theology' is precisely the ascent of the intellect, enlightened by faith, to union with God. J. *Gerson argued that 'mystical theology' concerns neither the will nor the intellect, but a union with God in the essence of the soul (*Ep.*, 55). This debate continued for several centuries.

Late medieval writers stressed that the height of the Christian life could be understood only by experience, and 'mystical theology' was increasingly taken to mean an experiential knowledge of God. Some writers specified particular subjective experiences as constituting or indicating the attainment of 'mystical theology' (generally identified, from the 16th cent. onwards, with *contemplation); this process reached its apogee in the Carmelite doctors, *Teresa of Ávila and St *John of the Cross, whose influence thereafter predominates.

From the late 16th cent. onwards the adjective 'mystic' tends to be used as a noun, so that certain people are called 'mystics', and *mystica, la mystique*, etc., begins to oust 'mystical theology'. The English word 'mysticism' is a rather later coinage.

Since the 17th cent. there has been debate among RC theologians as to whether 'mysticism' is to be regarded as the normal flowering of sanctifying grace, in principle open to all Christians, or whether it should be seen as a special grace reserved for the few. The latter opinion is esp. associated with the Jesuit G. B. *Scaramelli; the former has been upheld by A. Saudreau, the Dominicans J. G. Arintero and R. Garrigou-Lagrange, and many others.

Modern discussions of 'mysticism' have been dominated by the notion of 'mystical experience' and, on the one hand, by the quest for 'mystical' elements common to different religions and, on the other, by attempts to identify the essence of a specifically Christian 'mysticism'. The definitions proposed are usually arbitrary, and there is a marked lack of clarity. The attempt to identify Christian 'mystics' in earlier periods is anachronistic, and conventional phrases such as 'the German mystics' (esp. *Eckhart, *Henry Suso, and J. *Tauler) or 'the English mystics' (esp. R. *Rolle, W. *Hilton, and the author of the *Cloud of Unknowing*) can be misleading, since the writers concerned were not necessarily interested in the kinds of experience now regarded as constituting 'mysticism'.

There is an immense literature. Studies devoted to the subject include W. R. *Inge, *Christian Mysticism* (Bampton Lectures for 1899; 1899); id., *Mysticism in Religion* [1947]; A. Poulain, SJ, *Des grâces d'oraison* (1901; Eng. tr., 1910); A. Saudreau, *L'État Mystique: Sa nature, ses phases* (1903; 2nd edn., 1921; Eng. tr., 1924), and other works; W. *James, *The Varieties of Religious Experience* (Gifford Lectures for 1901–2; 1902), pp. 379–429; F. *von Hügel, *The Mystical Element of Religion as studied in Saint Catherine of Genoa and her Friends* (2 vols., 1908); E. *Underhill, *Mysticism* (1911); id., *The Mystics of the Church* [1925], and other works; [E.] C. Butler, OSB, *Western Mysticism: The Teaching of SS Augustine, Gregory and Bernard on Contemplation and the Contemplative Life* (1922; 2nd edn., with 'Afterthoughts', 1927); E. Brunner, *Die Mystik und das Wort: Der Gegensatz zwischen moderner Religionsauffassung und christlichen Glauben dargestellt an der Theologie Schleiermachers* (1924); E. A. Peers, *Spanish Mysticism: A Preliminary Survey* (1924); id., *Studies of the Spanish Mystics* (3 vols., 1927–60); J. G. Arintero, OP, *La Verdadera Mística Tradicional* (Salamanca, 1925; 2nd edn., 1980) and other works; E. Hendrikx, OESA, *Augustins Verhältnis zur Mystik: Eine patristische Untersuchung* (Cassicianum, 1; 1936); A. Stolz, OSB, *Theologie der Mystik* (1936; Eng. tr., 1938; rev. Fr. tr., Chevetogne, 1939); R. Garrigou-Lagrange, OP, *Les Trois Âges de la Vie Intérieure* (2 vols. [1938]; Eng. tr., 2 vols., St Louis, 1947–8), and other works; J. B. Collins, *Christian Mysticism in the Elizabethan Age with its Background in Mystical Methodology* (Baltimore and London, 1940); V. *Lossky, *Essai sur la théologie mystique de l'Église d'Orient* (Centre de recherches philosophiques et spirituelles, 1944; Eng. tr., 1957); R. C. Zaehner, *Mysticism Sacred and Profane: An Inquiry into some Varieties of Praeternatural Experience* (Oxford, 1957); C. Pepler, OP, *The Three Degrees: A Study of Christian Mysticism* (1957); H. [C.] Graef, *The Story of Mysticism* (1966); D. *Knowles, *What is Mysticism?* (1967), and other works; M. Andrés Martín, *Los Recogidos: Nueva Visión de la Mística Española (1500–1700)* (1975); S. T. Katz (ed.), *Mysticism and Philosophical Analysis* (1978); A. Louth, *The Origins of the Christian Mystical Tradition from Plato to Denys* (Oxford, 1981); A. de Libera, *Introduction à la Mystique Rhénane d'Albert le Grand à Maître Eckhart* (1984); M. de Certeau, *La Fable Mystique, XVIe–XVIIe Siècle* ([1982]; Eng. tr., Chicago and London, 1992); L. Bouyer, *Mysterion: Du mystère à la mystique* [1986]; B. McGinn, *The Presence of God: A History of Western Christian Mysticism* (4 vols., New York, 1991 ff.; London, 1992 ff.). L. Bouyer, Cong. Orat., ' "Mystique", Essai sur l'histoire d'un mot', *Supplément de la Vie Spirituelle*, 9 (May 1949) pp. 3–23; Eng. tr., 'Mysticism: An Essay on the History of a Word', in *Mystery and Mysticism: A Symposium* (1956), pp. 119–37; M. de Certeau, SJ, ' "Mystique" au xviie siècle. Le problème du langage "mystique" ', in *L'Homme devant Dieu: Mélanges offerts au Père Henri de Lubac*, 2 (Théologie, 57 [1964]), pp. 267–91. J. Vanneste, SJ, 'La théologie mystique du pseudo-Denys l'Aréopagite', in F. L. Cross (ed.), *Studia Patristica*, 5 (1962), pp. 401–15. A. Solignac, SJ, and others in *Dict. Sp.* 10 (1980), cols. 1889–1984, s.v. 'Mystique'; P. Gerlitz, A. Louth, and others in *TRE* 23 (1994), pp. 533–92, s.v. 'Mystik'.

N

Naassenes (or **Naasenes**) (Heb. נָחָשׁ, 'serpent'). A *Gnostic sect described by *Hippolytus (*Haer.* 5. 6–17). It has sometimes been held that the name represents the Hebrew equivalent of the Greek *Ophites (q.v.).

See bibl. s.v. OPHITES.

Nag Hammadi Papyri. A collection of papyrus codices found in 1945–6 near Nag Hammadi (the ancient Chenoboskion) in Upper Egypt, some 60 miles below Luxor on the Nile. Eleven of the codices still have their original leather bindings. The papyri are dated to the period between the 3rd and 5th cent. AD, and contain in various degrees of preservation over 40 (mainly *Gnostic) works, nearly all previously unknown. Written in *Coptic (predominantly in the Sahidic dialect), most, if not all, are translations from Greek. They vary widely in date and style, some being thought to go back to the 2nd cent. or earlier. Some of them are akin to the *Hermetic books, but most are at least superficially Christian and display Gnostic features in varying degree; thus the 'Apocryphon of *John' contains bizarre and fanciful theology, but some works, such as the 'Gospel of Truth' (see EVANGELIUM VERITATIS) and 'On the Resurrection', are not notably unorthodox. At least one, the 'Apocalypse of Adam', appears to show no distinctively Christian features, and may possibly be non-Christian. The library is a primary source for our knowledge of Gnosticism. The MSS are now all in the Coptic Library in Cairo.

The treatises found at Nag Hammadi include (with roman figures denoting the codex, and arabic figures the number within the codex): the 'Apocryphal Epistle of *James' (I, 2), the 'Gospel of Truth' (I, 3 and XII, 2), 'On the Resurrection' (also known as the 'Epistle to Rheginus', I, 4), the 'Tripartite Tractate' (I, 5), the 'Apocryphon of John' (II, 1, III, 1, and IV, 1), the 'Gospel of *Thomas' (II, 2), the 'Gospel of *Philip' (II, 3), the 'Hypostasis of the Archons' (II, 4), the 'Origin of the World' (untitled, also known as the 'Anonymous Revelation', II, 5 and XIII, 2), the 'Exegesis of the Soul' (II, 6), the 'Book of *Thomas' (II, 7), the 'Gospel of the Egyptians' (III, 2 and IV, 2), 'Eugnostos the Blessed' (III, 3 and V, 1), the '*Dialogue of the Redeemer' (III, 5), the 'Apocalypse of Paul' (V, 2), the 'Apocalypses of *James' (V, 3 and 4), the 'Apocalypse of Adam' (V, 5), the 'Paraphrase of Seth' (VII, 1), the 'Teaching of Silvanus' (VII, 4), 'Zostrianus' (VIII, 1), and the 'Letter of St *Peter to Philip' (VIII, 2).

There is a complete list of the Nag Hammadi treatises, with table showing the alternative numbering of J. Doresse and H.-C. Puech, and list of edns. and trs. to date, in *CPG* 1 (1983), pp. 68–104 (nos. 1175–222). *The Facsimile Edition of the Nag Hammadi Codices*, pub. under the Auspices of the Department of Antiquities of the Arab Republic of Egypt in Conjunction with UNESCO (12 vols., Leiden, 1972–84) supersedes earlier photographic edns. of individual texts. The main edns. of the texts are those pub. in Nag Hammadi Studies (NHS), with Eng. tr., Leiden, 1975 ff., in the Bibliothèque Copte de Nag Hammadi,

Section 'Textes' (BCNH), with Fr. tr., Quebec, 1977 ff., and a few in TU, 1967 ff. (vols. 101, 119, 132, 134, and 136). The following texts have been pub., with BCNH texts given only where the NHS edns. have not yet appeared: Codex I, ed. H. W. Attridge (NHS 22–3; 1985); II, 1: see JOHN, APOCRYPHON OF; II, 2–7, ed. B. Layton (NHS 20–1; 1989); III, 2 and IV, 2, ed. A. Böhlig and F. Wisse (NHS 4; 1975); III, 3, ed. D. Trakatellis (Athens, 1977); III, 5, ed. S. Emmel (NHS 26; 1984); V, 2–5 and VI [1–8], ed. D. M. Parrott (NHS 11; 1979); VII, 1, ed. M. Krause in F. Altheim and R. Stiehl, *Christentum am Roten Meer*, 2 (1973), pp. 2–105; VII, 2, ed. L. Painchaud (BCNH 6; 1982); VII, 4, ed. Y. Janssens (BCNH 13; 1983); VII, 5, ed. P. Claude (BCNH 8; 1983); VIII, 2: see PETER, LETTER OF ST, TO PHILIP; IX and X, ed. B. A. Pearson (NHS 15; 1981); XI, 2, ed. J. E. Ménard (BCNH 14; 1985); XII, 1 and 3, ed. P.-H. Poirier (BCNH 11; 1983); XIII, 1, ed. Y. Janssens (BCNH 4; 1978); and *Greek and Coptic Papyri from the Cartonnage of the Covers*, ed. J. W. B. Barns and others (NHS 16; 1981). Eng. tr. of all the codices, and similar material in Berlin MS 8502, ed. J. M. Robinson, *The Nag Hammadi Library in English* (Leiden, 1977; 3rd edn., 1988). For works on the significance of the Nag Hammadi material, see modern works cited s.v. GNOSTICISM. D. M. Scholer, *Nag Hammadi Bibliography 1948–1969* (Nag Hammadi Studies, 1; 1971); annual suppl. in *Novum Testamentum*, 1971 ff.

Nag's Head Story. This tale was apparently fabricated early in the 17th cent. to discredit the validity of M. *Parker's episcopal consecration. It alleged that when Parker found himself unable to obtain regular consecration, some clerics met at the Nag's Head tavern in Cheapside, and that there J. *Scory, the deprived Bp. of *Chichester, and himself affirmed not to have been properly consecrated, constituted Parker and the others bishops by placing a Bible on the neck of each in turn with the words 'Take thou authority to preach the Word of God sincerely'. The story was first put into circulation by C. Holywood, SJ, in 1604; and though soon discredited, it continued to reappear in the controversial literature on the validity of *Anglican Ordinations till beyond the middle of the 19th cent.

Christopher [Holywood], SJ, *De Investiganda Vera ac Visibili Christi Ecclesia Libellus* (Antwerp, 1604), pp. 17 f. The earliest attempt to discredit the story is that in F. *Mason, *Of the Consecration of the Bishops of the Church of England* (1613), pp. 123 f. See also bibl. to ANGLICAN ORDINATIONS and PARKER, M.

Nahum, Book of. One of the 12 '*Minor Prophets'. It consists of 3 chapters in all. The main subject is the fall of Nineveh (*c*.612 BC), which is described in such detail and is regarded as so certain and so imminent that it is generally supposed that the Book may be dated shortly before this. The opening verses, 1: 2–9 (or 1: 2–2: 2), contain a psalm which, although it forms a fitting introduction to what follows, has no reference to the main subject of the Book; and on this ground, combined with its (imperfectly preserved) acrostic form, some attribute the psalm to an independent source. Various theories have been advanced to explain the one fact stated in connection with the person of Nahum, that he was 'an Elkoshite' (1: 1). Some fix the site of Elkosh near Nineveh; others follow St *Jerome and place it in *Galilee (cf. the derivation of *Capernaum as 'village of Nahum'); most prefer a site in Judah.

Comm. by J. M. P. Smith (ICC on Mic., Zeph., Nah., Hab., Obad., and Joel, 1912, pp. 267–363), W. A. Maier (St Louis, 1959), and J. D. W. Watts (Camb. Bib., NEB, on Joel, Obad., Jon., Nah., Hab., and Zeph., 1975, pp. 98–120). W. R. Arnold, 'The Composition of Nahum 1–2: 3', *ZATW* 21 (1901), pp. 225–65. P. Humbert, 'Le Problème du Livre de Nahoum', *Revue d'Histoire et de Philosophie Religieuses*, 12 (1932), pp. 1–15. A. Haldar, *Studies in the Book of Nahum* (Uppsala Universitets Årsskrift, 1946, pt. 7; 1947), with bibl. H. Schulz, *Das Buch Nahum: Eine redaktionskritische Untersuchung* (Beiheft zur *ZATW*, 129; 1973). K. J. Cathcart, *Nahum in the Light of Northwest Semitic* (Biblica et Orientalia, 26; Rome, 1973). A. S. van der Woude, 'The Book of Nahum. A Letter Written in Exile', *Oudtestamentische Studiën*, 20 (1977), 108–26. A. George in *Dict. Bibl.*, Suppl. 6 (1960), cols. 291–301, s.v.; W. Dietrich in *TRE*, 23 (1994), pp. 737–42, both with bibl.

Name of Jesus. In consequence of the close relation between name and person, the Name of Jesus is used in the NT as a synonym for Jesus Himself, denoting His character and authority. The disciples perform miracles and exorcisms 'in the name of Jesus', i.e. by His power (Mk. 9: 38 ff., Acts 4: 30, etc.), and regularly baptize in it (Acts 2: 38, 8: 16, etc.), and St Paul esp. insists on its efficacy for our justification (1 Cor. 6: 11) and the obligation of Christians to venerate it above all other names (Phil. 2: 9 f.). This reverence for, and confidence in, the Name of Jesus has found expression in the Church from early times, e.g. in its use in exorcisms and the medieval custom of giving medals with the monogram 'IHS' (q.v.) to newly baptized infants. In the 15th cent. devotion to the Holy Name was popularized by the *Franciscans, St *Bernardino of Siena, and St *Giovanni Capistrano, to whom also the Litany of the Holy Name, used since the 15th cent. and approved for the universal RC Church by *Leo XIII in 1886, possibly owes its origin. See also foll. entry.

W. Heitmüller, '*Im Namen Jesu*' (Forschungen zur Religion und Literatur des Alten und Neuen Testaments, 1, Heft 2; 1903). F. J. Foakes Jackson and K. *Lake (eds.), *The Beginnings of Christianity*, pt. 1: The Acts of the Apostles, 5 (1933), pp. 121–40 ('The Name, Baptism, and the Laying on of Hands' by S. New). P. R. Biasiotto, OFM, *History of the Development of the Devotion to the Holy Name* (St Bonaventure, NY, 1943). A. Cabassut, OSB, 'La Dévotion au nom de Jésus dans l'Église d'occident', *La Vie spirituelle*, 86 (1952), pp. 46–69. J. Dupont, OSB, in *Dict. Bibl.*, Suppl. 6 (1960), cols. 514–41, s.v. 'Nom de Jésus'; I. Noye, PSS, in *Dict. Sp.* 8 (1974), cols. 1109–26, s.v. 'Jésus (Nom de)'.

Name of Jesus, Feast of the. This feast, which had been celebrated locally at the end of the Middle Ages, was officially granted to the *Franciscans in 1530 for commemoration on 14 Jan. The observance gradually spread until it was finally prescribed in 1721 by Innocent XIII for the whole RC Church on the Second Sunday after *Epiphany. The Office and Mass were composed by Bernardino dei Busti (d. 1500), while the celebrated office hymns, '*Jesu dulcis memoria', 'Jesu Rex admirabilis', and 'Jesu decus angelicum', were adapted from the work of a 12th cent. author. The date of the feast was again modified in the Latin Church by *Pius X, who fixed it for the Sunday between the *Circumcision (1 Jan.) and the Epiphany (6 Jan.) or, if in any year there was no such Sunday,

on 2 Jan. It was suppressed in the Roman Calendar of 1969. Acc. to late medieval practice in England, as embodied in the later forms of the *Sarum Rite, the feast was observed on 7 Aug., and this date is assigned to it in the calendar of the BCP. The American BCP (1979) places it on 1 Jan. Various other modern Anglican liturgies use the Naming of Jesus as an alternative title for the feast of the Circumcision.

R. W. Pfaff, *New Liturgical Feasts in Later Medieval England* (Oxford Theological Monographs, 1970), pp. 62–83. G. Löw, CSSR, in *EC* 8 (1952), cols. 1919 f., s.v. 'Nome di Gesù, Festa del'.

Nantes, Edict of. The edict signed at Nantes on 13 Apr. 1598 by *Henry IV, after the end of the French wars of religion, granting extensive rights to the *Huguenots (his former co-religionists), as well as confirming earlier edicts made in their favour in 1564 and 1570. The Huguenots were allowed free exercise of their religion, except in certain towns (incl. *Paris), civil equality with Catholics, and fair administration of justice, and they were given subsidies for their troops, pastors, and schools. They were also allowed to garrison certain towns. The terms were increasingly infringed in the 17th cent. until the edict was revoked by Louis XIV in the Edict of Fontainebleau on 18 Oct. 1685.

[E. Benoist], *Histoire de l'édit de Nantes* (24 books in 5 vols., Delft, 1693–5), with text of edict in vol. 1, pp. (62–94), and of revocation in vol. 5, pp. (184–6); Eng. tr. of Books 1–11 (2 vols., 1694), with Eng. tr. of text of edict, 1, pp. 526–62. Eng. tr. of main clauses of the edict, with comm., in S. Z. Ehler and J. B. Morrall, *Church and State through the Ages* (1954), pp. 183–8, and of the revocation, ibid., pp. 208–13. J. Orcibal, *Louis XIV et les Protestants* (Bibliothèque de la Société d'histoire ecclésiastique de France, 1951), esp. pp. 111–25. J. Garrisson, *L'Édit de Nantes et sa Révocation: Histoire d'une Intolérance* (1985); É. Labrousse, '*Une foi, une loi, un roi?': Essai sur la Révocation de l'Édit de Nantes* (Geneva and Paris, 1985); J. Quéniart, *La Révocation de l'Édit de Nantes: Protestants et Catholiques français de 1598 à 1685* [1985]; J.-R. Armogathe, *Croire en liberté: L'Église catholique et la Révocation de l'Édit de Nantes* (1985). R. Zuber and L. Theis (eds.), *La Révocation de l'Édit de Nantes et le protestantisme français en 1685: Actes du colloque de Paris (15–19 octobre 1985)* (Société de l'histoire du protestantisme français, supplément au Bulletin, 1986).

Narsai (also **Narses**) (d. *c.*503), poet and theologian of the *Church of the East. Born prob. in 399, he became head of the famous school of *Edessa, perhaps as early as 437. Owing to the growing hostility towards the followers of Theodore and *Nestorius, *c.*471 he fled to Nisibis, where the bishop, *Barsumas, asked him to stay and found a school. Narsai was one of the formative theologians of the Church of the East. He wrote an extensive set of commentaries on the OT, but these have been completely lost. There survive, however, a large number of metrical homilies and some hymns, whose beauty gained for him the epithet 'Harp of the Spirit'. Some of his homilies (the 'Liturgical Homilies') afford important evidence for the early history of the E. Syrian rites of *Baptism and the *Eucharist.

Syriac text of Works ed. A. Mingana (2 vols., Mosul, 1905; ed. partly in Syriac). 'Homilies on the Creation', ed., with Fr. tr. and introd., by P. Gignoux in *PO* 34 (1968), pp. 415–716; 'Metrical Homilies on the Nativity, Epiphany, Passion, Resurrection and Ascension' ed., with Eng. tr., by F. G. McLeod, SJ, ibid., 40

(1979), pp. 3–193. Text of further homilies pr. from one MS, with introd. and Fr. tr. by E. P. Siman, *Cinq homélies sur les paraboles évangéliques* (Paris, 1984). Eng. tr. of four of the 'Liturgical Homilies', with crit. discussions, by R. H. *Connolly (Texts and Studies, 8. 1; Cambridge, 1909). Fr. tr. of various homilies in *L'Orient Syrien* (12 vols., 1956–67), *passim*. A. Vööbus, *History of the School of Nisibis* (CSCO 266; 1965), pp. 57–121. A. *Baumstark, *Geschichte der syrischen Literatur* (1922), pp. 109–13. I. Ortiz de Urbina, SJ, *Patrologia Syriaca* (2nd edn., Rome, 1965), pp. 115–18. E. Tisserant in *DTC* 11 (pt. 1; 1931), cols. 26–30; P. Gignoux in *Dict. Sp.* 11 (1982), cols. 39–41, both s.v.

narthex (Gk. νάρθηξ, lit. 'a small case'). In a Byzantine church, the antechamber to the nave, from which it is separated by columns, rails, or a wall. *Catechumens, candidates for baptism, and penitents occupied the narthex. It is to be distinguished from the 'exonarthex', or porch, opening on to the street.

H. *Leclercq, OSB, in *DACL* 12 (1935), col. 888 f., s.v.; M. Zocca in *EC* 8 (1952), cols. 1659–61, s.v. 'Nartece'.

Nash Papyrus. A small fragment of papyrus which, until the discovery of the *Dead Sea Scrolls, was the oldest known MS of any portion of the Hebrew OT. It was acquired by W. L. Nash in 1902 and is in the Cambridge University Library (Or. 233). Perhaps to be dated in the 2nd cent. BC (and not, as was at first thought, in the 2nd cent. AD), it contains the Ten *Commandments in substantially the Deuteronomic text (Deut. 5: 6–21), with the 6th and 7th Commandments transposed (cf. Lk. 18: 20), followed by a brief introductory passage and then the *Shema.

S. A. *Cook, 'A Pre-Massoretic Biblical Papyrus', *Proc. of the Soc. of Biblical Archaeology*, 25 (1903), pp. 34–56 (with facsimile).

Nasorean. See NAZARENE.

Natalitia (Lat., 'birthday'). In the early cents, this word was used of the death-days of Christians, and esp. of martyrs, in the sense of their birthday into eternal life. In later Christian usage the word sometimes meant no more than 'anniversary', the *Gelasian Sacramentary, e.g., employing it of the anniversary of a bishop's consecration.

Nathanael. One of the first disciples of Jesus, who recommended him for his sincerity (Jn. 1: 47). He was a native of Cana (Jn. 21: 2) and his call is related in Jn. 1: 43–51. In spite of this his name is not included among those of the Twelve Apostles. From the 9th cent. he was identified with St *Bartholomew by Elias of Damascus, *Ebedjesus, and other writers of the *Church of the East. In the W. this conjecture is first mentioned by *Rupert of Deutz in the 12th cent. The identification is now widely accepted by biblical scholars.

See comm. to JOHN, GOSPEL OF ST.

National Anthem. See GOD SAVE THE KING/QUEEN.

National Apostasy, Sermon on. The sermon with this title preached by J. *Keble on 14 July 1833 in the church of St Mary the Virgin, Oxford, before the Judges of Assize and commonly regarded as the beginning of the *Oxford Movement (q.v.). Its aim was to promote action in defence

of the Church, esp. in view of the proposed suppression of ten Irish bishoprics. The text was 1 Sam. 12: 23.

The Sermon was pub. at Oxford in 1833 immediately after delivery; repr., with introd. by A. M. G. Stephenson (privately pr., Steventon, near Abingdon, 1983). Its traditional place as inaugurating the Oxford Movement appears to derive from a passage in J. H. *Newman's *Apologia*; cf. F. L. Cross, *John Henry Newman* (1933), Appendix IV, 'The Myth of July 14, 1833' (pp. 162 f.).

National Assembly of the Church of England. See CHURCH ASSEMBLY.

National Council of the Evangelical Free Churches. The formal title adopted in 1896 by the National Free Church Council. This association of Free Churches was formed in 1892 for mutual consultation, co-operation, and witness. In 1940 it united with the Federal Council of Evangelical Free Churches to form the *Free Church Federal Council.

National Covenant (1638). The Covenant of the Scottish *Presbyterians inaugurated in the Greyfriars churchyard at Edinburgh on 28 Feb. 1638, as an answer to the attempt to impose on the Scottish Church the 1637 BCP. It consisted of the *King's Confession of 1581, with many additions by A. *Henderson and others, and concluded with an oath. See also COVENANTERS.

Text pr. in S. R. Gardiner (ed.), *The Constitutional Documents of the Puritan Revolution* (3rd edn., Oxford, 1906), pp. 124–34. See also bibl. to COVENANTERS.

National Society. The popular name of the Society founded in 1811 by Joshua Watson (1771–1855; a leading member of the '*Hackney Phalanx') and incorporated in 1817 as 'The National Society for the Education of the Poor in the Principles of the Established Church'. Along with the British and Foreign Schools Society (founded in 1807), a mainly Nonconformist body, it was a pioneer in the provision of elementary education in England and Wales before there was any system of State education. It also undertook the training of teachers, the first college (St Mark's, Chelsea) being opened in 1841. After the establishment by the State in 1870 of Board Schools, the Society's schools (the 'National Schools') remained completely independent until 1902, when they began to receive financial aid from the Local Authorities. Though now part of the State system, those schools which survive retain a measure of independence, including scope for specifically Church teaching. A new charter, granted in 1934, extended the objects of the Society to promote Anglican religious education among all classes. This includes work in other than elementary schools, and much *Sunday School work comes under its auspices, together with concern for youth work and adult education. Until the formation of the C of E Council for Education in 1948, the National Society was recognized as the Church's central organization concerned with education; while no longer defining the Church's official educational policy, it is free to express views on all aspects of religious education. It supports Church schools and colleges of education; it manages a number of educational trusts, provides an information service on legal and other matters for school managers and others, and it publishes literature for religious education. It works closely both with the Division of Education of the Church in Wales and with the C of E General Synod of Education (the successor of the Council of Education) and its General Secretary is also the Secretary of the Board's Schools Council. Its headquarters is in *Church House, Westminster.

Much information in annual reports of the National Society (1811 ff.). C. K. F. Brown, *The Church's Part in Education, 1833–1941, with Special Reference to the Work of the National Society* (1942), with bibl. H. J. Burgess, *Enterprise in Education: The Story of the Work of the Established Church in the Education of the People prior to 1870* (1958); id. and P. A. Welsby, *A Short History of the National Society 1811–1961* (1961).

Nativity of St John the Baptist. A feast observed on 24 June, at any rate since the 4th cent., to commemorate the miraculous birth of the Baptist, recorded in Lk. 1. It was one of the earliest feasts to find a place in the Christian calendar. St *Augustine (*Serm.* 287. 4) explained the special appropriateness of the date selected, as after this feast the days begin to get shorter, whereas after the feast of Christ's Nativity they begin to grow longer (cf. Jn. 3: 30).

G. *Morin, 'La Date de la Saint-Jean. Solution d'un problème liturgique au IVᵉ siècle', *Le Messager des Fidèles* [later *R. Bén.*], 5 (1888), pp. 257–64. H. *Leclercq, OSB, in *DACL* 7 (pt. 2; 1927), cols. 2171–4.

Nativity of the Blessed Virgin. This feast, which is celebrated on 8 Sept., is attested for the 8th cent. in the E. by two sermons of St *Andrew of Crete. Though referred to in Rome by Pope *Sergius (687–701) and in some MSS of the *Gelasian and *Gregorian Sacramentaries, it was not generally observed in the W. until the 11th cent. It has survived in the calendar of the BCP. The choice of 8 Sept. for the feast is unexplained.

F. G. Holweck in *CE* 10 (1911), pp. 712 f.; G. Löw, CSSR, in *EC* 8 (1952), cols. 1678–80; J. Adriaense, MCS, in *LW* 2 (1968), cols. 1981–3, s.v. 'Onze Lieve Vrouw Geboorte', with extensive bibl.

Natural Law. An expression used with a wide variety of meanings, but in a theological context the law implanted in nature by the Creator which rational creatures can discern by the light of natural reason. It has been contrasted with the revealed law, though it was commonly held that the Commandments revealed in the *Decalogue (except that about Sabbath observance) were also precepts of the Natural Law. St *Paul refers to the Natural Law in Rom. 2: 14 f., where he says that the Gentiles 'show that what the law requires is written in their hearts' although they do not have the *Torah or Mosaic Law. *Stoics believed in the Law of Nature, and in the Middle Ages and in more recent times there have been philosophical doctrines that maintained the idea in some form. It has, however, often seemed that there was little agreement about the content of Natural Law other than that good is to be done and evil avoided, which would mean that Natural Law underwrites morality as such, rather than any particular moral code. The notion of 'human rights' (and 'animal rights'), understood as 'natural rights' and widely appealed to in modern times, has sometimes sought a philosophical foundation in the notion of Natural Law, and the growing importance

of international law has led to renewed attention to the concept.

O. Gierke, *Das deutsche Genossenschaftsrecht*, 4 (1913; Eng. tr., *Natural Law and the Theory of Society, 1500–1800*, 2 vols., 1934); C. G. Haines, *The Revival of Natural Law Concepts* (Harvard Studies in Jurisprudence, 4; 1930); H. A. Rommen, *Die ewige Wiederkehr des Naturrechts* (Leipzig, 1936; 2nd edn., Munich, 1947; Eng. tr., *The Natural Law*, 1949); N. Micklem, *The Theology of Law* (1943); C. H. *Dodd, 'Natural Law in the New Testament', *Theology*, 49 (1946), pp. 128–33 and 161–7; repr. in id., *New Testament Studies* (1953), pp. 129–142; J. Messner, *Das Naturrecht: Handbuch der Gesellschaftsethik, Staatsethik und Wirtschaftsethik* (Vienna, 1950; 4th edn., 1960; Eng. trs., 1952 and 1965). A. P. d'Entrèves, *Natural Law* (1951; 2nd edn., 1970); J. Fuchs, SJ, *Lex Naturae: Zur Theologie des Naturrechts* (Düsseldorf, 1955; Eng. tr., Dublin, 1965); E. Bloch, *Naturrecht und Menschliche Würde* (Frankfurt-am-Main, 1961; Eng. tr., *Natural Law and Human Dignity*, Cambridge, Mass., and London [1986]); I. Evans, OP (ed.), *Light on the Natural Law* [1965]; J. [M.] Finnis, *Natural Law and Natural Rights* (Oxford, 1980).

Natural Theology. The body of knowledge about God which may be obtained by human reason alone without the aid of Revelation and hence to be contrasted with 'Revealed Theology'. The distinction was worked out in the Middle Ages at great length, and is based on such passages as Rom. 1: 18 ff., acc. to which man is capable of arriving at certain religious truths by applying his natural powers of discursive thought. In a definition of the First *Vatican Council (*De fid. cath.*, cap. 2, can. 2) the possibility of this knowledge is explained by the dependence of the creature upon God. The chief objects of Natural Theology are God in so far as He is known through His works, the human soul, its freedom and immortality, and *Natural Law. Hence, strictly speaking, Natural Theology is part of philosophy and treated as such in the systems of Scholasticism. Reformation theology generally rejected the competence of fallen human reason to engage in Natural Theology; and in modern times this incompetence has been reasserted with emphasis by K. *Barth and the *Dialectical School. Modern theologians sympathetic towards the ideals of Natural Theology often present their views under the heading of '*Philosophy of Religion' (q.v.).

Naumburg Convention. A meeting of princes and representatives of the German Protestant leaders, held at Naumburg from 20 Jan. to 8 Feb. 1561, with a view to securing doctrinal unity, esp. in the matter of the *Eucharist. The proposed agreement on the basis of the *Augsburg Confession failed, as the *Calvinists stood by the 'variata' edition of 1540 and the *Lutherans by the 'invariata' of 1531. An invitation from the Pope to send legates to the Council of *Trent was rejected, nominally through objection to the form of address ('Dilecto filio') on the Papal letter, which was returned unopened.

The principal docs. were ed. J. H. Gelbke, *Der Naumburgische Fürstentag* (1793). R. Calinich, *Der Naumburgische Fürstentag, 1561* (1870). K. Schornbaum, 'Zum Tage von Naumburg 1561', *Archiv für Reformationsgeschichte*, 8 (1910–11), pp. 181–214; K. Braun, 'Nürnberg und die Naumburger Fürstentage 1561', *Zeitschrift für bayrische Kirchengeschichte*, 5 (1930), pp. 134–76. G. Kawerau in *PRE* (3rd edn.), 13 (1903), pp. 661–9.

nave. That part of a church, between the main front and the chancel and choir, which is assigned to the laity. It has often been separated from the sanctuary by a screen, and from the aisles by columns or pillars. The term is generally thought to be derived from the Lat. *navis*, 'ship', this being a symbol of the Church, but it may be a corrupt form of the Gk. *ναός*, 'temple'.

Nayler, James (*c*.1618–60), *Quaker. Born near Wakefield, W. Yorks, from 1643 to 1651 he served with some distinction in the Parliamentary army, in which he was noted as an Independent preacher. He retired, perhaps with tuberculosis, to a farm near his former home. When G. *Fox visited Wakefield at the end of 1651, Nayler heard him and was soon convinced of the Quaker doctrine of the *Inner (or Inward) Light. At the outset he was second only to Fox in the leadership of the movement. He was partially responsible for the conversion of the family of Judge Fell of Swarthmoor Hall, Cumbria, which soon became a noted centre of Quakerism. In 1652 he preached widely in the N. of England and was imprisoned at Appleby. From the summer of 1655 until the following spring, he was the chief spokesman of the movement in London. Soon afterward he came under the influence of a group of people with *Ranting views, led by one Martha Simmonds (1610–65), who, confusing the doctrine of the Inner Light with a belief in absolute unity with God, tried to worship him as Christ. At first Nayler resisted his devotees and set out to visit Fox, who was imprisoned in Launceston castle. Apprehended on the way as a Quaker, he was confined in the late summer of 1656 in *Exeter gaol. Here he was accredited with having raised a woman from the dead and in September, largely under the influence of Martha Simmonds, he quarrelled with Fox. As soon as he was released, he proceeded to Bristol, which he entered on 24 Oct. 1656 with his followers in the manner that the Lord entered Jerusalem. After examination by a Committee of the second Protectorate Parliament, he was very severely punished for blasphemy. He appears to have repented by *c*.1657, was released from prison by the Long Parliament in 1659, and in 1660, shortly before his death, was reconciled with Fox and regained some of his former popularity. He wrote many tracts, among them *How Sin is Strengthened and How it is Overcome* (1657).

A Collection of Sundry Books, Epistles and Papers written by James Nayler (1716). M. R. Brailsford, *A Quaker from Cromwell's Army* (1927); E. Fogelklou, *Koäkaren James Nayler: Ein Sällsam Gestalt i Religionens Historia* (1929; Eng. tr., 1931). G. F. Nuttall, *James Nayler: A Fresh Approach* (lecture, 1954). W. G. Bittle, *James Nayler 1618–1660: The Quaker Indicted by Parliament* (York and Richmond, Ind. [1986]). A. Gordon in *DNB* 40 (1894), pp. 130–3.

Nazarene. The term has been applied in a Christian context in various senses. In several of these the form 'Nasorean' is also found.

(1) In the NT Christ is called 'Jesus the Nazarene', which is usually understood as the equivalent of 'from *Nazareth', i.e. the place of his residence (cf. Mt. 21: 11, Jn. 1: 45, Acts 10: 38). In Mt. 2: 23 it is said to have been prophesied that the Christ should 'be called a Nazarene', but the original ref. and meaning of this prophecy, which is not found in the OT, is doubtful. Perhaps the original ref. here was not to Nazareth (so M. Lidzbarski, R. *Reitzenstein), though it is so understood by the Evangelist. In Mt., Jn., and Acts the form is *Ναζωραῖος*, in Mk. *Ναζαρηνός*, while in Lk. both forms occur.

(2) The 'Nazarenes' appears as a Jewish term for the early Christians in Acts 24: 5, and continued to be so used for some centuries. It is sometimes met with in Jewish literature in the form 'Noserim'.

(3) 'Nazarenes' occurs also as a name given by 4th-cent. writers to groups of Christians of Jewish race in Syria, who continued to obey much of the Jewish Law though they were otherwise orthodox Christians. The sect had no doubt existed from the earliest times of Christianity. See also the following entry.

(4) The *Mandaeans (q.v.) are described as Nasoreans in some of their earliest literature.

On (1) G. F. Moore, 'Nazarene and Nazareth', in F. J. Foakes Jackson and K. *Lake (eds.), *The Beginnings of Christianity*, 1. 1 (1920), pp. 426–32. J. A. Sanders, '*ΝΑΖΩΡΑΙΟΣ* in Matt. 2.23', *Journal of Biblical Literature*, 84 (1965), pp. 169–72. H. H. Schaeder in *TWB* 4 (1942), pp. 879–84; Eng. tr., 4 (1967), pp. 874–9, s.v. *Ναζαρηνός*, with extensive bibl. On (2) and (3), A. Pourkier, *L'hérésiologie chez Épiphane de Salamine* (Christianisme Antique, 4 [1992]), pp. 415–75, with bibl. p. 508. On (3) A. F. J. Klijn and G. J. Reinink, *Patristic Evidence for Jewish–Christian Sects* (Supplement to Novum Testamentum, 36; 1973), pp. 44–52.

Nazarenes, Gospel of the. A Gospel written in Aramaic, and, acc. to *Epiphanius and *Jerome, in use among the *Nazarenes of Beroea. The existence of such a Gospel seems to have been known earlier to *Hegesippus and *Eusebius. Epiphanius regarded it as an Aramaic version of Mt., while Jerome identified it with the 'Gospel acc. to the *Hebrews' (which he regarded as closely related to Mt.). Whether the Gospel, which was similar in content to Mt., represents an original Aramaic tradition earlier than the Synoptic Gospels, or is a translation from a Greek text, dependent on the Synoptics, is a subject of scholarly debate.

Eusebius, *HE* 4. 22. 8, and *Theophania*, 4. 12 (Syr. version); Epiphanius, *Haer.* 29 f.; Jerome, *De vir. ill.* 3, and *Dial. adv. Pel.* 3. 2. Ger. tr. of frags., with introd. by P. Vielhauer and G. Strecker in Schneemelcher, 1 (5th edn., 1987), pp. 128–38; Eng. tr., 1 (1991), pp. 154–65. Eng. tr. of frags. also in J. K. Eliott, *The Apocryphal New Testament* (Oxford, 1993), pp. 10–14. See also bibl. to HEBREWS, GOSPEL ACCORDING TO THE.

Nazareth. The village in Galilee which was the home of the BVM and St *Joseph, and where Christ was brought up and lived till the beginning of His ministry. It lies on a hill overlooking the valley of Esdraelon. It is not mentioned outside the NT. Today the town is a popular place of pilgrimage, many of its shrines having been rebuilt after their destruction by Muslims in the Middle Ages. Among its more important sanctuaries are the 'Church of the Annunciation', believed to be erected over the house of Mary, the 'Church of the Nutrition' (now the Church of St Joseph), on the traditional site of that of St Joseph, and the beautiful 'St Mary's Well'. See also NAZARENE.

T. Tobler, *Nazareth* (Berlin, 1868); G. Le Hardy, *Histoire de Nazareth et de ses sanctuaires: Étude chronologique des documents* (1905). B. Bagatti, OFM, *Gli Scavi di Nazaret* (Pubblicazioni dello Studium Biblicum Franciscanum, 17; 2 vols., 1967–84; Eng. tr., 1969 ff.). Id. in *Dict. Bibl.*, Suppl. 6 (1960), cols. 318–33; V.

Tzaferis and B. Bagatti in E. Stern and others (eds.), *The New Encyclopedia of Archaeological Excavations in the Holy Land*, 3 (Jerusalem and New York [1993]), pp. 1103–6, both s.v. See also bibl. to NAZARENE.

Nazarites. See NAZIRITES.

Nazarius, St. A martyr whose body St *Ambrose discovered in a garden outside Milan *c.*395 and translated to the Church of the Apostles in the city, which was afterwards rededicated to St Nazarius. In the same garden, St Ambrose later discovered the body of another martyr, St Celsus. Nothing else is known of the saints, the later '*Passions' being purely fictitious. The two saints appear together in the Ambrosian calendar on 28 July, and on 10 May there is also a feast of the 'Translation of St Nazarius'.

The primary source is Paulinus, *Vita S. Ambrosii*, 32 f. (*PL* 14. 38 f.). Text of 'Passions' in *AASS*, Jul. 6 (1729), pp. 503–34. Crit. edn. of 3 of the Gk. 'Passions' by U. Zanetti, SJ, in *Anal. Boll.* 105 (1987), pp. 303–84. Id., 'Les Passions des SS. Nazaire, Gervais, Protais et Celse', ibid. 97 (1979), pp. 69–88. H. *Leclercq, OSB, in *DACL* 11 (pt. 1; 1933), cols. 1057–60, s.v. 'Milan: xxvii, Saint-Nazaire'.

Nazirites (so modern translations of the Bible; AV 'Nazarites'). A body of Israelites specially consecrated to the service of God who were under vows to abstain from eating or drinking the produce of the vine, to let their hair grow, and to avoid defilement by contact with a dead body (Num. 6). Originally the vow seems to have been for life (e.g. that of *Samson), but later it was limited to a definite period (30 days, acc. to the *Mishnah, 'Nazir', 1. 3). If the Nazirite suffered defilement by the sudden death of someone beside him, he must undergo purification by shaving and burning his hair and renewing his vow. St *Paul demonstrated his loyalty to Judaism by joining with certain Jewish Christians who were completing such vows at Jerusalem (Acts 21: 23–6).

See comm. on Num. 6. G. B. *Gray, 'The Nazarite', *JTS* 1 (1899–1900), pp. 201–11. R. de Vaux, OP, *Les Institutions de l'Ancien Testament*, 2 (1960), pp. 361 f., with bibl. p. 456 (Eng. tr., 2nd edn., 1965, pp. 466 f., with bibl. p. 549). J. Milgrom and A. Rothkoff in *Encyclopaedia Judaica*, 12 (Jerusalem, 1972), cols. 907–10, s.v.

Neal, Daniel (1678–1743), historian of the *Puritans. After being educated at Merchant Taylors' School, he trained for the dissenting ministry, studying at Utrecht and *Leiden. He returned to London in 1703 to be assistant (1704), and two years later (1706) full, pastor of the Independent congregation in Aldersgate Street, a position he retained until his death. Here he was recognized as one of the best Puritan preachers of his day. Of great historical interest are his *History of New England, containing an Impartial Account of the Civil and Ecclesiastical Affairs of the Country to the Year of Our Lord 1700* (2 vols., 1720), and esp. his *History of the Puritans, 1517–1688* (1732–8), both valuable compilations, though the latter suffers from a strong Puritan bias. Neal also wrote a book defending inoculation against smallpox (1722).

Neal's *History of the Puritans* ed. J. Toulmin (5 vols., Bath, 1793–7; repr. London, 1822), with Life in vol. 1, pp. xvi–xxxiii. J. B. Mullinger in *DNB* 40 (1894), pp. 134–6.

Neale, John Mason (1818–66), Anglican author and hymn-writer. He was educated at Sherborne and Trinity College, Cambridge, where he became imbued with *High Church ideals, and in 1839, with his lifelong friend B. *Webb, was one of the founders of the *Cambridge Camden Society (q.v.). Ordained in 1842, he was presented to the living of Crawley, W. Sussex, but ill-health prevented his being instituted, and he spent the next three winters in Madeira. From 1846 till his death he held the wardenship of Sackville College, E. Grinstead, at a salary of £28 a year, dividing his activities between his manifold literary work and the Sisterhood of St Margaret which he founded in 1855. This community, whose rules were framed on those of St *Francis de Sales' Visitation and St *Vincent de Paul's Sisters of Charity, was founded esp. for the education of girls and the care of the sick, and though at first it met with violent opposition, and even rioting, from Protestant quarters, it developed into one of the leading religious communities in the C of E. Neale's ritualistic practices led to his inhibition by the Bp. of Chichester (A. T. Gilbert) from 1847 to 1863.

Neale excelled as a hymn-writer. Among the favourites of his own compositions are 'O happy band of pilgrims' and 'Art thou weary' and of his translations from Lat. and Gk. hymns, 'Jerusalem the golden', 'All glory, laud and honour', and 'Ye choirs of new Jerusalem'. His *Hymns of the Eastern Church* (1862) included many translations of Easter hymns which by their subsequent incorporation in English hymn-books introduced an important E. emphasis on the Resurrection into Anglican worship. In the *Hymnal Noted* (two parts, 1852 and 1854), 94 out of 105 hymns are from his pen, and *Hymns, Ancient and Modern* owes very much to his inspiration. In the *English Hymnal* more than one tenth of the hymns were Neale's compositions or translations. His *Commentary on the Psalms*, begun in Madeira and completed by R. F. *Littledale (4 vols., pub. 1860–74), is in essence a compilation from patristic and medieval authors. *The History of the Holy Eastern Church* (pub. in 5 vols., 1847–73) is a useful collection of material. Neale was also the author of numerous children's books, which were written to present Christian teaching in a simple and attractive form. The warmth of his devotional nature comes out clearly in his sermons, largely inspired by medieval models. Worn out by his labours, he died at the age of 48. In the American BCP (1979), feast day, 7 Aug.

Selections from the Writings of John Mason Neale was pub., London, 1884. Letters selected and ed. M. S. Lawson (daughter), ibid., 1910; Collected Hymns, Sequences, and Carols also ed. M. S. Lawson, ibid., 1914. Memoir by E. A. Towle, ibid., 1906. A. G. Lough, *The Influence of John Mason Neale* (1962); id., *John Mason Neale—Priest Extraordinary* (Newton Abbot, 1975); L. Litvack, *John Mason Neale and the Quest for Sobornost* (Oxford, 1994); M. Chandler, *The Life and Work of John Mason Neale 1818–1866* (Leominster, 1995). [D.] G. Rowell, *The Vision Glorious: Themes and Personalities of the Catholic Revival in Anglicanism* (Oxford, 1983), pp. 98–115. J. H. Overton in *DNB* 40 (1894), pp. 143–6, with further refs.

Neander, Joachim (1650–80), German hymn-writer. After a somewhat riotous student life, he was converted in 1670 by hearing T. Under-Eyck, the pastor of St Martin's church at Bremen. In 1673–4, during a winter at Frankfurt, where he made the acquaintance of P. J. *Spener, he became an ardent adherent of the *Pietist Movement. Most of his hymns date from the years 1674 to 1679, when he was rector of the Latin School of Düsseldorf. They reflect not only his deep Pietist faith but also his intense love of the beauties of nature. Many of them have been translated into English, perhaps the best known being 'Praise to the Lord, the Almighty'.

His 'Hymns' were first ed. at Bremen, 1680; later eds., with additional hymns, include those of Berlin, 1707, and Amsterdam, 1725. J. F. Iken, *Joachim Neander, sein Leben und seine Lieder* (1880). J. Mearns in J. Julian (ed.), *A Dictionary of Hymnology* (2nd edn., 1907), pp. 790–2. E. Simons in *PRE* (3rd edn.), 13 (1903), pp. 687–90, s.v.

Neander, Johann August Wilhelm (1789–1850), ecclesiastical historian.
David Mendel was a Jew by birth. After coming under the influence of F. D. E. *Schleiermacher, he was baptized in 1806 and took the name of Neander. At first interested in speculative theology, he soon turned to Church history and taught this subject at Berlin from 1813 till his death. His General Church History (6 vols., 1826–52), which went down to c.1450, was based on a wide study of original sources, somewhat uncritically treated however, and exercised great influence. Unlike J. L. von *Mosheim, whose interest was in institutions, Neander paid most attention to persons, and made it his aim to discover in Church history the interpenetration of human life by the Divine. A convinced Protestant, though eirenic in temper, he regarded outward ordinances, esp. the priesthood, as dangerous to Christian simplicity. Neander also wrote on the life of Christ (1837; in reply to D. F. *Strauss).

Collected edn. of Neander's works, 14 vols., Gotha, 1862–7. O. Krabbe, *August Neander: Ein Beitrag zu seiner Charakteristik* (Hamburg, 1852); P. *Schaff, *Saint Augustin, Melanchthon, Neander* (1886), pp. 128–68; A. F. J. Wiegand, *Neanders Leben* (Erfurt, 1889). Commemorative discourse by A. *Harnack (Berlin, 1889), repr. in his *Reden und Aufsätze*, 1 (1904), pp. 193–218. K. R. Hagenbach, 'Neander's Verdienste um die Kirchengeschichte', *Theologische Studien und Kritiken*, 24 (1851), pp. 543–94. K. Scholder in *RGG* (3rd edn.), 4 (1960), cols. 1388 f.; J. Mehlhausen in *TRE* 24 (1995), pp. 238–42, both s.v. with bibl.

Nectarius, St (d. 397), Bp. of *Constantinople.
He was born at Tarsus in Cilicia and rose to the office of *praetor* at Constantinople. Though unbaptized he was selected by *Theodosius I in 381 to succeed St *Gregory of Nazianzus in the imperial see. After Baptism he was consecrated Bp. and presided over the final stages of the (2nd) *Oecumenical Council, then in session. Despite his long episcopate, little is recorded of him. He died on 27 Sept. 397 and was succeeded by St John *Chrysostom. A sermon by him on a certain St Theodore, perhaps a martyr under *Julian (died 363), survives. Feast day, 11 Oct.

*Socrates, *HE* 5. 8, and *Sozomen, *HE* 7. 16. His Sermon on St Theodore will be found in J. P. Migne, *PG* 39. 1821–40 (from Cod. Nann. 134, 13th cent.; repr. from A. *Gallandi). V. Grumel, AA (ed.), *Les Regestes des Actes du Patriarcat de Constantinople*, 1, fasc. 1 (2nd edn., 1972), pp. 1–12 (nos. 1–12a). *CPG* 2 (1974), p. 490 (nos. 4300–1). W. M. Sinclair in *DCB* 4 (1887), pp. 11–14.

Nectarius (1605–c.1680), Patr. of *Jerusalem from 1661 to 1669.
Educated by the monks of *Sinai, he became a monk and later studied under the Neo-Aristotelian Theophilus Corydalleus at *Athens. He was a vigorous opponent of all W. theology, attacking at once the Roman claims and the Calvinist doctrines of Cyril *Lucar. In 1662 he expressed his warm approval of the 'Confession' of Peter *Mogila, and in 1672 he took a prominent part in the Synod of *Jerusalem. His treatise against the Papacy (Περὶ τῆς ἀρχῆς τοῦ πάπα ἀντίρρησις) was published by his successor, *Dositheus, in 1682.

V. Grumel, AA, in *DTC* 11 (pt. 1; 1931), cols. 56–8, with full bibl.

Negative Confession. See KING'S CONFESSION.

negative theology. See APOPHATIC THEOLOGY.

Nehemiah.
One of the most important Jewish leaders of the post-exilic period. The cup-bearer to the Persian king, Artaxerxes (probably the first of that name, 'Longimanus'), he obtained leave to visit Palestine on a mission of help, and, accompanied by an escort provided by the king, arrived in *Jerusalem as governor c.444 BC (Neh. 1 f.). Here, despite much hostility from the local officials and reports of a threatened attack from Samaria, he supervised the speedy completion of the rebuilding of the city walls (Neh. 2–6). Nehemiah's period of leave soon ended and he had to return to the Persian court. About 432 BC, however, he made a second journey to Jerusalem, and now introduced some important moral and religious reforms, insisting, e.g., on *Sabbath observance and denouncing intermarriage between Jews and non-Jews (Neh. 13). His own record of these events may be one of the sources drawn upon in the Book of Nehemiah. Nehemiah's work is closely related to that of *Ezra (q.v.), though their precise relationship is hard to judge because of uncertainties attaching to the dating of Ezra's activities.

For bibl. see comm. to EZRA AND NEHEMIAH, BOOKS OF, and other works cited s.v. H. H. Rowley, 'Nehemiah's Mission and its Background', *Bulletin of the John Rylands Library*, 37 (1955), pp. 528–61, repr. in *Men of God* (1963), pp. 211–45.

Nehemiah, Book of. See EZRA AND NEHEMIAH, BOOKS OF.

Nelson, Robert (1656–1715), *Nonjuring layman.
Convinced of pronounced Church principles by G. *Bull, who was his private tutor, he strongly disapproved of the Revolution of 1688 and went abroad to avoid it. When he returned in 1691, he made friends with many of the leading Nonjurors, and became one himself. He did not, however, altogether sever his connections with the 'Conformists', and eventually returned to the Established Church in 1710, though remaining a Jacobite in his political sympathies. Throughout his life he generously supported many philanthropic objects, notably the *SPCK and the *SPG. His publications include a *Companion for the Festivals and Fasts of the C of E* (1704), which had a wide circulation; a devotional work on the Eucharist, *The Great Duty of Frequenting the Christian Sacrifice* (1706); and a Life of Bishop Bull (1713).

C. F. Secretan, *Memoirs of the Life and Times of the pious Robert Nelson* (1860). C. J. Stranks, *Anglican Devotion* (1961), pp. 162–70. L. Stephen in *DNB* 40 (1894), pp. 210–12.

Nemesius of Emesa (*fl. c.*390), Christian philosopher. Beyond the fact that he was Bp. of Emesa in Syria, nothing is known of his life. His treatise Περὶ Φύσεως Ἀνθρώπου ('On Human Nature') is an attempt to construct on a mainly *Platonic basis a doctrine of the soul agreeable with the Christian revelation. Probably through confusion with the similar title of St *Gregory of Nyssa's anthropological treatise Περὶ Κατασκευῆς Ἀνθρώπου, Nemesius's book was often cited as Gregory's in the Middle Ages. It was much used by St *John of Damascus and, in Latin revisions, by several of the Schoolmen, notably Sts *Albertus Magnus and *Thomas Aquinas.

Gk. text first pub. by N. Ellebod (Antwerp, 1565; based on two inferior MSS). Later edns. by J. *Fell (Oxford, 1671; mainly reprod. of Ellebod) and C. F. Matthaei (Halle, 1802; this last repr. in J. P. Migne, *PG* 40. 504–817. Crit. edn. by M. Morani (Teub., 1987). Eng. tr., with introd. and notes, by W. Telfer in *Library of Christian Classics*, 4 (1955), pp. 201–466. Lat. tr. by N. Alfanus, Abp. of Salerno (1058–85), ed. C. Burkhard (Teub., 1917); that by *Burgundio of Pisa (d. 1193), ed. J., with full introd. and refs. to other trs., by G. Verbeke and J. R. Moncho (Corpus Latinum Commentariorum in Aristotelem Graecorum, Suppl. 1; Leiden, 1975). W. Jaeger, *Nemesios von Emesa: Quellenforschungen zum Neuplatonismus und seinen Anfängen bei Poseidonios* (1914). E. Skard, 'Nemesiosstudien', *Symbolae Osloenses*, 15–16 (1936), pp. 23–43; 17 (1937), pp. 9–25; 18 (1938), pp. 31–41; 19 (1939), pp. 46–56; 22 (1942), pp. 40–8. A. Kallis, *Der Mensch im Kosmos: Das Weldbild des Nemesios' von Emesa* (Münsterische Beiträge zur Theologie, 43; 1978). *CPG* 2 (1974), pp. 282 f. (no. 3550). J. Quasten, *Patrology*, 3 (Utrecht and Westminster, Md., 1960), pp. 351–5. E. Skard in *PW*, Suppl. 7 (1940), cols. 562–6, s.v. 'Nemesios'; W. Vanhamel in *Dict. Sp.* 11 (1982), cols. 92–9, s.v. 'Némésius d'Émèse'.

Neocaesarea, Council of. A Cappadocian Council of uncertain date (probably early 4th cent., before 325). It passed 15 canons concerned chiefly with disciplinary and marriage questions. Along with those of *Ancyra and *Gangra, the canons of this Council formed the earliest Greek *corpus canonum* (with the canons of *Nicaea prefixed). They were translated into Latin before AD 451, and thus became a constituent part of the canon law of both E. and W.

Hardouin, 1, cols. 281–6; Mansi, 2 (1759), cols. 539–52. Canons, with Fr. tr., also in Joannou, 1, pt. 2 (1962), pp. 74–82; crit. edn. of Lat. texts in *EOMIA* 2 (pt. 1; 1907). Hefele and Leclercq, 1 (pt. 1; 1907), pp. 326–34. *CPG* 4 (1980), pp. 3 f. (nos. 8504 f.).

Neo-Chalcedonianism. A modern term coined to describe the theological position of those 6th-cent. theologians (e.g. *John the Grammarian and *Leontius of Jerusalem) who sought to interpret the Christological teaching of the Council of *Chalcedon in the light of the Christology of St *Cyril of Alexandria (including the Anathemas appended to his Third Synodical Letter), in order to combat the *Monophysite claim that the Council had betrayed Cyril. This position involved an insistence that the one *hypostasis of the incarnate Christ is identical with the Second Person of the Trinity, and a consequent justification of the *Theopaschite formula. The use of the term 'Neo-Chalcedonianism' (in contrast to 'strict Chalcedonianism') might be taken to suggest the teaching of the Council of Chalcedon had been modified; those who want

to resist this suggestion prefer the term 'Cyrilline Chalcedonianism'.

neophyte (Gk. νεόφυτος, lit. 'newly planted'). The word occurs in 1 Tim. 3: 6 in the sense of 'newly converted' and was generally used in the early Church of the recently baptized. In acc. with the biblical admonition not to make a neophyte a bishop, the First Council of *Nicaea (AD 325, can. 2) postponed the admission of neophytes to holy orders until the bishop deemed them sufficiently strong in the faith.

Neoplatonism. The philosophical system of *Plotinus (*c.*205–70) and his successors. The Neoplatonists thought of themselves simply as *Platonists, but their thought owes its distinctiveness to the genius of Plotinus and inherits from the Platonists of the early Christian cents. deep religious interests. It was originally centred in *Alexandria, later spread to *Rome, where Plotinus taught from 244, and thence to the rest of the Roman world. Towards the end of the 4th cent. the Academy in *Athens became a centre of Neoplatonism and remained so until it was closed by the Emp. *Justinian in 529. The most outstanding representatives of Neoplatonism after Plotinus included *Porphyry (*c.*232–*c.*303; q.v.), *Iamblichus (*c.*250–330; q.v.), *Proclus (410 or 412–85; q.v.), and Damascius (b. *c.*480; head of the Academy in 529).

The main formative influences on Neoplatonism are somewhat obscure. Plotinus expresses his special indebtedness to *Ammonius Saccas, of whom, however, very little is known. While a sympathetic interest in Platonic doctrines had long existed among religious philosophers, both Jewish (*Philo) and Christian (*Pantaenus, *Clement of Alexandria, *Origen), at Alexandria, it is not clear that Plotinus himself drew directly on any of these thinkers. He has closer affinities with some of the later pagan philosophers, esp. Atticus and Albinus (2nd cent. AD) and Numenius of Apamea (*c.*150–200), a Neo-Pythagorean, for whom Plato was 'Moses writing Attic Greek' (Μωυσῆς Ἀττικίζων).

Characteristic of Neoplatonism is the doctrine of the three hypostases: the One, the ultimate unknowable source from which everything that exists emanates; Intelligence (or νοῦς), the realm of perfect intuitive knowledge; and Soul, the realm of discursive thought and activity. The outward movement of emanation (πρόοδος) is met by the ascending movement of return (ἐπιστροφή), which manifests itself as contemplation: everything that exists is a balance between these two forces. The contemplative movement of return seeks the One by purification, which for the intellect means a method of abstraction, and finds union with the One in a mystical experience of *ecstasy.

The more ardent and thoroughgoing Neoplatonists were necessarily hostile to Christianity, esp. its doctrine of an Incarnation in history and its rejection of the ancient philosophies. On the other hand, Neoplatonist influences gradually made themselves felt on Christian theology. They came in partly from their diffusive impact on the whole of the later Roman world; for outside the circle of its professed adherents it was scarcely possible to distinguish the Neoplatonist elements from those which were Platonist and idealistic in a broader sense. For the influence of the latter see the entry PLATONISM. Instances of more specifically Neoplatonist influences in Christianity may be seen in the writings of St *Augustine, *Synesius, Bp. of Ptolemais, in those of *Dionysius the Pseudo-Areopagite (who was esp. dependent on Proclus) and in the medieval thinkers who drew on the '*Liber de Causis' (q.v.).

E. R. Dodds, *Select Passages Illustrating Neoplatonism* (text, 1924; Eng. tr., 1923). T. Whittaker, *The Neo-Platonists* (1901); P. Merlan, *From Platonism to Neoplatonism* (The Hague, 1953; 2nd edn., 1960); W. Theiler, *Forschungen zum Neuplatonismus* (Quellen und Studien zur Geschichte der Philosophie, 10; 1966); *Le Néo-platonisme: Colloques internationaux du Centre National de la Recherche Scientifique. Sciences humaines* (1971); R. T. Wallis, *Neo-Platonism* (1972). H. J. Blumenthal and R. A. Markus (eds.), *Neo-platonism and Early Christian Thought: Essays in honour of A. H. Armstrong* (1981); *Néoplatonisme: Mélanges offerts à Jean Trouillard* (Les Cahiers de Fontenay, nos. 19–22; 1981); W. Beierwaltes, *Denken des Einen: Studien zur neuplatonischen Philosophie und ihrer Wirkungsgeschichte* (Frankfurt am Main, 1985); A. C. Lloyd, *The Anatomy of Neoplatonism* (Oxford, 1990). H. D. Saffrey, *Recherches sur le Néoplatonisme après Plotin* (Histoire des Doctrines de l'Antiquité Classique, 14; 1990 [collection of previously pub. essays]). A. H. Armstrong (ed.), *The Cambridge History of Later Greek and Early Medieval Philosophy* (Cambridge, 1967), with extensive bibl. E. R. Dodds, *Proclus' 'Elements of Theology'* (1933; 2nd edn., 1963). P. Hadot in *NCE* 10 (1967), pp. 334–6, s.v.; S. Lilla in *DPAC* 2 (1984), cols. 2356–88, s.v.; Eng. tr. in *Encyclopedia of the Early Church*, 2 (Cambridge, 1992), pp. 585–93. See also bibls. to PLOTINUS, PORPHYRY, IAMBLICHUS, and PROCLUS.

Neostadiensium Admonitio. The reply made by the members of the 'Reformed' (*Calvinist) church at Heidelberg to the Lutheran 'Formula of *Concord' (1577). It was issued in 1581 by Z. *Ursinus at Neustadt a.d. Haardt, whither the Heidelberg Calvinists had been forced to flee. It sets out in 12 chapters the more distinctive tenets of Calvinism.

Text pr. in Z. Ursinus's *Opera Theologica* (2nd edn. by Q. Reuter), 2 (Heidelberg, 1612), cols. 893–1138. E. F. K. Müller in *PRE* (3rd edn.), 13 (1903), pp. 709 f., s.v., with bibl.

Neot, St (*c.* 9th cent.), Cornish saint. He is known only from later English hagiography, acc. to which he was a monk of *Glastonbury who in search of solitude retired to the place now known as St Neot in Cornwall. He is said to have been visited and held in much honour by King *Alfred. After his death his relics are reputed to have found their way to St Neots, Cambridgeshire. Feast day, 31 July.

Four principal Lives survive: an 11th-cent. Anglo-Latin *Vita*, ed. D. Dumville and M. Lapidge, *The Annals of St Neots with Vita Prima Sancti Neoti* (The Anglo-Saxon Chronicle. A Collaborative Edition, 17; Cambridge, 1985), pp. 109–42; an Old English Life (MS Cotton Vespasian D. 14), pr. by R. D.-N. Warner, *Early English Homilies* (EETS, Orig. Ser. 152; 1917), pp. 129–34; a 12th-cent. Lat. *Vita* pr. in *AASS*, Jul. 7 (1731), pp. 319–29; and a 14th-cent. metrical Life, depending upon the last, pr. in J. Whitaker, *The Life of Saint Neot* (1809), pp. 317–38. Study by G. H. Doble in 'Cornish Saints' Series, no. 21 (Exeter, 1929). Hardy, 1 (pt. 2), pp. 538–49. M. Bateson in *DNB* 40 (1894), pp. 221 f.

Nepomuk, John of. See JOHN OF NEPOMUK.

nepotism. The bestowal of office or patronage on one's relations. The term is used esp. of the widespread abuse of the practice by certain 16th-cent. Popes, e.g. *Clement

VII and the Medici, *Paul III and the Farnese. The practice was condemned by St *Pius V in the bull 'Admonet Nos' (1567).

Nereus and Achilleus, Sts (perhaps 1st cent.), Roman martyrs. Their remains were buried in the Cemetery of St *Domitilla on the Via Ardeatina. Acc. to the inscription by Pope *Damasus on their tomb they were soldiers, acc. to their legendary 'Acta', eunuchs in Domitilla's household. These 'Acta' assert that all three were transported to the island of Terracina, where Nereus and Achilleus were beheaded and Domitilla burnt. The church built over their tomb dates from the later 4th cent. Feast day, 12 May (until 1969 in conjunction with St *Pancras and St Domitilla).

Early Lat. tr. of Acta in *AASS*, Mai. 3 (1680), pp. 6–13, with introd., pp. 4–6, and other material, pp. 13–16. Gk. text first ed. A. Wirth (Leipzig, 1890); also ed., with Ger. tr., by H. Achelis (TU 11, Heft 2; 1893). F. Schaefer, 'Die Acten der heiligen Nereus und Achilleus', *RQ* 8 (1894), pp. 89–119. G. B. *de Rossi, 'Scoperta della basilica di S. Petronilla. Col sepolcro dei martiri Nereo ed Achilleo nel cimitero di Domitilla', *Bullettino di archeologia cristiana*, 2nd ser. 5 (1874), pp. 5–35; id., 'Insigni scoperte nel cimitero di Domitilla: I, notizie preliminari sul sepolcro di S. Petronilla: scoperta d'un singolare monumento del sepolcro-altare dei martiri Nereo ed Achilleo', ibid. 6 (1875), pp. 5–11. A. Guerrieri, *La chiesa dei SS. Nereo ed Achilleo* (Collezione 'Amici delle Catacombe', 16; 1951); U. M. Fasola, *La Basilica dei SS. Nereo ed Achilleo e la Catacomba di Domitilla* [1958]. P. F. de' Cavalieri, *Note agiografiche*, 2 (ST 22; 1909), pp. 43–55 ('I SS. Nereo ed Achilleo nell'epigramma damasiano'). H. *Leclercq, OSB, in *DACL* 12 (pt. 1; 1935), cols. 1111–23, s.v. 'Nérée et Achillée'.

Neri, St Philip. See PHILIP NERI, ST.

Nero, Claudius (AD 37–68), Roman Emp. from 54. The last Emp. descended from Augustus, Nero was the son of the aristocrat Domitius Ahenobarbus and of Agrippina, sister of the Emp. Caligula. After her remarriage to the Emp. Claudius in 49 Nero was adopted by his stepfather, and after Claudius' murder was proclaimed Emp. at the age of 16 by the Praetorian Guard and accepted by the Senate. At first he ruled relatively well under the guidance of *Seneca and the Praetorian Prefect Burrus, but he soon scandalized public opinion at Rome by murdering his mother and his wife, Octavia, as well as possible competitors for the throne, and by appearing in public as a singer and charioteer; upper class discontent was repressed by terror. His extravagance and consequent exactions also turned many of his subjects against him; the best-known case is the revolt of Judaea in 66. In 68 he also provoked rebellion in Spain, Gaul, and Africa; the armies deserted him; and he finally committed suicide.

In Roman tradition Nero appears as a tyrant. Many believed that he had caused the great fire which burned down much of Rome in 64, with a view to rebuilding it to suit his artistic tastes; it was to divert his unpopularity on this score that he punished the Christians as scapegoats (see PERSECUTIONS, EARLY CHRISTIAN). Christian apologists could therefore attribute the persecutions to a ruler condemned by pagan opinion also. Yet 1 Peter (2: 11–17), traditionally written in his reign after persecution had begun, inculcates passive obedience ('honour the emperor'), cf. Romans 13: 1–6. Earlier, it had been to Nero that St *Paul appealed from the tribunal of Festus at Caesarea (Acts. 25: 11). It is unlikely that Nero personally heard the case, but acc. to a substantial tradition both St Peter and St Paul were executed at Rome in his time. After Nero's death there was a widespread belief that he would return, and 'false Neros' appeared in the E. provinces. The myth is perhaps indicated by the references to the Beast in Rev. 13: 11–18, where the '*Number of the Beast' corresponds to 'Neron Caesar' in Gk. notation. See also TACITUS and NUMBER OF THE BEAST.

The principal sources are Tacitus, *Annales*, 12–16; *Suetonius, 'Nero'; and Dio Cassius, *Hist.* 61–3. E. M. Smallwood (ed.), *Documents illustrating the Principates of Gaius, Claudius and Nero* (Cambridge, 1967). B. H. Warmington, *Nero: Reality and Legend* (1969); M. T. Griffin, *Nero: The End of a Dynasty* (1984). H. H. Scullard, *From the Gracchi to Nero* (1959), pp. 315–32 (5th edn., 1982, pp. 304–21); A. Garzetti, *From Tiberius to the Antonines* (rev. Eng. tr., 1974), pp. 146–89, with bibl. pp. 605–22 and 741–8. See also works cited s.v. PERSECUTIONS, EARLY CHRISTIAN.

Nerses, St (d. *c*.373), sixth *Catholicos of the *Armenian Church. A direct descendant of *Gregory the Illuminator, he was educated at Caesarea in Cappadocia and held office at the royal court. After the death of his wife he became an ecclesiastic, and, having been elected Catholicos (perh. *c*.363), undertook the reform of the Armenian Church. At the Council of Ashtishat (*c*.365) he promulgated a number of decrees, e.g. against marriages between relations and on fasting. He also founded many hospitals and orphanages. He was deposed and exiled for criticizing the dissolute life of King Arshak III. Though restored under Arshak's successor Pap (369), he also incurred the hostility of the new King, whom he censured for his immorality, and was poisoned by him during a meal. His son, St *Isaac the Great (q.v.), became one of his successors. Feast day, 19 Nov.

J. Markwart, *Die Entstehung der armenischen Bistümer: Kritische Untersuchung der armenischen Überlieferung* (Orientalia Christiana, 27. 2 [no. 80]; 1932, pp. 139–236), esp. pp. 223–33. F. Tournebize in *DHGE* 4 (1930), cols. 297 f., s.v. 'Arménie'; P. Ananian in *Bibliotheca Sanctorum*, 9 (1967), cols. 742–6, s.v. 'Narsete I'. See also works cited s.v. ARMENIA, CHRISTIANITY IN.

Nerses IV, St (1102–73), *Catholicos of the *Armenian Church. Nerses Shnornhali ('the Graceful') became Catholicos in 1166 (with his seat at Rhomkla in Cilician Armenia) and strove for union between the Armenian and Byzantine Churches, corresponding with the Emp. Michael I; his death prevented the project from being realized. His extensive writings, in both verse and prose, include many hymns and devotional works which have won him lasting fame; best known is his meditative poem on the history of salvation, called (after its first line) 'Jesus, only Son of the Father'. He is not to be confused with his great-nephew, Nerses of Lambron (1152/3–98), another prolific writer. Feast day, 13 Aug.

Fr. tr. of 'Jesus, only Son of the Father' by I. Kéchichian, SJ (SC 203; 1973), with introd. and bibl. P. Ananian in *Bibliotheca Sanctorum*, 9 (1967), cols. 746–59, s.v. 'Narsete IV'; B. L. Zekiyan in *Dict. Sp.* 11 (1982), cols. 134–50, s.v.

Nestle, Eberhard (1851–1913), biblical scholar. From 1883 to 1898 he taught at Ulm and *Tübingen, and from 1898 held appointments at the Evangelical Theological Seminary at Maulbronn. His early work was done on the text of the *Septuagint. He increasingly interested himself, however, in the NT, and in 1898 published the first edition of his Greek NT text, which, though somewhat mechanically constructed from the existing editions of C. *Tischendorf, B. F. *Westcott and F. J. A. *Hort, and B. *Weiss, came to be very widely used. In 1904 this text was adopted by the *British and Foreign Bible Society in place of the *Textus Receptus. Nestle also wrote many grammars and other aids to biblical study.

Nestle's Gk. text of the NT in its successive Ger. edns. has been constantly revised (ed. from the 10th edn., 1914, onwards, by his son E. Nestle, from the 22nd edn. (1956) by K. Aland, and from the 26th edn. (1979) by B. and K. Aland). The apparatus was radically altered in the 13th edn. (1927) and notable improvements were also made in the text in the 17th edn. (1941). Further revisions in the apparatus and text were made between the 22nd and 27th edns. (1994) to incl. readings from the *Bodmer Papyri. H. Haag in *Dict. Bibl.*, Suppl. 6 (1960), cols. 424–6, s.v.

Nestorian Stone. See SIGAN-FU STONE.

Nestorius (b. after 351; d. after 451), Patr. of *Constantinople and heresiarch. He gave his name to the doctrine (commonly called 'Nestorianism') that there were two separate Persons in the Incarnate Christ, the one Divine and the other Human (as opposed to the orthodox teaching that in the Incarnate Christ was a single Person, at once God and man); whether Nestorius ever taught this is disputed. A native of Germanicia in Syria Euphratensis, he entered a monastery at *Antioch, where he became imbued with the principles of the Antiochene theological school, and prob. studied under *Theodore of Mopsuestia. Soon he acquired a great reputation as a preacher; and in 428, when the see of Constantinople became vacant, *Theodosius II, overriding the claims of the local candidates, invited Nestorius to fill the see. Nestorius at once proclaimed himself a zealous upholder of orthodoxy, eager to rid the city of heretics and schismatics. When his chaplain Anastasius preached against the use of the term *Theotokos (q.v.) as savouring of heresy (*Apollinarianism), Nestorius gave him full support. A violent controversy developed round the propriety of a word which had long been used by theologians of the highest orthodoxy and was now gaining in popularity since it gave theological expression to the growing devotion to the Virgin as the Mother of God. Nestorius' opponents succeeded in winning the support of St *Cyril of Alexandria and the Egyptian monks to their cause. Both sides having appealed to Rome, at a Council held there in August 430, Nestorius' teaching was condemned by Pope *Celestine and Cyril was commissioned to pronounce sentence of deposition on Nestorius, if he would not submit. In Nov. 430 Cyril took action and on 7 Dec. 430 delivered his sentence into Nestorius' hands by legates sent to Constantinople, condemning Nestorius in a set of twelve anathemas and requiring him to retract within ten days. Meanwhile the Emp. had arranged a General Council to meet at *Ephesus in the following summer. It assembled on 22 June 431 and pronounced sentence of deposition on Nestorius (see EPHESUS, COUNCIL OF). Theodosius eventually acquiesced in its decision and Nestorius was sent back to his monastery at Antioch. In 435 Theodosius had his books condemned, and in 436 Nestorius was banished to Upper Egypt, where he died several years later (date unknown).

Nestorius' principal writings were his letters and sermons, which, however, for the most part, survive only in fragments. He was also the author of an extensive treatise, published in his last years and known as the 'Bazaar of Heracleides' (*Liber Heraclidis*). This was discovered *c.*1895 and first published in 1910. Written when the theological climate had completely changed, Nestorius is here claiming that his own beliefs were identical with those then being sustained (against the *Eutychians) by the orthodox. The twelve 'Counter Anathemas' long ascribed to Nestorius have been shown by E. *Schwartz to be of much later date.

Opinion is widely divided as to what the doctrine of Nestorius really was and how far it was heretical. His sustained objection to the term 'Theotokos' has traditionally been held to imply that he asserted not only two different natures, but also two different persons, in Christ, the one the man, born of Mary. But we must not overlook that he repeatedly affirmed the oneness of Christ, though he preferred to speak of conjunction (συνάφεια) rather than of union (ἕνωσις). His fear of the *Monophysite tendencies, which were actually to come into the open a few years later, led him to reject Cyril's conception of a hypostatic union (ἕνωσις καθ᾽ ὑπόστασιν), substituting for it a union of the will (κατ᾽ εὐδοκίαν). The latter term certainly savoured of *Adoptianism, of which he was actually, though unjustly, accused. Certainly his zeal for upholding the integrity of the two natures, which he believed to be both self-subsisting and therefore incapable of being physically united in the Person of the God-man, caused him to fall into unguarded language, and the fact that his own friends finally abandoned him supports the view that, by trying to defend, he actually compromised the Antiochene Christology. In the polemic surrounding the theological controversies of the later 5th and 6th cents., the term 'Nestorian' was applied by their opponents to all upholders of a strict Antiochene Christology; as a result the *Church of the East (q.v.) has come to be popularly called 'the Nestorian Church' even though its teaching has never been Nestorianism as defined above.

Collection of frags. (mainly in Gk.), ed. F. *Loofs, *Nestoriana* (Halle, 1905). Many of these frags. are preserved in the *acta* of the Council of Ephesus (q.v.) and can be found in the pr. edns. (J. *Hardouin, J. D. *Mansi, and others); crit. text by E. Schwartz in *ACO*. Syriac text of the *Liber Heraclides* first ed. P. Bedjan (Paris, 1910); Fr. tr. by F. Nau (ibid., 1910, incl. further frags. of Gk., not pr. by Loofs, pp. 335–58); Eng. tr., with introd. and studies, by G. R. *Driver and L. Hodgson (Oxford, 1925). On the true authorship of the Counter Anathemas, commonly ascribed to Nestorius, see E. Schwartz, *Die Gegenanathematismen des Nestorius* (*Sb.* (Bayr.), 1922, Heft 1). V. Grumel, AA (ed.), *Les Regestes des Actes du Patriarcat de Constantinople*, 1, fasc. 1 (2nd edn., 1972), pp. 41–53 (nos. 50–65b). On the historical course of the conflict with Cyril, L. *Duchesne, *Histoire ancienne de l'Église*, 3 (1910), pp. 313–88 (Eng. tr., 3 (1924), pp. 219–70) (very critical of Cyril's handling of Nestorius); M. Jugie, AA, *Nestorius et la controverse nestorienne* (1912; more sympathetic to Cyril). J. F. Bethune-Baker, *Nestorius and his Teaching* (1908; with extracts from the 'Bazaar' [tr. by R. H. *Connolly]). J. P. Junglas, *Die Irrlehre des Nestorius* (Trier, 1912); F. Loofs, *Nestorius and his Place in the History of Christian Doctrine* (1914). L. I. Scipioni, OP, *Ricerche sulla cristologia del 'Libro di Eraclide' di Nestorio: La formulazione*

teologica e il suo contesto filosofico (Paradosis, 11; 1956); id., *Nestorio e il consilio di Efeso* (Studia Patristica Mediolanensia, 1; 1974); L. Abramowski, *Untersuchungen zum* Liber Heraclidis *des Nestorius* (CSCO 242; Louvain, 1963). A. Grillmeier [SJ], *Jesus der Christus im Glauben der Kirche*, 1 (1979), pp. 642–60, 707–26. [This work is a much rev. and expanded edn. of the author's essay in his work on the Council of *Chalcedon, orig. pub. in 1951; Eng. tr. of one of the intermediate stages, *Christ in Christian Tradition*, 1 (2nd edn., 1975), pp. 447–63 and 501–19.] CPG 3 (1979), pp. 107–26 (nos. 5665–5766). Altaner and Stuiber (1978), pp. 336–8 and 619. A. J. Maclean in HERE 9 (1917), pp. 323–32, s.v. 'Nestorianism'; É. Amann in DTC 11 (pt. 1; 1931), cols. 76–157, s.v.; L. R. Wickham in TRE 24 (1995), pp. 276–86, s.v. See also bibl. to EPHESUS, COUNCIL OF.

Ne Temere.

The decree (2 Aug. 1907) of the Sacred Congregation of the Council, promulgated by *Pius X to come into force on 19 Apr. 1908, putting the matrimonial legislation of the RC Church on a new basis. It was designed to remedy the confusions created by the Tridentine *Tametsi* decree (q.v.) (1563). Earlier attempts at revision were Benedict XVI's *Matrimonia quae in locis* (4 Nov. 1741) exempting Belgium and the Netherlands from the operation of *Tametsi* and Pius X's constitution *Provida sapientiaque* (18 Jan. 1906) suspending its application in Germany for mixed marriages and the marriages of non-Catholics. The new regulations of *Ne Temere* were to be of universal application. No marriage between persons baptized as Catholics or who have been received into Catholic communion is valid unless celebrated before the parish priest or the Ordinary or a priest delegated by one or other of these. The same ruling holds if only one of the contracting parties is a Catholic (though in some *mixed marriages a Catholic may now be allowed to marry before a minister of another denomination). Hence, while the RC Church normally declines to recognize marriages in which a RC is involved, if solemnized before a minister of another denomination or merely by a civil contract, it does recognize such marriages between two non-Catholics. To make 'surprise marriages' (*mariages à la gaulmine*) impossible, *Ne Temere* also laid down that the parish priest must formally ask and receive the consent of the parties. The rulings of the decree, with important modifications, were taken over into the *Codex Iuris Canonici* (1983), cans. 1108–19.

Text in *ASS* 40 (1907), pp. 527–30. See also bibl. to MATRIMONY.

Netherlands, Christianity in the.

Christianity originally penetrated the territory now known as the Netherlands in Roman times, but the fall of the Empire and the establishment of the strongly pagan kingdom of Frisia delayed its effective conversion until the very end of the 7th cent. Chief among the Anglo-Saxon missionaries responsible for its evangelization were St *Willibrord, Bp. of Utrecht from 695 to 739, and St *Boniface, who was martyred by the Northern Frisians in 754. The range and success of their activities brought the whole country under the influence of the see of Utrecht, which was the only bishopric until modern times. Its Prince Bishop exerted a dominating influence on the subsequent history of the Church, though in the course of the later Middle Ages the see lost most of its political power to the Counts of Holland and Guelders, and the Bishop finally surrendered his temporal claims to *Charles V in 1526. In the 14th cent. the Netherlands saw the rise of an influential movement, known as the '*Devotio Moderna', which laid stress both on mystical piety and education. It found expression in the '*Brethren of the Common Life', whose school at Deventer numbered *Erasmus among its pupils.

Initially at the *Reformation both *Lutherans and *Anabaptists gained followers, and the latter especially were fiercely persecuted. The political revolt against Spanish rule became inextricably bound up with religion and the adherence of William the Silent to *Calvinism in 1573 was a significant step in underlining the role of that creed in the struggle. In 1574 William founded the University of *Leiden which quickly attained international importance, not least in the field of theology. By 1609 the Netherlands was effectively independent, but although the Reformed religion held sway, controversies arose within its ranks in the course of the 17th cent. The more notable of these concerned the disputes over free will and *predestination surrounding J. *Arminius, which led to the formal condemnation of his followers (*Remonstrants) at the Synod of *Dort (1618–19).

Though never formally established, the Reformed Church with its Calvinist orthodoxy continued to be the official religious body of the state until the political revolution of 1795. After the overthrow of French rule and the establishment of the kingdom of the Netherlands, William I introduced a system of Church government (1816) in which the state exercised very extensive powers. Objections to this arrangement and to the prevalent theological liberalism led to the Secession of 1834, when some of the stricter Calvinists set up the 'Christian Reformed Churches'. Further such disputes within the main body of the Reformed Church gave rise in 1886 to another major secession led by A. *Kuyper. During this period the foundations were laid of the distinctively Dutch system of 'pillarization', whereby society became divided into several distinct vertical blocks based on common ideologies: Catholic, Calvinist, socialist, and liberal. This arrangement dominated Dutch life between 1920 and 1960 and is still in evidence.

In an endeavour to find favour with the Catholics, *Philip II secured the creation of five new sees under Utrecht, which was now raised to an archbishopric (1560). But the experiment was overtaken by the Dutch revolt and the subsequent loss of the Netherlands, and from 1580 to 1853 the RC Church was without territorial bishops, being governed by *Vicars Apostolic or Papal *Legates. From 1583 to 1795 it was subjected by the government to severe penal restrictions. In 1697 accusations of *Jansenism were launched from Rome against the RCs of the Netherlands, notably against Petrus Codde (1648–1710), then Vicar General and titular Abp. of Philippi. In 1702 he was officially censured and a schism began. Codde's followers upheld the continuity of their communion with the national Catholic Church of the past. The support of the French Jansenists, who refused to accept the bull '*Unigenitus' (1713), secured for these '*Old Catholics', as they came to be called, the maintenance of the *Apostolic Succession; the group still survives as a branch of the Old Catholic Church. The main body of Dutch Catholics, however, accepted the condemnation of Jansenism. They looked largely to external (esp. *Jesuit) influ-

ence for guidance and protection until the archiepiscopal see of Utrecht was restored in 1853. In the modern Netherlands they are a vigorous body, esp. strong in the provinces of Limburg and North Brabant. In recent years there has been much advanced thinking among Dutch RCs, which has brought them near to conflict with the Papacy on such subjects as *contraception and clerical *celibacy.

Acc. to the 1989 census, c.36 per cent of the population belong to the RC Church, c.28 per cent are Protestant (mainly 'Dutch Reformed Church' and other Calvinist bodies), and c.32 per cent profess no religious allegiance.

The principal works are in Dutch. In English there is a general introduction by P. H. Ditchfield, *The Church in the Netherlands* (1892; dealing with Belgium and the Netherlands). Also W. E. Keeney, *Dutch Anabaptist Thought and Practice from 1539–1564* (Nieuwkoop, 1968); A. Duke, 'The Ambivalent Face of Calvinism in the Netherlands 1561–1618', in M. Prestwich (ed.), *International Calvinism 1541–1715* (Oxford, 1985), pp. 109–34; rev. repr. in Duke, *Reformation and Revolt in the Low Countries* (1990), pp. 269–93, with other material in this vol. (some not previously pub.); D. Nobbs, *Theocracy and Toleration: A Study of the Disputes in Dutch Calvinism from 1600 to 1650* (1938); J. H. Mackay, *Religious Thought in Holland during the Nineteenth Century* (Hastie Lectures, 1909–11; 1911); M. Wintle, *Pillars of Piety: Religion in the Netherlands in the Nineteenth Century 1813–1901* (Occasional Papers in Modern Dutch Studies, 2; Hull, 1987); E. C. Vanderlaan, *Protestant Modernism in Holland* (1924); and S. J. de Vries, *Bible and Theology in the Netherlands: Dutch Old Testament Criticism under Modernist and Conservative Auspices, 1850 to World War I* (Wageningen, 1968; 2nd edn., New York, 1989). S. Axters, OP, *La Spiritualité des Pays-Bas* (Bibliotheca Mechliniensis, 2nd ser. 1; 1948; Eng. tr., 1954); id., *Geschiedenis van de Vroomheid in de Nederlanden* (Antwerp, 1950 ff. [4 vols., covering the period to 1730, by 1960]). O. J. de Jong, *Nederlandse Kerkgeschiedenis* (Nijkerk, 1972; 3rd edn., 1985). R. R. Post, *Kerkgeschiedenis van Nederland in de Middeleeuwen* (2 vols., Utrecht, 1957). P. Brachin and L. J. Rogier, *Histoire du catholicisme hollandais depuis le xvie siècle* [1974]. L. J. Rogier, *Geschiedenis van het Katholicisme in Noord-Nederland in de 16e en de 17e Eeuw* (3 vols., Amsterdam, 1945–7); P. Polman, OFM, *Katholiek Nederland in de Achttiende Eeuw* (3 vols., Hilversum, 1968); L. J. Rogier, *Katholieke Herleving: Geschiedenis van Katholiek Nederland sinds 1853* (The Hague [1956]; 2nd edn., 1962). A. J. Rasker, *De Nederlandse Hervormde Kerk vanaf 1795: Haar geschiedenis en theologie in der negentiende en twintigste eeuw* (Kampen, 1974; 3rd edn., 1986). *Biographisch Lexicon voor de Geschiedenis van het Nederlandse Protestantisme*, ed. D. Nauta and others (3 vols., Kampen, 1978–88). *Archief voor Nederlandsche Kerkgeschiedenis* (The Hague, 1885–99), cont. as *Nederlandsch (Nederlands) Archief voor Kerkgeschiedenis* (ibid., 1900–66; Leiden, 1967 ff.). A. G. Weiler in *NCE* 10 (1967), pp. 354–62, s.v. 'Netherlands'; C. Augustijn in *TRE* 24 (1994), cols. 474–502, s.v. 'Niederlande', both with bibl. See also bibl. to ARMINIANISM, CALVINISM, DEVOTIO MODERNA, and OLD CATHOLICS.

Netter, Thomas (c.1375–1430), *Carmelite theologian. Born at Saffron Walden in Essex, he was sent by his superiors to study in Oxford, where he gained a reputation for sound scholarship ('Doctor praestantissimus'). In 1409 he was sent to the Council of *Pisa as the representative of King Henry IV, whose adviser he had become, and on his return to England took an active part in the struggle against the followers of J. *Wycliffe, acting at the trials of John Badby in 1410, John *Oldcastle in 1413, William Taylor in 1423, and William White in 1428. Henry V chose him for his confessor and, after Netter had been elected Provincial of the English Carmelites in 1414, appointed him one of his mandatories to the Council of *Constance. In 1419 he was sent on a political mission to Poland. Later he became spiritual adviser to *Henry VI, his former pupil. The latter part of his life appears to have been chiefly taken up with the composition of his main work, 'Doctrinale antiquitatum fidei ecclesiae catholicae', in which he sought to refute the doctrines of Wycliffe and the *Hussites from the teaching of the Bible and the Fathers. The 'Fasciculi Zizaniorum' (a collection of anti-Wycliffite documents) is traditionally associated with him, but it is unlikely that he was the author of any part of it.

The best edn. of his 'Doctrinale' is that of B. Blanciotti, Ord. Carm. (3 vols., Venice, 1757–9; repr. photographically, Farnborough, 1967), with introd., vol. 1, pp. ix–xviii. Life herein contained repr. in *Analecta Ordinis Carmelitarum*, 1 (1909), pp. 298–303, 329–35, and 361–5. Various letters, with brief introd., in B. Zimmerman, OCD (ed.), *Monumenta Historica Carmelitana*, 1 (Lérins, 1907), pp. 442–82. The 'Fasciculi Zizaniorum' is ed. in part by W. W. Shirley (RS, 1858). P. R. McCaffrey, Ord. Carm., *The White Friars: An Outline Carmelite History with Special Reference to the English-Speaking Provinces* (Dublin, 1936), pp. 143–51. J. A. Robson, *Wyclif and the Oxford Schools* (Cambridge, 1961), pp. 223–40. M. Hurley, SJ, 'A Pre-Tridentine Theology of Tradition: Thomas Netter of Walden (†1430)', *Heythrop Journal*, 4 (1963), pp. 348–66. J. Crompton, 'Fasciculi Zizaniorum', *JEH* 12 (1961), pp. 35–45 and 155–66. C. L. Kingsford in *DNB* 40 (1894), pp. 231–4; *BRUO* 2 (1958), pp. 1343–4.

Neumann, Therese (1898–1962), of Konnersreuth in Bavaria, *stigmatized visionary. After a normal childhood and youth, Therese Neumann lost her health in 1918 through overstrain in helping to put out a fire. Having become bedridden in the same year and blind in 1919, she regained her sight in 1923 on the day of the beatification of *Teresa of Lisieux. Two years later, on the day of the canonization of the same saint, she became able to walk again. During Lent 1926 she began to have visions of the Passion and received the stigmata, which remained visible and bled on Fridays. She was reputed to have taken no solid food after 1922, and after 1927 no nourishment whatever except daily Holy Communion. After her visions she was usually in an abnormal state of absorption during which she was credited with supernatural faculties such as ability to read consciences and to discern the authenticity of relics. The events of Konnersreuth, which soon became a place of pilgrimage for the curious as well as the devout, were for years a topic of lively discussion; but the RC ecclesiastical authorities have abstained from any pronouncement on the case.

L. Witt, *Das kleine Leben der stigmatisierten Jungfrau Therese von Konnersreuth* (1927); F. Gerlich, *Die stigmatisierte Therese Neumann* (2 vols., 1927); F. X. Huber, *Das Mysterium von Konnersreuth* (1950). Among the many other sympathetic works those available in Eng. incl. studies by R. W. Hynek (3rd edn., Prague, 1932; Eng. tr., 1932, with bibl.), C. E. Roy and W. A. Joyce (London, 1936), and J. Teodorowicz (Salzburg, 1936; Eng. tr., St Louis, 1940). More critical studies by J. Deutsch, *Aerztliche Kritik an Konnersreuth* (1938); B. Poray Madeyski, *Le Cas de la visionnaire stigmatisée: Thérèse Neumann de Konnersreuth* (1940). Other studies by H. C. Graef (Cork, 1950) and P. Siwek, SJ (Paris, 1950; Eng. tr., Dublin, 1954). P. Siwek in *NCE* 10 (1967), pp. 365 f., s.v.

neume. (1) From Gk. πνεῦμα, 'breath'. In plainsong, a prolonged group of notes, sung to a single syllable, esp. at the end of the '*Alleluia' and in the *responsories of the Mass. (2) From Gk. νεῦμα, 'sign'. The sign employed in the earliest plainsong to indicate the melody. These signs are probably derived from the accent-marks of the grammarians. They are thought to date from the 8th century.

Neutral text. The type of text of the Greek NT represented by the two MSS, *Codex Vaticanus and *Codex Sinaiticus, and so designated by F. J. A. *Hort because it was supposed to be less subject to corrupting influences of editorial revision than any other. There seems little doubt that the origin of the text is to be connected with Egypt (though either or both MSS may have been actually written elsewhere); and some scholars have believed it to be the work of *Hesychius, an Alexandrian who is said to have revised the *Septuagint. See also ALEXANDRIAN TEXT.

B. F. Westcott and F. J. A. Hort, *The New Testament in the Original Greek*, 1 (1881), esp. pp. 126–30 ('The Neutral Text and its Preservation').

Nevin, John Williamson (1803–86), American Protestant theologian. He was a native of Pennsylvania, of *Presbyterian upbringing and Scottish-Irish descent. From 1823 to 1828 he studied at Princeton Theological Seminary, being for part of the time in charge of the classes of Charles *Hodge. In 1828 he published his widely used *Summary of Biblical Antiquities* (2 vols.). From 1830 to 1840 he was professor of biblical literature at the Western Theological Seminary at Allegheny, Pa. Here, under the influence of the writings of J. A. W. *Neander, he gradually abandoned the dogmas of Presbyterianism for a more liberal theology, and became closely associated with P. *Schaff. In 1840 he became professor of theology in the Mercersburg (Pa.) Theological Seminary, a 'German Reformed' institution, where, having transferred his allegiance from the Presbyterian to this Reformed Church, he gained an increasing influence. In 1843 he attacked the then prevailing methods of revivalist preaching in *The Anxious Bench: A Tract for the Times*. In 1844 Schaff joined him from Germany, and the theological doctrines for which both stood became known as the '*Mercersburg Theology'. In 1846 he published *The Mystical Presence*, a defence of a doctrine of the Eucharist which conceded a 'Real Presence' and advocated a more sacramental conception of Christianity than is ordinarily held among Protestants. In 1853 he retired into private life on account of weak health, but from 1861 to 1866 he again lectured at, and from 1866 to 1876 was president of, the reorganized Franklin and Marshall College at Lancaster, Philadelphia.

Selected Theological Writings, ed. C. Yrigoyen and G. H. Bricker (Pittsburgh, 1978). T. Appel, *The Life and Work of John Williamson Nevin* (1889). J. H. Nichols, *Romanticism in American Theology: Nevin and Schaff at Mercersburg* (Chicago, 1961). W. W. Sweet in *Dict. Amer. Biog.* 13 (1934), pp. 442 f.

New Church. See SWEDENBORG, EMMANUEL.

New English Bible. See BIBLE (ENGLISH VERSIONS).

New Jerusalem Church. See SWEDENBORG, EMMANUEL.

Newman, Ven. John Henry (1801–90), *Tractarian leader and later Cardinal. He was brought up in the C of E under Evangelical influence. He entered Trinity College, Oxford, in June 1817, became Fellow of Oriel in 1822, and was ordained deacon in 1824. In 1825 he was appointed vice-principal of Alban Hall by R. *Whately, and in 1828 vicar of St Mary's, Oxford. In 1832–3 he toured S. Europe and on returning became intimately associated with the *Oxford Movement, in which he was the leading spirit. His sermons in St Mary's, published as *Parochial and Plain Sermons* (1834–42), had a profound influence on the religious life not only of Oxford but of the whole country. Their spirituality was based on a systematic study of the Fathers which bore fruit in *The Arians of the Fourth Century* (1833), whereas the *Tracts for the Times* (1833–41), 27 of which came from his pen, were popular statements of his religious position. Directed 'against Popery and Dissent', they defended his thesis of the 'via media', i.e. the belief that the C of E held an intermediate position, represented by the patristic tradition, as against modern Romanism on the one hand and modern Protestantism on the other. This belief received developed expression in his *Lectures on the Prophetical Office of the Church* (1837) and in his *Lectures on Justification* (1838). In the famous *Tract No. 90* (1841) he advocated the interpretation of the *Thirty-Nine Articles in a sense generally congruous with the decrees of *Trent. The Tract, which caused a violent controversy, was condemned by the Hebdomadal Board, and R. *Bagot, Bp. of Oxford, imposed silence on its author. Meanwhile, from 1839 onwards, Newman began to have doubts about the claims of the Anglican Church, and from 1841 onwards he gradually gave up his position in Oxford, living from 1842 at the neighbouring village of Littlemore, which was at that date part of the ecclesiastical parish of St Mary's. Here he set up a semi-monastic establishment and, during the next years, lived in retirement with a few friends. He resigned the incumbency of St Mary's on 18 Sept. 1843, preaching a few days later a celebrated sermon in Littlemore church on 'The Parting of Friends'. On 9 Oct. 1845 he was received into the RC Church. Almost immediately afterwards he issued his *Essay on the Development of Christian Doctrine* in defence of his change of allegiance.

Having been ordained in Rome, he established the *Oratorians at Birmingham in 1849 and was in Ireland as rector of the short-lived RC university in Dublin from 1854 to 1858. On his return to England he became for a few months editor of the *Rambler*, in which he published a controversial article 'On Consulting the Faithful in Matters of Doctrine', which was delated to Rome. His declared opposition to the retention of the Pope's Temporal Power was the occasion of his serious breach with his fellow-convert, H. E. *Manning. In 1864 a controversy with C. *Kingsley resulted in his *Apologia pro vita sua*, which, by its combination of frankness and delicacy, won him the sympathies of RCs and others alike. In the next year he wrote *The Dream of *Gerontius* depicting the journey of the soul to God at the hour of death, an almost Dantesque poem inspired by the Requiem Offices. In 1870 he published *A Grammar of Assent*, the work which contains much of his ripest thought. It is esp. remarkable for its differentiation between real and notional assent, its analysis of the function of the conscience in our knowledge of God and of the role of the 'illative sense', i.e. the faculty of judging from

given facts by processes outside the limits of strict logic, in reaching religious certitude. Although Newman never doubted Papal *Infallibility, he opposed the mounting *Ultramontanist pressure to obtain a conciliar definition in 1870. In his *Letter to the Duke of Norfolk* (1875) he supplied what has generally been acclaimed a masterly exposition of the implications of the Infallibility decree. In 1877 he was elected an Honorary Fellow of Trinity College, and two years later *Leo XIII made him Cardinal-Deacon of St George in Velabro.

Newman's thought was nourished by the Fathers rather than by the Schoolmen, and his main contribution to the thought of his age lay much more in the fields of psychological analysis and acute moral perception than in matters strictly theological. His fruitful use of the idea of development, in its application to the growth of Christian doctrine, and his profound insight into the nature and motives of religious faith, place him in the first rank of modern Christian thinkers. His ideals for Christian religious education were set forth in his *Idea of a University* (1852). Though unsuccessful in most of his undertakings in the RC Church during his lifetime, his genius has come to be more and more recognized after his death, and much of his teaching on liberty of conscience, the nature of biblical inspiration, and the role of the episcopate in the *magisterium* of the Church was to find official expression in the Second *Vatican Council. Proceedings for Newman's canonization were initiated in 1958; in 1991 he was declared Venerable.

Many of Newman's works have been repub. in crit. edns. The most notable are: the *Apologia*, ed. M. J. Svaglic (Oxford, 1967), *The Grammar of Assent*, ed. I. T. Ker (ibid., 1985); and *The Idea of a University*, ed. id. (ibid., 1976). Detailed aspects of Newman's theology in *The Theological Papers of John Henry Newman* on Faith and Certainty, ed. H. M. de Achaval, SJ, and J. D. Holmes (Oxford, 1976); *The Theological Papers of John Henry Newman* on Biblical Inspiration and on Infallibility, ed. J. D. Holmes (ibid., 1979). *Letters and Diaries*, ed. C. S. Dessain, Cong. Orat., and others (1961 ff. [vols. 11–22, London, 1961–72; other vols., Oxford, 1973 ff.]); *Sermons*, ed. P. Murray, OSB (Oxford, 1991 ff.). W. Ward, *The Life of John Henry Newman* (2 vols., 1912); I. [T.] Ker, *John Henry Newman: A Biography* (Oxford, 1988). Other biographical works include H. *Bremond, *Newman: Essai de biographie psychologique* ([1906]; Eng. tr. 1907); M. Ward, *Young Mr. Newman* (1948); L. Bouyer, Cong. Orat., *Newman: Sa vie, sa spiritualité* (1952; Eng. tr., 1958); C. S. Dessain, Cong. Orat., *John Henry Newman* (1966; 2nd edn., 1971); H. [C.] Graef, *God and Myself: The Spirituality of John Henry Newman* (1967). [W.] O. Chadwick, *From Bossuet to Newman: The Idea of Doctrinal Development* (Cambridge, 1957), *passim*; N. Lash, *Newman on Development* (1975); R. C. Selby, *The Principle of Reserve in the Writings of John Henry Cardinal Newman* (Oxford, 1975); P. Misner, *Papacy and Development: Newman and the Primacy of the Pope* (Studies in the History of Christian Thought, 15; Leiden, 1976). F. McGrath, SJ, *Newman's University: Idea and Reality* (1951); A. D. Culler, *The Imperial Intellect: A Study of Newman's Educational Ideal* (New Haven, Conn., and London, 1955). T. Kenny, *The Political Thought of John Henry Newman* (1957). J. Coulson, *Newman and the Common Tradition: A Study in the Language of Church and Society* (Oxford, 1970). S. Gilley, *Newman and his Age* (1990). D. [H.] Newsome, *The Convert Cardinals: John Henry Newman and Henry Edward Manning* (1993).

New Rome. A name for *Constantinople, which, acc. to *Sozomen (*Hist. Eccl.* 2. 3), was given to the city by the Emp. *Constantine himself. The Council of Constantinople of 381 lays down (can. 3) that 'the Bp. of Constantinople is to have honorary pre-eminence (ἔχειν τὰ πρεσβεῖα τῆς τιμῆς) after the Bp. of Rome, because Constantinople is new Rome (διὰ τὸ εἶναι αὐτὴν νέαν 'Ρώμην)'.

New Testament (Gk. Καινὴ Διαθήκη, Lat. *Novum Testamentum*). In the sense of 'new dispensation', a term denoting the Canonical Books belonging exclusively to the Church, in contradistinction to those styled *Old Testament (q.v.) which the Church shares with the Synagogue. The use of the word διαθήκη for the records of the OT dispensation has its roots in St *Paul (2 Cor. 3: 14) and from *Tertullian onwards 'Novum Testamentum' came to be accepted as a technical term. The NT contains the four Gospels, Acts, the Pauline and the 'Catholic' Epistles, and the Book of Revelation. See also CANON OF SCRIPTURE.

Newton, Isaac (1642–1727), mathematician and natural philosopher. He was elected a Fellow of Trinity College, Cambridge, in 1667 and in 1669 succeeded I. *Barrow as Lucasian Professor of mathematics. In 1688–9 and 1703–5 he represented the university in the House of Commons. After 1694 he moved to London, being appointed Master of the Mint in 1699 and knighted by Queen *Anne in 1705. He had been a member of the Royal Society since 1672 and was its president from 1703 until his death.

Newton was the most eminent physicist of his day, and his work is a landmark in the study of mathematics. Among his principal achievements are the formulation of the law of gravitation, the discovery of the differential calculus, and the first correct analysis of white light. In his celebrated *Philosophiae Naturalis Principia Mathematica* (1687) he gives expression also to his religious convictions. Belief in God rests for him chiefly on the admirable order of the universe. He acknowledges the Divine transcendence, omnipotence, and perfection, and combats the pantheistic idea of a world soul. God is the Supreme Being, with complete authority over the material universe as well as over human souls, which owe Him absolute submission.

Though a conforming Churchman, Newton was not orthodox. In private, he denied the doctrine of the Trinity on the ground that such a belief was inaccessible to reason. He was a friend of the *Cambridge Platonist, H. *More, whose millenarian interests he shared; some of his speculations in this field were embodied in his *Observations on the Prophecies of Daniel and the Apocalypse of St John* (posthumous, 1733). His concern with the problems of reconciling biblical with secular history is reflected in *The Chronology of Ancient Kingdoms Amended* (posthumous, 1728). His more exclusively scientific works include *Optics* (1704) and *Arithmetica Universalis* (1707).

Collected works ed. S. *Horsley (5 vols., London, 1779–85). Crit. edns. of *Papers and Letters on Natural Philosophy and Related Documents* by I. B. Cohen (Cambridge, 1958; 2nd edn., Cambridge, Mass., and London, 1978), of *Correspondence* by H. W. Turnbull and others (7 vols., Cambridge, 1959–77), of *Unpublished Scientific Papers* ed. and tr. by A. R. Hall and M. B. Hall (ibid., 1962), of *Mathematical Papers* by D. T. Whiteside (ibid., 1967 ff.), and of *Optical Papers*, ed. A. E. Shapiro (ibid., 1984 ff.). *Sir Isaac Newton's Theological Manuscripts* selected and ed. H. McLachlan (Liverpool, 1950). Classic Life by D. Brewster (2 vols., London, 1855). Modern account by R. S. Westfall, *Never at Rest: A Biography of Isaac Newton* (Cambridge, 1980), with full bibl. Other Lives by L. T. More (New York and London, 1934),

J. W. N. Sullivan (London, 1938), E. N. da C. Andrade (ibid., 1950), S. I. Wawilow (Berlin, 1951), and F. E. Manuel (Cambridge, Mass., 1968). F. Rosenberger, *Isaac Newton und seine physikalischen Principien* (Leipzig, 1895). H. Metzger, *Attraction universelle et religion naturelle chez quelques commentateurs anglais de Newton* (1938). *Newton Tercentenary Celebrations* (Cambridge, 1947). F. E. Manuel, *Isaac Newton Historian* (Cambridge, Mass., 1963); id., *The Religion of Isaac Newton* (Oxford, 1974). A. [A.] Koyré, *Newtonian Studies* (1965). I. B. Cohen, *The Newtonian Revolution* (1980).

Newton, John (1725–1807), *Evangelical divine. The son of a shipmaster, he was impressed into naval service, in the course of which he was converted on 10 Mar. (*NS* 21) 1748, though for some years he continued to be a slave-trader. From 1755 to 1764 he was Tide Surveyor at Liverpool. At this time he came under the influence of G. *Whitefield, and also began studying Latin, Hebrew, Greek, and Syriac. He considered entering the Dissenting ministry, but on being offered the curacy of Olney, he was ordained by the Bp. of Lincoln in 1764. Here he collaborated with W. *Cowper in the production of the *Olney Hymns* (1779). In 1780 he was appointed rector of St Mary Woolnoth, London, and held this post until his death. Among the better-known of his hymns, which are remarkable for their directness and simplicity, are 'Glorious things of Thee are spoken' and 'How sweet the Name of Jesus sounds'. He was also the author of several prose works, including letters and sermons. In theology he was a moderate *Calvinist and much influenced many leaders in the *Evangelical Revival, among them T. *Scott, W. *Wilberforce (whom he also aided in his campaign against slavery), C. *Simeon and Hannah *More.

Coll. edn. of his Works by R. Cecil (6 vols., London, 1808). Newton pub. much of his religious correspondence anonymously in *Omicron* (1774), *Cardiphonia* (2 vols., 1781), *Letters to a Wife* (2 vols., 1793), and *Letters to the Rev. W. Bull* (posthumous, 1847). *Journal of a Slave Trader (John Newton) 1750–1754* ed. B. [D.] Martin and M. Spurrell (1962). F. J. Hamilton (ed.), *'Out of the Depths', being the Autobiography of the Rev. John Newton* (1916). Memoir by R. Cecil (London, 1808). Other Lives by J. Bull (ibid., *c.*1868), B. [D.] Martin (ibid., 1950), and J. [C.] Pollock, *Amazing Grace* (ibid., 1981). D. E. Demaray, *The Innovation of John Newton (1725–1807): Synergism of Word and Music in Eighteenth Century Evangelism* (Texts and Studies in Religion, 36; Lewiston, NY, etc. [1988]). D. B. Hindmarsh, *John Newton and the English Evangelical Tradition* (Oxford, 1996). M. L. Loane, *Oxford and the Evangelical Succession* (1950), pp. 81–132. H. L. Bennett in *DNB* 40 (1894), pp. 235–8.

New Year's Day. In the pre-Christian era it was celebrated with great solemnity both by the Jews, who reckoned the year from the Feast of the New Moon at the end of Sept., and in the pagan empire. Acc. to the Julian Calendar, the Roman year began on 1 Jan., and the day was marked by the 'Saturnalia'. Christians were not only forbidden to participate in these festivities, but even had special fasts and Masses of expiation on the day, facts attested by the Second Council of Tours (567) and several Sacramentaries containing Masses and Offices *ad prohibendum ab idolis*. The later Christian practice of reckoning the beginning of the year varied acc. to the different countries. In England from early times the year began with the Feast of the *Annunciation (25 Mar.), in Germany with *Christmas, and in France and the Low Countries with

*Easter. Since *Gregory XIII's reform of the calendar in 1582, 1 Jan. came to be generally adopted as the first day of the year on the Continent, though this date was not accepted in England until 1752. In the E. *Orthodox Church, New Year's Day (here, 1 Sept.) is solemnized in many hymns, but in the W. until recent years the day had no liturgical significance, except for the fact of its coinciding with the Feast of the *Circumcision (q.v.). In the RC Church it was designated as the Octave of the Nativity of Christ in 1960; it is now also observed as the Solemnity of the Motherhood of the BVM. In England the custom of an informal 'watch-night' service, however, on the night of 31 Dec.–1 Jan. is often met with, esp. in the *Methodist Church.

M. Meslin, *La fête des kalendes de janvier dans l'empire romain* (Collection Latomus, 115; 1970), esp. pp. 95–129. F. Bünger, *Geschichte der Neujahrsfeier in der Kirche* (1911). R. L. Poole, 'The Beginning of the Year in the Middle Ages', *Proceedings of the British Academy*, 10 (1921–3), pp. 113–37; repr. in *Studies in Chronology and History* (Oxford, 1934), pp. 1–27.

New Zealand, Christianity in. The first Christian mission to the Maori of New Zealand was established in 1814 at the Bay of Islands by Samuel Marsden (1765–1838), an Anglican chaplain in New South Wales. Wesleyan *Methodists began a mission in 1822 and French RCs in 1838. By the 1840s the majority of the Maori population were attending Christian services. After the British annexation of New Zealand in 1840 there was extensive European colonization, which led to the introduction of a wide variety of denominations. *Presbyterians began as a settler Church in 1840 and members of the *Free Church of Scotland founded a colony at Otago in 1848. The Anglican see of New Zealand was set up in 1841, with G. A. *Selwyn as first bishop; by 1869 it had been subdivided to form six dioceses. In 1928 a Maori (F. A. Bennett, 1871–1950) was consecrated Bishop of Aotearoa to supervise work among the Maori, and in 1978 the see (previously suffragan to Waiapu) was raised to diocesan status. Women have been admitted to the Anglican priesthood in New Zealand since 1977. The first woman bishop was consecrated in 1990, for the diocese of Dunedin. The RC Church, predominantly Irish in membership, established two dioceses in 1848 and a Province (under the Abp. of Wellington) in 1887. The first Maori RC bishop was appointed in 1988. In the population as a whole Anglicans are the largest body (21 per cent in 1991), followed by Presbyterians (18 per cent), RCs (16 per cent) and Methodists (4 per cent). Among the Maori the RCs come second to the Anglicans, followed by the Ratana Church, an indigenous body founded by the Maori healer T. W. Ratana (1870–1939). Since the 1960s the *Charismatic Movement has become an influential force in traditional denominations and *Pentecostal Churches, imported and indigenous, have expanded rapidly. In the 1980s the major denominations began the creation of new structures for the Maori Church which reflect bicultural development in New Zealand society. Thus, in 1992 the Anglican Province of New Zealand became the Anglican Church in Aotearoa, New Zealand and Polynesia.

A. K. Davidson and P. J. Lineham (eds.), *Transplanted Christianity: Documents Illustrating Aspects of New Zealand Church History* (Auckland, 1987; 2nd edn., Palmerston North, 1989). W.

Yate, *An Account of New Zealand; and of the Formation and Progress of the Church Missionary Society's Mission in the Northern Island* (London, 1835; repr, with introd. by J. Binney, Shannon [1970]); W. Williams, *Christianity among the New Zealanders* (London, 1867); W. P. Morrell, *The Anglican Church in New Zealand: A History* (Dunedin, 1973); D. McEldowney (ed.), *Presbyterians in Aotearoa 1840–1990* (Wellington, 1990). E. R. Simmons, *A Brief History of the Catholic Church in New Zealand* (Auckland [1978]). B. Colless and P. Donovan (eds.), *Religion in New Zealand* (2nd edn., Palmerston North, 1985), pp. 9–142. P. Donovan (ed.), *Religions of New Zealanders* (ibid. [1990]); A. K. Davidson, *Christianity in Aotearoa: A History of Church and Society in New Zealand* (Wellington, 1991). P. J. Lineham and A. R. Grigg, *Religious History of New Zealand: A Bibliography* (Palmerston North, 1984; 2nd edn., 1987).

Nicaea, First Council of (325). The first *Oecumenical Council, summoned by the Emp. *Constantine within a few months of his conquest of the E. provinces, primarily to deal with the *Arian Controversy. The *acta* of the synod (if such ever existed) have been lost, the only authentic documents surviving from the Council being the Creed, the Synodal Letter, and the collection of twenty canons.

The Council, which had been orig. convened to Ancyra, assembled at Nicaea (now Iznik) in Bithynia in the early summer of 325 (traditionally 20 May). Shortly before there seems to have been a council at Antioch, held under the presidency of *Hosius of Córdoba, which condemned Arianism and its upholders (incl. *Eusebius of Caesarea). Constantine's main interest was to secure unity rather than any predetermined theological verdict. After the Emperor's opening speech, the presidency prob. passed to Hosius, though there is also some authority for the view that *Eustathius, Bp. of Antioch, presided. An Arian creed submitted by *Eusebius of Nicomedia was at once rejected. Eusebius of Caesarea then sought to vindicate himself by presenting the Baptismal Creed of his own Palestinian community, and this, supplemented by the word '*Homoousios', was received by the Council as orthodox. But the Creed formally promulgated by the Council was not this Creed but another, prob. a revision of the Baptismal Creed of *Jerusalem (see NICENE CREED). This Creed, with four anti-Arian anathemas attached, was subscribed by all the Bishops present except two (Theonas of Marmarica and Secundus of Ptolemais); and these last were deposed and banished. In the Arian struggle at the Council it would seem that *Athanasius, who was present as the deacon of his Bishop, *Alexander of Alexandria, was the leading champion of orthodoxy. The Council also reached decisions on the *Melitian Schism in Egypt and the *Paschal Controversy (qq.v.). It closed on 25 July. Some modern scholars (E. *Schwartz and others) have argued that this closure was only an adjournment, and that a second and concluding session of the Council met in 327.

The number of bishops who attended the Council is not known, since the signature lists are defective. The traditional number, which goes back to a late writing of Athanasius (*Ep. ad Afros*, 2), is 318, probably a symbolical figure, based on the number of *Abraham's servants (Gen. 14: 14). Between 220 and 250 is more likely. The Council, however, became generally known as 'the synod of the 318 Fathers'. Apparently the only representatives from the W. apart from Hosius were two priests representing the Pope of Rome, and the Bps. of Carthage, Milan, Dijon, and two others.

It is difficult to integrate what we learn from the 20 genuine surviving canons with our other information about the Council. Can. 6 laid down the precedence due to metropolitan sees, and was later constantly invoked in support of the claims of Rome; cans. 10–14 are a short penitential code, dealing with the treatment of the lapsed in the recent persecutions; can. 13 ordered that no one who sought it was to be refused the *viaticum; can. 19 dealt with the followers of *Paul of Samosata; can. 20 laid down that prayer should be said standing during the Paschal season. Before long these canons were universally accepted both in E. and W.; and several independent versions survive from the 4th and 5th cents. They were normally given pride of place in the canonical collections and, prob. through this cause, the canons of other Councils (notably *Sardica, q.v.) were apt to be cited as Nicene because they followed on without a break.

The genuine docs., together with a large collection of *spuria*, are pr. in all the principal Conciliar collections. Hardouin, 1 (1714), cols. 309–528; Mansi, 2 (1759), cols. 635–1082; Hefele and Leclercq, 1 (pt. 1; 1907), pp. 335–632. Text of Creed and canons also, with Eng. tr. and introd,, in Tanner, *Decrees* (1990), pp. 1–19; crit. text of Lat. versions in *EOMIA*, esp. 1. 2 (1904). W. *Bright, *Notes on the Canons of the First Four General Councils* (2nd edn., 1892), pp. 1–89. P. Batiffol, 'Les Sources de l'histoire du concile de Nicée', *ÉO* 24 (1925), pp. 385–402; 26 (1927), pp. 5–17. F. Haase, *Die koptischen Quellen zum Konzil von Nicäa: Übersetzt und untersucht* (Studien zur Geschichte und Kultur des Altertums, 10, Heft 4; 1920). G. Bardy in Fliche and Martin, 3 (1936), pp. 69–95, with good bibl. I. Ortiz de Urbina, SJ, *Nicée et Constantinople* (Histoire des Conciles Œcuméniques, 1; 1963), esp. pp. 15–136. C. Luibhéid, *The Council of Nicaea* (Galway, 1982). M. Aubineau, 'Les 318 Serviteurs d'Abraham (Gen., XIV, 14) et le Nombre des Pères au Concile de Nicée (325)', *RHE* 61 (1966), pp. 5–43; cf. H. Chadwick, 'Les 318 Pères de Nicée', ibid., pp. 808–11. R. Lorenz, 'Das Problem der Nachsynode von Nicäa (327)', *ZKG* 90 (1979), pp. 22–40; C. Luibhéid, 'The Alleged Second Session of the Council of Nicaea', *JEH* 34 (1983), pp. 165–74. *CPG* 4 (1980), pp. 5–10 (nos. 8511–27). G. Fritz in *DTC* 11 (pt. 1; 1931), cols. 399–417, s.v. 'Nicée (1ᵉʳ Concile de)'; I. O. de Urbina, SJ, in *NCE* 10 (1967), pp. 432–4, s.v.; H. C. Brennecke in *TRE* 24 (1995), pp. 429–41, s.v. 'Nicäa I', with bibl.

Nicaea, Second Council of (787). The Seventh General Council was convoked by the Empress Irene at the instigation of the Patr. *Tarasius of Constantinople in order to end the *Iconoclastic Controversy. Pope *Hadrian I accepted the invitation of the Empress and sent two legates on condition that the Iconoclastic Synod of Hieria (754) was condemned. The patriarchs of *Alexandria, *Antioch, and *Jerusalem, then subject to the Caliphs, were unable to come and were each represented by two monks. The Council met on 17 Aug. 786 in the church of the Holy Apostles at *Constantinople, but was immediately broken up by iconoclastic soldiers and did not reassemble till 24 Sept. 787, this time in the church of St Sophia at Nicaea, where Tarasius presided. The Council declared its adherence to the doctrine on the veneration (προσκύνησις) of images expounded by the Pope in his letter to the Empress, adding that such veneration is a matter of respect and honour (ἀσπασμὸν καὶ τιμητικὴν προσκύνησιν), whereas absolute adoration (ἀληθινὴ λατρεία) is reserved to God alone, the honour given to the image passing on to its prototype. The decree promulgating the doctrine was signed by all present and by the Empress and her son Constantine, and the iconoclasts were anathematized.

The 22 canons drawn up by the Council deal with disciplinary matters; they declare null the election by a secular authority of bishops, priests, and deacons, condemn simony, forbid priests to leave their diocese without permission of the bishop, enjoin simplicity of life on all clerics, and forbid the stay of women in bishops' houses and monasteries of men as well as the erection of double monasteries.

Hardouin, 4 (1714), cols. 3–820; Mansi, 12 (1766), cols. 951–1154, and 13 (1767), cols. 1–820. Doctrinal definition and canons, with Eng. tr. and introd., in Tanner, *Decrees* (1990), pp. 131–56. Eng. tr., with comm., of the material on the 6th session dealing with images, by D. J. Sahas, *Icon and Logos: Sources in Eighth-Century Iconoclasm* (Toronto Medieval Texts and Translations, 4 [1986]). G. Dumeige, SJ, *Nicée II* (Histoire des Conciles Œcuméniques, 4; 1978), esp. pp. 99–201. E. Boespflug and N. Lossky (eds.), *Nicée II, 787–1987: … Actes du Colloque international Nicée II tenue au Collège de France, Paris, les 2, 3, 4 octobre 1986* (1987). P. Henry, 'Initial Eastern Assessments of the Seventh Oecumenical Council', *JTS* NS 25 (1974), pp. 75–92. Hefele and Leclercq, 3 (pt. 2; 1910), pp. 741–98. V. Laurent, AA, in *NCE* 10 (1967), pp. 434 f., s.v.; H. G. Thümmel in *TRE* 24 (1995), pp. 441–4, s.v. 'Nicäa II', both with further bibl. See also bibl. to ICONOCLASTIC CONTROVERSY.

Nicene Creed. Two Creeds at present so named must be distinguished:

(1) The Nicene Creed properly so called, issued in 325 by the Council of *Nicaea (q.v.) and known to scholars as N. This Creed was drawn up at the Council to defend the Orthodox Faith against the *Arians and includes the word '*Homoousios'. Compared with later conciliar Creeds it is relatively short, concluding with the words 'And in the Holy Spirit'. Appended to it were four anathemas against Arianism, which came to be regarded as an integral part of the text. It was probably based on the Baptismal Creed of *Jerusalem (H. *Lietzmann), not, as older scholars held, through a misunderstanding of a statement of *Eusebius of Caesarea, on that of Caesarea in Palestine (F. J. A. *Hort).

(2) In common parlance, the 'Nicene Creed' more often means the considerably longer formula which bears this title in the *Thirty-Nine Articles and is in regular use in the *Eucharistic worship of the Church, both in East and West. It is also known as the 'Niceno-Constantinopolitan Creed', and is referred to as C. It differs from N. in that, *inter alia*, (1) the second section on the Person of Christ is longer; (2) the phrase in N. 'from the substance of the Father' (ἐκ τῆς οὐσίας τοῦ πατρός) as an explanation of 'Homoousios' is wanting; (3) the third section contains an extended statement on the status and work of the Holy Spirit; and (4) after this follow assertions of belief in the Church, Baptism, the Resurrection of the Dead, and Eternal Life. Also it has no anathemas. Since the time of the Council of *Chalcedon of 451 it has been regarded as the Creed of the Council of *Constantinople of 381; but the earliest authorities connecting it with that Council date from *c.*449–50. Furthermore the Creed is found in St *Epiphanius' *Ancoratus*, which was written in 374; its occurrence here would be decisive evidence that it was not drawn up by the Council if its position in this treatise were

established, but there are grounds for believing that N., not C., originally stood in the text here. The most likely theory is that the Creed, though not drawn up by the Council of Constantinople, was endorsed by it in the course of its (unsuccessful) deliberations with the *Pneumatomachi (so A. M. Ritter, followed by J. N. D. Kelly). Its origin is unclear, but it is probable that it was the Baptismal Creed of Constantinople.

Its use in Eucharistic worship after the Gospel apparently began at Antioch under *Peter the Fuller (476–88) and gradually spread through East and West, though it was not adopted at Rome until 1014. In the early Middle Ages the *Filioque (q.v.) was added to it in the W. In the Roman Rite its use at Mass is confined to Sundays and greater feasts. In the E. it is regularly used as a Baptismal Creed. It has been widely accepted in modern times as a proposed basis of Christian unity, e.g. in the *Lambeth Quadrilateral (1888).

Both Creeds, N. and C., are discussed in J. N. D. Kelly, *Early Christian Creeds* (1950; 3rd edn., 1972), pp. 205–62 and 296–367; J. Burnaby, *The Belief of Christendom: A Commentary on the Nicene Creed* (1959); G. L. Dossetti, *Il simbolo di Nicea e di Costantinopoli: Edizione critica* (1967). W.-D. Hauschild in *TRE* 24 (1995), pp. 444–56, s.v. 'Nicäno-Konstantinopolitanisches Glaubensbekenntis'.
On (1), see also F. *Loofs, 'Das Nicänum', in *Festgabe von Fachgenossen und Freunden Karl Müller zum siebzigsten Geburtstag dargebracht* (1922), pp. 68–82; H. Lietzmann, 'Symbolstudien XIII', *ZNTW* 24 (1925), pp. 193–202, with 'Kritischer Epilog' by A. *Harnack, p. 203. I. Ortiz de Urbina, SJ, *Il simbolo niceno* (Consejo Superior de Investigaciones Cientificas, 1947). Hefele and Leclercq, 1 (pt. 1; 1907), pp. 442–8.
On (2), F. J. A. Hort, *Two Dissertations* (1876), pp. 73–150 ('On the Constantinopolitan Creed and other Eastern Creeds of the Fourth Century'); A. M. Ritter, *Das Konzil von Konstantinopel und sein Symbol* (Forschungen zur Kirchen- und Dogmengeschichte, 15; 1965), pp. 133–208; R. Staats, *Das Glaubensbekenntnis von Nizää-Konstantinopel* (Darmstadt, 1996). T. F. Torrance (ed.), *The Incarnation: Ecumenical Studies in the Niceno-Constantinopolitan Creed A.D. 381* (1981).
On the use of the Nicene Creed [C.] at the Eucharist, cf. B. *Capelle, OSB, 'L'Introduction du symbole à la messe', in *Mélanges Joseph de Ghellinck*, 2 (Museum Lessianum, Sect. hist. 14; 1951), pp. 1003–27, repr. in his *Travaux Liturgiques*, 3 (1967), pp. 60–81; and Jungmann (1958 edn.), 1, pp. 591–606; Eng. tr., 1, pp. 461–74.

Nicephorus, St (758–828), Patr. of *Constantinople. His father had occupied high office under the Emp. Constantine Copronymus and suffered in the *Iconoclastic Controversy for his defence of images. Nicephorus inherited his father's beliefs and represented the Emperor at the Second Council of *Nicaea (787). Later he withdrew from court life and founded a monastery on the Propontis whither he retired, but without himself becoming a monk. The Emp. Constantine VI and his mother, Irene, recalled him to Constantinople, where the Emp. Nicephorus made him Patriarch on the death of *Tarasius (806), though he was not yet in holy orders. In recompense for the Imperial favour the Emperor demanded his reinstatement of the priest Joseph, who had been deposed in 797 for blessing the adulterous marriage of Constantine VI. After some hesitation Nicephorus gave way, and at a synod held in 806 or 807 rehabilitated Joseph. After the death of the Emperor and of his son Stauracius (811), he renewed the

original sentence against Joseph. In 813 he crowned the Emp. Leo V ('the Armenian'), who resumed the Iconoclastic policy of his predecessors in the 8th cent. Nicephorus resisted, but was abandoned by the majority of his bishops, who supported the Emperor. In 815 he was exiled and retired to his former monastery again, where he spent the remainder of his life. Despite the opposition of the *Studites, who could not forgive his weakness in the Adulterine Controversy, his relics were translated to Constantinople in 847, and he received the title of a confessor of the faith. Feast day in the Greek Church, 2 June; in the Latin Church, 13 Mar.

Among his writings on the Image controversy are 'Apologeticus Minor' (814/15), 'Apologeticus Major' and 'Libri Tres Antirrhetici' which belong together (816–20). Of particular value is his Ἱστορία σύντομος or 'Breviarium Nicephori', a Byzantine history from 602 to 770, highly praised by *Photius for its accuracy and literary excellence. He also compiled a Chronicle, Χρονογραφία σύντομος, reaching from Adam to the year of his own death.

V. Grumel, AA (ed.), *Les Régestes des actes du patriarcat de Constantinople*, 1, fascs. 2–3 (2nd edn. by J. Darrouzès, 1989), pp. 35–53 (nos. 374–407a). Collection of his works in J. P. Migne, *PG* 100. 169–1068; further works in J. B. *Pitra (ed.), *Spicilegium Solesmense*, 1 (1852), pp. 302–504, and 4 (1858), pp. 233–380; *Opuscula Historica* [i.e. his Ἱστορία σύντομος and Χρονογραφία σύντομος], ed. C. de Boor (Teub., 1880). 'Breviarium' ed., with Eng. tr. and comm., by C. Mango (Corpus Fontium Historiae Byzantinae, Dumbarton Oaks Texts, 10; Washington, DC, 1990). Life by his pupil, the Deacon Ignatius, pr. in *AASS*, Mar. 2 (1648), pp. 704–27, Gk. text, with Lat. tr., pp. 294–321, and introd., p. 293; repr. in J. P. Migne, op. cit., cols. 41–160; also in C. de Boor, op. cit., pp. 139–217. P. J. Alexander, *The Patriarch Nicephorus of Constantinople: Ecclesiastical Policy and Image Worship in the Byzantine Empire* (Oxford, 1958). A. J. Visser, *Nikephoros und der Bilderstreit: Eine Untersuchung über die Stellung des Konstantinopeler Patriarchen Nikephoros innerhalb der ikonoklastischen Wirren* (The Hague, 1952). V. Grumel, 'Les "Douze Chapitres contre les Iconomaques" de saint Nicéphore de Constantinople', *Revue des Études Byzantines*, 17 (1959), pp. 127–35, with refs. to texts. P. O'Connell, SJ, *The Ecclesiology of St Nicephorus I* (Orientalia Christiana Analecta, 194; 1972). Krumbacher, pp. 71–3. R. Janin, AA, in *DTC* 11 (pt. 1; 1931), cols. 452–5, s.v. 'Nicéphore de Constantinople'; D. Stiernon, AA, in *Dict. Sp.* 11 (1982), cols. 182–6, s.v. 'Nicéphore (1)'.

Nicephorus Callistus (c.1256–c.1335), 'Xanthopoulos', Byzantine historian. Little is known of his life. Apparently a native of *Constantinople and a priest of *Sancta Sophia, whose library he utilized for his works, at the end of his life he seems to have become a monk. He belonged to the party of the Emp. Andronicus II (reigned 1282–1328), whose ecclesiastical policy, in contrast to that of his father Michael Palaeologus, supported Greek Orthodoxy against the Latinizers. His principal work, a 'Church History', narrates in 18 books the events from the birth of Christ to the death of the Emp. Phocas (610). At the end of the introduction there is a summary of five more books, probably never executed, which were to continue the narrative to the death of *Leo VI, the Philosopher (912). The History has been held to rest on an anonymous 10th-cent. work, though this theory is now thought to be improbable; it is, however, a compilation of earlier sources, among them the Ecclesiastical Histories of *Eusebius, *Socrates, *Sozomen, *Theodoret, and *Evagrius. It is none the less an important source for certain of the early controversies and heresies as well as for the history of Byzantine legends, but its value throughout depends on that of the earlier material used. In 1555 it was translated into Latin and played an important part in the controversial literature of the time, furnishing material for the defence of images and relics. Among his other writings, several of them in iambics, are liturgical, exegetical, and hagiographical works.

His Church History was pub. in Lat. tr. by J. Lange, Basle, 1555; Gk. text with Lat. tr. by J. Lange, ed. F. *Ducaeus, 2 vols., Paris, 1630, repr. J. P. Migne, *PG* 145. 559–1332, 146, and 147. 9–448; other works repr. ibid. 147. 449–634, with note from J. A. *Fabricius, ibid. 145. 549–58. A. Papadopoulos-Kerameus, 'Νικηφόρος Κάλλιστος Ξανθόπουλος', *BZ* 11 (1902), pp. 38–49, incl. a few texts. *Progymnasmata*, ed. J. Gettner, ibid., 33 (1933), pp. 1–12 and 255–70 (text, pp. 7–12), with useful introd. G. Gentz, *Die Kirchengeschichte des Nicephorus Callistus Xanthopulus und ihre Quellen*, ed. F. Winkelmann (TU 98; 1966). Krumbacher, pp. 291–3. M. Jugie, AA, in *DTC* 11 (pt. 1; 1931), cols. 446–52, s.v.; D. Stiernon, AA, in *Dict. Sp.* 11 (1982), cols. 203–8, s.v. 'Nicéphore (5) Kallistos Xanthopoulos'.

Niceta, St (d. *c*.414), ecclesiastical writer. He was Bp. of Remesiana (Bela Palanka, SE of Niš) from *c*.370 onwards. His literary importance arises esp. from his contacts through his geographical situation with both E. and W. His writings, mainly ascribed to other authors in later times, have been largely restored to him by A. E. Burn (d. 1927). His *Explanatio Symboli* is a primary witness for the history of the *Apostles' Creed, containing, e.g., the oldest attestation for the words 'communio sanctorum'; *De Diversis Appellationibus* is a tract on the titles of Christ; *De Ratione Fidei* and *De Spiritu Sancto* are respectively directed against *Arianism and the *Pneumatomachi; *De Vigiliis* and *De Psalmodiae Bono* are of liturgical interest. The ascription to him of the '*Te Deum' (q.v.) has not been widely accepted. Feast day, 22 June.

Crit. edn. of principal texts in A. E. Burn, *Niceta of Remesiana: His Life and Works* (1905); of 'De Vigiliis' and 'De Psalmodiae Bono' by C. H. *Turner, *JTS* 22 (1920–1), pp. 305–20, and 24 (1922–3), pp. 225–50. *Instructio ad Competentes: Frühchristliche Katechesen aus Dacien*, ed. K. Gamber (Textus Patristici et Liturgici, 1; Regensburg, 1964); *Weitere Sermonen ad Competentes* ed. id. (ibid. 2, 5; 1965–6). Eng. tr. of his works by G. G. Walsh, SJ (Fathers of the Church, 7; 1949, pp. 3–76). W. A. Patin, *Niceta, Bischof von Remesiana, als Schriftsteller und Theologe* (1909). J. Zeiller, *Les Origines chrétiennes dans les provinces danubiennes de l'empire romain* (Bibliothèque des Écoles françaises d'Athènes et de Rome, 112; 1918), pp. 549–58. Z. Senjak, *Niceta von Remesiana* (Diss., Freiburg i.B., 1975). C. H. Turner, 'Niceta and Ambrosiaster, I', *JTS* 7 (1905–6), pp. 203–19. M. G. Mara in Quasten (cont.), *Patrology*, 4 (1986), pp. 190–4. *CPL* (3rd edn., 1995), pp. 228–30 (nos. 646–52). A. Solignac, SJ, in *Dict. Sp.* 11 (1982), cols. 214–9, s.v. See also bibl. to TE DEUM.

Nicetas Acominatos (1155/7–1217), Byzantine scholar. A native of Chonia (i.e. Colossae; hence also 'Nicetas Choniates') and of wealthy family, he studied at *Constantinople, where he rose rapidly in the Imperial service. He was governor of the province of Philippopolis when the Emp. *Frederick Barbarossa passed through on the Third *Crusade (1189). His dealings with the Crusaders at this time led him to become closely connected with the E. Court in the next years. On the Fall of Constantinople (1204) he fled to Nicaea, where he spent the rest of his life. His writings include a 'Treasury of Ortho-

doxy' (Θησαυρὸς Ὀρθοδοξίας), a comprehensive work in 27 books (written between 1204 and 1210) against contemporary heresies, intended to supplement *Euthymius Zigabenus' 'Panoplia Dogmatike'; and a History (Χρονικὴ Διήγησις) of the period 1118–1206 in 21 books covering the reigns of the last Comneni. The former is the main source for the Councils held between 1156 and 1166; the latter is esp. valuable for its account of the capture of Constantinople by the Latins in 1204. His elder brother, **Michael Acominatos** (*c*.1140–*c*.1215), who became Abp. of *Athens in 1175, was also a famous scholar, his writings including sermons, verses and a collection of letters.

Collection of Nicetas' writings in J. P. Migne, *PG* 139. 287–1444, and 140. 9–284; and of those of Michael, ibid. 299–382. Crit. edns. by J. A. [Lat. equivalent of J. L.] van Dieten of his History (Corpus Fontium Historiae Byzantinae, 11; 2 vols., Berlin, 1975); and of his Discourses and Letters (ibid. 3; 1972). *O City of Byzantium*, Eng. tr. of the History by H. J. Magoulias (Byzantine Texts in Translation; Detroit, 1984). J. L. van Dieten, *Zur Überlieferung und Veröffentlichung der Panoplia Dogmatike des Niketas Choniates* (Zetemata Byzantina, 3; Amsterdam, 1970); id., *Niketas Choniates: Erläuterungen zu den Reden und Briefen nebst einer Biographie* (Supplementa Byzantina, 2; 1971). On the History, H. Hunger, *Die hochsprachliche profane Literatur der Byzantiner*, 1 (Handbuch der Altertumswissenschaft, Abt. 12, Bd. 5; Munich, 1978), pp. 430–41, with bibl. V. Katsaros, 'A Contribution to the Exact Dating of the Death of the Byzantine Historian Nicetas Choniates', *Jahrbuch der Österreichischen Byzantinistik*, 32.3 (1982), pp. 83–91. Krumbacher, pp. 281–6 and 91–3 (on Nicetas); pp. 468–70 (on Michael). L. Petit, AA, in *DTC* 1 (1903), cols. 189 f., s.v. 'Acominatos, Nicétas'.

Nicetas Stethatos (*c*.1005–*c*.1085), Byzantine monk. As a young man he entered the monastery of *Studios in Constantinople, where he came to know St *Simeon the New Theologian (d. 1022). In about 1035 a vision renewed his devotion to Simeon, whose works he began to collect and whose Life he wrote. He may have earned the surname Stethatos ('courageous') for his opposition to the relationship between the Emp. Constantine IX Monomachus and his mistress Sclerina. In 1053–4 he was involved in the controversy between Cardinal *Humbert and the Patr. *Michael Cerularius which led to the mutual excommunications of 1054. He wrote three treatises against the Latins, though acc. to a Latin source he was personally reconciled to Humbert. Nothing more is known of Nicetas apart from his writings, though it appears from the inscription to his *Profession of Faith* that he became *hegoumen of Studios. If so, he must have died between 1076 and 1092. Many of his writings have a polemical edge: apart from the treatises against the Latins, there are treatises against the Armenians (largely unpublished) and against the Jews; several of his *opuscula*, with their interest in the soul and its fate after death, seem to envisage the controversy surrounding Michael *Psellus; and the *Life of Simeon* is conceived as a defence of the institution of spiritual fatherhood, even in laymen, against the hierarchy. His own spiritual teaching contained in his *Three Centuries of Practical, Physical and Gnostic Chapters* is indebted to Simeon: like him he ascribes importance to the gift of tears.

Crit. edn. of the Life of Simeon, with Fr. tr., by I. Hausherr, SJ (Orientalia Christiana, vol. 12, no. 45; 1928). Treatises against the Latins in A. Michel, *Humbert und Kerullarios*, 2 (Quellen und

Forschungen, 23; 1930), pp. 320–42, 371–409. *Opuscules et Lettres* (incl. treatise against the Jews), ed., with Fr. tr. and introd., by J. Darrouzès, AA (SC 81; 1961). Text of *Centuries* in **Philocalia* (Venice, 1782), pp. 785–851, repr. in J. P. Migne, *PG* 120. 852–1009; Eng. tr., with introd., in Eng. tr. of the *Philocalia* by G. E. H. Palmer and others, 4 (1995), pp. 76–174. W. Völker, *Praxis und Theoria bei Symeon dem Neuen Theologen* (Wiesbaden, 1974), pp. 456–89 ('Nicetas Stethatos als mystischer Schriftsteller und sein Verhältnis zu Symeon dem Neuen Theologen'). M. T. Disdier in *DTC* 11 (pt. 1; 1931), cols. 479–86, s.v.; A. Solignac, SJ, in *Dict. Sp.* 11 (1982), pp. 224–30.

Nicholas, St, Bp. of Myra in Lycia. Though one of the most popular saints in both the Greek and Latin Churches, scarcely anything is historically certain about him. Acc. to tradition, he was imprisoned during the *Diocletianic persecution and afterwards released and was present at the Council of *Nicaea. The latter supposition is most improbable, as he is not in any of the early lists of bishops present at the Council. The earliest evidence for his cult at Myra is found in the contemporary Life of St Nicholas of Sion, who lived in the reign of the Emp. *Justinian (d. 565). Episodes from the Life of St Nicholas of Sion were later transferred to the Life of his namesake. Justinian himself built a church in *Constantinople dedicated to St Priscus and St Nicholas. His cult became popular in the W. after the inhabitants of Bari claimed to have got possession of his remains on 9 May 1087.

St Nicholas is regarded as the patron saint of sailors, and churches under his dedication are often built so that they can be seen off the coast as landmarks. He is also the patron saint of children, bringing them gifts on 6 Dec. (whence 'Santa Claus', an American corruption of 'Sante Klaas', the Dutch for 'Saint Nicholas'). And he is also the patron saint of Russia. His symbol is sometimes three bags of gold, the dowry he is supposed to have given to three girls to save them from degradation, sometimes three children standing in a tub at his side, a representation which has been variously explained. Feast day, 6 Dec.

G. Anrich, *Hagios Nikolaos: Der heilige Nikolaos in der griechischen Kirche. Texte und Untersuchungen* (2 vols., 1913–17). 12th-cent. Life by Norman poet Wace, ed. M. S. Crawford (thesis, Philadelphia, 1923). The Life of St Nicholas of Sion is ed., with Eng. tr., by I. and N. P. Ševčenko (The Archbishop Iakovos Library of Ecclesiastical and Historical Sources, 10; Brookline, Mass. [1984]). K. Meisen, *Nikolauskult und Nikolausbrauch im Abendlande* (Forschungen zur Volkskunde, 9–12; 1931; repr. as Quellen und Abhandlungen zur Mittelrheinischen Kirchengeschichte, 41; 1981, with additional bibl, pp. xiv–xvi). C. W. Jones, *The Saint Nicholas Liturgy and its Literary Relationships (Ninth to Twelfth Centuries)* (University of California English Studies, 27; 1963). Less specialized treatment by id., *Saint Nicholas of Myra, Bari, and Manhattan* (Chicago and London, 1978). N. P. Ševčenko, *The Life of Saint Nicholas in Byzantine Art* (Centro Studi Bizantini, Monografie, 1; Turin, 1983). N. Del Re and M. C. Celletti in *Bibliotheca Sanctorum*, 9 (Rome, 1967), cols. 923–48, s.v. 'Nicola, vescovo di Mira'.

Nicholas I, St (d. 867), Pope from 858. He was one of the most forceful of the early medieval Popes. Of a noble Roman family, he entered the service of the Curia under Pope Sergius II (844–7) and was made subdeacon; having become deacon under *Leo IV (847–55), he gained a decisive influence in the affairs of the Holy See under Benedict III (855–8), and on his death he was elected to

succeed him (858). One of the chief events of his rule was the long-drawn-out struggle with the E. Church over the deposition of Ignatius by the Emp. Michael III and the appointment of *Photius to the see of Constantinople. The latter, though at first seeking Rome's approval of his accession, became more and more embittered when Nicholas, refusing to sanction the illegality of the proceedings, anathematized him and restored Ignatius at the Synod at Rome in 863. The situation was further aggravated by the readiness of the Pope to respond, in 866, to the advances of the newly converted Bulgars, whom he tried to win over to the see of Rome and for whom he wrote his famous 'Responsa Nicolai ad consulta Bulgarorum', a kind of summary of Christian faith and discipline. To this supposed encroachment on his rights, Photius replied in 867 by declaring the Pope deposed, but was himself deprived of his office in the same year. It was, however, in response to an invitation from Nicholas that Sts *Cyril and Methodius visited Rome, where they were welcomed by Nicholas's successor, Hadrian II. In the W. Nicholas had to contend with similar difficulties in upholding the Papal authority. He vigorously defended the sanctity of marriage in the divorce case of Lothair II of Lorraine, deposing the two Abps. of Cologne and Trier who had connived at his bigamous marriage, and effecting a temporary reconciliation between the king and his consort. He successfully asserted the supremacy of the see of Rome against Abp. John of Ravenna, who, counting on Imperial support, had violated the rights of property of the Holy See and tyrannized over his subjects. Similarly *Hincmar of Reims was obliged to acknowledge the right of the Papacy to intervene in disputes. There are grounds for believing that the '*False Decretals' were already received in Rome during his pontificate, though probably not before 864, and that Nicholas himself was influenced by them in his attitude to Hincmar. Apart from his decisive effect on the prestige of the Papacy in political matters, Nicholas was a man of high personal integrity, fully conscious of the responsibilities which he owed to his position. Feast day, 13 Nov.

Letters pr. in J. P. Migne, *PL* 119. 753–1212. Crit. edn. by E. Perels in *MGH*, Epistolae, 6 (1925), pp. 257–690. *LP* (Duchesne), 2, pp. 151–72; Eng. tr., with introd., by R. Davis, *The Lives of the Ninth-Century Popes* (Translated Texts for Historians, 20; Liverpool, 1995), pp. 189–247. Life by J. Roy ('Les Saints', 1899; Eng. tr., 1901). F. Dvornik, *The Photian Schism* (1948), *passim*. A. Greinacher, *Die Anschauungen des Papstes Nikolaus I über das Verhältnis von Staat und Kirche* (Abhandlungen zur mittleren und neueren Geschichte, 10; 1909); E. Perels, *Papst Nikolaus I und Anastasius Bibliothecarius* (1920); J. Haller, *Nikolaus I und Pseudo-Isidor* (1936). F. A. Norwood, 'The Political Pretensions of Pope Nicholas I', *Church History*, 15 (1946), pp. 271–85. L. Heiser, *Die Responsa ad Consulta Bulgarorum des Papstes Nikolaus I. (858–867)* (Trierer Theologische Studien, 36; 1979). L. *Duchesne, *Les Premiers Temps de l'état pontifical* (2nd edn., 1904), pp. 235–45 (Eng. tr., 1908, pp. 155–62). Mann, 3 (1906), pp. 1–148. É. Amann in *DTC* 11 (pt. 1; 1931), cols. 506–26.

Nicholas V (1397–1455), Pope from 1447. Thomas Parentucelli, the son of a doctor of Sarzana, studied theology at *Bologna, where Bp., later Cardinal, Nicholas Albergati became his protector. Appointed Bp. of Bologna after Albergati's death (1444), he was Papal Legate at the Diet of Frankfurt, where he worked so successfully for the recognition of *Eugenius IV by the German princes that he was created Cardinal in 1446. In 1447 he was elected Pope. By his conciliatory spirit and great diplomatic skill he obtained the recognition of the Papal rights in the matter of benefices and bishoprics by the Concordat of Vienna in 1448 and, in the following year, put an end to the schism by receiving the submission of the antipope, Felix V, and that of the Council of *Basle before its dissolution. In thanksgiving for the restoration of unity he decreed a *Jubilee in 1450, and immediately after sent out his legates to reform abuses—Cardinal *Nicholas of Cusa and St *Giovanni Capistrano to N. and S. Germany respectively, and Cardinal d'Estouteville to France. In 1452 he crowned Frederick III of Habsburg German Emperor (the last Imperial Coronation in Rome). At the same time he restored order in the States of the Church and suppressed the revolt of Stefano Porcaro (1453), who attempted to overthrow the papal régime and declare Rome a republic. After the fall of *Constantinople (1453) he tried in vain to incite the European princes to a crusade against the Turks, and anxiety for the state of Christendom probably hastened his death. An enthusiastic lover of arts and science, Nicholas restored many ruined churches, planned to rebuild the *Vatican and *St Peter's, and founded the Vatican Library. He was the first, and probably the best, of the Renaissance Popes, of blameless personal life, free from *nepotism and anxious to reconcile religion with the new learning.

The principal authorities are the Lives by Vespasiano da Bisticci (d. 1498) in *Vite di uomini illustri del secolo XV* (ed. P. d'Ancona and E. Aeschlimann, Milan, 1951, pp. 21–47; Eng. tr. by W. G. and E. Waters, *The Vespaniano Memoirs*, 1926, pp. 31–58) and B. *Platina, *Vitae Pontificum* (Venice, 1479; no pagination). J. Manetti (d. 1459), 'Vita Nicolai V' in L. A. *Muratori (ed.), *Rerum Italicarum Scriptores*, 3 (pt. 2; Milan, 1734), cols. 907–60. Modern Life by G. Sforza (Lucca, 1884; Ger. tr., 1887). K. Pleyer, *Die Politik Nikolaus V* (1927). Pastor, 2 (1891), pp. 3–314, with bibl. Fliche and Martin, 15 (1951), pp. 15–38. G. Mollat in *DTC* 11 (pt. 1; 1931), cols. 541–8, s.v. 'Nicolas V'; G. Schwaiger in *L.Th.K.* (2nd edn.), 7 (1962), cols. 979 f., s.v. 'Nikolaus V'; J. Gill, SJ, in *NCE* 10 (1967), pp. 443–5, s.v., all with further bibl.

Nicholas of Basle (d. *c*.1395), medieval heretic. He was a *Beghard who preached and propagated his opinions esp. in the district round Basle. Acc. to Martin of Mainz, a disciple of his who was burnt at Cologne in 1393, Nicholas claimed to understand the Gospels better than the Apostles, assumed ecclesiastical functions, and demanded obedience from his followers, whom he could release from their obedience to the Church into a state of primal innocence; the perfect did not need to pray to go to heaven, and the Lord's Prayer should read 'Lead us into temptation'. It is, however, not clear that his views were as radical as Martin's confession implies. For many years he evaded the *Inquisition but was eventually seized and burned at the stake in Vienna. At one time he was identified (esp. by K. Schmidt) with the mysterious 'Friend of God from the Oberland' who plays an important part in the writings of the Strasbourg ascetic, Rulman Merswin, but H. S. *Denifle has convincingly argued that this figure is a literary creation of Merswin himself.

K. Schmidt (ed.), *Nicolaus von Basel: Leben und ausgewählte Schriften* (1866); id., *Nicolaus von Basel: Bericht von der Bekehrung Taulers* (1875). H. S. Denifle, OP, 'Der Gottesfreund im Oberland und Nikolaus von Basel. Eine kritische Studie', *Historisch-politische Blätter für das katholische Deutschland*, 75 (1875), pp. 17–34, 93–122, 245–66, and 340–54. R. Haupt, 'Beiträge zur Geschichte der Sekte vom freien Geiste und des Beghardentums', *ZKG* 7 (1885), pp. 503–76, esp. pp. 508–11. R. E. Lerner, *The Heresy of the Free Spirit in the Later Middle Ages* (1972), pp. 151–4.

Nicholas Breakspear. See HADRIAN IV.

Nicholas Cabasilas, St. See CABASILAS, ST NICHOLAS.

Nicholas of Cusa (1401–64), German cardinal and philosopher. He was a native of the village of Cues, on the Moselle. After studying at Heidelberg (1416) and Padua (1417–23), where he became a doctor of canon law, he entered Cologne University in 1425. There he was in close touch with Heymericus de Campo, the Dean of the Faculty of Arts and chief proponent of the doctrines of *Albert the Great. Through Heymericus he became acquainted with the writings of Ramon *Llull. From 1426 he searched for manuscripts of the classics on behalf of Card. Giordano Orsini; his discoveries made him known to the Italian humanists. Having been ordained priest in 1426, he was made Dean of St Florin's at Coblenz in 1431. In 1433 he took part in the Council of *Basle as an advocate in a dispute concerning the possession of the archiepiscopal see of Trier. He also worked for the reconciliation of the *Hussites to the Church and in 1433 procured the acceptance of the *Calixtines by the Council. In the same year he wrote his famous work, *De Concordantia Catholica*, in which he outlined a comprehensive programme for the reform of Church and Empire. Though he originally favoured the *Conciliar Movement, the revolutionary proceedings of the Council and its failure to bring about a union with the Greeks estranged him from the majority of its supporters. From 1437 he devoted himself entirely to the cause of the Pope, being sent in that year by *Eugenius IV to *Constantinople in the interests of reunion. In the following years he worked for the Papal cause at the Diets of Mainz (1441), Frankfurt (1442), and Nuremberg (1444). When in 1448 a reconciliation was effected between the Pope and the Empire which culminated in the Concordat of Vienna, *Nicholas V rewarded him by creating him cardinal. In 1450 he was appointed Bp. of Brixen (in the Tyrol) and Papal legate for the German-speaking countries. As such, besides publishing the Jubilee Indulgences, he was authorized to hold provincial synods and to visit monasteries and remove abuses. In 1452 he took possession of his diocese, where he worked with great zeal for the reform of the morals of clergy and people. When a conflict with Duke Sigismund forced him to leave his diocese, he went to Rome, where *Pius II appointed him in 1459 his Vicar General with the task of reforming and governing Rome and the patrimony of St Peter. After an apparent reconciliation he returned to Brixen, but Sigismund soon declared war on him and besieged him in the fortress of Bruneck, which he was forced to surrender. He once more went to Rome, where he spent the rest of his life as Camerarius of the Sacred College.

In intellectual outlook Nicholas was a forerunner of the Renaissance. His principal work, *De Docta Ignorantia* (completed 1440), was a defence of his two celebrated principles, 'docta ignorantia' and 'coincidentia oppositorum'.

'Docta ignorantia' was the highest stage of intellectual apprehension accessible to the human intellect, since Truth, which is absolute, one, and infinitely simple, is unknowable to man. Knowledge by contrast is relative, multiple, complex, and at best only approximate. The road to Truth therefore leads beyond reason and the principle of contradiction; it is only by intuition that we can discover God, the 'coincidentia oppositorum', wherein all contradictions meet. This description is meant to indicate that God is at once infinitely great and infinitely small, the maximum and the minimum, the centre and the circumference of the world, everywhere and nowhere, neither One nor Three, but Triune.

Nicholas's general cast of thought has many affinities with *Neoplatonism; and among those who esp. influenced him were St *Augustine, *Proclus, and *Dionysius the Pseudo-Areopagite, and of medieval thinkers, esp. St *Bonaventure and Meister *Eckhart. He held the common Platonist view that mathematics is the supreme science. He also had considerable critical gifts as a historian, rejecting e.g. the authenticity of the *False Decretals and of the *Donation of Constantine.

His other writings incl. De Coniecturis (the first version, 1440), designed, by showing the underlying unity of all knowledge, to lead nearer to a truth which transcends the bounds of human reason; De Quaerendo Deum (1445); the Apologia Doctae Ignorantiae (1449), a reply to the charge of pantheism by Johann Wenck, professor of theology at Heidelberg; Idiota (1450), four dialogues on the human mind and on the ways that lead to wisdom; De Visione Dei (1453); De li Non Aliud (1462), using Proclus' term ('Not-Other') as the most suitable to characterize the nature of God; De Venatione Sapientiae (1462), and De Apice Theoriae (1464), a final summary.

Editio princeps of his Collected Works, 2 vols., Strasbourg, 1488; until the present century the standard edn. was that issued in 3 vols., Paris, 1514, repr., with some additions, one vol., Basle, 1565. Crit. edn. under the auspices of the Heidelberg Academy, by E. Hoffmann, R. Klibansky, and others (22 vols., 1932 ff.). Further collection of 'Cusanus-Texte' in the Sb. (Heid.), ed. E. Hoffmann and R. Klibansky (1928–9, Heft 3), G. Kallen (1935–6, Heft 3), J. Koch (1935–6, Heft 2), L. Bauer (1940–1, Heft 4), J. Koch (1941–2, Heft 1), id. (1942–3, Heft 2), id. (1944–8, Heft 3), G. von Bredow (1955, Heft 2), E. Maschke (1956, Heft 1), H. Hürten (1960, Heft 2); and by E. Meuthen in Abh. (Heid.), 1977, Heft 3. Eng. trs. by J. Hopkins, with facing Lat. texts, of 'De li Non Aliud' (God as Not-Other, Minneapolis [1979]; 2nd edn., 1983) and of 'De Visione Dei' (Nicholas of Cusa's Dialectical Mysticism, ibid. [1985]), and by J. Biechler and H. L. Bond of 'De Pace Fidei' (Nicholas of Cusa on Interreligious Harmony, Texts and Studies in Religion, 55; Lewiston, NY, etc. [1990]). Eng. trs. alone of 'De Visione Dei' by E. G. Salter (London, 1928), of 'De Docta Ignorantia' by J. Hopkins (Minneapolis [1981]), of 'De concordantia Catholica' by P. E. Sigmund (Cambridge Texts in the History of Political Thought, 1991), and of selected writings by J. P. Dolan, Unity and Reform (Notre Dame, Ind. [1962]). Substantial general studies by E. Vansteenberghe (Bibliothèque du XVᵉ siècle, 24; Paris, 1920, repr. Geneva, 1974) and M. Patronnier de Gandillac, La Philosophie de Nicolas de Cues (Paris thesis [1941], with further bibl.; rev. Ger. edn., Düsseldorf, 1953). Less technical introds. by H. Bett ('Great Medieval Churchmen', London, 1932), P. Mennicken (Leipzig, 1932; 2nd edn., Trier, 1950), and J. Hopkins (Minneapolis, 1978; 2nd edn., 1980). J. Uebinger, Die Gotteslehre des Nikolaus Cusanus (1888). E. Vansteenberghe, Autour de la docte ignorance (BGPM, 14, Hefte 2–4; 1915). J. Lenz, Die Docta Ignorantia oder die mystische Gotteser-

kenntnis des Nikolaus Cusanus in ihren philosophischen Grundlagen (Abhandlungen zur Philosophie und Psychologie der Religion, 3; 1923); 'Cusanus-Studien' in Sb. (Heid.), by E. Hoffmann and R. Klibansky (1929–30, Heft 3), M. Honecker (1937–8, Heft 2), E. Bohnenstädt (1938–9, Heft 1), R. Creutz (1938–9, Heft 3), M. Honecker (1939–40, Heft 2), O. Menzel (1940–1, Heft 6), E. Hoffmann (1941–2, Heft 4), G. Kallen (1963, Heft 2), and by H. G. Senger (1972, Heft 5). R. Klibansky, The Continuity of the Platonic Tradition (1939), esp. pp. 28–32; id., 'Plato's Parmenides in the Middle Ages and the Renaissance', Mediaeval and Renaissance Studies, 1 (1943), pp. 281–330, esp. pp. 304–10; these two works arc repr., with suppl. material, under the title of the former, Munich, 1981. R. Haubst, Das Bild des Einen und Dreieinen Gottes in der Welt nach Nikolaus von Kues (Trierer theologische Studien, 4; 1952); id., Studien zu Nikolaus von Kues und Johannes Wenck aus Handschriften der Vatikanischen Bibliothek (BGPM 38, Heft 1 [1955]), esp. pp. 1–32; id., Die Christologie des Nikolaus von Kues (Freiburg, 1956); id., Streitzüge in die cusanische Theologie (Münster, 1991). E. Meuthen, Die letzten Jahre des Nikolaus von Kues: Biographische Untersuchungen nach neuen Quellen (Wissenschaftliche Abhandlungen der Arbeitsgemeinschaft für Forschung des Landes Nordrhein-Westfalen, 3; 1958); id., Nikolaus von Kues 1401–1464: Skizze einer Biographie (Buchreihe der Cusanus-Gesellschaft, 1964). E. Colomer, SJ, Nikolaus von Kues und Raimund Lull: Aus Handschriften der Kueser Bibliothek (Quellen und Studien zur Geschichte der Philosophie, 2; 1961). M. Watanabe, The Political Ideas of Nicholas of Cusa, with special reference to his De concordantia catholica (Travaux d'humanisme et renaissance, 58; Geneva, 1963). P. E. Sigmund, Nicholas of Cusa and Medieval Political Thought (Cambridge, Mass., 1963). K. Jacobi, Die Methode der Cusanischen Philosophie (Munich, 1969). R. Klibansky, 'Die Wirkungsgeschichte des Dialogs "De pace fide" ', in R. Haubst (ed.), Der Friede unter den Religionen nach Nikolaus von Kues: Akten des Symposions in Trier vom 13. bis 15. Oktober 1982 (Mitteilungen und Forschungsbeiträge der Cusanus-Gesellschaft, 16; Mainz, 1984), pp. 113–25; see also other vols. in this series. C. Riccati, 'Processio' et 'Explicatio': La doctrine de la création chez Jean Scot et Nicolas de Cues (Istituto Italiano per gli Studi Filosofici, Serie Studi, 6; Naples, 1983). E. F. Jacob, 'Nicolas of Cusa', in F. J. C. Hearnshaw (ed.), The Social and Political Ideas of Some Great Thinkers of the Renaissance and Reformation (1925), pp. 32–59; id., 'Cusanus the Theologian', Bulletin of the John Rylands Library, 21 (1937), pp. 406–24. R. Klibansky, 'Nicholas of Cues', in id. (ed.), Philosophy in the Mid-Century, 4 (Florence, 1959), pp. 88–94. E. Vansteenberghe in DTC 11 (pt. 1; 1931), cols. 601–12, s.v. 'Nicolas (24) de Cusa'; R. Klibansky in Enciclopedia italiana, 24 (1934), pp. 761–3, s.v. 'Niccolà da Cusa'; J. Koch in NCE 10 (1967), pp. 449–52, s.v.

Nicholas of Flüe, St (1417–87), 'Brother Klaus', Swiss ascetic. The son of wealthy peasants, he distinguished himself as a soldier and later as a cantonal councillor and judge (1459). In 1467 he obtained the consent of his wife to leave her and their ten children, to lead the life of a hermit in the Ranft valley, near Sachseln, in Switzerland. Here, where he is said to have lived for 19 years with no food save the Eucharist, his reputation for sanctity attracted many visitors from all parts of Europe seeking his advice. His great influence showed itself in 1481, when a dispute between the delegates of the Swiss confederates at Stans that threatened to result in civil war was settled by his counsel. He was beatified in 1669 and canonized in 1947. The accounts of his visions have attracted much interest in modern times. Feast day, 21 Mar.; in Switzerland (of which he is the Patron Saint), 25 Sept.

Fundamental study by R. Durrer, Bruder Klaus: Die ältesten Quellen über den seligen Nikolaus von Flüe, sein Leben und seinen Einfluss (2 vols., Sarnen, 1917–21), orig. planned to mark the 5th centenary of his birth, with text of Life by Henry of Gundelfingen (d. 1490) and other primary material. Other studies incl. those of G. Méautis (Neuchâtel, 1940), C. Journet (Collection des Cahiers du Rhône, 5; 1942; 3rd edn., 1966) with texts, R. Centlivres (Geneva, 1947), A. Deuster (Bonn, 1950), G. R. Lamb (London, 1955), H. Stirnimann (Dokimion. Freiburger Zeitschrift für Philosophie und Theologie, Neue Schriftenreihe, 7; 1981), with texts, and (at a popular level) C. Yates, *Man of Two Worlds* (York [1989]). T. Boos in *NCE* 10 (1967), pp. 452 f., s.v., with refs.

Nicholas Hereford (d. *c.*1420), *Lollard writer. Neither the date of his birth nor that of his death is known, but he was ordained priest in 1370. While a Fellow of Queen's College, Oxford, he became an ardent supporter of J. *Wycliffe, and by 1382 he was preaching Wycliffite doctrines. For this he was condemned and excommunicated. An expedition to Rome to appeal against the sentence was unsuccessful, and imprisonment followed. Escaping, he returned to England and resumed his Lollard activities. After a further term of imprisonment, he seems to have recanted *c.*1391. He became a canon of *Hereford in 1394 and treasurer in 1397. In 1417 he resigned his preferment and was professed a *Carthusian monk. His name has been associated with the early Wycliffite translation of the Bible into English.

The principal chronicle sources include the *Fasciculi Zizaniorum* (ed. W. W. Shirley, RS, 1858, pp. 289–329), Henry Knighton, *Chronicon* (ed. J. R. Lumby, 2, ibid., 1895, pp. 170–4), and Thomas Walsingham, *Historia Anglicana* (ed. H. T. Riley, 2, ibid., 1864, pp. 159–60). M. Deanesly, *The Lollard Bible and Other Medieval Biblical Versions* (Cambridge, 1920), esp. pp. 232–6, 253–67, and 286–8; K. B. McFarlane, *John Wycliffe and the Beginnings of English Nonconformity* (1952), pp. 107–12 and 126–9; S. L. Fristedt, *The Wycliffite Bible*, 1 (Stockholm Studies in English, 4; 1953), pp. 115–18; H. Hargreaves in *The Cambridge History of the Bible*, 2, ed. G. W. H. Lampe (Cambridge, 1969), pp. 400–15; A. Hudson, 'A Neglected Wycliffite Text', *JEH* 29 (1978), pp. 257–79, esp. pp. 272–5. C. L. Kingsford in *DNB* 40 (1894), pp. 418–20; *BRUO* 2 (1958), pp. 913–15, s.v. 'Hereford, Nicholas'.

Nicholas of Lyre (*c.*1270–1349), biblical exegete. A native of Lyre (in the diocese of Evreux), Nicholas had become a *Franciscan and moved to *Paris by *c.*1300. There he shared in the administration of the Franciscan house of study, becoming minister of the provinces of France (1319) and Burgundy (1324). Although he was a regent master in the University of Paris (1309) and was instrumental in founding the Collège de Bourgogne, Nicholas was essentially a research scholar, who did not seek a following ('Nolo habere *caudam*'). He concentrated on the literal meaning of the Bible, writing analyses, or *Postillae*, on each verse or section of a chapter. These *Postillae* are based on the rich tradition of patristic and medieval Latin commentary, strengthened by Nicholas's unusually exact knowledge of the Hebrew text and of rabbinic exegesis. The *Postillae Litterales* (1322–33) were complemented by the *Postillae Morales* (1339). Long regarded as the definitive modern commentary, they ran to over 100 editions between 1471 and 1600. They were also adapted as sermons on the Sunday Gospels. Nicholas participated in the debates about apostolic poverty and the *Beatific Vision, but he was essentially an expositor rather than a theologian.

Convenient edn. of the *Postillae*, 4 vols., Nürnberg, 1487; also often pr. together with the *Glossa Ordinaria, e.g. Venice, 1495, Lyons, 1545. P. Glorieux, *Répertoire des maîtres en théologie de Paris au XIIIᵉ siècle*, 2 (1934), pp. 215–31, with details of MSS and edns. H. Labrosse, 'Sources de la biographie de Nicolas de Lyra', *Études Franciscaines*, 16 (1906), pp. 383–404; id., 'Biographie de Nicolas de Lyre', ibid. 17 (1907), pp. 489–505 and 593–608; id., 'Œuvres de Nicolas de Lyre. Sources bibliographiques', ibid. 19 (1908), pp. 41–52; id., 'Œuvres de Nicolas de Lyre. Catalogue des œuvres', ibid., pp. 153–75 and 368–79, and 35 (1923), pp. 171–87 and 400–32. H. Hailperin, *Rashi and the Christian Scholars* (Pittsburgh, 1963), pp. 137–246, with notes, pp. 282–357. H. Rüthing, 'Kritische Bemerkungen zu einer mittelalterlichen Biographie des Nikolaus von Lyra', *Archivum Franciscanum Historicum*, 60 (1967), pp. 42–54; E. A. Gosselin, 'A Listing of the Printed Editions of Nicolaus de Lyra', *Traditio*, 26 (1970), pp. 399–426. F. Stegmüller, *Repertorium Biblicum Medii Aevi*, 4 (Madrid, 1954), pp. 51–94 (nos. 5827–994). C. Schmitt in *Dict. Sp.* 11 (1982), cols. 291 f., s.v. 'Nicolas de Lyre', with bibl.

Nicholas of Oresme. See ORESME, NICOLAS.

Nicholas of Tolentino, St (*c.*1245–1306), *Augustinian friar. Born at Sant'Angelo in the March of Ancona, he made his profession as an Augustinian hermit *c.*1253. His life was pious but uneventful, devoted to preaching and pastoral work among the poor and destitute and, it is recorded, graced by frequent miracles. His last 30 years were spent at Tolentino, where fragments of his body, which are reputed to bleed shortly before great calamities (e.g. in 1452 before the Fall of *Constantinople, in 1510 before the Reformation), are interred. He was canonized by *Eugenius IV in 1446. Feast day, 10 Sept.

The principal authority is the contemporary Life by Pietro di Monte Rubiano, his fellow Augustinian hermit, written in 1326; repr. in *AASS*, Sept. 3 (1750), pp. 644–64, with other material, pp. 664–743, and introd., pp. 636–44. Popular modern Lives by A. Tonna-Barthet (Paris, 1896), E. A. Foran, OSA (London, 1920), and N. Concetti (Tolentino, 1932). D. Gentili in *Bibliotheca Sanctorum*, 9 (1967), cols. 953–68, s.v. 'Nicola da Tolentino'.

Nicholas, Henry (1502–*c.*1580), or **Hendrik Niclaes**, founder of the sect of '*Familists' (q.v.). His birthplace is unknown. He came of a devout RC family, and at an early age he began to have visions. By profession he was a merchant dealing mainly in cloth and he amassed a considerable fortune. About 1531 he went to Amsterdam, where he associated with the *Anabaptists. Here, *c.*1539, he believed he had Divine communications commanding him to found a new sect, 'The Family of Love' or 'Familia Caritatis'. In 1540 he went to Emden, where he lived for 20 years and wrote a large number of books, the best known being his *Spiegel der Gerechtigheid* (*Glass of Righteousness*), printed by C. *Plantin at Antwerp in the late 1550s. In 1560 the authorities at Emden took steps against his sectarian activities and he fled first to Kampen and then to Rotterdam; he spent the last ten years of his life in Cologne. Deeply influenced by the spirituality of the *Theologia Germanica* and S. *Franck, he was convinced that he would heal the schisms in Christendom and lead mankind to salvation in the 'last age of time'. His books, condemned by Protestants and Catholics alike, were placed on the *Index.

Cronica, Ordo Sacerdotis, Acta HN: Three Texts on the Family of Love [part of the first being the work of Nicholas, the rest of this and the other items being prob. based on texts by him if not his work], ed. A. [A. H.] Hamilton (Leiden, 1988). F. Nippold, 'Heinrich Niclaes und das Haus der Liebe', *Zeitschrift für die historische Theologie*, 32 (1862), pp. 323–402 and 473–563. I. Simon, 'Hendrik Niclaes. Biographische und bibliographische Notizen. Emden (1540–60)', *Niederdeutsches Wort*, 13 (1973), pp. 63–77. A. [A. H.] Hamilton, *The Family of Love* (Cambridge, 1981). See also bibl. TO FAMILISTS.

Niclaes, Hendrik. See NICHOLAS, HENRY.

Nicodemism. The term Nicodemite, derived from *Nicodemus who visited Jesus by night, generally denotes a secret or timid adherent. J. *Calvin, in his *Excuse à Messieurs les Nicodémites* (1544) and elsewhere, applied it to those converts to Protestantism in Catholic France who concealed their true sympathies and outwardly continued RC practices. In modern times Nicodemism has been taken to indicate all forms of religious simulation, and esp. that of certain Humanists, *Anabaptists, and sectaries such as the *Familists.

C. Ginzburg, *Il Nicodemismo: Simulazione e dissimulazione religiosa nell'Europa del '500* (Turin, 1970). C. M. N. Eire, 'Calvin and Nicodemism: A Reappraisal', *Sixteenth Century Journal*, 10 (1979), pp. 45–69, with bibl. refs.

Nicodemus. The Jew, learned in the Law and a member of the council of the *Sanhedrin, who came to Jesus by night and evoked the discourse narrated in Jn. 3: 1–15 on Christian rebirth. He is afterwards shown as a partial sympathizer with Christ (Jn. 7: 50) and as helping *Joseph of Arimathaea to give Him burial (Jn. 19: 39).

J. Graf, 'Nikodemus (Joh. 3. 1–21)', *Th.Q.* 132 (1952), pp. 62–86; S. Mendrer, 'Nikodemus', *Journal of Biblical Literature*, 77 (1958), pp. 293–323 [in Ger., with synopsis in Eng.]. See also comm. on John.

Nicodemus, Gospel of. See PILATE, ACTS OF.

Nicodemus of the Holy Mountain, St (c.1749–1809), Greek monk and spiritual writer. Born on Naxos, in 1775 he was professed on Mount *Athos, where he remained for almost all the rest of his life, devoting his energies to writing. His most important publications were the *Philocalia* (q.v.), on which he collaborated with St Macarius Notaras of Corinth; and a commentary on E. Canon Law entitled the *Pidalion* or 'Rudder' (Leipzig, 1800), which he produced with the help of Hieromonk Agapios of Dimitsana. He urged the necessity for frequent communion at a time when this was not usual in the Greek Church. Deeply rooted in the tradition of the Greek Fathers, he was at the same time ready to borrow from the W., and he published Greek editions of RC writers, including the *Spiritual Exercises* of St *Ignatius Loyola. He was proclaimed a saint in the Eastern *Orthodox Church in 1955; feast day (in the E.), 14 July.

Eng. trs. by D. Cummings of 'The Rudder' (Chicago, 1957) and by E. Kadloubovsky and G. E. H. Palmer of 'Unseen Warfare' (1952), with important introd. by H. A. Hodges, pp. 13–67; the 'Unseen Warfare' ('Αόρατος Πόλεμος; Venice, 1796) was the title given by Nicodemus to his tr. into Gk. of two Ital. works, the *Combattimento spirituale* of L. Scupoli (1589) and the *Sentiero*

del Paradiso attributed to Scupoli (1600); the Eng. tr. is based on the Russian revision of Theophan the Recluse (1815–94). C. Papoulidis, *Nicodème l'Hagiorite (1749–1809)* (Athens, 1967). C. [P.] Cavernos, *St Nicodemus the Hagiorite* (Modern Orthodox Saints, 3; Belmont, Mass., 1974). G. Podskalsky, *Griechische Theologie in der Zeit der Türkenherrschaft (1453–1821)* (Munich, 1988), pp. 377–82. D. Stiernon, AA, in *Dict. Sp.* 11 (1982), cols. 234–50, s.v. 'Nicodème l'Hagiorite', with bibl.

Nicolaitans. Sectaries mentioned in the NT only at Rev. 2: 6 and 2: 14 f., where they appear as the advocates of a return to pagan worship. It is possible that the word 'Nicolaitans' is allegorical, Nicolas being simply the Greek equivalent of Balaam (cf. Rev. 2: 14), arrived at by a fanciful etymology, and that the persons referred to in Rev. had no real existence as a sect. A *Gnostic sect of this name, however, is alluded to by *Irenaeus, *Clement of Alexandria, and Pseudo-*Tertullian; and Irenaeus affirms that they were founded by the Nicolas of Antioch mentioned in Acts 6: 5, though this is perhaps no more than a conjecture. Indeed, it is not impossible that all references to them in Christian tradition are merely deductions from Rev. At any rate, there is no trace of the sect after about the end of the 2nd cent. In the Middle Ages the term was sometimes applied to married priests by the upholders of clerical celibacy.

A. von *Harnack, 'The Sect of the Nicolaitans and Nicolaus, the Deacon in Jerusalem', *Journal of Religion*, 3 (1923), pp. 413–22, esp. pp. 413–17, with refs. to earlier lit.; A. Pourkier, *L'hérésiologie chez Épiphane de Salamine* (Christianisme Antique, 4 [1992]), pp. 291–341, with bibl. p. 506. See also comm. on Rev. 2. E. Amann in *DTC* 11 (pt. 1; 1931), cols. 499–506. D. F. Watson in *Anchor Bible Dictionary*, 4 (1992), pp. 1106 f.

Nicole, Pierre (1625–95), French theologian, controversialist, and moralist. A native of *Chartres, he studied in *Paris, but did not proceed beyond the degree of baccalaureus which he took in 1649. He went to teach in the 'Petites Écoles' at *Port-Royal, where he formed a close friendship with A. *Arnauld, in collaboration with whom many of his works were written, including the important *Logique ou l'Art de penser*, commonly known as the *Logique de Port-Royal* (1662; ed. P. Clair and F. Girbal, 1925); this was influenced by the ideas of St *Augustine, B. *Pascal, and R. *Descartes. A large number of his writings deal with the *Jansenist controversy, but they are more moderate in tone than most Jansenist works. In 1658 he published a Latin translation of Pascal's *Lettres provinciales*, with additional articles on *Probabilism and the Love of God. He opposed the signature of the formularies (see JANSENISM) in *L'Hérésie imaginaire* (1664). Against *Calvinist attack he defended Catholic teaching on the *Real Presence and *transubstantiation in two versions of *La Perpétuité de la foi de l'Église catholique touchant la Eucharistie* (that of 1664, known as *La petite Perpétuité*, and that in 3 vols., 1669–74, known as *La Grande Perpétuité*), both written in conjunction with Arnauld. In 1665 he published an *Apologie pour les religieuses de Port-Royal*. He continued his controversial writings with *Préjugés légitimes contre les calvinistes* (1671). The first version of his principal work, the *Essais de morale*, appeared from 1671 to 1678 (4 vols.). He had a pessimistic view of man's fallen nature, and generally advocated both outward and inward withdrawal from the world, though he accepted that those with positions in the world could live a serious Christian life. His spiritual works include the *Traité de l'oraison* (1679; slightly revised as the *Traité de la prière*, 1695), which is biased against mysticism. His last work, the *Réfutation des principales erreurs des quiétistes* (1695), undertaken at the instigation of J.-B. *Bossuet, was directed esp. against M. de *Molinos and Mme *Guyon. His *Traité de la grâce générale* (2 vols., posthumously pub., 1715), shows a turning away from Jansenist positions; he accepted the orthodox tenets of the universal saving will of God and the sufficiency of grace for all men. He also involved himself in the controversy over the theatre which he condemned on grounds of morality in the treatise 'De la Comédie' included in the combined edition of *Les imaginaires* and *Les Visionnaires* (1667; modern edn. of his *Traité de la Comédie* by G. Couton, 1961).

Life by C. P. Goujet in the *Continuation des essais de morale* [de P. Nicole], 14 (2 pts., 'Luxembourg', 1732). C. A. Saint-Beuve, *Port-Royal* (1840–59), bk. 5, chs. 7–8 (ed. M. Leroy, vol. 2, Bibliothèque de la Pléiade, 99 [1954], pp. 858–946). Modern studies by E. Thouverez (Paris, 1926), Le Breton Grandmaison (ibid., 1942), and E. D. James [in Eng.] (International Archives of the History of Ideas, Series Minor, 1; The Hague, 1972). D. Graham, ' "Courage, j'ai vaincu le monde": Retraite et Engagement dans les *Essais de Morale* de Pierre Nicole', in J.-J. Demorest and L. Leibacher-Ouvrard (eds.), *Pascal, Corneille, Desert, Retraite, Engagement: Actes de Tuscan* (Biblio, 17; 1984), pp. 239–58. Bremond, 4 (1920), pp. 418–588. J. Carreyre in *DTC* 11 (1931), cols. 634–46, s.v.; E. Chédozeau in *Dict. Sp.* 11 (1982), cols. 309–18, s.v. See also bibl. to JANSENISM and PORT-ROYAL.

Nicoll, William Robertson (1851–1923), editor. Ordained in 1874 to the Free Church of Scotland, he became minister at Kelso in 1877. In 1885, however, he was compelled through ill-health to resign his charge and go south, and for the rest of his life devoted his energies to successful editorial work, mainly with the assistance of the publishing house of Hodder & Stoughton. From 1885 till his death he edited the *Expositor*, a semi-popular monthly journal in which he enlisted the help of many leading scholars. From 1886 Nicoll also issued the *British Weekly*, a penny weekly in which current policy and affairs were discussed from a Christian (mainly Nonconformist) standpoint, Nicoll himself regularly contributing to its columns under the pseudonym of 'Claudius Clear'.

Life and Letters ed. by T. H. Darlow (1925), with bibl. J. *Denney, *Letters . . . to W. Robertson Nicoll, 1893–1917* [1920]. J. T. Stoddart in *DNB, 1922–1930*, pp. 636 f.

Nicolò de' Tudeschi. See PANORMITANUS.

Nicomedes, St, early Christian martyr. His name occurs in both the *Gelasian Sacramentary and the *Roman Martyrology under the date 15 Sept., but it is wanting from the oldest MSS of the *Hieronymian Martyrology. From refs. in three 7th-cent. itineraries, it would appear that he was buried in a catacomb on the Via Nomentana near the wall of *Rome. There is mention in the 5th cent. of a titular church at Rome dedicated to him. Nothing certain, however, is known of his date or the circumstances of his death. In the BCP calendar (here 'Nicomede') his feast is observed on 1 June, the date of the dedication of a church at Rome rebuilt in the 7th century.

AASS, Sept. 5 (1755), pp. 5–12. E. Josi in *EC* 8 (1952), cols. 1863 f., s.v. 'Nicomede, Cimitero di', with bibl. refs. to archaeological papers by G. B. *de Rossi, O. *Marucchi, and others.

Niebuhr, Helmut Richard (1894–1962), American theologian. The younger brother of Reinhold *Niebuhr, he was professor in the Yale Divinity School from 1938 until his death. His thinking was formed under the very diverse influences of K. *Barth and E. *Troeltsch. From Barth he learned to be dissatisfied with the superficialities of liberal theology and stressed the importance of historical revelation. From Troeltsch he learned that every revelation is conditioned by the historical and cultural media in which it finds expression and he analysed the correlations between religious belief and social group in the United States. His writings include *The Social Sources of Denominationalism* (1929), *The Kingdom of God in America* (1937), *The Meaning of Revelation* (1941), *Christ and Culture* (1951), *Radical Monotheism and Western Civilization* (1960).

P. Ramsey (ed.), *Faith and Ethics: The Theology of H. Richard Niebuhr* (New York, 1957), incl. list of his works, pp. 291–9. C. D. Grant, *The Center of Value: Value Theory in the Theology of H. Richard Niebuhr* (Fort Worth, Tex. [1984]); R. F. Thiemann (ed.), *The Legacy of H. Richard Niebuhr* (Harvard Theological Monographs, 36; Minneapolis [1991]).

Niebuhr, Reinhold (1892–1971), American theologian and writer on ethical and social problems. A native of Wright City, Mo., he was educated at Elmhurst College (1910) and Yale University (1914), and ordained in 1915. He was pastor at the Bethel Evangelical church of Detroit from 1915 to 1928, when he was appointed professor of Applied Christianity at the *Union Theological Seminary in New York City, remaining there until his retirement in 1960.

Influenced by K. *Barth and even more by E. *Brunner, Niebuhr sought to return to the categories of the biblical revelation and was critical both of liberal theology and of metaphysics. He reinstated the doctrine of original sin and aimed at expounding a 'vital prophetic Christianity'. He differed sharply from Barth in believing that Christianity has a direct prophetical vocation in relation to culture and for a generation his 'Christian realism' exercised an influential critique on American social and political institutions.

Niebuhr's principal work is *The Nature and Destiny of Man* (*Gifford Lectures for 1939; 2 vols., 1941–3). He also expounded his views in innumerable addresses and essays. His other writings (often collections of papers) include *Does Civilization need Religion?* (1928), *Moral Man and Immoral Society* (1932), *An Interpretation of Christian Ethics* (1936), *Beyond Tragedy* (1938), *Christian Realism and Political Problems* (1954), *The Self and the Dramas of History* (1955), and *Man's Nature and his Communities* (1965).

C. W. Kegley and R. W. Bretall (eds.), *Reinhold Niebuhr: His Religious, Social, and Political Thought* (New York, 1956), incl. his 'Intellectual Autobiography', pp. 3–23. R. W. Fox, *Reinhold Niebuhr: A Biography* (New York, 1986; London, 1988). G. Harland, *The Thought of Reinhold Niebuhr* (ibid., 1960). D. Lange, *Christlicher Glaube und soziale Probleme: Eine Darstellung der Theologie Reinhold Niebuhrs* (Gütersloh [1964]), with bibl. N. A. Scott, Jun. (ed.), *The Legacy of Reinhold Niebuhr* (Chicago and London,

1975); R. Harries (ed.), *Reinhold Niebuhr and the Issues of Our Time* [1986]. K. Durkin, *Reinhold Niebuhr* (Outstanding Christian Thinkers Series, 1989). G. Hammar, *Christian Realism in Contemporary American Theology: A Study of Reinhold Niebuhr, W. M. Horton, and H. P. Van Dusen* (Uppsala, 1940), pp. 167–253. Bibl. by D. B. Robertson (Boston, 1979).

Nieheim, Dietrich of. See DIETRICH OF NIEHEIM.

Niemöller, Martin (1892–1984), German *Lutheran pastor. The son of a Westphalian pastor, he served as a submarine commander during the war of 1914–18. In 1924 he was ordained minister of the Protestant church in Westphalia and in 1931 appointed pastor at Berlin-Dahlem. He at first welcomed National Socialism, but later opposed it on account of its pagan tendencies and supported the '*Confessing Church'. His anti-Nazi religious activities led to his arrest in 1937 and confinement in a concentration camp. Several offers of release were made to him on certain conditions, but he preferred imprisonment to giving up his convictions. A strong character as well as a picturesque personality, he became the symbolical figure of the Protestant opposition to National Socialism. After the Second World War, Niemöller took a leading part in the 'Declaration of Guilt' at Stuttgart. From 1945 to 1956 he was head of the Foreign Relations Department of the *Evangelical Church in Germany and from 1947 to 1964 *Kirchenpräsident* of the territorial Church of Hesse and Nassau. From the time of its foundation in 1948 he was a member of the Executive Council of the *World Council of Churches and from 1961 to 1968 one of the Presidents of the Council. He opposed the creation of the Federal Republic of Germany in 1949 and in the following decade excited criticism by his increasingly pacifist position.

J. Schmidt, *Martin Niemöller im Kirchenkampf* (Hamburg, 1971). J. Bentley, *Martin Niemöller* (Oxford, 1984). K. Robbins, 'Martin Niemöller, the German Church Struggle, and English Opinion', *JEH* 31 (1970), pp. 149–70.

Nietzsche, Friedrich Wilhelm (1844–1900), German philosopher. The son of a Lutheran pastor in the Prussian province of Saxony, he was educated at the public school of Schulpforta, near Naumburg. In 1864 he went to Bonn University and in the following year to Leipzig, where he studied philology. In 1869 he accepted a professorship at Basle which he resigned in 1879, owing to ill-health. He had already published several books, among them *Menschliches, Allzumenschliches* (1878; Eng. tr., *Human, All too Human*, 1911), and now devoted himself entirely to literary activities, writing in quick succession *Die fröhliche Wissenschaft* (1882); *Also sprach Zarathustra* (1883–91; Eng. tr., *Thus Spake Zarathustra*, 1896); *Jenseits von Gut und Böse* (1886; Eng. tr., *Beyond Good and Evil*, 1907); *Die Genealogie der Moral* (1887); *Der Antichrist* (1888); and *Der Wille zur Macht* (posthumous, 1901). In the beginning of 1889 Nietzsche lost his reason, and, nursed first by his mother, then by his widowed sister, he died on 25 Aug. 1900 after being an invalid for nearly 12 years.

Nietzsche was a prophet rather than a systematic thinker. His chief work, *Zarathustra*, written in fine poetic language, consists entirely of aphorisms. In his years at Leipzig he came under the influence of the works of A.

*Schopenhauer, whose atheism and depreciation of reason in favour of the will attracted him. On this atheistic and irrational foundation he constructed a philosophy of life by which he claimed to inaugurate a 'transvaluation of all values'. Acc. to this doctrine life is the will to power; but power, not as exercised collectively by the masses, but the power of the great individual whom he calls *Übermensch* ('superman'). The superman, though an ideal to be realized only in the future, has been adumbrated by personalities like Cesare Borgia and Napoleon; he may be described as a magnified man, disciplined and perfected in both mental and physical strength, serene and pitiless, ruthlessly pursuing his path of success and victory and without moral scruples. In order to make the superman possible the present values which are derived from Christianity must be abolished, since they are the portion of the weak and disinherited 'herd' who, by proclaiming humility, kindness, pity, and the like as virtues, have succeeded in putting themselves into power to the detriment of the strong.

There are several German edns. of Nietzsche's works, of which the best is the 'Musarionausgabe' (23 vols., Munich, 1920–9). Eng. tr. of 'Complete Works' ed. O. Levy in 18 vols., 1909–13. There are several collections of his Letters, from which a selection was pub. in Eng. tr. by O. Levy (New York, etc., 1921). Official Life by E. Förster-Nietzsche, his sister (2 vols. bound in 3, Leipzig, 1895–1904; shorter versions as *Der junge Nietzsche* (1912; Eng. tr., 1912) and *Der einsame Nietzsche* (1914; Eng. tr. [1915])). Best Life in Eng. by R. J. Hollingdale (London, 1965); see also that of R. Hayman (ibid., 1980). There are innumerable studies of his philosophy; they include those by F. [C.] Copleston, SJ (Bellarmine Series, 7, London, 1942), W. A. Kaufmann (Princeton, NJ, 1950), F. A. Lea (London, 1957), M. *Heidegger (2 vols., Pfullingen, 1961), J. P. Stern (London, 1978, more substantial, and Cambridge, 1979), and T. Meyer (Tübingen, 1991). P. Valadier, *Nietzsche et la critique du Christianisme* (1974). H. W. Reichert and K. Schlechta, *International Nietzsche Bibliography* (University of North Carolina Studies in Comparative Literature, 29; 1960; rev. edn., ibid. 45; 1968). H. Ellis in *HERE* 9 (1917), pp. 366–70; K. Schlechta in *RGG* (3rd edn.), 4 (1960), cols. 1475–9; W. [A.] Kaufmann in P. Edwards (ed.), *Encyclopedia of Philosophy*, 5 (1967), pp. 504–14.

Nigeria, Christianity in. Nigeria is the most populous country in Africa, with an estimated population of 80 millions, incorporating peoples diverse in language, ethnic group, culture, and religion. It has been a single entity since 1914, when two British protectorates, built up during the later 19th cent., were amalgamated.

The first Christian contact with peoples now included within Nigeria came with *Portuguese missions in coastal parts of Benin and Warri in the 1470s. The *Capuchins took responsibility for these missions in the 16th cent., but they faded with the Portuguese presence. The modern Christian phase dates from the 1840s. Between 1843 and 1845 the *Church Missionary Society and Wesleyan *Methodists entered Yoruba country at the request of Yoruba former slaves who had become Christians in *Sierra Leone and had returned home. In 1846 a mission from Jamaica, led by missionaries of the Scottish Secession (later *United Presbyterian) Church was established in Calabar. It was welcomed as a means to useful education for commerce. Calabar accepted some major social changes at its behest, but long hindered the mission's expansion to trade rivals. The most significant Christian development in Yorubaland was in the Egba state, Abeokuta. There CMS missionaries (incl. S. A. *Crowther, himself an Egba) and the American *Baptists (who arrived in 1850) assisted Egba self-defence and economic betterment. When European missionaries were expelled from Yorubaland in 1867, the Yoruba Church continued with its African missionaries. From 1857 Crowther headed a mission to the Niger and Benue riverine peoples, establishing Churches in the Niger Delta states and among the Niger Igbo. RC work resumed in 1868 when the Society of *African Missions arrived in the British colony of Lagos in 1868, and the *Holy Ghost Fathers in 1885. The former worked mostly W. of the Niger, the latter in Igbo areas E. of it. Between 1905 and 1920 the Igbo, who had strongly resisted British expansion, responded rapidly to Christianity, RCs and Protestants competing to open schools.

Christianity spread widely among S. Nigerian peoples. Disillusionment with missionary acts produced various 'African' Churches in the 1890s, but a major schism was averted. Since the First World War (1914–18) indigenous Churches stressing prophecy and healing (the Yoruba name for them is aladura, 'praying people') have developed a model of the Church distinct from that introduced by missions, but alert to the life-situation of Nigerian worshippers. The period since the Nigerian Civil War (1967–70) has produced many new *charismatic Churches and evangelistic movements. Various Nigerian Churches have missions abroad, incl. Britain and the USA.

By the late 19th cent. Muslim rulers dominated the area N. of the confluence of the rivers Niger and Benue, and most Hausa were Muslim. British imperial rule retained earlier structures, and sometimes excluded or restricted missions in N. Nigeria. Nevertheless CMS and RC missions extended their work to the N. and two major Protestant agencies came into being specifically for this area. The Sudan Interior Mission was non-denominational and international but N. American in ethos; the Evangelical Churches of W. Africa derive from it. The (originally British) Sudan United Mission had a federal structure which enabled Churches from *Denmark, *South Africa, and the *United States of America to work with it; the Fellowship of Churches of Christ in Nigeria comprises eight Churches deriving from it. Christians form a significant minority in N. Nigeria, esp. on the central plateau.

With Christians and Muslims holding dominance in different regions, religion frequently raises political and constitutional issues for the Nigerian secular state. These surfaced during the Civil War and in recurrent crises over shariah law.

J. F. A. Ajayi, Christian Missions in Nigeria 1841–1891: The Making of a new Élite (1965); E. A. Ayandele, The Missionary Impact on Modern Nigeria 1841–1914: A Political and Social Analysis (1966). G. Johnston, Of God and Maxim Guns: Presbyterianism in Nigeria, 1846–1966 (Waterloo, Ont., 1988). G. O. M. Tasie, Christian Missionary Enterprise in the Niger Delta 1864–1918 (Studies on Religion in Africa, 3; Leiden, 1978). F. K. Ekechi, Missionary Enterprise and Rivalry in Igboland 1857–1914 (1972). J. B. Webster, The African Churches among the Yoruba 1888–1922 (Oxford, 1964); H. W. Turner, History of an African Independent Church . . . (Aladura) (2 vols., ibid., 1967). E. P. T. Crampton, Christianity in Northern Nigeria (Zaria, 1975; 3rd edn., London, 1979). J. B. Grimley and G. E. Robinson, Church Growth in Central and Southern Nigeria (Grand Rapids [1966]). J. H. Boer, Missionary Messengers of Liberation in a Colonial Context: A Case

Study of the Sudan United Mission (Amsterdam Studies in Theology, 1; 1979). E. Isichei (ed.), Varieties of Christian Experience in Nigeria (1982). R. I. J. Hackett (ed.), New Religious Movements in Nigeria (African Studies, 5; Lewiston, NY [1987]). A. Hastings, The Church in Africa 1450–1950 (Oxford History of the Christian Church, 1994), passim (see index).

Night Office. Another name for *Mattins, the liturgical *Office formerly prescribed for the night.

Nightingale, Florence (1820–1910), reformer of hospital nursing. She was born at Florence, whence her Christian name. At an early age she began to interest herself in nursing, and from c.1844 undertook regular hospital visiting. On a journey to Egypt in 1849–50 she studied the nursing system of the Sisters of Charity of St *Vincent de Paul at *Alexandria, and soon afterwards visited T. Fliedner's deaconesses at *Kaiserswerth, where she was trained for several months in 1851. In 1853 she was made head of a hospital for invalid gentlewomen in Harley Street. In 1854 she offered to go out to the Crimea to organize the nursing of the sick and wounded English soldiers. She established her headquarters at Scutari, where the barrack hospital was in a state of indescribable neglect; but her indefatigable devotion soon improved conditions and considerably reduced the death-rate. She returned to England in 1856. In recognition of her services the Nightingale School and Home for Nurses was founded at St Thomas's Hospital in 1860, though owing to her weakened health she could take no more than an advisory part in its work. Her experience was also placed at the disposal of the governments concerned in the American Civil War of 1861–4 and the Franco-German War of 1870–1. She took an active interest in the establishment of several nursing societies and in the sanitary reforms carried out in the Indian army as well as among Indians. Her chief work, Notes on Nursing (1859), went through many editions.

Selections of her letters incl. those written in the Crimean War, 1854–6, 'I have done my duty', ed. S. M. Goldie (Manchester [1987]), and Ever Yours, ed. M. Vicinus and B. Nergaard (London, 1989). Lives by E. T. Cook (2 vols., ibid., 1913), M. [L.] Goldsmith (ibid., 1937), and C. [B.] Woodham-Smith (ibid., 1950). F. B. Smith, Florence Nightingale: Reputation and Power [1982]. W. J. Bishop and S. [M.] Goldie, A Bio-Bibliography of Florence Nightingale (1962). S. Paget in DNB, 1901–1911, 3, pp. 15–19.

Nihilianism. The Christological doctrine that Christ, in His human nature, was 'nothing', His essential Being being contained in His Godhead alone. It was defended by a number of 12th-cent. theologians (among them Peter of Poitiers, d. 1205) who claimed to deduce it from the teaching of *Peter Lombard. It was condemned by Pope *Alexander III in 1170 and 1177.

E. Portalié in DTC 1 (1903), cols. 413–18, s.v. 'Adoptianisme [au XIIᵉ siècle]'; G. H. Joyce, SJ, in HERE 9 (1917), pp. 370–2, s.v.

Nikon (1605–81), Patr. of Moscow. After a monastic education he married and became a secular priest, but separated from his wife, who entered a convent, and himself became a monk of the Solovetski monastery on the White Sea. A quarrel with the monks led him to transfer his membership to the Kozheozerski community, of which he became *hegumen (abbot) in 1643. On a journey to Moscow in 1646 the Tsar Alexis appointed him archimandrite of the Novospasskiy monastery at Moscow, and, three years later, Metropolitan of Novgorod; and when, in 1652, the Patr. of Moscow died, he was elected in his place by order of the Tsar. As Patriarch, Nikon at once began important reforms. One of his principal concerns was to carry through a much-needed revision of the Russian liturgy. He sought to bring the prescriptions of the service books into conformity with Greek usages and, taking expert advice, to eradicate many of their long-standing corruptions. He had such details settled as the making of the sign of the cross with three fingers instead of with two and the use of the threefold Alleluia. These reforms, which were carried out with the aid of the civil power, with great rigour, gained the Patriarch many enemies.

From 1652 to 1658 his influence with the Tsar was immense, but in the latter year, probably owing to his claims of complete independence in ecclesiastical matters, he fell from Imperial favour. After his resignation had been accepted by the Tsar, he retired to the monastery of the 'New Jerusalem' which he had founded. In the following years he tried to regain his position, but in 1667, at the Council of Moscow, he was finally deposed and sentenced to banishment. His liturgical reforms were sanctioned, however, and the formation of the schismatical sect of the *Old Believers followed. After 14 years of severe imprisonment Alexis' successor, Feodor II, recalled Nikon to Moscow, but he died on the way and was buried with patriarchal honours. Subsequently all decrees against him were revoked at the bidding of the Tsar.

W. *Palmer, *The Patriarch and the Tsar* (6 vols., 1871–6), with Eng. tr. of numerous primary docs. The main lit., which is extensive, is in Russian. In Eng. there is a brief Life [by R. Thornton] in *Lives of Eminent Russian Prelates* (1854), pp. 1–38. P. Meyendorff, *Russia, Ritual, and Reform: The Liturgical Reforms of Nikon in the 17th century* (Crestwood, NY, 1991). J. Ledit, SJ, in *DTC* 11 (pt. 1; 1931), cols. 646–55, s.v. 'Nicon (1)'. See also works cited under RUSSIA, CHRISTIANITY IN, and OLD BELIEVERS.

Nil Sorsky, St (1433–1508), Russian monk and mystic. Of noble Muscovite family, and for some years a monk of the monastery of St Cyril at Beloozero, in N. Russia, he visited Mt *Athos, where he found his vocation in the contemplative life of *Hesychasm. Returning to Russia, in a forest hermitage not far from Beloozero he introduced a new form of the ascetic monastic life, that of the small group (*skit*) guided by a spiritual father (*staretz*), for which he wrote a Rule. His ideals were poverty, simplicity, and contemplative prayer; though his influence was eclipsed at the time by that of *Joseph of Volokolamsk, he is regarded as the spiritual founder of the *skit* and *staretz* in 18th–19th cent. Russia.

F. v. Lilienfeld, *Nil Sorskij und seine Schriften* (1963), incl. Ger. tr. of his works. Fr. tr. by S. M. Jacamon, OSB, of his writings and of a 19th-cent. Life (Spiritualité orientale, 32; Bégrolles-en-Mauges, 1980). G. A. Maloney, SJ, *Russian Hesychasm: The Spirituality of Nil Sorskij* (The Hague, 1973; Fr. tr., Spiritualité orientale, 25; 1978).

Nilus the Ascetic, St (d. *c.*430), Bp. of Ancyra, also (erroneously) known as 'Nilus of Sinai'. Acc. to the traditional account (*Nicephorus Callistus; a set of 'Narrationes' attributed to Nilus; Byzantine *Synaxaria), Nilus

was a high officer at the *Constantinopolitan court who with his son, Theodulus, became a hermit on Mt *Sinai. In 410, when the monks were attacked by hordes of robbers, Nilus escaped, but Theodulus was captured and sold into slavery. After many adventures both were ordained by the Bp. of Eleusa in Palestine who sent them back to Sinai.

In modern times this account has been generally rejected (K. Heussi and others). It appears that Nilus was in fact a native of Ancyra who studied at Constantinople, where he became the disciple of St John *Chrysostom. He then became the founder and superior of a monastery near Ancyra, whence he conducted a large correspondence and exerted a wide influence on his contemporaries.

His writings deal mainly with ascetic and moral subjects. They include 'De Monachorum Praestantia', 'De Monastica Exercitatione', 'De Voluntaria Paupertate', and also a collection of 1,061 letters (mainly genuine in substance, but evidently edited in the 6th cent. and provided with often anachronistic headings). The 'Tractatus ad Eulogium' and the 'De Oratione' attributed to him appear to belong to *Evagrius Ponticus, while the 'De Octo Vitiosis Cogitationibus' is a compilation from *Cassian. Nilus' ideal of the spiritual life is a 'Christian philosophy' ($\varphi\iota\lambda o\sigma o\varphi\epsilon\tilde{\iota}\nu$ $\kappa\alpha\tau\dot{\alpha}$ $X\rho\iota\sigma\tau\acute{o}\nu$) based on a 'moderated poverty' ($\mu\acute{e}\sigma\eta$ $\dot{\alpha}\kappa\tau\eta\mu o\sigma\acute{\upsilon}\nu\eta$). Feast day, 12 Nov.

Works in J. P. Migne, *PG* 79 (unsatisfactory). Crit. edn. of 'Narrationes' by F. Conca (Teub., 1983). Part of a previously unpub. comm. on Songs of Songs, ed. S. Lucà, *Augustinianum*, 22 (1982), pp. 365–403. Syr. version of some of Nilus' works, ed., with Ital. tr., by P. Bettiolo (Publications de l'Institut orientaliste de Louvain, 30; 1983). Eng. tr. of 'De Monastica Exercitatione' in G. E. H. Palmer, P. Sherrard, and K. [T. R.] Ware, *The Philokalia*, 1 (1979), pp. 200–50. J. Gribomont, OSB, 'La Tradition manuscrite de saint Nil', *Studia Monastica*, 11 (1969), pp. 231–67; id., 'L'édition romaine (1673) des Tractatus de S. Nil et l'Ottobonianus gr. 25', in J. Dummer (ed.), *Texte und Textkritik* (TU 133; 1987), pp. 187–202. F. Degenhart, *Der hl. Nilus Sinaita: Sein Leben und seine Lehre vom Mönchtum* (Beiträge zur Geschichte des alten Mönchtums und des Benediktinerordens, 6; 1915); K. Heussi, *Untersuchungen zu Nilus dem Asketen* (TU 42, Heft 2; 1917); F. Degenhart, *Neue Beiträge zur Nilus-Forschung* (1918; reply to preceding work); K. Heussi, *Das Nilus Problem* (1921; a further reply). J. Henninger, 'Ist der sogenannte Nilus-Bericht eine brauchbare religionsgeschichtliche Quelle?', *Anthropos*, 1 (1955), pp. 81–148. Alan Cameron, 'The Authenticity of the Letters of St Nilus of Ancyra', *Greek, Roman and Byzantine Studies*, 17 (1976), pp. 181–96. Bardenhewer, 4, pp. 161–78; Altaner and Stuiber (1978), pp. 334 and 618. J. Quasten, *Patrology*, 3 (Utrecht and Westminster, Md., 1960), pp. 496–504. *CPG* 3 (1979), pp. 173–82 (nos. 6043–84). M. T. Disdier in *DTC* 11 (pt. 1; 1931), cols. 661–74; M.-G. Guérard in *Dict. Sp.* 11 (1982), cols. 345–56, s.v. 'Nil d'Ancyre'.

nimbus. See HALO.

Nimrod. Acc. to Gen. 10: 8–10 Nimrod was the first of the 'heroes' and a 'mighty hunter before the Lord', and founded the Assyrian Empire. In Babylonian mythology he is paralleled by the figure of *Gilgamesh, the tyrant of Erech. The only other references to him in the Bible are at 1 Chron. 1: 10 and Mic. 5: 6.

Nine Fridays. See FIRST FRIDAYS.

Nineveh, Fast of. A pre-*Lenten fast of three or four days kept esp. in several Eastern Churches (*Church of the East, *Syrian, *Coptic and *Armenian Orthodox). It is observed in the third week before Lent, except in the Armenian Church, where it immediately precedes the Lenten fast.

Ninian, St (5th or 6th cent.), British missionary. *Bede reports that before St *Columba (in Scotland 563–97) converted the N. Picts, Ninian had been active among the S. Picts. He describes Ninian as a bishop, 'a Briton who had received orthodox instruction at Rome', and states that he built a stone church dedicated to St *Martin of Tours (d. 397) at a place called 'Ad Candidam Casam' (At the White House), now Whithorn (S. of Wigtown), where he was buried. In the Middle Ages Ninian's tomb became a place of pilgrimage. His dates are uncertain. An 8th-cent. poem, the *Miracula Nynie Episcopi*, makes him contemporary with a local king called Tudwal, and there was a king of that name at Dumbarton *c*.550. The suggestion that Ninian visited St Martin on his way back from Rome derives from a largely unreliable Life by St *Ailred (d. 1167). Feast day, 16 Sept.

Bede, *HE* 3. 4 (notes in edn. by C. Plummer, 2, Oxford, 1896, pp. 128–30 or comm. by J. M. Wallace-Hadrill, Oxford, 1988, p. 92, with refs.). *Miracula Nynie Episcopi*, ed., with Eng. tr., by W. W. MacQueen in *Transactions of the Dumfriesshire and Galloway Natural History and Antiquarian Society*, 3rd ser. 38 (1961), pp. 21–57; Ailred's Life, ed. A. P. *Forbes, *Lives of S. Ninian and S. Kentigern* (Historians of Scotland, 5; 1874), pp. 137–57, with Eng. tr. pp. 3–26. W. D. Simpson, *Saint Ninian and the Origins of the Christian Church in Scotland* (1940); N. K. Chadwick, 'St. Ninian: A Preliminary Study of Sources', *Transactions of the Dumfriesshire and Galloway Natural History and Antiquarian Society*, 3rd ser. 27 (1950), pp. 9–53; J. MacQueen, *St Nynia: A Study of Literary and Linguistic Evidence* (1961); A. Macquarrie, 'The Date of Saint Ninian's Mission: A Reappraisal', *Scottish Church History Society Records*, 33 (1987), pp. 1–25.

Nisan. The opening month in the Jewish year, roughly corresponding to April. It was the month in which the *Passover was held, the Passover Lamb being slain in the afternoon of the 14th day of Nisan. The name appears to be Babylonian (Akkadian *nisannu*) and to have been substituted by the Jews from the time of the Exile (6th cent. BC) for its older Hebrew name of 'Abib' (found, e.g. in Exod. 13: 4).

Nitrian Desert. The region between *Alexandria and Cairo lying W. of the mouths of the Nile, and celebrated as a centre of early Christian monasticism. Since 1964 there have been excavations at the site of the Kellia (N. of Wadi Natroun). In the latter part of the 4th cent. an enormous colony of hermits was founded here, chiefly under the influence of Ammon, one of the *Tall Brothers. Of the still extant Coptic monasteries in Wadi Natroun, one, the 'Der es Suryan', i.e. the 'Monastery of the Syrians', formerly possessed a valuable collection of *Syriac MSS which were acquired partly by the *Assemani for the *Vatican Library (in 1707 and 1745), partly by H. *Tattam (1841 and 1843) and W. *Cureton (1847) for the British Museum.

H. G. E. White, *The History of the Monasteries of Nitria and of Scetis*, ed. W. Hauser (The Monasteries of the Wâdi 'n Natrûn,

2; Publications of the Metropolitan Museum of Art, Egyptian Expedition, 7; New York, 1932). F. Daumas and A. Guillaumont, *Kelia I, Kom 219* (Fouilles de l'Institut Français d'Archéologie Orientale de Caire, 28; 2 vols., 1969); further accounts of excavations at the Kellia by R. Kasser (Recherches Suisse d'Archéologie Copte, 1–2, Geneva, 1967–72; and 2 vols., Louvain, 1983). D. J. Chitty, *The Desert a City: An Introduction to the Study of Egyptian and Palestinian Monasticism under the Christian Empire* (Oxford, 1966), *passim*.

Nitzsch, Karl Immanuel (1787–1868), German *Lutheran theologian. Educated at Schulpforta and *Wittenberg, he became *Privatdozent* of theology in 1810 and assistant preacher at the Schlosskirche at Wittenberg in 1811. In 1822 he accepted a professorship at Bonn university, and in 1847 was called to Berlin to succeed P. K. *Marheineke; here he was made provost of the Nicolaikirche in 1854. His principal works are the *System der christlichen Lehre* (1829; Eng. tr. by R. Montgomery and J. Hennen, 1849) and *Praktische Theologie* (1847–1867). Nitzsch is one of the chief representatives of the German '*Vermittlungstheologie'. As an opponent of contemporary unbelieving rationalism he rejected a purely speculative interpretation of Christianity and emphasized esp. the immediacy of religious feeling, which, acc. to him, produces the foundations of religious knowledge. As a member of the Supreme Church Council he was an active promoter of the Evangelical Union of the Prussian Churches (1817).

Life by W. *Beyschlag (Berlin, 1872). H. Theurich, *Theorie und Praxis der Predigt bei Carl Immanuel Nitzsch* (Studien zur Theologie und Geistesgeschichte des Neunzehnten Jahrhunderts, 16; Göttingen, 1975). H. Theurich in *TRE* 24 (1995), pp. 576–81, s.v.

Noah (or Noe). A son of Lamech, and tenth in descent from *Adam. Acc. to the story in *Genesis (6–9), Noah and his family alone were saved in an ark of gopher-wood, when the rest of mankind were destroyed in the *Flood. He took with him into the ark specimens of all kinds of living creatures whereby the species were providentially preserved. From Noah, therefore, the entire surviving human race descended, through his three sons, Shem, Ham, and Japheth. To Noah is also attributed the discovery of viticulture (Gen. 9: 20).

Other races have traditions of a great flood in very early times. In Babylonian mythology the figure of Utnapishtim corresponds to Noah in the biblical account, while in classical literature the story of Noah is closely paralleled by the legend of Deucalion. See also GILGAMESH, EPICS OF.

J. Fink, *Noe der Gerechte in der frühchristlichen Kunst* (Beihefte zum Archiv für Kulturgeschichte, 4; 1955). J. P. Lewis, *A Study of the Interpretation of Noah and the Flood in Jewish and Christian Literature* (Leiden, 1968), esp. pp. 3–41, 121–55. L. R. Bailey, *Noah: The Person and the Story in History and Tradition* (Columbia, SC [1989]). P. Lundberg, *La Typologie baptismale dans l'ancienne Église* (Acta Seminarii Neotestamenticii Upsaliensis, 10; Leipzig and Uppsala, 1942), pp. 73–116; J. *Daniélou, SJ, *Sacramentum Futuri: Études sur les origines de la typologie biblique* (Études de Théologie Historique, 1950), pp. 55–94; Eng. tr. (1960), pp. 69–112. See also comm. to GENESIS cited s.v., and bibl. to ARK and FLOOD.

Noailles, L. A. de. See DE NOAILLES, L. A.

Nobili, Robert de. See DE NOBILI, ROBERT.

Nobis quoque peccatoribus (Lat., 'To us sinners, also'). The opening words of the section of the Roman *Canon of the Mass in which the celebrant prays for admission into the company of the saints, several of whom he mentions by name. In the *Ambrosian rite the words are in the variant form '*Nobis quoque minimis et peccatoribus*'.

V. L. Kennedy, CSB, *The Saints of the Canon of the Mass* (Studi di Antichità Cristiana, 14; 1938), pp. 34–8 and 189–199, who defends the improbable thesis that the *Nobis quoque peccatoribus*, like *Communicantes*, was first introduced into the Roman Canon by Pope *Gelasius I (492–6). N. J. Abercrombie, '*Nobis quoque* in the Roman *Canon Missae*', *JTS* NS 4 (1953), pp. 49 f. Jungmann (1958 edn.), 2, pp. 309–22; Eng. tr., 2, pp. 248–59.

Noble Guard. The bodyguard, consisting in all of 77 men of noble rank, which used to attend on the Pope at public functions. They were instituted by *Pius VII in 1801, but owing to political difficulties they did not come into effective being till later. They received the basis of their final constitution in 1815; they were disbanded in 1970. They wore impressive military uniform, and their commander was always a Roman prince. See PALATINE and SWISS GUARD.

G. Felice in *EC* 6 (1951), cols. 1203 f., s.v. 'Guardia nobile pontificia', with bibl. and illustr.

Nocturn. A division of the traditional 'night *office' (*Mattins, q.v.) of the W. Church. In the 1568 Roman Breviary, on Sundays and all feasts above the rank of a *Simple, and in the Office of the Dead, there were three Nocturns. The first Nocturn on Sundays consisted of twelve Psalms in groups of four with one *antiphon for each group, the second two of three Psalms with an antiphon for each Psalm; after the Psalms a versicle, Pater Noster, and a short prayer called 'Absolutio', and then three readings, each preceded by a blessing of the reader and followed by a *responsory (except for the last reading which was followed by the *Te Deum). The readings for the first Nocturn were always taken from the Bible, those of the second were patristic or from the Lives of the saints, and those of the third came from a homily on the Gospel of the day. On simple feasts and weekdays there was only one Nocturn of twelve Psalms, with an antiphon for every two Psalms (reduced by *Pius X to nine Psalms and nine antiphons), and three readings (from the Bible on weekdays and from the Bible and the Lives of saints on feasts); during the *Octaves of *Easter and *Pentecost there were only three Psalms and three readings. In the *Monastic Breviary there were two Nocturns with six Psalms each on weekdays, and on Sundays and feasts three Nocturns with twelve Psalms in all, three Canticles, and twelve readings, followed by a Gospel reading by the Abbot. In some monastic uses, the term 'Nocturn' was applied to the whole of the office known elsewhere as 'Mattins' or '*Vigils'.

Noetics (from Gk. νοητικός, 'pertaining to the mind or intellect'). A term applied to an early 19th-cent. group of thinkers, Whigs in politics, who were members of the Senior Common Room of Oriel College, Oxford. The chief were E. *Copleston and E. *Hawkins (successively Provosts of Oriel College), R. *Whately, and R. D. *Hampden. They freely criticized traditional religious orthodoxy, and sought to increase the comprehensiveness of the C of E. The later Noetics came into sharp conflict with the *Tractarians.

W. Tuckwell, *Pre-Tractarian Oxford: A Reminiscence of the Oriel 'Noetics'* (1909); R. Brent, *Liberal Anglican Politics: Whiggery, Religion, and Reform 1830–1841* (Oxford Historical Monographs, 1987), esp. pp. 144–83 and 247 f. H. C. G. Matthew, 'Noetics, Tractarians and the Reform of the University of Oxford in the Nineteenth Century', *History of Universities*, 9 (1991), pp. 195–225.

Noetus (*c*.200), heretic. Our knowledge of him comes chiefly from *Hippolytus (*Haer.* 9. 7–10; *Cont. Noetum*), acc. to whom he was a native of Smyrna. He was probably the first to teach *Patripassian doctrines—that it was God the Father who in the Incarnation was born, suffered, and died. He also rejected the Logos doctrine, admitted only a purely allegorical interpretation of the Prologue of St John's Gospel, and accused his opponents of ditheism. He was condemned by an assembly of presbyters at Smyrna *c*.200. Hippolytus asserts also that through his disciple, Epigonus, Patripassian teaching made its way from Asia Minor to Rome.

Further refs. in Hippolytus, *Haer.* 9. 2, and 10. 27; *Epiphanius, *Haer.* 57; and *Theodoret, *Haer. Fab.* 3. 3. Crit. text of Hippolytus, *Contra Noetum*, with discussion (much challenged), by P. Nautin (Paris, 1949); also ed., with Eng. tr., by R. Butterworth, SJ (Heythrop Monographs, 2; 1977). A. Pourkier, *L'hérésiologie chez Épiphane de Salamine* (Christianisme Antique, 4 [1992]), pp. 115–46. For further bibl. see under MONARCHIANISM.

Nolascans. An alternative name for the *Mercedarians (q.v.).

Nominalism. The theory of language which emphasizes the nature of universal concepts as names of human imposition. In the controversy on *universals, partly occasioned by the famous text in *Porphyry's 'Isagoge', which occupied medieval philosophers esp. in the 11th and 12th cents., a form of Nominalism was first evolved by *Roscelin and later by *Abelard. It was directed against the Platonist *Realists who held that universals, such as genus and species, had a separate existence apart from the individuals which are tributary to them. In opposition to this teaching, Roscelin carried the denial of the unity of species to a point which led him to be accused of *Tritheism. Abelard, on the other hand, though severely criticizing the doctrine of the separate existence of the universals, which he calls 'names' ('voces', 'nomina'), as opposed to 'things' ('res'), does not seem to have denied that the resemblances among individual things justify the use of universals for establishing knowledge, so that he has often been represented as a forerunner of Moderate Realism rather than as a Nominalist properly so called.

A different form of Nominalism appeared in the 14th cent.; this is usually associated with *William of Ockham. He asserted that the universal is not found at all in reality, but only in the human mind ('in anima'), for every substance is radically individual. Acc. to him the resemblance between two men does not lead to the conclusion that they share a common nature; universals are only ways of conceiving or knowing individual things. Thus our first knowledge is an intuition of the individual, accompanying sensation. In its application to theology, which was made by Ockham himself, but more esp. by Gabriel *Biel, Nominalism, which conceives God exclusively as omnipotence and mercy, denies the plurality of His attributes and the distinction between His Intellect and His Will. It simplifies His Being to such a degree that the reality of the Three Persons which depends on formal distinctions and real relations can be accepted only on the authority of faith. Nor can reason demonstrate that the First Cause of the existing universe is the One God. Thus Nominalism in its theological consequences withdrew almost all the data of faith from the realm of reason and paved the way for the disintegration of Scholasticism.

J. Reiners, *Der Nominalismus in der Frühscholastik* (BGPM 8. 5; 1910). M. H. Carré, *Realists and Nominalists* (Oxford, 1946). W. J. Courtenay, 'Nominales and Nominalism in the Twelfth Century', in J. Jolivet and others (eds.), *Lectionum Varietates: Hommage à Paul Vignaux* (Études de philosophie médiévale, 65; 1991), pp. 11–48. P. Vignaux, *Nominalisme au XIVe siècle* (Conférence Albert-le-Grand, 1948; Montreal and Paris, 1948). E. *Gilson, *History of Christian Philosophy in the Middle Ages* (1955), pp. 499–520. A. Vigneaux in *DTC* 11 (pt. 1; 1931), cols. 717–84; G. Küng in *NCE* 10 (1967), pp. 483–6, with bibl. See also bibl. to WILLIAM OF OCKHAM and BIEL, G.

Nomocanon (Gk. νόμος, 'a law', and κανών, 'canon'). In the E. Church, a collection of ecclesiastical canons and Imperial laws, arranged acc. to subject-matter. The earliest (*c*.600) derives from *John Scholasticus (q.v.). This is a later conflation (set out under 50 headings) of two legal collections, themselves compiled by John: (1) a collection of canons arranged in 50 tituli, the outline of which is preserved in all subsequent editions of the Nomocanon; (2) a collection of Imperial laws arranged in 87 capitula.

Non Expedit (Lat., 'It is not expedient'). The name given, from its opening words, to an official RC decree, issued on 29 Feb. 1868, forbidding Catholics in Italy to take part in the polling at civil elections. Its object was to counter the threat to the territorial possessions of the Papacy from the movement for a united Italy.

U. Benigni in *CE* 11 (1911), pp. 98 f., s.v.; R. Mori in *NCE* 10 (1967), pp. 486 f., s.v.; both with bibl., but neither gives ref. to text.

Nonconformists' Chapels Act 1844. In the face of disputes between *Presbyterians and *Unitarians, the Act laid down that where no particular religious doctrine or mode of worship was prescribed by the trust deed, the usage of the congregation for the past 25 years was to be taken as conclusive evidence of what might properly be done in meeting-houses. It was repealed by the Charities Act 1960. See also UNITARIANISM.

The Act, entitled 'An Act for the Regulation of Suits Relating to Meeting Houses and other such Property held for religious Purposes by Persons dissenting from the United Church of England and Ireland', is pr. in *The Statutes of the United Kingdom of Great Britain and Ireland*, 7 & 8 Victoria (1844), pp. 239 f. (cap. 45).

Nonconformity. Refusal to conform to the doctrines, polity, or discipline of any Established Church. The term was originally used in the 17th cent. of those who, while at first agreeing with the doctrines of the C of E, nevertheless refused to conform to its discipline and practice, esp. in matters of ceremony. The execution of the 1662 Act of *Uniformity (q.v.) led to the Bartholomean Exodus, which marked the formal beginnings of Nonconformity. The word is now applied generally to all dissenters, esp. those of Protestant sympathies. Among the groups to whom the term is commonly applied are the *Presbyterians (in England) and the *Congregationalists (now mainly united in the *United Reformed Church), the *Methodists, *Quakers, and *Baptists (qq.v.).

[D.] H. [M.] Davies, *The English Free Churches* (HUL, 1952); E. [R.] Routley, *English Religious Dissent* (Cambridge, 1960); P. Sangster, *A History of the Free Churches* (1983). G. L. Turner (ed.), *Original Records of Early Nonconformity under Persecution and Indulgence* (3 vols., 1911–14). A. G. Matthews, *Calamy Revised: Being a revision of Edmund *Calamy's Account of the Ministers and others ejected and silenced, 1660–2* (1934). M. R. Watts, *The Dissenters*, 1: *From the Reformation to the French Revolution* (Oxford [1978]); 2: *The Expansion of Evangelical Nonconformity* (ibid., 1995). E. A. Payne, *The Free Church Tradition in the Life of England* (1944); [J.] C. [G.] Binfield, *So Down to Prayers: Studies in English Nonconformity 1780–1920* (1977); J. Munson, *The Nonconformists: In Search of a Lost Culture* (1991). J. W. Grant, *Free Churchmanship in England, 1870–1940, with special reference to Congregationalism* [1955]. D. M. Thompson (ed.), *Nonconformity in the Nineteenth Century* (1972). H. McLachlan, *English Education under the Test Acts being the History of the Nonconformist Academies, 1662–1820* (Publications of the University of Manchester, no. 213; Historical Series, no. 59; 1931). N. H. Keeble, *The Literary Culture of Nonconformity in Later Seventeenth-Century England* (Leicester, 1987), passim. D. [A.] Davie, *A Gathered Church: The Literature of the English Dissenting Interest, 1700–1930* (Clark Lectures, 1976; 1978). W. F. Adeney in *HERE* 9 (1917), pp. 381–93, s.v.; T. F. Glasson in *DECH* (3rd edn., 1948), pp. 403–22, s.v. See also bibl. to SEPARATISTS and the various Nonconforming bodies.

None. The last of the 'Little Hours' of the Divine *Office, appointed to be recited at the ninth hour, i.e. 3 p.m. In many orders it came to be said either immediately after the principal Mass (hence 'noon') or together with the other Little Hours. For the structure of the service, see TERCE, SEXT, NONE.

Nonjurors, English. The title is used of members of the C of E who after 1688 scrupled to take the Oaths of Allegiance and Supremacy to William and Mary on the grounds that by so doing they would break their previous Oaths to *James II and his successors. They numbered nine bishops and some 400 priests, who were deprived of their livings, as well as a number of prominent laymen. The deprived bishops were Abp. W. *Sancroft of *Canterbury and Bps. T. *Ken of *Bath and Wells, F. Turner of *Ely, T. White of *Peterborough, W. Lloyd of *Norwich, R. Frampton of *Gloucester, J. Lake of *Chichester, W. Thomas of *Worcester, and T. Cartwright of *Chester, the last three of whom died before the sentence of deprivation against them could be carried out (1689). Since all were deprived by Act of Parliament and their successors appointed in the same way, with no attempt at canonical sentence, the Nonjuring clergy still regarded them as their lawful bishops, and many of the conforming clergy (including R. *South, J. *Sharp, and W. *Beveridge) refused to accept their sees as being irregularly vacated. To ensure the succession of Nonjuring Bishops, Sancroft delegated his archiepiscopal powers to Lloyd on 9 Feb. 1692, and in 1694 G. *Hickes and T. Wagstaffe were secretly consecrated (with the respective titles of Thetford and Ipswich) after the *congé d'élire had been received from the exiled James II. The *Abjuration Oath of 1701 and the Hanoverian succession in 1714 also helped to perpetuate the schism. Some Nonjurors, however, believed that legitimate grounds for schism ceased with the death of the last deprived bishop; these, led by H. *Dodwell, rejoined the C of E in 1711. The Nonjurors were divided on the question of the lawfulness of worshipping in their parish church; the majority preferred their own services, which were, of course, illegal. In 1716, after the death of Hickes, the controversy between *Usagers (q.v.) and Non-Usagers over questions of ritual produced a serious division which was not healed till 1732. From 1716 to 1725 they carried on abortive negotiations for union with the E. Churches. In addition to internal dissensions, the fear of a restoration of the Stuarts, esp. in the early Hanoverian period, considerably weakened their position. The last of the regular line of bishops, Robert Gordon, died in 1779, and, though an irregular line continued until the death of Charles Booth in 1805, during the latter part of the 18th cent. the Nonjurors virtually disappeared through absorption into the Established Church. Their guiding principles had been the sanctity of the Oath and the distinctive Anglican doctrine of the *Divine Right of Kings and the duty of passive obedience. They held a high conception of the Church as a spiritual society with its own laws, and laid particular emphasis on the external forms of worship, which tendencies link them with the *Caroline divines of the 17th and the *Tractarians of the 19th cents. They produced a number of good devotional writers. Among their more distinguished clergy were J. *Kettlewell, C. *Leslie, and W. *Law, well-known laymen being H. Dodwell and T. *Hearne.

T. Lathbury, A History of the Nonjurors (1845); J. H. Overton, The Nonjurors (1902); H. Broxap, The Later Nonjurors (1924). L. M. Hawkins, Allegiance in Church and State: The Problem of the Non-jurors in the English Revolution (Studies in Economics and Political Science, 97; 1928). M. Goldie, 'The Nonjurors, Episcopacy, and the Origins of the Convocation Controversy', in E. Cruickshanks (ed.), Ideology and Conspiracy: Aspects of Jacobitism, 1689-1759 (Edinburgh [1982]), pp. 15-35. Correspondence between the Orthodox patriarchs and the Nonjuring bishops, ed., with introd., by G. Williams, The Orthodox Church of the East in the Eighteenth Century (1868), and by L. Petit, AA, in Mansi, 37 (1905), cols. 369-624. The Nonjurors' liturgies of 1718 and 1734 are pr. by W. J. Grisbrooke, Anglican Liturgies of the Seventeenth and Eighteenth Centuries (*Alcuin Club Collections, 40; 1958), pp. 273-316, with comm., pp. 71-135. S. L. Ollard in DECH (1912), pp. 410-14, s.v.; C. J. B. Gaskoin in HERE 9 (1917), pp. 294-6, s.v.

Nonnus of Panopolis (b. c.400), poet. Beyond the fact that he came from Panopolis (the modern Akhmîn) in Egypt, nothing is known of his life. He seems to have written two Greek poems in hexameters, the one, Διονυσιακά, a descriptive account of the journey of the god Dionysus to India, and the other a 'Paraphrase' (μεταβολή) of the Fourth Gospel'. The latter, of which only part (3,750 lines) has survived, has a certain value for

the light it throws on the text of the Bible, but is otherwise of scant interest.

Crit. texts of 'Paraphrase' ed. A. Scheindler (Teub., 1881) and of 'Dionysiaca' ed. R. Keydell (2 vols., Berlin, 1959), and, with Fr. tr., by F. Vian and others (Collection des Universités de France, 1976 ff.); also with Eng. tr. by W. H. D. Rouse and notes by H. J. Rose and L. R. Lind (3 vols., Loeb, 1940); the 'Paraphrase', repr. from edn. by D. Heinsius (Leiden, 1627), also in J. P. Migne, PG 43. 749-920. W. Peek and others, Lexikon zu den Dionysiaka des Nonnos (Berlin, 1968-75). R. Janssen, Das Johannes-Evangelium nach der Paraphrase des Nonnus Panopolitanus (TU 23, Heft 4; 1903). J. Golega, Studien über die Evangelien-Dichtung des Nonnos von Panopolis (1930). G. d'Ippolito, Studi nonniani: L'epillio nelle Dionisiache (Palermo, 1964). W. Fauth, Eidos Poikilon: Zur Thematik der Metamorphose und zum Prinzip der Wandlung aus dem Gegensatz in den Dionysiaka des Nonnos von Panopolis (Hypomnemata, 66; Göttingen, 1981). C. A. Trypanis, Greek Poetry from Homer to Seferis (1981), pp. 392-5. J. Quasten, Patrology, 3 (Utrecht and Westminster, Md., 1960), pp. 114-16. R. Keydell in PW 17 (pt. 1; 1936), cols. 904-20.

Norbert, St (c.1080-1134), founder of the *Premonstratensians and Abp. of Magdeburg. The younger son of a noble family of Xanten, Norbert early became subdeacon and canon of St Victor's in his native town, but led a worldly life at the courts of Abp. Frederick I of Cologne and the Emp. Henry V. Having avoided the priesthood and declined the bishopric of Cambrai in 1113, he was converted in 1115 when in danger of death during a thunderstorm. After some time in retirement at the abbey of Siegburg near Cologne, whose Abbot Cuno became his spiritual director, he was ordained priest in the same year, and, having taken the monastic habit, endeavoured to reform his brother canons at Xanten. These, who resented his zeal, accused him at the Synod of Fritzlar in 1118 of making innovations and of preaching without authorization; and in reply he resigned his canonry, sold his property, and went to Pope Gelasius II at St-Gilles in Languedoc. After the Pope had given him permission to preach wherever he wished, he travelled as an itinerant preacher through N. France and soon became renowned for his eloquence and his miracles. In 1120, supported by Bartholomew, Bp. of Laon, he founded the Order of the Premonstratensians in the valley of Prémontré. He travelled in France, Belgium, and Germany, preaching everywhere, and successfully fighting the heresy of Tanchelm at Antwerp (1124). Early in 1126 he obtained at Rome the recognition of his order from Pope Honorius II, and in the same year was appointed Abp. of Magdeburg. His zeal for the reformation of his clergy and the recovery of alienated Church property made him many enemies and led to attempts against his life; but he won the confidence and favour of the Emp. Lothair II and accompanied him in 1132-3 to Rome, where he supported Innocent II against the antipope, Anacletus. He also prevented the outbreak of fresh quarrels about *Investiture, in recognition of which service the Pope extended his metropolitan jurisdiction to the whole of Poland. In 1133 Lothair made him Chancellor for Italy, but he remained in the country for only a short time. He died in the following year. In 1582 he was canonized by *Gregory XIII. Feast day, 6 June.

The principal authority is a Life written between 1157 and 1161, falsely attributed to Hugh of Prémontré, ed. R. Wilmans in MGH, Scriptores, 12 (1856), pp. 663-706; excerpts, from a later redaction, in *AASS*, Jun. 1 (1695), pp. 819–58. R. Rosenmund, *Die ältesten Biographieen des heiligen Norbert* (1874). Modern Lives by G. Madelaine, O.Praem. (Lille, 1886; 3rd edn., 2 vols., Tongerloo, 1928) and F. A. Žák, O.Praem. (Vienna, 1900). W. M. Grauwen, O.Praem., *Norbertus Aartsbisschop van Maagdenburg (1126–1134)* (Verhandelingen van de koninklijke Academie voor Wetenschappen, Letteren en Schone Kunsten van België, Klasse der Letteren, no. 86; 1978), with summary in Eng. and full bibl. F. Petit [O.Praem.], *Norbert et l'origine des Prémontrés* (1981). P. Lefèvre, O.Praem., 'L'Épisode de la conversion de S Norbert et la tradition hagiographique du "vita Norberti" ', *RHE* 56 (1961), pp. 813–26.

Noris, Henry (1631–1704), cardinal and theologian. The descendant of an English family, he studied with the *Jesuits at Rimini, where he entered the Order of *Augustinian Hermits out of devotion to St *Augustine. From the age of 27 he taught theology and Church history at Pesaro and Perugia, and from 1674 to 1692 at Padua. In 1692 Innocent XII called him to Rome, making him First Custodian of the *Vatican Library and, in 1695, creating him cardinal. His most important work is the *Historia Pelagiana et Dissertatio de Synodo V Oecumenica* (1673), a history of the *Pelagian controversy, followed by a defence of the Augustinian doctrine of grace (against that held by L. de *Molina). The book, though approved by the Holy See, raised a great deal of controversy, and, in 1676, was denounced to the Holy Office for renewing the errors of M. *Baius and C. O. *Jansen. Noris was acquitted of heresy, but 40 years after his death the Spanish *Inquisition renewed the accusation, placing the book on the *Index. His teaching was finally rehabilitated in 1748 by *Benedict XIV, who ordered Noris's books to be removed from the Index.

Collected works ed. P. and G. *Ballerini (4 vols., Verona, 1729–32), with Life in vol. 4, pp. xiii–xlii; suppl. of letters in Ital. (Padua, 1741). M. K. Wernicke, *Kardinal Enrico Noris und seine Verteidigung Augustins* (Cassiciacum, 28; Würzburg, 1973). F. Rojo, OSA, 'Ensayo bibliográfico de Noris, Bellelli y Berti', *Analecta Augustiniana*, 26 (1963), pp. 294–363, esp. pp. 296–330. F. Bonnard in *DTC* 11 (pt. 1; 1931), cols. 796–802.

Norris, John (1657–1712), English divine. He is generally reckoned the last of the *Cambridge Platonists. Educated at Winchester and Exeter College, Oxford, and later elected to a Fellowship at All Souls, he became rector of Newton St Loe, Somerset, in 1689. From 1692 until his death he was rector of Bemerton. His philosophy was mainly derived from the writings of N. *Malebranche, whose *Recherche de la vérité* (1674) made a great impression on him. Like Malebranche, he combined Cartesianism with a Platonic mysticism. His most elaborate work, his *Essay towards the Theory of the Ideal or Intelligible World* (2 vols., 1701, 1704), though tedious in its style, contained some penetrating criticisms of J. *Locke's *Essay* (1690). His other writings include an *Account of Reason and Faith* (1697), a reply to the *Deistic doctrines of J. *Toland's *Christianity not Mysterious* (1690).

In 1687 Norris issued *A Collection of Miscellanies*. Modern repr. of his *Cursory Reflections upon a Book call'd An Essay Concerning Human Understanding* (1690), with introd. by G. D. McEwen (Augustan Reprint Society, 93; 1961). R. Acworth, *The Philosophy of John Norris of Bemerton (1657–1712)* (Studien und Materialien zur Geschichte der Philosophie, Kleine Reihe, 6; Hildesheim and New York, 1979). [F.] J. Hoyles, *The Waning of the Renaissance*

1640–1740 (International Archives of the History of Ideas, 39; The Hague, 1971), pp. 75–139. L. Stephen in *DNB* 41 (1895), pp. 132–4.

'North End'. The position sometimes adopted at the Communion table by the celebrant of the *Eucharist in the C of E. It has been held to be required by certain rubrics in the BCP (see EASTWARD POSITION). It is now confined to pronounced Evangelicals; but where adopted, its use is generally defended with vigour on the ground that it rules out any ascription of a priestly or mediatorial function to the celebrant. Until comparatively recently, however, it was not a mark of doctrinal belief, such High Churchmen as C. *Wheatly and E. B. *Pusey having celebrated at the North End.

North India, Church of. The Church inaugurated on 29 Nov. 1970 by the union of six Christian bodies: the *Anglican Church of *India, Pakistan, and Ceylon in respect of 13 dioceses; the United Church of North India, itself a union of *Congregationalists and *Presbyterians dating from 1924; the circuits of the *Methodist Church linked with Britain and Australia; the *Baptists; the Church of the Brethren, which originated in Germany and was brought to India by American missionaries in 1895; and the *Disciples of Christ. The union, which was the fruit of negotiations extending back to a historic meeting at Tranquebar in 1919, was achieved by the act of a representative of each of the Churches involved reading his Church's resolutions of acceptance and assent to the Plan of Union. Thereafter, during the same inaugural Eucharist, six representative ministers from the united Church were joined by four ministers, one each from the *Mar Thoma Syrian Church, the Church of *South India, the Presbyterian Church of Assam, and a Baptist; these ten laid hands on each of three chosen ministers from the uniting Churches, who then jointly laid hands on all the other representative clergy present, thus uniting the ministries. Seven new bishops were consecrated next day by bishops from the Mar Thoma Church, the Church of South India, and a former Anglican bishop from the Church of North India. The C of E entered into full communion with the Church of North India in 1972. Though the Church of North India is not part of the Anglican Communion, it is a member of the Anglican Consultative Council, and its Moderator is invited to meetings of the Anglican Primates and to *Lambeth Conferences.

Norway, Christianity in. From about the middle of the 10th cent. Christianity seems to have been gradually introduced into the country, sometimes with royal support. This took the form of building churches, legislation, and securing conversions at the point of the sword. After the death of St *Olav (d. 1030), there is no record of 'heathen' opposition. The missionaries appear to have been mainly English, as the country's Christian vocabulary and liturgical books are of English origin. It was also an English legate, Card. Nicholas Breakspear (the future Pope *Hadrian IV) who made Nidaros (Trondheim) an archbishopric with jurisdiction over the other Norwegian dioceses and also over *Sodor and Man, the Orkneys, the Faeroe Islands, *Iceland, and Greenland. This arrangement was breaking down in the later Middle Ages, but it came to an end only in 1537, when the Reformation was imposed by Danish conquerors, who annexed the country. *Lutheranism became the state religion, in the radical form favoured by *Denmark rather than the more moderate form adopted by *Sweden, and no other form of religion was recognized until 1845. By then (since 1814) Norway was united with Sweden, recovering its independence in 1905. From the middle of the 19th cent. much of the country's religious activity has been influenced by a Low Church *Pietism, largely inspired by the lay preacher, Hans N. Hauge (1771–1824). Religious dissent has spread, finding expression particularly in groups of Anglo-Saxon origin (*Methodists, *Baptists, *Pentecostalists, and after the 1939–45 War also *Jehovah's Witnesses and *Mormons). During the German occupation of 1940–5, the Church was a focus of resistance under the leadership of E. *Berggrav, Bp. of Oslo. Since then, the importance of Christianity in Norway has been in decline, and Baptism is no longer sought as a matter of course. The RC Church was introduced into the country in 1843 and has gained some acceptance, esp. since 1945, thanks to intellectual converts and immigrant refugees.

J. R. Keyser, *Den Norske Kirkes Historie under Katholicismen* (2 vols., Kristiania, 1856–8). F. Siegmund-Schultze (ed.), *Ekklesia: Eine Sammlung von Selbstdarstellungen der christlichen Kirchen*, Bd. 2, fasc. 6 (1936). C. F. Wisløff and A. Aarflot, *Norsk Kirkehistorie* (3 vols., Oslo, 1966–71). E. Molland, *Fra Hans Nielsen Hauge til Eivind Berggrav* (ibid., 1951; 3rd edn., 1972; Eng. tr., *Church Life in Norway 1800–1950*, Minneapolis [1957]); id., *Norges Kirkehistorie i det 19. århundre* (2 vols., Oslo, 1979). B. Hoye and T. M. Ager, *The Fight of the Norwegian Church against Nazism* (New York, 1943). J. W. Gran and others (eds.), *Den Katoliske Kirke i Norge* (Oslo, 1993). H. Rieber-Mohn, OP, 'Catholicism in Norway since the Reformation (1537–1958)', *Month*, NS 21 (1959), pp. 69–88; O. Garstein, 'The Reformation in Norway', ibid., pp. 95–103. L. S. Hunter (ed.), *Scandinavian Churches: A Picture of the Development of the Life of the Churches of Denmark, Finland, Iceland, Norway and Sweden* (1965).

Norwich. Although Earpwald, King of East Anglia (d. *c.*628), embraced the Christian faith, the real conversion of the country dates from the reign (*c.*630–4) of his half-brother Sigeberht, when in 630 or 631 Honorius, Abp. of *Canterbury (*c.*627–53), sent St *Felix to evangelize the East Angles. About the same time St Fursey (d. *c.*650) founded a monastery, prob. at Burghcastle, on land provided by the King. In 672 St *Theodore, Abp. of Canterbury, divided the diocese between the North Folk and the South Folk, Dunwich remaining the see of the latter, while Elmham became a new see for Norfolk. There is a gap in the recorded succession of East Anglian bishops between *c.*870 and 957, when the area was perhaps under the episcopal jurisdiction of London. In 1071 Herfast (Bp. 1070–85) moved his see from Elmham to Thetford, whence in 1094 or 1095 Herbert of Losinga (Bp. 1091–1119) transferred it to Norwich. Here in 1096 he founded the Cathedral of the Holy and Undivided Trinity, poss. as a penance for simony, and constituted it a monastic church under the *Benedictine Rule. The limits of the diocese remained practically unchanged until 1837, when the archdeaconry of Sudbury was transferred to *Ely. In 1914 the archdeaconry of Suffolk was incorporated in the new diocese

of St Edmundsbury and Ipswich. The diocese of Norwich now corresponds roughly with the county of Norfolk.

The Cathedral is mainly a Norman building with a 15th-cent. spire and fine 15th- and 16th-cent. vaulted roofs. The nave has an altar at the E. end, behind which is the stone pulpitum, supporting the organ. The choir has an ambulatory with radiating chapels, and a semicircular apse. Here are the Jesus Chapel, the Bauchun Chapel, used as the Consistory Court, and St Luke's Chapel, which contains the fine late 14th-cent. paintings of Christ's Passion and Resurrection known as the 'Despenser retable'; this chapel is used as the parish church. A bridge on the N. side of the apse is believed to have led to a chapel for relics. The Lady Chapel, at the extreme E., built by Walter de Suffield (Bp. 1245–57), was later ruined, but rebuilt in 1930–2. The two-storeyed cloisters are 14th cent. and contain a remarkable series of roof-bosses. The late Norman Bishop's throne in the basilican position behind the altar is unique in England.

The Bp. of Norwich owes his unique position as a mitred Abbot to the fact that when *Henry VIII confiscated the episcopal revenues he substituted those of the Abbey of St Benet, together with those of Hickling. Notable Bishops include, besides Herbert of Losinga (1091–1119) and Henry Despenser, the 'fighting bishop' (1370–1406), J. *Overall (1618–19), F. *White (1629–31), M. Wren (1635–8; uncle of Christopher *Wren), R. *Montague (1638–41), J. *Hall (1641–56), E. *Reynolds (1661–76), and A. *Sparrow (1676–85).

H. T. Riley, 'Norwich: The Bishop's Registry', in the *First Report of the Royal Commission on Historical Manuscripts* (1874), Appendix., pp. 86 f.; id., 'Norwich: The Dean and Chapter', ibid., pp. 87–9. A. Jessopp (ed.), *Visitations of the Diocese of Norwich A.D. 1492–1532* (Camden Society, 2nd ser. 43; 1888). J. F. Williams (ed.), *Diocese of Norwich: Bishop Redman's Visitation, 1597* (Norfolk Record Society, 18; 1946); T. F. Barton (ed.), *The Registrum Vagum of Anthony Harison* [secretary to Bp. John Jegson, 1603–17] (ibid. 32–3; 1963–4). C. Harper-Bill (ed.), *English Episcopal Acta, 6: Norwich; 1070–1214* (Oxford, 1990). H. W. Saunders (ed.), *The First Register of Norwich Cathedral Priory* (Norfolk Record Society, 11; 1939); F. J. Williams and B. Cozens-Hardy (eds.), *Extracts from the Two Earliest Minute Books of the Dean and Chapter of Norwich Cathedral, 1566–1649* (ibid. 24; 1953). B. Dodwell (ed.), *The Charters of Norwich Cathedral Priory* (Publications of the Pipe Roll Society, NS 40 for 1965–66, and 46 for 1978–80; 1974–85). H. W. Saunders, *An Introduction to the Obedientiary and Manor Rolls of Norwich Cathedral Priory* (1930). Bartholomew de Cotton, 'Annales Ecclesiae Norwicensis' and continuation, in H. *Wharton, *Anglia Sacra*, 1 (1691), pp. 397–417. W. *Dugdale, *Monasticon Anglicanum*, 4 (1823 edn.), pp. 1–24. F. Blomefield, *An Essay towards the Topographical History of the County of Norfolk*, 3 (1806), pp. 445–671, and 4 (1806), pp. 1–64. A. Jessopp, *Norwich* (Diocesan Histories; 1884); D. H. S. Cranage (ed.), *Thirteen-Hundredth Anniversary of the Diocese of East Anglia* (Norwich, 1930). R. [A.] Houlbrooke, *Church Courts and the People during the English Reformation, 1520–1570* (Oxford Historical Monographs, 1979) focuses on the diocese of Norwich. H. Leeds, *Norwich Cathedral Past and Present* (1910); R. H. Mottram, *The Glories of Norwich Cathedral* (1948); E. Fernie, *An Architectural History of Norwich Cathedral* (Clarendon Studies in the History of Art, 8; 1993). I. Atherton and others (eds.), *Norwich Cathedral: Church, City, and Diocese, 1096–1996* (1996). J. C. Cox on 'The Cathedral Priory of the Holy Trinity, Norwich', *VCH*, Norfolk, 2, ed. W. Page (1906), pp. 317–28; also id. on the ecclesiastical history of the county, ibid., pp. 213–317. N. P. Tanner, *The Church in Late Medieval Norwich 1370–1532* (Pontifical Institute of Mediaeval Studies, Studies and Texts, 66; Toronto, 1984). Indices to wills in the Consistory Court and other similar material is pub. by the Norfolk Record Society and the Norfolk and Norwich Archaeological Society.

notaries. Specially appointed persons who confirm and attest the truth of any deeds or writings in order to render them authentic. It is a rule of RC canon law that certain kinds of evidence of one notary is equivalent to that of two witnesses; and unless the contrary is established, public documents, such as those authenticated by a notary, are acceptable evidence of what is directly and principally affirmed in them (*CIC* (1983), cans. 1541 and 1573). In the Middle Ages their appointment lay with the Pope or his delegates, and their work was and remains international. By the Ecclesiastical Licences Act 1533 (passed in 1534), the right of appointing notaries was transferred to the Abp. of *Canterbury who acted through his Master of Faculties. Nowadays the English notary, who is an ecclesiastical officer, is nominated by the judge of the provincial courts of Canterbury and *York.

G. Barraclough, *Public Notaries and the Papal Curia: A Calendar and Study of a Formularium Notariorum Curie from the Early Years of the Fourteenth Century* (1934), incl. text. C. J. Duerr, *The Judicial Notary. A historical Synopsis and a Commentary* (Catholic University of America Canon Law Studies, 312; 1951). C. R. Cheney, *Notaries Public in England in the Thirteenth and Fourteenth Centuries* (Oxford, 1972). R. Naz in *DDC* 6 (1957), cols. 1015–20, s.v. 'Notaire', with bibl.

Notes of the Church. The four characteristic marks of the Church first enumerated in the so-called *Nicene Creed, i.e. one, holy, catholic, and apostolic. Though forming the opening words of *Boniface VIII's bull '*Unam Sanctam', they were not generally discussed until the Reformation, when RC theologians utilized them to discern the true Church among the rival claims of the different Christian Communions. Since then they have been employed as a particular mode of apologetics ('via notarum'). From about the middle of the 16th cent. treatises 'De notis Ecclesiae' became very numerous, though the notes were not at first confined to the four of the Creed. Thus St Robert *Bellarmine enumerated as many as 15 notes, though he held that these 15 were ultimately reducible to four. Under the stress of controversy the positions were clarified and the exact meaning of the word defined. The term was taken over by the *Tractarians in order to demonstrate the Catholicity of the C of E, and a doctrine of the Church, based on its four notes, was elaborated with some fullness by W. *Palmer in his *Treatise on the Church of Christ* (2 vols., 1833). For a much earlier dispute about the notes of holiness and catholicity, see OPTATUS, ST.

D. *Stone, *The Notes of the Church* (1910). G. Thils, *Les Notes de l'Église dans l'apologétique catholique depuis la Réforme* (Gembloux, 1937).

Noth, Martin (1902–68), OT scholar. A native of Dresden, he was educated at the Universities of Erlangen, Rostock, and Leipzig. After serving as *Privatdozent* at Greifswald and Leipzig, he held chairs at Königsberg (1930–44) and Bonn (1945–65) and in the closing years of his life was Director of the *Institut für Wissenschaft des Heiligen Landes* in Jerusalem. He was a disciple of Albrecht

Alt (1883–1956; professor in Leipzig), from whom he derived his interest in the archaeology and geography of Palestine and the social and political structure of early Israel. In *Das System der zwölf Stämme Israels* (1930) he argued that, in the period before the establishment of the Israelite monarchy, the tribes were organized as an amphictyony similar to those known in classical antiquity, and that we have no reliable knowledge of Israel before the emergence of this amphictyony as a sequel to the invasion of Canaan by the 'house of Joseph'. This hypothesis was further developed in his *Geschichte Israels* (1950, 2nd edn., 1954; Eng. tr., 1958, 2nd edn., 1960). His *Traditio-Historical researches are best represented by *Überlieferungsgeschichtliche Studien*, 1 (all pub. under this title, 1943) and *Überlieferungsgeschichte des Pentateuch* (1948; Eng. tr., 1972). Of special importance is his contention that Jos., Jgs., 1 and 2 Sam., and 1 and 2 Kgs. form a '*Deuteronomistic History', to which the bulk of Deut. is the preamble rather than the concluding section of the Pentateuch. He also wrote important commentaries on Exod. (1959; Eng. tr., 1962), Lev. (1962; Eng. tr., 1965), Num. (1966; Eng. tr., 1968), and Jos. (1938, 2nd edn., 1953). Of his projected commentary on 1 and 2 Kgs., only 16 chapters were complete at the time of his death (5 fascs., 1964–8). His philological expertise is evident in *Die israelitischen Personennamen im Rahmen der gemeinsemitischen Namengebung* (1928); and his concern to relate Israel to its environment appears above all in *Die Welt des Alten Testaments* (1940, 4th edn., 1964; Eng. tr., 1966).

Many technical arts. by Noth appeared in *Zeitschrift des Deutschen Palästinavereins*, of which he was editor 1929–63. Some of his most important essays are collected in *Gesammelte Studien zum Alten Testament*, 1 (1957, 2nd edn., 1960; Eng. tr., *The Laws in the Pentateuch*, 1966); 2, ed. H. W. Wolff (1969), with memoir by R. Smend, pp. 139–65, and list of Noth's works by H. Schult, pp. 166–205; and *Aufsätze zur biblischen Landes- und Altertumskunde*, ed. H. W. Wolff (2 vols., Neukirchen, 1971). Eng. tr. of parts of his *Überlieferungsgeschichtliche Studien* as *The Deuteronomistic History* (Journal for the Study of the Old Testament, Supplement Series, 15; 1981) and *The Chronicler's History* (ibid. 50; 1987). B. W. Anderson, 'Martin Noth's Traditio-Historical Approach in the Context of Twentieth Century Biblical Research' in his tr. of Noth's *Überlieferungsgeschichte des Pentateuch* (*A History of Pentateuchal Traditions*, Englewood Cliffs, NJ, 1972), pp. xiii–xxxii. C. H. J. de Geus, *The Tribes of Israel: An Investigation into some of the Presuppositions of Martin Noth's Amphictyony Hypothesis* (Studia Semitica Neerlandica, 18; Assen and Amsterdam, 1976); O. Bächli, *Amphiktyonie im Alten Testament: Forschungsgeschichtliche Studie zur Hypothese von Martin Noth* (Theologische Zeitschrift, Sonderband 6; Basle, 1977). R. Smend, *Deutsche Alttestamentler in drei Jahrhunderten* (Göttingen, 1989), pp. 255–75.

Notker. Among several monks of the *Benedictine monastery of St *Gall of this name the two best known are:

(1) **Notker Balbulus** (c.840–912), 'the Stammerer'. He entered the monastery of St Gall in his youth, was made librarian in 890, then guest-master, and finally master of the monastic school, where Solomon III, later Bp. of Constance, was among his pupils. He is famous for his literary work, esp. his compilation of *Sequences, the *Liber Hymnorum*. He also continued the 'Breviarium Regum Francorum' attributed to Erchanbert, wrote a metrical 'Vita' of St Gall, and is the probable author of the 'Gesta Caroli Magni', an important and carefully contrived series of

exempla or moral tales about *Charlemagne which circulated under the designation of 'a monk of St Gall'. His biographer, Ekkehart IV, praises him as a vessel of the Holy Spirit, stammering of tongue but not of spirit. Soon venerated as a saint, his cult was approved by *Leo X for St Gall in 1512 and for the diocese of Constance a year later. Commemoration, 6 Apr. See also SEQUENCE.

(2) **Notker Labeo** (*c*.950–1022), called also 'Notker the German' and 'Notker III of St Gall'. He entered the monastery of St Gall as a boy and became a long-remembered master of the monastery school. To help his pupils in their study of Latin school texts and the Bible, he took the unprecedented step of composing a number of bilingual Latin-German versions, among them the 'Disticha Catonis', *Virgil's 'Eclogues', Terence's 'Andria', as well as the Book of Job (with glosses drawn from St *Gregory the Great's 'Moralia'). All, however, are now lost except the bilingual glossed Psalter, *Boethius' 'De consolatione philosophiae', Martianus Capella's 'De nuptiis Philologiae et Mercurii', and *Aristotle's 'De categoriis' and 'De interpretatione'. Several minor works in Latin and a short treatise on musical theory in German also survive. His vigorous style, his ability to translate philosophical terms into the as yet undeveloped Old High German, together with the quantity and range of his work, make him the most notable German vernacular writer of his time.

(1) Collection of his works in J. P. Migne, *PL* 131. 993–1178; Sequences also ed. C. Blume, SJ, and H. M. Bannister (AHMA 53; 1911); modern edn. of his poetical works, with full introd., by W. von den Steinen, *Notker der Dichter und seine geistige Welt* (Berne, 2 vols., 1948); *ed. minor* of his poetical works by id. (ibid., 1960). 'Vita S. Galli' also ed. K. Strecker in *MGH*, Poetae, 4 (pt. 2; 1923), pp. 1093–108. 'Gesta Caroli Magni' also ed. by P. Jaffé, *Monumenta Carolina* (Bibliotheca Rerum Germanicarum, 4; Berlin, 1867), pp. 628–700, and by H. F. Haefele (*MGH*, Scriptores Rerum Germanicarum, NS 12; 1959). Eng. tr. by L. Thorpe, *Two Lives of Charlemagne* (Penguin Classics, 1969), pp. 93–172, with notes, pp. 189–99. Life of Notker by Ekkehart IV is pr. in *AASS*, Apr. 1 (1675), pp. 579–96, with process of canonization, pp. 596–604. H. F. Haefele, 'Studien zu Notkers Gesta Karoli', *Deutsches Archiv*, 15 (1959), pp. 358–92. H. Löwe, 'Das Karlsbuch Notkers von St. Gallen und sein zeitgeschichtlicher Hintergrund', *Schweizerische Zeitschrift für Geschichte*, 20 (1970), pp. 269–302. H. W. Goetz, *Strukturen der spätkarolingischen Epoche im Spiegel der Vorstellungen eines Zeitgenössischen Mönchs: Eine Interpretation der 'Gesta Karoli' Notkers von Sankt Gallen* (Bonn, 1981). E. Lechner, *Vita Notkeri Balbuli: Geistesgeschichtlicher Standort und historische Kritik* (Mitteilungen zur Vaterländischen Geschichte, 47; 1972). Raby (1953), pp. 211–15; J. Szövérffy, *Die Annalen der lateinischen Hymnendichtung*, 1 (1964), pp. 282–99; R. L. Crocker, *The Early Medieval Sequence* (Berkeley, Calif., etc., 1977), esp. pp. 1–369. H. F. Haefele in *Verfasserlexikon* (2nd edn.), 6 (1987), cols. 1187–210, s.v. 'Notker I. von St Gallen'.

(2) Editions of his works by P. Piper (Germanischer Bücherschatz, 8–10; Freiburg i.B., and Tübingen, 1882–3), E. H. Sehrt and T. Starck (Altdeutsche Textbibliothek, 32–4, 37, 40, 42–3; Halle, 1933–55), and J. C. King and P. W. Tax (Altdeutsche Textbibliothek, 73–5, 80–1, 84, 87, 91, 93–4, 98, 100, 101, etc. [4 further vols. planned]; Tübingen, 1972 ff.). I. Schröbler, *Notker III von St Gallen als Übersetzer und Kommentator Boethius' De Consolatione Philosophiae* (Hermaea, NF 2; Tübingen, 1953). E. Hellgardt, 'Notkers des Deutschen Brief an Bischof Hugo von Sitten', in K. Grubmüller and others (eds.), *Befund und Deutung* [Festschrift for Hans Fromm] (Tübingen, 1979), pp. 169–92; id., 'Notker teutonicus: Überlegungen zum Stand der Forschung' [I–II], *Beiträge zur Geschichte der deutschen Sprache und Literatur*, 108 (1986), pp. 190–205; 109 (1987), pp. 202–21. J. K. Bostock, *A*

Handbook of Old High German Literature, 2nd edn. rev. by K. C. King and D. R. McLintock (Oxford, 1976), pp. 281–98. Manitius, 2 (1923), pp. 694–9. S. Sonderegger in *Verfasserlexikon* (2nd edn.), 6 (1987), cols. 1212–36, s.v. 'Notker III. von St Gallen'.

Notker (*c*.940–1008), Bp. of Liège. Of a noble Swabian family, he was perhaps educated by St *Bruno, Abp. of Cologne. The 'Annales Hildesheimenses' wrongly state that he was provost of St *Gall. Nominated Imperial chaplain in Italy in 969, he was made Bp. of Liège by the Emp. Otto I in 972 and throughout his life defended German interests both in Italy and Lorraine. He established the temporal sovereignty of the bishops of his diocese, which he embellished with many fine buildings. At the same time he improved the moral and intellectual standard of his clergy and reformed the abbey of Lobbes. He was a great benefactor of the Liège schools, to which he attracted celebrated scholars. The many Lives of saints attributed to him are the works of his friend Abbot Heriger of Lobbes, to which he lent his name. A fine *Evangeliary (Gospel lectionary) now in Musée Curtius at Liège is associated with him.

Works attributed to him in J. P. Migne, *PL* 139. 1135–68. Anonymous Life, written in the late 12th cent. and incorporated in the 13th cent. 'Gesta Episcoporum Leodiensium' of Giles of Orval, ed. J. Heller in *MGH*, Scriptores, 25 (1880), pp. 57–63; also ed., with detailed introd., by G. Kurth in *Compte Rendu des séances de la commission royale d'histoire, ou Recueil de ses bulletins*, 4th ser. 17 (Brussels, 1890), pp. 365–422. G. Kurth, *Notger de Liège et la civilisation au Xe siècle* (2 vols., 1905), with repr. of the Life in vol. 2, pp. 10–15. J. Philippe, *L'Évangéliaire de Notger et la chronologie de l'Art mosan des époques pre-romane et romane* (Académie royale de Belgique, Classe des beaux-arts, Mémoires, collection en 8°, 2nd ser. 10; 1956). C. E. Lutz, *Schoolmasters of the tenth century* (Hampden, Conn., 1977), pp. 93–9. Manitius, 2 (1923), pp. 219–22. É. Amann in *DTC* 11 (pt. 1; 1931), cols. 807–9, s.v.

Notre-Dame, Paris. The cathedral church of Paris. Built in the early French Gothic style on the Île de la Cité on the site of an 8th-cent. building of the same name and occupying a part of the old cathedral of St-Étienne, it was begun in 1163 and consecrated in 1182; and became an accepted model for several other French cathedrals. The W. front was added in 1200–20. The church was desecrated in the French Revolution, when the 'Feast of Reason' was celebrated in it in 1793, but it was reopened for use by the *Constitutional Church (1795–7) and restored to the RC Church in 1802. Victor Hugo's *Notre-Dame de Paris* (1831) awakened a fresh interest in the cathedral and restoration work was begun, from 1845 onwards, under E.-E. Viollet-le-Duc, who made considerable changes. Notre-Dame still has a role in national events.

B. Guérard (ed.), *Cartulaire de l'église Notre-Dame de Paris* (Collection de Documents inédits sur l'Histoire de France, 1st ser., Collection des Cartulaires de France, 4–7; 1850). F. de Guilhermy and E.-E. Viollet-le-Duc, *Description de Notre-Dame, cathédrale de Paris* (1856). *Huitième Centenaire de Notre-Dame de Paris (Congrès des 20 mai–3 juin 1964)*, preface by G. Le Bras (Bibliothèque de la Société d'histoire ecclésiastique de France, 1967). M. Aubert, *Notre-Dame de Paris: Sa place dans l'histoire de l'architecture du XIIe au XIVe siècle* (1920 and later edns.). A. Temko, *Notre-Dame of Paris: The Biography of a Cathedral* (1956); Y. Bottineau, *Notre-Dame de Paris et la Sainte-Chapelle* (1966), pp. 15–123. See also bibl. to PARIS.

Novalis. The pseudonym of **Friedrich Leopold Freiherr von Hardenberg** (1772–1801), the German Romantic poet. To his parents, who belonged to the *Moravian sect, he owed the deep religious strain in his character which he never lost. He was educated at the universities of Jena, Leipzig (where he made friends with F. *Schlegel), and *Wittenberg. His poetic genius, inspired by passion for the girl Sophie von Kühn, found its best expression in the beautiful *Hymnen an die Nacht* (1800), evoked by grief at her early death (1797). His marked leanings towards Catholicism became apparent in this, as also in his essay *Die Christenheit oder Europa* (1799; pub. 1826). Later he studied geology under Prof. A. G. Werner (1750–1817), whom he immortalized as the 'Meister' in one of his two great unfinished prose romances, *Die Lehrlinge zu Sais*. His other chief work, *Heinrich von Ofterdingen*, records much of his spiritual history under the allegory of a search for a mysterious 'blue flower'. He died of phthisis on 25 Mar. 1801.

His works, mostly frags., were ed. by his two associates, Ludwig Tieck and Friedrich Schlegel (2 vols., Berlin, 1802), often repr. Modern edn. by P. Kluckhohn (4 vols., Leipzig [1929]; 2nd edn. by id. and R. Samuel [1960–75]). Correspondence with Friedrich and August Wilhelm, Charlotte and Caroline Schlegel ed. J. M. Raich (Mainz, 1880). Novalis has been the subject of many studies in Germany, esp. from the literary standpoint. T. *Carlyle discusses him in a review of his many collected works in *The Foreign Review*, 3 (1829), pp. 97–141. In Eng., there is a useful introd by J. Neubauer, *Novalis* (Boston, 1980). Life by M. Seidel (Munich [1988]). H.-J. Mähl, *Die Idee des goldenen Zeitalters im Werk des Novalis* (Probleme der Dichtung, 7; Heidelberg, 1965); G. Schulz (ed.), *Novalis in Selbstzeugnissen und Bilddokumenten* (Reinbeck, 1973); N. Saul, *History and Poetry in Novalis and in the Tradition of the German Enlightenment* (Bithell Series of Dissertations, 8; 1984), esp. pp. 71–193. W. *Dilthey, *Das Erlebnis und die Dichtung* (1906), pp. 201–82; H. U. von *Balthasar, *Prometheus: Studien zur Geschichte des deutschen Idealismus* (Heidelberg, 1947), pp. 255–92; K. *Barth, *Die Protestantische Theologie im 19. Jahrhundert* (Zurich, 1947), pp. 303–42; Eng. tr. (1972), pp. 341–83. G. Kranz in *Dict. Sp.* 11 (1982), cols. 471–3; R. S. Furness in *TRE* 24 (1994), pp. 675–8, both s.v.

Novatianism. A rigorist schism in the W. Church which arose out of the *Decian persecution (AD 249–50). Its leader, Novatian, was a Roman presbyter and the author of an important (and completely orthodox) work on the doctrine of the Trinity. Details about the life of Novatian are limited and not entirely consistent. Apparently because he was disappointed by the election of *Cornelius as Pope (251), he joined the rigorist party, which deprecated concessions to those who had compromised with paganism, and was consecrated rival Bp. of Rome. Novatianist views were approved by *Antioch, but rejected by *Dionysius at Alexandria. Novatian himself suffered martyrdom under Valerian in 257–8.

Though doctrinally orthodox, the Novatianists were excommunicated. One of their bishops, Acesius, after accepting the *Nicene decisions on *Arianism and the *Paschal Controversy, was rebuked by *Constantine himself at the Council for persisting in schism. Can. 8 of Nicaea also elaborated the terms on which Novatianists could be received back into Catholic communion. A Novatianist Church persisted into the 5th cent. and, in isolated communities, even later.

The chief authority on Novatian is *Cyprian's 'Epistles'. Of the earlier edns. of the 'De Trinitate', the best is that of J. Jackson in his edn. of Novatian's works (London, 1728), pp. 1–250; this edn. repr. from A. *Gallandi, in J. P. Migne, *PL* 3. 911–82. Modern crit. edn. of Novatian's works by G. F. Diercks (CCSL 4; 1972). Eng. tr. by R. J. DeSimone, OSA (Fathers of the Church, 67; Washington, DC, 1974). A. d'Alès, SJ, *Novatien: Étude sur la théologie romaine au milieu du troisième siècle* (1924) H. J. Vogt, *Coetus Sanctorum: Der Kirchenbegriff des Novatian und die Geschichte seiner Sonderkirche* (Theophaneia, 20; 1968); R. J. DeSimone, OSA, *The Treatise of Novatian the Roman Presbyter on the Trinity* (Studia Ephemeridis 'Augustinianum', 4; Rome, 1970); H. Gülzow, *Cyprian und Novatian: Der Briefwechsel zwischen den Gemeinden in Rom und Karthago zur Zeit der Verfolgung des Kaisers Decius* (Beiträge zur historischen Theologie, 48; 1975). Altaner and Stuiber (1978), pp. 170–2 and 582. H. Koch in *PW* 33 (1936), cols. 1138–56; É. Amann in *DTC* 11 (pt. 1; 1931), cols. 816–49; R. J. DeSimone, OSA, in *Dict. Sp.* 11 (1982), cols. 479–83, s.v. 'Novatien'; id. in *DPAC* 2 (1984), cols. 2434–6, s.v. 'Novaziani'; Eng. tr. in *Encyclopedia of the Early Church*, 2 (1992), p. 604.

Novello, Vincent (1781–1861), Church musician. Born of mixed Italian and English parents, he was appointed organist of the Portuguese Embassy chapel as early as 1797, and from 1840 to 1843 was organist of the RC church in Moorfields. From 1849 till his death he lived at Nice. He was one of the founders of the London Philharmonic Society and of the Choral Harmonists' Society. He is esp. remembered for his editions of sacred music and for his introduction of such great works as the Masses of J. Haydn and W. A. Mozart and the music of G. P. da *Palestrina in England. Among his chief publications were: *A Collection of Sacred Music* (2 vols., 1811), *Twelve Easy Masses* (3 vols., 1816), *The Fitzwilliam Music* (i.e. the Musical MSS in the Fitzwilliam Museum, Cambridge; 5 vols., 1825), *Purcell's Sacred Music* (5 vols., 1828–32).

M. Cowden Clarke (daughter), *The Life and Labours of Vincent Novello* [1864]. *A Mozart Pilgrimage: Being the Travel Diaries of Vincent & Mary Novello in the Year 1829*, transcribed by N. M. di Marignano, ed. R. Hughes (1955). M. [J.] Hurd, *Vincent Novello—and Company* (1981). R. Hughes in S. Sadie (ed.), *The New Grove Dictionary of Music and Musicians*, 13 (1980), pp. 437 f., s.v.

Novena. In the W. Church, a term applied to a period of nine days' private or public devotion, by which it is hoped to obtain some special grace. The general observance of Novenas is quite modern, dating only from the 17th cent., though it is modelled on the nine days' preparation of the Apostles and the BVM for the descent of the Spirit at *Pentecost (Acts 1: 13 f.) and there are other instances of a nine days' preparation earlier. Novenas may be arranged either in circumstances of special peril or need, or as a recurrent devotion, and, in the RC Church, *indulgences have sometimes been attached to their observance.

J. Hilgers, SJ, in *CE* 11 (1911), pp. 141–4, s.v.; P. K. Meagher in *NCE* 10 (1967), pp. 543 f., s.v.

novice. A probationary member of a religious community. The period of probation generally lasts at least a year. During this time the novice is under the authority of the superior, and wears the dress and follows the rule of the community. A novice may be dismissed from the community at any stage of his or her novitiate, and may also leave at any time without incurring ecclesiastical penalties.

Admission to the novitiate, marked by the wearing of the habit of the community for the first time, is known as the 'clothing'. Usually admission to the novitiate takes place only after a period already spent as a '*postulant' (q.v.).

Novum Rubricarum (26 July 1960). The decree of the Sacred Congregation of *Rites instituting several liturgical reforms in the Roman rite, among them a new classification of the feasts and other days of the liturgical calendar, many details in the order and ceremonial of the Mass, and a revision of the regulations governing *Votive Masses. They mark an important stage in the general liturgical reform inaugurated by *John XXIII.

Text in *AAS* 52 (1960), pp. 593–740.

Nowell, Alexander (*c*.1507–1602), Dean of *St Paul's. He was educated at Brasenose College, Oxford, where he became a Fellow in 1536. In *Mary's first Parliament he was returned as the member for Looe, but was not allowed to take his seat on the ground that he was already a member of *Convocation. After some years in exile during Mary's reign he returned on *Elizabeth's accession and in 1560 was appointed Dean of St Paul's. He wrote three 'Catechisms'—the 'Large', the 'Middle', and the 'Small'. The last-named, published in 1573, so closely resembles that of the 1549 BCP that it has been argued that Nowell wrote this as well. The additions of 1604 to the BCP Catechism were certainly taken (by J. *Overall) in substance from Nowell's 'Small Catechism'. The 'Large Catechism' was probably approved by Convocation in 1563, though it was not printed till 1570.

His 'Large Catechism', with Eng. tr. by Thomas Norton, ed. G. E. Corrie (Parker Society, 1853), with biog. introd., pp. i–ix. Life by R. Churton (Oxford, 1809). W. P. Haugaard, 'John Calvin and the Catechism of Alexander Nowell', *Archiv für Reformationsgeschichte*, 61 (1970), pp. 50–65. *BRUO, 1501–1540*, pp. 419–21. W. Hunt in *DNB* 41 (1895), pp. 243–50.

Nubia, Christianity in. In the Nile Valley, from the First Cataract southwards to the area around the modern cities of Khartoum and Omdurman (the N. Sudan region formerly known as Nubia), there was a considerable Christian community from the later 6th to at least the 15th cent. There is some evidence that there were Christians in N. Nubia in the 4th cent., but the formal introduction of Christianity dates from the arrival of missionaries sent by the Emp. *Justinian and his wife *Theodora in 543. The rulers of the three kingdoms of Nobatia, Makuria, and Alodia (or Alwa) were converted, apparently soon to be followed by the greater part of the population; by *c*.580 all three kingdoms were officially Christian. In the 7th cent. they were able to resist the emergent Muslim armies. Early in the 8th cent. the two N. kingdoms of Nobatia and Makuria merged to form a stronger political unit; it was occasionally able to intervene on behalf of *Coptic Christians under Muslim rule in Egypt. From the time of their conversion to the late 12th cent. the Nubian kingdoms prospered. Hundreds of churches were built, mainly in the riverain area, but Christian remains have also been found in the desert at Zangkor, W. of Sennar, and there was possibly a monastery at Ain Farar in Darfur. Nubian artefacts, esp. pottery, were traded over a much wider area. The cathedrals at Faras, Qasr Ibrim, and Dongola are

among many churches excavated since 1960 when N. Nubia was about to be inundated as a result of building the High Aswan Dam. The magnificent frescoes at Faras, which include a list of 27 bishops and are echoed in many churches further south, and the remains of the library at Qasr Ibrim have led to a new appreciation of Nubian Christian culture. At Faras Nubian rulers and metropolitans are finely portrayed and show that in the 10th cent., when Nubia was at the height of its power, even in this most northerly area the leaders of Church and State were dark-skinned indigenous people, not, as was formerly claimed, immigrant Copts.

The Nubian Churches were *Monophysite (with the possible exception of Makuria, which may have been initially *Melchite), the bishops were appointed by the Patr. of *Alexandria, but very little is known of the details of Church life. Greek, Coptic, and Old Nubian seem all to have been used, increasingly the latter, but the form or language of the liturgy is not certain. Inscriptions on grave stelae testify to the presence of Coptic monks. Some pagan temples were converted to Christian use, and many of the churches were tiny, as in Egypt.

In 1172 the Fatimid dynasty in Egypt, which had been tolerant of Christianity and on good terms with Nubia, was overthrown, and a series of raids into Nubia followed. These events signalled the beginning of a long period of decline in Nubia which weakened both Church and State. From the early 14th cent. the kings at Dongola were Muslims but in the 15th cent. there were still Christian kings and bishops in a northern kingdom called Dotawo as well as in the southern kingdom of Alwa. The consecration and enthronement certificates of Timotheos, bishop of Qasr Ibrim, signed by Patriarch Gabriel IV of Alexandria in 1372, survive in Bohairic and Arabic, placed beneath his body in Qasr Ibrim. But by the early 16th cent. Muslim political control was complete and the Christian community slowly faded away. For modern Christianity, see SUDAN, CHRISTIANITY IN.

U. Monneret de Villard, *Storia della Nubia Cristiana* (Orientalia Christiana Analecta, 118; 1938); J. Vantini, *The Excavations at Faras: A Contribution to the History of Christian Nubia* (Museum Combonianum, 24; Bologna [1970]), with discussion of sources and bibl.; id. (ed.), *Oriental Sources concerning Nubia* [tr. into Eng.] (Heidelberg and Warsaw, 1975). P. L. Shinnie, 'Christian Nubia', in J. D. Fage (ed.), *The Cambridge History of Africa*, 2 (1978), pp. 556–88, with bibl., pp. 712–15 and 764–6. W. Y. Adams, *Nubia: Corridor to Africa* (1977), pp. 433–546. K. Michalowski, *Faras, die Kathedrale aus dem Wüstensand* (Zurich [1967]). E. Dinkler (ed.), *Kunst und Geschichte Nubiens in Christlicher Zeit* (Recklinghausen [1970]). C. J. Gardberg, *Late Nubian Sites: Churches and Settlements* (The Scandinavian Joint Expedition to Sudanese Nubia, 7; 1970), pp. 14–40. S. Jakobielski, *A History of the Bishopric of Pachoras on the Basis of Coptic Inscriptions* (Faras, 3; Warsaw, 1972); J. M. Plumley, *The Scrolls of Bishop Timotheos: Two Documents from Medieval Nubia* (Texts from Excavations, 1975 [incl. Eng. tr.]). W. Y. Adams, 'The twilight of Nubian Christianity', in K. Michałowski (ed.), *Nubia: Récentes Recherches. Actes du Colloque Nubiologique international au Musée National de Varsovie 19–22 Juin 1972* (Warsaw, 1975), pp. 11–17; J. M. Plumley, 'The Christian Period at Quasr Ibrim: Some Notes on the MSS Finds', ibid., pp. 101–7; L. P. Kirwan, 'Some Thoughts on the Conversion of Nubia to Christianity', in J. M. Plumley (ed.), *Nubian Studies: Proceedings of the Symposium for Nubian Studies, Selwyn College, Cambridge, 1978* (Warminster, Wilts. [1982]), pp. 142–5; A. Oman, 'Medieval Nubia: Retrospects and Introspects', in P. van Moorsel (ed.), *New Discoveries in Nubia: Proceedings of the Colloqium on Nubian Studies, The Hague, 1979* (Leiden, 1982), pp. 69–90; J. M. Plumley, 'The Christian Period in Nubia as Represented on the Site of Quasr Ibrim', ibid., pp. 99–110.

nullity. In law nullity generally means the absence of legal validity from an act or contract, owing to the omission of an integral requirement or the presence of a fatal flaw.

RC canon law has elaborate rules, and a world-wide system of ecclesiastical tribunals to decide on the nullity of marriages. Acc. to the *CIC* (1983), cans. 1156–60, a purported marriage can be declared null if certain formalities were not complied with, if a *diriment impediment was present, or if the consent of either party was substantially defective. Provided that at least one of the parties acted in good faith, the union remains, even after declaration of nullity, a 'putative marriage' and the children are considered 'legitimate'.

In England, since 1857 the civil courts have exercised jurisdiction in matrimonial causes, and the C of E has submitted, albeit sometimes reluctantly. By the Matrimonial Causes Act 1973, a marriage may be declared null if it is either void *ab initio* (within the *prohibited degrees, either party under 16, lacking certain formal requirements, bigamous, or the parties not respectively male and female), or voidable (not consummated through either incapacity or wilful refusal, defective consent, mental disorder, or undisclosed infectious venereal disease or pregnancy by another man at the date of the marriage). By the Matrimonial Causes Act 1937 (A. P. Herbert's Act), 'No clergyman of the Church of England . . . shall be compelled to solemnize the marriage of any person whose former marriage has been dissolved on any ground and whose former husband or wife is still living or to permit the marriage of any such person to be solemnized in the Church or Chapel of which he is Minister', thus considerably widening the conscience clause in the Divorce and Matrimonial Causes Act 1857. Four Resolutions of Convocation in 1938, promulgated as an Act of Convocation in 1957, converted this civil law dispensation into an ecclesiastical prohibition, and clergy are now forbidden as a matter of discipline from solemnizing such marriages, although in fact many do. The Resolutions provide that 'the Church should not allow the use of (the Marriage) service in the case of anyone who has a partner still living'. Although on the face of it this applies to those whose marriages have been annulled as well as dissolved, it has not in practice been applied to them, even though in the case of non-consummation the reason for annulment arose after the marriage. The report of the Commission appointed by the Abps. of *Canterbury and *York in 1949, *The Church and the Law of Nullity of Marriage* (1955) recommended that non-consummation be recognized as a ground for nullity by the Church, taking it as evidence of incapacity at the time of the marriage. The Law Commission has considered whether to recommend that voidable marriages be subsumed with *divorce cases, but in its 1970 report decided not to do so. See also MATRIMONY.

The RC position and practice, taking account of the changes incorporated in the 1983 revision of the *Codex Iuris Canonici*, is described by R. Brown, *Marriage Annulment in the Catholic Church* (3rd edn., Bury St Edmunds, 1990).

Number of the Beast. The number 666 (or, acc. to some MSS, 616) in Rev. 13: 18. As in both Gk. and Heb. each letter of the alphabet represented a figure as well as a letter, every name could be represented by a number corresponding to the sum of its letters. Innumerable explanations have been given of the cryptogram. The most prob. is that '*Nero Caesar' is intended. In Heb. letters it adds up to 666 (with the form 'Neron') or to 616 (with 'Nero'). This is esp. appropriate for the 'man of sin' (2 Thess. 2: 3) if 666 is read, since here each digit is one less than seven, the perfect number. St *Irenaeus proposed 'Euanthas', 'Lateinos' or 'Teitan' (*Adv. Haer.* 5. 30. 3). The many ingenious attempts to refer it to such persons as Muhammad, M. *Luther, Napoleon, or the Pope may be safely dismissed.

Numbers, Book of. The fourth Book of the *Pentateuch. Its English title, which follows that of the Greek and Latin versions, is explained by its two records of a census (1–4 and 26). The Hebrew title, 'Bemidhbar' (Heb. בְּמִדְבַּר, the fourth word, meaning 'in the wilderness'), is more appropriate, however, as the bulk of the Book narrates the experiences of the Israelites during their wilderness wanderings down to the time of *Joshua's appointment as *Moses' successor. The Book centres on the person of Moses and, besides its main narrative, contains large sections of miscellaneous laws and ceremonial directions. It includes the well-known episodes of the 12 spies (13), of the revolt of Korah, Dathan, and Abiram (16), and of Balaam's mission to Balak (22 f.). To the last of these there are references in the NT (2 Pet. 2: 15, Jude 11, Rev. 2: 14). The form of priestly blessing in 6: 24–6 is frequently used in the Christian Church.

Comm. by G. B. *Gray (ICC, 1903), M. *Noth (Das Alte Testament Deutsch, 7, 1966; Eng. tr., 1968), J. Sturdy (Camb. Bib., NEB, 1976), H. Jagersma (De Prediking van het Oude Testament; 3 vols., Nijkerk, 1983–90), P. J. Budd (Word Biblical Comm. 5; Waco, Tex. [1984]), and E. W. Davies (New Cent. Bib., 1995). J. Milgrom in *Anchor Bible Dictionary*, 4 (1992), pp. 1146–55, s.v.

numinous. A word coined by R. *Otto to denote the elements of a non-rational and amoral kind in what is experienced in religion as the 'holy'. The numinous is thus held to include feelings of awe and self-abasement (at the *Mysterium Tremendum*) as well as an element of religious fascination (the *fascinans*). Otto developed his psychological analyses for the first time in *Das Heilige* (1917; Eng. tr., 1923).

nun. In popular usage, a member of any Religious *Institute of women. In RC canon law, however, the term is correctly used only of members of enclosed orders whose members live in houses, which outsiders are not normally permitted to enter and which the members are only rarely permitted to leave (*CIC* (1983), can. 667).

Nun of Kent. See BARTON, ELIZABETH.

Nunc Dimittis. The Song of *Simeon (Lk. 2: 29–32), so named from its initial words in the *Vulgate version. It has formed part of daily prayers since the 4th cent., its use being already prescribed in the '*Apostolic Constitutions'

(7. 48). In the E. Rite it is said at *Vespers. In the Roman and many other W. breviaries its use is ordered at *Compline, whence it passed to the *Evensong of the BCP and Evening Prayer in modern Anglican liturgies. In the former *Monastic Breviary it found no regular place, but its use at Compline in monastic houses is now recommended in the *Thesaurus Liturgiae Monasticae Horarum* (1977). It is also part of the celebrant's final devotions in the Liturgy of St *Chrysostom, and in the Roman Rite it is sung at the *Candlemas Procession.

S. Farris, *The Hymns of Luke's Infancy Narrative* (Journal for the Study of the New Testament, Supplement Series, 9; Sheffield, 1985).

nuncio. A permanent diplomatic representative of the *Holy See accredited to a civil government, who also acts as a link between Rome and the Church in the State to which he is accredited. The nuncio was originally a fiscal officer, charged with the collection of Papal tithe and other monetary contributions, and only from the time of the *Counter-Reformation have his functions been diplomatic. Nuncios are traditionally deans of the diplomatic corps; where this precedence is not recognized, from 1965 the Holy See appointed a pro-nuncio, with ambassadorial status, but for appointments made after 1993 the distinction has been abolished. The first pro-nuncio in Great Britain was Abp. Bruno Heim, appointed on 22 Feb. 1982. See also APOSTOLIC DELEGATE; LEGATE, PAPAL.

Nuns' Rule. See ANCREN(E) RIWLE.

Nuptial Mass. The wedding Mass which includes the celebration of the marriage and contains the nuptial blessing. It is a *Ritual Mass, consisting of suitable lessons, chants and prayers. According to the present law of the RC Church, a Nuptial Mass may be celebrated even on Sundays and feast days; on these days the Mass of the day is said, though one lesson may be taken from the Nuptial Mass (except on a few feasts of the greatest liturgical importance) and the prayers of the nuptial blessing are inserted. Since 1966 a Nuptial Mass has been permitted at a *mixed marriage, in which both parties are baptized, though the non-RC partner generally may not receive Communion.

Nuremberg Declaration. The statement of belief issued by a group of 14 German Catholic professors and teachers which met at Nuremberg on 25–6 Aug. 1870 in protest against the decrees of the First *Vatican Council on the Papal claims (promulgated 18 July 1870). Those present included J. J. I. von *Döllinger (Munich), J. *Friedrich (Munich), W. C. Reischl (Munich), F. H. *Reusch (Bonn), J. F. von Schulte (Prague). The manifesto denied that the recent Vatican Council was a true *Oecumenical Council, repudiated the relevant chapters of *Pastor Aeternus*, maintained that Papal infallibility would destroy civil liberties, and demanded an unfettered General Council which should meet north of the Alps. The declaration was later signed by 33 professors and teachers, priests and laymen. Its signatories formed the nucleus of the *Old Catholic Movement (q.v.).

The text is in J. F. von Schulte, *Der Altkatholizismus* (1887), pp. 14–16. C. B. Moss, *The Old Catholic Movement* (1948), pp. 227 f.

O

Oak, Synod of the. The synod held under an Imperial order in July 403, at a suburb of *Chalcedon called 'The Oak'. Its object was to remove St *Chrysostom from his see of *Constantinople. Held under the presidency of Paul, the Exarch of Heraclea (390–403), it was attended by 36 (or possibly 45) bishops, of whom all but 7 were from Egypt and all were Chrysostom's enemies. After Chrysostom had been condemned on several fabricated counts, ranging from favouring *Origenism to eating lozenges in church, the Emp. Arcadius (395–408) accepted the synod's decision and exiled Chrysostom to Bithynia. The riotous indignation of the people of Constantinople, together with the occurrence of an earthquake, frightened the Empress and Chrysostom was recalled a few days later.

'Acta' (prob. genuine) survive in *Photius, Cod. 59 (*PG* 103. 105–13). Hardouin, 1, cols. 1037–42; Mansi, 3 (1759), cols. 1141–54; Hefele and Leclercq, 2 (pt. 1; 1908), pp. 137–54. P. Ubaldi, 'La sinodo "ad Quercum" dell'anno 403', *Memorie della Reale Accademia delle Scienze di Torino*, 2nd ser. 52 (1903), Scienze morali, storiche e filologiche, pp. 33–97. See also bibl. to ORIGENISM.

Oakeley, Frederick (1802–80), *Tractarian divine. Educated at Christ Church, Oxford, he was elected to a chaplain-fellowship at Balliol in 1827, where the influence of W. G. *Ward, who became a Fellow in 1834, led to his accepting Tractarian teaching. From 1839 to 1845 Oakeley was in charge of the Margaret Chapel, London, on the site of the present church of All Saints, Margaret Street, and under his ministry the chapel became a centre of Tractarian worship in London. When the rift began to appear in the Oxford Movement, Oakeley was on the pro-Roman side; and on 29 Oct. 1845, three weeks after J. H. *Newman, he was received into the RC Church. Ordained priest in that Church in 1847, he was a canon of the diocese of Westminster from 1852 until his death. His *Historical Notes on the Tractarian Movement* (1865) supplies detail about the Oxford Movement. He was a frequent contributor to the *British Critic* and *Dublin Review*.

In March 1880 Oakeley contributed 'Personal Recollections of Oxford from 1820 to 1845' to *The Month*, repr. in L. M. Q. Couch (ed.), *Reminiscences of Oxford* (Oxf. Hist. Soc. 22; 1892), pp. 301–45. There is no Life, but he figures extensively in the lit. of the Oxford Movement, e.g. in Wilfrid Ward, *W. G. Ward and the Oxford Movement* (1889), *passim*. C. R. Beazley in *DNB* 41 (1895), pp. 286 f.

O-Antiphons (also known as the **Greater Antiphons**). The *antiphons sung before and after *Magnificat at *Vespers, acc. to Roman use, on the seven days preceding Christmas Eve, i.e. from 17 to 23 Dec. The name is derived from their initial 'O'—'O Sapientia', 'O Adonai', 'O Radix Jesse', 'O Clavis David', 'O Oriens', 'O Rex gentium', and 'O Emmanuel'. The *Sarum Use began the Antiphons on 16 Dec., and provided an additional 'O' for 23 Dec. ('O Virgo virginum'), and this arrangement is reflected by the insertion of 'O Sapientia' for 16 Dec. in the calendar of the BCP. The authorship and date of composition of the Antiphons are alike unknown; but they were already in use by the 8th cent.

H. Thurston, SJ, 'The Great Antiphons. Heralds of Christmas', *The Month*, 106 (1905), pp. 616–31; A. Weber, 'Die sieben O-Antiphonen der Adventsliturgie', *Pastor Bonus*, 19 (1906–7), pp. 109–19; C. Callewaert, 'De groote Adventsantifonen O', *Liturgisch Tijdschrift*, 2 (1911–12), pp. 1–13, repr. in id., *Sacris Erudiri* (1940), pp. 405–18, with further bibl.; J. A. Cabaniss, 'A Note on the Date of the Great Advent Antiphons', *Speculum*, 22 (1947), pp. 440–2. A. Hollaardt, OP, in *LW* 2 (1968), cols. 1914–17, s.v., with further bibl.

Oates, Titus (1649–1705), conspirator. The son of a *Baptist preacher, Oates owes his notoriety to the part he played in the '*Popish Plot'. In the unsettled state of the times he managed to inflame public opinion by spreading stories of alleged RC intrigues to assassinate *Charles II and place his brother, *James, on the throne. The public panic lasted from 1678 to 1681, and many innocent persons were condemned and executed on his false testimony.

T. Seccombe, 'Titus Oates', in id. (ed.), *Lives of Twelve Bad Men* (1894), no. 5, pp. 95–154. J. Lane [pseudonym for E. Dakers], *Titus Oates* (1949), with refs. and bibl. T. Seccombe in *DNB* 41 (1895), pp. 296–303.

oath. Several Christian bodies, e.g. the *Waldensians, *Baptists, *Mennonites, and *Quakers, have interpreted Mt. 5: 33–7 as forbidding every oath; but the prohibition is more generally understood as primarily directed against the habit of promiscuous and unnecessary swearing such as prevailed among the Jews in the time of Christ.

Acc. to general Christian teaching, an oath, though not desirable, may be required by human weakness and is admissible for reasons of serious necessity. It must be concerned only with what one knows to be true, its object must be morally good, and in order to be valid it must be taken with the intention to swear. The taking of an oath is often surrounded with solemnity, ecclesiastical oaths, e.g., being sworn before the Crucifix and accompanied by the touching of the Gospel Book. An oath may be either assertory, i.e. referring to a fact past or present, or promissory, relating to the future; and in important matters it is held by moral theologians to be binding under grave sin.

J. E. Tyler, *Oaths: Their Origin, Nature and History* (1834). E. B. Tylor in *EB* (11th edn.), 19 (1911), pp. 939–43, s.v.; N. Iung in *DTC* 14 (pt. 2; 1941), cols. 1940–56, s.v. 'Serment'.

Oath of Allegiance. See ALLEGIANCE, OATH OF.

Obadiah, Book of. One of the *Minor Prophets and the shortest Book of the OT. It foretells the punishment of the Edomites, the traditional foes of the Jews, in the coming Day of the Lord. Reference to the destruction of *Jerusalem in v. 11 would seem to require a date later than 586 BC for the final compilation of the Book, but modern scholars tend to divide it into a number of sections, which are variously dated from the 9th to the 5th cent. BC. The similarities between vv. 1–15 and Jer. 49: 7–22 have suggested that one passage is dependent upon the other, unless both derive from an independent earlier prophecy.

Comm. by J. A. Bewer (ICC on Micah, Zeph., Nah., Hab., Obad., and Joel, 1912; sep. pagination), J. H. Eaton (on Obad., Nah., Hab., and Zeph., London, 1961, pp. 35–48), J. D. W. Watts (Camb. Bib., NEB, on Joel, Obad., Jon., Nah., Hab., and Zeph., 1975, pp. 51–71), and H. W. Wolff (*Dodekapropheton*, 3, Biblischer Kommentar, Altes Testament, 14/3, Neukirchen, 1977, on Obad. and Jon., pp. 1–51; Eng. tr., Minneapolis, 1986, pp. 17–71). W. Rudolph, 'Obadja' in *ZATW* 49 (1931), pp. 222–31; G. Fohrer, 'Die Sprüche Obadjas', in *Studia Biblica et Semitica Theodoro Christiano Vriezen . . . dedicata* (Wageningen, 1966), pp. 81–93. P. E. Bonnard in *Dict. Bibl.*, Suppl. 8 (1972), cols. 693–701, s.v. 'Prophètes d'Israël', with bibl.; P. R. Ackroyd in *Anchor Bible Dictionary*, 5 (1992), pp. 2–4, s.v.

obedience. The moral virtue which inclines a person to carry out the will of his lawful superior. Its exercise is necessary for the upholding of the order established in the world by both natural and positive law. Absolute obedience is due only to God, whereas obedience to men is limited by the bounds of authority and by the claims of conscience. Spiritual writers distinguish three degrees of lawful obedience: mere external obedience; willing submission to an order though its wisdom may be doubted; and blind obedience, i.e. submission of the personal judgement to that of the superior, except, of course, in cases of obviously sinful commands. Obedience is enjoined by Christ (Jn. 15: 10), who by His perfect obedience unto death (Phil. 2: 8, Heb. 5: 8) is its supreme example. It came to be one of the three *vows by which a religious binds himself to obey his superiors acc. to the rule and constitutions of his order or congregation. Acc. to RC canon law, an oath of fidelity is required from bishops, parish priests and others on taking up office to be exercised in the name of the Church. Anyone who persists in not obeying the lawful command of the Apostolic See or the Ordinary or Superior is to be punished. In the C of E every cleric before *institution to a benefice is required to take an oath of obedience to the Bishop of the Diocese in all things lawful and honest.

obedientiary. A now almost obsolete name of the permanent officials in a monastery, appointed by a superior. It was used, e.g., of the sacristan, the cantor, the cellarer, etc., but generally not of the prior and sub-prior.

Oberammergau, in Upper Bavaria. In 1633 the villagers vowed that if God would rid them of the plague, they would at 10-year intervals enact a play recalling Christ's Passion and Resurrection. Performances took place every 10 years from 1634 to 1674 and in the decimal years from 1680, except when war or political conditions led to postponement (1810 to 1811, 1870 to 1871, and 1920 to 1922) or prevented production in 1940. There were additional performances in 1801, 1815, 1934, and 1984. The play has been rewritten a number of times. The present text is based on the work of Othmar (1769–1843), written for the 1811 performance and revised for that of 1815, and further revised by Joseph Alois Daisenberger for the presentations of 1850 and 1860. Since 1815 the play has been accompanied by oratorio-style music, composed by

Rochus Dedler (1779–1850), rearranged in 1950. It became increasingly popular in the 19th cent., and is now seen by audiences of over 6,000, who are under cover, the stage being open. It is performed five times a week during the summer. In two parts, it takes over 5 hours to enact, with as many as 850 people on the stage, plus 100 musicians and some animals. It comprises recitation, music from choir and orchestra, and tableaux (incl. 17 from the OT), as well as straight acting.

The text of the play, which differs somewhat for each year's production, is issued at Oberammergau. Trs. into Eng. and other langs. are available. H. Diemer, *Oberammergau und seine Passionsspiele* (Munich and Oberammergau [1900]; Eng. tr., Munich, 1900; 4th edn., 1930). J. Bentley, *Oberammergau and the Passion Play: A Guide and History to mark the 350th Anniversary* (Harmondsworth, 1984). S. Schaller, OSB, *350 Jahre Passionsspiele Oberammergau* (Oberammergau, 1984; in Ger. and Eng., with 40 colour photographs). S. S. Friedman, *The Oberammergau Passion Play: A Lance against Civilization* (Carbondale and Edwardsville, Ill., 1984).

Oberlin, Jean Frédéric (1740–1825), *Lutheran pastor, educationist, and philanthropist. Born and educated at Strasbourg, Oberlin was pastor of Waldersbach (Ban de la Roche) in the Vosges from 1767 until his death. His people were poor, isolated, and demoralized; Oberlin ministered faithfully to them all, incl. the Reformed and the Catholics. Having won their trust, he transformed the parish, initiating schemes of road and bridge building, introducing lending and savings banks and promoting new agricultural techniques. He established schools in the five villages and was a pioneer in kindergarten work based on child psychology.

Eclectic in outlook and indebted to both the *Enlightenment (esp. J.-J. *Rousseau) and to mysticism (esp. E. *Swedenborg), he welcomed the French Revolution, with its republicanism and attack on privilege, and he tried to combine patriotic clubs with Christian worship; he was briefly imprisoned in 1794. His social and educational methods soon won international recognition; in particular, his principles of infant education were developed by Pestalozzi. He is commemorated by the Oberlin House in Potsdam and Oberlin College, Oberlin, Ohio.

Life and collected Works ed. E. Hilpert and others (4 vols. bound in 2, Stuttgart, 1843), with *Gedenkschrift* in vol. 1, Life by E. Stöber in vols. 2–3. The many other Lives incl. those by J. E. *Butler (London, 1882), A. Stein (Halle, 1899), C. Leenhardt (Montauban, 1911), W. Kambli (Zurich, 1927), A. Stucki (Basle, 1945), J. P. Benoit (Strasbourg, 1955), W. Heinsius (Lahr/Schwarzw., 1956), and A. Katterfeld (Berlin, 1960). E. Parisot, *Jean Frédéric Oberlin (1740–1826): Essai pédagogique* (Nancy thesis; Paris, 1905); H. Strohl, *Études sur Oberlin* (Cahiers de la Revue d'histoire et de philosophie religieuses, 13; 1926); M. Buch, *Die pädagogischen und sozialpädagogischen Ideen Johann Friedrich Oberlins* (1932).

oblate (Lat. *oblatus*, 'offered'). The word has several ecclesiastical senses. (1) In the early Middle Ages, it was esp. applied to children dedicated to a monastery by their parents and placed there to be brought up. (2) Later, after this practice had been abandoned, it became widely used of laity who lived at a monastery or in close connection with it, but who did not take full religious vows. (3) In modern times it has been adopted in the title of certain communities of the RC Church, e.g. the 'Oblates Regular of St Benedict' (see following entry), the 'Oblates of Mary Immaculate' (founded 1816) and the 'Oblates of St *Charles Borromeo' (founded by H. E. *Manning, 1857).

M. P. Deroux, *Les Origines de l'oblature bénédictine* (Vienne, 1927). U. Berlière, OSB, *La Familia dans les monastères bénédictins du Moyen Âge* (Académie Royale de Belgique, Classe des Lettres et des Sciences Morales et Politiques, Mémoires, Collection in-8°, 29, fasc. 2; 1931). J. Marchal, *Le 'Droit d'Oblat': Essai sur une variété de pensionnés monastiques* (Archives de la France monastique, 49; 1955). P. Hofmeister, OSB, 'Die Klaustral-Oblaten', *Studien und Mitteilungen zur Geschichte des Benediktiner-Ordens*, 72 (1961), pp. 5–45. J. Dubois, OSB, and others in *DIP* 6 (1980), cols. 654–76, s.v. 'Oblato'; G.-M. Oury, OSB, in *Dict. Sp.* 11 (1982), cols. 566–71, s.v. 'Oblature'. See also comm. on the Rule of St *Benedict, cited s.v., on ch. 59; also works cited s.v. LAY BROTHER.

Oblates Regular of St Benedict. The 'Oblates of Mary' were founded by St *Frances of Rome (q.v.) in 1425 as an association of noble Roman ladies, affiliated to the White *Benedictines ('*Olivetans') of Sta Maria Nuova (afterwards Sta Francesca Romana). In 1433, with the approval of *Eugenius IV, St Frances formed them into the Oblate Congregation of Tor de' Specchi, at the foot of the Capitol, Rome, where they still reside. Following her adaptation of the Benedictine Rule, they give themselves to prayer and good works, but without vows, strict enclosure, or giving up their property, and they make revocable promises of obedience to the Mother President.

M. B. Rivaldi in *DIP* 6 (1980), cols. 585–8, s.v. 'Oblate del Monastero di Tor de' Specchi'.

oblations (Lat. *oblationes, oblata*; Gk. προσφορά). In Christian usage, the term is applied both to the bread and wine offered for consecration in the Eucharist, and also to any other kind of gift (e.g. grapes, oil, cheese, altar cloths, etc.) presented by the faithful at Mass for the use of the clergy, the sick, the poor, the church, etc. In the Prayer for the Church Militant in the BCP, oblations, as distinguished from 'alms', originally meant money to be devoted to other purposes than the relief of the poor, but the authority of Bp. Simon *Patrick (1626–1707) can be invoked for interpreting 'oblations' here as meaning bread and wine. See also OFFERTORY.

J. Dowden, ' "Our Alms and Oblations": An Historical Study', *JTS* 1 (1899–1900), pp. 321–46; repr., with additions, in id., *Further Studies in the Prayer Book* (1908), pp. 176–222.

Obligation, Feasts of. See FEASTS OF OBLIGATION.

O'Bryan, William. See BIBLE CHRISTIANS.

obscurantism. Active opposition, esp. from supposedly religious motives, to intellectual enlightenment. Christians have sometimes been charged with it by secular critics, and professing Christians have also sometimes made the charge against one another, but it has rarely, if ever, been admitted. The word probably derives ultimately from the famous *Epistolae Obscurorum Virorum* (1515–17).

Observantines (Fratres de Observantia, also Observants). Those members of the *Franciscan Order who wanted to 'observe' the Rule of St *Francis strictly and with no relaxation. The movement started in Italy in 1368 as a protest against the decline in religious life and discipline and drew its inspiration largely from the *Spiritual Franciscans and early Papal pronouncements about the Rule. In 1517, after a protracted struggle, they were separated from the *Conventuals and declared the true Order of St Francis. In the 16th cent. they were further divided into the Reformed ('Riformati'), the *Recollects, and the *Discalced or Alcantarines, all of whom acknowledged the authority of the Minister General but kept their own constitutions. These were all incorporated in 1897 into the single Order of Friars Minor by *Leo XIII's bull 'Felicitate quadam'. A fourth group, the *Capuchins, broke away completely in 1528. See also CONVENTUALS, CAPUCHINS, and FRANCISCAN ORDER.

The other *Mendicant Orders had similar movements.

Bernardin of Aquila, OFM, *Chronica Fratrum Minorum Observantiae*, ed. L. Lemmens, OFM (Rome, 1902). D. Nimmo, *Reform and Division in the Medieval Franciscan Order from Saint Francis to the Foundation of the Capuchins* (Bibliotheca Seraphico-Capuccina, 33; Rome, 1987), pp. 109–658, *passim*. See also other works cited under FRANCISCAN ORDER.

Occam, William of. See WILLIAM OF OCKHAM.

Occasional Conformity Act. The commonly used name for the Toleration Act 1711, part of which was designed to restrain Nonconformists who had received Communion in the C of E in order to to qualify for Government posts from subsequently attending dissenting places of worship. It laid down that if after 25 March 1712 any civil or military officer in receipt of a salary, who had been obliged to receive Communion, should after admission to office be discovered at a conventicle, he should forfeit £40, cease to hold office, and no longer be eligible for any employment in England. If, however, the convicted person conformed to the C of E for one year after his conviction, then his eligibility for office was restored. An earlier bill against occasional conformity (imposing still larger penalties) had been introduced into the Commons in 1702 and succeeding years, but always rejected by the Whig Lords. The Act of 1711 proved a failure in operation; and in 1719, to conciliate the Nonconformists, the offending part was repealed by the Religious Worship Act 1718.

Principal clauses of the Act in W. C. Costin and J. S. Watson (eds.), *The Law and Working of the Constitution: Documents 1660–1914*, 1 (1952), pp. 118–21.

Occasional Offices. In the BCP, the services which, in distinction from the constant offices of the Church (namely *Mattins and *Evensong and the *Holy Communion), are used only as occasion may demand. They include *Baptism, *Confirmation, *Matrimony, *Visitation of the Sick, Communion of the Sick, Burial of the Dead, and the *Commination.

Occasional Prayers. In the BCP, the collection of 11 prayers prescribed for use 'upon several [i.e. appropriate] occasions' 'before the two final prayers of the Litany, or of Morning and Evening Prayer'. They include prayers for use in various times of adversity, two for the *Ember

Weeks, and the 'Collect and Prayer for all Conditions of Men'. They first appeared in their present position at the 1661 revision of the BCP. In modern Anglican liturgies the number of such occasional prayers is greater.

Occasionalism (Lat. *occasio*, 'event'). The philosophical theory of the relation of mind to matter which denies that finite things have efficient causality and postulates that God always intervenes to bring about a change in matter when a change occurs in mind and vice versa. Anticipated in medieval philosophy, it was formulated in the 17th cent. to avoid the difficulties confronting the dualism of R. *Descartes. Among its principal exponents were A. *Geulincx (d. 1669) and N. *Malebranche (d. 1715); in the latter it assumed a form very near to *pantheism. It never had any considerable following and soon suffered eclipse by G. W. *Leibniz's doctrine of 'Pre-established Harmony'. In the 19th cent. a form of Occasionalism was revived by Hermann Lotze (1817–81).

J. Prost, *Essai sur l'atomisme et l'occasionalisme dans la philosophie cartésienne* (1907). M. Fakhry, *Islamic Occasionalism and its Critique by Averroës and Aquinas* (1958). M. Gueroult, *Malebranche*, 2 (1959), esp. pp. 208–57. F. R. Tennant in *HERE* 9 (1917), pp. 443 f.; M. R. Holloway in *NCE* 10 (1967), pp. 624 f., both s.v. See also bibl. to GEULINCX, A., and MALEBRANCHE, N.

occurrence. The falling of two feasts (or other commemorations) on the same day in the ecclesiastical calendar, e.g. the coincidence of *Christmas Day with a Sunday. In the W. Church the feast of higher rank is kept in such cases. The inferior one used normally to be 'commemorated' by the recitation of its proper *collect after that of the greater feast, but in some cases, where the one feast was of very high rank, the lesser was always entirely unnoticed. When the feast displaced was a Sunday or other great holy day, its service was read on the first free day following. Commemorations are now made only when the feast of a saint of universal significance occurs during *Lent or the later part of *Advent (17–24 Dec.), and then only at the option of the celebrant.

Ochino, Bernardino (1487–1564), Protestant Reformer. A native of Siena, he joined the *Observantine Franciscans and rose to be their general. In 1534 he transferred to the still more austere *Capuchins, of whom he was twice (in 1538 and 1541) the vicar-general. His preaching was so eloquent and moving that *Charles V said of him, 'That man is enough to make the stones weep.' Contact with *Peter Martyr (Vermigli) led him to accept Protestant doctrines, and in 1541 he became a *Lutheran. He was cited before the *Inquisition, but escaped to Geneva. From 1545 to 1547 he was minister to the Italian Protestants at Augsburg. In the latter year T. *Cranmer invited him to England and secured for him a Prebend of *Canterbury and a royal pension, and Ochino gave himself up to writing *The Usurped Primacy of the Bishop of Rome* and the *Labyrinth*, the latter attacking the *Calvinistic doctrine of *Predestination. On *Mary's accession he returned to Switzerland and in 1555 was appointed a pastor at Zurich, but on account of his *Thirty Dialogues* (1563), which proved him unsound on the doctrine of the *Trinity and on monogamy, he was expelled from his office. He then

went to Poland, but was not allowed to remain there, and died at Slavkow (Austerlitz) in Moravia.

I 'Dialogi sette' e altri scritti del tempo della fuga, ed., with introd. and bibl., by U. Rozzo (Turin, 1985). Life by C. Benrath (Leipzig, 1875; 2nd edn., 1892; Eng. tr. by H. Zimmern, 1876); this work contains a full analysis and list of Ochino's writings. R. H. Bainton, *Bernardino Ochino* (Florence, 1940). P. McNair and J. Tedeschi, 'New Light on Ochino', *Bibliothèque d'Humanisme et Renaissance*, 35 (1973), pp. 289–301. C. Cargnoni in *Dict. Sp.* 11 (1982), cols. 575–91, s.v.

Ockham, William of. See WILLIAM OF OCKHAM.

O come, all ye faithful. See ADESTE FIDELES.

O come, O come, Emmanuel. See VENI, VENI, EMMANUEL.

O'Connell, Daniel (1775–1847), Irish statesman. Educated at the colleges of *St-Omer and *Douai (1792), he returned to England in 1793, entered Lincoln's Inn in the following year, and was called to the Irish bar in 1798. In 1800 he made his first appearance on a public platform, on behalf of the Irish Catholics, denouncing the Union. He soon became a successful lawyer, married in 1802, and from 1805 began to gain more and more influence as a Catholic leader. In 1813 he opposed the Bill of Emancipation introduced by H. Grattan which contained the royal veto for the election of bishops, a condition unacceptable to both Irish clergy and people though favoured by RCs in England. The next years saw a long-drawn-out struggle between O'Connell and the government, which suppressed all Catholic organizations. In 1823, however, O'Connell formed the *Catholic Association with the object of securing Catholic emancipation by legal means. It quickly spread throughout the country and became so powerful an instrument that it was proscribed in 1825. But it continued its work under other names and under the leadership of O'Connell, who, in 1828, was returned as MP for Clare by the disciplined votes of the 40-shilling freeholders. The Roman Catholic Emancipation Act (see CATHOLIC RELIEF ACTS) followed in the next year. O'Connell now led his own parliamentary party, while also conducting successive movements to repeal the Union. He fought against Lord Grey's Coercion Bill of 1833 and, in 1840, after five years of alliance with Lord Melbourne's government, founded his Repeal Association. In 1841–2, he was Lord Mayor of Dublin, an office he filled impartially. In 1843 he resumed his agitation for Repeal, holding 'monster meetings' of which the most famous was that on the Hill of Tara. In the same year he was arrested on a charge of conspiracy, and in 1844, after trial, condemned to a year's imprisonment. Though freed on appeal to the House of Lords, his health had suffered, and henceforward his policy, which wavered between Repeal and Federalism, lacked firmness. He also quarrelled with the Young Ireland Party. Acclaimed as the 'Liberator' by his countrymen, O'Connell's influence on Irish history was profound. A brilliant popular orator, he was also the skilful and pragmatic politician who created modern Irish constitutional nationalism.

Life and Speeches of Daniel O'Connell, ed. J. O'Connell (son) (2 vols., Dublin, 1846); *Correspondence of Daniel O'Connell*, ed.

M. R. O'Connell [great-great-grandson] (8 vols., Shannon, 1972–80). A. Houston, *Daniel O'Connell: His Early Life, and Journal, 1795–1802* (1906). S. O'Faoláin, *King of the Beggars: A Life of Daniel O'Connell . . .* (1938). A. [D.] Macintyre, *The Liberator: Daniel O'Connell and the Irish Party 1830–47* (1965). K. B. Nowlan, *The Politics of Repeal* (1965), *passim*. L. J. McCaffrey, *Daniel O'Connell and the Repeal Year* ([Lexington] Ky., 1966). K. B. Nowlan and M. R. O'Connell (eds.), *Daniel O'Connell: Portrait of a Radical* (Belfast, 1984). O. MacDonagh, *The Hereditary Bondsman: Daniel O'Connell 1775–1829* [1988]; id., *The Emancipist: Daniel O'Connell 1830–47* [1989]. R. Dunlop in *DNB* 41 (1895), pp. 371–89.

Octateuch (Gk. ὀκτα-, 'eight', + τεῦχος, 'book'). The first eight Books of the OT, i.e. the *Pentateuch with the three additional Books of *Joshua, *Judges, and *Ruth.

Octavarium. A collection of lessons, supplementary to those of the *Breviary, for use in the 2nd and 3rd *Nocturns of the *Mattins of *Octaves which were of only local observance.

Octave (Lat. *octava*, sc. *dies*, 'eighth day'; formerly used only in the plural). In Christian liturgical usage, the eighth day after a feast, reckoning inclusively, and so always falling on the same day of the week as the feast itself. The term is also applied to the whole period of these eight days, during which the observance of certain major feasts came to be continued.

The practice was prob. suggested by the OT usage of an eighth-day celebration of the 'Feast of Tabernacles' (Lev. 23: 36) and the 'Dedication of the Temple' (2 Chr. 7: 9), and first introduced under *Constantine (d. 337), when the dedication festivities of the basilicas at *Jerusalem and Tyre were extended over the same period. The first liturgical feasts to be dignified with an Octave were *Easter, *Pentecost, and, in the E., *Epiphany, the reason being possibly to provide a time of recollection for the newly baptized. From the 7th cent. saints' feasts also began to have Octaves, among the oldest being those of Sts *Peter and *Paul, St *Laurence, and St *Agnes, which were long observed in the Roman rite. From the 12th cent., however, the custom was introduced of observing also the days between the first and the eighth day as well as the eighth day itself. The number of feasts with Octaves was also greatly increased during the Middle Ages; they were reduced, however, by the Breviary reforms of Popes *Pius V and *Pius X. By a decree of the Congregation of *Rites dated 23 Mar. 1955, all Octaves were suppressed in the Latin rite except those of *Christmas, Easter, and Pentecost and the last of these was suppressed in 1969.

G. Löw, CSSR, in *EC* 9 (1952), cols. 451–3, s.v. 'Ottava'.

Octoechos (Gk. ὀκτώηχος [βίβλος], 'the book of eight tones'). A liturgical book in the E. Church which contains the variable parts of services on Sundays and weekdays when these services are not taken wholly from one of the other service books - the *Triodion, the *Pentecostarion, or the *Menaion. There are eight sets of tones (ὀκτὼ ἦχοι), one for each week, these variable parts recurring every eight weeks in the same order; hence the name. The cycle of tones begins on the Sunday after *Easter. This book is also known as the *Paracleticē* (Gk. παρακλητική, from παρακαλεῖν, to supplicate).

L. Tardo, *L'antica melurgia bizantina* (Grottaferrata, 1938), pp. 363–84. *The Hymns of the Octoechus* transcribed by H. J. W. Tillyard (Monumenta Musicae Byzantinae, 3, 5; Copenhagen, 1940–9). O. Strunk, 'The Antiphons of the Oktoechos', *Journal of the American Musicological Society*, 13 (1960), pp. 50–67. A. Cody, OSB, 'The early history of the Octoechos in Syria', in N. G. Garsoïan, T. F. Mathews, and R. W. Thomson (eds.), *East of Byzantium: Syria and Armenia in the Formative Period* (Dumbarton Oaks Symposium 1980; Washington, DC, 1982), pp. 89–113. I. Thomas in *NCE* 10 (1967), pp. 640 f., with bibl.

Oda, St (d. 959), 'Oda the Good', sometimes mistakenly also 'Odo', Abp. of *Canterbury. He is said to have been the son of a Dane and originally a pagan. In 927 he became Bp. of Ramsbury. On Abp. Wulfhelm's death in 942, Oda at first declined the see of Canterbury offered him by King Edmund, on the ground of not being a monk; but on the king's persistence he received the *Benedictine habit from *Fleury and accepted the office. He was very active in restoring the cathedral buildings and in raising the morals and discipline of the clergy. He was also a staunch defender of the privileges of the Church. Feast day, 4 July.

Text of the 'Constitutions', a set of 10 chapters dealing with matters of discipline and morals which Abp. Oda caused to be drawn up, and other material, are conveniently pr. in D. Whitelock, M. Brett, and C. N. L. Brooke (eds.), *Councils & Synods with other Documents Relating to the English Church*, I: A.D. 871–1204, 1 (Oxford, 1981), pp. 65–74. Life by *Eadmer is repr. in *PL* 133. 933–44, where, however, it is wrongly ascribed to Osbern. More reliable information is to be found scattered in the contemporary Life of his nephew, St *Oswald, Abp. of York (q.v.). N. Brooks, *The Early History of the Church of Canterbury* (Leicester, 1984), pp. 222–37.

ode. See CANTICLE.

Odes of Solomon. See SOLOMON, ODES OF.

Odilia, St (d. *c.*720), also 'Othilia', the patroness of Alsace. She is said to have been the daughter of Adalricus, a Frankish lord, and been born blind but later miraculously received her sight. Having been granted by Adalricus his castle at Hohenburg (now the Odilienberg) above Obernai in the Vosges Mountains, she founded a large nunnery which she ruled as Abbess. In the Middle Ages the abbey was granted exceptional privileges and became a famous centre of pilgrimage (visited by *Charlemagne, Pope *Leo IX and perhaps Richard I of England). In the last 100 years it has again been much visited. The water of the well is said to cure diseased eyes. Feast day, 13 Dec.

Crit. edns. of 10th-cent. Life (of little historical value) by C. Pfister in *Anal. Boll.* 13 (1894), pp. 5–32, and W. Levison in *MGH*, Scriptores Rerum Merovingicarum, 6 (1913), pp. 24–50, with useful introd. C. Pfister, *Pages alsaciennes* (Publications de la Faculté des Lettres de l'Université de Strasbourg, 40; 1927), pp. 87–119 ('La Légende de sainte Odile'), with refs. to the earlier works of the author. M. Barth, *Die heilige Odilia, Schutzherrin des Elsass: Ihr Kult in Volk und Kirche* (Forschungen zur Kirchengeschichte des Elsass, 4–5; 1938). H. *Leclercq, OSB, in *DACL* 12 (pt. 2; 1936), cols. 1921–34, s.v. 'Odile'; R. V. Doren and A. M. Raggi in *Bibliotheca Sanctorum*, 9 (1967), cols. 1110–16, s.v., with full bibl.

Odilo, St (961/2–1049), fifth Abbot of *Cluny. He entered the monastery in 991 and became abbot three years later. He was a man of high virtue as well as of great administrative abilities, under whose government the number of Cluniac houses rose from 37 to 65 and their influence spread throughout Christendom. The order was further strengthened by his plan of centralization, whereby most of the reformed monasteries were made directly dependent on Cluny. Odilo spent much of his time travelling in the interests of the Church and of his order, being highly esteemed by both Popes and Emperors; and the establishment of the '*Truce of God' for the South of France and Italy was largely his work. He has left a permanent mark on the Liturgy by introducing the commemoration of *All Souls' Day (2 Nov.), which, at first a local observance at Cluny, was soon extended to the whole W. Church. Though severe with himself he was gentle with others, and the great famines of the time, esp. between 1028 and 1033, gave scope to his charity, which saved many from death. He was canonized in 1063. Feast days, 1 or 2 Jan.; in the order, 29 Apr.

Collection of St Odilo's works in M. Marrier, OSB (ed.), *Bibliotheca Cluniacensis* (Paris, 1614; repr., 1915), cols. 338–408, with extracts of the Life by his disciple Iotsaldus, monk of Cluny, cols. 1813–24, and Life by *Peter Damian, cols. 315–32; works, with Life by Iotsaldus and other biog. material, repr. from L. *d'Achery, OSB, J. *Mabillon, OSB, and T. *Ruinart, OSB (eds.), *Acta Sanctorum Ordinis Sancti Benedicti*, 6 (pt. 1; Paris, 1701), pp. 631–710 (text of Life by Iotsaldus, pp. 679–710), in J. P. Migne, *PL* 142. 831–1038. E. Sackur, 'Handschriftliches aus Frankreich, II. Zu Iotsaldi *Vita Odilonis* und Verse auf Odilo', *NA* 15 (1889), pp. 117–26, with texts. Id., 'Ein Schreiben Odilo's von Cluni an Heinrich III vom Oktober 1046', ibid. 24 (1899), pp. 728–35, also with text. Crit. edn. of excerpts of Life by Iotsaldus by G. Waitz in *MGH*, Scriptores, 15 (pt. 2; 1888), pp. 813–20. *Liber tramitis aevi Odilonis Abbatis*, ed. P. Dinter (Corpus Consuetudinum Monasticarum, 10; Siegburg, 1980). J. Hourlier, OSB, *Saint Odilon, abbé de Cluny* (Bibliothèque de la Revue d'Histoire Ecclésiastique, 40; 1964). Id. in *Dict. Sp.* 11 (1982), cols. 608–13, s.v. 'Odilon'. See also bibl. to CLUNY.

odium theologicum (Lat., 'theological hatred'). A proverbial expression for the ill-feeling to which theological controversy frequently gives rise.

Odo, St (c.879–942), Abbot of *Cluny. The son of Abbo, a Frankish knight of Maine, he was born at Tours and brought up in the family of William, Duke of Aquitaine, who later (909/910) founded the abbey of Cluny. At the age of 19 he was instituted to a canonry at St Martin's, Tours, and then made his way to Paris, where he studied under *Remigius of Auxerre. After returning to Tours he was deeply affected by reading the Rule of St *Benedict and three years later gave up his canonry and was admitted by St Berno to the monastery of Baume (909). On the foundation of Cluny in the next year, Berno put Odo in charge of the monastery school at Baume. In 927 he succeeded Berno as Abbot of Cluny, where he was mainly instrumental in raising the monastery to the high position it held in the next centuries. During his abbacy the monastic church of SS. Peter and Paul was completed and the influence of Cluny over other monasteries was greatly extended, largely through a privilege of John XI (931). On his first visit to Rome (936) he took an important part in the conflict between Hugh, 'King of Italy', and the Patrician Alberic, and also won over several Italian monasteries

(S. Maria on the Aventine, *St Paul's outside the Walls, *Monte Cassino, *Subiaco) to Cluniac principles. His writings include a Life of Gerald of Aurillac, three books of moral essays ('Collationes'), some sermons, an epic ('Occupatio') on the Redemption, and twelve choral antiphons in honour of St *Martin. Feast day, 18 Nov. (by the Benedictines, 29 April).

Collection of his works pr. in M. Marrier, OSB (ed.), *Bibliotheca Cluniacensis* (Paris, 1614; repr. 1915), cols. 65–264, with Life of St Odo by his disciple, John, monk of Cluny, ibid., cols. 13–56; further collection of his works, from various sources, repr. in J. P. Migne, *PL* 133. 105–845, with Life by John, cols. 43–86, and 12th-cent. Life by Nalgodus, monk of Cluny, cols. 85–104 (both repr. from L. *d'Achery, OSB and J. *Mabillon, OSB (eds.), *Acta Sanctorum Ordinis Sancti Benedicti*, 5 (1685), pp. 150–99). Odo's 'Occupatio' was first ed. A. Swoboda (Teub., 1900). Eng. tr. of Odo's Life of Gerald of Aurillac and of John of Cluny's Life of Odo by G. Sitwell, OSB, *St Odo of Cluny* (1958). E. Sackur, 'Handschriftliches aus Frankreich', I. Zur Vita Odilo Abbatis Cluniacensis auctore Iohanne', *NA* 15 (1889), pp. 105–16. Modern Life by [A.] du Bourg, OSB ('Les Saints', 1905). A. Hessel, 'Odo von Cluni und das französische Kulturproblem im früheren Mittelalter', *HZ* 128 (1923), pp. 1–25. *A Cluny: Congrès scientifique. Fêtes et cérémonies liturgiques en l'honneur des saints abbés Odon et Odilon 9–11 juillet 1949. Travaux du congrès, Art, Histoire, Liturgie, publiés par la Société des Amis de Cluny* (Dijon, 1950), *passim*. B. [F.] Hamilton, 'The Monastic Revival in Tenth Century Rome', *Studia Monastica*, 4 (1962), pp. 35–68, esp. pp. 47–9; repr. in id., *Monastic Reform, Catharism and the Crusades* (1979), no. 2. J. Hourlier, OSB, in *Dict. Sp.* 11 (1982), cols. 620–4, s.v. 'Odon' (5), with bibl. See also bibl. to CLUNY.

Odo, St (d. 959). A corrupted form of *Oda, St (q.v.).

Odo (b. c.1030 or c.1035; d. 1097), Bp. of Bayeux. He was a uterine half-brother of *William I, the Conqueror, who gave him the see of Bayeux while Odo was still a young man (1049/50). He was present at the Battle of Hastings (14 Oct. 1066). In 1067 he became Earl of Kent and for several years he was an active and trusted minister of William I. He appropriated many ecclesiastical lands which he distributed among his supporters until *Lanfranc secured their restoration to the see of Canterbury. In 1080 Odo was sent north to punish the Northumbrians for the murder of Walcher, Bp. of *Durham. In 1082 he fell into disgrace, apparently for having planned a military expedition to Italy, and was kept in prison until William was on his deathbed (1087). After his release he returned to Kent and under Rufus organized a rebellion designed to put his nephew, Duke Robert, on the throne (1088). When it failed he finally left his English estates and returned to Normandy. He set out with Robert on the First *Crusade in Sept. 1096, but died at Palermo the following year.

Even in Normandy Odo was much engaged in temporal affairs, and in England his career was entirely that of a secular baron. But he had a good reputation as a bishop, and even *Ordericus Vitalis, though hostile to Odo, noted that virtues and vices were mixed in him. He developed the capitular organization and probably the cathedral school of his see, and supported monastic reform; he founded the priory of St Vigor outside Bayeux, colonizing it with monks from *Mont-St-Michel. He was a lavish patron of scholars and craftsmen; he rebuilt his cathedral (dedicated in 1077) and very probably commissioned the *Bayeux Tapestry.

There are references in E. A. Freeman, *The History of the Norman Conquest of England* (6 vols., 1867–79), F. M. Stenton, *Anglo-Saxon England* (1943; 3rd edn., 1971), and S. E. Gleason, *An Ecclesiastical Barony of the Middle Ages: The Bishopric of Bayeux, 1066–1204* (Harvard Historical Monographs, 10; 1936), esp. pp. 8–17. D. C. Douglas (ed.), *The Domesday Monachorum of Christ Church, Canterbury* (1944), esp. pp. 33–6, 54–8; id., 'The Norman Episcopate before the Norman Conquest', *Cambridge Historical Journal*, 13 (1957), pp. 101–15, *passim*; D. R. Bates, 'The Character and Career of Odo, Bishop of Bayeux (1049/50–1097)', *Speculum*, 50 (1975), pp. 1–20. C. L. Kingsford in *DNB* 41 (1895), pp. 424–6; J. Brownbill in G. E. Cockayne, *The Complete Peerage*, 2nd edn. by V. Gibbs and others, 7 (1929), pp. 124–9.

Oecolampadius, Johannes

Oecolampadius, Johannes (1482–1531), Reformer. His real name was 'Hussgen'. A native of Weinsberg in Württemberg, he studied in Heidelberg, Bologna, and Basle, acquiring a very good knowledge not only of theology but also of Greek and Hebrew. In 1515 he helped J. *Froben with the printing of *Erasmus' Greek–Latin New Testament and he wrote the notes at the end of it. In 1516 he was appointed cathedral preacher in Augsburg. In order to avoid having to take up a position on the ideas of M. *Luther, he entered a *Bridgettine monastery in 1520, but left it in 1522 to throw in his lot with the Reformers. On his return to Basle in the same year, his influence led to the adoption by the city of Reformation principles, which were accepted by the Canton of Berne in 1528. In the latter year he also married. At the Colloquy of *Marburg (1529) he defended the Eucharistic doctrine of U. *Zwingli. Of a retiring and tolerant disposition, Oecolampadius is thought to be the first Reformer to have advocated lay participation in Church government. His ideas on this subject were rejected in Basle; it is a matter of debate whether they had a direct influence on J. *Calvin.

E. Staehelin (ed.), *Briefe und Akten zum Leben Oekolampads* (vol. 1, 1499–1526, Quellen und Forschungen zur Reformationsgeschichte, 10; vol. 2, 1527–93, ibid. 19; 1927–34). Life by W. *Capito prefixed to his edn. of Oecolampadius' Comm. on Ezek. (Strasbourg, 1534 [no pagination]); also to the edn. of *Ioannis Oecolampadii et Huldrichi Zwinglii Epistolae* (Basle, 1536 [no pagination]); Eng. tr. in [H. Bennet], *A Famous and Godly History* (1561 [no pagination]). Modern Lives by J. J. *Herzog (2 vols., Basle, 1843) and K. R. Hagenbach (Leben und ausgewählte Schriften der Väter und Begründer der reformirten Kirche, 2, 1859, pp. 3–306). E. Staehelin, *Das theologische Lebenswerk Johannes Oekolampads* (Quellen und Forschungen zur Reformationsgeschichte, 21; 1939). [E.] G. Rupp, *Patterns in Reformation* (1969), pp. 1–46. K. Hammer, 'Oecolampads Reformprogramm', *Theologische Zeitschrift*, 37 (1981), pp. 149–63. H. R. Guggisburg 'Johannes Oekolampad', in M. Greschat (ed.), *Reformationszeit*, 1 (Gestalten der Kirchengeschichte, 5; 1981), pp. 117–28. E. Staehelin, *Oekolampad-Bibliographie* (2nd edn., Nieuwkoop, 1963). U. Gäbler in *TRE* 25 (1995), pp. 29–36, s.v. 'Oekolampad, Johannes', with bibl.

Oecumenical Councils

Oecumenical Councils (Gk. οἰκουμένη, 'the whole inhabited world'). Assemblies of bishops and other ecclesiastical representatives of the whole world whose decisions on doctrine, cultus, discipline, etc., are considered binding on all Christians. Acc. to the teaching of most Christian communions outside the RC Church there have been no Oecumenical Councils since the schism between E. and W., the last being the second of *Nicaea in 787. Acc. to present RC *canon law (*CIC* (1983), cans. 337–41, 749)

the Pope alone has the right to convene an Oecumenical Council, to preside over it (in person or through deputies), and to approve its decrees. As the oecumenicity of a Council is now held to depend on the co-operation of the Pope, the *Conciliar theory that there can be an appeal from the Pope to a Council is inadmissible. If the Apostolic See becomes vacant during a Council, it is interrupted until a new Pope orders it to be continued or dissolves it. Only bishops now have the right to take part in an Oecumenical Council with a deliberative vote; others may be called to it and the degree of their participation is then determined *ad hoc*. Under certain conditions the college of bishops gathered in an Oecumenical Council is held to possess infallible teaching authority.

Seven Councils are commonly held both in E. and W. to be oecumenical. These are, with their dates and the chief subjects dealt with: (1) *Nicaea I (325, *Arianism); (2) *Constantinople I (381, *Apollinarianism); (3) *Ephesus (431, *Nestorianism); (4) *Chalcedon (451, *Eutychianism); (5) *Constantinople II (553, *Three Chapters Controversy); (6) *Constantinople III (680–1, *Monothelitism); (7) Nicaea II (787, *Iconoclasm).

The RC Church reckons the following 14 further Councils as possessing oecumenical authority: (8) Constantinople IV (869–70, *Photian Schism); (9) *Lateran I (1123, *Investiture Controversy); (10) Lateran II (1139, *Arnold of Brescia, etc.); (11) Lateran III (1179, Papal elections, etc.); (12) Lateran IV (1215, *Waldenses, etc.); (13) *Lyons I (1245, *Frederick II); (14) *Lyons II (1274, Reunion, etc.); (15) *Vienne (1311–12, *Templars); (16) *Constance (1414–17, *Great Schism—the oecumenicity of the Council before the election of *Martin V is disputed); (17) *Basle–*Florence (1431–45, Reform and Union with the Greeks); (18) Lateran V (1512–17, Reform); (19) *Trent (1545–63, *Protestantism and Reform); (20) *Vatican I (1869–70, Papal Infallibility, etc.); (21) *Vatican II (1962–5, Renewal of the Church).

In the C of E the *Thirty-Nine Articles assert that General Councils 'may err, and sometimes have erred, even in things pertaining unto God', and that what they ordain is to be tested by reference to Scripture (Art. 21). The *Reformatio Legum Ecclesiasticarum* (1553) states that General Councils are regarded with honour and that the decisions of the first Four in particular are 'accepted and received with great reverence' (*De Summa Trinitate et Fide Catholica*, ch. 14). By s. 36 of the Act of *Supremacy 1558 the powers of those assigned to correct ecclesiastical abuses were limited in matters of heresy by the decisions of the first Four Councils and the authority of the Canonical Scriptures. R. *Hooker and L. *Andrewes uphold the authority of the first Four, while the *Book of Homilies* ('against Peril of Idolatry', pt. 2), R. *Field and H. *Hammond accept the first Six. It appears, however, that such Councils are ultimately revered in the C of E on the ground that their decisions are acceptable rather than vice versa.

Decrees of the Councils, with Eng. tr. and introd., in Tanner, *Decrees* (1990). G. Tangl, *Die Teilnehmer an den allgemeinen Konzilien des Mittelalters* (Weimar, 1932). H. Chadwick, 'The Origin of the Title "Oecumenical Council"', *JTS* NS 23 (1972), pp. 132–5. See also bibl. to individual Councils.

Oecumenical Patriarch

Oecumenical Patriarch (Gk. οἰκουμενικὸς πατριάρχης,

lit. 'patriarch of the whole inhabited world'). The style borne by the Abps. or Patrs. of *Constantinople since the 6th cent. It was occasionally used also of other prelates from the middle of the 5th cent. Its exact significance is nowhere officially defined, but the title has been attacked in the W. as incompatible with the claims of the see of Rome.

Oecumenius (6th cent.), author of the oldest extant Greek Comm. on Rev., to whom tradition has assigned the designations 'Rhetor' and 'Philosopher'. Little is known of his life, but he appears to have been a contemporary and supporter of *Severus of Antioch. His Comm., one of but three on the Apocalypse in Greek from the first millennium, was rediscovered by F. Diekamp and published by H. C. Hoskier in 1928. The exposition, vigorous, modest, but uneven, accepts the Apocalypse as a divinely inspired canonical Book, relevant not only for its immediate situation but for the understanding of the past and the future. It cites no earlier Comm., but its authorities include St *Athanasius, St *Basil, St *Gregory of Nazianzus, and *Evagrius Ponticus. This 6th-cent. expositor is not to be confused with Oecumenius, Bp. of Tricca in Thessaly (10th cent.), to whom Comm. on Acts and the Pauline and Catholic Epistles (printed in *PG* 118–19) have been ascribed. Fragments from Comm. on the Pauline Epistles in the *catenae*, ascribed to Oecumenius of Tricca, may, however, belong to the author of the Comm. on Rev.

H. C. Hoskier (ed.), *The Complete Commentary of Oecumenius on the Apocalypse* (University of Michigan Studies, Humanistic Series, 23; 1928). F. Diekamp, 'Mittheilungen über den neuaufgefundenen Commentar des Oekumenius zur Apokalypse', *Sb.* (Berl.) (1901) (2), pp. 1046–56; id., 'Neues über die Handschriften des Oekumenius-Kommentares zur Apokalypse', *Biblica*, 10 (1929), pp. 81–4. Frags. from *catenae* are pr. by K. Staab, *Pauluskommentare aus der griechischen Kirche* (Neutestamentliche Abhandlungen, 15; 1933), pp. 423–69. A. Spitaler, 'Zur Klärung des Ökumeniusproblems', *Oriens Christianus*, 3rd ser. 9 (1934), pp. 208–15; additional notes by J. Schmid, ibid., pp. 216–18. J. Schmid, 'Ökumenios der Apokalypsen-Ausleger und Ökumenios der Bischof von Trikka', *Byzantinisch-neugriechische Jahrbücher*, 14 (1938), pp. 322–30. *CPG* 3 (1979), pp. 394 f. (nos. 7470–5).

Oekonomos, Constantinos. See OIKONOMOS, CONSTANTINE.

Oengus, St (8th–9th cent.), Irish saint, commonly, though perhaps erroneously, called the *Culdee, author of the Félire, or verse *martyrology, known by his name. The traditional account of his career is based on a Middle Irish poem appended to one copy of this. He was educated and spent the later part of his life in the community at Clonenagh, Co. Laoise, and in the nearby hermitage of Dísert Bethech. At some point he joined the fraternity of Tallaght, nr. Dublin, where he collaborated with St Máel Rúain (d. 792) on the compilation of the Martyrology of Tallaght, a prose catalogue of saints, including many Irish ones, which is the oldest of the Irish martyrologies, and which was a major source for his own. Both martyrologies in their extant form can be dated *c.*800, or more likely *c.*830. Feast day, 11 March.

W. Stokes (ed.), *Félire Oengusso Céli Dé: The Martyrology of Oengus the Culdee* (HBS 29; 1905), with Eng. tr. and notes. Biog. poem, with Eng. tr., ibid., pp. xxiv–xxvi. 'The Life and Works of St Aengusius Hagiographus, or St Aengus the Culdee', *Irish Ecclesiastical Record*, 5 (1869), pp. 1–29, 73–81, and 97–108. R. Thurneysen, 'Die Abfassung des Félire von Oengus', *Zeitschrift für celtische Philologie*, 6 (1907), pp. 6–8; P. Ó Riain, 'The Tallaght Martyrologies, Redated', *Cambridge Medieval Celtic Studies*, 20 (1990), pp. 21–38.

Offa (d. 796), King of the Mercians from 757. He gained the Mercian throne after a short civil war which followed the death of Ethelbald, and he gradually secured dominion, either directly or as overlord, over other parts of England south of the Humber, including Kent, Sussex, and East Anglia. It seems that he lost control of Kent (and perhaps of Sussex as well) following the Battle of Otford in 776, but his authority in the south-east was reestablished by 785. Yet despite the extent of his power, he was styled no more than *rex Merciorum* in his charters and on his coins. The surviving portions of Offa's Dyke, constructed for the control of his frontier with the Welsh, are an index of the great resources at his disposal. He corresponded with *Charlemagne, and his dealings with Pope *Hadrian I led to a visit of two Papal legates to England in 786 and to the creation of a new archbishopric at *Lichfield in 787 (suppressed in 803); also in 787 his son Ecgfrith (d. 796) was anointed king—the first recorded consecration of an English king. Offa formed an enmity with Jaenberht, Abp. of *Canterbury (765–92), but he was remembered in many quarters as a generous benefactor of the Church; he is the reputed founder of the abbeys of *St Albans and *Bath.

Charters of King Offa are listed, with reference to their places of pub. and comments, in P. H. Sawyer, *Anglo-Saxon Charters: An Annotated List and Bibliography* (Royal Historical Society Guides and Handbooks, 6; 1968), pp. 98–109 (nos. 104–47); several are forgeries. Eng. tr. of docs. from his reign in D. Whitelock (ed.), *English Historical Documents c.500–1042* (2nd edn., 1979), pp. 836–51 (nos. 191–8), incl. the report of Hadrian's legates and letters of Charlemagne and Alcuin to Offa. F. M. Stenton, *Anglo-Saxon England* (Oxford History of England, 2; 3rd edn., 1971), pp. 202–38. N. Brooks, *The Early History of the Church of Canterbury* (Leicester, 1984), pp. 111–23.

Offertory. In the Eucharistic liturgy:

(1) The worshippers' offering of the bread and wine (and water) to be consecrated. In the Roman and derived rites, including the Anglican liturgy, it takes place at a relatively late point in the service (after the lections and the Creed), i.e. at what was originally the beginning of the 'Mass of the Faithful'. Until recently it was normally performed by the celebrant on behalf of the people; at Milan, however, representatives of the people (*Vecchioni) continued to offer the gifts, and in the current Roman rite a group of the laity bring the bread and wine, as well as other gifts including money, to the altar while a chant is sung. In the E. rites, the offertory, with its elaborate cutting up and arranging of the bread, takes place at the *prothesis at the outset of the whole service (see *Proskomide), the elements being solemnly brought to the altar at the '*Great Entrance' (ἡ μεγάλη εἴσοδος).

(2) The word is also used for the short anthem, first mentioned in St *Augustine (*Retract.* 2. 11), formerly sung in the Roman rite at the time of the act of offering. Originally a whole psalm, by the 8th cent. it had been reduced to one or two verses and it came to consist (except at

*Requiem Masses) of only an antiphon, proper to each Mass. It is now frequently replaced by a hymn or other chant.

Full discussion, with bibl. refs., in Jungmann (1958 edn.), 2, pp. 3–125; Eng. tr., 2, pp. 1–100. R. Cabie in A. G. Martimort, *L'Église en Prière* (édition nouvelle), 2 [1983], pp. 93–101, 174–181, and 219–23; Eng. tr. (1986), pp. 76–84, 157–64, and 203–7. A. Clark, 'The Function of the Offertory Rite in the Mass', *EL* 64 (1950), pp. 309–44. R. Berger, *Die Wendung 'Offerre pro' in der römischer Liturgie* (Liturgiewissenschaftliche Quellen und Forschungen, 41; 1964). K. [W.] Stevenson, 'L'Offrande Eucharistique. La Recherche sur les origines établit-elle une difference du sens?', *Maison Dieu*, 154 (1983), pp. 81–106. P. Tirot, OSB, 'Histoire des Prières d'Offertoire dans la liturgie romaine du VIIᵉ au XVIᵉ siècle', *EL* 98 (1984), pp. 148–97 and 323–91. F. *Cabrol, OSB, in *DACL* 12 (pt. 2; 1936), cols. 1946–62, s.v. 'Offertoire'; A. C. Clark in *NCE* 10 (1967), pp. 649–51, s.v. See also bibl. to SACRIFICE.

Office, Divine (*Officium Divinum*). The daily public prayer of the Church, also called in the RC Church since the Second *Vatican Council the 'Liturgy of the Hours'. Its recitation at stated times differentiates it from other liturgical services.

The Divine Office developed slowly and it is only in the 4th cent. that its main outlines can be clearly discerned. The practice of saying prayers at fixed hours was general among the Jews and was doubtless taken over by the first Christians, though the hours of prayer may not have been identical and the content would certainly have been different. It would seem from the first that parts of the Psalter were used in Christian prayer (cf. Acts 4: 23–30), and that such prayer was Christological cannot be doubted. The writer of the *Didache* (8) urged that the Lord's Prayer be recited three times a day, though he does not specify these times and his recommendation does not exclude the likelihood that other prayers were added to it. In the 2nd and 3rd cents. the practice of praying night and morning, as well as at the third, sixth, and ninth hours was known in both E. and W. (*Clement of Alexandria, *Origen, *Tertullian, *Cyprian, and perhaps *Hippolytus); if these were private prayers they were not individualistic and were sometimes at least said in families or small communities. Tertullian seems to have thought that morning and evening prayer was so customary as to be obligatory (*Orat.* 25).

The early monks ('Desert Fathers') sought to implement the NT injunction to pray constantly by making their prayer ceaseless. They used very long sections of the Psalter at a time, and different groups of monks sometimes took over from one another, so that prayer went on day and night. This practice influenced the organization of the Office by St *Basil in the E. and *Cassian in the W., and ultimately the whole Church. The monastic Offices of the hours of the night and day came into existence: namely *Mattins and *Lauds, *Terce, *Sext, *None, *Vespers, and *Compline. *Prime, it would seem, originated in the vicinity of *Bethlehem and was adopted by Cassian.

At the same time in cathedrals and non-monastic churches there was a simpler pattern of morning and evening prayer which the laity as well as the clergy were encouraged to attend. Fewer Psalms were used and they were chosen for their suitability to the time of day. In some places a reading from the Bible and/or a homily might be included. There were intercessions and a final prayer. From the 5th cent. the great basilicas of Rome were served by monastic communities; these added to morning and evening prayer both the other day hours and the Night Office or Vigils. It was on this Office of the Roman basilicas that St *Benedict based the Office of his Rule, in which he included *responsories, *antiphons, *hymns, and an ordered course of biblical readings, as well as redistributing the Psalms. This Benedictine Office in turn influenced the cathedral Office and led to a gradual development of liturgical prayer throughout the W. Church. By the 8th cent. the cycle of Day Hours and Mattins (or Night Office) had become the general pattern for all the clergy, secular as well as monastic. The Roman basilicas, however, retained much of their own tradition. Hymns were admitted into their Office only in the 12th cent. and the course of readings was different from that used elsewhere. The Papal Curia, however, developed a shorter Office. Because of the growing prestige of the Papacy and its Curia, by the end of the 12th cent. this curial Office came to be regarded as that of the Roman Church. St *Francis of Assisi adopted it for his friars and its use was propagated throughout Europe, though local traditions survived.

In principle the whole Psalter was to be recited each week and the course of readings was to include most of the Bible, but since various elements in the Office (antiphons, responsories, hymns, canticles, and prayers) differed acc. to the day or season, a large number of books was needed to recite the Office. The difficulty was partly overcome by arranging the texts in one, two, or three volumes; from this arrangement the *Breviary developed. The process led to the reduction in the length of biblical readings. The proliferation of saints' days (with their own Psalms) interfered with the recitation of the Psalter, while the 'legends' of saints tended to displace the Scripture readings. By the end of the Middle Ages the Office was in some confusion.

In the early 16th cent. attempts at reform were made, notably by Cardinal F. de *Quiñones, but his Breviary (*Breviarium S. Cruce*) was never formally adopted in the RC Church. The Council of *Trent ordered the abolition of the more apocryphal legends, and the *Breviarium Romanum* issued by *Pius V in 1568 made it possible to recite the whole Psalter in a week by reducing the number of saints' days which interrupted the ferial Office. In 1911 *Pius X shortened the Office by redistributing the Psalms and again altered the rubrics so that only the more important feasts were allowed to interfere with the regular recitation of the Psalter.

A complete reordering of the Offices in the RC Church was achieved by the *Liturgy of the Hours* issued by *Paul VI in 1971. This provides for an *Office of Readings, which may be said at any time during the day, Lauds, a midday Office (see TERCE, SEXT, NONE), Vespers, and Compline, which is to be said before retiring. The Psalter (apart from three Psalms omitted altogether) is distributed over a month, and most parts of the Bible (except the Gospels, which are included in the Mass lectionary) are read every year. There are also readings from the Fathers and later writers. The general shape of the Offices follows the traditional pattern, though the hymn now always comes at the beginning of the Office; in Lauds and Vespers a short responsory has been introduced after the reading and these two Offices now always include 'Preces' or Prayers, in the case of Vespers of an intercessory character.

All RC priests and deacons aspiring to the priesthood, as well as all professed religious whose rule requires it, are obliged to the daily recitation of the Office. Clerics with pastoral responsibility are urged to arrange that at least some of the Offices are recited in church and the laity are encouraged to attend. Various religious orders (now technically known as Religious *Institutes) have their own Offices which differ somewhat from the Roman, esp. in the matter of saints' days, and some religious are also bound to recite a Night Office. See also BREVIARY; MONASTIC BREVIARY; and under individual Offices.

In the C of E at the Reformation the traditional Offices were combined into Morning and Evening Prayer (Mattins and *Evensong). In addition to the changes introduced into these services by modern revisions of the BCP, in recent years there has been some restructuring of the Office in some parts of the Anglican Communion, e.g. provision for Noonday Prayer in the American BCP (1979). Anglican religious orders have used a number of Offices, largely based on those of the RC Church.

J. Grancolas, *Commentaire historique sur le bréviaire romain* (2 vols., 1727). F. *Probst, *Brevier und Breviergebet* (1854); P. *Batiffol, *Histoire du bréviaire romain* (1893; Eng. tr., 1898); S. *Bäumer, OSB, *Geschichte des Breviers* (1895; Fr. tr. with addition by R. Biron, OSB, 2 vols., 1905); C. Callewaert, *De Breviarii Romani Liturgia* (2nd edn.; Liturgicae Institutiones, 2; Bruges, 1939); J. Pascher, *Das Stundengebet der römischen Kirche* [1954]; J. A. Jungmann, SJ (ed.), *Brevier Studien* [1958]; P. Salmon, OSB, *L'Office divin: Histoire de la formation du bréviaire* (1959); id., *L'Office divin au moyen âge: Histoire de la formation du bréviaire du IX⁶ au XVI⁶ siècle* (1967). S. J. P. van Dijk, OFM, and J. Hazelden Walker, *The Origins of the Modern Roman Liturgy: The Liturgy of the Papal Court and the Franciscan Order in the Thirteenth Century* (1960); Mgr. Cassien, B. Botte, OSB, and others, *La Prière des heures* (Lex Orandi, 35; 1963); J. D. Crichton, *Christian Celebration: The Prayer of the Church* [1976]; C. [P.] Jones, G. Wainwright, and E. [J.] Yarnold, SJ (eds.), *The Study of Liturgy* (1978), pp. 350–402 (2nd edn., 1992, pp. 399–454); P. F. Bradshaw, *Daily Prayer in the Early Church: A Study of the Origin and Early Development of the Divine Office* (*Alcuin Club Collections, 63; 1981); id., 'Cathedral vs. Monastery: The Only Alternative for the Liturgy of the Hours?', in J. N. Alexander (ed.), *Time and Community: In Honor of Thomas Julian Talley* (Washington, DC [1990]), pp. 123–36. R. Taft, SJ, *The Liturgy of the Hours in East and West: The Origin of the Divine Office and its Meaning for Today* (Collegeville, Minn. [1986]). M. Righetti, UJD, *Manuale di storia liturgica*, 2 (2nd edn., 1955), pp. 471–715. P. Salmon in A. G. Martimort, *L'Église en Prière* (3rd edn., 1965), pp. 809–902, and A. G. Martimort in op. cit. (1983–4 edn.), 4, pp. 169–293 (Eng. tr., 1986, pp. 151–275), with bibl.

Office, Holy. See HOLY OFFICE.

Office Hymns. *Hymns appear as a fixed part of the Monastic Office already in the Rule of St *Benedict, though they were not generally used in the Roman liturgy until the 12th cent. The 1568 *Breviary provided a hymn to be sung at *Mattins (except during the last days of *Holy Week and a few other occasions) and at the Little Hours before, and at *Lauds, *Vespers, and *Compline after, the Psalms. The hymns of the Little Hours and Compline were substantially the same throughout the year; those of the other hours varied acc. to feast and season. The 1971 Breviary places the hymns before the Psalms in

all the offices; it provides two series of hymns for use at each office, which in the case of Lauds and Vespers are to be used on alternate weeks, in the case of the *Office of Readings acc. to whether the Office is said in the day or at night; and it allows conferences of bishops to introduce new hymns.

Many ancient Office Hymns are contained (in English versions) in modern hymnals, e.g. 'Lucis Creator Optime' ('O Blest Creator of the Light'; from Sunday Vespers), 'Te lucis ante terminum' ('Before the Ending of the Day'; from Compline), '*Pange lingua gloriosi Corporis mysterium' ('Of the glorious Body telling'; from the Vespers of *Corpus Christi).

Office of Readings. The Office in the 1971 *Breviary which replaced *Mattins. It may be said at any time of the day. It opens with a versicle and response, followed by the *Invitatory (if it is the first Office of the day). A hymn is recited; then come three Psalms (or one Psalm divided into three parts) with antiphons, and two Lessons or Readings. The first of these Readings is taken from Scripture, the second from the works of one of the Fathers or some other Christian writer; on the feast of a saint it may come from a Life of the saint commemorated. There are responsories after the Lessons. On Sundays and greater feasts the *Te Deum follows. The Office ends with the collect for the day.

Official Principal (also **Official**). In Anglican ecclesiastical law, the person to whom a bishop formerly entrusted the exercise of his coercive jurisdiction. Since the bishop had the right of sitting with the Official Principal in the court (a practice in fact seldom adopted), it became known as the '*Consistory Court' (the two together forming *unum consistorium*). Under the *Ecclesiastical Jurisdiction Measure 1963 the office is now combined with that of *Chancellor in a single judge. Against his sentence there is no appeal to the bishop.

Acc. to RC canon law, every diocesan bishop is normally bound to appoint (in addition to his *vicar general) an *officialis* or judicial vicar, who constitutes one tribunal with the bishop but cannot judge cases which the bishop reserves to himself (*CIC* (1983), can. 1420).

For bibl. See CHANCELLOR.

Oikonomos, Constantine (1780–1857), Greek scholar and theologian. A keen Greek patriot, his ecclesiastical career was more than once interrupted by political activities. He was the author of a very long and elaborate work on the *Septuagint entitled Περὶ τῶν ο΄ Ἑρμηνευτῶν (i.e. *On the Seventy Interpreters*, 4 vols., Athens, 1844–9) which, though setting out from wrong premisses (e.g. belief in the inspired character of the Septuagintal text as against the Hebrew), contains many valuable investigations. Oikonomos also wrote several works on philology and the history of literature. He made it one of his chief aims to oppose W. influences, which had assumed increasing prominence in Greek religious life since the middle of the 18th century.

Works partly repr. by his son, S. Oikonomos (3 vols., Athens, 1862–6). A. Papaderos, *Metakenosis: Griechenlands kulturelle Herausforderung durch die Aufklärung in der Sicht des Korais und des Oikonomos* (Archiv für vergleichende Kulturwissenschaft, 6;

Meisenheim am Glan, 1970). P. Meyer in *PRE* (3rd edn.), 14 (1904), pp. 299–304, s.v. 'Oekonomos'.

oils, holy. See CHRISM.

Olav, St (995?–1030), **Olav Haraldsson**, patron saint of *Norway and King from 1016 to 1028. After some years raiding the English and French coasts, he was baptized at Rouen. Shortly afterwards, in 1015, he returned to Norway and, by defeating Earl Svein at the battle of Nesjar in 1016, became King. At the time Christianity was still struggling to gain a foothold in the country. Olav's wholehearted support was to prove decisive in the long run, but the harshness of his methods provoked resistance; the nobles rallied around Canute the Great and Olav was forced to flee to Russia. When he tried to regain his kingdom in 1030, he was killed at the battle of Stiklestad (north of Trondheim). After only a year he was regarded as a saint. His shrine at Nidaros (Trondheim) was a famous place of pilgrimage in the Middle Ages. Feast day, 29 July.

He is not to be confused with **Olav Tryggvason**, King of Norway, 995–9.

Life by Øystein [Augustine], Abp. of Trondheim (1161–88), pr. in *AASS*, Jul. 7 (1731), pp. 113–15; more complete edn., with useful introd., by F. Metcalfe, *Passio et Miracula Beati Olaui* (Oxford, 1881). The Saga of St Olave written by Snorre Sturlason (1172–1241) has been pr. several times as part of his *Heimskringla*, e.g. in the edn. of F. Jónsson, as vol. 2 (Copenhagen, 1896); Eng. tr. by E. Monsen and A. H. Smith (Cambridge, 1932), pp. 218–474. An expanded version of various Olav Sagas was ed. O. A. Johnsen and J. Helgason (Norsk Historisk Kjeldeskrift-Institut, 2 vols., Oslo, 1941). Modern Life (in Norwegian) by V. Henriksen (Oslo, 1985). *St Olav, seine Zeit und sein Kult* (Acta Visbyensia, 6: Visbysympositet för historiska vetenskaper, 1979; Visby, 1981). F. B. Wallem and B. I. Larsen, *Iconographia Sancti Olavi* (Det kgl. Norske Videnskabers Selskabs Skrifter 1930, no. 1; Trondheim, 1947). B. Dickins, 'The Cult of S. Olave in the British Isles', *Saga-Book of the Viking Society*, 12 (1945), pp. 53–80, with refs. G. Turville-Petre, *The Heroic Age of Scandinavia* (1951), pp. 140–64.

Old Believers. The section of the Russian Orthodox Church which, under the leadership of the Archpriest Avvakum (1620/1–81), refused to accept the liturgical reforms of the patriarch *Nikon (d. 1681). They were excommunicated in 1667, called 'Raskolniki', i.e. schismatics, and violently persecuted, esp. during the first 80 years of the schism and again under Nicholas I (1825–55). They included a great body of peasants and many of the more devout priests, and received large reinforcements when Peter the Great (1682–1725), whom they believed to be the Antichrist, tried to Europeanize Russia. Since no bishops seceded from the Established Church, however, they were left without a hierarchy and split up into two sections: the one, called 'Popovtsy', who sought means of establishing their own priesthood, the other, 'Bezpopovtsy', who denied its necessity. The former had to be content with the ministrations of discontented priests coming to them from the Orthodox Church until, in 1846, a deposed bishop, Ambrose of Bosnia, joined them and established a hierarchy. From that time the Popovtsy steadily increased in number and importance (though some of them were reconciled to the Church) and they were officially recognized by the state in 1881. The Bezpopovtsy, on the other hand, split up into a great number of

sects, many of them adopting the most extravagant doctrines and practices, but they remained a comparatively small minority. Both factions survived the Revolution and still exist. The anathemas imposed on the Old Believers in 1667 were lifted by the Russian Orthodox Church in 1971, but the schism has not been healed.

The Life of the Archpriest Avvakum, written by himself in 1672 or 1673 [an *apologia* as well as a biog.], ed. from his autograph (Petrograd, 1916); Eng. tr. by J. Harrison and H. Mirrlees (London, 1924; repr. 1963). The main secondary lit. is in Russian. F. C. *Conybeare, *Russian Dissenters* (Harvard Theological Studies, 10; 1921), pp. 13–258, with refs.; P. Pascal, *Avvakum et les débuts du Raskol: La crise religieuse au XVIIe siècle en Russie* (Bibliothèque de l'Institut Français de Léningrad, 18; 1938; repr., with additional material, 1963). M. Cherniavsky, 'The Old Believers and the New Religion', *Slavic Review*, 25 (1966), pp. 1–39; A. Lambrechts, 'Les Vieux-Croyants en U.R.S.S.', *Irénikon*, 59 (1986), pp. 314–37. B. Marchadier in *Dict. Sp.* 13 (1988), cols. 127–34, s.v. 'Raskol', with bibl. See further bibl. to RUSSIA, CHRISTIANITY IN; also to NIKON.

Old Catholics. A group of small national Churches, consisting of Christians who have at various times separated from Rome. Since 1932 they have been in full communion with the C of E. They are composed of three sections:

(1) The Old Catholic Church in the *Netherlands, sometimes called the Church of Utrecht. This owed its origin to the papal handling of the *Jansenist controversy, and more particularly the deposition in 1702 of Petrus Codde (1648–1710), the Vicar Apostolic of the area, and the subsequent dispute as to whether the province and diocese of Utrecht had survived or ceased to exist at the Reformation. In 1723 the Chapter of Utrecht, acting independently of Rome, elected Cornelius Steenoven Abp. of Utrecht; he was consecrated in 1724 by Dominique Marie Varlet, Bp. of Babylon, who had fallen foul of the Roman authorities for exercising episcopal function when passing through the Netherlands, but whose own consecration had been perfectly regular; through him the Old Catholics maintained the *apostolic succession. On Steenoven's death Varlet consecrated his successor in 1725. To strengthen the Church two former bishoprics were re-established: Haarlem in 1740 and Deventer in 1758. The Old Catholic Church in the Netherlands enjoyed wide support in the 18th cent., but in the 19th cent. declined in importance as the RC Church regained the adherence of much of the Catholic population.

(2) The German, Austrian, and Swiss Old Catholic Churches. This group of Churches was created from those Christians who refused to accept the dogmas of the Infallibility and universal ordinary jurisdiction of the Pope, as defined by the *Vatican Council of 1870, and seceded from the RC Church shortly afterwards. The movement was temporarily strengthened by those who joined them for political reasons, owing to the strained relations between the Prussian Government and the Roman Curia (see KULTURKAMPF). Their organization was partly the work of Conferences, presided over by von *Döllinger at *Bonn in 1874 and 1875, and attended by members of the Old Catholic, Anglican, Orthodox, Lutheran, and other Churches, among the Anglican representatives being the Bp. of *Winchester (E. H. *Browne) and H. P. *Liddon. The Old Catholics received their episcopal succession from the Church of Utrecht; the first German bishop, J. H. *Rein-

kens (with see at Bonn), was consecrated in 1874, and the first Swiss bishop, E. Herzog (with see at Berne), in 1876. Owing to the opposition of the government, bishops were not consecrated for the Austrian communities till much later. A bishop of Warnsdorf (Bohemia) was consecrated in 1924 and of Vienna in 1925. In 1939 the three bishoprics of Bonn, Warnsdorf, and Vienna were united into one Church. They have since been separated.

(3) Some small groups of Slav origin. National Church movements among the Poles in the USA (1897) and the Croats (1924) resulted in the establishment of the 'Polish National Catholic Church', with four bishoprics in America and one in Poland, and of the 'Yugoslav Old Catholic Church' (see also MARIAVITES).

The doctrinal basis of the Old Catholic Churches is the 'Declaration of *Utrecht' (q.v.), agreed upon by the five Old Catholic bishops in 1889. The Old Catholics recognize the same seven *Oecumenical Councils as the E. Orthodox Church, and those doctrines accepted by the Church before the *Great Schism of 1054. The bishops, as well as the rest of the clergy, are permitted to marry. All services are in the vernacular. Communion is now generally given in both kinds. Auricular confession is not compulsory.

The Old Catholic communion formally recognized *Anglican Ordinations in 1925, and entered into full communion with the C of E in 1932, on the basis of an agreement reached at Bonn on 2 July 1931. The *Episcopal Church in the United States of America, and most other Anglican Churches, have since also established intercommunion. Old Catholic bishops have several times taken part in the consecration of Anglican bishops in London, using their own formula (*Accipe Spiritum Sanctum*, etc.), and in 1937 Anglican bishops took part in the consecration of Andreas Rinkel as Abp. of Utrecht. There are no Old Catholic communities in any English-speaking country except the USA, where their work is entirely among Poles and other foreigners. Various small sects which sometimes call themselves 'Old Catholic' are not recognized by the Old Catholic Churches referred to above.

The term 'Old Catholic' is also applied to RCs in England of older (esp. *recusant) background in contrast to converts from the *Oxford Movement and later and immigrants.

F. Siegmund-Schultze (ed.), *Ekklesia: Eine Sammlung von Selbstdarstellungen der christlichen Kirchen*, 3. 2 (1935), 'Die altkatholische Kirche'; C. B. Moss, *The Old Catholic Movement: Its Origins and History* (1948). J. M. *Neale, *History of the So-called Jansenist Church of Holland* (1853); J. F. von Schulte, *Der Altkatholicismus: Geschichte seiner Entwicklung, inneren Gestaltung und rechtlichen Stellung in Deutschland* (1887), with docs. and bibl.; P. Gschwind, *Geschichte der Entstehung der christkatholischen Kirche der Schweiz* (2 vols., Berne, 1904–10). G. Huelin (ed.), *Old Catholics and Anglicans 1931–1981* (Oxford, 1983). Quarterly periodical *Revue internationale de Théologie* (Berne, 1893–1910), with changed title *Internationale kirchliche Zeitschrift* (ibid., 1911 ff.). See also the Reports of Old Catholic International Conferences. J. F. von Schulte in *PRE* (3rd edn.), 1 (1896), pp. 415–25; W. Küppers in *TRE* 2 (1978), pp. 337–44, both s.v. 'Altkatholizismus'; L. Cristiani in *DTC* 15 (pt. 2; 1950), cols. 2980–8, s.v. 'Vieux-Catholiques'.

Oldcastle, Sir John (*c.*1378?–1417), *Lollard leader and rebel. He was a knight of Herefordshire who became, by his marriage in 1408, Lord Cobham. In 1413 he was accused of heresy before Convocation, and upheld Lollard opinions. He was given 40 days to recant, but escaped from the Tower of London before their expiration. He then put himself at the head of a conspiracy for a Lollard rebellion, which, however, collapsed. He remained in hiding till 1417, when he was captured and executed. He was reputed to have been the boon companion of the young Henry V, and this traditional figure of Sir John Oldcastle was the basis of Shakespeare's Falstaff.

W. T. Waugh, 'Sir John Oldcastle', *EHR* 20 (1905), pp. 434–56 and 637–58; H. G. Richardson, 'John Oldcastle in hiding, Aug.–Oct. 1417', ibid. 55 (1940), pp. 432–8. K. B. McFarlane, *John Wycliffe and the Beginnings of English Nonconformity* (1952), pp. 160–83. J. Tait in *DNB* 42 (1895), pp. 86–93. See also works cited s.v. LOLLARDS.

Oldham, Joseph Houldsworth (1874–1969), missionary statesman and leader of the *Ecumenical Movement. The son of Col. George Oldham, RE, he was born in India and educated in Scotland and at Trinity College, Oxford. After a year as General Secretary of the British Colleges Christian Union (1896–7), he was secretary of the *YMCA in Lahore (1897–1901). Invalided home, he studied theology at New College, Edinburgh, and at Halle in Germany. He was promoting missionary study for the *SCM when, in 1908, he was appointed organizing secretary of the World Missionary Conference which met in *Edinburgh in 1910. He was secretary of the Conference's Continuation Committee and edited the *International Review of Missions*, launched in 1912. He worked to rescue German missions from wartime extinction, to restore relationships with German Churchmen, and to inaugurate the International Missionary Council (1921), of which he was joint secretary. His work for Africa is considered by many the outstanding feature of his career. Called on by the missionaries to pursue with the government the question of indentured labour in East Africa, he became progressively involved in helping to create a missionary policy in education and in voicing a missionary opinion in the debate on the political future of colonial territories. In 1934 he became chairman of the Research Commission of the Universal Christian Council for '*Life and Work'; he thus initiated the preparations for the *Oxford Conference of 1937 (q.v.) and arranged the 1938 conference at Utrecht which set up the provisional committee for a *World Council of Churches. As secretary first of the Council on the Christian Faith and the Common Life (1939–42) and then of the Christian Frontier Council (1942–5), he edited the *Christian News Letter* throughout the Second World War. He became an Anglican in mid-career and remained a layman.

K. Bliss in *DNB, 1961–1970*, pp. 806–8, s.v.

Old Latin Versions. The Latin versions of the Scriptures in use in the Church before they were superseded by the *Vulgate. In S. Gaul and N. Africa a vernacular translation was needed sooner than in Rome (where the use of Greek continued until well into the 3rd cent. and all the earliest bishops bore Greek names), and the existence of the Scriptures in Latin in those two provinces is attested before the end of the 2nd cent. Several independent versions came into currency. One form, known as the 'African Old Latin', is very clearly defined. Its African *provenance* is proved by its use in the biblical quotations in St *Cyprian, and it is represented for example in the Gospels by the fragmentary 'Codex Bobiensis' ('*k*', 4th–5th cent., now at Turin; see BOBBIO), less exactly by the 'Palatinus' ('*e*', 5th cent., at Vienna). The MSS of the Old Latin differ greatly among themselves, and it was largely the desire to remedy the inconveniences arising out of such differences that led *Jerome (who asserted that there were almost as many different texts as MSS) to undertake his Vulgate. For large parts of the Bible no MSS are extant, and knowledge of the text derives entirely from such quotations as are preserved in the writings of the Fathers. See also ITALA and MANUSCRIPTS OF THE BIBLE.

The fullest presentation of the evidence for the whole Bible is still Pierre *Sabatier, OSB, *Bibliorum Sacrorum Latinae Versiones Antiquae, seu Vetus Italica* (3 vols., fol., Reims, 1743[–9]; repr. Paris, 1751). This is being superseded by B. Fischer, OSB, and others (eds.), *Vetus Latina* (Freiburg i.B., 1949 ff.); and for the Gospels only by A. *Jülicher and others (eds.), *Itala: Das Neue Testament in altlateinischer Überlieferung* (4 vols., Berlin, 1938–63; 2nd edn. of vols. 1–3, 1970–6). Several of the chief MSS were pr. separately by the Clarendon Press in the series of *Old Latin Biblical Texts* (7 vols., 1883–1923). I. Levin, *The Quedlinburg Itala: The Oldest Illustrated Biblical Manuscript* (Litterae textuales, codicologica, 4; Leiden, 1985). T. A. Marazuela, *La Vetus Latina Hispana* (Madrid, 1953 ff.). F. Stummer, *Einführung in die lateinische Bibel* (1928), pp. 4–76 ('Die lateinische Bibel vor Hieronymus'). H. Rönsch, *Itala und Vulgata* (1869; 2nd edn., 1875; mainly philological). B. Fischer, OSB, and others, *Aus der Geschichte der lateinischen Bibel* (Freiburg i.B., 1957 ff., esp. vol. 12: B. Fischer, *Beiträge zur Geschichte der lateinischen Bibeltexte*, 1986). B. M. Metzger, *The Early Versions of the New Testament* (Oxford, 1977), pp. 285–330. P.-M. Bogaert, 'La Bible latine des origines au moyen âge. Aperçu historique, état des questions', *Revue théologique de Louvain*, 19 (1988), pp. 137–59 and 276–314, with bibl. Current 'Bulletin de la bible latine' in *R. Bén.* B. Botte, OSB, in *Dict. Bibl. Suppl.* 5 (1957), cols. 334–47, s.v. 'Latines (versions) antérieures à S. Jérôme'. See also bibl. to VULGATE.

Old Roman Catholic Church.

A small community tracing its episcopal orders to A. H. *Mathew. It has congregations in Britain, USA, Canada, and the West Indies. It uses the *Tridentine liturgy current in the RC Church before the changes associated with the Second *Vatican Council. It is not under the authority of the Papacy.

Old Roman chant.

The musical repertory, which accompanies a form of the Roman rite with some special features, is found in five MSS dating from 1071 to the middle of the 13th cent. It is usually considered to be a precursor of the Gregorian chants, to which it is closely related, and to have been retained in the basilicas and title-churches after the latter had been adopted by the Papal court. However, neither repertory in its present form is now thought to be as old as Pope *Gregory I, and it may be that both are derived from a simpler original (see PLAINSONG).

The repertory of the Mass is ed. M. Landwehr-Melnicki (Monumenta Monodica Medii Aevi, 2; Kassel, etc., 1970), with introd. by B. Stäblein, pp. 3*–164*; facsimile of the 'Gradual' of Santa Cecilia in Trastevere (Cod. Bodmer 74), dated 1071 [containing the music of the Mass], ed., with introd. and comm., by M. Lütolf (Bibliotheca Bodmeriana, Texte, 2; 2 vols., Cologny and Geneva, 1987). R. J. Snow in W. Apel, *Gregorian Chant* [1958], pp. 484–505; S. J. P. van Dijk, OFM, 'The Urban and Papal Rites in Seventh and Eighth-Century Rome', *Sacris Erudiri*,

12 (1961), pp. 411–87; id., 'The Old Roman Rite', in F. L. Cross (ed.), *Studia Patristica*, 5 (1962), pp. 185–205.

Old Roman Creed.

An earlier and shorter form of the *Apostles' Creed (q.v.), which at least from the end of the 2nd cent. was the official baptismal creed of the Church of *Rome. It is first found, in an interrogatory form, in the *Apostolic Tradition* of St *Hippolytus (d. 235), and an almost identical text, but in a declaratory form, is attested in the 4th cent. by *Marcellus of Ancyra (ap. *Epiphanius, *Haer.* 72. 3) and *Rufinus of Aquileia (*Comm. in Symbol.*). It is also found in Codex E of Acts in the *Bodleian (Laud. gr. 35) and in an 8th cent. MS in the British Library (Royal 2 A XX).

The subject is necessarily discussed in all books dealing with the history of the Apostles' Creed (see bibl.). J. *Ussher, *De Romanae Ecclesiae Symbolo Apostolico Veteri, aliisque Fidei Formulis* (London, 1647). Modern studies dealing specifically with the Old Roman Creed include the brilliant essays by K. *Holl, 'Zur Auslegung des 2. Artikels des sog. apostolischen Glaubensbekenntnisses', *Sb.* (Berl.), 1919, pp. 2–11; A. *Harnack, 'Zur Abhandlung des Hrn. Holl: Zur Auslegung des 2. Artikels des sog. apostolischen Glaubensbekenntnisses', ibid., pp. 112–16; H. *Lietzmann, 'Die Urform des apostolischen Glaubensbekenntnisses', ibid., pp. 269–74. B. *Capelle, OSB, 'Le Symbole romain au second siècle', *R. Bén.* 39 (1927), pp. 33–45; id., 'Les Origines du symbole romain', *RTAM* 2 (1930), pp. 5–20. P. Smulders, SJ, 'The *Sitz im Leben* of the Old Roman Creed', in E. A. Livingstone (ed.), *Studia Patristica*, 13 (TU 116; 1975), pp. 409–21. J. N. D. Kelly, *Early Christian Creeds* (1950; 3rd edn., 1972), esp. pp. 100–66. Bardenhewer, 1, pp. 82–90; Altaner and Stuiber (1978), pp. 85–87 and 558.

Old Syriac Version.

The Syriac translation of the NT which circulated in the Syriac-speaking Church before the construction of the *Peshitta ('Vulgate') version early in the 5th cent. Only two MSS of the Old Syriac are known, both of the Gospels. The 'Curetonian' recovered by H. *Tattam from Egypt in 1842 was printed privately by W. *Cureton in 1848 and published in 1858. The 'Sinaitic' was found and photographed towards the end of the 19th cent. in the monastery of St Catherine on Mt. *Sinai by Mrs Lewis and Mrs Gibson of Cambridge. (The latter is not to be confounded with the Greek *Codex Sinaiticus discovered by C. *Tischendorf.) The existence of an Old Syriac text of Acts is attested by St *Ephraem Syrus' Commentary (which has survived, however, only in *Armenian). The readings of the Old Syriac NT are closely allied to those of the so-called *Western text, and in the Gospels are often under the influence of the *Diatessaron.

The best edn. of the Curetonian text (Sinaitic as *apparatus*) is in F. C. *Burkitt, *Evangelion Da-Mepharreshe* (2 vols., Cambridge, 1904), of the Sinaitic text (Curetonian as *apparatus*) that of Mrs A. S. Lewis (London, 1910). Facsimile edn. of the Sinaitic text by A. Hjelt (Helsingfors, 1930). I. Ortiz de Urbina, SJ (ed.), *Vetus Evangelium Syrorum et exinde excerptum Diatessaron Tatiani* (Biblia Polyglotta Matritensia, 4; Madrid, 1967). A. Hjelt, 'Die altsyrische Evangelienübersetzung und Tatians Diatessaron besonders in ihrem gegenseitigen Verhältnis', in T. *Zahn, *Forschungen zur Geschichte des neutestamentlichen Kanons*, 7 (pt. 1; 1903); Hjelt defends priority of Old Syriac over the Diatessaron. A. Vööbus, *Studies in the History of the Gospel Text in Syriac* (CSCO 128; 1951); id., *Early Versions of the New Testament* (Papers of the Estonian Theological Society in Exile, 6; Stockholm, 1954), esp. pp. 73–88; B. M. Metzger, *The Early Versions* of the New Testament (Oxford, 1977), pp. 36–48. Graphic account of the discovery of the 'Sinaitic' text in A. W. Price, *The Ladies of Castlebrae* (1985), pp. 125–35. C. van Puyvelde in *Dict. Bibl.*, Suppl. 6 (1960), cols. 870–2, s.v. 'Orientales de la Bible (Versions), III'.

Old Testament (Gk. Παλαιὰ Διαθήκη, Lat. *Vetus Testamentum*). Term denoting the collection of Canonical Books which the Christian Church shares with the Synagogue, together with (in Catholic and Orthodox Churches) certain other ancient Jewish Books not now accepted as canonical by the Jews (the *Apocrypha). In Jewish tradition the OT is divided into three parts: the Law, the Prophets, and the Writings. The Law (*Torah) consists of the first five Books, i.e. the *Pentateuch; the 'Prophets' are divided into the 'Former Prophets' (i.e. most of the historical Books) and the 'Latter Prophets' (Is., Jer., Ezek., and the *Minor Prophets); and the 'Writings' are the remainder of the OT (incl. Dan., Ezra–Nehemiah and 1 and 2 Chron.). Christian tradition, reflected in the conventional arrangement of English Bibles, divides it into 'historical' Books (the Pentateuch plus the 'Former Prophets'), 'didactic' Books (Job, Pss., Prov., etc.), and 'prophetic' Books (= the Hebrew 'Later Prophets'). Like the NT, the OT Books are regarded as inspired in the Church, which from the time of *Marcion has consistently defended them against attacks. The term 'Old Testament' is now sometimes regarded as unacceptably pejorative by both Jews and Christians, and 'Hebrew Bible' is then preferred.

Olier, Jean-Jacques (1608–57), founder of the Society and seminary of *Saint-Sulpice (q.v.). He studied philosophy and theology in his native Paris and was provided with ecclesiastical benefices at an early age. He went to Rome in 1630 to study Hebrew, but was threatened with the loss of his eyesight. On a pilgrimage to *Loreto he was cured and converted to a deeply religious life. In Paris he was ordained priest in 1633 and came under the influence of St *Vincent de Paul and then of C. de *Condren; he conducted missions in various parts of France. His main vocation, however, was the training of priests. After an unsuccessful attempt at *Chartres in 1641, he established a seminary at Vaugirard. When he became parish priest of Saint-Sulpice in Paris in 1642, he transferred the seminary there. He was responsible for the building of a new parish church as well as the seminary buildings; on the pattern of his seminary others were started. He sought to reform his parish which had a large population of libertines, atheists, *Huguenots, and *Jansenists. He also wanted to rid it of actors, including Molière who left for the provinces. The parish was divided into eight districts with a priest in charge of each; schools, catechism classes, homes for women, and charitable organizations for the poor ('Compagnie de charité') were established. Among the rich he led the movement against *duelling.

Both in his seminary and in the Society of Saint-Sulpice Olier adhered to the *Tridentine conception of the priesthood as totally dedicated and to the value of informed catechetical teaching. His was a community of secular priests, pursuing a common aim, but without religious vows. In 1657 he sent priests to start a seminary in Montreal.

Olier's spirituality was centred on the need for self-abasement, turning from a devotion to Christ's humanity to His divinity. His teaching owed much to St Vincent de Paul and to Condren. His published writings include *La Journée chrétienne* (1655; ed. F. Amiot, 1954); *Catéchisme chrétien pour la vie intérieure* (1656; ed. F. Amiot, 1954); *Explication des cérémonies de la grande messe de paroisse selon l'usage romain* ('1656'; really 1657); *Introduction à la vie et aux vertus chrétiennes* (1658; ed. F. Amiot, 1954); *Lettres spirituelles* (1672; ed. E. Levesque, 2 vols., 1935); and *Pietas Seminarii Sancti Sulpitii* (1815). His authorship of the *Traité des saints ordres*, published under his name in 1676, has recently been challenged.

Œuvres ed. J. P. *Migne (Paris, 1856). Modern Lives by E. M. Faillon (2 vols., ibid., 1841; Eng. Life by E. H. Thompson based entirely on that of Faillon, London, 1861), L. A. F. Monier, PSS (vol. 1 only; posthumously pub. by E. L[evesque], Paris, 1914), P. Pourrat, PSS (ibid., 1932), and A. Portaluppi (Milan, 1947). C. Letourneau, *La Mission de Jean-Jacques Olier et la fondation des grands séminaires en France* (1906). M. Dupuy, *Se Laisser à l'Esprit: Itinéraire spirituel de Jean-Jacques Olier* (1982). C. Chaillot, P. Cochois, and I. Noye, all PSS, *Traité des Saints Ordres (1676) comparé aux écrits authentiques de Jean-Jacques Olier (†1657)* (1984); incl. text. Bremond, 3 (1921), pp. 419–507; L. Cognet, *La Spiritualité Moderne*, 1 (1966), pp. 399–406. E. Levesque in *DTC* 11 (pt. 1; 1931), cols. 963–82; I. Noye and M. Dupuy in *Dict. Sp.* 11 (1982), cols. 737–51, s.v., both with detailed bibl.

Oliver Plunkett, St. See PLUNKETT, ST OLIVER.

Olives, Mount of. The highest point in the range of hills to the E. of *Jerusalem, rising to 2,600 ft. above sea-level, and separated from the city by the Valley of Jehoshaphat through which flows the brook *Cedron. Near its foot is the Garden of *Gethsemane (q.v.). It was aptly described by A. P. *Stanley as 'The Park' of Jerusalem in NT times. From the frequent refs. in the Gospels it would appear that Christ often resorted to the Mt. of Olives. He was met here by the crowd on *Palm Sunday (Mk. 11: 1 and 11: 7), and from this mount He ascended to Heaven (Acts 1: 2–12). The traditional site of the Ascension was marked by a church known as the 'Imbomon' (ἐν βωμῷ; prob. 'at the summit'), built by a matron Poemenia before 378. Another church on the slopes, the 'Eleona' (ὁ Ἐλαίων; 'the olive yard'), also dating from the 4th cent., was built over a grotto where Christ was believed to have discoursed to the disciples on the Last Things (Mk. 13).

The most comprehensive study is H. Vincent, OP, and F. M. Abel, OP, *Jérusalem: II, Jérusalem nouvelle* (1914), pp. 328–419 ('Les Sanctuaires du mont des Oliviers'). B. Bagatti, OFM, and J. T. Milik, *Gli scavi del 'Dominus Flevit'*, pt. 1 (Pubblicazioni dello Studium Biblicum Franciscanum, 13; 1958); S. J. Saller, OFM, *The Excavations at Dominus Flevit*, pt. 2 (ibid., 1964). W. J. Heard in *Anchor Bible Dictionary*, 5 (1992), pp. 13–15.

Olivetan (*c.*1506–38), Protestant Reformer. His real name may have been Pierre Robert. It used to be thought that he was dubbed 'Olivetanus' from burning the midnight oil, but this story has been discredited. A native of Noyon in Picardy and a cousin of J. *Calvin, he began his studies at Orléans in 1528. Here his adoption of *Lutheran doctrines forced him to flee to Strasbourg, where he became a competent Hebrew and Greek scholar. From 1532 to 1535 he preached Reformation doctrines to the

*Waldenses in Neuchâtel and for the purposes of his mission work translated the Bible into French. The OT was done direct from the Hebrew, but the *Apocrypha and NT were only a revision of the version of *Faber Stapulensis. Calvin contributed two prefaces, but is not now thought to have been involved in the work of translation. The version was published at Neuchâtel in June 1535. In his last years he helped Calvin in organizing the Reformation at *Geneva.

Short study by C. A. Négrier (Montauban Diss., 1891). G. Casalis and B. Roussel (eds.), *Olivétan: Traducteur de la Bible. Actes du colloque Olivétan, Noyon, mai 1985* (Paris, 1987), with bibl. pp. 191–6. M. Engammare, 'Quelques prénoms sans nom. A la recherche du patronyme de "l'humble et petit translateur" de la première Bible réformée en langue française', *Bulletin de la Société de l'Histoire du Protestantisme Français*, 133 (1987), pp. 413–31. G. Bonet-Maury in *PRE* (3rd edn.), 14 (1904), pp. 363 f., s.v.

Olivetans (The Congregation of Our Lady of Mount Olivet). A monastic *Congregation of *Benedictine monks founded in 1319 by Giovanni Tolomei (Bl Bernard Ptolomei, d. 1348) at Monte Oliveto, near Siena. They joined the Benedictine Confederation in 1960. They follow a strict interpretation of the rule, and for a period in their history they were total abstainers from wine. They wear a white habit. The Congregation is now international, and includes the well-known Abbey of *Bec.

S. Lancellotti, *Historiae Olivetae* (Venice, 1623). Anthony of Braga's *Chronicon Montis Oliveti* (1313–1450) ed. P. Lugano, OSB (Spicilegium Montolivetense, 1; Florence, 1901). P. Lugano, OSB, *Origine e primordi dell'ordine di Montoliveto, 1313–1450* (ibid. 2; 1903). M. Scarpini, OSB, *I Monaci Benedettini di Monte Oliveto* (Alessandria [1952]). *Saggi e ricerche nel VII centenario della nascita del B. Bernardo Tolomei (1272–1972)* (Monte Oliveto, 1972), incl. articles on the Olivetans. Life of Giovanni Tolomei by B. M. Maréchaux, OSB (Paris, 1888). J. C. Almond, OSB, in *CE* 11 (1911), p. 244, s.v.; G. Picasso, OSB, in *DIP* 2 (1975), cols. 1493–6, s.v. 'Congregazione Benedettina Olivetana', with bibl.

Olivi, Petrus Joannis (c.1248–98), *Spiritual Franciscan. Born at Sérignan in Hérault, Languedoc, at the age of 12 he entered the *Franciscan Order and studied at Paris. His zeal for the strict observance of the rule led him to be consulted by Nicholas III in 1279 about Franciscan poverty. As leader of the rigorists in the Order, he was accused of heresy in the General Chapter of Strasbourg in 1282; and after examination by seven masters his works were censured in 34 propositions (1283). At the General Chapter of Montpellier (1287), however, he established his orthodoxy, which was confirmed at Paris in 1292. He became lector in various convents (Nîmes, Florence, Montpellier). After his death the Spiritual Franciscans accorded him exaggerated veneration, and though in the decretal 'Fidei Catholicae Fundamento' at the Council of *Vienne in 1311 certain propositions believed to be his (on the moment at which the Lord's body was transfixed by the lance; on the manner of the soul's union with the body; on infant baptism) were repudiated, his name was not mentioned. In 1326 *John XXII condemned his *Postilla super Apocalypsim* (pub. 1700). His other works include *Quaestiones* on the *Sentences*, *Quodlibets*, Commentaries on Genesis, Job, the Psalms, the Proverbs, Ecclesiastes, the Song of Solomon, Lamentations, Ezekiel, the Minor Prophets, the Four Gospels, and the Epp. to the Romans and Corinthians, *Expositio Dionysii de Angelica Hierarchia* and various works on the Franciscan Order.

'Quaestiones in Secundum Librum Sententiarum', ed. B. Jansen (Bibliotheca Franciscana Scholastica Medii Aevi, 4–6; Quaracchi, 1922–6); 'Quaestio de Angelicis Influentiis', ed. F. Delorme, OFM, in his edn. of St *Bonaventure's 'Collationes in Hexaëmcron' (ibid. 8; 1934), pp. 363–417; 'Quaestiones de Incarnatione et Redemptione', ed. A. Emmen, OFM, and 'Quaestiones de Virtutibus', ed. E. Stadter (ibid. 24; Grottaferrata, 1981); 'Quaestiones Quatuor de Domina', ed. D. Pacetti, OFM (Bibliotheca Franciscana Ascetica Medii Aevi, 8; Quaracchi, 1954); his comm. on the Franciscan Rule ed., with full introd., by D. Flood (Veröffentlichungen des Instituts für Europäische Geschichte Mainz, 67; Wiesbaden, 1972); 'De emptionibus et venditionibus, de usuris, de restitutionibus', ed. G. Todeschini (Istituto Storico Italiano per il Medio Evo, Studi Storici, 125–6; 1980); extracts from further works ed. F. M. Delorme, 'Textes franciscains, I. L'Explication littérale du *Pater* selon Pierre-Jean Olivi', *Archivio italiano per la Storia della Pietà*, 1 (1951), pp. 181–203. F. *Ehrle, 'Petrus Johannis Olivi, sein Leben und seine Schriften', *Archiv für Litteratur- und Kirchengeschichte*, 3 (1887), pp. 409–552. R. Manselli, *La 'Lectura super Apocalipsim' di Pietro di Giovanni Olivi: Ricerche sull'escatologismo medioevale* (Istituto Storico Italiano per il Medio Evo, Studi Storici, 19–21; 1955). E. Bettoni, OFM, *Le dottrine filosofiche di Pier di Giovanni Olivi* (Pubblicazioni dell'Università Cattolica del S. Cuore, NS 73 [1959]). C. Partee, OFM, 'Petrus John Olivi: Historical and Doctrinal Study', *Franciscan Studies*, 20 (1960), pp. 215–60. D. Burr, *Olivi and Franciscan Poverty* (Philadelphia 1989). H. Lee, M. [E.] Reeves, and G. Silano, *Western Mediterranean Prophecy* (Pontifical Institute of Mediaeval Studies, Studies and Texts, 88; Toronto [1989]), pp. 17–26, with refs. S. Gieben, OFM Cap., 'Bibliographia Oliviana (1885–1967)', *Collectanea Franciscana*, 38 (1968), pp. 167–95. G. Gál, OFM, in *NCE* 11 (1967), pp. 219 f., s.v. 'Peter John Olivi'; P. Péano, OFM, in *Dict. Sp.* 11 (1982), cols. 751–62, s.v. 'Olieu'.

Ollé-Laprune, Léon (1839–98), French philosopher. From 1875 he was professor of philosophy at the École Normale Supérieure at Paris, where he became the leading lay exponent in France of a Catholic system of philosophy. He stressed the limits of a purely intellectual approach to the issues of philosophy along lines which had affinities with the teaching of J. H. *Newman in England, and in his emphasis on the part played by the will and the heart in cognition prepared the ground for such later influences in French culture as H. *Bergson, M. *Blondel, and the *Modernist Movement. His writings include *La Philosophie de Malebranche* (1870), *De la certitude morale* (1880), and *La Philosophie et le temps présent* (1890).

M. Blondel, *Léon Ollé-Laprune: L'achèvement et l'avenir de son œuvre* (Paris, 1923). E. Boutroux, 'Notice sur la vie et les œuvres de M. Léon Ollé-Laprune', *Mémoires de l'Académie des Sciences Morales et Politiques de l'Institut de France*, 25 (1907), pp. 207–42. G. Goyau in *CE* 11 (1911), pp. 246 f., s.v.; H. de Gensac in *Dict. Sp.* 11 (1982), cols. 782–4, s.v. See also bibl. to MODERNISM.

Oman, John Wood (1860–1939), *Presbyterian theologian. From 1889 to 1907 he was minister at Alnwick, Northumberland. From 1907 to 1935 he was professor at, and from 1925 to 1935 principal of, Westminster College, Cambridge. His early interest in F. D. E. *Schleiermacher, of whose *Speeches on Religion* he published a translation in 1893, indicates the direction of his thought.

Holding the uniqueness and independence of the religious consciousness as an immediate, self-authenticating awareness of the Supernatural, he nevertheless insisted that it should not be isolated from other spheres of experience. In *The Natural and the Supernatural* (1931) he set forth a powerful philosophic justification of his position. Esp. important in this work is his treatment of the idea of the sacred, which differed notably from, as it had in fact antedated in his class-room teaching, R. *Otto's treatment of the 'Holy'. On the side of doctrine, Oman's theology might be said to be the theology of 'sincerity'. The inner authority of truth determined his understanding of personality, of sin and grace, of the Church, sacraments, and ministry. His other writings include *Vision and Authority* (1902), *The Church and the Divine Order* (1911), *Grace and Personality* (1917).

Memoirs of the author by G. Alexander and H. H. Farmer prefixed to Oman's posthumously pub. *Honest Religion* (1941), pp. xv–xxv and xxvi–xxxii respectively. *A Dialogue with God and Other Sermons and Addresses* was also posthumously pub. by F. H. Ballard [son-in-law] (London [1952]). F. G. Healey, *Religion and Reality: The Theology of John Oman* (1965), with list of his works, pp. 153–5. S. Bevans, SVD, *John Oman and his Doctrine of God* (Cambridge, 1992). Obituary note by F. R. Tennant in *Proceedings of the British Academy*, 25 (1939), pp. 333–8, with portrait. H. H. Farmer in *DNB*, *1931–1940* (1949), pp. 657 f.

Omar, Mosque of. See DOME OF THE ROCK.

ombrellino. In the W. Church the small umbrella-like canopy of white silk sometimes carried over the Blessed Sacrament when it is moved informally from one place to another.

omophorion. The long scarf, originally of wool and now a piece of embroidered white silk or velvet, about 10 inches wide, worn in the E. Church by bishops round the shoulder and falling loose towards the ground. It corresponds to the *pallium in the Latin Church. It is worn at the Liturgy and when the bishop officiates at other rites. There are two forms, a larger one worn until the end of the Epistle (when it is laid aside as a sign of self-effacement for the reading of the Gospel) and a shorter one from the *Cherubicon until the end of the service.

Braun, *LG*, pp. 664–74.

Oneida Community. A Christian communist society established in 1848 at Oneida, Madison County, NY, by John Humphrey Noyes (1811–86). The body was also known as the **Perfectionists**, from their insistence that true sinlessness could be realized through communion with Christ. They also maintained that marriage was not a binding contract between husband and wife, but an arrangement under the control of the community. At first their activities were mainly agricultural, but later they included industry and the Community became a very prosperous body. In 1881 it was formed into a joint-stock company.

A. Estlake, *The Oneida Community* (1900); M. L. Carden, *Oneida: Utopian Community to Modern Corporation* (Baltimore, 1969); C. N. Robertson [granddaughter of J. H. Noyes] (ed.), *Oneida Community: An Autobiography, 1851–1876* (Syracuse, NY, 1970); id., *Oneida Community: The Breakup, 1876–1881* (ibid., 1972). J. McK. Whitworth, *God's Blueprints: A Sociological Study*

of Three Utopian Sects (1975), pp. 89–166. R. A. Parker, *Yankee Saint: J. H. Noyes and the Oneida Community* (1935).

Onesimus, St. The Phrygian slave on whose behalf St *Paul wrote his Ep. to *Philemon. St Paul perhaps plays on his name, which means 'profitable', in Philem. v. 11 ('which in time past was to thee unprofitable, ἄχρηστον, but now profitable, εὔχρηστον, to thee and to me'). Acc. to tradition, he suffered martyrdom. Feast day, in W., 16 Feb.; E., 15 Feb. (also 22 Nov.)

The NT Onesimus has often been identified with the Onesimus, Bp. of Ephesus, mentioned in *Ignatius, *Ad Eph.* i. 3; but the name is too common to make this more than a conjecture. P. Lampe in *Anchor Bible Dictionary*, 5 (1992), pp. 21 f., s.v., with bibl. See also comm. to PHILEMON, cited s.v.

Ontological Argument. A classical argument for God's existence holding that the concept of God entails the real existence of God. It was first elaborated by St *Anselm, who urged that God must exist since 'God' means 'that than which nothing greater can be conceived' (*id quo nihil majus cogitari possit*) and since nothing lacking extra-mental existence could be that than which nothing greater can be conceived. The argument was also championed by R. *Descartes and G. W. *Leibniz and it has been defended in the 20th cent. by certain exponents of modal logic (the logic of possibility and necessity), incl. C. Hartshorne and A. Plantinga. Major critics of it include St *Thomas Aquinas (who denied that we have a definitional knowledge of what God is), I. *Kant and G. Frege (who denied on logical grounds that existence can be part of the definition of anything).

The subject regularly finds a place in philosophical discussions of belief in God as well as in works on the philosophers mentioned above. Anselm's formulation of the argument can be found in his *Proslogion* (J. P. Migne, *PL* 158. 223–42); Eng. tr. with repr. of the text from the edn. of Anselm's works by F. S. Schmitt, OSB, and full discussion, by M. J. Charlesworth (Oxford, 1965). Eng. tr. of texts and some modern discussions in A. Plantinga (ed.), *The Ontological Argument from St Anselm to Contemporary Philosophers* (New York, 1965; London, 1968). G. Frege, *Die Grundlagen der Arithmetik* (Breslau, 1884; Eng. tr. by J. L. Austin, *The Foundations of Arithmetic*, Oxford, 1950), para. 53 (pp. 64 f.). K. *Barth, *Fides Quaerens Intellectum: Anselms Beweis der Existenz Gottes* (Forschungen zur Geschichte und Lehre des Protestantismus, Reihe 4, 3, 1931; 2nd edn., Zollikon, 1958; Eng. tr., 1960). C. Hartshorne, *The Logic of Perfection and other Essays in Neoclassical Metaphysics* (La Salle, Ill. [1962]), ch. 2: 'Ten Ontological or Modal Proofs for God's Existence', pp. 28–117; id., *Anselm's Discovery: A re-examination of the Ontological Proof for Existence* (ibid. [1965]). J. [H.] Hick and A. C. McGill (eds.), *The Many-Faced Argument: Recent Studies on the Ontological Argument for the Existence of God* (New York [1967]; London, 1968). A. Plantinga, *The Nature of Necessity* (Oxford, 1974), pp. 196–221.

Ontologism. A philosophical system favoured by certain Catholic philosophers, chiefly in Italy and France, during the 19th cent. The name first appears in the *Introduzione allo studio della filosofia* (1840) of the Italian statesman V. *Gioberti, who, with A. *Rosmini, may be regarded as the principal exponent of the system. Ontologism claims descent from *Plato and *Augustine, and positions akin to those of the ontologists are common to the whole Augustinian tradition of philosophers (e.g. St *Anselm, R. *Descartes, N. *Malebranche). In reaction from the sceptical trend of post-Kantian speculation, the ontologists asserted that God Himself is the guarantee of the validity of human ideas; that all human knowledge, itself a mode of truth, implies an immediate intuition of uncreated Truth; and that the idea of being, which is the first and simplest idea of all, is an immediate perception of absolute Being. A set of seven 'Errores Ontologistarum' was condemned by the *Inquisition on 18 Sept. 1861.

The condemned propositions are repr. in Denzinger and Hünermann (37th edn., 1991), pp. 783 f. (nos. 2841–7). Introduction by B. [M. G.] Reardon, *Liberalism and Tradition: Aspects of Catholic Thought in Nineteenth-Century France* (Cambridge, 1975), pp. 159–81; id., *Religion in the Age of Romanticism* (ibid., 1985), pp. 146–75. G. M. Sauvage in *CE* 11 (1911), pp. 259 f., s.v.; A. Fonck in *DTC* 11 (pt. 1; 1931), cols. 1000–61, s.v. 'Ontologisme', with full bibl.; D. Cleary in *NCE* 10 (1967), pp. 701–3, s.v. See also bibl. to GIOBERTI, V., and ROSMINI-SERBATI, A.

ontology (from Gk. τὸ ὄν, stem ὀντ-, 'that which is'; λόγος, 'discourse'). The branch of metaphysics which deals with being in general rather than this or that being. It investigates the nature of existence as such and the sense in which different things can be said to be. 'Ontology' also sometimes signifies the underlying presumptions about existence of any given world-view or conceptual scheme.

Ophites and **Naassenes** (Gk. ὄφις, Heb. נָחָשׁ, 'serpent'). *Gnostic sects which derived their names from the special importance which they attached to the serpent; it is not entirely clear whether they were connected. The Ophites (or Ophians) are mentioned by *Irenaeus and *Origen, the Naassenes only by *Hippolytus; the Ophite system recalls biblical accounts, and may be early, while the Naassene has a larger element of other material. The Naassenes were among the groups, like the Peratae and the Sethians, whose systems involved three primal principles. An Ophite diagram is described by Origen, and a Naassene hymn is quoted by Hippolytus. Since the serpent induced Adam and Eve to eat of the tree of knowledge (γνῶσις) (Gen. 3), it might be expected to have an honourable place among the Gnostics, but some sects saw it as a hostile power.

The principal sources are Hippolytus, *Haer.* 5; Irenaeus, *Adv. Haer.* 1. 30 Origen, *Contra Celsum*, 6. 24 ff. Convenient Eng. tr. in W. Foerster, *Gnosis*, 1 (tr. ed. R. McL. Wilson, Oxford, 1972), pp. 84–99, and 261–82. R. *Reitzenstein, *Poimandres* (1904), pp. 81–101. F. Legge, *Forerunners and Rivals of Christianity*, 2 (Cambridge, 1915, repr., New York, 1964), pp. 25–85; W. Foerster, 'Die Naassener', *Studi di storia religiosa della tarda antichità pubblicati dalla cattedra di storia delle religioni dell'Università di Messina* (Messina, 1968), pp. 21–33; J.-D. Kaestli, 'L'interprétation du serpent de Genèse 3 dans quelques textes gnostiques et la question de la gnose "ophite" ', in J. Ries (ed.), *Gnosticisme et monde hellénistique: Actes du Colloque de Louvain-la-Neuve, 11–14 mars 1980* (Publications de l'Institut Orientaliste de Louvain, 27; 1982), pp. 116–30. G. *Salmon in *DCB* 4 (1887), pp. 80–8; G. Bornkamm in *PW* 18 (pt. 1; 1939), cols. 654–8; G. Quispel in *L.Th.K.* (2nd edn.), 7 (1962), cols. 1178 f., all s.v.

Optatus, St (*fl.* 370), Bp. of Milevis in N. Africa. Nothing is known of him save his treatise against the Donatists, of which books 1–6 appeared about 367, and a revision, with book 7, about 385. The common title, 'Against Parmenian the Donatist' (Bp. of Carthage), is a deduction from the text, not found in any ancient writer or manu-

script. Book 1 relates the origins of *Donatism and 2–6 argue that the Donatist sect cannot be the One, Holy, Catholic Church. The argument turns mainly on the lack of 'catholicity' among the Donatists, but Optatus also attacks their claim to 'holiness'. Book 3 has some treatment of the problem of Church and State; 5 discusses Baptism; and 7 offers repentant Donatists readmission to the Church. An appendix ('dossier') of important historical documents has deservedly received much attention from modern scholars. Optatus' telling arguments formed the starting-point for St *Augustine's developed refutation of Donatism. Feast day, 4 June.

Editio princeps by J. *Cochlaeus (Mainz, 1549; based on a single indifferent MS). Best of earlier edns. by L. E. *Dupin (Paris, 1700); repr. in J. P. Migne, *PL* 11. 759–1556. Crit. edn. by C. Ziwsa (CSEL 26; 1893). Eng. tr. with introd. and notes by O. R. Vassall-Phillips, CSSR (London, 1917). S. Blomgren, *Eine Echtheitsfrage bei Optatus von Mileve* (Acta Academiae Regiae Scientiarum Upsaliensis, 5; 1959). A. C. de Veer, AA, 'A propos de l'authenticité du livre VII d'Optat de Milev', *Revue des Études Augustiniennes*, 7 (1961), pp. 389–91. M. Simonetti in Quasten (cont.), *Patrology*, 4 (1986), pp. 122–7. H. W. Phillott in *DCB* 4 (1887), pp. 90–3, s.v.; É. Amann in *DTC* 11 (pt. 1; 1931), cols. 1077–84, s.v. 'Optat de Milève'; A. Stuiber in *NCE* 10 (1967), pp. 706 f., s.v.

On the 'dossier', see also D. Völter, *Der Ursprung des Donatismus* (1883); O. Seeck, 'Urkundenfälschungen des 4. Jahrhunderts. I. Das Urkundenbuch des Optatus', *ZKG* 30 (1909), pp. 181–227; L. *Duchesne, 'Le Dossier du donatisme', *Mélanges d'Archéologie et d'Histoire publiés par l'École française de Rome*, 10 (1890), pp. 589–650; N. H. Baynes, 'Optatus', *JTS* 26 (1925), pp. 37–44 and 404–6. C. H. *Turner, 'Adversaria Critica: Notes on the Anti-Donatist Dossier and on Optatus, Books I, II', ibid. 27 (1926), pp. 283–96. J.-L. Maier, *Le Dossier du Donatisme*, 1 (TU 134; 1987), *passim*.

See also bibl. to DONATISM.

option. The right formerly possessed by an archbishop, when about to consecrate a bishop, of choosing within the latter's see some benefice to which he could act as patron at the next vacancy. The word is also used of the right of members of certain Cathedral or Collegiate chapters to secure at choice a particular benefice or title. *Cardinals may transfer by option, with Papal approval, to a title other than the one originally assigned to them.

Opus Dei (Lat., 'the work of God'). An old *Benedictine designation of the Divine *Office, to express the belief that this, the monk's special duty of prayer, is his first responsibility to God.

Opus Dei is also the name of a RC organization devoted to fostering the application of Christian principles to daily living by those engaged in all walks of life. Originally consisting exclusively of lay men, it was founded in Madrid on 2 Oct. 1928 by the Bl Josemaría Escrivá (1902–75), an Aragonese priest who became its president general. Two years later he set up a branch for women and in 1943 the Society of the Holy Cross for priests, inseparably united to Opus Dei. Opus Dei was approved by the Holy See in 1950 and in 1982 the *Personal Prelature of the Holy Cross and Opus Dei was established, giving the organization considerable independence of local bishops. Over a thousand priests are *incardinated in the Prelature. Lay members are encouraged to retain their social position and to pursue their profession, and esp. in Spain they have exercised considerable influence in public affairs, not without criticism. Corporately Opus Dei maintains a number of educational establishments, esp. residences for students and conference centres, in many parts of the world, notably the University of Pamplona.

D. le Tourneau, *L'Opus Dei* (Paris, 1984; Eng. tr., *What is Opus Dei?*, Cork [1987]).

opus operatum. See EX OPERE OPERATO.

Oracles, Sibylline. See SIBYLLINE ORACLES.

Orange, Councils of. Two synods held at Orange ('Arausio') in the S. of France in 441 and 529 respectively. The former, which took place under the presidency of St *Hilary of Arles, issued 30 canons, which deal mainly with disciplinary matters. The latter is of great importance for its 25 dogmatic *capitula*. These *capitula* upheld many of St Augustine's doctrines on the nature of grace as against the *Semipelagianism previously current in the region, though the Council repudiated any predestination of man to evil. Later these decrees were confirmed by Pope Boniface II (531).

On the Council of 441, Hardouin, 1, cols. 1783–8; Mansi, 6 (1761), cols. 433–52. C. Munier (ed.), *Concilia Galliae A. 314–A. 506* (CCSL 148; 1963), pp. 76–93. Hefele and Leclercq, 2 (pt. 1; 1908), pp. 430–54, with bibl. refs. See also bibl. to HILARY OF ARLES.
On the Council of 529, Hardouin, 2, cols. 1097–104; Mansi, 8 (1762), cols. 711–24; C. de Clercq (ed.), *Concilia Galliae A. 511–A. 695* (CCSL 148A; 1963), pp. 53–76, repr., with Fr. tr. and notes by J. Gaudemet and B. Basdevant, *Les Canons des Conciles Mérovingiens (VIᵉ–VIIᵉ siècles)*, 1 (SC 353; 1989), pp. 152–85; 'capitula' also ed. F. *Maassen in *MGH*, Legum Sectio III, Concilia, 1 (1893), pp. 44–54; Eng. tr. of principal clauses in Bettenson (2nd edn., 1963), pp. 86 f. On the vexed question of the relation between the *capitula* of the Council of Orange and the so-called *Capitula S. Augustini in urbem Romam transmissa*, see the edn. of the latter by F. Glorieux, *Maxentii ... Opuscula* (CCSL 85A; 1978), pp. 241–73, with comments of J.-P. Bouhot in *Revue des Études Augustiniennes*, 25 (1979), pp. 377–9, with further refs. M. Cappuyns, OSB, 'L'Origine des "Capitula" d'Orange 529', *RTAM* 6 (1934), pp. 121–42. O. Pontal, *Die Synoden im Merowingerreich* (1986), pp. 67–71 (rev. Fr. tr. [1989], pp. 94–99), with refs. G. Fritz in *DTC* 11 (pt. 1; 1931), cols. 1087–103, s.v. 'Orange (Deuxième Concile de)'.

Orangism. The movement defending the cause of Protestantism in *Ireland, maintained by the Orange Association (founded 1795). The word Orange in this connection probably derives directly or mediately from King William 'of Orange' (i.e. William III), and thus ultimately from the town of Orange in the S. of France (cf. previous entry). Members of the Orange Association are known as Orangemen.

orarion (Gk. ὠράριον). In the E. Church, the deacon's stole. It is a narrow band of material, worn over the left shoulder, and hangs straight down back and front; sometimes, before being left free to hang down in front, it is passed below the right arm, then attached once more to the left shoulder, and so hung down in front. While reciting prayers, the deacon holds it in his hand. At the time of Communion, it is crossed round the body.

Orate, fratres (Lat., 'Pray, brethren'). The opening words and hence the name of the sentence addressed by the celebrant to the people at *Mass, immediately after the *Offertory. It asks the prayers of the people before the *Eucharistic Prayer, and, with the response, emphasizes the unity of the congregation with the priest in the offering of the Sacrifice. The formula seems to have originated in Italy in the 11th century.

Jungmann (1958 edn.), 2, pp. 103–12; Eng. tr., 2, pp. 82–90.

Oratorians. (1) **The Oratory of St Philip Neri.** This, the original 'Oratory', grew out of the community of priests that had gathered round the saint (1564), the name being derived from the oratory at S. Girolamo, Rome, where they held their 'Exercises'. In 1575 they were erected into a congregation, and in 1612 their constitutions were sanctioned by *Paul V. The congregation spread quickly through Italy, Spain, South Germany, Poland, and South America. Though almost destroyed by the revolutions of the 18th and early 19th cents., they have revived in a number of countries. J. H. *Newman introduced them into England, in 1848 founding the Oratory at Old Oscott (later the Birmingham Oratory) and in 1849 that in London, which moved to its present site in Kensington in 1854 (the *Brompton Oratory).

St Philip's Oratory is a congregation of secular priests living in community without vows, those with private means supporting themselves. Each house is independent and elects its superior for three years. There is no central organization, though since 1958 there has been a 'Delegate of the Apostolic See' who acts as Visitor. The chief task of the Oratorians is to lead men to God by prayer, frequent popular preaching, and the Sacraments; and there is always a priest in the confessional. In conformity with the intentions of their founder, they lay stress not only on liturgy but also on attractive services, and esp. on good music; the modern 'oratorio' grew out of the *laudi spirituali* sung in their devotional exercises. The congregation has produced a number of scholars, among whom C. *Baronius and G. D. *Mansi are the best known.

(2) **The French Oratory** was founded in 1611 by P. de *Bérulle at Paris, and approved by Papal bull under the name of the 'Oratoire de Jésus-Christ' in 1613. It spread quickly through France and other European countries, esp. the Netherlands. Like the institute of St Philip, it was intended for the sanctification of secular priests and for the rehabilitation of the priestly office among the laity. Though formed on the Italian model, the French Oratory differs mainly in that it is a centralized organization governed by a Superior-General. One of its chief activities was the training of priests in *seminaries, run on the lines laid down by the Council of *Trent. The popularity of the French Oratory was temporarily eclipsed by the *Jansenist propensities of some of its members, esp. the two Superior-Generals, Père A. L. de Sainte-Marthe (1672–96) and Père de la Tour (1696–1733). The Oratory was dissolved in the French Revolution, but re-established in 1852 by L. P. Pététot and A. J. A. *Gratry as 'Oratoire de Jésus-Christ et de Marie Immaculée'.

The Oratorians, who have been excellent educationists and directors, have contributed much to the furtherance of popular devotion in France. Despite the Jansenist troubles, the Christ-centred spirituality of their founder, Bérulle, has been one of the chief characteristics of the congregation. Many of its members have been distinguished for their holiness and scholarship, e.g. C. de *Condren, N. *Malebranche, J.-B. *Massillon, and J. *Morin. St John *Eudes, though he later left the Oratory to found his own congregations, was deeply imbued with the Oratorian spirit.

(1) The principal material for the early history of the order is contained in the lives of St Philip Neri, cited s.v. A. George, *L'Oratoire* ('Les Grands Ordres monastiques', 1928), pp. 1–33, with bibl. pp. 231 f. C. Garbarri, *L'Oratorio Filippino* (1957). R. Addington, Cong. Orat., *The Idea of the Oratory* (1966). A. Cistellini, Cong. Orat., *San Filippo Neri, L'Oratorio e la Congregazione Oratoriana* (3 vols., 1989). P. Murray, OSB (ed.), *Newman the Oratorian* (1969), with text of Newman's papers on the Oratory. A. Cistellini, Cong. Orat., in *DIP* 6 (1980), cols. 765–75, s.v. 'Oratoriani'; id. in *Dict. Sp.* 11 (1982), 853–76, s.v. 'Oratoire Philippin'. In Eng. E. W. Wahl, Cong. Orat., in *NCE* 10 (1967), pp. 713 f., s.v. See also bibl. to foll. entry.

(2) L. Batterel (d. 1749), *Mémoires domestiques pour servir à l'histoire de l'Oratoire* (ed. A. M. P. Ingold and E. Bonnardet, 'Documents pour servir à l'histoire religieuse des XVIIᵉ et XVIIIᵉ siècles', 5 vols., 1902–11). M. Leherpeur, *L'Oratoire de France* (1926); A. George, op. cit., pp. 34–230, with bibl. pp. 232–7. R. Boureau, Cong. Orat., *L'Oratoire en France* (1991). A. M. P. Ingold, *L'Oratoire et la Révolution* (1883), and other works of this author. Id., *Essai de bibliographie oratorienne* (2 vols., 1880–2). *Bibliothèque oratorienne* (13 vols., Paris, 1880–92). Bremond, 3 (1921), esp. ch. 3, 'L'Oratoire', pp. 155–221. A. M. P. Ingold in *CE* 11 (1911), pp. 274 f., s.v.; A. Molien in *DTC* 11 (pt. 1; 1931), cols. 1104–38, s.v. 'Oratoire de Jésus (Congrégation de l')'; G. Rotureau in *Dict. Sp.* 11 (1982), cols. 847–853, s.v. 'Oratoire Bérullien'. See also bibl. to BÉRULLE, P. DE, and GRATRY, A. J. A.

oratorio. The musical setting of a religious libretto for soloists, chorus, and orchestra (or other accompaniment) without (in modern practice) the use of dramatic action, scenery, or dresses, though these adjuncts were sometimes employed until *c.*1730. Oratorio apparently derives from the dramatic services of St *Philip Neri (d. 1595) at the *Oratory in Rome. The first known oratorio in the present sense was performed at Santa Maria in Vallicella in Rome in 1600. The most important 17th-cent. oratorio composer was Giacomo Carissimi (1605–74), whose *Jephte* remains popular today. By the late 17th cent. the oratorio was commonly used as a Lenten substitute for opera. The English oratorio, with its characteristic emphasis on the chorus, was essentially the creation of G. F. *Handel, whose works include *Saul* (1738), *Israel in Egypt* (1738), *Samson* (1741), and *Messiah* (1741). In the 19th cent. the oratorio reached its greatest popularity, notably in England, but with few exceptions, such as F. Mendelssohn's *St Paul* (1836) and *Elijah* (1846), the compositions of the period were of little value. In more recent times England alone has maintained a considerable interest in oratorio, largely through the influence of annual musical festivals and local amateur choral societies. Among the more significant modern works are Sir E. *Elgar's *Dream of *Gerontius* (1900) and *Apostles* (1903), Sir W. Walton's *Belshazzar's Feast* (1931), and E. B. *Britten's *War Requiem* (1961).

The standard general work is H. E. Smither, *A History of the Oratorio* (Chapel Hill, NC, 1977 ff.; vol. 3 (1987) also pub. in Oxford). W. Dean, *Handel's Dramatic Oratorios and Masques* (1959), with general introd. P. Damilano and others in *Die Musik*

in Geschichte und Gegenwart, 10 (1962), cols. 120–68, s.v. 'Oratorium'; H. E. Smither in S. Sadie (ed.), *The New Grove Dictionary of Music and Musicians*, 13 (1980), pp. 656–78, s.v.

oratory (Lat. *oratorium*, 'place of prayer'). The term, used in antiquity for both churches and private chapels, has come to be restricted since the Middle Ages to places of worship other than the parish church. Their origin probably goes back to the chapels built over the tombs of the martyrs in early times. Their use became more frequent in the early Middle Ages, when churches tended to be restricted to cities, and places of worship were needed for the country districts.

In the RC Church the status of oratories is regulated by Canon Law. In place of the former categories of public, semi-public, and private oratories, current legislation (*CIC* (1983), cans. 1223–9) distinguishes (1) an oratory and (2) a private chapel, from a church, that is a sacred building to which all the faithful have access for divine worship. (1) The term oratory now signifies a place designated by permission of the *Ordinary for divine worship for the benefit of some community or assembly of the faithful who gather there. Other members of the faithful may also have access to it with the consent of the superior of the oratory. As a general rule, all sacred celebrations can be carried out there. (2) By the term private chapel is meant a place designated for divine worship for the advantage of one or several persons, with the permission of the local Ordinary. In addition, his permission is required for Mass and other celebrations to take place. It is fitting that both an oratory and a private chapel be blessed according to the prescribed liturgical rite. They must be reserved only for divine worship and be free of all domestic uses. With the permission of the local Ordinary, the Blessed Sacrament can be reserved in oratories and private chapels.

For the legal position of oratories in the C of E, see PRIVATE CHAPELS ACT 1871.

Oratory, The. The name is used absolutely of the *Oratorians (q.v.) or 'Congregation of the Oratory'. It is also often applied to churches belonging to the Congregation, e.g. the *Brompton Oratory, London.

ordeals. A method of judicial proof widely used in early medieval Europe in cases where sworn testimony and the evidence of witnesses was not thought sufficient to establish guilt or innocence. The accused was subjected to some physical test from a customary range which included walking on heated ploughshares, carrying hot iron, recovering an object from boiling water, and being lowered into cold water. Success or failure was demonstrated by the physical consequences, such as a 'clean' wound or a septic one. It would appear, however, that the result was often ambiguous and could be interpreted according to the preference of the local community, or its most powerful members. The ordeal was normally administered by the Church: the necessary equipment was often kept in the cathedral, and the blessing of a priest was required for its administration. It was seen as providing God's verdict upon the accusation, and the normal Latin term was 'the judgement of God', *iudicium Dei*; ordeal or *ordal* seems to be a distinctively English expression. Ordeals could be used outside the judicial process to establish the truth of important assertions: for example, relics were tested by fire, and a course of action could be justified by saying Mass or receiving Communion without mishap. The ownership of land was commonly settled by armed combat, or the 'judicial duel'. The Fourth *Lateran Council (1215) prohibited the participation of priests in the ceremony, and as a result the ordeal was rapidly abandoned in England and some other countries, and slowly disappeared from use in Europe as a whole.

Collection of primary material ed. P. Browe, SJ, *De Ordaliis* (Pontificia Universitas Gregoriana. Textus et Documenta in Usum Exercitationum et Praelectionum Academicarum, Series Theologica, 2 and 4; 1932–3); also K. Zeumer, 'Ordines Iudiciorum Dei' appended to his edn. of *Formulae Merowingici et Karolini Aevi* (*MGH*, Leges, Sectio 5; 1886), pp. 599–722, and S. L. Endlicher, *Rerum Hungaricarum Monumenta Arpadiana* (St Gall, 1849). C. Leitmaier, *Die Kirche und die Gottesurteile* (Wiener Rechtsgeschichtliche Arbeiten, 2 [1953]); K.-G. Cram, *Iudicium Belli: Zum Rechtscharakter des Krieges im deutschen Mittelalter* (Beihefte zum Archiv für Kulturgeschichte, 5; 1955); H. Nottarp, *Gottesurteilstudien* (Bamberger Abhandlungen und Forschungen, 2; 1956); J. W. Baldwin, 'The Intellectual Preparation for the Canon of 1215 against Ordeals', *Speculum*, 36 (1961), pp. 613–36; P. [R. L.] Brown, 'Society and the Supernatural: A Medieval Change', *Daedalus*, 104, no. 2 (1975), pp. 133–51, repr. in id., *Society and the Holy in Late Antiquity* (1982), pp. 302–32; C. Morris, '*Judicium Dei*: The Social and Political Significance of the Ordeal in the Eleventh Century', in D. Baker (ed.), *Church, Society, and Politics* (Studies in Church History, 12; 1975), pp. 95–111; P. R. Hyams, 'Trial by Ordeal: The Key to Proof in the Early Common Law', in M. S. Arnold and others (eds.), *On the Laws and Customs of England: Essays in Honor of Samuel E. Thorne* (Chapel Hill, NC [1981]), pp. 90–126; C. M. Radding, 'Superstition to Science: Nature, Fortune and the Passing of the Medieval Ordeal', *American Historical Review*, 84 (1979), pp. 945–69; R. Bartlett, *Trial by Fire and Water: The Medieval Judicial Ordeal* (Oxford, 1986); D. Barthélemy, 'Diversité des ordalies médiévales', *Revue Historique*, 280 (1988), pp. 3–25.

Order of the Communion, The. See COMMUNION, THE ORDER OF THE.

Order of Preachers. See DOMINICAN ORDER.

Ordericus Vitalis (1075–?1142), Anglo-Norman historian. He was the son of a French priest in the service of the first Norman earl of Shrewsbury and an English mother. Born near Shrewsbury in 1075, he went in 1085 as a novice to the Benedictine house of St-Évroul(t) in Normandy; here he remained (apart from a few journeys, including at least one to England) for the rest of his life. He called himself 'Angligena' and never lost his love of England. Orderic wrote (in a model hand) an Ecclesiastical History in 13 books: books 1 and 2, which were written last, are a conventional plagiarized account from the birth of Christ onwards; books 3–6, which were written first, began as a history of St-Évroul but have a long digression on the Norman conquest of England; the remainder is a history of Orderic's own time. His rhythmic style is complex and subtle, his vocabulary is at times unusual, the work is ill-arranged and its chronology often unclear; but Orderic's interpretation of 'ecclesiastical history' (a term borrowed from *Bede) was wide. He gives an inimitable account of the feudal politics of N. France and of Norman achievement throughout Christendom, and is altogether a prime source for the political and ecclesiastical history and customs of his time. His only rival among the historians of his day and region is *William of Malmesbury.

Editio princeps by A. Du Chesne (ed.), *Historiae Normannorum Scriptores antiqui* (Paris, 1619), pp. 319–925, repr. J. P. Migne, *PL* 188. 17–984. Crit. edn. in 5 vols. (admirably indexed) by A. Le Prévost (Société de l'Histoire de France, 1838–55), with important introd. in vol. 5 by L. Delisle; superseded by edn. with Eng. tr. by M. Chibnall (6 vols., Oxford, 1969–80). *Orderic Vital et l'abbaye de St-Évroul: Notice et travaux, publiés en l'honneur de l'historien normand* (Alençon, 1912); H. Wolter, SJ, *Ordericus Vitalis. Ein Beitrag zur Kluniazenischen Geschichtsschreibung* (Veröffentlichungen des Instituts für europäische Geschichte Mainz, 7; 1955). M. Chibnall, *The World of Orderic Vitalis* (Oxford, 1984). L. Delisle, 'Notes sur les manuscrits autographes d'Orderic Vital', in J. Lair (ed.), *Matériaux pour l'édition de Guillaume de Jumièges* (1910), pp. 7–27; E. Jamison, 'The Sicilian Norman Kingdom in the Mind of Anglo-Norman Contemporaries', *Proceedings of the British Academy*, 24 (1938), pp. 237–85, esp. pp. 242–7; P. Rousset, 'La Description du monde chevaleresque chez Orderic Vital', *Le Moyen Âge*, 75 (1969), pp. 427–44.

Orders, Anglican. See ANGLICAN ORDINATIONS.

Orders, Holy. See HOLY ORDERS.

Orders, Minor. See MINOR ORDERS.

Orders and Ordination. (1) ORIGINS. The Ministry of the Christian Church traces its beginnings to the Lord's commissioning of the Twelve (Mt. 10: 1–5; Mk. 3: 13–19, Lk. 6: 12–16) and the Seventy (Lk. 10: 1) to the work of the kingdom. This Ministry, so far from coming to an end at His death, received a new power and wider responsibilities after Pentecost (Acts 2: 1–13), though leadership of the *Jerusalem Church seems to have soon passed from St *Peter (Acts 1: 15; 2: 37; 4: 8, 5: 8; 10: 1–11 and 18; 15: 7; cf. Mt. 16: 16–18) to St *James, the Lord's brother (Acts 15: 19; 21: 18; *Eusebius, *HE* 2. 1).

Patterns of local ministry in the newly founded Churches varied, but comparison of St *Paul's first letter to the Corinthians with that of St *Clement of Rome indicates that the charismatic ministries of *prophets and teachers etc. (1 Cor. 12: 28) recognized by Paul in his Churches soon gave way to 'elders', i.e. *presbyters. Acts represents Paul as himself appointing them (14: 23; cf. 20: 17) and at 20: 28 takes *bishops (ἐπίσκοποι) to be broadly equivalent, as they also are in 1 Clement and the *Pastoral Epistles. Acts also assumes, perhaps correctly, that 'elders' existed early in Jerusalem (11: 30; 15: 2, etc.). That institution is not mentioned in Paul's genuine letters and was perhaps adopted by the Roman Church soon after the martyrdom of Peter and Paul. It is presupposed in the probably pseudonymous 1 Peter and James, and elsewhere (prob. Asia Minor) the author of 2 and 3 John calls himself 'the elder'. The further development to a monarchical episcopate, possibly reflected in 3 Jn. 9, is advocated and represented at *Antioch by St *Ignatius, in the face of the divisive effects of divergent beliefs.

The gradual transition from apostolic leadership and a variety of charismatic and non-charismatic ministries to that stronger Church order that provides a focus for unity is partly visible to the historian. If inferences about the Church in which Mt. originated can be drawn from such passages as 7: 15 and 23: 34, it seems that in Syria prophets and Jewish Christian scribes provided teaching. This pattern was overtaken by the evolution of the presbyterate and its fusion with the new orders of bishops and *deacons. The survival of prophets in the *Didache alongside bishops and deacons perhaps provides evidence for the transition. As early as 1 Cor. 12: 28 Paul had implied some gradations in ministry (cf. Eph. 4: 11), and the Pastoral Epistles' and Acts' appeal to him in legitimation of the development can be defended. But his own use of the word ἐπίσκοπος (Phil. 1: 1) is of uncertain meaning and διάκονος in his genuine letters (incidentally in Rom. 16: 1 with reference to a woman) does not sound like a definite order. That is first evident in 1 Tim. 3–4, which also adumbrates or envisages ordination (4: 14; cf. 5: 22). The local presbyters lay *hands on Timothy and the Spirit is understood to be conveyed by the rite (cf. also 2 Tim. 1: 6). The Jewish roots of this may be found in Num. 27: 15–23, where authority to lead the community is transmitted to Joshua (cf. Deut. 34: 9). The account in Acts 6: 1–6 of the appointment of the Seven echoes this passage. All these hints of later practice preserve the sense of God's choosing ministers (cf. 1 Tim. 1: 18), expressed also in the story of the election by lot of St *Matthias (Acts 1: 23–6).

(2) LATER DEVELOPMENT. By the middle of the 3rd cent. considerable evolution of the system is evident. At Rome under Pope *Cornelius (251–3) there were, besides the bishop, 46 presbyters, 7 deacons, 7 subdeacons, 42 acolytes and 52 exorcists, readers, and doorkeepers (*Eusebius, HE 6. 43. 11). But it was long before uniformity was reached. The *Statuta Ecclesiae Antiqua (prob. from Gaul, late-5th cent.) has nine distinct orders; St *John of Damascus has five; *Innocent III has six. By the later Middle Ages it was the prevalent view that there were seven Orders, but there were different methods of reckoning, largely through contending theories on the relation of the priesthood and the episcopate. For St *Thomas Aquinas, who held that the ultimate purpose of Holy Order lay in its relation to the Eucharist, the priesthood was the highest grade, since the priest possessed the power of consecrating the Sacrament; and this appears to be the view officially countenanced by the Council of *Trent, though since the Second *Vatican Council there has been an increased emphasis on the episcopate, in which the bishop is regarded as sharing pre-eminently in the priesthood of Christ. During the Middle Ages a distinction came to be drawn esp. in the W. between the '*Major Orders' (bishop, priest, deacon, subdeacon) and the *Minor Orders (acolytes, exorcists, readers, doorkeepers). The distinction in modern speech between 'consecration' to the episcopate and 'ordination' to the other Orders was unknown in early times and has been dropped in the current official RC documents.

(3) ORDER AS A SACRAMENT. Acc. to traditional Catholic theology the gift of Order is a Sacrament. The Council of Trent (Sess. 22) defines it as a Sacrament instituted by Christ (can. 3) and as conveying the Holy Spirit (can. 4). Like Baptism Order is held to impart an indelible *character. Hence a cleric if degraded does not lose the gift of Order and on restoration is not 're-ordained'; and though the civil law may treat an Anglican cleric who has executed a deed of relinquishment under the *Clerical Disabilities Act 1870 as a layman, from the standpoint of the Church he remains a priest or deacon. But where there

is grave doubt (e.g. through loss of records) whether ordination has been validly administered, it may be, and sometimes is, repeated 'conditionally'.

Despite the various grades in the ministry it is agreed that there is but a single Sacrament of Orders. It is widely denied, however, that the Orders lower than the diaconate can be reckoned a Sacrament. In the Middle Ages they were commonly so regarded (St Thomas, Summa Theolog., Suppl. 94, qu. 7, art. 3); but RC theologians now reject this view on the ground that they are of ecclesiastical (and not Divine) institution.

In the *Thirty-Nine Articles (art. 25) Orders is included among 'the five commonly called Sacraments' which 'are not to be counted for Sacraments of the Gospel'. In the Protestant Churches the Sacramental nature of Orders is commonly denied.

(4) THE RECIPIENT OF ORDERS. The traditional view is that only a baptized and confirmed male person can be validly ordained. However, in modern times many provinces of the Anglican Communion have admitted *women to the diaconate, and some to the priesthood and episcopate as well. The candidate must be of good moral character and convinced that he has a Divine call ('vocation') to the office (though a subjective interpretation of vocation does not appear to be ancient: several of the Fathers were ordained under protest). For the Ordination to be regular the candidate must also be of due age (in the C of E normally 24 years for the priesthood, 30 for the episcopate; see AGE, CANONICAL) and not be excommunicate; and (a matter esp. stressed by RC theologians) the *interstices must have been duly observed. The candidate also generally needs a '*title'. Further, an ordinand in the C of E is required by the *Clerical Subscription Act 1865 to take and subscribe the Oath of *Allegiance to the Sovereign, and by Canon to take and subscribe the Oath of Obedience to the bishop, and to make a Declaration of *Assent to 'the faith which is revealed in the Holy Scriptures and set forth in the catholic creeds and to which the historic formularies of the C of E bear witness'. The duties of the respective offices in the Anglican ministry are well set out in the *Ordinal. In the RC Church, the specific obligations incurred by the reception of Major Orders normally include, acc. to W. discipline, *celibacy (q.v.) and the recitation of the Divine *Office (q.v.).

(5) THE MINISTER OF ORDERS. Traditional theology also holds that the Sacrament of Orders can be validly conferred only by a duly consecrated bishop, acting as the minister of Christ and the successor of the Apostles. The episcopate is thus held to create a historical link between the Church of Apostolic times and that of today and is both the means and assurance of the continuity of office and of the transmission of grace (see APOSTOLIC SUCCESSION); and on these grounds the episcopate is held to be of the esse of the Church.

There is, however, a small body of evidence that in the early Church ordination was occasionally conferred by clerics other than bishops. The 13th can. of *Ancyra may provide for ordination by presbyters (but the text is disputed); and it was sometimes allowed that suffering for the faith in time of persecution was the equivalent of ordination (e.g. St *Hippolytus, Ap. Trad. 10. 1)

Since the purpose of Ordination is to qualify a person for office in the Church, it might seem that outside the

Church Orders could not be given. Such was the usual view of the early Church, and it is still that held in the E. But since the time of St *Augustine, whose influence here was paramount, it has been generally maintained in the W. that, even when in heresy or schism, a bishop can *validly ordain (as he can validly baptize and validly celebrate the Eucharist). Hence the RC Church does not 're-ordain' bishops and priests from the Orthodox Church should they be received into communion with the Pope, but accepts their previous Ordination as valid. Similarly Priests of the RC Church who join the C of E are not re-ordained, though for certain technical reasons (see ANGLICAN ORDINATIONS) the RC Church does not recognize Ordinations conferred in the C of E.

(6) RITES OF ORDINATION. The earliest known rite of Ordination is that in the *Apostolic Tradition of Hippolytus (c.215); and from the 4th cent. several such rites survive, e.g. the Liturgy of St *Serapion, and that in the *Apostolic Constitutions. Traditionally Ordination has always taken place in the context of the Eucharist, but for long, esp. in the E., the rite continued very simple. In both E. and W. it became the custom for the newly ordained presbyters to *concelebrate with the ordaining bishop. Gradually in the W. further elaborations were introduced esp. to signify the ordinand's new office. The Gospels were delivered to the deacon (in earlier times to the reader), while by the later Middle Ages the delivery of the paten and chalice with the elements prepared for the Mass to candidates for the priesthood had become sufficiently established for it to be regarded as the essence ('matter') of the rite (see INSTRUMENTS, TRADITION OF THE).

In 1968 the RC rites of ordination to the diaconate, priesthood and episcopate were all much simplified. In each case candidates are examined after the Gospel; when the diaconate and priesthood are both to be conferred the examination of the priests follows that of the deacons. The bishop lays hands on each candidate for the diaconate in silence and then says the ordination prayer over them all, seeking the gifts of the Holy Spirit to enable them to exercise their office faithfully. After each candidate has been vested in *dalmatic and *stole, the bishop gives him the book of the Gospels with a charge to proclaim and live by it. In the case of candidates for the priesthood, the bishop is joined by other clergy in the laying on of hands, and a different formula is used in the ordination prayer. The bishop then anoints the hands of each candidate with *chrism and delivers to him the paten and chalice with the bread and wine offered by the people. In the ordering of bishops, which is always a separate ceremony, the coconsecrators join with the consecrating bishop in saying that part of the consecratory prayer held to be necessary for validity. While this prayer is being said the book of the Gospels is held over the head of the candidate. The consecrating bishop then anoints his head, delivers the Gospels to him, puts a *ring on his finger and a *mitre on his head and gives him a pastoral staff or *crosier. The consecratory prayer used in the ordering of a bishop is substantially that found in the Apostolic Tradition of Hippolytus. In the new rite of ordination to the priesthood there is no mention of the power to forgive sins. For ceremonies of the ordination rites in the C of E, see ORDINAL.

It became usual in both E. and W. for bishops to be consecrated on a Sunday, e.g. the BCP orders that the rite is 'always to be performed upon some Sunday or Holyday'. In the W. the ordination of priests and deacons became customary at the *Ember (esp. December) seasons; and until very recently this remained the practice of the C of E; of recent years the feast of St Peter has tended to replace Trinity Sunday.

H. B. Porter, Jun., *The Ordination Prayers of the Ancient Western Churches* (Alcuin Club Collections, 49; 1967). J. *Morin, Cong. Orat., *De Sacris Ecclesiae Ordinationibus* (Paris, 1655); J. B. *Lightfoot, *St Paul's Epistle to the Philippians* (1868), pp. 179–267 ('The Christian Ministry'); E. *Hatch, *The Organization of the Early Christian Churches* (*Bampton Lectures for 1880; 1880); C. *Gore, *The Church and the Ministry* (1888; new edn. by C. H. *Turner, 1919); F. J. A. *Hort, *The Christian Ecclesia* (1897); R. C. *Moberly, *Ministerial Priesthood* (1897); A. *Harnack, *Die Entstehung und Entwicklung der Kirchenverfassung und des Kirchenrechts in den zwei ersten Jahrhunderten* (1910; Eng. tr., 1910); H. B. *Swete (ed.), *Essays on the Early History of the Church and the Ministry* (1918; esp. essay on 'Apostolic Succession' by C. H. Turner). J. Tixeront, *L'Ordre et les ordinations* (1924); G. *Dix, 'Jurisdiction, Episcopal and Papal, in the Early Church', *Laudate*, 15 (1938), pp. 45–55, 101–24, 157–73, and 232–50; 16 (1938), pp. 107–18, 166–81, and 231–43; repr. as a separate vol., with introd. by T. M. Parker (1975). B. H. *Streeter, *The Primitive Church studied with special reference to the Origins of the Christian Ministry* (1939); J. N. Ainslie, *The Doctrines of Ministerial Order in the Reformed Churches of the 16th and 17th Centuries* (1940); K. E. *Kirk (ed.), *The Apostolic Ministry* (1946); E. Lohse, *Die Ordination im Spätjudentum und im Neuen Testament* [1951]; H. von Campenhausen, *Kirchliches Amt und geistliche Vollmacht in den ersten drei Jahrhunderten* (Beiträge zur historischen Theologie, 41; 1953; Eng. tr., 1969); E. Schweizer, *Gemeinde und Gemeindeordnung im Neuen Testament* (Abhandlungen zur Theologie des Alten und Neuen Testaments, 35; Zurich, 1959; Eng. tr., Studies in Biblical Theology, 32; 1961); A. Lemaire, *Les Ministères aux origines de l'Église. Naissance de la triple hiérarchie: évêques, presbytres, diacres* (Lectio Divina, 68; 1971); K. Kertelge, *Gemeinde und Amt im Neuen Testament* (Biblische Handbibliothek, 10 [1972]); J. Delorme (ed.), *Le Ministère et les Ministères selon le Nouveau Testament* [1974]; A. Faivre, *Naissance d'une hiérarchie: Les premières étapes du cursus clérical* (Théologie historique, 40; 1977); J. Lécuyer, *Le Sacrement de l'Ordination: Recherche historique et théologique* (ibid. 65; 1983); P. Jounel in A. G. Martimort, *L'Église en Prière* (new edn., 3 [1984]), pp. 154–96; Eng. tr. (1988), pp. 139–84; E. [C. F. A.] *Schillebeeckx, OP, *Pleidooi voor Mensen in de Kerk: Christelijke Identiteit en Ambten in de Kerk* (Baarn, 1985; Eng. tr., 1985). M. V. MacDonald, *The Pauline Churches: A Sociohistorical Study of Institutionalization in the Pauline and Deutero-Pauline Writings* (Society for New Testament Studies, Monograph Series, 60; Cambridge, 1988), esp. pp. 46–60, 123–38, and 203–20; P. F. Bradshaw, *Ordination Rites of the Ancient Churches of East and West* (New York [1990]). See also bibl. to BISHOP, DEACON, PRIEST, and REUNION.

Ordinal (Lat. *ordinale*). (1) In the Middle Ages, a manual to acquaint the priest with the Office to be recited in acc. with variations in the ecclesiastical year.

(2) In the C of E, 'The Form and Manner of Making, Ordaining, and Consecrating of Bishops, Priests and Deacons, according to the Order of the Church of England'. This use of the word dates only from c.1600. There have been four English Ordinals. (i) The first was published in March 1550 ('1549'). It was the work of six bishops and six other scholars, appointed by an Order in Council of 31 Jan. 1550, as decreed by Act of Parliament (the Consecration of Bishops, etc., Act 1549). Though bound up with copies of the BCP, neither this nor the later Ordinals is

properly a part of the Book. It was modelled on the rite in the medieval *Sarum *Pontifical. Ordination was to take place on a Sunday or Holy Day. The Exhortation and Examination in the Ordering of Priests were mainly based on a draft by M. *Bucer. At the imposition of hands the formula was 'Receive the Holy Ghost. Whose sins thou dost forgive they are forgiven; whose sins thou dost retain they are retained. And be thou a faithful dispenser of the Word of God and of His Holy Sacraments. In the Name of the Father and of the Son and of the Holy Ghost. Amen'; and at the delivery of the Bible and the chalice with the bread, 'Take thou authority to preach the Word of God and to minister the Holy Sacraments in this congregation'. In the Consecration of Bishops the medieval ceremonies of anointing, putting on of gloves, and delivery of the ring and mitre were omitted. No provision was made for the Minor Orders. (ii) In 1552, the chief alterations were the omission of certain ceremonies, e.g., in the Ordering of Priests, the Tradition of the *Instruments. (iii) In 1559 the changes were negligible except in the wording of the Oath (now of 'the Queen's Sovereignty' instead of 'the King's Supremacy'). (iv) In 1662 some important modifications were made, notably in the Ordering of Priests, the change of the formula accompanying the imposition of hands to 'Receive the Holy Ghost *for the Office and Work of a Priest in the Church of God, now committed unto thee by the Imposition of our hands.* Whose sins, etc.' Subsequent attempts at revision throughout the Anglican Communion have generally been characterized by conservatism. See also ALTERNATIVE SERVICES.

The 1550 Ordinal is printed in *The Liturgies . . . of King Edward VI* (ed. *Parker Society by J. Ketley, 1844), pp. 159–186, and in the Everyman's Library edn. of the *First and Second Prayer Books of King Edward VI* (1910), pp. 291–317. F. E. *Brightman, *The English Rite* (1915), vol. 1, pp. cxxx–clxi; vol. 2, pp. 928–1017. P. F. Bradshaw, *The Anglican Ordinal: Its History and Development from the Reformation to the Present Day* (*Alcuin Club Collections, 53; 1971); id. in C. [P. M.] Jones and others (eds.), *The Study of Liturgy* (2nd edn., 1992), pp. 385–8.

Ordinary. In canon law, an ecclesiastic in the exercise of the jurisdiction permanently and irremovably annexed to his office. Such jurisdiction extends over his rights of teaching, governing, adjudicating, and administering the Sacraments. In the RC Church the term covers, besides the Pope, diocesan bishops and all who are, even temporarily, set over a diocese or other particular Church or community equivalent to it, and those in them who have ordinary general executive power, that is, *vicars general and episcopal vicars. It also includes, for their own members, the major superiors of clerical religious *institutes of pontifical right and of clerical societies of apostolic life of pontifical right who have at least ordinary executive power (*CIC* (1983), can. 134 § 1). The term 'local Ordinary' means all these except superiors of religious institutes and of societies of apostolic life (can. 134 § 2). The meaning of the term in the BCP is not precisely determined: it may refer either to the bishop or to the archdeacon. The parish priest may be regarded as possessing ordinary jurisdiction of an inferior kind, but he may not delegate it against the will of his superior ordinary.

Ordinary of the Mass (Lat. *Ordo Missae*). A term widely used until the recent liturgical reforms to describe

the invariable or almost invariable part of the *Mass, as distinguished from the parts which varied with the ecclesiastical calendar, called the *Proper. It comprised the preparatory prayers, the *Kyrie, *Gloria in Excelsis and *Creed, the *Preface and *Sanctus, the *Canon, the *Lord's Prayer, *Fraction and *Agnus Dei, part of the Communion and Post-Communion devotions, and (until 1965) the *Last Gospel. The Canon, however, was sometimes distinguished from the Ordinary, the two together being termed the 'Ordinary and Canon of the Mass'. The 1970 *Missale Romanum* uses the term 'Ordo Missae' to describe the whole service of the Mass.

Ordination. See ORDERS AND ORDINATION.

Ordinations, Anglican. See ANGLICAN ORDINATIONS.

Ordines Romani. The ancient collections of ceremonial directions for the performance of the Roman rite and thus the ancestors of the *Caeremoniale Romanum, the *Caeremoniale Episcoporum, and the *Pontifical. The first to be printed in modern times were edited by G. *Cassander in 1561 (Cologne) and more adequately by Melchior Hittorp in 1568 (also Cologne), but far more important was the collection of 15 Ordines published by J. *Mabillon in his *Musaeum Italicum*, vol. 2 (1689). The study of the Ordines was put on a new footing by M. Andrieu, who distinguished 50, which he arranged according to their content: I–X the Mass; XI Baptism; XII–XIV the Office; XV–XIX monastic and other rituals for the ecclesiastical year; XX–XXXIII feasts of the year, esp. the ceremonies of Holy Week; XXXIV–XL Ordinations; XLI–XLIV dedication of churches; XLV–XLVIII coronation of the Emperor; XLIX funerals; L is the Ordo from the Romano-Germanic Pontifical of the 10th cent. entitled by Hittorp 'Ordo Romanus Antiquus'. These 50 Ordines have survived in various collections which partly overlap, and which can be dated between the 8th and the 10th cents. They correspond to Mabillon's Ordines I–IX (his X–XV are of later date). The earliest Ordines originated in Rome; perhaps the oldest is Ordo XI (= Mabillon III), which is probably based on the *Gelasian Sacramentary. They provide the earliest evidence for the development of the Roman rite and illustrate its diffusion throughout Europe. They began to circulate north of the Alps at the end of the 8th cent. and were adapted and greatly enlarged. In the form in which they developed north of the Alps, seen in the Romano-Germanic Pontifical of the 10th cent. (Ordo L), they influenced the rite of Rome itself. See also PONTIFICAL.

Mabillon's text repr. in J. P. Migne, *PL* 78. 851–1408. Crit. edn. by M. Andrieu, *Les Ordines Romani du haut moyen âge* (SSL 11 [introd.], 23 [Ordines I–XIII], 24 [Ordines XIV–XXXIV], 38 [Ordines XXXV–XLIX], and 29 [Ordo L]; 1931–61). *Ordo Romanus Primus* also ed., with Eng. tr., by E. G. C. F. Atchley (LLE 6; 1905). M. Dykmans, SJ, 'Mabillon et les interpolations de son *Ordo Romanus XIV*', *Gregorianum*, 47 (1966), pp. 316–42. Vogel, *Sources*, pp. 135–224. T. A. Vismans, OP, in *LW* 2 (1968), cols. 2061–6, s.v.

Ordo Missae. See ORDINARY OF THE MASS.

Oresme, Nicholas (*c.*1320–82), French mathematician, natural philosopher, and economist, who is often somewhat misleadingly seen as foreshadowing later scientific theories developed by N. *Copernicus, G. *Galileo, R. *Descartes, and others. He was closely associated both with the University of *Paris and the French Court, and held a variety of academic and ecclesiastical positions culminating in his appointment as Bp. of Lisieux in 1377. Following Thomas *Bradwardine and others, he attempted to treat motion and other physical phenomena more mathematically, although still working within a basically *Aristotelian framework. He gave powerful arguments in favour of the Earth spinning daily on its own axis, but revealed that he did so as a sceptical and fideistic ploy against those who would use reason to attack the truths of Christianity. Both his sceptical stand and his use of sophisticated mathematical arguments were deployed in his attacks on astrologers, in writings intended mainly for use at the Court of Charles V. It was also for the Court that he produced several philosophical works in the vernacular, esp. Aristotelian translations and commentaries.

There are modern edns. of many of Oresme's works, incl. the foll. with Eng. tr., and in most cases, comm.: *De moneta* by C. Johnson (Medieval Texts, London, 1956); *De proportionibus proportionum* and *Ad pauca respicientes* by E. Grant (University of Wisconsin Publications in Medieval Science; Madison, Milwaukee, and London, 1966); *Tractatus de configurationibus qualitatum et motuum* by M. Clagett (ibid., 1968), with bibl. pp. 637–50; *Tractatus de commensurabilitate vel incommensurabilitate motuum celi* by E. Grant (ibid., 1971); *De causis mirabilium* by B. Hansen (Pontifical Institute of Mediaeval Studies, Studies and Texts, 68; Toronto [1985]). *Quaestio contra Divinatores Horoscopios*, ed. S. Caroti in *AHDLMA* 43 (for 1976; 1977), pp. 201–310. G. W. Coopland, *Nicole Oresme and the Astrologers: A Study of his Livre de Divinacions* (Liverpool, 1952), incl. text and Eng. tr. The French trs. and comm. on Aristotle (and Pseudo-Aristotle) are ed. by A. D. Menut: *Le Livre d'éthiques* (New York, 1940); *Le Livre de yconomique* in *Transactions of the American Philosophical Society*, NS 47 (1957), pp. 783–853 (with Eng. tr.); *Le Livre de politiques*, ibid. 60 (1970), pt. 6. *Le Livre de ciel et du monde*, ed. A. D. Menut and A. J. Demony, CSB (University of Wisconsin Publications in Medieval Science, Madison, etc., 1968, with Eng. tr.). P. Souffrin and A. P. Segonds (eds.), *Nicolas Oresme: Tradition et innovation chez un intellectuel du XIVᵉ siècle* (Paris and Padua [1988]); J. Quillet (ed.), *Autour de Nicole Oresme: Actes du Colloque Oresme organisé à l'Université de Paris XII* (1990). M. Clagett in *Dictionary of Scientific Biography*, ed. C. C. Gillispie, 10 (1981 edn.), pp. 223–30, s.v.

Organic Articles. The provisions of Napoleon (1802) to regulate public worship and the relations of Church and state in France. They included (1) governmental control over Papal documents entering France, and over the powers of ecclesiastical councils and synods; (2) a limited state control of seminaries and clergy, requiring *inter alia* the teaching of the *Gallican Articles; (3) state regulation of processions and clerical dress; and (4) state regulation of stipends and parish boundaries. Napoleon sought to defend this radical and sudden modification of the *Concordat (1801) on the ground that the Articles were supplementary and explanatory. The Pope objected to them from the first, and in fact the Articles were less and less enforced, though they were not finally repealed till the separation of Church and state in 1905.

The text is in C. Mirbt, no. 559, and J. E. C. Bodley, *The Church in France* (1906), pp. 121–34. Eng. tr. in F. Mourret, SS,

A History of the Catholic Church, tr. by N. Thompson, 7 (1955), pp. 565–74. See also works cited under CONCORDAT OF 1801.

organs. Known from the time of classical antiquity, the organ remained a purely secular instrument until the 10th cent., when it began to appear in major churches, such as *Glastonbury and *Winchester. What liturgical part, if any, it played remains largely unknown until *c*.1400, when the alternating of organ verses with *plainsong or polyphony sung by the choir became an established custom in both the Mass and Office. This continued as a common practice, esp. in France, until the 19th cent., but in *Lutheran churches in Germany in the 17th cent. it gave way to the development of the organ chorale with its subsequent rich repertoire. The organ also provided simple accompaniments for some choral music, such as the English verse *anthem, from the early 17th cent., a role which later evolved into more elaborate accompanimental styles. The organ's present predominant role, however, that of leading congregational singing, developed only gradually from the 17th cent. onwards. Even within the C of E organs found their way into many smaller parish churches only from about the mid-19th cent., whilst many of the more *Calvinistic churches remained inimical to them until modern times. In the 17th cent. English *Puritan opposition to organs in churches resulted in the destruction of almost all organs during the Commonwealth as a result of legislation in 1644. They were reintroduced after the Restoration (1660), among the most famous organ-builders being Bernard Smith (*c*. 1630–1708) and René (Renatus) Harris (?1640–?1715). Organs have always varied greatly in size, and been essentially individually designed to suit buildings and finances. In the late 18th and early 19th cent. the barrel organ, its barrels pinned with hymn tunes, enjoyed a brief popularity (no skilled performer being necessary), whilst in the second half of the 20th cent. the electronic organ has for economic reasons supplanted the pipe organ in many churches, although, despite technical advances, it remains a poor substitute for a quality pipe instrument.

W. L. Summer, *The Organ: Its Evolution, Principles of Construction and Use* (1952; 4th edn., 1973). P. [F] Williams, *The European Organ 1450–1850* (1966); id., *A New History of the Organ from the Greeks to the Present Day* (1980); id., *The Organ in Western Culture, 750–1250* (Cambridge, 1993); id., *The King of Instruments: How Churches came to have Organs* (1993). C. Clutton and A. Niland, *The British Organ* (1963; 2nd edn., 1982). O. [C.] Ochse, *The History of the Organ in the United States* (Bloomington, Ill., and London [1975]). F. Routh, *Early English Organ Music from the Middle Ages to 1837* (1973). N. Temperley, *The Music of the English Parish Church* (2 vols., Cambridge, 1979). P. [M.] Williams in S. Sadie (ed.), *The New Grove Dictionary of Music and Musicians*, 13 (1980), pp. 710–79, s.v.

Oriens Christianus. The title of two quite distinct publications.

(1) M. *Le Quien's work on the E. Church. It contains an enormous collection of geographical and historical material, arranged acc. to the four E. Patriarchates and, despite the inaccuracies incidental to a pioneer work of vast dimensions, has not been superseded. Le Quien worked on it from 1718 till his death in 1733, issuing a prospectus of the work in 1722; but it was not published till 1740, when it appeared in three folio volumes.

(2) A German periodical devoted to Oriental studies published at Leipzig under the direction of A. *Baumstark. It appeared in three series: the Original Series, 8 vols., 1901–10; a 'Neue Serie', 14 vols., 1911–25; and the Third Series, 14 vols., 1927 ['1926']–1941. The periodical was revived on new lines, under the auspices of the Görres-Gesellschaft, and a Fourth Series published at Wiesbaden, 1953 ff.

On (1), H. *Leclercq, OSB, in *DACL* 8 (pt. 2; 1929), cols. 2593–6, s.v. 'Le Quien'; S. Vailhé, AA, in *CE* 9 (1910), p. 188, s.v. 'Le Quien'.

Oriental Orthodox Churches. A modern designation for those Churches (i.e. the *Armenian, *Coptic, *Ethiopian, and *Syrian Orthodox) which rejected the Christological teaching of the Definition of *Chalcedon, and in particular the phrase 'in two natures'. The name distinguishes these Churches from the Eastern *Orthodox Church and avoids the ambiguous (and hence offensive) term *Monophysite.

P. Gregorios and others (eds.), *Does Chalcedon Divide or Unite? Towards Convergence in Orthodox Christology* (Geneva, 1981).

orientation. The construction of a church so that its longer axis runs E. and W. The earliest (4th cent.) basilicas in Rome had a façade to the E. and an *apse for the altar at the W., so that the celebrant at the Eucharist, standing behind the altar, faced E. The high altar of Byzantine churches, on the other hand, was placed in an E. apse, a practice followed later esp. in England, Germany, and Spain. Elsewhere custom has been more variable. Though orientation is derived historically from a pagan habit of praying towards the sunrise, Christians have seen in its adoption symbolic reference to Christ as the Rising Sun.

H. Nissen, *Orientation: Studien zur Geschichte der Religion* (3 Hefte, 1906–10), esp. pp. 391–459 ('Das Christentum'). F. J. Doelger, *Sol Salutis: Gebet und Gesang im christlichen Altertum mit besonderer Rücksicht auf die Ostung in Gebet und Liturgie* (Liturgische Forschungen, 4–5; 1920). O. Nussbaum, *Der Standort des Liturgen am christlichen Altar vor dem Jahre 1000: Eine archäologische und liturgiegeschichtliche Untersuchung* (2 vols., Theophaneia, 18; 1965). E. Weigand, 'Die Ostung in der frühchristlichen Architektur', in *Festschrift für Sebastian Merkle zu seinem 60. Geburtstage* (1922), pp. 370–85. E. Peterson, 'La croce e la preghiera verso oriente', *EL* 59 (1945), pp. 52–68; L. Voelkl, ' "Orientierung" im Weltbild der ersten christlichen Jahrhunderte', *Riv. A.C.* 25 (1949), pp. 155–70. M. J. Moreton, 'Εἰς ἀνατολὰς βλέψατε. Orientation as a Liturgical Principle', in E. A. Livingstone (ed.), *Studia Patristica*, 17 (Oxford, 1982), pp. 575–90. T. D. Atkinson in *HERE* 10 (1918), pp. 73–88, s.v. 'Points of the Compass'. H. *Leclercq, OSB, in *DACL* 12 (pt. 2; 1936), cols. 2665–9, s.v.

Origen (*c.*185–*c.*254), Alexandrian biblical critic, exegete, theologian, and spiritual writer. The facts of his life are recorded by *Eusebius. He was born in Egypt, prob. at *Alexandria, where he received a thoroughly Christian education in the house of his parents. During the persecution in Alexandria in 202 when his father, Leonidas, was killed, he was prevented from seeking martyrdom only by a ruse of his mother, who hid his clothes. He taught in Alexandria and, when peace was restored, was recognized by *Demetrius as head of the *Catechetical School (q.v.), in place of *Clement, who had fled the city. He now began

to lead a strictly ascetical life of fastings, vigils, and voluntary poverty, and even, acc. to Eusebius, mutilated himself, misinterpreting Mt. 19: 12 in a literal sense. He was well versed in the works of the Middle Platonists and studied pagan philosophy and literature under *Ammonius Saccas. He undertook several journeys, one to Rome, where he heard a sermon of St *Hippolytus, and one to Arabia. When, in 215, troubles broke out in Alexandria in connection with a visit of the Emp. Caracalla, he went to Palestine, where he was asked to preach by the Bps. of *Caesarea and *Aelia. As he was only a layman, this was regarded as a breach of the Alexandrian ecclesiastical discipline, in consequence of which he was recalled by his bishop, Demetrius. From *c.*218 to 230 he devoted himself almost without interruption to literary activities. In 230 he went again to Palestine, where he was ordained priest by the same bishops who had invited him to preach on his previous visit. As a consequence Bp. Demetrius deprived him of his chair and deposed him from the priesthood, more because of the irregularity of his ordination than, as later opponents asserted, for doctrinal reasons. Origen left Alexandria and found a refuge at Caesarea (231), where he established a school which soon became famous, and where he continued his literary work and devoted himself to preaching. In 250, in the persecution of *Decius, he was imprisoned and subjected to prolonged torture, which he survived only a few years.

Origen was a very fertile author. Many of his writings have perished and most of the others survive only in fragments or in Latin translations. The main reasons for this almost complete loss of the originals are the later condemnation of his teaching and the exorbitant length and diffusiveness of his works. His chief work on biblical criticism is his famous '*Hexapla' (q.v.). Among his many exegetical works are *scholia* on Exod., Lev., and Num., commentaries on almost all the books of the Bible, most of which survive only in small fragments, and many homilies, which are among the oldest examples of Christian preaching. Large portions of the Commentaries on Mt. and Jn., however, have been preserved, as well as considerable sections (in *Rufinus' Lat. tr.) of those on the Song of Solomon and Romans. Substantial sections of the Greek original of the commentaries on Rom. and Ex., and a homily on 1 Kgs., were discovered at Toura, near Cairo.

The most important of Origen's theological works is the 'De Principiis' (Περὶ Ἀρχῶν), which covers a wide range of doctrinal topics in four books treating of God and the heavenly beings, of man and the material world, of free will and its consequences, and of Holy Scripture. The original text has almost completely disappeared, and the work is extant only in the not very reliable Latin translation of Rufinus and the more faithful, but fragmentary, rendering of St *Jerome. Of his other theological works nearly all are lost. His two ascetical works, 'Exhortation to Martyrdom', written during the persecution of Maximin in 235, and 'On Prayer', were much read in antiquity. He also wrote an important apologetic work against *Celsus (q.v.).

Origen was essentially a biblical scholar whose thought was nourished on Scripture, the inspiration and integrity of which he affirmed esp. against the *Marcionites. He recognized a triple sense, literal, moral, and allegorical, of which he preferred the last. He justified this choice on many grounds, esp. the contention that the whole universe is pervaded with symbols and types of the invisible world. All things had a double aspect, one corporeal and sensible, which is accessible to all, the other spiritual and mystical, known only to the perfect. This led him to distinguish between two classes of Christians: the simple, who have to be satisfied with faith in Christ crucified, and the perfect, who ascend beyond this to the contemplation of the Word dwelling with the Father.

The point of departure of Origen's doctrinal teaching was faith in the unity of God, who is altogether transcendent. This unity in its fullest form is understood of God the Father. But the threefold nature of the godhead is also affirmed. The Son is eternally generated from the Father and manifests all His attributes. The Holy Spirit is also eternal, though His role in Origen's scheme of thought is far from clear and Origen is uncertain about His nature and His relation to the Father and to the Son. Origen's philosophical presuppositions ensure that for him the Son can be divine only in a lesser sense than the Father; the Son is θεός (god), but only the Father is αὐτόθεος (absolute God, God in himself). In his 'Treatise on Prayer' he taught that prayer ought to be addressed only to the Father through the Son. Yet his teaching and his faith are strongly positive with respect to the Son: He belongs eternally to the godhead: He is perfect mirror of the Father's goodness, love, truth, and all His other attributes, reflecting them in assimilable form to all the rest of the creation. Moreover in the more popular style of the homilies he himself addresses his prayers directly to Christ.

His philosophical speculations often issued in audacious theories, though, in the absence of the original texts, it is not always easy to say whether he held them as certain or merely stated them as hypotheses, or even simply repeated the ideas of other thinkers. He affirmed that creation was eternal in the belief that without an existing world God would have been inactive and not omnipotent. He held Him to be finite, because if He were infinite He could not think Himself. Among his most controverted theories was his teaching on souls and their destiny. All spirits were created equal, but through the exercise of their free will they developed in hierarchical order and some fell into sin and so became either demons or souls imprisoned in bodies. Death does not finally decide the fate of the soul, which may turn into a demon or an angel. This ascent and descent goes on uninterruptedly until the final '*Apocatastasis' (q.v.) when all creatures, even the devil, will be saved. There is also a strong current of mysticism in Origen. He held that true knowledge was the participation of the purified soul in the Wisdom of the Word and a way towards *deification and union with Christ. In the course of the disputes on *Origenism (q.v.) his teaching has often been misrepresented, and owing to the loss of the originals of most of his works, a satisfactory reconstruction of his authentic thought is not always possible.

The earliest pr. edns. were confined to Origen's Lat. works. Greek works ed. P. D. *Huet, Bp. of Avranches (2 vols., fol., Rouen, 1668; with important introd., repr. in J. P. Migne, PG 17. 633–1284). The best complete edn. (without, however, the Hexapla frags.) is still that of the *Maurist, C. de La Rue, OSB, 4 vols., fol., Paris, 1733–59 (vol. 4 completed by his nephew, C. Vincent de La Rue, OSB); repr. in J. P. Migne, PG 11–17. Modern crit. edn. of separate texts in GCS, incl. Contra Celsum (ed. P. Koetschau, 1899), Comm. in Jn. (ed. E. Preuschen, 1903),

De Principiis (ed. P. Koetschau, 1913), Comm. in Matt. (ed. E. Klostermann, E. Benz, and L. Früchtel, 1933–55), Hom. in Luc. (ed. M. Rauer, 1930; 2nd edn., 1959); also many vols., with Fr. tr., in SC, incl. Hom. in Jos., by A. Jaubert (SC 71; 1960), Hom. in Luc., by H. Crouzel, SJ, and others (SC 87; 1962), Comm. in Jn., by C. Blanc (SC 120, 157, 222, 290, 385; 1966–92); Contra Celsum, by M. Borret, SJ (SC 132, 136, 147, 150, 227; 1967–76); Hom. in Jer., by P. Nautin (SC 232 and 238; 1976–7), and De Princ., by H. Crouzel, SJ, and M. Simonetti (SC 252 f., 268 f., 312; 1978–84). De Princ., also ed. with Ger. tr., by H. Görgemanns and H. Karpp (Texte zur Forschung, 24; 1976). R. Cadiou, Commentaires inédits des psaumes (1936). Text of Origen's 'Dialogue with Heraclides', discovered in 1941 on Toura papyrus, ed. J. Scherer (Publications de la Société Fouad Iᵉʳ de Papyrologie. Textes et Documents, 9; Cairo, 1949; repr., with Fr. tr., SC 67; 1960). For the *Philocalia and the *Tractatus Origenis, see s.vv. Eng. tr. (incomplete) of his collected works in ANCL. Modern trs. of Contra Celsum by H. Chadwick (Cambridge, 1953), of De Principiis by G. W. Butterworth (London, 1936), of De Oratione and Exhortatio ad Martyrium by J. J. O'Meara (ACW 19; 1954), of De Oratione by J. E. L. Oulton and of 'Exhortatio ad Martyrium' and 'Dialogue with Heraclides' by H. Chadwick in Alexandrian Christianity (Library of Christian Classics, 2; 1954), pp. 169–458, incl. introd.; of Comm. and Homilies on the Song of Songs by R. P. Lawson (ACW 26; 1957); of Homilies on Gen. and Exod. by R. E. Heine (Fathers of the Church, 71 [1982]); of Comm. on John by id. (ibid. 80 and 89; 1989–94); and of the Homilies on Lev. 1–16 by G. W. Barkley (ibid. 83 [1990]).

There is an immense lit.; details in bibl. by H. Crouzel, listed below. Studies on Origen's life and work as a whole by E. de Faye (3 vols., Paris, 1923–8), J. *Daniélou, SJ (Paris, 1948; Eng. tr., 1955), P. Nautin (Paris, 1977), J. W. Trigg (Atlanta, Ga., 1983, London, 1985), and H. Crouzel, SJ (Paris, 1985; Eng. tr., 1989). R. Cadiou, Introduction au système d'Origène (1932); id., La Jeunesse d'Origène (1935). W. Völker, Das Vollkommenheitsideal des Origenes (1931); H. Koch, Pronoia und Paideusis: Studien über Origenes und sein Verhältniss zum Platonismus (Arbeiten zur Kirchengeschichte, 22; 1934); A. Lieske, Die Theologie der Logosmystik bei Origenes (1938). H. Crouzel, Théologie de l'image de Dieu chez Origène (Théologie, 34; 1956); id., Origène et la 'connaissance mystique' (Museum Lessianum, section théologique, 66; 1961), and other works of this author; M. Harl, Origène et la fonction révélatrice du Verbe Incarné (Patristica Sorbonensia, 2; 1958). P. Nemeshegyi, SJ, Paternité de Dieu chez Origène (Bibliothèque de Théologie, 4th ser. 2; 1960). J. Rius-Camps, El Dinamismo Trinitario en la Divinización de los seres racionales según Origenes (Orientalia Christiana Analecta, 188; 1970). H. J. Vogt, Das Kirchenverstandnis des Origenes (Bonner Beiträge zur Kirchengeschichte, 4; 1974). L. Lies, Wort und Eucharistie bei Origenes (Innsbrucker theologische Studien, 1; 1978). H. *Lubac, SJ, Histoire et esprit: L'Intelligence des Écritures d'après Origène (1950). R. P. C. Hanson, Origen's Doctrine of Tradition (1954); id., Allegory and Event: A Study of the Sources and Significance of Origen's Interpretation of Scripture (1959); K. J. Torjesen, Hermeneutical Procedure and Theological Method in Origen's Exegesis (Patristische Texte und Studien, 28; 1986); J. C. Smith, The Ancient Wisdom of Origen (Lewisburg and London [1992]). N. R. M. de Lange, Origen and the Jews (1976). The papers of a series of international conferences on Origen pub. under the title Origeniana: [1] held at Montserrat, 1973, ed. H. Crouzel and others (Quaderni di 'Vetera Christianorum', 12; 1975); 2, held at Bari, 1977, ed. H. Crouzel and A. Quacquarelli (ibid. 15; 1980); 3, held at Manchester, 1981, ed. R. [P. C.] Hanson and H. Crouzel (Rome, 1985); 4, held at Innsbruck, 1985, ed. L. Lies (Innsbrucker theologische Studien, 19; 1987); 5, held in Boston, 1989, ed. R. J. Daly (Bibliotheca Ephemeridum Theologicarum Lovaniensium, 105; 1992). H. Crouzel, Bibliographie critique d'Origène (Instrumenta Patristica, 8; 1971; suppl., ibid. 8A; 1982). CPG 1 (1983), pp. 141–86 (nos. 1410–525). Bardenhewer, 2, pp. 96–194; Altaner and Stuiber (1978), pp. 197–209 and 587–90. Important art. by B. F.

*Westcott in *DCB* 4 (1887; but art. dated 1882), pp. 96–142. G. Bardy in *DTC* 11 (pt. 2; 1932), cols. 1489–565; H. Crouzel in *DPAC* 2 (1984), cols. 2517–32, s.v. 'Origene'; Eng. tr. in *Encyclopedia of the Early Church*, 2 (1992), pp. 619–23. See also bibl. to ALEXANDRIAN THEOLOGY, CELSUS, HEXAPLA.

Origenism. The group of theories enunciated by, or attributed to, *Origen (q.v.). Among Origen's earliest opponents was *Methodius of Olympus, who rejected esp. his teaching on the pre-existence of souls and his denial of the identity between the mortal and the resurrection bodies. In the 4th cent. the attacks of the Anti-Origenists were directed mainly against the Trinitarian doctrine of the 'De Principiis'. He was further accused of teaching *metempsychosis and of interpreting the Scriptures only allegorically. But his supporters were also numerous. The martyr St *Pamphilus wrote in his defence, and later, Sts *Athanasius, *Basil, and *Gregory of Nazianzus esteemed him highly, and St *Didymus endeavoured to prove his Trinitarian orthodoxy. The first great controversy was inaugurated by St *Epiphanius (between *c.*375 and 377), who, in his 64th heresy, gives a very one-sided account of Origen's doctrines. Epiphanius's attack was taken up by St *Jerome. Having first been an ardent defender of Origen, Jerome changed his views in 395, on the occasion of a visit of Epiphanius to *Jerusalem, and attempted to obtain a condemnation of Origen from its bishop, John. In this he failed, and John even obtained a sentence of exile against Jerome from the secular authorities, which, however, was not carried out. For a time John and Jerome were reconciled through the good offices of *Theophilus of Alexandria, at that time an adherent of Origen. The peace was interrupted when, in 398, *Rufinus published in Rome his Latin translation of the 'De Principiis', in the preface of which he referred to Jerome's former Origenistic leanings. The controversy reached its climax when, in 400, a Council at Alexandria convoked by Theophilus, who had become an opponent, condemned Origenism. Pope Anastasius I and the Bps. of Palestine and Syria adhered to the condemnation, and Theophilus continued his campaign. In his Festal Letter of 402 he called Origen the 'hydra of heresies' and he expelled from their monasteries the famous '*Tall Brothers' (q.v.) and other supporters of Origenism, who found refuge with St *Chrysostom at *Constantinople.

The controversy flared up again in the 6th cent., being described in detail in the 'Life of St Sabas' by *Cyril of Scythopolis. Origenism had been propagated esp. in the New Laura, nr. Jerusalem, whose monks had separated from the Great Laura, but it found adherents also in the latter, and *c.*542 it had strong partisans throughout Palestine. Its Palestinian opponents, however, obtained from the Emp. *Justinian the famous letter to Mennas, Patr. of Constantinople, in which Origen is numbered among the most pernicious heretics. At the Emperor's command a Council was convoked at Constantinople in 543, and an edict drawn up in accordance with Justinian's views giving a long list of Origenistic errors and their refutation, which was signed by Pope *Vigilius and the E. patriarchs. The Origenist monks at Jerusalem split into two parties: the Isochrists, who held that at the Apocatastasis all men would become equal to Christ, and the Protoctists, who seem to have regarded the soul of Christ not as equal to the other souls but as the most excellent of creatures. These latter, after renouncing the doctrine of the pre-existence of souls, made common cause with the orthodox against the Isochrists. The Origenistic controversy was ended by the Second Council of *Constantinople (553), when Origen's teaching was condemned, though it is uncertain whether the Council examined his case afresh or simply adhered to the decision of the synods of 543. All the bishops submitted except Alexander of Abila, who was deposed.

L. B. Radford, *Three Teachers of Alexandria, Theognostus, Pierius and Peter: A Study in the Early History of Origenism and Anti-Origenism* (1908); K. *Holl, 'Die Zeitfolge des ersten origenistischen Streits', *Sb.* (Berl.), 1916, pp. 226–55, repr. in *Gesammelte Aufsätze*, 2 (1928), pp. 310–35. F. Diekamp, *Die origenistischen Streitigkeiten im sechsten Jahrhundert und das fünfte allgemeine Konzil* (1899). A. Guillaumont, *Les 'Képhalaia Gnostica' d'Évagre le Pontique et l'histoire de l'origénisme chez les Grecs et chez les Syriens* (Patristica Sorbonensia, 5; 1962). E. A. Clark, *The Origenist Controversy* (Princeton, NJ [1992]). Detailed account of the early stages of the controversy by P. Lardet, SJ, in his introd. to Jerome's *Apologia contra Rufinum* (SC 303; 1983), pp. 1*–75*. A. W. W. D. [prob. A. W. W. Dale] in *DCB* 4 (1887), pp. 142–56; A. d'Alès in *Dictionnaire apologétique de la foi catholique* (4th edn. by A. d'Alès), 3 (1926), cols. 1228–58, s.v. 'Origénisme', with bibl.; G. Fritz in *DTC* 11 (pt. 2; 1932), cols. 1565–88, s.v. 'Origénisme'; H. Crouzel, SJ, in *DPAC* 2 (1984), cols. 2533–8, s.v. 'Origenismo'; Eng. tr. in *Encyclopedia of the Early Church*, 2 (Cambridge, 1992), pp. 623 f.

Original Righteousness (*Justitia Originalis*). Acc. to Catholic theology, God's gratuitous impartation to man of perfect rectitude in his original condition before the *Fall. The state of Original Righteousness in which man was first created is held to have included freedom from concupiscence, bodily immortality and impassibility, and happiness.

Original Sin. In Christian theology, the state of sin in which mankind has been held captive since the *Fall (q.v.). Catholic theologians hold that its essential element is the loss of sanctifying grace. (It is also held by RCs that the BVM was by a special dispensation preserved from the stain of original sin: see IMMACULATE CONCEPTION.)

The scriptural foundation of the doctrine is the Pauline teaching that 'through one man [i.e. Adam] sin entered into the world', so that 'by the trespass of the one the many died' (cf. Rom. 5: 12–21 and 1 Cor. 15: 22). The doctrine, the significance of which was obscured by other preoccupations in the age of the *Apostolic Fathers and the *Apologists, began to be developed in the struggle against the *Gnostic errors by St *Irenaeus. As against the dualist systems of the heretics, he defended the teaching that evil came into the world through the sin of Adam. *Origen has the conception of man's fallen state, but in him it is bound up with speculations on the prenatal sins of souls. St *Athanasius in his treatise 'De Incarnatione' anticipated later developments by teaching that the chief result of the sin of Adam, which consisted in the abuse of his liberty, was the loss of the grace of conformity to the image of God, by which he and his descendants were reduced to their natural condition (ϵἰς τὸ κατὰ φύσιν) and became subject to corruption (φθορά) and death (θάνατος). The Greek Fathers emphasized the cosmic or metaphysical dimension of the Fall—men since Adam are born into a fallen world—but at the same time they held fast to the belief that man, though fallen, is free, seeing in any encroachment on man's freedom the threat of *Manichaeism. The Pseudo-*Macarian Homilies, however, paint a vivid picture of fallen man's bondage to sin.

The precise formulation of the doctrine was reserved to the W. Here *Tertullian, St *Cyprian, and St *Ambrose taught the solidarity of the whole human race with Adam not only in the consequences of his sin but in the sin itself, which is transmitted through natural generation, and the so-called '*Ambrosiaster' found its scriptural proof in Rom. 5: 12, translating ἐφ' ᾧ by in quo and referring it to Adam, 'in whom all have sinned'. In this he was followed by St *Augustine, who in his 'Quaestiones ad Simplicianum' (396–7) and other pre-Pelagian writings taught that Adam's guilt is transmitted to his descendants by concupiscence, thus making of humanity a massa damnata and much enfeebling, though not destroying, the freedom of the will. In the struggle against *Pelagianism the principles of the Augustinian doctrine were confirmed by many Councils, esp. the Second of *Orange (529).

With the existence of Original Sin firmly established the medieval theologians were particularly occupied with its nature and transmission. St *Anselm of Canterbury was the first to open up new ways of thought, in which he was followed by the great 13th-cent. Schoolmen. He defines Original Sin as the 'privation of the righteousness which every man ought to possess', thus separating it from concupiscence, with which the disciples of St Augustine had often identified it. It is transmitted by generation, because the whole human race was present in Adam seminaliter. His ideas were not immediately taken up. Whilst *Abelard was condemned by the Council of Sens (1140) for refusing to recognize Original Sin as guilt, other 12th-cent. theologians, e.g. *Peter Lombard, identified it with concupiscence. This latter conception was rejected in the next century by *Alexander of Hales and *Albert the Great, who distinguish a formal element, namely privation of original righteousness, from the material element of concupiscence. All of them hold that it is transmitted by the concupiscence accompanying the conjugal act. St *Thomas Aquinas, who treated the subject five times (esp. in 'De Malo' and in 'Summa Theol.' II (1), qq. 81–4), brought in a new element by distinguishing, in the state of Adam before the Fall, 'pure nature' (pura naturalia) from the supernatural gifts which perfected it. Hence Original Sin consists in the loss of these supernatural privileges which had directed man to his supernatural end and enabled him to keep his inferior powers in submission to reason, a rectitude not natural to a being compounded of soul and body such as man. This conception entails a more optimistic view of man than that of St Augustine and his successors in that it leaves to the reason, will, and passions of fallen man their natural powers. Acc. to St Thomas, Original Sin is transmitted not as the personal fault of Adam but as a state of human nature, yet constituting a fault inasmuch as all men are regarded as members of one great organism of which Adam was the first mover. Thus through his sin his descendants incur a culpability similar to that of the hand which executes a murder, moved by the human will. The instrument of transmission is generation, regardless of the accompanying concupiscence.

The Thomist synthesis was not at once accepted everywhere. The old rigorous Augustinianism persisted among the *Franciscans, and esp. in the religious family of St Augustine, whereas, on the other hand, the rationalist tendencies of Abelard were voiced by others who denied the guilt (reatus culpae), recognizing only its punitive consequences (reatus poenae). The more prominent Scholastics, however, such as *Duns Scotus, *William of Ockham, and their disciples, accepted the Thomist principles, but while defining Original Sin exclusively as lack of original righteousness (carentia justitiae originalis debitae), tended to eliminate the element of concupiscence.

In the subsequent controversy with the Reformers the teaching was made increasingly precise; to the exaggerated pessimism of M. *Luther and J. *Calvin, who equated Original Sin with concupiscence and affirmed that it completely destroyed liberty and persisted even after Baptism, the Council of *Trent opposed the teaching of the Schoolmen, without, however, pronouncing on points still disputed by Catholic theologians. In restating the doctrine of St Thomas, Dominic *Soto eliminated the element of concupiscence altogether from the definition and identified Original Sin with the loss of sanctifying grace. His views had a far-reaching influence, being accepted by authorities like F. *Suárez, R. *Bellarmine, and the *Salmanticenses. But the official decisions of the RC Church followed the teaching of the older theologians. In his condemnation of M. *Baius (1567), Pope *Pius V, going beyond Trent, sanctioned the Thomist distinction between nature and supernature in the state of Paradise, condemned the identification of Original Sin with concupiscence, and admitted the possibility of the right use of the freedom of the will in the unbaptized. In the 17th and 18th cents. the *Jesuits developed the doctrine along the lines of moderated optimism traced by the Schoolmen, whereas the French theologians of *Jansenist leanings, such as the circle of *Port-Royal and J.-B. *Bossuet, inclined towards the old Augustinian pessimism.

From about the 18th cent. there has been a tendency for the dogma of Original Sin to become increasingly attenuated. It conflicted with the *Enlightenment's confidence in human progress, and the accompanying individualism made the idea of being punished for the sins of another seem morally intolerable. The theory of evolution both cast doubt on the historicity of Gen. 2, and at the same time suggested that man's evil propensities might derive from his evolutionary origins. None the less, the doctrine of Original Sin in some form persisted. I. *Kant reaffirmed it in his conception of 'radical evil'; F. D. E. *Schleiermacher explained the state of sin and separation from God into which men are born as due to social heredity; G. W. F. *Hegel regarded Original Sin as evidence of the emergence of moral consciousness; and S. A. *Kierkegaard found it in man's Angst (dread or anxiety) in the face of moral possibility. The traditional doctrine has been strongly reaffirmed by K. *Barth and his followers. Modern treatments of Original Sin, however, tend to regard it as belonging to the nature of man rather than to the individual person; they derive it less from heredity than from the inescapably social character of man. This tendency is reflected in the emphasis of the Second *Vatican Council on the corporate aspects of sin and redemption.

F. R. Tennant, *The Origin and Propagation of Sin* (Hulsean Lectures for 1901–2; 1902); id., *The Sources of the Doctrines of the Fall and Original Sin* (1903); N. P. *Williams, *The Ideas of the Fall and of Original Sin* (Bampton Lectures for 1924; 1927), with formularies repr., pp. 537–50. E. *Brunner, *Der Mensch im Widerspruch* (1937; Eng. tr., *Man in Revolt*, 1939). F. H. Maycock, *Original Sin* (1948). L. Ligier, *Péché d'Adam et péché du monde* (Théologie, 43 and 48; 1960–1). K. Barth, *Christus und Adam nach Röm. 5* (Theologische Studien, 35; 1952; Eng. tr., Scottish Journal of Theology, Occasional Papers, 5; 1956): id., *Die kirchliche Dogmatik*, 4, pt. 1 (1953), pp. 531–73; Eng. tr. (1956), pp. 478–513. A.-M. Dubarle, OP, *Le Péché originel dans l'Écriture* (Lectio Divina, 20; 1958; Eng. tr., 1964). J. Gross, *Geschichte des Erbsündendogmas* (4 vols., 1960–72). H. Rondet, SJ, *Le Péché originel dans la tradition patristique et théologique* (1967; Eng. tr., 1972). P. Schoonenberg in *Mysterium Salutis*, ed. J. Feiner and M. Löhrer, 2 (Einsiedeln [1967]), pp. 899–941. E. W. Kemp (ed.), *Man: Fallen and Free* (1969). U. Baumann, *Erbsünde? Ihr traditionelles Verständnis in der Krise heutiger Theologie* (Ökumenische Forschungen, II. Soteriologische Abteilung, 2; 1970). A. Vanneste, *Le Dogme du Péché Originel* (Recherches Africaines de Théologie. Travaux de la Faculté de Théologie de Kinshasa, 1; Louvain and Paris, 1971). P. Grelot, *Péché originel et rédemption examinés à partir de l'épître aux Romains* [1973]. R. M. Martin (ed.), *La Controverse sur le péché originel au début du XIVᵉ siècle: Textes inédits* (SSL 10; 1930). S. A. Kierkegaard, *Begrebet Angest* (1844; Eng. tr., *The Concept of Dread*, 1944). A. Gaudel and M. Jugie, AA, in *DTC* 12 (pt. 1; 1933), cols. 275–623, s.v. 'Péché originel', with bibl. cols. 605 f. and 623; S. Lyonnet, SJ, in *Dict. Bibl.*, Suppl. 7 (1966), cols. 509–67, s.v. 'Péché (4)'; K. *Rahner in *Sacramentum Mundi*, 4 (1969), pp. 328–34, s.v. See also bibl. to AUGUSTINE, ST, SIN, and comm. on ROMANS, EPISTLE TO THE.

Ornaments Rubric. The common name for the ruling, inserted in the 1559 BCP at the beginning of the order for Morning and Evening Prayer, that the ornaments of the Church and the ministers should be those in use 'by the authority of Parliament in the second year of the reign of King *Edward VI'. The second Act of *Uniformity, to which this Book was attached, added the qualification that such use should continue 'until other order shall be therein taken by the authority of the Queen's Majesty, with the advice of her commissioners appointed and authorized under the great seal of England for causes ecclesiastical, or of the Metropolitan of this realm'. The interpretation of this rubric has been a vexed question since the 16th cent. The only explicit statement about the ornaments is contained in the Prayer Book of 1549, but it was long disputed whether the reference was to the provisions of this book. The *Judicial Committee of the Privy Council have twice ruled that Abp. M. *Parker's '*Advertisements' (1566) were the 'other order' foreshadowed in the Act; but their ruling has been widely contested, esp. since the Advertisements had no statutory authority, nor can they be regarded as overriding the later re-enactment of the rubric by Parliament in 1604 and 1662. The whole question seems too complex to permit of any certain solution.

The Ornaments of the Church and its Ministers. Convocation of Canterbury. Upper House Report No. 416. Report of the subcommittee appointed February 1907 to draw up a Historical Memorandum on the Ornaments of the Church and its Ministers (1908). J. T. Micklethwaite, *The Ornaments of the Rubric* (*Alcuin Club Tracts, 1; 1897). W. H. *Frere in *DECH*, pp. 425–7.

Orosius (early 5th cent.), Paulus Orosius, historian. A native of Braga, who as a young presbyter had written a 'Commonitorium' against *Priscillianism, in 414 he migrated to Africa, where he was befriended by St *Augustine. Shortly afterwards Augustine sent him to Palestine to enlist St *Jerome in the fight against *Pelagianism. When, however, the Council of Diospolis (in Palestine) of 415 upheld Pelagius, Orosius composed a 'Liber Apologeticus', defending himself against the charge of heresy. In 416 he returned to the W. and in 417 undertook, at Augustine's request and in the spirit of his 'City of God', a 'Historia adversus Paganos' which, by insisting on both the providential control of history and the calamities of the past, attacked the pagan complaint that Rome's troubles were due to her abandonment of the gods. Books 1–2 reach to the foundation of Rome, 3–4 to the birth of Christ, and 7 to AD 417. Only after AD 378 is it of any real historical value.

Ed. by S. Haverkamp (Leiden, 1738), repr. with additions in J. P. Migne, *PL* 31. Modern edn. of 'Historia' and 'Liber Apologeticus' by C. Zangemeister (CSEL 5, 1882; 'Historia' rev. for Teub. edn., 1889); of 'Commonitorium' by G. Schepss (CSEL 18, 1889, pp. 149–57) and by K.-D. Daur (CCLS 49, 1985, pp. 157–163). 'Historia' also ed., with Fr. tr., by M.-P. Arnaud-Lindet (Collection des Universités de France publiée sous le patronage de l'Association Guillaume Budé, 3 vols., 1990–1). Eng. tr. of 'Historia' and 'Liber Apologeticus' by I. W. Raymond (Records of Civilization. Sources and Studies, 26; 1936). J. Svennung, *Orosiana* (Uppsala, 1922); H. Hagendahl, *Orosius und Justinus* (Göteborg, 1941); B. Lacroix, OP, *Orose et ses idées* (Université de Montréal, Publications de l'Institut d'Études médiévales, 18; 1965); F. Fabbrini, *Paolo Orosio: Uno Storico* (1979); H.-W. Goetz, *Die Geschichtstheologie des Orosius* (Impulse der Forschung, 32; 1980). V. Grossi in Quasten (cont.), *Patrology*, 4 (1986), pp. 494–8. A. Solignac, SJ, in *Dict. Sp.* 11 (1982), cols. 965–9, s.v. 'Orose'.

Orsisius, St (d. *c.*380), also 'Orsiesius' and 'Horsi-isi', ascetic and Abbot of Tabenne (an island in the Nile). He was a disciple and close friend of St *Pachomius, who set him over the monastery of Chenobosci. On Pachomius' death (348) he succeeded him (after a few days' interval under Petronius) as *hegumen of Tabenne. The opposition to his strict rule led him to resign in favour of St Theodore (d. 368), but he resumed the oversight of the monastery on the latter's death. He wrote a 'Doctrina de Institutione Monachorum' (probably in Coptic), which was commended by *Gennadius of Marseilles; it survives in a Latin version, probably the work of St *Jerome. He was warmly supported by St *Athanasius, from whom two letters to Orsisius survive. Feast day, 15 June.

Jerome's text of 'Doctrina de Institutione Monachorum' repr. in J. P. Migne, *PG* 40. 869–94; also in *PL* 103. 453–76. Text of Athanasius' two Epp. to Orsisius in id., *PG* 26. 977–80. P. Ladeuze, *Étude sur le cénobitisme pakhômien* (Diss., Louvain, 1898), esp. pp. 155–255. J.-C. Guy in *Dict. Sp.* 7 (pt. 1; 1969), col. 763, s.v. 'Horsièse'.

Orthodox Church, also termed the Eastern, Greek, or Greco-Russian Church. A family of Churches, situated mainly in E. Europe: each member Church is independent in its internal administration, but all share the same faith and are in communion with one another, acknowledging the honorary primacy of the Patriarch of *Constantinople (or *Oecumenical Patriarch).

At present the Orthodox communion consists of the following self-governing or *autocephalous Churches: (1)

The four ancient *Patriarchates of Constantinople, *Alexandria, *Antioch, and *Jerusalem; (2) five Patriarchates of more recent origin: *Russia, *Serbia, *Romania, *Bulgaria, and *Georgia; (3) the Orthodox Churches of *Cyprus, *Greece, the Czech Republic and Slovakia, *Poland, and *Albania. To these must be added certain 'autonomous' Churches, which are self-governing in most respects but do not enjoy full independence: *Finland, *China, *Japan, and the monastery of *Sinai. An autocephalous Orthodox Church of America is in process of formation, but is not yet generally recognized as such.

Historically, what is today known as 'the Orthodox Church' developed from the Church of the E. Roman or Byzantine Empire; the predominant cultural influence upon Orthodoxy has thus been that of Greece. The Orthodox world first became limited on its E. side in consequence of the *Monophysite and *Nestorian schisms during the 5th–6th cents.; as a result the Patriarchates of Alexandria and Antioch were greatly reduced in numbers and importance. (It should be noted that the *Oriental Orthodox Churches also claim the title 'Orthodox'.) Then from the 9th cent. onwards (see PHOTIUS) there came an increasing estrangement between the two great sees of Rome and Constantinople, and this led eventually to an open and lasting schism. The final breach between Greek and Latin Christendom is usually assigned to the year 1054 (see MICHAEL CERULARIUS), but in fact the schism was a gradual and complicated process, and its beginning cannot be exactly dated. The chief doctrinal points at issue between the two sides were the Papal claims and the *Filioque; on the level of liturgical usage great tension was caused by the question of 'azymes' (see AZYMITES; BREAD, LEAVENED AND UNLEAVENED). Attempts at reconciliation were made by the Councils of *Lyons (1274) and *Florence (1438–9), but the Unions proclaimed at these two councils were never accepted by the Orthodox East at large and remained ineffective.

Bounded, as a result of these schisms, first on the eastern and subsequently on the western side, the Orthodox Church expanded to the north. A great missionary advance was inaugurated in the middle of the 9th cent. by Sts *Cyril and Methodius, the 'Apostles of the Slavs'. Bulgaria, Serbia, and subsequently Russia were converted to the Christian faith largely through the efforts of Byzantine missionaries. In due course these Slav countries acquired national Churches of their own, independent of the Mother Church of Constantinople. Since the fall of Constantinople to the Turks (1453), the Church of Russia has been the largest and most influential member of the Orthodox communion, but the Oecumenical Patriarch continues to retain his honorary primacy. During the past five centuries Orthodoxy suffered severely from outward oppression and persecution, first under the Ottoman Empire, and more recently under Communism. With the sudden collapse of Communist power around 1988, a new era of revival and expansion has begun for the Orthodox Churches in Russia and the rest of Eastern Europe.

The faith of the Orthodox Church is based primarily upon the dogmatic definitions of the seven *Oecumenical Councils. (The Orthodox do not recognize as Oecumenical any Council held since the Second of *Nicaea in 787.) Certain later Councils, although 'local' and not Oecumenical in character, have also exercised a decisive influence upon the expression of Orthodox doctrine. Most important among these are the Councils of Constantinople in 1341 and 1351, which endorsed the teaching of *Hesychasm concerning the Divine light; and the Councils of *Jassy (1642) and *Jerusalem (1672), which clarified Orthodox doctrine regarding the Eucharist and the nature of the Church. Orthodox teaching on many points has never been explicitly formulated by any Council, but is found embodied in the liturgical texts used by the Church in worship.

Orthodox theology attaches the utmost significance to the role of Councils in the life of the Church. The highest outward authority, alike in doctrine and discipline, is the Oecumenical Council, attended by representatives from the whole Church. Orthodox are willing to regard the Pope of Rome as the chief bishop in Christendom, but they look on him merely as the 'first among equals' in the episcopal college, and do not assign to him a universal supremacy of jurisdiction. While deeply respecting the episcopal and priestly office, Orthodoxy also allows an active place to the laity, who are often prominent as theologians and preachers, and even at times as spiritual directors (see STARETZ).

The Orthodox Church acknowledges the *seven sacraments, or 'mysteries' as they are termed: but Orthodox theologians attach less importance than RCs to the precise number seven, and no rigid distinction is drawn between these seven sacraments and other sacramental actions, such as monastic profession, the great blessing of the waters at *Epiphany, burial of the dead, the anointing of a monarch, etc. Baptism is performed by immersion; chrismation (confirmation) is administered by the priest immediately after baptism, and children are taken to communion from infancy. The bread and wine in the Eucharist are considered to become, at the consecration, the true and real Body and Blood of Christ: some Orthodox employ the term *transubstantiation, but others prefer to avoid it. Devout Orthodox normally communicate only four or five times a year, after careful preparation and confession; but in Greece and other parts of the Orthodox world there is now a movement in favour of more frequent communion. Services are in principle held in the language of the people, but in many places (e.g. Greece and Russia) an archaic form is used, not the modern vernacular.

The veneration of *icons plays a notable part in Orthodox worship, both private and public. Prayers to the Mother of God and the saints are common in the liturgical texts. Orthodox believe in the bodily *Assumption of the BVM—although it has never been formally defined or proclaimed as a dogma—but they usually deny the RC teaching on her *Immaculate Conception. Intercession for the departed is much emphasized in Orthodox spirituality, but the doctrine of *purgatory, as developed in RCism, is not accepted.

Monasteries have been highly influential throughout Orthodox history; since the 10th cent. the chief monastic centre has been Mount *Athos. From the 6th cent. onwards bishops in the E. have been drawn from the ranks of the celibate clergy. Parish priests, on the other hand, are generally married; the Orthodox Church has never insisted upon the *celibacy of the clergy. Any candidate for ordination, however, who wishes to marry, must do so before becoming deacon; and if a priest's wife dies, in principle he cannot marry again, although in practice exceptions to this rule are sometimes allowed.

Largely isolated from the West for many centuries, the Orthodox Church has now become better known in W. Europe and America, chiefly as a result of large-scale emigration by Greeks and Russians since *c.*1920. (There are today about 250,000 Orthodox in Britain, and some 3½ million in the United States.) The Patriarchate of Constantinople has from the start firmly supported the *Ecumenical Movement. Most other Orthodox Churches have been more reserved in their attitude towards reunion work, but virtually all of them are now represented on the *World Council of Churches. In recent years—and particularly since 1964—the Orthodox have begun to develop close and friendly contacts with the Oriental Orthodox Churches.

Modern introductions by Orthodox authors incl. N. [M.] Zernov, *Eastern Christendom: A Study of the Origin and Development of the Eastern Orthodox Church* [1961]; J. Meyendorff, *L'Église orthodoxe hier et aujourd'hui* (1960; Eng. tr., 1962); T. [R.] Ware, *The Orthodox Church* (Harmondsworth, 1963; repr. with revisions, 1993). See also E. von Ivánka, J. Tyciak, and P. Wiertz (eds.), *Handbuch der Ostkirchenkunde* (Dusseldorf, 1971). Older studies: L. *Allatius, *De ecclesiae occidentalis atque orientalis perpetua consensione* (Cologne, 1648); P. *Rycaut, *The Present State of the Greek and Armenian Churches, Anno Christi, 1678* (1679); T. Smith, *An Account of the Greek Church* (1680); J. *Covel, *Some Account of the Present Greek Church, with Reflections on their Present Doctrine and Discipline; Particularly in the Eucharist, and the Rest of their Seven Pretended Sacraments* (Cambridge, 1722); J. G. King, *The Rites and Ceremonies of the Greek Church, in Russia* (1772); J. M. *Neale, *A History of the Holy Eastern Church* (5 vols., 1847–73); W. *Palmer, *Dissertations on Subjects relating to the 'Orthodox' or 'Eastern-Catholic' Communion* (1853).

On theology and spirituality: G. *Florovsky, *Ways of Russian Theology* (Russ., Paris, 1937; Eng. tr. in *Collected Works*, 5–6; Belmont, Mass., 1979–87); V. *Lossky, *Essai sur la théologie mystique de l'Église d'Orient* (1944; Eng. tr., 1957); P. Sherrard, *The Greek East and the Latin West* (1959); F. [S. B.] Gavin, *Some Aspects of Contemporary Greek Orthodox Thought* (Hale Lectures for 1922; Milwaukee and London, 1923); S. *Bulgakov, *The Orthodox Church* (Eng. tr., 1935); P. Evdokimov, *L'Orthodoxie* (Bibliothèque Théologique, 1959); F. *Heiler, *Urkirche und Ostkirche* (Munich, 1937, expanded as *Die Ostkirchen*, posthumously pub., 1971); J. Meyendorff, *Byzantine Theology* (New York, 1974; London and Oxford, 1975). St *Nicodemus of the Holy Mountain (ed.), Φιλοκαλία τῶν ἱερῶν νηπτικῶν (Venice, 1782; Eng. tr., 1979 ff.). J. N. Karmiris, Τὰ δογματικὰ καὶ συμβολικὰ μνημεῖα τῆς Ὀρθοδόξου Καθολικῆς Ἐκκλησίας, 1–2 (Athens, 1952–3); P. N. Trembelas, Δογματικὴ τῆς Ὀρθοδόξου Καθολικῆς Ἐκκλησίας (3 vols., ibid., 1959–61; Fr. tr., 3 vols., Chevetogne [1966–8]). M. Jugie, AA, *Theologia Dogmatica Christianorum Orientalium ab Ecclesia Catholica Dissentium*, 1–4 (Paris, 1926–31). P. Hauptmann (ed.), *Unser ganzes Leben Christus unserm Gott überantworten: Studien zur ostkirchlichen Spiritualität. Fairy v. Lilienfeld zum 65. Geburtstag* (Kirche im Osten, 17; Göttingen, 1982). Worship: C. A. *Swainson (ed.), *The Greek Liturgies* (Cambridge, 1884); J. *Goar, Εὐχολόγιον *sive Rituale Graecorum* (Paris, 1647; 2nd edn., Venice, 1730; repr. Graz, 1960). P. N. Trembelas (ed.), Αἱ τρεῖς Λειτουργίαι (Texte und Forschungen zur Byzantinischneugriechischen Philologie, 15; Athens, 1935); id. (ed.), Μικρὸν Εὐχολόγιον (2 vols., Athens, 1950–5). E. Mercenier, OSB, and others, *La Prière des églises de rite byzantin* (vol. 1, Chevetogne, 1937, 3rd edn., 1975; vol. 2 in 2 pts., 1939–48, 2nd edn. of pt. 1, 1953; vol. 3, 1972). Partial Eng. trs. by Mother Mary and K. [T. R.] Ware of *The Festal Menaion* (1969) and *The Lenten Triodion* (1978). S. Salaville, AA, *Liturgies orientales:*

Notions générales, éléments principaux (1932; Eng. tr., 1938); A. Schmemann, *Introduction to Liturgical Theology* (Eng. tr. from Russian, 1966); H. [M.] Wybrew, *The Orthodox Liturgy: The Development of the Eucharistic Liturgy in the Byzantine Rite* (1989).

The question of reunion: W. J. Birkbeck, *Russia and the English Church during the Last Fifty Years*, 1 (all pub.; 1895); J. A. Douglas, *The Relations of the Anglican Churches with Eastern-Orthodox* (1921); V. T. Istavridis, Ὀρθοδοξία καὶ Ἀγγλικανισμός (1963; Eng. tr., 1966). J. Kotsonis, Ἡ κανονικὴ ἄποψις περὶ τῆς ἐπικοινωνίας μετὰ τῶν ἑτεροδόξων (*Intercommunio*) (1957); M. Fouyas, *Orthodoxy, Roman Catholicism, and Anglicanism* (1972).

Orthodoxy. As a religious system, right belief, as contrasted with heresy. The word is used esp. of those Churches in E. Christendom which are in communion with *Constantinople, collectively described in ancient times as 'the holy, orthodox, catholic, apostolic Eastern Church' (ἡ ἁγία ὀρθόδοξος καθολικὴ ἀποστολικὴ ἀνατολικὴ ἐκκλησία) and today as the 'Eastern Orthodox' to distinguish them from the separated bodies known collectively as the '*Oriental Orthodox Churches'. See also previous and following entries.

Orthodoxy, Feast of. The feast established in 843 to celebrate the final downfall of the *Iconoclastic party and the restoration of the icons. Since then it has been solemnly kept in the E. Church both by Orthodox and *Uniats on the First Sunday of *Lent, and has come to commemorate the triumph of the right faith not only over Iconoclasm but over all heresies. A list of heretics, and another of several saints and pious emperors, is read out in the *Synodicon, and old triumphal hymns, composed by martyrs of the Iconoclast persecution, are chanted during the procession of crosses and icons.

Orthros (Gk. ὄρθρος, 'dawn'). The name in the E. Church for the morning *office which corresponds to *Mattins and *Lauds in the West.

Ortlieb of Strasbourg (*c.* AD 1200), founder of a sect ('Ortlibarii'). Little is known of him beyond the fact that his teaching was condemned by *Innocent III. Like contemporary *Amalricians, he may have been influenced by a revived *Neoplatonism. His doctrine stressed a *pantheistic union of man with God, and his followers appealed against the external Church to the inner authority of the Spirit, maintaining the eternity of the world and unorthodox doctrines of the Trinity and the Incarnation. The sect had affinities with the later *Brethren of the Free Spirit but no historical connection has been established.

The principal source for the doctrines ascribed to the sect is the 'Anonymus of Passau contra Waldenses', pr. in the *Bibliotheca Maxima Veterum Patrum*, 25 (Lyons, 1677), pp. 262–77. W. Preger, *Geschichte der deutschen Mystik im Mittelalter*, 1 (1874), pp. 191–6; H. Reuter, *Geschichte der religiösen Aufklärung im Mittelalter*, 2 (1877), pp. 237–40, with notes, pp. 375 f. S. M. Deutsch in *PRE* (3rd edn.), 14 (1904), pp. 498–501, with bibl.; H. Grundmann in *L.Th.K.* (2nd edn.), 7 (1962), cols. 1256 f., s.v. 'Ortlieber'. See also works cited under WALDENSES.

O Salutaris Hostia. (Lat., 'O Saving Victim'). The last two verses of St *Thomas Aquinas's hymn 'Verbum Supernum Prodiens', written *c.*1263 for use on the Feast of *Corpus Christi. In the RC Church it is frequently sung during the service of *Benediction. There are many

English translations of the complete hymn, and still more of its two concluding verses, the most familiar being E. *Caswall's 'O Saving Victim! opening wide The gate of Heav'n to man below!' (1849).

Crit. edn. of text by C. M. Dreves (ed.), *Lateinische Hymnendichter des Mittelalters*, 2 (AHMA 1; 1907), pp. 588 f. Raby, pp. 409 f., with bibl. p. 483.

O Sapientia. (Lat., 'O Wisdom'). The initial apostrophe of the first of the *O-Antiphons. The words appeared in the *Sarum calendar as an entry against 16 Dec. Omitted from the calendar of the BCP of 1549, owing to the discontinuance of the Antiphons, they were restored in 1661. In non-English calendars the date is 17 Dec.

osculatorium. See PAX BREDE.

Osiander, Andreas (1496/8–1552), Reformation theologian. Ordained priest in 1520, he joined the *Lutherans *c.*1524 and took part in the *Marburg Colloquy of 1529 and the *Augsburg Diet of 1530. He collaborated with J. *Brenz and others in the Ansbach–Kulmbach–Nürnberg Church Order, adopted in 1533. In the same year he published his influential *Kinderpredigten* on the Catechism. He left Nürnberg in 1548 as a result of the *Augsburg Interim and soon afterwards became professor at Königsberg, where he published his *De Justificatione* (1550). A violent and bitter controversialist, he opposed M. *Luther's doctrine of *justification by faith, maintaining that justification was not a mere imputation of Christ's merits, but a substantial transference of His righteousness to the believer. His other writings include a revised edition of the *Vulgate and a 'Harmony' of the Gospels, the first of its kind. His niece, Margaret Osiander, became the wife of T. *Cranmer (1532).

Gesamtausgabe, ed. G. Müller and G. Seebass (Gütersloh, 1975 ff.). Standard study by W. Möller (Leben und ausgewählte Schriften der Väter und Begründer der lutherischen Kirche, ed. I. Hartmann and others, 5; Elberfeld, 1870; repr., Nieuwkoop, 1965). E. Hirsch, *Die Theologie des Andreas Osiander und ihre geschichtlichen Voraussetzungen* (1919); G. Seebass, *Das reformatorische Werk des Andreas Osiander* (Einzelarbeiten aus der Kirchengeschichte Bayerns, 44; 1967). M. Stupperich, *Osiander in Preussen 1549–1552* (Arbeiten zur Kirchengeschichte, 44; 1973). G. Müller, 'Andreas Osiander' in M. Greschat (ed.), *Die Reformationszeit*, 2 (Gestalten der Kirchengeschichte, 6; 1981), pp. 59–73, incl. bibl. D. Wünsch, *Evangelienharmonien im Reformationszeitalter* (Arbeiten zur Kirchengeschichte, 52; 1983), pp. 21–179. Bibl. of Osiander's works by G. Seebass (Nieuwkoop, 1971). Id. in *TRE* 25 (1995), pp. 507–15, s.v.

Osmund, St (d. 1099), Bp. of *Salisbury. Acc. to a late and historically impossible tradition, he was a nephew of *William I; the earliest established fact is that he was his chancellor in the 1070s. He became Bp. of Salisbury in 1078. He completed the cathedral at Old Sarum, dedicated in 1091 (not the present one at Salisbury which dates from 1225) and constituted a chapter of canons. He was a learned bibliophile and promoted the cult of St *Aldhelm. A document regulating chapter life ('institutio'), which influenced statutes at several cathedrals in the 13th cent., was traditionally ascribed to him, but the earliest parts of the text were probably not composed before 1150. The Sarum liturgical use, also attributed to him, is prob. not

older than Richard *Poore (dean and bishop, 1197/8–1228), who applied unsuccessfully for his canonization. Osmund was eventually canonized on 1 Jan. 1456. Feast day, 4 Dec.; of his translation, 16 July.

Vetus Registrum Sarisberiense alias dictum S. Osmundi Episcopi, ed. W. H. Rich Jones (2 vols., Rolls Series, 1883–4). A. R. Malden (ed.), *The Canonization of Saint Osmund from the Manuscript Records in the Muniment Room of Salisbury Cathedral ... with introduction and notes* (Wilts Record Society, 1901). W. J. Torrance, *The Story of Saint Osmund* (posthumous; Friends of Salisbury Cathedral Publications [1978]). D. E. Greenway, 'The false *Institutio* of St Osmund', in D. [E.] Greenway, C. [J.] Holdsworth, and J. [E.] Sayers (eds.), *Tradition and Change: Essays in Honour of Marjorie Chibnall* (Cambridge, 1985), pp. 77–101. See also bibl. s.v. SALISBURY OR SARUM, USE OF.

Osservatore Romano (Ital., 'The Roman Observer'). A newspaper founded in 1861 and owned by the *Vatican. It publishes the official text and authorized Italian translation of *encyclicals and other Papal documents, the Pope's speeches, appointments of bishops, the announcements of consistories and various other official acts. In addition to news of religious interest, it publishes reports and comments on political and social events. It is issued daily except on Mondays.

Ossius. Probably the correct spelling of the name of the celebrated 4th-cent. Bp. of Córdoba commonly known as *Hosius (q.v.).

C. H. *Turner, 'Ossius (Hosius) of Cordova', *JTS* 12 (1910–11), pp. 275–7.

ostensory (Lat. *ostensorium*). A receptacle for showing objects of religious devotion to the people. The word is now commonly restricted to the *monstrance (q.v.), used for the exposition of the Blessed Sacrament; but in earlier times it was applied to other vessels with a transparent casing, e.g. those for the exposition of relics.

Ostervald, Jean Frédéric (1663–1747), Swiss Reformed pastor of Neuchâtel. He became interested in the C of E, corresponded with G. *Burnet and W. *Wake, and in 1713 he published a Eucharistic liturgy in which J. *Calvin's rite was combined with elements from the BCP and the Roman Missal. It became widely known, remained in use until the 20th cent., and has been regarded as the first ecumenical liturgy.

The text of the liturgy is conveniently repr., with discussion, by B. Bürki, *Cène du Seigneur—Eucharistie de l'Église*, vol. A (Cahiers Œcuméniques, 17; Fribourg, 1985), pp. 14–24.

Ostian Way (Lat. *Via Ostiensis*). The ancient road which led from Rome to the seaport of Ostia, 14 miles distant at the mouth of the Tiber on its left bank. On its W. side, about two miles from the centre of Rome, lies the church of *St Paul's outside the Walls. This site has been held to be the resting-place of the remains of St *Paul at least from the end of the 2nd cent., for the presbyter *Gaius (*c.* AD 200) recorded that the tombs (τρόπαια) of Sts Peter and Paul were located (respectively) in his day at the *Vatican and on the Ostian Way. The Bp. of Ostia is the senior cardinal-bishop.

*Eusebius, *Hist. Eccl.* 2. 25. 6–7.

ostiarius. See DOORKEEPER.

Oswald, St (c.605–42), King of Northumbria, and martyr. The son of Ethelfrith, King of Northumbria, Oswald was forced to flee to Scotland when Edwin seized the kingdom after his father's death in 616. He was converted later to the Christian faith by the monks of St *Columba at *Iona. Edwin was killed in 633; Oswald returned in 634 and, after erecting a wooden cross on the battlefield and commanding his soldiers to pray, defeated the British king, Cadwallon, at Heavenfield, near Hexham. Encouraged by his victory, he began to establish Christianity in his kingdom and appealed to Iona for missionaries. St *Aidan was sent for the work, and having been given the isle of *Lindisfarne as his see, by his gentleness and with the co-operation of the king, who often acted as his interpreter, achieved the conversion of a large part of the country. In the eighth year of his reign Oswald was killed in battle by the pagan Penda of Mercia, who mutilated his body. His head, which was deposited in St *Cuthbert's coffin in 875, was found at *Durham in 1827. He was honoured as a martyr not only by the English but also on the Continent throughout the Middle Ages. Feast day, 5 Aug.; in some places, 8 or 9 Aug.

The principal authority is *Bede, HE 2. 5, 14, 20; 3. 1–3, 6 f., 9–14, 23 f.; and 4. 14; comm. by J. M. Wallace-Hadrill (Oxford, 1988), pp. 85, 88 f., 96–8, 102–6, 155, 230 f., with further refs. 11th-cent. Life by Drogo pr. in AASS, Aug. 2 (1735), pp. 94–103; Life by Reginald of Durham (1162), most of which is pr. among the works of *Simeon of Durham ed. T. Arnold, 1 (RS, 1882), pp. 326–85, with introd., p. xli. D. Townsend, 'Henry of Avranches: Vita Sancti Oswaldi', Mediaeval Studies, 56 (1994), pp. 1–65, incl. text. B. Colgrave in C. F. Battiscombe (ed.), The Relics of Saint Cuthbert (1956), pp. 116–18. R. Folz, 'Saint Oswald roi de Northumbrie. Étude d'hagiographie royale', Anal. Boll. 98 (1980), pp. 49–74. C. Stancliffe and E. Cambridge (eds.), Oswald: Northumbrian King to European Saint (Stamford, 1995). P. [A. M.] Clemoes, The Cult of St Oswald on the Continent (Jarrow Lecture, 1983). J. Raine in DCB 4 (1887), pp. 163 f., s.v. 'Oswald (1)'.

Oswald, St (d. 992), Abp. of *York. A Dane by birth, Oswald studied in the household of his uncle, Abp. *Oda of Canterbury, and later at the Benedictine monastery of *Fleury, where he was ordained. He returned to England in 959 and in 962 was consecrated Bp. of *Worcester by St *Dunstan. He took an active part in the reform of abuses and established many monasteries, the most famous of which was the abbey of Ramsey in Cambridgeshire. In 972 he was made Abp. of York, though he retained the see of Worcester in order to promote his monastic reforms. The latter were seriously endangered by Elfhere, earl of Mercia, who broke up many of Oswald's communities, though he spared Ramsey. Feast day, 28 Feb.

The principal authority is the anonymous Life, written between 995 and 1005, and now attributed to *Byrhtferth (q.v.); it is ed. J. Raine, The Historians of the Church of York and its Archbishops 1 (RS, 1879), pp. 399–475; crit. edn. by M. Lapidge (Oxford Medieval Texts, in preparation). The Life by *Eadmer, pr. by J. Raine, op. cit., 2 (RS, 1886), pp. 1–59, adds a certain amount of information. Other Lives, of little historical value, ibid., pp. 60–97 and 489–512, with introd., pp. ix–xi. J. Armitage *Robinson, St Oswald and the Church of Worcester (British Academy Supplementary Papers, 5; 1919); E. H. Pearce, St Oswald of Worcester and the Church of York (York Minster Historical Tracts, 4 [1928]). [M.] D. *Knowles, OSB, The Monastic Order in England

(Cambridge, 1940; 2nd edn., 1963), pp. 40–56. E. John, 'St. Oswald and the Tenth Century Reformation', JEH 9 (1958), pp. 159–172. W. Hunt in DNB 43 (1895), pp. 323–5, with further refs.

Oswine, St (d. 651), also 'Oswin', Anglo-Saxon King. After the murder of his father, Osric, King of Deira, by Cadwallon (634), Oswine was taken to Wessex for safety. Returning on the death of his kinsman St *Oswald, King of Northumbria (642), he became King of Deira, while Bernicia, the northern part of Northumbria, passed under the rule of Oswald's brother, Oswy. When open conflict broke out with Oswy, Oswine took refuge at Gilling, near Richmond, N. Yorks, where he was murdered. He was a devout Christian and a close friend of St *Aidan. His tomb at Gilling became a place of pilgrimage until, in the Danish invasions, it was removed to Tynemouth. Feast day, 20 Aug.

The principal authority is *Bede, HE 3. 14; comm. by J. M. Wallace-Hadrill (Oxford, 1988), pp. 106–8, with bibl. refs. There is a 12th-cent. Life by a monk of *St Albans resident at Tynemouth, based on the account of Bede, but with additional material on Oswine's translation and the miracles connected with him; it is mostly pr. in J. Raine (ed.), Miscellanea Biographica (Surtees Society, 8; 1838), pp. 1–59. Life [by F. W. *Faber] in The Lives of the English Saints [written at the suggestion of J. H. *Newman], 1844; ed. A. W. Hutton, 4 (1901), pp. 240–70. J. Raine in DCB 4 (1887), p. 165, s.v. 'Oswin (1)'; C. L. Kingsford in DNB 43 (1895), pp. 332 f.; W. Hunt in DECH, pp. 428 f., s.v.

Otfrid of Weissenburg (d. c.875), author of an Old High German biblical epic. He was a monk of Weissenburg (modern Wissembourg) in Alsace. Having studied under *Rabanus Maurus at *Fulda, he built up a library of biblical MSS and composed a poem in five books and of over 7,000 lines about the life of Christ (Evangelienbuch, c.863/71). It consists of a chronological narrative constructed from selected Gospel passages accompanied by theological commentary and culminating in the Last Judgement. Otfrid conceived his work as a revival of the tradition of ancient poetry, but now in the vernacular and to the glory of God and the Franks.

Editio princeps of the Evangelienbuch by M. *Flacius (Basle, 1571). Crit. edn. by O. Erdmann (Halle, 1882); editio minor rev. by L. Wolff (Altdeutsche Textbibliothek, 49; Tübingen, 1957). Selections, with modern Ger. tr., by G. Vollmann-Profe (Reclams Universal-Bibliothek, 8384; Stuttgart, 1987). W. Kleiber, Otfrid von Weissenburg (Bibliotheca Germanica, 14; Berne and Munich, 1971); id. (ed.), Otfrid von Weissenburg (Wege der Forschung, 419; Darmstadt, 1978). E. Hellgardt, Die exegetischen Quellen von Otfrids Evangelienbuch (Hermaea, NF 41; Tübingen, 1981). J. K. Bostock, A Handbook on Old High German Literature, 2nd edn., rev. by K. C. King and D. R. McLintock (Oxford, 1976), pp. 190–212. Johanna Belkin in id. and J. Meier, Bibliographie zu Otfrid von Weissenburg und zur altsächsischen Bibeldichtung (Heliand und Genesis) (Bibliographien zur deutschen Literatur des Mittelalters, 7 [1975]), pp. 5–59. W. Schröder in Verfasserlexikon (2nd edn.), 7 (1989), cols. 172–93, s.v.

Othilia, St. See ODILIA, ST.

Otto, St (1062/3–1139), Bp. of Bamberg, the 'Apostle of Pomerania'. Born of a noble family of Swabia, he entered the service of the Emp. *Henry IV before 1090, and was made chancellor in 1101. In 1102 Henry named him Bp. of Bamberg, but in 1105 he joined the party of Henry V and was consecrated in Rome in the following year. Though in the *Investiture Controversy his sympathies were with the Pope, he tried to maintain a neutral attitude which led to his temporary suspension by Adalbert of Mainz at the Synod of Fritzlar in 1118. At the Congress of Würzburg (1121) he endeavoured to restore peace, which was finally obtained by the Concordat of *Worms in 1122. Throughout these years Otto devoted himself to the reform of his diocese, taking part in the foundation of over 20 monasteries and completing the cathedral. In 1124 he went on a missionary journey to Pomerania at the instigation of Duke Boleslas III of Poland, who had obtained the Pomeranians' promise to accept the Christian faith as a condition of the peace made between the two peoples in 1120. He converted many of the most important towns and, on a second journey four years later, also the greater part of the nobles, though a bishopric was not established till after his death. He was canonized in 1189. Feast day, 30 Sept.; in the *Roman Martyrology, 2 July.

There are three primary Lives: (1) by a monk of Prüfening, prob. written between 1140 and 1146; (2) by Ebo, a monk of St Michael's, Bamberg, written in the 1150s; and (3) by Herbord, also a monk of Bamberg, 'Dialogus de Vita Ottonis', written in 1158–9. They are pr. by R. Köpke in *MGH*, Scriptores, 12 (1856), pp. 746–903, though the text of the Herbord Life is not complete. Complete text of all three ed. by I. Wikarjak (Monumenta Poloniae Historica, 2nd ser. 7: fasc. 1, the Prüfening Life, Warsaw, 1966; fasc. 2, the Life by Ebo, 1969; fasc. 3, Life by Herbord, 1974). Eng. tr. of Books 2 and 3 of Life by Ebo, with additional matter from Life by Herbord, by C. H. Robinson (Translations of Christian Literature, 2nd ser.; Latin Texts; 1920, not wholly satisfactory). *BHL* 2, pp. 923–6 (nos. 6392–407). E. Demm, *Reformmönchtum und Salwenmission im 12. Jahrhundert: Westsoziologisch-geistesgeschichtliche Untersuchungen zu den Viten Bischof Ottos von Bamberg* (Historische Studien, 419; 1970), with bibl. Id., 'Zur Interpretation und Datierung der Ottoviten', *Zeitschrift für bayerische Landesgeschichte*, 39 (1976), pp. 565–605. J. Petersohn, 'Otto von Bamberg und seine Biographen', ibid. 43 (1980), pp. 3–27; R. Bartlett, 'The Conversion of a Pagan Society in the Middle Ages', *History*, 70 (1985), pp. 185–201, with further refs. Modern study by M. Wehrmann (Pommersche Heimatkunde, 8; Greifswald, 1924). E. von Guttenberg, *Das Bistum Bamberg*, 1 (Germania Sacra, 2. 1; 1937), pp. 115–38. K. Löffler in *CE* 11 (1911), pp. 353 f., s.v.; J. Petersohn in *TRE* 25 (1995), pp. 552–5.

Otto of Freising (c.1114/15–58), Bp. of Freising. He was the son of Leopold III, Margrave of the Eastern March (Austria), and of Agnes, daughter of the Emp. *Henry IV, and thus *Frederick Barbarossa's uncle. He studied at Paris, possibly under *Hugh of St-Victor, and perhaps also at *Reims and *Chartres. He entered the Cistercian abbey of Morimond in Champagne c.1132 and became abbot c.1136. Appointed Bp. of Freising in 1138, he reformed his diocese, took part in the Second *Crusade (1147–8), and was one of the first theologians to introduce the study of *Aristotle into Germany. He is chiefly important as a historian, his principal works being 'Chronicon seu historia de duabus civitatibus' (1143–6) and 'Gesta Friderici' (1156–8). In the former he modified St *Augustine's conception of the 'two cities', seeing their union in the Catholic Church as the continuation of the Roman Empire. In the latter he described the history of the first part of Barbarossa's reign, largely on the basis of original documents.

Crit. edn. of his *Chronicon* by A. Hofmeister (Scriptores Rerum Germanicarum in Usum Scholarum, Hanover and Berlin, 1912); *Gesta Friderici* ed. G. Waitz and B. de Simson (ibid., 1912) and by F. J. Schmale (Ausgewählte Quellen zur deutschen Geschichte des Mittelalters, 17; 1965), with introd. and bibl. Eng. tr. of the *Chronicon* by C. C. Mierow (Records of Civilization, Sources and Studies [9]; 1928) and of the *Gesta* by id. (ibid. 49; 1953). A. Weissthanner, 'Regesten des Freisinger Bischofs Otto I', *Analecta Sacri Ordinis Cisterciensis*, 14 (1958), pp. 151–222, with other arts. on Otto in the same issue. A. Hofmeister, 'Studien über Otto von Freising', *NA* 37 (1912), pp. 99–161, 633–768. *Otto von Freising: Gedenkgabe zu seinem 800. Todesjahr*, ed. J. A. Fischer (Freising, 1958). H.-W. Goetz, *Das Geschichtsbild Ottos von Freising* (Beihefte zum Archiv für Kulturgeschichte, 19; Cologne and Vienna, 1984), with bibl. K. F. Morrison, 'Otto of Freising's Quest for the Hermeneutic Circle', *Speculum*, 55 (1980), pp. 207–36. C. Kirchner-Feyerabend, *Otto von Freising als Diözesan- und Reichsbischof* (Europäische Hochschulschriften, 3rd ser. 413 [1990]). F.-J. Schmale in *Verfasserlexikon* (2nd edn.), 7 (1989), cols. 215–23, s.v.

Otto, Rudolf (1869–1937), Protestant theologian. From 1904 to 1917 he was professor of systematic theology at Breslau, and from 1917 to 1929 at Marburg. His analysis of religion in *Das Heilige* (1917; Eng. tr., *The Idea of the Holy*, 1923) rested on a wide knowledge of *comparative religion, contemporary oriental thought, and the natural sciences. Its central theme was insistence on the part played by the *numinous in the religious consciousness. With its professed emphasis on the 'non-rational' moments in religion, Otto's understanding of religion had close affinities with that of F. D. E. *Schleiermacher (whose *Reden über die Religion* he edited, 1899). His other writings include *West-Östliche Mystik* (1926; Eng. tr., 1932) and *Reich Gottes und Menschensohn* (1934; Eng. tr., *The Kingdom of God and the Son of Man*, 1938).

H. Frick (ed.), *Rudolf Otto Festgruss* (1931); *Rudolf Otto Gedächtnisfeier* (1938). R. F. Davidson, *Rudolf Otto's Interpretation of Religion* (Princeton, NJ, 1947). A. Paus, *Religiöser Erkenntnisgrund: Herkunft und Wesen der Aprioritheorie Rudolf Ottos* (Leiden, 1966). P. C. Almond, *Rudolf Otto: An Introduction to his Philosophical Theology* (Chapel Hill, NC, and London [1984]).

Ouen, St (c.610–84) (also **Audoin** or **Owen**), Bp. of Rouen. He was a native of Sancy, nr. Soissons, and spent part of his youth at the court of King Clothair II. There he became the friend of St *Eligius, whose Life (no longer extant in its orig. form) may be his work. Under Dagobert I he became referendary or chancellor. In 634 he founded a monastery called Resbac, the present Rebais, but was prevented from becoming a monk there by King Dagobert. After being ordained priest he was consecrated Bp. of Rouen in 641. He encouraged scholarship, founded many monasteries, and fought simony and other serious abuses. He was employed on several political missions by the Merovingian kings, among them the arrangement of a peace between the Franks of Austrasia and Neustria. He is remembered esp. by the famous church dedicated to him at Rouen, where his body was interred. Feast day, 24 Aug.

Life of Eligius, ascribed to St Ouen, pr. in *PL* 87. 479–594; crit. edn. by B. Krusch in *MGH*, Scriptores Rerum Merovingicarum, 4 (1902), pp. 634–741. The earliest Life of St Ouen, dating from the 8th cent., ed. W. Levison, ibid. 5 (1910), pp. 536–67; earlier edn. in *AASS*, Aug. 4 (1739), pp. 805–9; one 9th-cent.

Life is also pr. ibid., pp. 810–19; a second was first ed. E. P. Savage in *Anal. Boll.* 5 (1886), pp. 67–146. Good modern study by E. Vacandard (Paris, 1902). F. Prinz, *Frühes Mönchtum im Frankenreich* (Munich, 1965; 2nd edn., Darmstadt, 1988), pp. 124–35. P. Fouracre, 'The Work of Audoenus of Rouen and Eligius of Noyon in extending episcopal influence from the town to the country in seventh-century Neustria', in D. Baker (ed.), *The Church in Town and Countryside* (Studies in Church History, 16; Oxford, 1979), pp. 77–91. G. Scheibelreiter, 'Audoin von Rouen: Ein Versuch über den Charakter des 7. Jahrhunderts', in H. Atsma (ed.), *La Neustrie: Les pays au nord de la Loire de 650 à 850*, 1 (Beihefte der *Francia*, 16/1; Sigmaringen, 1989), pp. 195–216.

Our Father. See LORD'S PRAYER.

Overall, John (1560–1619), Bp. of *Norwich. He was educated at Cambridge, where in 1581 he became a Fellow of Trinity College and from 1595 to 1607 was the Regius professor of divinity. In 1602 he succeeded A. *Nowell as Dean of St Paul's, and in 1605 became *prolocutor of the Lower House of *Convocation. He was consecrated Bp. of *Coventry and Lichfield in 1614 and translated to Norwich in 1618. The section on the Sacraments in the BCP Catechism was drawn up by Overall on the basis of that in Nowell's 'Small Catechism' of 1572. He was also responsible for a set of canons on the relations of Church and State, compiled in 1606 with the *Gunpowder Plot in view and known as his 'Convocation Book'. *James I, however, prohibited its acceptance by Convocation, as Overall defended teaching on the *Divine Right of Kings which appeared to justify a successful rebellion and permit the institution of 'new forms of government' (can. 28); and the publication of the book was delayed till 1690. Overall also assisted in the translation of the AV Bible.

His 'Convocation Book', orig. ed. W. *Sancroft, London, 1690, was repr. in the LACT, 1844. A. Gordon in *DNB* 42 (1895), pp. 375–7; B. Blaxland in *DECH*, p. 429, s.v.

Overbeck, Franz (1837–1905), Protestant theologian. He was born in St Petersburg and taught Church History at Jena (1864–70) and 'critical theology' at Basle (1870–97). Holding that the Christian Gospel was wholly eschatological and world-negating, he came to reject completely historic Christianity and expounded in his lectures a 'secular Church history' (*profane Kirchengeschichte*) in which the course of ecclesiastical history was understood as a radical departure from the original revelation in Scripture. Liberal and apologetic theology were also alike essentially unChristian. In his critique of immanental religious notions Overbeck has exercised considerable influence on the modern *dialectical theology. His writings include *Über die Christlichkeit unserer heutigen Theologie* (1873; 2nd edn., 1903), *Studien zur Geschichte der alten Kirche* (1875), and *Christentum und Kultur* (posthumous, 1919). He was for many years a close friend of F. *Nietzsche.

Correspondence with F. Nietzsche ed. R. Oehler and C. A. Bernoulli (Leipzig, 1916). C. A. Bernoulli, *Franz Overbeck und Friedrich Nietzsche: Eine Freundschaft* (2 vols., Jena, 1908; with list of writings, 1, pp. 439–44). E. Staehlin and M. Tetz (eds.), *Overbeckiana: Übersicht über den Franz-Overbeck-Nachlass der Universitätsbibliothek Basel* (Studien zur Geschichte der Wissenschaften in Basel, 12–13; 1962). Other studies by A. Pfeiffer (Studien zur Theologie und Geistesgeschichte des neunzehnten Jahrhunderts, 15; Göttingen, 1975) and R. Wehrli (Zurich

[1977]). K. *Barth, *Die Theologie und die Kirche: Gesammelte Vorträge*, 2 (1928), pp. 1–25; Eng. tr. (1962), pp. 55–73. J. C. O'Neill, *The Bible's Authority* (Edinburgh, 1991), pp. 179–90.

Overseas and Other Clergy (Ministry and Ordination) Measure (No. 3) 1967. This Measure, whose short title is the Overseas Clergy Measure 1967, supersedes the *Colonial Clergy Act 1874. Its main object is to regulate the exercise of their ministry within the Provinces of *Canterbury and *York by clergy ordained by bishops of Churches in communion with the C of E whose jurisdiction lies outside these two provinces, or by bishops of Churches whose *Orders are recognized by the C of E. Permission to officiate, either temporary or permanent, may be given by the Abp. of the *province concerned. If a priest is admitted to a benefice, the bishop may dispense with the Oath of *Allegiance.

Overseas Missionary Fellowship (OMF). An interdenominational and international mission to E. Asia. Founded by J. H. *Taylor in 1865 as the '*China Inland Mission', its name was changed in 1965. Following the withdrawal of missionaries from *China in 1951, the Mission extended its work to Singapore, Malaysia, *Indonesia, Thailand, Laos, Hong Kong, Taiwan, the *Philippines, South *Korea, and *Japan. The international headquarters is in Singapore.

Owen, John (1616–83), *Puritan divine and statesman. He was educated at Queen's College, Oxford, but ejected in 1637 under W. *Laud's Statutes. In 1642 he obtained the living of Fordham in Essex, and in 1647 became vicar of Coggeshall. Originally a Presbyterian, he had come to believe with J. *Milton that 'new presbyter was but old priest writ large', and took up the more tolerant Independent position. His preaching won the ear of O. *Cromwell, who in 1651 made him dean of *Christ Church and in the following year vice-chancellor of the university. In 1654 he sat for a short time in Parliament, was one of Cromwell's *Triers and a member of the *Savoy Conference. The Restoration drove him to London, where he continued to preach and write until his death. He was a voluminous author, often in controversy with R. *Baxter, *Arminians, and *Anglicans, but always tolerant and fair. Many of his writings show deep spiritual insight.

Works ed. by T. Russell with memoir by W. Orme (21 vols., 1826) and by W. H. Goold with Life by A. Thomson (24 vols., 1850–5). J. *Moffatt, *The Golden Book of John Owen* (1904). P. Toon, *God's Statesman: The Life and Work of John Owen* (Exeter [1971]); S. B. Ferguson, *John Owen on the Christian Life* (Edinburgh, 1987). J. M. Rigg in *DNB* 42 (1895), pp. 424–8.

Oxford. The ecclesiastical history of the city appears to begin with St *Frideswide (q.v.), whose father founded a convent there in the 8th cent. By 1002 the Priory of St Frideswide was occupied by secular canons, who in or before 1122 were replaced by *Augustinian Canons. In 1129 Oseney was founded outside the town, also for Augustinian Canons, and in 1281 Rewley Abbey ('de regali loco') for *Cistercians. Throughout the Middle Ages Oxford was in the diocese of *Lincoln, but in 1542 *Henry VIII created the See of Oxford, selecting the suppressed Oseney Abbey as the cathedral church and appointing Robert King, the last abbot, as the (first) bishop. In 1546 the seat of the bishopric was transferred to King's (previously 'Cardinal') College, founded by T. *Wolsey on the site of St Frideswide's Priory, which had been suppressed in 1524. The priory church then became the cathedral and the college was renamed '*Christ Church'. From 1635 to 1978 the bishop's official residence was in the village of Cuddesdon, some six miles to the east of the city. Among notable modern bishops of Oxford have been S. *Wilberforce (1845–69), W. *Stubbs (1889–1901), F. *Paget (1901–11), C. *Gore (1911–19), and K. E. *Kirk (1937–54).

The origins of the university go back to the 12th cent., when, in addition to schools attached to parish churches, there is fragmentary evidence for the existence of independent masters teaching Arts, Theology, and Civil and Canon Law in schools in the centre of the town. The earliest known masters were Theobald of Étampes in the 1120s and (shortly afterwards) Robert *Pullen. Thereafter, although academic activity no doubt continued, there is little evidence until the 1190s when Alexander Nequam taught Theology and several Masters were teaching Civil and Canon Law. During this decade the Oxford schools developed rapidly, partly because war with France made it dangerous for scholars to go to the Continent. This growth was interrupted in 1209 by a dispute between the scholars and the town over the jurisdictional privileges of the scholars who, as clerics, were subject only to ecclesiastical jurisdiction. The dispute was settled only in 1214 when the Papal legate, Nicholas de Romanis, drew up a constitution for the schools under which the scholars got their first chancellor, appointed by the Bp. of Lincoln, in whose diocese Oxford lay. From this date the university developed as a corporate institution with chancellor, proctors, and congregation of masters, who still form the framework of its constitution. Between 1220 and 1230 came the Friars—*Black, *Grey, *White, and *Augustinian. Out of the boarding-houses for masters and students emerged the colleges, of which the earliest were Merton (whose statutes date from 1264), Balliol, and University Colleges (all founded around the same time). In 1571 the University was incorporated by Act of Parliament, and from then until 1871 subscription to the *Thirty-nine Articles was required from all its members. In the 17th cent. its statutes were radically remodelled by W. *Laud; the next (and still continuing) era of far-reaching changes began with the institution of the first Honours Examinations in 1800 and the Report of a Royal Commission in 1852. The close and continuous links of the university with the life of the Church are shown by its connection with early *Lollardy, the trials of T. *Cranmer, N. *Ridley, and H. *Latimer in the University Church of St Mary (1555), the zeal of such men as J. *Fell and R. *South before and after the Restoration, the early history of the *Wesleys, and the development of the '*Oxford Movement' in the 19th cent.

In modern times Theology has ceased to hold a dominant position in Oxford, but important contributions were made to theological studies by such scholars as J. *Wordsworth, S. R. *Driver, H. B. *Swete, W. *Sanday, C. H. *Turner, H. J. White (d. 1934; see VULGATE), B. H. *Streeter, N. P. *Williams, R. H. *Lightfoot, G. R. *Driver, and A. M. Farrer (1904–68). In the field of Patristics, it was mainly the work of Oxford scholars which

went into the production of the *Patristic Greek Lexicon (q.v.), and Oxford has been the meeting-ground of the International *Patristic Conferences which have met since 1951.

For works on Oxford Cathedral see bibl. to CHRIST CHURCH. On the University, H. C. Maxwell Lyte, *A History of the University of Oxford from the Earliest Times to the Year 1530* (1886); C. E. Mallet, *A History of the University of Oxford* (3 vols., 1924–7); H. Rashdall, *The Universities of Europe in the Middle Ages*, 3 (ed. F. M. Powicke and A. B. Emden, 1936), pp. 1–273; T. H. Aston (ed.), *The History of the University of Oxford* (Oxford, 1984 ff.); A. B. Cobban, *The Medieval English Universities: Oxford and Cambridge to c.1500* (Aldershot, 1988). On a smaller scale, V. H. H. Green, *A History of Oxford University* (1974), and J. [M.] Prest (ed.), *The Illustrated History of Oxford University* (Oxford, 1993). A. B. Emden, *A Biographical Register of the University of Oxford to A.D. 1500* (3 vols., 1957–9; suppl. vol., *A.D. 1501 to 1540*, 1974). E. H. Cordeaux and D. H. Merry, *A Bibliography of Printed Works Relating to the University of Oxford* (Oxford, 1968). *VCH*, Oxford, 3, ed. H. E. Salter and M. Lobel (1954). *City of Oxford* (The Royal Commission on Historical Monuments, 1939). V. H. H. Green, *Religion at Oxford and Cambridge* (1964). C. Hibbert (ed.), *The Encyclopaedia of Oxford* (1988). The 'Oxford Historical Society', founded 1884 for the publication of material on the history of the University and City and neighbourhood, has issued over 130 vols. See also bibl. to BODLEIAN LIBRARY.

Oxford Conference (1937). The second Conference of the '*Life and Work' branch of the *Ecumenical Movement held at Oxford, 12–26 July 1937, under the general title of 'Church, Community, and State'. There were 425 delegates representing all the more important religious bodies except the RC Church and the German Evangelical Church (then under Nazi control). It was agreed to take steps for the fusion of the 'Life and Work' Movement with that of '*Faith and Order', which held a Conference at *Edinburgh (q.v.) a week or two later. The first assembly of the united bodies was held in 1948 at *Amsterdam (q.v.). See also WORLD COUNCIL OF CHURCHES.

The Report of the Conference, under the general title, 'The Church, Community, and State' series, comprised a preliminary volume on *The Church and its Function in Society*, by W. A. Visser 't Hooft and J. H. *Oldham (1937); *The Christian Understanding of Man*, by T. E. Jessop and others (1938); *The Kingdom of God and History*, by H. G. Wood and others (1938); *The Christian Faith and the Common Life*, by N. Ehrenström and others (1938); *Church and Community*, by K. S. Latourette and others (1938); *Church, Community, and State in Relation to Education*, by F. Clarke and others (1938); *The Universal Church and the World of Nations*, by the Marquess of Lothian and others (1938); and *The Churches Survey their Task*, with introd. by J. H. Oldham (1937).

Oxford Group. The religious movement founded by F. N. D. *Buchman, who in 1921 defined his aim as 'a programme of life issuing in personal, social, racial, national and supernational change'. Returning to England in 1920, Buchman visited Cambridge, and from there went to Oxford; here his preaching made a great impression on a post-war generation of students, but also aroused controversy in the following years. In 1928 a party from Oxford, including Rhodes scholars from South Africa, visited that country in the long vacation, and it was there that the name 'Oxford Group' was attached to them. Buchman himself went to South Africa with a team of people in 1929, and there were later campaigns in Canada (1932 and 1934), Norway (1934), Denmark (1935), and Switzerland.

Assemblies, or 'house-parties' as they were called, in Oxford each summer from 1930 to 1937 drew large numbers. In Britain there was animated debate over the name. Despite opposition, however, esp. from some members of Oxford University, in 1939 the Oxford Group was granted legal incorporation under this title. Meanwhile, in 1938, Buchman had issued from London his call for 'moral and spiritual re-armament', and the wider name, Moral Re-Armament or MRA, superseded the more local name, which remained the official title in Britain.

Moral Re-Armament was launched in Washington, DC, in 1939, when Harry S. Truman, the future President of the USA, read a message from President Roosevelt. Through its wartime programme in America, summarized as 'sound homes, teamwork in industry, national unity', Buchman sought to train an international force which would help him to rebuild after the end of the Second World War. He was joined in America by some Swiss supporters who decided to create a centre for reconstruction in their country and acquired the former Caux-Palace above Montreux. This opened in 1946, and between 1947 and 1951 some 4,000 Germans came to Caux, where much was done to heal relationships between former enemies. Delegations also came from Japan, India, and the newly emerging countries of Africa. In addition to Caux, there are training and conference centres at Tirley Garth in Cheshire; Panchgani near Pune in India; Petropolis, Brazil; Odawara, Japan; Melbourne, Australia; and Coolmoreen Farm, Gweru, Zimbabwe. The Westminster Theatre in London, acquired in 1946 as a memorial to the men and women of Moral Re-Armament who had died in the 1939–45 War, is the main centre in Britain; besides presenting plays it is a workshop and distribution centre for films and videos in many languages throughout the world.

Buchman, referred to inside the movement as 'Frank', was regarded as the leader and pioneer of a new and more authentic form of Christian life; his influence and that of his immediate associates was very great. He envisaged, however, 'a cabinet of like-minded friends around the world' leading the work, and since his death (1961) and that of Peter Howard (1965), a corporate leadership has emerged. The movement has several hundred full-time workers, all volunteers. It operates primarily through personal contact, its publications in book or magazine form, plays, films, and videos, and through conferences and seminars which often bring together people of opposing ideas.

The movement has met with considerable opposition on religious grounds, e.g. that the conversions it secured were spiritually unsound and often only temporary, that its 'sharing' and 'guidance' were pressed on converts indiscriminately without any real attempt at the cure of souls, and that its leaders were unqualified for the task they assumed. It was urged, however, that the Group presented Christianity in a language and manner which enabled it to reach many whom the Church failed to attract. Proscribed by the Nazis and attacked by the Communists, it has upheld absolute moral standards in an age when these were under open and covert attack.

Primary material is provided by the collection of Buchman's speeches, *Remaking the World* (1947; rev. edn., 1958); also G. [D.] Lean, *Frank Buchman: A Life* (1985); A. Wolrige Gordon, *Peter Howard: Life and Letters* (1969). Works on the Oxford Group emanating from its supporters incl. *The Oxford Group and its Work of Moral Re-Armament* (1954); G. Marcel (ed.), *Un Changement d'Espérance à la Rencontre du Réarmement Moral* (1958; Eng. tr., *Fresh Hope for the World*, 1960); P. Howard, *Frank Buchman's Secret* (1961); J. P. Thornton-Duesbery, *The Open Secret of MRA: An Examination of Mr. Driberg's 'critical examination' of Moral Re-Armament* (1964); P. Mottu, *Caux—de la belle époque au Réarmement Moral* (Neuchâtel, 1969; Eng. tr., 1970); T. Spoerri, *Dynamik aus der Stille* (Lucerne, 1971; Eng. tr., 1976); K. D. Belden, *Reflections on Moral Re-Armament* (1983). Works by outsiders incl. H. H. *Henson, *The Group Movement* (1933; 2nd edn., 1933; hostile); R. H. S. Crossman (ed.), *Oxford and the Groups* (1934); and W. H. Clark, *The Oxford Group: Its History and Significance* (New York, 1951).

Oxford Movement. The movement (1833–45) within the C of E, centred at Oxford, which aimed at restoring the *High Church ideals of the 17th cent. Several causes contributed to its growth. The progressive decline of Church life and the spread of 'Liberalism' in theology were causing grave misgivings among Churchmen; on the other hand, the works of C. *Lloyd and others, coupled with the Romantic Movement, had led to a new interest in many elements in primitive and medieval Christianity. Among the more immediate causes was the question of Anglican identity raised by the removal of religious tests for state office and by the modification of the confessional state signalled by the Roman *Catholic Relief Act 1829. The anxiety was increased by the passing of the Reform Bill (1832) and the plan to suppress ten Irish bishoprics. The latter proposal evoked from J. *Keble on 14 July 1833 a sermon delivered in the University pulpit at Oxford on '*National Apostasy', which is usually regarded as the beginning of the Movement.

Its chief object was the defence of the C of E as a Divine institution, of the doctrine of the *apostolic succession, and of the BCP as a rule of faith. These aims were realized esp. through the famous *Tracts for the Times*, begun by J. H. *Newman in 1833. The Movement, whose acknowledged leaders were Keble, Newman, and E. B. *Pusey, soon gained many articulate and able supporters, among them R. H. *Froude, R. W. *Church, R. I. *Wilberforce, C. *Marriott, and I. *Williams. The liberal party in the University and the bishops, however, soon began to attack it; among its early opponents were T. *Arnold, R. *Whately, and R. D. *Hampden. Within the Movement itself there gradually arose a party which found its inspiration in contemporary RCism rather than in the Church of the early centuries. In 1841 Newman published his famous *Tract 90*, which was condemned by many bishops, and in 1842 he retired to Littlemore.

After W. G. *Ward's book, *The Ideal of a Christian Church* (1844), had been censured by the Convocation of Oxford on 13 Feb. 1845, Ward, F. W. *Faber, and several of their circle were received into the Church of Rome, as was Newman in the autumn of the same year. But the majority remained in the C of E, and their views began to gain ground. In 1850 the *Gorham Case (q.v.) again brought about a number of conversions to RCism, among them being those of H. E. *Manning and R. I. Wilberforce. The Movement, however, continued to spread despite the hostility of the press and of the government, which chose the majority of bishops from the ranks of its opponents. Its influence was exercised esp. in the sphere of worship and ceremonial, which came to play a much larger part in the life of the C of E than in the 18th and early 19th cents. At the same time the dignity and responsibility of the ministry were emphasized, not only in the directly religious but also in the social sphere, the slum settlements being among its most notable achievements. The revival of monastic orders and religious community life (see RELIGIOUS ORDERS) in the C of E was a further expression of the Oxford Movement. As a movement with close associations with a university it made considerable contributions to scholarship. In 1836 Keble, Newman, and Pusey began to edit the *Library of the Fathers, and a few years later the Library of Anglo-Catholic Theology was begun as a corpus of *Caroline theology. The principles of the Movement, esp. its concern for a higher standard of worship, gradually influenced not only all groups within the C of E but even many Nonconformists, and had a decisive effect on the pattern of Church life in Britain and beyond.

There is an immense lit. Besides the writings, tracts, and innumerable controversial pamphlets of the leaders and their opponents, the biographies supply much primary material. The three fundamental historical sources are J. H. Newman, Apologia pro Vita Sua (1864); H. P. *Liddon, Life of E. B. Pusey (4 vols., 1893–7); and R. W. Church, The Oxford Movement: Twelve Years, 1833–45 (1891). A contemporary account (partly written in self-defence) is W. *Palmer, A Narrative of Events connected with the Publication of Tracts for the Times (1843). Collections of contemporary material by E. R. Fairweather (ed.), The Oxford Movement (New York, 1964) and E. Jay (ed.), The Evangelical and Oxford Movements (Cambridge, 1983), pp. 106–202, with notes pp. 209–15. Further studies include S. Baring-Gould, The Church Revival (1914); S. L. Ollard, A Short History of the Oxford Movement (1915); E. A. *Knox, The Tractarian Movement (1933). P. Thureau-Dangin, La Renaissance catholique en Angleterre au XIXᵉ siècle (3 vols., 1899–1906; Eng. tr., 2 vols., 1914); C. P. S. Clarke, The Oxford Movement and After (1932); C. Dawson, The Spirit of the Oxford Movement (1933). A. Härdelin, The Tractarian Understanding of the Eucharist (Acta Universitatis Upsaliensis: Studia Historico-Ecclesiastica Upsaliensia, 8; 1965). D. [H.] Newsome, The Parting of Friends: A Study of the Wilberforces and Henry Manning [1966]; P. Toon, Evangelical Theology, 1833–1856: A Response to Tractarianism (1979); [D.] G. Rowell, The Vision Glorious: Themes and Personalities of the Catholic Revival in Anglicanism (Oxford, 1983); id. (ed.), Tradition Renewed: The Oxford Movement Conference Papers (1986); [W.] O. Chadwick, The Spirit of the Oxford Movement: Tractarian Essays (Cambridge, 1990). L. N. Crumb, The Oxford Movement and its Leaders: A Bibliography of Secondary and Lesser Primary Sources (ATLA Bibliography Series, 24; 1988; with supplement, 1993).

Oxyrhynchus Papyri. The collection of many thousand papyri, mostly fragmentary, found from 1897 onwards at Oxyrhynchus, some 10 miles W. of the Nile, near the modern Behnesa. It includes, besides documents of all kinds ranging from the late 1st cent. BC to the 7th cent. AD, some very substantial fragments of Greek and Latin literary texts, both known and unknown, and of Christian literature. Among the last named the most celebrated are the MSS (nos. 1, 654 and 655) of '*Sayings of Jesus' (see THOMAS, GOSPEL OF); they also include, besides fragments of books of the Old and New Testaments and of apo-

cryphal works, a letter of *Peter, the martyred Bp. of Alexandria (d. 311), found together with an ecclesiastical calendar of AD 535–6 (no. 1357), and a Christian hymn with musical notation which is the oldest known piece of ecclesiastical music (no. 1786; late 3rd cent.).

The papyri are being ed., with Eng. tr. and notes, by B. P. Grenfell, A. S. Hunt, and others for the Egypt Exploration Fund, later Society, Graeco-Roman Branch (London, 1898 ff. [vols. 1–61 by 1995]). B. P. Grenfell and A. S. Hunt (eds.), Hellenica Oxyrhynchia (Oxford Classical Texts, 1909). See also works cited under PAPYROLOGY.

Ozanam, Antoine Frédéric (1813–53), French scholar and founder of the 'Society of St *Vincent de Paul'. At the age of 18 he wrote a pamphlet against C. H. *Saint-Simon, and two years later, while studying law and literature at Paris, founded the Society of St Vincent de Paul, an association of laymen for personal service among the poor. During his early years in Paris Ozanam made the acquaintance of F. R. de *Chateaubriand, C. R. F. *Montalembert, H.-D. *Lacordaire, and other progressive thinkers who became closely associated with the revival of Catholicism in France. In 1839 he published a brilliant thesis on the philosophy of *Dante; in 1841 he became assistant professor of foreign literature at the Sorbonne, and simultaneously professor of rhetoric at the Collège Stanislas, then under the direction of A. J. A. *Gratry; and in 1844 full professor at the Sorbonne. On the basis of research in Italian libraries (1846) he edited some early *Franciscan poetry (Poètes franciscains en Italie au XIIIᵉ siècle, 1852), of much importance for the history of medieval spirituality. Together with Lacordaire he founded the Ère nouvelle in 1848 as a mouthpiece of their ideas on Catholic socialism. In the next year he published his influential work La Civilisation chrétienne chez les Francs, in which he described the influence of the Church on the education of the Teutonic tribes. A keen advocate of political liberalism, he became the subject of many sharp attacks, and spent his last years away from public life in work for his Society and in travelling.

Collected edn. of his works, with preface signed J. J. Ampère, 8 vols., Paris, '1855', with Life by H. D. Lacordaire (dated '1856') appended to vol. 1 [separate pagination]. Letters: 1 (1819–40), ed. L. Celier and others (ibid., 1960); 2 (1841–4), ed. J. Caron (1971); 3 (1845–9), ed. D. Ozanam and others (1978). Life by his brother, C. A. Ozanam (ibid., 1879). The numerous other studies incl. those of K. O'Meara (Edinburgh, 1876), C. Huit (Lyons, 1888), L. Baunard (Paris, 1913; Eng. tr., Dublin [1925]), G. Goyau and others (Paris, 1913; to mark the centenary of his birth), H. L. Hughes (London, 1933), the vol. issued by the Society of St Vincent de Paul to mark the centenary of its foundation, L'Œuvre d'Ozanam à travers le monde, 1833–1933 (1933), L. Celier (Paris, 1956), and M. des Rivières (Montreal and Paris, 1984). L. Curnier, La Jeunesse de Frédéric Ozanam (1888). J. Méjecaze, Fr. Ozanam et l'Église catholique (Toulouse thesis; Lyons and Paris, 1932); id., Fr. Ozanam et les lettres (ibid., 1932). A. Foucault, La Société de Saint Vincent de Paul: Histoire de cent ans (1933). E. Galopin, Essai de bibliographie chronologique sur Antoine Frédéric Ozanam (1933). L. Chierotti in Bibliotheca Sanctorum, 9 (1967), cols. 1329–34; Y. Marchasson in Dict. Sp. 11 (1982), cols. 1078–84, both s.v.

P

'P'. A symbol widely used by scholars who follow the 'documentary hypothesis' of the origins of the *Pentateuch to denote the 'Priestly source'. This is marked by a preponderance of ritual and ceremonial enactments over narrative (e.g. Exod. 25–40, Lev., and much of Num.), a formal style (e.g. the first account of Creation, Gen. 1: 1–2: 4a), the avoidance of anthropomorphic ideas of God (contrast e.g. Gen. 3: 8, '*J'), the use of a historical framework linking events by means of genealogies (e.g. Gen. 5), and the inclusion of numerical information (e.g. Exod. 12: 37). The priesthood is conceived as limited to the sons of *Aaron (not merely to the tribe of *Levi as in '*D'), and the divine name *Yahweh (*Jehovah; AV and RV 'the LORD') is used only after its revelation to *Moses, related by 'P' in Exod. 6 (not from the first as in 'J'). Although 'P' may embody earlier matter, in its final redaction it is the latest element in the Pentateuch, dating from the Exile (c.586–c.538 BC) or after, though not later than c.400 BC. See also HOLINESS CODE.

For bibl. see PENTATEUCH.

Pacelli, Eugenio. See PIUS XII.

Pacem in Terris. The encyclical letter of Pope *John XXIII, dated 11 Apr. 1963, on peace among nations based on truth, justice, charity and liberty, and the right organization of society. Addressed to all men of goodwill, it includes a plea for the ending of the arms race, a ban on nuclear weapons, and eventual disarmament.

Text in *AAS* 55 (1963), pp. 257–304. Convenient Eng. tr. in D. J. O'Brien and T. A. Shannon (eds.), *Catholic Social Thought* (Maryknoll, NY [1992]), pp. 131–162. J. Newman, *Principles of Peace: A Commentary on John XXIII's Pacem in Terris* (Oxford, 1964).

Pachomius, St (c.290–346), the founder of *coenobitic Christian monasticism. Fact and legend are much confused in the many late Lives. Pachomius was born, apparently in Upper Egypt, of pagan parents, served as an army conscript and, after his discharge in 313, was converted and baptized. Having been for a time the disciple of the hermit Palaemon, he founded a monastery at Tabennisi in the Thebaid near the Nile about 320, where his fame soon attracted large numbers of monks. Other foundations followed and at his death Pachomius was ruling as abbot-general over nine monasteries for men and two for women. His 'Rule', which influenced St *Basil, John *Cassian, St *Caesarius of Arles, and St *Benedict, survives complete only in Latin translation. Feast day, 14 May in W.; 15 May in E.; in the Coptic Church, 9 May.

Coptic works ed. T. H. Lefort, *Œuvres de S. Pachôme et de ses disciples* (CSCO, Scriptores Coptici, 23; 1956), pp. 1–36, with Fr. tr., ibid. 24 (1956), pp. 1–37. His *Rule* and 11 letters tr. into Lat. by St *Jerome (*PL* 23. 61–99); crit. edn. by A. Boon, OSB, *Pachomiana Latina* (Bibliothèque de la *RHE*, 7; 1932), pp. 13–101, with Coptic frags. and Gk. excerpts of the *Rule*, ed. T. H.

Lefort, pp. 155–82; *Rule* also ed. P. B. Albers (Florilegium Patristicum, 16; Bonn, 1923). Lives in Greek ed. F. Halkin, SJ (Subsidia Hagiographica, 19; 1932; also, from MS in Athens, Cahiers d'Orientalisme, 2; Geneva, 1982). Fr. tr. of 'Vita Prima', with full introd., by A. J. Festugière, OP, *Les Moines d'Orient*, 4. 2 (1965); Coptic Lives ed. T. H. Lefort (*Bohairic in CSCO, Scriptores Coptici, 3rd ser. 7; 1925; with Lat. tr., ibid., 1936; *Sahidic, ibid. 8; 1933; with Lat. tr., 1934). Fr. tr. of Coptic Lives by L. T. Lefort, *Les Vies coptes de saint Pachôme et de ses premiers successeurs* (Bibliothèque du *Muséon*, 16; 1943). Arabic Life ed., with Fr. tr., by E. Amélineau, *Histoire de saint Pakhôme et de ses communautés* (Annales du Musée Guimet, 17; 1889), pp. 335–711; Syriac Life ed. P. Bedjan, *Acta Martyrum et Sanctorum*, 5 (Paris, 1895), pp. 122–76; Lat. Life, tr. from Gk. by *Dionysius Exiguus, ed. H. van Cranenburgh, OSB (Subsidia Hagiographica, 46; 1969). Eng. tr. of Life, from Coptic and Gk., of Rules, Letters, and other material, by A. Veilleux (Cistercian Studies, 45–47; Kalamazoo, Mich., 1980–2). There are also brief notices in *Palladius, *Historia Lausiaca*, 32, and *Sozomen, *HE* 3. 14. The considerable modern lit. incl. P. Ladeuze, *Étude sur le cénobitisme pakhômien pendant le quatrième siècle et la première moitié du cinquième* (1888); *Pachomiana: Commémoration du XVIᵉ centenaire de St Pachôme l'Égyptien (348–1948). Texte des conférences prononcées à Alexandrie et au Caire et relation de la séance de clôture* (Cairo, 1955). A. Veilleux, OCSO, *La Liturgie dans le cénobitisme pachômien au quatrième siècle* (Studia Anselmiana, 57; 1968). H. Bacht, *Das Vermächtnis des Ursprungs*, 2: *Pachomius—Der Mann und sein Werk* (Studien zur Theologie des geistlichen Lebens, 8; 1983), incl. Lat. text of the *Rule*, with Ger. tr. P. [H.] Rousseau, *Pachomius: The Making of a Community in Fourth-Century Egypt* (1985). J. E. Goehring, *The Letter of Ammon and Pachomian Monasticism* (Patristische Texte und Studien, 17; 1986). Altaner and Stuiber (1978), pp. 262 f. and 600 f., with extensive bibl. H. Bacht, SJ, in *Dict. Sp.* 12 (pt. 1; 1984), cols. 7–16, s.v.

Pacian, St (4th cent.), Bp. of Barcelona. A Spaniard by birth, he warmly defended the Catholic doctrine of the forgiveness of sins against the *Novatianists, then a flourishing body in Spain. Besides three letters a short treatise, *Paraenesis ad Poenitentiam*, survives. Pacian is esp. remembered for the epigrammatic passage which occurs in one of his letters (*Ep.* 1. 4), 'My name is Christian; my surname is Catholic' (*Christianus mihi nomen est, catholicus vero cognomen*). To his son, Flavius Dexter, who became pretorian prefect under Honorius, St *Jerome dedicated his *De Viris Illustribus*. Feast day, 9 Mar.

Works first ed. F. du Tillet (Paris, 1538), repr. in J. P. Migne, *PL* 12. 1051–94. Modern edns. by P. H. Peyrot (Zwolle, 1896), L. R. Fernández (Barcelona, 1958), and C. Granado, SJ, with Fr. tr. by C. Épitalon and M. Lestienne (SC 410; 1995). A. Gruber, *Studien zu Pacianus von Barcelona* (1901; philological); R. Kauer, *Studien zu Pacianus* (1902). Bardenhewer, 3, pp. 401–3; Altaner and Stuiber (1978), pp. 369 f. and 627, with bibl. É. Amann in *DTC* 11 (pt. 2; 1932), cols. 1718–21, s.v. 'Pacien'; G. Madoz, SJ, in *EC* 9 (1952), cols. 504 f. s.v.; A. Solignac, SJ, in *Dict. Sp.* 12 (pt. 1; 1984), cols. 17–20, s.v. 'Pacien de Barcelone', with bibl.

Pacific Islands. See SOUTH PACIFIC, CHRISTIANITY IN.

pacifism. See WAR, CHRISTIAN ATTITUDE TO.

Padre. Popular designation of a chaplain in the Army, Navy, and Air Force and also used of all clergymen. *Padre* is the Italian, Spanish, and Portuguese for 'Father', and hence became a common title for a priest. The term is supposed to have been picked up by the British army in India.

Paedobaptism. See INFANT BAPTISM.

Paenitemini. The opening word and hence the common name of the Apostolic Constitution of 17 Feb. 1966, which revised the rules of penitential observance in the RC Church. The days of *fasting were reduced to two: *Ash Wednesday or the first day of *Lent and *Good Friday. The penitential days were reduced to all Fridays (except when Holy Days of Obligation), Ash Wednesday or the first day of Lent, and Good Friday, and episcopal conferences were empowered to vary these days and to substitute for the traditional *abstinence other forms of penance, esp. works of charity and piety. With very slight modifications, its provisions were incorporated in *CIC* (1983), cans. 1249–53.

Text in *AAS* 58 (1966), pp. 177–98.

Paget, Francis (1851–1911), Bp. of *Oxford. Educated at Shrewsbury and *Christ Church, Oxford, he became a Senior Student of Christ Church in 1873, Vicar of Bromsgrove in 1883, Regius professor of pastoral theology at Oxford in 1885, Dean of Christ Church in 1892, and Bp. of Oxford in 1901. He warmly supported the reinterpretation of *Tractarian principles by the *Lux Mundi* group and himself contributed the essay on 'Sacraments' to the volume (1889). He also completed R. W. *Church's revision of J. *Keble's edition of R. *Hooker's *Ecclesiastical Polity* (1883–8) and wrote *An Introduction to the Fifth Book of Hooker's treatise* (1899). His fine spirituality is reflected in his *Spirit of Discipline* (1891), which contains a notable essay on '*Accidie'. He also took an important part in ecclesiastical politics, and was one of the most influential members of the Royal Commission on *Ecclesiastical Discipline (1904–6).

S. Paget and J. M. C. Crum, *Francis Paget* (1913). E. H. Pearce in *DNB*, *1901–11*, 3 (1912), pp. 62 f.

Paget, Henry Luke (1852–1932), Bp. of *Chester. Brother of the preceding, he was educated at Shrewsbury and *Christ Church, Oxford, ordained in 1877, and worked extensively in the East End of London, founding the Christ Church Mission at Poplar in 1879. Later he became Bp. of Ipswich (1906–9), of Stepney (1909–19), and of Chester (1919–32). Personal contact as a young man with E. B. *Pusey, J. H. *Newman, E. *King, and H. P. *Liddon had imbued him with the *Tractarian ideals; and he was a typical representative of the best Anglican pastors of his generation.

E. K. Paget (widow), *Henry Luke Paget: Portrait and Frame* (1939).

Pagi, Antoine (1624–99), French Church historian. A native of Rognes in Provence, he studied with the *Jesuits at Aix and entered the Order of Conventual *Franciscans in 1641. His principal work is the *Critica historico-*

chronologica, a learned attempt to correct the errors contained in the *Annals* of C. *Baronius. The first volume of it appeared in 1689; the complete work, in 4 vols., was edited posthumously by his nephew, François Pagi, in 1705. His other writings include a Latin edition of the sermons of St *Antony of Padua (1684).

A. Teetaert, OFM Cap., in *DTC* 11 (pt. 2; 1932), cols. 1728 f., s.v.

Pagnini, Santi (1470–1536), *Dominican scholar. A native of Lucca, he entered the Dominican Order in Fiesole in 1487 and soon, under the influence of G. *Savonarola, devoted himself to biblical and oriental studies. From *c.*1493 he was engaged in making a completely new Latin translation of the Bible from the original languages. At least the OT seems to have completed by 1518, but it was impossible to raise the money to print it in Italy. In 1525 he received permission to move to France, and his Bible was published at Lyons in 1528 (2nd edn., Cologne, 1541). A remarkably literal translation, it was widely drawn upon by M. *Coverdale. Pagnini also wrote textbooks on Greek and Hebrew, and compiled a Hebrew dictionary (Lyons, 1529). He was one of the theologians who supported *Henry VIII's case for the annulment of his marriage to Catherine of Aragon. See also BIBLE DIVISIONS AND REFERENCES.

G. Pagnino, *Vita di S. Pagnino Lucchese, dell'ordine de' predicatori* (Rome, 1653). I. Taurisano, OP, *Il Domenicani in Lucca* (Lucca, 1914), pp. 94–111. T. M. Centi, 'L'attività letteraria di Santi Pagnini nel campo delle scienze bibliche', *Archivum Fratrum Praedicatorum*, 15 (1945), pp. 5–51; J. D. Gauthier, SJ, 'Sanctes Pagninus, O.P.', *Catholic Biblical Quarterly*, 7 (1945), pp. 175–90. G. Bedouelle and P. Le Gal (eds.), *Le 'divorce' du roi Henry VIII* (Travaux d'Humanisme et Renaissance, 221; Geneva, 1987), pp. 393 f. I. Colosio, OP, in *Dict. Sp.* 12 (pt. 1; 1984), pp. 38 f.

pain bénit. The blessed bread often, until recent times, distributed to the people after Mass in French and Canadian churches. It has as its counterpart among the E. Orthodox the so-called 'antidoron' (ἀντίδωρον, 'instead of the gift'), i.e. what remains of the loaves from which the Eucharistic Bread is cut. The antidoron is distributed at the end of the Liturgy, in theory only to those who have not received Holy Communion (hence its name), but in practice to all those present. Although not consecrated, the antidoron is regarded as sharing in some measure in the Eucharistic blessing. The W. Church distinguished carefully between the Eucharistic Bread and the *pain bénit* by assigning to the latter a special blessing and regarding it as at most a symbol of charity and spiritual unity.

Paine, Thomas (1737–1809), political reformer and author of the *Rights of Man*. He was a native of Thetford in Norfolk and, though confirmed in the C of E, was greatly influenced by the principles of the *Quakers, of whom his father was a member. He was of an adventurous spirit, and after a chequered career as a sailor, staymaker, excise officer, and usher went to America in 1774 at the suggestion of Benjamin Franklin. There he became an editor, attacked slavery, and agitated for the emancipation of women. In 1776 he issued his pamphlet *Common Sense* in favour of American independence, which soon made him famous. During the American War he wrote a series of pamphlets entitled *The Crisis*. He also devoted himself to the invention of an iron bridge which he exhibited in England after his return in 1787. In 1791 he published the first part of his famous *Rights of Man* in reply to E. Burke's *Reflections on the Revolution in France*. After the publication of the second part (1792) he fled to Paris to escape arrest. Here he was received with enthusiasm, but he lost his influence after the fall of the Girondists in 1793 and was arrested in the same year, after completing the first part of his *Age of Reason* (1794). He was released in 1794, having written the second part of his work in prison (pub. 1795). *The Age of Reason*, which aroused fierce opposition in both Britain and America, reflected the Quaker influence of his youth as well as that of contemporary *Deism in its negative estimate of revealed religion, whose beliefs and institutions are ridiculed as full of superstition and bad faith. In 1802 he returned to America, where he spent his last years in disappointment, having lost most of his former friends through his political opinions and his hostility to Christianity.

Collected Works ed. M. D. Conway (4 vols., New York and London, 1894–6) and P. S. Foner (2 vols., New York, 1945), with biog. introd. in 1, pp. ix–xlvi. *Political Writings* (*Common Sense*, *The Crisis*, no. 1, *The Rights of Man* and pt. 1 of *The Age of Reason*), ed. B. Kuklick (Cambridge Texts in the History of Political Thought, 1989). The standard Life is that of M. D. Conway (2 vols., New York and London, 1892). Modern studies by W. E. Woodward (London, 1946), A. O. Aldridge (Philadelphia, 1959; London, 1960), E. Foner (New York, 1976), B. Vincent (Paris [1987]), and M. Philip (Past Masters, Oxford, 1989 [introductory]). I. M. Thompson, Jun., *The Religious Beliefs of Thomas Paine* (New York [1965]). G. Claeys, *Thomas Paine: Social and Political Thought* (Boston and London, 1989). L. Stephen in *DNB* 43 (1895), pp. 69–79, with refs. to earlier works.

Paisy Velichkovsky, St. See VELICHKOVSKY, ST PAISY.

Pakistan, Church of. The Church inaugurated on 1 Nov. 1970 by the union of four Christian bodies, namely the (*Anglican) Church of *India, Pakistan and Ceylon in respect of the dioceses of Lahore, Dacca, and Karachi; the United *Methodist Church in Pakistan; the Scottish and English *Presbyterians of the United Church in Pakistan; and the Pakistani *Lutheran Church. The union, which was the fruit of negotiations extending back to the historic meeting at Tranquebar in 1919, was achieved by a representative of the four Churches concerned each reading his Church's resolution and assent to the Plan of Union. At the same inaugural Eucharist they were then joined by representatives of their sister Churches abroad and all eight laid hands on three Pakistani clergy, who, in turn, laid hands on the representatives of the five dioceses of the new Church, thus uniting the ministries. The head of the Church of Pakistan has the title of Moderator. Though not part of the Anglican Communion, since 1972 the Church of Pakistan has been in communion with the C of E, and it has membership of the Anglican Consultative Council, the *Lambeth Conferences, and the Primates' Meeting.

Palamas. See GREGORY PALAMAS.

Palatine Guard. A corps of militia in the Papal service. It was created in 1850 by *Pius IX as the 'Guardia Palatina

d'Onore' out of two existing bodies, the *civici scelti* and the *capotori*; but after 1870 their numbers were greatly reduced. They were disbanded in 1970. A company used always to be stationed in the Cortile del Maresciallo during a Papal *conclave. Their dress was a uniform of dark blue and a peaked cap with a plume of feathers. See also NOBLE GUARD, SWISS GUARD.

G. Felici in *EC* 6 (1951), cols. 1204–6, s.v. 'Guardia palatina d'onore', with bibl. and illustr.

Palestine Exploration Fund. A fund and society founded in London in 1865 to provide 'for the accurate and systematic investigation of the archaeology, topography, geology and physical geography, natural history, manners and customs of the Holy Land, for biblical illustration.' Renowned initially for the survey of W. Palestine (1871–8) and pioneer excavations by Sir Charles Warren in Jerusalem, the Fund has continued to support all significant British research in the Holy Land. Its archives are of outstanding importance. From 1865 it has published a major journal on biblical archaeology and related subjects, called the *Quarterly Statement* until 1936 and since 1937 the *Palestine Exploration Quarterly*.

Palestinian Syriac text of the NT. A version of the NT in the Palestinian dialect of Syriac (properly called Christian Palestinian Aramaic). The date of the translation is disputed, but there are MSS surviving from the 6th–7th cent., albeit very fragmentary. The text is attested mainly in *lectionaries of the Byzantine type. The Greek underlying this version cannot be identified with any single type of text; in the Gospels some traces of *Diatessaron influence have been discerned. Parts of the OT also survive in this dialect.

Among the more important texts are A. S. Lewis and M. D. Gibson, *The Palestinian Syriac Lectionary of the Gospels* (1899); *Studia Sinaitica*, no. 6 (1897); H. Duensing, *Christlich-palästinisch-aramäische Texte und Fragmente nebst einer Abhandlung über den Wert der palästinischen Septuaginta* (Göttingen, 1906); and M. H. Goshen-Gottstein, *The Bible in the Syropalestinian Version*, 1. *Pentateuch and Prophets* (Hebrew University Bible Project, Monograph Series, 4; Jerusalem, 1973). C. Perrot, 'Un fragment christo-palestinien découvert à Khiret Mird', *R. Bibl.* 70 (1963), pp. 505–55. F. C. Burkitt, 'Christian Palestinian Literature', *JTS* 2 (1900–1), pp. 174–85. B. M. Metzger, *The Early Versions of the New Testament* (Oxford, 1977), pp. 75–82. C. van Puyvelde, OSB, in *Dict. Bibl.*, Suppl. 6 (1960), cols. 880–3 s.v. 'Orientales de la Bible (Versions), VI'.

Palestrina, Giovanni Pierluigi da (c.1525–94), Italian composer. He received his musical education at Rome and in 1544 became organist of the cathedral of his native town Palestrina. In 1551 Pope *Julius III appointed him musical instructor at the Capella Giulia of *St Peter's with the title of 'Magister Capellae', and then in 1554, although he was married, made him a member of the Papal choir; this office Palestrina lost a few months later under *Paul IV. In the same year he was appointed 'Maestro della Capella' of St John *Lateran, but he resigned in 1560. From 1561 to c.1567, however, he held a similar post at *Santa Maria Maggiore. The composition of his celebrated *Missa Papae Marcelli* probably belongs to this period. He may also have been associated with St *Philip Neri's *Oratory. In 1571 he was appointed choirmaster of St Peter's, a post he filled till his death. It was here that his famous *Improperia* were first performed in 1573. Among the enormous number of Masses and *motets he wrote during this last period of his life are the motets to words taken from the Song of Songs, published with a dedication to *Gregory XIII in 1584, and the Masses *Aeterna Christi munera* and *Assumpta est Maria*, which show him at the peak of his creative power.

Palestrina's music, coinciding with a time of vigorous ecclesiastical reforms, is suffused with a deep spirituality, although, compared with that of O. de *Lassus or W. *Byrd, its emotional range is restricted. The austere polyphony of Palestrina's work won the approval of the Church authorities and for centuries it came periodically to represent an 'ideal' of sacred music, never more so than in the 19th cent.

Complete Works ed. T. de Witt, F. Espagne, F. Commer, and F. X. Haberl (33 vols., Breitkopf-Härtel, Leipzig [1862–1907]); also ed. R. Casimiri, L. Virgili, and others (Rome, 1939 ff.). G. Baini, *Memorie storico-critiche della vita e delle opere di Giovanni Pierluigi Palestrina* (2 vols., 1828). R. Casimiri, *Nuovi documenti biografici* (2 fascs., 1918–22). H. Coates, *Palestrina* (Master Musicians, 1938). J. Roche, *Palestrina* (Oxford Studies of Composers, 7; London, 1971). K. G. Fellerer, *Der Palestrinastil und seine Bedeutung in der vokalen Kirchenmusik des achtzehnten Jahrhunderts* (1929); id., *Palestrina-Studien* (Sammlung musikwissenschaftlicher Abhandlungen, 66; 1982). K. Jeppesen, *Palestrinastil met scerligt henblik paa dissonansbehandlingen* (1923; Eng. tr., *The Style of Palestrina and the Dissonance*, 1927, rev. edn., 1946). H. K. Andrews, *An Introduction to the Technique of Palestrina* (1958). W. Kirsch (ed.), *Palestrina und die Kirchenmusik im 19. Jahrhundert* (Regensburg, 1989 ff.). L. Lockwood and J. A. Owens in S. Sadie (ed.), *The New Grove Dictionary of Music and Musicians*, 14 (1980), pp. 118–37, s.v.

Paley, William (1743–1805), author of the *Evidences of Christianity*. Educated at Christ's College, Cambridge, where his unusual abilities attracted attention, he was elected a Fellow in 1766. His clarity of style made him a highly regarded lecturer. His first book, *The Principles of Moral and Political Philosophy* (1785), was at once adopted at Cambridge as a standard textbook. It outlined a system of *Utilitarian ethics for most part identical with that of J. Bentham, though conceived independently; the main difference lay in Paley's somewhat strained attempt to take account of Christian belief in the afterlife. His *Horae Paulinae* (1790) was written to prove the historicity of the events recorded in the NT by comparison of the accounts of St *Paul in the Epistles and Acts; it is probably Paley's only original work. In 1794 followed the classic *A View of the Evidences of Christianity*. Though this work amounted to little more than a compilation of standard 18th-cent. arguments, its effective presentation of the facts and pellucid style made it extremely popular. In his last book, *Natural Theology* (1802), Paley sought to demonstrate the existence and attributes of God from the appearances of nature. Paley became Rector of Musgrave (Cumbria) in 1776 and Archdeacon of *Carlisle in 1782, and thereafter received a number of minor preferments in recognition of his literary achievements. Virtually all his major publications served in their day to provide accessible and cogent arguments for the defence of Church and State against the intellectual challenges which arose in the wake of the *Enlightenment and the French Revolution.

Edns. of his Works with Life by A. Chalmers (5 vols., London, 1819), by E. Paley (son, 7 vols., ibid., 1825), and by R. Lynam

with memoir (4 vols., ibid., 1825). G. W. Meadley, *Memoirs of William Paley* (1809). M. L. Clarke, *Paley: Evidences for the Man* (1974); D. L. LeMahieu, *The Mind of William Paley* (Lincoln, Nebr., 1976). J. B. Schneewind, *Sidgwick's Ethics and Victorian Moral Philosophy* (Oxford, 1977), esp. pp. 122–51, *passim*; P. Addinall, *Philosophy and Biblical Interpretation* (Cambridge, 1991), esp. pp. 35–55; A. M. C. Waterman, *Revolution, Economics and Religion: Christian Political Economy, 1793–1833* (ibid., 1991), esp. pp. 113–136. L. Stephen in *DNB* 43 (1895), pp. 101–7.

palimpsest (Gk. πάλιν, 'again'; ψάω, 'I rub'). A vellum or papyrus MS from which the original writing has been erased or obliterated and the surface then used for some (usually quite different) writing. Of biblical MSS, the best-known instance is the so-called *Codex Ephraemi ('C') of the Gk. NT. Many of the sheets of the original 5th-cent. MS (which appears to have contained a complete OT and NT) have been lost or thrown away, and the remainder cleaned and written over in the 12th cent. with some writings of St *Ephraem Syrus. Formerly chemical reagents were much used to reveal the underlying writings, but it is now possible to secure in many cases at least equally successful results by photography under ultraviolet light; this has the great advantage that there is no risk of damage to the MS. Instances are known of 'double palimpsests', where the MS has received three texts.

F. Mone, *De Libris Palimpsestis tam Latinis quam Graecis* (Carlsruhe, 1855). E. Chatelain, *Les Palimpsestes latins* (École Pratique des Hautes Études. Section des Sciences Historiques et Philologiques, 1904). A. Dold [OSB], 'Palimpsest-Handschriften. Ihre Erschliessung einst und jetzt; ihre Bedeutung', *Gutenberg-Jahrbuch* [25] (1950), pp. 16–24; also a number of other arts. by this author (list of his works in *Colligere Fragmenta: Festschrift Alban Dold zum 70. Geburtstag*, ed. B. Fischer, OSB, and V. Fiala (Texte und Arbeiten [the organ of the Palimpsest Institute founded by Dold at Beuron], 1, Heft 2; 1952), pp. ix–xx). E. A. Lowe, 'Codices Rescripti. A List of the Oldest Latin Palimpsests with stray observations on their origin', in *Mélanges Eugène Tisserant*, 5 (ST 235; 1964), pp. 67–112, repr. in Lowe's *Palaeographical Papers 1907–1965*, ed. L. Bieler, 2 (Oxford, 1972), pp. 480–519. K. Löffler and P. Ruf in *Handbuch der Bibliothekswissenschaft* begründet von F. Milkau, 1 (2nd edn. by G. Leyh, 1952), pp. 149–52.

pall. Originally the same word as *pallium, it has been applied to several kinds of cloth covering. In ecclesiastical usage it denotes esp. (1) the small linen cloth with which the chalice is covered at the Eucharist, stiffened in its modern form by a piece of cardboard; and (2) a cloth, commonly of black, purple, or white velvet, which is spread over the coffin at funerals.

Palladius (*c.*364—between 420 and 430), historian of early monasticism. Probably a native of Galatia, he spent several years with the monks of Egypt, where he was pupil of *Evagrius Ponticus. In 400 he returned to Asia Minor, where he became Bp. of Helenopolis in Bithynia. As a friend of St *Chrysostom he was forced into exile in 406, though he returned to Asia Minor later (*c.*413) and, acc. to *Socrates (*HE* 7. 36), became Bp. of Aspouma in Galatia. Both St *Jerome and St *Epiphanius accused him of *Origenism, but it is not clear that the charge was well founded. His famous 'Lausiac History' (so named from its dedication to Lausus, the chamberlain of *Theodosius II) of the 'Friends of God' (φιλόθεοι, i.e. the monks), composed *c*.419, is the most valuable single writing that survives for the history of early monasticism. If somewhat credulous about stories relating to the Egyptian monks, it is the work of a writer indubitably sincere and unquestionably religious. Palladius is also the author of a 'Dialogue' on the life of St Chrysostom.

Gk. text of 'Lausiac History' first ed. J. Meursius, Leiden, 1616. New edn. by F. *Ducaeus in his *Bibliotheca Veterum Patrum*, 2 (Paris, 1624), pp. 893–1053; repr. in J. P. Migne, *PG* 34. 991–1262. These are all interpolated texts. Crit. text, with introd. and discussion, in [E.] C. Butler (Texts and Studies, 6, nos. 1 and 2; Cambridge, 1898–1904). Eng. trs. by W. K. L. Clarke (Translations of Christian Literature, 1st ser., Greek Texts; 1918) and by R. T. Meyer (ACW 34; 1965). On the Syriac text, R. Draguet, *Les Formes syriaques de la matière de l'Histoire Lausiaque* (CSCO 389–90 and 398–9; Scriptores Syri, 169–70 and 173–4; 1978), incl. text and Fr. tr. The 'Dialogus' was first pr. by E. Bigot, Paris, 1680; repr. by B. de *Montfaucon in his edn. of Chrysostom, 13 (Paris, 1738), pp. 1–89, and in J. P. Migne, *PG* 47. 5–82. Crit. edns. by P. R. Coleman-Norton (Cambridge, 1928) and, with Fr. tr., by A.-M. Malingrey and P. Leclercq (SC 341–2; 1988). Eng. tr. by H. Moore (Translations of Christian Literature, 1st ser., Greek Texts; 1921). 'De Gentibus Indiae et Bragmanibus' attributed to Palladius [only partly his work], ed. W. Berghoff (Beiträge zur klassischen Philologie, 24; 1967).

E. Preuschen, *Palladius und Rufinus: Ein Beitrag zur Quellenkunde des ältesten Mönchtums* (1897); R. *Reitzenstein, *Historia Monachorum und Historia Lausiaca* (1916); W. *Bousset, 'Komposition und Charakter der Historia Lausiaca', *Nach.* (Gött.), 1917, pp. 173–217; E. *Schwartz, 'Palladiana', *ZNTW* 36 (1937), pp. 161–204; E. D. Hunt, 'Palladius of Helenopolis: a Party and its Supporters in the Church of the Late Fourth Century', *JTS* NS 24 (1973), pp. 456–80. *CPG* 3 (1979), pp. 168–72 (nos. 6036–8). Altaner and Stuiber (1978), pp. 238–40 and 595 f. (with bibl. of important arts. by R. Draguet and others); F. M. Young, *From Nicaea to Chalcedon* (1983), pp. 38–44. B. Flusin in *Dict. Sp.* 12 (pt. 1; 1984), cols. 113–26, s.v.

Palladius, St (5th cent.), first Bp. of the Irish. Acc. to *Prosper of Aquitaine, the deacon Palladius persuaded Pope *Celestine I (422–32) to send St *Germanus, Bp. of Auxerre, to stamp out the *Pelagian heresy in Britain and was later himself consecrated by the same Pope, who sent him to the Irish as their first bishop. Palladius has been variously regarded as an associate of Germanus of Auxerre, a delegate of the British Church, and a papal deacon close to Celestine I.

Lives of St *Patrick from the 7th cent. portray Palladius as an unsuccessful missionary, who abandoned his task or died, leaving the way open for Patrick. The fact that Irish sources gave Palladius no role independent of Patrick, and esp. the reference in the 'Book of *Armagh' to 'bishop Palladius who was by another name called Patricius', have given rise to the theory that his career has been subsumed within the legend of Patrick. The appearance of both St Germanus and Amator of Auxerre in Patrician texts has been supposed to derive from lost *Acta* of Palladius. Feast day, 7 July.

The only historical evidence comes from the Chronicle of Prosper of Aquitaine (for edns. of which see s.v. PROSPER); legendary material will be found in the Lives of Patrick (for which see PATRICK, ST). On the historical context, see R. P. C. Hanson, *Saint Patrick: His Origins and Career* (Oxford, 1968), pp. 52–6; on later traditions, pp. 192–4. The theory of two Patricks has a long history; on the equation of the 'elder Patrick' with Palladius, see, e.g., S. Malone, 'Sen (old) Patrick, who was he?', *Irish Ecclesiast-*

ical Record, 3rd ser. 12 (1891), pp. 800–809; T. F. O'Rahilly, *The Two Patricks* (Dublin, 1942), and criticism by D. A. Binchy, 'Patrick and his Biographers, Ancient and Modern', *Studia Hibernica*, 2 (1962), pp. 7–173, esp. pp. 115–46. See also L. Bieler, 'The Mission of Palladius. A Comparative Study of Sources', *Traditio*, 6 (1948), pp. 1–32, incl. texts. G. T. Stokes in *DCB* 4 (1887), pp. 176 f., s.v. See also bibl. to IRELAND, CHRISTIANITY IN.

pallium. In ecclesiastical usage, the circular band of white woollen material with two hanging strips and marked with six black crosses which is worn on the shoulders by the Pope and granted by him to *metropolitans (formerly also to some other bishops and archbishops) of the RC Church. The *Codex Iuris Canonici* (1983) describes the pallium as signifying the power which, in communion with the Roman Church, the metropolitan possesses by law in his own province. It must be requested within three months of episcopal consecration or canonical appointment of a new metropolitan (can. 437). It is made from the wool of lambs blessed on St *Agnes' day in the church of S. Agnese fuori le mura, and before dispatch, rests for a night on the tomb of St *Peter in the Vatican basilica. The early history of the pallium is very obscure. Derived from the imperial insignia, it seems to have been worn at first by archbishops and to have had no connection with Rome, still less with the investment of Papal authority. At a later stage, after the Pope had himself assumed it, he seems occasionally to have sent it to individual prelates as a mark of special honour, and in this way its reception became much coveted. Not until the 9th cent. were all metropolitans required to petition for it. The pallium naturally went out of use in the C of E at the *Reformation, though it still appears in some armorial bearings where it appears (as in a front or back view of the wearer) in the shape of the letter Y. See also OMOPHORION.

N. de Bralion, Cong. Orat., *Pallium Archiepiscopale* (Paris, 1648). P. de *Marca, *De Concordia Sacerdotii et Imperii*, ed. É. *Baluze, 2 (ibid., 1663), pp. 79–88. H. Thurston, SJ, *The Pallium* (Historical Papers, ed. J. Morris, SJ, 4 [*c*.1893]). H. Grisar, SJ, 'Das römische Pallium und die ältesten liturgischen Schärpen', in S. Ehses (ed.), *Festschrift zum elfhundertjährigen Jubiläum des Deutschen Campo Santo in Rom* (1897), pp. 83–114. J. W. Legg, 'The Blessing of the Episcopal Ornament called the Pall', *Yorkshire Archaeological Journal*, 15 (1898), pp. 121–41, repr. in id., *Essays Liturgical and Historical* (1917), pp. 108–56. T. Klauser, *Der Ursprung der bischöflichen Insignien und Ehrenrechte* (Bonner Akademische Reden, 1; Krefeld, 1948). P. Salmon, OSB, *Étude sur les insignes du pontife dans le rit romain* (Rome, 1955). A. A. King, *The Liturgy of the Roman Church* (1957), pp. 152–5. J. Mayo, *A History of Ecclesiastical Dress* (1984), pp. 22–4 and 124 f. Braun, *LG*, pp. 620–76; Braun, *LP*, pp. 143–51. J. Braun, SJ, in *CE* 11 (1911), pp. 427–9, s.v.; H. *Leclercq, OSB, in *DACL* 13 (pt. 1; 1937), pp. 931–40, s.v. with detailed bibl.; T. Klauser in *L.Th.K.* (2nd edn.), 8 (1963), cols. 7–9, s.v.

Pallottini Fathers. A society of RC priests, lay brothers, sisters, and associates, founded in 1835 by St Vincent Pallotti (1795–1850), a Roman by birth who, after ordination as priest (1818), devoted his life to pastoral work in the city. They were previously known as the 'Pious Society of Missions' (*Pia Societas Missionum*, PSM), but are now generally called the 'Society of the Catholic Apostolate' (*Societas Apostolatus Catholici*; SAC). The sisters were founded by Pallotti in 1843 as a separate congregation. He believed that all Christians, lay as well as ordained, had an equal status in working for the salvation of others, and *Pius XI saw in him a forerunner of *Catholic Action.

[J. Hettenkofer], *Historia Piae Societatis Missionum* (Rome, 1935); id., *Historia Societatis Apostolatus Catholici, 1935–1950* (ibid., 1950). H. Schulte, SAC, *Das Werk des Katholischen Apostolats* (3 vols., Limburg [an der Lahn], 1966–71), esp. vol. 3. Pallotti's *Opere Complete*, ed. F. Moccia, SAC (12 vols., Rome, 1964–85). Life by F. Frank, SAC (2 vols., Augsburg, 1952–63). F. Moccia, SAC, in *DIP* 8 (1988), cols. 1589–92, s.v. 'Società dell'Apostolato Cattolico'; A. Faller, SAC, ibid. 1 (1974), cols. 738 f., s.v. 'Apostolato Cattolico, Suore dell' '; A. Walkenbach, PSM, in *Dict. Sp.* 16 (1994), cols. 834–41, s.v. 'Vincent (6) Pallotti', all with bibl.

Palm Sunday (*Dominica in Palmis*). The Sunday before *Easter which introduces *Holy Week. The distinctive ceremonies of the day are the blessing of the palms and, in the W. Church and some E. Churches, the procession, representing the Lord's triumphal entry into *Jerusalem a week before the Resurrection. The Palm Sunday procession is attested for Jerusalem as early as the 4th cent. by the 'Pilgrimage of *Egeria'. In the W. the *Gallican *Bobbio Missal (8th cent.) contains a blessing of palms to be carried as symbols of the victory of Christ and protection against the devil; the wording seems to imply a procession, for which there is specific evidence in the 9th cent. In the Middle Ages the procession usually set out from one church and made its way to another, where the palms were blessed and distributed, and then returned to the church from which it had started. Frequently a representation of Christ, e.g. the Gospel book or a crucifix or a carved figure seated on a wooden ass, was carried in the procession. The use of the Blessed Sacrament for the purpose was ordered by Abp. *Lanfranc for the cathedral at *Canterbury *c.*1078, and thence spread to Rouen and several places in England.

A very elaborate rite for the blessing of the palms developed during the Middle Ages, similar in structure to the Mass. In the C of E the ceremony was abolished by an Order in Council in Jan. 1549, and only in recent times has a special rite for Palm Sunday been officially sanctioned within the Anglican Communion. In the RC Church the rite was radically simplified by the decree 'Maxima Redemptionis Nostrae Mysteria' of 16 Nov. 1955, and there have been a number of minor changes since. Acc. to the current rite there is a general blessing of the palms (or other greenery) held by the people, if possible in a different building from that in which the Mass is to be celebrated. After the reading of the account of the triumphal entry into Jerusalem in one or other of the Gospels, and a short homily, the clergy and people process into the church, singing Psalms or the traditional 'Gloria, Laus' ('All Glory, Laud and Honour' by *Theodulf of Orléans) or some other chant. If it is not possible to process outside, there is at least a procession in the church before the main Mass of the day. The Mass which follows begins with the collect (with no *Introit, etc.) and includes the chanting of the Passion from one of the Gospels. The colour for the Mass and the procession is red. The modern Anglican rites follow a similar pattern. In the Byzantine rite the palms or olive branches are blessed and distributed at Mattins after the reading of the Gospel account of the Lord's entry into Jerusalem. A procession is not usual.

The texts for the Latin Rite are pr. in the Roman Missal with the rest of the Palm Sunday proper. Those sanctioned for optional use in the C of E are in *Lent, Holy Week, Easter: Services and Prayers Commended by the House of Bishops of the General Synod of the Church of England* (1986), pp. 73–89; in other provinces of the Anglican Communion they are contained in modern revisions of the BCP. T. J. Talley, *The Origins of the Liturgical Year* (New York [1986]), esp. pp. 176–82, and 209–14. H. A. P. Schmidt, SJ, *Hebdomada Sancta* (2 vols in 3, Rome, etc., 1956–7), with texts of the 1955 rite, relevant decrees, and bibl. H. J. Gräf, SVD, *Palmenweihe und Palmenprozession in der lateinischen Liturgie* (Veröffentlichungen des Missionspriesterseminars St Augustin, Siegburg, 5; 1959), with extensive bibl. The pre-1955 rite is described in H. Thurston, SJ, *Lent and Holy Week* (1904), pp. 191–237. H. *Leclercq, OSB, in *DACL* 14 (pt. 2; 1948), cols. 2060–4, s.v. 'Rameaux (Dimanche des)'.

Palmer, Roundell (1812–95), First Earl of Selborne, Lord Chancellor, and High Churchman. Educated at Rugby, Winchester, and Trinity College, Oxford, he was elected a Fellow of Magdalen in 1835. His brilliant abilities led him to rise rapidly in his profession; he was Lord Chancellor in 1872–4 and again in 1880–5, being created Earl of Selborne in 1882. A devoted member of the C of E, he admired the leaders of the *Oxford Movement, actively supported I. *Williams's candidature for the Poetry Professorship, and expressed his belief that the condemnation of E. B. *Pusey's 1843 Sermon was illegal. Until 1869 he was opposed to the entrance of Dissenters to Oxford University. His writings include *The Book of Praise* (1863), a hymnal on historical principles, *Notes on Some Passages in the Liturgical History of the English Church* (1878), *A Defence of the Church of England against Disestablishment* (1886), and *Ancient Facts and Fictions concerning Churches and Tithes* (1888). He also contributed the art. 'Hymns' to the 9th edn. of the *Encyclopaedia Britannica*.

Palmer's *Letters to his Son on Religion* were posthumously pub. London, 1898; also *The Catholic and Apostolic Church: Letters to his Son*, ibid., 1899. Autobiographical *Memorials*, ed. by his daughter, S. M. Palmer (pt. 1, *Family and Personal*, 2 vols., London, 1896; pt. 2, *Personal and Political*, 2 vols., ibid., 1898). E. G. W. Bill, *Catalogue of the Papers of Roundell Palmer (1812–1895), first earl of Selborne* (1967). J. M. Rigg in *DNB* 43 (1895), pp. 150–4.

Palmer, William (1803–85), *Tractarian theologian. Of Irish extraction, he graduated at *Trinity College, Dublin, before coming to Oxford. From 1831 he was attached to Worcester College. His *Origines Liturgicae* (1832), a learned treatise on the history of the English liturgy, brought him into relations with J. H. *Newman, H. J. *Rose, and others who led the *Oxford Movement in the next years. A rigid High Churchman who was strongly opposed both to Popery and to Dissent, he expounded what he conceived to be the Anglican doctrine of the Church (roughly the so-called *branch theory) in his *Treatise on the Church of Christ* (2 vols., 1838) with learning and lucidity. When the Oxford Movement became less anti-Roman in its ideals, W. Palmer gave public expression to his misgivings in his *Narrative of Events connected with the Publication of Tracts for the Times* (1843). In 1846 he issued a reply to J. H. Newman's *Development of Christian Doctrine* in his *Doctrine of Development*. In the same year he became vicar of Whitchurch Canonicorum in Dorset.

The Jesuit theologian, G. *Perrone, described him as 'theologorum Oxoniensium facile princeps'.

G. Goodwin in *DNB* 43 (1895), pp. 168–70, with refs.

Palmer, William (1811–79), brother of Roundell *Palmer, Fellow of Magdalen College, Oxford (from 1832), and divine. Though for his day an extreme *High Churchman, he took little direct part in the *Oxford Movement. In 1840 and 1842 he paid visits to Russia, provided with letters of commendation from the revered president of his college (M. J. *Routh), to explore the possibilities of intercommunion between the Anglican and Orthodox Churches, and did much to foster interest in the E. Church in Great Britain. Between these two visits he made strong protests against the proposed Anglo-Lutheran *Jerusalem Bishopric plan. He corresponded with A. *Khomiakov, who visited him in Oxford in 1847, about Anglican–Orthodox relations. Distressed by the *Gorham Case, he tentatively considered seceding to the Orthodox Church; but deciding against this step because the Easterns insisted on his 'rebaptism', he eventually joined the RC Church in 1855. His writings include *Dissertations on Subjects relating to the Orthodox or Eastern-Catholic Communion* (1853), *Notes of a Visit to the Russian Church in the Years 1840, 1841* (ed. J. H. *Newman; 1882), and works on Russian Church history and archaeology.

His correspondence with Khomiakov, 1844–54, ed. by W. J. Birkbeck, *Russia and the English Church during the last fifty years*, 1 (1895; all pub.). J. M. Rigg in *DNB* 43 (1895), pp. 167 f.

Pammachius, St (*c.*340–410), Roman Christian. A senator of the Furian family, he was a friend of St *Jerome, who dedicated to him several works, among them the Commentaries on the Minor Prophets (406) and on Daniel (407). After the death of his wife, the daughter of St *Paula, he took the monastic habit and spent his possessions on works of piety, among them the famous hospital for pilgrims at Portus and the church of SS. Giovanni e Paolo (excavated in 1887) in Rome. Of a peace-loving character, he disapproved of the lack of moderation in Jerome's attack on *Jovinian and the violent controversy between Jerome and *Rufinus on the subject of *Origen. His intervention in the *Donatist schism in Numidia, where he owned estates, earned him a laudatory letter from St *Augustine (401). He died in the invasion of the Goths in 410. Feast day, 30 Aug.

The chief sources are St Jerome, *Epp.* 48 f., 57, 66, 83 f., and 98; St Augustine, *Ep.* 58, and *Palladius, *Historia Lausiaca*, 62. J. Pinius, SJ, in *AASS*, Aug. 6 (1743), pp. 555–63, incl. relevant texts of works cited above. On the *tituli S. Pammachii*, later *SS. Johannis et Pauli*, cf. J. P. Kirsch, *Die römischen Titelkirchen im Altertum* (Studien zur Geschichte und Kultur des Altertums, 9; 1918), pp. 26–33. A. H. M. Jones and others, *The Prosopography of the Later Roman Empire*, 1 (Cambridge, 1971), p. 663.

Pamphilus, St (*c.*240–310), disciple of *Origen. A native of Berytus (modern Beirut), he was a pupil of Pierius at *Alexandria; it was prob. from him that he derived his veneration for the teaching of Origen. Later he directed a theological school at *Caesarea in Palestine, where he was martyred. During imprisonment in the persecution of Maximinus Daza, he prepared an 'Apology for Origen'. In this work he was much assisted by *Eusebius of Caesarea,

who in turn held Pamphilus in immense veneration. Of the five books of the 'Apology' which are Pamphilus' own, only the first survives, and this in a Latin version of doubtful accuracy made by *Rufinus of Aquileia. After Pamphilus' martyrdom, Eusebius added a sixth book to the 'Apology', wrote Pamphilus' Life (now lost, except for a few fragments), and took for himself the name of 'Eusebius of Pamphilus' (ὁ τοῦ Παμφίλου). His large library survived at Caesarea until destroyed by the Arabs in the 7th cent. Feast day in the E., 16 Feb. (the day of his martyrdom); in the W., 1 June.

Rufinus' version of bk. 1 of Pamphilus' *Apology*, with 'Admonitio' of C. de La Rue, in J. P. Migne, *PG* 17. 521–616. Frag. of Eusebius' Life in *Jerome, *Adv. Rufin.* 1. 9. Eusebius, *HE* 7. 32. 25, and *De Mart. Pal.* 11. 3; Jerome, *De Vir. Illustr.* 75; *Photius, *Cod.* 118. P. Nautin, *Origène: Sa vie et son œuvre* (1977), pp. 99–153 ('L'"Apologie pour Origène et ses opinions" par Pamphile et Eusèbe'). Bardenhewer, 2, pp. 287–92. A. Solignac, SJ, in *Dict. Sp.* 12 (pt. 1; 1984), cols. 150–3, s.v.

panagia (Gk. παναγία, 'all holy'). A favourite title of the BVM in the E. Church. The word is also used (1) of an oval medallion depicting the BVM which Orthodox bishops wear on the breast suspended on a chain; and (2) of bread (ἄρτος τῆς παναγίας) which is solemnly blessed in honour of the BVM. See also ENCOLPION.

Pancras, St (d. 304), martyr. There are no reliable historical data about him. Acc. to an early tradition he was a Phrygian by race and a member of the Roman Church, who at the age of 14 was martyred on the Via Aurelia during the Diocletianic *persecution. Devotion to him became very popular, esp. in Rome, where his church gave one of the cardinals his title. Feast day, 12 May.

St Pancras railway station in London is named after the dedication of the church of the parish in which it is situated.

His 'Acta' survive in several recensions both in Lat. and Gk. A Lat. text from several MSS is pr., with discussion, in *AASS*, Mai. 3 (1680), pp. 17–22; other Lat. MSS in *Anal. Boll.* 2 (1883), pp. 289–91, and 10 (1891), pp. 53–6. P. Franchi de' Cavalieri, *Hagiographica* (ST 19; 1908), pp. 77–105 ('Della leggenda di S. Pancrazio Romano'), with Gk. text of 'Acta', pp. 109–12. J. Declerck, 'Les recensions grecques de la Passion de S. Pancrace, martyr à Rome', *Anal. Boll.* 105 (1987), pp. 65–85, incl. texts. *BHL*, pp. 928 f. (nos. 6420–8), and *novum supplementum* (1986), pp. 680 f. R. Krautheimer and others, *Corpus Basilicarum Christianarum Romae*, 3 (Vatican City, 1967), pp. 153–74 [in Eng.]. G. N. Verrando, 'Le Iscrizioni attribuite al Complesso di S. Pancrazio', *Riv.A.C.* 59 (1983), pp. 151–89, with refs. to earlier arts. H. *Leclercq, OSB, in *DACL* 13 (pt. 1; 1937), cols. 1001–14, with refs.

panentheism (Gk. πᾶν, 'everything'; ἐν, 'in'; θεός, 'God'). The belief that the Being of God includes and penetrates the whole universe, so that every part of it exists in Him, but (as against *pantheism, q.v.) that His Being is more than, and is not exhausted by, the universe. The word was coined by K. C. F. Krause (1781–1832) for his own system. The concept has gained some popularity in recent years, esp. among the exponents of *Process Theology and in the writings of John Macquarrie, who, in his *Gifford Lectures for 1983–4 (pub. as *In Search of Deity*, 1984) prefers the term 'dialectical theism'.

Pange Lingua. The title of two famous Latin hymns: the Passiontide hymn by *Venantius Fortunatus (d. *c.*610) (*Pange lingua gloriosi proelium certaminis*), and the *Corpus Christi hymn by St *Thomas Aquinas (d. 1274) (*Pange lingua gloriosi corporis mysterium*). On the latter see also TANTUM ERGO.

Panikhida. See PANNYCHIS.

Pannenberg, Wolfhart (1928–), German Protestant theologian. In 1950/51 he studied theology under K. *Barth in Basle, proceeding to doctoral work in Heidelberg in 1951. During his Heidelberg years he co-operated with a group of younger theologians in the development of a new approach, both exegetical and systematic, to the theology of revelation. This led to the book, *Offenbarung als Geschichte*, ed. by Pannenberg (1961; Eng. tr., *Revelation as History*, 1986). In 1961 he moved from his first teaching post at the Church seminary in Wuppertal to the Chair of Systematic Theology in Mainz; in 1968 he became Professor of Systematic Theology in the Protestant Faculty of Theology at Munich University. He is the author of a large number of articles and books.

Pannenberg's own contribution to *Offenbarung als Geschichte* marked a sharp break with the 'revelational positivism' (D. *Bonhoeffer's phrase) of Barth. Pannenberg had come to hold that Christian theology cannot protect itself against criticism by appeal to some privileged epistemology of faith. Faith, rather, is a manner of response to certain historical facts that, rationally speaking, suggest interpretation in revelatory terms. The key facts to which such an appeal is made were explored in detail in Pannenberg's first major work, *Grundzüge der Christologie* (1964; Eng. tr., *Jesus—God and Man*, 1968), remarkable especially for its defence of the historicity of the *Resurrection of Christ, in the context of a positive appreciation of Jewish *apocalyptic thought.

Such an argument, on Pannenberg's view, requires a wide understanding of historical rationality. This relies in part on an appeal to universal history in the manner of G. W. F. *Hegel (and creatively linked by Pannenberg with the apocalyptic framework of interpretation), in part on an assessment of the whole history of religions (here Panneberg engages critically with the historical relativism of E. *Troeltsch), and in part on a theological anthropology, which is again set out and defended rationally through critical engagement with all forms of reductionism. These themes were developed in a number of articles and form the substance of Pannenberg's next two major works, *Wissenschaftstheorie und Theologie* (1973; Eng. tr., *Theology and the Philosophy of Science*, 1976) and *Anthropologie in theologische Perspektive* (1983; Eng. tr., 1985). They illustrate, at length, Pannenberg's conviction that Christian theology must argue with *atheism in the shared context of critical rationality.

Pannenberg has written on many other theological topics, such as the *Apostles' Creed, the Kingdom of God, the Church, ethics, and spirituality. Notable features of his work include a powerful defence of reform (as opposed to revolution) in Christian social ethics, and a novel, if controversial, attempt to underpin the theology of hope with an ontology of God as the power of the future. The philosophical foundation of his theological work is briefly indicated in *Metaphysik und Gottesdanke* (1988; Eng. tr., 1990). In his *Systematische Theologie* (3 vols., 1988–93; Eng. tr., 1991 ff.) he presents in full his understanding of the doctrines of God, creation, Christ, the Church, and the Kingdom. It is notable throughout for its determination, at every level, to argue for the truth of Christian doctrine.

There are two collections of his essays: *Grundfragen systematischer Theologie* (2 vols., 1967–80; Eng. tr. of vol. 1 as *Basic Questions in Theology*, vols. 1–2, 1970–71; [vol. 3 of *Basic Questions*, 1973, is tr. from other sources] and *Ethik und Ekklesiologie* (1977; Eng. tr. of pt. 1, *Ethics*, 1981, and pt. 2, *The Church*, 1983). A. D. Galloway, *Wolfhart Pannenberg* (Contemporary Religious Thinkers Series, 1973); E. F. Tupper, *The Theology of Wolfhart Pannenberg* (Philadelphia, 1973; London, 1974). P. Warin, *Le Chemin de la Théologie chez Wolfhart Pannenberg* (Analecta Gregoriana, 224; 1981); C. E. Braaten and P. Clayton (eds.), *The Theology of Wolfhart Pannenberg* (Minneapolis [1988]); S. J. Grenz, *Reason for Hope: The Systematic Theology of Wolfhart Pannenberg* (New York and Oxford, 1990).

Pannychis (Gk. παννυχίς, literally: 'all-night [service]'), a Greek word for a *Vigil (q.v.), more usually known as ἀγρυπνία. It occurs already in St *Athanasius (*Apol. ad Const.* 25). The term 'Pannychis' came to be used mainly for vigils for the dead, hence the Slavonic word *Panikhida*, meaning a memorial service for the dead (which takes the form of a drastically curtailed vigil).

Panormitanus (1386–1445), also known as **Abbas Modernus** and **Siculus**, canonist. Born in Catania in Sicily, Nicolò de' Tudeschi entered the *Benedictine Order *c.*1400, and after studying under F. *Zabarella, he taught at *Bologna, Parma, Siena, and Florence. In 1425 he became abbot of Maniacio, near Messina, and in 1435 Abp. of Palermo (hence Panormitanus). In 1433 *Eugenius IV had sent him to the Council of *Basle as his representative, but in 1436 Panormitanus returned as the ambassador of Alfonso of Aragon, who was a contender for the throne of Naples against a nominee of Eugenius IV; consequently he usually supported the antipope, Felix V (by whom he was made a cardinal), defending in his *Tractatus de Concilio Basiliensi* the Pope's inferiority to a *General Council. Once Alfonso had obtained Naples in 1443, Panormitanus ceased to oppose Eugenius. His principal writings were his works on canon law, which included commentaries on the *Decretals of Gregory IX, on the *Sext, and on the *Clementines.

Many of his works were pr. in the 15th cent. Collected edns.: 8 vols., Venice, 1592, and 9 vols., ibid., 1617. K. W. Nörr, *Kirche und Konzil bei Nicolaus de Tudeschis (Panormitanus)* (Forschungen zur kirchlichen Rechtsgeschichte und zum Kirchenrecht, 4; 1964); A. Vagedes, *Das Konzil über dem Papst? Die Stellungnahmen des Nikolaus von Kues und des Panormitanus zum Streit zwischen dem Konzil von Basel und Eugen IV.* (2 vols., Paderborner Theologische Studien, 11; 1981). A. Black, 'Panormitanus on the Decretum', *Traditio*, 26 (1970), pp. 440–4. M. Watanabe, 'Authority and Consent in Church Government: Panormitanus, Aeneas Sylvius, Cusanus', *Journal of the History of Ideas*, 33 (1972), pp. 217–36. C. Lefebvre in *DDC* 6 (1957), cols. 1195–215, s.v., with extensive refs.

Panpsychism. The doctrine advocated by G. T. *Fechner (1801–87) and other 19th-cent. philosophers that everything in the universe is endowed with a measure of consciousness. It has found little favour with Christian theologians. A similar doctrine was expressly repudiated by St *Thomas Aquinas (*Summa Theol.* 1, q. 18, a. 1).

C. Hartshorne in V. Ferm (ed.), *A History of Philosophical Systems* [1950], pp. 442–53; P. Edwards in id. (ed.), *Encyclopedia of Philosophy*, 6 (1967), pp. 22–31, s.v., both with bibl.

Pantaenus, St (d. *c*. AD 190). He is described by *Eusebius (*HE* 5. 10 f.) as head of the *Catechetical School at Alexandria and one of the teachers of *Clement. Prob. a native of Sicily, he was converted from *Stoicism to the Christian faith and taught at Alexandria from *c*.180 until his death. Nothing of his work survives, and the fragments preserved under his name may be a record of his oral teaching. Eusebius also states that he preached the Gospel in 'India'. Feast day, 7 July; in the Coptic Church, 22 June.

Frags. in M. J. *Routh, *Reliquiae Sacrae*, 1 (2nd edn., Oxford, 1846), pp. 375–83. J. Munck, *Untersuchungen über Klemens von Alexandria* (Forschungen zur Kirchen- und Geistesgeschichte, 2; 1933), pp. 151–204 [critique of W. *Bousset's theory of a 'Pantaenus Source' in Clement]. J. Gwinn in *DCB* 4 (1887), pp. 181–4, s.v., with further primary refs.; S. Lilla in *DPAC* 2 (1984), cols. 2604–6, s.v. 'Panteno', with bibl.; Eng. tr. in *Encyclopedia of the Early Church*, 2 (Cambridge, 1992), p. 639.

Pantaleon, St (d. *c*.305), martyr. His name means 'the All-merciful' (παντελεήμων). Nothing is known with certainty about him. Acc. to one form of the legends, he was a physician to the Emp. Galerius at Nicomedia who, after having been converted to Christianity in his early years by his mother, was led into apostasy by the worldly attractions of court life. Reconverted by a Christian called Hermolaus, he suffered martyrdom when *Diocletian gave orders to purge the court of Christians. His cult has been very popular, esp. in the E.; and in the Middle Ages he was honoured as one of the patron saints of physicians, second only to St *Luke. He was accounted one of the 14 *Auxiliary Saints. Feast day, 27 July; also other dates.

Gk. text of 'Passio' in the works of *Simeon Metaphrastes pr. in J. P. Migne, *PG* 115. 448–77; Lat. tr. of this, and other material, with comm., in *AASS*, Jul. 6 (1729), pp. 397–427. Further refs. in *BHL*, pp. 929–32 (nos. 6429–48), and *novum supplementum* (1986), pp. 681 f.; *BHG* (3rd edn., 1957), pp. 166–9 (nos. 1412z–1418c); *BHO*, p. 183 (nos. 835–7). H. *Delehaye, SJ, *Les Origines du culte des martyrs* (Subsidia Hagiographica, 20; 1912), pp. 181 f. For popular account of the liquefaction of the relic of his blood, very similar to that recorded of St Januarius (q.v.), I. R. Grant, *The Testimony of Blood* (1929), pp. 17–44. J. M. Sauget in *Bibliotheca Sanctorum*, 10 (Rome, 1968), cols. 108–17, s.v.

pantheism (Gk. πᾶν, 'all', and θεός, 'God'). The belief or theory that God and the universe are identical. The word appears to have been coined by J. *Toland, the *Deist, in 1705 and to have been employed shortly afterwards by his opponents. Pantheistic systems, however, go back to very early times. It is a type of thought esp. found in Hinduism. Acc. as it interprets the universe in terms of God or God in terms of the universe, its attitude is religious or materialistic. Of the former type the most extreme representative in modern times was B. *Spinoza (1632–77) with his immanental formula, 'God or Nature' (*Deus sive Natura*). In the 19th cent. the German Idealists (F. W. J. von *Schelling, G. W. F. *Hegel) and the British *Absolute Idealists (F. H. *Bradley, B. *Bosanquet) taught

philosophical doctrines akin to pantheism. Mysticism, with its passionate search for God and desire for union with the Divine, has often been charged with pantheism. Among Christian thinkers accused of pantheistic tendencies may be named *Dionysius the Pseudo-Areopagite, *Erigena, and *Nicholas of Cusa; and such mystics as *Eckhart and Jakob *Boehme.

Collection of extracts from various authors, tr. into Eng., by C. Hartshorne and W. L. Rees, *Philosophers Speak of God* (Chicago, 1953). C. E. Plumptre, *History of Pantheism* (2 vols., 1881); W. S. Urquhart, *Pantheism and the Value of Life* (1919). A. E. Garvie, F. Thilly, and A. S. Geden in *HERE* 9 (1917), pp. 609–20, s.v.; F. A. Schalck in *DTC* 11 (pt. 2; 1932), cols. 1855–74, s.v. 'Panthéisme'; M. F. Sciacca in *EC* 9 (1952), cols. 686–93, s.v. 'Panteismo'; S. Pfürtner in *L.Th.K.* (2nd edn.), 8 (1963), cols. 25–9, s.v. 'Pantheismus'.

Papa Angelicus (also **Pastor Angelicus**). A belief which arose in Italy in the earlier half of the 13th cent. and is recorded by Roger *Bacon (*Opus Tertium*, 24), to the effect that a Pope would arise who would revive Apostolic simplicity and zeal in the Church and inaugurate a new age. It was developed in apocryphal writings and prophecies of the 14th cent., e.g. those of Telesphorus of Cosenza (1386). In the Prophecies of St *Malachy the 106th Pope, i.e. *Pius XII (1940–58), is so designated.

Papacy. While the term strictly denotes the office of the Pope, i.e. the Bp. of *Rome, it commonly refers to the system of centralized government in the Church exercised by him, along with the claim that by Divine appointment he has universal authority over Christendom. Acc. to RC doctrine, St *Peter was the first Bp. of Rome, and the Pope is not only his lineal successor in that office, but also inherits in its fullness the unique commission given to him by Christ (cf. esp. Mt. 16: 18 f. and Jn. 21: 17). Claims to the magisterial and jurisdictional primacy supposed to be contained in this commission, hinted at (it is held) as early as the First Epistle of St *Clement, the letters of St *Ignatius, and the writings of St *Irenaeus, were explicit in the teaching of *Leo I and *Gelasius I (the first Pope to be saluted as '*vicar of Christ'), and were eloquently developed by a succession of Popes, notably *Gregory VII, *Innocent III, and *Boniface VIII; for centuries Popes claimed supremacy over, and the right to depose, temporal rulers. The Papal primacy was never formally accepted by the E. Churches, and it was repudiated by the Protestant communions. From 756 to 1870 the Papacy itself was also a temporal power, ruling a large part of central Italy; since 1929 its sovereignty has been confined to the *Vatican City. But although it lost temporal power in 1870, the First *Vatican Council reinforced its spiritual authority by proclaiming the Pope *infallible and reaffirming that he was the absolute ruler of the Church. The Second *Vatican Council sought to balance the Papal monarchy by a declaration of the *collegiality of the bishops with the Pope in the government of the Church. See also ROMAN CATHOLICISM.

'Papal Aggression'. The name popularly given to the action of Pope *Pius IX making England and Wales, by Letters Apostolic, *Universalis Ecclesiae* (29 Sept. 1850), an ecclesiastical province of the RC Church, with a hierarchy consisting of an archbishop and 12 *suffragans all with territorial titles. The wording of the brief was provocative, e.g. by its reference to the C of E as 'the Anglican Schism'. An unexpected and almost fanatical storm of indignation spread through Great Britain under the leadership of Lord John Russell (1792–1878), culminating in the passing of the *Ecclesiastical Titles Act 1851 (q.v.).

Papal legate. See LEGATE, PAPAL.

Papal States. See STATES OF THE CHURCH.

Papebroch, Daniel (1628–1714) (or van Papenbroeck), *Bollandist hagiographer. In 1659 he became J. Bollandus's assistant and continued till his death to take an active part in the compilation of the *Acta Sanctorum, though he was forced to interrupt his work for a time by blindness. His name appears for the first time in 'Martius I' (1668), and for the last in 'Junius V' (1709), i.e. on 18 volumes in all. Bitter criticism from the *Carmelites, the foundation of whose order by *Elijah he denied, led to his denunciation at Rome and in Spain for heresy, and in 1695 14 volumes of the *Acta* were put on the *Index. In a long introduction to 'Aprilis II' (1675), Papebroch subjected Merovingian charters to drastic criticism, which called forth J. *Mabillon's De Re Diplomatica (1681).

J. Pien, SJ, in AASS, Jun. 6 (1715), pp. 3–21. H. *Delehaye, SJ, L'Œuvre des Bollandistes (1920), pp. 31–40; P. Peeters, SJ, L'Œuvre des Bollandistes (2nd edn., Académie Royale de Belgique. Classe des Lettres. Mémoires. Collection in-8°, 2nd ser. 54, fasc. 5; 1961), esp. pp. 17–34. Polgár, 2 (1992), pp. 619 f. H. Delehaye in Biographie nationale publiée par l'Académie Royale des Sciences, des Lettres et des Beaux-Arts de Belgique, 16 (1901), cols. 581–9, s.v. 'Papebrochius'; H. *Leclercq, OSB, in DACL 13 (pt. 1; 1937), cols. 1345–58, s.v. See also works cited under BOLLANDISTS.

Paphnutius, St (d. c.360), Bp. of the Upper Thebaid. He was an Egyptian monk, who had been a disciple of St *Antony. He suffered such hardship and cruelty during the persecution by Maximin Daza (305–13) that at the Council of *Nicaea his mutilated body was an object of wonder and veneration to the assembled bishops. Acc. to *Socrates (HE 1. 11) and *Sozomen (HE 1. 23), he dissuaded the Council from ordering all clergy to put away their wives. Feast day, 11 Sept.

Gk. text of 'Passio' ed. H. *Delehaye, SJ, in Anal. Boll. 40 (1922), pp. 328–43. Lat. tr. in AASS, Sept. 6 (1757), pp. 681–8. For his views on celibacy, G. *Bickell, 'Der Cölibat eine apostolische Anordnung', ZKT 2 (1878), pp. 26–64, esp. pp. 57–62. H. *Leclercq, OSB, in DACL 13 (pt. 1; 1937), cols. 1358–61, s.v. 'Paphnuce'.

Papias (c.60–130), Bp. of Hierapolis in Asia Minor. Nothing is known of his life, apart from the statement of St *Irenaeus that he was a 'man of long ago' (ἀρχαῖος ἀνήρ) and the disciple of one 'John' and a companion of St *Polycarp. His work, Λογίων Κυριακῶν Ἐξηγήσεις ('Expositions of the Oracles of the Lord'), in five books survives only in quotations in Irenaeus and *Eusebius, and seems to have contained many oral traditions and legends. In the famous fragments on the origin of the Gospels of St *Matthew and St *Mark he states, on the authority of 'the Elder', that Mark, having become the interpreter

of St *Peter, set down accurately (ἀκριβῶς), though not in order (οὐ μέντοι τάξει), everything that he remembered of the words and actions of the Lord, and that St Matthew composed 'the oracles' (τὰ λόγια) in Hebrew, and that everyone translated them as best he could. Of his theology we only know that he held *Millenarian views, believing that there would be a period of a thousand years after the Resurrection during which the Kingdom of Christ would be set up on earth in a material form.

The frags. have often been repr., e.g., with Eng. tr., in J. B. *Lightfoot, Apostolic Fathers (ed. J. R. Harmer, 1891), pp. 514–35. U. H. J. Körtner, Papias von Hierapolis: Ein Beitrag zur Geschichte des frühen Christentums (Forschungen zur Religion und Literatur des Alten und Neuen Testaments, 133; Göttingen, 1983), with detailed survey of lit. Various of his arts. collected by J. Kürzinger, Papias von Hierapolis und die Evangelien des Neuen Testaments (Eichstätter Materialien, 4; Ratisbon, 1983), incl. text and Ger. tr. of frags. R. Bauckham, 'Papias and Polycrates on the Origin of the Fourth Gospel', JTS NS 44 (1993), pp. 24–69, esp. pp. 44–63. CPG 1 (1983), pp. 20 f. (no. 1047). Altaner and Stuiber (1978), pp. 52 f. and 552. F. Wotke in PW 18 (pt. 3; 1949), cols. 966–76, s.v. 'Papias (2)'; M. Jourjon in Dict. Bibl., Suppl. 6 (1960), cols. 1104–9; W. R. Schoedel in Anchor Bible Dictionary, 5 (1992), pp. 140–2.

Papini, Giovanni (1881–1956), Italian author. In his early years he followed various trends of modern philosophy, esp. the *Pragmatism of W. *James, and in his own periodicals, Leonardo (1902) and Lacerba (1913), as well as in several volumes of essays, treated metaphysical and moral questions with originality and often with violence. In 1912 he published Un uomo finito, a novel reflecting his interior struggle between his philosophical speculations and the desire for faith, which he at last resolved by acceptance of the Catholic creed. The outcome of his conversion was the Storia di Cristo (1921; Eng. tr., The Story of Christ, 1923), his most successful book, in which he traces the earthly life of Christ, His effect on His contemporaries, and the uniqueness of His Person and message in the world of antiquity, with great poetical insight. It was followed in 1929 by a Life of St *Augustine (Eng. tr., 1930), a psychological study, but less successful than the earlier work.

Correspondence with Giuseppe Prezzolini ed., with introd. by Prezzolini, Storia di un'amicizia (2 vols., Florence [1966–8]); that with Pietro Pancrazi ed. S. Ramat, Le Ombre di Parnaso (ibid. [1973]); and that with Olga Signorelli ed. by her daughter, M. Signorelli (Quaderni dell'Osservatore, 19; Milan [1968]). A. Viviani, Gianfalco: Storia e vita (1934); M. Apollonio, Papini ('Guide di cultura contemporanea', 1944); R. Ridolfi, Vita di Giovanni Papini (1957). G. Fantino, Saggio su Papini [1981]; P. Bagnoli (ed.), Giovanni Papini: L'uomo impossibile [1982]. A. Santucci in P. Edwards (ed.), The Encyclopedia of Philosophy, 6 (1967), pp. 37 f., s.v.

papyrology. The science of dealing with MSS on papyrus. Papyrus is a writing material made out of the fibres of the stem of a water plant which formerly grew plentifully in the Nile. It was used in ancient Egypt and became the chief writing material in the Greco-Roman world from the 5th cent. BC (and probably earlier) to the 4th cent. AD, when it gradually gave way to vellum. It was manufactured in sheets, which were glued together to form rolls of any desired length up to about 35 feet. This was the form in which the books of the OT and possibly those of the NT were first written, and for pagan literature the roll predominates until the 4th cent. AD. Such a roll would not contain more than a single Gospel. But from the latter part of the first cent. an alternative form, that of the 'codex', which could contain much more matter, came into use, and this was predominantly used for Christian books. In the codex, sheets of papyrus were folded in two and formed into quires, as in a modern printed book. Early codices were often composed of single quires, consisting of any number of folded sheets, from 1 to 50 or more; eventually it was found more convenient to form quires of not more than 8 sheets, making 16 leaves or 32 pages, and (as in modern books) to make up the codex from several such quires. The writing on a roll was in columns of about $2\frac{1}{2}$ to $3\frac{1}{2}$ inches wide, and was normally on one side of the roll only; the references in Ezek. 2: 10 and Rev. 5: 1 to something written 'within and without' are to a sealed document, not to a book.

Papyrus manuscripts have survived in few areas apart from the dry soil of Egypt, where they were first found in 1778; but it is only since 1877 that they have been discovered in any large numbers, and still more recently that they have become important for the biblical text.

Useful directory to the many series of published papyri in H. G. *Liddell and R. *Scott, *A Greek–English Lexicon* (rev. edn., 1940), pp. xliii–xlv, with additions in Suppl. ed. E. A. Barber (1968), pp. x f.; J. van Haelst, *Catalogue des Papyrus Littéraires Juifs et Chrétiens* (1976); K. Aland, *Repertorium der Griechischen Christlichen Papyri*, 1: *Biblische Papyri* (Patristische Texte und Studien, 18; 1976). Large collection of historical and legal docs. assembled in L. Mitteis and U. Wilcken, *Grundzüge und Chrestomathie der Papyruskunde* (4 vols., 1912). A. S. Hunt and C. C. Edgar (eds.), *Select Papyri* (2 vols., Loeb, 1932–4); D. L. Page (ed.), *Select Papyri*, 3: *Literary Papyri, Poetry* (ibid., 1941; rev. edn., 1942). General introd. to subject by E. G. Turner, *Greek Papyri: An Introduction* (Oxford, 1968; enlarged repr., 1980). Lexicon by F. Preisigke, *Wörterbuch der griechischen Papyrusurkunden* (2 vols., 1925–7; suppl. ed. E. Kiessling, 2 vols., 1931–71). Grammar by E. Mayser (2 vols.; Bd. 2 in 3 parts; Berlin, 1906–34). *Archiv für Papyrusforschung und verwandte Gebiete* (begun by U. Wilcken, 1900 ff.). J. G. Winter, *Life and Letters in the Papyri* (University of Michigan Press, 1933). Vocabulary of NT Gk. usage by J. H. *Moulton and G. Milligan, *The Vocabulary of the Greek Testament Illustrated from the Papyri and other non-literary Sources* (1914–30). On the bearing of the papyri on NT studies, A. *Deissmann, *Licht vom Osten* (4th edn., 1923), pp. 18–38; Eng. tr. (1927), pp. 24–50. T. C. Skeat, 'Early Christian Book-Production: Papyri and Manuscripts', in G. W. H. Lampe (ed.), *The Cambridge History of the Bible*, 2 (1969), pp. 54–79; E. C. Turner, *The Typology of the Early Codex* (Philadelphia, 1977); C. H. Roberts and T. C. Skeat, *The Birth of the Codex* (1987). C. H. Roberts and A. F. Shore in J. R. *Harris (ed.), *The Legacy of Egypt* (2nd edn., Oxford, 1971), pp. 355–433. See also bibl. to BODMER PAPYRI, CHESTER BEATTY PAPYRI, NAG HAMMADI PAPYRI, OXYRHYNCHUS PAPYRI, and RYLANDS ST JOHN.

Parabalani (Gk. παραβαλανεύς; Lat. *parabolanus*; the etymology of the word, denoting a 'sick-nurse', is uncertain). The Parabalani were an association of men at *Alexandria, devoted to looking after the sick, who prob. originated in a period of epidemic. They are mentioned in two laws of the 'Codex Theodosianus', 16. 2 (*de episcopis* 42 and 43 of AD 416 and 418), reproduced in the 'Codex Justinianus', 1. 3 (*de episcopis* 18). Acc. to these laws, which fixed their number at 500, later at 600, we learn that the Parabalani were clerics under episcopal supervision and

exempt from public duties. They were forbidden to visit theatres and law courts. They seem to have played a considerable part in the public life of Alexandria and are believed to have had a share in the murder of the philosopher *Hypatia (415). They are also mentioned among *Dioscorus' supporters at the *Latrocinium of *Ephesus (449; *ACO* 2. 1. 1, p. 179, l. 28).

H. Grégoire, 'Sur le personnel hospitalier des Églises', *Byzantion*, 13 (1938), pp. 283–5; A. Philipsborn, 'La compagnie d'ambulanciers "parabalani" d'Alexandrie', ibid. 20 (1954), pp. 185–90; W. Schubart, 'Parabalani', *Journal of Egyptian Archaeology*, 40 (1954), pp. 97–101. E. Venables in *DCA* 2 (1880), pp. 1551 f., s.v. 'Parabolani'.

parable (Gk. παραβολή). In the *Synoptic Gospels, as in the OT tradition on which they draw, the word stands for a wide range of striking sayings, from well-known popular proverbs to little metaphors and elaborate *allegories. Mk., which is generally believed to be the earliest gospel, contains examples of all these, with the historical allegories of the Sower and the Wicked Husbandman dominating by size and importance. They alert the reader to the theological significance of the narrative. Among the teachings of Christ which Mt. added to Mk. is a wealth of new parables. They too range from the small pictures which illustrate the *Sermon on the Mount to the allegories in chapter 25, but they are given a more moral thrust than those in Mk. Lk. adds famous, realistic stories such as the *Good Samaritan and the Prodigal Son. Like Mt's parables, they have moral purpose but, while being long, they are distinctive in not being so strongly or solely allegorical. There are allegories in Jn. (the Sheepfold and the Vine), though these are not designated as parables.

Modern critics such as C. H. *Dodd and J. Jeremias, reacting against the dominance of allegory in patristic and medieval exegesis, have taken the Lukan parables to be the standard for recovering the Lord's own parables. Hence they have sought to clear away the allegory from other parables, taking it to be the accretion of early Christianity. There is, however, no reason why Christ should not have used allegorical parables and no sure criterion for distinguishing His parabolic teaching from that of the early Church or the evangelists. The more hospitable range of connotation of 'parable' remains valuable.

The most widely read of the older works was R. C. *Trench, *Notes on the Parables of Our Lord* (1841). Modern crit. works incl.: A. *Jülicher, *Die Gleichnisreden Jesu* (2 vols., 1888–99); P. Fiebig, *Die Gleichnisreden Jesu im Lichte der rabbinischen Gleichnisse des neutestamentlichen Zeitalters* (1912); C. H. Dodd, *The Parables of the Kingdom* (1935); J. Jeremias, *Die Gleichnisse Jesu* (Zurich, 1947; Eng. tr., 1954; 6th edn., Göttingen, 1962; Eng. tr., 1963); E. Linnemann, *Gleichnisse Jesu: Einführung und Auslegung* (Göttingen, 1961; 3rd edn., 1964; Eng. tr., 1966); E. Jüngel, *Paulus und Jesus* (Hermeneutische Untersuchungen zur Theologie, 2; 1962), pp. 87–174; D. O. Via, *The Parables: Their literary and existential dimension* (Philadelphia, 1967); C. E. Carlston, *The Parables of the Triple Tradition* (ibid. [1975]); H. Weder, *Die Gleichnisse Jesu als Metaphern* (Forschungen zur Religion und Literatur des Alten und Neuen Testaments, 120; 1978); J. [H.] Drury, *The Parables in the Gospels: History and Allegory* (1985); J. R. Donahue, SJ, *The Gospel in Parable: Metaphor, Narrative, and Theology in the Synoptic Gospels* (Philadelphia, 1988); B. B. Scott, *Hear Then the Parable: A Commentary on the Parables of Jesus* (Minneapolis [1989]). F. Hauck in *TWNT* 5 [1955], pp. 741–59 (Eng. tr., 1968, pp.

744–61), s.v. παραβολή; A. George in *Dict. Bibl.*, Suppl. 6 (1960), cols. 1149–77, s.v.

Parabolani. The Latin (apparently corrupt) form of Parabalani (q.v.). It was held to derive from the Gk. παρα-βολᾶνοι, 'those who disregard' *sc.* their lives; cf. Phil. 2: 30.

Paracelsus. The name coined for himself by Theophrast Bombast von Hohenheim (1493–1541), Swiss physician. While still young he came under the influence of Abbot J. *Trithemius' approach to alchemy and chemistry. In 1527, after studying at several universities in Germany, he was appointed city physician at Basle, but his open opposition to the prevailing system of medicine, based on Galen and *Avicenna, forced him to leave in 1528. For the rest of his life he was moving from place to place. His great advances in therapeutics rested on his belief that its principles were to be derived from the study of nature and not from scholastic disputations. Yet his empiricism did not prevent his elaborating a mystical theosophy on a *Neoplatonic basis, in which he held that, just as we know nature only to the extent that we are ourselves nature, so we know God only in so far as we are God. Paracelsus also made important contributions to the study of chemistry.

Collection of his works ed. J. Huser (11 parts, Basle, 1589–99). Crit. edn. by K. Sudhoff, W. Matthiesen, and K. Goldhammer (1. Abteilung: Medizinische, naturwissenschaftliche und philo-sophische Schriften, ed. K. Sudkoff, 14 vols., Munich, 1922–33; 2. Abteilung: Theologische und religionsphilosophische Schriften, vol. 1 ed. W. Matthiessen, Munich, 1923; vols. 2 ff. ed. W. Gold-hammer, Wiesbaden, 1955 ff.). Main works, in modernized form, ed. W.-E. Peuckert (5 vols., Darmstadt and Basle/Stuttgart, 1965–8). Eng. tr. of his *Hermetic and Alchemical Writings* by A. E. Waite (2 vols., London, 1894) and of his *Select Works* by N. Gut-erman (ibid., 1951). The very considerable lit. on Paracelsus incl. studies in Eng. by A. M. Stobbart (London, 1911), J. M. Stillman (Chicago and London, 1920), J. Hargrave (London, 1951; more popular), and W. Pagel (Basle and New York, 1958; 2nd edn., 1982). W.-E. Peuckert, *Theophrastus Paracelsus* (Stuttgart, 1941; 3rd edn., 1944, repr., Hildesheim and New York, 1976); B. Whiteside and S. Hutin, *Paracelse: l'homme, le médecin, l'alchimiste* [1966]; G. Bechtel, *Paracelse ou la naissance de la médecine alchi-mique* [1970]; G. Wehr, *Paracelsus* (Fermenta Cognitionis, 6; Freiburg i.B., 1979), with bibl. K. Goldammer, *Paracelsus in neuen Horizonten* (Salzburger Beiträge zur Paracelsusforschung, 24; Vienna, 1986). K. Biegger, 'De Invocatione Beatae Mariae Vir-ginis': *Paracelsus und die Marienverehrung* (Kosmosophie, 6; Stuttgart, 1990), incl. text. K. Sudhoff, *Versuch einer Kritik der Echtheit der paracelsischen Schriften* (1, Bibliographia Paracelsica; 2, Paracelsus-Handschriften, 1894–9). K.-H. Weimann, *Para-celsus-Bibliographie 1932–1960 mit einem Verzeichnis neu entdeckter Paracelsus-Handschriften (1900–1960)* (Kosmosophie, 2; Wiesbaden, 1963). W. Pagel in *Dictionary of Scientific Bio-graphy*, 10 (1981), pp. 304–13, s.v.; J. Wicks in *Dict. Sp.* 12 (pt. 1; 1984), cols. 182–7, s.v.

Paraclete (Gk. παράκλητος, 'advocate'), Johannine epi-thet of the Holy Spirit. It is traditionally translated 'Com-forter'. Though used of Christ in 1 Jn. 2: 1 and, by implication, in Jn. 14: 16, it is ordinarily applied to the Holy Spirit (Jn. 14: 16; 16: 7, etc.). *Origen interpreted the word as meaning 'Intercessor' where the reference is to the Lord, and as 'Consoler' (for the loss of Christ) where it is to the Holy Spirit. This latter meaning, though not found outside the NT, may be defended by the context, and was indeed that generally accepted by the Fathers. But

it describes the mission of the Holy Spirit, which is 'to strengthen and guide the Church into all truth' less fully than the renderings 'Helper', 'Counsellor', or the *Vulgate translation 'Advocate', preferred by many modern com-mentators. Several scholars are in favour of simply tran-scribing the Greek word as was done in several ancient versions of the NT.

Many important discussions will be found in comm., ad locc. O. Betz, *Der Paraklet: Fürsprecher im häretischen Spätjudentum, im Johannes-Evangelium und in neu gefundenen gnostischen Schriften* (Leiden and Cologne, 1963); R. E. Brown, 'The Paraclete in the Fourth Gospel', *New Testament Studies*, 13 (1967), pp. 113–32; E. Franck, *Revelation Taught: The Paraclete in the Gospel of John* (Coniectanea Biblica, New Testament Series, 14; Lund, 1985). A. Casurella, *The Johannine Paraclete in the Church Fathers* (Beiträge zur Geschichte der biblischen Exegese, 25; Tübingen, 1983). J. Behm in *TWNT* 5 (1954), pp. 798–812 (Eng. tr., 1967, pp. 800–814), s.v. παράκλητος; J. Ashton in *Anchor Bible Dictionary*, 5 (1992), pp. 152–4, s.v., both with bibl.

Paracletice. See OCTOECHOS.

Paradigm. The title given by M. *Dibelius and other *Form critics to passages in the Gospels which contain narratives woven round a particular saying of Christ in order to drive its teaching home. They are held to have received their present literary form from their use as illus-trations in preaching. They are called *Apophthegms by R. *Bultmann and *Pronouncement Stories by V. Taylor.

See bibl. to FORM CRITICISM.

paradise. The word is probably of Persian origin (Zend *pairidaêza*), denoting an enclosed park or pleasure-ground. It is found in the Hebrew of the OT in its primary mean-ing three times (Neh. 2: 8, Eccles. 2: 5 and Song of Songs 4: 13). In the LXX, in addition it occurs in Gen. 2 and 3 as the Greek rendering of the 'garden' planted by God in Eden. In later Jewish literature it came more and more to signify a state of blessedness whether material (much of the *Rabbinic literature) or spiritual (so Ecclus. 24: 25–30 and Pss. Sol. 14: 2), and with this latter meaning the word is used in the NT, where it occurs three times. In Lk. 23: 43 it has been variously interpreted as referring either to the intermediate state of the just before the Resurrection (*limbo) or as a synonym of the heaven of the blessed. In this second sense it is used in the two other NT passages, 2 Cor. 12: 4 and Rev. 2: 7. In patristic and medieval literat-ure there was much speculation both as to the conditions of the primeval paradise and, esp. in later times, on the intermediate state and the distinction between a terrestrial and a heavenly paradise. In modern popular usage paradise usually denotes the state of future bliss. See also BEATIFIC VISION.

For 'paradise' as an architectural term see PARVIS.

H. L. Strack and P. Billerbeck, *Kommentar zum Neuen Testa-ment aus Talmund und Midrasch*, 4 (pt. 2; 1928), pp. 1118–65. J. H. Tigay and B. J. Bamberger in *Encyclopaedia Judaica*, 13 (Jerusalem, 1972), cols. 77–85, s.v.; J. Jeremias in *TWNT* 5 (1954), pp. 763–71 (Eng. tr., 1967, pp. 765–73), s.v. παράδεισος. See also works cited s.v. HEAVEN.

Paradise Lost. The magnificent epic of J. *Milton (q.v.), describing the *Fall of Man and its consequences. It was the first original non-dramatic work of any importance to be written in English in blank verse. For vastness in conception and grandeur in treatment it is surpassed in modern literature only by *Dante's *Divina Commedia*. Its theology has been thought to show traces of Milton's *Arianism and his lack of sympathy with organized religion; but its main themes are those common to the mainstream of Christian doctrine. Milton prob. did not complete it until 1667, and on 27 Apr. 1667 he disposed of the copyright for the sum of £5, with the contingency of three further instalments of the same sum if additional editions were needed.

Facsimile of 1st edn. prepared by J. Isaacs, pr. at the Golden Cockerel Press [Waltham St Lawrence], 1937. Modern edn., with full notes, by A. W. Verity (Cambridge, 1910); cf. also edns. of Milton's Poetical Works, cited s.v. MILTON, esp. that of H. Darbishire, vol. 1 (Oxford, 1952). G. McColley, *Paradise Lost: An Account of its Growth and Major Origins* (Chicago, 1940); C. S. *Lewis, *A Preface to Paradise Lost* (1942); [J. N.] D. Bush, *Paradise Lost in Our Time* (Ithaca, NY, 1945); J. S. Diekhoff, *Milton's Paradise Lost: A Commentary on the Argument* (New York, 1946). B. Rajan, *Paradise Lost and the Seventeenth Century Reader* (1947); A. J. A. Waldock, *Paradise Lost and its Critics* (1947); A. H. Gilbert, *On the Composition of Paradise Lost* (Chapel Hill, NC, 1947); B. A. Wright, *Milton's 'Paradise Lost'* (1962); C. Ricks, *Milton's Grand Style* (Oxford, 1963); H. [L.] Gardner, *A Reading of Paradise Lost* (ibid., 1965); M. Fixler, *Milton and the Kingdoms of God* (1964); D. H. Burden, *The Logical Epic: A Study of the Argument of* Paradise Lost (1967); J. M. Evans, Paradise Lost *and the Genesis Tradition* (Oxford, 1968); D. R. Danielson, *Milton's Good God* (Cambridge, 1982); J. Leonard, *Naming in Paradise: Milton and the Language of Adam and Eve* (Oxford, 1990); L. Newlyn, Paradise Lost *and the Romantic Reader* (ibid., 1993). See also works cited s.v. MILTON, JOHN.

Paragraph Bibles. In 1755 a NT arranged in paragraphs (as opposed to the usual AV practice of arrangement in verses), with a revised text, was issued by J. *Wesley. In 1838 the *Religious Tract Society published an edition with the AV text in paragraphs; and other similar editions followed. It is the arrangement adopted in the RV and most other modern translations.

Paralipomenon (Gk. παραλειπομένων, 'of the things left out'), the name by which the two Books of *Chronicles are sometimes known to RCs. It is based on the *Vulgate title, which derives from the LXX, in which, e.g. in *Codex Vaticanus, the Books of Chronicles are entitled παραλειπομένων α´ and παραλειπομένων β´ respectively, a description which implies that the Books are supplementary to 1 and 2 Kings.

parallelism, poetic. This characteristic of Hebrew poetry was first analysed by R. *Lowth in his *De sacra poesi Hebraeorum* (Oxford, 1753). Such parallelism is not confined to the books of the Bible but it is also an essential element in other Near Eastern literature. Hebrew parallelism is ordinarily of three kinds:

(1) Synonymous parallelism, which is the most usual form, consisting in the simple repetition of the same thought in slightly different words, e.g. 'Hear my crying, O God: Give ear unto my prayer' (Ps. 61: 1).

(2) Antithetical parallelism, produced by contrasting the first member with the second. This form is very frequent in the Bk. of Prov., e.g. 'A merry heart doeth good like a medicine: But a broken spirit drieth the bones' (Prov. 17: 22).

(3) Synthetic parallelism, in which the first member is developed or completed by a similar thought in the second (or third, in the case of triplets), e.g. 'The kings of the earth stand up: And the rulers take counsel together: Against the Lord and against His Anointed' (Ps. 2: 2).

Apart from these chief forms some commentators have claimed to find others, such as 'climactic', 'introverted', 'stairlike', and 'emblematic' parallelism, but they are in general less easily discernible.

S. *Mowinckel, *Offersang og Sangoffer* (1951), pp. 418–35; Eng. tr., *The Psalms in Israel's Worship* (Oxford, 1962), vol. 2, pp. 159–75. R. Alter, *The Art of Biblical Poetry* (New York [1985]; Edinburgh, 1990), pp. 3–26; J. Muilenburg in *Encyclopaedia Judaica*, 13 (Jerusalem, 1972), cols. 671–81, s.v. 'Poetry'; A. Berlin in *Anchor Bible Dictionary*, 5 (1992), pp. 155–62.

Paraphrases of Erasmus, The. The Commentary on the Gospels written by *Erasmus which *Edward VI in his *Injunctions of 1547 ordered to be set up in all parish churches 'in some convenient place' where the 'parishioners may most commodiously resort unto the same and read the same'. The section on St John's Gospel was translated into English by the Princess *Mary.

Parasceve. See PREPARATION, DAY OF.

parclose. In ecclesiastical architecture, a screen or set of railings, usually standing at the E. end of the *aisle of a church, for enclosing a *chantry altar for *requiems and one or more seats for members of the family of the deceased. After the Reformation these enclosures developed into the 'family pew'.

Pardon. (1) Another name for an '*indulgence', found, e.g., in Art. 22 of the *Thirty-Nine Articles. In the later Middle Ages the right to share in an indulgence was hawked around Europe by the 'Pardoners', denounced by G. *Chaucer, W. Langland, and J. *Wycliffe. Such Pardons were a source of great profit to the ecclesiastical authorities and were frequently used to obtain money for building purposes, as for *St Peter's, Rome, and the completion of *York Minster.

(2) In Brittany, the feast of the patron saint of a church at which an indulgence may be gained. These Pardons are held in many places between *Easter and *Michaelmas. The celebrations are preceded by Confession on the night before and start early in the morning with Mass, and much of the day is given to prayer. The most dramatic element in the proceedings is the procession round the church or village in which relics or other votive objects are carried and the pilgrims assist in their best national costumes. They are commonly accompanied by a village fair. Among the more famous Breton Pardons are those of St-Jean-du-Doigt near Morlaix (24 June) and St-Anne d'Auray in Morbihan (24 July).

Paris. The city, which is first mentioned by Caesar as 'Lutetia Parisiorum', was a centre of Christianity at a very early date. Acc. to St *Gregory of Tours, St Denis (*Dionysius (3)), its first bishop, was one of the seven bishops sent out by Pope *Fabian c.250, and the Christian cemetery on the road to Sens and the episcopal buildings on the Île de la Cité date from the late 3rd to early 4th cents. The Huns were diverted from Paris in 451 by the pleading of St *Geneviève, who is still venerated as the city's patroness. In 507 *Clovis made it his capital, but its importance was diminished in the 7th cent. by the instability of Merovingian rule and in the 9th cent. by the Norman invasions. It began to revive as the centre of royal authority in the 11th cent., and most strongly under Louis VI (1108–37). At this time the re-establishment of Paris was linked with the association of the Crown with the abbey of *St-Denis. The beginnings of its famous University date from the 12th cent., when *Peter Lombard taught at the Cathedral School of Notre-Dame, *Hugh and *Richard at St-Victor, and *Abelard at Ste-Geneviève. The University as an established community of masters and pupils appears at the end of the 12th cent. It was styled 'Universitas magistrorum' in 1207 and received its statutes from *Innocent III in 1215. Many privileges were bestowed on it, making it a body independent of bishops, king, and Parliament. Between 1215 and 1225 developed the so-called 'nations', Gallicani, Normanni, Picardi, and Angli (the last being replaced by the Alemanni after the Hundred Years War), and soon afterwards the four faculties of theology, law, medicine, and arts. The early 13th cent. also saw the foundation of colleges, which originally provided lodging and food for poor students; the most famous of these was the *Sorbonne. Religious lived in the houses of their orders ('studia generalia'), the *Dominicans, e.g., at St-Jacques. In the 13th cent. Paris was the chief centre of *Scholasticism, counting among its teachers the *Franciscans *Alexander of Hales and St *Bonaventure, the Dominicans St *Albert the Great and St *Thomas Aquinas, and the seculars *William of Auxerre, *Henry of Ghent and the *Averroist *Siger of Brabant. St Albert, St Bonaventure, and St Thomas took part in the great controversy between the *Mendicant orders and the seculars, who, represented esp. by William of St-Amour (d. c.1273), were jealous of the growing influence of the religious, in whose favour the quarrel was decided by Alexander IV in 1256. The University continued to play an important part in the time of the W. Schism and of the Reform Councils, when some of its most learned men, such as J. *Gerson and Peter *d'Ailly, favoured the Conciliar party. At the end of the 14th cent. its decadence set in, caused by the general decline of Scholasticism as well as by the Schism and the war with England, in the course of which Paris was under English occupation from 1420 to 1436. Under Francis I and *Catherine de' Medici the city became the centre of the French Renaissance, supported by its bishop, (later Cardinal) Jean du Bellay (1532–51). From 1568 to 1662 the see was occupied by the Gondi family, under whom occurred the Massacre of St *Bartholomew's Day (1572). It became an archdiocese in 1622. During the 17th cent. the city witnessed a religious regeneration brought about by the activities of St *Francis of Sales, St *Vincent de Paul, P. de *Bérulle, and J.-J. *Olier, who counteracted *Jansenism and *Gallicanism, which numbered many adherents in the capital, esp. at the University. In the 18th cent. Paris became a centre of Rationalism and '*Enlightenment'; religion suffered its most serious eclipse during the Revolutions of 1789, 1830, and 1848. In the

first of these the old University was abolished; a new one was established in 1806 by the combination of the three faculties of arts, medicine, and law, but without theology, which, since 1875, has been represented by the *Institut Catholique. Under Napoleon III there was a faculty of theology supported by the state, but its degrees were not recognised by the Pope. The Orthodox Institut St-Serge (founded in 1925) has attracted a succession of distinguished Russian scholars, incl. S. *Bulgakov, V. *Lossky, and G. *Florovsky.

Paris has always been famous for its churches and monasteries. The old cathedral of St-Etienne was prob. built in the 6th cent., but in the 8th cent. its functions were taken over by *Notre-Dame. Other famous monasteries include the *Benedictine houses of *St-Germain-des-Prés, St-Denis and St-Maur-des-Fossés, the Augustinian monasteries of Ste-Geneviève and St-Victor (see VICTORINES), and the houses of Benedictine nuns, Montmartre and *Port-Royal, all of which perished in the Revolution of 1789, though the church of St-Germain-des-Prés is still an important centre of worship in Paris. Foremost among modern churches are *St-Sulpice with its 18 chapels, Notre-Dame-des-Victoires, a popular place of pilgrimage, La Madeleine, built in the form of a Greek temple, and the Sacré-Cœur on Montmartre, built in Byzantine-Romanesque style from 1875 to 1919.

See also SAINTE-CHAPELLE, SORBONNE.

Primary sources in Histoire générale de Paris: Collection des documents (65 vols., 1866–1963). M. Félibien, OSB, and G.-A. Lobineau, OSB, Histoire de la Ville de Paris (5 vols., 1725). The many modern general works incl. M. Poëte, Une vie de cité: Paris, de sa naissance à nos jours (4 vols., 1924–31); and three collections of essays in the series 'Colloques. Cahiers de civilisation', pub. under the direction of G. Michaud: Paris: Croissance d'une capitale (1961); Paris: Fonctions d'une capitale (1962); Paris: Présent et avenir d'une capitale [1964]. On the early history, M. Vieillard-Troïekouroff and others, 'Les anciennes églises suburbaines de Paris (ive–xe siècles)', Paris et Ile-de-France: Mémoires publiés par la Fédération des Sociétés Historiques et Archéologiques de Paris et de l'Ile-de-France, 11 (1960), pp. 17–282; J. Dubois, OSB, 'L'emplacement des premiers sanctuaires de Paris', Journal des Savants (1968), pp. 5–44; M. Fleury, 'La Cathédrale mérovingienne Saint-Etienne de Paris', in G. Droege and others (eds.), Landschaft und Geschichte: Festschrift für Franz Petri zu seinem 65. Geburtstag (Bonn, 1970), pp. 211–21; R.-H. Bautier, 'Quand et comment Paris devint capitale', Bulletin de la Société de l'Histoire de Paris et de l'Ile-de-France, 105 (for 1978; 1979), pp. 17–46; J. Boussard, Nouvelle Histoire de Paris: De la fin du siège de 885–886 à la mort de Philippe Auguste [1976]. A. Friedmann, Paris: Ses rues, ses paroisses du moyen âge à la révolution [1959].

On the University, H. [S.] *Denifle, OP, and A. Chatelain (eds.), Chartularium Universitatis Parisiensis (4 vols., Paris, 1889–97); idd. and others (eds.), Auctarium Chartularii Universitatis Parisiensis (4 vols., ibid., 1894–1964). C. E. Du Boulay, Historia Universitatis Parisiensis (6 vols., ibid., 1665–73). L. Halphen and others, Aspects de l'université de Paris (1949). S. d'Irsay, Histoire des universités françaises et étrangères des origines à nos jours (2 vols., 1933–5); J. Verger (ed.), Histoire des Universités en France [Toulouse, 1986], both passim. H. *Rashdall, The Universities of Europe in the Middle Ages, 1 (ed. F. M. Powicke and A. B. Emden, 1936), pp. 268–584. S. C. Ferruolo, The Origins of the University: The Schools of Paris and their critics, 1100–1215 (Stanford, Calif., 1985). P. Glorieux, Répertoire des maîtres en théologie de Paris au XIIIe siècle (Études de Philosophie médiévale, 16–18; 1932–4).; id., La Faculté des Arts et ses maîtres au XIIIe siècle (ibid. 59; 1971). G. [A.] Leff, Paris and Oxford Universities in the Thirteenth and Fourteenth Centuries (1968). L. W. B. Brockliss, French Higher Education in *the Seventeenth and Eighteenth Centuries* (Oxford, 1987), *passim*. S. Guenée, *Bibliographie de l'Histoire des Universités françaises des Origines à la Révolution*, 1 (1981), pp. 171–566.

On the ecclesiastical history, J. Lebeuf, *Histoire de la ville et de tout le diocèse de Paris* (15 vols., 1754–8). B. Plongeron and others, *Le Diocèse de Paris* (Histoire des diocèses de France, 20; 1987 ff.). P. Pisani, *L'Église de Paris et la Révolution* (4 vols., Bibliothèque d'histoire religieuse, 1908–11). A. Boinet, *Les Églises Parisiennes* (3 vols. [1958–64]).

P. Dollinger and P. Wolff, *Bibliographie d'histoire des villes de France* (1967), pp. 195–209. G. Goyau in *CE* 11 (1911), pp. 480–95, s.v. 'Paris, Archdiocese of'; P. Ferret, ibid., pp. 495–8, s.v. 'Paris, University of'; H. *Leclercq, OSB, in *DACL* 13 (pt. 2; 1938), cols. 1696–959, s.v. 'Paris [Histoire]', with bibl.; cols. 1959–2074, s.v. 'Paris (La Bibliothèque Nationale)'; cols. 2074–2160, s.v. 'Paris (Manuscrits liturgiques de)'. See also works cited under FRANCE, CHRISTIANITY IN.

Paris, Matthew. See MATTHEW PARIS.

parish. In England, an area under the spiritual care of a C of E clergyman (the '*incumbent' or, in the correct meaning of the word, the 'curate'), to whose religious ministrations all its inhabitants are entitled. The incumbent, who receives his income wholly or in part from funds specially allocated to the parish, is nominated by the *patron of the benefice, and can only be removed from his cure in very exceptional cases ('freehold of the clergy'). The word comes from the Gk. παροικία, 'district', via the Late Lat. *parochia*. Originally the παροικία was the ecclesiastical area under the bishop (the modern 'diocese'), but from the later 4th cent. it came to be applied to the subdivisions of the diocese, which the bishop put in the charge of resident presbyters. The earliest English parishes were large territories controlled from monastic churches, mostly founded in the late 7th and 8th cents. During the 10th cent. these parishes of 'old minsters' were starting to fragment, as private manorial lords built churches on their estates and diverted to them the *tithes and parochial allegiance of their tenants. By Domesday Book (1086) England contained many thousands of these manorial churches, and the transition from a system of minster parishes to one of local parishes had largely been achieved in fact, though not in name. During the 12th cent. the parochial network crystallised as bishops applied the principles of canon law at a local level, and restricted the rights of lay patrons. The compromise reached at the Third *Lateran Council of 1179, which gave the bishop the right of institution, strengthened the incumbent against his patron, and once instituted he still preserved his freehold against his bishop.

From a very early date the English parish has also been an important unit of civil administration. Except in the N. of England, where a parish might contain more than one town, the parish and the township were normally coterminous. To meet the growth and changing distribution of population, esp. since the Industrial Revolution, many new parishes have been formed. The New Churches in London and Westminster Act 1710 provided for 50 additional parishes in London; and the Church Building Acts 1818 to 1884 and the New Parishes Acts 1843 to 1884 enabled new parishes or districts to be created by Act of Parliament. The process, however, was slow and costly. It was drastically revised by the New Parishes Measure 1943, the relevant provisions of which have now been superseded by the

Pastoral Measure 1983. This provides for the establishment in every diocese of Pastoral Committees which can submit proposals to the Church Commissioners for the erection of new parishes or the alteration of existing ones, for the establishment, alteration, or termination of *team and *group ministries, and for making a church redundant, by means of a pastoral scheme or order. Such proposals, if approved, take effect on confirmation by an Order in Council. Since the abolition of Church Rates by the Compulsory Church Rate Abolition Act 1868, the civil importance of the parish has much declined.

The custom of marking the boundaries by '*beating the bounds' on the *Rogation Days or *Ascension Day is still observed in some parishes.

See also ADVOWSON.

E. Stolz, 'Παροικία, parochia und parochus', *Th.Q.* 89 (1907), pp. 424–48; id., 'Zur Geschichte des Terminus *Parochus*', ibid. 95 (1913), pp. 193–203; id., 'Parochus', ibid. 106 (1926), pp. 1–8. P. de Labriolle, 'Paroecia', *Rech. S.R.* 18 (1928), pp. 60–72. P. D. Thomson, *Parish and Parish Church: Their Place and Influence in History* (Baird Lecture for 1935; 1948). G. W. O. Addleshaw, *The Beginnings of the Parochial System* (St Anthony's Hall Publications, 3; 1953); id., *The Development of the Parochial System from Charlemagne (768–814) to Urban II (1088–1099)* (ibid. 6; 1954); id., *Rectors, Vicars and Patrons in Twelfth and Thirteenth Century Canon Law* (ibid. 9; 1956). C. N. L. Brooke, 'Rural Ecclesiastical Institutions in England: the Search for their Origins', in *Cristianizzazione ed Organizzazione Ecclesiastica delle Campagne nell'Alto Medioevo: Espansione e Resistenze, 10–16 aprile 1980* (Settimane di Studio del Centro Italiano di Studi sull'Alto Medioevo, 28; Spoleto, 1982), pp. 685–711. [W.] J. Blair, 'Local Churches in Domesday Book and Before', in J. C. Holt (ed.), *Domesday Studies: Papers read at the Novocentenary Conference of the Royal Historical Society and the Institute of British Geographers, Winchester, 1986* (Woodbridge, Suffolk, 1987), pp. 265–78. [W.] J. Blair (ed.), *Ministers and Parish Churches: The Local Church in Transition, 950–1200* (Oxford University Committee for Archaeology, Monograph 17; 1988). R. Morris, *Churches in the Landscape* (1989). [W.] J. Blair and R. Sharpe (eds.), *Pastoral Care before the Parish* (Studies in the Early History of Britain; Leicester, 1992). J. C. Cox, *The English Parish Church: An Account of the Chief Building Types and of their Material during Nine Centuries* (1914; with additional chs. by C. B. Ford, 1935). Id., *The Parish Registers of England* (The Antiquary's Books, 1910). E. G. Moore, *Introduction to English Canon Law* (3rd edn. by T. Briden and B. Hanson, 1992), pp. 29–39.

parish clerk. The church official, either a layman or in orders, but usually the former, who in England assists the priest, chiefly by making the responses of the congregation in the services, and sometimes in reading the epistle. He also helps in the general care of the church. The office, which is known from the time of St *Augustine of Canterbury, could be held only by men of some education. Until 1921 the office was freehold, but since then the parish clerk is appointed and dismissed by the incumbent and the *Parochial Church Council acting jointly. In the old 'three-decker' pulpits, the lowest stage was assigned to the clerk.

The conditions of the appointment of (lay) parish clerks were laid down in the *Canons of 1604, can. 91; of persons in Holy Orders by the Lecturers and Parish Clerks Act 1844. The present position is governed by Canon E 3 of 1969. J. Christie, *Some Account of Parish Clerks, more especially of the Ancient Fraternity (Brethren and Sisterne) of S. Nicholas, now known as the Worshipful Company of Parish Clerks* (privately pr. for the Company,

1893). J. Wickham Legg (ed.), *The Clerk's Book of 1549* (HBS 25; 1903), with good general introd., pp. xvii–lxii. P. H. Ditchfield, *The Parish Clerk* (1907). [E. G.] C. [F.] Atchley, *The Parish Clerk, and his Right to Read the Liturgical Epistle* (*Alcuin Club Tracts, 4; 1903).

Parker, Joseph (1830–1902), *Congregational divine. A native of Hexham, he was for a time a *Wesleyan local preacher, but in 1852 returned to Congregationalism and became an assistant to John Campbell at the Moorfields Tabernacle in London. After ministering at Banbury (1853–8) and Manchester (1858–69), he accepted in 1869 a call to the Poultry Street Chapel, where his power and dramatic oratory in the pulpit attracted a large congregation. By 1874 he had completed the City Temple on Holborn Viaduct, and here ministered with great influence until his death. His publications include *The People's Bible* (25 vols., 1883–95); *Ecce Deus* (1867), a reply to J. R. *Seeley's *Ecce Homo*; *A Preacher's Life* (1899), autobiographical; and many volumes of sermons. Throughout his life he was a strong advocate of *temperance.

Lives by A. Dawson (London, 1901), W. Adamson (Glasgow and London, 1902), and G. H. Pike (London, 1904). A. Gordon in *DNB, 1901–1911*, pp. 71–3, with further refs.

Parker, Matthew (1504–75), Abp. of *Canterbury. Educated at Corpus Christi College, Cambridge, where he was elected a Fellow in 1527, Parker soon identified himself with the groups of moderate reformers. Initially through the patronage of *Anne Boleyn, he received several preferments under *Henry VIII and *Edward VI, and in the latter reign took advantage of the permission to the clergy to marry. Under *Mary he was deprived, and lived in obscurity till 1559, when *Elizabeth I chose him for the vacant archbishopric of Canterbury. After accepting it with much reluctance, he was consecrated at *Lambeth Palace on 17 Dec. 1559 by four bishops who had held sees in Edward VI's reign. His main objects as primate were to preserve the settlement of 1559 from further change and to retain as far as possible the links with the past. To this end he took part in the issue of the *Thirty-Nine Articles and of the '*Bishops' Bible', and published in 1566 his '*Advertisements' on ritual matters, which commanded, *inter alia*, the use of the *surplice. Henceforward he had to face considerable opposition from the *Puritan party, which embodied its aims in the *Admonition to Parliament* (1572). Parker was a wise and tolerant, though hardly a forceful, archbishop, preferring scholarship to controversy. He issued editions of the works of many medieval chroniclers, among them Matthew of Westminster (1567–70), *Matthew Paris (1571), and Thomas of Walsingham (1574). The most considerable of his own writings was his *De Antiquitate Britannicae Ecclesiae et Privilegiis Ecclesiae Cantuariensis cum Archiepiscopis eiusdem 70* (1572). A large collection of the MSS collected by or for him survives in the library of his college at Cambridge.

Correspondence from 1535 to 1575 ed. J. Bruce and T. T. Perowne (*Parker Society, 1853). Episcopal Register transcribed by E. M. Thompson and ed., with introd., by W. H. *Frere (*Canterbury and York Society, 35, 36, 39; 1928–33). A *Florilegium Patristicum* in Corpus Christi College, Cambridge, compiled by M. *Bucer, with material added by Parker, is ed. by P. Fraenkel in Bucer's *Opera Latina*, 3 (Studies in Medieval and Reformation Thought, 41; Leiden, 1988). The primary authority

is the Life by J. *Strype (London, 1711). V. J. K. Brook, *A Life of Archbishop Parker* (Oxford, 1962). W. Haugaard, *Elizabeth and the English Reformation* (Cambridge, 1968), *passim*. *Matthew Parker's Legacy* [Exhibition Catalogue of his MSS, printed books, and plate in Corpus Christi College, Cambridge] (Cambridge, 1975). J. B. Mullinger in *DNB* 43 (1895), pp. 254–64; W. H. Frere in *DECH*, pp. 445 f. See also bibl. to ANGLICAN ORDINATIONS and other works cited under ELIZABETH I.

Parker, Theodore (1810–60), American *Unitarian preacher and reformer. The son of a New England farmer, he graduated at Harvard in 1836. Here he taught himself many oriental languages and began a translation of W. M. L. *de Wette's *Einleitung in das Alte Testament* (pub. 1843). In 1837 he was ordained first pastor of the parish (Unitarian) church in W. Roxbury, Mass. By 1841 he had come to hold much more liberal views than those of Unitarian orthodoxy and his associates consequently denounced him. In his *Discourse of Matters Pertaining to Religion* (1842) he maintained that the permanent essence of Christianity was the moral influence of Jesus and that belief in miracles was unnecessary. The work, which was widely read, won him some new followers esp. in Europe (among them J. *Martineau), but confirmed the orthodox Unitarians in their distrust of him. From 1845 till his death he ministered to a congregation at Boston, Mass. He became a fervent advocate of *temperance, prison reform, and education for women, and the leader in Boston of the Anti-Slavery Crusade.

Collected works ed. F. P. Cobbe (14 vols., London, 1863–71); also, better edn., but still incomplete, 15 vols., Boston, 1907–13. J. Myerson, *Theodore Parker: A Descriptive Bibliography* (New York and London, 1981). Lives by J. Weiss (New York, 1864), O. B. Frothington (Boston, 1874), J. W. Chadwick (ibid., 1900), H. S. Commager (ibid., 1936; 2nd edn., 1947), and R. C. Albrecht (New York [1971]). J. E. Dirks, *The Critical Theology of Theodore Parker* (ibid., 1948).

Parker Society. A society established in 1840 under the leadership of the Earl of *Shaftesbury and some other prominent *Evangelicals, including Edward *Bickersteth of the *CMS, to issue 'the works of the Fathers and early writers of the Reformed Church'. Its publications include editions of the works and letters of M. *Parker (from whom it took its name), T. *Cranmer, J. *Jewel, and others. Like the contemporary '*Library of the Fathers' (q.v.) and 'Library of Anglo-Catholic Theology' (1841 ff.), of which it was a kind of Protestant counterpart, these publications were of great service to historical and theological learning.

Parochial Church Council. A council set up in every parish in the C of E by the Church of England Assembly (Powers) Act 1919 to give the laity a share in parochial administration. Its functions were originally defined by the Parochial Church Councils (Powers) Measure 1921, passed under that Act, and the law has now been consolidated by the Parochial Church Councils (Powers) Measure 1956 as subsequently amended. At an annual parochial church meeting the qualified electors in every parish elect lay representatives to the Council, which also includes the incumbent and any clergy, deaconess, or stipendiary lay worker licensed in the parish, the churchwardens, and any lay members of a Deanery or Diocesan Synod, or the General

Synod. It must meet at least four times a year. Its primary duty is 'to co-operate with the incumbent in promoting in the parish the whole mission of the Church, pastoral, evangelistic, social and ecumenical'. Most of the powers formerly possessed by the vestry and the churchwardens which relate to the financial affairs of the church, as well as the maintenance of its fabric and ornaments, have been transferred to the Parochial Church Council.

K. M. Macmorran, *A Handbook for Churchwardens and Church Councillors* (1921; rev. as *A Handbook for Churchwardens and Parochial Church Councillors* by K. M. Macmorran, K. J. T. Elphinstone, E. G. Moore, and T. J. Briden, 1986).

Paroissien. The name for various prayer-books in the vernacular designed for the use of the laity which have been published in France since the 17th cent. They usually contain, besides private devotional exercises, a considerable amount of liturgical matter, such as translations of the *Masses and *Vespers for Sundays and feasts, as well as the Holy Week services, often together with the proper musical notation. Though lineally descended from the medieval *Primers, the popularity of the Paroissien in the 17th cent. was chiefly inspired by the desire for vernacular forms of worship.

Parousia (Gk. παρουσία, 'presence' or 'arrival'). In its English form, the word is employed (following 1 Cor. 15: 23 and Mt. 24, etc.) to denote particularly the future return of Christ in glory (later called the 'Second Coming') to judge the living and the dead, and to terminate the present world order. Primitive Christianity believed the event to be imminent and this belief has been revived from time to time in the history of the Church. The prevailing Christian tradition, while maintaining that the Lord's words attest the certainty of a final *General Judgement which will mark the end of the present order and the entry of redeemed humanity into the resurrection-life in heaven, has been opposed to speculation as to the exact time and manner of the Coming (cf. Mk. 13: 32). It is believed that in the Judgement humanity will be confronted by the risen and glorified Christ. The supposition that Christ, when He returned, would first reign for a long period on earth (the *Millennium, q.v.) was held in some early Christian circles, but it has not been generally followed.

A. L. Moore, *The Parousia in the New Testament* (Supplements to *Novum Testamentum*, 13; 1966), with bibl. A. Oepke in *TWNT* 5 (1954), pp. 856–69 (Eng. tr., 1967, pp. 858–71), s.v. παρουσία, πάρειμι; A. Feuillet in *Dict. Bibl.*, Suppl. 6 (1960), cols. 1331–419, s.v. 'Parousie', with extensive bibl. C. [C.] Rowland in *Anchor Bible Dictionary*, 5 (1992), pp. 166–70, s.v. See also bibl. to ESCHATOLOGY.

parson. Properly, the holder of an ecclesiastical benefice who has full possession of its rights, i.e. a *rector. This use was general until the 17th cent., e.g. E. *Stillingfleet wrote in a charge of 1691: 'A vicar cannot appoint a vicar, but a parson may.' Its current use for any (esp. C of E) clergyman has now completely superseded its orig. sense.

The ecclesiastical use of the Lat. *persona* appears to date from the 11th cent., e.g. Council of *Clermont (1095), can. 3. Acc. to English legal writers (E. Coke, W. Blackstone) it derives from the view of the parson as the legal 'person' by whom the property of God (or of the Patron Saint or of the church) in the *parish was actually held; he was the

person to sue or to be sued. C. D. *Du Cange, however, derives the usage from *persona* as equivalent to *dignitas*, meaning a 'personage' or 'dignitary', while H. Schaefer (*Pfarrkirche und Stift im deutschen Mittelalter*, 1903, para. 19), pointing out that *persona* was most frequently used of an absentee rector, often a layman, has suggested that the word is to be deduced from the use of *persona* as a role. The civil law sense seems the most likely origin of the English usage.

Parsons, Robert (1546–1610), also 'Persons', *Jesuit missionary. After holding a Fellowship at Balliol College, Oxford (1568–74), Parsons left England and was received into the RC Church at Louvain; and in 1575 became a Jesuit at Rome. Chosen with E. *Campion to lead the Jesuit Mission to England in 1580, he was soon (1581) forced to flee to the Continent, where he spent the rest of his life. His diplomatic ability made him a trusted counsellor of Popes and other Catholic rulers (esp. *Philip II of Spain); he negotiated for political intervention on behalf of the persecuted English RCs, and this earned him the particular hatred of the English government. Though his political efforts bore little fruit, his ideas played a major part in shaping *A Conference about the Next Succession to the Crown of England* ('1594' [1595]), which, despite *Elizabeth I's total ban on discussion, raised publicly the urgent problem of finding a Catholic successor, and the principles involved therein. Its plea for the rights of subjects led to its being reprinted in England in 1648 and 1681. Though Parsons was a skilled and trenchant controversialist, both against Anglicans and against opponents within the RC community, the most influential of his numerous published writings was a spiritual treatise, *The Christian Directory* (1582), which was adapted by E. Bunny and reprinted over 40 times before 1640 in England. His most enduring achievement was his work for education, notably his government of the *English College, Rome (1597–1610), and a major part in the foundation of the English Colleges at Valladolid, Seville, and *St-Omer.

'Memoirs', ed. by J. H. Pollen, SJ, in *Catholic Record Society Publications*, 2 (1906), pp. 1–161, and 4 (1907), pp. 1–161; 'Letters and Memorials', ed. L. Hicks, SJ, 1 [to 1588], ibid. 39 (1942). Id., 'Father Robert Persons S.J. and *The Book of Succession*', *Recusant History*, 4 (1958), pp. 104–37. J. E. Parish, *Robert Parsons and the English Counter-Reformation* (Rice University Studies, 52, no. 1; Houston, Tex., 1966). F. Eguiluz, *Robert Persons 'El Architraidor': Su vida y su obra (1546–1610)* (1990). J. Bossy, 'The Heart of Robert Persons', in T. M. McCoog, SJ (ed.), *The Reckoned Expense* (Woodbridge, Suffolk, 1996), pp. 141–58. See also pp. 159–77. Pre-1641 edns. of his works listed in A. F. Allison and D. M. Rogers, 'A Catalogue of Catholic Books in English ...', *Biographical Studies*, 3 (1956), pp. 245–52 (nos. 611–42); idd., *The Contemporary Printed Literature of the English Counter-Reformation*, 1 (Aldershot, 1989), pp. 120–23 (nos. 871–99). Polgár, 2 (1990), pp. 654 f. T. G. Law in *DNB* 43 (1895), pp. 411–18. See also bibl. to ALLEN, W.

Particular Baptists. The group of Baptists whose theology was essentially *Calvinistic as contrasted with the *Arminianism of the *General Baptists. Their polity was similar to that of the *Independents, but a considerable place was given to 'associations' of local Churches. The first Particular Baptist community in England was established at Southwark from 1633 onwards. In 1891 the General Baptists of the New Connexion joined the Baptist

Union which had been formed among the Particular Baptists.

Particular Judgement. In Catholic theology, the judgement on each individual soul immediately on its separation from the body. It is thus prior to and quite distinct from the *General Judgement (q.v.) on the Last Day. In the bull 'Benedictus Deus' (1336) *Benedict XII upheld the teaching that the Particular Judgement admits the soul at once either to the *Beatific Vision, to *purgatory, or to *hell, thus excluding an intermediate state of sleep or partial happiness or suffering between the day of death and the final resurrection of the body, such as had been envisaged by certain older theologians, e.g. St *Justin, *Tertullian, and St *Ambrose. The chief scriptural evidence for the doctrine is found in the Parable of Dives and Lazarus (Lk. 16: 19) and in Christ's words to the penitent thief (Lk. 23: 43). There is no universally accepted teaching as regards the circumstances of the Particular Judgement, but acc. to the common opinion of Catholic theologians, it occurs at the time of death and consists in an interior illumination which makes known to the separated soul its state in relation to God.

parvis (Fr., from Lat. *paradisus*). Originally the court in front of a cathedral or other large church, esp. when, as at *St Peter's, Rome, surrounded by a colonnade. The word came to be also used of the portico of a church porch. In modern times it is often erroneously applied to the room over such a porch, apparently through a misunderstood reference in F. Blomefield's *Norfolk* (2, p. 748; c.1744), which mentions a school kept in the parvis of St Martin's Church, Norwich, in 1300.

OED (2nd edn.), 9 (1989), p. 285, s.v.

Pascal, Blaise (1623–62), French scientist, polemicist, and Christian apologist. He was born at Clermont-Ferrand, and after the death of his mother when he was 4, was educated privately by his father together with his two sisters, Gilberte, his first biographer (b. 1620; in 1641 she married her cousin, Florin Périer) and Jacqueline (b. 1625). He showed great precocity, and engaged in various mathematical and physical experiments from an early age. He came into contact with the *Jansenists at Rouen in 1646 (his 'first conversion'), and later entered into direct communication with *Port-Royal, although he was never formally to become a 'solitaire'. In 1651 his father died, and shortly afterwards Jacqueline entered the convent of Port-Royal. Pascal continued his scientific pursuits (defending notably the possibility of the vacuum) and frequented the fashionable society of Paris. On 23 Nov. 1654 his 'definitive conversion' took place, when he discovered the 'God of Abraham, the God of Isaac, the God of Jacob, and not of the philosophers and men of science'; at the time he made a record of the experience (the 'Mémorial') which he carried on his person for the rest of his life. From 1655 he was a frequent visitor at Port-Royal-des-Champs. He was in bad health from 1658 until his death.

The condemnation of A. *Arnauld by the Sorbonne in 1655 promoted his famous attack on the *Jesuits in the *Lettres écrites à un provincial*, commonly known as the 'Lettres Provinciales' (18 in all). The first was printed on 23 Jan. 1656, the rest followed shortly afterwards (1656–

7). The first four and the last two were directly concerned with the immediate issue, which they identified satirically as being a purely personal quarrel. The remaining 12, attacking the Jesuit theories of grace (*Molinism) and moral theology (*Probabilism), were intended to expose the immoral character of casuistry and to oppose to it the rigorist morality of the Jansenists, with its aim of restoring the disciplinary practices and austerity of the primitive Church. The work was condemned by the Congregation of the *Index in 1657 but continued to provoke violent controversy. The literary history of the *Pensées* begins with the publication in 1670 of selections from the notes left at his death towards a Christian apology; the fragments have subsequently been frequently re-edited and a wide variety of possible arrangements proposed. The work had been intended as a vindication of the truth of Christianity against the indifference of free-thinking contemporaries; rather than depending on philosophical reasoning it seeks to persuade of the unique applicability of Christianity to the human condition as the apologist portrays it. Apart from its brilliant style, it owes its force to the wealth of psychological perception which it embodies.

Pascal's religion was centred on the person of Christ as Saviour and based on his own experience. Here, as in his scientific investigations, his thought was deeply influenced by his interest in empirical knowledge. Nourished on the *Augustinianism of Port-Royal, he stressed man's tragic situation between greatness and wretchedness, to escape from which he plunges into distractions. From this state only faith can free him, since human existence is confronted with the necessity of making a decision for or against God. The element of risk in the adoption of belief (encapsulated in the notorious 'wager' argument), and an emphasis on the heart and custom are characteristic of Pascal, who confesses that 'the heart has its reasons of which reason knows not'. He does not, however, thereby exclude the use of reasoned argument, and in particular biblical proofs, from demonstrating the truth of Christianity. Pascal was ridiculed by *Voltaire and the *Encyclopaedists of the 18th cent., but in the 19th cent. there came a revival of interest, which continues.

The standard edn. of Pascal's *Œuvres complètes* is still that of L. C. Brunschvicg, F. Boutroux and F. Gazier (14 vols., Grands Ecrivains de la France, Paris, 1904–14); modern edn. by J. Mesnard (Bruges, 1964 ff.). There is also a convenient edn. by L. Lafuma (Paris, 1963). Good edns. of the *Pensées* by L. Lafuma (3 vols., ibid., 1951; Eng. tr. by A. J. Krailsheimer, Penguin Classics, 1966) and P. Sellier (Paris, 1976); and of the *Lettres Provinciales* by L. Cognet (ibid. [1965]; Eng. tr. by A. J. Krailsheimer, Penguin Classics, 1967) and M. Le Guern (Paris, 1987). Photographic repr. of the original MS of the *Pensées*, with introd. by L. Lafuma, Paris, 1962. The large lit. incl.: J. Russier, *La Foi selon Pascal* (Bibliothèque de philosophie contemporaine, 2 vols., 1949); J. Mesnard, *Les Pensées de Pascal* [1976]; J. H. Broome, *Pascal* (London, 1965); J. Miel, *Pascal and Theology* (Baltimore and London [1969]); P. Sellier, *Pascal et Saint Augustin* (1970); A. W. S. Baird, *Studies in Pascal's Ethics* (International Archives of the History of Ideas, series minor, 16; The Hague, 1975); H. M. Davidson, *The Origins of Certainty: Means and Meaning in Pascal's 'Pensées'* (Chicago, 1979); D. Wetsel, *L'Écriture et le Reste: The Pensées of Pascal in the Exegetical Tradition of Port-Royal* (Columbus, Oh. [1981]); R. Parish, *Pascal's Lettres Provinciales: A Study in Polemic* (Oxford, 1989); V. Carraud, *Pascal et la Philosophie* [1992]. Introductory studies by A. [J.] Krailsheimer, *Pascal* (Past Masters; Oxford, 1980) and J. Cruickshank, *Pascal: Pensées*

(Critical Guides to French Texts, 24; 1983). J. Mesnard in *Dict. Sp.* 12 (pt. 1; 1984), cols. 279–91, s.v. See also bibl. to PORT-ROYAL.

Pasch (Aram. פַּסְחָא, Gk. πάσχα, 'passover'). A name formerly in fairly wide currency in England both for the Jewish *Passover and for the Christian festival of *Easter (qq.v.). See also PASSION.

Paschal II (d. 1118), Pope from 1099. Ranierus, who was prob. born at Bleda in the Romagna, entered an unknown monastery as a boy. He was made cardinal priest of San Clemente by *Gregory VII, served as legate in France and Spain under *Urban II, and became Abbot of *St Paul's outside the Walls in Rome. As Pope he renewed the Papal decrees against lay investiture in 1102, but died leaving the *Investiture Controversy still unsettled. By 1107 compromises had been reached with the kings of England and France, but with the Empire no settlement could yet be reached. Paschal supported the rebellion of the future Emp. Henry V against the latter's father *Henry IV, but Henry V in his turn practised investiture, and Paschal opposed him at successive councils; that of Troyes (1107) declared deposed those bishops who received investiture from laymen. At Rome in Feb. 1111 Paschal agreed to the renunciation by bishops of all regalia acquired since *Charlemagne, and Henry in return agreed to renounce investiture. This far-reaching proposal offended vested interests and was abortive; Henry took Paschal prisoner and at Ponte Mammolo (12 Apr. 1111) extorted concessions by which Paschal promised to forgive injuries, to grant investiture, and to crown Henry. This treaty aroused indignation, esp. among more advanced reformers; it was declared null and void by a council at Rome in 1112 and formally condemned by Paschal in 1116. Paschal took refuge from Henry at Benevento in 1117 and died at Rome on his return in January 1118.

Paschal maintained the links between *Cluny and the Papacy, and his councils at the Lateran and elsewhere, esp. Guastalla (1106), enacted important canons. On the other hand, the support which he gave to *Bohemond I's attack on the Eastern Emp. Alexius in 1107–8 caused bitter resentment in Byzantium. His pontificate leaves a mixed impression on historians, some of whom have thought him intransigent and even visionary but others inactive and inept. He has been thought lacking in leadership and consistency of purpose—a Pope who preferred to follow in the shadow of Gregory VII and Urban II rather than to meet new, 12th-cent., needs.

His Register has not survived; collection of letters in J. P. Migne, *PL* 163. 31–448. Jaffé, 1, pp. 702–72. *LP* (Duchesne), 2, pp. 296–310. C. Servatius, *Paschalis II. (1099–1118): Studien zu seiner Person und seiner Politik* (Päpste und Papsttum, 14; Stuttgart, 1979). U.-R. Blumenthal, *The Early Councils of Pope Paschal II 1100–1110* (Pontifical Institute of Mediaeval Studies, Studies and Texts, 43; 1978). G. M. Cantarella, *Ecclesiologia e politica nel papato di Pasquale II: Linee di una interpretazione* (Istituto storico italiano per il medio evo, Studi storici, 131; 1982) and other works of this author. J. G. Rowe, 'Pascal II, Bohemond of Antioch and the Byzantine Empire', *Bulletin of the John Rylands Library*, 49 (1967), pp. 165–202. M. J. Wilks, '*Ecclesiastica* and *Regalia*: Papal investiture policy from the Council of Guastalla to the First Lateran Council, 1106–23', *Studies in Church History*, 7 (1971), pp. 69–85. Mann, 8 (1910), pp. 1–119. A. Fliche in Fliche

and Martin, 8 (1944), pp. 338–75, with bibl.; É. Amann in *DTC* 11 (pt. 2; 1932), cols. 2057–74, s.v. 'Pascal II'. See also bibl. to INVESTITURE CONTROVERSY and HENRY IV.

Paschal Baylon, St (1540–92), *Franciscan lay brother. The son of peasant parents, he was born at Torre Hermosa, on the borders of Castile and Aragon, on Whitsunday 1540, and christened 'Pascua' after the feast. From his 7th to his 24th year he minded his father's sheep, leading a life of austerity and prayerfulness which was graced (it is recorded) by various miracles. In obedience to a vision he entered the neighbouring convent of the Franciscans of the Alcantarine reform where he practised extreme mortification. Throughout his life he was particularly devoted to the cult of the Blessed Sacrament. During a mission to *France he defended the doctrine of the *Real Presence at the risk of his life, and was roughly handled by the *Calvinists. He was canonized in 1690 and on 28 Nov. 1897 he was declared by *Leo XIII in the apostolic epistle 'Providentissimus Deus' (not to be confused with the encyclical of 1893 on the study of Scripture with the same title) patron of *Eucharistic Congresses and Associations. He is usually depicted in the act of adoration before the Host. Feast day, 17 May.

J. Sala, OFM (ed.), *Opúsculos de S. Pascual Bailón* (Toledo, 1911), with useful introd. The primary authorities are the Sp. *Chronicon del B. Fray P. Baylon de la Orden del P. S. Francisco* by his friend J. Ximénez, Valencia, 1601, and the account written in connection with his canonization by C. de Arta (It. tr., Venice, 1673). Lat. tr. of abstracts of these pr. in *AASS*, Mai 4 (1685), pp. 49–132. Modern studies by L. A. de Porrentruy, OMC (Paris, 1899), and A. Groeteken, OFM (Einsiedeln, 1909). P. M. Mansuy, OFM, *Le Patron des congrès et des œuvres eucharistiques, saint Pascal Baylon* (2nd edn., 1910). M. Acebal Luján, OFM, in *Dict. Sp.* 12 (pt. 1; 1984), cols. 275–8, s.v. 'Pascal Baylon'.

Paschal Candle. In the W. Church, the candle placed on a separate large candlestick in the N. side of the sanctuary which is lighted, esp. at liturgical functions, during Eastertide. During the *Paschal Vigil Service, after the blessing of the New Fire, the celebrant marks the candle with the sign of the Cross, the Greek letters *alpha and omega, and the date of the year, inserts five grains of incense in the cross, and then lights the candle from the New Fire. Since 1970 a simple blessing of the candle may be substituted. The deacon carries the lighted candle through the church, making three stations during which he sings 'Lumen Christi' ('Light of Christ'). When the deacon and celebrant reach the sanctuary, all the lights in the church are lit and the *Exultet is sung. The Paschal Candle is lit during services in Eastertide. It was formerly extinguished after the Gospel on *Ascension Day, but acc. to current RC practice, it remains in use in the sanctuary until the evening of *Whitsunday, when it is taken to the baptistery and lighted at all Baptisms throughout the year.

U. Berlière, OSB, 'Le Cierge pascal', *Le Messager des Fidèles* (later *Rev. Bén.*), 5 (1888), pp. 106–16; H. P. Feasey, OSB, 'The Paschal Candle', *Ecclesiastical Review*, 34 (1906), pp. 353–71; id., 'The Paschal Preconium', ibid. 36 (1907), pp. 248–61; H. J. Heuser, 'The Tenebrae and the New Light of the Holy Fire', ibid., pp. 225–31. H. *Leclercq, OSB, in *DACL* 13 (pt. 2; 1938), cols. 1559–71, s.v. 'Pâques'. See also bibl. to EXULTET.

Paschal Chronicle. See CHRONICON PASCHALE.

Paschal Controversies. Among the many controversies in the early Church over the complex question as to how to settle the date of *Easter (the Christian 'Passover' or 'Pasch') were:

(1) Whether Easter should be observed, after the Jewish manner, on a fixed day of the lunar month (14 *Nisan) or always on (the following) Sunday. The former practice was the ancient tradition in Asia Minor. On this dispute, see QUARTODECIMANISM.

(2) The divergences arising from the *Antiochene and *Alexandrian methods of determining the 'Paschal Moon', the Antiochenes being content to accept the Jewish reckoning, whereas at Alexandria an independent calculation was made. Acc. to Alexandrian practice, Easter was always put after the vernal equinox. The decision at *Nicaea (325) in favour of Alexandrian practice was generally accepted, except by a small group of schismatics (*Audiani, Protopaschites).

(3) Differences in the 4th and 5th cents. between the Roman and Alexandrian methods of computation, through the use of divergent 'paschal cycles', Alexandria having long accepted the *Anatolian 19-year cycle, whereas Rome used an older 84-year cycle. Further, while the Alexandrians allowed Easter to be kept on the 15th of the (lunar) month if a Sunday, it was never observed at Rome before the 16th; also the latest date for keeping Easter at Alexandria was 25 Apr., but at Rome 21 Apr. Such differences were mostly amicably resolved, usually in the Alexandrians' favour, as, e.g. in 455, when Pope *Leo I, after some correspondence, accepted their calculation. The Alexandrian method increasingly prevailed in the W.; it was accepted at Milan at least by 387 (cf. St *Ambrose, *Ep.* 23) and was formally adopted at Rome in the Easter cycle compiled by *Dionysius Exiguus (525).

(4) Until the time of *Charlemagne (*c.*742–814), considerable uncertainty existed in Gaul, owing to the adoption of Victorius of Aquitaine's Paschal Tables (drawn up in Rome in 457, but never much used in the City) with their cycle of 532 years.

(5) The possession by the Celtic Churches of their own method of computation led to a long quarrel in the British Isles after the arrival of the Roman missionaries. As late as 651 Queen Eanfleda, who followed the Roman rule, was keeping *Palm Sunday and fasting on the same day that her husband, Oswiu, King of Northumbria, was celebrating Easter (*Bede, *HE* 3. 25). The Roman custom was accepted for Northumbria by the Synod of *Whitby (664), and through the whole of England by the guidance of St *Wilfrid (ibid. 3. 28) and Abp. *Theodore (ibid. 4. 2).

With the introduction of the *Gregorian Calendar (1582), Easter was once again observed on divergent dates in different parts of Christendom. Easter calculated acc. to the Alexandrian method based on the Gregorian Calendar is nearly always astronomically correct (i.e. it falls on the Sunday following the full moon after the vernal equinox, though never on the day of the full moon itself); the Orthodox Churches, even though most of them have adopted the Gregorian Calendar for fixed feasts, still calculate Easter acc. to the Julian Calendar, and, as their calculation of the Paschal full moon is five days later than the astronomical full moon, their Easter sometimes coincides with the W. date, but is often one, four, or five weeks later.

B. Krusch, *Studien zur christlich-mittelalterlichen Chronologie: Der 84-jährige Ostercyclus und seine Quellen* (1880). L. *Duchesne, 'La Question de la Pâque au concile de Nicée', *RQH* 28 (1880), pp. 1–42. J. Schmid, *Die Osterfrage auf dem ersten allgemeinen Konzil von Nicäa* (Vienna, 1905). E. *Schwartz, *Christliche und jüdische Ostertafeln* (*Abh.* (Gött.), NF 8, Heft 6; 1905). Useful survey by C. W. Jones in his introd. to his edn. of Bede's *Opera de Temporibus* (Mediaeval Academy of America Publication, 41; 1943), pp. 3–122. V. Grumel, AA, 'Le Problème de la date pascale aux IIIe et IVe siècles', *Revue des Études Byzantines*, 18 (1960), pp. 163–78. A. Strobel, *Ursprung und Geschichte des frühchristlichen Osterkalenders* (TU 121; 1977). Id., *Texte zur Geschichte des frühchristlichen Osterkalenders* (Liturgiegeschichtliche Quellen und Forschungen, 64; 1984). M. Zelzer, 'Zum Osterfestbrief des heiligen Ambrosius und zur römischen Osterfestberechnung des 4. Jahrhunderts', *Wiener Studien*, NF 12 (1978), pp. 187–204. G. Fritz in *DTC* 11 (pt. 2; 1932), cols. 1948–70, s.v. 'Pâques, Les Controverses pascales'. See bibl. to EASTER and QUARTODECIMANISM.

Paschal lamb. Originally, the lamb eaten at the Jewish *Passover. The lambs were sacrificed in the *Temple on the afternoon of 14 *Nisan, then taken by the people to their homes and eaten during the night (cf. Exod. 12). The fulfilment of the Jewish Passover in Christ (cf. 1 Cor. 5: 7, 'Christ our Passover is sacrificed for us'; Jn. 1: 29, 'Behold the Lamb of God') has made Him for Christians the 'Paschal Lamb'. See also LAMB.

Paschaltide, the period in the ecclesiastical year immediately after *Easter. It is devoted to the celebration of the victory of the Risen Christ, who by His Passion has overcome sin and death and brought the Church into existence. In the W. the liturgy is characterized by the frequent recitation of *Alleluia, and there are certain other features peculiar to the season, such as the singing of *Vidi Aquam in place of Ps. 51 during the *Asperges. The proper colour for Paschaltide is white. In the RC Church it extends from Easter Sunday to *Pentecost; the C of E follows the practice, dating from the Middle Ages, of reckoning Eastertide from Easter Sunday to the Saturday before *Trinity Sunday. See also PENTECOST.

Paschal Vigil Service, the principal celebration of *Easter, traditionally observed during the night of *Holy Saturday/Easter Sunday. In the 2nd cent. there is clear evidence that there was a single festival celebrating both the Passion and the Resurrection of Christ, and the same situation is prob. reflected in various NT passages (e.g. 1 Cor. 5: 7 f.). The *Peri Pascha* of *Melito of Sardis supports the suggestion that this unitary feast developed out of a Christianized observance of the Jewish *Passover ritual. By the time of *Tertullian (d. *c.*225) the observance lasted throughout the night and was closely associated with *Baptism, an association prob. already discernible in Rom. 6. The elaborate description of the rite of Baptism in *Hippolytus' *Apostolic Tradition* is almost certainly that of a Paschal Vigil Service, in which the Baptism at cockcrow is followed by the Eucharist. In the 4th cent., with the development of the liturgical year and the separate observance of *Good Friday, the main emphasis of the Paschal Vigil Service came to centre upon the Resurrection. The *Paschal Candle, with its symbolism of light, was introduced in Italy (apart from Rome) about the same time, and later spread to Gaul. In the W. Church the service was put back to the Saturday afternoon in the 10th cent. and to the Saturday morning in the 14th, thereby losing the point of much of its symbolism. Only with the revision of the Holy Week liturgy in the RC Church in 1951 was the Paschal Vigil Service restored to the late evening of Holy Saturday.

The Paschal Vigil Service has been subjected to various modifications through the ages, but the basic pattern has remained. Acc. to the present RC rite, the celebrant blesses the New Fire outside the church, marks the Paschal Candle with the sign of the Cross, the Greek letters *alpha and omega, and the date of the year, and then lights it from the New Fire. (Since 1970 a simpler blessing of the Candle has been permitted.) The deacon (or in his absence the celebrant) carries the lighted Candle through a darkened church, making three stations during which he sings 'Lumen Christi' ('Light of Christ'); candles held by members of the congregation are lit from the Paschal Candle. When the procession reaches the sanctuary the lights in the church are lit. The deacon then sings the *Exultet, after which the people's candles are laid aside. Nine scriptural readings normally follow, interspersed with responsorial Psalms or periods of silence. Of the seven OT readings the first three record the story of creation, *Abraham's sacrifice of *Isaac, and the crossing of the Red Sea during the *Exodus; the other four are prophecies of redemption. (Some may be omitted.) The NT readings are the passage about Christ's resurrection and our Baptism in Rom. 6: 3-11, followed by a solemn *Alleluia, and one of the Gospel accounts of the Resurrection. A homily is then delivered. The next part of the service is connected with Baptism and normally takes place round the *font, to which a procession is made behind the Paschal Candle. During the procession the *Litany of the Saints is sung. The baptismal water is then blessed; during the blessing the Paschal Candle is lowered into the water and raised again. Baptism is administered to any candidates and if a bishop (or priest with a faculty to *confirm) is present, any newly baptized adults are confirmed. (If there are no candidates for Baptism, it is permitted to use a simple blessing of the water.) All present then renew their baptismal vows in answer to questions put by the celebrant, who sprinkles the people with the newly blessed water. The service concludes with the remaining parts of the Easter Eucharist, during which the newly baptized make their Communion. A form of Paschal Vigil Service (closely modelled on the current RC rite) was included in the Services and Prayers for Lent, Holy Week, and Easter commended by the House of Bishops of the General Synod of the C of E in 1986.

In the Byzantine rite the Paschal Vigil properly begins with *Vespers on Holy Saturday, which ends with 15 readings from the OT, similar to those in the W. rite. The Eucharist is then celebrated, the Liturgy of St *Basil being used, with Rom. 6: 3-11 and Mt. 28: 1-20 as the NT readings. These services are meant to begin late in the afternoon of Holy Saturday, but like most of those in Lent and Holy Week, are usually anticipated and celebrated in the morning. What is usually thought of as the Orthodox Easter Vigil consists of Mattins (beginning at midnight) and the Liturgy of Easter Day; it is preceded by the Midnight Office.

For bibliography see EASTER.

Paschasinus (c.440), Bp. of Lilybaeum (now Marsala) in Sicily. Pope *Leo the Great assisted him when his diocese was devastated by the Vandals. When asked by Leo his opinion in the *Paschal Controversy, he replied in favour of the Alexandrian as against the Roman usage. In 451 he was one of the Papal legates at the Council of *Chalcedon, where he vigorously objected to the presence of *Dioscorus. Nothing is known about him after the Council.

The chief source is his correspondence with Leo ('Leo', *Ep.* 3, 'De Paschate anni 444' and Leo, *Ep.* 88) and scattered references in the *Acta* of Chalcedon (q.v.).

Paschasius Radbertus, St (c.790-c.860), *Carolingian theologian. He entered the monastery at *Corbie under its abbot, Adalard, whom he accompanied into Saxony in 822. Elected abbot 843/4, he attended the Council of Paris in 847, but resigned in 849 and henceforth devoted himself entirely to study. His works include, besides a Life of Abbot Adalard, a Commentary on the Book of Lamentations, notable for its concentration on the literal sense, and a Commentary on St Matthew, in which he made careful use of earlier authorities. He is best known, however, for his treatise 'De Corpore et Sanguine Domini' (831/33, revised 844), which was composed for the monks of Corvey in Saxony. This work is the first doctrinal monograph on the Eucharist. In maintaining the real Presence of Christ in the Eucharist, Radbertus specified it further as the flesh born of Mary, which had suffered on the Cross and risen again, and which is miraculously multiplied by the omnipotence of God at each consecration. At the same time he insisted on the spiritual mode of this Presence, but without defining it. By eating this flesh the faithful are incorporated into Christ's mystical Body, which is the Church. Radbertus's doctrine was sharply attacked by *Ratramnus and *Rabanus Maurus, who opposed to his emphatic realism, which was sometimes marred by unfortunate comparisons and illustrations, their more spiritual conceptions of the Divine presence. It is now generally accepted that he was the author of Pseudo-*Jerome's *ep.* 9, 'Cogitis me', an important document in the history of the doctrine of the *Assumption of the BVM in the W. Feast day, 26 Apr.

Collection of his works ed. J. *Sirmond, SJ (Paris, 1618); repr. with additional works from other sources in J. P. Migne, *PL* 120. Crit. edns. of his Poems by L. Traube in *MGH*, Poetae, 3 (1896), pp. 38–53, with further notes, pp. 746 f.; of various 'Epistolae' (incl. extracts of his works) by E. Duemmler, ibid., Epistolae, 6 (1925), pp. 133–49; and of his 'Epitaphium Arsenii' by id. (*Abh.* (Berl.), aus den Jahren 1899 und 1900 (1900), Heft 2); of his 'De Corpore et Sanguine Domini' by B. Paulus, OSB (CCCM 16; 1969), and of his comm. on Mt. by id. (ibid. 56, 56 A, and 56 B; 1984); on Lam. by id. (ibid. 85; 1988); and on Ps. 44 by id. (ibid. 94; 1991); of *De fide, spe et caritate* by id. (ibid. 97; 1990); and of *De partu Virginis* by E. A. Matter and *De Assumptione Sanctae Mariae Virginis* by A. Ripberger (ibid. 56 C; 1985). Id. (ed.), *Der Pseudo-Hieronymus-Brief IX 'Cogitis Me': Ein erster marianischer Traktat des Mittelalters von Paschasius Radbert* (Spicilegium Friburgense, 9; 1962). Eng. tr. of Paschasius' Lives of Adalard and Wala, his brother and successor as Abbot of Corbie, by A. Cabaniss, *Charlemagne's Cousins* (Syracuse, NY, 1967). The 12th–13th-cent. Life of Paschasius, ed. O. Holder-Egger, *MGH*, Scriptores, 15 (pt. 1; 1887), pp. 452–4. H. Peltier, *Pascase Radbert, abbé de Corbie* (Strasbourg thesis; Amiens, 1938). C. Gliozzo, SJ, *La*

Dottrina della Conversione Eucaristica in Pascasio Radberto e Ratramno, monaci di Corbia (Palermo [1945]). D. *Stone, *A History of the Doctrine of the Holy Eucharist*, 1 (1909), pp. 216–22; G. Macy, *The Theologies of the Eucharist in the Early Scholastic Period* (Oxford, 1984), esp. pp. 21–35. H. Peltier in *DTC* 13 (pt. 2; 1937), cols. 1628–39, s.v. 'Radbert, Paschase'; R. Grégoire in *Dict. Sp.* 12 (1984), cols. 295–301, s.v. 'Paschase (2) Radbert'.

Passion, the (Lat. *passio*, lit. 'suffering'). The term is used absolutely of the Lord's Redemptive Suffering during the last days of His earthly life, and esp. of His Crucifixion. The word 'Pasch' or 'Passover' (Gk. Πάσχα), commonly applied in the early Church to the joint annual commemoration of the Redemptive Death and Resurrection of Christ (i.e. to 'Good Friday' and 'Easter' together), was often held by a false etymology to be derived from the Greek πάσχω ('to suffer'). See also following entry and PASCHAL VIGIL SERVICE, PASSION SUNDAY, PASSIONTIDE.

Passion, musical settings for the. From towards the end of the 4th cent. scriptural readings, incl. the Gospels, were recited to musical tones in church; the Gospel narratives of the Passion were thus recited during *Holy Week. The characters were early on differentiated by changes of pitch, and by the 13th cent. at latest this was emphasized by dividing the narrative between three or more singers; from the 15th cent. parts or all began to be composed polyphonically. About 1525 Johann Walther (1496–1570), M. *Luther's musical adviser, produced a Passion in German, the first to be written in a vernacular language, while in the next cent. H. *Schütz composed three notable settings in an austere but very expressive style. From the end of the 17th cent. lyric poems were sung in comment and chorales were added to be sung by the congregation; an orchestra was also introduced. The greatest examples of this *oratorio type of Passion were the *St John Passion* (1723) and esp. the *St Matthew Passion* (1727) of J. S. *Bach.

[L.] O. Kade, *Die ältere Passionskomposition bis zum Jahre 1631* (Gütersloh, 1893). W. Lott, 'Zur Geschichte der Passionskomposition von 1650–1800', *Archiv für Musikwissenschaft*, 3 (1921), pp. 285–320. B. Smallmann, *The Background of Passion Music: J. S. Bach and his Predecessors* (1957). B. Stäblein and others in *Die Musik in Geschichte und Gegenwart*, 10 (1962), cols. 886–933; K. von Fischer and W. Braun in S. Sadie (ed.), *The New Grove Dictionary of Music and Musicians*, 14 (1980), pp. 276–86. See also bibl. to ORATORIO, BACH and other individual composers.

Passion Plays. See DRAMA, CHRISTIAN and MYSTERY PLAYS; also OBERAMMERGAU.

Passion Sunday. Traditionally the name of the fifth Sunday in *Lent, which marked the beginning of *Passiontide. In the RC Church the special designation of this Sunday was suppressed in 1969 and the name is commonly used of *Palm Sunday (officially 'Dominica in Palmis de Passione Domini'). In the C of E the title (for the fifth Sunday in Lent) was printed in the 1928 BCP and became widely used, though some Provinces of the Anglican Communion have now followed the terminology of the RC Church. For the liturgical usage which began on this day, see PASSIONTIDE.

Passional (Lat. *Liber Passionarius*). The word is used for various Latin liturgical books:

(1) The series of lections from the Lives or Acts of the Saints read at *Mattins on their feast days.

(2) A book containing the narratives of the Lord's Passion from the four Gospels.

(3) The particular *Evangeliary, also known as 'King *Athelstan's Book', on which the English kings from Henry I to Edward III were at one time thought to have taken the Coronation Oath.

Passionists. The popular name for the members of the 'Congregation of Discalced Clerks of the Most Holy Cross and Passion of our Lord Jesus Christ'. The congregation was founded by St *Paul of the Cross, who drew up its rule in 1720 and erected the first house, the 'Retreat' on Monte Argentario, in 1737. After some mitigations the rule was approved by *Benedict XIV in 1741 and 1746, and in 1769 confirmed by *Clement XIV, who at the same time conferred the privileges of the old orders on the new congregation. It soon spread throughout Europe and beyond. In 1841 the Passionists came to England, where they were the first religious after the Reformation to lead a strict community life and wear their habit in public. Among them was Bl Dominic Barberi, who received J. H. *Newman into the RC Church. The Passionists stress the contemplative life as the foundation of their apostolic work; and they take a further fourth vow promising to further the memory of Christ's Passion in the souls of the faithful. Their chief activities are the giving of missions and retreats. Their habit is black with the badge of the Passion, a white heart with the inscription 'Jesu XPI Passio', surmounted by a cross. The Passionist nuns, founded by St Paul of the Cross together with Mother Mary Crucifixa in 1771, are strictly enclosed and contemplative; they, too, take a vow to practise devotion to the Passion.

Storia della Congregazione della Passione di Gesù Christo: vol. 1 (1720–75) by F. Giorgini, CP (Pescara, 1981); vol. 2. 1 (1775–96) by C. A. Naselli, CP (ibid., 1981); other vols. planned. F. Ward, CP, *The Passionists* (New York, 1923). E. Zoffoli, CP, *I Passionisti: Spiritualità, apostolato* (1955). C. J. Yuhaus, CP, *Compelled to Speak. The Passionists in America: Origin and apostolate* (New York [1967]). A. Devine, CP, in *CE* 11 (1911), pp. 521–5, s.v.; C. J. Yuhaus, CP, in *NCE* 10 (1967), pp. 1066–8, s.v.; F. Giorgini, CP, and C. A. Naselli, CP, in *DIP* 6 (1980), cols. 1236–47, s.v. 'Passionisti'. See also bibl. to PAUL OF THE CROSS, esp. art. in *Dict. Sp.*

Passions. The detailed and professedly contemporary accounts of the early Christian martyrdoms. They are commonly distinguished from the '*Acts' (q.v.), in which the narrative follows (or, at least, is intended to give the impression of following) the shorthand report taken down for official purposes.

Passiontide. Traditionally the last two weeks of Lent, extending from *Passion Sunday to *Holy Saturday. It was customary during this period for all crucifixes, pictures, and images in church to be veiled in purple (the crucifix only being unveiled on *Good Friday), and for the '*Gloria Patri' to be omitted from the Psalms, the *Introit, and the *Venite. Since 1969 in the RC Church

Passion Sunday as such has been dropped from the calendar and the observance combined with that of *Palm Sunday; the veiling of crucifixes etc. is optional and in any case confined to *Holy Week; and there are no observances peculiar to the period as a whole. In English pre-Reformation practice the Lenten array of unbleached linen gave place in Passiontide to a deep red as the liturgical colour, but in modern usage Lenten purple continues throughout, except on Palm Sunday, *Maundy Thursday, and Good Friday.

Passover. The Jewish festival celebrated every spring in connection with the *Exodus. Acc. to the account of its institution in Exod. 12, a lamb is to be slain in each household and its blood sprinkled on the lintel and doorposts of the house in memory of the fact that when the first-born in Egypt were slain, the Lord 'passed over' the houses which were so marked. In the Deuteronomic account (Deut. 16) the sacrifice is no longer to be performed in private houses but 'at the place where the Lord thy God shall place his name' [i.e. the *Temple]. In both these passages and elsewhere in the OT and the papyri in which the Passover is mentioned, the eating of the *Paschal lamb is associated with the use of unleavened bread. Many modern scholars, following J. *Wellhausen, have argued that the original setting of the Passover was the sacrifice of firstlings in a nomadic community; this festival is held to have become joined with an originally independent ceremony concerned with unleavened bread, which derived from an agricultural rite associated with the beginning of the barley-harvest. J. B. Segal, however, has argued, on the basis of certain similarities with the ritual of the feast of *Tabernacles, that the Passover itself was an agricultural feast celebrated at the time when the work begun at Tabernacles was reaching fruition. Whatever its origin, by later biblical times Passover had come to be the principal Jewish festival of the year, celebrated on the night of 14/15 Nisan. After the destruction of the Temple in AD 70, the Jews continued to observe the feast in a modified form which omitted the sacrifice of a lamb, using only a bone in its place. Details of the later observance were laid down in the *Mishnah tractate *Pesahim*.

Whether the *Last Supper was a Passover Meal (as the chronology of the Synoptic Gospels would suggest) or not (as St John), it is clear that the Eucharist was instituted at Passover time, and Christian writers from St *Paul (1 Cor. 5: 7) onwards have stressed that the death of Christ was the fulfilment of the sacrifice foreshadowed by the Passover. It is probable also that the earliest celebrations of the Christian Easter (the *Paschal Vigil Service) developed from the Jewish Passover rite, while the account of the Exodus and the institution of the Passover have from a very early date provided one of the readings in the Paschal liturgy of the W. Church. See also EUCHARIST, PASCHAL LAMB.

J. B. Segal, *The Hebrew Passover from the Earliest Times to A.D. 70* (London Oriental Series, 12; 1963). B. M. Bokser, *The Origins of the Seder: The Passover Rite and Early Rabbinic Judaism* [1984]. The early history is discussed in all comm. on Exodus and Leviticus. Good summary in G. B. *Gray, *Sacrifice in the Old Testament* (1925), esp. pp. 337–97. R. de Vaux, OP, *Les Institutions de l'Ancien Testament*, 2 (1960), pp. 383–94; Eng. tr., *Ancient Israel* (2nd edn., 1965), pp. 484–93; H.-J. Kraus, *Gottesdienst in Israel* (2nd

edn., Munich, 1962), pp. 61–72; Eng. tr., *Worship in Israel* (Oxford, 1966), pp. 45–55. L. Jacobs and others in *Encyclopaedia Judaica*, 13 (Jerusalem, 1972), cols. 163–73 (with illustrations). C. Mohrmann, 'Pascha, Passio, Transitus', *EL* 66 (1952), pp. 37–52. J. Jeremias in *TWNT* 5 (1954), pp. 895–903 (Eng. tr., 1968, pp. 896–904), s.v. πάσχα. For discussions on the relation of the Last Supper to the Passover, see LAST SUPPER.

pastophorion. (Gk. παστοφόριον). In the E. Church, the sacristy adjacent to the *apse, used at least from the end of the 4th cent. (*Apostolic Constitutions*, 8. 13) for the reservation of the Sacrament.

pastor. The title given by *Lutherans and some other Protestant bodies to their clergy, primarily those in charge of a church or congregation. The term derives from the Latin *pastor*, meaning 'herdsman' or 'shepherd', hence a 'shepherd of souls'. In this sense it is found in the Middle Ages and in the BCP (e.g. in the collect for the feast of St *Peter), and is occasionally used of RCs with cure of souls.

Pastor Aeternus. The title (from its opening words) of the 'First Dogmatic Constitution on the Church of Christ', issued at the concluding session of the First *Vatican Council on 18 July 1870. It defined the primacy and infallibility of the Pope.

Text in *ASS* 6 (1870), pp. 40–7, and in *Acta et Decreta Sacrorum Conciliorum Recentiorum: Collectio Lacensis*, 7 (Freiburg i.B., 1890), cols. 426–32; also pr. in Denzinger and Hünermann (37th edn., 1991), pp. 824–33 (nos. 3050–75) and, with Eng. tr., in [E.] Cuthbert Butler, OSB, *The Vatican Council*, 2 (1930), pp. 276–95.

Pastor of Hermas. See SHEPHERD OF HERMAS.

Pastor, Ludwig (1854–1928), historian of the Popes. He was a native of Aachen and, though his father had been a Protestant, was brought up a Catholic after his mother had become a widow. At the age of 19 he conceived the plan of writing a history of the Popes. After studying at Louvain, Vienna, and other universities he continued his researches at Rome. In 1881 he became lecturer at Innsbruck University, where he was appointed professor in 1887. In 1901 he became director of the Austrian Historical Institute in Rome, and in 1920 Austrian ambassador to the Holy See. His principal work is the *Geschichte der Päpste seit dem Ausgang des Mittelalters* (16 vols., 1886–1933), which has been translated into several languages. Based on extensive research in the archives of over 200 European cities, it aims at giving in vivid language a balanced representation of the history of Catholicism in modern times.

Diaries, Letters, and Memoirs ed. W. Wühr (Heidelberg, 1950), with bibl. pp. 918–20. Eng. tr. of his *Geschichte der Päpste* by F. I. Antrobus, Cong. Orat., and others (40 vols., 1891–1953). Appreciations by J. P. Dengel in *Hist. J.* 49 (1929), pp. 1–32; W. Goetz in *Historische Zeitschrift*, 145 (1932), pp. 550–63 (cf. ibid. 146, 1932, pp. 510–15); and A. Pelzer in *RHE* 46 (1951), pp. 192–201, with refs. F. Engel-Janosi, *Die diplomatische Mission Ludwig von Pastors beim heiligen Stuhle, 1920–1928* (Sb. (Wien), 254, Abh. 5; 1968). [W.] O. Chadwick, *Catholicism and History* (Cambridge, 1978), esp. pp. 116–27. F. Cognassi in *EC* 9 (1952), cols. 925–8, s.v.

Pastoral Epistles, the. A common designation for the Epistles to *Timothy and Titus, q.v.

pastoral letters (Lat. *litterae pastorales*). Official letters addressed by a bishop to all members of his diocese. Many RC bishops make a practice of publishing such letters to be read from the pulpit, e.g. at the beginning of *Lent and *Advent. They are commonly distinguished from 'encyclical letters' (*litterae encyclicae*) from a bishop, addressed only to his clergy.

pastoral staff. Another name for the *crosier (q.v.). The distinction drawn by many 19th-cent. antiquarians between the staff and the crosier was without authority. See CROSIER.

pastoralia. The branch of theology concerned with the principles regulating the life and conduct of the parish priest. Among the subjects which it normally includes are: (1) the methods of public worship and administration of the Sacraments; (2) preaching and sermon construction; (3) the care of the sick and dying; (4) the study of moral theology. All exponents of the subject are agreed that the personal training of the pastor himself in prayer and devotion to his calling are the pre-condition of all success.

Patarenes. The term 'Patareni' first appears in the 1050s at Milan as the designation of an extreme reforming movement enjoying considerable support at Rome; it contended first for clerical *celibacy and soon also for the extirpation of *simony. The derivation of the term is uncertain, but it is widely supposed to be from the name of the rag-pickers' quarter in Milan. Led initially by the clerks Arialdus and Landulf, the Patarenes played an important part in Milanese politics; they invited Roman intervention in the hitherto largely independent Ambrosian Church and violently resisted every manifestation of secular power over its affairs. Matters came to a head in 1071 when the Emp. *Henry IV invested a new archbishop. Under a new, lay leader, named Erlembald, the Patarenes demanded a free canonical election, propagated their movement elsewhere in Lombardy, and became Pope *Gregory VII's allies against Henry. With Erlembald's death in 1075 they suffered a crippling blow, but the movement persisted at Milan into the early 12th cent.

In the 1170s the name Patareni reappeared as a general label for heretics, especially the *Cathari in Italy, e.g. in can. 27 of the Third *Lateran Council (1179). It long remained current, with many variations of spelling, to describe both W. heretics and the *Bogomils of Bosnia and Dalmatia.

C. Violante, *La Pataria milanese e la riforma ecclesiastica*, 1 (Istituto storico italiano per il medio evo, Studi storici, 11–13; 1955). Id., 'I laici nel movimento patarino', in *I laici nella 'societas christiana' dei secoli xi e xii* (Miscellanea del Centro di studi medioevali, 5; 1968), pp. 597–697. E. Werner, *Pauperes Christi: Studien zu sozial-religiösen Bewegungen im Zeitalter des Reformpapsttums* (Leipzig, 1956), pp. 111–64. H. E. J. Cowdrey, 'The Papacy, the Patarenes and the Church of Milan', *Transactions of the Royal Historical Society*, 5th ser. 18 (1968), pp. 25–48, repr. in id., *Popes, Monks and Crusaders* (1984), no. 5; cf. also no. 6. J. P. Whitney, *Hildebrandine Essays* (Cambridge, 1932), pp. 80–2, 143–57. On the 12th-cent. Patarenes, A. Borst, *Die Katharer* (Schriften der Monumenta Germaniae Historica, 12; 1953), pp. 15–17, 81–9, 250. É. Amann in *DTC* 11 (pt. 2; 1932), cols. 224–6, s.v. 'Patarins', with details on sources; C. Violante in *NCE* 10 (1967), pp. 1084 f., s.v.

paten. The dish, now usually of silver or gold, on which the bread is placed at the celebration of the Eucharist. In the early centuries patens were of sufficient size to take the large loaves offered by the people and distributed at the Communion. Their modern counterparts in the W. are usually quite small, esp. where, as in the RC Church, wafer bread is used. In recent years, however, dishes to accommodate somewhat thicker altar-breads have come into use. The corresponding vessel in the E., the *discus (δίσκος), is larger and normally possesses a foot.

Rohault, 4 [1887], pp. 154–67, with plates cccxv–cccxvii. Braun, *AG*, pp. 197–246, with plates 41–7. W. W. Watts, *Catalogue of Chalices and other Communion Vessels* (Victoria and Albert Museum, 1922), pp. 39–46. H. *Leclercq, OSB, in *DACL* 13 (pt. 2; 1938), cols. 2392–414, s.v. 'Patène'.

Pater Noster. See LORD'S PRAYER.

Patmore, Coventry Kersey Dighton (1823–96), poet. He was educated privately and began to write poetry at an early age. In 1846 he was appointed supernumerary assistant in the printed book department of the British Museum and filled this post for nearly 20 years. He married the daughter of a *Congregational minister in 1847, and in 1854 and the following years there appeared the various parts of *The Angel in the House*, a set of poems forming a panegyric on married love. After the death of his wife in 1862, he went to Rome, where in 1864 he was received into the RC Church and in the same year married a second time. In 1877 he published *The Unknown Eros*, a collection of odes, some of them of great musical beauty and almost mystical depth. In 1880 he lost his second wife and in the following year married for the third time. His last book, *Rod, Root, and Flower* (1895), consists chiefly of meditations in prose on the same lines as the mystical poems in *The Unknown Eros*. As a religious poet Patmore is often of impressive beauty, though his conception of 'the relation of the soul to Christ as his betrothed wife' is sometimes unduly laboured.

Collected edns. of his Poems, 4 vols., London, 1879; repr., 2 vols., ibid., 1886; London, 1906, with introd. by B. Champneys, pp. xvii–xlvii, and ed. F. Page (Oxford Edition of Standard Authors, London, 1949). B. Champneys, *Memoirs and Correspondence of Coventry Patmore* (2 vols., 1900). Other studies by E. Gosse (London, 1905), O. [H.] Burdett (ibid., 1921), F. Page (ibid., 1933), D. [C.] Patmore (ibid., 1949), E. J. Oliver (ibid., 1956), and J. C. Reid (ibid., 1957). I. Anstruther, *Coventry Patmore's Angel: A study of Coventry Patmore, his wife Emily and* The Angel in the House (1992). R. Garnett in *DNB*, Suppl. 3 (1901), pp. 249–52. W. E. Fredeman in *NCBEL* 3 (1969), cols. 486–9.

Patmos. The small island in the Aegean off the coast of Asia Minor on which the author of Revelation (q.v.) received his vision (1.9; the sole NT ref.). Acc. to a tradition found in St *Irenaeus (*Adv. Haer.* 5. 30), *Eusebius (*HE* 3. 18) and St *Jerome (*De Vir. Ill.* 9), St. *John the Apostle was exiled to Patmos under *Domitian (AD 81–96) and returned to *Ephesus under Nerva (AD 96–8). The apocryphal 'Acts of *John' (q.v.) narrate several miracles which the Apostle performed at Patmos. In 1088 St Christodulus, who had been granted a bull by the Emp. Alexis Comnenus (1081–1118), founded a monastery on a peak in the middle of the island, which rapidly grew in importance; it has survived to the present day. The monastery amassed a valuable collection of MSS and, though many have since been dispersed (the famous 9th-cent. codex of *Plato is in the *Bodleian), a substantial number remain. The Abbot is directly subject to the Patr. of *Constantinople. A grotto in the hillside (τὸ σπήλαιον τῆς Ἀποκαλύψεως) is pointed out as the place where John received his vision.

Primary docs. in F. Miklosich and J. Müller (eds.), *Acta et diplomata graeca medii aevi*, 6 (Vienna, 1890). V. Guérin, *Description de l'île de Patmos et de l'île de Samos* (1856), pp. 1–120; W. E. Geil, *The Isle called Patmos* (1897). H. F. Tozer, *The Islands of the Aegean* (1890), pp. 178–98. G. Hofmann, SJ, *Patmos und Rom: Darstellung der Beziehungen zwischen dem griechischen Johanneskloster und der römischen Kirche* (Orientalia Christiana, fasc. 41; 1928). Catalogue of the MSS of the monastery by J. Sakkelion (Athens, 1890). F. C. *Conybeare in *HDB* 3 (1900), pp. 693 f., s.v.; H. *Leclercq, OSB, in *DACL* 13 (pt. 1; 1938), cols. 2424–40, s.v.; J. Schmidt in *PW* 18 (pt. 4; 1949), cols. 2174–91, s.v.; G. Campos, OSB, in *Dict. Bibl.*, Suppl. 7 (1966), cols. 73–81, s.v. See also comm. TO REVELATION, BOOK OF.

Paton, John Gibson (1824–1907), missionary to Vanuatu (then known as the New Hebrides). Born in Kirkmahoe, near Dumfries, of parents who belonged to the *Reformed Presbyterian Church of Scotland, he gained his education under great difficulties. Having worked for six years for the Glasgow City Mission, he was appointed as a missionary of the Reformed Presbyterian Church to Vanuatu and was ordained in 1858. He arrived with his wife at Aneityum on 30 Aug. 1858; shortly afterwards they moved to the island of Tanna. In the next year his wife gave birth to a child and both died. In 1862, his own life in danger, he fled from Tanna and went to the Australian colonies. Here he successfully aroused interest in missionary work in Vanuatu; after a visit to Scotland, where he married again, he returned to the Pacific on mission service in 1865. From 1866 to 1881 he was a missionary of the Presbyterian Church of Victoria on the island of Aniwa, near Tanna; from 1881 he was based in Melbourne as mission organizer and publicist. His autobiography, written in the form of notes, was put into shape by his brother, the Revd James Paton (1843–1906), and from its publication in 1889 did much to stimulate support for his cause.

The principal material is to be found in his own works. R. Adams, *In the Land of Strangers: A Century of European Contact with Tanna, 1774–1874* (Pacific Research Monograph, 9; Canberra, 1984), pp. 78–167. J. G. Miller, *Live: A History of Church Planting in the New Hebrides . . . to 1880*, 2 (Sydney, 1981), pp. 20–36 and 46–51. Sir Everard im Thurn in *DNB, 1901–1911*, 3 (1912), pp. 77 f.

Paton, William (1886–1943), *Presbyterian minister and writer on missionary subjects. Born in London, he was educated at Pembroke College, Oxford, and Westminster College, Cambridge. In 1911 he became Missionary Secretary to the *Student Christian Movement in England; he maintained a keen interest in missionary and ecumenical activities throughout his life. His earliest books on this subject are *Jesus Christ and the World's Religions* (1916) and *Social Ideas in India* (1919). From 1922 to 1927 he was General Secretary of the National Christian Council of India, Burma, and Ceylon, and subsequently held the position of Secretary to the International Missionary Council

and Editor of the *International Review of Missions*. Among his later publications are *Alexander Duff* (1922), *The Faiths of Mankind* (1932), *World Community* (1938), *The Message of the World-wide Church* (1940), and *The Church and the New Order* (1941).

Life by M. Sinclair (London, 1949). E. M. Jackson, *Red Tape and the Gospel: A Study of the Significance of the Ecumenical Missionary Struggle of William Paton (1886–1943)* (Birmingham [1980]). N. Micklem in *DNB, 1941–1950*, pp. 662–3.

patriarch (biblical). Literally the father or ruler of a family or tribe. The term is most commonly used of the three great forefathers of Israel, *Abraham, *Isaac, and *Jacob (cf. Gen. 12–50); the dating of these traditions has been the subject of continuing debate (on which see ABRAHAM). The term is also used of the ancestors of the human race before the *Flood and of the 12 sons of Jacob, to whom are attributed the pseudepigraphical *Testaments of the Twelve Patriarchs. In Acts 2: 29 the word is applied to *David.

The patriarchs have a major place in histories of *Israel (q.v.). A. Alt, *Der Gott der Väter* (Beiträge zur Wissenschaft vom Alten und Neuen Testament, Dritte Folge, 12; 1929; Eng. tr. in Alt's *Essays on Old Testament History and Religion*, Oxford, 1966, pp. 1–77). T. L. Thompson, *The Historicity of the Patriarchal Narratives* (Beihefte zur *ZATW*, 133; 1974); W. McKane, *Studies in the Patriarchal Narratives* (Edinburgh, 1979). H. Cazelles in *Dict. Bibl.*, Suppl. 7 (1966), cols. 81–156, s.v.; J. Van Seters in *The Interpreter's Dictionary of the Bible*, Suppl. Vol. (Nashville, 1976), pp. 645–8, s.v.

patriarch (ecclesiastical). A title dating from the 6th cent., for the bishops of the five chief sees of Christendom: *Rome, *Alexandria, *Antioch, *Constantinople, and *Jerusalem. Their jurisdiction extended over the adjoining territories, and included the right of ordaining the '*metropolitans', i.e. bishops of the principal sees under them, of trying the same when accused, and of hearing appeals from their judgements. The earliest bishops exercising such powers, though not so named, were those of Rome (over the whole or part of Italy), Alexandria (over Egypt and Libya), and Antioch (over large parts of Asia Minor). These three were recognized by the Council of *Nicaea (325). But at *Chalcedon (451) Jerusalem secured recognition as well as Constantinople, whose jurisdiction over Thrace, Asia, and Pontus was exercised henceforward in spite of protests from Rome. The title patriarch has been given in more recent times to the heads of certain other *autocephalous Churches in the E. (*Russia, *Serbia, *Romania, *Bulgaria, *Georgia). In the (Latin) RC Church the title is used in a purely honorific way for the bishops of certain sees, e.g. *Venice and Lisbon. See also OECUMENICAL PATRIARCH and CATHOLICOS.

Patriarchs, Testaments of the Twelve. See TESTAMENTS OF THE TWELVE PATRIARCHS.

Patrick, St (mid- or late 5th cent.), 'Apostle of the Irish'. Patrick was born in Britain, the son of a local *decurio* (member of a town council) called Calpornius, who was also a deacon of the church, and who had a property near the village (*vicus*) of Bannavem Taburniae, of which the site is unknown. Patrick was brought up as a Christian, though in no tradition of strong piety. At the age of 16 he was captured by Irish pirates and spent six years as a herdsman in Ireland. In his captivity he turned earnestly to God, and eventually received a Divine message that he was to escape. He made his way to some port 200 miles away, perhaps on the SE coast of Ireland, persuaded some sailors to give him a passage, and landed somewhere on the coast of Britain. After adventures in which he felt himself sustained and protected by Divine help, he returned to his kinsfolk, a changed man. He underwent training for the Christian ministry, which must have consisted mainly of learning a rather conservative rule of faith and acquiring an intimate knowledge of the Latin Bible. At some point he went from Britain as 'bishop in Ireland' (his own phrase, *Epistle* § 1), and he spent the rest of his life there, evangelizing, conciliating local chieftains and educating their sons, ordaining clergy, and instituting monks and nuns. One of his letters has survived, written in Latin to a British chieftain called Coroticus, whose identity is disputed. Towards the end of his life Patrick wrote, also in Latin, a moving personal account of his spiritual pilgrimage, called his *Confession*, perhaps in response to a serious attack on his character and career which was certainly made on him at some point during his episcopate.

Discussions on the chronology of Patrick's life have focused on the reference in the chronicle of *Prosper of Aquitaine to the sending of *Palladius by Pope *Celestine I (422–32) to be the 'first bishop to the Irish believing in Christ'. Though there is no certain connection between Palladius and Patrick, it is often argued that Patrick's mission to Ireland cannot have been much later than 431. The date of his birth is inferred from this date, and it is therefore held that the date of his death is not likely to have been later than *c*.460. Others argue that he lived a generation later and died *c*.490. There is no decisive evidence, and the Irish Annals, compiled two centuries later, admit both chronologies.

The few facts derived from Patrick's *Confession* were embellished by his biographers, of whom the earliest whose works are extant, Tírechán and Muirchú, lived in the second half of the 7th cent. The stories of his education in Gaul at *Lérins or Auxerre (under Amator or *Germanus), and of his being sent to Ireland by Pope Celestine, may perhaps have been transferred to Patrick from a lost source concerning Palladius. The story of his encounter with the 'High King' of Ireland, Loegaire, reflects the 7th-cent. political interests of *Armagh; the Church there had by then appropriated the legend of Patrick, which was propagated through a series of texts; many of them (including the works of Tírechán and Muirchú) are contained in the 'Book of *Armagh'. Dates between the 5th and 7th cents. are proposed for the two collections of canons formerly attributed to Patrick; the hymn 'Audite omnes amantes', on Patrick, perhaps dates from the 7th cent., and the vernacular '*Breastplate of St Patrick' from the early 8th cent. Feast day, 17 Mar. See also BELLS and ST PATRICK'S PURGATORY.

Crit. text by L. Bieler of Patrick's *Confession*, Letter to Coroticus, and some *dicta* attributed to him, *Libri Epistolarum Sancti Patricii Episcopi* (2 vols., Irish Manuscripts Commission, Dublin, 1952). These works, together with bk.1 of Life by Muirchú, also conveniently ed., with Eng. tr., by A. B. E. Hood (History from the Sources, 9; London and Chichester, 1978). The *Confession* and Letter to Coroticus ed., with Fr. tr., by R. P. C. Hanson and C. Blanc (SC 249; 1978). Convenient Eng. tr. of *Confession*, Letter to Coroticus, *dicta*, canons, Hymn on Patrick, and Breastplate by L. Bieler (ACW 17; 1953). The 7th-cent. *vitae* are ed., with Eng. tr. and comm., by id., *The Patrician Texts in the Book of Armagh* (Scriptores Latini Hiberniae, 10; Dublin, 1979); later Lat. texts ed. id., *Four Latin Lives of St Patrick* (ibid. 8; 1971). Further details on sources in M. Lapidge and R. Sharpe, *A Bibliography of Celtic-Latin Literature 400–1200* (Dublin, 1985), pp. 9–11, 103–5, and 107 f. (nos. 25 f., 354–60, and 365–8), and K. Devine and A. Harvey, *Clavis Patricii* (Dublin, 1989 ff.). Of the vast modern lit., the following are significant: J. H. Todd, *St Patrick, Apostle of Ireland* (1864); J. B. Bury, *The Life of St Patrick and his Place in History* (1905); T. F. O'Rahilly, *The Two Patricks* (Dublin, 1942); L. Bieler, *The Life and Legend of St Patrick: Problems of Modern Scholarship* (1949); J. Carney, *The Problem of St Patrick* (Dublin, 1961); D. A. Binchy, 'Patrick and his biographers: ancient and modern', *Studia Hibernica*, 2 (1962), pp. 7–173; R. P. C. Hanson, *Saint Patrick: His Origins and Career* (Oxford, 1968); D. N. Dumville and others, *Saint Patrick A.D. 493–1993* (Studies in Celtic History, 13; Woodbridge, Suffolk, 1993).

Patrick, Simon (1625–1707), Bp. of *Ely. A native of Gainsborough, Lincs., he was educated at Queens' College, Cambridge, where he came under the influence of the '*Cambridge Platonist', John *Smith. He was ordained a *Presbyterian minister in 1653; but the study of H. *Hammond and H. *Thorndike determined him to seek episcopal ordination. In 1654 he received holy orders from J. *Hall, Bp. of *Norwich, and became successively vicar of Battersea (1658), rector of St Paul's, Covent Garden (1662), and Dean of *Peterborough (1679), retaining at the same time his previous living. He was a prominent and sincere *Latitudinarian and prob. the author of *A Brief Account of the new Sect of Latitude-Men* (1662). In 1688 he resisted the reading of the *Declaration of Indulgence, and in 1689 took the Oath of Allegiance to William and Mary. In the same year he was appointed Bp. of *Chichester. He was translated to Ely in 1691. As bishop he was a warm supporter of the *SPCK, which he helped to found, and of the *SPG. He wrote extensively. In 1664 he published *The Parable of the Pilgrim*, an allegory similar to J. *Bunyan's *Pilgrim's Progress*. He commented on and paraphrased all the books of the OT from Genesis to the Song of Solomon (10 vols., 1695–1710), and wrote many controversial treatises against both *Nonconformists and RCs, among them *A Friendly Debate between a Conformist and a Nonconformist* (1669), *A Full View of the Doctrines and Practices of the Ancient Church* (1688), and *Texts Examined which Papists cite out of the Bible* (also 1688). In 1687 he edited an abridged version of W. *Chillingworth's *Religion of Protestants*. He also published a number of devotional books.

Works, incl. his autobiog., which was first pub. Oxford, 1839, but excluding his comms., ed. A. Taylor, 9 vols., Oxford, 1858. Facsimile repr. of 1st edn. of *A Brief Account of the new Sect of Latitude-Men*, with introd. by T. A. Birrell (Augustan Reprint Society Publication, 100; Los Angeles, 1963). H. R. McAdoo, *The Spirit of Anglicanism* (1965), pp. 189–98. J. H. Overton in *DNB* 44 (1895), pp. 45–7.

Patrimony of St Peter. The estates belonging to the Church of Rome. Although the Church of Rome had long been wealthy, persecutions had prevented the acquisition of permanent property until an edict of *Constantine (*Cod. Theod.* 16. 2. 4) made it legal to leave property to the

Church. In the following period, up to 600, economic conditions encouraged large donations of land and commendations. Parallels between the *patrimonium ecclesiae* and the *patrimonium principis* suggest that the *Donation of Constantine, though forged, represented the truth in substance and that much Imperial property was given to the Church. By gifts and inheritance the patrimony came to include lands in Sicily (confiscated by the Emp. *Leo III in 730), Illyria, Gaul, Corsica, Sardinia, around Hippo in Africa, as well as vast estates in Italy. They were governed by a centralized administration which facilitated the extension of Papal influence. The revenues were employed not only for administrative purposes, but widely for the relief of the poor, redemption of captives and later for defence. As the further patrimonies were conquered, Popes concentrated on the defence of the regions round Rome, esp. the exarchate of *Ravenna and the Duchy of Rome. When the castle of Sutri was captured in 727, the Lombard king Luitprand 'restored' it 'as a gift to the Blessed Apostles Peter and Paul'. In 753 *Stephen II appealed for protection to *Pepin, King of the Franks, who agreed to give the Pope certain lands to be conquered from the Lombards. By the Donations of 754 and 756 Pepin gave to St Peter territory in the exarchate of Ravenna, the Duchy of Rome, and the districts of Venetia and Istria, and, renouncing the Byzantine authority, founded the Papal states independent of any temporal power.

The term was applied in medieval usage to the environs of Rome. It is used loosely for the *States of the Church (q.v.) as a whole.

The primary sources include the *Liber Censuum* and the *Liber Pontificalis* (qq.v.). L. *Duchesne, *Les Premiers Temps de l'état pontifical* (1898; 2nd edn., 1904; Eng. tr., 1908). E. Spearing, *The Patrimony of the Roman Church in the Time of Gregory the Great* (posthumously ed. E. M. Spearing, 1918). P. Partner, *The Lands of St Peter: The Papal State in the Middle Ages and the Early Renaissance* (1972), pp. 1–41. T. F. X. Noble, *The Republic of St Peter: The Birth of the Papal State 680–825* (Philadelphia [1984]), with bibl. G. Schnürer in *CE* 14 (1912), pp. 257–61, s.v. 'States of the Church, 1'; O. Bertolini in *EC* 9 (1952), cols. 957–60, s.v. 'Patrimonio di S. Pietro'. See also works cited under PEPIN.

Patripassianism. A form of *Monarchianism (q.v.) which arose in the early 3rd cent. and held that God the Father suffered as the Son. It is also known as '*Sabellianism'.

Patristic Conferences. International Conferences on Patristic Studies have met in Oxford at four-year intervals beginning in 1951. The first five conferences were convened by F. L. Cross (1900–68), then Lady Margaret Professor of Divinity and canon of Christ Church. Besides fostering patristic scholarship on a broad basis, the conferences were of importance in bringing together scholars of different religious allegiance at a time when RCs were not taking part in ecumenical gatherings.

Proceedings of the second to seventh conferences have been pub. under the title *Studia Patristica* (TU 63–4, 1957; 78–81, 1961–2; 92–4, 1966; 107–8, 1970–2; 115–17, 1975–6; 128–9; 1984–5); those of the eighth conference pub. at Oxford, 3 vols., 1982; and those of the ninth and subsequent conferences mainly at Louvain.

patristics. The branch of theological study which deals with the writings of the *Fathers (*patres*) of the Church (q.v.). 'Patristics' normally embraces the Fathers in the more restrictive sense of the term, i.e. those who wrote between the end of the 1st cent., after the writing of most of the works that now comprise the NT, and the close of the 8th cent.; and this is the period commonly termed the 'Patristic Age'. The study of patristic literature is closely allied both with Church history and with the history of early doctrine, since this literature is the chief evidence both for the events and for the ideas of these times. The leading Fathers were the authors of much work vital to Christianity. They defended the Gospel against heresies and misunderstandings; they composed extensive commentaries on the Bible, explanatory, doctrinal, and practical, and published innumerable sermons, largely on the same subject; they exhibited the meaning and implications of the *Creeds; they recorded past and current events in Church history; and they related the Christian faith to the best thought of their own age.

The earliest essays in patristic study were the catalogues of Christian writers compiled by St *Jerome, *Gennadius of Marseilles, St *Isidore of Seville, St *Ildefonsus of Toledo, and *Photius. Later similar catalogues are due to *Sigebert of Gembloux, *Honorius 'of Autun', and the *Anonymus Mellicensis* (of Melk in Lower Austria, *c*.1135), and to (pseudo-) *Henry of Ghent. The more imp. early pr. collections include the *Bibliotheca SS. Patrum* (ed. M. de La Bigne, 8 vols., Paris, 1575, with later suppl.; more comprehensive new edn., 14 vols., Cologne, 1618, suppl. 1622; further extended as *Maxima Bibliotheca Veterum Patrum*, 27 vols., Lyons, 1677) and those of F. *Ducaeus, J. L. *d'Achery, J. *Sirmond, J. B. *Cotelier, and F. *Combefis. A new era in the editing of patristic texts was inaugurated by the *Maurists (q.v.). Later collections are due to J. E. *Grabe, B. de *Montfaucon, and A. *Gallandi, and, in the 19th cent., to M. J. *Routh, A. *Mai (cont. by J. Cozza-Luzi) and J. B. F. *Pitra. J. P. *Migne's vast *Patrologiae* ('Latina' and 'Graeca') incorporated nearly all the Gk. and Lat. texts hitherto in print. The chief recent collections, ed. on modern crit. principles, are the *Corpus Scriptorum Ecclesiasticorum Latinorum* (CSEL, Vienna, 1866 ff.), *Die griechischen christlichen Schriftsteller der ersten drei Jahrhunderte* (GCS, Leipzig, 1897–1941; Berlin and Leipzig, 1953; Berlin, 1954 ff.), the *Patrologia Orientalis* (ed. R. Graffin and F. Nau, Paris, 1907 ff.), the *Corpus Scriptorum Christianorum Orientalium* (CSCO, Paris, etc., 1903 ff.), and *Corpus Christianorum, Series Latina* (CCSL) and *Series Graeca* (CCSG), ed. under the initiative of the monks of Steenbrugge, Belgium (Turnhout, 1954 ff. and 1977 ff. respectively). Of Eng. trs. of the Fathers, the principal series are The *Library of the Fathers (48 vols., 1835–85), The Ante-Nicene Christian Library (28 vols., 1886–1900), A Select Library of the Nicene and Post-Nicene Fathers [1st ser.] (14 vols., New York, 1887–93), and NS (14 vols., Oxford and New York, 1890–1900), Ancient Christian Writers (Westminster, Md., and London, 1946–67; Westminster, Md., 1970 ff.), and Fathers of the Church (Washington, DC, 1947 ff.). Good Fr. edns. of many patristic texts in Sources Chrétiennes (Paris, 1942 ff.). For modern Patrologies, see foll. entry. J. de Ghellinck, Patristique et moyen-âge (3 vols., 1946–8); B. Altaner, 'Der Stand der patrologischen Wissenschaft und das Problem einer neuen altchristlichen Literaturgeschichte', Miscellanea Giovanni Mercati, 1 (ST 121; 1946), pp. 483–520. On the knowledge of Gk. patristic lit. in the W., see P. Courcelle, Les Lettres grecques en occident (1943), and A. Siegmund, Die Überlieferung der griechischen Literatur in der lateinischen Kirche bis zum 12. Jahrhundert (1949). For refs. to the Bible in the Fathers, see Biblia Patristica, ed. J. Allenbach and others (Paris, 1975 ff.). Bibliographia Patristica, ed. W. Schneemelcher and then K. Schäferdiek (35 vols., covering 1956–90; Berlin, 1959–97). On the Greek of the Fathers, see s.v. GREEK. See also PATRISTIC CONFERENCES and PATROLOGY.

patrology. In older English writers, the term patrology was synonymous with *patristics (q.v.), esp. in its doctrinal aspects, but it is now in current use for a systematically arranged manual on the patristic literature.

Among older works, the most ambitious are the *compendia* of J. A. *Fabricius (q.v.). The principal recent patrologies are A. *Harnack, *Geschichte der altchristlichen Literatur bis Eusebius* (3 vols., 1893–1904) and O. *Bardenhewer, *Patrologie* (1894; Eng. tr., 1908) and *Geschichte der altkirchlichen Literatur* (5 vols., 1902–31). The latter is suppl. by B. *Altaner, *Patrologie* (1938; 6th edn., 1960; Eng. tr., 1960; rev. A. Stuiber, 1966; 8th edn., with suppl. bibl., 1978). J. Quasten, *Patrology*, 1: *The Beginnings of Patristic Literature* (Utrecht, 1950); 2: *The Ante-Nicene Literature after Irenaeus* (ibid., 1953); 3: *The Golden Age of Greek Patristic Literature* (ibid., 1960); 4: *The Golden Age of Latin Patristic Literature*, ed. A. di Berardino (Westminster, Md., 1986; Eng. tr. of *Patrologia*, 3, Turin, 1978). Other works incl. B. Steidle, OSB, *Patrologia* (Freiburg i.B., 1937); F. L. Cross, *The Early Christian Fathers* (1960); F. [M.] Young, *From Nicaea to Chalcedon* (1983; on the Gk. Fathers only). For the Lat. Fathers, cf. also P. de Labriolle, *Histoire de la littérature latine chrétienne* (1920; new edn. by G. Bardy, 1947; Eng. tr., 1924). *Clavis Patrum Latinorum*, ed. E. Dekkers, OSB (Sacris Erudiri, 3; Steenbrugge, 1951; 3rd edn., 1995), and *Clavis Patrum Graecorum*, ed. M. Geerard (5 vols., Turnhout, 1974–87), are invaluable guides to the writings and edns. of individual Fathers.

patron. See ADVOWSON.

patron saint. A saint who, by tradition or otherwise, has been chosen as the special intercessor and advocate in heaven of a particular place, person, or organization. The custom of having patron saints for churches arose from the practice of building churches over the tombs of martyrs. The expression 'titular' is also used in the same sense. Since the middle of the 19th cent. the traditional celebration of the patronal feasts of churches has been widely revived in the C of E. See also DEDICATION OF CHURCHES.

Patteson, John Coleridge (1827–71), Bp. of Melanesia. A nephew of J. T. *Coleridge, he was educated at Eton (where he came under the influence of G. A. *Selwyn) and Balliol College, Oxford. Ordained in 1853, he was persuaded by Selwyn to sail for the *South Pacific in 1855 to assist in the work of the Melanesian Mission (founded by Selwyn in 1849 to extend the Anglican Church from *New Zealand to the islands northwards). Patteson toured the islands in the *Southern Cross*, learnt many of the languages, founded a college on Norfolk Island for the training of Melanesian boys, and was remarkably successful in his pastoral and educational work. In 1861 he was consecrated the first Bp. of Melanesia. On 20 Sept. 1871 he was murdered on the island of Nukapu, where he had landed alone; the killing was believed to be in revenge for the kidnapping of some of the inhabitants by white men a few months earlier. His fate made a deep impression in England and aroused much interest in missionary work and in the recruitment of Melanesians as indentured labourers for plantations in Fiji and Queensland. In the American BCP (1979) and various other Anglican calendars, feast day, 20 Sept.

The standard Life is that of C. M. *Yonge (2 vols., London, 1874 [1873]); modern Life by J. Gutch (ibid., 1971). D. [L.] Hilliard, 'The Making of an Anglican Martyr: Bishop John Coleridge Patteson of Melanesia', in D. Wood (ed.), *Martyrs and Martyrolo-*

gies (Studies in Church History, 30; Oxford, 1993), pp. 333–45. W. H. Fremantle in *DNB* 47 (1895), pp. 53–6.

Pattison, Andrew Seth Pringle- (1856–1931), until 1898 **Andrew Seth**, Scottish philosopher. He was educated at the Royal High School, Edinburgh, at Edinburgh University, and at Berlin, Jena, and Göttingen, where he studied under H. Lotze. After holding chairs at Cardiff (1883–7) and St Andrews (1887–91), he became Professor of Logic and Metaphysics at Edinburgh (1891–1919). He showed marked sympathy with German Idealism (I. *Kant, and esp. G. W. F. *Hegel) but he sought to free it from *pantheism and to safeguard the claims of the human person. He held that 'God or the Absolute', although not Himself an individual among others, was the source of individuation. His chief writings were *Scottish Philosophy* (1885), *The Idea of God in the Light of Recent Philosophy* (Gifford Lectures for 1912–13; 1917), and *Studies in the Philosophy of Religion* (1930).

Pattison's *The Balfour Lectures on Realism* was posthumously ed. by G. F. Barbour (1933), with memoir, pp. 3–46. Memoir by J. B. Cooper in *Proceedings of the British Academy*, 22 (1931), pp. 447–61; J. B. Baillie, 'Pringle Pattison as Philosopher', ibid., pp. 461–89. J. Laird in *DNB, 1931–1940*, pp. 678 f.

Pattison, Mark (1813–84), Rector of Lincoln College, Oxford. In 1832 he entered Oriel College, then suffering from E. *Hawkins's removal of J. H. *Newman, R. H. *Froude, and R. I. *Wilberforce from their tutorships, and, being mainly dependent on his own resources, came to assimilate a wide range of largely out-of-the-way knowledge. Before long he came under the religious influence of Newman, contributed to some of his translations for the *Library of the Fathers*, and from about 1838 to 1848 was a keen *Tractarian. Later his enthusiasm for the Oxford Movement declined and with it his faith in institutional Christianity. He became keenly interested, however, in educational and university reform, and did good work among his pupils and as a university examiner, after becoming a Fellow of Lincoln College in 1839. He was one of the contributors to *Essays and Reviews* (1860). In 1861 he was elected Rector of Lincoln College. His very extensive writing largely took the form of essays and articles on literary subjects, but his *Isaac *Casaubon* (1875) was an enduring contribution to the history of modern scholarship. His posthumous *Memoirs* (1885) reflect the fierce anti-Tractarianism of his last years.

A selection of his Essays was pub. by his friend, H. Nettleship (2 vols., 1889). L. A. Tollemache, *Recollections of Pattison* (1885). V. H. H. Green, *Oxford Common Room: A Study of Lincoln College and Mark Pattison* (1957); id., *Love in a Cool Climate: The Letters of Mark Pattison and Meta Bradley, 1879–1884* (Oxford, 1985). J. Sparrow, *Mark Pattison and the Idea of a University* (Cambridge, 1967). R. C. Christie in *DNB* 44 (1895), pp. 58–63.

Paul, St (d. prob. AD 62–5), the 'Apostle of the Gentiles'. Born during the first years of the Christian era, the future St Paul, originally 'Saul', was a Jew of the tribe of Benjamin, a native of *Tarsus in Cilicia, said by Acts to possess Roman citizenship. He was brought up a *Pharisee (Phil. 3: 5, Acts 26: 5) and perhaps had some of his education at *Jerusalem under *Gamaliel (so Acts 22: 3). This life in Judaism (Gal. 1: 14) gave him his trust in God, experience of the Law, and a thorough knowledge of the Scriptures, as well as his methods of arguing from Scripture. As a Jew of the *Diaspora he spoke and wrote Greek and shows some knowledge of rhetoric. Within a short time of the Crucifixion, he came in contact with the new 'Way' of the followers of Jesus, apparently in Palestine, and persecuted the Church (1 Cor. 15: 9, Gal. 1: 13). Acts 7: 58 represents him as present at the martyrdom of St *Stephen, and 9: 1–2 as authorized by the High Priest to arrest converts in *Damascus. As he drew near he was himself converted.

SOURCES. The account in Acts of Paul's early activities in Jerusalem and his subsequent Christian mission has been widely challenged. It was written from a later perspective when the conflict over Gentile converts and the Jewish law was no longer acute and reconciliation was needed. St *Luke therefore depicts Paul as a law-abiding Jew and omits the dispute with St *Peter recorded in Gal. 2: 11–14. He allows himself considerable freedom in the speeches and schematizes Paul's travels as missionary journeys. The primary source for Paul's life and missionary activity are the seven epistles generally agreed to be authentic. Col. and 2 Thess. are doubtful, and Eph. is widely thought to stem from a gifted follower; the Pastorals were almost certainly written later, though they contain some historical echoes and a few scholars still argue that they were written by Paul, after a postulated release from imprisonment in Rome. Rom., 1 and 2 Cor., Gal., Phil., 1 Thess., and Philem. are thought to be the work of Paul himself, but all except 1 Thess. and possibly Gal. were written within a few years' span in the mid-50s. They contain very little information about Paul's past. Acts is also fragmentary and leaves some uncertainties about even the best-documented parts of his life.

Paul's 18 months in *Corinth can be dated with some confidence by the reference in Acts 18: 12–17 to *Gallio who was procurator in Achaia in AD 51–2. Most scholars are accordingly also agreed that the vital Jerusalem meeting of Gal. 2: 1–10 (cf. Acts 15) took place in AD 49 or 50. Luke's account of Paul visiting Jerusalem at Acts 11: 27–30 cannot be fitted into this reconstruction unless, despite the discrepancies, it corresponds to the visit of Gal. 2. The epistle would then have been written before the council of Acts 15. But this is less likely than that Acts 11 is mistaken.

Paul's conversion can be dated to around AD 33 by his references in Gal. 1–2 to 3 and 14 years working backwards from the date of the council. That leaves gaps in our knowledge of his early missionary activity. The latter part of his life is much better documented, in Acts 20–8. But Luke's narrative ends with Paul's captivity in Rome and there is no solid evidence that he was released and fulfilled his ambitions for a Spanish mission (Rom. 15: 24 and 28). Other sources can scarcely be trusted to enlarge the historical picture beyond the reliable witnesses to his martyrdom in Rome under the Emp. *Nero. Writing some 30 years after his death St *Clement of Rome claims that he went 'to the limit (or goal) of the West (τὸ τέρμα τῆς δύσεως) (Ep. 1. 5). The Acts of St *Peter, several of the Fathers (e.g. *Cyril of Jerusalem, *Epiphanius, *Chrysostom, and *Jerome), and the *Muratorian Canon assume that he visited Spain, perhaps on the basis of Rom. 15. 1 Clement 6. 1 is sometimes taken to imply that he was martyred before the Neronian *persecution, but *Eusebius

dates his martyrdom as late as AD 67. *Tertullian (De Praescr. 36) adds that he was beheaded. *Gregory the Great and subsequent itineraries follow the Acts of St *Paul in identifying the spot (*Tre Fontane; see articles on APPIAN WAY, OSTIAN WAY, and ST PAUL'S OUTSIDE THE WALLS for legends of his burial). The sketch in the Acts of St Paul of a 'man small of stature, with a bald head and crooked legs, in a good state of body, with eyebrows meeting and nose somewhat hooked . . .' is probably imaginative, though Paul admits to his weak bodily presence (2 Cor. 10: 10) and a 'thorn in the flesh' (2 Cor. 12: 7).

MISSION. Despite these problems a partial outline can be constructed. Paul saw a vision of the risen Lord Jesus (1 Cor. 9: 1, narrated with some variations in Acts 9: 3–9, 22: 5–16, and 26: 4–18). He implies that his call and status as an apostle rested on this (1 Cor. 15: 8 f.). It seems from Gal. 1: 16 that from the outset his mission was to the Gentiles, though a few have questioned this. Some have inferred that his initial contact was with 'hellenists' who did not insist on Gentile converts observing the whole law of *Moses. Paul went first to Arabia and back to Damascus, then three years later to Jerusalem, where he came to know Peter and saw St *James, and on to Syria and Cilicia (Gal. 1).

Paul's 14 years, prior to the second visit to Jerusalem, include his journey with St *Barnabas (and John *Mark at first, Acts 15: 37 f.) from Antioch to *Cyprus, Pamphylia, S. Galatia (Pisidian Antioch, Iconium, Lystra, Derbe) and back, described in Acts 13–14. They may also possibly include (contrary to Acts) his subsequent travels with *Silas and *Timothy through Phrygia and N. Galatia (cf. Acts 16: 6), Troas (where perhaps Luke joined them, cf. Acts 16: 10: 'we') and Greece (Philippi, Thessalonica, and Beroea in Macedonia; *Athens and Corinth in Achaia). It is uncertain when the dispute in Antioch occurred. It may have preceded the second visit to Jerusalem, if Gal. 2: 1–14 is not chronological (so Lüdemann). The so-called council there allowed Paul to continue his Gentile mission on condition that he raised funds for the Jerusalem Church, but some Jewish Christians continued to oppose him.

Around AD 50–2 Paul spent 18 months in Corinth (Acts 18: 11), establishing the Church with the help of Silas and Timothy (2 Cor. 1: 19). The next major centre of his activity was *Ephesus (Acts 19), where he remained for 2–3 years (AD 52–4). There were disturbances (cf. 1 Cor. 15: 32) and perhaps imprisonment, but also successes. It is likely that the communities in the hinterland of Asia Minor (Colossae, *Philadelphia, Hierapolis, and *Laodicea) resulted from the work of Paul and his assistants in this period. After an enforced departure from Ephesus he went to Macedonia (2 Cor. 7: 5) before going S. to Achaia (prob. Corinth) for three months (Acts 20: 2 f.) in AD 56–7, prior to his final Jerusalem visit, with representatives of his Gentile congregations, bringing the 'collection'.

We know more about Paul's relations with the Corinthian 'saints' than any other congregation, thanks to the extensive correspondence contained in 1 and 2 Cor. Their practical problems in living the new life in a pagan environment, their doctrinal misunderstandings (including possibly incipient *Gnosticism), liturgical chaos, and challenges to Paul's authority explain his 'anxiety for all the Churches' (2 Cor. 11: 28). The earlier 1 Thess. reveals other problems in his Churches: persecution from Jews and pagans. But the most disruptive issue that Paul faced in this period came from other missionaries visiting his congregations and persuading his converts to observe the Jewish law. Gal. provides an angry but reasoned response; he argues from Scripture and experience against the necessity of observing the Torah. The issue here, as later in Phil. 3, was *circumcision rather than eating with Gentiles which had led to the earlier dispute at Antioch (Gal. 2: 11–14), but the principle on which the new community was based is the same: faith in Christ implies freedom from the ordinances of Moses.

The outcome of the dispute in Galatia is not known. For Paul himself in the 50s, the vital question was whether the Jerusalem Church would finally accept his law-free Gentile mission. He no doubt hoped that the money he had collected as promised (Gal. 2: 10, 1 Cor. 16: 1–4, 2 Cor. 8–9, and Rom. 15: 25–31) would help, and perhaps saw it as the fulfilment of the prophecies (Is. 60) about the nations bringing their wealth to Jerusalem. As he prepared to leave Greece for Jerusalem (Acts 20: 3) he wrote to the Jewish and Gentile believers in Rome, and asked for their prayers that he would be delivered from the unbelievers in Judaea and that his 'service' would be acceptable to the saints in Jerusalem (Rom. 15: 31). He explained that his work in the E. was complete, that he was planning a mission to Spain (15: 19 and 23 f.), and expected to visit them on the way.

Paul's concern was well grounded. However 'gladly' (Acts 21: 17) the Church in Jerusalem welcomed Paul and his Gentile party with their gift, it was apparently a proposal of James that led to his arrest. Paul's appearance in the *Temple caused a stir, and he escaped lynching by being taken into custody. There followed trials before the *Sanhedrin and the governor Felix in Caesarea, and two years' imprisonment until the new governor Festus reopened the case (AD 59). On appealing to Caesar, he was sent to Rome as a prisoner. After shipwreck (Acts 27), he probably arrived in AD 60, and spent two years under house arrest (Acts 28: 30).

The authentic epistles reveal more than Acts about Paul's character, though perhaps less than at first sight appears, because rhetorical conventions account for some of the pathos and Rom. 7 is no longer considered autobiographical. But a clear picture does emerge of Paul's apostolic self-consciousness, something of his religion, including *ecstacy (2 Cor. 12: 2–4), and especially his main convictions. These are coherent, though marshalled in different ways to argue a case or provide encouragement.

THEOLOGY. Paul was a phrase-maker, who wrote rhetorically powerful and theologically profound letters. Contrary to his own wishes, his understanding of what he called 'the gospel (of God)' accelerated the separation of the messianic sect from mainstream Judaism. His insistence that the crucified and risen Christ rather than Torah was decisive for all believers in their relationship to God made that schism inevitable and permanent. He maintained without question his earlier beliefs about God and the revelation of God in the Law and the Prophets, but the new factor was what God was doing now. Having sent His Son (Gal. 4: 4, Rom. 8: 3) God was rescuing Gentiles as well as Jews from the present evil age by transferring

them into the age to come which was dawning with the resurrection of the crucified *Messiah, and would soon transform the world. A variety of symbolism is used to describe this salvation event and process.

The decisive factor in Paul's messianic Judaism was thus the arrival and identity of the Messiah, 'Jesus Christ our Lord', whose death he understood as a sacrifice, as did those who were already followers before him (1 Cor. 15: 3), and whose resurrection was the first-fruits and beginning of the general resurrection inaugurating the new creation. Believers are through *Baptism (symbolically) united with Him (Rom. 6: 3–5), incorporated into Him, and so are 'in Christ'. This common phrase refers back to the person whose death and resurrection constitute the *eschatological event and describes the relationship between the believers and God through Christ in a quasi-spatial or locative way. That intimate unity of the believer and Lord can be described by other metaphors. Believers are Christ's body (1 Cor. 12: 27), one body in Christ (Rom. 12: 5), and this idea lends itself to expressing the unity and functional diversity of the Christian community (1 Cor. 12: 12 ff.). That unity in Christ can also be expressed through the metaphor of 'putting on' Christ like a garment. In Christ distinctions of race, gender, and social status are no longer germane (Gal. 3: 27 f.; cf. 1 Cor. 12: 13).

One who was baptized 'into' Christ had received the Spirit, another indicator of the new age fundamental to the self-understanding of the early Church. Paul so personalizes the *Holy Spirit that it is sometimes hard to distinguish between the Spirit and the risen Lord (Rom. 8: 9–11 and possibly 2 Cor. 3: 17). He draws out the moral significance of this experience of sonship by adoption and sees in the Spirit the basis and motor of the Christian life (Gal. 5, Rom. 8). The Spirit both sheds God's love in the believer's heart (Rom. 5: 5) and bears fruit in love, joy, peace, etc. (Gal. 5: 22). He is the guarantee of future glory and enables the believer to endure the sufferings of the present age in hope.

Because Paul's surviving letters are directed to believers, usually to Churches he has recently founded, they contain more moral admonition than doctrinal instruction. But it is typical of Paul the theologian that he rarely offers advice or encouragement without rooting it in the gospel and so giving expression to his fundamental convictions. He constantly roots the moral imperative in the reality of Christian experience and describes that as an unseen present and a future hope. He adds persuasive force to his moral exhortations by contrasting this 'now you are' with a 'once you were'.

Paul's picture of human existence outside Christ is negative. The world is under judgement and needs God's liberating intervention. This is explored in Rom. as part of an argument that all, Jews and Gentiles alike, are in the same predicament and rescued in the same way—by faith in Christ. Paul's language about God's 'putting right' on this basis (*justification) is drawn from Scripture, using language perhaps taken from Is. 53: 11 and already current among Jewish Christians. Paul combined this language about being 'right with God' with his basic Christian vocabulary of 'faith' (in Christ) by quoting Hab. 2: 4 and Gen. 15: 6 in order to construct an argument against those who insisted on Gentile converts becoming Jewish proselytes. All are put right, like *Abraham, on the basis of faith, not Jewish religious practice ('works of the law').

Although this terminology was drawn from Scripture for the purpose of a particular argument against Judaizers, it is clear from Gal. 2: 16–21 and Phil. 3: 5–11 how well it articulates Paul's own experience of God's saving action in Christ and the appropriate response of faith which includes hope, obedience, trust, confidence, and confession. What this gospel meant for the Law and the Jewish people was bound to be not only personally important for Paul but also theologically urgent. Nothing less than God's consistency was at stake. The discussion of these matters in Rom. is therefore the clearest expression of Paul's theology. Outside the sharply polemical context of Gal., he is able to insist on the positive function of the Law without loosening his central conviction that faith in Christ is alone decisive for salvation of Jews and Gentiles alike. He is also able to be positive about the privileges once given to Israel without leaving room for boasting in them, and he looks forward to God's ultimate inclusion of all Israel in salvation (Rom. 11: 26).

INFLUENCE. Paul's hope for historical Israel was soon lost and has only recently been retrieved as a basis for Jewish–Christian relations. His refusal to submit Gentile converts to circumcision, by contrast, contributed to the success of the Christian mission outside Judaism. His insistence that 'the truth of the gospel' required only faith in Christ and the life in the Spirit which flows from that secured Christianity's identity as a new religion worshipping the same God of Israel, only now 'through Jesus Christ our Lord'.

The collection of his surviving letters and their inclusion in Christian Scripture gave Paul a different kind of influence. His rhetoric has helped to shape the faith of millions who have not understood his arguments, and his arguments have proved fertile even when misunderstood. Many of his metaphors have lent themselves to doctrinal elaboration. For example, his genuine epistles barely make explicit an ecclesiology, but phrases such as 'body of Christ' were developed by others. Outside its original context Paul's scriptural argument associating righteousness with 'faith not works' attracted little attention except where 'works' were understood in new, not strictly Pauline ways.

The polemical contrast drawn by Paul between the old and the new way of salvation was usually weakened into a smooth development from promise to fulfilment. *Marcion, however, took it to cut out the Jewish roots of Christianity. Similarly, where Paul's realism about the constraints of living in a still unredeemed world was lost, his antithesis between faith and works could lead to *antinomianism. This claim that Christian community and the hope of salvation no longer depend on observing the Mosaic law taught St *Augustine that the gospel is a matter of grace or gift, and Christian morality life in the Spirit. That bulwark against moralism is true to Paul even if Paul himself did not intend 'works' to refer to morality. Augustine's anti-Pelagian theology of *grace was not generally followed to the extremes which threaten human free will and undercut morality, but it largely determined the course of W. medieval theology. The negative implications of Paul's 'apart from the works of the law' found their most powerful application in M. *Luther's doctrine of justification by faith alone. Augustine's doctrine of

*predestination, based on Rom. 9, was less influential, but was also continued by the Reformers, esp. in J. *Calvin's 'double predestination'. The E. Fathers reduced this element in Paul to divine foreknowledge, and W. humanism later agreed. But W. anthropology and notably the doctrine of *original sin still owe much to Augustine's interpretation of Rom. 5 and 7.

The W. Church's preoccupation with this part of Paul's vocabulary has brought its own distortions. It allowed legal categories an unwarranted centrality in medieval Christian thinking and has supported too easily the modern tendency to make humanity the centre of theology. In both cases the new historical exegesis advocated from the 17th cent. by H. *Grotius, J. *Locke, and others has introduced correctives from within Paul's own writing. As historical criticism was developed in the late 18th and esp. the 19th cent., notably by F. C. *Baur, Paul as known from his epistles has been the central figure in reconstructions of Christian origins. This shift of focus later weakened theological reflection on his teaching, and that in turn provoked the neo-Reformation reaction of K. *Barth, which R. *Bultmann and his successors fused with the 'history of religions' research (*Religionsgeschichtliche Schule) of their liberal Protestant teachers. Today intellectually responsible study of Paul is based on linguistic and historical study, sometimes enriched by literary and sociological insights. But the epistles are still most widely known through the conceptual frameworks provided by Christian tradition, and the Apostle himself through the idealized narrative of Acts.

A joint feast for SS Peter and Paul is observed in E. and W. on 29 June, in addition to the Feast of the *Conversion of St Paul on 25 Jan. in the W. A further commemoration of St Paul on 30 June was dropped from the RC Calendar in 1969.

The first modern treatment is F. C. Baur, *Paulus, der Apostel Jesu Christ* (1845; Eng. tr., 2 vols., 1873–5). W. M. *Ramsay, *St Paul the Traveller and the Roman Citizen* (1895) and other works; W. *Wrede, *Paulus* (1905; Eng. tr., 1907); A. *Deissmann, *Paulus* (1911; 2nd edn., 1925; Eng. tr., 1926); K. *Lake, *The Earlier Epistles of St Paul: Their Motive and Origin* (1911); P. Gardner, *The Religious Experience of St Paul* (1911); W. L. Knox, *St Paul and the Church of Jerusalem* (1925); id., *St Paul* (1932); A. D. Nock, *St Paul* (1938); W. L. Knox, *St Paul and the Church of the Gentiles* (1939); J. Knox, *Chapters in a Life of Paul* (1954; rev. edn., 1989); G. Ogg, *The Chronology of the Life of Paul* (1966); G. Bornkamm, *Paulus* (Stuttgart, 1969; Eng. tr., 1971). F. F. Bruce, *Paul: Apostle of the Free Spirit* (Exeter [1977]); L. E. Keck, *Paul and his Letters* (Philadelphia [1979]); R. Jewett, *Dating Paul's Life* (in USA and Canada, *A Chronology of Paul's Life*, 1979); G. Lüdemann, *Paulus, der Heidenapostel* (Forschungen zur Religion und Literatur des Alten und Neuen Testaments, 123, 130, etc.; 1980 ff.; Eng. tr., 1984 ff.); J. C. Beker, *Paul the Apostle: The Triumph of God in Life and Thought* (Philadelphia [1980]); W. A. Meeks, *The First Urban Christians: The Social World of the Apostle Paul* (New Haven, Conn., and London [1983]); H. W. Tajra, *The Trial of St Paul: A Juridical Exegesis of the Second Half of the Acts of the Apostles* (Wissenschaftliche Untersuchungen zum Neuen Testament, 2. Reihe, 35; 1989); A. F. Segal, *Paul the Convert: The Apostolate and Apostasy of Saul the Pharisee* (New Haven, Conn., and London [1990]); J. Becker, *Paulus: Der Apostel der Völker* (Tübingen, 1990; Eng. tr., Louisville, Ky., 1993); J. Murphy-O'Connor, *Paul: A Critical Life* (Oxford, 1996). Among studies in his theology: O. Pfleiderer, *Der Paulinismus* (1873; Eng. tr., 2 vols., 1877); C. A. A. Scott, *Christianity* according to St Paul (1927); A. *Schweitzer, Die Mystik des Apostels Paulus (1930; Eng. tr., The Mysticism of Paul the Apostle, 1931); R. Bultmann, Theologie des Neuen Testaments (3 parts, Tübingen, 1948–53; Eng. tr., 2 vols., 1952–5); C. K. Barrett, From First Adam to Last: A Study in Pauline Theology (1962); H. [N.] Ridderbos, Paulus: Ontwerp van zijn Theologie (Kampen, 1966; Eng. tr., 1977); K. Stendahl, Paul among Jews and Gentiles (Philadelphia [1976]; London, 1977); E. P. Sanders, Paul and Palestinian Judaism (1977); id., Paul, the Law and the Jewish People (Philadelphia [1983]; London, 1985); H. Räisänen, Paul and the Law (Wissenschaftliche Untersuchungen zum Neuen Testament, 29; 1983; 2nd edn., 1987); J. A. Ziesler, Pauline Christianity (Oxford Bible Series, 1983; rev. 1990). Studies on special subjects: O. Pfleiderer, The Influence of the Apostle Paul (1885, *Hibbert Lectures); A. Schweitzer, Geschichte der paulinischen Forschung von der Reformation bis auf die Gegenwart (1911; Eng. tr., Paul and his Interpreters, 1912). H. A. A. Kennedy, St Paul and the Mystery-Religions (1913); W. D. Davies, Paul and Rabbinic Judaism (1948); L. Cerfaux, Le Christ dans la théologie de saint Paul (1951; Eng. tr., 1959); J. Munck, Paulus und die Heilsgeschichte (Acta Jutland-ica, 26. 1; 1954; Eng. tr., 1959); H. J. Schoeps, Paulus: Die Theologie des Apostels im Lichte der jüdischen Religionsgeschichte (Tübingen, 1959; Eng. tr., 1961); V. P. Furnish, Theology and Ethics in Paul (Nashville [1968]); R. B. Hays, Echoes of Scripture in the Letters of Paul (New Haven, Conn., and London [1989]). See also bibl. to ACTS OF THE APOSTLES.

Paul, Acts of St. An apocryphal Book, written in Greek and put into circulation in the latter half of the 2nd cent. Unlike most apocryphal 'Acts', it appears to have been the work of an orthodox Christian. It was compiled in Asia Minor, and is contained in its completest form in Coptic in a Heidelberg papyrus which C. Schmidt pieced together in 1904 from some 2,000 fragments. Its reconstruction proved that a number of short treatises which had circulated independently and had been known to earlier scholars were all parts of this single work, among them the 'Martyrdom of St Paul', the 'Acts of *Paul and Thecla', and possibly the 'Third Ep. of St Paul to the *Corinthians' (qq.v.). Several passages of the Gk. text have long been known, the most important of them one pub. by C. Schmidt in 1936 from the Hamburg Public Library. It is now established that the work made use of the 'Acts of St *Peter'. The Acts, which were designed to glorify St Paul's achievements, incorporate legendary material circulating in the 2nd cent., as well as material which may reflect NT influence. The author, however, had little regard for historical truth, and it was doubtless the romancing character of the Acts rather than any heretical bias in their teaching that caused him, as *Tertullian relates (De Baptismo, 17), to be deprived of his office of presbyter. The Acts were used by *Origen, *Hippolytus, and *Cyprian.

Older edn. of texts in R. A. *Lipsius and M. Bonnet (eds.), Acta Apostolorum Apocrypha, 1 (Leipzig, 1891), pp. 23–44, 104–17, and 235–72. Coptic text ed. C. Schmidt, Acta Pauli aus der Heidelberger koptischen Papyrushandschrift Nr. 1 (1904; with facsimile in separate Tafelband, 1904, and Zusätze, 1905); id., 'Ein neues Fragment der Heidelberger Acta Pauli', Sb. (Berl.), 1909, pp. 216–20; id., ΠΡΑΞΕΙΣ ΠΑΥΛΟΥ (Veröffentlichungen aus der Hamburger Staats- und Universitäts-Bibliothek, NF 2; 1936). Further frag. ed. G. D. Kilpatrick and C. H. Roberts in JTS 47 (1946), pp. 196–9. Two further frags. among the *Bodmer papyri described by R. Kasser in Revue d'Histoire et de Philosophie religieuses, 40 (1960), pp. 45–57. Crit. edn. by W. Rordorf (CC, Series Apocrypha, in preparation). Eng. tr. in J. K. Elliott, The Apocryphal New Testament (Oxford, 1993), pp. 350–89. Ger. tr. in

Schneemelcher, 2 (5th edn., 1989), pp. 214–43, with introd. by W. Schneemelcher, pp. 193–214; Eng. tr., 2 [1992] pp. 213–70, incl. Eng. tr. of text. L. Vouaux, Les Actes de Paul et ses lettres apocryphes: Introduction, textes, traduction et commentaire (1913). E. Peterson, 'Einige Bemerkungen zum Hamburger Papyrusfragment der Acta Pauli', VC 3 (1949), pp. 142–62.

Paul, Apocalypse of St. An apocryphal apocalypse, written in Greek and dating from the latter half of the 4th cent., which describes in detail what St *Paul saw when he was taken up into the 'third heaven' (2 Cor. 12: 2). It narrates that St Paul was led into paradise, where in the city of God he met all the blessed—in one quarter the *Prophets, in another the *Holy Innocents, in another *Abraham, *Isaac, and *Jacob, and in the fourth those who had wholeheartedly devoted themselves to God. The treatise, which was known to St *Augustine (c.416), became very popular as a source for ideas about the afterlife, and it was translated into Latin, Syriac, Coptic, and Ethiopic. It also enjoyed a great vogue in the Middle Ages, being quoted by *Dante (Inferno, 2. 28). It is to be distinguished from both the 'Apocalypse of Paul' discovered in a Coptic version at *Nag Hammadi, and from the 'Ascension of Paul' mentioned by St *Epiphanius (Haer. 38. 2) as a *Gnostic writing; of this last nothing survives.

Gk. text in C. *Tischendorf, Apocalypses Apocryphae (Leipzig, 1866), pp. 34–69. Crit. edn. by M. R. James (ed.), Apocrypha Anecdota (Texts and Studies, 2, no. 3; Cambridge, 1893), pp. 11–42. Syr. text ed. G. Riciotti in Orientalia, 2 (Rome, 1933), pp. 1–25, 120–49. Lat. text ed. in several recensions, with full discussion, by T. Silverstein (Studies and Documents, ed. K. *Lake and S. Lake, 4; 1935); id., 'The Vision of Saint Paul: New Links and Patterns in the Western Tradition', AHDLMA 26 (for 1959; 1960), pp. 199–248, incl. further texts. Eng. tr. in J. K. Elliott, The Apocryphal New Testament (Oxford, 1993), pp. 616–44. Ger. tr., with introd. by H. Duensing and A. de Santos Otero, in Schneemelcher, 2 (5th edn., 1989), pp. 644–75; Eng. tr., 2 [1992], pp. 712–48. R. P. Casey, 'The Apocalypse of Paul', JTS 34 (1933), pp. 1–32. J. Quasten, Patrology, 1 (Utrecht, 1950), pp. 146–9. Ger. tr. of the Nag Hammadi Apocalypse of Paul, with introd. by W.-P. Funk, in Schneemelcher, 2 (5th edn., 1989), pp. 628–33; Eng. tr. 2 [1992] pp. 695–700.

Paul, Clerks Regular of St. See BARNABITES.

Paul, Martyrdom of St. An apocryphal account of the death of St *Paul dating from the latter part of the 2nd cent. It forms the concluding section of the 'Acts of St *Paul' (q.v.). It describes how Paul was brought into the presence of *Nero at Rome, sentenced to death, and led to execution by the prefect, Longus, and the centurion, Cestus (who were converted). Two of the Greek MSS containing the 'Martyrdom' also include the 'Acts of St *Peter'.

Two Gk. texts with a Lat. tr. in R. A. *Lipsius and M. Bonnet (eds.), Acta Apostolorum Apocrypha, 1 (Leipzig, 1891), pp. 104–17. Eng. tr. in J. K. Elliott, The Apocryphal New Testament (Oxford, 1993), pp. 385–8; also in Schneemelcher, 2 (Eng. tr. [1992]), pp. 260–3. For further items see bibl. to PAUL, ACTS OF ST.

Paul III (1468–1549), Pope from 1534. Alessandro Farnese was educated at Rome and Florence at the court of Lorenzo the Magnificent, and created cardinal-deacon by *Alexander VI in 1493. He held numerous benefices, among them the bishoprics of Parma and Ostia, became

Dean of the Sacred College under *Leo X, and was unanimously elected to the Papacy on 13 Oct. 1534. Though in his personal life a typical Renaissance Pope—he had three sons and a daughter, was much given to worldly pleasures, and indulged in unlimited nepotism—he was an efficient promoter of the inner reform of the Church. He created as cardinals men of virtue and scholarship such as R. *Pole, G. P. Carafa (later *Paul IV), and G. *Morone, established ecclesiastical commissions to draw up plans for the reform of the Church, and favoured the new orders, e.g. the *Ursulines, the *Barnabites, and esp. the *Jesuits which he approved in 1540 by the bull '*Regimini militantis Ecclesiae'. In 1542 he restored the *Inquisition, and above all fought hard against the opposition to a General Council which finally opened at *Trent in 1545. He was, however, less successful in his political efforts to check the spread of Protestantism. The religious colloquies in Germany and the wars of the Emperor whom he supported could not restore unity, and the bull which he published against *Henry VIII in 1538 alienated England still further from Rome. His last years were darkened by the death of his son and the revolt of his grandson, Ottavio, who took the part of the Emperor against him. Like his immediate predecessors, Paul III was a friend of art and scholarship. He appointed prominent theologians to the chairs of the Roman University, enriched the *Vatican Library with valuable MSS, and made *Michelangelo architect-in-chief of *St Peter's.

The best collection of his bulls is that in the *Bullarum Diplomatum et Privilegiorum Sanctorum Romanorum Pontificum Taurinensis Editio*, 6 (Turin, 1860), pp. 173–401. There is a good modern study by C. Capasso (2 vols., Messina, 1923–4 [on wrappers '1925']). L. Cardauns, 'Paul III, Karl V und Franz I in den Jahren 1535 und 1536', *Quellen und Forschungen aus italienischen Archiven und Bibliotheken herausgegeben vom koenigl. Preussischen Historischen Institut in Rom*, 11 (1908), pp. 147–244. L. Dorez, *La Cour du Pape Paul III d'après les registres de la Trésorerie Secrète* (*Collection F. de Navenne*) (2 vols., 1932). W. Friedensburg, *Kaiser Karl V und Papst Paul III* (Schriften des Vereins für Reformationsgeschichte, no. 153; 1932). W. H. Edwards, *Paulus III oder die geistliche Gegenreformation* (1933). Pastor, 11 and 12 (1912), with full bibl. J. F. Loughlin in *CE* 11 (1911), pp. 579–81, s.v.; L. Marchal in *DTC* 12 (pt. 1; 1933), cols. 9–20, s.v., with detailed bibl.; C. L. Hohl in *NCE* 11 (1967), pp. 13 f. See also bibl. to TRENT, COUNCIL OF.

Paul IV (1476–1559), Pope from 1555. Giovanni Pietro (Giampietro) Carafa came of a distinguished Neapolitan family. Having been brought by his uncle, Oliviero Carafa (1430–1511), into close relations with the *Curia, he became possessed from early life with a keen enthusiasm for the reform of abuses. From 1504 to 1524 he was Bp. of Chieti (Theate), sitting in 1520 on the commission at Rome appointed to deal with the affair of M. *Luther. In 1524 he resigned his bishopric in order to found, in conjunction with St *Cajetan, the *Theatine Order, which was named after him and in which he continued to be one of the chief movers. In 1536 he became Abp. of Naples and was created cardinal, and in 1542 he reorganized the *Inquisition. Finally in 1555 he was elected Pope. Despite his age he acted with great determination, though his actions in his later years seem to have been motivated more by the desire to advance his relatives than by devotion to the highest needs of the Church. His unpopularity was increased by his political sympathies, hatred of Spain making him quarrel with *Mary Tudor; and his opposition to anything savouring of *Protestantism was so violent that he even had cardinals brought before the Inquisition.

The best collection of his bulls is that in the *Bullarum Diplomatum et Privilegiorum Sanctorum Romanorum Pontificum Taurinensis Editio*, 6 (Turin, 1860), pp. 489–566. R. Ancel, OSB (ed.), *Nonciatures de France: Nonciatures de Paul IV* [to 4 July 1557] (Archives de l'Histoire Religieuse de la France, 2 vols., 1909–11). A. Caraccioli, *Collectanea Historica de Vita Pauli Quarti* (Cologne, 1612). C. Bromato, Theatine, *Storia di Paolo IV* (2 vols., Ravenna, 1748–53). G. M. Monti, *Ricerche su Paolo IV Carafa* (Benevento, 1923; repr. Turin, 1980). G. Duruy, *Le Cardinal Carlo Carafa (1519–1561): Étude sur le pontificat de Paul IV* (1882). L. Riess, *Die Politik Pauls IV und seiner Nepoten* (Historische Studien, 67; 1909). There is also a series of important arts. by R. Ancel, listed in *DTC* (see below). Pastor, 14 (1924), pp. 56–426, with full bibl. to date of German edn. G. Mollat in *DTC* 12 (pt. 1; 1933), cols. 20–3, s.v., with detailed bibl.; H. Jedin in *EC* 9 (1952), cols. 736–8, s.v. 'Paolo IV'; F. Andreu, Theatine, in *DIP* 2 (1973), cols. 256–61, s.v. 'Carafa, Gian Pietro', with bibl.

Paul V (1552–1621), Pope from 1605. Camillo Borghese was a descendant of a noble Sienese family. He studied law at Perugia and Padua, was created Cardinal in 1596, Papal Vicar in 1603, and elected and crowned Pope in May 1605. The first years of his reign were troubled by the conflict with *Venice, whose government had attacked ecclesiastical immunities and liberties by promulgating two laws (1604 and 1605) which forbade the erection of religious buildings without the consent of the Senate and the donation or sale of secular property to the Church. After a refusal to repeal these laws, the Pope excommunicated the Senate and put the city under the *interdict. In the theological controversy which ensued, he was defended by R. *Bellarmine and C. *Baronius against the *Servite, P. *Sarpi, who in the interests of Venice denied all temporal power and privileges to the Church. About the same time the English question became once more acute in consequence of the Oath of Allegiance required by *James I, which the Pope condemned in two Briefs in 1606 and 1607. This step gave rise to a dispute between the archpriest, G. *Blackwell, who defended the Oath, and the *Jesuits, who insisted on the right of the Pope to depose kings, and later between James I himself and Bellarmine. In his Continental policy Paul V preserved a neutral attitude between the two rival powers France and Spain, whom he tried to reconcile in order to present a united Christian front to the Turks. After futile efforts at re-establishing the Roman Church in Russia, he lived to see the beginnings of the *Thirty Years War in Germany. He died of a stroke soon after the celebrations of the Catholic victory in the Battle of the White Mountain. A man of blameless life (except for his nepotism) and a skilful canonist, he endeavoured from the beginning of his reign to enforce the decrees of the Council of *Trent. He fostered the work of the Congregations devoted to education and care of the sick as well as the missions, notably those in *Africa and *Canada; and many popular saints were canonized or beatified by him, among them *Charles Borromeo and *Frances of Rome. He was greatly devoted to the city of Rome, among the works which he carried through being the completion of *St Peter's and the extension of the *Vatican Library.

Life by A. Bzovius, OP (Rome, 1626). [C. P. Goujet], *Histoire du pontificat de Paul V* (2 vols., Amsterdam, 1765). E. Cornet, *Paolo e la Repubblica Veneta: Giornale dal 22 ottobre 1605–9 giugno 1607. Corredato di note e documenti* (Vienna, 1859). P. Pirri, SJ, *L'interdetto di Venezia del 1606 e i Gesuiti: Silloge di documenti con introduzione* (Bibliotheca Instituti Historici S.I., 14; 1959). A. Nürnberger, 'Papst Paul V und das venezianische Interdict', *Hist. J.* 4 (1883), pp. 189–209 and 473–515; id., 'Documente zum Ausgleich zwischen Paul V und der Republik Venedig', *RQ* 2 (1888), pp. 64–80, 248–76, and 354–67. C. P. de Magistris, *Per la storia del componimento della contesa tra la Repubblica Veneta e Paolo V, 1605–1607: Documenti* (posthumously pub., Turin, 1941). J. M. Pou y Marti, OFM, 'La intervención española en el conflicto entre Paulo V y Venecia (1605–1607)', *Miscellanea Pio Paschini*, 2 (Lateranum, NS 15; 1949), pp. 359–81. W. Reinhard, *Papstfinanz und Nepotismus unter Paul V.* (Päpste und Papsttum, 6; 2 vols., 1974). On his nepotism, see also V. Reinhardt, *Kardinal Scipione Borghese (1605–1633): Vermögen, Finanzen und sozialer Aufstieg eines Papstnepoten* (Bibliothek des Deutschen Historischen Instituts in Rom, 58; 1984). Pastor, 25 and 26 (1937), with full bibl. to date of Ger. edn. J. F. Loughlin in *CE* 11 (1911), pp. 581 f., s.v.; L. Marchal in *DTC* 12 (pt. 1; 1933), cols. 23–37, s.v., with detailed bibl. G. B. Picotti in *EC* 9 (1952), cols. 738–41, s.v. 'Paolo V'. See also bibl. to SARPI, P.

Paul VI (1897–1978), Pope from 1963. Giovanni Battista Montini, the son of a parliamentary delegate and editor of a Catholic newspaper, *Il Cittadino di Brescia*, was a delicate child; he was educated at home and attended the diocesan seminary only as circumstances permitted. After his ordination in 1920 he went to the Sapienza and then the *Gregorianum in Rome. Apart from a few months at the nunciature in Warsaw in 1923, he held office in the Papal Secretariat of State from 1922 for over 30 years. In 1931 he became a domestic prelate and in 1938 he accompanied E. Pacelli (the future *Pius XII) to the *Eucharistic Congress at Budapest. After the death of L. Maglione, the Secretary of State, in 1944, Pius XII appointed no successor and Montini, as pro-secretary for the internal business of the Church, discharged his business directly under the Pope. In this capacity he was responsible for Papal relief work, and he played a large part in the organization of the *Holy Year in 1950 and the Marian Year in 1954. His appointment as Abp. of Milan in 1954, involving his departure from Rome, is sometimes thought to have been due to internal Vatican politics. In Milan he did much to restore and rebuild churches destroyed during the Second World War, as well as trying to deal with the acute social problems of a highly industrialized diocese. In 1958, on the death of Pius XII, his name was widely mentioned as a candidate for the Papacy. Pope *John XXIII, shortly after his election, created Montini a Cardinal; he continually brought him forward at the Second *Vatican Council, and during the first session Montini was a member of the Secretariat appointed to examine the questions raised by members of the Council. On the death of John XXIII in 1963 he was elected Pope. He quickly promised to continue the Council and declared his intention of pursuing the same policy as his predecessor.

Within three weeks of his election he convened the Second Session of the Vatican Council, which he opened on 29 Sept. 1963. Before the opening of the Sessions he had issued a revised *Ordo Concilii* to expedite business, and he introduced a number of procedural reforms, such as the admission of laymen as auditors and the establish-ment of a press committee. In Nov. 1963 he enlarged the Conciliar Commissions to make them more representative. Before the meeting of the Third Session in 1964, he also admitted some women, both religious and lay, as auditors. He refused to intervene in the Third Session when he was asked to overrule a decision postponing a vote on the schema on religious liberty, but on his own authority he modified the Decree on Ecumenism and he declared the BVM 'Mother of the Church' despite the fact that the fathers of the Council had refused to attribute the title to her. He also directed that an explanatory note ('*nota praevia*') be added to the text of the 1964 constitution on the Church containing important clarifications. At the Fourth Session he announced that he was establishing a permanent 'Synod of Bishops', which would have deliberative as well as consultative powers at the Pope's discretion. At the close of the Council he proclaimed an extraordinary Jubilee or Holy Year, to be observed from 1 Jan. to *Whitsunday (29 May) 1966, in order that the faithful might be familiarized with the teaching of the Council and the life of the Church renewed. [For the decrees of the Council, see VATICAN COUNCIL, SECOND.]

Paul VI established a number of post-conciliar Commissions to put into effect the wishes of the Council and confirmed the permanent Secretariats for the Promotion of Christian Unity, for Non-Christian Religions, and for Non-Believers. The most far-reaching reforms of his pontificate were effected largely through the working of these Commissions, most notably the publication of a new *Missal in 1970, with its accompanying *lectionary, and a new *Breviary in 1971, which together involved a reordering of the Mass and *Office; these changes coincided with the introduction of the use of the vernacular. Other reforms, such as that of the *Codex Iuris Canonici, were put in hand, though this was completed only under *John Paul II. Paul VI's own encyclicals generally appeared more conservative; the most important include *Mysterium Fidei* (3 Sept. 1965) reaffirming the traditional doctrine of the Eucharist, *Sacerdotalis coelibatus* (24 June 1967), insisting on the need for priestly *celibacy, and *Humanae Vitae* (25 July 1968) condemning artificial methods of birth control. However, he also dealt with social, economic, and political issues in *Populorum Progressio* (16 March 1967). After 1968 he had to face growing tensions within the Church; the demand for celibacy was challenged and many religious sought secularization; there was widespread criticism of *Humanae Vitae*, and traditionalists, such as Abp. M. Lefebvre, refused to accept the conciliar reforms. In 1970 Paul VI proclaimed the first women, St *Teresa of Ávila and St *Catherine of Siena, *Doctors of the Church, but any idea of the ordination of women to the priesthood was firmly rejected. He also convened a number of episcopal synods on social and economic justice and on the priesthood (1971), evangelization (1974), and catechesis (1977).

In Jan. 1964 on a pilgrimage to the Holy Land he embraced *Athenagoras, the Oecumenical Patr. of Constantinople, in *Jerusalem, and at the close of the Vatican Council he took part in a historic gesture of friendship with the Eastern *Orthodox Church: before Mass on 7 Dec. 1965 a joint declaration was read in which Paul VI and Athenagoras expressed their mutual regret for the events of 1054, when Cardinal *Humbert of Silva Candida and Patr. *Michael Cerularius had excommunicated each other. After the Mass the Pope exchanged embraces with Athenagoras's envoy. With Anglicans and other Churches Paul VI fostered good relations. He received in Rome two Abps. of *Canterbury (A. M. *Ramsey and F. D. Coggan) and established the *Anglican–Roman Catholic International Commission. He also addressed the *World Council of Churches in Geneva in 1969. He was the first Pope to travel extensively abroad, going to New York to address the United Nations General Assembly in 1965 and visiting *Uganda in 1969 and the *Philippines and *Australia in 1970. He expanded the college of cardinals, making it a truly international body, and restricted the right of cardinals to vote in Papal elections to those under the age of 80. He also fixed a retirement age of bishops and clergy at 75. He reorganized the *Curia, reduced the ceremonial pomp of the Papacy and sold his tiara for the benefit of the poor. The cause for his beatification was opened on 11 May 1993.

Official docs. are pr. in the *AAS* for the years of his pontificate. *Insegnamenti di Paolo VI* (16 vols. + index to vols. 1–12, Vatican City, 1965–79; Fr. tr., *Documents Pontificaux de Paul VI*, 17 vols. + 3 vols. of index covering the whole pontificate, St-Maurice, Switzerland, 1967–83). N. Vian (ed.), *Anni e opere di Paolo VI* [1978]. *Paul VI et la modernité dans l'Église: Actes du Colloque organisé par l'École française de Rome (Rome 2–4 juin, 1983)* (Rome and Brescia, 1984). P. Hebblethwaite, *Paul VI: The First Modern Pope* (1993). P. Arató, SJ, and N. Vian, *Paulus PP. VI, 1963–1978: Elenchus Bibliographicus* (Pubblicazioni dell'Istituto Paolo VI, 1; Brescia, 1981). There are other specialized vols. in this series and in the series Quaderni dell'Istituto Paolo VI (ibid., 1981 ff.). A. Boland, SJ, in *Dict. Sp.* 12 (pt. 1; 1984), cols. 522–36, s.v.

Paul of Constantinople, St (d. 350). A native of
*Thessalonica, he succeeded Alexander in the see of *Constantinople in 336. He was soon displaced by the Arian *Macedonius, who had the support of the Emp. Constantius; and though he regained his see he was soon after removed again and went into exile in the W. Under pressure from Constans, the Emp. of the W., he again recovered his see, but after the death of Constans (350) he was once again exiled, first to Singara in Mesopotamia, then to Emesa, and finally to Cucusus in Armenia, where he was strangled. He was a zealous upholder of orthodoxy and a close associate of St *Athanasius and Pope *Julius. Feast day in E., 6 Nov.; in W., 7 June.

The literary refs. to Paul are scattered. W. Telfer, 'Paul of Constantinople', *HTR* 43 (1950), pp. 31–92, with refs.

Paul of the Cross, St (1694–1775), founder of the
*Passionists. Paul Francis Danei was the eldest son of a noble family whose fortunes had declined. He led a life of prayer and great austerity in the world until, in 1720, a vision inspired him to found a religious order in honour of the Passion of our Lord. In a 40-days' retreat he drew up its rule, which is in substance that still followed by his congregation. In 1725 *Benedict XIII encouraged him to receive novices and in 1727 ordained him and his brother priests. Paul then retired to Monte Argentario, where, faced with great difficulties (desertion of novices, threat of war), he laboured as a missionary among the people. In 1737 the first Passionist 'Retreat' was opened. The rule of the order was approved by *Benedict XIV in 1741. In

1744 Paul moved to the second house near Vetralla. By this time his position as Superior-General had been officially recognized. From 1769, apart from some visits to 'Retreats', he lived in Rome. He was one of the most celebrated preachers of his age, esp. on account of his stirring meditations on the Passion, and famous as a miracle-worker and spiritual director. He was canonized in 1867. Feast day, formerly 28 Apr., now 19 Oct.

Lettere di S. Paolo della Croce, ed. Amadeo della Madre del Buon Pastore, CP (4 vols., Rome, 1924). *Diario spirituale* also ed., with full introd., by E. Zoffoli, CP (Rome, 1964). Eng. tr. of extracts of his writings in M. Bialas, CP, *In this Sign . . .* (Ways of Prayer Series, 9; Dublin, 1984 [based partly on earlier Ger. tr.]). The primary Life is that by the Bl Vincenzo Maria Strambi, CP (Rome, 1786; Eng. tr., 'Saints and Servants of God', 2 vols., 1853). Modern studies incl. those by Pius a Spiritu Sancto [A. Devine], CP (Dublin and London, 1867; rev. edn., London, 1924), Gaëtan du S. Nom de Marie [J. Cajetan], CP (Tirlemont, 1934), Father Edmund [J. E. Burke], CP (Dublin, 1946), C. Almeras (Bruges, 1957; Eng. tr., New York, 1960), and E. Zoffoli, CP (3 vols., Rome, 1963–8). Gaëtan du S. Nom de Marie, *Oraison et ascension mystique de S. Paul de la Croix* (Museum Lessianum, 1930); id., *Doctrine de S. Paul de la Croix sur l'oraison et la mystique* (ibid., 1932). C. Brovetto, CP, *Introduzione alla Spiritualità di S. Paolo della Croce* (Studi e testi Passionisti, 1; 1955). M. Bialas, CP, *Das Leiden Christi beim hl. Paul vom Kreuz (1694–1775)* (Aschaffenburg, 1978; Eng. tr., San Francisco, 1990). A. Devine, CP, in *CE* 11 (1911), p. 590, s.v.; E. Zoffoli, CP, in *Bibliotheca Sanctorum*, 10 (Rome, 1968), cols. 231–57, s.v. 'Paolo della Croce'; F. Giorgini, CP, in *Dict. Sp.* 12 (pt. 1; 1984), cols. 540–60, s.v. 'Paul (5) de la Croix', the last two with extensive bibl. See also bibl. to PASSIONISTS.

Paul the Deacon (c.720–c.800), also 'Paulus Levita' or
'Warnefridi', 'Father of Italian History', chronicler. Of noble Lombard descent, he received an exceptionally good education, prob. at the court of Pavia, where he later taught Adelperga, the daughter of King Desiderius (756–74). At some time, perhaps c.760, Paul became a monk at *Monte Cassino. About 781 he visited *Charlemagne on behalf of a brother implicated in a revolt at Friuli in 776. Received with honour on account of his learning and culture, he remained in Francia until c.785 composing a history of the diocese of Metz ('Gesta Episcoporum Mettensium') and various didactic works. After his return to Monte Cassino he undertook his most important work, the 'Historia Gentis Langobardorum', an incomplete history in five books from 568 to the death of Luitprand (744). Based largely on documents no longer extant, it is the principal source for the Lombard history of the period, being esp. valuable for Franco-Lombard relations and its vivid picture of the life of the time. His 'Historia Romana', supplementing and continuing the 'Breviarium' of Eutropius to 553, which was undertaken at the request of Adelperga, is of much less historical value. In his later years he composed some important liturgical works, including a compilation of lessons for the Night Office and, at the request of Charlemagne, a collection of Homilies ('*Homiliary') which were ordered to be used throughout the Empire. He also wrote a Life of St *Gregory and various epitaphs and poems, although the famous hymn in honour of St John the Baptist ('Ut queant laxis', 'Let thine example', *EH* 223), ascribed to him, is prob. not his. An *Expositio super Regulam S. Benedicti* attributed to him has been shown to be the work of Hildemar (9th cent.).

Collection of his works in J. P. Migne, *PL* 95. 433–1710. Crit. edn. of his 'Historia Langobardorum' by L. Bethmann and G. Waitz in *MGH*, Scriptores Rerum Langobardicarum et Italicarum Saec. vi–ix (1879), pp. 12–187; and of Books 1–17 of his 'Historia Romana' by A. Crivellucci (Fonti per la Storia d'Italia, 51; 1914); of his poetry by K. Neff (Quellen und Untersuchungen zur lateinischen Philologie des Mittelalters, 3, Heft 4; 1908); and of his Life of Gregory I by H. Grisar, SJ, in *ZKT* 11 (1887), pp. 158–73. The Comm. on the Rule of St Benedict was first pub. by the monks of Monte Cassino (Monte Cassino, 1880). There is an Eng. tr. of his 'Historia Langobardorum' by W. D. Foulke (Philadelphia and New York, 1907). L. J. Engels, *Observations sur le vocabulaire de Paul Diacre* (Latinitas Christianorum Primaeva, 16; Nijmegen, 1961). [L.] Bethmann, 'Paulus Diaconus Leben und Schriften', *Archiv der Gesellschaft für ältere deutsche Geschichtkunde*, 10 (1851), pp. 247–334; id., 'Die Geschichtschreibung der Langobarden', ibid., pp. 335–414. P. S. Leicht, 'Paulo Diacono e gli altri scrittori delle Vicende d'Italia nell'età carolingia', in *Atti del 2° Congresso Internazionale di Studi sull'Alto Medioevo: Grado—Aquileia—Gorizia—Cividale—Udine, 7–11 settembre 1952* (Spoleto [1953]), pp. 57–74; see also contributions to this symposium by D. Bianchi, P. Lamma, A. Lentini, A. Pantoni, and I. Peri. D. A. Bullough, 'Ethnic History and the Carolingians: An Alternative Reading of Paul the Deacon's *Historia Langobardorum*', in C. Holdsworth and T. P. Wiseman (eds.), *The Inheritance of Historiography 350–900* (Exeter Studies in History, 12; 1986), pp. 85–105, repr., with emendations, in Bullough's *Carolingian Renewal: Sources and Heritage* (Manchester and New York, 1991), pp. 97–122. W. Goffart, *The Narrators of Barbarian History* (Princeton, NJ [1988]), pp. 329–431. K. Gamber, 'Il sacramentario di Paolo Diacono. La redazione del Gelasiano S. VIII in Pavia', *Rivista di storia della Chiesa in Italia*, 16 (1962), pp. 412–38. W. Hafner, *Das Basiliuskommentar zur Regula S. Benedicti: Ein Beitrag zur Autorenfrage karolingischer Regelkommentare* (Beiträge zur Geschichte des Alten Mönchtums und des Benediktinerordens, 23; 1959), *passim*. J. Szövérffy, *Die Annalen der lateinischen Hymnendichtung*, 1 (1964), pp. 186–9, with refs. J. Hourlier, OSB, in *Dict. Sp.* 12 (pt. 1; 1984), cols. 560–2, s.v.

Paul the Hermit, St. See PAUL OF THEBES, ST.

Paul of Samosata (3rd cent.), heretical Bp. of *Antioch. He was a native of Samosata, who acquired considerable wealth. About 260 he became Bp. of Antioch, though he preferred to be called, and perhaps was, a *procurator ducenarius*. His teaching on the Person of Christ was condemned at two, or possibly three, Synods of Antioch and in 268 he was deposed from his see. Although there are conflicting reports, he seems to have taught a form of Dynamic *Monarchianism, acc. to which the Word was simply an attribute of the Father, His reason or power (δύναμις). It is clear that in his Christology Paul was an *Adoptianist, holding that in the Incarnation the Word descended on and dwelt in the man Jesus, who thus became 'Son of God'. His use of the term '*Homoousios' to deny that the Word was a *hypostasis separate from the Father seems to have been condemned. Later he was regarded by the opponents of *Nestorius as his predecessor. The chief sources for the conflict are: (1) a synodal letter of the Antiochene Synod of 268, partly preserved by *Eusebius (*HE* 7. 30); (2) a stenographic report of a disputation at this Synod between Paul and an *Origenist presbyter of Antioch named Malchion; and (3) the so-called 'Hymenaeus Epistle', a letter addressed to Paul by Hymenaeus and five other bishops. The extant fragments of Paul's 'Addresses to Sabinus' are probably fabrications. Paul's followers ('*Paulianists'; q.v.) long survived his death.

G. Bardy, *Paul de Samosate: Étude historique* (SSL 4; 1923; new edn., 1929); F. *Loofs, *Paulus von Samosata* (TU 40, Heft 5; 1924); H. de Riedmatten, OP, *Les Actes du procès de Paul de Samosate: Étude sur la christologie du III° au IV° siècle* (Paradosis, 6; 1952). Collection of frags. in H. de Riedmatten, op. cit., pp. 135–58. E. *Schwartz, *Eine fingierte Korrespondenz mit Paulus dem Samosatener* (*Sb.* (Bayr.), 1927, Heft 3). P. Galtier [SJ], 'L'ὁμοούσιος de Paul de Samosate', *Rech. S.R.* 12 (1922), pp. 30–45. M. Richard, 'Malchion et Paul de Samosate. Le Témoignage d'Eusèbe de Césarée', *Ephemerides Theologicae Lovanienses*, 35 (1959), pp. 325–38, repr. in his *Opera Minora*, 2 (Turnhout and Louvain, 1977), no. 25. F. Millar, 'Paul of Samosata, Zenobia and Aurelian: The Church, Local Culture and Political Allegiance in Third-Century Syria', *Journal of Roman Studies*, 61 (1971), pp. 1–17; F. W. Norris, 'Paul of Samosata: Procurator Ducenarius', *JTS* NS 35 (1984), pp. 50–70. M. Simonetti, 'Per la Rivalutazione di alcune Testimonianze su Paolo di Samosata', *Rivista di Storia e Letteratura Religiosa*, 24 (1988), pp. 177–210. Altaner and Stuiber (1978), pp. 214 and 591. G. Bardy in *DTC* 12 (pt. 1; 1933), cols. 46–51; M. Simonetti in *DPAC* 2 (1984), cols. 2633–5, s.v.; Eng. tr. in *Encyclopedia of the Early Church*, 2 (Cambridge, 1992), p. 663.

Paul the Silentiary. See PAULUS SILENTIARIUS.

Paul of Thebes, St (d. *c*.340), traditionally the first Christian hermit. Acc. to St *Jerome's *Vita Pauli*, the sole authority, Paul was a native of the Thebaid. During the *Decian persecution (249–51) he fled to the desert, where he lived for some hundred years a life of prayer and penitence in a cave. St *Antony is said to have visited him when 113 years old and later to have buried him, wrapping him in the mantle which he had himself received from St *Athanasius.

The details of this narrative, which find no corroboration from other sources, are open to considerable suspicion. In later art, Paul is commonly represented with a palm tree or two lions. Feast day, 15 Jan.

Jerome's *Vita Pauli* (J. P. Migne, *PL* 23. 17–28) is prob. the source of the various Gk. and oriental Lives; cf. J. Bidez, *Deux versions grecques inédites de la vie de Paul de Thèbes, publiées avec une introduction* (Ghent, 1900). On his possible identification with a 'Paul of Oxyrhynchus' cf. H. *Delehaye, SJ, 'La Personnalité historique de S. Paul de Thèbes', *Anal. Boll.* 44 (1926), pp. 64–9.

Paul and Thecla, Acts of Sts. An apocryphal work describing the adventures of Sts *Paul and *Thecla, which was part of the 'Acts of St *Paul' (q.v.). Its great popularity in the early Church is shown by its existence not only in the original Greek, but also in five separate Latin translations, as well as in Syriac, Armenian, Slavonic, and Arabic. The 'Acts' describe how St Paul, after his flight from Antioch in Pisidia (Acts 13: 51), arrived at Iconium, where in the house of Onesiphorus he preached the benefits of chastity and thereby won St Thecla away from Thamyris, to whom she was betrothed. In consequence, Paul was charged before the civil authorities and beaten, while Thecla was condemned to death by burning, but miraculously saved. Other incidents in various parts of Asia Minor are described in the lives of both Paul and Thecla, and the 'Acts' conclude with the record of Thecla's death at Seleucia. It is not impossible that the 'Acts' contain some elements of historical truth.

Gk. text pr. in R. A. *Lipsius and M. Bonnet (eds.), *Acta Apostolorum Apocrypha*, 1 (Leipzig, 1891), pp. 235–72, Eng. tr. in

J. K. Elliott, *The Apocryphal New Testament* (Oxford, 1993), pp. 364–80. A frag. of a 4th-cent. Gk. papyrus was ed., with Eng. tr., by C. H. Roberts, *The Antinoopolis Papyri* (1950), pp. 26–8 (no. 15). Lat. texts ed. O. von Gebhardt (TU 22, Heft 2; 1902). Syr. text ed. W. Wright, *Apocryphal Acts of the Apostles* (1871), 1, pp. 128–69; Eng. tr., 2, pp. 116–45. Ethiopic text ed., with Eng. tr., by E. J. Goodspeed in *American Journal of Semitic Languages and Literatures*, 17 (1900–1), pp. 65–95. Armenian text pub. Venice, 1874; Eng. tr. of this text by F. C. *Conybeare, *The Apology and Acts of Apollonius and other Monuments of Early Christianity* (1894), pp. 61–88, with introd., pp. 49–60. Slavonic text ed. P. Vyncke, J. Scharpé, and J. Goubert (Centrale Bibliotheek van de Rijksuniversiteit te Gent, Mededeling 10; 1967). For important Coptic text, see PAUL, ACTS OF ST. Ger. tr., taking account of Coptic version, in Schneemelcher, 2 (5th edn., 1989), pp. 216–24; Eng. tr., 2 [1992], pp. 239–46. W. M. *Ramsay, *The Church in the Roman Empire before A.D. 170* (1893), pp. 375–428.

Paula, St (347–404), Roman matron. At the age of 33, then a mother of five children (among them St *Eustochium), this Roman lady of noble birth dedicated herself to a life of devotion. In 385 she and Eustochium both followed St *Jerome to Palestine; and after visiting the Holy Places and the hermits in the Egyptian deserts, from 386 she settled permanently in *Bethlehem, where she founded a convent of monks and another of nuns. Feast day, 26 Jan.

Her character is vividly described by Jerome in *Ep.* 108, written shortly after her death (J. P. Migne, *PL* 22. 878 ff.).

Paulianists. The followers of *Paul of Samosata. Presumably because they repudiated the *Trinity, the 19th canon of the Council of *Nicaea (325) required that they should be rebaptized on being received back into Catholic communion.

Paulicians. The members of a sect of the Byzantine Empire. Their name may be derived from St *Paul, whom they held in special veneration, or, more probably, from *Paul of Samosata, with whom they had affinities. The origins of the sect are obscure; their true founder seems to have been Constantine of Mananali, a *Manichaean village near Samosata, who established a community at Kibossa in Armenia under Constantius II (641–68). Under Constantine Pogonatus they were persecuted and their founder was stoned (*c.*684). In the 9th cent. they suffered again under Emp. Leo the Armenian, and the Empress Theodora tried to exterminate them. In consequence many of them assisted the Saracens in their raids on the Empire and adopted Islam. Those who sought refuge in Bulgaria seem to have amalgamated with the *Bogomils in the 10th cent. It seems that they ceased to exist as an independent sect in the 12th century.

The Paulicians professed a *dualistic doctrine, distinguishing between the good God, the Lord of Heaven and creator of souls, and the evil God, the Demiurge and ruler of the material universe. Holding all matter to be evil they denied the reality of Christ's Body and of the Redemption and considered Christ's most important work His teaching. From this contempt of His Body they were led to reject the Cross and all images. Instead they honoured the Book of the Gospels. Like *Marcion, they repudiated the OT and held St *Luke and the Pauline Epp. in particular esteem. Originally they were organized in four grades of

apostles, prophets, itinerants, and copyists, but later only the latter two remained, the itinerants being the superiors and the copyists being entrusted with transcribing the Sacred Books and keeping order in church. Their dualistic doctrines seem frequently to have led to grave moral disorders.

The primary sources incl. Petrus Siculus, 'Historia Haereseos Manichaeorum qui et Pauliciani' in J. P. Migne, *PG* 104. 1239–304; id., 'Sermones contra Paulicianos', ibid. 1305–50. *Euthymius Zigabenus, 'Panoplia Dogmatica, tit. xxiv', ibid. 130. 1189–244. The Greek sources are also ed., with Fr. tr., by C. Astruc and others in *Travaux et Mémoires*, 4 (1970), pp. 1–227. K. Ter-Mkrttschian, *Die Paulikianer im byzantinischen Kaiserreiche und verwandte ketzerische Erscheinungen in Armenien* (1893; with Armenian sources). N. G. Garsoïan, *The Paulician Heresy: A Study of the Origin and Development of Paulicianism in Armenia and the Eastern Provinces of the Byzantine Empire* (Publications in Near and Middle East Studies, Columbia University, Series A, 6; The Hague, 1967). P. Lemerle, 'L'Histoire des Pauliciens d'Asie Mineure d'après les sources grecques', *Travaux et Mémoires*, 5 (1973), pp. 1–144, with bibl. R. Janin, AA, in *DTC* 12 (pt. 1; 1933), cols. 56–62, s.v. 'Pauliciens'. See also works cited under MANI AND MANICHAEISM.

Pauline Privilege. The privilege conceded by St *Paul (1 Cor. 7: 15) to the partner of a heathen marriage to contract a new marriage on becoming a Christian, if the other (non-Christian) partner wished to separate or put serious obstacles in the way of the convert's faith and practice. There is little evidence of its exercise in the earliest times, but its use is attested by *Chrysostom and *Ambrosiaster. The right gradually became established in *canon law and is now provided for in the (1983) *Codex Iuris Canonici* (cans. 1143–9). See also DIVORCE.

G. H. Joyce, SJ, *Christian Marriage* (1933, 2nd edn., 1948), ch. 11. G. Oesterlé in *DDC* 7 (1965), cols. 229–80, s.v. 'Privilège paulin', with bibl.

Paulinus (4th–5th cent.), biographer of St *Ambrose. A deacon of the Church of Milan, he became Ambrose's secretary in his later years and was with him at the time of his death in 397. During a long stay in N. Africa on behalf of the Church of Milan, at the request of St *Augustine he wrote his *Life of St Ambrose* (*c.*422). It is modelled on earlier saints' Lives and, though full of interesting detail, ignores much that is now regarded as important and sets great store by the miraculous. Paulinus supported Augustine during the *Pelagian controversy and was prob. the author of the *libellus* sent to Pope *Zosimus listing the charges against *Celestius.

The *Vita S. Ambrosii* is pr. in edns. of Ambrose, e.g. in J. P. Migne, *PL* 14. 27–46. Modern edns. by M. Pellegrino (Verba Seniorum, 1; Rome, 1961) and A. A. R. Bastiaensen, *Vita di Cipriani . . .* (Vite dei Santi, 3; Milan, 1975, pp. 51–125, with notes and bibl., pp. 281–338), both with Ital. trs. Eng. tr. by F. R. Hoare, *The Western Fathers* (1954), pp. 145–88. The *Libellus adversus Caelestium Zosimo episcopo datus* is pr. in J. P. Migne, *PL* 20. 711–16. É. Lamirande, *Paulin de Milan et la 'Vita Ambrosii'* (1983), with bibl. M. G. Mara in *DPAC* 2 (1984), cols. 2607 f., s.v. 'Paolino'; Eng. tr. in *Encyclopedia of the Early Church*, 2 (1992), p. 660.

Paulinus, St (*c.*730–802), Bp. of *Aquileia. A native of Friuli, he became an assiduous and learned scholar. In 776 *Charlemagne summoned him to the Frankish court, where he made the close acquaintance of *Alcuin and other leading men of learning, and in 787 appointed him Patr. of Aquileia. Here he took a leading part in ecclesiastical affairs, notably in the relations between the Byzantine Church and the W. He also took a prominent share in the suppression of *Adoptianism, notably at the Councils of Regensburg (792), *Frankfurt (794), and Cividale (796), and in the conversion of the pagans in the Tyrol and adjacent provinces. His writings include two anti-Adoptianist works—'Libellus Sacrosyllabus contra Elipandum' and 'Libri iii contra Felicem'. He was a poet of no mean order, and was one of the first to give the rhythmical an equal place with metrical verse, as in the lament for Heric, Duke of Friuli. Feast day, 28 Jan. (otherwise, 11 Jan. and 2 Mar.).

Works ed. J. F. Madrisius, Cong. Orat. (Venice, 1737), repr. in J. P. Migne, *PL* 99. 9–683. Modern edn. of his Epp. by E. Dümmler in *MGH*, Epistolae, 4 (1895), pp. 516–27; of his Poems, with introd. and comm. in Fr., by D. Norberg (Stockholm, 1979); and of *Contra Felicem* by id. (CCCM 95; 1990). Lives by C. Giannoni (Vienna, 1896) and P. Paschini (Udine, 1906; repr. 1977). J. Szövérffy, *Die Annalen der lateinischen Hymnendichtung*, 1 (1964), pp. 194–202; id., *Weltliche Dichtungen des lateinischen Mittelalters*, 1 (1970), pp. 471–7. Raby (1953), pp. 168–71. A. Solignac, SJ, in *Dict. Sp.* 12 (pt. 1; 1984), cols. 584–8, s.v. 'Paulin d'Aquilée'. See also works cited under AQUILEIA.

Paulinus, St (353/5–431), Bp. of Nola. The son of a noble and wealthy Aquitaine family, he was educated at Bordeaux. He qualified for the senate by the exercise of a minor Roman magistracy and, as a young man, served as governor of Campania. After relinquishing this charge, he married a Spanish noblewoman, Therasia, and settled on his family estates in Aquitaine. Shortly afterwards he underwent some kind of spiritual conversion and was baptized (before 390); he and his wife then went to live in N. Spain. After the death of their only son they took a vow of continence and began distributing their fortune; at the same time Paulinus gave up secular poetry, a decision which he defended in a celebrated poetic correspondence with his former mentor *Ausonius. On Christmas Day 393 or 394 Paulinus was ordained priest in Barcelona. The next year he and his wife left Spain to lead a monastic life near the tomb of St Felix at Nola in Campania, where Paulinus was later made bishop (at some time between 403 and 413). Though a cause of scandal to certain members of his class, his renunciation of worldly interests was hailed as exemplary by advocates of monastic spirituality. He was acquainted with many of the most famous Christians of his time (e.g. St *Martin of Tours, St *Ambrose, St *Jerome, and St *Augustine) and conducted a wide-ranging correspondence, a large part of which survives. His poetic works have attracted special attention and place him beside *Prudentius as the foremost Christian Latin poet of the patristic period. Most of his poems were written for the annual celebrations in honour of St Felix and are of great interest as throwing light on the cult of saints and popular customs of the time. Feast day, 22 June. See also BELLS.

Early edns. of his works by F. *Ducaeus, SJ, and H. Rosweyde, SJ (Antwerp, 1622), J. B. Le Brun (2 vols., Paris, 1685), and L. A. *Muratori (Verona, 1736). Muratori's text is repr. in J. P. Migne, *PL* 61. Crit. edn. by W. Hartel (CSEL 29 and 30; 1894). Passages dealing with churches of Nola ed., with comm.

and Eng. tr., by R. C. Goldschmidt (Amsterdam, 1940). Eng. tr. by P. G. Walsh of his Letters (ACW 35–6; 1967) and of his Poems (ibid. 40; 1975). Life by A. Baudrillart ('Les Saints', 1905). P. Fabre, *Essai sur la Chronologie de l'Œuvre de Saint Paulin de Nole* (Publications de la Faculté des Lettres de l'Université de Strasbourg, 109; 1948); id., *Saint Paulin de Nole et l'amitié chrétienne* (Bibliothèque des Écoles françaises d'Athènes et de Rome, 167; 1949). J. T. Lienhard, SJ, *Paulinus of Nola and Early Western Monasticism* (Theophaneia, 28; Cologne and Bonn, 1977), with bibl. *Atti del Convegno XXXI Cinquantenario della morte di S. Paolino di Nola (431–1981), Nola, 20–21 marzo 1982* (Rome [1983]). J. Desmulliez, 'Paulin de Nole. Études chronologiques (393–397)', *Recherches Augustiniennes*, 20 (1985), pp. 35–64. D. E. Trout, 'The dates of the ordination of Paulinus of Bordeaux and of his departure for Nola', *Revue des études Augustiniennes*, 37 (1991), pp. 237–60. N. K. Chadwick, *Poetry and Letters in Early Christian Gaul* (1955), pp. 63–88; J. Fontaine, *Naissance de la poésie dans l'Occident chrétien* (Études Augustiniennes, 1981), pp. 143–54, 161–76, and bibl., pp. 297 f. J. T. Lienhard, SJ, in *Dict. Sp.* 12 (pt. 1; 1984), cols. 592–602, s.v., with bibl.

Paulinus, St (d. 358), Bp. of Trier. He was a disciple of St Maximin, whom he succeeded in the see of Trier. A strong opponent of *Arianism, he was banished after the Synod of *Arles of 353 to Phrygia, where he died in exile. His relics were brought back to Trier in 396, where they have since remained. Feast day, 31 Aug.

AASS, Aug. 6 (1743), pp. 668–79, with 8th–9th cent. Life, pp. 676–9. S. A. Bennett in *DCB* 4 (1887), p. 232, s.v. 'Paulinus (4), St'.

Paulinus, St (d. 644), Bp. of *York. In 601 he was sent to England by Pope *Gregory I to reinforce the mission of St *Augustine; and when in 625 *Edwin, King of Northumbria, married Ethelburga of Kent, Paulinus was consecrated bishop and went with her to York. As a result of his preaching, Edwin and his chiefs accepted Christianity at the assembly of Goodmanham (627). A cathedral was begun at York, and, assisted by *James the Deacon, Paulinus taught the faith there until 633, when, upon Edwin's defeat by the heathen Cadwallon, he returned with Ethelburga to Kent and became Bp. of *Rochester. Feast day, 10 Oct.

The principal authority is *Bede, *HE* 1. 29; 2. 9, 12–14, 16–18, 20; 3. 1; 4. 23; 5. 24; comm. by J. M. Wallace-Hadrill (Oxford, 1988), pp. 43, 65, 67–71, 74 f., 78 f., 81 f., and 84–6. Hardy, 1, pt. 1 (1862), pp. 229 f. R. H. Hodgkin, *A History of the Anglo-Saxons*, 1 (1935), pp. 273–80. H. M. R. E. Mayr-Harting, 'Paulinus of York', *Studies in Church History*, 4 (ed. G. J. Cuming) (Leiden, 1967), pp. 15–21; P. Hunter Blair, 'The Letters of Pope Boniface V and the Mission of Paulinus to Northumbria', in P. Clemoes and K. Hughes (eds.), *England before the Conquest: Studies in primary sources presented to Dorothy Whitelock* (Cambridge, 1971), pp. 5–13.

Paulists. The popular name for members of 'The Missionary Society of St Paul the Apostle in the State of New York', founded by I. T. *Hecker in 1858 to further the work and interests of the RC Church in the USA. Its members live under a rule based on that of the *Redemptorists, of which order Hecker had previously been a member. Through the supposed connection of Hecker with *Americanism, the Society was under suspicion for a time.

V. F. Holden in *NCE* 11 (1967), pp. 29 f., s.v.; J. McVann in *DIP* 8 (1988), cols. 10–12, s.v. 'Sacerdoti Missionari di San Paolo Apostolo'. See also bibl. to AMERICANISM and HECKER, I. T.

Paulus Orosius. See OROSIUS.

Paulus Silentiarius (6th cent.; a *silentiarius* was an usher who maintained silence in the Imperial Palace), Christian poet. He wrote during the reign of *Justinian (Emp. 527–65). His principal work, a hymn to mark the consecration of *Sancta Sophia at *Constantinople on 24 Dec. 562, gives a full description (ἔκφρασις) of the church and pulpit (ἄμβων) in fluent hexameters, and is of great interest for the history of Byzantine art. Paulus also wrote some 80 epigrams, preserved in the Greek anthology. A poem on the Baths of Pythia in Bithynia has also, but wrongly, been ascribed to him.

Paulus' *Ecphrasis* and *Ambo*, ed. I. Bekker (C.S.H.Byz., 1837); repr. in J. P. Migne, *PG.* 86. 2119–58 and 2251–64, with C. D. *Du Cange's comm. on the former, also repr. from Bekker, cols. 2159–252. Crit. edn. in P. Friedländer, *Johannes von Gaza und Paulus Silentiarius* (1912), pp. 225–65, with notes pp. 266–305, and, with Ger. tr., by O. Veh in his edn. of the works of *Procopius of Caesarea, 5 (Munich [1977]), pp. 306–75, with introd. on his life, pp. 376–80. Epigrams ed., with Ital. tr. and comm., by G. Viansino (Turin, 1963). W. von Christ, *Geschichte der griechischen Literatur*, 2 (6th edn. by W. Schmid and O. Stählin, 1924), pp. 977 f. and 980. *CPG* 3 (1979), p. 402 (nos. 7513–16). W. Peck in *PW* 18 (pt. 4; 1949), cols. 2363–72, s.v. 'Paulus 10'.

Pax. See KISS OF PEACE and following entry.

pax brede (also **pax** or **osculatorium**). A small plate of ivory, metal, or wood, with a representation of the Crucifixion or other religious subject on the face and a projecting handle on the back, formerly used at Mass for conveying the *Kiss of Peace (q.v.) esp. to those in choir and to the laity. It was kissed first by the celebrant and then by the others who received it in turn. Pax bredes came into general use in the later Middle Ages prob. under *Franciscan influence. They have been rendered obsolete by the current regulations concerning the Kiss of Peace.

Jungmann (1958 edns.), 2, pp. 408 f. (Eng. tr., 2, pp. 328 f.). F. *Cabrol, OSB, in *DACL* 2 (1910), cols. 128 f., s.v. 'Baiser. vi: *Osculatorium*'.

Peace of the Church, the. The term is applied:

(1) To the new situation in the Church when persecution ceased with the 'Edict of *Milan' in 313; also, in a more specialized sense,

(2) To the temporary cessation of the *Jansenist conflict in 1668, brought about when Pope Clement IX accepted the submission of the four French bishops (28 Sept.) and Louis XIV ordered all parties to the dispute to refrain from further conflict. The settlement, also known as the 'Clementine Peace' ('Pax Clementina'), was formally ratified by Clement IX in four briefs dated 19 Jan. 1669.

Peacock, Reginald. See PECOCK, REGINALD.

Peake, Arthur Samuel (1865–1929), biblical scholar. The son of a *Primitive Methodist minister, he was educated at St John's College, Oxford, and in 1890 elected a Fellow of Merton. In 1892 he was appointed tutor at the newly founded Hartley Primitive Methodist College, Manchester, where his influence was such that he raised the whole standard of ministry in the Methodist Church. In 1904 he also became the first occupant of the Rylands Chair of Biblical Criticism and Exegesis at Manchester University. An accurate, balanced, and cautious scholar, he possessed a vast knowledge of current biblical literature. The works by which he is best remembered are *The Bible, its Origin, its Significance, and its Abiding Worth* (1913), *The Problem of Suffering in the Old Testament* (1904), and esp. his editorship of a *Commentary on the Bible* in one volume (1919). He also took an active part in the ecclesiastical affairs of the Free Churches and the reunion movement among Methodist bodies and beyond. He was never ordained.

Supplement to Peake's Commentary, ed. A. J. Grieve (London, 1936). The so-called new edn. of *Peake's Commentary*, ed. M. Black and H. H. Rowley (1962), is a completely new work. A collection of his minor works, mainly obituary notices of other scholars, ed. W. F. Howard, under the title *Recollections and Appreciations* (London, 1938). Memoir of Peake by his eldest son, L. S. Peake (ibid., 1930). Life by J. T. Wilkinson (ibid., 1971); id. (ed.), *Arthur Samuel Peake 1865–1929: Essays in Commemoration* (1958). J. W. Rogerson, 'Progressive Revelation: Its History and Value as a Key to Old Testament Interpretation', *Epworth Review*, 9, pt. 2 (1982), pp. 73–86 (A. S. Peake Memorial Lecture, 1981). C. H. *Dodd in *DNB, 1922–1930*, pp. 657 f.

Pearson, John (1613–86), Bp. of *Chester. He was educated at Eton and Queens' College, Cambridge, and ordained in 1639. During the Civil War he supported the Royalist cause, under the Commonwealth lived in semi-retirement in London, and after the Restoration became Master successively of Jesus College (1660) and of Trinity College (1662), Cambridge, and also (from 1661) Lady Margaret professor of divinity. At the *Savoy Conference in 1661 he championed the cause of episcopacy. In 1673 he became Bp. of Chester. He was perhaps the most erudite and profound divine of a learned and theological age. His classical *Exposition of the Creed* (1659), in origin a series of lectures extending over several years at St Clement's, Eastcheap, reveals his firm grasp of fundamental principles, his delight in clear and accurate statement, and his judicious and sober temper, while the notes which illustrate the text reflect his remarkable knowledge, esp. of the Christian Fathers. Addressed to a more scholarly public is his *Vindiciae Epistolarum S. Ignatii* (1672), an elaborate defence of the authenticity of the Epp. of St *Ignatius against the attacks of J. *Daillé, of which the conclusions have only been strengthened by the intensive work of later scholars. Pearson also wrote a great number of minor works, largely concerned to uphold the position of the C of E against Rome and Nonconformity.

Life by E. Churton, prefixed to Pearson's *Minor Theological Works* (2 vols., Oxford, 1844), 1, pp. xiii–cxxxvi. S. Cheetham, 'John Pearson', in A. Barry (ed.), *Masters in English Theology* (1877), pp. 213–40. E. Fraenkel (ed.), Aeschylus, *Agamemnon*, 1 (Oxford, 1950), pp. 40–4 and 78–85. F. Sanders in *DNB* 44 (1895), pp. 168–73.

Pearson, John Loughborough (1817–97), architect. His work, which was mainly ecclesiastical and in the geometrical gothic style, was characterized by refined detail, elegant proportions, and noble vaulting. The best-known example is *Truro Cathedral (begun in 1880). Among his other notable churches are St Peter's, Vauxhall (1860–5), St Augustine's, Kilburn (1870–c.1877), St Michael's, Croydon (1876–85), and St Stephen's, Bournemouth (1881–98). He was a careful restorer of many ancient churches, and practically rebuilt the front of the north transept of *Westminster Abbey.

J. E. Newberry, 'The Work of John L. Pearson, R. A.', *Architectural Review*, 1 (1897), pp. 1–11 and 69–82; D. Lloyd, 'John Loughborough Pearson', in J. Fawcett (ed.), *Seven Victorian Architects* (1976), pp. 66–83, 144–5, 153. P. Waterhouse in *DNB*, Suppl. 3 (1901), pp. 255–8.

Peasants' War, formerly called the 'Peasants' Revolt'. A series of insurrections of the German peasants in 1524–6, often seen as a continuation of movements such as the *Bundschuh* on the Upper Rhine (from 1493) and the *Armer Konrad* in Württemberg. The immediate causes of the Peasants' War have been variously explained as religious, social, economic, or political; prob. a mixture of all these factors was at play. M. *Luther's theology, and notably his doctrine of the priesthood of all believers, could well have been interpreted as postulating greater social equality than it in fact did. Moreover, the economic distress of the German peasantry was real and several preachers who came in the wake of Luther advocated the abolition of *tithes and serfdom. T. *Müntzer's apocalyptic visions, although not responsible for the War, served as inspiration in the later stages. The rebels consisted of heterogeneous groups of serfs, farmers, townspeople, and minor clergy. Although they set out their grievances in the *Twelve Articles adopted at Memmingen (demanding *inter alia* the freedom to choose their pastors and the abolition of serfdom and certain taxes), they had few real leaders and experienced difficulties in carrying through a plan of action. In their attempt to destroy all authority the rebels looted and burned castles and monasteries. About a third of what was then German territory was affected, notably Swabia and Thuringia but also the Tyrol and Alsace. Most of the movement was brutally stamped out by the armies of the Swabian League, the union of Protestant princes, in 1525; the remnants survived for another year in Salzburg and the Tyrol. Luther's initial attitude to the risings was not hostile and he even attempted to mediate between the princes and the peasants with the pamphlet *Ermahnung zum Frieden* (April 1525). His second pamphlet containing an outright condemnation, entitled *Wider die räuberischen und mörderischen Rotten* and prob. written in May 1525, appeared later in the year just as the uprising was being suppressed. Although Luther's attitude to the rebels has been widely criticized by historians, it was little different from that of other Reformers such as P. *Melanchthon, M. *Bucer, and U. *Zwingli who also declared their allegiance to the established civil powers. The peasants' cause found more sympathy among some of the city authorities who appreciated their social and economic distress, apart from any religious issues.

G. Franz, *Der deutsche Bauernkrieg* (Munich and Berlin, 1933, with *Aktenband*, 1935; 12th edn., Darmstadt, 1984); id. (ed.), *Quellen zur Geschichte des Bauernkrieges* (Munich, 1963); A Laube and H. W. Seiffert (eds.) *Flugschriften der Bauernkriegszeit* (Berlin, 1975; repr. ('2nd edn.'), Vienna and Cologne, 1978). Eng. tr. of primary docs. ed. T. Scott and [R. W.] 'Bob' Scribner, *The German Peasants' War: A History in Documents* (Atlantic Highlands, NJ, and London, 1991). M. Bensing and S. Hoyer, *Der deutsche Bauernkrieg 1524–1526* (Berlin [1965]). P. Blickle, *Die Revolution von 1525* (1975; 2nd edn., 1981; Eng. tr., Baltimore and London [1981]). A. Friesen, *Reformation and Utopia: The Marxist Interpretation of the Reformation and its Antecedents* (Veröffentlichungen des Instituts für Europäische Geschichte, Mainz, 71; Wiesbaden, 1974), *passim*. [R. W.] 'Bob' Scribner and G. Benecke (eds.), *The German Peasant War of 1525—New Viewpoints* (1979); H. Buszello and others (eds.), *Der deutsche Bauernkrieg* (Paderborn, etc., 1984). G. Maron in *TRE* 5 (1980), pp. 319–38, s.v. 'Bauernkrieg', with full bibl.

Pecham, John (c.1225–92), also, in older works, 'Peckham', Abp. of *Canterbury. He was born at Patcham (formerly Pecham), E. Sussex, and prob. educated at Lewes. He proceeded to the University of *Paris, where he studied in the faculty of arts, and then transferred to *Oxford, where he joined the *Franciscans c.1250. Between 1257 and 1259 he returned to Paris to study theology, and here from c.1269 to c.1271 he occupied the Franciscan chair of theology. He played a prominent part in defending his Order against the attacks of secular masters. He returned to Oxford c.1272 as lector in theology in the Franciscan convent, and in 1274 he was appointed Provincial. From 1277 to 1279 he was *lector sacri palatii* in Rome. In 1279 he succeeded Robert *Kilwardby, OP, as Abp. of Canterbury, being the Papal candidate in opposition to Robert Burnell, Bp. of *Bath and Wells, who was the nominee of Edward I. He promptly inaugurated a vigorous policy of ecclesiastical reform. At a provincial Council at Reading on 30 July 1279 he legislated against pluralities and other abuses, in conformity with the decrees of the Second Council of *Lyons. At another Council at Lambeth (1281) he sought to suppress abuses concerning the Eucharist. At the parliament of 1285 he entered negotiations for a settlement of differences between ecclesiastical and secular authorities, esp. the question of disputed jurisdiction, which led to the issue of the writ 'Circumspecte agatis'. He also concerned himself with raising the standard of the clergy; took active steps to encourage preaching; and reformed the financial administration of many religious houses. He made visitations of all the dioceses in his Province, and his zeal brought him into conflict with some of his suffragans, e.g. St Thomas de *Cantilupe of Hereford.

In theology Pecham was an upholder of the Franciscan tradition; he strongly opposed the teaching of St *Thomas Aquinas on the unity of form in man, even going so far as to insist on its condemnation as heretical (1286). His writings include a commentary on Book 1 of the Sentences, three *Quodlibets, commentaries on Lamentations and on St John's Gospel, as well as works concerning the Franciscan Order. He also produced a French adaptation of *Dionysius the Pseudo–Areopagite for Queen Margaret of France. He had scientific interests and wrote a standard treatise on optics, the 'Perspectiva Communis', which was influenced by Roger *Bacon. He was a gifted poet; his best-known composition was the 'Philomena', a lyrical meditation arranged on the plan of the seven liturgical hours, which was translated into several vernaculars.

Registrum Epistolarum Fratris Johannis Peckham, ed. C. T. Martin (3 vols., RS, 1882–5); a more complete edn. of his Register [up to 1285; the part covering the remainder of his primacy is prob. lost] ed. F. N. Davis and others (*Canterbury and York Society, 64–5; 1968–9). His works are scattered; modern edns. incl. those of three treatises 'de paupertate' by C. L. Kingsford and others (British Society of Franciscan Studies, 2; Aberdeen, 1910), with list of his writings and edns. to date; 'Quaestiones Tractantes de Anima' by H. Spettmann, OFM (BGPM 19, Hefte 5–6; 1918); 'Quodlibet Romanum' by F. M. Delorme, OFM (Spicilegium Pontificii Athenaei Antoniani, 1; Rome, 1938); 'Tractatus de Anima' by G. Melani, OFM (Biblioteca di Studi Francescani, 1; Florence, 1948); and 'Perspectiva Communis', ed., with Eng. tr., by D. C. Lindberg (Madison etc., 1970); convenient edn. of 'Philomena' by G. M. Dreves, *Lateinische Hymnendichter des Mittelalters*, 2 (AHMA 50; 1907), pp. 602–10. A Life of St *Antony of Padua is attributed to Pecham by V. Gamboso (ed.), *Vita del 'Dialogus' e 'Benignitas'* (Fonti Agiografiche Antoniane, 3; Padua [1986]), pp. 251–616, incl. text and Ital. tr. Full list of works to date in A. Teetaert, Ord. Cap., in *DTC* 12 (pt. 1; 1933), cols. 100–40, s.v. 'Pecham', with bibl., esp. cols. 107–25. D. L. Douie, *Archbishop Pecham* (Oxford, 1952). C. Harkins, OFM, 'The Authorship of a Commentary on the Franciscan Rule published among the Works of St Bonaventure', *Franciscan Studies*, 29 (1969), pp. 157–248. C. L. Kingsford in *DNB* 44 (1895), pp. 190–7; *BRUO* 3 (1959), pp. 1445–7; I. Brady, OFM, in *Dict. Sp.* 8 (1974), cols. 645–9, s.v. 'Jean (165) Pecham'.

Pecock, Reginald (*c.*1393–1461), Bp. of *Chichester. A Welshman by birth, he was educated at Oriel College, Oxford, of which he became a Fellow. In 1431 he was appointed master of Whittington College, London, and subsequently, through court influence, Bp. of *St Asaph in 1444 and of Chichester in 1450. His antagonism to the Yorkist party and his theological writings having made him unpopular, he was accused of heresy in 1457, and although he recanted, he was deprived of his bishopric and confined in Thorney Abbey, where he died probably in 1461.

Pecock's thought, which is embodied in his best-known work *The Repressor of Overmuch Wijting* [i.e. *Blaming*] *of the Clergy*, written to controvert the *Lollards, is notable for its very marked emphasis on the 'law of kind', 'written in mennis soulis with the finger of God', to which the Scriptures are merely subordinate and supplementary. Much of his work is an apologia for the Church against the Lollards, of whose doctrines he gives a penetrating analysis. Although his writings were medieval in form, Pecock's critical faculty and his use of the English language make him one of the most significant figures of the 15th century.

There are modern edns. of 'The Repressor' by C. Babington (2 vols., RS, 1860), his 'Book of Faith' by J. L. Morison (Glasgow, 1909), 'The Donet' by E. V. Hitchcock (EETS 156; 1921), 'The Follower to the Donet' by id. (ibid. 164; 1924), and of 'The Rule of Christian Religion' by W. C. Greet (ibid. 171; 1927). V. H. H. Green, *Bishop Reginald Pecock: A Study in Ecclesiastical History and Thought* (Thirlwall Prize, 1941; 1945). J. F. Patrouch, *Reginald Pecock* (New York [1970]). C. W. Brockwell, *Bishop Reginald Pecock and the Lancastrian Church* (Texts and Studies in Religion, 25; Lewiston, NY [1985]). E. F. Jacob, 'Reynold Pecock, Bishop of Chichester', *Proceedings of the British Academy*, 37 (1951), pp. 121–53; R. M. Haines, 'Reginald Pecock: A Tolerant Man in an Age of Intolerance', in W. J. Sheils (ed.), *Persecution and Toleration* (Studies in Church History, 21; 1984), pp. 125–37. A. M. Cooke in *DNB* 44 (1895), pp. 198–202; *BRUO* 3 (1959), pp. 1447–9.

pectoral cross. A cross of precious metal worn on the breast and suspended by a chain which goes round the neck. In the C of E its use is almost exclusively confined to bishops; but in the RC Church cardinals and abbots also wear it. In the E. it is worn by *archimandrites, *archpriests, and in Russia even by simple priests: there, the distinctive emblem of the episcopate is not the pectoral cross but the *encolpion, although the bishop wears a pectoral cross as well as an encolpion on certain formal occasions, esp. when officiating in church.

Peculiar, a place exempt from the jurisdiction of the bishop of the diocese in which it is situated; it may be a parish, a group of parishes, or a chapel. At one time or another there have been six types of Peculiars: Monastic Peculiars, where great abbeys and certain religious orders were exempt from episcopal jurisdiction; Royal Peculiars, usually where churches were situated on lands connected with a royal castle or palace (e.g. St George's Chapel, *Windsor, and *Westminster Abbey), and which are exempt from any jurisdiction other than that of the Sovereign; Archiepiscopal Peculiars, linked with rights claimed by archbishops to exercise jurisdiction where they had manors or palaces; Episcopal Peculiars, where bishops owned residences in dioceses other than their own; and Cathedral Peculiars, in which cathedral chapters had jurisdiction over their property and instituted clerks. Apart from the Royal Peculiars, most of the rights and privileges of the others have been removed, so that they now come under the jurisdiction of the diocesan bishop, although the holders of some of them retain the title of Dean (e.g. Bocking, Battle, Stamford).

P. Barber, 'What is a Peculiar?', *Ecclesiastical Law Journal*, 3 (1995), pp. 299–312.

Peculiar People, the (also **Plumstead Peculiars**). A small sect of faith-healers, founded in Rochford, near Southend, in 1838. On the basis of Jas. 5: 14 f. they reject medical aid, and in cases of illness rely on anointing with oil and prayer. In 1956 they took the name of the Union of Evangelical Churches.

M. Sorrell, *The Peculiar People* (Exeter, 1979).

Pedilavium (Lat., 'washing of the feet'). The ceremony of the washing of the feet performed in the liturgy on *Maundy Thursday. It is attested by the 17th Synod of Toledo in 694 and for 13th-cent. Rome in (*Mabillon's) tenth *Ordo Romanus. When the Maundy Thursday Mass came to be celebrated in the morning, the Pedilavium remained as a separate service, confined to cathedral and abbey churches. Pope *Pius XII's Holy Week Ordinal placed it in the restored evening Mass immediately after the homily and recommended its observance in all churches. During the singing of antiphons, 12 men are led into the sanctuary, where the celebrant solemnly washes and dries the feet of each in turn. When the ceremony was observed apart from the Mass, it began with the recital of the Gospel narrative (Jn. 13). *Lent, Holy Week, Easter: Services and Prayers commended by the House of Bishops of the General Synod of the Church of England* (1986) includes a pedilavium in the Maundy Thursday liturgy after the sermon, and similar provision is made in modern liturgies of some other Provinces of the Anglican Communion. A similar ceremony in the Byzantine rite is still mainly confined to monasteries and cathedrals; here it follows the Eucharistic liturgy.

T. Schäfer, OSB, *Die Fusswaschung im monastischen Brauchtum und in der lateinischen Liturgie* (Texte und Arbeiten, Abt. 1, Heft 47; Beuron, 1956); P. F. Beatrice, *La lavanda dei piedi: Contributo alla storia delle antiche liturgie cristiane* (Bibliotheca Ephemerides Liturgicae, Subsidia, 28; 1983). A. Malvy, SJ, in *DTC* 9 (pt. 1; 1926), cols. 16–36, s.v. 'Lavement des pieds'; H. *Leclercq, OSB, in *DACL*. 8 (pt. 2; 1929), cols. 2002–9, s.v. 'Lavement (Lavage liturgique de la tête, des mains, des pieds)'.

Pedrog, St. See PETROCK, ST.

Peel parish. In the C of E, a term used for a *parish set up under the New Parishes Act 1843, passed when Sir Robert Peel was Prime Minister, or one of the subsequent Acts on this subject. Under this legislation a district not containing any existing parish church might be set up as a separate parish, with the consent of the bishop, under a scheme drawn up by the *Ecclesiastical (since 1948 *Church) Commissioners; the patronage is in the hands of the Crown and the bishop alternately.

Péguy, Charles Pierre (1873–1914), French poet and philosopher. He came of a peasant and artisan family in Orléans. He won scholarships to the local *lycée* and then to Paris, where he studied at the École Normale Supérieure and at the *Sorbonne. His philosophy was much influenced by H. *Bergson. An ardent socialist and Dreyfusard, he gave up his studies to manage a bookshop in the rue de la Sorbonne which became a centre of intellectual activity. In 1900 he founded the *Cahiers de la Quinzaine* in which he and a group of able young contributors he had brought together attacked the evils of the day. Their motto sums up the spirit of the *Cahiers*: 'The social revolution will be moral or nothing'. All Péguy's own works published in his lifetime appeared in the *Cahiers*. At one time a professed atheist, *c.*1907 he came back to the Catholic faith, without giving up his socialism. His attachment to France had found early expression in the drama *Jeanne d'Arc* (1897), and the Maid of Orléans remained a lifelong inspiration of his work. As an anticlerical who remained unreconciled to the Church because of domestic circumstances, he was estranged from his Catholic contemporaries, and he was distrusted by republicans and socialists because of his attacks on the modern world and its belief in progress. A solitary figure, a prophetic thinker, and a great poet, he lost his life in the Battle of the Marne on 5 Sept. 1914.

Œuvres complètes (19 vols., 1916–55). Convenient edn. of his *Œuvres poétiques* (Bibliothèque de la Pléiade, 60; 1948; rev. edn., 1975) and *Œuvres en Prose* (ibid. 122 and 140; 1957–9). Eng. trs. of selections of his works as *Basic Verities* (1943) and *Men and Saints* (1947); several of his individual works have also been translated, incl. *The Mystery of the Charity of Joan of Arc* (1950), *The Mystery of the Holy Innocents* (1956), and *The Portico of the Mystery of the Second Virtue* (Metuchen, NJ, 1970). Studies by D. Halévy (Paris, 1941; rev. edn., 1979; Eng. tr., 1946), R. Rolland (2 vols., Paris, 1944; rev. edn., 1972), Y. Servais (Cork and Oxford, 1953), M. Villiers (London, 1965), B. Guyon (Connaissance des Lettres, 55; 1960; rev. edn., 1973), S. Fraisse (Écrivains de toujours, 1979), and F. Laichter (Paris, 1985). P. Duployé, OP, *La Religion de Péguy* (Bibliothèque Française et Romaine, Série C: Études littéraires, 10 [1965]). S. Fraisse, *Péguy et le Monde Antique* (1973). *L'Amitié Charles Péguy: Bulletin d'informations et de recherches* (1978 ff.), incl. A. Barnes, 'Péguy et Mgr Batiffol', in vol. 9 (1986), pp. 137–77.

Pelagia, St (d. *c.*311), virgin and martyr. Her name occurs in the canon of the *Ambrosian Mass of Milan, and her fate is known from mentions of her in St *Ambrose (*PL* 16. 229–32 and 1093) and in St *Chrysostom (*PG* 1. 579–85). She was a 15-year-old girl of *Antioch who, when her house was surrounded by soldiers during one of the *persecutions (probably that under *Diocletian), threw herself out of a window into the sea to preserve her chastity. Feast day, 9 June.

To the name of this historical person a legend became attached of a 4th-cent. actress of Antioch who was suddenly converted by St Nonnus, Bp. of *Edessa, and went to *Jerusalem in men's clothes, where she lived as a recluse in a grotto of the Mt. of *Olives practising severe penances. Feast day, 8 Oct.

The story of a third Pelagia, a virgin martyr of *Tarsus, seems to be a combination of the former two. This Pelagia is supposed to have been burnt to death for refusing to become the mistress of the Emperor. Her feast is also on 8 Oct. in E. calendars, in the Roman martyrology on 4 May. H. Usener's attempt to explain the cultus of Pelagia as a Christian adaptation of the myth of Astarte was severely handled by H. *Delehaye.

The legend of St Pelagia appears to have close connections with that of St *Margaret (q.v.).

For the legends, besides the items cited in the text, see *BHG* (3rd edn., 1957), nos. 1478–80, and *BHL*, nos. 6605–11. H. Usener, *Legenden der hl. Pelagia* (1879); H. Delehaye, SJ, *Les Légendes hagiographiques* (1905), pp. 222–34; Eng. tr. (1907), pp. 197–206. P. Petitmengin and others (eds.), *Pélagie la Pénitente: Métamorphose d'une légende* (Études Augustiniennes, 3 vols., 1981 ff.), incl. texts. J. P. Kirsch in *CE* 11 (1911) pp. 601 f.; J. M. Sauget in *Bibliotheca Sanctorum*, 10 (Rome, 1968), cols. 432–7, both s.v.

Pelagianism. Theologically, Pelagianism is the heresy which holds that man can take the initial and fundamental steps towards salvation by his own efforts, apart from Divine *grace. Historically, it was an ascetic movement composed of disparate elements united under the name of the British theologian and exegete Pelagius, who taught in Rome in the late 4th and early 5th cents.

In essence, Pelagianism was a lay movement, aristocratic in tone and membership, which arose in the circles in Rome which admired St *Jerome in the 380s. It enjoyed considerable popularity in Sicily, where many of its Roman adherents had estates and where it produced a local theologian, the anonymous writer sometimes called the 'Sicilian Briton'. Pelagius' great contribution to the movement was to supply a theology vindicating Christian asceticism against the charge of *Manichaeism by emphasizing man's freedom to choose good by virtue of his God-given nature. He does not seem to have been greatly interested in the doctrine of *Original Sin; the denial of the transmission of Original Sin seems to have been introduced into Pelagianism by *Rufinus the Syrian, who influenced Pelagius' supporter *Celestius.

In 409 or 410, when Rome was menaced by the Goths, Pelagius and Celestius left Italy for Africa, whence Pelagius soon moved to Palestine. Celestius was subsequently accused by *Paulinus of Milan of denying the transmission of Adam's sin to his descendants. He was condemned by a Council at *Carthage in 411 and went to *Ephesus. Soon afterwards St *Augustine began to preach and write against Pelagian doctrine, though he continued to treat Pelagius himself with respect until 415. In that year Pelagius was accused of heresy by the Spanish priest *Orosius, who had been sent by Augustine to Jerome at Bethlehem. Pelagius, however, succeeded in clearing himself at a diocesan synod at *Jerusalem and at a provincial synod at Diospolis (Lydda). The African bishops, however, condemned Pelagius and Celestius at two councils at Carthage and Milevis in 416 and persuaded Pope *Innocent I (410–17) to excommunicate them. Celestius went to Rome and so impressed Innocent's successor, *Zosimus (417–19), that he reopened the case. The Africans stood firm and at the Council of Carthage on 1 May 418 they issued a series of nine canons affirming in uncompromising terms the so-called 'Augustinian' doctrine of the *Fall and Original Sin. Meanwhile, on 30 April the Emp. Honorius (395–423), perhaps under African pressure, had issued an imperial decree denouncing Pelagius and Celestius. Soon afterwards Pope Zosimus decided against them and by his 'Epistola Tractoria' (418) he reaffirmed the judgement of his predecessor.

Pelagius himself had little inclination to continue the struggle. He disappears from history and his subsequent fate is unknown. However, a new defender of Pelagianism appeared in *Julian of Eclanum, who conducted a literary debate of great bitterness with Augustine, which ended only with Augustine's death in 430. In 429 Celestius appealed to *Nestorius to intercede for him with Pope *Celestine I, but he and his supporters, like Nestorius, were condemned at the Council of *Ephesus in 431. Doctrines henceforth identified as Pelagian continued to find favour in Britain, where the intervention of *Germanus of Auxerre was needed to extirpate the heresy, while in Gaul the debate on grace gave rise to the movement misleadingly called '*Semipelagianism'. This was a rejection of Augustine's extreme predestinarian views without any corresponding approval of Pelagius. Controversy continued in Gaul during the 5th cent., and a satisfactory theological formula was reached only at the Second Council of *Orange in 529 through the influence of *Caesarius of Arles. The issues raised by Pelagianism, however, continually reappeared during the Middle Ages, only to break out afresh at the *Reformation.

See also SEMIPELAGIANISM.

Owing to Pelagius' condemnation his extensive writings have been largely lost or transmitted under other names. The most considerable surviving work is his 'Commentary on St Paul's Epp.' (on all 13, but not Heb.; written in Rome before 410), which has come down in a worked-over form ascribed to Jerome (*PL* 30. 645–902) and to *Primasius of Hadrumetum (ibid. 68. 413–686). The orig. text was discovered by A. *Souter and ed. by him with introd. (Texts and Studies, 9. 1–3; Cambridge, 1922–31; repr. in J. P. Migne, *PL*, Suppl. 1, ed. A. Hamman, OFM (1958), cols. 1110–374); Eng. tr. and comm. by T. de Bruyn (Oxford Early Christian Studies, 1993). Other works which are certainly the work of Pelagius are his 'Ep. ad Demetriadem', addressed to a Roman lady of high standing who became a nun (wrongly incl. among the works of Augustine and Jerome, *PL* 30. 15–45, and 33. 1099–120), and the short 'Libellus Fidei ad Innocentium Papam' (ibid. 48. 488–91). G. de Plinval has defended as indisputably the work of Pelagius a small collection of Epp. and other

writings brought together in C. P. *Caspari, *Briefe, Abhandlungen und Predigten* (Christiania, 1890), pp. 3–167 (with comm. pp. 223–389 and hence known as the 'Corpus Casparianum'), as well as a number of other lesser writings. Most of the other works attributed to Pelagius in modern times are repr. in *PL*, Suppl. 1, cols. 1375–570, with introd. cols. 1101–9; for further details see *CPL* (3rd edn., 1995), pp. 250–61 (nos. 728–66). Eng. tr. of 18 letters of Pelagius and his followers by B. R. Rees (Woodbridge, Suffolk, 1991).

The classic account of the subject is H. *Noris, *Historia Pelagiana* (Padua, 1673; with strong *Jansenist leanings). Modern studies include A. Souter, *The Earliest Latin Commentaries on the Epistles of St Paul* (1927), pp. 205–30; G. de Plinval, *Pélage: Ses écrits, sa vie et sa réforme* (Lausanne, 1943); id., *Essai sur le style et la langue de Pélage, suivi du traité inédit* De Induratione Cordis Pharaonis (Collectanea Friburgensia, NS 31; 1947); J. Ferguson, *Pelagius* (Cambridge, 1956); T. Bohlin, *Die Theologie des Pelagius und ihre Genesis* (Acta Universitatis Upsaliensis, 1957, no. 9); J. N. L. Myres, 'Pelagius and the End of Roman Rule in Britain', *Journal of Roman Studies*, 1 (1960), pp. 21–36; J. Morris, 'Pelagian Literature', *JTS* NS 16 (1965), pp. 26–60; id., 'The Literary Evidence', in M. W. Barley and R. P. C. Hanson (eds.), *Christianity in Britain, 300–700* (Leicester, 1968), pp. 55–73; R. F. Evans, *Pelagius: Inquiries and Reappraisals* (1968), and other works of this author; P. Brown, 'Pelagius and his Supporters: Aims and Environment', *JTS* NS 19 (1968), pp. 93–114; id., 'The Patrons of Pelagius', ibid. 21 (1970), pp. 56–72; G. Bonner, *Augustine and Modern Research on Pelagianism* (St Augustine Lecture, 1970; Villanova, Pa., 1972); G. Greshake, *Gnade als konkrete Freiheit: Eine Untersuchung zur Gnadenlehre des Pelagius* (Mainz, 1972); O. Wermelinger, *Rom und Pelagius* (Päpste und Papsttum, 7; Stuttgart, 1975); R. A. Markus, 'Pelagianism: Britain and the Continent', *JEH* 37 (1986), pp. 191–204; B. R. Rees, *Pelagius: A Reluctant Heretic* (Woodbridge, Suffolk, 1988). L. [R.] Wickham, 'Pelagianism in the East', in R. [D.] Williams (ed.), *The Making of Orthodoxy: Essays in honour of Henry Chadwick* (Cambridge, 1989), pp. 200–13. Useful collection of texts in A. Bruckner, *Quellen zur Geschichte des pelagianischen Streites* (Sammlung ausgewählter kirchen- und dogmengeschichtlicher Quellenschriften, Reihe 2, 7; 1906). H. J. Frede, *Pelagius, Der irische Paulustext, Sedulius Scottus* (Vetus Latina. Die Reste der Altlateinischen Bibel. Aus der Geschichte der lateinischen Bibel, 3; 1961), pp. 9–58. Bardenhewer, 4, pp. 513–15; Altaner and Stuiber (1978), pp. 374–7 and 628 f. F. *Loofs in *PRE* (3rd edn.), 15 (1904), pp. 747–74, s.v. 'Pelagius und der pelagianische Streit' [at end of the vol.]; R. Hedde, OP, and É. Amann in *DTC*, 12 (pt. 1; 1933), cols. 675–715; F. G. Nuvolone and A. Solignac, SJ, in *Dict. Sp.* 13 (pt. 2; 1986), cols. 2889–942, s.v. 'Pélage et Pélagianisme' [at end of the vol.]; G. Bonner in *TRE* 26 (1996), pp. 176–85, s.v. 'Pelagius/Pelagianischer Streit'. See also works cited under AUGUSTINE OF HIPPO, ST.

Pelagius. See PELAGIANISM.

pelican. The image of the pelican, 'vulning herself' with her beak to feed her young with her blood, has been widely used in Christian symbolism to typify the Lord's redeeming work, esp. as mediated through the Blessed Sacrament. Well-known instances are the first line of the 6th stanza of '*Adoro te devote', and the figure of the pelican on the column in the quadrangle of Corpus Christi College, Oxford. At *Durham the Blessed Sacrament used to be reserved in a silver pelican suspended over the high altar.

W. Lampen, OFM, ' "Pie Pelicane, Jesu Domine" ', *Antonianum*, 21 (1946), pp. 68–92. A. P. Frutaz in *EC* 9 (1952), cols. 1088 f., s.v. 'Pellicano'. See also works cited under ICONOGRAPHY.

penalties, ecclesiastical. The punishments which can be imposed upon an offender against the law of the

Church are divided into three categories: (1) 'censures' or 'medicinal penalties' designed to secure the correction of the offender and his reintegration into the life of the Church. They comprise *excommunication, *interdict, and *suspension of clerics from their office; (2) 'expiatory penalties' designed to punish the offender and safeguard the community; they include prohibition to live in a certain area and dismissal from the clerical life; (3) 'penal remedies' and penances. These remedies (i.e. warning and rebuke) are intended to prevent likely wrongdoing or to deal with the serious suspicion that an offence has been committed. Penances, imposed in the external *forum, may be given either as a substitute for, or in addition to, other penalties. Current RC legislation is contained in *CIC* (1983), cans. 1312–99.

T. J. Green in J. A. Coriden, T. J. Green, and D. E. Heintschel (eds.), *The Code of Canon Law: A Text and Commentary* (1985), pp. 893–941.

Penance. Of the earliest history of the Sacrament of Penance very little is known. By the 3rd cent. there had emerged a developed system of public Penance which was regarded as a 'second Baptism'. After the sinner, voluntarily or under threat of *excommunication, had asked the bishop for Penance, he was enrolled in the order of *penitents, excluded from Communion, and committed to a severe course of prayer, fasting, and almsgiving. At the end of a period whose length was determined by the gravity of the sin, the sinner was reconciled and rejoined the congregation of the faithful. Certain prohibitions, however, attached to him for life, e.g. he must not be a soldier and he might not marry. The outstanding characteristics of this system were: (1) the enrolment into the distinct order of penitents, (2) it could be undergone only once in a lifetime, and (3) the enforcement of lifelong continence. Because of these characteristics the system broke down, and Penance was usually postponed until the eve of death.

In consequence, a new system was developed in the W. through the influence of *Celtic or *Anglo-Saxon monk-missionaries, which was administered by means of the *Penitential Books (q.v.). This differed from the earlier system in the absence of the three features mentioned above; but the Penance remained public, long, and arduous, even in the new. Confession of the details of sin was secret. Absolution, at any rate at the start of the new system, was withheld until the completion of the Penance. Gradually it was pushed back until it was granted on confession and before the Penance was begun. From this developed the modern 'private Penance', with its confession, absolution, and light formal Penance. Although this procedure was established by the early 12th cent., its practice was systematically enjoined after the Fourth *Lateran Council (1215). Can. 25 of that Council, *Omnis utriusque sexus*, required every Christian to confess his or her sins in Penance to the parish priest at least once a year. The canon became both a charter and a stimulus to the further development of regular confession, a development witnessed by the birth, *c*.1200, of a burgeoning new literary genre, the confessor's handbook, and fostered by the appearance of an army of qualified confessors in the *mendicant orders. By 1500 the system was sufficiently ubiquitous to be a major target for the Church's more radical critics. In the E. a similar development took place.

Here, however, Penance was intimately bound up with spiritual direction which was not confined to the priesthood, but rather something sought from members of the monastic order. Absolution is not always mentioned in connection with such confession and it is certain that many confessors were lay, especially to other monks. By the 15th cent., private confession to a priest, followed by a prayer for forgiveness, was a generally accepted practice among lay people.

'Penance' means 'poena', i.e. punishment. In the W. it was apparently held that post-Baptismal sins must be atoned for in part by the punishment of the sinner, on the ground that it was better to endure the punishment in this world than in the next. Though the essential part played in the redemption of sin by Christ's *Atonement on the Cross was never overlooked, yet great weight was attached to the amends offered by the penitent, and the use of the word '*satisfaction' for the Penance, as well as its relative severity, reflected this belief. But from the first another idea was also present, namely that the practice of asceticism controlled and eradicated the passions that led to the sin, and by enforcing a semi-retirement from the world shielded the sinner from further temptations. These ideas were carried over into the Celtic system, together with the more secular purpose of enforcing obedience to the law and exercising over barbarians a moderating and civilizing influence. The Penance consisted generally of fasts (of greater or less severity), continence, pilgrimages, floggings, and imprisonment. Owing to the great inconvenience and interruption to ordinary life occasioned by long and arduous Penances, the system of commutation grew up. A Penance of years or a lengthy pilgrimage could be compressed into a single day by the payment of money or its place taken by the repeated recitation of the Psalter in a position of physical discomfort. The idea of commutation affected the later development of *indulgences. Their development also owed much to the greater doctrinal precision of the *Schoolmen, who distinguished between 'culpa' and 'poena', and between 'poena damnationis' and 'poena temporalis', the last alone being the object of Penance. 'Culpa' and 'poena damnationis' were held to be removed by contrition and absolution, whereas 'poena temporalis' required the Penance of the sinner or its equivalent drawn from the treasury of *merit. At every stage, the ability of the Church to intercede for sinners and the power of its ministers to absolve and reconcile them has lain behind the theology of Penance.

The Second *Vatican Council's 'Constitution on the Liturgy' (sect. 72; 1963) decreed that the rites and formulas of the Sacrament of Penance should be revised so that they might better express the nature and effect of the Sacrament. The *Ordo Poenitentiae*, issued in 1973, lays emphasis on the aspects of reconciliation and amendment of life rather than on confession, judgement, and punishment; it also stresses the social dimensions of sin and reparation. It provides three rites: (1) for the reconciliation of individual penitents, on the traditional pattern, though either the penitent or the confessor is urged to read a short passage of Scripture as an aid to conscience; (2) for the reconciliation of several penitents in a service of penitence, with prayers, Psalms, Bible readings, and a sermon, followed by individual private confession and absolution; and (3) for the reconciliation of many penitents in a service similar to (2) but without private confession; the service concludes with a general confession followed by a public act of reconciliation with absolution. The conditions for the use of this third rite are restricted: it may be used only when there is 'grave cause', i.e. where there is a considerable number of penitents and an insufficient number of confessors, so that those in need of the Sacrament would otherwise be deprived of it; and penitents who profit from this rite are obliged to confess their sins in due course, at least within the following 12 months.

In the C of E the use of Penance for those who wished for it was revived in the 19th cent. by E. B. *Pusey and other *Tractarians on the basis of the provisions in the BCP *Visitation of the Sick. Several modern Anglican liturgies (though not the ASB) include a separate rite for the Reconciliation of a Penitent.

See also SEAL OF CONFESSION and CONFESSION ROOMS.

Useful historical account in O. D. Watkins, *A History of Penance* (2 vols., 1920). J. A. Jungmann, SJ, *Die lateinischen Bussriten in ihrer geschichtlichen Entwicklung* (Forschungen zur Geschichte des innerkirchlichen Lebens, 3–4; 1932). B. Poschmann, *Busse und letzte Ölung* (Handbuch der Dogmengeschichte, 4, Fask. 3; 1951), pp. 1–123; Eng. tr. [1964], pp. 1–232, incl. additional bibl. The orig. Ger. of this last vol. has been partly superseded by the new vol. in the same series by H. Vorgrimler, *Busse und Krankensalbung* (ibid. 4, Fask. 3; 1978), pp. 1–214. P. Anciaux, *Le Sacrement de la pénitence* (Questions de Morale, 1957). W. Telfer, *The Forgiveness of Sins: An Essay in the History of Christian Doctrine and Practice* (1959). J. [T. A.] Gunstone, *The Liturgy of Penance* (Studies in Christian Worship, 7; 1966). J. Fitzsimons (ed.), *Penance: Virtue and Sacrament* (1969). Groupe de la Bussière [J.-C. Guy, SJ, and others], *Pratiques de la confession des pères du désert à Vatican II. Quinze études d'histoire* (1983), with bibl. M. Dudley and [D.] G. Rowell (eds.), *Confession and Absolution* (1990). J. Morinus [*Morin], *Commentarius Historicus de Disciplina in Administratione Sacramenti Poenitentiae* (Paris, fol., 1651). Collection of early texts ed., with Ger. tr., by H. Karpp, *Die Busse* (Traditio Christiana, 2 vols., Zurich, 1969; Fr. tr., 1970). Fr. tr. of primary texts also by C. Vogel, *Le Pécheur et la Pénitence dans l'Église ancienne* (1966); id., *Le Pécheur et la Pénitence au moyen âge* (1969). P. Galtier, SJ, *L'Église et la rémission des péchés aux premiers siècles* (1932); id., *Aux origines du sacrement de pénitence* (Analecta Gregoriana, 54; 1951), and other works by this author; R. C. Mortimer, *The Origins of Private Penance in the Western Church* (1939). C. Vogel, *La Discipline pénitentielle en Gaule des origines à la fin du VIIᵉ siècle* (1952). P. Anciaux, *La Théologie du sacrement de pénitence au XIIᵉ siècle* (Louvain, 1949). L. Braeckmans, SJ, *Confession et Communion au moyen âge et au concile de Trente* (Recherches et Synthèses, Section de Morale, 6; Gembloux [1971]). T. N. Tentler, *Sin and Confession on the Eve of the Reformation* (Princeton, NJ, 1977). M. Thurian, *La Confession* (Collection Communauté de Taizé, 1953; Eng. tr., 1958). D. Crichton, *The Ministry of Reconciliation: A Commentary on the Order of Penance 1974* (1974). J. A. Favazza, *The Order of Penitents: Historical Roots and Pastoral Future* (Collegeville, Minn. [1988]). É. Amann, A. Michel, and M. Jugie, AA, in *DTC* 12 (pt. 1; 1933), cols. 722–1138, s.v. 'Pénitence'; P. Palmer and P. E. McKeever in *NCE* 11 (1967), pp. 73–83, s.v.; P. Adnès, SJ, in *Dict. Sp.* 12 (pt. 1; 1984), cols. 943–1010, s.v. 'Pénitence'.

Penington, Isaac, the 'Younger'

Penington, Isaac, the 'Younger' (1616–79), also spelled 'Pennington', *Quaker. He was the eldest son of Sir Isaac Penington (c.1590–1661), Lord Mayor of London in 1642–3. Little is known of his education, but he matriculated at Cambridge in 1637. After years of religious perplexity, during which he attached himself for a time to the *Independents, he heard George *Fox speak near Luton in 1657 and, together with his wife, joined the Quaker body in 1658. His conversion was an important accession of strength to the Quakers, who hitherto had had no one of his station in their ranks. From 1658 Quaker worship took place at 'The Grange', his house at Chalfont St Peter. After 1660 he was imprisoned five times; his house and other property confiscated; and his health progressively undermined by the severity of prison life. At Jordans, Chalfont St Giles, where he was buried, a meeting-house that still survives was built on his property. He wrote many books and pamphlets, all of them in a spirit quite free from controversial bitterness, which were of great assistance in the building up of the new Quaker Society.

Works (2 parts, London, 1681, 1680). J. G. Bevan, *Memoirs of the Life of Isaac Penington; to which is added a review of his writings* (1807). M. Webb, *The Penns and Peningtons of the 17th Century* (1867). C. Fell-Smith in *DNB* 44 (1895), pp. 297–300.

Penitential Books. Books containing directions for confessors which included lists of sins with a set of graded *penances for each. They first appeared in the *Celtic Church in the 6th cent. Though the use of repeated and variable penances for specific sins was attacked as infringing the ancient discipline of public penance at the Council of Toledo in 589, the practice was commended at the Council of Chalon-sur-Saône (between 647 and 653), and the Penitentials which reflected it spread rapidly throughout the W. in the following cents. In a bewildering variety of forms they recommend inconsistent penalties; some allow commutation of penance for money, and even the employment of substitutes. The Carolingian reformers denounced their 'certain errors and uncertain authors' at Chalon-sur-Saône in 813, and the Council of Paris in 829 commanded bishops to burn all unauthorized texts of the kind. Several efforts to provide more orderly handbooks culminated in Book 19 of the *Decretum* of *Burckard of Worms (the 'Corrector'), which had an enormous influence. By the end of the 12th cent. this mechanistic discipline was giving way to a more individual approach, reflected in such handbooks for confessors as those of *Alan of Lille and St *Raymond of Peñafort.

Selection of texts, with discussion, pr. by F. W. H. Wasserschleben (Halle, 1851) and H. J. Schmitz (vol. 1, Mainz, 1883; vol. 2, Düsseldorf, 1898). Eng. trs. (various items) by J. T. McNeill and H. M. Gamer (Records of Civilization, 29; New York, 1938). *The Irish Penitentials*, ed. L. Bieler with appendix by D. A. Binchy (Scriptores Latini Hiberniae, 5; 1963). C. Vogel, *Les 'Libri Paenitentiales'* (Typologie des sources du moyen âge occidental, 27; 1978, with 'Mise à jour' by A. J. Frantzen, 1985). R. Kottje, *Die Bussbücher Halitgars von Cambrai und des Hrabanus Maurus* (Beiträge zur Geschichte und Quellenkunde des Mittelalters, 8; 1980). A. J. Frantzen, *The Literature of Penance in Anglo-Saxon England* (New Brunswick, NJ [1983]), with bibl. G. Le Bras in *DTC* 12 (pt. 1; 1933), cols. 1160–79, s.v. 'Pénitentiels'; P. J. Payer in *Dictionary of the Middle Ages*, 9 (1987), pp. 487–93, s.v. 'Penance and Penitentials', with extensive bibl.

Penitential Psalms. See SEVEN PENITENTIAL PSALMS.

Penitentiary. In the RC Church a Penitentiary in general is a cleric charged with certain aspects of the administration of the Sacrament of *Penance and related matters. A Canon Penitentiary is a member of a cathedral chapter who holds special powers to absolve in the sacramental *forum from certain automatically incurred censures (*CIC* (1983), can. 508). The 'Major Penitentiary' is the *cardinal who presides over a tribunal which deals with important matters to do with the internal and sacramental forum world-wide, as well as with the granting and uses of *indulgences.

E. Göller, *Die päpstliche Pönitentiarie von ihrem Ursprung bis zu ihrer Umgestaltung unter Pius V.* (Bibliothek des Kgl. Preussischen Historischen Instituts in Rom, 3–4 and 7–8; 1907–11). F. Tamburini, 'Per la Storia dei Cardinali Penitenzieri Maggiori e dell'Archivio della Penitenzieria Apostolica', *Rivista di Storia della Chiesa in Italia*, 36 (1982), pp. 332–80. R. Naz in *DDC* 6 (1957), cols. 1327–34, s.v. 'Pénitencerie'; P. Lumbreras in *NCE* 11 (1967), pp. 87 f., s.v.

penitents. In the ancient system of public *Penance (q.v.), penitents were segregated from the rest of the congregation by wearing a special robe, having close-cropped hair and worshipping apart in the church. Here, towards the W. end of the nave, placed between the *catechumens and the faithful, they received from the bishop special laying on of hands each Sunday. In the E. Church, though not in the W., the order of penitents may have been divided into four stages, though the prevalence of this procedure has been contested by F. X. Funk and E. *Schwartz. The penitent remained in the order till he was readmitted to Communion. Certain disabilities attached to him for life.

The disciplinary regulations controlling the exercise of Penance in the early Church will be found in the primitive collections of canons (for bibl. see CANON LAW). E. Vacandard, *La Pénitence publique dans l'Église primitive* (2 vols., 1903). C. Vogel, *Le Pécheur et la Pénitence dans l'Église ancienne* (1966), esp. pp. 34–41. F. X. Funk, *Kirchengeschichtliche Abhandlungen und Untersuchungen*, 1 (1897), pp. 155–209; E. Schwartz, *Bussstufen und Katechumenatsklassen* (Schriften der wissenschaftlichen Gesellschaft in Strassburg, 7; 1911). G. Mead in *DCA* 2 (1880), pp. 1591–6, s.v. 'Penitence, iii: The Penitential Stations' (useful collection of material, but assumes older view). See also bibl. to PENANCE.

Penn, William (1644–1718), *Quaker and founder of Pennsylvania. The eldest son of Admiral Sir William Penn (1621–70), who captured Jamaica from the Dutch (May 1655), he was for a time an undergraduate at Christ Church, Oxford, whence he was sent down in 1661 for refusal to conform with the restored Anglicanism. After some years of travel abroad he was admitted in 1665 a student at Lincoln's Inn. A sermon of Thomas Loe, an Oxford tradesman with whom he had been acquainted since boyhood, which he heard at Cork in 1666, had a decisive influence and in 1667 he attached himself to the Quakers. He soon began writing in defence of his newly won faith and in 1668 his *The Sandy Foundation Shaken*, an attack on the orthodox doctrines of the *Trinity and *Atonement and the *Calvinistic account of *justification, led to his imprisonment in the Tower. During his confinement he wrote *No Cross, No Crown* (1669), a recognized classic of Quaker practice. In 1670 the acquittal of him and William Meade at the Old Bailey by the jury, who gave a verdict against the ruling of the Court and were forthwith imprisoned, led to the famous 'Bushell's Case', in which 12 judges unanimously upheld the jury's rights and declared their imprisonment illegal. During the 1670s Penn became increasingly interested in the founda-

tion of a colony in America which would assure liberty of conscience for Quakers and others. From 1677 he and two other Friends were trustees of West New Jersey, which was given a constitution on Quaker principles, and in April 1681 he joined with 11 other Friends to purchase East New Jersey. Also in 1681 he obtained by letters patent a grant of Pennsylvania, confirmed the following year. He then founded the 'Free Society of Traders' to develop the colony economically, drew up a constitution which, like that of West New Jersey, permitted all forms of worship compatible with monotheism and religious liberty, and himself sailed for America. After establishing the colony he returned to England in 1684. Believing that *James II, with whom he had had relations from the days of his father's admiralship, was a true advocate of toleration, he expressed the Quakers' thanks for the *Declaration of Indulgence (1687) in a loyal address and followed it with a pamphlet, *Good Advice to the Church of England, Roman Catholic and Protestant Dissenter*. For a short time after the Revolution he was held to bail as one of James' adherents, and in 1692 he was deprived by an order in council of the Governorship of Pennsylvania. In 1693 he published *An Essay towards the Present and Future Peace of Europe*, advocating the establishment of a European Parliament. In the same year he resumed his practice of itinerant preaching and in 1696 wrote his *Primitive Christianity*, upholding the identity of Quaker principles with those of the early Church. In 1699 he paid a second visit to Pennsylvania, intending to settle there for good, but in 1701 the proposal to introduce legislation changing the status of the province into a Crown Colony brought him back to England, where he lived successively at Kensington, Knightsbridge, Brentford, and Field Ruscombe (near Twyford). He is buried at Jordans, near Chalfont St Giles. His prolific writings were almost all occasional.

Collected edn. of his works (2 vols., fol., London, 1726), with Life, written by Joseph Besse eight years after Penn's death, pr. anon. in vol. 1, pp. 1–150. Modern edn. under the title *The Papers of William Penn*, ed. M. M. Dunn and others (5 vols., Philadelphia, 1981–7, incl. as vol. 5: E. B. Bronner and D. Fraser, *William Penn's Published Writings 1660–1726: An Interpretive Bibliography*, 1986). Convenient edn. of *The Peace of Europe* and various other works in Everyman Library, 724 [1915]. Secondary Lives by T. Clarkson (2 vols., London, 1813); S. M. Janney (Philadelphia, 1851; 2nd edn., 1856; with many useful orig. docs.); Mrs. Colquhoun Grant (London, *c*.1907); M. R. Brailsford (ibid., 1930); B. Dobrée (ibid., 1932); C. E. Vulliamy (ibid., 1933); W. I. Hull (ibid., 1937); W. W. Comfort (Philadelphia, 1944); and C. O. Peare (ibid. and New York, 1957; London, 1959). V. Buranelli, *The King and the Quaker: A Study of William Penn and James II* (Philadelphia, 1962). M. M. Dunn, *William Penn: Politics and Conscience* (Princeton, NJ, 1967). M. B. Endy, *William Penn and early Quakerism* (ibid. [1973]). R. S. and M. M. Dunn (eds.), *The World of William Penn* (Philadelphia, 1986), pp. 3–84. J. M. Rigg in *DNB* 44 (1895), pp. 311–20; R. W. Kelsey in *Dict. Amer. Biog.* 14 (1934), pp. 433–7. See also bibl. to FRIENDS, SOCIETY OF.

Pennefather, William (1816–73), *Evangelical divine. Of Irish extraction, he was ordained priest in 1842; he was incumbent of Christ Church, Barnet (1852–64) and of St Jude's, Mildmay Park, Islington (1864–73), now both parts of London. His influence spread far beyond his parishes. In 1861 he founded what was to become the Mildmay Deaconess Institution, modelled on *Kaiserswerth.

Though originally devoted to various forms of social work, some of its members were to become *deaconesses; the Mildmay Institution, which in 1917 became St Catherine's Deaconess House, Highbury, was the only sizeable training institution in the Evangelical tradition, surviving until 1940. Pennefather invited D. L. *Moody and I. Sankey to conduct their first mission in Britain in 1873, but died before they arrived.

R. Braithwaite (ed), *The Life and Letters of the Rev. William Pennefather* (1878). A. R. Buckland in *DNB* 44 (1895), pp. 327 f.

Pennington, Isaac. See PENINGTON, ISAAC.

Penry, John (1559–93), *Separatist. Of Welsh descent, he was educated at Peterhouse, Cambridge, and St Alban's Hall, Oxford. After leaving Oxford, he quickly came into conflict with the bishops on account of his *Puritan ideas. His *Equity of an Humble Supplication in the behalf of the Country of Wales, that some Order may be taken for the Preaching of the Gospel among those People* (1587), an attack on the C of E, angered Abp. J. *Whitgift, who brought him before the Court of High Commission. In 1588, when the scurrilous *Marprelate tracts appeared, Penry was almost certainly unjustly suspected of being their author, and in consequence of these suspicions early in 1590 fled to Scotland, where he remained for nearly three years. On his return to England in the autumn of 1592 he became an adherent of the London Separatist congregation. Now considered a danger to the Church, he was hanged on 29 May 1593, on an ill-grounded charge of treason.

An Account of Penry's Trial, in Lat. (but with extracts from his works in Eng.), together with a collection of citations apparently collected for his trial and which Penry intended to present to Queen *Elizabeth I, the original MS of his defence against his first indictment and some of his final remarks to Lord Burghley on the day of his execution, were ed., with introd., by C. Burrage (Oxford, 1913). The Notebook containing the passages mainly responsible for his condemnation, ed. A. Peel (Camden Society, 3rd ser. 67; 1944). *Three Treatises concerning Wales*, by Penry are repr., with introd. by D. Williams (Cardiff, 1960). W. Pierce, *John Penry: His Life, Times and Writings* (1923). D. J. McGinn, *John Penry and the Marprelate Controversy* (New Brunswick, NJ, 1966). S. Lee in *DNB* 44 (1895), pp. 346–50. See also bibl. to MARPRELATE TRACTS.

Pentateuch (Gk. πεντα, 'five' + τεῦχος, 'book'). A title in general use among biblical scholars for the five 'Books of *Moses': *Genesis, *Exodus, *Leviticus, *Numbers, and *Deuteronomy. Traditionally, these Books were held to have been written, almost in their entirety, by Moses himself. However, during the 19th cent. the 'documentary hypothesis' was developed by scholars, notably J. *Wellhausen; according to this theory, the Pentateuch was compiled from previously written documents dating from the 9th to the 5th cent. BC. Following the work of H. *Gunkel early in the 20th cent., much research concerned itself with the oral traditions which lay behind these postulated documents; thus M. *Noth, G. von *Rad, and many others retained the 'documentary hypothesis', but supplemented it with insights from Gunkel's *form critical approach. Such a position is still widely accepted. An alternative approach has been to reject altogether the notion that previously independent written documents were combined to form the Pentateuch. Scholars who

favour this course have frequently emphasized the thematic unity of the Pentateuch and the importance of oral tradition, and have argued that cycles of tradition gradually evolved until something like the present form of the Pentateuch emerged. Rejection of Wellhausen's thesis long characterized Scandinavian scholarship (e.g. I. Engnell), but in recent years somewhat similar theories have found support elsewhere (including Germany, e.g. R. Rendtorff). See also entries 'J', 'E', 'D', 'P', and HOLINESS CODE.

J. Wellhausen, *Geschichte Israels*, 1 (1878; 2nd edn. as *Prolegomena zur Geschichte Israels*, 1883; Eng. tr., Edinburgh, 1885, repr. 1957). H. Gunkel, 'Die israelitische Literatur' in *Die Kultur der Gegenwart*, ed. P. Hinneberg, 1. 7 (1906), pp. 51–102. G. von Rad, *Das formgeschichtliche Problem des Hexateuchs* (Beiträge zur Wissenschaft vom Alten und Neuen Testament, 4. Folge, 26; 1938), repr. in his *Gesammelte Studien zum Alten Testament* (Munich, 1958), pp. 9–86; Eng. tr. in *The Problem of the Hexateuch and Other Essays* (1966), pp. 1–78; M. Noth, *Überlieferungsgeschichte des Pentateuch* (Stuttgart, 1948; Eng. tr., Englewood Cliffs, NJ, 1972); I. Engnell, 'Moseböckerna', *Svenskt Bibliskt Uppsalagsverk*, 2 (2nd edn., 1962), cols. 152–65; Eng. tr., 'The Pentateuch', in *Critical Essays on the Old Testament* (1970), pp. 50–67. R. Rendtorff, *Das überlieferungsgeschichtliche Problem des Pentateuch* (Beihefte zur *ZATW*, 147; 1977; Eng. tr., *The Problem of the Process of Transmission in the Pentateuch*, Journal for the Study of the Old Testament, Supplement Series, 89; Sheffield, 1990); cf. J. Van Seters, 'Recent Studies on the Pentateuch: a Crisis in Method', *Journal of the American Oriental Society*, 99 (1979), pp. 663–73. R. N. Whybray, *The Making of the Pentateuch: A Methodological Study* (Journal for the Study of the Old Testament, Supplement Series, 53; Sheffield [1987]). Soggin, pp. 91–163, with good bibl.

Pentecost (Gk. πεντηκοστή, the 'fiftieth day'). The Greek name given to the Feast of *Weeks (e.g. Tob. 2: 1; *Josephus, *Ant.* 17. 10. 2), so called because it fell on the 50th day after *Passover. At this feast the first-fruits of the corn harvest were presented (Deut. 16: 9) and, in most later times, the giving of the Law by Moses was commemorated. As the Holy Spirit descended on the Apostles on this day (Acts 2: 1), the name was applied by the Church to the feast celebrating this event, popularly called *Whitsunday (q.v.). In early times, e.g. in the *Nicene canons (can. 20), the word 'Pentecost' was also used for the whole period between Easter and Whitsunday, i.e. the Paschal time, during which no fast was allowed and prayer was only made standing. For further liturgical details see WHITSUNDAY.

F. Lohse in *TWNT* 6 (1959; Eng. tr., 1969), pp. 44–53, s.v. πεντηκοστή, with refs.; M. Delcor in *Dict. Bibl.*, Suppl. 7 (1966), cols. 858–79, s.v. 'Pentecôte (la Fête de la)'. For the Hebrew feast, see also WEEKS, FEAST OF; for the Christian, see WHITSUNDAY.

Pentecostalism. The modern Pentecostal movement is characterized by belief in the possibility of receiving the same experience and spiritual 'gifts' as did the first Christians 'on the day of Pentecost' (Acts 2: 1–4). Its adherents emphasize the corporate element in worship (often marked by great spontaneity) and lay special stress on the practice of the gifts listed in 1 Cor. and recorded in Acts (e.g. speaking in tongues or '*glossalalia', prophecy, divine [*spiritual] healing, and *exorcism), and on possession of these gifts by all true believers. Most of them claim that the 'power' to exercise these gifts is given initially in an experience known as '*baptism in the Holy Spirit', usually

regarded as distinct from conversion and from sacramental (or water) *Baptism, and the movement came to be distinguished by the claim (first made in 1900) that 'Spirit baptism' is normally signified by the recipient's breaking into tongues.

In the early years of the 20th cent. experiences of 'Spirit baptism' were reported among various denominational revivalist or *Holiness groups in America; those occurring in Los Angeles in 1906 attracted much attention and had widespread repercussions. Pentecostalism's origins were strongly apocalyptic, and its early adherents widely believed that it was to be preached throughout the world 'before the end came'. Of the many specifically Pentecostal Churches which came to be formed, one of the earliest was the 'Church of God', commonly designated of Cleveland, Tenn., to distinguish it from other bodies taking the same name. The structure of *Black slave religion contributed to the success of early Pentecostalism, but Pentecostals in America quickly segregated; the largest Black Pentecostal Church, the 'Church of God in Christ', was originally a Holiness body which adopted Pentecostal teaching in 1907. The largest Pentecostal body in America is the '*Assemblies of God', an affiliation of Churches formed in 1914.

Pentecostalism in Britain is usually dated from a visit to Sunderland in 1907 of T. B. Barratt, a *Methodist minister from Oslo who claimed to have received 'Spirit baptism' in New York. In 1915 the 'Elim Foursquare Gospel Alliance' came into being under George Jeffreys in Ireland, and in 1924 the 'Assemblies of God in Britain and Ireland' was constituted by c.70 independent assemblies. In 1953 immigrants from Jamaica established in Britain the 'New Testament Church of God', an offshoot of the Cleveland 'Church of God'. Pentecostalism also spread early to other W. European countries, above all through Barratt's influence. It is now expanding in the Third World, esp. in Latin America, *Indonesia, and among the African Independent Churches, but it is not always clear whether the 'pentecostal-type' features found in some Third-World Christianity have N. American origins or origins in the local culture; often the two have mingled.

Pentecostal Churches vary considerably, depending on the theology of their founders or the local culture, and since c.1960 the Pentecostal movement has come to be widely represented not only by the 'classical' Pentecostal Churches, but also within the main Christian denominations, where it is sometimes called 'Neo-Pentecostalism' (see CHARISMATIC RENEWAL MOVEMENT). Originally 'a religion of the poor', in N. America and Europe White Pentecostalism is becoming increasingly middle-class.

D. Gee, The Pentecostal Movement (1941; rev. edn., Wind and Flame, Croydon, 1967). W. J. Hollenweger, Enthusiastisches Christentum: Die Pfingstbewegung in Geschichte und Gegenwart (Wuppertal, 1969; Eng. tr., The Pentecostals, 1972). M. J. C. Calley, God's People: West Indian Pentecostal Sects in England (1965). [H.] V. Synan, The Holiness-Pentecostal Movement in the United States (Grand Rapids [1971]), pp. 95–224. R. Laurentin, Pentecôtisme chez les Catholiques ([1974] Eng. tr., 1977). R. M. Anderson, Vision of the Disinherited: The Making of American Pentecostalism (New York and Oxford, 1979). J. Sandige, Roman Catholic/Pentecostal Dialogue (1977–1982): A Study in Developing Ecumenism (Studien zur interkulturellen Geschichte des Christentums, 44; Frankfurt etc. [1987]). S. M. Burgess and G. B. McGee (eds.), Dictionary of Pentecostal and Charismatic Movements (Grand Rapids [1988]).

Pentecostarion (Gk. πεντηκοστάριον). In the E. rite the liturgical book which contains the variable portions of the services for the season between *Easter and the Sunday of All Saints (the Sunday after *Pentecost) inclusive. In Slav usage, it is known as the 'Flowery' or 'Festal' *Triodion (Tsvetnaya Triod).

Pepin (or more correctly **Pippin**) **III** (714–68), 'Pepin the Short', Frankish King. The son of *Charles Martel, he was educated by the monks of *St-Denis, near *Paris, and with his brother Carloman, succeeded to his father's office as Mayor of the Palace of the Frankish kingdom in 741. In 747 Carloman retired into a monastery, leaving Pepin sole ruler. With the assent of Pope *Zacharias he was elected King by the nobles in 751 in place of the purely nominal Merovingian King, Childeric III, and anointed by Frankish bishops. In 754 the ceremony was repeated by the Pope himself, *Stephen II (III), from whom he received the title 'patricius' in exchange for his promise to win back for him the exarchate of *Ravenna and the rights and territories of the Roman republic. Having defeated the Lombards under Aistulf in the same year and again in 756, Pepin fulfilled his promise by giving the Pope the territories specified in the no-longer-extant document known as the 'Donation of Pepin' and constituted himself and his successors protectors of the Holy See. Throughout his reign, in collaboration with Bp. *Chrodegang of Metz, he took an active part in furthering the ecclesiastical reforms begun by St *Boniface and thereby considerably increased the prestige of the Church among his people. He pursued a complex monastic policy, closely integrated with his political activities, which broke the power of aristocratic bishops. He also considerably extended Frankish dominion with campaigns in Saxony, Aquitaine, and Alemannia, and inaugurated a reform of the coinage under royal control. He died at St-Denis on 24 Sept. 768 and was succeeded by his son *Charlemagne. See also PATRIMONY OF ST PETER.

A. Dopsch, J. Lechner, M. Tangl, and E. Mühlbacher (eds.), Die Urkunden Pippins, Karlmanns und Karls des Grossen (MGH, Diplomata Karolinorum, 1; 1906), pp. 1–60. The Fourth Book of the Chronicle of Fredegar with its Continuations, tr. from Lat., with introd. and notes, by J. M. Wallace-Hadrill (1960), esp. pp. 97–121. E. Caspar, Pippin und die römische Kirche (1914; repr., Darmstadt, 1973); L. Levillain, 'L'Avènement de la dynastie carolingienne et les origines de l'État pontifical (749–757)', Bibliothèque de l'École des Chartes, 94 (1933), pp. 225–95. T. F. X. Noble, The Republic of St Peter: The Birth of the Papal State, 680–825 (Philadelphia [1984]), pp. 65–116 and 256–80 passim, with refs. to earlier studies on the subject. J. Semmler, 'Pippin III. und die fränkischen Kloster', Francia, 3 (for 1975; 1976), pp. 88–146. R. McKitterick, The Frankish Kingdoms under the Carolingians, 751–987 (1983), esp. pp. 33–59; J. M. Wallace-Hadrill, The Frankish Church (Oxford History of the Christian Church, 1983), pp. 162–80.

Perceval, Arthur Philip (1799–1853), *Tractarian theologian. He was educated at Oriel College, and from 1821 to 1825 held a fellowship at All Souls, Oxford. In 1824 he became rector of East Horsley in Surrey; from 1826 until deprived in 1850 he was a royal chaplain. In the early stages of the *Oxford Movement he was one of its chief supporters, being present at the celebrated conference at Hadleigh in July 1833. In his *Churchman's Manual*, a set of questions and answers conceived as a supplement to the Prayer Book *Catechism and issued shortly after the Conference, he stressed the *Apostolic Succession and thus produced a useful complement to No. 1 of the *Tracts for the Times*. In 1842 he published *A Collection of Papers Connected with the Theological Movement of 1833*, largely in defence of J. H. *Newman's 'Tract No. 90'. He had himself been the author of Tracts Nos. 23, 35, and 36. Queen Victoria deprived him of his chaplaincy because of his opposition to the *Gorham Judgement (1850).

A. F. Pollard in *DNB* 44 (1895), p. 368.

Percival, John (1834–1918), Bp. of *Hereford. Elected Fellow of Queen's College, Oxford, in 1858, he became successively first headmaster of Clifton College (1862), president of Trinity College, Oxford (1878), headmaster of Rugby (1887), and Bp. of Hereford (1895). He was keenly interested in religious and secular education, and did much to promote the university extension movement and the higher education of women; and as headmaster of Clifton exercised a great spiritual influence on his school. During his latter years he sought to further the cause of reunion between the C of E and the Nonconformist Churches, and met with the opposition both of *Convocation and of his own clergy when he invited Nonconformists to receive Communion in Hereford Cathedral.

W. *Temple, *Life of Bishop Percival* (1921). G. F. Bradby in *DNB, 1912–1921*, pp. 432 f.

Percy, John. See FISHER THE JESUIT.

Peregrinatio Egeriae (or Etheriae or Silviae). See EGERIA, PILGRIMAGE OF.

perfection. The primary meaning of the term is completeness and in an absolute sense it may be attributed only to God. In the OT, however, Job is described as a 'man that was perfect' (Job 1: 1) and in the NT perfection is frequently enjoined on the Christian. According to Mt. 5: 48 the perfection required of man is related to that of God ('Be ye therefore perfect as your heavenly Father is perfect'). In some passages (e.g. Phil. 3: 15 and Heb. 6: 1) it would appear that perfection is in some degree realizable even in this life. In Col. 3: 14 charity is described as 'the bond of perfection'. The close association of perfection and charity was developed in detail by later writers. The verb 'to perfect' was regularly used of the operation of the Sacraments, esp. *Baptism.

From early times *martyrdom was described as perfection (or fulfilment), and the term was soon also applied to the state of virginity. From the 4th cent. onwards, *monasticism came to be regarded as the way of perfection *par excellence*, and a double standard of perfection developed. This was held to be foreshadowed in Mt. 19: 11 f., 21 (cf. *Didache*, 6. 2). 'Religious Perfection', involving the practice of the so-called '*Counsels of Perfection', was distinguished from 'Christian Perfection' made possible by Baptism. In the W. the *Pelagian view of perfection as the crown of human endeavour led to a compensating emphasis on the need for Divine *grace. When

the Council of *Trent laid down that perfect obedience to the Divine Law was possible, it made it clear that the perfection envisaged was only that accommodated to the fallen state of man and to be distinguished from the perfect law of love.

In general, the Reformers held that perfection is possible in this life only through imputation of the perfection of Christ to the believer. Among the *Methodists, however, the idea of perfection has played a central part. The *Wesleys persistently sought perfection and held that every Christian believer could be perfected in the love of God and man and wholly delivered from sin. Acc. to Methodist spiritual writers the entrance on the way of perfection takes place some time after conversion; it is instantaneous, and those who receive the experience, known as the 'Great Salvation', are thereby convinced that all sin has been completely and permanently rooted out in them. Those that are made perfect in this way pray constantly without interruption, they feel nothing but love, and are restored to the original image of God.

R. Garrigou-Lagrange, OP, *Perfection chrétienne et contemplation* (1923); R. N. Flew, *The Idea of Perfection in Christian Theology* (1934); G. Feckes, *Die Lehre vom christlichen Vollkommenheitsstreben* (Freiburg i.B., 1949); I. Hausherr, SJ, *La Perfection du chrétien*, ed. M. Olphe-Galliard, SJ [1968]. J. Wesley, *Plain Account of Christian Perfection* (1766). G. S. Wakefield in id. (ed.), *A Dictionary of Christian Spirituality* (1983), pp. 297–9, s.v.; S. Legasse and others in *Dict. Sp.* 12 (pt. 1; 1984), cols. 1074–156, s.v. See also DEIFICATION.

Perfection, Counsels of. See COUNSELS OF PERFECTION.

Perfectionists. See ONEIDA COMMUNITY.

Pergamum. The town was situated *c.*50 miles north of *Smyrna and *c.*15 miles from the sea, on a hill 1,000 feet above the surrounding plain. In the 2nd cent. BC it became one of the greatest centres of art and culture in the ancient world, reaching the height of its glory in the reign of Eumenes II (197–159). This Eumenes erected the great altar of Zeus the Saviour (now in the Pergamon Museum, Berlin) with the frieze depicting the gods and goddesses of Hellas hurling back the earth-born giants, typifying the triumph of civilization over barbarism. To the same period belongs the invention of parchment ('pergamena carta') as a substitute for papyrus.

To the NT student the chief interest of Pergamum lies in its being one of the 'Seven Churches' in Rev. (2: 12–17). Here it is referred to as the place 'where Satan's throne is' and 'where Satan dwelleth' (2: 13). As Pergamum was the first city in Asia to receive permission to worship the living ruler, the allusion here is presumably to Emperor-worship. This permission had been granted by Octavian (Augustus) in 29 BC, although the temple was not erected until 19 BC. Pergamum was also one of the chief centres of the worship of the healing god Aesculapius, and a large 'Aesculapium' was uncovered by German excavators in 1928; further excavations began in 1958. The modern town is known as Bergama.

Inscriptions and other antiquities in *Altertümer von Pergamon*, pub. by the Königliches Museum at Berlin (10 vols. + plates, var. dates, 1885–1937; vols. 11 ff. pub. by the Deutsches Archäologisches Institut at Berlin, 1968 ff.). T. Wiegand, *Bericht über die Ausgrabungen in Pergamon in 1927* (*Abh.* (Berl.), 1928, Heft 3); id.,

Zweiter Bericht über die Ausgrabungen in Pergamon, 1928–32: Das Asklepieion (ibid., 1932, Heft 5). *Pergamenische Forschungen*, ed. E. Boehringer and others (1968 ff.). W. Radt, *Pergamon: Geschichte und Bauten, Funde und Erforschung einer antiken Metropole* (Cologne, 1988), with bibl. E. V. Hansen, *The Attalids of Pergamon* (Cornell Studies in Classical Philology, 29, Ithaca, NY, 1947; 2nd edn., ibid. 36, Ithaca, NY, and London, 1971). W. M. *Ramsay, *Letters to the Seven Churches of Asia and their Place in the Plan of the Apocalypse* (1904), pp. 281–315; C. J. Hemer, *The Letters to the Seven Churches of Asia in their Local Setting* (Journal for the Study of the New Testament, Supplement Series, 11; Sheffield [1986]), pp. 78–105. W. Zschietzschmann in *PW* 19 (pt. 1; 1937), cols. 1235–63 (Nachträge, s.v. 'Pergamon'); J. Schäfer in R. Stillwell (ed.), *The Princeton Encyclopedia of Classical Sites* (Princeton, NJ, 1976), pp. 688–92, s.v.

pericope (Gk. περικοπή, 'section'). A passage from the Scriptures, esp. one appointed to be read in the Church services. The use of such prescribed portions of Scripture in the Eucharist appears to date from the 4th–5th cents. In earlier times, both in E. and W., the passages were selected at choice by the officiating clergy. See also LEC-TIONARY.

Περικοπή for a section of the Bible occurs as early as St *Justin, *Dial. c. Tryph.* 65. 3. W. Caspari in *PRE* (3rd edn.), 15 (1904), pp. 131–59, s.v. 'Perikopen', where the writer shows that the word was first used as a liturgical term by Protestant writers of the 16th cent.

pericope adulterae, i.e. Jn. 7: 53–8: 11. These verses, which narrate the Lord's compassionate dealing with the woman taken in the act of adultery, are certainly not part of the original text of St John's Gospel. They are not found in any of the early Greek MSS, with the one exception of *Codex Bezae, and they are also wanting in many of the more important MSS of the Syriac, Latin, and Coptic versions. Nor does any Greek commentator before *Euthymius Zigabenus (c. AD 1118) discuss the passage. On the other hand, the story is very much in line with many of those in the Synoptic Gospels, and the facts that it is definitely referred to in a passage in the 3rd cent. *Didascalia Apostolorum* (2. 24; ed. R. H. *Connolly, p. 76), and was perhaps known to *Papias, point to its primitiveness. In the *Ferrar group of MSS the passage is placed after Lk. 21: 38; this fact, together with certain stylistic similarities, have led to the suggestion that the passage belongs to St Luke.

The passage is discussed in comm. on St John's Gospel, cited s.v. JOHN, GOSPEL OF ST. H. J. *Cadbury, 'A Possible Case of Lukan Authorship (John 7. 53–8. 11)', *HTR* 10 (1917), pp. 237–44. H. Riesenfeld, 'Perikopen de adultera i den fornkyrkliga traditionen', *Svensk Exegetisk Årsbok*, 17 (1953), pp. 106–18; Eng. tr. in *The Gospel Tradition* (Philadelphia, 1970; Oxford, 1971), pp. 95–110. U. Becker, *Jesus und die Ehebrecherin* (Beihefte zur ZNTW, 28; 1963). E. Bammel, 'The Cambridge Pericope. The Addition to Luke 6. 4 in Codex Bezae', *New Testament Studies*, 32 (1986), pp. 404–26.

peripatetic (Gk. περιπατητής, 'one who walks about'). A philosopher of the school of *Aristotle. The name was adopted in reference to Aristotle's practice of teaching while moving about in a covered walk (περίπατος) in the Lyceum at Athens.

Perkins, William (1558–1602), *Puritan theologian. Educated at Christ's College, Cambridge, where he was a Fellow from 1584 to 1594, he soon became prominent in the university by his preaching, lectures, and writings as a vigorous anti-Romanist theologian and a supporter of Puritan principles. His writings, mainly occasional, were marked by candour, an honest desire to understand his opponents, and, despite his use of the traditional scholastic methods which still survived at Cambridge, an evident concern for history. They include his *Reformed Catholike* (1597) on the Roman controversy, which W. Bishop, titular Bp. of Chalcedon (d. 1624), answered in his *Reformation of a Catholic Deformed by W. Perkins* (2 pts., 1604, 1607), and *De Praedestinationis Modo et Ordine* (1598), which evoked a reply from J. *Arminius in the same year. His works were held in high repute throughout the 17th cent. by theologians with Calvinist sympathies. They also include *An Exposition of the Lord's Prayer* (1592) and *An Exposition of the Symbol or Creed of the Apostles* (1595).

The numerous collected edns. of his works (all very incomplete) incl. those pub. Cambridge, 1603; ibid., 1605; 3 vols., fol., ibid., 1608–9, and 3 vols., fol., London and Cambridge, 1612–13. Modern collection of extracts, ed., with introd., by I. Breward (Courtenay Library of Reformation Classics, 3; Sutton Courtenay, Oxon, 1970). 'A Discourse of Conscience' (orig. pub. 1596) and 'The Whole Treatise of the Cases of Conscience' (pub. 1606) also ed. T. F. Merrill (Nieuwkoop, 1966), with introd. H. C. Porter, *Reformation and Reaction in Tudor Cambridge* (Cambridge, 1958), pp. 288–313; R. T. Kendall, *Calvin and English Calvinism to 1649* (Oxford Theological Monographs, 1979), pp. 51–76; R. A. Muller, *Christ and the Decree: Christology and Predestination in Reformed Theology from Calvin to Perkins* (Durham, NC, 1986), esp. pp. 142–73.

Perpetua, St (d. 7 Mar. 203), African martyr. The *Passion of St Perpetua and St *Felicity* tells how Perpetua and her slave, with other African catechumens, were imprisoned and, after their Baptism, condemned to execution in the arena at Carthage. It is a contemporary document, possibly edited by *Tertullian, which records, besides the story of their martyrdom, the interesting visions of Perpetua and the priest, Saturus. The basilica of Sts Perpetua and Felicity was among the most important in Carthage. Feast day, formerly 6 Mar. (transferred to make 7 Mar. free for St *Thomas Aquinas); since 1969, 7 Mar.

Crit. edn. of Lat. text of *Passio* by J. A. *Robinson (Texts and Studies, 1, no. 2; Cambridge, 1891). Gk. text first ed. from a Jerusalem MS by J. R. *Harris and S. K. Gifford, London, 1890 (Harris's defence of the priority of the Gk. text, however, has been generally rejected by later scholars). Lat. and Gk. texts also ed. by C. I. M. I. van Beek (Florilegium Patristicum, 43; Bonn, 1938). Lat. text repr., with Eng. tr. by H. Musurillo, *The Acts of the Christian Martyrs* (Oxford, 1972), pp. 106–31. P. Franchi de' Cavalieri, *La Passio SS. Perpetuae et Felicitatis* (RQ, Supplementheft, 5; 1896). Å. [J.] Fridh, *Le Problème de la Passion des saintes Perpétue et Félicité* (Studia Graeca et Latina Gothoburgensia, 26; 1968). E. R. Dodds, *Pagan and Christian in an Age of Anxiety* (Wiles Lectures, 1963; Cambridge, 1965), pp. 47–53, with refs. E. Corsini, 'Proposte per una lettura della "Passio Perpetuae" ', in *Forma Futuri: Studi in onore del Cardinale Michele Pellegrino* (Turin, 1975), pp. 481–541; other arts. by C. M. and V. Lamanto, ibid., pp. 542–86. L. Robert, 'Une vision de Perpétue martyre à Carthage en 203', *Comptes rendus de l'Académie des Inscriptions et Belles-Lettres* (1982), pp. 228–76. P. Habermehl, *Perpetua und der Ägypten* (TU 140 [1992]). J. Quasten, *Patrology*,

1 (Utrecht, 1950), pp. 181–3. J. P. Kirsch in *CE* 6 (1909), p. 29, s.v. 'Felicitas and Perpetua'; H. *Leclercq, OSB, in *DACL* 14 (pt. 1; 1939), cols. 393–444, s.v. 'Perpétue et Félicité (Saintes)'.

perpetual curate. The name formerly given to a clerk who officiated in a parish or district to which he had been nominated by the *impropriator and licensed by the Bishop. Exemption from the *Appropriation of Benefices Act 1402 was allowed to benefices granted to monasteries *ad mensam monachorum* and in certain other cases, which meant that no *vicar was endowed. When, after the *dissolution of the monasteries, such exempt parishes passed to *lay rectors, these rectors were obliged to discharge the spiritual duties by nominating some particular person to the *Ordinary for his licence to serve the cure on their behalf. Curates thus licensed became perpetual, removable only by revocation of the licence of the Ordinary. The ministers of new churches of separate parishes, ecclesiastical districts, consolidated chapelries and district chapelries were also perpetual curates (Church Building Act 1845) as were the ministers appointed to new parishes or districts created by the Church Building Acts 1831 and 1839, and the New Parishes Act 1843.

Because curacies had no corporate personality (unlike bishoprics, rectories and vicarages), property could not be settled on the office rather than the individual. To remedy this, curacies which were augmented from *Queen Anne's Bounty were declared perpetual benefices and the incumbents bodies politic by Queen Anne's Bounty Act 1714 s. 4. All other perpetual curacies were also classified as ecclesiastical *benefices in, but not before, the *Pluralities Act 1838 s. 124 and subsequent legislation, including the Interpretation Measure 1925 s. 3.

Perpetual curates obtained possession of their benefices by licence from the Bishop without *institution or *induction. They were styled vicars by the Incumbents Act 1868 for the purposes of title only, but they were not made vicars in fact. However, the Pastoral Measure 1968 s. 87 has now converted all perpetual curacies into vicarages and all perpetual curates at that date have become vicars in law without further formality. Perpetual curacies therefore ceased to exist on 1 April 1969, when the Measure came into force.

Perrone, Giovanni (1794–1876), Italian *Jesuit theologian. He joined the Society of Jesus in 1815 and in 1824 was made professor of dogmatic theology in the Roman College, a post which he held (not quite continuously) till his death. His *Praelectiones Theologicae* (9 vols., 1835–42) were one of the most widely used manuals on Catholic dogmatics in the 19th century.

Sommervogel, 6 (1895), cols. 558–71; Polgár, 2 (1990), p. 653. T. Lynch (ed.), 'The Newman–Perrone paper on Development', *Gregorianum*, 16 (1935), pp. 402–47; F. Cavallera, SJ, 'Le Document Newman–Perrone et le développement du dogme', *Bulletin de Littérature ecclésiastique*, 47 (1946), pp. 132–42. W. Kasper, *Die Lehre von der Tradition in der römischen Schule* (Freiburg, 1962), pp. 29–181.

per saltum (Lat., 'by a leap'). A term sometimes used of the conferring of a particular rank of orders when a candidate has not previously received the lower grades, e.g. the ordination to the priesthood of a man who is not already a deacon. In RC canon law it is held that such

ordinations are valid, but illicit. In early times, however, they were a common occurrence. See also INTERSTICES.

persecutions, early Christian. Christianity at first appeared to the Roman authorities as a form of *Judaism, which enjoyed toleration, but Jewish agitation against the Christians (e.g. Acts 17: 5; 18: 12) revealed its separate identity. The secrecy of the early Christian rites and misunderstandings of Christian language (e.g. Jn. 6: 35) and of the *agape and *Eucharist led pagans to suppose them guilty of *flagitia*, promiscuity, incest, and cannibalism. This fact explains why *Nero in 64 could make them scapegoats for the fire of Rome, which by popular report was his own doing; to *Tacitus, though guiltless on this charge, they were enemies of mankind. From then on, persecution prob. continued, though intermittently. It is, for instance, attested under *Domitian; St *Ignatius was martyred under Trajan, and in his reign *Pliny, as governor of Bithynia-Pontus, assumed that avowed Christians as such deserved death. No general enactment was directed against the faith before 249; the later Christian notion of ten persecutions initiated by particular emperors (analogous to the ten plagues of Egypt) has no foundation.

Pliny found no proof that the Christians were guilty of *flagitia* and was therefore disposed to pardon *apostates. Trajan accepted his findings, as if he were already aware of the truth, and confirmed his decision. He also ruled that Christians were not, like ordinary criminals, to be searched out, but to be punished only on information laid by private persons (not anonymously), if they would not recant. These rulings applied only to Bithynia-Pontus, but the evidence of Christian writings contemporary with later persecutions before *Decius shows that they came to be valid throughout the empire; the imperial rescripts affecting Christians collected *c.*215 by the jurist Ulpian and now lost cannot have introduced any essential change. Though *Apologists still found it necessary to demonstrate that the Christians were neither flagitious nor disloyal, the government, since it made no effort to exterminate them, evidently needed no convincing; humble folk, such as nearly all Christians were, taught to obey the authorities ordained of God (Rom. 13: 1–6), presented no political danger.

In general Rome practised religious toleration. Roman citizens, like the colonists at Philippi (Acts 16: 21), might not legally worship any god not recognized by the State, but the ban was seldom enforced, and in any case it cannot explain the punishment of those Christians who were not Roman citizens. Rome also protected the ancestral religions of all her subject peoples. Toleration extended to Judaism, as the ancestral religion of the Jews, even though the Jews denied the divinity of all pagan gods. As the Christians' claim to be 'the true Israel' was rejected, they did not benefit from the protection given to Judaism. They were regarded as atheists because they would take no part in the prescribed cults of the gods. These cults were widely supposed to be indispensable for maintaining peace with the gods (*pax deorum*); their neglect would entail divine retribution. Enlightened men did not all entertain this belief, but Trajan and his successors regarded traditional religious practices as the cement of society, and public order would have been at risk if they had withstood popular indignation against the Christians. This was aroused not only by their 'atheism', but by lingering credulity in their *flagitia*, and by their alienation from ordinary social life which was penetrated by civic and family cults; harmony in the household could be dissolved by the conversion of husband or wife. Disasters thought to betoken divine wrath exacerbated hostility. 'If the Tiber floods the city or the Nile does not inundate the fields, if there is an eclipse, or earthquake, or famine, or plague, men cry, "Christians to the lion" ' (Tertullian, *Apol.* 40). When St *Polycarp wished to justify his creed to the governor of Asia, the governor answered, 'convince the people'. The emperors would not protect men they saw as fanatics who irrationally set their private judgements against tradition and the wisdom of centuries, and some governors shared popular sentiments.

The persecutions, though attested in every reign of any length, were not yet initiated by the central government; they were sporadic and therefore ineffectual. *Martyrs were relatively few, but their impressive constancy made new converts. The Church grew in strength and respectability; as the new faith became more familiar, popular hostility abated: it played little part in later persecutions. But in the 3rd-cent. crisis of the empire, some emperors took more seriously the old conception that Rome's welfare rested on the favour of the gods; Christianity prob. seemed the more dangerous precisely because it was organized, and its adherents were more numerous and now included more persons of conspicuous station. In 249 Decius commanded all subjects to sacrifice and obtain certificates of their obedience. Those who refused were marked out as Christians and suffered accordingly. The persecution did not outlast Decius' defeat and death in 251. Valerian in 257 forbade Christian meetings and ordered the clergy to sacrifice; in 258 he subjected them to death, and high-ranking laymen to other severe penalties. After he was captured by the Persians in 260, his successor, Gallienus, allowed the Christians to resume their meetings and to receive back their property.

After a period of peace, lasting till *Diocletian's later years, systematic persecution was resumed. Diocletian apparently believed that the piety of the old religion was essential for divine protection, and that men were not entitled to set up their private judgement against traditional wisdom. On the latter principle he banned *Manichaeism *c*.298. The execution of the centurion Marcellus in Mauretania for refusing to participate in official cults prob. took place in 298. In 299 he took steps to purge the army and court of Christians, but only in 303, perhaps under the influence of *Galerius, did he issue edicts of general persecution. The first, in 303, was designed to avoid bloodshed: churches were to be demolished and the Scriptures seized and burnt, Christians were not to assemble, those of high rank were to lose their social and legal privileges, and sacrificing was required as a precondition of bringing legal suits. Then the Christians were held to have sought his life; and further edicts ordered first the incarceration of the clergy, and then their punishment on refusal to sacrifice; finally sacrifice was enjoined on all subjects. A fearful persecution ensued throughout the empire, though only the first edict was given effect in the W., and in Gaul and Britain Constantius Chlorus was content

merely to pull down the churches. After Diocletian and his co-Augustus Maximian had abdicated in 305, the persecution subsided in the W., but not in the E., where Galerius succeeded with Maximin Daia as his Caesar. At last in 311, frustrated generally in his political designs as well as in his efforts to extinguish Christianity, and dying of a painful illness, Galerius issued an edict of toleration, which permitted the Christians to meet and build churches and begged them to pray for his safety and that of the empire. On his death Maximin Daia promoted some persecution on a small scale, which lasted till his defeat by Licinius (313). *Constantine, an avowed convert, on acceding to power in Gaul and Britain in 306 had granted the Christians toleration and restitution of their possessions, and in Italy Maxentius had followed suit in 311; in the so-called Edict of *Milan (313) Licinius made the same concessions in the E. All men (including Christians) were to be free to worship as they pleased. Licinius' later measures against the Christians were terminated by Constantine's victory over him in 324. Christian emperors, from Constantine onwards, placed the Church in an increasingly privileged position; the anti-Christian policy of *Julian, Constantine's only pagan successor, hardly amounted to persecution; and from the time of *Theodosius I the State was to coerce pagans into conversion, with more fervour and success than it had shown in suppressing Christianity.

The victims of persecutions might be executed and, if of low degree, by the cruel methods authorized in Roman law; they enjoyed the fame of martyrs. But some governors were reluctant to shed blood. Many Christians were merely imprisoned for a time, or sent to the mines; survivors, who had often suffered hideous tortures (commonly used to induce apostasy) acquired great prestige in the Church as *confessors. Many too recanted, or persuaded the authorites that they had done so. Controversy about whether, and on what conditions, these *lapsi*, *libellatici*, or *traditores* might be reconciled gave rise to the *Novatian, *Melitian, and *Donatist schisms within the Church.

Apart from Pliny, Tacitus, unreliable statements in the *Historia Augusta*, and certificates of sacrifice preserved on papyri from Egypt from the Decian persecution (see bibl. to LIBELLATICI), the evidence for the persecutions comes from Christian sources; that which is not contemporary with the events must be used with caution. *Lactantius, *De Mortibus Persecutorum*, and *Eusebius, *Martyrs of Palestine* and *Ecclesiastical History*, were contemporary with the persecutions from 303, and Eusebius in the latter work preserves Christian writings relevant to earlier persecutions, for which further good evidence can be found (apart from scattered allusions) in the Apologists, in some *Acts of the Martyrs, and in St *Cyprian's letters and *De Lapsis*. The Christian writers had no direct knowledge and prob. no understanding of imperial policy, at least before Decius. Decius, and later persecutors, sometimes gave reasons for their actions in the general edicts against Christianity; cf. Diocletian's edict against the Manichees (*Mosaicarum et Romanarum Legium Collatio*, 15. 3; conveniently pr. in S. Riccobono and others (eds.), *Fontes Iuris Romani Antejustiniani*, pt. 2, 2nd edn., Florence, 1940, pp. 580 f.), which reveals his outlook. Lactantius and Eusebius give texts of imperial enactments of toleration from 311, which themselves cast light on the causes of persecution. What is known of pagan attitudes to Christians, esp. *Celsus and *Porphyry, analysed by P. de Labriolle, *La Réaction païenne: Étude sur la polémique antichrétienne du 1ᵉʳ au V1ᵉ siècle* (1934) is also relevant. See also bibl. to authors mentioned above.

All histories of the early Church and of Rome discuss the persecutions. Introductory account by H. B. Workman, *Persecution in the Early Church* (1906). J. Moreau, *La Persécution du christianisme dans l'Empire romain* (Mythes et Religions, 1956). W. H. C. Frend, *Martyrdom and Persecution in the Early Church* (Oxford, 1965), with bibl. R. Freudenberger, *Das Verhalten der römischen Behörden gegen die Christen im 2. Jahrhundert* (Münchener Beiträge zur Papyrusforschung und Antiken Rechtsgeschichte, 52; 1967). R. Lane Fox, *Pagans and Christians* (1986), pp. 419–92. A. N. Sherwin-White, 'The Early Persecutions and Roman Law Again', *JTS* NS 3 (1952), pp. 199–213; T. D. Barnes, 'Legislation against the Christians', *Journal of Roman Studies*, 58 (1968), pp. 32–50. G. E. M. de Ste Croix, 'Why were the Early Christians Persecuted?', *Past and Present*, 26 (1963), pp. 6–38; 'An Amendment' by A. N. Sherwin-White, ibid. 27 (1964), pp. 23–7, and a rejoinder by G. E. M. de Ste Croix, ibid., pp. 28–33; all repr. in M. I. Finley (ed.), *Studies in Ancient Society* (1974), pp. 210–62. P. A. Brunt, 'Marcus Aurelius and the Christians', in C. Deroux (ed.), *Studies in Latin Literature and Roman History*, 1 (Collection Latomus, 164; 1979), pp. 483–520. On the final phase, G. E. M. de Ste Croix, 'Aspects of the "Great" Persecution', *HTR* 47 (1954), pp. 75–113; T. D. Barnes, *Constantine and Eusebius* (Cambridge, Mass., and London, 1981), chs. 1–4 and 8–9; P. S. Davies, 'The Origin and Purpose of the Persecution of AD 303', *JTS* NS 40 (1989), pp. 66–94. J. Vogt and H. M. Last in *RAC* 2 (1954), cols. 1159–228, s.v. 'Christenverfolgung'; W. H. C. Frend in *DPAC* 2 (1984), cols. 2756–69; Eng. tr., *Encyclopedia of the Early Church*, 2 (1992), pp. 671–4, s.v.

perseverance. In addition to its general meaning, the word is used technically in connection with the doctrine of *predestination, to mean steady continuance, after conversion, in the faith and life proper to the attainment of eternal life. St *Augustine held that God bestowed on those elected to salvation, not only the initial call to be baptized and accept the Christian faith, but also the gift of such final perseverance. *Calvinism maintained that the elect could be certain that God would never allow them to fall away from Him. Outside Calvinism it would generally be held that none can be personally certain of persevering to the end and that the gift must be sought by prayer and effort.

Persia, Christianity in. See CHURCH OF THE EAST.

Person of Christ. See CHRISTOLOGY, also INCARNATION.

personal prelature. An institution established in 1982 with the creation of *Opus Dei into a personal prelature. Erected in each case by the Holy See, a personal prelature consists of priests and deacons of the secular clergy presided over by a prelate who can incardinate students and promote them to *Orders under the title of service to the prelature; by agreement lay persons may dedicate themselves to the work of a personal prelature. In each case it is governed by the statutes establishing it, which also regulate its relations with local bishops. Acc. to *CIC* (1983), can. 294, the purpose of personal prelatures is 'to promote an appropriate distribution of presbyters or to perform particular pastoral or missionary works for various regions or different social groups'.

P. Rodríguez, *Iglesias particulares y prelaturas personales* (Pamplona, 1985; Eng. tr., Blackrock, Co. Dublin [1986]). R. Ombres, OP, 'Opus Dei and Personal Prelatures', *Clergy Review*, 70 (1985), pp. 292–5.

Persons, Robert. See PARSONS, ROBERT.

Perth, Articles of (1618). Five articles forced on the Church in *Scotland at Perth in 1618 by *James I. They required (1) kneeling at Communion; (2) the observance of Easter and Christmas; (3) Confirmation; (4) provision for administering Communion to the dying in their houses; and (5) Baptism on the Sunday following the child's birth. In 1621, much to the horror of older Scottish Churchmen, the articles were carried with a majority through the Scottish parliament.

The text will be found in J. *Spottiswoode, *The History of the Church of Scotland* (1655), pp. 538 f. I. B. Cowan, 'The Five Articles of Perth' in D. Shaw (ed.), *Reformation and Revolution: Essays Presented to . . . Hugh Watt* (Edinburgh, 1967), pp. 160–77. W. R. Foster, *The Church before the Covenants* (Edinburgh and London, 1975), pp. 124 f., and 181–92. J. D. Ford, 'Conformity in Conscience: The Structure of the Perth Articles Debate in Scotland, 1618–38', *JEH* 46 (1995), pp. 256–77.

Perugino, Pietro Vannucci (*c.*1446–1523), Italian painter of the Umbrian school. He studied first at Perugia and afterwards at Florence under Verrocchio, where he learned the art of composition and perspective in which he became a master. In 1482 he painted the *Delivery of the Keys to St Peter* in the *Sistine Chapel. (His other frescoes in the Chapel gave way to *Michelangelo's *Last Judgement*.) The devotional warmth of his style soon caused a great demand for his religious pictures, and among his masterpieces were the *Adoration of the Holy Child* (1491; Torlonia Collection, Rome), the *Vision of St Bernard* (*c.*1494; Uffizi, Florence), and the *Lamentation* (1495; Pitti, Florence). In 1496 he completed his greatest work, the well-known fresco of the *Crucifixion* in Sta. Maria Maddalena dei Pazzi at Florence. In the same year he began work on the fresco cycle in the Sala del Cambio, Perugia (completed *c.*1500), in which *Raphael, then his apprentice, is generally thought to have had some part. After that his art showed a marked decline.

Good reprod. of his works ed. C. Castellaneta and E. Camesasca (Milan, 1969). F. Canuti, *Il Perugino* (2 vols., Siena [1931]); P. Scarpellini, *Perugino* (Milan [1984]), both with reprods. and bibl. P. J. Murray in *EB* (1974 edn.), Macropaedia, 14, pp. 136–8.

Peshitta, from the early 5th cent., the official text of the Bible in Syriac-speaking Christian lands. (The word 'Peshitta' means literally 'simple', or, as applied to a text, 'current'.) The NT portion was held by F. C. *Burkitt to have been the work of *Rabbula, Bp. of Edessa from 412 to 435. It now, however, seems more likely that the process of revision which produced the Peshitta NT had already begun before the end of the 4th cent. The NT did not include the Book of Rev. or the four lesser *Catholic Epistles (2 Pet., 2 and 3 Jn., and Jude). A large number of MSS have survived, the oldest dating from the 5th cent. The origins of the Peshitta OT are shrouded in obscurity, but in part it would seem to be the work of Jews, and in the Pentateuch, at least, there appear to be tenuous links with the *Targums.

Older edns. of NT by E. Widmanstadt (Vienna, 1555) and J. Leusden and C. Schaff (Leiden, 1709). Best edn. of Peshitta Gospels by P. E. *Pusey and G. H. Gwilliam (Oxford, 1901); complete edn. of NT ed. *British and Foreign Bible Society (London, 1905–20). Edns. of the OT incl. the London *Polyglot (1657) and that of S. Lee (London, 1823; reissued, with Apocrypha, by the United Bible Societies, ibid., 1979); a crit. edn. is in course of publication by the Peshitta Institute, Leiden (1966 ff.). L. Haefeli, *Die Peshitta des Alten Testaments* (Alttestamentliche Abhandlungen, 11, Heft 1; 1927); P. B. Dirksen, 'The Old Testament Peshitta', in M. J. Mulder (ed.), *Mikra* (Compendia Rerum Iudaicarum ad Novum Testamentum, 2. 1; Assen/Maastricht and Philadelphia, 1988), pp. 255–97. Id., *An Annotated Bibliography of the Peshitta of the Old Testament* (Monographs of the Peshitta Institute, 5; Leiden, 1989). M. Black, 'The New Testament Peshitta and its Predecessors', *Studiorum Novi Testamenti Societas*, Bulletin 1 (1950), pp. 51–62. Id., 'The Syriac versional tradition', in K. Aland (ed.), *Die alten Übersetzungen des Neuen Testaments, die Kirchenväterzitate und Lektionare* (Arbeiten zur neutestamentlichen Textforschungen, 5; 1972), pp. 120–59. B. M. Metzger, *The Early Versions of the New Testament* (Oxford, 1977), pp. 48–63. C. van Puyvelde in *Dict. Bibl.*, Suppl. 6 (1960), cols. 843–55 and 872–5, s.v. 'Orientales de la Bible (Versions)'; S. P. Brock and B. Aland in *TRE* 6 (1980), pp. 181–96, s.v. 'Bibelübersetzungen', 1. 4: 'Die Übersetzungen ins Syrische'. See also bibl. TO SYRIAC VERSIONS OF THE BIBLE.

Petavius, Dionysius (1583–1652), Denis Pétau, *Jesuit historian and theologian. A native of Orléans, he studied at Paris where I. *Casaubon aroused his interest in the Fathers. In 1605 he became a Jesuit. He taught rhetoric at Reims (1609–13), La Flèche (1613–18), and at the Collège de Clermont (1618–21), where he was given the chair of Dogmatic Theology in 1621. He lived at Paris for the rest of his life, one of the most brilliant and learned scholars of his age. His *Opus de Doctrina Temporum* (2 vols., 1627), in substance a thorough revision and expansion of J. J. *Scaliger's *De Emendatione Temporum* (1583), was a fundamental contribution to the study of ancient chronology; in 1633 he issued an abridged edition with the title *Rationarium Temporum*. He also published notable editions of the writings of *Synesius (1612; new edn., 1633) and St *Epiphanius (1622; not superseded until K. *Holl's edition of 1915–33).

Petavius was also an outstanding dogmatic theologian, strictly orthodox in doctrine but one of the first to accept the idea of doctrinal development (here he influenced J. H. *Newman) and to concede the imperfections of much patristic teaching judged by later standards. His vast and still valuable *De Theologicis Dogmatibus* (vols. 1–3, 1644; vol. 4, 1650) was unfinished at the time of his death. G. *Bull's famous *Defensio Fidei Nicaenae* (1685) was written primarily to defend the orthodoxy of pre-Nicene teaching on the Trinity against Petavius's criticisms. His *De la pénitence publique et de la préparation à la communion* (1644) was an attack on A. *Arnauld's *Fréquente Communion* (1643).

The primary source is the Life [by F. Oudin, SJ] in [J. P.] Nicéron, *Barnabite, *Mémoires pour servir à l'histoire des hommes illustres dans la république des lettres*, 37 (1737), pp. 81–234. Full Life by J. C. Vital Châtellain (Paris, 1884). Shorter study by J. Martin ('Science et religion. Les Grands Théologiens', fasc. 545; 1910). P. Di Rosa, SJ, 'Denis Petau e la cronologia', *Archivum Historicum Societatis Iesu*, 29 (1960), pp. 3–54. L. Karrer, *Die historisch-positive Methode des Theologen Dionysius Petavius* (Münchener theologische Studien, 2. Systematische Abteilung, 37; 1970). M. Hofmann, *Theologie, Dogma und Dogmenentwicklung im theologischen Werk Denis Petau's* (Regensburger Studien zur Theologie, 1; 1976). Sommervogel, 6 (1895), cols. 588–616; Polgár, 2 (1990), pp. 658–60. P. Galtier, SJ, in *DTC* 12 (pt. 1;

1933), cols. 1313–37; F. X. Murphy, CSSR, in *NCE* 11 (1967), pp. 199 f., both s.v. 'Petau'.

Peter, St, Prince of the *Apostles. Our knowledge of his life and personality is derived chiefly from the Gospels, Acts, St *Paul's Ep. to the *Galatians, and tradition. Acc. to the Gospel of St John (1: 44) he was a native of *Bethsaida, a village near Lake Tiberias, and in the Johannine account (1: 35–42) he is introduced to the Lord by his brother St *Andrew and given the name 'Cephas', the Aramaic equivalent of the Greek 'Peter' ($\pi \acute{\epsilon} \tau \rho \alpha$, 'rock'). In the Gospels of Sts Matthew (4: 18–20) and Mark (1: 16–18) he and Andrew, who are described as 'fishers', are together called from their fishing to follow Jesus. In St Luke's Gospel (5: 1–11) there is a variant account of this incident, in which Peter, at the Lord's command, catches a large draught of fishes. Some time later he is formally called to become one of the Twelve [Apostles] and in all the lists of the Twelve he is named first. He is present on all the occasions when only a small 'inner group' is admitted, namely at the raising of Jairus's daughter (Mt. 9: 18–26), at the *Transfiguration (Mt. 17: 1–8), and at the Agony in the Garden (Mt. 26: 37). He usually takes the lead and is the mouthpiece of the disciples, as when he says that they could not 'go away' (Jn. 6: 66–9). After his confession of faith at *Caesarea Philippi (Mk. 8: 27–30), when he professes his belief that Jesus is the Christ (in Mt. 16: 17, 'the Christ, the Son of the living God') and the disciples are silenced, Mt. adds the Lord's promise 'Thou art Peter, and on this rock will I build my church', together with the keys of heaven and the power of binding and loosing (16: 18 f.). (The precise interpretation of this passage, on which the claims of the Papacy have been based, has been the subject of much controversy.) Together with St *John, Peter is entrusted with the preparations for the *Last Supper, during which the Lord reaffirms his pre-eminence (Lk. 22: 31 f.). On the way to the Mount of Olives, his boast that he will never leave his Lord is answered by Christ's prediction that before the end of the night he will deny Him thrice (Mt. 26: 33 f.). At the arrest of Jesus, Peter strikes off the ear of a servant of the high priest (Jn. 18: 10). Having followed the Lord to the court of the high priest, he is accused of being one of His followers; he denies three times that he knows Him, then remembers His prediction and repents bitterly (Mt. 26: 69–75). After the Resurrection he goes to the Sepulchre as soon as the women report that it is empty (Lk. 24: 12; cf. Jn. 20: 2–6) and is later favoured with a special appearance of the risen Christ (Lk. 24: 34). At 1 Cor. 15: 5 Paul quotes a very early tradition that Peter was the first to receive a resurrection appearance. Acc. to the Johannine account, when the Lord appears to him and other disciples at the Sea of Tiberias, he makes a triple protestation of his love to Christ and receives the charge to feed His sheep and the prediction of his martyrdom (Jn. 21: 15–18).

After the Ascension Peter immediately takes the lead of the Apostles in designating the successor of Judas (Acts 1: 15–22) and throughout the first half of Acts he appears as their head. He speaks on the day of *Pentecost (Acts 2: 14–41); he is the first of the Apostles to perform a miracle in the name of Jesus (3: 1–10); he is the speaker when brought before the *Sanhedrin with John (4: 1–21); and he pronounces the condemnation of Ananias and Sapphira

(5: 1–11). He also is the greatest miracle-worker among the Apostles, whose shadow even heals the sick (5: 15); he opens the Church to the Gentiles by admitting Cornelius (10: 1–11: 18), and his authority is again evident at the Apostles' Council at Jerusalem (15: 7–11). Of the later years of his Apostolate outside Palestine very little is known. His visit to *Antioch is mentioned in Gal. 2: 11–21 by Paul, who sharply rebukes him for giving way to the demands of the Jewish Christians to dissociate himself from the Gentiles. Possibly he visited Corinth, as a party of 'Cephas' existed in that city (1 Cor. 1: 12).

The tradition connecting Peter with Rome (q.v.) is early and unrivalled. Against it can be placed only the silence of the NT; but even here Rom. 15: 20–2 may point to the presence of another Apostle in Rome before Paul wrote, while the identification of 'Babylon' in 1 Pet. 5: 13 (see PETER, EPISTLES OF ST) with Rome seems highly probable. St *Clement of Rome (I Clem. 5) conjoins Peter and Paul as the outstanding heroes of the Faith and prob. implies that Peter suffered martyrdom (μαρτυρήσας). St *Ignatius uses words (Rom. 4. 2) which suggest that Peter and Paul were the Apostles of special authority for the Roman Church, and St *Irenaeus (Adv. Haer. 3. 1. 2; 3. 3. 1) states definitely that they founded that Church and instituted its episcopal succession. Other early witnesses to the tradition are *Gaius of Rome and *Dionysius of Corinth, both cited by *Eusebius (HE 2. 25. 5–8), who also (HE 3. 1. 2 f.) quotes a statement of *Origen that Peter was crucified head downwards, having requested this form of death. The later tradition (first found in St *Jerome) which attributes to him an episcopate (or apostolate) in Rome of 25 years preceding his martyrdom is less well supported. His death is placed by Eusebius in the reign of *Nero (54–68) and was prob. in the *persecution of 64—not, as Eusebius himself asserts (Chron.), in 68. That he and St Paul suffered on the same day is perhaps a mistaken deduction from their common feast (prob. date of translation of their relics, not of martyrdom) on 29 June. Some modern Anglican calendars provide a feast of the Confession of St Peter on 18 Jan. See also LAMMAS DAY.

The tradition, which is found in *Papias, that Peter's memoirs lie behind the Gospel of St Mark, is still accepted by some scholars (see MARK, GOSPEL OF ST). For the Epistles, see PETER, EPISTLES OF ST. There are historical grounds for believing that his tomb in St Peter's, Rome, is authentic (see ST PETER'S, ROME). See also the following entries and QUO VADIS?

Modern studies with discussion of the main historical questions by F. J. Foakes Jackson, Peter, Prince of Apostles (1927), O. Cullmann, Petrus: Jünger, Apostel, Märtyrer (Zurich, 1952; Eng. tr., 1953), and R. Pesch, Simon-Petrus: Geschichte und geschichtliche Bedeutung des ersten Jüngers Jesu Christi (Päpste und Papsttum, 15; 1980). Works on the question of Peter's connection with Rome incl. H. *Lietzmann, Petrus und Paulus in Rom (1915; 2nd edn., Arbeiten zur Kirchengeschichte, 1; 1927); J. Munck, Petrus und Paulus in der Offenbarung Johannis (Copenhagen, 1950); K. Heussi, Die römische Petrustradition in kritischer Sicht (Tübingen, 1955), and other works of this author; T. Klauser, Die römische Petrustradition im Lichte der neuen Ausgrabungen unter der Peterskirche (Arbeitsgemeinschaft für Forschung des Landes Nordrhein-Westfalen. Geisteswissenschaften, 24 [1956]). See also other works cited under ST PETER'S, ROME. J. Dauvillier, Les Temps apostoliques (Histoire du droit et des institutions de l'Église en occident, publiée sous la direction de G. Le Bras; 1970), pp.

144–50 and 273–93; R. E. Brown and others (eds.), Peter in the New Testament: A Collaborative Assessment by Protestant and Roman Catholic Scholars (Minneapolis, etc., 1973). T. V. Smith, Petrine Controversies in Early Christianity: Attitudes towards Peter in Christian Writings of the First Two Centuries (Wissenschaftliche Untersuchungen zum Neuen Testament, 2. Reihe, 15; 1985). E. Fascher in PW 19 (pt. 2; 1938), cols. 1335–61, s.v. 'Petrus (121)'; P. de Ambroggi, E. Josi, and others in EC 9 (1952), cols. 1400–27, s.v. 'Pietro apostolo'; É. Cothenet in Dict. Sp. 12 (pt. 2; 1986), cols. 1452–86, s.v. 'Pierre (1)'.

Peter, Acts of St. An apocryphal Book composed in Greek c.180–90, perhaps in Asia Minor. Apart from the 'Martyrdom of St Peter' which forms part of it and survives in Greek as well as in several versions, most of it is preserved in Latin in a Vercelli MS. A Coptic fragment also survives which describes St Peter's miraculous treatment of his paralytic daughter. In the Martyrdom are recorded both the '*Quo Vadis?' incident and the crucifixion of St Peter head downwards. In places its teaching has a *Docetic ring, perhaps occasioned by the writer's limited theological capacities rather than by any connection with unorthodox circles.

The Lat. text, with Gk. text on the opposite pages where then available, in R. A. *Lipsius and M. Bonnet (eds.), Acta Apostolorum Apocrypha, 1 (Leipzig, 1891), pp. 45–103; corrections by C. H. *Turner in JTS 32 (1931), pp. 119–33. Coptic frag. ed. C. Schmidt, Die alten Petrusakten in Zusammenhang mit der apokryphen Apostelliteratur nebst einem neuentdeckten Fragment (TU 24, Heft 1; 1903), pp. 3–7, with Ger. tr., pp. 7–10. Further Gk. fragment in B. P. Grenfell and A. S. Hunt, The Oxyrhynchus Papyri, 6 (1908), pp. 6–12. Eng. tr. of the 'Martyrdom' from the Gk. text and the rest of the Acts from the Lat. and Coptic, in J. K. Elliott, The Apocryphal New Testament (Oxford, 1993), pp. 390–426. A Lat. paraphrase of the 'Martyrdom', attributed to St *Linus but dating from the 4th–6th cent., is pr. in R. A. Lipsius and M. Bonnet, op. cit., pp. 1–22. L. Vouaux, Les Actes de Pierre (1922; text, Fr. tr. and comm., with good bibl.). C. Schmidt, 'Studien zu den alten Petrusakten', ZKG 43 (1924), pp. 321–48; 45 (1926), pp. 481–513. Ger. tr., with introd. by W. Schneemelcher in Schneemelcher, 2 (5th edn., 1989), pp. 243–89; Eng. tr., 2 [1992], pp. 271–321. J. Quasten, Patrology, 1 (Utrecht, 1950), pp. 133–5. Bardenhewer, 1, pp. 550–4. É. Amann in Dict. Bibl., Suppl. 1 (1928), cols. 496–501.

Peter, Apocalypse of St. This, the most important of the apocryphal apocalypses, dates from the early 2nd cent. Small portions of it have survived in quotations in *Clement of Alexandria and others, and in some scattered fragments (e.g. those discovered at Akhmîm in Egypt in 1886–7); and an Ethiopic version, in a modified form, was published by S. Grébaut in 1910. The Apocalypse describes how the Lord granted to the Apostles a vision of their brethren in the next world and of their rewards. Both Clement and the *Muratorian Canon held it to be Scripture; and acc. to *Sozomen (HE 7. 19; 5th cent.) it was still read in his day on *Good Friday in some Palestinian churches. An 'Apocalypse of Peter' found at *Nag Hammadi has only the title in common.

Akhmîm frag. of Gk. text ed. A. Lods in Mémoires publiés par les membres de la Mission Archéologique Française du Caire, 9 (1893), pp. 224–8; repr. by E. Klostermann, Apocrypha, 1 (Kleine Texte, ed. H. *Lietzmann, 3, 1908), pp. 8–12. There is a small Gk. papyrus frag. in the *Bodleian Library (MS Gr. th. f. 4 (P)); cf. M. R. James, 'The Rainer Fragment of the Apocalypse of Peter', JTS 32 (1931–2), pp. 270–9, with text. Ethiopic text ed.

S. Grébaut in *Revue de l'Orient chrétien*, 15 (1910), pp. 199–208, 307–16, 425–33, with Fr. tr., pp. 208–14, 316–323, 433–9. Eng. tr. of the Patristic citations, the Akhmîm fragment, the Rainer fragment, and part of the Ethiopic text in J. K. Elliott, *The Apocryphal New Testament* (Oxford, 1993), pp. 593–612, with portion of the *Sibylline Oracles which appears to have been taken from the Apocalypse of Peter, pp. 613–5. M. R. James, 'The Recovery of the Apocalypse of Peter', *CQR* 80 (1915), pp. 1–36. Bardenhewer, 1, pp. 610–15; Altaner and Stuiber (1978), pp. 141 f. Ger. tr., with introd. by C. D. G. Müller in Schneemelcher, 2 (5th edn., 1989), pp. 562–78; Eng. tr., 2 [1992], pp. 620–38. On the Apocalypse found at Nag Hammadi, A. Werner in Schneemelcher, 2 (5th edn., 1989), pp. 633–43; Eng. tr., 2 [1992], pp. 700–12. É. Amann in *Dict. Bibl.*, Suppl. 1 (1928), cols. 525–7, with bibl.

Peter, Epistles of St. There are two Epistles ascribed to St *Peter in the NT.

(1) The First Epistle of Peter was written from *Rome (if this is the city referred to in 5: 13 as 'Babylon') to Christian communities in 'Pontus, Galatia, Cappadocia, Asia, and Bithynia' (1: 1), i.e. all lands in what is now Asia Minor, to encourage them under persecution. The author reminds his readers that, as the chosen people of God, they are heirs to the glorious promises made to Israel and insists on the central place of Christ's death and resurrection in the Christian plan of salvation (1: 2–25). As believers, they are called to love one another, to look for the coming of Christ, and esp. to witness by their good lives in their heathen surroundings, where trials are constantly awaited. It is widely accepted that Baptism is an important theme in the Epistle. It is specifically mentioned in 3: 20 f.; it is reflected in the imagery of rebirth (1: 23, 2: 2); and it is naturally connected with the overall stress on the new life of the Christian. The further claim that the Epistle was based on a Baptismal sermon or even liturgy has not won general approval. The apparent break after 4: 11 has led some critics to argue that separate elements have been combined in the one writing.

The Epistle was written 'through Silvanus' (5: 12), i.e. he was the scribe or messenger; he has sometimes been suggested as author. If tradition is correct in attributing it to Peter, its *terminus ad quem* is the date of his death, i.e. prob. *c*.65. Its Petrine authorship, however, has often been questioned. It is urged that its literary style is not that of a Galilean fisherman; that passages in the Epistle reflect Pauline teaching; and that *persecution of the Church in Asia Minor is not otherwise clearly attested before 112 (in *Pliny). What is envisaged in 1 Peter, however, may not be official persecution by the state. The arguments for and against Petrine authorship are inconclusive. External evidence for ascribing it to Peter goes back to St *Irenaeus (*Adv. Haer.* 4. 19. 1) and *Clement of Alexandria (*Strom.* 3. 18 [110]).

(2) The Second Epistle, though it is written as if by Peter, with a ref. to his presence at the *Transfiguration (1: 18; cf. Mk. 9: 2), is markedly different from the First in contents and manner, e.g. in the treatment of redemption with which it opens. Its main message is a warning against false and ungodly teachers, upon whom the future judgements of God are prophesied from the OT and Jewish writings. The chief passage in which this warning is given (2: 1–3: 3) is parallel to Jude 4–18, from which it is probably borrowed.

There are several indications that the Epistle is of a late date. Thus the passage (3: 3 ff.) dealing with the delay of

the Coming of the Lord presupposes that the first generation of Christians had passed away. The author classes the Epp. of St Paul as 'scripture' (3: 16), a position which they apparently did not attain until some considerable time after the Apostle's death. It is first definitely referred to by *Origen (in *Eusebius, *HE* 6. 25. 8) in the 3rd cent., and he writes of it as of disputed authenticity. It also has some close points of literary contact with the 'Apocalypse of St *Peter' (q.v.). These indications of date, and the difference in style and interest from 1 Peter, make it virtually impossible to hold that St Peter was the author. The Epistle was received into the *canon with considerable hesitation. Its date is probably the second or third Christian generation, perhaps *c*. AD 150.

Modern comm. on both Epp. incl. those of C. Bigg (ICC, 1901, with Jude, pp. 1–304), H. *Windisch (Hb. NT 4, Th. 2, 1911, on the Catholic Epp.; 2nd edn., 15, 1930, pp. 50–105; 3rd edn., by H. Preisker, 1951, with addenda, pp. 152–63), C. Spicq, OP (Sources Bibliques, 1966), and J. N. D. Kelly (Black's NT Comm., on Pet. and Jude, 1969). On 1 Pet. only, by F. J. A. *Hort (London, 1896; on 1 Pet. 1: 1–2: 17 only), E. G. Selwyn (ibid., 1946), F. W. Beare (Oxford, 1947, 3rd edn., 1970), C. E. B. Cranfield (London, 1950), E. Best (New Cent. Bib. [1971]), L. Goppelt (KEK 12/1, 8th edn., 1978; Eng. tr., Grand Rapids [1993]), N. Brox (Evanglisch-katholischer Kommentar zum Neuen Testament, 21, 1979), J. R. Michaels (Word Biblical Comm. 49, Waco, Tex. [1988]), and P. H. Davids (New International Comm. on the NT, Grand Rapids [1990]). On 2 Pet. only, by J. Chaîne (Études Bibliques, 2nd edn., 1939, on Catholic Epp., pp. 1–96), R. J. Bauckham (Word Biblical Comm. 50, on Jude and 2 Pet., Waco, Tex. [1983], pp. 131–342), H. Paulsen (KEK 12/2, on Jude and 2 Pet., 1992, pp. 89–175), and J. H. Neyrey (Anchor Bible 37 C, on Jude and 2 Pet., 1993, pp. 106–260). F. L. Cross, *1 Peter: A Paschal Liturgy* (1954). J. H. Elliott, *A Home for the Homeless: Sociological Exegesis of 1 Peter, Its Situation and Strategy* (Grand Rapids, 1981; London, 1982). Id. in *Anchor Bible Dictionary*, 5 (1992), pp. 269–78 (on 1 Pet.) and pp. 282–7 (on 2 Pet.).

Peter, Gospel of St. An early apocryphal Gospel of which the only surviving section is contained in an 8th-cent. MS discovered at Akhmîm in Egypt in 1886–7 (now in Cairo). A fragment of text in a late 2nd- or early 3rd-cent. *Oxyrhynchus papyrus (no. 2949) has affinities with it. Acc. to *Serapion, Bp. of Antioch (*c*.190), the Gospel of Peter was in use at Rhossus in his time, and in the next century *Origen knew of its existence. It seems to have been a largely legendary work, showing strong antipathy to the Jews and apparently with some *Docetic elements. It was prob. composed in Syria in the first half of the 2nd cent.

Editio princeps of the Akhmîm frag. by A. Lods in *Mémoires publiés par les membres de la Mission Archéologique Française du Caire*, 9 (1893), pp. 218–24, with facsimiles in plates II–VI. Text also ed., with introd., notes, and Eng. tr., by H. B. *Swete (London, 1893). Modern edn., with Fr. tr., introd. and comm., by M. G. Mara (SC 201; 1973). Eng. tr. in J. K. Elliott, *The Apocryphal New Testament* (Oxford, 1993), pp. 150–8. Fr. tr., with full comm. and bibl., by L. Vaganay (Études Bibliques, 1930). *The Oxyrhynchus Papyri*, 41 (1972), pp. 15 f. (no. 2949. 'Fragments of an Apocryphal Gospel(?)'); D. Lührmann, 'POx 2949: EvPt 3–5 in einer Handschrift des 2./3. Jahrhunderts', *ZNTW* 72 (1981), pp. 216–26. J. A. *Robinson in id. and M. R. James, *The Gospel according to Peter and the Revelation of Peter* (1892), pp. 13–36. J. Denker, *Die theologiegeschichtliche Stellung des Petrusevangeliums* (Europäische Hochschulschriften, Reihe 23, Bd. 36; 1975). C.

Maurer and W. Schneemelcher in Schneemelcher, 1 (5th edn., 1987), pp. 180–8; Eng. tr., 1 (1991), pp. 216–27.

Peter, Letter of St, to Philip. A *Coptic document contained in Codex VIII of the *Nag Hammadi library. The title strictly applies only to the first page or so of the text, which goes on to tell of St *Philip's response, a gathering of the Apostles on the Mount of *Olives, an appearance of the risen Christ, and the ensuing conversation. At the end Christ takes His leave in terms reminiscent of Jn. 20: 19–23 and Mt. 28: 20, and the Apostles disperse to preach. There are numerous NT echoes and parallels, although it is not always certain that there is any literary dependence. It is reported that another copy of the text has been found, but this has not so far been published.

Text ed., with Fr. tr. and comm., by J.-É. Ménard (Bibliothèque Copte de Nag Hammadi, Section 'Textes', 1; Quebec, 1977); also, with Eng. tr. and comm., by M. W. Meyer, (Society of Biblical Literature Dissertation Series, 53; Chico, Calif. [1981]). Eng. tr. by F. Wisse, with introd. by M. W. Meyer, in J. M. Robinson (ed.), *The Nag Hammadi Library in English* (3rd edn., Leiden, 1988), pp. 431–7. H.-G. Bethge, *Die Brief des Petrus an Philippus* (TU 141; 1996). Id. in Schneemelcher, 1 (5th edn., 1987), pp. 275–84; Eng. tr., 1 (1991), pp. 342–53.

Peter, Liturgy of St. A Mass combining elements from the Byzantine and Roman rites which was probably drawn up for the use of Greek communities in Italy, but may have been put together only as a literary experiment. The *canon is that of the Roman Mass. It was first published, apparently from Vat. graec. 1970 (12th cent.), by G. Linden in *Apologia pro Liturgia Petri Apostoli et Commentarius in eandem cum Missa Apostolica Petri Apostoli* (Antwerp, 1589, and Paris, 1595). It is to be distinguished from the *Maronite Third Anaphora of St Peter, which has affinities with the Liturgy of *Addai and Mari.

Text in C. A. *Swainson, *The Greek Liturgies* (1884), pp. 191–203. Brightman, *LEW* 1, p. 91, with refs. to other edns. H. W. Codrington, *The Liturgy of St Peter*, with Preface and Introduction by P. de Meester, OSB (Liturgiegeschichtliche Quellen und Forschungen, Heft 30; 1936). J. M. Hanssens, SJ, 'La Liturgie romano-byzantine de saint Pierre', *OCP* 4 (1938), pp. 235–58; 5 (1939), pp. 103–50.
The Third Anaphora of St Peter ed. J.-M. Sauget in *Anaphorae Syriacae*, 2, fasc. 3 (Rome, 1973), pp. 275–323.

Peter, Martyrdom of St. See PETER, ACTS OF ST.

Peter, Patrimony of St. See PATRIMONY OF ST PETER.

Peter, Preaching of St. (Gk. Κήρυγμα Πέτρου). A treatise, of which but few fragments survive, purporting to be the work of the Apostle St *Peter, but probably dating from the earlier half of the 2nd cent. It was very popular in the early Church and known in its entirety to *Clement of Alexandria. Apparently intended for missionary propaganda, it emphasized the superiority of Christian monotheism to the current beliefs of Greeks and Jews. *Origen thought that it was possibly genuine in whole or in part.

Frags. conveniently pr. in E. Klostermann, *Apocrypha*, 1 (Kleine Texte ed. H. *Lietzmann, 3; 1908), pp. 13–16; Eng. tr. in J. K. Elliott, *The Apocryphal New Testament* (Oxford, 1993), pp. 20–4. E. von Dobschütz, *Das Kerygma Petri kritisch untersucht*

(TU 11, Heft 1; 1893). J. N. Reagan, *The Preaching of Peter: The beginning of Christian apologetic* (Diss., Chicago, 1923). H. Paulsen, 'Die Kerygma Petri und die urchristliche Apologetik', *ZKG* 88 (1977), pp. 1–37. W. Schneemelcher in Schneemelcher, 2 (5th edn., 1989), pp. 34–41; Eng. tr., 2 [1992], pp. 34–41.

Peter of Alcántara, St (1499–1562), Spanish *Discalced Franciscan. Born Juan de Sanabria at Alcántara, in Extremadura, he studied at Salamanca from 1511 to 1515. He then immediately joined the Franciscans of the *custodia* (or sub-province) of Santo Evangelio, then attached to the Conventuals of the province of Santiago but transferred by *Leo X to the *Observantines in 1517. In 1519 it became the province of St Gabriel, regarded as the mother province of the Spanish Discalced Franciscans. Peter, who was ordained priest in 1524, was to remain in this province until 1557, serving as provincial from 1538 to 1541, though with numerous visits to Portugal, where he was guardian and novice master at Palhães from 1542 to 1544. In 1557 he became Commissary General of the reformed *Conventuals and founded the celebrated convent of El Pedroso del Acim. In 1560 St *Teresa met him at Ávila, receiving much valued spiritual guidance from him together with encouragement and help in her reform of the *Carmelite Order. Her *Life* records her admiration for his extreme asceticism. Thereafter, he devised Constitutions for the province of St Joseph, established through his efforts in 1561 and, though dependent on the Conventuals, strongly tending towards the Observance. These Constitutions are focused on the life of prayer and penitence. A small *Tratado de la oración y meditación* bearing Peter's name (earliest surviving edition, Lisbon *c*.1556) was much printed and translated. The question of the relation and indebtedness of this work to *Luis of Granada and his *Libro de la oración y meditación* (1554) has provoked long debate. According to Fr. Acerbal Luján's recent statement of the position, the *Tratado* is basically Peter's work: while it often summarizes and borrows substantially from the *Libro*, it contains much of Peter's own; it is more concentrated, more contemplative, more insistent on poverty, penitence, and prayer. Its treatment of the latter gives the treatise its particular value. Peter of Alcántara was canonized in 1669. Feast day, 19 Oct.

Eng. trs. of the *Tratado* by G. Willoughby (Brussels, 1632; 2nd edn., Liverpool, 1843), G. F. Bullock (ed. G. S. Hollings) (London, 1905), and D. Devas (ibid., 1926). Lives by F. Marchese (Rome, 1667), Juan de San Bernardo (Naples, 1710) and A. Barrado Manzano, OFM (Madrid, 1965). Cf. also *AASS*, Oct. 8 (1866), pp. 623–809. *Estudios sobre San Pedro de Alcántara en el IV centenario de su muerte (1562–1962)* (Archivo Ibero-Americano, 22; 1962), with full bibl. A. Huerga, OP, 'Génesis y autenticidad del "Libro de Oración y Meditación" ', *Rivista de Archivos, Bibliotecas y Museos*, 59 (1953), pp. 135–83; M. Ledrus, SJ, 'Grenade et Alcántara. Deux manuels d'oraison mentale', *Revue d'Ascétique et de Mystique*, 38 (1962), pp. 447–60; 39 (1963), pp. 32–44. E. A. Peers, *Studies in the Spanish Mystics*, 2 (1930), pp. 97–120, with bibl. pp. 411–16. M. Acerbal Luján, OFM, in *Dict. Sp.* 12 (pt. 2; 1986), cols. 1489–95, s.v. 'Pierre d'Alcántara', with bibl.

Peter of Alexandria, St (d. 311), Bp. of *Alexandria from 300. Peter is described by *Eusebius as 'a model bishop, remarkable alike for his virtuous life and for his keen study of the Scriptures'. He survived the persecution of

*Diocletian, and drew up rules governing the readmission to the Church of those who had lapsed from Christianity under the influence of fear or torture. While he was himself in hiding, another bishop, *Melitius, began to ordain priests and subsequently claimed authority over Alexandria. It seems that Peter came back to his see when peace was restored in 311, but was beheaded in the persecution of Maximin shortly afterwards. Little of his work survives except in fragments, from which it appears that he was a staunch opponent of *Origenism. Feast day in E., 24 Nov.; in W., 26 Nov.

Frags. in M. J. *Routh (ed.), *Reliquiae Sacrae* (2nd edn., Oxford, 1846), 4, pp. 19–82. J. P. Migne, *PG* 18. 449–522. Eng. tr. by J. B. H. Hawkins in ANCL 14 (1869), pp. 269–332, incl. introd. For more recently discovered frags., see *CPG* 1 (1983), pp. 202–9 (nos. 1635–62). Eusebius, *HE* 7. 32. 31; 8. 13. 7; and 9. 14. 2. L. B. Radford, *Three Teachers of Alexandria: Theognostus, Pierius and Peter* (1908), pp. 58–86. W. Telfer, 'St Peter of Alexandria and Arius', *Anal. Boll.* 67 (1949), pp. 117–30. P. Devos, 'Une Passion grecque inédite de S. Pierre d'Alexandrie et sa traduction par Anastase le Bibliothécaire', ibid. 83 (1965), pp. 157–87, incl. texts. T. Vivian, *St Peter of Alexandria, Bishop and Martyr* (Studies in Antiquity and Christianity, Philadelphia [1988]). J. Quasten, *Patrology*, 2 (Utrecht, 1953), pp. 113–18; Altaner and Stuiber (1978), pp. 212 f. and 591. F. H. Kettler in *PW* 19 (pt. 2; 1938), cols. 1281–8, s.v. 'Petros I'; A. Solignac, SJ, in *Dict. Sp.* 12 (pt. 2; 1986), cols. 1495–502, s.v. 'Pierre (5) d'Alexandrie'.

Peter de Bruys (d. prob. soon after 1130), medieval heretic. He is known through the writings of *Peter the Venerable and *Abelard. It would appear that he was a priest who was deprived of his office and then began to preach in Dauphiné and Provence. He rejected infant baptism, the Mass, church buildings (because every place is equally suitable for prayer), prayers for the dead, the veneration of the Cross (as being the instrument of crucifying Christ afresh), as well as large parts of the Scriptures and the authority of the Church. He gained a considerable number of followers, called 'Petrobrusians', who ill-treated priests and incited monks to marry. His teaching was frequently condemned, e.g. by the second *Lateran Council in 1139. He himself was thrown into the flames at St-Gilles, near Nîmes, by the people infuriated at his burning the crosses.

The principal sources are Peter the Venerable, 'Tractatus adversos Petrobrusianos Haereticos' (crit. edn. by J. Faerns (CCCM 10; 1968)), and Peter Abelard, 'Introductio ad Theologiam', 2. 4 (*PL* 178. 1056). J. Kramp, SJ, 'Chronologisches zu Peters des Ehrwürdigen *Epistola adversus Petrobrusianos*', in *Miscellanea Francesco Ehrle*, 1 (ST 37; 1924), pp. 71–9. J. C. Reagan, 'Did the Petrobrusians Teach Salvation by Faith Alone?', *Journal of Religion*, 7 (1927), pp. 81–91, with refs. R. Manselli, *Studi sulle Eresie del Secolo XII* (Istituto Storico Italiano per il Medio Evo, Studi Storici, 5; 1953), esp. pp. 25–43. J. Fearns, 'Peter von Bruis und die religiöse Bewegung des 12. Jahrhunderts', *Archiv für Kulturgeschichte*, 48 (1966), pp. 311–35. R. I. Moore, *The Origins of European Dissent* (1977), esp. pp. 102–5; M. D. Lambert, *Medieval Heresy: Popular Movements from Bogomil to Hus* (1977), pp. 51–5; 2nd edn. (1992), pp. 47–50.

Peter of Candia. See ALEXANDER V.

Peter Canisius, St. See CANISIUS, ST PETER.

Peter Celestine, St. See CELESTINE V, ST.

Peter the Chanter (d. 1197), medieval theologian. Prob. of a knightly family from Hodenc-en-Bray in the Beauvaisis, he was educated at *Reims and *Paris, where he taught theology from 1173 or earlier. In 1183 he became precentor of *Notre-Dame in Paris, and in 1197 dean of Reims. His works include glosses on all the books of the OT and NT, a collection of *quaestiones* known as the *Summa de Sacramentis*, and a work on virtues and vices, the *Verbum abbreviatum*. Peter was one of the most influential masters at Paris in the late 12th cent.; he concentrated on practical questions of ethics, and by his discussion of concrete cases for the guidance of confessors he contributed much to the elaboration of the doctrine of circumstances to be observed in the administration of *Penance. It is probable that Peter's views were influential in the reform programme of the *Lateran Council of 1215, notably in his strong condemnation of the use of *ordeals in the administration of justice. One respect in which his views did not prevail was his advocacy of life imprisonment and not the death penalty for heretics.

Verbum abbreviatum ed. G. Galpin, OSB (Mund, Switzerland, 1639), repr. in J. P. Migne, *PL* 205. 21–554. *Summa de Sacramentis* ed. J.-A. Dugauquier (Analecta Mediaevalia Namurcensia, 4, 7, 16, 21; 1954–67). For edns. of his other works to date, see F. Stegmüller, *Repertorium Biblicum Medii Aevi*, 4 (Madrid, 1954), pp. 248–75. An illustrated Prayer Manual attributed to Peter is ed., with a study of his *De Penitentia*, by R. C. Trexler, *The Christian at Prayer* (Medieval and Renaissance Texts and Studies, 44; New York, 1987). F. S. Gutjahr, *Petrus Cantor Parisiensis: Sein Leben und seine Schriften* (Graz, 1899). J. W. Baldwin, *Masters, Princes, and Merchants: The Social Views of Peter the Chanter and his Circle* (2 vols., Princeton, NJ, 1970). G. Dahan, 'Les interprétations juives dans les commentaires du Pentateuque de Pierre le Chantre', in *The Bible in the Medieval World: Essays in Memory of Beryl Smalley*, ed. K. Walsh and D. Wood (Studies in Church History, Subsidia, 4; 1985), pp. 131–55. J. W. Baldwin in *Dict. Sp.* 12 (pt. 2; 1986), cols. 1533–8, s.v. 'Pierre (16) le Chantre'.

Peter Chrysologus, St. See CHRYSOLOGUS, ST PETER.

Peter Claver, St (1581–1654), 'Apostle of the Negroes'. A native of Verdu in Catalonia, he entered the *Jesuit novitiate at Tarragona in 1601. While studying at Palma, Majorca, he was inspired by St Alphonsus Rodríguez with a longing to convert the heathen in the New World. In 1610 he landed at Cartagena in what is now Colombia and at once began ministering to the slaves who were brought over in terrible conditions from W. Africa. In 1615 he was ordained priest. He declared himself 'the slave of the negroes for ever' and, despite much opposition from slave-owners and people of fashion, he championed their cause and devoted himself for long years to their temporal and spiritual welfare. He is said to have instructed and baptized over 300,000 people. He was canonized by *Leo XIII in 1888. Feast day, 9 Sept.

J. Fernández, SJ, *Apostólica y penitente vida de el V. P. Pedro Claver* (Saragossa, 1666). The principal modern work is the Life by A. Valtierra, SJ, *El Santo que liberto una raza* (Bogota, 1954; rev. edn., *Pedro Claver: El Santo Redentor de los negros*, 2 vols., ibid., 1980; Eng. tr., 1960). G. Ledos, *Saint Pierre Claver* ('Les Saints', 1923); A. Lunn, *A Saint in the Slave Trade: Peter Claver* (1935). A. Astráin, SJ, *Historia de la Compañía de Jesús en la asistencia de España*, 5 (1916), pp. 479–95. Polgár, 1 (1990), pp. 493–500.

Peter Comestor (d. 1178/9), biblical scholar. Acc. to *Henry of Ghent he was a native of Troyes; he became dean of the cathedral there in 1147. By 1168 he was also Chancellor of *Notre-Dame in *Paris. He retained both offices when he retired to the *Victorine house in Paris towards the end of his life. A disciple of *Peter Lombard, he wrote Glosses on the four Gospels and on Lombard's Sentences, a treatise 'De Sacramentis' (a summary of the Sentences intended as a handbook for priests), a large number of sermons, and his best-known work, the 'Historia Scholastica'. Written towards the end of his life, the 'Historia' is a continuous history from Creation to the Ascension; a section on the Acts of the Apostles was added by Peter of Poitiers (d. c.1216). The work is based on the text of the OT, the Gospels, and Acts, with many scriptural quotations and literal and allegorical explanations frequently reflecting the tenets of contemporary science. The works of the Fathers and of pagan authors are used to fill up the gaps in the biblical narrative. It became the standard work on biblical history for the Middle Ages and was frequently annotated and commented on, e.g. by Stephen *Langton. Peter Comestor was known as the 'Magister Historiarum'.

The 'Historia Scholastica', first pr. Strasbourg, not later than 1473, is repr. from the edn. of E. Navarro, OSB (Madrid, 1699), in J. P. Migne, *PL* 198. 1049 (text 1053)–1722; the 'Sermons' are to be found ibid. 198, 1721–1844, and ibid. 171, *passim*; details of MSS and edns. in M. M. Lebreton, 'Recherches sur les manuscrits contenant des sermons de Pierre le Mangeur', *Centre National de la Recherche Scientifique. Publications de l'Institut de Recherche et d'Histoire des Textes. Bulletin d'Information*, 2 for 1953 (1954), pp. 25–44; 4 for 1955 (1956), pp. 35–6. Crit. text of the 'Tractatus De Sacramentis' with full bibl. by R. M. Martin, OP (as appendix in SSL 17; 1937). R. M. Martin, OP, 'Notes sur l'œuvre littéraire de Pierre le Mangeur', *RTAM* 3 (1931), pp. 54–66; A. Landgraf, 'Recherches sur les écrits de Pierre le Mangeur', ibid., pp. 292–306, 341–72; S. R. Daly, 'Peter Comestor: Master of Histories', *Speculum*, 32 (1957), pp. 62–73; B. Smalley, 'Some Gospel Commentaries of the Early Twelfth Century', *RTAM* 45 (1978), pp. 147–80; id., 'Peter Comestor on the Gospels and his Sources', ibid. 46 (1979), pp. 84–129; both repr. in id., *The Gospels in the Schools c.1100–c.1280* (1985), pp. 1–83; D. Luscombe, 'Peter Comestor', in *The Bible in the Medieval World: Essays in Memory of Beryl Smalley*, ed. K. Walsh and D. Wood (Studies in Church History, Subsidia, 4; 1985), pp. 109–29. J. Longère in *Dict. Sp.* 12 (pt. 2; 1986), cols. 1614–26, s.v. 'Pierre (39) le Mangeur'.

Peter Damian, St (1007–72), reformer and *Doctor of the Church. Born at Ravenna, he studied at Faenza and Parma. In 1035 he entered the hermitage at Fonte Avella, where he began to lead a life of extreme austerity. About 1043 he was chosen prior and spent the next years founding new monasteries and reforming old ones; before long he became famous as an uncompromising preacher against the worldliness and simoniacal practices of the clergy. In 1057, much against his will, he was made Cardinal Bishop of Ostia, and as such he took a prominent part in the work of ecclesiastical reform. Though he was relieved of his cardinalate by *Alexander II, he was sent several times on diplomatic missions to France and Germany.

During his life Peter enjoyed great authority in the Church, on account of his learning, zeal, and integrity. In his numerous writings he enjoined strict monastic discipline and severe mortification, and denounced immorality and simony. He campaigned for the creation of clerical communities living the 'apostolic life' without property. He was an important thinker in the spheres of theology and canon law; in particular his *Liber Gratissimus* defended the *validity of sacraments administered by priests guilty of *simony against the rigorist views of Cardinal *Humbert. He was never formally canonized, but since his death a local cult has existed in several places, and in 1828 Leo XII extended his feast to the universal Church, at the same time pronouncing him a 'Doctor of the Church'. Peter is said to have adopted the title Damian in gratitude to his brother of that name who had arranged for his education. His other writings include *Liber Gomorrhianus* (against *homosexuality) and *Disceptatio Synodalis*. Feast day, 21 Feb.

His works are listed, with details of edns., by C. Lucchesi, 'Clavis S. Petri Damiani', in *Studi su S. Pier Damiano in onore del Cardinale Amleto Giovanni Cicognani* (Faenza, 2nd edn., 1970), pp. 1–215. *Editio princeps* of Peter's collected works by C. Cajetan (4 vols., Rome, 1606–40), repr. in J. P. Migne, *PL* 144 and 145. Crit. edns. of his Sermons by I. Lucchesi (CCCM 57; 1983); of letters and treatises by K. Reindel (*MGH*, Briefe der deutschen Kaiserzeit, 1983 ff.); of *Liber Gratissimus* by L. de Heinemann in *MGH*, Libelli de Lite Imperatorum et Pontificum in Saeculis XI et XII, 1 (1891), pp. 15–75; of 'De Divina Omnipotentia' and other *opuscula* by P. Brezzi and B. Nardi (Florence, 1943); of 'Vita Beati Romualdi' by G. Tabacco (Fonti per la Storia d'Italia, 94; 1957); and of *Opera Poetica* by M. Lokrantz (Acta Universitatis Stockholmiensis, 12; 1964). The 'De Divina Omnipotentia' is also ed., with Fr. tr. and full introd., by A. Cantin (SC 191; 1972). Eng. trs. of *Selected Writings on the Spiritual Life* by P. McNulty (1959), of *Liber Gomorrhianus* by P. J. Payer (Waterloo, Ont., 1982), and of Letters by O. J. Blum, OFM (Fathers of the Church, Washington, DC, 1989 ff.). K. Reindel, 'Studien zur Überlieferung der Werke des Petrus Damiani', *Deutsches Archiv*, 15 (1959), pp. 23–102; 16 (1960), pp. 73–154; 18 (1962), pp. 317–417. Life by his disciple, John of Lodi, OSB, pr. in the edn. of his works by C. Cajetan, 1, op. cit., pp. v–xviii; repr. in *AASS*, Feb. 3 (1658), pp. 416–27, and in J. P. Migne, *PL* 144. 113–46. Modern studies by F. Dressler (Studia Anselmiana, 34; 1954, with bibl.) and J. Leclercq, OSB (Uomini e Dottrine, 8; 1960). J. J. Ryan, *Saint Peter Damiani and his Canonical Sources* (Pontifical Institute of Mediaeval Studies. Studies and Texts, 2; Toronto, 1956); J. Gonsette, SJ, *Pierre Damien et la culture profane* (Essais philosophiques, 7; 1965); R. Bultot, *La Doctrine du mépris du monde*, 4. *Le XIᵉ siècle*, 1: *Pierre Damien* (1963). *San Pier Damiano nel IX Centenario della Morte* (4 vols., Cesena, 1972–[1978]). C. Lohmer, *Heremi Conversatio: Studien zu den monastischen Vorschriften des Petrus Damiani* (Beiträge zur Geschichte des Alten Mönchtums und des Benediktinertums, 39; 1991). I. M. Resnick, *Divine Power and Possibility in St Peter Damian's De Divina Omnipotentia* (Studien und Texte zur Geistesgeschichte des Mittelalters, 31; Leiden, etc., 1992). *Studi Gregoriani*, 10 (1975) is devoted to him. J. P. Whitney, *Hildebrandine Essays* (1932), pp. 95–120. Raby, pp. 250–6; J. Szövérffy, *Die Annalen der lateinischen Hymnendichtung*, 1 (1964), pp. 393–8. Bibl. of works on Peter Damian, 1950–70, in *Studi su S. Pier Damiano in onore . . . Cicognani*, op. cit., pp. xxi–xxxi. B. Calati in *Dict. Sp.* 12 (pt. 2; 1986), cols. 1551–73, s.v. 'Pierre (25) Damien', with bibl.

Peter the Fuller (d. 488), Patr. of *Antioch. Acc. to an uncertain tradition, recorded by a 6th-cent. monk, Alexander of Cyprus, Peter had been a monk of the convent of the *Acoemetae at *Constantinople, where he practised the trade of a fuller. Expelled for his *Monophysite leanings, he went to Chalcedon, but after a brief stay returned and became known to the Emp. *Zeno the Isaurian, whom he accompanied to Antioch *c.*470. Here he joined the *Apollinarians and violently opposed Martyrius, Bp. of Antioch, a supporter of the *Chalcedonian Definition. During an absence of Martyrius, in search of assistance against the Apollinarians in Constantinople, Peter, backed by Zeno, had himself made bishop in his place (470). *Gennadius of Constantinople, however, obtained a decree of exile against him which was commuted to imprisonment in the convent of the Acoemetae. In 475 he succeeded in regaining his see, but in 477 he was once more deposed and interned, this time with the *Messalians. In 482 he gave his assent to Zeno's '*Henoticon' and again became Patr. of Antioch, where he remained till his death. At a Council he succeeded in inducing his bishops to assent to the Emperor's formula. He is chiefly remembered for his addition to the *Trisagion of the clause ὁ σταυρωθεὶς δι' ἡμᾶς ('who was crucified for us'). Acc. to *Theodore Lector he also introduced the recitation of the *Nicene Creed at the *Eucharist, the solemn blessing of the *chrism, and the commemoration of the *Theotokos at every service.

Theodore Lector, *HE* i. 20–2 (repr. in J. P. Migne, *PG* 86 (1). 175–8). *CPG* 3 (1979), pp. 253 f. (nos. 6522–5). E. Venables in *DCB* 4 (1887), pp. 338–40, s.v. 'Petrus (10)'; G. Fritz in *DTC* 12 (pt. 2; 1935), cols. 1933–5, s.v. 'Pierre le Foulon'; L. Perrone in *DPAC* 2 (1984), cols. 2794 f., s.v. 'Pietro il Fullone'; Eng. tr. in *Encyclopedia of the Early Church*, 2 (1992), p. 679, with bibl.

Peter Gonzales, St. See ELMO, ST.

Peter the Hermit (d. 1115), preacher of the First *Crusade. He was born at or near Amiens. Little is known of his early years, except that he was a hermit and may have had links with the 'poverty and preaching' movement of N. France. 12th-cent. sources report that he visited *Jerusalem as a pilgrim and returned with an appeal to Pope *Urban II to send help from the West. Historians have usually regarded this account as legendary, but it has recently been argued that it contains a kernel of historical truth. After the Council of *Clermont in 1095, Peter raised a considerable force which arrived at *Constantinople ahead of the rest of the First Crusade and was destroyed by the Turks on entering Anatolia. Peter himself then joined the main army. During the siege of Antioch (1098) he made an unsuccessful effort to escape but later apparently regained his reputation and entered Jerusalem with the victorious army. On his return to Europe he became prior of the *Augustinian monastery of Neufmoutier (Huy), which he had helped to found. He is commemorated on 8 July.

The standard study is H. Hagenmeyer, *Peter der Eremite* (1879; Fr. tr., 1883). E. O. Blake and C. Morris, 'A Hermit goes to War: Peter and the Origins of the First Crusade', in W. J. Sheils (ed.), *Monks, Hermits and the Ascetic Tradition* (Studies in Church History, 22; 1985), pp. 79–107; M. D. Coupe, 'Peter the Hermit—A Reassessment', *Nottingham Medieval Studies*, 31 (1987), pp. 37–45. See also works cited under CRUSADES.

Peter of Laodicea (*c.*7th–8th cent.), Gk. patristic writer and reputed Commentator on the Gospels. His name is attached to extracts from Gospel commentaries in two late MSS, though in others the passages are anonymous. In 1908 C. F. G. Heinrici argued that they were actually the

work of this author; but further investigation has made this improbable. The only undoubted work of Peter's to survive is a short 'Exposition of the Lord's Prayer'.

The 'Expositio in Orationem Domini' and other frags. in J. P. Migne, *PG* 86 (2). 3321–36. The surviving portions of his supposed Comm. on Mt., ed. C. F. G. Heinrici (Beiträge zur Geschichte und Erklärung des Neuen Testamentes, 5; 1908). M. Rauer, *Der dem Petrus von Laodicea zugeschriebene Lukaskommentar* (Neutestamentliche Abhandlungen, 8, Heft 2; 1920). Krumbacher, pp. 136 f. R. Devreesse in *Dict. Bibl.*, Suppl. 1 (1928), cols. 1165–7, s.v. 'Chaînes exégétiques grecques'.

Peter Lombard (*c.*1100–60), the 'Master of the Sentences'. He was born near Novara in Lombardy, and after studying in Italy went to *Reims and then to *Paris, where he taught at the Cathedral School from 1143 or 1144. In 1148 he opposed *Gilbert de la Porrée at the Council of Reims, and in 1159, shortly before his death, was appointed Bp. of Paris. His Commentaries on the Psalms and on the Pauline Epistles were written before and after 1148 respectively, and his chief work, the 'Sententiarum libri quatuor', probably 1155–8. This last work, to which he owes his fame, is arranged in four books, on (1) the Trinity, (2) the Creation and Sin, (3) the Incarnation and the Virtues, and (4) the Sacraments and the Four Last Things. It contains a wealth of quotations from the Latin Fathers, esp. Sts *Augustine and *Hilary, as well as (of the Greeks) from St *John of Damascus, hitherto almost unknown in the W. After Peter Lombard's death the book was violently attacked by *Walter of St-Victor on the ground of its *Abelardian Christological '*Nihilianism', i.e. the doctrine that Christ acc. to His humanity is nothing (*quod Christus secundum quod est homo non est aliquid*), which, however, was apparently given only as an opinion. Later, under the influence of *Joachim of Fiore's 'Liber de vera et falsa philosophia', which attacked Peter Lombard's Trinitarian teaching, efforts were made to have the work censured at the Fourth *Lateran Council in 1215, with the result that Joachim's doctrine was rejected and the 'Sentences' pronounced orthodox. After this rehabilitation it became the standard textbook of Catholic theology during the Middle Ages, despite the early rejection of several opinions advanced in it, e.g. the identification of the Holy Spirit with the virtue of charity. Its teaching on the Sacraments marked an important development; Peter Lombard is one of the first to insist on the number seven, to distinguish them (like *Alexander of Hales later) from the *sacramentals, and to clarify the conception by asserting the efficacity and causality of the sign. The book, which owed its success chiefly to its lucid arrangement, its comprehensiveness, and its absence of individuality, was commented on by nearly all theologians of repute and even versified. It was finally superseded as a textbook by the 'Summa Theologiae' of St *Thomas Aquinas, but in the 17th cent. commentaries were still produced, among the last being that of the *Jesuit, J. M. de Ripalda (1635).

Works collected in J. P. Migne, *PL* 191 and 192. Crit. edn. of the Sentences by the Franciscans of Grottaferrata [in fact by I. Brady] (Spicilegium Bonaventurianum, 4–5; Grottaferrata, 1971–81), incl. important survey of his life and works. J. N. Espenberger, *Die Philosophie des Petrus Lombardus und ihre Stellung im zwölften Jahrhundert* (BGPM 3, Heft 5; 1901). O. Baltzer, *Die Sentenzen des Petrus Lombardus* (Studien zur Geschichte der Theologie und der Kirche, 8, Heft 3; 1902). F. Stegmüller (ed.),

Repertorium Commentariorum in Sententias Petri Lombardi (2 vols., Würzburg, 1947). *Miscellanea Lombardiana pubblicata a chiusura delle celebrazioni centenarie organizzate in Novara per onorare Pietro Lombardo*, a cura del Pontificio Ateneo Salesiano di Torino (Novara, 1957), esp. D. Van den Eynde, OFM, 'Essai chronologique sur l'œuvre littéraire de Pierre Lombard', pp. 45–63. P. Delhaye, *Pierre Lombard* (Montreal and Paris, 1961). M. L. Colish, *Peter Lombard* (Brill's Studies in Intellectual History, 41; 2 vols., Leiden, 1994). J. de Ghellinck, SJ, *Le Mouvement théologique du XII⁴ siècle* (2nd edn., Museum Lessianum, Section Historique, 10; 1948), pp. 113–373. Id. in *DTC* 12 (pt. 2; 1935), cols. 1941–2019, s.v. 'Pierre Lombard', with good bibl.; I. Brady in *Dict. Sp.* 12 (pt. 2; 1986), cols. 1604–12, s.v. 'Pierre (37) Lombard'. J. de Ghellinck, SJ, in *CE* 11 (1911), pp. 768 f., s.v.

Peter Martyr, St (*c.*1200–52), *Dominican preacher and Inquisitor. Born at *Verona (hence known also as **Veronensis**), into a predominantly *Catharist family, he nevertheless grew up as a Catholic. He was sent to study in *Bologna, where he entered the Dominican Order, prob. *c.*1220–1. He was renowned as an eloquent and dedicated preacher and a successful controversialist against the Cathari. In Sept. 1251 he was appointed Inquisitor in Milan and Como by Pope *Innocent IV. He and his companion were assassinated on 6 Apr. 1252 between Como and Milan. As he died he prayed for his murderer, commended himself to God and began to recite the Creed. A late tradition asserts that he wrote the first words of the Creed on the ground in his own blood. Fra *Angelico depicted him in a famous painting in the convent of S. Marco, Florence, with wounded head, his finger to his lips. Feast day, 4 June, formerly 29 April.

Life by Thomas Agni de Lentino, OP, written before 1257, pr. from a redaction made *c.*1517 in *AASS*, Apr. 3 (1675), pp. 686–719; other material, pp. 678–86; Gerard de Fracheto, OP (d. 1271), *Vitae Fratrum Ordinis Praedicatorum*, ed. B. M. de Reichert, OP (Monumenta Ordinis Praedicatorum, 1; Rome, 1897), pp. 236–48 Life by P. T. Campana (Milan, 1741). F. T. Perrens, 'Saint Pierre Martyr et l'hérésie des Patarins à Florence', *Revue historique*, 2 (1876), pp. 337–66. G. Meersseman, OP, 'Études sur les anciennes confréries dominicaines, 2. Les confréries de saint Pierre Martyr', *Archivum Fratrum Praedicatorum*, 21 (1951), pp. 51–196, with docs. A. Dondaine, OP, 'Saint Pierre Martyr', ibid. 23 (1953), pp. 66–162, with refs. V. J. Koudelka and A. Silli in *Bibliotheca Sanctorum*, 10 (Rome, 1968), cols. 746–62, s.v. 'Pietro de Verona', with further bibl.

Peter Martyr (1499–1562), an Anglicized form of 'Pietro Martire Vermigli', Reformer. He was born at Florence, the son of Stefano Vermigli (a follower of *Savonarola), who, having lost several children, vowed to dedicate any that lived to St Peter Martyr (see previous entry). The traditional date for his birth (1500) rests upon a misreading of the Florence baptismal register. After education at Fiesole by the *Augustinians and joining that order, he became in 1530 abbot of the Augustinians at Spoleto, and in 1533 prior of St Petrus-ad-aram at Naples. He was now a serious student of the Bible, and was much impressed by a reading of M. *Bucer's Commentaries on the Gospels and Psalms, and U. *Zwingli's *De vera et falsa religione*. The sympathy with the Reformers which he displayed in his lectures led him to be accused of error and prohibited from preaching, though the prohibition was removed on appeal to Rome, through the help of R. *Pole and other friends. In 1542, however, he was forced to flee from Italy and take refuge at Zurich and Basle, and lastly at Strasbourg, where, with Bucer's help, he was appointed professor of theology (1542). Here he married Catherine Dammartin, a nun. At T. *Cranmer's invitation he came to England with B. *Ochino in 1547, was given a government pension of 40 marks, made Regius professor of divinity at Oxford (1548), and took part in a great disputation (1549) on the Eucharist. He was consulted on the BCP of 1552, and was one of the commissioners for the reform of canon law. In 1553 his wife died, and was buried in *Christ Church Cathedral, Oxford, near the tomb of St *Frideswide, but, at the order of Cardinal Pole, the body was subsequently disinterred. (In 1561 her remains were mingled with the supposed relics of St Frideswide and buried at the NE end of the cathedral; hence N. *Sanders' epigram 'hic requiescit religio cum superstitione'.) At *Mary's accession, Martyr was briefly put under house arrest, but in Sept. 1553 was allowed, through S. *Gardiner's influence, to go to Strasbourg, where he was reappointed professor of theology (1554). In 1556, owing to opposition to his Eucharistic views, he removed to Zurich, where he became professor of Hebrew, maintaining a long correspondence on English affairs with J. *Jewel, R. *Cox, John Parkhurst, and Edwin *Sandys.

Some of his correspondence is incl. in the *Zürich Letters*, ed. H. Robinson (*Parker Society, 4 vols., 1842–5). The primary source is J. Simler, *Oratio de Vita et Obitu* (Zurich, 1563; it was also appended to the collection of Martyr's miscellaneous works pub. under the title *Loci Communes Sacrarum Literarum*, Zurich, 1583; Eng. tr. of the latter, with the *Oratio* appended, by A. Marten, London, 1583). Eng. tr. of *Early Writings*, ed. J. C. McLelland (Sixteenth Century Essays & Studies, 30; Kirksville, Mo., 1994). Id., *The Visible Words of God: An Exposition of the Sacramental Theology of Peter Martyr Vermigli*, A.D. 1500–1562 (1957). P. McNair, *Peter Martyr in Italy: An Anatomy of Apostasy* (Oxford, 1967). K. Sturm, *Die Theologie Peter Martyr Vermiglis während seines ersten Aufenthalts in Strassburg 1542–1547* (Beiträge zur Geschichte und Lehre der Reformierten Kirche, 31; 1971). M. W. Anderson, *Peter Martyr: A Reformer in Exile (1542–1562)* (Bibliotheca Humanistica & Reformatorica, 10; Nieuwkoop, 1975). J. P. Donnelly, SJ, *Calvinism and Scholasticism in Vermigli's Doctrine of Man and Grace* (Studies in Medieval and Renaissance Thought, 18; Leiden, 1976). J. C. McLelland (ed.), *Peter Martyr Vermigli and Italian Reform* (Waterloo, Ont. [1980]), pp. 65–151. M. A. Overell, 'Peter Martyr in England 1547–1553: An Alternative View', *Sixteenth Century Journal*, 15 (1984), pp. 87–104. J. P. Donnelly, SJ, and R. M. Kingdon, *A Bibliography of the Works of Peter Martyr Vermigli* (Sixteenth Century Essays & Studies, 13; Kirksville, Mo. [1990]).

Peter Mogila. See MOGILA, PETER.

Peter Mongo (d. 490) (Gk. Μογγός, 'hoarse'), Patr. of *Alexandria. In 477 he was elected the successor of the *Monophysite *Timothy Aelurus. As both Rome and Constantinople recognized the Patriarchate of Timothy Salophaciolus (Patr. 460–82), Mongo, fearing the Emp. *Zeno, went into hiding. On the death of Salophaciolus in 482, however, Acacius, Patr. of *Constantinople (see ACACIAN SCHISM), persuaded the Emperor to recognize Mongo in return for his acceptance of the *Henoticon. While his acceptance of the Henoticon annoyed the extreme Monophysites in Alexandria, his endeavours to placate them by a Monophysite interpretation of it also offended the orthodox. The compromise served, however, to maintain peaceful relations with Constantinople during the patriarchate of Acacius. Euphemius, who became Patr. of Constantinople in 490, had his name erased from the *diptychs and intended to depose him, an action prevented by Mongo's death.

The sources incl. *Evagrius, *HE* 3, *Zacharias Scholasticus, *HE* 5, and Theophanes, *Chronogr.* 194. T. Niggl in *L.Th.K.* (2nd edn.), 8 (1963), cols. 370 f., s.v., with bibl.

Peter Nolasco, St (*c.*1180–*c.*1249), founder of the *Mercedarian Order. The hagiographical tradition, according to which he took part in the *Crusade against the *Albigensians and later achieved remarkable feats in ransoming captives, has been largely exploded by historians, leaving little that can be confidently asserted about his life. Even the authenticity of crucial documents is contested. He was prob. engaged in his life's work of ransoming captives by the mid-1220s, if not earlier. The focus of this work was Catalonia, but he was possibly of French extraction. When other people associated themselves with his activities, the Mercedarian Order began to take shape. The date of his death is disputed, but he was clearly no longer head of the Order after 1245. He was canonized by *Urban VIII in 1628. Feast day 28 (formerly 31) Jan., now suppressed from the universal calendar.

Lives by F. Zumel, Mercedarian, pr. in *AASS*, Jan. 2 (1643), pp. 981–8, F. Olignano, Mercedarian (Naples, 1668), F. Colombo (Madrid, 1674) and P. N. Pérez, Mercedarian (Barcelona, 1915; It. tr., 1921). For modern crit. appraisal, see recent works on the Mercedarians cited s.v., esp. art. by Y. Dossat. A. Rubino, Mercedarian, in *DIP* 6 (1980), cols. 1704–11, s.v. 'Pietro Nolasco'.

Peter of Spain. See JOHN XXI.

Peter of Tarentaise, St (d. 1175). (Not to be confounded with Pope Innocent V (1276), also 'Peter of Tarentaise'.) A native of the Dauphiné, at the age of 20 he became a *Cistercian monk at the Abbey of Bonnevaux, founded by St *Bernard, where he lived a life of great piety. In 1142 he was appointed Abp. of Tarentaise (Moutiers, in Savoy), and with great difficulty thoroughly reformed his diocese, founding many hospitals. His practice of distributing free bread and soup ('May Bread') in the weeks before harvest is said to have survived until the Revolution. In 1155 he sought release in flight, but being discovered as a lay brother in a Swiss monastery he was compelled to return to his see. He stood high in the confidence of the Popes and was commissioned to try to reconcile Prince Henry (later Henry II) of England and Louis VII of France. Feast day, 8 May.

AASS, Mai. 2 (1680), pp. 320–45, incl. Life by Godfrey, Abbot of Hauteville, written at the request of Pope Lucius III and completed before 1185. J. M. Chevray, *La Vie de saint Pierre II, archevêque de Tarentaise* (1841). H. Brultey, *Saint Pierre de Tarentaise: Ses miracles, ses reliques, son culte* (Besançon, 1874). Un Moine de Tamié [i.e. A. Dimier], *Saint Pierre de Tarentaise: Essai historique* (Ligugé, 1935). L. F. Barmann, SJ, 'Peter of Tarentaise. A Biographical Study of the Twelfth Century', *Revue de l'Université d'Ottawa*, 31 (1961), Section Spéciale, pp. 96*–125*.

Peter of Verona, St. See PETER MARTYR, ST.

Peter the Venerable (1092 or 1094–1156), eighth Abbot of *Cluny. A descendant of the noble family of Montboissier, he was educated at the monastery of Sauxillanges of the congregation of Cluny, and made his profession to its abbot, St *Hugh, shortly before the latter's death in 1109. After being prior at Vézelay and Domène (1120), he was elected abbot of Cluny in 1122. Against much opposition he carried through important reforms, esp. in the financial and educational spheres, in the two general chapters of 1132 and 1146 by enforcing the detailed constitutions which he had drawn up for the congregation. His interest in the pursuit of studies at Cluny brought about a controversy with his intimate friend, St *Bernard, who wished to see the monastic life confined to prayer and manual work. In 1130 Peter supported Innocent II against the antipope Anacletus II, himself a Cluniac monk, and in 1140 he gave shelter to *Abelard first at Cluny and later at the priory of St-Marcel-de-Chalon. Between his numerous journeys, which took him to Spain in 1142, to Germany in 1147, twice to England, and ten times to Italy, he frequently retired to a hermitage to devote himself to study and meditation. He was the first to have the *Koran translated into Latin (completed 1143) and himself wrote against the Muslims. His works, among which are treatises against *Peter de Bruys and against the Jews (1144–7), a number of sermons, and some poems, show comparatively little acquaintance with the Fathers but profound knowledge of the Scriptures, and a preference for the literal sense which causes him to avoid allegorical speculations. His moderation and gentleness earned him the veneration of his contemporaries, but in the eyes of posterity he was overshadowed by the great figure of his friend, St Bernard. Though honoured as a saint, he was never canonized. Commemoration in several martyrologies is on 29 Dec.

Collected edn. of his works, Paris, 1522 (very incomplete); further collection, incl. text of statutes of Cluny during his time, in M. Marrier, OSB (ed.), *Bibliotheca Cluniacensis* (Paris, 1614), cols. 621–1420; works repr., with additions from E. *Martène and elsewhere (details in *DTC*, see below), in J. P. Migne, *PL* 189. 61–1054. Crit. edns. of his letters, with introd., by G. Constable (2 vols., Cambridge, Mass., 1967); of his 'Contra Petrobrusianos Hereticos' by J. Fearns (CCCM 10; 1968); of his 'Adversus Iudaeorum inveteratam duritiem' by Y. Friedman (ibid. 58; 1985); of his 'De miraculis' by D. Bouthillier (ibid. 83; 1988); and of three of his sermons by G. Constable, in *R. Bén.* 64 (1954), pp. 224–72. Life by his friend, Rudolphus, pr. from a MS no longer known, in E. Martène, OSB, and U. Durand, OSB (eds.), *Veterum Scriptorum et Monumentorum Amplissima Collectio*, 6 (Paris, 1729), cols. 1187–202; repr. in J. P. Migne, op. cit., cols. 15–28. Further Life in M. Marrier, op. cit., cols. 589–602, repr. with other biog. material in J. P. Migne, op. cit., cols. 27–62. J. H. Pignot, *Histoire de l'ordre de Cluny depuis la fondation de l'abbaye jusqu'à la mort de Pierre-le-Vénérable*, 3 (1868), pp. 47–609. Good modern study by J. Leclercq, OSB ('Figures monastiques'; Abbaye S. Wandrille, 1946), with bibl. Festschrift commemorating the 8th centenary of his death, *Petrus Venerabilis*, ed. G. Constable and J. Kritzeck (Studia Anselmiana, 40; 1956); *Pierre Abélard—Pierre le Vénérable: Les courants philosophiques, littéraires et artistiques en Occident au milieu du XIIe siècle*, Abbaye de Cluny, 2 au 9 juillet 1972 (Colloques internationaux du centre national de la recherche scientifique, 546; 1975), esp. pp. 99–269. J. P. Torrell, OP, and D. Bouthillier, *Pierre le Vénérable et sa Vision du Monde* (SSL 42; 1986). J. Kritzeck, *Peter the Venerable and Islam* (Princeton Oriental Studies, 23; 1964), incl. text of his writings against the Muslims. A. *Wilmart, OSB, 'Le Poème apologétique de Pierre le Vénérable et les poèmes connexes', *R. Bén.* 51 (1939), pp. 53–69. H. Hoffmann, 'Zu den Briefen des Petrus Venerabilis', *Quellen und Forschungen aus Italienischen Archiven und Bibliotheken*, 49 (1969), pp. 399–441; 50 (1970), pp. 447–9. A. H. Bredero, *Cluny* *et Cîteaux au douzième siècle: L'Histoire d'une controverse monastique* (Amsterdam and Maarssen, 1985), *passim*. M. D. *Knowles, 'Peter the Venerable', *Bulletin of the John Rylands Library*, 39 (1956–7), pp. 132–45. Manitius, 3, pp. 136–44. P. Séjourné, OSB, in *DTC* 12 (pt. 2; 1935), cols. 2065–81; J. Hourlier, OSB, in *Dict. Sp.* 12 (pt. 2; 1986), cols. 1669–76, both s.v. 'Pierre le Vénérable'.

Peterborough. At the Saxon village of Medehamstede, which had existed on the site, a monastery was established *c.*655, Peada, son of Penda, King of the Mercians, being one of its founders. After the monastery church had been destroyed by the Danes in 870, it was rebuilt *c.*966 by *Ethelwold, Bp. of *Winchester, who dedicated it to St Peter, and hence the village came to be called 'Peterborough'. This church being accidentally burnt in 1116, the foundations of a new church were laid in the following year. It was completed in 1237 and consecrated by R. *Grosseteste, Bp. of *Lincoln, and in 1541 became the cathedral of the newly constituted diocese. Though containing architecture of every period from the Norman to the Perpendicular, it is fundamentally a Norman church, exceptionally well preserved, with a fine early 13th-cent. painted ceiling over the nave. Catherine of Aragon was buried here in 1536 and *Mary Queen of Scots in 1587, Mary's body being removed to *Westminster Abbey in 1612. In 1895 the site of a cruciform Saxon church was discovered under the south transept.

The Peterborough Chronicle, 1070–1154, ed. C. Clark (Oxford, 1958; 2nd edn., 1970). Chronicle of Hugh Candidus, ed. J. Sparke, *Historiae Anglicanae Scriptores Varii* (London, 1723), separate pagination; mod. edn. by W. T. Mellows (ibid., 1949); Eng. tr., Peterborough, 1941). Chronicles of Robert of Swaffham and Walter of Whittlesey also ed. J. Sparke, op. cit. *Chronicon Petroburgense,* ed. T. Stapleton (Camden Society, 47; 1849). *Account Rolls of the Obedientiaries of Peterborough,* ed. J. Greatrex (Northamptonshire Record Society, 33; 1984). Various docs. on the church of St John the Baptist, Peterborough, on the monastery, and on the cathedral, ed. W. T. Mellows, *Peterborough Local Administration* (ibid. 9, 12, and 13; 1939–47); id. and D. H. Gifford, *Elizabethan Peterborough* (ibid. 18; 1956). J. D. Martin, *The Cartularies and Registers of Peterborough Abbey* [A Handlist] (ibid. 28; 1978). S. Gunton, *The History of the Church of Peterborough* (1686). W. *Dugdale, *Monasticon Anglicanum,* 1 (1817 edn.), pp. 344–404. E. [J.] King, *Peterborough Abbey 1086–1310: A Study in the Land Market* (Cambridge, 1973). B. Willis, *A Survey of the Cathedrals of Lincoln, Ely, Oxford and Peterborough* (1730), pp. 475–540. W. D. Sweeting, *The Cathedral Church of Peterborough* (Bell's Cathedral Series, 1898). J. C. Cox in *VCH*, Northampton, 2, ed. R. M. Serjeantson and W. R. D. Adkins (1906), pp. 83–95, with refs. G. F. Assinder in *DECH*, pp. 455–7, s.v.

Peter's Chains, Feast of St. See LAMMAS DAY.

Peter's Pence (Lat. *denarii S. Petri*), also 'Rome-Scot', formerly an ecclesiastical tax in England paid to the Pope. It was first paid by King *Offa after the visit of the two Papal legates concerned in the establishment of the archbishopric of *Lichfield in 787, and appears to have been continued by Offa's successors. *William of Malmesbury records that it was paid by King Aethelwulf (d. 858), the father of *Alfred the Great. After a lapse it was renewed by *William I. At one time a levy, collected at midsummer on all but the poorest houses, in the 12th cent. it was commuted by the bishops to an annual sum of £199. 6s. 8d. As a tax it was finally abolished by *Henry VIII in 1534. After the restoration of the RC hierarchy in 1850,

however, the bishops agreed to resume more regularly constituted contributions to Rome, and from the 1860s Peter's Pence was collected on an informal diocesan basis; the practice received official sanction in 1871 and has continued.

Act forbidding the payment (Ecclesiastical Licences Act 1533) repr. in Gee and Hardy, pp. 209–32 (no. 53). P. Fabre, 'Recherches sur le denier de saint Pierre en Angleterre au moyen âge', in *Mélanges G. B. de Rossi* (Supplément aux Mélanges d'Archéologie et d'Histoire publiés par l'École française de Rome, 12; 1892), pp. 159–82; O. Jensen, 'The "Denarius Sancti Petri" in England', *Transactions of the Royal Historical Society*, NS 15 (1901), pp. 171–247. W. E. Lunt, *Papal Revenues in the Middle Ages* (Records of Civilization, 19; New York, 1934), 1, pp. 65–71, with docs., 2, pp. 55–81; id., *Financial Relations of the Papacy with England to 1327* (Studies in Anglo-Papal Relations during the Middle Ages, 1; Mediaeval Academy of America Publication, 33; 1939), pp. 3–84; id., *Financial Relations of the Papacy with England 1327–1534* (ibid. 2; Mediaeval Academy of America Publication, 74; 1962), pp. 1–53; 717–20, all with refs. E. W. Watson in *DECH*, pp. 457 f.

Petite Église. The body of French Catholics who refused to recognize the *Concordat of 1801 (q.v.) and separated themselves from the communion of the Pope. Its members, who were known by various names, such as 'Illuminés' and 'Fidèles', remained faithful to a number of exiled bishops who had resisted the Pope's order to resign their old dioceses, and met in private houses for worship. When at the restoration, between 1817 and 1818, all schismatic bishops were reconciled to the Holy See except the Bp. of Blois, he came to be regarded as the head of the Petite Église till his death in 1829, which left them without a bishop. From that date their number rapidly decreased, esp. after their last priest died in 1847. By 1900 the schism had practically ceased to exist.

C. De Clercq in *DDC* 6 (1957), cols. 1438–47, s.v.

Petrarch, Francesco (1304–74), Italian poet and humanist. He spent part of his youth at Carpentras, near *Avignon, where his father had settled after being exiled from Florence for embracing, like *Dante, the cause of the White Guelphs. After studying law at Montpellier from 1319 to 1323 and at *Bologna from 1323 to 1325, he received minor orders at Avignon in 1326 which enabled him to hold several benefices. In 1327 he first saw Laura, who was to inspire his most famous poems collected in the 'Canzoniere'. From 1330 to 1337 he journeyed through N. France, Germany, and Italy, visiting many scholars and copying classical MSS until, in 1337, he settled down to a life of solitude at Vaucluse, where most of his important works were written. His poems on Laura and his epic 'Africa' (begun in 1338) on Scipio Africanus won him the poet's crown in 1341. In the following year he wrote the treatise 'Secretum' (sometimes known as 'De Contemptu Mundi'), consisting of three dialogues between himself and St *Augustine, who seeks to turn the poet's mind from the transitory things of this world to thoughts of eternal life. In 1347 Petrarch supported the short-lived republican movement of Cola di *Rienzo and in 1350 began his famous friendship with Boccaccio. In the following years he was employed on several political embassies, e.g. to the Emp. Charles IV at Prague (1356). The last years of his life were spent again in retirement at Padua and the neighbouring village of Arquà. His religious nature, which was often in conflict with the sensuousness of the fame-loving poet and the passion of the scholar for pagan culture, found expression in several Latin treatises. 'De Otio Religioso' (begun in 1347), dedicated to the *Carthusians of Montrieu, is a panegyric on the contemplative life; 'De Vita Solitaria' (1356) is a praise of solitude; and in the 'De Remediis Utriusque Fortunae' (1358–66) the ageing poet meditates on the transitoriness of human life. His last great poetical work, the 'Trionfi', strongly influenced by Dante's *Divina Commedia, celebrates in allegorical form the triumph of the Divine over all things and the ultimate redemption of man from the dominion of the senses.

Editio princeps of his collected works, Basle, 1496 (Lat. works only); fuller edn. [by J. Herold] (4 vols. bound in 1, ibid., 1554). A. Hortis (ed.), *Scritti inediti di Francesco Petrarca* (Trieste, 1874). Crit. text in the *Edizione nazionale delle opere di Francesco Petrarca* by various eds. (Florence, 1926 ff.). Crit. edns. of *Prose*, with Ital. tr., by G. Martellotti and others (Letteratura Italiana, Storia e Testi, 7; 1955), incl. 'De Vita Solitaria', pp. 286–591, 'De Otio Religioso', pp. 594–603, and 'De Remediis Utriusque Fortunae', pp. 606–45; also of 'De Otio Religioso' by G. Rotondi (ST 195; 1958) and of 'Le Familiari', bks. 1–11, by U. Dotti (2 vols., Urbino, 1974). Eng. tr. of his 'De Vita Solitaria' by J. Zeitlin (Urbana, Ill., 1924); of his 'Letters on Familiar Matters' by A. S. Bernardo (bks. 1–8, Albany, NY, 1975; 9–24, 2 vols., Baltimore and London, 1982–5); of his 'Bucolicum Carmen' by T. G. Bergin (New Haven, Conn., and London, 1974); of his Lyric Poems by R. M. Durling (Cambridge, Mass., 1976), and of 'Africa' by T. G. Bergin and A. S. Wilson (ibid., 1977). The fullest account in Eng. is E. H. R. Tatham, *Francesco Petrarca . . .: His Life and Correspondence* (2 vols., 1925–6). The very extensive lit. incl. general studies by F. De Sanctis (Naples, 1869; ed. B. *Croce, 1907; also ed. among De Sanctis's works, by N. Gallo, Turin, 1952), U. Bosco (Turin, 1946; rev. edn., Bari, 1961), K. Foster [OP] (Edinburgh, 1984), and N. Mann (Past Masters; Oxford and New York, 1984). P. de Nolhac, *Pétrarque et l'humanisme* (Bibliothèque de l'École des Hautes-Études. Sciences Philologiques et Historiques, 91; 1892; rev. edn., Bibliothèque Littéraire de la Renaissance, NS 1 and 2; 1907). J. H. Whitfield, *Petrarch and the Renaissance* (1943). Collection of essays by E. H. Wilkins (Chicago, 1961); id., *Life of Petrarch* (ibid., 1961); U. Dotti, *Vita di Petrarca* (1987). M. O'R. Boyle, *Petrarch's Genius: Pentimento and Prophecy* (Berkeley and Los Angeles, Calif., and Oxford [1991]). A. S. Bernardo, *Petrarch, Scipio and the 'Africa'* (Baltimore [1962]); id., *Petrarch, Laura, and the Triumphs* (Albany, NY, 1974). H. Baron, *Petrarch's Secretum: Its Making and Meaning* (Cambridge, Mass., 1985). P. Hainsworth, *Petrarch the Poet: An Introduction to the* Rerum vulgarium fragmenta (1988). The *Catalogue of the Petrarch Collection Bequeathed by W. Fiske* [to the Cornell University Library], compiled by M. Fowler (1916), contains extensive bibl. to date. E. Carrara in *Enciclopedia italiana*, 27 (1935), pp. 8–23, s.v. 'Petrarca', with full bibl.; A. Niero in *Dict. Sp.* 12 (pt. 1; 1984), cols. 1208–17, s.v. 'Pétrarque', with more recent bibl.

Petri, Olaus (1493–1552), Swedish Reformer. The son of a blacksmith of Örebro, he studied at *Wittenberg (1516–18) and, returning home imbued with strict *Lutheran views, was made master of the chapter school at Strängnäs, and later appointed city clerk at Stockholm (1524). Gaining the favour of Gustavus Vasa, by whom he was made chancellor (1531–3), he became the leading exponent of doctrinal change in Sweden. After his marriage in 1525 he produced a continuous stream of tracts,

pamphlets, and a book of homilies, which were widely read. He published the first Swedish service book, *En handbok på svenska* (1529) and was almost certainly responsible for the Swedish translation of the NT (1526). The latter years of his life (after 1539) were spent in retirement.

His brother, **Laurentius Petri** (1499–1573), was also a leading Reformer. In 1551 he was appointed the first Protestant Abp. of *Uppsala. He was responsible for the Swedish Church Order of 1571.

Collected Works (4 vols., Uppsala, 1914–17). *The Manual of Olavus Petri* (ed. E. E. Yelverton, Church Historical Society, 1953). Lives by R. Holm (Uppsala, 1917), H. Schück (Stockholm, 1893) and R. Murray (ibid., 1952). S. Ingebrand, *Olavus Petris Reformatoriska Åskådning* (Acta Universitatis Upsaliensis. Studia Doctrinae Christianae Upsaliensia, 1; Lund, 1964); C. Gardemeister, *Den suveräne Guden: En studie i Olavus Petris teologi* (Studia theologica Lundensia, 43; 1989). C. J. I. Bergendoff, *Olaus Petri and the Ecclesiastical Transformation in Sweden* (New York, 1928). On Laurentius Petri there is a brief study by E. E. Yelverton, *An Archbishop of the Reformation* (1958). B. Ahlberg, *Laurentius Petris Nattvardsuppfattning* (Studia theologica Lundensia, 26; 1964).

Petrobrusians. See PETER DE BRUYS.

Petrock, St (6th cent.) also 'Pedrog', 'the captain of Cornish saints' (T. *Fuller). He is said to have been the son of a Welsh chieftain who after studying in Ireland (where he is said to have instructed St *Kevin) made his way to Cornwall and founded monasteries at Padstow (i.e. 'Petrockstowe') and Bodmin. It is almost impossible to disentangle the facts of his life from the extravagant embellishments of later times. In 1177 his relics were stolen from Bodmin by a Breton canon and given to the abbey of St-Méen, but Henry II secured their restoration. Many churches in Cornwall and Devon bear his dedication; and he is also venerated in Brittany as St Perreux. He is commonly represented with a stag. Feast day, 4 June.

14th-cent. Life by John of Tynemouth repr. in *AASS*, Jun. 1 (1695), pp. 400–2. P. Grosjean, SJ, 'Vies et miracles de S. Pétroc', *Anal. Boll.* 74 (1956), pp. 131–88 and 470–96, incl. texts and further refs. G. H. Doble, *Saint Petrock, Abbot and Confessor* ('Cornish Saints' Series, no. 11 [c.1929]), with Eng. tr. of Life in MS Bibl. Nat. Lat. 9889. C. W. Boase in *DCB* 4 (1887), pp. 326 f.

Petronius, St (early 5th cent.), Bp. of *Bologna c.432–50. He is briefly mentioned by contemporary historians. His Life describes him as a member of the imperial family, and says that he visited *Jerusalem, and that on becoming bishop he erected a church and monastery, dedicated to St *Stephen, modelled on the *Constantinian buildings at the *Holy Sepulchre. However, his cultus at Bologna developed rapidly after the finding of his relics in 1141, and the Life was apparently written between 1162 and 1180. It is largely legendary, and its statement about Petronius' buildings is highly controversial. Various writings have also been ascribed to him, mostly incorrectly. The present church of San Petronio, a vast Gothic structure, was begun in 1390 and completed in the 17th cent. Feast day, 4 Oct.

*Gennadius, *De Vir. Ill.* 41. G. *Morin, OSB, 'Deux petits discours d'un évêque Petronius, du Vᵉ siècle', *R. Ben.* 14 (1897), pp. 3–8. F. Lanzoni, *San Petronio vescovo di Bologna nella storia* *e nella legenda* (Rome, 1907) (text of Life, pp. 219–40); A. Testi Rasponi, 'Note Marginali al L. P. di Agnello', 4, 'Vita Sancti Petronii Episcopi et Confessoris', *Atti e Memorie della R. Deputazione di Storia Patria per le Provincie di Romagna*, 4th ser. 2 (1912), pp. 120–262; M. Corti, *Vita di San Petronio* (Bologna, 1962). W. Montorsi, *S. Stefano in Bologna* (Deputazione di Storia Patria per le Antiche Provincie Modenesi, Biblioteca, NS 52; 2 vols., Modena, 1980); L. Serchia (ed.), *Nel segno del S. Sepolcro* (Vigevano, 1987).

pew. At first the customary postures of the worshippers in the W., as to this day in E. churches, were standing and kneeling, and no seats were provided for the congregation. Later on, as a concession to the infirm, stone seats were attached to the walls, or, more rarely, to the piers of the nave; and by the end of the 13th cent. many English churches appear to have been equipped also with a number of fixed wooden benches. These were often known as 'pews' (probably derived from the Latin *podium* and meaning a seat raised up above floor-level). Such pews, even in village churches, were sometimes elaborately carved, at the ends and on the back, with figures of saints, symbols of the Passion of Christ, or grotesque animals. To finance the endowment of new churches and chapels built in the populous suburbs in the 19th cent., the Church Buildings Act 1818 and subsequent Acts allowed for payment for the exclusive use of certain pews. The pew-rents, as these payments were called, were normally to be used for the salary of a 'spiritual person' and clerk to serve in the church or chapel. Few, if any, now remain.

A. Heales, *The History and Law of Church Seats or Pews* (2 vols., 1872). J. C. Cox, *Bench Ends in English Churches* (1916). G. W. O. Addleshaw and F. Etchells, *The Architectural Setting of Anglican Worship* (1948), pp. 86–98. See also J. M. *Neale, *The History of Pews* (Paper read before the *Cambridge Camden Society, 22 Nov. 1841; 1841; suppl., 1842; 3rd edn., incl. suppl. and additions, 1843).

Pfaff Fragments of Irenaeus. Four fragments first pub. in F. S. *Maffei's *Giornale de' letterati d'Italia* in 1713 by C. M. Pfaff (d. 1760), who alleged that he had found them in the Turin library and believed them to be written by St *Irenaeus. Among other subjects they dealt with 'true Gnosis' and the 'new oblation' (i.e. the Eucharist). Though their Irenaean authorship was constantly challenged from the outset, they were regularly quoted and discussed down to the end of the 19th cent., when A. *Harnack showed convincingly that they were a fabrication of Pfaff himself. He proved that they made use of the (late) *Textus Receptus of the NT and of the defective printed editions of the Greek text of Irenaeus current in the early 18th cent., as well as reflecting Pfaff's own theological tenets, e.g. the *Lutheran doctrine of the Eucharist.

A. Harnack, *Die Pfaff'schen Irenäus-Fragmente als Fälschungen Pfaffs nachgewiesen* (TU 20, Heft 3; 1900), a magisterial monograph. On Pfaff himself, cf. E. Preuschen in *PRE* (3rd edn.), 15 (1904), pp. 233–7, with useful bibl.

Pflug, Julius von (1499–1564), Bp. of Naumburg. Of Saxon descent, he was educated at Leipzig, *Bologna, and Padua, and appointed Provost of Zeitz in 1522 and Dean of Meissen in 1537. His humanistic sympathies made him eager for peace with the Protestants and to that end he took part in several conferences, e.g. at Leipzig in 1534 and at *Ratisbon in 1541. He indicated his willingness even to tolerate a married clergy and communion in both kinds. In 1541 he was elected Bp. of Naumburg-Zeitz, but as the Elector Johann Friedrich of Saxony refused to acknowledge him, he was unable to take possession of his see till after the Elector's defeat at Mühlberg in 1547. The 'Interim of *Augsburg' (1548; q.v.) was largely Pflug's work. His rule was much disturbed by the Protestantism in his diocese. In his theology he was greatly influenced by G. *Contarini.

Correspondence, ed. J. V. Pollet, OP (5 vols in 6, Leiden, 1969–82). Id., *Julius Pflug (1499–1564) et la crise religieuse dans l'Allemagne du XVIe siècle* (Studies in Medieval and Reformation Thought, 45; Leiden, 1990). E. Neuss and J. V. Pollet (eds.), *Pflugiana: Studien über Julius Pflug (1499–1564)* (Reformationsgeschichtliche Studien und Texte, 129; 1990). J. Wicks, SJ, in *Dict. Sp.* 12 (pt. 1; 1984), cols. 1253–8, s.v. See also bibl. to AUGSBURG (INTERIM OF).

Phanar, the. The official residence and court of the *Oecumenical Patriarch at *Constantinople. It is in the Greek quarter of the city, on the Golden Horn.

Pharisees (Heb. פְּרוּשִׁין, 'separated ones'; Gk. Φαρισαῖοι). A Jewish religious party. The name occurs in *Josephus and in rabbinic sources, as well as in the NT. It is, however, far from certain that the *Perushin*, who are attacked in rabbinic sources as a separatist sect, are to be identified with the *Pharisaioi* of Josephus and the NT.

Josephus (*Ant.* 13. 5. 9) records the existence of the Pharisees as a distinct group in the time of Jonathan *Maccabaeus, *c.*145 BC, though some scholars hold that the term is here applied retrospectively. They opposed John Hyrcanus I (135–104 BC) for religious reasons and instigated a revolt against Alexander Jannaeus (103–76 BC), but they were favoured by Alexander's widow, Alexandra (76–67 BC). They refused to swear allegiance to *Herod on one occasion, but were respected by him. Unlike the *Sadducees, who tried to apply the Mosaic Law precisely as it was given, the Pharisees allowed some interpretation of it to make it more applicable to different situations. According to Josephus, they gradually secured a large following among the common people with regard to prayers and sacrifices, but modern scholars, reflecting the contradictory accounts in the ancient evidence, have reached no agreement either about the extent of the Pharisees' political and spiritual influence in 1st-cent. Palestine or about their main religious concerns.

In the Gospels the Pharisees appear as the chief opponents of the Lord, whom they attacked, e.g., for forgiving sins, breaking the Sabbath, and consorting with sinners. Christ repeatedly denounced what the Gospels describe as their purely external observance of the Law, their multitude of formalistic precepts which even they themselves could not keep (e.g. Mt. 23: 13–36), and their self-righteousness (Lk. 18: 9–14). During the Passion they remained in the background, when their place was taken by the Sadducees. After the Resurrection they appear less hostile to the nascent Church than the Sadducees; they share its belief in the resurrection and a retribution in the next world, in angels, in human freedom and Divine Providence; and it was a Pharisee, *Gamaliel, who publicly defended the Apostles before the Sanhedrin (Acts 5: 34–40).

After the fall of *Jerusalem (AD 70) the Pharisees disappear from history; but their influence survived in part in the teaching of the Rabbis and the *Mishnah. Several modern scholars have questioned whether the Pharisees depicted in the Gospels are representative of the party as a whole.

J. *Wellhausen, *Die Pharisäer und die Sadducäer* (1874). L. Finkelstein, *The Pharisees: The Sociological Background of their Faith* (2 vols., Philadelphia, 1938; 3rd edn., 1962). I. Abrahams, *Studies in Pharisaism and the Gospels* (2 vols., 1917–24). A. Finkel, *The Pharisees and the Teacher of Nazareth: A Study of their Background, their Halachic and Midrashic Teachings, the Similarities and Differences* (Arbeiten zur Geschichte des Spätjudentums und Urchristentums, 4; Leiden, 1964). J. Neusner, *The Rabbinic Traditions about the Pharisees before 70* (3 vols., Leiden, 1971); id., *From Religion to Piety: The emergence of Pharisaic Judaism* (Englewood Cliffs, NJ [1973]). J. W. Bowker, *Jesus and the Pharisees* (Cambridge, 1973). E. *Schürer, *The History of the Jewish People in the Age of Jesus Christ*, rev. Eng. tr. by G. Vermes and others, 2 (Edinburgh, 1979), pp. 381–403, incl. bibl. J. M. Baumgarten, 'The Name of the Pharisees', *Journal of Biblical Literature*, 102 (1983), pp. 411–28. E. P. Sanders, *Jewish Law from Jesus to the Mishnah* (1990), pp. 97–254. A. Michel and J. Le Moyne, OSB, in *Dict. Bibl.*, Suppl. 7 (1966), cols. 1022–115, s.v.; R. Meyer and H. F. Weiss in *TWNT* 9 (1973), pp. 11–51; Eng. tr. (1974), pp. 11–48, s.v. Φαρισαῖος, with full refs. A. J. Saldarini in *Anchor Bible Dictionary*, 5 (1992), pp. 289–303.

phelonion (Gk. φελόνιον). The E. form of the *chasuble. In shape it is somewhat like the W. Gothic vestment, but is gathered up in front instead of at the sides, so that when in use it looks more like a *cope.

Braun, *LG*, pp. 234–9.

phenomenalism. (1) The belief that what we term physical objects have no existence except as experienced as 'sense data' in men (or animals) who perceive them.

(2) The theory that such objects, though they may in reality exist, can be known only as the experiences ('sense data') which they occasion in us.

(3) As used by E. *Caird and N. Kemp Smith, the theory of knowledge expounded in, or implied by, *The Critique of Pure Reason* of I. *Kant, on the basis of his fundamental distinction between appearance and reality.

phenomenology (Gk. τὰ φαινόμενα, 'appearance', and λογία, 'discourse'), lit. 'the science of *phenomena*'. The term was occasionally employed by I. *Kant in its literal sense. By G. W. F. *Hegel, whose first large philosophical treatise bore the title *Phänomenologie des Geistes* (1807), it was applied to the description of the stages whereby the mind (*Geist*) develops from naïve consciousness (for Hegel, sense experience) to absolute knowledge. In recent times, however, it has been used esp. of the philosophical doctrines of Edmund Husserl (1859–1938) and his school. Acc. to Husserl phenomenology is a descriptive science concerned with the discovery and analysis of essences and essential meanings. It professes to exclude all metaphysical questions; but much in Husserl's first elaboration of the science tended towards a *Platonic realism. These Platonist elements were developed by his disciples and used e.g. by Max Scheler and Johannes Hessen for the defence of a Christian metaphysic of an *Augustinian (non-Thomistic)

type. Husserl himself in his later writings embraced a form of Subjective Idealism.

Husserl, who already employed the phenomenological method in parts of the *Logische Untersuchungen* (2 vols. in 3, 1900; Eng. tr., 2 vols., 1970), developed it in academic lectures in the years 1900–13 and systematically elaborated it in the programmatic *Ideen zu einer reinen Phänomenologie und phänomenologischen Philosophie* (1913; Eng. tr. by W. R. Boyce Gibson, *Ideas*, 1931). This book, which came to be known as *Ideen* 1, was the first part of a much larger work, of which the second and third parts were published only in 1952. The chief organ of the Phenomenological Movement was the *Jahrbuch für Philosophie und phänomenologische Forschung* (11 vols., 1913–30). Phenomenology was the most influential movement in German philosophy in the period 1910–33; but Husserl's Jewish ancestry brought it into disrepute under the Nazis and it had few followers at the time of his death, though these included Edith *Stein (q.v.). After the 1939–45 war, it was revived in a somewhat modified form by Maurice Merleau-Ponty (1908–61) in France, where it it still has disciples, notably Paul Ricoeur and the Jewish philosopher Emmanuel Levinas. Its influence has continued to be felt in RC circles, e.g. by the Jesuit philosopher, Bernard Lonergan (1904–84), and also by Pope *John Paul II, whose work *The Acting Person* was published in English translation in the series *Analecta Husserliana* (vol. 10; 1979). Phenomenology has also enjoyed renewed favour in America; the American periodical *Philosophy and Phenomenological Research* (1940 ff.) was founded by M. Farber as a successor to the *Jahrbuch*. See also EXISTENTIALISM.

Until his last years Husserl showed reluctance to publish. His later writings incl. *Vorlesungen zur Phänomenologie des inneren Zeitbewusstseins* (ed. M. *Heidegger, 1928; Eng. tr., The Hague, 1964), *Formale und transzendentale Logik* (1929; Eng. tr., ibid., 1969) and *Erfahrung und Urteil* (1939; Eng. tr., 1973). His works are being ed. from the Husserl Archiv at Louvain under the direction of H. L. Van Breda and others, *Husserliana* (The Hague, 1950 ff.); Eng. tr. of *Cartesianische Meditationen* from vol. 1, by D. Cairns (The Hague, 1960), of *Die Idee der Phänomenologie* from vol. 2, by W. P. Alston and G. Nakhnikian (ibid., 1964), and of *Ideen III* from vol. 5, by T. E. Klein and W. E. Pohl as *Phenomenology and the Foundations of the Sciences* (ibid., 1980; vol. 1 of an Eng. tr. of Husserl's *Collected Works*). Among Scheler's chief works were *Der Formalismus in der Ethik und die materiale Wertethik* (2 pts., 1913–16; Eng. tr., 1973), *Vom Ewigen im Menschen* (collected essays, 1921; Eng. tr., 1960), *Die Wissensformen und die Gesellschaft* (1926) and *Die Stellung des Menschen im Kosmos* (1928; Eng. tr. of *Selected Philosophical Essays* (Evanston, Ill., 1973). J. Hessen, *Augustins Metaphysik der Erkenntnis* (1931; 2nd edn., The Hague, 1960); M. Merleau-Ponty, *La Phénoménologie de la perception* (1945; Eng. tr., 1962); B. J. F. Lonergan, SJ, *Insight: A Study of Human Understanding* (1957); and E. Levinas, *Totalité et Infini* (Phaenomenologica, 8; The Hague, 1961; Eng. tr., Pittsburgh and The Hague [1969]).

M. Farber, *The Foundation of Phenomenology: Edmund Husserl and the Quest for a Rigorous Science of Philosophy* (Cambridge, Mass., 1943). H. Spiegelberg, *The Phenomenological Movement: A Historical Introduction* (Phaenomenologica, 5–6; The Hague, 1960, with suppl., 1965). J. J. Kockelmans, *A First Introduction to Husserl's Phenomenology* (Pittsburgh and Louvain, 1967); id., *Edmund Husserl's Phenomenological Psychology: A Historico-Critical Study* (ibid., 1967), and other works of this author. P. Ricoeur, *Husserl: An Analysis of his Phenomenology* (Evanston, Ill., 1967; Eng. tr. of a selection of articles). E. Pivčević, *Husserl and Phenomenology* (1970). T. de Boer, *The Development of Husserl's Thought*

(Phaenomenologica, 76; The Hague, 1978; rev. Eng. tr. of Dutch, orig. pub. 1966). E. Duplacy, *La Philosophie de Max Scheler* (2 vols., 1959); J. R. Staude, *Max Scheler 1874–1928: An Intellectual Portrait* (New York and London, 1967). R. Schmitt in P. Edwards (ed.), *The Encyclopedia of Philosophy*, 6 (1967), pp. 135–51, s.v.

Philadelphia. A city of the Roman province of Asia. It was the seat of one of the '*Seven Churches of Asia', addressed in Rev. 2–3, and was there commended for its faithfulness and given promises for the future (3: 7–13). The circumstances in which this Church was founded are unknown. In the 14th cent. the city was a Christian stronghold and withstood several sieges by the Turks.

W. M. *Ramsay, *The Letters to the Seven Churches of Asia* (1904), pp. 391–412, with notes, p. 446; C. J. Hemer, *The Letters to the Seven Churches of Asia in their Local Setting* (Journal for the Study of the New Testament, Supplement Series, 11; Sheffield [1986]), pp. 153–77. W. M. Ramsay in *HDB* 3 (1900), pp. 830–2, s.v.

Philadelphians. A religious sect which flourished at the end of the 17th cent. Their doctrines derived ultimately from J. *Boehme, whose notions were eagerly adopted by John Pordage (1607–81), rector of Bradfield, Berks. There gathered round Pordage, who was ejected from his living by the *Triers in 1655, but reinstated in 1660, a group of followers who shared his enthusiasm for Boehme, the chief of them being Mrs Jane Leade (1623–1704), who from her childhood had experienced visions which from 1670 she recorded in a diary entitled *A Fountain of Gardens*. In 1670 the group was organized as the Philadelphian Society for the Advancement of Piety and Divine Philosophy, the term 'Society' being preferred to 'Church' as its members were to retain their respective ecclesiastical allegiances. They professed a kind of nature pantheism, imbued with esoteric and pseudo-mystical teachings, and held that their souls were immediately illuminated by the Holy Spirit. Its headquarters later removed from Bradfield to London. A certain Francis Lee (1661–1719), who had been a Fellow of St John's College, Oxford, but refused the oaths on William III's accession, was much impressed by Mrs Leade's writings, which he had come across in the Netherlands, and, becoming an ardent disciple, was instrumental in spreading Philadelphian doctrines on the Continent. A formal confession of belief was drawn up in 1703; but the Society rapidly declined after Mrs Leade's death in 1704.

A number of Mrs Jane Leade's works were reissued in the 19th cent., incl. *The Wars of David* and other works, repr. 1816 and 1886; *The Revelation of Revelations*, repr. 1884, and *The Wonders of God's Creation*, repr. 1887. N. Thune, *The Behmenists and the Philadelphians* (Uppsala diss., 1948), pp. 68–216. S. Hutin, *Les Disciples anglais de Jacob Boehme aux XVIIᵉ et XVIIIᵉ siècles* [1960], pp. 81–123. [E.] G. Rupp, *Religion in England 1688–1791* (Oxford History of the Christian Church, 1986), pp. 214–7. W. T. Whitley in *HERE* 9 (1917), pp. 836 f., s.v.

Philaret, Theodore Nikitich Romanov (*c.*1553–1633), Patr. of Moscow and father of the first Romanov Tsar. Under his cousin, Theodore I (d. 1598), the last Tsar of the House of Rurik, he fought against the Swedes in 1590, and in 1593–4 conducted negotiations with the Emp. Rudolph II. Banished into a monastery by Boris Godunov (1598–1605), Theodore's successor, he was

released by Pseudo-Dimitri I, who made him Metropolitan of Rostov. In 1610 he was imprisoned by the Poles. On their expulsion his son Michael was elected Tsar (1613), but Philaret was not freed until the truce of Deulino in 1619. In the same year he was made patriarch and until his death remained the virtual ruler of Russia, introducing measures to stop the migration of the serfs from the land into the steppes and reorganizing the army. A zealous reformer, he made it his aim to establish a seminary in each diocese and to encourage the study of theology. He also founded the Patriarchal Library.

P. Pascal, *Avvakum et les débuts du Raskol: La crise religieuse au XVIIᵉ siècle en Russie* (Bibliothèque de l'Institut Français de Léningrad, 18; 1938), esp. pp. 25–30 (repr., with additional material, 1963). J. L. H. Keep, 'The Régime of Filaret, 1619–1633', *Slavonic and Eastern European Review*, 38 (1959–60), pp. 334–60. G. Vernadsky, *The Tsardom of Moscow 1547–1682* (History of Russia, 5, pt. 1; 1969), pp. 307–51 *passim*. See also bibl. to RUSSIA, CHRISTIANITY IN.

Philaret Drozdov (1782–1867), Russian theologian and Metropolitan of Moscow. Educated at the Trinity Monastery, near Moscow, he became lecturer at its academy in 1803, and in 1808 took the monastic habit. In the same year he was called to the academy at St Petersburg as professor of philosophy, and subsequently taught most branches of theology at the Ecclesiastical Academy. His rise to high office took place very rapidly. In 1818 he became a member of the Holy Synod, in 1820 Bp. of Jaroslav, and in 1821 he was transferred to Moscow with the title of Archbishop, which was changed into that of Metropolitan in 1826. He was an exemplary bishop, famous for his sermons and the wise administration of his diocese as well as for his profound influence in Church and State. He was the author of many theological works, but his best-known writing is his *Christian Catechism of the Orthodox Catholic Eastern Greco-Russian Church* (1823). It is composed of three parts, dealing with (1) the *Nicene Creed, (2) the *Lord's Prayer and the *Beatitudes, and (3) the *Decalogue. It underwent several redactions through the attempt of the procurator, Protasov, an opponent of the infiltration of *Lutheran teaching into the Russian Church, to eliminate its supposedly Protestant elements which Philaret had imbibed in his youth esp. through the works of T. Prokopovich (1681–1736). Though its doctrinal authority has been contested by other sections of the E. Church, it had a great influence on 19th-cent. Russian theology and has frequently been commented on.

Eng. tr. of his *Christian Catechism* conveniently repr. from the tr. of R. W. Blackmore in P. *Schaff, *The Creeds of Christendom*, 2 (1877), pp. 445–542. Fr. tr. of Selected Sermons by A. Serpinet (3 vols., Paris, 1866). C. Kern, 'Philarète, métropolite de Moscou. Cinquante ans de gloire épiscopale', *Istina*, 5 (1958), pp. 133–60, 261–82, 389–414. M. Rodes, *La Mariología de Filaret Drozdov, Metropolita de Moscú* (Milan, 1966). M. Jugie, AA, in *DTC* 12 (pt. 1; 1933), cols. 1376–95, with bibl. (mainly Russ.). See also bibl. to RUSSIA, CHRISTIANITY IN.

Philaster, St (d. *c.*397), more correctly 'Filaster', Bp. of Brescia and anti-heretical writer. After travel undertaken for the purpose of preaching the Gospel and confounding the *Arians and other heretics, he became Bp. of Brescia towards the end of the 4th cent. In 381 he took part in the Council of *Aquileia which deposed two Arian bishops. About 385 he wrote a treatise designed to refute 28 Jewish and 128 Christian heresies. This work, which was based largely on the similar compositions of *Irenaeus and *Epiphanius (and possibly also the 'Syntagma' of *Hippolytus), suffers from clumsy arrangement and a certain lack of proportion. Thus, the number of those stigmatized includes not only such notable heretics as *Simon Magus but also persons whose sole aberration was to believe that the stars occupied a fixed place in the sky instead of being set in position every evening by God. Despite its limitations, however, the book seems to have filled a real need in the W., and was freely used by St *Augustine. Philaster was succeeded in his see by St *Gaudentius. Feast day, 18 July.

Liber de Haeresibus first ed. by J. Sichard (Basle, 1528); later edns. by J. A. *Fabricius (Hamburg, 1721), P. Galeardi (Brescia, 1738; repr. in J. P. Migne, *PL* 12. 1111–302), F. Marx (CSEL 38; 1898), and F. Heylen in CCSL 9 (1957), pp. 207–324, with refs. The main source for his life is the 'Sermo de vita et obitu beati Filastrii' by Gaudentius, ed. A. Glueck in CSEL 68 (1936), pp. 184–9. R. A. *Lipsius, *Zur Quellenkritik des Epiphanios* (1865); id., *Die Quellen der ältesten Ketzergeschichte neu untersucht* (1875), pp. 91–137. P. C. Juret, 'Étude grammaticale sur le latin de S. Filastrius', *Romanische Forschungen*, 19 (1906), pp. 130–320. Bardenhewer, 3, pp. 481–5. M. Simonetti in Quasten (cont.), *Patrology*, 4 (1986), pp. 130–3. A. Rimoldi in *DHGE* 16 (1967), cols. 1473 f., s.v. 'Filastre'.

Phileas, St (d. 306/7), Bp. of Thmuis in Lower Egypt. Of noble birth and great wealth, he was imprisoned, tried before the prefect, Culcianus, and executed at *Alexandria. A Roman official, Philoromus, suffered at the same time. A letter to his flock from his dungeon is preserved by *Eusebius (*HE* 8. 10). The *acta* of his trial are prob. not so much a transcript of the official proceedings as an account based on them by a sympathetic eyewitness. A Latin translation has long been known; recently parts of the Greek text dating from the first half of the 4th cent. have been identified among the *Bodmer and *Chester Beatty Papyri. Feast day, 4 Feb.

Eusebius, *HE* 8. 9. 7 f. and 10 (with additions in *Rufinus' Lat. version). Latin text of the *acta* pr. in T. *Ruinart, OSB (ed.), *Acta Primorum Martyrum Sincera* (Paris, 1689), pp. 547–51; crit. text by P. Halkin (see below). The Bodmer Papyrus text of his Apology ed. V. Martin, *Papyrus Bodmer XX* (Geneva, 1964). Both are conveniently repr., with text of letter from Eusebius, and Eng. tr., in H. Musurillo, SJ, *The Acts of the Christian Martyrs* (Oxford Early Christian Texts, 1972), pp. 320–53. The Chester Beatty Papyrus, XV, is ed., with Eng. tr. by A. Pietersma, who also repr. the Bodmer Papyrus and the Lat. version of the Apology (Cahiers d'Orientalisme, 7; 1984). F. Halkin, SJ, 'L'"Apologie" du martyr Philéas de Thmuis (Papyrus Bodmer XX) et les Actes latins de Philéas et Philoromus', *Anal. Boll.* 81 (1963), pp. 5–27, incl. texts. H. *Delehaye, SJ, 'Les Martyrs d'Égypte', ibid. 40 (1922), pp. 5–154 and 299–364, esp. pp. 299–314. M. Simonetti, *Studi agiografici* (1955), pp. 109–32 ('Sugli Atti di Filea e Filoromo').

Philemon. The recipient of St *Paul's brief epistle of that name. He was a Christian of Colossae or the neighbourhood, whose slave, *Onesimus, had run away and somehow come to meet Paul, either in *Rome, or perhaps in *Ephesus. Paul sent Onesimus, now a Christian and therefore a 'beloved brother', back to his master with this epistle, which is a tactful plea for his forgiveness. Many of the personal references correspond closely with those in Col. 4: 9–14, suggesting that the Epistle to the *Colossians

is also authentic. The two letters would have been written and sent together. Acc. to tradition, Philemon and his wife, Apphia, were martyred at Colossae. Feast day, 22 Nov.

Modern comm. on the Ep. incl. those of J. B. *Lightfoot (London, 1875, with Col., pp. 369–412), C. F. D. Moule (Cambridge, 1957, with Col., pp. 1–42 and 140–9), E. Lohse (KEK 9, Heft 2, 14th edn., 1968, with Col., pp. 261–88; Eng. tr., Hermeneia, Philadelphia, 1971, pp. 185–208), J. H. Houlden (Pelican NT Comm. 1970, with Phil., Col., and Eph., pp. 223–32), R. P. Martin (New Cent. Bib., 1974, with Col., pp. 143–70), P. Stuhlmacher (Evangelisch-Katholischer Kommentar zum Neuen Testament [18]; Zurich and Neukirchen, 1975), G. B. Caird (New Clar. Bibl., 1976, with Eph., Phil., and Col., pp. 213–23), P. T. O'Brien (Word Biblical Comm. 44; Waco, Tex., 1982, with Col., pp. 263–308), and F. F. Bruce (New International Comm. on the NT, Grand Rapids [1984], with Col. and Eph., pp. 189–225). J. Knox, *Philemon among the Letters of Paul: A New View of its Place and Importance* (Chicago, 1935; 2nd edn., 1959; London, 1960). N. R. Petersen, *Recovering Paul: Philemon and the Sociology of Paul's Narrative World* (Philadelphia [1985]). G. S. Duncan, *St Paul's Ephesian Ministry* (1929), pp. 72–5. P. Benoît, OP, in *Dict. Bibl.*, Suppl. 7 (1966), cols. 1204–11, s.v., with extensive bibl.

Philibert, St (d. 684), founder and first abbot of *Jumièges. Under the influence of St *Ouen he took the monastic habit at Rebais, of which he became abbot. Led by the refractory character of his monks to retire to Neustria, he here founded the monastery of Jumièges on some land given him by Clovis II. In 674 his reproval of Ebroin, the mayor of the palace, for gross injustice was followed by his expulsion, and he retired first to Poitiers and later to the island of Her (now Noirmoutier, orig. 'Hermonasterium'), where he established another monastery. Feast day, 20 August.

The principal source is the 8th-cent. Life by an anonymous monk, pr. in *AASS*, Aug. 4 (1739), pp. 75–81; also ed. R. Poupardin, *Monuments de l'histoire des abbayes de Saint-Philibert* (Collection de textes pour servir à l'étude et à l'enseignement de l'histoire, 38; 1905), pp. 3–18; also ed. W. Levison in *MGH*, Scriptores Rerum Merovingicarum, 5 (1910), pp. 583–604, with discussion, pp. 568–83. The 9th-cent. 'Translationes et Miracula' by Ermentarius of Noirmoutier is pr. in *AASS*, loc. cit., pp. 81–95, and in R. Pouardin, op. cit., pp. 19–70. P. Antin, OSB, 'La critique de la *Vita* de saint Philibert', in *Jumièges: Congrès Scientifique du XIII' Centenaire*, 1 (Rouen, 1955), pp. 15–22. Modern Life by L. Jaud (Paris, 1910). P. Rouillard and C. Colafranceschi in *Bibliotheca Sanctorum*, 5 (1964), cols. 702–5, s.v. 'Filiberto', with bibl. See also bibl. to JUMIÈGES.

Philip, St. See PHILIPS IN THE NEW TESTAMENT.

Philip, Gospel of. A *Gnostic treatise preserved in *Coptic among the papyri found at *Nag Hammadi in 1945–6. It is a series of reflections on the quest for salvation, loosely linked by catch-phrases; it contains no narrative, and only a few incidents and sayings attributed to Christ. It shows marked Jewish influence, but also traces of Greek philosophy, and reflects *Valentinian doctrine in its references to the 'bridal chamber'. It dates from the 2nd, or perhaps the 3rd cent.; it is generally regarded as unconnected with the Gospel of Philip quoted by Epiphanius (*Haer.* 26. 13), but H.-M. Schenke has argued for their identity.

Edns. of the Coptic, with Fr. tr. and comm., by J.-E. Ménard (Paris, 1967), and, with Eng. tr. by W. W. Isenberg, in B. Layton (ed.), *Nag Hammadi Codex II, 2–7* (Nag Hammadi Studies, 20; Leiden, 1989), pp. 131–215; Eng. tr. also in J. M. Robinson (ed.), *The Nag Hammadi Library in English* (3rd edn.; Leiden, 1988), pp. 139–60. Eng. tr., with introd. and comm., by R. McL. Wilson (London, 1962). Sp. tr., with useful introd. and bibl., in A. de Santos Otero, *Los Evangelios Apócrifos* (6th edn.; 1988), pp. 706–47. H.-M. Schenke in Schneemelcher, 1 (5th edn., 1987), pp. 148–73; Eng. tr., 1 (1991), pp. 179–208. D. M. Scholer, *Nag Hammadi Bibliography 1948–1969* (Nag Hammadi Studies, 1; Leiden, 1971), pp. 165–71, with annual suppl. in *Novum Testamentum*.

Philip (1504–67), Landgraf of Hesse. He was the ablest of the German princes who supported M. *Luther. Declared of age in 1518, he led the suppression of the *Peasants' War (1525) and, though there seems to have been no popular sympathy for it, determined to introduce the Reformation into Hesse. In 1527 he founded the University of *Marburg as a school for Protestant theologians. Two years later he signed the Protest of *Speyer and summoned the Conference of Marburg, which failed, however, to bring about an understanding between M. Luther and U. *Zwingli on the subject of the Real Presence in the Eucharist. Philip's policy of uniting the Protestant princes was more successful. In 1530 the *Schmalkaldic League was founded with himself and the Elector of Saxony as leaders, but the dissension between the two Protestant parties largely hampered its striking power. This, as well as the whole cause of Protestantism, was further impaired by Philip's bigamous marriage (1540), which had been approved by Luther. Seriously compromised among his own followers, Philip now made peace with the Emperor and thereby lost his leadership of the Protestant party. His policy during the next years was wavering, resulting in the Schmalkalden War (1546–7), at the end of which he was imprisoned. Set free in 1552, he devoted his remaining years to the work of reunion between Catholics and Protestants.

Philip of Hesse figures prominently in all works on the *Lutheran Reformation. *Festschrift zum Gedächtnis Philipps des Grossmütigen* ed. Verein für hessische Geschichte und Landeskunde (Cassel, 1904). W. W. Rockwell, *Die Doppelehe des Landgrafen Philipp von Hessen* (1904). H. Grundmann, *Landgraf Philipp von Hessen auf dem Augsburger Reichstag 1530* (Schriften des Vereins für Reformationsgeschichte, no. 176; 1959). R. Hauswirth, *Landgraf Philipp von Hessen und Zwingli* (Schriften zur Kirchen- und Rechtsgeschichte, 35; 1968). Brief sketch (in Eng.) by H. J. Hillerbrand (Reformation Essays and Studies, 1; St Louis, 1967); also later assessment by id. (in Ger.) in M. Greschat (ed.), *Die Reformationszeit*, 2 (Gestalten der Kirchengeschichte, 6; Stuttgart, 1981), pp. 185–96. G. Müller in *TRE*, 26 (1996), pp. 492–7, with bibl.

Philip II (1527–98), of Spain. On the abdication of *Charles V in 1556 Philip inherited a composite monarchy which included all the Spanish kingdoms, Naples, Sicily and Milan, the Netherlands, and the Spanish empire in America and the Philippines. From 1554 to 1558, as husband of *Mary (Tudor) he was also titular king of England, though never crowned. After 1559 he stayed in Spain and ruled most of his dominions through viceroys and governors (where possible members of his family), maintaining his own influence through regular correspondence and through the control of local patronage. At first his polices were largely defensive: against France in W.

Europe and Italy, against the Turks in the Mediterranean, and against the enemies of the Catholic religion in all his dominions. By 1559 France, and its ally, Pope *Paul IV, were defeated, and from then onwards Philip helped to keep France paralysed by judicious intervention in its civil wars. Against the Turks he never launched a major offensive, in spite of the great naval victory of *Lepanto (1571). In Spain itself the *Inquisition was no longer mainly concerned with heresy (never very widespread) nor with converted Jews but rather with enforcing orthodox religious teaching and sexual morality on all Spaniards. In the Netherlands Philip's religious policies and disregard of local laws led to civil wars and foreign intervention. From c.1580 his policies became more aggressive and were financed by increasing imports of American silver and foreign loans. He conquered *Portugal (1580), reconquered the southern Netherlands (modern Belgium), organized the abortive *Armada against England (1588), and sent his armies into France, even claiming the French Crown for his daughter. When the Papacy proved unwilling to accept his identification of the good of Catholicism with the greatness of Spain, he used his ecclesiastical patronage to make three successive conclaves elect pro-Spanish Popes (1590–2); in 1592, however, the cardinals chose a more independent candidate as *Clement VIII. While Philip failed in his most ambitious aims, he successfully defended his many dominions (except for a few Netherlands provinces which he hoped would be reconquered), maintained his subjects' religion, neutralized the Turks, and had some part in forcing *Henry IV of France to renounce his Protestant faith. But the cost had been high: the squandering of American treasure, the overburdening of the Spanish economy, and the confirmation of an imperialist and military tradition which was to lead Spain to military and political disaster in the 17th cent. Personally, Philip was intelligent, hard-working, reserved, suspicious, and vengeful. The monastery-palace of El Escorial, with its austere façades and brilliant interior decoration, presents an idealized expression of his personality.

Much of his correspondence has been pub. in the *Colección de documentos inéditos para la historia de España*, esp. vols. 2–6, 27–43, 50 f., 68, and 87–102 (Madrid, 1843–92), *passim* (incl. the *Correspondencia de Felipe II con sus embajadores en la corte de Inglaterra 1558 á 1584* as vols. 87 and 89–92; 1886–8) and in [L. P.] Gachard, *Correspondance de Philippe II sur les affaires des Pays-Bas* (5 vols., 1848–79 + index, 1936), cont. by J. Lefèvre (4 vols., 1940–60). R. B. Merriman, *The Rise of the Spanish Empire in the Old World and the New*, 4: *Philip the Prudent* (New York, 1934). P. Pierson, *Philip II of Spain* [1975]; G. Parker, *Philip II* (1979). F. [P.] Braudel, *La Méditerranée et le monde méditerranéen à l'époque de Philippe II* (1949; 2nd edn., 2 vols., 1966; Eng. tr., 1972–3; abridged edn., 1992). H. [G.] Koenigsberger, *The Government of Sicily under Philip II of Spain* (1951); id., *The Habsburgs and Europe 1516–1660* (1971), pp. 63–217 *passim*; id., 'The Statecraft of Philip II', *European Studies Review*, 1 (1971), pp. 1–21; repr. with minor changes, in id., *Politicians and Virtuosi* (1986), pp. 77–96; see also other papers in this vol. J. H. Elliott, *Imperial Spain, 1469–1716* (1963), esp. pp. 200–295; J. Lynch, *Spain under the Habsburgs*, 1 (Oxford, 1964), pp. 167–348 (2nd edn., 1981, pp. 177–367), *passim*; I. A. A. Thompson, *War and Government in Habsburg Spain 1560–1620* (1976), *passim*. M. J. Rodríguez-Salgada, *The Changing Face of Empire: Charles V, Philip II and Habsburg Authority, 1551–1559* (Cambridge Studies in Early Modern History, 1988). C. Martin and G. Parker, *The Spanish Armada* (1988).

Philip the Arabian, Roman Emperor from 244 to 249, when he was killed in battle with *Decius. In 248 he celebrated the millennium of Rome's foundation with great magnificence and the customary religious ceremonies. This fact, and his coins, tell against the tradition that he was a Christian. This tradition is reported by *Eusebius (*HE* 6. 34), who gives an edifying story of his submission to a bishop (later identified with *Babylas of Antioch) who debarred him from church until he had made confession of his sins. That *Origen wrote a letter to him and one to his wife (ibid. 36) may suggest that they were thought to have an interest in religious questions. In any case Philip seems to have tolerated Christianity.

W. Ensslin in *C. Anc. H.* 12 (1939), pp. 87–95. E. Stein in *PW* 10 (pt. 1; 1917), cols. 755–70, s.v. 'Julius (Philippus) 386'.

Philip Neri, St (1515–95), the 'Apostle of Rome'. Son of a Florentine notary, he was educated by the *Dominicans of San Marco and later became a business apprentice. Resolving to give himself entirely to God, he went to Rome in 1533. Here he undertook the education of the two sons of a Florentine countryman, leading at the same time a very austere life. In 1535 he began to study philosophy and theology, but after three years sold his books and gave himself up to works of charity and instruction, spending the nights in prayer, mostly in the *catacomb of San Sebastiano on the *Appian Way. Here he experienced in 1544 the ecstasy which is believed to have miraculously enlarged his heart. In 1548 he became the co-founder of the Confraternity of the Most Holy Trinity for the care of pilgrims and convalescents which, in the year of the *Jubilee, 1575, assisted 145,000 pilgrims. In 1551, after being ordained, he went to live in a community of priests at San Girolamo, where his confessional soon became the centre of his apostolate and where he held spiritual conferences for men and boys often combined with visits to the Seven Churches. From these activities, which attracted more and more priests to the community, sprang the Congregation of the Oratory (see ORATORIANS), probably so called from the room at San Girolamo where the meetings were held. By 1575, when the Oratory was finally approved by *Gregory XIII, Philip Neri had become the most popular figure in Rome. His advice and direction were sought by Popes and cardinals no less than by the common people, and in 1593 he prevented a serious conflict between France and the Holy See by insisting on the absolution of *Henry IV. His chief characteristics were his gentleness and gaiety. Venerated as a saint during his lifetime, he was canonized by Gregory XV in 1622. Feast day, 26 May.

Il primo processo per San Filippo Neri, ed. G. Incisa della Rocchetta and N. Vian, with the collaboration of C. Gasbarri (ST 191, 196, 205, 224; 1957–63). The Canonization Process supplied the main material for the first and fundamental Life, written in Lat., by A. Gallonio, Cong. Orat. (Rome, 1600; repr. in *AASS*, Mai. 6 (1688), pp. 463–524). An Ital. tr., said to be clearer and more complete, pub. Rome, 1601. Other early Lives by P. J. Bacci, Cong. Orat. (Rome, 1622; ed. G. F. Ricci, 1678; Eng. tr., Paris, 1659; Eng. tr. of edn. of 1837 by F. W. *Faber (Saints and Servants of God, 2 vols., 1847); new edn. of Eng. tr. by F. I. Antrobus, Cong. Orat. (2 vols., 1902)), G. Crispino (Naples, 1675; Eng. tr. of last part by F. W. Faber, 1850) and J. Bernabei, Cong. Orat., pr. in *AASS*, loc. cit., pp. 524–649. The most important modern works are those by L. Poncelle and L. Bordet

(Paris, 1929; Eng. tr., 1932) and A. Cistellini (3 vols., Brescia, 1989). More popular accounts incl. [L.] M. Trevor, *Apostle of Rome: A Life of Philip Neri 1515–1595* (1966), with bibl., and P. Türks, Cong. Orat., *Philipp Neri oder das Feuer der Freude* (1986). Study by D. Fenlon (in preparation). C. Gasbarri, Cong. Orat., in *Bibliotheca Sanctorum*, 5 (Rome, 1964), cols. 760–99, s.v. 'Filippo Neri'. See also bibl. to ORATORIANS (1).

Philip Sidetes (early 5th cent.), historian. A native of Side, in Pamphylia, early in the 5th cent. he removed to *Constantinople, where he became the friend of St *Chrysostom, who ordained him deacon. After having become a priest he was three times an unsuccessful candidate for the patriarchate. He wrote a voluminous historical work, Χριστιανικὴ Ἱστορία, in 36 books which, to judge by *Socrates, appears to have been a hotch-potch of miscellaneous learning and to have dealt with the whole period from the creation of the world until AD 430. Only small fragments of this work remain, including the much-discussed assertion that *Papias had stated that *John the Apostle and his brother, *James, were martyred by the Jews. A defence of Christianity against *Julian the Apostate, mentioned by Socrates, seems to be wholly lost.

The frag. on the Alexandrian *Catechetical School was pub. by H. *Dodwell in his *Dissertationes in Irenaeum* (Oxford, 1689), p. 488; on this cf. C. de Boor, 'Zur Kenntnis der Handschriften der griechischen Kirchenhistoriker. Codex Baroccianus 142', *ZKT* 6 (1884), pp. 478–94, esp. p. 487 (variant readings). Id., *Neue Fragmente des Papias, Hegesippus und Pierius ... aus der Kirchengeschichte des Philippus Sidetes* (TU 5, Heft 2; 1888), pp. 165–84. E. Bratke, *Das sogenannte Religionsgespräch am Hof der Sasaniden* (ibid. 19, Heft 3; 1899), esp. pp. 157–64. E. Honigmann, *Patristic Studies* (ST 173; 1953), pp. 82–91 ('Philippus of Side and his "Christian History" (written about 434–439)'). *CPG* 3 (1979), p. 165 (no. 6026). J. Quasten, *Patrology*, 3 (Utrecht and Westminster, Md., 1960), pp. 528–30. [H. G.] Opitz in *PW* 19 (pt. 2; 1938), cols. 2350 f., s.v. 'Philippos 41'.

Philip, John (1771–1851), missionary and reformer in *South Africa. Born of weaving stock in Kirkcaldy, Fife, he underwent a conversion experience during a revival led by the *Congregationalists Robert and James Haldane. He entered the Congregational ministry and in 1804 became minister of Belmont Church in Aberdeen. A warm supporter of the *LMS, in 1819 he was sent by the Society to S. Africa on a commission of inquiry; he remained as Director of the Society resident in S. Africa.

Philip belonged to that wing of the evangelical movement which held that the transformation of society was, with individual conversion, the aim of evangelism, and he became for the rest of his life a passionate defender of native rights. He was especially concerned over the treatment of the Khoi or 'Hottentot' population and his campaign on their behalf prepared the ground for the 1828 Ordinance 50 which extended civil rights to all races. He defended the Xhosa people against those who wished to remove them from their lands, and tried to persuade the imperial authorities to protect the tribes to the north against the incursions of the Great Trek. He was responsible for bringing the Paris Evangelical Missionary Society to the Sotho people and the American Board of Missionaries to the Zulus.

Study by A. [C.] Ross (Aberdeen, 1986). W. M. MacMillan, *The Cape Colour Question: A Historical Survey* (1927), *passim*; id.,

Bantu, Boer and Briton: The Making of the South African Native Problem (1929; rev. edn., Oxford, 1963), *passim*.

Philips in the New Testament. (1) ST PHILIP THE APOSTLE. Mentioned in the Synoptic Gospels and in Acts 1: 13 as one of the Twelve, but Jn. alone supplies any details. Jn. 1: 43–51, where he is described as 'from *Bethsaida', relates how he obeyed the call of Jesus and then persuaded *Nathanael to appear before Jesus. In Jn. 6: 5–7 Philip, present at the feeding of the 5,000, observes that 200 pennyworth of bread would not provide even a scanty meal for those assembled. Philip is again referred to in Jn. 12: 21 f., and Jn. 14: 8 f. records his request to Jesus, 'Show us the Father', and its answer. The Apostle's subsequent career is obscure. *Polycrates of Ephesus connects him with Asia and declares that he died, apparently from natural causes, at Hierapolis; but other traditions describe him as having suffered crucifixion so that, in medieval art, his symbol—when not loaves, as suggested by Jn. 6—is a tall cross. He was confused with Philip the Evangelist, certainly by the time of *Eusebius. Feast day in the E., 14 Nov.; in the W. (jointly with St *James the Less), 1 May, transferred in the RC Church to 11 May in 1955 and to 3 May in 1969.

(2) PHILIP THE EVANGELIST. One of the 'seven men of honest report' whose appointment for the service of the poor and distribution of alms is recorded in Acts 6: 1–6 (later regarded as *deacons). According to Acts 8: 5–13, he preached in Samaria and was successful in winning over the Samaritans from belief in the sorceries of *Simon Magus to Christianity. After the conversion and baptism of the Ethiopian eunuch Philip went on a missionary tour from Ashdod northwards and settled at Caesarea (Acts 8: 26–40). Here at a later date he entertained St *Paul (Acts 21: 8). Uncertainty shrouds the latter years of Philip. One tradition makes him Bp. of Tralles, in Lydia. Feast day in E., 11 Oct.; in W., 6 June.

(3) PHILIP THE TETRARCH. One of the sons of *Herod the Great, he was ruler from 4 BC to AD 33 or 34 of 'the region of Ituraea and Trachonitis' (Lk. 3: 1). Acc. to *Josephus (*Antiq.* 18. 4. 6), he ruled with moderation, simplicity and good sense.

Philippians, Epistle to the. One of the so-called '*Captivity Epistles' of St *Paul, the authenticity of which is solidly attested by antiquity and almost unanimously accepted by modern scholars. It is addressed to the Christian community at Philippi in Macedonia, the first of the Churches founded by Paul in Europe, to which he was united by ties of particular affection and tenderness. According to the Apostle's own account (2: 25 and 4: 18), the Philippian Epaphroditus had come with presents from the community to relieve his needs during his imprisonment. This is generally held to refer to his captivity in *Rome, and the references to the Praetorian guard and to the members of Caesar's household would seem to favour this traditional opinion; but they would not be out of place in provincial capitals, and arguments can be maintained in favour of an origin in *Ephesus (so many, e.g. G. S. Duncan) or *Caesarea (so by E. Lohmeyer and e.g. W. G. Kümmel). Its date has also been a matter of discussion. Some, e.g. J. B. *Lightfoot, assign it to the beginning of his captivity, and there are similarities with Gal., 2 Cor., and Rom. which favour a date not long after these Epistles were written. On the other hand, a date at the end of his process of appeal would fit the internal indications that the Apostle has had a considerable period of time in prison, and that the issue of his trial is soon to be resolved. The unity of the Epistle has been contested, e.g. by A. F. *Loisy, because of the sudden attack on certain persons in 3: 1b ff.; the apparent break has been explained by others as due to the informal character of the letter (which follows the successive emotions of the writer) or on other grounds. The persons attacked have been variously identified as Jews or Christian Judaizers; they may be the same as those denounced in 1: 15 f. or 3: 18 ff., or there may be more than one group. It has also been argued that Paul's expression of thanks to the Philippians for a recent gift reads awkwardly in its present place (4: 11–18) and may be interpolated from an earlier letter.

After thanking the Philippians for their partnership (1: 1–11), Paul tells them of the success of his preaching in his captivity (1: 12–18) and asks them to make his joy perfect by charity, self-denial, and humility, of which Christ is the sublime example (1: 19–2: 11). He, too, wishes to give them joy and therefore promises to send them *Timothy and Epaphroditus (2: 12–30). After various warnings he again exhorts them to lead a blameless life of peace and concord (3: 1–4: 7) and ends with a doxology and salutations (4: 8–23).

The Epistle contains in 2: 5–11 a Christological passage of great importance. These verses present Christ, who 'being in the form of God' was 'found in fashion as a man' and 'humbled Himself' and was consequently exalted by God, as the sublime example of humility. In the traditional interpretation the 'humbling' consisted in the incarnation of the Son of God; but many modern scholars refer it to Christ's human obedience and see the passage as a strong contrast with *Adam, who snatched at equality with God (Gen. 3). The commentators discuss varying interpretations of a number of words, e.g. 'being' (ὑπάρχων), 'form' (μορφῇ), and esp. ἁρπαγμός ('robbery', AV; 'prey', RV; 'a thing to be grasped', RSV) in verse 6, and ἑαυτὸν ἐκένωσεν ('emptied himself') in verse 7. From the time of Lohmeyer it has commonly been held that the verses originally existed as a hymn, and that Paul has incorporated them with some changes. See also KENOTIC THEORIES.

Modern comm. incl. those of J. B. Lightfoot (London, 1868), E. Lohmeyer (KEK 9, Heft 1, 8th edn.; 1928), K. *Barth (Munich, 1928; 2nd edn., 1947; Eng. tr., 1962), F. W. Beare (Black's NT Comm., 1959; 2nd edn., 1969), J. Gnilka (Herders theologischer Kommentar zum neuen Testament, 10, fasc. 3; Freiburg, 1968), J.-F. Collange (Commentaire du Nouveau Testament, 10 A [1973]; Eng. tr., 1979), R. P. Martin (New Cent. Bib., 1976), G. B. Caird (New Clar. Bib., RV, on Eph., Phil., Col., and Philem., 1976, pp. 95–154), and G. F. Hawthorne (Word Biblical Comm. 43; Waco, Tex. [1983]). R. P. Martin, *Carmen Christi: Philippians ii. 5–11 in Recent Interpretation and in the Setting of Early Christian Worship* (Society of New Testament Studies Monograph, 4; Cambridge, 1967). Kümmel, pp. 320–335. J. T. Fitzgerald in *Anchor Bible Dictionary*, 5 (1992), pp. 318–27, with extensive bibl.

Philippines, Christianity in the. Christianity was introduced into the Philippines with the Spanish conquest and occupation of the archipelago which began in the 16th cent. The first Baptisms were conducted on the island of Cebu in 1521 by RC priests accompanying the explorer Ferdinand Magellan. From the beginning of Spanish rule in 1565 until the end of the 19th cent., the RC Church was supported and largely controlled by the Spanish Crown. The first episcopal see was founded at Manila in 1579. Missionary work among the Filipino people was undertaken by religious orders from Spain and Mexico. The *Augustinian friars arrived in 1565, and were later joined by *Franciscans, *Dominicans, *Jesuits, and Augustinian Recollects. The orders founded schools and universities, including the Dominican University of St Thomas in Manila (1611). They accumulated great wealth, esp. in land. By the end of the 18th cent. the majority of the population of the Philippines had been baptized, but indigenous secular priests held an inferior position. The first Filipino bishop was appointed in 1905. In the nationalist movement of the 1890s the resentment of many Filipinos against the continued domination of the RC Church by Spanish clergy and the wealth of the friars led to the emergence of a national Church, independent of Rome. The Philippine Independent Church, led by Gregorio Aglipay and I. de los Reyes, was founded in 1902. Initially it had wide popular support, but its membership rapidly dwindled and now comprises 5 per cent of the population. Since the Second World War it has established close links with the *Episcopal Church in the USA, and in 1961 the two Churches entered into full communion.

With the cession of the Philippines to the United States in 1898, and the resulting separation of Church and State, the way was opened for Protestant missionary activity. Between 1899 and 1901 American *Methodists, *Presbyterians, United Brethren, *Baptists, and Episcopalians began work in different parts of the Philippines. Because of continued schisms and the arrival of many new religious bodies, Protestantism in the Philippines became very fragmented. The *ecumenical movement found expression in a merger of several denominations to form the United Church of Christ in the Philippines (1948) and the foundation of the National Council of Churches of the Philippines (1963), but some 80 per cent of Evangelical Protestants belong to the large number of sects not affiliated to the National Council.

The Philippines, an independent republic since 1946, has the largest Christian population in Asia (49 million in 1980). More than 80 per cent of Filipinos are RCs and the RC Church has an influential role in national political life. It has over 60 dioceses, but an acute shortage of priests. As in Latin America, there is a sharp division between those in the Church who are influenced by *Liberation Theology and conservatives.

P. G. Gowing, *Islands under the Cross: The Story of the Church in the Philippines* (Manila, 1967); G. H. Anderson (ed.), *Studies in Philippine Church History* (Ithaca, NY, and London, 1969). M. A. Bernad, SJ, *The Christianization of the Philippines: Problems and Perspectives* (Manila, 1972). H. de la Costa, SJ, *The Jesuits in the Philippines 1581–1768* (Cambridge, Mass., 1961). P. S. de Archútegui, SJ, and M. A. Bernad, SJ, *Religious Revolution in the Philippines: The Life and Church of Gregorio Aglipay 1860–1960* (4 vols., Manila, 1960–72), incl. 2 vols. of docs. P. T. Giordano, *Awakening to Mission: The Philippine Catholic Church, 1965–1981* (Quezon City, 1988). R. L. Deats, *Nationalism and Christianity in the Philippines* (Dallas [1967]). R. C. Asedillo and B. D. Williams (eds.),

Rice in the Storm: Faith in Struggle in the Philippines (New York, 1989). K. J. Clymer, *Protestant Missionaries in the Philippines, 1898–1916: An Inquiry into the American Colonial Mentality* (Urbana, Ill. [1986]). H. de la Costa, SJ, in *NCE* 11 (1967), pp. 280–4, s.v.

Philippists. The followers of the *Lutheran theologian, Philip *Melanchthon ('Dr Philippus'), also known as '*Crypto-Calvinists' and '*Synergists' (qq.v.).

Philip's Lent, St. A name in use in the E. Church for the period from 15 Nov. to 24 Dec., i.e. the counterpart of *Advent in the W. Church. It is so named because it begins on the day following the Feast of St Philip (14 Nov. in the E.).

Phillimore, Robert Joseph (1810–85), English judge. Educated at Westminster and at Christ Church, Oxford, he became a prominent Anglican *High Churchman, numbering among his friends W. E. *Gladstone, G. A. *Denison, and H. P. *Liddon. In 1841 he was called to the bar at the Middle Temple. He held a succession of ecclesiastical appointments and in 1867 became *Dean of the Arches. In 1868, in the case against A. H. *Mackonochie, in which he had first appeared as defending counsel, he delivered judgement declaring the legality of altar lights and of kneeling during the prayer of consecration. The Judicature Act of 1875 caused him to resign his ecclesiastical judgeship. Deeply learned, he was the author of several legal writings, and his *Ecclesiastical Law of the Church of England* (2 vols., 1873; 2nd edn., 1895) long remained a standard treatise. His other writings include *Thoughts on the Law of Divorce in England* (1844) and *Commentaries upon International Law* (4 vols., 1854–61).

His son, **W. G. F. Phillimore** (High Court Judge, 1897–1913, and Lord Justice of Appeal, 1913–16), also appeared as counsel in many ritual cases.

R. J. Phillimore himself published a collection of *The Principal Ecclesiastical Judgements delivered in the Court of Arches, 1867 to 1875* [by himself] (1876). W. P. W. and W. G. F. Phillimore, *Genealogy of the Family of Phillimore* (Devizes, 1922), pp. 240–52. J. A. Hamilton in *DNB* 45 (1896), pp. 186–8; G. Crosse in *DECH*, p. 458.
On W. G. F. Phillimore, John, Baron Sankey, in *DNB, 1922–1930*, pp. 677 f.

Phillipps, Ambrose Lisle. See DE LISLE, AMBROSE LISLE MARCH PHILLIPPS.

Phillipps Manuscripts. The famous collection of MSS assembled at Cheltenham in the 19th cent. by the antiquary, Sir Thomas Phillipps (1792–1872). Phillipps, who had been educated at Rugby and University College, Oxford, began his collection by purchasing the bulk of the Meerman Collection at The Hague in 1824. Later acquisitions included the 9th-cent. MSS of Professor van Ess of Darmstadt, the Muschenbroek Collection of Chronicles and other documents on Dutch history, the Williams Collection (incl. Bp. Gundulf's Bible), the Knaresborough MSS on Mexico, many MSS on the history of Wales and of Ireland, as well as some Gk. MSS (incl. an illuminated 10th–11th cent. Dioscorides). His library was orig. located at Middle Hill, near Broadway, Worcs, whence Phillipps transferred it to Thirlestane House, Cheltenham, in 1862.

The collection passed at his death into the hands of his younger daughter, Mrs Fenwick. The MSS have since been gradually sold, the greater part of the Meerman Collection being now in the Staatsbibliothek at Berlin. See also MOMMSEN CATALOGUE.

Phillipps, who had installed a printing press at Middle Hill, pr. his own catalogue in fol., successive sections appearing as the collection grew: *Catalogus Librorum Manuscriptorum in Bibliotheca D. Thomae Phillipps* (1824–[1867]). A. N. L. Munby, *Phillipps Studies* (5 vols., 1951–60).

Phillpotts, Henry (1778–1869), Bp. of *Exeter. He was educated at Corpus Christi College, Oxford, and in 1795 elected a Fellow of Magdalen. From 1805 to 1826 he held a number of benefices in the diocese of *Durham. In 1828 he was appointed Dean of *Chester, and in 1830 Bp. of Exeter. An old-fashioned *High Churchman, he was sympathetic to the *Oxford Movement, although he disapproved of the more extreme activities of some of its adherents. He greatly desired to raise the standard of public worship and in 1844 ordered the surplice to be worn at all ministrations in his diocese, though the order raised so fierce a storm that it had to be withdrawn. His refusal to institute G. C. *Gorham (q.v.), who had been presented to the living of Brampford Speke, on the grounds of his denial of baptismal regeneration, gave rise to one of the most famous ecclesiastical lawsuits in the 19th cent. When the *Judicial Committee of the Privy Council decided that Gorham should be instituted and J. B. *Sumner, Abp. of Canterbury, directed that this should be done, Phillpotts declared that he would 'renounce and repudiate communion' with anyone instituting Gorham. He none the less remained in office. He was a champion of the revival of *religious orders in the Anglican Church and aided the efforts of E. B. *Pusey for the sisterhood at Devonport founded by Miss P. L. *Sellon.

A Life was begun by R. N. Shutte (vol. 1 only, London, 1863 [to 1832]; publication was suspended on an injunction granted to Phillpotts). Brief sketch by E. C. S. Gibson in W. E. Collins (ed.), *Typical English Churchmen* (1902), pp. 299–323. Full Life by G. C. B. Davies (CHS, 1954), with bibl. J. C. S. Nias, *Gorham and the Bishop of Exeter* (ibid., 1951). J. A. Hamilton in *DNB* 45 (1896), pp. 222–5.

Philo (*c.*20 BC–*c.* AD 50), Jewish thinker and exegete. He belonged to a prosperous priestly family of *Alexandria; but nothing is known of his life except that in 39 he took part in an embassy to *Rome, described in his *Legatio ad Caium*, to plead the religious rights of the Jews with Emp. Caligula. He was the most important figure among the Hellenistic Jews of his age and a fertile author. His numerous writings include: (1) Philosophical works, written in his youth, among them *De Aeternitate Mundi, Quod omnis probus liber sit*, and *De Providentia*; (2) Exegetical writings on the *Pentateuch, incl. *Quaestiones et Solutiones in Genesim et Exodum* and *Legum Allegoriae*; and (3) Historical and apologetic writings, incl. *De Vita Mosis, De Vita Contemplativa* (on the *Therapeutae, q.v.), and *Contra Flaccum* (against Flaccus, Procurator of Egypt, AD 32–8).

In his religious outlook Philo was essentially an eclectic. He reproduced a variety of doctrines, gathered from contemporary philosophical systems as well as from Jewish sources, without welding them into an harmonious whole. His most influential achievement was his development of the allegorical interpretation of Scripture which enabled him to discover much of Greek philosophy in the OT, and to combine the respect of his religion for the Pentateuchal law with his personal aspirations towards a more spiritual interpretation of it. In his theological ideas also, Greek and Jewish elements were interwoven. On the one hand he emphasized the complete transcendence of God, whom he asserted to be above virtue, above knowledge, and even above the Good, while on the other he maintained that God was the Father who governed the world as well as each individual soul by His Providence. He accorded a central place in his system to the *Logos, who was at once the creative power which orders the world and the intermediary through whom men know God. It was the Logos who spoke to *Moses in the burning bush, and who is represented in the OT under the figure of the *high priest. Many of Philo's ideas were taken up in the Christian mystical tradition, but whether he himself should be regarded as a mystic is much disputed.

Philo's influence was esp. strong in the *Alexandrian school of theology. *Clement and *Origen used him freely, and through them and later through St *Ambrose and other Latin Fathers his allegorical interpretation of Scripture became an accepted form of biblical exegesis in the Christian Church. His influence on the Logos doctrine of the Fourth Gospel and of the Apologists, notably St *Justin, has often been alleged, but in recent times the differences between the Christian and the Philonic conceptions have been very widely admitted.

Editio princeps of his collected works, Paris, 1522; much improved edn., with Lat. tr., by T. Mangey (2 vols., London, 1742); crit. edn. by L. Cohn, P. Wendland, and S. Reiter (6 vols., Berlin, 1896–1915; index by I. Leisegang, 2 pts., 1926–30); also ed. R. Arnaldez, J. Pouilloux, and C. Mondésert, SJ (36 vols. in 38, Paris, 1961–92). Eng. tr. by F. H. Colson, G. H. Whitaker, and R. Marcus (Loeb, 10 vols. + 2 suppl. vols., 1929–62). *De Vita Contemplativa* also ed., with full notes, by F. C. *Conybeare (Oxford, 1895). G. Mayer, *Index Philoneus* (Berlin and New York, 1974).

J. *Drummond, *Philo Judaeus* (2 vols., 1888); E. R. Goodenough, *An Introduction to Philo Judaeus* (New Haven, Conn., 1940; 2nd edn., Oxford, 1962); M. Pohlenz, 'Philon von Alexandreia', *Nachr.* (Gött.), 1942, pp. 409–87; H. A. Wolfson, *Philo: Foundations of Religious Philosophy in Judaism, Christianity and Islam* (2 vols., Cambridge, Mass., 1947); J. *Daniélou, SJ, *Philo d'Alexandrie* (1958); R. Arnaldez and others, *Philon d'Alexandrie: Colloques nationaux du Centre National de la Recherche Scientifique, Lyon, 11–15 septembre 1966* (1967). S. Sandmel, *Philo of Alexandria: An Introduction* (New York and Oxford, 1979). R. Williamson, *Jews in the Hellenistic World: Philo* (Cambridge, 1989). E. Bréhier, *Les Idées philosophiques et religieuses de Philon d'Alexandrie* (Paris thesis, 1907; 2nd edn., *Études de Philosophie médiévale*, 8; 1925). I. Heinemann, *Philos griechische und jüdische Bildung* (1932). R. Radice, *Platonismo e Creazionismo in Filone di Alessandria* (Metafisica del Platonismo nel suo Sviluppo Storico nella filosofia patristica, 7; Milan, 1989). E. R. Goodenough, *The Politics of Philo Judaeus* (New Haven, Conn., 1938), with general bibl. of Philo by H. L. Goodhart and E. R. Goodenough, pp. 127–321. W. Völker, *Fortschritt und Vollendung bei Philo von Alexandrien* (TU 49; 1938). D. T. Runia, *Philo of Alexandria and the Timaeus of Plato* (Philosophia Antiqua, 44; Leiden, 1986). E. Stein, *Die allegorische Exegese des Philo aus Alexandreia* (Beiheft zur *ZATW* 51; 1929); id., *Philo und der Midrasch* (ibid. 57; 1931). P. Katz, *Philo's Bible: The Aberrant Text of Bible Quotations in some Philonic Writings and its Place in the Textual Tradition of the Greek Bible* (1950). J.

Cazeaux, *La Trame et la Chaîne, ou les Structures littéraires et l'Exégèse dans cinq des Traités de Philon d'Alexandrie* (Arbeiten zur Literatur und Geschichte des hellenistischen Judentums, 15; Leiden, 1983); T. H. Tobin, SJ, *The Creation of Man: Philo and the History of Interpretation* (Catholic Biblical Quarterly Monograph Series, 14; Washington, DC, 1983). S. Sandmel, *Philo's Place in Judaism* (Cincinnati, 1956). E. *Schürer, *The History of the Jewish People in the Age of Jesus Christ*, rev. Eng. tr. by G. Vermes and others, 3 (pt. 2; Edinburgh, 1987), pp. 809–89. W. Haase (ed.), *Aufstieg und Niedergang der römischen Welt*, 2. 21 (pt. 1; 1984), with 'Bibliographia Philoniana 1935–1981' by F. Hilgert, pp. 47–97. R. Radice and D. T. Runia, *Philo of Alexandria: An Annotated Bibliography, 1937–1986* (Supplements to *Vigiliae Christianae*, 8; 1988). E. Schürer and C. Bigg in *EB* (11th edn.), 21 (1911), pp. 409–13, s.v.; H. Leisegang in *PW* 20 (pt. 1; 1941), cols. 1–50, s.v. 'Philon (41)'; C. Mondésert, SJ, and others in *Dict. Bibl.*, Suppl. 7 (1966), cols. 1288–351; R. Arnaldez in *NCE* 11 (1967), pp. 287–91; Y. Amir in *Encyclopaedia Judaica*, 13 (Jerusalem, 1972), cols. 409–15; V. Nikiprowetzky and A. Solignac, SJ, in *Dict. Sp.* 12 (pt. 1; 1984), cols. 1352–74, all s.v.

Philocalia. A title meaning 'Love of what is beautiful', applied in particular to two works:

(1) The *Philocalia* of *Origen: an anthology from his writings, compiled by Sts *Basil the Great and *Gregory of Nazianzus during 358–9, and containing many passages which would otherwise have been lost in the original Greek.

(2) The *Philocalia* of Sts Macarius Notaras and *Nicodemus of the Holy Mountain, first published at Venice in 1782. This is a collection of ascetic and mystical writings dating from the 4th to the 15th century, dealing in general terms with the teaching of *Hesychasm and more particularly with the *Jesus Prayer. Translated into Slavonic by St Paisy *Velichovksy (1793) and into Russian by St *Theophan the Recluse (enlarged edn. in 5 vols., 1876–90), the book has exercised an important influence throughout the modern Orthodox world.

Convenient edn. of the Greek text of (1) by J. A. *Robinson, *The Philocalia of Origen* (Cambridge, 1893). Chapters 1–20 also ed., with Fr. tr. and introd., by M. Harl (SC 302, 1983, pp. 7–468); chs. 21–7 ed., with Fr. tr., by E. Junod (ibid. 226; 1976). Eng tr. of (2) by G. E. H. Palmer, P. Sherrard, and K. [T. R.] Ware, *The Philokalia* (1979 ff.).

Philocalian Calendar, the. A name sometimes given to the list of Roman bishops (also known as the '*Liberian Catalogue') compiled by the '*Chronographer of 354' (q.v.). It takes this name from the fact that part of the document in which it occurs was illuminated by the artist, Furius Dionysius Philocalus (prob. better Filocalus).

On Filocalus, also known for his skilful incision of *Damasus' metrical inscriptions between 370 and 384, A. Ferrua, SJ, *Epigrammata Damasiana* (Sussidi allo Studio delle Antichità Cristiane, 2; 1942), pp. 21–35; and H. *Leclercq, OSB, in *DACL* 5 (pt. 2; 1923), cols. 1594–1600, s.v. For further bibl. see s.v. CHRONOGRAPHER OF AD 354.

Philomena, St. She was formerly held to be a virgin martyr of the early Church. Her cultus dates from 1802, when a *loculus was found in the Catacomb of St *Priscilla, near Rome, closed with three tiles on which were painted the letters LUMENA/PAX TE/CUM FI, which, arranged in the right order, read 'Pax tecum Filumena'. Taken in conjunction with an *ampulla supposed to have contained blood, the bones found in the tomb were held

to be those of a martyred Christian virgin. She came to be venerated as a saint when many miracles took place at the translation of her relics to Mugnano in 1805. A proper Office and Mass were granted to her by *Pius IX in 1855, and she temporarily became one of the most popular saints on account of the devotion to her of the *Curé d'Ars. Subsequent research, however, has cast grave doubt on the connection between the relics and the tiles, which seem to have belonged to another grave, so that nothing seems known about the saint venerated under this name. Feast day, 11 Aug.; suppressed 1961.

The identification was first made by F. di Lucia, *Relazione istorica della translazione del sacro corpo di Santa Filomena* (4th edn., 1833). It was refuted by A. de Waal, 'Die Grabschrift der Philumena aus dem Coemeterium der Priscilla', *RQ* 12 (1898), pp. 43–54; O. *Marucchi, 'Osservazioni archeologiche sulla iscrizione di S. Filomena', *Miscellanea di Storia ecclesiastica e di Studi ausiliari*, 2 (1904), pp. 365–86; id., 'Studio archeologico sulla celebre iscrizione di Filumena scoperta nel cimitero di Priscilla', *Nuovo Bullettino di Archaeologia cristiana*, 12 (1906), pp. 253–300. F. Trochu, *La 'Petite Sainte' du curé d'Ars: Sainte Philomène* (Lyons, 1924). In Eng. there is a popular, mainly devotional, account by C. Hallack (Dublin [1936]). H. *Leclercq, OSB, in *DACL* 5 (pt. 2; 1923), cols. 1600–2, s.v. 'Filumena', with detailed bibl.; D. Balboni in *Bibliotheca Sanctorum*, 5 (1964), cols. 796–800, s.v. 'Filomena'.

Philopatris. A Greek dialogue, formerly thought to be a veiled attack on Christianity by *Lucian of Samosata. The scene is laid at *Constantinople, where one Triephon, converted to the Christian faith, is transported into the third heaven and engages in a discussion on paganism, which concludes with reflections on the political situation of the time. The work, long assigned to the reign of *Julian (361–3), has been commonly put since B. G. Niebuhr in the time of Nicephorus Phocas (963–9).

The text is pr. in many edns. of the works of Lucian of Samosata (q.v.), e.g. that of C. Jacobitz, 3 (Teub. edn. of 1886, pp. 411–25); and ed. C. B. Hase appended to his edn. of the History of Leo the Deacon (C.S.H.Byz. 25; 1828), pp. 324–42. B. G. Niebuhr, *Kleine historische und philologische Schriften*, 2 (1843), pp. 73–8 ('Ueber das Alter des Dialogus Philopatris'). E. von Dobschütz in *PRE* (3rd edn.), 15 (1904), pp. 363–5, s.v.; there is a summary of this art. in Eng. in *EB* (11th edn.), 21 (1911), p. 439, s.v.

Philoponus, John. See JOHN PHILOPONUS.

philosophic sin. Acts of sin held to violate the natural order of reason without consciously transgressing the Divine law, and hence not to merit the punishments meted out to offences against the latter. The theory that sin under such conditions is possible presupposes the existence of a distinction between the Divine and natural moral law of contestable validity and was censured by Pope *Alexander VIII on 24 Aug. 1690.

Pope Alexander VIII's condemnation of 24 Aug. 1690 is pr. in C. Duplessis d'Argentré (ed.), *Collectio Judiciorum de Novis Erroribus*, 3 (Paris, etc., 1736), p. 365; main clauses repr. in Denzinger and Hünermann (37th edn., 1991), pp. 658 f. (nos. 2290 f.). H. Beylard, 'Le Péché philosophique. Quelques précisions historiques et doctrinales', *Nouvelle Revue théologique*, 62 (1935), pp. 591–616 and 673–98. T. Deman, OP, in *DTC* 12 (pt. 1; 1933), cols. 255–72, s.v. 'Péché. IX', with bibl. col. 275.

philosophy of religion. The notion of the philosophy of religion as a distinct discipline was the creation of the *Enlightenment. The term is first met with in Germany in the last years of the 18th cent. Early occurrences in titles are J. C. G. Schaumann, *Philosophie der Religion* (1793), and J. Berger, *Geschichte der Religionsphilosophie* (1800). Properly its aim, as the expression implies, is the philosophical investigation of the particular group of phenomena covered by the terms 'religion' and 'religious experience'. It studies the essence, content, origin, and, to some extent, value of religion as a factor in human life, and examines the claims of religion to be true. The '*natural theology' of earlier writers could be considered as philosophy of religion in the broadest sense, but whereas natural theology was regarded as the prelude to revealed theology, the philosophy of religion takes no cognizance of this distinction. Thus it is free to examine concepts found in any religion, not just Christianity. In so far as religions make conflicting claims to truth, the exploration of what kind of a conflict is entailed has become an increasing concern for the philosophy of religion, which thus overlaps with *comparative religion (q.v.).

The philosophy of religion has taken many forms. D. *Hume's *Dialogues concerning Natural Religion* (1779) and I. *Kant's *Religion innerhalb der Grenzen der blossen Vernunft* (1793) are two very different examples of the rationalist 18th-cent. approach to religion. G. W. F. *Hegel's posthumously published *Vorlesungen über die Philosophie der Religion* (1832, 2nd edn., 1840; Eng. tr., 1895) is the most celebrated of the many works on the philosophy of religion that have come out of the tradition of speculative idealism. In the latter part of the 19th cent. there was a tendency to move away from the speculative style of philosophy. Thus history is the controlling idea in O. Pfleiderer's *Religionsphilosophie* (1878), while H. *Høffding's *Religions Filosofi* (1901; Eng. tr., 1906) centres on the notion of value. In the 20th cent., still newer types of philosophy of religion have been developed. C. Hartshorne applied the insights of *process philosophy to the problems of religion, while K. *Jaspers constructed a 'philosophical faith' on the basis of an *existentialist type of thought. More recently still, esp. under the influence of post-war Oxford philosophy, the philosophy of religion has been understood as the analysis of religious language.

As a distinct discipline, the philosophy of religion has been cultivated for the most part by philosophers with religious leanings. Catholic theologians have more commonly envisaged the matters at issue from the standpoint of natural theology and *Thomist metaphysics. While some liberal Protestants have been attracted to the philosophy of religion, the more orthodox Protestant tradition, believing that the knowledge of God can be had only from revelation, has been suspicious of philosophical studies of religion.

Modern works incl. C. C. J. *Webb, *Problems in the Relations of God and Man* (1911); id., *Studies in the History of Natural Theology* (1915), and other writings of this author; E. *Troeltsch, *Gesammelte Schriften* (4 vols., 1912–25); F. *von Hügel, *Essays and Addresses on the Philosophy of Religion* (1921); id., 2nd ser. (1926); A. E. *Taylor, 'Theism', *HERE* 12 (1921), pp. 261–87; id., *The Faith of a Moralist* (Gifford Lectures [= 'GL']; 2 vols., 1930); id., *Philosophical Studies* (1934); J. W. *Oman, *The Natural and the Supernatural* (1931); F. R. Tennant, *Philosophical Theology*, 1: *The*

Soul and its Faculties (1935), 2: *The Word, the Soul and God* (1937); E. Bevan, *Symbolism and Belief* (1938); J. *Baillie, *Our Knowledge of God* (1939); V. A. Demant, *The Religious Prospect* (1939); C. Hartshorne, *Man's Vision of God and the Logic of Theism* (New York, 1941); E. L. Mascall, *He Who Is: A Study in Traditional Theism* (1943); id., *Existence and Analogy: A Sequel to* He Who Is (1949); id., *The Openness of Being: Natural Theology Today* (GL, 1971); D. M. Emmet, *The Nature of Metaphysical Thinking* (1945); A. [N. G.] Flew and A. MacIntyre (eds.), *New Essays in Philosophical Theology* (1955); C. A. Campbell, *On Selfhood and Godhood* (GL, 1957); B. [G.] Mitchell (ed.), *Faith and Logic: Oxford Essays in Philosophical Theology* (1957); id. (ed.), *The Philosophy of Religion* (Oxford, 1971); id., *The Justification of Religious Belief* (1973); K. Jaspers, *Der philosophische Glaube angesichts der Offenbarung* (1962; Eng. tr., 1967); N. Smart (ed.), *Historical Selections in the Philosophy of Religion* (1962); J. Hick, *Philosophy of Religion* (Englewood Cliffs, NJ, 1963); id., *God and the Universe of Faiths: Essays in the Philosophy of Religion* (1973); H. D. Lewis, *Philosophy of Religion* (1965); J. Macquarrie, *God-Talk: An Examination of the Language and Logic of Theology* (1967); F. [B.] Ferré, *Basic Modern Philosophy of Religion* (New York, 1967; London, 1968); R. G. Swinburne, *The Coherence of Theism* (Oxford, 1977); id., *The Existence of God* (ibid., 1979); S. R. L. Clark, *The Mysteries of Religion: An Introduction to Philosophy through Religion* (ibid., 1986); K. Ward, *Images of Eternity: Concepts of God in Five Religious Traditions* (1987); F. Kerr [OP], *Theology after Wittgenstein* (Oxford, 1986); G. Moore, OP, *Believing in God: A Philosophical Essay* (Edinburgh, 1988).

Philostorgius (*c*.368–*c*.439), *Arian ecclesiastical historian. A native of Borissus in Cappadocia Secunda, Philostorgius became a follower and warm admirer of *Eunomius (q.v.) and spent most of his active life in *Constantinople. His principal work, a 'History of the Church' from the Arian standpoint for the period *c*.300–430, survives only in fragments, esp. in the 'Passion of Artemius' (Artemius was an Arian martyr, *c*.362), and in an epitome by *Photius, who writes very disparagingly of its author. His work was inaccurate and biased, but what survives is of value through its use of excellent sources as well as on account of Philostorgius' descriptions of several of the chief Arian personalities.

Editio princeps of frags. by J. Gothofredus (Geneva, 1643); they are also pr. in J. P. Migne, *PG* 65. 459–624; crit. edn., with important introd., by J. Bidez (GCS 21; 1913; 3rd edn. rev. by F. Winkelmann, 1981). P. *Batiffol, *Quaestiones Philostorgianae* (thesis, Paris, 1891). J. Quasten, *Patrology*, 3 (Utrecht and Westminster, Md., 1960), pp. 530–32. G. Fritz in *DTC* 14 (pt. 2; 1935), cols. 1495–8, s.v.; G. Geutz in *PW* 20 (pt. 1; 1941), cols. 119–22, s.v.

Philoxenian Version of the NT. The Syriac version of the NT made from the Greek in 508 for *Philoxenus (q.v.) by Polycarp, a *chorepiscopus. Unlike the *Peshitta, it probably contained the four lesser Catholic Epistles (2 Pet., 2 and 3 Jn., Jude) and the Book of Rev. In 616 it was drastically revised throughout by Thomas of Harkel, and its original text has thus been almost completely lost, apart perhaps from that of the four lesser Catholic Epistles and Rev., for which a version different from, and earlier than, the *Harklean survives. For the rest of the NT, however, the surviving manuscripts do not take us back behind Thomas of Harkel's revision. J. White, the editor of this revised text (see HARKLEAN VERSION), was under the impression that Thomas confined his corrections to the margin, and so he called the text 'Versio Philoxeniana'; in this he has been followed (mistakenly) by several modern scholars.

Editio princeps of the four 'Philoxenian' Epp. by E. *Pococke, Leiden, 1630; modern edn. by J. Gwynn, Text and Translation Society, London and Oxford, 1909. 'Philoxenian' text of Rev. first discovered and pub. by J. Gwynn, *The Apocalypse of St John in a Syriac Version hitherto Unknown* (Dublin and London, 1897). A. Vööbus, 'New Data for the Solution of the Problem concerning the Philoxenian Version', in *Spiritus et Veritas* [Festschrift C. Kundzinš] (Eutin, 1953), pp. 169–86; S. [P.] Brock, 'The Resolution of the Philoxenian/Harclean Problem', in E. J. Epp and G. D. Fee (eds.), *New Testament Textual Criticism: Its Significance for Exegesis. Essays in Honour of Bruce M. Metzger* (Oxford, 1981), pp. 325–43; B. Aland, 'Die philoxenianisch-harklensische Übersetzungstradition', *Muséon*, 94 (1981), pp. 321–83. C. van Puyvelde in *Dict. Bibl.*, Suppl. 6 (1960), cols. 875–8, s.v. 'Orientales de la Bible (Versions)', v. 1, with bibl.

Philoxenus

Philoxenus (*c*.440–523), Bp. of Mabbug (Hierapolis), to which office he was appointed in 485 by *Peter the Fuller. Along with his contemporary, *Severus, he was one of the leading thinkers and writers of the nascent *Syrian Orthodox Church. His extensive writings, in Syriac, include a set of thirteen 'Discourses on the Christian Life', several works on the Incarnation and a number of exegetic and ascetic works. He also conducted a large correspondence which has partly survived. See also preceding entry.

The more important works incl. an edn. of his Discourses, with Eng. tr., by E. A. W. Budge (2 vols., London [1893]–1894); his 'Tractatus de Trinitate et Incarnatione' ed., with Lat. tr., by A. Vaschalde (CSCO, Scriptores Syri, 2nd ser. 27; 1907), and 'Dissertationes Decem de Uno e Sancta Trinitate Incorporato et Passo', ed., with Lat. or Fr. tr., by M. Brière and F. Graffin, SJ, in *PO* 15 (1927), pp. 441–542; 38 (1976–77), pp. 475–641; 39 (1978–9), pp. 541–764; 40 (1979–81), pp. 197–362; and 41 (1982–4), pp. 1–143. The more important letters incl. one sent to a friend, one to Patricius of Edessa, ed., with Fr. tr., by R. Lavenant, SJ, in *PO* 30 (1963), pp. 725–873 (a Gk. tr. of this is pub. among the works of *Isaac of Nineveh); one to the Monks of Senoun, ed. by A. de Halleux (CSCO 231, Scriptores Syri, 98; 1963, with Fr. tr., CSCO 232, Scriptores Syri, 99; 1963); and another to the monasteries of Beth Gaugal, ed., with Fr. tr., by id., in *Muséon*, 96 (1983), pp. 5–79. Verse Life by Eli of Qartamin, ed. by id. (CSCO 233, Scriptores Syri, 100; 1963; Fr. tr., CSCO 234, Scriptores Syri, 101; 1963), with further refs. A. de Halleux, OFM, *Philoxène de Mabbog: Sa vie, ses écrits, sa théologie* (Louvain, 1963). R. C. Chesnut, *Three Monophysite Christologies: Severus of Antioch, Philoxenus of Mabbug, and Jacob of Sarug* (Oxford Theological Monographs, 1976), pp. 57–112. A. Grillmeier, 'Die Taufe Christi und die Taufe Christen. Zur Tauftheologie des Philoxenus von Mabbug und ihrer Bedeutung für die christliche Spiritualität', in H. J. Auf der Maur and others (eds.), *Fides Sacramenti, Sacramentum Fidei: Studies in honour of Pieter Smulders* (Assen, 1981), pp. 137–75. G. Lardreau, *Discours philosophique et discours spirituel: Autour de la philosophie spirituelle de Philoxène de Mabbog* [1985] and R. G. Jenkins, *The Old Testament Quotations of Philoxenus of Mabbug* (CSCO 514, Subsidia, 84; 1989). I. Ortiz de Urbina, SJ, *Patrologia Syriaca* (2nd edn., Rome, 1965), pp. 157–61. E. Tisserant in *DTC* 12 (pt. 2; 1935), cols. 1509–32; R. Graffin, SJ, in *Dict. Sp.* 12 (pt. 1; 1984), cols. 1392–7, both s.v.

Philpot, John

Philpot, John (1516–55), Reformation divine. Few facts are known with certainty about Philpot's life. After being educated at *Winchester and New College, *Oxford, where he was in 1535 elected to a Fellowship which he had vacated by May 1541, he went abroad and developed doubts about the traditional Catholic doctrines. A controversial discussion with a *Franciscan friar near Padua almost led to his seizure by the *Inquisition. At an unknown date under *Edward VI (1547–53) he became Archdeacon of Winchester. An attack on *transubstantiation in the first Convocation of Mary's reign (1553) was followed by imprisonment. In Oct. 1555, despite E. *Bonner's defence, he was convicted, and on 18 Dec. burnt at *Smithfield. Besides many occasional writings dealing with current controversies he translated some of J. *Calvin's Homilies and *Chrysostom, 'Against Heresies'.

Extant works, with account of his 'Examination' taken mainly from J. *Foxe, *Acts and Monuments*, ed. R. Eden (*Parker Society, 1842), with biog. introd., pp. i–xxii. W. A. J. Archbold in *DNB* 45 (1896), pp. 226 f.; C. P. S. Clarke in *DECH*, p. 459; *BRUO, 1501–40*, pp. 449 f.

Phocas, St

Phocas, St (d. 117), Bp. of Sinope in Pontus. A martyr of this name who suffered under Trajan by suffocation in a bath is commemorated in the *Roman Martyrology on 14 July. He has constantly been confused with 'St Phocas the Gardener', commemorated in the W. Church on 23 July and in the E. on 22 Sept., who is stated to have been martyred in the *Diocletianic persecution, as well as with St Phocas of Antioch, named in the Roman Martyrology on 5 Mar. St Phocas the Gardener was the subject of a panegyric pronounced in 400 by Asterius, Bp. of Amasea. When the various traditions had become fused, the cult of St Phocas became very popular, esp. among seafaring people, perhaps through a superficial resemblance of his name to φώκη, 'seal'. Several attempts (for the most part unconvincing) have been made in recent times by students of folklore to connect the cultus of St Phocas with pagan myths.

Gk. text of Asterius' panegyric on Phocas the Gardener in *AASS*, Sept. 6 (1757), pp. 294–9. K. Lübeck, 'Der hl. Phocas von Sinope', *Hist. J.* 30 (1909), pp. 743–61. C. Van de Vorst, 'Saint Phocas', *Anal. Boll.* 30 (1911), pp. 252–72, with discussion of the relation of the various saints of this name and full refs. to earlier lit.; various primary texts, ibid., pp. 272–95. J.-M. Sauget in *Bibliotheca Sanctorum*, 5 (1964), cols. 948–50, s.v. 'Foca l'Ortolano'.

Phocylides, Pseudo-

Phocylides, Pseudo-. The name given to the author of 230 hexameters inserted into the work of Phocylides of Miletus (6th cent. BC). The strictly ethical character of the poem, combined with the absence of specifically Jewish allusions, and esp. of all ref. to Jewish ceremonial law, has suggested that the author was a Christian (A. *Harnack); on the other hand, there is no mention of Christ or of anything definitely Christian, while the moral teaching seems closely to follow that of the OT. The poem may have been written at any time within the period of the Judaeo-Hellenistic civilization up to *c*. AD 150. It was widely used as a school-book in the Byzantine period and has survived in many MSS.

Crit. edns. by D. [C. C.] Young, *Theognis* (Teub., 1971), pp. 95–112, and, with Fr. tr. and introd., by P. Derron (Collection des Universités de France, 1986). Young's edn. is repr., with Eng. tr. by P. W. van der Horst, *The Sentences of Pseudo-Phocylides* (Studia in Veteris Testamenti Pseudepigrapha, 4; Leiden, 1978), pp. 87–103. Further Eng. tr. by id. in J. H. Charlesworth (ed.), *The Old Testament Pseudepigrapha*, 2 (1985), pp. 565–82. J.

Bernays, *Ueber das phokylideische Gedicht: Ein Beitrag zur hellenistischen Litteratur* (1856); cf. review by A. Harnack in *TLZ* 10 (1885), col. 160. J. Thomas, *Die jüdische Phokylides: Formgeschichtliche Zugänge zu Pseudo-Phokylides und Vergleich mit der neutestamentlichen Paränese* (Novum Testamentum et Orbis Antiquus, 23; Göttingen, 1992). E. *Schürer, *The History of the Jewish People in the Age of Jesus Christ*, rev. Eng. tr. by G. Vermes and others, 3 (pt. 1; Edinburgh, 1986), pp. 687–92.

Phoebadius, St (d. *c.*395), also 'Fiari', Bp. of Agen (Agennum) in Guyenne. A friend of St *Hilary of Poitiers, he was a strong opponent of *Arianism and attacked the *Sirmian formula of 357 in his *Liber contra Arianos* (partly based on *Tertullian). In 359 he signed the formula of *Ariminum, but vigorously denounced the Council when he realized its import. A work, 'De Fide Orthodoxa contra Arianos', also passes under his name, but this probably belongs to *Gregory of Elvira. Feast day, 26 April.

Crit. edn. of his *Liber contra Arianos* by R. Demeulenaere (CCSL 64, 1985, pp. 3–52, incl. introd. [in Fr.] and bibl.). Text also in J. P. Migne, *PL* 20. 13–30. *Jerome, *De Vir. Ill.* 108. P. P. Gläser, *Phoebadius von Agen* (Augsburg Diss., 1978). V. C. De Clercq in *DHGE* 16 (1967), cols. 785–90, s.v. 'Fébade d'Agen', with bibl.

phoenix (Gk. φοῖνιξ), a gorgeously arrayed mythical bird which was the subject of several legends in antiquity, notably one to the effect that after living 500–600 years it burnt itself to ashes and then came back to life again with renewed youth. From St *Clement of Rome (I Clem. 25) and *Tertullian (*De Res. Carnis*, 13) onwards, Christian writers frequently regarded it as an image of the Resurrection. A poem on the religious significance of the phoenix, *De Ave Phoenice*, is prob. the work of *Lactantius; it enjoyed wide popularity and in its turn influenced the Anglo-Saxon poem, *The Phoenix*, contained in the *Exeter Book and at one time attributed to *Cynewulf. In Christian art the phoenix was occasionally used from *Constantinian times, representations of it being found, e.g., in the Roman churches of Sts *Cosmas and Damian, St Praxedes and St Cecilia, as well as on a variety of funerary monuments.

J. Hubaux and M. Leroy, *Le Mythe du phénix dans les littératures grecque et latine* (Bibliothèque de la Faculté de Philosophie et Lettres de l'Université de Liège, 82; 1939). R. van den Broek, *The Myth of the Phoenix according to Classical and Early Christian Traditions* (Eng. tr. by I. Seeger, Leiden, 1972). F. Bisconti, 'Aspetti e significati del simbolo della fenice nella letteratura e nell'arte del Cristianesimo primitivo', *Vetera Christianorum*, 16 (1979), pp. 21–40. Modern edns. of *De Ave Phoenice* by M. C. Fitzpatrick (Philadelphia, 1933) and of the Anglo-Saxon poem by N. F. Blake (Manchester, 1964); on its relationship with the *De Ave Phoenice*, O. F. Emerson, 'Originality in Old English Poetry', *Review of English Studies*, 2 (1926), pp. 18–31; J. E. Cross, 'The Conception of the Old English *Phoenix*', in R. P. Creed (ed.), *Old English Poetry* (Providence, RI, 1967), pp. 129–52. H. *Leclercq, OSB, in *DACL* 14 (pt. 1; 1939), cols. 682–91, s.v. 'Phénix'; F. Bisconti in *DPAC* 1 (1983), cols. 1350–2, s.v. 'Fenice'; Eng. tr. in *Encyclopedia of the Early Church*, 2 (1992), p. 685, s.v.

Phos Hilaron (Gk. Φῶς ἱλαρόν). In the E. Church, the hymn sung at 'Hesperinos' (the counterpart of the W. *Vespers) during 'the lighting of the lamps' and the central item in the office. It is found already in St *Basil (*De Spir. Sanct.* 73); he regarded it as ancient. Some modern

Anglican liturgies provide for its use in Evening Prayer. Translations include J. *Keble's 'Hail! gladdening light' and R. S. *Bridges' 'O gladsome light, O grace'.

Text pr., with Lat. tr., in M. J. *Routh, *Reliquiae Sacrae*, 3 (Oxford, 1815), p. 299, with notes, pp. 300–4; and in H. A. Daniel, *Thesaurus Hymnologicus*, 3 (Leipzig, 1846), p. 5, repr. by J. Julian in id. (ed.), *A Dictionary of Hymnology* (1892), p. 894, s.v., with list of Eng. trs. A. Tripolitis, 'Φῶς ἱλαρόν. Ancient Hymn and Modern Enigma', *VC* 24 (1970), pp. 189–96. *CPG* 1 (1983), pp. 131 f. (no. 1355).

Photinus (4th cent.), heretic. A pupil of *Marcellus of Ancyra, he became Bp. of Sirmium *c.*344. He was recognized as a man of learning and eloquence. Though involved in the condemnation of Marcellus by a Council of Antioch *c.*345, he retained his see until 351, when he was deposed and exiled after his errors had been exposed at a Council called by the Emp. Constantius at Sirmium. None of his writings have survived and his doctrine is variously described by his detractors. It was clearly a form of *Sabellianism. Acc. to St *Augustine, he denied the pre-existence of Christ, though he allowed that He was born of the Virgin and was endowed with superhuman excellences. His followers, the 'Photinians', were formally condemned at the Council of *Constantinople in 381.

The primary sources are scattered. D. *Petavius, *De Photino Haeretico eiusque Damnatione* (Paris, 1636). M. Simonetti, *Studi sull'Arianesimo* (Verba Seniorum, NS 5 [1965]), pp. 135–59. Bardenhewer, 3, pp. 123 f. F. *Loofs in *PRE* (3rd edn.), 15 (1904), pp. 372–4, and G. Bardy in *DTC* 12 (pt. 2; 1935), cols. 1532–6, both s.v.

Photius (*c.*810–*c.*895), Patriarch of *Constantinople. Of a noble Constantinopolitan family, he received a good education and gave up his original plan of entering a monastery for the career of a scholar and statesman. Close relations with the court made him the first Imperial Secretary and, in 838, Imperial Ambassador to Baghdad. When the Emp. Michael III deposed Ignatius, Patr. of Constantinople, in 858, Photius, still a layman, was appointed his successor. He was consecrated by his friend, Gregory Asbestas, Abp. of Syracuse, whom Ignatius had himself deposed. On Ignatius' refusal to abdicate, Michael and Photius sent an embassy to Pope *Nicholas I, asking for legates to a synod at Constantinople which, besides regulating the *Iconoclastic Controversy, should also settle the dispute of the two Patriarchs. Nicholas's legates exceeded their powers, probably under pressure from the E. court, and took part in the synod of 861, which deposed Ignatius. In 862 the Pope, in letters to Photius and to Michael III, blamed his legates' conduct and complained that his former letter had been tampered with at Constantinople; and, at a synod at Rome (863), annulled the proceedings at Constantinople. He maintained that Ignatius was still Patriarch; and after the arrival of an embassy from Ignatius declared Photius deposed and his friend, Gregory Asbestas, deprived of the priesthood and of all ecclesiastical offices. All clerics promoted by Photius were also deposed, and the deposition of Ignatius declared null and void. This assertion of Papal authority naturally gave great offence at Constantinople. Photius himself kept silence, but the Emperor wrote a strongly worded letter to the Pope, who in 865 declared himself ready to reopen the case. A reconciliation was prevented by the dispute whether Christianity in *Bulgaria, then being converted, was to depend on Rome or on Constantinople. In 867 Photius, in an encyclical, denounced the presence of Latin missionaries in Bulgaria as an intrusion, and also gave an exposition of his objections to the *Filioque clause in the creed. In the same year, at a Council at Constantinople, sentence of deposition was pronounced against the Pope, who was declared anathema and excommunicated.

With the accession of Basil (867), the murderer and successor of the Emp. Michael, the situation changed. Ignatius was reinstated, and a sentence of a Council at Rome in 869, anathematizing Photius, was confirmed by the Council of Constantinople of 869–70, later counted as the 8th General Council by the Latins. The restored harmony between E. and W. was of short duration. When Ignatius consecrated an archbishop and bishops for the Bulgarians (870) he was threatened by the Pope with excommunication. This action at Rome assured his continuance in his see, and it was only after Ignatius' death (877) that Photius, by order of the Emperor, once more became Patriarch. At a Council held at Constantinople in 879–80 the Papal legates seem to have approved Photius and annulled the decision of the Council of 869–70. Photius, however, still faced difficulties within the Byzantine Church, and when *Leo VI became Emperor (886), he resigned and disappears from history; he died at the monastery of Armeniaki towards the end of the 9th cent.

The Photian schism was only one among many similar incidents in the history of the relations between the Greek and Latin Churches, but it had grave consequences for the future. It accentuated the conflict between the Roman claim to be the centre of unity for Christendom and the Greek conception of the five patriarchates of almost equal status. Moreover, Photius was the first important theologian to accuse Rome of innovating in the matter of the Filioque. Hence in the 13th and 14th cents. the name of Photius became the watchword of those who opposed the union of the two Churches.

Photius was a scholar of wide interests and encyclopaedic knowledge. His most important work, his 'Bibliotheca' or 'Myriobiblion', is a description of several hundred books, often with exhaustive analyses and copious extracts. It is an invaluable mine of information, as a great number of the works mentioned in it are now lost. His 'Lexicon' provides further evidence of his great learning. The 'Amphilochia', written during his first exile, deals mainly with exegetical and doctrinal problems; his treatises against the *Manichaeans are chiefly concerned with the *Paulicians. The 'Treatise on the Holy Spirit', written after his resignation, has furnished all subsequent Greek theologians with their objections to the W. dogma. The 'Nomocanon', which is sometimes attributed to him, is not really his, though he may have re-edited it. A number of his homilies and letters have also been preserved. In the Orthodox Church Photius is venerated as a saint; feast day, 6 Feb.

The only collected edn. of Photius' writings is that of J. P. Migne, *PG* 101–4, which Migne prepared with the help of J. B. Malou, Bp. of Bruges, and J. *Hergenröther. Modern edns. of his 'Bibliotheca', with Fr. tr., by R. Henry (Collection Byzantine, 8 vols., 1959–77 + index by J. Schamp, 1991); of his 'Homilies' by B. Laourdas (Thessalonica, 1959); of his 'Lexicon' by C. Theodo-

ridis (Berlin and New York, 1982 ff.); and of his Letters and 'Amphilochia' by B. Laourdas and L. G. Westerink (6 vols. in 7 parts, Teub., 1983–8). Eng. tr. of his 'Homilies', with comm., by C. Mango (Cambridge, Mass., 1958). Other sources incl. J. Hergenröther, *Monumenta Graeca ad Photium eiusque Historiam Pertinentia* (Ratisbon, 1869), and A. Papadopoulos-Kerameus, Φωτιακά (St Petersburg, 1897). V. Grumel, AA (ed.), *Les Regestes des Actes du Patriarcat de Constantinople*, 1, fascs. 2–3, 2nd edn. rev. by J. Darrouzès, AA (1989), pp. 95–164 (nos. 456–589). Earlier works are now superseded by F. Dvornik, *The Photian Schism: History and Legend* (1948), with full bibl. R. Haugh, *Photius and the Carolingians: The Trinitarian Controversy* (Belmont, Mass. [1975]). W. T. Treadgold, *The Nature of the Bibliotheca of Photius* (Dumbarton Oaks Studies, 18; Washington, DC, 1980); D. S. White, *Patriarch Photios of Constantinople* (Brookline, Mass., 1981), incl. Eng. tr. of 52 letters; J. Schamp, *Photios, historien des Lettres* (Bibliothèque de la Faculté de Philosophie et Lettres de l'Université de Liège, 248; 1987). J. M. Hussey, *The Orthodox Church in the Byzantine Empire* (Oxford History of the Christian Church, 1986), pp. 72–90. Beck, pp. 520–8. É. Amann in *DTC* 12 (pt. 2; 1935), cols. 1536–604, with bibl.; K. Ziegler in *PW* 20 (pt. 1; 1941), cols. 667–737, s.v. 'Photios (13)'; F. Dvornik in *NCE* 11 (1967), pp. 326–9, s.v., with further bibl.

phylactery (Gk. φυλακτήριον; Heb. *tephillin*). A small leather case containing vellum strips inscribed with four passages from the OT, namely Exod. 13: 1–10, Exod. 13: 11–16, Deut. 6: 4–9, Deut. 11: 13–21. They have been worn by orthodox Jews from pre-Christian times on the forehead and arm during morning prayer on all days except the Sabbath and certain festivals, to remind them of their obligation to keep the law. The *Pharisees and scribes were condemned by Christ for their ostentatious broadening of their phylacteries (Mt. 23: 5).

There is a brief monograph by G. Langer, *Die jüdischen Gebetsriemen* (1931). H. L. Strack and P. Billerbeck, *Kommentar zum Neuen Testament aus Talmud und Midrasch*, 4 (1928), pp. 250–76 (Elfter Exkurs, 'Die Tephillin oder Gebetsriemen'). K. G. Kuhn, *Phylakterien aus Höhle 4 von Qumran* (Abhandlungen der Heidelberger Akademie der Wissenschaften, philosophisch-historische Klasse, Jahrgang 1957, Abh. 1; 1957). E. *Schürer, *The History of the Jewish People in the Age of Jesus Christ*, rev. Eng. tr. by G. Vermes and others, 2 (Edinburgh, 1979), p. 480 f. See also comm. to Exod., Deut., and Mt.

physico-theological argument. The name commonly applied in the 18th cent., e.g. by I. *Kant, to the *teleological argument for the existence of God. In 1713 William Derham (Canon of Windsor from 1716; d. 1735) published two series of *Boyle Lectures under the title *Physico-Theology; or, a Demonstration of the Being and Attributes of God from His Works of Creation*, which won great popularity and, through translations issued a few years later in Italian, French, and Dutch, probably did much towards bringing the expression into general currency.

Pia Desideria. P. J. *Spener's book which aimed at fostering a religious revival in German Protestantism and thus created the *Pietist Movement. Written in German, it was published in 1675 at Frankfurt, where Spener was then pastor. He stated his main immediate objectives under the head of six 'simple proposals' (*einfältige Vorschläge*): (1) an intensified study of the Bible, aiming at enhanced personal devotion as the chief end; (2) a fuller exercise by the laity of their spiritual priesthood; (3)

emphasis on the practical, as opposed to the merely intellectual, side of Christianity, culminating in the spirit of love; (4) the manifestation of charity in religious controversy, which by the sympathetic presentation of truth should seek to win the heart rather than to gain controversial victory; (5) the reorganization of theological studies at the universities and the establishment of higher standards of religious life among both professors and students; (6) the reform and revival of preaching with a view to edification. The author also looked forward to an age of prosperity for the Church when these ideals would be largely realized, after the conversion of the Jews and the fall of Papal Rome. Spener further developed his programme in *Das geistliche Priesterthum* (1677) and *Allgemeine Gottesgelehrtheit* (1680).

Convenient Eng. tr., with introd., by T. G. Tappert (Philadelphia, 1964). For other bibl. see SPENER, P. J.

Piarists. An order of *regular clergy devoted to the education of children and youths, esp. among the poor. The 'Regulares pauperes Matris Dei scholarum piarum', as they are officially called, derive their name from the 'Pious Schools', or free public schools, of which the first was opened in a poor district of Rome by St *Joseph Calasanctius in 1597. (In some countries they are called 'Scopoli' or 'Escolapios' from the Italian or Spanish for 'school'.) The teachers at Calasanctius's school were recognized as a congregation by *Paul V in 1617 and made into an order by Gregory XV in 1621. Though reduced to an association of independent houses in 1646, it was reinstated as an order in 1669. Its members live in community, adding a fourth vow dedicating themselves to education. They operate in many countries of Europe, N. and S. America, Africa, and Asia, running primary and secondary schools and a university (Veracruz) in Mexico. They did much to keep alive RC education when the *Jesuits were suppressed. The importance which Calasanctius attached to science is maintained by the Piarists, who are responsible for the Observatorio Ximeniano in Florence. The Superior General of the order, who resides in Rome, is elected by the General Chapter and holds office for six years; he is supported by four Assistants General. In each of the 29 provinces there is a Provincial General (elected for four years), with at least two Assistant Provincials.

L. Picanyol, Sch. P., *Brevis Conspectus Historico-Statisticus Ordinis Scholarum Piarum* (Rome, 1932); S. Giner Guerri, Sch. P., *Escuelas Pias: ser e historia* (Salamanca, 1978). J. M. Lesaga and others (eds.), *Documentos Fundacionales de las Escuelas Pías* (ibid., 1979). C. Rabaza, *Historia de las Esculas Pías de España* (4 vols., Valencia, 1917–18); G. Pelliccia, *La Scuola Primaria a Roma dal Secolo XVI al XIX* (Studi e fonti per la Storia dell'Università di Roma, 8; 1985). T. Viñas, *Index Bio-bibliographicus . . . [Scriptorum] Scholarum Piarum* (3 vols., Rome, 1908–11). *Diccionario Enciclopédico Escolapio*, ed. C. Vilá Pila, Sch. P., and L. M. Bandrés Rey (Salamanca, 1983 ff.). G. Ausenda, Sch. P., in *DIP* 2 (1975), cols. 927–45, s.v. 'Chierici regolari poveri della Madre di Dio delle Scuole Pie'.

Pica. See PIE.

Pico della Mirandola, Giovanni (1463–94), Italian nobleman, scholar, and writer on philosophy and theology. After studying at *Bologna he spent some years wandering among schools of learning in Italy and France and collecting a library. Besides being a good classic, he knew also

Hebrew, Aramaic, and Arabic; and he was the first to seek in the *Kabbala a clue to the Christian mysteries. His vivid imagination led him to many unorthodox views, several of which found expression in a set of 900 *Conclusiones* on a great variety of topics which he proposed to defend in Rome in 1487. As, however, some of them appeared to Innocent VIII definitely heretical, Pico abandoned the enterprise and withdrew briefly to France, then returned to Florence, where he spent the years 1488–94. He had earlier dedicated an *Apology* to Lorenzo de' Medici, and in Florence he presented to him the *Heptaplus*, an interpretation of Genesis; he also composed *De Ente et Uno* and the incomplete *Disputationes adversus Astrologiam*. Pico took a generous view of the existence of truth in non-Christian religions and was an early exponent of *syncretism. His *Oratio de Hominis Dignitate* asserted the unique position of man outside the *Neoplatonic hierarchy. On his deathbed he was clothed in the *Dominican habit by G. *Savonarola.

Collections of his works (2 parts, Bologna, 1495–6), with Life by his nephew G. F. Pico prefixed [no pagination]; also Basle, 1557, repr., with introd. by C. Vasoli (Hildesheim, 1969). Crit. edn. of his 'Oratio de Hominis Dignitate', 'Heptaplus', and 'De Ente et Uno' by E. Garin (Edizione Nazionale dei Classici del Pensiero Italiano, 1; Florence, 1942), of his 'Disputationes adversus astrologiam Divinatricem' by id. (ibid. 2 and 3; 1946–52), of his *Carmina Latina* by W. Speyer (Leiden, 1964), and of his *Conclusiones* by B. Kieszkowski (Travaux d'humanisme et renaissance, 131; Geneva, 1973). His 'Liber de Imaginatione' ed., with Eng. tr., by H. Caplan (Cornell Studies in English, 9; 1930). Eng. tr. of his *Commento* by S. Jayne (American University Studies, 2nd ser. 19; New York etc. [1984]). The Life by his nephew, three of his letters and certain other works were tr. into Eng. by Sir Thomas *More (London [*c*.1510]; modern edn. with introd. by J. M. Rigg, London, 1890; also among the works of Sir Thomas More). Modern studies by G. Semprini (Todi, 1921), E. Anagnine (Bari, 1937), E. Garin (Pubblicazioni della R. Università degli Studi di Firenze, Facoltà di Lettere e Filosofia, 3rd ser. 5; 1937), P. M. Cordier (Paris, 1957), E. Monnerjahn (Wiesbaden, 1960), and G. di Napoli (Collectio Philosophica Lateranensis, 8; Rome [1965]), H. de *Lubac (Paris [1974]), and F. Roulier (Bibliothèque Franco Simone, 17; Geneva, 1989). A. Dulles, *Princeps Concordiae: Pico della Mirandola and the Scholastic Tradition* (Harvard Phi Beta Prize Essay for 1940; Cambridge, Mass., 1941). A.-J. Festugière, OP, 'Studia Mirandulana' *AHDLMA* 7 (vol. for 1932; 1933), pp. 143–50, with text of 'De Ente et Uno', pp. 208–24, and Fr. tr., pp. 225–50. P. O. Kristeller, 'Giovanni Pico della Mirandola and his sources', in *L'Opera e il Pensiero di Giovanni Pico della Mirandola nella Storia dell'Umanesimo: Convegno Internazionale (Mirandola: 15–18 settembre 1963)*, 1 (Florence, 1965), pp. 35–133. P. Kibre, *The Library of Pico della Mirandola* (New York, 1936). H. Reinhardt, *Freiheit zu Gott: Der Grundgedanke des Systematikers Giovanni Pico della Mirandola (1463–1494)* (Weinheim [1989]). P. O. Kristeller in P. Edwards (ed.), *Encyclopedia of Philosophy*, 6 (1967), pp. 307–11; A. Niero in *Dict. Sp.* 12 (pt. 1; 1986), cols. 1420–6; C. Trinkaus in P. G. Bietenholz and T. B. Deutscher (eds.), *Contemporaries of Erasmus*, 3 (1987), pp. 81–4, all s.v.

Pie, or Pica. The name given in England in the 15th cent. to the *Ordinale* or *Directorium*, the book of directions for saying the service, and relating its various parts, esp. the *occurrence and *concurrence of *movable and immovable feasts. This work, which took the place of the modern *Ordo recitandi divini officii* or Calendar, is censured in the Preface to the 1549 BCP (since 1662 headed

'Concerning the Service of the Church') for 'the number and hardness of its rules'.

Pierre d'Ailly. See D'AILLY, PIERRE.

Pietà. A representation, often in sculpture, of the BVM lamenting over the dead body of Christ, which she holds on her knees. Of 13th-cent. German origin, this image is associated with devotion to the sufferings of the BVM during the Passion of Christ. The most famous Pietà is that of *Michelangelo in *St Peter's, Rome. In England there is a fine Pietà in a window in the church at Long Melford, Suffolk.

W. Passarge, *Des Deutsche Vesperbild im Mittelalter* (Cologne, 1924), E. Reiners-Ernst, *Das Freudvolle Vesperbild und die Anfänge der Pietà-Vorstellung* (Abhandlungen der Bayerischen Benediktiner-Akademie, 2; 1939); T. Dobrzeniecki, 'Mediaeval Sources of the Pietà', *Bulletin du Musée National de Varsovie*, 8 (1967), pp. 5–24. G. Schiller, *Ikonographie der christlichen Kunst*, 2 (1968), pp. 192–5 (Eng. tr., 2 (1972), pp. 179–81), with further refs. and figs. 622–37.

Pietism. A late-17th- and 18th-cent. movement within (primarily German) Protestantism which sought to supplement the emphasis on institutions and dogma in orthodox Protestant circles by concentrating on the 'practice of piety', rooted in inner experience and expressing itself in a life of religious commitment. The way for it was prepared by the writings of J. *Arndt and other mystical authors, as well as by translations of the works of English *Puritans such as L. *Bayly. At the same time, within Protestant orthodoxy there were movements towards a new reformation or revival of religious life ('Reformorthodoxie'). The word 'Pietist' came into use in the last quarter of the 17th cent., originally as a nickname. The *Lutheran minister P. J. *Spener had already published his *Pia Desideria, a set of six proposals for restoring true religion; the publication of this work in 1675 was a decisive moment in the development of the Pietist movement. Spener instituted devotional circles for prayer, Bible reading, etc.; he emphasized the universal priesthood of all the faithful, without, however, in essence deviating from Lutheran doctrine or intending to separate from the Church. Anti-establishment tendencies, sometimes combined with *millenarian expectations and more or less unorthodox doctrines, were to be found in the circle of 'radical Pietism' which, in its emphasis on the work of the Holy Spirit in the hearts of men, was heir to the mystical tradition. The relationship between mainstream Lutheran and Reformed Pietism on the one hand, and radical Pietism on the other, is a subject of current research. In its more orthodox and moderate form, as initially represented by Spener, the movement quickly won support from a large body of pastors, and in P. *Gerhardt it found a hymn-writer whose compositions did much to spread its ideals. But a clash with the orthodox became inevitable when his friend, A. H. *Francke, who through his 'Collegia Philobiblica' had been instrumental in bringing about a revival among the students in Leipzig, attacked the Leipzig theologians on account of their inquisitorial attitude. He had to leave Leipzig, but before long a new university at Halle was founded by Frederick III, Elector of Brandenburg and later King of Prussia, and in 1691

Francke received a professorship. For several years Halle was the centre of the movement. A body, chiefly of younger theologians, helped to carry the movement throughout Protestant Germany. It took on different aspects in different districts. In Halle it developed into a hard-and-fast system of penance, grace, and rebirth, while at *Herrnhut, in the settlement of Spener's godson, Count von *Zinzendorf, it consisted chiefly of personal devotion to the Redeemer. In the 18th cent. Pietism was characterized by various philanthropic activities (centred in Halle) and by its contribution to the missionary movement (the Danish-Halle mission in Tranquebar in S. *India, which started in 1706; *Moravian missionary activity in many parts of the world). In various forms Pietism has lasted into the 20th century, and has affected many similar movements in other countries, J. *Wesley's *Methodism among them.

H. [L. J.] Heppe, *Geschichte des Pietismus und der Mystik in der reformirten Kirche, namentlich der Niederlande* (Leiden, 1879); A. *Ritschl, *Geschichte des Pietismus* (3 vols., 1880–6). W. Goeters, *Die Vorbereitung des Pietismus in der reformierten Kirche der Niederlande bis zur Labadistischen Krisis 1670* (1911). A Lang, *Puritanismus und Pietismus: Studien zu ihrer Entwicklung von M. Butzer bis zum Methodismus* (Beiträge zur Geschichte und Lehre der Reformierten Kirche, 6; Neukirchen, 1941). F. E. Stoeffler, *The Rise of Evangelical Pietism* (Studies in the History of Religions, 9; Leiden, 1965); id., *German Pietism in the Eighteenth Century* (ibid. 24; 1973). H. Weigelt, *Pietismus-Studien*, 1 (Arbeiten zur Theologie, 2. Reihe, 4; 1965; all pub.). M. Schmidt, *Wiedergeburt und neuer Mensch: Gesammelte Studien zur Geschichte des Pietismus* (Arbeiten zur Geschichte des Pietismus, 2; 1969); id., *Pietismus* (Urban-Taschenbücher, 145; 1972). J. Wallmann, *Philipp Jakob Spener und die Anfänge des Pietismus* (Beiträge zur historischen Theologie, 42; 1970). H. Bornkamm and others (eds.), *Der Pietismus in Gestalten und Wirkungen: Martin Schmidt zum 65. Geburtstag* (Arbeiten zur Geschichte des Pietismus, 14; 1975). M. Greschat (ed.), *Zur neueren Pietismusforschung* (Wege der Forschung, 440; 1977); id. (ed.), *Orthodoxie und Pietismus* (Gestalten der Kirchengeschichte, 7; 1982). *Pietismus und Neuzeit: Ein Jahrbuch zur Geschichte des neueren Protestantismus*, ed. M. Brecht and others, 4: *Die Anfänge des Pietismus* (1977–8) and 8: *Der radikale Pietismus* (1982). J. van den Berg and J. P. van Dooren (eds.), *Pietismus und Reveil. Referate der internationalen Tagung: Der Pietismus in den Niederlanden und seine internationalen Beziehungen, Zeist 18.–22. Juni 1974* (Kerkhistorische Bijdragen, 7; 1978). E. Beyreuther, *Geschichte des Pietismus* (Stuttgart, 1978). D. Meyer (ed.), *Pietismus—Herrnhutertum—Erweckungsbewegung: Festschrift für Erich Beyreuther* (Schriftenreihe des Vereins für Rheinische Kirchengeschichte, 70; 1982). W. R. Ward, *The Protestant Evangelical Awakening* (Cambridge, 1992). G. Mälzer, *Die Werke der Württembergischen Pietisten des 17. und 18. Jahrhunderts* (Bibliographie zur Geschichte des Pietismus, 1; 1972). K. Aland in *Weltkirchen Lexikon* (1960), cols. 1151–6; M. Schmidt and M. Stallmann in *RGG* (3rd edn.), 5 (1961), cols. 370–83; E. W. Zeeden in *L.Th.K.* (2nd edn.), 8 (1963), cols. 499–501, all s.v. 'Pietismus'; B. Weber in *Dict. Sp.* 12 (pt. 2; 1986), cols. 1743–58, s.v. 'Piétisme'; M. Brecht in *TRE*, 26 (1996), pp. 606–31, s.v. 'Pietismus', with bibl. See also bibl. to SPENER, P. J., and FRANCKE, A. H.

Pighi, or **Pigge, Albert** (c.1490–1542), theologian. A native of Kampen in the Netherlands, he studied at Louvain and *Cologne and in 1522 was called to Rome by *Hadrian VI. Here he took a prominent part in writing on the main issues of his time. In 1525 he wrote a treatise *Adversus Graecorum Errores* (preserved in MS in the *Vatican Library) to pave the way for reunion with the

Orthodox Church. He also prepared a memorandum, since lost, on *Henry VIII's divorce project. His principal work, *Hierarchiae Ecclesiasticae Assertio* (Cologne, 1538) was an elaborate defence of *tradition as a source of Christian truth co-ordinate with Scripture; it defended a doctrine of Papal infallibility and denied the proposition that a pope might personally lapse into heresy. His emphasis on human free will in his opposition to M. *Luther and J. *Calvin led him to minimize the effects of *original sin, but under the influence of J. *Gropper he adopted the doctrine of '*double justice'. At the Colloquy of *Ratisbon (1541) he took part on the Catholic side.

Correspondence ed. W. Friedensburg in *ZKG* 23 (1902), pp. 110–55. H. Jedin; *Studien über die Schriftstellertätigkeit Albert Pigges* (Reformationsgeschichtliche Studien und Texte, 55; 1931). R. Bäumer, 'Albert Pigge (†1542)', in E. Iserloh (ed.), *Katholische Theologen der Reformationszeit*, 1 (Katholisches Leben und Kirchenreform im Zeitalter der Glaubensspaltung, 44; Münster, 1984), pp. 98–106. É. Amann in *DTC* 12 (pt. 2; 1935), cols. 2094–104, s.v., with useful bibl.

Pilate, Acts of. An apocryphal work giving an account of the trial, death, and resurrection of Christ. In some MSS an independent treatise on the *Descent of Christ into *Hades is attached to it. From the 13th cent. onwards, the two together have been sometimes known as the 'Gospel of Nicodemus'.

The first part, the 'Acts' proper, is generally held to be not earlier than the 4th cent., though references to the existence of Acts of Pilate in earlier writers, notably in *Justin Martyr (*Apol.* 1. 35, 48), have led some scholars to contend that the book is based on a 2nd-cent. original, and that this work may even have been founded on authentic records of Christ's trial. It seems more probable, however, that Justin was referring to an independent treatise. As it is known that fictitious accounts of the trial were put into circulation under the Emp. Maximin (early 4th cent.) in the interests of paganism, it is not impossible that the Acts of Pilate were compiled as a reply. The book draws extensively on the four canonical Gospels, to which it is evidently seeking to provide supplementary material, including fresh grounds for belief in Christ's *Resurrection.

The second part purports to have been written by the two sons of the aged *Simeon, Carinus and Leucius. It describes with much detail the effect of Christ's presence among the imprisoned souls in Hades (cf. 1 Pet. 3: 19, on which it is based).

The two documents were probably not united before the 5th cent. The work forms the basis of the medieval play-cycle on the *Harrowing of Hell and of the legends of St *Joseph of Arimathaea and the Holy *Grail.

Lat. and Gk. recensions ed. C. *Tischendorf, *Evangelia Apocrypha* (Leipzig, 1853), pp. 203–412 (2nd edn., 1876, pp. 210–434); also in A. de Santos Otero, *Les Evangelios Apócrifos* (6th edn., 1988), pp. 391–465; Eng. tr. in J. K. Elliott, *The Apocryphal New Testament* (Oxford, 1993), pp. 164–204; also in Schneemelcher (see below). Further edn. of Lat. and Gk. in parallel cols. by P. Vannutelli (Rome, 1938). Coptic text ed. E. Revillout in *PO* 9 (1913), pp. 57–132. Syriac text ed., with Lat. tr., by I. E. Rahmani, *Studia Syriaca*, 2 (Charfat, 1908). Armenian text, retranslated into Lat. and Gk., by F. C. *Conybeare in *Studia Biblica et Ecclesiastica*, 4 (Oxford, 1896), pp. 59–132. R. A. *Lipsius, *Die Pilatus-Acten kritisch untersucht* (1871). S. Brock, 'A Fragment of the *Acta Pilati* in Christian Palestinian Aramaic', *JTS* NS 22

(1971), pp. 157 f., with further refs. J.-P. Lémonon, *Pilate et le gouvernement de la Judée* (Études Bibliques, 1981), pp. 258–65. F. Scheidweiler in Schneemelcher, 1 (5th edn., 1987), pp. 395–424; Eng. tr., 1 (1991), pp. 501–36. incl. Eng. tr. of text. J. Quasten, *Patrology*, 1 (Utrecht, 1950), pp. 115–18; E. von Dobschütz in *HDB* 3 (1900), pp. 544–7, with bibl.

Pilate, Pontius. The governor ('prefect', not 'procurator') of Judaea from AD 26 to 36 under whom Christ was crucified. The Gospels represent him as at first well disposed towards Jesus, but as having finally yielded to the populace through fear of the consequences of an acquittal. The data as to his character contained in *Josephus and *Philo are in full accord with the NT narratives, their additional evidence showing him in anything but a favourable light. Lucius Vitellius, governor of Syria, removed him from his post for misgovernment. The tradition in *Eusebius (*HE* 2. 7) that he committed suicide may well be correct. Late legends embroidered this theme in the interest of Christianity, and also gave the name of his wife (Mt. 27: 19) as 'Claudia Procula'. In the *Coptic Church he is revered as a martyr (feast day, 25 June). See also previous entry.

The principal authorities, apart from the NT, include Philo, *Leg. ad Gaium*, 38; Josephus, *Antiquitates*, 18. 3–4, and *Bell. Jud.* 2. 8 f. An inscription discovered at *Caesarea in 1961 describes him as 'Prefect'; it was reported by A. Frova, 'L'iscrizione di Ponzio Pilato a Cesarea', *Rendiconti dell'Istituto Lombardo, Accademia di Scienze e Lettere*, Classe di Lettere e Scienze Morali e Storiche, 95 (1961), pp. 419–34. J.-P. Lémonon, *Pilate et le gouvernement de la Judée: Textes et Monuments* (Études Bibliques, 1981). E. *Schürer, *The History of the Jewish People in the Age of Jesus Christ*, rev. Eng. tr. by G. Vermes and others, 1 (Edinburgh, 1973), pp. 357–62. D. R. Schwartz in *Anchor Bible Dictionary*, 5 (1992), pp. 395–401, s.v. 'Pontius Pilate'.

Pilgrim Fathers. The English founders of the colony of Plymouth, Massachusetts, who sailed from Holland and England in the *Mayflower* in Sept. 1620. The title 'Pilgrim Fathers' is comparatively modern. In 1630 William Bradford, the Governor, wrote of his company as 'pilgrims' (with a ref. to Heb. 11: 13), and such language was gradually adopted in New England, e.g. on 22 Dec. 1798 a feast of the 'Sons' or 'Heirs of the Pilgrims' was held at Boston, at which the memory of 'the Fathers' was celebrated. In this way the phrase 'Pilgrim Fathers' eventually came into common use.

G. D. Langdon, *Pilgrim Colony: A History of New Plymouth 1620–1691* (Yale Publications in American Studies, 12; New Haven, Conn., and London, 1966).

Pilgrimage of Grace, the. A series of risings in Lincs, Yorks, and other counties of the N. of England, which took place between Oct. 1536 and Feb. 1537. The rising in Yorks, which was the most serious, was called by the participants 'this pilgrimage of grace for the commonwealth'. The religious element in the risings varied, and has been variously assessed. There was widespread hatred of T. *Cromwell and of government innovations in ecclesiastical matters (esp. the *dissolution of the lesser monasteries, and the attacks on the Sacraments and on saints' days in the *Ten Articles). In addition, there were economic and social grievances, such as resentment at new forms of taxation and at the threat to the rights of landowners posed by the Statute of Uses (1536). Dissatisfied conservative courtiers may also have had some part in fomenting unrest. In Lincs and Yorks some peers and gentry took the lead. R. *Aske, who led the Yorks rebellion, assembled c.30,000 men and treated with the government on equal terms; but promises of a parliament and a free pardon led him to disband his force and the King won him over at a private interview. Unrest, however, continued and might have become general, and it is unlikely that the King's intentions were at any stage honourable; a further outbreak in E. Yorks early in 1537 afforded a pretext for government action. At Henry's order over 200 rebels were hanged in the N. as a 'fearful spectacle' to others; Aske himself was charged with treason and hanged in chains.

M. H. and R. Dodds, *The Pilgrimage of Grace 1536–37 and the Exeter Conspiracy 1538* (2 vols., Cambridge, 1915). A. G. Dickens, *Lollards and Protestants in the Diocese of York 1509–1558* (1959; repr., with list of corrections, 1982), *passim*. C. [A.] Haigh, *The Last Days of the Lancashire Monasteries and the Pilgrimage of Grace* (Chetham Society, 3rd ser. 17; 1969). R. B. Smith, *Land and Politics in the England of Henry VIII: The West Riding of Yorkshire: 1530–46* (Oxford, 1970). S. M. Harrison, *The Pilgrimage of Grace in the Lake Counties, 1536–7* (Royal Historical Society Studies in History, 27; 1981). A. Ward, *The Lincolnshire Rising 1536* (Nottingham [1986]). C. S. L. Davies, 'The Pilgrimage of Grace Reconsidered', *Past and Present*, 41 (1968), pp. 54–76, repr. in P. Slack (ed.), *Rebellion, Popular Protest and the Social Order in Early Modern England* (Past and Present Publications, Cambridge, 1984), pp. 16–38; id., 'Popular Religion and the Pilgrimage of Grace', in A. Fletcher and J. Stevenson (eds.), *Order and Disorder in Early Modern England* (Cambridge, 1985), pp. 58–91; M. E. James, 'Obedience and Dissent in Henrician England: The Lincolnshire Rebellion 1536', *Past and Present*, 48 (1970), pp. 3–78, repr., id., *Society, Politics and Culture: Studies in Early Modern England* (Past and Present Publications, Cambridge, 1986), pp. 188–269; G. R. Elton, 'Politics and the Pilgrimage of Grace', in B. C. Malament (ed.), *After the Reformation: Essays in Honor of J. H. Hexter* (Philadelphia, 1980), pp. 25–56, repr. in id., *Studies in Tudor and Stuart Politics and Government*, 3 (Cambridge, 1983), pp. 183–215; R. W. Hoyle, 'Thomas Master's Narrative of the Pilgrimage of Grace', *Northern History*, 21 (1985), pp. 53–79; S. J. Gunn, 'Peers, Commons and Gentry in the Lincolnshire Revolt of 1536', *Past and Present*, 123 (1989), pp. 52–79; M. L. Bush, ' "Enhancements and Importunate Charges": An Analysis of the Tax Complaints of October 1536', *Albion*, 22 (1990), pp. 403–19; id., ' "Up for the Commonweal": The Significance of Tax Grievances in the English Rebellions of 1536', *EHR* 106 (1991), pp. 299–318.

pilgrimages. Generally, journeys to holy places undertaken from motives of devotion in order to obtain supernatural help or as acts of penance or thanksgiving. However, the word for a pilgrim (ξένος, πάροικος; *peregrinus*) meant a 'resident alien', and the notion that Christians were 'strangers and pilgrims on the earth' (Heb. 11: 13), whose true citizenship was in heaven (Phil. 3: 20; cf. Eph. 2: 19, Heb. 13: 14), is one firmly rooted in the NT and further developed in the Epistle to *Diognetus (5–6, esp. 5. 5) and in some early ascetic writers. In accordance with this ideal, pilgrimage could be seen essentially, not as a journey to a particular place, but as exile from one's native land voluntarily undertaken as a form of asceticism, in imitation esp. of *Abraham, who in obedience to God left his native land (Gen. 12: 1). Such an understanding of pilgrimage reached its full development among Irish monks in the 6th and following cents. in the

ascetic ideal of perpetual pilgrimage for the love of God which inspired men such as Sts *Columba, *Columbanus, and Fursey (d. c.650) to leave Ireland, so indirectly giving rise to extensive Irish influence upon W. Europe. From Carolingian times, however, monastic stability was emphasized and wandering monks discouraged, so gradually the practice lapsed, at least in the W. In the E. such pilgrimage continued and can be seen in the *stranichestvo* of 18th- and 19th-cent. Russia.

Meanwhile the idea of pilgrimage to special holy places had developed. The practice is common to most higher religions, e.g. Hinduism (Benares) and *Islam (Mecca) and is due to the natural desire of people to visit the places where their great heroes have lived and died and to the deep-seated conviction that certain localities are particularly favoured by the godhead. In Christianity the fact of the Incarnation is sufficient explanation of the early custom of visiting the places consecrated by the presence of Christ. The practice received a strong impulse from the conversion of *Constantine, followed by the visit of the Empress *Helena to *Jerusalem (326), and later in the 4th cent. from the example of St *Jerome. The 'Peregrinatio *Egeriae' (q.v.) is an illuminating account of one of these pilgrimages in the early Church. Almost on an equal footing with those to Palestine were pilgrimages to Rome, to the tomb of the Apostles, Sts *Peter and *Paul ('ad limina Apostolorum'), which came to be much frequented by Anglo-Saxon princes and nobles. To these the growing veneration of saints and images soon added many others, the most famous being Santiago de *Compostela. From the 8th cent. the practice of imposing a pilgrimage in the place of a public penance added to the number of pilgrims, so that throughout the Middle Ages they were organized on a grand scale and provided for by special ecclesiastical and civil legislation. Abuses which had already called forth the censure of St *Chrysostom and St Jerome increased with the popularity of the devotion and were satirized by *Erasmus in his 'Religious Pilgrimage'. The Reformation marked a notable setback, but the growth of popular piety in the period of the *Counter-Reformation led to a revival of the practice. In modern times *Lourdes has acquired an unrivalled fame as a place of pilgrimage, and in England the restoration of the shrines of the BVM at *Walsingham has once more attracted Anglican, RC, and Orthodox worshippers.

P. Geyer (ed.), *Itinera Hierosolymitana Saeculi iv–viii* (CSEL 39; 1898). Various texts also collected in *Itineraria et Alia Geographica* (CCSL 175–6; 1965). Convenient Eng. trs. by J. [D.] Wilkinson (ed.), *Jerusalem Pilgrims before the Crusades* (Warminster [1977]); id., with J. Hill and W. F. Ryan, *Jerusalem Pilgrimage 1099–1185* (Hakluyt Society, 2nd ser. 167; 1988). B. Kötting, *Peregrinatio Religiosa: Wallfahrten in der Antike und das Pilgerwesen in der alten Kirche* (1950). H. von Campenhausen, *Die asketische Heimatlosigkeit im altkirchlichen und frühmittelaltlichen Mönchtum* (Sammlung gemeinverständlicher Vorträge und Schriften aus der Gebiet der Theologie, 149; Tübingen, 1930; repr. in id., *Tradition und Leben* (Tübingen, 1960, pp. 290–317; Eng. tr., 1968, pp. 231–51). K. Hughes, 'The Changing Theory and Practice of Irish Pilgrimage', *JEH* 11 (1960), pp. 143–51. A. Angenendt, *Monachi Peregrini: Studien zu Pirmin und den monastischen Vorstellungen des frühen Mittelalters* (Münsterische Mittelalter-Schriften, 6; 1972). E. D. Hunt, *Holy Land Pilgrimage in the Later Roman Empire AD 312–460* (Oxford, 1982). P. Maraval, *Lieux saints et pèlerinage d'Orient: Histoire et géographie des origines à la conquête arabe* (1985). *Pellegrinaggi e Culto dei Santi in Europa fino alla 1ᵃ Crociata* (Convegni del Centro di Studi sulla Spiritualità medievale, 4; Todi, 1963); R. Oursel, *Les Pèlerins du moyen âge* (1963); L. Bonilla, *Los peregrinos: Sus origenes, ritus y religiones* (1965); A. Kendall, *Medieval Pilgrims* (1970); J. [P. C.] Sumption, *Pilgrimage: An Image of Mediaeval Religion* (1975). R. A. Fletcher, *Saint James's Catapult* (Oxford, 1984), pp. 78–101 (ch. 4: 'Pilgrimage and pilgrims, to Compostela and elsewhere'). L. de Sivry and M. Champagnac, *Dictionnaire géographique, historique, descriptif, archéologique des pèlerinages anciens et modernes, publié par l'Abbé *Migne* (2 vols., 1850–1). Bede Camm, OSB, *Forgotten Shrines: An Account of some old Catholic Halls and Families in England and of Relics and Memorials of the English Martyrs* (1910); id., *Pilgrim Paths in Latin Lands* (1923). L. Vázquez de Parga, J. M. Lacarra, and J. Uría Ríu, *Las peregrinaciones a Santiago de Compostela* (3 vols., 1948–9). V. and E. Turner, *Image and Pilgrimage in Christian Culture: Anthropological Perspectives* (Oxford, 1978). H. *Leclercq, OSB, in *DACL* 14 (pt. 1; 1939), cols. 65–176, s.v. 'Pèlerinages aux lieux saints', with bibl.; id. ibid., cols. 40–65, s.v. 'Pèlerinage à Rome'; S. M. Polan, M. C. McCarthy, and E. R. Labande in *NCE* 11 (1967), pp. 362–72, s.v.; A. Solignac, SJ, and others in *Dict. Sp.* 12 (pt. 1; 1984), cols. 888–940, s.v. 'Pèlerinages'.

Pilgrim's Progress, The. The First Part of the masterpiece of J. *Bunyan (q.v.), written either during his long imprisonment in Bedford gaol (1660–72) or during a second six months' imprisonment in 1676–7, was published in February 1678 (NS); a fresh edition, with many additions, appeared later in the same year; while the Second Part, depicting 'the manner of setting out of Christian's wife and children', did not appear until 1684. Attempts to identify an underlying medieval or Renaissance model have failed. Bunyan had but the most meagre historical knowledge and interests; and it is far more probable that the work owes everything to his own originality.

Its unrivalled place in the world's religious literature rests on its artless directness, its imaginative power, the homeliness and rusticity of its method and its plainness of style, which give it its universal appeal, even to the most simple-minded. The persons and incidents encountered by Christian on his journey from the 'City of Destruction' to the 'Heavenly City'—'Evangelist', 'Mr Worldly-Wiseman', 'Mr Legality' and his son 'Civility', Mr 'Talkative, the son of one Saywell, who dwelt in Prating Row', 'Mr Facing-both-ways', and 'Greatheart', and, of places, the 'Slough of Despond', the 'Hill Difficulty', the 'House Beautiful' (supposed to have been modelled on an actual house in Houghton Park), the 'Valley of the Shadow of Death', and 'Vanity Fair'—have become part and parcel of the language of religion in England.

The book, which circulated at first mainly in uneducated circles and whose supreme qualities were only gradually recognized, has appeared in a vast number of editions, and been translated into well over 100 languages. It has also been the subject of many adaptations (issued under similar titles), for the most part wholly without independent merit. The well-known hymn, 'He who would valiant be', is a modification of some lines sung by the pilgrims on the way to the 'Enchanted Ground'.

Good modern edn. by J. B. Wharey (Oxford, 1928; rev. by R. Sharrock, 1960), with full discussion of earlier edns. and bibl.; convenient edn., with introd. by N. H. Keeble (World's Classics, 1984). U. M. Kaufmann, *The Pilgrim's Progress and Tradition in Puritan Meditation* (Yale Studies in English, 163; 1966). V. Newey (ed.), *The Pilgrim's Progress: Critical and Historical Views*

(Liverpool English Texts and Studies, 1980). See also bibl. to BUNYAN, J.

Pilkington, James (*c.*1520–76), Bp. of *Durham. A native of Lancs, he went to St John's College, Cambridge, as an undergraduate; in 1539 he was elected a Fellow, and in 1559 became Master of it. In warm sympathy with the Reformation, he disputed at Cambridge, on 24 June 1549, against *transubstantiation. During the Marian Persecution he lived principally at Protestant centres on the Continent. Returning to England from Frankfurt after Mary's death in 1558, he now became a prominent member of the Protestant party in the C of E. He took an active part in the revision of the BCP and, as Master of St John's and Regius professor of divinity at Cambridge, upheld the tenets of Reformation theology in the university. Towards the end of 1560 he was appointed Bp. of Durham, thus becoming the first Protestant occupant of the see. His strong support of the Protestant cause in his diocese provoked much hostility and he and his family fled when the insurgents broke into Durham Cathedral during the Northern Rebellion of 1569. He upheld the temporal rights of his see with vigour, but failed as an administrator, allowing many of the buildings in his diocese to fall into decay. His writings include commentaries on *Haggai (*Aggeus*, 1560), *Obadiah (*Abdias*, pub. with a new edition of *Aggeus*, 1562), and *Nehemiah (1585, ed. posthumously by John Fox), as well as a treatise on 'The Burning of Paul's Church in London [4 June 1561] by Lightning'.

Works ed. J. Scholefield (*Parker Society, 1842), with biog. introd., pp. i–xvi. Episcopal Register ed. and calendared by G. Hinde (Surtees Society, 161, 1952, pp. 140–82). J. Pilkington, *The History of the Lancashire Family of Pilkington and its Branches from 1066 to 1600* (2nd edn., Liverpool, 1894), pp. 43–9, with portrait, and text of his will, pp. 94–7. C. W. Sutton in *DNB* 45 (1896), pp. 293–5.

Pillar Saint. See STYLITE.

Pin, L. E. Du. See DUPIN, L. E.

Pionius, St (d. 250), martyr. He was executed at Smyrna during the *Decian persecution, having been arrested while celebrating the anniversary of the martyrdom of St *Polycarp. The 'Acta Pionii', which describe his death, were known to *Eusebius, and are reliable documents. It was he who was responsible for the preservation of the 'Martyrium Polycarpi', but the attribution to him of the extant Life of St Polycarp is probably incorrect, though its authenticity has been defended (e.g. by C. J. Cadoux). Feast day in the E., 11 Mar.; in Latin martyrologies, 1 Feb.

Eusebius, *HE* 4. 15. 46 f. The Gk. 'Acta' (contemporary, but with slight 4th-cent. revision) discovered by O. von Gebhardt in 1896 in the Cod. Ven. Marc. 359. Text in id., *Acta Martyrum Selecta* (1902), pp. 96–114; repr., with Eng. tr., in H. Musurillo, *The Acts of the Christian Martyrs* (Oxford, 1972), pp. 137–67. J. den Boeft and J. Bremmer, 'Notiunculae Martyrologicae III. Some Observations on the Martyria of Polycarp and Pionius', *VC* 39 (1985), pp. 110–30, esp. pp. 113–30. Lat. text in *AASS*, Feb. 1 (1735), pp. 40–6. E. *Schwartz, *De Pionio et Polycarpo* (Göttingen, 1905); H. *Delehaye, SJ, *Les Passions des martyrs et les genres littéraires* (1921), pp. 28–59. H. Grégoire, P. Orgels, and J. Moreau, 'Les Martyres de Pionios et de Polycarpe', *Académie Royale de Belgique, Bulletin de la Classe des Lettres et des Sciences*

Morales et Politiques, 5th ser. 47 (1961), pp. 72–83. R. Lane Fox, *Pagans and Christians* (1986), pp. 460–92. L. Robert, *Le martyre de Pionios, prêtre de Smyrne*, posthumously ed. G. W. Bowersock and C. P. Jones (Washington, DC, 1994), incl. Greek text and Fr. tr. (pp. 21–45). C. J. Cadoux, *Ancient Smyrna* (1938), pp. 306–10 note. See also bibl. to POLYCARP, ST.

Pippin III. See PEPIN III.

Pirckheimer, Willibald (1470–1530), German humanist. Born at Eichstätt, he studied Greek at Padua (1489) and Law at Pavia (1492). In 1496 he became a town councillor at Nuremberg, where his house soon became a centre of learning. In 1499 he led the Nuremberg contingent in the Swiss War, of which he wrote a famous history, *Bellum Helveticum* (first pub. 1610). After his return he devoted himself to the translation of the Greek classics and Fathers into Latin, as well as to historical, astronomical, and artistic studies. He became a friend of A. *Dürer and a defender of J. *Reuchlin. At the beginning of the Reformation he favoured M. *Luther, whose chief opponent, J. *Eck, he attacked in the virulent pamphlet *Eccius Dedolatus*, now generally acknowledged to be his work. He regretted, however, Luther's break with the Church. In 1521, under the influence of his brilliant and devout sister, Charitas, abbess of the convent of *Poor Clares at Nuremberg, he asked to be absolved from the ban of excommunication which he had incurred as a follower of the Reformer. In his later years he completely abandoned Luther. His last work is an apology for the persecuted convent of his sister, entitled *Oratio Apologetica* (1529).

Collected edn. of Pirckheimer's works ed. M. Goldas (Frankfurt a.M., 1610). Modern edn. of *Eccius Dedolatus* by S. Szamatólski (Berlin, 1891); of his writings on the Swiss War (from the autograph in the Brit. Lib.) and his Autobiography by K. Rück (Munich, 1895). Correspondence ed. E. Reicke (vol. 1, Munich, 1940; vol. 2, ibid., 1956). Eng. tr. of *Eccius Dedolatus* by T. W. Best (Kentucky University Studies in the Germanic Languages and Literatures, 1; Lexington, Ky., 1971). Modern Life by E. Reicke ('Deutsche Volkheit', Jena, 1930). N. Holzberg, *Willibald Pirckheimer: Griechischer Humanismus in Deutschland* (Humanistische Bibliothek, Reihe 1, Band 41; 1981), with extensive bibl. P. Drews, *Willibald Pirckheimers Stellung zur Reformation* (1887). L. W. Spitz, *The Religious Renaissance of the German Humanists* (Cambridge, Mass., 1963), pp. 155–96. F. List in *PRE* (3rd edn.), 15 (1904), pp. 405–9; K. Löffler in *CE* 12 (1911), p. 109.

Pirminius, St (d. prob. 753), also 'Priminius', first Abbot of *Reichenau. His nationality is unknown but his monastic ideals seem to reflect a Frankish background, with strong Irish influences. He founded Reichenau (724) and other monasteries among the Alamanni in Baden and in Alsace, which became important centres of religious and cultural development. He is traditionally regarded as the author of the *Scarapsus* (called in one MS, *Dicta Pirminii*), a work of pastoral instruction which circulated widely in Carolingian times and which contains the earliest evidence for the present form of the *Apostles' Creed. Feast day, 3 Nov.

Life (9th cent.) and other material in *AASS*, Nov. 2 (pt. 1; 1894), pp. 2–56. G. Jecker, *Die Heimat des hl. Pirmin des Apostels der Alamannen* (Beiträge zur Geschichte des alten Mönchtums und des Benediktinerordens, 13; 1927), with text of 'Dicta', pp. 34–73. 'Dicta' also ed., with Ger. tr., by U. Engelmann, OSB,

Der heilige Pirmin und sein Missionsbuchlein (Constance [1959]; 2nd edn., with rev. introd. and slightly different title, Sigmaringen, 1976). A. Angenendt, *Monachi peregrini: Studien zu Pirmin und den monastischen Vortstellungen des frühen Mittelalters* (Münstersche Mittelalter-Schriften, 6; 1972). On his connections with the Apostles' Creed, see J. N. D. Kelly, *Early Christian Creeds* (1950; 3rd edn., 1972), esp. pp. 407–9. A. Angenendt in *DIP* 7 (1983), cols. 6–9, s.v.

Pirqe Aboth (Heb. פִּרְקֵי אָבוֹת, 'Sayings [lit. 'Sections'] of the Fathers'). A set of Jewish aphorisms assigned to some 60 different doctors ranging in date from the 3rd cent. BC to the 3rd cent. AD. Many are purely utilitarian, others are on a high moral level and constant stress is laid on the study of the *Torah. There are several points of contact with the sayings in the Gospels. The text is preserved as a tractate of the *Mishnah, and also in Jewish prayer books, where it is recommended for study on Sabbath afternoons in summer. An expanded form of the text is preserved in the so-called Aboth de Rabbi Nathan (one of the Minor Tractates of the Babylonian *Talmud), which exists in two versions (known as A and B).

Modern edns., with Eng. tr. and comm., by C. Taylor (Cambridge, 1877, 2nd edn., 2 vols., 1897–1900) and R. T. Herford (New York, 1925; 3rd edn., 1945). Eng. trs. also by R. T. Herford in R. H. *Charles, *The Apocrypha and Pseudepigrapha of the Old Testament*, 2 (Oxford, 1913), pp. 686–714, and in H. Danby, *The Mishnah* (ibid., 1933), pp. 446–61; also, with comm., by J. Neusner, *Torah from our Sages: Pirke Avot* (New York [1984]). Text of Aboth de Rabbi Nathan (both versions) ed. S. Schechter (Vienna, 1877); Eng. tr. of Version A by J. Goldin (Yale Judaica Series, 10; New Haven, Conn., and London, 1955); of Version B by A. J. Saldarini, SJ (Studies in Judaism in Late Antiquity, 11; Leiden, 1975).

Pisa, Council of. It was convoked by the cardinals in 1409 in order to end the *Great Schism which had divided W. Christendom since 1378. Though both Popes held rival councils, *Benedict XIII at Perpignan and Gregory XII at Cividale near *Aquileia, the assembly at Pisa was fairly representative, comprising besides a number of prelates the ambassadors of most European princes. After declaring itself canonically convoked and *oecumenical, the Council deposed both Popes as schismatics and heretics and elected Cardinal Peter Philargi, who took the name of *Alexander V, promised to work for the reform of the Church, and dissolved the Council.

The authority of the Council of Pisa has been much discussed. It is not normally recognized by the RC Church as oecumenical, partly on the ground of its not having been convoked by the Pope, but it was defended by J. *Gerson and P. *d'Ailly and later by the *Gallicans. Though it did not end the Schism, which, on the contrary, became worse than before by the existence of three Popes, it is generally admitted that it paved the way for the final solution found at the Council of *Constance (1417).

Hardouin, 8, cols. 1–204; Mansi, 26 (1784), cols. 1131–56, 27 (1784), cols. 1–502. Crit. edn. of the Acta by J. Vincke in *RQ* 46 (1941), pp. 81–331. Id., *Briefe zum Pisaner Konzil* (Beiträge zur Kirchen- und Rechtsgeschichte, 1; 1940); id., *Schriftstücke zum Pisaner Konzil: Ein Kampf um die öffentliche Meinung* (ibid. 3; 1942). Hefele and Leclercq, 7 (pt. 1; 1914), pp. 1–69. J. Lenfant, *Histoire du concile de Pise, et de ce qui s'est passé de mémorable depuis ce concile jusqu'au concile de Constance* (2 vols., Amsterdam, 1724). F. Bliemetzrieder, *Das Generalkonzil im grossen abendländischen*

Schisma (1904), esp. pp. 221–329. A. Landi, *Il Papa Deposto (Pisa 1409): L'idea conciliare nel Grande Scisma* (Turin [1985]). M. Harvey, 'England and the Council of Pisa: some new information', *Annuarium historiae conciliorum*, 2 (1970), pp. 263–83. J. Vincke in *L.Th.K.* (2nd edn.), 8 (1963), cols. 520 f., s.v.; L. E. Boyle, OP, in *NCE* 11 (1967), pp. 384 f., s.v. See also works cited under CONCILIAR THEORY.

piscina (Lat., 'basin'). A small bowl with a drain (*sacrarium*) connected with the earth, usually in a niche in the wall on the S. side of the altar; it is intended for the ablutions of the priest's hands and of the chalice and paten at Mass. The niche is often furnished with a shelf to hold the cruets. The piscina is of medieval origin; in a few English parish churches and in the crypt of *Gloucester Cathedral, piscinas date back to the Norman period. Sometimes two piscinas were set side by side, the one perhaps being reserved for the washing of the priest's hands, the other for the cleansing of the sacred vessels. They are often richly decorated.

Rohault, 3 (1883), pp. 140–4. F. Bond, *The Chancel of English Churches* (1916), pp. 143–63. I. McD. Jessiman, 'The Piscina in the English Medieval Church', *Journal of the British Archaeological Association*, 3rd ser. 20–1 (1958), pp. 53–71.

Pisgah (Vulg. 'Phasga'). The mountain or mountain-range to the E. of the river *Jordan where *Moses was granted a sight of the Holy Land at the end of his life and the promise made that his descendants would possess it (Deut. 34: 1–4). Scholarly opinion identifies Pisgah with Ras Siyagha, NW of Mount Nebo. This revelation to Moses is the source of such phrases as a 'Pisgah view', a 'Pisgah prospect', for any vision or hope of which a man will not himself see the realization.

Pistis Sophia. This curious work, a product of 3rd-cent. Egyptian Christianity, is contained in a solitary *Coptic MS in the British Library (Add. 5114), formerly the property of Dr Anthony Askew (d. 1774). It purports to record instruction given by Jesus to certain disciples at the end of a 12-year sojourn upon earth after the Resurrection. Among other things, it relates the salvation of the personi-fied 'Pistis Sophia' (i.e. 'Faith-Wisdom') from a demon named 'Self-Will'. The concluding chapters comprise a separate work of slightly earlier date. Both works appear to be translations from the Greek. Acc. to C. Schmidt, the MS dates from the later 4th cent.

Modern edn. of Coptic text by C. Schmidt (Copenhagen, 1925; repr., with Eng. tr., notes and bibl. by V. MacDermot, Nag Ham-madi Studies, 9; Leiden, 1978). Earlier Eng. tr. by G. Horner, with introd. by F. Legge (London, 1924). A. *Harnack, *Über das gnostische Buch* Pistis Sophia (TU 7, Heft 2, 1891, pp. 1–114). H.-C. Puech in Schneemelcher, 1 (5th edn., 1987), pp. 290–97; Eng. tr., 1 (1991), pp. 361–9. H. Leisegang in *PW* 20 (pt. 2; 1950), cols. 1813–21; P. Perkins in *Anchor Bible Dictionary*, 5 (1992), pp. 375 f., both s.v.

Pistoia, Synod of (1786). The synod met under the pres-idency of Scipione de' *Ricci, Bp. of Pistoia-Prato, to give support to the policy of Leopold I, Grand Duke of Tus-cany (1765–90), who was strongly in favour of a reform of the Church along the lines pursued by *Gallicanism in France and *Josephinism in Austria-Hungary. The synod adopted the Four *Gallican Articles of 1682, based the

authority of the Church upon the consent of the body as a whole, and that of bishops upon the assent of their clergy in synod, and held that the jurisdiction of a diocesan bishop is independent of the Pope. It exalted the civil power, and also decreed alterations in religious practice, requiring that there should be one altar only in each church, and one Mass only each Sunday; it also con-demned the use of Latin in services, and the cult of the *Sacred Heart. Not unnaturally the proposals aroused popular opposition as well as official displeasure. In 1791 Ricci resigned his see; but on the issue of the bull '*Auctorem Fidei', condemning 85 of the Pistoian articles, he recanted.

The acts of the synod were pub. in 1786 in Lat. and Ital. at Florence, and in Fr. at Pistoia; 2nd edn. of the Lat. and Ital., Florence, 1788, and of the Fr., Pistoia and Paris, 1789. Mansi (cont. by J. B. Martin and L. Petit, AA), 38 (Paris, 1907), cols. 989–1282. Much primary information in de' Ricci's *Memorie* and in his letters. M. Rosa, 'Italian Jansenism and the Synod of Pis-toia', *Concilium*, pt. 7 (Sept. 1966), pp. 19–26, with refs. C. Lamioni (ed.), *Il Sinodo di Pistoia del 1786: Atti del Convegno internazionale per il secondo centenario Pistoia-Prato, 25–27 settem-bre 1986* (Rome, 1991). In Eng., C. A. Bolton, *Church Reform in 18th Century Italy (The Synod of Pistoia, 1786)* (Archives Interna-tionales d'Histoire des Idées, 29; The Hague, 1969), esp. pp. 55–114. J. Carreyre in *DTC* 12 (pt. 2; 1935), cols. 2134–230, s.v. 'Pistoie (Synode de)', with bibl.; B. Matteucci in *NCE* 11 (1967), pp. 388–90, s.v. See also bibl. to RICCI, S. DE' and AUCTOREM FIDEI; also works on PIUS VI.

Pithou, Pierre (1539–96), *Gallican theologian. He came of a family of distinguished jurists. Brought up a Calvinist and called to the bar at Paris in 1560, he was converted to Catholicism in 1573. Later he received legal appointments from *Henry IV, whom he supported in his struggles with the League. Besides important political writings, which include his *Satire ménippée* (1593) and editions of several texts of the classics, he prepared for publication (in con-junction with his brother François) a text of the *Corpus Iuris Canonici* (issued in 1687). In his treatise, *Les Libertés de l'Église gallicane* (1594), the leading principles of Gal-licanism were formulated for the first time. His extensive collection of MSS, some of them of great value for the text of the early conciliar canons, is now in the Bibliothèque Nationale at Paris.

Collected edn. of Pithou's *Opera Sacra, Iuridica, Historica, Mis-cellanea*, Paris, 1609, with Life by I. Mercerus, dated 1597, pp. 819–27. [P. J.] Grosley, *Vie de Pierre Pithou; avec quelques mé-moires sur son père, et sur ses frères* (2 vols., 1756), vol. 1, and vol. 2, pp. 1–105. L. de Rosanbo, 'Pierre Pithou', *Revue du Seizième Siècle*, 15 (1928), pp. 279–305; id., 'Pierre Pithou érudit', ibid. 16 (1929), pp. 301–30. G. Goyau in *CE* 12 (1911), pp. 118 f., s.v.; J. Carreyre in *DTC* 12 (pt. 2; 1935), cols. 2235–8, s.v.

Pitra, Jean-Baptiste François (1812–89), *patristic scholar. He was ordained priest in 1836, and his reputation as an archaeologist was soon established by his decipherment (1839) of the 'Inscription of Autun', a (probably 3rd-cent.) grave-inscription. In 1843 he was professed as a Benedictine at *Solesmes, and for a short time he gave valuable co-operation to J. P. *Migne in the editing of his *Patrologiae*. He then travelled widely in search of MSS, in 1858 at the behest of *Pius IX visiting several Russian libraries. His knowledge of many branches of patristic and Byzantine literature was unrivalled.

Having been created cardinal in 1863, in 1869 he was appointed Librarian of the *Vatican, in which capacity *Leo XIII employed him to catalogue the Palatine Greek codices in the library. His publications include *Spicilegium Solesmense* (4 vols., 1852–8) and *Analecta Sacra* (8 vols., 1876–91), both containing many previously unpublished patristic texts, and an important collection of canonical material, *Iuris Ecclesiastici Graecorum Historia et Monumenta* (2 vols., 1864–8).

Lives by F. *Cabrol, OSB (Paris, 1893), and A. Battandier (ibid., 1896). There is also a short biog. introd. by A. Battandier prefixed to the posthumously pub. vol. 6 of the *Analecta Sacra* (Paris and Rome, 1891), pp. viii–xix. List of his works in F. Cabrol, OSB (ed.), *Bibliographie des Bénédictins de la Congrégation de France* (Solesmes, 1889), pp. 37–52 and 197. J.-P. Laurant, *Symbolisme et Écriture: Le Cardinal Pitra et la 'Clef' de Méliton de Sardis* (1988). M. Ott in *CE* 12 (1911), pp. 119 f.; P. Séjourné, OSB, in *DTC* 12 (pt. 2; 1935), cols. 2238–45, s.v.

Pius I, St (d. *c*.154), Bp. of *Rome from *c*.140. Acc. to the *Liber Pontificalis* he was a native of *Aquileia and acc. to the *Muratorian Canon he was the brother of *Hermas, the author of the 'Shepherd', but nothing certain is known of his pontificate. The tradition that he was a martyr has no early authority. Feast day, 11 July, suppressed in 1969.

LP (Duchesne), 1, pp. 132 f. J. Barmby in *DCB* 4 (1887), pp. 416 f., s.v.; É. Amann in *DTC* 12 (pt. 2; 1935), cols. 1612 f., s.v. 'Pie Iᵉʳ'.

Pius II (Aeneas Sylvius) (1405–64), Pope from 1458. Enea Silvio de' Piccolomini, born of a poor noble family at Corsignano (near Siena), studied at Siena and Florence, where he became one of the greatest representatives of the humanism of his age. In 1432 he went to the Council of *Basle as secretary of Cardinal D. Capranica, and later served several other prelates in the same capacity; and in 1435 he was sent on a secret mission to *Scotland by Cardinal N. Albergati. On his return to Basle in the following year his personal influence on the Council began to increase; he supported the adversaries of Pope *Eugenius IV and worked for the antipope, Felix V, who made him his secretary in 1439 after Enea had refused to take orders on account of his dissolute life. In the service of Felix he became an eloquent advocate of the *Conciliar Theory set forth in his *Libellus Dialogorum de Concilii Auctoritate* (1440). Crowned Imperial poet by the Emp. Frederick III in 1442, he became his secretary in the same year. In 1444 he wrote his much-admired love story, *Euryalus and Lucretia*. In 1445 he left the party of the antipope, was absolved of excommunication, and reconciled to Eugenius IV, to whom he now rendered valuable services by winning over the Emperor to his side and breaking up the Electors' League. At the same time he reformed his moral life and, in 1446, received holy orders. Appointed Bp. of Trieste by *Nicolas V in 1447, he was translated to Siena in 1450. From the fall of *Constantinople in 1453 he began to work enthusiastically for a *Crusade. In 1456 he was created cardinal by *Callistus III, whom, after a fierce conflict in the *conclave, he succeeded in 1458.

Pius II now subordinated all other interests to the war against the Turks, who became a daily increasing menace to Europe. When the Congress of Mantua (1459–60) had revealed the selfishness and lack of solidarity of the Euro-

pean princes, the Pope took the initiative in proclaiming a three-year Crusade. At the end of the Congress he promulgated the bull 'Execrabilis' (18 Jan. 1460), in which he condemned the practice of appealing to a General Council. He won a victory for these doctrines in Louis XI's repeal of the *Pragmatic Sanction of Bourges in 1461, but Bohemia under Podiebrad and a great number of German princes were in more or less open revolt against Pius, invoking his own former views in their support. This led him to publish his bull, 'In minoribus agentes' (26 Apr. 1463), in which occur the famous words 'Aeneam rejicite, Pium suscipite', retracting his earlier political doctrines. As he could not expect more than a strictly limited support from the European powers, Pius resolved, in 1463, to put himself at the head of the Crusaders, but he died at Ancona soon afterwards. His character and motives have been variously judged; but he was at least one of the best Popes of his age.

Opera, pub. Basle, 1551; *Orationes Politicae et Ecclesiasticae*, ed. G. D. *Mansi (3 pts. in 2 vols., Lucca, 1755–9); *Epistolae*, ed. R. Wolkan (Fontes Rerum Austriacarum, 61, 62, 67, and 68; 1909–18). 'Aeneae Silvii Piccolomini Senensis qui postea fuit Pius II Pont. Max. Opera Inedita descripsit ex codicibus Chisianis vulgavit notisque illustravit J. Cugnoni', *Atti della R. Accademia dei Lincei*, ser. 3, Memorie della Classe di Scienze morali, storiche e filologiche, 8 (1883), pp. 319–686. Selection of his writings ed. B. Widmer (Basle and Stuttgart, 1960). The standard (though incomplete) edn. of his Comm. on the memorable events of his times ist that pub. at Frankfurt, 1614; Eng. tr. by F. A. Gragg, with introd. and notes by L. C. Gabel (Smith College Studies in History, 22, nos. 1–2, 25, nos. 1–4, 30, 35, 43; Northampton, Mass., 1937–57). Abridged version ed. L. C. Gabel, *Memoirs of a Renaissance Pope* (London, 1960). Modern edns. of Lives by Giovanni Antonio Campano and B. *Platina ed. G. C. Zimolo (Raccolta degli Storici Italiani, nuova edizione, Tomo 3, Parte 2; Bologna, 1964) and by A. van Heck (ST 341; 1991); also, with Eng. tr., of his *De Gestis Concilii Basiliensis Commentariorum Libri II* by D. Hay and W. K. Smith (Oxford, 1967). G. Voigt, *Enea Silvio de Piccolomini, als Papst Pius der Zweite und sein Zeitalter* (3 vols., 1856–63). C. M. Ady, *Pius II . . .: The Humanist Pope* (1913). T. Buyken, *Enea Silvio Piccolomini: Sein Leben und Wirken bis zum Episkopat* (1931). G. Paparelli, *Enea Silvio Piccolomini: Pio II* (1950; 2nd edn. [1978]). R. J. Mitchell, *The Laurels and the Tiara: Pope Pius II 1458–1464* (1962). B. Widmer, *Enea Silvio Piccolomini in der sittlichen und politischen Entscheidung* (Basler Beiträge zur Geschichtswissenschaft, 88; 1963). D. Maffei (ed.), *Enea Silvio Piccolomini Papa Pio II: Atti del Convegno per il quinto centenario della morte e altri scritti* (Siena, 1968). G. Bernetti, *Saggi e Studi sugli Scritti di Enea Silvio Piccolomini Papa Pio II* (Florence, 1971). C. Ugurgieri della Berardenga, *Pio II Piccolomini con notizie su Pio III* (Biblioteca dell'Archivio Storico Italiano, 18; 1973), pp. 31–498. L. Totaro, *Pio II nei suoi Commentarii* (Bologna [1978]). M. Harvey, *England, Rome and the Papacy 1417–1464* (Manchester [1993]), esp. pp. 193–211. Pastor, 3 (1894), with full bibl. to date. Fliche and Martin, 15 (1951), esp. pp. 46–65, with bibl. E. Vansteenberghe in *DTC* 12 (pt. 2; 1935), cols. 1613–32, s.v. 'Pie II', with bibl.; G. B. Picotti in *EC* 9 (1952), cols. 1492–6, s.v. 'Pio II', with bibl.

Pius IV (1499–1565), Pope from 1559. Gian Angelo Medici, son of a Milanese family, after studying medicine and law at Pavia, came to Rome in 1527 where he held several offices at the Curia. Having been made Abp. of Ragusa in 1545, he was created cardinal by *Paul III in 1549, and under Julius III (1550–5) was Papal legate in Romagna. Elected Pope in 1559, he reversed the anti-

Imperial policy of his predecessor, *Paul IV, whose relatives he brought to trial. If he could be charged with nepotism this at least had beneficial results for the Church in the cardinalate of his nephew, St *Charles Borromeo. Probably his greatest achievement was the reassembling and successful conclusion of the Council of *Trent (1562–3), whose decrees he began to put into execution during the last two years of his reign. He published a new *Index in 1564, prepared the '*Roman Catechism', imposed the 'Professio Fidei Tridentina' on all holders of an ecclesiastical office, and reformed the *Sacred College. At the instance of the Emperor he conceded the chalice to the laity of Germany, Austria, Hungary, and several other countries (1564), to check the spread of Protestantism, a measure abolished by his successors. An unsuccessful attempt on his life was made in the last year of his pontificate, owing to the dissatisfaction of the heavily taxed subjects of the States of the Church. His artistic commissions contributed to the strains on the Papal finances.

Bullarum, Diplomatum et Privilegiorum S.R. Pontificum Taurinensis editio, 6 (Naples, 1860), pp. 489–566, and 7 (ibid., 1882), pp. 1–422. Docs. also in J. Šusta (ed.), *Die römische Kurie und das Conzil von Trient unter Pius IV* (4 vols., Vienna, 1904–14). P. Herre, *Papsttum und Papstwahl im Zeitalter Philipps II.* (Leipzig, 1907), pp. 33–102. G. Constant, *Concession à l'Allemagne de la communion sous les deux espèces: Étude sur les débuts de la réforme catholique en Allemagne, 1548–1621* (Bibliothèque des Écoles Françaises d'Athènes et de Rome, 128; 2 vols., 1923). J. Birkner, 'Das Konzil von Trient und die Reform des Kardinalkollegiums unter Pius IV', *Hist. J.* 52 (1932), pp. 340–55. G. Smith, *The Casino of Pius IV* (Princeton, NJ, 1977). Pastor, 15 and 16 (1928), with bibl.; Fliche and Martin, 17 (1948), pp. 148–222. G. Constant in *DTC* 12 (pt. 2; 1935), cols. 1633–47, s.v. 'Pie IV', with bibl.; H. Jedin in *EC* 9 (1952), cols. 1496–8, s.v. 'Pio IV', with bibl. See also bibl. to TRENT, COUNCIL OF.

Pius V, St (1504–72), Pope from 1566. Michele Ghislieri entered the *Dominican Order at the age of 14, was ordained priest in 1528, and subsequently lectured in philosophy and theology and held the offices of novice master and prior in his order. Conspicuous for his zeal and austerity of life, he was made Commissary General of the *Inquisition in 1551 by Cardinal G. P. Carafa who, having become Pope under the name of *Paul IV, appointed him Bp. of Nepi and Sutri in 1556 and created him cardinal in the following year, at the same time making him 'Inquisitor General of Christendom'. He opposed vigorously the nepotism of Paul's successor, *Pius IV (1559–1565), on whose death he was unanimously elected Pope (1566). Throughout his short but important pontificate he worked zealously for the reform of the Church. Continuing to observe the ascetical practices of the religious life—the Papal custom of wearing a white cassock is said to derive from the colour of his Dominican habit—he transformed his household into a model of regularity. In this task he was generously assisted by St *Charles Borromeo. He compelled bishops and clergy to accept the recommendations of the Council of *Trent, had the *Roman Catechism completed (1566) and translated into several languages, reformed the *Breviary (1568) and the *Missal (1570), and ordered a new complete edition of the works of St *Thomas Aquinas (1570), whom he had declared '*Doctor of the Church' in 1567. In his struggle against the spread of the Reformation he made successful use of the Inqui-

sition in Italy, but his excommunication of Queen *Elizabeth I in 1570 is generally considered a mistake, as it seriously aggravated the position of RCs in England. Politically his reign was marked by the decisive victory over the Turks of the combined Papal, Spanish, and Venetian fleets at *Lepanto in 1571. He was canonized in 1712. Feast day, 30 Apr. (formerly 5 May).

Bullarum, Diplomatum et Privilegiorum S.R. Pontificum Taurinensis editio, 7 (Naples, 1882), pp. 422–973. Epp. ed. F. Goubau (Antwerp, 1640); later collections of his Epp. ed. [J. L. A.] de Potter (Brussels, 1827), W. E. Schwartz (Paderborn, 1889), and L. Serrano, OSB (4 vols., Madrid, 1914). The oldest Life, anon. but almost certainly by Tommaso Porcacchi (d. 1585), ed., with other docs., by F. Van Ortroy in *Anal. Boll.* 33 (1914), pp. 187–215. Other early Lives by G. Catena (Rome, 1586), A. de Fuenmayor (Madrid, 1595; ed. L. Riber, ibid., 1953), and J. A. Gabutius (Rome, 1605; repr. in *AASS*, Mai. 1 (1680), pp. 617–714). Modern Lives by [A. F. P.] de Fallow (2 vols., Paris, 1844), G. Grente ('Les Saints', 1914), and L. Browne-Olf (Milwaukee, 1943). P. Herre, *Papsttum und Papstwahl im Zeitalter Philipps II.* (Leipzig, 1907), pp. 103–91. O. Braunsberger, SJ, *Pius V und die deutschen Katholiken* (Stimmen aus Maria-Laach, Ergänzungsheft, 108; 1912); C. Hirschauer, *La Politique de St Pie V en France, 1566–1572* (Bibliothèque des Écoles Françaises d'Athènes et de Rome, 120; 1922). Pastor, 17 and 18 (1929), with full bibl. and notes on sources. R. Hedde, OP, and É. Amann in *DTC* 12 (pt. 2; 1935), cols. 1647–53, s.v. 'Pie V'; H. Jedin in *EC* 9 (1952), cols. 1498–1500, s.v. 'Pio V'; A. Iszak, OP, and A. Silli, OP, in *Bibliotheca Sanctorum*, 10 (1968), cols. 883–901, s.v. 'Pio V', all with bibl.

Pius VI (1717–99), Pope from 1775. Giovanni Angelico Braschi, of a noble family of Cesena, was educated by the *Jesuits and, after having studied law, became secretary to Cardinal Raffo in 1740. Appointed Papal secretary and Canon of *St Peter's in 1755, he was ordained priest three years later. In 1766 *Clement XIII made him treasurer of the Roman Church, and his successor, *Clement XIV, created him cardinal in 1773. Elected Pope in 1775, his rule was marked by the struggle against the rising tide of atheism and secularism. Local Roman affairs, such as the draining of the Pontine marshes, the reorganization of the finances of the States of the Church, and the embellishment of the Vatican Museum and St Peter's, at first claimed his attention. Before long he became involved in a struggle against '*Febronianism' (q.v.); and though J. N. von *Hontheim made his submission in 1778, his ideas led to practical results in the ecclesiastical reforms of Joseph II (see JOSEPHINISM), who forbade the Austrian bishops to apply for dispensations to Rome and secularized a great number of monasteries. A visit of Pius to Vienna, in 1782, remained without result; Joseph's example was followed by his brother, Leopold, Grand Duke of Tuscany; and Febronianist doctrines were adopted in 1786 at the Synod of *Pistoia under the leadership of Bp. Scipione de' *Ricci. In 1794 Pius formally condemned Febronian teaching in the bull '*Auctorem fidei' (q.v.). Meanwhile, under pressure from Catherine II, Pius, who had already granted Frederick II an exemption from the decree of suppression for individual Jesuits in Silesia, permitted the continuation of the Jesuits in *Russia (1783–4). In 1791, after Louis XVI had sanctioned the *Civil Constitution of the Clergy, a decree subjecting the French clergy to the secular authorities (1790), Pius condemned it as schismatical and heretical and suspended all priests and prelates who had taken the civil oath. In the same year France annexed the Papal territories of *Avignon and the Venaissin. The strained relations between the two powers led to the occupation of the States of the Church by Napoleon, and the occupation was terminated only by the Peace of Tolentino (1797), which required the surrender of Ferrara, Bologna, and the Romagna, and, in addition, many valuable MSS and works of art. In the same year the French general, Duphot, was killed in an attempt to stir up revolution in Rome, whereupon Berthier occupied the city in the following year and declared it a republic. Pius VI was taken prisoner and, in spite of his age and infirmity, removed first to Siena and Florence, then (1799) to Bologna, and thence through several other places across the Alps to Briançon, Grenoble, and Valence, where he died. In his troubled reign Papal prestige was at its lowest before its regeneration in the 19th century.

Bullarii Romani Continuatio, coll. A. A. Barbèri, 5–10 (Rome, 1842–5). *Collectio Brevium atque Instructionum SS.D.N. Pii Papae VI quae ad Praesentes Gallicanarum Ecclesiarum Calamitates pertinent* (2 pts., Augsburg, 1796). [J. F. de Bourgoing], *Mémoires historiques et philosophiques sur Pie VI et son pontificat* (2 vols. [1799]; 2nd edn. [1800]; Eng. tr., 1799). P. P. Wolf, *Geschichte der römischkatholischen Kirche unter der Regierung Pius des Sechsten* (7 vols., 1793–1802). G. B. Tavanti, *Fasti del S.P. Pio VI* (3 vols., 1804). I. Bertrand, *Le Pontificat de Pie VI et l'athéisme révolutionnaire* (2 vols., 1879). J. M. Gendry, *Pius VI* (2 vols. [1906]). G. Soranzo, *Peregrinus Apostolicus: Lo spirito pubblico e il viaggio di Pio VI a Vienna* (Pubblicazioni della Università Cattolica del Sacro Cuore, 5th ser. 14; 1937). A. Latreille, *L'Église catholique et la Révolution française*, 1, *Le pontificat de Pie VI et la crise française, 1775–1799* (1946). E. E. Y. Hales, *Revolution and Papacy 1769–1846* (1960), pp. 45–129. Pastor, 39–40 (1952–3), with full refs. Fliche and Martin, 20 (1949), pp. 17–158. G. Bourgin in *DTC* 12 (pt. 2; 1935), cols. 1653–69, s.v. 'Pie VI', with bibl.; A. Latreille in *NCE* 11 (1967), pp. 398–400, s.v.

Pius VII (1742–1823), Pope from 1800. Luigi Barnaba Chiaramonti entered the *Benedictine Order in 1756, making his profession in 1758 and taking the name of Gregorio. In 1775 *Pius VI appointed him abbot of San Callisto at Rome and, in 1782, Bp. of Tivoli. Three years later he was translated to Imola and created cardinal, and in 1800 elected Pope at Venice. The main problem confronting him concerned the relations between Church and State in France. By the *Concordat of 1801 (q.v.), negotiated between Napoleon and Cardinal *Consalvi, religion had been restored in France; but the success of the plan was vitiated by the secretly drawn-up *Organic Articles (q.v.), published simultaneously, against the Gallican tendencies of which the Pope protested in vain. A concordat with the Italian republic followed in 1803; and at the same time the Church in Germany was seriously threatened by extensive secularizations. In 1804 Napoleon was proclaimed Emperor and the Pope accepted his invitation to consecrate him in Paris, but did not obtain the hoped-for concessions. In 1805 Napoleon occupied Ancona, despite the protests of the Pope, who had to dismiss Consalvi in the following year. When, in 1808, a French army entered Rome, Pius VII considered himself a prisoner and refused negotiations, and in 1809 the States of the Church were incorporated into the French Empire. When Pius in protest excommunicated the responsible parties by the bull 'Quum memoranda', he was arrested

and deported to Grenoble and thence to Savona. In 1811, separated from all his advisers, he assented to a new mode of the institution of bishops by the metropolitans without cognizance of the Pope, which had been propounded by the Council of Paris convoked by Napoleon in the same year. In 1812 he was brought to Fontainebleau, where, after a long illness and under pressure, he made far-reaching concessions to the Emperor, published by the latter in 1813 as the 'Concordat of Fontainebleau' and revoked by the Pope two months later. After the fall of Napoleon, Pius VII returned to Rome in 1814 and, in the same year, re-established the *Jesuits. The Congress of Vienna (1815) restored the States of the Church, which were reorganized by Consalvi. New concordats were concluded with Bavaria and Sardinia in 1817, with Naples and Russia in 1818, and with Prussia in 1821. In 1821 the Pope also published a bull against the *Carbonari, who were responsible for the revolution in Naples. Despite his political preoccupations, Pius VII favoured art and science; he made valuable additions to the *Vatican Library and established new chairs in the Roman College. His reign marks a transition between the troubles of the French Revolution and the quiet pontificates that were to follow.

Bullarii Romani Continuatio, coll. A. A. Barbèri, 11–15 (Rome, 1846–53). [A. F.] Artaud [de Montor], *Histoire du Pape Pie VII* (2 vols., 1836). M. H. Allies, *The Life of Pope Pius VII* ('Quarterly Series', 17; 1875). J. Leflon, *Pie VII: Des abbayes bénédictines à la papauté* [1958]. [J. O. B. de C.] d'Haussonville, *L'Église romaine et le premier empire, 1800–1814* (5 vols., 1868–9). A. Latreille, *L'Église catholique et la Révolution française*, 2, *L'Ère napoléonienne et la crise européenne, 1800–1815* (1950). E. E. Y. Hales, *Revolution and Papacy 1769–1846* (1960), pp. 130–312, *passim*; id., *Napoleon and the Pope: The Story of Napoleon and Pius VII* (1962). L. Pasztor, 'Per la storia del "Concordato" di Fontainebleau', in R. Aubert and others (eds.), *Chiesa e Stato nell'ottocento: Miscellanea in onore di Pietro Pirri*, 2 (Padua, 1962), pp. 597–603. M. Chappin, SJ, *Pie VII et les Pays-Bas: Tensions religieuses et tolérance civile 1814–1817* (Miscellanea Historiae Pontificiae, 49; Rome, 1984). Fliche and Martin, 20 (1949), pp. 161–376, with bibl. pp. 9 f. G. Bourgin in *DTC* 12 (pt. 2; 1935), cols. 1670–83, s.v. 'Pie VII', with bibl.; J. Leflon in *NCE* 11 (1967), pp. 400–4.

Pius IX (1792–1878), Pope from 1846. Giovanni Maria Mastai-Ferretti was ordained priest in 1819, took part in a Papal mission to Chile in 1823–5, was appointed Abp. of Spoleto in 1827, Bp. of Imola in 1832, and created cardinal in 1840. On the death of *Gregory XVI (1846), who had estranged the Italian people by his oppressive measures, he was elected Pope because of his reputation as a partisan of liberal ideas. He inaugurated his reign with a general amnesty of political prisoners and exiles and showed himself favourable to the movement of national unity; but his concessions came too late, and when, in 1848, he refused to make war on Austria, he lost popular favour and, in November of the same year, was besieged by the revolutionaries in the Quirinal. He escaped to Gaeta, whence he addressed an appeal to the Catholic European powers for the restoration of the Papal State; this was effected after the occupation of Rome by the French army in 1849. From his return to Rome in 1850, Pius abandoned his liberal attitude in politics. He saw his temporal power gradually decrease, as the Romagna was lost in 1859 and Umbria and the Marches in 1860, until, after the seizure of Rome by Victor Emmanuel on 20 Sept. 1870, he was virtually deprived of all temporal sovereignty by the Law of *Guarantees of 13 May 1871, against which the Pope solemnly protested.

Though an apparent failure from a political point of view, the pontificate of Pius IX was marked by its spiritual and ecclesiastical achievements. The erection of many new dioceses and missionary centres, as well as the restoration of the hierarchy in England (1850) and the Netherlands (1853) and the conclusion of *concordats with many European and American governments, testified to a vigorous life within the Church. His definition of the *Immaculate Conception of the BVM in 1854 provided a stimulus to Catholic devotion, while the issue of the *Syllabus Errorum and the encyclical *Quanta Cura in 1864 supported the traditional beliefs of Catholicism by condemning contemporary rationalism, pantheism, religious liberalism, and other forms of modern philosophy. His reign was marked by a tendency to centralize doctrinal and ecclesiastical authority in the Papacy. The most important event was the definition of Papal infallibility by the First *Vatican Council of 1869–70; though this gave rise to the *Old Catholic schism and the *Kulturkampf in Germany, it may be argued that the increased authority it added to the Papacy on the spiritual plane in the end more than compensated for the loss in temporal dominion that marked Pius IX's pontificate. He was the first Pope whose reign exceeded the 25 years traditionally ascribed to the rule of St Peter.

His *Acta* were pub., 7 vols., Rome [*c.*1854–78]; the official docs. for the latter part of his pontificate are also in *ASS*. G. Maioli (ed.), *Pio IX: Da vescovo a pontefice. Lettere al Card. Luigi Amat, agosto 1839–luglio 1848* (Collezione storica del Risorgimento, 2nd ser. 38; 1949). The numerous Lives incl. those by A. de Saint-Albin (Paris, 1860; 2nd edn., 1870; new edn., with continuation, 3 vols., 1878), J. M. Stepischnegg (2 vols., Vienna, 1879), F. Hayward (Paris, 1948), E. E. Y. Hales (London, 1954), A. Serafini (vol. 1 [covering 1792–1846] only pub., Vatican, 1958; based on unpub. sources), P. Fernessole (2 vols., Paris, 1960–3), G. Martina, SJ (Miscellanea Historiae Pontificiae, 38, 51, and 58; Rome, 1974–90), and A. Polverari (Studi Piani, 4–6; Vatican, 1986–88; see other vols. in this series connected with the cause for his beatification). R. Aubert, *Le Pontificat de Pie IX, 1846–1878* (Fliche and Martin, 21; 1952), C. Falconi, *Il Giovane Mastai: Il Futuro Pio IX dall'Infanzia a Senigallia alla Roma della Restaurazione 1792–1827* (Milan, 1981). A. M. Ghisalberti, *Nuove ricerche sugli inizi del pontificato di Pio IX e sulla consulta di stato* (Regio Istituto per la Storia del Risorgimento italiano, Biblioteca Scientifica, 2nd ser. 30; 1939). P. Pirri, SJ, *Pio IX e Vittorio Emanuele II dal loro carteggio privato* (Miscellanea Historiae Pontificiae, 8, 16, 17, 24, 25; 1944–61). D. Demarco, *Pio IX e la rivoluzione romana del 1848* (Collezione storica del Risorgimento italiano, 2nd ser. 36; 1947). A. B. Hasler, *Pius IX. (1846–1878), Päpstliche Unfehlbarkeit und I. Vatikanisches Konzil* (2 vols., Stuttgart, 1977); id., *Wie der Papst unfehlbar wurde* (Munich, 1979; Eng. tr., Garden City, NY, 1981). [W.] O. Chadwick, *A History of the Popes 1830–1914* (Oxford, 1998), esp. pp. 61–272. R. Aubert in *NCE* 11 (1967), pp. 405–8, s.v.

Pius X, St

Pius X, St (1835–1914), Pope from 1903. Giuseppe Melchior Sarto, born of a poor family at Riese in Upper Venetia, entered the seminary at Padua in 1850, was ordained priest in 1858, became chaplain at Tombolo in the same year, and, in 1867, archpriest of Salzano. In 1875 he was made canon of Treviso, where he was also chancellor to the bishop and spiritual director of the episcopal seminary, and, in 1884, he was appointed Bp. of Mantua. In 1893 *Leo XIII created him cardinal and Patr. of *Venice. Elected Pope in 1903, he chose as his guiding principle 'instaurare omnia in Christo' (Eph. 1: 10, quoted in his encyclical of 4 Oct. 1903), with the implication that, in contrast to his predecessor Leo XIII, he intended to be a religious rather than a political Pope. Events, however, frequently forced him into political action. When, in 1905, the French government effected the separation of Church and State and proposed the formation of the 'associations cultuelles', which were to take possession of the remaining Church property and to be responsible to the civil authorities, Pius X condemned them in two encyclicals (1906), a brave step which, at the price of material ruin, secured the independence of the Church in France from State interference. In 1911 *Portugal followed the example of the French government.

In the field of social policy, Pius X laid down the principles of '*Catholic Action' in his encyclical 'Il fermo proposito' (1905). Social action and the solution of the labour problem were only parts, though important parts, of the whole of Catholic Action, while its chief aim was to restore Christ to His rightful place within the home, the schools, and society in general. In 1910 he condemned the 'Sillon', a French social movement which seemed to be attempting to spread and adapt the ideas of the French Revolution. He saw another grave danger, threatening the purity of Catholic doctrine itself, in the spread of *Modernism, which he condemned in the decree '*Lamentabili' and the encyclical 'Pascendi' of 1907, and again by a *motu proprio* ('Sacrorum antistitum') three years later which introduced the anti-Modernist oath, and as an antidote to the new errors particularly recommended the study of *Thomism.

In addition to these protective measures, Pius X undertook a series of difficult reforms. Among them were the codification of the new *canon law (promulgated under *Benedict XV in 1917), which occupied almost the whole of his reign, and administrative changes which involved esp. the *Roman Congregations. His interest in liturgical matters showed itself in the Breviary Reform and in his decrees on sacred music, notably the *motu proprio* of 1903 restoring the Gregorian chant to its traditional place in the Liturgy. Pius X became particularly popular as the 'Pope of frequent Communion', and by recommending daily Communion in the decree of 1905 and children's Communion a year later, he gave a lasting stimulus to the spiritual life of the faithful and laid the foundations of the modern *Liturgical Movement. He was venerated as a saint even during his lifetime, and many miracles have been attributed to his intercession. He was beatified in 1951 and canonized in 1954. Feast day, 21 Aug.

Acta pub. Rome, 5 vols., 1905–14. Letters, collected by N. Vian (Rome [1955]). Lives by F. A. Forbes (London, 1918), R. Bazin (Paris [1928]; Eng. tr., 1928), K. Burton (Dublin, 1951), C. Ledré (Paris, 1952), P. Fernessole (2 vols., ibid. [1952–3]), and C. Maurras (ibid. [1953]). An Eng. tr. of Card. R. *Merry del Val's *Memories of Pope Pius X* was pub. London, 1939. P. Zovatto, *Ricerche su S. Pio X* (Pubblicazioni della Facoltà di Magistero dell'Università di Trieste, 3rd ser. 20; 1988). [W.] O. Chadwick, *A History of the Popes 1830–1914* (Oxford, 1998), esp. pp. 332–405. É. Amann in *DTC* 12 (pt. 2; 1935), cols. 1716–40, s.v. 'Pie X', with refs.; A. Niero in *Dict. Sp.* 12 (pt. 2; 1986), cols. 1429–32, s.v. 'Pie X'.

Pius XI (1857–1939), Pope from 1922. Achille Ambrogio Damiano Ratti was ordained priest in 1879, taught dogmatics at the Grand Seminary at Milan from 1883 to 1888, and in 1888 was elected to the College of Doctors at the *Ambrosian Library, of which he became prefect in 1907. While he was at Milan he applied himself to editing the *Ambrosian Missal and other texts. In 1912 he was made vice-prefect of the *Vatican Library. At the end of the war of 1914–18 he became Apostolic Visitor to Poland, in 1919 Nuncio and Titular Abp. of Lepanto, in 1921 Cardinal and Abp. of Milan, and in 1922 he was elected Pope. He made 'the restoration of all things in Christ', symbolized in the institution of the Feast of *Christ the King (1925), the chief object of his pontificate. His great encyclicals were directed to the same end: 'Divini illius magistri' (1929) deals with education; 'Casti connubii' (1930), which condemned *contraception, sought to restore a proper respect for married life; while the best known, '*Quadragesimo Anno' (1931), is concerned with social problems. The most important political event of his reign was the *Lateran Treaty (1929; q.v.). The spiritual life of the Church was fostered by the celebration of the Jubilee in 1925 which became the occasion of many canonizations (incl. that of St *Teresa of Lisieux and St Peter *Canisius), by his support of the apostolate of the laity in the *Catholic Action movement, and by several encyclicals recommending increased religious devotion. The last years of the Pope were overshadowed by the development of events in Europe, esp. the persecution of the Church in Germany (encyclical: '*Mit brennender Sorge') and the spread of atheism and neo-paganism.

His official acts are pr. in the *AAS* for the years of his pontificate. Eng. tr. of selected encyclicals to date, with introd., by J. H. Ryan (St Louis and London, 1927). A collection of his *Scritti storici* was pub., Florence [*c.*1932], with introd. by P. Bellezza, 'L'opera scientifica e letteraria di Achille Ratti', pp. vii–xlij; six of these essays were tr. into Eng. by E. Bulloch as *Essays in History written between the Years 1896–1912* (London [1934]). *Discorsi*, ed. D. Bertetto (3 vols., 1960–1). P. Hughes, *Pope Pius the Eleventh* (1937). C. Colombo and others (eds.), *Pio XI nel trentesimo della morte (1939–1969)* (Milan, 1969), incl. bibl. by A. Rimoldi, pp. 3–19. A. P. Frutaz in *EC* 9 (1952), cols. 1531–43, s.v. 'Pio XI'; G. Schwaiger in *NCE* 11 (1967), pp. 411–14, s.v. See also works cited under LATERAN TREATY.

Pius XII (1876–1958), Pope from 1939. Educated at the *Gregorian University and the Roman Seminary, Eugenio Pacelli was ordained priest in 1899 and entered the Papal Secretariat of State under *Leo XIII in 1901. In 1914 he was appointed Secretary of Extraordinary Ecclesiastical Affairs and, three years later, titular Abp. of Sardes and Apostolic *Nuncio to Bavaria. In this last capacity he took an active part in the peace efforts of *Benedict XV. In 1920 he became Nuncio to the German Republic at Berlin, where, as doyen of the Diplomatic Corps, he exercised considerable influence. In 1924 he concluded a favourable concordat with Bavaria, in 1929 a less satisfactory one with Prussia. In 1930 *Pius XI created him cardinal and appointed him Papal Secretary of State. In 1933 he promoted a concordat with the National Socialist German government, though its constant violations by Hitler and the deteriorating position of the Church in Germany soon created grave difficulties. Between 1934 and 1938 he undertook many journeys as Cardinal Legate to

*Eucharistic Congresses in Europe and America, and on other missions.

On 2 Mar. 1939 Pacelli was elected Pope and took the name of Pius XII. His elevation, contrary to the tradition against electing the Papal Secretary of State, reflected the need for an experienced politician and diplomat to guide the Church through the grave dangers that threatened. His first encyclical, '*Summi Pontificatus' (20 Oct. 1939), appealed to mankind to restore to God His due place in the life of the world and to unite in the defence of Natural Law, while his 'Christmas Allocution' (1939) laid down the principles of a lasting peace in 'Five Peace Points': (1) recognition of the right of every nation to life and independence; (2) true disarmament both material and spiritual; (3) institution of an international court to guarantee the peace; (4) recognition of the rights of minorities; and (5) the acquisition of a true Christian spirit among the nations. His alleged 'silence' in the face of Nazi atrocities has been the subject of criticism. The documents suggest that his experience of dealing with the German Government over Poland had convinced him that a public stand would only provoke worse persecution. Throughout the Second World War, and afterwards, he laboured to relieve distress, esp. among prisoners. In 1943 he issued the encyclical 'Mystici Corporis Christi' (29 June), emphasizing the unity of the Church as the Mystical Body of Christ. In the same year 'Divino Afflante Spiritu' (30 Sept.) stressed the need to follow the literal meaning of Scripture whenever possible, but, by also admitting the legitimacy of the study of literary forms, the encyclical opened the way for a more liberal approach to biblical criticism by Catholic scholars. The encyclical 'Mediator Dei' (20 Nov. 1947) expressed sympathy with the desire for the use of the vernacular in liturgy and gave conditional support to the *Liturgical Movement. In 1951 he restored the *Paschal Vigil Service and in the following years gradually reformed the entire liturgy for *Holy Week. His apostolic constitution 'Christus Dominus' (16 Jan. 1953) standardized the relaxations in the *Eucharistic fast which had been introduced during the War; together with the further relaxations permitted by his *motu proprio* 'Sacram Communionem' (19 Mar. 1957), this made possible the widespread introduction of *Evening Masses. Other important acts of his pontificate included the creation of an unprecedentedly large number of cardinals (32 in 1946 and 24 in 1953), drawn from a wide variety of countries, 33 canonizations, the initiation of the excavations under *St Peter's, Rome, the publication of the encyclical '*Humani Generis' (12 Aug. 1950) directed against certain modern tendencies in RC theology, and the definition of the doctrine of the *Assumption of the BVM in the apostolic constitution '*Munificentissimus Deus' (1 Nov. 1950). An instruction of the *Holy Office, 'Ecclesia Catholica', on 20 Sept. 1949 recognized that the desire for unity of those engaged in the *Ecumenical Movement was due to the inspiration of the Holy Spirit and under strict conditions allowed RC experts to join with other Christians in discussions on faith and morals. Pius also attempted to foster relations with the Eastern *Orthodox and *Uniat Churches in the encyclicals 'Orientalis Ecclesiae Decus' (9 Apr. 1944) and 'Orientales Omnes Ecclesiae' (23 Dec. 1945).

Official docs. are pr. in the *AAS* for the years of his pontificate. *Actes et documents du Saint Siège relatifs à la Seconde Guerre Mond-

iale, ed. P. Blet and others (11 vols., Rome, 1965–81; Eng. tr. of vol. 1, 1968). G. R. Pilote, *Guide de consultation des discours du Pape Pie XII* (Ottawa, 1963). Studies incl. those of O. Halecki (London, 1954), R. Galeazzi-Lisi (Paris, 1960), P. Rassinier (ibid., 1965), and M. O'Carroll (Dublin, 1980). S. Friedländer, *Pie XII et le IIIe Reich: Documents* (1964; Eng. tr., 1966); C. Falconi, *Il silenzio di Pio XII* (Milan, 1965; Eng. tr., 1970); V. Conzemius, 'Églises chrétiennes et totalitarisme national-socialiste', *RHE* 63 (1968), pp. 437–503, esp. pp. 459–503; I. Garzia, *Pio XII e l'Italia nella seconda guerra mondiale* (Biblioteca di Storia Contemporanea; Brescia, 1988). J. Chelini and J.-B. d'Onorio (eds.), *Pie XII et la Cité: ... Actes du Colloque d'Aix-en-Provence ...* (Aix and Marseilles [1988]), with preface by O. Rossi, 'Pie XII dans l'Église', pp. 11–31. R. Leiber, SJ, in *NCE* 11 (1967), pp. 414–18, s.v.

Placebo (Lat., 'I will please'). A traditional title for the *Vespers of the Dead, derived from the *antiphon (Ps. 116 [114]: 9; Vulg. *Placebo Domino in regione vivorum*) with which the office used to open. See also DIRGE.

Placet. See EXEQUATUR.

Placidia, Galla. See GALLA PLACIDIA.

plainsong. The traditional music of the Latin rite is generally known as Gregorian chant, after St *Gregory the Great, although in its surviving form it has little, if anything, to do with him. It was paralleled in the early Middle Ages by a number of other rites and their music, including the *Ambrosian (or Milanese), the ancient *Gallican, the *Mozarabic, and the *Old Roman, to which may be added that from Benevento in S. Italy, and perhaps others. Of these the Gallican has virtually disappeared, and the Mozarabic is mostly indecipherable; but substantial fragments of the Beneventan (suppressed in favour of the Gregorian in the 11th cent.) have been uncovered, while the Ambrosian and the Old Roman survive complete in fully legible form.

The origins of Gregorian chant and its relation to the Old Roman are disputed. Acc. to one view, it developed in the time of Pope *Vitalian (657–72) as a complement to a newly established Papal 'court' liturgy, leaving the Old Roman as the chant of the basilicas and titular churches; according to another, it emerged in Gaul as an unintended consequence of the imposition of the Roman rite there, and was subsequently exported back to Rome in that form. The former theory accords better with the liturgical and historical evidence, though it may be that the Roman chant of the 7th cent. was a much simpler affair from which the Old Roman and the Gregorian developed independently.

Plainsong as generally understood is entirely monophonic and was probably always sung in unmeasured time values, though this has been disputed. Its tonal organization is based on a system of modes, or scales corresponding to the white notes of the piano and centred for the most part on the notes D, E, F, or G. A form of staff-notation emerged in the 11th cent., from which period melodies are fully decipherable; those of the Gregorian chant can be shown to go back to *c.*900 in the form of neumes, which show the melodic contour but not the exact pitches. Before that, except for isolated examples, the oral tradition had sufficed.

The repertory of plainsong grew enormously in the later Middle Ages, but many additional melodies, particularly

*tropes and *sequences, were eliminated in the *Tridentine reform. The traditional plainsong was deliberately altered to make it conform to humanist ideals, for example by redistributing the notes so that lengthy melismas fell on accentuated syllables. In the 19th cent. a restoration of the medieval tradition was pursued, largely through the efforts of the monks of *Solesmes under the leadership of Dom Joseph Pothier (1835–1923) and his successors. The modern study of plainsong has resulted in numerous editions, both scholarly and practical, and a huge literature; but since the Second *Vatican Council plainsong has ceased to be the normal accompaniment of the Roman liturgy except in the few communities (such as *Beuron in Germany and Solesmes in France) where it is especially cultivated. However, the singing of plainsong to translated texts, already widely used in the Anglican Communion from the time of the *Tractarian movement, has in recent years also gained acceptance in the RC Church.

The corpus of plainsong is contained chiefly in two books, the *Gradual for the Mass and the *Antiphonal for the Choir Office; other chants are found in the *Manuale, the *Pontifical, and the *Processional.

Facsimiles of the principal musical MSS of the Gregorian, Ambrosian, Mozarabic, and Gallican chants are being pub. by the Benedictines of Solesmes in the series *Paléographie musicale* (Solesmes etc., 1889 ff.; since 1969 at Berne); the most reliable of the numerous modern practical edns. are the *Antiphonale monasticum* (Tournai etc., 1934) and the *Graduale Triplex* (Solesmes, 1979), both ed. by the monks of Solesmes. P. [J.] Wagner, *Einführung in die gregorianischen Melodien* (Freiburg, 1895; Eng. tr. of pt. 1 (from 2nd edn.) [1907]; expanded edn., 3 vols., Leipzig, 1911–21). W. Apel, *Gregorian Chant* [1958]; D. Hiley, *Western Plainchant: A Handbook* (Oxford, 1993). S. J. P. van Dijk, OFM, 'The Urban and Papal Rites in Seventh and Eighth-Century Rome', *Sacris Erudiri*, 12 (1961), pp. 411–87. P. Combe, OSB, *Histoire de la restauration du chant grégorien d'après des documents inédits* (Solesmes, 1969). H. Hucke, 'Toward a New Historical View of Gregorian Chant', *Journal of the American Musicological Society*, 33 (1980), pp. 437–67; D. G. Hughes, 'Evidence for the Traditional View of the Transmission of Gregorian Chant', ibid. 40 (1987), pp. 377–404. G. Reese, *Music in the Middle Ages* (New York, 1940; London, 1941), pp. 57–197. D. Hiley in D. Arnold (ed.), *The New Oxford Companion to Music* (1983), pp. 1447–56, s.v. 'Plainchant'.

planeta. An alternative name, found already in the Fourth Council of *Toledo (633; can. 28), for the *chasuble. The Lat. word perhaps comes from the Gk. πλανήτης, 'wanderer', signifying a garment originally worn when travelling.

Plantin Bibles. See following entry.

Plantin, Christopher (*c.*1520–89), printer. Born of humble parents, prob. in Touraine, Plantin was brought up in Lyons, became a bookbinder in Caen, and learned to print while living in Paris. Increasing pressure against printers suspected of heresy may account for his leaving France; in 1548 he settled in the wealthy commercial port of Antwerp. There, despite much competition and early difficulties arising from his connection with the *Familists, within a few years he built up the largest printing and publishing business in Europe. He established his commanding position through utilizing the best in all branches of publishing. The soundest texts, edited by some of the leading scholars of the age, printed with types and ornaments designed and cast by the most skilful craftsmen, and often illustrated by Flemish engravers, earned him fame. His most celebrated production was his Antwerp *Polyglot Bible in 8 folio volumes, 1569–72. He and his successors printed a great number of editions of the *Missal, *Breviary, and other liturgical books, in virtue of a monopoly granted to him within the dominions of the King of Spain. After his death the business descended by marriage to the Moretus family, which continued to operate it until 1876. Since then the establishment, with all its original contents—furniture, pictures, library, archives, and fully equipped printing works—has been preserved by the city of Antwerp as a museum.

C. Clair, *Christopher Plantin* (London, 1960). L. [B.] Voet, *The Golden Compasses: A History and Evaluation of the Printing and Publishing Activities of the Officina Plantiniana at Antwerp* (2 vols., Antwerp, etc. [1969–72]). B. Rekers, *Benito Arias Montano 1527–1598* (Amsterdam diss.; Groningen [1961]; Eng. tr., Studies of the Warburg Institute, 33; 1972), esp. chs. 3–4.

Platina, Bartolomeo (1421–81), Italian humanist. Born at Piadena (hence 'Platina', his family name was Sacchi), near Mantua, he went to Florence in 1457 to study Greek under Argyropolis. Proceeding to Rome in 1462, he was patronized by *Pius II, but when Paul II succeeded in 1464, he lost favour and was imprisoned. He again came into favour under *Sixtus IV, who made him librarian of the *Vatican (1475), and it was while holding this office that he compiled his *Lives of the Popes* (*Liber de vita Christi ac de vitis summorum pontificum omnium*, Venice, 1479). The work is written in a flowing, readable style, but is uncritical. A mention in its pages of the prayers and curses of *Callistus III in 1456 against the Turks, followed by a reference in the same context to the appearance of Halley's comet, gave rise to the fable, frequently repeated in the 19th cent., that the Pope had excommunicated the comet.

The original MS of his *Lives of the Popes*, which has often been ed., is preserved in the Vatican (Cod. 2044). Eng. tr. with continuation to date by P. *Rycaut (London, fol., 1685); more modern tr. by W. Benham (ibid., 2 vols. [1888]). G. J. Schorn, 'Die Quellen zu den *Vitae Pontificum Romanorum* des Bartolomeo Platina', *RQ* 27 (1913), pp. 3*–19* and 57*–84*. A. J. Dunston, 'Pope Pius II and the Humanists', *Journal of Religious History*, 7 (1973), pp. 287–306.

Plato (427–347 BC), Greek philosopher. He was a native of Athens, of a noble family, and destined for a political career. In his early years he was introduced to the doctrines of Heraclitus and in 407 (if not earlier) became a pupil of Socrates. Affection for his master and the love for philosophy turned him away from public life after Socrates' execution (399). He withdrew from Athens, taking refuge for a time with Eucleides at Megara. In the years 390–388 he travelled widely, perhaps to Egypt and Cyrene, certainly to Sicily and S. Italy, where he made the acquaintance of Pythagorean philosophers. Returning to Athens at a time which cannot certainly be fixed, he established a school on the outskirts of the city near the grove sacred to Academus; his school thus came to be known as the Academy, a tradition persisting until its dissolution by *Justinian in AD 529. At the age of 60 (367) Plato was unexpectedly invited to take a part in politics. Dion, a

leader at the court of the youthful Dionysius II (367–345), tyrant of Syracuse, was anxious to set up a liberal state on the model of the *Republic* and invited Plato to instruct Dionysius about the 'philosopher-king'. The enterprise met with small success and in 366 both Dion and Plato were forced to leave Syracuse. In 361 he paid a fruitless visit to Sicily to try to reconcile Dionysius with Dion. Apart from this Sicilian venture Plato seems to have spent the last 40 years of his life at the Academy.

With the exception of a small collection of *Epistles*, Plato's writings are in the form of Dialogues, often with Socrates as the principal speaker and various critics or pupils, after whom the Dialogues are usually named, taking part in the discussion. It is often uncertain how far the speeches represent the real or supposed teaching of the interlocutors, and how far they voice Plato's own beliefs. Their literary artistry (directness, dramatic tensions, irony), intellectual breadth, and moral seriousness are supreme. There is no contemporary record of their chronological arrangement, which must be determined mainly by internal criteria. Evidence is sometimes afforded by the historic setting of the Dialogues, though here again it is often uncertain how far Plato meant the history to be taken literally. More reliable criteria are the intrinsic probabilities of Plato's philosophic development, general considerations of subject-matter (e.g. the Dialogues in which Socrates is central are presumably to be put first), Plato's references back to earlier Dialogues (e.g. of the *Timaeus* to the *Republic*), and the growth of Plato's dramatic power. These evidences converge on conclusions about which there is a fair measure of agreement among scholars; these conclusions are confirmed by philological ('stylometric') considerations (W. Lutoslawski) and by an avoidance of stylistic hiatus in the later Dialogues, which probably shows Isocrates' influence.

The principal Dialogues, in their approximate order of composition, are:

(1) The *Socratic Dialogues*, a large group, including the *Gorgias, Meno, Euthyphro, Apology,* and *Crito*. Their common subject is the nature of virtue and whether or not it can be taught. The three last-mentioned are linked with the trial and death of Socrates. The *Euthyphro* deals with correct behaviour towards the gods (ὁσιότης), the *Apology* with Socrates' own life-style and activity as a teacher, and the *Crito* with the duty of loyalty to the State.

In the next four dialogues (2–5), Plato's philosophical and dramatic power is at its highest:

(2) *Phaedo*, on immortality. The divine and enduring soul which shares in the eternal Forms is here contrasted with the mutable human body.

(3) *Symposium*, on the nature of eros, true beauty, and the life of contemplation. The love of earthly beauty can lead the soul onwards to the love of wisdom and of the Form of beauty itself.

(4) *Protagoras*, on the nature of the good, whether virtue is one or many, and on the identity of knowledge and goodness.

(5) *Republic*, generally considered the supreme creation of Plato. Its twofold theme is the nature of right conduct and the ideal political state. Consideration of man's threefold psychological constitution leads to the famous description of the ideal city-state (the philosopher-king, the guardians, community of goods, etc.). The object of

the moral quest is no longer a particular ethical Form but the Form of the Good (ἰδέα τἀγαθοῦ) as such, held to underlie all the changing and particular facts in the world. Book 7 contains the well-known analogy of human life in which men who live in a cave see only the shadows of real objects (i.e. the Forms) cast on the opposite wall.

(6) *Phaedrus*, on persuasion and eros and their part in our perception of the Forms.

(7) *Theaetetus*, on the nature of knowledge (ἐπιστήμη), which is held to be judgement, i.e. the union of true opinion (δόξα) with reason (λόγος).

(8) *Parmenides*, on the relation of likeness and unlikeness, of the one and the many, expounded by the Eleatic philosophers. The first part reveals some of Plato's misgivings about the theory of Forms; the latter part seems to be a *reductio ad absurdum* designed to expose the failings of ill-defined arguments about unity and being.

(9) The pair *Sophistes* and *Politicus* (or *Statesman*). Their respective subjects (metaphysics; politics) differ widely, but the two Dialogues are closely connected and of the same date. The *Sophistes* examines the relation of being and becoming, posed by difficulties in the Eleatic teaching. It is argued that 'not being', no less than 'being', exists. The *Politicus* reiterates and develops the teaching of the *Republic* that good government should be left to experts.

(10) *Philebus*, on the nature of pleasure in its relation to the good life. The goodness of a thing lies in the unity of beauty, symmetry, and truth.

(11) *Timaeus*, on cosmology and natural science. Here, as in the *Laws*, the dialogue form has virtually been abandoned in favour of didactic exposition. The universe is described as a single living sphere, composed of soul and body. Besides the world and the model after which it was built there is a third entity, the receptacle (χώρα), in which the world becomes. The world itself is composed of the traditional four elements. Plato also gives an elaborate account of man and his various affections. Through a Latin translation by Chalcidius, known to the earlier Middle Ages, the *Timaeus* was for several centuries the best known of Plato's writings.

(12) *Laws*, on politics. This, the longest of the Dialogues, is in the form of a speech put into the mouth of an Athenian Stranger. The treatise, which was apparently left unfinished, reasserts the communistic teaching of the *Republic*, but with differences of detail. The constitution of the state must avoid the extremes of despotism and freedom. 'Examiners' and a 'Nocturnal Council' are to be in charge of the laws, which here occupy a more prominent place in the constitution than in the *Republic* and the *Politicus*. Great stress is laid on the importance of religious belief. Everyone is to be taught astronomy, since God's existence can be deduced from the study of the stars, while atheists who persist in their heresy are to be put to death. The perhaps inauthentic *Epinomis* develops the teaching of *Laws* 10; in this work astronomical interests are prominent.

In the earlier Dialogues the main emphasis is ethical. They insist *inter alia* that the cultivation of mind and will, 'goodness of soul', is the chief business of life; that this is attained by a rational insight into the nature of goodness, truth, and beauty; that morality and the claims of the enlightened conscience are to be respected in political life; and that the rational moral personality is created

by the 'recollection' (ἀνάμνησις) of what the soul knows of these values. Since the soul naturally aims at what it believes to be good, wrongdoing is the pursuit of a falsely conceived good.

These doctrines are all based on a metaphysic, developed esp. in the later Dialogues, which contrasts the world of sense and everyday experience with a true and higher world of 'Ideas' (or better 'Forms'). These 'Forms' are 'present to' individual entities, and by grasping the eternal Forms and participating in them the soul attains its true well-being and is lifted above the flux of 'becoming'. But the highest value, the 'Form of the Good', remains mysterious.

Plato's two principal discussions of theology in the narrower sense are in the *Timaeus* and book 10 of the *Laws*. The *Timaeus* describes how the divine Demiurge (δημιουργός, 'artisan' or 'craftsman') brings the world into being, how He makes it as an image (εἰκών) of an eternal archetype, and how He enables it to share in His perfection by putting into it mind (νοῦς) or soul (ψυχή). Time is described as a 'moving image of eternity'. *Aristotle criticized the Dialogue as teaching that the world had a beginning, whereas other members of the Academy held that Plato really agreed with Aristotle in making it eternal.

The *Laws* 10 embodies the earliest known exposition of natural theology, namely a form of the *cosmological argument based on the belief that all motions ultimately require at their head a 'perfectly good soul' (ἀρίστη ψυχή). The existence of a second maleficent world-soul, identified with necessity (ἀνάγκη), is also defended. (1) Atheism, (2) the view that the gods are indifferent to human conduct, and (3) the notion that the gods can be deterred from the execution of justice by human offerings, are all rejected as morally pernicious. The evil consequences of wrong belief make it the duty of the State to impose orthodoxy, where necessary by force.

It remains obscure how Plato related the highest of the Forms to God as the Supreme Soul. In the *Timaeus* the Forms are the thoughts of God (νοήματα Θεοῦ), but on the other hand, since God also created the universe after the pattern of the Forms, He would seem to be in some sense subordinate to them. On this matter Plato betrays no great concern for consistency; indeed θεός is sometimes better translated as 'the God' or as 'divinity'. It was only among the more theologically interested Platonists of later times that the problem became a matter of debate.

TEXT. *Editio princeps*: Aldine, Venice, 1513. H. *Stephanus (3 vols., 1578; still used for refs. to Plato); the effective ed. was Serranus, who also made the Lat. version. Other edns. by C. F. Herrmann and M. Wohlrab (6 vols., Teub., 1890–96), J. Burnet (Oxford Classical Texts, 5 vols. [1900–7]) and M. Croiset and others (14 vols. in 27 parts, Collection des Universités de France publiée sous le patronage de l'Association Guillaume Budé, Paris, 1920–64, incl. as vol. 14 a lexicon of Plato's philosophical and religious language by É. des Places, SJ, and Fr. tr.). Separate edns. incl. those of *Euthyphro, Apology*, and *Crito* by J. Burnet (Oxford, 1924), *Gorgias* by E. R. Dodds (ibid., 1959), *Meno* by R. S. Bluck (Cambridge, 1961), *Phaedo* by R. D. Archer-Hind (London, 1883; 2nd edn., 1894), J. Burnet (Oxford, 1911) and C. J. Rowe (Cambridge, 1993), *Republic* by J. Adam (2 vols., Cambridge, 1902; 2nd edn., with introd. by D. A. Rees, 1963), *Theaetetus* by L. Campbell (Oxford, 1861; 2nd edn., 1883), *Sophistes* and *Politicus* by id. (ibid., 1867), *Philebus* by R. G. Bury (Cambridge, 1897), and *Laws* by E. B. England (2 vols., Manchester and London, 1921).

TRANSLATIONS. Complete Eng. version by B. *Jowett (4 vols., 1871; 2nd edn., 5 vols., 1875; 4th edn., rev., 4 vols., 1953). Other Eng. trs., with comm., of *Euthyphro* by R. E. Allen (London and New York, 1970), of *Phaedo* by R. Hackforth (Cambridge, 1955), of *Republic* by F. M. Cornford (Oxford, 1941), of *Timaeus* by id., *Plato's Cosmology* (1937), of *Theaetetus* and *Sophist* by id., *Plato's Theory of Knowledge* (1935), of *Parmenides* by A. E. *Taylor (Oxford, 1934) and F. M. Cornford, *Plato and Parmenides* (1939), of *Politicus* by J. B. Skemp, *Plato's Statesman* (1952), of *Philebus* by R. Hackforth, *Plato's Examination of Pleasure* (Cambridge, 1945), and of *Phaedrus* by R. Hackforth (ibid., 1952). There are also versions by A. E. Taylor of the *Timaeus* and *Critias* (London, 1929), *Laws* (ibid., 1934), and *Philebus* and *Epinomis* (ibid., 1956, posthumously pub. with introd. by R. Klibansky and A. C. Lloyd) and of *Epistles* by J. Harward (Cambridge, 1932). See also G. R. Morrow, cited below.

LIFE. U. von Wilamowitz-Moellendorff, *Platon* (2 vols., Berlin, 1917–18; 5th edn., 1959); J. Stenzel, *Platon der Erzieher* (1928); P. Friedländer, *Platon* (2 vols., Berlin, 1928–30; 2nd edn., 3 vols., 1954–60; Eng. tr., 1958–69, with extensive refs.); G. C. Field, *Plato and his Contemporaries* (1930); G. R. Morrow, *Studies in the Platonic Epistles* (Illinois Studies in Language and Literature, 18, nos. 3–4; 1935; 2nd edn., New York, 1962, incl. Eng. tr. of text); H. Cherniss, *The Riddle of the Early Academy* (Berkeley, Calif., and Los Angeles, 1945); G. Ryle, *Plato's Progress* (Cambridge, 1966); L. Edelstein, *Plato's Seventh Letter* (Leiden, 1966); K. von Fritz, *Platon in Sizilien und das Problem der Philosophenherrschaft* (1968).

INTRODUCTIONS. These are numerous and incl. G. M. A. Grube, *Plato's Thought* (1935; repr. with introd. and new bibl. by D. J. Zeyl, 1980); G. C. Field, *The Philosophy of Plato* (1949; 2nd edn., 1969); J. E. Raven, *Plato's Thought in the Making: A Study of the Development of his Metaphysics* (Cambridge, 1965); P. Huby, *Plato and Modern Morality* (1972); R. M. Hare, *Plato* (Past Masters, Oxford, 1982).

INTERPRETATION AND CRITICISM. W. Lutoslawski, *The Origin and Growth of Plato's Logic* (1897); C. Ritter, *Platon* (2 vols., Munich, 1910–23); A. E. Taylor, *Plato: The Man and his Work* (1926; 4th edn., 1937); L. Robin, *Platon* (1935; rev. edn., 1968); J. Moreau, *La Construction de l'idéalisme platonicien* (1939); R. Robinson, *Plato's Earlier Dialectic* (Ithaca, NY, 1941; 2nd edn., Oxford, 1953); W. Jaeger, *Paideia: Die Formung des griechischen Menschen*, 2–3 (1944–7; Eng. tr., 1944–5); D. Ross, *Plato's Theory of Ideas* (Oxford, 1951); H. J. Krämer, *Arete bei Plato und Aristoteles* (Abhandlungen der Heidelberger Akademie der Wissenschaften, Philologisch-historische Klasse, Jahrgang 1959, 6. Abh.; 1959); W. Burkert, *Weisheit und Wissenschaft: Studien zu Pythagoras, Philolaos und Platon* (1962); I. M. Crombie, *An Examination of Plato's Doctrines* (2 vols., 1962–3); R. E. Allen (ed.), *Studies in Plato's Metaphysics* (1965); J. N. Findlay, *Plato: The Written and Unwritten Doctrines* (International Library of Philosophy and Scientific Method, 1974); G. Vlastos, *Plato's Universe* (Oxford, 1975); T. Irwin, *Plato's Moral Theory: The Early and Middle Dialogues* (ibid., 1977); I. Murdoch, *The Fire and the Sun: Why Plato Banished the Artists* (ibid., 1977); R. Kraut (ed.), *The Cambridge Companion to Plato* (Cambridge, 1992). On individual works, R. C. Cross and A. D. Woozley, *Plato's Republic: A Philosophical Commentary* (1964); J. Annas, *An Introduction to Plato's Republic* (Oxford, 1981); J. Pieper, *Begeisterung und göttlicher Wahnsinn: Über den platonischen Dialog 'Phaidros'* (Munich [1962]; Eng. tr., *Love and Inspiration*, 1965); A. D. Woozley, *Law and Obedience: The Arguments of Plato's Crito* (1979); D. Bostock, *Plato's Phaedo* (Oxford, 1986).

PLATO'S RELIGION. F. Solmsen, *Plato's Theology* (New York, 1942); O. Reverdin, *La Religion de la cité platonicienne* (1945); V. Goldschmidt, *La Religion de Platon* (1949); H. J. Krämer, *Ursprung der Geistmetaphysik: Untersuchungen zur Geschichte des Platonismus zwischen Platon und Plotin* (Amsterdam, 1964).

DICTIONARIES. A. E. Taylor in *EB* (14th edn.), 18 (1929), pp. 48–64; H. Leisegang in *PW* 40 (1950), cols. 2342–537; G. Ryle in

Encyclopedia of Philosophy, ed. P. Edwards, 6 [1967], cols. 314–33, all s.v. See also works cited under PLATONISM and NEOPLATONISM.

Platonism. After the death of *Plato (q.v.), his nephew, Speusippus, succeeded him as head of the Academy at Athens (347–339) which with varying fortunes persisted until its closure by *Justinian in AD 529. But in the Hellenistic age Plato's doctrines had a wide following which extended far beyond the direct influence of any institution. Their impact on later Judaism is to be seen in the Book of *Wisdom and the system of *Philo. In the 3rd cent. AD a thorough recasting of Plato's system ('*Neoplatonism') was elaborated by *Plotinus (205–70), whose disciple, *Porphyry (c.232–c.305), developed it in conscious opposition to Christianity. *Proclus, the last considerable head of the Academy and a celebrated commentator on Plato's writings, died in 485.

The beginnings of an interweaving of Platonism with Christian thought go back to *Clement of Alexandria and *Origen. Of perhaps even greater moment for the history of Christian theology was the fact that the thought of St *Augustine was radically influenced, largely through *Victorinus Afer, by Platonic doctrines. The authority accorded to his teaching throughout the Middle Ages did much to secure for many Platonic notions a permanent place in Latin Christianity. Henceforward the Platonic Forms were regularly reinterpreted as the creative thoughts of God, as they had been by pagan Platonists from shortly before the beginning of the Christian era. The relevance of Platonism for Christian mysticism was appreciated by *Dionysius the Pseudo-Areopagite and other spiritual writers, Eastern (St *John Climacus) and Western (St *Bernard of Clairvaux, the *Victorines). Other *media* through which Platonic doctrines reached the medieval Church were *Boethius, who translated Porphyry into Latin, John Scottus *Erigena (q.v.), and a Latin version by Chalcidius of Plato's *Timaeus*. Even the supposed eclipse of Plato by *Aristotle as 'the Philosopher' *par excellence* in the 13th cent. was only apparent, for, as A. E. *Taylor and others have pointed out, St *Thomas Aquinas's teaching remained fundamentally Platonist.

The Renaissance led to a revival of interest in Plato himself in such scholars as Marsilio *Ficino. In the 16th cent. there was a steady stream of Platonist influence on religion in England (J. *Colet, St John *Fisher, St Thomas *More, R. *Hooker). In the 17th cent. the *Cambridge Platonists urged the return of Christian theology to 'its old loving nurse, the Platonic philosophy' and found in its doctrine of the inwardness of morality and religion the best antidote to the controversial aridities of contemporary *Calvinism and the secularism of T. *Hobbes. Strong Platonist influences were also present in many English theologians of the 19th cent. (B. *Jowett, F. D. *Maurice, C. *Kingsley, the *Lux Mundi* School). Among recent philosophers A. N. Whitehead has defended a Platonist cosmology. On the other hand, Protestant orthodoxy on the Continent, with its distrust of natural reason, has commonly been hostile to Platonism and in the 20th cent. there has been much theological criticism of Greek metaphysics.

A. E. Taylor, *Platonism and its Influence* (1925); C. *Bigg, *The Christian Platonists of Alexandria* (Oxford, 1886; repr. with additions and corrections, 1913); R. Klibansky, *The Continuity of the

Platonic Tradition during the Middle Ages (1939); A. Fox, Plato and the Christians (1957; selected passages). E. Cassirer, Die platonische Renaissance in England und die Schule von Cambridge (1932; Eng. tr., 1953). E. Hoffmann, Platonismus und christliche Philosophie (Zurich, 1960). H. I. Marrou, 'Synesius of Cyrene and Alexandrian Neoplatonism', in A. Momigliano (ed.), The Conflict between Paganism and Christianity in the Fourth Century (Oxford, 1963), pp. 126–50; P. Courcelle, 'Anti-Christian Arguments and Christian Platonism: From Arnebius to St Ambrose', ibid., pp. 151–92. E. von Ivánka, Plato Christianus: Übernahme und Umgestaltung des Platonismus durch die Väter (Einsiedeln [1964]). A. H. Armstrong (ed.), The Cambridge History of Later Greek and Early Medieval Philosophy (1967), with extensive bibl. Le Néoplatonisme: Colloques Internationaux du Centre National de la Recherche Scientifique. Sciences humaines (1971). J. Dillon, The Middle Platonists: A Study of Platonism 80 B.C. to A.D. 220 (1977). R. Arnou in DTC 12 (pt. 2; 1935), cols. 2258–392, s.v. 'Platonisme des Pères'.

Plays, Passion. See MYSTERY PLAYS; also OBERAMMERGAU.

plenary indulgence. In modern RC theology an *indulgence which is held to remit the whole of the temporal punishment due to an individual's sins. The petitioner may apply it either to himself or to the profit of a soul, or souls, in purgatory. As it is held that its efficacy depends on the perfection of the soul's disposition (of which no one can ever be certain), there is always an element of doubt as to whether a soul has profited to the full by a particular plenary indulgence.

The earliest known example of the issue of a plenary indulgence was the promise of *Urban II at the Council of *Clermont (1095) that all penance incurred by Crusaders who confessed their sins should be remitted. As the issue of plenary indulgences became more common in the 12th and 13th cents. it was much debated (St *Albert the Great, St *Thomas Aquinas, Pope *Hadrian VI) whether or not plenary indulgences covered penances which ought to have been enjoined as well as those that had actually been imposed. It was the former view which gradually became accepted. Acc. to current RC regulations a plenary indulgence cannot be gained more than once on the same day except by someone on the point of death (in articulo mortis). It is normally granted for the recitation of certain prayers or other devotional exercises under prescribed conditions, namely the use of the Sacrament of *Penance, reception of Holy Communion, prayer for the Pope's intention, and the exclusion of all attachment to sin, incl. *venial sin. See also INDULGENCES.

Plethon, Georgius Gemistus. See GEMISTUS PLETHON, GEORGIUS.

Pliny. Gaius Plinius Caecilius Secundus (c.61–c.112), Roman senator and man of letters. His extant letters include those which, as governor of Bithynia and Pontus, he exchanged with the Emp. Trajan (Ep. 10. 96–7). In Pontus, he reported, Christianity had spread so widely in all social ranks, both in town and country, that the pagan cults were falling into neglect. The situation was new to him and he sought for guidance. Of those accused before him of Christianity, he had executed those who confessed and refused to sacrifice to the gods or emperor. But some who admitted to having been Christians in the past had proved their apostasy by taking this test. He did not know whether the offence consisted in the name alone or in criminal acts (flagitia) supposedly inherent in the Christian cult. His own investigations had produced no evidence of flagitia; his report throws valuable light on contemporary Christian practices, perhaps including the *agape. He suggests that apostates should not be punished. Trajan agreed; if they would sacrifice to the gods, they should be pardoned. He also prescribed that Christians were not to be 'sought out', implying that he too did not regard Christians as such as guilty of flagitia; they could still be accused of being Christians, though anonymous information was to be disregarded. See also PERSECUTIONS, EARLY CHRISTIAN.

Crit. edn. of Pliny's Letters by R. A. B. Mynors (Oxford, 1963); Eng. tr. by B. Radice (Penguin Classics, 1963). Eng. tr. of the letter to Trajan and the latter's reply also in J. Stevenson (ed.), A New Eusebius (1957), pp. 13–16. A. N. Sherwin-White, The Letters of Pliny: A Historical and Social Commentary (Oxford, 1966), esp. pp. 691–712 and 772–87.

Plotinus (c.205–70), *Neoplatonist philosopher and mystic. He was a native of Lycopolis, and acc. to his friend and pupil, *Porphyry, became interested in philosophy at the age of 28 and was for 11 years a disciple of *Ammonius Saccas. He later accompanied the Emp. Gordian (d. 243) on an expedition to Persia to make himself acquainted with E. thought. After his return he established his own school in Rome in 244. At the age of 51 he began to write, and after his death Porphyry published his 54 treatises, arranging them in six Enneads (Gk. ἐννεάδες, 'groups of nine').

Owing to the difficulty of his style and subject-matter Plotinus has been variously interpreted, and it is disputed whether his thought is fundamentally pantheistic or tending towards Theism. He rejects the *Gnostic dualism as vigorously as the Christian conception of a historic Redemption, opposing to either his system of an intellectualist *mysticism. Its main concern on the speculative side is with the relations between unity and multiplicity. At the summit of the hierarchy of beings there is the One (τὸ Ἕν) or the Good, the first principle, absolutely simple and self-sufficient, who transcends all thought and speech. Beneath it is the divine mind which is the world of ideas (Νοῦς). Next comes Soul (Ψυχή), the third member of the Plotinian Triad. This last is the intermediary between the intelligible and the material world, which, since matter holds the lowest place in the Plotinian system, is the furthest removed from the One. The World Soul is a particular soul, part of the hypostasis Soul on the same level as individual souls. It creates and orders the universe which other souls share in animating. All souls share in the unity of Soul and its capacity for contemplation.

Contemplation, which occupies a central position in Plotinus' system, is the most perfect activity, for by it souls can attain union with God. In order to reach this last end the soul must purify itself morally and intellectually, attaining to virtue and wisdom. Then it must pass not only beyond attachment to sensible things and discursive reasoning but beyond the highest intellectual contemplation to attain a vision of or union with the One which cannot be described but is likened to becoming the light one sees or to the union of lovers. The chief difference between this so-called 'natural mysticism' and that of the orthodox Christian mystics is that, in Plotinus' system, union is reached by the natural power of reason which the soul receives in its creation, whereas in Catholic teaching it is the work of Divine grace. Despite this fundamental difference Plotinus seems to have exercised indirectly much influence on Christian thought, esp. on St *Augustine and *Dionysius the Pseudo-Areopagite, and, through them, on the theologians and mystics of the Middle Ages.

Editio princeps of Gk. text of *Enneads*, Basle, 1580, with M. *Ficino's Lat. tr. Crit. text ed. P. Henry, SJ, and H.-R. Schwyzer (Museum Lessianum, Series Philosophica, 33–5; 1951–73; also 3 vols., Oxford, 1964–82); largely repr., with Eng. tr., by A. H. Armstrong (7 vols., Loeb, 1966–88). Eng. tr. of *Enneads*, with Porphyry's *Life*, by S. Mackenna (5 vols., London, 1917–30; 4th edn., rev. by B. S. Page, 1969). W. R. *Inge, *The Philosophy of Plotinus* (Gifford Lectures, 1918; subjective); R. Arnou, *Le Désir de Dieu dans la philosophie de Plotin* (1921; 2nd edn., 1967); E. Bréhier, *La Philosophie de Plotin* (1928; 3rd edn., 1961); J. Guitton, *Le Temps et l'éternité chez Plotin et saint Augustin* (1933; 3rd edn., 1959); P. Henry, SJ, *Plotin et l'Occident* (SSL 15; 1934); id., *Études plotiniennes* (2 vols., Museum Lessianum, Section philosophique, 20–1; 1938–41); A. H. Armstrong, *The Architecture of the Intelligible Universe in the Philosophy of Plotinus: An Analytical and Historical Study* (Cambridge, 1940); J. Trouillard, *La Purification Plotinienne* (Paris thesis, 1955); id., *La Procession Plotinienne* (Paris thesis, 1955); A. Dahl, *Augustin und Plotin: Philosophische Untersuchungen zum Trinitätsproblem und zur Nuslehre* (Lund, 1945); E. R. Dodds and others, *Les Sources de Plotin* (Entretiens sur l'Antiquité Classique, 5; Geneva, 1960); P. Hadot, *Plotin ou la simplicité du regard* (1963; 2nd edn., Études Augustiniennes, 1973); R. Ferwerda, *La Signification des images et des métaphores dans la pensée de Plotin* (Groningen, 1965); A. H. Armstrong in id. (ed.), *The Cambridge History of Later Greek and Early Medieval Philosophy* (Cambridge, 1967), pp. 195–268; J. N. Deck, *Nature, Contemplation and the One: A Study in the Philosophy of Plotinus* (Toronto, 1967); J. M. Rist, *Plotinus: The Road to Reality* (Cambridge, 1969); J.-M. Charrue, *Plotin, lecteur de Platon* (1978; 2nd edn., 1987); D. J. O'Meara, *Plotinus: An Introduction to the Enneads* (Oxford, 1993). D. O'Brien, *Théodicée Plotinienne, Théodicée Gnostique* (Philosophia Antiqua, 57; Leiden, 1993). A. H. Armstrong, *Plotinian and Christian Studies* (1979). P. E. More, *Hellenistic Philosophies* (The Greek Tradition, 2; Princeton, NJ, 1923), pp. 172–259. H.-R. Schwyzer in *PW* 41 (1951), cols. 471–591, and Supplementband, 15 (1978), cols. 310–28, both with bibl. See also bibl. to NEOPLATONISM.

Plumstead Peculiars. See PECULIAR PEOPLE.

Plunkett (or Plunket), St Oliver (1625–81), RC Abp. of *Armagh. Of noble family, he was born at Loughcrew, nr. Oldcastle, Co. Meath, and studied and later taught at Rome. In 1654 he was ordained priest, for some years acted as the representative of the Irish Bishops at Rome, and in 1669 was appointed Abp. of Armagh. Consecrated at Ghent, he returned to Ireland, where he administered his diocese energetically, raising the standards of education and morality in the face of constant hardship. During the persecutions which began in 1673 he remained in Ireland and in the fury engendered by the Titus *Oates Plot he was arrested (1679), tried in London, and executed for treason at Tyburn on 11 July (1 July, OS), 1681. His head, taken to Rome in 1684, has since 1722 been at Drogheda; most of his body is at *Downside. He was canonized in 1975. Feast day, 11 July.

Letters, ed. J. Hanly (Dublin, 1979). Report of his last speech and confession pub. London, 1681; repr., with other papers, by E. Horne, OSB, in *Downside Review*, 39 (1921), pp. 99–105. The

Trial and Condemnation of Edw. Fitz-Harris . . . as also . . . of Dr Oliver Plunket . . . (London, 1681), pp. 61–103. Another contemporary account of his martyrdom ('Vita et Mors Gloriosa Illustrissimi D. Oliverii Plunketti'), ed. by P. F. Moran in his *Spicilegium Ossoriense*, 3 (Dublin, 1884), pp. 102–8. Memoirs compiled from orig. sources, also by P. F. Moran (ibid., 1861). Other modern Lives by H. [Mrs T.] Concannon (London, 1935), E. Curtis, OCSO (Dublin and London, 1963), and T. Ó Fiaich (Dublin, 1975). A. Curtayne, *The Trial of Oliver Plunkett* (1953). R. Bagwell in *DNB* 45 (1896), pp. 442–5.

Pluralism. (1) The view that the world contains or consists of a plurality of things or states ultimately distinct, and hence the contradiction of '*Monism' (q.v.).

(2) For religious pluralism, see THEOLOGY OF RELIGIONS.

W. James, *A Pluralistic Universe* (1909); J. Ward, *The Realm of Ends, or Pluralism and Theism* (1911).

Pluralities Act 1838. An Act forbidding any clergyman in the C of E simultaneously to hold more than one ecclesiastical benefice with cure of souls except, by dispensation of the Abp. of *Canterbury, in the case of two livings with a population of under 3,000 where the travelling distance between the churches was less than ten miles and the joint annual income under £1,000. The Act also provided more stringent regulations for residence. It was modified by the Pluralities Act 1850, acc. to which the churches of benefices held in conjunction were to be under three miles apart and the annual value of one under £100; the Pluralities Acts Amendment Act 1885, which allowed the distance between the churches to be four miles and provided that the annual income of one should not exceed £200; and the Pluralities Measure 1930, which raised the annual income permissible in cases of plurality to £400. The Benefices Act 1898 and the Union of Benefices Measure 1923 were concerned with the administration of the Act. The terms of the Act are virtually abrogated by the Pastoral Reorganisation Measure 1949, and now benefices can be held in plurality only as part of a pastoral scheme made under the Pastoral Measure 1983. See also PARISH.

R. *Phillimore, *The Ecclesiastical Law of the Church of England*, 2 (2nd edn., 1895), pp. 898–906; H. W. Cripps, *A Practical Treatise on the Law relating to the Church and Clergy* (8th edn. by K. M. Macmorran, 1937), pp. 299–302.

pluvial (Lat. *pluviale*). An alternative name for the *cope, probably from its having been originally a rain-cloak. In its English form the word is now almost obsolete.

Plymouth Brethren. A Christian religious body, so named because its first centre in England was established by J. N. *Darby (1800–82), a former Anglican priest, at Plymouth in 1830. They had been founded two or three years earlier in *Ireland, where they were known as the 'Brethren', a title still widely used. Among their early converts was S. P. *Tregelles, the biblical scholar. Their teaching combines elements from *Calvinism and *Pietism and emphasis has often been laid on an expected *Millennium. Their moral outlook is *Puritanical and they renounce many secular occupations, allowing only those compatible with NT standards (e.g. medicine, handicrafts). They have no organized ministry, though great stress is laid on the Breaking of the Bread each Sunday, partly as a symbol of Christian union and partly as the appointed means of showing forth Christ's death. Their outlook on the Bible is conservative. They also stress the complete autonomy of the local church.

In spite of their emphasis on Christian unity as a principle, the Plymouth Brethren tended from the first to split into separate groups. Controversies on the human nature of Christ and subsequently on Church government led to the fundamental division in 1849 between the 'Open Brethren' and the 'Exclusive Brethren'; and within these groups there are several subdivisions. The second half of the 20th cent. has seen a sharp decline in the numbers of the Plymouth Brethren. Though numerically few, they are widely distributed, esp. in Great Britain and Ireland, on the Continent of Europe (esp. Switzerland, France, and Italy), and in the USA, and are very active in missionary work, esp. in India, E. Asia, Central Africa, and S. America.

W. B. Neatby, *A History of the Plymouth Brethren* (1901). D. J. Beattie, *Brethren: The Story of a Great Recovery* (Kilmarnock [1940]); H. H. Rowdon, *The Origins of the Brethren, 1825–1850* (1967); F. R. Coad, *A History of the Brethren Movement: Its Origins, its Worldwide Development and its Significance for the Present Day* ([Exeter] 1968); N. de L. Smith, *Roots, Renewal and the Brethren* (Pasadena, Calif., and Exeter [1986]). J. McCulloch in *HERE* 2 (1909), pp. 843–8, s.v. 'Brethren (Plymouth)'. See also works in bibl. to DARBY, J. N.

Pneumatomachi (Gk. πνευματομάχοι), 4th-cent. heretics who denied the full Godhead of the Holy Spirit. They are perhaps the 'Tropici' of St *Athanasius in his Epp. to *Serapion of Thmuis (between 355 and 361), but came to the fore only in 373, when *Eustathius of Sebaste became their head after breaking with his former friend St *Basil the Great. They were condemned by Pope *Damasus in 374, and their teaching was repeatedly attacked by the three great *Cappadocian Fathers and St *Didymus. The sect had reached its full development *c.*380, containing a more conservative section which, while rejecting the Divinity of the Holy Spirit, accepted the consubstantiality of the Son, and a radical party, which denied also the latter. At the Council of *Constantinople (381; can. 1) they were anathematized. The historians *Socrates and *Sozomen, as well as the Latin Fathers St *Jerome, *Rufinus, and others, regard *Macedonius (q.v.) as their founder, but as he disappeared from the forefront of theological controversy after his deposition in 360 and as his name does not occur in contemporary anti-Pneumatomachian writings, this statement seems to be unfounded. It is possible that after Macedonius's death his followers amalgamated with the Pneumatomachi, and that the identification is to be so explained. The sect disappeared after 383, when its adherents became victims of the Theodosian anti-heretical laws.

H. Dörries, *De Spiritu Sancto: Der Beitrag des Basilius zum Abschluss des trinitarischen Dogmas* (Abh. (Gött.), Dritte Folge, 39; 1956), esp. pp. 94–120. W.-D. Hauschild, *Die Pneumatomachen* (Hamburg diss., 1967). F. *Loofs in *HERE* 8 (1915), pp. 225–30, s.v. 'Macedonianism'; P. Meinhold in *PW* 21 (pt. 1; 1951), cols. 1066–1101, s.v.

Pococke, Edward (1604–91), orientalist. Educated at Magdalen Hall and Corpus Christi College, Oxford, he became a Fellow of the latter society in 1628 and was English chaplain at Aleppo from 1630 to 1635. Here he perfected his knowledge of Arabic, collected a large number of valuable MSS, and on his return was appointed by W. *Laud first professor of Arabic at Oxford. In 1648 he succeeded to the chair of Hebrew, but his royalist views led to his temporary suspension. His erudition was immense. He took an active part in the preparation of B. *Walton's '*Polyglot Bible' (1657), and in 1660, at the expense of R. *Boyle, published an Arabic edition of H. *Grotius's *De veritate christianae religionis* for the furtherance of Christianity among Muslims. In 1663 he issued the Arabic text (with a Latin translation) of the *Historia Compendiosa Dynastiarum* of *Bar Hebraeus (Abû-l-Faraǧ). He also published large parts of the BCP in Arabic.

L. Twells (ed.), *The Theological Works of the Learned Dr. Pocock* (2 vols., 1740), with full biog. and correspondence. P. M. Holt, *Studies in the History of the Near East* (1973), pp. 3–49. S. Lane-Poole in *DNB* 46 (1896), pp. 7–12.

Poimandres (Gk. ποιμάνδρης, apparently 'the Shepherd of Men'). The first treatise in the *corpus* of *Hermetic writings (q.v.), though in its text the name of Hermes does not occur. It describes a vision seen under the guidance of Poimandres, a semi-divine being who is termed 'the Mind of the Sovereignty' (ὁ τῆς αὐθεντίας νοῦς), and treats of the creation of the universe and man, the union of spirit with matter following the Fall, and the method of redemption by knowledge (γνῶσις). The writer's nearest associations are with *Gnosticism; but there are parallels with the NT, e.g. the description of the Divine as 'light' and 'life' and the doctrine that the Divine *Logos was active in creation (cf. Jn. 1: 2–4). At times the language closely approximates to that of the *Septuagint, which was certainly known to the author. The work was written in Egypt early in the Christian era, perhaps (C. H. *Dodd) not long after AD 100. A Latin translation by Marsilio *Ficino (finished in 1463/4), was the first printed text (Treviso, 1471).

Greek text in *Hermetis Trismegisti Poemander*, ed. G. Parthey, Berlin, 1854; and (with much highly conjectural emendation) in W. Scott, *Hermetica*, 1 (1924); also ed. A. D. Nock, with Fr. tr. by A. J. Festugière, *Corpus Hermeticum*, 1 (Collection des Universités de France, 1945), pp. 6–28. C. H. Dodd, *The Bible and the Greeks* (1935), pp. 99–248. R. *Reitzenstein, *Poimandres: Studien zur griechisch-ägyptischen und frühchristlichen Literatur* (1904). E. Haenchen, 'Aufbau und Theologie des "Poimandres" ', *Zeitschrift für Theologie und Kirche*, 53 (1956), pp. 149–91.

points, Hebrew. See VOWEL POINTS.

Poiret, Pierre (1646–1719), French Protestant spiritual writer. After being preacher at Heidelberg (1668) and Anweiler (1672), he resigned his office in 1676 and became the companion of the visionary, A. *Bourignon, whose ideas he subsequently interpreted in *L'Économie divine* (7 vols., 1687). After her death in 1680, he lived at Amsterdam and from 1688 at Rijnsburg. He was a keen student of mysticism, esp. as found in his contemporaries, J. *Boehme and Mme *Guyon (whose works he began editing in 1704), and, of earlier writers, of *Thomas à Kempis and J. *Tauler. Though he was critical of the Cartesian philosophy, he stressed its relevance to the study of mysticism. His most important work, *Bibliotheca mysticorum*

(1708), contains much valuable out-of-the-way information on minor writers on mystic subjects. After his death Poiret's influence was chiefly exercised through his disciple G. *Tersteegen, and, less directly, on the whole *Pietistic Movement.

M. Wieser, *Peter Poiret: Der Vater der romanischen Mystik in Deutschland* (1932); G. A. Krieg, *Der mystische Kreis: Wesen und Werden der Theologie Pierre Poirets* (Arbeiten zur Geschichte des Pietismus, 17; 1979). M. Chevallier, *Pierre Poiret* (Bibliotheca Dissentium. Répertoire des non-conformistes religieux des seizième et dix-septième siècles, 5; Baden-Baden, 1985). Id. in *Dict. Sp.* 12 (pt. 2; 1986), cols. 1831–6, s.v.

Poissy, Colloquy of (Disputatio Pussicena). A Conference held in 1561 at Poissy (on the Seine, not far from Paris) between the French bishops under Cardinal F. de Tournon and the Protestant ministers led by T. *Beza, to consider the religious situation created by the progress of the Reformed doctrines. It had been summoned by *Catherine de' Medici. Among the Catholic spokesmen was J. *Laínez, the General of the *Jesuits, and among the Protestants *Peter Martyr. Though it failed to secure dogmatic agreement between the two parties on the Eucharist, it prepared the way for the edict of Jan. 1562, which gave official recognition and a measure of freedom to French Protestants.

J. Roserot de Melin, 'Rome et Poissy (1560–61)', *Mélanges d'Archéologie et d'Histoire*, 39 (1921–2), pp. 47–151. H. O. Evennett, *The Cardinal of Lorraine and the Council of Trent* (Cambridge, 1930), esp. pp. 283–391. D. [G.] Nugent, *Ecumenism in the Age of The Reformation: The Colloquy of Poissy* (Cambridge, Mass., 1974). A. Dufour, 'Das Religionsgespräch von Poissy. Hoffnungen der Reformierten und der Moyenneurs', in G. Müller (ed.), *Die Religionsgespräche der Reformationszeit* (Gütersloh, 1980), pp. 117–26. M. Turchetti, *Concordia o tolleranza? François Bauduin (1520–1573) e i 'Moyenneurs'* (Travaux d'Humanisme et Renaissance, 200; Geneva, 1984), *passim* (see index). E. Lachenmann in *PRE* (3rd edn.), 15 (1904), pp. 497–504.

Poland, Christianity in. Poland received Christianity in the latter half of the 10th cent., probably from Moravia. In 966 the Prince Mieczysław I was baptized, and in 1000 Gniezno became a metropolitan see. (The alleged earlier dependence of the Church on the see of Magdeburg seems to have been disproved by modern research.) There were strong anti-Christian outbreaks between 1034 and 1040 and many martyrdoms. Throughout the 11th and 12th cents. the country was devastated by civil wars and disorders, and the Synod of Łęczyca (1180) had to take special measures against robbers of churches. The fact that the *Hildebrandine reforms (11th cent.) had been carried out by royal power in the teeth of the opposition of bishops and clergy had brought the Church strongly under State control, but early in the 13th cent. this control was shaken off and the Church was reorganized in conformity with current canon law. In the same century the Tartar invasions stirred up a revival of Christianity; this later manifested itself in missions to Lithuania, which was Christianized on its union with Poland in 1387.

In the early 15th cent. some of the nobility supported the *Hussites and the *Inquisition was introduced. In the 16th cent. the *Reformation also made headway, esp. among the nobility, who had long chafed at the dual control of the King and Church. *Calvinism was the strongest influence, though *Lutheran communities developed in German areas, and the country also became a haven for exiled *Bohemian Brethren and *Socinians. Religious tension grew, while internal reform of the Church was effectively prevented by the Papal legate, J. F. Commendone; but by the Confederation of Warsaw in 1573 mutual toleration was secured. After the Confederation the RCs, led by S. *Hosius, increased their influence by judicious reforms, while dissensions diminished the strength of their opponents. In 1595 the Ruthenian Church (see UKRAINIAN CHURCHES) renounced communion with *Constantinople and submitted to Rome, and shortly afterwards the *Armenians in Poland accepted *Uniat status.

In the 17th cent. the RC majority succeeded in making toleration almost a dead letter and in associating the revived and expanded Church with national values (esp. through the 'Black' Madonna of Częstochowa). The Protestants, though not often formally persecuted, remained under restrictions until the Confederation of Radom (1767) sought to reassert complete religious freedom. The continual wars hindered ecclesiastical organization, while the parlous state of the country opened the way for the growth of *Freemasonry, which fomented anti-Church feeling. The partition of Poland between Russia, Austria, and Prussia, begun in 1772 and completed in 1795, had serious consequences for the RC Church. Even though it gave little support to movements for national liberation, the Russians put endless restrictions upon RCs and in 1831 compelled the Uniat Easterns to give up their communion with Rome; Prussia also interfered with the freedom of its RC subjects; but Austria, while it placed the RCs under strict State supervision, and prevented control from Rome, often favoured their interests. With the independence of Poland in 1919 the influence of the RC Church revived, though the Orthodox retained their hold on many of the eastern parts.

Both Orthodox and RC Churches suffered severely under German and Russian occupation in 1939–45, and the setting up of a Communist-controlled government in 1945 led to the continuance of severe difficulties, esp. for the RCs who now, with the cession of eastern territories to the Soviet Union and the expulsion of most Germans, formed an overwhelming majority of the population. In the period since the Second World War relations between the Polish government and the RC Church have often been strained, but esp. after the election of a Pole as Pope *John Paul II in 1978, the RC Church enjoyed greater freedom in Poland than it did in other E. European countries, with active parochial life, flourishing monastic communities, and an autonomous university at Lublin. RC opposition, expressing itself esp. through the Solidarity movement, was a major factor in the collapse of the Communist regime in 1989, which allowed the Church to resume a central political role in Poland; but the strength of conservative attitudes in its ranks, allied to suspicion of the country's new liberal-capitalist arrangements, have made for a slow and painful process of accommodation. See also OLD CATHOLICS and MARIAVITES.

K. Völker, *Kirchengeschichte Polens* (1930), with bibl. W. F. Reddaway and others (eds.), *The Cambridge History of Poland* (2 vols., 1941–50), esp. vol. 1, chs. 2, 4, 16 and 19. J. Braun (ed.), *Poland in Christian Civilization* (London [1985]). B. Kumor and

Z. Obertyński (eds.), *Historia Kościoła w Polsce* (2 parts in 4 vols, Poznań and Warsaw, 1974–9 [up to 1914]). J. Kłoczowski (ed.), *Kościół w Polsce* (2 vols. + maps, Cracow [1968–70]). J. Dowiat, *Historia Kościoła katolickiego w Polsce do połowy XV wieku* (Warsaw, 1968). F. Siegmund-Schultze (ed.), *Ekklesia*, 5. 2 (Lfg. 21, Die evangelischen Kirchen in Polen; 1938), with bibl.; A. Rhode, *Geschichte der evangelischen Kirche in Posener Lande* (Marburger Ostforschungen, 4; Würzburg, 1956). V. Krasinski, *Historical Sketch of the Rise, Progress and Decline of the Reformation in Poland* (2 vols., 1838–40); T. Wotschke, *Geschichte der Reformation in Polen* (Studien zur Kultur und Geschichte der Reformation herausgegeben vom Verein für Reformationsgeschichte, fasc. 1; 1911); B. Stasiewski, *Reformation und Gegen-Reformation in Polen: Neue Forschungsergebnisse* (Katholisches Leben und Kämpfen im Zeitalter der Glaubensspaltung, 18; Münster i.W., 1960), and other works of this author; G. Schramm, *Der polnische Adel und die Reformation 1548–1607* (Veröffentlichungen des Instituts für Europäische Geschichte Mainz, 36; Wiesbaden, 1965); A. Jobert, *De Luther à Mohila: La Pologne dans la crise de la Chrétienté 1517–1648* (Collection historique de l'Institut d'études slaves, 21; Paris, 1974). J. Tazbir, *A State without Stakes: Polish Religious Toleration in the Sixteenth and Seventeenth Centuries* (New York and Warsaw [1973]; Eng. tr. of Polish work pub. in Warsaw, 1967). M. Rechowicz (ed.), *Dzieje teologii katolickiej w Polsce* (3 vols. in 5 parts, Lublin, 1974–7). T. Andrews, *The Polish National Church in America and Poland* (1953), *passim*. P. Walters (ed.), *World Christianity: Eastern Europe* (Keston Book, 29; Eastbourne, 1988), pp. 107–39. Much material is to be found in the periodicals *Nasza Przeszłość* (Warsaw, 1946 ff.; RC) and *Odrodzenie i Reformacja w Polsce* (ibid., 1956 ff.; Protestant). B. Stasiewski in *NCE* 11 (1967), pp. 471–86, s.v., K. Górski and others in *Dict. Sp.* 12 (pt. 2; 1986), cols. 1864–901, s.v. 'Pologne', both with bibl. See also UKRAINIAN CHURCHES.

Pole, Reginald

Pole, Reginald (1500–58), Abp. of *Canterbury. Of the blood royal by his mother, Margaret, Countess of Salisbury and niece of Edward IV, he was educated at the Sheen Charterhouse and Magdalen College, Oxford, and given ecclesiastical preferment by *Henry VIII while still in his teens and a layman. In 1519 he went to Padua, and for several years was in close contact with the later Italian Renaissance, corresponding with T. *More and *Erasmus, and visiting Rome and Paris. In 1530 Henry, anxious for help over his divorce, offered him the see of *York or *Winchester, but Pole declined both, and in 1534–6 wrote *Pro Ecclesiasticae Unitatis Defensione*, censuring the King's conduct. *Paul III summoned him in 1536 to confer about a general council, put him on a commission for the reform of discipline, and (after his ordination as deacon) created him a cardinal. In 1538 indignation at Rome over the destruction of *Becket's shrine caused Pole to be sent as legate on a fruitless mission to persuade Spain and France to break with England, and in 1539 an Act of Attainder was passed against him and his family. In 1541 G. *Contarini took counsel with Pole, before the Conference of *Ratisbon, with a view to conciliating the Protestants, whose views on justification were not unlike Pole's own; and in the following year he was one of the three legates appointed to preside at the Council of *Trent, which did not meet, however, until 1545. In 1547 he urged *Somerset to treat with the Holy See, and on Paul III's death (1549) was nearly elected Pope. On *Edward VI's death in 1553 *Julius III appointed him legate in England, and after the removal of his attainder he reached Dover in Nov. 1554, formally absolved Parliament from schism, and presided over a synod of both *Convocations. On 20 Mar.

1556 he was ordained priest at the Greyfriars, Greenwich, and consecrated Abp. of Canterbury two days later. With the outbreak of war between *Paul IV (Carafa) and *Philip II of Spain, the Queen became the Pope's enemy, and the Pope cancelled Pole's legation, accusing him also of doctrinal unsoundness. He died only 12 hours after the Queen. Pole was a man of pure morals, sincere piety, and ascetic habits, and animated by a remarkable singleness of purpose.

Standard edn. of his *Epistolae*, incl. some other writings, ed. Card. A. M. Quirini (Brescia, 5 vols., 1744–57). *Friedenslegation des Reginald Pole zu Kaiser Karl V. und König Heinrich II. (1553–1556)*, ed. H. Lutz (Nuntiaturberichte aus Deutschland, Abt. 1, Bd. 15; 1981). Lives by L. Beccadelli (Lat., Venice, 1563; Eng. tr., 1766), T. Phillips (Oxford, 1764), and W. Schenk (London, 1950). [F. A.] *Gasquet, *Cardinal Pole and his Early Friends* (1927). D. Fenlon, *Heresy and Obedience in Tridentine Italy: Cardinal Pole and the Counter Reformation* (Cambridge, 1972). P. Simoncelli, *Il Caso Reginald Pole: Eresia e Santità nelle Polemiche religiose del Cinquecento* (Uomini e Dottrine, 23; 1977). J. I. Tellechea Idígoras, *Fray Bartolomé Carranza y el Cardenal Pole: Un navarro en la restauración católica de Inglaterra (1554–1558)* (Pamplona, 1977). R. H. Pogson, 'Revival and reform in Mary Tudor's Church: a question of money', *JEH* 25 (1974), pp. 249–65, repr. in C. Haigh (ed.), *The English Reformation Revised* (1987), pp. 139–56; R. H. Pogson, 'Reginald Pole and the Priorities of Government in Mary Tudor's Church', *Historical Journal*, 18 (1975), pp. 3–20. T. F. Mayer, 'A Diet for Henry VIII: The Failure of Reginald Pole's 1537 Legation', *Journal of British Studies*, 26 (1987), pp. 305–31; id., 'A Fate Worse than Death: Reginald Pole and the Parisian Theologians', *EHR* 103 (1988), pp. 870–91. A. F. Allison and D. M. Rogers, *The Contemporary Printed Literature of the English Counter-Reformation between 1558 and 1640*, 1 (Aldershot, 1989), pp. 124–6 (nos. 911–24). *BRUO, 1501–1540*, pp. 453–5. J. *Gairdner in *DNB* 46 (1896), pp. 35–46. See also bibl. to HENRY VIII.

Polish National Church

Polish National Church. See OLD CATHOLICS (3).

politarchs

politarchs (Gk. πολιτάρχης). A comparatively rare title for magistrates in the Graeco-Roman world, used in the NT only of the city magistrates of Thessalonica (Acts 17: 6, 8; AV, 'the rulers of the city'). The accuracy of St *Luke's usage is proved by the occurrence of the word on several inscriptions which come from Thessalonica.

E. de W. Burton, 'The Politarchs', *American Journal of Theology*, 2 (1898), pp. 598–632. G. H. R. Horsley in *Anchor Bible Dictionary*, 5 (1992), pp. 384–9, s.v.

Politiques

Politiques. French political party which advocated religious toleration esp. after the Massacre of St *Bartholomew's Day (q.v.). They made an alliance with the *Huguenots and subsequently many of them supported *Henry IV.

Polycarp, St

Polycarp, St (traditionally *c.*69–*c.*155), Bp. of *Smyrna. He seems to have been the leading Christian figure in Roman Asia in the middle of the 2nd cent., and his long life (about which unfortunately little is known) is thus an important link between the *Apostolic Age and the great Christian writers (e.g. St *Irenaeus) who flourished at the end of the 2nd cent. A staunch defender of orthodoxy, he devoted much of his energy to combating such heretics as the *Marcionites and *Valentinians. A letter addressed to him by St *Ignatius has survived, as well as his own 'Ep.

to Philippians' (perhaps a combination of two epistles of different dates; so P. N. Harrison). The latter is full of echoes of the NT writings, esp. the *Pastoral Epistles. At the end of his life, when Polycarp paid a visit to Rome to see the bishop, Anicetus, and to discuss, among other things, the date of keeping the *Easter festival, it was agreed that each Church should maintain its own custom and that Asia should continue the *Quartodeciman practice. Soon after his return to Smyrna, Polycarp was arrested during a public (pagan) festival and, proclaiming that he had served Christ for 86 years, he refused to recant his faith and was burnt to death. The traditionally accepted date of his death is 23 Feb. 155 or 156, but as *Eusebius places it in the reign of *Marcus Aurelius (161–80), some scholars have argued for a later period and have put the date of his birth correspondingly later. The 'Martyrium Polycarpi', written from Smyrna by request of the Church at Philomelium, gives an account of his trial and martyrdom. St Irenaeus says that Polycarp 'had intercourse with John [the Apostle or Elder?] and with the rest of those who had seen the Lord'. Feast day, 23 Feb. (in W., formerly 26 Jan.).

Texts, incl. 'Martyrium Polycarpi', will be found in edns. of the Apostolic Fathers; with esp. valuable comm. and notes in ed. J. B. *Lightfoot (pt. 2, 3 vols., 1885); also conveniently ed., with Fr. tr., by P. T. Camelot, OP, in his edn. of the Letters of Ignatius (SC 10; 2nd edn., 1951), pp. 242–75; 4th edn. (1969), pp. 197–239. P. N. Harrison, *Polycarp's Two Epistles to the Philippians* (1936). On the date of the martyrdom, see C. H. *Turner in *Studia Biblica et Ecclesiastica*, 2 (1890), pp. 105–55 [defends 23 Feb. 155]; also H. Grégoire and P. Orgels, 'La Véritable Date du martyre de Polycarpe (23 févr. 177) et le *Corpus Polycarpianum*', *Anal. Boll.* 69 (1951), pp. 1–38 [much contested]; H. I. Marrou, 'La Date du martyre de S. Polycarpe', ibid. 71 (1953), pp. 5–20; T. D. Barnes, 'A Note on Polycarp', *JTS* NS 18 (1967), pp. 433–7; P. Brind'Amour, 'La date du martyre de saint Polycarpe (le 23 février 167)', *Anal. Boll.* 98 (1980), pp. 456–62. H. von Campenhausen, *Polykarp von Smyrna und die Pastoralbriefe* (Sb. (Heid.), 1951, Abhandlung 2; 1951); id., *Bearbeitungen und Interpolationen des Polykarpmartyriums* (ibid., 1957, Abhandlung 3; 1957); H. Conzelmann, *Bemerkungen zum Martyrium Polykarps* (Nachr. (Gött.), 1978, Heft 2); B. Dehandschutter, *Martyrium Polycarpi: Een literair-kritische studie* (Bibliotheca Ephemeridum Theologicarum Lovaniensium, 52 [1979]). G. Buschmann, *Martyrium Polycarpi—Eine formkritische Studie: Ein Beitrag zur Frage nach der Entstehung der Gattung Märtyrerakte* (Beihefte zur *ZNTW*, 70; 1994). Altaner and Stuiber (1978), pp. 50–2 and 552. G. *Salmon in *DCB* 4 (1887), pp. 423–31, s.v.; G. Fritz in *DTC* 12 (pt. 2; 1935), cols. 2515–20, s.v. 'Polycarpe'; P. Meinhold in *PW* 21 (pt. 2; 1952), cols. 1662–93; D. Van Damme in *Dict. Sp.* 12 (pt. 2; 1986), cols. 1902–8, s.v. See also PIONIUS, ST and bibl.

Polychronius (d. *c*.430), Bp. of Apamaea in Syria. He was the brother of *Theodore, Bp. of Mopsuestia. A biblical exegete of the *Antiochene school, he wrote commentaries on Job, Daniel, and Ezekiel, of which considerable fragments survive, chiefly in *catenae. It is probable that the fragments on other Books (Prov., Eccles., Song of Songs, etc.) come from another writer of the same name. He expressly condemned the *Alexandrian method of allegorical exegesis.

Frags. on Job ed. P. *Young in *Catena Graecorum Patrum in Jobum* (London, 1637); repr. in J. P. Migne, *PG* 93. 13–468. Other frags. ed. A. *Mai, whence repr. in J. P. Migne, *PG* 162 (very rare). O. *Bardenhewer, *Polychronius von Apamea* (1879).

CPG 2 (1974), pp. 361 f. (nos. 3878–82). Bardenhewer, 3, pp. 322–4.

Polycrates (2nd cent.), Bp. of *Ephesus. He was the leading *Quartodeciman of Asia who, after convening a synod *c*.190, sturdily opposed Pope *Victor in his attempts to secure that the feast of *Easter should be uniformly celebrated on a Sunday. In consequence, Victor withdrew from communion with Polycrates. The incident, which is all that is known of Polycrates, is an important illustration of the early claims of the Roman see.

Extracts from Polycrates' letter are preserved in *Eusebius, *HE* 5. 24. 2–8 and 3. 31. 3. E. Peterson in *EC* 9 (1952), cols. 1672 f.

Polyglot Bibles. A 'Polyglot Bible' is a single Bible containing the text in a number of languages. Such Bibles were issued esp. in the 16th and 17th cents. The most celebrated is the '*Complutensian Polyglot', in 6 vols. (1522), produced under the patronage of Cardinal *Ximénez, containing the OT in Hebrew, Latin, and Greek, and the NT in Greek and Latin. Other Polyglot Bibles are those of Antwerp (1569–72) in 8 vols., adding the Syriac NT, with a Latin translation; of Paris (1629–45) in 10 vols., adding the Syriac OT, Arabic, with a Latin translation, and the *Samaritan Pentateuch; and of London (1653–7), by B. *Walton, in six vols., containing the Hebrew, Greek, Latin, Syriac, Ethiopic, Arabic, and Persian, all with Latin translations, as well as the Samaritan Pentateuch, various *Targums, and selected readings of the *Codex Alexandrinus. Diglot biblical manuscripts (Graeco-Latin and Graeco-Coptic) are known from the 5th, and triglot from the 9th, cent. onwards. A few MSS with four or five languages, written in Egypt, come from the 14th cent.

B. Hall, *The Great Polyglot Bibles* (Book Club of California, 124; San Francisco, 1966). S. Brock, 'A Fourteenth-Century Polyglot Psalter', in G. E. Kadish and G. E. Freeman (eds.), *Studies in Philology in Honour of Ronald Jasper Williams* (Toronto, 1982), pp. 1–15. Darlow and Moule, 2 (1911), pp. 1–36.

Pomponazzi, Pietro (1462–1525). The most outstanding philosopher of the Italian Renaissance. He taught successively at Padua, Ferrara, and *Bologna. Under the influence esp. of the Aristotelian commentator, Alexander of Aphrodisias (*c*. AD 200; whence Pomponazzi's disciples were termed 'Alexandrists'), he expounded *Aristotle in a way at variance with that of the regnant *Scholasticism, maintaining, e.g., in his *De Immortalitate Animae* (1516) that it was possible to demonstrate by the natural reason the mortality of the human soul. He argued that the only sense in which one could speak legitimately of the immateriality and immortality of the soul was in reference to its capacity for reflective knowledge and conceiving universal concepts, a capacity which accorded it a status between the brutes on the one hand and the angelic beings on the other. Pomponazzi maintained, however, that these doctrines need cause no offence to the Christian, since they were merely the deductions of human reason and were transcended by the supernatural revelation made to the Church. Two later treatises, *De Incantationibus* and *De Fato*, were published posthumously at Basle.

Collections of a number of his works as *Tractatus Acutissimi* (Venice, 1525) and *Opera* (Basle, 1567). Modern edns. of *De

Immortalitate Animae, with Ital. tr., by G. Morra (Bologna, 1954) and of *De Fato*, by R. Lemay (Lugano, 1957). *Corsi inediti dell'Insegnamento Padovano*, 1. 'Super Libello de Substantia Orbis Expositio et Quaestiones Quattuor' (1507), ed. A. Poppi (Saggi e Testi, 6; Padua, 1966); 2. 'Quaestiones Physicae et Animasticae Decem' (1499–1500; 1503–4), ed. id. (ibid. 9; 1970). B. Nardi, 'Le opere inedite del Pomponazzi', *Giornale critico della filosofia italiana*, 29 (1950), pp. 427–42; 30 (1951), pp. 103–18, 363–81; 32 (1953), pp. 45–70, 175–91; 33 (1954), pp. 341–55; 34 (1955), pp. 186–98 and 385–403. P. O. Kristeller, 'A New Manuscript Source for Pomponazzi's Theory of the Soul from his Paduan Period', *Revue Internationale de Philosophie*, 5 (1951), pp. 145–57; id., 'Two Unpublished Questions on the Soul of Pietro Pomponazzi', *Medievalia et Humanistica*, 9 (1955), pp. 76–101, incl. text. Eng. tr. of *De Immortalitate Animae*, with introd., in E. Cassirer and others (eds.), *The Renaissance Philosophy of Man* (Chicago, 1948), pp. 257–381, with bibl. p. 400. F. Fiorentino, *Pietro Pomponazzi: Studi storici sulla scuola bolognese-padovana del sec. XVI* (Florence, 1868; still important); id., *Studi e ritratti della rinascenza* (Bari, 1911), pp. 1–79. A. H. Douglas, *The Philosophy and Psychology of P. Pomponazzi* (ed. C. Douglas and R. P. Hardie, 1910); B. Nardi, *Studi su Petro Pomponazzi* (Florence, 1965). A. Poppi, *Saggi sul Pensiero inedito di Pietro Pomponazzi* (Saggi e Testi, 8; Padua, 1970); P. O. Kristeller, *Aristotelismo e Sincretismo nel Pensiero di Pietro Pomponazzi* (ibid. 19; 1983). L. Ferri, *La psicologia di P. Pomponazzi, secondo un MS. della Bibl. Angelica di Roma* (1877). B. Nardi in *EC* 9 (1952), cols. 1731–4, s.v.

Pomponia Graecina (1st cent.), wife of Aulus Plautius, the conqueror of Britain, and thought by some scholars to have been an early convert to Christianity. Acc. to *Tacitus (*Annales*, 13. 32), she was accused by her husband of foreign superstition (*superstitio externa*), but acquitted. A Greek inscription to 'Pomponios Grecinos', perhaps a descendant, has been found in the catacomb of St *Callistus. She has been identified (not very convincingly) by G. B. *de Rossi and others with the Roman matron *Lucina (q.v.) of the 'Crypt of Lucina'.

G. B. de Rossi, *La Roma sotterranea cristiana*, 1 (1864), pp. 319 f., and 2 (1867), pp. 362–5. H. *Leclercq, OSB, in *DACL* 1 (pt. 2; 1907), cols. 2847 f., s.v. 'Aristocratiques (Classes), II', with bibl.

Pontifex Maximus (Lat., 'Supreme Pontiff'). Originally a pagan title of the chief priest at Rome, *Tertullian used it satirically in one of his *Montanist writings (*De pudicitia*, 1) of either the Pope or the Bp. of Carthage. In the 15th cent. it became a regular title of honour for Popes. Cf. the Italian 'Sommo Pontefice' and the French 'Souverain Pontife'.

R. Schieffer, 'Der Päpst als Pontifex Maximus. Bemerkungen zur Geschichte eines päpstlichen Ehrentitels' *Zeitschrift der Savigny-Stiftung für Rechtsgeschichte*, Kanonistische Abteilung, 57 (1971), pp. 300–9. I. Kajanto, '*Pontifex maximus* as the title of the Pope', *Arctos*, NS 15 (1981), pp. 37–52.

Pontifical, the liturgical book of the W. Church containing the prayers and ceremonies for rites used by a bishop, e.g. *Confirmation and *Ordinations, the consecration of churches, etc. It does not, however, contain the Pontifical Mass. Pontificals developed from a combination of the directions in the *Ordines with the relevant formulae from *Sacramentaries. The earliest attempts to combine these elements were made in the 9th cent. A very important stage was reached soon after the middle of the 10th cent., when a large collection of texts was put together,

prob. at St Alban's, Mainz; this has been named by its discoverer, M. Andrieu, the Romano-Germanic Pontifical. This book rapidly gained acceptance all over Europe and was received at Rome, where it came to be regarded as the *Ordo Romanus*. During the course of the 12th cent. it was adapted and brought up to date for use in the churches of Rome. Under *Innocent III a new recension was made, which was further developed under *Innocent IV. These books are known as the Pontificals of the Roman Curia. They gave way in the 14th cent. to a private compilation made *c.*1293–5 by the canonist, William *Durandus, Bp. of Mende. This was a marked improvement on them by reason of its clear organization. It was divided into three books: the first relates to persons: Confirmation, Ordination, Consecration of bishops, etc.; the second relates to things: consecration of churches, altars, etc.; and the third deals with rites for special functions, such as the consecration of holy oils, visitation, excommunication, etc. This compilation was the basis of the first printed Pontifical (Rome, 1485) and with minor modifications of the authoritative edition issued in 1596 by *Clement VIII, who forbade the use of any other Pontifical. A revision of part of the Pontifical was undertaken by a commission appointed by Pope *Pius XII; the revision of the remainder was ordained at the Second *Vatican Council. The new Pontifical (not as complete in its coverage) appeared in 1978. Some additional texts for the revised rites have been issued since.

The substance of the Roman Pontificals is largely taken from the *Ordines Romani* (q.v., incl. bibl.). C. Vogel and R. Elze (eds.), *Le Pontifical romano-germanique du dixième siècle* (ST 226–7; 1963); M. Andrieu (ed.), *Le Pontifical romain au Moyen Age* (ibid. 86–8, 99; 1938–41); M. Dykmans, SJ, *Le Pontifical Romain révisé au XVe siècle* (ibid. 311; 1985). W. H. *Frere, F. C. Ecles, and A. Riley, *Pontifical Services ... with descriptive Notes and a Liturgical Introduction* (*Alcuin Club Collections, 3, 4, 8, 12; 1901–8). P. de Puniet, OSB, *Le Pontifical romain* (2 vols., 1930–1; Eng. tr., 1932). Vogel, *Sources*, pp. 225–71. L. Brinkhoff, OFM, in *LW* 2 (1968), cols. 2225–9, s.v., with extensive list of pr. Pontificals.

pontificals (Lat. *pontificalia*). The insignia of the episcopal order worn by a prelate when celebrating Pontifical Mass. Those common to all prelates, as enumerated by *Pius VII in *Decet Romanos* (1823), are the buskins (silk leg-coverings), *sandals, *gloves, *dalmatic, *tunicle, *ring, *pectoral cross, and *mitre. The 1917 *Codex Iuris Canonici* (can. 337, §2), however, referred to the *pastoral staff and the mitre as the characteristic *insignia pontificalia*. Their use (and in some cases their suppression) is regulated by the *motu proprio* of *Paul VI and the Instruction of the Sacred Congregation of Rites, both of 1968. They are not specified in the 1983 *Codex*. The word is also applied to episcopal functions at which these insignia are worn.

T. Klauser, *Der Ursprung der bischöflichen Insignien und Ehrenrechte* (Lecture; 1948). P. Salmon, OSB, *Étude sur les insignes du pontife dans le rit romain* (Rome, 1955). M. Noirot in *DDC* 7 (1965), cols. 34–42, s.v. 'Pontificalia'.

Pontius, St (d. *c.*260), biographer of St *Cyprian. He was Cyprian's deacon at Carthage and followed him into exile at Curubis. His *Vita et Passio Cypriani*, more an edifying panegyric than a work of history, is the earliest Christian biography. Feast day, 8 Mar. (He is to be distinguished from the Roman martyr St Pontius [3rd cent.]; feast day, 14 May.)

Crit. text of *Vita Cypriani* ed. W. Hartel in CSEL 3 (1) (1868), pp. xc–cx; also ed. with full introd. by M. Pellegrino (Verba Seniorum, 3 [Alba, 1955]), and by A. A. R. Bastiaensen (Vite dei Santi, 3; Milan, 1975, pp. 1–49, with notes and bibl., pp. 249–79), both with Ital. tr. Eng. tr. in ANCL 8 (Writings of Cyprian, vol. 1), pp. xiii–xxxi. M. Pellegrino in *EC* 9 (1952), cols. 175 f., s.v. 'Ponzio'.

Pontius Pilate. See PILATE, PONTIUS.

Poor Clares (Fr., *Clarisses*), the 'Second Order' of St *Francis, founded by him and St *Clare between 1212 and 1214. It received its first rule in 1219 from Cardinal Ugolino (later *Gregory IX), and spread rapidly through Italy, and later all over Europe. In 1247 *Innocent IV sanctioned a second rule containing several modifications, esp. regarding poverty, and six years later a third and much stricter one, based on that of St Francis, which included the *privilegium paupertatis*, the right to practise corporate as well as personal poverty. This rule was not accepted by all convents, and in 1263 Urban IV sanctioned a milder one which was observed by the majority, those nuns who follow it being hence called 'Urbanists'. The order was thoroughly reformed in the 15th cent. by St Colette, who restored the principle of strict poverty in her houses. The *Capuchin Reform in the 16th cent. added the Capuchinesses to the family of Poor Clares. The Urbanists, *Colettines, and Capuchinesses are the chief branches of the order. The majority of Poor Clare convents are strictly contemplative, devoted to prayer, penance, and manual work. They have the strictest enclosure, practise severe fasts and other austerities, rise for the Night Office, and are regarded as the most austere women's order of the RC Church. Their habit, which, like that of the Franciscan Friars, has no *scapular, is of dark frieze with a cord girdle, and they wear a black veil and cloth sandals on bare feet.

Histoire abrégée de l'ordre de Sainte Clare d'Assise: Édition des Monastères des Clarisses Colettines à Lyon et à Tournai (1906). G. Daval, OFM, *Les Clarisses* (Les Grands Ordres religieux, 1924); J. Ancelot-Hustache, *Les Clarisses* (Les Grands Ordres monastiques, 1929). *Santa Chiara d'Assisi: Studi e cronaca del VII centenario 1253–1953* (Assisi [1954]), esp. pp. 311–516, with bibl. I. Omaechevarría, OFM, *Las Clarisas a través de los Siglos* [1972]. J. [R. H.] Moorman, *A History of the Franciscan Order from its Origins to the Year 1517* (Oxford, 1968), pp. 32–9, 205–15, 406–16, 548 f., with bibl. pp. 610 f. L. Oliger, OFM, 'De Origine Regularum Ordinis S. Clarae', *AFH* 5 (1912), pp. 181–209 and 413–47; I. Omaechevarría, OFM, 'La "Regla" y las Reglas de la Orden de Santa Clara', *Collectanea Franciscana*, 46 (1976), pp. 93–119. A. F. C. Bourdillon, *The Order of Minoresses in England* (Manchester University thesis; British Society of Franciscan Studies, 12; 1926); H. Concannon, *The Poor Clares in Ireland, A.D. 1629–A.D. 1929* (Dublin, 1929). F. Casolini in *Dict. Sp.* 5 (1964), cols. 1409–22, s.v. 'Frères Mineurs, vi. Sainte Claire et les Clarisses, 2. Les Clarisses'; I. Omaechevarría, OFM, in *DIP* 2 (1975), cols. 1116–32, s.v. 'Clarisse'. See also bibl. to CLARE, ST.

Poor Men of Lyons. The name under which Pope Lucius III condemned the *Waldenses (q.v.) in 1184.

Poore, Richard (d. 1237), Bp. of *Salisbury. His name also occurs in the forms **Poor, Poure,** and **Le Poer**. He came from a distinguished administrative family. He studied at the University of Paris under Stephen *Langton. Elected Dean of *Sarum, where his brother Herbert was bishop, in 1197/8, he was twice unsuccessful as a candidate for the sees of *Winchester (1204) and *Durham (1213), but became Bp. of *Chichester in 1215 and was translated to Salisbury two years later. In 1219 he removed his see from Old Sarum to its present site, and in the next year began the erection of the present cathedral, where he consecrated three altars at the E. End in 1225. About the same time he drew up the Salisbury Customary and probably gave the 'Use of Sarum' (q.v.) its final form. The diocesan statutes which he drew up as Bp. of Salisbury were the most widely influential of the English diocesan statutes of the 13th cent. In 1228 he was translated to the see of Durham. He was formerly, but quite erroneously, believed to be the author of the '*Ancren(e) Riwle'.

Crit. edn. of the statutes which he drew up for the diocese of Salisbury, and reissued at Durham, in F. M. Powicke and C. R. Cheney (eds.), *Councils & Synods with other documents relating to the English Church*, 2, pt. 1: 1205–1265 (Oxford, 1964), pp. 57–96. See also W. H. Rich Jones (ed.), *The Register of S. Osmund* (2 vols., RS, 1883–4), 1, pp. 284–379, and 2, pp. 4–100 *passim*, and introd., 2, pp. xcviii–cxxxi *passim*. C. R. Cheney, *English Synodalia of the Thirteenth Century* (1941), pp. 51–89. H. E. D. Blakiston in *DNB* 46 (1896), pp. 106–9; *BRUO* 3 (1959), p. 2189.

Pope (Gk. πάπ(π)ας, Lat. *papa*, 'father'). The title, though now in W. usage restricted to the Bp. of Rome in respect of his capacity as supreme head on earth of the universal Church, was from the early 3rd cent. used as an honorific designation of any bishop. In the E. it was apparently confined to the Bp. of *Alexandria, who is still regularly styled πάπας; however, from the 6th cent. the chancery at *Constantinople normally reserved it for the Bp. of Rome. In modern popular usage the term πάπας is applied in the *Orthodox Church to parish priests (cf. the use of 'Father', q.v., in the W.). As is illustrated by the writings of Magnus Felix *Ennodius and by the *Liber Pontificalis*, in the W. the word *papa* began from the early 6th cent. to be used esp. of the Bp. of Rome, first as a personal and soon as an official title; since the 8th cent. it was seldom used of any other Church dignitary. From the 11th cent. it was applied exclusively to the Bp. of Rome; thesis 11 of the *Dictatus papae* of Pope *Gregory VII (1075) is widely understood to be a statement of this by then established convention. See also PAPACY.

B. Labanca, 'Del nome Papa nelle chiese cristiane di Oriente ed Occidente', in *Actes du Douzième Congrès International des Orientalistes, Rome, 1899*, 3. 2 (Florence, 1902), pp. 47–101, with bibl. P. de Labriolle, 'Papa', *Bulletin Du Cange*, 4 (1928), pp. 65–75. J. Moorhead, '*Papa* as "bishop of Rome"', *JEH* 36 (1985), pp. 337–50.

Pope Joan. See JOAN, POPE.

Pope, William Burt (1822–1903), *Wesleyan theologian. He was born at Horton in Nova Scotia, and after studying privately entered the Methodist Theological Institution at Hoxton in 1840. From 1842 he was a minister in several large towns, including Dover, London, Manchester, and Leeds. In 1860 he became editor of the *London Quarterly Review* and in 1867 was appointed tutor of systematic theology at Didsbury. In 1876 he went to

America as delegate to the General Conference of the Methodist Episcopal Church at Baltimore, and in 1877 he presided over the Wesleyan Conference at Bristol. He resigned his tutorship at Didsbury College in 1886. He enjoyed a high reputation as a theologian in the Methodist Church. His principal work, the *Compendium of Christian Theology* (3 vols., 1875), contains an elaborate and sympathetic defence of the Methodist doctrine of Christian perfection. He also published several volumes of sermons and translations from the German.

Life by R. W. Moss (London, *c*.1909). C. H. Irwin in *DNB*, *1901–1911*, 3, p. 127.

Popery. This hostile designation for the specific doctrines and practices of the RC Church is already found in 1534 in W. *Tyndale and has been in common use since.

Popery, the Declaration against. The declaration imposed by the Parliament Act 1678 at the time of the *Popish Plot requiring all Members of Parliament except the Duke of York to denounce Transubstantiation, the Mass, and Invocation of Saints as idolatrous. It was abolished in 1778, when another and less exacting oath was substituted for it, allowing military recruits simply to take an oath of fidelity to the Crown.

Popish Plot. The supposed plot to murder *Charles II which T. *Oates (q.v.) claimed that he had discovered in 1678. Despite the great sensation it created, it seems to have been a pure invention of Oates.

[F.] J. Pollock, *The Popish Plot* (1903; 2nd edn., 1944). J. Kenyon, *The Popish Plot* (1972). R. L. Greaves, *Secrets of the Kingdom: British Radicals from the Popish Plot to the Revolution of 1688–89* (Stanford, Calif., 1992), pp. 5–32.

poppy heads. In ecclesiology, the ornamented finials at the tops of bench-ends, in form somewhat resembling a fleur de lys. They became common in the 15th cent., esp. in E. Anglia, where many fine examples can still be seen, and were widely copied. It is uncertain whether the name has any connection with the poppy flower. Possibly it derives from the Fr. *poupée*, a 'figure-head' or 'puppet'.

J. C. Cox, *Bench Ends in English Churches* (1916), esp. pp. 12–16. F. Bond, *Wood Carvings in English Churches*, 2 (1910), esp. pp. 6 f.

Porette, Margaret (d. 1310), also spelt 'Porete', author of *The Mirror of Simple Souls*. Prob. a native of Hainaut, she was burnt at the stake in Paris on 1 June 1310 for continuing to circulate copies of a book already condemned as heretical. Her name and details of her trial and death had been known since the events from contemporary documents, but it was only when Romana Guarnieri discovered that items from her teaching, quoted in the records, occur in their contexts in a French manuscript of *The Mirror of Simple Souls* (*Le Miroeur des simples âmes*) that her authorship of this treatise was recognized. The work, which has long been known anonymously, circulated, often in Latin, English, and Italian translation, as if it were harmlessly pious. It is one of few such writings which escaped destruction, and thus an important witness to the beliefs of the many in late medieval Europe who professed 'Liberty of the Spirit', freedom, that is, from the restrict-

ive teaching and practices of the Catholic Church. Today many exaggerated claims are made for the *Mirror*'s theological insights. Examination of her 'lyrics', such as 'Friend, what do you want from me?' shows that they are no more than dense series of scriptural allusions; and it seems that much of the 'preaching' in conventicles of the *Brethren of the Free Spirit was little else than devout repetition of Bible-excerpts. Externally, their evangelization may not have differed greatly from that of the early *Franciscans, but they were always accused of 'hypocritical' dissembling. Margaret's position is not entirely clear.

R. Guarnieri, 'Il Movimento del Libero Spirito', *Archivio Italiano per la Storia della Pietà*, 4 (1965), pp. 351–708, incl. Fr. text of the *Mirror*, pp. 513–635. Middle Eng. tr. ed. M. Doiron, ibid. 5 (1968), pp. 241–355. Fr. text ed. by R. Guarnieri, together with Lat. version, prob. made during Margaret's lifetime, ed. P. Verdeyen, SJ (CCCM 69; 1986). Modernized Eng. version by C. Kirchberger, *The Mirror of Simple Souls* ('Orchard Books', 1927; pub. before the authorship was known; it is repr., still without attribution, by C. Crawford, Dublin, 1981). E. Colledge, OSA, and J. C. Marler, ' "Poverty of the Will": Ruusbroec, Eckhart and *The Mirror of Simple Souls*' in P. Mommaers and N. de Paepe (eds.), *Jan van Ruusbroec: The Sources, Content and Sequels of his Mysticism* (Mediaevalia Lovaniensia, 1st ser., Studia, 12; 1984), pp. 14–47. P. Dronke, *Women Writers of the Middle Ages* (1984), pp. 217–28.

Porphyry (*c*.232–*c*.303), *Neoplatonist philosopher. Of pagan family, possibly orig. called 'Malchus', he was brought up at Tyre, and in his youth visited Syria, Palestine, and Alexandria. It is possible that he was at one time a Christian (so *Socrates and Aristocritus [5th cent.], followed by A. *Harnack; denied by J. Bidez), but he clearly did not hold the faith by the time of the persecution of the Emp. *Decius in 250. He studied philosophy at *Athens and was finally convinced of Neoplatonist principles by *Plotinus, whom he met at *Rome in 262. Just before the death of the latter (270) he went to Sicily, where he published many of his philosophical works, but towards the end of his life he returned to Rome and taught with considerable success, numbering *Iamblichus among his pupils.

After investigating with sympathetic interest the religious systems current in Asia, Porphyry adopted an attitude of scepticism towards all popular religion, marked by esp. bitterness against the Christians. In his Πρὸς Ἀνεβώ he pointed out the contradictions in popular superstition. Of more lasting significance was his treatise in 15 books against the Christians (Κατὰ Χριστιανῶν); it was condemned to be burnt in 448 and survives only in fragments in works written mainly to refute it. Porphyry seems to have observed a certain restraint in his remarks about Christ Himself, whom he admired as a teacher; but he considered the apparent failure of His life proof that He was not divine, and he launched his most bitter invective against the Apostles and leaders of the Church, which he finally condemned for its lack of patriotism in resisting the religious revival fostered by the Emps. Decius and Aurelian. His exposure of the alleged inconsistencies of the Gospels and his attack on the OT (e.g. the date of the Book of *Daniel) was sufficiently forceful to draw detailed refutations from St *Methodius of Olympus, *Eusebius of Caesarea, *Apollinarius of Laodicea, and others.

His numerous philosophical works, primarily intended to draw the soul from contact with the sensible world and turn it to the contemplation of intelligible reality, are important not so much for their originality as for their clear exposition, development and preservation of much that was obscurely put in Plotinus and others. They include popular expositions of his teaching, such as the Letter to Marcella, his wife, a treatise on abstinence from animal flesh, and a life of Pythagoras, besides various commentaries on the *Categories* of *Aristotle, Περὶ τῆς ἐκ λογίων φιλοσοφίας, Περὶ ἀγαλμάτων, Φιλόσοφος ἱστορία and Ἀφορμαὶ πρὸς τὰ νοητά. He also wrote a Life of Plotinus and edited his works (after 300), and composed various treatises on astronomy, mathematics, grammar, and rhetoric, a philological dissertation on Homer, a commentary on Ptolemy's *Harmonica*, and on various other technical subjects. His 'Introduction to the *Categories* of Aristotle' (Εἰσαγωγή) became a standard work in the medieval schools.

No collected edn. of Porphyry's works exists, the different items being pr. in a variety of places; careful list in J. Bidez, op. cit. infra, pp. 63*–73*. *Opuscula Selecta* ed. A. Nauck (Teub., 1886). Modern edns. of individual works incl. that of his 'Letter to Anebo' (reconstructed from Iamblichus' *de Mysteriis*) by A. R. Sodano (Naples, 1958); of 'Homeric Questions', bk. 1, by id. (ibid., 1970); of Ἀφορμαὶ πρὸς τὰ νοητά by E. Lamberz (Teub., 1975); of his 'Life of Pythagoras' and 'Letter to Marcella', with Fr. tr., by É. des Places, SJ (Collection des Universités de France, 1982); and 'Of Abstinence', with Fr. tr. by J. Bouffartigue and M. Patillon (2 vols., 1977–9). Eng. tr. of 'Isagoge' by E. W. Warren (Pontifical Institute of Mediaeval Studies, Toronto, Mediaeval Sources in Translation, 16; 1975). For Porphyry's life the chief sources are his own 'Life of Plotinus' (crit. edn. in *Plotini Opera*, ed. P. Henry, SJ, and H. R. Schwyzer, Paris, 1 (1951), pp. 1–41) and the entry in *Suidas'* Lexicon, s.v.; on the former see L. Brisson and others, *Porphyre, La Vie de Plotin* (Histoire des doctrines de l'antiquité classique, 6 and 16; 1982–92). The material is fully surveyed in J. Bidez, *Vie de Porphyre avec les fragments des traités Περὶ Ἀγαλμάτων et De Regressu Animae* (Université de Gand. Recueil de Travaux publiés par la Faculté de Philosophie et Lettres, 43; 1913). A. *Harnack, Porphyrius 'Gegen die Christen', 15 Bücher: Zeugnisse, Fragmente und Referate* (Abh. (Berl.), 1916, Heft 1; acc. to Harnack and others, Porphyry was the pagan philosopher extensively cited in *Macarius Magnes'* Apocriticus, but cf. T. D. Barnes in *JTS* NS 24 (1973), pp. 424–42). A. Smith, *Porphyry's Place in the Neoplatonic Tradition* (The Hague, 1974). F. Romano, *Porfirio di Tiro* (Università di Catania, Pubblicazioni della Facoltà di Lettere e Filosofia, 33; 1979). W. Theiler, *Porphyrios und Augustin* (Halle, 1933); repr. in *Forschungen zum Neuplatonismus* (Quellen und Studien zur Geschichte der Philosophie, 10; 1966), pp. 160–251. J. J. O'Meara, *Porphyry's Philosophy from Oracles in Augustine* (Paris, 1959). H. Dörrie and others, *Porphyre* (Fondation Hardt, Entretiens sur l'antiquité classiques, 12; 1966). P. Hadot, *Porphyre et Victorinus* (2 vols., Études Augustiniennes, 1968), incl. text, with Fr. tr., of frags. of a comm. on *Parmenides*, attributed by Hadot to Porphyry, in vol. 2, pp. 59–113. A. Benoit, 'Le "Contra Christianos" de Porphyre: où en est la collecte des Fragments?', in *Mélanges offerts à Marcel Simon: Paganisme, Judaïsme, Christianisme* (1978), pp. 261–75. P. de Labriolle, *La Réaction païenne* (1934), pp. 223–96. L. Vaganay in *DTC* 12 (pt. 2; 1935), cols. 2555–90, s.v. 'Porphyre', with bibl.; R. Beutler in *PW* 22 (pt. 1; 1953), cols. 275–313, s.v. 'Porphyrios'.

Porrectio Instrumentorum. See INSTRUMENTS, TRADITION OF THE.

Porta Santa. See HOLY DOOR.

Portas. See PORTIFORIUM.

porter. See DOORKEEPER.

Porteus, Beilby (1731–1808), Bp. of London. Of American descent, he was educated at Christ's College, Cambridge. In the 1760s he benefited from the patronage of T. *Secker, whose biography he wrote (1770). After holding various parochial appointments, he became Bp. of *Chester in 1776 and of London in 1787. He identified himself with the practical ideals of the rising *Evangelical school, energetically furthering many of their reforms, e.g. promoting mission work among negro slaves in America and securing the due observance of the Christian Holy Days. He was also an eager supporter of the *CMS and of the *British and Foreign Bible Society. A keen *Sabbatarian, he actively opposed the practice of Sunday concerts by professional performers in private houses, as well as Sunday debating societies. In 1767 he preached a sermon at Cambridge, some extracts from which, falling into the hands of John Norris (1734–77), moved him to found the Norrisian chair in divinity. Theologically he was out of sympathy with the *Calvinism currently upheld by the Evangelicals and to this extent did not fully accept all their teaching.

Collected edn. of his Works (35 Sermons, 24 Lectures and various Tracts) in 6 vols., London, 1811, with Life by R. Hodgson as vol. 1. J. H. Overton in *DNB* 45 (1896), pp. 195–7, with further refs.

Portiforium. A name used in England in the Middle Ages for the *Breviary. Other forms of the word are 'Portas', 'Portuary', and 'Portuis'.

Portiuncula. A small chapel, also known as Santa Maria degli Angeli, in the plain below *Assisi. Dating from *c.*11th cent., it was the favourite church of St *Francis and during his lifetime the headquarters of his order. In it he received his vocation and clothed St *Clare. The chapel and the cell in which he died are now enclosed by an imposing 16th-cent. church, largely rebuilt after an earthquake in 1832. The chapel gives its name to the 'Portiuncula *Indulgence', which can now be gained by visiting any parish or other designated church on 2 August or some other day fixed by the *Ordinary. The indulgence is said to have been granted by Pope *Honorius III in 1216 when he heard of a private revelation to St Francis. The documents connecting St Francis with the indulgence have been the subject of much controversy, but the practice of seeking the indulgence at the Portiuncula chapel (to which it was originally confined) is well attested before the end of the 13th cent.

L. Canonici, OFM, *La Porziuncola e gli inizi dell'Ordine Francescano* (Assisi, 1963). R. M. Huber, OFM, *The Portiuncula Indulgence from Honorius III to Pius XI* (New York, 1938). On the indulgence, also O. Englebert, *Saint Francis of Assisi*, Eng. tr., 2nd edn. rev. by I. Brady, OFM, and R. Brown (Chicago [1965]), pp. 203–11 and 475 f. R. Brown in *NCE* 11 (1967), pp. 601 f., with further refs.

Port-Royal, Convent of, *Jansenist centre. A convent of *Cistercian nuns was originally founded at Port-Royal, a marshy site some 18 miles SW of *Paris (hence

'Port-Royal-des-Champs'), in 1204. The appointment in 1602 of (Jacqueline Marie) Angélique *Arnauld as abbess at the age of 10 was the prelude to its emergence as a house of major importance. Converted (by a *Capuchin friar) to a new view of her responsibilities in 1608, she undertook far-reaching reforms and began to attract numerous novices (including several members of her own huge family). Owing to the unhealthy conditions, in 1625 the community reluctantly moved into Paris to a new house in the Faubourg St Jacques ('Port-Royal-de-Paris'). Under the direction of Sébastien Zamet, Bp. of Langres (Bp. 1615–55), in 1627 the community was removed from the jurisdiction of Cîteaux and formed an autonomous Ordre du St Sacrement, adding a large red cross to their white habit to signify their independence. The initial spirituality of Port-Royal was largely *Oratorian, but in 1635 Zamet handed over direction to *Saint-Cyran, Jansen's associate; his influence then became decisive, and was zealously maintained after his death in 1643 by Antoine *Arnauld, who became spokesman for what came to be called Jansenism. After 1637 some of Saint-Cyran's converts came to live near the convent (at first in Paris, then in the derelict Port-Royal-des-Champs) as 'Solitaires', without taking vows, but devoting themselves to the interests of the nuns, the education of a few boys (including Racine), and literary pursuits. By 1648 their labours had rendered Port-Royal-des-Champs habitable enough to receive some of the nuns, and henceforward the two houses existed with a single conventual organization, increasingly openly and militantly associated with the Jansenist cause. Blaise *Pascal, though never a 'Solitaire', was closely linked with Port-Royal, and his sister, Jacqueline, was professed there as a nun. Among the most famous 'Solitaires' were Antoine Singlin, Claude Lancelot, and Le Maître de Sacy.

When in 1661 the nuns of Port-Royal refused to subscribe the condemnation of Jansenism, certain measures affecting the prosperity of the convent were taken by the civil power and in 1664 a real persecution began; but very few of the nuns were persuaded to sign the 'formulary' until after the *Peace of the Church (1668). In 1669 the two houses were legally separated, Port-Royal-de-Paris being given over to the nuns who had submitted before 1668, while the Jansenist majority were established in Port-Royal-des-Champs. A period of prosperity followed, cut short in 1679, after the recrudescence of the Jansenist controversy, when the convent was forbidden to take boarders or receive any more novices. Subsequently further measures were taken to the prejudice of its temporalities. In 1705 *Clement XI published a bull condemning those who, in signing the anti-Jansenist formulary of *Alexander VII, used mental reservations: the nuns of Port-Royal refused to accept this new definition, and, after a short persecution, were finally dispersed in 1709. The buildings were subsequently destroyed, and the site desecrated (1710–13).

A. de Dion (ed.), Cartulaire de l'abbaye de Porrois au diocèse de Paris plus connue sous son nom mystique Port-Royal, 1: 1204–80 [all pub.] (1903). The fundamental modern crit. work is that of C. A. Sainte-Beuve, Port-Royal (5 vols., 1840–59, and index, 1861; modern edn. by M. Leroy, Bibliothèque de la Pléiade, 93, 99, 107; 1953–5). The more important earlier works incl. [C. Clémencet, OSB] Histoire générale de Port-Royal (10 vols., Amster-

dam, 1755–7); id., Histoire littéraire de Port-Royal, ed. [R. F. W.] Guettée (Paris, 1868); J. Racine (the poet), Abrégé de l'histoire de Port-Royal (1742–54; ed. A. Gazier, 1908); and C. *Beard, Port-Royal (2 vols., 1861). C. Gazier, Histoire du monastère de Port-Royal (1929); id., Les Belles Amies de Port-Royal (1930); id., Ces Messieurs de Port-Royal: Documents inédits (1932), and other works of this author. J. Laporte, La Doctrine de Port-Royal (1923; 2nd edn., enlarged, 2 vols., Bibliothèque d'Histoire de la Philosophie, 1951–2). L. Cognet, La Mère Angélique et son temps, 1: La Réforme de Port-Royal 1591–1618 (1950). F. E. Weaver, The Evolution of the Reform of Port-Royal: From the Rule of Cîteaux to Jansenism [1978]. F. Delforge, Les petites écoles de Port-Royal 1637–1660 (1985). A. Maulvault, Répertoire alphabétique des personnes et des choses de Port-Royal (1902). L. Rea, The Enthusiasts of Port-Royal (1912). Bremond, esp. vol. 4. E. Préclin in Fliche and Martin, 19 (pt. 1; 1955), pp. 193–219. L. Cognet in NCE 11 (1967), pp. 597–99, s.v.; E. E. Weaver in Dict. Sp. 12 (pt. 2; 1986), cols. 1931–52, s.v. See also bibl. to JANSENISM.

Portuary. See PORTIFORIUM.

Portugal, Christianity in. The independent history of Portugal began in the 12th cent., when the new country became free from Castile–León and a self-governing vassal of the Papacy. The presence of the *Cistercian Order in Portugal dates from 1140, and its influence was considerable in the early Middle Ages. Its great monastery at Alcobaça was one of the most important in the country. Under Sancho I (reigned 1185–1211) a strong nationalist and anti-Papal movement began which even *Innocent III could not crush. The submission of Sancho in 1210 produced only a temporary settlement and the disputes arising from the movement lasted through much of the 13th cent. The *Mendicant Orders which entered the country at that period proved valuable allies to the Popes in the quarrel. In the *Great Schism, anti-Castilian feeling kept the Portuguese bishops on the side of *Urban VI and his successors.

Early in the 15th cent. the Portuguese voyages of discovery began, and by the middle of the next cent. there had come into existence a great empire in Africa, America, and the East. Esp. after the mid-16th cent., missionaries were active throughout the new dominions, and partly by their preaching, and partly through the assistance of the secular power, they secured mass conversions. However, little trace of their activity now remains in the areas which were formerly under Portuguese influence, except in *Brazil.

In Portugal itself the reform of the bishops and clergy at the end of the 15th cent. had anticipated the *Reformation, which had no influence in the country. Persecution of Jews began later than in *Spain, and it was not until 1536 that, under the influence of the civil power, the *Inquisition was set up. Jews were expelled or converted by force, and for several generations there was discrimination against the so-called 'New Christians'.

Between 1580 and 1640 Portugal was annexed by Spain. From 1640 to 1668 a war of independence was waged in which the Papacy was openly allied with Spain, but in 1669 Portuguese independence was recognized by the Pope. The situation of the Church improved under the pious King João V (1706–50), but later in the 18th cent. the policies of the Marquis of Pombal resulted in the secularization of higher education and the expulsion of the *Jesuits (1759).

After the triumph of the liberals in the civil war of 1832–4, Portugal began to be further secularized. The property of the religious orders was confiscated, no novices were allowed, and the State took over many of the educational and charitable functions formerly exercised by the Church. By the concordat of 1886 the Church regained some of its influence, but the republican government which assumed power in 1910 was profoundly *anticlerical, and much of what had been regained was lost again. The RC Church was disestablished in Portugal in 1911, and in 1913 in the Portuguese colonies.

Under the rule of the dictator A. de O. Salazar (1928–68) and his successor, M. Caetano (1968–74), the relationship between the State and Church changed. In 1933 the religious orders were allowed to return (though the religious habit is rarely worn in public) and in 1940 a new concordat between the Portuguese government and the *Vatican was signed. The importance of the Church in national life continues to be considerable, even after the left-wing revolution of 1974, although there is disparity in religious practice between different parts of the country. The conference of bishops is a powerful political pressure group. The Church is exempted from certain taxes, and has great influence on religious education in schools. The Catholic University of Lisbon has expanded its activities in many Portuguese cities and the Church has its own radio station and television channel. A considerable and continuing impulse to religion was given by the occurrences in *Fátima in 1917.

The Lusitanian Church of Portugal is a small episcopal Church dating from c.1867. In full communion with the C or E since 1963, it was integrated into the Anglican Communion on 5 July 1980.

F. de Almeida, *História da Igreja em Portugal* (4 vols., 1910–22; rev. edn. by D. Peres, 1967–71); M. de Oliveira, *História Eclesiástica de Portugal* (1940; 4th edn., 1968). A. A. B. de Andrade and others (eds.), *Dicionário de História da Igreja em Portugal* (1980 ff.). J. Mattoso, *Religião e Cultura na Idade Média Portuguesa* [1982]. M. Gonçalves da Costa, *História do Bispado e Cidade de Lamego* (2 vols., Lamego, 1977–9). A. Herculano, *História da Origem e Estabelecimento da Inquisição em Portugal* (3 vols., 1852; with introd. by J. Borges de Macedo, 1975–6; Eng. tr., Stanford University Publications, University Series, vol. 1, no. 2; 1926). A. Brásio, C.S.Sp. (ed.), *Monumenta Missionária Africana: África Ocidental* (20 vols., Lisbon, 1952–88); A. da Silva Rego (ed.), *Documentação para a História das Missões do Padroado Português do Oriente* (18 vols., 1947–88). A. Brasio, C.S.Sp., *A Acção Missionária no Período Henriquino* (1958); A. da Silva Rego, *Les Missions Portugaises (Aperçu général)* (Lisbon, 1958); id., *O Padroado Português no Oriente e a sua Historiografia 1838–1950* (1978). C. R. Boxer, *The Church Militant and Iberian Expansion, 1440–1770* (Johns Hopkins Symposia in Comparative History, 10; Baltimore, 1978). L. de França, *Comportamento religioso da População Portuguesa* (Estudos para o Desenvolvimento, 4; 1981). There is also much information in the periodical *Lusitania Sacra* (10 vols., Lisbon, 1956–78; NS, 1989 ff.). J. Mattoso in *NCE* 11 (1967), pp. 607–14, s.v.; id. and others in *Dict. Sp.* 12 (pt. 2; 1986), cols. 1952–85, s.v., both with bibl.

Porvoo Agreement. See REUNION.

Positive Theology. The branch of theology which treats of matters of historic and particular fact, custom, or enactment, as opposed to '*Natural Theology' (or 'natural religion'), which deals with religious principles and laws

of universal validity. In RC theology, also historical as contrasted with speculative theology.

Positivism. In its orig. and narrower sense, the system of the French thinker Auguste *Comte (q.v.), which confined intellectual inquiry to observable ('positive') facts and their relations, and eschewed all consideration of ultimate issues, incl. those of philosophy and theology. Its most prominent English exponent was Frederic Harrison (1831–1923); but similar doctrines were taught by H. *Spencer and other defenders of *agnosticism. The term has now come to be used in a wider sense for any form of philosophical outlook which rejects metaphysics, esp. when the physical sciences are regarded as offering the norm of knowledge. Such an outlook was developed by the 'Vienna Circle' including R. Carnap and others, formed in 1922, which gave the name 'Logical Positivism' to its doctrines. They were influenced by L. *Wittgenstein, who published his *Tractatus Logico-Philosophicus* in German in 1921 (Eng. tr., 1922), but spent most of his working life in England. It was, however, chiefly through the work of A. J. Ayer (1910–89) and esp. his *Language, Truth and Logic* (1936) that Logical Positivism became known in Britain. In its original and radical form its influence was most widespread in the late 1930s, but it had a lasting effect on 20th-cent. philosophy and indirectly on theology by its demand for verifiability as a criterion of any statement being meaningful; all theologians thus had to meet the possible criticism of their statements not as false or unknowable but as unverifiable and therefore meaningless. Attention was devoted by a number of writers to the analysis of language and the meaningfulness or otherwise of religious forms of words (sometimes referred to as 'God-talk').

Possidius, St (c.370–c.440), biographer of St *Augustine. A converted pagan, he lived in the monastery at Hippo until he became Bp. of Calama in Numidia at some date between 397 and 403 (prob. closer to the latter). He helped Augustine in his struggle against *Donatism and *Pelagianism, was with him when he died, and left, besides a list of his works, a short but valuable sketch of his life.

His 'Vita Augustini', commonly pr. in the earlier edns. of St Augustine, is repr. in J. P. Migne, *PL* 32. 31–66. Crit. edns. by H. T. Weiskotten, Princeton, NJ, 1919, with Eng. tr.; A. Vega, Escurial, 1943; and M. Pellegrino, 'Verba Seniorum', Turin [c.1954]. Another Eng. tr. in *The Western Fathers*, ed. and tr. F. R. Hoare (1954), pp. 189–244. Study and Ger. tr. by A. *Harnack in *Abh.* (Berl.), 1930, Heft 1. Possidius' 'Operum S. Augustini Elenchus', ed. A. *Wilmart, OSB, in *Miscellanea Agostiniana*, 2 (1931), pp. 149–233. H. J. Diesner, 'Possidius und Augustinus', in F. L. Cross (ed.), *Studia Patristica*, 6 (TU 81; 1962), pp. 350–65. Bardenhewer, 4, pp. 428, 441, 443, 445; Altaner and Stuiber (1978), pp. 419 and 637. M.-F. Berrouard, OP, in *Dict. Sp.* 12 (pt. 1; 1986), cols. 1997–2008, s.v.

postcommunion. In the Roman *Mass the prayer, similar in structure to the *collect, which follows after the communion. In early times it was the last item in the Mass. In the past, when more than one collect was recited, there was a corresponding increase in the number of the postcommunions. The name postcommunion is first found in the *Gelasian Sacramentary.

Jungmann (1952 edn.), 2, pp. 520–7; Eng. tr., 2, pp. 419–25.

postil, also **apostil**. This word (Lat. *postilla*), which in the Middle Ages was used of a gloss on a scriptural text, came to be applied esp. to a homily on the Gospel or Epistle for the day or to a book of homilies. It is perhaps derived from *post illa*, meaning 'After those [words of scripture]'.

Postlapsarianism. See SUBLAPSARIANISM.

post-Sanctus. The prayer in the Eucharistic Liturgy which in the *Gallican rite followed the *Sanctus and varied according to the feast commemorated. It survives in the *Mozarabic rite.

postulant. One who is undergoing a preliminary stage of testing as a candidate for a religious order before admission to the *novitiate. The period of postulancy varies in length acc. to the religious order and the circumstances of the candidate, but it commonly extends over several months, which are spent at the religious house where the candidate expects later to be professed.

Potamius (d. after 359), the earliest known Bp. of Lisbon and a leading Churchman of the W. in the mid-4th cent. He originally professed and defended the orthodox *Nicene position, but at least for a period he aligned himself with the *Arianizing policy of the Emp. Constantius II, accepted the Second Creed of *Sirmium (357) with its repudiation of both ὁμοούσιος and ὁμοιούσιος and joined in putting pressure on Pope *Liberius to submit to the Emperor's demands. Four of his writings survive, all apparently orthodox, though a fragment of a letter written during his heretical period is preserved by *Phoebadius.

'De Lazaro', 'Epistula ad Athanasium' and 'De Martyrio Isaiae prophetae' are pr. in J. P. Migne. *PL* 8. 1411–18; 'Epistula de substantia Patris et Filii et Spiritus sancti' in A. Hamman, OFM (ed.), *Patrologiae cursus completus, Series latina, Supplementum*, 1 (1958), cols. 202–16. The last two also ed. A. C. Vega, *Scriptores Ecclesiastici hispanolatini veteris et medii aevi*, 2 (Madrid, 1934), pp. 25–54. A. M. Moreira, OFM, *Potamius de Lisbonne et la controverse arienne* (Louvain, 1969), with bibl. M. Simonetti in Quasten (cont.), *Patrology*, 4 (1986), pp. `>–3.

Potentiana, St. See PUDENTIANA, ST.

Pothinus, St (*c*.87–177), first Bp. of Lyons. He was probably a native of Asia Minor and a disciple of St *Polycarp, and if so would have brought Asian influences to early Christianity in the south of Gaul. The circumstances of his death are described in the 'Ep. of the Churches of Vienne and Lyons' (ap. *Eusebius, *HE* 5. 1). Feast day (with his companions in martyrdom), 2 June.

The text of the 'Epistle of the Churches' is conveniently pr., with Eng. tr., in H. Musurillo (ed.), *The Acts of the Christian Martyrs* (Oxford Early Christian Texts, 1972), pp. 62–85, the passage mentioning Pothinus, pp. 70–3, with introd. pp. xx–xxiii. T. Richoud, *Le Premier Évêque de Lugdunum* (Lyons, 1900). On the persecution of 177, see also H. Quentin, OSB, 'La Liste des martyrs de Lyon de l'an 177', *Anal. Boll.* 39 (1921), pp. 113–38, and various essays in *Les Martyrs de Lyon (177): Lyon, 20–23 septembre 1977* (Colloques Internationaux du Centre National de la Recherche Scientifique, 575; 1978). See also works cited under QUARTODECIMANISM.

Potter, John (*c*.1674–1747), Abp. of *Canterbury. Educated at Wakefield and University College, Oxford, Potter became successively Fellow of Lincoln (1694), Regius professor of divinity at Oxford (1707), and Bp. of Oxford (1715). He ordained J. *Wesley, with whom he remained on good terms. In 1737 he unexpectedly succeeded W. *Wake as Abp. of Canterbury (E. *Gibson's appointment being thought probable). A Whig, Potter was nevertheless a *High Churchman, as his *Discourse of Church Government* (1707) shows. His works include a long-used *Archaeologia Graeca* (2 vols., 1697–9), a fine edition of *Clement of Alexandria (1715), and writings against the views of B. *Hoadly.

Collected edn. of his *Theological Works* pub. in 3 vols., Oxford, 1753–4. Life by R. Anderson, MD (1750–1830), prefixed to the edn. of Potter's *Archaeologia Graeca* pub. London, 1818 (vol. 1, pp. i–xi), and subsequent edns. Short modern study by L. W. Barnard (Ilfracombe, Devon, 1989). J. H. Lupton in *DNB* 46 (1896), pp. 216 f.

Powers. Acc. to medieval angelology, the sixth order of angels in the celestial hierarchy. The word is also used more generally of any celestial being who exercises control or influence over other parts of creation (cf. the English version of the *Te Deum, 'To Thee all angels cry aloud: the heavens and all the powers therein').

Praedestinatus. A treatise, composed probably at Rome during the Papacy of Sixtus III (432–40), and directed against the more extreme forms of the doctrine of *predestination then being taught under the influence of certain passages in the writings of St *Augustine. Its standpoint, if not actually *Pelagian, is at least *Semipelagian. Of its three books, the first is mainly a plagiarized reproduction of St Augustine's 'De haeresibus'; the second purports to be the work of an upholder of St Augustine's predestination doctrines, though it is almost certainly a composition of the writer of the whole treatise; and the third is a refutation of the second book. It has been attributed to various authors: *Arnobius Junior, *Julian of Eclanum, or, with more probability, someone belonging to his circle. It was first edited in 1643 by J. *Sirmond, SJ.

J. Sirmond based his edn. on the MS Reims 40, once in the possession of *Hincmar. Rev. text by J. de La Baune, SJ, in his edn. of Sirmond's works (1696); repr. (via A. *Gallandi) in J. P. Migne, *PL* 53. 579–692. The work was much discussed in the *Jansenist controversies. H. von Schubert, *Der sogenannte Praedestinatus: Ein Beitrag zur Geschichte des Pelagianismus* (TU 24. 4; 1903); G. Morin, OSB, *Études, Textes, Découvertes* (Anecdota Maredsolana, 2nd ser. 1; 1913), pp. 315–24 ('Que le *Praedestinatus* est du même Arnobe qui a écrit le *Conflictus* et le Commentaire sur les Psaumes'); G. Bardy, 'Le Souvenir d'Arius dans le *Praedestinatus*', *R. Bén.* 40 (1928), pp. 256–61; M. Abel, 'Le *Praedestinatus* et le pélagianisme', *RTAM* 35 (1968), pp. 5–25. É. Amann in *DTC* 12 (pt. 2; 1935), cols. 2775–80, s.v.

Praemunire. The title of statutes (first passed in 1353, 1365, and 1393) which were designed to protect rights claimed by the English Crown against encroachment by the Papacy. The name can denote the statutes, the offence, the writ, and the punishment. The statute of 1353 forbade the withdrawal from England of cases which should be decided in the king's courts, and the penalties prescribed were in 1393 stiffened and extended to any who should promote any Papal bull translating to other sees bishops on whom the king depended as ministers of state and any Papal excommunication of bishops who enforced decisions of the king's courts regarding *advowsons. Appeals to Rome subsequently dwindled for a time. In 1529 *Henry VIII claimed that T. *Wolsey's activities as Papal legate infringed this statute, and in 1531 extracted a fine from the whole clergy on the ground that the jurisdiction of the Church courts contravened the Act. *Elizabeth I used Praemunire penalties to deal with purely civil offences and with RC recusants; and *James I's judges used Praemunire to assist the encroachments of temporal upon ecclesiastical courts. By the Criminal Law Act 1967 the statutes were repealed in entirety.

Eng. tr. of First Statute of Praemunire (1353) pr. Gee and Hardy, pp. 103 f. (no. 35); that of 1393, ibid., pp. 122–5 (no. 40). The latter is repr. in Bettenson, pp. 239–42. W. T. Waugh, 'The Great Statute of Praemunire', *EHR* 37 (1922), pp. 173–205. E. B. Graves, 'The Legal Significance of the Statute of Praemunire of 1353' in *Anniversary Essays in Mediaeval History by Students of Charles Homer Haskins* (Boston and New York, 1929), pp. 57–80. G. R. Elton, *The Tudor Constitution: Documents and Commentary* (2nd edn., Cambridge, 1982), pp. 24 f. and 339 f. G. Crosse in *DECH* (3rd edn., 1948), pp. 487 f., s.v.

Praepositinus (c.1140–c.1210), theologian and liturgist. Prob. a native of Cremona, he studied Arts and Theology in Paris at a time when *Peter Lombard's 'Sentences' were beginning to be established as a central theological text in the Parisian schools. Praepositinus' main theological work, his 'Summa Theologica', follows the pattern of Lombard's Sentences, being arranged in four books dealing respectively with God, the Creation and Fall, the Incarnation and Christian virtues, and the Sacraments. He expresses a distinctly personal view on several contested issues, and his work, though not very original, has an engaging spontaneity and clarity. It marks a stage in the development of logical and grammatical refinements and elaborations which later became the hallmark of scholastic theologians, and it had a wide circulation in the 13th cent.

At some stage he spent time trying to convert the *Cathars of S. France, apparently with little success. He was teaching Theology in Paris in 1194, when he accepted an invitation from Conrad of Wittelsbach, Abp. of Mainz, to take charge of the cathedral school of Mainz, and he held this post until Conrad's death in 1203. In a dispute between the cathedral chapter and *Innocent III over the appointment of Conrad's successor, Praepositinus took the side of the chapter, and he received a severe letter of personal rebuke from the Pope theatening him with dismissal, whereupon he gave up his position and returned to Paris. In 1206 he became head of the Parisian schools as chancellor of the cathedral, and he held this position until 1209. He died shortly afterwards, perhaps after entering a religious community.

In addition to his 'Summa Theologica', Praepositinus also (prob. while in Paris) wrote a 'Summa super Psalterium' and (prob. while in Mainz) a work on the liturgical year ('Tractatus de officiis'). The latter was largely borrowed from *Rupert of Deutz, and in its turn it was the main source of the standard work of William *Durandus. A 'Summa contra haereticos', ascribed to him in one MS, is prob. not by him.

Praepositinus was one of the ablest of the Parisian theologians of the second half of the 12th cent. Although he was not responsible for any major innovation, his work exemplifies the comprehensive aims of the generation of scholars who prepared the way for the more intensely intellectual theologians of the 13th cent.

Part of bk. 1 of the 'Summa Theologica', ed. G. Angelini, *L'Ortodossia e la grammatica: Analisi di struttura e deduzione storica della Teologia Trinitaria di Prepositino* (Analecta Gregoriana, 183; 1972), pp. 199–303; bk. 4, ed. D. E. Pilarczyk (Collectio Urbaniana, 3rd ser. 7; Rome, 1964). 'Tractatus de officiis' ed. J. A. Corbett (University of Notre Dame Publications in Mediaeval Studies, 31; 1969). The 'Summa contra haereticos' ascribed to Praepositinus, ed. J. N. Garvin and J. A. Corbett (ibid. 15; 1958). G. Lacombe, *La Vie et les œuvres de Prévostin* (Bibliothèque thomiste, 11; Kain, 1927; designed as *Opera Omnia*, 1, but all pub.). Id. in *DTC* 13 (pt. 1; 1936), cols. 162–9; J. Longère in *Dict. Sp.* 12 (pt. 2; 1986), cols. 2185–93, both s.v. 'Prévostin de Crémone'.

pragmatic sanction (Lat. *pragmatica sanctio*). A term orig. employed in later Roman law for an arrangement defining the limits of the sovereign power of a prince, esp. in the matter of royal succession. A pragmatic sanction, published by Philip V, introduced Salic Law into Spain, and another, issued later by Ferdinand VII, revoked it.

The Pragmatic Sanction of Bourges, issued by the French clergy on 7 July 1438 while the Council of *Basle (q.v.) was still in session, was a statement of *Gallicanist principles. It upheld the right of the French Church to administer its temporal property independently of the Papacy and disallowed Papal nominations to vacant benefices. In 1516 it was superseded by the Concordat of *Bologna (q.v.).

Text of the Pragmatic Sanction of Bourges in *Ordonnances des rois de France de la troisième race*, 13 (ed. M. de Vilevault, 1782), pp. 267–91; summary in Mirbt, no. 398, pp. 232 f.; Eng. tr. in S. Z. Ehler and J. B. Morrall (eds.), *Church and State Through the Centuries* (1954), pp. 112–21. N. Valois, *Histoire de la pragmatique sanction de Bourges sous Charles VII* (Archives de l'Histoire de la France; 1906). Hefele and Leclercq, 7 (pt. 2; 1916), pp. 1053–61. V. Martin, *Les Origines du gallicanisme*, 2 (1939), pp. 293–324. R. Hedde in *DTC* 12 (pt. 2; 1935), cols. 2781–6, s.v. 'Pragmatique Sanction, II'.

Pragmatism (Gk. πράγματα, 'ordinary things', 'affairs'). A system of belief devised by C. S. Peirce, H. *Bergson, F. C. S. Schiller, W. *James, J. Dewey, and others, on the principle that every truth has practical consequences, and that these are a test of its truthfulness. Truth is therefore relative, and the proof of a fact is not an act of the pure reason, but rather an account of how the fact has come to be accepted as justifying itself by practical results. The real is not to be investigated by metaphysical speculation, but rather acc. to the values developed through its being known. Pragmatism justifies and explains religions acc. as they satisfy psychological criteria and generate suitable values. In the RC Church the *Modernist Movement was much influenced by Pragmatist ideals, notably in the persons of L. *Laberthonnière and G. *Tyrrell, as well as F. *von Hügel in his earlier life. Pragmatist ideas also exercised a widely diffused influence on religious thought generally, esp. in the period 1901–30.

Personal Idealism (ed. H. Sturt, 1902); J. Dewey, *Studies in Logical Theory* (1903); F. C. S. Schiller, *Humanism* (1903); id.,

Studies in Humanism (1907); W. James, *Pragmatism* (1907); id., *The Meaning of Truth* (1909); H. Vaihinger, *Die Philosophie des Als Ob* (1911). A. J. Ayer, *The Origins of Pragmatism* (1968); F. C. S. Schiller in *HERE* 10 (1918), pp. 147–50, s.v., with bibl.

Prassede, St. See PRAXEDES, ST.

Praxeas (*fl. c.*200), heretic. The substance of his history and teaching is known only from the treatise 'Adversus Praxean' (*c.*213?) of his vigorous opponent *Tertullian and may thus be somewhat misrepresented. He is said to have arrived in Rome towards the end of the 2nd cent. from Asia, where he had suffered imprisonment for his faith, and to have succeeded in turning the Pope (*Victor or *Zephyrinus) against the *Montanists. He proclaimed himself a leader of the '*Patripassian Monarchians', i.e. of those who were concerned to maintain the unity of the Godhead even at the cost of declaring that God suffered. As Tertullian put it, he 'crucified the Father' (*Patrem crucifixit*) since he conceived of the Godhead as emptied into the person of Christ in order to assume the temporary role of Redeemer. Before the end of his life he recanted his heretical doctrines.

'Praxeas' is prob. a real name and not, as G. B. *de Rossi suggested, a pseudonym ('busybody') for *Noetus or Epigonus. Tertullian's *Adversus Praxean* is ed., with introd., Eng. tr. and comm., by E. Evans (London, 1948). P. Meinhold in *PW* 22 (pt. 2; 1954), cols. 1744–7, s.v. See also bibl. to MONARCHIANISM.

Praxedes, St (1st–2nd cent.), also 'Prassede', early martyr at Rome. Acc. to her (spurious) *acta*, she was a Roman virgin who sheltered Christians during the persecution under *Marcus Aurelius. She was buried in the Catacomb of *Priscilla next to the grave of St *Pudentiana and hence (on wholly insufficient grounds) was supposed to have been her sister. The well-known church of Santa Prassede on the Esquiline at Rome (which inspired R. Browning's 'Tomb at St Praxed's') was built by Paschal I (817–24) close to the site of an earlier structure supposed to have stood on the site of her house. Feast day, 21 July.

St Praxedes and St Pudentiana are first mentioned in 7th-cent. Roman Itineraries to the Catacombs; they occur only in interpolated texts of the *Hieronymian Martyrology. Later legends make them both daughters of St *Pudens (q.v.). *AASS*, Mai. 4 (1685), pp. 296–301. A. de Waal, 'Der Titulus Praxedis', *RQ* 19 (1905), pp. 169–80. J. P. Kirsch, *Die römischen Titelkirchen im Altertum* (1918), pp. 149–51. R. Krautheimer and S. Corbett in idd. and others, *Corpus Basilicarum Christianarum Romae*, 3 (Rome, 1967), pp. 232–59, with bibl. [in English].

prayer. 'Prayer, properly speaking, is a petition which we make to God for the things which pertain to our salvation; but it is also taken in another, broader sense to mean any raising of the heart to God' (*Luis of Granada). In its original sense of 'petition', prayer is a universal phenomenon, wherever people believe that they are in some way dependent on some higher power not subject to their control. 'Everyone has need of the gods' (Homer, *Od.* 3. 48). It is prayer in this strict sense whose scope and propriety is debated by the ancient philosophers, and in the Bible and in Christian literature until well into the Middle Ages no other meaning is normally envisaged, though a prayer, considered as a rhetorical construct, may include other elements such as thanksgiving and confession (cf. *Origen,

Orat. 33). The extended use of the word, taking in all kinds of 'raising of the heart to God', begins to appear in the W. in the late Middle Ages and in some 16th-cent. writers it is the primary sense. A consequent tendency to devalue petitionary prayer, if not to eliminate it entirely, is apparent in some circles, though both the Reformers and the *Roman Catechism of 1566 treat prayer as meaning essentially petition, and some modern theologians, such as K. *Rahner, insist on the primacy of petition. In the E., *Isaac of Nineveh notes an extension of 'prayer' to include 'all spiritual working', but, precisely because prayer is 'a beseeching for something', he prefers to say that prayer ceases once contemplation begins (*Discourse* 22, ed. Wensinck).

In antiquity prayer usually involved spoken words and gestures. The early Church took over from Judaism the posture of standing with hands upraised (1 Tim. 2: 8). Other gestures include kneeling (Lk. 22: 41) and prostration (Mt. 26: 39). The Church soon recognized that prayer need not be spoken aloud, but in the early cents. spoken prayer remained normative. The medieval monastic tradition increasingly stressed silent prayer and this became the common practice of the laity also.

Prayer may be offered privately by an individual (Mt. 6: 6) or publicly in a formal act of worship (Acts 3: 1) or by a community faced with some crisis (Acts 12: 5). There is early evidence for Christians assembling for public prayer on *Sundays and for saying regular prayers at set times each day; from this practice the Divine *Office (q.v.) developed.

Christ taught His disciples to call God 'Father', and some scholars connect this form of address with the special way in which He Himself addressed God; it is because Christians share in His Spirit that they cry out 'Abba, Father' (Rom. 8: 15, Gal. 4: 6). He also taught His disciples what to pray (Mt. 6: 9–13), though Christian tradition is unanimous in not confining prayer to the words of the *Lord's Prayer. Christians also believe that, in so much as they still do not know what they ought to pray, the Spirit helps them, praying within them with 'unutterable groanings' (Rom. 8: 26). Christ Himself intercedes for them (Heb. 7: 25) and it is in His name and through Him that Christians pray. Acc. to Origen (*Orat.* 16. 1) prayer should be made only to the Father through Christ, but in fact prayer to Christ has been common since early times and subsequently prayer to the Holy Spirit was introduced.

Because God is regarded as totally competent in all matters and because man is always dependent on Him, Christians are told to pray always (Phil. 4: 6, 1 Thess. 5: 17). If God does not immediately answer prayer, perseverance is recommended (Lk. 18: 1–8). God particularly hears the prayer of the righteous (Prov. 15: 29, James 5: 16), but He also hears the prayer of the repentant sinner (Lk. 18: 13 f.).

Ancient philosophers debated what could properly be prayed for. The *Stoics maintained that only spiritual benefits should be sought in prayer, and this view was accepted by Origen (*Orat.* 13. 4). The Middle Platonists denied that man can pray for virtue, since it is his responsibility to become virtuous, and they regarded prayer generally as of doubtful value; Maximus of Tyre suggested that it was significant only as 'converse with the gods' (ὁμιλία πρὸς τοὺς θεούς, 5. 8), a phrase adapted by *Clement of

Alexandria (*Strom.* 7. 39. 6), who shares the Platonist embarrassment. Later Platonists, from *Porphyry onwards, ascribe a higher value and more universal scope to prayer. St *Augustine maintains that it is proper to pray for anything that can be lawfully desired (*Ep.* 130. 9–13) and he complains about the *Pelagian elimination of prayer for virtue (*Spir. et Litt.* 13. 22). In general, the degree of emphasis placed on petition is proportionate to different thinkers' views of *grace and man's dependence on God.

There are conceptual difficulties about prayer, already noticed by Origen (*Orat.* 5): God knows what man needs better than man does, and from the beginning of time He has determined what He will do. The classic answer to this problem is given by St *Thomas Aquinas (*Summa Theol.* 2. 2. q. 83): in prayer man is not trying to force God's will; he is submitting his desires to Him (this is inherent in the very idea of petition); and he does not pray in the hope of changing God's mind, but in order to co-operate with Him in bringing about certain effects which He has foreordained; prayer is a secondary cause, itself caused by God. Some modern writers evade the difficulty either by denying that God's will is determined from the beginning or by reducing prayer to being only the expression of resignation to His will.

The early monastic tradition stressed the need for purity of prayer: in prayer the mind must be fixed on God without distraction. *Evagrius Ponticus extended this to mean that a person praying must dispel all thoughts from his mind, since God cannot be identified with anything that is thought. To facilitate this concentration short, intense prayer was recommended. Some E. writers recommend that a single formula of prayer, preferably containing the name of Jesus, should be adopted and used the whole time. This practice developed into the Byzantine 'prayer of the heart' (see HESYCHASM), in which a formula such as 'Lord Jesus Christ, Son of God, have mercy on me' (the '*Jesus Prayer') is recited continually; this practice, combined with the monastic discipline of guarding the heart against distracting thoughts, is believed to lead to the 'discovery of the Spirit' dwelling in the heart, so that human prayer becomes one with the prayer of the Spirit. In the W. the tradition of short, intense prayer persisted until near the end of the Middle Ages, but from the 15th cent. some people began to insist on longer, regular periods of private prayer.

In the course of the Middle Ages there was a tendency to reduce prayer to a seeking of God's gift of Himself, and so to a desire for God. Since a similar development was taking place with regard to *meditation and *contemplation, the words began to merge, so that from the 12th cent. some writers use the words more or less interchangeably and from the 14th cent. meditation and contemplation are sometimes treated as parts or forms of prayer. Thereafter various kinds of prayer came to be identified, such as 'discursive prayer', 'affective prayer', and 'contemplative prayer', and these are sometimes systematized as successive stages of prayer, which some writers connect with the *purgative, illuminative, and unitive ways. Praise, thanksgiving, and confession also came to be regularly seen as parts of prayer. The growing complexity of prayer led to the formulation of several 'methods' of prayer, such as those associated with St

*Ignatius Loyola, St *Francis de Sales, and J.-J. *Olier (the 'Sulpician method'); other writers oppose the idea of any such methods.

In the 20th cent. petition has continued to engage the attention of philosophers and theologians, and it is still the popular understanding of what prayer means. There has also been a lively interest in prayer in the enlarged sense, ranging from more or less technical methods of prayer, incl. the Jesus Prayer and practices adapted from E. non-Christian religions, to more simple notions of just 'being with God'.

Prayer to the BVM and to other *saints, and to angels, is attested from an early period; it is theologically distinct from prayer to God, being properly a request for the prayers of the saints and angels (cf. Thomas Aquinas, *Summa Theol.* 2. 2. qu. 83 a 4). The legitimacy of prayer to the saints and angels has traditionally been denied by Protestants.

There is an immense lit. on prayer; only a sample can be indicated here. In addition to works on Spirituality, cited s.v., there is a general survey by F. *Heiler, *Das Gebet* (1918; abbreviated Eng. tr., 1932). On the biblical texts, J. Herrmann and H. Greeven in *TWNT* 2 (1935), pp. 774–808, s.v. εὔχομαι (Eng. tr., 2 (1964), pp. 775–808); J. Jeremias, *The Prayers of Jesus* (Studies in Biblical Theology, 2nd ser. 6; 1967 [Eng. tr. of papers from *Abba*, 1966, and elsewhere]); also on the NT and early patristic period, A. [G.] Hamman, OFM, *La Prière* (2 vols. to date. Bibliothèque de Théologie [1959–63]; Eng. tr. of vol. 1, Chicago, 1971). The main patristic texts include Origen, *De Oratione*; *Cyprian, *De Oratione Dominica*; Evagrius Ponticus, *De Oratione*; and Augustine, *Ep. ad Probam* (*Ep.* 130). From the medieval period: *Hugh of St-Victor, *De Virtute Orandi*; John of Portes (d. *c*.1163), *De Modo Orandi* (ed., with Fr. tr., in *Lettres des Premiers Chartreux*, 2 (SC 274; 1980), pp. 150–71); Thomas Aquinas, *Summa Theol.* 2. 2. q. 83; Ludovic Barbo, OSB, Bp. of Treviso (d. 1443), *Forma Orationis et Meditationis* (ed. I. Tassi, OSB, *Ludovico Barbo* (Uomini e Dottrine, 1; 1952), pp. 143–52); G. *Savonarola, *Orazione Mentale*. 16th-cent. treatments of prayer in the strict sense incl. the 'Roman Catechism', pt. 4; J. *Calvin, *Institutio Christianae Religionis*, bk. 3, ch. 20; T. *Becon, *Catechism*, part 4; *Homilies, Book 2, homm. 7–8; of prayer in the wider sense, F. de Osuna, OFM, *Tercer Abecedario* (Toledo, 1527; modern edn., Madrid, 1972; Eng. tr., Classics of Western Spirituality, 1981); *Teresa of Ávila, *Castillo Interior o Moradas*; and Luis of Granada, *Libro de la Oración y Consideración*. Modern discussions of prayer are included in books on the spiritual life cited under SPIRITUALITY. On 'stages of prayer', J. G. Arintero, OP, *Grados de Oración* (1918; Eng. tr., 1957). On 'methods of prayer', G. Lercaro, *Metodi di Orazione Mentale* (Genoa, 1948; Eng. tr., 1957). On 'phenomena' of prayer, A. Poulain, SJ, *Des Grâces d'Oraison* (1901; Eng. tr., 1910). On petition, K. Rahner, SJ, 'Sendung zum Gebet', *Stimmen der Zeit*, 152 (1953), pp. 161–70, repr. in *Schriften zur Theologie*, 3 (1956), pp. 249–61 (Eng. tr., *Theological Investigations*, 3 (1967), pp. 209–19). Convenient anthology of Orthodox texts compiled by Igumen Chariton of Valamo, pub. Valamo, Finland, 1936; Eng. tr. by E. Kadloubovsky and E. M. Palmer, with introd. by T. [R.] Ware, *The Art of Prayer* (1966). On Orthodox traditions of prayer, see works cited under HESYCHASM and JESUS PRAYER. Philosophical discussions of prayer incl. D. Z. Phillips, *The Concept of Prayer* (1965); P. R. Baelz, *Prayer and Providence* (Hulsean Lectures for 1966; 1968); C. Fabro, *La Preghiera nel Pensiero Moderno* (1979); B. [E. A.] Davies [OP], *Thinking about God* (1985), pp. 307–34. Modern works, representing a variety of approaches, incl. H. E. *Fosdick, *The Meaning of Prayer* (1915); H. [W.] Northcott, CR, *The Venture of Prayer* (1950); H. U. von *Balthasar, SJ, *Das betrachtende Gebet* (1957; Eng. tr. 1961); M. Nédoncelle, *Prière humaine et prière divine: Notes phénoménolo-

giques (1962; Eng. tr., 1964); C. S. *Lewis, *Letters to Malcolm: Chiefly on Prayer* (1964); A. Bloom, *Living Prayer* (1966), and other works of this author; 'Abhishiktananda' [H. Le Saux, OSB], *Prayer* (Delhi, 1967); B. [A. F.] Basset, SJ, *Let's Start Praying Again* (1972); G. Lefebvre [OSB], *Simplicité de la Prière* (1973; Eng. tr., 1975); S. [C. ff.] Tugwell, OP, *Prayer* (2 vols., Dublin, 1974). M. Dupuy, PSS, in *Dict. Sp.* 11 (1982), cols. 831–46, s.v. 'Oraison'.

Prayer Book, the. A common designation of the Book of *Common Prayer (q.v.).

Prayer of Manasses. See MANASSES, PRAYER OF.

prayers for the dead. See DEAD, PRAYERS FOR THE.

Preachers, Order of. See DOMINICAN ORDER.

preaching. Preaching has always been regarded as an essential part of Christian ministry. The emphasis placed upon it has varied at different times and in different denominations because of the various views of the nature of the ministry that have been held, but it has always been looked upon as important. In the Anglican view of ministry it has taken equal part with the administration of the *sacraments. A visible sign of this is the prominent place that has been given to *pulpits in Anglican churches. In the *Calvinist tradition preaching has been accepted as the principal work of a minister, and correspondingly, in a Calvinist church the pulpit has been given pride of place in the centre of the building. The RC Church has at times subordinated preaching to the administration of the sacraments, but since the Second *Vatican Council (1962–5) greater emphasis has been given to the work of preaching. That Council declared that the homily (or sermon) was an integral part not only of the Eucharist but also of the other sacraments, and that preaching was central to the ministry of both bishops and priests.

The vehicle of preaching is human speech, and it is this fact which has given it its high place in ministry. For speech is that form of communication which is limited to human beings and therefore expresses human personality. It creates a relationship between persons. But preaching is not any speech; it is speech under the authority of God, and the communication of that authority is as important to preaching as speech itself. The sense of that authority carries with it the conviction, both for the preacher and the hearer, that the things of God are communicated through preaching.

The origins of preaching lie in the words of the *prophets of the OT. They saw themselves as God's spokesmen, directly commissioned by Him to declare His will to His people Israel, both in their corporate and individual lives; to influence the direction of life by encouragement, warning, and condemnation. Through this work of the prophets the idea of God relating to His people through His word became an important part of the OT tradition. In the NT St *John's Gospel used that tradition when the birth of Jesus Christ was there described as 'the Word was made flesh and dwelt among us' (Jn. 1: 14). There the claim is made that the incarnate life of Jesus is the fullest personal means of communication between God and humankind under the conditions of this world.

The ministry of Jesus Christ provides the ideal and pattern for Christian ministry; He is the model preacher. He is described in the gospels as a prophet who spoke with authority: one who fulfilled the work of the OT prophets. After His death and resurrection the *Apostles are shown exercising a similar but dependent ministry: dependent in the sense that the content of their preaching is witness to Jesus. So in Acts we are shown St *Peter and St *Paul in particular, winning converts to the new faith by their preaching. In this way the NT has set the standard for all subsequent ministry. Without preaching the ministry must be defective.

Since the 1st cent. the work of preaching has been principally, though not exclusively, directed to the Church. Its purpose has been to teach, strengthen, and enthuse congregations that they may become more effective witnesses to Christian truth and the Christian way of life. Where preaching has been directed to non-Christians its purpose has been so to move those who listen that they become a congregation of believers. All preaching is thus related to Christian community, and its content is always witness in some way to Jesus as the Son of God. Holy Scripture for the Christian has the same purpose, and so preaching and Scripture have always been closely related, as in the common practice of a sermon being seen as an exposition of a text taken from Scripture. Sermons extend the witness of Scripture by explaining its meaning and creating enthusiasm for its message.

Preaching has had a great influence on the character of ministry in that its effective performance has usually been seen as demanding an educated ministry. At times when there has been slackness in insisting on education as a requisite for ministry, the first casualty has been preaching, and at such times the work and witness of the Church has suffered. Revival in Church life has frequently been led by a revival in preaching and an insistence on the better education of the clergy. One example of this is the religious movement started by St *Francis of Assisi in the 12th cent. which led to a revival in preaching and the creation of two orders of preaching friars, the *Franciscans and the *Dominicans. Indeed the official title of the Dominicans is 'Ordo Praedicatorum', the 'Order of Preachers'. Later the Council of *Trent (1545–63) ordered the establishment of *seminaries for the education of the clergy in every RC diocese. Similar movements can be seen at various times in the history of the Church and all denominations.

In 17th-cent. *France J.-B. *Bossuet exercised great influence over the French court and the educated classes in general by the power of his preaching. In 18th-cent. England the preaching of John *Wesley led ultimately to the foundation of the *Methodist Church. In the *United States of America at much the same time there was a great revival of evangelical religious life inspired by the preaching of an Englishman, George *Whitefield. It became known as the *Great Awakening. Its most notable American leader was Jonathan *Edwards and it led to the development of what came to be dubbed 'New England Theology'. In the 19th cent. in the new territories opening up in the W. much preaching took place in tents; it was known as 'tent evangelism' and from it come the *Revival Movements of our own time led by such preachers as Billy *Graham. These are notable examples of the kind of influence that preaching has had on the life of the Church in most times and places.

Preaching has also influenced the study of theology. In the Graeco-Roman world much attention was paid to the study of rhetoric by lawyers, statesmen, and all who were concerned with public speaking. Christian preachers were influenced by this study. St *Augustine of Hippo is but one example. In time specifically Christian developments were added to this study such as *hermeneutics (the study of the proper interpretation of Scripture) and *apologetics (the study of the most effective way of commending the Gospel to those who do not know or accept it). In addition many preachers have in their sermons extended theological learning. Examples of such preachers are St Augustine of Hippo in the 5th cent., J. *Butler, Bp. of Durham, in the 18th cent., and F. D. *Maurice in the 19th. Other preachers have had considerable influence on the literary life of their times, such as John *Donne and Lancelot *Andrewes in 17th-cent. England and J. H. *Newman in 19th-cent. Oxford.

Preaching begins as speech by an authorized minister to a believing community or congregation but its influence has extended far beyond this to every aspect of Christian life.

See also ARS PRAEDICANDI; HOMILIES, THE BOOKS OF.

R. E. C. Browne, *The Ministry of the Word* (Studies in Ministry and Worship [3]; 1958). D. W. Cleverley Ford, *The Ministry of the Word* (1979). Y. T. Brilioth, *Predikans historia* (Lund [1946]); id., *Landmarks in the History of Preaching* (Donellan Lectures, 1949; 1950). C. H. *Dodd, *The Apostolic Preaching and its Developments* (1936). A. Olivar, *La Predicación Cristiana Antiqua* (Barcelona, 1991). C. [H.] Smyth, *The Art of Preaching: A Practical Survey of Preaching in the Church of England 747–1939* (1940). R. F. Bennett, *The Early Dominicans: Studies in Thirteenth Century Dominican History* (Cambridge Studies in Medieval Life and Thought, 1937), esp. pp. 75–127. G. R. Owst, *Preaching in Medieval England: An Introduction to Sermon Manuscripts of the Period c.1350–1450* (ibid., 1926); H. L. Spencer, *English Preaching in the Late Middle Ages* (Oxford, 1993); J. W. Blench, *Preaching in England in the late Fifteenth and Sixteenth Centuries* (ibid., 1964). *English Wycliffite Sermons*, ed. A. Hudson and P. Gradon (5 vols., ibid., 1983–96). *The English Sermon: An Anthology* (3 vols., Cheadle, 1976: vol. 1, ed. M. Seymour-Smith, 1550–1650; vol. 2, ed. C. H. Sisson, 1650–1750; vol. 3, ed. R. Nye, 1750–1850). P. [J.] Bayley, *French Pulpit Oratory 1598–1650: A Study in Themes and Styles, with a Descriptive Catalogue of Printed Texts* (Cambridge, 1980); id. (ed.), *Selected Sermons of the French Baroque (1600–1650)* (New York and London, 1983). L. [J.] Taylor, *Soldiers of Christ: Preaching in Late Medieval and Reformation France* (New York and Oxford, 1992). P. T. *Forsyth, *Positive Preaching and the Modern Mind* (1907). W. E. Sangster, *The Craft of Sermon Construction* (1949); W. J. Burghardt, SJ, *Preaching: The Art and the Craft* (Mahwah, NJ, 1987).

Preaching of Peter. See PETER, PREACHING OF ST.

prebend and **prebendary.** A *cathedral benefice and its holder. Though in the early Middle Ages reformers constantly aimed at maintaining the common life under rule for the *canons of cathedral and collegiate foundations, in the majority of such foundations this ideal was frankly abandoned and the endowment divided up into separate portions, each designed for the support of one member of the chapter. These acquired the name of 'prebends' from the fact that they supplied or furnished (*praebere*) a living to their holders, who in turn came to be known as 'prebendaries'. The prebend normally consisted of the revenue

from one manor of the cathedral estates, a fact which accounts for the territorial names still attached to the prebendal stalls in many English cathedrals. In English cathedrals of the 'Old Foundation' the ancient prebends have been kept in name, though the transference of their attached incomes to the *Ecclesiastical Commission by the 19th-cent. legislation has made them in nearly all cases honorary offices only. In the former monastic cathedrals, reorganized by *Henry VIII at the *Dissolution and known as cathedrals of the 'New Foundation', prebends in the proper sense do not exist, though 'prebendary' became the normal appellation of the members of the chapters of these churches until the 19th cent., when the title of 'canon' replaced it in general usage.

precentor. In *cathedrals, the cleric responsible for the direction of the choral services. In those of the 'Old Foundation' he is a member of the chapter who ranks next to the Dean, and commonly delegates his duties to a deputy known as the *succentor. In most cathedrals of the 'New Foundation', however, his status is the lower one of *minor canon or chaplain.

precept (Lat. *praeceptum*). In moral theology, a matter of obligation, as contrasted with a 'counsel', which is only a matter of persuasion. For Precepts of the Church, see COMMANDMENTS OF THE CHURCH.

preceptory. Among the Knights *Templar a community established on one of their provincial estates. The corresponding institution among the *Hospitallers was a '*commandery'.

preces feriales (Lat., 'ferial prayers'). In W. service books, a short series of prayers which used to be said esp. on ferial (non-festal) days, consisting of *Kyrie Eleison, the *Lord's Prayer, and versicles and responses. In the 1568 *Breviary they stood immediately before the collect; from 1955 their use was confined to *Lauds and *Vespers on the Wednesdays and Fridays of Lent and Advent and Ember Days. In the 1971 Breviary they have been replaced by a series of intercessions said every day at Lauds and Vespers. In the BCP the preces feriales are represented by the prayers at *Mattins and *Evensong between the Creed and the collects, and are said or sung throughout the year.

Preces Privatae. The Latin book of devotion issued by *Elizabeth I in 1564 with the title *Preces Privatae in Studiosorum Gratiam Collectae et Regia Autoritate Approbatae*. It was a manual of prayers largely based on the BCP, and thus carried on the tradition of the medieval English *Primers, which were compilations for private use based on the liturgical services. A later edition of 1573 contained additional devotions compiled by St John *Fisher. Apart from its title it has no connection with the celebrated 'Preces Privatae' of L. *Andrewes (q.v.).

It is pr. in *Private Prayers of the Reign of Queen Elizabeth* (Parker Society, 1851), pp. 209–428.

Precious Blood, devotion to the. The Blood of Christ, shed during the Passion, has been honoured and regarded as of redeeming virtue since the Apostolic Age, esp. in connection with the Eucharist. Beirut, Bruges, Saintes, the

English monasteries of Ashridge and Hailes, and various other churches have claimed to possess particles of it. Such relics have been greatly venerated, although St *Thomas Aquinas (*Summa Theol.* 3a., q. 54, a. 3) maintained that all the particles of the Blood of Christ shed during the Passion were reassumed by Him at His Resurrection, and that such relics must have flowed from an image of Christ. *Benedict XIV, admitting that some particles might not have been assumed, maintained that, not being united to the Godhead, they were to be venerated rather than adored. The *Dominicans held that the Precious Blood was an essential part of the Sacred Humanity; the *Franciscans that it was concomitant only. Since the Council of *Trent the former view has tended to prevail among RC theologians. Feasts in honour of the Precious Blood were celebrated by various orders in the 19th cent. In 1849 *Pius IX, while at Gaeta, extended the Feast to the whole Church, assigning to it the first Sunday in July, altered by *Pius X in 1914 to 1 July. It was raised to the rank of double of the first class in 1934, but suppressed altogether in 1969. *John XXIII inserted a clause about the Precious Blood in the *Divine Praises. The whole month of July is traditionally connected with the devotion. A number of religious orders are dedicated to the Precious Blood, and the dedication of the (RC) Cathedral Church of the Archdiocese of *Westminster is to the Most Precious Blood.

F. W. *Faber, *The Precious Blood, or the Price of our Salvation* (1860; devotional). G. Lefebvre, OSB, *La Rédemption par le sang de Jésus* (Bruges, 1942; Eng. tr., Westminster, Md., 1960). M.-D. Chenu, OP, in *DTC* 14 (pt. 1; 1939), cols. 1094–7, s.v. 'Sang du Christ'; R. Grégoire, OSB, in *Dict. Sp.* 14 (1990), cols. 319–33, s.v. 'Sang'.

Precisian. A name widely used of the *Puritans in the 16th and 17th cents. on account of their punctiliousness in observing external religious rules and forms.

predella. (1) The platform (foot-pace) on the uppermost of the steps to an altar, on which the priest formerly stood when celebrating Mass; it is now obsolete. (2) The lowest piece of a *reredos, immediately above the altar. The word is the Ital. *predella*, 'foot-stool', 'kneeling-stool'.

predestinarianism. The doctrine according to which human free will and co-operation are totally eliminated from the process of salvation by a thorough-going application of the principle of *predestination. It has always been regarded as heretical by the RC Church.

predestination (from Lat. 'praedestinare', Vulg. tr. of Gk. προορίζειν, 'foreordain'). The Divine decree acc. to which certain persons are infallibly guided to eternal salvation. The doctrine is not explicitly taught in the OT, but adumbrations of it may be found in the conception of the 'Book of Life' (Ps. 69: 29, Exod. 32: 32, Dan. 12: 1). Predestination is presupposed in the Gospels, e.g. Mt. 20: 23, where the Lord tells the Apostles that the sitting on His right or left is reserved 'for them for whom it hath been prepared of my Father', and in Jn. 10: 29, where He tells the Jews that no one can snatch from Him the sheep given Him by the Father. The most explicit teaching in the NT is in St *Paul, esp. in the crucial text Rom. 8: 28–30,

where he traces the process of the salvation of those 'that are called according to His purpose' from foreknowledge and predestination to vocation, justification, and glorification. The theme is resumed in Eph. 1: 3–14, where is added the factor of *election (q.v.), inserted between foreknowledge and predestination. In the same text great stress is laid on the gratuity of it, 'according to the good pleasure of His will'. This is still more emphasized in 2 Tim. 1: 9, where it is affirmed that God has called us 'not according to our works, but according to His own purpose and grace'.

In the W. the *Pelagian controversy caused a thorough investigation of the doctrine, which St *Augustine developed on the basis of St Paul's teaching. For him the mystery of predestination consists in the inaccessibility to the human mind of the reasons for the Divine choice, which, nevertheless, is made in perfect justice. In his view it is the vocation not only to grace but also to glory. It contains the gift of final perseverance (*donum perseverantiae*) and depends not on human acceptance but on the eternal decree of God and is therefore infallible, without, however, acc. to Augustine, violating free will. Evil enters into the plan of predestination in so far as it is permitted by God in view of a greater good.

In S. Gaul Augustine's teaching was questioned by John *Cassian and other so-called 'Semipelagians'. Though stoutly defended by St *Prosper of Aquitaine, it was attacked by *Faustus of Riez (d. *c.*490). In the early 520s, however, Faustus' views were condemned both at *Constantinople and at *Rome, and at the Council of *Orange (529) St *Caesarius of Arles secured the acceptance of the Augustinian position in France. In the 9th cent. the discussion was revived by *Gottschalk (q.v.); basing himself on Augustine, he took an extreme position, teaching a double predestination of some to eternal blessedness and others to eternal fire. This doctrine was condemned by the Synod of *Quiercy in 849.

The medieval teaching was based on Augustine, but took into account also the Greek doctrine, esp. as represented by St *John of Damascus, who followed *Origen and stressed the universal saving will of God. Acc. to him God 'antecedently' wills the universal salvation of all men, but, in consequence of their sins, He wills eternal punishment for some. The reconciliation of this view with the Divine omnipotence and the efficacy of grace, stressed by Augustine, was undertaken by the *Schoolmen. *Peter Lombard emphasized the absence, in God, of all passivity or dependence on the decisions of creatures, and St *Bonaventure asserted the principle of the Divine predilection, which is the cause, not the effect, of the greater or lesser goodness of creatures. St *Thomas Aquinas based the reconciliation of the universal saving will of God with the mystery of predestination on the same principle, namely that the love of God is the cause of the goodness of things (*Amor Dei est causa bonitatis rerum*).

Predestination emerged again as a significant issue at the *Reformation. M. *Luther revived the full Augustinian doctrine which he combined with a new stress on the total depravity of man. In his controversy with *Erasmus in 1525 he maintained that in an act of Divine sovereignty both the elect and the reprobate are predestined without reference to their merits or demerits. The *Gnesio-Lutheran party, centred around M. *Flacius, upheld this position, whereas the more moderate *Philippists, centered around Philip *Melanchthon, rejected it; they accepted the total depravity of man after the *Fall and *justification by faith alone, but denied that double predestination followed from either. This latter position was accepted in the Formula of *Concord (1577) and has remained Lutheran doctrine. J. *Calvin gave new vitality to the doctrine of double predestination, but it was his successors, prob. esp. T. *Beza, who made it a cornerstone of the Calvinist system. Going further than Calvin himself, they rejected belief in the universal saving will of God and held that Christ's atoning death was offered for the elect alone. Later Calvinists were divided into Ante- or *Supralapsarians and *Sublapsarians (qq.v.). The Calvinist doctrine of double predestination, which was not accepted by the *Arminians (q.v.) was imposed by the Synod of *Dort (1618–9) and by the *Westminster Assembly (1647), which declared that at least after the Fall God does not will the salvation of all men and that Christ died only for the elect.

The post-Tridentine RC theologians formulated their doctrine of predestination with particular emphasis on the freedom of the human will. Among the systems devised to reconcile the latter with the dogma of predestination was that of the Spaniard, L. de *Molina, who abandoned the principle of Divine predilection and taught predestination *post praevisa merita*. On the other side, F. *Suárez, R. *Bellarmine, and most *Jesuit theologians except the strict Molinists recognize the gratuity of predestination and its priority to the prevision of merits, though they seek to preserve the element of human consent and the reality of the Divine will that 'all men should be saved'.

In the 20th cent. K. *Barth sought to provide a Christological presentation of the doctrine of predestination within his treatment of God. In his view Christ is both the God who predestines man, and the man predestined; in communion with Him humans can discover their election. In so far as all men might be thought to be elected in Christ, some critics have seen Barth's position as involving *universalism rather than predestination in the more classical sense.

The number of the predestined has been a matter of speculation from early times. Acc. to the teaching of the majority of the Fathers and theologians, who based their belief on passages such as Mt. 22: 14, it was smaller than that of the reprobate.

See also ELECTION.

On the biblical teaching on predestination, see esp. comm. on the OT Prophets and Rom. and works on the theology of St Paul. The more important post-biblical discussions incl. Origen, *De Principiis*, 2 and 3; St Augustine, *De Praedestinatione Sanctorum*; and Calvin, *Institutes*, 3; K. Barth, *Die Kirchliche Dogmatik*, 2. 2 (1942), pp. 1–563; Eng. tr., 2. 2 (1957) pp. 1–506. Modern discussions will be found in treatises on dogmatic theology. J. B. *Mozley, *A Treatise on the Augustinian Doctrine of Predestination* (1855); W. A. Copinger, *A Treatise on Predestination, Election and Grace* (1889), with bibl. R. Garrigou-Lagrange, OP, *La Prédestination des saints et la grâce* (1936). H. H. Rowley, *The Biblical Doctrine of Election* (1950). P. Maury, *La Prédestination* (1957; Eng. tr., 1960). J. *Moltmann, *Prädestination und Perseveranz: Geschichte und Bedeutung der reformierten Lehre 'de perseverantia sanctorum'* (Beiträge zur Geschichte und Lehre der Reformierten Kirche, 12; Neukirchen, 1961). V. Boublík, *La predestinazione: S. Paolo e S. Agostino* (1961). G. G. Most, *Novum tentamen ad solu-* *tionem de Gratia et Praedestinatione* (Rome, 1963). M. J. Farrelly, OSB, *Predestination, Grace and Free Will* [1964]. A. Bsteh, *Zur Frage nach der Universalität der Erlösung unter besonderer Berücksichtigung ihres Verständnisses bei den Vätern des zweiten Jahrhunderts* (Wiener Beiträge zur Theologie, 14; 1966). J. S. Bray, *Theodore Beza's Doctrine of Predestination* (Bibliotheca Humanistica & Reformatorica, 12; Nieuwkoop, 1975). W. L. Craig, *The Problem of Divine Foreknowledge and Future Contingents from Aristotle to Suarez* (Brill's Studies in Intellectual History, 7; Leiden etc., 1988 [treats of *Aristotle, Augustine, *Boethius, Thomas Aquinas, *Duns Scotus, *William of Ockham, L. Molina, and F. Suárez]). M. Löhrer in *Mysterium Salutis*, ed. J. Feiner and M. Löhrer, 4 (pt. 2; Einsiedeln [1973]), pp. 773–830. J. Pohle in *CE* 12 (1911), pp. 376–84, s.vv. 'Predestinarianism' and 'Predestination'; A. S. Martin in *HERE* 10 (1918), pp. 225–35, s.v.; A. Lemonnyer, OP, H. D. Simonin, OP, R. Garrigou-Lagrange, OP, and B. Lavaud, OP, in *DTC* 12 (pt. 2; 1935), cols. 2809–3022, s.v. 'Prédestination'; H. Rondet, SJ, and K. *Rahner, SJ, in *Sacramentum Mundi*, 5 (1970), pp. 88–91; P. Gerlitz, R. Bergmeier, H. Hübner, G. R. Evans, and T. Mahlmann in *TRE*, 27 (1997), pp. 98–160, s.v. 'Prädestination', with extensive bibl.

Predestinatus. See PRAEDESTINATUS.

Pre-established Harmony. In the system of G. W. *Leibniz, the predetermined harmony between all the 'simple substances' (monads) in the universe. Leibniz believed that God had established such a harmony before creation, which explained the apparent interaction between mind and body in the world of experience. See also OCCASIONALISM.

Preface. In the Eucharist of the W. Church, the words which introduce the central part of the service. It begins with the '*Sursum Corda' and ends with the '*Sanctus'. The main part of it is an ascription of praise and thanksgiving to the Creator in union with the worship of the whole angelic company. It varies with the feast observed. There are 'proper' Prefaces for all the great seasons and feasts, ending with varying phrases leading into the Sanctus. The oldest surviving Roman *Sacramentary, the *Leonine, had a separate Preface for every Mass, the *Gelasian had 54, but in the *Gregorian their number had fallen to 10. The 1661 BCP provides 'Proper Prefaces' for *Christmas, *Easter, *Ascensiontide, *Whitsuntide, and on *Trinity Sunday; the ASB and other modern Anglican liturgies include considerably more, but nowhere near as many as the RC rite. There are no comparable variations in the rites of the E. Church. The Preface is the first part of the *Eucharistic Prayer, even though in the current Roman Missal (because of the number of proper Prefaces) it is printed in such a way that it appears to be a separate item, and in the BCP (and in a few modern Anglican liturgies) it is divided from the consecratory prayer by the 'Prayer of *Humble Access'.

E. Moeller, OSB (ed.), *Corpus Praefationum* (CCLS 161–161 D; 1980–1), with valuable introd. and bibl. in first vol. Jungmann (1958 edn.), 2, esp. pp. 145–61 (Eng. tr., pp. 115–28). C. Mohrmann, 'Sur l'histoire de Praefari-Praefatio', *VC* 7 (1953), pp. 1–15. H. *Leclercq, OSB, in *DACL* 14 (pt. 1; 1948), cols. 1704–16, s.v., with refs.

prelate. A term originally of wide connotation, it gradually acquired a purely ecclesiastical reference and still later came to be restricted to Church officials of high rank. In the C of E the title is restricted nowadays to bishops. In the RC Church it was long used of important ecclesiastics having an independent jurisdiction, but it is now also applied to a variety of officers attached to the Roman curia who may have only an honorary dignity. The term 'prelacy', which denotes the system of ecclesiastical government by bishops, is commonly used only in a hostile sense. See also PERSONAL PRELATURE.

Premonstratensian Canons, also 'Norbertines' and, in England, 'White Canons' from the colour of their habit, an order founded by St *Norbert (q.v.) at Prémontré, near Laon, in 1120. The basis of the rule was the so-called Rule of St *Augustine, with additional austerities, e.g. entire abstinence from meat. In its details, the Premonstratensian life also came under *Cistercian influences through Norbert's friendship with St *Bernard of Clairvaux. In 1126 the order received Papal approbation and quickly spread over W. Europe, their earliest English house being at Newhouse in Lincoln (c.1143). They became powerful in Hungary and also took an active part in evangelizing the lands between the Elbe and the Oder. Relaxation in the severity of the original rule led to several reforms and the creation of more or less independent congregations, notably in Spain, where a virtually self-contained body was established c.1573. The order suffered severely from the French Revolution and had become nearly extinct in the early 19th cent. More recently it has re-established its influence and is esp. strong in Belgium.

Numerous studies of primary importance in *Analectes de l'ordre de Prémontré*, ed. M. van Waefelghem (12 vols., Brussels, 1905–14); cont. as *Analecta Praemonstratensia* (1925 ff.; at Tongerloo and later at Averbode), and in the *Bibliotheca Analectorum Praemonstratensium* (1957 ff; some vols. at Louvain, some at Averbode). C. L. Hugo, *Sacri et Canonici Ordinis Praemonstratensis Annales* (2 vols., Nancy, 1734–5). F. Petit, O. Praem., *L'Ordre de Prémontré* ('Les Ordres religieux'; 1927); id., *Norbert et l'origine des Prémontrés* (1981), pp. 77–208. N. Backmund, O. Praem., *Monasticon Praemonstratense, id est Historia circariarum atque canoniarum candidi et canonici ordinis Praemonstratensis* (3 vols., Straubing, 1949–56; 2nd edn., Berlin, 1983 ff.). L. Milis and others, *Gedenkboek Orde van Prémontré 1121–1971* (Averbode, 1971). F. Petit, O. Praem., *La Spiritualité des Prémontrés aux XIIe et XIIIe siècles* (Études de Théologie et d'Histoire de Spiritualité, 10; 1947). B. Ardura, O. Praem., *Prémontrés: Histoire et Spiritualité* (Saint Etienne, 1995). J. Le Paige, *Bibliotheca Praemonstratensis Ordinis* (Paris, 1633). L. Goovaerts, *Écrivains, artistes et savants de l'ordre de Prémontré: Dictionnaire bio-bibliographique* (4 vols., bound in 3, 1899–1917). F. A. *Gasquet (ed.), *Collectanea Anglo-Premonstratensia: Documents drawn from the Original Register of the Order, now in the Bodleian Library, Oxford, and the Transcript of another Register in the British Museum* (Camden Society 3rd ser. 12; 1906). H. M. Colvin, *The White Canons in England* (1951), with bibl. R. van Waefelghem, *Répertoire des sources imprimées et manuscrites relatives à l'histoire et à la liturgie des monastères de l'ordre de Prémontré* (1930). R. J. Cornell, O. Praem., in *NCE* 11 (1967), pp. 737–9, s.v.; J.-B. Valvekens, O. Praem., and others in *DIP* 7 (1983), cols. 720–46, s.v. 'Premonstratensi', with bibl.

Preparation, the. In the W. Church the opening prayers at *Mass, formerly recited alternately by the priest and ministers (or *server) at the foot of the *altar. It usually consisted of Ps. 43 (Vulg. 42), a confession of sin, and two prayers preceded by four *versicles and responses. In the Roman Rite a shorter form dates from the 11th cent.; in

substantially its traditional form it is found from c.1300. In the current RC rite the Mass opens with the Rite of Entry, consisting of greeting, address, act of penitence and absolution.

Jungmann (1952 edn.), 1, pp. 377–409; Eng. tr., 1, pp. 290–311.

Preparation, Day of (Gk παρασκευή). A name given by the Jews to Fridays, i.e. the day preceding, and thus employed in 'preparation' for, the *Sabbath (hence also προσάββατον). The title was perhaps used occasionally also of the day before certain other of the greater feasts, e.g. the *Passover. In all four Gospels, the Crucifixion is recorded to have taken place on the Preparation (Mt. 27: 62, Mk. 15: 42, Lk. 23: 54, Jn. 19: 14, 31, 42).

Presanctified, Mass of the (Gk. λειτουργία τῶν προηγιασμένων). A shortened form of the Eucharistic Liturgy without consecration, a *Host consecrated at a previous Mass being used for Communion. It is attested as an approved custom for the E. by can. 52 of the *Quinisextum (692), and in the Byzantine Rite it was formerly celebrated on most weekdays in *Lent, though now it takes place ordinarily only on the *Wednesdays and *Fridays, and on Monday, Tuesday, and Wednesday in *Holy Week. The Byzantine Liturgy of the Presanctified (attributed to St Gregory 'the Dialogist', i.e. St *Gregory the Great) is a complex service combined with *Vespers and using a previously *intincted Host. The readings (which do not normally include a Gospel) are followed by litanies. Then, at the *Great Entrance, the consecrated elements are carried in procession and placed upon the altar. After the Lord's Prayer, there is Communion, first of the priests, then of the people. In the Latin Church, the Mass of the Presanctified is restricted to *Good Friday. It first appears in Gaul. It is described in the *Gelasian Sacramentary and was in general use in Rome by the 9th cent. According to the current Roman Missal, after the *Veneration of the Cross, the ciborium, containing Hosts consecrated on *Maundy Thursday, is brought from the Altar of *Repose to the High Altar. The priest says the Lord's Prayer, in which the people join, the *Embolism, a pre-Communion prayer, and the invitation to Communion (*Ecce Agnus Dei*); he then communicates himself and the people. The dismissal follows after a single collect. Before the reform of the Holy Week liturgy in 1955 the rite was very much more elaborate, and only the celebrant communicated; in that year General Communion, which was the custom in the early Middle Ages, was restored. At the same time the term 'presanctified' was dropped from the official documents.

The text of the various rites will be found in the standard edns. of the Liturgies. L. *Allatius, *De Missa Praesanctificatorum* (1648). G. *Dix, OSB, 'The Christian Passover', *Laudate*, 13 (1935), pp. 2–18; repr. sep. as *The Mass of the Presanctified*. D. N. Moraïtes, Ἡ Λειτουργία τῶν Προηγιασμένων (Thessalonica, 1955, with summary in Fr.). H. A. P. Schmidt, SJ, *Hebdomada Sancta* (2 vols. in 3, Rome etc., 1956–7), esp. 1, pp. 108–16, 2, pp. 797–806. M. Arranz, SJ, 'La Liturgie des Présanctifiés de l'ancien Euchologe byzantin', *OCP* 47 (1981), pp. 332–88, with refs. to earlier literature I. Ziadé in *DTC* 13 (pt. 1; 1936), cols. 77–111; H. Schmidt, SJ, in *LW* 1 (1962), cols. 892–5, s.v. 'Goede Vrijdag, VII', with bibl.

presbyter. The earliest organization of the Christian Churches in Palestine resembled that of the Jewish synagogues, each of which was administered by a board of 'elders' (πρεσβύτεροι, i.e. 'presbyters'). Acts 11: 30 and 15: 22 witness to this collegiate system of Church government at *Jerusalem, and Acts 14: 23 has St Paul appointing presbyters in the Churches he founded. At first the presbyters seem to have been identical with the 'overseers' (ἐπίσκοποι, i.e. 'bishops'), and such passages as Acts 20: 17 f. and Tit. 1: 5, 7 reveal the terms as interchangeable. But from the 2nd cent. the title of bishop is normally confined to the presidents of these councils of presbyters, and such 'bishops' came to be distinguished, both in honour and prerogative, from the presbyters, who were held to derive their authority by delegation from the bishops. The presbyterate, in its developed form, possesses both authority in administration and teaching and the sacerdotal functions foreshadowed by the Jewish priesthood. The English word 'priest' derives ultimately from this root. See also BISHOP, PRIEST, and ORDERS AND ORDINATION.

For discussion of the office of presbyter and its relation to that of the bishop in NT times see works on the early history of Orders; some listed in bibl. to BISHOP. G. Bornkamm in *TWNT* 6 (1959; Eng. tr., 1968), pp. 651–83, s.v. Πρέσβυς, etc.

Presbyterianism. Presbyterianism is a form of ecclesiastical polity in which the Church is governed by presbyters (Gk. πρεσβύτερος, 'elder'). Its proponents in the 16th and 17th cents. did not regard it as an innovation but as a rediscovery of the apostolic model found in the NT. Many of them held it to be the only permissible form of government and thus permanently binding upon the Church. However, the model has been adapted to suit a wide variety of regional variations. The pattern for the city-state of *Geneva required considerable emendation before it could be applied to the parochial system covering the whole of *Scotland. Today most Presbyterians recognize that the Church in NT times had episcopal and congregational as well as presbyterian elements and that Presbyterianism has no *jure divino* claim to be the only permissible or valid Church polity.

The normal pattern of government of Presbyterian Churches is a hierarchy of four interrelated bodies: the *Session* (Kirk session, consistory) of a local Church, consisting of the minister(s) and *elders who are the congregation's elected representatives; the *Presbytery* (colloquy, classis), consisting of ministers and representative elders from within a prescribed area, which oversees Sessions, congregations, and ministers in its area; *Synods*, which are geographically defined to include Presbyteries in a larger area and have important functions in the judicial process as a court of appeal; and the *General Assembly*, the Church's highest court of appeal, consisting of ministers and elders, usually in equal numbers, elected by the Presbyteries. It is responsible for the Church's mission, but has no legislative power over the lower bodies; it normally meets annually. Within all these bodies ministers and elders have an equal vote and decisions are made by majority voting. The powers of each body are limited by the Church's constitution.

Presbyterian concepts of the elder (q.v.) are based on J. *Calvin's recognition of the office as one of the four ministries of the Church, along with pastors, teachers, and

*deacons (*Institutes*, bk. 4, ch. 3, sections 4–9). Elders may participate in preaching, teaching, and administering the Sacraments. Calvin based his understanding of lay persons elected to share in the government of the Church on biblical passages such as Rom. 12: 8, 1 Cor. 12: 28, and 1 Tim. 5: 17. Ministers, who share in the government of the Church, have historically been seen as ordained as Ministers of the Word and Sacrament. Some Presbyterians regard *apostolic succession through presbyters as enhancing their position in this regard; others view the idea of lineal succession with indifference or even disfavour. Ministers are elected by the people, but their ordination is an act of the Presbytery. Presbyterians have traditionally stressed the need for an educated clergy, requiring college or university degrees, and additional seminary training, but Presbyteries may modify specific requirements. Most Presbyterian Churches ordain both men and women as ministers and elders. As in 16th-cent. Geneva, Church discipline as an aspect of Church government includes elements of guidance, education, and reconciliation within the Christian community, as well as censures such as rebuke and excommunication, but these no longer have power beyond the willingness of members to be bound by them.

The only Presbyterian State Church is the Church of Scotland, but it claims and exercises the spiritual independence which is a fundamental principle of all Presbyterians. As members of the Reformed theological tradition, all Presbyterians acknowledge the Bible as the supreme standard of faith and practice. The many Confessions of Faith produced by Reformed bodies at various times hold important but secondary positions as subordinate standards for the Church's doctrine and ministry. While many Presbyterian Churches retain the *Westminster Confession with the two *Westminster Catechisms of 1647 as their chief doctrinal standards, the United Presbyterian Church in the *United States of America, the largest Presbyterian body in the country, in 1967 adopted a *Book of Confessions* as its doctrinal base and this was accepted by the Presbyterian Church (USA) when that came into being in 1983. It contains the *Nicene and *Apostles' Creeds, the *Scottish Confession, the *Heidelberg Catechism, the Second *Helvetic Confession, the Westminster Confession and the two Westminster Catechisms, the *Barmen Declaration, and a new formula of confession drawn up in 1967. A 'Brief Statement of Faith' was added in 1991. Presbyterians interpret confessional standards within their Churches with varying decrees of latitude; the discretion permitted is illustrated by the terms of the *Declaratory Acts in Scotland.

Presbyterian worship is simple and dignified, with an emphasis on hearing and preaching the Word of God. There is a wide variety of liturgical practice, as well as differing degrees of formality. An increased appreciation of the place of the Sacraments has become apparent in the latter part of the 20th cent.; the Lord's Supper, formerly administered only quarterly in many churches, is now celebrated more frequently, often seven to 12 times a year.

Presbyterian Churches are found throughout the world. There are strong concentrations of Presbyterians in the United States of America, Scotland, *Hungary, the *Netherlands, Northern *Ireland, Switzerland, *France, the Cameroon, and *Korea; the largest single Presbyterian congregation is in Seoul. Some Presbyterian Churches have direct roots in the Reformed Churches of Europe. Others, esp. in the British Commonwealth and the USA, originated through emigration from countries such as Scotland, Ireland, and the Netherlands. Still others are the result of missionary efforts, particularly in *India, *Africa, and S. America.

Presbyterian Churches have been linked through the World Presbyterian Alliance (founded in 1875), which in 1970 merged with the International *Congregational Council (founded in 1891) to form the *World Alliance of Reformed Churches (q.v.). In America there have been notable unions of Presbyterian Churches in modern times. In 1958 the Presbyterian Church in the USA merged with the United Presbyterian Church of North America to form the United Presbyterian Church in the USA. This body in 1983 joined with the Presbyterian Church in the United States to form the Presbyterian Church (USA), thus uniting two streams of Presbyterianism divided since the Civil War. Some Presbyterian Churches have been involved in regional unions with other Churches. These have led, e.g., to the formation of the United Church of *Canada, the United Church of Christ in the *Philippines, the United Church of *Zambia, the Uniting Church in *Australia, and the Churches of *South India, *North India, and *Pakistan. In 1972 the Presbyterian Church of England united with the *Congregational Church of England and Wales to form the *United Reformed Church.

See also SCOTLAND, CHRISTIANITY IN; and, for the Presbyterian Church of *Wales, CALVINISTIC METHODISM.

J. N. Ogilvie, The Presbyterian Churches: Their Place and Power in Modern Christendom (1896; enlarged edn., 1925); W. M. Macphail, The Presbyterian Church: A Brief Account of its Doctrine, Worship, and Polity (1908); J. *Moffatt, The Presbyterian Church (1928); L. A. Loetscher, A Brief History of the Presbyterians (Philadelphia [1938]; 4th edn., 1983); J. M. Barkley, Presbyterianism (Belfast, 1951); G. D. Henderson, Presbyterianism (Chalmers Lectures, Aberdeen, 1954). E. W. Smith, The Creed of the Presbyterians (Toronto, 1901); H. J. Wotherspoon and J. M. Kirkpatrick, A Manual of Church Doctrine [1919], rev. T. F. Torrance and R. S. Wright (1960); J. Kennedy, Presbyterian Authority and Discipline (Chalmers Lectures; Edinburgh, 1960). E. A. Dowey, A Commentary on the Confession of 1967 and an Introduction to The Book of Confessions (Philadelphia [1968]); J. B. Rogers, Presbyterian Creeds: A Guide to the Book of Confessions (ibid. [1985]); W. C. Placher and D. Willis-Watkins, Belonging to God: A Commentary on A Brief Statement of Faith (Louisville, Ky. [1992]). E. A. McKee, Elders and the Plural Ministry: The Role of Exegetical History in Illuminating John Calvin's Theology (Travaux d'Humanisme et Renaissance, 223; Geneva, 1988). See also works cited under CALVINISM.

A. H. Drysdale, History of the Presbyterians in England: Their Rise, Decline and Revival (1889). O. M. Griffiths, Religion and Learning: A Study in English Presbyterian Thought from the Bartholomew Ejections [1662] to the Foundation of the Unitarian Movement (1935); C. G. Bolam and others, The English Presbyterians from Elizabethan Puritanism to Modern Unitarianism (1968). R. F. G. Holmes, Our Irish Presbyterian Heritage (Belfast, 1985). M. W. Armstrong, L. A. Loetscher, and C. A. Anderson (eds.), The Presbyterian Enterprise: Sources of American Presbyterian History (Philadelphia, 1956). C. A. *Briggs, American Presbyterianism: Its Growth and Early History (New York, 1885); R. E. Thompson, A History of the Presbyterian Church in the United States (American Church History Series, 6; New York, 1895). L. J. Trinterud, The Formation of an American Tradition: A re-examination of colonial Presbyterianism (Philadelphia [1949]). E. A. Smith, The Presby-
terian Ministry in American Culture: A Study in Changing Concepts, 1700–1900 (ibid. [1962]). L. A. Loetscher, The Broadening Church: A Study of Theological Issues in the Presbyterian Church since 1869 (ibid., 1954). B. J. Longfield, The Presbyterian Controversy: Fundamentalists, Modernists, and Moderates (New York and Oxford, 1991). E. T. Thompson, Presbyterians in the South (3 vols., Richmond, Va., 1963–73). W. N. Jamison, The United Presbyterian Story: A Centennial Study 1858–1958 (Philadelphia [1958]). J. S. Moir, Enduring Witness: A History of the Presbyterian Church in Canada [Toronto, 1974]. R. Macpherson, The Presbyterian Church in Kenya (Nairobi, 1970). M. Twagirayesu and J. van Butselaar (eds.), Ce don que nous avons reçu: Histoire de l'Église presbytérienne au Rwanda (1907–1982) (Kigali, 1982). J. Dall in HERE 10 (1918), pp. 244–70, s.v., with bibl. by J. Herkless, pp. 270 f. See also works cited under SCOTLAND, CHRISTIANITY IN, and WORLD ALLIANCE OF REFORMED CHURCHES.

Presbytery. (1) The sanctuary or E. part of the chancel of a church beyond the choir. (2) The residence of (esp.) RC priests. (3) Acc. to current Presbyterian usage, the Church court having oversight and jurisdiction over a certain area, the extent of which is decided by the *General Assembly, and consisting of the ministers and representative elders of the congregations within the bounds. A Presbyterian minister is ordained by it (the ministerial members only joining in the imposition of hands) and is subject to it, and not to his or her session. It belongs to the Presbytery, not to the court of a particular congregation (*Kirk session), to see that public worship is in accordance with the law and usage of the Church.

Presentation of Christ in the Temple. In the BCP an alternative name for the feast of the *Purification of the BVM or *Candlemas (q.v.), kept on 2 Feb. It is the sole title of the feast in the ASB and some other modern Anglican Prayer Books. In 1969 the RC Church adopted the title of 'the Presentation of the Lord' for this feast.

Presentation of the BVM (not to be confused with the preceding). A feast kept on 21 Nov. to commemorate the presentation of the Virgin in the Temple when 3 years old, as related in the apocryphal 'Book of *James'. The feast was first observed in the E. c. the 8th cent., and in the W. gradually established itself in the later Middle Ages. One of those who campaigned most vigorously in the 14th cent. for its observance in the W. was Philip de Mézières, a French knight who had lived in the E., and its observance was permitted in 1372. *Sixtus IV received it into the Roman *Breviary, St *Pius V removed it, and *Sixtus V made its observance universal in the RC Church in 1585. In the E. it is one of the *Twelve Great Feasts (q.v.).

Sr. Mary Jerome Kishpaugh, OP, The Feast of the Presentation of the Virgin Mary in the Temple (Catholic University of America, Diss., Washington, DC, 1941). R. W. Pfaff, New Liturgical Feasts in Later Medieval England (Oxford Theological Monographs, 1970), pp. 103–15. W. E. Coleman (ed.), Philippe de Mézières' Campaign for the Feast of Mary's Presentation (Toronto Medieval Latin Texts, 11; 1981 [docs. with introd.]). G. Löw, CSSR, in EC 9 (1952), cols. 1966–8.

Presentation of the Lord. The title given in the RC Church since 1969 to the feast of *Candlemas.

Prester John (i.e. 'Presbyter' John), legendary medieval Christian king of Asia. The story of an E. *Nestorian priest-king who had defeated the Muslims and would bring help to the Holy Land spread through Europe from the middle of the 12th cent. He is first mentioned in *Otto of Freising's Chronicle and soon afterwards in a letter full of fables, addressed by 'Prester John' to the German Emp. *Frederick I and to the E. Emp. Manuel and several other princes. In 1177 Pope *Alexander III wrote a letter, headed 'Indorum Regi, Sacerdotum Sanctissimo' ('to the King of the Indies, the most holy priest'), which was supposed to be addressed to Prester John. It has been argued, however, that it was meant for a real historical personage, namely the King of *Ethiopia, which country was commonly confused with India during the Middle Ages; and this contention gains weight from the fact that in the later Middle Ages Prester John was actually located in Ethiopia. Another theory, based on an account of the 13th-cent. *Franciscan missionary, William of Rubruck, identifies him with a Chinese prince, Gor Khan, who defeated the Sultan of Persia in 1141 and founded an empire in which lived a number of Nestorian Christians. The designation 'priest' is held to be due to a confusion of *khan*, 'king', with *kam*, 'priest'. The whole story seems to be a legend of Nestorian origin, but it probably contains a nucleus of historical fact.

Otto of Freising, *Chronicon*, 7. 33. F. Zarncke, 'Der Priester Johannes', *Abh.* (Säch.), 7 (1879), pp. 827–1030 (with Lat. text of the letter sent to the Emp., pp. 909–24); 8 (1883), pp. 1–186. F. Fleuret, 'La Lettre de Prêtre Jean, pseudo-roi d'Abyssinie', *Mercure de France*, 268 (1936), pp. 294–318, with Fr. tr. of the letter, pp. 298–309. E. D. Ross, 'Prester John and the Empire of Ethiopia', in A. P. Newton (ed.), *Travel and Travellers in the Middle Ages* (1926), pp. 174–94, with Eng. tr. of extract of the letter, pp. 174–8. G. Oppert, *Der Presbyter Johann in Sage und Geschichte* (1864). C. E. Nowell, 'The Historical Prester John', *Speculum*, 28 (1953), pp. 435–55. L. N. Gumilev, *Searches for an Imaginary Kingdom: The Legend of the Kingdom of Prester John* (Eng. tr. of work orig. pub. in Russ., 1970; Cambridge, 1987). U. Knefelkamp, *Die Suche nach dem Reich des Priesterkönigs Johannes* (Gelsenkirchen, 1986), with bibl. and discussion of lit., pp. 13–18.

prevenient grace. The species of actual *grace which, as an illumination or inspiration of the Holy Spirit, precedes the free determination of the will. It is held to mark the beginning of all activity leading to *justification, which cannot be achieved without it, but its acceptance or rejection depends on man's free choice. Belief in the existence of prevenient grace claims scriptural support in such texts as Ps. 59: 10 (Vulg.), Rom. 8: 30, and 2 Tim. 1: 9. It was defended by St *Augustine (who often uses the technical term, 'gratia praeveniens') against the *Pelagians, taught by St *Thomas Aquinas, formally defined by the Council of *Trent, and asserted in Article 10 of the *Thirty-Nine Articles.

Price, Richard (1723–91), Nonconformist minister, moral and political philosopher. In 1758 he published *A Review of the Principal Questions in Morals* (3rd edn., 1787), in which he defended a view of ethical action which had many affinities with the teaching later expounded by I. *Kant. He held that the rightness and wrongness of an action belonged to it intrinsically and criticized the 'moral sense' view of ethics which had secured popularity through such writers as Lord Shaftesbury (d. 1713) and F. Hutcheson (d. 1746). In the fields of politics and economics he

advocated the reduction of the National Debt, and strongly supported the cause of American Independence. Though holding opposite views on morals and metaphysics, he became an intimate friend of J. *Priestley. By 1778 both were '*Unitarians', and in 1791 Price became an original member of the Unitarian Society.

Modern edn. of Price's *Review of the Principal Questions in Morals* by D. D. Raphael (Oxford, 1948 [based on 3rd edn. of 1787, but repr. preface from first edn.]). Correspondence, ed. W. B. Peach and D. O. Thomas (3 vols., Durham, NC, and Cardiff, 1983–94); *Political Writings*, ed. D O. Thomas (Cambridge, 1991). The principal authority is the Memoir by his nephew, W. Morgan (London, 1815). Modern Life by R. Thomas (ibid., 1924); D. O. Thomas, *The Honest Mind: The Thought and Work of Richard Price* (Oxford, 1977), with bibl. C. B. Cone, *The Torchbearer of Freedom: The Influence of Richard Price on Eighteenth Century Thought* (Lexington, Ky., 1952). W. D. Hudson, *Reason and Right: A Critical Examination of Richard Price's Moral Philosophy* (1970). H. Laboucheix, *Richard Price: Théoricien de la révolution américaine; le philosophe et le sociologe; le pamphlétaire et l'orateur* (1970; partial Eng. tr., Oxford, 1982). D. O. Thomas and others, *A Bibliography of the Works of Richard Price* (Aldershot [1993]). T. Fowler in *DNB* 46 (1896), pp. 334–7. See also bibl. to UNITARIANISM.

pricket. A stand containing one or more upright spikes on which to fix votive candles.

pride. The first of the *seven deadly sins, being the inordinate love of one's own excellence. It is traditionally believed to have been the sin of the angels and the first man, and is denounced as a vice particularly repugnant to God throughout the OT and NT (e.g. Prov. 16: 18; 1 Pet. 5: 5).

Prideaux, Humphrey (1648–1724), Dean of *Norwich from 1702. He was educated at Westminster and at Christ Church, Oxford, where he came under the influence of J. *Fell, and from 1677 onwards held a succession of benefices. As a Low Churchman he welcomed the Revolution of 1688, and supported the proposed changes in the BCP with a view to the inclusion of dissenters. His fame rested on two treatises, his *Life of Mahomet* (1697), really a polemical tract against the *Deists, and *The Old and New Testaments connected in the History of the Jews* (2 vols., 1716–18), an account of the history of the Jewish people in the last centuries before the Christian era. He also issued *The Validity of the Orders of the C of E* (1688) and several other pamphlets.

Anon. Life (London, 1748, prob. by T. Birch), from information supplied by his son. *Bibliotheca Cornubiensis*, 2 (1878), pp. 527–33. His letters to John Ellis, Under-Secretary of State, 1674–1722, ed. E. M. Thompson (Camden Society, NS 15; 1875). P. M. Holt, 'The Treatment of Arab History by Prideaux, Ockley and Sale', in B. Lewis and P. Holt (eds.), *Historians of the Middle East* (1962), pp. 290–302, esp. pp. 290–4, repr. in Holt's *Studies in the History of the Near East* (1973), esp. pp. 51–4. A. Gordon in *DNB* 46 (1896), pp. 354–6.

prie-dieu (Fr., 'pray God'). A small prayer-desk for private use, usually constructed with a sloping ledge and sometimes also a shelf for books. The name appears to date from the early 17th cent.

Prierias, Sylvester (1456–1527), Sylvester Mazzolini, one of the earliest opponents of M. *Luther. A native of Priero in Piedmont, he entered the *Dominican Order at Savona in 1471. From 1492 to 1502 he served as Regent Master at *Bologna. In 1502 he was instituted Regent Master in *Venice and appointed professor of Thomistic theology in the university of Padua. He subsequently served as Prior in Milan, Verona, and Genoa, and Vicar General of the Congregation of Lombardy (1508–10). He was appointed *Inquisitor in Brescia in 1508 and in Milan in 1512. He was also Regent Master and Prior of Bologna (1510–12) and between 1512 and 1515 was Prior in Cremona and Venice. In 1512 *Leo X appointed him 'Master of the Sacred Palace', Inquisitor and censor of books for Rome, and professor of Thomistic theology at the Sapienza. He was involved in the juridical process against J. *Reuchlin and Luther and in the cases of P. *Pomponazzi and *Erasmus. He wrote numerous works on logic, theology, homiletics, spirituality and hagiography. His collection of sermons, *Rosa Aurea* (1503), his digest of moral theology, *Summa Silvestrina* (1514), and his manual on witchcraft, *De Strigimagarum, Daemonumque Mirandis* (1521), went into many editions. He left incomplete an anthology and commentary on the *Summa Theologiae* of St *Thomas Aquinas, *Conflatum ex S. Thoma* (Part 1, 1519). The procrastination of the Roman Curia mitigated against the impact of his polemical works against Luther: *Dialogus de Potestate Papae* (1518), *Replica ad Fratrum Martinum Luther* (1518), *Epitoma Responsionis ad Lutherum* (1519), and *Errata et Argumenta Martini Luteris* [sic] (1520). He died during the sack of Rome.

Modern edn. of his *Dialogus, Replica, Epitoma* and *Errata*, with introd. by P. Fabisch and E. Iserloh, *Dokumente zur Causa Lutheri (1517–1521)*, 1 (Corpus Catholicorum, 41; Münster, 1988), pp. 33–201. The brief study of his life and works by F. Michalski (Münster i.W., 1892; in Lat.) is unreliable. F. Lauchert, *Die italienischen literarischen Gegner Luthers* (Erläuterungen und Ergänzungen zu Janssens Geschichte des deutschen Volkes, ed. L. von *Pastor, 8; 1912), pp. 7–30. C. Lindberg, 'Prierias and his Significance for Luther's Development', *Sixteenth Century Journal*, 3, no. 2 (1972), pp. 45–64. U. Horst, OP, *Zwischen Konziliarismus und Reformation: Studien zur Ekklesiologie im Dominikanerorderen* (Institutum Historicum FF. Praedicatorum Romae ad S. Sabinae, Dissertationes Historicae, 22; 1985), pp. 127–62. P. Fabisch, 'Silvester Prierias' in E. Iserloh (ed.), *Katholische Theologen der Reformationszeit*, 1 (Katholisches Leben und Kirchenreform im Zeitalter der Glaubensspaltung, 44; 1984), pp. 26–36. J. Wicks, SJ, in *Dict. Sp.* 12 (pt. 2; 1986), cols. 2347–9, with bibl.; D. R. Janz in P. G. Bietenholz and T. B. Deutscher (eds.), *Contemporaries of Erasmus*, 3 (Toronto, etc., 1987), pp. 120 f., both s.v.

priest. The term 'priest' is etymologically a contraction of '*presbyter' (Gk. πρεσβύτερος, 'elder'), but while the AV and RV of the NT regularly render πρεσβύτερος by 'elder', they keep 'priest' and 'priesthood' for the purely sacerdotal terms ἱερεύς and ἱεράτευμα (Lat. *sacerdos* and *sacerdotium*). The latter words are never used in the NT specifically of Christian ministers, though they are applied to the Christian body as a whole (1 Pet. 2: 5 and 9; Rev. 5: 10). By the close of the Old English period the English term 'priest' had become the current word alike for 'presbyter' and 'sacerdos' and so an ambiguous term. The idea

and institution of priesthood is found in almost all the great religions, usually connected with the conception of *sacrifice. In some cases the duties attach to the father of the family or the ruler of the tribe or nation, but in most religions a separate order developed.

Acc. to the OT the priesthood before the age of *Moses was patriarchal. The father sacrificed for the family (*Noah, Gen. 8: 20; *Abraham, Gen. 22: 13), the sheik for his tribe (Jethro, Exod. 2: 16), and the prince for his people (*Melchizedek, Gen. 14: 18). Acc. to an early tradition, Moses himself was a priest. At the same time it appears that there was a separate class of priests (Exod. 19: 22), but it was not they whom Moses employed to offer sacrifice, but 'young men' and himself (cf. Exod. 24: 4–8). Later a more formal priesthood seems to have been established. On Mt. Sinai Moses was ordered to consecrate *Aaron and his three sons 'to minister in the priest's office' (Exod. 28: 1). In Exod. 32: 26–9 the tribe of Levi was chosen to be consecrated to the Lord; eventually the *Levites were given charge of the services of the Tabernacle, and only the sons of Aaron were to exercise the functions of the priesthood (Num. *passim*). All subsequent priests were held to be descendants of Aaron. It is likely, however, that the historical reality was very different: Zadok, the chief priest in *David's time (2 Sam. 8: 17 etc.), may represent the indigenous Jebusite priesthood. As the holiness of Israel centred on the Sanctuary, the importance of the priesthood, and esp. of the *High Priest (q.v.), increased with the enhanced place of the Temple in later Judaism. His position, exemplified in the Priestly Code of the Pentateuch, as mediator between God and man, came to be the predominant idea of the Jewish priesthood in the time of Christ.

In the NT the idea of Christ as High Priest finds clear expression in Heb. (2: 17; 3: 1; 4: 14 f., etc.). The Jewish priesthood is seen as the type of His priesthood, as the Jewish sacrifice was of His Sacrifice. By His Sacrifice as Priest He reconciles men and women to God, fulfilling what had been foreshadowed by the Jewish sacrifices. But though He was in the Sacrifice the Priest, He was also the Victim (Heb. 9: 12 ff.; 10: 5 ff.; cf. 'the Lamb slain from the foundation of the world', Rev. 13: 8); consequently, while He remains 'our Great High Priest', yet for the offering of the Sacrifice, a Christian priesthood was established in the Church.

The idea of priesthood as belonging to the Christian ministry was a gradual development arising from a sacrificial understanding of the Eucharist and based on OT ideas of priesthood; the term 'priest' does not appear to have been applied to Christian ministers until the end of the 2nd cent. The 'presbyters' of the NT were not commonly called 'sacerdotes' until the time of St *Cyprian (*Ep.* 61). At first the use of the term was commonly confined to bishops. It appears in St Cyprian that, while priests shared in the episcopal *sacerdotium*, could offer the Sacrifice of the Eucharist, and by the imposition of hands receive a penitent *lapsus, these functions were to be exercised only in the absence of the bishop and seem to have been regarded as delegated by him. With the spread of Christianity in the country and the establishment of parish churches, the presbyters adopted more fully the priestly functions of the bishop. A letter of *Innocent I to Decentius (AD 416) explains that in towns the Eucharist is to be consecrated by the bishop only and sent to parish priests, but in the outlying churches the priests are to consecrate themselves. When the priest thus independently obtained power to consecrate in the Eucharist and administer most other Sacraments, the way was opened for the fullest medieval doctrine of the priesthood. This was most fully developed in connection with the power conferred in *Ordination, esp. when, in the 11th cent., the custom spread of ordaining priests who had no benefice. As the parish priest came to be the normal celebrant of the Eucharist and customarily to exercise the power of absolution, esp. with the development of eucharistic theology and the obligation of confession (1215), increasingly he came to be regarded as the representative of God to the people rather than the converse. His supernatural powers and functions were emphasized, so that during the Middle Ages, vis-à-vis the laity, a priest acquired a position outside that of the feudal hierarchy. He remained, however, entirely subordinate to his bishop, who retained his superiority in such matters as Ordination and *Confirmation and his canonical jurisdiction, though there remained some doubt whether his office was of a different order from that of the priesthood. The *validity of the position of a priest always depended upon his Ordination.

The tendency of medieval theology to see the priesthood of the clergy almost exclusively in relation to the Mass led to its rejection by the Reformers. The term 'priest' was retained in the BCP apparently in order to make it clear that deacons were not to celebrate the Holy Communion. In general parlance, except in the N. of England, the term 'clergyman' was more frequently used in the C of E to avoid the implications of that of priest. With the revival of Catholic views, however, the term 'priest' has again come into common use. This revival of the term outside the RC Church prob. also reflects a more comprehensive view of the priesthood, which is seen in relation to the whole Church and to that extent ministerial rather than dominating, and a fresh recognition of its relation to the priesthood of Christ. See also ORDERS AND ORDINATION.

E. O. James, The Nature and Function of Priesthood: A Comparative and Anthropological Study (1955). E. Landtman, The Origin of Priesthood (University of Finland thesis; Ekenaes, 1905). On priesthood in the OT and Judaism, A. C. Welch, Prophet and Priest in the Old Israel (Oxford, 1953); A. Cody, OSB, A History of Old Testament Priesthood (Analecta Biblica, 35; 1969); R. de Vaux, OP, Les Institutions de l'Ancien Testament, 2 (1960; 4th edn., 1982), pp. 195–277; Eng. tr. (2nd edn., 1965), pp. 345–405; E. *Schürer, The History of the Jewish People in the Age of Jesus Christ, rev. Eng. tr. by G. Vermes and others, 2 (Edinburgh, 1979), pp. 227–313; M. Haran and others in Encyclopaedia Judaica, 13 (Jerusalem, 1972), pp. 1070–91, s.v. 'Priests and Priesthood'.

For the origins of the Christian Priesthood, see bibl. to ORDERS AND ORDINATION. Cf. also H. S. Box (ed.), Priesthood (1937); J. Lécuyer, C.S.Sp., Le Sacerdoce dans le mystère du Christ (1957); D. N. Power, OMI, Ministers of Christ and His Church: The Theology of the Priesthood (1969); N. Lash and J. Rhymer (eds.), The Christian Priesthood (9th Downside Symposium, 1970). B. Kleinheyer, Die Priesterweihe im römischen Ritus: Eine liturgiehistorische Studie (Trier theologische Studien, 12; 1962).

A. Michel in DTC 13 (pt. 1; 1936), cols. 138–61, s.v. 'Prêtre'; G. Schrenk in TWNT 3 (1938), pp. 257–84 (Eng. tr., 3, 1966, pp. 257–83), s.v. ἱερεύς, and G. Bornkamm, ibid. 6 (1959), pp. 651–83 (Eng. tr., 6, 1968, pp. 651–83), s.v. πρέσβυς; J. Haeckel and others in L.Th.K. (2nd edn.), 8 (1963), cols. 735–48, s.v. 'Priester'.

Priest, High. See HIGH PRIEST.

Priest in Absolution, The (1866; 1870). A privately printed manual for the use of Anglican confessors, compiled by the Revd J. C. *Chambers at the request of the *Society of the Holy Cross. The second part, dealing with certain sins which necessarily called for treatment in a technical manual, was sold only to *bona fide* confessors. On Chambers's death (1874), to prevent misuse of the work, the remaining stock and copyright were bought by the Society. The work created a storm of protest against the *High Church Movement when, on 14 June 1877, Lord Redesdale, into whose possession by some inadvertence a copy had come, drew attention to its contents in the House of Lords. The attack, in which A. C. *Tait, Abp. of Canterbury, took part, caused for a short time much annoyance to High Churchmen, but it passed without leaving any permanent mark and with Chambers's high character unstained.

R. T. *Davidson and W. Benham, Life of Archibald Campbell Tait (1891), 2, pp. 171–84. W. Walsh, The Secret History of the Oxford Movement (1897), pp. 93–146 (hostile); J. Embry, The Catholic Movement and the Society of the Holy Cross (1931), pp. 97–127.

Priestley, Joseph (1733–1804), *Presbyterian minister and scientist. A native of W. Yorkshire, he entered Daventry Academy to train for the Presbyterian ministry in 1751. In 1755 he became minister at Needham Market, Suffolk, and in 1758 at Nantwich, where he opened a school. His religious beliefs became increasingly unorthodox. He came to hold *Arian views on the Person of Christ, and rejected the doctrine of the *Atonement and the Inspiration of the Bible. In 1761 he became tutor of languages at the newly founded Academy at Warrington, and in 1767 was appointed minister of Mill Hill Chapel, Leeds, where he embraced *Socinianism. Here he brought out the *Theological Repository*, a critical periodical that appeared irregularly and aroused much hostility, favoured the autonomy of the individual congregation and an increase in the number of sects, and complete toleration for RCs; and he attacked the idea of a national Church. In 1772 the offer of a post as librarian to Lord Shelburne gave him sufficient leisure to pursue his scientific studies, which had already gained him a reputation. During this period he published his *Institutes of Natural and Revealed Religion* (3 vols., 1772–4), *Disquisitions relating to Matter and Spirit* (1777), and *A Harmony of the Evangelists* (also 1777). In 1780 he gave up his post with Lord Shelburne and settled at Birmingham, where he became junior minister of the New Meeting Society. In 1782 he published his widely read *History of the Corruptions of Christianity*. He denied the impeccability and infallibility of the Lord, views which he finally elaborated in his *History of Early Opinions concerning Jesus Christ* (1786). The book provoked a violent controversy, his chief orthodox critic being S. *Horsley. In 1791 he became one of the founders of the *Unitarian Society, and in the same year defended the French Revolution in his *Letters to Burke*. The hostility aroused was such that he had to escape to London, where he became morning preacher at Gravel Pit Chapel, Hackney. In 1794 he went to America, spending the remaining years of his life at Northumberland, Pennsylvania. During this period he adopted the doctrine of universal restitution and of moral progress in life after death. Despite his unorthodoxy on other points he was a firm believer in the mission of Moses and the Messiahship of the Lord. In the realm of science he is known chiefly for his 'discovery' of oxygen in 1774 and for his great work on *Experiments and Observations on Different Kinds of Air* (1774–86).

Theological and Miscellaneous Works, ed. J. T. Rutt (25 vols., London [1817–31]). Selections from his Writings ed. I. V. Brown (University Park, Pa., 1962). *Memoirs of Dr. Joseph Priestley, to the Year 1795, written by himself, with a Continuation . . . by his son, J. Priestley* (London, 1806); repr., with introd. by J. Lindsay (Bath, 1970). Modern Lives by A. Holt (London, 1931) and F. W. Gibbs (ibid. [1965]). L. Kieft and B. R. Willeford (eds.), *Joseph Priestley: Scientist, Theologian, and Metaphysician. A Symposium Celebrating the Two Hundredth Anniversary of the Discovery of Oxygen by Joseph Priestley in 1774* (Lewisburg and London [1980]). R. E. Crook, *A Bibliography of Joseph Priestley 1733–1804* (1966). Further bibl. by J. Stephens in preparation. A. Gordon and P. J. Hartog in *DNB* 46 (1896), pp. 357–76; R. E. Schofield in *Dictionary of Scientific Biography*, 11 (1970), pp. 139–47.

Primasius (6th cent.), Bp. of Hadrumetum in N. Africa. His commentary on Rev., which drew extensively on *Tyconius and *Augustine, is of great value for the light it throws on the history of the *Old Latin Version of the NT. A commentary on St *Paul's Epp. is also attributed to him, but this really belongs to the school of *Cassiodorus. In the *Three Chapters Controversy he was a strong supporter of Pope *Vigilius.

Comm. on Rev. ed. Cologne, 1535; Paris, 1544; Basle, 1544 (all purporting to be *editiones principes*). Works in J. P. Migne, *PL* 68. 407–936. Crit. edn. by A. W. Adams (CCSL 92; 1985). J. Haussleiter, *Leben und Werke des Bischofs Primasius von Hadrumetum* (1887); id., *Die lateinische Apokalypse der alten afrikanischen Kirche* (in T. *Zahn, *Forschungen zur Gesch. des NT Kanons*, 4, 1891, pp. 1–224); H. J. Vogels, *Untersuchungen zur Geschichte der lateinischen Apokalypse-Übersetzung* (1920), pp. 19–36 and 153–64. M. Dulaey in *Dict. Sp.* 12 (pt. 2; 1986), cols. 2351–3, s.v.

Primate. The title of the bishop of the 'first see' (*prima sedes*), used originally of the *metropolitan of a province, then for a time equated with the *patriarch, and later applied to the chief bishop of a single state or people. The Abp. of *Canterbury is 'Primate of All England', the Abp. of *York 'Primate of England'.

Prime. The *Office traditionally appointed for the first hour, i.e. 6 a.m. It has usually been held that it was introduced by *Cassian in his monastery at *Bethlehem *c.*395, as *altera matutina* ('Second Mattins'), but the meaning of this phrase has been disputed. Under the name of *Prima* it appears as first of the Little Hours (see TERCE, SEXT, NONE) in the *Regula Magistri and in the Rule of St *Benedict. At first recited in the dormitory, it was later transferred to the choir and thence passed into the Office of the secular clergy. In 1964 the recitation of Prime became voluntary for the secular clergy, and the Office has no place in the 1971 Breviary.

Prime consisted of two parts. The first, after the usual opening and the hymn 'Iam lucis orto sidere', contained three Psalms with antiphon to which a fourth was added on certain days; and on *Trinity and some other Sundays the 'Quicunque Vult' (see ATHANASIAN CREED) was recited as well. The Psalms were followed by a (little) *chapter with 'responsorium breve', the Sunday or ferial prayers, and a concluding prayer. The second part was the originally independent Chapter Office. It began with the reading of the *martyrology (if recited in choir), followed by several prayers, versicles, and the variable 'lectio brevis', and ended with a benediction.

J. Pargoire, 'Prime et complies', *Revue d'Histoire et de Littérature religieuses*, 3 (1898), pp. 281–8 and 456–67. J. Froger, OSB, *Les Origines de prime* (Bibliotheca 'Ephemerides Liturgicae', 19; 1946); crit. reviews by L. Brou in *JTS* 48 (1947), pp. 240 f., and by E. Cattaneo in *EL* 61 (1947), pp. 366–9; J. Froger, 'Note pour rectifier l'interprétation de Cassien, *Inst.* 3, 4: 6, proposée dans *Les Origines de prime*', *Archiv für Liturgiewissenschaft*, 2 (1952), pp. 96–102. J. M. Hanssens, SJ, *Aux origines de la prière liturgique: Nature et genèse de l'office des matines* (Analecta Gregoriana, 57; 1952), *passim*. See also works cited under OFFICE, DIVINE.

Primer or **Prymer** (Lat. *Primarium*). A devotional book popular among the educated laity from at least the early 14th cent. The etymology of the word is not entirely clear. It was often used as a synonym for 'Book of Hours' (*Horae*). The Primer contained the *Little Office of the BVM, followed by the *seven penitential Psalms, the 15 *Gradual Psalms, the *Litany of the Saints and the Office for the Dead. Until the beginning of the 16th cent. the prohibition against unauthorized English translations of any portion of the Bible (decreed because of the rise of *Lollardy) precluded an English version of the Primer. In the third decade of the 16th cent., however, some of the Reformers began to print abroad texts of the Primer in English adapted to their own doctrinal positions. Official attempts to prevent these books being smuggled into England were largely ineffective. From 1534 onwards various editions of the Primer were published in England with official sanction. In 1545 the first authorized Primer of *Henry VIII was issued, first in English and the following year in Latin; it was accompanied by the injunction that it was to be used by every schoolmaster next after the ABC in teaching children to read and know their Paternoster etc. The Primer came to be linked to elements in the BCP and continued for some years into the reign of *Elizabeth I in association with the *Catechism. In 1599 Richard Verstegan published an English translation of the post-Tridentine *Officium Beatae Mariae Virginis*; this Primer became one of the most popular works of devotion among RCs during the next two centuries, during which it was frequently revised, with new material and new translations being incorporated. The word Primer eventually lost its religious significance and came to be used also of any short introductory textbook, regardless of the subject.

E. Burton (ed.), *Three Primers put forth in the Reign of Henry VIII* (Oxford, 1834); W. Maskell, *Monumenta Ritualia Ecclesiae Anglicanae*, 3 (2nd edn., ibid., 1882), pp. i–lxvii and 1–260. Facsimile repr. of Verstegan's Primer (English Recusant Literature, 1558–1650, 262; Menston, Yorks, 1975). H. C. White, *The Tudor Books of Private Devotion* (Madison, Wis., 1951), pp. 53–133; C. C. Butterworth, *The English Primers (1529–1545): Their Publication and Connection with the English Bible and the Reformation in England* (Philadelphia, 1953); E. Duffy, *The Stripping of the Altars* (New Haven, Conn., and London, 1992), pp. 209–98. J. M. Blom, *The Post-Tridentine English Primer* (Catholic Record Society Publications, Monograph Series, 3; 1982). See also works cited under LITTLE OFFICE OF OUR LADY.

primicerius. The word, derived from 'primus in cera', i.e. 'the first on the waxed table' of names, was applied to the senior in rank of several classes of officials, both ecclesiastical and secular. In the Rule of St *Chrodegang he was the cleric next below the archdeacon and archpresbyter and charged with the liturgical functions and music of the monastery.

Primitive Methodist Church. One of the three *Methodist Churches which united in 1932. It came into being in 1811 in connexion with, but for the most part outside, the Wesleyan Methodist Church.

The new community developed out of some earlier unofficial Methodist movements. Hugh Bourne, a Methodist, had begun c.1800 an important evangelistic movement near Mow Cop, Staffs, but outside the official structure of Methodism. Another contributory element was the work of Lorenzo Dow, an American Methodist, who in 1807 introduced the *Camp Meeting into English Methodism at Mow Cop. This form of meeting, held for a whole day in the open and designed for those not attracted by the ordinary work of the Church, was pronounced by the Wesleyan Conference to be 'highly improper and likely to be of considerable mischief'. When these Camp Meetings were continued, Hugh Bourne, who was now mainly responsible for them, was expelled and in 1810 there came into being as a distinct community the 'Camp Meeting Methodists'. In the same year William Clowes, who had joined in evangelistic work at Tunstall and later at Hull, was also expelled from the Methodist Church. In 1811 the two bodies united under the name of the Primitive Methodists.

At first the policy of the new society was to cease mission work and consolidate itself; but soon they gave themselves to systematic and widespread evangelism. For several years they met with great success, in spite of persecution, but rapid growth and lack of discipline brought a serious decline in 1825–8. Bourne was able, however, to replace the original organization, whereby administration was carried out chiefly by District Meetings and each district was to a great extent autonomous, by a centralization of authority. In 1843 the Primitive Methodists founded missions in *Australia and *New Zealand; and in 1889 work was begun in Africa also. Their most notable member in later years was A. S. *Peake.

Notable features of the Church were its connexion with the Society of *Friends; its use of women as preachers, esp. in its earlier years; and its close relations with trades unions and the Labour Movement, esp. among miners and agricultural workers. In 1932 the Primitive Methodist Church united with the Wesleyan and *United Methodists to form the present Methodist Church.

H. B. Kendall, *The Origin and History of the Primitive Methodist Church* (2 vols. [1905]). J. Petty, *The History of the Primitive Methodist Connexion from its Origin to the Conference of 1859* (1860). J. S. Werner, *The Primitive Methodist Connexion: Its Background and Early History* (Madison, Wis., 1984). H. Bourne, *History of the Primitive Methodists, Giving an Account of their Rise and Progress to the Year 1823* (1823); J. Walford, ed. W. Antliff, *Memoirs of the Life and Labours of the late Venerable Hugh Bourne* (2 vols., 1855–6); J. T. Wilkinson, *Hugh Bourne 1772–1850* (1952). W. Clowes, *Journals* (1844); J. Davison [son-in-law], *The Life of the Venerable William Clowes* (1854); J. T. Wilkinson, *William Clowes*

1780–1851 (1951). H. B. Kendall, 'The Primitive Methodist Church and the Independent Methodist Churches, 1796–1908', in W. J. Townsend, H. B. Workman, and G. Eayrs (eds.), *A New History of Methodism*, 1 (1909), pp. 555–98; R. [E.] Davies, A. R. George, and [E.] G. Rupp, *A History of the Methodist Church in Great Britain*, 2 (1978), pp. 304–13. R. Currie, *Methodism Divided: A Study in the Sociology of Ecumenicalism* (1968), *passim*. R. [S.] Moore, *Pit-men, Preachers & Politics: The Effects of Methodism in a Durham Mining Community* (Cambridge, 1974). *The Christian Ambassador* (20 vols., 1854–78); cont. as *Primitive Methodist Quarterly Review* (31 vols., 1879–1909); cont. as *Holborn Review* (23 vols., 1910–32); in 1932 *Holborn Review* was amalgamated with *London Quarterly* to form *London Quarterly and Holborn Review* (37 vols., 1932–68). *Primitive Methodist Year Book* (ceased 1932).

Primus. In the Scottish Episcopal Church, the title of the presiding bishop. The first mention of the office is in 1731 in the 'Articles of Agreement amongst the Bishops of the Church of Scotland'. The principal function of the Primus, who has no metropolitical power, is to convene and preside at meetings of the Episcopal Synod. He is elected by the College of Bishops and the office is attached to no fixed see and not necessarily given by seniority. His title is 'The Most Revd the Lord Bishop of X, Primus of the Scottish Church'.

prior. The holder of an office found in certain male religious orders. In an abbey, the *abbot's deputy is usually designated prior; in a priory, the prior is the superior. Among the *mendicant friars (except the *Franciscans) and in a few of the monastic orders (esp. the *Carthusians), it is the general term by which all superiors are designated. See also PRIORY.

prioress. The holder of an office found in certain Religious *Institutes of women. In general the prioress fulfils the same functions as the *prior in the corresponding male order. While the office of *abbess in current RC usage is restricted to the superiors of certain houses of *nuns, the title of prioress is also used in certain Religious Institutes of women who are not nuns in the strict sense. See also ABBESS; PRIOR; and PRIORY.

priory. A religious house presided over by a *prior or a *prioress. It is the normal unit among most of the *mendicant friars; among orders following the Rule of St *Benedict a distinction is made between a conventual priory, which is autonomous, and a dependent priory, which depends on some other monastery. The multiplication of priories in the Middle Ages stemmed largely from the need to supervise properties owned by the monasteries, by installing a small community; these houses later became known as priories. In medieval England the cathedral monasteries, of which the bishop was the titular head but which were in practice ruled by the prior as his deputy, were also known as priories.

J.-L. Lemaître (ed.), *Prieurs et Prieurés dans l'Occident Médiéval: Actes du colloque organisé à Paris le 12 novembre 1984* (École Pratique des Hautes Études, IVe Section: Sciences historiques et philologiques, 5: Hautes Études mediévales et modernes, 6; 1987). J. Dubois, OSB, and others in *DIP* 7 (1983), cols. 828–61, s.v. 'Priorato'.

Prisca. The name given to an early Latin version of the canons of certain Greek Councils, namely those of

*Nicaea, *Sardica, *Ancyra, *Neocaesarea, *Gangra, *Antioch, *Chalcedon, and *Constantinople. The translation was made in Italy, almost certainly in the late 5th cent. The two chief MSS are the 'Chieti MS' (Vat. Reg. Lat. 1997; 9th cent.; this also includes some African canons) and the 'Justel MS' (Bod. e Mus. 100–2; 6th–7th cent.). The title 'Prisca', given it by Christopher Justel, its first editor, is taken from a (perhaps misunderstood) reference in *Dionysius Exiguus (confusione priscae translationis offensus). W. M. Peitz has argued that the translation is the work of Dionysius himself.

Text in G. Voellus and H. and C. Justel (eds.), Bibliotheca Iuris Canonici Veteris, 1 (Paris, 1661), pp. 275–304; repr. from the *Ballerini edn. of the works of St *Leo, in J. P. Migne, PL 56. 747–816. F. *Maassen, Geschichte der Quellen und der Literatur des canonischen Rechts im Abendlande, 1 (1870), pp. 87–100. C. H. *Turner, 'Chapters in the History of Latin MSS of Canons, 5 and 6', JTS 30 (1928–9), pp. 337–46, and 31 (1929–30), pp. 9–20. E. *Schwartz, 'Die Kanonessammlungen der alten Reichskirche', Zeitschrift der Savigny-Stiftung für Kirchengeschichte, Kanonistische Abteilung, 25 (1936), pp. 1–114, esp. pp. 95–108. W. M. Peitz, SJ, Dionysius Exiguus-Studien, ed. H. Foerster (Arbeiten zur Kirchengeschichte, 33; 1960), passim.

Prisca, St. See PRISCILLA, ST.

Priscilla, St (1st cent.), also 'Prisca', an early Christian convert. She is mentioned six times in the NT (Acts 18: verses 2, 18, and 26; Rom. 16: 3; 1 Cor. 16: 19; 2 Tim. 4: 19); in the Pauline Epp. the best attested form in all cases is 'Prisca'. She was the wife of Aquila, a Jew of Pontus and (like St *Paul) a tentmaker. They are mentioned in the NT at *Rome, *Ephesus, and *Corinth, and were clearly prominent members in the primitive Church. They were compelled to leave Rome by the Emp. Claudius' decree (Acts 18: 2), but, unless Rom. 16 is a fragment of an epistle sent by St Paul to Ephesus, returned later (Rom. 16: 3). The suggestion of A. *Harnack that she and her husband were the authors of the Ep. to the Hebrews has met with little favour. Feast day in E., 13 Feb.; in W., 8 July.

In later Roman tradition, a saint with one or other of her names is prominent in two connections:

(1) Since the 4th cent. a church has existed on the Aventine Hill known as the titulus S. Priscae. Acc. to the (late) Acta S. Priscae, this church enshrined the remains of the martyr St Prisca, whose relics had been translated hither from the *Ostian Way. This St Prisca, who was well known to the medieval hagiographers, is sometimes represented in art between two lions, who are reputed to have refused to attack her. Feast day, 18 Jan.

(2) The 'Coemeterium Priscillae' on the Via Salaria was one of the oldest of the *catacombs. It prob. takes its name from a Priscilla quite unconnected with the saint of the titulus S. Priscae and perh. a member of the senatorial family of the 'Acilii Glabriones'. It was in this catacomb that J. Wilpert discovered the well-known painting, 'Fractio Panis'. On the site Pope *Sylvester built a basilica in which he was himself buried.

There are no sufficient reasons for identifying either of these with the Priscilla of the NT.

A. Harnack, 'Ueber die beiden Recensionen der Geschichte der Prisca und des Aquila in Act. Apost. 18, 1–27', Sb. (Berl.), 1900, pp. 2–13.

On (1), J. P. Kirsch, Die römischen Titelkirchen im Altertum (Studien zur Geschichte und Kultur des Altertums, 9. 1–2; 1918), pp. 101–4, 162 f. F. Lanzoni, 'I titoli presbiterali di Roma antica nella storia e nella legenda', Riv. A.C. 2 (1925), pp. 195–257, esp. pp. 247–50; A. Amore, OFM, 'Note agiografiche sul calendario perpetuo della Chiesa Universale', Antonianum, 39 (1964), pp. 18–53, esp. pp. 27–29. R. Krautheimer and others in idd., Corpus Basilicarum Christianarum Romae, 3 (Rome, 1967), pp. 260–76 (in English).

On (2), see works cited s.v. CATACOMBS. J. Wilpert, Fractio Panis: Die älteste Darstellung des eucharistischen Opfers in der 'Cappella Greca' (1895). H. *Leclercq, OSB, in DACL 14 (pt. 2; 1948), cols. 1799–874, s.v. 'Priscille (Cimetière de)', with bibl.; E. Josi in EC 10 (1953), cols. 36–40, s.v. 'Priscilla, Cimitero di', with full bibl.

Priscillianism. The origins of this 4th–5th-cent. heresy are obscure; evidence for the sequence of events is mainly dependent on the somewhat biased testimony of *Sulpicius Severus. In the 370s, Priscillian, a devout Spanish layman of high (prob. senatorial) rank, called on his fellow Christians to take their vow of baptismal renunciation seriously and commit themselves to a strongly ascetical form of Christianity. As a person of education famous for his austerity, he soon found adherents, among them two bishops, *Instantius and Salvianus, and a large number of women. In 380 the doctrines attributed to him (though Priscillian was not mentioned by name) were condemned at Saragossa. The canons of this synod forbade mixed gatherings for the reading and interpretation of Scriptures, fasting on Sundays, absence from church during *Lent and the three weeks preceding *Epiphany, and similar unusual practices. Despite this condemnation Priscillian became Bp. of Ávila soon afterwards. In 381 his opponents obtained a decree of exile against him and his followers, who were now described as '*Manichaeans'. The exiles went to the S. of France and thence to Rome, where they sought Pope *Damasus' support but failed to obtain a hearing. At Milan they met with a similar rebuff from St *Ambrose. They succeeded, however, in getting the decree of exile annulled by the secular authorities and returned to Spain, where they won a large following.

Not long after this, the new Emperor, Maximus, seeking the support of the Catholic bishops, had Priscillian tried at an episcopal synod at Bordeaux. Priscillian, however, refused to recognize its authority and appealed to the Emperor. In 386 he was tried at Maximus' court at Trier on a charge of sorcery—a capital offence. Despite the pleadings of St *Martin of Tours, he was convicted and executed, together with several of his adherents. Although these executions were inflicted by a secular and not an ecclesiastical court, the religious motivation was obvious and in Spain the dead Priscillianists were venerated as martyrs. The fall of Maximus in 388 produced another change in imperial policy and Priscillianism flourished, esp. in the province of Galicia; it is possible that the shrine at *Compostela is on the site of Priscillian's burial-place. In 400 a Council at *Toledo decreed the deposition of those Priscillianist bishops who would not abandon the heresy and the confirmation in office of those who submitted. The movement, however, continued, being denounced by Pope *Leo I in 447, and it did not disappear until the end of the 6th cent.

Our knowledge of Priscillianist doctrine is derived principally from a collection of anonymous writings contained in a 5th/6th-cent. MS at Würzburg, attributed to Priscillian by G. Schepss, its first editor, in 1889; the ascription has been widely accepted, despite the doubts of some scholars, who regard the treatises as the work of Instantius or another of Priscillian's disciples. From these documents, it appears that Priscillianism was a movement of spiritual renewal. Priscillian, holding a sombre view of the earthbound condition of fallen humanity, set great store by asceticism and thought that spiritual aspirations released by it would be rewarded by the gift of prophecy and a deeper insight into Christian doctrine. Although he was accused of Manichaeism, there seems to be no reason to doubt his vehement rejection of this charge. None the less, several features of his teaching made him vulnerable to such an accusation: notably his deep interest in the cosmic dimensions of the ascetic struggle, his demand for celibacy, coupled with tolerance of the lower virtue of married Christians, his enthusiasm for the *Apocryphal NT, esp. the Apocryphal Acts, his taste for the occult, and his conviction that divine truth was not confined to the official Scriptures or to the Church. His trinitarian theology had marked signs of modalist *Monarchianism, but his real interest lay in Christian doctrine that bore on the ascetic struggle.

The Würzburg treatises ed. G. Schepss, *Priscilliani Quae Supersunt* (CSEL 18; 1889). Their ascription has been challenged by A. *Hilgenfeld, 'Priscillianus und seine neuentdeckten Schriften', *Zeitschrift für wissenschaftliche Theologie*, 35 (1892), pp. 1–85; G. *Morin, OSB, 'Pro Instantio, contre l'attribution à Priscillien des opuscules du manuscrit de Würzburg', *R. Bén.* 30 (1913), pp. 153–173; and M. Hartberger, 'Instantius oder Priscillian', *Th. Q.* 95 (1913), pp. 401–40; it has been defended by J. Martin, 'Priscillianus oder Instantius', *Hist. J.* 47 (1927), pp. 237–51, and H. Chadwick, op. cit. (below). D. de Bruyne, OSB, 'Fragments retrouvés d'apocryphes priscillianistes', *R. Bén.* 24 (1907), pp. 318–35, with text; G. Morin, OSB, 'Un Traité priscillianiste inédit sur la Trinité', ibid. 26 (1909), pp. 255–80, repr., with text, in his *Études, Textes, Découvertes*, 1 (Anecdota Maredsolana, 2nd ser., 1913), pp. 151–205. D. de Bruyne, OSB, 'La *Regula Consensoria*, une règle des moines priscillianistes', *R. Bén.* 25 (1908), pp. 83–8. J. *Chapman, OSB, *Notes on the Early History of the Vulgate Gospels* (1908), pp. 238–70, ch. 13, 'Priscillian the Author of the Prologues'. E. C. Babut, *Priscillien et le priscillianisme* (Bibliothèque de l'École des Hautes Études. Sciences Historiques et Philologiques, 169; 1909). A. Puech, 'Les Origines du priscillianisme et l'orthodoxie de Priscillien', *Bulletin d'ancienne Littérature et d'Archéologie chrétiennes*, 2 (1912), pp. 81–95 and 161–213. J. A. Davids, *De Orosio et Sancto Augustino Priscillianistarum Adversariis: Commentatio Historica et Philologica* (Diss., The Hague, 1930). A. d'Alès, SJ, *Priscillien et l'Espagne chrétienne à la fin du IVᵉ siècle* (1936). J. M. Ramos y Loscertales, *Priscilliano: Gesta rerum* (Acta Salmanticensia, Filosofia y Letras, 5, no. 5; 1952). B. Vollmann, *Studien zum Priszillianismus: Die Forschung, die Quellen, der fünfzehnte Brief Papst Leos des Grossen* (Kirchengeschichtliche Quellen und Studien, 7; 1965). R. López Caneda, *Priscilliano: Su pensamiento y su problema histórico* (Compostela, 1966), with bibl. H. Chadwick, *Priscillian of Avila: The Occult and the Charismatic in the Early Church* (Oxford, 1976). R. Van Dam, *Leadership and Community in Late Antique Gaul* (The Transformation of the Classical Heritage, 8; Berkeley, Calif., etc. [1985]), pp. 88–114 ('The Heresy of Priscillianism'). V. Burrus, *The Making of a Heretic: Gender, Authority, and the Priscillianist Controversy* (ibid. 24 [1995]). CPL (3rd edn., 1995), pp. 266–9 (nos. 178–97), and 609 (no. 1872). M. Simonetti in Quasten (cont.), *Patrology*, 4 (1986), pp. 138–43, with bibl. J. N. Hillgarth in NCE 11 (1967), pp. 790 f.; B. Vollmann in PW, Suppl. 14 (1974), cols. 485–559; H. Chadwick in *Dict. Sp.* 12 (pt. 2; 1986),

cols. 2353–69, all s.v. See also works cited under TOLEDO, COUNCILS OF.

Private Chapels Act 1871. This Act, which regulated the status of C of E chapels in schools, hospitals, and similar institutions, permitted the bishop of the diocese in which the chapel was situated to license a cleric to serve such chapels, with the right of administering the Lord's Supper. Such a cleric was not subject to interference from the incumbent of the parish, provided that the entire cure of souls, except of those within the institution, was safeguarded to the incumbent. All alms collected in such a chapel could be disposed of as the minister determined, subject to the *Ordinary's direction. The Act has now been superseded by the Extra-Parochial Ministry Measure 1967 which is in broadly the same terms, and Canon B 41 of the 1969 Canons lays down certain regulations for the conduct of divine service in private chapels.

privileged altar. An altar at which formerly, according to RC canon law, a *plenary indulgence could be secured for a soul in purgatory by the application of a Mass celebrated on it. All such privileges were abrogated by Pope *Paul VI's Constitution 'Indulgentiarum doctrina' (1 Jan. 1967).

Privileged Presses. The Oxford and Cambridge University Presses, so called in respect of their right, shared only with the King's (Queen's) Printer, of printing the Book of Common Prayer and, in England, the Authorized Version of the Bible, which are perpetual Crown copyright. The King's Printer holds this right by his Letters Patent of appointment, while the University Presses derive it from their respective Charters. That granted to Cambridge in 1534 conferred the right to print 'all manner of books' (*omnimodos libros*), and this was held to be unimpaired by the monopoly otherwise granted to the Stationers' Company in 1587, and was confirmed in 1628. A similar Charter was granted to Oxford in 1634. As a result, the Authorized Version, printed at first only by the then King's Printer, Robert Barker, was printed, with considerably improved accuracy, at Cambridge in 1629. At Oxford the same rights of printing Bibles and certain other books were claimed, but, by a 'covenant of forbearance' made with the members of the Stationers' Company (including the King's Printer), remained unexercised until 1675. Before 1839 the King's Printer for Scotland held similar exclusive rights in his territory; but an Order in Council of that year empowered the Lord Advocate to license any printer to produce an edition of the Authorized Version upon certain conditions.

J. Johnson and S. Gibson, *Print and Privilege at Oxford to the Year 1700* (1946).

Privy Council, Judicial Committee of the. See JUDICIAL COMMITTEE OF THE PRIVY COUNCIL.

Probabiliorism. The system of *moral theology based on the principle that, if the licitness or illicitness of an action is in doubt, it is lawful to follow the opinion favouring liberty only when it is more probable than the opinion favouring the law. The system was developed by opponents of *Probabilism (q.v.), adopted by the

*Dominican Order in 1656, and favoured by several Popes, esp. *Innocent XI. Though paramount in the first half of the 18th cent., it is today abandoned by most moral theologians. Chief among the objections to it is that the decision on the relative degrees of probability demanded by it requires more time and skill than are normally available in actual situations.

Probabilism. The system of *moral theology based on the principle that, if the licitness or illicitness of an action is in doubt, it is lawful to follow a solidly probable opinion favouring liberty, even though the opposing opinion, favouring the law, be more probable.

From the beginning of the 14th cent. the rights of the probable opinion began to be discussed, but Probabilist principles were first fostered esp. in the school of Salamanca in the 16th cent., where the *Dominican, B. *Medina, in his 'Commentary on the Summa of St *Thomas Aquinas' (1572), gave this teaching its classical form: 'Si est opinio probabilis, licitum est eam sequi, licet opposita probabilior sit.' From Medina down to 1656 the doctrine reigned almost without opposition, being accepted by both Dominicans (*John of St Thomas) and *Jesuits (G. *Vázquez, F. *Suárez) alike. The latter developed the 'principle of possession', acc. to which in case of doubt one is not obliged to change the present state of things, i.e. if a law is doubtful, human freedom remains 'in possession'. The system, however, was recognized to be open to the charge of *Laxism, since, under the pretext of making salvation easy, it would seem to allow men to act acc. to freedom even on a very slight chance of probability; and already in 1604 abuse of the principle was deplored by the Jesuit General, C. *Aquaviva.

It was not, however, till 1656 that a sharp conflict among moralists broke out. The Dominican general chapter in Rome required members of the order to follow more closely St Thomas and to adopt a system that came to be known as *Probabiliorism (q.v.). In the same year B. *Pascal began to publish his *Lettres provinciales* with their violent denunciations, inspired by *Jansenism, of the morality of the Jesuits, with whom, since then, Probabilism has increasingly been identified. Several Probabilist propositions savouring of Laxism were condemned by *Alexander VII in 1665 and 1666, and Laxism as a whole by *Innocent XI in 1679. In the following year the Pope ordered the Jesuit General, G. P. Oliva, to permit the teaching of Probabiliorism and to allow criticism of Probabilism in the Society, and in 1687 T. González (1624–1705), who favoured Probabiliorism, was elected General. His *Fundamentum Theologiae Moralis* (pub. 1694) further impaired the position of Probabilism in the order. On the other hand, '*Tutiorism', a more rigorist system, which had been taught by the Jansenists and J. Sinnich (1603–68) at Louvain, was condemned by *Alexander VIII in 1690. In 1700 the French clergy, under the leadership of J.-B. *Bossuet, censured Probabilism and adopted Probabiliorism, which, under Jansenist influence, held sway during the first part of the 18th cent. The vigorous advocacy of Probabiliorism by the Dominican, D. Concina (1687–1756), who attacked the rival teaching in his *Storia del probabilismo* (1743), provoked a long-drawn-out controversy between Dominicans and Jesuits.

The subsequent rehabilitation of Probabilism is due esp. to the authority of St *Alphonsus Liguori. After a short period of Probabiliorism, which he abandoned as too rigid, he became a Probabilist; and, though in 1762 he again modified his position and expounded his own theory of '*Equiprobabilism' (q.v.), this system rests at bottom on a Probabilist foundation. His great prestige as a moralist, esp. after he was canonized (1839) and declared a *Doctor of the Church (1871), reflected on the whole Probabilist position, which was further strengthened by the restoration of the Society of Jesus in 1814. Surrounded with safeguards to prevent it from degenerating into Laxism, Probabilism became the official teaching of the Society, and together with Equiprobabilism was the most generally accepted moral system of RC Church until the Second *Vatican Council. It is less in evidence in the work of moral theologians writing after the Council.

M. A. Potton, OP, *De Theoria Probabilitatis* (Paris, 1874); F. ter Haar, CSSR, *De Systemate Morali Antiquorum Probabilistarum* (Paderborn, 1894). Id., *Das Decret des Papstes Innocenz' XI über den Probabilismus* (1904). A. Schmitt, SJ, *Zur Geschichte des Probabilismus: Historisch-kritische Untersuchung über die ersten 50 Jahre desselben* (1904). T. Richard, OP, *Le Probabilisme moral et philosophique* (1922). T. Deman, OP, in *DTC* 13 (pt. 1; 1936), cols. 417–619, s.v.; Sisinio da Romallo, OFM, in *EC* 10 (1953), cols. 57–61, s.v., for further bibl. See also bibl. to MORAL THEOLOGY.

probationer. In the Presbyterian Churches, the status of one who, after examination and approval by his presbytery, receives a licence to preach. He is also known as a licentiate. The licence empowers him to act as an assistant to a minister, but he may not administer the Sacraments until he is ordained to a charge of his own. In Scotland a probationer who failed to be elected to a church used commonly to be called a 'stickit minister'. The title is also used in a similar sense in the Methodist Churches.

Probst, Ferdinand (1816–99), liturgical scholar. A pupil of K. J. *Hefele at Tübingen, he was ordained priest in 1840 and became Pastor at Pfärrich near Wangen in 1843, Professor of Pastoral Theology at Breslau in 1864, and Dean of Breslau Cathedral in 1896. Among Probst's long series of writings were *Die Liturgie der drei ersten christlichen Jahrhunderte* (1870), *Sakramente und Sakramentalien* (1872), *Die ältesten römischen Sakramentarien und Ordines* (1892), *Die Liturgie des vierten Jahrhunderts* (1893) and *Die abendländische Messe vom 5. bis 8. Jahrhundert* (1896). He was a scholar of great erudition and industry, but his conclusions were marked by an excessive conservatism, and his methods of argumentation were apt to be over-speculative.

W. Dürig, 'Ferdinand Probst (1816–1899)', in H. Fries and G. Schwaiger (eds.), *Katholische Theologen Deutschlands im 19. Jahrhundert*, 3 (Munich [1975]), pp. 87–105. H. *Leclercq, OSB, in *DACL* 9 (pt. 2; 1930), cols. 1731 f., s.v. 'Liturgistes, iv', and in 14 (pt. 2; 1948), cols. 1887–9, s.v.

Process Theology. A contemporary theological movement which emphasizes the processive or evolutionary nature of man and the world, and holds that God Himself is in process of development through His intercourse with the changing world. The name is derived from A. N. Whitehead's 1928–9 *Gifford Lectures, *Process and Reality* (1929), which gave considerable impetus to the movement. As a distinctive theological movement, it originated in the USA, especially in the University of Chicago during the 1920s and 1930s, but it soon spread elsewhere and is now represented in most W. denominations of Christianity. Its more important exponents include C. Hartshorne, S. M. Ogden, J. B. Cobb, P. N. Hamilton, and W. N. Pittenger.

Unlike other radical movements, process theology is theistic, but its concept of God emphasizes His relationships with creation, His capacity to 'surpass' Himself (but in respect of other entities to remain 'unsurpassable'), His 'bi-polar' nature, and His root attribute as love rather than uncreatedness. All process, natural, human, or divine, is regarded as social in nature, entailing inter-relationship, mutuality, and participation. Notions of 'substance' are rejected as outmoded relics of a static metaphysic; their place is taken by the concept of 'event'. Each event, including God, 'prehends' (grasps or actively receives) from all other events; it is a 'concrescence' of the past, which it inherits and remembers, its present relations, and its 'subjective aim' or future goal for self-fulfilment. Further, each event is given by God (in His 'primordial' aspect) its initial aim, which by free decision it seeks to satisfy, hence actualizing its possiblity. God is the ultimate recipient of all such realizations, which He harmonizes in accordance with His nature of love and then uses for further 'creative advance' in the cosmos. This affective nature of God is His 'consequent aspect'. Hence the bipolarity of God, who is thus seen, as Whitehead said, not as the 'exception to' but as the 'chief exemplification of' the metaphysical principles required to describe all elements in 'reality in process'.

Following this basic concept, process theologians see the Incarnation of Christ in a classical sense, and not as an anomaly in the world. In Him there is 'the disclosure in act' of what had elsewhere been 'divined in theory', namely that love and persuasion are more significant and effective than power or coercion. Sin is interpreted as deviation from creative advance, through the free decision of the creature to choose his own narrow self-realization instead of the wider shared good. Redemption is acceptance by God of the creature's achievement and the opening of future possibilities of true fulfilment in community with others. Heaven and hell are respectively the positive or negative acceptance by God of the creation's achievement, since God receives all accomplished good and rejects all that is not consonant with His nature as love-in-action.

Process theologians claim to take seriously the biblical portrayal of God as participating in and working through creation, but they hold that it is necessary to '*demythologize' the images in which this scriptural affirmation is made, and reject what they call 'classical theism' because of its supposedly static quality.

Other works expounding process theology include A. N. Whitehead, *Religion in the Making* (Cambridge, 1926); id., *Adventures of Ideas* (ibid., 1933); C. Hartshorne, *Man's Vision of God and the Logic of Theism* (New York [1941]); id., *The Divine Relativity* (New Haven, Conn., 1948); id., *A Natural Theology for our Time* (La Salle, Ill. [1967]); J. B. Cobb, Jun., *A Christian Natural Theology: Based on the thought of Alfred North Whitehead* (1966); S. M. Ogden, *The Reality of God and Other Essays* (1967); P. [N.] Hamilton, *The Living God and the Modern World* (1967); [W.] N. Pittenger, *God in Process* (1967); id., *Process-Thought and Christian Faith* (1968); id., *Christology Reconsidered* (1970); D. D. Williams,

The Spirit and the Forms of Love (1968); and D. A. Pailin, *God and the Processes of Reality* (1989). A critical approach is taken by I. Trethowan, OSB, *Process Theology and the Christian Tradition* (Studies in Historical Theology, 5; Still River, Mass. [1985]).

procession (liturgical). Processions are of two different kinds, festal and penitential. Acc. to strict W. use, there is a procession on all Sundays and principal festivals before the principal celebration of the *Eucharist, but in practice this takes place generally only on festivals. The ancient English use was for processions to be held after *Evensong on feasts and on all Saturdays from *Easter to *Advent. The order of procession, acc. to *Sarum Use, is thurifer, cross-bearer, candle-bearers, subdeacon, deacon, celebrant, choir, clergy, bishop (if present); but acc. to modern Roman use the choir walks before the celebrant. Processions are frequently held in the open air as acts of witness, e.g. on *Good Friday or before a parochial mission. Other traditional processions include those of *Palm Sunday, the *Rogation Days (often through the fields to pray for God's blessing on the fruits of the earth) and *Corpus Christi. Banners are often carried in procession both to excite devotion and to typify the Church's vocation to conquer like an army the powers of evil. In the Byzantine rite a procession, called the Lity (Gk., λιτή; Slavonic, *litia*) is prescribed for Vespers on the eves of Sundays and great feasts. In parish churches it goes only to the *narthex, but in monasteries it may well go round the outside of the church. There are also processions with the *epitaphion on Good Friday and *Holy Saturday, and a procession at the beginning of Mattins in the Midnight Easter Vigil. Open air processions with icons and relics are also common. See also PROCESSIONAL and STATION DAYS; for processions within the Eucharistic liturgy, see GOSPEL, OFFERTORY (1), and GREAT and LITTLE ENTRANCE.

N. Serrarius, *Sacri Peripatetici, sive de Sacris Ecclesiae Catholicae Processionibus libri duo* (Cologne, 1607). C. Dunlop, *Processions: A Dissertation together with Practical Suggestions* (*Alcuin Club Tracts, 20; 1932). T. Bailey, *The Processions of Sarum and the Western Church* (Pontifical Institute of Mediaeval Studies, Studies and Texts, 21; Toronto, 1971). *La Maison-Dieu*, no. 43 (1955), special number on processions, with arts. by F. Louvel, OP, P. Donceur, SJ, I. H. Dalmais, OP, A. G. Martimort, and J. Gelineau, SJ. J. Évenou in A. G. Martimort, *L'Église en prière* (édition nouvelle), 3 [1984], pp. 259–69; Eng. tr. (1988), pp. 241–50, with bibl. H. Thurston, SJ, in *CE* 12 (1911), pp. 446–8.

Procession (theological) (Gk. ἐκπόρευσις, Lat. *processio*). In Trinitarian doctrine, the attribute which distinguishes the Holy Spirit from the two Persons of the Father and the Son. This attribute of the Holy Spirit implied in the NT (cf. e.g. Jn. 15: 26) is asserted in the *Niceno-Constantinopolitan Creed, and is first developed at length by the *Cappadocian Fathers. See also DOUBLE PROCESSION OF THE HOLY SPIRIT and FILIOQUE.

Processional. The book containing the text of the litanies, hymns, and prayers formerly prescribed for use in processions. In the W. Church, the bulk of it was merely an extract from the '*Rituale, with some supplementary matter derived from the *Missal and the *Pontifical. In the later Middle Ages, 'Processionals' were often adapted to the requirements of local churches and uses, e.g. the widely used 'Sarum Processional'.

Proclus (410 or 412–85), *Neoplatonist philosopher. He was born in Lydia of wealthy parents. As a young man he went to *Athens, where, apart from a brief exile occasioned by his fervent paganism, he spent the rest of his life, at first as a pupil of Syrianus and later as head of the Academy (hence his title 'Diadochus'). His Life, written by one of his pupils, Marinus, portrays him as a pious, ascetic, and intellectual pagan. Although much of his vast literary output is lost, more of his writings survive than of any other late Neoplatonist; he is thus the principal source of our knowledge of late Athenian Neoplatonism. His philosophy is a systematization of the thought of *Plotinus, combined with an appreciation of the effectiveness of the pagan religious cult as a way of establishing contact with the Divine; this last he owed to *Iamblichus and ultimately to the Chaldean Oracles. His main contribution to Neoplatonism, apart from incorporating theurgy, lay in his detailed investigation of the system of causality implicit in Neoplatonic metaphysics; in this he developed the thought of Iamblichus and Syrianus. His influence on medieval and Renaissance thought was considerable, the earliest Christian thinker indebted to him being *Dionysius the Pseudo-Areopagite.

His principal extant works include the *Elements of Theology*, a concise summary of Neoplatonic metaphysics, his more elaborate *Platonic Theology*, commentaries on several of *Plato's dialogues, some scientific works, and a number of hymns, which, like those of *Synesius, are in the Doric dialect.

No collected edn. of his works exists; there is a useful (though dated) list in L. J. Rosán, op. cit. below, pp. 36–57. *Opera inedita*, ed. V. Cousin (2nd edn., Paris, 1864; repr. Hildesheim, 1961). Important edn. of the *Elements of Theology*, with introd., Eng. tr., and comm., by E. R. Dodds (Oxford, 1933; 2nd edn., 1963). *Platonic Theology*, ed. A. Portus (Hamburg, 1618); also, with Fr. tr., by H. D. Saffrey, OP, and L. G. Westerink (Collection des Universités de France, 1968 ff.). There are edns. of Proclus' commentaries on the following of Plato's works: *Parmenides* ed. V. Cousin, *Procli ... Opera Inedita* (2nd edn., Paris, 1864; repr., Hildesheim, 1961), cols. 603–1244; Lat. tr. by *William of Moerbeke, in which alone the final section survives, ed. by C. Steel (Ancient and Medieval Philosophy, de Wulf-Mansion Centre, 1st ser. 3–4; Louvain, 1982–5); final section also ed., with Eng. tr., by R. Klibansky and others, *Plato Latinus*, 3 (London, 1953), pp. 23–81; Eng. tr. by G. R. Morrow and J. M. Dillon (Princeton, NJ, 1987); on *Republic*, ed. W. Kroll (2 vols., Teub., 1899–1901; repr., 1965); Fr. tr. by A. J. Festugière (3 vols., Bibliothèque des Textes Philosophiques, 1970); on *Timaeus*, ed. E. Diehl (3 vols., Teub., 1903–6; repr., 1965); Fr. tr. by A. J. Festugière (5 vols., Bibliothèque des Textes Philosophiques, 1966–8); on *Cratylus*, ed. G. Pasquali (Teub., 1908); on *1 Alcibiades* by L. G. Westerink (Amsterdam, 1954) and, with Fr. tr., by A. P. Segonds (2 vols., Collection des Universités de France, 1985–6); Eng. tr. and notes by W. O'Neill (The Hague, 1965). *Tria Opuscula* (*de decem dubitationibus, de providentia, de malorum subsistentia*), ed. H. Boese (Quellen und Studien zur Geschichte der Philosophie, 1; Berlin, 1960); also, with Fr. tr., by D. Isaac (3 vols., Collection des Universités de France, 1977–82). 'On the Hieratic Art', ed., with Fr. tr., by J. Bidez, *Catalogue des manuscrits alchimiques grecs*, 6 (Union Académique Internationale; Brussels, 1928), pp. 148–51. *Eclogae de philosophia chaldaica*, ed., with Fr. tr., by É. des Places, SJ, *Oracles Chaldaïques* (Collection des Universités de France, 1971), pp. 202–12. *Hymni*, ed. E. Vogt (Klassisch-Philosophische Studien, 18; Wiesbaden, 1957). Marinus' Life of Proclus, ed., with Lat. tr., by J. F. Boissonade (Leipzig, 1814), repr. in V. Cousin, op. cit., cols. 1–66; Eng. tr.

in L. J. Rosán, op. cit. below, pp. 13–35. A. Severyns, *Recherches sur la Chrestomathie de Proclus* (Bibliothèque de la Faculté de Philosophie et Lettres de l'Université de Liége, 78 f., 132, and 170; 1938–63). L. J. Rosán, *The Philosophy of Proclus* (New York, 1949). W. Beierwaltes, *Proklos: Grundzüge seiner Metaphysik* (Philosophische Abhandlungen, 24; Frankfurt am Main, 1965). J. Trouillard, *L'Un et l'âme selon Proclos* (Collection d'études anciennes, 1972); id., *La Mystagogie de Proclos* (ibid., 1982). J. Pépin and H. D. Saffrey (eds.), *Proclus: Lecteur et Interprète des Anciens. Actes du colloque international du CNRS Paris (2–4 octobre 1985)* (1987); E. P. Bos and P. A. Meier (eds.), *On Proclus and his Influence in Medieval Philosophy* (Philosophia Antiqua, 53; Leiden, etc., 1992). A. E. *Taylor, *Philosophical Studies* (1934), pp. 151–91. R. Beutler in *PW* 23 (pt. 1; 1957), cols. 186–247, s.v. 'Proklos (4)'.

Proclus, St (d. 446 or 447), Patr. of *Constantinople. On the death of the Patr. Atticus (425), whose secretary he had been, he was an unsuccessful candidate for the patriarchate, but in 426 he was consecrated Abp. of Cyzicus. Unable to take possession of his see through ecclesiastical differences, he remained in Constantinople as a much-applauded preacher, and here delivered in 428 or 429 a famous sermon on the *Theotokos in the presence of *Nestorius, though Proclus did not take an active part in the subsequent controversy. When he became patriarch in 434, his moderation in the cause of orthodoxy gained him much sympathy and his popularity was enhanced by the solemn translation of the body of St *Chrysostom which he effected in 438. Among his writings, which consist for the most part of homilies and epistles, is the so-called 'Tome of St Proclus' (Ep. 2), an exposition of the doctrine of the one Christ in two natures, addressed to the *Armenians, and directed against *Theodore of Mopsuestia (but without naming him). Traditionally the formula 'One of the Trinity was crucified acc. to the flesh', destined to play an important part in the *Theopaschite Controversy (6th cent.), has been ascribed to him (but mistakenly). The introduction of the *Trisagion into the Liturgy has also been attributed to him. Feast day in E., 20 Nov.; in W., 24 Oct.

His writings, first ed. by V. Riccardus (1630), repr. in J. P. Migne, *PG* 65. 651–88. Crit. text of his Sermon on the Theotokos in *ACO* 1. 1. 1 (1927), pp. 103–7; of his *Tomus ad Armenios*, ibid. 4. 2 (1914), pp. 65–8, 187–205. E. *Schwartz, *Konzilstudien* (Schriften der wissenschaftlichen Gesellschaft in Strassburg, Heft 20; 1914), 2. *Über echte und unechte Schriften des Bischofs Proklos von Konstantinopel*, pp. 18–53. B. Marx, *Procliana: Untersuchungen über den homiletischen Nachlass des Patriarchen Proklos von Konstantinopel* (1940) (Marx ascribes, often on precarious grounds, more than 80 of the sermons preserved in the *spuria* of Chrysostom to Proclus). M. Richard, 'Proclus de Constantinople et le théopaschisme', *RHE* 38 (1942), pp. 303–31; repr. in id., *Opera Minora*, 2 (Turnhout and Louvain, 1977), no. 52. F. J. Leroy, SJ, *L'Homilétique de Proclus de Constantinople: Tradition manuscrite, inédits, études connexes* (ST 247; 1967). M. Aubineau, 'Bilan d'une enquête sur les homélies de Proclus de Constantinople', *Revue des Études grecs*, 85 (1972), pp. 572–96. V. Grumel, AA (ed.), *Les Regestes des Actes du Patriarcat de Constantinople*, 1, fasc. 1 (2nd edn., 1972), pp. 61–74 (nos. 76–93a). *CPG* 3 (1979), pp. 133–50 (nos. 5800–5915). Altaner and Stuiber (1978), pp. 338 f. and 619.

Procopius of Caesarea (mid-6th cent.), Byzantine historian. A native of *Caesarea in Palestine, in 527 he was appointed secretary to Belisarius, whom he accompanied in his campaigns against the Persians, the Vandals, and the Ostrogoths. At least from 542 he lived in *Constantinople.

His writings consist of his 'History of the Wars' (i.e. those which he had himself witnessed), his 'De aedificiis' (an account of the buildings of the Emp. *Justinian), and the so-called 'Anecdota' (or 'Secret History'), issued only after his death. The work of a careful and on the whole impartial author, they are of great historical value and stand in marked contrast to most of the poor compositions of his age. The 'De aedificiis', however, suffers from its excessive flattery of Justinian. On the other hand, the 'Anecdota', which were not intended for publication, are a bitter invective against Justinian and *Theodora.

Crit. edn. of his works by J. Haury (Teub., 3 vols., 1905–13; repr., with additions, 4 vols., 1962–4); also ed., with Eng. tr., by H. B. Dewing (Loeb, 7 vols., 1914–40). Other Eng. trs. of his 'Anecdota' by R. Attwater (Ann Arbor, Mich., 1961) and G. A. Williamson (Penguin Classics, 1966). F. Dahn, *Prokopius von Cäsarea* (1865). J. A. S. Evans, *Procopius* (New York, 1972); A. [M.] Cameron, *Procopius and the Sixth Century* (1985). Krumbacher, pp. 230–6. B. Rubin in *PW* 23. 1 (1957), cols. 273–599, s.v. 'Prokopius von Kaisareia'.

Procopius of Gaza (*c.*475–*c.*538), rhetorician and biblical exegete. He was perhaps the foremost figure of the 'School of Gaza', a group of Christian rhetoricians of the 5th–6th cent. His biblical works consist mainly of extensive extracts from older exegetes (*Philo, *Origen, *Basil, *Theodoret, *Cyril of Alexandria). Of his two Commentaries on the *Octateuch the shorter, which is preserved in Cod. Monac. gr. 358, has been published *in toto* in a Lat. translation and, in fragments, also in the Gk. He also commented on 1 and 2 Sam., 1 and 2 Kgs., and 1 and 2 Chron.; on Is.; and on Cant. His Epp., of which 166 survive, are in an affected and precious style (which, however, made them popular) and without theological interest, but remain, with the funeral oration of his pupil Choricius, the chief source for his life. Despite the doubts of some scholars, some fragments of a work against the Neoplatonist *Proclus are prob. to be assigned to Procopius of Gaza. He also wrote an account of a sequence of pagan pictures at Gaza.

Works first collected in J. P. Migne, *PG* 87. 1–2838 (pts. 1–3); new edns. of his *Epistolae et Declamationes* by A. Garzya and R. J. Loenertz, OP (Studia Patristica et Byzantina, 9; 1963); of *Catena in Ecclesiasten* by S. Leanza (CCSG 4, 1978, pp. 1–50, and suppl., 1983), and of his panegyric of the Emp. Anastasius I, with Fr. tr., by A. Chauvot (Antiquitas, Reihe 1, Band 35; Bonn, 1986). His *Descriptio imaginis*, ed. P. Friedländer (ST 89; 1939). The chief source for his life, apart from his Epp., is a funeral oration of Choricius of Gaza (*Opera*, ed. R. Foerster and E. Richtsteig, Teub., 1929, pp. 109–28). L. Eisenhofer, *Procopius von Gaza: Eine literarhistorische Studie* (1897). L. W. Westerink, 'Proclus, Procopius, Psellus', *Mnemosyne*, 3rd ser. 10 (1942), pp. 275–80. *CPG* 3 (1979), pp. 388–91 (nos. 7430–48). Bardenhewer, 5, pp. 86–91, with bibl.; Altaner and Stuiber (1978), p. 516, with bibl. J. van den Gheyn, SJ, in *Dict. Bibl.* 5 (1912), cols. 686–9, s.v.; W. Aly in *PW* 23 (pt. 1; 1957), cols. 259–73, s.v. 'Prokopius von Gaza'. See also bibl. to CATENA.

Proctors of the Clergy. In the C of E, the elected representatives of the clergy who, together with the *ex officio* members, constitute the Lower Houses of the *Convocations of *Canterbury and *York. Voting is carried out by electoral areas, each consisting of a diocese or part of a diocese, or a university or group of universities. The electors are assistant bishops; beneficed, cathedral and licensed clergy (excluding *suffragan bishops, deans, provosts and archdeacons); and, in the case of universities, qualifying clergy. The elections are governed by canon H 2, added to the 1969 canons in 1975. See also CONVOCATIONS OF CANTERBURY AND YORK.

profession, religious. The making of a public *vow promising, either explicitly or implicitly, to follow the three evangelical *counsels of poverty, chastity, and obedience necessary to the embracing of the 'religious life'. Profession follows upon the novitiate or training period. Acc. to RC canon law (*CIC* (1983), can. 657) there must first be a temporary profession of at least three years. At the end of this period the 'professed' may be allowed to renew his temporary profession for a set time. If he is not, he must either leave the Order or Congregation (technically known as the Religious *Institute), or make perpetual, that is lifelong, profession.

R. Yeo [OSB], *The Structure and Content of Monastic Profession: A Juridical Study, with particular regard to the practice of the English Benedictine Congregation since the French Revolution* (Studia Anselmiana, 83; Rome, 1982), with extensive bibl.

prohibited degrees. The relationships by blood or marriage which render it unlawful for two persons to marry. Certain relationships, e.g. mother and son, and a man and his wife's mother, prevent marriage in almost every state of society, however primitive. The reasons which underlie these prohibitions are partly biological, but mainly social, e.g. the maintenance of peace and purity in the home. Blood relationships are called '*consanguinity'; relationships by marriage '*affinity'.

In canon law such relationships are measured in degrees (cf. Lat. *gradus*, 'step'). Those of the 'direct line' are simply the number of steps between the persons related. Thus father to son is one step or the 'first degree', son to grandfather the second, and so on. For computing the 'collateral line', that is the relationship between the descendants of a common ancestor, two systems have been used, the Roman and the Germanic. The Roman system calculates on the basis of the number of generations between the relations, counting up to (but not including) the common ancestor, i.e. in the case of first cousins there are two generations on each side up to the ancestor; these are added together, making four generations or degrees. The Germanic system is based on the unity of the sibling group, the members of which are related in the first degree. This method counts only the generations from the common ancestor, so that, e.g., first cousins are related in the second degree. In both systems the degrees of affinity are calculated in the same way as those of consanguinity, the husband and wife being regarded as identical for this purpose, i.e. a man's wife's first cousin is regarded as related to him in the same degree as his own first cousin.

At first the Church followed the Roman system, and this has always been retained in the E. Orthodox Church. In the W., however, the Germanic system was generally adopted in the Middle Ages, though there were variations and much discussion; in 1983 the RC Church reverted to the Roman system. Though based on the prohibitions in Lev. 18, ecclesiastical legislation has at times extended the prohibitions to the seventh degree (on the Roman reckoning). Important legislative measures were taken at the Fourth *Lateran Council (1215) and in the 1917 *Codex Iuris Canonici. Acc. to the 1983 Code (can. 1091) marriage is invalid between those related by consanguinity in all degrees of the direct line, whilst in the collateral line it is invalid up to the fourth degree (first cousins). The impediment of consanguinity cannot be dispensed in any degree of the direct line or in the second degree of the collateral line. Affinity in any degree of the direct line invalidates a marriage (can. 1092). In the C of E the prohibited degrees are those listed in the Table of *Kindred and Affinity in the 1969 *Canons, can. B 31.

F. X. Wahl, *The Matrimonial Impediments of Consanguinity and Affinity* (Washington, DC, 1934), with bibl. J. Dauvillier and C. De Clercq, *Le Mariage en Droit Canonique Oriental* (1936), pp. 123–46. J. Goody, *The Development of the Family and Marriage in Europe* (Cambridge, 1983), esp. pp. 48–59. J. A. Brundage, *Law, Sex, and Christian Society in Medieval Europe* (Chicago and London, 1987), esp. pp. 140 f., 191–5, 355 f., and 373 f. F. Cimetier in *DTC* 11 (pt. 2; 1932), cols. 1995–2003, s.v. 'Parenté (Empêchements de)'. See also bibl. to AFFINITY, CONSANGUINITY, and MATRIMONY.

prokimenon (Gk. προκείμενον, 'placed before'). Verses from the Psalter, sung at the beginning of any series of readings from Scripture in the Byzantine rite. At *Vespers it is always sung after the *Phos Hilaron, even when no readings follow.

prolocutor. The title of the president and chairman of each of the Lower Houses of the *Convocations of *Canterbury and *York. He also acts as the representative of his House to the corresponding Upper House (of bishops). He is elected to his office by the House to which he belongs.

Promised Land, the. The land of *Canaan, promised to *Abraham and his descendants. Cf. Gen. 12: 7, 13: 15, etc.; and J. *Milton, *Paradise Lost*: 'Over the Promis'd Land to God so dear' (3. 531).

Promotor Fidei (Lat., 'promoter of the faith'), the foremost theologian of the Congregation for the *Causes of Saints in Rome. He was formerly responsible for critically examining the alleged virtues and miracles of a candidate for *beatification or *canonization, with a view to preventing any rash decision. Hence, he was popularly known as 'the Devil's Advocate' (*advocatus diaboli*). The first formal mention of the office seems to be in connection with the canonization of St Lawrence Justinian (d. 1456) by *Leo X. By the Apostolic Constitution 'Divinus Perfectionis Magister' (1983; see CANONIZATION), his functions have changed. He now presides over the meetings of the theological consultors who make the final assessment of a case and prepares their report for the session of Cardinals and Bishops who advise the Pope. The Cardinal Prefect of the Congregation for the Causes of Saints may appoint a special *Promotor Fidei* for a particular case.

Promotor Justitiae (Lat., 'promoter of justice'). The priest responsible for testing critically in the diocese in which he or she died the evidence adduced on behalf of a candidate for *beatification or *canonization in the RC Church. The creation of the office is due to the recent changes in the procedure for canonization under which the

Promotor Justitiae discharges tasks formerly assigned to the *Promotor Fidei*.

Prone. The name was given in medieval N. Europe, including Britain, to the vernacular office inserted into High Mass after the *Offertory on Sundays and other feast days. Its form was at the discretion of the preacher, but it ordinarily consisted of such items as the '*bidding of the bedes' (q.v.) and expositions of the Lord's Prayer and the Creed, as well as notifications of ensuing feasts and fasts and of banns of marriage and ordination. The name has also been used for sermons, esp. of an expository kind. The word is derived from the Fr. *prône*, orig. a grille which separated the chancel or place where notices were given out from the rest of the church.

Pronouncement Stories. The name proposed by V. Taylor for those passages in the Gospels which M. *Dibelius terms *Paradigms (q.v.) and R. *Bultmann *Apophthegms.

Propaganda Fide, Congregation of. The *Roman Congregation which is concerned with missionary activity throughout the world and with the administration of territories where there is no properly established hierarchy. It originated in the latter half of the 16th cent. to meet the spiritual needs of the newly discovered heathen populations, as one of the fruits of the general stimulus given to Church organization by the *Counter-Reformation. At first it took the form of a cardinalitial commission 'De propaganda fide', and it was not until 1622 that Gregory XV created the Congregation of Propaganda by the bull 'Inscrutabili Divinae Providentiae'. The Congregation was originally composed of 13 cardinals, 2 prelates, a secretary, and a consultor. *Urban VIII further gave the Congregation a prefect-general and a central missionary training seminary, the 'Collegium Urbanum', founded in 1627. Owing to the extensive range of its work the Congregation makes use of various pontifical organizations; the scope of its jurisdiction is regulated by the Apostolic Constitution 'Pastor Bonus' of 28 June 1988, arts. 85–92, which renamed it 'Congregatio pro Gentium Evangelizatione' (Congregation for the Evangelization of the Nations).

Bullarium Pontificium Sacrae Congregationis de Propaganda Fide (5 vols. bound in 3, Rome, 1839–41; appendix, 2 vols., ibid., no date); *Collectanea S. Congregationis de Propaganda Fide, seu Decreta, Instructiones, Rescripta pro Apostolicis Missionibus*, Ann. 1622–1906 (2 vols., ibid., 1907). *Sacrae Congregationis de Propaganda Fidei Memoria Rerum 1622–1972*, ed. J. Metzler (3 vols. in 5, ibid., 1971–6). The relevant sections of 'Pastor Bonus' are pr. in *AAS* 80 (1988), pp. 881–3. R. H. Song, *The Sacred Congregation for the Propagation of the Faith* (Catholic University of America, Canon Law Studies, 420; 1961). *Catalogus Editionum quae prodierunt ex Typographia Polyglotta Sacrae Congregationis de Propaganda Fide* (Rome, 1890). R. Hoffman in *NCE* 11 (1967), pp. 840–4, s.v. 'Propagation of the Faith, Congregation for the', with bibl. See also works cited under ROMAN CONGREGATIONS.

Proper. The part of the *Eucharist and *Offices which changes acc. to the festival or ecclesiastical season. It is thus contrasted with the rest of the service, the invariable '*Ordinary (or Order) of the Mass'. The 'Proper of Saints' ('Proprium Sanctorum' or, in the 1970 Missal, 'Proprium de Sanctis') is the Proper for festivals of a fixed date; the 'Proper of Time' ('Proprium Temporum', or, in the 1970

Missal, 'Proprium de Tempore') that for *Sundays, *ferias, and festivals which have no fixed date. Many saints' days share the same Proper with others, and where this is so their Proper is printed once for all in a separate part of the *Missal and *Breviary, under the title '*Common of Saints' ('Commune Sanctorum'). In the BCP the Proper consists of (1) the *Collect, *Epistle, and *Gospel (with the *Easter Anthems for use at *Mattins on Easter Day), which are arranged together in the order of the ecclesiastical year, the Proper of Time coming first, and then that of Saints (there being no Common), and (2) the *Prefaces, which are set out in the body of the Communion Service, as in the Roman Missal. The ASB also provides Proper Introductory and Postcommunion Sentences for Sundays, Festivals, and Holy Days and an OT reading in addition to the Epistle and Gospel.

prophecy. From the earliest times Christians have believed that already before the Incarnation God the Holy Spirit, as affirmed in the *Nicene Creed, 'spoke by the prophets'. Such prophetic inspiration was found esp. in the supernatural knowledge by which holy men were enabled to foresee and foretell, in part, the revelation which was to be given in Christ. It was extended to *Abraham (Jn. 8: 56) and *David (Mk. 12: 35 ff.), but it was pre-eminently the privilege of the prophets. It has also been generally recognized that the prophets were the inspired deliverers of God's message not only about the future, but to their contemporaries, to whom they declared His will, and whom they recalled to His righteousness.

At least since NT times the Jews have applied the term 'Prophets' to a large section of the OT Canon intermediate in authority between the ancient 'Law' and the more recent 'Writings' (*Hagiographa). In this connection it is customary to distinguish (1) the 'Former Prophets', namely Jos., Jgs., 1 and 2 Sam., 1 and 2 Kgs., and (2) the 'Latter Prophets', namely Is., Jer., Ezek. and the 12 (*Minor) Prophets. But the name of prophet could be applied personally in a wider sense, e.g. to *Moses and the future 'prophet like Moses' who was expected to appear (Deut. 18: 15 ff.), and to David (Acts 2: 29 f.). Christ Himself was considered by some as a prophet (Mk. 8: 28; Jn. 4: 19).

The beginnings of Hebrew prophecy can be traced to the early days of the monarchy. 1 Sam. 9 f. already attests the existence of two types of prophets, the Seer (Heb. *ro'eh*), possessed of clairvoyance, like Samuel who was able to show Saul the whereabouts of his lost asses, and the ecstatic (Heb. *nabi'*), associated with the local shrine, who under the stimulus of music and dancing fell into a frenzy and uttered words not his own, held to be Yahweh's (1 Sam. 10: 10 f., 19: 23 f.). In this ecstatic condition, the prophet gave the impression of madness (cf. 2 Kgs. 9: 11, Jer. 29: 26).

Gradually, however, the ecstatic features became of less importance and the conscious delivery of a Divine message or 'word' became the dominating feature of prophecy. Side by side with this was the use of symbolic action. Thus Zedekiah foretold the overthrow of the Syrians by equipping himself with horns of iron (1 Kgs. 22: 11); and, in the early period at least, such action was believed not merely to foretell but to influence the future (cf. 2 Kgs. 13: 14–19), being in its beginnings not far from sympath-

etic magic. Moreover, even among the later prophets words were reinforced by actions. *Isaiah went about naked 'for a sign' (Is. 20), *Jeremiah wore a 'yoke' (or fetters) on his shoulders (Jer. 27), and *Ezekiel performed various symbolic actions (e.g. Ezek. 12). A development can be traced in the message which prophets communicated through words and actions. *Amos proclaimed unrelieved divine judgement on Israel, but later prophets saw hope beyond judgement, and by the post-exilic age the prophetic message had turned to one of blessing and encouragement.

The prophetic Books of the OT Canon fall into four groups: (1) the 8th-cent. prophets, Amos, *Hosea, *Micah, and Isaiah; (2) the immediately pre-exilic prophets (late 7th–early 6th cent.), *Nahum, *Zephaniah, *Habakkuk, and Jeremiah; (3) the exilic prophets, Ezekiel and *Deutero-Isaiah; (4) the post-exilic prophets, *Haggai, *Zechariah, and *Malachi, together with (prob.) *Obadiah, *Joel, and *Jonah, which are less easy to date precisely.

Since it is in the prophets of the OT that most (though not all) of the passages concerning the *Messiah appear, Jews who looked for His coming had an especial interest in the prophets, who, with other inspired writers, had looked for the Messiah 'since the world began' (Lk. 1: 70; cf. Lk. 1: 55, 2 Pet. 1: 21). This interest can be clearly seen in the writings of the *Qumran community as well as in the NT. Christ Himself saw the fulfilment of OT prophecy in His own Ministry, saying, e.g., that 'many prophets and righteous men' had desired to see what the disciples were then seeing (Mt. 13: 17) and declaring that with His Coming the words of Is. 61: 1 were fulfilled (Lk. 4: 21). Similarly, the Evangelists point to the fulfilment of a number of OT prophecies in the events they describe, e.g. Christ's birth from a virgin (Mt. 1: 22; cf. Is. 7: 14) and its occurrence at *Bethlehem (Mt. 2: 6; cf. Mic. 5: 2), the ministry of *John the Baptist (Mk. 1: 2–3; cf. Mal. 3: 1 and Is. 40: 3), the Lord's entry into Jerusalem riding upon an ass (Jn. 12: 12–15; cf. Zech. 9: 9), and the piercing of His side at the Crucifixion (Jn. 19: 36 f.; cf. Zech. 12: 10).

Acc. to Acts, the Apostles began, immediately after *Pentecost, to see the fulfilment of OT passages in Christ's Resurrection and Ascension and the Coming of the Holy Spirit (Acts 2: 14–36, quoting Joel 2: 28–30, Ps. 16: 8–11 and Ps. 110: 1), and the appeal to OT prophecy was a constant feature of early Christian preaching (Acts 8: 26–35). St *Paul in writing to his converts not only reminds them of the universal Christian belief that 'Christ died for our sins acc. to the Scriptures' (1 Cor. 15: 3), but also uses many OT texts in a more individual manner, sometimes drawing on methods of interpretation known also from later rabbinic texts; thus he interprets the Rock which supplied the Israelites with water in the wilderness (Exod. 17: 6) as a type of Christ (1 Cor. 10: 4). The Ep. to the Hebrews is almost a continuous appeal to OT texts (predominantly in the Law and the Pss. rather than the Prophets) in support of teaching about Christ.

In Christian writers from the *Apostolic Fathers onwards the appeal to the OT is continued on the same general lines as in the NT. It is elaborated esp. in the Ep. of *Barnabas, for the author of which all the ceremonial enactments of the OT referred in a hidden manner to the

Christian revelation and had been misinterpreted by the Jews. Among the *Apologists it is found esp. in *Justin Martyr, whose 'Dialogue with Trypho, the Jew' is naturally much concerned with rival interpretations of the OT. Throughout the patristic and medieval periods all who sought to expound Christian doctrine (apart from dualist heretics such as *Marcion) assumed that the inspiration of Scripture guaranteed the prophetic foreknowledge of the Christian revelation, even in its details, so that OT texts might validly be used as arguments, e.g., for specific Christological teaching.

Wide application was given to the allegorical interpretation of OT texts, esp. by the *Alexandrian theologians. By the mystical interpretation of Scripture some Latin and medieval writers were able to find an appropriate relevance in one OT text or another to almost any conceivable subject. At the Reformation the traditionally accepted uses of OT texts in a Christian sense continued unchallenged; an example is afforded by the original chapter-summaries and page-headings of the *Authorized Version for such passages as Is. 40–66 and Ps. 110. It was only with the *Enlightenment and the rise of a critical approach to history that doubt was cast on the existence of any real anticipation of NT events in such texts as Is. 7: 14. Hence modern expositors of the OT tend to stress that the prophets were originally and primarily 'forth-tellers' of God's will to their contemporaries rather than 'foretellers' of the future.

Among the more important of the older discussions are J. Davison, *Discourses on Prophecy* (1824); H. G. A. *Ewald, *Die Propheten des Alten Bundes* (2 vols., 1840–1; Eng. tr. of 2nd edn., 5 vols., 1875–81); B. *Duhm, *Die Theologie der Propheten* (1875). In British theology, the modern critical view of the development of Hebrew Prophecy was popularized by W. R. *Smith, *The Prophets of Israel and their Place in History to the Close of the Eighth Century B.C.* (1882; 2nd edn., with notes by T. K. *Cheyne, 1895). B. Duhm, *Israels Propheten* (1916). More recent works incl. J. Lindblom, *Prophecy in Ancient Israel* (Oxford, 1962); P. D. Hanson, *The Dawn of Apocalyptic* (Philadelphia [1975]); K. Koch, *Die Profeten* (2 vols., Stuttgart, 1978–80; Eng. tr., 1982–3); R. [J.] Coggins and others (eds.), *Israel's Prophetic Tradition: Essays in Honour of Peter R. Ackroyd* (Cambridge, 1982); J. Blenkinsopp, *A History of Prophecy in Israel from the Settlement in the Land to the Hellenistic Period* (1984); J. Barton, *Oracles of God: Perceptions of Ancient Prophecy in Israel after the Exile* (1986).

On the Christian interpretation of prophecy, C. H. *Dodd, *According to the Scriptures* (1952); G. F. A. Knight, *A Christian Theology of the Old Testament* (1959); B. Lindars, SSF, *New Testament Apologetic: The Doctrinal Significance of the Old Testament Quotations* (1961); B. W. Anderson (ed.), *The Old Testament and Christian Faith* (New York, 1963; London, 1964); A. T. Hanson, *The New Testament Interpretation of Scripture* (1980); D. E. Aune, *Prophecy in Early Christianity and the Ancient Mediterranean World* (Michigan [1983]). See also works cited under ALLEGORY.

prophets (early Christian).

While prophecy as a phenomenon is well attested is the early Church (esp. 1 Cor. 12–14), the precise position of the prophets mentioned in the NT is unclear. Sometimes they appear as a distinct order of ministers (1 Cor. 12: 28 and Eph. 4: 11); other references suggest something less definite (e.g. Acts 11: 27), while women as well as men could prophesy (Acts 21: 9). The apocalyptic expectation that prophecy would be restored at the end of time seems to lie in the background. Several early Christian writers assume the authority of prophets (e.g. St *Ignatius and *Hermas), but prophecy seems to have died out, the *Didache perhaps witnessing to the period of transition. 'Prophets' once again found prominence in *Montanism, but they were unable to establish their authority against the developed episcopal authority of the Church.

Classic discussion of the position of prophets in the early Church by A. *Harnack, *Die Lehre der zwölf Apostel* (TU 2, Hefte 1–2; 1884), pp. 119–31. Wider treatments of prophecy include G. Dautzenberg, *Urchristliche Prophetie* (Beiträge zum Wissenschaften vom alten und neuen Testament, 6. Folge, Heft 4; 1975); D. E. Aune, *Prophecy in Early Christianity and the Ancient Mediterranean World* (Michigan [1983]). P. Veilhauer and E. Fascher in *RGG* (3rd edn.), 5 (1961), cols. 633–5; J. Schmid in *L.Th.K.* (2nd edn.), 8 (1963), cols. 798–800, both s.v.

propitiation.

The general meaning of the word is the appeasing of the wrath of the Deity by prayer or sacrifice when a sin or offence has been committed against Him. The word occurs three times in the AV, in connection with the death of Christ (Rom. 3: 25, 1 Jn. 2: 2, and 4: 10; to which RV adds Heb. 2: 17). Such a translation accurately represents the meaning in classical Greek of the words used (ἱλαστήριον, ἱλασμός). However, the Hebrew equivalent is never used with God as the object; this fact suggests that the primary biblical meaning is to expiate or remove an obstacle on man's part to his relationship with God. To say that the death of Christ is 'propitiatory' is, then, to say that it is effective in restoring the relationship between God and man, damaged by sin. Acc. to the Council of *Trent (Sess. 22, can. 3), the Sacrifice offered in the Eucharist is propitiatory (*propitiatorium*). See also ATONEMENT; MERCY SEAT.

proprietary chapel.

In the C of E a chapel built by subscription and maintained by private individuals, without constitutional existence or parochial rights. Such chapels were seldom episcopally consecrated, though their ministers were normally granted episcopal licences (revocable absolutely at the bishop's will) which could only be issued with the consent of the incumbent of the parish. They were established esp. in fashionable areas (London, watering-places); were commonly supported by pew rents, which were often high; and were sometimes centres of extreme Evangelicalism or (less frequently) High Church doctrine. Many such chapels existed in the 18th and early 19th cents.; but they are now almost, if not quite, extinct.

R. J. *Phillimore, *The Ecclesiastical Law of the Church of England* (2nd edn. by W. G. F. Phillimore, 1895), 1, pp. 250–2, 436, and 2, pp. 1459 and 1759; H. W. Cripps, *A Practical Treatise on the Law relating to the Church and Clergy* (8th edn., by K. M. Macmorran, 1937), pp. 104 f., esp. note m, 209, and 533.

Prose (Lat. *prosa*).

An alternative name, once common in England, for the *Sequence (q.v.). The word has occasionally been applied to other anthems of similar form which have no place in the Liturgy.

proselyte (Gk. προσήλυτος).

The word means literally 'stranger' or 'foreign sojourner', and, by an extension, a convert to Judaism. The NT mentions both 'proselytes' and 'God-fearers' (cf., e.g., Acts. 2: 10, 13: 43, 10: 2), the distinction being probably that the former underwent circumcision and were therefore reckoned full members of the Jewish Church, whereas the 'God-fearers' were more loosely attached to the Jewish communities. In a wider sense the word has come to be used of a convert to any faith or sect.

Proskomide (Gk. προσκομιδή). In the E. Church, the preparation of the bread and wine for the Eucharist which takes place before the beginning of the service at the table known as the *prothesis. The priest cuts the bread into pieces with the *lance, and then arranges it on the *discus in a fashion prescribed by the rubrics; then the deacon pours wine and water into the chalice; and the whole is afterwards veiled. At the end of the ceremony the bread and wine are censed and a prayer is said over them. In origin the Proskomide is the second part of the *Offertory, moved back to the beginning of the service. There are considerable variations in terminology among liturgical writers, the Proskomide being sometimes known as the Prothesis.

Prosper of Aquitaine, St (c.390–c.463), theologian. Prosper Tiro of Aquitania was living at Marseilles at the outbreak of the *Semipelagian controversy (426), probably as a lay monk. In 427/8 he wrote to St *Augustine, whose theology of grace and predestination he warmly accepted, informing him of the opposition which his teaching was encountering among the disciples of *Cassian. About the same time he wrote a letter to a certain Rufinus and the 'Carmen de ingratis', a poem of over 1,000 hexameters, both on the subject of grace. In 431, after St Augustine's death, he went to Rome to secure Pope *Celestine I's support for Augustinian doctrines and between 431 and 434 published a number of works in their defence, one of them directed perhaps against St *Vincent of Lérins and another against Cassian. After the latter's death (c.435), he became more conciliatory, as is borne out by his 'Expositio super Psalmos', and (if, as is now widely held, it be Prosper's) the 'Capitula Coelestini', written as an appendix to the Pope's letter to the bishops of Gaul, probably between 435 and 442, from Rome. In his last period, when he was closely associated with *Leo I, he collaborated with the Pope in some of his doctrinal statements and devoted himself to compilations and a 'Chronicle', which until 378 follows *Eusebius and St *Jerome, but is of value for his own time (425–455). It would seem that Prosper's theological opinions developed from the rigid Augustinianism of his earlier controversial writings to a milder view which rejected predestination to damnation and affirmed the will of God to save all men, though believing in fact in the reprobation of a great number. The canons of the Council of *Orange of 529 are partly based on his extracts from St Augustine, and later he exercised a considerable influence on the Carolingian theologians. Feast day, 7 July.

Works ed. J. B. Le Brun des Marettes, OSB, and D. Mangeant, OSB, Paris, 1711; repr. with addendum in J. P. Migne, PL 51 1–868. Crit. text of 'Chronicle' ed. T. *Mommsen in MGH, Auctores Antiquissimi, 9 (1892), pp. 341–499, and of 'Expositio super Psalmos' by P. Callens and of 'Liber Sententiarum' by M. Gastaldo (CCSL 68 A; 1972). The 'De Providentia Dei' attributed to Prosper, ed., with Eng. tr. and comm., by M. Marcovich (Suppls. to VC, 10; Leiden, 1989). Eng. trs. by P. De Letter, SJ, of Prosper's De Vocatione Omnium Gentium (ACW 14; 1952) and of various works in defence of St Augustine (ibid. 32; 1963). M. Cappuyns, OSB, 'Le premier réprésentant de l'augustinisme

médiéval, Prosper d'Aquitaine', RTAM 1 (1929), pp. 309–37; G. de Plinval, 'Prosper d'Aquitaine, interprète de saint Augustin', Recherches Augustiniennes, 1 (1958), pp. 339–55; R. Lorenz, 'Der Augustinismus Prospers von Aquitanien', ZKG 73 (1962), pp. 217–52, with bibl.; R. A. Markus, 'Chronicle and Theology: Prosper of Aquitaine', in C. Holdsworth and T. P. Wiseman (eds.), The Inheritance of Historiography 350–900 (Exeter Studies in History, 12; 1986), pp. 31–43. A. Hamman in Quasten (cont.), Patrology, 4 (1986), pp. 551–8. H. W. Phillott in DCB 4 (1887), pp. 492–7; R. Helm in PW 23 (pt. 1; 1957), cols. 880–97, s.v. 'Prosper (1)'; A. Solignac, SJ, in Dict. Sp. 12 (pt. 2; 1986), cols. 2446–56, s.v.

prosphora (Gk. προσφορά). In the E. Church, the altar bread. It takes the form of round leavened cakes about 3 inches in diameter and 2 inches thick, of which five are required for the service. They are solemnly cut up at the *Proskomide. From the first, which is divided by a cross into four quarters containing respectively the Greek letters IC ('Jesus'), XC ('Christ'), NI, KA (νικᾷ, 'conquers'), the principal particle (the 'seal', or the 'lamb') is cut out. From the second a particle is removed in honour of the BVM, from the third nine particles in honour of St John the Baptist, the Prophets, the Apostles and other Saints, from the fourth particles for the living to be prayed for, and from the fifth particles for the departed commemorated. Further particles are taken from the prosphoras offered by the people with names of living and departed to be prayed for. Only the 'lamb' is consecrated, the other particles are placed in the chalice after the distribution of communion, and the portions left over are distributed later among the congregation as the *antidoron. In the Greek Church today, outside monasteries, one large loaf stamped with five 'seals' is used, instead of five smaller loaves; but the Russian Church retains the older practice of the five loaves.

Protasius, St. See GERVASIUS AND PROTASIUS, STS.

Protestant Episcopal Church in the United States of America. See EPISCOPAL CHURCH IN THE UNITED STATES OF AMERICA.

Protestantism. The original 'Protestatio', from which the term derives, was a statement issued by five reforming princes and 14 cities of the Holy Roman Empire at the Diet of *Speyer in 1529. Divided among themselves and outnumbered by the Catholic powers, it seemed vital to produce a united declaration of faith. Their opponents wished to halt the reforming movement within the various territories of the empire, particularly the introduction of religious 'innovations' and the secularization of land which had belonged to the medieval Church. The signatories believed that to keep silent would touch 'God's honour and salvation and the eternal life of our souls'. The Protestation was, therefore, a stage in the development of a Lutheran system of faith and practice (the terms 'Protestant', for Lutheran, and '*Reformed', for Calvinist, were often contrasted with each other in the 16th cent.). Protestantism, therefore, originally had a much more positive sense than its modern anti-Roman flavour would suggest. This shift in meaning has led to the repudiation of the term by those non-Roman Christians who wish to emphasize their adherence to traditional 'Catholic' beliefs.

*Lutheranism, *Zwinglianism, and *Calvinism would now all be regarded as Protestant and there are, in fact, a large number of denominations, with a considerable variety of beliefs, which are in a general sense Protestant. Whether the C of E is Protestant is disputed. Strong Calvinist tendencies were intermingled with older traditions preserved after the Reformation but the term Protestant is not used in any edition of the BCP. In the 17th cent. it was used, e.g. by *Charles I in affirming his adherence to the Protestant religion, as a term opposed to both Roman Catholicism and Puritanism. After the Restoration its use was generally extended to include Nonconformists. There have always been some Anglicans anxious to insist that the C of E is not Protestant. The *Oxford Movement, which inherited much of the traditional orthodoxy of 18th cent. *High Churchmen, left its mark upon Anglicanism as a whole, not merely in the prevalence of more 'Catholic' forms of worship and practice, but in the existence of a strong movement within the communion which is concerned to preserve the traditional teaching of historical Christianity.

Because Protestantism has become such an inclusive term it is difficult to provide a precise definition in terms of beliefs; but the acceptance of the Bible as the sole source of revealed truth, the doctrine of *justification by faith alone, and the universal priesthood of all believers are characteristic. This last principle has led Protestants to reject any kind of two-tier spirituality (clerical/monastic and lay) and a lay spirituality based upon Bible-reading and a high standard of personal morality has been the norm. How the basic principles are worked out in terms of worship and devotion have varied considerably. Some have retained a liturgical form of worship while others (particularly the *Quakers) abandoned any formal structure. Lutherans and *Methodists have been characterized by the singing of hymns (and have written some great hymns), while Calvinists were, until quite late in the 19th cent., vigorously opposed to the singing of anything other than Psalms or metrical versions of them. In general Protestant worship has been marked by the participation of the whole congregation, by the public reading of the Bible in the vernacular, and by an emphasis on preaching. Celebration of the Eucharist has been infrequent in many Protestant churches, probably because the reformers were unwilling to encourage non-communicating attendance and the medieval habit of infrequent communion was impossible to break. On the other hand, in the 20th cent., the influence of the *Liturgical Movement has led to more frequent celebration of the Eucharist and to a renewal of liturgical forms of worship. One of the effects of both the emphasis on Bible-reading in personal devotional life and the importance of preaching in worship, has been the development of the principle of private judgement in interpreting the Bible which, in turn, has often encouraged an intense individualism. Charismatic, *Pentecostal Christianity has been an important element in modern Protestantism.

In the 18th cent. the influence of the *Enlightenment and a new sense of history (and particularly of the thought of G. E. *Lessing and I. *Kant) began to dissolve some of the earlier Protestant certainties, raising questions about the literal understanding of Scripture, emphasizing reason above revealed religion, and stressing the importance of an interior and subjective religion of the spirit. In the 19th cent. academic Protestantism was dominated by F. D. E. *Schleiermacher who contrived a systematic presentation of Christianity based upon feeling of absolute dependence (God-consciousness). Although Schleiermacher and G. W. F. *Hegel were each sharply opposed to the other's ideas, later theologians tended to combine Schleiermacher's subjectivism and Hegel's philosophical idealism to produce an unexciting, supposedly entirely rational religion which tended to be supportive of both State and society. This was, in turn, vigorously criticized by S. A. *Kierkegaard in *Denmark, though his ideas were not widely felt in Protestant theology until the beginning of the 20th cent. From 1870 to c.1920 the tone of Liberal Protestantism was set by the thought of A. *Ritschl, who reacted against Schleiermacher's emphasis on feeling, revived Kant's moralism and metaphysical scepticism, and strongly encouraged historical research. Among his followers was A. *Harnack, probably the most influential Protestant theologian at the turn of the century, whose influence was not confined to his religious ideas (that the earliest, 'simplest' Christianity preached the fatherhood of God and the brotherhood of humanity) and whose scholarly historical labours on early Christianity called in question many of the confident assumptions then made about the development of orthodox doctrine. Some scholars, like E. *Troeltsch, came to believe that the particularity of Christianity posed fundamental problems about its claim to be, alone amongst the religions of the world, the final and absolute truth. Others came to feel that the whole post-Enlightenment assumption that religious truth, like other truth, could be reached by the enquiring, questioning processes of human reason, was unsound. If God was to be known at all, it must be because He chose to reveal Himself.

The so-called theology of crisis, of which K. *Barth's *Römerbrief* (1919) was the beginning, was a marked reaction against the Liberal Protestantism of the 19th cent. Barth's own development led him to attempt a comprehensive restatement of classical dogmatic Protestantism founded upon his conviction that a belief in the Trinity necessarily followed from an acceptance of the premise that God reveals Himself. Others, notably R. *Bultmann, combined Reformation theology with the historical scepticism of the '*Religionsgeschichtliche Schule' and promoted Old and New Testament theologies more critical than the '*Biblical Theology' inspired by Barth. In Germany this hermeneutical interest was eclipsed by a revived concern with politics and society, while in America various secular theologies became briefly fashionable in the 1960s, including the '*Death of God' movement. After the *Holocaust in Nazi Germany Christian thinkers have been forced to face uncomfortable questions about incipient anti-Semitism within traditional teaching and about the action of a loving God in a world in which there is such cruelty and suffering. Among the most prominent Protestant theologians of the late 20th cent. are W. *Pannenberg, E. Jüngel (b. 1934), and J. *Moltmann (who has popularized an ecumenical and 'ecological' theology and is sensitive to the demand for *Feminist Theology).

In America Protestantism developed in a somewhat different way from that of Europe. It grew out of the 17th-cent. *Puritanism of New England, the 18th-cent. *Great

Awakening, and the *revivalism which inspired the Second Great Awakening in the early 19th cent. These elements fashioned a peculiar mixture of Calvinism and *Arminianism. In this form Protestantism has exerted a considerable impact on American culture. Thus Protestants were strongly motivated to reform society; this aspect was demonstrated in the anti-*slavery, *temperance, *Social Gospel, and Civil Rights movements. They concentrated just as intently on the moral and psychological improvement of individuals. American Protestantism also advanced the notion of rugged pioneer individualism and *laissez-faire* capitalism, promoted the 19th-cent. belief in American 'manifest destiny' to subdue and civilize the N. American continent, and in the later 20th cent. was active in championing human rights abroad and individual rights at home. American Protestantism's religious tolerance has bequeathed a proliferation of denominations, fostering a reductionist approach to the W. Church's historic liturgy and body of doctrine. Not all Protestants were in accord with these developments. Over against the prevailing Reformed religious ethos, some immigrant groups from Europe, e.g. certain Lutherans, have struggled to employ traditional forms of worship, piety, and theology, which were long held suspect by the Protestant mainstream as too Catholic and European.

The writings of many of the early leaders are pr. in the *Corpus Reformatorum*, ed. C. G. Bretschneider, H. E. Bindseil, and others (Halle, etc., 1834 ff.). Collection of the Protestant confessions tr. into Eng. in P. *Schaff, *The History of the Creeds*, 3 (1878), with discussion in vol. 1 (1878), pp. 203–930. R. W. *Dale, *Protestantism: Its Ultimate Principle* (1874). O. Ritschl, *Dogmengeschichte des Protestantismus: Grundlagen und Grundzüge der theologischen Gedanken- und Lehrbildung in den protestantischen Kirchen* (4 vols., 1908–27). E. Troeltsch, *Die Bedeutung des Protestantismus für die Entstehung der modernen Welt* (1906; 2nd edn., Beiheft 2 der Historische Zeitschrift, 1924; Eng. tr., *Protestantism and Progress*, 1912); id., *Die Soziallehren der christlichen Kirchen und Gruppen* (1912), pp. 427–986; Eng. tr., vol. 2 (1931). K. *Heim, *Das Wesen des evangelischen Christentums* (1925; Eng. tr., 1935). R. H. Tawney, *Religion and the Rise of Capitalism: A Historical Study* (Holland Memorial Lectures for 1922; 1926). K. Barth, *Die protestantische Theologie im 19. Jahrhundert: Ihre Vorgeschichte und ihre Geschichte* (Zurich, 1947; Eng. tr., 1972). P. *Tillich, *The Protestant Era* (Chicago, Ill., 1948; London, 1951). E. Hirsch, *Geschichte der neuern evangelischen Theologie* (5 vols., Gütersloh, 1949–54). J. Dillenberger and C. Welch, *Protestant Christianity interpreted through its Development* (New York, 1954). C. W. Kegley, *Protestantism in Transition* (New York, 1965). E. G. Léonard, *Histoire générale du protestantisme* (3 vols., 1961–4; 2nd edn., 1980 ff.; Eng. tr., 1965 ff.). M. E. Marty, *Protestantism* [1972]. C. Welch, *Protestant Thought in the Nineteenth Century* (2 vols., New Haven, Conn., and London, 1972-[85]). W. R. Ward, *The Protestant Evangelical Awakening* (Cambridge, 1992). E. Wolf and others in *RGG* (3rd edn.), 5 (1961), cols. 648–66; H. Fischer and F. W. Graf in *TRE*, 27 (1997), pp. 542–80, both s.v. 'Protestantismus'.

Protevangelium. A modern title of the apocryphal Infancy Narrative, also known as the Book of *James (q.v.). It was so described by G. Postel (d. 1581), whose Lat. of it was published by T. *Bibliander as *Protoevangelion Jacobi, fratris Domini, de natalibus Jesu Christi, et Virginis Mariae; cum Evangelio vitaque S. Marci Evangelistae* (Basle, 1552).

I. Backus, 'Guillaume Postel, Théodore Bibliander et le "Protévangile de Jacques"', *Apocrypha*, 6 (1995), pp. 7–65.

prothesis (Gk. πρόθεσις). In the E. Church the word is used (1) for the table on which the solemn preparation (*Proskomide) of the Eucharistic gifts takes place; (2) for the chamber to the left of the apse of the church, on the opposite side to the *diaconicon, in which the table just mentioned stands; and (3) for the Proskomide (q.v.) itself.

Proto-Luke. The name given by B. H. *Streeter to an early draft which he supposed St *Luke had composed from '*Q' and materials not found elsewhere ('L') before adding an infancy narrative and material drawn from Mk. Despite some initial following in England, this theory is now generally abandoned.

B. H. Streeter, 'Fresh Light on the Synoptic Problem', *Hibbert Journal*, 20 (1921–2), pp. 103–12; id., *The Four Gospels* (1924), ch. 8.

Protomartyr (i.e. First Martyr). A title commonly given to St *Stephen (Acts 7: 60), and also occasionally to the first martyrs of different countries, e.g. to St *Alban, the 'Protomartyr of England'.

protonotary apostolic. A member of the college of notaries attached to the Papal court. The office, which dates back to very early times, has undergone frequent changes. Until recently there were four grades, the highest being limited to seven members. In 1968, by the *motu proprio* 'Pontificalis Domus', the grades were reduced to two, *de numero* and *supra numerum*. The latter is purely honorary.

Proverbs, Book of. A poetical Book of the OT, part of the '*Hagiographa', and usually placed second after the *Psalms. The Book is divided into eight clearly marked sections: (1) chs. 1–9, headed 'The Proverbs of Solomon', comprising a series of counsels given by Divine Wisdom, and ending in a description of two feasts, of wisdom which leads to understanding (9: 1–6), and of folly which leads to '*Sheol' (9: 13–16); (2) 10: 1–22: 16, also headed 'The Proverbs of Solomon', consisting of simple unconnected distichs enunciating particular rules of conduct; (3) 22: 17–24: 22, entitled 'The Words of the Wise', consisting of small groups of practical counsels, more developed than the preceding ones; (4) 24: 23–34, 'The Sayings of the Wise', containing maxims of behaviour to one's neighbour; (5) chs. 25–9, 'Proverbs of Solomon, which the men of Hezekiah king of Judah copied out', also chiefly distichs but more popular in style than the two former Solomonic sections; (6) ch. 30, 'The Words of Agar'; (7) 31: 1–9, 'The Words of King Lemuel'; and (8) 31: 10–31, an acrostic poem in praise of the virtuous woman.

As it stands, the Book represents a compilation of various collections of proverbs, stemming from widely different periods and places, while the separate collections contain individual sayings of even more diverse origin. Section (3), for example, appears to be a variant version of the Egyptian Teaching of Amen-em-ope (which dates from c.1000 BC), though the precise relationship between the two is difficult to determine. It is possible that one or other of the sayings in the Book, or even of the small collections presupposed in the larger collections, may go back to *Solomon, but the tradition that he was the compiler of the Book is prob. best explained by the fact that he was known himself to have uttered proverbs and to have made his court a centre of Eastern wisdom (1 Kgs. 4: 29–34; 10: 23–4).

In the NT Proverbs is quoted as Scripture in Rom. 3: 15 and Jas. 4: 6. It was also a favourite source of quotations among the Fathers, and the passage in ch. 8, in which *Wisdom seems to be *hypostasized, was one of the key texts in the *Arian controversy. The Book as a whole, however, was little commented on either in antiquity or in the Middle Ages, but it was the subject of commentaries by P. *Melanchthon (1526), Card. T. *Cajetan (1542), and J.-B. *Bossuet (1693). Passages from the Book (esp. from the poem about the virtuous woman, 31: 10–31) are regularly used in the Roman liturgy. It is read daily at Vespers in Lent in the Byzantine rite.

Comm. by W. O. E. Oesterley (West. Comm., 1929), B. Gemser (HAT, Reihe 1, Abt. 16; 1937; 2nd edn., 1963), A. Barucq, SDB (Sources bibliques, 1964), R. B. Y. Scott (Anchor Bible, on Prov. and Eccles., 1965, pp. 3–187), W. McKane (London, 1970), R. N. Whybray (Camb. Bib., NEB, 1972), and O. Plöger (Biblischer Kommentar, Altes Testament, 17; Neukirchen, 1984). G. Boström, *Proverbiastudien: Die Weisheit und das Fremde Weib in Spr. 1–9* (Lunds Universitets Årsskrift, NF, Avd. 1, Bd. 30, Nr. 3; 1935); R. N. Whybray, *Wisdom in Proverbs: The Concept of Wisdom in Proverbs 1–9* (Studies in Biblical Theology, 45; 1965); C. Kayatz, *Studien zu Proverbien 1–9* (Wissenschaftliche Monographien zum Alten und Neuen Testament, 22; 1966). Soggin, pp. 445–8, with bibl. See also works cited s.v. WISDOM.

Providentissimus Deus (1893). The encyclical on the study of the Holy Scriptures issued by Pope *Leo XIII on 18 Nov. 1893. Its purpose was to give official guidance, esp. to the clergy, in the new situation in biblical studies brought about by recent discoveries in archaeology and literary criticism. While stressing the importance of the study of the new evidence, it condemned the use made of it in some quarters (with a clear ref. to such scholars as A. F. *Loisy and M. *d'Hulst, though they were not mentioned by name). It expressly reaffirmed the pronouncements of the *Tridentine and First *Vatican Councils on biblical inspiration and on the scriptural text and asserted that the whole of Scripture was written 'at the dictation of the Holy Spirit' (*Spiritu Sancto dictante*). Both conservatives and liberals appealed to the document; but in the next decade, owing to the spread of *Modernism (q.v.), the encyclical was increasingly interpreted in official quarters in a conservative sense. See also BIBLICAL COMMISSION.

Text pr. in *ASS* 26 (1893–4), pp. 269–92. Extracts in Denzinger and Hünermann (37th edn., 1991), pp. 884–91 (nos. 3280–94). A. M. Ambrozic in *NCE* 11 (1967), pp. 922 f., s.v.

province. A group of *dioceses, territorially contiguous, forming an ecclesiastical unit, so called because such groups were originally coincident with the provinces of the Roman Empire. See also ARCHBISHOP; METROPOLITAN; PRIMATE.

provincial. An official of a religious order subject to the superior-general. He exercises authority over all houses of the order within a given area, though a house may sometimes be geographically in one province, but subject to the provincial of another. The office of provincial, unknown to the old monastic orders, came into being with the more centralized *Mendicant orders, and from them was taken over by the majority of modern orders and congregations.

The provincial is normally either elected by the provincial chapter, subject to the approval of the superior-general, or is appointed by the superior-general. He holds office for a term of years, usually three to six, never for life. His chief duty is to make regular visitations of the houses of his jurisdiction and to supervise the life of the religious and the administration of their property.

Provisors, Statutes of. Four laws passed in England in the 14th cent. to check the practice of Papal 'provision', or nomination to vacant benefices over the head of the ordinary patron.

The first, the Provisors Act 1351, provided that 'the King and other lords shall present unto Benefices of their own, and not the Bishop of Rome'. The second, passed in 1353, imposed the penalties of '*Praemunire for suing in a foreign realm, or impeaching of Judgment given [*sc.* in the English courts]'. The third, passed in 1365, confirmed the law of 1351. The fourth, passed in 1389, enacted that benefices accepted contrary to the earlier Statutes of Provisors should be forfeited, and that proceedings should be taken against anyone attempting to enforce a provision by summons or excommunication, and against any prelate enforcing such a provision.

Despite these Statutes, the practice of provision continued down to the *Reformation, and was revived during the reign of *Mary.

See also PRAEMUNIRE.

Text, with Eng. tr., in A. J. Stephens, *The Statutes Relating to the Ecclesiastical and Eleemosynary Institutions of England, Wales, Ireland, India, and the Colonies* (1845), pp. 58–66, 67–70, and 84–7. Eng. tr. of the last, reciting in full the Statute of 1351, also in Gee and Hardy, pp. 112–21 (no. 39), mainly repr. in Bettenson (2nd edn., 1963), pp. 233–9. For general background see G. Barraclough, *Papal Provisions* (1935). F. Cheyette, 'Kings, Courts, Cures, and Sinecures: The Statute of Provisors and the Common Law', *Traditio*, 19 (1963), pp. 295–349, with further refs. G. Crosse in *DECH*, pp. 476 f.

provost (Lat. *praepositus*, Ger. *Probst*). In early Christian usage the official next in dignity to the abbot of a monastery, but now esp. the head of an ecclesiastical chapter. In England the title is used in the newer dioceses (e.g. Bradford, Derby, Portsmouth) of the head of the cathedral chapter where the cathedral is also a parish church and the provost is thus also an incumbent with cure of souls. The title is used in a non-ecclesiastical sense for the heads of certain colleges, e.g. of Oriel, Queen's, and Worcester Colleges at Oxford, King's College at Cambridge, and Eton College.

Prudentius, the common title of Aurelius Prudentius Clemens (348–c.410), Latin poet and hymn-writer. A Spaniard by birth, he practised at the bar and had a successful career in civil administration. The retirement of his later life was occupied in devout exercises and Christian writings. His didactic poems, 'Apotheosis' (on the theology of the Incarnation), 'Hamartigenia' (against *Marcion), and 'Contra Symmachum' (on the occasion of a temporary recrudescence of paganism), exhibit his distinction in abstract thought as well as in the imitation of classical models. The 'Psychomachia', an allegorical description of the struggle of the Christian soul and of the Christian Church, exercised a profound influence on later writers. These poems are written mainly in hexameters. His lyrical poems or 'hymns', rarely less than 100 lines long, are likewise composed in classical metres; extracts from them are found in most W. breviaries. One collection, the *Cathemerinon* (καθημερινῶν), consists of hymns designed for daily use; another, the *Peristephanon* (περὶ στεφάνων), sings the praises of a number of Spanish and Italian martyrs.

Of the older edns., the best is that of F. Arévalo (2 vols., Rome, 1788–9), with extended comm.; repr. in J. P. Migne, *PL* 59 and 60. Crit. edns. by J. Bergman (CSEL 61; 1926) and M. P. Cunningham (CCSL 126; 1966). Text with Fr. tr., also ed. M. Lavarenne in 'Collection des Universités de France' (4 vols., 1943–51); text with Eng. tr. by H. J. Thomson (2 vols., Loeb, 1949–53). Further Eng. tr. by M. C. Eagan, CCVI (Fathers of the Church, 43 and 52; 1962–5). R. J. Deferrari and J. Marshall Campbell, *A Concordance of Prudentius* (Cambridge, Mass., 1932). A. S. Walpole, *Early Latin Hymns* (1922), pp. 115–48. A. Puech, *Prudence* (1888); M. Lavarenne, *Étude sur la langue du poète Prudence* (1933), with bibl. I. Lana, *Due capitoli prudenziani: La biografia, la cronologia delle opere, la poetica* (Verba Seniorum, NS 2; 1962). L. Padovese, *La cristologia di Aurelio Clemente Prudenzio* (Analecta Gregoriana, 219; Rome, 1980). J. Fontaine, *Naissance de la poésie dans l'Occident chrétien* (Paris, 1981), pp. 143–60, 177–227, with bibl., pp. 297–301. A.-M. Palmer, *Prudentius on the Martyrs* (Oxford, 1989). A. di Berardino in Quasten (cont.), *Patrology*, 4 (1986), pp. 281–96. A. Kurfess in *PW* 23 (pt. 1; 1957), cols. 1039–71, s.v. 'Prudentius (2)'; C. Codoñer in *Dict. Sp.* 12 (pt. 2; 1986), cols. 2484–91, s.v. 'Prudence (1)'.

Prudentius, Galindo (d. 861), Bp. of Troyes. He was a native of Spain, became a chaplain at the court of *Louis the Pious, and, *c.*843, Bp. of Troyes. He played an important part in the controversy on *predestination between *Hincmar of Reims and the monk, *Gottschalk, defending the *Augustinianism of the latter, and denying the general saving will of God. In his 'Epistola ad Hincmarum' he taught the 'Augustinian' doctrine of the double predestination and, in 852, wrote a treatise 'De Praedestinatione contra Joannem Scotum', i.e. against John Scottus *Erigena, whom Hincmar had called to his aid. Acc. to Hincmar, he signed the four anti-Augustinian propositions of the Synod of *Quiercy (853). In 856, however, he wrote his 'Epistola Tractoria', addressed to Abp. Venilo of Sens, in which he opposed to the decisions of Quiercy four counter-propositions, teaching Augustinian doctrine of the strictest type. Prudentius also wrote a continuation of the 'Annales Bertiniani' for the years 835–61, valuable for the history of the Frankish Empire.

His writings on the predestination controversy were first pub. by G. Mauguin at Paris in 1650. Crit. edns. of his continuation of the 'Annales Bertiniani' by G. H. Pertz in *MGH*, Scriptores, 1 (1826), pp. 429–54, and by F. Grat, J. Vielliard, and S. Clémencet, *Annales de Saint-Bertin* (Société de l'histoire de France, 1964), pp. 17–84. Collected edn. in J. P. Migne, *PL* 115. 965–1458. J. Girgensohn, *Prudentius und die bertinianischen Annalen* (Riga, 1875). Manitius, 1, esp. pp. 344–8. H. Peltier in *DTC* 13 (pt. 1; 1936), cols. 1079–84, s.v. 'Prudence de Troyes'. See also works cited s.v. HINCMAR, esp. those of J. Devisse.

Prymer. See PRIMER.

Prynne, William (*c.*1602–69), *Puritan controversialist. Educated at Bath Grammar School and Oriel College, Oxford, he was admitted at Lincoln's Inn in 1621 and later

became a barrister. As a strong and unbending Puritan, he was soon in conflict with the *High Church party. In 1626 he published his first book, *The Perpetuity of a Regenerate Man's Estate*. A violent attack on the stage in *Histriomastix* ('1633' [1632]), thought to contain veiled attacks on both *Charles I and *Henrietta Maria, led to his sentence by the Star Chamber on 17 February 1634 to imprisonment for life, a fine of £5,000, expulsion from Lincoln's Inn, the loss of his university degree, and the pillory, where he was to lose both his ears. The whole sentence, except the permanence of the imprisonment and the fine, was carried out. His attacks on the 'Declaration of *Sports' led in 1637 to a fresh sentence by the Star Chamber and he was imprisoned first at Caernarvon and then in Mont Orgueil Castle in Jersey; but the unpopularity of ship-money and the metropolitical visitation had changed public opinion and Prynne now met with wide sympathy. When the Long Parliament met in 1640 he was liberated and defended the right of taking up arms against the King, notably in his *The Sovereign Power of Parliaments and Kingdoms* (1643). He also carried on a literary warfare with W. *Laud. On the other hand, his ideal of the supremacy of State over Church put him out of sympathy with the *Independents, whom he attacked in *Twelve Considerable Serious Questions touching Church Government* (1644); and he hated the notion of toleration. In 1648 he issued *The Levellers Levelled*, a defence of the House of Lords. Eventually on 7 Nov. 1648 he obtained a seat (Newport, Cornwall) in the Commons and unexpectedly argued for conciliation with the King and opposed his execution. In consequence he was included in 'Pride's Purge' (6 Dec.) and imprisoned. On 1 Jan. 1649 he published *A Brief Memento to the Present Unparliamentary Junto*. Later in the year he attacked the new tax imposed by the Commonwealth in *A Legal Vindication of the Liberties of England* and embarked on a large-scale work against the new Parliament; and in 1650 he was again imprisoned, without a trial. After his release (1653) he ceased from further attacks on O. *Cromwell's régime and wrote against the Papists and *Quakers. To his annoyance he was excluded from the Rump Parliament (1659) and fearlessly criticized it in a long series of controversial writings. He eventually resumed his seat in Parliament on 21 February 1660 and three days later brought in the bill for the dissolution preparatory to *Charles II's restoration. Shortly after his return, Charles appointed him Keeper of the Tower Records. His strong *Presbyterianism, however, soon brought him into conflict with the reviving *Anglicanism, which he attacked in a long series of publications, among them *A Short, Sober, Pacific Examination of Exuberances in the Common Prayer* (1661) and *A Moderate, Seasonable Apology for Tender Consciences touching Not Bowing at the Name of Jesus* (1662). But he continued to take a prominent part in Parliamentary affairs until his death. He also wrote extensively in his last years, defending on historical grounds the subjection of the clergy to the Crown.

S. R. Gardiner (ed.), *Documents Relating to the Proceedings against William Prynne in 1634 and 1637* (Camden Society, NS 18; 1877), with the beginning of a Life by J. Bruce (d. 1869) [up to 1624], pp. i–xxxv, and list of Prynne's works by Bruce, pp. 101–18. Modern studies by E. W. Kirby (Cambridge, Mass., 1931), with list of Prynne's works, pp. 194–207, and other bibl., pp. 207–19; and W. M. Lamont (London, 1963), also with bibl. M. W.

Helms and I. Cassidy in B. H. Henning (ed.), *The History of Parliament: The House of Commons 1660–1690*, 3 (1983), pp. 295–8; R. Spalding, *Contemporaries of Bulstrode Whitelocke 1605–1675* (British Academy Records of Social and Economic History, NS 14; Oxford [1990]), pp. 276–8. C. H. Firth in *DNB* 46 (1896), pp. 432–7.

Psalms, Book of (Gk. ψαλμοί, 'songs, accompanied by string music'), in the Hebrew Bible the first of the '*Hagiographa'. The Book contains 150 Psalms, variously enumerated. By combining Pss. 9 and 10 of the Hebrew *Massoretic text (followed by the BCP version, AV, and other non-Catholic English Bibles), the Gk. and Lat. (Vulg.) versions, up to Psalm 114, remain one number behind the Hebrew counting (e.g. Ps. 90 AV is Ps. 89 Vulg.); Pss. 114 and 115 (Heb.) are again conflated in Gk. and Lat., but as the following Ps. 116 is divided in two, the Gk. and Lat. numeration is again one behind that of the Heb. up to Ps. 147, which is divided in two in Gk. and Lat. Hence only the first eight and the last three Psalms agree in both enumerations.

The Psalms are traditionally divided into five Books, probably after the model of the Books of the *Pentateuch, namely 1–41, 42–72, 73–89, 90–106, 107–50, each except the last ending with a doxology. There are clear indications of earlier groupings which point back to independently existing collections, e.g. the concluding notice after 72 ('The prayers of David the son of Jesse are ended'). Similarly Pss. 3–41 are all (except 10, a continuation of 9, and 33) headed 'Of David'; 42–9 (except 43, a continuation of 42) 'Of the Sons of Korah'; and 73–83 (also 50) 'Of Asaph'. Evidence from the *Dead Sea Scrolls shows that the order of the Psalms was not firmly fixed until the Christian era.

The rubrics in the Massoretic text and in the Septuagint make it clear that in its present form the Psalter is essentially a liturgical book; it has often been described as the 'hymn-book of the Second *Temple' (a phrase coined by J. *Wellhausen). Being entirely composed of poems, the Book provides many excellent examples of the Hebrew device of *parallelism. Many attempts have been made to discover a definite metre in the Psalms, but with little success. Poetical conceits, such as refrains and acrostics, are frequent. Of 'Alphabetical Psalms', Ps. 119 is the most elaborate; it has 22 sections, one for each letter of the alphabet, and each of the eight lines in one of these sections begins with that letter.

The popular belief that *David was the author of the whole Psalter can no longer be sustained. It was held by many of the Latin Fathers, e.g. St *Ambrose and St *Augustine, and not seriously questioned during the Middle Ages or by the Reformers, except J. *Calvin; but it had been strongly opposed by St *Jerome. Most modern scholars believe that the Psalms come from a variety of authors and are of widely differing dates. The 20th cent. has, however, seen a reaction against the view, prevalent in the later 19th cent., that few, if any, of the Psalms are pre-exilic, and no serious scholar today would accept the thesis of B. *Duhm that the bulk of the Psalter belongs to the *Maccabean period. Many of the Psalms prob. come from the early years of the Monarchy and in their original form they may have been used in the worship of the First Temple. Uncertainty also prevails as to the date at which the various collections were made, but they are probably all post-exilic.

Traditionally the Psalms were held to be religious lyrics covering the whole range of the relations between God and man. The eternal, immutable, and omnipotent God is the Creator of the universe which He upholds and governs by His Divine Providence. Himself all-holy, He demands from His creatures holiness and penitence (see SEVEN PENITENTIAL PSALMS), but His supreme justice is tempered by His mercy. The Psalmists' zeal for the right often finds expression in a passionate desire to see God's vengeance on the wicked (see IMPRECATORY PSALMS). The conception of individual life after death is mainly confined to the shadowy realm of *Sheol, though a brighter hope at times emerges (Pss. 16: 9–11; 49: 15; 73: 23 f.). The nation's hope for the future is centred on a scion of the Davidic line, described as the great Priest-King (Ps. 110) and God's son (Ps. 2), who will cast down his enemies (Ps. 89) and unite the whole world in his worship (Ps. 22).

During the past 100 years this traditional exegesis has been challenged at several points. R. Smend and others maintained that the 'I' of the Psalms commonly refers not to an individual but to Israel as a nation, while for S. *Mowinckel the evil men about whom the Psalmists complain were frequently sorcerers and many of the Psalms themselves a kind of counter-charm. Such attempts to locate the Psalms in the corporate life of the nation rather than in the private spirituality of the individual have been influenced by comparative evidence from other ancient Near Eastern cultures, and by the methods of *Form Criticism pioneered by H. *Gunkel. Mowinckel's attention to both led him to argue that the so-called 'Accession Psalms', in which Yahweh is described as a king, find their origin in an otherwise unknown feast of the Enthronement of Yahweh, held to have been celebrated in Israel as a 'New Year Festival'; the grounds for the existence of such a festival are based on supposed parallels in Babylonian literature. Mowinckel's thesis has been severely criticized from many points of view, but continues to dominate scholarly discussion of the Psalms.

In the Christian Church the Psalter has been used both in public worship and private prayer from very early times. The Gospels record that Christ applied to Himself the metaphor of the 'stone which the builders rejected' (118: 22) and that on the Cross He voiced both His desolation and His supreme act of surrender in the words of Pss. 22: 1 and 31: 5 [BCP 31: 6]. Both St *Paul and the author of Heb. constantly see the Psalmists' aspirations fulfilled in Christ.

The patristic tradition follows the same lines as the NT. Jerome, Ambrose, and many others recommend the regular use of the Psalms, and Augustine, in his long commentary, finds Christ or His Church prefigured in almost every Psalm. As a book of devotion it has retained its position through the centuries. In the Divine Office of the RC Church, until the recent reordering of the Divine *Office, the whole Psalter was recited every week; in the C of E it has traditionally been said each month; while in the E. Church it is recited every week (twice a week in Lent). Both Continental Protestant and English Nonconformist piety have been nourished on it. The Psalms were an integral part of the spiritual life of men as widely apart as *Benedictines and *Puritans, M. *Luther and St *Francis

Xavier, Charles *Wesley and J. H. *Newman. See also PSALTER.

Comms. by B. Duhm (KHAT 14, 1899; 2nd edn., 1922); H. Gunkel (HKAT 2. Abt., Bd. 2, 4th edn., 1925–6); A. Weiser (Das Alte Testament Deutsch, 14–15; 5th edn., 1959; Eng. tr., 1962); H. J. Kraus (2 vols., Biblischer Kommentar, Altes Testament, 15; Neukirchen, 1960; 5th edn., 1978; Eng. tr., Minneapolis, 1988–9); M. Dahood, SJ (Anchor Bible, 3 vols., 1966–70); A. A. Anderson (New Cent. Bib., 2 vols. [1972]); J. W. Rogerson and J. W. McKay (Camb. Bib., NEB, 2 vols., 1977); and, on Pss. 1–50, P. C. Craigie (Word Biblical Comm. 19; Waco, Tex. [1983]), on Pss. 50–100 by M. E. Tate (ibid., 20; Dallas [1990]), and on Pss. 101–50, L. C. Allen (ibid. 21; Waco [1983]).

J. A. Sanders, *The Psalms Scroll of Qumrân Cave 11 (11QPs*)* (Discoveries in the Judaean Desert, 4; Oxford, 1965), S. Mowinckel, *Psalmenstudien* (6 parts, Kristiania, 1921–4); id., *Offersang og Sangoffer* (1951; rev. Eng. tr., 2 vols., Oxford, 1962); A. R. Johnson, *Sacral Kingship in Ancient Israel* (Cardiff, 1955); C. Westermann, *Die Loben Gottes in den Psalmen* (Göttingen, 1961; Eng. tr., 1965), H.-J. Kraus, *Gottesdienst in Israel* (2nd edn., Munich, 1962; Eng. tr., *Worship in Israel*, Oxford, 1966), *passim*; J. H. Eaton, *Kingship and the Psalms* (1976; 2nd edn., Sheffield, 1986); id., 'The Psalms and Israelite Worship', in G. W. Anderson (ed.), *Tradition and Interpretation* (Oxford, 1979), pp. 238–73; A. Aejmelaeus, *The Traditional Prayer in the Psalms* (Beihefte zur *ZNTW*, 167; 1986, pp. 1–119). S. E. Gillingham, *The Poems and Psalms of the Hebrew Bible* (Oxford Bible Series, 1994), esp. pp. 173–275. J. Day, *Psalms* (Old Testament Guides; Sheffield [1990]).

Psalms, imprecatory. See IMPRECATORY PSALMS.

Psalms, metrical. See METRICAL PSALTERS.

Psalms of Solomon. See SOLOMON, PSALMS OF.

Psalter. The term denotes: (1) the biblical Book of *Psalms as used, in appropriate translations, in the worship of the Church, and (2) the actual book containing the Psalms for such use.

(1a) *In the Western Church.* The earliest Latin Psalters were translated from the *Septuagint. The most ancient complete text of the *Old Latin Psalter is preserved in the Verona Psalter; the manuscript (Verona Capitular Library 1 (i)) dates from the 6th–7th cent., but the text was clearly used by St *Augustine in his Commentary on the Psalms. St *Jerome, in his Preface to the *Gallican Psalter, states that he had earlier worked on a translation of the Psalms from the Septuagint and this work has been traditionally equated with the *Roman Psalter (q.v.); but the identification has been largely abandoned. About 392 Jerome made a fresh translation of the Psalms from the *Hexaplaric text of the Septuagint (the Gallican Psalter, q.v.) and *c*.400 he made a further one from the Hebrew (the 'Psalterium iuxta Hebraeos' or 'Hebrew Psalter'). Conservatism in the practice of worship prevented this last Psalter from ever replacing the older version in public use; indeed, even in the *Vulgate the Gallican Psalter was ultimately preferred, although in many medieval manuscripts all three Psalters, Roman, Gallican, and Hebrew, are set out in parallel columns. In the *Breviary the Gallican Psalter was replaced in 1945 by a new Latin translation of the Psalms made direct from the Hebrew. The text in the 1971 Breviary, however, is an eclectic one which seeks to combine fidelity to the Hebrew with some of the felicities of style of the Vulgate. The vernacular versions of the Psalter

used in modern RC liturgy are normally based on the Hebrew text, as the Second *Vatican Council recommended that they should be.

The version of the Psalms in the BCP, which is almost identical with that of the '*Great Bible' (1539), was based on M. *Coverdale's translation from the Vulgate, i.e. from the Gallican Psalter; it thus embodies many Septuagintal readings not found in the Hebrew. The authors of the 'Revised Psalter' (1964) attempted to preserve the literary character of Coverdale's work while basing their translation on the Hebrew text. The version in the ASB is a fresh translation from the Hebrew into modern English, commissioned by the Liturgical Commission of the General *Synod in 1972 and published in 1977. Other modern Anglican liturgies contain new translations from the Hebrew.

(1b) *In the Eastern Church.* Greek-speaking Christians use the version of the Psalms in the Septuagint, and this formed the basis of the translation of the Psalter used in the Slavonic Churches (though there is evidence to suggest the influence of the Latin Psalter on the earliest Slavonic translations). The Syrian Churches used, and in some areas still use, the version of the Psalms from the *Peshitta, which is a translation from the Hebrew (though its numeration of the Psalms follows the Hebrew only up to Ps. 113, adopting the divisions of the LXX from Ps. 116). In most modern Orthodox Churches, where the Psalter is used in the vernacular, there is a preference for a translation made from the Septuagint.

(2) The book containing the Psalms for use in worship, in some instances elaborately illuminated. In the W., the Psalms were commonly arranged according to the requirements of the Divine *Office. Psalters thus often also contained the corresponding *antiphons, the *canticles recited in the Office, and other matter such as hymns, litanies, and prayers. When their contents were later incorporated into the Breviary, separate Psalters generally fell into disuse. In the E separate Psalters are still common. Here the Psalms are divided into 20 sections (see KATHISMA (1)); the book also contains the nine canticles (q.v.) or 'odes' (appended to Pss. in the LXX), a range of hymns (see KATHISMA (2)), and prayers associated with the recitation of the Psalms in the Office and in private devotion. See also METRICAL PSALTERS.

P. [later B.] *Capelle, *Le Texte du psautier latin en Afrique* (Collectanea Biblica Latina, 4; 1913). R. Weber, OSB (ed.), *Le Psautier romain et les autres anciens psautiers latins* (ibid. 10; 1953); H. de Sainte-Marie, OSB (ed.), *Sancti Hieronymi Psalterium iuxta Hebraeos* (ibid. 11; 1954); C. Estin, *Les Psautiers de Jérôme à la lumière des traductions juives antérieures* (ibid. 15; 1984). A. Allgeier, *Die altlateinischen Psalterien: Prolegomena zu einer Textgeschichte der hieronymianischen Psalmenübersetzungen* (Freiburg, 1928). See also works cited s.v. ROMAN PSALTER.

J. Mateos, SJ, 'La Psalmodie dans le rite byzantin', *Proche-Orient chrétien*, 15 (1965), pp. 107–26. K. Onasch, 'Der Psalter in der byzantinisch-slavischen Orthodoxie', in *Gottes ist der Orient: Festschrift für Prof. D. Dr. Otto Eissfeldt* [1959], pp. 106–28; J. Lépissier, 'La traduction vieux-slave du Psautier', *Revue des études slaves*, 43 (1964), pp. 59–72. H. *Leclercq, OSB, in *DACL* 14 (pt. 2; 1948), cols. 1950–67, s.v. 'Psautier'.

Psalter Collects. Prayers composed with reference to each of the 150 Psalms (and sometimes to each section of Ps. 119 as well). There are indications that in the late antique period some such collects were actually recited after their respective Psalms, e.g. references in *Egeria's account of the Sunday vigils at Jerusalem (24. 9), in *Cassian's description of monastic practice in Egypt (*Inst.* 2. 7), and in the *Regula Magistri* (33 and 55 f.). But the earliest MS evidence for any of the three series of collects published by L. Brou in 1949 goes back only to *c.*795, and there is no reason to think that such whole series were ever used liturgically (except perhaps in *Spain, where a profusion of these prayers has been traced). The nomenclature of 'African', 'Spanish', and 'Roman' series, adopted by Brou, derives from literary analysis of their putative origins, and bears little relation to the MSS in which they appear. Psalter collects continue to be found occasionally, mostly in luxury Psalters, throughout the Middle Ages, and are used in a limited way in some contemporary, esp. RC, liturgies.

The Psalter Collects . . . (Three Series), ed. L. Brou, OSB (using materials collected by A. *Wilmart, OSB) (HBS 83; 1949). Text also pr. by P. Verbraken, OSB, *Oraisons sur les cent cinquante psaumes* (Lex Orandi, 42; 1967), with Fr. tr. and full bibl. R. W. Pfaff, 'Psalter Collects as an Aid to the Classification of Psalters', in E. A. Livingstone (ed.), *Studia Patristica*, 18. 2 (Louvain, 1989), pp. 397–402.

psaltery (Lat. *psalterium*). (1) An ancient and medieval stringed instrument played by plucking the strings with the fingers or a plectrum. (2) An obsolete term for Psalter (2), sometimes used by Victorian liturgiologists.

Psellus, Michael (*c.*1019–*c.*1078), Byzantine philosopher, historian, theologian, and statesman. He was Imperial secretary to Michael V (1041–2), and secretary of state to his successor, Constantine IX (1042–54). A keen enthusiast for the revival of classical learning and esp. *Platonic philosophy, in 1045 he was appointed the first professor of philosophy at the newly founded University of *Constantinople. Having incurred the displeasure of the Emperor, he entered a monastery in 1054, but soon on Constantine's death returned to the court, where he took part in many intrigues until, in 1072, he fell from favour once more and spent the rest of his life in obscurity.

Psellus wrote a large number of treatises on a wide range of subjects as well as many speeches, letters, and poems. His Χρονογραφία remains an important source for the history of the years 976–1077 and was utilized by later historians such as *Anna Comnena and *Zonaras. His chief theological writings are expositions of various biblical books including an exegesis of 72 psalms in verse, a short treatise against the Latin theologians, and a dialogue Περὶ ἐνεργείας δαιμόνων against the *Messalians. His philosophical works include commentaries on the 'Timaeus' of *Plato and on the Περὶ ἑρμηνείας and other writings of *Aristotle.

There is no complete edn. of Psellus' works; many of them (mainly theological and philosophical) repr. from various sources in J. P. Migne, *PG* 122. 477–1358. His Χρονογραφία ('History') and various shorter works and epp., ed. C. N. Sathas, *Bibliotheca Graeca Medii Aevi*, 4–5 (Paris, 1874–6; repr. Athens, 1972). *Scripta Minora* [largely unpub.], ed. E. Kurtz and F. Drexl (Orbis Romanus, 5 and 12; Milan, 1936–41). Crit. edns. of *De Omnifara Doctrina* by L. G. Westerink (Nijmegen, 1948), of various *Oratoria Minora* by A. R. Littlewood (Teub., 1985), of *Orationes hagiographae* by E. A. Fisher (ibid., 1994), of *Orationes panegyricae*

by G. T. Dennis (ibid., 1994); *Philosophica minora*, ed. J. M. Duffy and D. J. O'Meara (2 vols., ibid., 1989–92); *Poemata*, ed. L. G. Westerink (ibid., 1992); and *Theologica*, ed. P. Gautier (ibid., 1989 ff.). Psellus' comm. on the Chaldean Oracles, and other related material, ed., with Fr. tr. and valuable introd., by É. des Places, SJ, *Oracles Chaldaïques* (Collection des Universités de France, 1971), pp. 153–201 and 218–26. Χρονογραφία also ed., with Ital. tr., by S. Impellizzeri and others (Scrittori Greci e Latini, 2 vols., 1984); Eng. tr. by E. R. A. Sewter (London, 1953). *Historia Syntomos* first ed., with Eng. tr., by W. J. Aerts (Corpus Fontium Historiae Byzantinae, 30; 1990). P.-P. Joannou, *Démonologie populaire—démonologie critique au XIe siècle: La vie inédite de S. Auxence par M. Psellos* (Schriften zur Geistesgeschichte des östlichen Europa, 5; Wiesbaden, 1971), pp. 41–150. C. Zervos, *Un Philosophe néoplatonicien du XI* siècle* (1919); P. [P.] Joannou, *Christliche Metaphysik in Byzanz*, 1: *Die Illuminationslehre des Michael Psellos und Joannes Italos* (Studia Patristica et Byzantina, 3; Ettal, 1956); G. Weiss, *Oströmische Beamte im Spiegel der Schriften des Michel Psellos* (Miscellanea Byzantina Monacensia, 16; 1973). N. G. Wilson, *Scholars of Byzantium* (1983), pp. 156–79. Krumbacher, pp. 433–44. M. Jugie, AA, in *DTC* 13 (pt. 1; 1936), cols. 1149–58, s.v. 'Psellos (Michel)'.

Pseudepigrapha. Writings ascribed to some other than their real author, generally with a view to giving them an enhanced authority. The term is used esp. of the pseudonymous Jewish works, dating from the centuries immediately before and after the beginning of the Christian era, which were not included in the Gk. *Canon of the OT. Among these writings are the 'Book of *Enoch', the 'Assumption of *Moses', the later 'Books of *Baruch', and the 'Psalms of *Solomon'. On the other hand, pseudonymous books which occur in the OT or *Apocrypha, e.g. 'the Rest of the Book of *Esther' and the '*Wisdom of Solomon', are by convention not ordinarily reckoned among the Pseudepigrapha.

Collections of these writings, in Eng. tr., with discussions of authorship, date, etc., ed. R. H. *Charles, *The Apocrypha and Pseudepigrapha of the Old Testament*, 2: *Pseudepigrapha* (Oxford, 1913); J. H. Charlesworth, *The Old Testament Pseudepigrapha* (2 vols., 1983–5); H. F. D. Sparks, *The Apocryphal Old Testament* (Oxford, 1984). Eissfeldt, pp. 603–37, with bibl. For further bibl. see also under separate treatises.

Pseudo-Clementines. See CLEMENTINE LITERATURE.

Pseudo-Isidorian Decretals. See FALSE DECRETALS.

psilanthropism (Gk. ψιλὸς ἄνθρωπος, 'a mere man'). The heretical doctrine that Christ was just a man and not God and man in one Person. In the '*Little Labyrinth', quoted by *Eusebius (*HE* 5. 28. 6), *Theodotus the Cobbler is said to have taught that He was a 'mere man' (ψιλὸς ἄνθρωπος). The single word, ψιλάνθρωπος, seems to occur for the first time in *Anastasius of Sinai (*Hodegos*, 13; J. P. Migne, *PL* 83. 216 c), while the noun 'psilanthropism' is apparently a 19th-cent. coinage.

psychology of religion. A field of study, dating from the late 19th cent., in which the concepts and methods of psychology are applied to religious experience and behaviour.

One of the first to investigate such possible applications of psychology was W. *James, whose work has since in some ways served as a model. The topics he chose for study included the experience of well-being or of conflict in human response to God, and the experiences of religious conversion and of saintliness and mysticism. His method was to collect written, and more rarely controlled, observations; his primary aim was a philosophical understanding of what he observed.

Many of the writings of S. Freud (1856–1939) on psychoanalysis significantly contributed to the psychological study of religion, though the critical and reductionist views of religion which he repeatedly expressed no longer command assent either among psychologists or among theologians. Similarly, the views of C. G. Jung (1875–1961), though by contrast tending to assign an almost indiscriminate validity to religious phenomena in human experience, have in turn led to critical restatements of permanent value for the psychology of religion.

Since the early 1960s there has been a considerable growth of interest in the subject, and much more sophisticated methods of analysis have been developed. These more precise methods have been applied not only to the topics studied by James, but more widely. With the help of tests, measurements, a few specifically devised questionnaires, and projective methods, religious behaviour and experience have been studied in relation to age, to cognitive style and other personal characteristics, and also with reference to pathological and drug-induced conditions. There is a growing interest in the contributions both of social psychology and of cognitive psychology in the exploration of religious phenomena. It is, however, now generally agreed in principle that merely psychological methods cannot fully answer questions about the validity of religious behaviour and experience, even if they can account for some aspects of both of these in non-religious terms.

W. James, *The Varieties of Religious Experience* (Gifford Lectures for 1901–2, 1902); S. Freud, *Totem und Tabu* (Vienna, 1913; Eng. tr., New York, 1918; London, 1919); id., *Die Zukunft einer Illusion* (Leipzig, 1927; Eng. tr., *The Future of an Illusion*, 1928); id., *Das Unbehagen in der Kultur* (Vienna, 1929; Eng. tr., *Civilization and its Discontents*, 1930); id., *Moses and Monotheism* (Eng. tr. of work previously partly unpub., 1939); R. H. Thouless, *An Introduction to the Psychology of Religion* (Cambridge, 1923; 3rd edn., 1971); C. G. Jung, *Psychology and Religion* (1938); G. W. Allport, *The Individual and his Religion: A Psychological Interpretation* (New York, 1950; London, 1951); V. White, OP, *God and the Unconscious* (1952); [J.] M. Argyle, *Religious Behaviour* (1958; rev., with B. Beit-Hallahmi as *The Social Psychology of Religion*, 1975); H. Faber, *Cirkelen om een geheim* (Meppel, 1972; Eng. tr., *Psychology of Religion*, 1976); W. E. Oates, *The Psychology of Religion* (Waco, Tex. [1973]); H. N. Malony (ed.), *Current Perspectives in the Psychology of Religion* (Grand Rapids [1977]); A. [C.] Hardy, *The Spiritual Nature of Man: A Study of Contemporary Religious Experience* (Oxford, 1979); J. R. Tisdale (ed.), *Growing Edges in the Psychology of Religion* (Chicago [1980]); J. W. Fowler, *Stages of Faith: The Psychology of Human Development and the Quest for Meaning* (San Francisco, etc. [1981]); D. Hay, *Exploring Inner Space: Scientists and Religious Experience* (Harmondsworth, 1982); C. D. Batson and W. L. Ventnis, *The Religious Experience: A Social-Psychological Perspective* (New York and Oxford, 1982); J. F. Byrnes, *The Psychology of Religion* (New York and London [1984]); M. J. Meadow and R. D. Kahoe, *Psychology of Religion: Religion in Individual Lives* (New York and London [1984]); B. Spilka and others, *The Psychology of Religion: An Empirical Approach* (Englewood Cliffs, NJ [1985]); D. S. Browning, *Religious Thought and the Modern Psychologies* (Philadelphia [1987]); F. Watts and M. Williams, *The Psychology of Religious Knowing*

(Cambridge, 1988); L. B. Brown, *The Psychology of Religion: An Introduction* (1988).

Ptolemaic system. The body of astronomical doctrines elaborated by Ptolemy (2nd cent. AD) in his Μαθηματικὴ σύνταξις, which explained the apparent motions of the sun, moon and planets on the assumption that the earth was stationary. It was commonly accepted throughout the Middle Ages and later until it was replaced by the *Copernican theory.

Public Worship Regulation Act 1874. An Act intended to suppress the growth of ritualism in the C of E. The Bill, drafted by Abp. A. C. *Tait, was drastically amended in Parliament in a more Protestant and *Erastian direction by Lord *Shaftesbury. It provided for the appointment, by the two Archbishops conjointly, of a barrister or ex-judge as Judge of the provincial courts of *Canterbury and *York to try ritual cases, with an appeal to the Privy Council. Tait secured (against Shaftesbury's wishes) provision for the bishop's veto of proceedings under the Act. The first judge was James Plaisted Baron Penzance, ex-judge of divorce. The imprisonment between 1877 and 1882 of four priests (Arthur Tooth, 1877; Thomas Pelham Dale, 1880; Richard William Enraght, 1880–1; Sidney Faithorn Green, 1881–2) for contumacy greatly discredited the Act and henceforward it was virtually obsolete. It was repealed by the *Ecclesiastical Jurisdiction Measure 1963.

J. Bentley, *Ritualism and Politics in Victorian Britain: The Attempt to Legislate for Belief* (Oxford, 1978), incl. text, pp. 129–42. P. T. Marsh, *The Victorian Church in Decline: Archbishop Tait and the Church of England 1868–1882* (1969), pp. 158–92. On the trial of A. Tooth and subsequent events, J. Coombs, *Judgement on Hatcham: The History of a Religious Struggle 1877–1886* (1969).

publican. The word used in the traditional English versions of the Bible to translate the Greek term τελώνης (Lat. *publicanus*), a member of one of the financial organizations which farmed the taxes in the service of the Roman government. In view of the abuses and corruptions to which the system led, the publicans were the objects of widespread hatred. In the Gospels they are commonly coupled with the 'sinners'. St *Matthew ('Levi'), one of their number, received the call to be an Apostle from his place of toll (τελώνιον) at *Capernaum (Mt. 9: 9 etc.). *Zacchaeus at *Jericho is described as a 'chief publican' (ἀρχιτελώνης) (Lk. 19: 2).

E. *Schürer, *The History of the Jewish People in the Age of Jesus Christ*, rev. Eng. tr. by G. Vermes and others, 1 (Edinburgh, 1973), pp. 374–6, with refs. E. Badian, *Publicans and Sinners: Private Enterprise in the Service of the Roman Empire* (Ithaca, NY, and London, 1972). F. Herrenbrück, *Jesus und die Zöllner* (Wissenschaftliche Untersuchungen zum Neuen Testament, 2. Reihe, 41; Tübingen [1990]), with refs. to earlier discussion. L. Fillion in *Dict. Bibl.* 5 (1912), cols. 858–61, s.v. 'Publicains'; O. Michel in *TWNT* 8 (1969), pp. 88–106; Eng. tr., 8 (1972), pp. 88–105, s.v. τελώνης, esp. part B.

Pudens, St (Gk. Πούδης). A Christian of *Rome who is mentioned in 2 Tim. 4: 21 as sending greetings along with Eubulus, *Linus, and Claudia to *Timothy. Tradition makes him St *Peter's host at Rome. There are no grounds for identifying the Pudens of the NT with the Pudens (prob. 3rd cent.) who gave his house on the Vicus

Patricius (*titulus Pudentis* or *ecclesia Pudentiana*) to the Roman Church. See also following entry. Feast day in E., 14 Apr.; in W., 19 May.

On the proposed identifications of the NT Pudens, see W. Lock in *HDB* 4 (1902), p. 173. A. Petrignani, *La basilica di S. Pudenziana in Roma* (Monumenti di antichità cristiana pubblicati dal Pontificio Istituto di Archeologia Cristiana, 2nd ser. 1; 1934); B. Vanmaele, O. Praem., *L'Église pudentienne de Rome (Santa Pudenziana)* (Bibliotheca Analecta Praemonstratensium, 6; 1965). R. Krautheimer and S. Corbett in idd. and others, *Corpus Basilicarum Christianarum Romae*, 3 (Rome, 1967), pp. 277–302, with bibl. [in Eng.]. C. Pietri, *Roma Christiana: Recherches sur l'Église de Rome . . . (311–440)* (Bibliothèque des Écoles françaises d'Athènes et de Rome, 224; 1976), pp. 468–70.

Pudentiana, St (also Potentiana).

Acc. to the *Roman Martyrology, she was a Roman virgin of the early Church, the daughter of St *Pudens and the sister of St *Praxedes. Probably the cultus rests on a mistaken popular notion which supposed that the '*ecclesia Pudentiana*' in Rome, really the church of St Pudens, presupposed a 'St Pudentiana'. The *Acta* of Sts Pudentiana and Praxedes, printed by the *Bollandists, are not earlier than the 8th cent. Feast day in W., 19 May.

AASS, Mai. 4 (1685), pp. 296–301. See also bibl. to preceding entry.

Pufendorf, Samuel (1632–94).

The first German professor of natural and international law. The son of a *Lutheran pastor, he became professor successively at Heidelberg (1661) and Lund (1670), historiographer to the court of Sweden (1677), and privy councillor to the Elector of Brandenburg (1688). Developing the system of H. *Grotius, he divided law into natural, civil, and moral, and maintained that while moral law was based on revelation and civil law on the positive enactments of the State, natural law had its basis in the instinct of society, and therefore ultimately in human reason. These ideas were developed in his chief book, *De Iure Naturae et Gentium* (1672), of which an Eng. tr. was published in 1710 (under the title, *Of the Law of Nature and Nations*) and also in *De Officio Hominis et Civis juxta legem naturalem* (1673) and in his *Dissertationes Academicae Selectores* (1675). In his *De Habitu Religionis Christianae ad Vitam Civilem* (1687), he expounded the theory of Church government known as '*Collegialism'. Pufendorf was also the author of many historical writings, among them *Einleitung zu der Historie der vornehmsten Reiche und Staaten . . . in Europa* (Frankfurt a.M., 1682), *Commentariorum de Rebus Suecicis Libri XXVI* (Utrecht, 1686; Eng. tr., with continuation, London, 1702), *De Rebus Gestis Friderici Wilhelmi Magni, Electoris Brandenburgici* (Berlin, 1695), and *De Rebus Gestis Friderici III Electoris Brandenburgici* (ibid., 1784).

Photographic reproductions of Pufendorf's *De Officio Hominis* [1682 edn.] with introd. by W. Schücking and Eng. tr. of text by F. G. Moore (The Classics of International Law, 10; 2 vols., New York, London, etc., 1927); of his *Elementorum Jurisprudentiae Universalis Libri Duo* [1672 edn.] with introd. by H. Wehberg and Eng. tr. of text by W. A. Oldfather (ibid. 15; 2 vols., Oxford and London, 1931); and of his *De Jure Naturae et Gentium* [1688 edn.] with introd. by W. Simons and Eng. tr. of text by C. H. and W. A. Oldfather (ibid. 17; ibid., 1934). The text of his 'De Statu Hominum Naturali' (originally part of his *Dissertationes Academicae Selectores* (Lund, 1675), pp. 582–632) was repr. from the 1678 edn., with Eng. tr. and introd. by M. Seidler (Studies in the History of Philosophy, 13; Lewiston, Queenston, and Lampeter [1990]). Correspondence with Christian Thomasius, 1687–93, ed. E. Gigas (Munich and Leipzig, 1897). F. Palladini, *Discussioni seicentesche su Samuel Pufendorf. Scritti latini: 1663–1700* (Pubblicazioni del Centro di Studio per la Storia della Storiografia Filosofica, 6 [1978]). Eng. tr. of the 1673 text of his *De Officio Hominis* by M. Silverthorne, with introd. and useful bibl. by J. Tully (Cambridge Texts in the History of Political Thought, 1991). L. Krieger, *The Politics of Discretion: Pufendorf and the Acceptance of Natural Law* (Chicago and London, 1965). P. Laurent, *Pufendorf et la loi naturelle* (1982). D. Döring, *Pufendorf-Studien: Beiträge zur Biographie Samuel von Pufendorfs und zu seiner Entwicklung als Historiker und theologischer Schriftsteller* (Historische Forschungen, 49; 1992). E. Wolf in P. Edwards (ed.), *Encyclopedia of Philosophy*, 7 (1967), pp. 27–9, s.v.

Pugin, Augustus Welby Northmore (1812–52),

architect and *ecclesiologist. He was the chief inspirer of the Gothic Revival. The son of Augustus Charles Pugin, a French *émigré*, he joined the RC Church in 1835, initially prompted by his ecclesiological studies. Among his numerous works are St Chad's (RC) Cathedral, Birmingham (1839–41); St Giles, Cheadle (1840–6); Killarney Cathedral (begun 1842); St Augustine's, Ramsgate (1845–51); and the chapel of St Edmund's College, Ware (1845–53). He also collaborated with C. Barry in his designs for the Houses of Parliament. His plans often had to be modified in execution through lack of money as the RCs by whom he was chiefly employed were a relatively poor body. Hence his designs and polemical writings provide a more adequate expression of his ideas than the buildings themselves. He also met with difficulties from RCs who rejected his identification of Gothic as the purest form of Christian architecture and preferred Italian prototypes. His most important writings are *Contrasts: or, A Parallel Between the Noble Edifices of the Fourteenth and Fifteenth Centuries, and Similar Buildings of the Present Day* (1836), *The True Principles of Pointed or Christian Architecture* (1841), *An Apology for The Revival of Christian Architecture in England* (1843), and *The Present State of Ecclesiastical Architecture in England* (1843). His sons **Edward Welby Pugin** (1834–75) and **Peter Paul Pugin** (1851–1904) were also church architects.

B. Ferrey, *Recollections of A. N. Welby Pugin, and his Father, Augustus Pugin* (1861; repr., with introd. by C. Wainwright, 1978). Modern studies by M. Trappes-Lomax (London, 1932) and P. Stanton (ibid., 1971). D. [R.] Gwynn, *Lord Shrewsbury, Pugin and the Gothic Revival* (1946). H.-R. Hitchcock, *Early Victorian Architecture in Britain* (2 vols., 1954), esp. 1, pp. 56–96, with illustrations in vol. 2, section 3. A. Wedgwood, *Catalogue of the Drawings Collection of the Royal Institute of British Architects: The Pugin Family* (Farnborough, 1977), pp. 38–112; id., *Catalogues of Architectural Drawings in the Victoria and Albert Museum: The Pugin Family* (1985), pp. 24–300; P. Atterbury and C. Wainwright (eds.), *Pugin: A Gothic Passion* (New Haven and London, 1994). D. Meara, *A. W. N. Pugin and the Revival of Memorial Brasses* (1991). M. Belcher, *A. W. N. Pugin: An Annotated Critical Bibliography* (1987). P. Waterhouse in *DNB* 47 (1896), pp. 6–10.

Pulcheria, St (399–453),

E. Empress from 450. She was the daughter of the Emp. Arcadius (395–408) and elder sister of *Theodosius II (408–50), and a woman of uncommon ability and deep piety. From 414 to 416 she was entrusted by the Senate, despite her youth, with the guardianship of her weak-minded brother, Theodosius;

and for several years she ran the Imperial palace at *Constantinople on strict and ascetic Christian principles. After Theodosius' marriage (421), she found life at court increasingly difficult, partly because of theological intrigues. A stalwart supporter of orthodoxy, she induced Theodosius to condemn *Nestorius. In 438 she put an end to the schism at Constantinople by bringing thither the bones of St *Chrysostom. In the *Monophysite controversy she was again on the orthodox side, and after the momentary triumph of Monophysitism at the *Latrocinium (449), she sought the support of Pope *Leo I. After the sudden death of Theodosius in 450 she became Empress, taking the aged general and senator, Marcian, as her consort. In the interests of orthodoxy, she forthwith arranged for a General Council to meet at *Chalcedon in 451, and herself attended the sixth session in person. Since the Middle Ages she has been commemorated as a saint. Feast day, 10 Sept.

The primary sources are cited in J. R. Martindale (ed.), *Prosopography of the Later Roman Empire* (Cambridge, 1980), pp. 929 f. *AASS*, Sept. 3 (1750), pp. 503–40. A. B. Teetgen, *Life and Times of the Empress Pulcheria* (popular; 1907). E. *Schwartz, 'Die Kaiserin Pulcheria auf der Synode von Chalkedon', in *Festgabe für Adolf Jülicher zum 70. Geburtstag 26. Januar 1927* (Tübingen, 1927), pp. 203–12; P. Goubert, SJ, 'Le Rôle de Sainte Pulchérie et de l'eunuque Chrysaphios', in A. Grillmeier, SJ, and H. Bacht, SJ (eds.), *Das Konzil von Chalkedon*, 1 (1951), pp. 303–21. J. P. Kirsch in *CE* 12 (1911), pp. 561 f., s.v.; W. Ensslin in *PW* 23 (pt. 2; 1959), cols. 1954–63, s.v. 'Pulcheria (2)'.

Pullen, Robert (d. 1146), theologian. He is one of the earliest known masters in the schools of *Oxford, where he began to teach the Scriptures in 1133. By 1139 he had moved to *Paris, where he taught logic and theology, counted *John of Salisbury among his pupils, and was highly esteemed by St *Bernard on account of his sound doctrine. He combined his teaching with holding the archdeaconry of *Rochester, despite the protests of the bishop. Called to Rome by Innocent II, he was created cardinal probably by Celestine II in 1143–4; c.1144 Lucius II appointed him Papal chancellor of the Holy Roman Church, an office he held also under St Bernard's disciple, *Eugenius III, who became Pope shortly afterwards. He left a collection of sermons, but his main surviving work is his 'Sentences', a compilation treating a wide range of theological subjects, soon to be superseded by the 'Sentences' of *Peter Lombard.

His *Sententiae*, repr. from the edn. of H. Mathoud, OSB (Paris, 1655), in J. P. Migne, *PL* 186. 625–1152. F. Courtney, SJ, *Cardinal Robert Pullen* (Analecta Gregoriana, 64; 1954). R. W. Southern in T. H. Aston (ed.), *The History of the University of Oxford*, 1 (Oxford, 1984), pp. 6–8. *BRUO* 3 (1959), p. 1525, s.v.; H. *Rashdall in *DNB* 47 (1896), pp. 19 f., s.v.

pulpit (Lat. *pulpitum*, 'platform'). An elevated stand of stone or wood for the preacher or reader. Pulpits first became general in the later Middle Ages. In early Christian times the bishop preached from his *cathedra. Later the *ambo was used for the sermon and in still later times the rood-loft. Except in cathedrals the N. side of the *nave is considered the proper place for the pulpit. Sometimes the workmanship of the pulpit is very elaborate, famous examples being the marble structures at Pisa and Siena and the wooden *baroque pulpits of the Netherlands. Pul-

pits are also generally found in monastic refectories, and sometimes outside but close to the wall of a church, e.g. at Magdalen College, Oxford. It is now customary to use the Latin word *pulpitum*, not for the preaching-stand, but for the stone choir-screen which sometimes separates the choir from the nave in cathedral and monastic churches.

F. T. Dollman, *Examples of Ancient Pulpits Existing in England* (1849); J. C. Cox, *Pulpits, Lecterns and Organs in English Churches* (1915), pp. 1–147. R. Grand, 'Les Chaires à prêcher au dehors des églises', *Bulletin Monumental*, 83 (1924), pp. 305–25.

Purcell, Henry (1659–95), English composer. He was born in London, and becoming a choirboy at the *Chapel Royal, began to study music at an early age. From 1674 he tuned the organ, and in 1679 was made organist, at *Westminster Abbey, to which in 1682 the office of one of the organists at the Chapel Royal was added. During the next few years he devoted himself chiefly to sacred music, though for the last six years or so of his life music for the theatre dominated his output. One of his most famous ecclesiastical works is the *Te Deum* and *Jubilate* in D (1694), written for St *Cecilia's day, which was regularly performed at *St Paul's Cathedral for over half a century. He also composed a complete setting for the Morning and Evening Service in B flat, and an Evening Service in G minor. His burial service for Queen Mary (d. 1694) contained the well-known anthem 'Thou knowest, Lord'. Although he wrote a number of 'full' *anthems in the older polyphonic style, including the highly expressive 'Hear my prayer', Purcell's outstanding contribution is to the development of the verse anthem, often with string accompaniments. In the spirit of the Restoration much of the music is elaborate and highly dramatic; the words are nearly always from the OT. They include 'In Thee, O Lord, do I put my trust', 'Rejoice in the Lord alway' (the 'Bell' anthem), 'O sing unto the Lord', 'My beloved spake', and the Coronation anthem, 'My heart is inditing of a good matter'. Finest among many non-liturgical pieces is perhaps his setting of William Fuller's 'Evening Hymn' ('Now that the sun hath veiled his light'). Even apart from his more extensive work in the sphere of secular composition, the technical skill, powers of expression, and the beauty of the melodies of his sacred music have deservedly maintained Purcell's reputation among the first rank of English composers.

Collected edn. of his works pub. by the Purcell Society (London, 1878 ff., 32 vols. to 1965; rev. edn., 1964 ff.). F. B. Zimmerman, *Henry Purcell 1659–1695: An Analytical Catalogue of his Music* (1963). J. A. Westrup, *Purcell* (Master Musicians Series, 1937; rev. N. Fortune, 1980); F. B. Zimmermann, *Henry Purcell, 1659–1695: His Life and Times* (1967; rev. edn., Philadelphia [1983]); P. Holman, *Henry Purcell* (Oxford Studies of Composers, 1994). M. Burden (ed.), *The Purcell Companion* (1995). F. B. Zimmermann, *The Anthems of Henry Purcell* (Special issue of the *American Choral Review*, 13, nos. 3–4; New York, 1971). Id., *Henry Purcell: A Guide to Research* (New York and London, 1989). J. [A.] Westrup in S. Sadie (ed.), *The New Grove Dictionary of Music and Musicians*, 15 (1980), pp. 457–76, s.v.

Purchas Judgement. The judgement by the *Judicial Committee of the Privy Council in 1871 that Eucharistic *Vestments, the *Eastward Position, the *Mixed Chalice, and Wafer *Bread were illegal. This decision, which was given when the Revd John Purchas (1823–72), vicar of St

James's, Brighton, had been charged with these and other ritualistic practices, reversed the previous judgement in Purchas's favour by the *Dean of the Arches. The verdict marks a turning-point in the ceremonial revival in the C of E in the 19th cent., because hitherto such practices had been regarded on nearly all sides as conforming with the letter of the law, whereas from now onwards ritualists were held to be law-breakers. The judgement was widely disobeyed, however, as without spiritual authority, and the Eastward Position was continued, e.g. in *St Paul's Cathedral.

The Law Report is to be found under *Hebbert v. Purchas* (1871), LR 3 PC 605.

purgative, illuminative, and unitive ways. The analysis of Christian development into these three 'ways' or phases derives from *Dionysius the Pseudo-Areopagite, who ascribed a rhythm of purification, illumination, and union (or perfection) both to the hierarchies of angels and to the Church on earth; in the latter case, the three phases are connected with the Sacraments, and a threefold hierarchy can also be identified of those being purged (*catechumens, penitents, etc.), 'contemplatives' (the baptized), and those leading the unitive life (monks). Medieval W. interpreters of Dionysius connected this scheme with the more traditional one (beginners, proficients, perfects) and turned it into an account of spiritual progress in terms of the three 'ways', beginning with the eradication of bad habits and the cultivation of the virtues, moving on to the illumination of the mind by meditation and contemplation, culminating in unitive love. Prob. through the influence of the late-13th-cent. *Carthusian, Hugh of Balma, these three 'ways' were adopted by later writers such as St *John of the Cross, and so became classic in systematic theories of Christian spirituality. St John of the Cross connected the illuminative way with contemplation in his strict sense of 'infused contemplation' (*Noche oscura*, 2. 14. 1), but some later writers maintained that it was possible to attain even to the unitive way without this. Other writers have questioned the usefulness of any rigid attempt to systematize spiritual progress.

purgatory. A term used only in W. Catholic theology for the state (or place) of punishment and purification where the souls of those who have died in a state of grace undergo such punishment as is still due to forgiven sins and, perhaps, expiate their unforgiven *venial sins, before being admitted to the *Beatific Vision.

In that explicit form the doctrine is not found before the 12th cent., but elements of it are much more ancient, esp. the notions that not all souls are condemned to Hell or are worthy of Heaven at the moment of death, and that prayer for the *dead (q.v.) is valuable. The former of these notions developed only gradually, partly because so long as the Church looked for an imminent end of the world there was little interest in an interim state: such souls were asleep or waiting (cf. 1 Thess. 4: 13), and partly because of a reluctance to encourage laxity by blurring the clear-cut alternative fates of Heaven and Hell. The E. Church came to admit of an intermediate state, but refrained from defining it so as not to blur this distinction; it combined with this doctrine a firm belief in the efficacy of prayer for the dead, which was a constant feature of both E. and W.

liturgies. Such prayer is held to be unintelligible without belief in some interim state in which the dead might benefit.

In the W. there was much more curiosity about the intermediate state. The visions of Dinocrates in the 'Passion of Sts *Perpetua and Felicity' (AD 203) give expression to the belief that sins can be purged by suffering in an afterlife, and that the process can be accelerated by prayer. St *Augustine's occasional remarks on a purifying fire after death (*De Civ. Dei*, 21. 26; *Enchiridion*, 68 f., etc.) and on the value of the Church's prayers for those who die in the communion of the Church (*De Civ. Dei*, 21. 24 etc.), combined with his implication that the ultimate fate of individual souls is decided at the moment of death (*Enchiridion*, 110), provides much fuel for later theology. Support for the notion of a purifying fire is sought in 1 Cor. 3: 11–15, and the idea that such fire is more painful than anything experienced in this life (*En. in Ps.* 37. 3) meets the suspicion of laxity. St *Gregory the Great in his *Dialogues* taught that 'light sins' will be purged in purgatorial fire (4. 41 [39]) and that it is proper to offer the Eucharist for the deliverance of the soul of a person who has died (4. 57 [55]). Scriptural texts cited or alluded to in support of this teaching include Mt. 12: 32 and Jn. 14: 2, as well as 1 Cor. 3: 11–15. Gregory's doctrine was expressed in visions and anecdotes in the *Dialogues* and such popular theology continued to elaborate on notions of punishment in the world to come. The establishment of the Commemoration of all the Faithful Departed (*All Souls' Day, 2 Nov.) through the influence of *Odilo of Cluny at the end of the 10th cent. and its adoption throughout the W. Church helped to concentrate imagination on the fate of departed souls and fostered a sense of solidarity between the living and the dead. In the 12th cent. the elaboration of theology in all spheres, and esp. of the theology of *penance, by the masters of *Paris and elsewhere, helped to fashion a notion of purgatory as a place where penances unfinished in this life could be completed. The classic formulation of the doctrine is found in St *Thomas Aquinas. He taught that in purgatory any unforgiven guilt (*culpa*) of venial sins is expiated and any punishment (*poena*) for sins, both mortal and venial, still remaining at the moment of death, is borne. Acc. to St Thomas and other scholastic theologians, the smallest pain in purgatory is greater than the greatest on earth, but is relieved by the certitude of salvation which establishes the holy souls, despite their sufferings, in deep peace. Moreover they may be helped by the prayers of the faithful, and esp. by the offering of the Eucharist on their behalf, a belief which St Thomas based on the doctrine of the *Communion of Saints, from which only the inhabitants of Hell and Limbo are excluded. The teaching of the W. Church on purgatory was defined at the Councils of *Lyons (1274) and *Florence (1439) with a view to reconciling the Greeks, who objected esp. to the conception of material fire and to the legalism of the W. approach (manifest, e.g., in the distinction between guilt and punishment), as well as suspecting the whole doctrine of *Origenism. But no lasting agreement was reached.

Supreme imaginative expression of the doctrine of purgatory is found in the second book of *Dante's *Divina Commedia*. Purgatory becomes a powerful symbol of all that the holiness of God requires of man and also of His mercy and His love for men; these find warm expression in St *Catherine of Genoa's *Treatise on Purgatory*. The doctrine also provided a context for the development of *indulgences, popularized by the *plenary indulgence granted by *Boniface VIII to all pilgrims to Rome in *Holy Year of 1300. In these ways belief in purgatory became a central part of late medieval religion.

In the W. the existence of purgatory had been denied in the Middle Ages by some heretical sects such as the *Cathars and the *Waldensians. Its rejection by the *Reformers is usually couched in terms of allusions to its weak support in Scripture and rejection of the mercenary aspects of late medieval religion in which purgatory was implicated, together with the way the doctrine seemed to extend Papal power into the afterlife. M. *Luther, for instance, in his 95 theses, allowed the existence of purgatory, but denied that it could be deduced from the Bible; he later denied it in the *Schmalkaldic Articles, but subsequent Lutheran Confessions do not expressly reject all ideas of purification after death, however much they object to *Requiem Masses and Papal claims to power to remit sins. An early reply to the Reformers' teaching was made by St John *Fisher, who in his *Assertionis Lutheranae Confutatio* (1523) based his defence of purgatory esp. on the Fathers and on the practice of prayer for the dead from the earliest times. The Council of *Trent defined RC doctrine by reaffirming the teaching propounded at Lyons and Florence, but confined itself to asserting the principles of purification after death and the value of prayers for the faithful departed. In the C of E Art. 22 of the *Thirty-Nine Articles condemns the 'Romish' doctrine of purgatory without further specification. In the second part of his *Considerationes Modestae*, Bp. W. *Forbes (d. 1634) rejected the doctrine of 'purgatory', but strongly affirmed the existence of an intermediate state in which purification takes place through the soul's fervent longing for God, and the value of prayer for the dead (deploring its absence at that time from official Anglican liturgies). In this he was followed by the *Tractarians and their successors, and in recent times by some Protestant theologians. Recent RC discussions of purgatory (Y. *Congar, K. *Rahner, H. U. von *Balthasar) respect the reserve of the Council of Trent, reinterpret some traditional aspects of the doctrine (e.g. fire as metaphorical, time as intensity) and leave many questions open, such as whether the guilt of unforgiven venial sins is forgiven in purgatory, or whether souls in purgatory can pray for the living. (The custom of seeking such prayers is a comparatively recent development, advocated in the W. by St Robert *Bellarmine and St *Alphonsus Liguori, among others.)

The doctrine of purgatory is one way of bridging the gap between the death of the individual and the general *resurrection of the dead. It may also be seen as bridging the gap between the individual and the Church, for while the Church may be presented to Christ at the end of time 'without spot or wrinkle', the individual Christian is likely to face his own death in a more ambiguous state. So purgatory represents the gap in which the individual as he was at the moment of death, faithful but imperfect, is rendered a worthy member of the Church as she will be at the Last Judgement. Whether the gap between death and resurrection is temporal for the individual is not clear, though it can hardly be imagined in any other way; and

the gap between the individual and the Church can be filled both by the individual's suffering and waiting (cf. Heb. 11: 40, though this more immediately envisages a *limbus patrum*) and by the corporate concern of the Church for its individual members expressed in prayer and esp. in the liturgy. In the traditional W. doctrine of purgatory, individuals are envisaged as attaining the Beatific Vision one by one in accordance with their deserts. In the teaching of the E. Church (which in this matter Forbes follows), the perfection of the whole Church awaits the individual, and so even the saints may be prayed for, as the fullness of beatitude will not be experienced by any until it is attained by all.

Besides the account in Aquinas (*Comm. in Lib. IV. Sent.*, dist. 21, qu. 1) there are classic treatises by R. Bellarmine, SJ, *Disputationes de Controversiis Fidei*, 3 (Ingoldstadt [1588]), pt. 2 (Primi Tomi Sexta Controversia: 'De Ecclesia, quae est in Purgatorio'), and F. *Suárez, SJ, *Commentarii ac Disputationes in Tertiam Partem Divi Thomae*, 4 (Lyons, 1603), pp. 618–55 ('De Purgatorio'). The Tridentine 'Decretum De Purgatorio' is repr., with Eng. tr., in Tanner, *Decrees*, 2 (1990), p. 774. *De Purgatorio disputationes in concilio Florentino habitae*, ed. L. Petit, AA, and G. Hofmann, SJ (Concilium Florentinum: Documenta et Scriptores, 8, fasc. 2; Rome, 1969). The subject is necessarily treated in all works on eschatology, q.v. There is an excellent art. by A. Michel and M. Jugie, AA, in *DTC* 13 (pt. 1; 1936), cols. 1163–357, s.v. 'Purgatoire'. Other general modern works incl.: A. J. Mason [Anglican], *Purgatory* [and other Lectures] (1901), esp. pp. 1–57; H. Rondet, SJ, *Le Purgatoire* (1948); Y. Congar, OP, 'Le Purgatoire', in *Le Mystère de la Mort et sa célébration* (Lex Orandi, 12; 1951), pp. 279–336; A. Piolanti, 'Il dogma del purgatorio', *Euntes docete*, 6 (1953), pp. 287–311; E. Fleischhack, *Fegfeuer* (Tübingen, 1969); R. Ombres, OP, *Theology of Purgatory* (Cork, 1979); J. Le Goff, *La Naissance du Purgatoire* (1981; Eng. tr., 1984). On the archaeological data, A. Stuiber, *Refrigerium Interim: Die Vorstellungen vom Zwischenzustand und die frühchristliche Grabeskunst* (Theophaneia, 11; Bonn, 1957); L. de Bruyne, 'Refrigerium Interim', *Riv. A.C.* 34 (1958), pp. 87–118. J. Gnilka, *Ist 1 Kor. 3, 10–15 ein Schriftzeugnis für das Fegfeuer? Eine exegetisch-historische Untersuchung* (Würzburg Inaugural diss., Düsseldorf, 1955). J. Ntedika, *L'Évolution de la Doctrine du Purgatoire chez saint Augustin* (Études Augustiniennes, 1966); id., *L'Évocation de l'au-delà dans la Prière pour les Morts: Étude de patristique et de liturgie latines (IVᵉ–VIIIᵉ S.)* (Recherches Africaines de Théologie. Travaux de la Faculté de Théologie de l'Université Lovanianum de Kinshasa, 2; Louvain and Paris, 1971). R. R. Atwell, 'From Augustine to Gregory the Great: an Evaluation of the Emergence of the Doctrine of Purgatory', *JEH* 38 (1987), pp. 173–86. R. Ombres, OP, 'The Doctrine of Purgatory according to St Thomas Aquinas', *Downside Review*, 99 (1981), pp. 279–87; id., 'Latins and Greeks in Debate over Purgatory, 1230–439', *JEH* 35 (1984), pp. 1–14; J. Gill, SJ, *The Council of Florence* (Cambridge, 1959), pp. 117–25, 285; C. Burgess, ' "A fond thing vainly invented": An Essay on Purgatory and Pious Motive in Later Medieval England' in S. J. Wright (ed.), *Parish, Church and People: Local studies in lay religion 1350–1750* (1988), pp. 56–84. P. Althaus, 'Luthers Gedanken über die letzten Dinge', *Luther-Jahrbuch*, 33 (1941), pp. 9–34, esp. pp. 22–8. E. Klinger in *Sacramentum Mundi*, 5 (1970), pp. 166–8, s.v.; P. Miquel, OSB, and C. de Seyssel in *Dict. Sp.* 12 (pt. 2; 1986), cols. 2652–76, s.v., both with further bibl.

Purgatory, St Patrick's. See ST PATRICK'S PURGATORY.

Purification of the BVM. The feast kept on 2 Feb. in commemoration of the BVM's purification in the Temple, recorded in Lk. 2: 21–39. The feast is also known as

*Candlemas (q.v.). In the RC Church since 1969 it has been called the 'Presentation of the Lord'.

purificator. A small piece of white linen used at celebrations of the Eucharist to cleanse the chalice after communion. Occasional references to purificators are found in the Middle Ages (e.g. in a Roman inventory of 1295), but they did not come into general use until the 16th cent.

Purim. A Jewish festival, celebrated in the spring (14 and 15 Adar), which commemorates the deliverance of the Jews from massacre under the Persian Empire (473 BC), as related in the Book of Esther (9: 26 ff.). The observance included the public reading of the Book, as regulated in the Tractate 'Megillah' of the *Talmud. The name was long thought to be of Persian or even Indian origin, but it has now been shown to be connected with the Assyrian *puru*, 'lot' (cf. Est. 3: 7). It used to be thought that the 'feast of the Jews' mentioned in Jn. 5: 1 was the Feast of Purim, but this identification is now rejected.

N. S. Doniach, *Purim or The Feast of Esther: An Historical Study* (Philadelphia, 1933). R. de Vaux, OP, *Les Institutions de l'Ancien Testament*, 2 (1960), pp. 425–9, with bibl. p. 460; Eng. tr. (2nd edn., 1965), pp. 514–17, with bibl. p. 552. H.-J. Kraus, *Gottesdienst in Israel* (2nd edn., 1962), pp. 111 f.; Eng. tr. (Oxford, 1966), pp. 91 f. L. Jacobs in *Encyclopaedia Judaica*, 13 (Jerusalem, 1972), cols. 1390–6, s.v. See also comms. on Esther.

Puritans, the more extreme English Protestants who, dissatisfied with the Elizabethan Settlement, sought a further purification of the Church from supposedly unscriptural and corrupt forms along the *Genevan model. Although never in the majority, they were powerful and influential, producing many able controversial writers and enjoying support from some royal councillors of *Elizabeth I, from some of the nobility and gentry, and among the mercantile classes. They demanded express scriptural warrant for all the details of public worship, believing that all other forms were Popish, superstitious, idolatrous, and anti-Christian. At first they attacked church ornaments, *vestments, *surplices, *rochets, *organs, the *sign of the Cross, and ecclesiastical courts, and put corresponding emphasis on preaching, Sunday observance, and the 'tablewise' position of the altar. From the early 1570s more extreme Puritans, such as T. *Cartwright, J. *Field, and W. *Travers, began to attack the institution of episcopacy itself, and to advocate a *Presbyterian polity. Elizabeth I bitterly opposed all Puritan attempts further to change the C of E. Abp. E. *Grindal was sympathetic to some Puritan grievances, but his successor, J. *Whitgift, enthusiastically aided the Queen in her resistance. His Articles of 1583 and the Act of 1593 against 'seditious sectaries' were aimed at the Puritans, who consequently formed extravagant hopes of her successor. On *James I's accession the Puritan *Millenary Petition led to the unsuccessful *Hampton Court Conference (1604). After the relative inactivity of Abp. G. *Abbot, the Puritans were among the chief targets of W. *Laud's ecclesiastical and political policy, which, for example, sought to thwart the Puritans' attempts to propagate their views by means of *Lecturers. By 1600 some Puritans, such as H. *Barrow and for a time R. *Browne, had come to advocate *Congregationalism. The Great Rebellion (sometimes called the 'Puritan Revolution') in

and after 1642 led not only to the temporary hollow triumph of Presbyterianism, but also to a rapid proliferation of sects. The term 'Puritan' never had a single precise meaning, and in the senses of the post-1559 period it ceased to be applicable after the Restoration in 1660.

W. *Perkins was a representative moderate Puritan of Elizabeth I's day; other more extreme later Puritans were W. *Prynne and J. *Milton. See also ADMONITION TO PARLIAMENT; PARKER, M.; MARPRELATE TRACTS; BANCROFT, R.; and 'ROOT AND BRANCH'.

Collections of Puritan docs. ed. H. C. Porter, *Puritanism in Tudor England* (1970), and L. J. Tinterud, *Elizabethan Puritanism* (New York, 1971). D. *Neal, *History of the Puritans from 1517 to 1688* (new edn. by J. Toulmin, 5 vols., 1793–7). C. E. Whiting, *Studies in English Puritanism, 1660–1688* (1931); W. Haller, *The Rise of Puritanism* (New York, 1938); M. M. Knappen, *Tudor Puritanism* (Chicago, 1939); [D.] H. [M.] Davies, *The Worship of the English Puritans* (1948); A. Simpson, *Puritanism in Old and New England* (Charles R. Walgreen Foundation Lectures; Chicago, 1955); G. S. Wakefield, *Puritan Devotion: Its Place in the Development of Christian Piety* (1957); G. R. Cragg, *Puritanism in the Period of the Great Persecution 1660–1688* (Cambridge, 1957); P. Collinson, *The Elizabethan Puritan Movement* (1967); id., *Godly People: Essays on English Protestantism and Puritanism* [Collected papers repr. from various sources] (1983); id., *English Puritanism* (Historical Association pamphlet, General Series, 106 [1983]); P. McGrath, *Papists and Puritans under Elizabeth I* (1967); W. M. Lamont, *Godly Rule: Politics and Religion 1603–1660* (1969); O. C. Watkins, *The Puritan Experience* (1972). J. S. Coolidge, *The Pauline Renaissance in England: Puritanism and the Bible* (Oxford, 1970); P. [G.] Lake, *Moderate Puritans and the Elizabethan Church* (Cambridge, 1982); id., *Anglicans and Puritans? Presbyterianism and English Conformist Thought from Whitgift to Hooker* (1988); J. Morgan, *Godly Learning: Puritan Attitudes towards Reason, Learning, and Education, 1560–1640* (Cambridge, 1986).

Purvey, John (*c.*1353–*c.*1428), *Wycliffite preacher. He was closely associated with John Wycliffe (d. 1384) in the last years of his life at Lutterworth in Leics. On account of his *Lollard activities, Purvey was brought to trial in 1401. After recanting under pressure, he was inducted to the vicarage of West Hythe, Kent; but he resigned in 1403 and, so far as records reveal, he reverted to Lollardy, and continued to disseminate Lollard doctrine. Various Lollard writings have been attributed to him, but the evidence for the ascriptions is inadequate. His name has traditionally been associated with the revision of the Wycliffite English translation of the Bible from its early, extremely literal version to the later idiomatic version; this association is not found until 1729, and is therefore dubious. See also BIBLE (ENGLISH VERSIONS).

H. Hargreaves, 'The Latin Text of Purvey's Psalter', *Medium Ævum*, 24 (1955), pp. 73–90; id. in *The Cambridge History of the Bible*, 2, ed. G. W. H. Lampe (Cambridge, 1969), pp. 408–11. M. Deanesly, *The Lollard Bible and Other Medieval Biblical Versions* (ibid., 1920), esp. pp. 266–85, 334–47, 437–67; id., *The Significance of the Lollard Bible* (Ethel M. Wood Lecture, 1951). A. Hudson, 'John Purvey: a Reconsideration of the Evidence for his Life and Writings', *Viator*, 12 (1981), pp. 355–80, repr. in id., *Lollards and their Books* (1985), pp. 85–110. *BRUO* 3 (1959), pp. 1526–7, with further refs. See also works on the Wycliffite Bible cited under BIBLE (ENGLISH VERSIONS).

Pusey, Edward Bouverie (1800–82), *Tractarian leader. He was educated at Eton and at *Christ Church, Oxford, and elected a Fellow of Oriel College in 1823. Not long afterwards he went to Göttingen and Berlin (1825), where he got to know many leading German biblical critics. During the next years he devoted himself to the study of Hebrew, Arabic, and other Semitic languages both at Oxford and in Germany. In 1828 he published *An Historical Enquiry into the Probable Causes of the Rationalist Character lately predominant in the Theology of Germany* (followed by Part 2 in 1830), in which he traced German rationalism to the dead orthodoxy of a Protestantism lacking in spiritual vitality; but the book was misunderstood to be a defence of his German masters and later he withdrew it. In 1828 he was ordained deacon and priest and also appointed Regius professor of Hebrew and Canon of Christ Church. He held this office for the rest of his life. At the end of 1833 he became formally attached to the *Oxford Movement by contributing a Tract (No. 18) on *Thoughts on the Benefits of the System of Fasting, Enjoined by our Church* (pub. 1834), his prestige and erudition proving of great benefit to the cause. In 1836 he published three further Tracts on *Scriptural Views of Holy Baptism* (Nos. 67–9), which taught a very rigorous doctrine on the forgiveness of post-baptismal sin, and which, in their form, were significant as altering the scope of the Tracts from pamphlets to learned treatises. He also gave whole-hearted support to the *Library of the Fathers*, supplying its first volume (St *Augustine's *Confessions*, 1838) with a notable preface on the significance of *patristic study. His most influential activity, however, was his preaching which drew on the Greek Fathers and the Christian mystical tradition. His sermons, while stressing the heinousness of sin and nothingness of the world, rise to contemplative rapture in their emphasis on the indwelling of Christ, salvation as participation in God, and the blessedness of heaven. The death of his wife, in 1839, left an indelible mark on his life; from that time he practised many austerities. His foundation of St Saviour's, Leeds, in memory of his wife and daughter, created a model Tractarian slum parish. When, in 1841, J. H. *Newman, whom he had vigorously defended, withdrew from the movement, the leadership devolved largely on Pusey. His sermon on *The Holy Eucharist, a Comfort to the Penitent*, preached before the university in 1843, was condemned by the vice-chancellor and six doctors of divinity as teaching error, and Pusey was suspended from the university pulpit for two years. The condemnation, however, secured for it wide publicity in its printed form and drew attention to the doctrine of the *Real Presence, of which Pusey remained a devoted defender. In 1845 he assisted in the establishment of the first Anglican sisterhood, and throughout his life he continued to encourage efforts in this direction, giving generously from his own quite substantial private income. In 1846 he preached another sermon before the university on *The Entire Absolution of the Penitent*, in which he claimed for the C of E the power of the keys and the reality of priestly absolution. This sermon was important in encouraging the revival of the practice of private confession in the modern Anglican Church. As the principal champion of the High Church Movement he had frequently to defend its doctrines, e.g. in the *Gorham Case (q.v.), which issued in a number of conversions to the RC Church, though Pusey then and later spared no effort to dissuade his followers from joining it. He took a leading part in the controversy on the reform of the university, defending the old tutorial system. In 1862 he accused B. *Jowett of teaching unsound doctrine, but the court of the chancellor of the university declined to hear the case. After the judgement of the Privy Council in favour of the authors of *Essays and Reviews (1860), he wrote his famous letter to J. *Keble on *The Church of England a Portion of Christ's One Holy Catholic Church, and a Means of Restoring Visible Unity: An Eirenicon* (1865). In it he expressed his belief that union with Rome was prevented not so much by the official teaching of the RC Church as by unofficial devotions, e.g. to the BVM, and by the popular conceptions of *purgatory and *indulgences. This letter was answered by Newman in 1866. From 1867 he took an active part in the Ritualist controversy. In his sermon *Will Ye also Go Away?* (1867) he again defended the doctrine of the Real Presence and the corresponding ceremonial. In 1869 he published his second *Eirenicon* in answer to Newman, which dealt chiefly with the *Immaculate Conception, and in 1870 he issued the third, entitled *Is Healthful Reunion Impossible?*, principally on the doctrine of purgatory, the deutero-canonical books, and the Roman supremacy. This he sent to many RC bishops who attended the First *Vatican Council, but his hopes were disappointed by the definition of Papal infallibility. From 1870 to 1873 he fought vigorously for the retention of the *Athanasian Creed, threatened by the Fourth Report of the Ritual Commission, which advocated its abandonment. In 1880 in *What is of Faith as to Everlasting Punishment?* he defended against F. W. *Farrar the eternity of hell, basing himself on scriptural and patristic teaching. He died at Ascot Priory, Berks, on 16 Sept. 1882 and is buried in the nave of Christ Church cathedral, Oxford. After his death his library was bought by his friends, who endowed for it the institution in Oxford known as Pusey House. In the American BCP (1979), feast day, 18 Sept.

Spiritual Letters, ed. J. O. Johnston and W. C. E. Newbolt (1898). *Monumental Life* by H. P. *Liddon (4 vols., London, 1893–7), with list of Pusey's writings, compiled by F. Madan, 4, pp. 395–446. Shorter Lives by M. Trench (anon.; ibid., 1900), G. W. E. Russell (ibid., 1907), and G. L. Prestige (ibid., 1933). P. Butler (ed.), *Pusey Rediscovered* (1983). D. [W. F.] Forrester, *Young Doctor Pusey: A Study in Development* (1989). H. C. G. Matthew, 'Edward Bouverie Pusey: From Scholar to Tractarian', *JTS* NS 32 (1981), pp. 101–24; A. Geck, 'The Concept of History in E. B. Pusey's First Enquiry into German Theology and its German Background', ibid. 38 (1987), pp. 387–408. [D.] G. Rowell, *The Vision Glorious: Themes and Personalities of the Catholic Revival in Anglicanism* (1983), pp. 71–97. J. O. Johnston in *DNB* 47 (1896), pp. 53–61. G. W. E. Russell in *DECH*, pp. 482–6. See also bibl. to OXFORD MOVEMENT.

Pusey, Philip Edward (1830–80), *patristic scholar. The only son of E. B. *Pusey, whom he assiduously assisted in his patristic and Semitic studies, he was an indefatigable student who, though deaf and a cripple, travelled all over Europe, working at MSS. He edited many of the writings of St *Cyril of Alexandria and laid the foundations for a critical edition of the four Gospels in the *Peshitta (pub., after further editing, by G. H. Gwilliam, 1901).

H. P. *Liddon, *Life of Edward Bouverie Pusey*, 4 (1897), pp. 346–9.

Puseyism. A contemporary title for the *Tractarian Movement, generally used in an opprobrious sense, from its leader, E. B. *Pusey. Pusey was prob. singled out as he was the first contributor to the *Tracts for the Times* to append his initials (to No. 18, 21 Dec. 1833), the earlier *Tracts* being anonymous.

OED 12 (2nd edn., 1989), p. 892, s.v.

Pye. See PIE.

Pyrrhonism. Properly, the system of sceptical philosophy expounded *c.*300 BC by the Greek thinker, Pyrrho of Elis. Its characteristic doctrine was the denial of all possibility of attaining to certain knowledge. Conceived in an ethical interest, it maintained that when a man had understood the futility of intellectual inquiry, he would not be perturbed or lose his happiness by disquietude at his inability to arrive at any certain truth. In a wider sense, the term has come to be applied to any sceptical system of thought.

Pyrrho himself left no writings; the propagation of his doctrines was due to his disciple, Timon of Phlius (*c.*320–230 BC), of whose satirical poems (Σίλλοι) a few fragments survive. *Pirrone Testimonianze*, ed. F. Decleva Caizzi (Elenchos 5 [1981]). L. Robin, *Pyrrhon et le scepticisme grec* (1944). G. Striker in *OCD* (3rd edn., 1996), p. 1283, s.v. 'Pyrrhon'.

pyx (Gk. πυξίς, 'box-wood vessel'). The word denoted formerly any receptacle destined to contain the reserved *Host, and is still so used officially in the *CIC* (1983), can. 939. Acc. to ordinary present terminology it is used esp. of a small, mostly flat, gold or silver-gilt box which is used for carrying the Blessed Sacrament to the sick. For this purpose it is wrapped in a small *corporal and placed in a pyx-bag hung round the priest's neck. The term is also used for the vessel in which the large Host for exposition is kept in the *Tabernacle.

Braun, *AG*, pp. 280–347 and 456 f. H. *Leclercq, OSB, in *DACL* 14 (pt. 2; 1948), cols. 1983–96, s.v. 'Pyxide'.

Q

'Q'. The symbol (usually held to come from the Ger. *Quelle*, 'source'), used by biblical critics in a strict sense for the hypothetical source of those passages in the Synoptic Gospels where Matthew and Luke show a close similarity to each other but not to any parallel passage in Mark. (See SYNOPTIC PROBLEM.) The passages consist largely of sayings of Jesus and some other material, e.g. on St *John the Baptist (Lk. 3: 17 f., cf. Mt. 3: 12; Lk. 7: 18–23, cf. Mt. 11: 2–6) and the account of the *Temptation of Christ (Lk. 4: 2–13, cf. Mt. 4: 2–11). The theory, elaborated on the basis of studies by Sir John Hawkins and A. *Harnack, was put into a widely accepted form by B. H. *Streeter, who held that (1) 'Q' was a document (not merely a group of oral traditions) written in Greek; (2) almost the whole of its content was used by either Matthew or Luke or both; and (3) that the order of the contents in Lk. is nearer to the original than in Mt. Attempts to reconstruct 'Q' have been made by A. Harnack and others, but certainty about its extent, order, and wording is not attainable. The existence of such a document has often been challenged, but the hypothesis (known as the 'two-document' hypothesis) that Mt. and Lk. are based on Mk. and 'Q', has retained wide support. In recent times some scholars have employed the symbol 'Q' or 'q' in a broader sense to denote not a common source of Mt. and Lk., but for their common material; and some have postulated a plurality of shorter sources, written or oral, all of which are collectively designated 'Q' or 'q'. More recently strenuous attempts have been made to determine stages in the composition of 'Q' and to characterize its theology and purpose.

J. C. Hawkins, *Horae Synopticae* (Oxford, 1899); A. Harnack, *Sprüche und Reden Jesu* (1907; Eng. tr., 1908); B. H. Streeter, *The Four Gospels* (1924), chs. 7–11. T. W. Manson in H. D. A. Major, T. W. Manson, and C. J. Wright, *The Mission and Message of Jesus* (1937), pp. 331–440; repr. as *The Sayings of Jesus* (1949), pp. 39–148. V. Taylor, 'The Order of Q', *JTS* NS 4 (1953), pp. 27–31; id., 'The Original Order of Q', in A. J. B. Higgins (ed.), *New Testament Essays: Studies in Memory of Thomas Walter Manson* (Manchester [1959]), pp. 246–69; both repr. in Taylor, *New Testament Essays* (1970), pp. 90–118. H. E. Tödt, *Der Menschensohn in der synoptischen Überlieferung* [1959], pp. 206–57; Eng. tr. (1965), pp. 224–83. F. G. Downing, 'Towards the Rehabilitation of Q', *New Testament Studies*, 11 (1964–5), pp. 169–81. G. N. Stanton, 'On the Christology of Q', in B. Lindars, SSF, and S. S. Smalley (eds.), *Christ and the Spirit in the New Testament: In Honour of Charles Francis Digby Moule* (Cambridge, 1973), pp. 27–42. R. A. Edwards, *The Theology of Q: Eschatology, Prophecy, and Wisdom* (Philadelphia [1976]). J. S. Kloppenborg, *The Formation of Q* (Studies in Antiquity and Christianity, ibid. [1987]). R. A. Piper, *Wisdom in the Q-Tradition* (Society for New Testament Studies, Monograph Series, 61; Cambridge, 1989). D. R. Catchpole, *The Quest for Q* (Edinburgh, 1993). See also works cited under SYNOPTIC PROBLEM.

QAB. See QUEEN ANNE'S BOUNTY.

Qaraites. See KARAITES.

Qoheleth. See ECCLESIASTES.

Qorban. See CORBAN.

Quadragesima. Another name for the 40 days of *Lent and, occasionally, for the First Sunday in Lent (six weeks before *Easter). The word 'Quadragesimale' has been sometimes used of a set of sermons delivered in Lent.

Quadragesimo Anno. The encyclical letter of *Pius XI, dated 15 May 1931, confirming and elaborating the theses of *Rerum Novarum (q.v.). Points esp. stressed are: the evil results of free competition and administrative centralization; the incompatibility of strict Socialism with Catholicism; and the need for a reorganization of society on the model of the 'guild' system.

Text in *AAS* 23 (1931), pp. 177–228. An Eng. tr. was pub. by the *Catholic Truth Society under the title *The Social Order* [1931]; also in D. J. O'Brien and T. A. Shannon (eds.), *Catholic Social Thought* (Maryknoll, NY [1992]), pp. 42–79, with introd. pp. 40 f.

Quadratus, St (2nd cent.), the earliest Christian '*Apologist'. About 124 he wrote in Asia Minor an apology for the Christian faith addressed to the Emp. Hadrian, of which a single fragment survives in *Eusebius (*HE* 4. 3. 2.). He is prob. to be identified with the evangelist and prophet of the same name mentioned by Eusebius (ibid. 3. 37. 1; 5. 17. 3); there is also perhaps no compelling reason for rejecting his identification with the Bp. of *Athens (mentioned by Eusebius, ibid. 4. 23. 3), first made by *Jerome (*De vir. ill.* 19; *ep.* 70). Feast day, 26 May.

G. Bardy, 'Sur l'apologiste Quadratus', in *Mélanges Henri Grégoire* (Annuaire de l'Institut de Philologie et d'Histoire orientales et slaves, 9; Brussels, 1949), pp. 75–86. R. M. Grant, 'Quadratus, the first Christian Apologist', in R. H. Fischer (ed.), *A Tribute to Arthur Vööbus* (Chicago [1977]), pp. 177–83. CPG 1 (1983), p. 25 (no. 1060). Bardenhewer, 1, pp. 183–7; Altaner and Stuiber (1978), pp. 61 f. É. Amann in *DTC* 13 (pt. 2; 1937), cols. 1429–31; V. Zangara in *DPAC* 2 (1984), cols. 2957 f., s.v. 'Quadrato'; Eng. tr. in *Encyclopedia of the Early Church*, 2 (Cambridge, 1992), p. 727.

Quadrilateral, Lambeth. See LAMBETH QUADRILATERAL.

quadrivium. The medieval name for the group of four sciences consisting of music, arithmetic, geometry, and astronomy, which together with the *trivium (q.v.) of the inferior sciences constituted the *seven liberal arts.

Quaker. A nickname first given by Justice Bennet in 1650 to George *Fox because he bade the Justice tremble at the Word of the Lord. The word had been used, however, at least as early as 1647 of a foreign religious sect. Early Quakers also explained it by the spiritual trembling sometimes experienced at their religious meetings. See FRIENDS, SOCIETY OF.

See *OED*, s.v.

Quam Singulari. The decree issued, on 8 Aug. 1910, by the Sacred Congregation of the Sacraments, recommending that children be admitted to receive Holy Communion as soon as they have reached the 'age of discretion' (*aetas discretionis*), i.e., by the tests there given, at the age of about 7 years.

Text in *AAS* 2 (1910), pp. 577–83.

Quanta Cura. The encyclical, issued by Pope *Pius IX on 8 Dec. 1864, to which the famous *Syllabus Errorum (q.v.) condemning the doctrines of *liberalism was attached.

Text in the *ASS* 3 (1867), pp. 160–7; excerpts repr. in Denzinger and Hünermann (37th edn., 1991), pp. 795–7 (nos. 2890–6).

Quarant' Ore. See FORTY HOURS' DEVOTION.

Quare Impedit. In the C of E a form of legal action in the temporal court by which a right of presentation to an ecclesiastical benefice is tried. It may be brought by a patron against the bishop on his refusal to institute his presentee to a living. Since the passing of the Benefices Act 1898 its use has been restricted to cases where the objection to presentation is on the grounds of doctrine or ritual. The name is from the opening words of the writ formerly issued to start proceedings; now an ordinary writ of summons is used. See also DUPLEX QUERELA.

Quarles, Francis (1592–1644), religious poet. He was born at Romford, Greater London, and educated at Christ's College, Cambridge (1606–9). In 1613 he went to Heidelberg in the retinue of the Princess Palatine, returning to England by 1615. He now began to publish many biblical paraphrases, among them *Job Militant* (1624) and *Sions Elegies wept by Jeremy* (1624). About 1626 he went to *Dublin, where he became private secretary to J. *Ussher, Abp. of Armagh. In 1630 a collection of his biblical paraphrases was published with the title *Divine Poems*, and in 1632 there appeared his *Divine Fancies*, a small volume of epigrams and meditations in verse. They were followed by his popular *Emblems* (1635), perhaps the most original of emblem-books, though it was partly derived from two Jesuit manuals, *Pia Desideria* (1624) and *Typus Mundi* (1627). In 1638 Quarles published another emblem-book, *Hieroglyphikes of the Life of Man*. In 1640 he was made chronologer to the city of London. In his later years he wrote chiefly devotional prose. His *Enchiridion* (1640), a collection of thoughts on religion and morals, achieved great popularity, and he also wrote *The Loyall Convert* (1644), a pamphlet defending the Royalist cause, of which he was an ardent partisan. His reputation increased after his death through the publication of his posthumous works, among them *The Shepherd's Oracles* (1646), a satire in verse on the contemporary religious disputes. Though often overladen with conceits and epithets in the style of his time, Quarles's poetry betrays deep religious feeling, coloured by a keen sense of sin and of the transitoriness of life.

Complete Works ed. A. B. Grosart (Chertsey Worthies' Library, 3 vols., privately pr., 1880–1), with biog. introd., 1, pp. ix–lxvi. The primary authority is the brief Life by U. Quarles,

widow, prefixed to Quarles's posthumously pub. *Solomon's Recantation, entitled Ecclesiastes Paraphrased* (1645) [no pagination]. K. J. Höltgen, *Francis Quarles* (Buchreihe der Anglia, Zeitschrift für Englische Philologie, 19; 1978), with summary in Eng. J. Horden, *Francis Quarles (1592–1644): A Bibliography of his Works to the Year 1800* (Oxford Bibliographical Society Publications, NS 2; 1953), with introd., pp. 1–16. Further bibl. in *NCBEL* 1 (1974), cols. 1199–201. S. Lee in *DNB* 47 (1896), pp. 92–6.

Quarr Abbey, near Ryde, Isle of Wight. In 1131 or 1132 Baldwin de Redvers founded a monastery on the site, which was originally colonized from *Savigny. With other houses dependent on Savigny, it was affiliated to the *Cistercians in 1147. It became the most considerable religious foundation on the island and survived until the *Dissolution in 1537. Soon afterwards the buildings were destroyed, and only a small part of the medieval structure remains. In 1908 the site was acquired by the *Benedictine monks exiled from *Solesmes (q.v.), who had previously (1901) settled at Appuldurcombe House, near Wroxall, in the centre of the island. A fine abbey in red brick in a Flemish style was erected (consecrated 1912). After the First World War many of the monks returned to Solesmes. The Abbey is now an independent house of the Solesmes Congregation. It was for some time an important centre of liturgical and historical studies.

S. F. Hockey, OSB, *Quarr Abbey and its Lands 1132–1631* (Leicester, 1970). S. C. Kaines-Smith in *VCH*, Hampshire, 5 (1912), pp. 152–4, with map and illustration of the medieval abbey.

Quartodecimanism. The early custom in some places of following Jewish practice in always observing *Easter, i.e. the Christian *Passover, on the 14th day of the month *Nisan, whatever the day of the week, and not (as elsewhere) on the following Sunday. The tradition was esp. rooted in Asia Minor, where it was believed to derive from St *John the Apostle, and upheld by *Melito of Sardis and *Apollinarius of Hierapolis. On a visit to Rome *c*.155 St *Polycarp, Bp. of Smyrna, sought to persuade Anicetus to conform to Quartodeciman usage. Though the Pope refused, he had no scruples about Polycarp's continuing his own custom. Thirty or forty years later a more rigid line was taken up by Pope *Victor, who tried to suppress Quartodecimanism; and when *Polycrates, Bp. of Ephesus, refused to comply, Victor forthwith excommunicated him. Despite this stern measure, which was met with a sharp rebuke from St *Irenaeus (*ap*. Eusebius, *HE* 5. 23–5), the Asiatic Churches retained their practice for the time being. At a later date the Quartodecimans organized themselves as a separate Church. They survived as a sect down to the 5th cent. See also PASCHAL CONTROVERSIES.

F. E. *Brightman, 'The Quartodeciman Question', *JTS* 25 (1923–4), pp. 254–70. B. Lohse, *Das Passafest der Quartadecimaner* (Beiträge zur Förderung christlicher Theologie, 2. Reihe, 54; Gütersloh, 1953). C. W. Dugmore, 'A Note on the Quartodecimans', in F. L. Cross (ed.), *Studia Patristica*, 4 (TU 79; 1961), pp. 411–21. C. Mohrmann, 'Le Conflit pascal au IIᵉ siècle', *VC* 16 (1962), pp. 154–71, with further refs. W. Huber, *Passa und Ostern: Untersuchungen zur Osterfeier der alten Kirche* (Beiheft zur *ZNTW* 35; 1969), esp. pp. 1–88. R. Cantalamessa, *La Pasqua della nostra Salvezza* [Turin, 1971], esp. pp. 116–32 and 147–56. C. C.

Richardson, 'A New Solution to the Quartodeciman Riddle', *JTS* NS 24 (1973), pp. 74–84. T. J. Talley, *The Origins of the Liturgical Year* (New York [1986]), pp. 5–33. See also bibl. to EASTER and PASCHAL CONTROVERSIES.

Quasimodo Sunday. A title in the W. Church for *Low Sunday, derived from the opening words of the *Introit at Mass on that day (*Quasi modo geniti*, 'As new-born babes', 1 Pet. 2: 2).

Quattro Coronati (i.e. 'the Four Crowned Ones'). A group of four saints, commemorated in the W. Church on 8 Nov., to whom a famous ancient basilica on the Celian Hill at *Rome is dedicated. Considerable doubt reigns as to which particular saints are intended. The *Roman Martyrology for 8 Nov. supposes the conflation of two groups of five and four martyrs respectively whose names it gives. It appears from other sources that the one group were five sculptors of Pannonia who were martyred for refusing to make a statue of Aesculapius for a heathen temple, and the other group four martyrs who were buried not at Rome but at Albano in the Alban Hills. They are the patrons of stonemasons.

AASS, Nov. 2 (2) (1931), pp. 590 f., and 3 (1910), pp. 748–84. C. Pietri, *Roma Christiana: Recherches sur l'Église de Rome . . . (311–440)* (Bibliothèque des Écoles françaises d'Athènes et de Rome, 224; 1976), 1, pp. 493–8. On the church, R. Krautheimer and S. Corbett in R. Krautheimer and others, *Corpus Basilicarum Christianarum Romae*, 4 (Rome, 1970), pp. 1–39 [in Eng.], with full bibl. A. Amore, OFM, and P. Cannata in *Bibliotheca Sanctorum*, 10 (Rome, 1968), cols. 1276–304, s.v., with bibl.

Queen Anne's Bounty (QAB). A fund incorporated by Queen *Anne in 1704 by letters patent pursuant to Queen Anne's Bounty Act 1703, to receive the first fruits (*annates) and tenths which the Appointment of Bishops Act 1533 had diverted from Rome to the Crown under *Henry VIII. On surrendering them for the benefit of the Church, she directed their use for the augmentation of the livings of the poorer Anglican clergy. Grants of capital (not income) were made to poorly endowed benefices; and later the fund was empowered to make loans (from 1777) and disbursements (from 1803) for the building and repair of parsonage houses, etc. Between 1809 and 1820 it received grants of over £1,000,000 from Parliament and at various times large private benefactions. By the Tithe Act 1925, QAB was charged with the collection of ecclesiastical tithe rentcharge and its distribution to benefices and ecclesiastical corporations. Annates and tenths, whose value had dwindled to almost nothing, were finally extinguished by the First Fruits and Tenths Measure 1926. When the Tithe Act 1936 extinguished tithe rentcharge, QAB received Government redemption stock as compensation, the amount being assessed by the Tithe Redemption Commission which was dissolved on 1 April 1960. On 1 April 1948, by the Church Commissioners Measure 1947, QAB and the *Ecclesiastical Commissioners were united in a new body, the *Church Commissioners for England (q.v.).

A. Savidge, *The Foundation and Early Years of Queen Anne's Bounty* (CHS, 1955); G. F. A. Best, *Temporal Pillars: Queen Anne's Bounty, the Ecclesiastical Commissioners, and the Church of England* (Cambridge, 1964).

Quentin, Henri (1872–1935), *Benedictine scholar. Professed at *Maredsous in 1895, he was transferred to *Solésmes in 1897 and ordained priest in 1902. Five years later *Pius X called him to Rome as a member of the commission on the revision of the *Vulgate, in which capacity he superintended the photographing of most of the important Vulgate MSS at Paris, Rome, London, and elsewhere, including the entire *Codex Amiatinus at Florence; and he was the principal editor of the text of the *Pentateuch (1926–36). His own writings include *J. D. Mansi et les grandes collections conciliaires* (1900) and *Les Martyrologes historiques du moyen âge* (1908), the latter containing discussions of the text of the *martyrologies of *Bede and other early medieval compilers. He also issued several writings in defence of his much-contested principles for establishing the Vulgate text. The new Office of the Feast of the *Sacred Heart (1928) was, for the most part, his work.

C. Mohlberg, OSB, 'Commemorazione dell'abbate Dom Enrico Quentin', *Atti della Pontificia Accademia Romana di Archeologia*, Serie 3, Rendiconti, 11 (for 1935; 1936), pp. 13–39, with list of his works, pp. 34–9.

Quesnel, Pasquier (1634–1719), French *Jansenist. Educated by the *Jesuits, he studied philosophy and theology at the *Sorbonne and entered the Congregation of the *Oratory in 1657, where he was soon entrusted with the direction of students and became the author of a number of spiritual books. In 1672 he published *Abrégé de la morale de l'Évangile*, with a commendatory preface by the Bp. of Châlons-sur-Marne; its subsequent editions, expanded and revised, became famous under the title of *Le Nouveau Testament en français, avec des réflexions morales sur chaque verset*, usually called *Réflexions morales*. As against the formalized methods of spirituality in the manuals, the work emphasized the value of the close study of the Scriptures in increasing true devotion. In 1675 he published a scholarly edition of the works of Pope *Leo I which, however, was placed on the *Index owing to the *Gallican theories developed in the notes. In 1681 he was removed to Orléans on the charge of upholding Jansenist views. Three years later he refused to subscribe to an anti-Jansenist formula imposed by his superiors and went to Brussels, where he lived together with A. *Arnauld. In 1703 he was imprisoned by the Abp. of Malines at the instigation of Philip V, but escaped and fled to the Netherlands the following year. His subsequent life was filled with defences of himself and his *Réflexions*, which, commended by the Abp. of *Paris, Cardinal L. A. *de Noailles, went through many editions, but was condemned by a brief of *Clement XI in 1708 and, five years later, by the bull '*Unigenitus'. Among his doctrines condemned by the bull are the theses that no grace is given outside the Church, that grace is irresistible, that without grace man is incapable of any good, and that all acts of a sinner, even prayer and attendance at Mass, are sins. Quesnel never accepted the condemnation, and though he asked for and received the Last Sacraments, he appealed to a future General Council for his vindication.

L. Batterel, *Mémoires domestiques pour servir à l'histoire de l'Oratoire* (ed. A. M. P. Ingold, 5 vols., 1902–11), with list of Quesnel's writings, 4, pp. 424–93. *Correspondance de Pasquier Quesnel*, ed. A. Le Roy (2 vols., 1900). *Causa Quesnelliana* (Brussels,

1704; docs. ed. by order of the Abp. of Malines). A. Le Roy, *Un Janséniste en exil* (1900; with selection of Quesnel's Letters). J. A. G. Tans, *Pasquier Quesnel et les Pays-Bas: Correspondance, publiée avec introduction et annotations* (Publications de l'Institut Français d'Amsterdam, Maison Descartes, 6; 1960); id. and H. Schmitz du Moulin, *Pasquier Quesnel devant la Congrégation de l'Index: Correspondance avec Francesco Barberini et mémoires sur la mise à l'Index de son édition des œuvres de saint Léon publiés avec introduction et annotations* (International Archives of the History of Ideas, 71; 1974). L. Ceyssens, 'Les Papiers de Quesnel saisis à Bruxelles et transportés à Paris en 1703 et 1704', *RHE* 44 (1949), pp. 508–51. J. A. G. Tans, 'Port-Royal entre le réveil spirituel et le drame gallican: le rôle de Pasquier Quesnel', *Lias*, 4 (1977) pp. 99–114. Id. and L. Ceyssens, 'Pasquier Quesnel (1634–1719). Autour de l'Unigenitus', *Ephemerides Theologicae Lovanienses*, 59 (1983), pp. 201–66, repr. in idd., *Autour de l'Unigenitus* (Bibliotheca Ephemeridum Theologicarum Lovaniensium, 56; 1987), pp. 583–648. J. Carreyre in *DTC* 13 (pt. 2; 1937), cols. 1460–535, s.v. 'Quesnel et le Quesnellisme'; J. A. G. Tans in *Dict. Sp.* 12 (pt. 2; 1986), cols. 2732–46, s.v.

Quest of the Historical Jesus. See HISTORICAL JESUS, QUEST OF THE.

Quicunque Vult (Lat., 'Whosoever wishes' [*salvus esse*, 'to be saved']). An alternative name for the '*Athanasian Creed' (q.v.) from its opening words.

Quien, Michel Le. See LE QUIEN, MICHEL.

Quiercy, Synods of. Of the several synods held in the 9th cent. at Quiercy (*palatium Carisiacum*), near Laon, the two most notable are:

(1) Synod of 849, under *Hincmar of Reims. It condemned the strict Augustinianism of *Gottschalk, who was sentenced to degradation and imprisonment at Hautvillers.

(2) Synod of 853, also under Hincmar. It repeated its condemnation of Gottschalk's doctrines, publishing four chapters ('capitula'), namely (*a*) that God has predestined to *life* only; (*b*) that human free will, lost by Adam, was restored to us by Christ; (*c*) that God would have all men to be saved; and (*d*) that Jesus Christ suffered for all. These articles were rejected by the Church of Lyons and formally repudiated in 855 by the Council of *Valence (q.v.).

(1) Hardouin, 5, cols. 17–20; Mansi, 14 (1769), cols. 919–22; W. Hartmann (ed.), *Die Konzilien der Karolingischen Teilreiche 843–859* (*MGH*, Concilia, 3; 1984), pp. 194–99. Hefele and Leclercq, 4 (pt. 1; 1911), pp. 150–6, and 4 (pt. 2; 1911), pp. 1308–10.

(2) Hardouin, 5, cols. 57 f.; Mansi, 14 (1769), cols. 995–8; W. Hartmann, op. cit, pp. 294–7. Hefele and Leclercq, 4 (pt. 1; 1911), pp. 197–9, and 4 (pt. 2; 1911), pp. 1324, 1390–8. B. Lavaud, OP, in *DTC* 12 (pt. 2; 1935), cols. 2920–2, s.v. 'Prédestination', with Lat. text and Fr. tr. of the *capitula*.

Quietism. The term 'Quietism', which is often used loosely of any system of spirituality minimizing human activity and responsibility, is usually restricted to the teaching of certain 17th-cent. writers, esp. that of M. de *Molinos, and, to a lesser degree, Mme *Guyon and Abp. *Fénelon.

The fundamental principle of Quietism is its condemnation of all human effort. Its exponents seem to have exaggerated earlier teaching, such as that of St *Teresa of Ávila, on the 'prayer of quiet'. In their view, man, in order to be perfect, must attain complete passivity and annihilation of will, abandoning himself to God to such an extent that he cares neither for Heaven nor Hell, nor for his own salvation. This state is reached by a certain form of mental prayer in which the soul consciously refuses not only all discursive meditation but any distinct act such as desire for virtue, love of Christ, or adoration of the Divine Persons, and simply rests in the presence of God in pure faith. As this passive prayer expresses the height of perfection, it makes any outward acts of mortification, almsgiving, going to confession, etc., superfluous. Once a man has attained to it, sin is impossible, for then all he does or thinks is the work of God. The devil may, indeed, tempt him and even compel him to commit actions that would be sinful in others, but when his will has become completely annihilated they cease to be sins in him; on the contrary, the man who has reached this state must carefully guard against being disquieted by such distractions, lest he should be disturbed in his state of mystic death.

Quietism was condemned in the person of M. de Molinos by *Innocent XI in his bull 'Coelestis Pastor' of 19 Nov. 1687. Sixty-eight propositions from Molinos' writings were condemned. Other notable exponents of Quietist teaching were P. M. Petrucci (1636–1701) and the *Barnabite, F. Lacombe, the director of Mme Guyon.

H. Heppe, *Geschichte der quietistischen Mystik in der katholischen Kirche* (1875). J.-R. Armogathe, *Le quiétisme* (Que sais-je?, 1545; 1973). M. Petrocchi, *Il quietismo italiano del seicento* (Storia e Letteratura, 20; 1948). J. Orcibal, *La Rencontre du Carmel thérésien avec les mystiques du nord* (Bibliothèque de l'École des Hautes Études, Section des Sciences Religieuses, 70; 1959), and other works. R. A. *Knox, *Enthusiasm* (1950), esp. pp. 231–87. Pourrat, 4 (2nd edn., 1928), pp. 128–295. E. Pacho, OCD, and J. Le Brun in *Dict. Sp.* 12 (pt. 2; 1986), cols. 2756–842, s.v., with bibl. See also works cited under FÉNELON, MOLINOS, and GUYON.

Quinisext Synod. See TRULLAN SYNOD.

Quiñones, Francisco de (d. 1540), reforming cardinal. ('Quignon', the French form of his name, is also used.) Born at León of a noble Spanish family, he entered the *Franciscan Order in 1498. In 1517 he became Definitor General and in 1523 and 1526 he was elected Minister *General of the *Observants, in which office he worked for a strengthening of discipline, promoted missions and studies, and induced many Conventuals to join the Observants. In 1526, and esp. in 1527 after the Sack of Rome and the imprisonment of *Clement VII, he mediated successfully between *Charles V and the Pope, who made him cardinal in the same year or early in 1528. From 1529 he took an active part in the question of the divorce of *Henry VIII, defending the interests of Queen Catherine.

It was then that Quiñones, by order of the Pope, devoted himself to the compilation of a new *Breviary, which *Paul III published in 1535, often called the 'Breviary of the Holy Cross' after the cardinal's titular church. It abolished almost entirely the difference of rank in the Feasts as well as *antiphons, *versicles, and *Little Office of Our Lady, and reduced to a minimum the readings from the Lives of the Saints. On the other hand, the whole *Psalter was recited during the week and nearly the whole of the Bible read during the year. The several Hours were almost equal in length, each containing only three Psalms, and Mattins on all days only three lessons. A second recension of it appeared in 1536. Although special permission was necessary for the recitation of Quiñones' Breviary, which was originally intended only for private use, it soon began to penetrate even into the public offices of the religious orders and more than 100 editions appeared between 1536 and 1566. In other quarters it was attacked for its disregard of tradition and it was eventually proscribed by *Paul IV in 1558.

Quiñones' Breviary considerably influenced T. *Cranmer, whose early drafts of a reformed Service Book and Calendar follow it closely; and with its uniformity, its continuous reading of Scripture, the recitation of the whole Psalter during a given period, and the general simplification by cutting out antiphons, responses, and the like, the BCP of 1549 and, through it, the final shape of the BCP, owe a good deal to the 'Breviary of the Holy Cross'.

Quiñones' Breviary of 1535 was repr. by J. Wickham Legg (Cambridge, 1888); the 2nd recension, of 1536, ed. id. (HBS 35 (text) and 42 (liturgical introd., Life of Quiñones, notes and indices); 1908–12). [Fernando] Marquis d'Alcedo, Le Cardinal Quiñones et la Sainte Ligue (Bayonne, 1910). J. A. Jungmann, SJ, 'Warum ist das Reformbrevier des Kardinals Quiñonez gescheitert?', ZKT 78 (1956), pp. 98–107; H. Boone Porter, 'Hispanic Influences on Worship in the English Tongue', in J. N. Alexander (ed.), Time and Community: In Honor of Thomas Julian Talley (Washington, DC [1990]), pp. 171–84, esp. pp. 171–4. See also works cited under BREVIARY and COMMON PRAYER, BOOK OF.

Quinquagesima. Properly the period of 50 days preceding *Easter which begins on the Sunday before *Ash Wednesday; but the word came to be generally applied only to the Sunday mentioned. In earlier times a new stage in the pre-Lenten discipline, e.g. abstinence from flesh-meat, began on this day. It ceased to have any liturgical significance and was suppressed in the RC Church in 1969. It has also been dropped in some modern Anglican liturgies. The word is occasionally used also of the 50 days which extend from Easter to *Pentecost.

A. Chavasse, 'Temps de préparation à la Pâque d'après quelques livres liturgiques romains', Rech. S.R. 37 (1950), pp. 125–45, esp. III, 'La "Cinquantaine" préparatoire au jour de Pâques ou Quinquagésime', p. 130. P. Siffrin, OSB, in EC 10 (1953), col. 421, s.v. See also bibl. to SEPTUAGESIMA and SEXAGESIMA.

Quinque Viae. The five 'ways' or arguments by which St *Thomas Aquinas (Summa Theol., 1, q. 2, art. 3) sought to prove the existence of God a posteriori, i.e. from effects of His which are known to us. Aquinas's arguments conclude that (1) change (motus) implies a first unchanging changer; (2) that a sequence of efficient causes, and their effects, such as we find in the world, implies an uncaused first cause; (3) that the existence of things able to be generated and to perish implies the existence of what is not generable and perishable (i.e. 'necessary') and that the existence of what is necessary ultimately implies the existence of something the existence of which derives from nothing apart from itself; (4) that the comparisons we make (more or less 'true', 'good', 'noble', etc.) imply a standard of comparison which is itself perfect in all these

qualities; (5) that the fulfilment by inanimate or unintelligent objects of an end to which they invariably tend implies the existence of a purpose or intelligence operative in nature.

A. [J. P.] Kenny, The Five Ways: St Thomas Aquinas' Proofs of God's Existence (Studies in Ethics and the Philosophy of Religion, 1969); F. Van Steenberghen, Le Problème de l'Existence de Dieu dans les Écrits de S. Thomas d'Aquin (Philosophes médiévaux, 23; 1980). See also works on the theology of Thomas Aquinas, cited s.v.

quire. The older spelling, still retained in the BCP, of the word now usually spelt **choir**.

Quirinus. The signature over which the series of 69 brilliantly written letters on the First *Vatican Council was published in the Augsburger Allgemeine Zeitung in 1869–70. The writer is now known to have been J. J. I. von *Döllinger, who relied on material supplied by informants residing in Rome, among them Lord *Acton and J. *Friedrich. The letters, which were directed against the dominant party at the Council which was pressing for the definition of the Pope's Infallibility, maintained that the anti-infallibilist cause suffered from the many non-theological factors working in favour of an early definition, e.g. the Pope's personal influence and the disproportionate representation of Italians at the Council. Admittedly the work of a strong partisan, they remain one of the primary sources for the history of the Council. See also JANUS.

An Eng. tr. was pub. in 1870. See also [E.] C. Butler, OSB, The Vatican Council (1930), 1, ch. 14, and V. Conzemius, 'Die Verfasser der "Römischen Briefe von Konzil" des "Quirinus"', Freiburger Geschichtsblätter, 52 (1963–64), pp. 229–56.

Qumran. The site of some ruins at the NW end of the *Dead Sea, c.8 miles S. of *Jericho. It was near here that the first of the so-called *Dead Sea Scrolls were discovered in 1947, to be followed by further finds in later years. Excavations carried out between 1951 and 1956 show that the site was occupied principally between c.130 BC and AD 68/9, probably with a break caused either by military aggression (c.40 BC) or an earthquake (31 or 24 BC) and lasting to the end of the reign of *Herod the Great. Subsequently the site was used as a Roman military outpost until the fall of Masada (AD 74); coin evidence also suggests that it was occupied by Jewish insurgents during the revolt of *Bar Cochba (AD 132–5).

R. de Vaux, OP, L'archéologie et les manuscrits de la Mer Morte (Schweich Lectures for 1959; London, 1961; rev. Eng. tr., 1973). J. T. Milik, Dix ans de découvertes dans le Désert de Juda (1957; Eng. tr., Studies in Biblical Theology, 26; 1959); E.-M. Laperrousaz, Qoumrân: L'établissement essénien des bords de la mer Morte (1976); P. R. Davies, Qumran (Cities of the Biblical World; Guildford, 1982); P. R. Callaway, The History of the Qumran Community (Journal for the Study of the Pseudepigrapha, Supplement Series, 3; Sheffield [1988]), pp. 29–51. E.-M. Laperrousaz and others in Dict. Bibl., Suppl. 9 (1979), cols. 737–805, s.v.

Qumran Scrolls. See DEAD SEA SCROLLS.

quoad omnia. The name given to parishes in *Scotland which were a unit of administration in respect of all things civil and ecclesiastical. If, however, through changed circumstances, e.g. owing to the growth of population, the parochial church was found insufficient and a portion of the original parish was erected by the Church of Scotland into a parish with a church of its own, the new parish was designated *quoad sacra*, i.e. as provided in respect of ecclesiastical matters alone. Historically, the stipend payable to the minister of a *quoad omnia* parish formed a burden on the *teinds related to the parish. Where a *quoad sacra* parish was erected, however, the stipend of the minister was secured by endowments acquired by the Church at the time and by the liberality of the members. With the standardization of stipend consequent upon the enactment of the Church of Scotland (Property and Endowments) Act 1925 and the later discontinuance of the parish as a unit of Local Government administration, all parishes of the Church of Scotland are now in effect *quoad sacra* ones.

quoad sacra. See QUOAD OMNIA.

quodlibet. The name of an academic exercise in medieval universities, chiefly Paris. Twice a year, before Christmas and Easter, a disputation was held in which the master undertook to deal with any questions (*disputatio de quolibet*) raised by any of the participants (*a quolibet*). The subjects ranged from abstruse questions of theology to the smallest details of daily life. The answers of the masters were afterwards drawn up in writing and published. Thus, for example, we possess eleven quodlibets of St *Thomas Aquinas and part of a twelfth. The exercise was not compulsory. The practice seems to have begun in the time of *Alexander of Hales and Guerric of St Quentin and was

at its height in the later 13th and early 14th cents. In the course of the 14th cent. its character changed, and it came to be part of the exercise required for a bachelor seeking the licentiate. One of the most famous encounters was between St Thomas Aquinas and John *Pecham on the doctrine of the soul.

P. Glorieux, *La Littérature quodlibétique* (Bibliothèque thomiste, 5 and 21; 1925–35); id., 'Où en est la question du Quodlibet?', *Revue du moyen âge latin*, 2 (1946), pp. 405–14. J. F. Wippel, 'The Quodlibetal Question as a Distinctive Genre', in *Les Genres Littéraires dans les Sources Théologiques et Philosophiques Médiévales: Actes du Colloque international de Louvain-la-Neuve 25–27 mai 1981* (Université Catholique de Louvain, Publications de l'Institut d'Études médiévales, 2nd ser. 5; 1982), pp. 67–84.

Quo Vadis? Acc. to a legend, first found in the 'Acts of St *Peter', the words 'Domine quo vadis?' (Lat., 'Lord, whither goest Thou?') were spoken by St *Peter when, fleeing from Rome, he met Christ on the *Appian Way. The Lord answered: 'I am coming to be crucified again', words which Peter took to mean that He was to suffer again in His disciple; so he turned back to Rome, where he was martyred. The legend is mentioned by St *Ambrose, though his text originally had 'Domine quo venis?', changed in later MSS. The small church of S. Maria delle Piante on the Appian Way, commonly called *Domine Quo Vadis*, which was rebuilt early in the 17th cent., commemorates the incident.

The development of the legend can be studied in 'Acts of St Peter', 35; *Origen, *Comm. in Joan.* 20. 12 (*PG* 14, 600B); Ambrose, *Ep.* 75a.13 (ed. M. Zelzer; CSEL 82 (pt. 3; 1982), p. 90; formerly pr. between *epp.* 21 and 22, *PL* 16. 1011).

R

Rabanus Maurus (*c*.780–856), poet, teacher, and ecclesiastical administrator. Entering the abbey of *Fulda as a child *oblate, he was sent *c*.800 for further study to *Alcuin at Tours. He returned to Fulda as master of the cloister school (818) and abbot (824–42). His pupils (818–42) included *Walafrid Strabo, *Lupus of Ferrières, and the pioneer vernacular scholar, *Otfrid of Weissenburg. As abbot Rabanus supervised extensive building work at Fulda and its dependencies and governed a total confraternity of over 600 monks. His active role in Carolingian politics was interrupted in 841 by the dynastic struggle which followed the death of *Louis I. Rabanus returned to public life as Abp. of Mainz (847–56), holding important synods in 847, 848, and 852. He was venerated as a saint in Fulda and Mainz, but never formally canonized. Feast day, 4 Feb.

As a schoolmaster Rabanus wrote textbooks on grammar and the reckoning of time. He wrote commentaries (many still unprinted) on nearly every Book of the Bible, and he enriched the Fulda liturgy with new hymns and a revised martyrology. As abbot he wrote several treatises on ecclesiastical law and practice, the best known being the *De institutione clericorum*, a vade-mecum for the clergy; as archbishop he addressed specific issues of discipline (e.g. *chorepiscopi) and theology (notably in his *De praedestinatione* against *Gottschalk). Over 50 of Rabanus' letters survive, a comprehensive series of sermons for Sundays and feast-days throughout the year, and about 100 poems. His earliest work, the *De laudibus sancti crucis*, in alternating prose and acrostic verse with superimposed drawings, had a wide and sustained success. The *De rerum naturis* (also called *De universo* and *De originibus rerum*), written in his enforced leisure *c*.842, is an encyclopaedic view of Christian belief and practice and of man in society and in the natural world.

Works ed. J. Pamelius and G. Colvenerius (6 vols., bound in 3, Cologne, 1626–7); repr. in J. P. Migne, *PL* 107–12. Modern edns. by E. Dümmler of his letters in *MGH*, Epistolae, 5 (1898), pp. 379–516, with appendix of frags. pp. 517–33, and of his poems, *MGH*, Poetae, 2 (1884), pp. 154–244, with 'Appendix Hymnorum Incertae Originis', pp. 244–58; by A. Koepler of his *De institutione clericorum* (Veröffentlichungen aus dem kirchenhistorischen Seminar München, no. 5; 1901); by J. McCulloh of his *Martyrologium* (CCCM 44, 1979, pp. 1–161), and by W. M. Stevens of his *De computo* (ibid., pp. 163–331). Facsimile edn. from MS Vienna, Nat. Bibl., lat. 652, of his *Liber de laudibus sanctae crucis*, with introd. by K. Holter (Codices Selecti, 33 and 33*; Graz, 1972–3). The only contemporary source for Rabanus' life is Rudolf of Fulda, *Miracula Sanctorum in Fuldenses Ecclesias translatorum*, ed. G. Waitz in *MGH*, Scriptores, 15 (pt. 1; 1887), pp. 328–41, concluding (pp. 340 f.) with a detailed list of Rabanus' writings. G. M. Dreves, *Hymnologische Studien zu Venantius Fortunatus und Rabanus Maurus* (Veröffentlichungen aus dem kirchenhistorischen Seminar München, III. Reihe, no. 3; 1908), pp. 55–136. P. Lehmann, 'Zu Hrabans geistiger Bedeutung', in *Sankt Bonifatius: Gedenkgabe zum zwölfhundertsten Todestag* (Fulda, 1954), pp. 473–87; repr. in his *Erforschung des Mittelalters*, 3 (Stuttgart, 1960), pp. 198–212. W. Böhne (ed.), *Hrabanus*

Maurus und seine Schule: Festschrift der Rabanus-Maurus-Schule 1980 (Fulda, 1980), with full bibl. by H. Spelsberg, pp. 210–28. R. Kottje and H. Zimmermann (eds.), *Hrabanus Maurus: Lehrer, Abt und Bischof* (Akademie der Wissenschaften und der Literatur, Abhandlungen der Geistes- und Sozialwissenschaftliche Klasse, Einzelveröffentlichungen, 4; Mainz [1982]). M. Reuter, *Text und Bild im Codex 132 der Bibliothek von Montecassino 'Liber Rabani de originibus rerum'* (Münchener Beiträge zur Mediävistik und Renaissance-Forschung, 34; 1984). Raby, pp. 179–81, with bibl. p. 474; J. Szövérffy, *Die Annalen der lateinischen Hymnendichtung*, 1 (1964), pp. 220–7. J. M. Wallace-Hadrill, *The Frankish Church* (Oxford History of the Christian Church, 1983), pp. 314–22. H. Peltier in *DTC* 13 (pt. 2; 1937), cols. 1601–20, s.v.; R. Kottje in *Verfasserlexikon* (2nd edn.), 4 (1983), cols. 166–96, s.v. 'Hrabanus Maurus'; id. in *Dict. Sp.* 13 (1988), cols. 1–10, s.v.

Rabbi (Heb., 'my master'). A Jewish title of respect given to honoured teachers by disciples and others (Mt. 23: 7). Christ is so addressed in the Gospels (Jn. 1: 38, etc.). Shortly after NT times it became added as a recognized title to the name of Jewish religious teachers, e.g. 'Rabbi Johanan'. The Romans invested the rabbis with delegated judicial powers which lasted in Europe until political emancipation in modern times. Today in the W. rabbis are little more than ministers of religion, but in Israel they are state functionaries.

Rabbula (d. 435), Bp. of *Edessa from 412. The leading figure in the Syrian Church in his day, he strongly opposed *Nestorianism, and attacked in particular the writings of *Theodore of Mopsuestia (d. 428). He translated into Syriac St *Cyril of Alexandria's 'De Recta Fide', and was also the author of some letters and hymns, a sermon against Nestorius, and a number of canons regulating the life of monks and clergy. It was once thought that he was responsible for producing the *Peshitta NT. His successor in the see was *Ibas.

Rabbula of Edessa is not to be confused with the scribe Rabbula, after whom the illuminated 'Rabbula Gospels' MS of 586 in Florence (Laur., Plut. I. 56) is named.

J. J. Overbeck (ed.), *S. Ephraemi Syri, Rabulae Episcopi Edesseni, Balaei aliorumque Opera Selecta* (Oxford, 1865), containing text of *Vita* (pp. 159–209), prose works (pp. 210–44), and some poetical and other texts (pp. 245–8, 362–78). Rabbula's canons ed., with introd. and Eng. tr., in A. Vööbus, *Syriac and Arabic Documents regarding Legislation relative to Syrian Asceticism* (Papers of the Estonian Theological Society in Exile, 11; Stockholm, 1960), pp. 24–50. P. Peeters, SJ, 'La Vie de Rabboula, évêque d'Édesse', *Rech. S.R.* 18 (1928), pp. 170–204 [very sceptical about the value of *Vita*]. G. G. Blum, *Rabbula von Edessa: Der Christ, der Bischof, der Theologe* (CSCO 300; 1969), with bibl. *CPG* 3 (1979), pp. 249 f. (nos. 6491–7). I. Ortiz de Urbina, SJ, *Patrologia Syriaca* (2nd edn., Rome, 1965), pp. 96–9. E. Venables in *DCB* 4 (1887), pp. 532–4, s.v. 'Rabbúlas'; I. Ziadé in *DTC* 13 (pt. 2; 1937), cols. 1620–6, s.v. 'Rabboula'. See also bibl. to PESHITTA.

Raccolta (Ital., 'collection'). An officially approved RC prayer book containing all the devotions to which Papal

1360

*indulgences were attached. The first Raccolta was published in 1807 at Rome by Telesforo Galli. The Raccolta has now been supplanted by the much briefer 'Enchiridion Indulgentiarum' of 1968, revised in 1986.

Racovian Catechism. The first statement of Socinian principles. Drawn up by Valentin Schmalz and Johannes Völkel on the basis of drafts by F. P. *Socinus, it was published in Polish in 1605 at Raków, an early stronghold of Socinianism in S. Poland. Versions in German (1608) and Latin (1609) followed. It was professedly not a formal confessional creed, designed to be dogmatically imposed on the Socinians, but a body of opinions which would point believers towards eternal life. In eight sections it dealt with (1) the Scriptures (the only source of truth), (2) the way of salvation (knowledge and a holy life), (3) the knowledge of God ('the Supreme Lord of all things', with rejection of the Trinity), (4) the Person of Christ (a man by his marvellous life and resurrection raised to divine power), (5) the Prophetic Office of Christ, (6) the Kingship of Christ, (7) the Priesthood of Christ, and (8) the Church (the body of Christians who uphold and profess the saving doctrines). A copy of the Latin version, sent to England with a dedication to *James I, was publicly burnt in 1614.

An Eng. version by J. *Biddle was pub. at Amsterdam in 1652; it was formally burnt in 1654 by order of O. *Cromwell. New Eng. edn. by Thomas Rees with Historical Introduction, London, 1818.

Rad, Gerhard von (1901–71), OT scholar. He was born at Nürnberg and educated at the Universities of Erlangen and Tübingen. After serving as *Privatdozent* at Leipzig (1930–4), he held chairs at Jena (1934–45), Göttingen (1945–9), and Heidelberg (1949–66). His most important writings are concerned with three main fields of study: Deuteronomy; the literary analysis, *form criticism, *traditio-historical criticism, and theological interpretation of the *Hexateuch; and the theology of the OT. On Deuteronomy he wrote his first substantial work, *Das Gottesvolk im Deuteronomium* (1929), *Deuteronomium-Studien* (1947; Eng. tr., 1953) and a commentary in *Das Alte Testament Deutsch* entitled *Das fünfte Buch Mose* (1964; Eng. tr., 1966). He attributed Deuteronomy to the preaching activity of priestly and Levitical circles who sought to restore the ancient traditions of the Israelite amphictyony, emphasized the influence of covenant formulas on its structure, and claimed that the idea of the 'Holy War' is an important element in its teaching. This last idea he also propounded in *Der Heilige Krieg im alten Israel* (1951). His principal writings on the Hexateuch were *Die Priesterschrift im Hexateuch* (1934), *Das formgeschichtliche Problem des Hexateuchs* (1938, repr. in his collected works), and his commentary on Genesis in *Das Alte Testament Deutsch* entitled *Das erste Buch Mose* (3 vols., 1949–53; Eng. tr., 1961). He applied form-critical methods to the entire structure of the Hexateuch and claimed that the short historical *credo* or cultic confession in Deut. 26: 5 f. was a miniature of the Hexateuch. He further maintained that the Exodus-Conquest traditions (the festival legend of the Feast of *Weeks at Gilgal) and the Sinai traditions (the festival legend of the renewal of the covenant at Shechem) were originally separate, and he emphasized the creative

unifying work of the compiler. His *Theologie des Alten Testament* (2 vols., 1957–60; Eng. tr., 1962–5) was also based on form-critical study and reflects important aspects of current contemporary German theological debate. He did not attempt to construct a unified system of OT theology, but expounded, first, Israel's confession of the *Heilsgeschichte* as proclaimed in the cult and transmitted in the historical traditions, second, the searching criticism of the older traditions by the prophets and their proclamation that new Divine acts were about to take place, and third, the relationship between the OT and the NT in terms of a modified typological interpretation. His *Weisheit in Israel* (1970; Eng. tr., 1972) is also important.

Collection of his more important essays in *Gesammelte Studien zum Alten Testament* (1958); Eng. tr., with additional essay, *The Problem of the Hexateuch and other Essays* (1966). Festschriften for his 60th birthday, ed. R. Rendtorff and K. Koch, *Studien zur Theologie der alttestamentlichen Überlieferungen* (Neukirchen, 1961), with list of his works, pp. 162–74; and for his 70th birthday, ed. H. G. Wolff, *Probleme biblischer Theologie* (Munich, 1971), incl. list of recent works, pp. 665–8. M. E. Andrew, 'Gerhard von Rad—A Personal Memoir', *Expository Times*, 83 (1971–2), pp. 296–30. J. L. Crenshaw, *Gerhard von Rad* (Waco, Tex. [1978]). R. Smend, *Deutsche Alttestamentler in drei Jahrhunderten* (Göttingen, 1989), pp. 226–54.

Radbertus, Paschasius. See PASCHASIUS RADBERTUS.

Radegunde, St (*c*.518–87), the Queen of Clothar I. The daughter of a prince of Thuringia, she fell into the hands of the Franks after a successful invasion of her country. She was a woman of great piety who did not wish to marry, but as an act of charity consented to become the wife of Clothar, a man of debased tastes and evil character (*c*. 540). His murder of her brother gave her an excuse to flee from court (*c*.550) and to persuade Médard, Bp. of Noyon, to ordain her a deaconess. Not long afterwards she founded a monastery of nuns outside Poitiers, where the rule of *Caesarius of Arles was adopted. Here she spent the remaining 30 years of her life in prayer, study, and good works. In 569 she obtained for her convent, from the Emp. Justin II, a large fragment of the true cross, which inspired *Venantius Fortunatus to write his famous '*Vexilla regis'. Feast day, 13 Aug.

Contemporary Lives by Venantius Fortunatus and the nun, Baudonivia, pr. in *AASS*, Aug. 3 (1737), pp. 67–83; crit. edn. by B. Krusch in *MGH*, Scriptores Rerum Merovingicarum, 2 (1888), pp. 358–95; Eng. tr. in *Sainted Women of the Dark Ages*, ed. and tr. J. A. McNamara and others (Durham, NC, and London, 1992), pp. 70–105; the former Life also ed., with Fr. tr., by R. Aigrain (Paris, 1910). On these Lives see C. Leonardi, 'Fortunato e Baudonivia', in H. Mordek (ed.), *Aus Kirche und Reich: . . . Festschrift für Friedrich Kempf* (Sigmaringen, 1983), pp. 23–32. Life by *Hildebert of Lavardin in *AASS*, loc. cit., pp. 83–92, repr. in J. P. Migne, *PL* 171. 967–88. Anon. Life attributed to Henry Bradshaw, OSB (d. 1513), pr. *c*. 1508–27, ed. F. Brittain (Cambridge, 1926). Modern Lives by E. Briand (Poitiers, 1898) and R. Aigrain ('Les Saints', 1918; 2nd edn., Poitiers, 1952). F. Brittain, *St Radegund: Patroness of Jesus College, Cambridge* (1925). L. Schmidt, *St Radegundis in Gross-Höflein: Zur frühmittelalterlichen Verehrung der heiligen Frankenkönigin im Burgenland und in Ostniederösterreich* (Burgenländische Forschungen, 32; 1956). G. Scheibelreiter, 'Königstöchter im Kloster. Radegund (†587) und der Nonnenaufstand von Poitiers (589)', *Mitteilungen des Instituts für Österreichische Geschichtsforschung*, 87 (1979), pp. 1–37. H. *Leclercq, OSB, in *DACL* 14 (pt. 2; 1948), cols. 2044–55, s.v.

Radewijns, Florentius. See FLORENTIUS RADEWIJNS.

Rahner, Karl (1904–84), RC theologian. Of Swabian extraction, Karl Rahner followed his elder brother into the *Jesuit Order in 1922. He was ordained in 1932. He continued his studies at Freiburg and Innsbruck, and was appointed to the theological faculty of the latter university in 1936. After the Second World War he returned to Innsbruck in 1948 and in the following year became Professor of Dogmatic Theology. He was Professor at Munich (1964–7) and then at Münster (1967–71). He was a *peritus* at the Second *Vatican Council.

Rahner was the author of a very large number of books and articles. The ultimate source of his thought is to be found in Joseph Maréchal's vast work *Le Point de départ de la métaphysique* (1923–49), which attempted to construct a revised system of Thomist metaphysics which would take account of and be immune to the criticism of I. *Kant. His literary and philosophical idiom was, however, largely that of the *existentialist philosopher Martin *Heidegger, under whom he studied in Freiburg; this renders his writing difficult to master. His basic position was expounded in detail in his major work, *Geist in Welt* (1939; 2nd edn., 1957; Eng. tr. as *Spirit in the World*, 1968) which, interpreting in existential terms St *Thomas Aquinas's doctrine of perception as the grasping of intelligible being through the medium of the sensible species, sees the human subjectivity as functioning within a horizon of being whose ultimate determinant is God. In a smaller work, *Hörer des Wortes* (1941), Rahner extended his argument to the realm of Christian revelation. In his later years he presented his approach to Christian doctrine in *Grundkurs des Glaubens* (1976; Eng. tr., *Foundations of Christian Faith*, 1978). From 1958 he also edited, with H. Schlier, the series *Quaestiones Disputatae* (Eng. tr. of 16 of the earlier volumes, 1961–7), and he was one of the editors of the second edition of the *Lexikon für Theologie und Kirche* (10 vols., 1957–65 + supplements on the Second Vatican Council) and of the six-volume encyclopaedia *Sacramentum Mundi* (1968–70), which was strongly influenced by his outlook.

In contrast to his technical writings Rahner's addresses to student and mixed audiences were direct and forceful, showing deep insight into the problems of the contemporary world and of the Church's pastoral and evangelistic task. He was one of the most influential RC theologians of the 20th cent., esp. in German-speaking countries.

Much of Rahner's vast output was in the form of articles; a collection of his most important theological essays was pub. under the title *Schriften zur Theologie* (16 vols., 1954–84; Eng. tr., *Theological Investigations*, 23 vols., 1961–92), and of his pastoral works as *Sendung und Gnade* (1959; Eng. tr., 3 vols., 1963–6). J. B. Betz and others (eds.), *Gott in Welt: Festgabe für Karl Rahner* (2 vols., Freiburg, etc., 1964), with list of his writings, 2, pp. 900–36; this was expanded and separately pub. as R. Bleistein and E. Klinger, *Bibliographie Karl Rahner 1924–1969* (Freiburg, 1969), with suppl. covering 1969–74 (ibid. [1974]); 1974–9 covered in H. Vorgrimler (ed.), *Wagnis Theologie: Erfahrungen mit der Theologie Karl Rahners* (ibid., 1979), pp. 579–97; E. Klinger and K. Wittstadt (eds.), *Glaube in Prozess: Christsein nach dem II. Vatikanum. Für Karl Rahner* (ibid., 1984), with bibl. 1979–84, pp. 854–71. C. J. Pedley, SJ, 'An English Bibliographical Aid to Karl Rahner', *Heythrop Journal*, 25 (1984), pp. 319–65, with additional note, ibid. 26 (1985), p. 310. K.-H. Weger, *Karl Rahner: Eine Ein-führung in sein theologisches Denken* (Freiburg, 1978; Eng. tr., 1980); H. Vorgrimler, *Karl Rahner verstehen: Eine Einführung in sein Leben und Denken* (ibid., 1985; Eng. tr., 1986); T. Sheehan, *Karl Rahner: The Philosophical Foundations* (Athens, Oh. [1987]); U. Möbs, *Das kirchliche Amt bei Karl Rahner: Eine Untersuchung der Amtsstufen und ihrer Ausgestaltung* (Beiträge zur ökumenischen Theologie; Munich, 1992). Introd. by W. V. Dych, SJ, *Karl Rahner* (Outstanding Christian Thinkers Series, 1992). Polgár, 3 (1990), pp. 8–38. K. H. Neufeld in *Dict. Sp.* 23 (1988), cols. 45–8, s.v.

Raikes, Robert (1736–1811), founder of *Sunday Schools. A native of *Gloucester, he was educated at the College (i.e. Cathedral) School. He became an advocate of many philanthropic causes which he supported in the *Gloucester Journal* (est. 1732), which he inherited from his father in 1757. Stimulated by the neglected condition of the local children and their behaviour on Sundays, he was led to assist in the establishment of a Sunday School in a neighbouring parish; and in 1780 he started a school in his own parish, open on weekdays and Sundays, for the teaching of Scripture, reading, and other elementary subjects. Although he had to face opposition at first from conservatives who felt that popular education spelled revolution, as well as from strict *Sabbatarians, his enthusiasm and use of new methods (phonetics, employment of monitors, etc.) triumphed. In 1783 he felt his school sufficiently established to draw attention to his achievement in his paper. His methods were soon followed by Hannah *More (q.v.) and others. Though Raikes was not the 'inventor' of Sunday Schools, his example and publicity stimulated their rapid expansion from the 1780s and by the time of his death they had become a major feature of Church life.

The basic Lives are those by A. Gregory (London, 1877) and that ed. J. H. Harris, with introd. by F. W. *Farrar (Bristol and London, 1899). Modern study by F. Booth, *Robert Raikes of Gloucester* (1980). Id. and S. Elliott in J. Ferguson (ed.), *Christianity, Society and Education* (1981), pp. 25–49. L. Stephen in *DNB* 47 (1896), pp. 168–70.

Rainolds, John (1549–1607), also 'Reynolds', Anglican divine. A native of Pinhoe, Devon, he was educated at Corpus Christi College, Oxford, where he was elected a Fellow in 1568. As reader in Greek in his college (1573–8), he became well known through his successful lectures on *Aristotle's *Rhetoric*. Resigning his Fellowship in 1586, probably through difficulties with William Coke, the president, he taught for a time at Queen's College. In 1593 he became Dean of *Lincoln and in 1598, by an arrangement welcome to Corpus, where Coke's rule was much disliked, exchanged this office with the president. By this time Rainolds had won a reputation as a skilled champion of *Calvinism, and at the *Hampton Court Conference (1604) he was the chief representative of the Puritan cause. Among the things in the BCP to which he objected were the *sign of the Cross in Baptism, the *ring in Marriage, the use of the *Apocrypha, and the *Churching of Women. Though the Puritan objections were overruled at the Conference, Rainolds did not fall from favour, and even escaped subscription to canon 36 of 1604. He was given a prominent part in preparing the *Authorized Version of the Bible, sitting in the company which translated the Prophets. His high character and wide learning won him respect even from his theological adversaries.

Rainolds's *Orationes Duodecim* were posthumously ed. by his friend and pupil, H. Jackson (London, 1614). The fifth of them, *Oratio in Laudem Artis Poeticae*, was repr. from a later edn., with introd. (pp. 1–23) and comm. by W. Ringler and Eng. tr. by W. Allen (Princeton Studies in English, 20; Princeton, NJ, 1940). His Oxford lectures on Aristotle's *Rhetoric*, ed., with Eng. tr. and comm., by L. D. Green (Newark, Del., and London [1986]). On them, see J. McConica, 'Humanism and Aristotle in Tudor Oxford', *EHR* 94 (1979), pp. 291–317, esp. pp. 302–9. C. M. Dent, *Protestant Reformers in Elizabethan Oxford* (Oxford, 1983), esp. pp. 227–31. T. Fowler in *DNB* 47 (1896), pp. 180–2.

Rainy, Robert (1826–1906), scholar and ecclesiastical politician. He was ordained to the ministry of the *Free Church of Scotland in 1851 and appointed professor of Church history at New College, Edinburgh, in 1862. From 1874, when he became principal of New College and leader of the General Assembly, he dominated the counsels of the Free Church, and later the *United Free Church; he was Moderator of the General Assembly in 1887, 1900, and 1905. Though essentially *Calvinist, he nevertheless exercised a liberalizing influence in theology, cautiously defending evolutionary biology and biblical criticism and promoting the Assembly's *Declaratory Act (1892) which helped to modify the Church's understanding of the *Westminster Confession and her relationship to it. Frequently involved in controversy, he joined forces with John Cairns of the *United Presbyterian Church to campaign for disestablishment of the Church of Scotland (*c.*1875–*c.*1895), played a major part in W. R. *Smith's removal from his chair in 1891, and defended A. B. *Bruce, Marcus Dods, and H. *Drummond from heresy proceedings in the 1890s. His last great achievement was the union of the Free and United Presbyterian Churches in 1900. When a tiny minority within the Free Church refused to enter the new United Free Church of Scotland and after a celebrated legal case retained all Free Church properties, Rainy played a leading role in the complicated negotiations which eventually resulted in the Church of Scotland Act 1905, which secured a more obviously equitable settlement. His writings include *Three Lectures on the Church of Scotland* (1872), controverting views expressed by A. P. *Stanley.

P. C. Simpson, *The Life of Principal Rainy* (2 vols., 1909).

Rambam. See MAIMONIDES, MOSES.

Rambler. A monthly RC periodical, founded by J. M. Capes in 1848, which became an organ of liberal English Catholicism. In 1859 (Lord) *Acton, then one of its proprietors, secured J. H. *Newman as editor. After four months, however, an article by Newman on the place of the laity in the Church was delated to Rome and he was compelled to retire. Acton himself nominally succeeded to the editorship, though in fact Richard Simpson, an earlier editor, did most of the work. The *Rambler* attacked the *Ultramontanism of W. G. *Ward and H. E. *Manning, and in 1862 the latter suppressed it. It was nominally merged in a quarterly, the *Home and Foreign Review* (itself suppressed for similar reasons in 1864).

J. L. Altholz, *The Liberal Catholic Movement in England: The 'Rambler' and its Contributors 1848–1864* (1962).

Ramon Llull. See LLULL, RAMON.

Ramsay, William Mitchell (1851–1939), NT scholar. Educated at Aberdeen, Oxford, and Göttingen, he became Fellow successively of Exeter (1882) and Lincoln (1885) Colleges, Oxford. From 1886 to 1911 he was Professor of Humanity at Aberdeen. He travelled extensively in Asia Minor, and became an eminent authority on its geography and history. He was also a keen student of the NT, making extensive use of his archaeological and other learning in defence of a moderate conservatism. His books include *The Historical Geography of Asia Minor* (1890), *The Church in the Roman Empire* (1893), *The Cities and Bishoprics of Phrygia* (2 vols., 1895, 1897), *St Paul, the Traveller and the Roman Citizen* (1895) and *Was Christ born at Bethlehem?* (1898).

Anatolian Studies presented to Sir William Mitchell Ramsay, ed. W. H. Buckler and W. M. Calder (Manchester, 1923). J. G. C. Anderson in *DNB, 1931–1940*, pp. 727 f.

Ramsey, Arthur Michael (1904–88), theologian and Abp. of *Canterbury. He came from a *Congregational background, but after education at Repton, Magdalene College, Cambridge, and Cuddesdon Theological College, he was ordained in the C of E in 1928. He spent only a short time in the parochial ministry before becoming subwarden of the theological college at *Lincoln in 1930. He was successively canon-professor at *Durham (1940–50), Regius Professor of Divinity at Cambridge (1950–52), Bp. of Durham (1952–6), Abp. of *York (1956–61), and Abp. of Canterbury (1961–74). While at Canterbury, he travelled widely to visit various branches of the Anglican Communion and also to promote relations with other Churches, esp. the Orthodox and RC. He formed personal links with *Athenagoras, Patr. of *Constantinople, and with Pope *Paul VI, whom he visited officially in 1966. At home he presided over the introduction of *synodical government in the C of E, gaining for the Church substantial control over its liturgy in the *Worship and Doctrine Measure of 1974, and he gave a strong lead in the abortive movement for the unification of the C of E and the *Methodist Church (see ANGLICAN–METHODIST CONVERSATIONS). He also took a prominent part in many of the public debates of the period, e.g. on *homosexuality, *abortion, *capital punishment, and race relations. As a theologian he was a representative of the *Biblical Theology movement, but is chiefly remembered for his writing on spirituality. He taught that *contemplative prayer was something to which all Christians could aspire, and he revived concern for the spiritual life, esp. among the clergy. His writings include *The Gospel and the Catholic Church* (1936), *The Glory of God and the Transfiguration of Christ* (1949), *Sacred and Secular* (1965), *God, Christ and the World* (1969), *The Christian Priest Today* (1972), and *Be Still and Know: A Study in the Life of Prayer* (1982).

Official Life by [W.] O. Chadwick (Oxford, 1990). J. B. Simpson, *The Hundredth Archbishop of Canterbury* (New York [1962]); M. De-la-Noy, *Michael Ramsey: A Portrait* (1990). [W.] O. Chadwick in *DNB, 1986–1990*, pp. 367 f.

Ramus, Petrus (Pierre de la Ramée) (1515–72), French humanist. A native of Picardy, he studied at the College of Navarre in Paris. Though doubt has been cast on the story that in his exercise for his Master of Arts at Paris in 1536 he defended the thesis that all *Aristotle's doctrines were false, it is clear that in his two works, *Aristotelicae Animadversiones* and *Dialecticae Institutiones*, which were published in 1543, he violently attacked Aristotle and the university curriculum, and a storm followed. In 1544 Francis I forbade him to teach, but through the influence of his patrons, the Cardinals de Bourbon and de Lorraine, he was appointed president of the College of Presles in 1545 and professor of rhetoric and philosophy at the Collège Royal in 1551. After becoming a *Calvinist in 1562 he went to Germany. He returned to Paris in 1571 and was killed in the Massacre of St *Bartholomew's Day in 1572. To Aristotle's system, which he accused of falsifying the innate logic of the human mind, he opposed his own, a development of Ciceronian topics which he presented in typographically schematic form (the so-called 'dichotomies'). His influence in philosophical teaching was strongest after his death, mainly in German-speaking parts of Europe, in which a struggle ensued between Ramists and supporters of P. *Melanchthon which lasted until the outbreak of the *Thirty Years War.

Facsimile of the 1543 edn. of his *Dialecticae Institutiones* and *Aristotelicae Animadversiones* with introd. by W. Risse (Stuttgart, 1964). Modern edn. of the Fr. version, *Dialectique*, orig. pub. in 1555, by M. Dassonville (Travaux d'Humanisme et Renaissance, 67; Geneva, 1964). Studies by C. Waddington-Kastus (Paris, 1848, in Lat.; ibid., 1855, in Fr.), W. J. Ong, SJ (Cambridge, Mass., 1958), with bibl., and R. Hooykaas (Leiden, 1958, in Fr., with Eng. summary). P. Lobstein, *Petrus Ramus als Theologe* (Strasbourg, 1878). N. Bruyère, *Méthode et dialectique dans l'œuvre de La Ramée* (De Pétrarque à Descartes, 45; 1984). W. J. Ong in *NCE* 12 (1967), pp. 77 f., s.v.

Rancé, Armand-Jean le Bouthillier de (1626–1700), reformer of *la Trappe. The son of a secretary of Marie de' Medici, and godson of A. J. P. du *Richelieu, by 1636 he held five benefices *in commendam*, including the *Cistercian abbey of la Trappe. A distinguished classical scholar, he went on to become a doctor of the *Sorbonne, and was ordained priest in 1651 by his uncle, the Abp. of Tours, whose successor he was expected to become. He led a worldly life, frequenting Parisian salons while pursuing a successful ecclesiastical career, until the sudden death of Mme de Monbazon in 1657 caused a dramatic conversion. Speculation as to the nature of their relationship continues; all that is certain is that he had known this much older woman since childhood, that her lovers were numerous, and that his emotional reaction to her loss was extreme. He immediately withdrew from Paris to his country house, put himself under the direction of *Oratorian priests, and followed a reading-programme prescribed by Arnauld d'Andilly, whom he visited at *Port-Royal, and through whom he seems to have been introduced to the Desert Fathers. Divesting himself of all his benefices except la Trappe, where he invited monks of the Strict Observance to take over in 1662, he only then found his vocation. After a year's novitiate at Perseigne, he was blessed as regular abbot of la Trappe in 1664. His fellow abbots of the Strict Observance almost at once delegated him to go to Rome to plead their cause against the Abbot of *Cîteaux. Returning unsuccessful in 1666, he began to build up his own community, and after 1675 only went beyond the *enclosure on four canonical visitations of an abbey of Cistercian nuns. To the existing rules of

the Strict Observance he added more stringent regulations, based, he always insisted, on the original uses of Cîteaux, and he always remained within the obedience of the Cistercian Order and Strict Observance (e.g. by accepting canonical visitations). It was only the unique survival of la Trappe through the Revolutionary era which led to the widespread adoption of his reform in the Order. Accused of poaching religious from other Orders, Rancé soon became involved in ceaseless polemic, esp. after the publication of his book *De la sainteté et des devoirs de la vie monastique* (1683). Rejecting study as a substitute for manual labour for 'true monks', Rancé provoked a lengthy and harmful dispute with the *Maurists, whose champion, J. *Mabillon, and he were eventually reconciled through royal intervention. *Lectio divina* was in fact compulsory at la Trappe, and Rancé's objection was to erudition for its own sake. For him penitence, rather than physical austerity as such, was the basis of monastic, and indeed Christian, life. Morally he was a rigorist, but despite many friends, and some monks at la Trappe with *Jansenist sympathies, he was theologically orthodox and explicitly disowned partisan sympathies. J.-B. *Bossuet enlisted his support in the *Quietist dispute in 1697. Among his other correspondents were Cardinal de *Retz and *James II.

A very inaccurate edn. of 220 of his letters appeared in 2 vols. (Paris, 1701–2); 220 more were ed. (reliably) by B. Gonod (ibid., 1846). Complete edn. of 2,000 letters by A. J. Krailsheimer (4 vols., ibid., 1993). They had previously been calendared (with 365 tr. in full) in Eng. by id. (Cistercian Studies Series, 80–1; Kalamazoo, Mich., 1984). Primary Lives by P. de Maupeou (2 vols., Paris, '1602' [1702]), J. Marsollier (ibid., 1703), and (far superior) by P. Le Nain (Prior of the Abbey, 2 vols., no place, 1715; 2nd dn., Paris, 1719). Other Lives incl. those by F. R. de *Chateaubriand (ibid., 1844; undertaken in fulfilment of a penance), L. Dubois (2 vols., ibid., 1866), H. *Bremond, *L'Abbé Tempête* (Paris, 1929; Eng. tr., 1930; unsympathetic), and A. J. Krailsheimer, *Armand-Jean de Rancé, abbot of La Trappe: His Influence in the Cloister and the World* (Oxford, 1974); id., *Rancé and the Trappist Legacy* (Cistercian Studies Series, 86; Kalamazoo, Mich., 1985 [1986]). *Collectanea Ordinis Cisterciensium Reformatorum*, 25 (1963), pp. 189–254, a special issue to mark the third centenary of his conversion; A. Mensáros, O. Cist., 'L'Abbé de Rancé et la règle bénédictine', *Analecta Cisterciensia*, 22 (1966), pp. 161–217. A. J. Krailsheimer in *Dict. Sp.* 13 (1986), cols. 81–90, s.v., with bibl.

Ranke, Leopold von (1795–1886), German historian. From 1825 till his death he was professor of history at Berlin. Ranke's work is characterized by emphasis on the primary importance of the study of original sources, by psychological penetration and by a fundamentally objective attitude to history, as well as by understanding of national tendencies in their relation to the history of their age. The most famous of his works was his History of the Popes in the 16th and 17th cents., *Die römischen Päpste, ihre Kirche und ihr Staat* (3 vols., 1834–6), which from the 6th edition (1874) was carried down to 1870. It was based on extensive researches in the libraries of Italy where he collected material for three years (1828–31). In this work he removed the history of the Papacy from denominational polemics and showed the development of the Papal power and its effects on the history of Europe, stressing, however, its political rather than its religious significance. This work was followed by a large-scale history of the Reformation, *Deutsche Geschichte im Zeitalter der Reformation* (6 vols.,

1839–47), which it studied in the setting of contemporary European history and with full appreciation of its religious values from the *Lutheran point of view.

Sämmtliche Werke (54 vols., Leipzig, 1867–90). *Das Briefwerk*, ed. W. P. Fuchs (Hamburg, 1949), with useful introd.; *Neue Briefe*, ed. B. Hoeft and H. Herzfeld (ibid., 1949); *Tagebücher*, ed. W. P. Fuchs (Aus Werk und Nachlass, 1; Munich, 1964). His principal works have been tr. into Eng. H. F. Helmolt, *Leopold von Rankes Leben und Wirken* (1921). T. H. Von Laue, *Leopold Ranke: The Formative Years* (Princeton, NJ, 1950), with bibl. C. Hinrichs, *Ranke und die Geschichtstheologie der Goethezeit* (Göttinger Bausteine zur Geschichtswissenschaft, 19; 1954); R. Vierhaus, *Ranke und die soziale Welt* (Neue Münsterische Beiträge zur Geschichtsforschung, 1; 1957); G. Berg, *Leopold von Ranke als akademischer Lehrer* (Schriftenreihe der historischen Kommission bei der Bayerischen Akademie der Wissenschaften, 9; 1968). L. Krieger, *Ranke: The Meaning of History* (Chicago and London [1977]). G. G. Iggers and J. M. Powell, (eds.), *Leopold von Ranke and the Shaping of the Historical Discipline* (Syracuse, NY, 1990).

Ranters. A grouping of people with *antinomian and *pantheistic tendencies in mid-17th-cent. England. There is controversy about whether they formed a coherent movement, but the likelihood is that a fairly disparate collection of individuals on the fringes of radical religious sects attracted popular suspicion and anxiety because of their wild behaviour and pronouncements, and were collectively labelled as Ranters. Commonly they are said to have relied on an inward experience of Christ and to have denied the authority of Scripture, Creeds, and the Ministry; hence the early *Quakers were often associated with them and suffered from the resulting confusion. They were fiercely attacked by R. *Baxter. In the 19th cent. the word was applied colloquially to Nonconformist (esp. *Primitive Methodist) preachers.

N. Smith (ed.), *A Collection of Ranter Writings from the 17th Century* [1983]. A. L. Morton, *The World of the Ranters: Religious Radicalism in the English Revolution* (1970), pp. 70–114. J. F. McGregor, 'Seekers and Ranters', in id. and B. Reay (eds.), *Radical Religion in the English Revolution* (Oxford, 1984), pp. 121–39, esp. pp. 121 f. and 129–39. J. C. Davis, *Fear, Myth and History: The Ranters and the Historians* (Cambridge, 1986), with appendix of docs., pp. 138–203; cf. G. E. Aylmer in *Past and Present*, 117 (1987), pp. 208–19, and [J. E.] C. Hill in *History Workshop*, 24 (1987), pp. 134–40; also 'Fear, Myth and Furore: Reappraising the "Ranters" ': comments by J. F. McGregor, B. Capp, N. Smith, and B. J. Gibbons, with a reply by J. C. Davis, *Past and Present*, 140 (1993), pp. 155–210. J. Friedman, *Blasphemy, Immortality, and Anarchy: The Ranters and the English Revolution* (Athens, Oh., and London [1987]).

Raphael, St, *archangel. In the Books of *Tobit and 1 *Enoch, Raphael figures as one of the seven archangels who stand in the presence of God. In Tobit (12: 12, 15) he hears the prayers of holy men and brings them before God. The name in Hebrew means 'God has healed', and in 1 Enoch (10: 7) he is said to have 'healed' the earth when it was defiled by the sins of the fallen angels. From these Jewish speculations the figure of Raphael passed into Christian tradition. Feast day, previously 24 Oct.; in 1969 combined with St Michael on 29 Sept.

In the C of E the Guild of St Raphael was founded in 1915 with the aim of restoring the Ministry of Healing as part of the normal function of the Church.

The principal lit. is to be found in comm. on 1 Enoch and Tobit, cited s.vv. On the Christian feast, L. Eisenhofer, *Handbuch der katholischen Liturgik*, 1 (1932), p. 602. J. T. Marshall in *HDB* 4 (1902), p. 201, s.v.; A. Penna, CRL, G Löw, CSSR, and M. Donati in *EC* 10 (1952), cols. 469–73, s.v. 'Raffaele'. See also works cited under ANGEL.

Raphael (1483–1520) **(Raffaello Sanzio)**, the most famous of the Renaissance painters. From 1499 to 1504 he worked under *Perugino at Perugia, and painted the *Crucifixion* (1502; National Gallery, London) and the *Espousals of the Virgin* (1504; Brera, Milan). In 1504 he migrated to Florence, where he was brought into contact with the greatest artists of the time, among them *Michelangelo, *Leonardo da Vinci, and the Dominican Fra *Bartolommeo. Here he painted the *Madonna del Granduca* (Pitti, Florence) and the *Ansidei Madonna* (National Gallery, London). In 1508 he was summoned to Rome by *Julius II to decorate the Vatican 'Stanze'. The series of famous paintings for their walls included the *Disputa* and *St Peter released from Prison*, while many biblical scenes depicted on the ceilings were very frequently reproduced in illustrations of the Bible. He also executed at Rome the celebrated *Sistine Madonna* (c.1512; Dresden) and the *Madonna della Sedia* (c.1513–14; Pitti, Florence). In 1514 *Leo X appointed him chief architect of *St Peter's in succession to Bramante. His last work, *The Transfiguration* (Vatican), was left unfinished and completed by his pupils.

V. Golzio, *Raffaello nei documenti nelle testimonianze dei contemporanei e nella letteratura del suo secolo* (Pontificia Insigne Accademia Artistica dei Virtuosi al Pantheon; Rome, 1936; repub., with 3 pages of corrections and additions, Farnborough, 1971). M. Salmi (ed.), *Raffaello: L'Opera, Le Fonti, La Fortuna* (2 vols., Novara, 1968; partial Eng. tr. as *The Complete Works of Raphael*, New York [1969]). Other modern general studies incl. those by O. Fischel (tr. into Eng. and posthumously pub., 2 vols., London, 1948, incl. one vol. of plates), J. Pope-Hennessy (Wrightsman Lectures; London [1970]), R. Jones and N. Penny (New Haven, Conn., and London, 1983), and L. D. and H. S. Ettlinger (Oxford, 1987). O. Fischel, *Raphaels Zeichnungen* (8 parts, Rome, 1913–41; pt. 9 by K. Oberhuber, Berlin, 1972); E. Knab and others, *Raphael: Die Zeichnungen* (Stuttgart, 1983). L. L. Dussler, *Raffael: Kritisches Verzeichnis der Gemälde, Wandbilder und Bildteppiche* (Munich, 1966; Eng. tr., 1971).

Rapp, Johann Georg (1757–1847), founder of the *Harmony Society (q.v.).

Ras Shamra Tablets. A collection of *cuneiform tablets with mythological poems and ritual prescriptions excavated by C. F. A. Schaeffer at Ras Shamra (anciently Ugarit) in N. Syria from 1929 onwards. The tablets, prob. dating from the 14th cent. BC or earlier, are in a hitherto unknown alphabetical script and in a Semitic language closely akin to Hebrew. They bear on the development of the alphabet and the language, literature, and religion of Canaan before the Israelite settlement. Their contents show some remarkable correspondences with the OT literature, throwing light on obscure Hebrew words and phrases, on OT religious practices and beliefs, and on the forms of Hebrew poems and their liturgical use. The key to the decipherment of the texts was discovered almost simultaneously by three scholars, H. Bauer, E. Dhorme, OP, and C. Virolleaud.

There are two standard edns. of the texts: A. Herdner, *Corpus des tablettes en cunéiformes alphabétiques découvertes à Ras Shamra-Ugarit de 1929 à 1939* (Mission de Ras Shamra, 10; 2 vols., 1963), and M. Dietrich, O. Loretz, and J. Sanmartín, *Die keilalphabetischen Texte aus Ugarit* (Alter Orient und Altes Testament, 24; 1976). Convenient collections by C. H. Gordon, *Ugaritic Textbook* (Analecta Orientalia, 38; 1965), J. C. L. Gibson, *Canaanite Myths and Legends* (2nd edn., Edinburgh, 1978, of work orig. by G. R. *Driver), and G. del Olmo Lete, *Mitos y Leyendas de Canaan segun la Tradicion de Ugarit* (Fuentes de la Ciencia Biblica, 1; 1981). On connections with the OT, J. Gray, *The Legacy of Canaan* (Supplements to *Vetus Testamentum*, 5; 1957; 2nd edn., 1965); L. Fisher and others (eds.), *Ras Shamra Parallels: The Texts from Ugarit and the Hebrew Bible* (Analecta Orientalia, 49–51; 1972–81); P. C. Craigie, *Ugarit and the Old Testament* (Grand Rapids, Mich. [1983]). J. Aisleiter, *Wörterbuch der ugaritischen Sprache*, ed. O. Eissfeldt (*Ber.* (Sächs.), 106, Heft 3; 1963; 3rd edn., Berlin, 1967). M. Dietrich, O. Loretz, P.-R. Berger, and J. Sanmartín, *Ugarit-Bibliographie 1928–1966* (Alter Orient und Altes Testament, 20/1–4; 1973); M. Dietrich, O. Loretz, and W. C. Delsman, *Ugarit-Bibliographie 1967–71* (ibid. 20/5; 1986). G. Saadé, *Ougarit: Métropole Cananéenne* (Beirut, 1979); G. D. Young (ed.), *Ugarit in Retrospect: Proceedings of the Symposium . . . held . . . at Madison, February 26, 1979* (Winona Lake, Ind. [1981]). J. C. de Moor in *Interpreter's Dictionary of the Bible*, Supplement (1976), pp. 928–31, s.v. 'Ugarit'; J.-C. Courtois and others in *Dict. Bibl.*, Suppl. 9 (1979), cols. 1124–466, s.v.

Rashdall, Hastings

Rashdall, Hastings (1858–1924), moral philosopher and theologian. Educated at Harrow and New College, Oxford, Rashdall taught philosophy at Oxford from 1888 to 1917, first at Hertford College and later (after 1895) at New College. From 1909 to 1917 he also held a canonry at *Hereford. From 1917 till his death he was Dean of *Carlisle. He won fame first as a historian by his *Universities of Europe in the Middle Ages* (3 vols., 1895; new edn. by F. M. Powicke and A. B. Emden, 1936). In 1907 he published an important treatise on moral philosophy, *The Theory of Good and Evil* (2 vols.), in which he expounded an ethical doctrine which he described as 'Ideal *Utilitarianism'. In his *Bampton Lectures for 1915, *The Idea of Atonement in Christian Theology* (1919), he upheld with much vigour the *Abelardian or '*exemplarist' theory of the Atonement. Rashdall possessed supreme confidence in the capacity of human reason, rightly employed, to arrive at the final truths of religion. He was in consequence an untiring controversialist, and a strong critic of all forms of *pragmatism, *modernism, sentimentalism, and *mysticism.

Three vols. of (largely unpub.) papers and sermons by Rashdall, ed. H. D. A. Major and F. L. Cross under the titles *Principles and Precepts* (Oxford, 1927), *Ideas and Ideals* (ibid., 1928), and *God and Man* (ibid., 1930). Life by P. E. Matheson (London, 1928). C. C. J. *Webb in *DNB, 1922–1930*, pp. 706–9.

Rashi

Rashi (1040–1105), Jewish biblical scholar, so called from the initials of his name Rabbi Solomon ben Isaac. After studying at Mainz and Worms he was appointed rabbi in his native city of Troyes. Among the Jews he is still one of the most highly reputed exegetes of the Hebrew Scriptures and the *Talmud. Although his work incorporated much traditional material, his scientific outlook and his evaluation of the literal sense marked the beginning of a new era in OT interpretation. His commentaries were influential from an early date; they were used by *Andrew of St-Victor as well as by *Nicholas of Lyre, through

whom they are commonly supposed to have influenced M. *Luther. His works were translated into Latin in the 17th and 18th cents., the most complete edition being that of F. Breithaupt (1710, 1713, 1714).

His Comm. on the Pentateuch is ed. with Eng. tr. and notes by M. Rosenbaum and A. M. Silbermann (5 vols., London, 1929–34). L. Zunz, 'Solomon ben Isaac genannt Raschi', *Zeitschrift für die Wissenschaft des Judentums*, 1 (1822), pp. 277–384. Vols. commemorating the 900th anniversary of his birth ed. H. L. Ginsberg (American Academy for Jewish Research, Texts and Studies, 1; New York, 1941) and commemorating the 850th anniversary of his death, ed. S. Federbush (New York, 1958). H. Hailperin, *Rashi and the Christian Scholars* (Pittsburgh, 1963). E. Shereshevsky, *Rashi, the Man and his World* (New York, 1982); cf. A. van der Heide, 'Rashi's Biblical Exegesis. Recent Research and Developments', *Bibliotheca Orientalis*, 41 (1984), pp. 292–318, with bibl. M. Banitt, *Rashi, Interpreter of the Biblical Letter* (Tel Aviv, 1985) [specialized]. E. I. J. Rosenthal, 'Rashi and the English Bible', *Bulletin of the John Rylands Library*, 24 (1940), pp. 138–67. Useful introd. by C. Pearl, *Rashi* (London, 1988).

Raskolniki

Raskolniki (Russ., 'schismatics'). A comprehensive name for the section of the Russian Church that refused to accept the reforms of the patriarch *Nikon (d. 1681). They are also known as the '*Old Believers' (q.v.).

Ratherius

Ratherius (*c.*887–974), Bp. of *Verona. A man of a very refractory and ambitious character, he took a prominent part in the ecclesiastical life of the 10th cent. Born in the neighbourhood of Liège, he at first became a monk at the abbey of Lobbes in the Hennegau. In 926 he accompanied his abbot, Hilduin, to Italy, where Hugo of Provence, Hilduin's cousin, was King. In 931 Ratherius received the see of Verona from Hugo, but he soon fell out with the King and was removed from his see. After many changes of fortune, he was made Bp. of Liège in 953, but forced to resign in 955. From 962 to 968 he was again in possession of the bishopric of Verona. His many writings, mostly of an occasional kind and often full of invective, throw important light on his age.

Works ed. J. and P. *Ballerini (Verona, 1765), with Life pp. xxvi–clxxiv; repr. in J. P. Migne, *PL* 136. 9–768. Letters ed. F. Weigle (*MGH*, Briefe der deutschen Kaiserzeit, 1; 1949); *Opera Minora* ed. P. L. D. Reid (CCCM 46; 1976); further works, incl. Ratherius' annotations on Martianus Capella and various canonical texts, ed. id. and others (ibid. 46A; 1984); Eng. tr. of *Complete Works* by P. L. D. Reid (Medieval & Renaissance Texts and Studies, 76; Binghamton, NY, 1991). Docs. relating to his episcopate at Verona ed. F. Weigle in *Quellen und Forschungen aus italienischen Archiven und Bibliotheken*, 29 (1938–9), pp. 1–40. A. Vogel, *Ratherius von Verona und das zehnte Jahrhundert* (2 vols., Jena, 1854; repr., Leipzig, 1977). G. Monticelli, *Raterio, vescovo di Verona, 890–974* (1938); V. Cavallari, *Raterio e Verona* (Biblioteca di Studi Storici Veronesi, 6; 1967); P. L. D. Reid, *Tenth-Century Latinity: Rather of Verona* (Humana Civilitas, 6; Malibu, Calif., 1981). F. Dolbeau, 'Ratheriana I. Nouvelles recherches sur les manuscrits et l'œuvre de Rathier', *Sacris Erudiri*, 27 (1984), pp. 373–431; 'Ratheriana II. Enquête sur les sources des *Praeloquia*', ibid. 28 (1985), pp. 511–56; 'Ratheriana III. Notes sur la culture patristique de Rathier', ibid. 29 (1986), pp. 151–221. C. Leonardi, 'Von Pacificus zu Rather. Zur Veroneser Kulturgeschichte im 9. und 10. Jahrhundert', *Deutsches Archiv*, 41 (1985), pp. 390–417. F. Dolbeau in *Dict. Sp.* 13 (1988), cols. 135–44, s.v. 'Rathier de Vérone'.

Ratio Studiorum (Lat., 'the method of the studies'). The abbreviated name for the 'Ratio atque Institutio Studiorum Societatis Jesu', the *Jesuit scheme of studies issued in 1599. After earlier drafts in 1586 and 1591, the original editions legislated for studies in the three divisions of letters (Latin and Greek), philosophy, and theology, but were chiefly concerned with the study of literature and philosophy. The success of Jesuit secondary education from the 16th to the 18th cent. was largely due to it. The Ratio is based on the best pedagogical theory and practice of the period. In the restored Society a revised edition was issued in 1832, but was never finally approved. It was no longer practical to regulate the Society's schools through such a document, and the term 'Ratio Studiorum' came to be used, until 1975, to denote the legislation regarding the philosophy and theology studied by Jesuit seminarians.

G. M. Pachtler, SJ (ed.), *Ratio Studiorum et institutiones scholasticae Societatis Jesu per Germaniam olim vigentes collectae* (Monumenta Germaniae paedagogica, 2, 5, 9, 16; Berlin, 1887–94). L. Lukács, SJ (ed.), *Monumenta Paedagogica Societatis Iesu* (Monumenta Historica Societatis Iesu, 92, 107, 108, 124, 129, 140, 141, etc.; Rome, 1965 ff.). E. A. Fitzpatrick, SJ, (ed.), *St Ignatius and the Ratio Studiorum* (New York, 1933), incl. Eng. tr. of the 1599 text, pp. 119–254. A. P. Farrell, SJ, *The Jesuit Code of Liberal Education* (Milwaukee, 1938). J. W. Donohue, SJ, *Jesuit Education: An Essay on the Foundations of its Idea* (New York, 1963).

rationale. The word has several ecclesiastical senses:
(1) Formerly, the breastplate worn by the Jewish high priest.
(2) A liturgical vestment of stuff which was sometimes worn by bishops over the shoulders. It seems to have been looked upon as a kind of substitute for the archiepiscopal *pallium, and to have been in use esp. in Germany. Its use is now confined to the bishops of Eichstätt, Paderborn, Toul, and Cracow.
(3) An ornament worked in gold sometimes worn by bishops on the breast over the *chasuble when celebrating Mass. Its adoption was never widespread, though its use survived at *Reims till the beginning of the 16th cent.
(4) It is also used in ecclesiastical contexts in the general sense of a reasoned exposition of principles, e.g. in the titles of W. *Durandus, *Rationale Divinorum Officiorum* (written 1286–91) and A. *Sparrow, *Rationale upon the Book of Common Prayer* (1657).

Ratisbon, Conference of (1541). A reunion conference of three Catholic and three Protestant theologians convened at Ratisbon (Regensburg) from 27 Apr. to 22 May by the Emp. *Charles V. The three Catholics were J. *Eck, J. von *Pflug, and J. *Gropper; the three Protestants P. *Melanchthon, M. *Bucer, and Pistorius (1503–83). G. *Contarini was present in Ratisbon while the Conference took place and as Papal legate he directed the work of the Catholic participants. The discussions followed the order of the 'Regensburg Book', a preliminary document produced in secret negotiations between Catholic and Protestant theologians. Though doctrinal agreement was reached at the Conference on some of the controverted subjects, including a basis of agreement on *justification, major issues on the Church and Sacraments remained unresolved. The subsequent hostility of M. *Luther, as well as political rivalries, prevented any reunion being effected.

The *Acta* were pub. by M. Bucer at Strasbourg in 1541 (Eng. tr. by M. *Coverdale [Geneva?], 1542). Kidd, pp. 340–6 [incl. docs. nos. 136–40]. C. Augustijn, *De Godsdienstgesprekken tussen Rooms-Katholieken en Protestanten van 1538 tot 1541* (Haarlem, 1967), pp. 73–131, with bibl., pp. 142–6. R. Stupperich, 'Der Ursprung des "Regensburger Buches" von 1541 und seine Rechtfertigungslehre', *Archiv für Reformationsgeschichte*, 36 (1939), pp. 88–116. P. Fraenkel, 'Les Protestants et le problème de la transsubstantiation au Colloque de Ratisbonne', *Oecumenica: Jahrbuch für ökumenische Forschung*, 1968, pp. 70–116, with texts and Eng. summary. K.-H. zur Mühlen, 'Die Einigung über die Rechtfertigungsartikel auf dem Regensburger Religionsgespräch von 1541—eine verpasste Chance?', *ZKT* 76 (1979), pp. 331–59. P. Matheson, *Cardinal Contarini at Regensburg* (Oxford, 1972). T. Kolde in *PRE* (3rd edn.), 16 (1905), pp. 542–52, s.v. 'Regensburger Religionsgespräch und Regensburger Buch, 1541'. See also bibl. to WORMS, CONFERENCE OF.

Ratramnus (9th cent.), *Carolingian theologian. He entered the monastery of *Corbie c.825 as a contemporary of *Paschasius Radbertus. His first and most influential work, the 'De Corpore et Sanguine Domini' (843) was a reaction to the realism of Paschasius' earlier treatise on the Eucharist. Ratramnus himself wrote at the request of Charles the Bald, King of the Franks, for whom he also composed the 'De Praedestinatione' (849–50), a contribution to the debate with *Gottschalk of Orbais. In this work he clarified the patristic basis for Gottschalk's belief in double predestination, to good or to evil. He went on to write two small works 'De Anima' and 'De Nativitate Christi' (853), and the longer 'De Anima ad Odonem', which was commissioned c.863 by Odo, Bp. of Beauvais, to refute an anonymous Irish monk who was affirming the existence of a single soul in all mankind. His last treatise, 'Contra Graecorum Opposita' (c.867) is a reply to a schedule of *Photius' criticisms of the W. Church that had been sent by Pope *Nicholas I to *Hincmar, Abp. of Reims. Ratramnus defends the *Double Procession of the Holy Spirit from the Father and the Son (see FILIOQUE) (books 1–3) and various differences in practice and jurisdiction (book 4).

Radical though his opinions were, Ratramnus attracted no formal condemnation in his own time. By the mid-11th cent. his Eucharistic treatise (wrongly attributed to *Erigena) was seen as incompatible with a change in the substance of the consecrated Bread and Wine, and it was condemned by Pope *Leo IX at the Synod of Vercelli on 1 Sept. 1050. But it was not until the *Reformation that Ratramnus' 'De Corpore et Sanguine Domini' was seriously read and quoted. First printed in 1531, it was a major source for N. *Ridley's formulations of Eucharistic doctrine. In 1559 it was put on the *Index, but removed in 1900.

Editiones principes of his 'De Corpore et Sanguine Domini', Cologne, 1531; of his 'De Praedestinatione' in G. Mauguin (ed.), *Veterum Auctorum qui IX. saeculo de Praedestinatione et Gratia scripserunt Opera et Fragmenta* (Paris, 1650), pp. 29–102. Collected edn. of his works repr. from various sources in J. P. Migne, *PL* 121. 11–346 and 1153–6. Crit. edns. of 'De Corpore et Sanguine Domini' by J. N. Bakhuizen van den Brink (Verhandelingen der koninklijke Nederlandse Akademie van Wetenschappen, Afd. Letterkunde, Nieuwe Reeks, 61, no. 1; 1954; 2nd edn., ibid. 87; 1974) and of his 'De Nativitate Christi' by J. M. Canal, *La Virginidad de María segun Ratramne y Radberto* (Rome, 1968; orig. pub. in *Marianum*, 16), pp. 32–60. The 'De Anima' was first pub. by A. *Wilmart, OSB, in *R. Bén.* 43 (1931), pp. 207–23; the 'De Anima ad Odonem' by C. Lambot, OSB (Analecta Mediaevalia Namurcensia, 2; Namur and Paris [1952]). Modern Eng. trs. of his 'De Corpore et Sanguine Domini' by 'H. W.' and 'W. C. C.' (London, 1838) and W. F. Taylor (ibid., 1880). J.-P. Bouhot, *Ratramne de Corbie: Histoire littéraire et controverses doctrinales* (Études Augustiniennes, 1976). D. *Stone, *A History of the Doctrine of the Holy Eucharist*, 1 (1909), pp. 226–33; J. Geiselmann, *Die Eucharistielehre der Vorscholastik* (Forschungen zur Christlichen Literatur- und Dogmengeschichte, 15, Hefte 1–3; 1926), esp. pp. 176–84; G. Macy, *The Theologies of the Eucharist in the Early Scholastic Period* (Oxford, 1984), esp. pp. 21 f. and 28–31. J. N. Bakhuizen van den Brink, 'Ratramn's Eucharistic Doctrine and its Influence in Sixteenth-Century England', *Studies in Church History*, 2 (1965), pp. 54–77. H. Peltier in *DTC* 13 (pt. 2; 1937), cols. 1780–7, s.v. 'Ratramne'. See also works cited under PASCHASIUS RADBERTUS, ST.

Rauschenbusch, Walter (1861–1918), exponent of the *Social Gospel in N. America. Born in Rochester, NY, and educated in Germany and the USA, Rauschenbusch graduated from the University of Rochester and Rochester Theological Seminary in 1886. For 11 years he served as pastor of the Second German *Baptist Church of New York, situated on the edge of a slum area known as Hell's Kitchen; here he encountered the human cost of escalating social evils. Finding few resources in his *Pietistic background for dealing with social questions, he probed biblical, historical, and theological materials seeking for answers, and in the Kingdom of God theology taught by A. *Ritschl and others he found a way to bring his inherited evangelical and his new social convictions together, and engaged in reform both actively and in his writings. Returning to Rochester in 1897 to teach Church history at the seminary, he wrote *Christianity and the Social Crisis* (1907). An eloquent, prophetic plea for the joining of Christian faith with social passion, it became one of the most influential religious books of the century and thrust its author into prominence as an internationally known leader of the burgeoning Social Gospel movement. His many other writings include *Prayers of the Social Awakening* (1910), *Christianizing the Social Order* (1912), *The Social Principles of Jesus* (1916), and *A Theology for the Social Gospel* (1917).

Selected Writings, ed. W. S. Hudson (Sources of American Spirituality; New York, 1984), with excellent introd., pp. 3–41.

Ravenna. Acc. to tradition the first Bp. of Ravenna was St *Apollinaris (q.v.). In the face of the Visigothic threat, in 402 the imperial court of the W. Empire moved from Milan to Ravenna, in order to take advantage of its secure position behind marshes. In 493 it fell to *Theodoric the Ostrogoth (d. 526), who also used it as his capital and who patronized the *Arian Church in the city. In 540 Ravenna was captured by the Byzantines. After 568, with the loss of much of Italy to the Lombards, its position declined, but it continued to serve as the capital of the beleaguered Byzantine province until it fell to the Lombards in 751. Following this capture, it lost all claims to be a secular capital, and sank to the status of an unhealthy and isolated provincial town.

Ravenna's importance in the later Roman and Byzantine periods elevated the status of its bishops who were placed over a newly created metropolitan province in the early 5th cent., and granted the title of 'archbishop' in the mid-6th cent. The claims of the Ravennate Church outlasted the decline of the city as a secular centre. In the early 9th cent. A. *Agnellus wrote his history of the Ravennate Church, in part as a defence of its privileges against Papal attacks. The Emp. Otto III made Abp. Gerbert Pope as *Sylvester II, and *Henry IV set up Abp. Wibert as (the antipope) Clement III against *Gregory VII.

In the 5th and 6th cents., on account of the wealth and importance of the city, a large number of splendid churches were built and decorated with mosaics. Because of the ravages of *Iconoclasm in the E., these mosaics are now the largest and finest collection surviving from this period. The principal monuments, all with mosaics, are: the Mausoleum of *Galla Placidia, the Orthodox Baptistery (*c.*458), the Arian Baptistery (prob. late 5th cent.), the archiepiscopal chapel (494/519), Theodoric's church of S. Apollinare Nuovo (493/526), and two remarkable churches paid for by a rich Ravennate banker, Julianus, S. Vitale (dedicated 547) and S. Apollinare in Classe (dedicated 549, some 3 miles from the city). Iconographically the most complex and interesting mosaics are the scenes from the life of Christ in the Arian church of S. Apollinare Nuovo.

The principal source for the history and buildings up to the 9th cent. is the *Liber Pontificalis Ecclesiae Ravennatis* of Agnellus (q.v.). The most comprehensive discussion of the history, buildings, and mosaics (with full illustrations in black and white) is F. W. Deichmann, *Frühchristliche Bauten und Mosaiken von Ravenna* (Baden-Baden, 1958) and id., *Ravenna, Hauptstadt des spätantiken Abendlandes* (2 vols. in 3 parts + plans, Wiesbaden, 1969–76). T. S. Brown, 'The Church of Ravenna and the imperial administration in the seventh century', *EHR* 94 (1979), pp. 1–28, is more wide-ranging than its title implies. G. Bovini, *Ravenna Mosaics* (Greenwich, Conn. [1956], London, 1957; repr. Oxford, 1978) is a useful introd. in Eng. L. von Matt and G. Bovini, *Ravenna* (Cologne [1971]) has superb plates of the mosaics in colour. G. Bovini (ed.), *'Corpus' della scultura paleocristiana bizantina ed altomedioevale di Ravenna* (3 vols., 1968–9). E. Dinkler, *Das Apsismosaik von S. Apollinare in Classe* (Wissenschaftliche Abhandlungen der Arbeitsgemeinschaft für Forschung des Landes Nordrhein-Westfalen, 29; 1964), with bibl. on Church history of Ravenna, p. 11. G. Bovini, *Saggio di bibliografia su Ravenna antica* (Bologna [1968]). Recent discoveries and research reported in the journals *Felix Ravenna* (Ravenna, 1911 ff.) and *Corsi di Cultura sull'Arte Ravennate e Bizantina* (ibid., 1955 ff.). See also following entry.

Ravenna Rotulus, the. An inscribed strip of material, prob. of Ravennate origin and now in the *Bodmer Stiftung at Geneva, containing a series of early Latin prayers. It is nearly four yards long and was made up by sewing together seven separate pieces of vellum. As it is mutilated at both ends, its original length is unknown. The writing (in large uncials) prob. dates from the second half of the 8th cent.; it is closest to that of a MS Life of St *Apollinaris now in St Petersburg. In its present mutilated form the MS contains 40 collects for the Advent season, together with a fragment of another collect and a further item which is prob. a 'Preface' for Christmas. The 27th item is found among the Christmas formularies in the '*Leonine', '*Gelasian' and '*Gregorian' Sacramentaries; but the rest are unique. The prayers may have been intended for use in the Office, not in the Mass.

On the back of the *rotulus* there are eight documents in a 10th-cent. minuscule hand. Prob. all these come from the metropolitan archives of Ravenna. The prayers have sometimes been attributed to St Peter *Chrysologus (d. 450), e.g. by F. *Cabrol; but on no sufficient evidence. They have also been ascribed (also improbably) to Marinianus, Bp. of Ravenna 595–?606.

Editio princeps by A. Ceriani and G. Porro, *Il rotolo opistografo del Principe Antonio Pio de Savoia* (Milan, 1883); conveniently in *DACL* 14 (pt. 2; 1948), cols 3028–33, s.v. 'Rome (liturgie)'. Text also ed. L. C. Mohlberg, OSB, *Sacramentarium Veronense* (Rerum Ecclesiasticarum Documenta, Series Maior, Fontes, 1; 1955), pp. 173–8. F. Cabrol, OSB, 'Autour de la liturgie de Ravenne. Saint Pierre Chrysologue et le *Rotulus*', *R. Bén.* 23 (1906), pp. 489–500. S. Benz, OSB, *Der Rotulus von Ravenna* (Liturgiewissenschaftliche Quellen und Forschungen, 45; 1967), also incl. text. E. A. Lowe, *Codices Latini Antiquiores*, 3 (Oxford, 1938), p. 30 (no. 371); cf. 11 (ibid., 1966), p. 8 (no. 1608).

Raymond Lull. See LLULL, RAMON.

Raymond Nonnatus, St (*c.*1204–40), *Mercedarian missioner. The accounts of his life rest on wholly unreliable sources written in the Mercedarian interest centuries later. Acc. to these he came into the world after his mother had died in labour (hence 'non natus', not born) at Portello in Catalonia. After a most pious childhood, he was given leave by his father to join the Mercedarians, to whom he was admitted at Barcelona by St *Peter Nolasco. Sent to N. Africa, he redeemed many slaves at Algiers and, when his funds were exhausted, gave himself up in ransom and for some years lived among the Muslims, converting many to the Christian faith. His trials are said to have culminated in an eight months' imprisonment, from which he was ransomed by members of his order. On his return to Spain in 1239, *Gregory IX nominated him cardinal, but in the next year on his way to Rome he died at Cardona, near Barcelona. Feast day, 31 Aug. He is the patron saint of midwives.

There is very little trustworthy information about the Saint. A 16th-cent. Life is pr. in *AASS*, Aug. 6 (1743), pp. 737–41, with introd., pp. 729–37, and account of the miracles attributed to him, pp. 741–76. See also histories of the MERCEDARIANS, cited s.v.

Raymond of Peñafort, St (*c.*1180–1275), Spanish canonist. He studied, and later taught, rhetoric and logic at Barcelona, but resigned his chair in 1210 in order to study law at *Bologna. Here he was made doctor in 1218 and lectured until 1220. He was persuaded by the Bp. of Barcelona to return and teach there, and was made canon and later provost of the cathedral. In 1222 he entered the *Dominican convent of Barcelona. Here he wrote his *Summa de casibus poenitentiae*, which exercised a profound influence on the development of the penitential system. In 1229 he was called away to accompany the Papal legate to Spain, and returned with him to Rome. In 1230 *Gregory IX appointed him chaplain and penitentiary, and charged him with the collection and arrangement of Papal decretals subsequent to *Gratian; this work was finished in 1234 and promulgated on 5 Sept. by the bull 'Rex Pacificus'. In 1236 Raymond went back to Spain for reasons of health, but two years later, much against his will, he was elected Master General of his order. In this capacity he rearranged the Dominican Constitutions into the form which they

essentially retained until 1924. After having resigned his generalship in 1240, he devoted himself esp. to the conversion of Jews and Moors, and for this purpose he founded schools of Hebrew and Arabic. Besides the *Summa* already mentioned, which he revised after 1234, Raymond wrote other works on canon law. He was held in high esteem by his contemporaries. James I of Aragon was among his penitents, and St *Thomas Aquinas wrote his *Summa contra Gentiles* possibly at his suggestion. He was canonized by *Clement VIII in 1601. Feast day, 7 (formerly 23) Jan.

Summa de casibus poenitentiae pr. at Rome 1603, and later edns.; modern edn. by X. Ochoa and A. Diez (Universa Bibliotheca Iuris, 1. B; Rome, 1976). *Summa de Matrimonio*, ed. idd. (ibid. 1. C; 1978). *Summa de Iure Canonico*, ed. J. Rius Serra (*Opera Omnia*, 1; Barcelona, 1945) and by X. Ochoa and A. Diez (Universa Bibliotheca Iuris, 1. A; 1975). Raymond's revision of the Dominican Constitutions ed. R. Creytens, OP, in *Archivum Fratrum Praedicatorum*, 18 (1948), pp. 5–68, with introd. *AASS*, Jan. 1 (1643), pp. 404–29, incl. material from the process of canonization. F. Balme, OP, C. Paban, OP, and J. Collomb, OP (eds.), *Raymundiana; seu Documenta quae pertinent ad S. Raymundi de Pennaforti Vitam et Scripta* (Monumenta Ordinis Fratrum Praedicatorum Historica, '4' [6], fascs. 1 and 2; 1898–1901); J. Rius Serra (ed.), *San Raimundo de Penyafort. Diplomatario: documentos, vida antigua, crónicas, procesos antiguos* (*Opera Omnia*, 3; Barcelona, 1954); A. Collell, OP, 'Raymundiana', *Analecta Sacra Tarraconensia*, 30 (1957), pp. 63–95; 31 (1958), pp. 341–66. Modern Life by F. Valls-Taberner (Colección pro Ecclesia et Patria, Barcelona, 1936; 2nd edn. in his *Obras Selectas*, 1. 2; 1953). Brief sketch in Eng. by T. M. Schwertner (Milwaukee [1935]). A special number of the periodical *Escritos del Vedat*, 7 (1977) was devoted to Raymond of Peñafort, incl. unpub. docs. P. Ribes Montané, *Relaciones entre la Potestad Eclesiástica y el Poder Secular, según san Ramón de Penyafort* (Publicaciones del Instituto Español de Historia Ecclesiástica, Monografías, 26; Rome, 1979). [D. A.] Mortier, OP, *Histoire des maîtres généraux de l'ordre des Frères Prêcheurs*, 1 (1903), pp. 255–85. S. Kuttner, *Repertorium der Kanonistik (1140–1234)*, 1 (ST 71; 1937), pp. 438–52. Kaeppeli, 3 (1980), pp. 283–7; 4 (1993), p. 248. A. Teetaert, OFM Cap., in *DTC* 13 (pt. 2; 1937), cols. 1806–23; A. Robles Sierra, OP, in *Dict. Sp.* 13 (1988), cols. 190–4, both s.v. 'Raymond de Penyafort'.

Raymond of Sebonde (d. 1436), Spanish philosopher. The date and place of his birth are unknown, but most modern scholars regard him as a Catalan. He became a professor at the University of Toulouse, where he taught theology, philosophy, and medicine. His book, 'Liber Naturae sive Creaturarum', in later printed editions *Theologia Naturalis*, written originally in Spanish, was first published in 1484, and achieved great fame in the 16th cent. through M. de *Montaigne, who translated and defended it (1569). Its Prologue gave offence because it over-emphasized the authority of the 'Book or Law of Nature' at the expense of Scripture and tradition, maintaining that it is possible for human reason to discover the contents of the Christian revelation in nature alone; and it was put on the *Index in 1559. The book itself, however, was highly esteemed, not only by his contemporaries but also by later authorities such as Cardinal Bona and St Peter *Canisius, for its able defence of the truth and reasonableness of Catholic doctrine on grounds appealing to those who do not accept revelation.

Raymond's *Theologia Naturalis* was often repr. in the 15th–17th cents. Best edn. (but without the preface) by J. Sighart, Sulzbach, 1852 (repr., with introd. by F. Stegmüller, Stuttgart, 1966). J. H.

Probst, *Le Lullisme de Raymond de Sebonde (Ramon de Sibiude)* (Toulouse, 1912); C. de Poer, *Montaigne als 'Apologeet' van Raymond Sebond* (Mededeelingen der Nederlandsche Akademie van Wetenschappen. Afd. Letterkunde, NR, dl. 3, no. 12; Amsterdam, 1940). T. and C. Carreras y Artau, *Historia de la Filosofía Española: Filosofía Cristiana de los Siglos XIII al XV*, 2 (1943), pp. 101–75. I. S. Révah, *Une Source de la spiritualité Péninsulaire au XVIème siècle: La 'Théologie naturelle' de Raymond de Sebond* (Lisbon, 1953). J. M. De Bujanda, 'L'Influence de Sebond en Espagne au XVIe siècle', *Renaissance and Reformation*, 10 (1974), pp. 78–84. C. C. J. *Webb, *Studies in the History of Natural Theology* (1915), pp. 292–312. A. Guy in *Dict. Sp.* 13 (1988), cols. 194–201, s.v. 'Raymond Sibiuda'.

reader. In the Anglican Communion, a lay person licensed to conduct religious services. The history of the office in its present form in the C of E dates from 1866, when the Bp. of *Gloucester and Bristol admitted the first reader. The number of readers gradually increased, and in 1905 the bishops issued rules governing their status, duties, forms of admission, etc. (The rules were revised in 1921 and 1940.) Since 1969 these matters have been regulated by *Canons E 4–6, revised in 1979, and, less directly, by Canons B 11 and 12. The duties which may be assigned to readers include the reading of *Morning and *Evening Prayer (except the Absolution) and of the *Litany, the publication of *Banns of Marriage, distributing the Bread and Wine at the Eucharist, officiating at the *Burial of the Dead, preaching; and generally giving an incumbent such assistance in his pastoral work as the bishop may direct. Readers are formally admitted to their office by a bishop, from whom they may also receive a licence either for a particular parish or for the diocese generally. Since 1969 women have been eligible for the office.

In the Episcopal Church of *Scotland the Canons of 1863 provided for lay readers and in the subsequent period many provinces of the Anglican Communion have established readers with duties similar to those exercised in the C of E. In a few places the office is sometimes stipendiary, as was formerly occasionally the case in England. See also LECTORS.

R. [A. S.] Martineau, *The Office and Work of a Reader* (1970; rev. edn., 1980). T. G. King, *Readers: A Pioneer Ministry* (1973).

Real Presence, the. In (esp. *Anglican) Eucharistic theology an expression used to cover several doctrines emphasizing the actual Presence of the Body and Blood of Christ in the Sacrament, as contrasted with others that maintain that the Body and Blood are present only figuratively or symbolically. The 16th-cent. English Reformers were so concerned to reject the doctrine of *transubstantiation that they were wary of speaking of real presence; when they used the phrase, it was usually in conjunction with expressions that would later be labelled *receptionist. Thus H. *Latimer in 1554 said that 'the same presence may be called a real presence, because to the faithful believer there is a real, or spiritual body of Christ'. T. *Cranmer in his earlier writings spoke of a 'real' or 'corporeal' presence, but later tended rather to refer to a 'true' or 'spiritual' presence. Subsequent Anglican writers, less close to the Reformation controversies, were more ready to use the phrase. It figures in the works of the *Caroline Divines (esp. W. *Laud and J. *Cosin), forms part of the title of Jeremy *Taylor's book, *The Real

Presence and Spirituall of Christ in the Blessed Sacrament proved against the Doctrine of Transubstantiation (1654), and comes in the hymns of Charles *Wesley.

H. Latimer, *Sermons and Remains*, ed. G. E. Corrie (*Parker Society, 1845), pp. 250–78 ('The Disputation had at Oxford, the 18th day of April, 1554, between Mr Hugh Latimer. . . and Mr Smith and others'). T. Cranmer, *Writings and Disputations . . . relative to the Sacrament of the Lord's Supper*, ed. J. E. Cox (ibid., 1844). P. [N.] Brooks, *Thomas Cranmer's Doctrine of the Eucharist* (1965; 2nd edn., 1992).

Realism. (1) Any form of belief which is chary of speculation and rooted in sober fact. In this sense, Christianity claims to be realistic as based not on abstract theorizing or symbolic myths, but on historical events known to have happened at a certain time and concerned with the concrete facts of human experience. Thus L. *Laberthonnière contrasted 'Christian Realism' with 'Greek Idealism'.

(2) The philosophical doctrine of the reality of the external world as against the idealistic view that it is constituted by consciousness. In reaction from the classical formulation of Idealism by I. *Kant and his successors (J. G. *Fichte, F. W. J. *Schelling, G. W. F. *Hegel), which exercised such a deep influence on speculative theology throughout the 19th cent., in the 20th cent. there has set in a strong reaction towards Realism. In philosophy the turning-point was G. E. Moore's 'Refutation of Idealism' in *Mind*, NS 12 (1903), pp. 433–53.

(3) In a more technical sense the doctrine that abstract concepts ('universals') have a real existence apart from the individuals ('particulars') in which they are embodied. The doctrine was developed in the Middle Ages on the basis of *Plato's metaphysic, largely out of a constantly discussed passage in *Porphyry's 'Isagoge' on the existence of genera and species. It was professed by *Erigena and *Remigius of Auxerre and, in a modified form, by St *Anselm in opposition to the *Nominalism (q.v.) of *Roscelin. It was carried further in the 12th cent. by *William of Champeaux, who recognized in the several individuals of the same species an identical reality (*eandem rem*), modified by *Abelard and, under the influence of *Aristotle, reconstructed by St *Thomas Aquinas, who, rejecting the view that universals exist apart from the individuals (*universalia ante res*), upheld a 'moderate realism' (*universalia in rebus*).

recapitulation (Lat. *recapitulatio*; Gk. ἀνακεφαλαίωσις, a 'summing-up', 'summary'). The term is used in its verbal form in Eph. 1: 10, where God is said to sum up all things in Christ, and from this passage was taken over by the Fathers. The conception of recapitulation was elaborated esp. by St *Irenaeus, who interpreted it both as the restoration of fallen humanity to communion with God through the obedience of Christ and as the summing-up of the previous revelations of God in past ages in the Incarnation. Besides these two meanings, which are common in patristic literature, there is a third found in St *Chrysostom, who applies the word to the reunion of both angels and men under Christ as their common head.

Recared (d. 601), King of the Visigoths. Having been associated with his father, the *Arian Leovigild, in the government of the country (most of Spain) from 573, he succeeded him on the throne in 586. In the next year, probably owing to the influence of St *Leander, Bp. of Seville, he and his family became Catholics. The step, though followed by several quickly suppressed insurrections on the part of the Arian bishops, helped considerably to pacify the country, in which the Catholic clergy and nobles were more powerful than the Arian Visigoths. The king's action was ratified in 589 by the Third Council of *Toledo, which regulated the religious situation in a number of canons. The remaining years of the king seem to have been peaceful; he is praised by St *Isidore of Seville for founding many churches and monasteries.

The main sources for his life are St Isidore's *Historia Gothorum* and the Chronicle of John of Biclara, both ed. T. *Mommsen in *MGH*, Chronica Minora, 2 (1894), pp. 217–20 and 288–90. E. A. Thompson, 'The Conversion of the Visigoths to Catholicism', *Nottingham Mediaeval Studies*, 4 (1960), pp. 4–35, esp. pp. 23–35. K. Schäferdiek, *Die Kirche in den Reichen der Westgoten und Suewen bis zur Errichtung der westgotischen katholischen Staatskirche* (Arbeiten zur Kirchengeschichte, 39; 1967), pp. 137–242, esp. pp. 192–233. T. González García in R. García Villoslada (ed.), *Historia de la Iglesia en España*, 1 (Biblioteca de Autores Cristianos, 1979), pp. 401–21, with full bibl.

reception. The informal process by which the whole Church gives subsequent assent to a conciliar or Papal decision in the light of its conformity with Scripture and tradition. Decisions of the early *Oecumenical Councils were accepted partly because they corresponded to the *sensus fidelium*. While the development of Papal *authority (esp. the definition of Papal *infallibility) has led reception to be comparatively neglected in the RC Church, Anglicans and Orthodox have emphasized it in modern times. Recently the idea has been used within the Anglican Communion to support experimentation, e.g. with the ordination of *women to the priesthood in some provinces, in the expectation that such innovations might come to be 'received'.

receptionism. A form of Eucharistic teaching acc. to which, while the bread and wine continue to exist unchanged after consecration, the faithful communicant receives together with them the true Body and Blood of Christ. Such a doctrine was common among Anglican divines in the 16th and 17th cent. Those who lean to such teaching have generally shrunk from giving it precise definition. The word itself is apparently not found before 1867.

Rechabites. A religious group in Israel, founded by Jehonadab, the son of Rechab, who persuaded Jehu to abolish Tyrian Baal worship (2 Kings 10). The Rechabites represented a protest against Canaanite luxury and ways of living and a return to the simplicity and even asceticism of the more nomadic life. Like the *Nazirites, they made it a rule to abstain from wine, and they were also opposed to agriculture and the cultivation of vineyards. The title has been adopted in modern times by a society of total abstainers.

S. Abramsky in *Encyclopaedia Judaica*, 13 (Jerusalem, 1972), cols. 1609–12, s.v.

recluse. A person who lives apart from the world, esp. for the purpose of religious meditation. In a stricter use,

the word is applied to those who have made definite vows to live in this way.

M.-C. Chartier in *Dict. Sp.* 13 (1988), cols. 217–28, s.v., with bibl.

Recognitions, Clementine. See CLEMENTINE LITERATURE.

recollection. A term used by modern spiritual writers to denote an attitude of attentiveness to God and to oneself. The idea that the soul becomes dissipated through its concern for worldly things and should 'collect itself' into itself to concentrate on its spiritual purpose is at least as old as *Plato (cf. *Phaedo*, 67 C), and it recurs in various forms in the Fathers and in medieval writers. The term 'recollection' itself first appears in Spanish in the mid-15th cent., meaning local 'withdrawal, seclusion'. In 16th-cent. writers it is common in the interiorized sense of 'living within oneself' (*John of Ávila, *Epistolario*, 109). The practice is recommended esp. by such writers as Francisco de Osuna (*c*.1492–*c*.1541) as a whole way of life. Other writers, such as *Teresa of Ávila, treat recollection as a kind or stage of prayer. Subsequently the term was extended to almost any kind of spiritual exercise, and 'recollected' came to be used independently of any technical definition.

M. Andrés Martín, *Los Recogidos: Nueva visión de la mística española (1500–1700)* (Publicaciones de la Fundacion Universitaria Española, Monografias, 13; 1975 [1976]). H.-J. Sieben and S. López Santidrián in *Dict. Sp.* 13 (1988), cols. 247–67, s.v. 'Recueillement'.

Recollects. The title of two separate religious orders:

(1) The Franciscan Recollects. A reformed branch of the Franciscan *Observants, started in France at the end of the 16th cent., which spread to Belgium, Germany, the Netherlands, Ireland, and the exiled English Friars on the Continent in the course of the 17th cent. In 1897 they were incorporated with the other Observants by *Leo XIII.

(2) The Augustinian Recollects. A strict branch of the *Augustinian Hermits, started in Spain. Their first house was founded at Talavera in 1589, and other monasteries were soon established in many parts of the country. They were erected into a separate province by a brief of *Clement VIII in 1602, and in 1621 formed a separate congregation. The congregation became successful as missionaries, esp. in Peru and the Philippines. In 1912 they were constituted into an independent order ('Ordo Eremitarum Recollectorum S. Augustini') with a prior-general at its head.

(1) P. Péano, OFM, in *DIP* 7 (1983), cols. 1307–22, s.v. 'Recolletti', with bibl. See also works cited under FRANCISCAN ORDER.

(2) *Bullarium Ordinis Recollectorum S. Augustini et Diplomatica Officialis* [to 1788], ed. I. Fernandez a S. Corde Iesu, ORSA (4 vols., Rome (1–3) and Salamanca (4), 1954–73). Andrés de San-Nicolas, *Historia general de los religios descalzos del orden de los Hermitanos del . . . Padre . . . San Agustín* (Madrid, 1644; cont. by other members of the Order, making 12 vols. to 1974, pub. Madrid and Barcelona). M. T. Disdier, AA, in *DHGE* 5 (1931), cols. 581–95, s.v. 'Augustin (Ier Ordre dit de saint-) (Ermites récollets)', with detailed bibl.; G. La Mountain in *NCE* 1 (1967), pp. 1061 f., s.v. 'Augustinian Recollects'. See also works cited under AUGUSTINIAN HERMITS.

Record, The. The first Anglican weekly newspaper, begun on 1 Jan. 1828. It was from the first strongly *Evangelical, among those concerned in its foundation being J. H. *Newman (then an Evangelical). During its early years it was controlled by Alexander Haldane (1800–82), who ensured that it remained Protestant in doctrine and Conservative in politics. On 1 Jan. 1949 it was amalgamated with the *Church of England Newspaper* (founded as the *Church Family Newspaper*, 1894).

rector. In the C of E the rector (Lat. 'ruler') was the person or *parson entitled to the whole *tithes of the parish. At first the rector was the incumbent, and it is when the two positions are still combined that the term is most familiar. Where, however, the tithes were *appropriated to a monastery or other spiritual body, the clergyman in the parish was merely the rector's *vicar (substitute) or *curate. The freehold of the church and churchyard is normally vested in the rector, whether or not he is the incumbent, but this does not allow him any special rights of access.

When tithes were *impropriated by laymen at the *Dissolution, they and their successors were known as *lay rectors (q.v.). Sinecure rectors are incumbent clergymen entitled to have a vicar in their own parish, thereby relieving them of the spiritual duties; most sinecure rectories have now been suppressed by the Ecclesiastical Commissioners Act 1840 and the Pastoral Measure 1983 s. 34.

A vicarage may be reunited with the rector's rights and converted into a rectory. Some parishes created by statute in the 19th cent. were also termed rectories, although there was no settled practice. A new benefice will be a rectory if it is formed by union with a rectory; a new benefice may also be a rectory if it replaces a rectory that is dissolved, but only if the pastoral scheme so provides.

In the Scottish universities the Rectors or Lord Rectors are elected officers. In English universities the title is used only of the heads of Exeter and Lincoln Colleges, Oxford. On the Continent the title is customary for the heads of universities or for the presidents of their administrative bodies. The heads of RC *seminaries and *Jesuit houses are also commonly styled rectors. Otherwise, RC rectors are normally priests with the care of churches which are not parochial, capitular, or attached to a religious community or society: *CIC* (1983), cans. 556–563.

See also TEAM MINISTRY.

recusancy. Refusal to submit to authority, and esp. refusal to attend the services of the established C of E. Though used particularly of RC recusants (esp. but not exclusively of the 16th and 17th cents.), it was also applied to Protestant *Separatists ('sectary recusants'). Until the Pope excommunicated *Elizabeth I in the bull '*Regnans in excelsis' (1570), recusancy had been rare, since conservative religious elements in the nation had received no clear guidance regarding their attitude to the Establishment. It received a powerful impetus with the arrival of *Jesuits and other priests from the Continent, esp. during the years around 1580. By Elizabethan and Jacobean statesmen it was considered a dangerous problem, since it had tenacious roots throughout the social structure in certain regions of England, notably in the N., where it was long thought likely to express itself in the form of armed rebellion. Lancashire and Durham, followed by certain regions of Yorkshire and Wales, took the lead in recusancy during the 16th and 17th cents. Derbyshire, Warwickshire, Staffordshire, Monmouthshire, Herefordshire, and even Hampshire and Sussex, also showed strong recusant parties among the landed gentry. That everywhere, except in Lancashire, actual recusants became a small percentage of the total populations was due partly to the eroding influence of the penal laws, and partly to the long-term success of Protestant evangelization, which could not be matched by the efforts of the hard-pressed RC clergy trained overseas. Nevertheless, the recusant minority preserved the continuity of RC practice in England, in contrast to its almost total disappearance in other northern European regions such as the Scottish Lowlands and Scandinavia. See also ROMAN CATHOLIC CHURCH IN ENGLAND AND WALES AFTER THE REFORMATION.

Much primary material is pub. by the *Catholic Record Society. The subject is also covered by *Recusant History* (Bognor Regis, 1951–64; London, 1965 ff.) and by *A Newsletter for Students of Recusant History*, ed. T. A. [C.] Birrell (9 vols., Nijmegen, 1958–70; from 1972 incorporated in *Recusant History*). The writings of recusants of the period 1558 to 1640 are being repr. in a facsimile series entitled English Recusant Literature, ed. D. M. Rogers (Leeds, 1969 ff.). A. O. Meyer, *England und die katholische Kirche unter Elisabeth* (Bibliothek des kgl. Preussischen Historischen Instituts in Rom, 6, pt. 1; 1911; Eng. tr., 1916). E. Rose, *Cases of Conscience: Alternatives open to Recusants and Puritans under Elizabeth I and James I* (Cambridge, 1975). There are also a number of journals devoted to regional research on recusancy. M. J. Havran in J. W. O'Malley, SJ (ed.), *Catholicism in Early Modern History: A Guide to Research* (Reformation Guides to Research, 2; St Louis [1988]), pp. 69–82. See also bibl. to ROMAN CATHOLIC CHURCH IN ENGLAND AND WALES AFTER THE REFORMATION.

Redaction Criticism (Ger. *Redaktionsgeschichte*). The name given by W. Marxsen and others to the investigation of the editorial work done by biblical authors on earlier material, e.g. the use made of the Marcan material by Matthew and Luke. It led to a more holistic interest in the Gospels as theological compositions and later pointed towards more literary approaches.

J. Rohde, *Die redaktionsgeschichtliche Methode* (1966; Eng. tr., *Rediscovering the Teaching of the Evangelists*, 1968). N. Perrin, *What is Redaction Criticism?* (1970). C. [M.] Tuckett, *Reading the New Testament: Methods of Interpretation* (1987), pp. 116–35.

Red Hat. The flat-crowned broad-brimmed hat, with two clusters of 15 tassels, traditionally distinctive of a *cardinal. Until recently the Pope invested the cardinal with the red hat at the first public *consistory after his appointment, and it was not worn again. After the cardinal's death, it was suspended over his tomb. Although cardinals are now invested with a red biretta, the expression 'red hat' is still often used for the cardinal's office.

red letter day. An important feast or saint's day, printed in ecclesiastical calendars in red ink. In the C of E the term is applied to those feasts for which the BCP provides a proper Collect, Epistle, and Gospel, as formerly these feasts were distinguished in the calendar in this way.

Red Mass. Acc. to W. usage, a *Votive Mass of the Holy Spirit, so named from the red vestments in which it is celebrated. Such Masses are customarily celebrated with some solemnity at the opening of councils, synods, etc., to invoke the aid and illumination of the Holy Spirit in the deliberations to follow. In England a Red Mass is celebrated at *Westminster Cathedral at the opening of the law term and attended by RC judges.

Red Sea. In the OT the Hebrew phrase rendered 'Red Sea' is usually taken to mean 'Reed' or 'Marsh Sea'; the change in terminology may be traced back to the LXX and Vulgate and no satisfactory explanation has been offered. In some cases the phrase seems to refer to the Gulf of Suez (e.g. Exod. 10. 19) and in others to the Gulf of Aqaba (e.g. 1 Kgs. 9: 26). However, its use to denote the site of the crossing of waters by the Israelites recorded in Exod. 14 and 15 has occasioned much debate. Some older scholars held that either the Gulf of Suez or the Gulf of Aqaba was intended here; more recently many critics have tended to favour a northern route for the Exodus, suggesting that the crossing took place in the eastern region of the Nile delta, perhaps on a southern extension of the present Lake Menzaleh, a lagoon adjacent to the Mediterranean Sea. The crossing of the Red Sea marked the end of the bondage of the Israelites in Egypt and was subsequently regarded as a turning-point in their destinies (e.g. Pss. 66: 6; 78: 53; 114: 3). In the NT (1 Cor. 10: 2) it is regarded as a type of Christian Baptism. See also EXODUS.

N. H. Snaith, 'יַם־סוּף: The Sea of Reeds: the Red Sea', *Vetus Testamentum*, 15 (1965), pp. 395–8. G. I. Davies, *The Way of the Wilderness: A Geographical Study of the Wilderness Itineraries in the Old Testament* (Society for Old Testament Study, Monograph Series, 5; Cambridge, 1979). J. R. Huddlestun in *Anchor Bible Dictionary*, 5 (1992), pp. 633–42, s.v., with bibl. See also bibl. to EXODUS.

redemption. The idea of redemption is common to many religions, being based on the desire of man to be delivered from sin, suffering, and death. Christianity claims that it has become a fact through the Incarnation and the Death of Christ. It is viewed by theologians under the double aspect of deliverance from sin and restoration of man and the world to communion with God. Both these aspects are developed in the NT, esp. in the Pauline Epistles, where the 'redemption (ἀπολύτρωσις) through His blood, the forgiveness of our trespasses' (Eph. 1: 7), and 'the dispensation of the fullness of the times, to sum up (ἀνακεφαλαιώσασθαι) all things in Christ' (Eph. 1: 10) are set forth as the interrelated effects of the work of the Redeemer. In patristic thought both sides were somewhat differently emphasized, the Greeks stressing more the restoration of man to the Divine life (see DEIFICATION), whereas the Latin Fathers gave primary importance to the expiation of our sins through the sacrificial death of Christ. In St *Augustine, and later in *Scholastic theology, Redemption was brought into more direct connection with *Original Sin, which it was held to remove by restoring man to his state of *Original Righteousness, lost by the *Fall of *Adam. From St *Anselm's *Cur Deus Homo* onwards, the question of the necessity of the Redemption was widely discussed. Anselm held that, given the Divine plan and the infinite damage incurred in its violation by sin, the justice of God which required adequate satisfac-

tion made redemption by the death of the God-man a necessity. This view was abandoned by the Schoolmen, notably St *Thomas Aquinas, who taught that, though God might have redeemed the world in many other ways, the manner in which He did so was highly 'congruous', because it showed forth His omnipotence, goodness, and wisdom, and the admirable harmony in His Being between Justice and Mercy. Consequently Redemption is the free gift of God to man, who could not have redeemed himself, because of the supernatural character of the gifts lost by Original Sin. He maintained that, though it was impossible that sin should be abolished as a physical reality, it could be repaired morally by the objective merits of the Redeemer which, applied to the repentant sinner, enabled him to co-operate with grace towards justification and sanctification.

The theologians of the Reformation claimed to return to the teaching of St Paul. They denied the idea of Redemption as a restoration to Original Righteousness and, consequently, the possibility of human co-operation with grace other than by faith alone, and placed the exclusive emphasis on the forgiveness of sin and justification by imputation of the righteousness of Christ. Through the teaching of J. *Calvin and, later, of C. O. *Jansen, the view that Redemption extends only to the predestined was advocated by a number of Protestant and Catholic theologians in the 16th and 17th cents. It was pronounced heretical by *Innocent X in the constitution '*Cum Occasione' (1653). Later, the proposition that Christ died for all the faithful, but for the faithful alone (*pro omnibus et solis fidelibus*), was also condemned by *Alexander VIII (1690). The universality of Redemption, taught already in the NT (e.g. 1 Jn. 2: 2), was thus safeguarded, without, on the other hand, prejudicing the fact that its actual application does not extend to the damned nor, as *Origen believed, to the fallen angels. See also ATONEMENT.

Redemptorists. The common name for the members of the 'Congregation of the Most Holy Redeemer', founded by St *Alphonsus Maria di Liguori at Scala, Italy, in 1732. The Congregation was instituted for mission work among the poor both in Europe and among the heathen, and it has steadily refused to engage in purely educational activities. The order received the sanction of *Benedict XIV in 1749, and a community of Redemptorist nuns received similar approval in 1750. Despite frequent persecution at the hands of secular governments, it has continued to flourish to the present time. It was introduced into England in 1843. The Congregation is governed by a 'Rector Major', who holds office for life and resides in Rome.

G. Stebbing, CSSR, *The Redemptorists* (1924); E. Hosp, CSSR, *Die Kongregation des allerheiligsten Erlösers: Ihr Werden und Wollen* (1924); and later works of this author; G. Brandhuber, CSSR, *Die Redemptoristen, 1732–1932* (1932). M. de Meulemeester, CSSR, *Histoire sommaire de la congrégation du T.S. Rédempteur* (Louvain, 1950; Eng. tr., ibid., 1956); id., *Origines de la Congrégation du Très Saint-Rédempteur: Études et Documents* (2 vols., ibid., 1953–7). F. Chiovaro, CSSR, *Storia della Congregazione del Santissimo Redentore*, 1: *Le Origini (1732–1793)* (Rome, 1993). J. B. Byrne, CSSR, *The Redemptorist Centenaries: 1732, Founding of the Congregation of the Most Holy Redeemer—1832, Establishment in United States* (1932). M. de Meulemeester, CSSR, E. Colet, CSSR, and C. Henze, CSSR, *Bibliographie générale des écrivains rédemptoristes* (3 vols., 1933–9). M. J. Curley, CSSR, in *NCE* 12

(1967), pp. 161–4, s.v.; T. Rey-Mermet, CSSR, in *Dict. Sp.* 13 (1988), cols. 268–81, s.v. 'Rédemptoristes'; F. Ferrero, CSSR, in *DIP* 8 (1988), cols. 808–19, s.v. 'Santissimo Redentore'.

Reformatio Legum Ecclesiasticarum (Lat., 'the Reform of the Ecclesiastical Laws'), the book which was designed to provide a system of order and discipline for the C of E in place of the medieval *canon law. Previous initiatives for reform by T. *Cromwell and T. *Cranmer had come to nothing, but the Canon Law Act 1549 empowered the king to appoint thirty-two persons to compile a *corpus* of ecclesiastical laws for the English spiritual courts. The work was actually begun in 1550 by a body of eight persons, and Cranmer presented the Book to Parliament in Mar. 1553. It was opposed by the Duke of Northumberland, and with Edward VI's death in the summer, it ceased to be possible to proceed with it. The Book was printed with a preface by J. *Foxe in 1571, but the Elizabethan government could not be persuaded to put it into use. Its provisions owed much to *Reformed ideas. It is of importance for its connections both in context and in language with the *Thirty-Nine Articles.

Modern edn. by E. *Cardwell (Oxford, 1850). Eng. tr. of an incomplete draft (British Library MS Harley 426), by J. C. Spalding, *The Reformation of the Ecclesiastical Laws of England, 1552* (Sixteenth Century Essays & Studies, 19; Kirksville, Mo., 1992), with introd.

Reformation, the. This loose term is sometimes used to describe an involved series of changes in W. Christendom between the 14th and 17th cents., but it is more commonly restricted to the early 16th cent. It is said to have begun with the attacks of the *Lollards and the *Hussites upon the hierarchical structure of the Church; at the same time Papal authority and finances were particularly criticized. The English statutes of *Provisors and *Praemunire and the French *Pragmatic Sanction of Bourges (1438) represented efforts of monarchies to expand their own influence over their national Churches. After the disruptions of the 'Babylonish Captivity' at *Avignon and the *Great Schism the Popes recovered sufficient authority to ride out the storms of the *Conciliar Movement, though the final collapse of the Council of *Basle in 1449 left critics dissatisfied with some aspects of the Papal monarchy in the Church. Until the early 16th cent. divergence from Catholic doctrine was uncommon, but there were more frequent attacks upon the financial exactions of the Papacy and Curia and upon their worldliness and involvement in the dynastic politics of Italy.

When M. *Luther protested against the corruption of Rome and the great abuses attending the sale of *indulgences, he was breaking no new controversial ground. Indeed most of the Reformation movements demanded not innovation, but a return to a primitive excellence. Luther's study of St *Augustine had led him to question devotional practices and the emphasis of late medieval theology on 'good works'; later his historical reading, based on the work of L. *Valla, raised doubts regarding the validity of Papal claims to supremacy. From these traditionalist origins were derived fundamental attacks upon *transubstantiation, clerical *celibacy and the religious orders, as well as his demands for the abolition of Papal power in Germany. Luther's views were vigorously

expressed and widely circulated in his celebrated treatises of 1520; his writings began to influence the literate laity of the German towns, as did the preaching of his colleagues and students from *Wittenberg. His advocacy of princely authoritarianism during the *Peasants' War helped to ensure the support of his cause by the German princes. The rulers of Saxony, Hesse, Brandenburg, and Brunswick, besides the kings of *Denmark and *Sweden, were won to the reformed beliefs before or shortly after their classic enunciation in the 'Confession of *Augsburg' (1530). These rulers reorganized and regulated the Churches within their territories, and the progress of the Lutheran Reformation lay in the hands of the 'godly prince', to whom the plenitude of power was explicitly confided, and in its adoption by a number of the imperial cities of Germany.

Meanwhile in 1523–5 the Swiss divine U. *Zwingli, motivated at first by studies and beliefs analogous to those of Luther, had captured the support of the civic authorities of Zurich and carried through anti-Papal, anti-hierarchic, and anti-monastic reforms in that city. Zwingli's theology, more radical and less scholastic in its Eucharistic and social doctrines than Luther's, rapidly affected many of the Swiss cantons and some cities in SW Germany, though the efforts of M. *Bucer at Strasbourg, J. *Oecolampadius at Basle, and G. *Farel at Neuchâtel and *Geneva were also significant. The influence of Zurich was restricted after its military defeat by the Catholic cantons and the death of Zwingli in 1531, and thereafter leadership of the Swiss Reformation passed to Geneva.

There, from 1541, J. *Calvin established an elaborately organized theocracy. In his hands reforming opinion was more systematically defined and organized. Emphasis upon *predestination, it is true, may be traced in the thought of J. *Wycliffe, while Luther himself denied man freedom or responsibility, as traditionally understood. Yet a coherent theological system based upon the doctrines of particular election and redemption first appeared in Calvin's *Institutio Christianae Religionis* (1536). This system, with its appeal to rising elements in European society, henceforth proved for several generations the driving force of the Reformation, esp. in W. Germany, *France, the *Netherlands, England, and *Scotland. Like that of Lutheranism, but upon a wider stage, the progress of the Calvinist Reformation became inextricably involved with a series of political struggles, notably the Wars of Religion in France, which temporarily secured the position of the *Huguenots, and the national revolt which freed the northern Netherlands from *Spain. In Scotland, too, the Calvinist cause, led by J. *Knox and the Lords of the Congregation, triumphed upon a wave of nationalist reaction against French control. Such Calvinist success, often against resistance by political authorities, owed much to the Genevan organizational pattern which made it an effective opposition movement.

Meanwhile, however, the English Reformation had remained an insular process responsive to peculiar political and social forces. *Henry VIII, a convinced traditionalist in both doctrine and Church government, accomplished the overthrow of Papal Supremacy and the *Dissolution of the Monasteries largely in pursuit of short-term political ends and the extension of royal controls. Despite his opposition, reforming Continental doctrines and native heresy became more widespread, and in the universities humanistic biblical studies undermined scholastic theology. During the reign of *Edward VI, political calculation and the influence of T. *Cranmer, J. *Hooper, and N. *Ridley led to a more wide-ranging alteration of doctrine and liturgy, culminating in the Prayer Book of 1552 and the *Forty-Two Articles of 1553. After *Mary's attempt to reverse a generation of ecclesiastical change, the accession of *Elizabeth I was followed in 1559–63 by the reimposition of the earlier Protestant formularies, somewhat tempered by the need for compromise. Although Calvinist doctrinal views came to be widely held among bishops, university theologians, parish clergy and the godly laity, demands for institutional reform were resisted by the Crown and its advisers. The English Reformation thus grafted elements of Reformed theology and worship upon a traditional Church structure, but the continuities ensured peaceful change and, ultimately, widespread public acceptance. In England, as on the Continent, the Reformation secured legal endorsement more easily than individual conversions: its spiritual impact was most obvious among those attracted by the new emphasis upon Bible-reading, while the illiterate majority conformed with less enthusiasm.

Useful primary material collected and tr. into Eng. in B. J. Kidd (ed.), *Documents Illustrative of the Continental Reformation* (1911); H. J. Hillerbrand (ed.), *The Reformation in its own words* (1964); id. (ed.), *The Protestant Reformation* (1968). Classic interpretations include: L. von *Ranke, *Deutsche Geschichte im Zeitalter der Reformation* (6 vols., 1839–47; Eng. tr. of vols. 1–3, 1845–7); J. Janssen, *Geschichte des deutschen Volkes seit dem Ausgang des Mittelalters* (8 vols., 1878–94; Eng. tr., 16 vols., 1896–1910, + index, 1925); P. [G. J. M.] Imbart de La Tour, *Les Origines de la réforme* (4 vols., 1905–1935; new edn. of vol. 2, with rev. bibl., by Y. Lanhers, 1946); J. P. Whitney, *The Reformation: Being an Outline of the History of the Church from A.D. 1503 to A.D. 1648* (1907; new edn. entitled 'The History of the Reformation', CHS, 1940); H. Hermelink, *Reformation und Gegenreformation* (Handbuch der Kirchengeschichte für Studierende, 3; 1911); P. Smith, *The Age of the Reformation* [1921]; N. Sykes, *The Crisis of the Reformation* (1938); J. Mackinnon, *The Origins of the Reformation* (1939); J. Lortz, *Die Reformation in Deutschland* (2 vols., 1939–40; Eng. tr., with new bibl., 1968). Modern scholarly studies incl.: R. H. Bainton, *The Reformation of the Sixteenth Century* (Kansas, 1952; London, 1953); H. J. Grimm, *The Reformation Era, 1500–1650* (New York, 1954; 2nd edn., 1973); G. R. Elton (ed.), *The Reformation 1520–1559* (New Cambridge Modern History, 2; 1958; 2nd edn., 1990); H. Holborn, *A History of Modern Germany* [1]: *The Reformation* (New York, 1959); H. Bornkamm, *Das Jahrhundert der Reformation: Gestalten und Kräfte* (Göttingen, 1961); E. G. Léonard, *Histoire générale du protestantisme*, 1: *La Réformation* (1961; Eng. tr., with additional bibl., 1965); J. Delumeau, *Naissance et affirmation de la Réforme* (Nouvelle Clio, 30; 1965; 2nd edn., 1968); A. G. Dickens, *Reformation and Society in Sixteenth-Century Europe* (1966); F. Lau and E. Bizer, *A History of the Reformation in Germany to 1555* (Eng. tr. of 2 separate works, 1969); E. Iserloh, J. Glazik, and H. Jedin, *Reformation, Katholische Reform und Gegenreformation* (Handbuch der Kirchengeschichte, ed. H. Jedin, 4, 1967), pp. 3–446 (Eng. tr., History of the Church, ed. H. Jedin and J. Dolan, 5; 1980, pp. 3–429); H. J. Hillerbrand, *Christendom Divided: The Protestant Reformation* (1971); S. E. Ozment, *The Reformation in the Cities: The Appeal of Protestantism to Sixteenth-Century Germany and Switzerland* (New Haven, Conn., and London, 1975); K. A. Oberman, *Werden und Wertung der Reformation* (Tübingen, 1977; abridged Eng. tr., 1981).

A. G. Dickens and D. Carr (eds.), *The Reformation in England to the Accession of Elizabeth I* (Documents of Modern History, 1967). P. Hughes, *The Reformation in England* (3 vols., 1950–4). T. M. Parker, *The English Reformation to 1558* (1950; 2nd edn., 1966). G. H. and K. George, *The Protestant Mind of the English Reformation 1570–1640* (Princeton, NJ, 1961). W. A. Clebsch, *England's Earliest Protestants 1520–1535* (1964). A. G. Dickens, *The English Reformation* (1964). P. Collinson, *The Religion of Protestants: The Church in English Society 1559–1625* (Ford Lectures for 1979; Oxford, 1982). C. Haigh (ed.), *The English Reformation Revised* (Cambridge, 1987). E. Duffy, *The Stripping of the Altars: Traditional Religion in England c.1400–c.1580* (New Haven, Conn., and London, 1992), pp. 377–593. C. Haigh, *English Reformations: Religion, Politics, and Society under the Tudors* (Oxford, 1993).

Extensive bibl. of works pub. since 1940 in *Bibliographie de la Réforme, 1450–1648*, pub. by the Commission Internationale d'Histoire Ecclésiastique Comparée au sein du Comité International des Sciences Historiques (Leiden, 1958 ff.). See also bibl. to CALVINISM and LUTHERANISM.

Reformed Churches. The term is sometimes taken to include all the Protestant Churches which have accepted the principles of the *Reformation, but in a narrower and more accurate sense it is used specifically of those Churches influenced by the theology of J. *Calvin, J. *Knox, and U. *Zwingli, among others (popularly called *Calvinist), as contrasted esp. with the *Lutherans. This restriction is almost universal, with the corresponding expressions in French (*Églises réformées*) and German (*reformierte Kirchen*). The designation of such Churches as 'ecclesiae reformatae' was already general before the end of the 16th century.

Reformed Presbyterian Church. The small body of Scottish Presbyterians, popularly known as *Cameronians, who declined to accept the settlement of 1690 which established the Church of Scotland. The Reformed Presbytery was formed in 1743. The majority joined the *Free Church of Scotland in 1876, but a remnant has continued to exist as a separate body. They are represented in N. Ireland, Canada, and the USA. J. G. *Paton, the missionary to Vanuatu (formerly the New Hebrides), was a member of this Church.

M. Hutchison, *The Reformed Presbyterian Church in Scotland: Its Origin and History 1680–1876* (Paisley, 1893). W. J. Couper, *The Reformed Presbyterian Church in Scotland: Its Congregations, Ministers and Students* (Edinburgh, 1925).

Refreshment Sunday. A name for the Fourth Sunday in Lent. The epithet has been explained as referring either to the miracle of the feeding of the five thousand which was until 1969 in the RC Church, and in the BCP is, the Gospel for the day (Jn. 6: 1–14) or to the relaxation of Lenten discipline allowed on this day (e.g. the consumption of simnel-cakes). It is also known as *Laetare Sunday and *Mothering Sunday.

Refuge, Cities of. See CITIES OF REFUGE.

Regale (Lat. *regale*, neut. of *regalis*, 'pertaining to the king'). In legal language esp., the right to the revenues of vacant bishoprics and abbeys and to presentation to their dependent benefices claimed by the kings of Europe during the Middle Ages. It was usually held to derive from their position as feudal lords, and taken as analogous to that enjoyed during the minority of a lay tenant. The claim, consistently denied by the Popes, became closely connected with the *Investiture Controversy. The earliest known trace of it is met with in *France towards the end of the Carolingian period (10th cent.). In England it was successfully asserted by King William II (1087–1100) on the death of *Lanfranc (1089), and later became one of the causes of rejection of the Constitutions of *Clarendon by *Alexander III. In 1176 King Henry II (1154–89) promised to limit the exercise of the right to one year, but it continued, with few exemptions, until the *Reformation. It is still enjoyed by the Crown over the temporalities of vacant sees (though the revenues are now restored untouched when the newly elected bishop does homage). In Germany the right was claimed and exercised by Henry V (1106–25) and his immediate successors, but practically ceased after the death of *Frederick II (1250). In France, where it was claimed not only by the king but also by certain of the more important territorial lords, it was a continual source of friction between the Papacy and the temporal power from the time of St *Bernard to the end of the 19th cent.

The term 'Regale' has also, since the 18th cent., been more properly used of the privileges and prerogatives of the Sovereign in general.

M. Howell, *Regalian Right in Medieval England* (1962), with refs. G. J. Campbell, SJ, 'Temporal and Spiritual Regalia during the Reigns of St. Louis and Philip III', *Traditio*, 20 (1964), pp. 351–83. J. Gaudemet in *DDC* 7 (1965), cols. 493–532, s.v., with full bibl. to date.

Regeneration. The spiritual rebirth (Gk. παλιγγενεσία), which, acc. to traditional theology, is effected in the soul by Christian Baptism (cf. Tit. 3: 5). See BAPTISM.

Regensburg, Conference of. See RATISBON, CONFERENCE OF.

Regimini militantis Ecclesiae. The bull issued by *Paul III on 27 Sept. 1540, instituting the Society of Jesus (*Jesuits) and authorizing St *Ignatius Loyola and the nine priests who had gathered round him to accept further recruits. The bull consists largely of the second version of a document drawn up by the early Jesuits themselves (the so-called 'Formula of the Institute'), summarizing the kind of religious life they hoped to lead. In 1550, *Julius III issued a further bull, 'Exposcit debitum', including a third version of the Formula, which had been subjected to additional revision in the light of the Society's accumulating experience. It is this version which is still in force.

Text, with draft material, in *Monumenta Ignatiana*, 3rd ser., vol. 1 (Monumenta Historica Societatis Jesu, 63; Rome, 1934), pp. 24–32; of 'Exposcit debitum', ibid., pp. 372–83; and of the first version of the Formula, ibid., pp. 14–21. Bull also in Mirbt and Aland (1967), pp. 539–42 (no. 817). Parallel Fr. tr. of all three versions of the Formula in Ignatius' *Écrits*, ed. M. Giuliani, SJ, and others [1991], pp. 293–309. Eng. trs. of 'Exposcit debitum' in *The Constitutions of the Society of Jesus*, ed. and tr. G. E. Ganss, SJ (St Louis, 1970), pp. 63–73; of the first version of the Formula in G. Schurhammer, SJ, *Francis Xavier*, 1 (Rome, 1973), pp. 462–5. Comm. on the Formula by A. M. de Aldama, SJ (in Spanish, Rome, 1981; Eng. tr., Anand, India, and St Louis, 1990).

Regina Coeli (Lat., 'Queen of Heaven'). The Eastertide anthem to the Blessed Virgin, so named from its opening words. In the Roman *Breviary its recitation after *Compline is prescribed from *Easter Day to *Whitsunday. It also takes the place of the *Angelus in Eastertide. Its authorship is unknown, but it probably dates from the 12th cent.

H. Thurston, SJ, 'The *Regina Cœli*', *The Month*, 121 (1913), pp. 384–8, repr. in his *Familiar Prayers*, ed. P. Grosjean, SJ (1953), pp. 146–51, with refs.

Reginald of Piperno (*c.*1230–1285/95), *Dominican friar. He was known as the 'lifelong' companion of St *Thomas Aquinas. He collected all Thomas's writings and took down several of his lectures, among them the Commentary on Jn. and part of that on the Pauline Epistles. It was prob. under his editorship that the Supplement to the Third Part of the 'Summa Theologiae' was compiled after Thomas's death.

A. Dondaine, *Secrétaires de saint Thomas* (Rome, 1956), esp. pp. 198–202. Id., 'Sermons de Réginald de Piperno (Un manuscrit de la Bibliothèque de Boniface VIII)', in *Mélanges Eugène Tisserant*, 6 (ST 236; 1964), pp. 357–94. Kaeppeli, 3 (1980), p. 291, s.v. 'Rainaldus de Piperno'.

regionarius. A name in use at Rome in the earlier Middle Ages for members of the clergy who filled offices dependent on the arrangement of the city into seven ecclesiastical 'regions' (*regiones*), and who were thus distinguished both from the 'Papal' and the 'titular' clergy. See TITLE.

Registers, Episcopal. Many English Episcopal Registers have been printed in the publications of the *Canterbury and York Society (q.v.) and elsewhere.

D. M. Smith, *Guide to Bishops' Registers of England and Wales: A Survey from the Middle Ages to the Abolition of Episcopacy in 1646* (Royal Historical Society Guides and Handbooks, 11; 1981). See also under separate dioceses and individual bishops.

Regium Donum (Lat., 'Royal Gift'). The grant from public funds formerly made to the ministers of certain English *Nonconforming bodies. It originated out of sums which *Charles II ordered to be paid to *Presbyterian ministers after the *Declaration of Indulgence of 1672; but the practice did not become established in England till 1723, when George I ordered £500 (soon increased to £1,000) be paid annually out of the Treasury for the relief of Dissenting ministers and their widows. By 1727 all the '*Three Denominations' (Presbyterians, *Baptists, *Congregationalists) were enjoying it, and it continued until 1851. In *Ireland a *regium donum* to Presbyterian ministers was paid almost continuously from 1690 until the disestablishment of the Church of Ireland in 1869.

R. W. *Dale, *History of English Congregationalism* (ed. A. W. W. Dale, 1907), pp. 524–7; B. L. Manning, *The Protestant Dissenting Deputies*, ed. O. Greenwood (Cambridge, 1952), pp. 22 f., 387 f., 444, and 447.

Regium Placet. See EXEQUATUR.

Regnans in Excelsis. The *bull of excommunication published by *Pius V on 25 Feb. 1570, against Queen *Elizabeth I. It was issued after a formal trial of the Queen at Rome, whither a number of English exiles had been summoned to testify to her heretical proceedings. The bull declares Elizabeth a usurper as well as a heretic, absolves her subjects of their allegiance, and orders them to disobey her laws. It thus placed the unfortunate English RCs between conflicting loyalties and evoked as a counterblast the Elizabethan penal laws.

Text in *Bullarum, Diplomatum et Privilegiorum Sanctorum Romanorum Pontificum Taurinensis Editio*, 7 (Naples, 1882), pp. 810 f.; operative clauses repr. in Mirbt, pp. 348 f. (no. 491), with refs. J. H. Pollen, SJ, *The English Catholics in the Reign of Queen Elizabeth* (1920), pp. 142–59. See also bibl. s.v. ELIZABETH I.

Regula Fidei. See RULE OF FAITH.

Regula Magistri. An anonymous monastic Rule written by 'the Master' in Italy SE of Rome *c.*500–25. It appears *c.*817 in the *Codex Regularum* of St *Benedict of Aniane. Being in part verbally identical with the prologue and chapters 1–7 of the Rule of St *Benedict, it was thought to be later than this until A. Génestout, OSB, in 1940 declared St Benedict to be the borrower. This assertion opened a lively and widespread debate which continued for 20 years; now practically all scholars give priority to the *Regula Magistri*. While textual and palaeographical evidence is inconclusive, liturgy and observance suggests the priority of the *Regula Magistri*, while vocabulary and grammar seem decisive in favour of separate authorship (i.e. the *Regula Magistri* is not a first recension of the Rule of St Benedict), though possibly the *Regula Magistri* may stand between two redactions of the Rule of St Benedict. The monastery of the Master, though similar to that of St Benedict, is smaller and simpler, with many homely details. The *Regula Magistri* is diffuse and disorderly; but if the prologue and chapters on the abbot, etc., were borrowed by St Benedict from the Master, the latter was a man of deep spiritual wisdom.

Diplomatic edn. by H. Vanderhoven, F. Masai, and P. B. Corbett (Publications de Scriptorium, 3; Brussels and Paris, 1953); text also ed., with Fr. tr. and introd., by A. de Vogüé, OSB, and others (SC 105–7; 1964–5). M. J. Cappuyns, OSB, *Lexique de la Regula Magistri* (Instrumenta Patristica, 6; 1964). A. Génestout, OSB, 'La Règle du Maître et la Règle de S. Benoît', *Revue d'Ascétique et de Mystique*, 21 (1940), pp. 51–122. The lit. of the subsequent controversy is considerable, mainly scattered in periodicals. B. Steidle, OSB (ed.), *Regula Magistri, Regula S. Benedicti: Studia Monastica* (Studia Anselmiana, 44; 1959), with extensive bibl. M. D. *Knowles, *Great Historical Enterprises* [1963], pp. 135–95. See also works cited s.v. BENEDICT, RULE OF ST, esp. introd. to edns. of R. Hanslik and of J. Neufville, OSB, and A. de Vogüé, OSB.

regular (from Lat. *regula*, rule). A general term for those members of the RC clergy who are bound by *vows of religion and live in community, following a rule. They are to be distinguished from the seculars, i.e. priests living in the world. In a narrower sense the expression was restricted to religious who had taken vows in an Order; the 1983 *Codex Iuris Canonici* does not use it. See *INSTITUTES OF CONSECRATED LIFE.

regular canons. See CANONS REGULAR.

regular clerks. See CLERKS REGULAR.

Regularis Concordia. The code of monastic observance in England, drawn up and approved by the Synod of *Winchester, which met some time between 970 and 973. Acc. to *Aelfric, it would appear that the compilation was the work of St *Ethelwold, though it was very prob. inspired by St *Dunstan, to whom it was long attributed. Its provisions follow the *Benedictine tradition of *Benedict of Aniane, greatly influenced by the customaries of *Fleury, Ghent, and elsewhere. Details are given of the liturgical functions of the day and year and the duties attached to various monastic offices. The important position accorded to the sovereigns as patrons of the monastic life, e.g. the intercession for the King and Queen after all parts of the Office, except *Prime, is peculiar to England. Other English traditions were the allowance of a fire in winter and processions through the streets; notable also is the encouragement given to daily Communion.

Text repr. in J. P. Migne, *PL* 137. 475–502. Crit. edns. by T. Symons, OSB ('Medieval Classics', 1953) and by K. Hallinger, OSB, *Consuetudinum saeculi X/XI/XII Monumenta Non-Cluniacensia* (Corpus Consuetudinum Monasticarum, 7, pt. 3; Siegburg, 1984), pp. 61–147. The 'Proem' is also pr., with introd., in D. Whitelock, M. Brett, and C. N. L. Brooke (eds.), *Councils & Synods . . .*, I: A.D. 871–1204, 1 (Oxford, 1981), pp. 133–41. T. Symons, OSB, '*Regularis Concordia.* History and Derivation', in D. Parsons (ed.), *Tenth-Century Studies* (1975), pp. 37–59, 214–7.

Reichenau (Lat. *Augia dives*). A small island in the W. arm of Lake Constance famous in the earlier Middle Ages for its Benedictine monastery, founded by St *Pirminius in 724. It was an important centre of culture when the neighbouring St *Gall was still insignificant; in the 9th cent. it numbered among its members *Walafrid Strabo and Hatto, Abp. of Mainz. Its collection of MSS (many of which have been at Karlsruhe since 1805) was already well established by the early part of the 9th cent. The churches still survive and contain interesting remains.

Quellen und Forschungen zur Geschichte der Abtei Reichenau herausg. von der Badischen historischen Kommission (2 vols., Heidelberg, 1890–3). J. Autenrieth and others (eds.), *Das Verbrüderungsbuch der Abtei Reichenau* (*MGH*, Libri memoriales et necrologia, 1; 1979). K. Beyerle (ed.), *Die Kultur der Abtei Reichenau: Erinnerungsschrift zur zwölfhundertsten Wiederkehr des Gründungsjahres des Inselklosters, 724–1924* (2 vols., 1925; repr. 1970). H. Maurer (ed.), *Die Abtei Reichenau: Neue Beiträge zur Geschichte und Kultur des Inselklosters* (Bodensee-Bibliothek, 20; Sigmaringen, 1974). A. Borst (ed.), *Mönchtum, Episkopat und Adel zur Gründungszeit des Klosters Reichenau* (Vorträge und Forschungen, 20; Sigmaringen, 1974). P. Classen (ed.), *Die Gründungsurkunden der Reichenau* (ibid. 24; 1977). A. Holder, *Die Reichenauer Handschriften beschrieben und erlaeutert* (Die Handschriften der Grossherzoglich Badischen Hof- und Landesbibliothek in Karlsruhe, 5–7; 1906–18); H. Hoffmann, *Buchkunst und Königtum im ottonischen und frühsalischen Reich* (Schriften der *MGH*, 30/1; 1986), pp. 303–55. U. Begrich in *Helvetia Sacra*, Abteilung 3, Band 1, Teil 2 (Berne, 1986), pp. 1059–100, with extensive bibl. E. Josi in *EC* 10 (1953), cols. 665–8, s.v.

Reichsbischof. The title adopted in May 1933 at the suggestion of a Committee of the German Evangelical Church Federation for the office of head of a united German Evangelical Church, incorporating all the provincial Churches. Its first holder was Friedrich von Bodelschwingh. When the state appointed a Commissar for Prussia, who dismissed many pastors, Bodelschwingh resigned and was succeeded by the *German-Christian, Ludwig *Müller.

Reimarus, Hermann Samuel (1694–1768), *Deist and biblical critic. A native of Hamburg, he joined the class of J. A. *Fabricius, whose son-in-law he was to become, and later studied theology, classical philology, and philosophy at Jena. For a time he was Privatdozent at *Wittenberg and rector of the Hochschule at Wismar; and from 1727 until his death Professor of Hebrew and Oriental languages at Hamburg. His light duties enabled him to pursue independent studies in many fields, and between 1744 and 1767 he composed the treatise from which G. E. *Lessing published the notorious *Wolfenbüttel Fragments (q.v.) in 1774–8. The complete work (which Reimarus kept back from publication during his lifetime) bore in the MS the title *Apologie oder Schutzschrift für die vernünftigen Verehrer Gottes*. It unreservedly rejected miracles and revelation and sought to convict the biblical writers of conscious fraud, innumerable contradictions, and fanaticism. The appearance of the fragments produced a sensation in Germany. Further portions were issued by C. A. E. Schmidt (a pseudonym) in 1787 and W. Klose in 1850–2, while D. F. *Strauss in his book on Reimarus gave an analysis of the complete work. It was published in full in 1972. Reimarus himself published a number of works on other subjects, including *Abhandlungen von den vornehmsten Wahrheiten der natürlichen Religion* (1754; Eng. tr., 1766), a defence of *Natural Theology on the principles of C. *Wolff, which became very popular, and a good edition of Dio Cassius (2 vols., 1750–2).

His *Apologie* was ed. by G. Alexander (2 vols., Frankfurt am Main, 1972). Eng. tr. of two extracts from his work, 'On the Resurrection' and 'On the Intention of Jesus', and of part of Strauss's work, ed., with introd., by C. H. Talbert, *Reimarus: Fragments* (1971). D. F. Strauss, *Hermann Samuel Reimarus und seine Schutzschrift für die vernünftigen Verehrer Gottes* (1862). A. C. Lundsteen, *Hermann Samuel Reimarus und die Anfänge der Leben-Jesu-Forschung* (Copenhagen, 1939), with bibl. A. *Schweitzer, *Geschichte der Leben-Jesu-Forschung* (2nd edn., 1913), pp. 13–26 (Eng. tr. of 1st edn., 1910, pp. 13–26). R. [C.] Morgan in R. J. Coggins and J. L. Houlden (eds.), *A Dictionary of Biblical Interpretation* (1990), pp. 585 f., s.v., with bibl.

Reims. Acc. to tradition, the episcopal see in the old capital of the *Remi* in Gaul was founded in the second half of the 3rd cent. by St Sixtus, who was succeeded by St Sinicius. The first bishop for whom there is historical evidence was Imbetausius (or Bethausius), who took part in the Council of *Arles in 314. The power of the see increased greatly under St *Remigius (d. *c.*533; q.v.), who baptized *Clovis and evangelized the surrounding districts, and under the famous *Hincmar (d. 882). Between 922 and 946 it was subject to the counts of Vermandois. From the middle of the 10th cent., the Abps. of Reims successfully claimed the right to crown the French kings; this claim was endorsed by Pope *Sylvester II in 999 and confirmed as their exclusive privilege by *Alexander III in 1179. One of the most famous consecrations was that of Charles VII in the presence of St *Joan of Arc in 1429. By the *Concordat of 1801 the archbishopric of Reims was abolished and its territories divided between the dioceses of Meaux and of Metz, but it was restored in 1821.

The cathedral, one of the finest examples of French Gothic, was begun in 1211 and completed in the 14th cent. In 1481 a fire destroyed the roof and spires, and during the First World War (1914–18) the famous western façade with its three portals richly decorated with statues suffered severely. Among the badly damaged parts were the beautiful rose window above the central portal, the statue of Christ (the 'beau Dieu'), and that of the smiling angel. The cathedral was restored after the war and reopened in 1927. It suffered further damage in the Second World War. Its rich treasury contains many famous relics, e.g. the chalice of St Remigius and the remains of the Sainte Ampoule (see AMPULLA). The tomb of St Remigius in the former Benedictine abbey of St-Rémi is a popular place of pilgrimage.

Flodoard (canon of Reims; d. 966), *Historia Remensis Ecclesiae* (ed. G. Colvener, Douai, 1617; ed. and cont. by G. Marlot, OSB, 2 vols., Lille and Reims, 1666–79). G. Marlot, OSB (d. 1667), *Histoire de la ville, cité et université de Reims* (ed. J. Lacourt, 4 vols., Reims, 1843–6). G. Boussinesq and G. Laurent, *Histoire de Reims depuis les origines jusqu'à nos jours* (2 vols. in 3 parts, 1933). *Gallia Christiana*, 9 (Paris, 1751 edn.), pp. 1–322. L. *Duchesne, *Fastes épiscopaux de l'ancienne Gaule*, 3 (1915), pp. 76–88. J. Leflon, *Histoire de l'Élise de Reims du Ier au Vme siècle* (Reims, 1942). R. McKitterick, 'The Carolingian Kings and the See of Rheims, 882–987', in *Ideal and Reality in Frankish and Anglo-Saxon Society: Studies Presented to J. M. Wallace-Hadrill*, ed. P. Wormald and others (Oxford, 1983), pp. 228–49. F. Poirier-Coutansais, *Les Abbayes bénédictines du diocèse de Reims* (Gallia Monastica, 1; 1974). The many architectural studies of the cathedral incl. those of C. Cerf (2 vols., Reims, 1861), P. Vitry (9 fascs., Paris, 1915–20; mainly plates), L. Bréhier (Paris, 1916), and H. Reinhardt (ibid., 1963), with bibl. M. Hollande, *Trésors de Reims* (Reims [1961]). G. Goyau in *CE* 12 (1911), pp. 725–30, s.v.

Reims New Testament. See DOUAI-REIMS BIBLE.

reincarnation. See METEMPSYCHOSIS.

Reinkens, Joseph Hubert (1821–96), *Old Catholic bishop. In 1850 he became professor of Church history at Breslau, where he published some monographs on *patristics. At the First *Vatican Council he was opposed to the definition of Papal infallibility, and in 1871 joined J. J. I. von *Döllinger in the *Nuremberg Declaration. After excommunication from the RC Church, Reinkens was elected the first bishop of the German Old Catholics at Cologne in 1873, and consecrated by Bp. Hermann Heykamp of Deventer. For the rest of his life he devoted himself to the Old Catholic cause by learned writing and in other ways. In 1874 and 1875 he took a prominent part in the *Bonn Reunion Conferences and in 1876 consecrated Edward Herzog the first Swiss Old Catholic bishop.

Letters which he wrote to his brother Wilhelm, 1840–73, ed. H. J. Sieben (Bonner Beiträge zur Kirchengeschichte, 10; 3 vols., 1979). His Life was written by his nephew, J. M. Reinkens (Gotha, 1906).

Reitzenstein, Richard (1861–1931), classical philologist and historian of religions. From 1889 onward he held professorships at several German universities, his final appointment being to Göttingen in 1914. His earlier work was chiefly philological, but later he applied the results of his philological studies to the religious and philosophical movements of the early cents. AD and their influence on the development of Christianity. In *Poimandres* (1904) he tried to prove that NT phraseology and ideas are largely derived from *Hermetic sources and that the Christian Churches were modelled on Hermetic communities, while in *Die hellenistischen Mysterien-religionen* (1910; 3rd edn., 1927; Eng. tr., 1978) and other later writings he sought to establish the direct dependence of early Christianity on Hellenistic, *Mandaean, and Iranian ideas. Similar methods were applied to the study of Christian monasticism in *Historia Monachorum und Historia Lausiaca* (1916). Though his brilliant and ingenious theories did not win much acceptance, they brought together much new material for the study of Christianity in relation to its primitive environment.

E. Fraenkel, H. Fränkel, M. Pohlenz, E. Reitzenstein, R. Reitzenstein, E. *Schwartz, and J. Stroux, *Festschrift Richard Reitzenstein zum 2. April 1931 dargebracht* (1931), with list of his works by R. Reitzenstein, pp. 160–8.

relics. In Christian usage the word is applied most commonly to the material remains of a saint after his death, as well as to sacred objects which have been in contact with his body; the most important relic, however, has been that of the True Cross (or fragments of it), according to tradition discovered by St *Helena during her pilgrimage to the Holy Land in 326. The veneration of relics is found in many religions, e.g. popular Buddhism, and is based on the natural instinct of men to treat with reverence what is left of the dead they loved. Traces of it may be found in the OT miracles worked through the mantle of *Elijah (2 Kgs. 2: 14) and the bones of *Elisha (2 Kgs. 13: 21), and, in the NT, in the healing power of handkerchiefs that had been in touch with St *Paul's body (Acts 19: 12). In post-NT times the martyrs' bodies were venerated from an early date, the first certain evidence occurring in the 'Martyrium Polycarpi' (*c.*156–7), where the relics of St *Polycarp are described as 'more valuable than precious stones and finer than refined gold' (ch. 18), to be carefully collected and honoured by a memorial service for the saint at the place where they were laid.

The cult of relics spread quickly both in the E. and in the W. In Rome it was bound up with the *catacombs, where prayer services were held and, from the 4th cent., the Eucharist celebrated over the tombs of the martyrs. The danger of exaggerated worship, caused by the great influx of pagans into the Church after the age of persecution, led *Vigilantius to oppose the cult. Against him St *Jerome enunciated the principle, already foreshadowed in the 'Martyrium Polycarpi', that the relics of the martyrs are honoured for the sake of Him whose martyrs they are. St *Augustine added the reason that the bodies served the saints while they lived as organs of the Holy Spirit, and that also the objects they used should be dear to Christians from motives of filial piety. *Gennadius held that they should be honoured as the members of Christ. At the same time the increasing demand for relics led, in the E., to the translating and even dismembering of the bodies, a practice strictly forbidden by the Roman civil law and not introduced into the W. till the 7th and 8th cents. In opposition to the *Iconoclasts, who rejected the veneration of relics as well as of *icons, the Second Council of *Nicaea (787) anathematized those who despised holy relics and laid down that no church should be consecrated

without them. The veneration of relics was confirmed for the E. Church by the Council of *Constantinople in 1084. In the W. the cult increased enormously, esp. during the *Crusades, when quantities of relics, often spurious, were brought to Europe from the Holy Land. They were kept in magnificent *reliquaries, carried in procession, and often gave rise to superstitious practices. After the end of the persecutions relics were placed under altars and the kissing of the *mensa* at the beginning of Mass came to be interpreted as a salutation of the relics. For current practice regarding the use of relics in the dedication of altars, see ALTAR.

The theological foundation of the cult of relics was worked out by the Schoolmen, esp. St *Thomas Aquinas, on the principles laid down by Jerome and Augustine. Stress was laid on the special dignity of the bodies of the saints as temples of the Holy Spirit destined to a glorious resurrection, and the sanction given by the Godhead in making them the occasion of many miracles. In the 16th cent. the doctrine was confirmed by the Council of *Trent against the Reformers. Post-Tridentine theologians have differed as to whether they are to be honoured with the same cult of '*dulia' as the saints or with an inferior one. Acc. to RC canon law, the sale of relics is strictly forbidden, and those which are significant or greatly revered cannot be validly alienated or permanently transferred without the permission of the *Holy See (*CIC* (1983), can. 1190). Among the most famous relics are those of Santiago de *Compostela, the Holy House of *Loreto, and the *Holy Coat of Trier. A feast of Holy Relics used to be observed in many English RC dioceses on 5 Nov.

See also MARTYRIUM.

S. Beissel, SJ, *Die Verehrung der Heiligen und ihre Reliquien in Deutschland* (Stimmen aus Maria-Laach, Ergänzungshefte, 47 and 54; 1890–2). H. Siebert, *Beiträge zur vorreformatorischen Heiligen- und Reliquienverehrung* (1907). U. Mioni, *Il culto delle reliquie nella chiesa cattolica* (1908). F. Pfister, *Der Reliquienkult im Altertum* (Religionsgeschichtliche Versuche und Vorarbeiten, 5; 2 vols., 1909–12). B. Lefeuvre, *Courte histoire des reliques* (1932). H. Fichtenau, 'Zum Reliquienwesen im früheren Mittelalter', *Mitteilungen des Instituts für österreichische Geschichtsforschung*, 60 (1952), pp. 60–89. B. Kötting, *Der frühchristliche Reliquienkult und die Bestattung im Kirchengebäude* (Arbeitsgemeinschaft für Forschung des Landes Nordrhein-Westfalen, Geisteswissenschaften, 123; 1965), with summary in Eng., pp. 38 f. N. Hermann-Mascard, *Les reliques des saints: Formation coutumière d'un droit* (Société d'histoire du droit. Collection d'histoire institutionnelle et sociale, 6; 1975). P. J. Geary, *Furta Sacra: Thefts of Relics in the Central Middle Ages* (Princeton, NJ, 1978). Popular treatment by J. Bentley, *Restless Bones: The Story of Relics* (1985). H. Thurston, SJ, in *CE* 12 (1911), pp. 734–8, s.v.; H. *Leclercq, OSB, in *DACL* 14 (pt. 2; 1948), cols. 2294–359, s.v. 'Reliques et reliquaires'; E. Josi, F. Antonelli, OFM, and P. Palazzini in *EC* 10 (1953), cols. 749–60, s.v. 'Reliquie'; F. Chiovaro in *NCE* 12 (1967), pp. 234–40, s.v. See also works cited under RELIQUARY.

Relief Acts. See CATHOLIC RELIEF ACTS.

Religionsgeschichtliche Schule. The 'History of Religion School', an influential group of German biblical scholars between 1880 and 1920 who advocated extensive use of data from the comparative study of religions in the interpretation of Christianity. In contrast to A. *Ritschl, who interpreted the NT in the light of modern doctrinal convictions and largely ignored its historical antecedents, this School reduced dogmatic considerations to a minimum. Further, religious documents must be understood not as isolated expressions of their authors' thoughts and aspirations, but as products of a long and often complex development of the tribe or community. In its philosophy the School was influenced by G. W. F. *Hegel and the concept of evolution, in its historical methods also by L. von *Ranke and T. *Mommsen. E. *Troeltsch regarded himself as the systematic theologian of the School.

At first the School confined itself to tracing historical developments inside Judaism and Christianity, but it soon came to search for parallels in Egyptian, Babylonian, and various Hellenistic religious systems. Thus H. *Gunkel, H. Gressmann (1877–1927), and W. *Bousset claimed that many biblical passages were based on the ancient myths not only of the Hebrews but also of, e.g., Babylon and Egypt. Bousset and J. *Weiss maintained that the eschatological ideas underlying the terms '*Messiah' and '*Kingdom of God' were largely of non-Jewish origin, while Bousset also claimed to have found extrabiblical antecedents for the term 'Lord'. R. *Reitzenstein, whose imagination admittedly far outran his critical sense, advanced similar claims for such terms as 'Man from Heaven', 'Holy Spirit', and 'Saviour', and he, A. Eichhorn (1856–1926), and W. Heitmüller (1869–1925) upheld the relevance of Gentile 'parallels' for the *Eucharist and *Baptism. Another prominent member of the school was H. *Windisch.

G. Lüdemann, 'Die Religionsgeschichtliche Schule', in B. Moeller (ed.), *Theologie in Göttingen* (Göttingen [1987]), pp. 325–61. J. Hempel in *RGG* (3rd edn.), 5 (1961), cols. 991–4; K. Rudolph in M. Eliade (ed.), *Encyclopedia of Religion*, 12 (1987), pp. 293–6, both s.v.

religious. The technical name for a member of a Religious *Institute of Consecrated Life (q.v.), some Institutes being Orders and some Congregations. In RC Canon law (*CIC* (1983), can. 607), religious are members of an Institute who bind themselves by public *vow to observe, in addition to the precepts, the evangelical *counsels of obedience, chastity, and poverty. They live a common life.

religious drama. See DRAMA, CHRISTIAN.

Religious Institutes. See INSTITUTES OF CONSECRATED LIFE.

religious orders in Anglicanism. The revival of religious orders in the Anglican Communion was one of the results of the *Oxford Movement. In 1839 E. B. *Pusey wrote to J. *Keble that he and J. H. *Newman had independently been led to recognize the desirability of some 'Sœurs de Charité' in the Anglican Church and on Trinity Sunday 1841 he received the vows of Marian Rebecca Hughes, who in 1849 became the first Superior of the Convent of the Holy and Undivided Trinity at Oxford. In 1845 he founded the first community at Park Village, Regent's Park, which was later merged in the Society of the Holy Trinity, founded at Devonport by Priscilla Lydia *Sellon in 1848 and now at Ascot. After this, communities followed in rapid succession. Among the most famous are the Community of St Mary the Virgin, founded in 1848 with the help of W. J. *Butler, vicar of Wantage; the Community of St John the Baptist, founded in 1852 at Clewer by T. T. *Carter, with Harriet Monsell as first superior; the Community of All Saints, founded in 1851 by W. Upton Richards, vicar of All Saints, Margaret Street, London; and the Community of St Margaret, founded in 1855 at East Grinstead by J. M. *Neale. All these were 'active' or 'mixed' communities, combining the monastic life (with its centre in the daily recitation of the Breviary Offices) with a life of service, and they were among the pioneers in the care for the poor in the slums of great cities which was one of the fruits of the Oxford Movement. The Deaconess Community of St Andrew, founded by Elizabeth Ferard in 1861, was unique in combining community life with admission to the order of *deaconess. It was not until 1907 that, with the foundation of the first enclosed community, the 'Sisters of the Love of God', at Fairacres, Oxford, the 'contemplative' life was revived. In the previous year, however, the Sisters of the Community of the Holy Comforter, founded at Edmonton, London, in 1891, decided to give up active work and adopt the rule of St *Benedict. After 10 years at Baltonsborough, Somerset, they moved to Malling Abbey, Kent, which had been vested in the English Abbey Restoration Fund before the secession to Rome of its donor.

Communities for men developed more slowly. J. H. Newman, after he had moved to Littlemore in 1842, lived a community life with some companions and on occasion referred to his establishment as a μονή, but there were no vows. Some of the ritualist slum priests, e.g. C. F. *Lowder, stressed the importance for mission of groups of celibate clergy living under rule, but the first religious order of men was the *Society of St John the Evangelist, founded in 1865 at Cowley by R. M. *Benson. The *Community of the Resurrection, founded in 1892 by C. *Gore, has been, since 1898, established at Mirfield, and the Society of the Sacred Mission, founded by H. H. Kelly in 1893 (a missionary brotherhood had existed since 1891), was at Kelham from 1903 to 1974; it is now based at Willen Priory, near Milton Keynes. One of the chief works of these two orders has been the training of ordinands. The Benedictine life for men was first revived by Joseph Leycester Lyne, Father *Ignatius, in 1869. The oldest surviving community, now at Elmore, near Newbury (from 1926 to 1987 at Nashdom), sprang from the Benedictine community at *Caldey. In 1981 the Benedictine Rule was formally adopted by the community at Alton Abbey (founded in 1884 in Rangoon as the Order of St Paul; the house at Alton dates from 1895. This had originally been a double order, but the women's side died out in 1952). The period immediately after the First World War saw the establishment of an Anglican *Franciscan Order (q.v.). In 1938 R. C. S. Gofton-Salmond retired to a woodland property near Crawley, Sussex, where the Community of the Servants of the Will of God now follow a contemplative vocation of a semi-eremitical type.

In recent years a decline in vocations both among men and women has led to the closure of some orders and to other communities moving out of over-large Victorian conventual and monastic buildings. At the same time there have been new ventures in community living (including attempts to turn small women's communities into double orders), as well as an increased interest in the eremitic life.

From England this revived religious life spread over much of the Anglican Communion. Many of the English orders have branch houses in other countries and new communities have grown up in America, Africa, India, and Australasia.

The early communities, though for the most part established in dioceses where the bishop was sympathetic, had no recognized place in the life of the Church and had to face much suspicion and at times active hostility. Since 1861, when the movement was first discussed in *Canterbury Convocation, their contribution to the life of the Church has been increasingly recognized. Following the recommendation made in a report to the *Lambeth Conference of 1930, an 'Advisory Council on the Relation of the Bishops and Religious Communities' was established for Canterbury and York, and it is now possible for communities to receive formal recognition. Can. H 2 of the 1969 *Canons (promulgated 7 Oct. 1969) provides for the clerical members of religious orders to have a representative in each of the Lower Houses of the *Convocations of Canterbury and York, and from the inception of *Synodical Government in 1970 the religious orders have been represented in both the House of Clergy and the House of Laity of the General Synod. In 1975 the Communities Consultative Council was established.

A Directory of the Religious Life (1943) and *Guide to the Religious Communities of the Anglican Communion* (1951), both issued by the Advisory Council on Religious Communities under the Chairmanship of the Bp. of Oxford [K. E. *Kirk]. A. T. Cameron (ed.), *Directory of Religious Communities of Men and Women and of Deaconess Communities and Institutions in the Anglican Communion* (1920; 2nd edn., enlarged, 1922). P. F. Anson, *The Call of the Cloister* (1955; rev. by A. W. Campbell, 1964). A. M. Allchin, *The Silent Rebellion: Anglican Religious Communities 1845–1900* (1958). M. Hill, *The Religious Order: A Study of Virtuoso Religion and its Legitimation in the Nineteenth-Century Church of England* (1973). S. L. Ollard in *DECH* (3rd edn., 1948), s.v. 'Religious Orders. II: Modern'.

Religious Tract Society (RTS). The Society was founded in 1799 (incorporated, 1899), with a committee of an equal number of Anglicans and Nonconformists, for the publication and dissemination of tracts and other Christian evangelical literature. It published in 200 languages for missionary purposes and established daughter societies in *India and *China. During the war of 1914–18 it gratuitously distributed many millions of books and magazines among soldiers, sailors, and prisoners of war. On 14 May 1935 it was absorbed in the *United Society for Christian Literature (q.v.).

W. Jones, *The Jubilee Volume of the Religious Tract Society: Containing a Record of its Origin, Proceedings, and Results. A.D. 1799–1849* (1850); S. G. Green, *The Story of the Religious Tract Society for One Hundred Years* (1899); G. Hewitt, *Let the People Read: A Short History of the United Society for Christian Literature, 1799; Christian Literature Society for India and Africa, 1858; Christian Literature Society for China (British Support), 1887* (1949). Annual Reports of the Religious Tract Society (London, 1799–[1936] for 1935).

reliquary. A receptacle for *relics. The oldest reliquaries took the form of caskets, capsules, *ampullas, also of crosses, esp. for relics of the True Cross, of rings and of purses, and from early times they have frequently been of precious material and richly decorated. For the reception of the whole remains of a saint the gabled shrine was a favourite form in the Middle Ages, among famous examples being the silver shrine of the Three Kings at *Cologne (c.1190–1225) and H. *Memling's reliquary of St *Ursula at Bruges. At the same period smaller relics were kept in reliquaries of the shape of arms, legs, and esp. heads and busts, while in the later Middle Ages the *monstrance form, which facilitated exposition, became frequent. Besides the varied formalized shapes, caskets and boxes of all sizes and materials have always served as receptacles for relics. See also MARTYRIUM.

J. Braun, SJ, *Die Reliquiare des christlichen Kultes und ihre Entwicklung* (1940). M. Andrieu, 'Aux origines du culte du Saint-Sacrement. Reliquaires et monstrances eucharistiques', *Anal. Boll.* 68 (1950), pp. 397–418. M.-M. [S.] Gauthier, *Les Routes de la Foi: Reliques et reliquaires de Jérusalem à Compostelle* [1983]. A series of arts. in *Ornamenta Ecclesiae: Kunst und Künstler der Romanik. Katalog zur Ausstellung des Schnütgen-Museums in der Josef-Haubrich-Kunsthalle*, ed. A. Legner, 3 (Cologne, 1985), pp. 19–184. H. Thurston, SJ, in *CE* 12 (1911), pp. 762 f., s.v.

Rembrandt (1606–69) **(Rembrandt Harmensz or Harmenszoon van Rijn)**, Dutch painter. The son of a wealthy miller of *Leiden, he showed an early inclination for his art and, at the age of 25, was one of the most famous portrait painters of his country. In 1631 he moved to Amsterdam, where he lived till his death. In 1634 he married the beautiful Saskia, who during the rest of her life was the inspiration of his art. His pictures on scriptural subjects in these years, which treat mostly of vivid scenes such as the story of *Samson, are full of vigour and imagination though they have not reached the spirituality of his later period. With the death of Saskia, in 1642, sorrow entered his life, and his troubles were increased by financial difficulties ending in bankruptcy and, in 1654, the scandal of having a child by his servant, Hendrickje, which brought him into conflict with the Reformed Church at Amsterdam. These sufferings, which threw him more and more into solitude, helped further to deepen and spiritualize his art and to give him an understanding of the Passion—a theme treated in about 90 paintings and etchings—such as few artists have possessed. Characteristic was his treatment of light and shade out of which his human figures appear to grow, thereby producing the impression of a happening beyond space and time. The supernatural atmosphere of the *Last Supper* and the *Disciples at Emmaus*, and the union of Divine majesty and redeeming love in the face of his Christ blessing the children or healing the sick, are unsurpassed in Christian art. Among his last great works is his famous *Return of the Prodigal Son* (Leningrad, c.1668), a painted confession of faith in the goodness of God expressed in the face and hands of the father, who receives the kneeling beggar with infinite love. Rembrandt has rightly been termed the painter of the soul.

Reproductions of his Paintings incl. edn. by A. Bredius (Utrecht, 1935; Eng. edn., 1937, rev. by H. Gerson, 1969); of his Drawings, ed. O. Benesch (6 vols., London, 1954–7; rev. by E. Benesch, 1973); of his Etchings, ed. L. Münz (2 vols., London, 1952), and K. G. Boon (ibid., 1963). The very extensive lit. incl. general studies by A. M. Hind (Charles Eliot Norton Lectures, 1930–1; London, 1932), J. Rosenberg (2 vols., Cambridge, Mass., 1948; rev. edn., London, 1964), B. Haak (Amsterdam, 1968; Eng.

tr., 1969), C. [J.] White (London, 1984), and S. Partsch (ibid., 1991). K. Clark, *Rembrandt and the Italian Renaissance* (Wrightsman Lectures, 1966), and other works by this author. C. [J.] White, *Rembrandt as Etcher* (2 vols., 1969). Id. and K. G. Boon, *Rembrandt's Etchings: An Illustrated Critical Catalogue* (2 vols., Amsterdam and New York [1970]). A. Bruyn and others, *A Corpus of Rembrandt's Paintings* (The Hague, Boston, and London, 1982 ff. [challenging the attribution of many paintings traditionally ascribed to Rembrandt]); cf. S. Alpers, *Rembrandt's Enterprise: The Studio and the Market* (1988).

Remigius, St (d. *c.*533), also 'Remi', 'Apostle of the Franks'. Born of a noble Gallo-Roman family in the region of Laon, he is reputed to have been elected bishop of the metropolitan see of *Reims at the age of 22, prob. *c.*458. His Baptism of *Clovis, with 3,000 of his subjects, greatly enhanced the position of the Frankish ruler and marked the beginning of a close co-operation between the Church and the ruler, the terms of which are set out in a famous letter of Remigius. He directed missions to the Morini and the *Arians of Burgundy and is associated with the foundation of bishoprics at Laon, Tournai, Térouanne, and Cambrai-Arras (where he appointed St *Vedast as bishop to promote the Christian mission in N. Gaul). Acc. to a legend, first mentioned by *Hincmar of Reims, the *ampulla of chrism traditionally used in the coronation of French kings was brought by a dove in answer to the prayers of Remigius at the Baptism of Clovis. He is said to have conferred upon Clovis the power of touching for the *King's evil. Feast day, 1 Oct., the anniversary of the translation of his relics to the abbey of St-Rémi by Pope *Leo IX in 1049, has now been dropped from the Universal Calendar of the RC Church. At Reims his death is commemorated on 13 Jan.

Letters, together with the Testament attributed to Remigius, pr. in J. P. Migne, *PL* 65. 963–76; crit. edn. of the letters by W. Gundlach in *MGH*, Epistolae, 3 (1892), pp. 112–16, and of the Testament by B. Krusch in *MGH*, Scriptores Rerum Merovingicarum, 3 (1896), pp. 336–47 (both repr. in CCSL 117 (1957), pp. 407–13, 473–87). Crit. edn. of early Life of Remigius, traditionally but wrongly ascribed to *Venantius Fortunatus, by B. Krusch in *MGH*, Auctores Antiquissimi, 4 (pt. 2; 1885), pp. 64–7, and of Life by Hincmar of Reims by id. in *MGH*, Scriptores Rerum Merovingicarum, 3 (1896), pp. 239–336. Important study of the latter by J. Devisse, *Hincmar, archevêque de Reims, 845–882*, 2 (Geneva, 1976), pp. 1004–54. The traditional account of the Baptism of Clovis is also found in *Gregory of Tours, *Historia Francorum*, 2. 31; the same author recounts the miracles of Remigius in his *In Gloria Confessorum*, 78 [79]. A. H. M. Jones, P. Grierson, and J. A. Crook, 'The authenticity of the "Testamentum S. Remigii"', *Revue Belge de Philologie et d'Histoire*, 35 (1957), pp. 356–73. Popular Life by R. Barroux ('Grandeurs et gloires de l'ancienne France', 1947). R. Kaiser, *Untersuchungen zur Geschichte der Civitas und Diözese Soissons im römischen und merowingischer Zeit* (Rheinisches Archiv, 89; Bonn, 1973), pp. 217–19. K. Schäferdiek, 'Remigius von Reims, Kirchenmann einer Umbruchszeit', *ZKG* 94 (1983), pp. 256–78. M. Heinzelmann, 'Gallische Prosopographie 160–527', *Francia*, 10 (1982), pp. 531–717, at p. 679, s.v. 'Remigius 2'. G. Bardy in *DTC* 13 (pt. 2; 1937), cols. 2379–81, s.v. 'Remi de Reims (Saint)'. See also bibl. to REIMS and CLOVIS.

Remigius of Auxerre (*c.*841–*c.*908), monk of St Germanus, Auxerre, scholar and teacher. The youngest member of the influential 'school of Auxerre', following Haimo and *Heiric, Remigius taught in Auxerre until 893,

when Abp. Fulc summoned him to restore the schools of *Reims. On Fulc's death (900) Remigius apparently moved to *Paris, where he taught *Odo, the future Abbot of *Cluny.

Remigius had the advantages of the libraries of St Germanus and Auxerre cathedral, and of the scholarly work of his predecessors. On that basis he taught a comprehensive programme of literary and moral texts. He commented on the grammarians Donatus, Priscian, Eutyches, and Phocas; on Terence (lost), *Virgil, Juvenal, and Persius; on the Christian poets *Sedulius and *Prudentius; on the *Dialectica* of St *Augustine, the *De Nuptiis* of Martianus Capella and both the *Opuscula Sacra* and the *De Consolatione Philosophiae* of *Boethius; on the schoolboy's ethical text, the *Distichs of Cato*, and on the *De Arte Metrica* of *Bede. Remigius' biblical exposition has been little studied. It prob. consisted of commentaries on Genesis and Psalms and twelve sermons on St Matthew's Gospel. Finally Remigius is credited with a brief exposition of the Mass. Although neither an original thinker in the mould of John Scottus *Erigena, nor achieving worldly promotion, Remigius did more than anyone else we know to make sound learning widely available to his contemporaries and successors. He 'lived in his pupils'.

Much the best account of Remigius' life and writings is Manitius, 1 (1911), pp. 504–19, with addenda in 2 (1923), p. 808, and 3 (1931), p. 1063. The texts of his comm. are scattered and in most cases not yet pr. in full. That on Donatus, *Ars minor*, ed. W. Fox, SJ (Teub., 1902); cf. L. Holtz, *Donat et la tradition de l'enseignement grammatical* (1981), pp. 440–1, with refs. Comm. on Martianus Capella, *De Nuptiis*, ed. C. E. Lutz (2 vols., Leiden, 1962–5), with introd. and edns. to date; q.v. for comm. on Virgil, Persius, Sedulius, and Prudentius. For comm. on other grammarians, see C. Jeudy, 'La tradition manuscrite des *Partitiones* de Priscien et la version longue du commentaire de Rémi d'Auxerre', *Revue d'histoire des textes*, 1 (1971), pp. 123–43; id., 'L'*Institutio de Nomine, Pronomine et Verbo* de Priscien. Manuscrits et commentaires médiévaux', ibid. 2 (1972), pp. 73–144; id., 'L'*Ars de Nomine et Verbo* de Phocas: manuscrits et commentaires médiévaux', *Viator*, 5 (1974), pp. 61–156; id., 'Les Manuscrits de l'*Ars de verbo* d'Eutychès et le commentaire de Rémi d'Auxerre' in *Études de Civilisation Médiévale (IXᵉ–XIIᵉ siècles): Mélanges offerts à Edmond-René Labande* (Poitiers [1974]), pp. 421–36. For comm. on Juvenal, see E. M. Sandford in P. O. Kristeller (ed.), *Catalogus Translationum et Commentariorum*, 1 (Washington, DC, 1960), pp. 176 f. His comm. on Augustine's *Dialectica* is mentioned by John of Cluny, *Vita S. Odonis*, 1. 19 (*PL* 133. 52A); cf. however, J. Marenbon, *From the Circle of Alcuin to the School of Auxerre* (Cambridge Studies in Medieval Life and Thought, 3rd ser. 15; 1981), pp. 173–9. For comm. on Boethius, see M. Cappuyns, 'Le plus ancien commentaire des "Opuscula Sacra" et son origine', *RTAM* 3 (1931), pp. 237–72, and P. Courcelle, *La Consolation de Philosophie dans la tradition littéraire* (Études Augustiniennes, 1967), pp. 241–99. For comm. on *Disticha Catonis*, see A. Mancini, 'Un commento ignoto di Remy d'Auxerre ai *Disticha Catonis*', *Rendiconti della Reale Accademia dei Lincei*, Classe di Scienze Morali, Storiche e Filologiche, 5th ser. 11 (1902), pp. 175–98, with further note, pp. 369–82. Comm. on Bede, *De Arte Metrica* and *De Schematibus et Tropis* pr. in full by M. H. King in Bede's *Opera*, Pars 6: *Opera didascalica*, 1 (CCSL 123A; 1975), pp. 77–171. Comm. on Gen. in J. P. Migne, *PL* 131. 51–134; cf. F. Stegmüller, *Repertorium Biblicum Medii Aevi*, 5 (Madrid, 1955), pp. 65 f. (no. 7194). For his comm. on Pss. (unpr.), see A. Vaccari, SJ, 'Il genuino commento ai Salmi di Remigio di Auxerre', *Biblica*, 26 (1945), pp. 52–99, repr., with additional material, in his collected *Scritti di Erudizione e di Filologia*, 1 (1955), pp. 283–329. (The comm. pr. under his name in J. P. Migne, *PL* 131.

133–844 is not genuine.) Sermons on Mt. in J. P. Migne, *PL* 131. 865–932; cf. F. Stegmüller, op. cit., pp. 75 f. (no. 7226). J.-P. Bouhot, 'Les sources de l'*Expositio missae* de Remi d'Auxerre', *Revue des Études Augustiniennes*, 26 (1980), pp. 118–69, incl. complete text. C. Jeudy and others in D. Iogna-Prat and others (eds.), *L'École Carolingienne d'Auxerre de Murethach à Remi 830–908: Entretiens d'Auxerre 1989* [1991], pp. 371–500. L. Scheffczyk in *L.Th.K.* (2nd edn.), 8 (1963), cols. 1223–5, s.v.

Remonstrance, the. The statement of *Arminian teaching drawn up in Jan. 1610 by J. Arminius' close friend, Johannes Uitenbogaert, very shortly after the former's death and signed by 44 of his followers. In a somewhat different version this declaration was presented a few months later to the States of Holland in a plea for greater theological toleration. It contains the celebrated five articles which, borrowed verbatim from Arminius' *Declaratio Sententiae* of 1608, briefly summarized the Remonstrants' doctrine and set the agenda for the ensuing controversies. Among the more extreme *Calvinist doctrines repudiated were both *Supralapsarian and *Sublapsarian forms of predestination, the doctrine that Christ died only for the elect, and the notion that, for the latter, grace was both irresistible and indefectible. The subsequent conflict was very bitter, for the Remonstrants were suspected of favouring the pro-Spanish party in politics, and the eventual alliance of the *Contra-Remonstrants with Prince Maurice of Orange led to the condemnation of the Remonstrants at the Synod of *Dort (1618–19). See also ARMINIANISM.

G. J. Hoenderdaal, 'Remonstrantie en Contraremonstrantie', *Nederlands Archief voor Kerkgeschiedenis*, NS 51 (1970–71), pp. 49–92 (incl. text, pp. 64–79). Text also, with Lat. and Eng. trs., in P. *Schaff, *The Creeds of Christendom*, 3 (1877), pp. 545–9. J. den Tex, *Oldenbarnevelt*, 3 (Haarlem, 1966), pp. 123–56; abridged Eng. tr., 2 (Cambridge, 1973), pp. 423–66.

Renan, Joseph Ernest (1823–92), French philosopher, theologian, and orientalist. A native of Tréguier in Brittany, he was invited in 1838 by F. A. P. *Dupanloup (whose attention had been drawn to Renan's brilliance through his sister, Henriette) to join his celebrated seminary of St-Nicolas-du-Chardonnet at Paris. His study of German theology and Semitic languages led him to have doubts of the truth of Christianity, and in Oct. 1845 he left the seminary of *St-Sulpice, where he then was. After a somewhat precarious and varied life for several years, he published in 1852 his *Averroès et l'averroïsme*, which at once established his reputation as a scholar. In 1860 he was sent by the Emperor on an archaeological mission to Phoenicia and Syria, and it was while in Palestine that he wrote his celebrated *Vie de Jésus*. In this book, written in an attractive and vivid style, but in a tone that hardly rang sincere, he repudiated the supernatural element in Christ's life, ignored its moral aspect, and portrayed Him as a charming and amiable Galilean preacher. Its publication in 1863 created an immediate sensation throughout Europe. In Jan. 1862 he had been appointed professor of Hebrew at the Collège de France, but the storm created by his *Vie de Jésus* led to his removal in 1864. For the rest of his life he held no further appointment. In 1866 he published a pioneer study on *Joachim of Fiore in the *Revue des Deux Mondes* (repr. in 1884 in *Nouvelles études d'histoire religieuse*). This essay reveals another side to Renan: the

combination of serious scholarship with a romantic vision of a new 'religion of humanity', prob. inspired by George Sand's Joachimist novel *Spiridion* (1839). His other writings include *Les Apôtres* (1866), *St Paul* (1869), *Les Évangiles* (1877), *Histoire du peuple d'Israël* (5 vols., 1887–93), and his widely popular *Souvenirs d'enfance et de jeunesse* (1883).

Collected edn. of his works by H. Psichari (10 vols., Paris, 1947–61). Many of his works were tr. into Eng., incl. his *Life of Jesus* (London, 1864, and many later edns.). Studies in Fr. incl. J. Pommier, *Ernest Renan d'après des documents inédits* (1923); id., *La Pensée religieuse de Renan* (1925), and id., *La Jeunesse cléricale d'Ernest Renan: Saint-Sulpice* (thesis, Strasbourg, 1933), with bibl.; R. Dussaud, *L'Œuvre scientifique d'Ernest Renan* (1951); J. Chaix-Ruy, *Ernest Renan* (Paris, 1956); and L. Retat, *Religion et Imagination religieuse: Leur formes et leur rapports dans l'œuvre d'Ernest Renan* (Paris thesis, 1979). M. J. *Lagrange, OP, *La Vie de Jésus d'après Renan* (1921; Eng. tr., 1928). P. Alfaric, *Les Manuscrits de la 'Vie de Jésus' d'Ernest Renan* (Publications de la Faculté des Lettres de l'Université de Strasbourg, 90; 1939), with introd., notes, and concordance. G. Pholien, *Les Deux 'Vie de Jésus' de Renan* (Bibliothèque de la Faculté de Philosophie et Lettres de l'Université de Liège, 239; 1983). H. Girard and H. Moncel, *Bibliographie des œuvres d'Ernest Renan* (Publication de la Société Ernest Renan. Histoire religieuse, 1; 1923). Studies in Eng. by H. W. Wardman (London, 1964) and R. M. Chadbourne (New York, 1968). H. W. Wardman in *EB* (1977 edn.), Macropaedia, 15, pp. 671–3, s.v.; Y. Marchason in *Dict. Bibl.*, Suppl. 10 (1985), cols. 277–344, s.v.

Renaudot, Eusèbe (1646–1720), orientalist and liturgist. He was a native of *Paris. After a short stay with the *Oratorians he devoted himself entirely to oriental studies and became a member of the Académie Française in 1689. A valued friend and adviser of the leading men of his time, among them J.-B. *Bossuet, he accompanied the Cardinal *de Noailles to the conclave of 1700. He never received more than minor orders.

Renaudot's two chief theological writings are his erudite *Historia Patriarcharum Alexandrinorum Jacobitarum* (1713) and his *Liturgiarum Orientalium Collectio* (2 vols., 1716). The latter contains the texts of a great number of E. liturgies with copious notes and commentaries, and is still indispensable for liturgical studies. Renaudot, who was a friend of several *Jansenists, was also the author of the fourth and fifth volumes of the famous *Perpétuité de la foi*, published under the direction of P. *Nicole and A. *Arnauld, in which, by rich documentation, he upheld the antiquity of the Eucharistic faith of the E. Churches against the *Calvinistic doctrine.

A corrected edn. of Renaudot's *Liturgiarum Orientalium Collectio* was pub., 2 vols., Frankfurt am Main, 1847. A photographic reprint of this was issued at Farnborough, 1970; of the *Historia Patriarcharum* at Brussels, 1969. Selections from his correspondence ed. F. Duffo (Paris, 1927 and 1931). H. Omont, 'Inventaire sommaire des manuscrits de la collection Renaudot, conservée à la Bibliothèque Nationale', *Bibliothèque de l'École des Chartes*, 51 (1890), pp. 270–97. A. Villien, *L'Abbé Eusèbe Renaudot: Essai sur sa vie et sur son œuvre liturgique* (1904). J. Carreyre in *DTC* 13 (pt. 2; 1937), cols. 2381–3, s.v.; H. *Leclercq, OSB, in *DACL* 14 (pt. 2; 1948), cols. 2369–72, s.v.

renegade. One who forsakes his religion for another faith. The term was formerly in current use esp. of Christians who apostatized to *Islam.

Renunciation of the Devil. The renunciation of Satan at *Baptism is attested in St *Hippolytus' *Apostolic Tradition*, St *Cyril of Jerusalem, and St *Ambrose's *De Mysteriis*, and has been a regular part of almost all Baptismal rites, E. and W. It was presumably designed originally to confirm the candidate in his intention to forsake all heathen worship and ways of life.

reordination. The repetition of an ordination to the priesthood which had been conferred either *extra ecclesiam*, i.e. by an heretical or schismatic bishop, or *intra ecclesiam* but not canonically, e.g. by a deposed or simoniacal bishop. Reordination was frequently practised in the Church down to the 12th cent., when the doctrine of the sacraments began to receive more precise formulation. The question of reordination first became a practical issue through the rise of schisms and heresies. Implicitly different answers were already given in the 3rd cent. by St *Cyprian of Carthage and St *Stephen of Rome, in that the one rejected and the other accepted the *validity of heretical Baptism.

In the following cents. the practice of the Church varied. Acc. to the Council of *Nicaea (325; can. 19) ordinations in the different sects were treated differently, whereas the *Apostolic Constitutions and the *Apostolic Canons are hostile to the sacraments of all non-Catholic bodies. In view of the new schisms of the 4th and 5th cents. the practice of reordination was attenuated and often replaced by a ceremony called χειροθεσία, which was mentioned in the Canons of Nicaea, and is apparently a supplementary rite distinct from ordination (χειροτονία). The Greek Church, though it repudiated reordination at the *Trullan Council (692; can. 95), has continued to waver in its practice. In the W. St *Augustine's doctrine of the validity of the sacraments administered by sinful, excommunicated, schismatic, or heretical priests, formed in the course of the *Donatist controversy, slowly gained ground against opposition. Though St *Gregory the Great expressed himself clearly against reordination, heretical sacraments were viewed with hostility by many subsequent theologians, and reordination was practised, e.g., by the Greek Abp. *Theodore of Canterbury, who, in 669, reordained Ceadda, who had been ordained by supposed *Quartodecimans. It was also practised in the case of priests ordained by the irregularly elected Pope Constantine II (767–9), by Pope *Formosus (891–6), and by the 9th-cent. *chorepiscopi, as well as on the simoniacal clergy of the 11th cent., many of whom were reordained by the Pope himself, St *Leo IX. From the period of *Gregory VII, however, when *Anselm of Lucca defended the validity of heretical sacraments, the Augustinian view became more and more general and was finally formulated by St *Thomas Aquinas, who rejected the practice of reordination because of the indelible *character bestowed by the sacrament of Holy Orders on its recipient. This doctrine was formally sanctioned by the Council of *Trent, provided that the sacrament was conferred in the prescribed form and with the right intention.

L. Saltet, *Les Réordinations* (1907); C. H. *Turner, 'Apostolic Succession', in H. B. *Swete (ed.), *Essays on the Early History of the Church and the Ministry* (1918), esp. pp. 161–79.

reparation. The making amends for damage done to another. In moral theology it is generally used in a sense similar to *restitution (q.v.) in cases of personal injury such as homicide, detraction, adultery, etc. For wrongs of this kind reparation cannot be made exactly corresponding to the loss, but takes the form of compensation, already prescribed in the Mosaic Law (Exod. 21: 22 ff.).

In modern devotional language the term is frequently used for the amends made to God for offences against Him by means of prayer and penance. Reparation plays a central part in the *Sacred Heart devotion, esp. with ref. to outrages committed against the Blessed Sacrament, and confraternities and congregations have been established with this and similar ends in view.

repentance. The acknowledgement and condemnation of one's own sins, coupled with a turning to God. True repentance or *contrition (as contrasted with mere *attrition) springs from love of God whom human sin rejects or offends. It includes sorrow for sin committed, confession of guilt, and the purpose of amendment. The Greek word μετάνοια, translated 'repentance' in the English NT, emphasizes the last aspect, while the Latin word *penitentia* (whence 'penance' and 'penitence') refers in origin to the first two aspects, esp. as expressed in the payment of a penalty. In accord with this distinction in language, Latin teaching has laid special emphasis on *Penance on acts of *reparation and *satisfaction for sin.

Repington, Philip (d. 1424), Bp. of *Lincoln. He was educated at *Oxford and became an *Augustinian canon of St Mary-de-Pré, Leicester. In early life he was a supporter of the doctrines of J. *Wycliffe, whose sacramental teaching he defended in several sermons. At the Council of Blackfriars (1382) he was suspended and a few weeks later excommunicated at *Canterbury, but he recanted his heresies and was restored to communion in the same year. In 1394 he became abbot of St Mary-de-Pré and three years later chancellor of the University of Oxford, an office he held again in 1400 and the two following years. Shortly after his accession in 1399 Henry IV made him his chaplain and confessor, and in 1404 he was appointed Bp. of Lincoln. Four years later Gregory XII created him cardinal, a dignity rendered doubtful by the deposition of Gregory by the Council of *Pisa in 1409 until it was revalidated in 1415 by the Council of *Constance. He resigned his bishopric in 1419, probably because Henry V had opposed the raising of Henry *Beaufort to the cardinalate.

Episcopal Register ed. M. Archer (Lincoln Record Society, 57, 58, 74; 1963–82). The primary source for his life is the *Fasciculi Zizaniorum*, ed. W. W. Shirley (Rolls Series, 1858), pp. 289 f., 296–329 *passim*. 'Cardinal Repyngdon and the Followers of Wycliffe', *CQR* 19 (1884), pp. 59–82. K. B. McFarlane, *John Wycliffe and the Beginnings of English Nonconformity* (1953), pp. 102 f., 108–15, and 120. C. L. Kingsford in *DNB* 48 (1896), pp. 26–8; *BRUO* 3 (1959), pp. 1565–7, s.v. 'Repyngdon'.

Repose, Altar of. An altar to which (acc. to W. use) the Blessed Sacrament is taken in procession after the evening Mass of *Maundy Thursday and reserved for communion on *Good Friday. Until 1955 it was customary to make the Altar of Repose as splendid as possible with lights and flowers and in many places the faithful kept watch before it in turns throughout the day and night. *Pius XII's Holy Week rite recommended a certain austerity and decreed that the watch need last only until midnight; in 1970 the length of the watch was left to the discretion of the parish priest. The Altar of Repose is first mentioned in the 15th century.

Reproaches, the (Lat. *Improperia*). The set of reproofs addressed by the Crucified Saviour to His ungrateful people, which form part of the *Good Friday Liturgy of the Latin Church. They are chanted by two choirs during the *Veneration of the Cross and consist of twelve verses, which set in parallel the Divine compassion for Israel and the outrages inflicted on Christ in His Passion. Each of the first three verses is followed by the *Trisagion sung alternately in Latin (or the vernacular) and Greek, and each of the other nine by the refrain 'Popule meus, quid feci tibi', etc. The Improperia are built up on OT passages, but their early history is obscure. The first three verses are found in documents of the late 9th and early 10th cents., the last nine are not found in their entirety before the 11th cent. There are, however, traces of the component parts in the 7th cent., and the use of the reproach as a homiletic device may go back to St *Cyril of Jerusalem.

H. A. P. Schmidt, SJ, *Hebdomada Sancta*, 2 (pt. 2; Rome, 1957), pp. 794 f. E. Werner, 'Zur Textgeschichte der Improperia', in M. Ruhnke (ed.), *Festschrift Bruno Stäblein zum 70. Geburtstag* (1967), pp. 274–86.

reprobation. The act by which God condemns sinners to eternal punishment, and the state of this punishment. In his struggle against *Pelagianism and *Semipelagianism, St *Augustine sometimes used expressions which might be understood as teaching that there is predestination, on the part of God, to everlasting death, as there is to eternal life. In the 9th cent. the question was agitated in the Frankish Church on account of the bold teaching of the monk *Gottschalk, who was accused of maintaining that God positively and irresistibly predestined certain men to sin and damnation. His doctrine, vigorously opposed by *Hincmar of Reims, was condemned by the Council of Mainz in 848 and by the first (849) and second (853) Councils of *Quiercy, which rejected all predestination to perdition. The Council of *Valence (855), though using the expression 'predestination to death', was none the less careful to point out that 'the evil deserts precede the just judgement of God'. The doctrine of predestination to eternal punishment was revived by many of the 16th cent. Reformers, esp. J. *Calvin, who taught positive and gratuitous reprobation. Acc. to Calvin God, by an inscrutable decree, Himself incites to sin those whom He has predestined to hell. This teaching was condemned by the Council of *Trent (Sess. VI, can. 6). Somewhat similar doctrines were taught later by M. *Baius and the *Jansenists.

Requiem. A Mass offered for the dead, so named from the first word of the *Introit which, until recently, was the common opening of all such Masses in the Roman rite ('Requiem aeternam dona eis, Domine'). The 1970 Roman Missal, which embodies a complete revision of these Masses, provides three formulas for *All Souls' Day (2 Nov.), which may be employed even on a Sunday; three formulas for use at funerals and three for anniversaries (in each case one for use in Eastertide and two for the rest of the year); and five for other occasions. There are also prayers for different categories of people, five *Prefaces, and a variety of Scriptural readings. Many of the characteristics previously distinctive of requiems have disappeared: vestments, which used to be black, may now be any colour determined by national conferences of bishops, and unbleached candles are no longer required. The *Paschal Candle is now usually placed at the head of the coffin. On the occasion of a burial, the Mass is followed immediately by a final commendation. In general, except on the most important feast days and a few other occasions, requiems are offered throughout the year, as occasion arises, e.g. on the day of burial of a member of the congregation (usually *praesente cadavere*) or of a public figure or by special request. In November, regarded acc. to modern RC custom as the month of Holy Souls, Masses for the dead used to be said with particular frequency. See also DIES IRAE.

J. Merk, *Die messliturgische Totenehrung in der römischen Kirche* (1926); E. Freistedt, *Altchristliche Totengedächtnistage und ihre Beziehung zum Jenseitsglauben und Totenkultus der Antike* (Liturgiegeschichtliche Quellen und Forschungen, 24; 1928). Jungmann, 1, pp. 275–7; Eng. tr., pp. 217–19. R. Rutherford, *The Death of a Christian: The Rite of Funerals* (Studies in the Reformed Rites of the Catholic Church, 7; New York, 1980), pp. 56–9; 2nd edn. by Rutherford and T. Barr (Collegeville, Minn., 1990), pp. 58–61 and 274–81. A. Hollaardt, OP, in *LW* 2 (1968), cols. 2382–9, s.v., with extensive bibl. on historical aspects.

reredos. Properly any decoration put up above and behind an altar. The earliest type of such decoration was the painting of scenes or symbols on the walls against which altars backed; but during the Middle Ages a reredos might consist of a rich silken hanging or a piece of jewelled metalwork, as, e.g., at St Mark's, *Venice. More commonly, painted wooden panels, either fixed or in the form of a triptych, made up the reredos, while another way of providing a reredos that represented biblical incidents or figures of the saints was to have it carved in stone or alabaster. Where there happened to be no east window behind the altar, a reredos might cover the whole wall, as at All Souls College, Oxford, or—a most elaborate example—at Burgos in Spain.

Braun, *CA* 2 (1924), pp. 277–544, with plates 192–336. F. Bond, *The Chancel of English Churches* (1916), pp. 51–100. H. Schindler, *Der Schnitzaltar: Meisterwerke und Meister in Süddeutschland, Österreich und Südtirol* (Regensburg, 1978).

Rerum Novarum. The encyclical issued by *Leo XIII on 15 May 1891 *De Conditione Opificum*. Its purpose was to apply to the new conditions created by the Industrial Revolution the traditional Catholic teaching on the relationship of a man to his work, profit, masters, and servants. On the ground that society originated in the family, it proclaimed private property a natural right and condemned 'socialism' as infringing it. It upheld wage-settlements by free agreement, the rightfulness of combinations of workers or employers, and above all the ideal of a just wage, defined as 'enough to support the wage-earner in reasonable and frugal comfort' with a family. It maintained that the natural place of women was in the home. It also emphasized the duty of the State to preserve justice and the responsibility of the Church in the moral aspects of employment.

This new concern of the Church for the condition of the workers was heralded as revolutionary and subversive of the established order; but the encyclical has since been widely acclaimed as among the most important modern pronouncements on social justice and has exercised wide influence. On 15 May 1931 *Quadragesimo Anno* (q.v.) was issued by *Pius XI to mark its fortieth anniversary, and on 1 May 1991 *John Paul II marked its hundredth anniversary with *Centesimus Annus*, which attacked the evils of both capitalism and Marxism.

Text in *Acta Leonis XIII*, 4 (1894), pp. 177–209. *L'Enciclica Rerum Novarum: Testo autentico e redazioni preparatorie dai documenti originali*, ed. G. Antonazzi (1957). Eng. tr. of text, with notes by J. Kirwan, pub. by the *Catholic Truth Society (1983). Eng. tr. also conveniently pr. in D. J. O'Brien and T. A. Shannon (eds.), *Catholic Social Thought* (Maryknoll, NY, 1992), pp. 14–39. Text of 'Centesimus Annus' in *AAS* 83 (1991), pp. 793–867; Eng. tr. in D. J. O'Brien and T. A. Shannon, op. cit., pp. 439–88. A. Luciani (ed.), *La 'Rerum Novarum' e il Problemi Sociali Oggi* (Milan, 1991).

Rescissory Act 1661. The Act passed by the Three Estates (the Parliament of Scotland) on 28 Mar. 1661 rendering null and void all actions in Church and State since 1633, when the Estates met under *Charles I. Since then the *National Covenant had been signed in 1638, the Church had been established as *Presbyterian, and Scotland had been governed under O. *Cromwell. The passing of the Act opened the way for *Charles II to decree the re-establishment of episcopacy. The 1690 Parliament did not rescind the Rescissory Act, but passed legislation which ratified the *Westminster Confession and again established the Church of Scotland as Presbyterian.

Text of Act pr. in *The Acts of the Parliaments of Scotland* [1124–1707], ed. T. Thomson and C. Innes for the Record Commission, 7 (1820), pp. 86 f.

Reservation. The practice of keeping the Bread (and occasionally also the Wine) consecrated at the Eucharist, primarily for the purpose of Holy Communion. The earliest mention of Reservation occurs in the First Apology of St *Justin Martyr (cap. 65). It is frequently referred to in the 2nd–4th cents., e.g. in *Tertullian, St *Cyprian and St *Basil. When Communion was frequent but Masses comparatively rare, the faithful kept the Bl Sacrament in their homes or carried It on their persons, as being the safest places, and this practice long survived; and among the hermits, who often lived at a great distance from a church, the custom survived until the 13th and 14th cents. But from the Constantinian era (4th cent.) the churches were increasingly the ordinary places for reservation. Here the Sacrament was kept either in the sacristy, as is attested for the 6th cent. in Gaul, and still in the 16th cent. for parts of N. Italy, or in the church itself, either in an *aumbry (q.v.) in the wall, or in a *pyx (q.v.) hanging over the altar, or in a *tabernacle (q.v.) on the altar, the last being until recently the normal modern RC practice as it still is in the E. Church. Current RC legislation favours reservation in a separate chapel apart from the centre of the church, but allows considerable latitude. A lamp is kept burning nearby as a sign of honour. From the beginning reservation under the Species of Bread only seems to have been the most common practice in both E. and W. But by the 11th cent. the modern E. custom had

developed, acc. to which the Host is marked with consecrated Wine from the communion spoon (λαβίς); it may then be artificially dried. The reserved Sacrament is used in the E. for the Communion of the sick as well as for the Liturgies of the *Presanctified in the season of *Lent, the Sacrament for the sick being reserved on *Maundy Thursday, that for the Liturgy of the Presanctified on the preceding Sunday.

In the 16th cent. the First BCP of 1549 provided for the Communion of the sick by reservation of the Sacrament at the open Communion and the carrying of It to the sick person as soon as convenient, though it also allowed the priest to celebrate in the sick person's house. In the Second BCP of 1552 the provision for reservation ceased, and it was not replaced in Elizabeth's English Book of 1559. In the Latin Prayer Book of Elizabeth (1560), however, the two provisions for sick Communions in the 1549 BCP came back. The (present) BCP of 1662 retained the regulations of 1559; but, apparently to prevent the use for profane purposes of any of the consecrated Sacrament left over, it ordered the reverent consumption of what remained immediately after the blessing. Anglican divines opposed to the practice have argued that this rubric, in conjunction with the statement in the *Thirty-Nine Articles that the Sacrament of the Lord's Supper was not commanded by Christ's ordinance to be kept, is prohibitive of reservation in the C of E. Those who defend it commonly maintain that in view of the circumstances mentioned the rubric is irrelevant to the issue. As a matter of history, the practice had died out in the C of E, except in very rare instances, before the beginning of the 19th cent., but it has now been widely restored. In the Scottish Episcopal Church it has remained customary and a note in the Scottish Liturgy of 1637 declares it to be lawful. The rubrics which would have permitted the practice in the proposed English Prayer Books of 1927 and 1928 largely contributed to the defeat of the Prayer Book Measure in Parliament. In a number of modern Anglican liturgies, however, the practice is implicitly recognized in rubrics permitting a deacon to administer Communion from the reserved Sacrament (e.g. in the *Welsh BCP of 1984) and in provisions for Communion from the reserved Sacrament in ministering to the sick and in the liturgy of *Good Friday (in the American BCP (1979) and authorized in the C of E in 1980 and 1986 respectively).

D. *Stone, *The Reserved Sacrament* (1917); W. H. Freestone, *The Sacrament Reserved* (Alcuin Club Collections, 21; 1917); *Reservation: Report of a Conference held at Farnham Castle on 24–27 Oct. 1925* (SPCK, 1926); G. *Dix, *A Detection of Aumbries* (1942); E. Maffei, *La Réservation eucharistique jusqu'à la Renaissance* (Brussels, 1942); S. J. P. van Dijk, OFM, and J. H. Walker, *The Myth of the Aumbry: Notes on Medieval Reservation Practice and Eucharistic Devotion with Special Reference to the Findings of Dom Gregory Dix* (1957); A. A. King, *Eucharistic Reservation in the Western Church* (1965); O. Nussbaum, *Die Aufbewahrung der Eucharistie* (Theophaneia, 29; 1979).

reservation, mental. See MENTAL RESERVATION.

reserved penalties. See RESERVED SINS.

reserved sins. In conformity with the early practice, which restricted the administration of penance to a bishop, bishops in the RC Church have retained the right to 'reserve' certain sins to their own jurisdiction. The reservation may be either as to the sin or as to the censure—excommunication etc.—imposed on the sin, a distinction corresponding to that between the internal and external *forum. In the 1983 *Codex Iuris Canonici* there are no longer any sins reserved by law. A penalty, however, can still be reserved, so that its remission can be obtained only through specified ecclesiastical authorities, such as diocesan bishops. A few very grave matters are reserved to the Pope, such as the throwing away of a consecrated *Host or the direct violation of the *seal of confession. A priest can absolve from any censures a penitent who is in danger of death, and any confessor can remit certain automatic censures under specific circumstances; in both these cases there may have to be recourse to a higher authority afterwards (cf. *CIC* (1983), cans. 976 and 1357). In the C of E the practice of such reservation of sins does not obtain.

residence. All clergy are under a grave obligation to reside personally in the place in which they are authorized to minister. From very early times, owing to the frequent abuse of non-residence, this injunction figures in the canons. Combined with the holding of livings in plurality, which non-residence makes possible, the abuse was at its worst during the Middle Ages. The Council of *Trent took reforming action (Sessions IV and XXIII). In RC *canon law, the place and time of residence for all grades of clergy are precisely laid down (*CIC* (1983), cans. 283, 356, 395, and 533). In the C of E residence is required by the English *Canons of 1969, cans. C 18, 20, 21 and 25.

responses. See VERSICLES.

responsory (Lat. *responsorium*), a liturgical chant traditionally consisting of a series of *versicles and responses, the text usually taken from Scripture. The arrangement was designed for the alternate singing of sentences or lines by different people. The 'cantus responsorius', which is already mentioned by *Tertullian, goes back to the worship of the Synagogue. Responsories were long found in the Mass at the *Gradual (this is now replaced by a Responsorial psalm sung by the cantor or choir and the people), and formerly also at the *Offertory. In the Divine *Office, responsories were already prescribed in the Rule of St *Benedict (*c.*540). They used to follow the Lessons at *Mattins and now follow them in the *Office of Readings. A shorter form, called the 'responsorium breve', follows the Little *Chapter at *Lauds, *Vespers, the Little Hours and *Compline in the Monastic Office; in the Roman *Breviary it used to follow only at Prime, the Little Hours and Compline, but in 1971 it was adopted at Lauds and Vespers. The 'responsorium breve' varies according to the Office and season.

restitution. In W. moral theology, the act of 'commutative justice' by which an injury done to the goods or person of another is repaired.

Restoration, the. A term used by English historians from the 18th cent. onwards to describe the restoration of the monarchy under *Charles II in 1660; by extension it is also applied to the period immediately following this event. For the C of E it was a turning-point leading to its political re-establishment and to its definition along strictly episcopalian lines during the primacies of G. *Sheldon and W. *Sancroft.

I. M. Green, *The Re-establishment of the Church of England, 1660–1663* (Oxford Historical Monographs, 1978); J. Spurr, *The Restoration Church of England, 1646–1689* (New Haven, Conn., and London, 1991).

Resurrection, Community of the. See COMMUNITY OF THE RESURRECTION.

Resurrection of Christ. The conviction that God not only sent His Son into the world but also vindicated Him after His death upon a cross, is fundamental to the NT witness and the corner-stone of Christian faith and theology. This certainty that God had reversed human judgement and established freedom from death in an event which inaugurated 'the age to come' found expression in the OT language of exaltation (Is. 52: 13) and heavenly session (Ps. 110: 1; see ASCENSION OF CHRIST), as well as in the Jewish eschatological vocabulary of a *resurrection of the dead (Dan. 12: 2). This last term linked what happened to Jesus Christ to what was expected to happen to Christians, a conjunction visible in St *Paul's claim that Christ is the first-fruits of them that slept (1 Cor. 15: 20) and the first-begotten from the dead (Col. 1: 18). The Christian hope is thus rooted in this event (1 Pet. 1: 3) and looks forward to the time when death shall be finally overcome (1 Cor. 15: 26).

One of the earliest Christian creeds, quoted by Paul at 1 Cor. 15: 3–5 (perhaps 15: 3–7) speaks of Christ being raised (i.e. by God) 'on the third day, according to the Scriptures' and appearing (ὤφθη) to Cephas (i.e. St *Peter) and to the twelve. The list continues with appearances to more than 500 brethren, to St *James, to all the *apostles, and, Paul adds, finally to himself. His instance (v. 11) that this belief was shared on all sides in the early Church is confirmed by the NT as a whole.

The Gospels report the discovery of Christ's empty tomb by St *Mary Magdalene either alone (Jn. 20: 1–9) or with one or more other women: with 'the other Mary' (Mt. 28: 1); with Mary the mother of James, and Salome (Mk. 16: 1); or with Joanna, Mary the mother of James, and the other women (Lk. 24: 10). The Gospels disagree over other details: whether it was one or two angels or young men who told of Christ's resurrection, whether Christ Himself then appeared (Mt., Jn.), whether He (Mt.) or the young man (Mk.) directed the disciples to *Galilee, and whether the women obeyed. Appearances follow, in *Jerusalem (Jn. 20) and nearby *Emmaus (Lk. 24), and/or Galilee (Mt. 28, Jn. 21). Attempts to harmonize these traditions have failed to persuade critics, but the testimony of the biblical witnesses to the Divine event itself is unanimous. There is also broad agreement among the Gospels about how, after some initial doubts, the disciples became convinced of what had happened. However, because Paul (writing earlier than the Evangelists) makes no mention of the empty tomb, some modern critics have disputed its historicity. Others have argued that his reference to Christ's burial implies that he assumed the tomb to be empty after the resurrection. While evidence of the empty tomb apart from the Christian tradition is not to be expected, there is equally no record of His body being produced, and the story about the bribing of the guards (Mt. 28: 11–15) might suggest that no such claim was ever made. It was mainly this story, designed to answer accusations that the disciples had stolen the body of Jesus, which led H. S. *Reimarus to revive the theory that the apostles had perpetrated a fraud, but subsequent historical investigations have discounted such speculations.

The nature of Christ's risen or 'spiritual body' (1 Cor. 15) has from the earliest days been a matter of debate, partly because the Church has always taught that God's saving action in Christ involves the material world, and also because the identity of the Risen Lord with the man from Nazareth is fundamental to orthodox Christianity. Believers have rightly resisted accounts which could undermine the reality of the event by dissolving it without remainder into the disciples' experience. One such early insistence on the objective reality of the event may be found at Lk. 24: 36–43. On the other hand the Gospels generally avoid implying that Jesus was restored to His previous earthly life; He is said to have passed through closed doors (Jn. 20: 19), a feat which suggests that these appearances were not material in the normal sense. But the reality of the conviction they engendered is confirmed by the way some of the fearful disciples (cf. Mk. 14: 50) became the bold leaders and missionaries depicted in Acts. Powerful transforming consequences ascribed to the Holy Spirit were from the beginning associated with the Resurrection (cf. Jn. 20: 22), but the event itself, like the *Incarnation, remains a mystery that cannot be analysed.

The subject is treated by St *Thomas Aquinas, *Summa Theologiae*, 3, qq. 54 ('De Qualitate Christi Resurgentis'), 55 ('De Manifestatione Resurrectionis'), and 56 ('De Resurrectionis Christi Causalitate'); also by the commentators on these questions, notably F. *Suárez, SJ. Modern works incl. B. F. *Westcott, *The Gospel of the Resurrection* (1866); W. Künneth, *Theologie der Auferstehung* (1933; 4th edn., 1951; Eng. tr., 1965); A. M. *Ramsey, *The Resurrection of Christ* (1945); F. X. Durrwell, *La Résurrection de Jésus, mystère de salut* (1950; 2nd edn., 1954; Eng. tr., 1960); M. C. Perry, *The Easter Enigma: An Essay on the Resurrection with special reference to the data of Psychical Research* (1959); S. H. Hooke, *The Resurrection of Christ as History and Experience* (1967); W. Marxsen, *Die Auferstehung Jesu von Nazareth* (Gütersloh, 1968; Eng. tr., 1970); C. F. Evans, *Resurrection and the New Testament* (Studies in Biblical Theology, 2nd ser. 12; 1970); R. H. Fuller, *The Formation of the Resurrection Narratives* (New York, 1971; London, 1972; 2nd edn., 1980); J. E. Alsup, *The Post-Resurrection Appearance Stories of the Gospel Tradition* (1975); P. Perkins, *Resurrection: New Testament Witness and Contemporary Reflection* (New York, 1984; London, 1985); P. Carnley, *The Structure of Resurrection Belief* (Oxford, 1987); J. I. H. McDonald, *The Resurrection: Narrative and Belief* (1989); G. Lüdemann, *Die Auferstehung Jesu* (1994; Eng. tr., 1994). P. Hoffmann and R. Staats in *TRE* 4 (1979), pp. 478–529, s.v. 'Auferstehung II. Auferstehung Jesu Christi'; J. Schmitt in *Dict. Bibl.*, Suppl. 10 (1985), cols. 487–582, s.v. 'Résurrection de Jésus'.

resurrection of the dead. The belief that at the *Parousia or 'Second Coming' of Christ departed souls will be restored to a bodily life and the saved will enter in this renewed form upon the life of heaven is a fundamental element in the Christian doctrine of man's final destiny. The doctrine of resurrection appears in a few late passages in the OT; it was held by many Jews at the time of Christ's ministry; and it was clinched for Christian believers by the *Resurrection of Christ Himself. It can be combined with

the Greek doctrine of the natural immortality of the soul, but the two doctrines are independent and different, since resurrection implies (1) that the full redeemed life of heaven must include a restoration of the whole psycho-physical organism, because man was created by God to be and to remain an embodied spirit; and (2) that the life after death is wholly the gift of God, and not due to the inherently immortal nature of man's soul. It has at times been the prevailing view that the resurrection will involve a collection and revivifying of the material particles of the dead body. Many theologians, however, following the principles of St *Paul, hold that the resurrection body will be new and 'spiritual' (1 Cor. 15: 35–54), i.e. a body of a new order, the perfect instrument of the spirit, raised above the limitations of the earthly body, with which it will be identical only in the sense that it will be the recognizable organism of the same personality. Commonly it is held that all the dead, whether saved or not, will rise to pass under judgement; but with some support in the NT it may be held that resurrection in any full sense will be confined to those destined to eternal life.

R. H. *Charles, *A Critical History of the Doctrine of a Future Life in Israel, in Judaism and in Christianity* (Jowett Lectures for 1898–9; 1899). H. Cornélius, OP, and others, *La Résurrection de la chair* (1962); J. Hick, *Death and Eternal Life* (1976); P. Badham, *Christian Beliefs about Life after Death* (1976); H. *Küng, *Ewiges Leben?* (Munich, 1982; Eng. tr., 1984); P. Perkins, *Resurrection: New Testament Witness and Contemporary Reflection* (1984); S. [C. ff.] Tugwell, OP, *Human Immortality and the Redemption of Death* (1990). A. Michel in *DTC* 13 (pt. 2; 1937), cols. 2502–71, s.v. 'Résurrection des morts'; H. Wissmann and others in *TRE* 4 (1979), pp. 441–77 and 529–75, s.v. 'Auferstehung', I, III and IV. See also bibl. to previous entry and to IMMORTALITY.

retable. A structure placed at the back of an altar in the form either of a ledge on which ornaments may be set or of a frame for decorated panels. The ledge form is also known as a *gradine, the form for panels also as a *reredos.

retreat. A period of days spent in silence, and occupied with meditation and other religious exercises. In essence the practice is older than Christianity, but the 40 days Christ spent in the wilderness have been considered to give the ultimate authority for its Christian use. As a formal devotion, retreats were introduced in the *Counter-Reformation period. The *Jesuits, who were the first religious order to include them in their rule, also counselled them to those outside their body. A little later St *Francis de Sales and St *Vincent de Paul became strong advocates of the practice. In the 17th cent. retreat houses were instituted, where those who wished to make a retreat might stay for short periods under the guidance of 'conductors'. In the RC Church the practice of annual retreat became widespread early in the 19th cent., at first for the clergy, both *regular and *secular, but soon also for many of the laity. In the C of E the practice of retreat was adopted under the influence of the *Oxford Movement, the first formal retreat being held in 1856 in Christ Church, Oxford.

R. Schofield (ed.), *Retreats: Their Value, Organisation and Growth* (1915); id., new work with same title but different contributors (1927). *Vision* (1920 ff., now issued annually by the National Retreat Association) includes current information about retreat houses in England, Wales, Scotland, Ireland, and the Channel Isles, and about organized retreats planned in them. P. Debuchy in *CE* 12 (1911), pp. 795–7, s.v.; D. *Stone in *HERE* 10 (1918), pp. 743 f., s.v., with bibl.

Retz, Cardinal de (Jean-François-Paul de Gondi) (1613–79), Abp. of *Paris. Of Italian stock, he was born and brought up in the château of Montmirail (Champagne) while St *Vincent de Paul was a member of the household. He was educated at the Collège de *Clermont and at the *Sorbonne. His family, in whose hands the see of Paris had been since 1570, forced him into an ecclesiastical career for which he had no inclination; he apparently approached his ordination with cynicism and continued to lead a life of immorality and intrigue. As a young man he wrote the *Conjuration de Fiesque* (pub. 1665), a thinly disguised attack on A. J. du P. *Richelieu. In 1643 he was appointed Coadjutor-Archbishop of Paris to his uncle, Jean-François de Gondi. He played an important, but unscrupulous role during the first and second Frondes (1648–9 and 1651–2), opposing J. *Mazarin but readily changing his allegiances. As a result of various intrigues in Rome and Paris, he was created a cardinal in 1652. Soon afterwards, however, at Mazarin's insistence, he was imprisoned in Vincennes. On the death of his uncle in 1654 he succeeded him; the cathedral chapter took possession of the see in his name. The King insisted on his signing a resignation of the archbishopric, but the Pope refused to accept it. Retz was transferred to Nantes and escaped from prison. He went to Rome and took part in the election of *Alexander VII in 1655. For the next few years he led a nomadic existence in various countries. At the request of the exiled *Charles II he tried, unsuccessfully, to win Papal support for the Stuart cause. In 1661, after Mazarin's death, he returned to Paris and resigned his see in exchange for the rich abbey of *St-Denis, held *in *commendam*. He took part in the conclaves which elected Clement IX, Clement X, and *Innocent XI, safeguarding French interests. Living on his estate at Commercy, he began to compose his *Mémoires* (prob. addressed to Mme de Sévigné and her daughter). A personal, if biased historical document on the period of the Frondes, written in a lively style, with interesting portraits of his contemporaries, it ranks as a considerable work of literature.

Œuvres, ed. A. Feillet, J. Gourdault, [F.] R. Chantelauze, and C. Cochin (11 vols., Paris, 1870–1920); also by M.-T. Hipp and M. Pernot (ibid. [1984]). *Mémoires*, first pub., 3 vols., Nancy, 1717; first ed. from autograph MSS by [A.] Champollion-Figeac and A. Champollion (Paris, 1837); modern edn. (with *La Conjuration de Fiesque*) by S. Bertière (2 vols., ibid. [1987]). *La Conjuration de Fiesque* also ed. D. A. Watts (Oxford, 1967). Eng. tr. of the *Mémoires* by P. Davall (4 vols., 1723; modernized by D. Ogg, Everyman Library, 735–6 [1917]). [F.] R. Chantelauze, *Le Cardinal de Retz et l'affaire du chapeau* (2 vols., 1878); id., *Le Cardinal de Retz et ses missions diplomatiques à Rome* (1879), D. Ogg, *Cardinal de Retz 1613–1679* (London, 1912); L. Batiffol, *Le Cardinal de Retz* (Paris [1927]); id., *Biographie du Cardinal de Retz* (1929); J. H. M. Salmon, *Cardinal de Retz: The Anatomy of a Conspirator* (1969); D. A. Watts, *Cardinal de Retz: The Ambiguities of a Seventeenth-Century Mind* (Oxford, 1980); S. Bertière, *La Vie du Cardinal de Retz* (1990), with bibl. Other studies by P.-G. Lorris (Paris [1956]), J. T. Letts (ibid., 1966), and J. Matrat (ibid., [1969]). F. J. Routledge, 'The Negotiations between Charles II and the Cardinal de Retz, 1658–59', *Transactions of the Royal Historical Society*, 5th ser. 6 (1955), pp. 49–68; A. J. Krailsheimer,

Studies in Self-Interest from Descartes to La Bruyère (Oxford, 1962), pp. 61–80; H. Carrier, 'Sincérité et création littéraire dans les *Mémoires* du cardinal de Retz', *Dix-septième Siècle*, 94–5 (1972), pp. 39–74. Six arts. based on a conference in Paris on 19 Feb. 1988 are pr. in the *Revue d'histoire littéraire de la France*, 89 (1989), pp. 4–70.

Reuchlin, Johannes (1454/5–1522), German humanist. He matriculated at Freiburg im Breisgau in 1470 and studied at *Paris in 1473 as tutor to a son of Charles I, Margrave of Baden. From 1474 to 1478 he studied at Basle, where he became Master of Arts in 1477. In 1478 he published a Latin lexicon, *Vocabularius*, which became very popular. He also began his study of Greek, which he continued briefly at Paris in 1478. He studied law at Orléans from 1479 and later at Poitiers, where he got his licentiate in law in 1481. The same year he took up a position as professor at *Tübingen. In 1482 he accompanied Count Eberhard of Württemburg to Rome first as his interpreter, later becoming his adviser and ambassador. Back in Tübingen in 1483 he taught Greek and there obtained his doctorate of laws in 1484/5. About 1485 he began to study Hebrew with the help of learned Jews and became interested in *Kabbalistic doctrines, expounding the latter in *De Verbo Mirifico* (1494) and later in *De Arte Cabbalistica* (1517), both full of abstruse speculations on sacred letters. Owing to the hostility of Eberhard's successor he fled to Heidelberg in 1496; here he wrote his spirited Latin comedies *Sergius* and *Henno* in imitation of Terence, and perfected his knowledge of Hebrew. After the deposition of Eberhard's son in 1498, he returned to Württemberg, where he became one of the three justices in the Swabian League in 1502. In 1506 he published his most important work, *De Rudimentis Hebraicis*. Consisting of a Hebrew grammar and lexicon, it placed on an entirely new basis the scientific study of the Hebrew language, which had hitherto been almost entirely neglected among Christians, and became a powerful incentive to the study of the OT in the original. It was supplemented by an edition of the *seven penitential Psalms in Hebrew, with a Latin translation (1512), and a treatise on Hebrew accents, *De Accentibus et Orthographia Linguae Hebraicae* (1518). The latter years of his life were troubled by controversy. Johann Pfefferkorn, a convert from Judaism, supported by the *Dominican friars of Cologne and in particular Jakob von Hochstraten (d. 1527), advocated the destruction of Jewish religious books. Among others Reuchlin was consulted by the Emp. Maximilian I, and he alone advised against such measures. This recommendation, combined with his interest in Kabbala, led to Reuchlin's being involved in a trial for heresy, initiated in 1513 by von Hochstraten. After repeated appeals by both sides, a final verdict was given in 1520 when *Leo X awarded costs against Reuchlin and banned his satirical *Augenspiegel* (1511). In the course of the controversy polemical pamphlets were produced on both sides. A famous contribution was the *Epistolae Obscurorum Virorum* (1515–17) written in defence of Reuchlin by Crotus Rubinanus and Ulrich von *Hutten. Though many of the Reformers took part in the controversy on the side of Reuchlin, he himself remained a loyal Catholic and endeavoured hard to detach his grandnephew, P. *Melanchthon, from his friendship with M. *Luther.

De Arte Cabbalistica is repr. photographically, with Eng. tr. by M. and S. Goodman (New York, 1983). The standard Life is that of L. Geiger (Leipzig, 1871). Correspondence ed. id. (Bibliothek des literarischen Vereins in Stuttgart, 126; 1875; repr. Hildesheim, 1962). A. Horawitz, 'Zur Biographie und Correspondenz Johannes Reuchlins', *Sb.* (Wien), 85 (1877), pp. 117–90. K. Christ, *Die Bibliothek Reuchlins in Pforzheim* (Beiheft zum Zentralblatt für Bibliothekswesen, 52; 1924). *Festschrift der Stadt Pforzheim zur Erinnerung an dem 400. Todestag Reuchlins* (Pforzheim [1922]); M, M. Krebs (ed.), *Johannes Reuchlin 1455–1522: Festgabe seiner Vaterstadt zur 500. Wiederkehr seines Geburtstages* (ibid. [1955]). M. Brod, *Johannes Reuchlin und sein Kampf: Eine historische Monographie* (1966). J. H. Overfield, 'A New Look at the Reuchlin Affair', *Studies in Medieval and Renaissance History*, 8 (1971), pp. 165–207. C. Zika, 'Reuchlin's *De Verbo Mirifico* and the Magic Debate of the Late Fifteenth Century', *Journal of the Warburg and Courtauld Institutes*, 39 (1976), pp. 104–38; H. Greive, 'Die hebräische Grammatik Johannes Reuchlins', *ZATW* 90 (1978), pp. 394–409. J. Benzing, *Bibliographie der Schriften Johannes Reuchlin im 15. und 16. Jahrhundert* (Bibliotheca Bibliographica, 18; Bad Bocklet, etc., 1955). H. Scheible in B. G. Bietenholz and T. B. Deutscher (eds.), *Contemporaries of Erasmus*, 3 [1987], pp. 145–50.

reunion. Desire for the visible unity of Christ's Church has increased in the 20th cent., as growing doctrinal agreement between the major Christian bodies has been reinforced by liturgical reforms derived from a wider knowledge of early Christian worship and a higher view of the status and functions of the laity. The problems involved in reunion vary according to the different groups between whom it is envisaged.

Reunion between the C of E and the RC Church has often been considered since the 17th cent., notably in the time of the *Oxford and post-*Tractarian movements and at the time of the *Malines Conversations (1921–5). Since the end of the Second World War (1945) there has been an increased openness in the attitude of the RC Church towards other communions. In 1960 Abp. G. F. *Fisher visited Pope *John XXIII, the first Abp. of *Canterbury since the Reformation to be received in Rome. In the same year non-RC Churches were invited to send observers to the Second *Vatican Council, and the Pope established a 'Secretariat [now Pontifical Council] for Promoting Christian Unity'. The Second Vatican Council's Decree on Ecumenism described members of other communions as being 'separated brethren' rather than outside the Church. A succession of documents (e.g. the 'Directory for the Application of Principles and Norms on Ecumenism', 1993) has encouraged, while defining current limits to, RC participation in ecumenical activities. The *Anglican–Roman Catholic International Commission (q.v.), set up in 1968, is now complemented by RC bilateral dialogues with many other Churches, e.g. the *Methodists and *Baptists.

Reunion with the *Orthodox Church has long been attempted by both Roman and non-Roman Churches. After the short-lived union effected by the Council of *Florence (1439), there were other less important *rapprochements*. Friendly relations with the C of E obtained until in 1725 Abp. W. *Wake disillusioned the Patr. of *Jerusalem about the status of the *Nonjurors, who had been in contact with the Orthodox since 1716. Several attempts in the 19th cent. came to nothing, including the Conferences at *Bonn in 1874 and 1875. In 1864 the 'Eastern Church Association' was founded, becoming in 1906 the '*Anglican and Eastern Churches Association'. The *Lambeth Conference of 1908 appointed a Committee to confer with the E. Patriarchs, and that of 1930 discussed the question of unity with Orthodox delegates. The first pan-Orthodox Conference at Rhodes in 1961 decided to open discussions with the RC Church and the C of E. Considerable progress has been made in many areas between Orthodox and Anglicans, though the ordination of *women to the priesthood and episcopate in some parts of the Anglican Communion has impeded the dialogue. Some Orthodox Churches sent observers to the Second Vatican Council, and in 1965 the mutual anathemas of 1054 between the E. and W. Churches were lifted. Much progress has been made in theological discussion between the Orthodox and RC Churches, though since c.1990 relations have been complicated by the question of the *Uniat Churches in E. Europe. Orthodox Churches are also involved in bilateral discussions with several other Churches, including the *Old Catholic and *Reformed.

Schemes for reunion between the C of E and foreign Protestant bodies were discussed in the 16th and 17th cents. In 1708 Frederick I of Prussia sought unsuccessfully to unite the *Lutheran and Reformed Churches in his kingdom and to introduce episcopacy by entering into union with the C of E. Negotiations continued until his death in 1713, and a fresh, but again unsuccessful attempt to introduce episcopacy was made in 1841 by the creation of the *Jerusalem Bishopric (q.v.). Further steps towards closer relationship between Anglican and Lutheran Churches include agreements to establish mutual Eucharistic hospitality between the C of E and the Churches of *Sweden (1922, but not ratified until 1954), *Finland (1934), Estonia and Latvia (1938), *Denmark, *Norway, and *Iceland (1951). In 1920 an Anglican bishop took part in the consecration of two Swedish bishops and from 1927 Swedish bishops have from time to time taken part in the consecration of bishops in the C of E. Similar arrangements for mutual participation in episcopal consecrations were included in the agreements with the Churches of Finland, Estonia and Latvia, who all expressed their understanding of episcopacy as within the framework of the historic succession. The Meissen Agreement (1988) between the C of E and the *Evangelical Church in Germany committed them to work towards full visible unity. The Porvoo Agreement, reached near Porvoo in Finland in 1992, went further. It envisaged a relationship of communion between the Anglican Churches in Britain and Ireland and the Nordic and Baltic Lutheran Churches, with a common membership and an interchangeable ministry. It was ratified by most of the Churches concerned, apart from Denmark. The 1990 Concordat between the Evangelical Lutheran Church in America and the *Episcopal Church in the United States of America (rejected by the Lutherans in 1997) would have brought them into a relationship described as 'full communion', with interchangeable ministries. Among the many other dialogues pursued by Protestant Churches, special significance attaches to the negotiations between the Reformed and Lutheran Churches in Europe which culminated in the *Leuenberg Concord of 1973. This emphasised the need for a 'reconciliation of memories' (a process of the Churches mutually facing, and moving beyond, the causes and painful results of their historic divisions). More than 80 Churches, including some in Latin America, have signed this text and declared themselves to be in full communion.

There have been several efforts to unite English dissenting bodies with the Established Church. At the *Restoration an attempt was made to 'comprehend' *Presbyterians and *Independents, but the *Savoy Conference (1661) failed, as did more private attempts in 1688 and in the mid-18th cent. In the 19th cent. reunion between the C of E and the Free Churches had several advocates, including W. T. Mowbray, founder of the Home Reunion Society (1873). The Lambeth Conference of 1888 laid down four conditions for such union (the '*Lambeth Quadrilateral', q.v.). An 'Appeal to all Christian People' by the Lambeth Conference of 1920 led to conversations with the Federal Council of the Evangelical Free Churches (1920–5). These were resumed after the Lambeth Conference of 1930. The main difficulties related to the question of the ministry. In 1946 G. F. Fisher, Abp. of Canterbury, suggested that the Free Churches might, without surrendering their identity, 'take episcopacy into their system' and thus prepare the way for intercommunion. Methodist response to the text 'Church Relations in England' (1946) led to the *Anglican–Methodist Conversations (q.v.). The 1964 '*Faith and Order' Conference at Nottingham resolved that the *British Council of Churches should work and pray together for unity by 1980. The English Churches Unity Commission, set up in 1974 in response to an invitation from the recently formed *United Reformed Church, in 1976 issued *Visible Unity: Ten Propositions*. This proposed a Covenant under which membership, ministers, and sacraments should be mutually recognized. The Churches' Council for Covenanting was set up in 1978 by five Churches; after being accepted by the Methodist and United Reformed Churches, the proposals were rejected by the C of E in 1982.

Despite numerous negotiations which have proved abortive, an impressive series of Church unions have taken place since the early 19th cent. The Lutheran and Reformed Churches which Frederick I of Prussia tried to unite in 1708 were finally brought together by King Frederick William III in 1817 in the United Evangelical Church of Prussia, or Old Prussian Union, reconstituted in the 1950s as the Evangelical Church of the Union. Similar arrangements were made elsewhere in Germany and in the Austro-Hungarian Empire later in the 19th cent. In 1918 the Evangelical Church of Czech Brethren united Czech Churches of the *Augsburg and *Helvetic Confessions, on the basis of their shared roots in the *Hussite Reformation. In subsequent stages of the movement towards union, Churches formed (or expanded) by interdenominational unions include the United Church of *Canada (1925); the Church of Christ in *China (1927); the Church of *Scotland (1929); the Church of Christ in Thailand (1934); the Reformed Church of *France (1938); the United Church of Christ in *Japan (a union originally imposed by the government in 1941); the Churches of *South India (1947), *North India (1970), *Pakistan (1970), and Bangladesh (1971); the United Church of Christ in the *Philippines (1948); the *United Church of Christ (1957); the United Church of *Zambia (1965); the United Congregational Church of Southern Africa (1967;

expanded 1972); the United Church of Jamaica and the Cayman Islands (1965; expanded 1993); the United Church in Papua New Guinea and the Solomon Islands (1968); the Church of Jesus Christ in Madagascar (1968); the United *Methodist Church (1968); the Church of Christ in *Zaire (1970); the *United Reformed Church in the United Kingdom (1972; expanded 1981); the Uniting Church in *Australia (1977), and the United Protestant Church of *Belgium (1979).

In these unions (which often include bodies formed by previous unions) Churches of the Presbyterian and *Congregationalist traditions are most often involved, followed by Methodists, *Disciples of Christ, and Brethren (see TUNKERS). Anglicans have entered only the United Churches of the Indian subcontinent. Probably the most comprehensive union has been that of North India, involving Anglican, Baptist, Congregational, Disciples, Methodist, Brethren, and Presbyterian Churches. Numerous unions have occurred among Churches within the same confessional family, such as those forming the Methodist Church of Great Britain (1932) and the Evangelical Lutheran Church in America (1988).

The unions in India and Pakistan, in including both episcopally and non-episcopally ordered Churches, have been most important ecclesiologically. Significantly bishops from 'all United Churches with which the Churches of the Anglican communion are in full communion' were invited to 'full membership' of the *Lambeth Conference of 1988. Unions have generally formed 'local' (i.e. national) Churches, and these were probably the inspiration behind the vision of the Fifth Assembly of the World Council of Churches at Nairobi in 1975 of a 'conciliar fellowship of *local churches truly united*'. In Africa and Asia they have played an important part in indigenizing the Church as, through union, several missionary-founded Churches, supported financially from overseas, have been succeeded by a single locally led and locally funded Church. Unions in which theological differences are minimal may still offer an important witness to the healing power of the Gospel, as when the Presbyterian Church (USA) was formed in 1983 by the reunion of two Churches which had been bitterly divided by the American Civil War. The failure of the union scheme in Ghana in 1983 emphasized the need for agreement on questions of theology and Church practice to be complemented by education to prepare local congregations for union.

Continuing interdenominational discussions include the Negotiating Churches Unity Council in *New Zealand; the Commission of the Covenanted Churches in *Wales; the Joint Council of the Church of South India, Church of North India and Mar Thoma Church. The *Consultation on Church Union (COCU), formed in 1962, includes nine major US denominations committed to 'becoming one in faith, sacraments, ministry, and mission' without, however, seeking 'consolidation of forms and structures'. Union discussions between Churches in the same confessional tradition are in progress, e.g. among several Methodist denominations in Ghana. In 1970 two world confessional organizations joined to form the *World Alliance of Reformed Churches, and this body has actively encouraged its member Churches to enter into unions (as also has the Disciples of Christ). The United Churches have not formed a world confessional body, but maintain contact through the Faith and Order Commission of the *World Council of Churches.

In recent years some have sensed a loss of momentum in the search for unity. The situation in the formerly Communist countries of E. Europe has fostered renewed rivalries as Churches and Christian groups centred in W. Europe and N. America have conducted missionary work in territory historically dominated by the Orthodox Church; the attitude of Pope *John Paul II is generally seen as more conservative than that of his immediate predecessors; and in some Churches a decline in membership and financial support has left fewer resources available for ecumenical work. Nevertheless most Churches remain committed to the search for visible unity and continue to address both the theological issues and the historical and social factors which divide them. See also ECUMENICAL MOVEMENT.

G. K. A. *Bell (ed.), *Documents on Christian Unity 1920–4* (1924): id., 2nd ser. [1920–30] (1930); id., 3rd ser. 1930–48 (1948); id., 4th ser. 1948–57 (1958); H. P. Douglass, *A Decade of Objective Progress in Church Unity 1927–1936* (1937); S. [C.] Neill, *Towards Church Union 1937–1952* (1952). A 'Survey of Church Union Negotiations' has been published in the *Ecumenical Review* at about 2-year intervals since 1954. On the Consultations of United and Uniting Churches, see *Mid-Stream*, 6 (1967), 9 (1970), and 14 (1975); *Growing Towards Consensus and Commitment: Report of the Fourth International Consultation of United and Uniting Churches, Colombo, Sri Lanka* (Faith and Order Paper, 110; Geneva, 1981); T. F. Best (ed.) *Living Today Towards Visible Unity: The Fifth International Consultation of United and Uniting Churches* (Faith and Order Paper, 142; ibid. [1988]). J. F. Puglisi and S. J. Voicu, *A Bibliography of Interchurch and Interconfessional Theological Dialogues* (Rome, 1984), with supplements in the bi-annual *Bulletin* of the Centro Pro Unione, 28, etc. (Rome, 1985 ff.).

Studies include A. C. *Headlam, *The Doctrine of the Church and Christian Reunion* (1920); J. T. McNeill, *Unitive Protestantism* (New York [1930]); [Y.] M.-J. *Congar, OP, *Chrétiens désunis* (Unam Sanctam, 1; 1937; Eng. tr., 1939); N. Sykes, *The Church of England and Non-Episcopal Churches in the Sixteenth and Seventeenth Centuries* (*Theology* Occasional Papers, NS 11; 1948); B. [G. M.] Sundkler, *Church of South India: The Movement Towards Union 1900–1947* (1954); A. Bea, *L'unione dei cristiani* ([1962]; Eng. tr., 1963); P. Bolink, *Towards Church Union in Zambia* (Franeker [1967]); P. A. Crow and W. J. Boney (eds.), *Church Union at Mid-Point* (New York [1972]); F. Engel, *Australian Christians in Conflict and Unity* (Melbourne, 1984); J. A. Burgess (ed.), *In Search of Christian Unity: Basic Consensus/Basic Differences* (Minneapolis [1991]); M. Cressey, 'Where and Whither? An Interpretive Survey of United and Uniting Churches', *Minutes of the Meeting of the Faith and Order Standing Committee, Rome, Italy, 1991* (Faith and Order Paper, 157; Geneva, 1992), pp. 57–64; also R. Rouse and S. C. Neill (eds.), *A History of the Ecumenical Movement, 1517–1948* (1954; 2nd edn. with rev. bibl., 1967; vol. 2: *The Ecumenical Advance, 1948–1968*, ed. H. E. Fey, 1970; both vols. repr., Geneva [1986], with bibl. covering the period 1968–85 in vol. 2, pp. 509–53), and other works cited under ECUMENICAL MOVEMENT.

Reusch, Franz Heinrich (1825–1900), *Old Catholic theologian. He taught at Bonn from 1854, holding a full professorship in OT exegesis from 1861 onwards. Throughout his life he was closely associated with his former teacher J. J. I. von *Döllinger, and shared his intellectual ideals as well as his liberal views of Church history. In 1870 he strongly opposed the infallibility decrees of the First *Vatican Council and in 1872 was excommunicated

on his refusal to subscribe. Thereafter he took a leading part in organizing in its earlier years the Old Catholic Church and in arranging the Reunion Conferences which were held at *Bonn in 1874 and 1875. When, however, the Old Catholics abolished clerical celibacy in 1878, Reusch objected and retired into lay communion. An untiring student, Reusch wrote many books, his earlier ones dealing with OT subjects and his later ones mainly with modern ecclesiastical history. Much of his best work was done in conjunction with Döllinger, notably a history of post-Tridentine moral theology (*Geschichte der Moralstreitigkeiten in der römisch-katholischen Kirche seit dem XVI. Jahrhundert*, 2 vols., 1889). His other writings include *Luis de Leon und die spanische Inquisition* (1873); *Der Prozess Galileis und die Jesuiten* (1879); and *Index der verbotenen Bücher* (2 vols., 1883–5).

Life by L. K. Götz, incl. list of Reusch's works (Gotha, 1901). [Dr] Menn, 'Fritz Heinrich Reusch als Schriftsteller', *Revue internationale de Théologie*, 14 (1906), pp. 38–72, 462–8, 729–44; 15 (1907), pp. 75–93, 462–80. In Eng. there is a brief sketch by J. E. B. Mayor (Cambridge, 1901). L. K. Goetz in *PRE* (3rd edn.), 16 (1905), pp. 689–91.

revelation. In Christian theology the word is used both of the *corpus* of truth about Himself which God discloses to us and of the process by which His communication of it takes place. Traditional theology has tended to conceive of revelation in the latter sense as taking place through propositions; but there has been an increasing tendency among many modern theologians to insist that Divine revelation reaches us largely, and even primarily, through God's activity (His 'mighty acts', *magnalia Dei*; cf. Acts 2: 11), rather than in propositional statements. Since it is commonly held that there are certain truths about God which can be learnt through man's natural endowments (e.g. His existence, which such philosophers as *Aristotle who were outside the Christian covenant believed that they could establish), while others, e.g. the Doctrine of the Holy *Trinity, are not knowable except by faith, Christian philosophers have often held that a sharp distinction must be drawn between 'truths of reason' and 'truths of revelation'. This distinction received its classic elaboration from St *Thomas Aquinas. It has its counterpart in the antithesis between 'natural theology' and 'revealed theology'. Over against this, there has been another school of theologians who have held that truths of revelation and truths of reason differ only in degree. When revelation has once been formulated, it is known as '*dogma' (q.v.). Christians of the Protestant tradition hold that all revelation is sufficiently contained in Scripture; Catholics on the other hand commonly maintain that part of it is also to be found in the unwritten traditions of the Church, but in recent years RC theologians have drawn a less sharp distinction between tradition and Scripture and have rather emphasized their ultimate unity. See also TRADITION.

Modern discussions incl. A. B. *Bruce, *The Chief End of Revelation* (1881); J. R. *Illingworth, *Reason and Revelation: An Essay in Christian Apology* (1902); J. *Baillie and H. Martin (eds.), *Revelation* (1927); R. *Bultmann, *Der Begriff der Offenbarung im Neuen Testament* (Sammlung gemeinverständlicher Vorträge und Schriften aus dem Gebiet der Theologie und Religionsgeschichte, 135; 1929); K. *Barth, *Die kirchliche Dogmatik*, 1, Heft 1 (1932), pp. 311–514; 1, Heft 2 (1938); and 2, Heft 1 (1940), pp. 1–287; Eng. tr., 1, pt. 1 (1975), pp. 295–489; 1, pt. 2 (1956); and 2, pt.

1 (1957), pp. 1–254; P. *Tillich, *Systematic Theology*, 1 (New York, 1951; London, 1953), pp. 79–177; J. Baillie, *The Idea of Revelation in the Light of Recent Discussion* (1956); W. *Pannenberg (ed.), *Offenbarung als Geschichte* (Göttingen, 1961; Eng. tr., New York and London, 1968); H. D. McDonald, *Theories of Revelation: An Historical Study 1860–1960* (1963); R. Latourelle, SJ, *Théologie de la Révélation* (Studia, 15; 1963; 2nd edn., 1966; Eng. tr., Statten Island, NY, 1966); K. *Rahner and J. Ratzinger, *Offenbarung und Überlieferung* (Quaestiones Disputatae, 17; 1965; Eng. tr., 1967); G. Moran, FSC, *Theology of Revelation* (New York, 1966; London, 1967), incl. Eng. tr. of the Dogmatic Constitution on Revelation at the Second Vatican Council, pp. 201–14. M. Seybold and others, *Die Offenbarung von der Schrift bis zum Ausgang der Scholastik* (Handbuch der Dogmengeschichte, 1, fasc. 1a; 1971); H. Waldenfels and others, *Die Offenbarung von der Reformation bis zur Gegenwart* (ibid. 1, fasc. 1b; 1978). A. [E. M.] Shorter, *Revelation and its Interpretation* (Introducing Catholic Theology, 1; 1983); A. Dulles, SJ, *Models of Revelation* (Garden City, NY, 1983; reissued, Maryknoll, NY, and Dublin, 1992). N. Iung in *DTC* 13 (pt. 2; 1937), cols. 2580–618, s.v. 'Révélation', with bibl. See also bibl. to TRADITION.

Revelation, Book of. The last Book of the NT and the only one which is an Apocalypse (see APOCALYPTIC LITERATURE). Its author, identified as 'John' in the title and 1: 9, and called 'the theologian' ('the divine') in later MSS of the title, was traditionally held to be St *John the Apostle.

At the time of writing, the author was in the island of *Patmos 'for the Word of God and the testimony of Jesus' (1: 9). He prefaces his Book with letters to the 'Seven Churches of Asia' (*Ephesus, *Smyrna, *Pergamum, *Thyatira, *Sardis, *Philadelphia, and *Laodicea). The remainder of the Book consists of a series of visions. In the first the author sees the glory of God (ch. 4) and the book sealed with seven seals which only Christ can open (5); as the first six seals are opened, four horsemen appear, presaging the approach of the end (6); the 144,000 faithful of Israel are sealed on the forehead and an innumerable multitude of the redeemed is seen in Heaven (7); the opening of the seventh seal begins a series of seven trumpet calls, heralding various disasters (8 f.); after the 'seven thunders', which the seer is bidden not to record, the angel's book is given him to eat (10: 1–11: 14); and the seventh trumpet call is followed by the proclamation of the kingdom of God and of Christ (11: 15–19). Then follow two general eschatological visions: the woman who is persecuted by a dragon, and war in heaven between *Michael and his angels and Satan (12); and then a pair of visions of a beast from the sea who blasphemes against God and a beast from the earth who compels all men to worship the first beast (13). The execution of judgement on 'Babylon the Great' is followed by world judgement, described under various images (14–16). The destruction of Babylon, now described as a harlot, is vividly portrayed (17 f.). Then comes the 'marriage supper of the Lamb'; the beast and the 'false prophet' are destroyed in a great battle and Satan is 'bound' for a thousand years (see MILLENARIANISM) and finally cast into the lake of brimstone for ever (19 f.). The Book ends with the general resurrection and judgement of souls, the 'New Heaven and the New Earth' and the 'New Jerusalem' (21: 1–22: 5), and an epilogue (22: 6–21).

The Book, which was prob. known to *Papias, is already ascribed by St *Justin to the Apostle John. This attribu-

tion was accepted in the *Muratorian Canon, and by *Tertullian and St *Hippolytus and (except by *Gaius, who assigned it to *Cerinthus) generally followed in the W. In the E., however, it was widely rejected, notably by the so-called *Alogi, St *Dionysius of Alexandria (who argued against its Apostolic authorship on the ground of differences in style and content from the Fourth Gospel and believed it to be the work of some other John) and *Eusebius. Some subsequent E. writers and Councils (St *Cyril of Jerusalem, Council of *Laodicea, St John *Chrysostom, *Theodore of Mopsuestia, *Theodoret) did not include it in the Canon, and it was omitted originally from the *Peshitta (Syriac) and *Armenian versions. This John from Asia Minor nowhere claims to be an eye-witness of the incarnate life of Christ, and he refers to the twelve Apostles in so reverential a manner (21: 14) that it is improbable that he was John the son of Zebedee.

Its bitterly hostile attitude to Rome indicates that the Book cannot be earlier than the persecution under *Nero in 64. If the '*Number of the Beast' is correctly interpreted as 'Nero Caesar', this would support a connection with that Emperor. But the Neronian persecution hardly affected Asia Minor and many date the Book from the time of the Emp. *Domitian (81–96). In that case the implication of the cryptogram may be that Domitian was regarded as a second Nero, reflecting the current superstition that Nero was not really dead, but would return (*Nero redivivus*) as the leader of barbaric hordes.

Many of the pictures and images with which the Book is filled doubtless have a historical reference, not always easy to disentangle. The labour that has been spent on explaining the predictions, however, has almost certainly been wasted. The aim of the Book, as of other Apocalypses, is to give assurance about God's power and purpose, in both salvation and judgement, rather than information about events to come. God's sovereignty and control of human destiny, already manifest in heaven, are guaranteed in the work of Christ and will be triumphantly effective in due time. God will preserve His servants, provided that they are faithful; the seer warns them against all idolatry, compromise with the pagan world, and slackness; and all God's enemies, heavenly and earthly, will be annihilated.

The Greek of the Book, both in grammar and vocabulary, is often uncouth. There are a few points of contact with St John's Gospel, notably in the use of the titles 'Word of God' (19: 13; cf. Jn. 1: 1) and 'Lamb of God' (Jn. 1: 29; cf. the different word at Rev. 5: 6) applied to Christ, neither of which appears elsewhere in the NT except in the Johannine Epistles. Such features could suggest a common theological background for the authors of the Gospel and Rev., but a common authorship is precluded by wide differences in eschatology, tone, and language. The political passion of the Book on behalf of the oppressed has attracted some modern readers and its social and historical background have been intensively studied in recent years. But its importance and potentially dangerous impact stem from its futuristic eschatology and the use made of it by millenarians of all periods, including *Jehovah's Witnesses and esp. fundamentalist Protestants today.

Patristic comm. incl. those by *Victorinus of Pettau, *Oecumenius of Tricca, and Andrew of Caesarea (J. P. Migne,

PG 106. 215–486); important medieval comm. by *Bede, *Richard of St-Victor, St *Albert the Great, and *Joachim of Fiore. Modern comm. incl. those of W. *Bousset (KEK 6, 5th edn.; 1896), R. H. *Charles (2 vols., ICC, 1920), E. B. Allo, OP (Études bibliques, 1921), A. *Loisy (Paris, 1923), T. *Zahn (Kommentar zum Neuen Testament, 18; 2 vols., 1924), E. Lohmeyer (Hb. NT 16; 1926; 2nd edn., 1953), E. Lohse (Das Neue Testament Deutsch, 11; 1960), A. M. Farrer (Oxford, 1964), T. F. Glasson (Cambridge, 1965), G. B. Caird (Black's NT Comm., 1966), H. Kraft (Hb. NT 16a; 1974), G. R. Beasley-Murray (New Cent. Bib., 1974), J. M. Ford (Anchor Bible, 1975), J. [P. M.] Sweet (SCM Pelican Commentaries, 1979) and D. E. Aune (forthcoming). Collations of Gk. MSS by H. C. Hoskier (2 vols., London, 1929). B. *Weiss, *Die Johannes-Apokalypse: Textkritische Untersuchungen und Textherstellung* (TU 7, Heft 1; 1891). A. S. *Peake, *The Revelation of John* (1919). A. M. Farrer, *The Rebirth of Images: The Making of St John's Apocalypse* (1949). S. Giet, *L'Apocalypse et l'histoire* (1957). T. Holtz, *Die Christologie der Apokalypse des Johannes* (TU 85; 1962). A. Feuillet. *L'Apocalypse: État de la question* (Studia Neotestamentica, Subsidia, 3; 1963). J. M. Court, *Myth and History in the Book of Revelation* (1979). L. L. Thompson, *The Book of Revelation: Apocalypse and Empire* (New York and Oxford, 1990). R. [J.] Bauckham, *The Theology of the Book of Revelation* (Cambridge, 1993). W. M. *Ramsay, *The Letters to the Seven Churches of Asia and their Place in the Plan of the Apocalypse* (1904). P. S. Minear, *I Saw a New Earth: An Introduction to the Visions of the Apocalypse* (Washington, DC, 1968). A. Y. Collins, *Crisis and Catharsis: The Power of the Apocalypse* (Philadelphia [1984]). E. Schüssler Fiorenza, *The Book of Revelation: Justice and Judgment* (Philadelphia [1985]; collected essays). R. K. Emmerson and B. McGinn (eds.), *The Apocalypse in the Middle Ages* (Ithaca, NY, and London, 1992). A. Y. Collins in *Anchor Bible Dictionary*, 5 (1992), pp. 694–708.

Reverend (Lat. *reverendus*, 'worthy of being revered'). An epithet of respect applied to the clergy since the 15th cent. Since the 17th cent. it has been used as a title prefixed to their names in correspondence. Archbishops and the Bp. of Meath (as the 'Premier Bp. of Ireland') are styled 'Most Reverend', other bishops 'Right Reverend', and deans 'Very Reverend'. Abbesses, prioresses, and other nuns who have the title of 'Mother', are also styled 'Reverend' (or sometimes 'Very Reverend' or 'Right Reverend'). The *Moderator of the General Assembly of the Church of Scotland is 'Right Reverend'. *Carthusian priests are an exception, all except the prior-general being styled not 'Reverend' but 'Venerable'. The legal right of Nonconformists to the title was established by the 'Keat Case' in 1876, when a faculty was ordered for the erection of a tombstone on which a *Wesleyan minister was styled 'Reverend', the incumbent having previously refused to allow it to be set up.

Revised Version of the Bible. See BIBLE (ENGLISH VERSIONS), 4.

revivalism. A type of religious worship and practice centring in evangelical revivals, or outbursts of mass religious fervour, and stimulated by intensive preaching and prayer meetings. It has been a common feature of the work of many religious bodies since the *Methodist movement of the 18th cent. under the *Wesleys, G. *Whitefield, and others. In the 19th cent. professional revivalists such as C. G. *Finney and D. L. *Moody developed techniques claimed to generate the recurrence of revivals, and some bodies, e.g. the *Salvation Army in its early days, made

revivalism the principal element of all their worship. In the 20th cent. notable revivalist campaigns have been led by 'Billy' *Graham. In the USA revivalism has been credited with a considerable influence on social reform.

T. L. Smith, *Revivalism and Social Reform in Mid-Nineteenth Century America* (Nashville [1957]; 2nd edn., with slightly different title and new afterword, Baltimore, 1980). W. G. McLoughlin, *Modern Revivalism: Charles Grandison Finney to Billy Graham* (New York [1959]). R. Carwardine, *Transatlantic Revivalism: Popular Evangelicalism in Britain and America 1790–1865* (Contributions in American History, 75, Westport, Conn., and London, 1978). J. [H. S.] Kent, *Holding the Fort: Studies in Victorian Revivalism* (1978). See also works cited under GREAT AWAKENING.

Revue Bénédictine. A Belgian periodical devoted esp. to the study of Christian Latin literature, issued quarterly from the abbey of *Maredsous. The first 6 vols., under the direction of Dom G. van Caloen, were issued as *Le Messager des fidèles* (1884–9).

Revue Biblique. The quarterly periodical on Biblical studies which is published (at Paris) by the *Dominicans established at the convent St-Étienne at *Jerusalem. It was founded by M. J. *Lagrange and its first issue appeared in Jan. 1892. Its contributions on matters of biblical archaeology tend to be of marked distinction.

Reynolds, Edward (1599–1676), Bp. of *Norwich. He was educated at Merton College, Oxford, and in 1628 appointed preacher at Lincoln's Inn. He had considerable sympathies with the *Puritan Movement, but, though a member of the *Westminster Assembly, did not take the Covenant until 1644. In 1647 he was one of the parliamentary visitors at Oxford, and in 1648–50 was Dean of *Christ Church; he returned briefly in 1660 as Dean before being obliged to move to Merton. He took a prominent part in the efforts made at the Restoration to effect a reconciliation between Episcopalians and Presbyterians; on deciding to conform, he was made Bp. of Norwich in 1661. He published many sermons and short devotional works which maintained a wide popularity down to the early 19th century.

Collected edns. of his works, London, 1658 and 1679; full edn. by A. Chalmers, 6 vols., ibid., 1826, with memoir in vol. 1, pp. xvii–lxxiv.

Reynolds, John. See RAINOLDS, JOHN.

Rhadagunde, St. See RADEGUNDE, ST.

Rheims. See REIMS.

Rhenanus, Beatus (1485–1547), German humanist. A native of Schlettstadt, he studied at *Paris from 1503 to 1507, where Jacob *Faber Stapulensis taught *Aristotelian philosophy. From 1511 to 1526 he lived at Basle, where he became interested in the publishing activities of J. *Froben, and from 1526 onwards at Schlettstadt, here pursuing his philosophical and historical studies. His earliest work was a biography of *Geiler von Kaisersberg (1510). Later he produced many editions of the classics and of the Fathers, e.g. of Velleius Paterculus, from a MS found by him at Murbach (1520), and of *Tertullian (1521). His studies of German antiquities resulted in the *Rerum Germanicarum Libri Tres* (1531), the best German work in critical historical research of the period. He wrote the earliest Life of his friend, *Erasmus, published first in Erasmus' translation of *Origen in 1536 and again in the first volume of his collected works (1540). Like him, Rhenanus at first favoured the Reformers, esp. their rejection of *indulgences and *auricular confession, but he changed his attitude when the revolutionary character of Protestantism became more apparent.

Correspondence ed. A. Horawitz and K. Hartfelder (Leipzig, 1866; repr. 1966). Selections from his Correspondence ed. R. Walter (Société Savante d'Alsace et des Régions de l'Est. Collection 'Grand Publications', 27; 1986). Eng. tr. of his Life of Erasmus in the tr. of the selected writings of Eramus, ed. J. O. Olin (1965), pp. 31–54. The primary authority is the Life by J. *Sturm (Basle, 1551). A. Horawitz, 'Beatus Rhenanus. Ein biographischer Versuch', *Sb.* (Wien), 70 (1872), pp. 189–244; id., 'Des Beatus Rhenanus literarische Thätigkeit in den Jahren 1508–1531', ibid. 71 (1872), pp. 643–90; id., 'Des Beatus Rhenanus literarische Thätigkeit in den Jahren 1530–1547', ibid. 72 (1872), pp. 323–76. W. Teichmann, 'Die kirchliche Haltung des Beatus Rhenanus', *ZKG* 26 (1905), pp. 363–81. H. Kaiser, 'Aus den letzten Jahren des Beatus Rhenanus', *Zeitschrift für die Geschichte des Oberrheins*, 70 (1916), pp. 30–52. J. F. D'Amico, *Theory and Practice in Renaissance Textual Criticism: Beatus Rhenanus between Conjecture and History* (Berkeley, Calif. [1988]). The *Annuaire de Les Amis de la Bibliothèque Humaniste de Sélestat*, 1985, was devoted to celebrating the 500th anniversary of Rhenanus' birth and incl. important arts. by H. Meyer and others. B. von Scarpatetti in P. G. Bietenholz and T. B. Deutscher (eds.), *Contemporaries of Erasmus*, 1 [1985], pp. 104–9, s.v. 'Beatus Rhenanus', with extensive bibl.

Rhodes, Knights of. See HOSPITALLERS.

Rhodo (2nd cent.), anti-*Gnostic apologist. A native of Asia Minor who became, for a time, a disciple of *Tatian at Rome, he wrote under the Emp. Commodus (180–192). *Eusebius tells us of the discussions he had with the aged *Apelles, a disciple of *Marcion. Rhodo's works included a treatise against the Marcionites and a commentary on the *Hexaemeron (Εἰς τὴν Ἑξαήμερον Ὑπόμνημα).

The few surviving frags., nearly all from Eusebius, *HE* 5. 13, are pr. in M. J. *Routh (ed.), *Reliquiae Sacrae*, 1 (2nd edn., Oxford, 1846), pp. 435–46; repr. in J. P. Migne, *PG* 5. 1331–8. Bardenhewer, 1, pp. 392–4. *CPG* 1 (1983), p. 109 (no. 1300). See also works cited under APELLES.

rhythmical office. A form of the Divine *Office, popular in the Middle Ages, in which besides the hymns almost all the other parts except the psalms and lessons were put into metre or rhyme. It developed from the practice of enlarging on the Lives of the saints in the *nocturns by additions in rhythm, and was thus also known as a 'Historia'. The construction of such rhythmical offices was a popular diversion for monks possessed of poetic gifts. Among the better-known writers of these offices are St *Odo (d. 942) and St *Odilo (d. 1048), abbots of *Cluny, and *Fulbert, Bp. of Chartres (d. 1028).

R. Jonsson, *Historia: Études sur la genèse des offices versifiés* (Acta Universitatis Stockholmiensis. Studia Latina Stockholmiensia, 15; 1968).

Ricaut, Paul. See RYCAUT, PAUL.

Ricci, Matteo (1552–1610), missionary in *China. He joined the *Jesuits at Rome in 1571, and his training included the study of mathematics and astronomy. He was sent to Goa in 1578 and from there to Macao in 1582, where he began to learn Chinese. After a long period of study and experimentation, during which he gradually moved northward, he settled in Beijing in 1601. Here he gained favour at court by displaying European scientific inventions and explaining astronomy, and influence among the scholarly élite by his assimilation of Confucian classics to Christian humanist ethics in a number of apologetic and catechetical works, especially his masterpiece, *T'iénchu Shih-i* (The True Meaning of the Lord of Heaven, 1595). Full Christian catechesis was kept for a later stage. Basic to his teaching was the conviction that the supreme deity of the Confucian classics was personal and could be assimilated to Christian theism. His method won converts among the Confucian scholarly class, but was less well adapted to Buddhism, Taoism, or popular Chinese religion. Criticism of his methods by other missionaries and the ensuing conflict was one of the factors in the Rites Controversy that erupted about a century later. See CHINA, CHRISTIANITY IN.

Opere storiche, ed. P. Tacchi Venturi, SJ (2 vols., Macerata, 1911–13). His journals of 1583–1610, ed. P. M. D'Elia, SJ, *Fonti ricciane* (Reale Accademia d'Italia, 3 vols., 1942–9); Eng. tr. by L. J. Gallagher, SJ (New York, 1953). *The True Meaning of the Lord of Heaven (T'ien-chu Shih-i)*, ed., with Eng. tr., by E. Malatesta, SJ (St Louis and Taipei, 1985). H. Bernard, SJ, *Le Père Matthieu Ricci et la société chinoise de son temps, 1552–1610* (2 vols., Tientsin, 1937). J. Bettray, SVD, *Die Akkommodationsmethode des P. Matteo Ricci S.I. in China* (Analecta Gregoriana, 76; Rome, 1955). J. D. Spence, *The Memory Palace of Matteo Ricci* (New York, 1984; London, 1985). V. Cronin, *The Wise Man from the West* (popular biog.; 1955). Sommervogel, 6 (1895), cols. 1792–5; Polgár, 3 (1990), pp. 65–78.

Ricci, Scipione de' (1741–1810) ecclesiastical reformer. In 1780 he was created Bp. of Pistoia-Prato in Tuscany at the instance of Leopold I. He took the initiative among the Tuscan prelates in introducing into N. Italy *Josephinist doctrines and a higher standard of morals. To this end he founded in 1783 a theological academy at Prato to which he appointed professors in sympathy with his views and carried through a plan of reform at the Synod of *Pistoia in 1786. He was esp. opposed to the excesses (as he held them) of the current devotions to the *Sacred Heart. His proposals however, met with much opposition and in 1791 he resigned from his see and retired into private life. Later he became reconciled to the RC Church.

His *Memorie* (ed. A. Gelli, 2 vols., Florence, 1865) is the chief authority. M. Vaussard (ed.), *Correspondance: Scipione de' Ricci–Henri Grégoire (1796–1807)* (Publications de l'Institut Français de Florence, 1ᵉ sér. Collection d'Études d'histoire, de critique et de philologie, 14; Florence and Paris, 1963). B. Bocchini Camaiani and M. Verga (eds.), *Lettere di Scipione de' Ricci a Pietro Leopoldo 1780–1791* (3 vols., Florence, 1990–2). Register of letters to de' Ricci from bishops and cardinals (1780–93), by C. Lamioni (Fonti Storiche Pistoiesi, 8; 1988). There is also a full Life by L. J. A. de Potter (3 vols., Brussels, 1825). B. Matteuci, *Scipione de' Ricci* (Studi e Documenti di Storia Religiosa; Brescia, 1941). E. Passerin, 'Il fallimento dell'offensiva riformista di Scipione de' Ricci secondo nuovi documenti (1781–1788)', *Rivista di Storia della*

Chiesa in Italia, 9 (1955), pp. 99–131, incl. texts. C. Fantappiè, *Reforme ecclesiastiche e resistenze sociali: La sperimentazione istituzionale nella diocesi di Prato alla fine dell'antico regime* (Religione e Società, 14; Bologna, 1986). See also works cited under PISTOIA, SYNOD OF, esp. arts. in work ed. C. Lamioni.

Richard of Chichester, St (*c.*1197–1253), Bp. of *Chichester. He was born at 'Wych' (i.e. Droitwich), and is hence sometimes known as 'Richard of Wych'. After studying at Oxford and Paris, he became chancellor of the University of Oxford *c.*1235 and a little later, under Abp. St *Edmund of Abingdon, chancellor of *Canterbury. He accompanied Edmund in his exile and was with him when he died (1242). In 1244 he was elected Bp. of Chichester but, on the refusal of Henry III, who favoured Richard Passelew, a rival candidate, to surrender the temporalities of the see, he obtained consecration from *Innocent IV at Lyons in 1245. Only under the threat of excommunication did Henry give way. Richard was a man of deep spirituality and an excellent administrator of his diocese, where he did much to raise the standard of clerical life. He was canonized by Urban IV in 1262. His shrine in Chichester Cathedral, where many cures are said to have been wrought, was destroyed by order of *Henry VIII in 1538. Feast day, 3 Apr.

His Statutes are pr. in F. M. Powicke and C. R. Cheney (eds.), *Councils & Synods with Other Documents relating to the English Church*, 2, pt. 1, 1205–1265 (Oxford, 1964), pp. 451–67; his will, with notes by W. H. Blaauw, in *Sussex Archaeological Collections*, 1 (1848), pp. 164–92. An almost contemporary Life by Ralf Bocking, with account of miracles and the bull of canonization, in *AASS*, April 1 (1675), pp. 282–318. Also ed., with Eng. tr., introd., and some other material, by D. Jones, *Saint Richard of Chichester: The sources for his life* (Sussex Record Society, 79 for 1993; 1995). E. F. Jacob, 'St. Richard of Chichester', *JEH* 7 (1956), pp. 174–88; C. H. Lawrence, 'St. Richard of Chichester', in M. J. Kitch (ed.), *Studies in Sussex Church History* (1981), pp. 35–55; D. Jones, 'The Medieval Lives of St. Richard of Chichester', *Anal. Boll.* 105 (1987), pp. 105–29. Mrs Tout in *DNB* 48 (1896), pp. 202–4. *BRUO* 3 (1959), pp. 2099–101, s.v. 'Wyche, Richard de'.

Richard of Middleton (b. *c.*1249), 'Richardus de Mediavilla', Franciscan philosopher and theologian. It is disputed whether he was French or English and very little is known of his life. As a bachelor of theology he was one of those charged to examine the writings of Petrus *Olivi at Paris in 1283. Records show him as a regent master there from 1284 to 1287, and he was in the household of Louis of Anjou, Bp. of Toulouse, *c.*1296. The date of his death is unknown. His chief writings are a Commentary on the 'Sentences' of *Peter Lombard, notable for its clarity and precision, *Quodlibets* and *Quaestiones disputatae*. He had a very free mind but at a number of points he followed the teaching of St *Thomas Aquinas. He rejected the thesis that there was an immediate bond of union between the human intellect and God, the uncreated Light, and also denied the validity of St *Anselm's *Ontological Argument for the being of God. In his 'Quodlibeta' he showed a keen interest in the phenomena of hypnotism. He also held that a plurality of worlds is possible.

His comm. on the Sentences, Book 4, was pr. at Venice, *c.*1477, 1489, and 1499; the whole comm., with the 'Quodlibeta', at Brescia, 1591. *Quaestio Disputata de Privilegio Martini Papae IV*, first ed. F. M. Delorme, OFM (Quaracchi, 1925). R. Zavalloni, OFM,

Richard de Mediavilla et la controverse sur la pluralité des formes: Textes inédits et étude critique (Philosophes médiévaux, 2; 1951). P. Glorieux, *La Littérature quodlibétique de 1260 à 1320*, 1 (Bibliothèque thomiste, 5; 1925), pp. 267–73, 2 (ibid. 21; 1935), p. 257. E. Hocedez, SJ, *Richard de Middleton: Sa vie, ses œuvres, sa doctrine* (SSL 6; 1925). J. Lechner, *Die Sakramentenlehre des Richard von Mediavilla* (Münchener Studien zur Historischen Theologie, 5; 1925). P. Rucker, OFM, *Der Ursprung unserer Begriffe nach Richard von Mediavilla* (BGPM 31, Heft 1; 1934). M. Schmaus, 'Die theologische Methode des Richard von Mediavilla', *Franziskanische Studien*, 48 (1966), pp. 254–65. E. *Gilson, *History of Christian Philosophy in the Middle Ages* (1955), pp. 347–50 and 696–8. É. Amann in *DTC* 13 (pt. 2; 1937), cols. 2669–75, s.v. 'Richard de Mediavilla'; V. Heynck in *L.Th.K.* (2nd edn.), 8 (1963), col. 1292, s.v. 'Richard v. Mediavilla'; *BRUO* 2 (1958), pp. 1253–5, s.v. 'Mediavilla, Richard de', each with detailed bibl.

Richard of St-Victor (d. 1173), *Victorine theologian and spiritual writer. Apparently a native of Scotland, he came as a young man to the Abbey of St-Victor in Paris. He became subprior in 1159, and prior in 1162. His most important theological treatise, 'De Trinitate', presented a complex argument, based on the nature of love, of necessary reasons for a triune deity. His other writings include many works devoted to the spiritual life (e.g. 'De praeparatione animi ad contemplationem, seu Liber dictus Benjamin minor', 'De gratia contemplationis, seu Benjamin maior', and 'De quattuor gradibus violentiae caritatis'), and to scriptural exegesis (e.g. 'Mysticae adnotationes in Psalmos', 'In visionem Ezechielis', and 'De Emmanuele'), as well as a compendium on the liberal arts, exegesis, and history ('Liber Exceptionum'), and a collection of sermons ('Sermones centum'). He followed *Hugh of St-Victor in incorporating ideas from *Dionysius the Pseudo-Areopagite into a theology that was basically Augustinian; at the same time he insisted on the importance of demonstration and argument in matters of theology, and emphasized the folly of contentment with a mere array of authorities. His spiritual teaching greatly influenced the Franciscan school, esp. St *Bonaventure.

Collected ed. of his *Opera*, Venice, 1506; also ed., with brief Life by John of Toulouse, a Victorine (Rouen, 1650; repr. in J. P. Migne, *PL* 196. 1–1378). Also by Richard are the 'Sermones centum' pr. as an appendix to the works of Hugh of St-Victor in *PL* 177. 899–1210; the exposition on Acts 12: 1–11 pr. under the name of *Fulbert of Chartres, ibid. 141. 277–306; *Sermons et opuscules spirituels inédits*, 1: *L'édit d'Alexandre ou les trois processions*, ed. J. Chatillon and W.-J. Tulloch, with Fr. tr. by J. Barthélemy (Bibliothèque de Spiritualité Médiévale [Bruges, 1951; all pub.]); and the *Liber Exceptionum*, ed. J. Chatillon (Textes Philosophiques du Moyen Âge, 5; 1958). *Opuscules théologiques* also ed. J. Ribaillier (ibid. 15; 1967); 'De quattuor gradibus violentiae caritatis', ed. G. Dumeige, with Ivo, *Épître à Séverin sur la charité* (ibid. 3; 1955), pp. 89–200; *De Trinitate*, ed. J. Ribaillier (ibid. 6; 1958) and, with Fr. tr., by G. Salet, SJ (SC 63; 1959); *Les Douze Patriarches ou Beniamin minor*, ed., with Fr. tr., by J. Châtillon and M. Duchet-Suchaux (ibid., 419; 1997). Eng. tr. of Selections from his Spiritual Writings, with introd. by C. Kirchberger (London, 1957); 'The Twelve Patriarchs' (*Benjamin minor*), 'The Mystical Ark' (*Benjamin maior*), and Book 3 of 'De Trinitate', tr., with introd., by G. A. Zinn (Classics of Western Spirituality [1979]). J. Ebner, *Die Erkenntnisse Richards von St Viktor* (BGPM 19, Heft 4; 1917). C. Ottaviano, 'Riccardo di S. Vittore. La vita, le opere, il pensiero', *Memorie della R. Accademia Nazionale dei Lincei*. Classe di scienze morali, storiche e filologiche, 6th ser. 4 (1933), pp. 411–541. A. M. Éthier, OP, *Le 'De Trinitate' de*

Richard de Saint-Victor (Publications de l'Institut d'Études Médiévales d'Ottawa, 9; Paris and Ottawa, 1939). L. Ott, *Untersuchungen zur theologischen Briefliteratur der Frühscholastik* (BGPM 34; 1937), pp. 549–657 ('Die theologischen Briefe Richards von St. Viktor'). G. Dumeige, *Richard de Saint-Victor et l'idée chrétienne de l'amour* (1952), with bibl. pp. 171–85. D. van den Eynde, OFM, 'Les Commentaires sur Joel, Abdias et Nahum attribués à Hugues de Saint-Victor', *Franciscan Studies*, 17 (1957), pp. 363–72. J. Châtillon in *Dict. Sp.* 13 (1988), cols. 593–654, s.v. 'Richard (10) de Saint-Victor'.

Richelieu, Armand Jean du Plessis (1585–1642), French cardinal, theologian, and politician. Destined at first for a miliary career, he took holy orders when his elder brother entered the *Grande Chartreuse, in order to secure the bishopric of Luçon to which his family had a claim. He was consecrated in 1607. On taking over his diocese, he enlisted the help of *Capuchins and *Oratorians, who preached missions in the parishes and sought to bring the *Huguenots back to the Church. Chosen to represent the clergy of Poitou in the States General in 1614, Richelieu gained influence with the Queen Mother and the young King, Louis XIII. In 1616 he was appointed Secretary of State, but he was dismissed on the downfall of C. Concini, whose patronage he had enjoyed. He retired to Blois and, in 1618, he was exiled to *Avignon. There he wrote *Les principaux points de la foi de l'Église catholique* (1617; Eng. tr. 1635) in answer to points raised by Protestant ministers, and the *Instruction du chrétien* (1621), the famous catechism written for his diocese, which was translated into many languages. He was recalled to Paris in 1619 through the influence of the Capuchin Father Joseph Leclerc du Tremblay, who became his close friend and adviser. In 1620 Richelieu reconciled Louis XIII with his mother and two years later he was created a cardinal by Gregory XV. He became President of the Council of Ministers in 1624, and from 1629 chief minister, a post which he held until his death. He aimed at the establishment of a centralized absolutism in France at every level and opposed both the feudal aristocracy and the political power of the Huguenots. The latter were defeated at La Rochelle in 1628 and their political privileges were abolished. In his foreign policy he aimed at securing France's frontiers and undermining the Habsburg predominance in Europe; he thus allied himself with the Protestant German princes and *Gustavus Adolphus of Sweden against the Emperor, thereby incurring the opposition of the devout Catholic party in France and incidentally impeding the progress of the *Counter-Reformation in Germany. He kept his political and religious commitments separate. In the controversy over *Gallicanism, he attempted to hold the balance between acceptance of the Pope's spiritual authority and rejection of his interference in French temporal affairs. He recognized the unorthodox character of the views put forward by the Abbé de *Saint-Cyran and his circle, who came to be known as the *Jansenists. He was Abbot General of *Cluny from 1629 and he encouraged the reform of the *Benedictine and other religious orders; he also fostered the renewal of religious practice and the training of priests. His theological position, expounded in the posthumously published *Traité de la perfection du chrétien* (1646), was based on reason and belief in the power of the will; although he recognized the value of the contemplative

life, he attached greater importance to the active. He was a patron of art and literature and, in 1635, founded the French Academy. See also THIRTY YEARS WAR.

Les Papiers de Richelieu: Section politique intérieure, correspondance et papiers d'État, ed. P. Grillon (Monumenta Europae Historica, Paris, 1975 ff.). Richelieu's *Testament Politique*, first pub. Amsterdam, 1688; crit. edn. by L. André (Paris, 1947). The best edn. of the *Mémoires du Cardinal de Richelieu* (written after his death from his papers, first pub. 1650) is that pub. by the Societé de l'Histoire de France (10 vols., 1907–31); see also *Rapports et notices sur l'édition des Mémoires du Cardinal de Richelieu*, by J. Lair and others (3 vols., 1905–22). G. Hanotaux and le Duc de la Force, *Histoire du Cardinal de Richelieu* (6 vols., 1893–1947). Other studies by C. J. Burckhardt (4 vols., Munich, 1935–67; abridged Eng. tr. of vols. 1, 2, and 3, 1940–71), C. V. Wedgwood ('Teach Yourself History', London, 1949), D. P. O'Connell (London, 1968), M. Andrieux and others (*Richelieu*; Collection Génies et Réalités, 1972), and R. J. Knecht ('Profiles in Power', London, 1991). G. Fagniez, *Le Père Joseph et Richelieu (1577–1638)* (2 vols., 1894). V.-L. Tapié, *La France de Louis XIII et de Richelieu* (1952; 2nd edn., 1967; Eng. tr., 1974; with additional matter and new bibl., Cambridge, 1984); O. A. Ranum, *Richelieu and the Councillors of Louis XIII* (Oxford, 1963); R. [J.] Bonney, *Political Change in France under Richelieu and Mazarin 1624–1661* (Oxford, 1978); J. H. Elliott, *Richelieu and Olivares* (Cambridge, 1984); J. Bergin, *Cardinal Richelieu: Power and the Pursuit of Wealth* (New Haven, Conn., and London, 1985). L. C. van Dijck, O.Praem., 'Pour une histoire du généralat prémontré du Cardinal de Richelieu', *Analecta Praemonstratensia*, 60 (1984), pp. 256–88; id., 'Le Cardinal de Richelieu, abbé de Prémontré', ibid. 62 (1986), pp. 150–233; 63 (1987), pp. 70–88 and 175–220. There is an attractive character study of Father Joseph Leclerc du Tremblay in A. Huxley, *Grey Eminence* (1941).

Ridley, Nicholas (*c.*1500–55), Bp. of London. After studying at Cambridge, the *Sorbonne, and Louvain, he became Fellow of Pembroke Hall, Cambridge (*c.*1530), chaplain to T. *Cranmer (1537), vicar of Herne in Kent (1538), and Master (1540) of Pembroke Hall. In 1547 he became Bp. of *Rochester and in 1550, upon E. *Bonner's deprivation, of London. From *c.*1535 he had had definite leanings towards the teachings of the Reformers, partly through the study of *Ratramnus' book on the Eucharist, and *c.*1546 he was a major influence in shifting T. *Cranmer's Eucharistic views away from *Real Presence doctrine. He assisted in the compilation of the BCP of 1549 and in the establishment of Protestantism at Cambridge University. Nevertheless, in 1550–1 he played the leading role in defeating J. *Hooper's attempt to avoid wearing *rochet and *chimere at his consecration as bishop. In 1553 he supported the claims of Lady Jane Grey to the Crown, and on Mary's accession was deprived of his see. After the Oxford disputations (1554) he was excommunicated, and, when heresy was made a capital offence, was burned with H. *Latimer at Oxford, 16 Oct. 1555. Like Latimer, he preached on the social injustices of his age, and a sermon he preached before the King was partly the occasion of the foundation of Christ's Hospital, St Thomas's Hospital, and Bridewell. In the American BCP (1979), feast day (with Latimer and Cranmer), 16 Oct.

Surviving works ed. H. Christmas (Parker Society, 1; 1841), with biog. notice, pp. i–xvi; selections also in *The Fathers of the English Church*, 4 (1809), pp. 31–267, with account of his life and martyrdom based on J. *Foxe, pp. 3–25; his *A Brief Declaration of the Lord's Supper*, ed. H. C. G. *Moule (1895), with biog. sketch, pp. 1–68. G. Ridley, *The Life of Nicholas Ridley* (1763).

Modern Life by J. G. Ridley (London, 1957). W. A. J. Archbold in *DNB* 48 (1896), pp. 286–90. See also bibl. to VESTIARIAN CONTROVERSY.

Ridsdale Judgement. The judgement of the *Judicial Committee of the Privy Council, pronounced on 12 May 1877, acc. to which Eucharistic vestments, 'alb and chasuble or cope, as distinguished from the surplice', were declared illegal in the C of E, except that copes were allowed in cathedrals and collegiate churches, and the *eastward position was permitted provided the *manual acts were not concealed from the congregation as a result. The defendant was the Revd C. J. Ridsdale, *Perpetual Curate of St Peter's, Folkestone.

The Judgement was fully reported as 'The Folkestone Ritual Case' in *The Times*, Monday, 14 May 1877, pp. 11–13; the official law report of the appeal is *Ridsdale* v. *Clifton* [1877], 2 PD, pp. 276–353.

Riemenschneider, Tilman (*c*.1460–1531), German wood-carver and sculptor. He was a native of Osterode (Harz) and lived from 1483 until his death at Würzburg, where he became Bürgermeister in 1520. He took a prominent part on the side of the insurgents in the *Peasants' War in 1525. His work, which was in both wood and stone, was marked by deep religious feeling; and now, after three centuries of neglect, it is considered among the most remarkable of the late Gothic style. In his altar-pieces he secured unity by focusing the design on a central point. In place of colour, he achieved his effects by the play of light, the texture of his material and the highly expressive faces of his figures. Among his most notable works are the Altar of the Blessed Sacrament in S. Jakobus, Rothenburg ob der Tauber (1499–1504); the tomb of Rudolf von Scherenberg (1496–9) and carvings in the Lady Chapel (1500–5) and on the High Altar (1508–10) in Würzburg Cathedral; and the tomb of the Emp. Henry II and his wife, Cunigunde, in Bamberg Cathedral (1499–1513).

J. Bier, *Die Jugendwerke Tilman Riemenschneiders* (1925), and other works of this author; K. Gerstenberg, *Tilman Riemenschneider* (Vienna, 1941; 6th edn., Munich, 1962); H. M. von Freeden, *Tilman Riemenschneider* (Frankfurt, 1954; 2nd edn., 1959). G. Poensgen (ed.), *Der Windsheimer Zwölfbotenaltar von Tilman Riemenschneider im kurpfälzischen Museum zu Heidelberg* (1955). M. [D. K.] Baxandall, *The Limewood Sculptors of Renaissance Germany* (New Haven, Conn., and London, 1980), pp. 172–90.

Rienzo, Cola di (*c*.1313–54), i.e. Nicolas, the son of Lorenzo, Tribune of the Roman People. The son of an innkeeper and a washerwoman, he passed his early years at Agnani, returning to Rome at the age of about 20. Intensive study of Roman classical authors, coupled with his own fertile imagination, led to a conviction that he was divinely inspired to liberate Rome from the tyranny of the patrician families and to bring about a rebirth of the Roman Empire. In 1343 he was part of a Roman embassy to *Clement VI which petitioned the Pope to return the Papacy from Avignon to Rome and to declare 1350 a *Jubilee Year. Clement was sufficiently impressed by Rienzo's abilities to make him a notary in 1344. In May 1347 Rienzo stirred up a popular revolution, as a result of which the people created him 'Tribune of the People'. While at first he ruled nominally in partnership with the Papal legate, he became

increasingly autocratic, and it soon became clear that he wished to unite all the Italian cities under his rule, and even that he had imperial aspirations. On 1 August he bathed in the font of the *Lateran Basilica, in which, acc. to tradition, the Emp. *Constantine had been baptized, and then had himself created a 'Knight of the Holy Ghost' in an extraordinary ceremony, and issued a revolutionary proclamation that the sovereignty of the world had returned to the Roman People. This was followed a fortnight later by his spectacular coronation as Tribune, a further proclamation, and a series of decrees. In his summons to Charles of Bohemia, Louis of Bavaria, and the Electors of the *Holy Roman Empire to appear before him the following Whit Sunday, he challenged the election of Charles IV (which had been engineered by Clement VI) and the Papal right to confirm imperial elections. The Roman people soon perceived that Cola was no longer their delegate, and their violent reaction forced him to flee from Rome in Dec. 1347 to the protection of the *Spiritual Franciscans of Monte Maiella, among whom he lived for two years. In 1350 he went to Prague to deliver a prophetic message to Charles IV, who arrested him and sent him to Clement VI, who imprisoned him. But when, in 1353, Cardinal Albornoz went to Rome to restore order, Innocent VI sent Rienzo with him. He was appointed senator, and triumphantly entered the city in 1354. Once again, however, his behaviour offended the people, who rose against him and killed him while he was trying to escape. A colourful figure, Cola was a skilful orator and letter writer, and among those with whom he corresponded were Clement VI, Charles IV, Ernest Pardubitz, Abp. of Prague, and the poet *Petrarch. He is the hero of one of Petrarch's odes and of the well-known opera by Richard Wagner (1842).

Epistolario di Cola di Rienzo, ed. A. Gabrielli (Rome, 1890); *Briefwechsel des Cola di Rienzo*, ed. K. Burdach and P. Piur (Vom Mittelalter zur Reformation. Forschungen zur Geschichte der deutschen Bildung, 2; 5 vols., 1912–29), includes as vol. 1, K. Burdach, *Rienzo und die geistige Wandlung seiner Zeit* (2 parts, 1913–28). Anon. contemporary Life, once attributed to T. Fortifiocca, pub. by A. Fei, Bracciano, 1624; modern edn. by A. M. Ghisalberti (Florence, 1928); Eng. tr. by J. Wright (Toronto, 1975). P. Piur, *Cola di Rienzo* (Vienna, 1931), with bibl. M. E. Cosenza, *Francesco Petrarca and the Revolution of Cola di Rienzo* (Chicago, 1913). J. Weider, 'Cola di Rienzo', in F. Seibt (ed.), *Karl IV und sein Kreis* (Lebensbilder zur Geschichte der böhmischen Länder, 3; 1978), pp. 111–44. Popular studies by I. Origo (*Tribune of Rome*, 1938) and V. Fleischer (London, 1938); anonymous novel, with much historical material, by Sir E. Bulwer-Lytton, *Rienzi, the Last of the Tribunes* (3 vols., 1835).

Rievaulx (i.e. Rye Vale), N. Yorks. One of the earliest *Cistercian foundations in England. At the invitation of Thurstan (d. 1140), Abp. of *York, a colony of Cistercians, under Abbot William, was sent by St *Bernard of Clairvaux to England to start a monastery, and in 1131 Walter Espec, who himself joined the community later, provided them with a site about 20 miles N. of York. The abbey was dedicated to the BVM. It soon gained repute as a centre of devotion, learning, and agriculture, and several other foundations such as Melrose sprang from it. By the time of St *Ailred (the 'Bernard of the North'), its third abbot (1147–67), the community numbered 600. Later its importance declined and at the *Dissolution there were only 23 religious beside the abbot. Today the abbey lies in ruins, but the greater part of the exquisite Early English cruciform church remains, with many of the altars *in situ*.

J. C. Atkinson (ed.), *Cartularium Abbatiae de Rievalle* (Surtees Society, 83; 1889). W. *Dugdale, *Monasticon Anglicanum*, 5 (1825 edn.), pp. 274–86. M. J. Parins, 'Rievaulx: the Architecture in its first hundred years', *Studia Monastica*, 22 (1980), pp. 89–99, with refs. T. M. Fallow in *VCH*, York, 3, ed. W. Page (1913), pp. 149–53; W. H. St J. Hope in *VCH*, North Riding, 1, ed. W. Page (1914), pp. 494–502. C. H. Talbot in *NCE* 12 (1967), pp. 494 f., s.v.

Righteousness, Original. See ORIGINAL RIGHTEOUSNESS.

rigorism. In a technical sense the word is used as another name for the system of moral philosophy known as *Tutiorism. Non-technically it is employed to denote the cult of extreme asceticism and self-denial and rigid keeping of the letter of the law, and thus approximates in meaning to *Puritanism and *formalism.

Rijswick Clause. See RYSWICK CLAUSE.

Rimini, Synod of. See ARIMINUM AND SELEUCIA, SYNODS OF.

rings. Of the ring, which is commonly considered an emblem of fidelity, there have been, and still are, several kinds in Christian use:

(1) Early Christian rings. In the 3rd–4th cents. rings with Christian emblems seem to have been often worn in ordinary life.

(2) Episcopal rings. Rings are first mentioned as an official part of a bishop's insignia of office in the early 7th cent., and their use became general in the 9th–10th cents. They were emblematic of the bishop's betrothal to his church. Worn on the third finger of the right hand, they were engraved with a signet and sometimes enclosed relics (e.g. the ring of St *Hugh of Lincoln). Today the bishop's ring is of gold and usually contains an amethyst. Cardinals, abbots, and some abbesses also wear similar rings. In the E. Church rings are not worn by bishops or abbots.

(3) Nuns' rings. In many female orders, e.g. the *Benedictine and *Cistercian, a ring is conferred at solemn profession.

(4) Wedding rings. Originating in the betrothal rings used by the Romans, they were adopted by Christians at an early date, but customs regarding their use have differed widely. In England down to the end of the 16th cent. the bride wore the ring on her right hand; since then it has been worn on the left hand. The custom of wearing it on the third finger is explained by the practice of pronouncing the Trinitarian formula over the thumb and first two fingers, so that the third was reached at the 'Amen' which sealed the marriage rite. The current RC marriage ceremony envisages the use of a ring for both husband and wife, providing forms of blessing for both. In the E. Church both husband and wife are given rings.

(5) The 'Fisherman's Ring' (*anulus piscatoris*). A gold seal-ring which the cardinal camerlengo places on the finger of a new Pope. Engraved on it is St *Peter in a boat fishing (cf. Lk. 5: 10), with the Pope's name round it. The earliest mention of it is in a letter of Clement IV (1265).

Since the 15th cent. it has been used for sealing Papal briefs. At the death of a Pope it is ceremonially broken up by a camerlengo.

(6) The 'Coronation Ring', in England placed by the Abp. of *Canterbury on the fourth finger of the Sovereign's right hand as 'the ensign of Kingly Dignity and of Defence of the Catholic Faith'.

(7) *Rosary rings. These have ten small knobs and are used for saying the rosary. They were in use in the 15th cent. and have been revived in modern times.

Ripalda, Juan Martínez de (1594–1648), *Jesuit theologian. One of the most famous theologians of his time, he taught philosophy at Monforte, theology at Salamanca, and, in the last years of his life, moral theology at the Imperial College at Madrid. His chief work is his treatise on the supernatural, *De Ente Supernaturali* (3 vols., 1634, 1645, and 1648, vol. 3 being mainly an attack on M. *Baius). Among his other published works are an exposition of the *Master of the Sentences, *Brevis Expositio Magistri Sententiarum* (1635), and the posthumous *De Virtutibus Fide, Spe, et Charitate* (1652). Several other treatises, among them 'De Visione Dei', 'De Voluntate Dei', and 'De Praedestinatione', are preserved in MS in the National Library at Salamanca.

A. Arbeloa Egüas, *La doctrina de la predestinación y de la gracia eficaz en Juan Martínez de Ripalda* (Pamplona, 1950); A. Kaiser, *Natur und Gnade im Urstand: Eine Untersuchung der Kontroverse zwischen Michael Bajus und Johannes Martinez de Ripalda* (Münchener Theologische Studien, Abt. 2, Bd. 30; 1965). Sommervogel, 5 (1894), cols. 640–3; Polgár, 3 (1990), p. 505. P. Dumont, SJ, in *DTC* 13 (pt. 2; 1937), cols. 2712–37, s.v.

ripidion. See FAN, LITURGICAL.

Ripon (Lat. *Ad Ripam*). Not long before 661, Ahlfrith, a son of Oswui, King of Northumbria, founded a monastery at Ripon which he peopled with monks from Melrose, but when shortly afterwards he required them to abandon their *Celtic customs and adopt Roman discipline, Eata, the abbot, St *Cuthbert, the guestmaster, and others returned to Melrose, and St *Wilfrid was made abbot (661). In 950 the monastery was destroyed by King Edred (d. 955) in his war with the Danes. It was rebuilt later by Abps. of *York. In the 11th cent. *Augustinian canons raised a new church, dedicated to Sts Peter and Paul, upon the ruins of that of St Wilfrid. This foundation was dissolved by *Henry VIII, but refounded in 1604 as a collegiate church. In 1836 the church became the cathedral of the new diocese of Ripon. Beneath it is the 7th-cent. crypt featuring the small aperture connecting the crypt with an adjacent passage, known as 'St Wilfrid's Needle'.

Primary material ed. J. T. Fowler, *Memorials of the Church of SS Peter and Wilfrid, Ripon* (Surtees Society, 74, 78, 81, and 115; 1881–1908). Id., *Acts of Chapter of the Collegiate Church of SS Peter and Wilfrid, Ripon, A.D. 1452 to A.D. 1506* (ibid. 64; 1875). W. *Dugdale, *Monasticon Anglicanum*, 2 (1819 edn.), pp. 131–3. M. F. Hearn, *Ripon Minster: The Beginning of the Gothic Style in Northern England* (Transactions of the American Philosophical Society, 73, pt. 6; 1983). Bill [i.e. W. A.] Forster and others, *Ripon Cathedral: Its History and Architecture* (York [1993]). G. G. *Scott, 'Ripon Minster', *The Archaeological Journal*, 31 (1874), pp. 309–18. R. L. Poole, 'St. Wilfred and the See of Ripon', *EHR* 34 (1919), pp. 1–24. A. H. Thompson in *VCH*, York, 3, ed. W.

Page (1913), pp. 367–72. G. Crosse in *DECH* (3rd edn., 1948), p. 536, s.v.

Rita of Cascia, St

Rita of Cascia, St (1381–1457), *Augustinian nun. Acc. to her biographers, she was a native of Roccaporena in the Apennines who wished from early childhood to become a nun, but was forced by her parents into marriage. For the next 18 years, despite tyrannical treatment from her husband, she behaved as an exemplary wife and mother. When after his death she sought admission to the Augustinian convent at Cascia, she was at first refused, as a widow, but later, owing (it is related) to supernatural intervention, was received and professed, and lived her last years with great austerity. Her symbol is roses, which are blessed in Augustinian churches on her feast day, 22 May.

There is very little early or reliable information. An Italian Life by A. Cevallucci is tr. into Latin in *AASS*, Mai. V (1694), pp. 224–9, with introd., pp. 223 f., and other material, pp. 230–2. The many popular Lives incl. those by J. Sicardo, AA (Madrid, 1701; modern edn., Naples, 1924), L. Tardi, AA (Foligno, 1805; modern edn., 1925; Eng. tr. by R. Connolly, OSB, 1903), M. J. Corcoran (New York, 1919), A. C. De Romanis, AA (Rome, 1923), and L. Vannutelli, OESA (Perugia, 1925). N. Del Re in *Bibliotheca Sanctorum*, 11 (Rome, 1968), cols. 212–18, with further bibl.

Rites, Congregation of Sacred

Rites, Congregation of Sacred. This Congregation was established by *Sixtus V in 1588 for the purpose of carrying out the decrees of the Council of *Trent with regard to the uniformity of public worship. It was responsible for the direction of the Liturgy of the Latin Church and everything relating to *canonization, *beatification, and the veneration of *relics, as well as for all *faculties, *indulgences, and *dispensations in liturgical matters. In 1930 *Pius XI imposed upon it the duty of correcting and improving liturgical books and established a historical section.

In 1969 the Congregation of Rites was divided into the Congregation for the *Causes of Saints and the Congregation for Divine Worship. The former deals with beatification and canonization procedures and the authentication and preservation of relics; the latter succeeded the *Consilium* set up in 1964 by the Second *Vatican Council for the reform of the liturgy, and liturgical documents are issued under its authority. It has already issued a new *Missal, *Lectionary and *Breviary, and new orders for administering the Sacraments. By the Apostolic Constitution 'Pastor Bonus' of 1988 it is again (as from 1975 to 1984) combined with the Congregation for the Discipline of the Sacraments.

The Decisions of the Congregation of Sacred Rites prior to 1926 are collected in *Decreta Authentica Congregationis Sacrorum Rituum . . . sub Auspiciis SS. Domini Nostri Leonis Papae XIII* (5 vols., Rome, 1898–1901; vols. 1–3, decisions issued from May 1588 to 15 Dec. 1899, nos. 1–4051, with enumeration of older collections in brackets; vol. 4, the 'Instructio Clementina' with comm. by A. Gardellini and further Suffragia and Adnotationes to decrees; vol. 5, index; vol. 6, Appendix I (1912), continuing the decrees to 1911 (nos. 4052–284), with index; and Appendix II (1927), containing the decrees (nos. 4285–404), issued 1912–26; later decrees are published in the *Acta Apostolicae Sedis*). An index of the archives placed in the Bibliothèque Nationale by order of Napoleon I was made by Amedeus Comes de Bourmont and pr. in *Anal. Boll.* 5 (1886), pp. 147–61. F. R. McManus, *The Congregation of Sacred Rites* (Catholic University of America, Canon

Law Studies, 352; 1954). B. Ojetti, SJ, in *CE* 13 (1912), pp. 144 f., s.v. 'Roman Congregations', with bibl.; F. R. McManus in *NCE* 12 (1967), pp. 518 f., s.v. See also works cited under ROMAN CONGREGATIONS and CANONIZATION.

Ritschl, Albrecht

Ritschl, Albrecht (1822–89), German Protestant theologian. He was the son of Georg Karl Benjamin Ritschl (1783–1858), a pastor in Berlin who later became bishop in the Prussian Church of the Union (*Lutheran and *Calvinist) in Stettin, Pomerania. After studying at Bonn, Halle, Heidelberg, and *Tübingen, he was successively extraordinary (1851–9) and full (1859–64) Professor of Theology at Bonn; and then, from 1864 until his death, Professor of Theology at Göttingen.

Ritschl began his career as a disciple of F. C. *Baur and the *Tübingen School (qq.v.), defending in *Das Evangelium Marcions und das kanonische Evangelium des Lukas* (1846) and *Die Entstehung der altkatholischen Kirche* (1st edn., 1850) Baur's thesis of the radical conflict in the primitive Church between Petrinism and Paulinism. But his partial independence of Baur was already clear in his *Entstehung*, and when in 1857 he issued a second edition of this work he had completely abandoned the Tübingen doctrines.

From 1852 onwards Ritschl lectured regularly on 'Systematic Theology'. He insisted on the irreducibility of religion to other forms of experience. We apprehend by faith, not by reason, and this faith rests not on the intellectual apprehension of a series of facts but on the making of value-judgements (*Werturtheile*). To take a concrete instance, the Lord's Divinity is to be understood not as an historical statement of fact but as an expression of the 'revelational-value' (*Offenbarungswert*) of Christ for the community which trusts in Him as God. The theologian will reject all forms of philosophical Idealism as irrelevant to the Christian faith. Ritschl believed that his doctrines were in essence a reaffirmation of the NT message, which, despite their serious endeavours, even the 16th-cent. Reformers did not wholly understand.

Ritschl insisted further that it was to a community, not to individuals, that the Gospel was, and still is, committed. The Church was the immediate subject of Divine revelation and of God's redemptive work. The forgiveness of sins ('justification') is primarily achieved in and through the community for which, in His priestly office and in loyalty to His vocation, Christ died; and the final purpose of God for redeemed man is the moral integration of humanity in the Kingdom of God. The 'faith' by which man receives this gift is totally different from every form of mystical experience, of which Ritschl and his followers showed a deep distrust.

Ritschl elaborated his main conceptions in *Die christliche Lehre von der Rechtfertigung und Versöhnung* (3 vols., 1870–4; Eng. tr. of vol. 1 by J. S. Black, 1872, of vol. 3 ed. H. R. Mackintosh and A. B. Macaulay, 1900). The work exercised an immense influence on the theology of Germany in the latter half of the 19th cent. Of his later writings the two most considerable were *Theologie und Metaphysik* (1881) and *Geschichte des Pietismus* (3 vols., 1880–6).

The so-called 'Ritschlian School' was characterized by its stress on ethics and on the 'community', and by its repudiation of metaphysics and religious experience. Its principal organs were the *Theologische Literaturzeitung*, founded by E. *Schürer in 1876, *Die christliche Welt* (1887 ff.), and the *Zeitschrift für Theologie und Kirche* (1891 ff.). Apart from a more rigidly 'Ritschlian' inner circle, the school counted a great number of important Protestant theologians among its members, among them J. W. M. *Kaftan, W. *Herrmann, F. *Kattenbusch, F. *Loofs, A. *Harnack, and E. *Troeltsch.

There is no collected edn. of Ritschl's works. Eng. tr. by P. Hefner of the 'Prolegomena' to *Geschichte des Pietismus, Theologie und Metaphysik*, and *Unterricht in der christlichen Religion* (pub. 1875), under the title *Three Essays* (Philadelphia [1972]), with introd., pp. 3–50. Life by O. Ritschl (son), 2 vols., Freiburg i.B. and Leipzig, 1892–6. W. Herrmann, *Der evangelische Glaube und die Theologie Albrecht Ritschls* (1890); F. Kattenbusch, *Von Schleiermacher zu Ritschl* (1892; rev. as *Die deutsche evangelische Theologie seit Schleiermacher*, 2 vols., 1926–34). P. Wrzecionko, *Die philosophischen Wurzeln der Theologie Albrecht Ritschls* (1964); P. Hefner, *Faith and the Vitalities of History* (New York, 1966); H. Timm, *Theorie und Praxis in der Theologie Albrecht Ritschls und Wilhelm Herrmanns* (Gütersloh, 1967), esp. pp. 29–88; R. Schäfer, *Ritschl: Grundlinien eines fast verschollenen dogmatischen Systems* (Beiträge zur historischen Theologie, 41; 1968); D. L. Mueller, *An Introduction to the Theology of Albrecht Ritschl* (Philadelphia [1969]); D. W. Lotz, *Ritschl & Luther: A Fresh Perspective on Albrecht Ritschl's Theology in the Light of his Luther Study* (Nashville and New York [1974]); J. Richmond, *Ritschl: A Reappraisal* (1978); H. Kuhlmann, *Die theologische Ethik Albrecht Ritschls* (Beiträge zur evangelischen Theologie, 112; 1992). C. Welch, *Protestant Thought in the Nineteenth Century*, 2 (New Haven, Conn., and London [1985]), esp. pp. 1–30, with bibl. pp. 303 f. O. Ritschl in *PRE* (3rd edn.), 17 (1906), pp. 22–34; R. Schäfer in *TRE*, 29 ('1998'), pp. 220–38.

ritual. Strictly, the prescribed form of words of a liturgical function. By common usage the word is also employed, often in a derogatory sense, of the accompanying ceremonial. In the 19th cent. the term 'Ritualist' was commonly used of those who introduced or reintroduced medieval or modern RC ceremonial practices into the C of E.

Ritual Commission. The Royal Commission created in 1867 to inquire into the differences of ceremonial practice in the C of E. Its appointment followed the creation of a Committee of the *Canterbury Convocation on the subject, set up on the motion of Harvey Goodwin, afterwards Bp. of *Carlisle, early in 1866. Among the Commissioners were Abp. C. T. *Longley, Bp. A. C. *Tait, Bp. S. *Wilberforce, Bp. C. *Thirlwall, Dean R. *Gregory, Dean A. P. *Stanley, and Sir Robert *Phillimore. The Commission published its evidence in four reports issued between 1867 and 1870. The first (1867) confined itself to the question of Eucharistic *vestments; the second (1868) dealt with *incense and lights; the third (1869) was concerned with the *lectionary; and the fourth (1870) dealt with Prayer Book revision and other subjects. The Commissioners were almost unanimous in their wish to forbid the use of vestments, but in the second and fourth reports there were great divergences of opinion. As a general rule, practices which had prevailed in the C of E for the last 300 years were to be the standard of Anglican usage, and the bishop, on receiving complaints relating to any variation from such established use from churchwardens or from five resident parishioners, was to enforce obedience. The proposals met with much criticism, esp. from *High

Churchmen, and failure to bring them into effect led ultimately to the *Public Worship Regulation Act 1874.

The reports, with appendices, are to be found respectively among the Parliamentary Papers, 1867, 20, pp. 719–896 (of the MS pagination of the vols. arranged for the House of Commons) (Cd. 3951); 1868, 38 (whole vol.; Cd. 4016); 1870, 19, pp. 437–59 (C. 17); and 1870, 19, pp. 461–742 (C. 218).

Ritual Masses. The Masses provided in the 1970 Roman Missal for use on the various occasions when Sacraments or other solemn acts are included in the Eucharist, e.g. at *Baptism, *Confirmation, *Ordination, the administration of *Viaticum, weddings, wedding anniversaries, the consecration of virgins, and the renewal of religious *vows. The Ritual Mass may take precedence over the Mass of the Day except on the most important Sundays and festivals. See also NUPTIAL MASS.

Rituale Romanum. The official service book of the Roman Rite, containing the prayers and formulas for the administration of the Sacraments and other liturgical actions of a priest apart from the Mass and the Divine Office. The first edition appeared under *Paul V in 1614; it was enlarged in 1752, revised in 1925, and has recently been under radical revision. The revised rites appeared separately between 1969 and 1976.

Before the pontificate of Paul V, various dioceses had issued their own Rituale. An *editio typica* of the *Rituale Romanum* was issued by Pope *Leo XIII (Ratisbon, 1884). F. A. Zaccaria, *Bibliotheca Ritualis*, 1 (Rome, 1776), pp. 137–60. L. Eisenhofer, *Handbuch der katholischen Liturgik*, 1 (1932), pp. 100–13, and, on the Rituale of the E. Churches, pp. 111–18. A. *Fortescue in *CE* 13 (1912), pp. 88–90, s.v. 'Ritual'; G. Löw, CSSR, in *EC* 10 (1953), cols. 1010–17, s.v. 'Rituale Romanum', with further bibl. On the Rituale of the E. Churches see also J. *Goar, Εὐχολόγιον sive *Rituale Graecorum* (Paris, 1647).

Ritus Servandus. Two liturgical items relating to the traditional RC Latin rite have this title.

(1) The rules about the customs and ceremonial of the Mass which, from the time of *Pius V until recent years, were printed at the beginning of the *Missal ('Ritus Servandus in Celebratione Missae'). It has now been replaced by the 'Instructio Generalis' issued in 1969 and attached to the 1970 Roman Missal.

(2) The book, formerly officially approved by the RC hierarchy in England, containing the directions and prayers for *Benediction of the Blessed Sacrament and certain other non-liturgical services (*Ritus Servandus in Solemni Expositione et Benedictione Sanctissimi Sacramenti*). This has now been replaced by the section of the *Rituale Romanum, *De Sacra Communione et de Cultu Mysterii Eucharistici extra Missam* (1973).

Robber Council of Ephesus (449). See LATROCINIUM.

Robbia, della. See DELLA ROBBIA.

Robert, St (*c.*1027–1111), Abbot of Molesme. A member of a noble family of Champagne, he entered the abbey of Moutier-la-Celle at the age of 15 and later became prior. After 1060 he was appointed abbot of St-Michel-de-Tonnerre, but failed to reform its greatly relaxed discipline and returned to Moutier-la-Celle. After a brief period as prior of St-Aiyoul, some hermits living in the forest of Colan asked to be placed under Robert's direction, and with the approval of the Pope he founded a monastery for them at Molesme (Burgundy) in 1075. The saintly life of its abbot and the original monks caused the house to flourish. But increasing wealth and the influx of unsuitable new members gradually brought about divisions in the community, and in 1098 Robert and several of his monks left Molesme and founded the monastery of *Cîteaux, to be made famous in the following century by St *Bernard of Clairvaux. When 18 months later the monks of Molesme asked to have their abbot back, Robert returned and under his government Molesme became a famous Benedictine centre. Permission for his cultus was granted by *Honorius III in 1222. Feast day, 29 Apr.

The principal authority is a 12th-cent. Life by a monk of Molesme, pr. in *AASS*, Apr. 3 (1675), pp. 668–76; Process of canonization, ibid., pp. 676–8. Life repr. in J. P. Migne, *PL* 157. 1269–94, with three letters, cols. 1293 f. Modern edn. of Life by K. Spahr, S. O. Cist. (Freiburg i.B., 1944), with bibl. M. F. Delehaye, 'Un Moine saint Robert fondateur de Cîteaux', *Collectanea Ordinis Cisterciensium Reformatorum*, 14 (1952), pp. 83–106; J. A. Lefèvre, 'Saint Robert de Molesme dans l'opinion monastique du XIIᵉ et du XIIIᵉ siècle', *Anal. Boll.* 74 (1956), pp. 50–83.

Robert Bellarmine, St. See BELLARMINE, ST ROBERT.

Robert of Holcot. See HOLCOT, ROBERT.

Robert of Melun (d. 1167), Scholastic theologian. An Englishman by birth, he studied at *Paris, where he became the successor of *Abelard at the school on Mont Ste-Geneviève and *John of Salisbury was among his pupils. In 1142 he went to Melun, where he directed a school, and in 1148 took part in the condemnation of *Gilbert de la Porrée at the Synod of *Reims. Recalled to England by Henry II *c*.1160, he was made Bp. of *Hereford in 1163. His works comprise 'Quaestiones de divina pagina', 'Quaestiones de epistolis Pauli' and the unfinished 'Sententiae'. His Trinitarian doctrine, which contradicted that of St *Bernard, came nearer to Abelard and was generally accepted by the 13th-cent. Schoolmen. Acc. to Robert, power is to be esp. attributed to the Father, wisdom to the Son, and goodness to the Holy Spirit, without, however, robbing the other two Persons of the quality predicated in a particular way of the one. Robert had a wide knowledge of the work of his contemporaries, and critically examined certain aspects of the Trinitarian doctrines of Gilbert de la Porrée and his followers, and theses of *Thierry of Chartres that tended to Pantheism. He used every known device of dialectic to maintain a conservative position.

'Quaestiones de divina pagina', 'Quaestiones de epistolis Pauli' and the first Book of the 'Sententiae' ed. R. M. Martin, OP, and R. M. Gallet, OP (SSL 13, 18, 21, 25; 1932–52), with series of arts. by Martin listed in vol. 2 (SSL 18), p. 326, and vol. 3 (pt. 1, SSL 21), p. 315. R. M. Martin, 'L'Œuvre théologique de Robert de Melun', *RHE* 15 (1920), pp. 456–89, with refs. and biog. introd. F. Anders, *Die Christologie des Robert von Melun* (Forschungen zur christlichen Literatur und Dogmengeschichte, 15, Heft 5; 1927). R. P. Nash, SJ, 'The Meaning of *Est* in the *Sentences* (1158–1160) of Robert of Melun', *Mediaeval Studies*, 14 (1952), pp. 129–42. U. Horst, OP, *Die Trinitäts- und Gotteslehre des Robert von Melun* (Walberger Studien des Albertus-Magnus-Akademie. Theologische Reihe, 1; 1964); id., *Gesetz und Evange-*

lium: Das Alte Testament in der Theologie des Robert von Melun (Veröffentlichungen des Grabmann-Institutes, NF 13; 1971). R. P. Nash, SJ, in *NCE* 11 (1967), pp. 533 f., s.v.

Robert of Winchelsea. See WINCHELSEA, ROBERT OF.

Robert, Pierre. See OLIVETAN.

Robertson, Archibald (1853–1931), Bp. of *Exeter. Educated at Trinity College, Oxford, of which he was elected a Fellow in 1876, he became Principal of Hatfield Hall, *Durham (1883–97), and later of *King's College, London (1897–1903). From 1903 to 1916 he was Bp. of Exeter. He was the principal Athanasian scholar of his generation. In 1882 and 1893 he issued editions of the text of the *De Incarnatione*, and in 1892 published the *Select Writings of Athanasius*, based on J. H. *Newman's translations, but with the addition of important prolegomena and notes. His other writings include *Regnum Dei* (1901; *Bampton Lectures).

C. Jenkins in *DNB*, *1931–1940* (1949), pp. 734 f., s.v.

Robertson, Frederick William (1816–1853), 'Robertson of Brighton', Anglican preacher. After abandoning an earlier intention of entering the army, he matriculated in 1837 at Brasenose College, Oxford, to prepare for the ministry. In 1840 he was ordained to a title at *Winchester and in 1842 became curate of Christ Church, Cheltenham. Here he gradually abandoned his earlier *Evangelicalism in favour of a *Broad Church type of theology. In 1846 he was for a short time minister of the English Church at Heidelberg. After returning to England and working for a brief space as rector of St Ebbe's, Oxford, he was appointed in 1847 minister of Trinity Chapel, Brighton, a small *proprietary chapel. Here his influence as a preacher extended far and wide. Though in no sense a scientific theologian, he appealed through his manifest sincerity, his great spiritual insight, and his remarkable capacity for analysing motive and character. He had a powerful influence with the working classes, at that time largely untouched by the C of E, and some of his best lectures were delivered to working men. The opposition he had to face throughout his time at Brighton, largely through his support of the revolutionary ideas of 1848, hastened his early death.

His sermons and lectures were pub. posthumously from shorthand notes: *Sermons Preached at Brighton* (1st and 2nd ser., 1855; 3rd ser., 1857; 4th ser., 1863); *Lectures and Addresses on Literary and Social Topics* (1858); *Expository Lectures on St Paul's Epistles to the Corinthians* (1859). Selection of Sermons in *Everyman's Library*, nos. 37–9 (1906). *Life and Letters*, ed. S. A. *Brooke (2 vols., London, 1865). Other Lives by F. Arnold (ibid., 1886) and H. H. *Henson (ibid., 1915). C. Beardsley, 'Frederick William Robertson of Brighton: Prince of Preachers', in M. J. Kitch (ed.), *Studies in Sussex Church History* (1981), pp. 157–71. R. Garnett in *DNB* 48 (1896), pp. 404–7.

Robertson, William (1721–93), a pivotal figure in the Scottish *Enlightenment. He was ordained in 1744 and came to prominence in the 1750s, when he helped to formulate the policies of the *Moderate party within the Church of Scotland and published the first of his widely acclaimed historical works, the *History of Scotland during the Reigns of Mary and James VI* (1759). Presented to the living of Old Greyfriars, Edinburgh, in 1761, he became principal of the University in the following year, holding both offices until his death. He enhanced his reputation as a philosophical historian with the *History of the Reign of Charles V* (1769) and the *History of America* (1777). As a university administrator he was extremely effective; he gathered a constellation of brilliant scholars and teachers, ended the imposition of religious tests for professors, and inspired the construction of new and impressive buildings. He was largely responsible for the foundation of the Royal Society of Edinburgh (1783). As leader of the General Assembly (1752–80) he helped to revolutionize the government and ethos of the Church. Unlike the leaders of the Popular party, who deplored the operation of the Patronage Act (1712) and supported opposition to it by parishes and presbyteries, Robertson and his friends insisted on obedience to civil and canon law. Their 'Reasons of Dissent' (1752), the manifesto of their emergent Moderate party, persuaded the Assembly to adopt more inflexible policies; conscientious scruples were henceforth disregarded, and dissenting ministers and congregations learned to submit or secede. He also turned his back on the controversial theology of the 17th cent., distrusting dogmatism and Puritanical other-worldliness, and freeing the clergy to contribute to the secular culture of their time. Though the upheavals of the late 18th cent. heralded the passing of his authoritarian and rational world, Scottish religion still bears the impress of his 'enlightened' regime.

Works pub. in 12 vols., London, 1812, incl. the Life by D. Stewart (orig. pub. in 1801). I. D. L. Clark, 'From Protest to Reaction: The Moderate Regime in the Church of Scotland, 1752–1805', in N. T. Phillipson and R. Mitchison (eds.), *Scotland in the Age of Improvement* (Edinburgh, 1970), pp. 200–24. R. B. Sher, *Church and University in the Scottish Enlightenment: The Moderate Literati of Edinburgh* (Princeton, NJ [1985]), *passim*.

Robinson, Henry Wheeler (1872–1945), theologian and OT scholar. Born in Northampton of humble parentage, he was educated for the *Baptist ministry in the universities of Edinburgh and Oxford. After short pastorates at Pitlochry and Coventry, he was appointed in 1906 to the staff of Rawdon Baptist College and quickly made his mark as teacher and writer. From 1920 to 1942 he was Principal of Regent's Park College and was chiefly responsible for its transference from London to Oxford. His main interests were in the fields of OT theology and the doctrines of the Holy Spirit and redemption. Among his principal writings were *The Christian Doctrine of Man* (1911), *The Religious Ideas of the Old Testament* (1913), *The Christian Experience of the Holy Spirit* (1928), *Redemption and Revelation* (1942), and *Inspiration and Revelation in the Old Testament* (1946). A man of wide intellectual interests and deep piety, his influence extended far beyond his own communion.

E. A. Payne (ed.), *Studies in History and Religion Presented to Dr. H. Wheeler Robinson . . . on his Seventieth Birthday* (1942), incl. list of his Works, pp. 254–7. Id., *Henry Wheeler Robinson: A Memoir* (1946). Id. in *DNB*, *1941–1950*, pp. 727–9.

Robinson, John (*c*.1575–1625), pastor to the *Pilgrim Fathers. Very little is known about his early life. He was a native of Lincs or Notts, probably studied at Cambridge, was ordained in the C of E, and seems to have held a curacy at *Norwich. He later became a *Puritan, joining

the 'gathered Church' at Scrooby Manor, Notts. In 1608, owing to severe measures against Nonconformity, Robinson and his congregation were forced to flee to the *Netherlands. In 1609 he settled at *Leiden, of which university he became a member in 1615. From 1617 he interested himself in the project of his Leiden community to emigrate to America, as their strict *Calvinism had brought them into conflict with the *Arminianism of which Leiden was a centre. Though he was prevented from joining the Pilgrim Fathers in the *Mayflower*, he assisted them in their preparations and encouraged them by his letters. He was an able controversialist: in 1610 he published *Justification of Separation from the Church*, and in his *Apologia* (1619) he defended the principles of Congregationalism. He also wrote *A Defence of the Doctrine Propounded by the Synod at Dort* (1624). His *Observations Divine and Moral*, a collection of 62 essays on spiritual and moral subjects, was published posthumously (1625).

Collected edn. of his works, 3 vols., London, 1851, with memoir by R. Ashton in vol. 1, pp. xiii–lxxiv. Modern studies by F. J. Powicke (London [1920]) and W. H. Burgess (ibid., 1920). T. George, *John Robinson and the English Separatist Tradition* (Macon, Ga. [1982]) A. C. Carter, 'John Robinson and the Dutch Reformed Church' *Studies in Church History*, 3, ed. G. J. Cuming (Leiden, 1966), pp. 232–41; S. Brachlow, 'John Robinson and the Lure of Separatism in Pre-Revolutionary England', *Church History*, 50 (1981), pp. 288–301. See also bibl. to CONGREGATIONALISM and SEPARATISTS.

Robinson, John Arthur Thomas (1919–83), Anglican theologian and bishop. Educated at Marlborough and at Jesus College and Westcott House, Cambridge, he was ordained to the parochial ministry but subsequently taught at *Wells Theological College (1948–51), and then was Dean of Clare College (1951–9) and later (1969–83) of Trinity College, Cambridge. In the intervening period he was Suffragan Bishop of Woolwich (1959–69). In 1963 he published a paperback, *Honest to God*, advocating new ways of interpreting traditional Christianity and conceiving the supernatural. It proved a best-seller and, although it deeply disturbed some and caused controversy, it helped many both inside and outside the Church to appreciate the need for a reformulation of religious faith in the light of the contemporary situation. The ideas were largely derived from the writings of P. *Tillich, R. *Bultmann, and D. *Bonhoeffer; the strong impact they made was partly due to the lively and original way in which they were synthesized and to the fact that the writer was a bishop. His more academic writings were mainly concerned with the NT; his study of Pauline theology (*The Body*, 1952) and his *Twelve New Testament Studies* (1962) established his reputation as a learned and original biblical scholar, though his later books, which argue that all the Gospels, incl. Jn., are very early, have not carried widespread conviction. His Hulsean Lectures for 1970 (published as *The Human Face of God*, 1973) revealed his continuing concern with the need to reformulate traditional doctrines, in this case the doctrine of the Incarnation, while *Truth is Two-Eyed* (1979) was an essay in the comparative study of religions; he also wrote on liturgy. His father, Arthur, and two of his uncles (J. Armitage *Robinson and Forbes Robinson) were theologians of an older generation and the influence of their way of thinking has been detected in his very conservative views on the origins of the NT. The radicalism of his other writings should not be exaggerated; he regarded himself as an exponent of historic Christianity.

Life by E. James (London, 1987). D. L. Edwards (ed.), *The Honest to God Debate* (1963). E. James in *DNB, 1982–1985*, pp. 347 f.

Robinson, Joseph Armitage (1858–1933), NT and patristic scholar. Educated at Christ's College, Cambridge, of which he was a Fellow from 1881 to 1899, he was ordained priest in 1882 and devoted himself to patristic studies. In 1891 he founded the series of monographs *Texts and Studies*, in which he edited the *Passion of Perpetua* in the same year. In 1893 he published an edition of *Origen's 'Philocalia'. In 1899 he became a canon, and in 1902 Dean, of *Westminster. In 1903 he published his commentary on *St Paul's Epistle to the Ephesians*, in which he defended the authenticity of the letter. In 1911 he resigned the Deanery of Westminster to become Dean of *Wells. Here he took a lively interest in the cathedral and the early history of the see and wrote *The Saxon Bishops of Wells* (1919) and *St Oswald at Worcester* (1919). In 1920 Robinson published an English translation of the recently recovered 'Apostolic Preaching' of St *Irenaeus and his Donnellan Lectures on *Barnabas, Hermas, and the Didache*, in which he attempted to prove a late date for the *Didache*. His later publications include *The Times of St Dunstan* (1923), which became a standard work. He was one of the Anglican participants in the *Malines Conversations.

Life by T. F. Taylor (Cambridge, 1991). C. Jenkins in *DNB, 1931–1940* (1949), pp. 743–5, s.v.

Roch, St (*c*.1295–1327), also **Rocco** (Ital.), healer of the plague-stricken. Very little is known of his life. Acc. to Francis Diedo, his Venetian biographer (1478), he was a native of Montpellier, who on a journey to Italy stopped at the plague-ridden town of Aquapendente, where he cured many by the sign of the cross. He afterwards performed similar miracles at Cesena, Mantua, Modena, Parma, and elsewhere, himself fell a victim at Piacenza, but recovered and returned to his native city. A miraculous cross is said to have been discovered on his body after his death. He was regularly invoked against the plague, notably in an outbreak in 1414 during the Council of *Constance. In 1485 his relics were moved to Venice, where they are still venerated. There is no sufficient evidence for the *Franciscan tradition that he was a *tertiary of the Order. Feast day, 16 Aug.

AASS, Aug. 3 (1727), pp. 380–415. Life by J. Phelipot, orig. pub. Brescia, 1494, re-ed. by M. Luthard (Paris, etc., 1917), with introd. and notes. Abbé Recluz, *Histoire de saint Roch et de son culte* (Avignon, 1858); G. Ceroni, *San Rocco nella vita, nel culto, nell'arte* (1927); M. Bessodes, *Saint Roch: Histoire et légendes* (Turin and Rome, 1931). A. Fliche, 'Le Problème de saint Roch', *Anal. Boll.* 68 (1950), pp. 343–61, with bibl. M.-T. Schmitz-Eichhoff, *St Rochus: Ikonographische und medizin-historische Studien* (Kölner medizinhistorische Beiträge, 3; 1977). A. P. Frutaz in *EC* 10 (1953), cols. 1054–9, s.v. 'Rocco'.

Rochester (Lat. *Durobrivae* or *Roffa*). This, the oldest and smallest of the suffragan sees of *Canterbury, was founded by St *Augustine, who consecrated St *Justus its first bishop in 604. The cathedral, which was dedicated to

St *Andrew and served in early times by a college of secular canons, was damaged in 676 by the Mercians and later by the Danes. Gundulf (Bp., 1077–1108) began a new cathedral, probably at the request of *Lanfranc, and in 1083 replaced the secular canons with *Benedictines. His nave is the oldest in England, and a fine example of rich and varied Norman work. The cathedral was consecrated in 1130 by the Abp. of Canterbury in the presence of Henry I, but a fire which occurred at the time damaged much of the cathedral and city. In 1343 the choir was rebuilt and a central tower added (replaced 1825–7) out of the offerings at the shrine of 'St William of Rochester' (a baker from Perth who was murdered here *c*.1201, while on pilgrimage; feast day, 23 May). At the *Dissolution, the priory surrendered in 1540; the secular foundation of a dean and six canons (now reduced to four) was established in 1541.

C. Johnson (ed.), *Registrum Hamonis Hethe, Diocesis Roffensis A.D. 1319–1352* (*Canterbury and York Society, 48 and 49; 1948). 'Ernulfi Episcopi Roffensis Collectanea', in H. *Wharton, *Anglia Sacra*, 1 (1691), pp. 329–40; 'Annales Ecclesiae Roffensis, ex Historia Ecclesiastica Edmundi de Hadenham', ibid., pp. 341–55; William de Dene, 'Historia Roffensis ab anno MCCCXIV. ad MCCCL.', ibid., pp. 356–83. T. *Hearne, *Textus Roffensis* (Oxford, 1720; a collection of docs. by Ernulf, many of them relating to the see of Rochester); facsimile of MS ed. P. Sawyer (Early English Manuscripts in Facsimile, 7 and 11; Copenhagen, 1957–62). J. Thorpe and J. Thorpe (son) (eds.), *Registrum Roffense: Or a Collection of Antient Records, Charters, and Instruments of Divers Kinds, necessary for illustrating the Ecclesiastical History and Antiquities of the Diocese and Cathedral Church of Rochester* (1769); J. Thorpe (ed.), *Custumale Roffense* (London, 1788). A. Campbell (ed.), *Charters of Rochester* (Anglo-Saxon Charters, 1; 1973). W. *Dugdale, *Monasticon Anglicanum*, 1 (1817 edn.), pp. 153–88. *The History and Antiquities of the Cathedral Church of Rochester* (anon., ascribed to J. Lewis, but generally supposed to have been written by Dr Rawlinson; 1717). A. I. Pearman, *Rochester* (Diocesan Histories; 1897); W. H. St J. Hope, *The Architectural History of the Cathedral and Monastery of St Andrew at Rochester* (1900). W. N. Yates (ed.), *Faith and Fabric: Rochester Cathedral 604–1994* (Woodbridge, Suffolk, 1996). R. A. L. Smith, 'The Early Community of St. Andrew at Rochester, 604–*c*.1080', *EHR* 60 (1945), pp. 289–99. R. C. Fowler in *VCH, Kent*, 2, ed. W. Page (1926), pp. 121–6. E. M. Blackie in *DECH* (1912), pp. 520–3, s.v.

rochet. A white linen vestment, resembling the *surplice but with tight sleeves, which is worn by bishops and occasionally by other ecclesiastical dignitaries. It is derived from the *alb, and until the 14th cent. was in use outside Rome by all clerics (and even sacristans). The rochet worn by Anglican bishops under the *chimere has wide lawn sleeves. In the 18th cent. these sleeves developed to such balloon-like dimensions that they were commonly detached from the rest of the garment and sewn on to the chimere separately.

Braun, *LG*, pp. 125–35. W. B. Marriott, *Vestiarium Christianum: The Origin and Gradual Development of the Dress of Holy Ministry in the Church* (1868), p. 226.

Rock, Daniel (1799–1871), ecclesiologist and antiquary. He was ordained to the RC priesthood in 1824. He took a keen interest in the English medieval religious ceremonial customs, and his chief work, *The Church of our Fathers* (3 vols. in 4, 1849–53), did much to spread knowledge of them, esp. of the *Sarum Rite. His other well-known work is his *Hierurgia, or the Holy Sacrifice of the Mass* (2 vols., 1833). He took an active part in furthering the restoration of the RC hierarchy in England, and in 1852 he was appointed one of the first canons of *Southwark RC Cathedral.

His *Church of our Fathers* ed. G. W. Hart and W. H. *Frere, CR (4 vols., London, 1903–4), with Life by B. W. Kelly, vol. 1, pp. xvii–xxvi; his *Hierurgia* was also ed. and rev. by W. H. J. Weale ('Catholic Standard Library', 2 vols., 1892).

rococo. A development of *baroque architecture and decoration, which originated in France and lasted from *c.*1715 to 1760. It endeavoured to substitute gracefulness for the dignity of the Louis XIV period, but was often overornate. The name is derived from the French *rocaille* ('shell-work'), the twisted curves of a shell typifying freedom and irregularity.

[S.] F. Kimball, *The Creation of the Rococo* (Philadelphia, 1943). *Rococo: Art and Design in Hogarth's England.* Exhibition Catalogue, Victoria and Albert Museum, ed. M. Snodin (1984).

Rogation Days (Lat. *rogare*, 'ask'). In W. Christendom certain prescribed days of prayer and fasting in the early summer, associated with intercession esp. for the harvest. The 'Major Rogation', which was on 25 April, was a Christianized version of the pagan observance of the 'Robigalia', which took the form of processions through the cornfields to pray for the preservation of the crops from mildew. Historically it had no connection with the Feast of St *Mark, of later institution, also kept on 25 Apr. The 'Minor Rogations' were kept on the Monday, Tuesday, and Wednesday before *Ascension Day. These rogations, which derived from the processional litanies ordered by St *Mamertus of Vienne (*c.*470), when his diocese was troubled by volcanic eruptions, spread through Gaul and later to other places. They are first found at Rome in the *Gregorian Sacramentary. In England they were adopted in 747 by the Council of *Clovesho (can. 16).

The outdoor Rogation processions were suppressed in England in 1547, but under Elizabeth I the Royal *Injunctions of 1559 (no. 19) ordered the perambulation of the parish at Rogationtide and the Second 'Book of *Homilies' contained two homilies for the Rogation Days. The observance is not mentioned in the earlier issues of the BCP. In that of 1662 the three (minor) Rogations (only) were ordered to be observed as 'Days of Fasting and Abstinence'.

In the RC Church the Rogation Days were replaced in 1969 by periods of prayer for the needs of mankind, the fruits of the earth, and the work of men's hands. The observance of these periods, which may be of one or several days' duration and may take place at different times of the year, is decided by conferences of local bishops. Suitable Masses are included in the 1970 Missal.

D. de Bruyne, OSB, 'L'Origine des processions de la chandeleur et des rogations à propos d'un sermon inédit', *R. Bén.* 34 (1922), pp. 14–26, esp. pp. 14–18. W. E. Scudamore in *DCA* 2 (1880), pp. 1809 f., s.v.; H. *Leclercq, OSB, in *DACL* 10 (pt. 2; 1932), cols. 1740 f., s.v. 'Marc (Procession de saint)'; id. ibid. 14 (pt. 2; 1948), cols. 2459–61, s.v. 'Rogations'; P. Siffrin, OSB, in *EC* 10 (1953), cols. 1084–6, s.v. 'Rogazioni'.

Roger Bacon. See BACON, ROGER.

Rogers, John (*c.*1500–55), editor of '*Matthew's Bible' and first British Protestant Martyr under *Mary. Educated at Pembroke Hall, Cambridge, in 1534 he became chaplain to the English merchants in Antwerp. Soon after meeting W. *Tyndale (d. 1536), then engaged on his translation of the Scriptures, he accepted the Protestant faith. In 1537 under the name of 'Thomas Matthew' he published the first complete version of the Bible in English, which was hence known as 'Matthew's Bible' (q.v.). Rogers's own share in it was confined to contributing some valuable prefaces and marginal notes. At about this time he gave evidence of his Protestantism by marrying. His wife was an Antwerp lady, Adriana de Weyden (later Anglicized as 'Pratt'). Having returned to London in 1548, he was given first the living of St Matthew, Friday Street, and then in 1550 the Crown livings of St Margaret Moses and St Sepulchre, all in London; in 1551 he became prebendary, and later divinity lecturer, at *St Paul's Cathedral. For preaching Protestant doctrine at Paul's Cross at the beginning of Mary's reign, he was first confined to his house, and then taken to Newgate prison, where he was kept for a year with J. *Hooper and others. In Jan. 1555 sentence of death was pronounced for denial of the Papal claims and of the Real Presence in the *Eucharist, and he was burnt at Smithfield on 4 Feb.

J. L. Chester, *John Rogers: The Compiler of the First Authorised English Bible; the Pioneer of the English Reformation; and its first Martyr* (1861). The attempt of W. T. Whitley ('Thomas Matthew's Bible', *Church Quarterly Review*, 125 (Oct. 1937), pp. 48–69) to deny that Matthew was an *alias* for John Rogers seems to have failed. Cf. J. F. Mozley, *William Tyndale* (1937), Appendix E, 'Thomas Matthew', pp. 354 f.; H. H. Hutson and H. R. Willoughby, *Decisive Data on Thomas Matthew Problems* [Chicago, 1938], with refs. S. Lee in *DNB* 49 (1897), pp. 126–9.

Rolle of Hampole, Richard (*c.*1300–49), English hermit and spiritual writer. The facts of his life have been much discussed in modern times. According to the account in the office drawn up in view of his (never realized) canonization, he was born at Thornton, near Pickering in N. Yorkshire, and studied at *Oxford under the patronage of Thomas Neville, Archdeacon of Durham. He broke off his studies at the age of 18 to become a hermit, first on the estate of his friend, John Dalton, and later in various other places, where he prayed, wrote, and gave guidance to others. Scholars disagree as to whether or not he studied for a time at the *Sorbonne. His last years were spent near the convent of Cistercian nuns at Hampole, where he died and was buried in 1349. He was held in considerable veneration as late as the 17th cent., when 'Blessed Richard, Confessor and Ermite' was commemorated in martyrologies of 1608 and 1672 (1 Nov. and 20 Jan.).

The canon of Rolle's writings, established by H. E. Allen, contains: (1) scriptural commentaries, incl. the popular commentary in English on the Psalter (some manuscripts of which were interpolated by the *Lollards); (2) Latin treatises, incl. 'Incendium Amoris' and 'Emendatio Vitae' (both later translated into English); (3) English treatises, incl. 'The Form of Living', written for the recluse Margaret Kirkby; and (4) a number of English poems. His authorship of the English 'Meditations on the Passion' is uncertain. His spiritual doctrine is greatly influenced by his own experience, to which he alludes several times. The contemplative life, in his view, begins with the experience of 'the opening of Heaven's door' and is thereafter characterized by 'heat', 'sweetness' and 'angelsong'. He was criticized by some of his contemporaries for teaching an unduly subjective religion. He defended the advantages of the solitary life in extreme and rather polemical terms.

Collections of his Lat. works were pr. at Antwerp, 1533; Cologne, 1535 and 1536; and in M. de la Bigne, *Magna Bibliotheca Veterum Patrum*, 15 (Cologne, 1622), pp. 817–38, and id., *Maxima Bibliotheca Veterum Patrum*, 26 (Lyons, 1677), pp. 609–32. His Comm. on the lessons from Job in the Office of the Dead was pr. at Oxford, 1483, and Paris, 1510. 'Incendium Amoris', ed. M. Deanesly (Publications of the University of Manchester, Historical Series, 26; 1915); 'Canticum Amoris', ed. A. *Wilmart, OSB, in *Revue d'Ascétique et de Mystique*, 21 (1940), pp. 131–48, and ed. G. M. Liegey in *Traditio*, 12 (1956), pp. 369–91; 'Melos Amoris', ed. E. J. F. Arnould (Oxford, 1957; repr., with introd. by F. Vandenbroucke, OSB, SC 168 f.; 1971); 'Contra Amatores Mundi', ed. P. F. Theiner (University of California Publications, English Series, 33; 1968); Comm. on Rev., ed. N. Marzac (Paris, 1968); 'Judica Me Deus' ed. J. P. Daly, SJ (Salzburg Studies in English Literature, Elizabethan & Renaissance Studies, 92. 14; 1984); and 'Tractatus super Psalmum Vicesimum' ed., with Eng. tr., by J. C. Dolan (Texts and Studies in Religion, 57; Lewiston, NY, etc. [1991]). Collections of his Eng. writings ed. G. G. Perry, *English Prose Treatises of Richard Rolle of Hampole* (EETS 20; 1866); C. Horstman (ed.), *Yorkshire Writers: Richard Rolle of Hampole . . . and his Followers* (2 vols., 1895–6); H. E. Allen (ed.), *English Writings of Richard Rolle* (Oxford, 1931; repr., Gloucester, 1988); and S. J. Ogilvie-Thomson (ed.), *Richard Rolle: Prose and Verse* (EETS 293; 1988). Modernized versions by G. E. Hodgson (ed.), *Some Minor Works* (1930), and *The English Writings*, tr. by R. S. Allen (Classics of Western Spirituality, New York, etc. [1988]). H. R. Bramley (ed.), *The Psalter or Psalms of David and Certain Canticles, with a Translation and Exposition in English by Richard Rolle of Hampole* (Oxford, 1884). 'Meditatio de Passione Domini' ed. H. Lindkvist (Skrifter utgifna af K. Humanistiska Vetenskaps-Samfundet i Uppsala, 19, no. 3; 1917).

The principal authority for his life is the office prepared for his canonization, ed. F. Procter, *Breviarium ad Usum Insignis Ecclesie Eboracensis*, 2 (Surtees Society, 75; 1883), Appendix 5, cols. 785–820; crit. edn. by R. M. Woolley (1919). H. E. Allen, *Writings ascribed to Richard Rolle Hermit of Hampole and Materials for his Biography* (Modern Language Association of America Monograph Series, 3; 1927). N. Watson, *Richard Rolle and the Invention of Authority* (Cambridge Studies in Medieval Literature, 13; 1991), with extensive bibl. E. J. F. Arnould, 'Richard Rolle of Hampole', *The Month*, NS 23 (1960), pp. 13–25, repr. in J. Walsh, SJ (ed.), *Pre-Reformation English Spirituality* (1966), pp. 132–44; D. Everett, 'The Middle English Prose Psalter of Richard Rolle of Hampole', *Modern Language Review*, 17 (1922), pp. 217–27, 337–50; 18 (1923), pp. 381–93; M. M. Morgan, 'Versions of the Meditations on the Passion ascribed to Richard Rolle', *Medium Ævum*, 22 (1953), pp. 93–103; G. M. Liegey, 'Richard Rolle's Carmen Prosaicum, an Edition and Commentary', *Mediaeval Studies*, 19 (1957), pp. 15–36; R. Allen, ' "Singuler Lufe": Richard Rolle and the Grammar of Spiritual Ascent', in M. Glasscoe (ed.), *The Medieval Mystical Tradition in England: Papers read at Dartington Hall, July 1984* (Cambridge [1984]), pp. 28–54, and other papers, pp. 55–103. R. Woolf, *The English Religious Lyric in the Middle Ages* (Oxford, 1968), pp. 159–79 and 380–382. W. Riehle, *Studien zur englischen Mystik des Mittelalters unter besonderer Berücksichtigung ihrer Metaphorik* (Anglistische Forschungen, 120; 1977; Eng. tr., 1981), *passim*. J. P. H. Clark, 'Richard Rolle: a theological re-assessment', *Downside Review*, 101 (1983), pp. 108–39. *BRUO* 3 (1959), pp. 1586–7. M. Sargent in *Dict. Sp.* 13 (1988), cols. 572–90, s.v. 'Richard (9) Rolle de Hampole'.

Rolls Chapel. A chapel which once stood on the site of the Public Record Office, London, and from the time of Edward III was annexed to the Keeper of the Rolls ('Custos Rotulorum'). The first chapel (begun in 1233) was part of a foundation by King Henry III for the reception of converted Jews; this was destroyed in the 17th cent. After extensive rebuilding and repairs in the 17th, 18th, and 19th cents., in 1895 it was decided to pull down the crumbling walls of the chapel and erect a museum incorporating any remains of historical value; these include fragments of the 13th cent. chancel arch. J. *Butler held the office of Preacher at the Rolls Chapel from 1718 to 1726 and delivered his famous sermons here. The records (Rolls) of Chancery were formerly kept in the chapel.

H. C. Maxwell Lyte, 'The Rolls Chapel', in *The Fifty-seventh Annual Report of the Deputy-Keeper of the Records* [C. 8271] (1896), pp. 19–47.

Romaine, William (1714–95), *Calvinist preacher. He was educated at Hart Hall (later Hertford College), and *Christ Church, Oxford, and was ordained in 1736. In his early years he followed the scholarly traditions of the C of E, to which he made an important contribution with his edition of the Hebrew Concordance of Marius de Calasio (1748). In 1749 he was appointed lecturer at St Dunstan's-in-the-West and in 1750 at St George's, Hanover Square. In 1755 he came under the influence of G. *Whitefield and became one of the principal representatives of rigid Calvinism. His preaching attracted vast crowds of the poor and uneducated, whose presence in church was resented by his fashionable parishioners, so that he had to give up his lectureships. After holding brief appointments at some other London churches he became incumbent of St Anne's, Blackfriars, in 1766, where his revivalist preaching continued to draw large congregations till his death. He was a powerful preacher; he held an extreme form of predestinationism which he expounded in several writings, e.g. *The Life of Faith* (1763), *The Walk of Faith* (1771), and *The Triumph of Faith* (1795).

Works ed. by his son (8 vols., bound in 4, London, 1796), with Life by W. B. Cadogan in vol. 7, pp. 9–111, and list of Romaine's works, ibid., pp. 112–16. The last three works mentioned in the text were repr., with introd. by P. Toon (Cambridge and London, 1970). A further contemporary Life, emphasizing his part in the Countess of *Huntingdon's Connexion, by T. Haweis (London, 1797). J. C. *Ryle, *The Christian Leaders of the Last Century* (1869), pp. 149–79. H. L. Bennett in *DNB* 49 (1897), pp. 175–7.

'Roman Catechism'. The *Catechismus ex Decreto Concilii Tridentini* (1566) is commonly known as the 'Roman Catechism'. Although a RC counterpart to the Protestant *catechisms was called for at the Council of *Trent as early as 1546, the text was produced only after the end of the Council and issued by Papal authority. It is not a catechism in the ordinary sense of a work arranged in question and answer form; it is a doctrinal exposition of the Creeds, Sacraments, Ten Commandments, and Prayer (incl. the *Lord's Prayer), intended for the use of parish priests. It owed much to earlier suggestions, including the controversial *Comentarios sobre el Catechismo Christiano* (1558) by the *Dominican Bartolomé de Carranza, Abp. of Toledo, which had been attacked by the Spanish *Inquisition, though it was approved by a group of bishops at the Council of Trent. Despite the authority of the Roman Catechism, difficulties over vernacular translations left room for local catechisms.

Crit. edns. of the Roman Catechism by P. Rodríguez, I. Adeva, F. Domingo, R. Lanzetti, and M. Merino (Vatican City and Pamplona, 1989), and of Carranza's *Comentarios* by J. I. Tellechea Idígoras (2 vols., Biblioteca de Autores Cristianos, 1972). Catechism pr. in Mirbt and Aland, pp. 655–93 (nos. 957–1094). P. Paschini, *Il Catechismo Romano del Concilio di Trento: Sue Origini e sua Prima Diffusione* (Lateranum, 1923), repr. in id., *Cinquecento Romano e Riforma Cattolica* (ibid., NS 24; 1958), pp. 33–91. G. [J.] Bellinger, *Der Catechismus Romanus und die Reformation* (Konfessionskundliche und Kontroverstheologische Studien, 27; 1970). P. Rodríguez and R. Lanzetti, *El Catecismo Romano: Fuentes e Historia del Texto y de la Redacción. Bases Críticas para el Estudio Teológico del Catecismo del Concilio de Trento* (Pamplona, 1982). G. J. Bellinger, *Bibliographie des Catechismus Romanus . . . 1566–1978* (Bibliotheca Bibliographica Aureliana, 87; Baden-Baden, 1983).

Roman Catholic Church in England and Wales after the Reformation.

Although there was strong Catholic sentiment in parts of the kingdom and some notable figures, including J. *Fisher and T. *More, were executed rather than agree to the royal *supremacy, the majority of the population acquiesced in the *Reformation of the *Church of England under *Henry VIII and *Edward VI. Legislation provided for the punishment of holders of benefices who refused to use the BCP, but much Catholic practice probably continued and the Papacy gave no clear guidance to Catholics regarding their attitude to the C of E. The restoration of Catholicism under *Mary made promising beginnings, but her early death prevented further progress, and her persecution of the Reformers created a legacy of bitterness which helped to ensure that under *Elizabeth I the breach between the C of E and the Papacy became complete. The distinction between RCs and Anglicans was made clear through the 1559 Act of *Uniformity's imposition of fines on those who failed to attend the services of the C of E, as well as fines and imprisonment on clergy who refused to accept the BCP. Over 400 clergy refused to conform to the Elizabethan settlement and many Catholics continued to practise their faith in secret, but at first there was little persecution. However, the presence of *Mary, Queen of Scots, in England from 1568, the Catholic leadership of the Northern Rebellion of 1569–70, and the excommunication of Elizabeth by *Pius V in 1570 led to a hardening in attitude. The arrival in 1574 of the first of the missionary priests from the Continent, to be followed by *Jesuits from 1580 onwards, strengthened the RC community, but was met with legislation making it treasonable to reconcile any of the Queen's subjects from the established Church, and in 1585 Jesuits and seminary priests were ordered to leave the realm within 40 days under penalty of death. The threat of the Spanish *Armada (1588) reinforced official fears of *recusancy and 189 RCs were executed during the reign of Elizabeth, including most of the *Forty Martyrs canonized in 1970. The foundation of *Douai (1568) was followed by other seminaries in Europe, but many of the missionary priests were at liberty only briefly in England, and their uneven distribution reduced their impact, esp. among the poor. Their training in seminaries throughout Europe, however, enabled the English RC clergy to con-

tribute to and absorb *Counter-Reformation ideals and practices. Nevertheless, disputes between the regular and secular clergy weakened the RC Church in England after the death of Card. W. *Allen in 1594. The appointment by *Clement VIII of an *archpriest (G. *Blackwell) over all the clergy brought into the open controversy about the proper attitude of RCs to the government. This dispute ended only when *Paul V deposed Blackwell for taking the Oath of Allegiance to *James I, an oath imposed in the aftermath of the *Gunpowder Plot (1605).

In the later part of James I's reign, the penal laws against RCs were often not strictly enforced, and their suspension was one of the conditions of *Charles I's marriage to *Henrietta Maria. Another was that she should have free exercise of her religion, and a considerable RC establishment developed around her court. In 1623 William Bishop had been consecrated Bp. of Chalcedon to serve the RCs in England, but his successor retired to France in 1631 and resigned after a dispute with the regular clergy. After the Civil War, in which many of the RC aristocracy and gentry supported the King, the penal laws were revived, but there was in fact a measure of toleration. *Charles II promised toleration in the Declaration of *Breda (1660) and sought to circumvent the legislation against RCs and Protestant Nonconformists by *Declarations of Indulgence in 1662 and 1672. Parliamentary opposition, heightened by the conversion to RCism of his brother, the future *James II, forced Charles to abandon his attempts to secure toleration and rather to accept the *Test Act and other legislation which excluded RCs from office and parliament. The strength of popular anti-Catholic feeling was further demonstrated in the *Exclusion Controversy. When James came to the throne (1685), he at first supported the C of E, while openly professing his personal allegiance to the RC Church. Soon, however, he claimed power to dispense from the provisions of the Test Act and promoted RCs to high office. This policy, culminating in his second Declaration of Indulgence and the Trial of the *Seven Bishops (1688) led to his replacement by William and Mary. The Bill of Rights 1688 and the Act of *Settlement 1700 debarred from the throne any RC or anyone who should marry a RC, and other legislation excluded RCs from the professions. The loyalty of many RCs to the exiled king and his successors in the early 18th cent. accentuated their alienation from the majority of the population.

In 1685 John Leyburn was appointed the first *Vicar Apostolic. Three other Vicars were appointed in 1688 and England and Wales was divided into four districts. This form of episcopal government survived until the restoration of the hierarchy in 1850. The most distinguished 18th-cent. Vicar Apostolic was R. *Challoner, whose *Garden of the Soul* (1740) influenced much subsequent RC piety. From the middle of the 18th cent. there was a shift in the pattern of RC Church life. Whereas previously the houses of the nobility and gentry had been the centres of RC worship, as they declined in number, the great Embassy chapels in London helped to provide for the needs of an expanding urban RC population, and chapels (similar in external appearance to the Dissenting chapels) were built here and in other towns. These last were technically illegal, but little action was taken. At the same time influence was passing from the regular to the secular clergy, and patterns of worship were affected by contemporary English culture. The need to recruit Irish and Scottish clansmen for the American War of Independence prompted the government to negotiate with a body of RC laymen who were ready to profess loyalty to the Crown and restrict Papal authority to spiritual matters; one result was the first *Catholic Relief Act of 1778. Despite the hostility manifested in the *Gordon Riots, subsequent legislation allowed for RC worship and schools (1791), made RCs eligible for commissions in the Army and Navy (1817), and in 1829 removed nearly all disabilities, so that RCs could stand for parliament and most public offices. The sufferings of the RC Church on the Continent as a result of the French Revolution (from 1789) created a degree of sympathy for Catholicism in England unprecedented since the Reformation; many French clergy arrived as refugees, and English religious communities and seminaries returned from abroad. In the 19th cent. the RC population was further increased by Irish immigrants. There were also some converts from the *Oxford Movement, such as J. H. *Newman.

In 1840 the number of Vicars Apostolic was increased from four to eight and ten years later a hierarchy of 12 *suffragan dioceses under an archbishop was established. This so-called '*Papal Aggression' aroused protest, but the *Ecclesiastical Titles Act 1851, which forbade RC bishops to assume territorial titles within the United Kingdom, was a dead letter from the start. N. P. S. *Wiseman was appointed first Abp. of Westminster and made a Cardinal. He introduced into England the *Ultramontanism which was further fostered by his successor, H. E. *Manning. This provoked some resentment among members of the older English RC families, such as Lord *Acton. Italianate devotions gained a foothold in the traditionally restrained worship of English Catholicism. Manning's radical social activity was not continued by Card. H. *Vaughan, who did, however, defend the denominational schools promoted by his two predecessors. He secured the removal of the ban placed by Manning on RC attendance at the Universities and began building *Westminster Cathedral.

Despite the presence in England of leading *Modernists such as F. *von Hügel and G. *Tyrrell, the Modernist crisis disturbed the RC Church here less than on the Continent. In 1908 England and Wales (for which a separate Vicar Apostolic had been appointed in 1895) ceased to be missionary territory, and in 1918 'missions' became legally constituted parishes under the *Codex Iuris Canonici. By 1924 the hierarchy of England and Wales consisted of 4 metropolitan sees (including Cardiff, created an archbishopric in 1916) and 14 suffragan sees. The bishops continued to defend denominational schools and to speak on matters of social justice. Card. A. *Hinsley became something of a national figure through his foundation in 1940 of the '*Sword of the Spirit' and his broadcasts in the early years of the Second World War.

The RC Church has undergone considerable change in the post-war period. In 1945, after a century of growth and consolidation, it was still widely regarded with hostility and had practically no official part in national life, while relations with other Churches in England and Wales were generally frosty. The educational expansion of the years following the 1944 Education Act resulted in a large growth in the numbers of RCs in higher education and the

professions. The Second *Vatican Council (1962–5) drew the whole RC Church into a new relationship with other Churches; dialogues were established, including the *Anglican–Roman Catholic International Commission, and from its inception in 1990 the RC Church in England and Wales has been a full member of the *Council of Churches in Britain and Ireland. The liturgical reforms foreshadowed by the Vatican Council met with some initial resistance from English RCs, but the introduction of the use of the vernacular in the liturgy made the RC Church appear less 'foreign'. After the Council another archdiocese (*Southwark) and four new dioceses were created and the organization of the national Bishops' Conference developed. (There are separate Conferences for Scotland and Ireland.) While here, as elsewhere, there has been a decline in vocations to the priesthood and the religious life, and a drop in Mass attendance since the 1960s, membership of the RC Church in England and Wales has steadily increased (esp. among the middle classes) and now exceeds four million. See also HUME, G. B.

D. Mathew, Catholicism in England: The Portrait of a Minority. Its Culture and Traditions (1936; 3rd edn., 1955); E. [R.] Norman, Roman Catholicism in England from the Elizabethan Settlement to the Second Vatican Council (Oxford, 1985). J. Bossy, The English Catholic Community 1570–1850 (1975); J. C. H. Aveling, The Handle and the Axe: The Catholic Recusants in England from Reformation to Emancipation (1976); A. Walsham, Church Papists: Catholicism, Conformity and Confessional Polemic in Early Modern England (Royal Historical Society Studies in History, 68; Woodbridge, Suffolk, 1993). A. Pritchard, Catholic Loyalism in Elizabethan England (1979); P. Holmes, Resistance and Compromise: The Political Thought of the Elizabethan Catholics (Cambridge, 1982). C. Haydon, Anti-Catholicism in Eighteenth-Century England, c.1740–80 (Manchester, 1993). J. D. Holmes, More Roman than Rome: English Catholicism in the Nineteenth Century (1978); E. R. Norman, The English Catholic Church in the Nineteenth Century (Oxford, 1984). G. A. Beck (ed.), The English Catholics 1850–1950 (1950). A. Hastings, A History of English Christianity 1920–1985 (1986), pp. 131–55, 273–87, 473–90, 561–79, and 630–48; 3rd edn., entitled A History of Christianity in England 1920–1990 (1991), with additional material pp. xix–xxv.
C. M. Hibbard, 'Early Stuart Catholicism: Revisions and Re-Revisions', Journal of Modern History, 52 (1980), pp. 1–34. C. [A.] Haigh, 'The Continuity of Catholicism in the English Reformation', Past and Present, 93 (1981), pp. 37–69, repr. in id. (ed.), The English Reformation Revised (Cambridge, 1987), pp. 176–208; P. McGrath, 'Elizabethan Catholicism: a Reconsideration', JEH 35 (1984), pp. 414–28; further discussion, ibid. 36 (1985), pp. 394–406. J. J. LaRocca, SJ, 'Time, Death and the Next Generation: The Early Elizabethan Recusancy Policy, 1558–1574', Albion, 14 (1982), pp. 103–17; id., ' "Who Can't Pray With Me, Can't Love Me". Toleration and the Early Jacobean Recusant Policy', Journal of British Studies, 23, pt. 2 (1984), pp. 22–36. L. Ward, 'The Treason Act of 1563: A Study of the Enforcement of anti-Catholic Legislation', Parliamentary History, 8 (1989), pp. 289–308. See also works cited under RECUSANCY and WALES, CHRISTIANITY IN.

Roman Catholicism. The term, which denotes the faith and practice of Christians who are in communion with the Pope, is used particularly of Catholicism as it has existed since the Reformation, in contradistinction to Protestant bodies. On its doctrinal side it has been characterized by strict adherence to tradition combined with acceptance of the living voice of the Church, which is held to expound infallibly the revealed truths contained in the deposit of faith. Whereas in the early centuries the Church had to clarify especially the great mysteries of the Trinity and the Incarnation, and in the Middle Ages doctrines concerning the relation of God and man through grace and the sacraments, post-Tridentine theologians have been especially concerned with the structure and prerogatives of the Church, the position of the BVM in the economy of salvation, and the function of the Pope as the Vicar of Christ on earth, culminating in the dogma of *Infallibility promulgated at the First *Vatican Council of 1870. In recent years there has been some reaction against the positions developed at the end of the 19th cent. and an attempt to bring the Church into closer communication with the modern world. This movement is closely connected with the Second *Vatican Council, with its doctrine of the *collegiality of bishops, the use of the vernacular in worship, and a more liberal attitude towards Christians of other denominations.

From an external point of view RCism presents itself as an organized hierarchy of bishops and priests with the Pope at its head. This structure has been built up during a long history and rests its claims on the powers entrusted by Christ to His Apostles in general (Jn. 20: 23) and to St *Peter in particular (Mt. 16: 18 f; Lk. 22: 32; Jn. 21: 15–17), as whose successors the Popes are traditionally regarded. Their supremacy over the Church, though sometimes contested by representatives of the *Conciliar theory and of *Gallicanism, was widely accepted in the W. from early times, as is shown by the appeals to Rome in the *Donatist and *Pelagian controversies of the 4th and 5th cents. Papal supremacy was positively accepted at the Council of *Trent and only slightly modified by the Second Vatican Council, which emphasized the position of the bishops. Acc. to RC teaching this hierarchy represents the Divine authority to whom obedience is due. Supernatural life is normally mediated to individual Christians by members of this hierarchy in the *seven sacraments. The emphasis in recent years on the part of the whole Church and the desirability of the participation of the community, e.g. in the administration of *Baptism, has not altered the essential position of the ordered episcopate and priesthood. An elaborate sacramental theology was developed by the Schoolmen and post-Tridentine theologians, and the sacramental system covers the whole life of RCs. The centre of the liturgical life of RCism is the Mass, which is regarded as a re-presentation of the redeeming work of Christ in His passion, death, and resurrection. Frequency of Communion has been encouraged by modern Popes, esp. *Pius X, and has been made easier by drastic relaxations in the *Eucharistic fast and by the introduction of *Evening Masses. Communion is, however, required only at Easter, and should then be preceded by the Sacrament of *Penance. Attendance at Mass on the other hand is compulsory on all Sundays and *Feasts of Obligation. Other devotions are left to the free choice of individuals and the traditional extra-liturgical exercises, such as *Benediction of the Blessed Sacrament, the *Rosary, and *Stations of the Cross, have recently come to play a less prominent part in RC life than formerly. This development may be partly explained by the introduction of the use of the vernacular in liturgical worship obviating the need for popular services, and more particularly by the increased emphasis on the liturgical life of the whole Church which is reflected not only in the new *Missal and *Breviary but also in the customary arrangement of services at times convenient for those engaged in secular life. The reformed liturgy has laid stress on the centrality of Sunday and drastically reduced the importance of saints' days. At the same time, devotion to the saints has been fostered by the large number of canonizations in modern times, such as those of St *Teresa of Lisieux and the *Forty Martyrs of England and Wales.

The religious life, confined in the Middle Ages to the comparatively few older orders of monks, friars, canons regular, and enclosed nuns, in post-Reformation Catholicism grew both in size and in scope. The most influential of the modern orders is the Society of Jesus (see JESUITS), beside which grew up a multitude of congregations and other associations of both men and women, often pursuing particular aims, such as teaching, nursing and social work. The period since the Second World War has seen the growth of 'lay congregations', such as the 'Little Brothers' and 'Little Sisters' inspired by the ideals of Charles *de Foucauld; they live in small communities in conditions prevailing among the poorest sections of the world, seeking to combine an element of contemplation with the discipline of earning their living, often in industrial society. Since the Second Vatican Council the traditional religious orders have also been undergoing considerable modernization and reform. But, despite all the apparent changes in the outward presentation of the RC faith, and despite the active interest of recent Popes and other RC agencies in social work throughout the world, the primary aim of the RC Church still remains the sanctification of its members and the conversion of souls. See also previous entry.

Introductions by RCs include K. *Adam, *Das Wesen des Katholizismus* (1924; Eng. tr., 1929); P. L. T. G Goyau, *Le Catholicisme* ('Les Religions'; 1931); P. Hughes, *The Faith in Practice: Catholic Doctrine and Life* (1938); T. Corbishley, SJ, *Roman Catholicism* (Hutchinson's University Library, 51; 1950); S. Bullough, OP, *Roman Catholicism* (Penguin, 1963); J. L. McKenzie, SJ, *The Roman Catholic Church* (1969); R. P. McBrien, *Catholicism* (2 vols., 1980; 3rd edn. in 1 vol., 1994). T. M. Gannon (ed.), *World Catholicism in Transition* (New York, etc. [1988]). A. Hastings (ed.), *Modern Catholicism: Vatican II and After* (1991). For works on RCism in England, see previous entry; for the history of the RC Church in other parts of the world, see bibl. to the various countries. For works on RC theology, see bibls. to MORAL THEOLOGY; TRENT, COUNCIL OF; VATICAN COUNCILS, etc. There is also abundant information in *CE*, *DTC*, *L.Th.K.*, *EC*, and *NCE*, also in W. E. Addis and T. Arnold, *A Catholic Dictionary* (1884; 16th edn. by T. B. Scannell and others, 1957), D. Attwater (ed.), *The Catholic Encyclopaedic Dictionary* (1931; rev. edn., 1949), and R. P. McBrien (ed.), *The Harper Collins Encyclopedia of Catholicism* [1995].

Roman Catholic Relief Acts. See CATHOLIC RELIEF ACTS.

Roman Congregations. The executive departments of the Roman *Curia responsible for the ordinary central administration of the RC Church. Established by *Sixtus V in 1588 and reorganized by *Pius X in 1908, their number was originally 14 but it was reduced to 11 in the 1917 *Codex Iuris Canonici* (cans. 242–57). In the complete reorganization of the Curia effected by the Apostolic Constitution 'Regimini Ecclesiae Universae' (15 Aug. 1967), nine congregations emerged, most of them with a modified title and redefined competence. After further changes in 1967, 1975, 1984, and 1988, there are now again nine congregations. The former *Holy Office, now styled *Congregatio de Doctrina Fidei*, still heads the list, with a wide-ranging competence. As formerly, each congregation consists primarily of cardinals under a cardinal-prefect, assisted by a secretary and lesser officials, but since 1967 each has attached to it as full members some diocesan bishops chosen by the Pope from various parts of the world, along with a panel of consultors similarly selected. Major appointments are for a five-year term. The official organ of the Roman Congregations is the *Acta Apostolicae Sedis*. See also CAUSES OF SAINTS, CONGREGATION FOR THE; PROPAGANDA FIDEI, CONGREGATION OF; and RITES, CONGREGATION OF SACRED.

V. Martin, *Les Congrégations romaines* (1930). The Apostolic Constitution 'Regimini Ecclesiae Universae' is pr. in *AAS* 59 (1967), pp. 885–928; that of 'Pastor Bonus' (effecting the changes made in 1988) is pr. ibid. 80 (1988), pp. 841–934. L. L. McReavy, 'The Reorganization of the Roman Curia', *Clergy Review*, 53 (1968), pp. 306–13; R. Ombres, OP, 'The Roman Curia Reorganised', *Priests and People*, 3 (1989), pp. 59–65. The names of the holders of the various posts are recorded in the *Annuario Pontificio*, the official Vatican yearbook. See also works cited s.v. CURIA.

Roman Martyrology (*Martyrologium Romanum*). The official *martyrology of the RC Church. It was compiled by a commission of ten scholars, among them C. *Baronius and A. Agellius (d. 1608), and issued by *Gregory XIII in 1584 to replace the various local adaptations of *Usuard's text current since the later Middle Ages. Several later Popes have subjected it to revisions demanded by the progress in historical knowledge and fresh canonizations. Of these the most radical was that of *Benedict XIV (1748), the principles of which are contained in a prefatory letter to John V, King of Portugal. More recent revisions are due to *Pius IX (1870), *Pius X (1913), and *Benedict XV (1922). A further revision is in progress.

The Roman Martyrology in which are to be found the eulogies of the saints and blessed approved by the Sacred Congregation of Rites up to 1961. An Eng. tr. from the 4th edn. after the Typical Edition (1956) approved by Pope Benedict XV (1922), ed. J. B. O'Connell [1962].

Roman Psalter. The text of the biblical Psalter which was used in all churches in Rome, as well as elsewhere in Italy, down to the time of Pope *Pius V (1566–72), when it was virtually replaced, except at *St Peter's, Rome, by the '*Gallican Psalter' (q.v.). Earlier scholarship equated it with revision of the Latin Psalter which St *Jerome says he compiled hastily ('cursim') on the basis of the *Septuagint. Few scholars now think that the Roman Psalter was produced by Jerome, though he may have used it as a basis for his first attempt to translate the Psalms. See also PSALTER.

Crit. edn. by R. Weber, OSB (Collectanea Biblica Latina, 10; Rome, 1953), with bibl. D. de Bruyne, 'Le Problème du psautier romain', *R. Bén.* 42 (1930), pp. 101–26; A. Allgeier, 'Die erste Psalmenübersetzung des hl. Hieronymus und das Psalterium Romanum', *Biblica*, 12 (1931), pp. 447–82.

Romania, Christianity in. Roman Dacia, which roughly covered the W. parts of present Romania, may have received Christianity through Roman soldiers and colonists by the 4th cent. or earlier, though evidence is scanty. Under Bulgarian rule its ecclesiastical affairs were placed under *Constantinople, and its worship gradually took on an E. character. In the 14th and 15th cent., when the Romanian Principalities stood in the outer line of defence of Europe against the Turks, they retained their national religion and culture. Under Turkish rule Christianity was not proscribed, but under the Phanariot hospodars (1721–1812), the episcopate was generally filled by Greeks, who upheld Greek customs in ecclesiastical matters. In the 19th cent. Romania gradually emerged as an independent state. In 1859 she claimed the independence of her national Church from the metropolitan jurisdiction of Constantinople, and in 1885 this claim was allowed by the *Oecumenical Patriarch and a Holy Synod was constituted. After the First World War (1914–18), Romania's territorial gains included Transylvania, where a *Uniat Church had existed since 1700, and whose large Hungarian and German minorities adhered to the RC, *Lutheran, *Calvinist, and *Unitarian Churches. In the 1923 constitution the Romanian Orthodox Church was recognized as the national Church. In 1935 the National Synod of the Romanian Orthodox Church recognized the Anglican Communion as part of the Catholic Church and its orders as valid.

After the Romanian surrender to Russia in 1944, a new constitution was enacted in 1948. In theory this guaranteed religious freedom and recognized the existence of the Romanian Orthodox Church, but until 1989 the Church was closely controlled by the communist government. Enforced retirement of bishops and other measures ensured that it supported government policy at home and abroad. A renewal movement within the Romanian Orthodox Church, the 'Lord's Army' (*Oastea Domnului*), which began in the 1920s, was legalized in 1989, and is active in schools and social work. All denominations have enjoyed greater freedom since 1989. The RC Church, which had suffered persecution, but whose position had eased earlier in the 1980s, has now received back some of its property. The Uniat Church, which had been forced to join the Orthodox Church in 1948, was legally reconstituted in 1990. *Baptists increased in number in the Communist period and have benefited from the new freedom. The Orthodox Church seeks to identify itself with Romanian nationality, posing a potential threat to other denominations. Ethnic discrimination affects the Hungarian minority in Transylvania, many of whom are Calvinist.

The main lit. is in Romanian. In Eng. there is a brief sketch by M. Beza, *The Rumanian Church* (1943). A. *Fortescue, *The Orthodox Eastern Church* (1907), pp. 328–34; D. Attwater, *The Catholic Eastern Churches* (Milwaukee, Wis. [1935]); id., *The Dissident Eastern Churches* (ibid. [1937]), pp. 110–18, both rev. as *The Christian Churches of the East* (2 vols., London, 1961), 1, pp. 105–11; 2, pp. 87–94. Ş. Meteş, *Istoria bisericii şi a vieţii religioase a românilor din Transilvani şi Ungaria*, 1 [to 1689] (Sibiu, 1935). M. Păcurariu, *Istoria Bisericii Ortodoxe Române* (3 vols., Bucharest, 1980–1). G. Rosu and others, 'Church and State in Romania', in V. Gsovski (ed.), *Church and State Behind the Iron Curtain* (New York, 1955; London, 1956), pp. 253–99. F. Popan and Č. Drašković, *Orthodoxie heute in Rumänien und Jugoslawien* (Vienna, 1960), pp. 9–135. Two books pub. by the Romanian Orthodox

Church: *De la Théologie Orthodoxe Roumaine des origines à nos jours* (Bucharest, 1974), and *The Romanian Orthodox Church yesterday and today* (ibid., 1979). P. Walters (ed.), *World Christianity: Eastern Europe* (Keston Book, 28; Eastbourne, 1988), pp. 247–70. G. K. A. *Bell (ed.), *Documents on Christian Unity*, 3rd ser., 1930–48 (1948), pp. 43–50 (nos. 158 f.). On the general history of the country, N. Iorga, *Histoire des Roumains et de leur civilisation* (Paris, 1920; 2nd edn., Bucharest, 1922; Eng. tr., 1925); R. W. Seton-Watson, *A History of the Roumanians from Roman Times to the Completion of Unity* (1934). M. Lacko in *NCE* 12 (1969), pp. 714–17, s.v.; L. Tautu, ibid., pp. 718–21, s.v. 'Rumanian Rite'.

Romanos, St (*fl. c.*540), 'Melodus' (ὁ μελῳδός), Greek religious poet, the most significant composer of the *kontakion, the metrical sermon chanted to music. A Syrian by birth, he made his way to Constantinople, where he achieved fame. Eighty metrical sermons have come down to us under his name, but not all are genuine. Some of these, like his celebrated *kontakia* 1 *On the Nativity*, 4 *On the Presentation in the Temple*, and 29 *On the Resurrection VI* (ed. Maas and Trypanis), are considered among the masterpieces of world literature. Feast day, 1 Oct.

Crit. edn. of his works by P. Maas and C. A. Trypanis (genuine *Cantica*, Oxford, 1963; *Cantica dubia*, Berlin, 1970). There is a much less satisfactory edn. by N. B. Tomadakes (4 vols. + suppl., Athens, 1952–9). Works also ed., with Fr. tr., by J. Grosdidier de Matons (SC 99, 110, 114, 128, 283; 1964–81). Eng. tr. of works, with comm., by M. Carpenter (2 vols., Columbia, Oh. [1970–3]). J. Grosdidier de Matons, *Romanos le Mélode et les Origines de la Poésie religieuse à Byzance* [1977]. W. L. Pedersen, *The Diatessaron and Ephraem Syrus as Sources of Romanos the Melodist* (CSCO 475, Subsidia, 74; 1985). S. P. Brock, 'From Ephrem to Romanos', in E. A. Livingstone (ed.), *Studia Patristica*, 20 (Louvain, 1989), pp. 139–51. M. Arranz, SJ, in *Dict. Sp.* 13 (1988), cols. 898–908, s.v. 'Romanos le Mélode'.

Romans, Epistle to the. The longest of St *Paul's Epistles and the most systematic. It was dispatched from *Corinth, prob. *c.* AD 58, when Paul was about to leave for *Jerusalem at the close of his 'Third Missionary Journey'; he is now proposing to go on from Jerusalem to *Rome, which he had not previously visited, and then on to *Spain. It is the only Epistle which Paul addressed to believers where he or one of his circle had not founded the Church. He writes as one conscious of his Apostolic commission from Christ, yet deferentially, as 'not wishing to build upon another man's foundation' (15: 20).

After a formal opening, Paul gives an epitome of the Gospel of salvation which he preaches (1: 16 f.). The universality of sin, both in the Gentile world with its idolatry and vice, and among the Jews, who have equally failed to keep the Mosaic law, is argued (1: 18–2: 29), and leads to the conclusion that 'by the works of the law no flesh is justified before God' (3: 20). On the contrary, *justification occurs 'apart from law' (3: 21) by 'the righteousness of God' which is revealed in the Gospel of His Son, whom God 'set forth to be a propitiation [or expiation]' to reconcile sinners to God (3: 25). This free gift is appropriated by faith, acc. to the example of *Abraham (4), whose trust in God, rather than any legal observance, was counted to him for righteousness (Gen. 15: 6). By such faith Christians obtain not only peace with God but also the hope of glory, God's love imparted through the gift of the Holy Spirit, and salvation mediated by the atoning death of Christ, the Second *Adam (5).

Paul next rebuts the objection that in such a situation we might as well continue to sin so that grace might abound. In reply he points to the accepted belief that *Baptism entails (i) a death to sin and a sharing in Christ's death and resurrection, (ii) a transfer, as of a slave, to a new ownership, that is, from sin to righteousness, or (iii), like the death of a spouse, the end of one marriage-bond and the beginning of another (6: 1–7: 4). Lest these analogies might seem to make the law equivalent to sin, he stresses that the law itself is good; it is human weakness which frustrates it. What the law achieves is to bring human sinfulness to light (7: 5–25 and cf. 8: 1–3). It is by the Spirit through Christ that we are freed from sin and the resulting condemnation, and that we walk not by flesh but by the Spirit. The life according to the Spirit, in which as 'joint heirs with Christ' we are led to eternal life, is celebrated in a hymn of confidence in the glory of our redemption (8).

The next section deals with the problem of the destiny of Israel. There is a new situation in which, while salvation is now offered freely also to the Gentiles, most Jews have rejected it. But, as in His dealings with the patriarchs and Pharaoh, God is sovereign in His choice or rejection of whom He will, even though only a remnant of Israel at present responds. Paul also claims that the falling-away of Israel is only temporary, to provide an occasion for the bringing in of the Gentiles, and that we can trustfully await the eventual restoration of 'all Israel' in God's providence (9–11).

Paul now turns to the practical obligations of the Christian life. We are to live not acc. to the fashion of this present world but acc. to the will of God in the unity of the Body of Christ, 'overcoming evil with good' (12). Due obedience must be given to the civil government, for the ruler is a 'minister of God' (13: 1–7). The whole law is summed up in the command to love one's neighbour. All this is the more urgent, as the *Parousia is at hand (13: 8–14). There must be mutual tolerance. Those who do not share the sensitiveness of others about foods and days must respect the consciences of the scrupulous, who in turn must not judge their brothers (14: 1–15: 13).

In the final section Paul treats of his personal plans, conveys his greetings to some 25 named persons, adds yet a word more on unity, and concludes with further greetings, the 'grace', and a doxology (15: 14–16: 27).

The integrity of the text of Romans has been much discussed. There is evidence of one ancient recension which ended at 14: 23 and of another ending at 15: 33, in each case followed immediately by the doxology (16: 25–27). The doxology thus appears in three different places in different MS traditions and in some MSS is lacking altogether; whatever their views on other matters, most scholars reject the Pauline authorship of the doxology. There are also texts which omit the name 'Rome' in 1: 7 and 1: 15. There is no completely satisfactory explanation of the existence of these recensions, but it seems more likely that the short recensions represent abbreviations of the full text rather than that the full text is an expansion of the recensions. A few modern scholars have contended (independently of the textual evidence) that the long list of personal greetings in ch. 16 suggests that this chapter at least was designed for some Church in which Paul had a number of friends (most prob. *Ephesus) rather than

Rome, which he explicitly states (1: 13) that he had never visited.

Why Paul wrote as he did, with far more quotation of the OT than usual, is much discussed. He perhaps envisaged Rome as a base for his planned mission to Spain (cf. 15: 24) and a full account of his strongly contested understanding of the Gospel and some specimens of his moral preaching would help prepare the way for this impending visit. There were both Jewish and Gentile believers in Rome and Paul may have hoped to improve relations between them (15: 7–9). Most importantly he will have wanted some understanding of his law-free Gentile mission as he went to Jerusalem with the collection for the poor, and to possible disaster (15: 25–31). Rom. is best read as a theological defence of his Gospel and mission, conciliatory to Jewish-Christians (unlike Gal.), but maintaining no less strongly that salvation is through faith in Christ, not by observance of *Torah.

Whatever the contingent historical circumstances that led Paul to unfold his message in this way, heavily dependent on scriptural language (notably the Greek Psalter which is quoted 33 times and echoed in the thematic statement of 1: 17), Rom. is a text of primary importance for the Christian theological tradition. Its influence is perhaps already to be traced in other Books of the NT (Eph., 1 Pet., Heb., Jas.) and it is quoted or alluded to by the Fathers from St *Clement of Rome onwards. From the 4th cent. it stood first in the Pauline corpus. From *Origen onwards it has been the subject of many commentaries and its teaching was esp. influential in St *Augustine's anti-*Pelagian works and has profoundly affected the W. Christian outlook on *sin, *grace, *merit, free will, justification, and *predestination. The strong interest of medieval theology in the 'righteousness of God' was intensified among the Reformers and continues in classical Protestantism. Meditation on Rom. 1: 16 f. strongly influenced M. *Luther's conviction of the truth of justification by faith, and J. *Wesley's conversion was also connected with his study of it. K. *Barth's theological revolution originated in his study of this Epistle, and recent attempts at rapprochement with Judaism take their start from Rom. 11. In addition to the religious (cf. Augustine's *Confessions*, 8.29) and theological impact of Paul's rhetoric, his advice at 13: 1–6 has been a force for social and political conversatism, esp. in German *Lutheranism.

The principal Gk. commentators are Origen (whose Comm., written at *Caesarea in his later life, survives, apart from frags., only in *Rufinus' paraphrase) and *Chrysostom (written during his Antiochene years). Lat. commentators incl. *Ambrosiaster, Pelagius, P. *Abelard, and St *Thomas Aquinas. Luther's early lectures on Rom. (1515–16), long thought lost, were pub. in a provisional edn. at Leipzig in 1908; also in the Weimar edn. of his works, vol. 56, 1938 (Eng. tr., Library of Christian Classics, 15; 1961). Important comm. of the Reformation period came from P. *Melanchthon (Nuremberg, 1522, on Rom. and Cor.; more fully on Rom. only, Wittenberg, 1532; enlarged edn., Strasbourg, 1540), H. *Bullinger (Zurich, 1533), and J. *Calvin (Strasbourg, 1540).

For English-speaking students, a new era in the study of Rom. was opened by the comm. of W. *Sanday and A. C. *Headlam (ICC, 1895). The many that have appeared since then incl. those by H. *Lietzmann (Hb. NT, 3, pt. 1; 1906; 3rd edn., 1928), T. *Zahn (Kommentar zum Neuen Testament, 6; Leipzig, 1910), E. Kühl (Leipzig, 1913), M. J. *Lagrange OP, (Études bibliques, 1916), C. H. *Dodd (Moff. Comm., 1932), K. E. *Kirk (Clar.

Bib., 1937), A. Nygren (Stockholm, 1944; Eng. tr., 1952), C. K. Barrett (Black's NT Comm., 1957), O. Michel (KEK, Abt. 4, 10th edn., 1955), F. J. Leenhardt (Neuchâtel, 1957; Eng. tr., 1961), E. Best (Cambridge, 1967), M. Black (New Cent. Bib., 1973), E. Käsemann (Hb. NT, 8a; 1973; Eng. tr., 1980), C. E. B. Cranfield (ICC, new edn., 2 vols., 1975–9), H. Schlier (Herders Theologischer Kommentar zum Neuen Testament, 6; 1977), U. Wilckens (Evangelisch-Katholischer Kommentar zum Neuen Testament, 6; Zurich, 3 parts, 1978–82), J. D. G. Dunn (Word Biblical Comm. 38A–B; Dallas, Tex. [1988]), and J. A. Fitzmyer (Anchor Bible, 33; 1993). K. Barth's comm., *Der Römerbrief* (1918; 2nd edn., 1921; Eng. tr., 1933), often throws flashes of illumination on the Epistle. Other influential studies incl. J C. Becker, *Paul the Apostle: The Triumph of God in Life and Thought* (Philadelphia and Edinburgh, 1980), and E. P. Sanders, *Paul, the Law, and the Jewish People* (Philadelphia [1983]; London, 1985). C. D. Myers in *Anchor Bible Dictionary*, 5 (1992), pp. 816–30, s.v.

Romanticism. The word is used for the movement in literature and art reasserting passion and imagination in reaction from the classicism and rationalism which marked the 18th cent. It is a vague term, and describes a mood or tendency rather than a system. Such a reaction against the *Enlightenment is found first in Germany, among such writers as Goethe, F. *Schlegel, F. D. E. *Schleiermacher, and *Novalis. Its influence spread to other countries and in England can be seen in the work of W. *Blake, W. *Wordsworth, S. T. *Coleridge, P. B. Shelley, and J. Keats, among others, and in France in *Chateaubriand, Victor Hugo, etc.

Romanus, St. A deacon and exorcist of a church of *Caesarea in Palestine, who was martyred at *Antioch (c.304) in the *Diocletianic Persecution. The contemporary account of *Eusebius (*De mart. Pal.* 2) was embellished by later writers. *Prudentius mentions a boy associated with him in martyrdom, whom later tradition, perhaps through some confusion with an authentic Syriac martyr Barlaha or Balaam, names Barulas. The two saints are mentioned together in the *Roman Martyrology. Feast day, 18 Nov.

H. *Delehaye, SJ, 'S. Romain martyr d'Antioche', *Anal. Boll.* 1 (1932), pp. 241–83, with text of sources. On the entry in the Roman Martyrology, id. in *AASS*, Nov. 2 (1931), pp. 650 f. Id., 'S. Barlaam, martyr à Antioche', *Anal. Boll.* 22 (1903), pp. 129–45, with text of 'Passio'. R. Henke, *Studien um Romanushymnus des Prudentius* (Europäische Hochschulschriften, Reihe 15, 27; 1983). J.-M. Sauget in *Bibliotheca Sanctorum*, 11 (1968), cols. 338–42, s.v. 'Romano e Barula'.

Romanus, St, 'Melodus'. See ROMANOS, ST.

Rome (early Christian). An early but not well-grounded tradition asserts that St *Peter reached Rome in AD 42. When the Ep. to the *Romans was written (c. AD 58), a large Christian community already existed at Rome, and *Suetonius almost certainly refers to Christians in *Claud. 25. 4 (*Judaeos impulsore Chresto tumultuantes Roma expulit*). St Paul arrived between AD 59 and 61 (Acts 28: 16) and many scholars hold that his 'Captivity Epistles', as well as Mk., Lk., Acts, and 1 Pet., were written in Rome. The burning of the City under *Nero (AD 64) was a pretext for a general *persecution of the Christians (*Tacitus, *Ann.* 15. 44; I Clem. 6). Ancient tradition held that both St Peter and St Paul were martyred at Rome in the 60s.

There may have been further persecution of Christians under the Emp. Domitian (81–96).

The early Roman bishops, of whom we have exceptionally reliable lists, were all Greek-speaking before *Victor I (c.189) and mostly administrators rather than theologians. In the first two cents. AD the most notable bishops were St *Clement I (c.88–97), author of an Ep. to the Church in Corinth; St *Telesphorus (c.126–36), prob. the only martyr among them; St *Pius I (c.141–54), said by the *Muratorian Canon to be the brother of the *Hermas who was author of 'The Shepherd'; Anicetus (c.155–66), who received St *Polycarp of Smyrna and discussed with him the dating of *Easter; and St Victor I, the first Latin-speaking bishop, whose action in the *Quartodeciman Controversy reflects the growing importance of the see. St *Ignatius of Antioch was martyred at Rome (c.110–17), as also was St *Justin Martyr (c.165). During the 2nd cent. Christians and semi-Christians of the most diverse views (*Tatian, *Hegesippus, *Valentinus and *Marcion) congregated in Rome.

During the early 3rd cent., a number of *Monarchians of varying schools taught in the capital and were opposed by the rigorist theologian, St *Hippolytus. Hippolytus' disputes with St *Callistus (Bp. 217–22) on disciplinary and dogmatic matters led to a serious schism, which continued until the episcopate of Pontian (230–5), when persecution issued in the exile of the leaders of both parties and their consequent reconciliation. During the persecution of *Decius (249–51) St *Fabian (Bp. 236–50) was martyred and the see kept vacant for 13 months. Another rigorist schism, led by the presbyter *Novatian, took place under Fabian's successor, *Cornelius (251–3), who died in exile, acc. to tradition a martyr. *Stephen I, the next Pope (253–7), is known for his controversy with St *Cyprian of Carthage about rebaptism. Persecution began once more under Valerian (253–60), who struck at both the clergy and the property of the Church, and in 258 the Bp., *Sixtus (Xystus) II, and all his deacons, incl. St *Laurence (q.v.), were martyred. Bp. *Dionysius of Rome (259–68) is best remembered for his intervention in a doctrinal dispute in the Church of Alexandria.

By this date the Roman Church was already highly organized. Under Cornelius there were 46 presbyters, seven deacons, and a large number of lesser ministers (*Eusebius, HE 6. 43. 11). The considerable property of the Church included private houses (tituli) in the City for worship and burial-places (*catacombs, q.v.) outside the walls. Both these would be made over to the Church by wealthy Christians who presumably held them in custody for the community. The administration of this property, together with the relief of a large number of poor, fell to the *deacons, each of whom had a district and a staff under him.

Little is recorded of the course taken at Rome of the persecution which broke out under *Diocletian in 303. Bp. Marcellinus (296–304) seems to have handed over copies of the Scriptures, and perhaps even offered incense to the gods; the later account of his being martyred is spurious. The Church's property was certainly confiscated and a number of other Christians fell away. With the accession of the Emp. Maxentius in 306, persecution in the W. ceased. The next two Bps. of Rome, Marcellus (306–8 or 308–9; the dates are disputed) and Eusebius (310) had to face opposition from the lapsed, who wished to be re-admitted to communion with little or no penance. The disorders which arose led to the exile of both bishops and their chief opponent, Heraclius. The re-establishment of the tituli by Marcellus and the return of the Church's property under Bp. *Miltiades (311–14) were the prelude to the grant of full toleration. This was achieved by *Constantine's victory at the *Milvian Bridge (312) and the so-called Edict of *Milan (313).

The period between the middle of the 4th and the end of the 5th cents. saw the steady growth of the authority of the bishops, or Popes, of Rome. They consistently intervened on the orthodox side in the theological disputes of the time. Their characteristics were common sense, firm adherence to traditional belief, distrust of theological niceties, and support of orthodox leaders in adversity, qualities which made appeal to their authority increasingly general. St *Athanasius was welcomed in Rome during his second exile (339–46). *Julius I (337–52) and *Liberius (352–66) upheld the Nicene faith against the *Arians, *Damasus I (366–84) condemned *Apollinarianism, *Innocent I (402–17) *Pelagianism, and *Celestine I (422–32) *Nestorianism, while the '*Tome' of *Leo I (the Great) (440–61), a masterly statement of the orthodox doctrine of the Incarnation, greatly assisted the defeat of *Eutychianism at the Council of *Chalcedon (451).

During this period the disciplinary authority of the Papacy increased steadily despite the exile of Liberius, the intrusion of the antipope Felix, and the tumults which accompanied the elections of Damasus and *Boniface (418–22). The Canons of *Sardica (343) and the legislation of Gratian (Emp., 375–83) and *Theodosius (d. 395) firmly established the Roman see as a court of appeal. The earliest genuine decretal dates from the reign of *Siricius (384–99), and Innocent I and Leo I frequently intervened in the affairs of other Churches.

Meanwhile paganism lingered on among the aristocracy in Rome. Not before 382 was Christian influence sufficiently strong to cause the removal, by Gratian, of the Altar of Victory from the Senate-house; but there soon followed the anti-pagan legislation of Theodosius and the decree of Honorius (408) denying the right of property to the pagan religions. The growth of Christianity in Rome in the period is reflected in the building of churches under Pope *Sylvester (314–35) and his successors (see ROME, CHURCHES OF), the restoration by Pope Damasus of the tombs of the martyrs, the introduction of monastic life by St Athanasius and St *Jerome, and the beginnings of the latter's new Latin version of the Bible (the *Vulgate) at the instance of Damasus.

In political significance Rome suffered greatly after the removal of the capital of the Empire to *Constantinople (330). Even in the W. Milan and later *Ravenna became the effective capitals rather than Rome. In the 5th cent. Italy was invaded by *Alaric, *Attila, and Gaiseric the Vandal king, and Rome was sacked twice before, with the end of the W. Empire, it came under the authority of barbarian rulers in 476. The policy of Odoacer and of *Theodoric was one of tolerance, and a far greater disaster was the long Gothic War (537–53) between the Goths and Byzantines, during which Rome changed hands several times, and at one point was almost completely abandoned by its inhabitants. The partial conquest of Italy by the

Lombards, some of whom were pagan and the rest Arian, and the decline of the Byzantine power, made it necessary for the Popes to assume political authority in Rome. Fortunately for the Papacy, this coincided with the pontificates of the able Pelagius II (579–90) and his greater successor St *Gregory I ('the Great') (590–604). The defence of the 'Roman Duchy' was assured by the Papal policy of holding the balance of power between Byzantines, Lombards, and (later) Franks. Gregory's missionary and pastoral zeal, united with his remarkable statesmanship, make his pontificate one of the outstanding eras in the history of the Papacy. In Rome he founded a monastery on the Celian Hill which gave refuge to monks whose houses had been destroyed in other parts of Italy. He also made important changes in the Roman liturgy and fostered the development of liturgical chant (see SCHOLA CANTORUM). From Rome, he sent St *Augustine to Britain.

Relations between the Papacy and the Byzantine Emperors, the nominal overlords of Rome, deteriorated during the 7th cent. Pope *Martin I (649–55) died a prisoner in exile because of his opposition to *Monothelitism and *Gregory II (715–31) was a prominent opponent of the *Iconoclast Emperor, *Leo III (the Isaurian). We have the beginnings of the Temporal Power of the Papacy in the Donation of Sutri to 'St Peter' (729) by the Lombard King, Liutprand. The growth of the Lombard power led Pope Stephen III (752–7) to appeal in 753 to the Frankish King *Pepin for support and in 773 *Hadrian I (772–95) followed his example with Pepin's son, *Charlemagne. The Frankish intervention led to the destruction of the Lombard kingdom, to the restoration of the Roman Duchy and the Exarchate of Ravenna not to the Byzantine Empire but to the Papacy, and, in 800, to the coronation by St *Leo III (795–816) in Rome of Charlemagne as Roman Emperor.

See also following entry, PATRIMONY OF ST PETER, and under individual Popes.

The most important single early source is the *Liber Pontificalis (q.v.). Much primary material is also to be found in the extant Papal Letters (conveniently catalogued in Jaffé, 1). The subject naturally occupies a place in all histories of the early Church, notably those of L. *Duchesne, P. *Batiffol, H. *Lietzmann, Fliche and Martin, and in C. *Baronius's Annales. Much information also in the earlier vols. of F. *Gregorovius, Geschichte der Stadt Rom im Mittelalter (8 vols., 1859–72; Eng. tr., 8 vols., 1894–1902). H. Grisar, SJ, Geschichte Roms und der Päpste im Mittelalter, 1: Rom beim Ausgang der antiken Welt (14 Lieferungen, [1898–] 1901; Eng. tr., 3 vols., 1911–12). H. Lietzmann, Petrus und Paulus in Rom: Liturgische und archäologische Studien (1915; 2nd edn., 1927). E. Caspar, Geschichte des Papsttums (2 vols., 1930–3). C. Pietri, Roma Christiana: Recherches sur l'Église de Rome, son organisation, sa politique, son idéologie de Miltiade à Sixte III (311–440) (Bibliothèque des Écoles Françaises d'Athènes et de Rome, 224; 2 vols., 1976). R. Krautheimer, Rome: Profile of a City 312–1308 (Princeton, NJ, 1980). On the transition to Medieval Rome, cf. also L. Duchesne, Les Premiers Temps de l'état pontifical, 754–1073 (1898), and T. F. X. Noble, The Republic of St Peter: The Birth of the Papal State, 680–825 (Philadelphia [1984]).

Rome, churches of. From the innumerable Roman churches of historic and ecclesiastical interest, only a selection, necessarily somewhat arbitrary, can be listed in this article. For the four 'Major *Basilicas'—(1) *St Peter's, (2) St John *Lateran, (3) *Santa Maria Maggiore, and (4) *St Paul's outside the Walls—see separate entries.

In addition to these Major Basilicas three further churches (here listed first, nos. 5, 6, and 7) also rank as 'Patriarchal Basilicas'.

(5) S. CROCE IN GERUSALEMME (Basilica Sessoriana). It was founded towards the middle of the 4th cent. within the precincts of an imperial residence (the Sessorian Palace) that had belonged to St *Helena, and endowed with relics of the Passion. Very little of the original building remains except a subterranean chapel and the pillars of the nave. From at least the 8th cent. Popes went barefoot on Good Friday from the Lateran to S. Croce, carrying a relic of the Cross. The church was rebuilt by Lucius II (1144), much restored at the end of the 15th and beginning of the 16th cent., and modernized under *Benedict XIV (1744).

(6) S. LORENZO FUORI LE MURA. In the Cemetery of S. Ciriaco where St *Laurence was buried. The original basilica, already mentioned by *Prudentius (d. c.410), was superseded by a nearby building constructed by Pelagius II (579–90); this in turn was remodelled and extended by *Honorius III (d. 1227), who transferred the façade and porch to the W. end. *Pius IX (d. 7 Feb. 1878) is buried in the crypt. The church was damaged by a bomb on 19 July 1943.

(7) S. SEBASTIANO FUORI LE MURA (4th–5th cent.). On the *Appian Way over the catacombs. The relics of St *Peter and St *Paul were possibly removed here during the Valerianic Persecution (258), and the basilica, built during the first half of the 4th cent., was initially known as the basilica apostolorum [sc. Petri et Pauli] and only later (from the 7th cent.) by the name of St *Sebastian. The present church is mainly the work of Card. Scipio Borghese (1612); it contains, in addition to the reputed remains of the saint, a statue of him designed by G. L. Bernini (1589–1680).

(8) S. AGNESE. On the Via Nomentana, adjoining the catacombs where St *Agnes was buried. The church (now subterranean) has a fine mosaic in the apse depicting St. Agnes between Popes *Symmachus (498–514) and *Honorius I (625–38); the latter was responsible for the present building, which replaced the original, mid 4th-cent. foundation. In a chapel is the shrine of St Emerentiana (feast day, 23 Jan.), Agnes's foster sister. Annually on 21 Jan. the lambs to provide wool for the archiepiscopal *pallia are blessed here. The church is served by *Canons Regular of the Lateran.

(9) S. CLEMENTE. Near the *Colosseum. The present church dates from the 12th cent. (*Paschal II, d. 1118); but excavations begun in 1858 revealed the existence of a much larger church (mentioned by St *Jerome in 392; the scene of a Council in 417) at a lower level, which was severely damaged at the sack of Rome under Robert Guiscard (1084). The latter has some highly interesting 9th–11th cent. mural paintings depicting the legends of Sts *Cyril and Methodius and of St *Clement. The white marble altar canopy, choir screen, and ambones of the present church no doubt belonged to this earlier structure. At a still lower level is a chapel of *Mithras dating from the Imperial Age. The church, with the adjacent priory, is now in the hands of Irish *Dominicans.

(10) SS. Cosmas and Damiano. On the edge of the Forum. One of the first Roman churches to be constructed from public buildings, it consists of a rectangular hall (probably the audience hall of the city prefect, built by Vespasian, d. AD 79) to which a rotunda has been added (perhaps to be identified with a temple of Romulus built by the Emp. Maxentius c.310). It was consecrated as a Christian church by Felix IV (528), who inserted the notable mosaics (subjects from the Apocalypse etc.) and dedicated it to Sts *Cosmas and Damian, the two 'anarguroi' who enjoyed great popularity at Rome in the 6th cent.

(11) S. Francesca Romana (S. Maria Nuova). In the Forum. *Leo IV (d. 855) erected the church, formerly known as Sta Maria Nuova, on a site partly occupied by a ruined Temple of Venus and Rome, to replace the ruined S. Maria Antiqua. The mosaics in the apse date from 1161; the beautiful campanile from the 13th cent. St *Frances of Rome (q.v.), whose labours were centred here, was buried in the church (1440), which was restored by Carlo Maderna (1556–1629) after her canonization (1608). It is served by *Oblates of the Order of St Benedict.

(12) The Gesù. The principal church of the *Jesuits and one of the most ornate in Rome, enshrining the body of St *Ignatius Loyola, their founder. It was built (1568–75) in the *baroque style by Card. Alessandro Farnese (1520–89, nephew of *Paul III) after designs by Vignola and Giacomo della Porta.

(13) SS. Giovanni and Paolo. On the Celian Hill. Built by *Pammachius over the supposed house of the two Roman saints, *John and Paul (4th cent.). Interesting remains of an ancient dwelling (discovered 1887) contain some famous frescoes (Christ between Sts Michael and Gabriel, Sts John and Paul). The church, which with other buildings on the Celian Hill was severely damaged by the Normans in the sack of Rome, was enlarged in 1154. It was extensively restored in the late 17th and early 18th cents. and again in the mid-20th. In a chapel lies the body of St *Paul of the Cross, founder of the *Passionists, who now serve the church.

(14) S. Gregorio Magno. Also on the Celian Hill, close to the site of a monastery established between 575 and 581 by St *Gregory the Great (Pope, 590–604) in his paternal house (gens Anicia) and dedicated to St *Andrew the Apostle. The present church, which claims to possess the stone bed and marble chair of Gregory (himself buried in St Peter's), was constructed in the 12th cent. It was extensively restored by G. B. Soria in 1633 under Card. Borghese and the interior modernized in 1725–34. St Gregory's has close connections with England as the orig. home of St *Augustine of Canterbury and the titular church of Cards. H. E. *Manning and H. *Vaughan, successive Abps. of *Westminster. There are some frescoes by Guido Reni (1574–1642). Since 1573 the church has been served by *Camaldolese.

(15) S. Maria in Ara Coeli (so named since the 14th cent.). On the site of the ancient Roman citadel and the Temple of Juno Moneta. A monastery of 'S. Maria in Capitolio' is already mentioned in the 10th cent.; the present church dates from the 13th and 14th cents. It was here that E. *Gibbon conceived the plan of his Decline and Fall. A chapel in the transept ('Cappella Santa di Sant'Elena')

contains an altar commemorating an early legend, acc. to which a vision of the BVM and the Christ Child on an altar in heaven (ara coeli) was granted to the Emp. Augustus (d. AD 14) when sacrificing. Beneath this altar in a porphyry sarcophagus are the reputed remains of St Helena. The church was the scene of Marcantonio Colonna's solemn thanksgiving for the victory of *Lepanto (5 Oct. 1571). Since c.1250 it has been served by *Franciscans.

(16) S. Maria in Cosmedin (also 'Bocca della Verità'). On the site of an ancient temple, perhaps the 'Temple of Fortune', and in a region formerly inhabited by Greek refugee Christians, it was prob. so named from its beauty (Gk. κοσμέω, 'adorn'; or perhaps from a square named 'Cosmedin' in *Constantinople). The present form of the church results from a 12th-cent. remodelling of a building erected in the time of *Hadrian I (d. 795) and itself based partly on a 6th-cent. structure. Acc. to a late tradition, St *Augustine of Hippo taught at a neighbouring house.

(17) S. Maria ad Martyres (also 'S. Maria Rotonda', the 'Pantheon') was prob. the first pagan temple in Rome to be turned into a Christian church. The foundations go back to a building erected by Marcus Agrippa, son-in-law of the Emp. Augustus, in 27 BC; the present round structure and vaulting are due to Hadrian (d. 138), who rebuilt it after it had been struck by lightning. On 13 May 609 it was dedicated as a Christian church by Boniface IV (608–15) under the name of 'S. Maria ad Martyres', large quantities of relics being brought from the catacombs to mark the event and the Feast of *All Saints (orig. 13 May) instituted. *Urban VIII (Maffeo Barberini) removed the bronze panels from the ceiling of the portico to provide metal for the spiral columns for the baldacchino of St Peter's (hence 'Quod non fecerunt barbari, fecerunt Barberini'). The church contains the tomb of *Raphael.

(18) S. Maria sopra Minerva. On the ruins of an ancient temple of Minerva which later became the site of a Greek monastery. The present church (completed 1453), the only Gothic Church in Rome, was begun c.1280 by Fra Sisto and Fra Ristoro, two *Dominicans, and has been continuously served by members of the Order. It contains statues, frescoes, and paintings by *Michelangelo, Filippino Lippi, Giacomo della Porta, and other famous artists.

(19) S. Pietro in Vincoli (also 'Basilica Eudoxiana'). The church, which may go back to c.400, was rebuilt as the titulus apostolorum by Sixtus III (432–40) and received the reputed chains of St Peter. At around the same time, or shortly afterwards, it was the object of a pious benefaction by the Empress Eudoxia, wife of Valentinian III. Among its monuments are the celebrated *Moses of Michelangelo, a relief of *Nicholas of Cusa, and the tomb of *Julius II (1503–13). It is served by Canons Regular of the Lateran.

(20) S. Prassede. On the Esquiline. The present church, which contains the reputed remains of St *Praxedes and St *Pudentiana, was built by Paschal I (817–24) near an earlier church of the same dedication. A chapel near the W. end contains some furniture which belonged to St *Charles Borromeo, titular Card. of this church. The 9th-cent. mosaics, among the best in Rome, depict subjects from the Apocalypse. A column in the chapel of St *Zeno

is traditionally reckoned that to which Christ was bound. The church, which is served by *Vallumbrosans, inspired R. Browning's 'Tomb at St Praxed's'.

(21) S. PUDENZIANA. Near the foot of the Esquiline. It is traditionally believed to have been founded on the site of the mansion of the senator, Pudens, whose daughters, Praxedes and Pudentiana, are said to have given it to *Pius I (d. 154?). Excavations have revealed the remains of a 2nd-cent. house and adjacent bath building; the latter was converted into a Christian church in the time of *Siricius (d. 395). The apse has a fine early mosaic (c.400, but much restored; incl. Christ enthroned with the Apostles, and two female figures, prob. representing the Jewish and Gentile Churches). A table in the church is venerated as that on which St Peter celebrated Mass.

(22) SS. QUATTRO CORONATI. On the Celian Hill. Perhaps as early as the 4th cent. a church (titulus Aemilianae) existed on or near the site; this was later rebuilt, incorporating the walls of a large secular reception hall, and was dedicated to the *Quattro Coronati whose bodies it enshrines. After its destruction by Robert Guiscard (1084), it was rebuilt in 1111 by Paschal II, who reduced its size. It is served by *Capuchins.

(23) S. SABINA. On the Aventine. Founded by an Illyrian priest, Petrus, during the pontificate of *Celestine I (423–32), it is one of the most impressive Roman basilicas (admirably restored in the first half of the 20th cent.). It contains a fine series of columns of Proconnesian marble and, between the vestibule and nave, a large wooden door (5th–6th cent.) with a series of remarkable wood-carvings (incl. a very early Crucifixion). The church has been served by Dominicans since the time of *Honorius III (d. 1227).

(24) S. STEFANO ROTONDO. On the Celian Hill not far from the Lateran. It was built by Pope *Simplicius (468–83), decorated with marbles in the 6th cent., and adorned with mosaics (Christ above a jewelled cross; Sts Primus and Felicianus, martyrs from the age of the Persecution of Diocletian) in the 7th cent. Under Innocent II (1130–43) a third outside circle of pillars was demolished and the church correspondingly reduced in size; but it is said to be still the largest circular church in existence. It contains an ancient episcopal throne from which St Gregory I (d. 604) delivered one of his homilies.

M. Armellini, Le chiese di Roma dalle loro origini fino al secolo XVI (1887; new edn., continuing history to 19th cent., ed. C. Cecchelli, 2 vols., 1942). O. *Marucchi, Basiliques et églises de Rome (1902). J. P. Kirsch, Die römischen Titelkirchen im Altertum (Studien zur Geschichte und Kultur des Altertums, 9, Hefte 1–2; 1918). Id., Die Stationskirchen des Missale Romanum (Ecclesia Orans, 19; 1926). C. Hülsen, Le chiese di Roma nel medio evo: Cataloghi ed appunti (1927). F. X. Zimmermann, Die Kirchen Roms (1935). R. Krautheimer and others, Corpus Basilicarum Christianarum Romae (Monumenti d'Antichità cristiana pubblicati dal Pontificio Istituto di Archeologia Cristiana, 2nd ser. 2; 5 vols., 1937–77). R. Vielliard, Recherches sur les origines de la Rome chrétienne: Les Églises romaines et leur rôle dans l'histoire et la topographie de la ville depuis la fin du monde antique jusqu'à la formation de l'état pontifical (Mâcon, 1941; repr. with illustrations, Rome, 1959). É. Mâle, Rome et ses vieilles églises ([1942]; Eng. tr., 1960). F. W. Deichmann, Frühchristliche Kirchen in Rom (Basle, 1948). C. G. Paluzzi (ed.), Roma cristiana; vol. 2: P. Testini, Le catacombe e gli antichi cimiteri cristiani in Roma [1966]; vol. 3: G. Matthiae, Le chiese di Roma dal IV al X secolo [1962]; vol. 4: V. Golzio and G. Zander, Le chiese di Roma dall'XI al XVI secolo [1963]; vol. 5: V. Mariani, Le chiese di Roma dal XVII al XVIII secolo [1963]; vol. 6: C. Cheschi, Le chiese di Roma dagli inizi del neoclassico al 1961 [1963]; vol. 7: M. Dejonge, Roma Santuario Mariano [1969]. H. Brandenburg, Roms frühchristliche Basiliken des 4. Jahrhunderts (Munich, 1979). R. Krautheimer, Rome: Profile of a City, 312–1308 (Princeton, NJ, 1980), passim. J. Wilpert, Die römische Mosaiken und Malereien kirchlicher Bauten vom IV. bis XIII. Jahrhundert (4 vols., 1916); section on mosaics rev. by W. N. Schumacher, Die römischen Mosaiken der kirchlichen Bauten vom IV.–XIII. Jahrhundert (1976). Popular surveys in Eng. by E. Hutton, Rome (1909; 7th edn., 1950); R. Thynne, The Churches of Rome (1924); R. Lanciani, Wanderings through Ancient Roman Churches (1925); and R. Beny and P. Gunn, The Churches of Rome (1981). U. Benigni in CE 13 (1912), pp. 164–79, s.v. 'Rome', esp. pp. 169–75; E. Josi in EC 10 (1953), cols. 1208–45, s.v. 'Roma V: topografia'.

Romero, Oscar Arnulfo (1917–80), Abp. of San Salvador. He was born into a poor family at Ciudad Barrios in El Salvador. When he was 12 years old his non-believing father arranged for him to be apprenticed as a carpenter, but through the intervention of a visiting priest he was accepted for a seminary and at the age of 18 he went to the *Gregorianum in Rome. Ordained priest in 1942, he was made an auxiliary bishop in 1970 (to his predecessor as Abp, Luis Chávez). At this stage he had a member of *Opus Dei as a confessor and in 1972, when he took charge of the country's national theological seminary, he attempted to reverse many of the liberalizing changes that had taken place under the previous *Jesuit management. In 1974 he was appointed a diocesan as Bp. of Santiago de María, an area that included his home town. Even as late as 1976 he was still attacking *Liberation Theology as expounded by Jon Sobrino, SJ, the country's leading theologian, and it was thus as a noted conservative that he was appointed Abp. of San Salvador in 1977. But, partly as a result of the murder of his friend, Fr. Rutilio Grande, and partly because of the general polarization caused by the worsening situation in the country, he soon espoused the principles of Liberation Theology and became an opponent of the then dictator of El Salvador, also called Romero. While the majority of the clergy supported him and his broadcast sermons attracted large audiences, all but one of his fellow bishops opposed him. Among his more controversial acts were the use of a single archdiocesan Mass as a form of protest and two apparent exceptions to his normal advocacy of peaceful means of opposition, his agreement to conduct a public funeral for one of his priests, generally acknowledged to have been a terrorist (Ernesto Barrera), and the endorsement in his fourth pastoral letter of proportionate counter-violence. After the overthrow of his namesake he tried to negotiate between the three main factions in the country, but he was assassinated on 24 Mar. 1980 while celebrating Mass at the Divine Providence (cancer) Hospital in San Salvador.

Four Pastoral Letters and other statements were pub. as La Voz de los sin voz (San Salvador, 1980; Eng. tr., Maryknoll, NY, 1985), with introd. essays by I. Martín Baró and J. Sobrino. P. Erdozaín, Monseñor Romero: Mártir de la Iglesia Popular (San Jose, 1980; Eng. tr., 1981). J. R. Brockman, The World Remains: A Life of Oscar Romero (Maryknoll, NY, and London, 1982).

Romuald, St (c.950–1027), founder of the *Camaldolese Order. A nobleman of *Ravenna, he entered the abbey of

Sant'Apollinare in Classe through horror at his father's having killed a man in a duel. In 998 he was appointed abbot, but the life not proving sufficiently severe, he resigned in the next year and retired to the neighbouring marshes to practise rigid asceticism. In his later years he wandered round Italy, founding hermitages and monasteries, that at Campus Malduli becoming the centre of the Camaldolese Order. Feast day, formerly 7 Feb., now 19 June.

Frag. of exposition on Ps. 68 attrib. to Romuald in J. P. Migne, *PL* 140. 1125–8. Life by St *Peter Damian (*c.*1040); repr. from A. *Mai's edn. of Damian's works in J. P. Migne, op. cit., 144. 953–1008; and ed. G. Tabacco (Fonti per la Storia d'Italia, 94; 1957). F. M. da Napoli, O. Camald., *Delle notizie storiche della vita di San Romoaldo* (Naples, 1716). B. Collina, *Vita di San Romualdo, fondatore della religione camaldolese* (2 pts., Bologna, 1752). W. Franke, *Quellen und Chronologie zur Geschichte Romualdo von Camaldoli und seiner Einsiedlergenossenschaften im Zeitalter Ottos III* (Diss., Halle, 1910); id., *Romuald von Camaldoli und seine Reformtätigkeit zur Zeit Ottos III* (Historische Studien, 107; 1913). Modern Lives by A. Pagnani (Sassoferrato, 1927; 2nd edn., 1967) and T. Ciampelli (Ravenna, 1927). J. Leclercq, OSB, 'Saint Romuald et le monachisme missionnaire', *R. Bén.* 72 (1962), pp. 307–23. G. Tabacco, 'Romualdo di Ravenna e gli inizi dell'eremitismo camaldolese', *L'eremitismo in occidente nei secoli XI e XII* (Miscellanea del Centro di Studi Medioevali, 4; Pubblicazioni dell'Università Cattolica del Sacro Cuore, Contributi, Serie Terza, Varia, 4 [1965]), pp. 73–119. L. A. St L. Toke in *CE* 13 (1912), p. 179. G. Tabacco and P. Cannata in *Bibliotheca Sanctorum*, 11 (1968), cols. 365–84, s.v.

Roncalli, Angelo Giuseppe. See JOHN XXIII.

'Root and Branch'.

An expression originally taken from the wording of the London Petition of 11 Dec. 1640 (itself modelled on Mal. 4: 1) in which it was demanded 'that the said government [i.e. the episcopal system] with all its dependencies, roots, and branches, be abolished'. The petition thus became known as the Root and Branch Petition, and the bill of 1641 embodying its demands the Root and Branch Bill; and the expression hence came to be applied to any thoroughgoing policy.

Ropes, James Hardy

(1866–1933), NT scholar. Born at Salem, Mass., he was educated at Harvard and Andover and in Germany. From 1903 until his death he was a professor at Harvard University. His principal writings were *Die Sprüche Jesu* (Texte und Untersuchungen, 14. 2; 1896), an edition of the uncanonical sayings of Christ; a Commentary on the Ep. of St James (ICC, 1916); and an edition of the texts (based on *Codex Vaticanus and *Codex Bezae) of the Acts of the Apostles (*Beginnings of Christianity*, ed. F. J. Foakes-Jackson and K. *Lake, vol. 3; 1926).

E. C. Moore in *Dict. Amer. Biog.* 16 (1935), pp. 151 f.

rosary.

A form of prayer in which 15 *decades of *Hail Marys are recited, each decade being preceded by the *Lord's Prayer and followed by the *Gloria Patri; the prayers are counted on a string of beads or sometimes on a ring. Each decade is accompanied by meditation on one of a sequence of *Mysteries running from the *Annunciation of the BVM. Usually only five decades (the so-called *chaplet) or less are recited at a time. The practice of saying a prayer a set number of times, often with some device to help keep count, is attested in early Christian monasticism. In the E. it developed into the '*Jesus Prayer'. In the W. at first the dominant equivalent was the repeated recitation of the Lord's Prayer which came to be seen as equivalent to the recitation of the Psalter for people who could not read. In the 12th–13th cent. some people began adding or substituting Hail Marys; 150 Hail Marys came to be known as the Marian Psalter, recited whole or in part. The development of the cycle of meditations owes much to the *Carthusians in Trier in the early 15th cent.; they influenced the *Dominican Alain de la Roche (*c.* 1428–75), who used this devotion to revive the Dominican Confraternity of the BVM. The tradition that the BVM gave the rosary to St *Dominic as a weapon against the *Albigensian heresy derives from revelations which Alain claimed to have received. The rosary was propagated by the establishment of rosary confraternities, which were increasingly under Dominican control; in 1559 *Pius V gave the Dominican Master General exclusive control over them. As a consequence, until 1984 the blessing of rosaries came to be reserved to Dominicans or priests having special faculties. Besides the Dominican rosary, there are various other forms. The *Servite rosary, for instance, has seven sections in memory of the *Seven Sorrows of the BVM, each consisting of the Lord's Prayer and seven Hail Marys; it apparently dates from the 17th cent. and was approved by the General Chapter of the Servites in 1646. The feast of the BVM of the Rosary on 7 Oct. was instituted by *Pius V in 1572 in memory of the Christian victory over the Turks at *Lepanto (1571); in 1573 it was moved to the first Sunday in Oct., but in the present RC calendar it has returned to 7 Oct. See also FRATERNITIES.

J. M. Larroca, OP (ed.), *Acta Sanctae Sedis necnon Magistrorum et Capitulorum Generalium Sacri Ordinis Praedicatorum pro Societate SS. Rosarii* (2 vols. in 4, Lyons, 1890–91). E. Wilkins, *The Rose-Garden Game: The Symbolic Background to the European Prayer-Beads* (1969). G. G. Meersseman and G. P. Pacini, *Ordo Fraternitatis: Confraternite e pietà dei laici nel medioevo* (Italia Sacra, 24–6; Rome 1977), pp. 1144–232. K. J. Klinkhammer, SJ, *Adolf von Essen und seine Werke: Der Rosenkranz in der geschichtlichen Situation seiner Entstehung und in seinem bleibendem Anliegen* (Frankfurter Theologische Studien, 13; 1972). On the Servite rosary, *Corona dell'Addolorata*, issued by the General Curia of the Servites (Rome, 1986; Eng. tr., *Rosary of our Lady of Sorrows*, Chicago, 1986). W. A. Hinnebusch, OP, in *NCE* 12 (1967), pp. 667–70, s.v.; A. Duval, OP, in *Dict. Sp.* 13 (1988), cols. 937–80, s.v. 'Rosaire'.

Roscelin

(d. 1125), *Scholastic philosopher and theologian. The facts of his life are very imperfectly known. Probably a native of Compiègne, he studied at Soissons and *Reims. He was accused of *Tritheism at a Council at Soissons *c.*1092, but denied having taught it and went to England, where his doctrines were opposed by St *Anselm. After his return to France he taught at Loches, Besançon, and Tours (where he held canonries), his most famous pupil being P. *Abelard, who attacked his teaching *c.*1120.

Roscelin's theories have been known principally through the works of his opponents Anselm, Abelard, and *John of Salisbury. He was one of the first and most outstanding defenders of *Nominalism. He stressed that universal terms were *voces*, claiming to establish that a being can have no parts. These philosophical tenets led him to identify the three Persons of the Trinity as distinct things (*res*), on the consideration that if they were identical in substance, the Father and the Holy Spirit would have become incarnate together with the Son.

His letter to Abelard ed. J. A. Schmeller in *Abh.* (Bayr.), 5 (Heft 3; 1849), pp. 189–210; repr. in J. P. Migne, *PL* 178. 357–72; crit. edn. by J. Reiners, *Der Nominalismus in der Frühscholastik* (BGPM 8, Heft 5; 1910), pp. 62–80, with discussion of his position, pp. 25–41. Two essays on the Trinity and a Psalm comm. are attributed to him by C. J. Mews, 'Nominalism and Theology before Abaelard: New Light on Roscelin of Compiègne', *Vivarium*, 30 (1992), pp. 5–37. Letter from Walter of Honnecourt to Roscelin ed. G. *Morin, OSB, *R. Bén.* 22 (1905), pp. 172–5. F. Picavet, *Roscelin, philosophe et théologien, d'après la légende et d'après l'histoire* (École pratique des Hautes Études. Section des sciences religieuses. Rapports annuels, 1896; greatly enlarged edn., 1911). M.-M. Gorce, OP, in *DTC* 13 (pt. 2; 1937), cols. 2911–15, s.v.

Rose of Lima, St (1586–1617), the first canonized saint of America. She lived all her life in Lima, Peru, and from childhood practised the severest austerities. In her 20th year she joined the *Third Order of St *Dominic. A vow of virginity and her strictness of life incurred persecution from her family and friends, and she also suffered intensely from interior desolation. Long sickness and early death crowned her self-sought mortifications. She was canonized by Clement X in 1671 and is the Patroness of S. America and the *Philippines. Feast day, 23 Aug.

AASS, Aug. 5 (1741), pp. 892–1029, incl. text of Life by L. Hansen, OP, pr. at Louvain, 1668, pp. 902–84, and bull of canonization, pp. 1027–9. Short Life by J. B. Feuillet (Paris, 1671; Eng. tr. in *The Lives of St Rose of Lima, the Blessed Columba*, etc., ed. F. W. *Faber, London, 1847, pp. 3–195). M. T. de Bussierre, *Le Pérou et sainte Rose de Lima* (1863); F. M. Capes, *The Flower of the New World: Being a Short History of St Rose of Lima* (1899); R. Vargas Ugarte, SJ, *Vida de Santa Rosa de Santa María* (Lima, 1951). F. Parkinson Keyes, *The Rose and the Lily* (1962), pp. 55–138.

Rose, Golden. See GOLDEN ROSE.

Rose, Hugh James (1795–1838), pre-*Tractarian Anglican High Churchman. He was educated at Trinity College, Cambridge, and after ordination as priest in 1819 held the vicarage of Horsham, W. Sussex, from 1821 to 1830, and of Hadleigh, Suffolk, from 1830 to 1833. A year's absence in Germany from May 1824 bore fruit in *The State of the Protestant Religion in Germany* (1825), warning of the dangers of contemporary rationalism in German theology and attributing this to laxity in relation to creeds and Church formularies and the absence of episcopacy having an authoritative teaching office. It provoked a reply from E. B. *Pusey, who in his early years was more sympathetically disposed than later towards German theology. Rose responded to Pusey in *A Letter to the Lord Bishop of London* (1829). In 1832 he founded the *British Magazine* to further High Church doctrines. A meeting in July 1833 in his rectory at Hadleigh, attended by W. *Palmer (of Worcester College), A. P. *Perceval, and R. H. *Froude, was an important landmark in the beginnings of the Tractarian Movement. Later Rose became somewhat more critical of the Tractarian ideals. In 1833–4 he held the chair of divinity at *Durham University and

in 1836 he was appointed Principal of *King's College, London.

J. W. *Burgon, *The Lives of Twelve Good Men*, 1 (1888), pp. 116–283 (no. 2: 'The Restorer of the Old Paths'). J. M. Rigg in *DNB* 49 (1897), pp. 240–2. See also bibl. to OXFORD MOVEMENT.

Rosetta Stone, the celebrated basalt stele which provided J. F. Champollion (1790–1832) and others with the key to the Egyptian hieroglyphics. Discovered in 1799 by a party of French soldiers in the neighbourhood of Rosetta on the W. bank of the western mouth of the Nile, it records in Egyptian (both hieroglyphic and demotic) and in Greek a decree of the priests assembled at Memphis in favour of Ptolemy V Epiphanes, dated 27 March 196 BC. At the fall of *Alexandria in 1801 it passed into the hands of the British Government and is now in the British Museum. The interpretation of the demotic text was mainly the work of Thomas Young (1773–1829), who published his conclusions in 1815.

E. A. W. Budge, *The Rosetta Stone and the Decipherment of Egyptian Hieroglyphs* (1929), with Gk., Demotic, and Egyptian texts, Eng. trs., and full bibl. Popular booklet by C. Andrews, *The Rosetta Stone* [1981]. H.-J. Thissen in W. Helck and W. Westendorf (eds.), *Lexikon der Ägyptologie*, 5 (1984), cols. 310 f., s.v. 'Rosette, Stein von', with bibl.

Rosicrucians. The name assumed by certain secret societies similar to the *Freemasons, who venerated the emblems of the Rose (or perhaps the Dew, *ros*) and the Cross as twin symbols of the Lord's Resurrection and Redemption. Early in the 17th cent. two anonymous writings, the so-called 'Rosicrucian Manifestos' were published in Germany, the *Fama Fraternitatis* (1614) and the *Confessio Fraternitatis* (1615). They were followed in 1616 by the *Chymische Hochzeit Christiani Rosenkreutz*, now ascribed to the *Lutheran pastor J. V. Andreae (1586–1654), to whom the earlier works are also sometimes attributed. The ideas in these writings derive from the occult philosophy of the British mathematician and astrologer John Dee (1527–1608), as expressed in his *Monas hieroglyphica* (1654). The *Chymische Hochzeit* narrates the fabulous story of a certain Christian Rosenkreutz, who, having learned the wisdom of the Arabs in the E., became the founder of a secret society devoted to the study of the hidden things of nature and an esoteric and anti-catholic kind of Christianity, which acc. to the author was still in existence. The books were taken seriously and aroused a very wide interest. A flood of literature about the mysterious society followed, and the curiosity kindled was so great that even men like R. *Descartes and G. W. *Leibniz tried in vain to get into touch with its genuine members, while a number of new societies with alchemistic tendencies actually came into being under their influence. The best-known English representative of these tendencies was Robert Fludd (1574–1637), a London physician who spread Rosicrucian ideas in a number of medico-theosophical books. In the 18th cent. the name 'Gold- und Rosenkreuzer' ('Gold- and Rosicrucians') was adopted by a society started in Vienna which, spreading rapidly through Germany, Russia, and Poland, received only Freemasons of the master grade and generally followed masonic ideas. One of its most famous members was the Prussian minister, J. C. von Wöllner (1732–1800), through whom Rosicrucian ideas exercised a strong influence on Friedrich Wilhelm II of Prussia; but this society became extinct before the end of the 18th century.

The *Fama Fraternititis, Confessio Fraternitatis*, and *Chymische Hochzeit*, ed., with introd., by R. van Dülmen (Quellen und Forschungen zur Württembergischen Kirchengeschichte, 6; 1973). Fr. tr. of these works, with introd., by B. Gorceix, *La Bible des Rose-Croix* (1970). F. A. Yates, *The Rosicrucian Enlightenment* (1972), with Eng. tr. of the 'Manifestos', pp. 238–60 (and bibl. note, pp. 235–8). Most other lit. is uncritical, being mainly the work of authors of Rosicrucian leanings or profession, incl.: A. E. Waite, *The Real History of the Rosicrucians* (1887), with refs. to earlier Eng. lit.; id., *The Brotherhood of the Rosy Cross* (1924); W. E. Peuckert, *Die Rosenkreutzer: Zur Geschichte einer Reformation* (1928); and P. Arnold, *Histoire des Rose-Croix et les origines de la Franc-Maçonnerie* (1955); id., *La Rose-Croix et ses rapports avec la Franc-Maçonnerie* (1970). R. Kienast, *Johann Valentin Andreae und die vier echten Rosenkreutzer-Schriften* (Palaestra, 152; 1926); J. W. Montgomery, *Cross and Crucible: John Valentin Andreae (1586–1654), Phoenix of the Theologians* (International Archives of the History of Ideas, 55; 2 vols., Leiden, 1973), incl. photographic repr. of (1690) Eng. tr. of *Chymische Hochzeit*, vol. 2, pp. 288–486. A. C. Jones in *HERE* 10 (1918), pp. 856–8, s.v., with bibl.; H. Hermelink in *PRE* (3rd edn.), 17 (1906), pp. 150–6, s.v. 'Rosenkreuzer'.

Rosmini-Serbati, Antonio (1797–1855),

Italian philosopher and founder of the 'Institute of Charity'. Born at Rovereto of a noble family, he studied at Padua and was ordained priest in 1821. With the aid of Pius VIII, *Gregory XVI, and *Pius IX, he undertook the renewal of Italian philosophy, beginning with the systematic study of St *Thomas Aquinas, a translation of whose *Summa Theologiae* he had attempted in 1819. Following a suggestion of the Bl. Maddalena di Canossa, the foundress of a society of Daughters of Charity, he established, in 1828, his congregation of the 'Fathers of Charity' (see ROSMINIANS), without, however, relaxing his efforts to construct a satisfying philosophical synthesis. His first and most important work, *Nuovo saggio sull'origine delle idee*, appeared in 1830 and was supplemented by *Il rinnovamento della filosofia in Italia* in 1836. Through his attack on *Probabilism in his *Trattato della coscienza morale* (1839) he incurred the hostility of the *Jesuits, and in the following years was repeatedly accused of *Jansenist and *pantheistic teaching. In 1848 he proposed ecclesiastical reforms in the *Costituzione secondo la giusticia sociale*, which, along with his *Cinque piaghe della Chiesa*, was condemned by the Congregation of the *Index in 1849. Rosmini submitted at once and retired to Stresa, where, a year before his death, he had the satisfaction of seeing his works, which had been denounced to the Index in their entirety, returned with a *dimittantur*, i.e. without censure. After his death, however, and esp. after the posthumous publication of his voluminous synthesis *La teosofia* (5 vols., 1859–74), the accusations against his teaching continued and a second examination of his works resulted in a mild condemnation of 40 propositions by *Leo XIII in 1887–8. The cause for the beatification was opened in 1994.

Rosmini's system, which is a form of Idealism, is founded on the leading idea of indeterminate being, innate in the human soul. If analysed this idea divides itself into a plurality of other ideas which are identical with those that are in the mind of God. Rosmini distinguished between degrees of being acc. to their completeness, God alone being absolutely complete. The being, however, which actualizes finite nature and which is the object of human intuition, is 'something of God', though not God Himself. Among the 40 condemned propositions were several on this metaphysical doctrine of the idea. Others related to the mystery of the *Trinity, which Rosmini thought capable of rational explanation, to *transubstantiation, and to *Original Sin, which he seems to have believed to be only a physical infection of the human flesh.

His influence, though negligible outside Italy, was considerable in his own country. A number of periodicals were founded after his death with the object of defending his teaching, and A. Manzoni, M. Minghetti, and G. Cavour were among those who came under his influence.

Edizione Nazionale of Rosmini's *Opere edite e inedite* (49 vols., Rome, 1934–77); new crit. edn. by the Istituto di Studi Filosofici, Rome, and the Centro (Internazionale) di Studi Rosminiana, Stresa (ibid., 1979 ff.). Works tr. into Eng. incl. Eng. trs. by D. Cleary and T. Watson, of *Cinque piage della Chiesa* as *The Five Wounds of the Church* (Leominster, 1987); of *Nuovo saggio sull'origine delle idee*, vol. 2 (abridged) as *The Origin of Thought* (ibid., 1987) and vol. 3 as *Certainty* (Durham [1991]); of *Principi della scienze morali* as *Principles of Ethics* (Leominster, 1988); of *Antropologia in servizio della scienza morale* as *Anthropology as an Aid to Moral Science* (Durham [1991]); and *Filosofia del Diretto*, 1, as *The Philosophy of Right* (ibid. [1993 ff.]). For his correspondence, *Epistolario completo* (13 vols., Cassale Monferrato, 1887–94); Eng. tr. of *A Selection of Ascetical Letters* by J. Morris, Inst.Ch. (Loughborough, 1993 ff.). Lives incl. those by G. B. Pagani (2 vols., Turin, 1880–4; Eng. tr., 1907; and the anonymous Life which he pub. as *La vita di Antonio Rosmini scritta da un sacerdote dell'Istituto della Carità*, 2 vols., ibid., 1897, rev. by G. Rossi, 2 vols., Rovereto, 1959), G. S. Macwalter (vol. 1 only, London, 1883) and W. Lockhart (2 vols. [vol. 1 being a reissue of the previous item without the author's name], London, 1886), B. Brunello (Milan, 1941), and C. Leetham (London, 1957). A. Luciani [*John Paul I], *L'Origine dell'anima umana secondo Antonio Rosmini* (Rome diss., 1950; 2nd edn., Padua, 1958). F. Evain, *Être et Personne chez Antonio Rosmini* (Bibliothèque des Archives de Philosophie, NS 32; 1981). B. M. G. Reardon, *Religion in the Age of Romanticism* (Cambridge, 1985), pp. 156–75. Bibl. by C. Bergamaschi (2 vols., Milan, 1967). G. Bozzetti in *EC* 10 (1953), cols. 1359–71, s.v.; F. Évain in *Dict. Sp.* 13 (1988), cols. 987–91, s.v.

Rosminians,

the 'Fathers of Charity'. The congregation was founded by A. *Rosmini in 1828 and formally approved by *Gregory XVI in 1838. Its chief aim is the sanctification of its members, combined with such works of charity as they may be called upon to perform, e.g. teaching, preaching, popular missions, and literary activities. There are the two grades of presbyters and coadjutors, the presbyters taking a special fourth vow of obedience to the Pope; and persons living in the world may be affiliated to the Institute. The congregation, which was introduced into England by A. Gentili in 1835, now has houses in Italy, England, Ireland, America, Tanzania, New Zealand, and Venezuela. The women's branch of the congregation, the 'Sisters of Providence', was founded in 1831–2 and has houses in Italy, England, Tanzania, and Venezuela; they devote themselves esp. to the instruction of converts.

Modern edn. of Rosmini's *Constitutions* by A. Valle (Stresa, 1974). Eng. tr., from Latin MS, by D. Cleary and T. Watson (Durham [1989]). C. J. Emery, IC, *The Rosminians* (1960). C. R. Leetham, IC, in *NCE* 12 (1967), p. 679, s.v.; C. Riva, IC, in *DIP* 5 (1978), cols. 133–6, s.v. 'Istituto della Carità'; A. Franchi, ibid.

7 (1983), cols. 1091–3, s.v. 'Provvidenza (Rosminiane), Suore della'. See also Lives of ROSMINI-SERBATI, A., cited s.v.

Rossetti, Christina Georgina

Rossetti, Christina Georgina (1830–94), poetess. She was a younger sister of M. F. *Rossetti and D. G. *Rossetti, and closely associated with the Pre-Raphaelite Brotherhood. The first of her poems to be published (some had been privately printed earlier) appeared in the *Germ* (1850), the organ of the Brotherhood, under the pseudonym of 'Ellen Alleyne'. Marked by great beauty and care in the selection of words and pervaded by a deep melancholy (not, as is sometimes asserted, morbidity), they are the expression of a strong Christian faith. Besides those dealing with definitely religious subjects, many give expression to the agonies that come from disappointed love. She also wrote a number of religious books, among them *Seek and Find* (1879) and *Time Flies, a Reading Diary* (1885). Her hymns include 'What are these that glow from afar?' and the well-known carol 'In the bleak mid-winter'.

Poetical Works ed. with memoir and notes by W. M. Rossetti, brother (London, 1904; memoir, pp. xlv–lxxi); Variorum edn. of *Poems* by R. W. Crump (3 vols., Baton Rouge, La., and London [1979–90]). *Family Letters*, ed. W. M. Rossetti (London, 1908). Further letters in J. C. Troxell (ed.), *Three Rossettis: Unpublished Letters to and from Dante Gabriel, Christina, William* (Cambridge, Mass., 1937), esp. pp. 138–80, and in L. M. Packer (ed.), *The Rossetti–Macmillan Letters: Some 133 Unpublished Letters written to Alexander Macmillan, F. S. Ellis, and Others, by Dante Gabriel, Christina, and William Michael Rossetti, 1861–1889* (Berkeley, Calif., and Cambridge, 1963). Brief memoir by E. A. Proctor (London, 1895); much fuller Life by M. Bell (ibid., 1898). Modern studies by L. M. Packer (Berkeley, Calif., and Cambridge, 1963) and [E.] G. Battiscombe (London, 1981). D. A. Kent (ed.), *The Achievement of Christina Rossetti* (1987). R. Garnett in *DNB* 49 (1897), pp. 282–4. Further bibl. by W. E. Fredeman in *NCBEL* 3 (1969), cols. 496–500. See also bibl. to following entry.

Rossetti, Dante Gabriel

Rossetti, Dante Gabriel (1828–82), English Pre-Raphaelite poet and painter. He was for a short time a pupil of Ford Madox Brown, and with J. E. Millais, Holman *Hunt, and T. Woolner founded the Pre-Raphaelite Brotherhood in 1848. In 1860 he married Elizabeth Siddal, whose death in 1862 marked a turning-point in his life. The principal influence of Rossetti's early years was *Dante, whom he began to translate in 1845. In his own poetry of this period Christian themes abound, and his ideal of womanhood is expressed by the BVM and Beatrix. Among his poems of this period are 'Ave', a beautiful prayer to the Blessed Virgin, the well-known 'The Blessed Damozel' (1847) with its Dantesque conception of heaven, and the weird 'Sister Helen' (1850–1), characteristic of his love for mystery and magic. Of his paintings *The Girlhood of Mary Virgin* (1849), and *Ecce Ancilla Domini* (1850), both in the Tate Gallery, London, recall something of the spiritual beauty of medieval pictures, but this simplicity is lacking in most of his work, including the triptych *The Seed of David* in *Llandaff Cathedral and *Beata Beatrix* (c.1863–70; Tate Gallery, London). In the second period, from c.1863 to his death, religious motives disappear, and the inherent sensuality of his poetry and art, which now came more and more to the fore, brought upon him the charge of being a 'fleshly poet'. The eroticism of these years was coupled with a pessimistic outlook

on life and an intensified interest in its morbid aspects which comes out, e.g., in his poem 'Rose Mary'.

Collected Works [prose and poetry], ed. W. M. Rossetti, brother (2 vols., London, 1886; enlarged edn., 1911); *Family Letters*, ed. id. (2 vols., ibid., 1895), with memoir as vol. 1. Further material in id. (ed.), *Præraphaelite Diaries and Letters* (1900), esp. pp. 3–47 ('Some Early Correspondence of Dante Gabriel Rossetti'), and id., *Rossetti Family Papers, 1862 to 1870* (1903). Modern edn. of *Letters* by O. Doughty and J. R. Wahl (5 vols., Oxford, 1965 ff.). L. M. Packer (ed.), *The Rossetti–Macmillan Letters: Some 133 Unpublished Letters written to Alexander Macmillan, F. S. Ellis, and William Michael Rossetti, 1861–1889* (Berkeley, Calif., and Cambridge, 1963). Correspondence of D. G. Rossetti and J. Morris, ed. J. Bryson and J. C. Troxell (Oxford, 1976). W. M. Rossetti, *Dante Gabriel Rossetti as Designer and Painter* (1889). W. Sharp, *Dante Gabriel Rossetti: A Record and a Study* (1882); T. H. Caine, *Recollections of Dante Gabriel Rossetti* (1882; fuller edn., 1928). Later general studies incl. those of A. C. Benson ('English Men of Letters', 1904), E. Waugh (London, 1928), R. L. Mégroz (ibid., 1928), O. Doughty, *A Victorian Romantic* (London, 1949; 2nd edn., 1960), H. R. Angeli (niece; ibid., 1949), and R. G. Grylls (ibid., 1946). [L.] J. Rees, *The Poetry of Dante Gabriel Rossetti: Modes of Self-Expression* (Cambridge, 1981); D. G. Riede, *Dante Gabriel Rossetti and the Limits of Victorian Vision* (Ithaca, NY, and London, 1983). Works dealing specifically with his art, incl. reproductions, by H. C. Marillier (London, 1899) and V. Surtees, *The Paintings and Drawings of Dante Gabriel Rossetti (1828–1882): A Catalogue raisonné* (2 vols., incl. plates, Oxford, 1971). J. Savarit, *Tendances mystiques et ésotériques chez Dante-Gabriel Rossetti* (1961). G. H. Fleming, *Rossetti and the Pre-Raphaelite Brotherhood* (1967). W. E. Fredeman, *Pre-Raphaelitism: A Bibliocritical Study* (Cambridge, Mass., 1965), pp. 90–132; id. in *NCBEL* 3 (1969), cols. 490–96.

Rossetti, Maria Francesca

Rossetti, Maria Francesca (1827–76), Anglican religious. The eldest of the Rossetti family, she was, in the opinion of her agnostic brother William (W. M.), 'more warmly and spontaneously devotional than any person I have ever known'. Feeling herself free from domestic responsibilities on his marriage in 1874, she joined the sisterhood of All Saints', Margaret Street, London, but died shortly afterwards. In 1871 she published *A Shadow of Dante*.

The principal sources are W. M. Rossetti's Lives of C. G. and D. G. Rossetti, cited s.vv. R. D. Waller, *The Rossetti Family, 1824–1854* (Manchester, 1932), pp. 171–80. See also other works cited in the two previous entries.

Rosvitha

Rosvitha. See HROSVIT.

Rosy Sequence

Rosy Sequence. A part of the hymn '*Jesu, dulcis memoria' (q.v.), used as a sequence for the Feast of the *Name of Jesus in the *Sarum Gradual. A form of the hymn in 50 stanzas was formerly used as a kind of *rosary in five decades.

Rota Romana

Rota Romana. The normal RC appeal tribunal for judging cases brought before the *Holy See. It dates from the reorganization of the Papal administration by *John XXII in 1331 and derives from the *audientia sacri palatii* and other judicial arrangements employed to decide causes by the Papacy since the 12th cent. Its name appears to derive from the circular table used by the judges at *Avignon. Its power was at a maximum in the 15th and 16th cents., but under Pope *Gregory XVI its duties were restricted, and with the cessation of the temporal power of the Papacy in 1870 they almost ended altogether. In its present form it was created by *Pius X in 1908 by the Apostolic Constitution 'Sapienti Consilio'; since then it has been reorganized a number of times, notable changes being introduced with the new Norms of 18 Apr. 1994. Basically it is the court of appeal for all ecclesiastical cases first heard in the diocesan and other courts and then coming under the Roman *Curia, unless they are reserved for others. It also deals with ecclesiastical appeal cases in the *Vatican City state. In addition it judges at first instance cases reserved to the Holy See or set aside by the Pope. The judges, who are known as auditors (*auditores*) and form a college, must be priests who are at least doctors in civil and canon law. The President is called the 'Dean' and is *primus inter pares*. It is prob. best known as the court to which certain *nullity of marriage cases are referred.

Its decisions for various periods from the mid-14th cent. onwards survive in MSS and pr. collections; cf. J. H. Baker, 'Dr. Thomas Fastolf and the History of Law Reporting', *Cambridge Law Journal*, 45 (1986), pp. 84–96. Modern decisions are reported, until recently after an interval of 10 years now of 5 years, in *S. Romanae Rotae Decisiones seu Sententiae* (Rome, 1912 ff.). The Norms issued by *John Paul II in 1994 are pr. in *AAS* 86 (1994), pp. 508–40; the Rota is also governed by *CIC* (1983), cans. 1405 and 1443–4. D. Bernini, *Il tribunale della S. Rota Romana* (1717). E. Schneider, *Die römische Rota nach geltendem Recht auf geschichtlicher Grundlage*, 1. Die Verfassung der Rota (all pub. Görres-Gesellschaft. Veröffentlichungen der Sektion für Rechts- und Sozialwissenschaft, 22; 1914), with bibl. to date. E. Cerchiari, *Capellani Papae et Apostolicae Sedis Auditores Causarum Sacri Palatii Apostolici seu Sacra Romana Rota ab Origine ad diem usque 20 Septembris 1870: Relatio historica-juridica* (4 vols., Rome, 1919–21). E. Schneider, 'Über den Ursprung und die Bedeutung des Namens *Rota* als Bezeichnung für den obersten päpstlichen Gerichtshof', *RQ* 41 (1933), pp. 29–43, with further refs. C. Lefebvre in *DDC* 7 (1965), cols. 742–71, s.v. 'Rote Romaine (Tribunal de la Sainte)', with bibl.; E. A. Fusin in *NCE* 12 (1967), pp. 683–5, s.v. See also works cited s.v. CURIA.

Rothe, Richard

Rothe, Richard (1799–1867), *Lutheran theologian. He taught successively at *Wittenberg (from 1828), Bonn (from 1849), and Heidelberg (from 1854). A disciple of F. D. E. *Schleiermacher and J. A. W. *Neander, he combined a devout and even pietistic spirit with a keenly critical and historical sense. He emphasized the inseparable relation between religion and morals in his great work *Theologische Ethik* (3 vols., 1845–8; 2nd edn., 5 vols., 1867–71). He also wrote a book on the beginnings of the Christian Church (1837). He is best known in Britain by his *Stille Stunden* (1872), a collection of devotional essays and reflections translated under the title *Still Hours* (1886).

Several treatises, based on Rothe's unpub. papers, were issued posthumously. There is a brief sketch by J. Macpherson prefixed to Rothe's *Still Hours* (Eng. tr. by J. T. Stoddart, 1886), pp. 9–41. Studies on Rothe incl. W. Hoenig, *Richard Rothe* (Berlin, 1898); A. Hausrath, *Richard Rothe und seine Freunde* (2 vols., 1902–6); and H. J. Birkner, *Spekulation und Heilsgeschichte: Die Geschichtsauffassung Richard Rothes* (Forschungen zur Geschichte und Lehre des Protestantismus, Zehnte Reihe, 17; 1959). A. E. F. Sieffert in *PRE* (3rd edn.), 17 (1906), pp. 169–78; E. Schott in *RGG* (3rd edn.), 5 (1961), cols. 1197–9, s.v.

Rothmann, Bernt

Rothmann, Bernt (or Bernhard) (*c*.1495–*c*.1535), German *Anabaptist preacher and theologian. He was educated by the *Brethren of the Common Life and in 1529 appointed chaplain of St Maurice's church in Warendorf near Münster. He visited *Wittenberg and Strasbourg, where he met P. *Melanchthon and W. *Capito in 1531. On his return he supported the cause of the Reformation, and in the autumn of 1531 he debated the doctrine of *Purgatory with Johannes à Daventria, Guardian of the *Minorites in Hamm. He was then silenced by his bishop, but he had the support of the town Council and guilds of Münster and an Imperial mandate gave him safety and freedom of movement. In Jan. 1532 he moved into Münster and was given the pulpit of the large church of St Lambert. In the same year he published his confession of faith which was *Lutheran in most respects but *Zwinglian in regard to the Sacraments. In a public disputation in Münster in Aug. 1532 he was opposed by Lutherans from *Marburg; at this he won the continued support of the civic officials as well as the people of Münster and he and his fellow ministers were able to occupy the leading churches. His position was strengthened by the arrival of the 'Wassenberg preachers', a group of six clerics from Wassenberg in Jülich, who were also *Sacramentarian in their view of the Eucharist. Rothmann now replied to the Marburg theologians and wrote his *Bekenntnisse van beyden Sacramenten* (1533). This confession showed that Rothmann and his circle had not only rejected M. *Luther but had moved beyond U. *Zwingli to repudiate *Infant Baptism. In Jan. 1534 they were rebaptized by followers of Melchior *Hoffmann and Münster became an Anabaptist city-state. Under the fanatical leadership of John of Leiden (d. 1536), and while the city was under siege, community of goods and polygamy were established. Rothmann's role in this is uncertain, but he became 'court preacher' and wrote *Restitution rechter und gesunder christlicher Lehre* and *Bericht von der Wrake* (both 1534) in an attempt to justify the 'New Jerusalem' of Münster. The town fell to the prince-bishop and his allies in June 1535; many of the Anabaptists were killed and their leaders tried and executed, but the fate of Rothmann is not known.

Die Schriften Bernhard Rothmanns, ed. R. Stupperich (Veröffentlichungen der Historischen Kommission Westfalens, 32: Die Schriften der Münsterischen Täufer und ihrer Gegner, 1; 1970), with introd. See also bibl. to ANABAPTISTS.

Rousseau, Jean-Jacques

Rousseau, Jean-Jacques (1712–78), French author. He was the son of a French refugee family at Geneva, and, though brought up a Calvinist, became a Catholic in 1728 through the influence of Mme de Warens, his benefactress and later his mistress, herself a convert from Protestant Pietism. She had a large share in his religious formation, combining *Deistic beliefs, which excluded doctrines such as Hell and Original Sin, with a kind of *Quietist sentimentalism. During the years spent with her (1731–40), Rousseau completed his sketchy education by omnivorous reading, including the works of R. *Descartes, G. W. *Leibniz, J. *Locke, B. *Pascal, and others. In 1741 he went to Paris, where he met Thérèse Levasseur, a servant girl, by whom he had five children whom he placed in a foundlings' hospital. Through D. *Diderot he was introduced to the circle of the *Encyclopaedists, for whom he wrote several contributions, all but one of them on musical subjects. In 1750 he published his *Discours sur les sciences et les arts*, a prize essay for Dijon Academy, in which he defended the thesis that technical progress and material goods corrupt human morals. In 1754 he returned to Geneva and once more became a Calvinist, and in the same year wrote his *Discours sur l'origine et les fondements de l'inégalité parmi les hommes*. Inspired by H. *Grotius, S. *Pufendorf, and others, he treated the subject regardless of historical reality, and, on the gratuitous assumption that the primitive man was a free and happy being living in acc. with his instincts, without virtue or vice, alleged that human inequalities arose from the undue development of his social and proprietary instincts. In 1756 Rousseau settled near Montmorency, where he wrote the works which made him world-famous. In *Julie, ou La Nouvelle Héloïse* (1761), a passionate love story, he condemned a society which for the sake of convention divorced love from marriage, and put forward a defence of a natural religion based on an undogmatic personal interpretation of the Gospels which, he maintained, is necessary for morality. In *Émile, ou de l'Éducation* (1762) he developed a Utopian programme of an education far from the corrupting influence of society and in acc. with nature. In the famous chapter entitled 'La Profession de foi du vicaire savoyard' he summed up his religious ideas. He advocated a Deism which, although similar to that of the Philosophes in affirming belief in the existence of God, the soul, and a future life, found its ultimate justification in the individual's sense of a personal relationship with God through the conscience, of which He is the source and inspiration. *Du contrat social* (1762) set out his theory of the just state, resting on the general will of the people, the expression of which are the laws. This too, contained a chapter on religion, 'De la religion civile', in which 'civic religion' was distinguished from natural religion. The articles of this civic religion, which are fixed and enforced by the state, bear on the same subjects as natural religion, forbid all dogmatic intolerance, and admit only those religions which do not claim to possess the absolute truth. *Émile*, put on the *Index in 1762, and *Du contrat social* were condemned in France and at Geneva, and Rousseau fled first to Neuchâtel, then to an island in the Canton of Berne, and, in 1766-7, he was the guest of D. *Hume in England. But, suffering from persecution mania, he went back to France, where he married Thérèse Levasseur 'before nature' in 1768, and in 1772 completed his *Confessions*, with their curious mixture of vanity and self-accusation.

After his death Rousseau became one of the most powerful influences in Europe. In France his ideas were taken up by the Revolution, in Germany by the 'Storm and Stress' movement. His religious impact was the deeper as, unlike *Voltaire, he offered man a substitute for revealed religion which was not only doctrinally simple and unelaborate in its moral prescriptions, but also addressed to his emotional as well as his intellectual needs. It has sometimes been asserted that he served Christianity by propagating its fundamental truths among his unbelieving contemporaries. A more just estimate might point out that, by eliminating the idea of original sin and replacing the need for grace by belief in the complete adequacy of reason, conscience, and free-will, he removed the foundations of sound religion and became a forerunner of humanistic liberalism.

Many edns. of his collected works, incl. that of V. D. Musset-Pathay (24 vols., Paris, 1823-6). Convenient edn. by B. Gagnebin, M. Raymond, and others (Bibliothèque de la Pléiade, 4 vols., 1959-69), but this does not incl. correspondence. *Religious Writings*, ed. R. Grimsley (Oxford, 1970). *Correspondance complète*, ed. R. A. Leigh (vols. 1-14, Geneva, 1965-71; 15-24, Thorpe Mandeville, Banbury, 1972-5; 25-53, Oxford, 1976-97). There have been innumerable edns. of individual works; useful edns. of his Political Writings, with full introd. and notes in Eng., by C. E. Vaughan (2 vols., Cambridge, 1915). His more important works were tr. into Eng. soon after publication; there have been many reprs. and new trs., incl. that of *The Social Contract* by M. Cranston (Penguin Classics, 1968), and also, with *The Discourses*, by G D. H. Cole (Everyman's Library, 660 [1913]); of *Émile* by B. Foxley (ibid. [1911]); of his *Confessions* by J. M. Cohen (Penguin Classics, 1953). The numerous studies incl. those of J. Morley (2 vols., London, 1873) and J. H. Broome (ibid., 1963); also M. Cranston, *Jean-Jacques: The Early Life and Work of Jean-Jacques Rousseau 1712-1754* (1983); id., *The Noble Savage: Jean-Jacques Rousseau 1754-1762* (1991). A. Schinz, *La Pensée de Jean-Jacques Rousseau* (2 vols., Northampton, Mass., 1929). R. Derathé, *Jean-Jacques Rousseau et la science politique de son temps* (1950). S. Baud-Bovy and others, *Jean-Jacques Rousseau* (Université Ouvrière et Faculté des Lettres de l'Université de Genève, Neuchâtel, 1962). *Études sur le* Contrat social *de Jean-Jacques Rousseau: Actes des journées d'étude organisées à Dijon pour la commémoration du 200ᵉ anniversaire du* Contrat social (Publications de l'Université de Dijon, 30; 1964). R. A. Leigh (ed.), *Rousseau after Two Hundred Years: Proceedings of the Cambridge Bicentennial Colloquium* (Cambridge, 1982). P. M. Masson, *La Religion de J.-J. Rousseau* (3 vols., 1916); R. Derathé, *Le Rationalisme de J.-J. Rousseau* (1948); J. F. Thomas, *Le Pélagianisme de J.-J. Rousseau* (1956); R. Grimsley, *Rousseau and the Religious Quest* (Oxford, 1968). J. Starobinski, *Jean-Jacques Rousseau: La transparence et l'obstacle* (1957; 2nd edn., 1971); R. Grimsley, *Jean-Jacques Rousseau: A Study in Self-awareness* (Cardiff, 1961). H. Roddier, *J.-J. Rousseau en Angleterre au XVIIIᵉ siècle* (Études de Littérature étrangère et comparée [1950]). J.-A. E. McEachern, *Bibliography of the Writings of Jean Jacques Rousseau to 1800* (Oxford, 1989 ff.). *Annales de la Société Jean-Jacques Rousseau* (Geneva, 1905 ff.).

Routh, Martin Joseph (1755-1854), patristic scholar and president of Magdalen College, Oxford. A strong supporter of the traditional High Church position in Anglican theology, he was much respected and revered by the *Tractarians, J. H. *Newman in dedicating to him his *Lectures on the Prophetical Office of the Church* (1837) declaring that he had 'been reserved to report to a forgetful generation the theology of their fathers'. It was he who advised S. *Seabury, when sent to Europe to inaugurate an episcopal succession in the American (Anglican) Church, to seek it from the Scottish Episcopal Church.

Elected a demy at Magdalen College in 1771, he was ordained deacon in 1777, and, after holding College appointments, was elected president in 1791 (in succession to G. *Horne), to hold the office for 63 years. His *Reliquiae Sacrae*, an edition of scattered pre-Nicene patristic texts first announced in 1788, was published in 4 vols., Oxford, 1814-1818; a complete revision ('ed. altera'), with an additional volume, was issued in 5 vols., 1846-8. Routh also published *Scriptorum Ecclesiasticorum Opuscula Praecipua Quaedam* (2 vols., 1832).

Life by R. D. Middleton (London, 1938). J. W. *Burgon, *Lives of Twelve Good Men*, i (1888), pp. 1-115. G. C. Boase in *DNB* 49 (1897), pp. 324-7.

Rowites. The disciples of J. McLeod *Campbell, who was in charge of the parish of Row, near Cardross, Dumbarton, from 1825 to 1830. They are also known as 'Campbellites'.

Rowntree, Joseph (1836–1925), *Quaker philanthropist and social reformer. Educated at Bootham School, *York, he entered the grocery business established by his father in the city in 1822, and eventually, on the death of his elder brother, Henry Isaac Rowntree, in 1883, became head of the cocoa business of Rowntree & Co. He was a pioneer in the movement for securing for workpeople reasonable hours and conditions of labour, higher wages, and provision against old age and unemployment. He established three trusts to carry some of his ideals into effect and in 1904 founded the model village of New Earswick. He was an ardent *temperance reformer, did much to promote adult education, esp. in the Society of Friends, and took a prominent part in the civic life of York.

A. Vernon, *A Quaker Business Man: The Life of Joseph Rowntree 1836–1925* (1958). A. E. Watkin in *DNB, 1922–1930* (1937), pp. 731 f., s.v.

Royal Chapels. See CHAPEL ROYAL.

Royal Declaration. See DECLARATION OF THE SOVEREIGN.

Royal School of Church Music (RSCM). An organization founded in 1927 as the School of English Church Music, and granted its present title in 1945. Till his death in 1947 its Director was Sydney H. Nicholson (b. 1875; organist of *Westminster Abbey, 1918–27). Its work has consisted in advice to choirs affiliated to the School, provision of suitable music, and the organization of choral festivals. In 1929 the College of St Nicholas was founded at Chislehurst, London, to provide courses for organists, choristers, clergy, and ordinands, with both resident and non-resident students. In 1945 the work, interrupted by the War since 1939, was resumed at *Canterbury, and in 1954 was removed to Addington Palace (an archiepiscopal residence 1807–96) near Croydon, London.

Royal Supremacy. See ESTABLISHMENT, para. 2.

Rubric, Black. See BLACK RUBRIC.

Rubric, Ornaments. See ORNAMENTS RUBRIC.

rubrics. Ritual or ceremonial directions, printed at the beginning of service-books, or in the course of the text. The word originated from the fact that in medieval books they were written in red (Lat. *ruber*), to distinguish them from the text of the services.

Rucherat (or Ruchrat), John. See JOHN OF WESEL.

Rufinus, Tyrannius or **Turranius** (*c.*345–411), monk, historian, and translator. Born near *Aquileia in N. Italy, he went to a school in Rome, where he became friends with St *Jerome. About 373 he went to Egypt; here he met *Melania the Elder and visited the monks of the desert. He also studied for several years in *Alexandria under *Didymus the Blind, and was deeply influenced by his *Origenism. In 381 he was in Jerusalem. With Melania he founded a *double monastery on the Mount of *Olives.

After the outbreak of the controversy about the teaching of *Origen, he returned to Italy in 397.

Though he was also an original writer, Rufinus is mainly important as a translator of Greek theological works into Latin at a time when knowledge of Greek was declining in the W. His free translation of Origen's 'De Principiis', the only complete text now surviving, was intended to vindicate Origen's orthodoxy, and involved Rufinus in bitter controversy with his former friend, St Jerome, who criticized the tendentious character of his rendering. He also translated some of Origen's scriptural commentaries, the 'Sentences' of Sextus (which he attributed to Pope *Sixtus II), the '*Clementine Recognitions', some works of *Basil and *Gregory of Nazianzus, the 'Historia Monachorum' (long thought to be his own original work) and, in a free rendering, the 'Ecclesiastical History' of *Eusebius, with two additional books (possibly based on the lost history of *Gelasius of Caesarea), bringing the narrative up to the death of the Emp. *Theodosius I (395). His commentary on the *Apostles' Creed, which is partly based on the 'Catechetical Discourses' of St *Cyril of Jerusalem, gives the earliest continuous Latin text of the 4th-cent. form of the creed, as used at Aquileia and Rome. At the invitation of *Paulinus of Nola, he wrote a commentary on the Benedictions of the Twelve Patriarchs in Gen. 49 which, though not original, is of some importance in the history of exegesis.

D. *Vallarsi projected a collected edn. in 2 vols., fol., but only vol. 1, containing Rufinus' independent works, appeared (Verona, 1745); this is repr. in J. P. Migne, *PL* 21. Works ed. M. Simonetti (CCSL 20; 1961). The 'De Benedictionibus' is repr., with Fr. tr. by H. Rochais and P. Antin and introd. by M. Simonetti (SC 140; 1968). Rufinus' *Historia Monachorum*, ed. E. Schulz-Flügel (Patristische Texte und Studien, 34; 1990). Rufinus' other trs. are to be sought in the edns. of their corresponding Gk. authors. Eng. tr. of his 'Commentary on the Apostles' Creed', with crit. introd. and notes, by J. N. D. Kelly (ACW 20; 1955). The most comprehensive study is F. X. Murphy, CSSR, *Rufinus of Aquileia, 345–411* (Catholic University of America. Studies in Mediaeval History, NS 6; 1945). Id., 'Rufinus of Aquileia and Paulinus of Nola', *Revue des Études Augustiniennes*, 2 (1956), pp. 79–91. R. *Reitzenstein, *Historia Monachorum* [by Rufinus] *und Historia Lausiaca* [by *Palladius] (Forschungen zur Religion und Literatur des Alten und Neuen Testaments, NF 7; 1916). J. E. L. Oulton, 'Rufinus's Translation of the Church History of Eusebius', *JTS* 30 (1928–9), pp. 150–74; F. Thelamon, *Païens et Chrétiennes au IVe Siècle: L'apport de l'Histoire ecclésiastique' de Rufin d'Aquilée* (Études Augustiniennes, 1981); T. Christensen, *Rufinus of Aquileia and the Historia Ecclesiastica, Lib. VIII–IX, of Eusebius* (Kongelige Danske Videnskabernes Selskab, Historisk-filosofiske Meddelelser, 58; 1989). H. Chadwick, 'Rufinus and the Tura Papyrus of Origen's Commentary on Romans', *JTS* NS 10 (1959), pp. 10–42; C. P. H. Bammel, *Der Römerbrieftext des Rufin und seine Origenes-Übersetzung* (Vetus Latina. Aus der Geschichte der lateinischen Bibel, 10; 1985). Id., 'The Last Ten Years of Rufinus' Life and the Date of his Move South from Aquileia', *JTS* NS 28 (1977), pp. 372–429. CPL (3rd edn., 1991), pp. 63–8 (nos. 195–201). J. Gribomont, OSB, in Quasten (cont.), *Patrology*, 4 (1986), pp. 247–54. M. Simonetti in *NCE* 12 (1967), pp. 702–4, s.v.; F. Thelamon in *Dict. Sp.* 13 (1988), cols. 1107–17, s.v. 'Rufin d'Aquilée'.

Rufinus (*fl.* 399–401?), commonly called the Syrian, author of a *Liber de Fide* which is described in the only known surviving MS (St Petersburg, Public Library MS Q. v. 1. 6) as the work of Rufinus, priest of the province of Palestine. This work, formerly ascribed to Tyrannius *Rufinus, is marked by hostility to *Arianism, to *Origen, and to the doctrine of *Original Sin; these features have led to the identification of the author with the Rufinus *natione Syrus*, said by *Marius Mercator to have corrupted the theology of *Pelagius at Rome during the pontificate of Anastasius (399–401), and with the deceased priest mentioned by *Celestius in his trial in *Carthage in 411. Further attempts to clarify Rufinus' identity remain controversial.

Editio princeps of the *Liber de Fide* by J. *Sirmond, SJ, Paris, 1650. Modern edn., with Eng. tr., by M. W. Miller (Catholic University of America Patristic Studies, 96; Washington, DC, 1964). B. *Altaner, 'Der Liber de Fide, ein Werk des Pelagianers Rufinus des "Syrers" ', *TQ* 130 (1950), pp. 432–49; H.-I. Marrou, 'Les attaches orientales de Pélagianisme', *Comptes Rendus des Séances de l'Académie des Inscriptions et Belles-Lettres*, 1968 (1968), pp. 459–72; G. Bonner, 'Rufinus of Syria and African Pelagianism', *Augustinian Studies*, 1 (1970), pp. 31–47; id., *Augustine and Modern Research on Pelagianism* (St Augustine Lecture, 1970; Villanova, Pa., 1972), esp. pp. 19–31, repr. in id., *God's Decree and Man's Destiny* (1987), nos. 10 and 11; W. Dunphy, 'Rufinus the Syrian's "Books" ', *Augustinianum*, 23 (1983), pp. 523–9. *CPL* (3rd edn., 1995), pp. 67 f. (no. 200).

Ruinart, Thierry (1657–1709), *Maurist scholar. From 1674 he was a monk of St-Rémi at *Reims and from 1682 an assistant to J. *Mabillon at *St-Germain-des-Prés. The most celebrated of his writings is his *Acta Primorum Martyrum Sincera et Selecta* (1689), a collection to which he admitted only those *acta* which seemed to him authentic, though some of its contents are no longer regarded as genuine. Among his other works were an edition of St *Gregory of Tours (1699) and a life of Mabillon (1709).

V. Thuiller, OSB (ed.), *Ouvrages posthumes de D. Jean Mabillon et de D. Thierri Ruinart* (3 vols., Paris, 1724; repr. Farnborough, 1967), vol. 2, pp. 399–554, and vol. 3. His Journal for 1698–9 is pr. in A.-M.-P. Ingold, *Histoire de l'édition bénédictine de saint Augustin* (Documents pour servir à l'histoire religieuse des XVIIᵉ et XVIIIᵉ siècles, 1903), pp. 155–93. Modern edn. of his *Acta Martyrum* (Ratisbon, 1859). H. Jadart, *Dom Thierry Ruinart (1657–1709): Notice suivie de documents inédits sur sa famille, sa vie, ses œuvres, ses relations avec D. Mabillon* (1886). H. *Leclercq, OSB, in *DACL* 15 (pt. 1; 1950), cols. 163–82, s.v., with bibl.; J. Daoust in *NCE* 12 (1967), pp. 704 f., s.v.

Rule, Golden. See GOLDEN RULE.

Rule of Faith (*Regula Fidei*). One of the names used to describe outline statements of Christian belief which circulated in the 2nd-cent. Church and were designed to make clear the essential contents of the Christian faith, to serve as guides in the exegesis of Scripture (e.g. *Irenaeus, *Adv. Haer.* 1. 9. 4), and to distinguish the orthodox tradition from traditions to which heretics appealed. Alternative names were the 'rule of truth', the 'law of faith' or the 'norm (κανών) of truth'. Unlike *creeds, which came later, these formularies varied in wording, though it was claimed that they faithfully reflected NT teaching, and did not differ from one another in their essential content. This content was held to have descended unchanged from apostolic times, in contrast to the spurious traditions of the heretics, which were taken to be later developments and mutually incompatible.

Gal. 6: 16 is the biblical origin of this terminology. Other patristic instances include Irenaeus, *Demonstration*, 3 and 6, and

Tertullian, *De Pud.* 8. 15, *De Virg. Vel.* 1. 4. D. van den Eynde, *Les Normes de l'Enseignement Chrétien dans la littérature patristique des trois premiers siècles* (1933), pp. 281–313, with full refs. J. N. D. Kelly, *Early Christian Creeds* (1950; 3rd edn., 1972), pp. 76–88. G. H. Tavard, *Holy Writ or Holy Church* [1959], pp. 3–11. J. Quasten in *L.Th.K.* (2nd edn.), 8 (1963), cols. 1102 f., s.v. 'Regula Fidei'.

Rule of St Benedict. See BENEDICT, RULE OF ST.

ruler. A name formerly applied to those who presided in cathedrals over the singing in the choir, esp. over the psalms. The office, which goes back to medieval times, when the rulers frequently wore copes, was revived in a few places in the C of E in the 19th cent.

Rumania, Christianity in. See ROMANIA, CHRISTIANITY IN.

Rupert of Deutz (*c*.1075–1129 or 1130), monastic theologian. At an early age he entered the Abbey of St Laurent in Liège. In 1092 he went into exile for three years with his abbot, who was expelled during the troubles of the *Investiture Controversy. Rupert himself was not made priest until 1106, because he refused to accept ordination from a bishop who was excommunicated. His first work, 'Liber de divinis officiis' (*c*.1111), was concerned to expound the ecclesiastical year; it made much use of *allegory. In it he used language about the Real Presence in the Eucharist which provoked a fatherly rebuke from *William of St-Thierry, who accused him of holding the doctrine later known as *Impanation. There followed long Homilies on the Gospel of St John. Then came the 'De Trinitate' in 42 books. This work is in effect concerned with the history of salvation. It is based on an analysis of the historical books of the Bible. In 1116 a fellow monk returned from a period of study under *Anselm of Laon and proclaimed that he had taught that God willed that evil should happen. Rupert was scandalized and wrote a rejoinder, 'De voluntate Dei', which created a storm. Rupert had to retire to the monastery of Siegburg in the Rhineland. From here he was summoned to Liège in 1117 for examination of his thesis. He emerged unscathed and wrote his treatise 'De omnipotentia Dei'. At Siegburg he came to the notice of the Abp. of Cologne, who secured his election as abbot of Deutz in 1120. He continued his writing and produced a Commentary on the Twelve Minor Prophets, the 'De victoria Verbi Dei', and a Commentary on the Song of Songs in which he interprets the bride as the BVM, providing an early example of this interpretation. He also engaged in controversy, defending the historical Benedictine way of life against the new orders (*Cistercians and *Canons Regular). Rupert's work demonstrates the interaction between the older monastic theology and the nascent scholastic way of thinking. When his writings were printed in the 16th cent., the Reformers sought to find in them support for their own doctrines, esp. on the Eucharist.

Opera Omnia, ed. M. Pleunich (4 vols. bound in 2, Venice, 1748–51), repr. in J. P. Migne, *PL* 167–170. Crit. edns. by R. Haacke, OSB, of his *Liber de divinis officiis* (CCCM 7; 1967); of his Commentary on St John's Gospel (ibid. 9; 1969); of *De Sancta Trinitate et operibus eius* (ibid. 21–4; 1971–2); of his Commentary on the Song of Songs (ibid. 26; 1974); of *De gloria et honore filii hominis super Mattheum* (ibid. 29; 1979); and of *De victoria Verbi Dei* (*MGH*, Quellen zur Geistesgeschichte des Mittelalters, 5; 1970), and by P. Dinter of his *Vita Heriberti* [Abp. of Cologne, 999–1021] (Veröffentlichungen des Historischen Vereins für den Niederrhein, 13; 1976). Part III of *De Trinitate* also ed., with Fr. tr., by É. de Solms, OSB, and useful introd. and notes by J. Gribomont, OSB (Les Œuvres du Saint-Esprit, 1–2; SC 131 and 165; 1967–70). The *Chronicon Sancti Laurentii Leodiensis* is no longer attributed to Rupert; cf. H. Silvestre, *Le Chronicon Sancti Laurentii Leodiensis dit de Rupert de Deutz: Étude critique* (Université de Louvain. Recueil de Travaux d'histoire et de philosophie, 3rd ser. 43; 1952). W. Beinert, *Die Kirche Gottes Heil in der Welt: Die Lehre von der Kirche nach den Schriften des Rupert von Deutz, Honorius Augustodunensis und Gerhoch von Reichersberg* (BGPM, NF 13; 1973), with introd. on his life and works, pp. 12–37. M. L. Arduini, *Ruperto di Deutz e la Controversia tra Cristiani ed Ebrei nel Secolo XII*, with text of 'Anulus seu dialogus inter Christianum et Iudaeum', ed. R. Haacke, OSB (Istituto Storico Italiano per il Medio Evo, Studi Storici, 119–21; 1979); id., *Rupert von Deutz (1076–1129) und der 'Status Christianitatis' seiner Zeit* (Beihefte zum Archiv für Kulturgeschichte, 25; 1987), and other works of this author. J. H. van Engen, *Rupert of Deutz* (Berkeley, Calif., and London [1983]). Id. in *Dict. Sp.* 13 (1988), cols. 1126–33, s.v. 'Rupert (1) de Deutz'.

rural dean. In the C of E, the head of a group of parishes in a given area ('rural deanery'). He is appointed by the bishop of the diocese, usually, but not necessarily, from among the beneficed clergy of the deanery, and may be removed by the bishop at any time. The boundaries of a rural deanery can, if necessary, be modified under the Archdeaconries and Rural Deaneries Act 1874.

The office is ancient and formerly the duties were important, but they were gradually absorbed by the *archdeacons. The office was revived in 1836; and since the later 19th cent. rural deans have again come to play a considerable part in the life of the diocese, e.g. as a channel of communication between the smaller parishes and the bishop. The rural dean is president of the ruridecanal chapter, i.e. the incumbents and clergy licensed under seal in the deanery, and co-chairman of the deanery synods established by the *Synodical Government Measure 1969.

In the RC Church rural deans are technically known as 'vicars forane'. See DEAN.

W. Dansey, *Horae Decanicae Rurales* (2 vols., London, 1835). J. B. Hughes, *Deans Rural: The History of their Office and Duties* (rev. edn., 1889). F. Makower, *Die Verfassung der Kirche von England* (1894), pp. 334–9; Eng. tr. (1895), pp. 321–6. A. H. Thompson, 'Diocesan Organization in the Middle Ages. Archdeacons and Rural Deans', *Proceedings of the British Academy*, 29 (1943), pp. 153–94, esp. pp. 184–94. E. W. Watson in *DECH*, pp. 527–9, s.v.

Ruskin, John (1819–1900), art critic and social reformer. The son of a puritanical mother and an art-loving father, Ruskin was brought up at home. From 1836 to 1840 he studied at *Christ Church, Oxford, where he retained a simple *Evangelical piety and was completely untouched by the *Tractarian Movement. The first book that established his fame was *Modern Painters* (1843; four more volumes appeared at intervals to 1860, treating not only contemporary artists such as J. M. W. Turner, but also the old Italian masters, esp. Fra *Angelico and *Tintoretto). It was followed by *The Seven Lamps of Architecture* (1849). In these and later works Ruskin expounded his spiritual interpretation of art in which moral and aesthetic ideals were closely linked; he held that the art and architecture

of a people are the expression of its religion and morality. From 1851 to 1853 appeared his *Stones of Venice*, with the famous chapter on 'The Nature of Gothic' which became an important influence in the growth of the Gothic Revival in architecture. About the same time he became connected with the Pre-Raphaelites, whom he defended in his work on *Pre-Raphaelitism* (1851). His interest in Protestant reunion resulted in his pamphlet *Notes on the Construction of Sheepfolds* (1851), in which he proposed as a basis a simple NT Christianity, though retaining the episcopate. After the completion of the series *Modern Painters* in 1860, he devoted himself almost entirely to social and economic problems. In *Unto This Last* (1862) he defended the dignity and moral destiny of man. He stressed nobility of character and aesthetic development as the only true wealth of humanity and upheld national education, organization of labour, old-age pensions, and other social institutions as against the *laissez-faire* principles of the age. In *Time and Tide* (1867), *Munera Pulveris* (1872), and other works, he further elaborated his views. By this date his early Evangelicalism had given place to a vague Theism, and among his ideas for social reforms was the plan of a completely dependent State Church with state-salaried officials and with a minimum of dogma. From 1871 onwards he attempted to put his principles into practice, and he established the 'Guild of St George', comprising agricultural and also industrial settlements; but they did not succeed. From Brantwood on Coniston Water he wrote monthly letters 'to the workmen and labourers of Great Britain' which are collected in the volumes of *Fors Clavigera* as a means of propagating his ideas. In 1870 he was elected the first professor of fine arts in Oxford. Here he also worked out his social programme, which was among the main influences leading to the establishment of university settlements. From *c.*1875 he returned to a more Christian standpoint, his partiality for the Middle Ages and his friendship with H. E. *Manning at one time giving rise to the rumour that he was about to become a RC. But the religion of his last period seems to have been rather an undogmatic kind of Bible Christianity without attachment to any Church. From 1884 he lived in retirement.

Best edn. of his Works by E. T. Cook and A. Wedderburn (39 vols., 1903–12). J. H. Whitehouse (ed.), *The Solitary Warrior: New Letters by Ruskin* (1929); J. L. Bradley (ed.), *Ruskin's Letters from Venice 1851–1852* (Yale Studies in English, 129; 1955); H. I. Shapiro (ed.), *Ruskin in Italy: Letters to his Parents 1845* (Oxford, 1972); V. A. Burd (ed.), *The Ruskin Family Letters: The Correspondence of John James Ruskin, His Wife, and Their Son John, 1801–1843* (2 vols., Ithaca, NY, and London, 1973). There are also various collections of his correspondence with individuals. Selections from *Diaries* ed. J. Evans and J. H. Whitehouse (3 vols., Oxford, 1956–9). W. G. Collingwood, *The Life and Work of John Ruskin* (2 vols., 1893); id., *The Life of John Ruskin* (1900); E. T. Cook, *The Life of John Ruskin* (2 vols., 1911). Other studies by R. H. Wilenski (London, 1933), P. Quennell (ibid., 1949), J. Evans (ibid., 1954), J. D. Rosenberg (New York and London, 1961), G. P. Landow (Princeton, NJ, 1971), E. K. Helsinger (Cambridge, Mass., and London, 1982), P. L. Sawyer (Ithaca, NY, and London, 1985), W. Kemp (Munich, 1983; Eng. tr., *The Desire of my Eyes*, New York, 1990; London 1991) and T. Hilton (New Haven, Conn., and London, 1985 ff.). P. Walton, *The Drawings of Ruskin* (Oxford, 1972). R. Hewison (ed.), *New Approaches to Ruskin* (1981). Useful introd. by G. P. Landow, *Ruskin* (Past Masters, Oxford, 1985). H. G. Pollard in *NCBEL* 3 (1969), cols. 1340–64.

Russell, Charles Taze (1852–1916), 'Pastor Russell', founder of Zion's Watch Tower Tract Society in 1881, the forerunner of the organization now popularly known as *Jehovah's Witnesses (q.v.). He worked in his father's drapery business in Pennsylvania, and was active in the *Congregational Church before he encountered *Adventism. His intensive but untutored study of the Bible led him to reject the doctrine of eternal punishment, to believe that the Second Coming of Christ had already taken place, invisibly, in 1874, and to expect the end of the world in 1914. His first pamphlet, *The Object and Manner of Our Lord's Return* (1873), and his collaboration with another Adventist publisher, helped to attract many fellow students of biblical prophecy to the groups who regarded Russell as their Pastor, though he had never received any formal ordination. He began publishing the magazine *Zion's Watch Tower and Herald of Christ's Presence* in 1879, and his articles and pamphlets eventually formed the basis for his *Studies in the Scriptures* (6 vols., 1886–1904). Under Russell's presidency, the Watch Tower Bible and Tract Society, as it was renamed in 1896, quickly developed into a flourishing business, publishing numerous books, pamphlets, magazines, and tracts. At the same time Russell became a controversial figure in the *United States of America not only because of his involvement in several personal and business scandals but also on account of the attacks against Churches that he launched in his widely syndicated newspaper column.

The number of Bible Students, as Russell's followers were called, continued to grow in many countries in spite of the fact that the outbreak of war in 1914 did not appear to be an unequivocal confirmation of his interpretation of prophecy. The succession crisis which followed his death in 1916 brought J. F. *Rutherford (q.v.) to the presidency of the Bible Students and split the organization into various groups, some of which dispute the claim of Jehovah's Witnesses to be Russell's true successors.

E. S. Bates in *Dict. Amer. Biog.* 16 (1935), p. 240. See also bibl. to JEHOVAH'S WITNESSES.

Russia, the Soviet Union, and the Commonwealth of Independent States, Christianity in. Christian missionaries first preached extensively in Russia in the 9th and 10th cents. About 988 Prince *Vladimir (canonized, 13th cent.) was baptized and established Christianity as the official religion in his dominions. Anxious to bring Russia into closer relationship with Europe, he brought priests from the Byzantine Empire and established a Greek hierarchy under a metropolitan. From the first the Slav tongue was used in worship and gradually a Russian clergy replaced the Greeks. At the *Great Schism of 1054 the Russian Church took the E. side. Monastic life began with the coming from Mount *Athos in the first half of the 11th cent. of the monk Antony, who established himself in a grotto near Kiev and laid the foundations of the great Kiev Monastery of the Caves, organized (c.1062–74) by his disciple Theodosius. Monasticism spread rapidly, so that by the 12th cent. in Kiev alone there were 17 monasteries.

During the invasions of the Tartars from Mongolia, which began in 1237, several Russian princes suffered martyrdom for their faith. The monastic movement continued to grow, and in 1329 two Russian monks, Sergius

and Germanus, founded the famous monastery of Valamo on an islet in Lake Ladoga. Later St *Sergius of Radonezh (c.1314–92), one of the most honoured saints in Russia, began a reform of monastic life. He founded the monastery of the Most Holy Trinity at Sergievo, and gave the impulse to the wave of monasticism which in the following cent. resulted in the building of monasteries all over Russia. Monasteries supplied bishops, while the secular clergy were commonly married. When the Church eventually emerged from the ruins left by the invasions she had become the embodiment of the Russian people.

During the early years of the 14th cent. the metropolitical see was moved from Kiev to Moscow. In 1461 the Russian Church was divided between two Metropolitans, centred at Moscow and Kiev, the former entirely Russian and rigidly Orthodox, the latter more exposed to pressure and influences from the W. During the 15th and 16th cents. the missionary activity of the Russians continued to the south and east of their borders.

Russia wholly refused the findings of the Council of *Florence (1439). Since the official Church at Constantinople for a time accepted the Florentine Union, in 1448 a Council of Russian bishops elected a Metropolitan of Moscow without reference to the Greek ecclesiastical authorities, and in this way the Russian Church became *autocephalous. Two outstanding religious leaders in the see of Moscow during this period were St *Macarius (1542–63) and St Philip II, the latter slain by the order of Ivan the Terrible (1533–84) in 1569.

In 1503 a famous dispute broke out concerning the monastic ownership of property. One group of monks, the 'Possessors', led by St *Joseph of Volokalamsk (1439/40–1515), stressed the social responsibilities of the monasteries—their duty to provide schools, orphanages, hospitals, and relief for the poor—and therefore insisted on the need for adequate endowments. The other party, the 'Non-Possessors', led by St *Nil Sorsky (1433–1508), underlined the more spiritual and mystical aspects of monasticism, and demanded a stricter interpretation of the vow of poverty. The Non-Possessors, who came into conflict with the Tsar, were largely suppressed and their centres closed, to the grave impoverishment of Russia's future religious development. In 1551 the celebrated Council of the Hundred Chapters was called to reform the clergy. In the reign of Theodore (1584–98), the second son of Ivan the Terrible, the Russian Church realized her greatest ambition in the creation of the Patriarchate of Moscow by Jeremias II, Patriarch of Constantinople (1589). The first Patriarch was St Job (1589–1605; canonized in 1989).

Since the Council of Florence RCs had been severely repressed in the Moscow Tsardom, but Russians in the metropolis of Kiev to the south, falling as they did within the territory of *Poland and Lithuania, found themselves under constant pressure from their RC masters. A large part of the Russian Church in this area acknowledged the Papacy at the Synod of *Brest-Litovsk in 1596. The Orthodox metropolis of Kiev, however, despite persecution, still continued in existence, organizing a vigorous opposition to the *Uniats, and attaining considerable intellectual brilliance in the 17th cent., esp. under Peter *Mogila, Metropolitan from 1632 to 1646. In 1606–12 a determined effort was made by the Poles to impose a RC Tsar at Moscow itself, but this was eventually repulsed.

Outstanding among the Patriarchs of Moscow during the 17th cent. was *Nikon (q.v.; d. 1681). A man of great ability and sincerity but of autocratic temper, he pushed forward too hastily with the work of revising the service-books, inaugurated under his predecessors, esp. Patriarch *Philaret (Romanov), and his liturgical reforms precipitated the schism of the 'Old Believers' (q.v.). This tragic division grievously weakened the Church in Russia.

Peter the Great (1672–1725), anxious to secure the subjugation of the Church to his authority, abolished the office of Patriarch, and in his 'Spiritual Regulation' of 1721 he replaced it with the *Holy Synod, the members of which were nominated by the Emperor and could be dismissed by him at any time. All its meetings were attended by a lay official, the Chief Procurator, who wielded considerable influence over Church affairs.

From the inclusion of part of Poland in the Russian Empire, which took place by stages at the end of the 18th cent., RC activity was intensified and sternly repressed by imperial ukases. In the reign of Catherine the Great (d. 1796) the *Jesuits, after their suppression by *Benedict XIV in 1773, found a home in Russia, but, proving unwelcome guests, they were shortly afterwards expelled. The RC cause was bound up with Polish and Lithuanian nationalism while these countries were under Russian rule, and even the edict of toleration to all faiths, issued by Nicholas II in 1905, had almost at once to be modified and limited in respect of the RCs.

In 1917–18 a council of bishops, parish clergy, and laity met in Moscow and initiated a thorough reorganization of all aspects of Church life. In particular, the office of Patriarch was restored with the election of Metropolitan *Tikhon of Moscow. The Revolution of 1917, however, completely disrupted its work. Except for granting some latitude to the scattered Protestants, who had suffered under Tsars, the Bolshevik government persecuted the 'progressive' and 'conservative' elements in the Church indiscriminately. Public worship was never forbidden by law, but it became difficult after Lenin's decree of 1918 had removed the legal right of the Church to own property. During the famine of 1921–2 the State appropriated all Church valuables, including priceless *icons; resistance provided a pretext for the arrest of many clergy and large numbers were condemned to death or banished to prison camps. Lenin's decree had also made the formal teaching of religion to anyone under 18 a criminal offence; monasteries and all theological schools (except one for the *Baptists) were closed, and the Church's public role ceased. Islam, Judaism, and Buddhism suffered equally, and the RC Church virtually ceased to exist in the Soviet Union. In the early 1920s a reform movement began within the Orthodox Church, known as the 'Living' or 'Renovationist Church', which had the backing of the government; it formed a schismatic body but lacked general support and its membership dwindled until it died out during the Second World War. When Patr. Tikhon died in 1925, no successor could be elected. In 1927 Metropolitan Sergius of Moscow reached a limited understanding with the government, but this occasioned sharp opposition among the remaining bishops and further persecution resulted. Stalin's 'Law on Religious Associations' (1929) formalized the situation and prepared the way for the suppression of virtually all religion during the Great Purge

(1934–7). The Constitution of 1936 proclaimed 'freedom of religious worship', but this was a paper guarantee only, while State organs enjoyed to the full the 'freedom of anti-religious propaganda' also embodied in the Constitution. In practice, by 1939 in the whole of the USSR only a few hundred churches remained open and the ranks of the clergy were depleted to a critical degree. Underground and in exile the faith survived, ready to emerge when Sergius supported the war effort after the German invasion in 1941. The resulting concessions by the Soviet government allowed the reopening of some 20,000 Orthodox churches, eight seminaries for the training of clergy, two academies for advanced study, and some monasteries, as well as the election of Sergius as Patriarch. After his death in 1944, a synod of 44 bishops elected Metropolitan Alexis of Leningrad as Patriarch in 1945.

With the defeat of Germany and increasing tension between the USSR and the W., anti-religious propaganda was resumed. The Orthodox Church in the Soviet Union (as in other countries of E. Europe) retained a limited degree of freedom, but it was required to support the Government position. At home, Church leaders justified the suppression of the *Ukrainian Eastern-rite Catholic (Uniat) Churches in 1946 and the incorporation of the remnants into the Russian Orthodox Church. At the same time there was widespread persecution of the *Lutheran and RC Churches in the newly conquered western territory, including the Baltic states. Abroad, the Moscow Patriarchate supported Soviet foreign policy. A conference held at Moscow in 1948, attended by delegates from most of the Orthodox Churches, displayed considerable reserve towards the W., passing resolutions hostile to the *Vatican and the *World Council of Churches; it also reached an unfavourable (though qualified) decision on *Anglican Ordinations, but a constructive dialogue between Anglican and Russian theologians took place in Moscow in 1956 and relations between the Churches have been maintained. Under Khrushchev there was a further wave of persecution (1959–64), with the closure of two thirds of the churches still in use, five of the eight seminaries, and most of the monasteries, and widespread imprisonment of religious activists. In 1961 the major denominations in Russia (except the RCs) joined the World Council of Churches, though the Moscow Patriarchate was forced to conceal the new persecution. While the closure of churches slowed after 1964, pressure remained severe until the accession of President Gorbachev in 1985. Until then the Council for Religious Affairs (reconstituted in 1965) kept a tight grip on religious activity. In the early 1960s one group of Baptists formally seceded from the registered 'All-Union Council of Evangelical Christians and Baptists' on the ground that the movement was under the control of secular rather than Christian authority. The subsequent imprisonment of Baptist and *Pentecostal leaders became internationally known, largely through the works of the emergent Soviet human rights movement, in which the Council of Baptist Prisoners' Relatives was prominent. Under President Gorbachev these prisoners were freed. In June 1988 on the occasion of the celebrations of the millennium of the conversion of the Eastern Slav lands to Christianity, a Council of the Russian Orthodox Church was held at Zagorsk, near Moscow. This Council, which was attended by delegates from all the dioceses of the Russian Orthodox Church both in the Soviet Union and abroad, accepted new statutes governing the Church and canonized nine saints. In April of that year President Gorbachev had received Patr. Pimen (elected 1971; d. 1991) and promised concessions and new legislation in return for help in rebuilding society. The restored Danilov monastery became the headquarters of the Moscow Patriarchate, plans were made for the opening of new churches and monasteries by the Orthodox Church, while in the Baltic states RC and Lutheran cathedrals began to reopen, and in W. Ukraine there were demands for the restoration of the Eastern-rite Catholic (Uniat) Church, which was finally achieved in Dec. 1989. In Oct. 1990 a new law on religious freedom was adopted (for which significant revisions were discussed in 1992–3) and the Council for Religious Affairs was disbanded. With the advent of religious freedom, however, interdenominational hostility increased. There was much resentment both of Protestant missionary groups from the W. and of the establishment of parallel RC dioceses. Within the Orthodox community the long-standing conflict between the Moscow Patriarchate and the Russian Orthodox Church Abroad (ROCA) was aggravated in 1990 by the formation on Russian soil of the Free Russian Orthodox Church, whose parishes give their allegiance to the ROCA. In 1991 Committees to Liaise with Religious Organizations were established in Moscow and St Petersburg and in April 1992 a Government decree placed a new Commission on Religious Denominations at the head of this new structure for state regulation of religion; its members include many who served earlier on the Council for Religious Affairs.

The principal material is in Russian. The best general history in a W. European language is A. M. Ammann, SJ, *Storia della Chiesa russa e dei paesi limitrofi* (Turin, 1948). Other general works incl.: N. *Zernov, *The Russians and their Church* (1945); G. P. Fedotov, *The Russian Religious Mind* (2 vols., Cambridge, Mass., 1946–66); É. Behr-Sigel, *Prière et sainteté dans l'Église russe* (1950; rev. edn., Bégrolles-en-Mauges, 1982); M. Rouët de Journel, SJ, *Monachisme et monastères russes* (1952); I. Kologrivof, *Essai sur la sainteté en Russie* (Bruges, 1953); I. Smolitsch, *Russisches Mönchtum: Entstehung, Entwicklung und Wesen 988–1917* (Das Östliche Christentum, NF 10–11; 1953); N. Zernov, *The Russian Religious Renaissance of the Twentieth Century* (1963); A. Schmemann (ed.), *Ultimate Questions: An Anthology of Modern Russian Religious Thought* (New York, 1965); and K. C. Felmy and others (ed.), *Tausend Jahre Christentum in Russland: Zum Millennium der Taufe der Kiever Rus'* (Göttingen, 1988).

L. K. Goetz, *Staat und Kirche in Altrussland . . . 988–1240* (1908). G. Podskalsky, *Christentum und theologische Literatur in der Kiever Rus' (988–1237)* (Munich, 1982). P. Pierling, SJ, *La Russie et le saint-siège: Études diplomatiques* (5 vols., 1896–1912). I. Smolitsch, *Geschichte der russischen Kirche, 1700–1917*, I (Studien zur Geschichte Osteuropas, 9; Leiden, 1964). G. L. Freeze, *The Russian Levites: Parish Clergy in the Eighteenth Century* (Cambridge, Mass., and London, 1977); id., *The Parish Clergy in Nineteenth Century Russia: Crisis, Reform, Counter-Reform* (Princeton, NJ [1983]). J. S. Curtiss, *Church and State in Russia: The Last Years of the Empire, 1900–1917* (New York, 1940); id., *The Russian Church and the Soviet State, 1917–1950* (Boston, 1953). M. Spinka, *The Church in Soviet Russia* (New York, 1956); W. Kolarz, *Religion in the Soviet Union* (1961); N. Struve, *Les Chrétiens en U.R.S.S.* (1963; enlarged Eng. tr., 1967). Johannes Chrysostomus [Blaschkewitz], *Kirchengeschichte Russlands der neuesten Zeit* (3 vols., Munich and Salzburg, 1965–8). W. C. Fletcher, *A Study in Survival: The Church in Russia 1927–1943* (1965); id., *The Russian Orthodox Church Underground, 1917–1970* (1971); id., *Religion and*

Soviet Foreign Policy 1945–1970 (1973). M. [A.] Bourdeaux, *Opium of the People: The Christian Religion in the U.S.S.R.* (1965); id., *Religious Ferment in Russia: Protestant Opposition to Soviet Religious Policy* (1968); id., *Patriarch and Prophets: Persecution of the Russian Orthodox Church Today* [1969]; id., *Land of Crosses: The Struggle for Religious Freedom in Lithuania, 1939–78* (Keston Book, 12; Chulmleigh, Devon, 1979); id., *Gorbachev, Glasnost & the Gospel* (1990). H. Fireside, *Icon and Swastika: The Russian Orthodox Church under Nazi and Soviet Control* (Cambridge, Mass., 1971). R. H. Marshall (ed.), *Aspects of Religion in the Soviet Union 1917–1967* (Chicago and London, 1971). G. Simon, *Church, State and Opposition in the U.S.S.R.* [1974; Eng. tr. of *Die Kirchen in Russland*, pub. 1970, with rev. documentation]. D. [V.] Pospielovsky, *The Russian Church under the Soviet Regime 1917–1982* (2 vols., Crestwood, NY, 1984); id., *A History of Soviet Atheism in Theory and Practice, and the Believer* (3 vols., Basingstoke, 1987–8). J. Ellis, *The Russian Orthodox Church: A Contemporary History* (1986). T. [R.] Beeson, *Discretion and Valour: Religious Conditions in Russia and Eastern Europe* (2nd edn., 1982), pp. 23–153; P. Walters (ed.), *World Christianity: Eastern Europe* (Keston Book, 29; Monrovia, Calif., and Eastbourne, Sussex, 1988), pp. 15–106.

K. K. Grass, *Die russischen Sekten* (2 vols., 1907–9); F. C. *Conybeare, *Russian Dissenters* (Harvard Theological Studies, 10; 1921). S. Bolshakoff, *Russian Nonconformity* (Philadelphia [1950]). W. Sawatsky, *Soviet Evangelicals since World War II* (Kitchener, Ont., and Scottdale, Pa., 1981). M. Rowe, *Russian Resurrection: Strength in Suffering—A History of Russia's Evangelical Church* (1994). S. Bolshakoff, *The Foreign Missions of the Russian Orthodox Church* (1943). J. Glazik, MSC, *Die russisch-orthodoxe Heidenmission seit Peter dem Grossen* (Missionswissenschaftliche Abhandlungen und Texte, 19; 1954); id., *Die Islammission der russisch-orthodoxen Kirche* (ibid. 23; 1959).

Ruth, Book of. The Book tells the story of Ruth, a Moabitess, who had married a Hebrew when he was compelled during a famine in the land of Judah to take refuge in Moab. It is narrated how, after the death of her husband, Ruth determined to return to Judah with her mother-in-law, and how Boaz, a kinsman of her former husband, took her under his protection and married her. The incident is set in the later days of the Judges (before 1000 BC), and this explains the position of the Book in the English Bible (as in the Greek and Latin Versions) after *Judges. The Book itself, however, is evidently of a relatively late date, certainly not earlier than the Exile (6th cent. BC); and in the Hebrew Bible it appears as one of the 'Five *Megilloth', i.e. in the third and latest division of the Hebrew OT, the *Hagiographa. The genealogy at the end (4: 18–22) indicates one of the apparent aims of the book, that is, to record the Moabite strain in *David's ancestry. This shows that the writer had a broader view on the legitimacy of the marriage of Jews with foreigners than was inculcated by *Nehemiah and *Ezra, and the story may point to his disapproval of the exclusive attitude of many of the Jews of his time. He probably also wished to insist on the duty of marriage on the part of the next-of-kin with a widow left without male offspring. In St *Matthew's genealogy, Ruth is specifically mentioned as the great-grandmother of David, and so as an ancestress of Christ (1: 5–16).

Comm. by H. W. Hertzberg (Das Alte Testament Deutsch, 9, on Jos., Jgs., and Ruth, 1953; 2nd edn., 1959, pp. 257–83), E. Würthwein (HAT, Reihe 1, Bd. 18, 2nd edn., on Ruth, Song of Songs, Est., Eccles., and Lam., 1969, pp. 1–24), J. Gray (New Cent. Bib. on Jos., Jgs., and Ruth, 1967, pp. 397–424; 2nd edn.,

1986, pp. 365–403), E. F. Campbell (Anchor Bible, 1975), and E. Zenger (Zürcher Bibelkommentare, Altes Testament, 8; 1986). J. M. Myres, *The Linguistic and Literary Form of the Book of Ruth* (Leiden, 1955). H. H. Rowley, 'The Marriage of Ruth', *HTR* 40 (1947), pp. 77–99, repr. in *The Servant of the Lord* (2nd edn., Oxford, 1965), pp. 171–94, with bibl. D. R. G. Beattie, *Jewish Exegesis on the Book of Ruth* (Journal for the Study of the Old Testament, Supplement Series, 2; Sheffield, 1977).

Ruthenian Churches. See UKRAINIAN CHURCHES.

Rutherford, Joseph Franklin (1869–1942), 'Judge Rutherford', second President of the *Adventist organization popularly known as the '*Jehovah's Witnesses' (q.v.). Of *Baptist family, he practised law in his native Missouri. In 1906 he joined the Bible Students of C. T. *Russell and quickly became the organization's legal counsel. The succession crisis following Russell's death led to Rutherford's election as President of the Watch Tower Bible and Tract Society in 1917. With other Directors of the Society he was imprisoned in 1918 on a charge of inciting insubordination, disloyalty, and refusal of duty in the American armed forces, but the conviction was overturned in 1919. Rutherford then moulded the Society into a *theocratic organization, known as Jehovah's Witnesses, which questioned the authority of sovereign states. He vilified religion as a 'snare and a racket' in his many publications, but at the same time he succeeded in welding Jehovah's Witnesses into an expansive religious organization resilient enough to withstand persecution in many countries during the Second World War.

H. Stroup in *Dict. Amer. Biog.*, Suppl. 3 (1973), pp. 678 f. See also bibl. to JEHOVAH'S WITNESSES.

Rutherford, Mark, pseudonym of **William Hale White** (1831–1913), author of religious works. The son of William White, a Nonconformist bookseller who was later a doorkeeper of the House of Commons and author of *The Inner Life of the House of Commons* (1897), Hale White had orig. intended to enter the *Congregational ministry. He spent most of his life as a civil servant. He won recognition as a religious author by *The Autobiography of Mark Rutherford* (1881), marked by its unusual combination of spiritual depth, irony, and humour. It was followed by *Mark Rutherford's Deliverance* (1885) and other works, incl. *Catharine Furze* (1893), *Pages from a Journal* (1900), *More Pages from a Journal* (1910), and *Last Pages from a Journal* (posthumous, 1915). He also issued under his real name an Eng. tr. of B. de *Spinoza's writings. Though he has never made more than a limited appeal, the freshness and penetration of his books have won him an assured place among English religious writers.

W. R. *Nicoll, *A Bookman's Letters* (1913), pp. 364–412; repr. separately as *Memories of Mark Rutherford* (1924). Lives by C. M. Maclean (London, 1955) and I. Stock (ibid., 1956). S. Merton, *Mark Rutherford (William Hale White)* (New York [1967]). W. Stone, *Religion and Art of William Hale White ('Mark Rutherford')* (Stanford University Publications, University Series. Language and Literature, 12; Stanford, Calif., 1954). H. W. Massingham in *DNB, 1912–1921*, pp. 573 f.

Rutherford, Samuel (c.1600–61), also 'Rutherfurd', Scottish *Presbyterian divine. After studying at Edinburgh University, he was elected regent of humanity in

1623, but deprived in 1626 for a pre-nuptial scandal. Soon afterwards he became fervently religious. In 1627 he was appointed minister at Anwoth, Dumfries and Galloway. His *Exercitationes Apologeticae pro Divina Gratia* (Amsterdam, 1636), written from a rigidly *Calvinist standpoint, led to his prosecution before the High Commission, and in 1636 he was deposed and exiled at Aberdeen till 1638. In 1639 he became professor of divinity at, and in 1647 principal of, St Mary's College, St Andrews. His *Plea for Presbytery* appeared in 1642. In 1643 he was one of the eight Scottish Commissioners at the *Westminster Assembly and for four years he defended the Presbyterian cause at London. His *Lex Rex, a Dispute for the Just Prerogative of King and People* (1644), which was an attack on monarchical absolutism, brought him considerable repute as a constitutional theorist. There followed *The Divine Right of Church Government and Excommunication* (1646), on behalf of Presbyterian Church polity, and *A Free Disputation against Pretended Liberty of Conscience* (1649), a vigorous defence of religious persecution in reply to Jeremy *Taylor, on the ground that the advocacy of toleration put conscience in the place of God and the Bible. Several devotional writings also belong to these years. At the Restoration (1660) his *Lex Rex* was publicly burnt and a charge of high treason was preferred against him, but he died shortly afterwards.

Collection of his letters pub. under the title *Joshua Redivivus or Mr Rutherford's Letters* [ed. by R. McWard], no place, 1664; the best edn. is that of A. A. Bonar (London, 1848), with sketch of Rutherford's life, pp. v–xxxiii, frequently repub.; in edn. of 1891 there is also a list of Rutherford's works, pp. 31 f.; modern selection ed. H. Martin (London, 1957). A collection of his Sermons also ed. A. A. Bonar (ibid., 1885). Lives by T. Murray (Edinburgh, 1828), A. Thomson ('Men Worth Remembering', London, 1884), and R. Gilmour (Edinburgh and London, 1904). A. Whyte, *Samuel Rutherford and some of his Correspondents* (Lectures delivered in St George's Free Church, Edinburgh; 1894). G. W. Sprott in *DNB* 50 (1897), pp. 7–9; B. Hall in *Dict. Sp.* 13 (1988), cols. 1190–3.

Rutilius Claudius Namatianus (5th cent.), Latin poet. In 416 or 417 he returned to his native Gaul after some time spent in Rome; in his 'De Reditu Suo' he described the journey homewards. By religion he was almost certainly a pagan, despite H. Schenkl's attempt (1911) to prove him a Christian. He was conservative in his outlook, despised all religious innovations and was esp. critical of the monastic movement which, under St *Jerome's influence, had then become very popular at Rome. Stilicho (the Roman general and virtual ruler of the W. Empire) he regards not as a restorer of traditional pagan practices (the usual Christian conception of him), but as their uncompromising enemy. His poem throws important light on the background of the Church in the period.

Editio princeps by J. B. Pius, Bologna, 1520. Crit. texts by J. Vesserau, with full study (Paris, 1904), id. and F. Préchac (Collection des Universités de France, Paris, 1933; with Fr. tr.), P. van de Woestijne (Rijksuniversiteit te Gent. Werken uitgegeven door de Faculteit van de Wijsbegeerte en Letteren, Afl. 76; Antwerp, 1936), and E. Castorina (Florence, 1967). Further frag. ed. M. Ferrari in *Italia Medioevale e Umanistica*, 16 (1973), pp. 15–30. Convenient edn., with Eng. tr. and introd., by J. W. and A. M. Duff, *Minor Latin Poets* (Loeb, 1934), pp. 753–829. I. Lana, *Rutilio Namaziano* (Turin, 1961); F. Corsaro, *Studi Rutiliani* (Bologne, 1981). H. Schenkl, 'Ein spätrömischer Dichter und sein

Glaubensbekenntnis', *Rheinisches Museum für Philologie*, NF 66 (1911), pp. 393–416. A. Cameron, 'Rutilius Namatianus, St. Augustine, and the Date of the *De Reditu*', *Journal of Roman Studies*, 57 (1967), pp. 31–9.

Ruysbroeck or more correctly **Ruusbroec, Bl Jan van** (1293–1381), mystic. His name derives from his birthplace, a small village in Brabant. About 1304 he went to Brussels for his education, living in the house of his relative, J. Hinckaert, a canon of St-Gudule, and remaining there after his ordination, *c.*1317. His biographer, Pomerius, states that he opposed a woman heretic (Bloemardinne), who seems to have been connected with the *Brethren of the Free Spirit; this assertion has been questioned in recent years. In 1343 he retired with Hinckaert and another priest to a hermitage at Groenendaal, near Brussels, where they were joined by others. In 1350 the group became a community of *Canons Regular, with Ruysbroeck as prior until his death. Groenendaal became prominent in the religious movement later known as *Devotio Moderna*, with which were also associated the *Brethren of the Common Life and the Canons Regular of *Windesheim, and such eminent spiritual writers as *Thomas à Kempis.

Ruysbroeck wrote almost entirely in the vernacular of the country, Middle Dutch. His works (with their titles in English) include *The Spiritual Espousals* (later criticized on doctrinal grounds by J. *Gerson), *The Kingdom of the Lovers of God*, *The Book of Supreme Truth*, *The Mirror of Eternal Salvation*, *The Seven Steps of the Ladder of Spiritual Love*, *The Sparkling Stone* (also known as *The Treatise of Perfection of the Sons of God*), and *The Book of the Spiritual Tabernacle*. Several of these works were translated into Latin during the 14th cent., and all of them by L. Surius in the 16th cent. His writings show the influence of St *Augustine, *Bede, St *Bernard, *Dionysius the Pseudo-Areopagite, *Eckhart (though some of his opinions were rejected), *Hadewijch, and *Peter Comestor; their authority has endured. He was beatified in 1908. Feast day, 2 Dec.

Works ed. J. [B.] David (6 vols., Ghent, 1858–68); also under the auspices of the Ruusbroec-Genootschap at Antwerp by J. B. Poukens, SJ, and others (4 vols., Malines and Amsterdam, 1932–4; rev. edn., Tielt, 1944–8) and by G. de Baere, SJ, and others (10 vols., Tielt and Leiden, 1981 ff.); this last edn. repr. the Lat. tr. of L. Surius, orig. issued at Cologne in 1552, and a fresh Eng. tr. There are separate modern Eng. trs. of many of his works. The Life by H. Pomerius (1382–1469) is pr. in *Anal. Boll.* 4 (1885), pp. 257–308. A. Auger, *De Doctrina et Meritis Johannis van Ruysbroek* (Louvain, 1892). *Jan van Ruusbroec: Leven, Werken, onder de redactie van het Ruusbroec-Genootschap, Antwerpen* (Malines and Amsterdam, 1931). P. Mommaers, *Waar naartoe is nu de gloed van de liefde?* (Antwerp and Utrecht, 1973; Eng. tr., *The Land Within: The Process of Possessing and being Possessed by God according to the Mystic Jan van Ruysbroeck*, Chicago [1975]). A. Ampe, SJ, *Ruusbroec: Traditie en werkelijkheid* (Studiën en Tekstuitgaven van Ons Geestelijk Erf, 19; 1975). P. Mommaers and N. de Paepe (eds.), *Jan van Ruusbroec: The Sources, Content and Sequels of his Mysticism* (Mediaevalia Lovaniensis, Series 1, Studia 12; 1984). *Jan van Ruusbroec, 1293–1381: Tentoonstellingscatalogus . . . georganiseerd door het Comité-Jan van Ruusbroec, 1981* (Brussels, 1981), with detailed bibl. E. Colledge, OSA, in *NCE* 12 (1967), pp. 763–5, s.v.; A. Ampe, SJ, in *Dict. Sp.* 8 (1974), cols. 659–97, s.v. 'Jean Ruusbroec'.

Rycaut, Paul (1628–1700), also 'Ricaut', traveller and author. Born at Aylesford, Kent, after studying at Trinity College, Cambridge, he spent most of his life abroad. In 1661 he was appointed secretary to the British Embassy at *Constantinople, where he collected extensive materials on the life and customs of Turkey and the Muslim religion, which were published later as *The Present State of the Ottoman Empire* (1668; acc. to S. Pepys, the original edition was almost completely destroyed in the Great Fire). From 1667 to 1679 he was consul to the Levant Company at Smyrna. On his return to England he issued an essay on *The Present State of the Greek and Armenian Churches* (1679), which remains an important contemporary source of information on the E. Churches. He was also the author of *The History of the Turkish Empire from the Year 1623 to the Year 1677* (2 parts, 1679–80), and translated a large number of Latin and Greek treatises into English, incl. B. *Platina's *Lives of the Popes* (1685).

S. P. Anderson, *An English Consul in Turkey: Paul Rycaut at Smyrna, 1667–1678* (Oxford, 1989).

Ryder, Henry (1777–1836), Bp. of *Gloucester and then of Coventry and *Lichfield. The younger son of the first Lord Harrowby, he was educated at Harrow and St John's College, Cambridge. In 1801, the year after his ordination, he became rector of Lutterworth. At first he stood aloof from the *Evangelicals, attacking their principles as at variance with those of the C of E, but he was soon won over and became one of their most prominent leaders and the first Evangelical to be made a bishop. He was a canon of *Windsor (1808–12) and Dean of *Wells (1812–15) before he became Bp. of Gloucester in 1815, an appointment aided by the influence of his brother. Though his ecclesiastical position at first made him suspect among the clergy of the diocese, his personal qualities made him greatly loved both in Gloucester and in Lichfield, to which he was translated in 1824. He was one of the earliest bishops to introduce reforms into his dioceses, including the more careful administration of *Confirmation. He preached much more frequently than most bishops, and he worked hard to recover the masses, building a number of new churches. He had a special concern for the industrial areas of his Lichfield diocese which included Birmingham and the Potteries. He was a friend and confidant of Hannah *More.

T. D. Ryder (son), *A Memoir of the Hon. and Rt. Rev. Henry Ryder* (pr. for private circulation, 1886). G. C. B. Davies, *The First Evangelical Bishop: Some Aspects of the Life of Henry Ryder* (Tyndale Church History Lecture, 1957; 1958). J. H. Overton in *DNB* 50 (1897), pp. 45–7.

Rylands St John. Part of one page of a papyrus codex (P. 52), now in the John Rylands University Library of Manchester. It contains on the recto chapter 18, verses 31–3, and on the verso verses 37–8, of St John's Gospel. It is written in a clear quasi-documentary hand and may be assigned to the first half of the second cent. and prob. to the early part of it. It is thus both the earliest known MS of any part of the NT and the earliest distinct evidence for the existence of the Fourth Gospel. It was found in Egypt, prob. either in *Oxyrhynchus or the Fayum. The text exhibits no striking divergences from the known text. The complete Gospel would have occupied some 150 pages, and it may be assumed that the codex contained no other work.

Text first pub. by C. H. Roberts, *An Unpublished Fragment of the Fourth Gospel in the John Rylands Library* (Manchester, 1935); also in *Catalogue of the Greek and Latin Papyri in the John Rylands Library, Manchester*, 3, ed. id. (ibid., 1938), pp. 1–3. H. I. Bell, *Recent Discoveries of Biblical Papyri* (lecture; Oxford, 1937), esp. pp. 20 f. B. M. Metzger, *The Text of the New Testament* (2nd edn., Oxford, 1968), pp. 38 f.

Ryle, Herbert Edward (1856–1925), Dean of *Westminster. The son of J. C. *Ryle, he was educated at Eton and King's College, Cambridge, where in 1881 he was elected a Fellow. Apart from a short period as principal of St David's College, Lampeter (1886–8), he remained at Cambridge until his appointment to the see of *Exeter in 1900. Translated in 1903 to the see of *Winchester, he resigned this office to become Dean of Westminster in 1911. From 1919 to 1925 he was *Prolocutor of the Lower House of Convocation of Canterbury. His writings include *The Early Narratives of Genesis* (1892), *The Canon of the OT* (1892), and *Genesis* (Camb. Bible, 1914).

Memoir by M. H. FitzGerald (London, 1928). Id. in *DNB, 1922–1930*, pp. 733–5.

Ryle, John Charles (1816–1900), Bp. of Liverpool. He was born at Macclesfield and educated at Eton and Christ Church, Oxford. When his wish to become a Member of Parliament had been frustrated by lack of financial means, he decided to take orders. He was ordained priest in 1842, and after holding several parochial cures, was consecrated bishop of the newly created Anglican see of Liverpool in 1880, which he held till shortly before his death. A strong Evangelical in his beliefs, he defended his convictions in forceful and simple language in a number of tracts which had a wide circulation. Among his publications are *The Bishop, the Pastor, and the Preacher* (1854; studies on H. *Latimer, R. *Baxter, and G. *Whitefield), *The Christian Leaders of the Last Century* (1869), *What do we owe to the Reformation?* (1877), and *Principles for Churchmen* (1884).

Life by P. Toon and M. Smout (Cambridge, 1976). J. M. Rigg in *DNB*, Suppl., 3 (1901), pp. 334 f., s.v.

Rynsburgers. See COLLEGIANTS.

Ryswick (or Rijswick) Clause. The clause 'Religione tamen Catholica Romana in locis sic restitutis, in statu quo nunc est, remanente', inserted into Article IV of the Treaty of Ryswick (30 Oct. 1697). It modifies the general rule that the religious frontiers should revert to their position at the time of the Treaty of Nijmegen (1679) in favour of the Catholic communities in those places where they had been re-established by Louis XIV in the interval.

Text of the Treaty of Ryswick between the Emp. Leopold and Louis XIV, pr., with comm., in H. Vast, *Les Grands Traités du règne de Louis XIV*, 2 (1898), pp. 228–53, this stipulation occurring on p. 232; most imp. sections of Treaty repr. in E. Reich (ed.), *Select Documents Illustrating Mediaeval and Modern History* (1905), pp. 25–32, with this stipulation, pp. 26 f. C. T. G. von Scheurl in *PRE* (3rd edn.), 17 (1906), pp. 273 f., s.v. 'Ryswicker Klausel'.

S

Sá, Manoel de (*c.*1530–96), Portuguese theologian. He entered the *Jesuit novitiate at Coimbra in 1545. In 1551 he became professor of philosophy at Alcalá and in 1557 was called to teach theology at the Roman College. *Pius V appointed him a member of the *Septuagint Commission. The last years of his life he spent in pastoral work at *Loreto and Genoa. Besides several scriptural Commentaries he published, in 1595, *Aphorismi Confessariorum*, a manual of casuistry in dictionary form which was temporarily placed on the *Index in 1603 for allowing confession and absolution to be made by letter, but in its corrected edition of 1607–8 enjoyed great authority among moral theologians.

G. Barbieri, 'Spunti sociali ed economici nell'opera del gesuita portoghese Manuel Sà', *Estudos italianos em Portugal*, 23 (1964), pp. 25–41. Sommervogel, 7 (1896), cols. 349–54; 9 (1900), col. 829; and 12 (1911–31; repr. 1960), cols. 775 f. R. Brouillard, SJ, in *DTC* 14 (pt. 1; 1939), cols. 425–8, s.v. 'Sa (Emmanuel)', with bibl.

Sabaoth (Heb. צְבָאוֹת; Gk. Σαβαώθ). This Hebrew word, which denotes 'armies' or 'hosts', is preserved untranslated in the phrase 'Lord of Sabaoth' in older translations of the NT (Rom. 9: 29, Jas. 5: 4) and in the traditional English version of the *Te Deum. See also LORD OF HOSTS.

Sabas, St (439–532), monk. A native of Mutalaska in Cappadocia, after leading the life of a monk and solitary in several places in the E., in 478 he founded a large *lavra (still extant as 'Mar Saba') in Palestine in the wild country between *Jerusalem and the Dead Sea (the Wadi en-Nar). With reluctance he accepted ordination to the priesthood (then not usual for monks) in 490, and in 492 the Patr. of Jerusalem created him superior of all the hermits in Palestine. A strong supporter of theological orthodoxy, he took a prominent part in the campaign against *Origenism and *Monophysitism. A *typicon circulates under his name in the E. Church. Feast day, 5 Dec.

The principal authority is the Life by *Cyril of Scythopolis, pr., with Lat. tr., by J. B. *Cotelier, *Ecclesiae Graecae Monumenta*, 3 (Paris, 1686), pp. 220–376; modern edn. by E. *Schwartz in *TU* 49 (Heft 2; 1939), pp. 85–200. Fr. tr. by A. J. Festugière, OP, *Les Moines d'orient*, 3, pt. 2 (1962). *BHG* (3rd edn., 1957), 2, pp. 228 f. (nos. 1608–10). D. J. Chitty, *The Desert a City* (Oxford, 1966), esp. pp. 105–24. History of the Lavra of St Sabas (in Gk.) by J. Phocylides (Alexandria, 1927). H. *Leclercq, OSB, in *DACL* 15 (pt. 1; 1950), cols. 189–211, s.v., with full bibl. on the churches and monastery.

Sabas, St, Patron of Serbia. See SAVA, ST.

Sabatier, Auguste (1839–1901), French Protestant theologian. He was professor of reformed dogmatics at Strasbourg University from 1868 to 1873, and from 1877 at the newly established Protestant theological faculty at *Paris. He propagated the theories of F. D. E. *Schleiermacher

and A. *Ritschl in France, applied the methods of historical criticism to the NT, and, esp. by his interpretation of Christian dogma as the symbolism of religious feelings, exercised a profound influence not only on French Protestantism but also in Catholic theological circles, thus helping to prepare for the *Modernist Movement. Among his best-known works are *L'Apôtre Paul* (1870; Eng. tr., 1891), *La Vie intime des dogmes* (1890), *Esquisse d'une philosophie de la religion* (1897; Eng. tr., 1897) and his posthumous *Les Religions d'autorité et la religion de l'esprit* (1903; Eng. tr., 1904).

T. Silkstone, *Religions, Symbolism and Meaning: A Critical Study of the Views of Auguste Sabatier* (Oxford, 1968). B. Reymond, *Auguste Sabatier et le procès théologique de l'autorité* (Lausanne [1976]), with bibl., pp. 307–27.

Sabatier, Paul (1858–1928), *Calvinist pastor and Franciscan scholar. After completing his theological studies at Paris, where he had Auguste *Sabatier and E. *Renan among his teachers, he held pastoral cures in Strasbourg, where he had been born, and then at St-Cierge-le-Serre. At the latter he began his studies on St *Francis. Soon compelled by frail health to give up his pastoral work, he devoted the rest of his life to his research, spending long periods in Italy, esp. at *Assisi. His *Vie de S. François* (1893; Eng. tr. 1894), depicting the mission of Francis as a renewal of the medieval Church in the light of the 'pure Gospel', was based on a close study of the sources, brilliant in presentation and penetrating in its psychological understanding. The work was widely read, but, on account of its liberal outlook, was soon put on the *Index (8 June 1894).

Sabatier's further researches brought to light much important new material, notably the *Speculum Perfectionis*, the *Tractatus de Indulgentia S. Mariae de Portiuncula*, and the *Regula Antiqua* of the Franciscan *Third Order, though some of his contentions on the primitive sources turned out to be mistaken. He also directed two series of publications, *Collection de documents pour l'histoire religieuse et littéraire du moyen âge* (1898–1909) and *Opuscules de critique historique* (1901–19). In 1902 he founded the 'Società Internazionale di Studi Francescani' at Assisi and in 1908 the British Society of Franciscan Studies at London. He was also an active sympathizer with the RC *Modernist Movement, on which he delivered a course of Jowett Lectures in London in 1908 (pub. later in the year).

A. G. Little, *Franciscan Papers, Lists and Documents* (Publications of the University of Manchester, no. 284; 1943), pp. 179–88 ('Paul Sabatier, Historian of St Francis'; lecture delivered in 1929); C. [N. L.] Brooke, *Medieval Church and Society* (1971), pp. 197–213 ('Paul Sabatier and St Francis of Assisi'; composed 1957–8); R. Manselli, 'Paul Sabatier e la "Questione Francescana"', in *La 'Questione Francescana' dal Sabatier ad oggi: Atti del I Convegno Internazionale, Assisi, 18–20 ottobre 1973* (Società Internazionale di Studi Francescani, Assisi, 1974), pp. 51–70.

Sabatier, Pierre (1682–1742), *Maurist scholar. After joining the *Benedictine Order at *Reims in 1700, he went to *St-Germain-des-Prés, where he was trained in historical method by T. *Ruinart. His monumental work, the fruit of many years' research, was a virtually exhaustive collection of the material then available for the *Old Latin (i.e. pre-*Vulgate) text of the Bible. It was published posthumously as *Bibliorum Sacrorum Latinae Versiones Antiquae* (3 vols., fol., 1743[-9]) at Reims, whither the author had been transferred in 1727 on account of his supposed *Jansenist tendencies. The importance of his work is acknowledged by the fact that his name still occurs in the title of the edition in process of publication by the Vetus Latina Institute at the Archabbey of *Beuron.

[R. P. Tassin, OSB,] *Histoire littéraire de la congrégation de Saint-Maur* (1770), pp. 617–21. P.-M. Bogaert, OSB, in *Dict. Bibl.*, Suppl. 10 (1985), cols. 1127–30, s.v., with further refs. In English, L. F. Hartman in *NCE* 12 (1967), p. 777.

Sabbatarianism. Excessive strictness in the observance of the Divinely ordained day of rest. Although there is evidence of a similar rigidity in the observance of *Saturday among the *Anabaptists of E. Europe in the 16th cent., the rigorous observance of *Sunday is a peculiar development of the English and Scottish Reformation, being unknown on the Continent even among *Calvinists. The beginning of 17th-cent. Sabbatarianism is connected with the publication in 1595 of Nicholas Bound's *True Doctrine of the Sabbath*, which advocated its strict enforcement on OT lines. The book caused a lively controversy, which assumed political importance when *James I issued his *Book of *Sports* (1618), enjoining cessation of work but allowing lawful recreation. When reissued by *Charles I in 1633, the *Book* roused a storm of protest, and was burned by Parliament in 1643. The Puritan Sabbath was imposed by successive Acts of legislation (1644, 1650, 1655) prohibiting any kind of recreation on Sunday, even going for a walk. After the Restoration observance was slightly relaxed when under *Charles II the Act for the Better Observance of the Lord's Day (1677) was passed which, though it forbade all work and travel by horse or boat on Sunday, was silent on recreations. Under the influence of the *Evangelical Revival at the end of the 18th cent. rigorism took a new lease of life by the Lord's Day Observance Act, drawn up by Bp. B. *Porteus in 1781, which laid down that any place of entertainment or debate where admission was gained by payment of money should be closed to use on Sunday. In Scotland Sabbatarianism was carried to extremes from the beginning of the 17th cent., all recreation including even books and music not strictly religious being disallowed. Here, as well as in England, relaxation has been progressive since the latter part of the 19th cent. The Puritan point of view is today represented by the *Lord's Day Observance Society. See also SUNDAY.

Full bibl. of the older literature (which, though abundant, is very repetitive) in R. Cox, *The Literature of the Sabbath Question* (2 vols., Edinburgh, 1865). K. L. Sprunger, 'English and Dutch Sabbatarianism and the Development of Puritan Social Theology (1600–1660)', *Church History*, 51 (1982), pp. 24–38. D. S. Katz, *Sabbath and Sectarianism in Seventeenth-Century England* (Studies in Intellectual History, 10; Leiden, 1986). K. L. Parker, *The English Sabbath: A Study of the Doctrine and Discipline from the Reformation to the Civil War* (Cambridge, 1988; cf. review by A. Milton in *JEH* 41 (1990), pp. 491–4). B. W. Ball, *The Seventh-day Men: Sabbatarians and Sabbatarianism in England and Wales, 1660–1800* (Oxford, 1994). See also bibl. to SUNDAY.

Sabbath. The seventh day of the Jewish week. It is sanctified by complete abstinence from work (Exod. 20: 10) and in OT times it was marked by the doubling of the daily sacrifices (Num. 28: 9 f.) and special gatherings for worship (Lev. 23: 2 f.). The particular distinction of the seventh day may be connected with the phases of the moon. No exact parallels are known from other ancient Near Eastern cultures; the word may be connected with the Akkadian *shapattu*, the day of the full moon, but there are no resemblances to the way this day was observed in Mesopotamia. In the Bible its origin is accounted for in a double way. Acc. to Exod. 20: 11 and 31: 17 it represents the rest God took on the seventh day from His work of Creation (cf. Gen. 2: 2–3), whereas acc. to Deut. 5: 15 it is apparently kept in remembrance of the deliverance from Egypt. The Sabbath served the twofold purpose of being a day set apart for the worship of God (Exod. 31: 13–17) as well as for the rest and recreation of man, esp. slaves, and cattle (Deut. 5: 14). The prohibition of work was regulated by detailed prescription, forbidding e.g. the gathering of manna, cooking (Exod. 16: 22–30), and the lighting of fire (Exod. 35: 3). In the *Maccabaean period there was a tendency for regulations to become increasingly strict, and some pious Jews let themselves be killed rather than defend their lives on the Sabbath (1 Macc. 2: 32–8). In NT times activities such as healing (e.g. Mt. 12: 10) and plucking of ears of corn (Mt. 12: 1 f.) were sometimes considered forbidden, but debate about the precise definition of the work to be prohibited continued until rabbinic times. One of the Pharisees' chief grievances against Christ was that He declared the Sabbath to have been made for man and not vice versa (Mk. 2: 27). Though the primitive Christians largely continued to keep the seventh day as a day of rest and prayer, the fact that the Resurrection and Coming of the Holy Spirit had taken place on the first day of the week soon led to the observance of that day (i.e. *Sunday), to the exclusion of the Jewish Sabbath on Saturday. In modern times a few sects, such as the *Seventh-day Adventists, observe Saturday in literal fulfilment of the Fourth Commandment rather than the Sunday adopted by most Christian bodies.

The details of rabbinic Sabbath observances are set out in the *Mishnah tractate 'Shabbath'; Eng. tr. with notes by H. Danby, *The Mishnah* (1933), pp. 100–21. R. de Vaux, OP, *Les Institutions de l'Ancien Testament*, 2 (1960), pp. 371–82, with bibl. pp. 456 f. (Eng. tr., 2nd edn., 1965, pp. 475–83, with bibl. p. 550). E. P. Sanders, *Jewish Law from Jesus to the Mishnah* (1990), pp. 6–23. R. North, SJ, 'The Derivation of Sabbath', *Biblica*, 35 (1955), pp. 182–201. E. Lohse in *TWNT* 7 (1964; Eng. tr., 1971), pp. 1–35, s.v. σάββατον. M. Greenberg in *Encyclopaedia Judaica*, 14 (Jerusalem, 1972), cols. 557–62, s.v.; J. Briend in *Dict. Bibl.*, Suppl. 10 (1985), cols. 1132–70, s.v. 'Sabbat'; G. F. Hasel in *Anchor Bible Dictionary*, 5 (1992), pp. 849–56, s.v.

Sabbatical Year. The one year in seven which the *Mosaic legislation (Exod. 21: 2–6; Deut. 15: 1–3; 15: 12–18; 31: 10–13; Lev. 25, etc.) ordered to be observed as a 'Sabbath', i.e., requiring the land to remain fallow and all debtors and Israelite slaves to be freed. In Lev. 25 a simultaneous fallow year is prescribed, and its observance is attested in Neh. 10: 31 and 1 Macc. 6: 49, 53; cf. *Josephus, *Antiquities*, 14. 202, where Julius Caesar is said to have exempted the Jews from taxes in the sabbatical year. In the older strata of the *Pentateuch it seems to have been intended that each husbandman and slave-owner should be at liberty to decide which seventh year he would observe, so that the whole land should not go out of cultivation at once. See also JUBILEE, YEAR OF.

R. de Vaux, OP, *Les Institutions de l'Ancien Testament*, 1 (1958), pp. 264–7, with bibl. pp. 338 f. (Eng. tr., 2nd edn., 1965, pp. 173–5, with bibl. p. 532). E. Neufeld, 'Socio-Economic Background of Yōbēl and Šemittā', *Rivista degli Studi Orientali*, 33 (1958), pp. 53–124. M. Greenberg and others in *Encyclopaedia Judaica*, 14 (Jerusalem, 1972), cols. 574–86, s.v. 'Sabbatical Year and Jubilee'. See also comm. on Deut., ad loc.

Sabbatine Privilege. An indulgence granted to the *Carmelite Order. On the basis of a bull, 'Sacratissimo uti culmine', ascribed to *John XXII (1322), which was held to rest on an apparition of the BVM, certain privileges were granted to the Carmelite Order and its confraternit-ies. They include unfailing salvation and early release from Purgatory through the intervention of the BVM (esp. release on *Saturdays, Our Lady's day), provided certain conditions such as wearing the brown *scapular, keeping certain fasts, and reciting the *Little Office of Our Lady, are observed. The Sabbatine Privilege has been confirmed by several Popes, e.g. by *Pius XI in 1922. The authenti-city of the original bull was widely contested in the 16th and 17th cents., esp. by the Jesuit D. *Papebroch, and some violent controversies ensued. Its spuriousness is now admitted even by Carmelites themselves, such as B. Zimmerman. It prob. dates from the latter half of the 15th cent.

A note of the bull of John XXII occurs in G. Mollat (ed.), *Jean XXII (1316–1334): Lettres communes analysées d'après les registres dits d'Avignon et du Vatican*, 4 (1910), p. 169 (no. 16193). B. Zimmerman, ODC, *Monumenta Historica Carmelitana* (Lérins, 1907), pp. 356–63. See also bibl. to SIMON STOCK, ST.

Sabellianism. An alternative title for the Modalist form of *Monarchianism (q.v.). It is so named from Sabellius, of whom, however, very little is known. He was perhaps, like his fellow-Monarchians *Noetus and *Praxeas, an early 3rd-cent. theologian of Roman origin, though he is described by later 4th–5th-cent. Gk. writers (*Basil, *Timothy of Constantinople) as belonging to Libya or the Pentapolis.

Sabina, St (*c*.126), Roman martyr. Acc. to her late and untrustworthy *acta*, she was a widow of Umbria who was converted by the virtuous life of her servant, Serapia, a native of Antioch in Syria. Both Sabina and Serapia were arrested in the persecution under Hadrian, and Serapia beaten to death, while Sabina was discharged on account of her rank. A year later, however, Sabina was again appre-hended and martyred at Rome. There seems no probability even of the existence of such a saint. The *acta* were per-haps fabricated to account for the church of Sta Sabina (originally 'titulus Sabinae', later 'titulus Sanctae Sabinae') on the Aventine Hill, which is believed to contain her relics. Feast day, 29 Aug. She is commemorated by name

in the canon (now the first Eucharistic Prayer) of the *Ambrosian rite.

On SS Sabina and Serapia, *AASS*, Aug. 6 (1743), pp. 496–504; cf. also H. *Delehaye, SJ, in his edn. of the *Hieronymian Martyrology (*AASS*, Nov. 2 (pt. 2; 1931), p. 475). J. P. Kirsch, *Die römischen Titelkirchen im Altertum* (Studien zur Geschichte und Kultur des Altertums, 9, Hefte 1–2; 1918), pp. 163–6. On the church, J. J. Berthier, *L'Église de Sainte-Sabine à Rome* (Rome, 1918); id., *Le Couvent de Sainte-Sabine à Rome* (ibid., 1912). A. Muñoz, *Il restauro della basilica di Santa Sabina* (1938). F. Darsy, OP, *Santa Sabina* (Le chiese di Roma illustrate, 63–4; 1961). Id., *Recherches archéologiques à Sainte-Sabine* (Monumenti dell'Antichità Cristiana, 2nd ser., Monumenti, 9; 1968). R. Kraut-heimer and S. Corbett in R. Krautheimer and others, *Corpus Basilicarum Christianarum Romae*, 4 (Rome, 1970), pp. 72–98 [in Eng.]. J. P. Kirsch, op. cit., pp. 96–100. H. I. Marrou, 'Sur les origines du titre romain de Sainte-Sabine', *Archivum Fratrum Praedicatorum*, 2 (1932), pp. 316–25. M. D. Darsy, OP, in *DACL* 15 (pt. 1; 1950), cols. 218–38, s.v. 'Sabine (Basilique de Sainte-)'.

Saccas, Ammonius. See AMMONIUS SACCAS.

saccos. See SAKKOS.

Sacheverell, Henry (1674–1724), *High Church divine and pamphleteer. Born at Marlborough, he was educated at the Grammar School and at Magdalen College, Oxford, where he became a Fellow in 1701. In 1705 he was elected chaplain of St Saviour's, Southwark (now *Southwark Cathedral). On 15 Aug. 1709 he preached the assize sermon at Derby and on 5 Nov. 1709 before the Lord Mayor at *St Paul's. On both these occasions he upheld the doctrine of non-resistance and emphasized in violent language the perils facing the Church from the Whig gov-ernment's policy of toleration and allowance of *Occasional Conformity. In the latter sermon (*The Perils of False Brethren*) he also openly attacked G. *Burnet, Bp. of *Salisbury. In Dec. 1709 the Commons condemned the sermons as seditious and, despite the opposition of the Tories and of many Whigs, as well as strong feeling in the country, Sacheverell was impeached for high crimes and misdemeanours. The sentence (suspension from preaching for three years) was so light as to be a triumph for the accused and he became a popular hero. When the three years had passed, Sacheverell preached on Palm Sunday, 1713, to a packed gathering at St Saviour's, Southwark. The sermon, *The Christian Triumph; or, The Duty of Pray-ing for Our Enemies*, sold for £100 and had a very wide circulation. In 1713 he was presented by Queen *Anne, who had openly shown him sympathy, to the living of St Andrew's, Holborn.

Although the fall of the Whigs in 1710 was largely the result of the impeachment of Sacheverell, he would prob. not have made his mark in history had he not become the champion of the High Church and Tory parties. Among his pamphlets were *Character of a Low Churchman* (1701) and *The Rights of the Church of England* (1705; with Edmund Perkes).

Perils of False Brethren was repr. in facsimile (Exeter, 1974). J. R. *Bloxam, *Register* of Magdalen, 6 (1879), pp. 98–110. F. Madan, *A Bibliography of Dr. Henry Sacheverell* (1884). A. T. Scudi, *The Sacheverell Affair* (New York, 1939). G. Holmes, *The Trial of Doctor Sacheverell* (1973). W. Hunt in *DNB* 1 (1897), pp. 80–3.

Sacrament. The word is derived from the Lat. *sacramentum*, which was used to translate the Gk. μυστήριον ('mystery') in the Lat. NT; sacraments are thus means by which Christians partake in the 'mystery of Christ' (cf. Col. 1: 26 f.; Eph. 3: 4, 9; 6: 19, etc.). The fundamental mystery is the *Incarnation of Christ, and, depending on that, the Church, His Body, through which He communicates Himself to mankind. This communication is accomplished through certain symbolic acts (e.g. the washing of *Baptism, the meal of the *Eucharist) interpreted by the Gospel and the response of faith.

In Christian theology the scope of what the word comprises has varied widely. St *Augustine, who defined it as the 'visible form of invisible grace' or 'a sign of a sacred thing', applied it to *formulae* such as the Creed and the *Lord's Prayer, and such a wide application was commonplace for the first 1,000 years of the history of the Church. The earliest attempt to classify the sacraments was made by *Dionysius the Pseudo-Areopagite (*c.*500), who distinguished three 'rites' (τελεταί)—Baptism, the Eucharist, and *Unction—to which he added priestly *ordination, monastic consecration, and the funeral service. The same combination is found as a list of six sacraments in St *Theodore of Studios (d. 826), and the threefold classification is presupposed in the *De Vita in Christo* by N. *Cabasilas (14th cent.).

In the W. a general connotation of the term is still found in *Hugh of St-Victor (d. 1142), who has a large number of sacraments divided into three groups. Very soon, however, W. theology narrowed the connotation by regarding institution by Christ as an essential characteristic. In *Peter Lombard (*Sentences*, Bk. 4, dist. 1, num. 2) the seven which have become traditional in the W., i.e. Baptism, *Confirmation, the Eucharist, *Penance, Extreme Unction, Orders, and *Matrimony, are enumerated. Other symbolic rites came to be called 'sacramentals' (q.v.). The list was accepted by St *Thomas Aquinas and formally affirmed at the Councils of *Florence (1439; in the 'Decretum pro Armenis') and *Trent (1545–63). Despite the importance of the notion of institution, in several cases no occasion of explicit institution by Christ is apparent, so such institution had to be held to be implicit. Clearly the symbolic significance of the number seven played a part in the formation of the list. A more critical attitude to the Gospels in modern times has increased these difficulties and led to more emphasis on the Church as the fundamental sacrament of Christ in which all the commonly enumerated sacraments are implicit. The W. list of seven sacraments was imposed on the Emp. Michael Palaeologus in 1267, but such a list is rarely found in Orthodox circles until the 16th cent. It was never formally adopted by the Orthodox Church and is rejected by many modern Orthodox authorities.

From early times a special rank among the sacraments was given to Baptism and the Eucharist, both of which are clearly referred to in the Gospels (Mt. 28: 19 and 26: 26–9). In the *Thirty-Nine articles (Art. 25) of the C of E they are differentiated as the 'two Sacraments ordained of Christ our Lord in the Gospel' as distinct from the other 'five commonly called Sacraments'.

In the Middle Ages, under the influence of *Aristotelian *hylomorphism, a distinction was made between the 'matter' (*materia*) and the 'form' (*forma*) of the sacraments, the matter being the undetermined material element (in Baptism, water; in the Eucharist, the bread and the wine) and the form the consecratory words (in Baptism, the pronouncement of the Triple Formula; in the Eucharist, the words 'This is My Body', 'This is My Blood'). This distinction is first found in *William of Auxerre (d. 1231). Despite problems such as that of determining the 'matter', in e.g. Penance and Matrimony, such hylomorphism became the norm in W. theology until the middle of the 20th cent. According to such an approach the right matter and the right form, used with the right *intention, are among the minimal conditions for the *validity of the sacrament. Where these conditions are all present the due performance of the act is sufficient to ensure that the sacrament will normally convey grace, since, acc. to Catholic theology, the validity of the sacraments is independent of the worthiness or unworthiness of the minister and hence their working is normally *ex opere operato*. Nevertheless they do not convey grace to the recipient if he is not rightly disposed. In the absence of faith and repentance he may put an impediment (*obex*) in the way of the grace which would normally flow from the sacrament. In such cases the sacramental act, though 'valid' is not 'efficacious'.

The theological significance of the sacraments lies in: (1) The exhibition of the principle of the Incarnation. By the embodiment of spiritual reality in material form an appropriate counterpart of the union of God with man in the Person of Christ is made patent. (2) Their expression of the objectivity of God's action on the human soul. The reception of God's gifts is normally dependent not on changing subjective feelings, but on obedience to the Divine will. (3) As ordinances mediated through the Church, their essentially social structure. They are the means whereby the union of God and man consequent on the Incarnation is perpetuated in Christ's mystical Body of His Church, its members incorporated in Him, and through Him united to one another.

Recent theology has reaffirmed the primary NT and patristic understanding of the sacraments as a way of participating in the mystery of Christ through symbolic actions. This was reflected in the documents of the Second *Vatican Council (1962–5) and the rites which have been subsequently authorized. There has been an increased emphasis on the word in the celebration of the sacraments, so that the reading of Scripture and a homily have come to form a normal part of sacramental celebration. The 'word' is thus more than the 'form' of the sacrament; rather it effects an encounter with the Word of Christ by which the mind and heart of the Christian is opened to the incoming grace of God. The suspicion, often aroused by traditional RC theology, of a 'mechanical' understanding of the sacraments with its hylomorphism and notion of *ex opere operato* causality, is thus dispelled; the Christian can rely on the sacraments because Christ is faithful in His sacraments, not simply because certain rules are observed.

Three of the sacraments, namely Baptism, Confirmation, and Orders, are held to imprint an abiding mark or *character (*character indelibilis*) on the soul and therefore cannot be repeated. When there is uncertainty as to whether a person has already received these sacraments, they are administered 'conditionally'.

Among the Protestant Churches the *Quakers and the *Salvation Army are the only two large bodies which make no use of sacraments. In Protestantism in general, though the technicalities of sacramental theology are less developed, the greatest importance is often attached to Baptism and the Lord's Supper. The comparative rarity of celebrations of the latter in Protestant Churches in the past, which has survived in some cases, is often matched by a correspondingly high degree of seriousness and devotion in its reception. Great emphasis has always been laid on the belief that the sacraments are expressive of the Word of God.

See also the entries on separate sacraments; also '*Baptism, Eucharist and Ministry'.

Introductory modern studies incl. P. T. *Forsyth, *Lectures on the Church and the Sacraments* (1917); O. C. Quick, *The Christian Sacraments* (1927); J. W. C. Wand, *The Development of Sacramentalism* (1928). F. *Probst, *Sakramente und Sakramentalien in den drei ersten christlichen Jahrhunderten* (1872). W. Knoch, *Die Einsetzung der Sakramente durch Christus: Eine Untersuchung zur Sakramententheologie der Frühscholastik von Anselm von Laon bis zu Wilhelm von Auxerre* (BGPM, NF 24 [1983]). J. B. *Franzelin, SJ, *Tractatus de Sacramentis in Genere* (Rome, 1868); P. Schanz, *Die Lehre von den heiligen Sakramenten der katholischen Kirche* (1893); N. Gihr, *Die heiligen Sakramente der katholischen Kirche* (Theologische Bibliothek, 2 vols., 1918–21). [E.] H. *Schillebeeckx, OP, *De Sacramentele Heilseconomie: Theologische bezinning op S. Thomas' sacramentenleer in het licht van de traditie en van de hedendaagse sacramentsproblematiek* (Antwerp, 1952). Id., *Christus, Sacrament van de Godsontmoeting* (Bilthoven, 1960; Eng. tr., 1963); B. Leeming, SJ, *Principles of Sacramental Theology* (1956; new edn., 1960). D. M. Baillie, *The Theology of the Sacraments and Other Papers* (1957), pp. 37–124. K. *Rahner, SJ, *Kirche und Sakramente* (Quaestiones Disputatae, 10; 1960; Eng. tr., 1963). J. D. Crichton, *Christian Celebration: The Mass* (1971); id., *Christian Celebration: The Sacraments* [except the Eucharist] (1973). H. Rondet, SJ, *La Vie Sacramentaire: Théologie, histoire et dogme* [1972]. B. Spáčil, SJ, *Doctrina Theologiae Orientis Separati de Sacramentis in Genere* (Orientalia Christiana Analecta, 113; 1937). A. Schmemann, *Introduction to Liturgical Theology* (Eng. tr. from Russ., 1966; Orthodox). J. de Ghellinck, SJ, and others, *Pour l'histoire du mot 'Sacramentum'* (SSL 3; 1924). A. Michel in *DTC* 14 (pt. 1; 1946), cols. 485–644, s.v. 'Sacrements', with further bibl. See also bibls. to separate sacraments.

sacrament house. A shrine-like receptacle for the *reservation of the Blessed Sacrament. It developed from the stone niche in the wall ('*aumbry'), and in Scotland it always retained this form. Elsewhere, after the introduction of the Feast of *Corpus Christi (1264), it began to take the shape of a small tower, the central part of which was often done in open-work. These sacrament houses, which were popular esp. in Germany, Belgium, and France, were frequently decorated with reliefs depicting the Last Supper, the Passion, or other subjects. From the 16th cent. onwards they were largely displaced by *tabernacles, but current RC legislation permitting reservation away from the altar has led to the revival in some places of receptacles similar to the medieval sacrament houses.

J. Hertkens, *Die mittelalterlichen Sakraments-Häuschen* (Frankfurt am Main [1908]); E. Maffei, *La Réservation eucharistique jusqu'à la Renaissance* (Brussels, 1942), pp. 91–122. A. Macpherson, 'Scottish Sacrament Houses', *Proceedings of the Society of Antiquaries of Scotland*, 25 (1891), pp. 89–116. Braun, *CA* 2, pp. 585–97 *passim*. F. X. Noppenberger in *L.Th.K.* (2nd edn.), 9 (1964), col. 244, s.v. 'Sakramentshäuschen'. See also works cited under RESERVATION.

sacramentals. Acc. to RC theology, sacred signs with spiritual effects, resembling the *sacraments. When the theology of the sacraments was defined and their number limited to seven in the W. Church in the 12th cent., analogous religious practices, not held to have been instituted by Christ, came to be known as 'sacramentals'. In contrast to the sacraments, which are held to convey grace primarily through the power of the rite itself (*ex opere operato*), sacramentals do so *ex opere operantis ecclesiae*, that is through the intercession of the Church. Some are closely associated with sacraments (e.g. the blessing of baptismal water, holy oils, or the ring in marriage), and by them men and women are prepared to receive the chief fruit of the sacrament; by others (such as *grace at meals or religious *profession), various human activities are rendered holy. In the nature of the case there is no definitive list of sacramentals.

For current formulas, see the section of the *Rituale Romanum, *De Benedictionibus* (1984). The subject is treated in the *Catechism of the Catholic Church* (1992), nos. 1667–79. Popular account in M. Donovan, *Sacramentals* (1925). F. *Probst, *Sakramente und Sakramentalien in den drei ersten christlichen Jahrhunderten* (1872), pp. 16–96. J. R. Quinn in *NCE* 12 (1967), pp. 790–2, s.v. See also s.v. BLESSING.

Sacramentarians. The name which M. *Luther gave to those theologians (esp. U. *Zwingli and J. *Oecolampadius) who maintained that the Bread and Wine of the *Eucharist were the Body and Blood of Christ in only a 'sacramental', i.e. metaphorical, sense. The word thus came to be commonly used in the 16th cent. for all those who denied the doctrine of the *Real Presence of Christ in the Eucharist. It has occasionally been applied also in other senses.

Sacramentary (Lat. *Liber Sacramentorum*). In the W. Church, the liturgical book in use down to the 13th cent. for the celebrant at Mass; it contained the *Canon of the Mass and the proper *Collects, *Prefaces, and other prayers for use throughout the year, but not the *Epistles or *Gospels, nor those parts of the rite (e.g. the *Gradual) which were sung. Sacramentaries also contained *Ordination formularies, blessings, and other prayers used by priests and bishops. From the 10th cent. onwards, the desirability of having all the parts of the service in a single book led to the gradual replacement of the Sacramentary by the *Missal and *Pontifical.

Older edns. of the texts incl. G. M. *Tommasi, *Codices Sacramentorum* (Rome, 1680); id., *Antiqui Libri Missarum* (ibid., 1691); L. A. *Muratori, *Liturgia Romana Vetus* (2 vols., Venice, 1748); J. A. *Assemani, *Codex Liturgicus Ecclesiae Universae* (13 vols., Rome, 1749–66; repr. in facsimile, Farnborough, Hants, 1968–9). For more recent edns., see GELASIAN, GREGORIAN and LEONINE SACRAMENTARIES, MISSALE FRANCORUM, MISSALE GALLICANUM VETUS, and MISSALE GOTHICUM. L. Delisle, *Mémoire sur d'anciens sacramentaires* (1886); F. *Probst, *Die ältesten römischen Sakramentarien und Ordines* (1892); E. Bourque, *Étude sur les sacramentaires romains* (1, Studi di Antichità Cristiana, 20, 1948; 2. 1, Bibliothèque Théologique de Laval, Quebec; 1952; 2. 2, Studi di Antichità Cristiana, 25, 1958), with extensive bibl. C. Vogel, *Medieval Liturgy: An Introduction to the Sources*, rev. Eng. tr. by W. G. Storey and N. K. Rasmussen, OP (Washington, DC [1988]), pp. 61–134. K. Gamber (ed.), *Sakramentartypen: Versuch einer Gruppierung der Handschriften und Fragmente bis zur Jahrtausendwende* (Texte und Arbeiten, 1. Abteilung, Heft 49/1; 1958);

id., *Codices Liturgici Latini Antiquiores* (Spicilegii Friburgensis Subsidia, 1; Fribourg, 1963; with Suppl., ibid. 1A; 1988) [both books are useful but inaccurate]. V. Leroquais, *Les Sacramentaires et les missels manuscrits des bibliothèques publiques de France* (1924; with plates). M. Andrieu, 'Quelques remarques sur le classement des sacramentaires', *JLW* 11 (1931), pp. 46–66. H. *Leclercq, OSB, in *DACL* 15 (pt. 1; 1950), cols. 242–85, s.v. 'Sacramentaires'; A. Bugnini in *EC* 10 (1953), cols. 1558–69, s.v. 'Sacramentario'; H. Ashworth, OSB, in *NCE* 12 (1967), pp. 792–800, s.v. See also bibl. to MISSAL and to ORDINES ROMANI.

Sacred College (Lat. *Sacrum Collegium*). The former and still commonly used designation of the college of *cardinals (q.v.), though, in common with other such bodies, 'sacrum' has now been dropped from the official title.

Sacred Heart. Devotion to the physical heart of Jesus, though theologically defined and officially practised only since the 18th cent., can be traced back to the Middle Ages. It seems to have sprung from the cult of the Wound in the Side. It is to be met with in two treatises of St *Bonaventure, 'Vitis mystica' (formerly attributed to St *Bernard) and 'De ligno vitae'. Extracts from the latter are incorporated in the present Office of the feast, and the devotion appears richly developed in the visions attributed to St Mechtild of Hackeborn (d. 1299) and St *Gertrude (d. c.1302), both at the convent of Helfta. But the devotion was long confined to a relatively small number of mystics and saints, e.g. *Julian of Norwich and St *Frances of Rome. A new departure was made in the 16th cent., when the devotion extended from the visions of the mystics to the regular practice of many given to the ascetic life, and it was fostered esp. by the *Carthusians. A little later the *Jesuits became its most ardent advocates in France and St *Francis of Sales imbued with it his *Visitandines, and these two orders worked together to obtain for the Sacred Heart a place in the official as well as the popular life of the Church. The first to provide an elaborate theological and liturgical foundation for both devotion and feast, however, was St John *Eudes (q.v.). But his efforts remained without much response until the famous visions (1673–1675) of the Visitandine nun, St *Margaret Mary Alacoque, which gave a definite shape to the object of the devotion and its practices. Its most prominent feature was reparation for the outrages committed against the Divine Love, esp. in the Blessed Sacrament. From that time it became one of the most popular RC devotions, though its liturgical observance was not permitted until 1765, when *Clement XIII authorized the Mass and Office of the feast. It is observed on the Friday in the week after *Corpus Christi. In 1856 *Pius IX extended the feast to the universal Church; in 1889 *Leo XIII raised it to a *Double of the First Class, and ten years later solemnly consecrated all mankind to the Sacred Heart. The Mass and Office of the feast were revised by *Pius XI in 1928 when it received a privileged octave. The octave was dropped in 1960. In the 1969 Roman calendar the observance is now classed as a '*solemnity'.

J. Croiset, *La Dévotion au Sacré-Cœur de N.S. Jésus-Christ* (Lyons, 1691; 3rd and definitive edn., 1694; Eng. tr. from Ital., London, 1863; modern Eng. tr. from 1694 edn., Dublin and London, 1949). J.-B. Terrien, SJ, *La Dévotion au Sacré-Cœur de Jésus d'après les documents authentiques et la théologie* (1893). J. V.

Bainvel, *La Dévotion au Sacré-Cœur de Jésus* (1906; Eng. tr., 1924). D. Chastelain, *De Cultu Eucharistici Cordis Jesu: Historia—Doctrina—Documenta* (Paris, 1928). Useful material in the Encyclical of Pius XI revising the Mass and Office (8 May 1928), pr. in *AAS* 20 (1928), pp. 165–78. P. Debongnie, CSSR, 'Commencement et recommencements de la dévotion au Coeur de Jésus', in *Le Coeur: Les Études Carmélitaines* (1950), pp. 147–92; K. *Rahner, SJ, ' "Siehe dieses Herz!" Prolegomena zu einer Theologie der Herz-Jesu-Verehrung', *Schriften zur Theologie*, 3 (1956), pp. 379–90; id., 'Einige Thesen zur Theologie der Herz-Jesu-Verehrung', ibid., pp. 391–415; Eng. tr. of both arts. in *Theological Investigations*, 3 (1967), pp. 321–52. G. de Becker, SSCC, *Les Sacrés-Cœurs de Jésus et de Marie* (Études Picpuciennes, 5; 1959), pp. 9–235; J. Le Brun, 'Politics and Spirituality: The Devotion to the Sacred Heart', *Concilium*, 9, no. 7 (1971), pp. 29–43. J. Bainvel in *CE* 7 (1910), pp. 163–7, s.v. 'Heart of Jesus. Devotion to the'; id. in *DTC* 3 (1908), cols. 271–351, s.v. 'Cœur Sacré de Jésus (Dévotion au)', with bibl.; L. Penzo in *EC* 4 (1950), cols. 1059–64, s.v. 'Cuore di Gesù', with bibl.

Sacred Heart of Mary. Devotion to the heart of the BVM was first seriously fostered in the 17th cent. by St John *Eudes (q.v.), who linked it closely with the cult of the Sacred Heart of Jesus. In 1805 *Pius VII allowed the observance of a feast of the Pure Heart of Mary; in 1855 a proper Mass, based on texts proposed by Eudes, was authorized for use in some places, and an Office followed in 1857. Words attributed to the BVM at *Fátima popularized the cult; in 1942 *Pius XII consecrated the world to the Immaculate Heart of Mary and in 1944 he made universal a corresponding feast to be observed on 22 Aug., the *Octave day of the *Assumption. In the 1969 RC calendar this observance became an optional '*memoria'.

Pius XII's Oratio consecrating the world to the Immaculate Heart of Mary is pr. in *AAS* 34 (1942), pp. 345 f.; the new Office and Mass provided for the feast in Aug. 1944 are pr. ibid. 37 (1945), pp. 44–52. G. de Becker, SSCC, *Les Sacrés-Cœurs de Jésus et de Marie* (Études Picpuciennes, 5; 1959), pp. 239–437, with bibl. pp. 243–5. J. Arragain, 'La Dévotion au Cœur de Marie' in H. du Manoir, SJ (ed.), *Maria*, 5 (Paris, 1958), pp. 1007–48. See also works of St John Eudes.

sacrifice. Sacrifice is fundamentally the offering to the Deity of a gift, esp. a living creature. It is a widespread feature of religion, incl. that of the Hebrews. Early in the OT there is the record of the sacrifice of Cain and *Abel (Gen. 4: 3–5), while the demand for the sacrifice of *Isaac (Gen. 22) underlies the need for the offering to be a costly one and may be taken to suggest that human sacrifice was not excluded (cf. Jephthah's daughter, Jgs. 11: 32–40; also Exod. 22: 29 and Mic. 6: 7). From the earliest times also sacrifice was particularly associated with the making of covenants; the most important of these were God's covenants with *Noah after the Flood (Gen. 8: 20–9: 17), with *Abraham (Gen. 15), and with Israel at *Sinai (Ex. 24: 4–8). After the settlement in Canaan sacrificial observances became increasingly elaborate and they provoked considerable criticism from some of the 8th–7th-cent. Prophets (e.g. Amos 5: 21–5, Hos. 6: 6, and Jer. 7: 21–3). At the end of the 7th cent. King Josiah (c.640–c.608 BC) prohibited sacrifices except at the *Temple in Jerusalem, and when the city was destroyed at the Exile (c.586) the regular round of official sacrifices temporarily ceased. After the Exile, when the Temple was rebuilt, an even more elaborate system of sacrifices was devised; it is described in detail in the final form of the *Pentateuch, and esp. in Leviticus. Apart from a brief interruption by *Antiochus Epiphanes (168), this sacrificial system was practised in the restored Temple until its destruction in AD 70. The chief annual sacrifices were those of the *Paschal Lamb sacrificed for each household at the Passover in memory of the deliverance of the Israelites from Egypt (Exod. 12: 1–28) and those of the Day of *Atonement (q.v.).

In the NT Christ appears to have tolerated the current practice of sacrifice (cf. Matt. 5: 23 f., 8: 4); but He quoted with approval the teaching of Hosea subordinating 'sacrifice' to 'mercy' (Matt. 9: 13, 12: 7: cf. Hos. 6: 6). At the Institution of the *Eucharist, which took place in the sacrificial context of the Passover (whether on 14 Nisan or 15 Nisan) and with reference to the covenant-sacrifice of Exod. 24: 4–8, He pointed to the sacrificial quality of His death (cf. Mk. 10: 45), speaking of the shedding of His blood in a New Covenant. Both St *John the Baptist (Jn. 1: 29) and the Evangelist (Jn. 19: 14 and 36) appear to imply that Christ, as the 'Lamb of God', is Himself a Sacrificial Victim, a doctrine endorsed by St *Paul in 1 Cor. 5: 7, and made more explicit in Eph. 5: 2 (cf. also 1 Pet. 1: 19), while Rev. 13: 8 emphasizes the eternal nature of the Lord's Sacrifice. The author of *Hebrews (q.v.) stresses the High Priesthood of Christ, who by His perfect obedience in the voluntary offering of Himself (9: 26, cf. 10: 5 ff.) made 'one sacrifice for sins for ever' (10: 12), in contrast to the deficiencies of the OT sacrifices, and he compares the Lord's Passion to the sin-offering (13: 11 f.).

The implications of these biblical ideas are developed by the Fathers, who stress esp. the uniqueness of Christ's sacrifice in that He was (1) a voluntary victim, (2) a victim of infinite value, and (3) also Himself the Priest. See also ATONEMENT.

The chief development of the patristic and medieval period was in regard to the *Eucharist (q.v.). From early times the Eucharistic Offering was called a sacrifice in virtue of its immediate relation to the Sacrifice of Christ (e.g. by *Serapion of Thmuis). While it can also be said that in the Eucharist Christ is sacrificed 'again', yet St *Thomas Aquinas insisted that the Mass was itself an 'immolation' only in so far as it was an 'image' of the Passion which was the 'real immolation' (Summa Theol. III. 83. 1). In rejecting the doctrine of 'the sacrifices of Masses' the Anglican *Thirty-Nine Articles (Art. 31) is perhaps more concerned to deny the idea, current in the Middle Ages, of the repeated 'immolation' of Christ than to repudiate belief in the Eucharistic Sacrifice altogether. See also EUCHARIST.

In accordance with such passages as Ps. 40: 6–8 and Rom. 12: 1, Christian theology has commonly asserted that the individual's conscious obedience, active or passive, to the will of God may be a form of sacrifice which can be offered to God the Father in imitation of, and in union with, the Sacrifice of Christ.

E. O. James, *Origins of Sacrifice* (1933). W. R. *Smith, *Lectures on the Religion of the Semites* (1889), pp. 196–419; 3rd edn. by S. A. *Cook (1927), pp. 213–440, with full notes; S. C. Gayford, *Sacrifice and Priesthood* (1924); G. B. *Gray, *Sacrifice in the Old Testament* (posthumous, 1925); W. O. E. Oesterley, *Sacrifices in Ancient Israel* (1937); R. de Vaux, OP, *Les Sacrifices de l'Ancien Testament* (Cahiers de la *Revue Biblique*, 1; 1964; Eng. tr., Cardiff, 1964). J. Lécuyer, CSSP, *Le Sacrifice de la nouvelle alliance* (1962).

F. M. Young, *Sacrifice and the Death of Christ* (1975). R. J. Daly, SJ, *The Origins of the Christian Doctrine of Sacrifice* (1978). G. [W. E. C.] Ashby, *Sacrifice: Its Nature and Purpose* (1988). S. W. Sykes (ed.), *Sacrifice and Redemption: Durham Essays in Theology* (Cambridge, 1991). L. Sabourin, SJ, 'A Bibliography of Sacrifice in the Bible and the Ancient Near East', in S. Lyonnet, SJ, and L. Sabourin, *Sin, Redemption, and Sacrifice: A Biblical and Patristic Study* (Analecta Biblica, 48; 1970), pp. 299–333, incl. a section on the Eucharistic Sacrifice. On the Eucharist as Sacrifice, as well as works cited s.v. Eucharist, K. [W.] Stevenson, *Eucharist and Offering* (New York [1986]), with bibl.; id., *Accept This Offering: The Eucharist as Sacrifice Today* (1989). A. Gaudel in *DTC* 14 (pt. 1; 1939), cols. 662–92, s.v., with bibl.

sacrilege. Strictly a violation or contemptuous treatment of a person, thing, or place, publicly dedicated to the worship of God. Moral theologians hold that it may be either personal, i.e. directed against a person in holy orders or a religious (e.g. ill-treatment or sins against chastity), or real, i.e. committed against a thing, esp. the Sacraments (e.g. treating irreverently the Blessed Sacrament or administering or receiving the Sacraments in a state of mortal sin), or local, i.e. committed in a holy place (e.g. homicide in a church). Sacrilege is held to be a grave sin in itself, though venial if the matter is trivial. In everyday language the term is used more vaguely, though in a sense similar to that of moral theology.

The subject is regularly treated in works on moral theology. N. Iung in *DTC* 14 (pt. 1; 1939), cols. 692–703, s.v. 'Sacrilège'.

sacring bell. A bell, also known as a 'Sanctus bell', rung at Mass to focus the people's attention. The use of a bell, esp. at the *Elevation of the Elements, dates from the 12th cent. The *Ritus Servandus required the bell to be rung at the *Sanctus and at the Elevation, and it became customary to ring it at certain other moments as well. Where bells are used at all, they are now usually rung at the Elevation and before the communion of the celebrant.

H. Thurston, SJ, 'The Bells of the Mass', *The Month*, 123 (1914), pp. 389–401. Braun, *CA*, pp. 573–80. Jungmann (1958 edn.), 2, pp. 261 f.; Eng. tr., 2, p. 131, with refs.

sacristan. The term is used either (1) for a *sexton or (2), more commonly, for the sacrist or official who has charge of the contents of a church, esp. those used in Divine worship such as sacred vessels, vestments, etc. He may be in holy orders, as is usual in a cathedral, or a layman.

sacristy (Lat. *sacristia*, *sacrarium*, or *secretarium*; Gk. διακονικόν). A room annexed to a church or chapel for keeping the sacred vessels and for the vesting of priests and other clerics. Sacristies were introduced *c.*400 in Syria as annexes to the apse; in the Middle Ages they came to be built behind or on either side of the high altar. In large conventual churches and cathedrals they often consist of a suite of separate rooms for the higher and the lower clergy and for lay servers. They are furnished with chests, cupboards, and a table for vestments, liturgical books, and vessels, a basin for the washing of hands, a *prie-dieu*, and a crucifix. In early times the sacristy was often used for the permanent reservation of the Blessed Sacrament, and it is commonly still so used for the purpose when the Blessed Sacrament is removed from the church between Good

Friday and the Paschal Vigil Service. In current Anglican usage, the room where the clergy vest is often known as the (priests') vestry, the term sacristy tending to be restricted to vestries in churches with an elaborate ceremonial, where a larger number of liturgical objects need to be stored.

Sadducees. A Jewish politico-religious sect, opposed to the '*Pharisees'. The name is probably derived from the high priest Zadok (2 Sam. 8: 17). The party originated at the time of the *Hasmonaeans. Its members were never numerous, but they included wealthy men of high standing, such as some *High Priests. Though their teachings were never popular, individual Sadducees exercised great political influence from the reign of John Hyrcanus (135–104 BC) onwards, and in the time of Christ they were of particular importance in *Jerusalem and in the *Temple. Little can be recovered of their beliefs, but they rejected the traditional interpretations accepted by the Pharisees and accepted the written Law only. Thus they rejected belief in retribution in an afterlife and in the resurrection of the body (Mt. 22: 23), and also the existence of angels and spirits (Acts 23: 8). In the NT they appear to have taken a leading part against Jesus, perhaps because they feared trouble with the Roman power, and in any case because they opposed His doctrines (Mt. 22: 23–33, etc.). They also repeatedly attacked the Apostles for teaching the Resurrection of Christ (Acts 4: 1–3; 5: 17; cf. 23: 6–10). After the fall of Jerusalem they disappear from history.

For works dealing with the Pharisees and the Sadducees, together, see also bibl. to PHARISEES. G. Hölscher, *Der Sadduzäismus* (1906); R. Leszynsky, *Die Sadduzäer* (1912); J. Le Moyne, OSB, *Les Sadducées* (Études Bibliques, 1972), with good bibl. T. W. Manson, 'Sadducee and Pharisee—The Origin and Significance of the Names', *Bulletin of the John Rylands Library*, 22 (1938), pp. 144–59, esp. pp. 144–53. J. Jeremias, *Jerusalem zur Zeit Jesu* (3rd edn., Göttingen, 1962), pp. 259–64; Eng. tr., *Jerusalem in the Time of Christ* (1969), pp. 228–32. E. *Schürer, *The History of the Jewish People in the Age of Jesus Christ*, rev. Eng. tr. by G. Vermes and others, 2 (Edinburgh, 1979), pp. 404–14, with bibl. pp. 381 f. H. L. Strack and P. Billerbeck, *Kommentar zum Neuen Testament aus Talmud und Midrash*, 4 (1928), pp. 339–52. K. Kohler in *JE* 10 (1905), pp. 630–3, s.v.; R. Meyer in *TWNT* 7 (1964; Eng. tr. 1971), pp. 35–54, s.v. Σαδδουκαῖος, with bibl.

Sadhu, the. See SUNDAR SINGH, SADHU.

Sadoleto, Jacopo (1477–1547), cardinal. A classical and philosophical scholar and favourite of Card. O. Carafa, he was appointed secretary to *Leo X in 1513, and in 1517 Bp. of Carpentras. A man of pure and blameless character and unselfish zeal, he soon became one of the most influential ecclesiastics of his time, one of his chief concerns being the reconciliation of the Protestants. In 1536 he was made cardinal by *Paul III together with R. *Pole, and in 1537 he became a member of the special commission for the reform of the Church and the preparation of a General Council. At the same time he endeavoured unsuccessfully to win back P. *Melanchthon (1537) and the city of *Geneva (1539) to the Catholic faith. In 1542 as Papal legate he failed to effect a reconciliation between the French King Francis I and the Emp. *Charles V. During his last years he was among the most trusted advisers of Paul III, constantly advocating reform. Among his writings are the treatise *De Peccato Originali* and *De Exstructione Ecclesiae Catholicae* as well as a commentary on Romans, which was forbidden at Rome until its doctrine of grace, which was suspected of *Semipelagianism, had been corrected in the *Augustinian sense.

Works [ed. D. Raustius] (Mainz, 1607), with Life by A. Florebelli prefixed [no pagination]; also ed. in 4 vols., Verona, 1737–8. Eng. tr. of his *De Pueris Recte Instituendis* by E. T. Campagnac and K. Forbes (London, 1916) and of his letter to the city of Geneva, along with Calvin's reply, by J. C. Olin, *A Reformation Debate* (New York, 1966). Modern studies by G. von Schulthess-Rechberg (Zurich, 1909), S. Ritter, *Un umanista teologo* (Rome, 1912), and R. M. Douglas (Cambridge, Mass., 1959). W. Reinhard, 'Jacopo Sadoleto' in E. Iserloh (ed.), *Katholische Theologen der Reformationszeit*, 4 (Katholisches Leben und Kirchenreform im Zeitalter der Glaubensspaltung, 47; 1987), pp. 29–42, with bibl. J. E. Sandys, *A History of Classical Scholarship*, 2 (1908), pp. 115 f. F. Gagliuolo in *EC* 10 (1953), cols. 1611 f., s.v.; R. M. Douglas in *NCE* 12 (1967), p. 846, s.v.

Sahdona (or, from the Gk., 'Martyrius'), 7th-cent. spiritual writer. A native of the Persian Empire, he was educated at Nisibis and about 615/20 entered a monastery. About 635/40 he became Bp. of Mahoze in the *Church of the East. He was, however, expelled from that Church because of his teaching on the Person of Christ and fled to *Edessa. It was very probably here that he wrote 'The Book of Perfection', one of the masterpieces of Syriac spiritual writing.

Œuvres spirituelles, ed., with Fr. tr., by A. de Halleux, OFM (CSCO, Scriptores Syri, 86–7, 90–1, 110–13; 1960–5). S. P. Brock, 'A further fragment of the Sinai Sahdona Manuscript', *Muséon*, 81 (1968), pp. 139–54; A. de Halleux, 'Un chapitre retrouvé du *Livre de Perfection* de Martyrius', ibid. 88 (1975), pp. 253–96. L. Leloir, OSB, in *Dict. Sp.* 10 (1980), cols. 737–42, s.v. 'Martyrius (Sahdona)'.

Sahidic. One of the principal dialects of Coptic (q.v.; see also BOHAIRIC and FAYUMIC). Among older scholars it was known as 'Thebaic', from Thebes, the chief city of Upper (i.e. Southern) Egypt, where Sahidic was used early in the Christian era. The Scriptures were translated into Sahidic prob. as early as the 3rd or even the end of the 2nd cent. In recent times a large number of papyrus fragments and parchment manuscripts have been discovered. Notable biblical MSS include *Bodmer Papyrus 23 (4th cent.), containing Is. 47: 1–66: 24, an almost complete Acts (also containing Deut. and Jonah; early 4th cent., British Library Or. 7594), and the Gospels of Sts Mark, Luke, and John in Barcelona (P. Palau Rib. Inv. no. 181–3; 5th cent.). The text of the NT in the Sahidic version has both '*Neutral' and '*Western' elements, though the extent of the W. elements is less considerable than used to be supposed. Sahidic was the principal literary dialect from the 4th to the 10th cent. and has an extensive body of ecclesiastical literature, mostly translated from Greek; native writers include *Pachomius, *Shenoute, and his disciple Besa.

The edn. of the Sahidic NT by G. Horner (7 vols., Oxford, 1911–24) now needs to be supplemented; the Barcelona texts of Mk., Lk., and Jn., with variants from certain other MSS, ed. H. Quecke (Papyrologica Castroctaviana, 4, 6, and 11, respectively;

Barcelona, 1972, 1977, and 1984). B. M. Metzger, *The Early Versions of the New Testament* (Oxford, 1977), pp. 99–152. T. Orlandi, *Elementi di lingua e letteratura copta* (Milan [1970]). For works on grammar and dictionaries, see COPTIC (LANGUAGE).

St Albans. A church has existed at Verulam on the site of the reputed martyrdom of St *Alban from at least the time of *Bede; and *c.*794 King *Offa endowed a monastery here in expiation of the murder of St *Ethelbert, King of the East Angles, which soon became one of the most famous in the country. In 1077 Paul of Caen, the first Norman abbot, began to rebuild it. Its wealth continued to increase, esp. after *Hadrian IV gave it precedence over all other English monasteries and exempted it from episcopal jurisdiction. At the Reformation the church was bought from *Edward VI (1553) for use as a parish church. In 1877 a see of St Albans was constituted, by taking Hertfordshire and Essex from London and N. Woolwich from *Rochester to make the new diocese; and the abbey became the new cathedral church. In 1914 Essex and N. Woolwich were transferred to the new see of Chelmsford, while the county of Bedford was taken from *Lincoln and added as compensation to St Albans. See also MATTHEW PARIS.

Thomas Walsingham, *Gesta Abbatum Monasterii Sancti Albani*, ed. H. T. Riley (3 vols., RS, 1867–9); fuller text of the St Albans Chronicle, 1406–1420, ed. from Bodley MS 462 by V. H. Galbraith (Oxford, 1937). John Amundesham, *Annales Monasterii S. Albani*, ed. H. T. Riley (2 vols., RS, 1870–1). *Chronica Monasterii S. Albani: Registra Quorundam Abbatum Monasterii S. Albani, qui Saeculo XVmo floruere*, ed. id. (2 vols., ibid., 1872–3). W. *Dugdale, *Monasticon Anglicanum*, 2 (1819 edn.), pp. 178–255. P. Newcome, *The History of the Ancient and Royal Foundation, called the Abbey of St Alban ... from the Foundation thereof in 793, to its Dissolution in 1539* (2 pts., bound in one, 1793–5); J. C. and C. A. Buckler, *A History of the Architecture of the Abbey Church of St Alban, with especial reference to the Norman Structure* (1847). L. F. R. Williams, *History of the Abbey of St Alban* (1917). Royal Commission on Historical Monuments (England), *A Guide to Saint Albans Cathedral* (1952; 2nd edn., 1982). E. Toms, *The Story of St Albans* (1962). R. [A. K.] Runcie (ed.), *Cathedral and City: St Albans Ancient and Modern* (1977). C. R. Peers, W. Page, and others in *VCH*, Hertfordshire, 2, ed. W. Page (1908), pp. 469–515. W. Levison, 'St. Alban and St. Albans', *Antiquity*, 15 (1941), pp. 337–59. The St Albans Psalter, a richly illuminated 12th-cent. MS prob. written at St Albans for Christina, anchoress of Markyate, ed. O. Pächt, C. R. Dodwell, and F. Wormald (Studies of the Warburg Institute, 25; 1960).

St Asaph. The church of St Asaph (called Llanelwy in earlier Welsh sources) was in origin a monastic settlement, traditionally held to be founded by St *Kentigern in the late 6th cent. According to a 12th-cent Life of the saint, he was succeeded at Llanelwy by his disciple, St *Asaph, from whom the church later took its name. It became a territorial diocese in the early 12th cent. The present Anglican diocese comprises the whole or parts of the counties of Conwy, Flintshire, Denbighshire, and Wrexham. The present cathedral is largely the work of Bp. Redman (*c.*1480); the choir was rebuilt *c.*1770; and the whole restored by G. G. *Scott (1869–75). Notable Bishops of St Asaph include *Geoffrey of Monmouth (1152–4), Adam Parvipontanus (1175–80), R. *Pecock (1444–50), W. *Morgan (1601–4), I. Barrow, the elder (1670–80), W. *Beveridge (1704–8), and S. *Horsley (1802–6).

'Summi Libri Rubei Asaphensis communiter dicti "Llyfr Coch Asaph", exscrpt. ex Originali 26° Octobris 1602', in *Collectanea Topographica et Genealogica*, 2 (1835), pp. 255–79; 'Index to "Llyfr Coch Asaph" copied out of a MS. in the Bishop's Library at St. Asaph', ed. G. Roberts in *Archaeologia Cambrensis*, 3rd ser. 14 (1868), pp. 151–66, 329–40, with notes pp. 433–43. The Registers of the 13 ancient parishes of the Diocese in the County of Shropshire, ed. W. P. W. Phillimore, W. G. D. Fletcher, and D. R. Thomas (Shropshire Parish Register Society, 8 vols. bound in 11, 1899–1922). B. Willis, *A Survey of the Cathedral Church of St Asaph and the Edifices belonging to it* (1720; enlarged edn. by E. Edwards, 2 vols., 1801). D. R. Thomas, *Esgobaeth Llanelwy: A History of the Diocese of St Asaph* (1874; enlarged edn., 3 vols., Oswestry, 1906–13). Id., *St Asaph* (Diocesan Histories, 1888); P. B. I. Bax, *The Cathedral Church of Saint Asaph* (Bell's Cathedral Series, 1904). J. Fisher in *DECH* (1912), pp. 532–5, s.v. See also works cited s.v. WALES, CHRISTIANITY IN.

Saint-Cyran, Abbé de (1581–1643), Jean Duvergier de Hauranne, one of the authors of *Jansenism. A protégé of Justus Lipsius at the *Jesuit College at Louvain, and then a fellow-student at Paris (1604–10) and Bayonne (1611–17) with C. *Jansen, with whom he made a close friendship, he was attracted to St *Augustine's writings, the theology of which he preferred to the prevailing scholasticism. In 1617 he settled for a time at Poitiers, where he was secretary to the Bishop, de la Rocheposay. In 1620 he was created commendatory Abbot of Saint-Cyran and thenceforward lived mainly in Paris, seeking out all the chief personalities of the time (*Vincent de Paul, J.-J. *Olier, G. Tarisse, P. de *Bérulle). He made it his object to reform Catholicism on Augustinian lines, largely in the hope of defeating Protestantism with its own weapons. From 1623 he became closely associated with the influential *Arnauld family and with *Port-Royal, and from 1633 as spiritual counsellor of the convent exercised an immense religious influence. Between 1617 and 1635 he was the recipient of a long series of letters from Jansen (pub. Louvain, 1654). His power led *Richelieu to consider him a dangerous character, and from 1638 until 1643 after Richelieu's death he was incarcerated in the fortress of Vincennes, where he wrote his *Lettres chrétiennes et spirituelles* (pub. 1645). He was held in great veneration by later Jansenists, who looked up to him as a martyr. His writings include *Somme des fautes ... du P. Garasse* (1626), an attack on the *Jesuits; *Petrus Aurelius de Hierarchia Ecclesiastica* (1631), a plea for the rights of the episcopate against the Papacy, partly based on M. Antonio *de Dominis's *De Republica Christiana*; and *Théologie familière* (1642).

C. Lancelot, *Mémoires touchant la vie de M. de S. Cyran* (2 vols., Cologne, 1738). J. Lafferière, *Étude sur Jean Duvergier de Hauranne, abbé de Saint-Cyran* (Louvain, 1912). J. Orcibal, *Les Origines du jansénisme* (Bibliothèque de la RHE, 16), 2 and 3, *Jean Duvergier de Hauranne, abbé de Saint-Cyran et son temps*, 4, *Lettres inédites de Jean Duvergier de Hauranne, abbé de Saint-Cyran*, ed. A. Barnes, and 5, *La Spiritualité de Saint-Cyran avec ses écrits de piété inédits* (1947–62). J. Orcibal in *DHGE* 14 (1960), cols. 1216–41, s.v. 'Duvergier de Hauranne (Jean-Ambroise)'; B. Chédozeau in *Dict. Sp.* 14 (1990), cols. 140–50, s.v. See also bibl. to JANSENISM and PORT-ROYAL.

St Davids. Acc. to tradition a monastery was founded in Menevia by St *David (6th cent.), the Patron of *Wales, which was thereafter called St Davids. The early history is fragmentary and uncertain, but a succession of bishops followed. The Life of St David, written by Rhygyfarch in the late 11th cent., was designed to bolster the claims of the Welsh bishops to independence from *Canterbury. On the death of the last native Welsh bishop in 1115, however, King Henry I forced on the *claswyr* or clergy as their bishop Bernard, chaplain of Queen Matilda, who was prepared to recognize the authority of the Archbishop. Some time between 1124 and 1130 the Chapter of St Davids addressed to Pope Honorius II a letter claiming metropolitan status. In the latter part of his episcopate Bp. Bernard also tried to secure Papal recognition of this claim, but without success, even though in 1140 two other Welsh bishops were ready to recognize his primacy. The attempts of *Giraldus Cambrensis to secure metropolitan status for St Davids in 1198–1203 were equally unsuccessful. Meanwhile, the shrine of St David became famous, and was visited by *William I, Henry II, Edward I and his Queen Eleanor; and, acc. to an inscription found on the shrine by Abp. *Pecham (1240–92), two pilgrimages to St Davids were the equivalent of one to Rome. Today only the stone base of the shrine survives, but the reputed relics of St David are preserved close by. The present beautiful cathedral was begun by Bp. Peter de Leia (1176–98). Among his successors were Henry Gower (1328–47), the 'Menevian [*William of] Wykeham', who built the stone rood-screen and the fine episcopal palace (now in ruins); Henry *Chichele (1408–14), afterwards Abp. of Canterbury; W. *Barlow (1536–48), the chief consecrator of Abp. M. *Parker (1559); and W. *Laud (1621–6). The official title of the Bishop of St Davids is 'Episcopus Menevensis'.

The Episcopal Registers of the Diocese of St David's, 1397 to 1518, ed., with Eng. tr., by R. F. Isaacson (Cymmrodorion Record Series no. 6, vols. 1 and 2, 1917; vol. 3, A Study of the Published Registers by R. A. Roberts, 1920). J. W. Willis-Bund (ed.), *An Extent of all the Lands and Rents of the Lord Bishop of St David's, made by Master David Fraunceys, Chancellor of St David's ... in the Year of Our Lord 1326: Usually called the Black Book of St David's* (ibid., no. 5; 1902). J. C. Davies (ed.), *Episcopal Acts and Cognate Documents relating to Welsh Dioceses 1066–1272*, 1 (Historical Society of the Church in Wales, 1; 1946), pp. 233–413. B. Willis, *A Survey of the Cathedral Church of St David's, and the Edifices belonging to it as they stood in the Year 1715* (1717). W. B. Jones and E. A. Freeman, *The History and Antiquities of Saint David's* (1856). [J.] W. Evans and R. Worsley, *Eglwys Gadeiriol Tyddewi, St Davids Cathedral, 1181–1981* (Aberystwith, 1981). D. W. James, *St Davids and Dewisland: A Social History* (Cardiff, (1981), esp. chs. 2, 3, 6, 7, and 8. F. Morgan in *DECH* (1912), pp. 535–9, s.v. See also works cited under DAVID, ST, and WALES, CHRISTIANITY IN.

St-Denis. The *Benedictine abbey at St-Denis, four miles N. of *Paris, which was founded c.625 and contained the reputed shrine of St Denis (see DIONYSIUS, ST [3]), was for centuries the richest and most important in France. As it became the regular burying-place of the kings of France and other French princes and nobles, it long enjoyed royal favour, and over the high altar was suspended the 'Oriflamme' of the kings of France (originally the banner of the abbey). Here St *Joan of Arc hung up her arms in 1429, and *Henry IV renounced his Protestantism in 1593. Early in the 17th cent. it was constituted the chief abbey of an independent Benedictine congregation, but in 1633 it was attached to the *Maurists. The abbey (which had been reduced to the rank of a priory in 1691 by Louis

XIV) was dissolved and sacked at the Revolution (1792–3), but the buildings were restored under Napoleon III, and are now a 'national monument'.

The best edn. of the book of Abbot *Suger (q.v.), *Sugerii Abbatis Sancti Dionysii Liber*, is that, with Eng. tr. and introd., by E. Panofsky (Princeton, NJ, 1946). G. G. Meersseman, OP (ed.), *Les Capitules du Diurnal de Saint-Denis (Cod. Verona Cap. LXXXVIII, Saec. IX)* (Spicilegium Friburgense, 30; 1986); E. B. Foley (ed.), *The First Ordinary of the Royal Abbey of St-Denis in France (Paris, Bibliothèque Mazarine 526)* (ibid. 32; 1990). J. Doublet, OSB, *Histoire de l'abbaye de S. Denys en France* (1625); M. Félibien, OSB, *Histoire de l'abbaye royale de Saint-Denys en France* (1706). [F.] de Guilhermy, *Monographie de l'église royale de Saint-Denis: Tombeaux et figures historiques* (1848). J. Formigé, *L'Abbaye royale de Saint-Denis: Recherches nouvelles* (1960). S. McK. Crosby, *The Royal Abbey of Saint-Denis from its Beginnings to the Death of Suger, 475–1151*, ed. P. Z. Blum (Yale Publications on the History of Art, 37 [1987]), and earlier works of this author. L. Grodecki, *Les Vitraux de Saint-Denis*, 1 (Corpus Vitrearum Medii Aevi, France, Études, 1; 1976). *Le Trésor de Saint-Denis* (Catalogue of exhibition at the Musée du Louvre, Paris, 12 mars–17 juin 1991).

St Gall. See GALL, ST.

St-Germain-des-Prés. An abbey in Paris on the S. bank of the Seine, founded in the 6th cent. St *Germanus of Paris dedicated the church to the Holy Cross and St Vincent on a 23 Dec. between 557 and 559, but it later assumed his name. In the 17th cent. it gained great celebrity when it adopted the *Maurist reform and became the headquarters of such scholars as J. *Mabillon and B. de *Montfaucon. Most of the abbey was destroyed by fire during the French Revolution, but its fine collection of MSS was saved, and mostly passed in 1795–6 to the Bibliothèque Nationale.

J. Bouillart, OSB, *Histoire de l'abbaye royale de Saint-Germain-des-Prez* (1724). F. Ribadeau Dumas, *Histoire de Saint Germain des Prés, abbaye royale* (1958). M. Ultee, *The Abbey of St Germain des Prés in the Seventeenth Century* (1981). J. B. Vanel (ed.), *Nécrologe des religieux de la Congrégation de Saint-Maur décédés à l'Abbaye de Saint-Germain-des-Prés* (1896). H. *Leclercq, OSB, in *DACL* 6 (pt. 2; 1925), cols. 1102–50, s.v. 'Germain-des-Prés (Saint-)', with refs. L. H. Cottineau, OSB, *Répertoire topo-bibliographique des abbayes et prieurés* (Mâcon, 1935), cols. 2710 f. See also bibl. to MAURISTS.

St-Maur, Congregation of. See MAURISTS.

St-Omer. The *Jesuit college of St-Omer in Artois was founded by R. *Parsons c.1592 for the education of the English RC laity and, in the first ten years of its existence, numbered already over 100 pupils. After a fire in 1684 it was rebuilt on a large scale. When, in 1762, the Parlement of Paris ordered the expulsion of the Jesuits and the Society transferred its school to Bruges, the buildings at St-Omer were used for the preparatory school of the English clergy at *Douai until they removed to England in 1795. The house at St-Omer was afterwards sold to the French Government and used for secular purposes.

Hubert Chadwick, SJ, *St Omers to Stonyhurst* (1962), pp. 1–311. G. Holt, SJ, *The English Jesuits in the Age of Reason* (Tunbridge Wells, Kent, 1993), esp. pp. 110–13 and 127–41.

St Patrick's Purgatory. Since the 12th cent., a place of pilgrimage on Station Island, Lough Derg, Co. Donegal, where Christ is supposed to have revealed to St *Patrick an entrance to *purgatory and the earthly paradise. The earliest recorded visit, by an Irish knight named Owein *c.* 1146/7, is reported by the *Cistercian H[enry] of Sawtrey (or Saltrey) *c.*1180–4 in the *Tractatus de Purgatorio Sancti Patricii*. Widely copied and translated, this text motivated occasional visits to the Purgatory by knightly pilgrims from different countries in the late 14th and 15th cents. and influenced their accounts of what they experienced. This knightly pilgrimage, initially fostered by R. *FitzRalph, Abp. of *Armagh, led to a popular pilgrimage to the site in the 16th cent. and later. Drawn by Patrick's promise of a *plenary indulgence to those who visited the sanctuary in penitence and faith, pilgrims continue to come to the island, which is now dominated by a modern basilica.

Various MSS containing the legend in different forms have been ed., mainly in specialized periodicals; details to date are given in a collection of the legends, tr. into Eng. by [J. R.] S. Leslie, *Saint Patrick's Purgatory: A Record from History and Literature* (1932), with bibl. pp. 195–215. The best available Lat. text is that ed. K. Warnke, *Das Buch vom Espurgatoire S. Patrice der Marie de France und seine Quelle* (Bibliotheca Normannica, 9; Halle/Saale, 1938). Eng. tr. of this text by J.-M. Picard, *Saint Patrick's Purgatory* (Blackrock, Co. Dublin [1985]), with introd. by Y. de Pontfarcy, pp. 9–40. For list of MSS see R. J. Hayes (ed.), *Manuscript Sources for the History of Irish Civilization*, 2 (Boston, 1965), pp. 455 f., and *First Supplement 1965–75*, 1 (1979), pp. 673–6. Two medieval Eng. trs., with one recension of the Lat. text, ed., with full introd., by R. [B.] Easting, *St Patrick's Purgatory* (EETS, OS 298; 1991). M. Haren and Y. de Pontfarcy (eds.), *The Medieval Pilgrimage to St Patrick's Purgatory: Lough Derg and the European Tradition* (Clogher Historical Society, Enniskillen [1988]).

St Paul's Cathedral, London. A church was built *c.*607 by *Ethelbert, King of Kent, as a cathedral for St *Mellitus, first Bp. of London. This was rebuilt in stone between 675 and 685 by St *Erconwald, whose shrine attracted pilgrims throughout the Middle Ages. The Saxon building, the scene of many of the early synods of the English, was burnt in a great fire which destroyed much of London in 1087. The new Norman cathedral was begun in the same year and completed in 1240. In the later 13th cent. the Norman apse was replaced by a Gothic choir and presbytery, completed in 1313. The largest building in England, it was 690 ft. long and covered an area of $3\frac{1}{2}$ acres. The spire was 498 ft. high. The Bishop's Palace adjoined the NW corner of the Close. In the NE part of the Close stood 'St Paul's Cross', originally a rallying-place for Folkmoots, but from the mid-13th cent. until 1633 the national centre for religious and political proclamations, sermons, and disputations. It was destroyed in 1643. During W. *Laud's episcopate (1628–33) a restoration of St Paul's was begun with Inigo *Jones as architect, but this ceased under the Commonwealth, when the Nave became a cavalry barrack and the Lady Chapel a preaching-house. The old building, already ruinous, perished in the Great Fire of 1666.

The present Cathedral, designed by Sir Christopher *Wren, combines with much success the classical style and a traditionally Gothic ground-plan. Rebuilding began in 1675, the choir was opened for service in 1697, and the whole was completed by 1710. The restrained Baroque of the interior was enriched considerably by the woodwork

of Grinling Gibbons (1648–1720) and the iron-work of Jean Tijou (*fl.* 1690–1711). Later generations have removed Wren's fine organ-screen and filled the vaulting and saucer-domes of the E. end with mosaics. Since 1906 the SW chapel, formerly the *Consistory Court, has been the religious centre of the Most Distinguished Order of St Michael and St George. The chapel of the Most Excellent Order of the British Empire is in the crypt. Also in the crypt are the tombs of Lord Nelson and the Duke of Wellington and of Wren, with its famous inscription *Lector si monumentum requiris circumspice*. Because of its position St Paul's is frequently the scene of great national services. Very many buildings in the surrounding area were destroyed by bombing in 1940, but St Paul's escaped serious damage. Notable Deans include J. *Colet, A. *Nowell, J. *Overall, J. *Donne, W. *Sancroft, E. *Stillingfleet, J. *Tillotson, H. H. *Milman, H. L. *Mansel, R. W. *Church, R. *Gregory, and W. R. *Inge. Among the residentiary canons Sydney Smith (1771–1845) and H. P. *Liddon are outstanding.

W. *Dugdale, *The History of St Paul's Cathedral in London from its Foundation Untill these Times* (1658; 3rd edn., with continuation by H. Ellis, 1818). W. Sparrow Simpson (ed.), 'The Charter and Statutes of the College of the Minor Canons in S. Paul's Cathedral, London', *Archaeologia*, 43 (1871), pp. 165–200; id. (ed.), *Registrum Statutorum et Consuetudinum Ecclesiae Sancti Pauli Londinensis* (London, 1873); id. (ed.), *Documents Illustrating the History of S. Paul's Cathedral* (Camden Society, NS 26; 1880); M. Gibbs (ed.), *Early Charters of the Cathedral Church of St Paul, London* (ibid., 3rd ser. 58; 1939). J. *Le Neve, *Fasti Ecclesiae Anglicanae*: 1066–1300, 1, rev. by D. E. Greenway (1968); 1300–1542, 5, rev. by J. M. Horn (1963); 1541–1857, 1, rev. by id. (1969). H. H. Milman, *Annals of S. Paul's Cathedral* (1868); W. Longman, *A History of the Three Cathedrals Dedicated to St Paul in London* (1873); W. Sparrow Simpson, *Chapters in the History of Old S. Paul's* (1881); id., *Gleanings from Old S. Paul's* (1889); id., *S. Paul's Cathedral and City Life: Illustrations of Civil and Cathedral Life from the Thirteenth to the Sixteenth Centuries* (1894); W. M. Sinclair, *Memorials of St Paul's Cathedral* (1909); C. H. Cook, *Old S. Paul's Cathedral* (1955). W. R. Matthews and W. M. Atkins (eds.), *A History of St Paul's Cathedral and the Men associated with it* (1957). G. L. Prestige, *St Paul's in its Glory: A Candid History of the Cathedral 1831–1911* (1955). J. Lang, *Rebuilding St Paul's after the Great Fire of London* (1956). [J.] K. Downes, *Sir Christopher Wren: The Design of St Paul's Cathedral. Introduction and Catalogue* (1988). S. A. Warner, *St Paul's Cathedral* (1926); P. [A. T.] Burman, *St Paul's Cathedral* (New Bell's Cathedral Guides, 1987).

St Paul's outside the Walls, Rome (San Paolo fuori le Mura). The church, one of the four 'Major *Basilicas', lies on the W. side of the *Ostian Way about $1\frac{1}{2}$ miles beyond the Porta S. Paolo. The *Liber Pontificalis* states that the original building was erected over the relics of St *Paul by the Emp. *Constantine. While there are difficulties about this assertion, the rebuilding of a large basilica was planned at the end of the 4th cent. and completed by the Emp. Honorius (395–402/3); this latter suffered little change until it was destroyed by fire on 15 July 1823, with only the triumphal arch and its mosaics surviving. The present building, which conforms closely to the plan of the earlier basilica, was consecrated on 10 Dec. 1854, two days after the Definition of the *Immaculate Conception. Until the Reformation the kings of England were honorary members of the Chapter and the Abbot of the monastery a Prelate of the Order of the Garter (hence the insignia of the Garter incorporated in the arms of the church). The basilica has long been served by *Benedictines.

N. M. Nicolai, *Della basilica di S. Paolo* (1815). I. Schuster, *La basilica e il monasterio di S. Paolo fuori le Mura: Note storiche* (1934). S. Pesarini, 'La basilica di S. Paolo sulla *Via Ostiense* prima delle innovazioni del sec. XVI', *Studi romani*, 1 (1913), pp. 386–427. L. de Bruyne, *L'antica serie di ritratti papali della basilica di S. Paolo fuori le Mura* (Studi di antichità cristiana, 7; 1934). R. Krautheimer and others, *Corpus Basilicarum Christianarum Romae*, 5 (Rome, 1977), pp. 93–164 [in Eng.], with full bibl. See also works cited under ROME, CHURCHES OF.

St Peter's, Rome. The present 16th-cent. building replaced a much older basilican structure, erected by *Constantine (d. 337) on the supposed site of St *Peter's crucifixion. After it had fallen into serious disrepair by the later Middle Ages, *Nicholas V (1447–55) planned to replace it by a new church in the form of a Latin cross, selecting Bernardo Rosselino (1409–64), the restorer of the church of St *Francis at *Assisi, as architect. Little had been done when the work was suspended on Nicholas's death. It was resumed under *Julius II (1503–13), who laid the first stone on 18 April 1506, and continued by a succession of architects—Bramante (d. 1514), *Raphael (d. 1520), Peruzzi (d. 1536), Sangallo (d. 1546)—all in turn making drastic changes in the design. The dome followed closely a design of *Michelangelo (d. 1564). By a radical change in plan the nave was lengthened under *Sixtus V to accommodate a vast congregation; the effect of this extension was to spoil the view of the dome from the Piazza. The building was finished in 1614 and consecrated by *Urban VIII on 18 Nov. 1626. Excavations carried out under the basilica since 1940 have revealed the existence of a Christian shrine dating from the first part of the 3rd cent., if not earlier.

St Peter's, which is the largest church in Christendom (length, 619 ft.; *St Paul's Cathedral, London, c.517 ft.), contains the remains of over 130 Popes. The traditional burial-place of St Peter is the *confessio* under the high altar. The baldachino over the high altar, supported on four massive spiral columns of bronze, is the work of G. L. Bernini (1598–1680). Around the base of the dome are inscribed the words *Tu es Petrus . . . cœlorum* (from Mt. 16: 18 f.). See also VATICAN.

Modern studies incl. [S.] Schüller-Piroli, *2000 Jahre Sankt Peter: Die Weltkirche von den Anfängen bis zur Gegenwart* (Olten, 1950); J. Lees-Milne, *Saint Peter's: The Story of Saint Peter's Basilica in Rome* (1967); C. Galassi Paluzzi, *La Basilica di S. Pietro* (Roma Cristiana, 17 [1975]). R. Krautheimer and others, *Corpus Basilicarum Christianarum Romae*, 5 (Rome, 1977), pp. 165–279 [in Eng.], with bibl. J. H. Jongkees, *Studies on Old St Peter's* (Archaeologica Traiectina, 8; Groningen, 1966); E. Francia, *1505–1606: Storia della costruzione del nuovo San Pietro* (Rome [1977]). The official report of the modern excavations was issued under the title *Esplorazioni sotto la confessione di San Pietro in Vaticano eseguite negli anni 1940–1949*, relazioni a cura di B. M. Apollonj Ghetti, A. Ferrua, SJ, E. Josi, and E. Kirschbaum, SJ (2 vols., 1951). J. [M. C.] Toynbee and J. [B.] Ward-Perkins, *The Shrine of St Peter and the Vatican Excavations* (1956). J. Carcopino, *Études d'histoire chrétienne* [1953]; 2nd edn., with rev. subtitle: *Les Fouilles de Saint-Pierre et la tradition* [1963]; id., *Études d'histoire chrétienne*, 2: *Les Reliques de saint Pierre à Rome* [1965]. T. Klauser, *Die römische Petrustradition im Lichte der neuen Ausgrabungen unter der Peterskirche* (Arbeitsgemeinschaft für Forschung des Landes Nordrhein-Westfalen. Geisteswissenschaften, 24 [1956]). E. Kirschbaum, SJ, *Die Gräber der Apostelfürsten* (Frankfurt a.M. [1957]; 3rd edn., 1974; Eng. tr., 1959). M. Guarducci, *I graffiti sotto la Confessione di San Pietro in Vaticano* (3 vols., 1958 [conclusions largely contested; cf. A. Ferrua, SJ, in *Rivista di Archeologia Cristiana*, 35 (1959), pp. 231–47; M. Guarducci in *Archeologia Classica*, 13 (1961), pp. 183–239]. Id., *Pietro in Vaticano* (1983). D. W. O'Connor, *Peter in Rome: The Literary, Liturgical and Archeological Evidence* (New York and London, 1969). J. Ruysschaert, 'Les premiers siècles de la tombe de Pierre. Une discussion dégagée d'une hypothèse', *Revue des Archéologues et Historiens d'Art de Louvain*, 8 (1975), pp. 7–47. C. Pietri, *Roma Christiana: Recherches sur l'Église de Rome . . . (311–440)* (Bibliothèque des Écoles françaises d'Athènes et de Rome, 224; 1976), pp. 51–69. A. Arbeiter, *Alt-St. Peter in Geschichte und Wissenschaft: Abfolge der Bauten, Rekonstruktion, Architekturprogramm* (Berlin, 1988), with full bibl. A. G. Martimort, 'Vingt-cinq ans de travaux et recherches sur la mort de saint Pierre et sur sa sépulture (1946–1971)', *Bulletin de Littérature Ecclésiastique*, 73 (1972), pp. 73–101, with refs. H. I. Marrou in *DACL* 15 (pt. 2; 1953), cols. 3290–334, s.v. 'Vatican (Fouilles du)', with refs.; E. Josi in *EC* 12 (1954), cols. 1053–97, s.v. 'Vaticano. III: Zona archeologica e basilica', with further bibl. See also bibl. to ROME, CHURCHES OF.

Saint-Simon, Claude Henri de Rouvroy (1760–1825), one of the earliest exponents of French socialism. Of noble family, he fought on the American side in the War of Independence and then led a life of adventure in various European countries. In the French Revolution of 1789 he abandoned his titles and changed his name. In the following years he took part in various financial enterprises designed to further his ideal of service to humanity, but was reduced to great poverty. From 1797 his interest in science and the reorganization of society rapidly increased, and he worked out the ideas which he later embodied esp. in *L'Industrie* (1817), *L'Organisateur* (1819; a periodical), *Du système industriel* (1821), and *Catéchisme des industriels* (1823–4). In these works he developed and expounded his thesis that only the industrial classes work for the moral and physical welfare of mankind and that they should be preferred to those who have hitherto been privileged. In the last years of his life his thought turned into more religious channels and was expressed in the *Nouveau Christianisme* (1825). The one Divine principle in Christianity is that men must behave as brothers towards each other, i.e. must organize society in the way that will be most advantageous to the majority. Religion, therefore, ought to provide a speedy amelioration of the lot of the poorest. A truly Christian priest will regard dogma and cult as negligible accessories and give his chief attention to morals and social betterment.

This teaching, which won little following in Saint-Simon's lifetime, was later propagated by his disciples, esp. O. Rodrigues, S. A. Bazard, and B. P. Enfantin. In the two collective volumes, *Exposition de la doctrine de Saint-Simon* (1829 and 1830), Bazard and Enfantin sought to substitute for the traditional structure of society a religious system of social solidarity with the object of the progressive disappearance of the leisured classes and the abolition of all privileges, including interest and inheritance. This Saint-Simonian tendency to generalize and unify everything eventually led his disciples, esp. Enfantin, to a pantheism that divinized the universe and the carnal instincts of man and resulted in a semi-religious sect given to immorality. In 1832 Enfantin was imprisoned; but the ideas of his master exercised a great influence not only in France but also in other Continental countries and in England.

Saint-Simon was one of the first representatives of *Positivist science, industrialism, and socialism as well as the apostle of a new humanitarian lay religion, whose suggestions were destined to have a great future in the 19th and early 20th cents. For a time A. *Comte, the Positivist leader, was under his influence.

Works in Œuvres de Saint-Simon et d'Enfantin publiées par les membres du conseil institué par Enfantin (47 vols., Paris, 1865–78), vols. 15, 18–23, 37–45, and 47, with Notice Historique in vol. 1, pp. 1–133. Eng. trs. of Selected Writings [on politics], by F. M. H. Markham (Oxford, 1952), and on science, industry, and social organization by K. Taylor (London [1975]). P. A. Janet, Saint-Simon et le saint-simonisme (Bibliothèque de Philosophie contemporaine, 1876); [J.] G. Weill, Saint-Simon et son œuvre (1894); S. Charléty, Essai sur l'histoire du saint-simonisme (Paris thesis, 1896; rev. edn., 1931); M. Leroy, La Vie véritable du Comte Henri de Saint-Simon (1925); E. Durkheim, Le Socialisme, ed. M. Mauss (1928; Eng. tr. as Socialism and Saint-Simon, Yellow Springs, Oh., 1958; London, 1959); F. E. Manuel, The New World of Henri Saint-Simon (Cambridge, Mass., 1956); id., The Prophets of Paris (ibid., 1962), pp. 103–93; P. Ansart, Sociologie de Saint-Simon (1970); T. Petermann, Claude-Henri de Saint-Simon: Die Gesellschaft als Werkstatt (Beiträge zur politischen Wissenschaft, 34 [1979]). J. Tonneau in DTC 14 (pt. 1; 1939), cols. 769–99, s.v. 'Saint-Simon et saint-simonisme'.

St Sophia. See SANCTA SOPHIA.

Saint-Sulpice, Society of.
The congregation of secular priests founded by J.-J. *Olier in the parish of St-Sulpice, *Paris, in 1642 with the aim of forming a zealous clergy, esp. suited to be directors of seminaries. The Society, which spread to Canada in 1657, was granted Papal approbation in 1664. Under its second Superior General, A. de Bretonvilliers (1657–76), it received its constitutions, which were further elaborated by his successor, L. Tronson (1676–1700), who also developed the Sulpician method of prayer and asceticism. Acc. to their rule, modelled on that of the French *Oratory and adapted to the double purpose of studies and spiritual formation, the members of the Society take no vows, keep their property, which they are expected to use in the spirit of poverty, and live in close community with their pupils, whose spiritual and other exercises they share.

St-Sulpice soon gained a profound influence on the ecclesiastical life of France, to which it gave a great number of bishops. After a period of partial eclipse during the French Revolution, it was restored soon after the *Concordat of 1801 by its resolute Superior General J. A. Emery, who, in 1791, had opened a house in Baltimore. Though again hard hit by the anti-ecclesiastical legislation in France of 1903 and 1906, the Society still trains many of those destined for the French priesthood and has provinces in Canada and the USA and missions in the Far East, Central Africa, and Central and S. America.

The theology of St-Sulpice, which, until at least the 1930s, was considered solid and traditional, has been deeply imbued with *Thomism. Its spirituality followed the lines of the French School, professed by its founder, Olier, and laid down in the ascetical textbooks of Tronson. Past members of the Society include B. Joubert, who pre-

pared new editions of the *Missal (1777) and the *Breviary (1778), F. Vigouroux, the author of La Bible et les découvertes modernes (1877) and editor of the Dictionnaire de la Bible (1895–1912), A. A. *Tanquerey, P. Pourrat, whose La Spiritualité chrétienne (1917) is a standard work on the history of spirituality, and F. Amiot, author of L'Enseignement de Saint Paul (1938) and numerous other works.

H. Joly, La Compagnie de Saint-Sulpice (1914); J. Montval, Les Sulpiciens (1934); J. Gautier, PSS, Ces Messieurs de Saint-Sulpice (Bibliothèque Ecclesia, 33; 1957). C. G. Herbermann, The Sulpicians in the United States (New York, 1916). L. Bertrand, PSS, Bibliothèque sulpicienne, ou Histoire littéraire de la compagnie de Saint-Sulpice (3 vols., 1900). Bremond, 3, pp. 419–507. C. Hamel, Histoire de l'église de Saint-Sulpice (1900). E. Levesque, PSS, in DTC 14 (pt. 1; 1939), cols. 802–32, s.v.; I. Noye, PSS, in DIP 8 (1988), cols. 24–8, s.v. 'Sacerdoti di San Sulpizio'; id. in Dict. Sp. 14 (1990), cols. 170–81, s.v.

St-Victor, Abbey of. See VICTORINES.

Sainte-Chapelle, *Paris.
The chapel was built by St *Louis IX of France to house the *Crown of Thorns. Begun c.1245, it was consecrated in 1248, and forms part of the Palais de Justice, formerly the royal residence. It was desecrated in 1791, restored to religious use in 1837, and again secularized and dismantled in 1906. This masterpiece of Gothic architecture is traditionally ascribed to Pierre de Montereau, and though zealously restored in the 19th cent. by E. E. Viollet-le-Duc (1814–79) and J. B. A. Lassus (1807–57), in the upper chapel it still contains notable medieval glass.

H. Stein, Le Palais de Justice et la Sainte-Chapelle de Paris (1912), pp. 191–239; F. Gebelin, La Sainte-Chapelle et la Conciergerie (Petites Monographies des Grands Édifices de la France, 1931), pp. 1–86; L. Grodecki, Sainte-Chapelle (Caisse Nationale des Monuments historiques [1964]). Y. Bottineau, Notre-Dame de Paris et la Sainte-Chapelle [1966], pp. 155–221. M. Aubert and others, Les Vitraux de Notre-Dame et de la Sainte-Chapelle de Paris (Corpus Vitrearum Medii Aevi, France, 1; Paris, 1959), pp. 71–328. R. Branner, Saint Louis and the Court Style in Gothic Architecture (1965), pp. 56–84. See also works cited s.v. PARIS.

saints, devotion to the.
The practice of venerating and invoking the saints has long been a regular element in Catholic devotion. Its justification rests on the beliefs that the saints are both close to God (because of their holiness) and accessible to man (whose nature they share), and in the efficacy of intercessory prayer.

A Jewish anticipation of the conception is found in 2 Macc., where *Judas Maccabaeus sees Onias and *Jeremiah in a dream 'with outstretched hands invoking blessings on the whole body of the Jews' (15: 12). In the NT the gift of special privileges for certain persons in the next world is held to be indicated in Christ's promises to the Apostles (Mt. 19: 28), while support for the idea that the dead may intercede on behalf of the living has been found in the parable of Dives and Lazarus (Lk. 16: 19–31). Other NT references commonly invoked are the description of the saints of the Old Covenant as a 'cloud of witnesses' (Heb. 12: 1), which Christians are to imitate (13: 7), and the martyrs who pray before the throne of God (Rev. 6: 9 f.) and receive white robes (7: 14–17) as a reward of their martyrdom. But the principal theological basis of the practice is the Pauline doctrine of the Body of Christ, in which all members have their particular office (Rom. 12: 4–8) as 'fellow citizens with the saints, and of the household of God' (Eph. 2: 19). It is the implications of this teaching about the Church rather than specific references to the subject that are commonly held by its advocates to constitute the biblical foundation of devotion to the saints.

For the pre-Nicene period, literary evidence for the practice continues scanty, though the 'Odes of *Solomon' (2nd cent.) and the (largely *Gnostic) Apocryphal Acts of the Apostles attest a developing cult. The first incontrovertible documentary witness is the 'Martyrium *Polycarpi' (c.156), where his followers express their intention of 'celebrating the birthday of his martyrdom' in days to come. The practice was furthered by the growing cultus of the relics of those who had suffered death for their faith. Besides the actual martyrs, those who had survived their sufferings ('confessores') were also paid special honours, and their power of intercession after death was asserted e.g. by St *Cyprian. *Origen was apparently the first of the Fathers to give the cult of martyrs an express theological foundation. He placed it within the doctrine of the Communion of Saints and taught that the prayer of the saints is efficacious in so far as the faithful follow in their footsteps.

From the 4th cent. devotion to the saints spread rapidly. St *Cyril of Jerusalem distinguished the saints commemorated at the Eucharistic Sacrifice who offer our prayer to God from the ordinary dead who would be benefited by the sacrifice. The same distinction is found in St *Chrysostom, who exhorted his hearers to have confidence in the intercession of the martyrs. About the same time the ranks of those accounted saints were enlarged by the addition of 'confessors' and 'virgins', on the ground that a life of renunciation and holiness might equal the devotion of those who had actually died for Christ. Thus ascetics such as St *Antony and bishops such as St *Athanasius and St Chrysostom were soon venerated in the E., and in the W. St *Augustine was honoured as a saint at Carthage before 475. The abuses connected with the cultus met, however, with occasional opposition, e.g. from *Vigilantius (q.v.). Later theologians sought to rebut the charge of idolatry by a distinction between the worship of God, expressed in the Gk. word λατρεία, and the cult of honour and imitation due to the saints, expressed in the term δουλεία. Among later Fathers who contributed to the theology of the cultus were St *Leo, St *Gregory the Great, and St *John of Damascus. St Leo affirmed that the saints as our special intercessors obtain for us the mercy of God by their prayers; St Gregory, who did much to further the cultus, exhorted the faithful in his 'Dialogues' to place themselves under the protection of the saints; and St John of Damascus stressed the theocentric character of the cult.

Liturgical developments followed popular devotion and the current of patristic teaching. The mention of saints in the Mass is already attested by St Augustine (De Civ. Dei, 22. 10). From the 5th cent. onwards *diptychs of martyrs and confessors found a place in the *Gallican, *Mozarabic, and *Celtic liturgies, and from the early 6th cent. also in the *Roman Mass. From the 8th cent. the Lives of the saints were read at *Mattins. At the beginning of the Middle Ages their cult was greatly extended through the

conversion of the barbarians. The Irish monks, themselves influenced by the E., spread it to England, and thence to the Continent. From the 9th cent. saints' Lives and edificatory sermons, often resting on very slender historical evidence, enjoyed increasing popularity and Councils frequently found it necessary to curb the excesses and superstitions of popular devotion. The fervour of even such preachers as St *Peter Damian, St *Anselm, and St *Bernard attracted the disapproval of the great 13th-cent. Scholastics.

The large amount of superstition surrounding the practice in the later Middle Ages had led the *Bogomils and *Waldensians to attack the practice, and at the Reformation it was fiercely repudiated, esp. by the *Zwinglians and *Calvinists, on the ground that it was not explicitly recommended in Scripture. In the *Thirty-Nine Articles (Art. 22) of the C of E the 'Romish Doctrine' on the subject is designated 'a fond thing vainly invented'; but it is debated by modern Anglican theologians whether the Article forbids the invocation of saints altogether, or only condemns exaggerations in the RC Church. Under the influence of the *Oxford Movement the practice has been widely revived in the C of E in modern times, though the early Tractarians viewed the veneration of the saints with considerable misgivings.

In the RC Church the practice is everywhere upheld. The Council of *Trent, however, treated the subject with studied moderation, the bishops being merely asked to remind the faithful to address themselves to the saints to obtain their assistance in winning the favours of God and Christ. The post-Tridentine theologians carried on and developed the teaching of the Schoolmen. The modern cult of the saints in the RC Church is regulated by canon law (CIC (1983), cans. 1186–7), which recommends the veneration of the saints and esp. of the BVM. The attitude of the E. Churches to the subject is closely akin to that of Rome. See also BEATIFICATION, CANONIZATION.

On the history of the cult of the saints: I. C. Trombelli, De Cultu Sanctorum (2 vols., Bologna, 1740–3); H. *Delehaye, SJ, Les Origines du culte des martyrs (Brussels, 1912; 2nd edn., Subsidia Hagiographica, 20; 1933); id., Sanctus: Essai sur le culte des martyrs dans l'antiquité (Subsidia Hagiographica, 17; 1927). P. Dörfler, Die Anfänge der Heiligenverehrung nach den römischen Inschriften und Bildwerken (Veröffentlichungen aus dem Kirchenhistorischen Seminar München, 4. Reihe, 2; 1913). L. Bieler, Θεῖος ἀνήρ. Das Bild des 'göttlichen Menschen' in Spätantike und Frühchristentum (2 vols., Vienna, 1935–6). A.-J. Festugière, OP, La Sainteté (1949). A. Vauchez, La Sainteté en Occident aux derniers siècles du moyen âge d'après les procès de canonisation et les documents hagiographiques (Bibliothèque des Écoles Françaises d'Athènes et de Rome, 241; 1981). P. [R. L.] Brown, The Cult of the Saints: Its Rise and Function in Latin Christianity (1981); cf. J. Fontaine in Anal. Boll. 100 (1982), pp. 17–41. S. Wilson (ed.), Saints and their Cults: Studies in Religious Sociology, Folklore and History (1983). On the theological principles involved J. P. Kirsch, Die Lehre von der Gemeinschaft der Heiligen im christlichen Altertum (1900; Eng. tr. [1911]); M. Perham, The Communion of Saints: An Examination of the Place of the Christian Dead in the Belief, Worship and Calendars of the Church (Alcuin Club Collections, 62; 1980). H. Thurston, SJ, in HERE 11 (1920), pp. 51–9, s.v. 'Saints and Martyrs (Christian)'; P. Séjourné, OSB, in DTC 14 (pt. 1; 1939), cols. 870–978, s.v. 'Saints (Culte des)'; T. Baumeister in RAC 14 (1988), cols. 96–150, s.v. 'Heiligenverehrung I.' Much material will be found also in the *Analecta Bollandiana (q.v.). See also bibls. to MARTYR and MARTYROLOGY.

sakkos (Gk. σάκκος). In the E. Church, an embroidered liturgical vestment similar in form to the *dalmatic in the W. It prob. dates from the 11th cent. It is the chief Eucharistic vestment of those of high rank and was orig. confined to archbishops and metropolitans. It is now normally worn instead of the *phelonion (q.v.) by all bishops.

Salamanca, School of. See SALMANTICENSES.

Salesians. Of the many orders known under this name, the principal is the 'Society of St *Francis de Sales', founded near Turin in 1859 by St John *Bosco for the Christian education of boys and young men of the poorer classes, esp. with a view to their ordination. In 1846 Bosco began to gather them together in what he termed 'festive oratories' and night schools; the first 'festive oratory' was established in Turin, but similar foundations soon followed in other parts of Italy. A religious congregation of priests and teachers under the patronage of St Francis de Sales came into being to develop the work, and in 1859 began to live by a rule drawn up by Bosco two years earlier. In 1874 the rule was approved by *Pius IX, and the Society spread rapidly to many parts of the world, including England. It now has about 17,500 members—priests and lay brothers. A sister congregation of Daughters of Our Lady Help of Christians was founded by Bosco in 1872, out of a small community started independently in 1852 by St Mary Mazzarello at Mornese, for similar work among girls. This congregation now has just under 17,000 members with houses in England and many other parts of the world.

E. Ceria, *Annali della Società Salesiana* [1841–1921] (4 vols., Turin, 1941–51); also other specialized works by the same author. E. J. Doherty, *Lambs in Wolfskins* (New York, 1953). A. M. Gonzalez, SDB, *Origen de las Misiones Salesianas: La Evangelizacíon des las gentes según el pensamiento de San Juan Bosco* (Guatemala, 1978), with docs. W. Kelley in *NCE* 12 (1969), pp. 982 f., s.v.; R. Alberdi, SDB, and C. Semeraro, SDB, in *DIP* 8 (1988), cols. 1689–714, s.v. 'Società Salesiana di San Giovanni Bosco'; G. Capetti, FMA, ibid. 3 (1976), cols. 1609–13, s.v. 'Figlie di Maria Ausiliatrice'. J. Struś, SDB, ibid. 8 (1988), cols. 383–5, s.v. 'Salesiane, Salesiani', for refs. to other orders inspired by St Francis de Sales. See also Lives of BOSCO, ST JOHN, cited s.v.

Salette, La. See LA SALETTE.

Salisbury. From the see originally founded in 634 by St *Birinus at *Dorchester in Oxfordshire sprang the later sees of *Winchester, *Sherborne, Ramsbury, and Salisbury. Herman, Bp. of Ramsbury, who united the dioceses of Ramsbury and Sherborne in 1058, transferred the see to Old Sarum in 1075. Here his successor, St *Osmund, completed a cathedral, constituted a chapter, and drew up offices, which perhaps formed the basis of the Sarum rite. Richard *Poore, the seventh Bp. of Old Sarum, moved the see to New Sarum or Salisbury in 1219, and laid the foundation of the new cathedral (of the BVM) on 28 Apr. 1220. Three altars at the E. End were consecrated in 1225 in the presence of Stephen *Langton, Abp. of Canterbury (St *Edmund, afterwards Abp. of Canterbury, was also there). The whole cathedral was consecrated in 1258 and completed when the roof was finished in 1266. Built throughout in the Early English style, it is a rare example

of architectural unity. Cloisters and chapter-house were added later in the 13th cent. The spire, built between 1334 and 1350, is the highest in England. See following entry.

Registers of Simon of Ghent, Bp. 1297–1315, ed. C. T. Flower and M. C. B. Dawes (*Canterbury and York Society, 40 and 41; 1934); of Roger Martival, Bp. 1315–30, ed. K. Edwards, C. R. Elrington, and others (ibid. 55, 57–59; 1959–75); of Robert Hallum, Bp. 1407–17, ed. J. M. Horn (ibid. 72; 1982); and of Thomas Langton, Bp. 1485–93, ed. D. P. Wright (ibid. 74; 1985). W. H. Rich Jones (ed.), *Vetus Registrum Sarisberiense alias dictum Registrum S. Osmundi Episcopi* (2 vols., RS, 1883–4); id. and W. D. Macray, *Charters and Documents Illustrating the History of the Cathedral, City and Diocese of Salisbury in the Twelfth and Thirteenth Centuries, selected from the Capitular and Diocesan Registers* (RS, 1891). E. A Dayman and W. H. Rich Jones (eds.), *Statutes of the Cathedral Church of Sarum* (privately pr., Bath, 1883); C. Wordsworth and D. Macleane (eds.), *Statutes and Customs of the Cathedral Church of the Blessed Virgin Mary of Salisbury* (1915), incl. Eng. tr. C. Wordsworth (ed.), *Ceremonies and Processions of the Cathedral Church of Salisbury* (Cambridge, 1901). J. *Le Neve, *Fasti Ecclesiae Anglicanae*: 1066–1300, 4, rev. by D. E. Greenway (1991); 1300–1541, 3, rev. by J. M. Horn (1962); 1541–1857, 6, rev. by id. (1986). R. L. Poole, 'The Muniments of the Dean and Chapter of Salisbury', *Historical Manuscripts Commission Report on Manuscripts in Various Collections*, 1 (1901), pp. 338–88; id., 'The Records of the Bishop of Salisbury', ibid. 4 (1907), pp. 1–12. S. M. Lakin, *A Catalogue of the Library of the Cathedral Church of Salisbury* (1880). T. Webber, *Scribes and Scholars at Salisbury Cathedral c.1075–c.1125* (Oxford, 1992). [R. Rawlinson,] *The History and Antiquities of the Cathedral-Church of Salisbury and the Abbey-Church of Bath* (1719), pp. iii–xvi, 1–161, and 269–351. W. Dodsworth, *An Historical Account of the Episcopal See and Cathedral Church of Salisbury* (1814). R. Spring, *Salisbury Cathedral* (New Bell's Cathedral Guides, 1987). id., *Salisbury Cathedral* (Salisbury, 1991). S. H. Cassan, *Lives and Memoirs of the Bishops of Sherborne and Salisbury, from the Year 705 to 1824* (ibid., 1824). K. Edwards in *VCH*, Wilts. 3, ed. R. B. Pugh and E. Crittall (1956), pp. 156–210. G. Crosse in *DECH* (1912), pp. 539–43, s.v.

Salisbury or **Sarum, Use of.** The local medieval modification of the Roman rite in use at the cathedral church of Salisbury, traditionally ascribed to St *Osmund (d. 1099) but really much later. The *Customary, i.e. the cathedral statutes and customs and a complete directory of services, were compiled by Richard *Poore (d. 1237). The 'New Use of Sarum' was a further (14th-cent.) revision, effecting certain changes in the Calendar. In the later Middle Ages the Sarum Use was increasingly followed, in whole or in part, in other dioceses, and in 1457 stated to be in use in nearly the whole of England, Wales, and Ireland. In 1543 the *Canterbury Convocation imposed the Sarum *Breviary on the whole province, and the books of the Sarum rite furnished the Reformers with their main material for the First (1549) BCP of *Edward VI, in the Preface to which (the section now headed 'Concerning the Service of the Church') the Sarum Use appears as one of the local variations which the new standard order was to replace. In the years preceding the Reformation the output of Sarum books was enormous. The much increased knowledge which followed their discovery and re-editing in modern times led to the revival of Sarum customs and ornaments in many English cathedral and parish churches.

Missale ad Usum Insignis et Praeclarae Ecclesiae Sarum, ed. F. H. Dickinson (Burntisland, 1861–83); *The Sarum Missal*, tr. into English [by A. Harford Pearson] (1868; 2nd edn., 1884); F. Procter and C. Wordsworth (eds.), *Breviarium ad Usum Insignis*

Ecclesiae Sarum (3 vols., 1879–86); W. H. *Frere, *The Use of Sarum*, 1: *The Sarum Customs* (1898), 2: *The Ordinal and Tonal* (1901); C. Wordsworth, *Ceremonies and Processions of the Cathedral Church of Salisbury* (1901); J. W. Legg, *The Sarum Missal edited from Three Early Manuscripts* (1916); *Manuale ad usum percelebris ecclesie Sarisburiensis*, ed. J. Collins (HBS 91; 1960). R. W. Pfaff, *New Liturgical Feasts in Later Medieval England* (Oxford Theological Monographs, 1970).

Salmanticenses. The customary name for the authors of the *Cursus theologicus Summam d. Thomae complectens*, a group of Discalced *Carmelites who taught at Salamanca between 1600 and 1725. The authors were anonymous, but their identity is now well established: they were Antonio de la Madre de Dios (1583–1637), Domingo de Sta Teresa (1604–60), Juan de la Anunciación (1633–1701), and three others. The *Cursus*, which took 70 years to complete (1631–1701), is a gigantic Commentary on the *Summa Theologiae* of St *Thomas Aquinas, undertaken to provide a sound basis of theological teaching for the friars of the *Teresian reform. It was conceived on the same lines as the philosophical course (*Cursus Complutensis*) done by their college at Alcalá, and was supplemented by the *Cursus Salmanticensis Theologiae Moralis* (pub. in its complete form, 1717–24).

O. Merl, OCD, *Theologia Salmanticensis: Untersuchung über Entstehung, Lehrrichtung und Quellen des theologischen Kurses der spanischen Karmeliten* ([Regensburg] 1947). T. Deman, OP, in *DTC* 14 (pt. 1; 1939), cols. 1017–31, s.v. 'Salamanque (Théologiens de)', with bibl.; R. A. Couture in *NCE* 12 (1967), pp. 987 f., s.v.; E. Llamas in Q. Aldea Vaquero and others (eds.), *Diccionario de Historia Eclesiastica de España*, 4 (1975), pp. 2151–3, s.v. 'Salmanticenses Dogmaticos'; T. del Santísimo Sacramento, ibid., pp. 2153 f., s.v. 'Salmanticenses Morales'.

Salmasius, Claudius (1588–1653), **Claude Saumaise,** French classical scholar. At Paris, where he studied from 1604, he became a friend of I. *Casaubon and was converted to *Calvinism. In 1608 he edited two 14th-cent. tracts against the primacy of the Pope. After publishing various classical works, including an edition of Solinus' 'Polyhistor' (1629), he succeeded to the chair of J. J. *Scaliger (d. 1609) at *Leiden in 1632. Here he wrote two books defending the compatibility of *usury with Christian principles, *De usuris liber* (1638) and *De modo usurarum* (1639), and a *Defensio regia pro Carolo I* (1649) which provoked J. *Milton's celebrated and successful reply, *Pro populo anglicano defensio* (1651). In 1650 he accepted an invitation to visit the court of Queen *Christina of Sweden, but soon afterwards returned to the Netherlands.

Letters ed. A. Clément (Leiden, 1656), with Life of Salmasius prefixed (pp. iii–lxiv). There also exists a MS Life by Philibert de la Mare, which was used by P. Papillon, *Bibliothèque des auteurs de Bourgogne* (Dijon, 1745), pp. 247–87 [incl. full list of Salmasius' works]. E. and E. Haag, *La France Protestante*, 9 (1859), pp. 149–73, s.v. 'Saumaise, Claude'. Unsigned art. in *EB* (11th edn.), 24 (1911), p. 81, s.v.

Salmon, George (1819–1904), mathematician and theologian. He was educated at *Trinity College, Dublin, of which he became a Fellow in 1841, Regius Professor of Divinity in 1866, and Provost in 1888. He was ordained priest in 1845. A strong Protestant, Salmon co-operated with R. *Whately in writing the *Cautions for the Times* (1853), intended as a reply to the *Tracts for the Times*

(1833–41). His lectures on the *Infallibility of the Church*, first published in 1888, were a defence of Protestant principles against the tenets of the Church of Rome, and well illustrate at once his skill, his vigour, and his humour, as a controversialist. In his widely read *Introduction to the New Testament* (1885), he was more concerned to refute critical theories than to produce a handbook of reference. His distinguished work as a mathematician cannot be described here. Salmon also took a prominent part in the reconstruction of the Church of *Ireland after its disestablishment in 1870.

J. H. *Bernard in *DNB, 1901–1911*, 3 (1912), pp. 251–4.

Salome. (1) A woman who followed Jesus to Jerusalem, Mk. 15: 40; 16: 1. Matthew (27: 56) appears to identify her with the mother of St *James and St *John, the sons of Zebedee (Mt. 27: 56; cf. Mk. 15: 40). She is sometimes also identified with the sister of the BVM (Jn. 19: 25). See MARYS IN THE NT (4).

(2) The name given by *Josephus (*Ant.* 18. 136) to the daughter of Herodias, who is mentioned without a name at Mt. 14: 6 and Mk. 6: 22.

Salonica. See THESSALONICA.

salos (Gk. σαλός, silly, mad). One who practised a pecular form of asceticism in the E., presenting himself as a holy fool in society. The best known is the 6th-cent. Simeon, of whom there is an excellent 7th-cent. Life by Leontius of Neapolis. It is, however, uncertain whether the Life of Andrew Salos (date disputed: 7th or 10th cent.) reflects a historical or a fictional character. The practice gained popularity and extended later into the Russian Church with the *Yurodivy*. Similar characteristics appear independently in the Life of St Benedict Joseph *Labre.

Gk. text of the Lives mentioned pr. in J. P. Migne, *PG* 93. 1669–748 (Simeon), and ibid. 111. 621–888 (Andrew). Crit. edn. of Life of Simeon by L. Rydén (Studia Graeca Upsaliensia, 4; 1963). S. [C.] Murray, *A Study of the Life of Andreas, the Fool for the Sake of Christ* (Munich Diss.; Borna and Leipzig, 1910). J. Grosdidier de Matons, 'Les thèmes d'édification dans la Vie d'André Salos', *Travaux et Mémoires*, 4 (1970), pp. 277–328. L. Rydén, 'Style and historical fiction in the Life of St. Andreas Salos', *Jahrbuch der österreichischen Byzantinistik*, 32/3. XVI. Internationaler Byzantinistenkongress, Wien, 4.–9. Oktober 1981, Akten 2/3 (1982), pp. 175–83. J. [N.] Saward, *Perfect Fools: Folly for Christ's Sake in Catholic and Orthodox Spirituality* (1980), pp. 19–21 (on Simeon and Andrew). Beck, pp. 140, 456, 567 f., with bibl.

salt. Owing to its preservative quality salt was a sign of purity and incorruptibility, esp. among the Semitic peoples. As such, it served to confirm contracts and friendship, the covenant between Yahweh and Israel on *Sinai, e.g., being called a 'covenant of salt' in Num. 18: 19. This symbolism, taken together with its seasoning properties, explains the Lord's saying 'Ye are the salt of the earth' (Mt. 5: 13, cf. also Mk. 9: 50), where the salt represents Christian wisdom and integrity, as also in Col. 4: 6. The ritual use of salt is very old and widespread. It was prescribed in the OT for every oblation (Lev. 2: 13) and played an important part in the sacrifices of the Greeks and Romans. The old pagan Roman custom of placing a few grains of salt on the lips of an infant on the 8th day after his birth to chase away the demons prob. lay behind the offering of blessed salt to *catechumens which formerly formed part of the RC rite of *Baptism. Salt may also be used for the preparation of *Holy Water.

V. Hehn, *Das Salz: Eine kulturhistorische Studie* (1873; 2nd edn. by O. Schader, 1901). J. E. Latham, *The Religious Symbolism of Salt* (Théologie Historique, 64 [1982]). F. Hauck in *TWNT* 1 (1933), p. 229 (Eng. tr., 1 (1964), pp. 228 f.), s.v. ἅλας, with bibl.

Saltmarsh, John (d. 1647), preacher and writer. He crowded much controversy into a short life of some 35 years. About 1639 he became rector of Heslerton, N. Yorks, and was at first an ardent supporter of episcopacy and conformity; but his opinions gradually changed and he became equally ardent in advocating complete religious liberty. In 1644 he was appointed to the sequestered rectory of Brasted, Kent, and in 1646 became a chaplain in Fairfax's army. All the time he was pouring forth a stream of books and pamphlets of which the best known are *Holy Discoveries* (1640) and *Sparkles of Glory* (1647).

L. F. Solt, 'John Saltmarsh: New Model Army Chaplain', *JEH* 2 (1951), pp. 69–80. A. L. Morton, *The World of the Ranters* (1970), pp. 45–69. A. Gordon in *DNB* 50 (1897), pp. 220–2.

saltum, per. See PER SALTUM.

salutary act. In RC theological terminology a human act which contributes to the salvation of the person performing it. To be 'salutary', it must be carried out in a state of grace and with the co-operation of the will, i.e. it must not be a purely instinctive reaction.

Salvation Army. An extensive international Christian organization for evangelistic and social work. It was founded by W. *Booth (q.v.) in 1865, received its present form and title in 1878, and from that time spread rapidly all over the world. It is organized on a strictly military basis, with a 'General' at its head. On W. Booth's death (1912), his son, William Bramwell Booth, succeeded to the Generalship on his father's nomination, but since 1931 the General has been elected by the High Council, consisting of commanders and other leading officers. 'Unquestioning obedience' is required from all members of the Army, which is divided into 'territories', acc. to the national frontiers of the respective countries, which, in their turn, are subdivided into 'provinces' and 'divisions'. The religious teaching of the Salvation Army is largely in harmony with traditional evangelical belief, but rejects all Sacraments and stresses esp. the moral side of Christianity. The technique of producing conversions is aggressive and emotional and makes extensive use of public testimony and penance; its realistic methods of presenting religion to the people, in which open-air meetings with brass bands and banners play an important part, differ greatly from those of other Christian bodies. The Army carries on a great variety of social activities, including all kinds of rescue work, care of criminals and drunkards, soup kitchens, workers' hostels and night shelters, as well as hospitals and schools. The Army, which is esp. strong in the USA, has its headquarters in London.

R. Sandall, A. R. Wiggins, and F. Coutts, *The History of the Salvation Army* (7 vols., 1947–86). G. K. Horridge, *The Salvation Army: Origins and Early Days. 1865–1900* (Godalming, 1993). See also Lives of W. Booth, cited s.v.

Salvator Noster. The bull of *Sixtus IV, dated 3 Aug. 1476, granting an indulgence to the church of Saintes. It is the first instance of the issue of an indulgence granting plenary remission of sins for the dead (*plenariam remissionem per modum suffragii*).

Text in *Archives historiques de la Saintonge et de l'Aunis*, 10 (1882), pp. 56–69. The clauses concerning the souls in purgatory also pr. in H. Lea, *A History of Auricular Confession and Indulgences in the Latin Church*, 3 (1896), pp. 585 f., with discussion, pp. 345–51, and extracts from other allied docs., pp. 586–96; extracts of the text repr. in Kidd, pp. 3 f. (no. 2). A. Teetaert, OFM Cap., in *DTC* 14 (pt. 2; 1941), cols. 2210 f., s.v. 'Sixte IV'. See also works cited under INDULGENCES.

Salve Regina (Lat., 'Hail, Holy Queen'). One of the oldest Marian *antiphons, sometimes recited in the W. Church at the end of the canonical hours. It is among the most widely used Catholic prayers to the BVM, owing its popularity to its tender devotional language and beautiful plainsong. The earliest MS evidence is usually dated at the end of the 11th cent. The chronicle of Alberic of Trois-Fontaines (d. 1241) mentions the Salve Regina under the year 1130 in connection with a story about St *Bernard, who is said to have referred to it as the antiphon of Le Puy ('Antiphona de Podio'), the famous pilgrim shrine of Le Puy-en-Velay. The authorship is unknown. It has been variously ascribed to Adhémar, Bp. of Le Puy (d. 1098), Peter, Bp. of Compostela (d. 1003), *Herimannus Contractus, and St Bernard.

From the middle of the 12th cent. the Salve Regina was used by the *Cistercians as an antiphon for either the *Benedictus or the *Magnificat on the four great feasts of the BVM and from early in the 13th cent. they sang it daily. It was adopted by both the *Franciscans and the *Dominicans. The *Breviary of *Pius V in 1568 made it generally obligatory to recite the Salve Regina after Compline, and after Lauds on Sunday, from Trinity to Advent; in the 1971 Breviary it is one of five antiphons which may be used at the end of Compline. From 1884 to 1964 its recitation was also required after Low Mass.

Crit. edn. of text by G. M. Dreves, *Lateinische Hymnendichter des Mittelalters*, 2 (AHMA 50; 1907), pp. 318 f. J. de Valois, *En marge d'une antienne: Le 'Salve Regina'* (1912); J. Maier, *Studien zur Geschichte der Marienantiphon 'Salve regina'* (Regensburg, 1939); J. M. Canal, *Salve Regina Misericordiae: Historia y leyendas en torno a esta antifona* (Temi e Testi, 9; Rome, 1963). H. Thurston, SJ, 'The Salve Regina', *The Month*, 128 (1918), pp. 248–60 and 300–14; text (without illustrations) repr. in his *Familiar Prayers*, ed. P. Grosjean, SJ (1953), no. 7, pp. 115–45, with refs. I. Cecchetti in *EC* 10 (1953), cols. 1719–21, with bibl.

Salvian (*c*.400–*c*.480), 'of Marseilles', ecclesiastical writer. Born in the vicinity of *Cologne or Trier, of noble family, he married one Palladia. After the birth of a daughter, he and his wife decided to adopt a life of asceticism, thereby alienating her parents who were still pagans. After a period spent at *Lérins (from *c*.424), Salvian moved (prob. in the 430s) to Marseilles, where he appears to have spent the rest of his life. He was already a priest in 431. The author of numerous works, many of which are now lost, he is best known for his treatise *De Gubernatione Dei*, in which, by contrasting the vices of decadent Roman civilization with the virtues of the victorious barbarians, he used the latter as a witness to God's judgement on society and as an incentive for Christians to purity of life and faith in Providence. Also extant are a treatise *Ad Ecclesiam* (against avarice), issued under the pseudonym of 'Timothy', and 9 letters. Written in a clear and vigorous style, his works provide valuable evidence of contemporary attitudes and social conditions.

Works repr. from edn. of S. *Baluze in J. P. Migne, *PL* 53. 25–238; crit. edns. by F. Pauly (CSEL 8; 1883), by C. Halm in *MGH*, Auctores Antiquissimi, 1 (pt. 1; 1887), and, with Fr. tr., by G. Lagarrigue (SC 176 and 220; 1971–5). Eng. tr. of his works by J. F. O'Sullivan (Fathers of the Church, 3; 1962) and of his *De Gubernatione Dei* by E. M. Sandford (Records of Civilization, Sources and Studies; New York, 1930), with notes on early edns. of his works. M. Pellegrino, *Salviano di Marsiglia* (Lateranum, NS 6, fascs. 1–2; 1940). P. Badot, 'La Notice de Gennade relative à Salvien', *R. Bén.* 84 (1974), pp. 352–66; S. Prococo, 'Una nota biografica su Salviano di Marsiglia', *Siculorum Gymnasium*, NS 29 (Catania, 1976), pp. 351–68. J. Badewien, *Geschichtstheologie und Sozialkritik im Werk Salvians von Marseille* (Forschungen zur Kirchen- und Dogmengeschichte, 32; Göttingen, 1980). A. Hamman in Quasten (cont.), *Patrology*, 4 (1986), pp. 528–37. G. Lagarrigue in *Dict. Sp.* 14 (1990), cols. 290–7, s.v., with bibl.

Samaria. The capital of the kingdom of *Israel, i.e. of the 'Ten [northern] Tribes', founded by King Omri (*c.*880 BC) and in *c.*721 BC captured by the Assyrians, who resettled the territory with pagans from other parts of their empire (2 Kgs. 18: 9–12 and ch. 17). According to Jewish tradition, the Samaritans known to later Judaism and the NT were the descendants of these settlers, though precisely when they became a separate religious sect with a temple of their own on Mt. Gerizim is disputed; opinions vary between the 5th and the 1st cent. BC, most scholars favouring a date in the 4th cent. The hostility of the Jews to the Samaritans was proverbial (Jn. 4: 9 and 8: 48). The Lord's sympathy to them is shown in the parables of the Good Samaritan (Lk. 10: 33) and the Ten Lepers (Lk. 17: 16). Apparently St *Philip the Evangelist was the first to preach the Gospel to them. A small Samaritan community survives at Nablus.

G. A. *Smith, *The Historical Geography of the Holy Land* (25th edn., 1931), pp. 323–63. J. A. Montgomery, *The Samaritans* (Philadelphia, 1907); M. Gaster, *The Samaritans* (Schweich Lectures for 1923; 1925); J. Macdonald, *The Theology of the Samaritans* (1964); A. D. Crown, (ed.), *The Samaritans* (Tübingen, 1989). Id., *A Bibliography of the Samaritans* (American Theological Library Association Bibliography Series, 10; Metuchen, NJ, and London, 1984). J. Jeremias in *TWNT* 7 (1960–4), pp. 88–94 (Eng. tr., 7 (1971), pp. 88–94), s.v. Σαμάρεια, with bibl.; J. Macdonald and others in *Encyclopaedia Judaica*, 14 (Jerusalem, 1971), cols. 725–58; R. T. Anderson in *Anchor Bible Dictionary*, 5 (1992), pp. 940–7, these last two both s.v. 'Samaritans'. R. W. Hamilton, *Guide to Samaria-Sebaste* (Jerusalem, 1944). A. Alt, *Der Stadtstaat Samaria* (Ber. (Sächs.), 101, Heft 5; 1954). A. Parrot, *Samarie, capitale du royaume d'Israël* (Cahiers d'Archéologie Biblique, 7; 1955; Eng. tr., 1958). K. [M.] Kenyon, *Royal Cities of the Old Testament* (1971), pp. 71–89. J. D. Purvis in *Anchor Bible Dictionary*, 5 (1992), pp. 914–21, s.v.; N. Avigad in E. Stern and others (eds.), *The New Encyclopedia of Archaeological Excavations in the Holy Land*, 4 (Jerusalem and New York [1993]), pp. 1300–10, s.v. 'Samaria (City)'; E. Hovers and others, ibid., pp. 1310–18, s.v. 'Samaria (Region)'. See also bibl. to following entry.

Samaritan Pentateuch. A slightly divergent form of the *Pentateuch in Hebrew, current since pre-Christian times among the Samaritans and the only part of the OT accepted by them. Where it differs from the *Massoretic (i.e. the standard Jewish) text, it seems usually to be inferior in value. Though the differences for the most part are only verbal, it is worth noting that they not infrequently agree with divergent readings found in the LXX, and they sometimes accord with the more developed ideas of reverence of a later date, e.g. in the substitution of 'the angel of God' for 'God' in the sentence 'God met Balaam' (Num. 23: 4). A notable difference is the name of the Samaritan holy mountain, Mt. Gerizim, for Mt. Ebal in Deut. 27: 4. No extant MS appears to be older than the 11th cent. AD, apart from a fragment of Num. 26: 62–27: 11 in Manchester, which is dated in the 9th century. There is an Aramaic translation, whose origins may go back to about the 2nd cent. AD; it is known as the Samaritan Targum.

The text was first made known in Europe in 1616 by the traveller Pietro della Valle, who brought home a copy from Damascus, now preserved in the *Vatican Library. The text was first pub. in the Paris *Polyglot of 1645 and repr. by B. *Walton in the London Polyglot of 1657; also ed. separately by B. Blayney (Oxford, 1790) and by A. von Gall (5 pts., Giessen, 1914–18; eclectic text, which makes no use of older MSS preserved at Nablus). Crit. edn. of the Samaritan Targum by A. Tal (3 vols., Tel Aviv, 1980–3). W. *Gesenius, *De Pentateuchi Samaritani Origine, Indole et Auctoritate* (Halle, 1815; denies its usefulness for OT text). P. Kahle, 'Untersuchungen zur Geschichte des Pentateuchtextes', *Theologische Studien und Kritiken*, 88 (1915), pp. 399–439, esp. 'I. Der Pentateuch der Samaritaner', pp. 402–10. J. D. Purvis, *The Samaritan Pentateuch and the Origin of the Samaritan Sect* (Harvard Semitic Monographs, 2; Cambridge, Mass., 1968). Id. in *The Interpreter's Dictionary of the Bible*, Suppl. vol. (Nashville, 1976), pp. 772–5, s.v.; B. K. Waltke in *Anchor Bible Dictionary*, 5 (1992), pp. 932–40, s.v., with bibl.

Samson (prob. 11th cent. BC), Hebrew hero, enemy of the Philistines and traditionally the last of the great 'judges'. Acc. to Jgs. 13: 2–16: 31 he was the son of Manoah, of the tribe of Dan, born in answer to prayer and bound throughout his life by a *Nazirite vow. He was endowed with prodigious strength, which enabled him to perform various remarkable exploits (e.g. slaying a lion and moving the gates of Gaza). After marrying a Philistine woman who betrayed him, he wrought havoc among the Philistines, from whom he escaped by his own strength both when surrendered by the men of Judah and when surrounded while visiting a harlot at Gaza. He at last fell victim to his consuming passion for Delilah, to whom he revealed that the secret of his strength lay in his hair. The Philistines put out his eyes, but Samson was granted his revenge in pulling down the pillars of the temple when 3,000 Philistines were assembled.

The name 'Samson' is almost certainly connected with the Hebrew word for 'sun' (*shemesh*), and some have seen in Samson the hero of a solar myth, derived from either the form of his name or that of his burial-place (Bethshemesh). Recent scholarship thinks of the Samson stories as originally independent tales, perhaps concerning a variety of local heroes, which have been skilfully woven together by the editors of the *Deuteronomistic History. In acc. with the scheme of the Book of Judges, he is said to have 'judged' Israel for 20 years (15: 20 and 16: 31), but the account in general contains nothing to suggest that he was a deliverer of Israel. He was, however, regarded as a recipient of divine favour and in the NT his faith is commended (Heb. 11: 32). In later literature he is the hero of J. *Milton's *Samson Agonistes* (1671) and one of G. F. *Handel's oratorios (1741).

See comm. on JUDGES, cited s.v., notably C. F. *Burney, *The Book of Judges* (1918), with bibl. p. 335, and additional note pp. 391–408 ('The Mythical Element in the Story of Samson'), and J. A. Soggin, *Judges* (1981), pp. 225–59. H. *Gunkel, 'Simson', in *Reden und Aufsätze* (Göttingen, 1913), pp. 38–64. G. von *Rad, 'Die Geschichte von Simson' [talk broadcast in 1953], in *Gottes Wirken in Israel: Vorträge zum alten Testament*, ed. O. H. Steck (Neukirchen, 1974), pp. 49–52. J. Blenkinsopp, 'Structure and Style in Judges 13–16', *Journal of Biblical Literature*, 82 (1963), pp. 65–76. J. L. Crenshaw, *Samson: A Secret Betrayed, a Vow Ignored* (Atlanta [1978]; London, 1979). Id. in *Anchor Bible Dictionary*, 5 (1992), pp. 950–4, s.v.

Samson, St (*c*.486–after 557), Bp. of Dol in Brittany. Born in S. Wales, he was ordained by St *Dubricius and then entered the monastery on *Caldey Island, in due course becoming abbot. He is said to have visited *Ireland and on his return to have sent his uncle Umbraphel to take charge of a monastery which had been given to him. He retired for a while to a cave near the R. Severn and attended a synod at which he was made a bishop. Instructed in a vision to leave his monastery, he went first to Cornwall and then to Brittany. There he founded the monastery of Dol which became a centre of missionary activity. He attended the councils of Paris in 553 and 557, signing the decrees as *Samson peccator episcopus*.

His Life, which perhaps dates from the 7th cent., seems to have been the model of many later Lives. His cult became popular soon after his death. Dol was the centre of the Church in Brittany, preserving its independence from Tours from the 6th to the 9th cent. Only in 1199 did Pope *Innocent III finally reject its claim to metropolitan status. Feast day, 28 July.

Life, first pr. by J. *Mabillon, also in *AASS*, Jul. 7 (1729), pp. 573–93; and ed. by R. Fawtier (Bibliothèque de l'École des Hautes Études, 197; 1912); Eng. tr. of text by T. Taylor ('Translations of Christian Literature'; 1925). F. Duine, 'La Vie de saint Samson, à propos d'un ouvrage récent', *Annales de Bretagne*, 28 (1913), pp. 332–56; J. Loth, 'La Vie la plus ancienne de saint Samson de Dol d'après des travaux récents: remarques et additions', *Revue Celtique*, 35 (1914), pp. 269–300; 39 (1922), pp. 301–33; and 40 (1923), pp. 1–50; R. Fawtier, 'Saint Samson abbé de Dol. Réponse à quelques objections', *Annales de Bretagne*, 35 (1923), pp. 137–70, with reply, pp. 171–86. F. C. Burkitt in *JTS* 27 (1926), pp. 42–57. G. H. Doble, *Saint Samson in Cornwall* (Cornish Saints Series, 36 [1935]), J.-C. Poulin, 'Hagiographie et politique. La première vie de saint Samson de Dol', *Francia*, 5 for 1977 (1978), pp. 1–26; B. Merdrignac, 'La première vie de saint Samson: étude chronologique', *Studia Monastica*, 30 (1988), pp. 245–89. Further bibl. in M. Lapidge and R. Sharpe, *A Bibliography of Celtic-Latin Literature 400–1200* (Dublin, 1985), pp. 261 f. (nos. 950 f.).

Samuel, Books of. The two Books of Samuel were originally a single Book, which was divided for convenience by the compilers of the *Septuagint, who also grouped the Books of Samuel with those of *Kings under the one single title of the '[Four] Books of the Reigns'. The English title follows the Hebrew, and is due to the import-

ant part played in the opening chapters by the prophet Samuel, in the establishment of the monarchy in Israel. After relating the history of Samuel, the writer sets down a description of the reigns of Saul (*c*.1025–*c*.1010 BC) and *David (*c*.1010–*c*.970). Three ancient poems lie embedded in the narrative: Hannah's prayer (1 Sam. 2: 1–10), David's lament (2 Sam. 1: 19–27), David's song of triumph (2 Sam. 22). As might be expected in such a work, various sources have been used by the compilers. It is widely believed that 2 Sam. 9–20, together with 1 Kgs. 1–2, originally formed an independent work concerned with the succession to the throne of David and accordingly often referred to as the 'Succession Narrative'. There is also evidence of the use of fragmentary sources, ranging from prophetic legends to excerpts from books of annals. The older view, that the Pentateuchal sources '*J' and '*E' continue into the Books of Samuel, is now less commonly held. Many modern scholars have been less interested in the sources than in the religious and theological standpoint of the compilers and regard the Books as an important constituent of the so-called '*Deuteronomistic History' (q.v.).

Comm. by H. W. Hertzberg (Das Alte Testament Deutsch, 10; 1956; 2nd edn., 1960; Eng. tr. 1964), J. Mauchline (New Cent. Bib., 1971), P. K. McCarter (Anchor Bible, 2 vols., 1980–4), R. P. Gordon (Exeter [1986]); on 1 Sam. by R. W. Klein (Word Biblical Comm. 10; Waco, Tex. [1983]), and on 2 Sam. by P. R. Ackroyd (Cam. Bib., NEB, 1977) and A. A. Anderson (Word Biblical Comm. 11 [1989]). S. R. *Driver, *Notes on the Hebrew Text and the Topography of the Books of Samuel* (1890); O. Eissfeldt, *Die Komposition der Samuelisbücher* (1931). R. A. Carlson, *David, the Chosen King: A Traditio-Historical Approach to the Second Book of Samuel* (Eng. tr., Stockholm, 1964). A. Weiser, *Samuel: Seine geschichtliche Aufgabe und religiöse Bedeutung. Traditionsgeschichtliche Untersuchungen zu 1. Samuel 7–12* (Göttingen, 1962). R. N. Whybray, *The Succession Narrative* (Studies in Biblical Theology, 2nd ser. 9; 1968); D. M. Gunn, *The Story of King David: Genre and Interpretation* (Journal for the Study of the Old Testament, Supplement Series, 6; Sheffield 1978). Brief introd. by R. P. Gordon, *1 & 2 Samuel* (Old Testament Guides, Sheffield [1984]). A. Caquot in *Dict. Bibl.*, Suppl. 11 (1991), cols. 1048–98, s.v.

sanatio in radice (Lat., 'healing at the root'). In canon law, the process whereby an invalid 'marriage' is validated retrospectively, i.e. from the moment at which the 'marriage' was solemnized. Unless special provision is made for *sanatio in radice*, the marriage is validated only from the moment at which the *impediment is dispensed and valid consent exchanged. In the absence of such retrospective validation, the full legitimacy of children born before validation would not be secured. Under RC canon law (*CIC* (1983), can. 1165) *sanatio in radice* can be granted by the Pope, and by diocesan bishops in certain types of cases. See also VALIDATION OF MARRIAGE.

T. P. Doyle, OP, in J. A. Coriden and others (eds.), *The Code of Canon Law: A Text and Commentary* (1985), pp. 822–9, with bibl. p. 833. See also bibl. to discussions in RC handbooks of moral theology.

sanbenito. The penitential garment which the medieval and later the Spanish *Inquisition ordered to be worn, either for life or for a specified period, by those who had been sentenced for heresy. It was normally yellow, with one or two crosses on it, but in the case of those to be handed over to the secular authorities at an *auto de fe, it was black, with flames, demons, and other decorative matter painted or embroidered on it.

Sánchez, Thomas (1550–1610), Spanish *Jesuit moral theologian. He entered the Society of Jesus in 1567 and was appointed master of novices at Granada, where he also taught moral theology and canon law. He became famous for his *Disputationes de sancto matrimonii sacramento* (1602), a comprehensive work on the moral and canonical aspects of matrimony which enjoyed high authority in the 17th cent. One volume of its Venetian edition was placed on the *Index because of the omission of a passage, displeasing to the Venetian Republic, defending the legitimization of illegitimate children by the Pope without interference of the civil authorities. In the *Opus Morale in Praecepta Decalogi* (1613), published posthumously, he undertook to expound a system of casuistry based on the Decalogue, but he did not go beyond the Second Commandment. Much later Sánchez was attacked as a *laxist by B. *Pascal in his *Lettres provinciales*, but he seems only to have shared some erroneous opinions, e.g. on *mental reservation, with other *probabilists of his time.

Collected edn. of his works, 7 vols., Venice, 1740. H. Zapp, *Die Geisteskrankheit in der Ehekonsenslehre Thomas Sanchez'* (Forschungen zur kirchlichen Rechtsgeschichte und zum Kirchenrecht, 11; Cologne and Vienna, 1971); M. Bajén, *Pensamiento de Tomas Sanchez S.I. sobre Moral Sexual* (Granada, 1976). Sommervogel, 7 (1896), cols. 530–7; Polgár, 3 (1990), pp. 152 f. R. Brouillard, SJ, in *DTC* 14 (1939), cols. 1075–85, s.v.

Sancroft, William (1617–93), Abp. of *Canterbury. He was educated at Emmanuel College, Cambridge, where he was a Fellow from 1642 till 1651, when he was ejected by the *Puritans. At the *Restoration he was appointed chaplain to *Charles II, Prebendary of *Durham (1662), Master of Emmanuel College (1662), and Dean of *York (1664). As chaplain to Bp. J. *Cosin of Durham he acted as secretary to the revisers of the 1662 BCP, which he also saw through the press. In Dec. 1664 he became Dean of *St Paul's, where he reordered the capitular finances; after the disastrous fire of 1666 he collaborated with C. *Wren in rebuilding the cathedral. In 1678 he succeeded G. *Sheldon in the see of Canterbury. His primacy was distinguished by a major effort to renew the strength of the Anglican establishment, both politically, in alliance with the Tory party, and spiritually. He raised the standard of ordination requirements; conducted a Metropolitical Visitation in 1682, and suspended Thomas Wood, Bp. of *Lichfield and Coventry, for negligence in 1684. The accession of the RC *James II caused him to alter the *Coronation rite radically in 1685, so that the Communion could be omitted. James's attack on the inherited position of the C of E soon pushed Sancroft into opposition to the royal policies. His action as leader of the *Seven Bishops who opposed the *Declaration of Indulgence in 1688 led to his imprisonment in the Tower, but on trial he was acquitted. After James's flight he refused, however, to recognize William of Orange as rightful king, was suspended from office on 1 Aug. 1689, and on 1 Feb. 1690 deprived of his archbishopric as a '*Nonjuror'. His later years were spent in retirement in Suffolk, where he came to support schemes to perpetuate the Nonjuring succes-

sion. In 1692 he formally delegated his archiepiscopal authority to William Lloyd, the deprived Bp. of *Norwich.

A small collection of his *Occasional Sermons* was pub., London, 1694. Life by G. D'Oyly (2 vols., London 1821). C. R. L. Fletcher, 'Some Troubles of Archbishop Sancroft', *Proceedings of the Huguenot Society of London*, 13 (1926), pp. 209–61, with calendar of some of his correspondence in the Tanner Collection [Bodleian Library], pp. 255 f. N. Sykes, *From Sheldon to Secker* (Ford Lectures, 1958; Cambridge, 1959), esp. pp. 16–18, 82–9, 134 f., 188–92. R. [A.] Beddard, 'The Commission for Ecclesiastical Promotions, 1681–4: An Instrument of Tory Reaction', *Historical Journal*, 10 (1967), pp. 11–40; id., 'The Guildhall Declaration of 11 December 1688 and the Counter-Revolution of the Loyalists', ibid. 11 (1968), pp. 403–20. W. H. *Hutton in *DNB* 1 (1897), pp. 244–50; id. in *DECH*, pp. 543 f. See also works cited under SEVEN BISHOPS and NONJURORS.

Sancta Clara, Franciscus a. See DAVENPORT, CHRISTOPHER.

Sancta Sophia. The famous church at *Constantinople, dedicated to the 'Holy *Wisdom' (i.e. the Person of Christ), was built under *Justinian by Anthemius of Tralles and Isidore of Miletus between 532 and 537 and consecrated in 538. One of the most perfect examples of Byzantine architecture, its chief feature is the enormous dome, supported by piers, arches, and pendentives, and pierced by 40 windows, which crowns the basilica. In 1453 the church was converted into a mosque by the Turks, and the mosaics which adorned its interior were covered up and partly destroyed. Discovered during restoration work in 1847–9, they have been laid bare and restored during the 20th cent. The church has been a museum since 1935.

W. R. Lethaby and H. Swainson, *The Church of Sancta Sophia, Constantinople: A Study of Byzantine Building* (1894). E. M. Antoniades, Ἔκφρασις τῆς Ἁγίας Σοφίας (3 vols., Athens, 1907–9). V. R. Zalozciecky, *Die Sophienkirche in Konstantinopel und ihre Stellung in der abendländischen Architektur* (Studi di Antichità Cristiana, 12; 1936). A. M. Schneider, *Die Hagia Sophia zu Konstantinopel* (Bilderhefte Antiker Kunst herausgegeben vom Archäologischen Institut des Deutschen Reiches, 6 [1938]). E. H. Swift, *Hagia Sophia* (New York, 1940). H. Kähler, *Die Hagia Sophia* (1967; Eng. tr., 1967, incl. a section by C. Mango on the mosaics). R. J. Mainstone, *Hagia Sophia: Architecture, Structure and Liturgy of Justinian's Great Church* [1988]. R. Mark and A. Ş. Çakmak, *Hagia Sophia from the Age of Justinian to the Present* (Cambridge, 1992). T. Whittemore, *The Mosaics of St Sophia at Istanbul* (Byzantine Institute, 4 vols., 1933–52); C. Mango, *Materials for the Study of the Mosaics of St Sophia at Istanbul* (Dumbarton Oaks Studies, 8; 1962). See also works cited under CONSTANTINOPLE.

Sanctorale. The section of a *Missal, *Lectionary, or *Breviary (sometimes made into a separate book) which supplies the variable parts of the Mass or Offices peculiar to the festivals of particular saints.

sanctuary (Gk. ἱερατεῖον, or, more commonly, βῆμα). The part of the church containing the altar (or, if there be several altars, the high altar). In Byzantine churches it is enclosed by the *iconostasis. It is sometimes termed the 'presbytery', as being the portion of the church properly reserved to the clergy.

sanctuary, right of. In the Middle Ages this was of two kinds, ecclesiastical and secular. The former had developed out of the usage that a criminal who had taken refuge in a church might not be removed from it, but was allowed to take an oath of abjuration before the coroner and proceed to a seaport appointed by the latter. If within 40 days he refused to adopt this procedure, he might be forcibly extricated for justice. The privilege was understood not to extend to sacrilege or high treason. Sometimes those claiming the privilege of sanctuary had to touch a particular object in the church (in early times, often the altar). The sanctuary-stool ('frith-stool') survives at *Hexham, the sanctuary-knocker at *Durham and elsewhere.

Secular and jurisdictional sanctuary relied upon royal grant, and in theory at least might be held to apply to every franchise where the lord had *jura regalia* and the king's writ did not run. This institution is frequently confused with ecclesiastical sanctuary, since criminals commonly repaired to a church in a franchise, esp. in the great ecclesiastical liberties like *Beverley, Durham, and Tynemouth. Such sanctuaries as these latter certainly promoted social disorder in the later Middle Ages. At the Reformation the privilege of sanctuary was drastically curtailed. In 1540 *Henry VIII limited it to seven cities, namely, *Wells, *Westminster, Northampton, Manchester, *York, Derby, and Launceston. A petition from Manchester against the nomination led to *Chester being substituted. By an act of *James I (1623), sanctuary for crime was finally abolished altogether, though it lingered on for civil processes until 1723.

S. Pegge, 'A Sketch of the History of the Asylum, or Sanctuary, from its Origin to the Final Abolition of it in the Reign of James I', *Archaeologia*, 8 (1787), pp. 1–44. N. M. Trenholme, *The Right of Sanctuary in England* (University of Missouri Studies, vol. 1, no. 5; 1903). J. C. Cox, *The Sanctuaries and Sanctuary Seekers of Mediaeval England* (1911). J. H. Baker, 'The English Law of Sanctuary', *Ecclesiastical Law Journal*, 2 (1990), pp. 8–13. G. Le Bras in *DHGE* 4 (1930), cols. 1035–47, s.v. 'Asile'; E. Herman and L. R. Misserey in *DDC* 1 (1935), cols. 1084–9 and 1089–1104, s.vv. 'Asile dans l'Église orientale (Le Droit de)' and 'Asile en Occident' respectively, all with detailed bibl.

Sanctus. The hymn of praise which follows the *Preface in the Eucharist and begins with the words 'Holy, holy, holy' (Is. 6: 3). It appeared in some synagogue prayers, and, though used by Christians from an early date, it was not apparently part of the earliest Eucharistic rite; the allusion to it in St *Clement of Rome (1 Clem. 34: 6 f.) need not be liturgical. By 350, however, its use in the Eucharist in most E. and some W. Churches is reported in the treatise *De Spiritu Sancto* (PL 17. 1010) attributed to St *Ambrose. Its use in the E. is also attested by sermons ascribed to *Asterius (15. 16 and 29. 10), by St *Gregory of Nyssa (*De Baptismo*) and St John *Chrysostom (*In Eph.* 14. 4). It may have been introduced in Rome by Sixtus III (432–40), but it was slow to become established in the W. and as late as 529 the Council of *Vaison had to direct that it be always included. To the angelic cry 'Sanctus' was soon added the human acclamation '*Benedictus qui venit' ('Blessed is he who comes in the name of the Lord, Hosanna in the highest'). This is found in the 8th-cent. Latin rite, the E. liturgies of St *James and St *Chrysos-

tom, in the 1549 Book of *Common Prayer, and in modern RC and Anglican texts. Originally the Sanctus and Benedictus were not separated from the *Canon which followed immediately afterwards, but the practice of the congregation and choir joining in the words of the Sanctus led to a division here, and the Canon came to be looked on as a separate item. In sung Masses, the Sanctus and Benedictus were at one time separated, with the Benedictus being sung after the *Elevation. In modern liturgies the Sanctus and Benedictus form part of the *Eucharistic Prayers.

A. *Baumstark, 'Trishagion und Qeduscha', *JLW* 3 (1923), pp. 18–32. E. C. Ratcliff, 'The Sanctus and the Pattern of the Early Anaphora', *JEH* 1 (1950), pp. 29–36 and 125–34. W. C. van Unnik, 'I Clement 34 and the "Sanctus"', *VC* 5 (1951), pp. 204–48. H. Auf der Maur, *Die Osterhomilien des Asterius Sophistes als Quellen für die Geschichte des Osterfeier* (Trierer theologische Studien, 19; 1967), pp. 74–94. B. D. Spinks, *The Sanctus in the Eucharistic Prayer* (Cambridge, 1991). Jungmann (1958 edn.), 2, pp. 161–73 (Eng. tr., 2, pp. 128–38), with refs. to ancient sources and older bibl.

Sanctus bell. See SACRING BELL.

Sanctus candle. The rubrics of the Roman Missal long required that at the Epistle side of the altar an additional candle should be lighted at the *Sanctus, and that it should be left burning until after the Communion. The custom seems to have originated at the end of the Middle Ages; but, despite the rubric, it was not generally observed in modern times.

sandals, episcopal. The low shoes with leather soles and the upper part of embroidery which before 1984 could be worn by bishops in the W. Church only at solemn Pontifical Masses and other functions (e.g. Ordination) performed during them. Except in Rome they were usually adorned with a small cross. Their use certainly goes back to the 5th cent. Liturgical stockings (*caligae*), in modern times of the liturgical colour of the day, were worn with them.

Braun, *LG*, pp. 384–424. J. Braun, SJ, in *CE* 13 (1912), pp. 434 f., s.v.

Sanday, William (1843–1920), English NT scholar. He was educated at Repton and at Balliol and Corpus Christi Colleges, Oxford. In 1876 he was appointed principal of Hatfield Hall, *Durham, and in 1882 recalled to Oxford as Dean Ireland's professor of exegesis, where he remained for the rest of his life. From 1895 to 1919 he was Lady Margaret professor of divinity. His influence went far to winning Anglican clergy to the acceptance of modern methods of NT study. Though his long-projected Life of Christ was never achieved, the plan bore fruit in a large number of books conceived as subsidiary studies. He is now known mainly for his *Commentary on Romans* (1895, in conjunction with A. C. *Headlam) and his *Christologies, Ancient and Modern* (1910).

Obituary notice by W. Lock in *JTS* 22 (1921), pp. 97–104, with bibl. of his published works by A. *Souter, pp. 193–205. M. D. Chapman, 'The Socratic Subversion of Tradition: William Sanday and Theology, 1900–1920', ibid., NS 45 (1994), pp. 94–116. C. H. *Turner in *DNB, 1912–1921*, pp. 482–4.

Sandemanians. See GLASITES.

Sanders, Nicholas (*c*.1530–81), also 'Sander', RC controversialist and historian. Educated at Winchester and New College, Oxford, he graduated in 1551 and lectured on canon law. After the accession of *Elizabeth I he fled to the Continent (1559) and was ordained priest at Rome in 1560. In 1561 he accompanied Cardinal S. *Hosius to the Council of *Trent and later on missions to Poland, Prussia, and Lithuania. In 1565 he went to Louvain, where he became professor of theology and, in connection with the controversy aroused by Bp. J. *Jewel's *Apology*, published *The Supper of Our Lord* (1565), *A Treatise of Images* (1567), *The Rock of the Church* (1567), and *De Visibili Monarchia Ecclesiae* (1571). The last of these, resuming the general ideas of St *Augustine's *De Civitate Dei*, gives a comprehensive view of the Church from its first adumbrations at the beginnings of humanity and defends its monarchical government; it also throws much incidental light on the sufferings endured by RCs under Elizabeth. Called to Rome in 1572, he became consultor to *Gregory XIII on English affairs. In 1573 he went to Spain to induce *Philip II to make war on Elizabeth, and in 1579 he went to Ireland as Papal agent to cause an insurrection against the government. After two years of continual failure he died as a fugitive, probably of exhaustion. His unfinished work *De Origine ac Progressu Schismatis Anglicani* was edited by E. Rishton in 1585 and translated by D. Lewis in 1877. Though sharply criticized at the time, it is now admitted to be accurate in some of its controverted statements.

J. H. Pollen, SJ (ed.), 'Dr Nicholas Sander's Report to Cardinal Moroni *N.d.* [? May, 1561.]', *Catholic Record Society Miscellanea*, 1 (*Catholic Record Society, 1; 1905), pp. 1–23, with Eng. tr. pp. 24–47. J. B. Wainewright (ed.), 'Some Letters and Papers of Nicholas Sander, 1562–1580', *Catholic Record Society Miscellanea* 13 (ibid. 26; 1926), pp. 1–57. J. H. Pollen, SJ, 'Dr. Nicholas Sanders', *EHR* 6 (1891), pp. 36–47. T. M. Veech, *Dr Nicholas Sanders and the English Reformation, 1530–81* (Université de Louvain, Recueil de Travaux publiés par les Membres des Conférences d'Histoire et de Philologie, 2nd ser., fasc. 32; 1935), with bibl. A. F. Allison and D. M. Rogers, *The Contemporary Printed Literature of the English Counter-Reformation between 1558 and 1640*, 1 (Aldershot, 1989), pp. 135–40 (nos. 966–1022). T. G. Law in *DNB* 50 (1897), pp. 259–62.

Sanderson, Robert (1587–1663), Bp. of *Lincoln. Educated at Rotherham Grammar School and Lincoln College, Oxford, of which he became a Fellow in 1606, he was ordained in 1611 and held several livings, as well as prebendal stalls at *Southwell and Lincoln. Gaining the favour of W. *Laud, he was appointed a royal chaplain in 1631 and Regius professor of divinity at Oxford in 1642. During the Civil War he was deprived of his professorship and for a time imprisoned. In 1660 he was reinstated and soon afterwards consecrated to the see of Lincoln. He took a leading part in the *Savoy Conference of 1661 and drafted the preface to the new (1662) Prayer Book. His best-known work is his *Nine Cases of Conscience Occasionally Determined* (1678), one of the most notable contributions to moral theology in its age. His other writings include: *Logicae Artis Compendium* (1615); *De Juramenti Promissorii Obligatione* (1647); and *De Obligatione Conscientiae* (lectures in 1647; pub. 1660).

Facsimile of his *Logicae Artis Compendium*, with introd. by E. J. Ashworth (Instrumenta Rationis, 2; Bologna, 1985). An Eng.

tr. of his *De Obligatione Conscientiae* by R. Codrington was also pub., London, 1660; Eng. tr. with preface by C. *Wordsworth, Lincoln, 1877. Collected edn. of his works by W. Jacobson (6 vols., Oxford, 1854), with repr. of the famous Life by I. *Walton, orig. pub. London, 1678, in vol. 6, pp. 265–350. Modern study by G. Lewis (London, 1924). P. G. Lake, 'Serving God and the Times: The Calvinist Conformity of Robert Sanderson', *Journal of British Studies*, 27 (1988), pp. 81–116. J. H. Legge in *DNB* 50 (1897), pp. 265 f., with further refs.

Sandys, Edwin (*c*.1516–88), Abp. of *York. A graduate of St John's College, Cambridge, he became master of St Catharine's Hall in 1547, vicar of Caversham in 1548, canon of *Peterborough in 1549, and vice-chancellor of Cambridge University in 1553, in all these posts doing his utmost to further the principles of the English Reformation. A supporter of Lady Jane Grey, he was imprisoned in the Tower in July 1553, but eventually escaped to the Continent. On *Elizabeth I's accession he returned, and was appointed subsequently to the sees of *Worcester (1559), London (1570), and York (1577). A fervent and learned opponent of Romanist practices, with personal leanings towards *Puritanism, he came on several occasions into collision with his clergy. He was one of the translators of the *Bishops' Bible.

Sandys issued a collection of his sermons, London, 1585; ed. T. Whitaker (ibid., 1812), with Life, pp. i–lxiv; also ed., with other miscellaneous pieces, by J. Ayre (*Parker Society, 1841), with biographical introduction, pp. i–xxxii. Further letters in H. Robinson (ed.), *The Zürich Letters*, 1 (Parker Society, 1842), pp. 3–6, 72–5, 145 f., 264–6, 294–7, 311–13, and 331–3. H. Trevor-Roper, *Catholics, Anglicans and Puritans* (1987), pp. 195–8. W. A. J. Archbold in *DNB* 50 (1897), pp. 283–6.

Sanhedrin. The Jewish supreme council and court of justice at *Jerusalem in NT times. The surviving evidence is confused and conflicting as to its precise name, function, composition, competence, and procedures, and it is possible that it was not at all times a formal, clearly identifiable, constitutional body. The name is a Heb. form of the Gk. συνέδριον, 'council', but in Gk. sources the main council of Jerusalem is also designated by the words βουλή (*Josephus, *Bell. Jud.* 2. 15. 6), γερουσία (Acts 5: 21) and πρεσβυτέριον (Lk. 22: 66, Acts 22: 5). The origin of such a council is obscure, but an assembly of this type in operation is attested before Roman times. Acc. to rabbinic texts, the Sanhedrin consisted of 71 members (cf. Num. 11: 16). Acc. to the NT and Josephus, it included both priests and laymen, and both *Sadducees and *Pharisees. The NT implies that it was presided over by the *High Priest (Mt. 26: 57, Acts 24: 1). Rabbinic sources, however, make no mention of such a position belonging to the High Priest and refer to its president by such expressions as 'Nasi' ('Prince') or 'the Father of the House of Judgement'. It is debated whether it had the right to try capital cases (Josephus, *Antiq.* 14. 9. 3 f.; Mt. 26: 3 f.; Acts 4: 5, 6: 12, 22: 30), but such a right may be presupposed by the tradition that it pronounced sentence of death on Christ. After the destruction of Jerusalem in AD 70, when it came to an end in its original form, the *rabbis at *Jamnia claimed the right to take over some of its duties and authority.

Much information is contained in the Tractate 'Sanhedrin' of the *Mishnah (q.v.), but the relevance of this material to the period before AD 70 is disputed. S. B. Hoenig, *The Great Sanhedrin: A Study of the Origin, Development, Composition and Functions* of the Bet Din ha-Gadol during the Second Jewish Commonwealth (Philadelphia, 1953). H. Mantel, *Studies in the History of the Sanhedrin* (Harvard Semitic Series, 17; 1961). G. Alon, *The Jews in their Land in the Talmudic Age (70–640 C.E.)*, 1 (Jerusalem, 1980; Eng. tr. of Heb. rev. edn., pub. Tel Aviv, 1967), pp. 185–205; E. *Schürer, *The History of the Jewish People in the Age of Jesus Christ*, rev. Eng. tr. by G. Vermes and others, 2 (Edinburgh, 1979), pp. 199–226; M. Goodman, *The Ruling Class of Judaea* (Cambridge, 1987), pp. 112–16. On the disputed right of the Sanhedrin to inflict the death sentence, and its relevance to the Passion Narrative, cf. also A. N. Sherwin-White, *Roman Society and Roman Law in the New Testament* (Sarum Lectures, 1960–1, Oxford, 1963), esp. pp. 32–47, with refs.; P. Winter, *On the Trial of Jesus* (Studia Judaica, 1; Berlin, 1961; 2nd edn., with addenda, by T. A. Burkill and G. Vermes, 1974); D. R. Catchpole, *The Trial of Jesus* (Studia Post-Biblica, 18; Leiden, 1971). An ingenious solution to some of the problems is proposed by the suggestion that there were two separate bodies, A. Büchler, *Das Synedrion in Jerusalem und das grosse Beth-din in der Quaderkammer des Jerusalemischen Tempels* (Vienna, 1902). E. Lohse in *TWNT* 7 (1964), pp. 858–69 (Eng. tr., 7 (1971), pp. 860–71), s.v. συνέδριον; A. J. Saldarini in *Anchor Bible Dictionary*, 5 (1992), pp. 975–80, s.v.

Sankey, Ira David (1840–1908). See MOODY, DWIGHT LYMAN.

Santa Claus. An American corruption of the Dutch form of St *Nicholas, Bp. of Myra, widely venerated as the patron of children. The custom of making Christmas gifts in his name was introduced in America by the Dutch Protestants at New Amsterdam and thence into England. In some countries, e.g. parts of Germany, small presents are given to children on his feast day, 6 Dec.

Santa Maria Maggiore, Rome. The celebrated *basilica on the Esquiline Hill was founded by Pope *Liberius (352–66). The present structure was erected under Sixtus III (432–40). Acc. to a medieval tradition the site was indicated by the BVM, who one August night left her footprints in a miraculous fall of summer snow. This legend was formerly commemorated in the Feast of Our Lady of the Snows (5 Aug.; now renamed as the Dedication of the Basilica of St Mary). Though smaller than the other early basilicas (Old St Peter's, S. Paolo fuori le Mura, and the *Lateran), it is the largest of the 80 churches in Rome dedicated to the BVM. Among the treasures of the church are the reputed remains of parts of the manger in which Christ was born.

A. Valentini, *La patriarcale basilica liberiana illustrata* (Rome, 1839). A. Schuchert, *S. Maria Maggiore zu Rom*, 1. *Die Gründungsgeschichte der Basilika und die ursprüngliche Apsisanlage* (Studi di Antichità Cristiana, 15; 1939). R. Krautheimer, S. Corbett, and W. Frankl, *Corpus Basilicarum Christianarum Romae*, 3 (Rome, 1967), pp. 1–60, with full bibl. [in Eng.]. B. Brenk, *Die frühchristlichen Mosaiken in S. Maria Maggiore zu Rom* (Wiesbaden, 1975). See also ROME, CHURCHES OF.

Santa Sophia. See SANCTA SOPHIA.

Santiago de Compostela. See COMPOSTELA.

Santiago, Order of. A military order under the patronage of St *James founded in 1170 for the protection of pilgrims and the expulsion of the Moors. Its constitution was closely modelled on that of the *Templars; it was

approved by Pope *Alexander III 1175. A distinctive feature of the Order was that the knights were allowed to marry under certain conditions, a right obtained by the other military Orders only at the end of the Middle Ages. The Order rapidly acquired property in Castile and Portugal as well as León, and in 1523 its administration was annexed to the Spanish crown.

J. López Arguleta, *Bullarium Equestris Ordinis Sancti Jacobi de Spatha* (Madrid, 1719). Lat. and Sp. texts of the rule ed., with Eng. tr. and preliminary study, by E. Gallego Blanco (Medieval Iberian Peninsula Texts and Studies, 4; Leiden, 1971). D. W. Lomax, *La Orden de Santiago (1170–1275)* (1965), with bibl.

sarabaites. A name, of doubtful derivation, given in the early Church to a class of ascetics who dwelt either in their own houses or in small groups near cities and acknowledged no monastic superior. Their mode of life seems to have been regarded with disfavour, notably by St *Benedict, who refers to them adversely in the first chapter of his Rule.

Comm. on Rule of St Benedict (q.v.), esp. that by P. Delatte, OSB (Eng. tr., 1921), pp. 30–2. J. *Bingham, *Origines Ecclesiasticae*, 7. 2. 4.

Saracens (Lat. Saraceni, Gk. Σαρακηνοί). A term prob. originally applied to the nomads of N. Arabia, who claim descent from Ishmael; hence St. *John of Damascus, *De Haeresibus Compendium*, 101 (*PG* 94. 764 AB) calls them Ishmaelites. From at least the 9th cent. it came to be applied to all Muslims, esp. those against whom the *Crusaders fought. Two theories of the origin of the name (which is never used by Muslims themselves) have been advanced: one connects it with Arabic *sharqi*, 'Easterner', the other with an early use of Arabic *sharika* in the sense of 'tribal confederacy'.

Sarapion, St. See SERAPION, ST.

Saravia, Hadrian a (c.1532–1613), Protestant divine. Born at Hesdin in Artois of Hispano-Flemish parents, he entered the *Franciscan Order at St-Omer as a youth but left it on his conversion to Protestantism in 1557. From 1559 to 1562 he was in London as a member of the Dutch Reformed Church at Austin Friars. During this time he was consulted over the drafting of the the the *Belgic Confession and, on becoming a minister of the Walloon congregation at Antwerp, was instrumental in commending this to William of Orange and other Dutch noblemen. In 1563 Saravia was appointed as the first master of Elizabeth College, Guernsey, and, after being granted English nationality in 1568, settled in Southampton as master of King Edward VI School (1572–8). Returning to the Netherlands, he served as a minister in Ghent (1578–82) and *Leiden (1582–4), before becoming professor of theology at the latter university in 1584. In 1587, his devoted support of the Governor General, the Earl of Leicester, led to his dismissal and flight to England, where he was appointed rector of Tatenhill (1588–95) and later a prebendary of *Gloucester (1591–5). He resigned these offices on becoming a canon of *Canterbury and vicar of Lewisham (1595–1604). In 1601 he added a canonry at *Westminster and, in 1610, the living of Great Chart. With the publication in 1590 of his chief theological work,

De Diversis Ministrorum Evangelii Gradibus, Saravia emerged as a zealous champion of episcopacy and as the first Protestant theologian to base this position upon an appeal to the 'ius divinum'. Evidently directed against T. *Beza's teaching on Church government, the work provoked a response from Beza in 1592 to which Saravia replied in 1594. Incidentally his book was among the earliest Protestant writings to urge the apostolic commission to preach the Gospel to the heathen. A cultured and studious man, he was a close friend of R. *Hooker and I. *Casaubon. He was also one of the translators of the AV of the Bible.

A collection of some of his writings was pub. as *Diversi Tractatus Theologici* (London, 1611). His treatise *De Sacra Eucharistica* first pub., with Eng. tr. by G. A. *Denison (1885). W. Nijenhuis, *Adrianus Saravia (c.1532–1613)* (Studies in the History of Christian Thought, 21 [in Eng.]; Leiden, 1980).

sarcophagus. Sarcophagi, i.e. stone coffins, usually adorned with bas-reliefs, were much used down to the Byzantine period for the burial of both pagans and Christians. Till a late date Christians continued to adorn them with pagan designs; but from the 4th cent. Christian designs also became common. The Christian subjects illustrated were, however, strictly limited in number, the most popular being *Jonah and the whale, *Moses striking the rock, the apprehension of *Peter, and one or two of the Lord's miracles. Most of the extant Christian sarcophagi are to be found in Italy, esp. in the *Vatican Museum and at *Ravenna. There are also many at Arles.

G. Wilpert, *I sarcofagi cristiani antichi* (3 vols., bound in 5, 1929–36); F. Gerke, *Die christlichen Sarkophage der vorkonstantinischen Zeit* (Studien zur spätantiken Kunstgeschichte, 11; 1940); G. Bovini, *I sarcofagi paleocristiani: Determinazione della loro cronologia mediante l'analisi dei ritratti* (Monumenti di Antichità Cristiana, 2nd ser. 5; 1949). R. [L. P.] Milburn, *Early Christian Art and Architecture* (Aldershot, 1988), esp. pp. 58–80. H. *Leclercq, OSB, in *DACL* 15 (pt. 1; 1950), cols. 778–888, s.v.; M. Sotomayor in *DPAC* 2 (1984), cols. 3097–102, s.v.; Eng. tr. in *Encyclopedia of the Early Church*, 2 (1992), pp. 755 f., with bibl.

Sardica (or Serdica), Council of (mod. Sofia). A Council summoned c.343 by Emps. Constans and Constantius principally to settle the orthodoxy of St *Athanasius. It was intended that it should be an Oecumenical Council, but the E. bishops on arrival refused to attend on the ground that Athanasius, whom the E. had deposed, was being regarded by the W. as a proper member of the synod. The W. bishops therefore met by themselves, under the presidency of *Hosius of Córdoba. They confirmed the restoration of Athanasius, acquitted *Marcellus of Ancyra of heresy, and also restored Asclepas, Bp. of Gaza, who had been deposed by a Synod of *Antioch. The Council is famous for the disciplinary canons which it passed, chief among which are the provisions constituting the Bp. of Rome a court of appeal for accused bishops in certain circumstances. The canons of Sardica were at one time held to be canons of *Nicaea and were quoted as such by Pope *Zosimus in a letter sent in 418 to a Council of *Carthage.

The docs. connected with the Council, incl. the text of the canons (both Gk. and Lat. versions), will be found in Hardouin, 1, cols. 635–84, and Mansi, 3 (Florence, 1759), cols. 1–140. Crit. edn. of Lat. text of canons [incl. Gk. text in parallel column] in

EOMIA 1. 2. 3 (1930), pp. 441–560. Lat. and Gk. text also pr., with Fr. tr., in Joannou, 1, pt. 2 (1962), pp. 159–89. Hefele and Leclercq, 1 (pt. 2; 1907), pp. 733–823. H. Hess, *The Canons of the Council of Sardica*, A.D. 343 (Oxford, 1958). L. W. Barnard, *The Council of Serdica 343 A.D.* (Sofia, 1983). *CPG* 4 (1980), pp. 16–18 (nos. 8560–71). G. Bardy in Fliche and Martin, 3 (1936), pp. 122–30. Id. in *DTC* 14 (pt. 1; 1939), cols. 1109–14, s.v. 'Sardique (Concile de)'. On the Sardican Creed, F. *Loofs, *Das Glaubensbekenntnis der Homousianer von Sardika* (*Abh.* (Berl.), 1909, Heft 1); M. Tetz, 'Ante omnia de sancta fide et de integritate veritatis. Glaubensfragen auf der Synode von Serdika (342)', *ZNTW* 76 (1985), pp. 243–69; and S. G. Hall, 'The Creed of Sardica', in E. A. Livingstone (ed.), *Studia Patristica*, 19 (Louvain, 1989), pp. 173–84.

Sardis, city in Lydia, Asia Minor. The Christian community is one of the '*Seven Churches' addressed in Rev. 3: 1–6. Having a reputation for being alive, though in fact dead, its members are exhorted to repent, as Christ will return without warning. *Melito, Bp. of Sardis in the 2nd cent., also had apocalyptic concerns. The classical city's principal cult was that of Cybele, the ancient mother goddess of Anatolia; there was also a large and ornate synagogue in use c. AD 200–616. In Late Antiquity Sardis was a prosperous city. Despite severe damage in the early 7th cent., it was a significant centre and bishopric in the Middle Ages. However, W. travellers in the 17th cent. found a Turkish village with few Christians and no priest or church building.

The results of the Archaeological Exploration, organized by the Fogg Art Museum of Harvard University and other institutions from 1958 to 1975, are summarized in G. M. A. Hanfmann and others, *Sardis from Prehistoric to Roman Times* (Cambridge, Mass., and London, 1983), with full bibl. There is a popular account by id., *Letters from Sardis* (Cambridge, Mass., 1972). The series of monographs and reports issued in connection with the Archaeological Exploration incl. J. G. Pedley, *Ancient Literary Sources on Sardis* (Monograph, 2; ibid., 1972); C. Foss, *Byzantine and Turkish Sardis* (ibid. 4; 1976); A. R. Seager and others, *The Synagogue and its Setting* (Report, 4; forthcoming), and R. Thomas and others, *A Bibliography of Lydia and Sardis* (Monograph, 11; forthcoming). C. J. Hemer, *The Letters to the Seven Churches of Asia in their Local Setting* (Journal for the Study of the New Testament, Supplement Series, 11; Sheffield [1986]), pp. 129–52. J. G. Pedley in *Anchor Bible Dictionary*, 5 (1992), pp. 982–4.

Sarpi, Paolo (1552–1623), **Fra Paolo**, *Servite jurist and theologian. A native of *Venice, he entered the Servite Order in 1565 or 1566, and was elected Provincial in 1579. From 1585 to 1588 he was Procurator-General. His relations with leading Protestants aroused the suspicion of the Curia, which opposed several times his appointment to an episcopal see. In the struggle between Venice and *Paul V (1606–7) he defended the interests of the Republic, which appointed him its theological consultor in 1606. Largely owing to his influence the interdict placed on Venice remained without effect, and his violent anti-Papal activities resulted in his excommunication in 1607. In the same year an abortive attempt to murder him was made, possibly by his ecclesiastical enemies. Despite his excommunication he remained theological counsellor to the Republic and exercised his priestly functions until his death. His most important work is the *Historia del Concilio Tridentino*, first published, at London in 1619, under the name of 'Pietro Soave Polano' (an anagram of 'Paolo Sarpi

Veneto'). It is based on much authentic material but, lacking in objectivity, it represents the Council as being solely a conspiracy against the reform of the Church. Sarpi's general attitude favoured the Protestants, and he was also keenly interested in the new scientific movement.

Works collected in 5 vols., bound in 6 (Venice, 1677), with Life by F. Micanzio, Ord. Serv. (orig. pub. Leiden, 1646) in vol. 1, pp. 1–326; standard edn., 8 vols. (Helmstadt and Verona, 1761–8); modern edn. by M. D. Busnelli, G. Gambarin, and R. Amerio in the series 'Scrittori d'Italia' (7 vols. in 9, Bari, 1931–51 [incomplete]); *Opere* [Selections] ed. G. and L. Cozzi (La Letteratura Italiano, Storia e Testi, 35, vol. 1; Milan and Naples [1969]). There are also modern edns. of *Lettere ai Gallicani* by B. Ulianich (Veröffentlichungen des Instituts für Europäische Geschichte Mainz, 26; Wiesbaden, 1961), *La Repubblica di Venezia, la Casa d'Austria e gli Uscocchi*, aggiunta e supplimento all'Istoria degli Uscocchi trattato di pace et accommodamento, by G. and L. Cozzi ('Scrittori d'Italia', 231; Bari, 1965), and *Istoria del Concilio Tridentino* by C. Vivanti (2 vols., Turin, 1974). A. Bianchi-Giovini, *Biografia di Frà Paolo Sarpi* (2 vols., Brussels, 1836). F. A. Yates, 'Paolo Sarpi's "History of the Council of Trent"', *Journal of the Warburg and Courtauld Institutes*, 7 (1944), pp. 123–44. L. Salvatorelli, 'Le idee religiose di Fra Paolo Sarpi', *Atti della Accademia Nazionale dei Lincei*, Classe di scienze morali, storiche e filologiche, 8th ser. 5 (1954), pp. 311–60; G. Cozzi, 'Fra Paolo Sarpi, l'anglicanesimo e la "Historia del Concilio Tridentino"', *Rivista Storica Italiana*, 68 (1956), pp. 559–619. G. Getto, *Paolo Sarpi* (Biblioteca della Rivista di Storia e Letteratura Religiosa, Studi e Testi, 1; 1967). G. Cozzi, *Paolo Sarpi tra Venezia e l'Europa* (Turin, 1979). D. Wootton, *Paolo Sarpi: Between Renaissance and Enlightenment* (Cambridge, 1983). É Amann in *DTC* 14 (pt. 1; 1939), cols. 1115–21, s.v.; H. Jedin in *EC* 10 (1953), cols. 1928 f., s.v. with further bibl.

Sartre, Jean Paul. See EXISTENTIALISM.

Sarum; Sarum rite. See SALISBURY; SALISBURY, USE OF.

Satan. In the Judaeo-Christian tradition, the supreme embodiment of evil, also the *devil (q.v.). The word is from the Heb. שָׂטָן (satan), 'adversary', esp. one who plots against another. In the OT it is used of an angelic being hostile to God, esp. in the later Books (Job, Chr., Zech., Ps. 119). The older form of the word ('Satanas', Gk. Σατανᾶς), usual in the Greek NT and the *Vulgate, is found in J. *Wycliffe, but was abandoned in the English Bible from W. *Tyndale onwards.

For bibl., see DEVIL.

Satis Cognitum. The encyclical issued by Pope *Leo XIII on 29 June 1896, on the subject of religious unity. While professing an ardent desire for the reunion of Christendom, it insisted that it was possible only on the basis that the Pope was recognized as the sole source of jurisdiction in the Church and hence the necessary centre of unity. The bull '*Apostolicae Curae' (13 Sept.), pronouncing *Anglican Ordinations invalid, followed shortly afterwards.

The text is in *Leonis Papae XIII Allocutiones, Epistolae, Constitutiones*, 6 (1900), pp. 156–89. Eng. tr. in C. Carlen, IHM, *The Papal Encyclicals 1878–1903* (Salem, NH [1981]), pp. 387–404. Critique in E. Denny, *Papalism: The Claims of the Papacy as set forth in the Encyclical* Satis Cognitum (1912).

satisfaction. An act of reparation for an injury committed. In Christian theology it is usually applied to the payment of a penalty due to God on account of sin. St *Anselm first gave the term theological currency in reference to the *Atonement (q.v.) by interpreting Christ's death as a sufficient vicarious satisfaction for the sins of the world, which was possible because of the sinlessness of His human nature and its hypostatic union with the Second Person of the Trinity.

In Catholic moral theology satisfaction is held to be a necessary element of the virtue and Sacrament of *Penance, in addition to contrition and confession. The term was used by *Tertullian and *Cyprian of the reparation made for sin by fasting, almsgiving, and other good works, which were already in Scripture regarded as means of averting Divine punishment (cf. Dan. 4: 27, Lk. 16: 9). It became part of the penitential practice of the early Church, which enjoined such works before giving absolution. With the gradual attenuation of penances and the practice of giving absolution before satisfaction was made, the distinction between the forgiveness of the fault and the satisfaction due to it after forgiveness was worked out more clearly, the classic example, adduced by St *Augustine, being the penance inflicted on David after Nathan had pronouced God's forgiveness (2 Sam. 12: 13, 14). Thus *satisfactio operis* came to be regarded as a necessary means of avoiding punishment in purgatory after the sin itself had been remitted by sacramental absolution, and this doctrine, which had been repeatedly formulated by *Peter Lombard and the later Schoolmen, was defended by the Council of *Trent.

P. Eder, *Sühne: Eine theologische Untersuchung* (Vienna, 1962), with bibl. On the place of satisfaction in the Sacrament of Penance, cf. St *Thomas Aquinas, *Summa Theologiae*, Suppl. qqu. 12–15. Also R. S. Franks in *HERE* 11 (1920), pp. 207–10, s.v.; P. Galtier, SJ in *DTC* 14 (pt. 1; 1939), cols. 1129–210, s.v. See also bibl. to PENANCE.

SATOR. See INSCRIPTIONS, EARLY CHRISTIAN.

Satornilus. See SATURNINUS.

Saturday. The Jewish '*Sabbath' (q.v.) and the day of the week on which Christ's body rested in the tomb. In the W. Saturday was observed as a fast day as early as the 3rd cent., but never so in the E. (apart from *Holy Saturday). The reason for the fasting was probably the extension of the Friday fast (*superponere jejunium*) which was subsequently reduced to a semi-fast on both days. In modern times the Saturday fast, except during *Lent and on the *Ember Days, became more and more restricted to Italy and Rome, where it was eventually abolished in 1918. Down to the 5th cent. Mass was not celebrated on that day at Rome and Alexandria, or apparently elsewhere in the W. In most of the E. Church, on the other hand Saturday was marked from the 4th cent. onwards by the celebration of the Liturgy, which in Lent is still confined to Saturday and Sunday.

The special connection of Saturday with the BVM is a W. medieval development. Usually mystical reasons are are given for it, such as the Sabbath rest of the Word in Mary. It found liturgical expression in the recitation of the 'Office of Our Lady' on Saturday, a practice supposed to have been introduced by *Urban II at the Council of Clermont in 1096. Acc. to pre-Tridentine MS breviaries this office (*Officium BMV in Sabbato*) was said in addition to the ferial office; since the time of *Pius V (1566–72), however, it replaced the ferial office. In the 1971 Breviary an optional memorial of the BVM is provided for use on Saturdays throughout the year, except in Lent and Advent and on certain feasts. On the same occasions a Mass of the BVM may be said in place of the ferial Mass. In the E. Church Saturday is associated with the commemoration of the departed.

G. Schreiber, *Die Wochentage im Erlebnis der Ostkirche und des christlichen Abendlandes* (Wissenschaftliche Abhandlungen der Arbeitsgemeinschaft für Forschung des Landes Nordrhein-Westfalen, 11; 1959), pp. 207–20. W. Rodorf, *Der Sonntag: Gesichte des Ruhe- und Gottesdiensttages im ältesten Christentum* (Abhandlungen zur Theologie des Alten und Neuen Testaments, 43; 1962), pp. 79–151; Eng. tr. (1968), pp. 80–153.

Saturday, Holy. See HOLY SATURDAY.

Saturninus (2nd cent.), also 'Satornilus', Syrian *Gnostic. Apparently the only authority is St *Irenaeus (*Haer.* 1. 24), on whom later references to this heretic (*Hippolytus, *Ref.* 7. 28; *Tertullian, *De Anima*, 23. 1; *Epiphanius, *Haer.* 23; *Philaster, *Haer.* 31; etc.) depend He is said to have been a pupil of Menander, the Samaritan heretic (himself the disciple of *Simon Magus), and to have taught in *Antioch. He held that the origin of things was to be sought in a Father unknown to all, who created a series of angels and other supernatural beings who in turn created man. As originally formed, man was a powerless entity who wriggled on the ground like a worm (ὡς σκώληκος σκαρίζοντος) until a divine spark set him on his feet. The God of the Jews was one of the creator angels, and the Supreme Father sent the Saviour to destroy this God and to redeem such as were endowed with the divine spark. These cosmological speculations have affinities with those of the *Ophites, with which they are perhaps historically linked. In ethics Saturninus rejected marriage and the use of animals as food.

A. Pourkier, *L'hérésiologie chez Épiphane de Salamine* (Christianisme Antique, 4 [1992]), pp. 167–204. G. *Salmon in *DCB* 4 (1887), pp. 587 f., s.v.; G. Bardy in *DTC* 14 (pt. 1; 1939), cols. 1310 f., s.v. 'Satornil'. See also bibl. to GNOSTICISM.

Satyrus, St (d. 375 or 377), elder brother of St *Ambrose, whose household and property he administered. He was evidently a much-loved and gentle character. When Satyrus died, Ambrose preached the funeral orations 'De Excessu Fratris'. Feast day, 17 Sept.

Crit. edn. of 'De Excessu Fratris' by O. Faller, SJ, in Ambrose, *Opera*, 7 (CSEL 73; 1955), pp. 207–325. A. Palestra and C. Perogalli, *San Satiro* (Milan, 1980).

Saumaise, Claude. See SALMASIUS, CLAUDIUS.

Sava, St (c.1175–1235), also 'Sabas', patron of *Serbia. Rastko was the third son of Stephen Nemanja, founder of a strong Serbian dynasty who united the Serbs into a nation. In 1191 he secretly went to Mt. *Athos, where he became a monk under the name of Sava. In 1197 his father followed him, after abdicating in favour of Sava's elder brother, Stephen. Here on Mt. Athos father and son founded the Serbian monastery of Hilandar which became

one of the leading centres of Serbian culture in the Middle Ages. In 1206 Sava returned to Serbia, where, as archimandrite of the monastery of Studenica, he took an active part in the political and religious life of the country. He seems to have accepted the policy of his brother, who, c.1217, had himself crowned king with the help of the Pope, and in 1219 Sava succeeded in establishing an independent Serbian Church, of which he was consecrated the first archbishop by the Patr. of Nicaea. He organized the Church by establishing several bishoprics, devoted himself to the education of the country, and built and embellished many churches. In 1229 he made a pilgrimage to Palestine, and c.1234 went there again, and then went on to Egypt, Asia Minor, and *Constantinople. He died in Tŭrnovo in Bulgaria. Feast day in the Serbian Church, 14 Jan.

D. Obolensky, *Six Byzantine Portraits* (Oxford, 1988), pp. 115–72, with refs.; I. Dujčev in *Bibliotheca Sanctorum*, 11 (1968), cols. 522–9, s.v. 'Saba'.

Savigny, Abbey of, Normandy. In 1093 Vitalis of Mortain, a canon of the collegiate church of St-Évroul, established a hermitage in the Forest of Savigny. After a time some of the hermits felt a call to follow the *Benedictine Rule in its primitive strictness and by 1112 Vitalis had obtained from Ralph, lord of Fougères, some grants of land. The new house, established by 1115, preserved some distinctive practices, e.g. the wearing of grey habits. It rose to high repute, esp. under the Abbots Geoffrey (1122–38) and Serlo (1140–53); and daughter monasteries were founded in France (*la Trappe), England (Furness, *Quarr), Ireland, and elsewhere. In 1147 Serlo aggregated the houses into the *Cistercian Order (confirmed by Pope *Eugenius III, 10 Apr. 1148), though they continued to retain certain peculiarities. In the later Middle Ages the orig. Abbey of Savigny declined and community life finally came to an end during the French Revolution.

'Vitae BB. Vitalis et Gaufridi, primi et secundi abbatum Saviniacensium', ed. E. P. Sauvage, *Anal. Boll.* 1 (1882), pp. 355–410. C. Auvray, OSB, *Histoire de la congrégation de Savigny*, ed. A. Laveille (3 vols., Rouen, 1896–8). B. D. Hill, *English Cistercian Monasteries and their Patrons in the Twelfth Century* (1968), pp. 80–115. L. H. Cottineau, OSB, *Répertoire topo-bibliographique des abbayes et prieurés* (Mâcon, 1935), cols. 2065–7, with full bibl. E. M. Obrecht, OCR, in *CE* 13 (1912), p. 489, s.v.; F. R. Swietek in *DIP* 8 (1988), cols. 991–4, s.v., with bibl.

Savile, Henry (1549–1622), Warden of Merton College, Oxford, and Provost of Eton. He was educated at Brasenose College, became a Fellow of Merton in 1565, and soon acquired a wide reputation as a Greek scholar, mathematician, historian, and antiquarian. In 1578 he travelled in Europe, collecting MSS, and on his return was appointed Greek tutor to Queen *Elizabeth I. In 1585 he was elected Warden of Merton, which greatly flourished under his rule. In 1596 he asked for, and obtained from the Queen, the provostship of Eton, although, not being in holy orders, he was not qualified under the statutes. In 1604 he was named as one of the scholars appointed to prepare the AV of the Bible. In 1610–13 he published in 8 folio vols. his celebrated edition of the works of St *Chrysostom, based on a collation of the best available MSS and earlier editions, and still of great value for determining the correct text of many of St Chrysostom's treatises. It was printed at Savile's private press at Eton, at his own charges (£8,000), in type imported from the Netherlands. He also helped in the foundation of the *Bodleian Library, to which he afterwards presented many MSS and printed books; and he founded at Oxford professorships of geometry and astronomy.

S. L. Greenslade, 'The Printer's Copy for the Eton Chrysostom, 1610–13', in F. L. Cross (ed.), *Studia Patristica*, 7 (TU 92; 1966), pp. 60–4. W. Carr in *DNB* 50 (1897), pp. 367–70, s.v., with refs.

Savonarola, Girolamo (1452–98), Italian preacher and reformer. Born and educated at Ferrara, he entered the *Dominican Order at *Bologna in 1475. He was soon in demand as a preacher, but his first positions were mostly academic. He was appointed lector at San Marco, Florence, in 1482; he was Master of Studies at Bologna, 1487–8; and in 1490 he was again appointed lector at San Marco. During this period he wrote some competent, if unoriginal, textbooks on philosophy. He emphasized the importance of biblical studies, based on knowledge of the original languages, and he succeeded in making San Marco a centre for oriental studies, as well as being a meeting-place for some of the leading Humanist scholars of Florence. In 1491 he became prior of San Marco. From about this time he adopted an apocalyptic style of preaching, prophesying an impending divine chastisement of the corruption of Church and society and claiming to receive special revelations from God. Wanting to go beyond the existing Dominican reform in recalling his Order to its original fervour and austerity, he secured the independence of San Marco from the reformed Congregation of Lombardy in 1493, thus launching a new Congregation, of which he soon became Vicar General, and to which other priories were successively added. Politically, he called for radical social and moral reform and, after the death of Lorenzo de' Medici in 1492, established a kind of theocratic democracy in Florence. He supported Charles VIII of France in his Italian campaign of 1494–5, seeing in him God's instrument for reform. He sought to create a Christian culture, based on the Bible and Christian morality and asceticism, in opposition to the 'pagan' culture of the Humanists. His prophecies and his extremism won him both fervent supporters and determined opponents, and in 1495 *Alexander VI summoned him to Rome to give an account of himself. He pleaded that he was unable to leave Florence. Alexander then tried to return San Marco to the jurisdiction of the Congregation of Lombardy, and forbade Savonarola to preach until his case had been decided by the superior of the Congregation. On the ground that the Pope was acting on false information and that it would be wrong to obey instructions contrary to the commandments of God and the Church, Savonarola, after a brief silence, resumed his preaching, and, with the support of the Dominican authorities, San Marco retained its independence. In 1496 the Pope attempted to create a new reformed Congregation, of which San Marco would be only a part and of which Savonarola would not be superior, but this scheme too was not put into operation until after Savonarola's death. On 13 May 1497 he was excommunicated, but he decided that the excommunication was invalid and continued to preach and to defend the authenticity of his revelations. In the same year he published an impressive

apologia for orthodox Catholicism, *Triumphus Crucis*. Despite conciliatory gestures on both sides, the conflict between Savonarola and the Pope worsened and, in 1498, on the grounds that Alexander was not even a Christian and could therefore not be deemed a legitimate Pope, Savonarola wrote to the major Christian princes asking them to convoke a council. Popular opinion began to turn against him and, abandoned by the Florentine authorities, he was arrested and condemned for schism and heresy. He was hanged and burned on 23 May 1498. After his death an attempt was made to eliminate his influence, but some people, such as St *Catherine de' Ricci, venerated him as a martyr. It is still debated whether he was a prophet and saint or a misguided and fanatical trouble-maker. Steps are now being taken to secure his canonization.

Edizione nazionale of his Works (Rome, 1955 ff.). Poetry and sermons in *Ambrosiana, MS SP II.5 (codex Borromeo), ed. G. Cattin, *Il Primo Savonarola* (Biblioteca di 'Lettere Italiane', 12; Florence, 1973). Convenient Ital. tr. of his correspondence with Alexander VI between 1495 and 1498 pub. by the Accademia d'Oropa, *Alessandro VI e Savonarola* (Serie Collegiale, 1; Turin, 1950). *Le Procès de Savonarola*, ed. R. Klein [1957]. P. Villari, *La storia di Girolamo Savonaroli e de' suoi tempi* (2 vols., 1859–61; rev. edn. of 1887–8, repr. 1930; Eng. tr., 1863); J. Schnitzer, *Savonarola* (2 vols., Munich, 1924); R. Ridolfi, *Studi Savonaroliani* (Florence, 1935); id., *Vita di Girolamo Savonarola* (2 vols., 1952; 6th edn., 1981; Eng. tr., 1959); M. Ferrara, *Savonarola* (2 vols., Florence, 1952); R. de Maio, *Savonarola e la Curia Romana* (Uomini e Dottrine, 15; 1969); D. Weinstein, *Savonarola and Florence* (Princeton, NJ, 1970); A. Huerga [OP], *Savonarola, reformador y profeta* (Biblioteca de Autores Cristianos, 397; Madrid, 1978); F. Cordero, *Savonarola* (4 vols., Rome, 1986–8). R. Ridolfi, *Cronologia e Bibliografia delle Prediche* (Bibliografia delle Opere del Savonarola a cura del Principe Piero Ginori Conti, 1; Florence, 1939); M. Ferrara, *Bibliografia Savonaroliana: Bibliografia ragionata degli scritti editi dal principio del secolo XIX ad oggi* (Biblioteca di Bibliografia Italiana, 31; ibid., 1958). A. F. Verde, OP, in *Dict. Sp.* 14 (1990), cols. 370–88, s.v.

Savoy Conference. The conference which sat by royal warrant, dated 25 March 1661, at the Savoy in the Strand from 15 April until 24 July 1661, to review the BCP. It consisted of 12 bishops, 12 Presbyterian divines, and 9 assessors from each party. The Presbyterians vainly hoped to gain concessions which would enable them to remain members of the Established Church. The bishops, led by G. *Sheldon, Bp. of London (though Accepted Frewen, Abp. of York, was nominal president), ignored R. *Baxter's alternative service-book and his appeal that ministers not episcopally ordained should not be required to seek reordination. In reply to the Presbyterian *Exceptions (q.v.) to the BCP, the bishops made only 17 trivial concessions, 15 of which were embodied in the BCP of 1662. The Presbyterians could not accept the 1662 Book and were deprived of their livings, bringing the total of clergy ejected between 1660 and 1662 to over 2,000.

Proceedings of the Commission for the Revision of the Book of Common Prayer (1661). E. *Cardwell, *A History of Conferences and other Proceedings connected with the Revision of the Book of Common Prayer from the Year 1558 to the Year 1690* (1840), chs. 6 and 7. R. Baxter, *A Petition for Peace* (1661). E. C. Ratcliff, 'The Savoy Conference and the Revision of the Book of Common Prayer', in G. F. Nuttall and [W.] O. Chadwick (eds.), *From Uniformity to Unity* (1962), pp. 89–148. F. E. *Brightman in *DECH*, pp. 548–50, s.v.

Savoy Declaration. A statement of *Congregational principles and polity of a moderate type, drawn up at a Conference held at the Chapel of the old Savoy Palace in 1658 by representatives of 120 churches. It consists of a Preface, a Confession of Faith closely akin to the *Westminster Confession, and a Platform of Discipline. The first is largely an apology for the divisions of the Reformed Churches as contrasted with the 'dull and stupid peace' of the Church of Rome and a plea for toleration of the Congregational form of Church government side by side with Presbyterianism. The second professes the modified *Calvinism of the Westminster Confession, with a few alterations, e.g. rejecting the power of the civil authority to punish heresy. The third part, which treats of the Institution of Churches, declares that all necessary power is vested in each individual Church and repudiates the institution, by Christ, of a wider organization.

Text repr. in P. *Schaff, *A History of the Creeds*, 3 (1877), pp. 707–29, with introd. in vol. 1 (1877), pp. 829–33. Modern edn., with introd., by A. G. Matthews (London, 1959). See also works cited under CONGREGATIONALISM.

Sawtrey, William (d. 1401), *Lollard. As a priest at Lynn, Norfolk, he was summoned before his bishop in 1399 to answer charges of heresy; and after ministering in London, he was charged before Abp. T. *Arundel in 1401 with heresies concerning the adoration of the cross, *transubstantiation, and other matters. He appealed to the King in Parliament, and also made a defence from the NT and St *Augustine. On the ground that he had relapsed into heresies which he had abjured in 1399, he was burned, shortly before the statute '*De Haeretico Comburendo' was passed.

K. B. McFarlane, *John Wycliffe and the Beginnings of English Nonconformity* (1952), pp. 150–2. A. M. Cooke in *DNB* 50 (1897), pp. 380 f.

Saxa Rubra, Battle of. See MILVIAN BRIDGE, BATTLE OF THE.

Saxon Confession (1551). The Protestant Confession of Faith drawn up in 1551 for the Council of *Trent by P. *Melanchthon at the request of the Elector Maurice of Saxony, who wished to strengthen his position in relation to other Protestant princes. It followed the main lines of the *Augsburg Confession of 1530, but was less conciliatory. The distinctive Protestant doctrines were elaborated round the two articles in the *Apostles' Creed on the forgiveness of sins and the Church. The former article was held to exclude merit and justification by works, the latter to prove the Church to be a spiritual though visible communion of believers in Christ. Unlike the Augsburg Confession, the Saxon Confession bore the signatures of theologians only, among them, besides Melanchthon himself, J. *Bugenhagen and G. *Major.

Lat. and Ger. texts pr. among P. Melanchthon's collected works ed. E. H. Bindseil, 28 (Corpus Reformatorum, 28; Brunswick, 1860), cols. 369–568, with introd. cols. 327–68; Lat. text also in his selected works ed. R. Stupperich, 6 (Gütersloh, 1955), pp. 80–167. P. *Schaff, *A History of the Creeds of Christendom*, 1 (1877), pp. 340–3. H. Jedin, *Geschichte des Konzils von Trient*, 3 (1970), esp. pp. 301–11.

Sayce, Archibald Henry (1845–1933), English oriental scholar. He was elected a Fellow of Queen's College, Oxford, in 1869, and from 1891 to 1915 was professor of Assyriology at Oxford. He was a member of the company which produced the RV of the OT. After 1885 he was almost wholly absorbed in the history of religion, particularly of Egypt, Babylon, and Israel, and in this connection he travelled and explored extensively in the E. His many publications included works on the Hittites, Hebrews, Assyrians, Babylonians, and Egyptians. In several of them, notably *The 'Higher Criticism' and the Verdict of the Monuments* (1894), he defended the Mosaic authorship of the *Pentateuch.

A. H. Sayce, *Reminiscences* (1923). B. Gunn in *DNB, 1931–1940*, pp. 786–8.

Sayers, Dorothy Leigh (1893–1957), novelist, religious playwright and apologist. The daughter of an Anglican clergyman, she qualified for a first class honours degree in modern languages at Somerville College, Oxford, in 1915. For a number of years she worked as a copywriter in an advertising agency until the success of her detective novels, of which the last was published in 1937, gave her financial independence. She established her reputation as a religious writer with *The Zeal of Thy House* (1937) and *The Devil to Pay* (1939), plays written for the *Canterbury Festival; it was subsequently extended by her radio dramatization of the life of Christ, *The Man Born to be King*. This was broadcast at monthly intervals between 21 Dec. 1941 and 18 Oct. 1942, and caused widespread controversy by its representation of Christ by an actor and because the dialogue in which he took part was in modern English. From 1940 she published a number of volumes containing studies, lectures, and essays on theological topics. In these writings, as in her plays, she combined a high degree of professional competence with fresh and penetrating insights into the meaning of the Christian faith in the modern world. Her major work was an annotated English verse translation of *Dante's *Divine Commedy*. *Hell* was published in 1949 and *Purgatory* in 1955, but at the time of her death she had only made a start on *Heaven*, which was completed by Barbara Reynolds and published in 1962.

J. Hitchman, *'Such a Strange Lady': An Introduction to Dorothy L. Sayers* (1975); R. E. Hone, *Dorothy L. Sayers: A Literary Biography* (Kent, Oh., 1979); J. Brabazon, *Dorothy L. Sayers: The Life of a Courageous Woman* (1981); C. Kenney, *The Remarkable Case of Dorothy L. Sayers* (Kent, Oh., and London [1990]); B. Reynolds, *Dorothy L. Sayers: Her Life and Soul* (1993). C. B. Gilbert, *A Bibliography of the Works of Dorothy L. Sayers* (Hamden, Conn., 1978; London, 1979); R. T. Youngberg, *Dorothy L. Sayers: A Reference Guide* (Boston [1982]).

Sayings of Jesus. The name given by their first editors to the texts preserved in two *Oxyrhynchus papyri (nos. 1 and 654). It is now clear that these texts, together with those in no. 655, if not portions of the Greek original of passages in the Gospel of *Thomas (q.v.), are very closely related to it.

B. P. Grenfell and A. S. Hunt, *ΛΟΓΙΑ ΙΗΣΟΥ. Sayings of Our Lord from an early Greek Papyrus* (1897); idd., *New Sayings of Jesus and Fragments of a Lost Gospel* (1904). See bibl. to THOMAS, GOSPEL OF.

Sayings of the Jewish Fathers. See PIRQE ABOTH.

Scala Sancta (also known as the **Scala Pilati**). A staircase of 28 Tyrian marble steps near the *Lateran church at *Rome. Tradition affirms that they were the steps descended by Christ after His condemnation to death and brought to the W. by St *Helena from the palace of *Pilate in *Jerusalem. Now covered with wood, they are a popular place of *pilgrimage in Rome, pilgrims making the ascent on their knees. At the top of the steps is the 'Sancta Sanctorum' chapel (1278), the only surviving piece of the old Lateran Palace.

H. Thurston, SJ, *The Holy Year of Jubilee* (1900), pp. 185–91, A. Cempanari, CP, and T. Amodei, CP, *La Scala santa* (Le Chiese di Roma illustrate, 72; 1963), with bibl. L. Oliger, OFM, in *CE* 13 (1912), pp. 505 f., s.v.

Scaliger, Joseph Justus (1540–1609), French scholar. He was a native of Agen and studied Greek and oriental languages at Paris, where he became a *Calvinist in 1562. After travelling in Italy (1565) and England and Scotland (1566), between 1567 and 1570 he fought on the side of the *Huguenots. From 1572 to 1574 he was professor at *Geneva. The following years he spent in private research until, in 1593, he became the successor of J. Lipsius at *Leiden University, which he made a European centre of philological studies, though he did not lecture himself. His editions of Latin authors such as Festus (1575), Catullus, Tibullus, Propertius (1577), and others were a new departure in the field of textual criticism. His greatest claim to fame, however, is his *De Emendatione Temporum* (1583), by which he established the modern science of chronology, though his attacks on the newly introduced *Gregorian Calendar and on the genuineness of *Dionysius the Pseudo-Areopagite earned him the hostility of the *Jesuits. In 1606 followed the *Thesaurus Temporum*, containing a brilliant partial reconstruction of the 'Chronicon' of *Eusebius of Caesarea. D. *Petavius' great work, *De Doctrina Temporum* (1627), directed against Scaliger, whom it corrected, carried on his ideas.

The chief sources for his life are his *Epistolae* (Leiden, 1627) and his *Lettres françaises inédites* (ed. P. Tamizey de Larroque, Agen and Paris, 1879). *Autobiography of Joseph Scaliger: With autobiographical Selections from his Letters, his Testament and the Funeral Orations by Daniel Heinsius and Dominicus Baudius*, tr. . . . with introd. and notes by G. W. Robinson (Harvard Translations, Cambridge, Mass., 1927; good collection of material. 'Autobiography', however, very brief, on pp. 29–33). Life by J. Bernays (Berlin, 1855). Full modern study by A. T. Grafton (2 vols., Oxford, 1983–93). C. M. Bruehl, 'Josef Justus Scaliger. Ein Beitrag zur geistesgeschichtlichen Bedeutung der Altertumswissenschaft', *Zeitschrift für Religions- und Geistesgeschichte*, 12 (1960), pp. 201–18; 13 (1961), pp. 45–65. A. T. Grafton and H. J. de Jonge, *Scaliger: A Bibliography 1852–1982* (The Hague, 1982).

Scandinavia, Christianity in. See DENMARK; NORWAY; and SWEDEN, CHRISTIANITY IN.

scapular (Lat. *scapulare*, from *scapulae*, 'shoulderblades'). A garment consisting essentially of a piece of cloth worn over the shoulders and hanging down in front and behind. It is usually from 14 to 18 inches wide with its two ends reaching almost to the feet, and forms part of the regular monastic habit. The Rule of St *Benedict (cap.

55) prescribes its use for the monks when engaged in manual labour and the rules of some religious orders require it to be worn also throughout the night. By a natural symbolism it is taken to denote the 'yoke of Christ' (*jugum Christi*, cf. Mt. 11: 29 f.). A vesture of very much smaller dimensions (known as 'the smaller scapular') is worn by persons living in the world who have become affiliated to the religious orders, e.g. *Tertiaries. In the RC Church important privileges have been attached to wearing the smaller scapular.

Comm. on Rule of St Benedict (q.v.), esp. by P. Delatte, OSB (Eng. tr., 1921), pp. 349 f. P. Oppenheim, OSB, *Das Mönchskleid im christlichen Altertum* (RQ Supplementheft 28; 1931), esp. pp. 139–42. P. E. Magennis, Ord. Carm., *The Scapular Devotion: Origin, Legislation and Indulgences attached to the Scapular* (Dublin, 1923). H. Thurston, SJ, 'Scapulars', *The Month*, 149 (1927), pp. 481–8, and 150 (1927), pp. 44–58. J. Hilgers, SJ, in *CE* 13 (1912), pp. 508–14, s.v.; P. N. Zammit in *NCE* 12 (1969), pp. 1114–16, s.v.; L. Saggi in *Dict. Sp.* 14 (1990), cols. 390–6, s.v. 'Scapulaire'.

Scaramelli, Giovanni Battista (1687–1752), Italian *Jesuit spiritual writer. He entered the Society of Jesus in 1706 and was ordained priest in 1717. From 1722 onwards he was chiefly engaged in giving missions and retreats in the Pontifical States. He expounded his spiritual teaching in three works, *Direttorio ascetico* (1752), *Discernimento de' spiriti* (1753), and *Direttorio mistico* (1754). In his Ascetic Directory, which has long been regarded as a classic, Scaramelli examines the nature of Christian perfection and the means of attaining it. His books were designed primarily for the use of spiritual directors.

Eng. tr. of *Direttorio ascetico* by W. Eyre (4 vols., Dublin, 1870; 2nd edn., London, 1879–81). O. Marchetti, SJ, 'Un' opera inedita su di una mistica del 700 attribuita al P. Scaramelli, S.J.', *Archivum Historicum Societatis Jesu*, 2 (1933), pp. 230–57. L. A. Hogue, SJ, 'The *Direttorio mistico* of J. B. Scaramelli, S.J.', ibid. 9 (1940), pp. 1–39. Sommervogel, 7 (1896), cols. 689–94; 9 (1900), cols. 840 f.; Polgár, 3 (1990), p. 168. Pourrat, 4, pp. 439–42.; G. Mellinato in *Dict. Sp.* 14 (1990), cols. 396–402, s.v.

Scete. The southern portion of the *Nitrian Desert which lies to the west of the mouths of the Nile, celebrated in the 4th and 5th cents. as a centre of monasticism. Among the most celebrated of its monks were Pambo and *Macarius of Egypt.

D. J. Chitty, *The Desert a City* (Oxford, 1966), esp. pp. 33–6, 56–61, 66–74, and 144–9. H. *Leclercq, OSB, in *DACL* 15 (pt. 1; 1950), cols. 994–1002.

Schaff, Philip (1819–93), German American theologian and Church historian. Born in Switzerland, he was educated at *Tübingen, Halle, and Berlin, and became professor first in the German Reformed Seminary at Mercersburg, Pennsylvania (1844), and later in *Union Theological Seminary, New York (1870). He saw through the press an immense body of theological literature. The most extensive of his original writings was his *History of the Christian Church* (12 vols., 1883–93), a popular work from the standpoint of Evangelical liberalism, hortatory rather than scientific in tone. He edited, among other compendious works, the *Religious Encyclopaedia* (3 vols., 1882–4), an American adaptation of J. J. *Herzog's *Realencyclopädie* (22 vols., 1854–68), and the sets of patristic translations known as the *Nicene and post-Nicene Fathers* (Series I, 14 vols., 1886–9; Series II, 14 vols., of varying merit, 1890–1900); and he compiled a valuable collection of credal documents in *The Creeds of Christendom* (3 vols., 1877). From 1870 he was president of the American committee which co-operated with the British committee responsible for the Revised Version of the Bible. As an exponent of the '*Mercersburg Theology', he was closely associated in outlook with J. W. Nevin (q.v.).

Selected Historical and Theological Writings, ed. C. Yrigoyen and G. 'M' [H.] Bricker (Pittsburgh, 1979). D. S. Schaff (son), *The Life of Philip Schaff* (New York, 1897). J. H. Nichols, *Romanticism in American Theology: Nevin and Schaff at Mercersburg* (Chicago, 1961). G. H. Shriver, *Philip Schaff: Christian Scholar and Ecumenical Prophet* (Macon, Ga. [1987]). D. W. Lotz, 'Philip Schaff and the Idea of Church History', in H. W. Bowden (ed.), *A Century of Church History: The Legacy of Philip Schaff* (Carbondale, Ill. [1988]), pp. 1–35; other art. on Schaff, pp. 148–67. D. S. Schaff in *PRE* (3rd edn.), 17 (1906), pp. 515–22, s.v.; H. E. Starr in *Dict. Amer. Biog.* 16 (1935), pp. 417 f.

Scheeben, Matthias Joseph (1835–88), German Catholic theologian. He was educated at the *Gregorian University in Rome (1852–9), ordained priest in 1858, and was professor of dogma at the seminary at *Cologne from 1860 to his death. Already in his first speculative work *Natur und Gnade* (1861) he outlined his doctrine of the supernatural, which he describes as a participation in the Being of God, and popularized this conception in *Die Herrlichkeiten der göttlichen Gnade* (1863, an independent version of a work of the 17th-cent. author, E. Nieremberg), which had an immediate success and was translated into many languages. In his profound, though sometimes obscure, *Mysterien des Christenthums* (1865) he attempted to build up the whole organism of Christian doctrine, viewed as a supernatural cosmos with the mystery of the Blessed Trinity as its centre. In the following years his dogmatic work was interrupted by the controversies raised by the impending *Vatican Council, in which he took a vigorous part as one of the chief opponents of J. J. I. von *Döllinger and a passionate defender of Papal *Infallibility. Between 1873 and 1887 he wrote his *Handbuch der katholischen Dogmatik*, a work of immense erudition, based on Thomist principles but also making extensive use of the Fathers as well as of modern theologians. Scheeben stood for the rights of supernatural faith against the rationalist and naturalist tendencies of 18th- and 19th-cent. theology which had been rife esp. in Germany and Austria.

Gesammelte Schriften, ed. J. Höfer (8 vols., Freiburg i.B., 1941–67). Eng. trs. of *Die Mysterien des Christentums* by C. Vollert, SJ (St Louis, 1946), and of *Natur und Gnade* by id. (ibid. and London, 1954). J. Hertkens, *Professor M. J. Scheeben: Leben und Wirken eines katholischen Gelehrten im Dienste der Kirche* (1892). K. Feckes and others, *M. J. Scheeben* (Mainz, 1935). F. S. Pancheri, OFM, *Il pensiero teologico di M. J. Scheeben e S. Tommaso* (1956), with bibl.; B. Fraigneau-Julien, PSS, *L'Église et le caractère sacramentel selon M.-J. Scheeben* (1958); W. Bartz, *Die lehrende Kirche: Ein Beitrag zur Ekklesiologie M. J. Scheebens* (Trierer theologische Studien, 9; 1959). N. Hoffmann, SSCC, *Natur und Gnade: Die Theologie der Gottesschau als vollendeter Vergöttlichung des Geistgeschöpfes bei M. J. Scheeben* (Analecta Gregoriana, 160; 1967). E. Paul, *Denkweg und Denkform der Theologie von Matthias Joseph Scheeben* (Münchener theologische Studien, II. Systematische Abteilung, 60; 1970), with extensive bibl. T. F. O'Meara, OP, *Church and Culture: German Catholic Theology, 1860–1914*

(Notre Dame, Ind., and London [1991]), pp. 53–67. K.-H. Minz in *Dict. Sp.* 14 (1990), cols. 404–8, s.v.

Scheffler, Johannes. See ANGELUS SILESIUS.

Schelling, Friedrich Wilhelm Joseph von (1775–1854), German Idealist philosopher. He was the son of a Württemberg pastor and was educated at the *Tübingen Stift, where G. W. F. *Hegel was one of his elder contemporaries. From 1798 to 1803 he taught at Jena, where he was brought into close contact with the leaders of the *Romantic Movement, and from 1803 at the University of Würzburg. Difficulties with the government led him to retire to Munich in 1806. From 1820 to 1826 he lectured at Erlangen, and in 1827 he became professor at the newly founded University of Munich. In 1841 he was called to Berlin to counteract the influence of Hegel's disciples.

Schelling never elaborated a consistent philosophical system. His constantly changing views owed much to his vivid imagination and were also greatly influenced by current scientific doctrines which, however, he only imperfectly understood. In his early years he was under the influence of J. G. *Fichte and thus mediately of I. *Kant. In his first important work, *Vom Ich als Prinzip der Philosophie* (1795), he acknowledged only one reality, the infinite and absolute Ego, of which the universe was the expression. In his *Ideen zu einer Philosophie der Natur* (1797) and *Von der Weltseele* (1798), this abstract pantheism was modified in favour of his conception of 'Naturphilosophie', acc. to which nature was an absolute being which works unconsciously, though purposively. The problem of the relation of nature to spirit later gave rise to his 'Identitätsphilosophie', expounded esp. in *Darlegung des Systems der Philosophie* (1802) and *Bruno, oder über das göttliche und natürliche Prinzip der Dinge* (1802). Acc. to this philosophy, which shows strong traces of B. *Spinoza, both nature and spirit are but manifestations of one and the same being, absolute identity being the ground of all things. In his subsequent speculations he became more and more influenced by *Neoplatonist and *theosophist speculations, esp. by J. *Boehme. Thus in *Philosophie und Religion* (1804) he explained the universe as a Fall of the ideas into matter and redemption as a return to the world of ideas. His attempt in *Philosophische Untersuchungen über das Wesen der menschlichen Freiheit* (1809) to reconcile Christianity with his philosophy was carried on later in his Berlin lectures (pub. 1856–8). Here he distinguished three elements in God: (1) the blind primeval necessary being; (2) the three potentialities of the Divine Essence, namely unconscious will (material cause), rational will (efficient cause), and unity of the two (final cause of creation); (3) the Three Persons who evolve from the three potentialities by overcoming the primeval being. In the history of Christianity he also distinguished three periods—the Petrine or Catholic, the Pauline or Protestant, and the Johannine or the Church of the future.

Schelling exercised a profound influence on German thought. His earlier teaching was the point of departure of Hegel's system, and many elements of his nature and religious philosophy were taken up and transformed by E. von *Hartmann. His general philosophical position had a great influence on P. *Tillich and on the Catholic Tübingen School.

Collected works ed. by his son, K. F. A. von Schelling (14 vols., Stuttgart, 1856–61) and ed. M. Schroter (6 vols., Munich, 1927–8, + 6 extra vols., 1943–59) Crit. edn. by H. M. Baumgartner and others (Stuttgart, 1976 ff.). His Munich lectures 'Zur Geschichte der neueren Philosophie' ed. A. *Drews (Leipzig, 1902). *Briefe und Dokumente, 1775–1809*, ed. H. Fuhrmans (3 vols., Bonn, 1962–75). Among the many studies of his system may be mentioned: J. Watson, *Schelling's Transcendental Idealism* (1882); E. von Hartmann, *Schelling's Philosophisches System* (Leipzig, 1897); H. Sueskind, *Der Einfluss Schellings auf die Entwicklung von Schleiermachers System* (Tübingen, 1909); W. Metzger, *Die Epochen der Schellingschen Philosophie v. 1795–1802* (Heidelberg, 1911); E. Bréhier, *Schelling* ('Les Grands Philosophes', 1912). R. Kroner, *Von Kant bis Hegel*, 1 (1921), pp. 535–612, 2 (Tübingen, 1924), pp. 1–141. N. Hartmann, *Die Philosophie des deutschen Idealismus*, 1 (1923), pp. 123–186, with bibl. pp. 279 f. H. Fuhrmans, *Schellings letzte Philosophie* (Neue Deutsche Forschungen, Abteilung Philosophie, 1940); id., *Schellings Philosophie der Weltalter* (Düsseldorf, 1954). K. *Jaspers, *Schelling: Grösse und Verhängnis* (Munich [1955]). E. D. Hirsch, *Wordsworth and Schelling: A Typological Study of Romanticism* (Yale Studies in English, 145; 1960). X. Tilliette, SJ, *Schelling: Une philosophie en devenir* (Bibliothèque d'histoire de philosophie, 2 vols., 1970). R. F. Brown, *The Later Philosophy of Schelling: The Influence of Boehme on the Works of 1809–1815* (Lewisburg, Pa., and London [1977]). J. L. Esposito, *Schelling's Idealism and Philosophy of Nature* (ibid. [1977]). T. F. O'Meara, OP, *Romantic Idealism and Roman Catholicism: Schelling and the Theologians* (Notre Dame, Ind., and London [1982]). M. Maesschalck, *Philosophie et révélation dans l'itinéraire de Schelling* (Bibliothèque philosophique de Louvain, 33; 1989). Bibl. by G. Schneeberger (Berne, 1954). A. Margoshes in P. Edwards (ed.), *Encyclopedia of Philosophy*, 7 (1967), pp. 305–9, s.v. R. Kroner in *EB* (1968 edn.), 19, pp. 1153 f., s.v.

Schelstrate, Emmanuel (1649–92), Belgian Church historian and canonist. A native of Antwerp, he early specialized in the study of Christian antiquities. Through his publications, in which he defended the rights of the Holy See, he attracted the attention of *Innocent XI, who made him Prefect of the *Vatican Library and later canon of the *Lateran and of *St Peter's. Among his writings are *Antiquitas Illustrata circa Concilia Generalia et Provincialia* (1678), in which he undertook to prove the antiquity of the Roman primacy, and the *Acta Constantiensis Concilii* (1683), defending the supremacy of the Pope over the Council against the *Gallican Articles of 1682. In the considerable controversy created by the latter, J. B. *Bossuet and A. *Arnauld took sides against the author. In the *De *disciplina arcani* (1685) he developed the view that the 'discipline of the secret', i.e. the secrecy exacted by Christ, the Apostles and their successors, explained the relative weakness of the evidence for the doctrines of the Person of Christ and the Sacraments in the primitive Church.

The primary authority for Schelstrate's life is the introd. to vol. 2 of his *Antiquitas Illustrata* (Rome, 1697; i.e. five years after his death), written by an unknown Roman friend of the author. L. Ceyssens, OFM, *La Correspondance d'Emmanuel Schelstrate, préfet de la bibliothèque vaticane, 1683–1692* (Bibliothèque de l'Institut historique Belge de Rome, fasc. 1; 1949); this vol. has a valuable study of Schelstrate with full bibl. refs. in its introd. (esp. pp. 18–90). J. Ruysschaert, 'Annotations marginales à la biographie d'Emmanuel Schelstrate', *Bulletin de l'Institut historique Belge de Rome*, 28 (1953), pp. 137–56. J. Mercier in *DTC* 14 (pt. 1; 1939), cols. 1278–80, s.v., also with bibl. refs.

Schenudi. See SHENOUTE.

Schillebeeckx, Edward Cornelis Florentius Alfons (1914–), RC theologian. Born in Antwerp, the son of a prosperous accountant, he entered the *Dominican Order in 1934. From 1935 he studied philosophy and theology at Louvain, and, with interruptions for military service, remained there until the end of the Second World War, becoming lecturer in dogmatic theology. After further study in Paris, he returned to Louvain as professor in 1947. From 1958 until his retirement in 1982 he was Professor of Dogmatics and the History of Theology in the University of Nijmegen. Under growing suspicion from Rome, he attended the Second *Vatican Council as adviser to the Dutch bishops, but not as a *peritus*; he was subsequently a key figure in the foundation of the RC journal *Concilium* (1965 ff.). His writings came under investigation by the Congregation for the Doctrine of the Faith (see HOLY OFFICE) in 1968 and again in 1979, but the outcome was inconclusive. By contrast, he received numerous academic honours and in 1982 was awarded the European Erasmus prize and made a Commander in the Order of Orange Nassau.

His book *Jezus, het verhaal van een levende* (1974; Eng. tr., *Jesus*, 1979), marks a watershed in his writing. Before that he was known primarily within RC circles for collections of articles and a major book, *Christus, sacrament van de Godsontmoeting* (1959; Eng. tr., *Christ the Sacrament of the Encounter of God*, 1963), in which he sought to bring out the personal dimension in the Eucharist by means of *existentialist philosophy while remaining within official teaching. *Jezus*, with its interpretation of the Lord as an eschatological prophet, taking account of modern developments in biblical criticism, caused a furore in Rome and made him an international figure. Its sequel, *Gerechtigheid en liefde: Genade en brevrijding* (1977; Eng. tr., *Christ*, 1980), which analyses the nature of experience and relates early Christian experience of salvation to contemporary Christian and non-Christian experience, shows him moving into the centre of mainstream theological discussion. The increasing conservatism of the RC Church in the 1980s led him to postpone the completion of a planned trilogy and instead to call for changes in the RC theology of ministry, on the basis of the pattern of the first millennium and modern needs (*Kerkelijk ambt*, 1980; Eng. tr., *Ministry*, 1981; expanded and rewritten as *Pleidooi voor Mensen in de Kerk*, 1985; Eng. tr., *The Church with a Human Face*, 1985). This concern, and increasing intervention from Rome in the Dutch Church, cast a shadow over the last volume of his trilogy, *Mensen als verhaal van God* (1989; Eng. tr., *The Church: The Human Story of God*, 1990), in which a vision of the future influenced by *liberation theology and inter-faith dialogue is darkened by actual experience of the hierarchical Church.

His numerous works are listed in *Tijdschrift voor Theologie*, 14 (1974), pp. 491–501, supplemented (to 1982) in H. Häring, T. Schoof, and A. Willems, *Meedenken met Edward Schillebeeckx* [1983], pp. 320–5, with an account of his teaching method, pp. 11–39. J. [S.] Bowden, *Edward Schillebeeckx: Portrait of a Theologian* (1983); R. J. Schreiter, CPPS, and M. C. Hilkert, OP (eds.), *The Praxis of Christian Experience: An Introduction to the Theology of Edward Schillebeeckx* (San Francisco [1989]). P. Kennedy, OP, *Schillebeeckx* (Outstanding Christian Thinkers Series, 1993).

schism (Gk. σχίσμα, 'tear' or 'rent'). Formal and wilful separation from the unity of the Church. In a technical sense the word is first met with in St *Irenaeus (*Adv. Haer.* 4. 33. 7). The *Novatians and *Donatists are early instances of schismatic bodies. Schism is distinguished from heresy in that the separation involved is not at basis doctrinal; whereas heresy is opposed to faith, schism is opposed to charity, though in the early Church this distinction was not at all clear-cut. RC theologians account all those out of communion with the Pope, the supreme head of the Church, in a state of schism, though the Decree of the Second *Vatican Council on Ecumenism stated that those baptized into other Christian communions were established in 'a certain, albeit imperfect, communion with the Catholic Church'. The term 'schism' is also often used by Anglican and Protestant theologians of divisions within the Church, e.g. of that between Anglicanism and Roman (or Orthodox) Catholicism. See also ECUMENICAL MOVEMENT and REUNION; also GREAT SCHISM.

T. A. *Lacey, *Unity and Schism* (1917); S. L. Greenslade, *Schism in the Early Church* (1953; 2nd edn., 1964).

Schism Act. The popular name for the Established Church Act 1713, passed in 1714 by the English Parliament under the Tory leadership of Bolingbroke, which forbade dissenters to keep schools or engage in tuition. It was repealed by the Religious Worship Act 1718.

The principal clauses of the Act are pr. in W. C. Costin and J. S. Watson (eds.), *The Law and Working of the Constitution: Documents*, 1 (1952), pp. 121–3.

Schlatter, Adolf (1852–1938), Protestant theologian. Born at St *Gall in Switzerland, he taught first at Berne (1880–8), and later was professor at Greifswald (1888–93), Berlin (1893–98), and Tübingen (1898–1922). He held that the only sound foundation of Systematic Theology lay in biblical exegesis, and wrote commentaries on every book of the NT, the most notable being those on Mt. (*Der Evangelist Matthäus*, 1929), and on 1 and 2 Cor. (1934) and Rom. (1935). He vigorously opposed all idealistic interpretations of the Christian faith. In these and other respects he anticipated the *Dialectical Theology of K. *Barth. His work on the Fourth Gospel exercised considerable influence on E. C. *Hoskyns. His writings (none tr. into English during his lifetime) include *Der Glaube im Neuen Testament* (1885), *Erläuterungen zum Neuen Testament* (3 vols., 1887–1904), *Die philosophische Arbeit seit Cartesius* (1906; 4th edn., 1959, entitled *Die philosophische Arbeit seit Descartes*), the classic *Die Theologie des Neuen Testaments* (2 vols., 1909, of which vol. 1 was revised as *Die Geschichte des Christus*, 1920, and vol. 2 as *Die Theologie der Apostel*, 1922), and *Das Christliche Dogma* (1911).

Collection of his 'Kleine Schriften', *Zur Theologie des Neuen Testaments und zur Dogmatik*, ed., with introd., by U. Luck (Munich, 1969). Eng. tr. of 'Die Theologie des Neuen Testament und die Dogmatik' (orig. pub. in *Beiträge zur Förderung christlicher Theologie*, 13, Heft 2 (1909), pp. 7–82) by R. [C.] Morgan, *The Nature of New Testament Theology* (Studies in Biblical Theology, 2nd ser. 25; 1973), pp. 117–66, with introd. pp. 27–33. T. Schlatter (ed.), *Adolf Schlatters Rückblick auf seine Lebensarbeit: Zu seinem hundertsten Geburtstag* (Beiträge zur Förderung christlicher Theologie, Sonderheft; 1952). Memorial vol. to A. Schlatter and W. Lütgert by P. Althaus, G. *Kittel, and H. Strathmann (Beiträge zur Förderung christlicher Theologie, 40, Heft 1; 1938). U. Luck, *Kerygma und Tradition in der Hermeneutik Adolf Schlatters* (Arbeitsgemeinschaft für Forschung des Landes Nordrhein-Westfalen, 45; 1955); A. Bailer, *Das systematische Prinzip in der Theologie Adolf Schlatters* (Arbeiten zur Theologie, II. Reihe, 12 [1968]); I. Kindt, *Der Gedanke der Einheit: Adolf Schlatters Theologie und ihre historischen Voraussetzungen* (Stuttgart [1978]). List of his writings by R. Brezger (Beiträge zur Förderung christlicher Theologie, 40, Heft 2; 1938).

Schlegel, Friedrich (1772–1829), *Romantic author and Catholic apologist. From 1793 onwards he devoted himself entirely to literary pursuits. His early leanings were towards Greek ideals, as revealed in his *Von den Schulen der griechischen Poesie* (1794). Before long, however, he abandoned classicism and became an enthusiast for medieval poetry and the reigning German idealism, esp. the ideas of J. G. *Fichte and F. W. J. *Schelling. In 1797 he settled in Berlin, where he became one of the leaders of the Romantic Movement. His next years were devoted to lectures at Jena, Dresden, and Paris, and the study of oriental languages and literature. In 1808 he and his wife, Dorothea, a daughter of Moses Mendelssohn, were converted to the RC Church. From now on Schlegel became an advocate of Catholic principles. In lectures on literature and modern history which he gave at Vienna (1810–12) he defended the medieval Imperial idea against the Napoleonic state; and, in association with F. X. von Baader and St Clement Maria *Hofbauer, he sought to restore the national life of Austria and Germany on a Catholic basis. When circumstances led him to despair of a reform of the state on these lines, he looked to literature and philosophy for a renewed Catholicism. His *Philosophie der Geschichte* (2 vols., 1829; Eng. tr., 1835) contained the lectures given to these ends at Vienna in 1828. Philosophically, Schlegel after he became a Catholic was a severe critic of the *pantheism of G. W. F. *Hegel. His own philosophy, based on *Plato rather than *Aristotle, had affinities with some forms of *Ontologism.

Collected works ed., 10 vols., Vienna, 1822–5; crit. edn. by E. Behler and others (Munich and Zurich, 1958 ff.); also of his *Literary Notebooks 1797–1801* by H. Eichner (London, 1957). Eng. tr. of selected writings by E. J. Millington (Bohn's Standard Library, London, 1849), and of 'Dialogue on Poetry' and 'Literary Aphorisms' by E. Behler and R. Struc (University Park, Pa., and London, 1968). F. [D. E.] *Schleiermacher, *Vertraute Briefe über Lucinde* (1800). C. Enders, *Friedrich Schlegel: Die Quellen seines Wesens und Werdens* (Leipzig, 1913). O. Mann, *Der junge Friedrich Schlegel: Eine Analyse von Existenz und Werk* (1932). L. Wirz, *Friedrich Schlegels philosophische Entwicklung* (Grenzfragen zwischen Theologie und Philosophie, 13; 1939). J. J. Anstett, *La Pensée religieuse de Friedrich Schlegel* (Strasbourg thesis; Lyons, 1941), with extensive bibl. Useful introd. by H. Eichner, *Friedrich Schlegel* (New York [1970]). G. Fritz in *DTC* 14 (pt. 1; 1939), cols. 1492–5; R. Anchor in P. Edwards (ed.), *The Encyclopedia of Philosophy*, 7 (1967), pp. 315 f., s.v.

Schleiermacher, Friedrich Daniel Ernst (1768–1834), German theologian. A native of Breslau in Silesia, he was the son of a Reformed army chaplain, and, after his parents' conversion to the *Herrnhuter Brethren, was educated at their college at Niesky and their seminary at Barby. Finding the teaching imparted at Barby too narrow for his independent intellect, he entered the University of Halle in 1787, where he was introduced to the philosophy of I. *Kant and *Aristotle. In 1790 he accepted a post as tutor to a noble family in W. Prussia. Ordained to the ministry in 1794, he was appointed Reformed preacher at the Charité at Berlin, where he came into close contact with representatives of the *Romantic Movement, esp. F. *Schlegel. In 1799 he published his famous *Reden über die Religion* (Eng. tr., *Religion: Speeches to its Cultured Despisers*, 1893). In this work, which shows the influence of B. *Spinoza, G. W. *Leibniz, and I. Kant, he attempts to win the educated classes back to religion, which he defines romantically as 'a sense and taste for the infinite'. Contending that religion was based on intuition and feeling (*Anschauung und Gefühl*) and independent of all dogma, he saw its highest experience in a sensation of union with the infinite. In 1800 followed the *Monologen*, a preliminary to his later work on ethics. In 1804 he became professor of theology at Halle, but left it in 1807, after the Prussian defeat, and went to Berlin, where he was appointed preacher at the Dreifaltigkeitskirche in 1809 and dean of the Theological Faculty of the newly founded university in 1810. As such he played an influential part in the Prussian war against Napoleon, esp. through his stirring sermons. From 1819 he was chiefly occupied with his most important work, published in 1821–2 under the title *Der christliche Glaube nach den Grundsätzen der evangelischen Kirche im Zusammenhang dargestellt*, which is the chief source for his theology. Here he defines religion as the feeling of absolute dependence, which finds its purest expression in monotheism. The variety of forms which this feeling assumes in different individuals and nations accounts for the diversity of religions, of which Christianity is the highest, though not the only true one.

Schleiermacher's strong emphasis on feeling as the basis of religion, inherited from his Herrnhut education, was at once a reaction from contemporary German rationalism and from the ruling formalist orthodoxy. His influence on Protestant thought was enormous; generations of theologians, among whom were authorities such as A. *Ritschl, A. von *Harnack, and E. *Troeltsch, built on, developed, and modified his ideas. There was a powerful reaction against his influence, connected especially with the names of K. *Barth and E. *Brunner, who opposed to Schleiermacher's 'feeling' the scriptural principle of the Reformers. The pendulum has now begun to swing the other way and Schleiermacher's importance is again being recognized.

Crit. edn. of his works by H.-J. Birkner and others (Berlin, 1980 ff.). Older collected edn. of his writings, Berlin, 32 vols., 1834–64. Collected correspondence, ed. L. Jonas and W. *Dilthey, 4 vols., Berlin, 1858–63; Eng. tr. of vols. 1 and 2, 1860; selected correspondence [ed. M. Rade], Jena, 1906. Crit. edns. of his *Reden über die Religion* by R. *Otto (Jubiläumsausgabe), Göttingen, 1899; of the *Monologen* by F. M. Schiele, Philosophische Bibliothek, 84; Leipzig, 1902; and of *Der christliche Glaube* by M. Redeker, 2 vols., Berlin, 1960. *Friedrich Schleiermachers Aesthetik*, ed. from unpub. sources by R. Odebrecht (Berlin and Leipzig, 1931); *Friedrich Schleiermachers Dialektik*, also ed. from unpub. sources by id. (Leipzig, 1942). Eng. tr. of Schleiermacher's essay on St Luke's Gospel by C. *Thirlwall, London, 1825; of his *Reden über die Religion* (from 3rd edn., 1831) by J. *Oman, ibid., 1893, and (from 1st edn., 1799) by R. Crouter, Cambridge, 1988; of 'Selected Sermons' by M. F. Wilson, London, 1890; of the *Monologen* by H. L. Friess, Chicago, 1926; and of *Der christliche Glaube* by H. R. Mackintosh and J. S. Stewart, Edinburgh, 1928.

Apart from edns. of Schleiermacher's correspondence, the primary source for his life is the biog. by W. Dilthey (pt. 1, Berlin, 1870; 3rd edn. by M. Redeker, 2 vols., 1970; pt. 2 first pub., ed.

id., 2 vols., 1966). M. Redeker, *Friedrich Schleiermacher, Leben und Wirken* (1968; Eng. tr., Philadelphia [1973]). Studies on Schleiermacher in Eng. by R. R. Niebuhr (New York, 1964; London, 1965), G. E. Spiegler (New York, 1967), S. W. Sykes (London, 1971), R. R. Williams (Philadelphia [1978]), and B. A. Gerrish (London, 1984). E. Troeltsch and others, *Schleiermacher, der Philosoph des Glaubens* (Moderne Philosophie, 6; 1910). K. Barth, *Die Theologie Schleiermachers* (lectures given in 1923/4; ed. D. Ritschl in Barth's *Gesamtausgabe*, Reihe 2, Band 5; 1978; Eng. tr., Grand Rapids, Mich., and Edinburgh, 1982); id., *Die protestantische Theologie im 19. Jahrhundert* (Zurich, 1947), pp. 379–424; Eng. tr (1972), pp. 425–73. E. Brunner, *Die Mystik und das Wort: Der Gegensatz zwischen moderner Religionsauffassung und christlichem Glauben dargestellt an der Theologie Schleiermachers* (1924). R. Odebrecht, *Schleiermachers System der Aesthetik* (1932). E. Herms, *Herkunft, Entfaltung und erste Gestalt des Systems der Wissenschaften bei Schleiermacher* (Gütersloh [1974]); T. H. Jørgensen, *Das religionsphilosophische Offenbarungsverständnis des späteren Schleiermacher* (Beiträge zur historischen Theologie, 53; 1977). J. O. Duke and R. F. Streetman (eds.), *Barth and Schleiermacher: Beyond the Impasse?* (Philadelphia [1988]). R. D. Richardson (ed.), *Schleiermacher in Context: Papers from the 1988 International Symposium on Schleiermacher at Herrnhut* (Lewiston, NY, etc. [1991]). G. Meckenstock and J. Ringleben (eds.), *Schleiermacher und die wissenschaftliche Kultur des Christentums* (Theologische Bibliothek Töpelmann, 51; 1991). T. N. Rice, *Schleiermacher Bibliography* (Princeton, NJ, 1966). *Schleiermacher-Archiv*, ed. H. Fischer and others (Berlin and New York, 1985 ff.). W. B. Selbie in *HERE* 11 (1920), pp. 236–9; R. Hermann and E. Weniger in *RGG* (3rd edn.), 5 (1961), cols. 1422–36, s.v.

Schmalkaldic Articles (1537). The doctrinal statement drawn up by M. *Luther at the behest of Johann Friedrich, Elector of Saxony, for presentation to the projected General Council convoked by *Paul III to Mantua for 23 May 1537. It consisted of (1) a statement of the doctrines of the Creeds, very brief, as outside controversy; (2) a long section on 'the office and work of Christ, or our redemption', attacking such practices and institutions as the *Mass ('the greatest and most horrible abomination'), *purgatory ('a Satanic delusion'), the *Pope ('Antichrist'), the invocation of *saints, and *monasticism; and (3) a final section on matters on which Protestants were themselves divided, e.g. the *Eucharist. On 23 Feb. 1537 an assembly of Lutheran princes and theologians at Schmalkalden in Thuringia approved the Articles as well as a much more moderate Appendix, added by P. *Melanchthon at the Assembly's request, conceding to the Pope as a matter of human right jurisdiction over the other bishops of Christendom and adopting a markedly conciliatory attitude towards the Papacy. The Articles were issued from the press by Luther (but without Melanchthon's Appendix, which had exposed its author to violent abuse from the stricter *Lutherans) as *Artikel christlicher Lehre* in 1538, and in 1580 were incorporated in the 'Book of *Concord'. The title *Articuli Smalcaldici* is first met with in 1553.

Text pr. among the works of Luther, e.g. in the Weimar edn., 1 (1914), pp. 192–254, with introd., pp. 160–91; also ed., with Melanchthon's Appendix, by H. Volz in the *Bekenntnisschriften der evangelisch-lutherischen Kirche* (Göttingen, 1930; 10th edn., 1986), pp. 405–98 (with additional bibl. in 10th edn., pp. 1226–8). Eng. tr. by T. G. Tappert, *The Book of Concord* (Philadelphia [1959]), pp. 287–335. H. Volz, 'Luthers Schmalkaldische Artikel und Melanchthons *Tractatus de Potestate Papae*', *Theologische Studien und Kritiken*, 103 (1931), pp. 1–70. Id. (ed.), *Urkunden und Aktenstücke zur Geschichte von Martin Luthers Schmalkaldischen Artikeln (1536–1574)* (Kleine Texte, 179; 1957). E. Bizer, 'Zum geschichtlichen Verständnis von Luthers Schmalkaldischen Artikeln', *ZKG* 67 (1955–6), pp. 61–92. H. Volz, 'Luthers Schmalkaldische Artikel', ibid. 68 (1957), pp. 259–86; id., 'Zur Entstehungsgeschichte von Luthers Schmalkaldischen Artikeln', ibid. 74 (1963), pp. 316–20. P. *Schaff, *A History of the Creeds*, 1 (1877), pp. 253–7. T. Kolde in *PRE* (3rd edn.), 17 (1906), pp. 640–5, s.v. 'Schmalkaldische Artikel'.

Schmalkaldic League. The alliance concluded in Schmalkalden on 27 Feb. 1531 between several German Protestant princes and cities in opposition to *Charles V's 'Recess of Augsburg' (23 Sept. 1530) which suppressed their religious autonomy. The League united *Lutherans and *Zwinglians and by 1537 it included 35 states. In the years 1534–41 it was a considerable anti-Habsburg force and T. *Cromwell wanted England to join it. This wish was never realized and the League was destroyed by Charles V in 1547.

E. Fabian, *Die Entstehung des Schmalkaldischen Bundes und seiner Verfassung 1529–1531/33* (Schriften zur Kirchen- und Rechtsgeschichte, 1; 1956); id. (ed.), *Die Schmalkaldischen Bundesabschiede 1530–1532* (ibid. 7; 1958); id. (ed.), *Die Schmalkaldischen Bundesabschiede 1533–1536* (ibid. 8; 1958); G. Dommasch, *Die Religionsprozesse der rekusierenden Fürsten und Städte und die Erneuerung des Schmalkaldischen Bundes 1534–1536* (ibid. 28, 1961). T. A. Brady, 'Phases and Strategies of the Schmalkaldic League: A Perspective after 450 Years', *Archiv für Reformationsgeschichte*, 74 (1983), pp. 162–81. H. R. Schmidt, 'Der Schmalkaldische Bund und die oberdeutschen Städte bis 1536', *Zwingliana*, 18 (1989), pp. 36–61, with further refs.

Schola Cantorum (Lat., 'a school of singers'). In the worship of the early Church all music was rendered by the clergy with the assistance of the congregation, but gradually the practice of having a body of trained singers was introduced. At *Rome the Schola was established on a sound basis by *Gregory the Great (d. 604), and several of his successors were trained in it. From Rome the custom spread rapidly over W. Christendom, the Roman chant being brought to England by St *Benedict Biscop (d. 690) and St *Wilfrid (d. 709). The modern descendant of the Schola is the cathedral choir school and, in certain monasteries (notably *Solesmes), those monks whose special work is the study of the ecclesiastical chant. The term 'Schola Cantorum' is also used for the place where the chant is taught.

Scholarius, George. See GEORGE SCHOLARIUS.

Scholastica, St (*c.*480–*c.*543), sister of St *Benedict of Nursia. The only early source for her life is a brief passage in St *Gregory the Great's 'Dialogues' (2. 33 f.). She is said to have established a convent at Plombariola, a few miles from *Monte Cassino, where brother and sister met annually for the discussion of spiritual matters. Feast day, 10 Feb. She is invoked against storms.

B. Heurtebize, OSB, and R. Triger, *Sainte Scholastique, patronne du Mans* (Solesmes, 1897). W. Goffart, 'Le Mans, St. Scholastica and the literary tradition of the translation of St. Benedict', *R. Bén.* 77 (1967), pp. 107–41. A. Pantoni, OSB, 'Sulla località del convegno annuale di S. Benedetto e S. Scolastica, e sul monastero di Piumarola', *Benedictina*, 15 (1968), pp. 206–28; A. de Vogüé, OSB, 'La rencontre de Benoît et de Scholastique. Essai d'interprétation', *Revue d'histoire de la spiritualité*, 48 (1972), pp. 257–73; P. A. Cusack, O. Cist., 'St Scholastica: Myth or real

person?', *Downside Review*, 92 (1974), pp. 145–59. A. Lentini, OSB, in *Bibliotheca Sanctorum*, 11 (Rome, 1968), cols. 742–9, s.v. 'Scolastica', with extensive bibl. See also Lives of ST BENEDICT, s.v.

Scholasticism. A method of scholarly inquiry which proceeds by way of questioning ancient and authoritative texts, legal, medical, philosophical, and theological; first by drawing up lists of contradictory statements in these texts and then applying to them the rules of logic to reveal their underlying agreement, thus attaining what the scholastics saw as the one inner truth of things (*veritas rerum*) to which in the end all these texts bore witness. Originally the scholastic method was a teaching device developed in the schools and universities of W. Europe from the end of the 11th cent. It flourished until the 16th cent., when it came under severe criticism from Humanist scholars, who favoured a more literary and historical approach to ancient literature. Its use then became increasingly restricted to theology. As such scholasticism underwent a revival in the RC Church between 1850 and 1960, which gave rise to the assumption that scholasticism and medieval theology were synonymous. Originally, however, the scholastic method was applied to all branches of scholarship. At the same time not all medieval theology was scholastic, although this entry treats only the area of overlap.

The man who provided the tools which medieval scholars later used to develop the art of logical argument was *Boethius, particularly in his translations of, and commentaries on, *Porphyry's *Isagoge* and part of *Aristotle's logical works, a collection later known as the *logica vetus*. Grammatical instruction in the Middle Ages was based on the manuals of Donatus and Priscianus' *Instructiones grammaticae*. *Charlemagne and *Alcuin created an institutional framework of monastic and cathedral schools in which learning could be cultivated and material collected. From Martianus Capella's *De nuptiis Philologiae et Mercurii* and *Cassiodorus' *Institutiones divinarum et humanarum litterarum* the *Carolingians took over the classical plan of studies based on the *seven liberal arts, the *trivium* (grammar, rhetoric, and dialectic or logic) and the *quadrivium* (music, arithmetic, geometry, and astronomy). Within the schools the *quadrivium* was never developed, as medieval scholarship remained firmly based on the study of texts and thus on the two arts which could help in understanding and explaining texts: grammar and logic, which throughout the Middle Ages formed the heart of the academic curriculum. Already the works of late Carolingian schoolmasters, such as *Remigius of Auxerre, showed a clear preoccupation with logic and its possible use in theology, although their interest did not yet go beyond collecting glosses on the standard texts. The exception was John Scottus *Erigena, whose *Periphyseon* was the first independent effort to apply logic and *Neoplatonism to the realm of faith. In the 10th cent. the work of collecting and glossing was continued in monastic schools such as *Fleury and St *Gall, so that by 1050 important collections of logical material were at hand to be explored and developed.

By the mid-11th cent. the growth of literacy was making its impact felt and the social and economic environment was improving so rapidly that a more rational approach to life and its problems became feasible for the first time since Late Antiquity. A generation arose which was confident that 'man could control his environment through his mind' (A. Murray). Such was their trust in the written word that the study of grammar and logic was seen as the way to achieve this lofty purpose, in the hope that by laying bare the structure of language and thought they would ultimately be able to unravel the structure of reality itself.

An early example of this confidence is provided in the controversy between *Berengar of Tours and *Lanfranc of Bec about the mystery of the Eucharist. Grammatical analysis of the sacramental formula forced Berengar to state that Christ's presence in the Eucharist was real and spiritual, whereas his adversary, Lanfranc, using the logical categories of *substance and *accident, came to the conclusion that it must be physical, involving a change of substance, a *transubstantiation. Lanfranc's pupil, St *Anselm of Canterbury, went one step further in trying to establish a coherent logical language beyond ordinary speech (*usus loquendi*) which would enable him to trace the grammar of reality. Thus he thought he could prove the necessity of God's existence and of the Incarnation without appealing to biblical authority. Important as this new beginning was, Anselm's influence on subsequent generations was limited, as his outlook remained monastic in an age when the schools were emerging from the shadow of the monastery to become independent intellectual centres.

Through the Gregorian Reform (see GREGORY VII) formal education and no longer only inheritance or social origin had become a route to preferment in Church and society. And it was in the schools that the scholastic method was fully developed. One of the most important was the school of Laon, where *Anselm and his brother, in order to facilitate their lectures on Scripture, collected authoritative statements from the Church Fathers and attached them to the matching texts of the Bible, beginning the *Glossa Ordinaria*. When two Fathers differed in their interpretation of a biblical passage, their contradictory statements were compared in the classroom and became the subject of a *quaestio*.

This technique, probably inspired by similar procedures in canon law, was perfected by Peter *Abelard in his *Sic et Non*, a random collection of 150 theological puzzles. This was a pioneering work in two respects. First, by simply collecting contradictory *auctoritates* without attaching them to the appropriate biblical passages, Abelard showed a way for later generations of theologians to separate systematic questioning from lecturing on Scripture. In this his example was followed and improved upon by *Robert of Melun and *Peter Lombard, who both composed similar anthologies of contradictory texts, called *Sententiae*, which were carefully arranged by subject and thus formed a much better framework for questioning than the text of a glossed Bible. Secondly, in the prologue Abelard formulated two key doctrines of scholasticism: (1) that questioning is the key to the perception of truth, and (2) that difficulties which arise in questioning can usually be resolved by determining the meaning of terms used by different authors in varying ways. Thus he gave logic and semantics pride of place in theology. This programme immediately met with strenuous opposition from the monastic spokesman of the 12th cent., St *Bernard of Clairvaux, who accused Abelard of arguing about that which could only be accepted in faith. By defending the tradition of theology as a meditation on God's word in Scripture,

Bernard inaugurated a form of mystical theology which acted as a constant counterpoint to the rational clarity of scholastic theology. It was unobtrusive at first, but came to the fore in the different social and economic circumstances of the 14th cent. in the works of Meister *Eckhart, *Henry Suso, and John *Tauler.

The introduction from 1150 onwards of the full Aristotelian corpus of logical works, the *logica nova*, provided a new impulse but did not add any essentially new elements to the scholastic technique. By the end of the 12th cent. *Alan of Lille had devised a complete set of rules for the proper use of language and logic in theology, the *Regulae caelestis iuris*, which summed up the methodological progress of the century.

The 13th cent. saw the coming of age of the universities and confrontation with the contents of Greek and Arabic learning, which was an altogether different challenge, with fewer consequences for methodology but with many more repercussions on Church doctrine. In the universities the teaching methods of the schools were further developed. *Paris was the first university to separate speculative questioning from lectures on the Bible. Under *Alexander of Hales's influence Peter Lombard's *Sententiae* was chosen as the textbook for this new lecture course, and remained so until the 16th cent. Robert *Grosseteste, who disliked speculative methods in theology, tried to stem the tide by forbidding *Oxford theologians any textbook but the Bible, but in 1253 lectures on the *Sentences* were officially introduced in Oxford as well. A last vociferous protest came from Roger *Bacon, who complained unavailingly that modern scholars no longer had any knowledge of Scripture. Besides ordinary lectures, special days in the university calendar were set aside for disputations, in which either the master broached a controversial question or someone in the audience could ask him anything (*quaestiones de quodlibet*). It was in these *quaestiones disputatae* and *quodlibetales* that the scholastic technique could be exploited most fully, because the master was not hemmed in by *auctoritates* but free to explore all possible sides to a question. The final stage in the development of the scholastic method in the 13th cent. was reached with the *Summae*, freely composed works in which the sequence of questions was not dictated by the text used in the classroom but by the internal progress of the argument.

The chief controversy of the 13th cent. revolved on the contents of Aristotle's natural philosophy and his Arab and Jewish commentators, such as *Avicenna, *Averroes, *Avicebron, and *Maimonides. Using the methods developed in the 12th cent., the great generation of friar scholars, headed by St *Bonaventure, St *Albertus Magnus, and St *Thomas Aquinas, tried to cope with the huge quantity of new information and to prove that there could be no fundamental contradiction between secular learning and theology. At first it seemed as if these daring syntheses were to succeed, but doubts about a possible reconciliation between faith and reason grew as knowledge of Aristotle's natural philosophy, as interpreted by Averroes and other commentators, increased and the full consequences of his naturalism and determinism were drawn out by venturous scholars such as *Siger of Brabant and Boethius of Dacia. In 1277 Étienne Tempier, Bp. of Paris, encouraged by *Henry of Ghent, and Robert *Kilwardby, Abp. of Canterbury, both issued a list of condemnations which voiced some of these doubts.

Although the immediate consequences of this episcopal intervention have often been exaggerated—the scholastic method as such had not been condemned—it was a sign of a profound change in outlook. When after 1300 the economic and political horizon darkened and catastrophes, such as the Black Death, hit the population, the optimism of the previous centuries seemed vacuous. What stood out was the sheer fortuity of man's fate rather than the regularity of nature and the harmony between all its constituent parts. The result was that, although the scholastic technique was, if possible, even more highly developed in the 14th cent., its scope became more narrowly defined.

This apparent paradox is first seen in the work of John *Duns Scotus, perhaps the most subtle mind scholasticism produced. With him even the ordinary *quaestio* became not so much an attempt to reconcile contradictory authorities as a debate with contemporary scholars and with himself. Problems of the present superseded preoccupation with ancient books, as the connection between text and question, though maintained, became a mere formality. Duns Scotus was also the first theologian to limit the universal validity of logic by stating that the structure of this world, a result of God's *potestas ordinata*, represented only one possibility of God's *potestas absoluta*, which was bound by nothing but His will and the law of contradiction. *William of Ockham went even further; he severed the link between logic and reality, maintaining that logic is not about reality, as represented by words, but just about words. It is a science of language studying the ways in which the human mind devises universal concepts to organize its intuitive perceptions of individual things, the only things that really exist. Ockham thought logic of little use in theology, because it obscured the fundamental truth of God's absolute freedom and loving care for mankind with pseudo-explanations. Although often denounced as the destroyer of the medieval synthesis, Ockham had apparently expressed a central concern of his age; he had a host of followers, from *Gregory of Rimini to Gabriel *Biel, who proudly named their way the *via moderna*, as against the *via antiqua* of those who followed 13th-cent. theologians.

In the Renaissance Italy of the 15th cent. scholasticism was frontally attacked by L. *Valla who in his *Dialecticae disputationes* argued that not certainty but persuasion was the central concern of the study of language, that rhetoric was therefore more important than logic. His influence made itself felt in the early 16th cent. At that time most European universities gradually replaced the medieval arts course with the study of Greek and Latin literature and thus put an end to the long reign of logic in the world of scholarship. Later 'scholastic' revivals did not so much try to revive the scholastic methods as to draw attention to the actuality of the contents of medieval philosophy and theology.

The background of scholasticism is portrayed in R. W. Southern, *The Making of the Middle Ages* (1953), pp. 170–257; id., *Scholastic Humanism and the Unification of Europe* (3 vols., Oxford, 1995 ff.); A. Murray, *Reason and Society in the Middle Ages* (Oxford, 1978); and B. Stock, *The Implications of Literacy: Written Language and Models of Interpretation in the Eleventh and Twelfth Centuries* (Princeton, NJ [1983]), pp. 241–454. See also A. B.

Cobban, *The Medieval Universities: Their Development and Organization* (1975), and S. C. Ferruolo, *The Origins of the University: The Schools of Paris and their critics, 1100–1215* (Stanford, Calif., 1985).

The scholastic method is discussed by L. M. de Rijk, *Middeleeuwse Wijsbegeerte* (Assen, 1977; Fr. tr., *La Philosophie au Moyen Âge*, Leiden, 1985). M. [J.] Haren, *Medieval Thought: The Western Intellectual Tradition from Antiquity to the Thirteenth Century* (Basingstoke, 1985); J. [A.] Marenbon, *Early Medieval Philosophy (480–1150): An Introduction* (1983); id., *Later Medieval Philosophy (1150–1350): An Introduction* (1987); H. Liebeschütz in A. H. Armstrong (ed.), *The Cambridge History of Later Greek and Early Medieval Philosophy* (1967), pp. 538–639; N. Kretzmann and others (eds.), *The Cambridge History of Later Medieval Philosophy from the Rediscovery of Aristotle to the Disintegration of Scholasticism 1100–1600* (1982); [E.] P. [M.] Dronke (ed.), *A History of Twelfth-Century Western Philosophy* (Cambridge, 1988), all with bibl. Classic works still of value incl. M. *Grabmann, *Die Geschichte der scholastischen Methode* (2 vols., Freiburg i.B., 1909–11), and E. *Gilson, *History of Christian Philosophy in the Middle Ages* (1955).

On medieval logic, J. Pinborg, *Logik und Semantik im Mittelalter: Ein Überblick* (Stuttgart [1972]); S. Ebbesen and others in N. Kretzmann, op. cit., pp. 99–381; and A. [R.] Broadie, *Introduction to Medieval Logic* (Oxford, 1987). On theology, B. Smalley, *The Study of the Bible in the Middle Ages* (Oxford, 1941; 3rd edn. [1983]), with discussion of the development of the *quaestio* technique; M.-D. Chenu, OP, *La Théologie au douzième siècle* (Études de philosophie médiévale, 45; 1957; partial Eng. tr. as *Nature, Man and Society in the Twelfth Century*, Chicago and London, 1968); id., *La Théologie comme science au XIIIe siècle* (3rd edn., Bibliothèque Thomiste, 33; 1957; orig. pub. in *AHDLMA* 2 (1927), pp. 31–71); id., *Introduction à l'étude de Saint Thomas d'Aquin* (Université de Montréal, Publications de l'Institut d'études médiévales, 11; 1950; Eng. tr., *Toward Understanding Saint Thomas*, Chicago [1964]; wider than its title suggests). Also valuable are J. de Ghellinck, SJ, *Le Mouvement théologique du XIIe siècle* (1914; 2nd edn., Museum Lessianum, section historique, 10; 1948); J. [J.] Pelikan, *The Christian Tradition: A History of the Development of Doctrine, 3: The Growth of Medieval Theology (600–1300)* (Chicago and London [1978]). H. A. Oberman, *Forerunners of the Reformation: The Shape of Late Medieval Thought* (New York, 1966; London, 1967); id., 'Fourteenth-Century Religious Thought. A Premature Profile', *Speculum*, 53 (1978), pp. 80–93.

There are important collections of texts in J. P. Migne, *PL* (authors up 1200) and in *CCCM*; also O. Lottin, OSB, *Psychologie et morale aux XIIe et XIIIe siècles* (6 vols., Louvain and Gembloux, 1942–60; 2nd edn. of vol. 1, 1957). For other edns. of texts see under individual authors mentioned above; also A. M. Landgraf, *Einführung in die Geschichte der theologischen Literatur der Frühscholastik* (Regensburg, 1948; Fr. tr., rev. by A.-M. Landry, OP, *Introduction à l'histoire de la littérature théologique de la scolastique naissante*, Université de Montréal, Publications de l'Institut d'études médiévales, 22; 1973); F. Stegmüller, *Repertorium Commentariorum in Sententias Petri Lombardi* (2 vols., Würzburg, 1947), supplemented by V. Doucet, OFM, in *AFH* 47 (1954), pp. 88–170, and by J. van Dijk in *Franciscan Studies*, 39 (1979), pp. 255–315; P. Glorieux, *La Littérature quodlibétique* (Bibliothèque Thomiste, 5 and 21; 1925–35). Id., *Répertoire des maîtres en théologie de Paris au XIIIe siècle* (Études de philosophie médiévale, 17–18; 1933–4); id., *La Faculté des arts et ses maîtres au XIIIe siècle* (ibid. 59; 1971).

Important periodicals, with bibls. of current lit., incl. the *Revue thomiste* (Paris, 1893 ff., with separate *Bulletin thomiste*, ibid., 1924–68, cont. as *Rassegna di letteratura tomistica*, Naples, 1969 ff.); *Revue néo-scolastique (de philosophie)* (Louvain, 1894–1945; cont. as *Revue philosophique de Louvain*, 1946 ff.; with separate *Répertoire bibliographique de la philosophie*, Louvain, 1934 ff.); *Revue d'histoire ecclésiastique* (Louvain, 1900 ff.); *Ephemerides théologicae Lovanienses* (ibid., 1924 ff.); and *Recherches de théologie ancienne et médiévale* (ibid., 1929 ff., with separate *Bulletin*). Work in progress is reported in the *Bulletin de la Société internationale pour l'étude de la philosophie médiévale* (Louvain, 1959–63; cont. as the *Bulletin de philosophie médiévale*, ibid., 1964 ff.).

I. C. Brady, J. E. Gurr, J. A. Weisheipl in *NCE* 12 (1967), pp. 1153–70, s.v.

scholia (plur. of Gk. σχόλιον). Notes, esp. of a critical, grammatical, or explanatory kind, inserted in the margins of an ancient MS. Their use was a regular practice in the Greek schools of later classical antiquity, and, probably through the contact between pagan and Christian culture at Alexandria, they were introduced by Christian scholars into the MSS of biblical and ecclesiastical texts. Scholia were often collected and published as a kind of commentary.

School of English Church Music. See ROYAL SCHOOL OF CHURCH MUSIC.

Schoolmen. The teachers of philosophy and theology at the medieval European universities, then usually called 'schools', of which *Paris and *Oxford were pre-eminent. From the 13th cent. many of their greatest representatives belonged to the *Mendicant Orders, among the most famous being the Dominicans St *Albert the Great and St *Thomas Aquinas, and the Franciscans St *Bonaventure and *Duns Scotus. See SCHOLASTICISM.

schools, cathedral. See CATHEDRAL SCHOOLS.

Schools, Sunday. See SUNDAY SCHOOLS.

Schopenhauer, Arthur (1788–1860), German philosopher. The son of a wealthy Danzig merchant, he was apprenticed to a Hamburg firm by his father in 1804, but went to Göttingen University in 1809 and to Berlin in 1811, where he attended the lectures of J. G. *Fichte and F. D. E. *Schleiermacher. He was a great admirer of I. *Kant, whose only authentic interpreter he professed himself to be, and was also influenced by the nature philosophy of J. W. Goethe and F. W. J. *Schelling. The problem of combining Kant's criticism with the positive view of life of Goethe and Schelling led him to construct a philosophical system which he expounded in his chief work, *Die Welt als Wille und Vorstellung* ('1819' [really 1818]; 2nd edn., 1844). After its completion he travelled in Italy and in 1820 accepted a lectureship at Berlin University which, however, proved a failure. In 1831 he fled from the cholera to Frankfurt, where he spent the latter part of his life in embittered seclusion, publishing only a few works, the chief of which were *Die beiden Grundprobleme der Ethik* (1841) and *Parerga und Paralipomena* (1851).

Schopenhauer may be regarded as the classic exponent of Pessimism. The ultimate Reality was Will (Gk. θέλημα, 'impulse', 'striving'; rather than βούλησις, 'the capacity to determine'), which extends far beyond the range of conscious life. Its extinction by pity for creatures and the mortification of the passions was the sovereign remedy for the ills of existence; and Schopenhauer claimed that his teaching was so far essentially at one with that of the Christian mystics. Meanwhile, as a stage towards this goal, he found a transient place of rest in the realms of art, poetry, and above all music. In the formulation of his ethical doctrines he was considerably influenced by Buddhism, though he never made any pretence of himself practising the Buddhist maxims.

Schopenhauer's philosophy, which achieved recognition only at the end of his life, influenced R. Wagner and F. *Nietzsche (in his early years), and was continued and modified by E. von *Hartmann and A. *Drews. It was one of the chief anti-Christian systems in Germany in the 19th century.

Collected works ed. by his pupil, J. Frauenstädt, 6 vols., Leipzig, 1873–4; 2nd edn. by A. Hübscher, 7 vols., Wiesbaden, 1946–50. The most complete edn. of his posthumous writings is that ed. A. Hübscher, 5 vols., Frankfurt am Main, 1966–75; Eng. tr., 4 vols., Oxford, etc., 1988–90. Letters ed. id., Bonn, 1978; 2nd edn., 1987. Eng. tr. of his principal work by R. B. Haldane and J. Kemp, *The World as Will and Idea* (3 vols., 1883–6; 8th edn., 1937), and by E. F. J. Payne, *The World as Will and Representation* (2 vols., Indian Hill, Colo., 1958). Many of his other works have also been tr. Studies in Ger. by W. von Gwinner (Leipzig, 1862; 2nd edn., much enlarged, 1878), J. Volkelt (Stuttgart, 1900; 5th edn., 1923), H. Hasse (Munich, 1926), W. Schneider (Vienna, 1937), A. Hübscher, *Denker gegen den Strom* (Bonn, 1973; Eng. tr., Lewiston, Lampeter, and Queenston [1989]), and R. Malter (Stuttgart and Bad Cannstatt [1991]). Studies in Eng. by H. Zimmern (London, 1876; rev. edn., 1932), W. Wallace (ibid., 1890 and 1913), W. Caldwell (Edinburgh, 1896), F. Copleston, SJ (Bellarmine Series, 11; 1946; repr. 1975), P. [L.] Gardiner (Harmondsworth, 1963), and B. Magee (Oxford, 1983). G. Simmel, *Schopenhauer und Nietzsche* (1907; 2nd edn., 1920). *Schopenhauer-Lexikon*, ed. J. Frauenstädt (2 vols., Leipzig, 1871). *Jahrbuch der Schopenhauer-Gesellschaft* (1912 ff.). C. Gebhardt, *Schopenhauer-Bilder* (1913). A. Hübscher, *Schopenhauer-Bibliographie* (Stuttgart and Bad Cannstatt, 1981). P. [L.] Gardiner in *Encyclopedia of Philosophy*, 7 (1967), pp. 325–32, s.v.

Schürer, Emil (1844–1910), German NT scholar. After lecturing in theology at Leipzig from 1869 to 1878, he was appointed professor at Giessen in 1878, went to Kiel in 1890, and held a chair of NT exegesis at Göttingen from 1895. In 1876 he founded the *Theologische Literaturzeitung*, which he edited together with A. *Harnack from 1881. His principal work is the *Lehrbuch der Neutestamentlichen Zeitgeschichte* (1874), published since its 2nd edition (1886–7) under the title *Geschichte des jüdischen Volkes im Zeitalter Jesu Christi* (Eng. tr., *A History of the Jewish People in the Time of Jesus Christ*, 5 vols., 1890–1). This monumental treatise gives a detailed and carefully substantiated account of the political history and the religious and social customs and beliefs as well as of the religious and profane literature of the Jewish people from the time of the *Maccabees to the wars under Trajan. There is a completely revised English version, taking account of later scholarship, by G. Vermes, F. Millar, and M. Black (3 vols. in 4 parts, 1973–87).

Obituary notice by A. Harnack in *TLZ* 35 (1910), cols. 289–92. A. B. Titius in *PRE* (3rd edn.), 24 (1913), pp. 460–6.

Schütz, Heinrich (1585–1672), German composer. The Latin form 'Henricus Sagittarius' is also found. From 1609 to 1612 he studied music at *Venice, became court organist at Kassel in 1612, and from 1617 was court Kapellmeister at Dresden, where, apart from short periods in Copenhagen during the *Thirty Years War, he remained for the rest of his life. Most of his surviving music was composed for the *Lutheran Church both for Latin and German texts. He is esp. famous for his *Passion music, which is remarkable for its dramatic qualities. He was one of the greatest exponents of the musical *baroque, blending German traditions with Italian innovations in a powerfully expressive manner. His works include the *Symphoniae Sacrae*, 1 (1629), 2 (1647), and 3 (1650), the *Kleine Geistliche Konzerte* (1636–9), and *Geistliche Chormusik* (1648).

Collected edn. of his musical works by P. Spitta and others (18 vols., Leipzig, 1885–1927); Neue Ausgabe, herausgegeben im Auftrag der Neuen Schütz-Gesellschaft, by F. Schöneich and others (Kassel, 1955 ff.); letters and other writings ed. E. H. Müller (Ratisbon, 1931). Annotated Eng. tr. of *Letters and Documents 1656–1672* by G. Spagnoli (London [1990]). Modern studies by A. Pirro (Paris, 1913), H. J. Moser (Kassel, 1936; 2nd edn., 1954; Eng. tr., St Louis, 1959; also a shorter study, Kassel, 1940; 3rd edn., 1952; Eng. tr., 1967), and F. Civra (Turin, 1986). W. Bittinger (ed.), *Schütz-Werke-Verzeichnis* (1960); A. B. Skei, *Heinrich Schütz: A Guide to Research* (Garland Composer Resource Manuals, 1; New York and London, 1981). J. Rifkin and others in S. Sadie (ed.), *The New Grove Dictionary of Music and Musicians*, 17 (1980), pp. 1–37, s.v.

Schwabach, Articles of (1529), the first of the *Lutheran Confessions. These 17 Articles were based on the collection of 15 Articles considered and, with one exception (that on the Eucharist), adopted at the Colloquy of *Marburg (3 Oct. 1529). The revision was due to M. *Luther, assisted by P. *Melanchthon, J. *Jonas, J. *Brenz, and others. On 16 Oct. 1529 they were accepted at Schwabach by the Elector and George, Margrave of Brandenburg-Ansbach, as admitting to membership of the Lutheran League of the N. German States, but they failed to win over the S. German Protestants. They were later taken as the basis of the *Augsburg Confession.

Text of the Articles pr. among the works of P. Melanchthon in the *Corpus Reformatorum* founded by C. G. Bretschneider, 26, ed. H. E. Bindseil (Brunswick, 1857), cols. 151–60, with introd. cols. 129–50. They are also pr. in a way which shows their relationship to the Augsburg Confession in *Die Bekenntnisschriften der evangelisch-lutherischen Kirche herausgegeben im Gedenkjahr der Augsburgischen Konfession 1930* (10th edn., Göttingen, 1982), pp. 52–83d. P. *Schaff, *The History of the Creeds*, 1 (2nd edn., London, 1878), pp. 228 f. Schottenloher, 4 (1938), p. 599 (nos. 42437–44). T. Kolde in *PRE* (3rd edn.), 18 (1906), pp. 1 f., s.v. 'Schwabacher Artikel'.

Schwartz, Eduard (1858–1940), classical philologist and *patristic scholar. A native of Kiel, he was educated at Göttingen, Bonn (under H. Usener), and Greifswald (under U. von Wilamowitz-Moellendorff). He held a succession of professorships in German universities, among them Strasbourg (1897–1902; 1913–18), Göttingen (1902–9; here he was closely associated with J. *Wellhausen), and Munich (1919 onwards). His early training, philological rather than theological, gave the stamp to his patristic work. He published editions of *Tatian's 'Oratio ad Graecos' (1888), *Athenagoras (1891), and *Eusebius' 'Ecclesiastical History' (1903–9, in collaboration with T. *Mommsen), the Pseudo-*Athanasian *Sermo Major de Fide* (1924), *Cyril of Scythopolis (1939), and other patristic texts. His main work, the *Acta Conciliorum Oecumenicorum* (1914–40), was a grandly planned edition of the

Greek Councils; it was mostly completed at the time of his death. It provided, for the first time, a critical edition of the 'Acts' of *Ephesus (431) and *Chalcedon (451), besides portions of the later Councils. It was in many respects the Greek counterpart of C. H. *Turner's *Monumenta*, the last part of which, after Turner's death (1930), Schwartz saw through the press (1939). His important collection of papers on Athanasius in the *Nachrichten* of the Göttingen Gesellschaft (1904–11) inaugurated a new era in Athanasian studies. His other writings include a paper maintaining the early death of *John, the son of Zebedee (1904), *Kaiser Konstantin und die christliche Kirche* (1913; 2nd edn., 1936), and a paper on the so-called 'Counter-Anathemas' of *Nestorius (1923). Among the many papers subsidiary to his edition of the Councils was an important study of the *Theodosian Collection.

Gesammelte Schriften, ed. E. Schwartz, K. Aland, W. Eltester, and H. D. Altendorf (5 vols., 1938–63). There is much autobiog. material in Schwartz's own *Vergangene Gegenwärtigkeiten* (1938). A. Rehm, *Eduard Schwartz' wissenschaftliches Lebenswerk* (*Sb.* (Bayr.), 1942, Heft 4), with list of his works, pp. 67–75. C. H. Turner, 'Eduard Schwartz and the *Acta Conciliorum Oecumenicorum*', *JTS* 30 (1929), pp. 113–20. A. Momigliano, 'Premesse per una discussione su Eduard Schwartz', *Rivista Storica Italiana*, 90 (1978), pp. 617–26; id., *New Paths of Classicism in the Nineteenth Century* (History and Theory, Beiheft, 21; 1982), pp. 59–63, with bibl. p. 64.

Schwartzerdt, Philipp. See MELANCHTHON, PHILIPP.

Schwegler, Albert (1819–57), German patristic scholar and philosopher. At the University of Tübingen, which he had entered in 1836, he came under the influence of F. C. *Baur, and from the standpoint of the *Tübingen School published *Der Montanismus und die christliche Kirche des zweiten Jahrhunderts* (1841). His other writings in the field of patristics, all written from the same point of view, include a *Geschichte des nachapostolischen Zeitalters* (2 vols., 1846) and an edition of the '*Clementine Homilies' (1847). He also wrote extensively on the history of philosophy and on Roman history.

E. Zeller, *Vorträge und Abhandlungen*, 2 (1877), pp. 329–63 ('Drei deutsche Gelehrte: 1. Albert Schwegler'). H. Harris, *The Tübingen School* (Oxford, 1975), esp. pp. 78–88. W. S. Teuffel in *Allgemeine Deutsche Biographie*, 33 (1891), pp. 327 f.

Schweitzer, Albert (1875–1965), German theologian, physician, and organist. Born at Kaisersberg in Alsace, he was educated at Strasbourg University, completing his studies at Berlin and Paris. In 1899 he became pastor at Strasbourg. In *Das Messianitäts- und Leidensgeheimnis* (1901; Eng. tr., *The Mystery of the Kingdom of God*, 1914, repr. 1925) he expounded what was to be the leading idea of his theological work, that the Lord's teaching centred in His conviction of the imminent end of the world. The book made a great stir, and shortly after its publication he became lecturer at Strasbourg University (1902) and principal of a theological college. In 1906 appeared his brilliant *Von Reimarus zu Wrede* (Eng. tr., *The Quest of the Historical Jesus*, 1910). After a review of previous attempts at interpreting the Life of Christ (G. E. *Lessing, D. F. *Strauss, J. E. *Renan, O. Pfleiderer, and W. *Wrede), all of which he held to be inadequate, he expounded an interpretation on the basis of 'thoroughgoing eschatology'.

He held that Christ shared with His contemporaries the expectation of a speedy end of the world and, when this proved a mistake, concluded that He Himself must suffer in order to save His people from the tribulations preceding the last days. In 1911 there followed *Die Geschichte der paulinischen Forschung* (Eng. tr., *Paul and his Interpreters*, 1912), in which Schweitzer applied similar eschatological principles to the theology of St *Paul. In the same year he took his medical degree, and in 1913 gave up a career of great academic distinction to devote himself at Lambaréné, Gabon (then French Equatorial Africa) to the care of the sick and to missionary activities. Having been interned in France in 1917, he returned to Strasbourg in 1918. In 1921 he published his widely read reminiscences, *Zwischen Wasser und Urwald* (Eng. tr., *On the Edge of the Primeval Forest*, 1922). In 1923 appeared his *Kulturphilosophie*, summing up his views on ethics as 'reverence for life'. In 1924 he went back to Lambaréné and restored his destroyed hospital, which was his principal concern for the rest of his life. He nevertheless completed his work on St Paul, *Die Mystik des Apostels Paulus* (1930, Eng. tr., 1931), which is built on the thesis that 'Being in Christ', interpreted as the 'physical union between Christ and the elect', is the centre of the Pauline teaching and is to be distinguished from 'God mysticism', which attains to God directly without the mediation of Christ. At the time of his death he was working on the posthumously published *Reich Gottes und Christentum*, ed. by Ulrich Neuenschwander (1967; Eng. tr. as *The Kingdom of God and Primitive Christianity*, 1968).

Schweitzer exercised a very considerable influence on Continental as well as on English and American Protestant theology, though his view of the Lord's Person aroused much opposition not only among conservative, but also among liberal Protestant theologians. He was also an accomplished musician and interpreter of J. S. *Bach, on whom he wrote a monograph (1908; Eng. tr., 1911), and his organ recitals found an enthusiastic public. In 1953 he was awarded the Nobel Peace Prize for the previous year.

Collections of autobiog. reminiscences pub. as *Aus meiner Kindheit und Jugendzeit* (1924; Eng. tr. by C. T. Campion as *Memoirs of Childhood and Youth*, 1924); *Aus meinem Leben und Denken* (1931; Eng. tr. by id. as *My Life and Thought*, 1933); and *Afrikanisches Tagebuch, 1939–45* (1946). Sermons preached at Strasbourg between 1900 and 1919, ed. U. Neuenschwander, *Strassburger Predigten* (Munich [1966]; Eng. tr., *Reverence for Life*, 1970). Collected edn. of his works by R. Grabs (5 vols., Berlin, 1971). Lives by G. Seaver (London, 1947; 6th edn., 1969) and J. Brabazon (ibid., 1976). The numerous other substantial studies incl. R. Grabs, *Albert Schweitzer* (Berlin, 1949); W. Picht, *Albert Schweitzer: Leben und Bedeutung* (1960; Eng. tr., 1964); H. W. Bähr (ed.), *Albert Schweitzer: Sein Denken und sein Weg* (Tübingen, 1962); H. Clark, *The Ethical Mysticism of Albert Schweitzer* (Boston, 1962; London, 1964, as *The Philosophy of Albert Schweitzer*); E. Grässer, *Albert Schweitzer als Theologe* (Beiträge zur historischen Theologie, 60; Tübingen, 1979). J. C. O'Neill, *The Bible's Authority* (Edinburgh, 1991), pp. 248–65.

Schwenckfeldians. The followers of the Silesian Reformation theologian, Caspar Schwenckfeld (1490–1561).

Schwenckfeld, essentially a mystic by temperament, was much impressed by the writings of J. *Tauler and M. *Luther, and in 1522 made a pilgrimage to *Wittenberg.

He soon found, however, that he could not give unreserved assent to many of the Protestant doctrines. He believed that the tenet of justification by faith created serious moral dangers; he was unable to accept the Lutheran doctrine of the Eucharist; and he sought to introduce among his followers a strict rule of Church discipline. The opposition which his teaching met with from both Catholics and Protestants led him to leave his native Silesia in 1529 for Strasbourg and other cities in S. Germany. He gradually came to hold also a doctrine of the deification of Christ's humanity, and in 1540 issued an elaborate account (*Konfession und Erklärung*) of his beliefs on the subject, with a reply to his opponents. Its theses were at once repudiated by the main body of orthodox Protestants, and a few years later Schwenckfeld finally withdrew from the Lutheran Church. After much further persecution from both Church and State he died at Ulm on 10 Dec. 1561.

After his death his small band of disciples, who called themselves the 'Confessors of the Glory of Christ', continued to propagate his teaching, publishing many of his writings from his MSS. They continued to exist in Silesia till 1826, and a branch of their disciples, which established itself at Philadelphia, in 1734, still survives.

Their writings and letters are collected in the *Corpus Schwenckfeldianorum*, ed. C. D. Hartranft and others (vols. 1–15; Leipzig, 1907–39; vols. 16–19; Pennsburg, Pa., 1959–61). Schwenckfeld's correspondence with *Philip of Hesse, ed. J. L. French (London, 1908). K. [T. C. G.] Ecke, *Schwenckfeld, Luther und der Gedanke einer apostolischen Reformation* (1911; new edn. as *Kaspar Schwenckfeld, ungelöste Geistesfragen der Reformationszeit* (Gütersloh, 1952). S. G. Schultz, *Caspar Schwenckfeld von Ossig* (Pennsburg, Pa., 1946). F. M. Weber, *Kaspar Schwenckfeld und seine Anhänger in den freybergischen Herrschaften Justingen und Öpfingen* (Stuttgart, 1962). A. Sciegienny, *Homme charnel, homme spirituel: Étude sur la christologie de Caspar Schwenckfeld (1489–1561)* (Wiesbaden, 1975). P. C. Erb, *Schwenckfeld in his Reformation Setting* (Valley Forge, Pa. [1978]). Id. (ed.), *Schwenckfeld and Early Schwenkfeldianism: Papers Presented at the Colloquium on Schwenckfeld and the Schwenkfelders, Pennsburg, Pa., September 17–22, 1984* (Pennsburg, Pa., 1986). R. E. McLaughlin, *Caspar Schwenckfeld, Reluctant Radical: His Life to 1540* (New Haven, Conn., and London [1986]). H. W. Kriebel, *The Schwenkfelders in Pennsylvania* (Lancaster, Pa., 1904). W. K. Meschter, *Twentieth Century Schwenkfelders* (Pennsburg, Pa., 1984). R. H. Grützmacher in *PRE* (3rd edn.), 18 (1906), pp. 72–81; G. Maron in *RGG* (3rd edn.), 5 (1961), cols. 1620–3.

Science, Christian. See CHRISTIAN SCIENCE.

scientia media (Lat., 'mediate knowledge'), A term coined by the *Jesuit theologian, L. *Molina, in his attempt to reconcile God's foreknowledge with human free will. It designates the knowledge which God has of 'futuribilia', i.e. of things which are not, but which would be if certain conditions were realized, and thus are *intermediate* between mere possibilities and actual future events. Acc. to Molinist teaching this mediate knowledge is independent of the decree of the Divine Will. This thesis was keenly contested by the *Thomists and remains one of the chief differences between the systems of theology in the Jesuit and *Dominican Orders. See also MOLINA, LUIS DE.

G. de Henao, SJ, *Scientia Media Historice Propugnata* (Lyons, 1655); id., *Scientia Media Theologice Defensata* (ibid., 1674). F. Stegmüller in *L.Th.K.* (2nd edn.), 9 (1964), col. 551, s.v., with bibl.

Scillitan Martyrs, the. Seven men and five women of Scillium in N. Africa who were executed in 180, by order of the proconsul Saturninus, for refusal to renounce Christianity and to swear by the 'genius' of the Roman Emperor. Their 'Passio', which is authentic, is a valuable document for the *persecutions of the 2nd cent. It shows the pagan authorities eager to obtain a recantation and the martyrs steadfast in their refusal; and it is the first documentary evidence of Christianity in N. Africa. Later a basilica was built over their tomb where St *Augustine preached three sermons. Feast day, 17 July.

Orig. Lat. text of the 'Acta', with Gk. version and later Lat. recension, ed. J. A. *Robinson, *The Passion of S. Perpetua* (Texts and Studies, 1, no. 2; Cambridge, 1891), pp. 106–21. Original Lat. text repr., with Eng. tr., by H. Musurillo, *The Acts of the Christian Martyrs* (Oxford, 1972), pp. 86–9. J. den Boeft and J. Bremmer, 'Notiunculae Martyrologicae', *VC* 35 (1981), pp. 43–56, esp. pp. 44–8. P. Franchi de' Cavalieri, 'Le reliquie dei martiri scillitani', *RQ* 17 (1903), pp. 209–21. H. Karpp, 'Die Zahl der Scilitanischen Märtyrer', *VC* 15 (1961), pp. 165–72. G. Lanata, *Gli Atti dei Martiri come Documenti Processuali* (Studi e Testi per un Corpus Iudiciorum, 1; Milan, 1973), pp. 137–44, with further bibl.

scintilla animae (Lat., 'spark of the soul'). A metaphorical expression current in mystical literature, esp. in the writings of Meister *Eckhart, for the element in the soul (also 'ground' or 'apex') in which its union with God is achieved.

SCM. See STUDENT CHRISTIAN MOVEMENT.

Scone, Perthshire, an ancient Scottish religious centre and once the capital of a Pictish kingdom. At an assembly held here in 908, the Scottish king, Constantine, swore to protect the Church and recognized the Bp. of St Andrews as primate. An abbey of *Augustinian canons, succeeding an earlier foundation, was settled there *c.*1115 by King Alexander I (1107–24); it was sacked by a Protestant mob in 1559, and the last Commendator Abbot died in 1573. Kings of Scotland from Malcolm IV (1153) onwards were crowned at Scone. The Stone of Destiny, on which the Celtic kings were crowned, was brought to *Westminster Abbey by Edward I in 1296. It was traditionally believed to be that on which *Jacob laid his head at *Bethel (Gen. 28: 11). In 1996 the British Government announced that it would be returned to Scotland; on 30 Nov. it was transferred to Edinburgh castle.

The *Liber Ecclesie de Scon* was ed. by W. Smythe for the Bannatyne Society, vol. 82, Edinburgh, 1843. M. E. C. Walcott, *Scoti-Monasticon: The Ancient Church of Scotland* (1874), esp. pp. 313–16. W. F. Skene, *The Coronation Stone* (1869). J. Hilton, 'The Coronation Stone at Westminster Abbey', *Archaeological Journal*, 54 (1897), pp. 201–24. See also bibl. to CORONATION RITE IN ENGLAND.

Scory, John (d. 1585), successively Bp. of *Chichester and *Hereford. Originally a Cambridge *Dominican, he became a secular clerk in 1538 at the *Dissolution of the Monasteries and was appointed in 1551 to the see of *Rochester and in 1552 to that of Chichester. At the accession of *Mary Tudor, Scory was deprived of his see, but submitted and recanted. Nevertheless he left England, going first to Emden and then to Geneva. In 1558 he returned and was in the next year appointed Bp. of Here-

ford, which see he held until his death. He was a wealthy, able, and not over-scrupulous prelate. He assisted at M. *Parker's consecration (and hence figured prominently in the *Nag's Head Story) and is thus held to be one of the channels through which the episcopal succession was preserved in the C of E.

W. A. J. Archbold in *DNB* 51 (1897), pp. 8 f., s.v., with further refs. See also H. N. Birt, OSB, *The Elizabethan Religious Settlement* (1907), pp. 241, 246, 248, 362–70 and *passim*.

Scotism. The system of Scholastic philosophy expounded by the *Franciscan teacher, *Duns Scotus (q.v.), and defended in the later Middle Ages, esp. in the Franciscan Order.

Scotland, Christianity in. In the early Middle Ages the territory of what is now Scotland was occupied by four different nations. The earliest evidence for Christianity is a number of inscribed monuments of the 5th and 6th cents. in the British area of SW Scotland at sites such as Kirkmadrine (Wigtownshire). The early Christian centre at Whithorn, *Bede's *Ad Candidam Casam* (*HE* 3. 4), associated with St *Ninian, lies in the same region. The kingdom of Dalriada in the area of Argyll and northwards was already settled from *Ireland, and by the later 6th cent. St *Columba was one of several Irish saints active here, apparently ministering to a Christian population. His encounters with the Picts suggests that these people were still pagan, but by the beginning of the 8th cent. Pictish tradition asserted that the community of Columba had established many churches in E. Scotland. *Iona had also been largely responsible for the conversion of the Northumbrian kingdom of Bernicia, where St *Aidan's foundation at *Lindisfarne (635) was a major centre of Irish influence in England. From here English bishops were sent to Whithorn (8th–9th cent.) and one to Abercorn (681–5). The Columban Church lost influence in Northumbria after King Oswiu's adoption of the Roman date of Easter in 664, and Northumbrian influence among the Picts led to their adopting Roman practice in 710. Soon afterwards, in 717, the Columban clergy were expelled from Pictish territory. The union of Pictland and Dalriada in the 9th cent. and the gradual settling of the frontier with the English led to the creation of the Scottish kingdom. In the 10th and 11th cents. there is evidence for bishops at St Andrews. Jurisdiction over the originally British see at Glasgow was disputed between the Bps. of St Andrews and the Abps. of *York. Topographical evidence suggests that the 12th cent. dioceses based on Brechin, Dunblane, and Dunkeld, whose territories are intermingled with those of St Andrews, had a comparatively ancient origin based on a proprietory rather than a jurisdictional role.

The *Investiture Controversy had little impact on Scotland, but the English and Anglo-Norman connections of Queen *Margaret (d. 1093) and her three sons who were successively kings in the first half of the 12th cent. (esp. David I, reigned 1124–53) brought new Church leaders with reformed ideas who transformed the structure of the Scottish Church. A territorial episcopate in 11 mainland dioceses with clearly defined boundaries of jurisdiction controlled a system of *c.*1,000 parishes now supported by royally imposed teind (*tithe). But attempts by the Abp.

of *York during much of the 12th cent. to extend his metropolitan authority over the Scottish sees led in 1192 to a compromise unique in the W. Church whereby all of them except Galloway (which remained under York) were exempted from any superior authority except that of *Rome. The Popes regarded themselves as Scotland's metropolitans; and despite the difficulties of travel from the 13th cent. to the 16th there was a regular flow of Scots to the Papal court to take advantage of this Papal interest in Scottish business. The lack of any single pre-eminent bishop in Scotland until changes made at the end of the 15th cent. also meant that the Scottish Church was normally under royal control, with little signs of organized resistance. King and Pope seldom disagreed.

The change of direction among the regular clergy from Irish to reformed Continental models was fostered by King David. He showed special interest in Tironensian monks (a small congregation of reformed *Benedictines centered on Tiron (now Thiron) in France) and *Augustinian canons, who were both more dominant in Scotland than in England. *Cistercians also became important in due course, but the more traditional Benedictines had little support. The friars had warm royal support from 1230 onwards. At first it was bishops appointed from among the regular clergy who kept the Scottish Church abreast of changing ideals in France and England. Then from the late 12th cent. onwards the more ambitious secular clergy sought university education abroad (since there was no university in Scotland until the founding of St Andrews in 1410). They had much Papal support in this movement and ensured on their return that Scotland was kept in touch with current trends in thought and practice. *Duns Scotus was a product of this background.

In the absence of a profession of lay common lawyers, university-trained *canon lawyers played an exceptionally important part in Scottish society. The Church courts of the various dioceses provided a vital service in resolving disputes at a popular level. In general the clergy served the country satisfactorily by the standards of the time. Though they formed only a small group of between 3,000 and 4,000 in a population of some half a million, they were so well renumerated that by the later Middle Ages they were able to pay two-fifths of the national taxation.

The early 15th cent. brought fear of contamination by *Lollardy, and two heretics from England and Bohemia were condemned and burned (Resby in 1408 and Crawar in 1433). But these were the only cases, for the threat to the established order was not a serious or continuing one in Scotland and heresy was long contained. One reason for this was the late spread of literacy and individualistic devotional attitudes among laymen in Scotland compared with some other countries. There was therefore for long little open criticism of the clerical sins of concubinage and pluralism, and enthusiastic acceptance of the attractions of *pilgrimages and *indulgences, along with widespread endowment at all social levels of Masses for the dead. Yet the later 15th cent. was for most people a time of mechanical and perfunctory attitudes to religion: the thoughtful and devout were still a small minority.

The first wave of the Reformation proper was *Lutheran, the second *Calvinist. Heretical books were smuggled into Scotland in spite of an Act of Parliament (1525) against their importation. Patrick *Hamilton, who

had been in Germany, was burnt at the stake in St Andrews (1528) for his advocacy of Lutheran principles and his death increased the number of reformers. The policy and campaigns of England under *Henry VIII and *Edward VI added to the pro-Reformation forces but also created patriotic opposition. Cardinal *Beaton led the anti-English party, but his responsibility for the martyrdom of G. *Wishart (1546) led to his murder shortly afterwards. Wishart's mantle fell upon the shoulders of J. *Knox, who, after his labours in England, Frankfurt, and Geneva, ultimately returned to lead the Calvinistic party, now strongly supported by the Lords of the Congregation.

In 1560 the reformed Church of Scotland was established on *Presbyterian lines. It prepared a Confession of Faith (see SCOTTISH CONFESSION) and a 'Book of *Discipline' (1560) and soon adopted the Anglo-Genevan 'Book of *Common Order' as its liturgical directory, but not until 20 years afterwards were presbyteries systematically erected. To make up for the dearth of ministers at first, it was deemed expedient to appoint *superintendents and readers. Soon after the death of Knox (1572) the mantle of leadership was borne by the doughty advocate of high Presbyterianism, A. *Melville. Intimate associations existed between Scottish Presbyterians and the English *Puritans, who, led by T. *Cartwright and W. *Travers, sought by 'Scottizing for Discipline'—to use R. *Bancroft's phrase—to presbyterianize the C of E, but were frustrated by *Elizabeth I and her agent J. *Whitgift.

For more than 100 years the fortunes of Scottish Presbyterians ebbed and flowed owing to the determination of the Stuart kings to make the Kirk episcopal. Now the Crown was dominant and pro-episcopal Acts were passed (1584); now the Kirk came into power again and Presbyterianism was ratified (1592). For some decades the policy of *James VI and I prevailed, Episcopacy being established by the Scottish Parliament in 1612. The Five Articles of *Perth, which enjoined such usages as kneeling at Communion and the observance of holy days, were passed by a packed Assembly in 1618. The imposition of the Prayer Book, known as W. *Laud's liturgy, brought the conflict between the Kirk and *Charles I to a head in 1637. In the following year the pro-Presbyterian *National Covenant was subscribed and the Glasgow General Assembly, the first free assembly for 30 years, swept Episcopacy away. In 1643 the alliance between the Scottish Covenanters and the Long Parliament was cemented by the *Solemn League and Covenant, and the southern Parliament, aiming, under Scottish influence, at Presbyterian uniformity for the British Isles, convened the *Westminster Assembly (q.v.). The *Directory of Church Government, the Directory of Public *Worship, the *Westminster Confession, and the *Westminster Catechisms (qq.v.) were formally accepted as standards by the Church of Scotland.

After the Restoration Episcopacy was re-established and a bitter and bloody struggle between Scottish Episcopalians and Presbyterians ensued. At the Revolution the Church of Scotland became Presbyterian once more (1690) and has remained so ever since. Chiefly owing to the infringement of popular rights by the Patronage Act of 1712 the Church was weakened by secessions in the 18th cent. (Original Secession, 1733; Relief, 1761) and by the *Disruption (q.v.) of 1843, when nearly a third of its ministers and members left the Establishment and formed the

*Free Church of Scotland. Among notable modern features of Scottish Presbyterian history may be mentioned foreign and colonial missionary enterprise, Church extension at home, increased interest in worship and Church architecture, the transfer of Church schools to the civil authorities (1872), the abolition of patronage (1874), and the relaxation of the terms of credal subscription. The 19th cent. witnessed a growing movement in favour of the union of the different Presbyterian Churches in Scotland. The chief unions took place in 1847 (Secession and Relief to form *United Presbyterian), 1900 (United Presbyterian and Free to form *United Free), and 1929 (United Free and Church of Scotland under the name of the latter). Each union had its unyielding remnant who continued in their former ways, e.g. Free Church, 1900, and United Free Church, 1929. Attempts to bring about a *rapprochement* between the Church of Scotland and the (Anglican) Episcopal Church in Scotland were accompanied in the 20th cent. by conversations between the Church of Scotland and the C of E, but the 1957 Report advocating 'Bishops in Presbytery' was defeated by a small majority in the General Assembly, as was the proposal in 1971 that the Episcopal Church should form a Synod of the General Assembly. Negotiations for organic unity have continued in the 1990s through multilateral conversations of which both the Church of Scotland and the Scottish Episcopal Church are members.

After the 1929 reunion among the Presbyterians, the majority of the population of Scotland belonged to the Church of Scotland, which is Presbyterian, national, endowed, and free. Its spiritual independence has been recognized and its patrimony secured by Acts of Parliament (1921, 1925). From those who adhered to Episcopacy after the Revolution settlement (1690) arose the Episcopal Church in Scotland (since 1979 called the Scottish Episcopal Church). Subject because of its Jacobite loyalty to Penal Laws from 1715 to 1792, it was reduced in numbers, but since their repeal it has won growing acceptance. It is an autonomous Province of the *Anglican Communion. Through it the (then Protestant) *Episcopal Church in the United States of America received episcopal *Orders by the consecration of S. *Seabury in 1784. The Church is governed by a General Synod, of which one House comprises the seven diocesan bishops. They elect from among themselves a *Primus who is their chairman, but metropolitical authority resides with the College of Bishops, not an individual. It has maintained a distinctive liturgical tradition (see COMMON PRAYER, BOOK OF). The Prayer Book of 1929, while remaining an authorized liturgy, is being superseded by contemporary revisions. Women have been ordained as deacons since 1986, as priests since 1994. The RC Church always retained its hold on those in some remote parts of the Highlands and Islands who were never much influenced by the Reformation. It has also long been influential among those of Irish extraction in the industrial Lowland areas. In recent years it has attracted a wider following and now comprises c.20 per cent of the population, roughly the same proportion as the Church of Scotland. See also CONGREGATIONALISM.

J. H. S. Burleigh, *A Church History of Scotland* (1960). G. Donaldson, *Scottish Church History* (Edinburgh, 1985); id., *The Faith of the Scots* (1990). F. T. Wainwright (ed.), *The Problem of the Picts* (Edinburgh, 1955). [A.] C. Thomas, *The Early Christian Archaeology of North Britain* (Oxford, 1971); id., *Christianity in Roman Britain to A.D. 500* (1981), pp. 275–94. A. Macquarrie, 'Early Christian Religious Houses in Scotland: Foundation and Function', in J. Blair and R. Sharpe (eds.), *Pastoral Care before the Parish* (Leicester, 1992), pp. 110–33. J. Dowden, *The Medieval Church in Scotland: Its Constitution, Organisation and Law* (Glasgow, 1910); id., *The Bishops of Scotland: Being Notes on the Lives of all the Bishops under each of the Sees prior to the Reformation* (Glasgow, 1912). D. E. R. Watt and others (eds.), *Ecclesia Scoticana* (Series Episcoporum Ecclesiae Catholicae Occidentalis, 6th ser. 1; Stuttgart, 1991). R. Somerville (ed.), *Scotia Pontificia: Papal Letters to Scotland before the Pontificate of Innocent III* (Oxford, 1982). *Concilia Scotiae: Ecclesiae Scoticanae Statuta tam provincialia quam synodalia quae supersunt, MCCXXV–MDLIX*, ed. J. Robertson (Bannatyne Club, 2 vols., 1866); Eng. tr., with introd., by D. Patrick, *Statutes of the Scottish Church 1225–1559* (Scottish History Society, 54; 1907). I. B. Cowan, *The Parishes of Medieval Scotland* (ibid. 93; 1967), and other vols. in this series. G. W. S. Barrow, *Kingship and Unity: Scotland 1000–1306* (1981), pp. 61–83; id., *The Kingdom of the Scots: Government, Church and Society from the Eleventh to the Fourteenth Century* (1973), pp. 165–254. A. Grant, *Independence and Nationhood: Scotland 1306–1469* (1984), esp. pp. 89–119; J. Wormald, *Court, Kirk and Community: Scotland 1470–1625* (1981), esp. pp. 75–139. D. E. R. Watt, *A Biographical Dictionary of Scottish Graduates to A.D. 1400* (Oxford, 1977).

The primary authorities for the period of the Reformation are the histories of J. Knox, J. *Spottiswode, and D. *Calderwood (qq.v.). G. D. Henderson, *The Burning Bush: Studies in Scottish Church History* [from the Reformation onwards] (Edinburgh, 1957). W. M. Campbell, *The Triumph of Presbyterianism* (ibid., 1958). G. Donaldson, *The Scottish Reformation* (Cambridge, 1960). I. B. Cowan, *The Scottish Reformation: Church and Society in Sixteenth Century Scotland* [1982]. J. Kirk, *Patterns of Reform: Continuity and Change in the Reformation Kirk* (Edinburgh, 1989). D. Shaw, *The General Assemblies of the Church of Scotland 1560–1600: Their Origins and Development* (ibid., 1964). W. R. Foster, *The Church before the Covenants: The Church of Scotland 1596–1638* (ibid., 1975). D. G. Mullan, *Episcopacy in Scotland: The History of an Idea, 1560–1638* (ibid. [1986]). J. Buckroyd, *Church and State in Scotland 1660–1681* (ibid. [1980]). R. B. Sher, *Church and University in the Scottish Enlightenment: The Moderate Literati of Edinburgh* (Edinburgh, 1985). A. L. Drummond and J. Bulloch, *The Scottish Church 1688–1843: The Age of the Moderates* (ibid., 1973); id., *The Church in Victorian Scotland 1843–1874* (ibid., 1975); id., *The Church in Late Victorian Scotland 1874–1900* (ibid., 1978). J. R. Fleming, *A History of the Church in Scotland, 1843–1874* (ibid., 1927); id., *A History of the Church in Scotland, 1875–1929* (ibid., 1933). C. G. Brown, *The Social History of Religion in Scotland since 1730* (1987). A. C. Cheyne, *The Transforming of the Kirk: Victorian Scotlands Religious Revolution* (Edinburgh, 1983). H. Scott, *Fasti Ecclesiae Scoticanae: The Succession of Ministers in the Church of Scotland from the Reformation* (3 vols., Edinburgh, 1866–71; new edn., 7 vols., Edinburgh, 1915–28, + 3 additional vols., 8–10, 1950–81). J. T. Cox, *Practice and Procedure in the Church of Scotland* (1934; 6th edn. by D. F. M. Macdonald, 1976). F. Lyall, *Of Presbyters and Kings: Church and State in the Law of Scotland* (Aberdeen, 1980). H. J. Wotherspoon and J. M. Kirkpatrick, *A Manual of Church Doctrine* [1919], revised by T. F. Torrance and R. Selby Wright (1960). D. B. Forrester and D. M. Murray (eds.), *Studies in the History of Worship in Scotland* (Edinburgh, 1984). G. B. Burnet, *The Holy Communion in the Reformed Church of Scotland 1560–1960* (1960). F. Goldie, *A Short History of the Episcopal Church from the Restoration to the Present Time* (1951). The Scottish liturgies of 1637 and 1764 are pr. in W. J. Grisbrooke, *Anglican Liturgies of the Seventeenth and Eighteenth Centuries* (Alcuin Club Collections, 40; 1958), pp. 163–82 and 333–48, with comm. pp. 1–18 and 150–9. M. Lochhead, *Episcopal Scotland in the Nineteenth Century* [1966]. D. Maclean, *The Counter-Reformation in Scotland, 1560–1930* [1931]; P. F.

Anson, *The Catholic Church in Modern Scotland, 1560–1937* (1937); id., *Underground Catholicism in Scotland 1622–1878* (Montrose, 1970); C. Johnson, *Developments in the Roman Catholic Church in Scotland 1789–1929* (Edinburgh [1983]); series of essays in the *Innes Review*, 29 (1978), repr. as *Modern Scottish Catholicism 1878–1978*, ed. D. McRoberts (Glasgow, 1979). H. Escott, *A History of Scottish Congregationalism* (Glasgow, 1960).

Scott, George Gilbert (1811–78), ecclesiastical architect. The grandson of T. *Scott, the biblical commentator, he was born at Gawcott, Bucks, and brought up as an *Evangelical. After studying architecture under James Edmeston and Henry Roberts, he began work in partnership with W. B. Moffatt as a designer of workhouses in various styles. His acquaintance with A. W. N. *Pugin and Benjamin *Webb, the secretary of the (High Church) *Cambridge Camden Society, led him to an intensified study of the principles of Gothic art. In 1840 he was selected as architect for the Martyrs' Memorial, Oxford. His first notable church in Gothic style was St Giles, Camberwell (1842–4), and from this time he became the most prominent ecclesiastical architect in England. In 1844 he won a competition for the *Lutheran church of St Nicholas, Hamburg, executed in 14th-cent. German Gothic. He frequently travelled on the Continent, utilizing his studies, esp. of French Gothic, for his work in Britain, e.g. for the chapel of Exeter College, Oxford (1857–9). His later works include the Albert Memorial (1864–71), St Mary Abbots, Kensington (1870–2), and St Mary's (Episcopal) Cathedral, Edinburgh (1874–80). Among the many buildings where he was entrusted with the work of restoration were *Westminster Abbey and the cathedrals at *Ely, *Hereford, *Salisbury, and *Chester. In his 'restorations' he met with resistance owing to his too ready preference for his own designs to existing work, and the Society for the Protection of Ancient Buildings was founded to oppose the methods of restoration of which Scott was the leading promoter. Well-known ecclesiastical architects who were trained in his office include G. E. *Street and G. F. *Bodley.

His grandson, **Giles Gilbert Scott** (1880–1960), was also a distinguished architect. His works include the Anglican cathedral at *Liverpool (begun in 1904; completed in 1978 on a modified plan), the University Library at Cambridge (1931–4), the New Bodleian Library (1937–40) and the Deneke Building and Chapel (1931) at Lady Margaret Hall, Oxford.

George Gilbert Scott, *Personal and Professional Recollections*, ed. by his son, G. Gilbert Scott (1879); D. Cole, *The Work of Sir Gilbert Scott* (1980). P. Waterhouse in *DNB* 51 (1897), pp. 19–23. On Giles Gilbert Scott, A. S. G. Butler in *DNB, 1951–1960*, pp. 870–72.

Scott, Robert (1811–87), Greek lexicographer. Educated at Shrewsbury and at *Christ Church, Oxford, he was elected a Fellow of Balliol in 1835 and Master (with B. *Jowett, who succeeded him at the next election, as rival candidate) in 1854. From 1861 to 1870 he was also Dean Ireland's professor of exegesis, and from 1870 till his death Dean of *Rochester. He is remembered esp. through the famous Lexicon which he edited in conjunction with H. G. *Liddell (q.v. for particulars).

Various letters to and from Scott ed. J. M. Prest, *Robert Scott and Benjamin Jowett* (Suppl. to Balliol College Record, 1966). H. Craik in *DNB* 51 (1897), pp. 65 f.

Scott, Thomas (1747–1821), biblical commentator. The son of John Scott (d. 1777), a grazier, Thomas was apprenticed to a surgeon at Alford, Lincs, but after quick dismissal for some misconduct was employed for some nine years in menial work on the land. Eventually he was ordained deacon in 1772 by the Bp. of *Lincoln and held a succession of curacies, in 1781 succeeding John *Newton, whose acquaintance he had made earlier, at Olney. From 1801 till his death he was rector of Aston Sandford, Bucks. In his *Force of Truth* (1779) he set out the stages in which his theological beliefs developed from a *Unitarian rationalism to a fervent *Calvinism. His chief work, however, was his *Commentary on the Bible*, issued in weekly numbers between 1788 and 1792. It was remarkable for its endeavour to discover the message of each section of the Bible for his own soul and a persistent refusal to shirk difficulties by falling back on historical or pietistic disquisitions. It had an enormous circulation, though Scott, who shared but few of the financial profits, continued a poor man. J. H. *Newman in the *Apologia* testifies to Scott as the influence 'to whom (humanly speaking) I almost owe my soul'. See also CMS.

Collected edns. of his works pub. Buckingham, 1805–8 (5 vols.), and 1823–5 (10 vols.). M. L. Loane, *Oxford and the Evangelical Succession* (1950), pp. 135–92. J. E. Marshall, *Thomas Scott (1747–1821) and 'The Force of Truth' (1779)* (lecture, 1979). A. Gordon in *DNB* 51 (1897), pp. 73–5.

Scottish Confession (Lat. *Confessio Scotica*). The first Confession of Faith of the reformed Church of Scotland. It was adopted by the Scottish Parliament in 1560 and remained the confessional standard until superseded by the *Westminster Confession in 1647. It had been drawn up in four days by J. *Knox and five other ministers in 25 articles, and is a typical Calvinistic document. *Justification by faith is assumed; the doctrine of *election is affirmed; the Real Presence in Communion is emphasized and *transubstantiation and the view that the elements are bare signs are condemned. The Kirk is defined as Catholic; it consists of the elect, and outside of it there is no salvation. The notes of the true Kirk on earth are not lineal descent or numbers, but the true preaching of the Word and the right administration of the sacraments and of discipline. Civil magistrates are stated to be the lieutenants of God, whose duty it is to conserve and purge the Church when necessary; but supreme authority is ascribed to the Word of God.

A supplement to the Confession was issued and subscribed in 1581; it is commonly known as the *King's Confession (q.v.).

Lat. and Scots text repr., with introd. by G. D. Henderson, *Scots Confession, 1560 ...* (Edinburgh, 1937); Scots text, with introd. by G. D. Henderson, *The Scots Confession 1560* (ibid., 1960), has also modern Eng. rendering by J. Bulloch, pp. 57–80. Further modern Eng. version in W. Croft Dickinson (ed.), *John Knox's History of the Reformation in Scotland*, 2 (1949), pp. 257–72. K. *Barth's *Gifford Lectures (*The Knowledge of God and the Service of God according to the Teaching of the Reformation*, 1938) are in the form of a comm. on the 1560 Confession. J. Kirk, 'The Influence of Calvinism on the Scottish Reformation', *Records of* the *Scottish Church History Society*, 18 (1974), pp. 157–79, esp. pp. 157–61. W. I. P. Hazlett, 'The Scots Confession 1560: Context, Complexion and Critique', *Archiv für Reformationsgeschichte*, 78 (1987), pp. 287–320.

Scottish Episcopal Church. See SCOTLAND, CHRISTIANITY IN.

Scottus Erigena. See ERIGENA, JOHN THE SCOT.

Scotus, Duns. See DUNS SCOTUS.

'Scourge of God', the. See ATTILA.

screens. Partitions of wood, stone, or metal, often with painted or sculptural decoration, dividing a church into two or more parts. Chancel- or choir-screens, separating the *choir from the *nave, may be high, solid, and elaborate, as the 13th-cent. German examples at Naumburg and Wechselburg and the 15th-cent. ones at *Canterbury and *York, or, as in Italy in early times, quite low. In the latter form they were sometimes provided with *ambones on either side. When a chancel-screen is surmounted by a cross ('rood') it is termed a 'rood-screen'. See also ICONOSTASIS.

A. W. [N.] *Pugin, *A Treatise on Chancel Screens and Rood Lofts, their Antiquity, Use and Symbolic Significance* (1851). F. B. Bond and B. Camm, OSB, *Roodscreens and Roodlofts* (2 vols., 1909). F. Bond, *Screens and Galleries in English Churches* (1908); [W. H.] A. Vallance, *English Church Screens* (1936); id., *Greater English Church Screens*, posthumously ed. E. T. Long (1947). G. W. O. Addleshaw and F. Etchells, *The Architectural Setting of Anglican Worship* (1948), pp. 37–63. J. Mogin, *Les Jubés de la Renaissance* (Brussels, 1946). J. Mallion, *Chartres: Le Jubé de la Cathédrale* (Chartres, 1964); E. Hütter and H. Magirius, *Der Wechselburger Lettner: Forschungen und Denkmalpflege* (Weimar, 1983).

scriptorium. The room, esp. in a monastery, which was set apart for the scribes to copy MSS. The necessary utensils were provided by a person known as the 'armarius'. As the scriptorium of a particular monastery (or group of monasteries) often adopted a characteristic script, its affiliations can be of great value to palaeographers in assigning the date and place to a MS. A good instance of such a characteristic style of writing is the school of Tours, and of illumination that of *Winchester.

Scrivener, Frederick Henry Ambrose (1813–91), NT textual critic. Educated at Trinity College, Cambridge, he held a number of parochial appointments. From 1846 to 1856 he was headmaster of Falmouth School. He made a very comprehensive study of the text of the NT, publishing collations and detailed descriptions of a large number of (esp. minuscule) MSS, some of them hitherto unexamined. His *Plain Introduction to the Criticism of the NT*, of which the 1st edition appeared in 1861 (listing some 1,170 MSS) and the 4th (posthumous, ed. E. Miller) in 1894 (listing over 3,000), is still a valuable book of reference, despite the attempt made in it to defend the *textus receptus.

E. C. Marchant in *DNB* 51 (1897), p. 126, s.v.

scrofula, touching for. See KING'S EVIL, TOUCHING FOR THE.

Scrope, Richard le (c.1346–1405), Abp. of *York. Of noble family, he was ordained priest in 1377, became chancellor of Cambridge University in 1378, and in 1382 went to Rome, where he was made auditor of the Curia. He was appointed Bp. of Coventry and *Lichfield in 1386 and, at the request of Richard II, was translated to the archbishopric of York in 1398. Though he assisted in forcing the abdication of the King in 1399 and took part in the enthronement of Henry IV, he soon grew discontented with the latter's government and favoured Northumberland's revolt, to which his reputation for holiness gave additional weight. He also composed a manifesto demanding justice, security, and lighter taxation, and gathered an army which included dissatisfied citizens whom he led against the royal troops. He was tricked, however, into disbanding his followers by the Earl of Westmorland, who feigned compliance with his demands for reform, and was arrested and irregularly sentenced to death at the command of the King. At his tomb in York Minster miracles were soon believed to take place, and he was popularly venerated as a saint, though his cult was never formally approved.

Miscellanea relating to Abp. Scrope in J. Raine (ed.), *The Historians of the Church of York and its Archbishops*, 2 (RS, 1886), pp. 292–311; account of the proceedings against him, ibid. 3 (1894), pp. 288–91, and letters deprecating the worship at his shrine, pp. 291–4. Life by continuator of chronicle of Thomas Stubbs (perh. William Melton, 1496–1528), ibid. 2, pp. 428–33. Short Life by N. H. Nicolas in his edn. of the Scrope and Grosvenor Roll, *The Controversy between Sir Richard Scrope and Sir Robert Grosvenor in the Court of Heraldry, MCCCLXXXV–MCCCXC*, 2 (1832), pp. 121–6. J. Solloway, *Archbishop Scrope* ('York Minster Tracts', no. 15 [1928]). J. W. McKenna, 'Popular Canonization as Political Propaganda: The Cult of Archbishop Scrope', *Speculum*, 45 (1970), pp. 608–23; P. McNiven, 'The Betrayal of Archbishop Scrope', *Bulletin of the John Rylands Library*, 54 (1972), pp. 173–213. J. Hughes, *Pastors and Visionaries: Religion and Secular Life in Late Medieval Yorkshire* (Woodbridge, Suffolk [1988]), passim [see index]. J. Tait in *DNB* 51 (1897), pp. 144–7, s.v., with refs. to orig. sources. *BRUO* 3 (1959), pp. 1659–60; *BRUC*, pp. 513–14.

scruples (Lat. *scrupulus*, 'small sharp stone'). In *moral theology, unfounded fears that there is sin where there is none. Scrupulosity may be the result of much ascetic reading of a rigorist tendency, but more often is the outcome of nervous disturbances. It usually manifests itself in the fear of having consented to sinful imaginations and desires, of having made incomplete confessions, and of being unworthy of the reception of the sacraments. It may also err with regard to duties which it is prone to see where they do not exist. Scrupulosity, which often inclines the penitent to refuse submission to the judgement of his confessor, may lead to the sins of obstinacy and despair, or, conversely, to self-indulgence. The scrupulous, who are discouraged from making minute confessions, are usually counselled to disregard their scruples and to act in obedience to the advice of a prudent spiritual director.

scrutiny (Lat. *scrutinium*). A term applied to the formal testing of *catechumens before their Baptism in the early Church. The 1972 RC Order for Adult Baptism includes three 'scrutinies' of catechumens; these comprise a homily, prayers, and laying on of hands, and take place after the *Gospel at the Eucharist on the third, fourth, and fifth Sundays in Lent (or, if necessary, in the week following). The word also came to be used for the examination of candidates for holy orders.

See works cited s.v. CATECHUMENS.

Sea, Forms of Prayer to be used at. In the BCP, a small collection of prayers and anthems for use in various circumstances at sea. The forms include a prayer to be used daily in the Royal Navy, prayers for use in a storm and before battle, thanksgivings for deliverance from storm and for victory, and directions for general confession and absolution in serious danger. The first special prayers for use at sea were put out as a supplement to the Directory of Public *Worship, issued by the Long Parliament in 1645, and the forms now prescribed were first included in the BCP of 1662.

F. Procter and W. H. *Frere, *A New History of the Book of Common Prayer* (1901), pp. 162, 199, 246, and esp. 644 f. F. S. Horan in *PBD*, pp. 745 f., s.v.

Seabury, Samuel (1729–96), first bishop of the *Episcopal Church in the USA. After studying theology at Yale University and medicine at Edinburgh, he was ordained priest by the Bp. of *Lincoln in 1753 and served as a missionary in New Brunswick, later holding livings near New York. Remaining loyal to the British Government in the War of Independence, he engaged in controversy in the three 'Farmer's Letters' with Alexander Hamilton and for a time (in 1775) suffered imprisonment. He was elected bishop in 1783; but as his inability, now that the States were independent, to take the Oath of Allegiance precluded his consecration by English bishops, arrangements were made that he should obtain his episcopal Orders from Scotland. Seabury was accordingly consecrated at Aberdeen on 14 Nov. 1784. Later, by his co-operation in the consecration of Bp. T. J. Claggett of Maryland, the Scottish and English successions were united. An able organizer and administrator, he secured for the Episcopal Church in America a structure and a liturgy in which the native High Church tradition could grow and develop. His influence on the history of his Church was immense. His consecration is commemorated on 14 Nov. in the American BCP (1979).

E. E. Beardsley, *Life and Correspondence of the Right Reverend Samuel Seabury* (Boston, 1881; abridged edn. as *The Life of Samuel Seabury*, London, 1884). Other Lives by his great-grandson, W. J. Seabury (New York and London, 1908), H. Thoms (Hamden, Conn., and London, 1963), and B. E. Steiner (Athens, Oh. [1971]). C. K. Vance in *Dict. Amer. Biog.* 16 (1935), pp. 528–30.

Seal of Confession. The absolute obligation not to reveal anything said by a penitent using the Sacrament of *Penance. The obligation includes not only the confessor, but interpreter, bystander, eavesdropper, persons finding and reading lists of sins obviously drawn up for the purpose of the confession, and indeed everyone except the penitent himself. It covers all sins, *venial as well as *mortal, and any other matter the revelation of which would grieve or damage the penitent, or would lower the repute of the sacrament. The obligation arises from a tacit contract between penitent and confessor, from its necessity for the maintenance of the use of the sacrament by the faithful, and from canon law. The obligation covers direct and indirect revelation, e.g. unguarded statements from which matters heard in confession could be deduced or recognized, and admits of no exception, no matter what urgent reasons of life and death, Church or State, may be advanced. The RC ruling on the seal (*Sacramentale sigillum*) is to be found in *CIC* (1983), can. 983. In the C of E the relevant proviso in the 1604 *Canons (can. 113) was left unrepealed by the 1969 Canons, which superseded the earlier collection in almost every other respect.

B. Kurtscheid, OFM, *Das Beichtsiegel in seiner geschichtlichen Entwicklung* (1912; Eng. tr. as *A History of the Seal of Confession*, 1927). L. Honoré, SJ, *Le Secret de la Confession* (Museum Lessianum, Section théologique, 10; 1924). [J.] P. Winckworth, *The Seal of the Confessional and the Law of Evidence* (1952).

Sebaldus, St, patron saint of Nürnberg. His date (9th–11th cent.) is disputed, but he is prob. to be placed within the eremetical movement of the 11th cent., and seems to have lived in the woods near Nürnberg. His tomb is attested as a place of pilgrimage from 1072, when miracles were reported to have taken place at it and a church was built over it. From 1300 to 1377 the famous Sebalduskirche was built, and in 1425 the city obtained his formal canonization from Pope *Martin V. His relics rest in the celebrated shrine of Peter Vischer (1508–19), and his name was inserted in the *Roman Martyrology in 1927. Feast day, 19 Aug.

His Acta, of uncertain date, mainly recording miracles, pr., with introd., together with the proper of the Mass for his feast, in *AASS*, Aug. 3 (1737), pp. 762–77. A. Feulner, *Peter Vischers Sebaldusgrab in Nürnberg* (Munich, 1924). A. Borst, 'Die Sebaldslegenden in der mittelalterlichen Geschichte Nürnbergs', *Jahrbuch für fränkische Landesforschung*, 26 (1966 [1967]), pp. 19–178. A. Bauch, 'Der heilige Sebald', in G. Schwaiger (ed.), *Bavaria Sancta*, 3 (Regensburg, 1973), pp. 156–69. S. Sprusansky and others, *Der heilige Sebald, seine Kirche und seine Stadt: Ausstellung des Landeskirchlichen Archivs im Stadtmuseum Nürnberg Fembohaus 24. August–28. Oktober 1979* (Nürnberg [1979]). K. Kunze in *Bibliotheca Sanctorum*, 11 (Rome, 1968), cols. 754–67, with extensive refs.

Se-Baptists (Lat. *se baptizare*, 'to baptize oneself'). In the 17th cent. a name occasionally given to the followers of John *Smyth (the 'Se-Baptist', q.v.), who after baptizing himself established a church at Amsterdam in 1609.

Sebaste, the Forty Martyrs of. Forty Christian soldiers of the '*Thundering Legion' who were martyred at Sebaste in Lesser Armenia during the Licinian persecution (*c.*320) by being left naked on the ice of a frozen pond, with baths of hot water on the banks as a temptation to apostatize. The place of one who gave way was taken by a heathen soldier of the guard, who was immediately converted. Their martyrdom is narrated by St *Basil of Caesarea and St *Gregory of Nyssa and in works attributed to St *Ephraem Syrus; and their ashes, which were recovered by the Empress *Pulcheria, were very greatly venerated in the E. Feast day in the E., 9 Mar.; in the W., formerly 10 Mar.

Besides the descriptions in Basil, *Hom.* 19 ('In sanctos quadraginta Martyres'; J. P. Migne, *PG* 31. 507–26), Greg. Nyss., 'In Laudem SS. Quadraginta Martyrum' (J. P. Migne, *PG* 46. 749–88), the 'Encomium in Sanctos Quadraginta Martyres' attributed to Ephraem (*Opera omnia*, 2 (Rome, 1743), pp. 341–56) and the hymns on the 40 martyrs attributed to him (*Hymni et Sermones*, ed. T. J. Lamy, 3 (Mechlin, 1889), cols. 937–58), there survive an ancient Gk. *Passio* (not contemporary; ed. O. von Gebhardt, *Acta Martyrum Selecta*, Berlin, 1902, pp. 171–81) and a *Testamentum* (διαθήκη; Gk. and Old Slavonic; ed. N. Bonwetsch, *Das Testament der vierzig Märtyrer*, 1897); the 'Testament' is repr., with Eng. tr., by H. Musurillo, *The Acts of the Christian Martyrs* (Oxford, 1972), pp. 354–61. M. [E.] Mullett and A. [M.] Wilson (eds.), *The Forty Martyrs of Sebasteia* (Belfast Byzantine Texts and Translations, 2; 2 vols., 1997), incl., as vol. 2, Eng. tr. of the primary texts. P. F. de' Cavalieri, 'I quaranta martiri di Sebastia', in *Note agiografiche*, 7 (ST 49; 1928), pp. 155–84 (retracting his earlier views).

Sebastian, St, Roman martyr who is believed to have suffered death during the *Diocletianic Persecution. He is mentioned by the *Chronographer of 354 and in the *Hieronymian Martyrology, and his remains probably gave the name to the Basilica San Sebastiano on the *Appian Way. Acc. to later legend, he was sentenced by the Emp. Diocletian to be shot by archers (hence the representations of him in late medieval and renaissance art as a young man transfixed by arrows), but through the attentions of a widow, named Irene, he recovered from this ordeal and unexpectedly presented himself before the Emperor, who caused him to be clubbed to death. Feast day, 20 Jan.

Gk. text of Martyrium in J. P. Migne, *PG* 116. 793–816. *AASS*, Jan. 2 (1643), pp. 257–96. B. Pesci, OFM, 'Il culto di san Sebastiano a Roma nell'antichità e nel medioevo', *Antonianum*, 20 (1945), pp. 177–200. On the Basilica, A. Ferrua, SJ, *S. Sebastiano fuori le mura e la sua catacomba* (Le Chiese di Roma illustrate, 99; 1968), and R. Krautheimer and S. Corbett in R. Krautheimer and others, *Corpus Basilicarum Christianarum Romae*, 4 (Rome, 1970), pp. 99–147, with extensive bibl. [in Eng.]. A. Amore in *L.Th.K.* (2nd edn.), 9 (1964), cols. 557 f.; G. D. Gordini and P. Cannata in *Bibliotheca Sanctorum*, 11 (Rome, 1968), cols. 776–801, both s.v.

Secker, Thomas (1693–1768), Abp. of *Canterbury. He qualifed in medicine at *Leiden, but, having been won over from Dissent to the C of E, he was passed with celerity through Exeter College, Oxford, and deacon's orders, and was ordained priest in 1723. Standing in high favour with Queen Caroline, he was made rector of St James's, *Westminster, in 1733, and Bp. of Bristol in addition in 1735. In 1737 he became Bp. of *Oxford, in 1750 Dean of *St Paul's, and from 1758 till his death was Abp. of Canterbury. Secker was among the better prelates of his age. Though he disliked the enthusiasm of the *Methodists, he admired their piety, and he favoured the dispatch of bishops to the American colonies. He stood for tolerance and good sense in general, and thoroughly eschewed the theology of B. *Hoadly. He published a large number of his sermons, which though of no outstanding merit reflect his sober and judicious outlook.

Best edn. of Secker's *Works* (6 vols., London, 1811), with Life by B. *Porteus (orig. pub. 1770), repr. in vol. 1, pp. i–lxiv. *Articles of Enquiry Addressed to the Clergy of the Diocese of Oxford at the Primary Visitation of Dr. Thomas Secker, 1738*, ed. H. A. Lloyd Jukes (Oxfordshire Record Society, 38; 1957). *Correspondence*, ed. A. P. Jenkins (ibid. 57; 1991). His autobiog., written in the last

years of his life, was first ed. by J. S. Macauley and R. W. Greaves (Lawrence, Kan., 1988). N. Sykes, *From Sheldon to Secker* (Ford Lectures, 1958; Cambridge, 1959), esp. pp. 216–23. J. R. Guy, 'Archbishop Secker as a Physician', in W. J. Sheils (ed.), *The Church and Healing* (Studies in Church History, 19; Oxford, 1982), pp. 127–35. J. H. Overton in *DNB* 51 (1897), pp. 170–3.

SECM. See ROYAL SCHOOL OF CHURCH MUSIC.

Second Adam. A title of Christ, the new Head of redeemed humanity, as contrasted with the 'first Adam', the original member and type of fallen man. The conception goes back to St *Paul (Rom. 5: 14, 1 Cor. 15: 45), whose expression, however, is not the 'second' but the 'last Adam' (ὁ ἔσχατος Ἀδάμ).

Second Coming. See PAROUSIA.

Secret (Lat. *Oratio secreta*). The name long given to a prayer to which the 1970 Roman Missal restores the earlier designation 'Oratio super oblata'. It is said or sung by the celebrant at Mass after the offering of the bread and wine. Until 1964 it was customarily said silently, a practice first recorded in France in the middle of the 8th cent.; it is prob. from this circumstance that the name derived. The prayer varies with the *Proper. It can be traced back to the *Gelasian Sacramentaries.

Secrétan, Charles (1815–95), Swiss Protestant philosopher and theologian. A native of Lausanne, he studied at Munich under F. W. J. *Schelling and Franz Baader (1765–1841), under whose joint influence he was led to a speculative and mystical view of religion. He held professorships at Lausanne (1839–45; there he lost his post in the latter year for political reasons), Neuchâtel (1850–66), and again at Lausanne (from 1866). With his older contemporary, A. R. *Vinet (1797–1847), he was one of the leaders of liberal Swiss Protestant thought in the 19th cent. As his outlook matured he increasingly emphasized, under I. *Kant's influence, the moral significance of faith and the importance of freedom. Among his works were *Philosophie de la liberté* (2 vols., 1849; later edns., much altered, 1866, 1879), *La Raison et le christianisme* (1863), *La Civilisation et la croyance* (1887), and *Essais de philosophie et de littérature* (1896; posthumous).

L. Secrétan, *Charles Secrétan: Sa vie et ses œuvres* (1911). F. Pillon, *La Philosophie de Charles Secrétan* (1898). U. Perone, *La filosofia della libertà in Charles Secrétan* (Memorie della Accademia delle Scienze di Torino, serie 4, no. 16; 1968). E. Plasshoff-Lejeune in *PRE* (3rd edn.), 18 (1896), pp. 114–18.

Secrets of Enoch, Book of the. One of the names sometimes given to 2 Enoch. See ENOCH, BOOKS OF.

sectary. The term was applied in the 17th and 18th cents. esp. to Protestant Nonconformists in England. Occasionally it is used in modern writers of those whose zeal for their own religious body is considered excessive.

secular arm. In *canon law, a term used to describe the state or any lay power when intervening in ecclesiastical cases. This intervention was generally of two kinds, (1) unsought, (2) sought, by the Church. (1) Resort was often made by individuals to the lay authorities to interfere with or hinder the process of ecclesiastical jurisdiction. It was frequently invoked as an appeal *tamquam ab abusu*, i.e. an appeal to the secular arm to see that justice was done, on the grounds that the ecclesiastical authorities had been guilty of a miscarriage of justice. Until recently, such action was punished in the RC Church by excommunication. (2) The Church did not feel justified in imposing in her own tribunals penalties which involved mutilation or death, but the Church courts had to deal with some cases, chiefly those of heresy, in which it was felt that sterner punishments were needed than they could impose. The assistance of the secular arm was therefore sought and, after trial by an ecclesiastical judge, the condemned prisoner was handed over to the secular authorities for punishment. In the Middle Ages this course of action, which was common, was a fruitful source of dispute between the two powers as to the proper method of procedure, and in particular as to whether there should be a second trial in a secular court.

For the action of the secular arm in the trial and punishment of clerks see *Benefit of Clergy.

R. Naz in *DDC* 2 (1937), cols. 980 f., s.v. 'Bras séculier (Appel au)'; R. Laprat, ibid., cols. 981–1060, s.v. 'Bras séculier (Livraison au)'. See also works cited under INQUISITION.

secular clergy. The term, which seems to have been first used in the 12th cent., is used of priests living in the world, to distinguish them from the 'regular clergy', i.e. members of religious orders, who live acc. to a rule. Secular priests are bound by no vows, may possess property, and owe canonical obedience to their bishops. Acc. to RC canon law those of the Latin Church are normally bound to *celibacy.

Secular Institute. See INSTITUTES OF CONSECRATED LIFE.

secularism. The term, which was first used *c.*1850 by G. J. Holyoake (1817–1906), denotes a system which seeks to interpret and order life on principles taken solely from this world, without recourse to belief in God and a future life. Holyoake's ideas were later developed into extreme atheism by being cast into a more logical form by C. *Bradlaugh. Apart from its negative attitude to Christianity and religion in general, secularism advocated on the positive side social progress and the amelioration of material conditions for the working classes. The term is now widely used in a more general sense for the modern tendency to ignore, if not to deny, the principles of supernatural religion in the interpretation of the world and existence.

sede vacante (Lat., 'the see being vacant'). The period during which a diocese is without its bishop. In the C of E during such vacancy the archbishop of the province is *guardian of the spiritualities of the diocese, which are administered under his commission. The temporalities are in the custody of the sovereign. During a vacancy in the Papal See, the administration of the RC Church is in the hands of the College of Cardinals headed by the 'Cardinale Camerlengo', the Chamberlain at the Vatican, and the Major Penitentiary.

sedia gestatoria. The portable throne on which until recently the Pope used to be carried by 12 footmen (*palafrenieri*), dressed in red uniforms, on certain prescribed solemn occasions.

sedilia (Lat., 'seats'). The seats, usually three in number, for the celebrant, deacon, and subdeacon, on the south side of the chancel. They were introduced in England about the middle of the 12th cent., and used during those parts of the service at which it was customary for the ministers to sit. In medieval England they were usually stone benches built into a niche in the wall, often richly carved and surmounted by arches or canopies. On the Continent and in modern England wooden seats (*scamna*) have been more common. Since 1964 sedilia have largely been replaced by a chair for the celebrant placed in the centre of the sanctuary.

F. Bond, *The Chancel of English Churches* (1916), pp. 176–203.

Sedulius (5th cent.), Christian poet. Little is known of his life. In his early years he devoted himself to pagan literature. Later (perhaps after conversion to Christianity), he was ordained priest and lived in some kind of religious community. His great poem, the *Paschale Carmen*, after an introductory book drawing on the OT, in four books traces the life of Christ from His virginal conception to His Resurrection and Ascension, at all points emphasizing the miraculous. He also wrote a prose version, the *Opus Paschale*. Of his two surviving hymns, one provides two hymns in the Roman Divine *Office (known also in English versions, 'From east to west, from shore to shore' and 'Why, impious Herod shouldst thou fear', *EH* 18 and 38).

Crit. edn. of his works by J. Huemer (CSEL 10; 1885). Eng. tr. of the *Paschale Carmen* (into rhyming couplets) by G. Sigerson (Dublin and London, 1922). T. Mayr, OSB, *Studien zu dem Paschale Carmen des christlichen Dichters Sedulius* (Diss., Augsburg, 1916). F. Corsaro, *Sedulio Poeta* (Pubblicazioni dell'Istituto Universitario di Magistero di Catania, Serie Letteraria, 2; 1956). C. P. E. Springer, *The Gospel as Epic in Late Antiquity: The Paschale carmen of Sedulius* (Supplements to *VC*, 2; 1988). *CPL* (3rd edn., 1995), pp. 474 f. (nos. 1447–54). Altaner and Stuiber (1978), pp. 411 and 636. W. Lock in *DCB* 4 (1887), pp. 598–600, s.v. 'Sedulius (1)'.

Sedulius Scottus (9th cent.), poet, teacher, and biblical critic. Born and educated in Ireland, Sedulius typifies the wandering Irish scholar in Carolingian Europe. Arriving in France between 840 and 851, he was active in Liège and other N. cities as he followed the itinerant royal court. His occasional poems (many of high quality and metrically skilled) show the range of his royal and clerical patrons. The *De Rectoribus Christianis* (written between 855 and 859) may arise from a formal position as tutor to the future King Lothair II; certainly the extensive grammatical commentaries testify to his work as a teacher. His *Collectaneum* is further proof of wide reading in sacred and secular texts, both ancient and modern. He commented on Mt. and the Pauline Epistles, drawing for the latter on the genuine commentary of *Pelagius; and he may have provided the Latin gloss to a Greek Psalter now in Basle.

J. P. Migne, *PL* 103. 9–352, prints the *De Rectoribus Christianis*, the comm. on the Pauline Epistles and the prolegomena to the Synoptic Gospels (cf. F. Stegmüller, cited below, nos. 7597–605) and to St *Jerome's Prefaces. Crit. edns. of the poems by I. Meyers (CCCM 117; 1991); of *De Rectoribus Christianis* by S. Hellmann, *Sedulius Scottus* (Quellen und Untersuchungen zur lateinischen Philologie des Mittelalters, 1, Heft 1; 1906), pp. 19–91; of comm. on Donatus Major and Minor, Priscian, *Institutiones*, 1. 1–3. 1 (fragmentary) and Eutyches, by B. Löfstedt, *Grammatici Hibernici Carolini Aevi*, 3 (CCCM 40B–C; 1977); of *Collectaneum* by D. Simpson (ibid. 67; 1988, with suppl. by F. Dolbeau, 1990); of a perhaps authentic letter on the Psalter by E. Duemmler in *MGH*, Epistolae, 6 (1925), pp. 201–5; of comm. on Eph. by H. J. Frede, *Pelagius, Der irische Paulustext, Sedulius Scottus* (Vetus Latina. Die Reste der Altlateinischen Bibel. Aus der Geschichte der lateinischen Bibel, 3; 1961), pp. 107–55, and of comm. on Mt. by B. Löfstedt (ibid. 14 and 19; 1989–91). Facsimile of Graeco-Latin Psalter (Codex Basiliensis A. VII. 3), ed. L. Bieler (Umbrae Codicum Occidentalium, 5; Amsterdam, 1960). Six of his poems are pr., with Eng. tr., by P. [J.] Godman, *Poetry of the Carolingian Renaissance* (1985), pp. 282–301. J. Gross, 'Sedulius Scottus, ein verspäteter Semi-Pelagianer', *ZKG* 68 (1957), pp. 322–32. R. Düchtung, *Sedulius Scottus: Seine Dichtungen* (Munich, 1968). P. [J.] Godman, *Poets and Emperors: Frankish Politics and Carolingian Poetry* (Oxford, 1987), pp. 155–70. Raby (1953), pp. 193–6; F. J. E. Raby, *A History of Secular Latin Poetry in the Middle Ages*, 1 (2nd edn., Oxford, 1957), pp. 242–7. Manitius, 1, pp. 315–23; F. Stegmüller, *Repertorium Biblicum Medii Aevi*, 5 (Madrid, 1955), pp. 202–9 (nos. 7595–621); F. Brunhölzl, *Geschichte der lateinischen Literatur des Mittelalters* (Munich, 1975), pp. 449–66 and 568; W. Berschin, *Griechisch-Lateinisches Mittelalter* (Berne, 1980), pp. 172 f. J. F. Kenney, *The Sources for the Early History of Ireland*, 1 (Records of Civilization, 1929), pp. 553–69; M. Lapidge and R. Sharpe, *A Bibliography of Celtic-Latin Literature 400–1200* (Dublin, 1985), pp. 177–80 (nos. 672–86).

see. Properly, the official 'seat' (*sedes*) or 'throne' (*cathedra*) of a *bishop. This seat, which is the earliest of the bishop's insignia, normally stands in the *cathedral of the diocese; hence the town or place where the cathedral is located is also itself known as the bishop's see. See also HOLY SEE.

Seekers. A loose grouping of defectors from the C of E and esp. from the *Puritan congregations in early 17th-cent. England. They believed that no true Church had existed since the spirit of *Antichrist became uppermost in the Church, and that God would in His own time ordain new Apostles or Prophets to found a new Church. They did not think it right to hasten on this process, with the result that they were vehemently opposed by the *Anabaptists. In their quietistic outlook they had many affinities with the *Quakers. Bartholomew Legate (*c*.1575–1612), one of their preachers, was burnt at Smithfield for heresy. During the Commonwealth period the word was used very loosely to describe people dissatisfied with the existing religious sects. Many of these Seekers were absorbed into the Society of *Friends.

R. M. *Jones, *Studies in Mystical Religion* (1909), pp. 452–67; W. C. Braithwaite, *The Beginnings of Quakerism* (1912), esp. pp. 25–7, 58–65, and 78–97. J. F. McGregor, 'Seekers and Ranters', in id. and B. Reay (eds.), *Radical Religion in the English Revolution* (Oxford, 1984), pp. 121–39, esp. pp. 121–9. R. M. Jones in *HERE* 11 (1920), pp. 350 f., s.v., with refs. See also bibl. to FRIENDS, SOCIETY OF.

Seeley, John Robert (1834–95), historian. The son of R. B. Seeley, an author and publisher (1798–1886), J. R. Seeley was educated at Christ's College, Cambridge, and in 1863 appointed professor of Latin at University College,

London. His book **Ecce Homo* (1865; q.v.) at once made him famous. Later he supplemented this by an essay, *Natural Religion* (1882), which was designed to reconcile the claims of Christianity with those of natural science, though he denied that the supernatural was an integral part of the Christian faith. In 1869 he was appointed professor of modern history at Cambridge, where he exercised a stimulating influence as a teacher. His later writings were on purely historical subjects, among them his widely read *Expansion of England* (1883). He was knighted in 1894.

Memoir by G. W. Prothero prefixed to Seeley's *The Growth of British Policy*, 1 (1895), pp. vii–xxii. D. Wormell, *Sir John Seeley and the Uses of History* (Cambridge, 1980). G. W. Prothero in *DNB* 51 (1897), pp. 190–3, s.v.

Segneri, Paolo (1624–94), Italian *Jesuit preacher. Having entered the Society of Jesus in 1637, he was ordained priest in 1653. He is reckoned the greatest pulpit orator of Italy after St *Bernardino of Siena and *Savonarola. Though his sermons show occasional lapses in taste, he was very successful in uniting a vigorous and ordered exposition of his argument with a powerful emotional appeal. His most famous collection of sermons is his *Quaresimale* (i.e. those delivered in *Lent), first published at Florence in 1679. In the matter of moral theology he opposed both *Probabiliorist and *Quietist doctrines.

Early collected edns. of his works in 2 vols., Parma, 1700–1701; 4 vols., Venice, 1712; and 3 vols., Parma, 1714; several later edns. *Lettere inedite*, ed. G. Boero (Naples, 1848); further *Lettere inedite di P. Segneri al granduca Cosimo Terzo* [ed. S. Giamini] (Florence, 1857). P. T. Venturi, SJ (ed.), 'Lettere inedite di Paolo Segneri di Cosimo III e di Giuseppe Agnelli intorno la condanna dell'opera segneriana la "Concordia"', *Archivio storico italiano*, 5th ser. 31 (1903), pp. 127–65. The brief Life by G. Massei, SJ (Venice, 1701), is also pr. in the edns. of his works; Eng. tr. ed. F. W. *Faber, Cong. Orat., London, 1851. G. Minozzi, *Paolo Segneri* (Il pensiero cristiano, 1; 2 vols., Amatrice, 1949). V. Socini, *Il p. Paolo Segneri (1624–1694) nella storia farnese a Parma con lettere e documenti inediti* (Parma, 1924). A. Marzot, *Un classico della controriforma, Paolo Segneri* (Saggi di letteratura ital. 10; Palermo, 1950). Sommervogel, 7 (1896), cols. 1050–89, and 9 (1900), col. 849; Polgár, 3 (1990), pp. 191–3. C. Testore, SJ, in *EC* 11 (1953), cols. 239–41, s.v.; G. Mellinato, SJ, in *Dict. Sp.* 14 (1990), cols. 519–22, s.v.

Séguier, Pierre (1588–1672), Chancellor of France from 1635 (with some interruptions) until his death. A keen patron of literature, he possessed one of the finest private collections of (esp. Greek) MSS then in existence. Séguier's great-grandson, H. C. du Cambout de Coislin, Bp. of Metz from 1697 to 1732, into whose hands his library had passed, commissioned the *Maurist scholar, B. de *Montfaucon, to make a catalogue of it, which he issued in 1715 as *Bibliotheca Coisliniana olim Segueriana*. In 1735 the MSS came into the possession of the abbey of *St-Germain-des-Prés; they passed to the Bibliothèque Nationale during the winter of 1794–5.

Lettres et mémoires adressés au Chancelier Séguier (1633–1649), ed. R. Mousnier (Publications de la Faculté des Lettres et Sciences Humaines de Paris, Série 'Textes et Documents', 6–7; 1964). Modern catalogue of the MSS by R. Devreesse, *Bibliothèque Nationale: Département des Manuscrits. Catalogue des Manuscrits grecs, 2. Le Fonds Coislin* (1945). Life by R. Kerviler (Paris, 1874).

Seises, Dance of the. The religious dance performed before the Blessed Sacrament in Seville Cathedral in the course of the celebrations of *Corpus Christi and the *Immaculate Conception of the BVM. It is executed by a group of boys, of whom there were formerly (as their name implies; *seis* = 'six') only six, but are now ten.

Selborne, First Earl of. See PALMER, ROUNDELL.

Selden, John (1584–1654), author of *The History of Tithes*. Educated at Hart Hall, Oxford, he was admitted to the bar at the Inner Temple in 1612. Although on several occasions he gave professional opinions to both Houses of Parliament (e.g., in his *Privileges of the Baronage of England* (1642)) as well as to private individuals, he never made the practice of law more than incidental to his life. He sat in several parliaments, being MP for Oxford University in the Long Parliament. A moderate *Puritan, he became in 1643 a member of the *Westminster Assembly of Divines during whose deliberations he sometimes confounded other members by referring them to the Hebrew and Greek texts of the Bible. His learning was prodigious. In his *History of Tithes* (1618) he upheld their legal, but denied their Divine, right, and in consequence the book was suppressed and its author forbidden to reply to any of his antagonists. Among his other historico-legal writings are *Jani Anglorum Facies Altera* (1610), *The Duello* (1610; a history of trial by combat), *Mare Clausum* (1635, but for the most part written much earlier; it argued, against H. *Grotius's *Mare Liberum* (1609), that the sea was capable of sovereignty), and *Uxor Ebraica* (1646; on Jewish marriage law). Selden was also one of the foremost oriental scholars of his day and the author of *De Diis Syris* (1617). The greater part of his valuable collection of books passed to the *Bodleian Library. His *Table Talk* (1689), the utterances of his last twenty years which show a buoyant anticlericalism, was compiled by his amanuensis, Richard Milward.

Opera Omnia, ed. D. *Wilkins (3 vols. bound in 6, London, 1726), with Life by id. in vol. 1, pt. 1, pp. i–lvi. Modern edn. of his *Table Talk* by F. Pollock (ibid, 1927), with account of his life by E. Fry (repr. from *DNB* 51 (1897), pp. 212–24, s.v.), pp. 153–85, and introd., pp. vii–xxiv. Eng. tr. of *Uxor Ebraica*, with comm., by J. R. Ziskind (Leiden, 1991). J. Aikin, *The Lives of John Selden, Esq., and Archbishop Usher* (1812), pp. 1–199. G. W. Johnson, *Memoirs of John Selden and Notices of the Political Contest during his Time* (1835). D. S. Berkowitz, *John Selden's Formative Years* (Washington, DC, and London [1988]). H. D. Hazeltine, 'Selden as Legal Historian: A Comment in Criticism and Appreciation', in *Festschrift Heinrich Brunner zum siebzigsten Geburtstag dargebracht von Schülern und Verehrern* (Weimar, 1910), pp. 579–630. A. W. Ward, 'Selden's Table Talk', in A. W. Ward and A. R. Waller (eds.), *The Cambridge History of English Literature*, 8 (1912), pp. 321–7. I. Herzog, 'John Selden and Jewish Law', *Journal of Comparative Legislation*, 3rd ser. 13 (1931), pp. 236–45. D. M. Barratt, 'The Library of John Selden and its later History', *Bodleian Record*, 3 (1951), pp. 128–42, 208–13, and 256–74. E. [G. M.] Fletcher, *John Selden 1584–1654* (Selden Society Lecture, 1969). M. J. Mulder, 'Von Selden bis Schaeffer: Die Erforschung der kanaanäischen Götterwelt', *Ugarit-Forschungen*, 11 (1979), pp. 655–71, esp. pp. 655–8.

Seleucia, Synod of. See ARIMINUM AND SELEUCIA, SYNODS OF.

Sellon, Priscilla Lydia (1821–76), a restorer of the religious life in the C of E. She was the daughter of W. R. B. Sellon, Commander RN. When about to leave England for her health on New Year's Day, 1848, she was led to change her plans at the last moment by a public appeal of H. *Phillpotts, Bp. of Exeter, for work among the degraded and destitute of Plymouth, Devonport, and Stonehouse. Here she was gradually joined by others, who, with the help of E. B. *Pusey, created a community life (the 'Devonport Sisters of Mercy'), set up schools and orphanages and heroically tended the sick in the cholera epidemic of 1848. Their conventual mode of life soon provoked local opposition, but the support of Phillpotts (who, however, withdrew from the office of 'visitor' in 1852) enabled them to continue. In 1856 Miss Sellon united her community with the Sisters of the Holy Cross at Osnaburgh Street, Regent's Park, and assumed the title of Abbess of the combined sisterhood of the 'Society of the Most Holy Trinity' (present headquarters at Ascot Priory, Berks). In her last years Miss Sellon was severely paralysed. In 1867 she visited Honolulu, where she founded St Andrew's Priory.

T. J. Williams, *Priscilla Lydia Sellon* (1950; rev. edn., 1965); id. and A. W. Campbell, *The Park Village Sisterhood* (1965), *passim*. P. F. Anson, *The Call of the Cloister* (1955; 2nd edn., rev. by A. W. Campbell, 1958), pp. 259–79. S. Gill, 'The Power of Christian Ladyhood: Priscilla Lydia Sellon and the Creation of Anglican Sisterhoods', in S. Mews (ed.), *Modern Religious Rebels: Presented to John Kent* (1993), pp. 144–65.

Selwyn, George Augustus (1809–78), first Bp. of *New Zealand. Educated at Eton and St John's College, Cambridge, he was ordained deacon in 1833 and made missionary Bishop of New Zealand in 1841. He was a *Tractarian in his convictions, whose formal protest against a clause in the civil Letter Patent professing to 'give him power to ordain' signalled the beginnings of a less Erastian conception of the Colonial Episcopate. He had a very marked effect on the future of the New Zealand Church, for settling the constitution of which he was himself largely responsible. Returning to England in 1867, he was appointed in 1868 to the see of *Lichfield. In the American BCP (1979), feast day, 11 April.

His son, **John Richardson Selwyn** (1844–98), was Bp. of Melanesia (1877–89) and master of Selwyn College, Cambridge (1890–98), which had been founded in memory of his father in 1881.

Lives by H. W. Tucker (2 vols., London, 1879), G. H. Curteis (ibid., 1889), L. Creighton (ibid., 1923) and J. H. Evans (ibid., 1964). W. E. Limbrick (ed.), *Bishop Selwyn in New Zealand, 1841–68* (New Zealand Academic Monographs, General Series, 1; Palmerston North [1983]). R. Bayne in *DNB* 51 (1897), pp. 232 f.; R. H. Codrington in *DECH*, pp. 550 f.
On J. R. Selwyn, Life by F. D. How (London, 1899). R. Bayne in *DNB*, Suppl. 3 (1901), pp. 338 f.

Semiarianism. The name given to the teaching of the theologians who gathered round *Basil of Ancyra from c.356 onwards and upheld a doctrine of Christ's Sonship intermediate between that of orthodoxy and *Arianism. Other members of the group were *Macedonius of Constantinople, *George of Laodicea, *Eustathius of Sebaste, and Eleusius of Cyzicus. Over against ὁμοούσιος, they took as their watchword ὁμοιούσιος; but the whole tendency of the group was towards orthodoxy. They were sympathetically treated by St *Athanasius at the Alexandrine Council of 362, and by their theological influence on the '*Cappadocian Fathers' contributed largely to the re-affirmation of orthodoxy at the Council of *Constantinople in 381.

The chief work is J. Gummerus, *Die homöusianische Partei bis zum Tode des Konstantius: Ein Beitrag zur Geschichte des arianischen Streites in den Jahren 356–61* (1900). Much useful material also in H. M. Gwatkin, *Studies of Arianism* (2nd edn., 1900). M. Simonetti, *Studi sull'arianesimo* (Verba Seniorum, NS 5 [1965]), pp. 160–86 ('Sulla dottrina dei Semiariani'). G. Rasneur, 'L'Homoiousianisme dans ses rapports avec l'orthodoxie', *RHE* 4 (1903), pp. 189–206, 411–31. F. J. Foakes Jackson in *HERE* 11 (1920), pp. 374–6, s.v.; É. Amann in *DTC* 14 (pt. 2; 1941), cols. 1790–6, s.v. 'Semi-Ariens'. See also bibl. to ARIANISM.

Semi-Doubles. Feasts in the RC Calendar which ranked below *Doubles and above *Simple Feasts. By a decree of the Sacred Congregation of *Rites dated 23 Mar. 1955, the rank of Semi-Double was abolished, feasts which had ranked hitherto as such being reduced to Simples.

seminary. In ecclesiastical usage, a school or college devoted to the training of the clergy, esp. used of such institutions in the RC Church. The Council of *Trent ordered the establishment of a seminary in every diocese and this remained roughly the rule in the RC Church. The rules concerning seminaries were revised by the Second *Vatican Council's decree on priestly formation, 'Optatam totius' (28 Oct. 1965) whose principles underlie the regulations on seminaries and the formation of clerics contained in *CIC* (1983), cans. 232–64. This provides for minor and major seminaries. The former are to assist a young man in his spiritual formation while he engages in the same course of arts and sciences as other young men. The purpose of the major seminaries is to form men spiritually, academically, and pastorally for the priesthood.

J. A. O'Donohoe, *Tridentine Seminary Legislation: Its Sources and its Formation* (Bibliotheca Ephemeridum Theologicarum Lovaniensium, 9; 1957). P. L. Golden, CM, in J. A. Coriden, T. J. Green, and D. E. Heintschel (eds.), *The Code of Canon Law: A Text and Commentary* (1985), pp. 174–90. J. A. O'Donohoe in *NCE* 13 (1967), pp. 72–5, s.v.

Semipelagianism. The name given to doctrines on human nature upheld in the 5th cent. by a group of theologians who, while not denying the necessity of *grace for salvation, maintained that the first steps towards the Christian life were ordinarily taken by the human will and that grace supervened only later. Their position was roughly midway between the radically opposed doctrines of St *Augustine and *Pelagius.

These teachings were first given expression *c*.425 by representatives of the monastic movement in S. Gaul, the most prominent of whom was J. *Cassian. They were developed mainly in opposition to St Augustine's later writings, which taught an extreme form of *predestination, infallible perseverance, and a 'numerus clausus' of the elect. Augustine's opinions were championed in Gaul by St *Prosper of Aquitaine, whose writings constitute our chief source of information on the early stages of the controversy; they include a treatise 'Contra Collatorem' (directed against Cassian) and another entitled 'Responsiones ad Capitula Objectionum Vincentiarum'

(replying to a work almost certainly by *Vincent of Lérins). Although the initial dispute seems to have died down by *c*.435, Semipelagianism continued to be the dominant teaching on grace in Gaul for several generations. The Gallic position was set out in detail in the 'De Gratia' of *Faustus of Riez, a work composed *c*.472 to combat predestinarianism. In the early 520s Faustus' views were denounced as heretical both at *Constantinople and at Rome by a group of Scythian monks led by John Maxentius, who also gained the support of St *Fulgentius of Ruspe. Shortly afterwards a series of *capitula* condemning key Semipelagian (as well as Pelagian) doctrines was promulgated by a Council convened at *Orange in 529 by St *Caesarius of Arles. From then onwards the Augustinian teaching on grace was generally accepted in orthodox W. theology.

The term 'Semipelagian' appears to have been coined by Dominican opponents of the Jesuit L. *Molina during the controversy *De Auxiliis*, and quickly to have been applied to Cassian and those who followed him. It is used cautiously by modern scholars who have come to recognize that these theologians owed little or nothing to Pelagius.

For an extended treatment, see the classic study of H. *Noris, *Historia Pelagiana* (Padua, 1673), pp. 158–338. F. Wörter, *Beiträge zur Dogmengeschichte des Semipelagianismus* ('1898' [1897]); id., *Zur Dogmengeschichte des Semipelagianismus* (Kirchengeschichtliche Studien, 5, Heft 2; 1899). M. Jacquin, OP, 'A quelle date apparaît le terme "Semipélagien"?', *RSPT* 1 (1907), pp. 506–8. J. Chéné, 'Le semipélagianisme du Midi de la Gaule d'après les lettres de Prosper d'Aquitaine et de Hilaire à saint Augustin', *Rech. S.R.* 43 (1955), pp. 321–41; C. Tibiletti, 'Rassegni de studi e testi sui "semipelagiani"', *Augustinianum*, 25 (1985), pp. 507–22, and other arts. by this author; R. A. Markus, 'The Legacy of Pelagius: Orthodoxy, Heresy and Conciliation', in R. [D.] Williams (ed.), *The Making of Orthodoxy: Essays in Honour of Henry Chadwick* (Cambridge, 1989), pp. 214–34. F. A. *Loofs in *PRE* (3rd edn.), 18 (1906), pp. 192–203, s.v. 'Semipelagianismus'; É. Amann in *DTC* 14 (pt. 2; 1941), cols. 1796–1850, s.v. 'Semi-Pélagiens'. See also bibl. to ORANGE, COUNCILS OF, and to the Semipelagians mentioned in the text.

Semi-Quietism. A name sometimes applied to the doctrines of Abp. *Fénelon and other spiritual writers who, though not sufficiently unorthodox to come under the censures attaching to *Quietism and quite free from its anti-ecclesiastical and anti-moral elements, manifest certain quietist tendencies.

Semler, Johann Salomo (1725–91), *Lutheran theologian and biblical critic. Born at Saalfeld in Thuringia, he studied at Halle, where he later became Professor of Theology (1753–91). He soon rejected the *Pietism of his youth for a rationalistic position which he termed 'liberalis theologia'. One of the first German theologians to apply the critico-historical method to the study of the biblical *canon and text, he reached many novel, and often unorthodox, conclusions, at some points anticipating F. C. *Baur. He held, however, that Christian ministers should be required to make external profession of all traditional doctrine. In this matter, finding himself at variance with G. E. *Lessing in the controversy over the *Wolfenbüttel Fragments, he directed against Lessing his *Beantwortung der Fragmente eines Ungenannten* (1779). In his last years he interested himself in scientific, alchemistic, and theosophical studies. His principal treatises are *Historiae Ecclesiasticae Selecta Capita* (3 vols., Halle, 1767–9), *Abhandlung von freier Untersuchung des Canon* (4 parts, ibid., 1771–5), *Commentarii Historici de Antiquo Christianorum Statu* (2 vols., ibid., 1771–2), and *Versuch eines fruchtbaren Auszugs der Kirchengeschichte* (3 vols., ibid., 1773–8).

Autobiog., 2 vols., Halle, 1781–2, with list of his writings. Crit. edn. of pt. 1 of his *Abhandlung von freier Untersuchungen des Canons* by H. Scheible (Texte zur Kirchen- und Theologiegeschichte, 5; 1967). H. Hoffmann, *Die Theologie Semlers* (1905); P. Gastrow, *Johann Salamo Semler in seiner Bedeutung für die Theologie* (1905); L. Zscharnack, *Lessing und Semler: Ein Beitrag zur Entstehungsgeschichte des Rationalismus und der kritischen Theologie* (1905); G. Hornig, *Die Anfänge der historisch-kritischen Theologie: Johann Salomo Semlers Schriftverständnis und seine Stellung zu Luther* (Forschungen zur systematischen Theologie und Religionsphilosophie, 8; Göttingen, 1961). J. C. O'Neill, *The Bible's Authority* (Edinburgh, 1991), pp. 39–53.

Sempringham. In S. Lincolnshire, the mother-house of the Order founded by St *Gilbert of Sempringham (d. 1189; q.v.). Gilbert was in early life the incumbent of the parish.

Seneca, Lucius Annaeus (*c.*4 BC–AD 65), Roman moralist and tragic poet. The son of a rhetorician of Córdoba, prob. of Italian descent, he embarked on a senatorial career at Rome, but was banished by the Emp. Claudius to Corsica (41–9) and then, through the influence of the Empress Agrippina, recalled to become tutor to her son, the future Emp. *Nero. After Nero's accession in 54, Seneca was the chief adviser of state, but he lost favour, retired from public life in 62, and in 65 he was charged with complicity in Piso's conspiracy and forced to take his own life. His brother *Gallio (q.v.) is mentioned in Acts 18: 12.

Seneca was the author of several surviving tragedies, prob. of the *Apocolocyntosis* (a skit on the *apotheosis of the late Emp. Claudius), of essays couched as letters to his friend Lucilius, and of various treatises (some now lost); both the treatises and the letters are mostly concerned with ethics, but some bear on physics, psychology, and logic. Seneca was a professed *Stoic, though he took some ideas from other schools, and his writings are one of the chief sources of our knowledge of Stoicism. Both ancient and modern critics have contrasted their moral austerity with his life as a very rich man and a courtier ready to preserve his influence by compromise. Apart from his letters, perhaps the most notable of his writings are the *De Clementia*, outlining his ideal of the good emperor, and the *De Beneficiis*, which examines in detail our duty to do good to others and to requite benefits received. The Stoic morality which he mediated has often since *Lactantius been compared and contrasted with that of Christianity.

There is also in existence an apocryphal correspondence of 14 letters between Seneca (8 letters) and St *Paul (6 letters). Their commonplace manner and colourless style show that they cannot be the work either of the moralist or of St Paul. They are prob. the same letters as those known to St *Jerome (*De Vir. Ill.* 12), who on the strength of them reckons Seneca a Christian, and to St *Augustine (*Ep.* 153. 14), though some critics have denied the identification and assigned the extant letters to a much later

date. The oldest MSS date from the 9th cent., and the text is transmitted in a corrupt state.

There have been innumerable edns. of Seneca's works, beginning with the *editio princeps* of B. Romerus, Naples, 1475. Modern Lives by R. Waltz (Paris, 1909), C. Marchesi (Messina, 1920; 3rd edn., 1944), and P. Grimal (Paris, 1948). M. T. Griffin, *Seneca: A Philosopher in Politics* (Oxford, 1976). M. Baumgarten, *Lucius Annaeus Seneca und das Christenthum* (1895). E. Albertini, *La Composition dans les ouvrages philosophiques de Sénèque* (1923). W. Trilltzsch, *Seneca im literatischen Urteil der Antike* (2 vols., Amsterdam, 1971). M. Spanneut in *NCE* 13 (1967) pp. 80 f., s.v.; L. D. Reynolds, M. T. Griffin, and E. Fantham in *OCD* (3rd edn., 1996), pp. 96–8, s.v. 'Annaeus Seneca' (2).

Edns. of Seneca's correspondence with St Paul by F. Haase in *Senecae Opera*, Suppl. (Teub., 1902), pp. 74–9, and by C. W. Barlow (Rome, 1938), repr. in J. P. Migne, *PL*, Suppl. 1. 673–8. Eng. tr. in J. K. Elliott, *The Apocryphal New Testament* (Oxford, 1993), pp. 547–53. Ger. tr., with introd. by C. Römer in Schneemelcher, 2 (5th edn.; 1989), pp. 44–50; Eng. tr., 2 [1992], pp. 46–53. A. Momigliano, 'Note sulla leggenda del cristianesimo di Seneca', *Rivista Storica Italiana*, 62 (1950), pp. 325–43, with extensive refs.; repr. in his *Contributo alla storia degli studi classici* (1955), pp. 13–32. On the relations between St Paul and the real Seneca see J. B. *Lightfoot, 'St Paul and Seneca', *Philippians* (1868), pp. 268–331; K. Deissner, *Paulus und Seneca* (Beiträge zur Förderung christlicher Theologie, Bd. 21 (2); 1917); and J. N. Sevenster, *Paul and Seneca* (Supplements to *Novum Testamentum*, 4; 1961).

Sens, Councils of. Of the many provincial Councils held at Sens (e.g. in AD 601(?), 833, 845, 1140, 1225, 1461, 1485), the most renowned is that of 1140 under Abp. Henri le Sanglier, which condemned *Abelard for heresy. Abelard forthwith appealed to Pope Innocent II against its sentence.

On the council of 1140 (formerly dated 1141), Hardouin, 6 (pt. 2), cols. 1219–24; Mansi, 21 (Venice, 1776), cols. 559–70. Hefele and Leclercq, 5 (pt. 1; 1912), pp. 747–90. E. Vacandard, 'Chronologie abélardienne; la date du concile de Sens: 1140', *RQH* 1 (1891), pp. 235–45. C. J. Mews provides useful background in his introd. to Abelard's 'Theologia "Scholarium" ' in the edn. of Abelard's *Opera Theologica*, 3 (CCCM 13; 1987), pp. 277–92. See also other works cited under ABELARD, P., and BERNARD, ST.

Sentences (Lat. *Sententiae*), short reasoned expositions of the principal truths of Christian doctrine. The Lat. word 'sententia' orig. meant any exposition of thought. During the early Middle Ages it came to be used esp. of general impersonal maxims, and then later took on a new technical meaning in relation to exegesis. *Hugh of St-Victor distinguished three elements in the explanation of texts: (1) *littera*, which studied words and their connection with each other; (2) *sensus*, the obvious meaning; and (3) *sententia*, which provided understanding of the meaning underlying the text. Collections of Sentences then became systematized, reasoned compilations of opinions; the most famous of these collections was the 'Sententiarum libri quattuor' of *Peter Lombard, which was the subject of numerous commentaries. By the 13th cent. *sententia* had come to mean an accepted proposition or theological conclusion. See also FLORILEGIUM.

G. Paré, A. Brunet, and P. Tremblay, *La Renaissance du XIIe siècle: Les écoles et l'enseignement* (Publications de l'Institut d'Études Médiévales d'Ottawa, 3; 1933), pp. 240–74.

Separatists. As a title, first applied to the followers of R. *Browne and later to the *Independents (*Congregationalists) and others who separated from the C of E. See also CONGREGATIONALISM, BARROW, H., BROWNE, R., and PENRY, J.

B. R. White, *The English Separatist Tradition from the Marian Martyrs to the Pilgrim Fathers* (Oxford Theological Monographs, 1971); S. Brachlow, *The Communion of Saints: Radical Puritan and Separatist Ecclesiology 1570–1625* (ibid., 1988).

Septuagesima (Lat., 'the seventieth [day before Easter]'). The third Sunday before *Lent and hence the ninth before *Easter. The name, which first occurs in the *Gelasian Sacramentary, seems not very appropriate, as the Sunday indicated is in fact only 64, and not 70, days before Easter; but perhaps it was coined by reckoning back the series 'septuagesima', 'sexagesima', 'quinquagesima', from Quinquagesima Sunday, which is exactly 50 days from Easter. In the RC Church it was suppressed in 1969. Previously in the liturgical cycle it marked a stage towards the Lent fast; purple vestments were worn from that day onwards until *Holy Week and the word 'Alleluia' was not used again in the offices or at Mass until the end of Lent. The name passed into the BCP but has been dropped from some modern Anglican liturgies.

C. Callewaert, 'L'Œuvre liturgique de S. Grégoire. La septua-gésime et l'alléluia', *RHE* 33 (1937), pp. 306–26; G. *Morin, OSB, 'La Part des papes du sixième siècle dans le développement de l'année liturgique', *R. Bén.* 52 (1940), pp. 1–14, pp. 1–8 being relevant; J. Froger, OSB, 'Les Anticipations du jeûne quadragés-imal', *Mélanges de Science religieuse*, 3 (1946), pp. 207–34; A. Chavasse, 'Temps de préparation à la Pâques d'après quelques livres liturgiques romains', *Rech. S.R.* 37 (1950), pp. 125–45, esp. V, 'La "Septantaine" ou Septuagésime', pp. 143–5. H. *Leclercq, OSB, in *DACL* 15 (pt. 1; 1950), cols. 1262–6, s.v.

Septuagint ('LXX'). The most influential of the Greek versions of the Heb. OT. Jewish tradition attributes its origin to the initiative of Ptolemy Philadelphus (285–246 BC), who desired a translated copy of the Hebrew Law for his famous Library at Alexandria (see ARISTEAS, LETTER OF) and engaged 72 translators (hence the title 'Septuagint') for the work. Gradually the story was improved, and Ptolemy's name was connected not only with the Pentateuch, but with all the OT. Internal evidence indicates that the LXX was really the work of a number of translators (in some cases more than one scholar sharing the responsibility for a single Book), that not all of it was translated at Alexandria, and that the work of translation extended over a considerable period. A passage in the preface to the Greek version of Ecclus. suggests that at the time the author of the preface was writing (132 BC) the Greek OT as we now know it was virtually complete.

The LXX differs from the Hebrew Bible both in the order of the biblical Books and in the fact that it includes more Books. The threefold division into the 'Law', the 'Prophets', and the 'Writings' is abandoned, and several other Books, which are not found in the Hebrew, are included. These, known as the '*Apocrypha' in the English Bible, include Wisdom, Ecclesiasticus, Judith, Tobit, and Baruch. Also the text of the LXX differs considerably at many points from the corresponding Hebrew. The original LXX of Job is about one-sixth shorter than the Hebrew; there are several interesting passages in the

LXX of 1 Kings that are not in the Hebrew; and there are considerable differences in order between the Hebrew and the LXX in Jeremiah.

The early Christian Church inherited the LXX, and the NT writers commonly quoted the OT Books from it. In Mt. 1: 23, where the *Immanuel prophecy of Is. 7: 14 is cited in approximately the LXX form, the Greek is particularly relevant since it here renders the Hebrew word *'almah* ('a young woman of marriageable age') by παρθένος ('a virgin'). Commonly, however, the differences between the Hebrew and LXX are only verbal. It must also be noted that in a number of NT passages the Hebrew is followed against the LXX.

In post-NT times, the Christian Fathers down to the later 4th cent. almost all regarded the LXX as the standard form of the OT and seldom referred to the Hebrew. *Origen, however, was greatly interested in the relation of the LXX to the Hebrew and the other Greek versions. The LXX was also the basis of the '*Old Latin Version(s)' of the OT. It was St *Jerome's *Vulgate that first provided Christians with a Latin version of the OT direct from the original, and did most to dispel the belief, common in the early Church, that the LXX was verbally inspired. It is still the canonical text of the OT in the E. Orthodox Church.

The LXX exists in a large number of MSS, uncial and minuscule, as well as in a number of important, though not very extensive, papyrus fragments (esp. the *Chester Beatty Papyri). The MSS include the *Codex Sinaiticus, where, however, only about a third of the OT survives; the *Codex Vaticanus (with Gen. 1: 1–46: 28, and a few other portions, wanting); *Codex Alexandrinus (1 Sam. 12: 18–14: 9, Pss. 49 (50): 19–79 (80): 10, and a few short passages in Gen. 14–16, wanting); and the *Codex Ephraemi, of which only 64 leaves from the poetical Books remain.

The complete LXX was printed for the first time in Cardinal *Ximénez's *Complutensian Polyglot (1514–17), the Latin Vulgate being placed between the Hebrew on the left and the LXX on the right ('*tanquam duos hinc et inde latrones, medium autem Jesum*'). Later editions are those of Aldus Manutius (1518); '*Auctoritate Sixti V Pont. Max.*' (Rome, 1587); J. E. *Grabe (Oxford, 1707–20); R. Holmes and J. Parsons (ibid., 1798–1827); H. B. *Swete (Cambridge, 1887–94); A. E. Brooke, N. McLean, and H. St J. Thackeray (ibid., 1906–40 [Gen.–Tobit only]); the Göttingen Academy (Stuttgart, 1926 ff.); A. Rahlfs (Stuttgart, 1935).

E. *Hatch and H. A. Redpath, *A Concordance to the Septuagint* (2 vols., 1897; suppl., 1906; repr. Graz, 1954). J. Lust and others, *A Greek–English Lexicon of the Septuagint* (Stuttgart, 1992 ff.). H. St J. Thackeray, *A Grammar of the Old Testament in Greek according to the Septuagint* (vol. 1, all pub., 1909). H. B. Swete, *An Introduction to the Old Testament in Greek* (1900, rev. by R. R. Ottley, 1914). A. Rahlfs, *Septuaginta-Studien* (3 vols., 1904–11; reissued, Göttingen, 1965). J. Ziegler, *Die Septuaginta: Erbe und Auftrag* (lecture, Würzburg, 1962, repr. in his *Sylloge: Gesammelte Aufsätze zur Septuaginta* (Göttingen, 1971), pp. 590–614, with other specialized articles. D. Barthélemy, OP, *Les Devanciers d'Aquila* (Supplements to *Vetus Testamentum*, 10; Leiden, 1963). S. Jellicoe, *The Septuagint and Modern Study* (Oxford, 1968). P. Walters, *The Text of the Septuagint*, ed. D. W. Gooding (Cambridge, 1973). Id. (ed.), *Studies in the Septuagint: Origins, Recensions, and Interpretations* (New York [1974]). N. Fernández

Marcos, *Introducción a las versiones Griegas de la Biblia* (Textos y estudios 'Cardinal Cisneros', 23; 1979). E. Tov, *The Text-Critical Use of the Septuagint in Biblical Research* (Jerusalem Bible Studies, 3; Jerusalem, 1981). G. Dorival, M. Harl, and O. Munnich, *La Bible grecque des Septante: Du judaïsme hellénisitique au christianisme ancien* (1988). M. Alexandre, *Le Commencement du Livre Genèse I–V: La version grecque de la Septante et sa réception* (Christianisme Antique, 3 [1988]). E. Tov, 'The Septuagint' in M. J. Mulder (ed.), *Mikra* (Compendia Rerum Iudaicarum ad Novum Testamentum, 2. 1; Assen/Maastricht and Philadelphia, 1988), pp. 161–88. M. Hengel and A. M. Schwemer (eds.), *Die Septuaginta zwischen Judentum und Christentum* (1994). *Mitteilungen des Septuaginta-Unternehmens der Gesellschaft der Wissenschaften zu Göttingen* (Berlin, 1910–32; Göttingen, 1958 ff.). E. *Schürer, *The History of the Jewish People in the Age of Jesus Christ*, Eng. tr. rev. by G. Vermes and others, 3 (pt. 1; Edinburgh, 1986), pp. 474–93. S. P. Brock and others, *A Classified Bibliography of the Septuagint* (Arbeiten zur Literatur und Geschichte des Hellenistischen Judentums, 6; Leiden, 1973). E. *Nestle in *HDB* 4 (1902), pp. 437–54, s.v.; S. P. Brock in *TRE* 6 (1980), pp. 163–8, with bibl., pp. 170 f., s.v. 'Bibelübersetzungen', I. 2: 'Die Übersetzungen des Alten Testaments ins Griechische'; M. K. H. Peters in *Anchor Bible Dictionary*, 5 (1992), pp. 1093–104, s.v.; B. Botte and P.-M. Bogaert, OSB, in *Dict. Bibl.*, Suppl. 12 ('1993'), cols. 536–691, s.v. 'Septante et versions grecques'.

Sepulchre, Holy. See HOLY SEPULCHRE.

Sequence (Lat. *sequentia*). In the liturgy, a chant sung on certain days until 1970 after (now before) the *Alleluia of the Mass. Originally the word seems to have denoted a purely melodic extension of the word 'Alleluia', sung to its final vowel; during the 9th cent. a custom arose of providing a syllabic text (usually called a *prosa*) for the melody. In due course the term *sequentia* came to be applied to the resulting musical–textual entity, and hence eventually to the text alone, and in this sense its English equivalent has gained widespread currency.

In the application of a syllabic text to an existing melody (a practice that was also adopted in other types of chant), the word 'Alleluia' might be retained or discarded. The first author to make a systematic collection of such texts was *Notker Balbulus (d. 912); its title, *Liber Hymnorum*, suggests that the term *sequentia* was not yet applicable to syllabically texted chants, and also, perhaps, that they were not intended at that stage for liturgical performance. The authenticity of his famous preface, in which he claims to have derived his method of fitting texts to 'melodiae longissimae' from a priest from Jumièges, cannot reasonably be doubted. Later authors of sequences include *Hildegard of Bingen and *Adam of St-Victor; by their day texts had become increasingly rhymed and scanned, and were set to melodies either specially composed or previously devised for poems of similar metrical form. In medieval times a large number of sequences were in popular use, but only five remain. These are the well-known '*Victimae paschali' (at *Easter), the '*Veni, Sancte Spiritus' (at *Whitsun), the 'Lauda Sion' (at *Corpus Christi), the '*Dies Irae' (at *All Souls'), and the '*Stabat Mater' (on the feast of the *Seven Sorrows of the BVM). Acc. to the rubrics of the 1970 *Missale Romanum* only the first two of these need to be used, and the sequence comes before, instead of after, the Alleluia. See also TROPE.

The principal Sequences ed. C. Blume, SJ, and H. Bannister in *AHMA* 53–5 (1911–22); further *Sequentiae Ineditae* are pub.

ibid. 8, 9, 10, 34, 37, 39, 40, 42, and 44 (1890–1904). Notker's *Liber Hymnorum* ed. W. von den Steinen, *Notker der Dichter und seine geistige Welt* (2 vols., Berne, 1948); Hildegard of Bingen, *Sequences and Hymns*, ed. C. Page (Newton Abbot, 1983), incl. all pieces labelled *sequentia* in the two MS sources of her songs. For edns. of the sequences of Adam of St-Victor, see s.v. R. L. Crocker, *The Early Medieval Sequence* (Berkeley, Calif., etc., 1977). Jungmann (1958 edn.), 1, pp. 557–64; Eng. tr., pp. 436–41. Raby (1953), pp. 210–19, with bibl. p. 479. J. Szövérffy, *Die Annalen der lateinischen Hymnendichtung* (2 vols., 1964–5), esp. 1, pp. 282–359, 409–16; 2, pp. 99–121. R. L. Crocker and J. Caldwell in S. Sadie (ed.), *The New Grove Dictionary of Music and Musicians*, 17 (1980), pp. 141–56, s.v., with detailed bibl.

Seraphic Order, the. Another name for the *Franciscan Order (q.v.). The name commemorates St Francis's vision on Mount Alverna in which he saw a seraph from heaven impressing the stigmata on his body.

Seraphim. The supernatural creatures, each with six wings, which *Isaiah in his inaugural vision saw standing above the throne of Yahweh (Is. 6: 2–7). Unless they are to be identified with the 'fiery serpents' mentioned in Num. 21: 6 ff., Deut. 8: 15, Is. 14: 29, and Is. 30: 6, they are not mentioned elsewhere in the OT.

From an early date Christian interpreters held the 'Seraphim' to be a category of *angels, and considered them counterparts of the '*Cherubim'; hence their occurrence together in the *Preface of the Roman Mass and also in the *Te Deum. The further view, which was widely accepted among Christian exegetes, that the Heb. word 'seraphim' was connected with a root meaning 'to burn' led to the notion that they were esp. distinguished by the fervour of their love. As such they came to be ranked highest in the nine orders of angels (the Cherubim filling the next place).

OED (2nd edn., 1989), 15, pp. 2 f., s.v. See also comm. to Isaiah, cited s.v.

Seraphim of Sarov, St (1759–1833), Russian monk and *staretz. He was born at Kursk, into a family of provincial merchants. At 19 he entered the monastery of Sarov, and spent 15 years in the ordinary life of the community, being ordained deacon and then priest. From 1794 to 1825 he lived in seclusion, first as a hermit in the forest close to the monastery, and then enclosed in a small cell within the monastic building itself. In 1825 he opened the door of his cell, and during the remaining eight years of his life he devoted his entire energies to the work of spiritual direction, receiving a constant stream of visitors from all parts of Russia. Astonishingly severe in his personal ascetic practices, towards others he was always gentle, stressing the importance of joy and cheerfulness in the spiritual life, and the need for the transforming presence of the Holy Spirit. His teaching is best summed up in a conversation recorded by his friend Nicolas Motovilov. He was canonized in 1903. Feast day, 2 Jan.

Eng. tr. of extracts from his Life, and also the conversation with Motovilov, in G. P. Fedotov (ed.), *A Treasury of Russian Spirituality* (1950), pp. 246–79. V. Zander, *St Seraphim of Sarov* (Eng. tr. from unpub. Fr., 1975). I. de Beausobre, *Flame in the Snow* (1945; a popular account).

Serapion, St (d. 211), Bp. of *Antioch from 199. Though one of the chief theologians of his age, little is known of him. His writings, of which only a few fragments survive, include a letter to Caricus and Pontius against *Montanism, a work addressed to one Domninus who had lapsed during persecution, and a letter withdrawing his earlier permission to the Church of Rhossus to read the 'Gospel of St *Peter', on the ground that he had now discovered it to be *Docetic. Feast day, 30 Oct.

The principal ancient authorities are *Eusebius, *HE* 5. 19 and 6. 12, and *Jerome, *De Vir. Ill.* 31. The frags. are collected in M. J. *Routh, *Reliquiae Sacrae*, 1 (2nd edn; Oxford, 1846), pp. 447–62.

Serapion, St (d. after 360), Bp. of Thmuis in the Nile delta from *c*.339. He was the close friend and protégé of St *Athanasius, probably his junior in age; and before he became bishop had been a monk and a companion of St *Antony, who left in his will one of his two sheepskin cloaks to Serapion and the other to Athanasius. Athanasius selected him for a difficult mission to the Emp. Constantius, and addressed to him a series of important doctrinal letters on the Divinity of the Holy Spirit. Serapion composed some literary works, notably a treatise against the *Manichees; and an early 'Sacramentary' which has come down under his name was probably his compilation. He also corresponded with the heresiarch *Apollinarius, then still orthodox. Feast day, 21 Mar.

Crit. edn. of 'Serapion of Thmuis against the Manichees' by R. P. Casey (Harvard Theological Studies, no. 15; Cambridge, Mass., 1931); older uncrit. text, with other items of Serapion, in J. P. Migne, *PG* 40. 895–942 (from A. *Gallandi). 'Sacramentary' (or 'Euchologion'), which survives in the single 11th-cent. MS Athos Laura 149, ed. G. Wobbermin, *Altchristliche liturgische Stücke aus der Kirche Ägyptens nebst einem dogmatischen Brief des Bischofs Serapion von Thmuis* (TU 17. 3b; 1898); also ed. F. E. *Brightman, *JTS* 1 (1899–1900), pp. 88–113, 247–77. Eng. tr. (based on Wobbermin's edn.) by J. *Wordsworth (*Bishop Sarapion's Prayer-Book*; Early Church Classics, 1899). R. Draguet, 'Une Lettre de Sérapion de Thmuis aux disciples d'Antoine (A.D. 356) en version syriaque et arménienne', *Muséon*, 64 (1951), pp. 1–25, incl. text and Lat. tr. Eng. edn. of Athanasius' Epp. to Serapion, with introd. and notes, by C. R. B. Shapland (1951). A. Peters, OFM, 'Het Tractaat van Serapion van Thmuis tegen de Manichaeën', *Sacris Erudiri*, 2 (1949), pp. 55–94. B. *Capelle, OSB, 'L'Anaphore de Sérapion. Essai d'exégèse', *Muséon*, 59 (1946), pp. 425–43, repr. in his *Travaux Liturgiques*, 2 (1962), pp. 344–58; B. Botte, OSB, 'L'Eucologe de Sérapion est-il authentique?', *OC* 48 (1964), pp. 50–6. G. J. Cuming, 'Thmuis Revisited: Another Look at the Prayers of Bishop Serapion', *Theological Studies*, 41 (1980), pp. 568–75. K. Fitschen, *Serapion von Thmuis: Echte und unechte Schriften sowie die Zeugnisse des Athanasius und anderer* (Patristische Texte und Studien, 37; 1992). *CPG* 2 (1974), pp. 97–100 (nos. 2485–504). Bardenhewer, 3, pp. 98–102. G. Bardy in *DTC* 14 (pt. 2; 1941), cols. 1908–12; H. Dörrie in *PW*, Suppl. 8 (1956), cols. 1260–7, both s.v.

Serbia, Church of. Systematic missionary work in Serbia was first undertaken by the Byzantines during the second half of the 9th cent., in particular by followers of Sts *Cyril and Methodius from Moravia. With the baptism of Prince Mutimir (reigned *c*.860–91) Christianity became the official religion of the country. For some time the Serbs wavered between Constantinople and Rome, and it was not until the start of the 13th cent. that their attach-

ment to E. Christendom became definite. In the closing years of the 12th cent. the Serbian monastery of Hilandar was founded on Mt *Athos by St *Sava and his father; it became an important centre of Serbian spirituality and culture. In 1219 Sava established an *autocephalous Serbian Church, of which he was consecrated the first archbishop by the *Oecumenical Patriarch in Nicaea (Constantinople being at this time in the hands of the Latins). The Serbian medieval empire, and with it the Church, attained its period of greatest brilliance under Stephen Dushan (1331–55). In 1346 the head of the Serbian Church assumed the title '*Patriarch', with his seat at Peć: the Serbian Patriarchate was recognized by Constantinople in 1375. Along with the *Bulgarians and the *Romanians, during the Ottoman period the Serbs passed increasingly under Greek ecclesiastical control, and the Patriarchate of Peć was eventually suppressed in 1766. The Church of Serbia became autocephalous once more in 1879, with the approval of Constantinople. In 1920 the Serbian Patriarchate was restored, its seat being transferred from Peć to Belgrade. The Church of Serbia has always been closely identified with the national aspirations of the people, and in the break up of the old Yugoslavia in the early 1990s it was unable to do more than deplore the violence with which the government pursued its aim of a 'Greater Serbia'.

R. M. French, *Serbian Church Life* (1942); L. Hadrovics, *Le Peuple serbe et son Église sous la domination turque* (1947). S. Alexander, *Church and State in Yugoslavia since 1945* (1979). J. Kondrinewitsch in *L.Th.K.* (2nd edn.), 9 (1964), cols. 684–6, with bibl.; V. J. Pospishil in *NCE* 13 (1967), pp. 107–11, s.v. 'Serbian Rite'.

Serdica. See SARDICA.

Sergeant, John (1622–1707), RC controversialist. He was educated at St John's College, Cambridge, and afterwards became secretary to T. *Morton, Bp. of *Durham. Later he became a RC. After study at the English College, Lisbon, he was ordained to the priesthood, and in 1652 was attached to the English Mission. The remainder of his life was spent in controversy, for which he had marked gifts. Indeed there was hardly any Protestant writer of standing whose views Sergeant did not attack. The titles of some 34 pamphlets by Sergeant are listed under his name in the *DNB*.

His 'Literary Life' written by himself is pub. in *Catholicon*, 2 (1816), pp. 132–6, 169–76, 217–24; 3 (1816), pp. 9–16, 55–64, 97–104, and 121–7, with introd. in 2, pp. 129–31. J. Warner, *The History of English Persecution of Catholics and the Presbyterian Plot*, ed. T. A. Birrell, with tr. by J. Bligh, SJ (Catholic Record Society, 47–8; 1953), 1, pp. 230–2 (nos. 208–13), pp. 277 f. (nos. 328–30), 2, pp. 456 f. (nos. 606–8), and pp. 527–32. T. Cooper in *DNB* 51 (1897), pp. 251–3, s.v.

Sergius (d. 638), Patr. of *Constantinople from 610 and the most influential exponent of *Monothelitism. He was of Syrian origin. After elevation to the Patriarchal See he became the trusted adviser of the Emp. *Heraclius, who confided the capital to his care during his absence in his wars with the Persians. To reconcile the disaffected Monophysites Sergius, in his search for a Christological formula acceptable both to them and to the adherents of the Dyophysite *Chalcedonian orthodoxy, began to teach Two Natures but only one 'activity' (ἐνέργεια) in Christ. On being opposed by St *Sophronius of Jerusalem, he issued the 'Psephos' (633) which forbade mention of either one or two 'activities' in Christ. Sergius also appealed to Pope *Honorius I, and together they agreed that there was only one will (ἓν θέλημα) in Christ. This doctrine was promulgated by the Emperor in the famous '*Ecthesis' (q.v.), of which Sergius was the author. Two synods held at Constantinople in 638 and 639 approved this teaching, which was, however, condemned by the Council of *Constantinople in 681. Sergius is believed to have introduced several liturgical innovations, and an old tradition ascribes to him the authorship of the famous hymn known as the '*Acathistus'.

V. Grumel, AA, *Les Régestes des actes du patriarcat de Constantinople*, 1, fasc. 1 (2nd edn., 1972), pp. 211–22 (nos. 278c–293b), with refs. J. L. van Dieten, *Geschichte der Patriarchen von Sergios I. bis Johannes VI. (610–715)* (Enzyklopädie der Byzantinistik, 24; Amsterdam, 1972), pp. 1–56. L. Magi, *La Sede Romana nella corrispondenza degli imperatori e patriarchi bizantini (VI–VII sec.)* (Bibliothèque de la *RHE*, 57; 1972), pp. 196–205. F.-X. Murphy, CSSR, and P. Sherwood, OSB, *Constantinople II et Constantinople III* (Histoire des Conciles Œcuméniques, 3; 1974), pp. 133–62 and 305–8. *CPG* 3 (1974), pp. 418 f. (nos. 7604–8). Krumbacher, pp. 671–3. See also bibl. to MONOTHELITISM, esp. arts. by V. Grumel.

Sergius, St (d. 701), Pope from 687. A native of *Antioch, he was educated at Palermo. On the death of his predecessor, Pope Conon (686–7), Sergius was elected in the face of two rival candidates with the support of the mass of the clergy and people. He took an active part in several English matters. He baptized Caedwalla, King of the West Saxons (689), consecrated St *Willibrord, Bp. of the Frisians (Nov. 695), and ordered St *Wilfrid to be restored to his see (c.700). He strongly resisted the attempt of the Emp. Justinian II (685–95) to secure his support for the *Trullan Council (692), which would have placed Constantinople on an ecclesiastical level with Rome, and was saved by the Roman populace from being forcibly conveyed to the E. capital. He made various liturgical innovations, notably the singing of *Agnus Dei in the Mass and the introduction of a litany and processions on the four chief feasts of the BVM. He also did much for the restoration of the Roman basilicas. Feast day, 8 Sept.

Jaffé, 1, pp. 244 f. *LP* (Duchesne), 1, pp. 371–82. F. Görres, 'Justinian II und das römische Papsttum', *BZ* 17 (1908), pp. 432–54, esp. pp. 440–54. J. Gay, 'Quelques Remarques sur les papes grecs et syriens avant la querelle des iconoclastes (678–715)', *Mélanges offerts à M. Gustave Schlumberger*, 1 (1924), pp. 40–54. O. Bertolini, *Roma di fronte a Bisanzio e ai Longobardi* (Bologna, 1941), esp. pp. 399–408. P. Conte, *Chiesa e Primato nella lettere dei Papi del secolo VII* (Milan, 1971), pp. 494–504; see also index. Mann, 1 (pt. 2; 1902), pp. 77–104. E. Caspar, *Geschichte des Papsttums*, 2 (1933), pp. 624–36; Fliche and Martin, 5 (1938), pp. 407–9. É. Amann in *DTC* 14 (pt. 2; 1941), cols. 1913–16, s.v. 'Serge Iᵉʳ'. See also bibl. to TRULLAN SYNOD.

Sergius, St (c.1314–92), Russian monastic reformer and mystic. His original name was Bartholomew. He was born at Rostov, and when a boy, fled with his family to Radonezh, nr. Moscow. He founded in the neighbourhood, with his brother Stephen, the famous monastery of the Holy Trinity, and thereby re-established the community life which had been lost in Russia through the Tartar

invasion. When his brother opposed his reforms, Sergius, though abbot, retired into seclusion, but was later restored. He had great influence over all classes, stopped four civil wars between Russian princes, and inspired the resistance of Prince Dmitri which saved Russia from the Tartars (1380). In 1378 he refused the metropolitan see. Altogether, Sergius founded 40 monasteries. He was canonized before 1449, and is regarded as the greatest of Russian saints. Feast day, 25 Sept.

The primary authority is the Life written by Epiphanius the Wise, one of his monks, shortened and rev. in the 15th cent. by a Serbian monk, Pachomius. Abridged Eng. tr. in G. P. Fedotov (ed.), *A Treasury of Russian Spirituality* (1950), pp. 54–83, with introd. pp. 50–3, and notes pp. 487–9. Complete Eng. tr. by M. Klimenko (Houston, Tex. [1980]). N. Zernov, *St Sergius: Builder of Russia* (New York, 1939), also with Eng. tr. of Life, by A. Delafeld, as pt. 3 (pts. 1 and 2 also pub., London [1939]). P. Kovalevsky, *Saint Serge et la spiritualité russe* ([1958]; Eng. tr., Crestwood, NY, 1976). G. P. Fedotov, *The Russian Religious Mind*, 2 (Cambridge, Mass., 1966), pp. 195–229. J. Meyendorff, *Byzantium and the Rise of Russia* (Cambridge, 1981), esp. pp. 132–6.

Sergius Paulus. The proconsul of *Cyprus who, acc. to Acts 13: 4–12, having invited St *Paul and St *Barnabas to preach before him on their first missionary journey and seen the miracle done by Paul on the sorcerer Bar-Jesus, 'believed' (ἐπίστευσεν). He is perhaps the Paulus mentioned as proconsul in a Cypriot inscription of this time.

J. Devreker, 'Les Sergii Paulli: problèmes généalogiques d'une famille supposée chrétienne', in M. Van Uytfanghe and R. Demeulenaere (eds.), *Aevum inter Utrumque: Mélanges offerts à Gabriel Sanders* (Instrumenta Patristica, 23; 1991), pp. 109–19, with refs. J. E. Roberts in *DAC* 2 (1918), p. 471, s.v. 'Sergius Paulus'.

Seripando, Girolamo (1492/3–1563), *Augustinian friar. Born in Naples, he took the Augustinian habit in 1507 and was ordained in 1513. He gained a reputation as a teacher and a preacher and rose to high office; he was General of the Order from 1539 to 1551. Internal troubles, partly connected with the defection of M. *Luther, led him to organize a visitation of the whole Order, which resulted in administrative and educational reforms. He himself undertook the visitation in Italy, *France, *Spain, and *Portugal. From the start he played a significant part in the debates of the Council of *Trent; he was made a legate to the Council in 1561. Anxious to avoid a complete break with the Lutherans, he took a moderate position on *justification, adopting the theory of '*double justice', but he failed to win sufficient support. He became Abp. of Salerno in 1554 and was made a Cardinal in 1561.

Crit. edn. of his treatise *De Justitia et Libertate Christiana* by A. Forster, OSB (Corpus Catholicorum, 30; 1969). 'Diarium de vita sua' (1513–62), ed. D. Gutiérrez, OSA, in *Analecta Augustiniana*, 26 (1963), pp. 5–193; *Registrum Generalatus*, ed. id. (Fontes Historiae Ordinis Sancti Augustini, Prima Series, 25–30; Rome, 1982–90). H. Jedin, *Girolamo Seripando: Sein Leben und Denken im Geisteskampf des 16. Jahrhunderts* (Cassiciacum, 2–3; Würzburg, 1937; Eng. tr., with abbreviated documentation, *Papal Legate at the Council of Trent: Cardinal Seripando*, St Louis and London, 1947). A. Forster, OSB, *Gesetz und Evangelium bei Girolamo Seripando* (Konfessionskundliche und kontroverstheologische Studien, 6 [1963]). J. Mercier in *DTC* 14 (pt. 2; 1941), cols. 1923–

40, s.v., with extensive bibl.; D. Gutiérrez, OSA, in *Dict. Sp.* 14 (1990), cols. 655–61, s.v.

sermo generalis. The ceremony at which the final decision in trials of heretics by the *Inquisition was pronounced, usually with great solemnity. After a short sermon, from which the ceremony took its name, sentences were pronounced: those found innocent were acquitted; those who recanted were sentenced to the penances prescribed by canon law, incl. imprisonment by the Inquisition; and unrepentant heretics were handed over to the secular authorities for punishment. This invariably took the form of *burning at the stake. The term *sermo generalis* has come to be replaced in more recent usage by *auto de fe*.

Sermon on the Mount. The compilation of the Lord's sayings in Mt. 5–7 provides an epitome of His moral teaching; it shows Christ as the true interpreter of the *Mosaic Law (5: 17–48) and has always been a central element in Christian ethics. It includes the *Beatitudes (5: 3–12) and the *Lord's Prayer (6: 9–13). The admonition not to resist the evil one but rather to 'turn the other cheek' (5: 39) has been one of the main sources of Christian *pacificism. There is a somewhat parallel, though shorter, discourse of similar content, sometimes known as the 'Sermon on the Plain', in Lk. 6: 20–49 [cf. 6: 17].

The only patristic treatment of the subject as a separate work is St *Augustine, 'De Sermone Domini in Monte' (*PL* 34. 1229–1308); Eng. tr. by J. J. Jepson, with introd. and notes (ACW 5; 1948). H. *Windisch, *Der Sinn der Bergpredigt* (1929; 2nd edn., 1937); M. *Dibelius, *The Sermon on the Mount* (New York, 1940); T. Soiron, OFM, *Die Bergpredigt Jesu: Formgeschichtliche, exegetische und theologische Erklärung* (Freiburg i.B., 1941); J. Jeremias, *The Sermon on the Mount* (Ethel M. Wood Lecture; 1961); W. D. Davies, *The Setting of the Sermon on the Mount* (1964); id., *The Sermon on the Mount* (1966); G. Strecker, *Die Bergpredigt: Ein evangelischer Kommentar* (Göttingen, 1984; 2nd edn., 1985; Eng. tr., Edinburgh, 1988); H. D. Betz, *Essays on the Sermon on the Mount*, tr. by L. L. Welborn (Philadelphia [1985]); R. A. Guelich, *The Sermon on the Mount: A Foundation for Understanding* (Waco, Tex. [1982]); H. D. Betz, *The Sermon on the Mount: A Commentary . . .*, ed. A. Y. Collins (Hermeneia; Minneapolis, 1995). C. W. Votaw in *HDB*, Extra vol. (1904), pp. 1–45; H. D. Betz in *Anchor Bible Dictionary*, 5 (1992), pp. 1106–12. See also comm. to LUKE and MATTHEW, GOSPELS OF.

serpent, brazen. See BRAZEN SERPENT.

Servant Songs. The four passages in *Deutero-Isaiah (Is. 42: 1–4; 49: 1–6; 50: 4–9; and 52: 13–53: 12) describing the person and character of the 'Servant of the Lord'. They were first isolated from their contexts and seen as an entity by B. *Duhm. In his commentary on Isaiah, Duhm challenged the prevalent view that Yahweh's servant in these and other passages in Is. referred to the nation of Israel, or some element in it; he held that the Servant in these four passages was an otherwise unknown individual and that the author of the poems was one of his disciples. There have since then been many attempts to identify the Servant with some historical individual, e.g. Zerubbabel, Jehoiachin, Cyrus, or even *Moses, while in 1921 S. *Mowinckel contended (though he abandoned the theory later) that it was the Prophet himself. Among British OT scholars prevalent opinion still identifies the Servant with Israel in some form. Christian theology has traditionally

interpreted the Servant in Isaiah as a prophecy of the Incarnate Christ.

There is a vast lit. Among the more important items are B. Duhm, *Die Theologie der Propheten als Grundlage für die innere Entwicklungsgeschichte der Israelitischen Religion dargestellt* (Bonn, 1875), pp. 287–301; id., *Das Buch Jesaia* (KAT 3. 1; 1892), esp. pp. 284–7, 339–43, 351–3, and 365–78; S. R. *Driver and A. Neubauer, *The Fifty-Third Chapter of Isaiah according to the Jewish Interpretation* (2 vols., 1876–7); S. Mowinckel, *Der Knecht Jahwäs* (Giessen, 1921); C. R. North, *The Suffering Servant in Deutero-Isaiah* (1948; 2nd edn., 1956); [C.] J. Lindblom, *The Servant Songs in Deutero-Isaiah: A New Attempt to Solve an Old Problem* (Lunds Universitets Årsskrift, NF, Avd. 1, Bd. 47, Nr. 5; 1951): H. H. Rowley, *The Servant of the Lord and Other Essays* (1952), pp. 1–88; G. R. *Driver, 'Isaiah 52, 13–53, 12: the Servant Song of the Lord', in M. Black and G. Fohrer (eds.), *In Memoriam Paul Kahle* (Beihefte zur *ZATW*, 103; 1968), pp. 90–105; R. N. Whybray, *Thanksgiving for a Liberated Prophet* (Journal for the Study of the Old Testament, Supplement Series, 4; Sheffield, 1978). The subject is also discussed in all comm. on Isaiah (qq.v.).

Servatus Lupus. See LUPUS, SERVATUS.

server. In the W. Church, a minister in the sanctuary. The principal duties of the server are to make the responses, bring the bread and wine to the altar, wash the celebrant's hands, and ring the *sacring bell at the Elevation if it is used. Until 1994 only boys or adult men could act as servers in the RC Church, though when no male person was available a woman could answer a Mass from outside the sanctuary.

Servetus, Michael (c.1511–53), physician and anti-Trinitarian writer. Prob. born in Tudela in Navarre, he studied law in Toulouse, and then, after travelling in Italy, went to Basle and Strasbourg, where he met J. *Oecolampadius and M. *Bucer. In 1531 at Hagenau he published a treatise, *De Trinitatis Erroribus Libri VII*, in which he attacked the current formulation of the doctrine of the *Trinity, arguing that the term itself was unbiblical. The book shocked his Protestant friends, and he worked for a time as a proof-corrector in Lyons (c.1535–7). He then studied medicine at Paris and Montpellier and in 1542 he was appointed physician to the Abp. of Vienne. In the same year he published an edition of S. *Paginus' Latin translation of the Bible, adding his own annotations. In 1546 he entered into correspondence with J. *Calvin, submitting to him the manuscript of his principal work, *Christianismi Restitutio*, which was to appear anonymously in 1553. In this Servetus not only rejected the traditional doctrine of the Trinity but also developed unorthodox views of the Incarnation; he maintained that an essentially unknowable divinity was manifest as Word and communicated as Spirit, the supreme manifestation of the Word being the historical Jesus, the Son of God, whose existence was limited to His earthly life. With Calvin's collaboration, Servetus' authorship was denounced to the *Inquisition. He was imprisoned but escaped to Geneva; here he was arrested and, refusing to recant, was burnt as a heretic at Champel (near Geneva) on 27 Oct. 1553. This event gave rise to heated controversy among Protestants as to whether heretics should be condemned to death. Servetus himself had argued against the use of force in defence of Christian truth, as well as expressing *millenarian views and rejecting *Infant Baptism. He also promoted belief in the pulmonary circulation of the blood.

Eng. tr. of his *Two Treatises on the Trinity* by E. M. Wilbur (HTS 16; 1932) and of his *Geographical, Medical and Astrological Writings* by C. D. O'Malley (Philadelphia, 1953). Sp. tr. of *Christianismi Restitutio* by A. Alcalá and L. Betés, with introd. and notes by A. Alcalá (Madrid, 1980). R. H. Bainton, *Hunted Heretic: The Life and Death of Michael Servetus* (Boston, 1953); B. Becker (ed.), *Autour de Michael Servetus et de Sébastien Castellion* (Haarlem, 1953), pp. 29–157; C. Manzoni, *Umanesimo ed eresia: Michele Serveto* (Esperienze, 26; Naples [1974]); J. Friedman, *Michael Servetus: A Case Study in Total Heresy* (Travaux d'Humanisme et de Renaissance, 163; Geneva, 1978). Full bibl. of Servetus' works and of lit. since the 16th cent. by A. G. Kinder, *Michael Servetus* (Bibliotheca Dissidentium, 10; Baden-Baden, 1989). J. C. Godbey in M. Eliade (ed.), *The Encyclopedia of Religion*, 13 (1987), pp. 176–8; J.-G. Margolin in *Dict. Sp.* 14 (1990), cols. 672–9, s.v.

service, Divine. See DIVINE SERVICE.

servile work (Lat. *opus servile*, Lev. 23, Num. 28 and 29 *passim*, Vulg.), a term applied specifically to work which is forbidden on *Sundays or Holy Days, as the work of slaves, in contrast with liberal work, that of free men. Taken in early times to cover agricultural and mechanical work, by the 13th cent., when the prohibition was becoming increasingly unpopular, attempts were made to define it (after St *Augustine, *In Jo.* 3. 19; J. P. Migne, *PL* 35. 1404) as work which made a man the slave of sin or had the appearance of making him such. In modern times it has often been interpreted as work in which the body plays a greater part than the mind, or as gainful work. The term was still used in the 1917 *Codex Iuris Canonici* (can. 1248) but it does not figure in the 1983 *Codex*. For details of current requirements, see SUNDAY.

Servites, Order of (*Ordo Servorum BVM*). The Order was founded by seven wealthy Florentine city councillors who abandoned their worldly positions to devote themselves entirely to the service of the BVM, traditionally in 1233. They adopted a black habit and the Rule of St *Augustine, with some additions from the *Dominican constitutions. The Order developed rapidly, esp. after it had been officially sanctioned by a bull of Benedict XI in 1304. Its most influential member in early days was St Philip Benizi (1233–85), under whose generalship Servite missionaries were sent as far as India. The Servite nuns (Second Order) were founded by two of Benizi's penitents about the time of his death; they are chiefly contemplative. The sisters of the *Third Order were founded by St Juliana Falconieri in 1306; they devote themselves to the care of the sick and the poor and to the education of children. The principal Servite devotion is to the Sorrowful Virgin, in whose honour they recite the *Rosary of the *Seven Sorrows. The Feast of the Seven Founders is on 17 (formerly 12) Feb.

A. Gianius, OSM, *Annales Sacri Ordinis Fratrum Servorum B. Mariae Virginis* (Florence, 1618; 2nd edn. with continuation by A. M. Garbio, OSM, 3 vols., Lucca, 1719–25). *Monumenta Ordinis Servorum Sanctae Mariae*, ed. A. Morini, OSM, P. Soulier, OSM, and others [to 1750] (20 vols., Brussels and Rome, 1897–1930). A. P. M. Piermejus, *Memorabilia Sacri Ordinis Servorum B.M.V.* (4 vols., Rome, 1927–34). A. M. Rossi, OSM, *Manuale di storia dell'Ordine dei Servi di Maria (MCCXXXIII-MCMLIV)* (1956). F. A. dal Pino [OSM], *I frati Servi di S.*

Maria dalle origini all'approvazione 1233 ca.-1304 (Université de Louvain, Recueil de travaux d'histoire et de philologie, 4th ser. 49–50; in 3 vols., 1972). V. Benassi and others, *A Short History of the Servite Order* (Rome, 1987). *Studi storici sull'Ordine dei Servi di Maria* (ibid., 1933 ff., incl. bibl. by G. M. Besutti, OSM, in vol. 21, 1971, pp. 90–151). J. M. Ryska, OSM, in *NCE* 11 (1967), pp. 131–5, s.v.; F. dal Pino and others in *DIP* 8 (1988), cols. 1398–423; E. M. Casalini, OSM, and others in *Dict. Sp.* 14 (1990), cols. 695–730.

Servus Servorum Dei (Lat., 'the servant of God's servants'). A title of the Pope employed in official documents. It was first used by St *Gregory the Great (590–604) and has been in general use since the time of *Gregory VII (1073–85).

K. Schmitz, *Ursprung und Geschichte der Devotionsformeln bis zu ihrer Aufnahme in die fränkische Königsurkunde* (Kirchenrechtliche Abhandlungen, ed. U. Stutz, Heft 81; 1913), ch. 5, 'Servus Servorum Dei', pp. 120–39. W. Levison, 'Zur Vorgeschichte der Bezeichnung Servus Servorum Dei', *Zeitschrift der Savigny-Stiftung für Rechtsgeschichte*, Kan. Abt. 6 (1916), pp. 384–6.

session. See KIRK SESSION.

Seth, Andrew. See PATTISON, ANDREW SETH PRINGLE-.

Settlement, Act of. The Act of Settlement 1700 was passed in 1701 to settle the Crown on the Electress Sophia of Hanover. Since William III had no children, Princess *Anne's only surviving child had died in childhood, and the son of *James II was a RC, the hereditary rights of the descendants of *Charles I were set aside and the succession vested in Sophia of Hanover, daughter of Elizabeth of Bohemia, who was the daughter of *James I. Thus the title of the present monarch rests not so much on hereditary right as on Parliamentary settlement. The opportunity was also taken to extend the provisions of the Bill of Rights (which had debarred RCs and anyone who should marry a RC from the Crown) by positively ordaining that all future sovereigns should 'join in Communion with the Church of England as by law established'.

Text in Gee and Hardy, no. 124, pp. 664–70; C. G. Robertson, *Select Statutes, Cases and Documents* (1904), no. 20, pp. 87–92; and in W. C. Costin and J. S. Watson, *The Law and Working of the Constitution*, 1 (1952), no. 36, pp. 92–6.

Seuse, Bl Heinrich. See HENRY SUSO, BLESSED.

Seven Bishops, Trial of the. The trial arose out of *James II's order that his *Declaration of Indulgence should be read in all churches on 20 and 27 May 1688 (London) or 3 and 10 June (elsewhere). W. *Sancroft, Abp. of *Canterbury, summoned a meeting and a protest was drawn up and signed by Sancroft and six other bishops, namely W. Lloyd of *St Asaph, F. Turner of *Ely, J. Lake of *Chichester, T. *Ken of *Bath and Wells, T. White of *Peterborough, and J. Trelawney of Bristol. Their petition was presented on 18 May. The protest, received with approval throughout the country, seemed to James 'a standard of rebellion'. The seven bishops were imprisoned in the Tower on 8 June and tried in Westminster Hall on 29 June on a charge of seditious libel. By ten o'clock on the next day even the King's Brewer (to his sorrow a juryman) had consented to the verdict of 'Not

Guilty'. The case marked the limits of Anglican obedience to a RC king; James's authority never recovered, even though five of the bishops remained constant in their allegiance and became *Nonjurors.

Full account in T. B. Howell, *A Complete Collection of State Trials and Proceedings for High Treason and other Crimes and Misdemeanours*, 12 (1812), cols. 183–434, with other docs. cols. 433–524. Chief relevant docs. in C. G. Robertson, *Select Statutes, Cases and Documents to Illustrate English Constitutional History, 1660–1832* (1904), Case 9, pp. 249–67; extracts of the case also in W. C. Costin and J. S. Watson, *The Law and Working of the Constitution: Documents, 1660–1914*, 1 (1952), pp. 258–71. R. Thomas, 'The Seven Bishops and their Petition, 18 May 1688', *JEH* 12 (1961), pp. 56–70; G. V. Bennett, 'The Seven Bishops: A Reconsideration', in D. Baker (ed.), *Religious Motivation: Biographical and Sociological Problems for the Church Historian* (Studies in Church History, 15; Oxford, 1978), pp. 267–87.

Seven Churches. The Churches in Asia Minor to which the letter of St *John, incorporated in Rev. (1–3), was addressed, namely *Ephesus, *Smyrna, *Pergamum, *Thyatira, *Sardis, *Philadelphia, and *Laodicea. A separate message for each of these Churches, appropriate to its particular temporal and spiritual condition, was revealed to John.

W. M. *Ramsay, *The Letters to the Seven Churches of Asia and their Place in the Plan of the Apocalypse* (1904); C. J. Hemer, *The Letters to the Seven Churches of Asia in their Local Setting* (Journal for the Study of the New Testament, Supplement Series, 11; Sheffield, 1986). See also comm. on Revelation, cited s.v.

seven corporal acts of mercy. See CORPORAL WORKS OF MERCY.

Seven Deacons. The title traditionally given to the 'seven men of honest report, full of the Holy Ghost and wisdom' who, as related in Acts 6: 1–6, were appointed to 'serve tables', i.e. to administer the temporal concerns of the Church. Their names were *Stephen, *Philip, Prochorus, Nicanor, Timon, Parmenas, and Nicolas. Their appointment has traditionally been regarded as instituting the order of *deacons in the Christian Church, and for many centuries the practice obtained at Rome of restricting the number of its deacons to seven.

S. Bibel, OFM, 'De Septem Diaconis (Act. 6, 1–7)', *Antonianum*, 3 (1928), pp. 129–50. See also comm. on Acts, cited s.v.

seven deadly sins. They are: (1) *pride; (2) covetousness; (3) lust; (4) envy; (5) gluttony; (6) anger; (7) sloth ('*accidie').

*Cassian, *Coll.* 5. 10, gives a list of eight sins (dejection and accidie counting as two); the traditional number of seven is found in St *Gregory the Great, *Moralia in Job*, 31. 45 (where *tristitia* takes the place of *accidie*). St *Thomas Aquinas, *Summa Theol.* II (1), qu. 84, art. 4. O. Zöckler, *Askese und Mönchtum*, 1 (1897), pp. 253–6. K. E. *Kirk, *Some Principles of Moral Theology and their Application* (1920), pp. 265–7; id., *The Vision of God* (1931), pp. 201 f. (nn. 4 f.). M. W. Bloomfield, *The Seven Deadly Sins: An Introduction to the History of a Religious Concept, with Special Reference to Medieval English Literature* ([E. Lansing, Mich.], 1952). S. Wenzel, 'The Seven Deadly Sins: some Problems of Research', *Speculum*, 43 (1968), pp. 1–22. R. Staats in *RAC* 13 (1986), cols. 734–70, s.v. 'Hauptsünden'.

seven gifts of the Holy Spirit. They are: (1) wisdom; (2) understanding; (3) counsel; (4) fortitude; (5) knowledge; (6) piety; (7) fear of the Lord. The list is taken from Is. 11: 2 (*Vulgate text, which adds *pietas* to the six in the AV and RV).

K. Schlütz, *Is. 11. 2: Die sieben Gaben des Heiligen Geistes in den ersten vier Jahrhunderten* (Alttestamentliche Abhandlungen, 11, Heft 4; 1932). A. Gardeil, OP, in *DTC* 4 (1911), cols. 1728–81; G. Bardy and others in *Dict. Sp. 3* (1957), cols. 1579–641, both s.v. 'Dons du Saint-Esprit'.

seven liberal arts. The group of sciences which formed the staple of secular education esp. in the earlier Middle Ages, consisting of the elementary *trivium (grammar, rhetoric, and dialectic) and the more advanced *quadrivium (music, arithmetic, geometry, and astronomy). This grouping derived from Martianus Capella (early 5th cent.), who drew it up on the basis of the ninefold arrangement of Varro by excluding architecture and medicine, but it did not become generally established until the time of *Alcuin. In practice considerably more was covered by the three disciplines of the trivium than their titles might suggest, e.g. classical and philological study as well as the technical rules of grammar were comprised under 'grammar'. It was not till the student had completed his studies in the 'liberal arts' that he was held competent to proceed to theology. See also SCHOLASTICISM.

Seven Penitential Psalms, the. Psalms 6, 32, 38, 51, 102, 130, and 143. They were in liturgical use from early Christian times, and in the later Middle Ages they were ordered to be recited after *Lauds on Fridays in *Lent. The BCP appoints them as Proper Psalms for *Ash Wednesday, the first three at *Mattins, Ps. 51 at the *Commination, and the last three at *Evensong. They were also used in the English *Coronation Service before the revision of 1603.

Seven Sacraments, the. Since the 12th cent. the RC Church has held the number of the sacraments to be seven, namely *Baptism, *Confirmation, *Eucharist, *Penance, Extreme *Unction, *Ordination, and *Matrimony. Though the beginnings of these rites can all be traced back to very much earlier times, it was through the teaching of *Peter Lombard in his 'Sentences' (*c.*1150) that the belief gained general credence that these particular seven constituted a set different in kind from all other religious rites (see SACRAMENTALS). Their sevenfold number was given formal definition at the Council of *Trent (Sess. 7, can. 1). Most of the Reformed Churches rejected this enumeration, coming to hold that there were only two sacraments, viz. Baptism and the Eucharist. The E. Church, however, has generally accepted the W. enumeration. For further discussion, see SACRAMENT.

Seven Sleepers of Ephesus. Seven Christian young men who are said to have been walled up in a cave when taking refuge during the *Decian persecution (*c.* AD 250) and to have been awakened under the Emp. *Theodosius II (d. 450), as a proof of the *resurrection of the dead. The legend was certainly known in the E. and the W. in the 6th cent., as both *Jacob of Sarug (d. 521) and St *Gregory of Tours record it. It probably arose in a

Syriac-speaking Church in connection with the *Origenist controversies over bodily resurrection. The alleged tomb of the Sleepers was much visited by pilgrims from all parts of the world before the Turkish conquest of Asia Minor. Feast day, 27 July.

I. Guidi (ed.), 'Testi orientali inediti sopra i Sette Dormienti di Efeso', *Atti della R. Accademia dei Lincei. Memorie della classe di scienze morali, storiche e filologiche*, 3rd ser. 11 (1884), pp. 343–445, with It. tr.; crit. edn. of the version of Gregory of Tours by B. Krusch in *Anal. Boll.* 12 (1893), pp. 371–87. M. Huber, OSB, 'Textbeiträge zur Siebenschläferlegende des Mittelalters', *Romanische Forschungen*, 26 (1909), pp. 462–583 and 825–36. Id., *Die Wanderlegende von den Siebenschläfern: Eine literargeschichtliche Untersuchung* (1910), with refs. *Forschungen in Ephesos* veröffentlicht vom Österreichischen Archaeologischen Institute, 4 (Heft 2; 1937): *Das Cömeterium der Sieben Schläfer*. E. Honigmann, *Patristic Studies* (Studi e Testi, 173; 1953), no. 17, 'Stephen of Ephesus (April 15, 448–Oct. 29, 451) and the Legend of the Seven Sleepers', pp. 125–68. I. Guidi in *HERE* 11 (1920), pp. 428–30, with refs.; H. *Leclercq, OSB, in *DACL* 15 (pt. 1; 1950), cols. 1251–62, s.v. 'Sept Dormants d'Éphèse'; V. Saxer in *Bibliotheca Sanctorum*, 11 (1968), cols. 900–7, s.v. 'Sette Dormienti'.

Seven Sorrows of the BVM. Acc. to the former Roman Breviary, the Sorrows were the following: (1) at the prophecy of *Simeon; (2) at the flight into Egypt; (3) at the loss of the Holy Child; (4) on meeting the Lord on the way to Calvary; (5) at standing at the foot of the Cross; (6) at the taking down of Christ from the Cross; (7) at His burial. Until 1960 the Seven Sorrows were commemorated on two feast days: the Friday after *Passion Sunday (dating locally from the 15th cent., made of universal observance by *Benedict XIII in 1729, but reduced to a commemoration in 1960 and dropped entirely in 1969) and 15 Sept. The September feast, originally observed on the third Sunday in September, was granted to the *Servites in 1668 and extended by *Pius VII to the whole RC Church. In 1913 it was fixed on 15 September, except for the Servites who retain the Sunday. In the 1969 Calendar it was called the feast of Our Lady of Sorrow.

seven virtues. They are (1) faith; (2) hope; (3) charity; (4) justice; (5) prudence; (6) temperance; (7) fortitude. The first three are the '*theological virtues', the remaining four the '*cardinal virtues'.

Seven Words from the Cross. They are (1) 'Father, forgive them; for they know not what they do' (Lk. 23: 34); (2) 'Today shalt thou be with me in paradise' (Lk. 23: 43); (3) 'Woman, behold thy son! . . . Behold thy mother' (Jn. 19: 26 f.); (4) 'Eli, Eli, lama sabachthani? [that is to say] My God, my God, why hast thou forsaken me?' (Mt. 27: 46; cf. Mk. 15: 34); (5) 'I thirst' (Jn. 19: 28); (6) 'It is finished' (Jn. 19: 30); (7) 'Father, into thy hands I commend my spirit' (Lk 23: 46).

Seventh-day Adventists. One of the groups of *Adventists who originally expected the Second Coming of Christ in 1844. Later in that year they began to observe the seventh day as the Sabbath, although the name 'Seventh-day Adventist' was not adopted until 1861. In England their beginnings as an organized community go back to a mission started at Southampton by W. Ings in 1878. They are a staunchly Protestant body, believing that

the Scriptures provide the unerring rule of faith and practice and that the return of Christ is imminent, although they set no date for that event. Emphasizing that the human body is a temple of the Holy Spirit (1 Cor. 6: 19), they require of their members a life of strict temperance; abstinence from alcohol and tobacco is mandatory and that from tea, coffee, and meat is recommended. Members observe the Sabbath from sunset on Friday to sunset on Saturday. They are expected to pay tithe on their income in addition to freewill offerings. They are Trinitarian in belief and adhere to the doctrine of salvation by grace through faith alone. They practise adult Baptism by total immersion. Their current world membership (1994) is over eight million (*c.*18,500 in the British Isles).

D. F. Neufeld and others (ed.), *Seventh-day Adventist Encyclopedia* (Washington, DC, 1966). A. W. Spalding, *Origin and History of Seventh-day Adventists* (4 vols., ibid., 1961–2); L. E. Froom, *Movement of Destiny* (ibid., 1971); G. Land (ed.), *Adventism in America: A History* (Grand Rapids, Mich. [1986]). On their early history, F. D. Nichol, *The Midnight Cry* (Washington, DC, 1944); P. G. Damsteegt, *Foundations of the Seventh-day Adventist Message and Mission* (Grand Rapids, Mich., 1977); R. L. Numbers and J. M. Butler (eds.), *The Disappointed: Millerism and Millenarianism in the Nineteenth Century* (Bloomington, Ind. [1987]); on their doctrine, *Seventh-day Adventists Answer Questions on Doctrine* (Washington, DC, 1957), a compilation; B. W. Ball, *The English Connection: The Puritan Roots of Seventh-day Adventist Belief* (Cambridge [1981]); R. Rice, *The Reign of God* (Berrien Springs, Mich., 1985); *Seventh-day Adventists Believe. . .* (Washington, DC, 1988), a compilation; M. Bull and K. Lockhart, *Seeking a Sanctuary: Seventh-day Adventism and the American Dream* (San Francisco and London [1989] [sociological]).

Seventh Day Baptists. See BAPTISTS.

Severian (*fl. c.*400), Bp. of Gabala. A strong opponent of St *Chrysostom, he played a leading part at *Constantinople in the events leading up to the Synod of the *Oak in 403. He is chiefly important as an exegete of the *Antiochene School. His writings include a collection of six Homilies on the *Hexaemeron*, other sermons on Genesis, a set of nine Homilies which have come down in Armenian, and several catena fragments. Many of these survive under the name of St Chrysostom.

His writings have not been collected. His six Homilies on the *Hexaemeron* are repr. in J. P. Migne, *PG* 56. 429–500; Hom. de Serpente, ibid., cols. 499–516; Hom. de Sigillis, ibid. 63. 531–44. Catena frags. from Severian's Comm. on the Pauline Epp. in K. Staab, *Die Pauluskommentare aus der griechischen Kirche* (1933), pp. 213–351. Fifteen Armenian Homilies ed. J. B. Aucher, Venice, 1827 (several of these, however, are spurious). Further homily, ed., with Ger. tr., by B. M. Weischer, *Qērellos IV 3: Traktate des Severianos von Gabala, Gregorios Thaumaturgos und Kyrillos von Alexandrien* (Äthiopistische Forschungen, 7; Wiesbaden, 1980), pp. 19–67. M. Aubineau, *Un Traité inédit de Christologie de Sévérien de Gabala In Centurionem et contra Manichæos et Apollinaristas: Exploitation par Sévère d'Antioche (519) et le Synode du Latran (649)* (Cahiers d'Orientalisme, 5; Geneva, 1983), incl. text. C. Datema, 'Towards a Critical Edition of the Greek Homilies of Severian of Gabala', *Orientalia Lovaniensia Periodica*, 19 (1988), pp. 107–15. J. Zellinger, *Die Genesishomilien des Bischofs Severian von Gabala* (Alttestamentliche Abhandlungen, 7, Heft 1; 1916); id., *Studien zu Severian von Gabala* (Münsterische Beiträge zur Theologie, 8; 1926). H. D. Altendorf, *Untersuchungen zu Severian von Gabala* (Tübingen diss., 1957). B. Marx ascribed other homilies among the Chrysostomica to Severian in '*Severiana* unter der *Spuria Chrysostomi* bei Montfaucon-Migne', *OCP* 5 (1939), pp. 281–367. *CPG* 2 (1974), pp. 468–88 (nos. 4185–295). Altaner and Stuiber (1978), pp. 332 and 618. E. Venables in *DCB* 4 (1887), pp. 625 f.; S. J. Voicu in *Dict. Sp.* 14 (1990), cols. 752–63, s.v. 'Sévérien de Gabala'.

Severinus, St (d. 482), 'Apostle of Austria'. He was in early life a monk in the East. After the death of *Attila in 453, he came to Noricum Ripense, then overrun by barbarian invaders, and though never himself a bishop, he rallied the Church, founded two monasteries, and organized relief work, in this way winning the respect of the barbarians (particularly Odoacer) and moderating their cruelty. His body was taken to Lucullanum, nr. Naples, where his companion *Eugippius wrote his Life *c*.511. Feast day, 8 Jan. He is the patron of vine-dressers.

Acc. to the Roman Martyrology, his feast day, Jan. 8, is also observed as that of another Severinus, Bp. of Naples, 'brother of Bl Victorinus, Martyr'. As no Bishop of Naples of this name is known to have existed, there is perhaps some confusion with St Severinus, the Apostle of Austria.

The principal authority is the Life by Eugippius, pr. J. P. Migne, *PL*. 62. 1167–2000; crit. edns. by P. Knoell (CSEL 9, pt. 2; 1886), T. *Mommsen (*MGH*, Scriptores Rerum Germanicarum in usum scholarum; Berlin, 1898), R. Noll (Schriften und Quellen der alten Welt, 11; 1963), and, with Fr. tr. and introd., by P. Régerat (SC 374; 1991). Eng. tr. by L. Bieler and L. Krestan (Fathers of the Church, 55; 1965). P. Dörfler, *Severin, der Seher von Norikum* (2nd edn., Freiburg i.B., 1947). K. Kramert and E. K. Winter, *St Severin* (2 vols., Klosterneuburg [1958–9]). F. Lotter, *Severinus von Noricum* (Monographien zur Geschichte des Mittelalters, 12; Stuttgart, 1976). J. Haberl, *Wien ist älter: Der Heilige Severin und die Frühgeschichte Wiens* (Vienna, 1981). R. Bratož, *Severinus von Noricum und seine Zeit* (Österreichische Akademie der Wissenschaften, Phil.-hist. Klasse, Denkschriften, 165; 1983). Popular study by R. Zinnhobler (Linz [1982]), with good illustrations. V. Pavan in *DIP* 8 (1988), cols. 1456–9, s.v. 'Severino'.

Severus (*c*.465–538), *Syrian Orthodox Patr. of *Antioch. He studied at *Alexandria and Beirut, was baptized in 488, and later became a monk. About 508 he went to *Constantinople, where he succeeded in securing the support of the Emp. Anastasius (491–518) for the persecuted *Monophysite monks, and in 512 was made Patr. of Antioch in place of the deposed Flavian II. On Justin I's accession (518), he was deposed, took refuge with Timothy IV, the Monophysite Patr. of Alexandria, and after the failure of an attempted reconciliation under *Justinian, was excommunicated by a synod at Constantinople in 536. Severus was the leading theologian of the moderate Monophysites. Many of his works, still not completely edited, survive, including 125 homilies and 400 letters. They are mainly preserved in Syriac translations. His Life to the year 512 was written by his friend *Zacharias Scholasticus.

Severus' *Liber contra Impium Grammaticum* [*sc*. against *John the Grammarian] ed. J. Lebon (CSCO, Scriptores Syri, 4. 4–6; 1929–38); his *Orationes ad Nephalium* ed. id. (ibid. 4. 7; 1949) (incl. his correspondence with Sergius Grammaticus); his *Philalethes* ed. R. Hespel (ibid., Scriptores Syri, 68–69; 1952); other writings against the extreme Monophysite, *Julian of Halicarnassus, ed. id. (ibid. 104–5, 124–7, 136–7; 1964–71). Of his 125 Cathedral Homilies, dating from 512–518, the first, in Coptic, and the rest of the collection in Syr. tr., mainly by *Jacob of Edessa, ed., with Fr. tr., in *PO* 4–38 (1906–76); for details see *PO* 38

(1976–7), p. 250 (fasc. 2, p. 6). His 'Sixth Book of Letters', ed. E. W. Brooks (2 vols., Text and Translation Society, 1902–4); further Letters, ed. id., with Eng. tr., in *PO* 12 (1919), pp. 165–342 (fasc. 2), and 14 (1920), pp. 1–310 (fasc. 1). His Hymns, in the tr. of Jacob of Edessa, ed., with Eng. tr., by E. W. Brooks, ibid. 6 (1911), pp. 5–179 (fasc. 1); 7 (1911), pp. 597–802 (fasc. 5). Eng. tr. of his correspondence with Sergius the Grammarian by I. R. Torrance, *Christology after Chalcedon* (Norwich, 1988). The 'Anaphora' traditionally (but wrongly) ascribed to Severus ed. H. W. Codrington, *Anaphorae Syriacae*, 1, fasc. 1 (Rome, 1939), pp. 51–96, with introd. by A. Raes, SJ, pp. v–xlix. Lives by Zacharias Scholasticus and by John of Beith Aphthonia, with other relevant documents, ed. M. A. Kugener, with Fr. tr., in *PO* 2 (1907), pp. 5–115 and 203–400 (fascs. 1 and 3). There is also a verse Life by *George, Bp. of the Arabians, ed., with Eng. tr., by K. E. McVey (CSCO, Scriptores Syri, 216–17; 1993). The most important modern study is J. Lebon, *Le Monophysisme sévérien* (Louvain, 1909). A. Grillmeier, SJ, and H. Bacht, SJ (eds.), *Das Konzil von Chalkedon* (3 vols., 1951–4), *passim* (see index, 3, pp. 968 f.). R. C. Chesnut, *Three Monophysite Christologies: Severus of Antioch, Philoxenus of Mabbug, and Jacob of Sarug* (Oxford Theological Monographs, 1976), pp. 9–56. A. Grillmeier, SJ, *Jesus der Christus im Glauben der Kirche*, 2 (pt. 2; Freiburg, etc., 1989), pp. 20–185; Eng. tr. (1995), pp. 19–175. A. *Baumstark, 'Das Kirchenjahr in Antiocheia zwischen 512 und 518', *RQ* 11 (1897), pp. 31–66; 13 (1899), pp. 305–23. *CPG* 3 (1979), pp. 327–45 (nos. 7022–81). A. Baumstark, *Geschichte der syrischen Literatur* (1922), see index, p. 376; Altaner and Stuiber (1978), pp. 505–7 and 658. G. Bardy in *DTC* 14 (pt. 2; 1941), cols. 1988–2000; F. Graffin, SJ, in *Dict. Sp.* 14 (1990), cols. 748–51, s.v.

Severus, Gabriel, Metropolitan of Philadelphia. See GABRIEL SEVERUS.

Severus, Sulpicius. See SULPICIUS SEVERUS.

Sewell, William (1804–74), Anglican divine. Educated at *Winchester and Merton College, Oxford, where he had a brilliant academic career, he was elected a Fellow of Exeter College in 1827. From 1836 to 1841 he was Professor of Moral Philosophy, publishing in 1840 a significant work, *Christian Morals*, and in 1845 his popular novel, *Hawkstone*. He was one of the ablest and most learned of those in general sympathy with the *Tractarian movement in its earlier days, though he dissociated himself from it after the publication of *Tract 90* in 1841. He remained a *High Churchman with a particular interest in education in accordance with Anglican principles. He founded St Columba's College, Rathfarnham, near Dublin, in 1843, in association with a group of Irish High Churchmen, and in 1847, St Peter's College, Radley. He was also the author of many theological and classical writings.

L. James, *A Forgotten Genius: Sewell of St Columba's and Radley* (1945). G. C. Boase in *DNB* 51 (1897), pp. 290 f.

Sexagesima (Lat., 'the sixtieth [day before Easter]'). The second Sunday before *Lent and hence the eighth before *Easter. Its name, formed on the analogy of *Quinquagesima and *Septuagesima (qq.v.), goes back certainly to the 6th cent. It was suppressed in the RC Church in 1969, and it does not figure in some modern Anglican liturgies. In the W. the Sunday was also known, from the opening words of the *Introit, as Exsurge Sunday.

A. Chavasse, 'Temps de préparation à la Pâques d'après quelques livres liturgiques romains', *Rech. S.R.* 37 (1950), pp.

125–45, esp. IV, 'La "Soixantaine" ou Sexagésime', pp. 130–43. See also bibl. to SEPTUAGESIMA.

Sext (1). 'Liber Sextus Decretalium', the book of *canon law promulgated by *Boniface VIII in 1298. This 'Sixth Book' contains the *decretals posterior to the five books issued by *Gregory IX (1234), the material being similarly arranged. The bulk of the texts are from the decretals of Boniface VIII himself, notably the bull '*Clericis laicos' (under the title 'De immunitate)', the rest from those of the successors of Gregory IX and the two Councils of *Lyons in 1245 and 1274. The legislation in the Sext, as in most collections of canon law, covers a wide range of miscellaneous subjects and also reflects the growing tendency to centralization in the later medieval Church.

The standard text is that of E. Friedberg (ed.), *Corpus Juris Canonici*, 2 (Leipzig, 1881), cols. 929–1124. P. Torquebiau in *DDC* 4 (1949), cols. 632–5, s.v. 'Corpus Juris Canonici III', with list of principal commentators and other bibl. refs.

Sext (2). The 'Little Hour' of the Breviary Office appointed to be recited at noon. See also TERCE, SEXT, NONE.

sexton. Traditionally the sexton was the assistant of the *parish clerk. His principal duties consisted of cleaning the church fabric, ringing the bell, and digging graves: he thus combined the ancient offices of *fossor, *doorkeeper, and *sacristan. With the division of these duties the title has become obsolescent. The office may be held by a woman. The sexton is appointed by the minister and parochial church council, who determine the nature of the duty and terms of employment (can. E 3 of 1969).

J. Wickham Legg (ed.), *The Clerk's Book of 1549* (HBS 25; 1903), esp. pp. xlvii–xlviii and 78–80.

Seymour, Edward. See SOMERSET, DUKE OF.

Shaftesbury, Anthony Ashley Cooper (1801–85), Seventh Earl of Shaftesbury, social reformer and factory legislator. He was educated at Harrow and Christ Church, Oxford, and in 1826 entered on his Parliamentary career as a member of the Conservative Party. His main concern was with the amelioration of the conditions of the working classes, in whose interest he often pursued an independent line of policy. A personal investigation of the London slums in 1846 bore fruit in the Ten Hours Bill of 1847 and the Factory Act of 1874, for both of which he was largely responsible. He also took up the cause of women and children in the mines and collieries, as well as young chimney sweeps, for whose protection he introduced the Climbing Boys Act. He was for a long time chairman of the Ragged School Union, and in 1872 he laid the foundation stone of Shaftesbury Park Estate at Battersea. He was a fervent *Evangelical, who hated Ritualism and attacked Rationalism. Though a supporter of *Catholic Emancipation, he opposed the *Maynooth Endowment. He was for many years president of the *British and Foreign Bible Society. He was also the first president of the *CPAS; it was in company with Scripture readers from this society and the London City Mission that he went into the slums. He took a deep interest in the work of the *CMS and the *YMCA. He was the trusted adviser of Lord Palmerston

for the appointment of bishops and other high preferment in the C of E.

E. Hodder, *The Life and Work of the Seventh Earl of Shaftesbury* (3 vols., 1886), with extracts from his diaries *passim*. J. L. and B. Hammond, *Lord Shaftesbury* (1923); G. B. A. M. Finlayson, *The Seventh Earl of Shaftesbury* (1981). Other studies by G. F. A. Best (London, 1964), G. Battiscombe (ibid., 1974), and J. Pollock (ibid., 1985). J. W. Bready, *Lord Shaftesbury and Social-Industrial Progress* (1926). W. G. Blaikie in *DNB* 12 (1887), pp. 133–7, s.v. 'Cooper'.

Shakers, also 'The United Society of Believers in Christ's Second Appearing' or 'The Millennial Church', an early communistic body which originated in 1747 in an eccentric group known as 'Shaking Quakers' in Bolton, Lancs; their connection with the main body of *Quakers is unclear. They may have been influenced by survivors of the French Prophets or *Camisards. The original leaders, James and Jane Wardley, were succeeded by Ann Lee, wife of a Manchester blacksmith, known later as 'Mother Ann'. She came to be regarded as 'The female principle in Christ', Jesus being the 'Male principle'; in her the Second Coming was fulfilled. After a period of persecution, in 1774 she led a band of six men and two women to the USA, where they settled near Albany, NY. They were joined by members of existing *revivalist movements in the 1780s and soon founded further communities. After Mother Ann's death in 1784 the leadership passed to Joseph Meacham and Lucy Wright who instituted a more tightly regulated community life.

The name 'Shakers' derived from the shaking by which under the stress of spiritual exaltation they were possessed during their meetings; this later developed into formal ritual dances. They were organized in large 'families' within each community and full members practised community of goods under a hierarchical form of government. They insisted on confession to the Elders before admission, and enjoined it on those conscious of faults thereafter. A minute discipline was exercised over dress and personal behaviour; the use of alcohol and tobacco was severely limited, and herbal medicine was practised along with *spiritual healing. Underlying Shaker teaching and practice was the belief that celibacy was the way to the holy life; it was secured by careful monitoring of relations between the sexes. Relations with the outside world were also restricted, though Shaker opinion was divided on the extent to which separation should be observed. The principle of 'simplicity' was exemplified in Shaker artefacts which are now admired for their aesthetic qualities. The Shakers probably achieved a maximum of 6,000 members at their peak in the 1840s, but by 1994 only one community remained.

Testimonies of the Life, Character, Revelations, and Doctrines of our blessed Mother Ann Lee (Hancock, Mass., 1816; 2nd edn., Albany, NY, 1888; repr., New York, 1975). Extracts from this and other Shaker writings ed., with introd., by R. E. Whitson, *The Shakers: Two Centuries of Spiritual Reflection* (Classics of Western Spirituality, 1983). A. White and L. S. Taylor, *Shakerism, its meaning and message* (Columbus, Oh. [1904]); M. F. Melcher, *The Shaker Adventure* (Princeton, NJ, and London, 1941); E. D. Andrews, *The People called Shakers* (New York, 1953; repr., with additional notes [1963]). H. Desroche, *Les Shakers américains: D'un néo-Christianisme à un pre-socialisme?* (1955; Eng. tr., Amherst, 1971). J. McK. Whitworth, *God's Blueprints: A Sociological Study* of *Three Utopian Sects* (1975), pp. 13–88 and 242 f. C. Garrett, *Spirit Possession and Popular Religion: From the Camisards to the Shakers* (Baltimore, 1987), pp. 14–241. S. J. Stein, *The Shaker Experience in America: A History of the United Society of Believers* (New Haven and London [1992]). D. W. Patterson, *The Shaker Spiritual* (Princeton, NJ [1979]). J. Sprigg, *Shaker Design* (New York and London [1986]). J. P. MacLean, *A Bibliography of Shaker Literature* (privately pr., Columbus, Oh., 1905).

Shakespeare, John Howard (1857–1928), *Baptist preacher and organizer. After a 15-year pastorate at *Norwich, he became secretary of the Baptist Union in 1898 and gradually won for himself a leading position in the religious world. He made the Baptist Union a highly influential organization, and was mainly responsible for founding the Baptist World Alliance (1905) and the Federal Council of the Evangelical Free Churches (1919; see FREE CHURCH FEDERAL COUNCIL) and for securing the appointment of Baptist and Congregational chaplains in the army. His book, *The Churches at the Cross Roads* (1918), is a moving and powerful plea for the reunion of Christendom.

G. Shakespeare (son), *Let Candles Be Brought* (1947), ch. 17, pp. 335–47.

Shammai, School of. The disciples of Shammai, a leading Jewish teacher of the time of Christ. In contrast with the School of *Hillel, the Shammaites interpreted the Mosaic Law strictly and rigidly, following the unbending attitude of their founder, and during the reorganization of rabbinic Judaism after AD 70 generally the moderation of the School of Hillel prevailed.

Bibl. as for School of Hillel, q.v.

Sharp, James (1618–79), Abp. of St Andrews. He was educated at King's College, Aberdeen, where he remained until at least 1638. He seems to have identified himself with the Aberdeen doctors who opposed the *National Covenant, and, acc. to early sources, went to England. By early 1642 he was employed as a regent in St Andrews University, and in 1648 became minister of Crail (in Fife). When the Scottish Kirk was divided into resolutioners and protestors he took sides with the former and soon became one of their leaders. In 1660 he joined General G. Monck, who was then planning to effect the Restoration, and began to work secretly for the re-establishment of Episcopacy while outwardly protesting his loyalty to the Kirk. The services he thus rendered to the King's cause were rewarded by his appointment to the see of St Andrews in 1661. As Archbishop he took severe measures to abolish Presbyterianism and supported the oppressive policy of the Earl of Lauderdale, an attitude which roused the bitter resentment of his opponents. In 1668 James Mitchell made an attempt to shoot him, and when, in 1678, Mitchell was finally executed, the hatred against Sharp increased, and in the next year he was brutally murdered by a party of Fife lairds and farmers.

'Thirty Four Letters written to James Sharp ... by the Duke and Duchess of Lauderdale and by Charles Maitland, Lord Hatton, 1660–1672', ed. J. Dowden in *Miscellany of the Scottish History Society*, 1 (Scottish History Society, 15; 1893), pp. 229–92. A number of polemical accounts of his murder were pub. at the time of his death; further contemporary account by James Russell appended to J. Kirkton, *The Secret and True History of the Church of Scotland from the Restoration to the Year 1678* (1817), pp. 403–82. J. Buckroyd, *Church and State in Scotland 1660–1681* (Edinburgh, 1980), *passim*; id., *The Life of James Sharp, Archbishop of St Andrews 1618–1679* (ibid. [1987]). T. F. Henderson in *DNB* 51 (1897), pp. 404–7.

Sharp, John (1645–1714), Abp. of *York. Educated at Christ's College, Cambridge, he became rector of St Giles-in-the-Fields in 1675 and Dean of *Norwich in 1681. A strong High Churchman, he refused to read the *Declaration of Indulgence of 1688. In 1689, however, he took the oaths to William and Mary, but announced that he would not accept any bishopric vacated by a *Nonjuror during the lifetime of the former occupant. In 1691 he accepted the see of York on the death of Thomas Lamplugh, and his episcopate was notable for the high standard of duty which marked it (e.g. in his distribution of patronage). Queen *Anne, who greatly respected him, made him her spiritual adviser.

Life by Thomas Sharp (son), ed. T. Newcome, pub. 2 vols., London, 1825. A. T. Hart, *The Life and Times of John Sharp, Archbishop of York* (CHS, 1949). G. Le G. Norgate in *DNB* 51 (1897), pp. 408–11.

Shaxton, Nicholas (*c*.1485–1556), Bp. of *Salisbury. Educated at Cambridge, he was one of the committee appointed by the university in 1530 to consider the royal divorce. He thereby obtained the patronage of *Anne Boleyn, while the favour of T. *Cromwell and his own advocacy of the Royal Supremacy enabled him to survive her downfall unharmed. He soon developed pronounced Protestant views. In 1535 he was made Bp. of Salisbury, but resigned his see in 1539, in protest against the *Six Articles. During the rest of the reign his position was precarious, and in 1546 he was arrested with Anne *Askew and others and charged with heretical views on the Eucharist. He saved himself from the stake by a recantation, apparently quite sincere, since he maintained a Catholic position throughout the reign of *Edward VI. Under *Mary he was appointed a suffragan to the Bp. of *Ely, and took part in the examination of certain Protestants on trial for heresy.

His Injunctions for the Archdeaconry of Dorset in 1538 were pr. in London and pub. at Salisbury. J. *Gairdner in *DNB* 51 (1897), pp. 452–4, s.v., with refs.

Sheer Thursday. An old name for *Maundy Thursday, perhaps from 'skere' or 'sheer' (= 'clean', 'free from guilt'), with reference to the practice of receiving absolution or (alternatively) of ceremonially washing the altars of the church on that day.

Shekinah (Heb. שְׁכִינָה, 'dwelling'). The word (not found in the OT) is used by the Jews of God's visible Presence, conceived as 'dwelling' among men. The *Rabbis often employed it as one of the circumlocutions for the name of 'God' in cases where it was desired to avoid *anthropomorphism. Hence in the *Targum, Is. 6: 5 becomes 'Mine eyes have seen the glory of the Shekinah of the King of the Ages'. Similarly, in the NT the ideas of God's glory and His dwelling among men are associated in Jn. 1: 14 ('And the Word became flesh, and dwelt among us, and we beheld his glory'), and in a number of other passages the word 'glory' (δόξα) occasionally seems to convey the overtones associated with the Jewish Shekinah.

M. Kadushin, *The Rabbinic Mind* (New York, 1952; 3rd edn., 1972), esp. pp. 222–61. E. E. Urbach, *The Sages: Their Concepts and Beliefs*, 1 (Jerusalem, 1975; Eng. tr. from Heb. pub. 1969), pp. 37–65.

Sheldon, Gilbert (1598–1677), Abp. of *Canterbury. Educated at Trinity College, Oxford, he was elected Fellow of All Souls in 1622 and ordained in the same year. In 1626 he was made Warden of All Souls and became an active supporter of W. *Laud's reforms at Oxford. During this period he also held in plurality several country livings. In 1638 he was put on the reforming commission which visited Merton College. A strong Royalist, he took part in the negotiations for the Uxbridge treaty of 1644 and in 1647 was with the King at Newmarket and Carisbrooke. In 1648 he was ejected from All Souls and spent some months in prison. During most of the Commonwealth he lived in retirement in the Midlands. Eventually, in 1659, he was restored to his Wardenship. In 1660 he became Bp. of London and Master of the Savoy, and in 1661 the *Savoy Conference met at his lodgings. While W. *Juxon lived he was virtually primate and succeeded him at Canterbury on his death in 1663. As Archbishop he worked hard for the re-establishment of Laudian religious principles. He also carried through the arrangement with Clarendon whereby the Convocations ceased to tax the clergy (1664). After Clarendon's fall in 1667 he was in disfavour at Court for most of the rest of his primacy, and he strongly opposed *Charles II's *Declaration of Indulgence of 1672. Throughout his life he was devoted to his university, and from 1667 to 1669 he was Chancellor. The Sheldonian Theatre at Oxford was built at his expense. Many of his papers are preserved in the *Bodleian Library.

N. Salmon (anon.), *The Lives of English Bishops from the Restauration to the Revolution* (pt. 1; 1731), pp. 10–47. V. Staley, *The Life and Times of Gilbert Sheldon* [1913]. N. Sykes, *From Sheldon to Secker* (Ford Lectures, 1958; Cambridge, 1959), *passim*. V. D. Sutch, *Gilbert Sheldon, Architect of Anglican Survival, 1640–1675* (International Archives of the History of Ideas, Series Minor, 12; The Hague, 1973; cf. review by R. A. Beddard in *Historical Journal*, 19 (1976), pp. 1005–17). P. Seaward, 'Gilbert Sheldon, the London Vestries, and the Defence of the Church', in T. Harris and others (eds.), *The Politics of Religion in Restoration England* (Oxford, 1990), pp. 49–73. W. H. *Hutton in *DNB* 52 (1897), pp. 24–6.

Shema, the (Heb. שְׁמַע, 'hear'). The Jewish confession of faith. Its name is derived from the first word of the first of the three scriptural passages of which it consists, namely Deut. 6: 4–9, 11: 13–21, Num. 15: 37–41. These are preceded and followed by a number of benedictions. The Shema, which is mentioned as a well-known observance in the *Mishnah (*Berakoth*, 1) and was doubtless known to Christ (cf. Mk. 12: 29), is to be recited every morning and evening by all Jewish men and is included among the passages inscribed in the *phylacteries.

A. Z. Idelsohn, *Jewish Liturgy and its Development* (New York [1932]), pp. 88–92; L. A. Hoffman, *The Canonization of the Synagogue Service* (Notre Dame, Ind., and London [1979]), pp. 24–49. L. Jacobs in *Encyclopaedia Judaica*, 14 (Jerusalem, 1972), cols. 1370–74, s.v.

Shemone Esre. See EIGHTEEN BENEDICTIONS.

Shenoute (d. prob. 466), or 'Shenudi', Abbot of Athribis in Egypt. In 370 he entered the White Monastery, nr. Schâg, under his uncle Pgôl, where he became superior *c*.388. His community greatly increased, the numbers being given as 2,200 monks and 1,800 nuns. His government was very severe, esp. in the punishments, which included flogging and imprisonment for light faults, and he added many austerities to the more humane rule of *Pachomius. One of his most important innovations was the introduction of a written profession of obedience for his religious, probably elicited by the frequent cases of revolt and insubordination. He also allowed his older monks to live apart as hermits. An organizer rather than a theologian, Shenoute accompanied St *Cyril of Alexandria to the Council of *Ephesus in 431, where he played an important part opposing *Nestorius. He knew Greek, but wrote in Coptic. The letters, homilies, and apocalypses attributed to him, of which many are spurious, are written in a fiery style and deal chiefly with monastic concerns and with exhortations to practise virtue and avoid vice. Feast day in the Coptic Church, 1 July.

Works ed., with Fr. tr., by E. Amélineau (2 vols. in 3 parts, Paris, 1907–14), and by W. E. Leipoldt and W. E. Crum (CSCO, Scriptores Coptici, 2nd ser. 4–5; 1908–13; with Lat. tr. by H. Weismann, SJ, 1931–6). Some sermons and letters also ed. É. Chassinat (Mémoires publiés par les membres de l'Institut Français d'Archéologie Orientale du Caire, 23; 1911). Previously unpublished frags. in the British Library ed., with Eng. tr., by A. Shisha-Halevy in *Orientalia*, NS 44 (1975), pp. 149–85, with comm., pp. 469–82; others from a work against Origenism ed., with Eng. tr., by id. in *Enchoria*, 5 (Wiesbaden, 1975), pp. 53–108, with comm., ibid. 6 (1976), pp. 29–61; frags. of the same work in Italian libraries ed., with Ital. tr., by T. Orlandi (Rome, 1985). Pseudo-Shenoute, *On Christian Behaviour* ed. K. H. Kuhn (CSCO, Scriptores Coptici, 29; 1960, with Eng. tr., ibid. 30; 1960). Life by his pupil Besa, ed. J. Leipoldt and W. E. Crum (CSCO, Scriptores Coptici, 2nd ser. 2; 1906; Lat. tr. by H. Wiesmann, SJ, ibid., Scriptores Coptici, 16; 1951). Eng. tr. by D. N. Bell (Cistercian Studies Series, 73; Kalamazoo, Mich., 1983), with introd. and bibl. J. Leipoldt, *Schenute von Atripe und die Entstehung des national-ägyptischen Christentums* (TU 25, Heft 1; 1903). D. W. Young, 'The Milieu of Nag Hammadi: Some Historical Considerations', *VC* 24 (1970), pp. 127–37. J. Horn, *Studien zu den Märtyrern des nördlichen Oberägypten, 1: Märtyrerverehrung und Märtyrerlegende im Werk des Schenute* (Göttinger Orientforschungen, Reihe IV, Band 15; 1986). J. Quasten, *Patrology*, 3 (Utrecht and Westminster, Md., 1960), pp. 185–7.

Sheol (Heb. שְׁאוֹל), in the OT, the underworld, the place of the departed spirits. The derivation of the word is not known. In the AV it is translated variously as 'hell', 'grave', or 'pit'; more recent translations usually leave it untranslated as a proper noun. The notion reflects an undeveloped and shadowy belief in the future life which was gradually superseded by the more defined beliefs of later Judaism. The conception was widely held in early Semitic mythology and descriptions of Sheol in the OT can frequently be paralleled from Assyrian and Babylonian sources.

F. *Delitzsch, *Das Land ohne Umkehr: Die Gedanken der Babylonier-Assyrer über Tod und Jenseits* (1911). P. Dhorme, OP, 'Le Séjour des morts chez les Babyloniens et chez les Hébreux', *R. Bibl.* 16 (1907), pp. 59–78; id., 'L'Idée de l'au-delà dans la religion hébraïque', *Revue de l'Histoire des Religions*, 113 (1941), pp. 113–42. H. H. Rowley, *The Faith of Israel* (1956), pp. 157–60, 171–5. W. Eichrodt, *Theologie des Alten Testaments*, Teile 2 und 3 (5th edn., 1964), pp. 143–7; Eng. tr., vol. 2 (1967), pp. 210–16. N. J. Tromp, MSC, *Primitive Conceptions of Death and the Nether World in the Old Testament* (Biblica et Orientalia, 21; 1969), *passim*. R. H. *Charles, *A Critical History of the Doctrine of a Future Life* (1899), see index p. 426.

Shepherd of Hermas, The. The treatise of the sub-Apostolic Christian writer, *Hermas (q.v.). It was so named from the angel who, in the form of a shepherd, is recorded to have communicated to Hermas some of its contents. The identification of Hermas himself with the Shepherd, found in some later writers, seems to have arisen from mere confusion.

For bibl. see HERMAS.

Sheppard, Hugh Richard Lawrie (1880–1937), popularly 'Dick Sheppard', vicar of St Martin-in-the-Fields, London. He was educated at Marlborough, Trinity Hall, Cambridge, and Cuddesdon, ordained deacon in 1907 to Oxford House, Bethnal Green, and in 1911 became curate of St George's, Hanover Square, London. In 1914 he was appointed vicar of St Martin-in-the-Fields. His religious enthusiasm and personal attractiveness won the affection of innumerable people in all stations of life, esp. after the growth of *broadcasting, of which he was the first to sense the full possibilities as a Christian influence. He made his church, with its unique 'parish magazine', the *St Martin's Review*, the best-known parish church in the British Empire. A keen enthusiast for ecclesiastical reform on unconventional lines, Sheppard identified himself with the Life and Liberty Movement in its earlier stages, and later his ideals for reform were embodied in *The Human Parson* (1924) and the very widely read *The Impatience of a Parson* (1927). Ill-health compelled his resignation of St Martin's in 1926. From 1929 to 1931 he was Dean of *Canterbury and for a brief space (1934–5) Canon of *St Paul's. In his last years he was an ardent upholder of the Pacifist cause and devoted his chief energies to its propagation.

R. Ellis Roberts, *H. R. L. Sheppard: Life and Letters* (1942). C. Scott, *Dick Sheppard: A Biography* (1977). C. Jenkins in *DNB, 1931–1940*, pp. 809 f.

Sherborne. St *Aldhelm established the seat of the Bp. of W. Wessex here in 705, and founded a church and school. In 978 Bp. Wulfsige introduced the Benedictine Rule, himself becoming the first abbot. In 1058 the see was united with Ramsbury, and in 1075 moved to Old *Sarum. The church was rebuilt in the 12th cent., and again, after a serious fire, in the 15th. At the *Dissolution in 1536, the parishioners purchased the abbey for a parish church, while the conventual buildings (13th, 14th, and 15th cents.) were handed over to the school, which was refounded (1550), with a new charter from *Edward VI. The church is a fine example of the Perpendicular style, with notable fan-tracery in the choir. A bishopric of Sherborne, suffragan to *Salisbury, was founded in 1928.

M. A. O'Donovan (ed.), *Charters of Sherborne* (Anglo-Saxon Charters, 3; Oxford, 1988). J. H. P. Gibb, *The Book of Sherborne* (Buckingham, 1981). On the abbey, see also W. *Dugdale, *Monasticon Anglicanum*, 1 (1817 edn.), pp. 331–41; M. M. C. Calthrop in *VCH*, Dorset, 2, ed. W. Page (1908), pp. 62–70; Royal Commission on Historical Monuments of England, *Dorset*, 1 (1952), pp. 200–9.

Sherlock, Thomas (1678–1761), Bp. of London. He was educated at Eton and Catharine Hall, Cambridge, where he was elected Fellow in 1698, and was Master from 1714 to 1719. In 1704 he had succeeded his father as Master of the Temple and held the office till 1753. Here he established a great reputation as a preacher. In the *Bangorian Controversy he was strongly opposed to B. *Hoadly, thereby temporarily losing his influence at court. Remarkably, his *High Church and Tory principles nevertheless did not prevent his promotion as Bp. in turn of *Bangor (1728–34), of *Salisbury (1734–48), and of London (1748–61). The most celebrated of his writings was his *Trial of the Witnesses of the Resurrection of Jesus* (1729, anon.), a highly characteristic apologetic writing of its age.

Extracts in J. M. Creed and J. S. Smith (eds.), *Religious Thought in the Eighteenth Century* (Cambridge, 1934), pp. 61–4 and 67–75. E. F. Carpenter, *Thomas Sherlock* (CHS, 1936). W. H. *Hutton in *DNB* 52 (1897), pp. 93–5.

Sherlock, William (1641–1707), Dean of St *Paul's. He was a native of Southwark, educated at Eton and Peterhouse, Cambridge, and in 1669 became rector of St George's, Botolph Lane, London. In 1674 he published *The Knowledge of Jesus Christ, and Union with Him*, in which he attacked Puritan spirituality, esp. the contention of J. *Owen that the mercy of God can be known only through Christ. In his *Case of Resistance* (1684) he upheld the *Divine Right of Kings and inculcated the duty of passive obedience. In 1685 he was made Master of the Temple. In the Revolution of 1688 he originally sided with the *Nonjurors. In 1690 he published the *Vindication of the Doctrines of the Trinity and of the Incarnation*. A violent controversy with R. *South and others followed, in which he was charged with teaching Tritheism. In the same year he took the oath, an action which he defended in the *Case of Allegiance* (1691), and in 1691 he was made Dean of St Paul's. In 1695 his Trinitarian views, propagated at Oxford by J. *Bingham, were condemned by the Hebdomadal Council, and in his *Present State of the Socinian Controversy* (1698) Sherlock abandoned most of his earlier theological doctrines. He is now best remembered for his *Practical Discourse concerning Death* (1689).

Sermons Preached upon Several Occasions (1700; 4th edn., 2 vols., 1755); several repr. in T. S. Hughes, *Summaries of the Sermons and Discourses of the Most Eminent British Divines* (1834), pp. 1–276. Sherlock's *Practical Discourse of Religious Assemblies* (1681), ed. H. Melvill (1840). C. F. Mullett, 'A Case of Allegiance: William Sherlock and the Revolution of 1688', *Huntington Library Quarterly*, 10 (1946–7), pp. 83–103. G. Every, *The High Church Party, 1688–1718* (CHS, 1956), esp. pp. 79–81; J. P. Kenyon, *Revolution Principles: The Politics of Party 1689–1720* (Ford Lectures, 1975–6; Cambridge, 1977), pp. 26–9. A. Gordon in *DNB* 52 (1897), pp. 95–7.

Shewbread (Heb. לֶחֶם הַפָּנִים; Gk. ὁ ἄρτος τῆς προθέσεως. The English word was adopted by W. *Tyndale from M. *Luther's *Schaubrot*. Modern translations generally prefer 'Bread of the Presence' (thus RSV, NEB, REB), or 'bread of offering' (JB)). The 12 loaves which, acc. to the practice of the Jewish *Temple, were prepared from the finest flour and, arranged in two piles, set out weekly beside the altar of incense 'before the Lord'. When they were removed for renewal at the end of the week, only the priests might eat them (cf. Lev. 24: 9, Mk. 2: 26). The practice, which is first referred to in 1 Sam. 21: 2–6 (*David at the sanctuary of Nob), was perhaps a survival from the custom of putting out food for the god (cf. Bel and the Dragon; also the Roman *lectisternia*). Acc. to 1 Kgs. 7: 48, the Table of Shewbread was among the furnishings of *Solomon's Temple. The use of the Shewbread was restored by *Judas Maccabaeus after Antiochus Epiphanes' desecration of the Temple (2 Macc. 10: 3). At the destruction of the Temple under Titus in AD 70, the Table was rescued and its transport to Rome by captured Jews is prominently depicted on the Arch of Titus. It eventually reached *Constantinople, whence it was sent back to *Jerusalem under *Justinian (d. 565). It probably perished in the sack of Jerusalem by Chosroes in 614.

M. Haran in *Encylopaedia Judaica*, 14 (Jerusalem, 1972), cols. 1394–6, s.v.

shibboleth (Heb. שִׁבֹּלֶת). A word used by Jephthah as a test to distinguish the Gileadites from the Ephraimites, whose local pronunciation of it as 'sibboleth' betrayed their identity (Jgs. 12: 4 ff.). In modern usage it denotes a sectarian or party catchword.

Shortened Services Act. See UNIFORMITY AMENDMENT ACT 1872.

Shorthouse, Joseph Henry (1834–1903), author of *John Inglesant*. Born at Birmingham, the son of *Quaker parents, he was attracted to Anglicanism under the influence of J. *Ruskin and the Pre-Raphaelites and baptized at St John's, Ladywood, in 1861. From 1866 to 1876, in the intervals of an active business life, he was constantly brooding over and working on *John Inglesant*, which he wrote down piecemeal. Finishing it at Llandudno in 1876, he was unable to find a publisher and had it printed privately in 1880. Shortly afterwards Mrs Humphry Ward brought it to the notice of A. Macmillan, who published it in 1881. It at once attracted very wide interest, among its admirers being W. E. *Gladstone, C. M. *Yonge, T. H. *Huxley, H. E. *Manning, and E. S. *Talbot. The delicacy and charm with which John Inglesant's spiritual pilgrimage is portrayed, its sympathetic understanding of the religious life of the 17th cent., and its vivid delineation of the community at *Little Gidding made it, apart from its high literary qualities, a powerful *apologia* for Anglicanism.

Shorthouse also wrote some other works, but they were without merit and have long been forgotten.

Life and Letters of J. H. Shorthouse, ed. by his Widow (2 vols., 1905). T. Seccombe in *DNB*, *1901–1911*, 3, pp. 309 f.

shrine (Lat. *scrinium*, 'chest'). In its original sense the word is applied to *reliquaries (q.v.), but is now commonly used either of sacred images of special importance usually kept in a church, or of any holy place, esp. one connected with *pilgrimages (q.v.). Among famous English medieval shrines are those of Our Lady of *Walsingham (recently rebuilt), of St *Edward the Confessor at *Westminster Abbey, of St Thomas *Becket at *Canterbury, and of St *Cuthbert at *Durham.

Shroud, Holy. See HOLY SHROUD.

Shrove Tuesday. The day immediately preceding *Ash Wednesday, so named from the 'shriving', i.e. confession and absolution, of the faithful on that day.

Sian-Fu Stone. See SIGAN-FU STONE.

Sibylline Oracles. An amorphous collection of oracles worked up by Jewish and Christian authors in imitation of the pagan 'Sibylline Books'. They consist of 14 books, two of which (9–10) duplicate material in earlier books. Books 1 and 2 give an account of the history of the world, in prophetic form, from the beginning of the world to the fall of Rome. Book 3 contains a defence of Jewish monotheism, together with another history of the world and apocalyptic prophecies. Books 4 and 5 deal with Roman history of Neronian times from the Jewish point of view, whereas Book 6 is a hymn to Christ. Book 7 is a conglomeration of eschatological prophecies and moral and ritual precepts. Book 8 treats of the nature of Christ and of His Incarnation. Books 11 to 14 (transmitted separately from 1–8) are of less religious interest, giving yet another account of world history of more or less imaginative character. The whole collection, which is written in hexameters, is preceded by a prose prologue affirming that the oracles are utterances of Greek Sibyls of various periods.

Many of the Fathers, e.g. *Theophilus of Antioch and *Clement of Alexandria, accepted this view of the Oracles and drew from them arguments in defence of Christianity. Modern critics, however, assign them to Jewish and Christian authors; for, though genuine Greek oracles are inserted in some places, the tendency of the whole is monotheistic and Messianic. They are evidently cast in their particular form to gain the pagan world to Jewish or Christian doctrines. The dates of the definitely Jewish portions of the collection range from the *Maccabaean period to the time of Hadrian, and these were freely used by the Christian *Apologists of the 2nd cent. The Christian additions seem to date from the late 2nd cent. onwards. Books 3–5 in their present form are probably mainly Jewish, of which the third, the oldest, is generally attributed to an Egyptian Jew writing *c.*140 BC, whilst the contents of Books 4 and 5 demand a date after the destruction of Jerusalem in AD 70. The other books are either of Christian origin or heavily interpolated in a Christian sense. Their dates are much disputed. Apart from Books 11–14, which are usually assigned to the 4th cent., or later, the latest seems to be Book 7 (generally dated 3rd cent.). The earliest are the Christian elements in Books 1 and 2, which are prob. to be dated in the second half of the 2nd cent. Books 6 and 8 used to be assigned to the 3rd cent., but most scholars now argue for a 2nd-cent. date for Book 8, and the hymn to Christ (Book 6) is often held to be *Gnostic and 2nd cent. The work, which reflects contemporary popular theology, had considerable influence on *Lactantius and was known to St *Augustine, who quotes a short passage in his 'De Civitate Dei' (18. 23).

Crit. edn. by J. Geffcken (GCS, 1902); more recent edn., with Ger. tr., by E. A. Kurfess [Munich, 1951]. Eng. tr., with introd., by J. J. Collins in J. H. Charlesworth (ed.), *The Old Testament Pseudepigrapha*, 1 (1983), pp. 317–472. Eng. tr. of considerable extracts from Books 1–2 and 6–8 by R. McL. Wilson, with tr. of introd. by U. Treu, in Schneemelcher, 2 (5th edn., Eng. tr., [1992]), pp. 652–80. J. Geffcken, *Komposition und Entstehungszeit der Oracula Sibyllina* (TU 23, Heft 1; 1902). B. Bischoff, 'Die lateinischen Übersetzungen und Bearbeitungen aus den *Oracula Sibyllina*', in *Mélanges Joseph de Ghellinck*, 1 (Museum Lessianum, Section Historique, 13; 1951), pp. 121–47; repr. in his *Mittelalterliche Studien*, 1 (1966), pp. 150–171. E. *Schürer, *A History of the Jewish People in the Age of Jesus Christ*, rev. Eng. tr. by G. Vermes and others, 3 (pt. 1, Edinburgh, 1986), pp. 618–54, with bibl. [A.] Rzach in *PW*, Zweite Reihe, 2 (pt. 2; 1923), cols. 2117–69, s.v. 'Sibyllinische Orakel'; J. J. Collins in *Anchor Bible Dictionary*, 6 (1992), pp. 2–7, s.v.

Sicard (*c.*1155–1215), Bp. of Cremona, historian, canonist, and liturgist. A native of Cremona, he was appointed Canon of Mainz in 1183 and Bp. of Cremona in 1185. Having won the confidence of *Frederick I, he played a considerable part in Lombard politics and was entrusted with several missions to Rome. In 1212–13 he was employed by the Pope on behalf of *Frederick II against Otto IV. His principal works are his *Chronicon*, a history of the world orig. up to 1201, revised and continued up to 1213, which is a primary authority for the Crusade of Frederick I; his *Summa* on the Decretum of *Gratian; and his *Mitrale*. The last of these, a moralistic and allegorical interpretation of places, ceremonies and vestments, throws important light on contemporary liturgical practice.

The best edn. of his *Chronicon* is that of O. Holder-Egger in *MGH*, Scriptores, 31 (1904), pp. 22–181, with bibl. refs.; the *Mitrale* is pr. in J. P. Migne, *PL* 213. 13–436. S. Kuttner, 'Zur Biographie des Sicardus von Cremona', *Zeitschrift der Savigny-Stiftung für Rechtsgeschichte*. Kanonistische Abteilung, 25 (1936), pp. 476–8, with valuable refs. E. Brocchieri, *Sicardo di Cremona e la sua opera letteraria* (Annali della Biblioteca Governativa e Libreria Civica di Cremona, 11, fasc. 1; 1958). O. Holder-Egger, 'Einiges zur Quellenkritik der Chronik Sicards', *NA* 26 (1900), pp. 471–555; id., 'Ueber die verlorene grössere Chronik Sicards von Cremona', ibid. 29 (1904), pp. 177–245. P. G. Ficker, *Der Mitralis des Sicardus nach seiner Bedeutung für die Ikonographie des Mittelalters* (Leipzig Diss., 1889; also pr. as Beiträge zur Kunstgeschichte, NF 9; 1889). J. Sauer, *Symbolik des Kirchengebäudes und seiner Ausstattung in der Auffassung des Mittelalters* (1902), passim, esp. pp. 22–8. A. Franz, *Die Messe im deutschen Mittelalter* (1902), pp. 448–52. G. Picasso, OSB, in *Dict. Sp.* 14 (1990), cols. 810–14, s.v.

Sicilian Vespers, the. A general massacre of the French in Sicily on 30 March 1282, the signal for which was the tolling of the bell for *Vespers. The number of the victims was prob. between 3,000 and 4,000.

S. Runciman, *The Sicilian Vespers* (Cambridge, 1958), with bibl.

Sick, Visitation of the. See VISITATION OF THE SICK.

Sickingen, Franz von (1481–1523), German knight. A native of Ebernburg near Worms, he became the leader of bands of 'Landsknechte' with whose help he conducted many feuds, ostensibly in the cause of the weak and oppressed, but always accompanied by plunder and cruelty. He warred against the cities of Worms and Metz and also fought in the service of Francis I of France and the German Emp. Maximilian I. Having supported the election of *Charles V, he was made Imperial Councillor in 1519. Under the influence of Ulrich von *Hutten he embraced the Reformation, defended J. *Reuchlin, and

offered his castles as places of refuge to the Protestants. He also aided the Reformers by literary activities and supported M. *Luther in the hope of wresting their power from the spiritual princes and of increasing the strength of the knights. In 1522 he led an army against the Abp. of Trier, but the campaign was a failure, and in 1523 the archbishop and other princes laid a siege against his castle of Landstuhl. In the defence he was mortally wounded and capitulated shortly before his death.

Studies by E. de Bouteiller (Metz, 1860), H. Ulmann (Leipzig, 1872), and K. H. Rendenbach (Historische Studien, 225; 1933). W. R. Hitchcock, *The Background of the Knights' Revolt 1522–1523* (University of California Publications in History, 61; 1958), pp. 42–52. Further bibl. in Schottenloher, 2 (1935), pp. 274–276 (nos. 20010–67), and 7 (1966), p. 216 (nos. 58243–55).

sidesmen. The 1604 Canons (can. 90) ordered that two, three or more persons in each parish be chosen as 'Sidemen or Assistants' to the *churchwardens, by agreement between minister and parishioners if possible, or otherwise by the bishop. Their function was to ensure the attendance of parishioners at divine service. They are now optional, but by the 1969 Canons (can. E 2 as amended) if there are to be sidesmen they are elected by the annual parochial church meeting. They must be on the electoral roll, and it is their duty to promote the cause of true religion in the parish, and to assist the churchwardens.

Sidetes, Philip. See PHILIP SIDETES.

Sidgwick, Henry (1838–1900), moral philosopher. A cousin of Abp. E. W. *Benson, he was educated at Rugby and Trinity College, Cambridge, and in 1859 elected a Fellow of his college. Here he taught classics and (after 1869) moral philosophy. He gave strong support to the movement for abolishing religious tests at Cambridge, and in 1869, through feeling no longer able to subscribe himself, resigned his fellowship as a public protest. From 1883 till his death he held the Knightbridge professorship at Cambridge. Sidgwick took a keen and active interest in many fields—university administration, psychical research, morality, politics, and the admission of women students to the university. His *Methods of Ethics* (1874), a thorough, if inconclusive, study of moral philosophy on mainly *hedonistic lines, exercised considerable influence, e.g. on H. *Rashdall and C. D. Broad. Sidgwick's other writings include *The Ethics of Conformity and Subscription* (1871), *The Principles of Political Economy* (1883), *Outlines of the History of Ethics* (1886), and *The Elements of Politics* (1891).

His posthumous writings include *Lectures on the Ethics of T. H. Green, Mr. H. Spencer, and J. Martineau* (1902), *The Development of European Polity* (1903), *Miscellaneous Essays and Addresses* (1904) and *Lectures on the Philosophy of Kant and other Philosophical Lectures and Essays* (ed. J. Ward, 1905). A. Sidgwick (brother) and Mrs E. M. Sidgwick, *Henry Sidgwick: A Memoir* (1906). L. Stephen, 'Henry Sidgwick', *Mind*, 10 (1901), pp. 1–17. F. H. Hayward, *The Ethical Philosophy of Sidgwick* (1901); C. D. Broad, *Five Types of Ethical Theory* (1930), ch. 6 (pp. 143–256); D. G. James, *Henry Sidgwick* (Riddell Memorial Lectures [not delivered]; posthumously pub., 1970); J. B. Schneewind, *Sidgwick's Ethics and Victorian Moral Philosophy* (Oxford, 1977). B. Schultz (ed.), *Essays on Henry Sidgwick* (Cambridge, 1992). L. Stephen in *DNB*, Suppl. 3 (1901), pp. 342–5.

Sidonius Apollinaris, St (*c.*430–*c.*486), statesman, author and Bp. of Clermont. A member of an aristocratic family of the Lyonnais, he received a good classical education at Arles (and perhaps also at Lyons). About 450 he married Papianilla, a daughter of the future Emp. Avitus (455–6), and about the same time entered upon a political career. In 456 he published an elaborate panegyric on his father-in-law for which he was rewarded by a statue in the Forum of Trajan. After the overthrow of Avitus by Ricimer and the Emp. Majorian, he obtained the favour of the latter through another panegyric. On Majorian's fall he retired for a time from public life, but resumed it in 467 with a mission to the Emp. Anthemius, being soon made prefect of Rome (468–9). In 470 or 471, when possibly still a layman, he was elected Bp. of Clermont, partly in order to defend the country against the Goths. He accepted the episcopal office with reluctance and humility, abandoned poetry, became a benefactor of monks, and distributed much of his wealth in charities. His strenuous efforts did not avert the occupation of Clermont by the Visigoths under Euric in 475 after repeated sieges, and he himself was exiled and imprisoned. Freed in 476 and reinstated in his diocese, he spent the leisure of his remaining years in making a collection of his letters.

Sidonius was one of the last representatives of classical culture in Gaul. His poems, of which 24 are still extant, lack poetical inspiration but show great technical skill. They are formed on the models of *Virgil and Horace and filled with pagan mythology. His letters, though often marred by verbosity, are a valuable source for the social, ecclesiastical, and intellectual history of his time; his correspondents included such major figures as *Faustus of Riez, *Lupus of Troyes, and *Claudianus Mamertus. *Gregory of Tours (*Hist. Franc.* 2. 22) records that Sidonius composed 'missae'; these are perhaps to be identified with the 'contestatiunculae' (commonly thought to be *Contestationes or Eucharistic *Prefaces) to which he himself refers. He is venerated as a saint in Gaul. Feast day, 23 (in modern editions of the Roman Martyrology, 21) Aug.

Editio princeps by E. Vinetus (Lyons, 1552). Improved edn. by J. *Sirmond, SJ, Paris, 1614; new edn., 1652; repr. in J. P. Migne, *PL* 58. 435–752. Crit. edns. by C. Luetjohann (completed by F. Leo and T. *Mommsen; *MGH*, Auctores Antiquissimi, 8; 1887) and A. Loyen (Collection des Universités de France, 3 vols., 1960–70). There is also an edn., with Eng. tr., by W. B. Anderson (Loeb, 2 vols., 1936–65). C. E. Stevens, *Sidonius Apollinaris and his Age* (1933), with bibl. A. Loyen, *Sidoine Apollinaire et l'esprit précieux en Gaule aux derniers jours de l'Empire* (1943), and other works of this author. R. P. C. Hanson, 'The Church in Fifth-Century Gaul. Evidence from Sidonius Apollinaris', *JEH* 21 (1970), pp. 1–10; repr. in id., *Studies in Christian Antiquity* (Edinburgh, 1985), pp. 332–46. P. Rousseau, 'In Search of Sidonius the Bishop', *Historia*, 25 (Wiesbaden, 1976), pp. 356–77. I. Gualandri, *Furtiva Lectio: Studi su Sidonio Apollinare* (Testi e Documenti per lo Studio dell'Antichità, 62; Milan, 1979). Altaner and Stuiber (1978), pp. 498 and 656 f. A. Klotz in *PW*, 2te Reihe, 2 (pt. 2; 1923), cols. 2230–8, s.v. 'Sidonius (1)'; S. Pricoco in *DPAC* 2 (1984), cols. 3189–92, s.v. 'Sidonio Apollinare'; Eng. tr. in *Encyclopedia of the Early Church*, 2 (1992), pp. 778 f.

Sierra Leone. The modern republic's borders reflect those of a British protectorate, declared in 1896. Previously the name denoted a much smaller area around Free-

town, with a special role in African Church history. In 1787 associates of the *Clapham Sect bought land for a self-supporting Christian settlement for poor Blacks. This soon collapsed, but was refounded in 1792 with Black soldiers from America who had supported Britain in the War of Independence. They brought a vigorous Church life, *Methodist, *Baptist, and the Countess of *Huntingdon's Connexion. In 1808, following the abolition of the slave trade, Sierra Leone became a British colony and the landing place for intercepted slave cargoes from all over W. Africa. Uprooted and diverse in origin, most of those who had been recaptured gradually entered the new model of society offered by the missionaries (esp. the *Church Missionary Society) and the 1792 settlers. The resultant Christian, literate, English-speaking Krio community was one of the early Protestant missionary successes. Sierra Leonians travelled extensively in W. Africa, sometimes re-establishing contact with their places of origin and taking Christianity with them. S. A. *Crowther was among the many missionaries, lay or ordained, who served abroad from the 1840s. Fourah Bay College, a CMS institution, was affiliated to Durham University in 1876, and Sierra Leone was the centre of an educated African community. From the 1890s, however, colonial and missionary policy eclipsed the Krio community. The incorporation of the Protectorate changed Sierra Leone's demographic basis; the hinterland dominated as the modern state emerged in 1961.

Hinterland missions began in the 1790s; they were renewed after Mende slaves brought a slave ship to the waters of the United States of America. The Mendi Mission (1841) and United Brethren in Christ (1855) initiated increasing American involvement. Anglican and Methodist missions spread from the colony and the *Holy Ghost Fathers began work in 1895, but everywhere the response was slow, and the Mende rising of 1898 brought attacks on the missions and Krio. Today the United Methodist Church (incorporating the United Brethren in Christ) and the RC Church are the leading Christian bodies in the hinterland. African prophet-healing Churches have been less common than in *Ghana and *Nigeria, but *charismatic movements are becoming increasingly prominent in Freetown.

C. Fyfe, *A History of Sierra Leone* (Oxford, 1962), *passim*, and other works of this author. J. Peterson, *Province of Freedom: A History of Sierra Leone 1787–1870* (1969), *passim*. G. W. Olson, *Church Growth in Sierra Leone: A Study of Church Growth in Africa's Oldest Protestant Mission Field* (Grand Rapids, Mich. [1969]). A. F. Walls, 'Christian Experiment: The Early Sierra Leone Colony', in G. J. Cuming (ed.), *The Mission of the Church and the Propagation of the Faith* (Studies in Church History, 6; 1970), pp. 107–29; id., 'A Colonial Concordat: Two Views of Christianity and Civilisation', in D. Baker (ed.), *Church Society and Politics* (ibid. 12; 1975), pp. 293–302; id., 'Black Europeans. White Africans: Some Missionary Motives in West Africa', in id. (ed.), *Religious Motivation* (ibid. 15; 1975), pp. 339–48. A. Hastings, *The Church in Africa 1450–1950* (Oxford History of the Christian Church, 1994), esp. pp. 179–88, 247, and 338–43. D. B. Barrett (ed.), *World Christian Encyclopedia* (Nairobi, etc., 1982), pp. 609–12 [to be used with caution].

Sigan-Fu Stone. An early monument of the *Church of the East, discovered in 1625 (or perhaps 1623) at Sigan-Fu (Sian-fu, Hsi-an-fu, or Xian) in NW China, where it remains. It is a slab, $7\frac{1}{2}$ ft. high by 3 ft. wide, which was set up in AD 781. The inscription, mainly in Chinese, contains (1) an allusive statement of Christian doctrine; (2) a description of the arrival in 635 from Tuts' in (or the land of Ta-ch' in) of a missionary named Olopan (in Chinese characters, A-lo-pên, believed by some to be a version of the name 'Abraham') and the imperial privileges which he was granted. After relating how Olopan became a 'Guardian of the Empire' and 'Lord of the Great Law', there follows an account of the fortunes of the Church down to the reign of Tih-tsung (780–3); (3) an epitome of (2) in octosyllabic verse; and (4) a series of short additions in *Syriac in the Estrangelo character. The stone is the most considerable extant witness to the growth of Christianity in the Far East before the 13th cent. In 1907 a replica of the stone was made by the Danish traveller, Frits v. Holm, and deposited in 1908 in the Metropolitan Museum of Art, New York.

F. v. Holm, *The Nestorian Monument* (Chicago, 1909); P. Y. Saeki, *The Nestorian Monument in China* (1916): id., *The Nestorian Documents and Relics in China* (Tokyo, 1937); P. Pelliot, *Recherches sur les chrétiens d'Asie centrale et d'Extrême Orient*, 2. 1: *La stèle de Si-ngan-fou*, ed. J. Dauvillier and A. Guillaumont (Œuvres posthumes, Paris [1984]).

Sigebert of Gembloux

Sigebert of Gembloux (*c.*1030–1112), medieval chronicler. He was a monk of the *Benedictine abbey of Gembloux, taught for more than 20 years at the school of St Vincent at Metz, and returned to Gembloux *c.*1071. His principal works are the *De Viris Illustribus* (an ecclesiastical literary history in biographies), the recently identified *Liber Decennalis*, in which (following the attempts of *Dionysius Exiguus and *Bede) he endeavoured to fix the dates of Christ's Incarnation and Passion in the overall chronology of the world, and the *Chronicon* (from 381 to 1111), which uses some first-hand material for the period after 1024. He is also the author of a history of the early abbots of Gembloux (*Gesta Abbatum Gemblacensium*), as well as of a number of hagiographical works mainly intended for edification and of little historical value. In the great struggle between the Empire and the Papacy he took the side of *Henry IV against *Gregory VII, whose reforms he thought inopportune and whose policy he attacked in several pamphlets. He also wrote against Pope *Paschal II.

Collection of his works in J. P. Migne, *PL* 160. 57–834 (incl. repr. edn. of the *Chronicon* from L. C. Bethmann in *MGH*, Scriptores, 6 (1844), pp. 300–74). *Apologia contra eos qui calumniantur Missas Coniugatorum Sacerdotum* first pr. by E. Sackur in *MGH*, Libelli de Lite Imperatorum et Pontificum Saeculis XI et XII, 2 (1892), pp. 436–464; *Passio Sanctae Luciae Virginis* and *Passio Sanctorum Thebeorum* pr. in full by H. Dümmler in *Abh.* (Berl.), 1893, Abh. 1; *Liber Decennalis* first pr. by J. Wiesenbach (*MGH*, Quellen zur Geistesgeschichte des Mittelalters, 12; 1986); see also id., 'Der Liber decennalis in der HS. Rom, Biblioteca Angelica 1413, als Werk Sigeberts von Gembloux', *Deutsches Archiv*, 33 (1977), pp. 171–81. Crit. edn. of *De Viris Illustribus* by R. Witte (Lateinische Sprache und Literatur des Mittelalters, 1; 1974). The attribution to Sigebert of a treatise 'On the Investiture of Bishops' is uncertain: J. Beumann, *Sigebert von Gembloux und der Traktat de investitura episcoporum* (Vorträge und Forschungen, Sonderband 20 [1976]), with useful bibl.; id., 'Der Traktat "De investitura episcoporum" von 1109', *Deutsches Archiv*, 33 (1977), pp. 37–83, incl. text. E. Dekkers, OSB, 'Sigebert van Gembloux en zijn "De viris illustribus" ', *Sacris Erudiri*, 26 (1983), pp. 57–102. E. de Moreau, SJ, *Histoire de l'Église en Belgique*, 2 (2nd edn.,

Museum Lessianum, Section Historique, 2; 1945), pp. 83–6, 95–9, 156–8, 277–81, and 285 f. L. Brigué in *DTC* 14 (pt. 2; 1941), cols. 2035–41, s.v.

Siger of Brabant (*c.*1240–*c.*1284), *Averroist philosopher. All that is known of his earlier career is that in 1266 he was a master of arts in the University of *Paris, where he was teaching, and that he was a member of the 'Picard' nation and a canon of St Paul, Liège. He must therefore have come to Paris not later than 1260. He was involved in the condemnation of 13 errors by Stephen Tempier, Bp. of Paris (10 Dec. 1270), and in the same year *Thomas Aquinas wrote the 'De Unitate intellectus contra Averroistas', which is chiefly directed against him. He may have somewhat modified his radicalism, but dissension continued in the Faculty of Arts until 1275, when a Papal legate acted as arbitrator. In 1276 Siger was cited for heresy with two others by Simon du Val, inquisitor of France. It is not known whether he was acquitted, as was one of those associated with him in the charge, or whether he had already fled the kingdom. According to a letter of John *Pecham, written in 1284, he was killed at Orvieto by his *clericus* in a fit of insanity.

When Siger arrived in Paris the Faculty of Arts had recently revised the curriculum to include the study of the *Metaphysics* of *Aristotle and his works on natural philosophy. The most substantial works of Siger were commentaries and *quaestiones* on books of Aristotle, notably *quaestiones* on the *Metaphysics*, books 2–7, on the *Physics*, and *De Anima*, book 3. He also wrote shorter treatises, including 'De aeternitate mundi' and 'De anima intellectiva'. An early 16th-cent. Italian writer quotes from a 'De intellectu', not known to be extant, which was apparently a reply to Thomas Aquinas. Siger regarded it as his task not to conceal Aristotle's views, even if they were contrary to revealed truth; and, like all medieval interpreters, his views on Aristotle were coloured by study of the works of *Proclus, *Avicenna, and Averroes. The chief doctrines in question were the eternity of the world and the unity of the intellect in the human race, which involved the denial of personal immortality and of rewards and punishments in a future life. Theological critics accused him of holding the position known as the doctrine of the 'double truth', i.e. that the same tenet might be true in theology but false in philosophy. This he would have disputed. He maintained that in cases of conflict, truth was on the side of faith. How far he resolved the status of philosophical truths is not clear from his writings. *Dante (*Paradiso*, 10. 133–7) did not regard him as a heretic, and placed him among the twelve sages.

Edns. of his treatises in P. Mandonnet, OP, *Siger de Brabant et l'averroisme latin au XIIIème siècle* (Collectanea Friburgensia, 8, 1899; 2nd edn. enlarged in 2 vols., 'Les Philosophes belges', 6, 1911, and 7, 1908). Crit. edn. of two texts of his 'Quaestiones in Metaphysicam' by W. Dunphy (Philosophes médiévaux, 24; Louvain etc., 1981) and A. Maurer (ibid. 25; 1983); of his 'Quaestio de necessitate et contingentia causarum' by J. J. Duin (ibid. 3; 1954); of his 'Quaestiones super Librum de Causis' ed. A. Marlasca (ibid. 12; 1972); of his 'Quaestiones in Tertium de Anima', 'De Anima Intellectiva', and 'De Aeternitate Mundi', ed. B. Bazán (ibid. 13; 1972); and of his other nine smaller treatises, ed. B. Bazán (ibid. 14; 1974, incl. 'Quaestiones in Physicam', ed. A. Zimmermann, pp. 141–84). Eng. tr. of 'De Aeternitate Mundi' by L. H. Kendzierski (Mediaeval Philosophical Texts in Translation, no. 16, Milwaukee, 1964, pp. 75–98, incl. introd.). F. van Steenberghen, *Maître Siger de Brabant* (Philosophes médiévaux, 21; 1977), incl. list of his works, with edns., pp. 184–91; id., *La Philosophie au XIIIᵉ siècle* (2nd edn., Philosophes médiévaux, 28; 1991), pp. 325–60. B. Nardi, *Sigieri di Brabante nel pensiero del rinascimento italiano* [1945]. A. Dondaine, OP, and L. J. Bataillon, OP, 'Le Manuscrit Vindob. Lat. 2330 et Siger de Brabant', *Archivum Fratrum Praedicatorum*, 36 (1966), pp. 153–261, incl. attributions of new works. R. A. Gauthier, 'Notes sur Siger de Brabant', *RSPT* 67 (1983), pp. 201–32; 68 (1984), pp. 3–49. Z. Kuksewicz in N. Kretzmann and others (ed.), *The Cambridge History of Later Medieval Philosophy* (1982), pp. 611–22, with further refs.; see also pp. 885 f., and index.

sign of the Cross. From the time of *Tertullian Christian writers testify to the use of the 'sign of the Lord', partly as sanctifying every action in daily life from rising in the morning to retiring at night, partly as an encouragement in temptation and trial, and partly as a means of mutual recognition in times of persecution. From early times the sign was also employed in *Baptism and *Confirmation, and its use was then extended to the liturgical blessing of persons and things. In the early centuries the sign was drawn upon the forehead by the thumb or finger of the right hand. In later times it has been made by drawing the right hand from forehead to breast, and then from shoulder to shoulder. It is usual in the W. Church to make the cross-stroke from left to right, in the E. from right to left.

H. Thurston, SJ, 'The Sign of the Cross', *The Month*, 118 (1911), pp. 586–602, repr. in his *Familiar Prayers*, ed. P. Grosjean, SJ (1953), pp. 1–21, with refs. E. Beresford-Cooke, *The Sign of the Cross in the Western Liturgies* (*Alcuin Club Tracts, 7; 1907), with refs. F. Dölger, 'Das Segnen der Sinne mit der Eucharistie', *Antike und Christentum*, 3 (1932), pp. 231–44. A. Rücker, 'Die Kreuzzeichen in der westsyrischen Messliturgie', in *Pisciculi: Studien zur Religion und Kultur des Altertums Franz Joseph Dölger zum sechzigsten Geburtstag dargeboten von Freunden, Verehren und Schülern* (Antike und Christentum, Ergänzungsband, 1; 1937), pp. 245–51. F. J. Dölger, 'Beiträge zur Geschichte des Kreuzzeichens', *Jahrbuch für Antike und Christentum*, 1 (1958), pp. 5–19; 2 (1959), pp. 15–29; 3 (1960), pp. 5–16; 4 (1961), pp. 5–17; and 5 (1962), pp. 5–22. E. Dinkler, *Signum Crucis: Aufsätze zum Neuen Testament und zur Christlichen Archäologie* (Tübingen, 1967), esp. pp. 1–76.

Silas, St. St *Paul's companion on his first visit to Greece is called Silas in Acts. 15: 22–18: 5 (13 times). Paul calls him 'Silvanus' at 2 Cor. 1: 19 (as does 1 Pet. 5: 12) and associates him with himself in writing to the Thessalonians (1 and 2 Thess. 1: 1). This led some of the Fathers to distinguish between the two, making Silas Bp. of Corinth and Silvanus Bp. of Thessalonica. Acc. to tradition Silas died in Macedonia. Feast day, 13 July; in the Greek calendar, 30 July.

E. G. Selwyn, *The First Epistle of St Peter* (1946), pp. 9–17. B. N. Kaye, 'Acts' portrait of Silas', *Novum Testamentum*, 21 (1979), pp. 13–26. F. F. Bruce, *The Pauline Circle* [1985], pp. 23–8.

silence, the argument from (Lat. *argumentum e silentio*). The deduction from the absence of any known reference to a subject in the extant writings of a particular author that he was ignorant of it. Many 19th-cent. critics of historic Christianity carried it to extreme lengths. In

a famous set of articles (1874–7) criticizing *Supernatural Religion* (anon., by W. R. Cassels; 3 vols., 1874–7), in which the argument had been extensively used, J. B. *Lightfoot showed that it is unsafe to employ it, except in the most compelling cases.

Silesius, Angelus. See ANGELUS SILESIUS.

Siloam, Pool of. A pool or reservoir at *Jerusalem, mentioned several times in the OT, and almost certainly the modern *Birket Silwān*. In the NT it is referred to only twice, namely in the incident of the man born blind (Jn. 9: 1 ff.), whom Christ told to go and wash in this pool, and in Christ's mention of the fall of a tower 'in Siloam' (Lk. 13: 4). In the latter reference, part of the city wall, which ran near the pool, may be intended.

The pool *Birket Silwān* receives its waters from the 'Virgin's Spring' (*Ain Sitti Maryam*) on the E. side of Ophel through a tunnel in the rock. The tunnel and the pool are universally identified with the waterworks of King Hezekiah (2 Kgs. 20: 20; 2 Chron. 32: 30). Kathleen Kenyon's argument that the pool was originally a subterranean cistern outside the contemporary city wall, not an open reservoir within it, has not been widely accepted. Since the 4th cent. it has been a place of pilgrimage for Christians.

T. Tobler, *Die Siloahquelle und der Oelberg* (1852), pp. 1–58. H. Vincent, OP, and F. M. Abel, OP, *Jérusalem*, 2 (1914), pp. 861–4, with refs. K. [M.] Kenyon, *Digging up Jerusalem* (1974), pp. 156–9; cf. D. R. Ap-Thomas in D. W. Thomas (ed.), *Archaeology and Old Testament Study* (Oxford, 1967), pp. 283–5 and 290 f.; N. Avigad, *Discovering Jerusalem* (Oxford, 1984), p. 60.

Silvester. See SYLVESTER.

Silvia of Aquitaine. A relative of the Roman prefect, Rufinus. Her sole interest to the Church historian lies in the fact that she was considered to be the authoress of the 'Pilgrimage of *Egeria' (q.v.), by F. Gamurrini, who discovered the work in MS in 1884. In 1903, however, Dom M. Férotin identified the writer with a Spanish nun, Etheria (now more usually called Egeria), and this view is now generally accepted.

Simeon. (1) In the OT, one of the Hebrew patriarchs, the ancestor of the tribe of the same name. (2) In the NT, the aged and devout Jew who took the infant Christ in his arms in the *Temple at *Jerusalem and spoke the words known as the '*Nunc Dimittis' (Lk. 2: 25–35). (3) In Acts 15: 14, apparently for St *Peter (elsewhere 'Simon Peter'), though St *Chrysostom, perhaps correctly, sees here a reference to the Simeon of Lk. 2. (4) Simeon that was called Niger, a prophet at Antioch (Acts 13: 1).

Simeon, the New Theologian, St (949–1022), Byzantine mystic and spiritual writer. In youth he entered the imperial service at *Constantinople, but in 977 he embraced the monastic life at *Studios. Within a few months he transferred to the monastery of St Mamas, also at Constantinople, becoming priest in 980 and a year later abbot. Because of the fierce opposition which certain aspects of his teaching aroused, in 1005 he was forced to resign from his position as superior, and four years later he was sent into exile in Asia Minor. Although this sentence was quickly revoked, he preferred to remain in voluntary retirement for the rest of his life. He is the greatest of Byzantine mystical writers, with a vivid and highly personal style. In his teaching he assigned a central place to the vision of Divine Light, while being at the same time strongly Christocentric, and underlining the importance of the Eucharist. He combined the contemplative tradition of *Isaac of Nineveh with the *coenobitic tradition of *Basil the Great and *Theodore of Studios. He was much influenced by the Homilies attributed to *Macarius of Egypt, and in his turn he exercised a formative influence upon the rise of *Hesychasm. His appellation 'the New Theologian' implies a comparison with St *Gregory Nazianzen, known in the E. as 'Gregory the Theologian'. Alternatively, but with less probability, it has been understood to mean 'Simeon the Younger, the Theologian'. Feast day in the E., 12 Mar.

'Catecheses' ed. B. Krivochéine, with Fr. tr. by J. Paramelle, SJ (SC 96, 104, 113; 1963–5); Eng. tr. by C. J. deCatanzaro (Classics of Western Spirituality, 1980); 'Kephalaia', ed. *Nicodemus of the Holy Mountain and Macarius of Corinth, in *Philocalia* (Venice, 1782; 2nd edn., Athens, 1893); repr. in J. P. Migne, PG 120. 604–688; crit. edn., with Fr. tr., by J. Darrouzès, AA (SC 51; 1957); Ethical and Theological Treatises, also ed., with Fr. tr., by id. (ibid. 122, 129; 1966–7); Eng. tr. of the 'Kephalaia' and Theological Treatises by P. McGuckin, CP (Cistercian Studies Series, 41; Kalamazoo, Mich., 1982); Hymns ed. J. Koder, with Fr. tr. by J. Paramelle, SJ (SC 156, 174, 196; 1969–73) and by A. Kambylis (Supplementa Byzantina, 3; Berlin and New York, 1976); Eng. tr. by G. A. Maloney, SJ (Denville, NJ [1975]). Life by *Nicetas Stethatos ed. I. Hausherr, SJ, with Fr. tr. by G. Horn, SJ (Orientalia Christiana, 12; 1928; fasc. 45). K. *Holl, *Enthusiasmus und Bussgewalt beim griechischen Mönchtum: Eine Studie zu Symeon dem Neuen Theologen* (Leipzig, 1898). W. Völker, *Praxis und Theoria bei Symeon dem neuen Theologen* (1974). G. A. Maloney, SJ, *The Mystic of Fire and Light: St Symeon the New Theologian* (Denville, NJ, 1975). B. Krivochéine, *Dans la lumière du Christ: Saint Syméon le Nouveau Théologien, 949–1022. Vie, Spiritualité, Doctrine* (Chevetogne, 1980; Eng. tr., Crestwood, NY, 1986). B. Fraigneau-Julien, *Les sens spirituels et la vision de Dieu selon Syméon le Nouveau Théologien* (Théologie Historique, 67 [1985]). H. J. M. Turner, *St Symeon the New Theologian and Spiritual Fatherhood* (Byzantina Neederlandica, 11; 1990). J. Gouillard, AA, in *DTC* 14 (pt. 2; 1941), cols. 2941–56, s.v. 'Syméon le Jeune'; T. Špidlík, SJ, in *Dict. Sp.* 14 (1990), cols. 1387–401, s.v. 'Syméon le Nouveau Théologien'.

Simeon of Durham (c.1060–c.1130), chronicler. He was a monk of the *Benedictine monastery of *Durham, where he was professed in 1085 or 1086 and later became precentor. His first work, inspired by *Bede, was his 'Historia Ecclesiae Dunelmensis', written between 1104 and 1107, which brings the history of the see of Durham down to 1096. It was prob. he who later wrote a general history of England, 'Historia regum Anglorum et Dacorum', wholly based on earlier writers, except for the contemporary period between 1119 and 1129. The latter was continued by Richard and John of *Hexham.

Opera Omnia, ed. T. Arnold (RS, 2 vols., 1882–5), with biog. introd. pp. ix–xv. Eng. tr. of his Historical Works by J. Stevenson (The Church Historians of England, 3, pt. 2; 1855). Preface by I. H. Hinde to his edn. of *Symeonis Dunelmensis Opera et Collectanea*, 1 (all pub.; Surtees Society, 51; 1868), pp. v–lv. H. S. Offler, *Medieval Historians of Durham* (Inaugural lecture, Durham, 1958), pp. 6–10. P. H. Blair, 'Some Observations on the "Historia Regum" attributed to Symeon of Durham', in K. [H.] Jackson

and others, *Celt and Saxon* (Cambridge, 1963), pp. 63–118; M. Lapidge, 'Byrhtferth of Ramsey and the Early Sections of the *Historia Regum* attributed to Symeon of Durham', *Anglo-Saxon England*, 10 (1982), pp. 97–122. C. L. Kingsford in *DNB* 52 (1897), pp. 254 f.

Simeon of Mesopotamia (5th cent.). A leader of the *Messalians, mentioned by *Theodoret (*HE* 4. 11. 2), sometimes identified with the Simeon to whom some MSS attribute the writings of Pseudo-Macarius. See MACARIUS/ SIMEON.

Simeon Metaphrastes, St (fl. c.960), Byzantine hagiographer. Nothing is known of his life. He owes his fame to his collection of saints' Lives ('Menologion') compiled, it is said, at the bidding of the Emperor. A few of the Lives were simply copied from older collections, but most of them were worked over ('metaphrased', hence his name) to make them acceptable in style and manner of presentation to the taste of his time. They were not, however, subjected to criticism, the historical errors of the models being reproduced in the new versions, as the interest of the author was chiefly moral and devotional. His work was frequently added to in later times. The continuation of the Chronicle of *George Hamartolus to the death of the Emp. Romanus Lecapenus (948) is ascribed in some Greek manuscripts and in the Old Church Slavonic translation to Simeon Logothetes, who has often been identified with Simeon Metaphrastes, though this identification is now disputed. Also ascribed to him are collections of sayings of St *Basil and other Fathers. The Orthodox Church honours him as a saint. Feast day in the E., 9 or 28 Nov.

Texts (many only in mod. Lat. trs.) collected in J. P. Migne, PG 114–16. Old Church Slavonic tr. of the Chronicle, ed. V. I. Sreznevskij (St Petersburg, 1905; repr., London, 1971, with an art. on the subject by G. Ostrogorsky (in Russian), orig. pub. 1932). On Lives of Simeon, see *BHG* 2 (3rd edn.; 1957), pp. 255 f. (nos. 1675 f.); on works by Simeon, see refs. in index, 3, pp. 263 f. H. *Delehaye, SJ, 'La Vie de saint Paul le Jeune et la chronologie de Métaphraste', *RQH* 54 (1893), pp. 49–85; id., *Les Saints stylites* (1923; Lives of St Alypius, pp. lxxvi–lxxxv and 148–94). A. Ehrhard, *Überlieferung und Bestand der hagiographischen Literatur der griechischen Kirche*, 2 (TU 51; 1938), pp. 306–717; Krumbacher, pp. 200–3 and 358–61; Beck (1959), pp. 570–5; H. Hunger, *Die hochsprachliche profane Literatur der Byzantiner*, 1 (Byzantinisches Handbuch, Teil 5, Bd. 1; Munich, 1978), pp. 354–7. J. Gouillard, AA, in *DTC* 14 (pt. 2; 1941), cols. 2959–71, s.v. 'Syméon Logothète'; B. Kötter, OSB, in *L.Th.K.* (2nd edn.), 9 (1964), cols. 1214 f., s.v. 'Symeon Metaphrastes'.

Simeon Stylites, St (c.390–459). The first of the *Stylites or pillar ascetics. He was born on the Syrian border of Cilicia. After some time as a monk in the monastery of Eusebona (at Tell 'Ada, between *Antioch and Aleppo) he moved to Telanissos, which was not far away. Here, after several years of anchoretic life, he mounted a pillar, at first low, but gradually increased to a height of forty cubits; he lived on the top of it until his death, occupied in adoration and intercession. This novel austerity attracted to him a continuous stream of pilgrims, and was widely imitated. Both by personal intercourse and by correspondence, Simeon exercised considerable influence upon the world of his time, converting pagans, awakening the careless, reconciling enemies, and urging the cause of *Chalcedonian orthodoxy. There are still extensive

remains of the church and monastery that were built around his pillar (modern Qal'at Sim'ān). He is not to be confused with his 6th-cent. namesake, also a Stylite, who took up residence on Mons Admirabilis, just to the W. of Antioch. Feast day, 1 Sept. in the E. Orthodox Church; 27 July among the *Syrian Orthodox; 5 Jan. in the W.

Of the early Lives, the most trustworthy is the account in *Theodoret (*Hist. Rel.* 26). This was used, and the narrative carried to a later date, in the less reliable Gk. Life by a monk Antony (to which a Coptic Life is nearly related). Its Gk. text was first pr. from a St Petersburg MS by A. Papadopoulos-Keramevs (St Petersburg, 1907). Coptic text ed., with Fr. tr., by M. Chaîne (Publications de l'Institut Français d'Archéologie Orientale, Bibliothèque des Études Coptes, 3; Cairo, 1948). Syriac Life ed. P. Bedjan, *Acta Martyrum et Sanctorum*, 4 (Paris, 1894), pp. 507–644; Eng. tr. by F. Lent in *Journal of the American Oriental Society*, 35 (1915–17), pp. 103–98. This is closely followed by a Georgian Life, ed. G. Garitte (CSCO 171, Scriptores Iberici, 7, 1957, pp. 1–77, with Lat. tr. in CSCO 172, Scriptores Iberici, 8, 1957, pp. 1–53), with suppl. in *Muséon*, 76 (1963), pp. 79–93. H. *Lietzmann, *Das Leben des heiligen Simeon Stylites* (TU 32. 4; 1908), with texts and full crit. discussion. H. *Delehaye, SJ, *Les Saints stylites* (1923), pp. i–xxxix. P. Peeters, SJ, 'S. Syméon Stylite et ses premiers biographes', *Anal. Boll.* 61 (1943), pp. 29–71, repr., with revisions, as 'Un saint hellénisé par annexion: Syméon Stylite', in his *Le Tréfonds oriental de l'hagiographie byzantine* (Subsidia Hagiographica, 26; 1950), pp. 93–136. A. J. Festugière, OP, *Antioche païenne et chrétienne* (Bibliothèque des Écoles françaises d'Athènes et de Rome, 194; 1959), pp. 347–401 and 493–506, incl. Fr. tr. of texts. A. Leroy-Molinghen, 'A propos de la "Vie" de Syméon Stylite', *Byzantion*, 34 (1964), pp. 375–84. A. Vööbus, *History of Asceticism in the Syrian Orient*, 2 (CSCO 197, Subsidia, 17; 1960), pp. 208–23. J. Lassus, *Sanctuaires chrétiens de Syrie* (Institut Français d'Archéologie de Beyrouth. Bibliothèque archéologique et historique, 42; 1947), pp. 129–32. *CPG* 3 (1979), pp. 277 f. (nos. 6640–50). D. Stiernon in *Bibliotheca Sanctorum*, 11 (1968), cols. 1116–38, s.v., with extensive bibl.

On the younger Simeon Stylites, P. van den Ven (ed.), *La vie ancienne de S. Syméon Stylite le Jeune (521–592)* (Subsidia Hagiographica, 32; 2 vols., 1962–70), incl. full introd.

Simeon of Thessalonica, St (d. 1429), Abp. of Thessalonica. Little is known of his life except that he favoured the Venetians who had bought Thessalonica in 1423 and opposed the surrender of the city to the Turks. He was one of the most influential authors of his age. His principal work is a 'Dialogue against all Heresies and on the One Faith' (Διάλογος κατὰ πασῶν τῶν αἱρέσεων καὶ περὶ τῆς μόνης πίστεως), which reflects his predominating interest in the mystical interpretation of the Byzantine cultus. It consists of a shorter treatise on doctrine, dealing chiefly with the Trinity and with Christology, and a longer second part on the Liturgy and the Sacraments. The polemical passages envisage the Jews, *Bogomils, Muslims, and the Church of Rome; these polemical interests are developed in a recently discovered collection of treatises by Simeon. Among his other works are a treatise 'On the Holy Temple' (Περὶ τοῦ θείου Ναοῦ), also mainly a symbolical explanation of the ritual, and an exposition of the *Niceno-Constantinopolitan Creed ('Ερμηνεία συνοπτική). He was canonized in the Greek Church in 1981; feast day, 15 Sept.

His writings, ed. by *Dositheus (Jassy, 1683), are repr. in J. P. Migne, *PG* 155. Liturgical works also ed. I. M. Phountoules (Thessalonica, 1968 ff.). 20 previously unpub. works ed. D. Balfour: *Politico-Historical Works* (Wiener byzantinische Studien, 13;

1979); *Theological Works* (Analecta Vlatadon, 34; Thessalonica, 1981). I. M. Phountoules, Τὸ λειτουργικὸν ἔργον Συμεὼν τοῦ Θεσσαλονίκης (ibid., 1966), with summary in French R. Bornert, OSB, *Les Commentaires byzantins de la divine liturgie du VIIe au XVe siècle* (Archives de l'Orient Chrétien, 9; 1966), pp. 245–63. M. Kunzler, *Gnadenquellen: Symeon von Thessaloniki († 1429) als Beispiel für die Einflussnahme des Palamismus auf die orthodoxe Sakramententheologie und Liturgik* (Trierer theologische Studien, 47; 1989). In Eng. there is a convenient introd. by D. Balfour, 'St Symeon of Thessalonica: A Polemical Hesychast', *Sobronost*, 4 (1982), pp. 6–21. M. Jugie, AA, in *DTC* 14 (pt. 2; 1941), cols. 2976–94, s.v. 'Syméon de Thessalonique'.

Simeon, Charles (1759–1836), leader of the *Evangelical Revival. He was educated at Eton and King's College, Cambridge, where he became a Fellow in 1782. In 1783 he was ordained priest, and in the same year was appointed vicar of Holy Trinity, Cambridge, holding this incumbency till his death. At an early date he had come under the influence of the two *Venns and his whole future ministry was strongly coloured by his Evangelical experience. At first he was met by hostility both in the university and among his congregation, but his pastoral zeal broke down all opposition and he exercised a significant influence among Evangelical undergraduates and ordinands. He became a leading figure in the Missionary Movement, being one of the founders of the *CMS (1799) and a prominent supporter of the *British and Foreign Bible Society; and he was frequently consulted by the East India Company on the choice of their chaplains. He was also the founder of a body of trustees (the Simeon Trustees) for securing and administering Church patronage in accordance with his principles. In the ASB, feast day, 13 Nov.; in the American BCP (1979), 12 Nov.

W. Carus, *Memoirs of the Life of the Rev. Charles Simeon, ... with a selection from his writings and correspondence* (1847). H. C. G. *Moule, *Charles Simeon* (1892); C. Smyth, *Simeon and Church Order* (1940). A. Pollard and M. Hennell (eds.), *Charles Simeon ... : Essays Written in Commemoration of his Bi-Centenary* (1959); H. E. Hopkins, *Charles Simeon of Cambridge* (1977).

Similitudo Dei (Lat., 'likeness of God'). Acc. to a distinction based on a traditional exegesis of Gen. 1: 26, that element in man's being as originally constituted which he lost through the Fall. See IMAGO DEI.

Simon, St, 'the Less', Apostle. One of the 12 Apostles, called in Mt. 10: 4 and Mk. 3: 18 'the Canaanite' (AV) or 'the Cananaean' (RV and RSV). The Greek word is probably a transcription of the Aramaic, meaning 'zealous', which would account for St *Luke's translation '*zealot' (Lk. 6: 15, Acts 1: 13), though this could imply that he had once been a member of the Zealots, if that party existed at the time. The apocryphal 'Passion of Simon and Jude' related the preaching and martyrdom of these two Apostles in Persia. In the W. the two are always coupled in the ecclesiastical calendar and in dedications of churches. Feast day in E., 10 May; in W. (with St Jude), 28 Oct. See also SIMONS IN THE NT.

AASS, Oct. 12 (1867), pp. 421–36.

Simon of Cyrene. A passer-by who was compelled by the Roman soldiers to carry Christ's cross on the way to the crucifixion (Mt. 27: 32 etc.). Mark (15: 21) describes him as the father of Alexander and Rufus, implying that these were figures known in the early Church. According to *Irenaeus (*Adv. Haer.* 1. 24. 4) the *Basilideans held that Simon not only carried Christ's cross but was crucified in His place. In modern times Simon of Cyrene has been claimed as patron by groups of people working among outcasts.

See comm. on Mk. 15: 21, etc.

Simon Magus. Acc. to Acts 8: 9–24, a sorcerer, known as 'the Power of God which is called Great', who practised in *Samaria in the time of the Apostles. Having professed Christianity and been baptized, he was later rebuked by St *Peter for trying to obtain spiritual powers from the Apostles for money (hence the term '*simony'). This in substance is all that is recorded in the NT. *Justin Martyr, followed by other writers, suggests that he was a native of Gitta in Samaria, who came to Rome in the time of the Emp. Claudius (AD 41–54). He also affirms that Simon was regarded by his disciples as a god and describes a statue in his honour on an island in the Tiber inscribed 'Simoni Deo Sancto'; but the base of a statue recovered in 1574, and usually regarded as the statue in question, shows by its inscription (Semoni Sanco Deo Fidio) that it was really dedicated not to Simon but to a Sabine god. Simon was said by St *Hippolytus and others to have come into conflict with St Peter again at Rome, and to have perished dramatically there through a failure of his magic powers. He later figures in the '*Clementine Homilies' and 'Recognitions', and also in ancient and medieval legends from which, perhaps, that of Faust evolved.

The Christian fathers of the 2nd–3rd cent. who opposed Gnosticism regarded Simon as its founder. He is said to have been accompanied by a former prostitute called Helen whom he redeemed and whom he called his 'First Thought' (Ἔννοια) the 'Mother of All'. Hippolytus also ascribes to him a short treatise, the *Apophasis Megale* (the text of which survives only in the *Refutatio*, 6. 9–18). There is much dispute about Simon Magus' relationship to Gnosticism and, in particular, to the 2nd-cent. sect of Simonians, to whom, rather than to Simon himself, the *Apophasis* is prob. to be ascribed.

On the NT account see comm. on Acts, cited s.v. For a brief account of the ancient evidence about Simon, with Eng. tr. of relevant texts, see W. Foerster, *Gnosis*, 1 (Eng. tr., Oxford, 1972), pp. 27–32. The text of the *Apophasis Megale* (incl. in edns. of Hippolytus) is also in J. M. A. Salles-Dabadie, *Recherches sur Simon le Mage*, 1 (Cahiers de la *Revue Biblique*, 10; 1969), pp. 12–39 [the work has been much criticized in other respects]. Convenient Eng. tr. in W. Foerster, op. cit., 1, pp. 251–60. J. Frickel, SJ, *Die 'Apophasis Megale' in Hippolyts Refutatio (VI 9–18)* (Orientalia Christiana Analecta, 182; Rome, 1968); K. Beyschlag, *Simon Magus und die christliche Gnosis* (Wissenschaftliche Untersuchungen zum Neuen Testament, 16; Tübingen, 1974); G. Lüdemann, *Untersuchungen zur simonianischen Gnosis* (Göttinger Theologische Arbeiten, 1 [1975]). K. Rudolph, 'Simon—Magus oder Gnosticus? Zum Stand der Debatte', *Theologische Rundschau*, NF 42 (1977), pp. 279–359. C. [J.] Osborne, *Rethinking Early Greek Philosophy: Hippolytus of Rome and the Presocratics* (1987), pp. 212–27. J. [E.] Fossum, 'Samaritan Sects and Movements', in A. D. Crown (ed.), *The Samaritans* (Tübingen [1989]), pp. 293–389, esp. pp. 357–89. *CPG* 1 (1983), pp. 59 f. (no. 1120). G. *Salmon in *DCB* 4 (1887), pp. 681–8; H. *Lietzmann in *PW*, Zweite Reihe, 3 (1929), cols. 180–4; É. Amann in *DTC* 14 (pt. 2; 1941), cols. 2130–40, s.v. 'Simon le Magicien'.

Simon Peter, St. See PETER, ST.

Simon Stock, St (*c.*1165–1265), also 'Simon Anglus' or 'Simon of England', Prior General of the *Carmelites. The details of his career are very obscure. He may have been elected Prior General at a chapter held in London in 1254; it is at least clear that he did not (as used to be thought) hold this office in 1247 when Pope *Innocent IV approved changes in Carmelite practices. Acc. to a later tradition, in 1251 Simon received a vision of the BVM which gave rise to the 'Scapular devotion', a devotion based on the belief that all who wore the small Carmelite *scapular would be saved. The name 'Stock' is also of late date. Feast day, 16 May. See also SABBATINE PRIVILEGE.

J. Smet, O. Carm., *The Carmelites*, 1 (rev. edn., Darien, Ill., 1988), pp. 22–4. B. Zimmerman, ODC (ed.), *Monumenta Historica Carmelitana*, 1 (Lérins, 1907), pp. 313–22. F. M. Xiberta, O. Carm., *De Visione Sancti Simonis Stock* (Bibliotheca Sacri Scapularis, 1; Rome, 1950). *BRUO* 3 (1959), p. 1779, s.v. 'Stock, Simon', with further refs. L. Saggi, O. Carm., and C. M. Carpano in *Bibliotheca Sanctorum*, 11 (1968), cols.1187–92, s.v. 'Simone Stock'.

Simon of Sudbury (d. 1381), Abp. of *Canterbury. Born at Sudbury in Suffolk, he studied at the University of *Paris, and later became chaplain to Innocent VI, who appointed him Bp. of London in 1361. He was very soon playing a prominent part as a diplomatist and politician, being an adherent of John of Gaunt, Duke of Lancaster. In 1375 he was translated to Canterbury, and two years later crowned Richard II. He seems to have been reluctant to take proceedings against J. *Wycliffe until ordered to do so by the Pope, and then was not extreme in his measures. In 1380 he became chancellor and was responsible for the imposition of a poll tax. When in 1381 a great rising took place (the Peasants' Revolt), the Kentish rioters spoiled the archbishop's lands, released from prison John *Ball, the excommunicated priest, and attacked the Tower, where Sudbury had taken refuge with the King. He resigned the chancellorship, but this did not avail to save him, and on Friday, 14 June 1381, the mob captured and beheaded him. The archbishop met his death bravely and was by many regarded as a martyr.

R. C. Fowler (ed.), *Registrum Simonis de Sudbiria, Diocesis Londoniensis* A.D. 1362–1375 (*Canterbury and York Society, 34 and 38; 1927–38), with introd. by C. Jenkins in vol. 2, pp. v–lxv. W. L. Warren, 'A Reappraisal of Simon Sudbury, bishop of London (1361–75) and archbishop of Canterbury (1375–81)', *JEH* 10 (1959), pp. 139–152. G. [A.] Holmes, *The Good Parliament* (Oxford, 1975), esp. pp. 18 f., 47–9, and 140–4. W. Hunt in *DNB* 55 (1898), pp. 146–9, s.v. 'Sudbury, Simon of'; W. H. *Hutton in *DECH* (1912), p. 575, s.v. 'Sudbury, Simon of'.

Simon, Richard (1638–1712), biblical scholar. From 1662 to 1678 he was a member of the French *Oratory. After extensive studies in oriental languages, he published in 1678 his *Histoire critique du Vieux Testament*, in which he denied that *Moses was the author of the *Pentateuch, arguing from the existence of duplicate accounts of the same incident and the variations of style. He is thus generally regarded as the founder of OT criticism. For his boldness Simon was expelled from his order. Much of his work, however, was written in the interests of orthodoxy against B. *Spinoza's OT theories, and Simon continued throughout his life to have the interests of Catholicism at heart. He was strongly opposed to *Jansenism. He lived later at Rouen and at Dieppe, where he wrote several works on the NT.

Of older books the best is the Life by K. H. Graf (Jena, 1847). J. Steinmann, *Richard Simon et les origines de l'exégèse biblique* (1960). P. Auvray, *Richard Simon 1638–1712: Étude bio-bibliographique avec textes inédites* (1974). W. McKane, *Selected Christian Hebraists* (Cambridge, 1989), pp. 111–50, with notes pp. 231–38 and bibl. pp. 250 f. A. Molien in *DTC* 14 (pt. 2; 1941), cols. 2094–118, s.v., with bibl.

Simons, Menno. See MENNONITES.

Simons in the NT. Besides (1) Simon *Peter the Apostle, (2) *Simon 'the Less', Apostle, called 'the Cananaean' or 'the Zealot', (3) *Simon Magus, and (4) *Simon of Cyrene, there is mention in the NT of (5) Simon, one of the *Brethren of the Lord, who has been identified with (2) but is almost certainly distinct; (6) Simon the *Pharisee, in whose house Christ was anointed by 'a woman which was a sinner' (Lk. 7: 36–50); (7) Simon the leper, in whose house at *Bethany Christ was anointed by an unnamed woman (Mk. 14: 3–9), sometimes identified with Mary of Bethany (see MARYS IN THE NT); (8) Simon, the father of *Judas Iscariot (Jn. 6: 71); and (9) Simon, a tanner, with whom St Peter lodged at Joppa (Acts 9: 43).

simony. The term, which is derived from *Simon Magus (cf. Acts 8: 18–24), denotes the purchase or sale of spiritual things. The legislation of the early Councils shows that simony became frequent in the Christian Church after the age of the persecutions. The Council of *Chalcedon (451) forbade ordination to any order for money. St *Gregory the Great later vigorously denounced the same evil. It came to be very widespread in the Middle Ages, esp. in its form of traffic in ecclesiastical preferment, which was frequently forbidden, e.g. by the Third *Lateran Council (1179). It was treated in detail by St *Thomas Aquinas and again strenuously opposed by the Council of *Trent. Acc. to current RC canon law, anyone who resorts to simony to celebrate or receive a sacrament is to be punished by an *interdict or *suspension (*CIC* (1983), can. 1380), while the simoniacal provision of an office is invalid (can. 149). In post-Reformation England the English *Canons of 1604 exacted an oath from all ordinands and recipients of benefices to the effect that their offices had not been obtained by simoniacal transactions. The system of ecclesiastical patronage led almost inevitably to simony in a large number of cases, an evil partly remedied by the English Benefices Act of 1898, initiated by Abp. E. W. *Benson, which, among other anti-simoniacal provisions, forbade sales of next presentations. The form of the Declaration against Simony now required from the recipients of benefices in the C of E is incorporated in Canon C 16 of the 1969 Canons.

A. Leinz, *Die Simonie: Eine kanonistische Studie* (1902); N. A. Weber, *A History of Simony in the Christian Church from the Beginning to the Death of Charlemagne, 814* (Baltimore, 1909); R. A. Ryder, *Simony: An historical Synopsis and Commentary* (Catholic University of America Canon Law Studies; 65; 1931). H. Meier-Welcker, 'Die Simonie im frühen Mittelalter', *ZKG* 64 (1952–53), pp. 61–93. J. Weitzel, *Begriff und Erscheinungsformen der Simonie bei Gratian und den Dekretisten* (Münchener Theologische

Studien, 3. Kanonistische Abteilung, 25; 1967). A. Nothum, SCJ, *La Rénumération du travail inhérent aux fonctions spirituelles et la simonie de droit divin* (Analecta Gregoriana, 176; 1969). A. Bride in *DTC* 14 (pt. 2; 1941), cols. 2141–60, s.v. 'Simonie'.

Simple Feasts. Feasts of the lowest rank in the pre-1960 RC Calendar. They were characterized by having no Second Vespers and only one *nocturn with three lessons at *Mattins. For the classification of feasts, see DOUBLE FEASTS.

Simplicianus, St (d. 400), Bp. of Milan. He is first heard of at *Rome between 350 and 360, where he was instrumental in bringing about the conversion of *Victorinus. Later he played an important part in St *Augustine's conversion by recounting the story, and some of Augustine's early treatises are addressed to him. Augustine refers to him as St *Ambrose's 'father in receiving grace'; this phrase has been variously interpreted, sometimes being taken to suggest that he prepared him for baptism. In 397 he succeeded Ambrose as Bp. of Milan. Feast day, 16 (sometimes 13) Aug.

The chief early sources are Augustine, *Confessions*, 8. 1–12, and *Gennadius, *De Viris Illustribus*, 36. Useful note on Simplicianus by A. Solignac in the edn. of Augustine's *Confessions* in his *Œuvres*, 14 (Bibliothèque Augustinienne, 1962), pp. 530–33. H. W. Phillpott in *DCB* 4 (1887), pp. 688 f. with further refs.

Simplicius, St (d. 483), Pope from 468. He was born at Tivoli. During his pontificate, which was marked by the deposition of the last western emperor (476), followed by the rule of Odoacer (an *Arian) as king of Italy, and the spread of the *Monophysite heresy, he considerably advanced the jurisdictional claims and prestige of the Roman see. In the E. he successfully intervened in defence of the *Chalcedonian formula against its Monophysite critics. He also ably organized the ecclesiastical affairs of the city, where he established several new churches, including S. Stefano Rotondo on the Celian Hill. See ROME, CHURCHES OF. Feast day (local), observed at different times on 2 or 10 Mar.

Several of his letters are repr. from the conciliar collections in J. P. Migne, *PL* 58. 35–62; fourteen from the Collectio Avellana also ed. O. Guenther in CSEL 25 (pt. 1; 1895), pp. 124–55. P. Jaffé, *Regesta Pontificum Romanorum*, 1 (2nd edn. by W. Wattenbach, Leipzig, 1885), pp. 77–80. V. Grumel, AA, *Les Regestes des actes du patriarcat de Constantinople*, 1, fasc. 1 (2nd edn., 1972), pp. 112–19 (nos. 149–160a). *LP* (Duchesne), 1 (1886), pp. 92 f. and 249–51. É. Amann in *DTC* 14 (pt. 2; 1941), cols. 2161–4, s.v.; J. Chapin in *NCE* 13 (1967), p. 232, s.v., both with refs.

simultaneum. The term was originally used in the 16th cent. in Germany for the authorization of two or more religious communions in the same territory. It gradually came to be restricted to the simultaneous right of two congregations differing in their faith to use a single ecclesiastical building. Special provisions for this practice were made in the Peace of *Ryswick (1697). Fresh arrangements for the joint use of churches were drawn up by the Prussian state after the First *Vatican Council in 1870 for the newly formed *Old Catholics and the RCs, but on 12 Mar. 1873 *Pius IX expressly forbade RCs to use the churches given by the government to the Old Catholics.

sin. The purposeful disobedience of a creature to the known will of God. Unlike moral evil it is a fundamentally theological conception.

In the OT sin is represented as a constant factor in the experience both of God's people and of the world from the first transgression of *Adam and *Eve in the Garden of Eden (Gen. 3) onwards. Its power was aggravated rather than diminished by the moral and ceremonial precepts in the Law of *Moses, which both increased the occasions of sin and developed a keener sense of moral responsibility (cf. Rom. 7: 13). The teaching of the Prophets with its emphasis on the heinousness of injustice (Am. 5: 11–24), lack of mercy (Hos. 4: 1), and idolatry (Am. 5: 4–5, Is. 1: 10–17) deepened the sense of sin in another way; in addition, Ezekiel (18: 1–4) and Jeremiah (31: 29–30) proclaim the personal responsibility of each man for his own sins. The Pss., by their stress on the heart as the seat of sin, are marked by their penetrating insights into its personal and emotional effects.

In the NT the Hebrew and Jewish teaching on sin is summed up and deepened by the clear recognition that its roots lie in a man's character (Mt. 5: 21–5; 15: 18). St *Paul expounds it as a breach of the natural law written in the conscience of man (Rom. 2: 14–16) and asserts its universality. The Epistle of St *James stresses its origin in the human will and again emphasizes personal responsibility. In the Johannine writings sin is seen to consist esp. in disbelief in Christ and the consequent judgement.

Later theology, though it introduced many formal distinctions, has added little if anything to what is implicit in the NT. In the 2nd cent. an acute problem was raised by the question of serious post-Baptismal sins which certain theologians held to be never, or only once (*Tertullian, *Hermas) forgivable; this rigorism, though eventually abandoned, left its mark on the development of the Sacrament of *Penance (q.v.). The Fathers held varying beliefs in the universality or otherwise of sin, e.g. St *Athanasius believed that there were sinless lives both before and after Christ. In the early 5th cent. *Pelagius raised the fiercest of all controversies on the nature of *original sin and grace. St *Augustine's part in the conflict, combined with his own religious experience, issued in an intense personal perception of the gravity of sin. Yet on the theological issue St Augustine emphatically rejected the *Manichaean doctrine that evil was a substance and the created universe inherently wicked, opposing to it the *Platonic view that sin was in essence privative (*privatio boni*). In this teaching he exercised a decisive influence on the medieval doctrine of sin.

In the 8th–9th cents. the prevalence of feudal notions and the development of the penitential system fostered in many quarters a somewhat external view of sin. For each sin due satisfaction was to be paid in a measurable quantity of penance. But under the influence of such teachers as St *Anselm and the *Victorines a fundamentally personal view of sin reasserted itself. The regularization of confessional practice also led to the elaboration of a *corpus* of *moral theology in St *Thomas Aquinas and other writers. For the long dispute as to whether or not the BVM was conceived without sin, see IMMACULATE CONCEPTION.

The Reformers were largely concerned to reject the external view of sin which they saw in the later Middle Ages. The doctrine of *justification by faith alone was held by M. *Luther to be the one solvent for every external view of sin. The *Calvinistic teaching on *predestination brought vividly before the imagination of countless Protestants the terrifying consequences of sin. In the 17th cent. the doctrine of sin in the *Jansenist movement in the RC Church had close affinities with the teaching of the Reformers, while in the Protestant Churches certain *Arminian tenets had much in common with Catholic teaching. Among Catholic theologians, the intensive cultivation of moral theology since the 16th cent. has led to such precise distinctions as those currently drawn between *mortal and *venial, and between *formal and *material, sin (qq.v.).

Since the end of the 17th cent. there has been little further development of the doctrine of sin. Under the secularizing influences of the *Enlightenment attempts were made to remove sin from its religious setting and interpret it as moral evil ('philosophic sin'). The liberalistic optimism of the 19th cent. led to the virtual elimination of the notion of sin from much popular religious teaching. Early in the present century the Freudian psychology was invoked in attempts to explain sin in non-moral terms. At a later date the recognition of demonic forces in contemporary civilization led to a renewed theological emphasis on the gravity of sin in the spirit of St Augustine and the Reformers (*Dialectical Theology, etc.).

See also ATONEMENT, ORIGINAL SIN, PENANCE, REDEMPTION, SEVEN DEADLY SINS.

Modern works in Eng. directly on the subject incl. J. *Tulloch, *The Christian Doctrine of Sin* (1877); F. R. Tennant, *The Concept of Sin* (1912); T. A. *Lacey, *Nature, Miracle and Sin* (1916); P. Green, *The Problem of Evil* (1920); R. S. Moxon, *The Doctrine of Sin* (1922); C. R. Smith, *The Biblical Doctrine of Sin and the Ways of God with Sinners* (1953); F. Greeves, *The Meaning of Sin* (Fernley-Hartley Lecture, 1956; 1956); J. Hick, *Evil and the God of Love* (1966). Other modern works incl. H. Rondet, SJ, *Notes sur la théologie du péché* (1957); S. Lyonnet, SJ, *De Peccato et Redemptione*, 1 (Rome, 1957), largely in Eng. tr. in id. and L. Sabourin, SJ, *Sin, Redemption, and Sacrifice: A Biblical and Patristic Study* (Analecta Biblica, 48; 1970); P. Delhaye and others, *Théologie du péché* (Bibliothèque de Théologie, Série 2. Théologie Morale, 7; 1960); P. Ricœur, *Finitude et Culpabilité* (Philosophie de l'Esprit, 2 vols., 1960; Eng. tr. of vol. 1, as *Fallible Man*, Chicago, 1965; vol. 2, *The Symbolism of Evil*, New York, 1967); C. Journet, *Le Mal: Essai théologique* (1961; Eng. tr., 1963). P. Palazzini (ed.), *Il peccato* (1959; Eng. tr., Dublin, 1964). P. Schoonenberg in *Mysterium Salutis*, ed. J. Feiner and M. Löhrer, 2 (Einsiedeln [1967]), pp. 845–941. P. H. Simon, *La Littérature du péché et de la grâce: Essai sur la constitution d'une littérature chrétienne depuis 1880* [1957]. Arts. in *HERE* 11 (1920), pp. 528–71, esp. H. R. *Mackintosh on 'Sin (Christian)', pp. 538–44; T. Deman, OP, in *DTC* 12 (pt. 1; 1933), cols. 140–275, s.v. 'Péché'; G. Quell, G. Bertram, G. Stählin, and W. Grundmann in *TWNT* 1 (1933), pp. 267–320 (Eng. tr., 1 (1964), pp. 267–316), s.v. ἁμαρτάνω, ἁμάρτημα, ἁμαρτία, with extensive bibl. refs.; P. Schoonenberg and K. *Rahner, SJ, in *Sacramentum Mundi*, ed. K. Rahner and others, 6 (1970), pp. 87–94, s.v.; S. Lyonnet, SJ, and P. Gervais, SJ, in *Dict. Sp.* 12 (pt. 1; 1984), cols. 790–853, s.v. 'Péché-Pécheur'. See also works cited under ORIGINAL SIN.

Sinai. The mountain in the desert between Egypt and Palestine where the Law was given by *Moses (Ex. 19: 1 ff.). From very ancient times it was regarded as the sacred mountain of *Yahweh (Deut. 33: 2, Jgs. 5: 5). The region of the traditional Sinai (now Jebel Musa) became an early centre of Christian *monasticism, the present monastery dedicated to St *Catherine of Alexandria claiming to have been built on the site to which her body was miraculously transported. The name is also used for the whole peninsula in which the sacred mountain was located.

A. P. *Stanley, *Sinai and Palestine in connection with their History* (1856), ch. 1, 'The Peninsula of Sinai', pp. 3–62. D. Nielsen, 'The Site of the Biblical Mount Sinai', *Journal of the Palestine Oriental Society*, 7 (Jerusalem, 1927), pp. 187–208; L. H. Vincent, OP, 'Un Nouveau Sinaï biblique', *R. Bibl.* 39 (1930), pp. 73–83. L. Prévost, *Le Sinaï hier-aujourd'hui: Étude topographique, biblique, historique, archéologique* (1937). G. I. Davies, *The Way of the Wilderness* (Society for Old Testament Study, Monograph Series, 5; Cambridge, 1979), pp. 63–9. A. Legendre in *Dict. Bibl.* 5 (1908), cols. 1751–83, s.v., with bibl.; E. Lohse in *TWNT* 7 (1960–4), pp. 281–6 (Eng. tr., 7 (1971), pp. 282–7), s.v. Σινᾶ. C. N. Papamichalopoulos, Ἡ μονὴ τοῦ Ὄρους Σινᾶ (Athens, 1932), with docs. M. H. L. Rabino, *Le Monastère de Sainte-Catherine du Mont Sinaï: Souvenirs épigraphiques des anciens pèlerins* (Cairo, 1935). G. H. Forsyth, K. Weitzmann, and others, *The Monastery of Saint Catherine at Mount Sinai: The Church and Fortress of Justinian* (Ann Arbor, Mich. [1974 ff.]). J. Galey, *Sinai and the Monastery of St Catherine* (1980), with contributions by K. Weitzmann and G. Forsyth. D. J. Chitty, *The Desert a City* (Oxford, 1966), pp. 168–78.

Sinai, Church of, the smallest independent Church of the Orthodox Communion. It is ruled by the 'Archbishop of Mount Sinai', the abbot of the monastery of St Catherine on the mountain, who has jurisdiction over a few daughter-houses and cells and a small number of Arabs who live in the vicinity of the monastery. The independence of the Church was proclaimed in 1575 and confirmed in 1782. The archbishop must always be consecrated by the Patr. of *Jerusalem, who in consequence has often tried, though with little success, to assert a certain supremacy over the Church.

Sinaiticus, Codex. See CODEX SINAITICUS.

Sinodos. An Ethiopic collection of canons, the first two sections of which are now often referred to as the 'Sinodos Alexandrina', since they are also preserved together in *Sahidic and Arabic; these items are assumed to go back to a lost Greek collection of the 5th cent. The 'Sinodus Alexandrina' contains four distinct documents, the first three of which are run together: the *Apostolic Church Order, the *Apostolic Tradition*, parts of Book 8 of the *Apostolic Constitutions, and the *Apostolic Canons. The first and second of these also feature together in the Latin *Verona palimpsest lv [53].

The edns. of the Sahidic, Arabic, and Ethiopic versions are listed, with further refs., in *CPG* 1 (1983), pp. 222 f. (no. 1732). Eng. tr. of the first three texts in these versions by G. [W.] Horner, *The Statutes of the Apostles* (1904), pp. 127–363. Fr. tr. of the Arabic version of the Apostolic Canons in the edn. of the Arabic text by J. and A. Périer in *PO* 8 (1912), pp. 664–93. A. Faivre, 'La documentation canonico-liturgique de l'église ancienne', pt. 1, *Rev. S.R.* 54 (1980), pp. 204–19.

Sion. See ZION.

Sion College, London. An ecclesiastical institution founded by Thomas White (*c.*1550–1624), who left £3,000

to purchase premises for a 'college' for a 'corporation' or guild of the clergy of London and its suburbs, with almshouses for 20 people attached. To the original hall, chapel, and almshouses in London Wall, a library was added by the donation of John Simson, White's executor. The College moved to the Victoria Embankment in 1886 and until 1996 functioned chiefly as a theological and historical library. It was then agreed to sell this building and divide most of the books between *Lambeth Palace Library and *King's College, London.

E. H. Pearce, *Sion College and Library* (1913); G. Huelin, *Sion College and Library 1912–1990* (1992).

Si quis (Lat., 'if anyone'). The public notice until 1976 issued on behalf of a candidate for a benefice, holy orders, etc., in the C of E, requiring any objectors to come forward.

Siricius, St (*c.*334–99), Bp. of *Rome from 384. His pontificate is of importance as marking a new stage in the development of Papal authority. His epistle to Himerius, Bp. of Tarragona (385), advocating a relatively lenient treatment of public penitents, is the first of the Papal *decretals. He held a synod at Rome in 386 which passed nine canons on matters of ecclesiastical discipline that were sent to the African Church. He also took active steps towards preventing the Church in E. Illyria from becoming subject to the jurisdiction of *Constantinople. In 390 he dedicated the new *basilica of St Paul on the *Ostian Way, and in 392 condemned *Jovinian. Feast day, 26 Nov.

Letters ed. P. *Coustant, OSB, *Epistolae Romanorum Pontificum*, 1 (Paris, 1721), cols. 623–700; repr. in J. P. Migne, *PL* 13. 1131–96. Jaffé, 1, pp. 40–2. *LP* (Duchesne), 1, pp. 216 f. J. Janini, *S. Siricio y las cuatro temporas: Una investigación sobre las fuentes de la espiritualidad seglar y del Sacramentario Leoniano* (Valencia, 1958). C. Pietri, *Roma Christiana: Recherches sur l'Église de Rome . . . de Miltiade à Sixte III* (Bibliothèque des Écoles Françaises d'Athènes et de Rome, 224; 1976), pp. 888–909. J. Barmby in *DCB* 4 (1887), pp. 696–702, s.v.; P. T. Camelot, OP, in *NCE* 13 (1969), pp. 258 f., s.v.; J. N. D. Kelly, *Oxford Dictionary of Popes* (1986), pp. 35 f., s.v.

Sirmium, Blasphemy of. The doctrinal formula published in Latin by the Council of Sirmium of 357, setting forth the teaching of the extreme *Arian party. All mention of the term 'substance' (*substantia, quae Graece usia appellatur*) and its compounds (including the *Homoousion) in Trinitarian speculation was forbidden, and the subordination of the Son to the Father asserted. Its promulgation marked the turning-point in the history of the Arian controversy. It takes its name from the description of it in St *Hilary of Poitiers' 'De synodis' as the *Exemplum blasphemiae apud Sirmium*.

The text is in A. Hahn, *Bibliothek der Symbole und Glaubensregeln der alten Kirche* (3rd edn., 1897), §161, pp. 199–201; convenient Eng. tr. in J. Stevenson (ed.), *Creeds, Councils, and Controversies* (1966), pp. 35–7 (no. 23).

Sirmond, Jacques (1559–1651), French *Jesuit scholar. Having entered the Society of Jesus in 1576, he was professor of literature and rhetoric from 1581 to 1590 at the Collège de *Clermont in Paris, where he numbered St *Francis de Sales among his pupils. From 1590 to 1608 he was secretary to the General of the Jesuits, C. *Aquaviva, at Rome, and while there assisted C. *Baronius in his historical works. After returning to France he became rector of the Paris College (1617) and later confessor to Louis XIII (1637–43). From 1610 onwards he published the works which established his fame as one of the greatest scholars of his century. Esp. important are his editions of the Fathers, which include St *Fulgentius' 'De veritate praedestinationis et gratiae' (1612), the works of *Paschasius Radbertus (1618) and *Theodoret of Cyrrhus (1642), the 'Opuscula' of *Eusebius of Caesarea (now thought to be by *Eusebius of Emesa, q.v.; 1643), and *Rufinus' 'De Fide' (1650). His other writings include *Concilia Antiqua Galliae* (1629), a dissertation *Dionysii Parisiensis et Dionysii Areopagitae discrimen* (1641) which raised a long-drawn-out controversy owing to its attack on the traditional identification of the two *Dionysii, and various polemical works.

Opera Varia nunc primum collecta (not quite complete), ed. J. de La Baune, SJ (5 vols., fol., Paris, 1696, with brief biog; repr. Venice, 1728). H. *Valesius, Oratio in Obitum J. Sirmondi (Paris, 1651). H. Mordek, 'Der Codex Andegavensis Jacques Sirmonds', Traditio, 25 (1969), pp. 485–98. Sommervogel, 7 (1896), pp. 1237–61. P. Galtier, SJ, in DTC 14 (pt. 2; 1941), cols. 2186–93.

Sisters of Mercy.
(1) A name widely used in the 19th cent. of members of any (esp. Anglican) religious community engaged in nursing or similar work. A penitentiary conducted by such sisters was known as a 'House of Mercy'. (2) A RC sisterhood founded in *Dublin in 1827.

Sistine Chapel.
The principal chapel of the *Vatican Palace, so called because it was built for Pope *Sixtus IV (1471–84). It is used for the principal Papal ceremonies and also by the cardinals for the election of a new Pope when there is a vacancy. The chapel is celebrated for the frescoes by *Michelangelo and other artists on its walls and ceiling, chief among them being Michelangelo's *Last Judgement* covering the altar wall. The decorations of the chapel also included a set of tapestries commissioned from *Raphael by Pope *Leo X illustrating scenes from the lives of St *Peter and St *Paul (now elsewhere in the Vatican Palace).

E. Steinmann, Die Sixtinische Kapelle (2 vols., 1901–5), with plates (2 vols., 1901–5). C. de Tolnay, Michelangelo, 2: The Sistine Ceiling (Princeton, NJ, 1945), incl. full bibl. L. D. Ettlinger, The Sistine Chapel before Michelangelo: Religious Imagery and Papal Primacy (Oxford, 1965). M. Giacometi (ed.), The Sistine Chapel: Michelangelo Rediscovered (1986). F. Hartt and others, The Sistine Chapel (2 vols., 1991). J. Shearman, Raphael's Cartoons in the Collection of Her Majesty the Queen and the Tapestries for the Sistine Chapel [1972].

Sistine Madonna (Madonna di S. Sisto).
One of *Raphael's most famous altarpieces, now in Dresden. It shows the BVM and Child floating on the clouds of heaven, between Pope *Sixtus II and St *Barbara, as a transcendent vision, quite different from the realistic treatment of the theme normal in the 15th cent. It was painted in Rome in 1512–13 for Pope *Julius II, whose features are given to St Sixtus, and presented by him to the Benedictine abbey of San Sisto at Piacenza. It has no connection with the *Sistine Chapel.

M. Putscher, Raphaels Sixtinische Madonna (Tübingen, 1955). L. Dussler, Raphael: A Critical Catalogue (1971; rev. Eng. tr. of work pub. in Munich, 1966), pp. 36–8, with plate 83.

Sitz im Leben
(Ger., 'place in life'). A term used particularly in biblical criticism, to signify the circumstances (most often in the life of a community) in which a particular story, saying, etc., was either created or preserved and transmitted.

Six Articles.
The Articles imposed in June 1539 at the King's bidding by the Religion Act 1539 (sometimes called 'the Whip with Six Strings'), to prevent the spread of Reformation doctrines and practices. They (1) maintained *transubstantiation and (2) *Communion in one kind, (3) enforced clerical *celibacy, (4) upheld *monastic vows and (5) defended private *Masses and (6) *auricular confession. The bill was introduced into the Lords by the Duke of Norfolk, and all the lay peers were subservient. A minority of the bishops, however, resisted. Nicholas *Shaxton, Bp. of *Salisbury, and H. *Latimer, Bp. of *Worcester, resigned their sees, and T. *Cranmer sent his wife back to Germany. In operation the act turned out to be less severe than its critics feared, as its requirements were widely ignored even by those holding high ecclesiastical office. It was repealed in 1547.

Text in Gee and Hardy, pp. 303–19 (no. 65); the Articles, without the rest of the Act, repr. in Bettenson, pp. 328 f. G. Redworth, 'A Study in the Formulation of Policy: The Genesis and Evolution of the Act of Six Articles', JEH 37 (1986), pp. 42–67.

Six Points, the.
The *Eastward Position, *Eucharistic Vestments, the *Mixed Chalice, *Altar Lights, Unleavened *Bread at the *Eucharist, and *Incense. Their introduction into the C of E followed a campaign, set on foot c.1870 under the indirect influence of the *Oxford Movement, to restore these and many similar ceremonial usages. Their crystallization into 'six points' dates from a resolution of the *English Church Union, proposed by T. T. *Carter and passed at the annual meeting of the Union on 15 June 1875. See also PURCHAS JUDGEMENT, LINCOLN JUDGEMENT.

Six Preachers.
In *Canterbury Cathedral, six preachers were part of the New Foundation of 1541, appointed by T. *Cranmer 'to preach against the Pope and his supremacy'. Supplied with an income of £24 a year, lodgings in the Precincts, a horse, and firewood, they were required to preach every saint's day, not being a Sunday, and to travel round the diocese. Still appointed by the Abp. of Canterbury (normally for a period of five years), they now receive no emoluments and are only required to preach once a year at Evensong in the cathedral on a Sunday afternoon.

D. I. Hill, The Six Preachers of Canterbury Cathedral 1541–1982 (Ramsgate, 1982).

Sixtus II, St
(d. 258), or 'Xystus', Pope. On his accession in 257 to the Roman see, he resumed relations with St *Cyprian and the Churches of Africa and Asia Minor, which had been broken off under his predecessor St *Stephen I on account of the controversy on the validity of heretical baptism. Sixtus himself, however, continued the Roman practice of not rebaptizing heretics. He suffered martyrdom under the second edict of the Emp. Valerian (Aug. 258) and was buried in the catacomb of St *Callistus. He was one of the most highly venerated of early martyrs. His name is found in the Roman calendar

of the middle of the 4th cent. and still stands in the *Canon of the Mass. Feast day, 7 (formerly 6) Aug.

He is to be distinguished from an earlier St Sixtus (I), who was Bp. of Rome *c.*117–*c.*127. Feast day, 3 (before 1922, 6) Apr. (in the *Roman Martyrology).

Jaffé, 1, pp. 21 f. *LP* (Duchesne), 1, pp. 155 f. *AASS*, Aug. 2. (1735), pp. 124–42; also Nov. 2 (pt. 2; 1931), pp. 420 f., with full refs. P. Corssen, 'Der Schauplatz der Passion des römischen Bischofs Sixtus II', *ZNTW* 16 (1915), pp. 147–166, with refs.; P. F. de' Cavalieri, *Note agiografiche*, 6 (ST 33; 1920), no. 4, 'Un recente studio sul luogo del martirio di S. Sisto II', pp. 145–78. É. Amann in *DTC* 14 (pt. 2; 1941), cols. 2194–6, s.v. 'Sixte II'; H. *Leclercq, OSB, and M. Combet-Farnoux in *DACL* 15 (pt. 1; 1950), cols. 1501–15, s.v. 'Sixte II', with bibl.; S. Carletti and C. M. Carpano in *Bibliotheca Sanctorum*, 11 (1968), cols. 1256–62, s.v. 'Sisto II'.

The Sayings of a pagan moralist Sextus, wrongly ascribed to the Pope by *Rufinus, ed. H. Chadwick (Texts and Studies, 5; Cambridge, 1959); id., 'The Sentences of Sextus and of the Pythagoreans', *JTS* NS 11 (1960), p. 349.

Sixtus IV (1414–84), Pope from 1471. Born of a poor family, Francesco della Rovere entered the *Franciscan Order, where he became a successful lecturer, General in 1464, and Cardinal in 1467. Elected Pope in 1471, he undertook a crusade against the Turks, but with little success, and soon turned almost entirely to Italian politics and the aggrandizement of his family. With him the nepotism of the Renaissance Popes entered its worst stage and the spiritual interests of the Church were almost wholly relegated to the background. His nephews, one of whom was the later Pope *Julius II, implicated the Pope in political intrigues with the Italian cities, esp. in the conspiracy of the Pazzi, which resulted in the murder of Giuliano de' Medici and a war with Florence (1478–80). His nepotism also led to considerable confusion of the Papal finances and troubles in the Pontifical States. Besides increasing the privileges of the Franciscans and other Mendicant Orders and furthering the cult of the BVM, Sixtus was a great protector of arts and scholarship. He founded the Sistine Choir, built the *Sistine Chapel, and enriched the *Vatican Library. Sixtus was unfortunate in his training and his circumstances. His extravagance arose from his inexperience as a member of a Mendicant Order and from the want of any worthy relatives on whom to exercise his natural generosity. In his personal life he appears to have been blameless and also a passable theologian.

P. M. Sevesi, OFM (ed.), 'Lettere autografe di Francesco della Rovere da Savona. . .', *AFH* 28 (1935), pp. 198–234 and 477–99. Account of his life to 1474 by B. *Platina (d. 1481) in L. A. *Muratori (ed.), *Rerum Italicarum Scriptores* (2nd edn.), 3, pt. 1 (Città di Castello [1932]), pp. 398–420. E. Lee, *Sixtus IV and Men of Letters* (Temi e Testi, 26; Rome, 1978), with further docs. M. Miglio and others (eds.), *Un Pontificato ed una Città, Sisto IV (1471–1484): Atti del Convegno, Roma, 3–7 dicembre 1984* (Scuola Vaticana di Paleografia, Diplomatica e Archivistica, Littera Antiqua, 5; 1986). C. Bauer, 'Studi per la storia delle finanze papali durante il pontificato di Sisto IV', *Archivio della R. Società di Storia Patria*, 50 (1927), pp. 314–404. A. Matanić, OFM, 'Xystus Pp. IV scripsitne librum "de conceptione beate Virginis Marie"?', *Antonianum*, 29 (1954), pp. 573–8. Pastor, 4 (1894), pp. 197–471; Fliche and Martin, 15 (1951), esp. pp. 74–90. A. Teetaert, OFM Cap., in *DTC* 14 (pt. 2; 1941), cols. 2199–217, s.v. 'Sixte IV', with bibl.

Sixtus V (1521–90), Pope from 1585. The son of a gardener, Felice Peretti was educated by the *Franciscans of Montalto, where he took the habit at the age of 12. Ordained priest in 1547, he soon became a famous preacher and a friend of St *Ignatius Loyola and St *Philip Neri. He was appointed Consultor of the *Inquisition and professor at the Roman University in 1560, and General of his order and Bp. of S. Agata in 1566. In 1570 he was created cardinal by *Pius V, whose confessor he was. He was Bp. of Fermo from 1571 to 1577 and in 1585 was elected Pope. His pontificate was devoted to far-reaching reforms in the government of the Church and of the Papal States, ruthlessly implemented. He suppressed brigandage in his territories and put the Papal finances on a sound basis by the sale of certain offices, the setting-up of more '*montes', and additional taxes. Continuing the reform of the Curia, he fixed the number of cardinals at 70, and by the bull 'Immensa Aeterni' of 1588 established 15 congregations (see ROMAN CONGREGATIONS). In his European policy he endeavoured to uphold the balance of the Catholic powers, and thus distrusted the ambitions of *Philip II, who wished to split up France. A patron of art and scholarship, Sixtus V was esp. concerned with the embellishment of Rome, though he had scant appreciation of its antiquities. He built the *Lateran Palace and the *Vatican Library, had the cupola of St Peter's finished, and supplied the city with drinking water, the 'Acqua Felice', which was conducted over a distance of 20 miles. He also inaugurated an edition of the *Vulgate (q.v.), which, after the corrections made under *Clement VIII, long remained the standard text.

Bullarum, Diplomatum et Privilegiorum Sanctorum Romanorum Pontificum Taurinensis Editio, 8 (Naples, 1883), pp. 563–1025, and 9 (Turin, 1865), pp. 1–381. 'Acta Consistorialia', *Analecta Juris Pontificii*, 9 (Rome, Paris, and Brussels, 1872), cols. 841–74. G. Cugnoni, 'Documenti chigiani concernenti Felice Peretti, Sisto V', *Archivio della Società Romana di Storia Patria*, 5 (1882), pp. 1–32, 210–304, and 542–89. G. Leti, *Vita di Sisto V* (3 vols., Amsterdam, 1721; Eng. tr., 1724); J. A. de Hübner, *Sixte-Quint* (2 vols., 1870; Eng. tr., 1872; rev. Ger. tr., 1932). S. Klein, *Sixtus der Fünfte nach dem grösseren Werke des Barons von Hübner bearbeitet* (Sammlung historischer Bildnisse, 10; 1873). L. M. Personé, *Sisto Quinto: Il genio della potenza* (Florence, 1935). I. de Feo, *Sisto V: Un grande papa tra Rinascimento e Barocco* (Storia e documenti, 75; Milan, 1987). E. A. Segretain, *Sixte-Quint et Henri IV* (1861). M. de Boüard, *Sixte-Quint, Henri IV et la Ligue. La Légation du Cardinal Caetani en France (1589–1590)', *RQH* 116 (1932), pp. 59–140. R. Schiffmann, *Roma felix: Aspekte der städtebaulichen Gestaltung Roms unter Papst Sixtus V.* (Europäische Hochschulschriften, Reihe 28, 36; 1985). H. Gamrath, *Roma Sancta Renovata: Studi sull'urbanistica di Roma nella seconda metà del sec. XVI con particolare riferimento al pontificato di Sisto V (1585–1590)* (Analecta Romana Instituti Danici, Suppl. 12; 1987). U. Balzani in *CMH* 3 (1904), pp. 422–55. Pastor, 21 (1932) and 22 (1932), pp. 1–312. A. Teertaert, OFM Cap., in *DTC* 14 (pt. 2; 1941), cols. 2217–38, s.v. 'Sixte-Quint'; G. B. Picotti in *EC* 11 (1953), cols. 780–7, s.v. 'Sisto V'; D. R. Campbell in *NCE* 13 (1969), pp. 273–5, s.v.

slavery. A state of servitude by which a man is the property of another man. It is opposed on the one hand to human dignity, which does not allow a person to be treated as a chattel, and violates a man's rights to liberty of conscience, integrity of soul and body, and the stability of family life, and, on the other hand, tends to breed vice and cruelty in the owner. In the OT, however, a mitigated form of slavery was tolerated by the Mosaic Law (Exod. 21: 1–11, Lev. 25: 44–55), and in NT times it was an integral part of the social system whose sudden abolition would have reduced the Roman Empire to chaos. There is no explicit teaching on the subject in the Gospels, but the spiritual equality of men as children of the same Father, together with the *Golden Rule and the Lord's affection for the poor and oppressed, provided the principles which were slowly to penetrate the nascent Christian society. They were formulated by St *Paul, who recognized neither bond nor free in Christ (Gal. 3: 28, 1 Cor. 12: 13, Col. 3: 11), though he did not condemn slavery but rather strove to imbue both masters and slaves with the new Christian spirit of charity which was finally to abolish the institution itself. This teaching is most conspicuous in his Ep. to Philemon and in the exhortations of Col. 3: 22–4: 1 (cf. Eph. 6: 5–9). A similar attitude was prevalent in the early Church until the 3rd cent., Christian masters and slaves, who shared in the same sacraments, being still more closely drawn together by their common sufferings and experience of martyrdom. From *Constantine onwards the Imperial legislation followed the Christian sentiment and many mitigations were introduced, esp. in the 6th cent., by *Justinian. Slaves who, with the consent of their masters, became priests were automatically freed, whereas entrance into the religious life did not even presuppose this consent. After the christianization of N. and E. Europe slavery was gradually transformed into the much milder institution of serfdom, which in its turn slowly disappeared in and after the Renaissance. A cruel form of slavery, however, re-appeared after the fall of *Constantinople in 1453, when the Turks reduced large numbers of Christians to a servitude which was only mitigated by the devoted work of the religious orders such as the *Trinitarians, the *Mercedarians, and St *Vincent de Paul's 'Congregation of the Mission'. A renewed outbreak of slave-owning among Christians took place after the discovery of America, when the Spanish, Portuguese, and British settlers made slaves of the Indians and later also introduced negro slaves from Africa despite the steady resistance of the missionaries, esp. the *Dominicans and the *Jesuits, who set up a model colony without slaves in Paraguay, and despite the condemnations of successive Popes, e.g. *Paul III in 1537, *Pius V in 1567, and *Urban VIII in 1639. In the 18th cent. the movement against slavery was taken up by the *Quakers, esp. W. *Penn, who abolished slavery in Pennsylvania, and philanthropists like T. Clarkson and W. *Wilberforce. The slave trade was made illegal in 1808, and slavery was finally suppressed in the British Empire in 1833. In the USA, at the conclusion of the Civil War in Dec. 1865, a constitutional amendment for ever prohibited slavery throughout the States.

The question of slavery has been much discussed by theologians. Acc. to several of the Fathers, e.g. St *Gregory of Nazianzus and St *Augustine, it was a state of life which was consequent on the Fall; acc. to St *Thomas Aquinas it was a chastisement. It has been admitted as, theoretically, not contrary to the natural law by later theologians such as L. *Lessius and J. de *Lugo, if arising from contract, birth, in punishment for a crime, or as the result of a just war. It is now generally condemned on account of the almost inevitable abuses accompanying it

and of its opposition to the spirit of the Gospel. The *Catechism of the Catholic Church (1992; no. 2414) regards the enslavement or sale of people as contravening the seventh Commandment ('Thou shalt not steal').

T. Clarkson, The History of the Rise, Progress, and Accomplishment of the Abolition of the African Slave-Trade by the British Parliament (2 vols., 1808; new edn. with prefatory remarks on the subsequent abolition of slavery, 1839); W. L. Mathieson, British Slavery and its Abolition 1823–1838 (1926); id., British Slave Emancipation 1838–1849 (1932); id., Great Britain and the Slave Trade 1839–1865 (1929); C. W. W. Greenidge, Slavery (1958), and other works of this author. A. Katz, Christentum und Sklaverei (Vienna [1926]); J. F. Maxwell, Slavery and the Catholic Church: The History of Catholic Teaching concerning the Moral Legitimacy of the Institution of Slavery (Chichester and London, 1975). P. Allard, Les Esclaves chrétiens, depuis les premiers temps de l'Eglise jusqu'à la fin de la domination romaine en Occident (1876); H. Wallon, Histoire de l'esclavage dans l'antiquité (3 vols., 1879); J. Vogt, Sklaverei und Humanität (Historia, Einzelschriften 8; Wiesbaden, 1965; 2nd edn., 1972; Eng. tr., Ancient Slavery and the Ideal of Man (Oxford [1974]); M. I. Finley, Ancient Slavery and Modern Ideology (1980); C. W. Weber, Sklaverei im Altertum (Düsseldorf and Vienna [1981]). H. Langenfeld, Christianisierungspolitik und Sklavengesetzgebung der römischen Kaiser von Konstantin bis Theodosius II (Antiquitas, Reihe I, 26; 1977). F Laub, Die Begegnung des frühen Christentums mit der antiken Sklaverei (Stuttgarter Bibelstudien, 107; 1982). R. Klein, Die Sklaverei in der Sicht der Bischöfe Ambrosius und Augustinus (Forschungen zur Antiken Sklaverei, 20; Stuttgart, 1988). J. Heers, Esclaves et domestiques au Moyen-Age dans le monde méditerranéen [1981]. J. Höffner, Christentum und Menschenwürde: Das Anliegen der spanischen Kolonialethik im goldenen Zeitalter (Trier, 1947). D. B. Davies, The Problem of Slavery in Western Culture (Ithaca, NY, 1966; Harmondsworth, 1970), and other works of this author; E. D. Genovese, Roll, Jordan, Roll: The World the Slaves Made (New York [1974]; London, 1975); C. D. Rice, The Rise and Fall of Black Slavery (1975); R. Anstey, The Atlantic Slave Trade and British Abolition 1760–1810 (1975); C. Bolt and S. Drescher (eds.), Anti-Slavery, Religion, and Reform: Essays in Memory of Roger Anstey (Folkestone, 1980). For the history of the abolition of slavery in the British Empire see also lives of W. Wilberforce, etc. J. D. Dutilleul in DTC 5 (1913), cols. 457–520, s.v. 'Esclavage'; L. D. Agate in HERE 11 (1920), pp. 601–12, s.v. 'Slavery, Christian'; J. Weeger, SJ, and A. Derville, SJ, in Dict. Sp. 4 (pt. 1; 1960), cols. 1067–80, s.v. 'Esclave'.

Slavonic Book of Enoch. See ENOCH, BOOKS OF.

Sleidanus, Johannes (1506–56), historian of the German Reformation. Born at Schleiden near Aachen, he studied classics at Liège and *Cologne and jurisprudence at *Paris and Orléans. Adopting Protestant views (exact date unknown), in 1536 he entered the service of the Bellay brothers, who were in correspondence with the *Schmalkaldic League, and in 1540–1 he was employed in diplomatic missions for the French crown. In 1545, thanks to the efforts of M. *Bucer and J. *Sturm, he was commissioned by the Schmalkaldic League to write the history of the Protestant cause in Germany. When war interrupted his work, *Edward VI at T. *Cranmer's intercession gave him a stipend in England (1551). But he soon returned to the Continent, where he represented a group of S. German cities at the Council of *Trent (1551–2) and took part in the negotiations of the German Protestants with Henry II of France in 1552. In 1554 he was appointed Professor of Law at Strasbourg, where he completed his De Statu Religionis et Reipublicae Carolo V Caesare Commentarii (2 vols.

[Strasbourg], 1555; Eng. tr. by J. Daws, 1560), now valued chiefly for the many official documents included in it. His other works include a Latin version of Bucer's *Shorter Catechism* (1544).

Briefwechsel ed. H. Baumgarten (Strasbourg, 1881). Id., *Über Sleidans Leben und Briefwechsel* (1878); W. Friedensburg, *Johannes Sleidanus* (Leipzig, 1935), with refs. A. G. Dickens, 'Johannes Sleidan and Reformation History', in R. B. Knox (ed.), *Reformation, Conformity and Dissent: Essays in honour of Geoffrey Nuttall* (1977), pp. 17–43. Further bibl. in Schottenloher, 2 (1935), pp. 279–81 (nos. 20151–78).

Slessor, Mary (1848–1915), missionary of the *United Presbyterian Church. Born in Aberdeen, she spent her early life in work in a factory. In 1875 she offered herself for service in Africa to the Foreign Missions Board of her Church, and the next year sailed for the Calabar coast of W. Africa. Here she gained great influence with the native population, not least in successfully bringing to an end many tribal abuses (twin murder, human sacrifice, witchcraft, cruelty). In 1905 the Government, recognizing her authority, invested 'Ma Slessor' (as she was popularly called) with the powers of a magistrate, which she continued to exercise until her death.

Life by W. P. Livingstone (London, 1915). C. Christian and G. Plummer, *God and one Redhead: Mary Slessor of Calabar* (1970); J. Buchan, *The Expendable Mary Slessor* (Edinburgh, 1980).

Smaragdus (d. after 825), abbot of St-Mihiel. Of Spanish or Aquitaine origin, he became abbot of Castellion (near the source of the tiny R. Marsoupe), and was responsible for transferring the community to St-Mihiel, some 5 miles distant, where the Marsoupe flows into the R. Meuse. He took part in the Council of Aachen in 809 and formulated its conclusions in a letter sent by *Charlemagne to Pope *Leo III. He wrote a commentary on the grammarian Donatus and a number of theological and ascetical works, incl. the 'Via Regia', on the spiritual formation of a prince, addressed to either Charlemagne or *Louis the Pious, and, most importantly, an 'Expositio' on the Rule of St *Benedict, composed after 817 and connected with the monastic reforms of St *Benedict of Aniane.

Works collected in J. P. Migne, *PL* 102. 15–976. Crit. edns. of his 'Carmina' by E. Duemmler in *MGH*, Poetae, 1 (1881), pp. 605–19; of *Expositio in Regulam S. Benedicti* by A. Spannagel and P. Engelbert, OSB (Corpus Consuetudinum Monasticum, 8; Siegburg, 1974), and of *Liber in partibus Donati* by B. Löfstedt and others (CCCM 68; 1986). F. Rädle, *Studien zu Smaragd von Saint-Mihiel* (Medium Aevum, Philologische Studien, 29; Munich, 1974). O. Eberhardt, *Via Media: Der Fürstenspiegel Smaragds von St Mihiel und seine literarische Gattung* (Münsterische Mittelalter-Schriften, 28; 1977). J. Leclercq, OSB, 'Smaragdus', in P. E. Szarmach (ed.), *An Introduction to the Medieval Mystics of Europe* (Albany, NY [1984]), pp. 37–51.

Smalkaldic Articles, League. See SCHMALKALDIC ARTICLES, LEAGUE.

Smart, Peter (1569–*c.*1652), *Puritan. He was educated at Broadgates Hall and *Christ Church, Oxford. In 1598 he was appointed Headmaster of *Durham Grammar School, following the move of William James from the Deanery of Christ Church to that of Durham. When James became Bp. of Durham (1607–17), Smart's rise was swift; from 1609 he was James's chaplain and a prebendary of Durham Cathedral, and from 1612 Master of Gateshead Hospital. By 1625 he was a member of the *High Commission for Durham. He strongly resisted the introduction by Richard Neile (Bp. of Durham, 1617–28) of High Church ornaments into the cathedral, and on 27 July 1628 he preached a sermon against J. *Cosin, one of the chief promoters of the advanced ceremonial, which was published as *The Vanity and Downfall of Superstitious Popish Ceremonies* (1628). Smart was brought before the Durham High Commission and on 2 Sept. sequestered from his prebend. Early in 1629 the case was removed to the Southern High Commission, but referred to the *York High Commission; in 1630 Smart was fined £400 (or possibly £500), and on refusing to pay, imprisoned and degraded. He was released in Nov. 1640, when the Long Parliament ordered the prosecution of Cosin, and in Jan. 1641 he was restored to his preferments. In 1643 he took the *Solemn League and Covenant. In his last years he was given various sequestered benefices.

W. H. D. Longstaffe (ed.), *The Acts of the High Commission Court within the Diocese of Durham* (Surtees Society, 34; 1858), pp. 197–250 (Appendix A). G. W. Kitchin, *Seven Sages of Durham* (1911), pp. 97–132. A. Gordon in *DNB* 52 (1897), pp. 392 f.; L. Pullan in *DECH*, pp. 560 f., s.v.

'Smectymnuus'. The professed writer of a book pub. in March 1641 to defend the *Presbyterian theory of the Christian ministry in reply to Bp. J. *Hall's *Humble Remonstrance*. The name was made up of the initials of its five real authors, namely Stephen Marshall, Edmund *Calamy, Thomas Young, Matthew Newcomen, and William Spurstow. The form 'Smectymnuan' was used both of the actual composers of the treatise and of others who accepted its views. On its publication J. Hall replied with a *Defence of that Remonstrance*; in May 1641 J. *Milton, who had prob. had a hand in the orig. Smectymnuan work, defended 'Smectymnuus' in *Of Reformation touching Church Discipline in England and the Causes that hitherto have hindered it*, and there were several further polemical exchanges.

Smith, George Adam (1856–1942), OT scholar. Born at Calcutta and educated at Edinburgh, *Tübingen, and Leipzig, he became minister of Queen's Cross Free Church, Aberdeen in 1882, professor of OT at the United Free Church College at Glasgow in 1892 and Principal of the University of Aberdeen in 1909. He travelled extensively in Egypt, Syria, and Palestine. His writings include *The Book of Isaiah* (Expositor's Bible, 2 vols., 1888–90); *Historical Geography of the Holy Land* (1894, 25th edn., 1931, still unsurpassed); *The Twelve Prophets* (Expositor's Bible, 2 vols., 1896–7); *Life of Henry *Drummond* (1899); *Jerusalem* (2 vols., 1907–8); *The Early Poetry of Israel* (Schweich Lectures, 1912); *Deuteronomy* (Cambridge Bible, 1918); and *Jeremiah* (1923).

L. Adam Smith, *George Adam Smith: A Personal Memoir and Family Chronicle* (1943). W. Manson in *DNB, 1941–1950*, pp. 792–4.

Smith, John (?1570–1612), the 'Se-Baptist'. See SMYTH, JOHN.

Smith, John (1618–52), *Cambridge Platonist. He was educated in the *Puritan foundation of Emmanuel College, Cambridge, where B. *Whichcote was his tutor. In 1644 he was transferred to Queens' College and here lectured. Under the influence of Whichcote and the study of *Plato and *Plotinus he became one of the leading Cambridge Platonists, upholding spiritual religion against the acrimonious theological disputes of his age. His work was cut short by his early death. S. *Patrick, a warm admirer, preached his funeral sermon.

His *Select Discourses*, ed. J. Worthington (London, 1660), with the sermon preached at his funeral and a short account of his life and death by S. Patrick, pp. 483–526; 4th edn. rev. by H. G. Williams (Cambridge, 1859). M. Micheletti, *Il Pensiero Religioso di John Smith, Platonico di Cambridge* (Centro Internazionale di Studi di Filosofia della Religione. Filosofia e Religione, 12; Padua, 1976). E. I. Watkin, *Poets and Mystics* (1953), pp. 238–56. See also works cited under CAMBRIDGE PLATONISTS.

Smith, William Robertson (1846–94), Scottish theologian and Semitic scholar. Educated at Aberdeen, Edinburgh, Bonn, and Göttingen, he became professor of oriental languages and OT exegesis at the Free Church College, Aberdeen, in 1870. In 1875 he was made a member of the company for the RV of the OT. About the same time his articles in the 9th edition of the *Encyclopaedia Britannica* began to appear, and henceforward Smith was in the centre of the storm provoked by the *Higher Criticism of the OT. His writings having been severely criticized by a committee of the General Assembly of the Free Church as undermining belief in the inspiration of the Bible, in 1881 he was removed from his chair. He spent the rest of his life at Cambridge, where he was elected in 1885 a Fellow of Christ's College. Of his two celebrated books, *The OT in the Jewish Church* (1881) and *The Prophets of Israel* (1882; 2nd edn., by T. K *Cheyne, 1895), both series of lectures, the former popularized among English readers J. *Wellhausen's theory of the structure and date of the Pentateuch and of the development of the Israelite religion; the latter work expounded on this basis the life and teaching of the early prophets. Later Smith extended his researches into the whole field of Semitic religion. Through *The Religion of the Semites* (1889; 3rd edn., by S. A.*Cook, 1927) his thesis that the original leading idea in sacrifice was that of communion with the Deity rather than propitiation became widely known and accepted, though it is now generally recognized to be an over-simplification.

Collection of his *Lectures and Essays* (mainly unpub.) ed. J. S. Black and G. Chrystal (London, 1902). Idd., *The Life of William Robertson Smith* (1912). T. O. Beidelman, *W. Robertson Smith and the Sociological Study of Religion* (Chicago and London, 1974). J. [W.] Rogerson, *Old Testament Criticism in the Nineteenth Century: England and Germany* (1984), pp. 275–81. J. S. Black in *DNB* 53 (1898), pp. 160–2, s.v.

Smithfield, in London, originally Smoothfield. The place was noted formerly as the site of executions, esp. during the Reformation period, when in the 'fires of Smithfield' during *Mary Tudor's reign about 300 heretics were burnt there. It is now famous as a meat market.

Smyrna. One of the principal cities of Roman Asia, now Izmir on the W. coast of Turkey. The Christian community there was one of the '*Seven Churches' addressed in Rev. (2: 8–11); it was warned of coming persecution and of hostility from the Jewish community, which was numerous in this mercantile port. Later it was visited by St *Ignatius, who afterwards addressed letters to the Church and its bishop, St *Polycarp. The martyrdom of Polycarp in the city's stadium was abetted by a mob of Jews and pagans. St *Irenaeus was prob. a native of Smyrna; later martyrs from Smyrna included St *Pionius.

In Late Antiquity Smyrna's traditional rivalry with *Ephesus was expressed in competition over the relative status of their bishoprics, but the Bp. of Smyrna achieved metropolitan status only in the 9th cent. The city was held by various powers during the Byzantine era. It passed to the Ottoman Turks in 1414, but continued to have a substantial Christian population.

From the 17th cent. Christian numbers were augmented by W. merchants; in the 19th cent. there were also American Protestant missionaries. There was a Muslim majority only after the Greco-Turkish war of 1922–3 and the exchange of population which followed it.

C. J. Cadoux, *Ancient Smyrna: A History of the City from the Earliest Times to 324 A.D.* (Oxford, 1938). C. J. Hemer, *The Letters to the Seven Churches of Asia in their Local Setting* (Journal for the Study of the New Testament, Supplement Series, 11; Sheffield [1986]), pp. 57–77. H. Ahrweiler, 'L'histoire et la géographie de la région de Smyrne entre les deux occupations turques (1081–1317), particulièrement au XIIIᵉ siècle', *Travaux et Mémoires*, 1 (1965), pp. 1–204. H. *Leclercq, OSB, in *DACL* 15 (pt. 2; 1953), cols. 1519–48, s.v. See also bibl. to POLYCARP, ST, and comm. on REVELATION, BOOK OF.

Smyth, or **Smith, John** (?1570–1612), the 'Se-Baptist' and reputed founder of the *General Baptists. Educated at Christ's College, Cambridge, of which he became a Fellow in 1594, he was ordained in the C of E. He became a *Puritan preacher at *Lincoln (1600–2) and later (by 1607) was a *Separatist pastor in Gainsborough. He led a company of exiles to Amsterdam c.1608 and there, after baptizing himself (hence the name Se-Baptist), established in 1609 the first modern *Baptist Church. He styled his community 'The Brethren of the Separation of the Second English Church at Amsterdam'. Membership consisted of such as had confessed their faith in Baptism. From now onwards Smyth passed increasingly under *Mennonite influence. He died in Amsterdam in 1612. In the same year a company of his associates returned to London to establish the first Baptist Church in Great Britain. Among Smyth's writings were *A Pattern of True Prayer* (1605; on the *Lord's Prayer) and *The Differences of the Churches of the Separation* (1608).

Collected edn. of his works by W. T. Whitley (Tercentenary edn. for the Baptist Historical Society, 2 vols., Cambridge, 1915), with Life, vol. 1, pp. xvii–cxxii. W. H. Burgess, *John Smith, Se-Baptist, Thomas Helwys, and the First Baptist Church in England* (1911). B. R. White, *The English Separatist Tradition from the Marian Martyrs to the Pilgrim Fathers* (Oxford Theological Monographs, 1971), pp. 116–41; S. Brachlow, *The Communion of Saints: Radical Puritan and Separatist Ecclesiology 1570–1625* (ibid., 1988), passim. J. R. Coggins, *John Smyth's Congregation: English Separatism, Mennonite Influence, and the Elect Nation* (Studies in Anabaptist and Mennonite History, 32; Scottdale, Pa. [1991]).

sobornost. A Russian term with no exact English equivalent. It signifies (1) 'catholicity' (the word *soborny* is used in Slavonic to translate 'catholic' in the *Niceno-Constantinopolitan Creed); (2) 'conciliarity' (the word *sobor* in Russian means 'assembly' or 'council'). In modern Russian theology (e.g. of A. S. *Khomiakoff and S. *Bulgakov), the word denotes primarily the unity of many persons within the organic fellowship of the Church. In this unity each member retains his full freedom and personal integrity, while at the same time sharing in the common and corporate life of the whole. Russian writers claim 'sobornost' as a special characteristic of the Orthodox Church, contrasted with the emphasis on juridical authority in the RC Church and the excessive individualism of the Protestant communions.

Social Gospel. The most conspicuous movement representing the social aspects of Christianity in American and Canadian Protestantism in the late 19th and early 20th cents. The impact of the industrial revolution and urbanization led to the emergence of various movements of Christian social thought in W. Europe (e.g. *Christian Socialism), and the work of such British leaders as F. D. *Maurice, C. *Kingsley, and H. S. *Holland was well known to those who shaped the Social Gospel in America. They protested against the injustices suffered by the working classes, championed the rights of labour, and criticized the excessive individualism of prevailing social and economic views. Washington Gladden (1836–1918), a prominent *Congregational minister and prolific author who defended the right of working people to form unions in a time of intense strife between capital and labour, became known as the 'father' of the Social Gospel. Josiah Strong (1847–1916), author of *Our Country* (1885), organized interdenominational gatherings that promoted the movement while he was secretary of the (American) Evangelical Alliance; the economist Richard T. Ely (1854–1943) contributed two significant books, *Social Aspects of Christianity* (1889) and *The Social Law of Service* (1896); while W. *Rauschenbusch became the foremost prophet of the movement. In Canada, Salem Bland (1859–1950) was the leading interpreter of Social Gospel thought and J. S. Woodsworth (1874–1942) its most conspicuous practitioner. The Social Gospel was esp. influential in the Congregational, *Episcopal, *Baptist, *Methodist, and *Presbyterian Churches. It also stimulated the growth of interdenominational organizations, such as the Federal Council of the Churches of Christ in America (1908).

Though the Social Gospel was not theologically homogeneous, it was based largely on liberal theology, with its characteristic emphases on the immanence of God, the organic nature of society, human brotherhood, the teaching of Christ as the primary source of ethics, and the progressive, post-millennial coming of the Kingdom of God on earth in the near future. The movement had a high view of human nature and its potentiality, stressed the idea of progress, was reformist in tone, and had a somewhat utopian cast. As an aggressive, advancing movement it passed its zenith after the First World War, but it left a legacy of continuing importance in the theological, ecumenical, and social thought of many Churches.

R. T. Handy (ed.), *The Social Gospel in America, 1870–1920: Gladden, Ely, Rauschenbusch* (Library of Protestant Thought; New York, 1966). C. H. Hopkins, *The Rise of the Social Gospel in American Protestantism, 1865–1915* (Yale Studies in Religious Educa-

tion, 14; 1940); [A.] R. Allen, *The Social Passion: Religion and Social Reform in Canada, 1914–1928* (Toronto, 1971); R. C. White, Jun., and C. H. Hopkins, *The Social Gospel: Religion and Reform in Changing America* (Philadelphia, 1976); D. K. Gorrell, *The Age of Social Responsibility: The Social Gospel in the Progressive Era 1900–1920* (Macon, Ga. [1988]); S. Curtis, *A Consuming Faith: The Social Gospel and Modern American Culture* (Baltimore and London [1991]); R. E. Luker, *The Social Gospel in Black and White: American Racial Reform, 1885–1912* (Chapel Hill, NC, and London [1991]).

Socialism, Christian. See CHRISTIAN SOCIALISM.

Society for Promoting Christian Knowledge. See SPCK.

Society for the Propagation of the Gospel. See SPG.

Society of Friends. See FRIENDS, SOCIETY OF.

Society of Jesus. See JESUITS.

Society of St John the Evangelist (SSJE). The Anglican society of mission priests and laymen, popularly known as the '*Cowley Fathers'. It was founded in 1865 by R. M. *Benson, then vicar of St James's, Cowley, and is thus the oldest Anglican community for men religious. While a life of prayer under the monastic vows is its first object, the society is also occupied in missionary and educational works. It is now constituted in three congregations—English, American, and Canadian—each with its own superior and chapter, and there are houses in Oxford and London; Cambridge (Mass.) and Boston; and Bracebridge (Ontario).

H. E. W. Slade, SSJE, *A Work Begun: The Story of the Cowley Fathers in India, 1874–1967* (1970).

Society of the Holy Cross (SSC from the Latin form, 'Societas Sanctae Crucis'). An *Anglo-Catholic society of clergy founded in 1855 by C. F. *Lowder and others. Modelled on the Mission Priests established by St *Vincent de Paul, it aimed to promote a stricter rule of life among the clergy, home missions to the poor, and the publication of works in defence of Catholic faith and practice. Members were to follow one of three rules of life of varying strictness, the white, the red, and the green. A year after its foundation it began the revival of *retreats in the C of E. In the 1890s the Society pressed for the 1549 Book of *Common Prayer to be made the model for liturgical revision, and it encouraged the revival of sacramental *confession. Lord Redesdale's denunciation in the House of Lords of a privately printed manual for confessors (*The *Priest in Absolution*, q.v.) whose compilation the Society had encouraged, brought it to public notice and provoked a hostile reaction in *Convocation.

J. Embry, *The Catholic Movement and the Society of the Holy Cross* (1931).

Socinianism. See the following entry, and UNITARIANISM.

Socinus. The Latinized name of two Italian religious teachers, uncle and nephew.

(1) Lelio Francesco Maria Sozini (1525–62), a native of Siena, came of a cultivated family. He was educated by his

father, Mariano Sozini, junior (1482–1556), himself a jurist, at *Bologna, to be a lawyer. Finding that his real interests were in theology he made his way to *Venice, then the headquarters of Protestantism in Italy. In 1547 he came also under the influence of Camillo, a Sicilian mystic of liberal views, at Chiavenna. Between 1547 and 1550 he was received by the Reformers in several countries (Switzerland, France, England, and the Netherlands), and from 1548 to 1550 settled in Switzerland. Later he visited *Wittenberg, where for a time he was the guest of P. *Melanchthon, and later Poland. Changed political conditions in 1552 drew him back to Italy, where he endeavoured to win his nephew (see below) over to his beliefs. Early in 1554 he left Italy again for Switzerland. After brief visits to Basle and Geneva (where he made the acquaintance of J. *Calvin and was challenged on the doctrine of the Trinity), later in the year he settled for the rest of his life at Zurich. Here he found it easier to satisfy H. *Bullinger, though he reserved to himself the right to further inquiry. His surviving writings include a Confession of Faith (1555) and De Sacramentis Dissertatio (1560).

(2) Fausto Paolo Sozzini (1539–1604; he spelled his name with two z's), nephew of the preceding, was also a native of Siena. His early education was neglected. Moving to Lyons in 1561, he there published a work on St John's Gospel (1562) in which he denied the essential divinity of Christ. By 1563 he had also rejected the natural immortality of man. He returned to Italy in 1563 and was in the service of Isabella de' Medici (daughter of the Grand Duke of Tuscany) until 1574; outwardly he conformed to Catholicism. He left Italy after the death of Isabella's father and settled in Basle, where in 1578 he composed his De Christo Servatore (pub. in 1594), directed against the Reformers' teaching on salvation. Later in the year he went to Klausenburg in Transylvania (now Cluj in Romania) in the hope that his liberal teachings would be welcomed under the anti-Trinitarian ruler, John Sigismund. In fact his services were enlisted to moderate the extreme anti-Trinitarianism of the Bishop, Francis David (1510–79). In 1579 he moved to Poland, where he spent the rest of his life and did much to spread moderate *Unitarian doctrines among the upper classes. Several of his writings were now published for the first time. After five years in Cracow, in 1583 he went to Pawlikowice, where he married. He returned to Cracow in 1588, but was forced to flee ten years later when, on Ascension Day 1598, a crowd of students unsympathetic to his teachings was narrowly prevented from lynching him. He spent his last years at Lusławice. See also RACOVIAN CATECHISM and UNITARIANISM.

(1) C. F. Illgen, Vita Laelii Socini (Leipzig, 1814); E. Burnat, Lelio Socin (Vevey, 1894). J. A. Tedeschi (ed.), Italian Reformation Studies in honor of Laelius Socinus (Florence, 1965), esp. pp. 215–41 ('Four Letters from the Socinus–Calvin Correspondence' tr. and ed. R. Lazzaro, and D. Willis, 'The Influence of Laelius Socinus on Calvin's Doctrines of the Merits of Christ and the Assurance of Faith'). G. H. Williams, The Radical Reformation (Philadelphia and London [1962]), pp. 566–70 and 630–34; 2nd edn. (Sixteenth Century Essays & Studies, 15; Kirksville, Mo., 1992), pp. 876–83 and 965–72. (2) The works of F. Socinus [ed. by his grandson, A. Wiszowaty] (Bibliotheca Fratrum Polonorum quos Unitarios vocant, 1–2; Amsterdam, 1656), with Life by S. Przipcovius written in 1636 prefixed to vol. 1 [no pagination]; this Life was repr.,

with Eng. annotations by 'E.S.' (Manchester, 1912). G. Pioli, Fausto Socino: Vita, opere, fortuna (Modena, 1952). Other modern studies by D. M. Cory (Boston, 1932), L. Chmaj (Warsaw, 1963), and M. Martini, Fausto Socino et la pensée socinienne (Paris [1967]). G. H. Williams, The Radical Reformation (Philadelphia and London [1962]), pp. 749–63; 2nd edn. (Sixteenth Century Essays & Studies, 15; Kirksville, Mo., 1992), pp. 978–89. Z. Ogonowski, 'Faustus Socinus', in J. Raitt (ed.), Shapers of Religious Traditions in Germany, Switzerland, and Poland, 1560–1600 (New Haven, Conn., and London [1981]), pp. 195–209.

On the two Socini, L. Cristiani in DTC 14 (pt. 2; 1941), cols. 2326–34, s.v. 'Socinianisme'. See also bibl. to UNITARIANISM.

Socrates (c.380–450), 'Scholasticus', Greek Church historian. He was a native of *Constantinople, where he became a lawyer (σχολαστικός). His Church History, in seven books, each covering the life of one of the emperors, was designed as a continuation of *Eusebius' treatise and extends from the abdication of *Diocletian (305) to 439. It draws on *Rufinus and also on *Gelasius of Caesarea. After publishing it, Socrates became possessed of the writings of St *Athanasius, which apprised him of Rufinus' historical blunders, and he accordingly drastically revised the work. Only this later edition survives. For information about the ecclesiastical Councils he made extensive use of a collection of documents issued c.375 by the *Macedonian, Sabinus of Heraclea. In general Socrates' history is objective and lucidly written, but its treatment is rather colourless and the author has few theological interests. He shows a certain sympathy with the *Novatianists and gives special attention to events connected with Constantinople. See also SOZOMEN.

Ed. princeps by R. *Stephanus (Paris, 1544). An excellent edn. for its date by H. *Valesius (ibid., 1668); rev. by W. Reading (Cambridge, 1720; repr. J. P. Migne, PG 67. 9–842) and R. Hussey (3 vols., Oxford, 1853). Hussey's text was repr. by W. *Bright (Oxford, 1878). Crit. ed. by G. C. Hansen (GCS, NF 1; 1995). Eng. tr. by A. C. Zenos in NPNCF, 2nd ser., vol. 2, 1890. F. Geppert, Die Quellen des Kirchenhistorikers Sokrates Scholasticus (1898). G. F. Chesnut, The First Christian Histories (Théologie historique, 46 [1978]), pp. 167–89. CPG 3 (1979), pp. 166 f. (no. 6028). W. Eltester in PW, 2te Reihe, 3 (pt. 1; 1927), cols. 893–901; G. Bardy in DTC 14 (pt. 2; 1941), cols. 2334–6, s.v.; A. Labate in DPAC 2 (1984), cols. 3248–50 (Eng. tr. in Encyclopedia of the Early Church, 2 (1992), p. 785), all s.v., with bibl.

sodality (Lat. sodalis, 'companion'). In the RC Church, a common designation for a guild established for the furtherance of some religious purpose by mutual action or assistance.

Söderblom, Nathan (1866–1931), *Lutheran Abp. of *Uppsala and chief promoter of the '*Life and Work' Movement. A native of Trönö, nr. Söderhamn, he studied at Uppsala and was ordained in 1893. In the same year he published a study of M. *Luther's religion. In 1894 he was appointed chaplain to the Swedish legation in *Paris and in 1901 he became a professor at Uppsala. He was appointed Abp. of Uppsala in 1914 despite the opposition of the more conservative elements in the Swedish Church. He was a prominent supporter of the reunion movement and the leading figure in the *Stockholm Conference (1925), his aim being to organize the practical co-operation of the Christian Churches esp. in social questions without consideration of doctrinal differences. His own theological beliefs were largely influenced by A. *Sabatier, A. *Ritschl, and other representatives of Liberal Protestantism.

Söderblom's religious outlook was essentially constructive, despite its challenge to the older orthodoxy. His sense of personal religion went deep. Of his books, comparatively few have been translated into English. In *The Nature of Revelation* (1903; Eng. tr., 1933) he defended the position of '*Higher Criticism', maintaining that the scientific study of the history of religion will lead to a sure knowledge of God. He criticized here the dogma of the two natures of Christ as unacceptable for modern men and also formulated one of his leading ideas—that God's Revelation is restricted neither to the Bible nor to the Church but continues in history throughout the ages. In his treatise *Gudstrons Uppkomst* (1914) he argued that the idea of holiness rather than the conception of God was at the basis of religion. Among his other works are *Christian Fellowship* (Eng. tr., 1923) and *The Living God* (1933; Gifford Lectures for 1931). He encouraged the liturgical movement in the Swedish Church and was also influenced by Catholic modernist authors such as A. *Loisy and F. *von Hügel.

Tal och Skrifter (5 vols., Stockholm, 1933). Correspondence with F. von Hügel and F. *Heiler, ed. P. Misner (Paderborn [1981]). Good modern study by B. [G. M.] Sundkler, *Nathan Söderblom: His Life and Work* (1968). Earlier Lives in Swedish by T. Andrae (Uppsala, 1931), in Danish by M. Neiiendam (Copenhagen, 1933). Brief sketch by Y. [T.] Brilioth prefixed to Söderblom's (posthumous) Gifford Lectures (1933). J. G. H. Hoffmann, *Nathan Soederblom: Prophète de l'œcuménisme* (Geneva, 1948); E. Ehnmark, *Religionsproblemet hos Nathan Söderblom* (Lund [1949]); H. Åkerberg, *Omvändelse och kamp: En empirisk religionspsykologisk undersökning av den unge Nathan Söderbloms religiösa utveckling 1866–1894* (ibid., 1975), with Eng. summary. N. Karlström in R. Rouse and S. C. Neill (eds.), *A History of the Ecumenical Movement 1517–1948* (1954), pp. 519–42.

Sodom and Gomorrah. Acc. to Gen. 19: 24 two 'Cities of the Plain' which were destroyed by fire from heaven for their wickedness. They were prob. S. of the *Dead Sea, perhaps at Bab ed-Dra' and Numeira, now in Jordan. Initial claims that the 'Cities of the Plain' are mentioned in the archive of mid-third millennium BC cuneiform tablets found in 1974–5 at Tell Mardikh, ancient Ebla, near Aleppo in Syria, have proved to be erroneous. Sodom and Gomorrah became proverbial both for their sinfulness (see Is. 1: 10–17) and for the scale of their destruction (Is. 1: 5–9); both aspects are present in Christ's saying that in the Day of Judgement even more severe punishment would be meted out to those cities which rejected the Gospel than to Sodom and Gomorrah (Mt. 10: 15). The association of Sodom with *homosexual practice rests only on Gen. 19: 1–14, where the men of Sodom attempt to exploit Lot's hospitality to two angels by seeking to assault them sexually; elsewhere the sin of Sodom is not specified.

On the question of the location of Sodom, F. M. Abel, OP, 'Histoire d'une controverse', *R. Bibl.* 40 (1931), pp. 388–400, with refs. to earlier lit.; cf. also other arts. by the same author in earlier numbers of the review; M. J. *Lagrange, OP, 'Le Site de Sodome d'après les textes', ibid. 41 (1932), pp. 489–514; F. C. Clapp, 'The Site of Sodom and Gomorrah', *American Journal of Archaeology*, NS 40 (1936), pp. 323–44, also with refs.; J. P. Harland, 'Sodom and Gomorrah', *Biblical Archaeologist*, 5 (1942), pp. 17–32, and 6 (1943), pp. 41–54. D. N. Freedman, 'The real story of the Ebla Tablets. Ebla and the Cities of the Plain', ibid. 41 (1978), pp.

143–64; A. Archi, 'Further concerning Ebla and the Bible', ibid. 44 (1981), pp. 145–54, esp. pp. 151 f., pointing out the misreading. J. A. Loader, *A Tale of Two Cities: Sodom and Gomorrah in the Old Testament, early Jewish and early Christian Traditions* (Contributions to Biblical Exegesis and Theology, 1; Kampen [1990]).

Sodor and Man. The present Anglican diocese of Sodor and Man consists of the Isle of Man. Traditions credit St *Patrick with the establishment of episcopal authority there in the 5th cent. After the arrival of Norwegian rulers in the late 8th cent., Man came to be associated by them with the many islands to the west of the Scottish mainland as part of the Southern Isles ('Sudreys', 'Sodor') as they called them to distinguish them from the Northern Isles of Orkney and Shetland. Before 1134 there was a plurality of bishops under the sub-king of the Isles (*rex Insularum*); thereafter for two centuries there was one see for the whole island area, which the Norwegians transferred to Scottish rule in 1266. Some of the early bishops were consecrated at York; but after 1154 the see was by Papal authority made part of the province of Nidaros (Trondheim) in Norway. 1331 (by which time the English Crown was assuming control of the Isle of Man) saw the last Scot appointed to the see based there. Then during and after the *Great Schism (1378–1417) there emerged parallel to the bishops on Man a continuous line of Scottish bishops of the Isles resident in the Scottish section of the old unitary diocese. Since 1542 the diocese of Sodor has been in the province of York, but it has its own *Convocation. The termination 'and Man' was apparently added in error by a 17th-cent. legal draughtsman. The Prayer Book was issued in Manx in 1765, the Bible in 1772. In 1895 a *chapter was constituted with four canons, the bishop being dean. The bishop, who is a member of the Upper House of the Tynwald in the Isle of Man, has no seat in the House of Lords. Of the bishops of Sodor and Man the most renowned is the saintly T. *Wilson (bishop 1698–1755). The 13th-cent. cathedral on St Patrick's Isle (now united to the mainland at Peel) fell into disuse in the 18th cent. and is now in ruins. In 1980 the parish church of St German in Peel became the cathedral of the diocese.

The principal source for the early history of the Isle of Man is the *Chronica Regum Manniae et Insularum* (ed. P. A. Munich, Manx Society, 22 and 23; 1874, with Eng. tr.); facsimile edn. from Cod. Julius A. VI in Brit. Library (Douglas, 1924). W. Harrison (ed.), *The Old Historians of the Isle of Man: Camden, Speed, Dugdale, Cox, Wilson, Willis and Crosse* (Manx Society, 18; 1871). A. W. Moore and J. Rhŷs (eds.), *The Book of Common Prayer in Manx Gaelic: Being translations made by Bishop Phillips in 1610, and by the Manx Clergy in 1765* (2 vols., 1895). A. W. Moore, *Sodor and Man* (Diocesan Histories, 1893). A. Ashley, *The Church in the Isle of Man* (St Anthony's Hall Publications, 13; 1958). C. R. Cheney (ed.), 'Manx Synodal Statutes, A.D. 1230(?)–1351', *Cambridge Medieval Celtic Studies*, no. 7 (1984), pp. 63–89; no. 8 (1984), pp. 51–63. D. E. R. Watt, 'Bishops in the Isles before 1203: Bibliography and Biographical Lists', *Innes Review*, 45 (1994), pp. 99–119. P. M. C. Kermode, *Manx Crosses* (1907). E. W. Watson in *DECH* (1912), pp. 346–9, s.v. 'Man, Isle of, Church in'.

Sohm, Rudolph (1841–1917), jurist and Protestant Church historian. He taught law first at Göttingen, and later as professor at Freiburg i.B. (1880), Strasbourg (1872), and Leipzig (1887). His chief theological works were *Verhältnis von Staat und Kirche* (1873), *Kirchenrecht* (vol. 1, 1892; vol. 2, posthumously ed. E. Jacobi and O. Mayer, 1923), and *Wesen und Ursprung des Katholizismus* (1909). In these and other writings he developed the view that, while the Church was wholly spiritual, law was wholly secular; hence the development of canon law ('Catholicism') was an abandonment of the primitive ideal of the Church, which was a fundamentally '*charismatic' body. Sohm also compiled a manual, *Kirchengeschichte im Grundriss* (1888; Eng. tr., *Outlines of Church History*, 1895). His ideas attracted considerable interest, esp. in their implications for the relationship of Church and State.

Festgabe für Rudolph Sohm (Munich, 1914). W. Lowrie, *The Church and its Organisation in Primitive and Catholic Times: An Interpretation of Rudolph Sohm's* Kirchenrecht (1904); critique of Sohm's theses in A. *Harnack, *Entstehung und Entwicklung der Kirchenverfassung und des Kirchenrechts* (1910; Eng. tr., 1910). H. Barion, *Rudolf Sohm und die Grundlegung des Kirchenrechts* (1931); E. Foerster, *Rudolph Sohms Kritik des Kirchenrechtes* (Haarlem, 1942). W. A. Hauck, *Rudolf Sohm und Leo Tolstoi: Rechtsordnung und Gottesreich* (Heidelberg, 1950), pp. 11–156. D. Stoodt, *Wort und Recht: Rudolf Sohm und das theologische Problem des Kirchenrechts* (Forschungen zur Geschichte und Lehre des Protestantismus, Reihe 2, 33; 1962). A. Bühler, *Kirche und Staat bei Rudolph Sohm* (Basler Studien zur historischen und systematischen Theologie, 6; 1965). H.-J. Schmitz, *Frühkatholizismus bei Adolf von Harnack, Rudolph Sohm und Ernst Käsemann* (Düsseldorf, 1977), pp. 94–144.

Soissons, Councils of. The two principal Councils are:

(1) *c.*1092. The Council was convened by Raynaldus, Abp. of *Reims, against the *nominalist, *Roscelin, who was accused of teaching *Tritheism. Roscelin asserted that *Lanfranc and *Anselm, then abbot of Bec, shared his views; but the latter sent a letter to be read at the Council, denying the charge and professing the Catholic faith. Roscelin was condemned by the Council and recanted, though he later declared that he had done so only through fear of the populace.

(2) 1121. The Council was held by the Papal legate, Conon, Bp. of Palestrina, in order to censure Peter *Abelard's work, 'Theologia Summi Boni'. Conceived as an attack on Roscelin's Tritheistic teaching, it was condemned, according to *Otto of Freising, for the opposite error of *Sabellianism. Abelard's account in his 'Historia Calamitatum' however, shows that he thought he was defending orthodoxy against both these heresies. He was not allowed to dispute about the book at the Council, but forced to burn it.

(1) Hardouin, 6 (pt. 2), cols. 1695–1700; Mansi, 20 (Venice, 1775), cols. 741–4. Hefele and Leclercq, 5 (pt. 1; 1912), pp. 365–7.
(2) Hardouin, 6 (pt. 2), cols. 1103–6; Mansi, 21 (Venice, 1726), cols. 265–70. Hefele and Leclercq, 5 (pt. 1; 1912), pp. 593–602. See also bibl. to ABELARD, P.

soleas (Gk. σωλέας). In the E. Church, the platform immediately in front of the *iconostasis, raised above the nave floor by one or more steps, and on the same level as the sanctuary.

Solemn League and Covenant. The agreement between the Scots and the English Parliament in 1643. Its professed aims were the maintenance of the *Presbyterian Church of Scotland, the reformation of the Church of England, the uniformity of the Churches of the British Isles, the extirpation of Popery and prelacy (i.e. episcopacy), the preservation of the rights of Parliaments and the liberties of the kingdoms, the defence of the King's just power and the suppression of the malignants who sought to divide him from his people. It was also a pact of mutual defence and a covenant of penitents with their God. The English Parliamentarians in their struggle with the Royalists were specially anxious for a civil league; the Scots emphasized the religious side of the agreement. It was formally accepted by the Scottish Convention of the Estates and the General Assembly of the Church of Scotland on 17 Aug. 1643, and by the English Commons and the *Westminster Assembly on 25 Sept. 1643. Shortly afterwards, the proceedings of the Westminster Assembly took a pro-Presbyterian turn and for a time the English allies became nominal 'Covenanters'; but after the Scottish army had helped to turn the tide at Marston Moor (2 July 1644) and the rise of O. *Cromwell and the *Independents to power the Covenant became a dead letter in England. It continued longer, however, to be a living document in Scotland, where it was renewed in 1648 and subscribed by *Charles II in 1650 and 1651.

Text in Gee and Hardy, pp. 569–74 (no. 107). See also bibl. to WESTMINSTER ASSEMBLY.

Solemnitas (Lat., commonly rendered in English 'Solemnity'), the name given in the 1969 Calendar and subsequent liturgical documents of the RC Church to feasts of the greatest importance.

Solesmes. The seat of a famous Benedictine monastery, dedicated to St Peter, in the department of Sarthe, France. It was founded in 1010, but in modern times its history goes back to Dom Prosper *Guéranger, who settled there with five other priests in 1833. In 1837 *Gregory XVI constituted it an abbey and head of the French Benedictine congregation, with Guéranger as its first abbot. Under his influence it became, and has remained, a centre of the *Liturgical Movement in France, taking a notable part in the revival and development of liturgical music. After being several times ejected by force by the French Government, the monks were finally expelled from France under the anticlerical legislation in 1901, and for several years *Quarr Abbey in the Isle of Wight was their headquarters. They returned to Solesmes in 1922. Solesmes has numbered among its members many eminent scholars, notably Dom J. B. F. *Pitra (1812–89), Dom P. Cagin (1847–1923), Dom F. *Cabrol (1855–1937), Dom H. *Quentin (1872–1935), and Dom A. *Wilmart (1876–1941). See also PLAINSONG.

H. Quentin, OSB, *Notice historique sur l'abbaye de Solesmes, suivie d'une courte description de l'église abbatiale et ses sculptures* (Tours, 1924). J. Hourlier, OSB, *Les Églises de Solesmes* (1951). A. des Mazis, OSB, *L'Entrée de Solesmes dans la Congrégation de Saint-Maur* (Solesmes, [1950]), and other works of this author. L. Soltner, OSB, *Solesmes & Dom Guéranger (1805–1875)* (ibid., 1974). N. Rousseau, *L'École grégorienne de Solesmes, 1833–1910* (Tournai, 1910). F. Cabrol, OSB, 'L'Œuvre historique et littéraire de Solesmes et de la Congrégation de France (1833–1933)', *Revue Mabillon*, 23 (1933), pp. 249–65.

Solifidianism. The *Reformation doctrine of *justification by faith alone (*per solam fidem*), as found esp. in the writings of M. *Luther, who translated πίστει in Rom. 3: 28 as *allein durch den Glauben* ('only by faith').

Solipsism (Lat. *solus*, 'alone', and *ipse*, 'oneself'). The philosophical belief that the individual self is the only existent and that all other selves are illusions. It is doubtful whether any philosopher has ever held this extreme form of theoretical egotism; its chief use in philosophical debate is to reduce opponents to absurdity. The word is less commonly applied to the doctrine that the self is the only object of real knowledge, without prejudice to the existence of other selves. Either doctrine is a particular form of 'Subjective Idealism'.

Solomon (d. *c*.930 BC), King of *Israel from *c*.970 BC. No such clear picture of his personality is to be found in the OT as we have of his father, *David, whom he succeeded. The impression made by the account in 1 Kgs. 1–11 is of an oriental despot, honoured for his wealth and wisdom and round whose name much legendary material has gathered. This reputation, which is responsible for the later attribution to him of the Books of *Proverbs, the Song of *Solomon, *Ecclesiastes, and the *Wisdom of Solomon, has probably coloured the history in 1 Kings. His reign marked the zenith of ancient Israel's prosperity and saw the organization of the kingdom on new lines. The *Temple, with the erection of which his name is esp. associated in subsequent history, was part of a grandiose building scheme intended to make *Jerusalem a worthy capital for a kingdom which he determined should rank among the great powers. With such ends in view, he made a marriage alliance with the reigning Pharaoh and, by strengthening the friendly relations established by David with Hiram, King of Tyre, obtained from Phoenicia the skill and materials needed for his building schemes (1 Kgs. 5: 1–12) and also the experienced sailors to direct a short-lived naval experiment (9: 26–8). His other enterprises include a trade in horses with Egypt (10: 28–9), the fortifying of strategic cities (9: 15–19), and the establishment of a standing army (10: 26). But to finance his projects Solomon had to impose on his subjects a system of levies and forced labour, and the resulting discontent led, after his death, to the secession of the ten northern tribes under Jeroboam I. In this the compiler of the Books of Kings saw Divine retribution for Solomon's apostasy in his later years, which is ascribed to the influence of his foreign wives. His son Rehoboam ruled over the kingdom of *Judah (1 Kgs. 11: 43–14: 31).

The main discussions will be found in Histories of Israel and comm. on 1 Kgs. F. Thieberger, *King Solomon* (1947). B. Porten, 'The Structure and Theme of the Solomon Narrative (1 Kings 3–11)', *Hebrew Union College Annual*, 38 (1967), pp. 93–128. E. W. Heaton, *Solomon's New Men: The Emergence of Ancient Israel as a Nation State* (1974). E. Lohse in *TWNT* 7 (1964; Eng. tr., 1971), pp. 459–65, s.v. Σολομών, with bibl.; J. Briend and others in *Dict. Bibl.*, Suppl. 11 (1991), cols. 431–85, s.v. 'Salomon'; T. Ishida in *Anchor Bible Dictionary*, 6 (1993), pp. 105–13.

Solomon, Odes of. This pseudepigraphical work contains 42 short hymns of a lyrical character. Mention of it occurs in lists of Christian books from the 6th cent.

onwards, but until the discovery (1908) by J. R. *Harris of a Syriac MS containing the Odes and Psalms of Solomon, the only known fragments of it were (1) five of the Odes included in the *Gnostic *Pistis Sophia* (where the Odes are treated as of almost equal authority with the Pss. of David) and (2) a short quotation in *Lactantius. The Greek text of Ode 11 is preserved in a *Bodmer papyrus. The Odes are prob. Christian in origin, and though containing thoughts and expressions which lend themselves to a Gnostic interpretation, they are not unorthodox. Their composition is variously assigned to dates ranging from the 1st to the 3rd cent. AD; the late 2nd cent. seems most likely. They were prob. written in Syria, but it is disputed whether their original language was Greek or Syriac. In these Psalms, the terms used of '*Wisdom' in the Wisdom literature are freely applied to Christ. Though there are few references to the Lord's life, the *Descent into Hell is described in some detail in more than one place; but the doctrine of the Holy Spirit is undeveloped and the word 'Church' nowhere occurs. Although there are many allusions to Baptism, it is unlikely that they were specifically baptismal hymns, as J. H. *Bernard suggested.

Syriac text of Odes and Psalms of Solomon ed., with Eng. tr., by J. R. Harris (Cambridge, 1909; 2nd edn., with facsimile, 1911); also ed., with facsimile of the whole MS, by id. and A. Mingana (Manchester, etc., 1916; Eng. tr. and notes, 1920); Syriac text also ed., with Eng. tr., by J. H. Charlesworth (Oxford, 1973). Greek text of 11th Ode ed. from Bodmer Papyrus XI by M. Testuz, *Papyrus Bodmer X–XII* (Geneva, 1959), pp. 49–69. Eng. tr. of Syriac, with notes, by [J.] R. Harris, *An Early Christian Psalter* (London, 1909). Further Eng. trs., with introd. and notes, by J. H. Bernard (Texts and Studies, 8, no. 3; Cambridge, 1912); by J. A. Emerton in H. F. D. Sparks (ed.), *The Apocryphal Old Testament* (Oxford, 1984), pp. 683–731; and by J. H. Charlesworth in id. (ed.), *The Old Testament Pseudepigrapha*, 2 (1985), pp. 725–71, the last two both with recent bibl. M. Lattke, *Die Oden Salomos in ihrer Bedeutung für Neues Testament und Gnosis* (Orbis Biblicus et Orientalis, 25; 4 parts in 5, 1979 ff., incl. full bibl. in vol. 3 [1986]). M. Franzmann, *The Odes of Solomon: An Analysis of the Poetical Structure and Form* (Novum Testamentum et Orbis Antiquus, 20; Göttingen, 1991). H. J. W. Drijvers, 'Die Oden Salomos und die Polemik mit den Markioniten im Syrischen Christentum', in *Symposium Syriacum 1976* (Orientalia Christiana Analecta, 205; 1978), pp. 39–55; repr. in id., *East of Antioch: Studies in Early Syriac Christianity* (1984), no. 7; cf. also nos. 8–10.

Solomon, Psalms of. Mention of this Jewish *pseudepigraphical collection of 18 Psalms occurs after the list of OT and NT Books in the catalogue at the beginning of *Codex Alexandrinus (A), as well as in later lists of canonical Books, but the Psalms had little influence on early Christian literature. Though extant only in Greek (and in a Syriac translation of the Greek), almost all scholars are agreed that they were written in Hebrew. Certain historical allusions indicate the date. A period of prosperity has been brought to an end by foreign invasion and the capture of Jerusalem; Jewish kings are condemned as usurpers; and the description of the invader seems most readily to apply to Pompey; thus the Psalms can be assigned with considerable confidence to the post-*Maccabean age and probably to the years 70–40 BC. The Psalms depict the nation as divided into two classes, 'the righteous' (almost entirely the *Pharisees, to which party the author belongs) and the 'sinners' (the *Sadducees), while the writer sees in the catastrophes that have overcome his country Divine retribution for national sin. The last two Psalms are esp. significant as predicting the coming of a Messiah of the house of David who will cleanse *Jerusalem, punish sinners, subdue the nations hostile to Israel and rule in righteousness.

Crit. edn. of Gk. text with Eng. tr. by H. E. *Ryle and M. R. James (Cambridge, 1891); also by O. von Gebhardt (TU 13, Heft 2; 1895). Gk. text also pr. in H. B. *Swete, *The Old Testament in Greek*, 3 (4th edn., Cambridge, 1912), pp. 765–87, and in A. Rahlfs (ed.), *Septuaginta*, 2 (Stuttgart [1935]), pp. 471–489 Syriac text first ed , along with that of the Odes of Solomon, with Eng. tr., by J. R. *Harris (Cambridge, 1909; 2nd edn., with additions, 1911); also ed., with facsimile, by [J.] R. Harris and A. Mingana (Manchester, etc., 1916, with Eng. tr. and notes, 1920); standard edn. by W. Baars, *The Old Testament in Syriac according to the Peshitta Version*, pt. 4, fasc. 6 (Leiden, 1972), separate pagination. Gk. text also pr., with notes of main Syriac variations, Fr. tr. and comm., by J. Viteau (Documents pour l'Étude de la Bible, 1911). Eng. trs. and comm. by G. B. *Gray in R. H. *Charles (ed.), *The Apocrypha and Pseudepigrapha of the Old Testament*, 2 (Oxford, 1913), pp. 625–52; S. P. Brock in H. F. D. Sparks (ed.), *The Apocryphal Old Testament* (ibid., 1984), pp. 649–82; and R. B. Wright in J. H. Charlesworth (ed.), *The Old Testament Pseudepigrapha*, 2 (1985), pp. 639–70. J. Schüpphaus, *Die Psalmen Salomos: Eine Zeugnis Jerusalemer Theologie und Frömmigkeit in der Mitte der vorchristlichen Jahrhunderts* (Arbeiten zur Literatur und Geschichte des hellenistischen Judentums, 7; 1977). R. R. Hann, *The Manuscript History of the Psalms of Solomon* (Septuagint and Cognate Studies, 13; Chico, Calif., 1982). J. L. Trafton, *The Syriac Version of the Psalms of Solomon* (ibid. 11; Atlanta [1985]). E. *Schürer, *A History of the Jewish People in the Age of Jesus Christ*, rev. Eng. tr. by G. Vermes and others, 3 (pt. 1; Edinburgh, 1986), pp. 192–7, with bibl.

Solomon, Song of (also known as **Song of Songs** or as **Canticles**), OT Book included among the *Hagiographa. It is prob. an anthology of love poems of varying length, ascribed to *Solomon and his beloved (the 'Shulamite') and their friends. The Book, however, must be much later than the time of Solomon; its vocabulary and place in the *Canon suggest that it may date from as late as the 3rd cent BC, though some of the individual poems may be earlier. In the Hebrew Bible it is the first of the five *Megilloth and it is read by the Jews on the eighth day of *Passover.

From an early date Jewish and Christian exegetes alike have interpreted the Book allegorically. Rabbi *Akiba (d. 132) already protested strongly against a literal interpretation of its contents. In the *Talmud it is interpreted as an allegory of God's dealings with the congregation of Israel. Christian exegetes from St *Hippolytus onwards have seen in it a description of God's relations with the Church or the individual soul; and it was already the subject of a commentary in this sense by *Origen. This interpretation became esp. congenial to a long succession of spiritual writers; it received classical form in St *Bernard's 86 homilies on Canticles. Others who have interpreted the Book on the same lines include R. *Rolle, St *Teresa of Ávila, and St *John of the Cross (esp. in his 'Spiritual Canticle'). Indeed among Christian interpreters *Theodore of Mopsuestia seems to have been alone until modern times in upholding a literal exegesis. This was revived in the 16th cent. by S. *Castellio and the *Anabaptists and it is now very generally allowed that the original character of the work was erotic.

Comm. by H. Ringgren (Das Alte Testament Deutsch, 16/2, on Song of Songs, Lam., Est., 1958, pp. 1–37; 2nd edn., on Prov., Eccles., Song of Songs, Lam., Est., 1967, pp. 257–93), W. Rudolph (KAT 17. 1–3, on Ruth, Song of Songs, Lam., 1962, pp. 73–186), G. Gerleman (Biblischer Kommentar (Altes Testament), 17, on Ruth and Song of Songs, 1965, pp. 43–227), E. Würthwein (HAT, Reihe 1, Bd. 18, on Ruth, Song of Songs, Eccles., Lam., and Est., 2nd edn., 1969, pp. 25–71), M. H. Pope (Anchor Bible, 1977), and O. Keel (Zürcher Bibelkommentare, Altes Testament, 18; 1986). H. H. Rowley, 'The Interpretation of the Song of Songs', *JTS* 38 (1937), pp. 337–63; id., 'The Song of Songs. An Examination of Recent Theory', *The Journal of the Royal Asiatic Society*, 1938, pp. 251–76. A. Feuillet, PSS, *Le Cantique des Cantiques: Étude de théologie biblique et réflexions sur une méthode d'exégèse* (Lectio Divina, 10; 1953). M. D. Goulder, *The Song of Fourteen Songs* (Journal for the Study of the Old Testament, Supplement Series, 36 [1986]). H. Riedlinger, *Die Makellosigkeit der Kirche in den lateinischen Hoheliedkommentaren des Mittelalters* (BGPM 38, Heft 3; 1958); F. Ohly, *Hohelied-Studien: Grundzüge einer Geschichte der Hoheliedauslegung des Abendlandes bis um 1200* (Schriften der wissenschaftlichen Gesellschaft an der Johann Wolfgang Goethe-Universität Frankfurt am Main. Geisteswissenschaftliche Reihe, 1; Wiesbaden, 1958). E. A. Matter, *The Voice of My Beloved: The Song of Songs in Western Medieval Christianity* (Philadelphia [1990]).

Solomon, Wisdom of. See WISDOM OF SOLOMON.

Solovyov, Vladimir (1853–1900), Russian philosopher and theologian. After lecturing on philosophy at Moscow in 1875 and holding a post in the ministry of education at St Petersburg from 1877 to 1881, he devoted himself entirely to writing. In 1877 he became an intimate friend of F. *Dostoevsky, on whose religious ideas he exercised considerable influence. Down to 1881 he shared the ideas of the religiously minded Slavophils, including their antipathy to the RC Church; but further study and the desire for visible unity led him to modify his attitude, and from that time he regarded the union of the Churches as the main task of Russia, desiring to conserve the characteristic values of E. and W. During this period he wrote a profound ascetical book on the spiritual foundations of life (1882–4) and carried on negotiations with Bp. J. G. *Strossmayer for reunion between the Orthodox and RC Churches. In 1889 he published *La Russie et l'Église universelle* in which he proclaimed his Catholic ideal. It met with violent opposition in Russia, and when forbidden by the Holy Synod to write on religious questions he confined himself to politics and philosophy. In 1896 he received Communion in a RC church in Moscow, an act, he believed, of adhesion to the universal Church.

In his philosophical and religious ideas he was strongly influenced by B. *Spinoza and the German Idealists, esp. G. W. F. *Hegel. He sought to combine their pantheism with the Christian doctrine of the Incarnation. He admitted into his system, however, Gnostic elements and upheld the existence of a female principle, 'Sophia' or the worldsoul. Solovyov also wrote fine religious poetry. His influence, esp. among the refugees from the 1917 Revolution, did much to turn the Russian intellectuals from their 19th-cent. materialism and nihilism to a definitely religious and Christian view of the world.

2nd edn. of his works, pub. in 10 vols., St Petersburg, 1911–14. Letters pub. ibid., 4 vols., 1908–23. All repr., with 2 additional vols., Brussels, 1966–70. *La Sophia et les autres écrits français*, ed.

F. Rouleau (Lausanne, 1978), with introd. pp. vii–lxxii. There are Eng. trs. of *War and Christianity* with introd. by S. Graham (London, 1915); *The Justification of the Good*, by N. A. Dudding-ton (ibid., 1918); *Plato*, by R. Gill (ibid., 1935), with note by J. Lavrin, pp. 5–21; *God, Man and the Church*, by D. Attwater (ibid. [1938]); *Lectures on Godmanhood*, by P. Zouboff (New York, 1944), with introd. pp. 11–77; *The Meaning of Love*, by J. Marshall (London, 1945); and *Russia and the Universal Church*, by H. Rees (ibid., 1948). There is also *A Solovyov Anthology* arranged by S. L. Frank, tr. N. [A.] Duddington (1950), with introd. pp. 9–31.

D. Strémooukoff, *Vladimir Soloviev et son œuvre messianique* (1935; Eng. tr., Belmont, Mass., 1980). F. Muckermann, SJ, *Wladimir Solowiew* (Olten, 1945). L. Müller, *Das religionsphilosophische System Vladimir Solovjevs* (1956). E. Munzer, *Solovyev: Prophet of Russian-Western Unity* (posthumously pub., 1956). E. Klum, *Natur, Kunst und Liebe in der Philosophie Vladimir Solov'evs* (Slavistische Beiträge, 14; 1965). A. Paplauskas-Ramunas, *Dialogue entre Rome et Moscou: Vladimir Soloviev, porte-parole du mouvement œcuménique en Russie* (Ottawa, 1966). M. George, *Mystische und religiöse Erfahrung im Denken Vladimir Solov'evs* (Forschungen zur systematischen und ökumenischen Theologie, 54; Göttingen [1988]). J. Sutton, *The Religious Philosophy of Vladimir Solovyov* (1988). K. Pfleger, *Geister die um Christus ringen* (1934; Eng. tr., 1936), ch. 7 (pp. 223–65 of Eng. tr.); N. *Zernov, *Three Russian Prophets* (1944), pp. 116–51; F. C. Copleston, SJ, *Philosophy in Russia* (1986), pp. 201–40. F. Rouleau, SJ, in *Dict. Sp.* 14 (1990), cols. 1024–33, s.v.

Somaschi. An order of clerks regular in solemn vows who follow the Rule of St *Augustine. They were founded in 1532 by St *Jerome Emiliani at Somasca in N. Italy to work among the poor and afflicted, and formally constituted by Pope *Pius V in 1568. They still flourish in Italy and have houses in Central and South America as well as the USA. They run schools and orphanages.

L'ordine dei Chierici Regolari Somaschi nel IV centenario della sua fondazione (Rome, 1928). M. Tentorio, CRS, 'I Somaschi', in M. Escobar (ed.), *Ordini e Congregazioni Religiose*, 1 (1951), pp. 609–30, and other works of this author. P. Bianchini, CRS, in *NCE* 13 (1969), pp. 424 f., s.v.; id. in *DIP* 2 (1975), cols. 975–8, s.v. 'Chierici Regolari Somaschi'.

Somerset, Duke of (*c*.1506 [or perhaps *c*.1500]–1552), Protector of England. Edward Seymour, Earl of Hertford (1537) and Duke of Somerset (1547), was a brother of Jane Seymour, third wife of *Henry VIII. From 1524 onwards he held a succession of offices in the royal household. He played an important part in the Scottish campaign of 1544, and in 1546 successfully commanded the English forces in France. The fall of the Howards left him the leading figure in the Council when his nephew succeeded as *Edward VI. As protector to the young King he pressed on the reforming cause in the English Church, while attempting to coerce the Scots into co-operation. The offence given by his agrarian policy and his failure to prevent the risings of 1549 contributed largely to his deprival of the protectorship in Oct. 1549 and his ultimate execution on a charge of conspiracy against his rival and successor, Warwick.

W. K. Jordan, *Edward VI: The Young King. The Protectorship of the Duke of Somerset* (1968); M. L. Bush, *The Government Policy of Protector Somerset* (1975). A. F. Pollard in *DNB* 51 (1897), pp. 299–310, s.v. 'Seymour, Edward', with notes on unpub. material. See further bibl. s.v. EDWARD VI.

Son of Man. In the NT, a designation applied to Jesus. With one exception (Acts 7: 56), it is found only in the Gospels and here always on His own lips. The uses of the term in the Gospels are frequently classified as: (1) passages where Jesus refers to Himself in His earthly ministry, e.g. Mt. 11: 19 and Lk. 7: 34. In some other parallel passages one Gospel has 'I' or 'Me' (cf. Lk. 12: 8 and Mt. 10: 32; Mt. 16: 13, Mk. 8: 27, and Lk. 9: 18); (2) passages foretelling suffering, death, and resurrection for the Son of Man, e.g. Mt. 17: 22, Mk. 8: 31, Jn. 3: 14; and (3) passages in which the Son of Man is to appear at the End (Doomsday), 'coming with the clouds of heaven' (Mk. 14: 62), with 'authority to execute judgement' (Jn. 5: 27). In addition the Fourth Gospel uses the phrase in its 'man from heaven' Christology (3: 13 and 6: 62).

In the Aramaic of NT times it seems that the phrase could be used almost as a paraphrase for 'I'. In the OT the corresponding Hebrew expression is often a synonym for 'man', i.e. a human being (e.g. Num. 23: 19; Ps. 8: 4), and in Ezekiel (e.g. 2: 1) the Prophet is addressed by God as 'Son of man', perhaps emphasizing his humanity. This usage may be reflected in some passages in the Gospels (e.g. Mt. 8: 20). In Dan. 7: 13, however, the phrase 'one like a son of man' occurs in the context of the final establishment of God's *kingdom and the vindication of His people, and is used as a symbol representative of God's elect. In Dan. it denotes some angelic being; the identification with an individual leader or Messiah is not found until the Similitudes of *Enoch and 2 Esdras, in passages prob. too late to have influenced the Gospels.

In the Gospels there is an element of mystery about the phrase which confirms the view that it was not an established Messianic title before the time of Jesus. Whether He made the identification Himself either implicitly or explicitly remains a matter of dispute. Some argue that He used it as a personal pronoun, and that the passages echoing Dan. and giving Him the status of judge or redeemer were later Christian developments; others that He spoke of the final vindication through the Son of Man without casting Himself for that role. Perhaps He saw His role as representative of the people of God, and having a crucial part to play in God's drama of salvation.

Later readers of the Gospels have seen 'Son of Man' as denoting esp. the humility of Christ's incarnate manhood as contrasted with the majesty of His Divinity denoted by 'Son of God', and as emphasizing His universalist role as 'son of Adam' in contrast with the nationalist conceptions associated with the title 'Son of David'.

H. *Lietzmann, *Der Menschensohn* (1896); H. E. Tödt, *Der Menschensohn in der synoptischen Überlieferung* (Gütersloh, 1959; 2nd edn., 1963; Eng. tr., 1965); A. J. B. Higgins, *Jesus and the Son of Man* (1964); M. D. Hooker, *The Son of Man in Mark: A Study of the Background of the Term 'Son of Man' and its Use in St Mark's Gospel* (1967); F. H. Borsch, *The Son of Man in Myth and History* (1967); id., *The Christian and Gnostic Son of Man* (Studies in Biblical Theology, 2nd ser. 14; 1970); [P.] M. Casey, *Son of Man: The Interpretation and Influence of Daniel 7* (1979); B. Lindars, SSF, *Jesus Son of Man: A Fresh Examination of the Son of Man Sayings in the Gospels in the Light of Recent Research* (1983). W. *Bousset, *Kyrios Christos* (1913), esp. pp. 1–27; T. W. Manson, *The Teaching of Jesus* (1931), pp. 211–36; R. *Otto, *Reich Gottes und Menschensohn* (1934), pp. 124–220 (Eng. tr., pp. 159–261); W. Manson, *Jesus the Messiah* (1943), esp. Appendix D ('The Heavenly Man Redemption Myth'), pp. 174–90; J. A.

Emerton, 'The Origin of the Son of Man Imagery', *JTS* NS 9 (1958), pp. 225–42; S. S. Smalley, 'The Johannine Son of Man Sayings', *New Testament Studies*, 15 (1969), pp. 278–301; G. Vermes, 'The Use of נש בר/בר נשא in Jewish Aramaic', in M. Black, *An Aramaic Approach to the Gospels and Acts* (3rd edn., Oxford, 1967), pp. 310–30; id., 'The Present State of the "Son of Man" Debate', *Journal of Jewish Studies*, 29 (1978), pp. 123–34; C. F. D. Moule, 'Neglected Features in the Problem of the "Son of Man"', in J. Gnilka (ed.), *Neues Testament und Kirche: Für Rudolf Schnackenburg* (1974), pp. 413–28; repr. in his *Essays in New Testament Interpretation* (Cambridge, 1982), pp. 75–90; id., *The Origin of Christology* (ibid., 1977), pp. 11–22. M. D. Hooker, 'Is the Son of Man Problem really insoluble?', in E. Best and R. McL. Wilson (eds.), *Text and Interpretation: Studies in the New Testament presented to Matthew Black* (Cambridge, 1979), pp. 155–68. W. G. Kümmel, 'Jesusforschung seit 1965', 5: 'Der Persönliche Anspruch Jesu', *Theologische Rundschau*, NF 45 (1980), pp. 40–84. C. Colpe in *TWNT* 8 (1969), pp. 403–81; Eng. tr., 8 (1972), pp. 400–77, s.v. υἱὸς τοῦ ἀνθρώπου, with further bibl., 10/1 (1979), pp. 1283–6; G. W. E. Nickelsburg in *Anchor Bible Dictionary*, 6 (1992), pp. 137–50, s.v.

Song of Songs. See SOLOMON, SONG OF.

Song of the Three Children (now often called the 'Song of the Three Young Men'). A short 'Book' of the *Apocrypha. In the *Septuagint and *Vulgate, where its 68 verses are treated as part of the canonical Book of *Daniel (into which they are inserted after Dan. 3: 23), the Song of the Three Children is part of the story of the three young Hebrew exiles thrown into the fiery furnace by Nebuchadnezzar. It consists of (1) the Prayer of Azarias, a petition for national deliverance (which is prescribed as the seventh daily canticle in the Byzantine *Orthros), and (2) the canticle used in Christian worship in both the E. and W. Church under the name of the '*Benedicite'. Neither of these, however, apart from a single verse (66) in the Benedicite, seems to have any immediate relevance to the story of the three young men of Dan., and hence they are both generally supposed to have been written originally for some other occasion or occasions.

Gk. text in H. B. *Swete, *The Old Testament in Greek*, 2 (1912 edn.), pp. 515–23; also in A. Ralphs (ed.), *Septuaginta*, 2 (Stuttgart [1935]), pp. 885–94, and, without the introd., among the Odes, pp. 174–7. Eng. trs. and comm. by W. H. Bennett in R. H. *Charles (ed.), *The Apocrypha and Pseudepigrapha of the Old Testament*, 1 (Oxford, 1913), pp. 625–37, J. C. Dancy, *The Shorter Books of the Apocrypha* (Camb. Bib., NEB, 1972), pp. 211–23, and C. A. Moore, *Daniel, Esther and Jeremiah: The Additions* (Anchor Bible, 44; 1977), pp. 23–76. W. H. Daubney, *The Three Additions to Daniel: A Study* (1906), pp. 17–99. C. Kuhl, *Die drei Männer im Feuer* (Beiheft zur *ZATW* 55; 1930). R. H. Pfeiffer, *History of New Testament Times with an Introduction to the Apocrypha* (New York, 1949; London [1954]), pp. 444–8. E. *Schürer, *The History of the Jewish People in the Age of Jesus Christ*, rev. Eng. tr. by G. Vermes and others, 3 (pt. 2; Edinburgh, 1987), pp. 722–30 (on the additions of Daniel). See also RC comm. on Daniel and bibl. to BENEDICITE and APOCRYPHA.

Songs of Ascent or **Songs of Degrees.** See GRADUAL PSALMS.

Songs of Praise, a 'national' hymnal designed for the use of Christians of all denominations, first published in 1925. The General Editor was P. *Dearmer (1867–1936) and the Musical Editors Martin Shaw (1875–1958) and R. *Vaughan Williams (1872–1958). It aimed at an improved literary and artistic quality in the words, introducing many poems which had hitherto not found a place in hymnals. Theologically its standpoint was markedly liberal; considerable place was found for the social aspects of religion; and a high standard of musical taste was set. In 1931 it was superseded by a second edition in which the liberal element in the book was carried to a much greater extreme. Many of the hymns were altered, and sometimes rewritten, to eliminate expressions of dogmatic faith, esp. those concerned with the Atonement, and references to penitence, fasting, and the sterner side of Christian practice generally were removed. Though *Songs of Praise* continues to be used for interdenominational purposes, e.g. in schools, its use in Anglican churches has very largely ceased.

P. Dearmer, *Songs of Praise Discussed: A Handbook to the Best-known Hymns and to Others Recently Introduced* (1933), with notes on the music by A. Jacob.

Sophia, St. See SANCTA SOPHIA.

Sophronius, St (*c*.560–638), Patr. of *Jerusalem from 634. His identity with Sophronius 'the Sophist' seems now beyond dispute. He was a monk first in Egypt (*c*.580), later near the Jordan, and finally (from 619) at *Jerusalem. From 633 onwards he was the chief opponent of *Monothelitism, then being defended by Cyrus, Patr. of Alexandria. He wrote extended Lives of the two Alexandrian saints, Cyrus and John, believed to have been martyred in the *Diocletianic Persecution, and some of his sermons, as well as several poems, have also survived. Shortly before his death he negotiated the surrender of Jerusalem to the Arabs under Caliph 'Umar in 638. Feast day, 11 Mar.

Collection of his works in J. P. Migne, *PG* 87 (3). 3147–4014, with Life (repr. from *AASS*), 3125–46. Modern edn. of his 'Anacreontica' by M. Gigante (Rome, 1957). C. von Schönborn, *Sophrone de Jérusalem: Vie monastique et confession dogmatique* (Théologie historique, 20; 1972). H. Chadwick, 'John Moschus and his Friend Sophronius the Sophist', *JTS* NS 25 (1974), pp. 41–74, repr. in *History and Thought of the Early Church* (1982), no. 18. *CPG* 3 (1979), pp. 422–31 (nos. 7635–81). C. Schönborn in *Dict. Sp.* 14 (1990), cols. 1066–73, s.v.

Sorbonne. The most famous college of the old University of *Paris, originally known as the Collegium Pauperum Magistrorum. It was founded *c*.1257 by Robert de Sorbon, confessor of St *Louis, for the education of advanced students aspiring to the theological doctorate. Among its many benefactors was St Louis himself, who gave part of the site. It was favoured by the Popes, and Clement IV granted it Papal approbation in 1268. The house was governed by a 'provisor', assisted by the 'bursars', to whom were added the 'socii' without a 'burse' and the 'hospites'. In addition to these were the 'beneficiarii', supported by the college to perform menial offices for the Fellows. The reputation of the Sorbonne, whose examinations were famous for their severity, soon became such that its membership was sought not only by most theological doctors of Paris but also by many otherwise prominent personalities. The college also came to be consulted on theological and even political questions from all parts of Christendom. From 1554 it was the regular meeting-place of the Theological Faculty, and from this date the name Sorbonne was popularly applied to this faculty. From the later Middle

Ages the Sorbonne had favoured *Gallican tendencies, and in the 17th and 18th cents., when the royal authority allowed it to do so, it vigorously defended Gallican ecclesiastical views and a typically French approach to ecclesiastical scholarship. It opposed the bull '*Unigenitus' (1713), thus losing its influence with Rome, and also fought the *probabilist moral theology and the educational and missionary aims of the *Jesuits. On the other hand, it stoutly defended Catholic principles against the Reformation theology and the Rationalist philosophy of the 18th cent. The Sorbonne was suppressed in 1793, but re-established as the Theological Faculty of the University of Paris by Napoleon in 1808. Its professors and graduates, however, were theoretically obliged to subscribe to the Gallican Articles, a condition which drew away most theological students to *St-Sulpice and the diocesan seminaries. The faculty was finally abolished in 1885, but the name 'Sorbonne' continued in use for the University of Paris as a whole. Since the latter's reorganization into 13 separate universities in 1969, the term has been attached to those still connected with the original site: Paris I ('Panthéon-Sorbonne'), Paris III ('la Nouvelle Sorbonne'), and Paris IV ('Paris-Sorbonne').

Important docs. in the *Chartularium Universitatis Parisiensis*, ed. H. [S.] *Denifle, OP, and A. Chatelain (4 vols., Paris, 1889–97). J. Duvernet, *Histoire de la Sorbonne dans laquelle on voit l'influence de la théologie sur l'ordre social* (2 vols., bound in one, 1790). O. Gréard, *Nos Adieux à la vieille Sorbonne* (1893), with docs. J. Bonnerot, *La Sorbonne: Sa vie, son rôle, son œuvre à travers les siècles* (1927). P. Glorieux, *Aux origines de la Sorbonne* (Études de Philosophie Médiévale, 53–4; 1965–6), incl. text of Cartulary of the college in vol. 2. A. Franklin, *La Sorbonne: Ses origines, sa bibliothèque, les débuts de l'imprimerie à Paris et la succession de Richelieu* (1875). P. Feret, *La Faculté de théologie de Paris et ses docteurs les plus célèbres: Moyen Âge* (4 vols., 1894–7); *Époque moderne* (7 vols., 1900–10). J. K. Farge, *Biographical Register of Paris Doctors of Theology 1500–1536* (Pontifical Institute of Mediaeval Studies, Subsidia Mediaevalia, 10; Toronto, 1980). See also bibl. to PARIS.

Sorrowful Mysteries, the Five. The second chaplet of the *Rosary, consisting of (1) the Agony in Gethsemane, (2) the Scourging, (3) the Crowning with Thorns, (4) the Carrying of the Cross, and (5) the Crucifixion.

soteriology (Gk. σωτηρία, 'salvation'). The section of Christian theology which treats of the saving work of Christ for the world. It includes not only the doctrines of the *Atonement and of *Grace, but also (1) the doctrine of human nature as affected by the *Fall and by *sin, which is the presupposition of Christ's work, and (2) the doctrine of man's final destiny as the result of that work (see RESURRECTION OF THE DEAD, HEAVEN, HELL).

Soto, Dominic de (1494–1560), *Dominican theologian. A native of Spain who was a student at Alcalá and at Paris, he entered the Dominican Order at Burgos in 1524. Here he taught in his convent for 7 years until appointed in 1532 to a chair of theology at Salamanca University. This office he continued to hold until 1545, when *Charles V chose him as Imperial Theologian for the Council of *Trent, where he ably expounded the *Thomistic teaching on grace and original sin. After spending some time in Germany as confessor to Charles V, in 1550 he returned to Salamanca, where he was elected in 1552 to the prin-

cipal chair of theology in succession to Melchior *Cano. His principal writings are treatises *De Natura et de Gratia* (Venice, 1547, repr., Ridgewood, NJ, 1965) and *De Justitia et Jure* (Salamanca, 1553–4).

V. Beltrán de Heredia, OP, *Domingo de Soto: Estudio biográfico documentado* (1961). C. Gutiérrez, SJ, *Españoles en Trento* (Corpus Tridentinum Hispanicum, 50; Valladolid, 1951), pp. 314–38. F. Stegmüller, 'Zur Gnadenlehre des spanischen Konzilstheologen Domingo de Soto', in G. Schreiber (ed.), *Das Weltkonzil von Trient*, 1 (1951), pp. 169–230. K. J. Becker, SJ, *Die Rechtfertigungslehre nach Domingo de Soto* (Analecta Gregoriana, 156; 1967). B. Hamilton, *Political Thought in Sixteenth-Century Spain: A Study of the Political Ideas of Vitoria, De Soto, Suárez, and Molina* (Oxford, 1963). M. Andrés [Martín], *La teología española en el siglo XVI* (Biblioteca de Autores Cristianos, 13–14; 1976–7), esp. 2, pp. 362–5, 483–5, and 504–7. Quétif and Échard, 2, pp. 171–4. V. Beltrán de Heredia, OP, in *DTC* 14 (pt. 2; 1941), cols. 2423–31, s.v.

Soubirous, Bernadette. See BERNADETTE, ST.

soul. The idea of a distinction between the soul, the immaterial principle of life and intelligence, and the body is of great antiquity, though only gradually expressed with any precision. Hebrew thought made little of this distinction, and there is practically no specific teaching on the subject in the Bible beyond an underlying assumption of some form of afterlife (see IMMORTALITY). Greek thought, on the other hand, developed various ways of understanding the relation of body and soul: from the *Platonic idea that the immortal soul is the true self, imprisoned for a time in an alien body, to the *Stoic view of the soul as the 'leading element' (ἡγεμονικόν) of a unity which includes the body. No precise teaching about the soul received general acceptance until the Middle Ages.

This uncertainty is reflected in the writings of the Fathers. *Tertullian, supporting his view by the material imagery of the parable of Dives and Lazarus and influenced by Stoic notions, held the corporeity of the soul, an error from which even St *Irenaeus does not seem to have been entirely free. *Origen, on the other hand, was led by his strongly Platonist leanings to affirm its pre-existence and explained its confinement in a body as a punishment for sins committed in its previous incorporeal state. In the post-Nicene period these divergences largely disappeared, and a modified Platonic view, seeing the soul as the true self, immortal but not pre-existent, won acceptance. The soul came to be universally regarded as an image of God (cf. Gen. 1: 26). St *Augustine gave this doctrine a novel turn by seeing the soul (consisting of *memoria, intelligentia*, and *voluntas*) as an image of the Trinity; this formulation was destined to have great influence in the W. *Nemesius and St *Maximus the Confessor provide the most elaborate statement of the Greek patristic position.

Acc. to St *Thomas Aquinas, who follows *Aristotle in his definition of the human soul, the soul is an individual spiritual substance, the 'form' of the body. Both, body and soul together, constitute the human unity, though the soul may be severed from the body and lead a separate existence, as happens after death. The separation, however, is not final, as the soul, in this differing from the angels, was made for the body. As it is purely spiritual, the soul is not, as *Traducianism affirms, a product of the generative, and therefore entirely material, powers of man, but each individual soul is a new creation of God, infused into the body destined for it ('Creationism').

From the 17th cent. R. *Descartes's oversimplified dichotomy between soul and body (*res cogitans* and *res extensa*) has had a marked effect on subsequent theological thought. In more recent times, philosophical perplexities over such a dichotomy and the recovery of the biblical insight into the unity of man have meant that the doctrine of the soul, if considered at all, is thought of in relation to the whole biblical doctrine of man.

Source Criticism. See HIGHER CRITICISM.

Souter, Alexander (1873–1949), NT and patristic scholar. He was educated at Aberdeen and Gonville and Caius College, Cambridge, where he came under the influence of the Latinist, J. E. B. Mayor. From 1903 to 1911 he was professor of NT Greek at Mansfield College, Oxford, and from 1911 to 1937 Regius Professor of Humanity (in succession to W. M. *Ramsay) at Aberdeen. He came to acquire an unrivalled knowledge of early Christian Latin. His works in the patristic field include *A Study of *Ambrosiaster* (1905), an edition of the Pseudo-Augustinian *Quaestiones Veteris et Novi Testamenti* (CSEL, 1908), and, most important of all, his identification of the text of *Pelagius' Commentary on St Paul's Epistles, which he edited (Texts and Studies, 1922–31). He co-operated with W. *Sanday in studies on the text of the NT. He also argued for a late date (370–420) for the Latin version of *Irenaeus. His valuable *Glossary of Later Latin* (1949) was published posthumously.

R. J. Getty, 'Alexander Souter, 1873–1949', *Aberdeen University Review*, 33 (1950), pp. 117–24; repr. with expansions in *Proceedings of the British Academy*, 28 (1952), pp. 255–68.

South, Robert (1634–1716), English divine. Educated at Westminster under R. Busby and at Christ Church, Oxford, he was for a time in sympathy with *Presbyterianism. In 1658, however, he secretly took Orders. He held a varied succession of offices, becoming Public Orator of Oxford (1660), domestic chaplain to Lord Clarendon (1660), Prebendary of *Westminster (1663), chaplain to the Duke of York (1667), canon of Christ Church (1670), and rector of Islip, Oxon (1678). His sermons, smart, witty, and often sarcastic, became exceedingly popular, but his outspokenness precluded him from higher preferment, though in 1713 he was apparently offered, but declined, the see of *Rochester. In 1689 he opposed the *Toleration Act and for a time hesitated before taking the Oath, and in 1710 he sided with H. *Sacheverell. For several years he controverted with vigour W. *Sherlock's dubiously orthodox teaching on the *Trinity, publishing in 1693 some *Animadversions* on Sherlock's *Vindication* (1690) and in 1695, in answer to a reply by Sherlock, *Tritheism Charged* (both anonymous).

South himself began pub. of his *Sermons Preached on Several Occasions* (Oxford, 1679; new edns., with further sermons, London, 1692, and 3 vols., ibid., 1697–8). Posthumous works, Lat. and Eng., pub. 2 vols., London, 1717, incl. his will and memoir of his life and writings. The many later edns. of his sermons incl. five additional vols., London, 1744; also collected edn., 7 vols., Oxford, 1823. G. Reedy, SJ, *Robert South (1634–1716):*

An Introduction to his Life and Sermons (Cambridge, 1992). A. Gordon in *DNB* 53 (1898), pp. 275–7, s.v.

South Africa, Christianity in. The first Christian missions to Africa south of the Zambezi river were Portuguese. Their effect on what is now S. Africa was very limited, and Christianity was really introduced by the Dutch, who began to settle in 1652. There was no organized mission to the indigenous inhabitants until some *Moravians went to the Cape in 1737, but the authorities were suspicious and the mission was soon closed; it did not reopen until 1792 at Genadendal, as a complete, self-contained community living a semi-monastic life. During the Napoleonic Wars the British twice occupied the Cape, and they retained the colony at the Peace of Paris (1814). Though they expelled two RC missionaries whom they found, many other agencies began work in this period. The *LMS arrived in 1799 and provided many of the most famous missionaries, including the pioneers J. *van der Kemp, J. *Philip, R. *Moffat, and D. *Livingstone. Among the earliest African converts was the Xhosa poet Ntsikana (died 1821) who, though never baptized, established through his hymns and his example a tradition which has remained central to black Christianity ever since.

The character of Christian work in S. Africa during the past 200 years has been determined by two principal facts. The existence of a large white community (though not large in proportion to the indigenous population) caused the establishment and organization of a settler Church in many places, with duties other than those of missionary propaganda. And the immensity of the field provided room for the missionary activity of religious bodies and societies from almost every part of W. Christendom. *Methodists arrived in 1814; under William Shaw (1798–1872) they established a thriving mission in the E. Cape and came to have the largest number of African adherents in the country. American, German, French, Finnish, Swiss, Scandinavian, Scottish, and English Protestant missions have all been at work for varying periods. The *SPG arrived in 1821. Outstandingly influential was the Church of Scotland mission centred around the educational institution at *Lovedale in Ciskei. From it many of the country's leading African Christians have come, including Tiyo Soga (d. 1871), translator into Xhosa of *Pilgrim's Progress* and of parts of the Bible, and Tengo Jabavu (d. 1921), the first black professor at Fort Hare.

The Great Trek (1837) resulted in the establishment as the State Church in the Transvaal of the Hervormde Kerk, separate from the Dutch Reformed Church. A further separation led to the creation of a free Gereformeerde Kerk. The Dutch Reformed Church was subjected to considerable tensions not unlike those of the controversy surrounding Bp. J. W. *Colenso in the Anglican Church. It later experienced a renewal of missionary zeal as a result of the *pietistic revival led by Andrew Murray (1828–1917). RC missions particularly have grown since the latter part of the 19th cent., the Oblates of Mary Immaculate (founded 1816) playing a leading part. German *Trappists established themselves at Mariannhill in Natal in 1882 and developed one of the great monastic missions of modern Africa but its work proved irreconcilable with the Trappist rule and they became instead a separate order, Missionaries of Mariannhill, in 1909.

The multiplication of missions led to the creation of the first official *ecumenical organization in S. Africa, the General Missionary Conference founded in 1904. It was replaced in 1932 by the Christian Council of South Africa, which was, in turn, reorganized in the early 1960s and became the South African Council of Churches. In 1963 the Anglican, *Congregational, Methodist, and *Presbyterian Churches established a federal theological seminary at Alice in Cape Province, later closed by the government, reopened at Umtata in the Transkei and now at Pietermaritzburg. Racially discriminatory government policies have brought tension with the Churches ever since the time of van der Kemp. The Dutch Reformed Church, whose theology in the 20th cent. for a time backed a policy of 'separate development', left the *World Council of Churches after the Sharpeville crisis of 1960. The other Churches were all more or less opposed to the policies of the State and their work in black education was almost eliminated following the Bantu Education Act of 1954. With the establishment of the Christian Institute in Johannesburg by Beyers Naudé in 1963, Christian criticism of, and opposition to, racialism became more systematic and was led increasingly by black Christians such as Desmond Tutu (Anglican Abp. of Cape Town 1986–96). Some leading churchmen were deported; others, such as Naudé, Gonville ffrench-Beytagh, and Patrick Mkatschwa, tried or imprisoned.

African Independent Churches have been more numerous in S. Africa than elsewhere on the continent, perhaps because of racial tensions. There are thought to be over 3,000 of these bodies. They include at least 30 per cent of African Christians. While some derive from schisms, or sub-schisms, from a mainline mission Church whose doctrine and order they retain (these are frequently described as 'Ethiopian'), others (generally called 'Zionist') have developed their own rituals, especially of healing, and were often founded by a 'prophet' figure. The most famous of these is the Amanazaretha, founded by Isaiah Shembe in Zululand.

The Church of the Province of Southern Africa (as the former province of South Africa became in 1982) is an independent province of the Anglican communion. The archiepiscopal see at Cape Town was founded in 1847, with R. *Gray as its first bishop. The Province as a whole has been strongly influenced by the *Tractarian Movement, and religious communities, both of men and of women, are perhaps more active in S. Africa than in any other Anglican province. An Alternative *Eucharistic Liturgy was approved by the Provincial Synod in 1919; a complete provincial Prayer Book was issued in 1954 and another in 1989.

J. du Plessis, *A History of Christian Missions in South Africa* (1911); G. B. A. Gerdener, *Recent Developments in the South African Mission Field* (1958); P. [B.] Hinchliff, *The Church in South Africa* (CHS, 1968). C. Lewis and G. E. Edwards, *Historical Records of the Church of the Province of South Africa* (1934). A. T. Wirgman, *The History of the English Church and People in South Africa* (1895); P. [B.] Hinchliff, *The Anglican Church in South Africa: An Account of the History and Development of the Church of the Province of South Africa* (1963). W. E. Brown, *The Catholic Church in South Africa from its Origins to the Present Day*, ed. M. Derrick [1960]. G. B. A. Gerdener (ed.), *Boustowwe vir die Geskiedenis van die Nederduits-Gereformeerde Kerk in die Transgariep* (Cape Town, 1930). H. D. van Broekhuizen, *Die Wordingsgeskiedenis van die Hollandse Kerke in Suid-Afrika, 1652–1804* (Amsterdam, 1922); A. Moorrees, *Die Nederduitse Gereformeerde Kerk in Suid-Afrika 1652–1873* (Cape Town, 1937). J. Whiteside, *History of the Wesleyan Methodist Church of South Africa* (1906); L. A. Hewson, *An Introduction to South African Methodists* (Cape Town [1951]). B. G. M. Sundkler, *Bantu Prophets in South Africa* (1948; 2nd edn., 1961). J. Sales, *Mission Stations and the Coloured Communities of the Eastern Cape 1800–1852* (Cape Town and Rotterdam, 1975). B. [G. M.] Sundkler, *Zulu Zion and some Swazi Zionists* (1976). J. W. de Gruchy, *The Church Struggle in South Africa* (Grand Rapids, Mich., and London, 1979); P. Walshe, *Church versus State in South Africa* (1983). J. W. Hofmeyr and K. E. Cross, *History of the Church in Southern Africa*, vol. 1: *A select bibliography of published material to 1980* (Pretoria, 1986). Latourette, 3, pp. 245 f.; 5, pp. 319–81, with bibl. pp. 471–506 *passim*; and 7, pp. 224–31, with bibl. notes.

South India, Church of. The Church inaugurated on 27 Sept. 1947 by the union of three religious bodies: (1) the (*Anglican) Church of India, Burma, and Ceylon, in respect to four of its dioceses, namely Madras, Tinnevelly, Travancore and Cochin, and Dornakal; (2) the South India Province of the *Methodist Church; (3) the South India United Church, itself the result of a movement which brought *Presbyterian, *Congregational, and Dutch Reformed bodies into organic union in 1908 and was joined in 1919 by the Malabar District of the Basel Mission, which drew its foreign workers from Continental *Lutheran and *Reformed Churches. The Church of South India, which numbers somewhat over one and a half million, is based doctrinally on the *Lambeth Quadrilateral (1888) and claims to be a united and visible Church, in which the Congregational, Presbyterian, and Episcopal elements are preserved. The union was achieved by the acceptance of ministers ordained in each of these traditions into a united ministry (without requiring any reordinations), combined with the introduction of an episcopate in the historic succession (from Anglicanism) and its maintainance for the future, with the assurance that all future ordinations would be episcopal. It was expected that at the end of 30 years all presbyters would have been episcopally ordained.

The creation of the Church of South India was the fruit of negotiations which began at a historic conference at Tranquebar in May 1919, when the 33 participants (31 Indians, 1 American, and 1 Englishman, almost all ministers of varying denominations) determined to remedy the evils arising from divisions to Christian mission work in India. The 1920 *Lambeth Conference *Appeal to all Christian People* quickened hopes, and a Joint Committee of the three bodies concerned was set up. The challenge to traditional Catholic order in the proposed arrangement led to much controversy and many delays; but the 1930 Lambeth Conference gave general encouragement to the scheme, believing that Catholic principles would be sufficiently safeguarded. The scheme was later subjected to considerable revision, and in 1947, if one vote had been differently cast, the union would have been delayed. In the Nandyal district of S. India some 40,000 Anglicans refused to join the Church. It has subsequently been joined by various other small groups, including the Basel Mission Council of Bombay–Karnatik in 1958.

The 1948 Lambeth Conference gave the union a measure of qualified approval, and in 1955 a state of 'limited inter-communion' between the Church of South India and the C of E was approved by the Convocations of Canterbury and York. This was somewhat extended by the General Synod in 1972. The Church of South India is now a member of the Anglican Consultative Council, the *Lambeth Conference, and the Primates' Meeting.

The method of uniting the ministries adopted by the Church of South India has been widely advocated in union negotiations in various parts of the world, but usually rejected in favour of the imposition of hands by bishops on all uniting ministries at the time of union.

G. K. A. *Bell, *Documents on Christian Unity* (4 vols., 1924–58; nos. 71–81, 139–43, 147, 204–8 and 267–74). B. [G. M.] Sundkler, *Church of South India: The Movement towards Union, 1900–1947* (1954). [A.] M. Ward, *The Pilgrim Church: An Account of the First Five Years in the Life of the Church of South India* (1953).

South Pacific, Christianity in. In 1776 a RC mission was sent by the Viceroy of Peru to Tahiti, but withdrew after a few months. The *LMS sent out evangelists who started work in Tahiti in 1797, and rapidly extended it. Later pioneers included John *Williams, who suffered martyrdom at Erromanga in Vanuatu (formerly the New Hebrides) in 1839. The work of the LMS in the area was more persistent and more widespread than that of any other society, but many other bodies have taken part in attempts to evangelize the Pacific Islanders. In 1822 the Wesleyan *Methodists sent their first missionaries to Tonga; they later went on to the Fiji Islands. In 1854 the control of this mission passed from the Methodists in Britain to those of *Australia. From 1848 onwards *Presbyterians came from Nova Scotia and Scotland, while in 1886 and 1887 two *Lutheran societies took up work in the German part of New Guinea. The South Sea Evangelical Mission began work in the Solomon Islands in 1904. When the Society Islands and the Loyalty Islands came under French colonial rule, the LMS was replaced by the Paris Evangelical Missionary Society. For the missionary work performed by the *Reformed Presbyterian Church, see PATON, J. G.

RC missions entered the field in many places early in the 19th cent. The work was largely undertaken by the newer missionary orders, notably the Picpus Society or Fathers of the Sacred Hearts of Jesus and Mary (approved in 1817), who were given responsibility for work in Oceania in 1825, and the *Marists (q.v.). In 1835 the area was divided between the two orders, East Oceania being assigned to the Picpusians and West Oceania to the Marists. The Picpusian mission included the heroic work of Father *Damien in the leper colony at Molokai, Hawaii. The Hawaiian Islands were annexed to the USA in 1898 and created the 50th state of the Union in 1959; but for a long period most of the missionary work in that part of the Pacific had originated in the USA.

Anglican work in the S. Pacific began under G. A. *Selwyn, appointed first Bp. of New Zealand in 1841. One of his disciples, J. C. *Patteson, first Bp. of Melanesia (1861), was killed in 1871. The diocese of Melanesia formed part of the Province of New Zealand until it became an independent Province in 1975. The Anglican mission in Papua, founded from Australia in 1891, developed into the Province of Papua New Guinea, formed in 1977. The South Pacific Anglican Council comprises the Provinces of Melanesia and Papua New Guinea and the diocese of Polynesia, which is part of the Province of New Zealand.

The task which confronted missionaries in the S. Pacific was one of the hardest in missionary history. In addition to the difficulties of communication over a vast area, many of the inhabitants had a reputation for savagery; even to modern times missionaries have suffered martyrdom in the SW Pacific. Here, as elsewhere, during the 20th cent. there has been a marked diminution of hostility between Protestant and RC missionaries, which in the 19th cent. was aggravated by the support given to the latter by French naval power. In the *ecumenical sphere notable events have included the foundation of the Pacific Literature Society, formed in 1943 to prepare literature on an interdenominational basis, the Pacific Theological College in 1965, and the Pacific Conference of Churches in 1966. There has also been an example of interconfessional union in the inauguration in 1968 of the United Church of Papua New Guinea and the Solomon Islands, which brought together Methodists and the Papua Ekalesia, which had grown out of the work of the LMS. Another major trend in the later 20th cent. is the creation of self-governing Churches and the advance towards indigenous leadership. In the RC Church a hierarchy was set up in the South Pacific in 1966. The majority of the inhabitants of the Pacific Islands now profess Christianity. The largest non-Christian population is in Fiji, where descendants of Indian immigrants are mainly Hindus or Muslims.

Primary accounts incl. J. Williams, *A Narrative of Missionary Enterprises in the South Sea Islands* (1837), and C. E. Fox, *Kakamora* (1962). J. Colwell (ed.), *A Century in the Pacific* (1914), pt. 4, 'Missionary', pp. 409–585. J. Garrett, *To Live among the Stars: Christian Origins in Oceania* (Geneva [1982]) [covers period to 1900, with some material on the 20th cent.]; id., *Footsteps in the Sea: Christianity in Oceania to World War II* (Suva and Geneva, 1992). C. W. Forman, *The Island Churches of the South Pacific: Emergence in the Twentieth Century* (American Society of Missiology Series, 5; Maryknoll, NY [1982]). J. A. Boutilier and others (eds.), *Mission, Church, and Sect in Oceania* (Association for Social Anthropology in Oceania, Monograph, 6; Ann Arbor, Mich. [1978]). [W.] N. Gunson, *Messengers of Grace: Evangelical Missionaries in the South Seas, 1797–1860* (Melbourne, 1978). D. [L.] Hilliard, *God's Gentlemen: A History of the Melanesian Mission, 1849–1942* (St Lucia, Queensland [1978]). A. H. Wood, *Overseas Missions of the Australian Methodist Church*, 1–3 (Melbourne, 1975–8) and 5, in conjunction with M. Reeson (Sydney [1987]). R. M. Wiltgen, *The Founding of the Roman Catholic Church in Oceania 1825 to 1850* (Canberra, London, and Norwalk, Conn., 1981). A. R. Tippett, *Solomon Islands Christianity: A Study in Growth and Obstruction* (1967). H. [M.] Laracy, *Marists and Melanesians: A History of Catholic Missions in the Solomon Islands* (Canberra, 1976). H. Wagner and H. Reiner (eds.), *The Lutheran Church in Papua New Guinea: The First Hundred Years, 1886–1986* (Adelaide, 1986). R. Lovett, *The History of the London Missionary Society, 1795–1895*, 1 (1899), pp. 117–474; N. Goodall, *History of the London Missionary Society, 1895–1945* (1954), esp. pp. 352–411, and bibl. refs., p. 592; Latourette, 5, pp. 198–263, with bibl. pp. 471–506 passim, and 7, pp. 192–9, with bibl. notes. J. L. Dunstan in S. [C.] Neill and others (eds.), *Concise Dictionary of the Christian World Mission* (1970), pp. 459–65, s.v. 'Pacific Islands'.

Southcott, Joanna (1750–1814), self-styled prophetess. She began work as a dairymaid and then became a domestic servant. In 1791 she joined the *Methodists 'by Divine command', and in the following year proclaimed that she was the 'woman clothed with the sun' of Rev. 12. By 1814 she was expecting to give birth to a messianic child, the 'Shiloh'. In the meantime she had been 'sealing' those who hoped to be among the 144,000 elect. Some 20,000 are believed to have been sealed and her total following (largely artisan but with some genteel persons) may have been much larger. She published over 60 pamphlets containing her revelations. The movement survived in the 19th cent. under a variety of leaders who claimed to be her successors but now appears to be extinct. R. T. *Davidson, when Abp. of Canterbury, was constantly pressed to summon the bishops to open a box of her prophecies for the well-being of the country, and the Panacea Society still makes similar demands.

Her own writings are the primary source for her life. *A General Index to the Writings of Joanna Southcott* (London [1805]). G. R. Balleine, *Past Finding Out: The Tragic Story of Joanna Southcott and her Successors* (1956). A. Seymour, *The Express* (2 vols., 1909; sympathetic, with extensive summaries and extracts of her writings). J. K. Hopkins, *A Woman to deliver her People: Joanna Southcott and English Millenarianism in an Era of Revolution* (Austin, Tex., 1982). J. F. C. Harrison, *The Second Coming: Popular Millenarianism 1780–1850* (1979), pp. 86–160. A. Gordon in *DNB* 53 (1898), pp. 277–9, s.v., with further bibl.

Southwark. The Anglican diocese of Southwark was created in 1905, comprising the deaneries of Greenwich, Lewisham, and Woolwich in Kent and the Parliamentary Divisions of East and Mid-Surrey. In 1877 these deaneries had been taken away from the diocese of *Winchester and added to that of Rochester. Anthony Thorold (Bp. of Rochester 1877–91; Bp. of Winchester 1891–5) worked for the establishment of a separate diocese for S. London and Surrey and for the restoration of St Saviour's, Southwark, as the future cathedral for a new diocese. In 1905, through the efforts of E. S. *Talbot, the diocese of Southwark was created and Talbot translated from Rochester as its first bishop.

The priory of St Mary Overie ('Overie' means 'over the water from the City of London') was founded in 1106, when it was served by *Augustinian canons. The church was severely damaged by fire in 1212. A new Gothic church was built during the next 200 years, though a few traces of the Norman church can still be seen. In 1469 the roof of the nave collapsed and was rebuilt. The priory was surrendered to *Henry VIII in 1539, and it became the parish church of St Saviour, Southwark. By 1815 the church had fallen into disrepair and much work was undertaken between 1818 and 1827. After the roof of the nave was found to be unsafe in 1831, it was removed and the walls were taken down, and in 1841 a new nave was completed. In 1890 the foundation stone was laid for the fourth nave to be built since the Conquest. When the diocese of Southwark was created the church became 'The Collegiate Church of St Saviour and St Mary Overie'. Lancelot *Andrewes, Bp. of Winchester, was buried in the church in 1626.

The RC diocese of Southwark dates from the restoration of the hierarchy in 1850; it was created an archdiocese in 1965.

W. Taylor, *Annals of St Mary Overy: An Historical and Descriptive Account of St Saviour's Church and Parish* (1833); F. T. Dollman, *The Priory of St Mary Overie, Southwark* (1881); [W.] Thompson, *History and Antiquities of the Collegiate Church of St Saviour (St Marie Overie), Southwark* (1904): G. Worley, *Southwark Cathedral . . .: A Short History and Description of the Fabric, with some account of the College and See* (Bell's Cathedral Guides, 1905); T. P. Stevens, *The Story of Southwark Cathedral* [1922]; F. [M. G.] Higham, *Southwark Story* (1955). Royal Commission on Historical Monuments (England), *An Inventory of the Historical Monuments in London, 5: East London* (1930), pp. 58–66.

Southwell. St *Paulinus is said to have founded a collegiate church here *c*.630. The present cathedral church of St Mary the Virgin was begun in the reign of Henry I and has a fine Norman nave and transepts, and a 13th-cent. *chapter house. The early collegiate foundation developed into a college of secular canons, which was dissolved by *Henry VIII in 1540, refounded in 1585, and again dissolved in 1841. In 1884 the church became the cathedral of the new Diocese of Southwell, consisting roughly of the counties of Derbyshire and Nottinghamshire. In 1927 the former was separated off when the Diocese of Derby was constituted. In 1935 the Diocese was transferred from the Province of *Canterbury to that of *York.

A. F. Leach (ed.), *Visitations and Memorials of Southwell Minster* (Camden Society, 2nd ser. 48; 1891); T. M. Blagg (ed.), *Seventeenth Century Parish Register Transcripts Belonging to the Peculiar of Southwell* (Thoroton Society, Record Series, 1; 1903); A. H. Thompson (ed.), 'The Certificates of the Chantry Commissioners for the College of Southwell in 1546 and 1548', *Transactions of the Thoroton Society*, 15 (1900), pp. 63–158. W. D. Macray, 'The Manuscripts of Southwell Cathedral', in *Twelfth Report of the Historical Manuscripts Commission, Appendix*, pt. 9 (1891), pp. 539–52. W. *Dugdale, *Monasticon Anglicanum*, 6 (pt. 3, 1830 edn.), pp. 1312–23. W. Dickinson Rastall, *A History of the Antiquities of the Town and Church of Southwell* (1787). A. Dimock, *The Cathedral Church of Southwell* (Bell's Cathedral Series, 1898). A. H. Thompson, 'The Cathedral Church of the Blessed Virgin Mary, Southwell', *Transactions of the Thoroton Society*, 15 (1900), pp. 15–62. J. C. Cox in *VCH*, Nottingham, 2, ed. W. Page (1910), pp. 152–61. G. Crosse in *DECH* (3rd edn., 1948), pp. 582 f., s.v.

Southwell, St Robert (*c*.1561–95), poet and RC martyr. He was a native of Norfolk, educated by the *Jesuits at *Douai and *Paris, and entered the Society in 1580 after a two-year novitiate. In 1584 he was ordained priest and made prefect of studies at the English College in Rome. In 1586 he was sent on the English mission. He first stayed with Lord Vaux of Harrowden and, though closely watched, gained many conversions through his piety and winning manner. In 1589 he became chaplain to Anne, Countess of Arundel, and established relations with her husband, imprisoned in the Tower. He spent much of his time in hiding in London or in RC country houses, where he stayed in disguise and under assumed names. In 1592 he was betrayed by Anne Bellamy, the daughter of Richard Bellamy, a Catholic whom he had visited at Harrow. He was confined first at the gatehouse at *Westminster and later in the Tower. After three years of imprisonment he was hanged and quartered as a traitor. He was beatified in 1929 and was among the *Forty Martyrs of England and Wales canonized in 1970. Feast day, formerly 21 Feb.

Collections of his verse were published immediately after his death entitled *St Peter's Complaint with other*

Poems and *Maeoniae* (both 1595). Among his prose treatises are *An Epistle of Comfort*, *The Triumphs over Death*, *Mary Magdalen's Funerall Teares*, and *An Humble Supplication to Her Majestie*, all written in 1591 and at first circulated in manuscript. They were designed esp. to encourage Catholics under persecution. His poems, most of which were probably written in prison, soon became popular with both Catholics and Protestants. They give utterance to deep religious feeling, though his vivid imagination led him to use extensively the fanciful conceits favoured by the poets of his time.

Southwell's *Prose Works* ed. W. J. Walter (London, 1828); *Poems* ed. A. B. Grosart ('The Fuller Worthies Library', ibid., 1872) and by J. H. McDonald and N. P. Brown (Oxford, 1967). His *Spiritual Exercises and Devotions* (Lat. text) first ed. J. M. de Buck, SJ, with Eng. tr. by P. E. Hallett (London, 1931). Modern edn. of *An Humble Supplication to her Maiestie* by R. C. Bald (Cambridge, 1953). Modern Life by C. Devlin (London, 1956). P. Janelle, *Robert Southwell the Writer: A Study in Religious Interpretation* (Paris thesis, Clermont-Ferrand; also London, 1935); J. D. Scallon, SJ, *The Poetry of Robert Southwell, S.J.* (Salzburg Studies in English Literature, Elizabethan & Renaissance Studies, 11; 1975). A. D. Cousins, *The Catholic Religious Poets from Southwell to Crashaw* (1991), pp. 38–71. N. P. Brown, 'Robert Southwell: The Mission of the Written Word', in T. M. McCoog, SJ (ed.), *The Reckoned Expense* (Woodbridge, Suffolk, 1996), pp. 193–213. J. H. McDonald, *The Poems and Prose Writings of Robert Southwell, S.J.: A Bibliographical Study* (Roxburghe Club, 1937). S. Lee in *DNB* 53 (1898), pp. 294–9, with refs. to orig. sources. Polgár, 3 (1990), pp. 239–44.

Sozomen (early 5th cent.), Salmaninius Hermias Sozomenus, Church historian. Little is known of his life beyond the facts that he was a native of Bethelia, nr. Gaza in Palestine, that he was educated by monks, and that, after travelling extensively, he settled at *Constantinople as a lawyer. Here he conceived the idea of continuing *Eusebius of Caesarea's 'Church History' down to his own day. His work, in nine Books, covers the period 323 to 425. He drew extensively upon his elder contemporary, *Socrates; his historical grasp was weaker, but he reports certain subjects, e.g. the spread of Christianity among the *Armenians, Saracens, and Goths, much more fully. Also, he had more sense of style than Socrates. Though orthodox in intention, he reveals little understanding of the issues at stake in the dogmatic controversies.

Text ed. R. *Stephanus, H. *Valesius, and W. Reading, as for Socrates (q.v.). W. Reading's edn. repr. in J. P. Migne, *PG* 67. 843–1630. Revision by R. Hussey (3 vols., Oxford, 1860). Modern crit. edn. of Sozomen by J. Bidez and G. C. Hansen (GCS 50; 1960; repr., with Fr. tr. by A.-J. Festugière, OP, and introd. by B. Grillet and G. Sabbah, SC 306, 418, etc., 1983 ff.). G. Schoo, *Die Quellen des Kirchenhistorikers Sozomenos* (1911). P. *Batiffol, 'Sozomène et Sabinos', *BZ* 7 (1898), pp. 265–84. *CPG* 3 (1979), p. 167 (no. 6030). W. Eltester in *PW*, 2te Reihe, 2 (pt. 1; 1927), cols. 1240–8; G. Bardy in *DTC* 14 (pt. 2; 1941), cols. 2469–71; A. Labate in *DPAC* 2 (1984), cols. 3261–3; Eng. tr., *Encyclopedia of the Early Church*, 2 (1992), p. 790, all s.v.

Spain, Christianity in. Tradition ascribes the evangelization of Spain to St *Paul and St *James, but the earliest record of Spanish ecclesiastical organization is a letter of St *Cyprian of 254. The spread of Christianity in the peninsula by the end of the 3rd cent. is attested by Spanish martyrdoms in the *persecution under *Diocletian (many of them commemorated in verse by *Prudentius) and by

the set of disciplinary measures enacted by the Council of *Elvira (*c.*306). In the 4th cent. the Spanish bishops *Hosius of Córdoba and *Gregory of Elvira won distinction as opponents of *Arianism, while *Priscillian (d. 386) and his followers became notorious as adepts of an asceticism bordering on heterodoxy.

In the course of the 5th cent. most of Spain fell under the rule of Arian Visigoths. The conversion of that people to Catholicism, officially proclaimed by King *Recared at the Third Council of *Toledo (589), inaugurated an era of exceptional brilliance in the religious and cultural life of the region; it is illustrated in the writings of such men as *Leander and *Isidore of Seville, *Ildefonsus and *Julian of Toledo. The movement towards reform and order in the Spanish Church is reflected in an important series of national Visigothic councils held at Toledo, in the progressive elaboration of the collection of canon law known as the *Hispana*, and in the emergence of the so-called *Mozarabic rite. Monasticism also flourished and several Spanish Rules date from the Visigothic period.

Early in the 8th cent. the Visigothic kingdom was conquered by the forces of *Islam from N. Africa. In accordance with the precepts of the *Koran, the new Muslim rulers tolerated Christianity, though there were occasional episodes of persecution, e.g. at Córdoba in the mid-9th cent. Christian principalities emerged in N. Spain in the 8th and 9th cents. as nuclei of opposition to Islamic rule. Their slow expansion to the south was seen by later generations as a sustained war of reconquest, but perhaps owed more to opportunism and social factors such as demographic pressure. From the 12th cent. this southward drift was influenced by the spirit of the *Crusades. Most of the Iberian peninsula had come under Christian rule by *c.*1250, though a small Islamic enclave survived in the vassal-state of Granada until its incorporation into Castile in 1492. Franco-Papal influences upon the medieval Spanish Church were pronounced from *c.*1050; they may be seen in the foundation of *Cluniac and *Cistercian monasteries and in the disappearance of some distinctively Spanish uses such as the Mozarabic rite proscribed at the Council of Burgos in 1080. Military orders modelled on the *Templars, incl. those of Calatrava and *Santiago, were founded in the 12th cent. In the 13th cent. three Spaniards made outstanding contributions to the Christian life of Europe: St *Dominic, St *Raymond of Peñafort, and Ramon *Llull (qq.v.).

In the *Great Schism Castile and Aragon played a leading part on the side of the antipopes until shortly before the Council of *Constance (1415). Yet the Middle Ages were also marked by the expansion of the eremitical orders, such as the *Carthusians and esp. the Jeronimites (founded in 1373). The *mendicants also, notably the *Dominicans and *Franciscans, experienced a growing popularity. Both these orders saw a movement towards reform which brought about the birth of branches of '*Observants'; though this led to rivalry it also meant that the Franciscans, with the Observant Abp. of Toledo, Card. F. *Ximénez de Cisneros at their head, were in a good position to take advantage of the opportunities offered in the mission field with the discovery of America. The Spanish *Inquisition, which, in answer to popular hostility towards Jews and converted Muslims, was established by *Ferdinand and *Isabella in 1480 in Andalusia (with some reluctance on the Papal side), was gradually to spread to the rest of Castile, though not to Aragon until the 16th cent.

In 1492, after the union of the Crowns of Aragon and Castile and the expulsion of all professed Jews, the title of '*Catholic Majesty' was conferred by Pope *Alexander VI upon the King of Spain. Considerable reforms of the religious orders took place during the reigns of Ferdinand and Isabella. Under the Emp. *Charles V, who was King of Spain from 1516 to 1556, the power of the country reached its height. Not only was its influence in Europe unparalleled, but it had won an Empire in the New World equalled only by *Portugal (over which the Spanish King ruled from 1580 to 1640). The adhesion of Spain to the Papacy in the conflicts of the 16th cent. thus became a political factor of the first importance. Charles V, as *Holy Roman Emperor, was involved in the conflicts produced by the *Reformation in Germany, while his son *Philip II (1556–98) was faced with the revolt of the Spanish *Netherlands. Groups of *Alumbrados and *Protestants within Spain were suppressed, but undercurrents of heterodoxy remained, and the Inquisition was very active. This was a period of greater vigour and variety in Spanish religious life than has commonly been supposed. Sharp differences existed between the theological traditions of some religious orders. The influence of Spanish bishops at the Council of *Trent did much to shape the *Counter-Reformation. It was also an age of unparalleled mystics and spiritual writers (St *Teresa of Ávila, St *John of the Cross, Luis de *León, and *Luis of Granada), who nevertheless faced ecclesiastical suspicion and hostility in their own day.

Philip V, the Bourbon king named as the successor of the childless Charles II in 1700, strove to enforce the authority of the Crown over the Church. The position of the Church in Spain, as the one serious threat to royal absolutism, was uneasy, and relations between the Spanish Court and the Papacy, broken off during the War of Spanish Succession (1701–15), were not healed until the 1753 Concordat between the Holy See and Ferdinand VI. The *Jesuits, who were one focus of resistance to the extension of royal authority, were expelled in 1767; a second, the Inquisition, was to survive until 1808. Political and religious liberalism appeared again under French influence; hostility between liberalism and the Church continued through the 19th cent., a period of unrest, conflict and alternating extremes in which the Church was firmly allied to the conservative side. Thus the ecclesiastical censorship of the reactionary Ferdinand VII in the 1820s was followed by the expropriation of Church assets during the regime of the radical Juan Alvarez Mendizabal in the 1830s. *Anticlericalism, expressed in the 'monk murders' of 1835, together with the dissolution of many convents and monasteries and the widespread destruction of churches, helped polarize attitudes. Meanwhile, the early 19th-cent. 'Neo-Catholic Revival', partly inspired by F. R. de *Chateaubriand, produced the RC apologists Juan Donoso Cortes (1809–53) and Jaime Luciano Balmès (1810–48), and was influential in Spanish intellectual life well into the middle of the 19th cent.

The overthrow of Ferdinand VII's daughter, Isabel II, in 1868 was followed in 1869 by the proclamation of freedom of conscience by a secularizing parliament. The position of the Church was under threat until the monarchy was restored in the person of Isabel's son, Alfonso, in 1874. The moderate constitution agreed in 1876 was to remain the framework of Spanish politics for nearly 50 years. This again recognized Catholicism as the State religion, subsidized clergy stipends and the upkeep of RC churches, and strictly limited the activities of other religious bodies. Under this settlement there was a noteworthy Catholic revival, including the spectacular growth of the religious *congregations of men and esp. women, and their network of schools, clinics, hospitals, and orphanages. The revival, however, was more a bourgeois than a popular phenomenon, and it had little effect in the poor rural south or in the new industrial areas of the cities. Nor did it prevent many Spanish intellectuals from embracing *deism or *agnosticism, and resenting Church tutelage.

When the monarchy fell in 1931, the Second Republic committed itself to the laicizing agenda of the anticlerical intellectuals as well as to the radical social measures expected of it by the working masses. It separated Church and State, ended State subsidies, dissolved the Jesuits, and attempted to close the schools run by the religious orders. It also introduced civil marriage and *divorce and secularized cemeteries. Defence of the Church became identified with hostility both to the laicizing initiatives of the Republic and to its social reforms. Consequently, when a group of generals took up arms against the Republic in July 1936, most bishops and conservative Catholic politicians greeted the attempted coup with relief. This was intensified when in many Republican areas anticlerical violence on a scale unprecedented in modern W. Europe resulted in the killing of almost 7,000 priests and religious and the destruction of hundreds of churches and other ecclesiastical buildings. In Republican Spain, except in the Basque country, RCism was driven underground, while the insurgent generals assumed the role and rhetoric of a crusade to save the Church.

General Franco's victory in 1939 gave the Church a powerful position. The Republic's laicizing changes were swept away and the old closeness of Church and State re-established. Moreover the Church's main opponents— socialists, anarchists, communists, and free-thinking intellectuals—had been killed, imprisoned, or driven into exile. Until the 1960s the alliance of Church and State was unchallenged. In that decade, however, criticism of the dictatorship began to mount within the ranks of the clergy and was encouraged by the adoption of the language of civil rights and social justice by Pope *John XXIII and the Second *Vatican Council. By the time of Franco's death in 1975, the Church had distanced itself far enough from the dictatorship, and established good enough democratic credentials, to find a secure place relatively easily in the new democratic order which gradually emerged and which was finally enshrined in the 1978 Constitution. Spain now has no State religion, respects freedom of conscience, and has reintroduced civil marriage and divorce. Protestantism in any form, numerically of little importance in Spain, no longer involves any legal disabilities.

H. Florez, cont. by M. Risco, A. Merino, J. de la Canal, S. de Barnanda, V. de la Fuente, and C. R. Fort, *España sagrada: Theatro geográphico-histórico de la Iglesia de España* (56 vols., 1747–1961; index by A. González Palencia, 1918; 2nd edn., 1946). P. B. *Gams, *Die Kirchengeschichte von Spanien* (3 vols., 1862–

79); R. García-Villoslada (ed.), *Historia de la Iglesia en España* (Biblioteca de Autores Cristianos, Maior, 16–22; 1979–82). S. G. Payne, *Spanish Catholicism: An Historical Overview* (Madison, Wis., 1984). Z. García Villada, SJ, *Historia eclesiástica de España* [to 1085] (3 vols. bound in 5, 1920–36). R. [J. H.] Collins, *Early Medieval Spain: Unity in Diversity, 400–1000* (1983). E. A. Thompson, 'The Conversion of the Spanish Suevi to Catholicism', in E. James (ed.), *Visigothic Spain: New Approaches* (Oxford, 1980), pp. 77–92. J. Orlandis and D. Ramos-Lissón, *Die Synoden auf der Iberischen Halbinsel bis zum Einbruch des Islam (711)* (Paderborn, 1981). K. B. Wolf, *Christian Martyrs in Muslim Spain* (Cambridge, 1988). M. Defourneaux, *Les Français en Espagne aux XIe et XIIe siècles* (1949). P. Linehan, *The Spanish Church and the Papacy in the Thirteenth Century* (Cambridge Studies in Medieval Life and Thought, 3rd ser. 4; 1971). J. Vincke, *Staat und Kirche in Katalonien und Aragon während des Mittelalters*, 1 (1931). Id., 'Kirche und Staat in Spanien während des Spätmittelalters', *RQ* 43 (1935), pp. 35–53. J. García Oró, OFM, *Cisneros y la Reforma del Clero Español en tiempo de los Reyes Catolicos* (1971). J. M. Revuelta Somalo, 'Renovación de la vida espiritual', in *Historia General de España y América*, 5 (1981), pp. 189–270. M. Bataillon, *Érasme et l'Espagne: Recherches sur l'histoire spirituelle du XVIe siècle* (Bibliothèque de l'École des hautes études hispaniques, 21; 1937; 2nd edn. by D. Devoto and C. Amiel, Travaux d'Humanisme et Renaissance, 250; 3 vols., Geneva, 1991). M. Andrés, *La teología española en el siglo XVI* (Biblioteca de Autores Cristianos, Maior, 13–14; 1976–7). W. A. Christian, Jun., *Local Religion in Sixteenth-Century Spain* (Princeton, NJ, 1981). R. Herr, *The Eighteenth-century Revolution in Spain* (ibid., 1958), esp. pp. 11–36 and 400–33. W. J. Callahan, *Church, Politics, and Society in Spain, 1750–1874* (Harvard Historical Monograph, 73; 1984); F. Lannon, *Privilege, Persecution, and Prophecy: The Catholic Church in Spain 1875–1975* (Oxford, 1987). J. Iribarren (ed.), *Documentos colectivos del Episcopado español 1870–1974* (Biblioteca de Autores Cristianos, 1974). J. C. Ullman, *The Tragic Week: A Study of Anticlericalism in Spain, 1875–1912* (Cambridge, Mass., 1968). C. A. García and K. G. Grubb, *Religion in the Republic of Spain* (1933; evangelical survey). J. Delpech, *The Oppression of Protestants in Spain* (Eng. tr. by T. and D. Johnson, Boston, 1955; London, 1956). C. J. Bartlett, 'The Question of Religious Toleration in Spain in the Nineteenth Century', *JEH* 8 (1957), pp. 205–16. A. Ferreiro, *The Visigoths in Gaul and Spain A.D. 418–711: A Bibliography* (Leiden, 1988), esp. pp. 171–413. A. G. Kinder, *Spanish Protestants and Reformers in the Sixteenth Century: A Bibliography* (1983). Q. Aldea Vaquero and others (eds.), *Diccionario de historia eclesiástica de España* (4 vols. + suppl., 1972–87). C. Baraut, OSB, and others in *Dict. Sp.*, 4 (1960), cols. 1089–192, s.v. 'Espagne'; J. Fernández Alonso in *DHGE* 15 (1963), cols. 892–944, s.v. 'Espagne'.

Spalatin, Georg (1484–1545), German humanist and reformer. Georg Burkhardt was born at Spalt (hence his name) near Nürnberg, studied at Erfurt and *Wittenberg, and from 1505 to 1507 taught at the monastery of Georgenthal. In 1508 he was ordained priest and in 1509 was appointed tutor to the sons of the Prince Elector, *Frederick the Wise of Saxony. He soon won the Elector's confidence and became his secretary and librarian. In 1511 he was sent back to Wittenberg, where he became acquainted with M. *Luther, under whose guidance he began to study the Bible. His scholarship came to be much valued at the Saxon court, and it was mainly through Spalatin's influence that the hesitating Elector was gained to the ideas of the Reformer. In 1518 he accompanied Frederick to the Diet of *Augsburg, and in 1521 to *Worms. In 1525 he married and went to Altenburg, where he carried through the change from Catholicism to Lutheranism. Under Frederick's successor, John (1525–32), he continued to

foster the Reformation, being chiefly engaged in the visitation of schools and churches. His later years were darkened by melancholy. Besides translations of writings of Luther, P. *Melanchthon, and *Erasmus, he compiled *Annales Reformationis* (ed. 1718) and *Chronicon et Annales* [1463–1525]. He also conducted an extensive correspondence with Luther, whose confidant he was, but only Luther's replies survive.

An edn. of his *Historischer Nachlass und Briefe* was undertaken by C. Neudecker and L. Preller (vol. 1 only, the Life of Frederick the Wise, pub. Jena, 1851). I. Höss, *Georg Spalatin, 1484–1545* (Weimar, 1956; repr., with new introd. and other revisions, 1989). H. Volz, 'Bibliographie der im 16. Jahrhundert erschienenen Schriften Georg Spalatins', *Zeitschrift für Bibliothekswesen und Bibliographie*, 5 (1958), pp. 83–119. F. Müller in *Allgemeine deutsche Biographie*, 35 (1893), pp. 1–29; I. Höss in *Contemporaries of Erasmus*, ed. P. G. Bietenholz and T. B. Deutscher, 3 (1987), pp. 266–8, both s.v. Further bibl. in Schottenloher, 2 (1935), pp. 284–6 (nos. 20266–96), and 7 (1966), p. 217 (nos. 58271–82).

Spalatrensis. See DE DOMINIS, MARCO ANTONIO.

Spanish Armada. See ARMADA, SPANISH.

Sparrow, Anthony (1612–85), Bp. of *Norwich. He was a Fellow of Queens' College, Cambridge, from 1633 till his expulsion by the *Puritans in 1644. For a sermon preached on confession and absolution in 1637, he was brought into the Vice-Chancellor's court, but successfully defended by W. *Juxon, Bp. of London. At the Restoration he became Archdeacon of Sudbury. In 1662 he was appointed President of his college, in 1667 was made Bp. of *Exeter, and in 1676 translated to Norwich. He was a keen High Churchman throughout his life, best known through his *Rationale upon the Book of Common Prayer* (1655; many times reprinted), the object of which was to show that the C of E service was neither 'old superstitious Roman dotage' nor 'schismatically new'.

Rationale, with some of his minor works, ed. by S. Downes (London, 1722), and repr. by J. H. *N[ewman] (Oxford, 1839), with preface, pp. i–iv; extracts in P. E. More and F. L. Cross (eds.), *Anglicanism* (1935), nos. 220 and 234, pp. 501 f. and 521 f. W. P. Courtney in *DNB* 53 (1898), pp. 313 f., s.v.

SPCK. The 'Society for Promoting Christian Knowledge'. It was founded by T. *Bray and four laymen in 1698 'to promote and encourage the erection of charity schools in all parts of England and Wales; to disperse, both at home and abroad, Bibles and tracts of religion; and in general to advance the honour of God and the good of mankind, by promoting Christian knowledge both at home and in the other parts of the world by the best methods that should offer'. Much of its original educational and missionary work was in due course taken over by the *National Society and the *SPG. The Society now operates in three divisions: SPCK Worldwide, which by funding helps to make books available in countries overseas; publishing (the SPCK is the third oldest publisher in Great Britain), and bookselling, with its own bookshops in Britain. History, ethos, and constitution link the SPCK closely with the C of E, but it is a voluntary society serving a wide Christian constituency.

W. O. B. Allen and E. McClure, *Two Hundred Years: The History of the Society for Promoting Christian Knowledge, 1698–1898*

(1898); W. K. Lowther Clarke, *A History of the S.P.C.K.* (1959). E. McClure (ed.), *A Chapter in English Church History: Being the Minutes of the Society for Promoting Christian Knowledge for the Years 1698–1704, together with Abstracts of Correspondents' Letters during Part of the same Period* (1888). M. Clement, *The S.P.C.K. and Wales, 1699–1740: The History of the S.P.C.K. in Wales from its Foundation to the Early Years of the Welsh Methodist Movement* (CHS, 1954), with bibl. C. Rose, 'The origins and ideals of the SPCK 1699–1716', in J. Walsh and others (eds.), *The Church of England c.1689–c.1833* (Cambridge, 1993), pp. 172–90.

Speaker's Commentary, the. A Commentary on the whole Bible, edited by F. C. Cook (1810–89), at the instance of J. E. Denison (1800–73), who was Speaker of the House of Commons from 1857 to 1872. It was published in 10 vols. between 1871 and 1881. Its object was the defence of a conservative attitude to Scripture, to combat the liberalism of *Essays and Reviews* (1860) and similar writings. Cook was assisted by many eminent scholars and theologians, but his work suffered from the somewhat narrow purpose for which it was conceived.

species. A Latin word meaning 'form' or 'kind', employed in scholastic theology to designate the material elements used in the sacraments, esp. the bread and wine in the *Eucharist, and in that sense taken over into theological English.

Speier, Diets of. See SPEYER, DIETS OF.

Spencer, Herbert (1820–1903), philosophical and scientific thinker. The son of a schoolmaster, he was practically self-taught. From 1837 to 1846 he was a civil engineer on the railway. Two years later he became connected with the *Economist* and afterwards with the *Westminster Review*. His two earliest writings were *Social Statics* (1851) and *Principles of Psychology* (1855). In 1860 he announced a systematic series of philosophical treatises; they included *First Principles* (1862), *Principles of Biology* (1867), *Principles of Psychology* (1872), and *Principles of Sociology* (1877). From 1886 to 1891 Spencer's health prevented his writing, but in 1893 he completed *Principles of Ethics*.

Spencer was the chief exponent of *agnosticism in 19th-cent. England. He divided all reality into the knowable (the province of science) and the unknowable (that of religion). He asserted that man could not only be conscious of the unknowable, but that knowledge itself was finally dependent upon the unknowable, and that the Absolute is the fundamental reality behind all things. Nevertheless the Absolute could not be known in the strict sense of the word. Spencer also affirmed his belief in progress as a supreme law of the universe. All his writings were characterized by an extreme individualism.

Autobiography (2 vols., 1904; posthumous). D. Duncan, *The Life and Letters of Herbert Spencer* (1908, with full bibl.). F. H. Collins, *An Epitome of* The Synthetic Philosophy (1889; suppl., 1894; Pref. by H. Spencer). Other studies incl. those by H. Macpherson (London, 1900) and J. Royce (New York and London, 1904). W. H. Hudson, *An Introduction to the Philosophy of Herbert Spencer* (New York, 1894; London, 1895; rev. edn., 1904); H. *Sidgwick, *Lectures on the Ethics of T. H. Green, Mr. Herbert Spencer, and J. Martineau* (1902), pp. 135–312. J. Rumney, *Herbert Spencer's Sociology* (1934); J. D. Y. Peel, *Herbert Spencer: The Evolution of a Sociologist* (1971); D. Wiltshire, *The Social and Political Thought of Herbert Spencer* (Oxford, 1978).

M. W. Taylor, *Men versus the State: Herbert Spencer and Late Victorian Individualism* (ibid., 1992). M. Thiel, *Methode VII*, pt. 3: H. Spencer (Heidelberg, 1983). H. S. R. Elliot in *DNB, 1901–1911*, 3, pp. 360–9.

Spencer, John (1630–93), English Hebraist. He was a native of Bocton, Kent. In 1645 he became a scholar of Corpus Christi, Cambridge, of which he was elected a Fellow c.1655 and Master in 1667. In 1677 he became Dean of *Ely. After publishing a treatise on the *Urim and Thummim (1669), which he believed to be of Egyptian origin, he devoted himself chiefly to Hebrew studies. The result was his principal work, *De Legibus Hebraeorum Ritualibus et earum Rationibus, libri tres* (1685). Though, owing to the state of contemporary oriental studies, he had to rely almost entirely on second-hand information furnished mainly by the Bible, the classical authors, and the Fathers, he can claim to be the founder of the study of *comparative religion. He endeavoured to trace the connections between the religious rites of the Hebrews and those of other Semitic peoples, and his work remains a permanent contribution to the subject. His new departure in OT scholarship caused his orthodoxy to be suspected, and his opinions, being too far in advance of his time, were severely criticized and exercised no immediate influence. His work, however, was taken up in the 19th cent. by such scholars as J. *Wellhausen and W. Robertson *Smith.

His Works were reissued at Cambridge (rev. by L. Chappelow), 2 vols., 1727. H. Reventlow, *Bibelautorität und Geist der Moderne* (Forschungen zur Kirchen- und Dogmengeschichte, 30; 1980), pp. 475–7; Eng. tr., *The Authority of the Bible and the Rise of the Modern World* (1984), pp. 291 f. T. Cooper in *DNB* 53 (1898), pp. 359 f.

Spener, Philipp Jakob (1635–1705), early leader of German *Pietism. Born of devout Protestant parents at Rappoltsweiler in Alsace, he studied history and philosophy at Strasbourg (1651–3). Influenced by J. *Arndt's *Vier Bücher von wahren Christentum*, by the works of English *Puritan authors, and, on a visit to Geneva, by J. de Labadie (see LABADISTS), he became increasingly aware of a call to revivify the *Lutheran Church with evangelical fervour. At Frankfurt, where he was appointed minister in 1666, he introduced 'Collegia Pietatis', devotional meetings which gathered twice weekly in his house, and also issued his *Pia Desideria* (1675, q.v.). While he remained essentially loyal to the Lutheran tradition, the personal and interior turn of his religion made him critical of a sterile and polemical form of orthodoxy. At the same time he tried to give the laity an active part in Church life. In 1686 he accepted an invitation to Dresden as court preacher. Here in Saxony he gained the warm support of A. H. *Francke (q.v.) and P. Anton, who instituted their 'Collegia Philobiblica'; but he came into conflict with the theological faculty at Leipzig. In 1691 he migrated to Berlin, where he was appointed Rector of the Nikolaikirche, finding an influential ally in the Elector of Brandenburg (King Frederick I of Prussia from 1701). His movement, by this time known as 'Pietism', made rapid progress, and in 1694 the University of Halle was founded, largely under his influence. Though he met with ever increasing opposition from Lutheran orthodoxy, the movement won many ardent supporters. In 1695 J. Deutschmann's *Christus-

lutherische Vorstellung, composed for the theological faculty at *Wittenberg, charged Spener with 283 heads of heretical teaching. In 1698 Spener withdrew from the struggle and devoted his last years mainly to pastoral work. He was a prolific writer, whose theology was marked by a biblical, anti-*scholastic orientation, by a strong emphasis on the notion of new birth, and by a moderate *millenarianism ('Hoffnung besserer Zeiten'). His enthusiasm for the reform of the Lutheran Church, from which he never wanted to dissociate himself, and his insistence on the inner religious life of the individual had a deep and mainly beneficent influence on German Protestantism.

Briefe aus der Frankfurter Zeit 1666–1686, ed. J. Wallmann and others (Tübingen, 1992 ff.). Facsimile repr. of *Schriften*, ed. E. Beyreuther (Hildesheim and New York, 1979 ff.). Life by P. Grünberg (3 vols., Göttingen, 1893–1906). J. Wallmann, *Philipp Jakob Spener und die Anfänge des Pietismus* (Beiträge zur historischen Theologie, 42; 1970). Other studies by K. Aland (Arbeiten zur Kirchengeschichte, 28; 1943), D. Blaufuss (Europäische Hochschulschriften, Reihe 23, Bd. 46; 1975), and K. J. Stein (Chicago [1986]). K. Aland, *Kirchengeschichtliche Entwürfe* (Gütersloh, 1960), pp. 523–42, 'Philipp Jakob Spener. Sein Lebensweg von Frankfurt nach Berlin (1666–1705) dargestellt an Hand seiner Briefe nach Frankfurt'. J. Wallmann in M. Greschat (ed.), *Orthodoxie und Pietismus* (Gestalten der Kirchengeschichte, 7; Stuttgart, 1982), pp. 205–23, with bibl. P. Grünberg in *PRE* (3rd edn.), 18 (1906), pp. 609–22; R. Pietsch in *Dict. Sp.* 14 (1990), cols. 1121–4, s.v.

Speyer (Spires), Diets of (1526 and 1529). (1) The Diet of June 1526 marked a new stage in the consolidation of reforming influences in Germany. Instructions sent by *Charles V from Spain in the previous March forbidding all innovations and requiring the enforcement of the Edict of *Worms (1521) were set aside on the ground of his war with the Papacy which had broken out in the interval. The Diet determined that each Prince should order ecclesiastical affairs in his state in acc. with his own conscience.

(2) By the end of 1528 a Catholic reaction had set in, provoked by *Philip of Hesse's repressive measures and his invocation of foreign (French and Hungarian) aid. In response to an appeal from the Pope, Charles V issued a mandate on 30 Nov. 1528 summoning the Diet to Speyer on 21 Feb. 1529. The proceedings were controlled by a strong and well-organized Catholic majority who passed legislation to end all toleration of *Lutherans in Catholic districts. On 19 April five Princes and 14 cities made a formal 'protest' addressed to the Archduke Ferdinand, defending freedom of conscience and the right of minorities. Henceforward the Reformers were known as 'Protestants'.

(1) W. Friedensburg, *Der Reichstag zu Speier 1526 im Zusammenhang der politischen und kirchlichen Entwicklung Deutschlands im Reformationszeitalter* (Historische Untersuchungen herausgegeben J. Jastrow, 5; 1887; repr., Nieuwkoop, 1970). J. Ney, *Der Reichstag zu Speier 1526* (Sammlung gemeinverständlicher wissenschaftlicher Vorträge, 75; 1889). R. Wohlfeil, 'Der Speyrer Reichstag von 1526', *Blätter für pfälzische Kirchengeschichte*, 43 (1976), pp. 5–20. T. J. Ney in *PRE* (3rd edn.), 18 (1906), pp. 589–94, s.v. 'Speier, Reichstage in, 1'. Further bibl. in Schottenloher, 3 (1936), pp. 15 f. (nos. 27960b–74).

(2) J. Ney, 'Geschichte des Reichstages zu Speier im Jahre 1529', *Mittheilungen des historischen Vereins der Pfalz*, 8 (1879), pp. 1–368; also issued separately, Halle, 1880, with primary docs., pp. 291–362. Some of these docs. tr. into Eng. in Kidd, pp. 239–45

(no. 32). The formal 'protest' ed. J. Ney (Quellenschriften zur Geschichte Protestantismus, 5; 1906; repr., Darmstadt, 1967). J. Kühn, *Die Geschichte des Speyer Reichstags 1529* (Schriften des Vereins für Reformationsgeschichte, 47, Heft 1; 1929). E. Mayer, *Der Speierer Reichstag 1529* (Speyer, 1929). M. Brecht, 'Die gemeinsame Politik der Reichsstädte und die Reformation', *Zeitschrift der Savigny-Stiftung für Rechtsgeschichte*, Kanonistische Abteilung, 63 (1977), pp. 180–263, esp. pp. 233–50. T. J. Ney in *PRE*, loc. cit., pp. 594–603, s.v. 'Speier, Reichstage in, 2'. Further bibl. in Schottenloher, 3 (1936), pp. 16–18 (nos. 27975–8010).

SPG The 'Society for the Propagation of the Gospel in foreign parts'. This Anglican society was formed in 1701 by Thomas *Bray and his associates to assist in the missionary work initiated by the *SPCK. Authorized by Convocation, and incorporated by Royal Charter, it had two main objects: (1) to provide the ministrations of the Church for British people overseas; and (2) to evangelize the non-Christian races subject to the Crown. In the 18th cent. its work was carried out mostly in the American colonies, *Canada, and the *West Indies. Its sphere of activity increased in the 19th cent., esp. in *India, *South and *West Africa, *Australia, and the Far East. In most of the areas where the SPG worked the Churches are now independent provinces and their bishops and clergy are largely nationals, but some financial assistance and some of the staffing, especially in Africa, still comes from Britain.

In 1965 the SPG joined with the *UMCA to form the United Society for the Propagation of the Gospel (*USPG).

C. F. Pascoe, *Two Hundred Years of the S.P.G. . . . 1701–1900: Based on a Digest of the Society's Records* (1901). H. P. Thompson, *Into All Lands: A History of the Society for the Propagation of the Gospel in Foreign Parts, 1701–1950* (1951). M. Dewey, *The Messengers: A Concise History of the United Society for the Propagation of the Gospel* (1975).

Spinckes, Nathaniel (1653–1727), *Nonjuror. The son of a Northamptonshire rector, he was educated locally and at Trinity and Jesus Colleges, Cambridge. Ordained priest in 1678, he became chaplain to the first Duke of Lauderdale (d. 1682), curate and lecturer at St Stephen's, Walbrook (1682–5), rector of Peakirk-cum-Glinton (now Cambs) and in 1687 a prebendary and rector of St Martin's, *Salisbury. On his refusal to take the oath of allegiance to William and Mary he was deprived in 1690. In 1713 he was consecrated Bishop by G. *Hickes, assisted by two Scottish bishops, but he took no title. In the dispute about the *Usages, he advocated the retention of the BCP as it then was rather than a return to the First Book of *Edward VI. A man of considerable learning, proficient in Greek, Latin, Anglo-Saxon, and French, with some knowledge of oriental languages, he was much revered for his personal sanctity. He wrote five treatises on the Roman controversy, one against the French prophets, one against B. *Hoadly, and several against the Usagers, but he is esp. remembered for his sermons and devotional works, which include *A Sick Man Visited* (1712) and a collection of prayers and meditations from L. *Andrewes, W. *Laud, T. *Ken, and others entitled '*The True Church of England Man's Companion to the Closet* with a preface by N. Spinckes' (1721), commonly known as 'Spinckes's Devotions'. He was a close friend of G. Hickes, R. *Nelson, and J. *Kettlewell.

J. Blackbourne, *The Life of the R. Reverend Mr. Nathanael Spinckes* (1731). J. H. Overton, *The Nonjurors* (1902), pp. 129–33 and 384 f.; id. in *DNB* 53 (1898), pp. 405 f.

Spinoza, Benedictus de (also **Baruch**) (1632–77), Dutch Jewish philosopher. He was born in Amsterdam of Portuguese parents. From an early age he was probably familiar with the works of G. *Bruno, *Maimonides, R. *Descartes, T. *Hobbes, and others who fostered in him religious unorthodoxy, and in 1656 he was expelled by the Synagogue and compelled to leave Amsterdam. He went to Rijnsburg and several other places, and last to The Hague (1670), earning his living by grinding lenses. During his lifetime only a treatise on Descartes (1663) and the *Tractatus Theologico-politicus* (1670) were published. His principal work, the *Ethica ordine geometrico demonstrata*, appeared posthumously (Amsterdam, 1677). It is in five parts: on 'God'; 'the nature and origin of the mind'; 'the origin and nature of the emotions'; 'human bondage, or the powers of the emotions'; and 'the power of the intellect, or human freedom'. Spinoza also wrote a *Tractatus Politicus* and a *Tractatus de Intellectus Emendatione* (both first pub. with the *Ethica*, 1677). Several of his letters have also survived.

Spinoza is commonly described as a *pantheist, since there is a sense in which he regards all things as part of God. The foundation of his system is his idea of God as a single all-embracing substance which is *causa sui* (contains within itself the reason for its existence) and which may be thought of either as creator (*natura naturans*) or as creation (*natura naturata*). This substance is infinite, with an infinite number of attributes of which, however, only two, thought (*cogitatio*) and extension (*extensio*), are known to man. All individual things are modes of these two attributes, being either bodies or ideas, between which there is a perfect parallelism. The human mind is part of the Divine impersonal intellect which works acc. to necessity. Thus Spinoza denies 'absolute' or contra-causal free will, the permanence of personality, and immortality. The highest human activity is the loving contemplation of God (*amor Dei intellectualis*) which becomes possible in so far as one can master the passions and live in accordance with reason. In his political writings, Spinoza champions tolerance, rationality, and a purely scientific or 'naturalistic' approach to political theory. His studies on the Bible, carried on from the same point of view, have made him one of the fathers of the modern historical criticism of the Bible. Spinoza's influence on European philosophy was at its height in the 19th cent., esp. in Germany, where F. D. E. *Schleiermacher, F. W. J. *Schelling, G. W. F. *Hegel, and others owed much to his teaching.

Modern edn. of his works by C. Gebhardt (4 vols., Heidelberg [1924–6]). The best Eng. tr. of his works is that of E. Curley (Princeton, NJ, 1985 ff.). Separate Eng. trs. of the *Ethics* and other works by R. H. M. Elwes (Bohn's Philological Library, 1883); of *Ethics* also by S. Shirley (Indianapolis, 1982); of his *Political Works* (*Tractatus Theologico-politicus* in part and *Tractatus Politicus* in full) by A. G. Wernham (Oxford, 1958). Correspondence tr. and ed. A. Wolf (London, 1928). Earliest Life, usually attributed to J. M. Lucas, and prob. written between 1677 and 1678 (orig. pr. at Amsterdam, 1719), also ed., with Eng. tr., by A. Wolf (London, 1927). Studies in Eng. by F. Pollock (London, 1880), J. *Caird (Blackwood's Philosophical Classics, 1888), R. MacKeon (New York, 1928), L. Roth (Leaders of Philosophy, London, 1929),

H. A. Wolfson (2 vols., Cambridge, Mass., 1934), S. Hampshire (Pelican Books, 1951), R. J. Delahunty (London, 1985), and others. L. Brunschvicg, *Spinoza* (Paris, 1894; 4th edn., extended, with title *Spinoza et ses contemporains*, 1951). H. H. Joachim, *A Study of the Ethics of Spinoza* (1901); id., *Spinoza's Tractatus de Intellectus Emendatione: A Commentary* (1940; posthumous). H. F. Hallett, *Aeternitas: A Spinozistic Study* (1930); id., *Benedict de Spinoza: The Elements of his Philosophy* (1957); id., *Creation, Emanation and Salvation: A Spinozistic Study* (The Hague, 1962). L. Strauss, *Die Religionskritik Spinozas als Grundlage seiner Bibelwissenschaft: Untersuchungen zu Spinozas Theologisch-Politischem Traktat* (1930; rev. Eng. tr., New York [1965]). P. Siwek, SJ, *Spinoza et le panthéisme religieux* (1937; 2nd edn., 1950). G. H. R. Parkinson, *Spinoza's Theory of Knowledge* (Oxford, 1954). E. M. Curley, *Spinoza's Metaphysics* (Cambridge, Mass., 1969). N. Altwicker (ed.), *Texte zur Geschichte des Spinozismus* (1971), with bibl. S. P. Kashap (ed.), *Studies in Spinoza* (Berkeley, Calif., and London, 1972). J. [F.] Bennett, *A Study of Spinoza's Ethics* (Cambridge, 1984). Y. Yovel, *Spinoza and Other Heretics* (2 vols., Princeton, NJ [1989]). E. Giancotti (ed.), *Spinoza nel 350° Anniversario della Nascita: Atti del Congresso (Urbino 4–8 ottobre, 1982)* (Saggi Bibliopolis, 19; Naples [1985]; E. Curley and P.-F. Moreau (eds.), *Spinoza Issues and Directions: The Proceedings of the Chicago Spinoza Conference* (Brill's Studies in Intellectual History, 14; Leiden, etc., 1990). W. I. Boucher, *Spinoza in English: A Bibliography from the Seventeenth Century to the Present* (ibid. 28; 1991). G. Rabeau in *DTC* 14 (pt. 2; 1941), cols. 2489–506, s.v., with extensive bibl. There is a 'Societas Spinozana' at The Hague which issues a *Chronicon Spinozanum* (The Hague, 1921 ff.).

Spires, Diets of. See SPEYER, DIETS OF.

Spiridion, St. See SPYRIDON, ST.

Spirit. In Christian theology the word denotes: (1) The intelligent and immaterial part of man or the human *soul in general, whether united with the body in life or separated from it in death, and esp. that aspect of it which is concerned with religious truth and action and is directly susceptible to Divine influence. (2) An order of being which is superhuman in the sense that it is not subject to the limits of time, space, and a bodily frame. In this sense God Himself is said in Scripture to be spirit (in contrast with 'flesh', i.e. humanity). (3) One of the creatures belonging to this order, whether good or evil, i.e. angels or demons. In accord with popular beliefs of the time, certain forms of disease, esp. lunacy and epilepsy, were attributed in the early Christian centuries to the presence of evil or 'unclean' spirits in the human body (see EXORCISM). (4) The Third Person of the *Trinity (see HOLY SPIRIT).

Spirit, Brethren of the Free. See BRETHREN OF THE FREE SPIRIT.

Spiritism. See SPIRITUALISM.

Spiritual Exercises, The. The famous treatise of St *Ignatius Loyola, originating from his spiritual experiences at Manresa in 1522–3, and substantially completed by 1541. The book is a manual for those giving *retreats. It provides for a structured, individually guided programme of mainly imaginative prayer lasting, in its full form, for about a month. The first week is devoted to reflection on sin and its consequences. The second focuses on the life of Christ, beginning with consideration of the kingdom and centring on the 'Two Standards' (Christ's and Satan's—standard being understood in a military sense). The third week concentrates on the Passion, and the fourth on the Resurrection. Reflection on what is experienced—normally with the help of the director of the retreat—is crucial to the process, and may lead to decisions regarding one's way of life. Ignatius requires the director always to be sensitive, adapting the instructions to the circumstances of individuals. Themes from the *Exercises* have often been taken up in retreats of shorter duration, both within and outside the RC Church. The *Exercises* may also be followed in daily life by devoting to them about an hour a day over a lengthy period.

Crit. edn., with introd., notes, and bibl., by J. Calveras, SJ, and C. de Dalmases, SJ (Monumenta Historica Societatis Jesu, 100; Rome, 1969). Eng. trs. by E. Mullan, SJ (New York, 1914), W. H. Longridge, SSJE (London, 1919), and a modernized adaptation by D. L. Fleming, SJ, *A Contemporary Reading of the Spiritual Exercises* (St Louis, 1976; rev. text pr. in parallel with the more literal tr. of E. Mullan, ibid., 1978). Other edns. and trs. listed in Sommervogel, 5 (1894), cols. 59–75; L. Polgár, SJ, *Bibliographie sur l'histoire de la Compagnie de Jésus 1901–1980*, I (Rome, 1981), pp. 269–77; and M. Ruiz Jurado, SJ, *Orientaciones bibliográficas sobre San Ignacio de Loyola*, 3 (Subsidia ad Historiam S.I., 10; Rome, 1990), pp. 30–33. Comm. by S. Arzubialde (Bilbao and Santander, 1991). I. Iparraguirre, SJ, *Historia de la práctica de los ejercicios espirituales de san Ignacio de Loyola* (Bibliotheca Instituti Historici S.I., 3, 7, and 36; Rome, 1946–73). D. L. Fleming, SJ (ed.), *Notes on the Spiritual Exercises of St Ignatius of Loyola* (St Louis, 1981); P. Sheldrake, SJ (ed.), *The Way of Ignatius Loyola: Contemporary Approaches to* The Spiritual Exercises (1991). M. Schneider [SJ], '*Unterscheidung der Geister': Die ignatianischen Exerzitien in der Deutung von E. Pryzwara, K. Rahner und G. Fessard* (Innsbrucker theologische Studien, 11; 1983). Further bibl. in L. Polgár, op. cit., pp. 265–8 and 277–373, and M. Ruiz Jurado, op. cit., pp. 33–100. See also bibl. to IGNATIUS LOYOLA, ST.

Spiritual Franciscans. Before St *Francis's death two groups of Franciscans could be distinguished: (1) those led by *Elias of Cortona who wished to mitigate the rule of poverty and remodel the order, and (2) those later to be known as 'Zealots' or 'Spirituals' who wished to maintain the original manner of life. The latter group became more apparent as the original simplicity of the Franciscan rule was modified, with the decretal 'Quo elongati' (1230), e.g., allowing anyone to give alms to the order provided it was given to a *nuncius*, chosen by the donor or the order, who would buy the goods required, whilst any surplus money was given into the administration of a so-called 'spiritual friend'. While an apocalyptic sense of mission was widespread in the whole order, for the Spirituals this was reinforced by the prophetic doctrines of *Joachim of Fiore, partly through the extracts of his works published in 1254 as the *Eternal Gospel* by a Franciscan, Gerard of San Donnino, and partly through the dissemination of pseudo-Joachimist prophecies. Rigid adherence to the Rule and Testament of St Francis became, esp. during the generalship of *John of Parma (1247–57), the hallmark of the Joachimist programme for the last age.

By the end of the 13th cent. a compromise, implicit in the teaching of St *Bonaventure, who held that all property left to the friars was the property of the Church and that they were permitted to use things necessary for their life and work (*usus pauper*), had been arrived at and was embodied in Nicholas III's decretal 'Exiit qui Seminat' (1279). The solution proved unacceptable, however, to the Spirituals, esp. as the Constitutions of the Chapter-Generals of the time indicate that the abuses denounced by the Spirituals were spreading. The conflict was renewed under *Clement V (1310–12; see UBERTINO OF CASALE), as a result of which Nicholas's decretal was re-affirmed and further specified in 'Exivi de Paradiso' (1312). Meanwhile the Spirituals, now led by Angelo Clareno in the March of Ancona and by disciples of P. J. *Olivi in Provence, maintained an intransigent position. Pope *John XXII, in consequence, resorted to rigorous measures, enjoining them to obey authority under penalty of excommunication and burning four of their number as heretics (1318). He also issued the bulls 'Sancta Romana' (1317), in which the Spirituals were first called '*Fraticelli', and 'Gloriosam Ecclesiam' (1318) condemning their theology. Shortly afterwards the order was threatened with schism over what was originally a separate issue, the theoretical question of the poverty of Christ, on which the Minister General, Michael of Cesena, clashed with the Pope. Though Michael had opposed the Spirituals, the doctrine of Christ's poverty had a connection with the poverty to which the Spirituals aspired, and both were condemned by John XXII. The decretals 'Ad Conditorem Canonum' (1322) affirmed that complete renunciation of possessions did not constitute the perfect life, and 'Cum Inter Nonnullos' (1323) declared the doctrine of the absolute poverty of Christ and the Apostles, both individually and corporately, heretical. The conflict continued. The Fraticelli and the Beguins of Provence continued to hold the Spirituals' views, while the whole question of *usus facti* and *dominium* gave rise to R. *FitzRalph's 'De Pauperie Salvatoris', perhaps the best-argued attack on their position. In face of persecution the numbers dwindled, but the movement gave an impetus to the rise of more rigorous groups in the Franciscan Order, first to the Friars of the Strict Observance (*Observantines) and later to the *Capuchins.

F. *Ehrle, SJ, 'Die Spiritualen, ihr Verhältniss zum Franciscanerorden und zu den Fraticellen', *Archiv für Litteratur- und Kirchengeschichte des Mittelalters*, 1 (1885), pp. 509–69; 2 (1886), pp. 106–64; 3 (1887), pp. 553–623; and 4 (1888), pp. 1–190, with full refs. K. Balthasar, *Geschichte des Armutsstreites im Franziskanerorden bis zum Konzil von Vienne* (Vorreformationsgeschichtliche Forschungen, 6; 1911). D. L. Douie, *The Nature and the Effect of the Heresy of the Fraticelli* (Publications of the University of Manchester, 220; Historical Series, 61; 1932). M. D. Lambert, *Franciscan Poverty: The Doctrine of the Absolute Poverty of Christ and the Apostles in the Franciscan Order 1210–1323* (CHS, 1961). E. R. Daniel, *The Franciscan Concept of Mission in the High Middle Ages* (Lexington, Ky. [1975]), esp. pp. 1–36 and 76–100. L. Oliger, OFM, in *DTC* 14 (pt. 2; 1941), cols. 2522–49, s.v. 'Spirituels', with detailed bibl.; C. Schmitt, OFM, in *DHGE* 18 (1977), cols. 1063–108, s.v. 'Fraticelles'. See also bibl. to FRANCISCAN ORDER.

spiritual healing. The expression, occasionally used as a synonym of psychotherapy, is properly confined to the attempt to heal the whole personality by prayer and sacramental means, sometimes combined with religious suggestion. Among the methods in general use are *Unction and the laying on of hands. Most of those who practise such methods believe that the patient should at the same time make full use of medical skill, but a minority holds that spiritual means should alone be sufficient. It is a common practice among Anglicans to give Absolution and Communion immediately before the anointing. Although bodily healing is not normally expected as a result of Unction in the Roman Communion, many miraculous cures are claimed at *Lourdes and other places of pilgrimage. The laying on of hands as a '*sacramental' should be distinguished from the use of a natural gift of healing which does not depend on its possessor being a Christian; but it may be added that such a gift may most profitably be used when combined with Christian suggestion. The possession of the gift of healing was regarded in the early Church as a recommendation in candidates for Holy Orders. Spiritual healing (often called 'faith healing' or 'divine healing') plays a prominent part in modern *Pentecostalism and in the *Charismatic Renewal Movement.

The *Lambeth Conference of 1920 (Resolution 63) asked the Abp. of *Canterbury to appoint a committee to consider and report upon 'the use with prayer of the Laying on of Hands, of the Unction of the Sick, and other spiritual means of Healing'; the report of the committee was pub. under the title *The Ministry of Healing* (1924), with 'Forms of Service suggested for use at the Anointing of the Sick', pp. 38–43. A further commission was appointed by the Abps. of Canterbury and York at the request of the Convocations in 1953 to 'consider the theological, medical, psychological and pastoral aspects of "Divine Healing"'; the report of this commission was issued under the title *The Church's Ministry of Healing* (1958). The Alternative Services *Ministry to the Sick* (1983) makes provision for the Laying on of Hands and Anointing, as do most modern liturgies. The subject is treated historically in G. G. Dawson, *Healing, Pagan and Christian* (1935), pp. 112–308 on the Christian period. E. Frost, *Christian Healing: A Consideration of the Place of Spiritual Healing in the Church of Today in the Light of the Doctrine and Practice of the Ante-Nicene Church* (1940); id. (now Dame Raphael Frost, OSB), *Christ and Wholeness: An Approach to Christian Healing* (Cambridge, 1985). L. D. Weatherhead, *Psychology, Religion and Healing* (1951). M. T. Kelsey, *Healing and Christianity* (1973). C. W. Gusmer, *The Ministry of Healing in the Church of England: An Ecumenical-Liturgical Study* (Alcuin Club Collections, 56; 1974), with bibl. M. Maddocks, *The Christian Healing Ministry* (1981; 2nd edn., 1990). J. [T. A.] Gunstone, *The Lord is our Healer: Spiritual Renewal and the Ministry of Healing* (1986). See also bibl. to UNCTION and VISITATION OF THE SICK.

spiritual works of mercy. There are traditionally seven: (1) converting the sinner; (2) instructing the ignorant; (3) counselling the doubtful; (4) comforting the sorrowful; (5) bearing wrongs patiently; (6) forgiving injuries; (7) praying for the living and the dead. See also CORPORAL WORKS OF MERCY.

Spiritualism, also 'Spiritism'. A system of (often superstitious) beliefs and practices the purpose of which is to establish communication with the spirits of the dead. Necromancy is an element common to most primitive and many higher religions, an early example occurring in 1 Sam. 28: 8. In its modern form Spiritualism dates from the occult experiences of the American Fox family in 1848, and soon spread to England and the Continent as a reaction against the prevalent materialism. It professes to make contact with the souls of the departed chiefly by means of mediums, accompanied by table-turning, automatic writing, and other devices. It has found adherents, also, among recognized scholars such as O. Lodge, F. W. H. Myers,

and W. F. Prince. The scientific study of these phenomena has been extensively pursued in Great Britain by the Society for Psychical Research (founded 1882). After ruling out conscious or unconscious fraud, of which almost all famous mediums have been convicted, and phenomena susceptible of a natural explanation, e.g. by the abnormal qualities of the medium, there remains a certain number of striking cases such as the foreseeing of free actions and otherwise incalculable events. The theory that such phenomena are due to preternatural, i.e. demonic, agencies has been advanced by certain Christian theologians who point to the fact that the alleged messages from the beyond are generally hostile to Christian doctrine and of no moral or spiritual value. The practice of Spiritualism is denounced by Scripture (Deut. 18: 11) and by all parts of the Christian Church. In England, and esp. in USA, the cult is highly organized, and has been much exploited for commercial ends.

The Christian Spiritualist Churches profess acceptance of the leadership of Jesus Christ, but their understanding of Him is very different from that of the orthodox Churches.

There is an immense lit. on the subject. More serious studies in Eng. incl. E. Gurney, F. W. H. Myers, and F. Podmore, *Phantasms of the Living* (2 vols., 1886); F. Podmore, *Modern Spiritualism: A History and Criticism* (2 vols., 1902); F. W. H. Myers, *Human Personality and its Survival after Bodily Death* (2 vols., 1903); O. J. Lodge, *Raymond, or Life and Death, with examples of the evidence for survival of memory and affection after Death* (1916); A. C. Doyle, *The History of Spiritualism* (2 vols., 1926); A. Gauld, *The Founders of Psychical Research* (1968); id., *Mediumship and Survival: A Century of Investigations* (1982); G. K. Nelson, *Spiritualism and Society* (International Library of Sociology and Social Investigations, 1969). H. Thurston, SJ, *The Church and Spiritualism* (Milwaukee, Wis., 1933); G. W. Butterworth, *Spiritualism and Religion* (1944). F. C. S. Schiller in *HERE* 11 (1920), pp. 805–8, s.v. 'Spiritism'; L. Roure, SJ, in *DTC* 14 (pt. 1; 1941), cols. 2507–22, s.v. 'Spiritisme', both with further bibl.; L. Price in *A Dictionary of Christian Spirituality*, ed. G. S. Wakefield (1983), pp. 360 f., s.v. See also the *Proceedings of the Society for Psychical Research* (London, 1882 ff.) and the *Journal* of the same body (ibid., 1884 ff.).

spirituality. The term has come into very widespread use in many languages during the 20th cent., though its meaning has not been satisfactorily defined. It is used to refer to people's subjective practice and experience of their religion, or to the spiritual exercises and beliefs which individuals or groups have with regard to their personal relationship with God. It is usual to regard *prayer, *meditation, *contemplation, and *mysticism as major factors in spirituality. Where certain groups have a characteristic set of spiritual practices and beliefs, they may be regarded as constituting a 'school of spirituality' (e.g. '*Cistercian spirituality', '*Carmelite spirituality', '*Jesuit spirituality'), and this usage has come to be generalized, so that there is an increasing interest in 'lay spirituality', 'married spirituality', etc.

The word *spiritualitas* is first attested in the 5th cent., referring to the quality of life which should result from the spiritual gifts imparted to all who believe in Christ. During the Middle Ages it occurs in a variety of senses, but a narrowing of its application and of related expressions such as 'spiritual life' and 'spiritual exercises' is discernible from the 12th cent. onwards, so that a 'spiritual life' came to be regarded as more or less identical with interior religion and the explicitly devotional practices used to foster it. As such, it was sometimes considered unsuitable for lay Christians. As a result of this development, a distinction became possible between the moral life, incumbent on all believers, and the spiritual life, reserved to those specially called or specially fervent. Thus in the 17th cent. 'ascetical theology' (the science of the spiritual life) was differentiated from '*moral theology'. A distinction was also made between 'ascetical theology' (the science of human spiritual endeavour to attain to perfection) and 'mystical theology' (now regarded as the science of those special experiences accorded purely by God's grace), though some writers have treated the two terms as interchangeable; both are now generally treated as parts of 'spiritual theology' or 'spirituality'. In modern times the term 'spirituality' is often extended to apply to believers in religions other than Christianity.

On the history, P. Pourrat, PSS, *La Spiritualité chrétienne* (4 vols., 1918–28; Eng. tr. of vols. 1–3, 1922–7); A. Saudreau, *La Piété à travers les âges* (1927); *Histoire de la Spiritualité chrétienne*: 1: L. [C.] Bouyer, Cong. Orat., *La Spiritualité du Nouveau Testament et des Pères* (1960; Eng. tr., 1963); 2: J. Leclercq, OSB, and others, *La Spiritualité du moyen âge* (1961; Eng. tr., 1968); 3. 1: L. [C.] Bouyer, *La Spiritualité Orthodoxe et la Spiritualité Protestante et Anglicane* (1965; Eng. tr., 1969); 3. 2: L. Cognet, *La Spiritualité moderne*, 1: *1500–1650* (1966). M. García Cordero, OP, and others, *Historia de la Espiritualidad* (4 vols., Barcelona, 1969). B. McGinn and J. Meyendorff (eds.), *Christian Spirituality: Origins to the Twelfth Century* (World Spirituality, 16; New York, 1985; London, 1986); J. Raitt (ed.), *Christian Spirituality: High Middle Ages and Reformation* (ibid. 17; New York, 1987; London, 1989); L. [K.] Dupré and D. E. Saliers (eds.), *Christian Spirituality: Post-Reformation and Modern* (ibid. 18; New York, 1989; London, 1990). C. [P. M.] Jones, G. Wainwright, and E. [J.] Yarnold, SJ (eds.), *The Study of Spirituality* (1986). R. [D.] Williams, *The Wound of Knowledge: Christian Spirituality from the New Testament to St John of the Cross* (1979; 2nd edn., 1990); S. [C. ff.] Tugwell, OP, *Ways of Imperfection: An Exploration of Christian Spirituality* (1984).

The many more or less systematic treatises on spirituality include G. B. *Scaramelli, SJ, *Direttorio ascetico* (Naples, 1752; Eng. tr., 4 vols., 1870–71); A. Saudreau, *Les Degrés de la vie spirituelle* (2 vols., Angers, 1896; Eng. tr., 1926); A. *Tanquerey, *Précis de théologie ascétique et mystique* (2 parts, 1923–4; Eng. tr., Tournai, 1930); K. E. *Kirk, *The Vision of God* (1931); F. P. Harton, *The Elements of the Spiritual Life* (1932); R. Garrigou-Lagrange, OP, *Les Trois Âges de la vie intérieure* (2 vols. [1938]; Eng. tr., 2 vols., St Louis, 1947–8); L. [C.] Bouyer, Cong. Orat., *Introduction à la vie spirituelle* (1960; Eng. tr., 1961); M. [S. F.] Thornton, OGS, *English Spirituality: An Outline of Ascetical Theology according to the English Pastoral Tradition* (1963); J. Aumann, OP, *Spiritual Theology* (Huntingdon, Ind., and London [1980]). On the word, J. Leclercq, OSB, ' "Spiritualitas" ', *Studi Medievali*, 3rd ser. 3 (1962), pp. 279–96; W. Principe [CSB], 'Toward Defining Spirituality', *Studies in Religion*, 12 (1983), pp. 127–41. Periodicals specially devoted to the subject include *Revue d'Ascétique et de Mystique* (Toulouse, 1920–71, continued as *Revue d'Histoire de la Spiritualité*, 1972–7); *Zeitschrift für Aszese und Mystik* (Innsbruck, 1926–44, continued as *Geist und Leben*, Würzburg, 1947 ff.), and *Life of the Spirit* (1946–64, supplement to *Blackfriars*; incorporated in *New Blackfriars*, 1964 ff.). *Dictionnaire de spiritualité ascétique et mystique* (ed. M. Viller, SJ, F. Cavallera, and others, 16 vols. + index, 1937–95); *A Dictionary of Christian Spirituality*, ed. G. S. Wakefield (1983).

spirituals. American religious folk songs. They originated (as 'spiritual songs') in the White *revivalist Churches of the 18th cent., and their large-scale *camp meetings in the 19th cent. The Black form ('Negro spiritual'), although it appears to have derived from the early White style, acquired its own character, with texts identifying the sufferings of Christ with the Blacks' own conditions of slavery, and a typical emphasis on the desire for release from the troubles of the world. 'Michael, row the boat ashore', 'Steal away', and 'Deep river' are examples of songs which became internationally known after being popularized by Black singing groups on concert tours from the 1870s onwards. Other forms of *Gospel Music developed out of both styles of spiritual from the later part of the 19th cent.

W. F. Allen, C. P. Ware, and L. McK. Garrison (eds.), *Slave Songs of the United States* (New York, 1867). G. P. Jackson, *White and Negro Spirituals* (ibid., 1943), incl. text of 116 songs. J. Lovell, *Black Song: The Forge and the Flame; the Story of how the Afro-American Spiritual was Hammered out* (ibid. [1972]). E. J. Lorenz, *Glory Hallelujah! The story of the Camp-meeting Spiritual* (Nashville [1980]). J. C. Downey and P. Oliver in S. Sadie (ed.), *The New Grove Dictionary of Music and Musicians*, 18 (1980), pp. 1–7, s.v.; rev. in H. W. Hitchcock and S. Sadie (eds.), *The New Grove Dictionary of American Music*, 4 (1986), pp. 284–90, s.v.

Spitta, Friedrich (1852–1924), German Protestant theologian. Born at Wittingen in Hanover, he became lecturer at Bonn in 1880, professor of NT and pastoral theology at Strasbourg in 1887, and professor at Göttingen in 1919. He was keenly interested in Church music and the renewal of liturgical life in German Protestantism, and from 1895 was joint editor with J. Smend (1857–1930) of the *Monatsschrift für Gottesdienst und kirchliche Kunst*. Most of his books were on the Gospels and the early Church. The best-known is *Zur Geschichte und Litteratur des Urchristentums* (3 vols., in 4 parts, 1893–1907).

A. Meyer in *RGG* (2nd edn.), 5 (1931), col. 704, s.v.

sponsor. Another name for a *godparent at a *Baptism.

spoon, liturgical. In the E. rites, a spoon is used for giving communion, a portion of the consecrated Host being dipped in the chalice and the two species then conveyed on the spoon to the communicant. In the RC Church the use of a spoon for administering the consecrated Wine was sanctioned in 1965. In the W. spoons are also sometimes used to measure the water at the mixing of the chalice. Mention of them, however, in inventories of Church property is not proof that they have any liturgical significance. See also FISTULA.

Rohault, 4 [c.1887], pp. 185–8. Braun, *CA*, pp. 265–79, and plate 142, fig. 565. H. *Leclercq, OSB, in *DACL* 3 (pt. 2; 1914), cols. 3172–83, s.v. 'Cuiller', with bibl.

Sports, Book of. A declaration defining the recreations permissible on Sunday first issued in 1617 by *James I for the use of the magistrates in Lancs, and extended in the following year to the whole country with instructions to ministers to read it from the pulpit. It was reissued in 1633 by *Charles I, who deprived all clergy who refused to publish it. It permitted archery and dancing, and was designed to counteract the extreme and growing *Sabbatarianism fostered by the *Puritans. It derived such legal force as it possessed from the ecclesiastical supremacy conferred on the Crown in 1559; its publication aroused considerable opposition, culminating in its being publicly burnt by order of Parliament in 1643.

Modernized version of text in E. *Cardwell, *Documentary Annals of the Reformed Church of England*, 2 (1839), pp. 188–93; repr. in P. E. More and F. L. Cross (eds.), *Anglicanism* (1935), no. 261, pp. 565–8. R. W. Henderson, *The King's Book of Sports in England and America* (repr. from the Bulletin of the New York Public Library of November 1948). J. Davies, *The Caroline Captivity of the Church* (Oxford Historical Monographs, 1992), pp. 172–204. See also bibl. to SABBATARIANISM and Lives of James I cited s.v.

Spottiswoode, John (1565–1639), Abp. of St Andrews and historian. He was educated at Glasgow University and was originally a staunch supporter of strict Presbyterianism. When, however, at the end of the century the relations between King and Kirk deteriorated he became an adherent of the royal policy. In 1603 he accompanied *James I to London and was appointed Abp. of Glasgow. He did not receive episcopal consecration, however, until 1610, when, with two other Scottish bishops, he was consecrated (**per saltum*, on High Anglican principles) at London House. He became the chief agent of the King for suppressing the political influence of the Kirk, being a convinced advocate of *Erastian principles. In 1610 he was Moderator of the Assembly which limited the presbyteries, and in 1615 was translated to St Andrews. At the General Assembly of the Kirk in 1618 he made himself Moderator without election, and succeeded in imposing the so-called Five Articles of *Perth (q.v.), heavy penalties being inflicted on ministers who refused to conform. In 1635 *Charles I appointed him Chancellor, and as such he gave loyal, if reluctant, support to the introduction of the Liturgy which he regarded as inexpedient. After the riots in 1637 he petitioned the King to desist from his policy, and when, in 1638, the *National Covenant had been signed, he fled to Newcastle. He was deposed by the Assembly some months later on a series of unjustified charges, including adultery, incest, and sacrilege. His chief works are *Refutatio Libelli de Regimine Ecclesiae Scoticanae* (1620) and *The History of the Church of Scotland* [to 1625] (1655; rev. edn. by G. *Burnet, 1677; new edn., 3 vols., 1847–51), an amply documented official history reflecting the writer's position in the struggle.

Life prefixed to the 1st edn. of his *History* (1655), ascribed in the 4th edn. (1677) to B. *Duppa, and another by M. Russell prefixed to the latter's edn. of the *History* pub. for the Spottiswoode Society (3 vols., 1847–51), 1, pp. xxix–cxxxvi. The 4th edn. of his *History* (1677) contains an appendix by G. Burnet, with additional information to date. Study by I. Dunlop in R. S. Wright (ed.), *Fathers of the Kirk* (1960), pp. 48–61. J. Kirk, *Archbishop Spottiswoode and the See of Glasgow* (Glasgow Cathedral Lecture Series, 3 [1988]), repr. in id., *Patterns of Reform* (Edinburgh, 1989), pp. 426–48. T. F. Henderson in *DNB* 53 (1898), pp. 412–15.

Spurgeon, Charles Haddon (1834–92), *Baptist preacher. The descendant of two generations of *Independent ministers, he was born at Kelvedon, Essex, and became a Baptist in 1850. In the same year he preached his first sermon, and in 1852 he was appointed pastor of the Baptist congregation at Waterbeach. In 1854

he went to Southwark, where his sermons drew such crowds that a new church, the Metropolitan Tabernacle in Newington Causeway, had to be built for him. Apart from his preaching activities, he founded a pastors' college, an orphanage, and a colportage association for the propagation of uplifting literature. Spurgeon was a strong *Calvinist. He had a controversy in 1864 with the *Evangelical party of the C of E for remaining in a Church that taught Baptismal Regeneration, and also estranged considerable sections of his own community by rigid opposition to the more liberal methods of biblical exegesis. These differences led to a rupture with the Baptist Union in 1887. He owed his fame as a preacher to his great oratorical gifts, humour, and shrewd common sense, which showed itself esp. in his treatment of contemporary problems. Among his works are *The Saint and his Saviour* (1857), *Commenting and Commentaries* (1876) and numerous volumes of sermons (translated into many languages).

Spurgeon's Autobiography, compiled from his Diary, Letters, and Records, by his wife [S. Spurgeon] and private secretary [Revd W. J. Harrald] (4 vols., London, 1897–1900). Letters ed. C. Spurgeon, son (ibid. [1923]). Full Life by G. H. Pike (3 vols., ibid. [1892–3]). The many other studies incl. those of W. Williams (ibid., 1895), W. Y. Fullerton (ibid., 1920), J. C. Carlile (ibid., 1933), P. S. Kruppa (New York and London, 1982), A. Dallimore (Chicago [1984]; Edinburgh, etc., 1985), and M. Nicholls (Didcot, Oxon., 1992). A. R. Buckland in *DNB* 53 (1898), pp. 433–5.

Spy Wednesday. The Wednesday before *Good Friday, so named as the day on which *Judas Iscariot arranged to betray Christ (Mt. 26: 14–16).

Spyridon (also **Spiridion**), **St** (d. *c.*348), Bp. of Tremithus in *Cyprus. He was a simple peasant who acc. to tradition had suffered in the *Diocletianic Persecution, and after becoming bishop had attended the Council of *Nicaea (though his name is not found in the episcopal lists of signatures). He was certainly present at the Council of *Sardica (*c.*343). His life gathered to it many legends. Acc. to one, some thieves trying one night to rob him of his sheep discovered their hands tied miraculously behind their backs and were set free by Spyridon the next morning; acc. to another, he recovered a valuable ornament by the prayers of his deceased daughter, Irene (*Socrates, *HE* 1. 12; *Sozomen, *HE* 1. 11). Later writers attribute to him the recitation of the Creed at Nicaea that converted the heathen philosopher who had mocked at the Christian faith. Feast day, in the E., 12 Dec.; in the W., 14 Dec.

P. van den Ven, *La Légende de S. Spyridon, évêque de Trimithonte* (Bibliothèque du *Muséon*, 33; 1953), incl. crit. edn. of basic texts; review art. by G. Garitte in *RHE* 50 (1955), pp. 125–40. *BGH* (3rd edn., 1957), pp. 246 f. (nos. 1647 f.); *Novum Auctarium* (1984), pp. 192 f.

Sri Lanka, Christianity in. Sri Lanka (formerly known as Ceylon) is inhabited by two main ethnic groups, Sinhalese and Tamil, the latter having migrated from S. India. Acc. to *Cosmas Indicopleustes, there were *Nestorian Christians in Sri Lanka in the 6th cent., but their Churches appear to have died out.

From 1505 Sri Lanka was brought within the Portuguese seaborne trading empire; within this empire the Portuguese propagated Christianity, and the first RC priests arrived in Colombo in 1518. In 1543 missionary work was begun by *Franciscan friars, who in the early 17th cent. were joined by *Jesuits, *Augustinian friars, and *Dominicans. As a result of mass Baptisms, the Christian community grew rapidly. In 1658 the Portuguese were finally driven out by the Dutch, who attempted to suppress the RC Church and expelled the Portuguese priests. Protestantism was introduced by the Dutch East India Company, which supported and controlled the Dutch Reformed Church and brought ministers from the Netherlands. The RC Church, nevertheless, survived, and from 1687 RC ministry was provided by *Oratorian priests from Goa in India. In 1796 the Dutch were in turn displaced by the British and in 1802 Ceylon became a Crown colony. In 1806 the laws against RC activity were abolished and the fortunes of that Church revived. The apostolic *vicariate of Ceylon was created in 1834 and a hierarchy in 1886. The first indigenous RC bishop was appointed in 1940.

Under British rule missionary work was begun by English societies: *Baptist (1812), Wesleyan *Methodist (1814), *CMS (1818), and *SPG (1840). The American Board of Commissioners for Foreign Missions founded a mission at Jaffna in the north of Sri Lanka in 1816. The Anglican diocese of Colombo was created in 1845. A Sinhalese bishop, H. L. J. De Mel (1902–76) was appointed to the new see of Kurunagala in 1950. D. T. Niles (1908–70), a Tamil Methodist, achieved international prominence in the *Ecumenical Movement as first general secretary of the East Asia Christian Conference (1957–68) and a member of the presidium of the *World Council of Churches (1968–70). Meanwhile, since the achievement of political independence in 1948, all the Churches have had to face the challenge of a revived and militant Buddhism. In 1961 Christian schools receiving state aid were nationalized and in 1972 Buddhism was recognized as the state religion. Some Christians have been involved in inter-faith dialogue with Buddhists. A long proposed union, in which Anglicans, Baptists, Methodists, *Presbyterians, and the Church of *South India would have formed a united Church of Sri Lanka, was abandoned in the 1980s. Christians comprise about 8 per cent of the population; nine-tenths of them are RCs.

J. E. Tennent, *Christianity in Ceylon: Its Introduction and Progress under the Portuguese, the Dutch, the British, and the American Missions* (London, 1850). W. L. A. D. Peter, *Studies in Ceylon Church History* (Colombo, 1963). V. Perniola, SJ, *The Catholic Church in Sri Lanka: Original Documents translated into English* (Dehiwala, 1989 ff.). S. G. Prakasar, OMI, *A History of the Catholic Church in Ceylon*, 1 . . . 1505–1602 (Colombo, 1924). R. Boudens, OMI, *The Catholic Church in Ceylon under Dutch Rule* (Bibliotheca Missionalis, 10; Rome, 1957); id., *Catholic Missionaries in a British Colony: Successes and Failures in Ceylon 1796–1893* (Immensee, Switzerland, 1979). J. W. Balding, *One Hundred Years in Ceylon; or, the Centenary Volume of the Church Missionary Society in Ceylon, 1818–1918* (Madras, 1922). F. L. Beven (ed.), *A History of the Diocese of Colombo* (Colombo [c.1946]; on the Anglican diocese). H. J. Charter, *Ceylon Advancing* (London, 1955; on the Baptist Mission). S. D. Franciscus, *Faith of our Fathers: History of the Dutch Reformed Church in Sri Lanka (Ceylon)* (Colombo, 1983). F. Houtart, *Religion and Ideology in Sri Lanka* (ibid., 1974), esp. pp. 155–72, 212–24, 265–300, and 365–90.

SSJE. See SOCIETY OF ST JOHN THE EVANGELIST.

Stabat Mater dolorosa. A hymn of unknown date descriptive of the Sorrows of the BVM at the Cross. Suggested authors are *Innocent III (d. 1216), St *Bonaventure (d. 1274), and *Jacopone da Todi (d. 1306). It gradually came into liturgical use in the later Middle Ages, and in 1727 the Roman Missal prescribed it as a *sequence for the two feasts of the *Seven Sorrows of the BVM and in the corresponding Breviary offices. It survives as a sequence for optional use at Mass on 15 September, and may be used at the devotions of the *Stations of the Cross. Its popularity is reflected in the many English translations (among them 'At the Cross her station keeping') and the variety of musical settings (e.g. of G. P. da *Palestrina, F. J. Haydn, A. Dvořák, etc.). Another hymn, 'Stabat Mater speciosa', apparently modelled on the 'dolorosa', which describes the sorrows of the BVM at the manger in *Bethlehem, was also widely popular, though this hymn was never used liturgically.

Crit. edn. of text in C. Blume, SJ, and H. M. Bannister (eds.), *Liturgische Prosen des Übergangsstiles und der zweiten Epoche insbesondere die dem Adam von Sanct Victor zugeschriebenen* (AHMA 54; 1915), pp. 312–18. C. Carbone, *L'inno del dolore mariano 'Stabat Mater': Studi critico-dogmatico-litterari* (1911). C. Blume, SJ, 'Der Sänger der Sequenz auf die "Schmerzensreiche Mutter" ', *Stimmen der Zeit*, 89 (1915), pp. 592–8. G. Hasehohr, 'Les traductions françaises du "Stabat mater dolorosa". Textes et contextes (XIVᵉ–XVIᵉ siècles)', *Recherches Augustiniennes*, 24 (1989), pp. 243–355. Raby, pp. 437–40, with bibl. pp. 484 f.; J. Szövérffy, *Die Annalen der lateinischen Hymnendichtung*, 2 (1965), pp. 287–90.

stability (Lat. *stabilitas*). Part of the commitment made by monks and nuns following the Rule of St *Benedict. The 4th- and 5th-cent. Egyptian monks insisted on the importance of not leaving one's cell; St Benedict required the monk making profession to promise stability, but he did not define the word. Later writers interpreted it variously as staying in one place, staying with one community, or perseverance in the monastic life. Modern writers tend not to ascribe a specific legal obligation to this promise, but all agree that it has exercised a strong influence in moulding the character of W. monasticism.

Rule of St Benedict, cap. 58. See also comm. cited under BENEDICT, RULE OF ST.

staff, pastoral. See CROSIER.

Stafford, Anthony (1587–1645?), devotional writer. He was educated at Oriel College, Oxford. He is known as the author of *The Female Glory; or the Life and Death of Our Blessed Lady, the Holy Virgin Mary, God's Own Immaculate Mother* (1635), of which the language of exalted adulation addressed to the BVM and an engraving depicting the *Assumption gave great offence to the *Puritans, esp. when the work was licensed and defended by W. *Laud.

The book was ed. and repr. in 1860 by O. Shipley (4th edn., 1869). G. C. M. Smith, 'Anthony Stafford', *Notes and Queries*, 152 (1927), pp. 219–21, 239–43, 431. G. Le G. Norgate in *DNB* 53 (1898), pp. 444 f.

Stainer, Sir John (1840–1901), organist and composer. Born in *Southwark, he was a chorister of *St Paul's, and obtained his first post as an organist in 1854. In 1872 he was appointed organist of St Paul's Cathedral, where he carried out reforms in its service music, which became famous for its beauty and reverence under his direction. He was knighted in 1888 when he resigned because of failing eyesight. From 1889 to 1899 he was Professor of Music in the University of Oxford. His principal works were oratorios and cantatas, among them *St Mary Magdalen*, performed at the *Gloucester Festival of 1887, *The Crucifixion* (1887), and *The Story of the Cross* (1893). His anthems include 'Lead, kindly Light', 'O clap your hands', and 'I saw the Lord'. He also composed hymn tunes, many of which are reproduced in *Hymns, Ancient and Modern*. His compositions are typical and often good examples of their period, showing influences from various schools, notably F. Mendelssohn and C. F. Gounod, but his distinction lies more in his work as an organist and choirmaster, and as an all-round musician and scholar.

P. Charlton, *John Stainer and the Musical Life of Victorian Britain* [1984]. W. G. McNaught in *DNB, 1901–1911*, pp. 377–9, s.v.; N. Temperley in S. Sadie (ed.), *The New Grove Dictionary of Music and Musicians*, 18 (1980), pp. 57 f., s.v.

stalls. The fixed seats for the clergy and others on both sides of the choirs of cathedral and certain other churches. They are usually separated by high projecting arms, often richly carved, and sometimes surmounted by canopies. The seats can frequently be turned back, disclosing a bracket called a '*misericord' (sometimes carved with a grotesque design). Knightly orders have stalls for their members, the Knights of the Garter, e.g., having stalls assigned to them in St George's Chapel, Windsor. See also INSTALLATION.

F. Bond, *Wood Carvings in English Churches*, 2 (1910), pp. 1–100. C. Tracy, *English Gothic Choir-Stalls 1200–1400* (Woodbridge, Suffolk, 1987).

stake. A post upon which persons were bound for execution, esp. by burning, and hence the punishment of death by burning. See BURNING.

Stanford, Sir Charles Villiers (1852–1924), composer and teacher. Born in Ireland, and showing early musical gifts, Stanford was a choral scholar at Queens' College, Cambridge, and studied in Leipzig and Berlin. From 1873 to 1882 he was organist at Trinity College, Cambridge, and from 1883 Professor of Composition at the Royal College of Music in London, to which he added the duties of conductor of the London Bach Choir in 1885 and the Cambridge Professorship of Music in 1887. He was knighted in 1902. An all-round composer, he was immensely influential as a teacher of the generation of R. *Vaughan Williams (1872–1958) and his contemporaries. His numerous settings of the Morning, Evening, and Holy Communion services, with their striking melodic ideas and rhythmic drive, gave Victorian church music much-needed freshness, so that they have retained a firm place in the English cathedral repertoire. Also well known are the anthems 'The Lord is my shepherd' and 'Ye choirs of new Jerusalem', and the *motets, op. 38 (including 'Justorum animae'). In addition, he wrote much organ music.

Studies by J. F. Porte (London, 1921) and H. P. Greene (ibid., 1935). G. Norris, *Stanford, the Cambridge Jubilee and Tchaikovsky* [1980], pp. 7–60 and 538–76. F. Hudson in S. Sadie (ed.), *The*

New Grove Dictionary of Music and Musicians, 18 (1980), pp. 70–4, s.v.

Stanislaus, St (1030–79), in Polish 'Stanisław', Patron of *Poland. The son of a noble family, he was educated at Gniezno, and perhaps at *Paris, and became Bp. of Cracow in 1072. In imposing strict discipline in his diocese, he soon came into conflict with King Boleslaw II, whom he repeatedly reproved for his scandalous conduct. Eventually he excommunicated the King, and Boleslaw, acc. to tradition, slew him with his own hand while he was offering Mass. He was canonized by *Innocent IV in 1253, and his first biography, which is full of purely legendary material, dates from that time. There are evident parallels with the subsequent martyrdoms of St Thomas *Becket and of St *John of Nepomuk in neighbouring Bohemia. In 1904 the Polish historian, T. Wojciechowski, provoked much discussion by alleging that Stanislaus had rightly been put to death for treason. Feast day, 11 April (formerly 7 May; at Cracow, 8 May).

Two early Lives, with miracles cited in procedure for canonization, ed. W. Ketrzyński in *Monumenta Poloniae Historica*, 4 (Lvóv, 1884), pp. 238–438; excerpts ed. M. Perlbach in *MGH*, Scriptores, 29 (1892), pp. 501–17. 15th-cent. Life by J. Dlugossius pr. in *AASS*, Mai 2 (1680), pp. 200–80. *BHL* (pt. 2; 1901), pp. 1134 f. (nos. 7832–43). T. Wojciechowski, *Szkice Historyczne Jedenastego Wieku* (3rd edn., 1950), pp. 221–340, *passim*, and introd. by A. Gieysztor, pp. 17–19. K. W. Schenk, *Kult liturgiczny Św. Stanisława Biskupa na Śląsku* (Lublin, 1959), with summary in Ger. and extensive bibl.

Stanley, Arthur Penrhyn (1815–81), Broad Church Anglican divine. He was educated at Rugby under T. *Arnold and felt his master's influence all his life. In 1834 he went up to Balliol College, Oxford, and in 1838 was elected a Fellow of University College. In the ecclesiastical struggles of the period he consistently advocated toleration for both *Tractarian and liberal extremes. He was Canon of *Canterbury from 1851 to 1858, professor of ecclesiastical history at Oxford from 1856 to 1864, and Dean of *Westminster from 1864 till his death. He made it his aim at Westminster to make the Abbey a national shrine for all, irrespective of dogmatic creed, and gave much offence to conservative Churchmen by his invitation to all the scholars who had produced the RV, among them a Unitarian, to receive Holy Communion in the Abbey. Though he did not share J. W. *Colenso's opinions in all particulars, he was strongly opposed to disciplinary action against him. Despite the atmosphere of unorthodoxy that hung about Stanley during his life, he was an extremely influential figure, and was more widely read than were most divines. His publications include *Life and Correspondence of Thomas Arnold* (1844), *Memorials of Canterbury* (1854), *Sinai and Palestine* (1856), *Lectures on the History of the Eastern Church* (1861), *Lectures on the History of the Jewish Church* (3 parts, 1863–76), and volumes of sermons.

Letters and Verses of Arthur Penrhyn Stanley, D.D., between the Years 1829 and 1881, ed. R. E. Prothero (London, 1895). R. E. Prothero and G. G. Bradley, *The Life and Correspondence of Arthur Penrhyn Stanley* (2 vols., 1893). Modern memoir, with further letters, ed. A. V. Baillie and H. Bolitho, *A Victorian Dean* (1930). P. Hammond, *Dean Stanley of Westminster* (Worthing, 1987). R. E. Prothero in *DNB* 54 (1898), pp. 44–8.

Stanley, Henry Morton (1841–1904), explorer, administrator, author, and journalist. His original name was John Rowlands, but in 1859 he took the name of Henry Morton Stanley, after his adoptive father. Appointed in 1868 foreign correspondent to the *New York Herald*, he left Zanzibar on 21 Mar. 1871 to seek D. *Livingstone, and they met on the following 10 Nov. This expedition led to various other journeys of exploration between 1873 and 1889, in the course of which he discovered and reported on the nature of over two million sq. miles of the interior of Africa. His communications with the *CMS during his crossing of Africa from east to west in 1874–7 led to the beginning of mission work in *Uganda, and, whatever his character, his discoveries made possible Christian missionary work in much of Central Africa.

Autobiography ed. by D. Stanley, widow (London, 1909), with Life cont. from his Journal and Notes, pp. 219–539, and list of his works, which contain much autobiog. material, p. 540. Authorized Life by F. Hird (London [1935]). Other Lives by H. W. Little (ibid., 1890), J. Wassermann (Berlin, 1932; Eng. tr., 1932), and R. Hall (London, 1974). F. McLynn, *Stanley: The Making of an African Explorer* (1989); id., *Stanley: Sorcerer's Apprentice* (1991). J. A. Casada, *Dr. David Livingstone and Sir Henry Morton Stanley: An Annotated Bibliography* (1976), pp. 103–94. C. L. Skinner in *Dict. Amer. Biog.* 17 (1935), pp. 509–13.

Stanton, Arthur Henry (1839–1913), *Anglo-Catholic priest. He was educated at Trinity College, Oxford, and in 1862 ordained to the title of St Alban's, Holborn, where he remained as a curate for 50 years. The depth and sincerity of his religious faith, combined with his personal attractiveness, won him the confidence of thousands of men in one of the roughest parts of London, while his eloquent and powerful preaching made a great appeal to people of all classes. Like many other Anglo-Catholic priests of that time, he met with much opposition at the hands of the more official elements in the Church.

Faithful Stewardship and other Sermons, ed. E. F. Russell (London, 1916), and *Last Sermons in S. Alban's, Holborn*, ed. id. (ibid. [1916]), both ed. from reports of a shorthand writer. Further collection of *Sermon Outlines* from his own MSS. ed. id. (2 vols., ibid., 1917–19). Life by G. W. E. Russell (ibid., 1917). E. F. Russell in *DNB, 1912–1921*, pp. 506 f.

Stapeldon, Walter de (*c.*1261–1326), Bp. of *Exeter. Coming from a prosperous family in NW Devon, he became professor of canon law at Oxford and chaplain to *Clement V. In 1308 he was consecrated to the see of Exeter. As Lord Treasurer (from 1320) he reformed the royal exchequer; he helped to rebuild Exeter Cathedral, and founded Stapeldon Hall, which became Exeter College, Oxford. He was murdered by the London mob for his association with the misgovernment of Edward II.

Register ed. F. C. Hingeston-Randolph (1892). M. Buck, *Politics, Finance and the Church in the Reign of Edward II: Walter Stapeldon, Treasurer of England* (Cambridge Studies in Medieval Life and Thought, 3rd ser. 19; 1983). F. C. Hingeston-Randolph in *DNB* 54 (1898), pp. 92 f., s.v.; *BRUO* 3 (1959), pp. 1764–5.

Stapleton, Thomas (1535–98), RC controversialist. He was born at Henfield in W. Sussex and educated at Winchester and New College, Oxford, of which he was a Fellow. He became a prebendary of *Chichester under *Mary in 1558, but on *Elizabeth's accession fled to Louvain, where he studied theology. Returning to England, he declined to renounce the authority of the Pope, was deprived of his prebend in 1563, and went back to Louvain. In 1569 he moved to *Douai and began to teach there in the university faculty of theology, and from 1585 also in the Jesuit college. In 1590 he was given by *Philip II the professorship of Scripture at Louvain as the successor of M. *Baius. Shortly afterwards he became Dean of Hilverenbeck, and in 1597 *Clement VIII made him *protonotary apostolic. Stapleton was an able, skilful, and erudite controversialist. The circumstances of his time led him to treat esp. of the relation of the Pope to the temporal power, a matter in which he ascribed more limited rights to the Pope than many RC writers. He was a prolific author. Among his more important works are the *Principiorum Fidei Doctrinalium Demonstratio* (1578); *Tres Thomae* (1588; namely, the Apostle, St Thomas *Becket, and St Thomas *More); and *Auctoritatis Ecclesiasticae Defensio* (1592), directed against W. *Whitaker.

Lat. tr. of his Eng. works pub. 4 vols., Paris, 1620, with brief Life by T. Holland in vol. 1 (no pagination). Mod. edn. of his Eng. tr. of *Bede's *Historia Ecclesiastica* (orig. pub. Antwerp, 1565; Oxford, 1930; also ed. P. Hereford, London, 1935); Eng. tr. of his Lat. Life of Sir Thomas More from *Tres Thomae* (orig. pub. Douai, 1588) by P. E. Hallett (London, 1928). M. R. O'Connell, *Thomas Stapleton and the Counter Reformation* (Yale Publications in Religion, 9; 1964). H. Schützeichel, *Wesen und Gegenstand der kirchlichen Lehrautorität nach Thomas Stapleton* (Trierer theologische Studien, 20; 1966); M. Seybold, *Glaube und Rechtfertigung bei Thomas Stapleton* (Konfessionskundliche und kontroverstheologische Studien, 21; 1967). M. Richards, 'Thomas Stapleton', *JEH* 18 (1967), pp. 187–99. A. F. Allison and D. M. Rogers, *The Contemporary Printed Literature of the English Counter-Reformation between 1558 and 1640*, 1 (Aldershot, 1989), pp. 154–64 (nos. 1129–243). T. Cooper in *DNB* 54 (1898), pp. 101–4, s.v.

Star of Bethlehem. The star seen by the wise men 'in the east' at the birth of Christ and which 'went before them till it came and stood over where the young child was' [i.e. at *Bethlehem] (Mt. 2: 1–11). Several attempts have been made to connect the star with unusual astronomical phenomena at the time, e.g. J. *Kepler calculated that there was a conjunction of the planets, Jupiter and Saturn, in 7 BC.

A modern suggestion, with refs. to other recent lit., was made by C. J. Humphreys, 'The Star of Bethlehem—a Comet in 5 BC—and the Date of the Birth of Christ', *Quarterly Journal of the Royal Astronomical Society*, 32 (1991), pp. 389–407.

staretz. In the Russian Church a person who is sought out as a spiritual counsellor because of his exceptional personal holiness. He has no formal position in the ecclesiastical hierarchy, but owes his authority to his spiritual gifts. A staretz is usually a monk, but may on occasion be a lay person. The Russian word means an 'elder' and is a translation of the Greek word γέρων, used since the 4th cent. for a spiritual father.

Starovery. Another name for the Russian sect of the *Old Believers (q.v.).

State Prayers. In the BCP, the prayers for the Sovereign and the Royal Family towards the end of *Mattins and *Evensong.

F. Streatfeild, *The State Prayers and other Variations in the Book of Common Prayer* (1950), pp. 9–30. C. L. Berry, ' "... and all the Royal Family" ', *History Today*, 16 (1966), pp. 276 f.

State Services. In the C of E, the services appointed to commemorate days of national rejoicing or deliverance. Since the Reformation the rubrics have required the anniversary of the reigning sovereign's accession to be so observed. In the 17th cent., services to mark the *Gunpowder Plot (5 Nov.), the beheading of *Charles I (30 Jan.), and the birth and return of *Charles II (both 29 May) were drawn up. Though these services have never been an integral part of the BCP, and thus did not fall under the provisions of the Acts of *Uniformity, they were formerly printed at the end of the Book. In 1859 all except the 'Accession Service' were withdrawn.

States of the Church. Those parts of Italy and the territory of *Avignon and Venaissin in France which at one time acknowledged the temporal sovereignty of the Papacy. Some of these lands, which were a special gift to the Basilica of *St Peter at Rome, were also known as the '*Patrimony of St Peter' (q.v.). Their beginnings date from the edict of *Constantine in 321, which declared the Church capable of holding and transmitting property, but their possession constantly involved the Popes in temporal disputes, which added nothing to their spiritual authority. See also STEPHEN II and DONATION OF CONSTANTINE.

In 1791 the Papal territories situated in France were lost to the new republic, and by 1861 the Papacy was left with Rome alone, all the rest having been absorbed in the kingdom of Italy. In 1870 Rome itself was lost and the Pope withdrew into the *Vatican. By the Law of *Guarantees the new secular state allotted to the Pope a pension and declared the basilicas and palaces of the *Lateran and the Vatican and the country seat of *Castel Gandolfo to be extraterritorial. The Popes refused to accept this settlement, but in 1929 the *Lateran Treaty between *Pius XI and Fascist Italy contained an agreement on much the same lines and constituted the 'Vatican City' a separate state.

For the early history of the Papal States see bibl. to PATRIMONY OF ST PETER. C. Morris, *The Papal Monarchy: The Western Church from 1050–1250* (Oxford History of the Christian Church, 1989), pp. 82–108, 191 f., 420–6, 450 f., 563–6, with bibl. pp. 585 f. D. [P.] Waley, *The Papal State in the Thirteenth Century* (1961). P. Toubert, *Les Structures du Latium médiéval: Le Latium méridional et la Sabine du IX⁰ siècle à la fin du XII⁰ siècle* (Bibliothèque des Écoles françaises d'Athènes et de Rome, 221; 2 vols., Rome, 1973). L. Dal Pane, *Lo Stato pontificio e il movimento riformatore del Settecento* (Milan, 1959). P. Partner, *The Papal State under Martin V: The Administration and Government of the Temporal Power in the Early Fifteenth Century* (1958); id., *The Lands of St Peter: The Papal State in the Middle Ages and Early Renaissance* (1972). M. Brosch, *Geschichte des Kirchenstaats* [1500–1800] (Geschichte der europäischen Staaten, 41 and 43; 1880–2). D. Demarco, *Il Tramonto dello Stato pontificio: Il papato di Gregorio XVI* ([Turin] 1949); id., *Pio IX e la Rivoluzione Romana del 1848: Saggio di Storia economico-sociale* (Modena, 1947); id., *Una Rivoluzione Sociale: La Reppublica Romana del 1849* (Naples [1944]; all repr., Naples, 1992). A. C. Jemolo, *Chiesa e Stato in Italia negli ultimi cento anni* (1948; 2nd edn., Turin [1963]; Eng. tr. of abridged edn., *Church and State in Italy 1850–1950*, Oxford, 1960). N. Miko, *Das Ende des Kirchenstaates* (Veröffentlichungen des Österreichischen Kulturinstitutes in Rom. Abteilung für historische Studien, 1–4; 1962–70). G. Schnürer in *CE* 14 (1912), pp. 257–68, s.v.; P. Partner and others in *NCE* 13 (1969), pp. 655–62, s.v. See also bibl. to LATERAN TREATY and under individual Popes.

Station Days. Certain days, until 1970 marked in the Roman Missal, on which the Pope formerly celebrated Mass in the so-called 'station churches' in Rome. There is early evidence (for Rome: *Hermas; for N. Africa: *Tertullian and *Victorinus of Pettau) for the observance of *stationes*, but apart from the fact that such observance involved fasting, it is unclear of what it consisted. At Rome, from the 4th cent., the solemnity was enhanced by processions of clergy and people from one church, called 'collecta', to the station church, where the Pope was to offer Mass, while litanies and other prayers were recited on the way. Acc. to tradition it was St *Gregory the Great who assigned its special church to each of the station days. In the Würzburg *comes* (probably 8th cent., but reflecting practices going back to the time of Gregory), the station days comprised the Marian feasts, the *Ember Days, Christmas Eve and Christmas Day, *Septuagesima and *Sexagesima Sundays, most of the Sundays and ferias in Lent (except the Thursdays), Easter Sunday and the following weekdays, and Whitsunday and the following weekdays. Certain other days came to be added later, including the missing Thursdays in Lent, and various other feasts and vigils, eventually making 87 days in all. The Papal station Masses fell into disuse esp. during the exile of the Popes at *Avignon, but traces of the ancient custom survive in the indulgences attached to visits to the station churches under certain conditions. Among the most famous of the station churches are *Santa Maria Maggiore for the First Sunday in Advent, the First and Third Mass on Christmas Day, and Easter Day, the church of St John *Lateran for Holy Saturday, and Santa Sabina, established by *Urban VIII for Ash Wednesday, where the Popes distributed the ashes to the people. The station Masses were also imitated by some churches outside Rome, e.g. at Milan. See also ROME, CHURCHES OF.

H. Grisar, SJ, 'Die Stationsfeier und der erste römische Ordo', *ZKT* 9 (1885), pp. 385–422. Id., *Das Missale im Lichte römischer Stadtgeschichte: Stationen, Perikopen, Gebräuche* (1925). J. P. Kirsch, 'Origine e carattere primitivo delle stazioni liturgiche di Roma', *Atti della Pontificia Accademia Romana di Archeologia*, ser. 3, Rendiconti, 3 (1925), pp. 123–41. Id., *Die Stationskirchen des Missale Romanum* (Ecclesia Orans, 19; 1926). R. Hierzegger, 'Collecta und Statio. Die römischen Stationsprozessionen im frühen Mittelalter', *ZKT* 60 (1936), pp. 511–54. C. Mohrmann, 'Statio', *VC* 7 (1953), pp. 221–45. R. Zerfass, 'Die Idee der römischen Stationsfeier und ihr Fortleben', *Liturgisches Jahrbuch*, 8 (1958), pp. 218–29. G. G. Willis, *Further Essays in Early Roman Liturgy* (Alcuin Club Collections, 50; 1968), pp. 1–87 ('Roman Stational Liturgy'). A. A. Häussling, *Mönchskonvent und Eucharistiefeier* (Liturgiewissenschaftliche Quellen und Forschungen, 58; 1973), esp. pp. 186–201 and 316–19. J. F. Baldovin, SJ, *The Urban Character of Christian Worship: The Origins, Development, and Meaning of Stational Liturgy* (Orientalia Christiana Analecta, 228; 1987), esp. pp. 105–66.

Stations of the Cross. A series of 14 pictures or carvings, designed for devotional purposes, which depict incidents in the last journey of Christ from *Pilate's house to His entombment. They are commonly arranged round the walls of a church, and it is a popular devotion, esp. during

*Lent and *Passiontide, to visit the Stations in order, reciting prayers and meditating on each incident. The devotion probably arose out of the practice, attested from an early date, of pilgrims at *Jerusalem following the traditional route from Pilate's house to *Calvary and wishing to reproduce an analogous devotion at home. Its currency dates from the later Middle Ages, when it was popularized esp. by the *Franciscans, but the final selection of incidents was not settled until the 18th–19th cents. In the RC Church an *indulgence is attached to the devotion. The 14 incidents of which the Stations usually consist are: (1) Christ is condemned to death; (2) Christ receives the cross; (3) His first fall; (4) He meets His Mother; (5) *Simon of Cyrene is made to bear the cross; (6) Christ's face is wiped by *Veronica; (7) His second fall; (8) He meets the women of Jerusalem; (9) His third fall; (10) He is stripped of His garments; (11) He is nailed to the cross; (12) Christ dies on the cross; (13) His body is taken down from the cross; (14) His body is laid in the tomb.

H. Thurston, SJ, *The Stations of the Cross: An Account of their History and Devotional Purpose* (1906), with refs. B. [A.] Brown, OFM, in *NCE* 14 (1967), pp. 832–5, s.v. 'Way of the Cross'. M.-J. Picard in *Dict. Sp.* 2 (1953), cols. 2576–606, s.v. 'Croix (Chemin de)'.

Statuta Ecclesiae Antiqua

Statuta Ecclesiae Antiqua (Lat., 'The Ancient Statutes of the Church'). A document comprising a profession of faith, disciplinary canons, and a ritual for *Ordination. It is preserved in very many ancient MSS, which can be divided into Gallican, Italian, and Spanish families. Acc. to the *Hispana collection of canons, the Statuta were the decrees of the Fourth Council of Carthage of 398; it was from this source that they were first known and were long cited. It was not until 1757 that the *Ballerini brothers showed that the Statuta originated from S. Gaul and were composed in the second half of the 5th cent. Some scholars tried to connect them with *Caesarius of Arles, but this attribution has now been rejected. More recently C. Munier has suggested that they were compiled by *Gennadius of Marseilles.

The canons are found in all the principal edns. of the Councils under 'Council of Carthage of 398'. The Hispana form is pr. in J. P. Migne, *PL* 84. 199–208; the Ballerini edn., ibid. 56. 879–89. Crit. edn., with full discussion, by C. Munier (Bibliothèque de l'Institut de Droit Canonique de l'Université de Strasbourg, 5; 1960); text repr. in his *Concilia Galliae A. 314–A. 506* (CCSL 148; 1963), pp. 162–88. M. Coquin, OSB, 'Le sort des "Statuta Ecclesiae antiqua" dans les Collections canoniques jusqu'à la "Concordia" de Gratien', *RTAM* 28 (1961), pp. 193–224. J. Gaudemet, *Les Sources du Droit de l'Église en Occident du IIe au VIIe Siècle* (1985), pp. 84–6. Hefele and Leclercq, 2 (pt. 1; 1908), pp. 102–20. A. Malnory, *Saint Césaire, évêque d'Arles* (Paris thesis, 1894; also pub. in the Bibliothèque de l'École des Hautes Études, 103; 1894), pp. 50–62. B. Botte, OSB, 'Le Rituel d'ordination des Statuta Ecclesiae antiqua', *RTAM* 11 (1939), pp. 223–41.

Statutes of Provisors. See PROVISORS, STATUTES OF.

Steen, Cornelis Cornelissen van den. See CORNELIUS A LAPIDE.

Stein, Bl Edith (1891–1942), in religion Teresa Benedicta of the Cross, *Carmelite nun. A native of Breslau, of Jewish family, she studied at Göttingen and Freiburg i.B.

under E. Husserl and became a leading figure of the *Phenomenological School. Having abandoned Jewish practice in childhood, she was received into the RC Church in 1922, and from then on sought to interpret Phenomenology from a Thomist standpoint. She took the Carmelite habit at Cologne in 1934; in 1938 to escape arrest by the Nazis she was transferred to the Netherlands, but when that country was occupied she was taken to Auschwitz and put to death in a gas chamber. Her philosophical publications include 'Beiträge zur philosophischen Begründung der Psychologie und der Geisteswissenschaften' in *Jahrbuch für Philosophie und phänomenologische Forschung*, 5 (1922), pp. 1–283, and 'Eine Untersuchung über den Staat', ibid. 7 (1925), pp. 1–123. Most of her later works remained unpublished at her death. She was beatified in 1987. Feast day, 9 Aug.

Collected works ed. L. Gelber and R. Leuven, OCD (10 vols., Louvain, 1950–83, incl., as vol. 10, a Life by R. Leuven; Eng. tr., Washington, DC, 1986 ff.). Earlier Eng. tr. of Selected Writings by H. [C.] Graef (1956) and of *Kreuzeswissenschaft* (vol. 1 of Collected Works) as *The Science of the Cross* by id. (1960). Biog. by Sr. Teresa Renata de Spiritu Sancto, Prioress of Carmelite Convent, Cologne (Nuremberg, 1948; Eng. tr., 1952). H. C. Graef, *The Scholar and the Cross: The Life and Work of Edith Stein* (1955). W. Herbstrith, *Das Wahre Gesicht Edith Steins* (Munich [1971]; 5th edn., 1983; Eng. tr., San Francisco [1985]).

Steiner, Rudolf (1861–1925), founder of *anthroposophy (q.v.). The son of a station-master and apparently given a Catholic upbringing, he studied natural science at Vienna University and from 1890 to 1897 he was engaged on the Weimar edn. of the works of J. W. Goethe. In the next years he sought to elaborate a scientific method of studying the world of spirit and lectured widely on his conclusions. He was co-editor for a time of a literary magazine, and in 1902 he became the leader of a German section of the *Theosophical Society, but rejected the predominantly eastern associations of the main body. In 1913 Steiner founded the Anthroposophical Society as an independent association, building the Goetheanum at Dornach near Basle as its headquarters. His aim was to develop the faculty of spirit cognition inherent in ordinary people and to put them into touch with the spiritual world from which materialism had long estranged them. He taught the original nobility of the human spirit and a doctrine of immortality, supporting his teaching by a claimed clairvoyance. His extensive writings, which were mostly founded on his lectures, include *Die Philosophie der Freiheit* (1894; Eng. tr., 1916), *Theosophie: Einführung in übersinnliche Welterkenntnis und Menschenbestimmung* (1904; Eng. tr., 1910), and *Die Geheimwissenschaft im Umriss* (1910; Eng. tr., 1914).

The principal authority for his life is Steiner's autobiog., written when he was about 60; it was pub. Dornach, Switzerland, 1925; Eng. tr., London, 1928. Details of his lectures by A. Arenson, *Ein Führer durch die Vortragszyklen Rudolf Steiners* (1–50) (3 vols., 1930). A. P. Shepherd, *A Scientist of the Invisible: An Introduction to the Life and Work of Rudolf Steiner* (1954). A. W. Harwood (ed.), *The Faithful Thinker: Centenary Essays on the Work and Thought of Rudolf Steiner* (1961). F. Hiebel, *Rudolf Steiner im Geistesgang des Abendlandes* (Bern and Munich [1965]). C. Wilson, *Rudolf Steiner: The Man and his Vision* (Wellingborough, Northants, 1985). P. M. Allen, *The Writings and Lectures of Rudolf Steiner: A Chronological Bibliography of his Books, Lectures,*

Addresses, Courses, Cycles, Essays and Reports as published in English translation (New York, 1956); *Rudolf Steiner: Das literarische und künstlerische Werk. Eine bibliographische Übersicht*, herausgegeben von der Rudolf Steiner-Nachlassverwaltung (Dornach, Switzerland, 1961).

'Stephanus' (Estienne). A family of scholar-printers who worked at *Paris and *Geneva in the 16th and 17th cents.

HENRI [I] ESTIENNE (d. 1520), principal printer and publisher to Jacobus *Faber and his circle.

ROBERT [I] ESTIENNE (1503–59), Printer to Francis I. He is famous chiefly for his editions of the Scriptures and for his *Thesaurus Linguae Latinae*, first published in 1532, and for long a standard work. In his Latin Bibles, of which those of 1528, 1532, and 1540 are of special importance, he tried to follow as closely as possible the original text of St *Jerome. Of his editions of the Hebrew OT the chief are those of 1539 and 1544–6. In 1544 he began to print Greek, first using the famous Garamond type in his *editio princeps* of *Eusebius' *Historia Ecclesiastica*. Among his later editions of the Fathers is that of *Justin Martyr (1551). His most important edition of the Greek NT is that of 1550. It was the earliest to contain a critical apparatus, and its text is almost identical with the '*textus receptus' (q.v.). His annotations to his Bibles provoked severe attacks from the *Sorbonne, which led him to move to Geneva in 1551 where he became a *Calvinist. In his NT, published at Geneva in the same year, he introduced the division into verses arranged by himself, which is still used today. He subsequently published many of J. Calvin's works.

HENRI [II] ESTIENNE (1528–98), Robert's eldest son, who took over his father's establishment at Geneva. He published several *editiones principes*, including works by *Athenagoras, *Athanasius (spurious), and *Synesius. His fame rests chiefly on his *Thesaurus Linguae Graecae* (5 vols., 1572), a work of outstanding erudition which remained indispensable to generations of Greek scholars and was twice republished in the 19th cent. (London, 1815–25; Paris, 1831–63).

Two of Robert's other sons were of some importance: Robert [II] Estienne (1530–71), who returned to France and the RC Church, and in 1561 succeeded his father as Printer to the King; and François Estienne (b. *c*.1539), who supplemented the work of Henri at Geneva. Both printed Bibles.

A. A. Renouard, *Annales de l'imprimerie des Estienne, ou histoire de la famille des Estienne et de ses éditions* (2 vols., 1837–8; 2nd edn., 1843). M. *Pattison in *Quarterly Review*, 117 (1856), pp. 323–64, repr. as 'The Stephenses', in *Essays*, ed. H. Nettleship (Oxford, 1889), 1, pp. 67–123. H. Stein (ed.), 'Nouveaux Documents sur les Estienne, imprimeurs parisiens (1517–1665)', *Mémoires de la Société de l'Histoire de Paris et de l'Ile-de-France*, 22 (1895), pp. 249–95. L. Clément, *Henri Estienne et son œuvre française* (Paris thesis, 1898). J. Bompaire and others, *Henri Estienne* (Collection de l'École Normale Supérieure de Jeunes Filles, 43; Cahiers V. L. Saulnier, 5; 1988). [A.] E. Armstrong, *Robert Estienne, Royal Printer* (Cambridge, 1954; rev. edn., Courtenay Studies in Reformation Theology, 6; 1986). DeW. T. Starnes, *Robert Estienne's Influence on Lexicography* (Austin, Tex. [1963]). A. E. Tyler, 'Jacques Lefèvre d'Étaples and Henry Estienne the Elder 1502–20', in W. [G.] Moore and others (eds.), *The French Mind: Studies in honour of Gustave Rudler* (Oxford, 1952), pp. 17–33; R. M. Kingdon, 'The Business Activities of Printers Henri et

François Estienne', in G. Berthoud and others, *Aspects de la propagande religieuse* (Travaux d'Humanisme et Renaissance, 28; Geneva, 1957), pp. 258–75; [A.] E. Armstrong, 'Robert (II) Estienne à Paris (1556–1570)', *Bibliothèque d'Humanisme et Renaissance*. Travaux et documents, 20 (1958), pp. 349–69.

Stephen, St (d. *c*.35), protomartyr and, acc. to tradition, the first *deacon. Most probably a Hellenistic Jew, he was one of 'the seven' who, acc. to Acts 6: 5, were appointed by the Apostles to 'serve tables' in *Jerusalem. It is reported that he also took part in the preaching and performed miracles (Acts 6: 8 ff.), thus incurring the hostility of the Jews, who accused him to the *Sanhedrin; there he delivered a great discourse, setting out by a recapitulation of Israel's history that God does not depend on the Temple, which he had been accused of blaspheming, and that Christ was the prophet announced by *Moses, whom the Jews had killed (Acts 7: 2–53). Incensed at his denunciations, his accusers, apparently without formal trial, had him stoned acc. to the Mosaic Law, the witnesses laying their clothes at the feet of Saul, the future St *Paul. He died confessing Christ and asking forgiveness for his persecutors, and was buried by 'devout men' (Acts 8: 2). His tomb was not known until its alleged discovery by the priest Lucian in 415. His feast has been celebrated on 26 Dec. from the end of the 4th cent., while at one time a second feast, 'Inventio S. Stephani', commemorating the finding of his relics, was also kept on 3 Aug. A church containing his relics and dedicated to him was built outside the Damascus Gate by the Empress Eudoxia; it was dedicated in 439 and completed by 460. Its ruins were discovered by the *Dominicans in 1882 and a new church erected on the site. St Stephen was one of the most popular saints of the Middle Ages, esp. on the Continent. He is also commemorated in the *Canon of the Roman Mass. In the E. Church his feast is kept on 27 Dec.

For St Stephen himself the main material is to be found in comm. on Acts, cited s.v., e.g. that of E. Haenchen (Eng. tr., 1971), pp. 270–93. M. Simon, *St Stephen and the Hellenists in the Primitive Church* (1958). J. Bihler, *Die Stephanusgeschichte im Zusammenhang der Apostelgeschichte* (Münchener Theologische Studien. I. Historische Abteilung, 16; 1963). M. H. Scharlemann, *Stephen: A singular saint* (Analecta Biblica, 34; Rome, 1968). On the church at Jerusalem, M. J. *Lagrange, OP, *Saint Étienne et son sanctuaire à Jérusalem* (1894); C. Mommert, *Saint Étienne et ses sanctuaires à Jérusalem* (Jerusalem, etc., 1912); [L.] H. Vincent, OP, and F. M. Abel, OP, *Jérusalem*, 2 (1914), pp. 743–804; P. Devos, SJ, 'L'année de la dédicace de Saint-Étienne à Jérusalem: 439', *Anal. Boll.* 105 (1987), pp. 265–79. H. *Leclercq, OSB, in *DACL* 5 (1922), cols. 624–71, s.v. 'Étienne (Martyre et sépulture de saint)'; F. M. Abel, OP, in *Dict. Bibl.*, Suppl. 2 (1934), cols. 1132–46, s.v. 'Étienne (Saint)'; M.-É. Boismard [OP] in *Anchor Bible Dictionary*, 6 (1992), pp. 207–10, s.v. with further bibl.

Stephen I, St (d. 257), Pope from 12 May 254. He was a Roman by birth of the *gens Julia* and successor to Pope Lucius I. On his accession he (with St *Cyprian) was at once pressed by Faustinus, Bp. of Lyons, to intervene in the affairs of S. Gaul where Marcian, Bp. of Arles, had embraced *Novatianist doctrines. About the same time he also intervened in *Spain in another dispute arising out of the *Decian Persecution. Later he became involved in a long and bitter dispute with Cyprian over the validity of Baptism by heretics, which Cyprian, with the support of three African councils and Firmilian, Bp. of Caesarea in

Cappadocia, held to be null and void; and Stephen even refused to see a delegation from Carthage in 256. Acc. to the (unreliable) *Liber Pontificalis*, he introduced the rule that clerics should wear special clothes at their ministrations. He is traditionally reckoned a martyr, but on insufficient evidence. Feast day, formerly 2 Aug.

Two letters ascribed to Pope Stephen I are pr. in J. P. Migne, *PL* 3. 1033–44. Jaffé, 1, pp. 20 f. The principal sources are Cyprian, *Epp.* 67–75; *Eusebius, *HE* 7. 2–5; and *LP* (Duchesne), 1, pp. 68 and 154. *AASS*, Aug. 1 (1733), pp. 112–46, incl. Lat. text of 'Acta', pp. 139–46; 'Acta' tr. into Lat. from Armenian text by P. Martin in *Anal. Boll.* 1 (1882), pp. 470–84. J. Ernst, *Stephan I und der Ketzertaufstreit* (Forschungen zur christlichen Literatur- und Dogmengeschichte, 5, Heft 4; 1905); id., 'Die Stellung der römischen Kirche zur Ketzertauffrage vor und unmittelbar nach Papst Stephan I', *ZKT* 29 (1905), pp. 258–98. H. Koch, 'Zwei Erlasse Papst Stephans I in sprachgeschichtlicher Beleuchtung', *Philologus*, 86 (1930), pp. 128–32. S. G. Hall, 'Stephen I of Rome and the Baptismal Controversy of 256', in B. Vogler (ed.), *Miscellanea Historiae Ecclesiasticae*, 8 (Bibliothèque de la *Revue Ecclésiastique*, 72; 1987), pp. 78–82. A. Clerval in *DTC* 5 (1913), cols. 970–3, s.v. 'Étienne (1) I⁰ (Saint)'; J. N. D. Kelly, *The Oxford Dictionary of Popes* (1986), pp. 20 f.

Stephen II (III) (d. 757), Pope from 752. (He is sometimes counted the third of his name, 'Stephen II' having died four days after his election.) Under him the Papacy became allied with the Carolingian dynasty, a fact which was to influence the relations between the Church and the kingdoms of W. Europe for several centuries. When the Lombard king, Aistulf, in defiance of a treaty concluded with Stephen shortly before, besieged Rome, the Pope, after turning in vain to the Byzantine Emperor for help, crossed the Alps to ask the assistance of the Frankish king, *Pepin. After obtaining from him the much discussed 'Donation' of Quiercy (now often called the 'Donation of Pepin', 754), Stephen returned to Rome, which was finally delivered from the Lombard threat by Pepin's second campaign in 756. It was possibly in Stephen's curia that the '*Donation of Constantine' was produced. See also PATRIMONY OF ST PETER.

Letters preserved in the Codex Carolingus (ed. W. Gundlach in *MGH*, Epistolae, 3 (1892), pp. 487–507). Jaffé, 1, pp. 271–7. *LP* (Duchesne), 1 (1886), pp. 440–62 (Eng. tr. by R. Davis, Liverpool, 1992, pp. 51–76). E. Caspar, *Pippin und die römische Kirche* (1914; repr., Darmstadt, 1973). C. Rodenburg, *Pippin, Karlmann und Papst Stephan II* (Historische Studien, 152; 1923). L. Levillain, 'L'Avènement de la dynastie carolingienne et les origines de l'état pontifical (749–757)', *Bibliothèque de l'École des Chartes*, 94 (1933), pp. 225–95. M. Buchner, *Das Vizepapsttum des Abtes von St-Denis: Studien zur 'Offenbarung des Papstes Stephan II.' ('Revelatio') und ihrem Anhang ('Gesta')* (1928); O. Bertolini, 'Il problema delle origini del potere temporale dei papi nei suoi presupposti teoretici iniziali: il concetto di "Restitutio" nelle prime cessioni territoriali (756–757) alla Chiesa di Roma', *Miscellanea Pio Paschini*, 1 (Lateranum, NS 14; 1948), pp. 103–71. L. *Duchesne, *Les Premiers Temps de l'état pontifical* (2nd edn., 1904), pp. 52–78. T. F. X. Noble, *The Republic of St Peter: The Birth of the Papal State, 680–825* (Philadelphia [1984]), esp. pp. 71–88 and 90–8. A. Dumas in *DHGE* 15 (1963), cols. 1184–90, s.v. 'Étienne II'; J. N. D. Kelly, *The Oxford Dictionary of Popes* (1986), pp. 91 f.

Stephen III (IV) (d. 772), Pope from 768. Elected after the expulsion of the usurper Constantine II, he held a synod at the *Lateran (769) to regularize the situation

created by Constantine's irregular election and ordinations, which were declared null. The same synod excluded laymen from the Papal elections, confirmed the veneration of images, and anathematized the *iconoclastic Synod of 754. In the following years the Pope tried in vain to prevent a marriage between *Charlemagne and the daughter of the Lombard king, Desiderius, but finally abandoned the Franks and allied himself with the Lombards, a policy revoked by his successor *Hadrian I.

Letters preserved in the Codex Carolingus (ed. W. Gundlach in *MGH*, Epistolae, 3 (1892), pp. 558–67). Jaffé, 1, pp. 284–8. *LP* (Duchesne), 1, pp. 468–85 (Eng. tr. by R. Davis, Liverpool, 1992, pp. 85–106). O. Bertolini, 'La caduta del primicerio Cristoforo (771) nelle versioni dei contemporanei, e le correnti anti-longobarde e filolongobarde in Roma alla fine del pontificato di Stefano III (771–772)', *Rivista di Storia della Chiesa in Italia*, 1 (1947), pp. 227–62 and 349–78. J. T. Hallenbeck, 'Pope Stephen III: why was he elected?', *Archivium Historiae Pontificia*, 12 (1974), pp. 287–99. L. *Duchesne, *Les Premiers Temps de l'état pontifical* (2nd edn., 1904), pp. 123–33. T. F. X. Noble, *The Republic of St Peter: The Birth of the Papal State, 680–825* (Philadelphia [1984]), esp. pp. 120–7. Hefele and Leclercq, 3 (pt. 2; 1910), pp. 952–73. A. Dumas in *DHGE* 15 (1963), cols. 1190–3, s.v. 'Étienne III'; J. N. D. Kelly, *The Oxford Dictionary of Popes* (1986), pp. 95 f.

Stephen, St (975–1038), first king of *Hungary. He became a Christian, with his father, in 985, and on his accession to the Hungarian throne in 997 set out to Christianize his country, a work which was partly undone by his pagan successors. A strong supporter of the Papacy, he obtained in 1001 a royal crown from the Pope, though it appears later to have been returned to Rome, and is no longer believed to form part of the Hungarian crown preserved at Budapest. At about the same date he established episcopal sees throughout Hungary. He was canonized in 1083 together with his son, St Emeric. His feast (now an optional memorial) is kept on 16 Aug. (formerly 2 Sept.); but in Hungary 20 Aug., the day of the translation of his relics, is his principal festival.

Two early Lives (prob. 11th cent.), known as the Vita Major and the Vita Minor, ed. W. Wattenbach in *MGH*, Scriptores, 11 (1854), pp. 224–42. A 12th-cent. Life by Hartwick, perh. Bp. of Veszprém, pr. in *AASS*, Sept. 1 (1746), pp. 562–75, with other material, pp. 456–562. Vita Major and Vita Minor, and Life by Hartwick, also ed. E. Bartoniek in *Scriptores Rerum Hungaricarum*, ed. E. Szentpétery, 2 (Budapest, 1938), pp. 363–440, with material on his son, Emeric, pp. 441–60. T. von Bogyay, *Stephanus Rex: Versuch einer Biographie* (Vienna and Munich [1975]). G. Györffy, *István király és műve* (Budapest, 1977). Z. J. Kosztolnyik, *Five Eleventh Century Hungarian Kings: Their Politics and their Relations with Rome* (East European Monographs, 79; New York, etc., 1981), pp. 14–55 and 110–16. G. Klaniczay, *The Uses of Supernatural Power: The Transformation of Popular Religion in Medieval and Early-Modern Europe*, tr. by S. Singerman (Cambridge, 1990), esp. pp. 87–90. P. J. Kelleher, *The Holy Crown of Hungary* (Papers and Monographs of the American Academy in Rome, 13; 1951), with bibl. On his son Emeric, *AASS*, Nov. 2 (pt. 1; 1894), pp. 477–91, incl. discussion of sources for the history of the father. J. Szalay in *DHGE* 15 (1963), cols. 1235–7, s.v. 'Étienne (51)'.

Stephen Harding, St (d. 1134), third abbot of *Cîteaux. He was educated at the abbey of *Sherborne in N. Dorset. After travelling in Scotland and France, he underwent a conversion and went to Rome. Upon returning to Burgundy, he became a monk at Molesme; in 1098, he went with part of the community to Cîteaux. There, after being in turn sub-prior and prior, he was elected abbot in 1109. Owing to poverty and the severity of the rule, the monastery was faced with the danger of dying out when, in 1112, St *Bernard with 30 followers joined the monks, whose sudden increase of numbers soon necessitated other foundations. In order to maintain the original austerity and uniform government, Stephen drew up the nucleus of the '*Carta Caritatis', which established the system of regular visitations and General Chapters. The oldest history of the Order, the 'Exordium Cisterciensis Coenobii', has in part been ascribed to him, but the attribution is questionable. Besides being a great organizer, he is credited with responsibility for the text of the Latin Bible used at Cîteaux, correcting the OT with the help of Jews. The Cistercian General Chapter of 1623 prescribed his feast; that of 1683 transferred it from 17 Apr. to 16 July, though 17 Apr. stands in the *Roman Martyrology.

Works ascribed to him, with Life from *AASS*, repr. in J. P. Migne, *PL* 166. 1361–510. Life [by J. B. *Dalgairns] (The Lives of English Saints written at the suggestion of J. H. *Newman, 1844; 2nd edn. by A. W. Hutton, 1, 1900, pp. 3–214; also pub. separately, with notes by H. Thurston, SJ, London, 1898). There is no modern biog.: the best study is that of M.-A. Dimier in *DHGE* 15 (1963), cols. 1226–34, s.v. 'Étienne Harding', with extensive bibl. to date. Y. Załuska, *L'Enluminure et le Scriptorium de Cîteaux au XIIᵉ siècle* (Cîteaux, Studia et Documenta, 4; Cîteaux, 1989), *passim*. See also bibl. to CARTA CARITATIS and CISTERCIAN ORDER.

Stercoranists. Persons who asserted that the Blessed Sacrament is digested and evacuated by the recipient. Although they are written of as a sect, there appears to be no evidence that such a sect ever existed. The name, prob. of 12th-cent. origin (from Lat. *stercus*, 'dung'), is found in connection with the *Berengarian controversies.

C. M. *Pfaff, *Dissertatio Theologica de Stercoranistis Medii Aevi, tam Latinis, quam Graecis* (Tübingen, 1750). O. Zöckler and A. Hauck in *PRE* (3rd edn.), 19 (1907), pp. 9 f., s.v. 'Sterkoranisten', with further bibl.; also *OED*, s.v.

Stern, Henry Aaron (1820–85), missionary to the Jews. Born of Jewish parents at Unterreichenbach in Hesse-Cassel, he was educated at Frankfurt and Hamburg. Having entered on a commercial career he went to London, where he received Christian Baptism in 1840, and in 1842 began to prepare for service as a missionary. In 1844 he was ordained deacon by M. S. *Alexander, Bp. in *Jerusalem, on his way to Baghdad, and for some ten years he conducted itinerant missionary work among the Jews of Mesopotamia, Persia, and Kurdistan. He was ordained priest in 1849 on a visit to London. From 1853 to 1856 and again from 1857 to 1859 he was at *Constantinople. In 1859 and 1862 he made journeys to Ethiopia, where he did notable work among the Falashas, the so-called 'black Jews'. Anti-European feeling led to the imprisonment of Stern and his fellow-Europeans by King Theodore of Ethiopia in 1864, and only the approach of a British army secured his release in 1868. Somewhat broken in health, he spent the rest of his life in missionary activity in London, where many conversions and Baptisms took place. His publications include *Dawning of Light in the East* (1854), *Wanderings among the Falashas in Abyssinia* (1862) and *The Captive Missionary* (1868).

His *Wanderings among the Falashas* was repr., with introd. by R. L. Hess (1968). Life by A. A. Isaacs (London, 1886). Popular sketch by E. C. Dawson ('Splendid Lives Series', ibid. [1904]). W. G. D. Fletcher in *DNB* 54 (1898), pp. 195–7.

Sternhold, Thomas (d. 1549), versifier of the Psalms. Supposedly educated at Oxford, he entered the King's service and became a court favourite as one of the grooms of the robes. In 1545 he was elected MP for Plymouth. His claim to fame rests on his metrical version of the Psalms. A first (undated) edition, containing 19 Pss., appeared probably in 1549; it was dedicated to *Edward VI. A third edition, with 37 Pss., was issued posthumously in 1549; it contained seven further Pss. by 'J. H.' (John Hopkins, probably a Suffolk clergyman who died in 1570), and the collection, in the complete edition printed by John *Day in 1562, became generally known as 'Sternhold and Hopkins'. For the most part Sternhold used the familiar ballad metre of 'Chevy Chase', a fact which partly accounts for the popularity of psalm-singing in Elizabethan times.

J. Holland, *The Psalmists of Great Britain*, 1 (1843), pp. 91–105. R. Virgoe in S. T. Bindoff (ed.), *The History of Parliament: The House of Commons 1509–1558*, 3 (1982), p. 383, s.v. *BRUO, 1501–1540*, p. 539, s.v. See also bibl. to METRICAL PSALTERS.

Sterry, Peter (?1613–72), *Puritan divine. He was a native of Surrey and educated at Emmanuel College, Cambridge, where he was elected a Fellow in 1636. In 1643 he was one of the 14 divines proposed by the House of Lords for the *Westminster Assembly, and from 1645 preached frequently before the Houses of Parliament. In 1649 he was appointed one of O. *Cromwell's chaplains. After the Protector's death he retired to Hackney, where he took pupils and devoted himself to literary work. Sterry's theology was a mixture of *Calvinism and *Neoplatonism. The former is to be seen in his emphasis on the will of God to the virtual exclusion of secondary causes and human free will, the latter in his conception of the world as emanating from God and, through the Fall and Redemption by Christ, returning to God and to its own original beauty. He was influenced by *J. Boehme, and in an age of sectarian strife was an ardent advocate of mutual tolerance founded on Christian love. Among his more important works, all written in a fine prose, are *A Discourse of the Freedom of the Will* (1675) and *The Rise, Race and Royalty of the Kingdom of God in the Soul of Man* (1683).

V. de Sola Pinto, *Peter Sterry, Platonist and Puritan, 1613–1672: A Biographical and Critical Study with Passages selected from his Writings* (1934). F. J. Powicke, *The Cambridge Platonists: A Study* (1926), ch. 5, pp. 174–92. C. Fell-Smith in *DNB* 54 (1898), pp. 224 f.

Stevens, William (1732–1807), Anglican religious writer. He was born at Southwark, and educated at Maidstone together with his cousin, G. *Horne. He later became partner of a hosier and studied theology in his leisure time. He belonged to the circle of '*Hutchinsonians' and acquired an extensive knowledge of the Scriptures, the early Fathers, and such Anglican divines as L. *Andrewes and Jeremy *Taylor. His works were chiefly pamphlets, collected as Οὐδενὸς Ἔργα ('Nobody's Works') in 1805. One of his best-known studies is *An Essay on the Nature and Constitution of the Church*

(1773), in which he defended episcopacy and the legislative power of the Church. He also edited the works of W. *Jones of Nayland (12 vols., 1801) to which he prefixed a Life written by himself in the style of I. *Walton.

J. A. Park, *Memoirs of William Stevens, Esq.* (anon., 1812; enlarged edn. with name of author, 1859). G. Le G. Norgate in *DNB* 54 (1898), p. 233.

stewardship. The management of property by a servant on behalf of its owner, and more particularly in modern times, the organized pledging of a specific amount of money to be given regularly to the Church, often designated 'Christian stewardship'. In its general sense the term (οἰκονομία and its cognates) occurs frequently in the NT. In the early Church, though the word itself was rarely used, it was widely taught that the Christian ought to regard the holding of property as a trust to be administered on behalf of the needy. In subsequent ages exhortations to give alms to the poor were less closely connected with the concept of stewardship, though this continued to have an important role in the distribution of charity by monastic and other ecclesiastical institutions. The concept of stewardship again came to the fore with the 'success' preachers in N. America in the late 17th cent.; disbursement of one's income to pious causes 'as a steward of the Lord' was extolled both as a Christian virtue and a key ingredient in business success. It was, however, the need to fund missionaries which brought about what is called the 'Stewardship Awakening' in the second quarter of the 19th cent. in the USA.

Essential to the emerging doctrine of stewardship was the idea that all people, and not just the affluent, could be benefactors of religion. As methods of church funding (such as pew rents) which drew class distinctions between members were increasingly disliked, 'systematic finance' was hailed as an acceptable alternative. Drawing on developments in fund-raising pioneered by the *YMCA in the United States, American Protestant Churches developed the 'Every Member Canvass' (RC interest came later) and many established denominational stewardship agencies which would assist parishes' annual stewardship programmes. The system was refined by commercial fund-raising agencies, including the Chicago-based Wells Organizations, founded in 1946 by Herbert Wells. This introduced triennial stewardship programmes, first to *Australia (1954) and then to other Commonwealth countries, including England, where the decline in the value of endowments necessitated contributions from the laity as never before. Wells canvassers stressed both the Church's need for money to finance its work and the need of individuals to promise regular financial support as part of their personal Christian stewardship. The canvassers relied on the presence of a full-time director to train and motivate local leaders. The programmes featured elaborate brochures and parish dinners, sermons on generosity and individual solicitation by Church members who had already made a significant financial pledge. The results of the stewardship campaigns were astonishingly successful, often with huge increases in parish income, but after the initial success, many Churches wanted to reduce the cost of such programmes and to eliminate the peer-pressure which was inherent in the Wells method. They then set up their own departments of stewardship.

In Europe the *Lutheran Churches have shown practical interest in stewardship (usually *Haushalterschaft*), interpreting the concept as pastoral support and evangelism through home visitation.

From 1920, perhaps in response to a perceived overemphasis on financial stewardship, stewardship theology was applied to all aspects of life, often defined as time, talents, and treasure. More recently, 'stewardship of creation' has been a theme of theological response to environmental issues.

See also TITHES.

H. Brattgård, *God's Stewards: A Theological Study of the Principles and Practices of Stewardship*, tr. by G. J. Lund (Minneapolis [1963]); D. J. Hall, *The Steward: A Biblical Symbol Come of Age* (Library of Christian Stewardship; New York, 1982; rev. edn. [1990]). P. De Vos and others, *Earthkeeping: Christian Stewardship of Natural Resources* (Grand Rapids, Mich. [1980]). *A Stewardship Bibliography*, pub. by the Commission on Stewardship of the National Council of the Churches of Christ in the USA (3rd edn., New York, 1985).

sticharion (Gk. στιχάριον). The liturgical tunic, usually of coloured stuff, worn in the E. Church and comparable with the *alb in the W.

Braun, *LG*, pp. 92–101.

sticheron (Gk. στιχηρόν). In the E. Church a brief liturgical hymn which is attached to a verse (στίχος) of a Psalm or other scriptural passage.

stichometry. The practice, dating from at least 300 BC, of computing the length of a MS from the number of lines. In the MSS of the Greek classics the standard line (στίχος) contained 16 syllables; but when stichometric reckoning came to be applied to biblical MSS, it seems that a 15-syllable line was sometimes used for the Gospels. Among the oldest extant biblical stichometric tables is the list of the Pauline Epistles in the *Codex Sinaiticus.

Stigand (d. ?1072), Abp. of *Canterbury. A king's priest under Cnut, he was made Bishop of Elmham in his native E. Anglia in 1043, translated to *Winchester in 1047, and appointed Abp. of Canterbury in 1052 in succession to the Norman Robert of Jumièges, who had been expelled and outlawed. He nevertheless retained the see of Winchester, thus combining the two richest bishoprics in England. He did not secure Papal recognition until 1058, and then from Benedict X, who next year was himself deposed as a schismatic Pope. Stigand, a patron of the arts but greedy for lands and monasteries, exemplified some of the weaknesses of the English Church before 1066. His uninspiring leadership and dubious status at Canterbury cast a shadow over his province. Although his position provided a pretext for *William I's invasion in 1066, he was honoured by the Conqueror until the throne was secure. In 1070 William had him deposed on various charges by Papal legates; he was succeeded by *Lanfranc and died in custody at Winchester.

*William of Malmesbury, *De Gestis Pontificum Anglorum*, ed. N. E. S. A. Hamilton (Rolls Series, 1870), pp. 35–7, gives the critical view of the next generation. F. Barlow, *The English Church 1000–1066* (1963), esp. pp. 76–81, 302–7. F. M. Stenton, *Anglo-Saxon England* (3rd edn., Oxford, 1971), esp. pp. 465 f., 623 f., 659–61. N. Brooks, *The Early History of the Church of Canterbury*

(Leicester, 1984), pp. 305–13. W. Hunt in *DNB* 54 (1898), pp. 369 f., with refs.

stigmatization. The reproduction of the wounds of the Passion of Christ in the human body. It is a phenomenon usually accompanied by other manifestations of the same category, such as levitation, *bilocation, and telepathic faculties, as well as by abnormal physical states such as lameness or blindness not due to organic causes, and almost complete abstinence from food and sleep. Stigmata may either be invisible, i.e. the stigmatized person experiences only the pain without any exterior signs, or visible, in which case they normally consist of wounds or blood blisters on hands, feet, and near the heart, also on the head (Crown of Thorns) or shoulders and back (carrying of the Cross and Scourging). They do not become septic and resist ordinary treatment, but are liable to periodical bleedings, mostly on Fridays and during Lent and Passiontide. Various natural explanations have been advanced; and though it is widely held that supernatural influences have to be admitted in many cases, a certain abnormal physical predisposition, acted upon by a deeply religious mind imbued with an extraordinary devotion to the Passion of the Lord, would seem to account for much in these phenomena. The official attitude of the RC Church has always been guarded, and stigmatization has never been made a reason for *canonization; among the known stigmatized, who are estimated to number over 300, there are only some 60 saints and beati. None of them appear before the 13th cent., when the growing devotion to the suffering Christ seems to have occasioned their appearance. The first saint known to have received the stigmata is St *Francis of Assisi; but since then cases have been numerous, predominantly among women. Some of the best known are St *Catherine of Siena (invisible), St *Catherine of Genoa, Anna Katharina *Emmerick, St Gemma *Galgani, and Therese *Neumann. The Stigmata of St Francis are commemorated in the Franciscan Order on 17 Sept.

A. Imbert-Gourbeyre, *La Stigmatisation, l'extase divine et les miracles de Lourdes* (2 vols., 1894), esp. vol. 1, and vol. 2, pp. 1–231. A series of arts. in *Études Carmélitaines*, 21, vol. 2 (Oct. 1936) ('Douleur et Stigmatisation'). H. Thurston, SJ, *The Physical Phenomena of Mysticism* (posthumously ed. J. H. Crehan, SJ, 1952), pp. 32–129 (various essays repr. from scattered sources, with corrections). R. Biot, *L'Énigme des stigmatisés* (1955; Eng. tr., 1962). G. Wunderle, *Zur Psychologie der Stigmatisation* (1938). Octavianus a Rieden [O. Schmucki], OFM Cap., 'De Sancti Francisci Assisiensis Stigmatum Susceptione. Disquisitio historico-critica luce testimoniorum saeculi XIII', *Collectanea Franciscana*, 33 (1963), pp. 210–66, 392–422; 34 (1964), pp. 5–62 and 241–338; Eng. tr., with additional bibl. and notes, *The Stigmata of St Francis of Assisi* (Franciscan Institute Publications, History Series, 6; St Bonaventure, NY [1991]). J. Danemarie [pseudonym for M. Ponet-Bordeaux], *Le Mystère des stigmatisés de Catherine Emmerich à Thérèse Neumann* (1933; Eng. tr., 1934). É. Amann in *DTC* 14 (pt. 2; 1941), cols. 2616–24, s.v. 'Stigmatisation'; P. Adnès, SJ, in *Dict. Sp.* 14 (1990), cols. 1211–43, s.v. 'Stigmates'.

Stillingfleet, Edward (1635–99), Bp. of *Worcester. He was born at Cranborne in Dorset and educated at St John's College, Cambridge, of which he became a Fellow in 1653. In 1657 he was appointed rector of Sutton, Bedfordshire, and in 1665 rector of St Andrew's, Holborn, where he soon made a name as a preacher. Having won the favour of *Charles II he was given several preferments, becoming

Archdeacon of London in 1677 and Dean of *St Paul's in 1678. He was less esteemed under *James II, but after the Revolution of 1689 he was immediately appointed Bp. of Worcester.

Stillingfleet was a man of *Latitudinarian views. His first book, the *Irenicum* (1659), advocated a union between *Episcopalians and *Presbyterians. While opposing Nonconformity, it treated forms of Church government as inessential and led to his being accused of following T. *Hobbes. The work was re-edited in 1662 with an appendix, in which Stillingfleet propounded the view that the Church was a society distinct from the State with its own rights and privileges. In the same year he published *Origines Sacrae*, an apologetic work dealing with the Divine authority of Scripture. In 1664 he replied to the *Jesuit account of the controversy between W. *Laud and J. *Fisher in his *Rational Account of the Grounds of the Protestant Religion*. The book had a great success and was followed by other controversial writings against RCs, *Socinians, and J. *Locke. Stillingfleet held Locke's *Essay Concerning Human Understanding* (1690) to be detrimental to the Trinitarian faith and published three pamphlets in reply (1696–7). His famous *Origines Britannicae* (1685) deals with the sources of the British Church. His *Sermons*, of which several volumes were published, enjoyed a long popularity.

Works (6 vols., London, 1709–10), with Life [by R. Bentley] in vol. 1, pp. 1–46. J. [W. H.] Nankivell, 'Edward Stillingfleet, Bishop of Worcester 1689–99', *Transactions of the Worcestershire Archaeological Society*, 22 for 1945 (1946), pp. 16–34; sep. pub. with list of his ordinations appended (1946). R. T. Carroll, *The Common-Sense Philosophy of Religion of Bishop Edward Stillingfleet, 1635–1699* (International Archives of the History of Ideas, 77; The Hague, 1975). G. Reedy, SJ, *The Bible and Reason: Anglicans and Scripture in Late Seventeenth-Century England* (Philadelphia [1985]), *passim*. J. Marshall, 'The Ecclesiology of the Latitude-men 1660–1689: Stillingfleet, Tillotson and "Hobbism"', *JEH* 36 (1985), pp. 407–27. W. H. *Hutton in *DNB* 54 (1898), pp. 375–8; id. in *DECH* (1912), pp. 574 f.

Stock, St Simon. See SIMON STOCK, ST.

Stockholm Conference (1925). It grew out of an appeal for peace and fellowship sent out by Christian leaders in several neutral countries at the outset of the First World War (1914), followed by a further appeal by N. *Söderblom, Abp. of Uppsala, in June 1917 for an immediate conference. After the end of the war plans were made, and the Universal Christian Conference on *Life and Work eventually met at Stockholm, 19–30 Aug. 1925, to promote Christian influences on political, social, and economic life in the modern world. Over 500 representatives, drawn from most of the larger Christian bodies except the RC Church, took part. The subjects of the discussions were: The Purpose of God for Humanity and the Duty of the Church; The Church and Economic and Industrial Problems; The Church and International Relations; The Church and Christian Education; and Methods of Cooperative and Federative Efforts by the Christian Communions. The conference issued a 'Message', but no official findings. Its work was carried further in the conferences of *Oxford (1937) and *Amsterdam (1948).

G. K. A. *Bell (ed.), *The Stockholm Conference 1925: The Official Report of the Universal Christian Conference on Life and Work held in Stockholm, 19–30 August, 1925* (1926).

Stoicism. A Graeco-Roman school of philosophy, founded at *Athens by Zeno of Citium (335–263 BC). His chief pupil was Cleanthes of Assos (331–232), whose work was carried on by Chrysippus of Soli (c.280–207). The system may be described as a form of materialistic pantheism or monism in contrast to *Platonic idealism on the one hand and *Epicurean hedonism on the other. The Stoics believed in law—the law of nature and the law of conscience or duty. To them God is the immanent all-pervading energy by which the natural world is created and sustained. He is also the world reason or '*Logos' which manifests itself in the order and beauty of the world. To the Stoics the good man is the wise man, and his wisdom consists in conformity to nature, i.e. in living according to the law of the universe embodied in the Divine reason. This 'life according to nature' was open to all men, even to slaves. Stoic ethics had a wide and tonic influence in the Graeco-Roman world, and its religious spirit is well illustrated in the famous 'Hymn to Zeus' of Cleanthes. The Stoic *Seneca was reputed to have engaged in correspondence with St *Paul.

Frags. of earlier Stoics collected in H. von Arnim, *Stoicorum Veterum Fragmenta* (4 vols. [vol. 4, index], Teub., 1903–24). For the edns. of Seneca, Epictetus, and Marcus Aurelius, see s.vv. Studies in Eng. incl. J. M. Rist, *Stoic Philosophy* (Cambridge, 1969); F. H. Sandbach, *The Stoics* (1975); J. M. Rist (ed.), *The Stoics* (Berkeley and Los Angeles, Calif., and London [1978]); G. Verbeke, *The Presence of Stoicism in Medieval Thought* (Washington, DC, 1983); M. L. Colish, *The Stoic Tradition from Antiquity to the Early Middle Ages* (Studies in the History of Christian Thought, 34–5; Leiden, 1985); B. Inwood, *Ethics and Human Action in Early Stoicism* (Oxford, 1985). M. Pohlenz, *Die Stoa: Geschichte einer geistigen Bewegung* (2 vols., Göttingen, 1948–9; vol. 1, repr. 1970; vol. 2, with bibl. suppl. by H.-T. Johann, 1972); M. Spanneut, *Le Stoïcisme des pères de l'Église de Clément de Rome à Clément d'Alexandrie* (Patristica Sorbonensia, 1; 1957; 2nd edn., 1969); id., *Permanence du Stoïcisme de Zénon à Malraux* (Gembloux, 1973); M. Forschner, *Die stoische Ethik: Über den Zusammenhang von Natur-, Sprach- und Moralphilosophie im altstoischen System* (Stuttgart, 1981). For works on the reputed correspondence of Seneca and St Paul, see bibl. to SENECA.

Stolberg, Friedrich Leopold, Graf zu (1750–1819), poet. A member of the German poets' circle, Goettinger Hain, he was an admirer and imitator of F. G. *Klopstock and a friend of J. W. Goethe, and became a translator of Homer, Aeschylus, and other classical authors. After filling the posts of envoy of the Protestant Prince Bp. of Lübeck to the Danish court (1777), of Danish envoy to Berlin (1789), and other offices, he was received into the RC Church in 1800. His most important work after his conversion is the *Geschichte der Religion Jesu Christi* in 15 vols. (1806–18), an influential though not always scholarly history of Christianity from OT times to the death of St *Augustine. Among his numerous poetical and prose works a Life of *Alfred the Great (1817) and the devotional *Büchlein von der Liebe* (1819) became popular among his contemporaries.

Gesammelte Werke der Brüder Christian und Friedrich Leopold Grafen zu Stolberg (20 vols., Hamburg, 1820–5; 2nd edn., 1827). *Briefe* [a selection], ed. J. Behrens (Kieler Studien zur deutschen Literaturgeschichte, 5; Neumünster, 1966). Facsimile repr. of *Streitschriften über Stolbergs Konversion*, ed. id. (Berne and Frankfurt am Main, 1973). J. Janssen, *Friedrich Leopold Graf zu Stolberg: Sein Entwicklungsgang und sein Wirken im Geiste der Kirche* (1882; 4th edn. by L. von *Pastor, 1910). L. Scheffczyk, *Friedrich Leopold zu Stolbergs 'Geschichte der Religion Jesu Christi'* (Münchener theologische Studien, I. Historische Abteilung, 3; 1952). E. Schmidt in *Allgemeine Deutsche Biographie*, 36 (1893), pp. 350–67, s.v. 'Stolberg-Stolberg: Friedrich Leopold', with lit. to date; P. Wittmann in *CE* 14 (1912), pp. 299 f., s.v.

stole. A liturgical vestment consisting of a long strip of coloured material. Its origin is doubtful. It was possibly first used in the manner of a scarf or a handkerchief in the E., where the deacon's stole is first mentioned in the 4th cent. In the W. it is first attested for Spain in the 6th cent. When it came to Rome in the 8th cent. it was worn under the *dalmatic, whereas in the *Ambrosian rite it has always been worn outside it. In the E., where it is called an *orarion, it is worn on top of the *sticharion. The priest's stole is not mentioned in the E. (where it is called an *epitrachelion) until the 8th cent., but was in general use in the W. from the 9th, when the priests of the Frankish Empire were bidden always to wear it as a sign of their calling, e.g. by the Synod of Mainz in 813. At Rome the stole was originally called 'orarium', the word *stola* being Gallican and introduced into Italy c. 11th cent.

In the W. Church the stole has become the distinctive vestment of the deacon, who wears it like a sash over the left shoulder, its ends being fastened together under the right arm. It is, however, also a regular vestment of the priest, who in the RC Church now always wears it round the neck, with its ends falling straight down in front, as does the bishop. Besides its use at Mass, it is also worn when touching the Blessed Sacrament, when administering the Sacraments, and very generally when preaching. Its colour depends on that of the other vestments and on the occasion, e.g. when hearing confessions the priest wears a purple stole. In the C of E the use of the stole was revived in the middle of the 19th cent. The 1969 Canons (B 8) make provision for either a stole or a scarf to be worn by the minister at the Occasional Offices and by the celebrant, gospeller, and epistoler at the Eucharist. See also BROAD STOLE.

Braun, *LG*, pp. 562–620. J. Braun, SJ, *Handbuch der Paramentik* (1912), pp. 154–64. Id. in *CE* 14 (1913), pp. 301 f., s.v.

Stone, Darwell (1859–1941), *Anglo-Catholic theologian. Educated at Merton College, Oxford, he was ordained deacon in 1883, and after a short period of parish work at Ashbourne (1883–4) was priested and became vice-principal (1885) and later principal (1888) of Dorchester (Oxon) Missionary College. From 1909 to 1934 he was principal of Pusey House, Oxford. Throughout his adult life he was a strenuous upholder of High Church principles, defending the more traditional theology of R. W. *Church and H. P. *Liddon against the teaching of the *Lux Mundi School. In later life he became increasingly the leader of the Anglo-Catholic Movement in the C of E. Stone's writings were characterized by wide and accurate learning and fairness towards his opponents. Among the chief were *Holy Baptism* (1899), *Outlines of Christian Dogma* (1900), *The Christian Church* (1905), *A*

History of the Doctrine of the Holy Eucharist (1909), and *The Reserved Sacrament* (1917). From 1915 till his death he was editor of the projected *Lexicon of *Patristic Greek*.

F. L. Cross, *Darwell Stone, Churchman and Counsellor* (1943). Id. in *DNB*, *1941–1950*, pp. 842–3.

Stonyhurst College. One of the largest RC schools in England. Conducted by the *Jesuit Fathers, it traces its origin back to Elizabethan days, when a college for English boys was founded at *St-Omer (1592) and subsequently transferred to Bruges (1762) and Liège (1773). In 1794 it moved to Stonyhurst Hall in Lancashire. The standard of education is that of the great public schools. Stonyhurst Observatory has been made famous by many astronomers of European reputation. Though closed as a professional observatory in 1947, it was reopened for amateur use by the school and local community in 1980.

A. Hewitson, *Stonyhurst College, Past and Present* (Preston, 1870). J. Gerard, SJ, *Stonyhurst College: Its Life Beyond the Seas, 1592–1794, and on English Soil, 1794–1894* (Centenary Record; Belfast, 1894). G. Gruggen, SJ, and J. Keating, SJ, *Stonyhurst: Its Past History and Life in the Present* (1901). H. Chadwick, SJ, *St Omers to Stonyhurst* (1962). A. Henderson, *The Stone Phoenix: Stonyhurst College 1794–1894* (Worthing, 1986). T. E. Muir, *Stonyhurst College 1593–1993* (1992). F. Irwin, SJ, in *CE* 14 (1912), pp. 309 f., s.v.

Storch, Nicolas (d. after 1536), *Anabaptist. A Saxon wool-weaver, he became leader of the *Zwickau Prophets (q.v.) during T. *Müntzer's sojourn in the city (1520–51). Later, he and his associates, having been compelled to leave Zwickau, arrived late in 1521 at *Wittenberg, where their biblical learning impressed both P. *Melanchthon and N. von *Amsdorf. Thereafter his movements are obscure, until his stay in W. Thuringia in 1523. After the defeat of the rebels in the *Peasants' War in central Germany, Storch emerged as the leader of an Anabaptist sect in N. Franconia. In 1536 he was once more rumoured to be in Zwickau. The date of his death is unknown. His teaching was essentially spiritualist, with a chiliastic expectation of the imminent purification of the Church. The influence upon Storch of *Hussite ideas from Bohemia has been refuted, but he may have embraced the libertine doctrines of the *Brethren of the Free Spirit.

S. Hoyer, 'Die Zwickauer Storchianer—Vorläufer der Täufer?', *Jahrbuch für Regionalgeschichte*, 13 (1986), pp. 60–78 (repr. in J.-G. Rott and S. L. Verheus (eds.), *Anabaptistes et dissidents au XVIᵉ siècle* (Bibliotheca Dissidentium, scripta et studia, 3; Baden-Baden and Bouxwiller, 1987), pp. 65–83). S. C. Karant-Nunn, *Zwickau in Transition, 1500–1547: The Reformation as an Agent of Change* (Columbus, Oh., 1987), *passim*. A. Friesen, *Thomas Muentzer, a Destroyer of the Godless* (Berkeley, Calif., etc, 1990), pp. 73–99. See also bibl. to ZWICKAU PROPHETS.

stoup (OE *stéap*). A basin near the entrance of a church containing *holy water with which the faithful may sprinkle themselves. Holy-water fonts were perhaps originally derived from the fountains in the *atriums of the old basilicas, in which those who entered washed their hands and faces. They began to come into more general use with the custom of sprinkling the people with holy water at the Sunday Mass, which was introduced in the middle of the 9th cent. The stoups are of various forms, either let into the wall or standing on a socle, and often

richly ornamented. In England they were usually of stone and built into a small niche, and many specimens are preserved in pre-Reformation churches. Their use is universal in RC churches and has been revived in the C of E in modern times.

F. Bond, *The Chancel of English Churches* (1916), Appendix, 'The Holy Water Stoup', pp. 255–8. H. *Leclercq, OSB, in *DACL* 2 (pt. 1; 1910), pp. 758–71, s.v. 'Bénitier'.

Stowe Missal. An early Mass-book of the Irish Church, formerly preserved at Stowe House in Bucks, and now in the Library of the Royal Irish Academy at Dublin (D. II. 3). In its present state it contains, besides extracts from St John's Gospel, an *Ordinary and *Canon of the Mass, propers for three special Masses, an office of Baptism and of the Visitation of the Sick, a treatise in Irish on the ceremonies of the Mass, and three Irish spells. The main interest lies in the Ordinary and Canon, in which various peculiarities in the text suggest that the book was originally made for a specific occasion, perhaps the dedication of a church in a largely pagan district of N. Ireland. The last name in the series of bishops enumerated in the *diptychs is 'Maileruen', who is usually identified with St Maelruain of Tallaght, who died in 792; the earliest part of the MS cannot have been written before this date. This nucleus was considerably revised and extended at a later date by a scribe called Moelcaich. In the 11th cent. the MS was encased in a *cumdach*, or case of precious metal.

The most convenient edn. of the text is still that of B. Mac-Carthy in *Transactions of the Royal Irish Academy*, 27 (1886), pp. 135–268. It is also ed., with facsimiles, by G. F. Warner (HBS 31–2; 1906–15).

Strabo, Walafrid. See WALAFRID STRABO.

Stratford, John (*c.*1275/80–1348), Abp. of *Canterbury. He was a native of Stratford-upon-Avon. After being Archdeacon of *Lincoln and Dean of the Court of *Arches, he became Bp. of *Winchester in 1323, an appointment which temporarily lost him the favour of Edward II. In 1327 he drew up the six articles against Edward II and counselled him to abdicate. From 1330, the year in which he was first appointed Chancellor by Edward III, he was the chief adviser of the young King, and in 1333 became Abp. of Canterbury. The following years were mainly spent in political affairs, including repeated negotiations with France. When, in 1340, Edward returned from an unsuccessful expedition to Flanders, Stratford's enemies attributed to him the failure and the King brought a series of charges against him. Stratford, however, inspired by the example of St Thomas *Becket, stood firm and finally obtained recognition of the principle that peers should be tried only by their equals in full Parliament. Though soon reconciled to the King, he retired from political life and devoted himself to his ecclesiastical duties. He was a benefactor of Stratford-upon-Avon, where his devotion to Becket led him to establish a chantry in his honour in the parish church and to endow a college of priests.

W. D. Macray, 'Sermons for the Festivals of St. Thomas Becket, etc. probably by Archbishop Stratford', *English Historical Review*, 8 (1893), pp. 85–91, incl. extracts. G. Lapsley, 'Archbishop Stratford and the Parliamentary Crisis of 1341', ibid. 30

(1915), pp. 6–18, 193–215; N. M. Fryde, 'John Stratford, Bishop of Winchester, and the Crown, 1323–30', *Bulletin of the Institute of Historical Research*, 44 (1971), pp. 153–61. R. M. Haines, *Archbishop John Stratford* (Pontifical Institute of Mediaeval Studies, Studies and Texts, 76; Toronto [1986]). D. Hughes, *A Study of Social and Constitutional Tendencies in the Early Years of Edward III* (1915), *passim*. BRUO 3 (1959), pp. 1796–8.

Strauss, David Friedrich (1808–74), German theologian. A native of Ludwigsburg in Württemberg, in 1821 he entered the seminary at Blaubeuren, where he was a pupil of F. C. *Baur, and in 1825 went to the *Tübingen Stift. Here he came under the influence of F. D. E. *Schleiermacher (with whose doctrines he later lost sympathy) and of G. W. F. *Hegel's philosophy. After studying in Berlin, he was appointed in 1832 'Repetent' at the Stift and lecturer on Hegelian philosophy at Tübingen University. His famous *Leben Jesu*, in which he applied the 'myth theory' to the life of Christ, appeared in 1835. The book denied the historical foundation of all supernatural elements in the Gospels, which were assigned to an unintentionally creative legend (the 'myth'), developed between the death of Christ and the writing of the Gospels in the 2nd cent. The growth of primitive Christianity was to be understood in terms of the Hegelian dialectic. The work, which exercised a deep influence on subsequent Gospel criticism, roused a storm of indignation and led to Strauss's dismissal from his post at Tübingen. In 1839 an attempt to obtain for him a Professorship of Theology at Zurich came to nothing. His next work, *Die christliche Glaubenslehre* (2 vols., 1840–1), is a polemical history of Christian doctrine from the NT and the Fathers to its dissolution in Hegelian philosophy. Strauss now turned his attention to politics and, in the literary sphere, to biography. His writings of this period include *Ulrich von Hutten* (3 vols., 1858–60) and *Hermann Samuel Reimarus* (1862). In 1864 he published a slightly more positive version of his first work, *Leben Jesu für das deutsche Volk*, and in 1865 *Der Christus des Glaubens und der Jesus der Geschichte* (1865), an attack on Schleiermacher's attempt to combine the 'historical Jesus' with the 'Christ' of dogma. His last work, *Der alte und der neue Glaube* (1872; Eng. tr., *The Old Faith and the New*, 1873), is essentially a negation of Christianity in favour of scientific materialism and rejects human immortality.

Gesammelte Schriften (incomplete), ed. E. Zeller (12 vols., Bonn, 1876–8); *Ausgewählte Briefe*, ed. id. (ibid., 1895); *Briefwechsel zwischen Strauss und Vischer*, ed. A. Rapp (Veröffentlichungen der deutschen Schillergesellschaft, 18 and 19; 1952–3). The 1892 edn. of George Eliot's tr. of Strauss's *Life of Jesus* (orig. pub. 1846) was repr., with introd. by P. C. Hodgson (Philadelphia [1972]; London, 1973). Modern Eng. trs. of *The Christ of Faith and the Jesus of History*, with introd. by L. E. Keck (Philadelphia [1977]) and of the work which Strauss wrote *In Defence of My Life of Jesus against the Hegelians*, with introd. by M. C. Massey (Hamden, Conn., 1983; the orig. Ger. was pub. in 1837). E. Zeller, *David Friedrich Strauss in seinem Leben und seinen Schriften* (1874; Eng. tr., 1874); A. Hausrath, *David Friedrich Strauss und die Theologie seiner Zeit* (2 vols., 1876–8); T. Ziegler, *David Friedrich Strauss* (2 vols., Strasbourg, 1908). G. Müller, *Identität und Immanenz: Zur Genese der Theologie von David Friedrich Strauss* (Basler Studien zur historischen und systematischen Theologie, 10; 1968); J. F. Sandberger, *David Friedrich Strauss als theologischer Hegelianer* (Studien zur Theologie und Geistesgeschichte des neunzehnten Jahrhunderts, 5; 1972); H. Harris, *David Friedrich Strauss and his Theology* (Cambridge, 1973); F. W. Graf, *Kritik und Pseudo-Spekulation: David Friedrich Strauss als Dogmatiker im Kontext der positionellen Theologie seiner Zeit* (Münchener Monographien zur historischen und systematischen Theologie, 7; 1982); M. C. Massey, *Christ Unmasked: The Meaning of* The Life of Jesus *in German Politics* (Chapel Hill, NC, and London [1983]). A. *Schweitzer, *Von Reimarus zu Wrede* (1906), pp. 67–119 (Eng. tr., *The Quest of the Historical Jesus*, 1910, pp. 68–120). T. Ziegler in *PRE* (3rd edn.), 19 (1907), pp. 76–92, s.v.

Street, George Edmund (1824–81), architect. Born at Woodford, now part of N. London, he was educated at Mitcham and Camberwell. He soon developed an enthusiastic interest in ecclesiastical architecture and obtained an appointment under G. G. *Scott. In 1849 he set up an office of his own and, after making the acquaintance of B. *Webb, became a member of the Ecclesiological Society (see CAMBRIDGE CAMDEN SOCIETY). His first successes were several churches in the West Country, esp. Cornwall. After some good work for W. J. *Butler at Wantage, where he resided from 1850 to 1852, he was appointed diocesan architect by S. *Wilberforce, Bp. of Oxford. He was also diocesan architect to *York, *Ripon, and *Winchester. He travelled extensively to study French, German, N. Italian, and Spanish churches, and in 1855 his design for the new cathedral at Lille only just missed acceptance. He was the architect of the Crimea Memorial Church at *Constantinople (1864–9). At home he became a leader in the Gothic revival, designing a number of churches and institutional buildings, among them Cuddesdon Theological College; St Peter's, Bournemouth; St James the Less, Westminster; St Philip and St James's, Oxford; St Margaret's Convent, East Grinstead; the nave of Bristol cathedral; St Mary Magdalene, Paddington; and Kingston, Dorset. In *Some Account of Gothic Architecture in Spain* (1865) he made students of architecture aware of the glories of the church of Santiago de *Compostela. The height of his career was the invitation to design the new Law Courts in the Strand, which he did not live to see completed.

A. E. Street (son), *Memoir of George Edmund Street, RA, 1824–1881* (1888; with complete list of Street's works). *Victorian Church Art*. Exhibition Catalogue, Victoria and Albert Museum (1971), pp. 46–54. P. Waterhouse in *DNB* 55 (1898), pp. 42–5.

Streeter, Burnett Hillman (1874–1937), theologian and NT scholar. He was educated at Queen's College, Oxford, and was a Fellow from 1905 to 1933 and Provost from 1933 to 1937. From 1915 to 1934 he was also a canon of *Hereford Cathedral. His researches into the *Synoptic Problem, notably in *Oxford Studies in the Synoptic Problem* (ed. W. *Sanday, 1911), helped to establish among English Churchmen belief in the priority of St Mark's Gospel and the existence of '*Q'. In *The Four Gospels* (1924) he set out his conclusions on the Gospels as a whole and expounded his theses on the '*Caesarean text' and '*Proto-Luke'. In *Reality* (1926) he sought to correlate science with theology. His other publications included *The Primitive Church* (1929) and essays in *Foundations* (1912), *Concerning Prayer* (1916), *Immortality* (1917), *The Spirit* (1919), and *Adventure* (1926), all of which he edited. In 1932 he delivered a course of *Bampton Lectures on *The Buddha and the Christ*. He was an active supporter of the *Student Christian Movement and of the *Modern

Churchmen's Union, and also (at the end of his life) of the *Oxford Group movement.

P. [B.] Hinchliff, *God and History: Aspects of British Theology 1875–1914* (Oxford, 1992), pp. 223–47. L. W. Grensted in *DNB, 1931–40*, pp. 836–8, s.v.

Strigel, Victorinus (1524–69), Reformation theologian. A native of Kaufbeuren in Swabia, in 1538 he went to school in Freiburg im Breisgau and from 1542 studied at *Wittenberg, where he was much influenced by P. *Melanchthon. After teaching for a time at Erfurt, in 1548 he became first professor and rector of the new school at Jena, founded by the followers of J. A. *Ernesti. Here he expounded, in opposition to the strict Lutheranism of M. *Flacius, more moderate and conciliatory doctrines and defended a form of *synergism. At Weimar in Aug. 1560 he found himself involved in a disputation in the presence of the court on the relation of the human will to divine grace in the work of conversion. The five heads of discussion—*de libero arbitrio, de definitione legis et evangelii, de *Majorismo, de *Adiaphorismo*, and *de academica ἐποχή*—indicate the points at which Strigel's teaching departed from the stricter Lutheranism, it being opposition to Strigel at Weimar that led Flacius to the formula that original sin is the substance of the natural man. In 1563 he was appointed professor at Leipzig, but four years later opposition to the *Calvinistic tendencies of his Eucharistic doctrine led to his withdrawal, and he became a professor at Heidelberg. He wrote extensively on philological and historical as well as on theological subjects, though many of his works were not published till after his death. They include a commentary on almost the whole Bible.

Collection of his *Opuscula Quaedam Theologica*, pub. Hanover, 1598. V. A. Nordman, *Victorinus Strigelius als Geschichtslehrer* (Helsingfors thesis, Åbo, 1930), with refs. to earlier lit. G. Kawerau in *PRE* (3rd edn.), 19 (1907), pp. 97–102, s.v.

Strossmayer Joseph Georg (1815–1905), Bp. of Djakovo in Croatia. Born in Osijek to a family of Austrian descent, he was ordained priest in 1838 and in 1847 became chaplain at the imperial court in Vienna. He was consecrated Bp. of Djakovo in 1850. Here he promoted the cause of pan-Slavism, worked for reunion with the Orthodox Church of *Serbia and *Russia (negotiating with V. *Solovyov), and spent large sums on education, regardless of the denominational allegiance of the recipients of his bounty. At the First *Vatican Council in 1869–70 he was one of the most outstanding opponents of the definition of Papal infallibility, and on 22 Mar. 1870 occasioned a 'scene' at the Council by his ill-timed defence of Protestantism. Until Oct. 1871 he continued to maintain relations with J. J. I. v. *Döllinger and J. H. *Reinkens, but on 26 Dec. 1872 finally published the Vatican decrees in his official diocesan journal.

F. Šišić (ed.), *Korespondencija Rački-Strossmayer* (Zagreb, 4 vols., 1928–31); id., *Josi Juraj Strossmayer: Dokumenti i Korespondencija*, 1 (all pub., ibid., 1933). I. Sivrić, OFM, *Bishop J. G. Strossmayer: New Light on Vatican I* (Chicago and Rome, 1975), with useful discussion of earlier works. K. Milutinović, *Štrosmajer i Jugoslovensko Pitanje* (Institut za Izučavanje Istorije Vojvodine, Monografije, 15; Novi Sad, 1976). [E.] C. Butler, OSB, *The Vatican Council*, 1 (1930), pp. 134 f., 189 f., 270–5, and 2 (1930), p. 175, and *passim*. R. Schutz in *DTC* 14 (pt. 2; 1941), cols. 2630–5, s.v.

Strype, John (1643–1737), English Church historian. He was a native of London, educated at St Paul's School and at Jesus College and Catharine Hall, Cambridge, and in 1669 was appointed curate and lecturer at Leyton, London. From 1689 to 1724 he was also lecturer at Hackney, and in 1711 he was given the sinecure of West Tarring, W. Sussex. He formed a very fine collection of Tudor documents, now in the Harleian and Lansdowne MSS of the British Library. His historical works deal chiefly with the Reformation period, the principal one being the *Memorials of Thomas Cranmer* (1694, ed. for the Eccl. Hist. Soc. in 3 vols., 1848–54). Among the others are *Annals of the Reformation in England* (4 vols., 1709–31), *Life and Acts of Matthew Parker* (1711), and *Ecclesiastical Memorials* (3 vols., 1721). The wealth of documentary material on which his works are based renders them invaluable to the student of the period, despite their bad arrangement, cumbersome style, and frequent errors. He also edited J. Stow's *Survey of London* (1720).

Modern repr. of historical and biog. works, 19 vols. bound in 25, Oxford, 1812–24; index to this edn. [by R. F. Laurence] (2 vols., ibid., 1828). W. D. J. Cargill Thompson, 'John Strype as a Source for the Study of Sixteenth-Century Church History', in D. Baker (ed.), *The Materials, Sources and Methods of Ecclesiastical History* (Studies in Church History, 11; 1975), pp. 237–47, repr. in Cargill Thompson, *Studies in the Reformation: Luther to Hooker*, ed. C. W. Dugmore (1980), pp. 192–201. R. O'Day, *The Debate on the English Reformation* (1986), pp. 42–53. G. Goodwin in *DNB* 55 (1898), pp. 67–9.

Stubbs, John (*c.*1543–90), also 'Stubbe', *Puritan writer. A native of Norfolk, he was drawn into Puritan circles while studying at Trinity College, Cambridge, and at Lincoln's Inn; his sister married T. *Cartwright in 1577. In 1574 Stubbs probably had some part in the publication of a parodic English version of Abp. M. *Parker's biographical study of the Archbishops of Canterbury, *De Antiquitate Britannicae Ecclesiae* (1572). In Aug. 1579 he published *The Discovery of a Gaping Gulf whereinto England is like to be swallowed by another French marriage*, an attack on *Elizabeth I's proposed marriage to the Catholic Francis, Duke of Anjou. Stubbs, his publisher, and his printer were all sentenced and the first two had their right hands cut off (3 Nov. 1579), though they both continued to protest their loyalty to the Queen. After 18 months' imprisonment in the Tower he was set free, and subsequently commissioned by Lord Burghley to write a reply (1587, now apparently lost) to W. *Allen's *Defence of the English Catholics* (1584). In 1589 he became MP for Great Yarmouth, but died during his patron Lord Willoughby's military expedition to France. His other writings include an English version of some of T. *Beza's Meditations on the Psalms (pub. 1582).

L. E. Berry (ed.), *John Stubbs's* Gaping Gulf *with Letters and Other Relevant Documents* (Folger Documents of Tudor and Stuart Civilization; Charlottesville, Va., 1968), with biog. introd. A. F. Scott Pearson, *Thomas Cartwright and Elizabethan Puritanism* (Cambridge, 1925), pp. 183 f. and 305 f.; A. G. R. Smith, *Servant of the Cecils: The Life of Sir Michael Hickes, 1543–1612* (1977), pp. 92–8. Id. in P. W. Hasler (ed.), *The History of Parliament: The House of Commons 1558–1603*, 3 (1981), pp. 460 f., s.v. 'Stubbe, John'.

Stubbs, William (1825–1901), ecclesiastical historian and Bp. of *Oxford. He was born at Knaresborough, N.

Yorks, educated at Ripon Grammar School and through C. T. *Longley's influence nominated a servitor at *Christ Church, Oxford. In 1848 he was elected a Fellow of Trinity College. While rector of Navestock (1850–66) he laid the basis of his immense historical learning. From 1866 to 1884 he was Regius professor of modern history at Oxford, and from 1879 to 1884 also a Canon of *St Paul's. Later he became Bp. of *Chester (1884–9) and of Oxford (1889–1901).

Stubbs was the greatest British historian of his time. He contributed 19 volumes to the Rolls Series of *Chronicles and Memorials*, among them the *Gesta Regum* of *William of Malmesbury (1867), the *Gesta Regis Henrici II* (1867), Roger Hoveden's *Chronica* (4 vols., 1868–71), the *Memorials of St Dunstan* (1874), and the *Historical Works of Gervase of Canterbury* (1879–80). His *Constitutional History of England* (3 vols., 1873–8), which takes its subject down to 1485, and the companion vol. of *Select Charters* (1870) became classics. His other works included *Registrum Sacrum Anglicanum* (1858, 2nd edn., 1897; chronological lists of the English Bishops) and *Councils and Ecclesiastical Documents relating to Great Britain and Ireland* (3 vols., 1869–73, with A. W. Haddan). A collection of his ordination addresses was published posthumously in 1901.

W. H. *Hutton (ed.), *Letters of William Stubbs, Bishop of Oxford* (1904). J. G. Edwards, *William Stubbs* (Historical Association Pamphlet G. 22; 1952), with further refs. H. G. Richardson and G. O. Sayles, *The Governance of Mediaeval England from the Conquest to Magna Carta* (Edinburgh, 1963), pp. 1–21 ('William Stubbs: The Man and the Historian'). T. F. Tout in *DNB, 1901–1911*, pp. 444–51.

Studd, Charles Thomas (1862–1931), missionary. He was the son of a retired planter, Edward Studd, who was converted in 1877 at a mission of D. L. *Moody and I. D. Sankey. He was educated at Eton and Trinity College, Cambridge, where he was famed for his cricketing prowess. Edward Studd's conversion influenced his three sons and 'C. T.' (as he came to be called) volunteered for missionary work in China. As one of the 'Cambridge Seven' his intentions aroused much interest and enthusiasm, and laid the seeds of the Student Volunteer Movement. Sailing for China under the *China Inland Mission in 1885, he followed the early practice of that Mission by living in Chinese fashion. Ill-health compelled him to return in 1894. In 1900 he sailed for India, where he was the pastor of an undenominational Church at Ootacamund until he was again forced to return through sickness. Stirred by the need of missionary pioneer work in Central Africa, he sailed, contrary to medical advice, for the heart of Africa in 1910, and continued to work there till his death. On being joined by recruits in 1912, he founded the 'Heart of Africa Mission'. As this work developed, 'C. T.' conceived the idea of a 'World Evangelization Crusade' for the occupation by missionaries of the unevangelized areas of the world; the Crusade later extended its activities to S. America and elsewhere.

Lives by T. B. Walters (London, 1930), N. P. Grubb (ibid., 1933), and E. Buxton [daughter] (ibid., 1968). E. Vincent, *C. T. Studd and Priscilla* (Bromley, Kent, 1988). N. [P.] Grubb, *After C. T. Studd* (1939).

Studdert Kennedy, Geoffrey Anketell (1883–1929),

Anglican priest. Of Irish descent, he was educated at Leeds Grammar School, Trinity College, Dublin, and Ripon Clergy College, and in 1908 was ordained deacon. After holding curacies at Rugby and Leeds, he became vicar of St Paul's, *Worcester (1914–21), and Chaplain to the Forces (1916–19). His vivid faith, the fruit of a deep sacramentalism, was reflected in a warmth of character which endeared him to the men in the trenches (where he won the affectionate title of 'Woodbine Willie', from a brand of cigarettes he distributed) and made him the best-known padre in the First World War (1914–18). The unconventionality of his views (e.g. his belief in God's passibility and his dissatisfaction with certain elements in the traditional Christian moral code), which helped to gain him a wide hearing, were the expression of a solid theology. In 1922 he was appointed rector of St Edmund, King and Martyr, Lombard Street. He continued his mission preaching, constantly travelling about and working in association with the *Industrial Christian Fellowship. His books, popular in form, include *Rough Rhymes* (1918), *The Hardest Part* (1918), *The Wicket Gate* (1923), and *The Word and the Work* (1925).

J. K. Mozley (ed.), *G. A. Studdert Kennedy. By his friends* (1929); W. Purcell, *Woodbine Willie: An Anglican Incident. Being some account of the life and times of Geoffrey Anketell Studdert Kennedy, poet, prophet, seeker after truth, 1883–1929* (1962).

Student Christian Movement (SCM). The British section of a world-wide fellowship of students desiring 'to understand the Christian faith and live the Christian life'. It developed out of several independent movements at Cambridge and elsewhere in the later years of the 19th cent. By study-circles, conferences, and camps, it sought to bring Christian students of all denominations together, to instruct them in the Christian faith and to enable them to witness to the outside world. From the first an integral part of its work was the 'Student Volunteer Missionary Union', which aimed at fostering missionary work abroad, and it took its full share in the international association known as the World Student Christian Federation. From its activity in promoting the issue of literature addressed to students, originally publications of small cost and of practical purpose, there developed a religious publishing house (SCM Press, Ltd., London). As a body drawing membership from all Christian communions (since the Second *Vatican Council incl. the RC) the Movement cultivated an outlook closely akin to that of the *Ecumenical Movement, many of whose leaders had earlier been associated with the SCM. Its slow decline began after the Second World War, when it failed to find a real role in the new universities and allied itself with ephemeral radical movements. The SCM Press, on the other hand, developed into a major international publisher and in 1989 became independent of the SCM. By the 1990s the SCM had virtually disappeared.

T. Tatlow, *The Story of the Student Christian Movement of Great Britain and Ireland* (1933). E. Fenn, *Learning Wisdom: Fifty Years of the Student Christian Movement* (1939). R. Rouse, *The World's Student Christian Federation: A History of the First Thirty Years* [i.e. 1895–1924] (1948). D. L. Edwards, *Movements into Tomorrow: A Sketch of the British SCM* (1960).

Studios. The famous monastery of *Constantinople, dedicated to St *John the Baptist. It stood in the west of the city, not far from the Golden Horn. Acc. to tradition founded in 463 by the former Roman consul, Studios, its monks followed the rule of the '*Acoemetae', who organized their psalmody so as to ensure its perpetual recitation by part of the community. They became famous as zealous upholders of orthodoxy, and defended the decrees of *Chalcedon against the Monophysite patriarch, *Acacius (484–519). Driven from their monastery by the persecution of Constantine Copronymus (Emp. 741–75), only a few of them returned after his death.

A new period began for Studios under St *Theodore, who became its abbot in 799. He introduced a new rule, based on that of St *Basil, in which manual work played a far greater part than hitherto, and a strict discipline, esp. in regard to enclosure, poverty, and the exclusion of women from the monastery, was introduced. From his time Studios became the centre and model of E. monasticism and the monks of Mount *Athos, e.g., formed their life on its basis. It became esp. famous for its school of copyists and artists, and very many of its ancient hymns are still in use in the Greek Church. During the *Iconoclastic Controversy it supplied the most ardent defenders of images. Destroyed by the *Crusaders in 1204, the monastery was rebuilt in 1290, but again severely damaged by the Turks in 1453. The church, once a mosque, is now in ruins. The religious life of Studios, however, was revived by A. Szeptyckij, metropolitan of Lvov (in the Ukraine), who founded an organization of *Uniat monks acc. to the Rule of St Theodore of Studios in 1906.

Extracts from the Rule ('Constitutiones Studianae') from Vat. gr. 2029 in J. P. Migne, *PG* 99. 1703–20. E. Marin, *De Studio Constantinopolitano* (Paris, 1897). On the form of the name, H. *Delehaye, SJ, 'Studion-Studios', *Anal. Boll.* 52 (1934), pp. 64 f. J. Leroy, OSB, 'La vie quotidienne du moine studite', *Irénikon*, 27 (1954), pp. 21–50. *Oriente Cattolico: Cenni storici e statistiche*, issued by the Sacra Congregazione per le Chiese Orientali (4th edn., Vatican City, 1974), pp. 523–7. E. Candal, SJ, in *EC* 11 (1953), cols. 1441 f., s.v. 'Studiti'.

studium generale. A name widely current from the middle of the 13th cent. for higher educational establishments of more than purely local significance, notably (1) universities attracting students from different regions and, usually, different countries and (2) international colleges run by religious orders, such as the *Dominicans, along university lines and often in association with universities. With reference to (1) the term acquired ever greater legal precision from the late 13th cent. onwards and *studia generalia* were thenceforth normally characterised by their right to confer the *licentia ubique docendi* ('licence to teach anywhere') on the authority of the pope or the emperor.

O. Weijers, *Terminologie des Universités au XIIIᵉ siècle* (Rome, 1987), pp. 34–45, with full refs.

Stundists (Russ. *štundisty*; cf. Ger. *Stunde*, 'devotional hour'). Certain Russian evangelical sects which emerged in the Ukraine *c.*1858–62, under the direct influence of *Lutheran and *Reformed pastors and *Mennonite preachers. In the last quarter of the 19th cent. the Stundists became increasingly Baptist in orientation, and their present-day descendants form part of the 'All Union Council of Evangelical Christians and Baptists', established in Russia in 1944.

W. Gutsche, *Westliche Quellen des russischen Stundismus* (Cassel, 1956).

Sturm, Johannes (1507–89), Protestant Reformer and educationalist. Educated at Liège at the School of the *Brethren of the Common Life and at Louvain University, he joined himself to the French humanists and lectured on the classics at *Paris from 1530 to 1536. Having become a Protestant under M. *Bucer's influence, he went to Strasbourg in 1537, where he took an active part in furthering the Reformation. His interest in education did much to make the city one of the foremost educational centres of Europe, and in 1538 a gymnasium on a humanistic model devised by Sturm was established with himself as rector. In 1566 an academy followed. In 1581 Sturm was expelled from Strasbourg for his liberalism and inter-confessional sympathies by the strict *Lutherans, but eventually allowed to return. His writings included a Life of the German humanist, B. *Rhenanus.

W. Sohm, *Die Schule Johannes Sturms und die Kirche Strassburgs in ihren gegenseitigen Verhältnis* (Historische Bibliothek, 27; 1912). J. Rott, 'Le recteur strasbourgeois Jean Sturm et les Protestants français', *Actes du Colloque L'Amiral de Coligny et son temps (Paris, 24–28 octobre 1972)* (1974), pp. 407–425; id., 'Bibliographie des œuvres imprimées du recteur strasbourgeois Jean Sturm (1507–1589)', *Actes du 95ᵉ Congrès National des Sociétés Savantes (Reims, 1970). Section de philologie et d'histoire jusqu'à 1610*, 1 (1975), pp. 318–404; both repr. in id., *Investigationes Historicae*, ed. M. de Kroon and M. Lienhard, 2 (Strasbourg, 1986), pp. 43–61 and 471–559. A. Schindling, *Humanistische Hochschule und freie Reichsstadt* (Veröffentlichungen des Instituts für europäische Geschichte Mainz, 77; Wiesbaden, 1977), *passim*. C. Schmidt and J. Ficker in *PRE* (3rd edn.), 19 (1907), pp. 109–13. Schottenloher, 2 (1935), pp. 315 f. (nos. 20926–52).

Stylite (Gk. στῦλος, 'pillar'). In the early Church a solitary who lived on the top of a pillar. Their pillars would vary in height, and the platforms, sometimes made more habitable by a small hut, were generally provided with a parapet against which the Stylite would lean for his scanty sleep. Food was usually supplied by disciples or admirers. Apart from prayer Stylites gave much time to spiritual instruction, to reconciling enemies, and often to theological controversies. They considered St *Simeon Stylites (q.v.) their founder. There are many instances of such ascetics from the 5th to the 10th cents., and isolated examples down to modern times. They flourished esp. in Syria, Mesopotamia, Egypt, and Greece.

H. *Delehaye, SJ, *Les Saints stylites* (Subsidia Hagiographica, 14; 1923), with general bibl. in note to pp. cxvii f. B. Kötting, *Peregrinatio Religiosa* (Münster, 1950), pp. 113–31. I. Peña, OFM, and others, *Les Stylites Syriens* (Publications du 'Studium Biblicum Franciscanum', Collectio Minor, 16; Milan [1975]). H. *Leclercq, OSB, in *DACL* 15 (pt. 2; 1953), cols. 1697–718, s.v.; T. Špidlík, SJ, in *Dict. Sp.* 14 (1990), cols. 1267–75, s.v.

Suárez, Francisco (1548–1617), Spanish *Jesuit theologian. From 1564 to 1570 he studied philosophy and theology at Salamanca, and then taught at several Spanish colleges of his order. From 1580 to 1585 he lectured on the 'Summa Theologiae' of St *Thomas Aquinas at the Roman College, and from 1585 to 1593 on the Incarnation and the Sacraments at the Jesuit College at Alcalá. Here he wrote his first work, *De Verbo Incarnato* (1590), a commentary on the first 26 questions of the third part of the

'Summa', noted esp. for its attempt to reconcile the Thomist view of the Redemption as the final cause of the Incarnation with that of *Duns Scotus, who held the manifestation of the perfection of the Divine work of creation to be its final cause, so that even without the Fall the Incarnation would have taken place. *De Mysteriis Vitae Christi* followed in 1592, and in 1597 appeared his *Disputationes Metaphysicae*, one of the principal textbooks on the subject, in which he combined the teaching of *Aristotle with that of St Thomas. The work, which exercised a considerable influence also on Protestant contemporary philosophers, is important esp. for its new method, as it no longer closely follows Aristotle in the sequence of thought but gives an independent systematic treatment adapted to the needs of the modern Christian thinker. In 1597 *Philip II called Suárez to the University of Coimbra, where he lectured until 1616. In 1599 he published his *Varia Opuscula Theologica*, occasioned by the controversy on grace (*de Auxiliis*) between the Jesuits and *Dominicans. In it, as in his *De vera intelligentia auxilii efficacis* of 1605 (pub. 1655), he proposed in the system called *Congruism a solution of the problem of the relation between human freedom and Divine grace on *Molinist lines. Acc. to Suárez, God does not, as the Thomists teach, cause man's free acts, but, foreseeing them by His special knowledge called '*scientia media', brings about the salvation of the elect by giving them those graces ('gratia congrua') of which he foresees that they will make good use in certain given circumstances. The teaching provoked much opposition but became the prevalent doctrine among non-Thomist RC theologians. In 1608–9 he published *De Virtute et Statu Religionis*, a fundamental work on the religious state with special reference to the Society of Jesus, and in 1612 *De Legibus* (which became of paramount importance for jurists and legislators in Continental Europe and in America) in the form of a Commentary on the 19 relevant questions of the 'Summa', in which he expounded the principles of natural and international law. It was followed, in 1613, by the *Defensio Fidei*, directed against the C of E, which was burned in London and banned by the Parlement of Paris for teaching doctrines prejudicial to the power of the state. His last great works on grace, published posthumously in three parts as *De necessitate gratiae* (1619), *De gratia habituali* (1619), and *De gratia actuali* (1651), elaborated and systematized the teaching given in his earlier writings.

The salient points in which Suárez departs from Thomism are regarded by some scholars as forming a system of his own, called 'Suárezianism'. Among its chief features are the conception of the individual as the object of direct Divine and human intellectual cognition, the pure potentiality of matter, and the conceptual, not real, distinction in created beings of essence and existence. Suárez is usually considered the greatest theologian of the Society of Jesus and was called by *Paul V 'Doctor eximius et pius'.

Collected edn. of his *Opera*, 23 vols., Venice, 1740–51; new edn. by D. M. André, 28 vols., Paris, 1856–78. Photographic reprods. from orig. edns. of *Selections from Three Works*: De Legibus ac Deo Legislatore, 1612; Defensio Fidei Catholicae et Apostolicae adversus Anglicanae Sectae Errores, 1613; De Triplici Virtute Theologica, Fide, Spe, et Charitate, 1621, with list of errata and Eng. tr. by G. L. Williams, A. Brown, J. Waldron, and H. Davis, SJ, and introd. by J. B. Scott (2 vols., Classics of

International Law, 20; 1944). Modern edns., with Sp. tr., of his *Disputaciones metafísicas*, by S. Rabade Romeo and others (7 vols., Madrid, 1960–6), of *Defensio Fidei* by E. Elorduy and L. Pereña (ibid., 1965), and of *De Legibus* by L. Pereña and others (Corpus Hispanorum de Pace, 11–17, 21–2, etc.; 1971 ff.). Good general modern study by R. de Scorraille, SJ, *François Suarez de la Compagnie de Jésus d'après ses lettres, ses autres écrits inédits et un grand nombre de documents nouveaux* (2 vols. [1912–13]). J. H. Fichter, *Man of Spain: Francis Suarez* (New York, 1940) C. Larrainzar, *Una introducción a Francisco Suárez* (Pamplona, 1980). The vast number of more specialized studies, of which there is an extensive list in Polgár, cited below, incl. L. Mahieu, *François Suarez: Sa philosophie et les rapports qu'elle a avec sa théologie* (1921); P. Dumont, SJ, *Liberté humaine et concours divin d'après Suarez* (1936), and J. J. O'Brien, *Reparation for Sin: A Study of the Doctrine of Francis Suarez* (Mundelein, Ill., 1960). B. Hamilton, *Political Thought in Sixteenth-Century Spain: A Study of the Political Ideas of Vitoria, De Soto, Suárez, and Molina* (Oxford, 1963). Sommervogel, 7 (1896), cols. 1661–87, s.v.; P. Múgica, SJ, *Bibliografía Suareciana, con una introducción sobre el estado actual de los estudios suarecianos* by E. Elorduy, SJ (Granada, 1948); Polgár, 3 (1990), pp. 268–329. P. Monnot, SJ, P. Dumont, SJ, and R. Brouillard, SJ, in *DTC* 14 (pt. 2; 1941), cols. 2638–728, s.v.

subcintorium. An ecclesiastical vestment resembling the *maniple. In the Middle Ages it was worn by bishops (a usage which persisted at Milan until the 16th cent.) and occasionally by priests, but its use came to be restricted to the Pope and has now been dropped entirely. It was worn on the left side, attached to the *girdle, when celebrating a solemn pontifical Mass; its purpose was to secure the *stole to the girdle.

Braun, *LG*, pp. 117–24.

subdeacon. In the RC Church, formerly a person in the lowest of the three *Major Orders. The subdiaconate was not thought to be instituted by Christ but by the Church, and the conferring of the order was thus regarded as a *sacramental rather than a true *Sacrament. The earliest mention of a 'subdeacon' is in a letter of Pope *Cornelius to Fabius of Antioch (251), while the correspondence of St *Cyprian attests the existence of subdeacons in Africa at the same time. Until the 13th cent. the subdiaconate was regarded as a *minor, not a major, order.

A subdeacon was one of the three sacred ministers at *High Mass, when his functions were to prepare the bread and wine and the vessels, to chant the Epistle, to present the chalice and paten at the offertory and to remove the vessels from the altar after the communion. In recent times, however, the part of the subdeacon at High Mass was generally taken by a person in deacon's or priest's orders. In the RC Church, until the office was suppressed in 1972, candidates had to be over 21 years of age and were bound to *celibacy and the recitation of the Divine *Office. In the E. Church the subdiaconate still exists as a minor order. It was given up in the C of E with the other minor orders in the 16th cent., though in recent times proposals have occasionally been made to restore it. It has been restored in certain Anglican missionary dioceses.

H. Reuter, *Das Subdiakonat: Dessen historische Entwicklung und liturgisch-kanonische Bedeutung* (1890). F. Wieland, *Die genetische Entwicklung der sog. Ordines Minores in den drei ersten Jahrhunderten* (*RQ*, Supplementheft, 7; 1897), pp. 18–48. A. Michel in *DTC* 14 (pt. 2; 1941), cols. 2459–66, s.v. 'Sous-diacre'; H. *Leclercq, OSB, in *DACL* 15 (1953), cols. 1619–26, s.v.

'Sous-diacre', with refs. See also works cited under ORDERS AND ORDINATION.

Subiaco. (Lat. *Sublacum*). A town some 40 miles E. of Rome, famous as the site of the grotto where St *Benedict settled on his retirement from the world. Before his death St Benedict founded 12 separate monasteries in the vicinity, two of which exist today. See also SUBIACO CONGREGATION.

P. Egidi, G. Giovannoni, F. Hermanin, and V. Federici, *I monasteri di Subiaco* (2 vols., 1904). B. Cignitti and L. Caronti, *L'Abbazia nullius Sublacense: Le origini. La commenda* [1956]. P. Carosi, *Il primo monastero benedettino* (Studia Anselmiana, 39; 1956). C. Mirzio, OSB, *Cronaca Sublacense* (ed. L. Allodi, OSB, Rome, 1885). 'Chronicon Sublacense, sive Catalogus Abbatum Monasterii Sublacensis ab Anno circiter DXCV usque ad MCCCXC', by an anonymous monk, ed. L. A. *Muratori, *Rerum Italicarum Scriptores*, 24 (Milan, 1738), pp. 927–66; new edn. by R. Morghen in G. Carducci, V. Fiorini, and P. Fedele's edn. of Muratori, 24, pt. 6; Bologna, 1927. L. Allodi and G. Levi (eds.), *Il Regesto Sublacense del secolo XI* (Biblioteca della R. Società Romana di Storia Patria, 1885). J. F. Angerer, O. Praem. (ed.), *Caeremoniae Sublacences* (Corpus Consuetudinum Monasticarum, 11; 2 pts., Siegburg, 1985–7). B. Trifone, OSB (ed.), 'Documenti Sublacensi', *Archivio della R. Società Romana di Storia Patria*, 31 (1908), pp. 101–20. L. H. Cottineau, OSB, *Répertoire topo-bibliographique des abbayes et prieurés* (Mâcon, 1935), cols. 3099 f., s.v. S. Andreotta, OSB, in *NCE* 13 (1967), pp. 756 f., s.v.

Subiaco Congregation. A monastic *Congregation of *Benedictine monks formerly known as the Cassinese Congregation of the Primitive Observance. It originated in 1851 within the *Cassinese Congregation, led by Abbot Peter Casaretto, and became a separate Congregation in 1872. It was officially renamed the Subiaco Congregation in 1967. It is international in character, with the majority of its monasteries situated in W. Europe (esp. France, Italy, Spain, Belgium); its English province has abbeys in Ramsgate in Kent, Prinknash in Glos., and Pluscarden in Scotland.

I Monasteri Italiani della Congregazione Sublacence (1843–1972) (Parma, 1972). A series of arts. in *Studia Monastica*, 14 (Montserrat, 1972), pp. 347–525, a special number to mark the centenary of the congregation. In Eng., P. Ievers, OSB, 'The Cassinese Congregation of the Primitive Observance', *Pax*, 28 (1939), pp. 225–9. G. Lunardi, OSB, in *DIP* 2 (1975), cols. 1503–7, s.v. 'Congregazione Benedettina Sublacense'.

subintroductae (Gk. συνείσακται). In the early Church, women who lived associated with men in spiritual marriage; in the 4th cent. they were also called *agapetae* (ἀγαπηταί, 'beloved'). *Hermas seems to be familiar with the practice, and later *subintroductae* existed at *Antioch under *Paul of Samosata and at *Constantinople under St *Chrysostom. The practice, with its obvious dangers, was opposed by St *Cyprian, St Chrysostom, and others, and forbidden by the canons of the Councils of *Elvira (can. 27), *Ancyra (can. 19), and *Nicaea (can. 3; AD 325). There is a certain analogy with the practice centuries later in the *double monasteries of monks and nuns. *Philo attests the existence of a similar institution among the *Therapeutae (q.v.).

H. Achelis, *Virgines Subintroductae: Ein Beitrag zu 1 Kor. 7* (1902). H. Koch, *Virgines Christi* (TU 31, Heft 2; 1907, pp. 59–112). P. de Labriolle, 'Le "Mariage spirituel" dans l'antiquité chrétienne', *Revue historique*, 137 (1921), pp. 204–25. A. Guillaumont, 'Le Nom des "Agapètes"', *VC* 23 (1969), pp. 30–7. H. Achelis in *HERE* 1 (1908), pp. 177–80, s.v. 'Agapetæ'; E. Magnin in *DDC* 1 (1935), cols. 311–15, s.v. 'Agapètes'.

Sublapsarianism. Also known as 'Infra-' or 'Post-lapsarianism'. In contrast to *Supralapsarianism (q.v.), the form of the *Calvinistic doctrine of *predestination which holds that it was only after the *Fall that God decreed the election or non-election of individual men to salvation. This less rigid teaching on predestination has been commonly current among Calvinists, esp. since the Synod of *Dort (1618).

submersion (also 'total immersion' or, loosely, 'immersion'). The form of *Baptism in which the water completely covers the candidate's body. Though *immersion is now also common, submersion is practised in the Orthodox and several of the other E. Churches, as well as in the *Ambrosian rite. It is one of the methods provided in the 1969 RC rite for the Baptism of Infants. On the basis of Rom. 6: 3–11 it has been generally supposed to have been the custom of the early Church, but this view has been challenged by C. F. Rogers from the evidence of primitive pictorial representations and measurements of surviving early baptismal fonts.

C. F. Rogers, 'Baptism and Christian Archaeology', *Studia Biblica et Ecclesiastica: Essays chiefly in Biblical and Patristic Criticism by Members of the University of Oxford*, 5 (1903), pp. 239–361; id., 'Baptism by Affusion in the Early Church', *JTS* 6 (1905), pp. 107–10, with refs. See also bibl. to BAPTISM.

Submission of the Clergy. The act whereby the English *Convocations surrendered, on 15 May 1532, to the demands made by *Henry VIII. The clergy promised to make no new *canon without royal licence, and to submit the existing canons to a committee of 32, half lay and half clerical and all to be chosen by the King, for revision. Its effect was to make the King supreme in all ecclesiastical causes. Less than two years later (Jan. 1534), the submission of the clergy was incorporated into the Submission of the Clergy Act 1533, which coupled it with the restraint of appeals to Rome. See also REFORMATIO LEGUM ECCLESIASTICARUM and JUDICIAL COMMITTEE OF THE PRIVY COUNCIL.

Text in Gee and Hardy, pp. 176–8 (no. 48); also repr. in Bettenson, pp. 305 f.

subordinationism. Teaching about the Godhead which regards either the Son as subordinate to the Father or the Holy Spirit as subordinate to both. It is a characteristic tendency in much Christian teaching of the first three centuries, and is a marked feature of such otherwise orthodox Fathers as St *Justin and St *Irenaeus. Various reasons may be given for this tendency: the stress on the absolute unity and transcendence of God the Father, which is common to all forms of theology using the existing categories of Greek thought; the fear of compromising monotheism; and the implications of one strand of biblical teaching, represented by such texts as Jn. 14: 28. By the standards of orthodoxy established in the 4th cent., such a position came to be regarded as clearly heretical in its denial of the co-equality of the Three Persons of the Trinity. The issue was most explicitly dealt with in the conflict with *Arius and his followers, who held that the Son was God not by nature but by grace and was created by the Father, though in a creation outside time. In relation to the Holy Spirit the issue came to the fore later in the 4th cent., with the teaching of the *Pneumatomachi (q.v.). Subordinationism was condemned by the Council of *Constantinople in 381.

W. Marcus, *Der Subordinatianismus* (Munich, 1963), with bibl.

substance (Lat. *substantia*). (1) The word has played a continuous and important part in philosophy since *Aristotle, who in the *Categories* distinguished between first and second substances (πρώτη οὐσία, δευτέρα οὐσία). The former was the individual, which can neither exist in another nor be predicated of another; the latter was the universal, which does not as such exist in another, though it may be predicated of another. These distinctions were taken over by the *Scholastic philosophers. In general *substantia* was the permanent, underlying reality as contrasted with its changing and perceptible accidents. In modern times R. *Descartes defined substance as that which needed nothing else for its existence; there were two kinds of substances—absolute substance, i.e. God, and created substances (unextended mind and extended matter). For B. *Spinoza substance was whatever needed nothing else for its conception. The sole substance was the eternal and infinite substance, God, whose essence implied His existence. For G. W. *Leibniz the monads were substances. In England J. *Locke conceived of substance as an unknowable underlying stuff in which qualities inhere: a view ridiculed by G. *Berkeley in the case of matter (though he retained the notion of spiritual substance). D. *Hume held the Scholastic notion of substance to be wholly dispensable, a view largely shared by later empiricists. In modern German *Existentialist philosophy, e.g. by M. *Heidegger, substance (or 'being') is conceived from the viewpoint of an existing individual and thus understood as a form of presence, bounded by death and threatened by finitude, which threat is experienced as anxiety (*Angst*).

(2) In the Christian doctrine of the Godhead, the word is used to express the underlying Being, by which all Three Persons are One. The earliest theologian to make extensive use of the word *substantia* in this connection was *Tertullian; but the common view that he was largely influenced by its legal meaning ('a piece of property') is exaggerated. At first, besides οὐσία, the Greek-speaking Church widely used ὑπόστασις in a closely similar sense, a usage favoured by the apparent etymological equivalence of ὑπο-στασις and *sub-stantia*; and this identity was accepted at *Nicaea (325) and is common in *Athanasius. But under the influence of the *Arian controversy, and esp. the *Cappadocian Fathers, οὐσία and ὑπόστασις became generally distinguished, οὐσία being confined to the meaning 'substance', whereas ὑπόστασις became the accepted equivalent of the Latin *persona*. See also HOMO-OUSION.

(3) In the Middle Ages the word filled an important place in the theology of the *Eucharist, where the substance of the Eucharistic species was contrasted with their '*accidents' (q.v.). For the history of the doctrine see TRANSUBSTANTIATION.

Subunists. The party in Bohemia in the 15th cent. which defended against the *Utraquists the practice of communion in one kind (*sub una specie*).

Suburbicarian Dioceses (Lat. *suburbium*, 'suburb'). The seven dioceses in the immediate vicinity of Rome, namely Albano, Frascati, Ostia, Palestrina, Porto and Santa Rufina (united in 1120), Sabina and Poggio Mirteto (divided in 1841, reunited in 1925), and Velletri. The six '*Cardinal Bishops' take their episcopal titles from these sees, but, since 1962, they no longer have pastoral charge of them. The Dean and Sub-Dean of the College of Cardinals are elected by them from their own number. The Suburbicarian Dioceses are very small, but very ancient. Their bishops had the right of taking part in the election of the Pope probably as early as the 11th century.

P. F. Kehr, *Regesta Pontificum Romanorum: Italia Pontificia sive Repertorium Privilegiorum et Litterarum a Romanis Pontificibus ante Annum MCLXXXXVIII Italiae Ecclesiis, Monasteriis, Civitatibus Singulisque Personis Concessorum*, 2 (Berlin, 1907), pp. 14–74. G. Phillips, *Kirchenrecht*, 4 (1864), pp. 145–220. U. Benigni in *CE* 14 (1912), pp. 324 f., s.v.; F. C. Bouuaert in *DDC* 4 (1949), cols. 1267–71, s.v. 'Diocèses suburbicaires'. See also works cited under CARDINAL.

succentor. In *cathedral churches of the 'Old Foundation', the title usually given to the deputy of the *precentor. He is generally a *minor canon. At *York there are two succentors, the one subject to the canons and the other the principal member of the corporation of vicars-choral. At *Lichfield the holder of the office is called the 'subchanter'.

succession, apostolic. See APOSTOLIC SUCCESSION.

Sudan, Christianity in. The ancient Church of *Nubia, in Northern Sudan, died out in the 16th cent. Christianity returned to the Upper Nile in the 19th cent. From 1846, when a *Vicariate Apostolic of Central Africa was created by the *Propaganda Fide, until the Mahdist rising in 1881, RC missionaries struggled to establish the Church in Khartoum and up the Nile, succeeding in reaching as far south as Gondokoro. Two outstanding missionaries were the Austrian Ignaz Knoblecher (1819–58), who held the mission together for its first ten years in highly adverse circumstances, and D. *Comboni, who first reached the Sudan in 1857. The author of a remarkable work, *Piano per la rigenerazione dell'Africa* (1864), in 1867 he established a training institute in Verona out of which the *Verona Fathers Mission developed. In 1881, when Muhammad Ahmad ibn Abdullah declared himself to be the Mahdi, the Restorer of Justice promised by the Prophet Muhammad, work came to an abrupt end. Missions were overrun and missionaries killed or imprisoned.

Evangelism began again when an Anglo-Egyptian condominium over Sudan was established in 1899. No direct evangelism was permitted in the mainly Muslim North, though Christian schools and hospitals were established in Khartoum, but the Verona Fathers returned to their mission in the South and were joined by the *CMS and American *Presbyterian Mission. In 1920 the interdenominational Sudan Interior Mission started educational work in the Nuba Mountains, and the Sudan United Mission and the Africa Inland Mission (both interdenominational) each opened small missions. Under the Condominium Government's policy of developing the South separately from the North, English, not Arabic, was the language of education, and education remained entirely in the hands of missionaries. The first ordination of Sudanese in the (Anglican) Episcopal Church took place only in 1941 when Daniel Deng Atong and Andereya Apaya were made deacons. In 1955 the former became Sudan's first indigenous bishop. By 1941 there were some 18,600 members of the Episcopal Church; by 1950 the RCs numbered 100,000. The other Churches were numerically smaller.

In 1946 government policy changed: the South was to be more closely integrated with the Muslim North in preparation for independence, which came ten years later. The South was severely disadvantaged by lack of development and trust quickly broke down, with the Sudan gradually drifting into civil war. In 1957 all Church schools were nationalized. In 1962 an attempt was made to abolish Sunday as the day of rest in the South. Missionaries were increasingly harassed and restricted, and in 1964 all those still remaining were expelled. By this time the southern population was thought to be about 10 per cent Christian. Most of the southern politicians and leaders had been educated in mission schools, and the Christian presence was therefore disproportionately important. Although the churches were deprived of clergy outside the main government controlled towns, Church membership grew apace as southerners began to find a Christian identity over against the Muslim North.

The *World Council of Churches and the All Africa Conferences of Churches played a crucial role in the peace process which resulted in the 1972 Addis Ababa Agreement. In the subsequent years of reconstruction Church membership continued to grow and its leadership was almost entirely indigenized, both the RC and the Episcopal Church appointing archbishops. The Addis Ababa Agreement, however, was steadily abandoned by the central government, and in 1985 hostilities were resumed. By the end of the 1980s southern fear of Sharia Law and Muslim fundamentalist plans for Sudan to be united as a Muslim state had become central factors in the conflict. In the 1990s civil war and famine have rendered the position of the Christians desperate.

W. B. Anderson, *Ambassadors by the Nile: The Church in North-East Africa* (1963; brief). E. Pezzi, *La Missione Cattolica nel Sudan dall'Inizio fino alla Ripresa dopo la Rivoluzione Mahdista* (Verona, 1972). F. Morlang, *Missione in Africa Centrale: Diario 1855–1856*, tr. with notes by O. Huber and V. Dellagiacomo (Museum Combonianum, 28; Bologna, 1973). R. O. Collins, *Land Beyond the Rivers: The Southern Sudan 1898–1918* (New Haven, Conn., and London, 1971), pp. 281–323. R. Hill, 'Government and Christian Missions in the Anglo-Egyptian Sudan, 1899–1914', *Middle Eastern Studies*, 1 (1964–5), pp. 113–34; V. M. Battle, 'The American Mission and Educational Development in Southern Sudan, 1900–1929', in id. and C. H. Lyons (eds.), *Essays in the History of African Education* (New York, 1970), pp. 63–83; L. P. and N. Sanderson, *Education, Religion & Politics in Southern Sudan 1899–1964* (1981). E. Stock, *The History of the Church Missionary Society*, 3 (1899), pp. 746–50; 4 (1916), pp. 105–14; G. Hewitt, *The Problems of Success: A History of the Church Missionary Society 1910–1942*, 1 (1971), pp. 319–49. On the Episcopal Church, also O. C. Allison, *A Pilgrim Church's Progress* (1966); id., *Through Fire and Water* (1976). The 'Memorandum' on the expulsion of missionaries from Southern Sudan in 1964 and an answer to its allegations was issued by the Verona Fathers, *The Black Book of the Sudan* [Milan, 1964]. D. McEwan, *A Catholic Sudan: Dream, Mission, and Reality. A Study of the Roman Catholic Mission to Central Africa and its Protection by the Hapsburg Empire from 1846 to 1900 (1914) as revealed in the Correspondence of the Imperial and Royal Austro-Hungarian Consulate Khartoum* (Rome, 1987). *Denying 'the Honor of Living': Sudan a Human Rights Disaster* (An Africa Watch Report, New York and London, 1990).

Sudbury, Simon. See SIMON OF SUDBURY.

Suetonius, Roman writer, until 121/2 secretary to the Emp. Hadrian. He was apparently one of the first pagan writers to mention Christianity. His 'Lives of the Caesars' refers to the expulsion by Claudius (d. 54) of the Jews from Rome on the ground that they had made disturbances 'at the instigation of Chrestus' (Claudius, 25. 4); this is prob. a garbled account of trouble between Jews and Christians. He seems to have approved of *Nero's persecution of the Christians, 'a class of men given to a new and mischievous superstition' (Nero, 16).

'Lives of the Caesars' ed. M. Ihm (Teub., 1908), repr., with Eng. tr. by J. C. Rolfe (Loeb, 2 vols., 1914); other works ed. A. Reifferscheid (Leipzig, 1860). Convenient Eng. tr. of 'Lives of the Caesars' by R. Graves (Penguin Classics, 1957; rev. by M. Grant, 1979). A. Wallace-Hadrill, *Suetonius: The Scholar and his Caesars* (1983); J. Gascou, *Suétone historien* (Bibliothèque des Écoles françaises d'Athènes et de Rome, 255; 1984). K. R. Bradley in *OCD* (3rd edn., 1996), pp. 1451 f. s.v. 'Suetonius (Gaius Suetonius Tranquillus)'.

sufficient grace. In the RC theology of grace, grace which, in contrast to *efficacious grace (q.v.), does not meet with adequate co-operation on the part of the recipient, and hence fails to achieve the result for which it was bestowed. In the *Dominican view (D. *Bañez), it required a further Divine motion ('efficacious grace') to produce a salutary act. The *Jesuit view (L. *Molina), on the other hand, was that 'sufficient grace' was really adequate to produce such a result, needing only the consent of human free will to become efficacious. Both sufficient and efficacious grace are different forms of 'actual grace'.

suffragan bishop. The title is used in two senses:

(1) Any bishop in relation to his *archbishop or *metropolitan, by whom he may be summoned to assist at synods and give his 'suffrage'.

(2) An assistant bishop appointed to help the bishop of the diocese. The first instance of this office in England is from 1240. From the end of the 14th cent. to the Reformation appointments of such assistant bishops were frequent and made by the Pope. The Suffragan Bishops Act 1534 named 26 specific places (Thetford, Ipswich, Colchester, Dover, Guildford, and so on) as sees from which bishops suffragan should take their titles. When a diocesan bishop was desirous of a suffragan, he was to recommend two candidates to the Sovereign, who was to have power to nominate one of them to any see in the list specified within the same province and to present him to the archbishop, in letters patent under the great seal, for consecration within three months. The suffragan depended for his authority and fees on the commission of the diocesan, which was presumed to lapse on the death or translation of the latter and was renewable only at the

pleasure of his successor. The Act was repealed under *Mary by the See of Rome Act 1554, but restored under *Elizabeth I in 1559 by the Act of Supremacy 1558. After the consecration of 17 suffragan bishops in the 16th cent. the office lapsed in 1592, though the existence of bishops suffragan is assumed in the 1604 *Canons. In 1870, in the face of strong demands, suffragan bishops were consecrated under the same Act for Nottingham (for the diocese of *Lincoln) and Dover (for that of *Canterbury). The Suffragans Nomination Act 1888 empowered the Crown, by Order in Council, to make additions to the list of places from which suffragan bishops might take their titles. By the Dioceses Measure 1978, if a new suffragan see is to be created or an existing one has been vacant for five years or more, a diocesan bishop may petition the Crown for a suffragan only with the approval of the Diocesan and the General Synods. See also AREA BISHOP.

The Suffragan Bishops Act 1534 is repr. in Gee and Hardy, pp. 253–6. (no. 59). W. *Stubbs, *Registrum Sacrum Anglicanum: An Attempt to Exhibit the Course of Episcopal Succession in England from the Records of the Church* (1858), esp. pp. 142–9 (Appendix 5: 'Suffragans and Bishops in Partibus'). R. Phillimore, *The Ecclesiastical Law of the Church of England*, 1 (2nd edn. by W. G. F. Phillimore, 1895), pp. 75–86 ('Bishops without Sees').

Suger (*c*.1081–1151), Abbot of *St-Denis, near Paris. Of humble origin, *c*.1091 he entered the abbey of St-Denis, where he was a fellow-student of King Louis VI. From 1106 onwards, he was active in the affairs of the abbey. In 1107 he was nominated Provost of Berneval in Normandy and in 1109 of Toury. He was sent by the King on embassies to the Papal Curia, and he was returning from a visit to *Callistus II in 1122 when he was elected Abbot of St-Denis. In the next year he went to Rome again to attend the (Ninth) General Council at the *Lateran. Throughout much of his life he was an influential adviser of the French Crown, an active administrator of the lands of his monastery, and a friend of monastic reformers. During Louis VII's absence on the Second *Crusade he was one of the regents, discharging his duties with such success that Louis on his return rewarded him with the title of 'Father of the Country'.

Suger's 'Vita Ludovici Grossi' is a primary historical source for his age. His new church at St-Denis (choir consecrated 1144), of which he has left an account in his 'Libellus de Consecratione Ecclesiae S. Dionysii', was a crucial step in the development of Gothic architecture. His methods of monastic government are set out in his 'Liber de Rebus in Administratione sua gestis'.

Œuvres complètes, ed. A. Lecoy de La Marche (Société de l'Histoire de France; 1867), with 12th-cent. Life by Père Guillaume, OSB, pp. 377–411. Modern edn., with Fr. tr., of his Life of Louis VI by H. Waquet (Paris, 1929). Eng. tr. of his 'Sancti Dionysii Liber' (comprising the 'Liber de Rebus' and the 'Libellus de Consecratione') by E. Panofsky, *Abbot Suger on the Abbey Church of St-Denis and its Art Treasures* (Princeton, NJ, 1946). F. A. Gervaise, OSB, *Histoire de Suger* (3 vols., 1721). M. Aubert, *Suger* ('Figures monastiques'; 1950), with refs. P. L. Gerson (ed.), *Abbot Suger and Saint-Denis: A Symposium* (New York [1986]). O. von Simson, *The Gothic Cathedral: The Origins of Gothic Architecture & the Medieval Concept of Order* (1956), esp. pp. 64–141. P. Kidson, 'Panofsky, Suger and St Denis', *Journal of the Warburg and Courtauld Institutes*, 50 (1987), pp. 1–17; C. Rudolph, *Artistic*

Change at St-Denis: Abbot Suger's Program and the Early Twelfth-Century Controversy over Art (Princeton, NJ [1990]).

Suicer, Johann Kaspar (1620–84), author of the *Thesaurus Ecclesiasticus*. He was a Reformed theologian, a native of Frauenfeld in Switzerland. Educated at the French academies of Montauban and Saumur (1640–3), he taught Latin, Greek, and Hebrew at Zurich from 1644 and was professor of Greek at the Collegium Carolinum from 1660 to 1683. After publishing several works on Greek linguistics, he brought out his famous *Thesaurus Ecclesiasticus e Patribus Graecis Ordine Alphabetico* in 1682 (2 vols., Amsterdam), of which a second enlarged edition appeared in 1728. The work, which shows immense erudition and extensive reading of patristic literature, is still indispensable to students of the vocabulary of the Greek Fathers and of Greek ecclesiastical institutions. He is generally considered to have exercised a liberal influence in the compilation of the *Consensus Helveticus*, a confession of faith drawn up by all the Swiss Protestant Churches in 1675.

A. Schweizer, 'Die Entstehung der helvetischen Consensus-Formel', *Zeitschrift für die historische Theologie*, 30 (1860), pp. 122–48. Id. and P. Schweizer in *PRE* (3nd edn.), 19 (1907), pp. 149 f.

suicide. The intentional taking of one's own life is condemned in the Bible by no text more specific than the Sixth *Commandment ('Thou shalt not kill') unless, with rabbinic tradition, we read Gen. 9: 5 in this sense ('Your life-blood will I require'). However, with the exception of Maccabees, where a heroic suicide in 2 Macc. 14: 16 echoes contemporary Roman ideals, the six clear biblical suicides are associated with God's disfavour: namely those of Abimelech (Jgs. 9: 53–5), Achitophel (2 Sam. 17: 23), Zimri (1 Kgs. 16: 15–20), Saul (1 Chron. 10: 3–13), and *Judas Iscariot (acc. to Mt. 27: 5). The case of *Samson (Jgs. 16: 30) is complicated by the fact that his own death was not the main motive for his action. In Tob. 3: 10 a person in trouble rejects suicide as an option because of its effect on other people. The Bible similarly makes no mention of posthumous sanctions against suicide, even though, acc. to *Josephus, normal Jewish practice of his time included the shameful burial of suicides after dusk (*Bel. Jud.* 3. 8. 5[377]). Evidence of similar measures survives from elsewhere in the ancient world, notably among the Greeks (cf. *Plato, *Laws*, 9. 873) and in Sanskrit law.

Roman law, like much articulate Roman tradition, opposed any moral condemnation of suicide and hence provided no sanctions. Christian authority took the opposite position, but gradually. While *Origen criticized the suicide of Judas in his commentary on Mt., it was left to *Lactantius (*Inst. Div.* 3. 18) and later 4th-cent. Fathers to condemn suicide forcibly and at length. The treatment which for centuries remained the fullest was that by St *Augustine, *City of God*, book 1, chapters 16–27, which exposed alleged contradictions in the current Roman position, with the aim of dissuading Christian women, threatened by barbarians, from preferring suicide to rape. At about the same date, though with no traceable connection, posthumous sanctions make their first Christian appearance in the context of Egyptian monasticism. Possibly under influence from Egypt the sanctions entered canon law in the acts of Visigothic and Gallican Councils of the 6th cent., in particular, the first Council of Braga (561), can. 16, which refers to an older, apparently unwritten, rule that suicides are to be denied normal burial and prayers. This text became the basis for a widespread exercise of the same sanctions in medieval Europe. Most medieval secular law, both written and customary, augmented the canonical penalties with its own, by (for instance) putting suicide among crimes entailing forfeiture of goods, and in some places by ritual maltreatment of the corpse.

These sanctions were applied with a degree of rigour which varied according to period and local circumstances. Despite such variations the status of suicide as a secular crime persisted in most countries of Europe at least until the French Revolution, and in England until 1961 (although long before this date jurors had tended to acquit many suicides as being 'of unsound mind'). The erosion of the sanctions can be traced to two sources. One was the simple view that suicide is intrinsically innocent: a view held wherever Roman law and tradition have been strong, as in medieval urban Italy, during the Renaissance and *Enlightenment, and in modern currents of thought acknowledging their influence. The second source of erosion is the more complex view that while suicide is wrong, it is proper to feel pity for the suicide and hope for God's mercy on his behalf. While explicit Christian doctrine has since the 4th cent. normally shunned this view, signs survive from the Anglo-Saxon period onwards—as in the Braga canon itself—that a minority of priests, singly or in religious orders, did give suicides normal burial and prayers, apparently from motives of pious sympathy. In the late 20th cent. this covert tradition has come to the surface in canon law. RC canons no longer expressly exclude suicides from Christian burial (*CIC* (1983), can. 1184), while those of the C of E allow burial with a special form of service (can. B 38 § 2). The *Catechism of the Catholic Church* (1992), while condemning suicide, now states positively that 'The Church prays for those who have taken their own lives' (no. 2283). Unless dispensed, attempted suicide nevertheless remains a bar to RC ordination (*CIC* (1983), can. 1041) and is an impediment to the exercise of orders already conferred (ibid., can. 1044).

Debates about suicide include the empirical one as to whether suicide-rates are lower among Christians than others. A marked under-average incidence among Church members was first brought to public attention by Émile Durkheim in 1897 and can still, after reformulation in response to modern conditions, find statistical backing. Another such debate is on the nature and effect of the work of the Samaritans, a voluntary organization founded in 1953 by the Revd Eric Chad Varah (then Vicar of St Stephen's Walbrook in the City of London) to give help anonymously to persons tempted to suicide. Moral debate, for Christians, centres exclusively on the question how far God may, or the Church should, make allowance for human frailty or confusion, not on the wrongness of the act itself. Of the many grounds adduced to establish this wrongness, the most specifically Christian is the antithesis that suicide presents to the Passion of Christ, who suffered the extremes of pain and loss (including the loss of a conscious sense of God's presence) in loving acceptance of the Father's will, and precisely by doing so did His work of redeeming mankind. See also DYING, CARE OF THE.

[D.] E. Durkheim, *Le Suicide: Étude de sociologie* (1897; Eng. tr., Glencoe, Ill. [1951]; London, 1952); A. Bayet, *Le Suicide et la morale* (1922); M. Halbwachs, *Les causes du suicide* (1930; Eng. tr., 1978). A. J. L. van Hooff, *From Autothanasia to Suicide: Self-killing in Classical Antiquity* (1990); O. Anderson, *Suicide in Victorian and Edwardian England* (Oxford, 1987); M. MacDonald and T. R. Murphy, *Sleepless Souls: Suicide in Early Modern England* (ibid., 1990); A. Murray, *Suicide in the Middle Ages* (ibid., 1998 ff.). [E.] C. Varah (ed.), *The Samaritans: To help those tempted to suicide or despair* (1965).

Suidas (*c.* AD 1000), 'Greek lexicographer'. The traditional supposition that the Greek Lexicon which passes under this name was the work of a certain 'Suidas' is, however, prob. mistaken, the name (properly ἡ Σοῦδα) being apparently derived from a Lat. word meaning 'fortress', i.e. an armoury of information. The Lexicon, both a dictionary and an encyclopaedia, was compiled *c.*1000 from many ancient texts, abridgements, and scholia (Homer, Aristophanes, the Palatine Anthology, an epitome of Hesychius of Miletus), including several sources now lost, and also drew, for its lexical entries, on glossaries and word-lists. Much of its historical material came from the Chronicle of *George Hamartolos (9th cent.) and the Excerpts of Constantine Porphyrogenitus (912–59). Its contents are largely of indifferent merit, but certain items stand apart as of great historical value. The whole work is an important witness to the interests and learning of late Byzantine culture.

Editio princeps of the Lexicon [by D. Chalcondyles], Milan, 1499; modern crit. edn. by A. Adler (5 vols., Lexicographi Graeci, Leipzig, 1928–38). F. Dölger, *Die Titel des sog. Suidaslexikons* (*Sb.* (Bayr.), 1936, Heft 6); P. Lemerle, *Le Premier Humanisme Byzantin* (Bibliothèque Byzantine, Études 6; 1971), pp. 297–300; Eng. tr. (Byzantina Australiensia, 3; Canberra, 1986), pp. 343–6. N. G. Wilson, *Scholars of Byzantium* (1983), pp. 145–7. A. Adler in *PW*, Zweite Reihe, 4 (pt. 1; 1931), cols. 675–717, s.v.

Sulpice, St. See SAINT-SULPICE, SOCIETY OF.

Sulpicius Severus (b. *c.*360, d. perhaps *c.*430), historian and hagiographer. Sulpicius was a rising advocate in Aquitaine until his wife's death, his friend *Paulinus of Nola's example, and *Martin of Tours's exhortations led to his conversion to asceticism (*c.*394). He established a community on his estate of Primuliacum in SW Gaul, where he lived a gentlemanly version of the religious life. His *Life of Martin* (396), a literary *tour de force*, was highly influential on later hagiography. Although composed within Martin's lifetime, it portrays him as a man of God, attested by miracles. Later Sulpicius added 3 letters, and then the *Dialogues* (*c.*405), where Martin's thaumaturgical powers are compared favourably with those of the Egyptian ascetics. Sulpicius also wrote a *Chronicle*, which summarizes OT and then early Church history from the Creation to AD 400 in classical style, utilizing both Christian and pagan sources. It evinces a critical regard for chronology, and is an important source for the *Priscillianist movement. Acc. to *Gennadius, Sulpicius was a priest, and in his old age he was temporarily inclined towards *Pelagianism. This statement suggests that he was still alive during the *Semipelagian controversy of the 420s, though we have no contemporary information about him after *c.*404.

Editio princeps of his collected works by V. Giselinus (Antwerp, 1574); also ed. Hieronymus de Prato (2 vols., Verona, 1741–54), repr. in J. P. Migne, *PL* 20. 95–222. Crit. edn. by C. Halm (CSEL 1; 1866). Eng. tr. by A. Roberts (NPNCF, 2nd ser., vol. 11, 1894, pp. 3–122), and of *Life of St Martin, Letters,* and *Dialogues* by B. M. Peebles (Fathers of the Church, 7, New York, 1949, pp. 101–251). *Life of St Martin* ed., with Fr. tr., introd. and comm., by J. Fontaine (SC 133–5; 1967–9), and, with Ital. tr., by J. W. Smit and L. Canali (Vite dei Santi, 4, 1975, pp. 1–67). *Dialogues* ed., with Ital. tr., by G. Augello (Palermo, 1969); note also E. C. Babut, 'Sur trois lignes inédites de Sulpice Sévère', *Le Moyen Âge,* 19 (1906), pp. 205–13. The chief source for Sulpicius' life is Paulinus of Nola's letters; also Gennadius, *De vir. ill.* 19. C. [E.] Stancliffe, *St Martin and his Hagiographer: History and Miracle in Sulpicius Severus* (Oxford Historical Monographs, 1983). F. Ghizzoni, *Sulpicio Severo* (Università degli Studi di Parma. Istituto di Lingua e Letteratura Latina, 8 [1983]). A. Rous[s]elle-Estève, 'Deux exemples d'évangélisation en Gaule à la fin du IVᵉ siècle: Paulin de Nole et Sulpice Sévère', *Fédération historique du Languedoc méditerranéen et du Roussillon, XLIIIᵉ Congrès (Béziers, 30–31 Mai 1970)* (Montpellier, 1971), pp. 91–8. G. K. van Andel, 'Sulpicius Severus and Origenism', *VC* 34 (1980), pp. 278–87. J. Bernays, *Ueber die Chronik des Sulpicius Severus* (1861); S. Prete, *I Chronica di Sulpicio Severo* (Collezione 'Amici delle catacombe', 24; 1955); G. K. van Andel, *The Christian Concept of History in the Chronicle of Sulpicius Severus* (Amsterdam, 1976); F. Murru, 'La concezione della storia nei *Chronica* di Sulpicio Severo. alcune linee di studio', *Latomus,* 38 (1979), pp. 961–81. J. Fontaine in *Dict. Sp.* 14 (1990), cols. 1301–8, s.v. See also bibl. to MARTIN, ST.

Summa. Originally a title of reference books on various subjects, the term, as used by medieval writers, came to denote a compendium of theology, philosophy, or canon law. These compendia were normally used as handbooks in the Schools, much like the earlier *Sentences. The 'Summae' divide their subjects into a great number of questions, usually following a more or less generally accepted order, and use the dialectical method of evolving a theme by affirmation and contradiction. The most famous 'Summae' are the 'Summa Theologiae' and the 'Summa contra Gentiles' of St *Thomas Aquinas; but well-known Summae were also produced by *William of Auxerre, St *Albertus Magnus, and many others.

Summa Theologiae. The chief dogmatic work of St *Thomas Aquinas (q.v.), until recently generally known as the 'Summa Theologica'. It is a vast structure of treatises, questions, and articles, which falls into three parts. The First Part ('Prima') treats of God considered in Himself and as the principle of creation, the first half of the Second Part ('Prima Secundae') of God as the end of man, its second half ('Secunda Secundae') of man's return to God, and the Third Part ('Tertia') of Christ as the way of man to God. The concluding sections of the Tertia, which deal with the Sacraments and the Last Things, were left unfinished, the missing parts being supplied on the basis of Thomas's 'Commentary on the Sentences', presumably under the editorship of *Reginald of Piperno.

For bibl. see THOMAS AQUINAS, ST.

Summi Pontificatus. The *encyclical issued by *Pius XII on 20 Oct. 1939 expounding the bearing of Catholic principles on such matters as the growth of secularism, the brotherhood of man, the state and the family, state-worship and international confidence, and *Catholic Action, and summoning Christians to a renewed devotion to the *Sacred Heart.

Lat. text in *AAS* 31 (1939), pp. 413–53, with Eng. tr., pp. 538–64. Further Eng. tr. in C. Carlen, IHM, *The Papal Encyclicals 1939–1958* (Salem, NH [1981]), pp. 5–22, with bibl.

Sumner, Charles Richard (1790–1874), Bp. of *Winchester. A younger brother of J. B. *Sumner (q.v.), he was educated at Eton and Trinity College, Cambridge, and ordained deacon in 1814. In 1820 he was introduced to George IV through the good offices of Lady Conyngham (the King's mistress), to whose son he had been tutor; he owed his subsequent rapid preferment to her influence. Having been appointed Chaplain to the King, he was made Canon of *Worcester in 1822 and of *Canterbury in 1825. In 1826 he was consecrated to the see of *Llandaff, which he held in plurality with the deanery of *St Paul's, and in 1827 he was translated to Winchester by order of the King. He lost the royal favour by voting for the *Catholic Emancipation Bill in 1829, an action he regretted in later life. He was an *Evangelical in his sympathies and as such opposed R. D. *Hampden's appointment to the see of *Hereford, though he patronized some High Churchmen, esp. S. *Wilberforce. In 1850 he strongly protested against the restoration of the RC hierarchy. A very capable and successful administrator, he furthered in his diocese the establishment of Poor Schools, better conditions for the agricultural labourers, and the building of churches and parsonages. His literary works include *The Ministerial Character of Christ Practically Considered* (1824) and an annotated translation of J. *Milton's *De Doctrina Christiana* (2 vols., 1825). In 1869 he resigned his see through ill-health, to be succeeded by S. Wilberforce.

Life by his son, G. H. Sumner (London, 1876). W. P. Courtney in *DNB* 55 (1898), pp. 165–8.

Sumner, John Bird (1780–1862), Abp. of *Canterbury. Elder brother of C. R. *Sumner, he was born at Kenilworth and educated at Eton and King's College, Cambridge, of which he was elected a Fellow in 1801. In 1802 he became assistant master at Eton, and was ordained in 1803. After holding several benefices he was nominated Bp. of *Chester in 1828. Though a convinced *Evangelical, he voted for the *Catholic Emancipation Bill in 1829. Later he opposed the *Oxford Movement. He was an able administrator of his diocese, which he enriched by causing many churches and schools to be built. In 1848 he was appointed Abp. of Canterbury. Though unsympathetic towards the theology of R. D. *Hampden's Bampton Lectures, he did not oppose his consecration as Bp. of *Hereford, in which he himself took part. In the controversy concerning the *Gorham Case he denied that Baptismal Regeneration was a fundamental doctrine of the C of E. In 1852 it fell to him to preside over the Upper House of *Convocation when, for the first time for 135 years, it met again for business. His numerous writings, which were highly esteemed in Evangelical circles, include *Apostolical Preaching* (1815), based on the Pauline Epp.; *A Treatise on the Records of the Creation* (2 vols., 1816), founded on the Mosaic account in Genesis; and *The Evidence of Christianity* (1824), in which he argued from the vitality of Christianity to its Divine origin; as well as several volumes of sermons.

N. Scotland, *John Bird Sumner: Evangelical Archbishop* (Leominster, 1995). W. P. Courtney in *DNB* 55 (1898), pp. 168–70, s.v.

Sun, The Canticle of the. See CANTICLE OF THE SUN, THE.

Sundar Singh, Sadhu (1889–*c*.1929), an Indian Christian and mystic. Born of wealthy Sikh parents, he was converted to Christianity by a vision on 18 Dec. 1904, baptized in the C of E at Simla in 1905, and donned the robe of a Sadhu (i.e. 'holy man') in an endeavour to present Christianity in a Hindu form. In his early travels he covered the Punjab, Kashmir, Baluchistan, and Afghanistan, and in 1908 made his first visit to evangelize Tibet. A visit to Madras in 1908 introduced him to the world at large, and his fame was enhanced by travels in the W. in 1920 and 1922. He expected death at 33, the age at which Christ died, and was disappointed that he lived on. Despite ill-health, he persisted in his strenuous work in Tibet. He was last heard of in April 1929.

A collection of his writings, ed. T. Dayanandan Francis, *The Christian Witness of Sadhu Sundar Singh* (Madras, 1989), with full introd. B. H. *Streeter and A. J. Appasamy, *The Sadhu* (1921); C. F. Andrews, *Sadhu Sundar Singh* (1934); A. J. Appasamy, *Sundar Singh* (1958); P. Thompson, *Sadhu Sundar Singh* (Bromley, 1992).

Sunday. Its English name derives from the old pagan 'dies solis' (Gk. ἡλίου ἡμέρα), the day consecrated to the sun, which was given a Christian interpretation and referred to Christ, the Sun of Righteousness (Mal. 4: 2). In Rev. it is called the Day of the Lord, κυριακὴ ἡμέρα (1: 10), the Latin translation of which, 'Dominica', is the name used in the calendars of the W. Church. Already in NT times Sunday began to replace the Jewish *Sabbath. St *Paul and the Christians of Troas assembled on the first day of the week 'to break bread' (Acts 20: 7) and the Apostle bids his converts put by their alms on this day (1 Cor. 16: 2). The chief reason for the substitution of Sunday for the Sabbath was the commemoration of the Resurrection, mentioned already by St *Ignatius, which gives the day its joyful character; thus there is to be no fasting or kneeling on this day. *Justin Martyr connects it also with the first day of Creation, and St. *Isidore of Seville, much later, with the Coming of the Holy Spirit. Sunday also came to be associated with the Three Divine Persons and esp. dedicated to the Trinity, so that, e.g., the *Preface of the Trinity came to be used on all Sundays without a Preface of their own—a custom now abandoned in the RC Church.

The observance of Sunday as a day of rest consecrated esp. to the service of God began to be regulated by both ecclesiastical and civil legislation from the 4th cent. It was enjoined by the Council of *Elvira (*c*.306; can. 21), and by *Constantine in a law promulgated in 321, commanding abstention from work, including legal business, for townspeople, though permitting farm labour; *Oxyrhynchus papyrus 3759 affords evidence of the operation of this law in 325. The Council of *Laodicea (*c*.380; can. 29) enjoined abstention from work as far as possible. From the 6th to the 13th cents. the ecclesiastical legislation became more

and more strict, enforcing also assistance at Mass, and was helped by the infliction of severe penalties by the civil authorities, e.g. by the Anglo-Saxon king Ine and by *Alfred the Great. From the 13th cent. onwards the custom of allowing dispensations became widespread. Acc. to current RC canon law, the faithful are normally obliged to hear Mass on Sunday, or on the previous evening, and to abstain from 'work or business that would inhibit the worship to be given to God, the joy proper to the Lord's Day, or the due relaxation of mind and body'. If it is impossible to attend Mass, the faithful are to attend other forms of worship or 'spend an appropriate time in prayer' (*CIC* (1983), cans. 1247–8).

The Protestant Churches did not at first introduce special Sunday legislation; but the abuse of Sunday soon led to a reaction. In England the new attitude to Sunday was much influenced by Nicholas Bound's *True Doctrine of the Sabbath* (1595), which identified the Christian Sunday with the Jewish Sabbath. Despite King *James's defence of the traditional Sunday pleasures in his *Book of *Sports* (1618), rigorist views gained ground and found classic expression in the legislation of the Long Parliament and the *Westminster standards. While the Restoration brought much relaxation, the Act of 1677, by reducing Sunday labour, furthered its rigorist observance. The early 18th cent. was marked by greater liberty, but through the influence of the *Evangelical Revival stricter observance was once more enforced by the Act of 1781. In the 19th cent. Sunday was still a day mainly devoted to duties of piety, but the secularization of life in the 20th cent. has considerably reduced its religious observance. For some time considerations of social well-being led the civil authorities to encourage the cessation of work on Sundays, but increased leisure in the Western world has been accompanied by pressure to abolish restrictions on both recreational and commercial activities on Sundays. See also SABBATARIANISM.

J. A. Hessey, *Sunday: Its Origin, History and Present Obligation* (Bampton Lectures for 1860; 1860). T. *Zahn, *Geschichte des Sonntags vornehmlich in der alten Kirche* (1878). W. Rordorf, *Der Sonntag: Geschichte des Ruhe- und Gottesdiensttages im ältesten Christentum* (Abhandlungen zur Theologie des Alten und Neuen Testaments, 43; 1962; Eng. tr., 1968). B. Botte, OSB, and others, *Le Dimanche* (Lex Orandi, 39; 1965). S. Bacchiocchi, *From Sabbath to Sunday: A Historical Investigation of the Rise of Sunday Observance in early Christianity* (Rome, 1977). D. A. Carson (ed.), *From Sabbath to Lord's Day: A Biblical, Historical and Theological Investigation* (Grand Rapids, Mich., 1982). E. Haag, *Vom Sabbat zum Sonntag: Eine bibeltheologische Studie* (Trierer theologische Studien, 52; 1991). A. Barry in *DCA* 2 (1880), pp. 1042–53, s.v. 'Lord's Day'; J. Gaillard, OSB, in *Dict. Sp.* 3 (1957), cols. 948–82, s.v. 'Dimanche'.

Sunday letter. In ecclesiastical calendars that one of the seven letters A to G, allotted to the days of the year in rotation (1 Jan. = A, etc.), which coincides with the Sundays in a given year. Knowledge of it enables the user to discover at a glance on what day of the week any calendarial date in that year will fall. It is ascertained by a simple arithmetical calculation, as described, e.g., in the 'Table to Find Easter Day' prefixed to the BCP. A leap year necessarily has two Sunday letters, the change in the BCP calendar falling on 29 Feb., but in older forms of the calendar on 25 Feb. (vi. Kal. Mar.; hence 'bissextile years').

Sunday Schools. Schools, mainly for children, in which instruction, now primarily religious instruction, is given on Sunday; they are usually held in conjunction with a parish or congregation. Although there are isolated earlier examples of schools for poor children on Sundays, the movement owed its success to Robert *Raikes (q.v.), who, along with the local incumbent (T. Stock), engaged four women in 1780 to instruct the children of *Gloucester in reading and the Church Catechism on Sundays. Partly owing to the publicity which Raikes gave to the enterprise in his *Journal*, his example was soon followed elsewhere, both in Europe and America. Most schools at first used paid teachers. In England two national societies were founded on an interdenominational basis: the Sunday School Society (1783) to give financial support to individual schools and the Sunday School Union (1803) to help to provide books and materials. Most schools, however, were locally supported and after the early 1800s interdenominational co-operation tended to be replaced by denominational rivalry. There were also disputes about clerical and ministerial control and over the teaching of writing and other 'secular' subjects on Sunday. Some schools, independently of the Churches, developed into important centres for working-class culture and self-improvement, though frequently under middle-class supervision.

With the increase of general education in the 19th cent. the Sunday Schools devoted themselves more exclusively to religious education. Partly as a result of the *Oxford Movement, there grew up a desire among Anglicans to introduce more specifically C of E teaching, and in 1843 a new society, the Sunday School Institute, was formed. It was incorporated into the *National Society in 1936.

As standards of education advanced after the 1870 Act, more education was needed for the Sunday School teachers, who, from c.1840, were mainly voluntary workers. Under the auspices of the Sunday School Union a training college for teachers was founded in 1907 at Selly Oak, Birmingham (Westhill); the Sunday School Institute opened St Christopher's College, Blackheath, in 1909 for similar purposes. This latter has become the St Christopher's College Education Trust, which exists to promote religious education. In 1966 the (National from 1921) Sunday School Union became the National Christian Education Council.

The Sunday Schools of the C of E are partly organized on a diocesan basis; those sponsored by the National Christian Education Council are on a national basis. The Church of England Board of Education and the National Society offer advice and material assistance.

B. C. Cliff, *The Rise and Development of the Sunday School Movement in England 1780–1980* (Redhill, Surrey [1986]). T. W. Laqueur, *Religion and Respectability: Sunday Schools and Working Class Culture 1780–1850* (1976). J. Ferguson (ed.), *Christianity, Society and Education: Robert Raikes, Past, Present and Future* (1981). A. M. Boylan, *Sunday School: The Formation of an American Institution 1790–1880* (New Haven, Conn., and London [1988]).

supererogation, works of. In RC *moral theology, acts which are not enjoined as of strict obligation, and therefore are not simply good as opposed to bad, but better as opposed to good ('opera meliora'). Thus the '*Counsels of Evangelical Perfection' are held to be not of duty but of supererogation. The term, which goes back to the Latin translation of Lk. 10: 35 ('quodcumque supererogaveris'), was probably not used in its present technical sense until the Middle Ages, when 'opera supererogationis' were treated in the *Summa* attributed to *Alexander of Hales and in the works of St *Thomas Aquinas, and others. The doctrine, for which the story of the rich young ruler (Mt. 19: 16–22) and St Paul's teaching on virginity (1 Cor. 7) are usually adduced in evidence, was repudiated by the Reformers and in the Anglican *Thirty-Nine Articles (Art. XIV), which asserts that 'Works of Supererogation cannot be taught without arrogancy and impiety'.

D. Heyd, *Supererogation: Its Status in Ethical Theory* (Cambridge Studies in Philosophy, 1982). Comm. on the Thirty-Nine Articles, cited s.v., Art. XIV, esp. E. C. S. Gibson, *The Thirty-Nine Articles*, 2 (1897), pp. 424–38.

superintendents. In the reformed Church of Scotland, the officials appointed under the *First Book of *Discipline* (1560) to oversee the districts roughly corresponding to the old dioceses. It has been much disputed whether their appointment implies that the Church of Scotland was originally Episcopalian, and in particular whether their appointment was originally regarded as a temporary measure. While they enjoyed a measure of superiority over other ministers, they differed from diocesan bishops in being admitted to office by fellow-presbyters, in not possessing exclusive power of ordination, and in being subject to the control and censure of the other ministers regularly associated with them.

In the *Lutheran Churches, which in this matter supplied a model for the Scottish superintendents, Church officials of this name were created from an early date for similar reasons and with similar functions. In the Scandinavian countries the title of 'Bishop' was retained. In accordance with the principles of Lutheran polity they were to be appointed by, and responsible to, the civil powers. See also GENERAL SUPERINTENDENT.

In English *Methodism, in J. *Wesley's lifetime, senior travelling preachers with the title of 'Assistant', supervised a 'Circuit' (localized group of societies). Since the 1790s these ministers have been called 'Superintendents'. In American Methodism, the title of Superintendent or General Superintendent was originally applied to the two supervising ministers of the whole Church, but was soon replaced by that of 'Bishop'. Since 1908 District Superintendents have supervised Districts within the American regional Conferences.

On the Scottish superintendents, G. Donaldson, *The Scottish Reformation* (Cambridge, 1960), pp. 108–29; D. G. Mullan, *Episcopacy in Scotland: The History of an Idea, 1560–1638* (Edinburgh [1986]), pp. 17–32; J. Kirk, *Patterns of Reform: Continuity and Change in the Reformation Kirk* (ibid., 1989), esp. pp. 154–231.

superior. One who has authority over others by virtue of his ecclesiastical rank. The term is commonly used of the heads of the religious orders and congregations, though it is not in general use in those (esp. older) orders of monks and canons which consisted originally of independent houses. In some of the more recent bodies of religious, esp. of women, it has become a title.

Supper, Last. See LAST SUPPER.

Suppression of the Monasteries. See DISSOLUTION OF THE MONASTERIES.

Supralapsarianism (or 'Antelapsarianism'). The form of the *Calvinistic doctrine of *predestination which maintains that God decreed the election and non-election of individual men before the *Fall of *Adam. *Calvin himself regarded Divine predestination as an inscrutable mystery; for though he held that the elect, being sinners, were favoured beyond their merit, and that the non-elect, being also sinners, received just treatment acc. to their merit, he did not presume to elaborate the whole subject. It was his followers who boldly asserted such doctrines as supralapsarianism. Though logical consistency may appear to favour the supralapsarian position, the milder *sublapsarian doctrine (q.v.) has been generally dominant among Calvinists, esp. since the Synod of *Dort (1618).

Supremacy, Acts of. The Supremacy of the Crown Act 1534 confirmed to *Henry VIII and his successors the title of 'the only supreme head in earth of the Church of England, called *Anglicana Ecclesia*'. It was repealed under *Mary by the See of Rome Act 1554, and the repeal was confirmed by *Elizabeth I. But Elizabeth's Act of Supremacy 1558, the first Act of her reign (1559), restored the Henrician legislation in a revised form. The monarch's title just quoted was dropped, however, and the Queen declared to be 'the only supreme governor of this realm, and of all her highness's dominions and countries, as well in all spiritual and ecclesiastical things or causes as temporal'. The election of bishops by *congé d'élire was restored, and an oath of obedience to the Crown in things ecclesiastical as well as temporal imposed on all clergymen and public officials. The Act was an assertion of the monarch's responsibility before God for the welfare of the Church, and annexed 'for ever' the power of reforming abuses to the Crown.

The text of the Supremacy of the Crown Act 1534 is repr. in Gee and Hardy, pp. 243 f. (no. 55); the repeal by Mary of this and other ecclesiastical legislation of the previous reigns is repr. ibid., pp. 385–415 (no. 76), esp. p. 390; and the Act of Supremacy 1558 is repr. ibid., pp. 442–58 (no. 79).

Surin, Jean-Joseph (1600–65), *Jesuit mystic and spiritual writer. The eldest son of a Bordeaux magistrate, in 1616 he entered the Society of Jesus, where he came under the influence of the teaching on mysticism of Louis Lallemant (1587–1635). Of frail health, but endowed with great intellectual and spiritual gifts, he was sent to Loudun in 1634 to exorcise some *Ursulines believed to be possessed by the devil. He acted as spiritual director to the superior, Jeanne des Anges, and she recovered. Surin experienced some 20 years of mental trials, alternating between believing himself to be damned (with an attempt at *suicide) and to be receiving Divine graces; modern scholars suspect manic depressive illness. At the same time, Surin seems to have had genuine mystical experiences and eventually regained his mental powers and some

stability. In his autobiographical writings, he describes his trials and how he overcame them. He also composed a number of spiritual writings; *Catéchisme spirituel* (1657; published without his knowledge), *Les Fondements de la vie spirituelle* (1667; based on the *Imitation of Christ), *Dialogues spirituels* (1700–9), and other works. He advocated the practice of the presence of God and the prayer of contemplation in which the soul, abandoned to the Holy Spirit, loses itself in the love of God. He was sought after as a spiritual director, a task to which he gave much thought, as his letters of direction show. An Italian translation of his *Catéchisme* was placed on the *Index in 1695 during the controversy between F. *Fénelon and J.-B. *Bossuet, but his *Fondements* was published by E. B. *Pusey in a version 'adapted' for C of E readers in 1844.

List of his works with notices of edns. and trs. to date in Sommervogel, 7 (1896), cols. 1704–16; 9 (1900), col. 868; and 12 (1911–30, repr. 1960), cols. 826–30; Polgár, 3 (1990), pp. 331–5. His autobiog. is incl. in the edn. of his *Lettres spirituelles*, ed. L. Michel and F. Cavallera (Bibliothèque de la *Revue d'Ascétique et de Mystique*, 2 vols., 1926–8), 2, pp. 1–151. Modern edns. of his *Poésies spirituelles* and *Contrats spirituels* by É Catta (Études de théologie et d'histoire de la spiritualité, 15; 1957), of his *Guide spirituel pour la perfection* (unfinished at Surin's death and first pub. 1801) by M. de Certeau, SJ (Paris [1963]), and of his *Correspondance*, by id. (ibid. [1966]). E. de Greeff, 'Succédanés et Concomitances psychopathologiques de la "Nuit obscure" (le cas du père Surin)', *Études Carmélitaines*, 23. 2 (1938), pp. 152–76, esp. 160–76, with other arts. on Surin by M. Olphe-Galliard, SJ, J. de Guibert, SJ, and F. Achille-Delmais, pp. 177–89 and 235–9; F. de Dainville, SJ, 'Une étape de la "Déroute des Mystiques". La révision romaine du "Catéchisme Spirituel" (1661)', *Revue d'Ascétique et de Mystique*, 33 (1957), pp. 62–87; M. de Certeau, 'Jean-Joseph Surin', *The Month*, 210 (1960), pp. 340–53; id., 'Les Œuvres de Jean-Joseph Surin', *Revue d'Ascétique et de Mystique*, 40 (1964), pp. 443–76; 41 (1965), pp. 55–78 [discusses edns.; no more pub.]; id. (ed.), *La Possession de Loudun* (Collection Archives [1970]), pp. 289–306; F. P. Bowman, 'Suffering, Madness, and Literary Creation in Seventeenth-Century Spiritual Autobiography', *French Forum*, 1 (1976), pp. 24–48. A. Louth, *The Wilderness of God* (1991), pp. 104–22. Bremond, 5 (1920), pp. 148–310. M. Olphe-Gailliard, SJ, in *DTC* 14 (pt. 2; 1941), cols. 2834–42, s.v.; M. Dupuy, PSS, in *Dict. Sp.* 14 (1990), cols. 1311–25, s.v.

surplice (Lat. *superpelliceum*, 'over a fur garment'). A liturgical vestment of white linen, with wide sleeves. It was originally a loose choir vestment substituted for the narrow-sleeved alb because it was better suited for wear over the fur coats customary in northern countries, hence its name. From the 12th cent. it came to be the distinctive dress of the lower clergy and to be used by priests outside Mass. At first a tunic reaching to the feet, it became steadily shorter until, in the 18th cent. on the Continent, it just covered the hips, the sleeves also being reduced in size. This form, usually called the *cotta, was until recently widely used in the RC Church beside the older, wide-sleeved form, reaching to the knees. The surplice is worn by all clerics and is also used by laymen, e.g. in choir, when serving Mass, acting as acolytes, etc. In the C of E the BCP of 1552 made it the only prescribed vestment of the clergy, but the '*Ornaments Rubric' ordering it was removed in later editions. Its use caused much controversy in the reign of *Elizabeth I, but was insisted upon by Abp. M. *Parker in his *Advertisements*. Can. 58 of 1604 ordered the wearing of the surplice by ministers during Divine service and when administering the sacraments, and can. 17 enjoined it also on students in colleges other than clerics on certain days. Can. B 8 of 1969 prescribes its use by ministers at Morning and Evening Prayer and for the Occasional Offices and gives it as one of the alternative vestments of the celebrant at the Eucharist. The question whether a surplice should be worn by a cleric when preaching in the pulpit was widely agitated in the 19th cent. in connection with the Ritualist Movement. Its use in the C of E is now almost, if not quite, universal. See also VESTIARIAN CONTROVERSY.

Braun, *LG*, pp. 135–48. J. Braun, SJ, in *CE* 14 (1912), pp. 343 f., s.v. V. Staley in *PBD* (1912), pp. 774 f., s.v. See also bibl. to ORNAMENTS RUBRIC.

surplice fees. The fees which are payable to the incumbent of a parish for marriages and burials. They are his by right, whoever performs the service, and he pays income tax on them as part of the income of the benefice, unless he has assigned his fees to the Diocesan Board of Finance by deed.

surrogate. In ecclesiastical usage, the word is applied esp. to a clergyman or other person appointed by the bishop as his deputy to grant licences for marriages without banns.

Sursum Corda (Lat., 'Lift up your hearts'). In the Eucharistic liturgy the words addressed by the celebrant to the congregation immediately before the *Preface. The reply is: 'Habemus ad Dominum', traditionally translated, 'We lift them up unto the Lord'. Its use, which is universal, is attested as early as St *Hippolytus of Rome (*c.*215) and St *Cyprian (252) in the W. and as St *Cyril of Jerusalem (*c.*350) in the E.

Jungmann (1958 edn.), 2, pp. 138–44; Eng. tr., 2, pp. 110–15. C. A. Bouman, 'Variants in the introduction to the Eucharistic Prayer', *VC* 4 (1950), pp. 94–115. E. Ferguson, 'The Liturgical Function of the "Sursum Corda" ', in E. A. Livingstone (ed.), *Studia Patristica*, 13 (TU 116; 1975), pp. 360–3.

Susanna, Book of. In the English Bible one of the smaller Books of the *Apocrypha. In the LXX it follows the Book of Daniel (of which the *Vulgate reckons it the thirteenth chapter); in the *Old Latin it comes immediately before Daniel. There is no agreement among scholars as to whether it was originally written in Greek, Hebrew, or Aramaic. The Book tells in 64 verses of the false accusation of adultery brought against Susanna by two elders, her condemnation, and her final deliverance by the sagacity of Daniel. In the Christian era the incident became the symbol of the saved soul, and as such is to be met with already in the paintings of the *catacombs and on early *sarcophagi. It became again a favourite subject of art in the Renaissance, esp. the bathing scene, which has also been painted by P. P. Rubens, *Rembrandt, and others, as well as by many modern artists.

Gk. texts in H. B. *Swete (ed.), *The Old Testament in Greek*, 3 (1912 edn.), pp. 576–85, and A. Rahlfs (ed.), *Septuaginta*, 2 (Stuttgart, 1935), pp. 864–70. Eng. tr., with comm. and refs. to other edns. of texts, by D. M. Kay in R. H. *Charles (ed.), *The Apocrypha and Pseudepigrapha of the Old Testament*, 1 (1913), pp. 638–51; J. C. Dancy, *The Shorter Books of the Apocrypha* (Camb. Bib., NEB, 1972), pp. 224–34; and C. A. Moore, *Daniel, Esther,*

and Jeremiah: The Additions (Anchor Bible, 1977), pp. 77–116. Ger. tr. and comm. by H. Engel, *Die Susannah-Erzählung* (Orbis Biblicus et Orientalis, 61; Freiburg, Switz., and Göttingen, 1985). E. *Schürer, *The History of the Jewish People in the Age of Jesus Christ*, rev. Eng. tr. by G. Vermes and others, 3 (pt. 2, Edinburgh, 1987), pp. 722–30, with bibl. On early representations in art, H. *Leclercq, OSB, in *DACL* 15 (pt. 2; 1953), cols. 1742–52, s.v. 'Suzanne', with refs. See also Catholic comm. to Daniel and bibl. to APOCRYPHA.

Susanna, St (3rd cent.), Roman martyr. Acc. to legend, she was a woman of noble birth and great beauty, a niece of Pope Caius (283–96), and was put to death for refusing to marry a pagan relative of *Diocletian. Her 'Acta' seem to be a working-over of what was orig. an edifying tale. Since the 5th cent. her name has been attached to one of the *tituli* (see TITLE) at Rome. Feast day, 11 Aug.

AASS, Aug. 2 (1734), pp. 624–32, with pt. 2 of the Acta and other material; pt. 1, ibid., Feb. 3 (1658), pp. 61–4, L. *Duchesne, 'Les Légendes de l'Alta Semita', *Mélanges d'Archéologie et d'Histoire*, 36 (1916–17), pp. 27–56, esp. pp. 33–42; J. P. Kirsch, *Die römischen Titelkirchen im Altertum* (Studien zur Geschichte und Kultur des Altertums, 9, Hefte 1 and 2; 1918), pp. 70–4; P. Franchi de' Cavalieri, *Note agiografiche*, 7 (ST 49; 1928), pp. 185–202. C. Pietri, *Roma Christiana: Recherches sur l'Église de Rome ... (311–440)* (Bibliothèque des Écoles françaises d'Athènes et de Rome, 224; 1976), 1, pp. 498–501.

Suso, Bl Henry. See HENRY SUSO, BL.

suspension. In the RC Church, one of the censures or 'medicinal' *penalties. Suspension, which only affects clerics, prohibits the exercise of some or all of the functions of *Orders, the powers of governance, and the rights and functions attaching to an office. A suspension prohibiting the receipt of benefits (stipends, pensions, etc.) carries with it the obligation to restore whatever has been unlawfully received, even in good faith (*CIC* (1983), can. 1333 § 1 and § 4).

In the C of E, suspension is one of the five censures which the Diocesan *Chancellor may impose on a cleric following a conviction in the *Consistory Court for an offence against ecclesiastical law other than one in respect of doctrine, ritual, or ceremonial under the *Ecclesiastical Jurisdiction Measure 1963. The other four are deprivation, inhibition, monition, and rebuke.

Sutton, Christopher (*c.*1565–1629), devotional writer. Educated at Hart Hall and Lincoln College, *Oxford, he held several livings in the E. counties. In 1605 he became a Canon of *Westminster and in 1618 of *Lincoln. His devotional books, written with much fervour, enjoyed great popularity. The most used was *Godly Meditations upon the Most Holy Sacrament of the Lord's Supper* (1601), in which, deprecating controversy, he sought to defend a doctrine of Christ's presence in the Eucharist midway between *transubstantiation and the teaching of H. *Zwingli, maintaining that while consecration effected no change in the substance of the elements it radically altered their use. The book was reissued by J. H. *Newman with a fresh preface in 1838 and became popular for some years with the *Tractarians. Sutton's *Disce Mori* (1600) and *Disce Vivere* (1602) were also reissued in the 19th cent.

His *Disce Vivere* was repr. from the 1602 ed. with a Memoir of his life by J. E. Tyler (1847), pp. iii–xxii. B. Hall in *Dict. Sp.* 14 (1990), cols. 1352–4, s.v. [dating of Sutton's works is inaccurate].

Suvermerian. A word applied by the Saxon Reformers to certain Swiss Protestant extremists. It arose from an attempted Latinization (*Swermeros*) of the Ger. *Schwärmer* ('fanatical enthusiasts'). In modern times it was brought to general notice through its use (mistakenly, as he later acknowledged) by C. H. Smyth to describe the Eucharistic doctrine of T. *Cranmer in *Cranmer and the Reformation under Edward VI* (1926).

On the term see C. Hopf, *Martin Bucer and the English Reformation* (Oxford, 1946), pp. 35–40, and review of Hopf by Smyth, *Cambridge Review*, 69 (1947), p. 54.

Swainson, Charles Anthony (1820–87), English theologian. A native of Liverpool, he was educated at Trinity College, Cambridge, and became a Fellow of Christ's College in 1841. He was ordained priest in 1844 and was appointed principal of the theological college at *Chichester in 1854. In 1864 he became Norrisian professor of divinity at Cambridge, was elected master of Christ's College in 1881, and vice-chancellor of the university in 1885. In 1858 he published his *Hulsean Lectures on *The Creeds of the Church*. It was followed in 1875 by his important work, *The Nicene and Apostles' Creeds*, which was the fruit of many years' work on MSS in Continental libraries. It included an account of the *Athanasian Creed, which Swainson dated between 860 and 870 and believed to consist of two separate documents. He also produced a standard collection of texts, *The Greek Liturgies* (1884).

S. Cheetham in *DNB* 55 (1898), pp. 191 f., s.v.

swastika (Skt. *svastika*, 'well-being', 'fortune'; Lat. *crux gammata*; Fr. *croix gammée*; Ger. *Hakenkreuz*). A symbol of great antiquity, in the form of a cross of equal arms each of which is bent at right angles. It was probably in origin a charm for attracting good luck and averting misfortune and has also been explained as a symbol of fertility or as representing the wheel of the sun, though the latter interpretation has been commonly rejected in recent times. It appears already on the vases of Mussiân Tepe (nr. Susa, in Elamite country) *c.*4000–3000 BC, among the German tribes *c.*1000 BC, and is found as a widespread ornament in China, Japan—esp. in Buddhist art—and America in the Christian era. From the middle of the 3rd cent. AD it appears in the Roman catacombs, but apparently without any symbolic or Christian reference. It is also to be found on medieval embroidery and brasses, e.g. at Lewknor, Oxfordshire. In modern times, owing to the mistaken idea that it is an old Teutonic sign confined to the Aryan peoples, it was adopted as the official symbol of the National Socialist Party in Germany, with special emphasis on its anti-Semitic significance.

T. Wilson, 'The Swastika. The earliest known Symbol and its Migrations', *Annual Report of . . . the . . . Smithsonian Institution for the Year ending June 30, 1894* (Washington, DC, 1896), pp. 757–1011, with bibl. J. Lechler, *Vom Hakenkreuz: Die Geschichte eines Symbols* (Leipzig, 1921; 2nd edn., 1934). O. Hupp, *Runen und Hakenkreuz: Eine archäologische Studie mit heraldischen Schlussfolgerungen* (Munich, 1921).

Sweden, Christianity in. The effective evangelization of Sweden dates from the 11th cent. About 830 St *Anskar established a Church at Birka, near Stockholm, but this did not survive. A more lasting mission was initiated by St Sigfrid, a monk from England, who baptized King Olov Skötkonung *c.*1000. Despite heathen resistance, the conversion of the country was virtually completed in the early 12th cent. In 1104 Asker, Bp. of *Lund, became Abp. of the newly constituted Nordic province, and in 1164 *Uppsala was made an archbishopric, independent of Lund (then in *Denmark). The first monasteries were founded by the *Cistercians at Alvastra and Nydala in 1143. The outstanding figure in later medieval Swedish Church history was St *Bridget (*c.*1303–73), who founded the *Bridgettine Order with its mother house at Vadstena.

The Reformation in Sweden was gradual and closely connected with political events. Gustav Vasa, leader of the movement for independence from Denmark and King of Sweden 1523–60, was badly in need of funds and anxious to curb the power of the bishops. Under his protection, Olaus *Petri, a pupil of M. *Luther, was appointed city clerk at Stockholm in 1524, while his friend Laurentius Andreae became the King's chancellor. At the Diet of *Västerås in 1527 the 'superfluous' revenue of the bishops, cathedrals, and monastic houses was vested in the King, who was entreated that 'God's Word might be purely preached'. At this stage there was no overt attack on the Papacy. In 1531, however, Olaus Petri's brother Laurentius was consecrated Abp. of Uppsala without Papal sanction and without the *pallium, though the *Apostolic Succession was maintained through the participation of Petrus Magni, Bp. of Västerås. The majority of the population remained Catholic in sympathy. Services in the vernacular were provided by the Swedish Handbook of 1529 and the Swedish Mass of 1531, but their use remained optional until 1536. The NT had been translated into Swedish in 1526 (almost certainly by Olaus Petri); it was followed by the whole Bible in 1541. By then most of the monasteries had disappeared and the bishops had become state officials. It was not, however, until 1593 that the Swedes adopted the *Augsburg Confession and thus committed themselves to *Lutheran dogma, after the attempts of King John III (reigned 1569–92) to reunite the Swedish Church with Rome had failed. With the participation of *Gustavus Adolphus in the *Thirty Years' War (1618–48), Sweden became one of the leading Protestant powers. The abdication of his daughter *Christina (1654) and her subsequent conversion to RCism was followed by a wave of anti-Catholic feeling.

In the last decades of the 17th cent. *Pietism became an influence in Sweden; its appeal was strengthened by military defeats followed by the imprisonment of Swedish soldiers in Siberia in the early 18th cent. To combat it the Conventicle Proclamation of 1726 restricted meetings for religious purposes. From the 1730s the *Moravians gained ground. Under the influence of the *Enlightenment, E. *Swedenborg sought to combine rationalism and mysticism to form a new moral religion. The 1781 Act of Toleration gave freedom of religion to foreigners. This more liberal attitude was extended in the 1809 Constitution and various later measures, notably the 1860 Dissenter Act which provided freedom of worship and allowed the formation of Christian denominations. Within the Church of Sweden the *revivalism which accompanied the social dislocation of the industrial revolution, was fostered not only by the repeal of the Conventicle Proclamation in 1858, but also by the establishment two years earlier of the *Evangeliska Fosterlands-Stiftelsen* (Evangelical Fosterland Society). Divisions appeared in this body, and in 1878 P. P. *Waldenström broke with the Church of Sweden and founded a free Lutheran Church, the *Svenska Missionsförbundet* (Swedish Mission Society), which now has its own ministers and sacraments. Meanwhile the first *Methodist congregations were founded in 1868, and the *Salvation Army began work in Sweden in 1882. The *temperance movement was strong. In the early years of the 20th cent. there was a revival of theological scholarship in Sweden. It was led by Abp. N. *Söderblom, who also played a leading part in the early history of the *Ecumenical Movement, culminating in the *Stockholm Conference of 1925. A High Church Movement, perhaps influenced by contacts with England, spread throughout the country in the 1930s. Since 1951 it has been possible to renounce membership of any Church. The majority of the population still belongs to the Church of Sweden. Thanks to modern immigration the RC Church is the next largest denomination, followed by the Swedish Mission Society and the *Pentecostalists. The state, while tolerating all religions, gives special, if decreasing, protection to the Established Church, which has its own Kyrkomöte, or Convocation, without the consent of which no laws on Church matters may be passed by Parliament.

Survey in Eng. by J. *Wordsworth, *The National Church of Sweden* (Hale Lectures, 1910; 1911); shorter accounts by H. M. Waddams, *The Swedish Church* (1946) and R. Murray, *A Brief History of the Church of Sweden* (Stockholm, 1961). I. Andersson, *A History of Sweden*, tr. by C. Hannay (1955), *passim*. H. Holmquist and H. Pleijel (eds.), *Svenska Kyrkans Historia*, 2 [1274–1521] (1941); 3 [1521–1611] (1933); 4 (1) [1611–32] (1938); 5 [1680–1772] (1935); 6 (2) [1809–23] (1946). P. G. Lindhardt, *Skandinavische Kirchengeschichte seit dem 16. Jahrhundert* (Die Kirche in ihrer Geschichte: Ein Handbuch, ... ed. B. Moeller, Band 3, Lieferung M3; Göttingen [1982]), pp. 276–302. Eng. tr. of the *Handbok för Svenska Kyrkan* (the service book containing the orders for administering the Sacraments, the forms for Morning and Evening Prayer and the Occasional Offices) by E. E. Yelverton, *The Swedish Rite* (Translations of Christian Literature, Series 3, Liturgical Texts, 1921). Id., *The Mass in Sweden: Its Development from the Latin Rite from 1531 to 1917* (HBS 57; 1920). M. Roberts, *The Early Vasas: A History of Sweden, 1523–1611* (Cambridge, 1968), esp. pp. 59–91, 107–24, 273–96, 412–26. H. Holmquist, *Die schwedische Reformation 1523–1531* (Schriften des Vereins für Reformationsgeschichte, 139; Leipzig, 1925); J. G. H. Hoffmann, *La Réforme en Suède 1523–1527 et la succession apostolique* (1945); I. Montgomery, 'La Réforme en Suède, une libération nationale de politique', *Revue d'Histoire et de Philosophie Religieuses*, 63 (1983), pp. 113–24. H. Pleijel, *Der schwedische Pietismus in seinen Beziehungen zu Deutschland* (Lunds Universitets Årsskrift, NF, Avd. 1, Bd. 34, Nr. 4; 1935); id., *Das Kirchenproblem der Brüdergemeine in Schweden* (ibid. 1. 33. 6; 1938). C. H. Lyttkens, *The Growth of Swedish–Anglican Intercommunion between 1833 and 1922* (Bibliotheca Theologiae Practicae, 24; Lund [1970]). L. Österlin, *Svenska Kyrkan i Profil: Ur engelskt och nordiskt perspektiv* (1994; Eng. tr., *Churches of Northern Europe in Profile*, Norwich, 1995). A. Palmquist, *Die römisch-katholische Kirche in Schweden nach 1781*, 1 [1783–1820] (Publications of the Swedish Society of Church History, NS 8; Uppsala, 1954), 2 [1870–73] (Uppsala Universitets Årsskrift, 1958, pt. 8).

Swedenborg, Emanuel (1688–1772), orig. 'Swedberg',

Swedish scientist and mystical thinker. He was the son of Jesper Swedberg, who later became professor of theology at *Uppsala and Bp. of Skara. After studying at Uppsala and extensive travels in England (where he was influenced by Henry *More, J. *Locke, and I. *Newton) and elsewhere, he was appointed by Charles XII to a post on the Swedish Board of Mines (1716). Endowed with considerable inventiveness and mathematical ability, he anticipated many subsequent hypothcses and discoveries (nebular theory, magnetic theory, machine-gun, acroplane). As time went on he became increasingly concerned to show by purely scientific (esp. physical) analysis that the Universe had a fundamentally spiritual structure, notably in *Prodromus Philosophiae Ratiocinantis de Infinito et Causa Finali Creationis* (1734).

In 1743–5 Swedenborg's outlook underwent a sudden development. He became conscious of direct contact with the angels and the spiritual world, partly in dreams and supernatural visions, but also in his normal waking life. He felt that the Lord was commissioning him to make known his doctrines to mankind at large. The agency was to be the New Church, organized not as a body separate from the existing Churches, but as a spiritual fraternity of all those of whatever ecclesiastical allegiance who accepted his doctrines. In 1747 he resigned his position on the Board of Mines and embarked on intensive study of the Scriptures. He spent the rest of his life in Sweden, the Netherlands, and London, writing assiduously in defence of his teachings, but also maintaining his purely scientific interests to the end. He died in London and was buried in the Swedish Church in Princes Square. In 1908 his remains were removed to Stockholm by arrangement with the Swedish Government.

Among the earliest disseminators of his teaching were two C of E clergymen, Thomas Hartley (d. 1784), rector of Winwick, Northants (though apparently non-resident in later years), and John Clowes (1743–1831), vicar of St John's, Manchester. Lancashire has remained a centre of Swedenborgian influence in England. The formal creation of a separate body, known as the New Jerusalem Church, was, however, the work of five ex-Wesleyan preachers in London (7 May 1787). Since 1815 conferences have been held annually. In USA, the first congregation was formed in Baltimore in 1792, and a General Convention of the New Jerusalem met in 1817 at Philadelphia. In 1890 a smaller, separate body of Swedenborgians, which in 1897 took the name of General Church of the New Jerusalem, was established, with headquarters at Bryn Athyn, Pa. There are also bodies of Swedenborgians on the Continent of Europe, in Africa, *Australia, *Canada, *Japan, and in South America. They claim world membership of about 65,000.

The basis of Swedenborg's system was a 'doctrine of correspondence' between the physical and spiritual worlds. He envisaged the spiritual world as containing various groupings of deceased human beings which made up a single great human being. He accepted Christ as the greatest manifestation of humanity, but rejected the doctrine of the *Atonement. Of his voluminous expositions the most comprehensive was *Arcana Coelestia* (8 vols., 1756). Among others were *The Earths in the Universe* (1758), *The New Jerusalem and its Heavenly Doctrine* (1758), *Heaven and Hell* (1758), *Divine Love and Wisdom* (1763; perhaps the best epitome of his system), *The Apocalypse Revealed*

(1766), and *The True Christian Religion* (1771). W. *Blake was much influenced by him. His earliest critics included I. *Kant, whose *Träume eines Geistersehers* (1766) was directed against him.

Photolithographed edn. of his works by R. L. Tafel (10 vols., Stockholm, 1869–70); also ed. in 18 vols., ibid., 1901–16. *Posthumous Tracts* tr. from Lat. into Eng. by J. J. G. Wilkinson (London, 1847). A facsimile edn. of his *Memorabilia seu Diarium Spirituale ab Anno 1747 ad Annum 1765* was pub. at Stockholm (3 vols., 1901–5); Eng. tr. of the Diary by G. Bush and J. H. Smithson (5 vols., London, 1883–1902). 3rd edn. of *Arcana Coelestia*, by P. H. Johnson and others (8 vols., ibid., 1949–73); Eng. tr. by J. H. Elliott (1983 ff.). W. R. Woofenden, *Swedenborg Researcher's Manual* (Bryn Athyn, Pa., 1988). Concordance to his theological works compiled and translated into Eng. by J. F. Potts (6 vols., London, 1888–1902). R. L. Tafel (ed. and tr.), *Documents Concerning the Life and Character of Emanuel Swedenborg* (2 vols., bound in 3, 1875–7). G. Trobridge, *A Life of Emanuel Swedenborg: With a Popular Exposition of his Philosophical and Theological Teachings* (1912). E. Benz, *Swedenborg in Deutschland: F. C. Oetinger und Immanuel Kants Auseinandersetzung mit der Person und Lehre Emanuel Swedenborgs* (Auflage 2000; 1947); id., *Emanuel Swedenborg: Naturforscher und Seher* (1948). C. O. Sigstedt, *The Swedenborg Epic: The Life and Works of Emanuel Swedenborg* (New York, 1952). I. Jonsson, *Swedenborgs Korrespondenslära* (Acta Universitatis Stockholmiensis. Stockholm Studies in Literature, 10; 1969), with summary in English. Id., *Emanuel Swedenborg* (Twayne's World Authors, 127; New York [1971]). W. van Dusen, *The Presence of Other Worlds: The Psychological/Spiritual Findings of Emanuel Swedenborg* (1975). E. J. Brock and others (eds.), *Swedenborg and his Influence* (Bryn Athyn, Pa., and London, 1988). L. B. de Beaumont in *HERE* 12 (1921), pp. 129–32. s.v.; S. Lindroth in *Dictionary of Scientific Biography*, 13 (1976), pp. 178–81, s.v.

Swete, Henry Barclay (1835–1917), biblical and patristic scholar. He was educated at King's College, London, and Gonville and Caius College, Cambridge. From 1882 to 1890 he was professor at King's College, London, and from 1890 until 1915 Regius professor of divinity at Cambridge. He achieved great success in fostering theological study, esp. at Cambridge; and among the many co-operative projects with which he was directly concerned were the *Journal of Theological Studies* (1899 ff.), the series of Cambridge Patristic Texts and the Cambridge Handbooks of Liturgical Study, the Central Society of Sacred Study (CSSS, for the encouragement of theological study among Anglican clergy), and *A *Patristic Greek Lexicon* (eventually pub. 1961–8). His own writings include 2 vols. on the history of the doctrine of the Holy Spirit (1909, 1912), editions of *Theodore of Mopsuestia's commentary on the Minor Epistles of St Paul (1880–2) and of the text of the *Septuagint (3 vols., 1887–94), and commentaries on St Mark (1898) and the Apocalypse (1906). He also edited *Essays on the Early History of the Church and the Ministry* (posthumous, 1918).

'M. B. K.', 'H. G.', and 'J. F. B.-B.', *Henry Barclay Swete....: A Remembrance* (1918); this repr., with additions, on pp. 163–92, a bibl. of Swete's pub. works by C. H. *Turner and A. Rogers, orig. pub. in *JTS* 19 (1918), pp. 1–19. J. H. Srawley in *DNB, 1912–1921*, pp. 520–2.

Swift, Jonathan (1667–1745), Dean of St Patrick's, *Dublin (from 1713), and English satirist. Only the more definitely religious aspects of his career can be noted here. Ordained priest in Ireland in 1695, he remained faithful to the C of E and opposed alike to the N. Irish and Scottish *Presbyterians and to English Dissenters. In politics he was a Whig, but was persuaded to write against the *Occasional Conformity Act (1708) and frequently found difficulty in supporting his party in its leanings towards Nonconformists. His great powers of satire were used to religious ends in his *Argument to Prove the Inconvenience of Abolishing Christianity* (1708). He hated injustice and condemned the English misgovernment of Ireland, attacking even the Irish Bishops, but retaining the confidence of the common people. He wrote pamphlets against G. *Burnet, Bp. of *Salisbury, and A. *Collins, the *Deist. He is most popularly remembered as the author of *Gulliver's Travels* (1726). His works (nearly 100) were, with one exception, published anonymously.

Early edns. of his works by J. Hawkesworth (14 vols., London, 1755–79), with Life in vol. 1, pp. 9–40; and by T. Sheridan (17 vols., ibid., 1784), with Life as vol. 1, also issued separately. Crit. edns. of his prose works by H. Davis (14 vols., Oxford, 1939–68); of his poems by H. Wilson (3 vols., ibid., 1937; 2nd edn., 1958), with bibl.; and of his correspondence by H. Williams (5 vols., ibid., 1963–5). Lives and studies by L. Stephen ('English Men of Letters'; 1882), W. D. Taylor (London, 1933), R. Quintana (ibid., 1936; rev. 1956), J. M. Murray (ibid., 1954), I. Ehrenpreis (3 vols., ibid., 1962–83), D. Donoghue (Cambridge, 1969), P. Steele (Oxford, 1978), D. Nokes (ibid., 1985), and K. Craven (Brill's Studies in Intellectual History, 30; Leiden, etc., 1992). C. Rawson (ed.), *The Character of Swift's Satire* (Newark, Del., etc. [1983]). R. W. Jackson, *Jonathan Swift, Dean and Pastor* (1939); L. A. Landa, *Swift and the Church of Ireland* (Oxford, 1954). H. Teerink, *A Bibliography of the Writings in Prose and Verse of Jonathan Swift* (The Hague, 1937; rev. by A. H. Scouten, Philadelphia, 1963). J. J. Stathis, *A Bibliography of Swift Studies, 1945–1965* (Nashville, 1967); R. H. Rodino, *Swift Studies, 1965–1980: An Annotated Bibliography* (New York and London, 1984). O. W. Ferguson in *NCBEL* 2 (1971), cols. 1054–91. L. Stephen in *DNB* 55 (1898), pp. 204–27.

Swiss Brethren. A group of *Anabaptists who reintroduced believers' Baptism as the basis of Church fellowship at Zollikon (near Zurich) in Jan. 1525. The name originally designated congregations in the German-speaking areas of Switzerland, but it came to be applied also to similar groups in the Austrian Tyrol, S. Germany, and Alsace. In contrast to T. *Müntzer, the Brethren believed in non-resistance and rejected participation in the magistracy. They established visible and ordered Churches but disagreed with the *Hutterites about community of possessions. Their religious tenets were formulated in the 7 articles of the Schleitheim Confession or 'Brotherly Union of a Number of the Children of God' (*Brüderliche Vereinigung etlicher Kinder Gottes'*, 1527); this document, perhaps drafted by Michael Sattler (*c.*1490–1527), was controverted by U. *Zwingli as well as J. *Calvin. Other early leaders included Conrad Grebel (*c.*1498–1526) and George Blaurock (*c.*1492–1529). In spite of persecution lasting into the 18th cent. they survived, esp. in the mountain fastness of the Canton of Berne, but the majority migrated to Germany, the *Netherlands, and the *United States of America, where they form a major part of the *Mennonites. Their modern descendants in Switzerland number *c.*3,000 baptized members and are organized as the 'Conference of Mennonites in Switzerland', which is a member of the Mennonite World Conference.

Quellen zur Geschichte der Täufer in der Schweiz, ed. L. von Muralt and others (Zurich, 1952 ff.). Eng. tr. of some of the works of M. Sattler by J. H. Yoder, *The Legacy of Michael Sattler* (Classics of the Radical Reformation Series, 1; Scottdale, Pa., 1973), incl. the Schleitheim Confession, pp. 34–43. Eng. tr. of 'The Grebel Letters and Related Documents' by L. Harden, *The Sources of Swiss Anabaptism* (ibid. 4; 1985). H. S. Bender, *Conrad Grebel c.1498–1526: The Founder of the Swiss Brethren Sometimes Called Anabaptists* (Studies in Anabaptist and Mennonite History, 6; Goshen, Ind., 1950). F. Blanke, *Brüder in Christo: Die Geschichte der ältesten Täufergemeinde (Zollikon 1525)* (Zurich, 1955; Eng. tr., Scottdale, Pa., 1961). H. Fast, *Heinrich Bullinger und die Täufer* (Schriftenreihe des Mennonitischen Geschichtsvereins, 7; Weierhof, 1959). See also works cited under ANABAPTISTS.

Swiss Guard (*Guardia Svizzera Pontificia*).
The military guardians of the Papal Palace. The corps was instituted by Pope *Julius II (1503–13), with whom the cantons of Zurich and Lucerne entered into an agreement to supply 250 guardsmen. It now consists of about 100 men, recruited from all the Swiss cantons. The parade uniform of the Guard, which was designed by *Michelangelo, is composed of tunic, breeches, and stockings of wide and gaily coloured red, yellow, and dark blue stripes. See also NOBLE GUARD, PALATINE GUARD.

P Krieg, *Die päpstliche Schweizergarde* (Zurich, 1948). J. Repond, *Le Costume de la garde suisse pontificale et la renaissance italienne* (Rome, 1917). E. Hampoole, OP, 'The Papal Swiss Guards', *The American Catholic Quarterly Review*, 37 (1912), pp. 286–309 and 369–87. Information about the Swiss Guard is incl. in the section 'Note Storiche' of the *Annuario Pontificio*. E. D. McShane in *NCE* 13 (1967), pp. 840 f., s.v., with illustr.

Swithun, St (d. 862),
also 'Swithin', Bp. of *Winchester. Little is certainly known of his life, contemporary evidence attesting only his existence as Bp. of Winchester from 852. Originally buried 'humbly' outside the walls of the minster, in 971 his body was translated to a shrine in the cathedral which had been rebuilt by *Ethelwold, and his cult seems to date from this period. In 1093 his relics were again translated, but they disappeared when his shrine was destroyed at the Reformation (1538). The popular belief that the weather on St Swithun's day (15 July) will be that of the next 40 days may have arisen from a similar attribution to the feast of SS. Processus and Martinian, which coincides with the anniversary of Swithun's death (2 July).

The principal sources for the legends are the works emanating from the milieu of the Winchester community after its reform by Ethelwold, notably the Lives by Lantfred, Wulfstan, and *Aelfric, and a Life of uncertain date formerly attributed to *Goscelin. Part of Lantfred's Life is pr. in *AASS*, Jul. 1 (1719), pp. 328–30; the remainder is ed. E. P. Sauvage in *Anal. Boll.* 4 (1885), pp. 367–410; Wulfstan's Life ed. A. Campbell, *Frithegodi Monachi breviloquium vitae beati Wilfredi et Wulfstani Cantoris narratio metrica de Sancto Swithuno* (Zurich, 1950), pp. 63–177. Aelfric's Old English Life ed. and tr. W. W. Skeat, *Aelfric's Lives of Saints* (EETS 76 and 82; 1881–5), pp. 440–73. The Life attributed to Goscelin ed. E. P. Sauvage in *Anal. Boll.* 7 (1888), pp. 373–380. Crit. edn. of early Lives, with Eng. tr. and full introd. by M. Lapidge, *The Cult of St Swithun* (Winchester Studies, 4. 2; in preparation). On the 971 translation see also R. N. Quirk, 'Winchester Cathedral in the tenth century', *Archaeological Journal*, 114 (for 1957; 1959), pp. 28–68; M. Biddle, '*Felix Urbs Winthonia*: Winchester in the Age of Monastic Reform', in D. Parsons (ed.), *Tenth-Century Studies* (1975), pp. 123–40, esp. pp. 136–8; D. J. Sheerin, 'The Dedication of the Old Minster, Winchester, in 980', *R. Bén.* 88 (1978), pp. 261–73.

Sword of the Spirit.
A RC social movement inaugurated by Card. A. *Hinsley in 1940. It was designed as an organization for unifying international Catholic social efforts by 'prayer, study, and action' with a view to promoting justice in war and in the peace which would follow, on the basis of *Pius XII's 'Five Peace Points' and the requirements of the *Natural Law. These aims were shared by Christians of other denominations and were stated in a letter to *The Times* (21 Dec. 1940) signed by the Abps. of Canterbury (C. G. *Lang) and York (W. *Temple), Card. Hinsley, and the Moderator of the Free Churches (W. H. Armstrong). The collaboration between RCs and other groups was, however, restricted in 1941, when full membership of the 'Sword' was confined to RCs and the non-RC communions set up a separate organization under the title 'Religion and Life', the two movements being connected by a Joint Committee. In 1965 the 'Sword of the Spirit' became the Catholic Institute for International Relations.

S. Mews, 'The Sword of the Spirit: a Catholic cultural crusade of 1940', in W. J. Sheils (ed.), *The Church and War* (Studies in Church History, 20; Oxford, 1983), pp. 409–30.

Syllabus Errorum.
A set of 80 theses, already condemned in earlier pronouncements (encyclicals, allocutions, etc.) of *Pius IX and promulgated as erroneous with '*Quanta Cura' (q.v.) on 8 Dec. 1864. The suggestion of a comprehensive attack on modern errors seems to have originated with V. G. Pecci, Bp. of Perugia (later *Leo XIII), at the Council of Spoleto in 1849. The basis of the Syllabus was a list of 85 errors in a Pastoral Instruction (1860) of O. P. Gerbet, Bp. of Perpignan (1853–64), which, modified in turn into a catalogue of 61 theses with corresponding censures, was approved by an assembly of Bishops at Rome in 1862.

The Syllabus was disposed under ten heads dealing with: (1) Pantheism, Naturalism, and Absolute Rationalism (1–7); (2) Moderate Rationalism (8–14); (3) Indifferentism and Latitudinarianism (15–18); (4) Socialism, Communism, secret societies, Bible societies, and Liberalclerical societies (various earlier documents); (5) The Church and its Rights (19–38); (6) Civil Society and its relation to the Church (39–55); (7) Natural and Christian Ethics (56–64); (8) Christian Marriage (65–74); (9) The Temporal Power of the Pope (75–6); and (10) Modern Liberalism (77–80). The last (the 80th) of the rejected propositions is the (often misunderstood) thesis that the 'Roman Pontiff can and ought to reconcile and adjust himself with progress, liberalism and modern civilization' (80). The covering letter issued with the Syllabus and 'Quanta Cura' seemed to make it dogmatically binding.

Its issue was greeted with a storm of protest, e.g. from W. E. *Gladstone. In France publication of the Syllabus and Encyclical was forbidden on 1 Jan. 1865, though the prohibition was withdrawn shortly afterwards. F. A. P. *Dupanloup's *La Convention du 15 septembre et l'encyclique du 8 décembre* (1865), which purported to interpret each condemnation in the light of its original context, did much to mitigate consternation. Many of its fundamental doctrines were embodied in the Dogmatic Constitution, 'De Fide Catholica' at the First *Vatican Council in 1870. In the later years of the 19th cent. the Syllabus was the bulwark of the *Ultramontane party in the RC Church.

Text in *ASS* 3 (1867), pp. 168–76, and in *Pii IX Pontificis Acta*, Pars Prima, 3 (no date), pp. 701–17; repr. in Denzinger and Hünermann (37th edn., 1991), pp. 798–809 (nos. 2901–80). D. McElrath, OFM, *The Syllabus of Pius IX: Some Reactions in England* (Bibliothèque de la *Revue d'Histoire Ecclésiastique*, 39; 1964). J. B. Bury, *History of the Papacy in the Nineteenth Century* (ed. R. H. Murray, 1930), esp. Lectures 1 and 2, pp. 1–46. L. Brigué in *DTC* 14 (pt. 2; 1941), cols. 2877–923, s.v.

Sylvester I, St, Bp. of Rome from 314 to 335. He filled the see of Rome at a very important era in the history of the Church, but very little is known of him. He occupies, however, an important place in later legend, which asserts that he baptized the Emp. *Constantine (cleansing him from physical leprosy) at the Baptistery of the *Lateran and established the Lateran church as the cathedral of Rome on territory given him by the Emperor. He is also the reputed recipient of the *Donation of Constantine, which provided him with wide temporal rights over the Church. Though he did not himself attend the Council of *Nicaea (325), he was represented by two legates, Vitus and Vincentius. Feast day in the W., 31 Dec.; in the E., 2 Jan.

Jaffé, 1, pp. 28–30. *LP* (Duchesne), 1, pp. 170–201; see also pp. cix–cxx. W. Levison, 'Konstantinische Schenkung und Silvester-Legende', in *Miscellanea Francesco Ehrle*, 2 (ST 38; 1924), pp. 159–247, with full refs.; H. Fuhrmann, 'Konstantinische Schenkung und Silvesterlegende in neuer Sicht', *Deutsches Archiv*, 15 (1959), pp. 523–40. C. Pietri, *Roma Christiana: Recherches sur l'Eglise de Rome … (311–440)* (Bibliothèque des Écoles Françaises d'Athènes et de Rome, 224; 2 vols., 1976), esp. 1, pp. 168–87; see also index, p. 1699, s.v. 'Silvestre'. A. Amore, OFM, and C. M. Carpano in *Bibliotheca Sanctorum*, 11 (Rome, 1968), cols. 1077–82, s.v. 'Silvestro I'. See also bibl. to DONATION OF CONSTANTINE.

Sylvester II (*c*.940–1003), Pope from 999. Gerbert is important both as a Churchman and as a scholar. Educated at the *Benedictine monastery of Aurillac (in the département of Cantal), Gerbert enjoyed the patronage of the Bp. of Vich (Catalonia), with whom he went to Rome in 970 or 971. His encounter there with the Emp. Otto I (962–73) was decisive for his future life, which was to be spent within the orbit of the German Empire. In 972 Gerbert went to *Reims, first as a student and then as a master in the cathedral school. He was made abbot of *Bobbio (*c*.982), but in the face of local opposition he soon returned to Reims. On the deposition of his predecessor, he became Abp. of Reims from 991 to 997; in 998 he became Abp. of Ravenna and a year later Pope. He owed these promotions to the Emps. Otto II (973–83) and Otto III (983–1002), who both regarded him as a loyal servant of the Empire in the troubled country outside Germany, while his difficulties at Reims reflected the decline of the imperial influence in Eastern France after the last of the Carolingian kings had been replaced by Hugh Capet in 987.

His choice of the name Sylvester on his election as Pope was a conscious imitation of *Sylvester I, who had long been regarded as the pattern of Papal co-operation with the Emperor. Otto III, as the new Constantine, would restore the universal Roman Empire, while the Church under Sylvester would recover its original purity. The reality of his rule was not wholly divorced from this ideal. He opposed *simony and upheld clerical *celibacy and did much to strengthen the Church in E. Europe. Archbishop-

rics were established in Gniezno (Poland) and Esztergom (Hungary), and *Stephen of Hungary was given Papal recognition as King.

Gerbert's scholarly interests covered both the *trivium and the *quadrivium. The chronicler Richer asserts that he taught the complete *logica vetus* in the school of Reims; if this is so, Gerbert was the first master in Europe to use a substantial part of the logical works of *Aristotle and *Boethius as a practical system of education. Richer also describes his victory over a master from Magdeburg in a court debate before Otto II at Ravenna. Gerbert's surviving work consists of a short logical tractate, *De rationali et ratione uti*, and a considerable body of mathematical material, some of which may well be derived from his stay in Vich, which was close to the resources of Arabic Spain. The Eucharistic treatise attributed to him is almost certainly the work of Heriger of Lobbes. Gerbert's pupils at Reims included *Abbo of Fleury and *Fulbert of Chartres, who gave his teaching further currency in the 11th cent.

Opera Omnia in J. P. Migne, *PL* 139. 57–338; *Opera Mathematica* ed. N. Bubnov (Berlin, 1899). *Die Briefsammlung Gerberts von Reims* ed. F. Weigle (*MGH*, Die Briefe der Deutschen Kaiserzeit, 2; 1966), with introd. Eng. tr. of Letters by H. P. Lattin (Records of Civilization, Sources and Studies, 60; New York, 1961). Jaffé, 1, pp. 496–501. Richer, *Historia*, esp. 3. 43–65, and 4. 99–108 (ed. R. Latouche, vol. 2: Les Classiques de l'histoire de France au Moyen Age, 17, 1964, pp. 50–80 and 312–32). P. Riche, *Gerbert d'Aurillac: Le Pape de l'an mil* (1987). P. E. Schramm, *Kaiser, Rom und Renovatio* (Studien der Bibliothek Warburg, 17; 1929; repr. with additional notes, Darmstadt, 1957), 1, pp. 96–101, 161–76; 2, pp. 64–7. On his scholastic achievement, besides the *Opera Mathematica*, cited above, see A. van de Vyver, 'Les Œuvres inédites d'Abbon de Fleury', *R. Bén.* 47 (1935), pp. 125–69, esp. pp. 158–69, and R. W. Southern, *The Making of the Middle Ages* (1953), esp. pp. 65 f., 175–8, 208. U. Lindgren, *Gerbert von Aurillac und das Quadrivium: Untersuchungen zur Bildung im Zeitalter der Ottonen* (Sudhoffs Archiv, Beiheft 18; 1976). M. Oldoni, 'Gerberto e la sua storia', *Studi Medievali*, 3rd ser. 18 (1977), pp. 1195–270; 21 (1980), pp. 493–622; and 24 (1983), pp. 167–245. *Gerberto, scienza, storia e mito: Atti del Gerberti Symposium (Bobbio 25–27 luglio 1983)* (Archivum Bobiense, Studia, 2; Bobbio, 1985). Mann, 5 (1910), pp. 1–120. É. Amann in *DTC* 14 (pt. 2; 1941), cols. 2075–83, s.v. 'Silvestre II'; H. P. Lattin in *NCE* 13 (1967), pp. 858–69, s.v., both with bibl.

Sylvestrines. A monastic *Congregation which follows the Rule of St *Benedict, but with special emphasis on the vow of poverty. It was founded in 1231 by St Sylvester Gozzolini (d. 1267, feast day, 26 Nov.). It joined the Benedictine Confederation in 1973. It has houses in Italy, the USA, Asia, and Australia.

[P. Helyot], *Histoire des ordres monastiques, religieux et militaires*, 6 (1718), pp. 170–8. M. Papi in *NCE* 2 (1967), pp. 302 f., s.v. 'Benedictines, Sylvestrine'; I. Di Nicola, Silvestrine, and others, in *DIP* 8 (1988), cols. 1507–19, s.v. 'Silvestrini', with bibl.

Symeon. See SIMEON.

Symmachus (prob. later 2nd cent.), translator of the Gk. version of the OT reproduced in the 4th column of *Origen's *Hexapla. Hardly anything is known of his life. According to *Eusebius (*HE* 6. 17) and *Jerome (*De Vir. Ill.* 16) he was an *Ebionite, but *Epiphanius (*De Mensuris et Ponderibus*, 16) speaks of him as a Samaritan who became a Jewish proselyte. From *Irenaeus' silence it has been argued that Symmachus was later than his time, and it is a matter of dispute whether Symmachus' translation or that of *Theodotion was the earlier. Unlike *Aquila, Symmachus preferred a readable style and palatable rendering to verbal accuracy, and he modified the anthropomorphic expressions of the Hebrew text. The extant fragments of his work are therefore of limited value for critical purposes.

G. *Mercati, *L'età di Simmaco l'interprete e S. Epifanio* (Modena, 1892). H. B. *Swete, *Introduction to the Old Testament in Greek* (1900), pp. 49–53. H. J. Schoeps, 'Symmachusstudien. [1.] Der Bibelübersetzer Symmachus als Ebionitischer Theologe', *Coniectanea Neotestamentica*, 6 (Uppsala, 1942), pp. 65–93; 2. 'Mythologisches bei Symmachus', *Biblica*, 26 (1945), pp. 100–11; 3. 'Symmachus und der Midrasch', ibid. 29 (1948), pp. 31–51; all repr. in *Aus frühchristlicher Zeit* (Tübingen, 1950), pp. 82–119. D. Barthélemy, OP, *Les Devanciers d'Aquila* (Supplements to *Vetus Testamentum*, 10; Leiden, 1963), esp. pp. 261–5; id., 'Qui est Symmaque?', *Catholic Biblical Quarterly*, 36 (1974), pp. 451–65, repr. in his *Études d'histoire du texte de l'Ancien Testament* (Orbis Biblicus et Orientalis, 21; 1978), pp. 307–21. S. Jellicoe, *The Septuagint and Modern Study* (Oxford, 1968), pp. 94–9. J. R. Busto Saiz, *La Traducción de Símaco en el libro de los Salmos* (Textos y estudios 'Cardinal Cisneros', 22; 1978), incl. text. A. Salvesen, *Symmachus in the Pentateuch* (Journal of Semitic Studies, Monograph 15; Manchester, 1991). J. Gwynn in *DCB* 4 (1887), pp. 748 f., s.v. 'Symmachus (2)'.

Symmachus, St (d. 514), Pope from 498. A native of Sardinia, Symmachus was appointed Pope by the majority to oppose the concessions to the Emp. and Patr. of *Constantinople advocated by the party of his predecessor, Anastasius II, which elected against him the archpriest Laurentius. As the validity of the election of Symmachus was confirmed by the Gothic King, *Theodoric, the partisans of Laurentius cast suspicion upon the Pope's personal character, accused him of simony and of celebrating Easter at the wrong date, and occupied most of the Roman churches. In 501 the King summoned a council of bishops (the 'Palmary Synod') to Rome to deal with these charges, but Symmachus, who had been attacked on the way, refused to appear. The synod, on the other hand, declared itself incompetent to pronounce him guilty and asserted him to be the rightful Pope. Theodoric, however, allowed Laurentius to return to Rome, and Symmachus was restricted to St Peter's, though he had the support of the majority of the people and, among others, the Abps. of Milan and *Ravenna. The troubles, which led to much bloodshed in the city, lasted till 506. In 507, owing to the good offices of the Alexandrian deacon Dioscurus, Theodoric withdrew his opposition. During the latter part of his reign Symmachus devoted himself to the defence of the Catholic faith against the *Henoticon of *Zeno, upheld by Emp. Anastasius, and against the *Manichaeans, whom he expelled from Rome. He confirmed the primatial rights of *Arles over the Gallican and Spanish Churches and sent the pallium to *Caesarius, its archbishop, who was thus the first bishop outside Italy to receive the privilege. He also liberally assisted the poor and the African Catholics who were persecuted by the *Arians, and embellished many Roman churches, esp. St Peter's. Among his liturgical innovations were the singing of *Gloria in excelsis* on Sundays and the feasts of martyrs (but only by bishops).

During his reign *Dionysius Exiguus compiled his collection of Latin canons, and the so-called 'Symmachian Forgeries', a collection of writings intended to prove from spurious precedents that the Pope cannot be judged by any man, were also issued. Feast day, 19 July.

Epistolae et Decreta in A. Thiel (ed.), *Epistolae Romanorum Pontificum Genuinae*, 1 (Brunswick, 1867), pp. 641–738; Acts of the synods held in Rome in 499, 501, and 502 also ed. T. *Mommsen in *MGH*, Auctores Antiquissimi, 12 (1894), pp. 395–455. Jaffé, 1, pp. 96–100. *CPL* (3rd edn., 1995), pp. 546 f. (nos. 1678–82). *LP* (Duchesne), 1, pp. 260–8; see also pp. cxxxiii–cxl. A. Alessandrini, 'Teodorico e Papa Simmaco durante lo scisma laurenziano', *Archivio della R. Deputazione Romana di Storia Patria*, 67 (1944), pp. 152–207; G. B. Picotti, 'I sinodi romani nello scisma laurenziano', *Studi storici in onore di Gioacchino Volpe*, 2 (Florence, 1958), pp. 741–86; C. Pietri, 'Le sénat, le peuple chrétien, et les partis du cirque sous le pape Symmaque (498–514)', *Mélanges d'archéologie et de l'histoire de l'École française de Rome*, 78 (1966), pp. 123–39; P. A. B. Llewellyn, 'The Roman Church during the Laurentian Schism: Priests and Senators', *Church History*, 45 (1976), pp. 417–27. E. Caspar, *Geschichte des Papsttums*, 2 (1933), pp. 87–129. É. Amann in *DTC* 14 (pt. 2; 1941), cols. 2984–90, s.v. 'Symmaque (Saint)'; J. N. D. Kelly, *Oxford Dictionary of Popes* (1986), pp. 50–2.

synagogue (Gk. συναγωγή). The origins of the Jewish institution of the synagogue are debated. It is possible that Jews introduced synagogues as regular meeting-places for worship during the Babylonian exile (6th cent. BC), when they could no longer take part in the *Temple worship at Jerusalem, but the first clear evidence for synagogue buildings comes from Egypt in the Hellenistic period. At any rate, in NT times synagogues were well established, and they have remained a characteristic feature of Jewry down to the present day.

The worship of the synagogue, unlike that of the Temple, has always been non-sacrificial. It consists chiefly of readings from Scripture, accompanied by prayers, canticles, and sometimes a sermon. The most important piece of furniture is the 'Ark', a kind of cupboard in which the sacred rolls of the Law are kept. At least ten adult males are required for public worship, and certain officials are responsible for the various duties.

There is ample evidence in the Gospels that the Lord took part in synagogue worship and frequently taught or preached in the synagogue (e.g. Lk. 4: 16: 'as his custom was, he went into the synagogue on the sabbath day'; also Mt. 13: 54 and Jn. 6: 59). In the early Church, St *Paul is reported as going into the synagogue (e.g. Acts 17: 1–2), and according to the account of his mission presented in Acts, it was his normal practice to preach the Gospel in the synagogue first in the places he visited on his missionary journeys, and to turn to the Gentiles only after the Jews had failed to respond to his teaching (Acts 13: 46). In James 2: 2 the Greek word συναγωγή is still applied to the assembly in which Christians gathered for worship, but in post-biblical times it came to be used of Jewry in general, as contrasted with the Christian Church. The ruins of many synagogues have been excavated in Palestine. Most date from the 3rd cent. AD or later (e.g. that at Tell Hûm, the site of *Capernaum), but the buildings identified at Masada and Herodium date to the 1st cent. AD and that at Gamala goes back to the 1st cent. BC. Important synagogues have been excavated outside Palestine at *Dura Europos and *Sardis (qq.v.).

I. Elbogen, *Der jüdische Gottesdienst in seiner geschichtlichen Entwicklung* (1913), pp. 444–510 ('Organisation des jüdischen Gottesdienstes'); S. Krauss, *Synagogale Altertümer* (1922). H. Kohl and C. Watzinger, *Antike Synagogen in Galiläa* (1916); E. L. Sukenik, *Ancient Synagogues in Palestine and Greece* (Schweich Lectures for 1930; 1934). E. *Schürer, *The History of the Jewish People in the Age of Jesus Christ*, rev. Eng. tr. by G. Vermes and others, 2 (Edinburgh, 1979), pp. 423–54. L. I. Levine (ed.), *Ancient Synagogues Revealed* (Jerusalem, 1981); id. (ed.), *The Synagogue in Late Antiquity* (Philadelphia [1987]). L. L. Grabbe, 'Synagogues in Pre-70 Palestine: a Re-Assessment', *JTS* NS 39 (1988), pp. 401–10. J. Gutmann (ed.), *Ancient Synagogues: The State of Research* (Brown Judaic Studies, 22; Chico, Calif. [1981]). R. Krautheimer, *Mittelalterliche Synagogen* (1927). W. Schrage in *TWNT* 7 (1964), pp. 798–850 (Eng. tr., 1971, pp. 798–852), s.v. συναγωγή, with extensive bibl.; L. I. Rabinowitz and others in *Encyclopaedia Judaica*, 15 (Jerusalem, 1972), cols. 579–629, s.v.

Synagogue, Great. Acc. to Jewish tradition, a legislative body of 120 members which was established in *Jerusalem in the time of *Ezra and *Nehemiah (5th cent. BC). Its activities were held to have included the fixing of the *canon and text of the Hebrew Scriptures. The grounds for supposing that such a permanently constituted body ever existed, however, are dubious, the oldest reference to it being in the Jewish treatise *Pirqe Aboth (3rd cent. AD).

S. Krauss, 'The Great Synod', *JQR* 10 (1898), pp. 347–77. L. Finkelstein in W. D. Davies and L. Finkelstein (eds.), *The Cambridge History of Judaism* 2 (1989), pp. 229–44. J. A. Selbie in *HDB*, 4 (1902), pp. 643 f., s.v.; W. Bacher in *JE* 11 (1905), pp. 640–3, s.v.; D. Sperber in *Encyclopaedia Judaica*, 15 (Jerusalem, 1972), cols. 629–31, s.v.

Synapte (Gk. συναπτή, 'joined together'). In the E. Church, a prayer constructed in the form of a *litany (i.e. a series of suffrages 'linked together'), used in the Liturgy and other services. It consists of short petitions said by the deacon, to which choir or congregation respond with *Kyrie eleison, while at the end there is a closing prayer by the priest.

Synaxarion (Gk. συναξάριον). (1) In the E. Church, a short account of a saint or feast appointed to be read at the early morning service of *Orthros. (2) The book which contains, *inter alia*, these passages, arranged acc. to the calendar ('The Greater Synaxarion'). (3) Another book which merely enumerates the feasts to be observed every day, with a reference to the appropriate biblical lessons ('The Lesser Synaxarion'). Confusion arises through these various uses, and H. *Delehaye recommends that the word be confined to senses (1) and (2). See also MENOLOGION.

synaxis (Gk. σύναξις, 'an assembly' or 'congregation', a word cognate with and equivalent to συναγωγή, 'synagogue', the use of which was avoided by Christian writers, doubtless on account of its Jewish associations). The term is applicable to any assembly for public worship and prayer, inclusive of the Eucharist or 'liturgical synaxis', and is so used in the E. Church. In the W. it was used in early times esp. of the 'aliturgical synaxis', or non-Eucharistic service, consisting of Psalms, lessons from Scripture, and prayers. Some scholars hold that the opening part of the Eucharist (the pre-anaphoral rite) developed out of this 'aliturgical synaxis'; others that it was an alternative service used when the Eucharist was not

celebrated. It was also at one time regarded as the precursor of the Divine *Office, but this view has generally been abandoned.

syncellus (a hybrid word: Gk. σύν + Lat. *cella*; i.e., literally, a person who shares a cell with someone else). In the Byzantine Church, an ecclesiastic who lived continually with a bishop, esp. in the capacity of a domestic chaplain and in order to bear witness to the purity of the bishop's moral life. In the W. St *Augustine of Canterbury is said by *Leo III to have been the *syncellus* of St *Gregory the Great. In later times the word was used of a dignitary associated as counsellor with a prelate who subsequently succeeded to his office.

Syncellus, George (*fl. c.*800). See GEORGE SYNCELLUS. He is often referred to simply as 'Syncellus'.

syncretism. The attempt to combine different or opposite doctrines and practices, esp. in reference to philosophical and religious systems. The term came into prominence in the 17th cent., when it was applied to the teaching of G. *Calixtus, who undertook to unite the Reformation Churches in Germany with each other and with the Catholic Church on the basis of the Apostles' Creed and the doctrine of the first five centuries. It is also frequently applied to the unifying cultural forces in the Mediterranean civilization of the Hellenistic and Roman periods, and in the history of religion to any fusion of various beliefs and practices, e.g. to some tendencies in pre-Christian Judaism. In the RC theology of grace the term is used of attempts to combine *Thomist and *Molinist teaching.

synderesis. See SYNTERESIS.

synergism. The teaching of P. *Melanchthon that in the act of conversion the human will can co-operate with the Holy Spirit and God's grace. By insisting that the primary cause of such conversion is the Holy Spirit and not the will Melanchthon rebutted the charge of *Pelagianism which his opponents raised against him. His teaching had many points of contact with the *Semipelagianism (*Cassian, etc.) of the 5th cent. The long controversy provoked by Melanchthon ended only with the publication of the 'Formula of *Concord' in 1577.

Synesius (*c.*370–*c.*413), Bp. of Ptolemais. A native of Cyrene and descended from an ancient family, perhaps now Christian, he studied at *Alexandria under the celebrated *Neoplatonist philosopher *Hypatia. In 403/4 he married a Christian wife, with the blessing of *Theophilus, Patr. of Alexandria. Having won the confidence and affection of his fellow-countrymen by a successful embassy to the Imperial court at *Constantinople, *c.*410 he was chosen Bp. of Ptolemais. At first he hesitated, wishing to continue living with his wife and to retain certain of his philosophical beliefs, e.g. in the pre-existence of the soul and the eternity of the world; but eventually, without engaging himself to give up either his wife or his doctrines, he was consecrated by Theophilus. A series of domestic and other tragedies marked his episcopate, though he did not survive to witness the murder of Hypatia in 415. He was succeeded in the see by his younger brother Euoptius.

Before he became a bishop, Synesius wrote a number of short treatises; they are typical of cultivated, but non-professional, philosophy, and none of them betray anything distinctively Christian. His collection of hymns in the Doric dialect (nine in all; the tenth, the well-known 'Lord Jesus, think on me' (*EH* 77) is the work of a copyist who called himself George the Sinner) expresses a complex doctrine of the Trinity and Incarnation, deeply influenced by a form of *Neoplatonism which has marked parallels with that of Marius *Victorinus. His 156 surviving letters are an entertaining and important source for the study of provincial Church life.

Works ed. D. *Petavius (Paris, 1612), repr. in J. P. Migne, *PG* 66. 1021–756; crit. edn. of Hymns and *Opuscula* by N. Terzaghi (2 vols., Rome, 1939–44) and of his Letters by A. Garzya (ibid., 1979). Hymns also ed., with Ital. tr., by A. dell'Era (Classici Greci, 3; Rome, 1968), and, with Fr. tr., by C. Lacombrade (Collection des Universités de France, Paris, 1978). A. dell'Era, *Appunti sulla tradizione manoscritta degli inni di Sinesio* (Temi et Testi, 16; 1969). Eng. tr. of Letters by A. FitzGerald (London, 1926); of Essays and Hymns by id. (2 vols., ibid., 1930). On Synesius' life and works, studies by G. Grützmacher (Leipzig, 1913), J. C. Pando (Catholic University of America, Patristic Studies, 63; 1940), C. Lacombrade (Paris, 1951), J. Bregman (Berkeley, etc., and London, 1982), S. Vollenweider (Forschungen zur Kirchen- und Dogmengeschichte, 35; 1985), D. Roques (Études d'Antiquités Africaines, 1987), and A. Cameron and J. Long, *Barbarians and Politics at the Court of Arcadius* (Berkeley, etc., and Oxford [1993]). K. Treu, *Synesios von Kyrene: Ein Kommentar zu seinem 'Dion'* (TU 71; 1958). D. Roques, *Études sur la Correspondance de Synésios de Cyrène* (Collection Latomos, 205; Brussels, 1989). J. H. W. G. Liebeschuetz, 'Why did Synesius become bishop of Ptolemais?', *Byzantion*, 56 (1986), pp. 180–95; id., *Barbarians and Bishops* (Oxford, 1990), esp. pp. 228–35 and 253–72. *CPG* 3 (1979), pp. 98–101 (nos. 5630–40). Altaner and Stuiber (1978), pp. 282 f. and 605. T. R. Halcomb in *DCB* 4 (1887), pp. 756–80, s.v. 'Synesius (2)'; E. Cavalcanti in *DPAC* 2 (1984), cols. 3217–19, s.v. 'Sinesio di Cirene'; Eng. tr. in *Encyclopedia of the Early Church*, 2 (1992), p. 806.

Synod. See COUNCIL.

Synod, General, of the C of E. See the following entry.

Synodical Government. The system of government of the C of E introduced by the Synodical Government Measure 1969, which took effect the following year. This was designed to achieve a more effective and coherent system, to give a greater part to the laity, and to avoid the delays caused by the dual control of the *Convocations and the *Church Assembly.

Under the Measure a General Synod took over the powers of the Church Assembly, which ceased to exist, and also some of those the Convocations, though these remained in being. It is comprised of the members of the Upper Houses of the Convocations of Canterbury and York, a House of Clergy consisting of the two Lower Houses of the Convocations, somewhat reduced in size, and a House of Laity of not more than 250 elected members. The House of Laity of the General Synod is elected by members of the Houses of Laity of the deanery synods. The General Synod is required to meet at least twice a year. Matters concerning doctrinal formulae, the services

of the Church and the administration of the Sacraments can be approved only in terms proposed by the House of Bishops.

Diocesan conferences were replaced by diocesan synods, each consisting of the Bishop, the House of Clergy, and the House of Laity. Members of the two latter are elected by the respective Houses of deanery synods. In 1980 a House of Bishops was constituted; it consists of the diocesan Bishop, every *suffragan Bishop, and such other Bishops working in the diocese as the diocesan Bishop may nominate. The functions of the diocesan synods remain the same as those of the previous diocesan conferences, but the number of members is considerably smaller, so that not all parishes are directly represented. The former ruridecanal conferences were replaced by deanery synods, which became the connecting link between the diocese and the parish. The lowest of the deliberative bodies remain the parochial church councils, the functions of which are fundamentally unchanged, though the relationships with the diocese and diocesan and deanery synods are emphasized. The base of the whole system continues to be the electoral roll maintained by every parish, from which elections are made, to the deanery synod triennially and to the parochial church council annually, at the annual parochial church meeting held on or before 30 Apr. each year.

Synodicon. The term is applied:

(1) In a general sense to a synodal act or a collection of such acts (e.g. W. *Beveridge's *Synodicon*, 1672).

(2) To a liturgical text for use in the E. Church on the 'Feast of *Orthodoxy'. Composed by Patr. Methodius I c.843 for the new feast, it was worked over by Sergius II c.1000 and since then has been frequently modified by excising old names and inserting new ones. Its form is akin to a litany, and it contains a series of praises for the heroes of orthodoxy and for Emperors and bishops, followed by anathemas against numerous heresies. In modern times it is not customary to recite it publicly *in extenso*.

(2) Crit. edn. and comm. by J. Gouillard, *Le Synodikon de l'Orthodoxie* (Centre de Recherche d'Histoire et Civilisation Byzantines, Travaux et Mémoires, 2; 1967). Earlier edns. in Mansi, 13 (Florence, 1767), cols. 812–20 (under the year 1027); and in J. P. Migne, *PG* 120. 728–36. In its current official form it is contained in edns. of the *Triodion for the First Sunday in Lent.

Synoptic Problem. The problem of the literary relationship between the three 'Synoptic Gospels' (Mt., Mk., Lk.), posed by the amount of subject-matter which they share and the many similarities in wording and order. Common dependence on oral traditions (including *Aramaic ones) may account for some of the phenomena, but there are such close parallels in the Greek that a direct literary connection is generally accepted.

In modern times most scholars have held (1) that Mk. was the earliest of the three Synoptic Gospels and that it was used as a source by Mt. and Lk., and (2) that for the considerable non-Marcan material common to Mt. and Lk. their authors drew independently on a lost common source (or sources) known to critics as '*Q' (q.v.). The priority of Mk., which fits well with his comparative brevity and vivid narrative, his unpolished language, and the fact that the Marcan material appears in substantially the same order in Mt. and Lk., is generally accepted; a detailed comparison of parallel passages offers strong support to this judgement. The 'Q'-hypothesis is widely thought to account more easily than the alternative theories (that the author of Lk. utilized Mt. or *vice versa*) for the variations in order of the relevant material and also for the cases where it is Lk. (and not, as is usual, Mt.) that appears to preserve the older version of a particular saying. This 'two-document' hypothesis (that Mt. and Lk. are based on Mk. and 'Q'), which was worked out mainly in Germany in the 19th cent., was given classic expression and amplified by B. H. *Streeter; it came to be almost universally accepted and is still widely held.

In the second half of the 20th cent. a few scholars have challenged the priority of Mk., and several the existence of 'Q'. The view that Mt. was the oldest Gospel and Mk.'s chief source, which is found in St *Augustine and was officially upheld by the RC *Biblical Commission in 1912, has in modern times been defended by B. C. Butler, OSB, and others. An Aramaic Matthew has also been postulated as the earliest Gospel. More recently W. R. Farmer and others have revived the theory of J. J. *Griesbach that Mk. was the latest of the three Gospels and utilized both Mt. and Lk.; in that case it is hard to see why Mk. should ever have been written.

J. C. Hawkins, *Horae Synopticae* (Oxford, 1899); [Oxford] *Studies in the Synoptic Problem*, ed. W. *Sanday (ibid., 1911); B. H. Streeter, *The Four Gospels* (1924); B. C. Butler, OSB, *The Originality of St Matthew* (Cambridge, 1951); W. R. Farmer, *The Synoptic Problem: A Critical Analysis* (New York, 1964); E. P. Sanders, *The Tendencies of the Synoptic Tradition* (Society for New Testament Studies Monograph Series, 9; Cambridge, 1969); D. G. Miller (ed.), *Jesus and Man's Hope*, 1 (Pittsburgh [1970]); F. Neirynck, *The Minor Agreements of Matthew and Luke against Mark, with a Cumulative List* (Bibliotheca Ephemeridum Theologicarum Lovaniensium, 37; 1974); H.-H. Stoldt, *Geschichte und Kritik der Markushypothese* (Göttingen, 1977; Eng. tr., 1980); R. M. Rist, *On the Independence of Matthew and Mark* (Society for New Testament Studies Monograph Series, 32; 1978); G. M. Styler, 'The Priority of Mark', in C. F. D. Moule, *The Birth of the New Testament* (Black's NT Comm., 3rd edn., 1981), pp. 285–316; W. R. Farmer (ed.), *New Synoptic Studies: The Cambridge Gospel Conference and Beyond* (Macon, Ga. [1983]); E. P. Sanders and M. Davies, *Studying the Synoptic Gospels* (1989), pp. 51–119; D. L. Dungan (ed.), *The Interrelations of the Gospels: A Symposium led by M.-É. Boismard and others, . . . Jerusalem, 1984* (Bibliotheca Ephemeridum Theologicarum Lovaniensium, 95; 1990). C. M. Tuckett in *Anchor Bible Dictionary*, 6 (1992), pp. 263–70, s.v. For parallel texts of the three Gospels in English see H. F. D. Sparks, *A Synopsis of the Gospels: The Synoptic Gospels with Johannine Parallels* (1964); for the Greek text, A. *Huck, *Synopse der drei ersten Evangelien* (1892 and later; 13th edn., with introd. in Ger. and Eng., by H. Greeven, Tübingen, 1981). K. Aland, *Synopsis Quattuor Evangeliorum locis parallelis evangeliorum apocryphorum et patrum adhibitis* (Stuttgart, 1964).

synteresis, also 'synderesis'. A technical term used by St *Thomas Aquinas (e.g. 'De Veritate', q. 17. a. 2) and other Scholastic theologians for our knowledge of the first principles of moral action. It appears to derive from a scribal error in St *Jerome's 'Commentary on Ezekiel' (on Ezek. 1: 7), where συντήρησις (not attested elsewhere in this sense) occurs as a corruption of συνείδησις, the normal Greek word for 'conscience'. The medieval mystics, e.g. Meister *Eckhart, sometimes identify it with the myster-

ious ground of the soul where the mystic union takes place.

O. Renz, *Die Synteresis nach dem heiligen Thomas von Aquin* (1911); O. Lottin, OSB, *Psychologie et morale aux xiiᵉ et xiiiᵉ siècles*, 2 (1948), pp. 103–349. A. Solignac, SJ, in *Dict. Sp.* 14 (1990), cols. 1407–12, s.v. 'Synderesis'.

Syriac. The Syriac language is a branch of Aramaic which was spoken in *Edessa and its neighbourhood from shortly before the beginning of the Christian era. It was extensively used in the early Church owing to the active Christian communities in those parts. From an early date it was employed in translations of the Bible (see DIATESSARON; OLD SYRIAC VERSION; PESHITTA; SYRO-HEXAPLA), translations of other works from the Greek, and for original Syriac compositions. After the religious divisions in the 5th cent. it continued in general use in both the *Church of the East and the *Syrian Orthodox Church. Like *Hebrew, its alphabet is derived from the so-called Phoenician alphabet and is fundamentally consonantal. There are three forms of script: Estrangelo, East Syrian (or 'Nestorian'), and Serto (or 'Jacobite').

The surviving literature, which dates mainly from the 2nd to the 13th cents. AD, is almost wholly Christian. The Syriac Versions of the Bible are of exceptional value to the textual critic of the Scriptures on account of their early date and the natural accuracy of Syriac scholars. A large number of Gk. patristic works survive only in Syriac. These (generally very literal) versions sometimes make it possible to recover the Greek with an approach to certainty. Among the most important Syriac authors were *Aphrahat, St *Ephraem Syrus, *Philoxenus, *Jacob of Edessa, *Isaac of Nineveh, *Moses bar Kepha, and *Bar Hebraeus. One of the outstanding literary genres was that of liturgical poetry: besides Ephraem, *Jacob of Sarug and *Narsai are pre-eminent in this field. When Arabic became the current vernacular, Syriac increasingly became an artificial language, though it continues in restricted use to the present day. Various modern Syriac (neo-Aramaic) dialects also survive.

The most important collections of Syriac MSS are now preserved in the *Vatican and the British Library. Notable editors of Syriac texts include the *Assemani, W. *Cureton, W. Wright, G. *Bickell, R. Duval, P. Bedjan, Cong. Orat., I. E. Rahmani, E. W. Brooks, R. Graffin, F. Nau, J. B. Chabot, A. *Baumstark, E. Beck, A. de Halleux, OFM, F. Graffin, SJ, and A. Vööbus.

The chief modern collections of pr. texts incl. many items in the series *Horae Semiticae* (London, 1903 ff.); others issued by the Text and Translation Society (ibid., 1902 ff.); others in *PO*; *Patrologia Syriaca* (3 vols., Paris, 1894–1926); *CSCO*, Scriptores Syri (Paris, etc., 1907–19; Louvain, 1919 ff.); also texts and trs. in *Woodbrooke Studies: Christian Documents in Syriac, Arabic, and Garshūni*, ed. and tr. by A. Mingana (7 vols., Cambridge, 1927–34). C. Moss, *Catalogue of Syriac Printed Books and Related Literature in the British Museum* (posthumously pub., London, 1962). S. P. Brock, 'Syriac Studies 1960–1970', *Parole de l'Orient*, 4 (1973), pp. 393–465; id., 'Syriac Studies 1971–1980', ibid. 10 (1981–2), pp. 291–412; id., 'Syriac Studies 1981–1985', ibid. 14 (1987), pp. 289–360. *Thesaurus Syriacus* by R. P. Smith (2 vols., Oxford, 1879; suppl. by J. P. Margoliouth, 1927); *Lexicon Syriacum* by C. Brockelmann (Edinburgh and Berlin, 1895; 2nd edn., Halle, 1928). *Compendious Syriac Dictionary* by J. P. Margoliouth (Oxford, 1903). *Dictionary of the Dialects of Vernacular Syriac* by

A. J. Maclean (ibid., 1901). Lexicon to Syriac NT by W. Jennings and U. Gantillon (ibid., 1926). *Kurzgefasste syrische Grammatik* by T. Nöldeke (Leipzig, 1880; Eng. tr. as *Compendious Syriac Grammar* by J. A. Crichton, 1904); shorter *Syrische Grammatik* by C. Brockelmann (Berlin, etc., 1899; many subsequent edns.); *Grammatik der neusyrischen Sprache* by T. Nöldeke (Leipzig, 1868); *Grammar of the Dialects of Vernacular Syriac* by A. J. Maclean (Cambridge, 1895). R. Duval, *Traité de grammaire syriaque* (1881; repr. Amsterdam, 1969). J. S. Assemani, *Bibliotheca Orientalis* (3 vols. in 4 parts, Rome, 1719–28; repr., Hildesheim, 1975). W. Wright, *A Short History of Syriac Literature* (1894); R. Duval, *La Littérature syriaque* (1899); A. Baumstark, *Geschichte der syrischen Literatur mit Ausschluss der christlich-palästinischen Texte* (1922); J. B. Chabot, *Littérature syriaque* (1935). J. Ortiz de Urbina, SJ, *Patrologia Syriaca* (Rome, 1958; 2nd edn., 1965); R. Macuch, *Geschichte der spät- und neusyrischen Literatur* (1976). W. S. McCullough, *A Short History of Syriac Christianity to the Rise of Islam* (Chico, Calif. [1982]). S. [P.] Brock, 'An Introduction to Syriac Studies', in J. H. Eaton (ed.), *Horizons in Semitic Studies* (Birmingham, 1980), pp. 1–33. P. Bettiolo, 'Lineamenti di Patrologia Siriaca', in A. Quacquarelli (ed.), *Complementi interdisciplinari di Patrologia* (1989), pp. 503–603. M. Albert, 'Langue et littérature syriaques', in id. and others (eds.), *Christianisme orientaux* (1993), pp. 297–372. W. Heinrichs (ed.), *Studies in Neo-Aramaic* (Atlanta, Ga., 1990), with bibl. by G. Krotkoff, pp. 3–26. *L'Orient syrien* (12 vols., Paris, 1956–67). A. Vööbus in *EB* (1968 edn.), 21, pp. 586–90, s.v. 'Syriac Literature'.

Syriac Versions of the Bible.

(1) *Old Testament.* The principal are: (*a*) The *Peshitta version, perhaps in part made by Jews, probably in the early 2nd cent., for the Jewish community at *Edessa. Apart from Proverbs (where the Jewish *Targum derives from the Peshitta), this version was used solely by Syriac-speaking Christian communities. (*b*) The *Syro-Hexapla, a close rendering of *Origen's text of the Septuagint made at Alexandria c.616–17 by the *Syrian Orthodox bishop, Paul of Tella.

(2) *New Testament.* In early times the Gospels were known in two forms: (*a*) The *Evangelión da-Mĕhallĕtĕ*, or 'Gospel of the Mixed', a Syriac version of *Tatian's *Diatessaron; and (*b*) the *Evangelión da-Mĕpharrĕshĕ*, or 'Gospel of the Separated' (i.e. the four Gospels), known as the '*Old Syriac'. It is probable that the 'Gospel of the Separated' was made not earlier than 200, and that the 'Syriac Diatessaron' is prior to and independent of it. The Old Syriac NT was the basis of the NT Peshitta revision.

Subsequent to the Peshitta, two further versions of the NT were made: (*c*) the *Philoxenian, in 508, which included the Books omitted from the Peshitta canon, and (*d*) the *Harklean, in 616, a revision of the Philoxenian and more literal than its predecessor in rendering the Greek. With the exception of the Books omitted from the Peshitta, the Philoxenian version has perished.

The Peshitta remains the authorized version of the Syriac-speaking Churches. See also PESHITTA.

Introductory account in B. M. Metzger, *The Early Versions of the New Testament* (Oxford, 1977), pp. 3–98, incl. contribution by S. P. Brock. A. Vööbus, *Studies in the History of the Gospel Text in Syriac* (CSCO 128 and 496, Subsidia, 3 and 79; 1951–78). M. Black, 'The Syriac Versional Tradition', in K. Aland (ed.), *Die alten Übersetzungen des Neuen Testaments, die Kirchenväterzitate und Lektionare* (Arbeiten zur Neutestamentlichen Textforschung, 5; 1972), pp. 120–59, with full refs. C. van Puyvelde in *Dict. Bibl.*, Suppl. 6 (1960), cols. 834–84, s.v. 'Orientales de la Bible (Versions)', 6: 'Versions syriaques'; A. Vööbus in *The Interpreter's Dictionary of The Bible*, Suppl. Vol. (Nashville, 1976), pp. 848–54, s.v.; S. P. Brock and B. Aland in *TRE* 6 (1980), pp. 181–96, s.v. 'Bibelübersetzungen', I. 4: 'Die Übersetzungen ins Syrische'; S. P. Brock in *Anchor Bible Dictionary*, 6 (1992), pp. 794–9, s.v. 'Versions, Ancient (Syriac)'. For further bibl. see arts. on separate items cited above.

Syrian Catholics. A body of *Uniat Christians descended from the *Syrian Orthodox. In the latter part of the 16th cent. relations were established between the Syrian Orthodox Church and the Papacy, which led to some conversions in the 17th cent., and the election of a Catholic, Andrew Akhijan, to the see of Aleppo in 1656. The Catholics had, however, a precarious existence and seem to have virtually disappeared soon after 1700. The present Church traces its existence to the accession of Mar Michael Garweh, who had become a RC, to the archbishopric of Aleppo in 1783, since when a Catholic minority has coexisted with the Syrian Orthodox in Syria. In 1830 their existence as a separate body was formally recognized by the Turks. The Patr., Ignatius Ephrem II Rahmani (1898–1929), became known in the W. as a scholar of distinction through his edition of the *Testamentum Domini* (1899). The seat of the patriarchate is Beirut. Their membership in the Middle East is about 90,000, with a further 7,000 in Europe and N. and S. America.

D. Attwater, *The Catholic Eastern Churches* (Milwaukee, Wis., rev. edn., 1935), pp. 163–79; further rev. as *The Christian Churches of the East*, 1 (1961), pp. 147–57. W. de Vries, SJ, 'Dreihundert Jahre syrisch-katholische Hierarchie', *Ostkirchliche Studien*, 5 (1956), pp. 137–57. C. Sélis, *Les Syriens orthodoxes et catholiques* (Turnhout [1988]). S. Vailhé, AA, in *DTC* 1 (1903), cols. 1430–3, s.v. 'Antioche, V. Patriarcat syrien catholique'; I. Ziade, ibid., 14 (pt. 2; 1946), cols. 3017–88, s.v. 'Syrienne (Église)', esp cols. 3023 f. (Droit Canonique), 3025–8 (Liturgie, with refs. to edns. of texts), and 3078–80 (Hiérarchie); G. Khouri-Sarkis in *NCE* 13 (1969), pp. 901–5, s.v. 'Syrian Rite'. For edns. of liturgical texts see also A. *Baumstark, *Liturgie comparée* (3rd edn., 1953), pp. 244 f.; Eng. tr. (1958), pp. 221 f.

Syrian Orthodox Church. One of the *Oriental Orthodox Churches; its adherents are often called *Jacobites (after *Jacob Baradaeus) or *Monophysites (because of their rejection of *dyophysite Christology). The Syrian Orthodox Church emerged as a separate Church in the aftermath of the Council of *Chalcedon (451), which it does not recognize; an independent hierarchy under a Patriarch of *Antioch was built up in the 6th cent. In the 7th–9th cents. Syrian Orthodox scholars, such as *Jacob of Edessa, *George, 'Bp. of the Arabians', and *Moses bar Kepha, played an important role in transmitting Greek learning to the Arab world. *Bar Hebraeus was an outstanding scholar and ecclesiastic of the Middle Ages.

During the 14th cent. the numbers of Syrian Orthodox were greatly reduced by the Mongol invasions; at the end of the 18th cent. they were further diminished by the establishment of a separate *Uniat patriarchate of Antioch (see SYRIAN CATHOLICS); at the turn of the 20th cent. they suffered from massacres at the hands of the Turks. They may number c.200,000 in the Middle East, 100,000 in Europe and N. and S. America, and perhaps something over a million in S. *India (*Malabar Christians), where the local head of the Church has, since 1964, had the title

'Catholicos of the East'. The seat of the patriarchate, after many peregrinations over the centuries, is now in Damascus. There are 23 archdioceses, including one in America and one in Europe. In the Middle East *Tur 'Abdin has been one of the main centres of Syrian Orthodox culture; since the 1960s, however, large numbers of Syrian Orthodox have emigrated to W. Europe, and the monastery of St Ephrem in the Netherlands (consecrated in 1984) is active in publishing Syriac liturgical and other texts. Since 1960 the Syrian Orthodox Church has been a member of the *World Council of Churches.

The liturgical language is Syriac, the normal anaphora being that of St *James, and the Church has a rich literary heritage (see SYRIAC). Ignatius Ephrem Barsaum (Patriarch, 1933–57) was the author of a valuable history of Syrian Orthodox literature in Arabic (Aleppo, 2nd edn., 1956; Syriac translation, Qamishlieh, 1967).

E. Honigmann, Évêques et évêchés monophysites d'Asie antérieure au VIᵉ siècle (CSCO, Subsidia 2; 1951); id., Le couvent de Barsaumā et Patriarcat Jacobite d'Antioche et de Syrie (ibid. 7; 1954). W. Hage, Die syrisch-jakobitische Kirche in frühislamischer Zeit nach orientalischen Quellen (Wiesbaden, 1966). P. Kawerau, Die jakobitische Kirche im Zeitalter der syrischen Renaissance (Berliner Byzantinische Arbeiten, 3; 1955). B. Spuler, Handbuch der Orientalistik, Abteilung 1, Band 8, Abschnitt 2 (Leiden, 1961), pp. 170–216. D. Attwater, The Christian Churches of the East, 2 (London, 1961), pp. 204–18; A. K. Arvanites, Ἐπίτομος ἱστορία Συρο-Ιακωβιτικῆς Ἀρμενικῆς καὶ Αἰθιοπικῆς Ἐκκλησίας (Athens, 1967), pp. 5–51; A. S. Atiya, A History of Eastern Christianity (1968), pp. 167–235. C. Sélis, Les Syriens orthodoxes et catholiques (Turnhout [1988]). J. Joseph, Muslim–Christian Relations and Inter-Christian Rivalries in the Middle East: The case of the Jacobites in an age of transition (Albany, NY, 1983). W. de Vries, SJ, Sakramententheologie bei den syrischen Monophysiten (Orientalia Christiana Analecta, 125; 1940). J. M. Fiey, Pour un Oriens Christianus Novus: Répertoire des diocèses syriaques orientaux et occidentaux (Beiruter Texte und Studien, 49; 1993). Current information in the annual 'Chronique' in Proche-Orient Chrétien (Jerusalem, 1951 ff.). See also bibl. to MONOPHYSITISM, SYRIAC, and TUR 'ABDIN.

Syrian text of the NT. The name applied by B. F. *Westcott and F. J. A. *Hort to an edition of the Greek text of the NT which was made, as they held, in or near *Antioch in Syria c. AD 300, and of which *Lucian of Antioch was the probable author. See also LUCIANIC TEXT.

Syro-Chaldaeans. An alternative name for the *Chaldean Christians, i.e. the descendants of the ancient *Church of the East now in communion with the see of Rome.

Syro-Hexapla. The translation into *Syriac of the Greek text of the *Septuagint contained in *Origen's *Hexapla, which was made in 616–17 by Paul, the *Syrian Orthodox Bp. of Tella in Mesopotamia. It was produced with great care and accuracy, preserving Origen's critical symbols, which have disappeared from nearly all the Greek MSS copied from the original Hexapla. It is thus an important witness to the text of the OT.

The complete text, in 2 vols., was still known to A. Masius in the 16th cent., but of these only vol. 2 (Job–Mal.) survives, in the *Ambrosiana; it was ed. by A. M. Ceriani, Monumenta Sacra et Profana, 7 (Milan, 1874; photolithographic text). Most of the surviving remnants of other Books are ed. by P. de *Lagarde, Bibliothecae Syriacae (Göttingen, 1892), pp. 1–256. Further texts in W. Baars, New Syro-Hexaplaric Texts, edited, commented on and compared with the Septuagint (Leiden, 1968); A. Vööbus, The Pentateuch in the Version of the Syro-Hexapla: A fac-simile Edition of a Midyat MS. Discovered 1964 (CSCO 369, Subsidia 45; 1975), with useful introd. R. J. V. Hiebert, The 'Syrohexaplaric' Psalter (Septuagint and Cognate Studies, 27; Atlanta, Ga. [1989]). CPG 1 (1983), pp. 175–7 (no. 1501). On the liturgical use of the Syro-Hexapla, cf. A. *Baumstark, Nichtevangelische syrische Perikopenordnungen des ersten Jahrtausends (Liturgiegeschichtliche Forschungen, 3; 1921), pp. 88–100. C. Van Puyvelde in Dict. Bibl., Suppl. 6 (1960), cols. 879–80, s.v. 'Orientales de la Bible (Versions)', VI. v. 5.

Syro-Malabar Church. See MALABAR CHRISTIANS.

syzygy (Gk. συζυγία, 'pair'). A word current among the *Gnostics, notably *Valentinus, for a pair of cosmological opposites, e.g. male and female. It was held that the universe had come into being through the interaction of such opposites (somewhat after the fashion of the *Hegelian doctrine of thesis and antithesis).

T

Tabernacle (Jewish), sometimes also called the 'tent of meeting'. The portable shrine said to have been constructed under *Moses' direction during the wilderness wanderings.

The fullest account of its structure is contained in Exod. 25–31 and 35–40, where it is described as consisting of an inner shrine (the 'Holy of Holies') which housed the *Ark and an outer chamber (the 'Holy Place') which contained the seven-branched lampstand, the table for the *shewbread, and the altar of incense. These were surrounded by an enclosure in which stood the altar of sacrifice and the whole was set up in the midst of the camp. Acc. to modern biblical critics this description is the work of the Priestly school of scribes (*P). Many hold that it is of far later date than Moses and reflects the structure of the Temple of *Solomon, though some argue that it is based on memories of a real pre-monarchic shrine, perhaps at the sanctuary of Shiloh (cf. 1 Sam. 3).

There is an independent and briefer account in Exod. 33: 7–10, which critics attribute to one of the earlier, pre-Exilic sources (*E). Acc. to this account it was set up outside the camp and was the centre towards which the people directed their worship; at its door was to be seen the pillar of cloud, the symbol of the Divine presence. There is no reason why such a simple tent-sanctuary should not have existed before the Israelites settled in Palestine.

Theologically the Tabernacle was held to embody the presence of God in the midst of His people, the symmetry and harmony of its parts to express the Divine perfection, and the careful gradation of the courts and of the service to reflect the Divine holiness. In the NT the imagery of the Tabernacle was used by the writer of the Ep. to the Hebrews to explain the meaning of the atoning work of Christ (cf. Heb. 9: 1–10: 25).

The principal material is to be found in comm. on Exodus, cited s.v., ad locc., and in discussions on the *Pentateuch, q.v. Studies devoted to the Tabernacle incl. J. Morgenstern, 'The Tent of Meeting', *Journal of the American Oriental Society*, 38 (1918), pp. 125–39; id., 'The Ark, the Ephod and the Tent', *Hebrew Union College Annual*, 17 (1942–3), pp. 153–265, and 18 (1943–4), pp. 1–52, esp. pp. 17–47 of the latter vol. [G.] von *Rad, 'Zelt und Lade', *Neue kirchliche Zeitschrift*, 42 (1931), pp. 476–98. F. M. Cross, 'The Tabernacle. A Study from an Archaeological and Historical Aspect', *Biblical Archaeologist*, 10 (1947), pp. 45–68. K. Koch, *Die Priesterschrift von Exodus 25 bis Leviticus 16* (Forschungen zur Religion und Literatur des Alten und Neuen Testament, NF 53; 1959), pp. 7–45; M. Haran, 'The Priestly Image of the Tabernacle', *Hebrew Union College Annual*, 36 (1965), pp. 191–226; id., *Temples and Temple-Service in Ancient Israel* (Oxford, 1978), esp. pp. 149–204; R. E. Friedman, 'The Tabernacle in the Temple', *Biblical Archaeologist*, 43 (1980), pp. 241–8. C. R. Koester, *The Dwelling of God: The Tabernacle in the Old Testament, Intertestamental Jewish Literature, and the New Testament* (Catholic Biblical Quarterly Monograph Series, 22; Washington, DC, 1989). There is also a popular reconstruction in Eng. by R. E. Friedman, *Who Wrote the Bible?* (1988), pp. 174–87. A. Rothkoff in *Encyclopaedia Judaica*, 15 (Jerusalem, 1972), cols. 679–88, s.v.; R. E. Friedman in *Anchor Bible Dictionary*, 6 (1992), pp. 292–300, s.v.

Tabernacle (Christian). The ornamental receptacle for the vessels containing the Blessed Sacrament in RC churches. Derived from the Lat. *tabernaculum* (= 'tent') and used of a variety of canopied structures in the church building, the word came to be applied esp. to the box set in the middle of the altar which, from the 16th cent. onwards, gradually superseded earlier types of receptacles used for this purpose, e.g. hanging *pyxes and *sacrament houses. Acc. to current RC legislation, the Tabernacle may stand on the High Altar, but an altar in a side chapel is preferred. A lamp is kept burning before it. It is normally covered with a veil, but this requirement is no longer universally enforced.

F. Raible, *Der Tabernakel einst und jetzt: Eine historische und liturgische Darstellung der Andacht zur aufbewahrten Eucharistie* (1908). Braun, *CA* 2 (1924), pp. 632–47. E. Maffei, *La Réservation eucharistique jusqu'à la Renaissance* (1942). J. Braun, SJ, in *CE* 14 (1914), p. 424. See also other works cited under RESERVATION.

Tabernacles, Feast of. With the *Passover and *Pentecost, one of the great feasts of the Jewish year. By some critics it is supposed to have been originally a New Year festival, but in the earliest biblical accounts it is described as 'the feast of ingathering, at the end of the year' (Exod. 23: 16), i.e. the harvest-home. It lasted for seven days (Deut. 16: 13–15) and was followed by a solemn eighth day of 'holy convocation' (Lev. 23: 33–6). During the feast the people dwelt in booths (i.e. 'tabernacles') in commemoration of the sojourn in the wilderness (Lev. 23: 42–3; cf. Neh. 8: 14–15). The last and greatest feast of the year in pre-exilic times, it was sometimes referred to simply as 'the feast' (cf. 1 Kgs. 8: 2). By the NT period it had lost its primacy to the Feast of Passover; in modern Judaism it is less important among the autumnal 'High Holidays' than the New Year and Day of *Atonement.

G. F. Moore, *Judaism in the First Centuries of the Christian Era, the Age of the Tannaim*, 2 (Cambridge, Mass., 1927), pp. 43–51. R. de Vaux, OP, *Les Institutions de l'Ancien Testament*, 2 (1960), pp. 397–407, with bibl. p. 458 (Eng. tr., 2nd edn., 1965, pp. 495–502, with bibl. p. 551). S. *Mowinckel, *Psalmenstudien*, esp. vols. 2 and 3 (Skrifter utgiv av Videnskapsselskapet i Kristiania, II. Hist.-Filos. Klasse, 1921, no. 6 (1922), and 1922, no. 1 (1923)); id., *Offersang og Sangoffer* (1951), esp. pp. 143–71 (Eng. tr., *The Psalms in Israel's Worship* (Oxford, 1962), esp. 1, pp. 118–30). N. H. Snaith, *The Jewish New Year Festival: Its Origins and Development* (1947), passim; A. R. Johnson, *Sacral Kingship in Ancient Israel* (Cardiff, 1955). H.-J. Kraus, *Gottesdienst in Israel* (2nd edn., Munich, 1962), pp. 79–86; Eng. tr., *Worship in Israel* (Oxford, 1966), pp. 61–8. W. H. Schmidt, *Alttestamentlicher Glaube in seiner Geschichte* (6th edn., Neukirchen, 1987), pp. 149–51; Eng. tr. (of 4th edn.), *The Faith of the Old Testament* (Oxford, 1983), pp. 124–6. E. Kutsch and others in *Encyclopaedia Judaica*, 15 (Jerusalem, 1972), cols. 495–502, s.v. 'Sukkot'.

table, Communion. See COMMUNION TABLE.

Table Prayers. A term apparently first found in the 19th cent. for the prayers from the Communion service said at the altar (or 'Holy Table') when there was no administration of the Communion. In all the forms of the English BCP provision is made (in slightly varying form) for such prayers. The term seems to be no longer in use.

Tablet. RC weekly, founded in 1840 in London by Frederick Lucas, a barrister and recent convert. It was later edited by the Revd H. (later Cardinal) *Vaughan. Apart from the *Dublin Review (founded in 1836) it is the oldest RC periodical in England.

M. Walsh, *The Tablet 1840–1990: A Commemorative History* [1990].

Taborites. The extreme party of *Hussites, so called from their fortified stronghold south of Prague to which they gave the OT name of Mount Tabor (Jgs. 4: 6–14). They gained ascendancy after the death of King Wenceslaus (1419) and, under their leader Žižka, began to spread the 'Kingdom of God' by force of arms. Through Žižka's military genius and the fanatical devotion of his followers the far superior armies sent against them were repeatedly defeated. After Žižka's death (1424) they split into two main parties, the more moderate of which joined the Catholics after the Compactata of Prague (1433; see UTRAQUISM); the radicals, under Procopius the Bald, suffered a crushing defeat at Lipany in 1434.

The Taborites scorned all reasoned theology. They had no churches and kept no feast days; they rejected *transubstantiation; their priests wore lay clothes and blessed bread and wine at an ordinary table while the people said the Lord's Prayer. They professed extreme social doctrines, demanding the abolition of oaths, courts of justice, and all worldly dignities. Though the militant Taborites lost influence steadily after 1434, and Tabor itself was conquered by their enemies in 1452, the pacific and sectarian elements in their tradition were inherited by the *Bohemian Brethren.

F. C. Heymann, *John Žižka and the Hussite Revolution* (Princeton, NJ, 1955). J. Macek, *Tábor v husitském revolučním hnutí* (2 vols., 1955–6); id., *The Hussite Movement in Bohemia* (Eng. tr., 1965). H. Kaminský, *A History of the Hussite Revolution* (Berkeley, Calif., and Los Angeles, 1967), esp. pp. 278–494. P. de Vooght, 'L'Hérésie des taborites sur l'eucharistie (1418–1421)', *Irénikon*, 35 (1962), pp. 340–9. M. Lambert, *Medieval Heresy* (2nd edn., 1992), pp. 327–48. See also bibl. to HUSS, J.

Tacitus, Cornelius (born *c.* AD 55), Roman historian. A senator and the chief orator of his day, he was last heard of as governor of Asia, *c.*113. His surviving writings are: (1) a life of his father-in-law, Agricola, who was governor of Britain, 78–85; (2) the *Germania*, an ethnographic work; (3) a dialogue *De Oratoribus*; (4) large parts of the *Histories* and (5) of the *Annals* (written later than the *Histories*), which recounted events year by year from 69 to 96 and from 14 to 68 respectively.

In his *Annals*, 15. 44, the earliest non-Christian reference to the Crucifixion, Tacitus describes *Nero's persecution of the Christians at Rome as scapegoats for the fire in the city (AD 64); they were thrown to the dogs, crucified, or burnt alive. Though Tacitus holds them innocent of the charge of arson, he regarded Christianity as a 'pernicious

superstition' (*exitiabilis superstitio*) and seems to have shared the popular belief that its adherents were guilty of atrocious crimes, of which his friend *Pliny and the Emp. Trajan exonerated them.

Modern edns. of his works by E. Koestermann (2 vols., Teub., 1936; 3rd edn., 3 vols., 1965–70), H. Heubner and others (2 vols. in 5 parts, ibid., 1978–83) and by K. Wellesley and others (ibid., 1986 ff.); also of *Annals* and *Histories* by C. D. Fisher (Oxford, 1906 and 1911 respectively) and of *Opera Minora* by M. Winterbottom and R. M. Ogilvie (ibid., 1975). Eng. tr. by A. J. Church and W. J. Brodribb (3 vols., 1864–9; frequently repr.). Comm. on the *Annals* by H. Furneaux (2 vols., Oxford, 1884–91; 2nd edn., 1896–1907) and E. Koestermann (4 vols., Heidelberg, 1963–8). R. Syme, *Tacitus* (2 vols., Oxford, 1958).

Tait, Archibald Campbell (1811–82), Abp. of *Canterbury. Of *Presbyterian upbringing, he was educated at Glasgow University and Balliol College, Oxford, where he was confirmed in 1830. He became a Fellow of the college in 1834. In 1841 he was one of the four Oxford tutors who publicly protested against Tract 90 (see TRACTARIANISM), and henceforth, despite personal friendship with many of its leaders, he was strongly opposed to the *Anglo-Catholic movement. In 1842 he succeeded T. *Arnold as headmaster of Rugby and in 1849, suffering from ill-health, became Dean of *Carlisle. In 1856, at the personal request of the Queen, he was appointed Bp. of London, where his *Broad Church sympathies became more prominent. In 1858 he withdrew the licence of Alfred Poole, curate of St Barnabas, Pimlico, for his practice of hearing confessions, and in 1860 by personal intervention he resolved the conflict that had led to riots over Anglo-Catholic practices at St George's-in-the-East (see LOWDER, C. F.). He joined with other bishops in publicly deprecating *Essays and Reviews (1860), but in 1864 he sided with the majority of the *Judicial Committee of the Privy Council (against the Abps. of Canterbury and *York) in favour of two of the essayists. In 1868 he became Abp. of Canterbury. A staunch upholder of *Establishment, when he came to view W. E. *Gladstone's policy in *Ireland as inevitable, he used his considerable gifts of statesmanship to secure the best terms possible for the disestablished Church of Ireland. He was a member of the *Ritual Commission and the *Public Worship Regulation Act 1874 was mainly his creation, though he objected to its final form and was convinced that its practical working was a failure. He tried, unsuccessfully, to end the recitation of the *Athanasian Creed in Divine Service (1871–2). In 1877 he brought R. T. *Davidson to Lambeth as his chaplain. He championed the Burial Laws Amendment Act 1880, which granted to Nonconformists the right to be buried in their parish churchyards, and he presided ably over the second *Lambeth Conference in 1878.

Life by R. T. Davidson (son-in-law) and W. Benham (2 vols., London, 1891). P. T. Marsh, *The Victorian Church in Decline: Archbishop Tait and the Church of England 1868–1882* (1969). W. H. Fremantle in *DNB* 55 (1898), pp. 292–9.

Taizé Community, an international and ecumenical monastic community founded in 1940 by Roger Schutz-Marsauche (b. 1915). His aim was to open up ways of healing the divisions between Christians and through the reconciliation of Christians to overcome conflicts within humanity. Acquiring a house in Taizé, near *Cluny, in SE France, he began by sheltering Jews and other refugees in his home. After the end of the Second World War, he obtained permission to welcome German prisoners of war from a nearby camp. The first brothers took life-vows in 1949. They were all Protestants, of various backgrounds, but since 1969 they have been joined by RCs. There are now c.90 brothers, from some 20 countries and every continent. In addition to those at Taizé, there are small groups living in poor areas of Africa, Asia, and N. and S. America.

Since 1958 the community has welcomed to Taizé young adults in increasing numbers. Weekly intercontinental meetings bring together youths from numerous countries, those in the summer drawing up to 6,000 participants at a time. The meetings are centred on the three set times of prayer each day in the Church of Reconciliation; the themes for reflection are based on 'inner life and human solidarity'. Songs from Taizé are used in groups and parishes around the world. At the end of each year the Taizé brothers lead a 'European Meeting', where many thousands of young people from E. and W. Europe are welcomed for several days by parishes of a major city. Similar meetings have been held in N. America and Asia.

Brother Roger [Schutz] has published a number of books, including vols. of journals under various titles; there is a collection of extracts, *Son Amour est un Feu* (1988; Eng. tr., *His Love is a Fire*, 1990). J. L. González Balado, *El Desafío de Taizé* (1976; rev. Eng. tr., *The Story of Taizé*, 1980; 3rd edn., 1988). K. Spink, *A Universal Heart: The Life and Vision of Brother Roger of Taizé* (1986). *Songs and Prayers from Taizé* (1991). É. Marchant in *Dict. Sp.* 15 (1991), cols. 9–12, s.v., with detailed bibl.

Talbot, Edward Stuart (1844–1934), Bp. of *Winchester. He was educated at Christ Church, Oxford, where in 1866 he was elected a Student. In 1870 he became first Warden of Keble College, Oxford. Nearly 20 years later he exchanged academic for parish work; and from 1888 to 1895 he had a very successful incumbency as vicar of Leeds. In 1895 he became Bp. of *Rochester, where his main work was the division of the diocese and the creation of the see of *Southwark, of which he was enthroned bishop in 1905. From 1911 to 1923 he was Bp. of *Winchester. Closely associated in his earlier years with C. *Gore, he was theologically a member of the school of *Lux Mundi* (1889), to which he had contributed the essay on 'The Preparation in History for Christ', and throughout his life exercised great influence in furthering moderate High Church principles. Like other members of the *Lux Mundi* school, he was a keen advocate of social reform.

His three sons were:

(1) **Edward Keble Talbot** (1877–1949), who joined the *Community of the Resurrection at Mirfield in 1910 (Superior, 1922–40).

(2) **Neville Stuart Talbot** (1879–1943), who, after army service in the Boer War, became Chaplain of Balliol College, Oxford (1909), Bp. of Pretoria (1920), and Vicar of St Mary's, Nottingham (1933). He contributed an essay on 'The Present Situation' to *Foundations*.

(3) **Gilbert Talbot** (1891–1915), who was killed in action (30 July 1915) on the Ypres salient. 'Talbot House' (popularly '*Toc H', q.v.) was founded in his memory.

There is much autobiog. material in E. S. Talbot's *Memories of Early Life* (1924). Life by G. Stephenson (London, 1936). A.

Mansbridge, *Edward Stuart Talbot and Charles Gore* (1935), pp. 1–27 and 71–90. J. Sankey in *DNB, 1931–1940*, pp. 844 f.

Edward Keble Talbot's *Retreat Addresses*, ed. L. Menzies (London, 1954), with introd., pp. 7–16; miscellaneous writings in G. P. H. Pawson, CR (ed.), *Edward Keble Talbot: His Community and his Friends* (ibid., 1954), with memoir, pp. 11–33. Memoir of Neville Stuart Talbot by F. H. Brabant (ibid., 1949).

Tall Brothers (Gk. ἀδελφοὶ μακροί). The four monks, Dioscorus (Bp. of Hermopolis Minor), Ammonius, Eusebius, and Euthymius, who led the *Origenist Movement in Egypt at the end of the 4th cent. In 399 they made their way from the *Nitrian Desert to Alexandria to defend Origenist views against their new opponent, Theophilus, Patr. of Alexandria. Failing to get satisfaction, they proceeded to *Constantinople, where they continued their propaganda and even gained the support of St *Chrysostom.

The chief source is *Sozomen, *Hist. Eccl.* 8. 12.

Talleyrand-Périgord, Charles Maurice de (1754–1838), Prince of Benevento, Bp. of Autun, and statesman. Ordained priest in 1779, he was made Bp. of Autun in 1789. After a short hesitation, he joined the cause of the Revolution and became a member of the Constitutional Assembly, taking the oath to the *Civil Constitution and consecrating persons prepared to do likewise to fill the vacated bishoprics. In 1791 he was constrained to resign his see, and in 1792 was excommunicated. The same year he undertook an embassy to London to win support for the Revolution, but shortly afterwards lost the favour of the Government and had to flee to the USA. Regaining favour, in 1796 he became Foreign Minister. After the *Concordat of 1801 *Pius VII readmitted him to lay communion. Henceforward he was Napoleon's principal agent in making treaties, except between 1809 and 1814, when he was in disgrace. In 1814 he took charge of the provisional Government, and in that year and the next he was instrumental in preserving the territorial integrity of France in the peace treaties. He retired from active political life in 1815, but later lent his support to Louis Philippe (1830–48) in his bid for the throne, and was by him made Ambassador to England, a post which he held from 1830 to 1834. On his deathbed he signed, in the presence of the Abbé F. A. P. *Dupanloup, a solemn repudiation of his errors and misdeeds against the Church.

[C. J. V. A.] de Broglie (ed.), *Mémoires du Prince de Talleyrand* (5 vols., 1891–2; Eng. tr., 5 vols., 1891–2). *Mémoires* also ed. P. Léon (7 vols., 1953–5) and P.-L. Couchoud (1957; rev. by J.-P. Couchoud, 1982). G. Pallain (ed.), *Correspondance inédite du Prince de Talleyrand et du Roi Louis XVIII pendant le congrès de Vienne* (1881; Eng. tr., 2 vols., 1881); id. (ed.), *Correspondance diplomatique de Talleyrand: La mission de Talleyrand à Londres en 1792* (1889); id. (ed.), *Correspondance diplomatique de Talleyrand: Le ministère de Talleyrand sous le Directoire* (1891); id. (ed.), *Correspondance diplomatique de Talleyrand: Ambassade de Talleyrand à Londres, 1830–1834* (pt. 1; 1891). P. Bertrand (ed.), *Lettres inédites de Talleyrand à Napoléon, 1800–1809* (1889). Full Life by G. Lacour-Gayet (3 vols., Paris, 1928–32; repr. 1991). Other modern studies incl. those of A. Duff Cooper (London, 1932; repr, 1987), A. F. Saint-Aulaire (Paris, 1936; Eng. tr., 1937), L. Madelin (Paris, 1944; Eng. tr., 1948), and J. F. Bernard (London, 1973). G.-A. Morlot and J. Happart, *Talleyrand, une mystification historique* [1991]. C. Brinton, *The Lives of Talleyrand* (1937), with *bibliographie raisonnée*.

Tallis, Thomas (*c*.1505–85), organist and composer. He was organist of Waltham Abbey before its dissolution in 1540, and soon afterwards was appointed a Gentleman of the *Chapel Royal. By this time his unprinted compositions were already in use, but his first works to be printed were five anthems which appeared in 1560. He lived in his later years largely on the income of leases granted to him by Queens *Mary (1557) and *Elizabeth I (1577). In 1575 Elizabeth also granted to Tallis and W. *Byrd a monopoly of music printing for 21 years, but this apparently brought little financial benefit. His vocal works are his principal compositions. They are mostly set to Latin words, but also include a number of settings of the Anglican service, responses, and anthems which, in their simplicity of form, are a clear reflection of T. *Cranmer's desire for intelligible word-setting. His most outstanding work is the 40-part *motet *Spem in alium*, a unique achievement, apparently composed for the Duke of Norfolk in 1571. He also composed 9 Psalm tunes for M. *Parker's Psalter (1567), which include the tunes now known (in adapted form) as 'Tallis's Canon' and 'Tallis's Ordinal'.

P. Doe, *Tallis* (Oxford Studies of Composers, 4; London, 1968). P. [G.] Le Huray, *Music and the Reformation in England, 1549–1660* (1967), esp. pp. 193–9. P. Doe in S. Sadie (ed.), *The New Grove Dictionary of Music and Musicians*, 18 (1980), pp. 541–8, s.v.

Talmud. The Jewish compilations which embody the *Mishnah, or oral teaching of the Jews, and the *Gemara, or collection of discussions on the Mishnah. The two main forms of Talmud, the Babylonian and the Palestinian, are similar in method and construction, but by no means identical in content. Neither contains Gemara (commentary) on all Tractates of the Mishnah. The material in the Gemara is extremely varied, and comprises both *Halachah and *Haggadah (whereas the Mishnah on which it comments is primarily Halachic). The so-called Minor Tractates and Additional Tractates are a kind of appendix to the Babylonian Talmud, and they contain material of great importance. The Palestinian and Babylonian Talmuds were formed during the 5th cent. (the Palestinian earlier than the Babylonian), but work continued on the Babylonian Talmud after that time, and both include material that went back much earlier.

Best standard edns. of texts, *Talmud Babli* in 20 vols., Vilnius, 1880–6; Eng. tr. ed. I. Epstein (35 vols., London, 1935–52), with Eng. tr. of Minor Tractates ed. A. Cohen (2 vols., 1965); Ger. tr. of the Talmud, with *variae lectiones*, by L. Goldschmidt (9 vols., Berlin, 1897–1935); *Talmud Yerushalmi* in 8 vols., Vilnius, 1922; Eng. tr. by J. Neusner and others (Chicago Studies in the History of Judaism, 1982 ff.). H. L. Strack, *Einleitung in Talmud und Midrasch* (1887; 7th edn. by G. Stemberger, 1982; Eng. tr., Edinburgh, 1991). A. Goldberg and M. B. Lerner in S. Safrai (ed.), *The Literature of the Sages*, 1 (Compendia Rerum Iudaicarum ad Novum Testamentum, Section 2, vol. 3, pt. 1; Assen and Philadelphia, 1987), pp. 303–409. D. Goodblatt, 'The Babylonian Talmud' in *Aufstieg und Niedergang der römischen Welt*, Reihe II, Bd. 19, ed. W. Haase (2. Halbband, 1979), pp. 257–336. B. M. Bokser, 'An Annotated Bibliographical Guide to the Study of the Palestinian Talmud', ibid., pp. 139–256. M. Berlin and S. J. Zevin, *Ensiklopedia Talmudith* (Heb., 21 vols., Jerusalem, 1948–93; Eng. tr., Jerusalem, 1969 ff.). G. G. Porton in *Anchor Bible Dictionary*, 6 (1992), pp. 310–15, s.v.

Tambaram Conference. The Missionary Conference, convened by the International Missionary Council, which met at Tambaram, nr. Madras, from 12 to 29 Dec. 1938. Its membership of 471, drawn from 69 different countries and all the more important non-RC communions, was esp. remarkable for its strong representation from the younger Churches, the white delegates being actually in a slight minority. The chairman of the Conference was John R. *Mott, with Dr William Paton as Secretary.

The Tambaram Series: 1. *The Authority of the Faith*; 2. *The Growing Church*; 3. *Evangelism*; 4. *The Life of the Church*; 5. *The Economic Basis of the Church*; 6. *The Church and the State*, 7. *Addresses and other Records* [with list of members]. 7 vols. (all 1939).

Tametsi. The *Tridentine decree (Sess. 24, cap. 1; 1563) prescribing the formal mode of celebrating matrimony, it aimed at suppressing clandestinity and was passed after long debates by a majority of 133 to 59. It laid down that in places where the decree was promulgated, a marriage between baptized persons (whether Catholics or not) was valid only when it took place in the presence of the parish priest or of the local Ordinary, or a priest appointed by one of these, and at least two witnesses. As its effect in Protestant countries would have been to reduce all unions between men and women to illicit cohabitations, it was prescribed that before coming into operation in any parish the decree had to be formally published in that parish. Hence it was normally not published in Protestant countries, e.g. it was never brought into operation anywhere in England, Scotland, or Wales. None the less it led to many complications and in 1908 it was finally superseded by other provisions of *Ne Temere* (q.v.).

The text is pr. in the edns. of the decrees of the Council of Trent, e.g. in *Concilium Tridentinum: Diariorum, Actorum, Epistularum, Tractatuum Nova Collectio. Edidit Societas Goerresiana*, 9, ed. S. Eshes (Freiburg i.B., 1924), pp. 968 f.; also, with Fr. tr., in Hefele and Leclercq, 10 (pt. 1; 1938), pp. 554–8, and, with Eng. tr., in Tanner, *Decrees*, 2 (1990), pp. 755–9. See also works on MATRIMONY by RC authors and bibl. to TRENT, COUNCIL OF.

Tammuz. The Akkadian (Babylonian) name for the ancient Sumerian deity, Dumuzi, who is commonly regarded as the equivalent of the Greek Adonis. Originally associated with Sun-worship, the deity became the Divine personification of the annual decay and revival of vegetation in autumn and spring. The chief feature of the cultus was ceremonial lamentation, a reference to which occurs at Ezek. 8: 14.

S. [H.] Langdon, *Tammuz and Ishtar* (1914). M. Witzel, OFM, *Tammuz-Liturgien und Verwandtes* (Analecta Orientalia, 10; 1935). A. Moortgat, *Tammuz: Der Unsterblichkeitsglaube in der altorientalischen Bildkunst* (1949). S. H. Hooke, *Babylonian and Assyrian Religion* (1953), esp. pp. 36–46. K. Preisendanz in *PW*, Reihe 2, 4 (pt. 2; 1932), cols. 2139–48, s.v.; T. Jacobsen in *Encyclopedia of Religion*, ed. M. Eliade, 4 (1987), pp. 512 f., s.v. 'Dumuzi'.

Tanner, Thomas (1674–1735), English antiquary and divine. Born at Market Lavington, Wilts, he was educated at Queen's College, Oxford, where he formed a lifelong friendship with E. *Gibson; he was elected a Fellow of All

Souls in 1696. In 1695 he published his *Notitia Monastica*, an erudite account of the medieval religious houses in England and Wales (enlarged edition pub. by his brother, John Tanner, in 1744). In 1698 he became private chaplain to John Moore, then Bp. of *Norwich, who appointed him chancellor of his diocese in 1701. Having become Canon of *Ely in 1713, he returned to Oxford as Canon of *Christ Church in 1724. In 1732 he became Bp. of *St Asaph. His second great work, the *Bibliotheca Britannico-Hibernica*, an enlargement of J. Leland's *De Scriptoribus*, was published posthumously by D. *Wilkins in 1748. Based on extensive research into medieval bibliography, it aims at giving a comprehensive account of all British writers down to the beginning of the 17th cent., and long remained the standard work on the subject. He bequeathed to the *Bodleian Library a choice of his printed books and the whole of his valuable collection of MSS, a large number of which had formerly belonged to Abp. W. *Sancroft. His MSS include a number of important papers relating to the time of the civil wars.

A. Hackman (ed.), *Catalogi Codicum Manuscriptorum Bibliothecae Bodleianae Pars Quarta: Codices Viri Admodum Reverendi Thomae Tanneri* (1860). C. McNeill, *The Tanner Letters: Original Documents and Notices of Irish Affairs in the Sixteenth and Seventeenth Centuries Extracted from the Collection in the Bodleian Library, Oxford* (Dublin, 1943). Microfilm of the Tanner MSS in the Bodleian Library, ed. M. Hawkins (Hassocks, W. Sussex, 1977). D. C. Douglas, *English Scholars* (1939), pp. 199–207 (2nd edn., 1951, pp. 156–64), and *passim*. W. P. Courtney in *DNB* 55 (1898), pp. 359–62.

Tanquerey, Adolf Alfred (1854–1932), dogmatic theologian. Born at Blainville, Normandy, he was educated at Saint-Lô, Coutances, *Saint-Sulpice de Paris, and Rome. In 1878 he was ordained priest and entered the Society of Saint-Sulpice. He taught at Rodez from 1879 to 1887, at Baltimore, USA, from 1887 to 1902, and at Saint-Sulpice de Paris from 1902 to 1905. From 1915 to 1926 he was superior of the Solitude (a training centre for novices) at Issy, retiring to Aix in 1927.

His *Synopsis Theologiae Dogmaticae* (3 vols., 1894–6) and his *Synopsis Theologiae Moralis et Pastoralis* (3 vols., 1902–5), condensed in his *Brevior Synopsis Theologiae Dogmaticae* (1911) and his *Brevior Synopsis Theologiae Moralis et Pastoralis* (1913), had a wide circulation. They provided a large body of useful and generally reliable information within a manageable compass. His other published works include *Précis de théologie ascétique et mystique* (1923–4) and contributions to various Catholic periodicals.

I. Noye, PSS, in *Dict. Sp.* 15 (1991), cols. 25–7, s.v.

Tantum ergo. The last two verses of St *Thomas Aquinas's Eucharistic hymn '*Pange lingua gloriosi', and the principal hymn often used at *Benediction in the RC Church. The practice of inclining the head at the words 'veneremur cernui' is general, but not laid down in any rubrics. There are several English translations, the best-known beginning 'Therefore we, before Him bending'.

Tarasius, St (d. 806), Patr. of *Constantinople from 784. He was an uncle or great-uncle of *Photius and chief secretary of the Empress Irene II, at whose instigation,

though only a layman, he was uncanonically elected patriarch. He at once embarked on a policy of restoring good relations between the Byzantine Church and the W. and persuaded the Empress to convoke, in concert with the Pope, *Hadrian I, a General Council which sat at *Nicaea in 787 under his own presidency. After its successful conclusion he became involved in a series of difficulties, consequent on his supposed tolerance of simony and his lack of energy in the divorce affair of Irene's son, Constantine VI. On being violently attacked for laxity by *Theodore of Studios and his rigorous monks, he excommunicated the priest who had performed the ceremony of Constantine's second marriage. In 802 he crowned as Emperor Nicephorus, who had dethroned Irene. After his death he was venerated as a saint. Feast day, 25 Feb.

A few of his letters and a sermon which have survived are repr. from J. D. *Mansi in J. P. Migne, *PG* 98. 1423–500. V. Grumel, AA, *Les Regestes des actes du patriarcat de Constantinople*, vol. 1, fascs. 2–3 (2nd edn. by J. Darrouzès, 1989), pp. 21–34 (nos. 350–73e). Lat. tr. of Life by his disciple Ignatius, pr. in *AASS*, Feb. 3 (1658), pp. 576–90, repr. in J. P. Migne, op. cit., 1385–424; Gk. text first ed. by I. A. Heikel in *Acta Societatis Scientiarum Fennicae*, 17 (Helsingfors, 1891), pp. 389–439. Theophanes, *Chronographia* (ed. C. de Boor, 1, Leipzig, 1885, pp. 457–63, 470 f., 480 f., 500). J. M. Hussey, *The Orthodox Church in the Byzantine Empire* (Oxford History of the Christian Church, 1986), pp. 45–52. R. Janin, AA, in *DTC* 15 (pt. 1; 1946), cols. 54–7, s.v. 'Taraise'; D. Stiernon in *Bibliotheca Sanctorum*, 12 (Rome, 1969), cols. 127–31, s.v. 'Tarasio', with further bibl. See also works cited under NICAEA, SECOND COUNCIL OF.

Targum. The name, meaning 'translation', given to the Aramaic interpretative translations of the OT made when Hebrew had ceased to be the normal medium of speech among the Jews. They were the outcome of the explanatory oral matter which for a long time had been added to the Scripture lections in the worship of the *synagogue. The Targum of Onkelos (on the *Pentateuch) and the Targum of Jonathan (on the Prophets), which were to become the official Targums, emerged in Babylonia in about the 3rd cent. AD. Unofficial and more expansive Targums were also current in Palestine, perhaps from about 1st cent. AD; the MSS of these, however, are all late and mainly confined to the Pentateuch, on which only one (Neofiti I in the *Vatican), dated AD 1504, is complete; other witnesses are: fragments from the Cairo *Geniza, the 'Fragment Targum', and the Targum of Pseudo-Jonathan (which has many elements in common with that of Onkelos). The nature of the relationship between the Babylonian and the Palestinian Targums is disputed. The Targums to the *Hagiographa are all late, apart from fragments of a (different) Targum to Job found at *Qumran. There is no Targum to Ezra, Nehemiah, or Daniel, the first and third of which already contained sections in Aramaic.

The Targum of Onkelos was first pr. in Italy, prob. in 1480. Both that of Onkelos and of Jonathan are pr. in the London *Polyglot. The Targums of Onkelos and Jonathan and the Targums to the Hagiographa apart from Pss., Prov., and Job, ed. A. Sperber, *The Bible in Aramaic* (4 vols. in 5, Leiden, 1959–73). A. Diez Macho, MSC (ed.), *Neophyti I* (Textos y Estudios, 7–12; Madrid, 1968–79; incl. Eng. tr.). M. L. Klein, *The Fragment-Targums of the Pentateuch* (2 vols., Analecta Biblica, 76; Rome, 1980; incl. Eng. tr.). Fr. tr. of Neofiti I and the Targums of Pseudo-Jonathan by R. Le Déaut, *Targum du Pentateuque* (SC 245, 256, 261, 271,

282; 1978–81). Modern edns. of the Targum of Pseudo-Jonathan by D. Rieder (Jerusalem, 1974) and E. G. Clarke (Hoboken, NJ, 1984); A. Diez Macho and others, *Biblia Polyglotta Matritensia*, 4th ser.: *Targum Palestinense in Pentateuchum. Additur Targum Pseudojonatan* (Madrid, 1977 ff.). J. F. Stenning (ed.), *The Targum of Isaiah* (1949; incl. Eng. tr.). M. Sokoloff, *The Targum to Job from Qumran Cave XI* (Ramat-Gan [1974]; incl. Eng. tr.). M. L. Klein, *Genizah Manuscripts of Palestinian Targum to the Pentateuch* (2 vols., Cincinnati, 1986). P. E. Kahle, *The Cairo Geniza* (Schweich Lectures, 1941; 2nd edn., Oxford, 1959), pp. 191–208. M. McNamara, MSC, *The New Testament and the Palestinian Targum to the Pentateuch* (Analecta Biblica, 27; Rome, 1966). R. Le Déaut, *Introduction à la littérature targumique*, 1 [all pub.] (Rome, 1966). J. [W.] Bowker, *The Targums and Rabbinic Literature: An Introduction to Jewish Interpretations of Scripture* (Cambridge, 1969). E. *Schürer, *The History of the Jewish People in the Age of Jesus Christ*, rev. Eng. tr. by G. Vermes and others, 1 (1973), pp. 99–114, with bibl. M. Jastrow, *A Dictionary of the Targumim, the Talmud Babli and Yerushalmi and the Midrashic Literature* (2 vols., 1886–1903; repr., New York, 1971). B. Grossfeld, *A Bibliography of Targum Literature* (Bibliographica Judaica, 3 and 8; Cincinnati and New York, 1972–7). Id. in *Encyclopaedia Judaica*, 4 (Jerusalem, 1971), cols. 841–51, s.v. 'Bible, Translations, Ancient Versions, Aramaic: the Targumim'; P. S. Alexander in *Anchor Bible Dictionary*, 6 (1992), pp. 320–31, s.v.

Tarsicius, St (3rd–4th cent.), martyr. Tradition states that he was killed in *Rome by the mob while bearing the Blessed Sacrament rather than surrender it to profanation. He is first mentioned in one of *Damasus' *Epigrammata*, where a comparison with St *Stephen (Acts 6) suggests that he may have been a deacon. Acc. to a 6th-cent. tradition, he took the Sacrament as an acolyte to certain Christian prisoners. His relics were originally located in the catacombs of S. Callisto, though they were later claimed by San Silvestro in Capite. Feast day, 15 Aug. A fraternity dedicated to him, fostering the cult of the Blessed Sacrament, received Papal approval in 1920. The incident of his death figures in N. *Wiseman's *Fabiola*.

AASS, Aug. 3 (1737), p. 201. A. Ferrua, SJ (ed.), *Epigrammata Damasiana* (Rome, 1942), Elogium 15, pp. 117–19, with refs. J. M. Lambert, *Étude historique et critique sur saint Tharsicius, acolyte* (Rome, 1890). J. Wilpert, *Die Papstgräber und die Cäciliengruft in der Katakombe des hl. Kallistus* (1909), pp. 92–4 and 96–8; O. *Marucchi, 'La questione del sepolcro del papa Zeffirino e del martire Tarsicio in seguito ad una ultima scoperta', *Nuovo Bullettino di Archaeologia cristiana*, 16 (1910), pp. 205–25.

Tarsus. Pompey made this ancient city of Asia Minor the capital of the Roman province of Cilicia in 67 BC. It became the seat of a famous *Stoic philosophical school and was the birthplace of St *Paul (Acts 9: 11; 21: 39; 22: 3). In Christian times it was an episcopal see, and included among its bishops Helenus (*fl. c.*250), the opponent of *Paul of Samosata, and *Diodore (Bp. 378–*c.*390), the Antiochene exegete and theologian.

H. Goldman (ed.), *Excavations at Gözlü Kule, Tarsus* (3 vols. of text + 3 vols. of plates, Princeton, NJ, 1950–63). W. M. *Ramsay, *The Cities of St Paul* (1907), pp. 85–244. W. C. van Unnik, 'Tarsus of Jeruzalem. De Stad van Paulus' Jeugd', *Mededelingen der koninklijke Nederlandse Akademie van Wetenschappen*, Afd. Letterkunde, Nieuwe Reeks, 15 (1952), pp. 141–89; Eng. tr. as *Tarsus or Jerusalem: The City of Paul's Youth* (1962). C. Bradford Welles, 'Hellenistic Tarsus', *Mélanges de l'Université Saint Joseph*, 38 (1962), pp. 43–75. W. Ruge in *PW*, Zweite Reihe, 4 (pt. 2; 1932), cols. 2413–39, s.v. 'Tarsos (3)'.

Tasso, Torquato (1544–95), Italian poet. Educated at *Venice and Padua, he published his first poem *Rinaldo* in 1562, and in 1565 entered the service of Cardinal Luigi d'Este at Ferrara. Here most of his time was given to his great epic *Gerusalemme liberata*, a poem on the First *Crusade, written in the grave style characteristic of the *Counter-Reformation and completed in 1574. From that time he suffered much from religious scruples as well as from the criticisms directed against his work. As he became increasingly tormented by a kind of persecution mania and subject to violent outbursts, the Duke of Ferrara had him confined in an asylum in 1579. During this imprisonment he composed numerous prose dialogues on philosophical subjects. On his liberation in 1586, he went to Mantua and from there to various other Italian cities, spending his last years in writing *Gerusalemme conquistata* (1592), an attempt to satisfy the critics of the earlier work, to which it is much inferior, and the *Sette giornate*, a blank-verse epic of the Creation. He died shortly before receiving the crown of the Poet Laureate intended for him by *Clement VIII.

The best collected edn. of his works is that of G. Rosini, 33 vols., Pisa, 1821–32. Crit. edns. by A. Solerti of *Le rime* (4 vols., Bologna, 1898–1902); by L. Bonfigli of *Gerusalemme conquistata* (Scritti d'Italia, 2 vols., Bari, 1934) and of *Rinaldo* (ibid., 1936); and by G. C. Baiardi of *Aminta* (Urbino [1976]) and of *Gerusalemme liberata* (Ferrara [1991]). A number of his works have been tr. into Eng. A. Solerti, *Vita di Torquato Tasso* (3 vols., Turin, 1895); E. Donadoni, *Torquato Tasso: Saggio critico* (2 vols., Florence, 1920); A. Banfi and others, *Torquato Tasso: Comitato per le celebrazioni di Torquato Tasso Ferrara 1954* (Milan, 1957); L. Caretti, *Ariosto e Tasso* (Turin, 1961; 2nd edn. [1967]), pp. 47–121; rev. repr. [1970], pp. 55–149 and 165–82; C. P. Brand, *Torquato Tasso: A Study of the Poet and his Contribution to English Literature* (Cambridge, 1965). C. Previtera, *La poesia e l'arte di Torquato Tasso* (Messina and Milan, 1936); G. Getto, *Interpretazione del Tasso* (Naples, 1951); B. Basile, *Poëta Melancholicus: Tradizione classica e follia nell'ultimo Tasso* (Pisa [1984]). On his religion and spirituality, see L. Firpo's introd. in his edn. of Tasso's *Tre scritti politici* (Turin, 1980), pp. 7–82, esp. pp. 42–59. G. Getto in *EC* 11 (1953), cols. 1784–94; G. Crupi in A. Asor Rosa (ed.), *Letteratura Italiana. Gli Autori. Dizionario bio-bibliografico*, 2 (Turin, 1991), pp. 1698–703, both s.v.

Tate, Nahum (1652–1715), and **Brady, Nicholas** (1659–1726), authors of the *New Version of the Psalms* (1696). Both were Irish Protestants, educated at Trinity College, Dublin, Brady also at Christ Church, Oxford. Tate, who had written the second part of *Absalom and Achitophel* (1682) under J. *Dryden's direction, besides a large number of works of indifferent merit, including alterations of some of Shakespeare's plays, became Poet Laureate in 1692. Brady who was ordained by 1688, was chaplain to William III, Mary, and Queen *Anne, and held a number of benefices; among his works was a translation of *Virgil's *Aeneid* in blank verse (1726). Their joint work, the *New Version*, is a versification of the Psalter acc. to the artificial taste of the period, sacrificing the literal method of previous versions to the principle of contemporary literary refinement. There are, however, a number of simpler and more poetical pieces, such as 'Through all the changing scenes of life' (Ps. 34) and 'As pants the hart' (Ps. 42), which have made their way into modern hymn-books. Two slightly differing editions of the version, which were both printed in 1698, were the standard texts of later reissues. This *New Version*, though at first not favourably received, gradually supplanted the older rendering of T. *Sternhold and J. Hopkins. It was constantly reprinted during the next 100 years and down to the early 19th cent. was in almost universal use.

W. Hunt in *DNB* 6 (1886), pp. 192 f., s.v. 'Brady'; H. L. Bennett, ibid. 55 (1898), pp. 379 f., s.v. 'Tate'. W. J. Austin and J. Ralf, *The Lives of the Poets-Laureate* (1853), pp. 196–222, esp. pp. 214–19; on the other works of Tate, E. K. Broadus, *The Laureateship: A Study of the Office of Poet Laureate in England with some account of the Poets* (1921), pp. 88–101, and *NCBEL* 2 (1971), cols. 774–6. Nicholas Brady's sermon *Church-Musick Vindicated*, preached on St Cecilia's day, 1697, is repr., with introd. by J. E. Phillips, Jun., *Two St Cecilia's Day Sermons* (Augustan Reprint Society, 49; Los Angeles, 1955). On the New Version, see N. Temperley, *The Music of the English Parish Church*, 1 (Cambridge Studies in Music, 1979), pp. 120–4. See also bibl. to METRICAL PSALTERS.

Tatian (*c*.160), Christian *Apologist and rigorist. A native of Assyria, he was educated in Greek rhetoric and philosophy. He became a Christian in Rome between 150 and 165 and was a pupil of St *Justin Martyr, but soon showed leanings to independent opinions. About 172 he went into the E., where he is said to have founded the ascetic sect of the *Encratites. He is the author of an apology, usually called 'Oratio ad Graecos'. It is a passionate defence of the venerable age and Divine purity of Christianity combined with a violent attack on Greek civilization, which is represented as a mass of evil, incompatible with the Christian Faith. His chief claim to fame is the '*Diatessaron' (q.v.), a history of the life of Christ compiled from the four gospels which was used in the Syriac Church until the 5th cent., when it was replaced by the *Peshitta version because its author was considered a heretic. Among his literary opponents were St *Irenaeus, *Tertullian, *Clement of Alexandria, St *Hippolytus, and *Origen.

The best edns. of Tatian's 'Oratio ad Graecos' are those by J. C. T. Otto (Corpus Apologetarum Christianorum, 6; Jena, 1851), E. *Schwartz (TU 4, Heft 1; 1888), E. J. Goodspeed (*Die ältesten Apologeten* (1914), pp. 266–305) and, with Eng. tr., by M. Whittaker (Oxford, 1982; incl. other frags.). M. Elze, *Tatian und seine Theologie* (Forschungen zur Kirchen- und Dogmengeschichte, 9; 1960), with full bibl. *CPG* 1 (1983), pp. 44–53 (nos. 1104–6). J. Quasten, *Patrology*, 1 (Utrecht, 1950), pp. 220–8; Altaner and Stuiber (1978), pp. 71–4 and 555 f. E. Fascher in *PW*, Zweite Reihe, 4 (pt. 2; 1932), cols. 2468–71, s.v. 'Tatianus (9)'; G. Bardy in *DTC* 15 (pt. 1; 1946), cols. 59–66, s.v. 'Tatien'; F. Bolgiani in *DPAC* 2 (1984), cols. 3354–7, s.v. 'Taziano'; Eng. tr. in *Encyclopedia of the Early Church*, 2 (1992), p. 815. See also bibl. to DIATESSARON.

Tattam, Henry (1789–1868), Coptic scholar. He held a succession of Anglican benefices, and in 1845 was appointed Archdeacon of Bedford. On travels in Egypt he recovered from the *Nitrian Desert several important Coptic and Syriac MSS, now in the British Library, among them the 5th-cent. codex of the *Old Syriac text of the Gospels which W. *Cureton identified in 1847 and published in 1858.

Miss Platt (stepdaughter), *Journal of a Tour through Egypt, the Peninsula of Sinai, and the Holy Land in 1838, 1839* (2 vols., privately pr., 1841–2). W. Wright, *Catalogue of the Syriac Manu-*

scripts in the British Museum, acquired since the Year 1838, 3 (1872), esp. pp. xi–xiii and xvi–xxv. T. Cooper in *DNB* 55 (1898), pp. 386 f., s.v., for full list of his works.

Tauler, John (d. 1361), German *Dominican spiritual teacher. Little is known of his life. Born prob. near the end of the 13th cent., he entered the Order of Preachers in Strasbourg and possibly studied in Cologne. He may have known *Eckhart and *Henry Suso personally; he was certainly influenced by Eckhart and the *Neoplatonism current among the German Dominican disciples of St *Albertus Magnus. When Strasbourg was placed under an interdict he moved to Basle (1339–42); he also visited Medingen (1339 and 1347), Cologne (1339 and 1346), and prob. Paris (1350). He died in Strasbourg. He was famous as a preacher and director of nuns, and his popularity caused many spurious works to be ascribed to him; apart from the sermons and one letter, the authenticity of all the other works is now rejected. The canon of his sermons is still not entirely established. His spirituality is notable for its balance between inwardness (detachment, the birth of God in the soul, and living in the 'ground' of the soul) and the external practice of the virtues and of pious exercises. His notion of 'suffering' (*leiden*) holds together the imitation of Christ Crucified by patient endurance and a more radical stance of receptiveness towards God's acting upon the soul. He had a lasting influence on later German piety, both Catholic and Protestant, and, esp. after the Latin translation by L. Surius (1548), he was frequently cited also by Spanish spiritual writers, though the reference is sometimes to spurious works.

Editio princeps of his sermons, Leipzig, 1498. First crit. edn. by F. Vetter (Deutsche Texte des Mittelalters, 11; 1910); also ed. from two important Vienna MSS (2744 and 2739) by A. L. Corin (Bibliothèque de la Faculté de Philosophie et Lettres de l'Université de Liège, 33 and 42; 1924–9). Modern Ger. version by G. Hofmann (Freiburg i.B., 1961). Eng. tr. by W. Elliott (Washington, DC, 1910); of selected passages by E. Strakosch (London, 1958), and by E. Colledge and M. Jane [Ciantar], OP (St Louis and London, 1961). Fr. tr. by E. Hugueny, C. Théry, and A. L. Corin (1930; ed. J.-P. Jossua, with note on 'Jean Tauler et Maître Eckhart' by E. H. Weber, OP, 1991). C. Schmidt, *Johannes Tauler von Strassburg: Beitrag zur Geschichte der Mystik und des religiösen Lebens im vierzehnten Jahrhundert* (Hamburg, 1841). H. S. *Denifle, OP, *Taulers Bekehrung kritisch untersucht* (Quellen und Forschungen zur Sprach- und Culturgeschichte der germanischen Völker, 36; 1879). K. Grunewald, *Studien zu Johannes Taulers Frömmigkeit* (Beiträge zur Kulturgeschichte des Mittelalters und Renaissance, 44; 1930). E. Filthaut, OP (ed.), *Johannes Tauler: Ein deutscher Mystiker. Gedenkschrift zum 600. Todestag* (with substantial bibl.; Essen, 1961). I. Weilner, *Johannes Taulers Bekehrungsweg: Die Erfahrungsgrundlagen seiner Mystik* (Regensburg, 1961). C. Pleuser, *Die Benennungen und der Begriff des Leides J. Tauler* (Philologische Studien und Quellen, 38; 1967); J. A. Hernández, *Studien zum religiös-ethischen Wortschatz der deutschen Mystik: Die Bezeichnung und der Begriff des Eigentums bei Meister Eckhart und Johannes Tauler* (ibid. 105; 1984). J. M. Clark, *The Great German Mystics* (Oxford, 1949), pp. 36–54, with bibl. pp. 114–17. R. Kieckhefer, 'The role of Christ in Tauler's spirituality', *Downside Review*, 96 (1978), pp. 176–91; id., 'John Tauler', in P. Szarmach (ed.), *Introduction to the Medieval Mystics of Europe* (Albany, NY, 1984), pp. 259–72. Kaeppeli, 3 (1980), pp. 20 f. L. Gnädinger in *Dict. Sp.* 15 (1991), cols. 57–79, s.v.

taurobolium. A rite which seems to have originated in the sacrifice of a bull to the Great Mother goddess, which was later associated with the cult of Cybele; by the 4th cent. it involved a ceremony (described by *Prudentius, *Peristephanon*, 10. 1011–50), in which a 'high priest' (*summus sacerdos*) descended into a ditch and was bathed in the blood of a bull slain above him. Despite many references to the rite in inscriptions, it is hard to be clear about the nature and stages of its development, but the view that it influenced the Christian theology of *Baptism is unfounded.

R. Duthoy, *The Taurobolium: Its Evolution and Terminology* (Études préliminaires aux religions orientales dans l'Empire romain, 10; Leiden, 1969).

Tausen, Hans (1494–1561), Reformer, the 'Danish Luther'. A peasant's son, he became a *Hospitaller at Antvorskov. He then studied at Rostock, Copenhagen, Louvain, and (from 1523) at *Wittenberg, where he came under the influence of M. *Luther. The result was that on his return to *Denmark he was imprisoned for teaching novel doctrines. After his release he preached reform at Viborg, discarded his religious habit, and, on becoming chaplain to King Frederick I (1526), he married and proceeded to employ Danish in the Church services. In 1529, following his appointment by the King to preach at Copenhagen, he secured the support of the Danish National Assembly (*Herredag*) against J. Rönne, Bp. of Roskilde. A Confession of Faith in 43 articles was then drawn up by Tausen and his supporters. Three years later, when Rönne had turned the *Herredag* against him, Tausen was convicted of heresy, but as he saved the bishop from the enraged mob, his only punishment was a warning to modify his opinions. In the following years Tausen's Confession was replaced by the more moderate *Augsburg Confession, which became the basis of the Danish Reformation. In 1535 Tausen published a Danish translation of the Pentateuch and in 1537 he became Hebrew lecturer at Copenhagen University. He became cathedral preacher at Roskilde in 1538 and in 1542 was made Bp. of Ribe.

Selections of his Writings ed. H. F. Rördam (Copenhagen, 1870). L. Schmitt, SJ, *Johannes Tausen oder der dänische Luther* (Cologne, 1894). N. K. Andersen, *Confessio hafniensis: Den kobenhavnske Bekendelse af 1530* (thesis; Copenhagen, 1954). K. E. Bugge (ed.), *Tro og tale: Studier over Hans Tausens Postil* (ibid., 1963). F. Nielsen in *PRE* (3rd edn.), 19 (1907), pp. 459–62; M. S. Lausten in *Dansk Biografisk Leksikon*, 14 (1983), pp. 378–85, s.v., with bibl. [in Danish].

Taverner's Bible. The English translation of the Bible issued in 1539 by Richard Taverner (1505?–75). It was a revision of *Matthew's Bible of 1537. As Taverner was a good Greek scholar, but not a Hebraist, his work was far better in the NT than in the OT. The edition never became popular, as M. *Coverdale's officially sponsored '*Great Bible' (1539) appeared in the same year.

H. H. Hutson and H. R. Willoughby, 'The Ignored Taverner Bible of 1539', *The Crozer Quarterly*, 16 (1939), pp. 161–76. B. F. *Westcott, *A General View of the History of the English Bible* (1868), pp. 110–13, 269–71, with Taverner's variants collated with other edns. of the Bible, pp. 408–13. Darlow and Moule, ed. A. S. Herbert, 1 (1968), p. 24. On Taverner himself, S. M. Thorpe in S. T. Bindoff (ed.), *The History of Parliament: The House of Commons 1509–1558*, 3 (1982), pp. 424 f.; *BRUO, 1501–1540*, pp. 557 f.

tax-collector, tax-gatherer. Terms used in the modern versions of the Bible to replace *publican (q.v.).

Taylor, Alfred Edward (1869–1945), Anglican philosopher. Educated at New College, Oxford, he was successively Fellow of Merton College (1891–8), Lecturer in Greek and philosophy at Owens College, Manchester (1896–1903), professor of logic and metaphysics at McGill University, Montreal (1903–8), and professor of moral philosophy at St Andrews (1908–24) and at Edinburgh (1924–41). Though a commentator and philosophical man of letters rather than an original systematic thinker he became a considerable intellectual and religious power. His writings, most of which are packed with information and suggestive judgements, include *Plato: The Man and his Work* (1926), *The Faith of a Moralist* (2 vols., 1930; *Gifford Lectures at St Andrews for 1926–8), *Philosophical Studies* (1934; with studies of Aeschines, *Proclus, St *Thomas Aquinas, Francis *Bacon, and others); *The Christian Hope of Immortality* (1938), and *Does God Exist?* (1945). He also contributed the art. 'Theism' to J. *Hastings's *Encyclopedia of Religion and Ethics* (vol. 12, 1921) and that on 'The Vindication of Religion' to *Essays Catholic and Critical* (1926).

W. D. Ross, 'Alfred Edward Taylor, 1869–1945', *Proceedings of the British Academy*, 31 (1945), pp. 407–22, with bibl of his works, pp. 422–4. G. Galea, *Il pensiero morale di Alfredo Edoardo Taylor* (Sguardi su la filosofia contemporanea, 70; Turin, 1965). D. M. MacKinnon in *DNB, 1941–1950*, pp. 864 f., s.v.

Taylor, James Hudson (1832–1905), founder of the *China Inland Mission. He was a medical man who felt the call to be a missionary (1849) and sailed for China in 1853 under the auspices of the Chinese Evangelization Society. Despite many obstacles, among them ill-health which forced him to return in 1860, he carried on his work for China, and in 1865 founded the interdenominational China Inland Mission (q.v.). In 1866, accompanied by his family and a small staff, he went back to China, where he travelled extensively, heroically facing many difficulties, and conforming as much as possible to Chinese habits of life. A man of indomitable faith and great personal devotion, he carried the missionary work into the heart of the country and ensured its continuance by recruiting a large number of helpers. His books include *China: Its Spiritual Need and Claims* (1865), *A Retrospect* (1894), and *Union and Communion* (1894).

H. and G. Taylor (son and daughter-in-law), *Hudson Taylor in Early Years: The Growth of a Soul* (1911); idd., *Hudson Taylor and the China Inland Mission: The Growth of a Work of God* (1918); abridged edn., *Biography of James Hudson Taylor* (1965). Idd., *Hudson Taylor's Spiritual Secret* (1932). Exhaustive study, based on previously unpub. material, by A. J. Broomhall, *Hudson Taylor & China's Open Century* (7 vols., 1981–89). Popular account by R. Steer, *J. Hudson Taylor* (Singapore and Sevenoaks, Kent, 1990).

Taylor, Jeremy (1613–67), Anglican bishop and writer. He was a native of Cambridge and educated at Gonville and Caius College, of which he was elected a Fellow in 1633. Having been ordained in the same year he went to London to preach in the place of a friend; there he attracted the notice of Abp. W. *Laud, who nominated him to a fellowship at All Souls, Oxford, in 1635. Shortly afterwards he was appointed chaplain to *Charles I. Owing to his friendship with the Franciscan, Christopher *Davenport, he was suspected of Roman tendencies, of which he cleared himself in a 'Gunpowder Sermon' at Oxford in 1638. In the same year he was made rector of Uppingham, which he left in 1642 to become a chaplain in the Royalist army. After imprisonment for a short time he retired in 1645 to Wales, where he lived as chaplain to Lord Carbery at Golden Grove. Many of Taylor's best works were written here, among them *The Liberty of Prophesying* (1647), a plea for *toleration; the two devotional treatises, *The Rule and Exercise of Holy Living* (1650) and *The Rule and Exercise of Holy Dying* (1651); *The Golden Grove* (1655); and the *Unum Necessarium* (1655), a treatise on sin and repentance. In 1658 he went to Lisburn in NE Ireland as a lecturer, and in 1660 was appointed Bp. of Down and Connor and vice-chancellor of Dublin University, which he restored to order. In the same year he published his *Ductor Dubitantium*, a comprehensive manual of *moral theology. In 1661 he received the further see of Dromore. His episcopate was much troubled by the *Presbyterians, who refused submission and whom he treated with considerable harshness, as also the RCs, against whom he wrote his *Dissuasive from Popery* (1664), a violent invective against Roman Catholicism.

Taylor's fame today rests mainly on his devotional writings, esp. *Holy Living* and *Holy Dying*. They are characteristic expressions of Anglican spirituality in their balanced sobriety and their insistence on a well-ordered piety which stresses temperance and moderation in all things. They have become classics esp. for their beautiful prose, combining transparent lucidity with rhetorical vigour and powerful imagery, qualities which also made him one of the most celebrated preachers of his day. He was less felicitous as a theologian. The *Unum Necessarium* roused a violent controversy by reason of its alleged *Pelagianism and minimizing treatment of Original Sin. In his controversial writings he defended Episcopalianism against the Presbyterians (*Of the Sacred Order and Offices of Episcopacy*, 1642) and attacked the RC doctrine of *transubstantiation (*The Real Presence . . . proved against . . . Transubstantiation*, 1654), himself holding a view of the *Real Presence which comes near to the *Receptionist or *Virtualist doctrines. The work he accounted of most value was his *Ductor Dubitantium*, a compendium of casuistry based on both RC and Continental Protestant authors, and intended to guide the Anglican clergy in the practice of confession. Feast day in some Anglican Churches, 13 Aug.

Whole Works, ed. R. *Heber (15 vols., London, 1822), with Life by id., vol. 1, pp. ix–ccciii; rev. by C. P. Eden (10 vols., ibid., 1847–54), with Life by R. Heber, vol. 1, pp. ix–ccl. Crit. edn. of *Holy Living* and *Holy Dying* by P. G. Stanwood (2 vols., Oxford, 1989). Modern Lives by E. Gosse ('English Men of Letters', 1904), W. J. Brown ('English Theologians', 1925), and C. J. Stranks (London, 1952). T. Wood, *English Casuistical Divinity During the Seventeenth Century with Special Reference to Jeremy Taylor* (1952). F. R. Bolton, *The Caroline Tradition of the Church of Ireland with special reference to Bishop Jeremy Taylor* (1958). H. T. Hughes, *The Piety of Jeremy Taylor* (1960). F. L. Huntley, *Jeremy Taylor and the Great Rebellion: A Study of his Mind and Temper in Controversy* (Ann Arbor, Mich. [1970]). H. B. Porter, *Jeremy Taylor Liturgist (1613–1667)* (Alcuin Club Collections, 61; 1979). H. R. McAdoo, *The Eucharistic Theology of Jeremy Taylor*

Today (Norwich, 1988). The liturgy which Taylor composed for Anglican congregations under the Commonwealth is repr. by W. J. Grisbrooke, *Anglican Liturgies of the Seventeenth and Eighteenth Centuries* (Alcuin Club Collections, 40; 1958), pp. 183–200, with comm., pp. 19–36.

Taylor, John (1694–1761), Dissenting divine and Hebrew scholar. After studying at the academy at Whitehaven for the training of Presbyterian and Congregational ministers, he was ordained by dissenting ministers and worked at *Norwich, where he founded the Octagon Chapel (1754). In 1757 he was appointed divinity tutor at Warrington Academy. His greatest work of scholarship was his *Hebrew Concordance*, pub. by subscription in 1754–7. Based on that of J. Buxtorf, it was designed to serve also the purpose of a lexicon, and marked an important advance in the study of Hebrew roots. In matters of theology, Taylor tended increasingly towards an *Arian view of the Person of Christ and to a denial of the fact of Original Sin. His influential *Scripture Doctrine of Original Sin* (1740), which had a wide circulation in England, Scotland, and America, did much by undermining the foundations of the *Calvinistic system to prepare the way for the *Unitarian Movement in American Congregationalism.

A. Gordon in *DNB* 55 (1898), pp. 439 f., with refs.

Teaching of the Twelve Apostles, The. See DIDACHE.

team ministry. In the C of E since 1968, where a pastoral scheme has been made, the cure of souls in the area of a benefice or plurality may be shared by a team consisting of the incumbent of the benefice, known as the team rector, and one or more other ministers, with the title of vicar and the status of an incumbent of a benefice. Other lay or ordained ministers may share in the parochial care. The team rector may, depending on the scheme, be appointed to a freehold or for a term of years, while team vicars are always appointed for a term of years. The provisions are now consolidated in the Pastoral Measure 1983.

Te Deum. A Latin hymn to the Father and Son, in rhythmical prose. Since the 9th cent. tradition has assigned its composition to Sts *Ambrose and *Augustine at the latter's baptism, but this account of its authorship is almost universally rejected by modern scholars.

On the basis of an attribution to Bishop 'Nicet' in some MSS, Dom G. *Morin and A. E. Burn ascribed it to *Niceta of Remesiana; more recently E. Kähler has followed P. Cagin in emphasizing its liturgical character and has argued that it derives from the text of a *Paschal Vigil Service. Verses 22 ff. are suffrages, appended at an early date to the original. Its use in the offices is already referred to in the Rules of St *Caesarius of Arles and of St *Benedict, and in the RC Church it has remained an integral part of *Mattins (now of the *Office of Readings), at least on greater festivals. The BCP prescribed its use daily at Mattins, with the *Benedicite as an alternative. In the ASB and other modern Anglican liturgies its use at Morning Prayer is retained, at least on some occasions, in some cases without the concluding verses. The central section is included in some modern Anglican *burial services. It has often been set to music for use on occasions of thanksgiving, e.g. G. F. *Handel's 'Dettingen Te Deum'.

J. *Wordsworth, The 'Te Deum' (1902). A. E. Burn, The Hymn Te Deum and its Author (1926). E. Kähler, Studien zum Te Deum und zur Geschichte des 24. Psalms in der alten Kirche (Göttingen, 1958). P. Cagin, OSB, L'Euchologie latine, 1: Te Deum ou Illatio? Contribution à l'histoire de l'euchologie latine à propos des origines du Te Deum (Solesmes, 1906). G. Morin, OSB, 'Nouvelles recherches sur l'auteur du Te Deum', R. Bén. 11 (1894), pp. 49–77; id., 'Notes additionnelles à l'étude sur l'auteur du Te Deum', ibid. 337–45; id.; 'Le Te Deum, type anonyme d'anaphore latine préhistorique?', ibid. 24 (1907), pp. 180–223. M. Huglo in NCE 13 (1967), pp. 954 f., s.v.

Te Igitur (Lat., 'Thee, therefore'), the first words of the prayer which was long regarded as the opening section of the *Canon of the Roman Mass, and hence also the name for the first section of the canon. It asks God to accept and bless the Eucharistic offerings, and offers intercession for the whole Church, including the Pope, the Diocesan Bishop (these two mentioned by name), and all the faithful. The representation of the Crucifixion immediately preceding it in *Missals was apparently in origin a pictorial elaboration of the initial T of Te igitur.

A. Ebner, Quellen und Forschungen zur Geschichte und Kunstgeschichte des Missale Romanum im Mittelalter (1896), pp. 443–9; V. Leroquais, Les Sacramentaires et les missels manuscrits des bibliothèques publiques de France (4 vols., 1924), esp. vol. 1, pp. xxxiii–xxxvii, with refs. Jungmann (1958 edn.), 2, pp. 185–90; Eng. tr., 2 (1955), pp. 147–52.

Teilhard de Chardin, Pierre (1881–1955), French theologian and scientist. Born near Clermont in central France, he entered the *Jesuit novitiate at Aix-en-Provence in 1899, and was ordained priest in 1911. During this long training he studied theology but was also strongly attracted to the natural sciences, especially geology and palaeontology. After service in the First World War, he was able to devote himself to his scientific studies. For many years he worked in China and gained a notable reputation as a palaeontologist. His last years were spent in the USA. At the time of his death he had published only scientific papers, for he had not been able to obtain permission for the publication of his religious and theological works. These appeared from 1955 onward and at once made a powerful impression as a new synthesis of science and religion. Le Phénomène humain (1955; Eng. tr., The Phenomenon of Man, 1959) is probably his best-known work and contains the essence of his ideas. The universe is seen as an evolutionary process in which the movement is always towards systems of greater complexity. Correlated with this movement towards complexity is the movement towards higher levels of consciousness. The whole process has included several critical moments or thresholds at which leaps to new levels have been made. Such thresholds were the emergence of life on earth and then the emergence of rational self-consciousness in man. This latter emergence has special significance, since it means that evolution no longer takes place in accordance with the laws of nature only, but that man now takes part in directing it. The whole process moves towards a fulfilment in which all things will be gathered up in God. Teilhard's philosophical theology is reflected in his devotional writings, notably Le Milieu divin (1957; Eng. tr., 1960). For him, matter has a sacramental character, and the whole universe is in process of 'Christification' as a consequence of the Incarnation. Though he has been criticized for the philosophical weaknesses of his work and for an uncritical optimism, Teilhard's thought is a remarkable effort to relate the Christian tradition to the contemporary scientific understanding of nature.

Collected edn. of his works, 13 vols., Paris, 1955–76. Eng. tr. of other individual works incl. Letters from a Traveller (1962); The Future of Man (1964), and Hymn of the Universe (1965). The standard biog. is C. Cuénot, Pierre Teilhard de Chardin: Les grands étapes de son évolution (1958; Eng. tr., 1965). Other studies incl. H. de *Lubac, SJ, La Pensée religieuse du Père Pierre Teilhard de Chardin (1962; Eng. tr., 1967); id., La Prière du Père Teilhard de Chardin (1964; Eng. tr., 1965); R. W. Kropf, Teilhard, Scripture, and Revelation: A Study of Teilhard de Chardin's Reinterpretation of Pauline Themes [1980]; T. M. King, Teilhard's Mysticism of Knowing (New York, 1981); J. A. Lyons, The Cosmic Christ in Origen and Teilhard de Chardin (Oxford Theological Monographs, 1982); A. Hunt Overzee, The Body Divine: The Symbol of the Body in the Works of Teilhard de Chardin and Rāmānuga (Cambridge, 1992). J. E. Jarque, Bibliographie générale des œuvres et articles sur Pierre Teilhard de Chardin parus jusqu'à fin décembre 1969 (Fribourg, 1970). Works on Teilhard de Chardin have also been listed annually since 1956 in the Archivum Historicum Societatis Iesu. Polgár, 3 (1990), pp. 359–553. P. Noir, SJ, in Dict. Sp. 15 (1991), cols. 115–26, s.v.

Teilo, St (6th cent.), patron saint and Bp. of *Llandaff. It is difficult to deduce from the mass of mutually conflicting later traditions anything certain about his life. He is credited with having been consecrated bishop at *Jerusalem while on a pilgrimage to Palestine and (a less unlikely tradition) with having visited St *Samson at Dol. He is also said to have succeeded St *Dubricius in the see of Llandaff when the latter retired to Bardsey in 495. His reputation for piety and pastoral devotion was such that three churches laid claim to possess his bones. The dispute was settled (it is said) when two additional identical corpses were provided supernaturally. Feast day, 9 Feb.

An account of his life is incl. in the Liber Landavensis (first pub. by W. J. Rees for the Welsh MSS Society, 1840, pp. 92–111; re-ed. by I. G. Evans from the Gwysaney MS, 1893, pp. 97–117). Lat. text also pub. with crit. notes by J. Loth, 'La Vie de saint Teliau d'après le livre de Llandaf', Annales de Bretagne, 9 (1893), pp. 81–5, 277–86, 438–46, and 10 (1894), pp. 66–77. G. H. Doble, Saint Teilo ('Welsh Saints', 3; Lampeter, 1942), repr. in his Lives of the Welsh Saints, ed. D. S. Evans (Cardiff, 1971), pp. 162–206. C. [N. L.] Brooke in N. K. Chadwick and others, Studies in the Early British Church (Cambridge, 1958), esp. pp. 214 f., 219 f., 224–6, and 236–8.

teinds. The Scottish equivalent of *tithes. Historically, teinds were that proportion of the produce of lands in the parish available for the support of the clergy. The stipend payable to the parish minister formed a burden on the teinds and generally fluctuated from year to year, depending on the price of victual. That system of payment of stipend came to an end with the enactment of the Church of Scotland (Property and Endowments) Act 1925 in terms of which stipend was standardized, i.e. the amounts due became fixed annual payments known as standard charges and were secured as real burdens on the lands involved. The landowner has the option (and on a sale of the relevant property the obligation) to redeem such charges; most have in fact been redeemed.

Telemachus, St. Acc. to *Theodoret (*HE* 5. 26), Telemachus was an E. monk who, seeking to put an end to the gladiatorial shows at Rome, entered the arena in person on 1 Jan. 391 to separate the combatants, and was killed by the spectators. The act is said to have led the Emp. Honorius to abolish the games. In the *Hieronymian Martyrology he is called 'Almachius'. Feast day, 1 Jan.

The sole sources are Theodoret, *HE* 5. 26, and a note in the Hieronymianum. H. *Delehaye, SJ, 'Saint Almachius ou Télémaque', *Anal. Boll.* 33 (1914), pp. 421–8. G. *Morin, 'Le Dragon du Forum romain, sa légende et son histoire', *R. Bén.* 31 (1919), pp. 321–6. J. P. Kirsch in *DHGE* 2 (1914), cols. 630 f., s.v. 'Almachius', with further bibl. St Telemachus is also the subject of a poem by C. G. *Rossetti.

teleology (Gk. τέλος, 'end'). The word, probably coined by C. *Wolff in 1728, denotes the science of ends or final causes. It is esp. applied to the doctrine, inherent in every organic and non-mechanistic interpretation of the universe, that it embodies design and purpose. This doctrine, implicit in much classical philosophy, was taken over by Christian theology and forms the basis of the modern argument from design (also known in the 18th cent. as the 'physico-theological argument' and by recent philosophers as the 'teleological argument') for the existence of God. In its classic form (e.g., in W. *Paley's *Evidences*), it sets out from the observation that every biological species is apparently designed to serve its own needs, and argues therefrom to an intelligent Creator. Under the influence of C. *Darwin, E. *Haeckel, and the general trend of 19th-cent. science, the traditional form of the argument has been abandoned. While teleological arguments for the existence of God are no longer fashionable among philosophers, there has in recent times been a renewal of interest in teleological explanations in science, after a long period when only mechanistic explanations were tolerated.

For modern presentations of the teleological argument see F. R. Tennant, *Philosophical Theology* (2 vols., Cambridge, 1928–30); A. R. Peacocke, *Creation and the World of Science* (Bampton Lectures, 1978; Oxford, 1979); T. F. Torrance, *Divine and Contingent Order* (Oxford, 1981). A. Woodfield, *Teleology* (Cambridge, 1976).

Telesio, Bernardino (1509–88), Italian humanist. A native of Cosenza, nr. Naples, he studied philosophy, mathematics, and natural science at Padua and Rome, becoming a strong critic of the *Aristotelian philosophy. At Rome he enjoyed for a while the patronage of *Paul IV, who offered him the archbishopric of Cosenza. In 1566 he returned to Naples and founded a scientific society ('Academia Telesiana'). His doctrines, much influenced by the early Greek nature philosophers (esp. Parmenides), were based on an extreme empiricism; but he gradually built up a speculative system in which the Aristotelian doctrine of matter and form was replaced by one of matter and force. His principal treatise was *De Rerum Natura iuxta Propria Principia* (pt. 1, Rome, 1565; pt. 2, Naples, 1586); others were *De Somno, De Cometis et Lacteo Circulo,* and *De Iride* (ed. together, A. Persius, Venice, 1590). Among his disciples were T. *Campanella and G. *Bruno (qq.v.). In 1600 most of his writings were placed on the *Index.

Modern edn. of *De Rerum Natura* by V. Spampanato (vol. 1, Modena, 1910; vol. 2, Genoa, 1913; vol. 3, Rome, 1923); also ed. L. de Franco (vols. 1 and 2, Cosenza, 1965–74; vol. 3, Florence, 1976); *Varii de naturalibus rebus libelli,* ed. id. (Florence, 1981). Studies by F. Fiorentino (2 vols., Florence, 1872–4), E. Troilo (Modena, 1910; 2nd edn., Rome, 1924), G. *Gentile (Bari, 1911; 2nd edn., 1923), N. C. Van Deusen (New York, 1932), and G. Soleri (Brescia, 1944). N. Abbagnano, *Bernardino Telesio e la filosofia del rinascimento* (1941). E. Zavattari, *La visione della vita nel rinascimento e Bernardino Telesio* (1923). N. Van Deusen, 'The Place of Telesio in the History of Philosophy', *Philosophical Review*, 44 (1935), pp. 417–34. B. M. Bonansea, OFM, in P. Edwards (ed.), *Encyclopedia of Philosophy,* 8 (1967), pp. 92 f., s.v.

Telesphorus (d. *c.*137), Bp. of Rome from *c.*127. St *Irenaeus (ap. Eusebius, *HE* 5. 24. 14) mentions that he always observed Easter on Sundays, as against the *Quartodeciman practice, and that he suffered death by martyrdom (*Haer.* 3. 3. 3). He is thus the only 2nd-cent. Pope whose martyrdom is well attested. Feast day, in the E., 22 Feb.; in the W., 2 or 5 Jan., suppressed in 1969.

Jaffé, 1, p. 6. The principal authority is *LP* (Duchesne), 1, pp. 129 f. J. N. D. Kelly, *Oxford Dictionary of Popes* (1986), p. 9.

Tell el-Amarna Tablets. A collection of ancient inscribed clay tablets, discovered in 1887 at Tell el-Amarna, the site of the former royal city of Akhenaton, Egyptian ruler of the 14th cent. BC. They are written in *cuneiform script, mostly in Akkadian, and consist chiefly of letters, many of them from Canaanite kings to their Egyptian suzerain, complaining of the attacks on Palestine of invading forces from the north and the east. Among the letters are some from an early ruler of Urusalim (i.e. *Jerusalem) named Abdi-Ḫiba.

The standard edn. of the Tablets, in transliteration, is that of J. A. Knudtzon, *Die El-Amarna Tafeln* (Vorderasiatische Bibliothek, 2; 1908–15), incl. Ger. tr.; suppl. by A. F. Rainey, *El Amarna Tablets 359–379* (Alter Orient und Altes Testament, 8; 1970), with Eng. tr. Eng. tr., with introd., by W. L. Moran, *The Amarna Letters* (Baltimore and London [1992]). Convenient Eng. tr. of selections in J. B. Pritchard (ed.), *Ancient Near Eastern Texts relating to the Old Testament* (2nd edn., 1955), pp. 483–90. E. F. Campbell, *The Chronology of the Amarna Letters* (Baltimore, 1964). On the site, T. E. Peet and C. J. Woolley, *The City of Akhenaten,* 1 (Egyptian Exploration Society, 1923), 2 (ibid., 1933) and 3 (in 2 parts, ibid., 1951). W. F. Albright in *C. Anc. H.* (3rd edn.), 2, ch. 20 [no. 51 in fascicle edn. (1966), pp. 3–23], with full bibl.

temperance (Lat. *temperantia,* used by Cicero to render *Plato's σωφροσύνη), restraint of the appetites and passions in accordance with reason. One of the four *cardinal virtues, and indeed, acc. to the moralists, the most fundamental of them as that on which the other three depend, it was inculcated by the Gk. philosophers, esp. Plato and the *Stoics. In the NT, the Gk. noun σωφροσύνη, translated in the AV by 'soberness' or 'sobriety', occurs three times (Acts 26: 25, 1 Tim. 2: 9 and 15), in each case as an adjunct to godliness. The adjective σώφρων, translated indiscriminately as 'sober', 'temperate', or 'discreet', is listed among the attributes proper to a bishop (1 Tim. 3: 2 and Tit. 1: 8), to old men (Tit. 2: 2) and aged women (Tit. 2: 5). (Elsewhere in the NT, the AV 'temperance' is a rendering of ἐγκράτεια, 'self-control'.)

For the Christian, temperance in its physical aspects is linked with the need for self-control of the body, regarded as a 'temple of the Holy Spirit'. The Gk. teaching influenced *Origen and the *Cappadocian Fathers, while the conception was developed, under the influence of Cicero, esp. by St *Ambrose and St *Augustine; it was further elaborated by St *Thomas Aquinas. Moral theologians commonly subdivide it into several other virtues, e.g. abstinence, chastity, and modesty.

The 'temperance societies', founded to foster abstinence from alcohol, date from the 19th cent. Though the first American temperance society, that of Moreau and Northumberland, was founded at Saratoga, NY, in 1808, the formation of a nationwide movement was largely due to the work of L. *Beecher. The American Society for the Promotion of Temperance was established at Boston in 1829. In an attempt to co-ordinate the numerous local societies that had grown up, in 1833 it held a convention which created the United States Temperance Union, in 1836 renamed the American Temperance Union (to accommodate the Canadian societies). There were divisions as to whether the aim should be temperance or total abstinence, but the latter view was accepted. In the middle of the 19th cent. several states followed Maine in prohibiting the manufacture or sale of intoxicating liquor. This legislation was soon either declared unconstitutional or repealed, but pressure continued, and in 1919 the Eighteenth Amendment to the Constitution, forbidding the manufacture, sale, or transportation of intoxicating liquor throughout the USA was accepted by Congress. Intensely unpopular, it was repealed in 1933. The failure of the national experiment in prohibition tended to discredit the (mainly Protestant) leaders of the temperance societies. More recently the temperance societies (including the International Temperance Society founded in 1947) have concerned themselves broadly with problems associated with alcohol, tobacco, and drugs.

Similar temperance societies were established in Britain, but their influence was never as great as those in America. The first British society, the Ulster Temperance Society, was formed in 1829 and soon had branches in Lancashire and Yorkshire. The nucleus of the Church of England Temperance Society dates from 1862, though it adopted this title only when it amalgamated with a regional diocesan society in 1873. It not only encouraged its supporters to take the pledge of total abstinence (sometimes for a limited period) or to a general agreement to be abstemious with regard to alcohol, but it also sought to provide alternatives to the public houses by establishing coffee taverns and engaged in other preventative work. In 1967 it joined with the National Police Court Mission (concerned esp. with the effects of alcohol on prisoners), and the Church of England Council for Social Aid was formed; it now deals with a wide range of problems. Elsewhere in Europe there have been similar manifestations of the temperance movement.

On the virtue of temperance, A. Michel in *DTC* 15 (pt. 1; 1946), cols. 94–9, s.v. On the temperance movements, D. Burns, *Temperance History: A Consecutive Narrative of the Rise, Development, and Extension, of the Temperance Reform. 1826–1880* (2 vols. in 4 parts [1889–91]); E. H. Cherrington, *The Evolution of Prohibition in the United States of America* (Westerville, Oh. [1920]); P. E. Prestwich, *Drink and the Politics of Social Reform: Antialcoholism in France since 1870* (Palo Alto, Calif., 1988). H. D. Langley in *NCE* 13 (1967), pp. 987–92, s.v. 'Temperance Movements'.

Templars (or **Knights Templar**). The 'Poor Knights of Christ and of the Temple of Solomon', one of the two chief Military Orders of medieval Christendom, with headquarters successively in *Jerusalem, Acre, and *Cyprus. The original nucleus consisted of Hugh de Payens, a knight of Champagne, and eight companions, who in *c.*1119 bound themselves by a solemn vow to protect pilgrims from bandits on the public roads of the Holy Land. They were given quarters at the site of Solomon's *Temple. At first they lived on alms, but in 1127 Hugh journeyed to the W. to obtain ecclesiastical approbation and recruits, and their fortunes (then perhaps at a low ebb) quickly improved. At the Council of Troyes (1129) approval was given to the Rule of the Order, said to have been drawn up by St *Bernard, who dedicated to Hugh his treatise 'De laude novae militiae'. The Order contained four ranks of 'knights', 'serjeants', 'squires' and 'chaplains'.

The Templars soon rose in influence and wealth, acquiring property and setting up their organization in most parts of Christendom. The new Order gained the support of the Papacy which, in a series of bulls, granted it extensive privileges, the most important being contained in 'Omne Datum Optimum' (1139). In the 12th-cent. *Crusader states, the professional forces of the Templars and *Hospitallers played an increasingly important part in campaigns, and from the late 1130s onwards various castles came into the Templars' hands. The Grand Master of the Temple was partly responsible for the disaster which overtook the Crusaders in 1187, but then and later the knights of the Order fought bravely. The Order became still more important in the 13th cent., providing an even higher proportion of troops and acquiring even more castles; in 1217–18 they built Castle Pilgrim, and in 1240–3 they rebuilt Safed, the largest Christian fortress in the East, bought by the Templars in 1168. However, the Military Orders increasingly acted independently of the rulers, and they were sometimes at odds with each other. At the fall of Acre (1291) the Templars fought fiercely and their Grand Master was killed.

Meanwhile great wealth had been accumulated by the Templars; this was deposited in their 'temples' in Paris and London, and the integrity and credit of the Order led it to be much trusted as a banking house. The same wealth led to its early ruin after the loss of Acre. Already the Council of *Lyons (1274) had witnessed an attempt to end the rivalry of the Templars and Hospitallers by incorporating them into a single Order; but even in 1306 the last Grand Master, James de Molay, opposed such a scheme. In 1303, Hugh de Pairaud, the Visitor of the Templars in France, was among those who supported Philip the Fair, the King of France, against Pope *Boniface VIII, but the King soon found the temptation of the Order's great wealth too strong. Aided by a renegade Templar, he brought charges of sodomy, blasphemy, and heresy against the Order, and enlisted the reluctant aid of Pope *Clement V. Both the King and the *Inquisition used torture freely to obtain confessions; many knights died under torture or at the stake. Philip IV, in his later years increasingly preoccupied by a rather morbid piety, may have become convinced of the Templars' guilt, as well as seeking to gain material profit from the downfall. Clement V finally suppressed the Order at the Council of *Vienne in 1312;

James de Molay was burnt in Paris in 1314, and the Order's possessions (except those in Spain and Portugal) were given to the Hospitallers. The innocence of the Templars, vigorously championed by *Dante, has been a matter of prolonged controversy, but is now generally admitted.

The headquarters of the English branch of the Order was for a long time in London, S. of the Strand (now the Inner and Middle Temple). The Temple Church, dating from 1185, was, in common with some other churches of the Templars, a round structure on the model of the Church of the *Holy Sepulchre in Jerusalem. A nave (or choir) was added in 1240.

The standard edn. of the Rule is that of H. de Curzon (Société de l'Histoire de France, 1886), to be used in conjunction with G. Schnürer, *Die ursprüngliche Templerregel* (Studien und Darstellungen aus dem Gebiete der Geschichte. Im Auftrage der Görres-Gesellschaft und in Verbindung mit der Redaktion des Historischen Jahrbuches, 3, Hefte 1–2; 1903). Eng. tr. of the Rule, with introd., by J. M. Upton-Ward (Woodbridge, Suffolk [1992]). St Bernard's 'De laude novae militiae' is pr. in his *Opera*, 3, ed. J. Leclercq, OSB, and H. M. Rochais, OSB (Rome, 1963), pp. 207–39; Eng. tr. by C. Greenia, OCSO, in St Bernard's *Works*, 7 (Cistercian Fathers Series, 19; Kalamazoo, Mich., 1977), pp. 125–67, with introd. by R. J. Z. Werblowsky, pp. 115–23. The Marquis d'Albon began to make a general collection of Templar docs., part of which he pub. as *Cartulaire général de l'Ordre du Temple, 1119?–1150* (1913; fasc. complémentaire, 1922), but the bulk of the material is in the Bibliothèque Nationale in Paris; E. G. Léonard, *Introduction au cartulaire manuscrit du Temple (1150–1317) constitué par le marquis d'Albon* (1930) is a detailed guide. R. Röhricht (ed.), *Regesta Regni Hierosolymitani* (2 vols., Innsbruck, 1893–1904) contains summaries of docs. and their sources in the Latin Kingdom of Jerusalem, incl. those concerning the Templars. Privileges and bulls ed. R. Hiestand, *Papsturkunden für Templer und Johanniter* (Abh. (Gött.), Dritte Folge, 77 and 135; 1972–84). The most important chronicler of the Templars' activities in the East is *William of Tyre (q.v.), while the rebuilding of Safed is described in a text ed. by R. B. C. Huygens in *Studi medievali*, 3rd ser. 6 (1965), pp. 355–87. There is a wide range of material for the Templars' western lands, of which good examples are the inquest of 1185 in England, ed. B. A. Lees, *Records of the Templars in England in the Twelfth Century* (1935), and P. Gérard and É. Magnou (eds.), *Cartulaires des Templiers de Douzens* (Collection de documents inédits sur l'histoire de France, sér. in 8°, 3; 1965). A good selection of docs. on the trial can be found, with Fr. tr., in G. Lizerand (ed.), *Le Dossier de l'Affaire des Templiers* (Les classiques de l'histoire de France au moyen âge, 1923), but the most substantial collections are contained in [J.] Michelet (ed.), *Procès des Templiers* (Collection de documents inédits sur l'histoire de France, 1st ser., Histoire politique, 2 vols., 1841–51), H. Finke, *Papsttum und Untergang des Templerordens* (Vorreformationsgeschichtliche Forschungen, 4–5; 1907), and K. Schottmüller, *Der Untergang des Templer-Ordens*, 2 (1887). The use of these materials is facilitated by the tables in J. Gmelin, *Schuld oder Unschuld des Templerordens* (Stuttgart, 1893). These materials are concerned largely, though not exclusively, with the trial in France. Sources for other countries incl. A. Gilmour-Bryson, *The Trial of the Templars in the Papal State and the Abruzzi* (ST 303; 1982).

Secondary lit. is extensive, but of variable quality and often tendentious. General histories incl. H. Prutz, *Die Geistlichen Ritterorder: Ihre Stellung zur kirchlichen, politischen, gesellschaftlichen und wirtschaftlichen Entwicklung des Mittelalters* (1908); G. A. Campbell, *The Knights Templars* (1937); M. Melville, *La Vie des Templiers* (1951); A. Demurger, *Vie et mort de l'Ordre du Temple, 1118–1314* [1985]; and M. [C.] Barber, *The New Knighthood: A History of the Order of the Temple* (Cambridge, 1994). Various arts.

in J. Fleckenstein and M. Hellmann (eds.), *Die Geistlichen Ritterorden Europas* (Vorträge und Forschungen, 26; Sigmaringen, 1980). Particular aspects are covered by L. Delisle, *Mémoire sur les opérations financières des Templiers* (Mémoires de l'Institut National de France, Académie des Inscriptions et Belles-Lettres, 33, pt. 2; 1889); J. Piquet, *Des Banquiers au moyen âge: Les Templiers* (1939); É. Lambert, *L'Architecture des Templiers* (1955); and M. L. Bulst-Thiele, *Sacrae Domus Militiae Templi Hierosolymitani Magistri: Untersuchungen zur Geschichte des Templerordens 1118/9–1314* (Abh. (Gött.), Dritte Folge, 86; 1974). Regional studies incl. V. Carrière, *Histoire et cartulaire des Templiers de Provins* (1919); T. W. Parker, *The Knights Templars in England* (Tucson, Ariz., 1963); and A. J. Forey, *The Templars in the Corona de Aragón* (University of Durham Publications; London, 1973). For the trial, H. Prutz, *Entwicklung und Untergang des Tempelherrenordens* (1888), incl. docs.; H. C. Lea, *A History of the Inquisition of the Middle Ages*, 3 (New York, 1887; London, 1888), pp. 238–334; H. Finke, op. cit., 1; G. Lizerand, *Clément V et Philippe IV le Bel* (1910), also with docs.; and M. [C.] Barber, *The Trial of the Templars* (Cambridge, 1978). For the controversies over the Order, see P. [D.] Partner, *The Murdered Magicians: The Templars and their Myth* (Oxford, 1982). Works up to 1965 are listed in M. Dessubré, *Bibliographie de l'Ordre des Templiers* (Bibliothèque des Initiations Modernes, 5; 1928) and H. Neu, *Bibliographie des Templer-Ordens 1927–1965* (Bonn [1965]).

Temple, the. Although tradition ascribes the idea of a national Israelite shrine at *Jerusalem to *David (2 Sam. 7), the first Temple dates from the reign of *Solomon (c.970–c.930). The building of this 'house of God' is described in 1 Kgs. 5–8. It became the central sanctuary of the nation, and here alone, acc. to the legislation of Deuteronomy, could sacrificial worship be offered. It was destroyed by the Babylonians c.586 BC; its rebuilding was envisaged in Ezekiel (chs. 40–8) and effectively undertaken at the instigation of *Haggai and *Zechariah c.520. This structure (the 'Second Temple') suffered desecration at the hands of *Antiochus Epiphanes in 167 BC, but in 164 BC it was rededicated under *Judas Maccabaeus. The Temple buildings were reconstructed and richly adorned by *Herod the Great, his chief motive being a bid for popular approval. This was the Temple standing in Christ's time, the scene of the Cleansing, and of His teaching during the days before the Betrayal. In Roman times the custody of the Temple was left in the hands of the *High Priest, assisted by priests officiating by rota. With the destruction of Jerusalem by the Romans in AD 70 the Temple worship ceased. The site, one of the most sacred in *Islam, is now occupied by two mosques. See also JERUSALEM; DOME OF THE ROCK.

All attempted reconstructions of the Temple are necessarily highly conjectural. The more important reliable modern discussions incl. K. Möhlenbrink, *Der Tempel Salomos: Eine Untersuchung seiner Stellung in der Sakralarchitektur des alten Orients* (Beiträge zur Wissenschaft vom Alten und Neuen Testament, Folge 4, 7; 1932); J. Parrot, *Le Temple de Jérusalem* (Cahiers d'Archéologie Biblique, 5; 1954; Eng. tr., 1957); and T. A. Busink, *Der Tempel von Jerusalem von Salomo bis Herodes: Eine archäologisch-historische Studie unter Berücksichtigung des Westsemitischen Tempelbaus* (2 vols., Leiden, 1970–80). M. Barker, *The Gate of Heaven: The History and Symbolism of the Temple in Jerusalem* (1991 [popular in style]). E. *Schürer, *The History of the Jewish People in the Age of Jesus Christ*, rev. Eng. tr. by G. Vermes and others (3 vols. in 4, Edinburgh, 1973–87), esp. 1, pp. 162 f., 237–313; see also index, 3, pt. 2, pp. 999 f. R. E. Clements, *God and Temple* (Oxford, 1965). Y. Yadin and others in *Encyclopaedia*

Judaica, 15 (Jerusalem, 1972), cols. 942–88; C. Meyers in *Anchor Bible Dictionary*, 6 (1992), pp. 350–69, s.v. 'Temple, Jerusalem'.

Temple, Frederick (1821–1902), Abp. of *Canterbury. Born at Santa Maura in the Ionian Islands, he was educated at Blundell's School, Tiverton, and at Balliol College, Oxford, where B. *Jowett, A. C. *Tait, and W. G. *Ward were among his tutors. He was much interested in the *Tractarian Movement, but never attached himself to it; and, gradually welcoming liberal principles, he condemned the attempted censure of both W. G. Ward and R. D. *Hampden. In 1846 he was ordained deacon and in 1847 priest, both by S. *Wilberforce. He continued to teach for a time at Balliol, where he became an advocate of educational reform. From 1848 to 1857 he worked for the Committee of the Council of Education before he succeeded A. C. *Tait as Headmaster of Rugby (1857–69). He did much to enhance the prestige of the school, as well as becoming increasingly prominent in the education movement. In 1860 he wrote on 'The Education of the World' for *Essays and Reviews* (q.v.). This paper, though wholly inoffensive from the standpoint of orthodoxy, brought him much obloquy through the extremism of some of his fellow-contributors. Hence, when in 1869 he was offered the bishopric of *Exeter, the nomination was received with fierce opposition, but he was consecrated on 21 Dec. 1869 and, characteristically, only consented to withdraw his essay from future editions of *Essays and Reviews* after the event. In his diocese he did much to foster Church Schools and was a leading figure in the *temperance movement. He was also influential in the establishment of the diocese of *Truro. In 1885 he was translated to London; here he played an important part in the *Lincoln Judgement (1890). In his later years he became increasingly involved in conflict with the High Church party. In 1897 he was translated to *Canterbury. His primacy was marked by the issue in 1897 of the 'Responsio' of the Abps. of Canterbury and York to '*Apostolicae Curae', the *Lambeth Conference of 1897, and the issue of the *Lambeth Opinions (q.v.) of 1899–1900. He was responsible for the restoration of the Old Palace at Canterbury as a residence for the Archbishop. His writings include an impressive set of *Bampton Lectures on *The Relations between Religion and Science* (1884) and several vols. of sermons.

M. Barber, *Index to the Letters and Papers of Frederick Temple . . . in Lambeth Palace Library* (1975). E. G. Sandford (ed.), *Memoirs of Archbishop Temple by Seven Friends* (2 vols., 1906); last section (Editor's Supplement), with extracts from other parts, repr. as E. G. Sandford, *Frederick Temple: An Appreciation* (1907). P. [B.] Hinchliff, *Frederick Temple, Archbishop of Canterbury: A Life* (Oxford, 1998). H. M. Spooner in *DNB, 1901–1911*, pp. 488–93.

Temple, William (1881–1944), Abp. of *Canterbury. The second son of F. *Temple, he was successively Exhibitioner of Balliol College (1900), Fellow of Queen's College, Oxford (1904), Headmaster of Repton (1910), Rector of St James's, Piccadilly (1914), Canon of Westminster (1919), Bp. of Manchester (1921), Abp. of *York (1929), and Abp. of Canterbury (1942). While still a layman, he formed lasting interests in educational and social work, esp. through the Workers' Educational Association and the *Student Christian Movement. He contributed to *Foundations* (1912; q.v.) and was among the leaders of the 'Life and Liberty Movement', calling for a degree of autonomy for the C of E which was substantially granted by the *Enabling Act (1919). In 1923 he became a member (from 1925, Chairman) of the Archbishops' Commission which in 1938 produced the report on *Doctrine in the Church of England*. As Abp. of York (1929–42) he became increasingly prominent in national life, esp. through his lively concern with social, economic, and international questions, though remaining independent of organized parties, both political and religious. In 1924 he was the main inspiration behind the Conference on Politics, Economics, and Citizenship (COPEC), a seminal discussion of contemporary social needs which was resumed at the *Malvern Conference, over which he presided in 1941. He also gave whole-hearted support to the *Faith and Order and *Life and Work Movements and to the *Ecumenical Movement generally. His short period as Abp. of Canterbury (23 Apr. 1942–26 Oct. 1944) was overshadowed by the War of 1939–45 and by ill-health, but it was remarkable, *inter alia*, for his participation, with Card. A. *Hinsley and the Moderator of the Free Church Council, in the issue of a statement of principles which should guide a post-war settlement, and for his public speeches and broadcasts.

Temple was trained as a philosopher under E. *Caird, and the Neo-*Hegelian position from which he set out coloured all his later thinking, though he gradually developed into an independent thinker and philosopher of some significance. His principal works include *Mens Creatrix* (1917), *Christus Veritas* (1924), and *Nature, Man and God* (*Gifford Lectures for 1932–3 and 1933–4; 1934), *Readings in St John's Gospel* (1939; 2nd ser., 1940; devotional studies), and *Christianity and Social Order* (Penguin Special; 1942). Of his other published works, many originated as lectures or addresses.

Life by F. A. Iremonger (London, 1948). *Some Lambeth Letters, 1942–1944* (selected from W. Temple's correspondence), ed. F. S. Temple (1963). O. C. Thomas, *William Temple's Philosophy of Religion* (1961); R. Craig, *Social Concern in the Thought of William Temple* (1963); J. D. Carmichael and H. S. Goodwin, *William Temple's Political Legacy* (1963); A. M. Suggate, *William Temple and Christian Social Ethics Today* (Edinburgh, 1987). J. Kent, *William Temple* (Cambridge, 1993). F. A. Iremonger in *DNB, 1941–1950*, pp. 869–73.

Temporale. The section of a *Missal, *Lectionary, or *Breviary which supplies the variable parts of the *Masses, *Offices, and a few other closely connected services, for the whole of the ecclesiastical year, except in so far as they are provided for in the *Sanctorale.

temptation. The etymology of the Lat. word (*temptatio*), of which the Heb. (מַסָּה) and Greek (πειρασμός) equivalents are neutral in flavour, suggests 'trying' or 'proving'. This primary sense is retained in the ideas of the children of Israel's tempting God (Exod. 17: 2) and of God's tempting *Abraham (Gen. 22: 1), and in Jas. 1: 2 f.: 'Count it all joy when ye fall into divers temptations, knowing this, that the trial of your faith worketh patience'. Perhaps it was by an extension of this usage that the word was applied to the persecutions of the early Christians. It is also possible that this is the meaning of the word in the *Lord's Prayer.

Elsewhere in the NT, as in present-day usage, the word has the implication of incitement to sin. St *Augustine distinguished temptation which tended to issue in sin (tentatio deceptionis or seductionis) from temptation which merely put to the proof (tentatio probationis). Both he and St *Gregory the Great divided the former into the three stages of suggestion, delight, and consent (suggestio, delectatio, consensus). In this, the classical sense, temptation seems to be part of universal experience which already attacked our first parents before the *Fall. But, although St *Paul warns his readers against committing acts which though innocent in themselves might be a temptation to others, he nowhere implies that inclination to wrongful action is sinful before consent. Acc. to the author of the Epistle of St *James, temptation is inherent in free will, but God does not permit it beyond what the soul can bear. He warns his readers against regarding God as its author (1: 13). The three traditional sources of temptation are the world, the flesh, and the devil. Although in the OT the tempter is regularly regarded as personal, the Lord also points to the weakness of the flesh as the cause of temptation (Mt. 26: 41), while James holds that lust is its main source (1: 14 f.).

Modern psychologists, who frequently interpret sin mainly as psychological disorder, often teach that the forms of temptation rooted in the appetites are primarily natural instincts, which as such ought, at least to some extent, to be satisfied. They are apt to regard many forms of mental temptation, notably those which may lead to scruples and illusions, as of a much more serious nature. Since temptation is heightened by resistance, they frequently advocate circumvention rather than direct defence as the best means of avoiding repression. For the Christian moralist, the fundamental ethical facts remain unaffected by these psychological analyses. Rightly appreciated, these analyses can be of positive service to him in assisting him to a better estimation of the roots of moral action and enabling him to see where moral responsibility really lies. See also the following entry.

The subject is regularly treated in works on Moral Theology. J. H. Horn, Πειρασμός: Die Versuchung des Gläubigen in der griechischen Bibel (Beiträge zum Wissenschaft vom Alten und Neuen Testament, Vierte Folge, 20; 1937). R. Brouillard in DTC 15 (pt. 1; 1946), cols. 116–27, s.v. 'Tentation', with bibl.; H. Seesemann in TWNT 6 (1959), pp. 23–37 (Eng. tr., 1968, pp. 23–36), s.v. πεῖρα κτλ., with further bibl.; S. Légasse, OFM, and others in Dict. Sp. 15 (1991), cols. 193–251, s.v. 'Tentation', with bibl.

Temptation of Christ. The Temptation of Christ in the wilderness after His baptism is recorded in Mk. 1: 13, Mt. 4: 1–11, Lk. 4: 1–13. Three particular temptations are described in Mt. and Lk.: (1) to use His power as Son of God to turn stones into bread to satisfy His hunger; (2) to cast Himself down from a pinnacle of the Temple, i.e. to put God to an arbitrary test and to stage a spectacular miracle; and (3) to obtain from the devil power over all the kingdoms of the world by falling down and worshipping him, i.e. to desert His true mission for the sake of power unworthily obtained. In Lk. the last two temptations are related in the reverse order. It is a matter of Christian faith that though Christ was 'tempted in all points like as we are', He was 'yet without sin' (Heb. 4: 15). The Fathers understood the narrative of the Temptation of Christ both retrospectively as a typological recapitulation of Adam's temptation and prospectively as linked to the coming Passion. They also saw it as foreshadowing the continuing conflict between the Lord and Satan in the mission of the Church. The theme has long been a subject of special meditation in Lent, and in the W. Church an account of the Temptation has provided the Gospel for the First Sunday in Lent from the 5th cent. onwards.

F. *Spitta, Zur Geschichte und Literatur des Urchristentums, 3 (pt. 2; 1907), pp. 1–108 ('Die Versuchung Jesu'); P. Ketter, Die Versuchung Jesu nach dem Berichte der Synoptiker (Neutestamentliche Abhandlungen, 6, Heft 3; 1918); E. Fascher, Jesus und der Satan: Eine Studie zur Auslegung der Versuchungsgeschichte (Hallische Monographien herausgegeben O. Eissfeldt, 10; 1949); K.-P. Köppen, Die Auslegung der Versuchungsgeschichte unter besonderer Berüksichtigung der Alten Kirche (Beiträge zur Geschichte der biblischen Exegese, 4; Tübingen, 1961); E. Best, The Temptation and the Passion: The Markan Soteriology (Society for New Testament Studies, Monograph Series, 2; Cambridge, 1965), pp. 3–60; M. Steiner, OFM, La Tentation de Jésus dans l'interprétation patristique de saint Justin à Origène (Études bibliques, 1962). H. Seesemann in TWNT 6 (1959), pp. 33–7 (Eng. tr. (1968), pp. 33–6) s.v. 'πεῖρα κτλ. C. III. Die Versuchungen Jesu', with further bibl. in 10/2 (1979), cols. 1226–8. See also comm. to the Gospels.

tempus clausum (Lat., 'closed time'). The seasons in the Christian year in which, owing to their penitential or solemn character, marriages might not normally be celebrated with solemnity or at all. In the 4th cent. the 52nd canon of the Council of *Laodicea prohibited the celebration of marriage in *Lent. Later, at the Council of Beneventum in 1091, celebration was also forbidden in the periods between the beginning of *Advent and the end of the *Octave of the *Epiphany and from *Septuagesima Sunday to the Sunday after *Pentecost (*Easter in some MSS). Until the Council of *Trent, however, there was in practice no agreement as to whether the marriage ceremony itself or only the solemnities were forbidden; that Council defined the closed season for solemnities as extending from the first Sunday of Advent to the Epiphany and from *Ash Wednesday to *Low Sunday (Sess. 24, cap. 10), implying that marriages could take place at any time. In the 1917 *Codex Iuris Canonici (can. 1108) the closed season for solemnities extended only from the first Sunday in Advent to *Christmas Day and from Ash Wednesday to Easter Day; there is no similar restriction in the 1983 Code. In the E. Church, however, comparable restrictions remain.

A. Bride in DTC 15 (pt. 1; 1946), cols. 110–15, s.v. 'Temps prohibé'.

Ten Articles (1536). The first Articles of faith issued by the C of E during the Reformation period. They were adopted by *Convocation in 1536 at the desire of *Henry VIII. The three Sacraments of Baptism, Penance, and the Eucharist are upheld. The Eucharistic presence is called both corporal and substantial, but *transubstantiation is not mentioned. Justification is said to be attained by contrition and faith joined with charity. Images are to be retained as representative of virtue, but are not to be worshipped. The intercession of the saints may be sought. Prayers and Masses for the dead are enjoined. The Articles were superseded in 1537 by the *'Bishops' Book' (q.v.).

Text in C. Hardwick, *A History of the Articles of Religion* (1851), pp. 231–48, with discussion, pp. 39–59.

Ten Commandments, the. See COMMANDMENTS, THE TEN.

Ten Thousand Martyrs.

Two groups of 'Ten Thousand Martyrs' are named in the '*Roman Martyrology': (1) On 22 June, *In monte Ararath, passio sanctorum martyrum decem millia crucifixorum*. The reference here is a purely legendary record of 10,000 soldiers, crucified with their leader, Acacius, on Mount Ararat. Some of their reputed relics were brought to the W. at the time of the *Crusades. (2) On 18 Mar., *Nicomediae sanctorum decem millium martyrum qui pro Christi confessione gladio percussi sunt*. This entry would seem to relate to those who suffered at the beginning of the *Diocletianic Persecution (303). Though the number has doubtless been rounded to a conventional figure and is almost certainly exaggerated, both *Eusebius (*HE* 8. 6) and *Lactantius (*De Mortibus Persecut.* 15) indicate that it was very large.

The legends will be found with commentary in *AASS*, Jun. 4 (1707), pp. 175–88, and Mar. 2 (1668), p. 617.

Ten Tribes, the.

Ten of the twelve Hebrew tribes at the death of *Solomon (*c*.930 BC) separated from the tribes of Judah and Benjamin to form the kingdom of Israel, while the two latter formed the kingdom of Judah. When Israel was conquered by the Assyrians *c*.721, though the bulk of the population remained in Palestine, many were deported to Assyria (2 Kgs. 17: 1–6). The descendants of those who were deported doubtless became merged in the Gentile population of the Assyrian Empire, though some of them at a later date may have accounted themselves part of the Jewish *Diaspora. The theory upheld by '*British Israelites' that the lost Ten Tribes were the ancestors of the British nation has no sound basis.

Ten Years' Conflict (1834–43).

The struggle in the Church of *Scotland (and beyond it) which culminated in the *Disruption of 1843. Lay patronage (reintroduced by the United Kingdom Parliament in 1712) had long been a grievance in Scotland, but after the extension of the franchise in 1832, and the gradual eclipse of the *Moderate party in the Church by their Evangelical opponents, opinion strengthened in favour of giving congregations a greater say in ministerial settlements. In the General Assembly of 1834, therefore, the Evangelical (or 'Popular') party carried the Veto Act, which obliged presbyteries to reject a patron's presentee if he was vetoed by a majority of the 'male heads of families'. The application of this 'non-intrusion' policy, e.g. at Auchterarder and Marnoch, led to conflict with the civil courts. Disappointed patrons and presentees, supported by the Moderates, appealed to the Court of Session in Edinburgh and ultimately to the House of Lords, both of which condemned the Veto Act and its companion the Chapels Act as *ultra vires*. While the Moderates advised the Church to retract, their Evangelical brethren stood firm—deposing ministers in Strathbogie presbytery who had acted in accordance with the law of the land, and affirming the Church's spiritual independence in the Claim of Rights (1842). With Government and Parliament refusing all the

Assembly's appeals for help, the 'Non-intrusionists', led by T. *Chalmers, concluded that the State connection was no longer in the interests of true religion, and in May 1843 more than one third of the ministers of the Church withdrew from the Establishment to form the *Free Church of Scotland (q.v.).

R. Buchanan, *The Ten Years' Conflict* (2 vols., 1849). G. I. T. Machin, *Politics and the Churches in Great Britain 1832 to 1868* (Oxford, 1977), pp. 112–47. See also works cited under CHALMERS, T.

Tenebrae.

The popular name for the special form of *Mattins and *Lauds provided for the last three days of *Holy Week. Until 1955 it was sung by anticipation on the three preceding evenings. The name (*lit.* darkness) prob. derived from the ceremony of extinguishing the lights in church one by one during the service. The only light was provided by a set of 15 (since the later Middle Ages) candles fitted on a '*hearse' placed before the altar; one candle was extinguished at the end of each Psalm until only that at the apex remained; this was hidden behind the altar at the end of the *Benedictus (signifying Christ's death). After 1955 Tenebrae was no longer anticipated, and certain modifications were introduced, notably the omission of the *Miserere (Ps. 51), with which the service had previously closed. Several of the Tenebrae texts have survived in the offices provided for the mornings of *Good Friday and *Holy Saturday in the 1971 Breviary.

H. Thurston, SJ, *Lent and Holy Week* (1904), pp. 238–73. M. Andrieu, *Les Ordines Romani du haut moyen âge*, 3 (SSL 24; 1951), pp. 313–20. H. Thurston, SJ, in *CE* 14 (1912), p. 506, s.v.

Tenison, Thomas (1636–1715), Abp. of *Canterbury.

Educated at *Norwich and Corpus Christi College, Cambridge, he was ordained privately in 1659 by B. *Duppa, and after other parochial work was appointed in 1680 to St Martin-in-the-Fields, where he gained a considerable reputation as a preacher. In 1687 he engaged in a public controversy with Fr. Andrew Pulton, SJ. At the same time he made zealous efforts to reunite the more moderate Protestant Nonconformists with the C of E, though he supported the protest of the *Seven Bishops against the *Declaration of Indulgence. In 1692 he became Bp. of *Lincoln, and in 1695 Abp. of Canterbury, where he at once revived the Archbishop's Court. In 1701 he took a prominent part in the foundation of the *SPG. He fell into disfavour under *Anne, because of his pronounced Whig and *Low Church views, and for the same reasons was a zealous supporter of the Hanoverian succession. J. *Evelyn wrote in praise of his generosity, modesty, prudence, and piety, while J. *Swift spoke of him as 'a very dull man who had a horror of anything like levity in his clergy, especially of whist'. Besides sermons and pamphlets, he wrote *The Creed of Mr. Hobbes examined* (1670) and *Baconia, or Certain Genuine Remains of Lord Bacon* (1679).

Memoirs of the Life and Times of the Most Reverend Father in God, Dr. Thomas Tennison [1715]. E. [F.] Carpenter, *Thomas Tenison, Archbishop of Canterbury: His Life and Times* (CHS, 1948). W. H. *Hutton in *DNB* 56 (1898), pp. 57–60.

tephillin (תְּפִלִּין).

The Jewish name for *phylacteries. It is the plural of *tephillah*, a 'prayer'.

teraphim. Religious images, mentioned in Gen. 31: 19 and 31: 30–5, which were popularly venerated by the Israelites in pre-exilic times. The narrative of 1 Sam. 19: 13 would imply that at least their upper part had human shape. They are now generally held to have been household gods of some kind, used also for purposes of divination (Ezek. 21: 21, Zech. 10: 2). In Jgs. 17: 5 and Hos. 3: 4 they are associated with the *ephod, and are perhaps regarded as legitimate implements of religion, but in 2 Kgs. 23: 24 their use is condemned by Josiah. There is no mention of them in later times.

See comm. to biblical passages cited and works cited s.v. EPHOD. P. R. Ackroyd, 'The Teraphim', *Expository Times*, 62 (1950–1), pp. 378–80.

Terce, Sext, None. Together with *Prime, the 'Little Hours' of the Divine *Office, appointed to be recited at the third, sixth, and ninth hours respectively. The old Jewish times for prayer played some part in the devotion of the early Christians (cf. Acts 3: 1, 10: 9), but it is difficult to establish any link between those times and the hours of private prayer attested by *Clement of Alexandria, *Cyprian, and others. It was not until the 5th cent. that, under the influence of monasticism, the public recitation of prayers at these three times became general. Acc. to the *Breviary of *Pius V (1568), Terce, Sext, and None, which were all of like structure, consisted of three Psalms, preceded by Pater, Ave, versicle, and (almost) unchanging hymn, and followed by a chapter with responsory, prayer, and the usual concluding versicles. Since 1971, however, only one midday office has been obligatory, and the time of day at which it is said dictates which of the three offices (Terce, Sext, or None) should be chosen. Supplementary Psalms are provided for any who wish to say all three offices.

The principal work is contained in histories of the Office, q.v. C. Callewaert, 'De Parvis Horis Romanis ante Regulam S. Benedicti', *Collationes Brugenses*, 29 (1929), pp. 481–92, repr. in his *Sacris Erudiri* (Steenbrugge, 1940), pp. 119–26. J. Pinell, 'El numero sagrado de las horas de Oficio', in *Miscellanea Liturgica in onore di . . . Cardinale Giacomo Lercaro*, 2 [1967], pp. 887–934. L. Eisenhofer, *Handbuch der katholischen Liturgik*, 2 (1933), pp. 527–37 ('Die kleinen Horen'); M. Righetti, *Manuale di storia liturgica*, 2 (2nd edn., Milan, 1955), pp. 655–8. F. *Cabrol, OSB, in *CE* 11 (1911), pp. 97 f., s.v. 'None'; id., ibid. 13 (1912), pp. 747 f., s.v. 'Sext'; id., ibid. 14 (1912), pp. 514 f., s.v. 'Terce'; H. *Leclercq, OSB, in *DACL* 12 (pt. 2; 1936), cols. 1554–7, s.v. 'None'; id., ibid. 15 (pt. 1; 1950), cols. 1396–9, s.v. 'Sexte et Tierce'.

Teresa, Mother (1910–97), nun and founder of the Missionaries of Charity. Agnes Gonxha Bojaxhiu was born in Skopje, Macedonia, of Albanian parents. Early attracted to work in *India, in 1928 she joined the Sisters of Loretto at Rathfarnham in Ireland and was sent to Darjeeling to begin her novitiate; she took the name of *Teresa (of Lisieux). In 1929 she went to Calcutta to teach in St Mary's, a school of her Order which catered for the well-to-do. She felt herself drawn towards the very poor, and in 1948 she was given permission to leave her Order. Dressed in a blue-edged sari, she went to live in the slums of Calcutta, teaching the children of the poor and caring for the destitute and hopeless. Others joined her and in 1950 her new Order, the Missionaries of Charity (Sisters),

was approved. Its foundation was followed in 1963 by that of the Missionary Brothers of Charity and in 1969 by that of the International Co-Workers of Mother Teresa. Their activities, which are now world-wide, embrace the care of all manner of deprived and diseased people and victims of hatred and neglect. Mother Teresa's selfless love and devotion (esp. to the dying) caught the imagination of the world and she received many honours, among them the Nobel Peace Prize for 1979.

E. Egan, *Such a Vision of the Street: Mother Teresa—The Spirit and the Work* (1985).

Teresa of Ávila, St (1515–82), the commonly used name of **St Teresa of Jesus,** Spanish *Carmelite nun and mystic. Teresa was descended from an old Spanish family. She was educated by *Augustinian nuns and in 1535 entered the Carmelite monastery of the Incarnation ('mitigated observance') at Ávila. A mysterious illness obliged her to return to her family, but on her recovery she re-entered her convent, where she began to lead a rather lax life. On the advice of her confessor she resumed mental prayer, but it was not until 1555 that she was finally converted to a life of perfection, while praying before a statue of Christ scourged at the pillar. Her mystic life began soon afterwards with Divine locutions, her first ecstasy, and an intellectual vision of Christ. In 1560 she received much valued spiritual counsel from St *Peter of Alcántara. In order to lead a more mortified life she wanted to found a house where the primitive rule would be strictly observed. This plan she carried out in the face of strong opposition and in 1562 the convent of St Joseph was founded at Ávila. Here she began *The Way of Perfection* (for her nuns), having recently completed her *Life*, a spiritual autobiography written under obedience. The subsequent years from 1567 to her death were filled with labours for the establishment of houses of the primitive rule ('Discalced Carmelites') both for nuns and for friars, an undertaking in which she received much assistance from St *John of the Cross (q.v.). Despite violent opposition from the Calced Carmelites and several of the ecclesiastical authorities, her work proceeded, and at the same time her religious life deepened until it reached the state of 'spiritual marriage' (1572). In the intervals between her foundations she wrote, under obedience to her confessors, *Foundations*, *The Interior Castle*, several smaller works, and some poetry. Her style, personal, colloquial, and vivid, has been widely admired. After her last foundation at Burgos (1582) under the greatest difficulties and privations, she fell ill and died at Alba de Tormes on 4 Oct. She was canonized in 1622 and her feast is kept on 15 Oct. In 1970 she was declared a *Doctor of the Church.

St Teresa's importance is twofold. Her work in reforming the Carmelite Order has survived in the great number of Discalced houses which venerate her as their foundress. She was a woman of strong character, shrewdness, and great practical ability. As a spiritual writer her influence was epoch-making, because she was the first to point to the existence of states of prayer intermediate between discursive meditation and ecstasy ('quiet' and 'union') and to give a scientific description of the entire life of prayer from meditation to the so-called mystic marriage. Her combination of mystic experience with ceaseless activity as a reformer and organizer makes her life the classic instance for those who contend that the highest contemplation is not incompatible with practical achievements.

Editio princeps of her works by L. de *León (Salamanca, 1588; incomplete); crit. edns. by Silverio de Santa Teresa, OCD (6 vols., Burgos, 1915–19; Letters, 3 vols., 1922–4, in 'Biblioteca Mística Carmelitana', 1–9; Eng. tr. by E. A. Peers of the Works, 3 vols., 1946, and of the Letters, 2 vols., 1951) and by Efrén de la Madre de Dios, OCD, Otilio del Niño Jesús, OCD, and O. Steggink, O. Carm. (Biblioteca de autores cristianos, 74, 120, and 189; 1951–9; with editio minor, ibid. 212, 1962; 2nd edn., 1967). Eng. tr. of her main works also by K. Kavanaugh, OCD, and O. Rodriguez, OCD (2 vols., Washington, DC, 1976–80; based on edn. by Tomás de la Cruz [Alvarez], Burgos, 1971). Autobiog. also tr. into Eng. by J. M. Cohen (Penguin Classics, 1957). Early Lives by Diego de Yepes (Madrid, 1587) and F. de Ribera, SJ (Salamanca, 1590; Lat. tr., Cologne, 1620). *AASS*, Oct. 7 (1845), pp. 109–790, with Lat. tr. of Life by F. de Ribera, pp. 539–725. Crisógono de Jesús, OCD, *Santa Teresa de Jesús: Su vida y su doctrina* (1936; 2nd edn., 1942); E. A. Peers, *Mother of Carmel: A Portrait of St Teresa of Jesus* (1945); id., *Saint Teresa of Jesus and other Essays and Addresses* (1953), pp. 15–135; id., *Handbook to the Life and Times of St Teresa and St John of the Cross* (1954); O. Leroy, *Sainte Thérèse d'Ávila: Biographie spirituelle* (Études Carmélitaines, 1962); E. W. T. Dicken, *The Crucible of Love: A Study of the Mysticism of St Teresa of Jesus and St John of the Cross* (1963). Fr. Thomas, ODC, and Fr. Gabriel, ODC (eds.), *St Teresa of Ávila: Studies in her Life, Doctrine and Times* (1963); Efrén de la Madre de Dios, OCD, and O. Steggink, O. Carm., *Tiempo y vida de Santa Teresa* (Biblioteca de autores cristianos, 283; 1968); *Sancta Teresia a Iesu, Doctor Ecclesiae: Historia, Doctrina, Documenta* (Ephemerides Carmeliticae, 21, nos. 1–2; 1970), with introd. by G. M. Garrone. G. Etchegoyen, *L'Amour divin: Essai sur les sources de sainte Thérèse* (Bibliothèque de l'École des Hautes Études Hispaniques, 4; 1923). A. Vermeylen, *Sainte Thérèse en France au XVIIᵉ siècle 1600–1660* (Louvain, 1958). E. Llamas Martínez, OCD, *Santa Teresa de Jesus y la Inquisición Española* (1972). V. G. de la Concha, *El Arte literario de Santa Teresa* (Barcelona, 1978). Popular account in V. Sackville-West, *The Eagle and the Dove* (1943), pp. 7–100. Brief account of her thought by R. [D.] Williams, *Teresa of Ávila* (1991). M. Jiménez Salas, *Santa Teresa de Jesús: Bibliografía fundamental* (Cuadernos bibliográficos, 6; 1962). Pourrat, 3, pp. 187–268. O. Steggink, O. Carm., in *NCE* 13 (1967), pp. 1013–16, s.v.; T. Alvarez, O. Carm., in *Dict. Sp.* 15 (1991), cols. 611–58, s.v. 'Thérèse (5) de Jésus'.

Teresa of Lisieux, St (1873–97), *Carmelite nun. The youngest daughter of Louis Martin, a devout watchmaker of Alençon, she was drawn towards religious perfection at an early age. In spite of opposition, she obtained permission to enter the Carmelite convent at Lisieux at the age of 15. She was professed in 1890, and was assistant novice-mistress from 1893. In 1896 she was prevented from joining the Carmelites in *China by the first of a series of haemorrhages. She died of tuberculosis on 30 Sept. 1897.

At the command of her superiors she wrote her autobiography, *L'Histoire d'une âme*. The spread of her fame was largely due to the decision of the prioress to circulate a revised version of this, together with details of her death, to all Carmelite houses. Miracles of healing and prophecy were soon reported in sufficient number to realize her promise, 'Je vais faire tomber un torrent de roses.' By 1907 an account of them was appended to her biography. Proceedings for her beatification were initiated in the court of Bayeux in 1910 and moved to Rome in 1918, her cause being exempted from the 50 years' delay imposed by

Canon Law. On 25 Apr. 1923 her beatification was proclaimed by *Pius XI and her bones solemnly translated to the convent. On 17 May 1925 she was canonized under the name of 'St Teresa of the Child Jesus and the Holy Face' (her name in religion). In 1997 she was declared a '*Doctor of the Church'. Feast day, 1 (formerly 3) Oct.

Owing to the continued increase in the number of pilgrims of all nations, it was decided in 1926 to erect a large basilica at Lisieux. The popularity of her cult was largely due to the appeal to the ordinary people of her age, to whom her life showed that the attainment of sanctity was practicable, not only through extreme mortification, but through continual renunciation in small matters. She is popularly known in England as 'The Little Flower' from the subtitle of her autobiography. In 1927 Pius XI named her patroness of foreign missions (along with St *Francis Xavier). In 1947 she was joined with *Joan of Arc as patroness of France.

Crit. edn. of her works (Édition du Centenaire) by D. Delalande, OCD, and others, pub. Paris from 1971; all the texts had been pub. by 1989, but the later vols. appeared as separate items. Eng. tr., Washington, DC, 1975 ff. The first reliable text of her autobiog. was the facsimile of it and other related documents, + 3 vols. of Introd., Notes et Tables, Table des Citations, pub. Lisieux, 1956. Eng. tr. of autobiog., based on the facsimile, by R. [A.] *Knox, London, 1958. Letters ed. A. Combes, Lisieux, 1948; Eng. tr., New York, 1948. *Pluies des roses* (6 vols., Lisieux, 1913–25). Collection of photographs, with comm. by François de Sainte-Marie, OCD, *Le Visage de Thérèse de Lisieux* (2 vols., 1961; Eng. tr. as *The Photo Album of St Thérèse of Lisieux*, 1962). *Procès de Béatification et Canonisation*: 1: *Procès Informatif Ordinaire* [1910–11]; 2: *Procès Apostolique* [1915–17] (Bibliotheca Carmelitica, Series 1, Textus, 2–3; Rome, 1973–6); partial Eng. tr. of the former by C. O'Mahony, OCD (Dublin, 1975). A. P. Laveille, *Sainte Thérèse de l'Enfant Jésus (1873–1897), d'après les documents officiels du Carmel de Lisieux* (1925; Eng. tr., 1928). The large number of other Lives incl. studies by H. Petitot, OP (1922; Eng. tr., 1927), H. U. von *Balthasar (Olten, 1950; Eng. tr., 1953), V. Johnson (London, 1953), I. F. Görres (Freiburg, 1958; Eng tr., 1959), P. Descouvement (Paris, 1962), J. Norbury (London, 1966), and G. Gaucher [OCD] (Paris, 1982). A. Combes, *Introduction à la spiritualité de sainte Thérèse de l'Enfant Jésus* (1946; enlarged edn., 1948; Eng. tr. of 1946 edn., 1950); id., *Sainte Thérèse de Lisieux et sa mission* (1954; Eng. tr., 1956), and other works by this author; J.-F. Six, *La Véritable Enfance de Thérèse de Lisieux* (1972); id., *Thérèse de Lisieux au Carmel* (1973); B. Bro, OP, *La Gloire et le Mendiant* (1974; Eng. tr., 1979). P. Descouvement in *Dict. Sp.* 15 (1991), cols. 576–611, s.v. 'Thérèse de l'Enfant Jésus'.

Teresian reform. The reform of the *Carmelite Order begun by St *Teresa of Ávila.

Terminism. (1) The doctrine that God has ordained a definite period or 'term' in the life of every individual at the end of which he loses his opportunity of achieving salvation. The belief was defended by J. G. Böse (*c.*1662–1700) in his *De Termino Salutis* (1698) and much cherished in *Pietist circles, and also upheld by Adam Rechenberg (1642–1721); but it met with fierce opposition from orthodox *Lutherans. (2) By philosophers, the word is occasionally used as another name for *Nominalism (q.v.).

Territorialism. A theory of Church government formerly held by certain Protestant theologians, acc. to which the civil authority had the right to determine the religious doctrines of its subjects. It is summarized in the formula *cuius regio eius religio*. The opposite view was often known as *Collegialism.

Tersanctus. An alternative name for the *Sanctus ('Holy, Holy, Holy'), sung or recited in the *Eucharistic Liturgy. The word is sometimes used also for the *Trisagion in the *Reproaches on *Good Friday.

Tersteegen, Gerhard (1697–1769), German Protestant devotional writer. Born at Moers, near Düsseldorf, he underwent a conversion in a circle of *Pietists at the age of 20. Under the influence of ascetic and *Quietist ideas, he retired into solitude and earned his living as a ribbon weaver. Having established in 1727 his Pilgrims' Hut at Otterbeck, near Mülheim, in order to realize his spiritual ideals in a kind of religious community, he abandoned his profession in 1728 and devoted himself entirely to the career of a director of souls and devotional meetings. Besides many translations, chiefly from French Quietist writers, he published poems and hymns under the title *Geistliches Blumen-Gärtlein inniger Seelen* (1729) and, from 1733 to 1753, *Auserlesene Lebensbeschreibungen heiliger Seelen*, a set of selected biographies of Catholic mystics, in which, however, he explicitly denounced their 'sensual religion'. His influence spread throughout Germany, the Netherlands, and Scandinavia, though his activities were temporarily hampered by the Prussian anti-conventicle laws of 1740. His piety was highly individualistic, e.g. he refused to partake of Holy Communion together with worldly or godless people. Today he is chiefly known for his hymns, remarkable for their poetical charm and a deep spirituality which expresses itself esp. in adoration of the Divine Majesty and a tender love for the Saviour. Many of them, e.g. '*Brunn alles Heils*' ('Thee fount of blessing') and '*Gott ist gegenwärtig*' ('Lo, God is here!'), have been translated into English.

Gesammelte Schriften, 8 vols., Stuttgart, 1844–6; modern edn. of his *Werke* by W. Zeller (Texte zur Geschichte des Pietismus, Abt. 5; Göttingen, 1979 ff.). Anthology ed. T. Klein (Munich, 1925). Various of his hymns tr. into Eng. by F. Bevan, *Hymns of Ter Steegen, Suso and Others* (1895); id., *Hymns of Ter Steegen and Others* (1897). The basic study is that of G. Kerlen (Mülheim a.d. Ruhr, 1851). W. Blankenagel, *Tersteegen als religiöser Erzieher* (Emsdetten, 1934). C. P. van Andel, *Gerhard Tersteegen: Leben und Werk. Sein Platz in der Kirchengeschichte* (Schriftenreihe des Vereins für Rheinische Kirchengeschichte, 46; Dusseldorf, 1973). H. Ludewig, *Gebet und Gotteserfahrung bei Gerhard Tersteegen* (Arbeiten zur Geschichte des Pietismus, 24; 1986). In Eng. there is a Life by H. E. Govan (London, 1898, with selections of his writings) and a popular sketch by W. E. Oliphant (pub. by the *Salvation Army, London, 1905). B. Jaspert in *Dict. Sp.* 15 (1991), cols. 260–71, s.v.

tertianship. In the *Jesuit Order a 'third year' of probation (the *novitiate constitutes the first two) before admission to final vows; it is usually undergone a few years after ordination. It is intended to rekindle and deepen the candidate's spirituality after long years of study, and includes the full 30 days' *Spiritual Exercises*. Study of the Jesuit Constitutions and a variety of pastoral experiences form part of the course. It has sometimes been described as the 'Schola Perfectionis'.

Tertiary. See THIRD ORDERS.

Tertullian, Quintus Septimius Florens (*c*.160–*c*.225), African Church Father. Brought up in Carthage as a pagan, Tertullian received a good education in literature and rhetoric; he may have practised as a lawyer, though identification with the jurist Tertullian is improbable. He was converted to Christianity before 197. Acc. to St *Jerome he became a priest, but there are other indications that he remained a layman. Eventually he joined the *Montanist sect. The detailed chronology of his life and works has recently been much disputed.

Tertullian was the author of a long list of apologetic, theological, controversial, and ascetic works in Latin, as well as of a few writings in Greek. In the 'Apologeticum' (*c*.197) and other early apologetic writings he appeals for the toleration of Christianity, attacking pagan superstition, rebutting charges against Christian morality, and, to him the chief point, claiming that Christians were no danger to the state but good and useful citizens. In these works he is less concerned with theology than with the Greek Apologists whom he had read, though 'De testimonio animae' affirms the witness of natural instinct to the existence of God. In moral and disciplinary works addressed to Christians (e.g. 'De spectaculis', 'De corona militis', 'De idololatria', 'De paenitentia'), he emphasizes rather the separation from pagan society, which was necessary in order to escape contamination from its immorality and idolatry. Many occupations (including military service) and social institutions are barred, and in the last resort martyrdom must be accepted; the blood of martyrs is the seed of the Church. Tertullian may well be the editor of the 'Passio SS Perpetuae et Felicitatis'.

His theological writings are mostly polemical in origin and form. In the early 'De praescriptione haereticorum' he disposes of all heresy in principle: the one true Church, visible in history through the episcopal succession (here he follows *Irenaeus), alone possesses the authentic tradition from Christ and the apostles, and alone has authority to interpret Scripture. It need not argue. Yet he himself frequently argued against Gnostic dualism and spiritualism: against Hermogenes, the *Valentinians, *Marcion, and in 'De carne Christi', 'De resurrectione mortuorum', and 'Scorpiace'. Against Marcion he defended the identity of the one God of the Old and New Testaments and His activity throughout history, both just and loving, and the identity of Jesus Christ, truly the incarnate Word of God, with the Messiah of prophecy. Against the unidentified '*Praxeas' he tried to expose the unscriptural and unhistorical implications of *modalism and to formulate a positive doctrine of the Trinity without falling into the opposite error of *subordinationism. In these respects his thought and language powerfully influenced Christianity. 'De baptismo', which is liturgically valuable, also raises the problem of *Infant Baptism, which Tertullian disliked. But his later 'De anima', a pioneer work in Christian psychology, which advocated *Traducianism, prepared the way for that pessimistic doctrine of the Fall and *Original Sin which came, through *Augustine, to dominate Latin theology.

The rigorist strain in Tertullian, and the opposition which it evoked in Carthage, took him into Montanism, with its heightened eschatological expectations, its emphasis upon the immediacy of the Spirit (Paraclete) and ecstatic prophecy, its asceticism, and, at least by implication, a perfectionist and potentially sectarian doctrine of the Church which challenged the more institutional one that he had earlier helped to establish against *Gnosticism. All this, but especially the rigorism, is evident in the extant Montanist works, e.g. 'De monogamia', 'De exhortatione castitatis', 'De jejunio' and 'De pudicitia'. This last was written in the 220s against the disciplinary leniency with sexual sin of a Bp. of Carthage. His understanding of the other aspects of Montanism might have been clearer if 'De ecstasi', 'De paradiso', and 'De spe fidelium' had survived.

Tertullian's style is brilliant, masterful, and difficult. In argument he employs every rhetorical and sophistical device (his ambience is the elaborate Second Sophistic); he devastates opponents with ridicule and cleverly undermines their reasoning. Yet, though often unfair and superficial in controversy, he grapples thoughtfully with the moral and religious problems of his time. Legal knowledge may have helped him to formulate, but did little to determine, his theology, except perhaps in his legalistic conception of reward and punishment. Though influenced by *Stoicism and willing to use philosophy as a tool, he distrusted it as a source of truth. Christianity is revelation, act and gift of God. So his theology is fundamentally scriptural, and, while his exegesis can be perverse in attack, for theological construction he generally prefers a literal and historical interpretation to an allegorical one. If, as seems probable, a Latin Bible was available to him, the creation of a Latin theological terminology must not be too readily attributed to him. But his influence upon language and thought was sufficient to justify the title of Father of Latin theology.

Except for the *Apologeticum*, MSS are scarce. The damaged 'Codex Agobardinus' (Par. lat. 1622; 9th cent.) contains 13 of the 31 extant works; 'Codex Trecensis' (Troyes, Bibliothèque Municipale, 523; 12th cent.) is important for 5 works. The 16th-cent. eds. used several MSS now lost. Collected writings containing 22 works, by Beatus *Rhenanus (Basle, 1521); edn. by J. Gagnaeus (Paris, 1545) added 9. Good notes in edn. of N. Rigaud (ibid., 1634). Modern edns. by F. Oehler (3 vols., Leipzig, 1853–4, with comm.), A. Reifferscheid and others (CSEL 20, 47, 69, 70, 76, etc.; 1890 ff.) and E. Dekkers, OSB, and others (CCSL 1–2; 1954). Eng. tr. of works by P. Holmes and others (ANCL 7, 11, 15, and 18; 1868–70). Comm. on individual works, with edns. of text, incl. *De anima*, ed. J. H. Waszink (Amsterdam, 1947; valuable for Tertullian generally); and the edns. by E. Evans (all with Eng. trs.) of *Adversus Praxean* (London, 1948), *De oratione* (ibid., 1953), *De carne Christi* (ibid., 1956), *De resurrectione mortuorum* (ibid., 1960), *De baptismo* (ibid., 1964), *Adversus Marcionem* (Oxford Early Christian Texts, 2 vols., 1972). There are also comm. in the Eng. trs. of *Adversus Hermogenem* by J. H. Waszink (ACW 24; 1956), of *Ad Uxorem, De exhortatione castitatis*, and *De monogamia* by W. P. Le Saint, SJ (ibid. 13; 1951), of *De paenitentia* and *De pudicitia* by id. (ibid. 28; 1959), and of *De praescriptione* and *De idololatria* by S. L. Greenslade, *Early Latin Theology* (Library of Christian Classics, 5; 1956), pp. 21–110. Several works are also ed. with comm. and Fr. tr., in SC.

A. d'Alès, SJ, *La Théologie de Tertullien* (1905); J. Lortz, *Tertullian als Apologet* (Münsterische Beiträge zur Theologie, 9–10; 1927–8); E. Dekkers, OSB, *Tertullianus en de Geschiednis der Liturgie* (1947); C. Becker, *Tertullians Apologeticum: Werden und Leistung* (Munich, 1954); G. Säflund, *De Pallio und stilistische Entwicklung Tertullians* (Skrifter utgivna av Svenska Institutet i Rom, 8°, 8; Lund, 1955); S. Otto, *'Natura' und 'dispositio': Untersuchung zum Naturbegriff und Denkform Tertullians* (Münchener Theologische Studien, Abt. 2, Bd. 19; 1960); R. Cantalamessa, OFM Cap.,

La Cristologia di Tertulliano (Paradosis, 18; Fribourg, 1962); R. Braun, *'Deus Christianorum': Recherches sur le vocabulaire doctrinale de Tertullien* (Paris thesis; 1962; 2nd edn., with much suppl. material, Études Augustiniennes, 1977); J. Moingt, SJ, *Théologie trinitaire de Tertullien* (Théologie, 68–70; 1966); T. P. O'Malley, SJ, *Tertullian and the Bible* (Latinitas Christianorum Primaeva, 21; 1967); D. Michaélidès, *Sacramentum chez Tertullien* (Études Augustiniennes, 1970); T. D. Barnes, *Tertullian: A Historical and Literary Study* (Oxford, 1971; repr., with corrections and postscript, 1985); R. D. Sider, *Ancient Rhetoric and the Art of Tertullian* (Oxford Theological Monographs, 1971); J.-C. Fredouille, *Tertullien et la conversion de la culture antique* (Études Augustiniennes, 1972); C. Aziza, *Tertullien et le judaïsme* (Nice, 1977); C. Rambaux, *Tertullien face aux morales des trois premiers siècles* (1979); D. Rankin, *Tertullian and the Church* (Cambridge, 1995); E. [F.] Osborn, *Tertullian, First Theologian of the West* (ibid., 1997). G. Claesson, *Index Tertullianeus* (3 vols., Études Augustiniennes, 1974–5). Bardenhewer, 2, pp. 377–442; Altaner and Stuiber (1978), pp. 148–63 and 577–80; J. Quasten, *Patrology*, 2 (Utrecht, 1953), pp. 246–340; *CPL* (3rd edn., 1995), pp. 1–10 (nos. 1–36), all with further bibl. P. Siniscalco in *DPAC* 2 (1984), cols. 3413–24, s.v. 'Tertulliano'; Eng. tr. in *Encyclopedia of the Early Church*, 2 (1992), pp. 818–20; C. Munier in *Dict. Sp.* 15 (1991), cols. 271–95, s.v. 'Tertullien'.

Test Act. The Popish Recusants Act 1672, passed in 1673, requiring all holders of office under the Crown (*inter alia*) to receive the sacrament of the Eucharist acc. to the usage of the C of E, to take the Oaths of Supremacy and Allegiance to the King, and to make the *Declaration against Transubstantiation. Among its first effects was the resignation by *James (II), Duke of York, of his post of Lord High Admiral. The Act was in force until the Roman *Catholic Relief Act 1829 was passed, and it was not finally repealed until 1863.

Text in Gee and Hardy, pp. 632–40 (no. 120); part also in Bettenson, pp. 405–7 (2nd edn., pp. 418–20).

Testament, Old and **New.** See OLD TESTAMENT and NEW TESTAMENT.

Testament of Our Lord in Galilee, also known as the **Epistle of the Apostles** (*Epistula Apostolorum*). This *apocryphal document, dating from *c.*150 and written in the form of an encyclical sent out by the eleven Apostles after the Resurrection, purports to record conversations between the Apostles and the Risen Christ. It was written in Greek, but survives, as far as is known, only in Ethiopic, *Coptic (in an incomplete form), and, in the case of a single leaf, in Latin. It was apparently directed against the *Gnostics and probably emanated from Egypt or Asia Minor. It is to be distinguished from the *Testamentum Domini* (q.v.).

C. Schmidt, *Gespräche Jesu mit seinen Jüngern nach der Auferstehung* (TU 43; 1919); review by G. Bardy in *R. Bibl.* 30 (1921), pp. 110–34. Eth. text, ed., with introd. and Fr. tr., by L. Guerrier and S. Grébaut in *PO* 9 (1913), pp. 141–236 (fasc. 3). Eng. tr. with short introd. in J. K. Elliott, *The Apocryphal New Testament* (Oxford, 1993), pp. 555–88. Ger. tr., with introd. by C. D. G. Müller in Schneemelcher (5th edn., 1987), 1, pp. 205–33; Eng. tr., 1 (1991), pp. 249–84. A. A. T. Ehrhardt, 'Judaeo-Christians in Egypt, the Epistula Apostolorum and the Gospel to the Hebrews', in F. L. Cross (ed.), *Studia Evangelica*, 3 (TU 68; 1964), pp. 360–82. M. Hornschuh, *Studien zur Epistula Apostolorum* (Patristische Texte und Studien, 5; 1965). J. Quasten, *Patrology*, 1 (Utrecht, 1950), pp. 150–3.

Testaments of the Twelve Patriarchs. A pseud-epigraphical writing modelled on the 'Testament of *Jacob' in Gen. 49. It professes to relate in its 12 books the message that each of the 12 sons of Jacob gave to his descendants on his deathbed. Its purpose is chiefly to give moral encouragement and spiritual consolation to its readers, whose confidence is claimed by revelations *ex post facto* prophetic of the later history of the different Israelite tribes. The work survives in Greek, and also in Armenian and Slavonic versions. It is a matter of dispute whether the Greek was the original or was itself a translation from Hebrew or Aramaic. Also disputed is the question whether the work was Christian in origin or Jewish (in which case the obviously Christian passages are explained as interpolations). The most prominent exponent of the latter point of view in modern times is R. H. *Charles, who argued that the work was originally written in Hebrew and that the bulk of it dates from the latter part of the 2nd cent. BC. Of the view that the Testaments were Christian in origin, adapting and incorporating traditional Jewish material, the outstanding modern representative is M. de Jonge, who dates them *c.* AD 200. The question of the date of the work is of importance, since it can be maintained that if it is pre-Christian, 'the book . . . has achieved a real immortality by influencing the thought and diction of the writers of the New Testament, and even those of our Lord' (Charles). On the other hand, if the Testaments are Christian, 'what they illustrate is not the preparation of Christianity, but the social and religious life of the early Christian Church' (de Jonge).

Editio princeps of Gk. text by J. E. *Grabe (ed.), *Spicilegium SS. Patrum*, 1 (Oxford, 1698), pp. 145–253; the edn. of A. *Gallandi is repr. in J. P. Migne, *PG* 2. 1037–150. Crit. edns. by R. Sinker (Cambridge, 1869, with appendix, ibid., 1879), R. H. Charles (Oxford, 1908), and M. de Jonge and others (Pseudepigrapha Veteris Testamenti Graece, 1, pt. 2; Leiden, 1978). Eng. trs. by R. H. Charles (London, 1908); also, with notes and other material, in id., *The Apocrypha and Pseudepigrapha of the Old Testament*, 2 (1913), pp. 282–367; by H. C. Kee in J. H. Charlesworth (ed.), *The Old Testament Pseudepigrapha*, 1 (1983), pp. 775–828; and by M. de Jonge in H. F. D. Sparks (ed.), *The Apocryphal Old Testament* (Oxford, 1984), pp. 505–15. Comm. [in Eng.] by H. W. Hollander and M. de Jonge (Studia in Veteris Testamenti Pseudepigrapha, 8; Leiden, 1985). M. de Jonge, *The Testaments of the Twelve Patriarchs* (Theologische Bibliotheek, 25; Assen, Holland, 1953; also pub. by Manchester University Press), with detailed bibl. pp. 170 f. C. Burchard, J. Jervell, and J. Thomas, *Studien zu den Testamenten der Zwölf Patriarchen: Drei Aufsätze*, ed. W. Eltester (Beiheft zur *ZNTW* 36; 1969). J. Becker, *Untersuchungen zur Entstehungsgeschichte der Testamente der zwölf Patriarchen* (Arbeiten zur Geschichte des antiken Judentums und des Urchristentums, 8; 1970). M. de Jonge (ed.), *Studies on the Testaments of the Twelve Patriarchs* (Studia in Veteris Testamenti Pseudepigrapha, 3; Leiden, 1975). E. *Schürer, *A History of the Jewish People in the Age of Jesus Christ*, rev. Eng. tr. by G. Vermes and others, 3 (pt. 2; Edinburgh, 1987), pp. 767–81. M. de Jonge in *Anchor Bible Dictionary*, 5 (1992), pp. 181–6, s.v. 'Patriarchs, Testaments of the Twelve'.

Testamentum Domini. A short early Christian treatise professing to be in the words of Christ Himself. It contains detailed regulations on matters of ecclesiastical order and church building, and a complete liturgy. It was originally written in Greek, probably in the 4th–5th cents., but survives only in a Syriac translation made in the 7th cent.

apparently by *Jacob of Edessa. It was probably a private compilation and hence does not represent the official practice of any Church. Later it became incorporated in a collection known as the 'Clementine Octateuch' which circulated among the *Syrian Orthodox; extracts were also included in their *Synodicon.

The work has close literary connections with Hippolytus' *Apostolic Tradition*, the *Apostolic Constitutions, and other early Church Orders. *Editio princeps* of complete Syr. text in the Clementine Octateuch by Mgr. Ignatius Ephraem II Rahmani (Mainz, 1899; with Lat. tr.). J. Cooper and A. J. Maclean, *The Testament of the Lord* (1902; Eng. tr. with useful notes). Extracts in the Synodicon ed., with Eng. tr., by A. Vööbus, *The Synodicon in the West Syrian Tradition*, 1 (CSCO 367–8, Scriptores Syri, 161–2; 1975), pp. 1–49; Eng. tr., pp. 27–64. F. X. Funk, *Das Testament unseres Herrn und die verwandten Schriften* (1901). CPG 1 (1983), pp. 234 f. (no. 1743). É. Amann in *DTC* 15 (pt. 1; 1946), cols. 194–200.

Tetragrammaton. The technical term for the four-lettered Hebrew name of God יהוה (i.e. YHWH or JHVH). Owing to its sacred character, from *c.*300 BC the Jews tended to avoid uttering it when reading the Scriptures, and substituted 'Adonai' (i.e. the Hebrew word for 'Lord'), whence the rendering Κύριος of the *Septuagint, *Dominus* of the *Vulgate, and 'the LORD' in most English Bibles. When *vowel points were put into Hebrew MSS those of 'Adonai' were inserted into the letters of the Tetragrammaton, and since the 16th cent. the bastard word 'Jehovah', obtained by fusing the vowels of the one word with the consonants of the other, has become established. The original pronunciation is now commonly thought to have been 'Yahweh' or 'Jahveh' and both these forms (but nowadays esp. the former) are frequently found in scholarly works. The name is undoubtedly very ancient and was certainly in use by *c.*850 BC, as it occurs on the *Moabite Stone. Some scholars have held that its original form was 'Yah' (cf. Exod. 15: 2 [RV margin] and Ps. 68: 4). The traditional explanation of the meaning of the name as connected with the verb 'to be' is given in Exod. 3: 14 f. (cf. 6: 2 f.).

S. R. *Driver, 'Recent Theories on the Origin and Nature of the Tetragrammaton', in *Studia Biblica: Essays in Biblical Archaeology and Criticism*, 1 (1885), pp. 1–20. G. R. *Driver, 'The Evidence for the Name "Yahweh" outside the Old Testament', in D. C. Simpson (ed.), *Old Testament Essays: Papers read before the Society for Old Testament Studies . . .* (1927), pp. 18–24. W. F. Albright, *From the Stone Age to Christianity* (Baltimore, 1940), esp. pp. 197–9. O. Eissfeldt, 'El and Yahweh', *Journal of Semitic Studies*, 1 (1956), pp. 27–37; F. M. Cross, Jun., 'Yahweh and the God of the Patriarchs', *HTR* 55 (1962), pp. 225–59; E. C. B. Maclaurin, 'YHWH. The Origin of the Tetragrammaton', *Vetus Testamentum*, 12 (1962), pp. 439–63, with refs.; R. de Vaux, OP, 'The Revelation of the Divine Name YHWH', in J. I. Durham and J. R. Porter (eds.), *Proclamation and Presence: Old Testament Essays in Honour of Gwynne Henton Davies* (1970), pp. 48–75; G. H. Parke-Taylor, *Yahweh: The Divine Name in the Bible* (Waterloo, Ont. [1975]).

Tetrapolitan Confession. A Protestant Confession of Faith drawn up by M. *Bucer and W. *Capito conjointly at the Diet of Augsburg (1530) and presented to the Emperor on 9 July 1530, in the name of the four S. German cities of Strasbourg, Memmingen, Lindau, and Constance. Its purpose was to prevent a rupture in

German Protestantism. Its doctrinal formulae, though they had some *Zwinglian affinities, were based on those of the *Augsburg Confession, a copy of which had been secretly transmitted to its compilers.

Crit. edn. by M. Moeller in Bucer's *Deutsche Schriften*, ed. R. Stupperich, 3 (Gütersloh and Paris, 1969), pp. 13–185, with introd. and bibl. Eng. tr., with brief introd., in A. C. Cochrane (ed.), *Reformed Confessions of the 16th Century* (1966), pp. 51–88.

Tetrateuch (Gk. τετρα- 'four' + τεῦχος 'book'). The name often given to the first four books of the *Pentateuch (Gen.–Num.), all of which appear to have been compiled from the same three sources and on the same editorial principle, i.e. '*P' has been taken as the framework and material from '*J' and '*E' fitted into it. In Deut. this is plainly not so. Thus, on this view, the major dividing line in the earlier part of the OT is to be placed at the end of Num. and Deut. is to be regarded as the first volume of a '*Deuteronomistic History' which extends as far as II Kings.

M. Noth, *Überlieferungsgeschichtliche Studien*, 1 (Halle/Saale, 1943), pp. 180–216. The name 'Tetrateuch' appears to have been coined by I. Engnell, *Gamla Testamentet: En traditionshistorisk inledning*, 1 (Stockholm, 1945), p. 209. See also S. *Mowinckel, *Tetrateuch—Pentateuch—Hexateuch* (Beihefte zur *ZATW*, 90; 1964).

Tetzel, Johann (*c.*1464–1519), German *Dominican preacher of *indulgences. He graduated at the University of Leipzig in 1487 and entered the Dominican Order soon afterwards. He seems to have enjoyed a reputation both as a teacher and a preacher, and for much of his life served as an *inquisitor; in 1515 he was appointed a professor at the Dominican *studium* in Leipzig. In 1505 he was deputed to preach the indulgence for the campaign of the *Teutonic Order in Livonia; he continued with this task until at least 1510. In 1516 he was appointed to preach the indulgence for the rebuilding of *St Peter's, Rome, joining the team of the Abp. of Mainz for this purpose early in 1517. Following the instructions issued to this team, Tetzel maintained the controversial thesis that indulgences could be obtained for the benefit of souls in *purgatory even by people not themselves in a state of grace, simply on the strength of their financial contribution. The enthusiasm with which he raised money on this basis provoked considerable criticism, and it was his preaching that prompted M. *Luther to issue his 95 theses on 31 Oct. 1517. Tetzel conducted a disputation against these theses in the University of Frankfurt an der Oder in 1518 and returned to the attack twice more in the same year; he saw that Luther had raised important ecclesiological issues transcending the particular question of indulgences. Wild stories about alleged financial irregularities circulated, with the support of C. von *Miltitz, whose conciliatory attitude to Luther was very different from that of Tetzel. From the end of 1518 Tetzel feared that his life was in danger and did not appear in public.

Primary docs. relating to his dispute with Luther in P. Fabisch and E. Iserloh (eds.), *Dokumente zur Causa Lutheri (1517–1521)*, 1 (Corpus Catholicorum, 41; 1988), pp. 310–75. The best modern study is that of N. Paulus (Mainz, 1899), with other works of this author cited in Schottenloher, see below. P. Mandonnet, OP, 'Jean Tetzel et sa prédication des indulgences', *Revue thomiste*, 7 (1899), pp. 481–496, and 8 (1900), pp. 178–93. H. G. Ganss in

CE 14 (1912), pp. 539–41, s.v. Further bibl. in Schottenloher, 2 (1935), pp. 324–6 (nos. 21132–74). See also works cited s.v. INDULGENCES.

Teutonic Order. The order of German knights (ordo fratrum domus hospitalis Sanctae Mariae Theutonicorum Ierosolymitani) grew out of a hospital community founded outside Acre in 1190. In 1198 it was converted into a military order with the rule of the *Templars and confirmed as such by the Papacy. In 1245 it received a rule of its own. The order, made up of knights, priests, and lay brothers, was active and richly endowed in Palestine and Syria, but soon it also sought to advance the frontiers of Christendom elsewhere. After a brief and abortive interlude in Hungary (1211–25) the fourth Grand Master, Hermann of Salza, planned a new sphere of action for his knights in Prussia, having received an invitation from Duke Conrad of Masovia to fight and subdue the heathen Prussians. In the Golden Bull of Rimini (1226) the Emp. *Frederick II conferred princely powers on the Grand Master and gave almost limitless rights over future conquests to the order. In 1231 the knights crossed the Vistula and set about building their first castles. From the very beginning their missionary enterprise was compromised by their aristocratic interest in lordship and government. From 1236 onwards the order also expanded in Livonia, but the heathen Lithuanians remained an unconquered threat to its land-communications. The seat of the Grand Masters, at first at Montfort in Palestine, was moved from Acre to Venice in 1291 and to Marienburg on the Nogat in 1309. From the later 13th cent. onwards the order gave itself more and more to the administration of its territories, their colonization by German immigrants—not always at the expense of the subject Prussians—and the development of prosperous towns. When Lithuania accepted Latin Christianity and entered into a personal union with the Polish kingdom in 1386 the knights' crusading task finally lost its meaning. They succumbed to a Polish–Lithuanian army at the battle of Tannenberg (1410) and henceforth had to face increasing disaffection from their noble vassals and towns. In 1525 the Grand Master, *Albert of Prussia, resigned his office and became the first ecclesiastical prince to secularize his territory for dynastic ends when he embraced *Lutheranism. Soon afterwards the order also lost its possessions in Livonia and the Grand Masters now resided at Mergentheim in Swabia supervising their S. German bailiwicks. The order still met needs, if only to provide a suitable abode for the younger sons of RC nobles. Suppressed by Napoleon, it survived under the protection of the Habsburgs in Austria and until 1918 the Grand Master was usually one of the Archdukes. From about 1840 it found its vocation once more in hospital work, especially military hospitals, but also in schools. The institution of serving sisters, who had held a humble place in the order's medieval statutes, was revived. Clerical rather than knightly, the community resumed its charitable work after 1945. It has, however, remained conscious of its long martial past.

E. Joachim and W. Hubatsch (eds.), *Regesta Historico-Diplomatica Ordinis S. Mariae Theutonicorum: 1198–1525* (4 vols., Göttingen, 1948–50; *Register zu Pars I und zu Pars II*, 1965). For details of other pr. sources see Mayer and Lampe, cited below. E. Caspar, *Hermann von Salza und die Gründung des Deutschor-*

densstaats in Preussen (Tübingen, 1924). M. Tumler, Der Deutsche Orden im Werden, Wachsen und Wirken bis 1400 (Vienna [1955]). K. Wieser, OT (ed.), Acht Jahrhunderte Deutscher Orden in Einzeldarstellungen (Quellen und Studien zur Geschichte des Deutschen Ordens, 1; Bad Godesberg [1967]; also other vols. in this series, mostly specialized, but some more general, such as vol. 36: U. Arnold (ed.), Beiträge zur Geschichte des Deutschen Ordens, 1; 1986). M.-L. Favreau, Studien zur Frühgeschichte des Deutschen Ordens (Kieler Historische Studien, 21; 1977). H. Boockmann, Der Deutsche Orden: Zwölf Kapitel aus seiner Geschichte (Munich, 1981). B. Schumacher, 'Die Idee der geistlichen Ritterorden im Mittelalter', Altpreussische Forschungen, 1 (1924), pp. 5–24, repr. in H. Beumann (ed.), Heidenmission und Kreuzzugsgedanke in der deutschen Ostpolitik des Mittelalters (Wege der Forschung, 7; Darmstadt, 1963), pp. 364–85; other arts. repr. ibid., pp. 389–485. K. Górski, 'The Teutonic Order in Prussia', Medievalia et Humanistica, 17 (1966), pp. 20–37. W. Urban, The Baltic Crusade DeKalb, Ill., 1975), pp. 157–259 passim. E. Christiansen, The Northern Crusades: The Baltic and the Catholic Frontier 1100–1525 (New Studies in Medieval History, 1980), passim. M. Biskup, 'Polish Research Work on the History of the Teutonic Order State Organization in Prussia (1945–1959)', Acta Poloniae Historica, 3 (Warsaw, 1960), pp. 89–113. H. E. Mayer, Bibliographie zur Geschichte der Kreuzzüge (Hanover, 1960), p. 4 (no. 57), p. 6 (nos. 118–20), p. 87 (no. 1624), and pp. 169 f. (nos. 3622–47), with addenda in HZ, Sonderheft, 3 (1969), p. 708; K. H. Lampe, Bibliographie zur Geschichte des Deutschen Ordens bis 1959, 1, Quellen und Studien zur Geschichte des Deutschen Ordens, 3 (Bad Godesberg, 1970). K. Wieser in DIP 6 (1980), cols. 796–806, s.v. 'Ordine Teutonico'.

Tewkesbury Abbey. Notwithstanding the tradition of an 8th-cent. foundation by Theoc, a hermit, modern scholars give the derivation of the name as 'Twixtbury', the fortified place between the rivers. A cell of Cranborne since 980, Tewkesbury was refounded as a *Benedictine abbey in 1087 by Robert Fitzhamon with Giraldus, Abbot of Cranborne, who moved his community there. The magnificent abbey church was consecrated in 1121 and extensively remodelled in the early 14th cent. In 1540, at the *Dissolution, it became the parish church of Tewkesbury. It was restored by Sir G. G. *Scott in 1875–9.

Annales Monasterii de Theokesberia, 1066–1263, ed. H. R. Luard, Annales Monastici, 1 (Rolls Series, 1864), pp. 43–180, with introd. pp. xv–xxvii. W. *Dugdale, *Monasticon Anglicanum, 2 (1819 edn.), pp. 53–87. A Cursory Disquisition on the Conventual Church of Tewkesbury and its Antiquities (1818). J. H. Blunt, Tewkesbury Abbey and its Associations (1875); H. J. L. J. Massé, The Abbey Church of Tewkesbury with some Account of the Priory Church of Deerhurst, Gloucester (1900), pp. 3–102. R. Graham in W. Page (ed.), VCH, Gloucester, 2 (1907), pp. 61–6, with refs.

Texte und Untersuchungen. The abbreviated title of Texte und Untersuchungen zur Geschichte der altchristlichen Literatur, a famous series of texts and studies of early Christian literature, published since 1882, originally under the editorship of O. von Gebhardt and A. *Harnack. From 1897 to 1961 it was the organ for publishing studies subsidiary to the edition of the Greek Fathers issued by the Prussian (later Berlin) Academy (Die Griechischen Christlichen Schriftsteller).

Textual Criticism. The critical study of the text of an ancient writer whose work has come down in MS from the period before the invention of printing. Few scribes are able to copy a text exactly; it follows that the more often a text is copied and the greater the number of resulting MSS, the greater variation there is likely to be between them. The work of the textual critic is therefore to compare and evaluate the differences in the MSS (usually known as different 'readings') in order to reconstruct the history of the text through its various stages and ultimately to establish the original text as it left the hands of the author.

The great majority of the extant Hebrew MSS of the OT, representing the so-called *Massoretic text, have relatively few variations, and these are for the most part only minor. But there is good reason to suspect that this situation is due to an authoritative text having been decided on at the beginning of the Christian era and having subsequently been copied with the very greatest care. The *Septuagint Greek MSS, however, display not only considerable differences among themselves, but also a large number of instances in which they agree in differing from the Hebrew; from this observation critics have deduced that the LXX translation was made from a different (and prob. earlier) text than that which has survived in the Massoretic text. This deduction has been confirmed by the discoveries at Qumran (see DEAD SEA SCROLLS). Among the Hebrew MSS there discovered are several representing a type of text which lies behind the LXX, as well as others of pre-Massoretic type.

In the NT the problems are of another kind. The variations between the MSS are both very numerous and in some instances very considerable, occasionally involving whole passages, e.g. the end of Mark, q.v. Study of the MSS has revealed that in general (but only very generally) three main types of text are to be distinguished; and by using the evidence of the ancient versions (Latin, *Syriac, *Coptic, etc.) and quotations in the early Fathers it has been possible to a great extent to localize and date these types. They are: (1) a type associated with *Alexandria, which goes back to an archetype which must be put early in the 2nd cent.; (2) a *Western type (so called by F. J. A. *Hort because the chief witnesses to it are the Latin versions and Fathers), which can be traced back to c. AD 150; and (3) a type associated with *Antioch and *Constantinople (the so-called 'Koine' or *Byzantine or *Syrian text) which appears to be a systematic revision undertaken towards the end of the 3rd cent. This last type of text became standard in the Greek-speaking Church of the medieval period. It is found in the majority of the extant Greek MSS of the NT and was the text of the first printed edition (see TEXTUS RECEPTUS).

Some of the works of ancient and medieval Christian writers have survived in many MSS; others only in a few or even a single MS; but in these cases the problems confronting the textual critic and the methods used in dealing with them resemble those encountered in the NT.

Modern editors of texts, whether biblical or otherwise, are accustomed to print as the text of their edition either the text of a single MS or a text which they themselves have constructed from the total material available; in either case it is usual to accompany the text with a statement of variant readings found in other MSS and elsewhere (e.g. versions and quotations). This is normally printed at the foot of the page and is known as a '*critical apparatus'.

In the broadest sense, the history of textual criticism may be said to have started in the pre-Christian period with the labours of the Alexandrian critics on the texts of the classical authors. Of the early Christian critics the most outstanding was *Origen, whose *Hexapla was a landmark in OT text-critical history. At the Renaissance, Robert *Stephanus I edited and printed a number of editions of the Bible in Latin, in Greek, and in Hebrew, and also of some of the Fathers. In the 17th and 18th centuries the *Maurists were justly famous for their editions of many patristic texts. J. J. *Griesbach (1745–1812) is often regarded as the founder of NT textual criticism as the term is understood today; and he was followed by C. *Tischendorf (1815–74), whose edition of the NT, although published in its final form in 1894 and so pre-dating the major *papyrus finds, is still a standard work of reference. In the development of the textual criticism of the OT important stages were marked by the publication of B. *Kennicott's *Vetus Testamentum Hebraicum cum variis lectionibus* (1776–80) and R. Kittel's *Biblia Hebraica* (Leipzig, 1905–6; 3rd edn. by P. Kahle, Stuttgart, 1929–37); *Biblia Hebraica Stuttgartensia*, ed. K. Elliger and W. Rudolph (1977; rev., 1983), the standard scholarly text, is the 4th edn. of Kittel. The later years of the 19th cent. witnessed the inauguration of two large-scale undertakings in editing the Fathers on the most modern critical principles, namely the Berlin corpus of Greek Fathers ('GCS') and the Vienna corpus of Latin Fathers ('CSEL'), to be followed in the earlier years of the 20th cent. by the first volumes in the two oriental series, *CSCO* and *PO*, and in the second half of the cent. by the various series of the *Corpus Christianorum* (CCLS, CCSG, CCCM, etc.) and *Sources Chrétiennes*.

The belief that textual criticism has radically altered the text lying behind the traditional translations of the Bible has been one of the factors prompting the production of modern versions in recent times. An example of the results of textual criticism in the NT is afforded by Mk. 9. 29. The AV, based on the *textus receptus*, reads: 'And he said unto them, This kind can come forth by nothing, but by prayer and fasting'. It now seems clear that the words 'and fasting' were not part of the original Gk. text, and they are therefore omitted from the English text of scholarly versions from the RV onwards. But the resulting changes in the text, at least so far as the NT is concerned, are by no means so fundamental as is often supposed.

Useful introd. to biblical textual criticism by F. C. *Burkitt in *E.Bi.* 4 (1903), cols. 4977–5031, s.v. 'Text and Versions'. On the OT, B. J. Roberts, *The Old Testament Text and Versions: The Hebrew Text in Transmission and the History of the Ancient Versions* (Cardiff, 1951); E. Würthwein, *Der Text des Alten Testaments: Eine Einführung in die Biblia Hebraica von Rudolf Kittel* (1952, Eng. tr., Oxford, 1957; 4th edn., 1973, Eng. tr., Grand Rapids, Mich., 1979, London, 1980); J. Weingreen, *Introduction to the Critical Study of the Hebrew Bible* (Oxford, 1982); E. Tov, *Textual Criticism of the Hebrew Bible* (Minneapolis and Assen [1992]: expanded Eng. tr. of work publ. in Heb., Jerusalem, 1989). S. Talmon, 'The Old Testament Text', in P. R. Ackroyd and C. F. Evans (eds.), *The Cambridge History of the Bible*, 1 (1970), pp. 159–99. Eissfeldt, pp. 669–719. On the NT, F. H. *Scrivener, *A Plain Introduction to the Criticism of the New Testament* (1861; 4th edn., by E. Miller, 2 vols., 1894); C. R. Gregory, *Textkritik des neuen Testamentes* (3 parts, Leipzig, 1900–9); id., *Canon and Text of the New Testament* (1907), pp. 297–528; F. G. Kenyon, *Handbook to the Textual Criticism of the New Testament* (1901; 2nd edn., 1912); id., *The Text of the Greek Bible* (1937; 3rd edn. by A. W. Adams, 1975); B. M. Metzger, *The Text of the New Testament: Its Transmission, Corruption, and Restoration* (Oxford, 1964; 3rd

edn., 1992); J. Finegan, *Encountering New Testament Manuscripts* (Grand Rapids, Mich., 1974; London, 1975). J. N. Birdsall, 'The New Testament Text', in P. R. Ackroyd and C. F. Evans (eds.), *The Cambridge History of the Bible*, 1 (1970), pp. 308–77. E. Tov and E. J. Epp in *Anchor Bible Dictionary*, 6 (1992), pp. 393–435, s.v., on OT and NT respectively. See also bibl. to GREEK (BIBLICAL AND PATRISTIC).

Textus Receptus (Lat., 'the Received Text'). The Greek text of the NT ordinarily contained in printed editions down to the later decades of the 19th cent. It takes its name from a casual phrase in the preface of the 2nd (1633) *Elzevir edition ('Textum *ergo habes, nunc ab omnibus receptum, in quo nihil immutatum aut corruptum damus*'). This text, which closely followed that of T. *Beza (1565), was substantially that of *Erasmus (1516), the *Complutensian Polyglot (NT printed 1514, pub. 1522) and esp. R. *Stephanus I (1550). It is in substance the *Byzantine text contained in the great majority of the MSS and underlies the AV of the English Bible. See TEXTUAL CRITICISM.

Thaddaeus, St. Mentioned in Mt. 10: 3 and Mk. 3: 8 (some MSS read *Lebbaeus), he is usually identified with the Apostle *Jude (q.v.). He is, however, sometimes identified with *Addai, one of the Seventy, who plays an important part in the *Abgar legend. Feast day of the latter, in the E. Church, 21 August.

Passio, which purports to be the work of Abdias, a disciple of St Thaddaeus and first Bp. of Babylon, pr. in R. A. *Lipsius and M. Bonnet, *Acta Apostolorum Apocrypha*, 1 (Leipzig, 1891), pp. 273–8, with introd. pp. cvi–cx.

Thaddaeus, Doctrine of. See ADDAI, DOCTRINE OF.

Thanksgiving, General. See GENERAL THANKSGIVING.

theandric activity (Gk. θεανδρικὴ ἐνέργεια). The term was popularized by *Dionysius the Ps.-Areopagite (*Ep.* 4) to denote the characteristic activity of the God-man. Although used by *Monophysites (esp. *Severus of Antioch) and *Monothelites in support of their theories of the one nature and one will in Christ, it was defended by St *Maximus the Confessor as presupposing the two natures, whose union and interaction it was meant to emphasize.

Theatines, religious order. Founded in Rome in 1524, as 'Clerks Regular of the Divine Providence', by two members of the Roman Oratory of Divine Love, St *Cajetan and Gian Pietro Carafa (Bp. of Chieti, or 'Theate'; afterwards Pope *Paul IV), the order aimed at the reform of the Church from the grave abuses and scandals then corrupting it. The Theatines were not allowed to have any property, or to beg; they observed the strictest austerity of life; and their habit was distinguished from that of the secular clergy only by their white socks. Within ten years other houses of Theatines had been established in Italy, and the order soon spread into Spain and Central Europe. By their zeal and piety they played an important part in the *Counter-Reformation. In 1583 a congregation of Theatine nuns was founded in Italy under the direction of the Theatine fathers; but the order never obtained wide extension.

G. B. del Tufo, *Historia della religione de' padri chierici regolari* (2 vols., 1609–16); G. Silos, CR, *Historia Clericorum Regularium a Congregatione Condita* (3 parts, Rome and Parma, 1650–66). B. Ferro, CR, *Istoria delle missioni de' chierici regolari teatini* (2 vols.,

Rome, 1704–5). Heimbucher, 2, pp. 97–106. F. Andreu, CR, in *DIP* 2 (1975), cols. 978–99, s.v. 'Chierici Regolari Teatini', with bibl. See also Lives of St Cajetan and Pope Paul IV, cited s.vv.

Thebaic Version. See SAHIDIC.

Thebaid, the. The upper part of the Nile valley (named after its capital, Thebes) which from the 3rd cent. onwards was the cradle of Christian monasticism. Acc. to St *Jerome the first ascetic in the region was St *Paul of Thebes (*c.*230–341). The monks, who at first practised the most extreme asceticism and lived as solitaries, became increasingly organized into communities, mainly through the efforts of St *Antony and St *Pachomius.

Theban Legion, the. The Christian legion from the *Thebaid which acc. to tradition was massacred under the Emp. Maximian at St-Maurice-en-Valais. See MAURICE, ST.

Thecla, St. An early Christian virgin. The tradition concerning her derives from the 'Acts of Sts *Paul and Thecla' (q.v. for details), acc. to which she was converted by St Paul at Iconium. W. M. *Ramsay and others have contended that these 'Acts' contain a nucleus of genuine history, though it is difficult to separate fact from legend. A large church was built over Thecla's supposed tomb at Meriamlik, near Seleucia, and she was greatly venerated in both E. and W. Feast day in the W., 23 Sept. (suppressed in the RC Church in 1969); in the E., 24 Sept.

'De Vita et Miraculis S. Theclae', attributed in the MSS to *Basil of Seleucia, but now held to be the work of an unknown 5th-cent. author, ed., with Fr. tr. and full introd., by G. Dagron (Subsidia Hagiographica, 62; 1978). C. Holzhey, *Die Thekla-Akten: Ihre Verbreitung und Beurtheilung in der Kirche* (Veröffentlichungen aus dem kirchen-historischen Seminar München, Reihe 2, 7; 1905). L. Radermacher, *Hippolytus und Thekla: Studien zur Geschichte von Legende und Kultus* (*Sb.* (Wien), 182; 1916), pp. 51–69 and 121–6. R. Albrecht, *Das Leben der heiligen Makrina auf dem Hintergrund der Thekla-Traditionen* (Forschungen zur Kirchen- und Dogmengeschichte, 38; 1986), pp. 239–326. U. M. Fasola, 'Il Complesso catacombale di S. Tecla', *Riv. A.C.* 40 (for 1964; 1966), pp. 19–50; id., 'La Basilica sotterranea di S. Tecla e le regioni cimiteriali vicine', ibid. 46 (1970) pp. 193–288. H. *Leclercq, OSB, in *DACL* 15 (pt. 2; 1953), cols. 2225–36, s.v. 'Thècle (Sainte)', with refs. See also works cited under PAUL AND THECLA, ACTS OF STS.

Theism (from Gk. Θεός, 'God'). The term, prob. first employed by R. *Cudworth in the preface to his *Intellectual System* (1678), was originally used as an opposite to 'atheism', and only later acquired its present definite meaning to denote a creed distinct also from *pantheism and esp. from *Deism (q.v.). Theism, as the word is currently employed, may be said to denote a philosophical system which accepts a transcendent and personal God who not only created but also preserves and governs the world, the contingency of which does not exclude miracles and the exercise of human freedom. Theism, therefore, leaves room for the Christian revelation and is in various forms the view of the world common to all orthodox Christian philosophers; it is also required by *Judaism and *Islam. Apart from certain aberrations, usually of a pantheistic character, Theism was the basis of Christian philosophy down to modern times. Relegated to the background by the Deistic philosophy of the 18th cent. and the

*Hegelianism and materialism of the 19th, it has again found many competent and convinced exponents in the modern world. See also PANENTHEISM.

Modern works defending Theism incl. F. *von Hügel, *Eternal Life* (1912), *passim*; C. C. J. *Webb, *Studies in the History of Natural Theology* (1915), and other works; W. R. Sorley, *Moral Values and the Idea of God* (Gifford Lectures, 1914–15; 1918); E. L. Mascall, *He Who Is: A Study in Traditional Theism* (1943; with new introd. and appendix, 1966); A. M. Farrer, *Finite and Infinite* (1943); D. J. B. Hawkins, *The Essentials of Theism* (1949); H. D. Lewis, *Our Experience of God* (1959); E. L. Mascall, *The Openness of Being: Natural Theology Today* (Gifford Lectures, 1970–1; 1971); A. C. Ewing, *Value and Reality: The Philosophical Case for Theism* (1973); R. [G.] Swinburne, *The Coherence of Theism* (Oxford, 1977); B. [L.] Hebblethwaite, *The Ocean of Truth: A Defence of Objective Theism* (Cambridge, 1988). A. E. *Taylor in *HERE* 12 (1921), pp. 261–87, s.v. See also bibl. to GOD and PHILOSOPHY OF RELIGION.

Themistians. See AGNOETAE.

Theobald (d. 1161), Abp. of *Canterbury. The son of a knight of Thierville (Eure) in Normandy, he became a monk at *Bec, prior in 1127, and abbot in 1137. In 1139, as King Stephen's choice, he became Abp. of Canterbury. The disappointed *Henry of Blois, Bp. of *Winchester, whom Innocent II made a Papal legate, became a rival and, for a time, dominant power in the English Church. Theobald tried to prevent the election as Abp. of *York of the future St *William, a kinsman of Stephen and Henry, and he struggled against the rebellious monks of Christ Church and St Augustine's, Canterbury. He assembled a distinguished household of clerks, many of whom became bishops and archbishops. They included his brother Walter (later Bp. of *Rochester), John of Canterbury (Bp. of Poitiers, Abp. of Narbonne and Lyons), Roger of Pont-l'Évêque (Abp. of York), *John of Salisbury, and Thomas *Becket. The great civilian and canonist Master Vacarius was also in his household. During the civil war, although sympathetic to the Angevin cause, he loyally supported Stephen. When in 1148 he defied the King and attended the Council of *Reims, his property was seized and he was exiled. In consequence *Eugenius III laid England under an *interdict, but the King and the country were reconciled in the same year. At the end of 1149 he was made a Papal legate and in 1151 held an important legatine Council in London. In 1152 he refused to crown Stephen's son Eustace and had to flee to Flanders. Soon recalled, he reconciled Stephen and Henry of Anjou in 1153. On Stephen's death (1154), he crowned Henry King and recommended to him Thomas Becket as chancellor. His own secretary, John of Salisbury, was his chief adviser during his last years. With his defeat of the schemes of Henry of Blois, his championship of episcopal authority over monasteries, his encouragement of greater administrative and judicial efficiency, and his attempts to withstand royal 'tyranny', he did much to give the English Church a new identity and purpose.

Some of his letters are pr. among the correspondence of John of Salisbury (q.v.). Brief 'Compendium Vitae', written at Bec, pr. among the works of *Lanfranc (q.v.); ed. J. A. Giles, 1 (Oxford, 1844), pp. 337–9, repr. in J. P. Migne, *PL* 150. 733 f.). A. Saltman, *Theobald of Canterbury* (University of London Historical Studies,

2; 1956), with text of charters, etc. W. Hunt in *DNB* 56 (1898), pp. 113–18, with refs.

theocracy (Gk. θεοκρατία, 'government by God'). The term was coined by Flavius *Josephus (*Contra Apionem*, 2. 16) to denote the political organization of the Jewish people, as the purest example of a theocracy. Before the institution of the kingship in Israel, Yahweh was regarded as the supreme ruler of the Hebrews, whose laws constituted at the same time religious and civil obligations, and even after the election of a king, the kings were vice-gerents of Yahweh, though (in Judah at least) they claimed a status which some prophets saw as derogating from the authority of Yahweh (cf. Hos. 8: 4). A more complete theocracy was created after the Exile, when the monarchy disappeared. A theocratic form of government was also known to many ancient peoples, e.g. in Egypt and Tibet, where kings appeared as representatives or even incarnations of the Deity, and it is intrinsic in *Islam. In the history of Christianity attempts at the realization of the theocratic ideal were made by the medieval Popes, esp. *Gregory VII, and again by J. *Calvin at *Geneva. The influence of the OT model of government on Calvinist political doctrines is the source of the theocratic features in O. *Cromwell's Commonwealth and in Scottish Presbyterianism.

Theodicy (Gk. Θεός, 'God', and δίκη, 'justice'), etymologically the justification of God. The word was coined by G. W. *Leibniz, who used it as the title of his *Essais de théodicée sur la bonté de Dieu* (1710), and since then it has been applied to that part of natural theology which is concerned to defend the goodness and omnipotence of God against objections arising from the existence of evil in the world. The question itself, i.e. the origin and meaning of evil, has occupied philosophers and theologians from early times. Attempts at solving it have been made in many religions, e.g. in Hinduism, Buddhism, and *Manichaeism, both on dualistic and on pantheistic lines, and in the philosophic systems of *Plato and the *Stoics. *Origen explained it by the abuse of the freedom of the creatures, an interpretation since then developed in many forms, notably by St *Thomas Aquinas. The problem, less prominent in very religious eras, was much discussed in the period of the *Enlightenment, and Leibniz's work was an answer to P. *Bayle's brilliantly developed thesis that the existence of evil is incompatible with the goodness and omnipotence of God. Leibniz, who, in contrast to St Thomas, regarded this world as the best of all possible worlds, held that evil is a necessary element like the shade in a picture, throwing into relief the beauty and harmony of the whole. This optimistic view was shared by most 18th-cent. thinkers, e.g. by Lord Shaftesbury and Alexander Pope. In the 19th cent. Theodicy came to be more and more regarded in connection with the entire complex of *Natural Theology, of which it is now sometimes used as a synonym.

Theodora I (*c.*500–47), wife of *Justinian I, who married her in 523. Solemnly crowned co-regnant Empress in 527, she exercised a very great influence upon the complicated theological controversies of the time. Her sympathies were on the side of the *Monophysite party, and it was probably mainly through her influence that Justinian adopted his reactionary religious policy, which, esp. in the dispute over the *Three Chapters, sought to conciliate the Monophysites even at the expense of the *Chalcedonian decrees. Although, acc. to the (unreliable) evidence of the 'Anecdota' of *Procopius, she had lived a very dissolute life in her earlier years, she was undoubtedly a woman of outstanding intellect and learning, and as Empress she is said to have been a moral reformer. Her firm character was shown in her vigorous support of her husband in the Nika insurrection (532). Her portrait in mosaic is to be seen in the church of San Vitale at *Ravenna.

C. Diehl, *Théodora: Impératrice de Byzance* (Paris, 3rd edn., *c.*1904); H. Stadelmann, *Theodora von Byzanz* (2 vols., Dresden, 1927). W. G. Holmes, *The Age of Justinian and Theodora*, esp. 1 (1905), pp. 321–49, and 2 (1907), *passim*; R. Browning, *Justinian and Theodora* (1971; rev. edn., 1987), *passim*. A. Cameron, *Procopius and the Sixth Century* (1985), pp. 67–83, with further refs. L. *Duchesne, 'Les Protégés de Théodora', *Mélanges d'Archéologie et d'Histoire*, 32 (1915), pp. 57–79.

Theodore the Lector (early 6th cent.), Church historian who lived at *Constantinople. He wrote two historical treatises: (1) a 'Tripartite History', composed of extracts from the Histories of *Socrates, *Sozomen, and *Theodoret; and (2) a work composed by himself carrying the history down to the time of Justin I (d. 527). The former work has survived in part, but of the latter only fragments have been preserved.

Of the 'Tripartite History' (4 Books), Bks. 1 and 2 survive in Cod. Marc. 344 and excerpts in Cod. Bodl. Barocc. 142. In the 7th–8th cent. an Epitome of the Church History (2, above) was compiled; frags. of this are embodied in the Byzantine Chronographers. Frags. of Theodore, first pub. by H. *Valesius (1673), repr. from 1720 edn. (Valesius and Reading) in J. P. Migne, *PG* 86 (1). 165–228. Complete crit. text, incl. further frags., ed. G. C. Hansen (GCS, 1971; 2nd edn., 1995). J. Bidez, *La Tradition manuscrite de Sozomène et la Tripartite de Théodore le Lecteur* (TU 32. 2b; 1908), pp. 35–72 and 76–80. *CPG* 3 (1979), pp. 398 f. (nos. 7502 f.). H. G. Opitz in *PW*, Zweite Reihe, 5 (pt. 2; 1934), cols. 1869–81, s.v. 'Theodorus (48)'.

Theodore of Mopsuestia (*c.*350–428), Antiochene theologian and biblical exegete. He studied rhetoric at *Antioch under Libanius; but in 369, with his friend St John *Chrysostom, he entered the school of *Diodore in a monastery at Antioch, where he remained for nearly ten years. In 392 he became Bp. of Mopsuestia. The rest of his life he spent in his see, gaining a wide reputation for learning and orthodoxy. In his biblical commentaries he used scientific, critical, philological, and historical methods, following Diodore in rejecting the Alexandrian use of allegorical interpretations. His account of the Fall of man includes positions superficially like those of *Pelagianism. His doctrine concerning the Incarnation was condemned at the Councils of *Ephesus (431) and *Constantinople (553). But the recovery in modern times of certain of his works, which have been preserved in Syriac, has shown that he has sometimes been judged unjustly. His terminology, as is only to be expected in one who wrote before the Council of *Chalcedon, is not always precise on questions of Christology. His psychological analysis of human personality, influenced by a hostile reaction against *Apollinarianism, seems to have dictated certain

*Nestorian formulae; however, he tried sincerely to explain them in a Catholic sense. See also THREE CHAPTERS, THE.

The texts of Theodore's works are scattered. Collection of his comm. on NT ed. O. F. Fritzsche (Zurich, 1847), repr., together with comm. on the Minor Prophets and others, from A. *Mai (ed.), *Nova Patrum Bibliotheca*, 7, pt. 1 (Rome, 1854), and other material, in J. P. Migne, *PG* 66. 9–1020. Crit. edns. of his Commentaries on Minor Epp. of St Paul (fragmentary) by H. B. *Swete (2 vols., Cambridge, 1880–2); frags. on St Paul collected in K. Staab, *Pauluskommentare aus der griechischen Kirche aus Katenenhandschriften gesammelt* (Neutestamentliche Abhandlungen, 15; 1933), pp. 113–212; frags. of comm. on Pss. 1–80 [81], ed. R. Devreesse (ST 93; 1939); of comm. on Jn., ed. id., *Essai sur Théodore de Mopsueste* (ST 141; 1948 [a major work]), appendix, pp. 287–419; and crit. edn. of comm. on the Minor Prophets by H. N. Sprenger (Göttinger Orientsforschungen, 5. Reihe, Bd. 1; Wiesbaden, 1977). Syr. text of comm. on Jn., ed., with Lat. tr., by J. M. Vosté, OP (CSCO, Scriptores Syri, 4th ser. 3; 1940); of frags. of comm. on Pss. 118 [119] and 138 [139]–48, ed., with Lat. tr., by L. van Rompay (CSCO 435–6, Scriptores Syri, 189–90; 1982) (for edn. of tr. by *Julian of Eclanum, see s.v.); and of frag. of comm. on Eccles. by W. Strothmann (Göttinger Orientsforschungen, 1. Reihe, Bd. 28; Wiesbaden, 1988). Catecheses (Syr. text and Eng. tr.) ed. A. Mingana (Woodbrooke Studies, 5 (on Nicene Creed), 1932; and 6 (on the *Lord's Prayer and the Sacraments of Baptism and the Eucharist), 1933); also photographically repr. from MS Mingana Syr. 561 (Selly Oak Colleges' Library, Birmingham) with Fr. tr. and introd. by R. Tonneau, OP, and R. Devreesse (ST 145; 1949). R. P. Vaggione, 'Some Neglected Fragments of Theodore of Mopsuestia's *Contra Eunomium*', *JTS* NS 31 (1980), pp. 403–70. U. Wickert, *Studien zu den Pauluskommentaren Theodors von Mopsuestia als Beitrag zum Verständnis der Antiochenischen Theologie* (Beiheft zur *ZNTW* 27; 1962). More general studies by F. A. Sullivan, SJ (Analecta Gregoriana, 82; 1956), R. A. Greer (London, 1961), R. A. Norris (Oxford, 1963), G. Koch (Münchener Theologische Studien, 2. Systematische Abteilung, 31; 1965), J. McW. Dewart (Catholic University of America, Studies in Christian Antiquity, 16; 1971), and D. Z. Zaharopoulos (New York etc. [1989]). *CPG* 2 (1974), pp. 344–61 (nos. 3827–73). Altaner and Stuiber (1978), pp. 319–22 and 615. H. B. Swete in *DCB* 4 (1887), pp. 934–48, s.v. 'Theodorus (26)'; É. Amann in *DTC* 15 (pt. 1; 1946), cols. 235–79, s.v.; J. M. Lera, SJ, in *Dict. Sp.* 15 (1991), cols. 385–400, s.v. 'Théodore (3) de Mopsueste'.

Theodore of Pharan. See THEODORE OF RAÏTHU.

Theodore of Raïthu

Theodore of Raïthu (*fl.* after 550, perhaps 7th cent.), monk at the monastery of Raïthu on the Gulf of Suez. It has been argued that he later became Bp. of nearby Pharan, and as such was involved in the early stages of the *Monothelite controversy as a proponent of monenergism. He was the author of a Προπαρασκευή (*Praeparatio*), defending the Christological formulae of St *Cyril of Alexandria (d. 444) and of the *Chalcedonian Council (451) alike and attacking the doctrines of *Severus of Antioch and *Julian of Halicarnassus. The treatise outlines the chief Christological heresies from *Mani to Severus, while in its later sections it deals with specifically philosophical problems. J. P. Junglas and others have argued that Theodore was also the author of the 'De Sectis' traditionally ascribed to *Leontius of Byzantium.

The only complete pr. text of the 'Praeparatio' is the crit. edn. in F. Diekamp, *Analecta Patristica* (Orientalia Christiana Analecta, no. 117; 1938), pp. 185–222, with introd. pp. 173–84. Portions of the text in J. P. Migne, *PG* 91. 1484–504. J. P. Junglas, *Leontius*

von Byzanz (Paderborn, 1908), pp. 15–20. W. Elert, 'Theodore von Pharan und Theodor von Raithu', *TLZ* 76 (1951), cols. 67–76; id., *Der Ausgang der altchristlichen Christologie: Eine Untersuchung über Theodor von Pharan und seine Zeit als Einführung in die alte Dogmengeschichte* (1957). *CPG* 3 (1979), pp. 417 f. (nos. 7600–2). Beck (1959), pp. 382 f. and 430 f. M. Richard in *DTC* 15 (pt. 1; 1946), cols. 282–4, s.v.; É. Amann, ibid., cols. 279–82, s.v. 'Théodore de Pharan'.

Theodore of Studios

Theodore of Studios, St (759–826), monastic reformer. The son of pious parents of *Constantinople, he early came under the influence of his uncle, St Plato, abbot of Saccudium, under whose direction he embraced the religious life *c.*780. He was ordained priest by the patriarch *Tarasius in 787, and in 794 was made abbot of Saccudium in the place of Plato, who resigned in his favour. In 796 he was one of the most influential opponents of the adulterous marriage of Constantine VI and separated from the communion of Tarasius who had tolerated it. The result was that his monks were scattered and he himself was banished to Thessalonica; but in the next year he was recalled after the Emperor's mother, Irene, had deposed her son. In 799 he and the greater part of his community went from Saccudium, where they had been exposed to the raids of the Saracens, to the old monastery of *Studios at Constantinople which had become almost extinct. The energy and organizing genius of Theodore soon made it the centre of the monastic life of the E. The sermons in which he expounded to his monks the principles of the religious life embody his austere and noble ideals. In the controversy under the next Emp., Nicephorus I (802–11), about the reinstitution of the priest Joseph, who had blessed Constantine's second marriage, by the new patriarch, Theodore was again banished (809). From his exile he appealed to Pope *Leo III, but without success. After the Emperor's death in 811 Theodore returned.

In 813 Leo V ascended the throne and, reviving the *Iconoclastic policy of Constantine V, exiled Theodore, its most vigorous opponent. In 815 Theodore was taken to Metopa in N. Phrygia, and subsequently to Boneta in Anatolia and to Smyrna, where he was closely confined and frequently ill-treated, though he succeeded in writing numerous letters (many of them still extant) to encourage his followers. He also sent appeals to the Pope, Paschal I, who wrote to the Emperor on the question of image-worship. After Leo's assassination in 820, Theodore was recalled by his successor, Michael, who pursued a policy of toleration, but prohibited image-worship in the capital. Theodore therefore could not permanently return to his monastery and spent his last years outside Constantinople, largely on the peninsula of Tryphon. A man of austere sanctity and iron will, a vigorous defender of the independence of the Church, and a genius in religious legislation, Theodore of Studios was one of the finest representatives of Byzantine monasticism. His writings include a 'Short' and a 'Long Catechesis', an Exposition of the Liturgy of the *Presanctified, a number of spiritual orations, a list of canonical penances, several polemical works directed against the Iconoclasts, and poetry and correspondence. He is widely venerated esp. in the E. Feast day, 11 Nov.

There is no complete edn. of his works, that projected by the *Maurists not having been carried through. His letters and various dogmatic works ed. J. *Sirmond, *Opera Varia*, 5 (Venice, 1696); further texts ed. A. *Mai, *NPB* 5 (Rome, 1849), with notice by L. *Allatius in vol. 6 (ibid., 1853), pt. 2, pp. 158–68; these items are repr. in J. P. Migne, *PG* 99 (repr., with introd. by G. D. Dragas, Athens, 1988). Further letters and frags. ed. J. P. Cozza Luzi, *NPB* 8 (Rome, 1871), pt. 1, pp. 1–244, and sermons, ibid. 9 (1888), pt. 1, pp. 1–318 ('Short Catechesis'), and pt. 2, pp. 1–217 ('Long Catechesis'); a second bk. of this 'Long Catechesis' was ed. by A. Papadopoulos-Kerameus (St Petersburg, 1904); hymns ed. J. B. *Pitra, *Analecta Sacra Spicilegio Solesmensi*, 1 (Paris, 1876), pp. 336–80. Crit. edn. of some of his poetry, with Ger. tr. and comm., by P. Speck (Supplementa Byzantina, 1; 1968), and of his letters by G. Fatouros (Corpus Fontium Historiae Byzantinae, 31; 2 vols., 1992). Eng. tr. of his writings against the Iconoclasts: *On the Holy Icons*, tr. by C. P. Roth (Crestwood, NY, 1981). Modern studies by A. Gardner (London, 1905), [B.] E. Marin ('Les Saints'; 1906), and A. P. Dobroklonskij (in Russian; 2 vols., Odessa, 1913–14). I. Hausherr, SJ, 'Saint Théodore Studite, l'homme et l'ascète', *Orientalia Christiana*, 6 (1926), pp. 1–87. C. von Schönborn, OP, *L'Icône du Christ: Fondements théologiques* (Paradosis, 24; Fribourg, 1976), pp. 217–34 (on his theology of icons). Beck (1959), pp. 491–5, with bibl. M.-H. Congourdeau in *Dict. Sp.* 15 (1991), cols. 401–14, s.v. 'Théodore (6) Stoudite'.

Theodore of Tarsus, St (*c*.602–90), Abp. of *Canterbury. He was an Asiatic Greek, living as a monk in one of the Greek-speaking monasteries in Rome when he was recommended to Pope *Vitalian for the Archbishopric of Canterbury by *Hadrian, an African monk to whom the see had been offered. Vitalian consecrated him in 668; but the Pope, fearing that his orthodoxy might be corrupted by his Greek upbringing, arranged for *Benedict Biscop and Hadrian to accompany him to Britain. After a visitation of the whole of England, he set about reforming the government of the Church by dividing dioceses and extending the episcopate. In 672 or 673 he summoned, and presided over, the first important synod of the whole English Church at *Hertford, and in 679 he held another great synod at *Hatfield, where a declaration of orthodoxy was drawn up and forwarded to Rome at the request of Pope *Agatho. By such methods he unified the English Church and established the metropolitical authority of the see of Canterbury. He also did much to prepare the way for the parochial system. His active interference in the diocese of York created serious difficulties with St *Wilfrid (q.v. for details). His few writings, some only recently identified, comprise the *Iudicia* (which preserves his opinions on matters of ecclesiastical discipline and penance), the *Laterculus Malalianus*, a brief treatise which is partly chronological and partly exegetical, and a Latin translation of the Greek *Passio S. Anastasii*, as well as a corpus of commentaries on the Pentateuch and Gospels. The 'Penitential' attributed to him also reflects his views. Feast day, 19 Sept.

The principal sources are *Bede, *HE*, esp. 4. 1–5. 8; cf. notes in edn. by B. Colgrave and R. A. B. Mynors (Oxford, 1969), ad locc. and comm. by J. M. Wallace-Hadrill (ibid., 1988), pp. 38, 40, 51, 101, 136–40, 142–5, 148, 150, 161, 178–80, 190, and 194; and Eddius' life of St Wilfrid, ed., with Eng. tr., by B. Colgrave (Cambridge, 1927; repr. 1985). The 'Penitential' was first pr. in full by F. W. H. Wasserschleben, *Die Bussordnungen der abendländischen Kirche* (Halle, 1851), pp. 182–219, with other decrees, pp. 145–81; the best edn. is that of P. W. Finsterwalder, *Die Canones Theodori Cantuariensis: Über ihre Überlieferungsformen* (Untersuchungen zu den Bussbüchern des 7., 8., und 9. Jahrhunderts, 1; 1929). Text of the 'Penitential' (though incomplete) is also conveniently pr. in A. W. Haddan and W. *Stubbs (eds.),

Councils and Ecclesiastical Documents Relating to Great Britain and Ireland, 3 (1871), pp. 173–213; other decrees of his archiepiscopate, pp. 114–72. B. Bischoff and M. Lapidge (eds.), *Biblical Commentaries from the Canterbury School of Theodore and Hadrian* (Cambridge Studies in Anglo-Saxon England, 10; 1994), with Eng. tr., and full account of Theodore, pp. 5–81 and 133–89. J. Stevenson, *The 'Laterculus Malalianus' and the School of Archbishop Theodore* (ibid., 14; 1995), incl. text and Eng. tr. M. Lapidge (ed.), *Archbishop Theodore: Commemorative Studies on his Life and Influence* (ibid., 11; 1995). A. J. Frantzen, *The Literature of Penance in Anglo-Saxon England* (New Brunswick, NJ, 1983), pp. 62–78. N. Brooks, *The Early History of the Church of Canterbury* (Leicester, 1984), pp. 71–6 and 94–9. M. Lapidge, 'The School of Theodore and Hadrian', *Anglo-Saxon England*, 15 (1986), pp. 45–72; id., 'The Study of Greek at the School of Canterbury in the Seventh Century', in M. W. Herren (ed.), *The Sacred Nectar of the Greeks: The Study of Greek in the West in the Early Middle Ages* (King's College, London, Medieval Studies, 2; 1988), pp. 169–94. W. Stubbs in *DCB* 4 (1887), pp. 926–32, s.v. 'Theodorus (7)'.

Theodoret (*c*.393–*c*.460), Bp. of Cyrrhus. A native of *Antioch, he was educated in its monastery schools. After distributing his property among the poor, he entered the monastery of Nicerte *c*.416. Consecrated Bp. of Cyrrhus in Syria against his will in 423, he governed his diocese with great wisdom and munificence, at the same time indefatigably fighting paganism and heresy. He soon became involved in the Christological controversy between *Nestorius and *Cyril of Alexandria, in the latter of whose anathematisms he believed he detected a new version of *Apollinarianism. As a personal friend and admirer of Nestorius, he became one of the foremost defenders of the Antiochene Christology, and in a polemical work against Cyril maintained a duality in Christ and accepted the title '*Theotokos' only in a figurative sense. After the Council of *Ephesus (431) he continued to oppose Cyril and the decision of the Council, though Cyril accepted (433) a declaration of faith which had prob. been composed (432) by Theodoret himself. In 448, when accused by Cyril's successor, *Dioscorus, of dividing Christ 'into two Sons', he drew up another confession of faith in which he plainly asserted the unity of Christ and anathematized anyone who did not recognize the BVM as θεοτόκος. In spite of this, Dioscorus anathematized him and obtained Imperial edicts forbidding him to leave his diocese (448) and to come to the Council held at Ephesus in 449 unless summoned. This council, the so-called '*Latrocinium', deposed Theodoret, who was forced into exile. The new Emp., Marcian, summoned him to the Council of *Chalcedon (451), where he reluctantly anathematized Nestorius. It seems that he spent his last years in the peaceful administration of his diocese. A century later his writings against Cyril became the subject of the '*Three Chapters Controversy' and were condemned by the Council of *Constantinople in 553.

Only a comparatively small number of Theodoret's works has come down to us. In his 'Graecarum Affectionum Curatio', one of the finest Christian apologies, he places side by side the Christian and the pagan answers to the fundamental religious questions such as the nature of God and of man, sacrifice, the end of the world, etc. The 'Eranistes' is a treatise against the *Monophysites which asserts the immutability and impassibility of the Divine nature in Christ and the unconfused co-existence of the

Divine and human natures in Him. His exegetical works, which deal with a large number of OT Books, e.g. the *Octateuch, Kings and Chronicles, Psalms, Song of Solomon, and the Major and Minor Prophets, are among the finest specimens of the Antiochene School and remarkable for their lucidity and erudition. His historical works include a 'Religious History', i.e. a collection of biographies of monks, a 'Church History', which continues the work of *Eusebius down to 428, and is esp. valuable for the numerous authentic documents used in it, and a 'Compendium of Heretical Fables', which gives information on *Arianism, Nestorianism, and *Eutychianism.

Theodoret's Christological opinions have been a matter of controversy, but it seems to be conceded by most scholars that he held Nestorian views at least till 434–5 and possibly until Chalcedon, but abandoned them at the latest after 451.

Collected works ed. J. *Sirmond, SJ (4 vols., Paris, 1642); suppl. vol. ed. J. *Garnier, SJ (ibid., 1684), repr. with additions by J. L. Schulze and J. A. Noesselt in J. P. Migne, *PG* 80–4. There are separate edns. of the *Graecarum Affectionum Curatio* by J. Raeder (Teub., 1904), and, with Fr. tr., by P. Canivet, SJ (SC 57; 2 vols., 1958); *Eccl. Hist.* by T. *Gaisford (Oxford, 1854) and L. Parmentier (GCS, 1911; 2nd edn. by F. Scheidweiler, 1954); Comm. on Is. by A. Möhle (Mitteilungen des Septuaginta-Unternehmens der Gesellschaft der Wissenschaften zu Göttingen, 5; 1932; repr., with Fr. tr. by J.-N. Guinot, SC, 276, 295, and 315; 1980–4); Correspondence, with Fr. tr., by Y. Azéma (SC 40, 98, 111, and 429; 1955–98); *Eranistes* by G. H. Ettlinger (Oxford, 1975); *Historia religiosa*, with Fr. tr. by P. Canivet and A. Leroy-Molinghen (SC 234, 257; 1977–9); *Quaestiones in Octateuchum* by N. Fernández Marcos and A. Sáenz-Badillos (Madrid, 1979); and *Quaestiones in Regis et Paralipomena* by N. Fernández Marcos and J. R. Busto Saiz (ibid., 1984). There is an Eng. tr. of *De Providentia Orationes* by T. [P.] Halton (ACW 49 [1988]) and of *Historia religiosa* by R. M. Price (Cistercian Studies Series, 88; Kalamazoo, Mich., 1985). M. Richard, 'L'Activité littéraire de Théodoret avant le Concile d'Éphèse', *RSPT* 24 (1935), pp. 83–106; id., 'Notes sur l'évolution doctrinale de Théodoret', ibid. 25 (1936), pp. 459–81; id., 'Théodoret, Jean d'Antioche et les moines d'Orient', *Mélanges de Science Religieuse*, 3 (1946), pp. 147–56; and other works of this author. G. W. Ashby, *Theodoret of Cyrrhus as Exegete of the Old Testament* (Grahamstown, 1972). G. Koch, *Strukturen und Geschichte des Heils in der Theologie des Theodoret von Kyros* (Frankfurter Theologische Studien, 17; 1974). P. Canivet, *Le Monachisme Syrien selon Théodoret de Cyr* (Théologie Historique, 42; 1977). M. Ninci, *Aporia ed entusiasmo: Il mondo materiale e i filosofi secondo Teodoreto e la tradizione patristica greca* (Temi i Testi, 24; 1977). J.-N. Guinot, *L'Exégèse de Théodoret de Cyr* (Théologie Historique, 100; 1995). *CPG* 3 (1979), pp. 201–19 (nos. 6200–88). Altaner and Stuiber (1978), pp. 339–41 and 620. Y. Azéma in *Dict. Sp.* 15 (1991), cols. 418–35, s.v.

Theodoric (*c.*455–526), King of the Ostrogoths from 475, and ruler of Italy from 493. He spent his early years as a hostage at *Constantinople, and subsequently, as leader of his people in the Balkans, was at times allied with the E. Empire and at times at war with it. In 487 he was commissioned by the Emp. *Zeno to overthrow the usurper Odoacer who was then ruling in Italy. Theodoric defeated and killed Odoacer, and ruled Italy until his death, paying only lip-service to their imperial overlords in Constantinople. His rule gave Italy a period of prolonged peace. Although he and his people were *Arians in a country that was solidly Catholic, he pursued a policy of toleration of the religious and cultural traditions of his Roman subjects,

allowing the Catholic Church to retain all its churches, property, and privileges. In his capital, *Ravenna, and in other towns with Gothic settlers, two rival hierarchies, Arian and Catholic, coexisted. Such a policy was in marked contrast to the intolerance of religious dissent in contemporary Byzantium or in some other Arian kingdoms.

The chief source for his life is Jordanes, *Getica* (ed. T. *Mommsen, *MGH*, Auctores Antiquissimi, 5 (pars 1; 1882), pp. 53–138) and for his rule in Italy, *Cassiodorus, *Variae* (ed. id., ibid. 12 (1884) and by Å. J. Fridh, CCSL 96 (1973), pp. 1–499; Eng. tr. by S. J. B. Barnish (Translated Texts for Historians, 12; Liverpool, 1992)). Studies by M. Brion (Paris, 1935) and W. Ensslin (Munich [1947]). Good modern account of his life and rule by H. Wolfram, *Geschichte der Goten* (Munich, 1979; 2nd edn., 1980), esp. pp. 326–411; rev. Eng. tr. (Berkeley, Calif., and London [1988]), pp. 261–332. J. Moorhead, *Theodoric in Italy* (Oxford, 1992). For his churches in Ravenna, see F. W. Deichmann, *Ravenna: Hauptstadt des spätantiken Abendlandes* (2 vols. in 3 parts + plans, Wiesbaden, 1969–76); for his mausoleum, with its extraordinary monolithic dome, also R. Heidenreich and H. Johannes, *Das Grabmal Theodorichs zu Ravenna* (ibid., 1971).

Theodoric of Chartres. See THIERRY OF CHARTRES.

Theodosian Code. A collection of Roman imperial constitutions of general application from the time of *Constantine I to that of *Theodosius II, assembled and edited according to instructions given by Theodosius himself in 429 and 435. Compiled in Latin, the Code was promulgated to the E. on 15 Feb. 438, with effect from 1 Jan. 439; it was accepted as authoritative in both E. and W. and was still used in the W. after its supersession in the E. by *Justinian. The laws are arranged chronologically under topical *tituli* in 16 books. Book 16, which deals with religious affairs, contains the laws that banned paganism and penalized heresy, as well as those regulating the position of the clergy and determining the relation between Church and State.

The standard edn. is that of T. *Mommsen and P. M. Meyer (2 vols., Berlin, 1905); Books 1–8 also ed. P. Krüger (ibid., 1923–6). Eng. tr., with comm., by C. Pharr (Princeton, NJ, 1952). W. K. Boyd, *The Ecclesiastical Edicts of the Theodosian Code* (New York, 1905). G. G. Archi, *Teodosio II e la sua codificazione* (Naples [1976]), esp. pp. 151–90. L. de Giovanni, *Chiesa e Stato nel Codice Teodosiano* (ibid., 1980). Tony [i.e. A. M.] Honoré, 'The Making of the Theodosian Code', *Zeitschrift der Savigny-Stiftung für Rechtsgeschichte*, Romanische Abteilung, 103 (1986), pp. 133–222. J. Gaudemet in *DDC* 7 (1965), cols. 1215–46, with bibl.

Theodosian Collection. The compilation of esp. canonical documents in the *Verona Chapter MS LX (58), subscribed with the name of Theodosius the Deacon. It contains *inter alia* an epistle from a Roman synod under *Damasus in 372 to the Catholic bishops in the E., 10 canons of the Council of *Carthage of 421, a Paschal cycle, some letters sent from the Council of *Sardica to Egypt, the 'Historia Acephala' relating to St *Athanasius, and some important documents concerning the *Melitian Schism at Alexandria. As none of these items is found elsewhere, the collection is one of unique interest. Among other items (27 in all, acc. to the usual reckoning) are the canons of *Nicaea and other Councils in various Latin versions. Some of its contents were published by S. *Maffei, its discoverer, and later instalments have been issued by the *Ballerini, F. *Maassen, C. H. *Turner, and E. *Schwartz. The thesis, first propounded by Turner, that the Collection goes back to the mission sent by Carthage to the E. in 419 in connection with the Apiarius affair has received a wide measure of acceptance.

[F.] S. Maffei, 'Monumenti ecclesiastici del quarto secolo Cristiano non più venuti in luce: conservati in Codice antichissimo del Capitolo Veronese', *Osservazioni letterarie*, 3 (Verona, 1738), pp. 7–92, text repr. in Maffei's *Istoria teologica* (Trent, 1742), pt. 2, pp. 254–72, with description, pp. 75–7. P. and G. Ballerini (eds.), *Leonis Magni Opera*, 3 (Venice, 1757), pp. cxxiv–cxxix, 105–27, 434–46, 581–622, 649–53. F. Maassen, *Geschichte der Quellen und der Literatur des canonischen Rechts im Abendlande*, 1 (1870), pp. 546–51. C. H. Turner, 'The Verona Manuscripts of Canons: The Theodosian MS. and its Connection with St. Cyril', *The Guardian*, 50 (pt. 2; 1895), pp. 1921 f.; cf. also *EOMIA* 1 (fasc. 2, pt. 3; 1930), pp. 623 f. E. Schwartz, 'Zur Geschichte des Athanasius', pt. 2, *Nachr.* (Gött.), 1904, pp. 357–91; id., 'Ueber die Sammlung des Cod. Veronensis LX', *ZNTW* 35 (1936), pp. 1–23. W. Telfer, 'The Codex Verona LX (58)', *HTR* 36 (1943), pp. 169–246. Crit. edn. of 'Historia Acephala', with Fr. tr., by A. Martin (SC 317, 1985, pp. 11–213, incl. introd. and bibl.). See also works cited s.v. VERONA.

Theodosius I (the 'Great'), Roman Emperor from 379 to 395. After repelling barbarian attacks on Britain and suppressing revolt in Africa, his father, the Spanish general, Count Theodosius, was executed, for reasons now unknown, in 376. In 379, however, his son was created co-Augustus by Gratian. In secular affairs he defeated and pacified the Goths after their victory at Hadrianople (378). Ecclesiastically he continued Gratian's policy and founded the orthodox Christian state. *Arianism and other heresies became legal offences, sacrifice was forbidden, and paganism almost outlawed. The Emperor's penitent submission to St *Ambrose after the massacre at Thessalonica (390) foreshadows *Canossa. The senatorial attempt to restore at Rome the 'Altar of Victory' (384) failed, and Theodosius sealed his work by defeating Arbogast's puppet-king, Eugenius, who would have tolerated paganism.

The principal sources incl. Aurelius Victor, *Epitome*, 48; Pacatus, *Panegyricus Theodosio Aug. dictus*; and St Ambrose, *De Obitu Theodosii Oratio* and *Ep.* 51. 4; and the 5th-cent. Church historians. Eng. tr. of Pacatus' Panegyric, with introd., by C. E. V. Nixon (Translated Texts for Historians, Latin Series, 2; Liverpool, 1987). G. Rauschen, *Jahrbücher der christlichen Kirche unter dem Kaiser Theodosius dem Grossen* (1897). A. Güldenpenning and J. Ifland, *Der Kaiser Theodosius der Grosse* (1878). E. Stein and J. R. Palanque, *Histoire du Bas-Empire*, 2 (1949), pp. 107–56. W. Ensslin, *Die Religionspolitik des Kaisers Theodosius d. Gr.* (*Sb.* (Bayr.), 1953, Heft 2). N. Q. King, *The Emperor Theodosius and the Establishment of Christianity* (1961). J. H. W. G. Liebeschuetz, *Barbarians and Bishops* (Oxford, 1990), esp. pp. 157–65. G. T. Stokes in *DCB* 4 (1887), pp. 959–64, s.v. 'Theodosius (2) I'; A. Lippold in *PW*, Suppl. 13 (1973), cols. 837–961, with suppl. bibl. cols. 1043 f.

Theodosius II (401–50), grandson of *Theodosius I, E. Roman Emperor from 408. He is significant in religious history by his foundation of the University of Constantinople (425), his summoning of the Council of *Ephesus (431), and his enactment of the *Theodosian Code (q.v.). Though pious by nature, he was politically incompetent, being dominated at one stage by *Simeon Stylites, and later in his reign by his minister, Chrysaphius, who

secured his support for the *Monophysites. He died on 28 July 450 after a fall from his horse.

The primary sources are listed by J. R. Martindale, *The Prosopography of the Later Roman Empire*, 2 (Cambridge, 1980), p. 1100, s.v. 'Theodosius (6)'. A. Güldenpenning, *Geschichte des oströmischen Reiches unter den Kaisern Arcadius und Theodosius II* (1885). G. T. Stokes in *DCB* 4 (1887), pp. 964–7, s.v. 'Theodosius (3) II'; A. Lippold in *PW*, Suppl. 13 (1973), cols. 961–1044. See also bibl. to THEODOSIAN CODE.

Theodotion (prob. 2nd cent.), translator or reviser of the Gk. version of the OT placed in *Origen's *Hexapla next after the LXX. Hardly anything is known of his life. St *Irenaeus (*Haer.* 3. 21. 1) refers to him as a Jewish proselyte; St *Jerome (*De Vir. Ill.* 54) as an *Ebionite Christian; and *Epiphanius (*De Mensuris et Ponderibus*, 17) as a follower of *Marcion. Excerpts attributed to Theodotion in the Hexapla may include the work of earlier revisers; this is particularly likely in the text of Dan., which was used by the Church from the 4th cent. onwards in preference to the LXX. Acc. to D. Barthélemy, Theodotion worked in the middle of the 1st. cent. and was the author of a Hebraizing revision of the LXX of which fragments of the Minor Prophets have been found in the Judaean desert and further elements identified in the textual tradition of other Books (the *kai ge* recension, so named after a distinctive feature). The text of Theodotion in the Hexapla has special value for Jer. and Job, as it was used by Origen to make good the many gaps in the LXX text.

H. B. *Swete, *An Introduction to the Old Testament in Greek* (1900), pp. 42–9. D. Barthélemy, OP, *Les Devanciers d'Aquila* (Supplements to *Vetus Testamentum*, 10; Leiden, 1963), esp. pp. 144–67. S. Jellicoe, *The Septuagint and Modern Study* (Oxford, 1968), pp. 83–94. A. Schmitt, 'Stammt der sogenannte "θ"-Text bei Daniel wirklich von Theodotion?', *Nachr.* (Gött.), 1966, pp. 279–392; K. G. O'Connell, SJ, *The Theodotionic Revision of the Book of Exodus* (Harvard Semitic Monographs, 3; Cambridge, Mass., 1972). J. Gwynn in *DCB* 4 (1887), pp. 970–9, s.v.; K. G. O'Connell in *The Interpreter's Dictionary of the Bible*, suppl. vol. (Nashville, 1976), pp. 377–81, s.v. 'Greek Versions (minor)'.

Theodotus (2nd cent.), *Gnostic. A follower of *Valentinus, he is known from the fragments preserved by *Clement of Alexandria in the *Excerpta ex Theodoto* found among Clement's writings.

The *Excerpta* are pr. in all the edns. of Clement. Separate edns. by R. P. Casey ('Studies and Documents', 1934) and F. M. M. Sagnard, OP (SC 23; 1948; excellent notes). *CPG* 1 (1983), p. 64 (no. 1139).

Theodotus, the Cobbler or Leather-seller (2nd cent.), Adoptionist *Monarchian. He came from Byzantium to Rome under Pope *Victor (*c.*189–198), proclaiming that Jesus was a man who was anointed with the Holy Spirit at His baptism and thus became Christ. He was excommunicated by Victor. His disciples, who were known as 'Theodotians', included his namesake, 'Theodotus the Money-changer' (early 3rd cent.).

The primary sources are *Hippolytus, *Haer.* 7. 35 f. and 10. 23 f., and *Eusebius, *HE* 5. 28. See also *Epiphanius, *Haer.* 54 f., where the sect is described under the name of 'Melchisedekians'. A. *Harnack in *PRE* (3rd edn.), 13 (1903), pp. 311–18, s.v. 'Monarchianismus'; G. Bardy in *DTC* 10 (pt. 1; 1928), cols. 513–16, s.v. 'Melchisédéciens'.

Theodotus (d. *c*.445), Bp. of Ancyra. At first a supporter of *Nestorius, he became one of his most determined adversaries, taking a prominent part on the Cyrilline side at the Council of *Ephesus (431). At the (Nestorian) Council of Tarsus (432) he was anathematized. Among his writings were: (1) Six books against Nestorius (lost); (2) an 'Explanation of the Creed of Nicaea', maintaining that Nestorian teaching was already condemned by the Creed of 325; and (3) various 'Sermons' (partly lost), incl. two for *Christmas (which were read at the Council of Ephesus) and another for the *Purification (εἰς τὰ φῶτα). These last are important early witnesses to the existence of these two Feasts. Recently another sermon on Christmas has been discovered. A long panegyric ascribed to him on 'The Martyrdom and Miracles of St *George' is certainly spurious.

He is not to be confused with St Theodotus of Ancyra, a martyr in the *Diocletianic Persecution, commemorated in the *Roman Martyrology on 18 May.

Works in J. P. Migne, *PG* 77. 1309–1432 (from A. *Gallandi). M. Aubineau, SJ, 'Une Homélie de Théodote d'Ancyre sur la Nativité du Seigneur', *OCP* 26 (1960), pp. 221–50, incl. text. *CPG* 3 (1979), pp. 192–6 (nos. 6124–41). Bardenhewer, 4, pp. 197–200. G. Bardy in *DTC* 15 (pt. 1; 1946), cols. 328–30.

Theodulf (*c*.750–821), Bp. of Orléans, poet, and textual critic. A Visigothic refugee from the Islamic invasion of Spain, Theodulf was welcomed at the court of *Charlemagne. By 798 he was Bp. of Orléans and Abbot of nearby *Fleury. As an ecclesiastical magnate, he joined Abp. Leidrad of Lyons (also a good scholar) when they went as royal legates on a visitation in the south of France (798–9), and he was present at Charlemagne's coronation in Rome (800). After 20 years as a powerful aristocrat at court, he was deposed from all his offices for alleged conspiracy against *Louis I, the Pious (816–40) and exiled to Angers (818) where he died.

Theodulf is a witness to the life and intellectual concerns of the imperial court at Aachen. His 79 poems, epigrams, and hymns include verses referring to *Alcuin, *Einhard, and Charlemagne himself. The 'Versus contra Judices' record his impressions of the visitation of 798–9 and sharply criticize the harshness of Frankish law. His treatise 'De Spiritu Sancto' is a collection of patristic excerpts on the *Double Procession of the Holy Spirit; the 'De ordine baptismi' (812) is one of a number of responses to Charlemagne's letter to his bishops asking how they understood the practice of Baptism. The '*Caroline Books' (*c*.790–2, now attributed mainly to Theodulf) concern the use of visual images in private devotion and in the liturgy; they were a reaction to recent Byzantine legislation at the Second Council of *Nicaea (787; see ICONOCLASTIC CONTROVERSY). Theodulf's own taste may be seen in his chapel at Germigny-des-Prés, a hunting-lodge between Fleury and Orleans. There the apse mosaic (*c*.806)—angels guarding the Ark of the Covenant—reflects older models seen presumably in Italy; it is the only such mosaic work surviving north of the Alps.

Theodulf's two series of episcopal statutes, regulating Christian practice and the life of the clergy, had an influence far beyond his own diocese. His hymn 'All glory, laud and honour' became the *Palm Sunday processional of the W. Church. But his most distinctive achievement is his scholarly revision of the *Vulgate, drawing on MSS from Spain, Italy, and Gaul, and even referring back to the original Hebrew. Six contemporary MSS of Theodulf's edition of the Bible survive, two (in Paris and Le Puy) with sumptuous decoration.

His works, ed. J. *Sirmond, SJ (Paris, 1646), repr. in J. P. Migne, *PL* 105. 191–380. Crit. edns. of his poems by E. Duemmler, *MGH*, Poetae, 1 (1881), pp. 437–581; some of them repr., with Eng. tr., by P. Godman, *Poetry of the Carolingian Renaissance* (1985), pp. 150–75. Crit. edn. of his statutes by P. Brommer, *MGH*, Capitula Episcoporum, 1 (1984), pp. 73–184. C. Cuissard, 'Théodulfe, évêque d'Orléans, sa vie et ses œuvres', *Mémoires de la Société Archéologique et Historique de l'Orléanais*, 24 (1892), pp. 1–351; H. Liebeschütz, 'Theodulf of Orleans and the Problem of the Carolingian Renaissance', in D. J. Gordon (ed.), *Fritz Saxl 1890–1948* (1957), pp. 77–92; E. Dahlhaus-Berg, *Nova Antiquitas et Antiqua Novitas: Typologische Exegese und isidorianisches Geschichtsbild bei Theodulf von Orléans* (Kölner historische Abhandlungen, 23; 1975) [discusses his biblical text, 'De ordine baptismi', and the 'Caroline Books']; R. McKitterick, *The Frankish Church and the Carolingian Reforms, 789–895* (1977), pp. 52–7; J. M. Wallace-Hadrill, *The Frankish Church* (Oxford History of the Christian Church, 1983), pp. 217–25. For 'Theodulf Bibles', see B. Fischer [OSB], 'Bibeltext und Bibelreform unter Karl dem Grossen', in W. Braunfels (ed.), *Karl der Grosse: Lebenswerk und Nachleben*, 2 (Düsseldorf, 1965), pp. 156–216, esp. pp. 175–83, repr. in B. Fischer, *Lateinische Bibelhandschriften im frühen Mittelalter* (Vetus Latina, 11; Freiburg, 1985), pp. 101–202, esp. pp. 135–47, the Hebrew variants, n. 37, and further refs. Raby, pp. 171–7; Manitius, 1 (1911), pp. 537–43; F. Brunhölzl, *Geschichte der lateinischen Literatur des Mittelalters*, 1 (1975), pp. 288–99.

Theognostus (2nd half of 3rd cent.), *Alexandrian ecclesiastical writer. *Philip Sidetes states that he was head of the *Catechetical School in succession to Pierius (*c*.300), but no other ancient authority gives him such a position. He elaborated a system of theology on *Origenist lines in seven books of Hypotyposes, ('Υποτυπώσεις), of which an account is preserved by *Photius (Cod. 106). Quotations also survive in St *Athanasius (*Ep.* 4 *ad Serapionem*, 11; *De Decretis*, 25) and St *Gregory of Nyssa (*Contra Eunom.* 3. 3). Despite his subordinationist language on the Son (derived from Origen), Athanasius could appeal to his support against the *Arians.

Frags. pr. in J. P. Migne, *PG* 10. 235–42. A. *Harnack, 'Die Hypotyposen des Theognost' (TU 24. 3; Leipzig, 1903). L. B. Radford, *Three Teachers of Alexandria: Theognostus, Pierius, Peter* (1908), pp. 1–43. G. Anesi, 'La notizia di Fozio sulle *Hypotyposeis* di Teognosto', *Augustinianum*, 21 (1981), pp. 491–516. *CPG* 1 (1983), p. 200 (nos. 1626 f.).

theologia crucis (Lat., 'theology of the cross'). The name given by Martin *Luther to the theological principle that our knowledge of the Being of God must be derived from the study of Christ in His humiliation and the sufferings He underwent on the cross. He opposed it to a *theologia gloriae* ('theology of glory') which would maintain with the *Scholastic theologians that a true knowledge of God can be obtained from the study of nature.

Theologia Deutsch. See THEOLOGIA GERMANICA.

Theologia Germanica. An anonymous medieval spiritual treatise, written in German by a priest of the *Teutonic Order at Sachsenhausen, near Frankfurt am Main. Martin

*Luther published an incomplete text in 1516 and the full text in 1518, giving it the title *Deutsch Theologia*. In 1851 F. Pfeiffer published a longer version on the basis of a newly discovered manuscript, in which the work is entitled *Der Franckforter*. The discovery of several new manuscripts and the publication of a critical edition in 1982 seem to show that the text published by Luther is closer to the original than the longer version and to have confirmed the view that the work comes from the milieu of the *Friends of God associated with *Eckhart and J. *Tauler, whose doctrines it reflects; it must therefore be dated in the late 14th cent.

The treatise counsels radical poverty of spirit and renunciation of self as the way of union in and with God. Luther was much impressed by the work in his early period and found in it support for his own opposition to good works and for his views on individual religion. Later it was admired by the *Pietists, and it has been translated into many languages. In 1612 it was placed on the *Index; J. *Calvin too had been suspicious of it, but it is now generally recognized as perfectly orthodox.

Crit. edn. by W. von Hinten, *'Der Franckforter' ('Theologia Deutsch')* (Münchener Texte und Untersuchungen zur Deutschen Literatur des Mittelalters, 78; 1982), with bibl. Eng. trs. by S. Winkworth, with preface by C. *Kingsley (London, 1854) and by B. Hoffman (Classics of Western Spirituality, 1980). G. Baring, 'Neues von der "Theologia Deutsch" und ihrer weltweiten Bedeutung', *Archiv für Reformationsgeschichte*, 48 (1957), pp. 1–11, with summary in Eng.; A. M. Haas, 'Die "Theologia Deutsch". Konstitution eines mystologischen Texts', *Freiburger Zeitschrift für Philosophie und Theologie*, 25 (1978), pp. 304–50. S. E. Ozment, *Mysticism and Dissent: Religious Ideology and Social Protest in the Sixteenth Century* (New Haven, Conn., and London, 1973), pp. 14–60. G. Baring, *Bibliographie der Ausgaben der 'Theologia Deutsch' (1516–1961)* (Baden-Baden, 1963). U. Mennecke-Haustein in *Dict. Sp.* 15 (1991), cols. 459–63, s.v. 'Theologia Deutsch'.

Theological Colleges (Anglican). In these Colleges candidates receive their final preparation for ordination. Before the 19th cent. various attempts were made to establish theological colleges in England, notably by Matthew Sutcliffe, Dean of Exeter, in 1609, by G. *Burnet, Bp. of Salisbury (d. 1715), and by T. *Wilson, Bp. of Sodor and Man, in 1700; but nothing in the way of a permanent foundation was accomplished. Edinburgh Theological College was founded in 1810 and is thus the oldest surviving theological college in the Anglican Communion. In England, G. H. Law, Bp. of *Chester, founded St Bees' College for non-university men in 1816, and in 1825 the *CMS started a college at Islington for those of its candidates who were not graduates. Neither of these colleges has survived. The oldest existing seminary in England is the Queen's College, Birmingham, which was founded in 1828 for medical and theological students, and in 1934 was reconstituted for theology alone. Chichester Theological College was established in 1839, and after that date others followed rapidly. In recent years, however, owing to the decline in the number of ordination candidates and a desire to conserve resources, some theological colleges have closed (e.g. Ely in 1964, and St Aidan's, Birkenhead, and Bishop's College, Cheshunt, in 1969) and some have amalgamated (e.g. Ripon Hall and Cuddesdon College to form Ripon College, Cuddesdon, in 1975). There have also been amalgamations with theological colleges of other denominations, notably the amalgamation in Birmingham between the Queen's College and Handsworth College (Methodist).

F. W. B. Bullock, *A History of Training for the Ministry of the Church of England in England and Wales from 1800 to 1874* (St Leonards-on-Sea, 1955). Id., *The History of Ridley Hall, Cambridge* (2 vols., 1941–53), with much general information, esp. Introduction on 'Theological Colleges of the Church of England before 1875' in vol. 1, pp. 1–17. *Theological Colleges for Tomorrow: Being the Report of a Working Party appointed by the Archbishops of Canterbury and York, to consider the problems of the Theological Colleges of the Church of England* (1968). A notable history of a particular foundation is [W.] O. Chadwick, *The Founding of Cuddesdon* (1954). S. L. Ollard in *DECH*, pp. 587–91, s.v.

theological virtues. A title given to the three virtues of *faith, *hope, and *charity, which are grouped together by St *Paul (1 Cor. 13: 13; cf. 1 Thess. 1: 3, Gal. 5: 5–6, Col. 1: 4–5) as the bases of the Christian life. They are so named in contradistinction to the 'natural' or 'cardinal virtues' (q.v.). Their place in the life of grace and their relations to each other were much studied by the Schoolmen, esp. St *Thomas Aquinas.

A. Michel in *DTC* 15 (pt. 2; 1950), cols. 2739–99, s.v. 'Vertu', esp. cols. 2782–4 ('vii, Vertus théologales').

Theologische Literaturzeitung. A German theological periodical, founded in 1876 by E. *Schürer and A. *Harnack largely in the interests of *Ritschlian theology and devoted entirely to reviews of current theological literature. It was published fortnightly till the end of 1938, and from 1939 monthly.

theology (Gk. θεολογία), lit. the 'science of God'. Among the Greek Fathers it comes to have two specific references: it can denote either the doctrine of the *Trinity (i.e., of God's being, as opposed to his dealings with the created order), or it can mean prayer (as it is only in prayer that God is truly known). Later, in the W. it came to mean the science of the Divinely revealed religious truths. Its theme is the Being and Nature of God and His creatures and the whole complex of the Divine dispensation from the Fall of Adam to the Redemption through Christ and its mediation to men by His Church, including the so-called natural truths of God, the soul, the moral law, etc., which are accessible to mere reason. Its purpose is the investigation of the contents of belief by means of reason enlightened by faith (*fides quaerens intellectum*) and the promotion of its deeper understanding. In the course of time theology has developed into several branches, among them dogmatic, historical, and practical theology. The methods of classification of the sub-disciplines, however, fluctuate in different theological systems.

See also NATURAL THEOLOGY; REVELATION; TRADITION; and CATHOLIC (5).

theology of religions. The interpretation of how God (or ultimate Divine reality) may be operative for salvation through religions other than Christianity. Early belief in Jesus Christ as God's final agent of salvation (later embodied in the doctrine of the *Incarnation) encouraged the view that He either fulfilled or was destined to replace the religious aspirations within other traditions. This attitude of superiority was qualified by unresolved puzzlement about the availability of salvation in the time before the coming of Christ and in places where the Christian message had not penetrated.

The *Apologists of the 2nd and 3rd cents. held a positive view of other religions based on the doctrine of the universal presence of the divine *Logos, which was manifest not only in Greek religions and ancient Judaism but also in Buddhists and Brahmins (so, e.g. *Clement of Alexandria). After *Constantine, the maxim 'no salvation outside the Church', which had hitherto been applied to Christian heretics and schismatics, was extended to pagans and Jews, because it was assumed that in the Empire everyone would have had a chance to hear the Christian message. The encounter in the 7th cent. with *Islam, an alternative universal missionary religion, confirmed Christianity in its exclusivist tendency. The Fourth *Lateran Council (1215) and the Council of *Florence (1442) both endorsed the belief that salvation was confined to the Church.

After the European expansion of the late 15th and 16th cents., the encounter with peoples beyond the known world deepened the unresolved puzzlement about salvation beyond the Church. Protests against the ill-treatment of native peoples in the colonized territories rekindled earlier debates about the culpability of such people in respect of salvation. Taking up hints in the writings of St *Thomas Aquinas, some *Dominicans at Salamanca (e.g. F. de *Vitoria and M. *Cano) and some Jesuits (e.g. R. *Bellarmine and F. *Suárez) in the 16th cent. argued that salvation outside the Church was possible by virtue of a 'baptism of desire' or 'implicit faith' in Christ. In the 18th and 19th cent., though their actions were motivated by belief in the supremacy of Christianity, some missionaries (both Protestant and RC) came to doubt exclusivist views as an adequate response to the perceived ethical aspirations and depth of spirituality in other religions. A number of inter-faith organizations which came into being in the 20th cent., trace the beginnings of the inter-faith movement to the first conference of the World's Parliament of Religions held in Chicago in 1893.

In the second half of the 20th cent. a new global consciousness brought about by decolonization, increased travel, and the enormously enhanced ease of communication, form the background for the further promotion of an encounter between Christianity and other religions based on mutual respect and dialogue. While there is little agreement about its motivations and expectations, this dialogue none the less implies a more open theological approach. The Second *Vatican Council (notably in *Nostra Aetate*, 1960) encouraged RCs to value what is holy, good, and true in other religions, and in 1979 the *World Council of Churches established the Sub-Unit on Dialogue with People of Living Faiths and Ideologies. The Orthodox Church, through its membership of the World Council of Churches, is now beginning to value the dialogue with other religions. In general, these movements have been motivated by an inclusivist understanding of salvation, utilizing such notions as the 'cosmic Christ' (Orthodox), 'anonymous Christ' (K. *Rahner, SJ) and 'normative Christ' (Anglican and Protestant) which is thought to be somehow effective for other believers within their own traditions.

Conservative theologians, anxious to counter any ambiguity over belief in the absolute uniqueness of the Person of Christ, stress the discontinuity between Christianity and other religions, while at the same time respecting cultural differences. In this respect the influence of the Dutch missionary theologian Hendrik Kraemer, through his contribution to the third International Missionary Council at *Tambaram in 1938, has been considerable among Protestants. Greater emphasis on historical-cultural relativism, the symbolic nature of theological concepts, and philosophical perspectivism, have motivated other Catholic and Protestant theologians (notably John Hick, Wilfred Cantwell Smith, Stanley Samartha, and Paul Knitter) to argue that each religion provides its own effective context for salvation/liberation/enlightenment (formulated as a generic concept), and that each tradition has its own validity before the one ultimate Divine reality. In a different vein, *Liberation theologians stress the concept of the '*Kingdom of God' as a focus for sharing insights on justice. *Feminist theologians have pointed to structural similarities between the oppression of women in Christianity and the treatment of other religions by the Church. Global problems of war, poverty, and ecological survival are leading some to formulate a shared global ethic. This aspect is reflected in the 'Declaration Towards a Global Ethic' commended by leaders from the world religions which met at Chicago in 1993 to commemorate the centenary of the World's Parliament of Religions.

Convenient collection of key passages from various writers ed. J. Hick and B. Hebblethwaite, *Christianity and other Religions* (1980). A. *Schweitzer, *Christianity and the Religions of the World* (1923). H. Kraemer, *The Christian Message in a Non-Christian World* (1938). [R.] N. Smart, *A Dialogue of Religions* (1960). S. J. Samartha, *Courage for Dialogue: Ecumenical Issues in Inter-Religious Relationships* (Geneva [1981]). A. Race, *Christians and Religious Pluralism: Patterns in the Christian Theology of Religions* (1983), with bibl. H. *Küng and others, *Christentum und Weltreligion* (Munich, [1984]; Eng. tr., 1987); id., *Projekt Weltethos* (ibid., 1990; Eng. tr., *Global Responsibility*, 1991). P. F. Knitter, *No other Name? A Critical Survey of Christian Attitudes Toward the World Religions* (1985). J. Hick and P. F. Knitter (eds.), *The Myth of Christian Uniqueness* (1987); G. D'Costa (ed.), *Christian Uniqueness Reconsidered: The Myth of a Pluralist Theology of Religions* (Maryknoll, NY [1990]). S. W. Ariarajah, *Hindus and Christians: A Century of Protestant Ecumenical Thought* (Amsterdam and Grand Rapids, Mich., 1991). M. Braybrooke, *Pilgrimage of Hope: One Hundred Years of Global Interfaith Dialogue* (1992). F. A. Sullivan, SJ, *Salvation Outside the Church? Tracing the History of the Catholic Response* (New York and London, 1992). M. [F.] Wiles, *Christian Theology and Inter-Religious Dialogue* (1992).

Theopaschites (Gk. θεοπασχῖται, i.e. 'those who hold that God suffered'), a name applied to those in the 5th and 6th cents. who held that, in virtue of the unity of the Incarnate Christ, it could be said that God had suffered. Controversy over theopaschism had two focal points. The first arose when *Peter the Fuller added the phrase 'who was crucified for us' to the '*Trisagion'. This addition had the support of his fellow *Monophysites (who agreed with him in regarding the 'Trisagion' as a Christological hymn), but was condemned by the Catholics (who regarded it as addressed to the Trinity). The second centred on the formula 'One of the Trinity suffered in the flesh', first defended in *Constantinople in 519 by a group of Scythian monks, including John Maxentius. The formula was rejected by the Patr. of Constantinople and (with some hesitation) by Pope *Hormisdas, but gained the support of the Emp. *Justinian who eventually (in 534) secured the agreement of Pope John II. The Second Council of *Constantinople in 553 anathematized those who denied that Christ, who was crucified in the flesh, was one of the Trinity (Session 8, anathema 10). Theopaschism is to be distinguished from *Patripassianism, which confounds the Persons of the Father and the Son.

See works cited s.v. TRISAGION.

Theophany. An appearance of God in visible form, temporary and not necessarily material (cf. e.g. Exod. 33: 20 ff.). Such an appearance is to be contrasted with the *Incarnation, in which there was a permanent union between God and complete manhood (body, soul, and spirit). In early Christian times the word was in regular use in an orthodox sense, e.g. for the Feast of the *Epiphany in the *Gelasian Sacramentary.

Theophan (in Russian, Feofan) the Recluse, St (1815–94), bishop and spiritual writer. George Vasilievich Govorov, the son of a Russian priest, was ordained and became a monk in 1841, taking the name of Theophan. He spent the first part of his ministry teaching in various theological seminaries, with a break of seven years (1847–54) working with the 'Russian Spiritual Mission' in *Jerusalem, and a further period in *Constantinople (1856–7). In 1859 he was consecrated Bp. of Tambov and was translated to Vladimir in 1863. In 1866 he retired and spent the rest of his life as a monk, later as a hermit, in the small monastery of Vyshi. He played an important part in making the fruits of the 18th-cent. *Hesychast revival known in Russia and, in particular, popularized the use of the *Jesus Prayer among Russian Orthodox Christians. He translated into Russian various Greek spiritual writings, incl. the *Philocalia (1876–90) and *Nicodemus of the Holy Mountain's 'Unseen Warfare'; he also wrote numerous letters to those who turned to him for spiritual counsel. He was canonized by the 1988 Synod of the Russian Orthodox Church; feast day, 10 Jan.

There is a partial Eng. tr. of his version of the *Philocalia* by E. Kadloubovsky and G. E. H. Palmer, *Writings from the* Philokalia *on Prayer of the Heart* (1951) and idd., *Early Fathers from the* Philokalia (1954). Eng. trs. by idd. of his version of Nicodemus of the Holy Mountain's 'Unseen Warfare' (1952) and of an anthology containing much of his correspondence compiled by Igumen Chariton of Valamo (pub. Valamo in Finland, 1936), as *The Art of Prayer* (1966), with introd. by T. Ware, pp. 9–38, and by E. Williams of selected works and a contemporary Life as *The Heart of Salvation* (Newbury, Mass., and Robertsbridge, E. Sussex [1992]). T. Špidlík, SJ, *La Doctrine spirituelle de Théophane le Reclus* (Orientalia Christiana Analecta, 172; 1965). Id. in *Dict. Sp.* 15 (1991), cols. 517–22, s.v. 'Théophane (3) le Reclus'.

Theophilanthropists. A *Deistic sect founded in France during the reign of the Directory under the patronage esp. of the Director L. M. La Réveillère-Lépeaux (1753–1824). Its tenets were set forth in a pamphlet by J. B. Chemin-Dupontès (Paris, Sept. 1796) under the title of *Manuel des théophilanthropes*, the three articles of its creed being belief in God, virtue, and immortality. At first the movement seemed likely to spread and was given the use of ten churches in Paris by the Directory; but after

the re-establishment of Catholicism by the *Concordat of 1801 it soon lost ground, and in 1802 Napoleon restored its churches to Catholic worship. Some attempts were made to revive it later in the 19th cent., but without success.

J. Brugerette in *DTC* 15 (pt. 1; 1946), cols. 518–23, s.v.

Theophilus (later 2nd cent.), Bp. of *Antioch and one of the 'Christian *Apologists'. Of his writings, only his 'Apology', in three books addressed to Autolycus, has survived. Its purpose was to set before the pagan world the Christian idea of God and the superiority of the doctrine of *Creation over the immoral myths of the Olympian religion. Theophilus developed the doctrine of the *Logos a stage further than any of his Christian predecessors, distinguishing between the λόγος ἐνδιάθετος, the intelligence of the Father, and the λόγος προφορικός, the Word brought forth externally in order to create. He is also the first theologian to use the word '*Triad' (τριάς) of the Godhead. Among his (lost) treatises were writings against *Marcion and Hermogenes. F. *Loofs endeavoured to show that considerable portions of his work against Marcion were incorporated in *Irenaeus' 'Treatise Against Heresies', but his contention has won little support.

The sole MS authority for the 'Ad Autolycum' is Cod. Marcianus 496 (11th cent.), all other known MSS being direct descendants. *Editio princeps* by J. Frisius and C. Gesner (Zurich, 1546). Crit. edns. by J. C. T. Otto, *Corpus Apologetarum*, 8 (3rd edn., Jena, 1861) and R. M. Grant, with Eng. tr. (Oxford Early Christian Texts, 1970). J. P. Migne, *PG* 6. 1023–168. F. Loofs, *Theophilus von Antioch und die anderen theologischen Quellen bei Irenäus* (TU 46 (2); 1930). *CPG* 1 (1983), pp. 53 f. (nos. 1107–9). Altaner and Stuiber (1978), pp. 75–7 and 556. G. Bardy in *DTC* 15 (pt. 1; 1946), cols. 530–6; P. Nautin in *DPAC* 2 (1984), cols. 3405 f.; Eng. tr. in *Encyclopedia of the Early Church*, 2 (1992), pp. 831 f., all s.v.

Theophilus (d. 412), Patr. of Alexandria from 385. He was the uncle of St *Cyril, who succeeded him. In his first years as patriarch he took an active part in suppressing the remnants of paganism in his city, in 391 destroying the temple of Serapis; but later his main ambition seems to have been the furtherance of the prestige of his see. Originally a supporter of *Origenism, he became a fierce opponent of the Origenist monks. When the *Tall Brothers fled to *Constantinople and were sheltered by St John *Chrysostom, Theophilus seized the opportunity to bring about his deposition at the Synod of the *Oak. The Copts and Syrians, who consider him a saint, celebrate his feast on 15 and 17 Oct. respectively.

Works ed. A. *Gallandi in *Bibliotheca Veterum Patrum*, 7 (1770), pp. 601–53, repr. in J. P. Migne, *PG* 65. 29–68 and 401–4. Further letters, id., *PL* 22. 758–69, 773–90, 792–812, and 813–28. M. Richard, 'Une Homélie de Théophile d'Alexandrie sur l'institution de l'Eucharistie', *RHE* 33 (1937), pp. 46–56; id., 'Nouveaux fragments de Théophile d'Alexandrie', *Nachr.* (Gött.) (1975), pp. 55–65; both repr. in id., *Opera Minora*, 2 (Turnhout and Louvain, 1977), nos. 37 and 39. A. Favale, SDB, *Teofilo d'Alessandria (345 c.–412): Scritti, vita e dottrina* (Biblioteca del 'Salesianum', 41; 1958). *CPG* 2 (1974), pp. 112–34 (nos. 2580–2684). H. G. Opitz in *PW*, 2. Reihe, 5 (pt. 2; 1934), cols. 2149–65. R. Delobel and M. Richard in *DTC* 15 (pt. 1; 1946), cols. 523–30, s.v., with further refs.

Theophylact (b. *c.*1050/60; d. after 1125), Byzantine exegete. A native of Euboea, he was a pupil of Michael *Psellus, and for a time tutor to Constantine Doukas, son of the former Emp. Michael VII. About 1090 he was made Abp. of Ohrid in the country of the Bulgarians; his letters suggest that their lack of civilization was a source of constant suffering to him. His principal work is a series of commentaries on several OT Books and on the whole of the NT except Rev. They are marked by lucidity of thought and expression and closely follow the scriptural text. At the same time they insist on practical morality in the manner of St John *Chrysostom, whom Theophylact took as a model. In matters of exegesis Theophylact was largely influenced by earlier writers such as the so-called '*Oecumenius', esp. in Acts and the Catholic Epistles, as well as by his contemporary, *Euthymius Zigabenus. In his turn he influenced *Erasmus. He adopted a conciliatory position in the matter of the Schism, defending in his Περὶ ὧν ἐγκαλοῦνται Λατῖνοι the Orthodox rejection of the *Filioque, the veneration of images, and also the use of unleavened *bread in the Eucharist. Among his other works are a formal address to Constantine when he was co-emperor (formerly, through a misunderstanding, known as the παιδεία βασιλική), a panegyric addressed to the Emp. Alexis Commenus, 15 poems, and almost certainly a biography of St Clement of Ohrid (one of the principal disciples of Sts *Cyril and Methodius; his authorship of this last work has, in the past, been disputed).

Works [ed. F. Foscari], 4 vols., Venice, 1754–63, repr. in J. P. Migne, *PG* 123–6; prefaced by useful 'Dissertatio' by J. F. Bernard María de Rubeis, OP, repr. in *PG* 123. 9–130. Crit. edn., with Fr. tr. and introd., by P. Gautier, of his Orations, Treatises, and Poems (Corpus Fontium Historiae Byzantinae, Series Thessalonicensis, 16/1; Thessalonica, 1980) and of his Letters (ibid. 16/2; 1986). D. Obolensky, *Six Byzantine Portraits* (Oxford, 1988), pp. 34–82. Beck (1959), pp. 649–51. R. Janin, AA, in *DTC* 15 (pt. 1; 1946), cols. 536–8, s.v.; G. Podskalsky, SJ, in *Dict. Sp.* 15 (1991), cols. 542–6, s.v.

theosophy. The Greek term θεοσοφία, denoting knowledge of divine things (from θεός, 'God' or 'Divine being', + σοφία, 'wisdom') is found in magical papyri and was taken up by the *Neoplatonists. *Porphyry (*De Abstinentia*, 4. 17) associates it with Indian philosophy; this connection suggests that it could be understood to be the Greek equivalent of the Sanskrit *brahmavidya* (Divine knowledge). It is found in Christian Neoplatonists such as *Dionysius the Pseudo-Areopagite and John Scottus *Erigena, who introduced the term into Latin. It was revived in the 17th cent. in both Latin and vernacular forms to denote the kind of speculation, based on intuitive knowledge, which is found in the Jewish *Kabbala. It is often applied to the system of J. *Boehme (the 'Teutonic Theosopher').

In modern times the term has been used to denote the supposed hidden essence of all religions, and in this sense has been regarded as identical with Esoteric Buddhism. It is believed to be an empirical philosophy handed down by wise men of all cultures and religious traditions. It is held that knowledge of the truth, obtained by direct perception, results from the development of powers latent in all men, but fully realized only in the few who choose to fulfil strict conditions of discipline. Truth is one and indivisible; the patent similarities in different traditions and practices stem from their common origin in the Divine Wisdom. The primary tenet of theosophy is that all existence is a unity; the essence of everything, physical and spiritual, is one life. Manifestation, or the emanation of universes, is a periodic process, without beginning or end, involving an alternation of periods of activity and rest. Theosophists thus admit no ultimate distinction between man and the source of all being. They see the cosmic process as evolutionary, latent possibilities finding increasing expression through the kingdoms of nature. In man the process becomes self-conscious and is consummated in the Divine union of mysticism or the self-realization of yoga. Theosophical philosophy does not admit the existence of a personal God, personal immortality, or the validity of the Christian revelation.

The Theosophical Society (which exists to promote the principles of theosophy in the modern sense) was founded in New York in 1875 by Mme H. P. Blavatsky and Col. H. S. Olcott. They left the United States of America in 1878, arriving in Bombay in 1879; a few years later the headquarters of the Society were established at Adyar, near Madras. After the death of Col. Olcott in 1907, Mrs Annie Besant was elected President of the Society. It spread to Europe, Australia, and New Zealand before the end of the 19th cent. and now has adherents in many countries of the non-communist world. It is not a religion and has no creed; it is based on the recognition of the universal brotherhood of all mankind and advocates toleration of all differences.

Primary material on the modern Theosophical Movement includes H. P. Blavatsky, *Isis Unveiled* (New York, 1877); id., *The Secret Doctrine* (1888); id., *The Key to Theosophy* (1889); id., *Collected Writings* [excluding the major works] (Los Angeles, Wheaton, Ill., and more recently, Adyar, Madras, 1950 ff.); A. P. Sinnett, *The Occult World* (1881); id., *Esoteric Buddhism* (1883); *The Mahatma Letters to A. P. Sinnett*, ed. A. T. Baker (1923); G. A. Barborka, *The Divine Plan written in the form of a commentary on H. P. Blavatsky's* Secret Doctrine (Adyar, 1961); K. Prem [R. H. Nixon] and M. Ashish, *Man, The Measure of All Things* (1969); idd., *Foundations of Esoteric Philosophy from the Writings of H. P. Blavatsky*, arranged by I. H. Hoskins [1980]. Expositions by Theosophists include W. Q. Judge, *The Ocean of Theosophy* (New York, 1893); A. Besant, *The Ancient Wisdom: An Outline of Theosophical Teachings* (1897); W. Kingsland, *The Real H. P. Blavatsky: A Study in Theosophy, and a Memoir of a Great Soul* (1928); and J. O. Fuller, *Blavatsky and her Teachers* [1988]. Critical studies incl. R. Guénon, *Le Théosophisme: Histoire d'une pseudo-religion* (Bibliothèque Française de Philosophie; 1921); T. Mainage, OP, *Les Principes de la théosophie: Étude critique* (1922; Eng. tr., 1927); L. de Grandmaison, *La Théosophie et l'anthroposophie* (1939). A. Taylor, *Annie Besant: A Biography* (Oxford, 1992), pp. 222–332. P. Oltramare, *L'Histoire des idées théosophiques dans l'Inde* (Annales du Musée Guimet. Bibliothèque d'Études, 23 and 31; 1906–23). A. Besant in *HERE* 12 (1921), pp. 300–4, s.v. 'Theosophical Society'; P. Oltramare, ibid., pp. 304–15, s.v.; R. K. MacMaster in *NCE* 14 (1967), pp. 74 f.

theotokion (Gk. θεοτοκίον). In the E. Church, a stanza of liturgical hymnography referring to the BVM (*Theotokos). The concluding verse in a series of *troparia usually takes the form of a theotokion.

Theotokos (Gk. Θεοτόκος, Lat. *Deipara*), the 'one who gave birth to God', title of the BVM. The word was used of the Virgin by the Greek Fathers (perhaps by *Origen and possibly even by *Hippolytus) and increasingly became a popular term of devotion. In 429 it was attacked by *Nestorius and his supporters as incompatible with the full humanity of Christ, and the word 'Christotokos' proposed in its place. It found, however, a zealous champion in St *Cyril of Alexandria and was formally upheld at the Councils of *Ephesus (431) and *Chalcedon (451). Henceforward its orthodoxy was generally undisputed in the Church. In the W. the usual equivalent in practice was not *Deipara*, which corresponded to it etymologically, but *Dei Genitrix* ('Mother of God'), with its somewhat different emphasis.

J. H. *Newman, *Select Treatises of St Athanasius* (2nd edn., 1881), 2, pp. 204–15. F. J. Dölger in *Antike und Christentum*, 1 (1929), pp. 118–23 ['Zum Theotokos-Namen']; H. Rahner, SJ, 'Hippolyt von Rom als Zeuge für den Ausdruck Θεοτόκος', *ZKT* 59 (1935), pp. 73–81; cf. id., ibid., 60 (1936), pp. 577–90. M. Starowieyski, 'Le titre Θεοτόκος avant le concile d'Ephèse', in E. A. Livingstone (ed.), *Studia Patristica*, 19 (Louvain, 1989), pp. 236–42. G. W. H. Lampe (ed.), *A Patristic Greek Lexicon* (Oxford, 1961), pp. 639–41, s.v.

Therapeutae (Gk. θεραπευταί, 'physicians', 'devotees', hence 'those who worship God'), a pre-Christian monastic community of Egyptian Jewish ascetics. The only real authority for their practice and beliefs is *Philo's *De Vita Contemplativa*, where they are contrasted with the *Essenes, who lived a more active life. They were severe in their discipline, abjured money, and lived in seclusion near Alexandria and above Lake Mareotis. They prayed at sunrise and at sunset; devoted themselves assiduously to the allegorical study of the OT; and met together only for Sabbath-worship and during the great festival corresponding to Pentecost, when bands of men and women danced and sang throughout the night. Virtually nothing is known of their history. Their interest lies largely in their being an example of a pre-Christian monastic system. *Eusebius (*HE* 2. 17) mistakenly regarded them as a Christian sect.

F. C. *Conybeare (ed.), *Philo: About the Contemplative Life, or the Fourth Book of the Treatise concerning Virtues* (1895; text, with defence of its genuineness). The *De Vita Contemplativa* is also ed., with important introd. on the Therapeutae, by F. Daumas (*Les Œuvres de Philon d'Alexandrie*, ed. R. Arnaldez and others, 29; 1963). E. *Schürer, *The History of the Jewish People in the Age of Jesus Christ*, rev. Eng. tr. by G. Vermes and others, 2 (Edinburgh, 1979), pp. 591–7, with refs.

Theresa of Ávila, St. See TERESA OF ÁVILA, ST.

Thérèse of Lisieux, St. See TERESA OF LISIEUX, ST.

thermarion (Gk. θερμάριον). In the E. Church, a vessel for the warm water used in the Eucharistic rite for mixing with the species of wine after its consecration and in the washing of altars at their dedication.

Thessalonians, Epistles to the. The First Epistle was most probably written by St *Paul from Corinth on his first visit to the city (*c.*51) and is the earliest of his letters, unless it be argued that Gal. was written before it. A notable feature of this First Epistle, remarkable for the affectionate solicitude of the Apostle for his converts, is his desire to set their minds at rest on the fate of the dead

members of the community. He assures them that, at the Second Coming of Christ, those who have died in the Lord will rise first and then, together with the living, be united to Christ; he declines, however, to make pronouncements on the time and circumstances of these events, except that the day of the Lord will come 'like a thief in the night' (5: 2), and he bids his readers watch and be sober.

The Second Epistle, apparently following shortly afterwards, was also occasioned by the eschatological preoccupations of the Thessalonians, many of whom had become over-excited by their belief in the immediately impending *Parousia and neglected their ordinary duties. Paul reminds them of his former teaching, according to which the apostasy and the 'Son of Perdition' (see ANTICHRIST) must come first, but teaches that there is still something or someone 'that restraineth' (2: 6, τὸ κατέχον; 2: 7, ὁ κατέχων). This has been very differently interpreted; the most widely accepted critical explanation regards the term as referring to the Roman Empire under Claudius, whereas in the more traditional view it applies to a supernatural power, such as e.g. St *Michael.

The authenticity of the First Epistle, once questioned by F. C. *Baur, is now generally accepted. That of the Second Epistle is still rejected by many scholars, despite its early attestation as one of Paul's letters by the time of St *Irenaeus and its place in the *Muratorian Canon as well as in *Marcion's collection. The chief objections are the differences in the eschatological teaching of the two Epp., at some points hard, if not impossible, to reconcile, and their different tone, particularly in view of the fact that, if both are genuine, they must have been written the one shortly after the other.

The more valuable patristic comm. incl. those of St John *Chrysostom (*PG* 62. 391–500); *Theodore of Mopsuestia (frags., ibid. 66. 931–6); *Theodoret (ibid. 82. 628–73) and *John of Damascus (ibid. 95. 905–29); further list in *DTC*, cited below. Modern comm. incl. those of J. *Calvin (Strasbourg, 1540; modern Eng. tr., 1961) and J. *Jewel (London, 1583); also those of M. *Dibelius (Hb. NT 3, pt. 2, 1911, with Philippians, pp. 1–43), J. E. Frame (ICC, 1912), A. Plummer (2 vols., London, 1918), B. Rigaux, OFM (Études Bibliques, 1956), C. Masson (Commentaire du Nouveau Testament, 11a; Neuchâtel, 1957), L. Morris (New London Commentaries, 1959), A. L. Moore (New Cent. Bib., 1969), E. Best (Black's NT Comm., 1972), F. F. Bruce (Word Biblical Comm. 45; Waco, Tex., 1982), and on 1 Thess., T. Holtz (Evangelisch-Katholischer Kommentar, 13; Zurich, 1986). F. C. Baur, *Paulus, der Apostel Jesu Christi: Sein Leben und Wirken, seine Briefe und seine Lehre* (1845), pp. 480–99 (Eng. tr., vol. 2, 1875, pp. 85–97). W. *Wrede, *Die Echtheit des zweiten Thessalonicherbriefs* (TU 24, Heft 2; 1903). C. H. Giblin, SJ, *The Threat to Faith: An Exegetical and Theological Re-examination of 2 Thessalonians 2* (Analecta Biblica, 31; 1967). R. F. Collins, *Studies on the First Letter to the Thessalonians* (Bibliotheca Ephemeridum Theologicarum Lovaniensium, 66; 1984). R. Jewett, *The Thessalonian Correspondence: Pauline Rhetoric and Millenarian Piety* (Philadelphia [1986]); A. J. Malherbe, *Paul and the Thessalonians: The Philosophic Tradition of Pastoral Care* (ibid. [1987]). D. Buzy and A. Burnot in *DTC* 15 (pt. 1; 1946), cols. 573–610, s.v. 'Thessaloniciens (Épîtres aux)'.

Thessalonica. The city in Macedonia, now called Thessaloniki, but long known as Salonica, was founded *c.*315 BC by Cassander, perhaps on the site of the ancient Thermae, and called after his wife, Thessalonica (step-sister of

Alexander the Great). Under the Romans it became the virtual capital of the province and an important centre of trade. In the first Civil War it was the headquarters of Pompey and the Senate. Its rulers were known as 'politarchs' (cf. Acts 17: 6). In AD 50 or 51 St *Paul visited the city, preached on three 'Sabbaths' in the synagogue, and founded the second Christian community in Europe, chiefly from the Greeks and proselytes (Acts 17), which was renowned for its orthodoxy and steadfastness in the succeeding period. (For his two letters to the *Thessalonians, see previous entry.) Their early martyrs included St Agape, with her sisters Chionia and Irene, St Agathopus, and St Demetrius (later the patron of the city). Acc. to *Origen (on Rom. 16: 23), the first Bp. of Thessalonica was Gaius (cf. 1 Cor. 1: 14, Acts 19: 29). In the late 4th or early 5th cent. the creation of a Papal Vicariate of Thessalonica enabled Rome to retain ecclesiastical control of Illyria, which had been transferred politically to the E. Empire. In 732 *Leo III, the Isaurian, made Thessalonica and all Illyrian sees dependent on the Patriarchate of *Constantinople.

Notable archbishops of later date included St Joseph, brother of St *Theodore of Studios, Basil of Achrida (1145–c.1169), Eustathius of Thessalonica (d. c.1193), St *Gregory Palamas, and St *Simeon of Thessalonica. From 1430 to 1912 Thessalonica was governed by the Turks, and many of its beautiful churches, which still preserve much of their old mosaic work, were turned into mosques. Since 1912 the city has again been Greek. It is the seat of a Greek Orthodox metropolitan. A Latin Vicariate Apostolic was established in 1926.

C. Diehl, M. Le Tournai, and H. Saladin, *Les Monuments chrétiens de Salonique* (Monuments de l'art byzantin, 4; text + vol. of plates, 1918); J.-M. Spieser, *Thessalonique et ses Monuments du IVᵉ au VIᵉ Siècle* (Bibliothèque des Écoles françaises d'Athènes et de Rome, 254; 1984). P. Lemerle, *Les plus anciens recueils des miracles de Saint Démétrius et la pénétrations des Slavs dans les Balkans* (2 vols., 1979–81; text and comm.). S. L. Greenslade, 'The Illyrian Churches and the Vicariate of Thessalonica, 378–95', *JTS* 46 (1945), pp. 17–30. R. Janin, AA, *Les Églises et les Monastères des Grands Centres Byzantins* (1975), pp. 341–419. A. E. Vacalopoulos, *A History of Thessaloniki*, tr. into Eng. by T. F. Carney (Thessalonica, 1963). E. Oberhummer in *PW*, 2te Reihe, 6 (pt. 1; 1936), cols. 143–63; H. L. Hendrix in *Anchor Bible Dictionary*, 6 (1992), pp. 523–7, s.v.

Theudas. The leader of an unsuccessful insurrection, mentioned in a speech attributed to *Gamaliel in Acts 5: 36. The reference raises two difficulties: (1) Josephus (*Ant.* 25. 5. 1), the only other ancient writer to mention Theudas, describes an insurrection by a leader of this name in AD 45 or 46; this is considerably later than the time at which Gamaliel is represented as speaking. (2) The passage in Acts clearly states that Theudas raised his rebellion before the rebellion of Judas of Galilee, which was 'in the days of the taxing', i.e. AD 6 or 7. Biblical critics sometimes explained this mistake as due to an inaccurate use by St Luke of the passage in Josephus which describes the execution of the sons of Judas of Galilee after the rebellion of Theudas. This hypothesis involves supposing that Acts was written after the publication of Josephus' *Antiquities*, c. AD 94, unless St Luke was following a source later used by Josephus.

M. Krenkel, *Josephus und Lukas* (1894), pp. 162–74. E. *Schürer, *The History of the Jewish People in the Age of Jesus Christ*, rev. Eng. tr. by G. Vermes and others, 1 (Edinburgh, 1973), pp. 456 f., with refs. C. N. Jefford in *Anchor Bible Dictionary*, 6 (1992), pp. 527 f. See also comm. on Acts, cited s.v.

Thierry of Chartres (*c.*1100–*c.*1155), philosopher and teacher. A Breton by birth and a younger brother of *Bernard of Chartres, he was present at the Council of *Soissons (1121) which condemned one of Peter *Abelard's works. He made his name as a teacher in Paris *c.*1125–41, becoming Archdeacon of Dreux (in the diocese of *Chartres) *c.*1137 and Chancellor of Chartres prob. in 1141. He took part in the Papal examination of *Gilbert de la Porrée at *Reims in 1148. He is thought to have retired in his last years to a *Cistercian monastery.

Thierry is characterized by *John of Salisbury as 'a most devoted student of the liberal arts'. Of his logical and rhetorical teaching all that survives is commentaries on Cicero, *De Inventione*, and the anonymous *Rhetorica ad Herennium*; he also expounded (with some distaste) the newly recovered *Topics* of *Aristotle. Thierry's most original work was in the application of the liberal arts to Christian doctrine. His analysis of the *Opuscula Sacra* of *Boethius circulated in several versions as a more conservative, and perhaps less difficult, interpretation of the *Trinity than that proposed by Gilbert de la Porrée (q.v.). For Thierry the doctrine of the Trinity might be deduced from a consideration of the unity, the Father, which leads to equality, the Son, and thence to the bond between the two, the Holy Spirit. The treatise *De Sex Dierum Operibus* (*On the Six Days of Creation*) is a bold interpretation of Gen. 1 in the light of his study of *Plato and Aristotle. He assigned the four Aristotelian causes to the Persons of the Trinity, the Father being the efficient cause, the Son the formal, and the Holy Spirit the final cause, whereas divinely created matter was the material cause. The range of Thierry's learning is illustrated in his prologue to the 'Heptateuchon', a compendium of major texts of the seven liberal arts. Bernard Sylvestris' *Cosmographia* and a Latin translation from Arabic of Ptolemy's *Planisphere* (1143) were both dedicated to Thierry.

His comm. on Cicero's *De Inventione* and on *Ad Herennium*, ed. K. M. Fredborg, *The Latin Rhetorical Commentaries by Thierry of Chartres* (Pontifical Institute of Mediaeval Studies, Studies and Texts, 84; Toronto, 1988); his exposition of the *Opuscula Sacra*, ed. N. H. Häring, *Commentaries on Boethius by Thierry of Chartres and his School* (ibid. 20; Toronto, 1971), with his treatise *De sex dierum operibus* in the same vol., pp. 553–75. His prologue to the 'Heptateuchon' ed. E. Jeauneau in *Mediaeval Studies*, 16 (1954), pp. 171–5, repr. in his '*Lectio Philosophorum*': *Recherches sur l'École de Chartres* (Amsterdam, 1973), pp. 87–91, with other material on Thierry, pp. 75–86 and 93–9. For Thierry's career see N. [M.] Häring, 'Chartres and Paris revisited', in J. R. O'Donnell (ed.), *Essays in honour of Anton Charles Pegis* (Toronto, 1974), pp. 268–329, esp. pp. 279–94. For the Councils of Soissons and Reims respectively, see Abelard, *Historia Calamitatum* (J. P. Migne, *PL* 178. 150 B) and J. Leclercq, OSB, 'Textes sur Saint Bernard et Gilbert de la Porrée', *Mediaeval Studies*, 14 (1952), pp. 107–11. John of Salisbury, *Metalogicon*, 1. 5; 2. 10; and 4. 24. A. Vernet, 'Une Épitaphe inédite de Thierry de Chartres', in *Recueil de travaux offert à M. Clovis Brunel*, 2 (Mémoires et Documents publiés par la Société de l'École des Chartes, 12; 1955), pp. 660–70. R. W. Southern and S. Gersh in R. L. Benson and G. Constable (eds.), *Renaissance and Renewal in the Twelfth Century* (Oxford,

1982), pp. 129–33 and 512–34; see also index; [E.] P. [M.] Dronke in id. (ed.), *A History of Twelfth-Century Western Philosophy* (Cambridge, 1988), pp. 358–85, with biographical bibl., p. 455. Manitius, 3, pp. 198–202.

Third Orders. Religious organizations affiliated usually to one of the *Mendicant Orders. They are so called to distinguish them from the First and Second Orders, now normally of professed men and women respectively. Their origins lie in the practice, which developed in the 12th cent., of voluntarily adopting the status of *penitent. In 1175 *Alexander III made it possible for married men and women to be associated with the religious life by declaring that obedience, not continence, was essential. In the 13th cent. various attempts were made to clarify the canonical position of these penitents and gather them into regular institutions, with proper statutes governing their way of life. Though they lived in their own homes, the penitents wore distinctive dress and benefited from some of the same privileges as religious. The seculars associated with the *Humiliati were formed into a 'Third Order' (in this case to distinguish them from the First Order of Clerics and the Second Order of enclosed men and enclosed women). Later many penitents attached themselves to the *Franciscans and *Dominicans. St *Francis of Assisi, who began his religious life as a penitent, contributed greatly to the penance movement, and was later regarded as having 'founded' the Order of Penance, which in fact existed before his time. In 1284 the Master of the Dominican Order, Munio of Zamora, established a Dominican Order of Penance subject to his own jurisdiction; shortly afterwards the Franciscans were given official responsibility for the groups of penitents under their care, and these penitents began to be known as the Third Order of St Francis. In the late 13th cent. informal communities of men and women, including some of the Beghards and *Beguines, established houses and began to attach themselves to the Mendicants. In the 15th cent. some of these communities began to take religious vows. From these developed the Third Orders Regular, which proliferated in the 19th cent. Their members are sometimes known as Regular Tertiaries. Some of the women's houses are strictly enclosed. They are all formally regarded as *religious and, despite some differences, their life is broadly similar to that of the First or Second Orders of their respective societies.

Members of Third Orders who do not take religious vows are now known as Secular Tertiaries. Modern RC canon law describes these Secular Third Orders as 'associations whose members lead an apostolic life and strive for Christian perfection while living in the world and who share in the spirit of some religious institute under the higher direction of that same institute' (*CIC* (1983), can. 303). The most important are the Franciscan, Dominican (technically known as Lay Fraternities and Fraternities of Priests), and the *Carmelite ones. Each Secular Third Order has its own rules, and its aims vary according to the spirit of the Order to which it is attached. Members usually have to make a novitiate, observe a rule and say certain prescribed prayers. Though they do not take religious vows, they usually make a promise, and they normally enjoy some of the spiritual privileges of the professed religious.

G. G. Meersseman, OP, *Dossier de l'Ordre de la Pénitence au XIIIᵉ siècle* (Spicilegium Friburgense, 7; 1961; 2nd edn., 1982).

Third Rome. A title given esp. by Russian Christians to Moscow in the belief that the privileges which formerly belonged to *Rome and *Constantinople (the 'New Rome') had been committed to the city. The first instance of its use appears to be in a letter of the monk Philotheus to the Grand Duke Basil III (1505–33).

Thirlby, Thomas (1506?–70), successively Bp. of *Westminster (1540), *Norwich (1550), and *Ely (1554). A Cambridge man who was favoured by T. *Cranmer, he became a chaplain to *Henry VIII, and first and only bishop of the new see of Westminster (suppressed 1550). In 1549 he spoke against the First Prayer Book of *Edward VI and the Act of *Uniformity, but accepted them when passed, despite his strong Catholic sympathies. He was naturally in high favour under *Mary, but under *Elizabeth I refused the Oath of Supremacy and was deposed and afterwards imprisoned.

T. F. Shirley, *Thomas Thirlby, Tudor Bishop* (CHS, 1964). T. Cooper in *DNB* 56 (1898), pp. 135–8, s.v., with refs.

Thirlwall, Connop (1797–1875), historian and Bp. of *St Davids. After a very precocious childhood he was educated at Trinity College, Cambridge, where he became a Fellow in 1818. After studying law in Lincoln's Inn he entered on an ecclesiastical career, and in 1828 was ordained priest. In 1832 he was appointed assistant tutor at Trinity College, but in 1834 was compelled to resign owing to his denunciation of compulsory attendance at chapel in the course of the controversy over the admission of Dissenters to the universities. In the same year he was offered the living of Kirby Underdale, Humberside, where he began his chief work, the *History of Greece* (8 vols., 1835–44). In 1840 Lord Melbourne appointed him Bp. of St Davids. He learned Welsh, restored Church life in his diocese, and took part in all the ecclesiastical questions of the day in a liberal and unbiased spirit. He supported the grant to *Maynooth (1845) and the removal of the civil disabilities of the Jews (1848), and urged the disestablishment of the Irish Church (1869). He and A. C. *Tait were the only bishops in the C of E who refused to issue an interdict against Bp. J. W. *Colenso preaching in their dioceses when such a ban was organized in 1868. His important 'Charges', delivered between 1842 and 1872 (pub. in *Remains Literary and Theological*, 3 vols., 1877–8), deal with these and other subjects such as the question of *Essays and Reviews*, the *Ritualist controversy, and the First *Vatican Council.

Thirlwall's *Letters, Literary and Theological*, ed. J. J. S. Perowne and L. Stokes (London, 1881); his *Letters to a Friend* [now identified as Miss Betha Johnes], ed. A. P. *Stanley (ibid., 1881). Excellent obituary notice [by E. H. Plumptre] in *Edinburgh Review*, 143 (1876), pp. 281–316. Life by J. C. Thirlwall (great-great-great-nephew) (London, 1936). G. Rees, 'Connop Thirlwall: Liberal Anglican', *Journal of the Historical Society of the Church in Wales*, 14 (1964), pp. 66–76. J. W. Clark in *DNB* 56 (1898), pp. 138–41.

Thirteen Articles (1538). A MS in Latin entitled *A Book containing Divers Articles de Unitate Dei et Trinitate Personarum, de Peccato Originali, etc.* which was discovered among some papers that belonged to Abp. T. *Cranmer. It appears to have been drawn up as a basis for negotiations, or was perhaps a record of doctrines actually agreed upon, between a small body of conservative *Lutheran divines, invited to England by *Henry VIII in 1538, and an English committee of three bishops and four doctors. The articles were closely modelled upon the *Augsburg Confession.

Text in C. Hardwick, *A History of the Articles of Religion* (1851), pp. 251–63, with discussion, pp. 60–73. Eng. tr. of text in N. S. Tjernagel, *Henry VIII and the Lutherans: A Study in Anglo-Lutheran Relations from 1521 to 1547* (St Louis, 1965), pp. 287–306, with discussion, pp. 184–9. See also bibl. to CRANMER, T.

Thirty-Nine Articles. The set of doctrinal formulae finally accepted by the C of E in its attempt to define its dogmatic position in relation to the controversies of the 16th cent. The earlier stages were the *Ten Articles (1536), the *Bishops' Book (1537), the *Six Articles (1539), the *King's Book (1543), and the *Forty-Two Articles (1553). In 1563 *Convocation, by slightly revising the last named, issued the first text of the Thirty-Nine Articles. But, before they were printed, no. 29 ('Of the Wicked which eat not the Body of Christ') was excised, probably in a move to facilitate diplomatic negotiations with the *Lutheran princes of Germany, and a preamble to no. 20, asserting the authority of the Church to decree rites and ceremonies, was added. Both alterations may have been due to personal intervention by *Elizabeth I. In 1571 no. 29 was restored. In their final form the Articles gained synodical approval through Convocation.

The Thirty-Nine Articles are not a statement of Christian doctrine in the form of a creed, nor the exposition of a creed already accepted. They are, rather, short summaries of dogmatic tenets, each article dealing with some point raised in current controversies and laying down in general terms the Anglican view. Though not ostensibly vague, they avoid unduly narrow definition. Much variety of interpretation has been put upon many of them without improperly straining the text, and probably this licence was deliberately intended by their framers. They seek esp. to define the Anglican position with regard to medieval corruptions of Catholic teaching, to orthodox RC doctrine, to *Calvinism, and to *Anabaptist teachings. Among typical points it may be noticed that Art. 28 excludes *transubstantiation (in the sense in which it is there defined) and *Zwinglian Eucharistic doctrine, but can be interpreted in terms either of a doctrine of the *Real Presence or of *receptionism. Art. 6 declares that 'Holy Scripture containeth all things necessary to salvation'; the Creeds are to be accepted because they may be proved by Scripture (Art. 8); and General Councils are declared to be not of themselves infallible (Art. 21). Predestination is discussed in Art. 17, the masterly ambiguity of which is seen when it is compared with other professions of faith such as the Presbyterian *Westminster Confession (1647). The position of the Sovereign and civil power in relation to the Church is set out in the concluding Articles.

Subscription to the Articles has never been required of any but the clergy and, until the 19th cent., members of the universities of Oxford and Cambridge. From 1865 the clergy were required only to affirm that the doctrine of the C of E as set forth in the BCP and the Articles was agree-

able to the Word of God, and to undertake not to teach in contradiction of them, instead of giving a more particular subscription as before. Since 1975 they have been required simply to acknowledge the Thirty-Nine Articles as one of the historic formularies of the C of E which bear witness to the faith revealed in Scripture and set forth in the catholic creeds (Can. C 15). See also CLERICAL SUBSCRIPTION ACT.

E. C. S. Gibson, *The Thirty-Nine Articles* (2 vols., 1896–7); B. J. Kidd, *The Thirty-Nine Articles* (2 vols., 1899). E. J. Bicknell, *A Theological Introduction to the Thirty-Nine Articles* (1919; 3rd edn. by H. J. Carpenter, 1955; chiefly of doctrinal interest). W. P. Haugaard, *Elizabeth and the English Reformation* (Cambridge, 1968), pp. 62–7 and 233–90, *passim*. H. Horie, 'The Lutheran Influence on the Elizabethan Settlement, 1558–1653', *Historical Journal*, 34 (1991), pp. 519–37. For *Tractarian views on the Articles, J. H. *Newman, *Tract 90* (1841), and A. P. *Forbes, *The Thirty-Nine Articles* (1867).

Thirty Years War (1618–48). The series of religious and political wars fought out in Central Europe in the 17th cent. Foremost among its manifold causes were the decay of the *Holy Roman Empire and the continued religious unrest after the Peace of *Augsburg in 1555. The war began with the revolt of the Bohemians against the Emperor, and the '*Defenestration of Prague'. The first part of the war (1618–23) was carried on chiefly in Bohemia and the Palatinate. The Bohemians, who had set up Frederick V of the Palatinate, the so-called 'Winter King', in opposition to Emp. *Ferdinand II, were defeated in the Battle at the White Hill (1620) by the armies of the Catholic League under the Imperial general, Tilly, and Maximilian of Bavaria. Frederick was put to the ban of the Empire, Maximilian conquered the Upper Palatinate, and this stage of the war ended with the capture of the Calvinistic stronghold of Heidelberg by Tilly (1622) and the restoration of Catholicism in the conquered territories.

War broke out anew in 1623. Shifting to Lower Saxony, it was conducted with Dutch and English support, with Wallenstein as the chief leader on the Imperial side. After his victory, in 1626, over Ernest of Mansfeld, and Christian IV of Denmark's defeat at the hands of Tilly (1626), the Peace of Lübeck was concluded in 1629. In the same year the Emperor issued the Edict of Restitution which ordered the restoration of all ecclesiastical property unlawfully appropriated by the Protestants since 1552. Its strict execution roused much opposition among the Protestants, while many Catholics were alienated from the Emperor by the extravagances of Wallenstein's army. In 1630 Wallenstein himself was dismissed.

The third stage of the war, which now became a European conflict, began with the landing of *Gustavus Adolphus in Pomerania in 1630. Encouraged by Cardinal A. J. du P. *Richelieu, whose anti-Habsburg policy led him to support all opponents of the Imperial power at Vienna, the Swedish invasion was a mainly political adventure, though it incidentally saved German Protestantism. In 1631 Tilly conquered Magdeburg, but he was defeated in the same year at Breitenfeld and killed in 1632. Wallenstein, who had been recalled by the Emperor, was defeated in the battle at Lützen, but Gustavus Adolphus himself was killed (1632). The next two years were taken up with negotiations, while the Protestant leader, Bernard of Weimar, took Ratisbon and laid waste Bavaria without opposition from Wallenstein, who was murdered in 1634. In the same year Imperial and Bavarian troops gained a decisive victory at Nördlingen, which led to the treaty of Prague (1635) between the Emperor and the majority of the Protestant estates.

The Swedes, however, continuing to resist, were now openly joined by France and the war entered on its final and most violent stage (1635–48). After years of fighting with varying success in E. and W. Germany, the French position became increasingly advantageous, esp. owing to the weakening of Spain by internal discord. The demand for peace in Germany grew increasingly insistent and in 1644 negotiations were opened with the French at Münster and with Sweden at Osnabrück, and the Peace of *Westphalia (q.v.) was at last concluded in 1648. As a result the ecclesiastical state of the Empire as it was in 1624 was restored, except for the secularization—a term then used for the first time—of a considerable part of ecclesiastical property, which was distributed among the several powers as compensation for their participation in the war. The decrees of the Religious Peace of Augsburg were reinforced and extended to the *Calvinists, and Catholics and Protestants given equal political rights.

Among the chief effects of the Thirty Years War was an enormous strengthening of the power of France. The corresponding weakening of Germany and Spain hastened the final breaking-up of the Empire and decided the future of Europe in succeeding centuries. The religious, moral, and economic anarchy which it produced in Central Europe had the same far-reaching consequences, and accounts for much in the subsequent religious and social developments on the Continent.

Important docs. pr. in the collections of *Briefe und Acten zur Geschichte des Dreissigjährigen Krieges* . . . herausgegeben durch die histor. Commission bei der Königl. (later Bayerischen) Academie der Wissenschaften (11 vols., Munich, 1870–1909; NF, 1966 ff.), and *Documenta Bohemica Bellum Tricennale Illustrantia*, ed. J. [V.] Polišenský and others (7 vols., Prague, 1971–81; Eng. tr. of vol. 1 as *War and Society in Europe, 1618–1648*, Cambridge, 1978). Classic studies incl. A. Gindely, *Geschichte des Dreissigjährigen Krieges* (4 vols., 1869–80); also a shorter study by the same author with the same title (Das Wissen der Gegenwart, 1, 3, 5; 1882; Eng. tr., 2 vols., New York, 1884; London, 1885); S. R. Gardiner, *The Thirty Years War* (Epochs of Modern History, 1874); A. W. Ward in *CMH* 4 (1906), pp. 1–255 and 364–433, with bibl. to date, pp. 801–72, incl. good discussion of sources; M. Ritter, *Deutsche Geschichte im Zeitalter der Gegenreformation und des Dreissigjährigen Krieges (1555–1648)*, 3 (1908); C. V. Wedgwood, *The Thirty Years War* (1938); G. Pagès, *La Guerre de Trente Ans* (1939; Eng. tr., 1970); G. Franz, *Der Dreissigjährige Krieg und das deutsche Volk* (1940; 3rd edn., 1961). Recent accounts incl. J. V. Polišenský, *The Thirty Years War* (Eng. tr., 1971, of orig. Czech pub. at Prague in 1970); H. Langer, *Hortus Bellicus* (Leipzig, 1978; Eng. tr., *The Thirty Years' War*, Poole, Dorset, 1980 [mainly cultural]); R. Bireley, SJ, *Religion and Politics in the Age of the Counterreformation: Emperor Ferdinand II, William Lamormaini, S.J., and the Formation of Imperial Policy* (Chapel Hill, NC [1981]); G. Parker [and others], *The Thirty Years' War* (1984), with excellent bibl.; K. Repgen (ed.), *Krieg und Politik 1618–1648: Europäische Probleme und Perspektiven* (Schriften des Historischen Kollegs, Kolloquien 8; Munich, 1988). See also bibl. to WEST-PHALIA, PEACE OF.

Tholuck, Friedrich August Gottreu (1799–1877), German Protestant theologian. He was educated at Breslau

and Berlin, where he studied esp. oriental languages, but under the influence of *Pietist friends and J. A. W. *Neander he turned to theology. From 1820 to 1826 he lectured at Berlin and in 1826 became professor at Halle University, where he remained to his death, except for a short appointment as embassy chaplain at Rome from 1827 to 1829. In 1823 appeared his influential work *Die Lehre von der Sünde und dem Versöhner, oder die wahre Weihe des Zweiflers*, which was widely translated and did much to check the spread of Rationalism in Germany. It was followed by a commentary on Romans (1824), a collection of the writings of oriental mystics (*Blütensammlung aus der morgenländischen Mystik*, 1825), and further commentaries on St John (1827), the Sermon on the Mount (1833), and Hebrews (1836), which are written from a moralist and apologetic rather than an exegetical point of view. His other works include the devotional *Stunden christlicher Andacht* (1839), *Die Propheten und ihre Weissagungen* (1861), and a history of Rationalism (1865). Tholuck, who through his pastoral work among the students exercised a profound influence on his contemporaries, was a representative of the '*Vermittlungstheologie' (q.v.), combining personal piety with far-reaching disregard of dogma. Despite their theological divergences, he was a lifelong friend of E. B. *Pusey, who had become acquainted with Tholuck in 1825, and whose first work, *The Theology of Germany* (1828), is largely based on Tholuck's ideas.

Gesammelte Werke (11 vols., Gotha, 1862–73). Life by L. Witte (2 vols., Bielefeld and Leipzig, 1884–6). M. Schellbach, *Tholucks Predigt: Ihre Grundlage und ihre Bedeutung für die heutige Praxis* (Theologische Arbeiten, 3; 1956). K. Toiviainen, *August Tholuckin Teologinen Antropologia* (Suomalaisen Teologisen Kirjallisuusseuran Julkaisuja, 80; Helsinki, 1968), with summary in Ger. J. [W.] Rogerson, *Old Testament Criticism in the Nineteenth Century: England and Germany* (1984), pp. 83–5. M. Kähler in *PRE* (3rd edn.), 19 (1907), pp. 695–702.

Thomas, St, Apostle. He is mentioned as one of the Twelve in all four Gospels. In St John, where his name is translated as Δίδυμος (Gk., 'twin'), he appears in three episodes, namely offering to die with Jesus on His way to Bethany (Jn. 11: 16), interrupting the last discourse with his question 'We know not whither thou goest, how know we the way?' (14: 5), and, lastly, doubting the Resurrection unless he were to touch the wounds of the Risen Lord (20: 25–8). After Christ's appearance he confesses his faith in the words 'My Lord and my God' and is thus the first to confess explicitly His Divinity. Acc. to an early tradition mentioned by *Eusebius (*HE* 3. 1) and others, he evangelized the Parthians, whereas another tradition, derived from the Gnostic 'Acts of *Thomas' (where he is called 'Judas Thomas', as generally by the Syrians), asserts that he brought the Gospel to *India, where he was martyred. The Syrian Christians of *Malabar, who call themselves 'Christians of St Thomas', have a tradition which they strongly defend that they were evangelized by the Apostle, who later was martyred and buried at Mylapore, nr. Madras. The 'Thomas Cross', an ancient stone cross (6th–8th cent.) with a problematical inscription, is preserved in the church which marks the place where his body is held to have rested before its translation to *Edessa in the 4th cent. His relics are now supposed to be at Ortona in the Abruzzi, where they are still venerated. In the *Roman

Martyrology the place where he died is given as Calamina. As yet it has not been identified, but it has sometimes been connected with Mylapore. Feast day: 3 July in the RC Church, the ASB, and the Syrian Church; 21 Dec. in the BCP and some modern Anglican rites (and formerly in the RC Church); 6 Oct. in the Greek Church.

For the several apocryphal writings that have circulated under his name, see the following entries.

For discussions of the evidence in the NT, see comm. on the Gospels. For later traditions, see bibl. to THOMAS, ACTS OF.

Thomas, Acts of (Περίοδοι Θωμᾶ). An apocryphal book of great length which recounts in 13 'Acts' the missionary activities of the Apostle Thomas ('Judas Thomas'). It tells how Gundaphorus, one of the kings of India, wishing for a magnificent palace, sent his merchant Abbanes to Syria to obtain a skilled architect. At *Jerusalem Abbanes met Jesus, the carpenter's son, who recommended to him His 'slave', Thomas, and Thomas agreed to go back with him to Syria. Thomas gave away to the poor the large sums of money with which Gundaphorus provided him, and soon convinced him that his money was being used to build a far nobler palace in heaven than the earthly building for which it had been intended. Gundaphorus and many others were thereupon converted. After further missionary work, accompanied by healing miracles, in the neighbouring lands of King Misdaeus, Thomas was persecuted for his success in persuading Mygdonia to cease marriage relationships with her husband, Charisius, and finally was pierced with spears. The Apostle's bones were taken back shortly afterwards to Mesopotamia. Contained in the 'Acts' are two hymns, the 'Hymn on the Daughter of Light' (6–7; sometimes called an 'Ode to Sophia') and the famous Hymn to the Redeemer (108–13; now usually known as the 'Hymn of the Pearl' but formerly sometimes called the 'Hymn of the Soul'), and two hymnic invocations relating to Baptism (27) and the Eucharist (50).

The work, which was in origin a *Gnostic composition and apparently written before the middle of the 3rd cent., survives in several Syriac and Greek MSS. The complicated relation of the Syriac and Greek texts is held by most scholars to point to a Syriac original. Parts of the Acts survive also in Latin and Ethiopic; and there exists also an Armenian version. It would appear that from the surviving texts most of the Gnostic elements have been removed to make the work acceptable to Catholic readers, though its origin is betrayed, e.g., by its continual depreciation of marriage.

Syriac text ed. W. Wright, *Apocryphal Acts of the Apostles* (1871), 1, pp. 171–333; Eng. tr., 2, pp. 146–298; Eng. tr. of older frags. by Mrs A. S. Lewis, *The Mythological Acts of the Apostles* (Horae Semiticae, 4; 1904), pp. 223–41. Further Eng. tr., based on that of Wright, with introd. and comm., by A. F. J. Klijn (Supplements to *Novum Testamentum*, 5; 1962). Best edn. of the Gk. text in R. A. *Lipsius and M. Bonnet, *Acta Apostolorum Apocrypha*, 2 (pt. 2; Leipzig, 1903), pp. 99–291. Eng. tr. in J. K. Elliott, *The Apocryphal New Testament* (Oxford, 1993), pp. 439–511. Ger. tr., with introd., by H. J. W. Drijvers in Schneemelcher (5th edn., 1989), 2, pp. 289–367; Eng. tr., 2 [1992], pp. 322–411. Lat. text ed. K. Zelzer, *Die alten lateinischen Thomasakten* (TU 122; 1977). P.-H. Poirier, *L'Hymne de la Perle des Actes de Thomas: Introduction, texte, traduction, commentaire* (Louvain, 1981). F. C. *Burkitt, 'The Original Language of the Acts of Judas Thomas', *JTS* 1 (1900), pp. 280–90; id., 'Another Indication of the Syriac

Origin of the Acts of Thomas', ibid. 3 (1902), pp. 94–6. G. E. Medlycott, *India and the Apostle Thomas: An Inquiry, with a Critical Analysis of the* Acta Thomae (1905), pp. 213–97. F. Wilhelm, *Deutsche Legenden und Legendare: Texte und Untersuchungen zu ihrer Geschichte im Mittelalter* (1907). J. Dahlmann, SJ, *Die Thomas-Legende und die ältesten historischen Beziehungen des Christentums zum fernen Osten im Lichte der indischen Altertumskunde* (Stimmen aus Maria Laach, Ergänzungsheft, 107; 1912). J. N. Farquhar, 'The Apostle Thomas in North India', *Bulletin of the John Rylands Library*, 10 (1926), pp. 80–111; id., 'The Apostle Thomas in South India', ibid. 11 (1927), pp. 20–50. G. Bornkamm, *Mythos und Legende in den apokryphen Thomas-Akten* (1933). R. H. *Connolly, 'A Negative Golden Rule in the Syriac Acts of Thomas', *JTS* 36 (1935), pp. 353–7. A. Dihle, 'Neues zur Thomas-Tradition', *Jahrbuch für Antike und Christentum*, 6 (1963), pp. 54–70. Bardenhewer, 2, pp. 579–84; J. Quasten, *Patrology*, 1 (Utrecht, 1950), pp. 139 f., with bibl.; I. Ortiz de Urbina, SJ, *Patrologia Syriaca* (2nd edn., Rome, 1965), pp. 37–41. H. W. Attridge in *Anchor Bible Dictionary*, 6 (1992), pp. 531–4.

Thomas, Apocalypse of. An apocryphal eschatological treatise, probably written by a *Manichaean at the end of the 4th cent. and referred to in the *Gelasian Decree. It had long been lost, but two recensions, both in Latin, were rediscovered in a number of MSS early in the 20th cent. The shorter, edited by P. Bihlmeyer in 1911 on the basis of MS Monacensis Clm 4563, is probably the original. There are signs of its influence in Anglo-Saxon and Irish texts.

P. Bihlmeyer, OSB, 'Un Texte non interpolé de l'Apocalypse de Thomas', *R. Bén.* 28 (1911), pp. 270–82, incl. text. It was also ed. by M. Förster from two Anglo-Saxon revisions of the text in 'Der Vercelli-Codex CXVII nebst Abdruck einiger altenglischer Homilien der Handschrift', in *Festgabe für Lorenz Morsbach* (Studien zur englischen Philologie, 50; 1913), pp. 20–179; this text being pr. pp. 116–37. A reconstructed text is the basis of the trs. in J. K. Elliott, *The Apocryphal New Testament* (Oxford, 1993), pp. 645–51. Ger. tr. of the shorter text, with introd. by A. de Santos Otero in Schneemelcher (5th edn., 1989), 2, pp. 675–9; Eng. tr., 2 [1992], pp. 748–52. M. McNamara, MSC, *The Apocrypha in the Irish Church* (Dublin, 1975), pp. 119–21.

Thomas, Book of. One of the Coptic documents discovered at *Nag Hammadi in 1945–6, sometimes known from its subscript title as the 'Book of Thomas the Contender' (a designation not apparently given elsewhere to St *Thomas). It professes to contain the 'secret words' spoken by Jesus to Judas Thomas and written down by St *Matthias (or perhaps St *Matthew). Its main themes are ethics and eschatology, and it is strongly ascetic in character. It was probably written in Syria, the homeland of the traditions about Thomas, and its original language was probably Greek.

Text ed., with Ger. tr., M. Krause and P. Labib, *Gnostische und hermetische Schriften aus Codex II und Codex VI* (Abhandlungen des Deutschen Archäologischen Instituts Kairo, Koptische Reihe, 2; Glückstadt, 1971), pp. 88–106; also, with Eng. tr., by J. D. Turner, *The Book of Thomas the Contender* (Society of Biblical Literature, Dissertation Series, 23; Missoula, Mont. [1975]), and by B. Layton, *Nag Hammadi Codex II, 2–7* (Nag Hammadi Studies, 21; 1989), pp. 173–205, incl. Eng. tr. by J. D. Turner. Turner's tr. also in J. M. Robinson (ed.), *The Nag Hammadi Library in English* (3rd edn., Leiden, 1988), pp. 199–207. Further edn. of text, with Ger. tr. and comm. by H.-M. Schenke (TU 138; 1989). Id., in Schneemelcher (5th edn., 1987), 1, pp. 192–204; Eng. tr., 1 (1991), pp. 232–47.

Thomas, Gospel of. An apocryphal Gospel, originally written in Greek, of which a *Coptic version was discovered among the papyri found at *Nag Hammadi in 1945–6; it is now in the Coptic Museum at Cairo. The Greek original perhaps dates from *c*.150, the Coptic, which contains some additions, from *c*.350. In its heading, the Gospel professes to have been written down by 'Didymus Judas Thomas'. It is not, like the canonical Gospels, historical in form, but consists of a series of pithy sayings and parabolic discourses of Jesus. Some of its 114 items have points of contact with sayings in Mt. and Lk.; where parallels exist the sayings in Thomas often appear to be secondary, but it has been thought possible that it may preserve a few words of Christ not found in the canonical Gospels which ultimately go back to genuine tradition. The Greek *Oxyrhynchus papyri, nos. 1, 654, and 655, preserve fragments of a Greek text which agrees closely, though not exactly, with the Coptic version of the Gospel of Thomas found at Nag Hammadi. The work is apparently of *Gnostic provenance.

Coptic text ed., with Eng. tr., by A. Guillaumont and others (London, 1959); also by B. Layton, *Nag Hammadi Codex II, 2–7* (Nag Hammadi Studies, 20; Leiden, 1989), pp. 38–93, incl. introd. by H. Koester and Eng. tr. by T. O. Lambdin; Oxyrhynchus frags. ed. H. W. Attridge, pp. 96–128, incl. introd. and patristic *testimonia*. Eng. tr., with brief introd., also in J. M. Robinson (ed.), *The Nag Hammadi Library in English* (3rd edn., Leiden, 1988), pp. 124–38; and in J. K. Elliott, *The Apocryphal New Testament* (Oxford, 1993), pp. 123–47. G. Quispel, 'The Gospel of Thomas and the New Testament', *VC* 11 (1957), pp. 189–207, repr. with other relevant arts., id., *Gnostic Studies*, 2 (Istanbul, 1975), pp. 3–112. R. McL. Wilson, *Studies in the Gospel of Thomas* (1960); B. Gärtner, *The Theology of the Gospel of Thomas* (1961); G. Quispel, *Makarius, das Thomasevangelium und das Lied von der Perle* (Supplements to *Novum Testamentum*, 15; 1967). B. Blatz in Schneemelcher (5th edn., 1987), 1, pp. 93–113; Eng. tr., 1 (1991), pp. 110–33. Useful introd. and extensive bibl. in the Sp. tr. of the text by A. de Santos Otero, *Los Evangelios Apócrifos* (6th edn., 1988), pp. 678–705. *CPG* 1 (1983), pp. 76 f. (no. 1181). R. Cameron in *Anchor Bible Dictionary*, 6 (1992), pp. 535–40, s.v.

Thomas, Infancy Gospel of. An apocryphal writing extant in two Greek recensions as well as in Armenian, Ethiopic, Georgian, Latin, Syriac, and Slavonic versions (the last being esp. important). It is prob. not the work mentioned by St *Hippolytus (*Ref.* 5. 7) and *Origen (*Hom. 1 in Luc.*). It professes to record miracles performed by Christ in His childhood (in Greek text A between the ages of 5 and 12; other versions vary considerably). The alleged miracles are primarily displays of power, often without theological point or moral justification, so that the Lord appears callous and irresponsible. They are probably drawn from folk-tales; one incident was reproduced by *Marcosian Gnostics (*Irenaeus, *Adv. Haer.* 1. 20. 1) but appears also in the *Testament of Our Lord in Galilee* (4) and so gives no certain clue to the date of the work.

The two Gk. texts and the Lat. version ed. C. *Tischendorf, *Evangelia Apocrypha* (Leipzig, 1853), pp. 134–70; 2nd edn. (1876), pp. 140–80; Eng. tr. in J. K. Elliott, *The Apocryphal New Testament* (Oxford, 1993), pp. 68–83. See also Schneemelcher, cited below. Ger. tr. of Gk. text A, with some other matter, and introd. by O. *Cullmann, in Schneemelcher (5th edn., 1987), 1, pp. 349–60; Eng. tr., 1 (1991), pp. 439–53. Syriac text ed., with Eng. tr., by W. Wright, *Contributions to the Apocryphal Literature of the*

New Testament (1865), pp. 1–16 of the Syriac; Eng. tr., pp. 6–11. Gk. text also ed., with Fr. tr., by C. Michel and P. Peeters, SJ (eds.), *Évangiles apocryphes*, 1 (Textes et Documents pour l'Étude du Christianisme; 1911), pp. 162–189, with introd., pp. xxiii–xxxii; Fr. tr. of Lat. and Syriac texts ibid. 2 (1914), pp. 290–311. A. de Santos Otero, *Das Kirchenslavischen Evangelium des Thomas* (Patristische Texte und Studien, 6; 1967). P. A. Mirecki in *Anchor Bible Dictionary*, 6 (1992), pp. 540–4, s.v.

Thomas Aquinas, St (*c*.1225–74), also 'Doctor Communis' and 'Doctor Angelicus', *Dominican philosopher and theologian. Born at Roccasecca, near Aquino, in the kingdom of Naples, Thomas was the youngest son of Landolfo d'Aquino, the head of a large and aristocratic family. At the age of 5 he was given to the *Benedictine abbey of *Monte Cassino, in the expectation that he would eventually become abbot. When the troops of *Frederick II occupied the abbey in 1239, Thomas was sent to the University of Naples; here he was attracted to the newly founded Dominican Order. After his reception into the Order, he was sent to *Paris, so that he might be out of reach of his powerful family's opposition; on his way there he was seized by an armed party north of Rome (Mar./Apr. 1244) and confined in the family castle for nearly two years. On his release he began his theological studies in the Dominican priory of St-Jacques in the University of Paris. Here he came under the influence of St *Albertus Magnus, with whom he continued his studies at *Cologne (1248–51). After his return to Paris, he lectured, as *cursor biblicus*, on Isaiah and Jeremiah, and then as bachelor, on the *Sentences* of *Peter Lombard. His *De Ente et Essentia* (against *Avicebron) dates from this period. In 1256 he wrote the *Contra Impugnantes Dei Cultus* defending the *mendicant orders against the attacks of the secular doctors, notably against William of St-Amour's *De Periculis Novissorum Temporum*. In July 1256 Thomas became a Master of Theology and for the next three years served as a Regent Master of St-Jacques. His *Quaestiones Disputatae de Veritate* derive from this teaching activity. Just before he left Paris, Thomas began composing the *Summa contra Gentiles*, a treatise apparently designed for the use of Dominican missionaries in their dealings with non-Christians.

Thomas returned to Italy in 1259 and served as *lector* in various Dominican houses, but his exact movements are not clear. Prob. by 1261 he was in Orvieto, where he produced several works at the request of Pope Urban IV. He examined a collection of Greek patristic writings (some of them forged) which purported to support W. doctrinal teaching, and replied cautiously in *Contra Errores Graecorum*. In the *Catena Aurea*, a continuous gloss on the Gospels compiled from patristic sources, he included various previously unknown Greek texts which were to influence his own theology profoundly. He composed a liturgy for the feast of *Corpus Christi which Urban intended to institute throughout Latin Christendom (his authorship of these texts has been disputed but is now increasingly accepted). While at Orvieto he also wrote a literal exposition of Job. In 1265 he was sent to Rome to direct a Dominican *studium* at Santa Sabina. Here he began the *Summa Theologiae*, originally designed as a handbook for friars not bound for university study. Throughout his time in Italy he held regular disputations, incl. those on power, on evil, and on spiritual creatures.

In 1268 Thomas returned to Paris; he held one of the Dominican chairs of theology in the university until 1272. He was involved in controversy not only with Gerard d'Abbeville and other secular masters over the rights of the mendicants, but also with *Siger of Brabant and radical Aristotelians in the Arts Faculty as well as conservative theologians opposed altogether to the use of *Aristotle in theology. During this period, which was his most productive, Thomas lectured on Mt., Jn., and part at least of the Pauline corpus, and he held disputations on the soul, on the virtues, on whether the union in Christ was one of nature or of person, as well as the *quodlibetal disputations 1–6 and 12. He again defended the mendicants in *Contra Doctrinam Retrahentium a Religione*, and he expounded his views on perfection, against both *Franciscan and secular critics, in *De Perfectione Vitae Spiritualis*. He also continued work on the *Summa Theologiae*, completing the Second Part, and he prepared for publication literal expositions of some of the major works of Aristotle used in the schools, incl. the 'Ethics', 'Posterior Analytics', and 'Metaphysics'. He also finished a commentary on *Dionysius the Pseudo-Areopagite's 'Divine Names'. At Easter 1272 he returned to Italy. Commissioned by his Provincial Chapter to establish a *studium* somewhere within the Roman Province of the Dominican Order, he chose his own priory at Naples. There he continued the Third Part of the *Summa Theologiae* and his expositions on other philosophical works of Aristotle and on the Platonist *Liber de Causis*, lectured on the Pauline Epistles, and preached to the people of Naples during Lent 1273; these sermons were recast in the form of commentaries on the Creed, the *Lord's Prayer, and '*Hail Mary'. On 6 Dec. 1273, while saying Mass, he underwent some mysterious traumatic experience, which abruptly ended his teaching and writing. 'Everything I have written seems like straw by comparison with what I have seen and what has been revealed to me', he reported. In Feb. 1274, on his way to the Second Council of *Lyons, he suffered a head injury; he died on 7 Mar. 1274 at the *Cistercian abbey of Fossanuova, where he was buried.

Although Thomas accorded primacy to revelation, he recognized an autonomy proper to human reason and clearly delineated the spheres of faith and reason, maintaining the importance of philosophy and the sciences even for theology. Despite a profound influence from *Neoplatonism, his philosophical thought, contained in commentaries on Aristotle and independent treatises, is basically Aristotelian, empirical, and realist, or what G. K. *Chesterton called 'organized common sense'. Following Aristotle's maxim that knowledge presupposes an essential likeness between the knower and thing known, and because human nature is both corporeal and intellectual, he held that knowledge necessarily begins with sense perception (*nihil in intellectu quod non prius fuerit in sensu*). This conviction that valid arguments must start with facts of the natural world gave his proofs for the existence of God their characteristic form (for these see QUINQUE VIAE). He emphasized the notion of 'scientific' knowledge based on 'first principles', which are acquired either by experience or education, and deemed Aristotelian logic basic to an understanding of all other disciplines. Also running through his thought is the antithesis of potency and act. He held that the idea of 'primary matter' or pure potency,

existing without form, was self-contradictory, while God, on the other hand, was 'pure act' (*actus purus*), in whom every perfection was fully realized. Intermediate in the scale of being were created things, composed of potency and act. Closely related is his distinction of matter and form. While all individuals in a species have the same form, the matter is proper to each individual. (*Angels, however, as non-material beings, he held to be individuated by their form.) Fundamental, too, is his distinction between essence and existence.

Distinct from philosophy was sacred doctrine or theology. Thomas declared this to be a science, in as much as it is an ordered body of knowledge, even though it depends for its first principles on a higher knowledge that it cannot itself test or prove, namely the knowledge which God has, in which man has some share by means of divine revelation. The fundamental truths revealed by God are the Trinity of Persons in the Godhead and the Incarnation of the Word as a Person of human nature born of the BVM. But Thomas held that revelation was also necessary for truths, such as the existence of God and the divine attributes of creative power and providence, which reason can attain unaided, because without revelation such truths 'would be known only by a few, and that after a long time, and with an admixture of error' (*Summa Theol.* 1. 1. 1). He treated sacred doctrine as a single discipline, at a time when it was often presented in a fragmented way which obscured its connection with the practice of religion; in Thomas's teaching theology embraces the whole life of the Church, including worship, morals, and spiritual practice. All this is illustrated in his great theological synthesis, the *Summa Theologiae*, whose three parts treat respectively of God and creation, of the human person as a free moral agent, and of Christ as the way of man to God.

Thomas's most striking insight, acc. to E. *Gilson, is that whereas all creatures are composed of a nature and a borrowed existence, God alone is subsistent being, the necessary being, the necessary being who cannot not be. Seeing God as subsistent being, Thomas resolved the dichotomy between immanence and transcendence, positing God's intimate presence at the centre of every creature as the cause of its being. Perhaps his most controversial proposition was that the rational soul is the only form of the human body, which Thomas insisted on, in spite of the difficulty it caused in explaining the continuity of Christ's dead body with His living body; one consequence is that the human person has to be treated as a composite whole, rather than as a soul using a body. Thomas identified God's *image in human beings with their capacity to know and direct their own activity. His moral theology is theological, dealing first with happiness as the end of human existence and then with the soul's faculties and powers, which can be directed by virtue and guided by law and grace, as a means to this end. The first principles of moral knowledge (the *Natural Law) are part of human nature; the 'law' of the Gospel is the grace of the Holy Spirit which transforms and elevates (but does not negate) human nature.

Thomas emphasized the role of Christ's humanity in the Incarnation, insisting on His human emotions and acquired knowledge. More importantly, he showed that Christ's humanity had a causal relationship to the work of redemption. As the head of redeemed humanity, Christ continues the work of redemption through the sacraments which are an extension of His humanity, mediating His fullness of grace to His members. Thomas held that all seven sacraments were instituted by Christ, that the Eucharist was the highest of them all (*sacramentum sacramentorum*), and that as the ultimate purpose of the sacrament of *Order was the Eucharist, the Priesthood was the highest of the orders, and the Episcopate therefore not a separate order. He explored in a highly original way the possibility of exploiting the Aristotelian philosophy of *substance and *accidents to develop a systematic understanding of *transubstantiation. The *concomitance of the Body and Blood of Christ in both Eucharistic species afforded a theological justification for *Communion in one kind.

Various of his teachings were attacked before and after his death, and a formal condemnation by Étienne Tempier, Abp. of Paris, was averted only by the intervention of the Roman Curia in 1277. Propositions condemned by the Dominican R. *Kilwardby, Abp. of Canterbury, in 1277, and by his successor, the Franciscan J. *Pecham in 1284, appeared to involve his teaching, while theologians hostile to Thomas tried to implicate him in Tempier's 1277 condemnation of a long list of propositions allegedly being taught in the Arts Faculty at Paris. From 1278 General Chapters of the Dominican Order insisted that his writings be respected and defended within the Order. In 1323 he was canonized by *John XXII, and the Parisian condemnation 'in so far as it touched or seemed to touch him' was lifted in 1325. His body was translated to the Dominican church in Toulouse on 28 Jan. 1369. Feast day, 28 Jan. (formerly, 7 Mar.).

Apart from the 15th-cent. Dominican John *Capreolus, who used Thomas's thought in his critique of *Nominalism, it was not until the 16th cent. that Thomism was revived by Thomas *Cajetan, Sylvester of Ferrara (1474–1528), *John of St Thomas, and others. By the time of the Council of *Trent, the RC Church had accepted the substance of his teaching as an authentic expression of doctrine. In 1567 *Pius V declared him a '*Doctor of the Church' and ordered the first complete printed edition of his works. After another period of eclipse, a new era for Thomism was inaugurated by *Leo XIII's bull *Aeterni Patris (1879), which enjoined the study of Aquinas on all theological students as a clear, systematic philosophy capable of defending Christian tradition from contemporary attack. In 1880 Thomas was declared patron of all Catholic universities and in 1923 his authority as a teacher was reiterated by *Pius XI in *Studium Ducem*. In his encyclical *Lumen Ecclesiae* (1974), *Paul VI proposed Thomas as a model for theologians not only for his doctrinal position, but also for his openness to the world of his day. The period since the Second *Vatican Council (1962–5) has witnessed a critical reappraisal of neo-scholasticism and has opened up new areas of research, notably on the value of Thomas's thought on moral development.

The most important edns. of his works are the 'Piana' in 17 vols., Rome, 1570–1; that issued in 25 vols., Parma, 1852–73; and the 'Vivès' in 34 vols., Paris, 1871–80. All previous edns. are being superseded by the Leonine edn., Rome, 1882 ff. Where this is not yet available, the 'standard' edns. remain those pub. at different times by Marietti, Turin, containing all the works except the

Scriptum super Libros Sententiarum. There are many edns. and trs. of individual works. Important edn., with Eng. tr., of the *Summa Theologiae* (60 vols. + index, London [1964–81]; the 'Blackfriars *Summa*'). Incomplete edn. of the *Scriptum super Libros Sententiarum* by P. Mandonnet, OP, and M. F. Moos, OP (4 vols., Paris, 1929–47). Good edns. of *Super Librum de Causis Expositio* by H. D. Saffrey, OP (Textus Philosophici Friburgenses, 4–5; Fribourg and Louvain, 1954); of *Expositio super Librum Boethii de Trinitate* by B. Decker (Studien und Texte zur Geistesgeschichte des Mittelalters, 4; Leiden, 1955; rev. edn., 1959); and of *Quaestiones de Anima* by J. H. Robb (Pontifical Institute of Mediaeval Studies, Studies and Texts, 14; Toronto, 1968). The Leonine text of *Summa contra Gentiles* is repr., with Fr. tr. by B. Bernier [OP] and others (4 vols., Paris [1951–64]), with introd. by [R.] A. Gauthier [OP] in vol. 1, pp. 7–123. Selections of texts in Eng. tr. incl. his *Basic Writings*, by A. C. Pegis (2 vols., New York [1945]); *Philosophical Texts*, by T. Gilby [OP] (London, 1951); *Theological Texts*, ed. id. (ibid., 1955); V. J. Bourke (ed.), *The Pocket Aquinas* (New York, 1960); C. Martin (ed.), *The Philosophy of Thomas Aquinas: Introductory Readings* (London, 1988); and S. [C. ff.] Tugwell, OP, *Albert & Thomas: Selected Writings* (Classics of Western Spirituality, New York, 1988), pp. 353–632.

On the MSS, H. F. Dondaine [OP] and H. V. Shooner [OP], *Codices Manuscripti Operum Thomae de Aquino* (Rome, 1967–73; Montreal and Paris, 1985 ff.); see also A. Dondaine [OP], *Secrétaires de Saint Thomas* (Rome, 1956). On the corpus of Thomas's work, P. Mandonnet, OP, 'Des écrits authentiques de Saint Thomas d'Aquin', *Revue Thomiste*, 17 (1909), pp. 38–55, 155–81, 257–74, 441–55, 562–73, 678–91; 18 (1910), pp. 62–82, 289–307 (also pub. separately, Fribourg, 1910); M. Grabmann, *Die echten Schriften des hl. Thomas von Aquin* (BGPM 22, Hefte 1–2; 1920; 2nd edn. as *Die Werke des hl. Thomas von Aquin*, 1931; 3rd edn., 1949); I. T. Eschmann, OP, 'A Catalogue of St. Thomas's Works', in Eng. tr. of E. *Gilson, *The Christian Philosophy of St Thomas Aquinas* (1957), pp. 381–439; J. A. Weisheipl, OP, *Friar Thomas d'Aquino* (Garden City, NY, 1974; Oxford, 1975; repr., with corrections and additions, Washington, DC, 1983), pp. 355–405; also L. S. Bataillon, OP, 'Les sermons attribués à Saint Thomas: questions d'authenticité', in A. Zimmermann (ed.), *Thomas von Aquin, Werk und Wirkung im Licht neuerer Forschungen* (Miscellanea Mediaevalia. Veröffentlichungen des Thomas-Instituts der Universität zu Köln, 19; Berlin, 1988), pp. 325–41. Index and concordance of all the writings, prepared by computer, *Index Thomisticus*, ed. R. Busa, SJ (50 vols., Stuttgart, 1974–80); simpler *Lexicon of St Thomas Aquinas based on the Summa Theologica and selected passages of his other works* by R. J. Deferrari and M. I. Barry, CDP (5 fascs., Washington, DC [1948–9]).

The sources for the life of Thomas are ed. D. Prümmer, OP, and M.-H. Laurent, OP, *Fontes Vitae S. Thomae Aquinatis* (6 fascs., Toulouse and then Saint-Maximin, [1912]–1937). Eng. tr. of main sources in K. Foster, OP, *The Life of Saint Thomas Aquinas: Biographical Documents* (1959). Important modern biogs. incl. A. M. Walz, OP, *San Tommaso d'Aquino* (1945; Eng. tr., Westminster, Md., 1951; rev. Fr. tr. by P. Novarina, Philosophes Médiévaux, 5; 1962); J. A. Weisheipl, op. cit.; S. Tugwell, op. cit., pp. 199–351. Useful introds. to the study of his thought incl. E. Gilson, *Le Thomisme* (Strasbourg, 1919; 5th edn., Études de Philosophie Médiévales, 1; 1944; Eng. tr., *The Christian Philosophy of St Thomas Aquinas*, 1957); M.-D. Chenu, OP, *Introduction à l'Étude de Saint Thomas d'Aquin* (Université de Montréal, Publications de l'Institut d'Études Médiévales, 11; 1950; Eng. tr., *Toward Understanding Saint Thomas*, Chicago [1964]); F. C. Copleston [SJ], *Aquinas* (Harmondsworth, 1955); J. Pieper, *Hinführung zu Thomas von Aquin* (Munich [1958]; Eng. tr., New York, 1962; London, 1963); R. McInerny, *Ethica Thomistica: The Moral Philosophy of Thomas Aquinas* (Washington, DC [1982]); A. Patfoort, OP, *Thomas d'Aquin: Les Clés d'une Théologie* [1983]; O. H. Pesch, *Thomas von Aquin* (Mainz, 1988; 2nd edn., 1989); B. Davies [OP], *The Thought of Thomas Aquinas* (Oxford, 1992); and J. P. Torrell, OP, *Initiation à saint Thomas d'Aquin: Sa personne et son œuvre* (Vestigia, 13 [1993]). The many collections of papers incl. A. Kenny (ed.), *Aquinas: A Collection of Critical Essays* (New York, 1969; London, 1970); A. A. Maurer, CSB, and others (eds.), *St Thomas Aquinas 1274–1974: Commemorative Studies* (2 vols., Toronto, 1974); A. Lobato, OP (ed.), *L'Anima nell'Antropologia di S. Tommaso d'Aquinas* (Studia Universitatis S. Thomae in Urbe, 28; Milan, 1987); A. Zimmermann, op. cit.; and N. Kretzmann and E. Stump (eds.), *The Cambridge Companion to Aquinas* (1993). F. Van Steenberghen, *La Philosophie au XIIIᵉ siècle* (2nd edn., Philosophes Médiévaux, 28; 1991), esp. pp. 277–320. The immense lit. is recorded in P. Mandonnet, OP, and J. Destrez, OP, *Bibliographie Thomiste* (Bibliothèque thomiste, 1; Kain, 1921; 2nd edn. by M.-D. Chenu [OP], Paris, 1960); V. J. Bourke, *Thomistic Bibliography 1920–1940* (St Louis, 1945); T. Miethe and V. J. Bourke, *Thomistic Bibliography, 1940–1978* (Westport, Conn., and London, 1980); R. Ingardia, *Thomas Aquinas International Bibliography 1977–1990* (Bowling Green, Ohio [1993]). Current bibl. in *Bulletin Thomiste* (12 vols., 1924–68) and its continuation, *Rassegna di Letteratura Tomistica* (Naples, 1969 ff.). L. A. Kennedy, CSB, *A Catalogue of Thomists, 1270–1900* (Houston, Tex. [1987]). P. A. Walz, OP, and others, in *DTC* 15 (pt. 1; 1946), cols. 618–761, s.v. 'Thomas d'Aquin'; R. Garrigou-Lagrange, OP, ibid., cols. 823–1024, s.v. 'Thomisme'; W. A. Wallace and J. A. Weisheipl in *NCE* 14 (1967), pp. 102–15, s.v.; all with extensive bibl.

Thomas Becket of Canterbury, St. See BECKET, ST THOMAS.

Thomas Bradwardine. See BRADWARDINE, THOMAS.

Thomas de Cantilupe, St. See CANTILUPE, ST THOMAS DE.

Thomas of Celano (*c*.1190–1260), the earliest of St *Francis's biographers. Having joined St Francis's band of friars *c*.1214, he wrote two Lives of the saint (d. 1226), the first in 1228 at the command of *Gregory IX and the second in 1246–7 at the instance of the General of his order. They were followed in 1250–3 by the 'Tractatus de Miraculis S. Francisci'. Written in the rhythmical prose that delighted his age, these biographies were deservedly admired for their elegance, but their historicity has been challenged in modern times. Thomas was also the author of the 'Legend' of St *Clare and, acc. to an uncertain tradition, of the *Dies Irae (q.v.).

Crit. edn. of Thomas's two Lives and miracles of St Francis by the Franciscans of Quaracchi in *Analecta Franciscana*, 10 (1926–41), pp. 1–331, with introd. pp. iii–xlii. Eng. tr. of the two Lives of St Francis and selections from the miracles by P. Hermann, OFM (Chicago, 1963; also in St Francis of Assisi, *Writings and Early Biographies: English Omnibus of the Sources for the Life of St Francis*, ed. M. A. Habig, ibid. [1973], 3rd edn., London, 1979, pp. 177–611). For further edns. see bibl. to FRANCIS, ST, and for edns. of Legend of St Clare, see bibl. to CLARE, ST. J. R. H. Moorman, *The Sources for the Life of St Francis of Assisi* (Publications of the University of Manchester, no. 274, Historical Series, no. 79; 1940), esp. pp. 61–81 and 110–28. M. Bihl, OFM, 'Disquisitiones Celanenses', *AFH* 20 (1927), pp. 433–96; 21 (1928), pp. 3–54 and 161–205. A. G. Little, 'Some Recently Discovered Franciscan Documents and their Relation to the Second Life of Celano and the *Speculum Perfectionis*', *Proceedings of the British Academy*, 12 (1926), pp. 147–78. T. Desbonnets, OFM, 'Recherches sur la Généalogie des Biographies primitives de Saint François', *AFH* 60 (1967), pp. 273–316; Lorenzo di Fonzo, OFM Conv., 'L'Anonimo Perugino tra le Fonti Francescane del Secolo XIII. Rapporti, Letterari e Testo Critico', *Miscellanea*

Francescana, 72 (1972), pp. 117–483, esp. pp. 117–48 and 466. G. Mailleux [OFM], *Thesaurus Celanensis* (Corpus des Sources Franciscaines, 1; 1974). See also bibl. to DIES IRAE.

Thomas Christians. See MALABAR CHRISTIANS.

Thomas Gallus (d. 1246), mystical theologian. A canon of St-Victor in Paris (see VICTORINES), in 1219 he was sent to Vercelli to help establish a new foundation, of which he was prior by 1224 and received the title of abbot in 1224/5. For political reasons he spent the last three years of his life in exile.

He wrote commentaries on Isaiah and the Song of Songs and two treatises on contemplation, but he is chiefly known for his work on *Dionysius the Pseudo-Areopagite, whose work he helped to make known in the W. He seems to have been the first to link Dionysius' *apophatic theology with the idea that the deepest part of the human personality is a non-intellectual mystical faculty for apprehending God. He compiled glosses on the 'Celestial Hierarchy' and 'Mystical Theology' and more substantial commentaries on both these works and on the 'Divine Names'; his most influential work was an *Extractio* or synopsis of the whole Dionysian corpus, which came to be included in the Dionysian corpus used in the University of *Paris. The author of the '*Cloud of Unknowing' and Jean *Gerson were among those influenced by him.

His *Explicatio* is conveniently repr. in the Carthusian edn. of the Works of *Dionysius the Carthusian, 15–16 (Tournai, 1902) (*Commentaria in Libros S. Dionysii Areopagitae*) at the end of each ch. of Dionysius the Pseudo-Areopagite's works. His commentaries on the Song of Songs are ed. J. Barbet (Textes philosophiques du moyen âge, 14; 1967), with introd., pp. 15–61. His other works are largely unpr.; details of those pub. to date are given by J. Barbet in *Dict. Sp.* 15 (1991), cols. 800–16, s.v. J. Walsh, SJ, 'The "Expositions" of Thomas Gallus on the Pseudo-Dionysian Letters', *AHDLMA* 30 (for 1963; 1964), pp. 199–220, incl. text. G. Théry, OP, 'Thomas Gallus: Aperçu biographique', ibid. 12 (1939), pp. 141–208. M. Capellino, *Tommaso di S. Vittore, abate Vercellese* (Vercelli, 1978).

Thomas of Hereford, St. See CANTILUPE, ST THOMAS DE.

Thomas a Jesu (1564–1627), spiritual author. Influenced by the writings of St *Teresa, Díaz Sánchez de Ávila entered the *Carmelite Order in 1587, and he soon held the offices of professor of theology at Seville, prior at Saragossa, and provincial of Old Castile. After establishing a strictly eremitical life in several Carmelite monasteries, he was called to Rome in 1607 by *Paul V, in order to further the missionary activities in his order; but his efforts were frustrated by the opposition of the Spanish and Italian superiors. The literary results of the enterprise, however, the treatises *Stimulus Missionum* (1610) and *De Procuranda Salute omnium Gentium* (1613), in which he outlined his missionary theory, contributed largely to the foundation of the Congregation 'De *Propaganda Fide' (1622). His works on mysticism, *De Contemplatione Divina* (1620) and *Divinae Orationis Methodus* (1623), are remarkable for the clarity and sureness of their doctrine, presenting the teaching of St Teresa in the form of Scholastic treatises.

Opera Omnia, pub. in 2 vols. bound in 1, Cologne, 1684. B. M. Zimmerman, CD, *Les Saints déserts des Carmes déchaussés* (1927), pp. 46–60. E. A. Peers, *Studies of the Spanish Mystics*, 2 (1930), pp. 279–306, with bibl. pp. 447–452. S. Salaville, AA, 'Un Précurseur de la Propagande et un apôtre des missions, le P. Thomas de Jésus', *Études carmélitaines*, 5 (1920), pp. 301–23. José de Jesús Crucificado, OCD, 'El Tomás de Jesús, escritor místico', *Ephemerides Carmeliticae*, 3 (1949), pp. 305–49, and 4 (1950), pp. 149–206; Gabriel de Ste-Marie-Magdaleine, OCD, 'Thomas de Jésus et la contemplation acquise', *Revue d'Ascétique et de Mystique*, 25 (1949), pp. 3–17. M. A. Diez, OCD, in *Dict. Sp.* 15 (1991), cols. 833–44, s.v. 'Thomas (22) de Jésus'.

Thomas à Kempis (*c.*1380–1471), ascetical writer. Thomas Hemerken, acc. to the usual and most probable tradition the author of the '*Imitation of Christ*' (q.v.), was born at Kempen, nr. Krefeld, of poor parents. After education at Deventer at the school of the *Brethren of the Common Life, he entered in 1399 the house of the *Canons Regular at the Agnietenberg, nr. Zwolle (one of the daughter-houses of *Windesheim), of which his elder brother, John, was co-founder and prior, and in 1406 took the habit. Here he lived for almost the whole of the rest of his life, writing, preaching, and copying MSS. and widely sought after as a spiritual adviser. His writings, though of many different kinds—ascetical, homiletic, poetical, biographical, etc.—are all pervaded by the devotional spirit which finds its classic expression in the 'Imitation'. They include *Orationes et Meditationes de Vita Christi*, *Vallis Liliorum*, and *Soliloquium Animae*. Feast day in the American BCP (1979), 24 July.

Opera et Libri Vite Fratris Thome a Kempis by H. Rosweyden [ed. P. Danhausser] (Nuremberg, 1494); rev. edn. by H. Sommalius, SJ, (Antwerp, 1601); crit. edn. by M. J. Pohl (7 vols., Freiburg i.B., 1902–22; vol. 8 wanting). Eng. tr. from edn. by M. J. Pohl of *Prayers and Meditations on the Life of Christ* by W. Duthoit (London, 1904); of *The Founders of the New Devotion* by J. P. Arthur (ibid., 1905); of *The Chronicle of the Canons Regular of Mount St Agnes* by id. (ibid., 1906); of *Sermons to the Novices Regular* by V. Scully, CRL (ibid., 1907); and of *Meditations and Sermons on the Incarnation, Life and Passion of Our Lord* by id. (ibid., 1907). S. Kettlewell, *Thomas à Kempis and the Brothers of the Common Life* (2 vols., 1882). *Thomas von Kempen: Beiträge zum 500. Todesjahr 1471–1971* . . . Herausgegeben von der Stadt Kempen (Kempen and Niederrhein, 1971). E. Iserloh, *Thomas von Kempen und die Kirchenreform im Spätmittelalter* (ibid., 1971). R. T. M. van Dijk in *Dict. Sp.* 15 (1991), cols. 817–26, s.v. 'Thomas (16) Hemerken'. See further bibl. to IMITATION OF CHRIST, more esp. works of those authors who accept the attribution to Thomas à Kempis.

Thomas of Marga (9th cent.), historian of the *Church of the East. In 832 he entered the celebrated monastery of Beth-'Abhe, *c.*40 miles NE of Mosul. Later he became secretary to the Patr. Abraham (837–50), by whom he was created Bp. of Marga. Finally he became Metropolitan of Beth-Garmai. He wrote *c.*840 his *Book of Governors*, a history of his monastery, but embodying also biographies of monks from various places in Mesopotamia; it is one of the chief authorities for the monastic history of the Church of the East.

Thomas's 'Book of Governors' (Liber Superiorum), ed. E. A. W. Budge (2 vols., London, 1893; Syr. text with Eng. tr. in vol. 2) and P. Bedjan, Cong. Miss. (Paris, 1901). W. Wright, *A Short History of Syriac Literature* (1894), pp. 219 f.; A. *Baumstark, *Geschichte der syrischen Literatur* (1922), p. 233 f. A. Solignac, SJ, in *Dict. Sp.* 15 (1991), cols. 847–9, s.v. 'Thomas (26) de Marga'.

Thomas More, St. See MORE, ST THOMAS.

Thomism. The systematized expression of the (esp. philosophical) doctrines of St *Thomas Aquinas (q.v.), particularly as developed in the RC Church in the *Dominican Order.

Thompson, Francis (1859–1907), RC poet. A native of Preston, he was originally intended for the priesthood and educated at Ushaw, but later unsuccessfully studied medicine at Manchester. In 1885 he went to London, where he lived for three years in almost complete destitution, occasionally selling newspapers and matches. In 1888 his poetic gifts were discovered by Wilfrid Meynell, then editor of the Catholic magazine *Merry England*, who remained his friend and benefactor throughout his life. His first volume of *Poems*, published in 1893, contained the fine cycle 'Love in Dian's Lap', dedicated to Alice *Meynell, and his best-known poem, 'The Hound of Heaven', with its arresting description of the pursuit of the soul by God. It was followed by *Sister Songs* (1895) and *New Poems* (1897). His poetry, though sometimes marred by an excessive use of neologisms, archaic words, and difficult allusions, has affinities with that of the '*Metaphysical School' of the 17th cent. Its occasional obscurity rarely prevents it from conveying the central thought, and in its profound spirituality and love of children and the simple things of life it has a genuine Franciscan ring, fostered by the poet's long stay (1893–7) near the Franciscan monastery at Pantasaph. After 1897 he wrote almost no more poetry. Among his prose works are *Health and Holiness; A Study of the Relations between Brother Ass the Body and his Rider the Soul* (1905; with Preface by G. *Tyrrell), a *Life of St *Ignatius Loyola* and an *Essay on Shelley* (the last two both posthumous, 1909).

Works (3 vols., London, 1913). Further material by Thompson was identified and ed. by T. L. Connolly, SJ: *Literary Criticisms* (New York, 1948); *The Real Robert Louis Stevenson and Other Critical Essays* (ibid., 1959), incl. full bibl. of Thompson's works, pp. 353–98; and *The Man has Wings: New Poems and Plays* (Garden City, NY, 1957); *Letters* ed. J. E. Walsh (New York, 1969). E. Meynell, *The Life of Francis Thompson* (1913); R. L. Mégroz, *Francis Thompson* (1927); V. Meynell, *Francis Thompson and Wilfrid Meynell* (1952); J. C. Reid, *Francis Thompson: Man and Poet* (1959); P. Danchin, *Francis Thompson: La vie et l'œuvre d'un poète* (1959); P. van K. Thompson, *Francis Thompson: A Critical Biography* (1961); J. [E.] Walsh, *Strange Harp, Strange Symphony: The Life of Francis Thompson* (New York, 1967; London, 1968); B. M. Boardman, *Between Heaven and Charing Cross: The Life of Francis Thompson* (New Haven, Conn., and London, 1988). E. Meynell in *DNB, 1901–1911*, pp. 502 f.

Thoresby, John (d. 1373), Abp. of *York. After executing several missions for W. Melton, Abp. of York (1317–40), and holding a number of ecclesiastical positions, he became Master of the Rolls in 1341 and Keeper of the Privy Seal in 1345, and was employed by Edward III to treat with France in 1346 and with Scotland in 1357, and to be guardian of the kingdom in 1355. In 1347 he became Bp. of *St Davids, and in 1349 of *Worcester. From 1349 to 1356 he was Chancellor of England, and from 1352 to 1373 Abp. of York. It was mainly through his instrumentality that the ancient dispute as to the respective privileges of Canterbury and York was settled, the Pope directing, on 22 Feb. 1354, that the Abp. of York should be the 'Primate of England' and the Abp. of Canterbury the 'Primate of All England'.

A few of his Constitutions are pr. in D. *Wilkins (ed.), *Concilia Magnae Britanniae et Hiberniae*, 3 (1737), pp. 663, 666–79; his will in J. Raine (ed.), *The Historians of the Church of York and its Archbishops*, 3 (RS, 1894), pp. 281–4. W. H. Dixon and J. Raine (eds.), *Fasti Eboracenses: Lives of the Archbishops of York*, 1 (1863), pp. 449–94, with eight of his letters, pp. 377–80. Life by T. Stubbs (14th cent.) in J. Raine, op. cit., 2 (RS, 1886), pp. 419–21. J. Hughes, *Pastors and Visionaries: Religion and Secular Life in Late Medieval Yorkshire* (Woodbridge, Suffolk, 1988), esp. pp. 127–73 [to be used with caution]. C. L. Kingsford in *DNB* 56 (1898), pp. 280–2, s.v.; *BRUO* 3 (1959), pp. 1863 f.

Thorn, Conference of (1645). A conference (*colloquium caritativum*), of 26 *Catholic, 28 *Lutheran, and 24 *Calvinist theologians, convened in the Rathaus at Thorn (Toruń) on 28 Aug. 1645 on the proposal of Władysław IV, King of Poland (1632–48), to bring about religious reunion. Among the participants were J. A. *Comenius, A. *Calovius, and G. *Calixtus (who on being rejected by the Lutherans ranked himself a Calvinist). Though discussions continued until 21 Nov., no result was achieved, largely because the Lutherans believed that the Catholics' only interest was to sever them from the Calvinists and the Protestant cause. Hence it was described as in fact *colloquium irritativum*.

Acta Conventus Thoruniensis Celebrati Anno 1645 (Warsaw, 1646); F. Jacobi, 'Das liebreiche Religionsgespräch zu Thorn 1645', *ZKG* 15 (1895), pp. 345–63; expanded edn. issued separately, Gotha, 1895. K. E. J. Jørgensen, *Ökumenische Bestrebungen unter den polnischen Protestanten bis zum Jahre 1645* (Copenhagen, 1942), pp. 377–87; A. Jobert, *De Luther à Mohila: La Pologne dans la crise de la Chrétienté 1517–1648* (Collection historique de l'Institut d'Études Slaves, 21; 1974), pp. 384–94, with bibl. pp. 430 f. B. Tschackert in *PRE* (3rd edn.), 19 (1907), pp. 745–51.

Thorndike, Herbert (1598–1672), Anglican theologian. Probably a native of Suffolk, he was educated at Trinity College, Cambridge, of which he became a Fellow in 1620. Ordained priest c.1627, he held various offices in his college. In 1642 he became rector of Barley in Herts, but was ejected in 1643, as also from his fellowship at Trinity in 1646. In 1660 he was reinstated in both offices, and in the following year was appointed Prebendary of *Westminster. His first important theological work was his *Discourse of the Government of Churches* (1641), in which he defended the Apostolic origin of episcopal government against the Presbyterians. It was followed by the treatise *Of Religious Assemblies and the Public Service of God* (1642), upholding the worship of the C of E against the Puritans. In *A Discourse of the Right of the Church in a Christian State* (1649) he endeavoured to elucidate the relations between Church and State, stressing the supranational character of the former but conceding to the latter a certain authority over it. From 1652 to 1657 he helped in editing B. *Walton's *Polyglot Bible*, working chiefly on the Syriac texts. His principal work is *An Epilogue to the Tragedy of the Church of England* (1659), which consists of three parts: 1, The Principles of Christian Truth; 2, The Covenant of Grace; 3, The Laws of the Church. In it he looks for a unified Christendom on the basis of the first six General Councils, conceding a certain superiority to the Pope with

prescriptive rights over the W. Church. The third part contains his Eucharistic teaching. He rejects what he calls the 'Socinian' (=*Zwinglian), *Calvinistic, and *Lutheran doctrines as well as *transubstantiation, to which, however, he is more sympathetic than most of his contemporaries. Acc. to his own view, the mystical but objective Presence of the Body and Blood of Christ is added to the substance of bread and wine by the consecration, which, however, is not effected by the words of Institution, but by the use of prayer. Thorndike's significance was for long forgotten, until he was rediscovered by the *Tractarians.

Works in LACT (6 vols., bound in 9, 1844–54; with Life in vol. 6 by A. W. Haddan, pp. 153–266). T. A. *Lacey, *Herbert Thorndike, 1598–1672* (1929). J. B. Mullinger in *DNB* 56 (1898), pp. 290–2.

Thorvaldsen, Bertel (1770–1844), Danish sculptor. Educated at the School of Art at Copenhagen, in 1797 he went to Rome, where he lived until 1838. His art is saturated with the classical ideal of beauty, which is prominent also where he deals with Christian subjects. His most famous religious work is the monumental group of Christ and His Apostles (1821–42) in the Frue Kirke at Copenhagen; the beautiful figure of the Transfigured Christ, His hands extended in blessing, has often been imitated. Among his other religious works are the tomb of Pope *Pius VII in St Peter's (1830) and an Entrance of Christ into Jerusalem. All his works, originals or casts or copies, are collected in the Thorvaldsen Museum in Copenhagen.

J. M. Thiele, *Den Danske Billedhugger Bertel Thorvaldsen og hans Vaerker* (4 vols., Copenhagen, 1831–50); id., *Thorvaldsens Biographi* (4 vols., ibid., 1851–6; much abridged Eng. adaptation by M. R. Bernard, 1865); T. Oppermann, *Thorvaldsen* (3 vols., Copenhagen, 1924–1930); E. K. Sass, *Thorvaldsens Portrætbuster* (3 vols., ibid., 1963–5); J. B. Hartmann, *Bertil Thorvaldsen* (Quaderni di Storia dell'Arte, 19; Rome, 1971); id., *Antike Motive bei Thorvaldsen*, ed. K. Parlasca (Tübingen [1979]). Catalogues of the Thorvaldsen Museum, ed. B. Jørnaes (in Danish, Copenhagen, 1975) and by id. and A. S. Urne (in Eng. tr., ibid., 1985).

Thou, Jacques Auguste De. See DE THOU, JACQUES AUGUSTE.

Three Chapters, the (τὰ τρία κεφάλαια). The three subjects condemned by the Emp. *Justinian in an edict of 543–4, namely (1) the person and works of *Theodore of Mopsuestia, (2) the writings of *Theodoret against *Cyril of Alexandria, and (3) the letter of *Ibas of Edessa to Maris. As all three were considered sympathetic to *Nestorius, Justinian issued the edict in the hope of conciliating the *Monophysites by a display of anti-Nestorian zeal. The E. patriarchs assented, but in the W. the Emperor's interference was unpopular, and on the ground that it was opposed to the *Chalcedonian decrees, Pope *Vigilius refused at first to approve the edict. After being summoned to *Constantinople, however, Vigilius eventually issued in 548 his 'Iudicatum' to *Menas, the Patr. of Constantinople; this condemned the Three Chapters, but upheld the Chalcedonian decisions. After a storm of protest in the W., Vigilius deemed it best to withdraw his 'Iudicatum' and await a General Council. At the Fifth General Council, which met at *Constantinople in 553, the Three Chapters, and indirectly Vigilius, were condemned, though the Council also asserted the intention of the E. to remain in communion with Rome. In a 'Constitutum', issued in 554, Vigilius declared his submission to the Council's decision and his successor, Pelagius I, followed his example, though a serious schism in the W. resulted. Justinian's policy, which was in fact an attack on the *Antiochene theology and the decisions of Chalcedon, failed even of its purpose of reconciling the Monophysites.

The main docs. will be found with the Acta of the Fifth General Council, pr. in the Conciliar collections. Latin theologians who wrote expressly in defence of the 'Three Chapters' incl. *Facundus of Hermiane and Fulgentius *Ferrandus [Ep. 6], qq.v., also Pope Pelagius I (556–61). L. *Duchesne, *L'Église au sixième siècle* (1925), pp. 185–218. Hefele and Leclercq, 3 (pt. 1; 1909), pp. 1–156, *passim*. R. Devreesse, *Essai sur Théodore de Mopsueste* (ST 141; Rome, 1948), pp. 194–272. C. Moeller, 'Le Chalcédonisme et le néochalcédonisme en Orient de 451 à la fin du VIᵉ siècle', in A. Grillmeier, SJ, and H. Bacht, SJ (eds.), *Das Konzil von Chalkedon*, 1 (Würzburg, 1951), pp. 637–720. H. M. Diepen, OSB, *Les Trois Chapitres au Concile de Chalcédoine: Une étude de la christologie de l'Anatolie ancienne* (Oosterhout, 1953). Id., *Douze Dialogues de christologie ancienne* (Rome, 1960), *passim*. É. Amann in *DTC* 15 (pt. 2; 1950), cols. 1868–1924, s.v. 'Trois-Chapitres (Affaire des)'. See also bibl. to CONSTANTINOPLE, SECOND COUNCIL OF.

Three Children, Song of the. See SONG OF THE THREE CHILDREN.

Three Denominations, the. A title applied to the *Presbyterian, *Congregationalist, and *Baptist Churches, the ministers of which in London and Westminster formed an association in 1727 for the purpose of joint political action. See also REGIUM DONUM.

Three Hours' Service. An extra-liturgical service on Good Friday. It is held during the three hours of the Lord's Passion from noon till 3 p.m., and usually consists of seven sermons on the Seven Words from the Cross, with the intervals filled with hymns and prayers. The service was instituted by the *Jesuits on the occasion of an earthquake at Lima in 1687.

It appears to have been introduced in the C of E by A. H. *Mackonochie in the 1860s; there is a record of such a service in *St Paul's Cathedral, London, in 1876. It came to be widely observed esp. in Anglican churches as well as in some RC churches, though since the middle of the 20th cent. its popularity has declined.

A. Mesia, SJ, *Devoción á las Tres Horas de Agonia de Nuestro Redentor Jesú Cristo* (1687; Eng. tr., London, 1806, repr. with historical introd. by H. Thurston, SJ, as *The Devotion of the Three Hours' Agony on Good Friday*, 1899). G. M. Bosworth, 'A Note on the History of the Three-Hour Devotion', *CQR* 154 (1953), pp. 86–91.

Three Witnesses, the. See JOHANNINE COMMA.

Thundering Legion. When in the Danubian campaigns of the Emp. *Marcus Aurelius (172) a sudden rainstorm saved the Roman army from drought and defeat, Christians, such as *Tertullian (*Apol.* 5. 6) and *Eusebius (*HE* 5. 5, who also mentions Claudius *Apollinarius), attributed this to the prayers of Christian members of the 'Legio XII Fulminata', claiming that the Emperor had admitted this in a letter to the Senate. The miracle is also referred to by pagan writers, e.g. Dio Cassius, though without ref-

erence to the Christian setting. On the column of M. Aurelius, in Rome, Jupiter Pluvius is represented as the benefactor. The mistranslation 'thundering' for 'thunderstruck' led to the elaboration that a thunderbolt had destroyed the enemy. As the name 'Fulminata' for the Legion dates from the time of Augustus (d. AD 14), it had no connection originally with the incident here mentioned. The 'Thundering Legion' again appears in the legend of the Forty Martyrs of *Sebaste (q.v.).

Good discussion of the legend, with text and Eng. tr. of the letter of Marcus Aurelius to the Senate and further refs., in J. B. *Lightfoot, *The Apostolic Fathers*, pt. 2. 1 (1885), pp. 469–76. G. T. Stokes in *DCB* 4 (1887), pp. 1023 f., s.v.; H. *Leclercq, OSB, in *DACL* 5 (pt. 2; 1923), cols. 2692–703, s.v. 'Fulminata (Légion XIIᵉ)'.

thurible (Lat. *thus* or *tus*, 'incense'). A metal vessel for the ceremonial burning of *incense. In the usual form of thurible the container is suspended on chains from which it can be swung during the incensation. The thurible is also known as a 'censer'.

Rohault, 5 (1887), pp. 149–69. Braun, *AG*, pp. 598–632, with plates 126–37. H. *Leclercq, OSB, in *DACL* 5 (pt. 1; 1922), cols. 21–33, s.v. 'Encensoir'; A. Weckwerth in *L.Th.K.* (2nd edn.), 8 (1963), cols. 1012 f., s.v. 'Rauchfass'.

thurifer. A person appointed to carry the *thurible at religious ceremonies and services. He is sometimes attended by a boy bearing the incense-boat (the 'boat boy'), sometimes he carries this also himself.

Thurneysen, Eduard (1888–1974), Swiss Protestant theologian. A native of Wallenstadt, after working among the Christian youth at Zurich he was pastor successively at Leutwil in Aargau (1913), Bruggen near St Gall (1920), and the Münster at Basle (1927). From 1913 onwards he was intimately associated with K. *Barth, and largely contributed to the elaboration of the *Dialectical Theology, with the pastoral and social applications of which he was esp. concerned. His writings include *Dostojewski* (1921; Eng. tr., 1964), *Komm' Schöpfer Geist* (sermons, in collaboration with K. Barth, 1924; Eng. tr., 1934), *Christoph Blumhardt* (1926), *Das Wort Gottes und die Kirche* (collected essays, 1927), and *Die Lehre von der Seelsorge* (1948). He was also one of the editors of the Barthian periodical *Zwischen den Zeiten* (1923 onwards).

Gottesdienst—Menschendienst: Eduard Thurneysen zum 70. Geburtstag am 10. Juli 1958 (Zollikon, 1958), with bibl. of his works to date, pp. 333–50, and correspondence between Thurneysen and Barth 1921–5 and introd. by Barth, pp. 7–173; Eng. tr. of correspondence and Barth's introd. by J. D. Smart, *Revolutionary Theology in the Making* (1964), pp. 65–249. *Wort und Gemeinde: Probleme und Aufgaben der praktischen Theologie. Eduard Thurneysen zum 80. Geburtstag* (Zurich, 1968), with bibl. of his works, 1958–68, pp. 521–6. H. J. Ponsteen, *Karl Barth en Eduard Thurneysen (de theologische relevantie van een levenslange vriendschap)* (Oosterbeek [1989]), with Eng. summary.

Thursday, Holy or Maundy. See MAUNDY THURSDAY.

Thyatira, city in N. Lydia, now W. Turkey. It is one of the 'Seven Churches' addressed in Rev. (2: 18–29) and the birthplace of St Paul's convert Lydia, 'a seller of purple' (Acts 16: 14), one of the industries for which the town was noted. In Rev. its Christian community is upbraided for tolerating a 'Jezebel' in their midst who teaches them 'to commit fornication and to eat things sacrificed to idols' (2: 20), probably an adherent of the sect of the *Nicolaitans who introduced pagan elements into Christian worship. In the beginning of the 3rd cent. Thyatira was a stronghold of *Montanism. Its bishop, Sozon, took part in the Council of *Nicaea (325), and another bishop, Basil, is mentioned in 879. The modern city, named Akhisar, had a small Christian community until the 1920s.

In 1922 the head of the newly-founded Orthodox Exarchate of W. Europe was given the title 'Metropolitan of Thyatira' by the Patr. of *Constantinople. In 1963 the Exarchate was divided into four and since 1968 the spiritual leader of the Greek Orthodox communities in Britain has been styled 'Abp. of Thyatira and Great Britain'.

W. M. *Ramsay in *HDB* 4, pp. 757–9, s.v.; id., *The Letters to the Seven Churches of Asia* (1904), pp. 316–53; C. J. Hemer, *The Letters to the Seven Churches of Asia in their Local Setting* (Journal for the Study of the New Testament, Supplement Series, 11; Sheffield [1986]), pp. 106–28.

tiara, extra-liturgical Papal headdress. First mentioned in the 'Vita' of Pope Constantine (708–15), it was in its original form a kind of white Phrygian cap, called 'camelaucum', worn as a sign of the Papal prerogative. Not later than the 11th cent. a coronet was placed round its lower rim, to which were added in the 13th cent. two lappets hanging down at the back. Under *Boniface VIII the tiara was adorned with a second coronet, possibly to symbolize the twofold power of the Papacy, and under Benedict XI (1303–4) or *Clement V (1305–14) a third coronet was added. At the same time the tiara increased in bulk, and in the 15th cent. it attained its modern shape resembling a beehive. It was worn by, or carried in front of, the Pope at important non-liturgical functions such as Papal processions and at solemn acts of jurisdiction, e.g. solemn dogmatic definitions, but it has not been used since the death of *Paul VI.

Braun, *LG*, pp. 498–508. E. Müntz, 'La Tiare pontificale du VIIIe au XVIe siècle', *Mémoires de l'Institut National de France. Académie des Inscriptions et Belles-Lettres*, 36 (1898), pp. 235–324; C. Sachsse, 'Tiara und Mitra der Päpste', *ZKG* 35 (1914), pp. 481–501; P. E. Schramm, 'Zur Geschichte der päpstlichen Tiara', *HZ* 152 (1935), pp. 307–12. J. Braun, SJ, in *CE* 14 (1913), pp. 714 f., s.v.

Ticonius. See TYCONIUS.

Tiele, Cornelis Petrus (1830–1902), Dutch theologian. A *Remonstrant pastor, he became professor of religious history, a chair specially founded for him, at *Leiden University, and here during the years of his professorship (1877–1901) exercised a great influence on the development of the study of comparative religion, esp. in the Netherlands. Among the best known of his many books are *Geschiedenis van den Godsdienst tot aan de Heerschappij der Wereldgodsdiensten* (1876; Eng. tr. by J. E. *Carpenter as *Outlines of the History of Religion*, 1877) and his *Gifford Lectures on *The Elements of the Science of Religion* (1897–9). The fruit of a vast knowledge of ancient languages and history and prodigious industry, they

became widely used on account of their lucid and orderly arrangement.

P. D. Chantepie de la Saussaye, 'Cornelis Petrus Tiele, 16 December 1830–11 Januari 1902', *Koninklijke Akademie van Wetenschappen*, Jaarboek 1902, pp. 125–54. L. Leertouwer, 'C. P. Tiele's Strategy of Conquest', in W. Otterspeer (ed.), *Leiden Oriental Connections 1850–1940* (Leiden, 1989), pp. 153–67.

Tierce. See TERCE, SEXT, NONE.

Tigurinus, Consensus. See CONSENSUS TIGURINUS.

Tikhon, St (1866–1925), Basil Ivanovitch Belavin, the first Patriarch of the Russian Church since 1700. The son of a village priest, he studied theology at the ecclesiastical academy of St Petersburg and was successively Bp. of Lublin in 1897, of N. America in 1898, of Yaroslav in 1907, and of Vilna in 1914. In Apr. 1917 he became metropolitan of Moscow, and in Nov. 1917 was elected Patriarch, though with very circumscribed powers, by the Panrussian Council. Though not an eminent scholar or Church politician, his courage and humility gave him the moral authority needed in the subsequent difficult years. In 1919 he anathematized all who persecuted the Church and called upon the people to resist, but in the same year he imposed neutrality on the clergy in the civil war between the Reds and the Whites and refused to give his blessing to the latter. Owing to resistance to the State policy of confiscating Church property during the famine of 1921–2 he was placed under arrest, but, due to English political pressure, he was not brought to trial. During his absence the State-supported schismatic 'Living Church' was set up, which called a council in 1923 to depose him and gained many adherents. In the same year Tikhon signed a declaration professing loyalty to the Soviet Government, which gained him less intolerable conditions, and he was allowed to live in the Don monastery at Moscow and to officiate in the churches of the capital. Owing to his personal influence many schismatics returned to the Patriarchal Church, and his death was the occasion of great popular demonstrations of veneration and affection. He was canonized in 1989. Feast day, 9 Oct.

Prince P. M. Volkonsky, 'La Reconstitution du patriarcat en Russie. Mgr Tykhon, patriarche de Moscou et de toute la Russie', *ÉO* 20 (1921), pp. 195–219. M. d'Herbigny, SJ, *Après la mort du patriarche Tykhon: Les patriarcats de Constantinople et de Moscou. Projects anglo-orthodoxes de Concile Œcuménique. Grecs et Russes en Europe et en Amérique* (Orientalia Christiana [Analecta], 15, vol. 4, no. 2; 1925). A. Wuyts, SJ, *Le Patriarcat russe au concile de Moscou de 1917–1918* (Orientalia Christiana Analecta, 129; 1941). M. Spinka, *The Church in Soviet Russia* (New York and London, 1956). R. Rössler, *Kirche und Revolution in Russland: Patriarch Tichon und der Sowjetstaat* (1969).

Tikhon of Zadonsk, St (1724–83), Russian bishop and spiritual writer. The son of a village sexton, his childhood was passed in extreme poverty. He studied at the seminary in Novgorod, where he subsequently became professor, taking monastic vows in 1758. In 1761 he was appointed assistant bishop in the Novgorod diocese, and in 1763 Bp. of Voronezh. He resigned in 1767 and retired into seclusion, settling in 1769 at the Zadonsk monastery, where he remained for the rest of his life. Both as diocesan bishop and in retirement Tikhon displayed a vivid pastoral concern and spent much of his time helping those in distress and destitution. Like many members of the Russian Church in the 18th cent., he was considerably influenced by the W., and among his favourite authors included the Lutheran Johann *Arndt and the Anglican Joseph *Hall; but he possessed at the same time a deep understanding of the ascetic and mystical traditions of E. Orthodoxy. He was canonized in 1861. Feast day, 13 August.

Modern edn. of his Works (in Russ.) pub. in 4 vols., St Petersburg, 1912 (repr., with introd. in Eng. and bibl. by N. Gorodetzky, 2 vols., Farnborough, 1970). Eng. tr. of extracts from his Life and writings in G. P. Fedotov (ed.), *A Treasury of Russian Spirituality* (1950), pp. 182–241. N. Gorodetzky, *Saint Tikhon Zadonsky, Inspirer of Dostoevsky* (1951), with full bibl. E. Behr-Sigel, *Prière et Sainteté dans l'Église Russe* (2nd edn., Spiritualité orientale et vie monastique, 33; Bégrolles-en-Mauges, 1982), pp. 131–57 ('Tikhon de Zadonsk'). T. Špidlík, SJ, in *Dict. Sp.* 15 (1991), cols. 960–4, s.v.

Tillemont, Louis Sébastien Le Nain de (1637–98), French Church historian. He was educated at *Port-Royal under P. *Nicole, showed an early interest in history, and was guided into research. He left Port-Royal in 1656, lived in Paris and continued to study. He entered the seminary of Beauvais in 1661 and stayed until 1669, but was not ordained until 1676. He then returned to Port-Royal, but had to leave in 1679, when he retired to his country house at Tillemont, east of Paris. He had close relationships with the *Jansenists, but did not take part in the controversy. He lived an austere life of Augustinian-inspired spirituality. His fame rests on the *Mémoires pour servir à l'histoire ecclésiastique des six premiers siècles* (16 vols., 1693–1712), a work of enormous erudition, covering the development of the Church from the beginning of Christianity to the year 513. Its narrative consists almost entirely of patristic material, linked by a minimum of connecting text, with discussion of chronology, authorship, etc., relegated to the critical notes appended to each volume. For comprehensiveness the work has not been surpassed, though it lacks elegance of style. It was much used by E. *Gibbon in his *Decline and Fall of the Roman Empire* and by J. H. *Newman in *The Arians of the Fourth Century*. Tillemont concurrently wrote a *Histoire des Empereurs et des autres princes qui ont régné dans les six premiers siècles de l'Église* (6 vols., 1690–1738). His materials for a Life of St *Louis were not pub. until 1847–51 (6 vols.).

B. Neveu, *Un Historien à l'École de Port-Royal: Sébastien Le Nain de Tillemont 1637–1698* (International Archives of the History of Ideas, 15; The Hague, 1966). In Eng., M. R. P. McGuire, 'Louis-Sébastien Le Nain de Tillement', *Catholic Historical Review*, 52 (1966–7), pp. 186–200. Bremond, 4 (1920), pp. 258–80. J.-R. Armogathe in *Dict. Sp.* 9 (1976), cols. 590–3, s.v. 'Le Nain de Tillemont'.

Tillich, Paul (1886–1965), Protestant theologian. The son of a *Lutheran pastor, he studied at Berlin, Tübingen and Halle (1904–8). During the First World War he served as an army chaplain. In 1924 he became professor of theology at Marburg, in 1925 at the Technical Hochschule at Dresden, and in 1929 professor of philosophy at Frankfurt. Compelled by his connection with the Religious Socialists to leave Germany in 1933, he settled in the USA, where he was appointed professor of philosophical theology at the *Union Theological Seminary, New York.

In 1940 he became an American national. He became professor at Harvard Divinity School in 1955 and in 1962 Nuveen Professor of Theology at the Divinity School of the University of Chicago.

Tillich was a prolific writer and exercised great influence. His aim was to bridge the gap between Christian faith and modern culture. To do this he employed the 'method of correlation', acc. to which the content of the Christian revelation is stated as answering the questions arising out of the cultural situation. This situation was interpreted by Tillich in terms of *existentialism, ontology, and Jungian psychology. His works include *Das System der Wissenschaften* (1923), *Kirche und Kultur* (1924), *Die religiöse Lage der Gegenwart* (1926; Eng. tr., 1932), *The Interpretation of History* (1936), *The Protestant Era* (1948), *The Shaking of the Foundations* (sermons, 1948), *The Courage to Be* (lectures, 1952), *Love, Power, and Justice* (lectures, 1954), *The New Being* (sermons, 1955), *The Eternal Now* (sermons, 1963), and *Morality and Beyond* (1963); the most important is prob. his *Systematic Theology* (3 vols., 1951–64).

Works ed. R. Albrecht (14 vols., Stuttgart, 1959–75). W. Leibrecht (ed.), *Religion and Culture: Essays in Honor of Paul Tillich* (New York, 1959); K. Hennig (ed.), *Der Spannungsbogen: Festgabe für Paul Tillich zum 75. Geburtstag* (1961). Studies ed. C. W. Kegley and R. W. Bretall (New York, 1952), by K. Hamilton (London, 1963), G. H. Tavard (ibid. [1963]), J. H. Thomas (ibid., 1963), A. J. McKelway (Richmond, Va., 1964; London, 1966), ed. T. A. O'Meara, OP, and C. D. Weisser, OP (Dubuque, Iowa [1965]), J. L. Adams (New York, 1965), D. H. Kelsey (New Haven, Conn., and London, 1967), C. J. Armbruster, SJ (New York, 1967), A. M. Macleod (London, 1973), W. and M. Pauck (ibid., 1977 ff.), J. P. Clayton (Berlin and New York, 1980 [in Eng.]), and L. Gilkey (New York, 1990). *Religion et Culture: Actes du colloque international du centenaire Paul Tillich, Université Laval, Québec, 18–22 août 1986*, ed. J. Richard (Laval, 1987). N. Ernst, *Die Tiefe des Seins: Eine Untersuchung zum Ort der analogia entis im Denken Paul Tillichs* (Fuldaer Studien, 2; St Ottilien, 1988). W. Schüssler, *Jenseits von Religion und Nicht-Religion: Der Religionsbegriff im Werk Paul Tillichs* (Athenäum Monografien, Theologie, 4; Frankfurt am Main [1989]). R. F. Bulman and F. J. Parrella (eds.), *Paul Tillich: A New Catholic Assessment* (Collegeville, Minnesota [1994]). R. C. Crossman, *Paul Tillich: A Comprehensive Bibliography and Keyword Index to ... Writings ... in English* (American Theological Library Association Bibliography Series, 9; Metuchen, NJ, and London, 1983). B. Jaspert in *Dict. Sp.* 15 (1991), cols. 964–83, s.v.

Tillotson, John (1630–94), Abp. of *Canterbury. He was educated at, and later Fellow of, Clare Hall, Cambridge. In 1661 he was present at the *Savoy Conference, as a watcher on the Nonconformist side. In 1688 he helped the *Seven Bishops to draw up their reasons for refusing to read the *Declaration of Indulgence of *James II. In 1689 he was appointed Dean of *St Paul's, and in the same year became a member of the commission for revising the BCP and the *Canons. He wished to be rid of the *Athanasian Creed and held *Zwinglian doctrines about the *Eucharist. The advocates of the policy of comprehension for Nonconformists proposed him in 1689 as *Prolocutor of the Lower House of Convocation, but he was heavily defeated. In 1691, with some reluctance through the circumstances of W. *Sancroft's deposition, he accepted the see of Canterbury. His archiepiscopate was undistinguished. His policy was dictated by hatred of the RC

Church and a desire to include all Protestant dissenters other than *Unitarians in the C of E. A famous preacher, he was a pattern on which the 18th-cent. divines modelled their sermons. He was the first married Abp. of Canterbury since M. *Parker.

Sermons, ed. R. Barker (14 vols., 1695–1704), and as *Works*, ed. with Life by T. Birch (3 vols., 1752). *The Golden Book of Tillotson*. Selection ed. by J. *Moffatt (1926). L. G. Locke, *Tillotson: A Study in Seventeenth-Century Literature* (Anglistica, 4; Copenhagen, 1954). G. Reedy, SJ, *The Bible and Reason: Anglicans and Scripture in Late Seventeenth-Century England* (Philadelphia [1985]), *passim*. J. Marshall, 'The Ecclesiology of the Latitudemen 1660–1689: Stillingfleet, Tillotson and "Hobbism" ', *JEH* 36 (1985), pp. 407–27. A. C. Clifford, *Atonement and Justification: English Evangelical Theology 1640–1790* (Oxford, 1990), pp. 32–49. A. Gordon in *DNB* 56 (1898), pp. 392–8.

Timothy, St. St *Paul's companion on his Second Missionary Journey and later apparently one of his most intimate friends. Two of the *Pastoral Epistles are addressed to him (see following entry). A native of Lystra, he was the son of a mixed marriage between a Jewess, Eunice, and a heathen, and was, acc. to Acts 16: 3, circumcised by Paul out of respect for the Jews. Among the missions with which the Apostle entrusted him were that to the *Thessalonians to encourage them under persecution (1 Thess. 3: 2) and that to *Corinth to confirm the converts in the faith (1 Cor. 4: 17). His name appears joined with that of Paul in the salutations of seven of the Epistles. 1 Tim. 1: 3 suggests that he became Paul's representative at *Ephesus, and *Eusebius saw him as the first bishop of that city. The 4th-cent. *Acta S. Timothei* narrate his martyrdom on 22 Jan. 97 at the hands of the pagans when he opposed the 'Katagogia', the licentious festivities of Diana. His supposed relics were translated to *Constantinople in 356. Feast day, 26 (formerly 24) Jan.; in the Greek and Syrian Churches, 22 Jan.

Gk. text of *Acta* ed. H. Usener (Bonn. diss. [1877]). R. A. *Lipsius, *Die apokryphen Apostelgeschichten und Apostellegenden*, 2 (pt. 2; 1884), pp. 372–400, with further notes in Ergänzungsheft (1890), pp. 86 f. W. Michaelis, *Die Gefangenschaft des Paulus in Ephesus und das Itinerar des Timotheus* (Neutestamentliche Forschungen, Reihe 1, Heft 3; 1925). H. *Delehaye, SJ, 'Les Actes de saint Timothée', in *Anatolian Studies Presented to William Hepburn Buckler*, ed. W. M. Calder and J. Keil (Manchester, 1939), pp. 77–84, repr. in *Mélanges d'hagiographie grecque et latine* (Subsidia Hagiographica, 42; 1966), pp. 408–15. F. F. Bruce, *The Pauline Circle* [1985], pp. 29–34. E. Fascher in *PW*, Zweite Reihe, 6 (pt. 2; 1937), cols. 1342–54, s.v. 'Timotheus (20)'; J. Gillman in *Anchor Bible Dictionary* (1992), pp. 558–60, s.v. See also introds. to comm. cited in following entry, and comm. to Acts, etc.

Timothy and Titus, Epistles to. The term 'Pastoral Epistles', under which these three Epistles attributed to St *Paul are generally known, dates from the 18th cent.; it was used of Titus by D. N. Barbot in 1703 and of all three by Paul Anton in lectures delivered at Halle in 1726–7 and published as his *Exegetische Abhandlungen* (1753–5). The First to Timothy professes to have been sent from Macedonia, that to Titus while its author was on a journey to Nicopolis, and the Second to Timothy during another imprisonment in Rome, shortly before the author's death. But since F. D. E. *Schleiermacher disputed the authenticity of 1 Tim. in 1807 and F. C. *Baur in 1835 argued that all three stem from a later period, their Pauline

authorship has been increasingly denied. The few scholars who still argue for it propose a date beyond the narrative of Acts, suggesting that Paul was released from imprisonment in Rome, travelled East as well as to *Spain, developed strong views on an organized ministry, and used a secretary, thus accounting for the differences in style and vocabulary from the earlier Epistles. P. N. Harrison, following E. *Renan and others, argued that 5 (later 3) genuine fragments from Paul had been incorporated, but this idea has found little support, and despite problems about pseudonymity and the universal witness of tradition since St *Irenaeus and *Tertullian, the critical view has prevailed. The absence of these Epistles from *Marcion's canon may support a second-century dating, but hints about heresies combated are vague and it is impossible to identify even the 'antitheses of the so-called gnosis' (1 Tim. 6: 20). These Epistles contain earlier traditions ('the saying is reliable', e.g. 2 Tim. 2: 11) but themselves reflect a period of consolidation in which orthodoxy was more valued than theological exploration, and error in doctrine and morals was to be denounced rather than discussed.

The chief subject of these Epistles is the organization of a Christian ministry able to combat the false doctrine that Timothy (1 Tim. 1 and 4, 2 Tim. 2: 15–4: 8) and Titus (3: 9–11) are told to confront. It seems that these teachings included some element of Jewish speculation, as well as an asceticism incompatible with belief in God's creation; it is often held that they contained elements later prominent in *Gnosticism. 1 Tim. orders the institution of public prayers (2: 1–8), regulates the position of men and women in the community (2: 9–15), describes the qualities necessary for bishops and deacons (3), gives instructions for the enrolment of widows and the rule of elders (5), and concludes with various moral exhortations. In 2 Tim. the author encourages the disciples not only to stand fast against false teachers but also to endure every difficulty and to preach the word 'in season [and] out of season'. The Ep. to Titus deals with the qualities required in elders (1), the duties of various classes in society (2), and motivates Christian life by reference to Baptism (3). The witness of the Pastorals to the development of Church organisation is important but ambiguous. 'Bishops' (ἐπίσκοποι) appear to be synonymous with 'elders' (πρεσβύτεροι) in Tit. 1: 5–7, but the reference to 'the bishop' (in the singular) in 1: 7 may be an indication of a development in the direction of the monarchical bishop found in St *Ignatius (e.g. *Smyrn*. 8. 1–9. 1). 'Deacon' (διάκονος) may still be a non-technical term meaning 'helper, assistant', but to many scholars it already seems to denote a grade in the order of ministry (1 Tim. 3: 8–13). In each case, interest centres on the moral qualifications of the officials and not on their function.

The Epp. were the subject of comm. by St John *Chrysostom (*PG* 62. 501–700), *Ambrosiaster (*PL* 17. 461–503), and J. *Calvin (Geneva, 1563; modern Eng. tr., 1964). Important modern comm. incl. those of B. *Weiss (KEK, NT 11, 5th edn., 1885), J. H. *Bernard (Camb. Bib., Gk. text, 1899), M. *Dibelius (Hb. NT 3, pt. 2, 1913, pp. 133–222; 4th edn. rev. by H. Conzelmann, ibid., 13; 1966; Eng. tr., Hermeneia [1972]), W. Lock (ICC, 1924), C. Spicq, OP (Études bibliques, 1947; 4th edn., 2 vols., 1969), with detailed bibl., C. K. Barrett (Oxford, 1963), J. N. D. Kelly (Black's NT Comm., 1963), G. Holtz (Theologischer Handkommentar zum Neuen Testament, 13; 1965), A. T. Hanson (Cambridge, 1966), J. Roloff (on 1 Tim.,

Evangelisch-katholischer Kommentar zum Neuen Testament, 15; Neukirchen, 1988). F. D. E. Schleiermacher, *Ueber den soge-nannten ersten Brief des Paulos an den Timotheos* (1807); F. C. Baur, *Die sogenannten Pastoralbriefe des Apostels Paulus* (1835). P. N. Harrison, *The Problem of the Pastoral Epistles* (1921), with full bibl., pp. 179–84; id., *Paulines and Pastorals* (1964); W. Michaelis, *Pastoralbriefe und Gefangenschaftsbriefe: Zur Echtheitsfrage der Pas-toralbriefe* (Neutestamentliche Forschungen, Reihe 1, Heft 6; 1930). A. T. Hanson, *Studies in the Pastoral Epistles* (1968). D. C. Verner, *The Household of God: The Social World of the Pastoral Epistles* (Society of Biblical Literature, Dissertation Series, 71; Chico, Calif. [1983]). C. F. D. Moule, 'The Problem of the Pas-toral Epistles: A Reappraisal', *Bulletin of the John Rylands Library*, 47 (1965), pp. 430–52, repr. in his *Essays in New Testament Inter-pretation* (1982), pp. 113–32. C. Spicq, OP, in *Dict. Bibl.*, Suppl. 6 (1966), cols. 1–73, s.v. 'Pastorales (Épîtres)'; J. D. Quinn in *Anchor Bible Dictionary*, 6 (1992), pp. 560–71, s.v.

Timothy (d. 518), Patr. of *Constantinople. He was in charge of the cathedral ornaments of Constantinople till 511 when, on the deposition of Macedonius II, the Emp. Anastasius I made him patriarch. After some initial hesita-tion, he became a strong defender of the *Monophysite doctrine and in 512 provoked a riot through adding to the '*Trisagion' the Monophysite formula 'Who was crucified for us'. At a synod in 515 he formally condemned the Chalcedonian teaching and afterwards worked in conjunc-tion with *Severus of Antioch. The regular use of the *Nicene Creed in the Liturgy at Constantinople is ascribed by *Theodore the Lector to Timothy; it had probably been introduced earlier at Antioch by *Peter the Fuller.

V. Grumel, AA (ed.), *Les Regestes des actes du patriarcat de Con-stantinople*, 1. *Les Actes des patriarches*, fasc. 1 (2nd edn., 1972), pp. 143–8 (nos. 193–205a). Id., in *L.Th.K.* (2nd edn.), 10 (1965), col. 200, s.v.

Timothy (6th or 7th cent.), priest of the 'Great Church' (*sc.* *Sancta Sophia) in Constantinople. He wrote a treatise on the reception of heretics into the Church, dividing them into three categories: those who require Baptism (e.g. *Eunomians and *Pelagians), those who require *Confirmation (Chrismation) only (e.g. *Quartodecimans and *Arians), and those who are required simply to renounce their errors (esp. *Messalians and *Monophysites, on the variety of whom he displays detailed knowledge). He is first cited by the Patr. *Niceph-orus (806–15).

The Gk. text of his work Περὶ τῶν προσερχομένων τῇ ἁγίᾳ ἐκκλησίᾳ ('De Receptione Haereticorum') was first pr. by J. Meursius, *Varii Divini*, 1 (Leiden, 1619), pp. 111–30; also pr., with Lat. tr., by J. B. *Cotelier, *Ecclesiae Graecae Monumenta*, 3 (Paris, 1686), pp. 377–424, repr. in J. P. Migne, *PG* 86 (1). 11–74. *CPG* 3 (1979), p. 326 (no. 7016). D. Stiernon, AA, in *DPAC* 2 (1984), cols. 3455 f., s.v. 'Timoteo di Constantinopoli'; Eng. tr. in *Encyclopedia of the Early Church*, 2 (1992), p. 841.

Timothy Aelurus (d. 477), Patr. of *Alexandria. His name 'Aelurus' (Gk. αἴλουρος, 'cat') was given him by his opponents because of his small stature. He became patri-arch in 457 after his predecessor Proterius had been lynched by the mob, but, being unacceptable to the major-ity of bishops on account of his *Monophysite views, he was banished by the Emp. Leo I in 460 and replaced by

Timothy Salophaciolus. During his exile he wrote much to propagate Monophysitism, but also anathematized *Eutyches because, unlike Eutyches, he held that the human nature of Christ was of the same substance as other human beings. He was recalled to Alexandria by the Emp. Basiliscus in 475, where he died before another decree of banishment by the Emp. *Zeno could be carried out. Of his writings several letters are extant in a Syriac transla-tion. A collection of treatises and letters against the Council of *Chalcedon, also in Syriac, goes under his name, as well as an Armenian version of a similar work. In the *Coptic Church he is venerated as a saint, his feast day being 31 July.

R. Y. Ebied and L. R. Wickham, 'A Collection of Unpublished Syriac Letters of Timothy Aelurus', *JTS* NS 21 (1970), pp. 321–69; idd., 'Timothy Aelurus: Against the Council of Chalcedon', in C. Laga and others (eds.), *After Chalcedon: Studies in Theology and Church History offered to Professor Albert van Roey for his Sev-entieth Birthday* (Orientalia Lovaniensia Analecta, 18; 1985), pp. 115–66, both with text and Eng. tr. Details of other works surviv-ing in versions in *CPG* 3 (1979), pp. 62–5 (nos. 5475–91). J. Lebon, 'La Christologie de Timothée Aelure, archevêque mono-physite d'Alexandrie, d'après les sources syriaques inédites', *RHE* 9 (1908), pp. 677–702; id. in A. Grillmeier, SJ, and H. Bacht, SJ (eds.), *Das Konzil von Chalkedon*, 1 (Würzburg, 1951), pp. 425–580. G. Bardy in Fliche and Martin, 4 (1937), pp. 279–87. W. *Bright in *DCB* 4 (1887), pp. 1031–3, s.v. 'Timotheus (18)'; H. G. Opitz in *PW*, Zweite Reihe, 6 (pt. 2; 1937), cols. 1355–7, s.v. 'Timotheos (24)'.

Tindal, Matthew (1655–1733), one of the leading *Deists. Educated at Lincoln and Exeter colleges, Oxford, he was elected a Fellow of All Souls in 1678. For a short time in *James II's reign he became a RC, but returned to the C of E at Easter 1688. He called himself a 'Christian Deist', and his book, *The Rights of the Christian Church asserted against the Romish and all other Priests who claim an Independent Power over it* (1706), written in defence of a rationalistic and *Erastian position, created a consider-able stir. Author, publisher, and printer were prosecuted, but four editions were printed. Tindal then issued *A Defence of the Rights of the Christian Church* (1709), which was burned, together with H. *Sacheverell's sermon, in 1710 by the common hangman, by order of the House of Commons. It was denounced for several years, as it was thought to undermine the Christian religion. He replied at the end of his life by *Christianity as old as the Creation, or the Gospel a Republication of the Religion of Nature* (1730), which became the 'Bible' of Deism. It sought to show that, common to all rational creatures 'there's a law of nature or reason, absolutely perfect, eternal, and unchangeable; and that the design of the Gospel was not to add to, or take from this law', but to free men from superstition.

E. C[urll], *Memoirs of the Life and Writings of Matthew Tindal ... with a History of the Controversies wherein he was engaged* (1733); *The Religious, Rational, and Moral Conduct of Matthew Tindal ... in a letter to a Friend* by a Member of All Souls College (1735). J. Leland, *A View of the Principal Deistical Writers that have Appeared in England in the Last and Present Century*, 1 (1754), pp. 144–76. L. Stephen, *History of English Thought in the Eight-eenth Century*, 1 (1876), pp. 134–63. G. C. Joyce in *HERE* 4 (1911), pp. 535–7, s.v. 'Deism'. L. Stephen in *DNB* 56 (1898), pp. 403–5.

Tindal, William. See TYNDALE, WILLIAM.

Tintern Abbey, on the River Wye. It was founded by
Walter de Clare in 1131 for French *Cistercian monks
from the Abbey of L'Aumône. The magnificent abbey
church was built in the late 13th cent., but the subsequent
history of the monastery was uneventful, and when it was
dissolved in 1536 there were only 13 monks left. The ruins
of Tintern Abbey, in scenery which inspired W. *Wordsworth to one of his finest poems, are among the most beautiful in England. The roofless church, with its delicately
traced windows, shows the transitional Gothic style to perfection. The rest of the abbey has, for the most part, disappeared.

W. *Dugdale, *Monasticon Anglicanum*, 5 (1825 edn.), pp. 265–
73. [C. Heath,] *Descriptive Accounts of Tintern Abbey: Selected from
the Most Esteemed Writers on that Beautiful Ruin: with . . . a correct
translation of the charters of the Earls of Pembroke and Norfolk,
whose ancestors founded the Monastery in the Year 1131* (1798).
O. E. Craster, *Tintern Abbey, Monmouthshire* (1956). On the
daughter house of the same name in Co. Wexford, see P. H. Hore,
History of the Town and County of Wexford (1901), pp. 3–151.

Tintoretto (1518–94), Venetian Mannerist painter.
Jacopo Robusti was known as Tintoretto on account of his
father's occupation as a dyer. He was born in Venice and
spent his life there. He is known to have been a Master
by 1539, but his first certainly datable work is *The Last
Supper* in S. Marcuola, Venice (1547), a theme which he
often repeated and which is already treated in characteristically dramatic fashion. His reputation was established in
1548 with his even more dramatic *St Mark liberating a
Slave* (Venice, Accademia). His most important religious
work was undertaken for the Scuola di San Rocco, a charitable and religious body in Venice of which he was a leading member. He began work for their church and meeting
hall in 1564, and in 1576, in return for a small annuity, he
embarked on a series of 64 canvases to cover the entire
walls and ceilings of the Lower Hall and the two rooms of
the upper floor of the Hall; they were completed in 1588.
The Lower Hall has a series of scenes from the life of the
BVM and pictures of St *Mary Magdalene and St *Mary
of Egypt, all about 12 ft. high. On the upper floor the
paintings are over 17 ft. high and consist of scenes from
the life and passion of Christ (including an enormous
Crucifixion). All these works, which concentrate on the
dramatic moment, have sharp perspectives and contrasts of
light and shade, as well as strong colour. Like his younger
contemporary *El Greco in Spain, he expresses in the
highest degree the artistic ideals adopted by the RC
Church in the 16th cent.

The primary source is the Life by C. Ridolfi (Venice, 1642),
virtually repr. in id., *Le Maraviglie dell'Arte, overo Le Vite de gl'illustri Pittore Veneti e dello Stato*, 2 (ibid., 1648), pp. 2–64; Eng.
tr. by C. and R. Enggass, *The Life of Tintoretto and his children*
(University Park, Pa., and London [1984]), pp. 11–84. R. Pallucchini and P. Rossi, *Tintoretto: L'Opere sacre e profane* (2 vols.,
Milan [1982]). Other works by H. Tietze (London, 1948), C.
Bernari and P. de Vecchi (Classici dell'Arte, Milan, 1970), and by
F. Valcanover and T. Pignatti (Milan, 1985; Eng. tr., New York,
1985). R. Pallucchini in *Encyclopedia of World Art*, 14 (1967), cols.
112–33, s.v., with extensive bibl.

tippet (Lat. *liripipium*). A broad black scarf worn by Anglican clergy in choir over the surplice. It may be of silk if
its wearer is a graduate, but in other cases is of stuff. It

was evolved, it seems, from the long ends of the hood
which hung down from the shoulders in front, and was
not originally confined to the clergy. There has been much
dispute as to what vesture was denoted by the word in the
16th and 17th cents., some antiquarians holding that it was
then used of a garment identical with the ordinary graduate's hood, except in the matter of shape and material.
Can. 74 of 1604 ordered all the clergy to wear the tippet
as part of their ordinary apparel, and can. 58 allowed non-
graduates to wear it as a substitute for the hood. The word
is not used in the 1969 canons, which order the minister
to wear a scarf at Morning and Evening Prayer, and a
scarf or stole for the Occasional Offices and the Eucharist,
adding that when a scarf is worn, the minister may also
wear the hood of his degree (B 8). The custom of confining
the tippet to dignitaries and chaplains has never had any
authority.

Tischendorf, Constantin (1815–74), NT textual critic.
From 1859 he was professor of theology at Leipzig.
Between 1840 and 1860 he visited many libraries in
Europe and the Near East in search of MSS, the most
famous of his finds being his dramatic discovery of the
*Codex Sinaiticus (q.v.). Besides careful editions of several
important biblical MSS (e.g. of *Codex Ephraemi, 1843–
5; *Codex Amiatinus, 1850; Codex Claromontanus, 1852),
he published between 1841 and 1869 eight editions of the
Greek text of the NT with a full critical apparatus of the
variant readings. The last edition of this work, the '*octava
critica maior*', remains by reason of the abundance of its
data a standard book of reference for the text of the NT.

C. R. Gregory, 'De Tischendorfio', prefixed to the *editio octava
critica maior* of Tischendorf's Gk. NT, 3 (1894), pp. 3–22, with
list of his works. L. Schneller (son-in-law), *Tischendorf-
Erinnerungen: Merkwürdige Geschichte einer verlorenen Handschrift*
(1927; Eng. tr., 1939 [popular]). I. Ševčenko, 'New Documents
on Constantine Tischendorf and the *Codex Sinaiticus*', *Scriptorium*, 18 (1964), pp. 55–80. K. Aland, *Konstantin von Tischen-
dorff (1815–1874): Neutestamentliche Textforschung damals und
heute* (Sb. (Bayr.), 133, Heft 2; 1993). Popular account in J.
Bentley, *Secrets of Mount Sinai: The Story of Codex Sinaiticus*
(1985). G. Bertheau in *PRE* (3rd edn.), 19 (1907), pp. 788–97, s.v.

Tissot, James Joseph Jacques (1836–1902), French
Bible illustrator. He was a painter of fashionable women
in Paris before he fled to England in 1871. Here he became
known by his caricatures for *Vanity Fair* and as a portrait
and genre painter. Later he returned to Paris, where his
art underwent a complete change owing to an experience
of conversion, and henceforth he devoted himself to the
illustration of the Life of Christ, for which purpose he
made comprehensive studies in Palestine. His *Vie de
Notre-Seigneur Jésus-Christ* (1896) is a series of some 350
watercolours, representing the scenes of the Gospel in a
fresh and unconventional style which abandons the traditional types. It was followed by an unfinished sequence of
illustrations to the OT which, however, are inferior in
quality to the earlier work.

An edn. of the OT (Gen.–Job, with some additions) in Fr.,
incorporating Tissot's illustrations, was pub., with preface by
A. D. Sertillanges, 2 vols., Paris, 1904; with text in Eng., 2 vols.,
London, 1904. J. Laver, '*Vulgar Society': The Romantic Career
of James Tissot, 1836–1902* (1936); M. Wentworth, *James Tissot*

(Oxford, 1984); K. Matyjaszkiewicz (ed.), *James Tissot* (1984); C. Wood, *The Life and Work of Jacques Joseph Tissot* (1986).

tithes. The tenth part of all fruits and profits due to God and thus to the Church for the maintenance of its ministry. The payment of tithes has been held to be enjoined not merely by ecclesiastical law but by *natural and divine law—by natural law because it is essential to the maintenance of religion, which is enjoined by natural law; by divine law because the payment of tithes is specifically ordered in the OT (Lev. 27: 30–2, Deut. 14: 22–4). It is, however, only implied in the NT (Mt. 5: 17–19, 23: 23) which places much greater emphasis on voluntary giving (e.g. 2 Cor. 9: 6–7).

The early Church depended on offerings. In the 4th cent. payment of the tenth part of all the produce of lands began to be taught as a Christian duty and in the following cents. this gradually became established. In England the payment of tithes was strongly enjoined by the legatine synod of 786 and legally enforced by King *Athelstan's Ordinance *c*.930. Once received, tithes were subject to canonical division into four parts between the bishop, the clergy, the fabric of the church, and the relief of the poor. However, this was not universally observed and the poor and the bishop were sometimes denied their share. In England a tripartite division excluding the bishop survived until the 11th cent. but eventually tithes were left at the entire disposal of the clergy who received them.

At first, the owner of the land might pay the tithe to what clergy he pleased. Probably they were usually paid to the bishop, who distributed them among his clergy. But, as the parochial system developed, the tithes of each parish were allotted to its own '*parson', often by the action of the lord of the manor, who in this way provided the endowment necessary for securing the right to build a church on his estate. In time, the allocation of tithes became the general law.

Tithes were of three sorts: praedial, mixed, and personal. Praedial tithes came immediately from the ground, such as grain, timber, and fruit. Mixed tithes came from things nourished by the ground, such as calves, lambs, chickens, milk, cheese, and eggs. Personal tithes arose from the net profits of labour and industry. Wild animals were not subject to tithe, nor was barren, uncultivated land. Tithes were further divided into great tithes (chiefly corn, hay, and wood) and small tithes (all others). The amount actually produced was irrelevant to this distinction. Tithe was payable annually even if the fruits had grown without being collected—as in the case of saffron, gathered only once in three years. The BCP provides for payment of tithes, with other ecclesiastical dues, at the time of communion on *Easter Day.

The incumbent, when entitled to the whole tithes of a parish, was termed a *rector. But tithes could be appropriated to a spiritual person or corporation (and, after the *dissolution of the monasteries, to lay people as well) who were then normally compelled to provide and endow a clergyman to reside in the parish and perform the ecclesiastical duties, under the name of *vicar. The vicar's endowment usually took the form of a portion of the *glebe, together with the small tithes, because they were troublesome to collect, while the rector (or appropriator) retained the great tithes for himself. Strictly,

*impropriation was the term correctly applied to lay people, and *appropriation to bishops, colleges, religious houses, and the like.

Originally all land in England was theoretically subject to tithe, but there were a number of exceptions, including land held or derived from certain privileged orders (e.g. the *Cistercians, *Templars, and *Hospitallers), Church or glebe land occupied by the incumbent himself, and forest land occupied or leased by the Crown. The right to tithe could also lapse after non-payment over many years. However, the most important means of freeing land from tithe were: (1) the composition real, whereby until 1571 real property was given in exchange for the exemption of other property, and (2) the *modus decimandi*, or *modus*, whereby tithe was commuted to some other, more convenient, annual payment. Tithes were also commuted by statute to 'corn rents' or rent-charges on land, particularly when common or waste land was enclosed; the value of these charges fluctuated with the price of corn.

The desire to obtain exemption from tithe was prompted as much by the inconvenience of a levy in kind as by a wish to fix or limit its value. By the 19th cent. the anomalous nature of tithes was widely felt, and the Tithe Act 1836 established a procedure for the commutation of all tithes into tithe rent-charges on land. This was further refined until by the Tithe Act 1936 all tithe rent-charges were extinguished and replaced by an annuity payable for 60 years by the landowner to the Crown, while the Crown compensated the owner of the rent-charge in turn with an appropriate amount of 3 per cent redemption stock charged on the Consolidated Fund. The Finance Act 1977 finally ended payment of the annuity by the landowner, and in 1988 all the remaining stock created under the 1936 Act was redeemed from the beneficiaries by the Treasury. Tithes have therefore ceased to exist in England altogether.

In Scotland, tithes were collected under the name of *teinds until their abolition in 1925. In Ireland, tithes were abolished in 1871. They have never been part of the law of the United States of America, although similar payments were sometimes made.

See also STEWARDSHIP.

Early Christian refs. to tithes are conveniently collected by J. Sharpe in *DCA* 2 (1893), pp. 1963–6, s.v. The classic study is J. *Selden, *The History of Tithes* (1618). H. W. Clarke, *A History of Tithes* (1891). G. Constable *Monastic Tithes from their Origins to the Twelfth Century* (Cambridge, 1964). E. Le Roy Ladurie, *Tithe and Agrarian History from the Fourteenth to the Nineteenth Centuries*, tr. by S. Burke (ibid. and Paris, 1982). English law of tithe is described in *Halsbury's Laws of England* (4th edn.), 14 (1975), pp. 661–72 (paras. 1209–23) and legislation (1548–1977) is pr. in *Halsbury's Statutes of England and Wales* (4th edn.), 14 (1986), pp. 1166–1285.

Titian (d. 1576), **Tiziano Vecellio** or **Vecelli**, Venetian painter. Acc. to tradition, he was 99 years old when he died, but modern scholars think it more likely that he was born *c*.1487/90 than in 1476/7. Titian was a pupil of Gentile and Giovanni Bellini and in his early years much influenced by Giorgione, though he cultivated a more monumental style. To this period belongs the *Tribute Money* (*c*.1515; Dresden), which is famous for the face of Christ with its impressive blending of sweetness and majesty. After Bellini's death (1516) Titian became the acknowledged head of the Venetian school and was connected with many European monarchs, e.g. *Charles V and Francis I. His most famous painting of this time is the huge *Assumption* (completed in 1518) for the High Altar of Santa Maria dei Frari in Venice, where it remains; though of high craftsmanship, it is without deeper religious feeling. On the other hand, his stirring *St Peter Martyr* (1528–30; destroyed in 1867, but known from copies), *Crowning with Thorns* (c.1542; Louvre), and *Ecce Homo* (1543; Vienna) are all fraught with tragic emotion. In his later years his compositions are remarkable for an increasing emphasis on dramatic effects. His *St Sebastian* (c.1570/75; St Petersburg), the *Entombment* (1525; Louvre; another, 1559, at the Prado) and the *Annunciation* (c.1564; S. Salvatore, Venice) are all vivid scenes of much beauty in colouring and form, though lacking the interior spirit characteristic of medieval religious painting.

H. Tietze, *Tizian: Leben und Werk* (2 vols., Vienna, 1936, vol. 2 being plates with reprods., some in colour; this latter vol. also pub., with introd. in Eng., London, 1937; 2nd edn. (abbreviated), 1950). F. Valcanover, *Tutta la pittura di Tiziano* (2 vols., Milan, 1960; Eng. tr., 4 vols., 1965). R. Pallucchini, *Tiziano* (2 vols., Florence [1969]). H. E. Wethey, *The Paintings of Titian* (3 vols., 1969–75). E. Panofsky, *Problems in Titian, mostly iconographic* (Wrightsman Lectures, 1969).

title (Lat. *titulus*). At least since the 3rd cent., this term has been used to designate the older churches of *Rome. As several clergy were attached to each *titulus*, all of whom were provided with revenues for their personal maintenance, allocation to a 'title' at ordination came to mean the provision of maintenance, which otherwise was the personal responsibility of the Pope or ordaining bishop. From this, the term has acquired the general sense of a definite spiritual charge or office with guarantee of maintenance, without appointment to which a bishop may not ordinarily ordain a man (or woman), unless he is prepared to support that person until he can prefer him (or her) to a 'living'. The C of E rules are contained in can. C 5 of the 1969 Canons. In the RC Church there were detailed provisions concerning title, but they do not appear in the 1983 *Codex Iuris Canonici*. See also BENEFICE.

J. P. Kirsch, *Die römischen Titelkirchen im Altertum* (Studien zur Geschichte und Kultur des Altertums, 9, Hefte 1 and 2; 1918); L. *Duchesne, 'Les Titres presbytéraux et les diaconies', *Mélanges d'Archéologie et d'Histoire*, 7 (1887), pp. 217–43.

Titus, St. A Gentile disciple of St *Paul, who first appears on the journey to the Apostles' Council at *Jerusalem (Gal. 2: 1) and was later sent on difficult missions to *Corinth (2 Cor. 8: 6, 16 f., and 23). Acc. to the Pauline traditions of the *Pastoral Epistles he was left behind in Crete to organize the Church there (Tit. 1: 5), summoned to meet Paul at Nicopolis in Epirus (Tit. 3: 12) and afterwards sent by him to Dalmatia (2 Tim. 4: 10). He is assumed to have returned to Crete, of which, acc. to *Eusebius, he was the first bishop. His body was reputed to rest at Gortyna, the ancient capital of the island. After the invasion of the Saracens in 823, the head was brought to *Venice, where it has since been venerated in St Mark's. Feast day in the Greek and Syrian Churches, 25 Aug.; in the Latin Church, 4 Jan. In the RC Church the

feast was transferred to 6 Feb. by *Pius IX to avoid coincidence with the Octave of the Holy Innocents, but has now been joined with that of St Timothy on 26 Jan.

The main lit. is to be found in comm. to the Epistle addressed to Titus, cited s.v. TIMOTHY AND TITUS, EPISTLES TO. C. K. Barrett, 'Titus', in E. E. Ellis and M. Wilcox (eds.), *Neotestamentica et Semitica: Studies in honour of Matthew Black* (1969), pp. 1–14. F. F. Bruce, *The Pauline Circle* [1985], pp. 58–65. On the apocryphal letter of Titus to Paul, R. A. *Lipsius, *Die apokryphen Apostelgeschichten und Apostellegenden*, 2 (pt. 2; 1884), pp. 401–6; A. von *Harnack, 'Der apokryphe Brief des Paulusschülers Titus "De Dispositione Sanctimonii" ', in *Sb.* (Berl.), 1925, pp. 180–213; A. de Santos Otero in Schneemelcher (5th edn., 1989), 2, pp. 50–70; Eng. tr., 2 (1992), pp. 53–74. E. Fascher in *PW*, 2. Reihe, 6 (pt. 2; 1937), cols. 1579–86, s.v. 'Titus (4)'; J. Walker in *Anchor Bible Dictionary*, 6 (1992), pp. 581 f.

Titus, Epistle to. See TIMOTHY AND TITUS, EPISTLES TO.

Titus (4th cent.), Bp. of Bostra. Little is known of his life except that he was involved in a controversy with the Emp. *Julian, who ordered his expulsion, and that he took part in a synod at *Antioch, in 363, which sent a letter to the Emp. *Jovian recognizing the Nicene Creed. His name has survived through his authorship of a voluminous treatise against the *Manichaeans. In its first part he gives the Christian solution of the problem of evil based on the ideas of Divine Providence and human free will; in the second he defends the OT and denounces the Manichaean falsifications of the NT. The first half of the treatise is preserved in the Greek original, but the whole now exists only in a Syriac version. Both were edited in 1859 by P. A. de *Lagarde, who recognized in the Greek text an interpolation which has been identified as a work of *Serapion of Thmuis. Titus is also the author of a work on St Luke in the form of homilies, fragments of which have survived in later *catenae*.

Gk. text first pub. by J. *Basnage, *Thesaurus Monumentorum Ecclesiasticorum et Historicorum*, 1 (Antwerp, 1725), pp. 56–162; repr. from A. *Gallandi in J. P. Migne, *PG* 18. 1065–204; crit. edn. by P. A. de Lagarde (Berlin, 1859). Syriac text ed. id. (ibid., 1859). P. Nagel, 'Neues griechisches Material zu Titus von Bostra (Adversus Manichaeos III 7–29)', in J. Irmscher and P. Nagel (eds.), *Studia Byzantina*, 2: *Beiträge aus der byzantinistischen Forschung der Deutschen Demokratischen Republik zum XIV. Internationalen Byzantinistenkongress Bukarest 1971* (Berliner Byzantinische Arbeiten, 44; Berlin, 1973), pp. 285–350. J. Sickenberger, *Titus von Bostra: Studien zu dessen Lukashomilien* (TU 21, Heft 1; 1901). R. P. Casey, 'The Text of the Anti-Manichaean Writings of Titus of Bostra and Serapion of Thmuis', *HTR* 21 (1928), pp. 97–111. A. *Baumstark, 'Der Text der Mani-Zitate in der syrischen Übersetzung des Titus von Bostra', *Oriens Christianus*, 28 (1931), pp. 23–42. *CPG* 2 (1974), pp. 286–8 (nos. 3575–81). R. P. Casey in *PW*, 2. Reihe, 6 (pt. 2; 1937), cols. 1586–91, s.v. 'Titus (5) v. Bostra'; A. Solignac, SJ, in *Dict. Sp.* 15 (1991), cols. 999–1006, s.v. 'Titus (1) de Bostra'.

Tobit, Book of. One of the apocryphal books of the OT. It relates the story of Tobit, a pious Jew taken captive to Nineveh after the fall of *Samaria to the Assyrians. In pursuit of his good works, Tobit became poor and blind in his old age. He prayed to God to deliver him, and, remembering a debt due to him from a friend in Media, sent his son Tobias there with a companion who later revealed himself as the angel *Raphael. With the assistance of the angel, Tobias rescued his kinswoman, Sarah, from the power of a demon, and married her. Raphael recovered the debt and then enabled Tobias to heal the aged Tobit of his blindness.

The chief purpose of the story is to inculcate that God is faithful to such Jews as are faithful to Him and to recommend virtue, esp. almsgiving and the burial of the dead. The book exists in Greek, Latin, Syriac, Aramaic, and Hebrew versions. Its original language was Aramaic or Hebrew, and its date probably c.200 BC. There is a copy among the *Dead Sea Scrolls. Until modern times it was generally regarded as historical, but many now consider it a piece of folklore and find in it traces of Persian demonology. It also draws on traditions about *Ahikar (who appears in the book as Tobit's nephew), a familiar hero of many ancient Near Eastern tales. Owing to its intrinsic charm Tobit has been one of the most popular books of the Bible. It was frequently quoted by the Fathers from the time of St *Polycarp (*Phil.* 10), and was a favourite subject of Christian art, its principal scenes being represented in the Catacombs.

The Gk. text is pr. in edns. of the Septuagint (q.v.); for edns. of the Lat. text see bibl. to OLD LATIN VERSIONS, also A. Neubauer, cited below; Heb. text ed. S. *Münster (Basle, 1542); Heb. and Syriac text also in B. *Walton's London Polyglot of 1657; Aramaic text ed. A. Neubauer (Oxford, 1878). R. Hanhart, *Text und Textgeschichte des Buches Tobit* (*Abh.* (Gött.), Dritte Folge, 139; 1984). Modern comm. incl. those of D. C. Simpson in R. H. *Charles (ed.), *The Apocrypha and Pseudepigrapha of the Old Testament*, 1 (Oxford, 1913), pp. 174–241, F. Zimmermann (Jewish Apocryphal Literature; New York, 1958), and J. C. Dancy, *The Shorter Books of the Apocrypha* (Camb. Bib., NEB, 1972), pp. 1–66. D. C. Simpson, 'The Chief Recensions of the Book of Tobit', *JTS* 14 (1913), pp. 516–30. J. Gamberoni, *Die Auslegung des Buches Tobias in der griechisch-lateinischen Kirche der Antike und der Christenheit des Westens bis 1600* (Studien zum Alten und Neuen Testament, 21; 1969). M. Rabenau, *Studien zum Buch Tobit* (Beihefte zur ZATW, 220; 1994). R. H. Pfeiffer, *History of New Testament Times with an Introduction to the Apocrypha* (New York [1949]; London [1954]), pp. 258–84, with bibl. p. 534. G. W. E. Nickelsburg, *Jewish Literature Between the Bible and the Mishnah* (Philadelphia [1981]), pp. 30–35. E. *Schürer, *The History of the Jewish People in the Age of Jesus Christ*, rev. Eng. tr. by G. Vermes and others, 3 (pt. 1; Edinburgh, 1986), pp. 222–32. C. A. Moore in *Anchor Bible Dictionary*, 6 (1992), pp. 585–94, s.v., with bibl.

Toc H. A Christian fellowship embracing men of all ages over 16, of all classes, denominations, and political opinions. Its Women's Association covers the same ground among women. It originated in Talbot House, a soldiers' club opened in 1915 at Poperinghe in Belgium under the Revd P. T. B. Clayton, MC, a C of E chaplain, and named after Lt. Gilbert Talbot, son of E. S. *Talbot (q.v.). In 1920 Toc H (the army signallers' method of pronouncing T H) was refounded in London and spread rapidly through Britain and English-speaking countries. It was incorporated by Royal Charter, 14 Dec. 1922. It is organized in branches and has a number of residential houses ('Marks'). The close fellowship finds its natural outlet in a great variety of Christian social service.

P. T. B. Clayton, *Tales of Talbot House: Everyman's Club in Poperinghe and Ypres, 1915–1918* (1919); P. W. Monie, *Toc H under Weigh* [1927]; J. Rice and K. Prideaux-Brune, *Out of a Hop Loft: Seventy-five years of Toc H* (1990). M. Harcourt, *Tubby Clayton: A Personal Saga* (1953).

tokens, Communion. See COMMUNION TOKENS.

Toland, John (1670–1722), *Deistical writer. He was a RC Irishman who became a Protestant at the age of 16. In 1687 he entered Glasgow University, and after spending some time in English Protestant families, probably as tutor, was sent to *Leiden, where he studied Divinity under F. Spanheim. In 1694 he went to Oxford, where in 1695 he finished his *Christianity not Mysterious* (pub. 1696). In it he asserted that neither God Himself nor His revelation is above the comprehension of human reason, and attributed the mysteries of Christianity to the intrusion of pagan conceptions and the machinations of priestcraft. The work roused great indignation and was condemned and caused to be burned by the Irish Parliament in 1697, and Toland fled from Ireland, whither he had returned, to England to avoid imprisonment. In 1698 he published a *Life of Milton*. A passage of this book, which was believed to cast doubt on the authenticity of the NT, caused great scandal, and Toland replied in his *Amyntor, or a Defence of Milton's Life* (1699), stating that the passage in question referred to the apocryphal writings, of which he gave a remarkable list. In 1701 he defended the Act of Succession in his book *Anglia Libera*, which won him the favour of the Electress Sophia, and during the next years he several times visited the courts at Hanover and Berlin. He was admitted to the intimate circle of the Prussian Queen Sophie Charlotte, to whom he addressed several letters (*Letters to Serena*, 1704), one of which became famous through its attempt to prove that motion is essential to matter. From 1707 to 1710 he travelled on the Continent and, after returning to England, wrote many polemical pamphlets, directed esp. against *High Churchmen and Jacobites. In 1718 appeared his *Nazarenus*, a treatise on the *Ebionites, and in 1720 *Tetradymus*, a collection of essays dealing, among other things, with the natural explanation of Scripture miracles. In the same year he published his *Pantheisticon*, a kind of pagan liturgy in imitation of Christian services, in which he expounded a *pantheistic creed, the term 'pantheist' having apparently first been used by him in 1705. Though not an original thinker, Toland was one of the most influential representatives of Deism, and his books largely contributed to later discussions on the relations between reason and revelation and the genuineness of the NT Books.

A Collection of Several Pieces of Mr. John Toland, now first published from his Original Manuscripts (2 vols., 1726), with Memoir of his Life and Writings [by P. Desmaizeaux], vol. 1, pp. iii–xcii. *An Historical Account of the Life and Writings of the late Eminently Famous Mr. John Toland by one of his most intimate friends* (1722). C. Giuntini, *Panteismo e ideologia repubblicana: John Toland (1670–1722)* (Bologna [1979]); R. E. Sullivan, *John Toland and the Deist Controversy: A Study in Adaptations* (1982); S. H. Daniel, *John Toland: His Methods, Manners and Mind* (Kingston, Ont. [1984]). G. R. Cragg, *From Puritanism to the Age of Reason: A Study of Changes in Religious Thought within the Church of England 1660 to 1700* (Cambridge, 1950), pp. 136–55; P. Harrison, 'Religion' and the religions in the English Enlightenment (Cambridge, 1990), esp. pp. 86–91, 156 f., and 164–7. G. Carabelli, *Tolandiana: Materiali bibliografici per lo studio dell'opera e della fortuna di John Toland (1670–1722)* (2 vols., Florence, 1975–8). L. Stephen in *DNB* 56 (1898), pp. 438–42.

Toledo, Councils of. Some 30 ecclesiastical Councils

took place at Toledo (*Concilia Toletana*) between the 5th and 16th cents., the canons of the earlier of which are preserved in the *Hispana Collection. They include the 'First' (400), directed against *Priscillianism; the 'Third' (589), when King *Recared formally renounced the *Arian Creed; the 'Fourth' (633), under St *Isidore of Seville, which affirmed the Christian significance of kingship and issued important liturgical regulations; and the 'Twelfth' (681), which established the primacy of the See of Toledo in the Spanish Church. For the liturgy of Toledo, see MOZARABIC RITE.

Crit. edn. of the canons of the earlier Councils (1–17) in J. Vives (ed.), *Concilios visigóticos e hispano-romanos* (España Cristiana: Textos, 1; 1963), pp. 19–33, 42–52, 107–45, 186–324, 344–69, 380–474, 482–537. An earlier edn. is repr. in J. P. Migne, *PL* 84. 327–562. Eng. tr. of some of the canons, with introd., in E. H. Landon, *A Manual of the Councils of the Holy Church* (2nd edn. by P. Landon), 2 [1893], pp. 151–69. On the first, third, fourth, and twelfth councils, Hefele and Leclercq, 2 (pt. 1; 1908), pp. 122–5; 3 (pt. 1; 1909), pp. 222–8, 279–81, and 540–6. J. Orlandis and D. Ramos-Lissón, *Die Synoden auf der Iberischen Halbinsel bis zum Einbruch des Islam* (1981), pp. 39–51, 61–5, 95–117, 144–223, 233–40, 248–93, and 299–323. J. A. de Aldama, SJ, *El Símbolo Toledano I* (Analecta Gregoriana, 7; 1943); J. Madoz, SJ, 'Le Symbole du IVᵉ concile de Tolède', *RHE* 34 (1938), pp. 5–20. A. Michel in *DTC* 15 (pt. 1; 1946), cols. 1176–208, s.v. 'Tolède (Conciles de)'; I. Escribano Alberca in *NCE* 14 (1967), pp. 189–91, s.v. See also works cited under SPAIN, CHRISTIANITY IN.

Toledo, rite of. An alternative name for the *Mozarabic rite (q.v.).

tolerati (Lat., 'tolerated persons'). The technical term formerly used in *canon law for those *excommunicated persons with whom the faithful were permitted to have some measure of intercourse. They were thus distinguished from the *vitandi* (q.v.). These categories are no longer used in RC canon law.

Toleration Act. The Toleration Act 1688, passed in 1689, granting freedom of worship to Dissenters on certain prescribed conditions. Its real purpose was to unite all Protestants under William III against the deposed RC *James II. It exempted from the penalties of existing statutes against conventicles persons who took the Oaths of Allegiance and Supremacy (though Dissenters continued to be barred from civil office until 1828; see CORPORATION ACT and TEST ACT) and relieved dissenting ministers from religious disabilities provided that, in addition to the oaths, they signed the *Thirty-Nine Articles (except two requiring Infant Baptism). *Quakers might make an *affirmation instead of taking the oaths. RCs and disbelievers in the Trinity did not benefit under this Act.

Text in Gee and Hardy, pp. 654–64 (no. 123).

Toleration, Edict of (313). See MILAN, EDICT OF.

toleration, religious. Christianity, which claims to be the only true religion, is in principle dogmatically intolerant of other religions, and *heresy within its own ranks has been repeatedly anathematized. In practice, however, Christian Churches and Christian rulers have often suffered or 'tolerated' a non-Christian presence and Christian diversity and dissent, their power being insufficient to coerce infidels or dissenters into conformity. Sometimes they have made a virtue of necessity and claimed to be tolerating an evil because not to do so would provoke a greater evil. Sometimes they have argued that faith should not or could not be compelled and that charitable admonition is more appropriate than force in converting infidels or in persuading heretics back within the fold. To call all these diverse actions 'toleration' and to give them a continuous history would be entirely false.

Christians in the pagan world of late antiquity did not invariably experience intolerance at the hands of non-Christians (see PERSECUTIONS, EARLY CHRISTIAN), but they almost always practised it among themselves. This tendency was accelerated after the rise of the Emp. *Constantine by the increasingly close connection between ecclesiastical authority and the civil power. Persistence in superstition or in unorthodoxy became an offence in canon and civil law.

Throughout the Middle Ages mainstream ecclesiastical opinion followed St *Augustine's demand for the punishment of heretics and schismatics, but, as the preaching of St *Bernard illustrates, it never entirely silenced the voice of eirenic reconciliation, whose tradition was of equal antiquity. It was this tradition that furnished *Erasmus with many of the arguments that were to be debated and taken further in the bitter disputes of the 16th cent. about the location and limits of authority in matters of faith.

Although leading Protestant Reformers (M. *Luther, J. *Calvin, T. *Beza, and H. *Bullinger) seem at first sight to be arguing for a novel and subjectivist individual liberty of conscience, they prove on further scrutiny to be resolute defenders of the right and duty of the ecclesiastical and civil powers to co-operate in the extirpation of heresy within the area of their joint jurisdiction. Like Augustine, they regarded persistence in error as an affront to God. They demanded freedom to worship in their own way, but where they enjoyed this freedom, they pursued dissenters with relentless zeal, regarding with abhorrence the mystical conception of Christianity put forward by S. *Castellio, who argued that the way to God lay not through dogma but through the annihilation of self-will. He argued that there is much in Scripture that is enigmatic and obscure; instead of struggling with thorny points we should listen to the voice of reason, which every man experiences as 'an interior and eternal word of truth always speaking'. For Castellio, the disintegration of the earthly Church could be contemplated with equanimity, for its disappearance would leave revealed the inward fellowship of the faithful, recognizable by the fruits of the spirit and of love. For minister and magistrate no persecuting duty would be left.

These arguments had some appeal in *Remonstrant circles in the Netherlands (D. *Coornhert and J. *Arminius). In 17th-cent. England *Baptists, *Congregationalists, and *Quakers insisted on their religious independence of Church and State. Experiments in practical toleration took place in N. America, in Maryland and Rhode Island, whose founders Lord Baltimore (a RC) and Roger *Williams (a *Baptist) saw no responsibility for religious coercion resting on the civil power. Castellio's assertion that belief in a merciful God entailed acceptance of the liberty of the individual Christian was developed further by J. *Milton, while J. *Locke in his *Letters on Toleration* (1689–92) explored the implication of a restricted definition of the rights and duties of the civil power, arguing that the Church was a voluntary association having the right only to expel dissenters and no right to hound them thereafter, and that civil society had the duty to concern itself only with life, liberty, property, and the pursuit of happiness.

Intellectuals of the *Enlightenment, including *Voltaire and J.-J. *Rousseau, transformed the debate by using the arguments in favour of toleration in attacks not only on ecclesiastical authority, but on the very notion of the Christian religion. They thus struck, as J.-B. *Bossuet had predicted, at the heart of Christianity itself. During the 19th cent. the division deepened. On the one hand stood the heterogeneous defenders of religious liberty, including liberals and free-thinkers, who advocated religious toleration by the State, in many countries securing its embodiment in law. On the other stood the resolutely dogmatic and defensive RC Church, whose authoritarianism was exemplified in the *Syllabus Errorum* of 1864 and the condemnation of *Modernism in 1907.

Between 1900 and 1965 there was profound debate within the RC Church between those who emphasized the responsibility of the Church in defending revealed truth and those who laid stress on the God-given duty of the human individual to govern his behaviour by an interior light. This discussion came to a head at the Second *Vatican Council. The 'Declaration on Religious Freedom' (*Dignitatis Humanae*) of 7 Dec. 1965 states that 'all men ought to be immune from compulsion . . . so that in the sphere of religion no one is compelled to act against his *conscience and no one is prevented from acting in accordance with his conscience in private or public'. The right to religious freedom is said to be founded upon the dignity of the human person as it is made known both by the revealed will of God and by reason. It should become a civil right. *Dignitatis Humanae* thus transformed the RC concept of toleration into something more closely aligned with the view that had long prevailed elsewhere in the Christian world.

See also CONSCIENCE and THEOLOGY OF RELIGIONS.

Collection of extracts, in Fr. tr., from writers defending religious toleration from the Reformation onwards, with introd., ed. J. Leclerc, SJ, and M. F. Valkhoff, *Les Premiers Défenseurs de la liberté religieuse* (2 vols. [1969]). Further collection of primary material ed. H. R. Guggisberg, *Religiöse Toleranz: Dokumente zur Geschichte einer Forderung* (Neuzeit im Aufbau, 4; Stuttgart, 1984). J. Locke, *A Letter Concerning Toleration*. Latin and English texts ed., with introd. by M. Montuori (The Hague, 1963); other edns. listed in bibl. to Locke. R. H. Bainton, 'Sebastian Castellio, Champion of Religious Liberty', in id. and others, *Castellioniana: Quatre études sur Sebastien Castellion et l'idée de la tolerance* (Leiden, 1951), pp. 25–79. Id., *The Travail of Religious Liberty* (Philadelphia [1951]; London, 1953). J. Leclerc, SJ, *Histoire de la tolérance au siècle de la réforme* (Théologie, 31; 2 vols., 1955; Eng. tr., 1960). A. Momigliano, 'Empietà ed eresia nel mondo antico', *Rivista Storica Italiana*, 83 (1971), pp. 771–91. M. Firpo, *Il Problema della Tolleranza Religiosa nell'età moderna della riforma protestante a Locke* (Documenti della Storia, 13; Turin [1978]). W. J. Sheils (ed.), *Persecution and Toleration* (Studies in Church History, 21; 1984). M. Turchetti, *Concordia o Tolleranza? François Bauduin (1520–1573) e i 'Moyenneurs'* (Milan and Geneva, 1984). V. Roeser, *Politik und religiöse Toleranz vor dem ersten Hugenottenkrieg in Frankreich* (Basler Beiträge zur Geschichtswissenschaft, 153; 1985). S. Mendus (ed.), *Justifying Toleration: Conceptual and Historical Perspectives* (Cambridge, 1988).

Tolstoy, Leo (1828–1910), Russian novelist and social reformer. From 1844 to 1847 he studied at the University of Kazan, but did not take a degree. Under the influence of J.-J. *Rousseau's writings he became an enthusiast for social reform, anxious to relieve the miseries of the serfs. In 1851 he joined the Russian army. His *Tales from Sebastopol* (1855) at once attracted literary notice. In this period he also began the serial publication of his autobiographical fragments (1852–6), describing the mental struggles of his youth. He left the army in 1855 and in 1857 and 1860/1 he travelled in Germany, France, Italy, Switzerland, and England, studying educational methods and writing in support of reforms; he also established a school on his estate at Yasnaya Polyana and others in the neighbourhood, all run on enlightened principles. In 1862 he married Sophia Behrs, by whom he had 13 children. In the next years there followed his two most famous novels, *War and Peace* (1864–9) and *Anna Karenina* (1873–7). After 1877 he renounced his literary ambitions, believing them to be incompatible with his deepest convictions. All his later works were on moral and religious subjects and his output was considerable. He was deeply influenced by a close study of A. *Schopenhauer's writings and became very critical of the formalism of the Orthodox Church, which eventually excommunicated him in 1901. He sought to live in great simplicity, renouncing his property and the happiness of family life, engaging in manual labour and striving ceaselessly for the relief of social distress during the great famine of 1891–2. In 1895 he actively took up the cause of the persecuted *Doukhobors, writing in their defence his last great novel, *Resurrection* (1899).

Tolstoy's religious teaching in its latest phase claimed to be a following of the Gospels when the miraculous and other irrelevancies are set aside. The key was to be found in the *Sermon on the Mount, which could be resolved into five wholly new commandments: (1) the suppression of anger, even righteous indignation, and living in peace with all men; (2) the complete exclusion of sexual relationships outside marriage; (3) the wrongfulness of oaths; (4) non-resistance to evil and the consequent refusal to act as judges or police officers; (5) unreserved love of one's enemies. These, and not the doctrines of the Atonement, the Resurrection, the Trinity, and personal immortality, were the central tenets of the Christian message. He did not accept the divinity of Christ and he believed that man's greatest good consisted in the fulfilment of God's will that men should love one another. The increase of love in individuals would do away with the evils of the existing order and lead to the establishment of the *kingdom of God in the world.

Eng. tr. of his works ed. L. Wiener (24 vols., London and Boston, 1904–5; incl. Life by the translator in vol. 24, pp. 205–317, and bibl. to date of works in Eng., Ger., and Fr., pp. 403–35; but incl. some works not by Tolstoy); better Eng. tr., mainly by A. and L. Maude (Tolstoy Centenary Edition, ed. A. Maude, 21 vols., London, 1928–37). Life by A. Maude, 2 vols., London, 1908–10; abridged edn., ibid., 1918; full Life also repr. in Centenary edn., vols. 1–2. Many of his works have since been repr. separately. C. A. Behrs's *Recollections of Count Tolstoy* tr. into Eng. by C. E. Turner (London, 1893); the *Reminiscences of Tolstoy* by his son, Count I. Tolstoy, tr. into Eng. by G. Calderon (ibid., 1914);

a number of arts. on Tolstoy by members of his family collected by R. Fülöp-Miller tr. into Eng. under the title *Family Views of Tolstoy*, ed. A. Maude (1926); *Tolstoy Remembered* by his son S. Tolstoy, orig. pub. in Moscow, 1949, tr. into Eng., 1961. A Life, written with Tolstoy's co-operation, by P. Birukoff was pub. 4 vols., Moscow, 1906–23; Eng. tr. of vol. 1, 1906; an abridged version tr. into Eng., 1911. There is a wide range of studies on Tolstoy; those available in Eng., incl. the works of R. Rolland (Paris, 1911; Eng. tr., 1911), D. Leon (London, 1944, also with bibl.), E. J. Simmons (Boston, 1946; London, 1949), H. Troyat (orig. 'L. Tarassov'; Paris, 1965; Eng. tr., New York, 1967; London, 1968; Penguin edn., 1970), R. F. Christian (Cambridge, 1969), and A. N. Wilson (London, 1988). I. Berlin, *The Hedgehog and the Fox: An Essay on Tolstoy's View of History* (1953). G. Steiner, *Tolstoy or Dostoevsky: An Essay in Contrast* (1960). G. W. Spence, *Tolstoy the Ascetic* (1967). E. J. Simmons, *Introduction to Tolstoy's Writings* (1969). R. V. Sampson, *Tolstoy: The Discovery of Peace* (1973), esp. pp. 108–67. D. Matual, *Tolstoy's Translation of the Gospels: A Critical Study* (Lewiston, Queenston, and Lampeter [1992]).

Tomasi, St Giuseppe Maria. See TOMMASI, ST GIUSEPPE MARIA

Tome of Damasus. A collection of 24 canons endorsed by a Roman synod (prob. in 377) and subsequently sent by Pope *Damasus to Paulinus, then recognized at Rome as the legitimate Bp. of Antioch. In some MSS the canons are appended to the Creed of *Nicaea. Twenty-three of them are dogmatic, anathematizing the principal Trinitarian and Christological heresies of the 4th cent. (without, however, naming *Apollinarius or *Marcellus of Ancyra). The ninth is disciplinary, condemning the translation of bishops, and was directed against *Melitius of Antioch.

The text is first found in *Arnobius Junior, *Conflictus de deo trino et uno*, 2. 32 (repr. in *PL* 53. 319–22), and (in Gk.) in *Theodoret, *HE* 5. 11. The Latin and Greek texts are critically edited in *EOMIA* 1. 2 (1), 1913, pp. 281–96. Lat. text also repr. in Denzinger and Hünermann (37th edn., 1991), pp. 85–8 (nos. 152–77). G. L. Dossetti, *Il Simbolo di Nicea e di Costantinopoli* (Testi e Ricerche di Scienze Religiose, 2; 1967), pp. 94–111. C. Pietri, *Roma Christiana: Recherches sur l'Église de Rome . . . (311–440)* (Bibliothèque des Écoles Françaises d'Athènes et de Rome, 224; 1976), pp. 833–44 and 873–80.

Tome of Leo. The letter sent by Pope *Leo I (*Ep.* 28) to *Flavian, Patr. of *Constantinople, on 13 June 449, also called **Epistola Dogmatica**. Basing himself on the teaching of the Fathers, esp. *Tertullian and St *Augustine, St Leo expounds with remarkable clarity, precision, and vigour the Christological doctrine of the Latin Church. Acc. to it Jesus Christ is One Person, the Divine Word, in whom are two natures, the Divine and the human, permanently united, though unconfused and unmixed. Each of these exercises its own particular faculties, but within the unity of the Person. Hence follows the '*communicatio idiomatum', so that it can truly be said that the Son of Man descended from heaven, and that the Son of God was crucified. The letter, which was directed esp. against the heresy of *Eutyches, was given formal authority by the Council of *Chalcedon (451) as the classic statement of the Catholic doctrine of the Incarnation: 'Peter has spoken through Leo'. Later it was constantly used in the controversies with the Monophysites.

Text in P. and H. *Ballerini's edn. of Leo, 1 (1753), cols. 793–838, repr. in J. P. Migne, *PL* 54. 755–82. Crit. edn. in *ACO* 2. 2. 1 (1932), pp. 24–33; also by C. Silva-Tarouca, SJ (Rome, 1932). Eng. tr. in Tanner, *Decrees* (1990), pp. 77*–82*. Gk. text in *ACO* 2. 1. 1 (1933), pp. 10–20; on this cf. G. L. Prestige, 'The Greek Translation of the *Tome* of St Leo', *JTS* 31 (1929–30), pp. 183 f. P. Mouterde, SJ, 'Les Versions syriaques du tome de saint Léon', *Mélanges de l'Université Saint-Joseph, Beyrouth*, 16 (1932), pp. 121–65, with Syr. text, pp. 146–65. H. Arens, *Die christologische Sprache Leos des Grossen: Analyse des Tomus an den Patriarchen Flavian* (Freiburger theologische Studien, 122; 1982).

Tommasi, St Giuseppe Maria (1649–1713), liturgical scholar. The eldest son of the Duke of Palma, he resigned his claims as heir in favour of his younger brother in 1664 and entered the Order of the *Theatines, in which he was professed in 1666. After studying at Messina, Rome, and Palermo, he was ordained priest in 1673 and henceforth devoted himself completely to biblical, patristic, and above all liturgical studies, leading a life of great austerity. Of his numerous publications, many of them under the pseudonym of 'J. M. Carus', his editions of the ancient *Sacramentaries and *Missals are esp. valuable. They include the *Codices Sacramentorum Nongentis Annis Vetustiores* (1680), which comprises Gallican books and contains the *editiones principes* of the '*Missale Gothicum' and the '*Missale Francorum', the *Responsalia et Antiphonaria Romanae Ecclesiae a Sancto Gregorio Magno disposita* (1686), and *Antiqui Libri Missarum Romanae Ecclesiae* (1691), as well as several editions of the Psalter and of biblical texts used in the liturgy of the first ten centuries. A project for a reformed and much simplified *Breviary was probably compiled in 1706. Tommasi was made a cardinal in 1712. He was canonized in 1986; feast day, 3 Jan.

An edn. of his works was begun by J. Bianchini (Rome, 1741; vol. 1 (in parts) only pub.); new ed. by A. F. Vezzosi, Theatine (7 vols., ibid., 1747–54); cont. with *Institutiones Theologicae*, ed. id. (4 vols., ibid., 1769), with Life prefixed to vol. 1. *Opuscoli inediti*, ed. G. *Mercati (ST 15; 1905). The reformed Breviary ed., with Eng. tr. and introd. by J. W. Legg (CHS 80; 1904). Lives by A. Borromeo (Venice, 1713) and D. Bernino (Rome, 1714). I. Scicolone, OSB, *Il Cardinale Giuseppe Tomasi di Lampedusa e gli Inizi della Scienze Liturgica* (Studia Anselmiana, 82; Rome, 1981). F. Andreu, Theatine, in *Dict. Sp.* 8 (1974), cols. 1414–16, s.v. 'Joseph-Marie Tomasi'.

tongues, gift of. See GLOSSOLALIA.

tonsure. The shaving of all or part of the head, traditionally a distinctive feature of monks and clerics in the RC Church; it was formerly prescribed by Canon Law (cf. *CIC* (1917), can. 136) for all clerics, except in places where, as in England and USA, it was not in accordance with popular usage. The cutting of the hair, a religious ceremony of many E. peoples, became a generally received custom in 4th- and 5th-cent. monasticism and thence was introduced into the W. as the form of admission to the clerical state, distinct from Minor Orders, in the 6th and 7th cents. From the 16th cent. onwards it became customary to shave only a small space on the crown of the head of the secular clergy and in modern times the shaving of some hair during the admission of a layman to the clerical state became purely symbolic. It has no place in the 1972 rite of *Admission to Candidacy for Ordination of

Deacons and Priests. Among monks various congregations now follow different customs in the matter.

Classic study by G. Chamillard, *De Corona, Tonsura et Habitu Clericorum Locuples cum veterum tum recentiorum Canonum, Pontificarumque Constitutionum etc. Collectio* (Paris, 1659). E. *Martène, *De Antiquis Ecclesiae Ritibus*, 2 (Rouen, 1700), pp. 294–301 (Lib. 1, cap. 8, art. 7: 'De Tonsura Clericali'); id., *De Antiquis Monachorum Ritibus* (Lyons, 1690), pp. 723–35 (Lib. 5, cap. 7: 'De Tonsura et Rasura Fratrum'). There is a useful appendix by J. Smith to his edn. of *Bede, *HE* (Cambridge, 1722), pp. 705–15 (Appendix no. IX. b. 'De Tonsura Clericorum'), repr. in J. P. Migne, *PL* 95. 327–32. P. Gobillot, 'Sur la tonsure chrétienne et ses prétendues origines païennes', *RHE* 21 (1925), pp. 399–451; E. James, 'Bede and the Tonsure Question', *Peritia*, 3 (1984), pp. 85–98; L. Trichet, *La Tonsure: Vie et mort d'une pratique ecclésiastique* (1990), with bibl. F. E. Warren in *DCA* 2 (1880), pp. 1989 f., s.v.; A. Michel in *DTC* 14 (pt. 1; 1946), cols. 1228–35, s.v.; H. *Leclercq, OSB, in *DACL* 15 (pt. 2; 1953), cols. 2430–43, s.v. See also comm. on the 1917 *Codex Juris Canonici*, ad loc.

Tophet. A place or object in the valley of Hinnom, immediately to the SW of *Jerusalem, where human sacrifices were burned by idolatrous Israelites in the worship of Molech (2 Kgs. 23: 10, Jer. 7: 31, etc.).

Toplady, Augustus Montague (1740–1778), author and hymn writer. He was a native of Farnham, Surrey, and educated at Westminster School and *Trinity College, Dublin. He was ordained priest in 1764 and in 1768 became vicar of Broad Hembury in Devonshire. At first he fell under J. *Wesley's influence, but in 1758 he was converted to extreme *Calvinist opinions and henceforward bitterly attacked Wesley. His position was set out in his most important prose work, *The Historic Proof of the Doctrinal Calvinism of the Church of England* (1774), in which he developed his subject from the *Apostolic Fathers downwards. He also wrote on the same subject *The Church of England Vindicated from the Charge of *Arminianism* (2 vols., 1769). Toplady, however, is remembered esp. for his hymns, of which he published several collections. His well-known 'Rock of Ages' first appeared in the *Gospel Magazine* in 1775, though the tradition that he wrote it while sheltering in the Mendips from a storm is without foundation.

Works pub. 6 vols., London, 1794, with memoir [by W. Row] in vol. 1, pp. 1–125; new edn., 6 vols., ibid., 1825. Separate edn. of his *Hymns and Sacred Poems on a Variety of Divine Subjects* (London, 1860). Life by T. Wright ('The Lives of British Hymnwriters', 2; 1911). G. Lawton, *Within the Rock of Ages: The Life and Work of Augustus Montague Toplady* (Cambridge [1983]). H. L. Bennett in *DNB* 57 (1899), pp. 57–9.

Torah. The English equivalent of the Heb. תּוֹרָה, usually translated 'Law'. The word probably comes from a root meaning 'throw', 'shoot', 'direct', 'instruct'. Although it could be used of the teaching of the Prophets (e.g. Is. 8: 16), of the precepts of parents (e.g. Prov. 1: 8 and 4: 2), and of the utterances of wise men (e.g. Prov. 13: 14), for all of which the OT writers characteristically claim a Divine origin, it was pre-eminently the function of the priests to give 'torah' or instruction on the Will of God (e.g. Jer. 18: 18), and it was for their failure in, or misuse of, this aspect of the priestly office that the Prophets denounced them (e.g. Mic. 3: 11, Zeph. 3: 4). By a natural development, 'torah' came to be used also of written col-

lections of such priestly decisions (e.g. Hos. 8: 12), and so of the Pentateuch as containing the Mosaic legislation, as well as of individual laws within that legislation (e.g. Lev. 7: 1). Rabbinic Judaism ascribes equal and Divine authority to the written and oral Torah (see MISHNAH).

Torgau Articles. A memorandum summarizing the disciplinary and ceremonial demands of the four Reformers, M. *Luther, P. *Melanchthon, J. *Bugenhagen, and J. *Jonas. It was compiled in Mar.–Apr. 1530, and handed in to the Diet of *Augsburg by John, Elector of Saxony. The name is misleading, as no gathering at Torgau of the four theologians mentioned ever took place.

They are to be distinguished from the Torgau Book of 1570, produced by a conference of theologians at Torgau called to reconcile the Swabian-Saxon Confession and the Maulbronn Formula. J. *Andreae's summary of the Book, known as the Epitome, was incorporated in the Formula of *Concord (q.v.).

Text in *Corpus Reformatorum*, 26 (1858), pp. 171–200. T. Brieger, 'Die Torgauer Artikel', in *Kirchengeschichtliche Studien Hermann Reuter zum 70. Geburtstag gewidmet* (1888), pp. 265–320. See also bibl. to AUGSBURG CONFESSION.

Torquemada, Juan de (1388–1468), 'Turrecremata', Spanish theologian. In 1404 he entered the *Dominican Order. In 1417 he accompanied his provincial to the Council of *Constance and from there went to Paris to finish his studies. Having been prior of the houses of his order at Valladolid and Toledo, from 1432 to 1437 he attended the Council of *Basle, and in 1435 *Eugenius IV made him master of the Sacred Palace. He took an active part in the negotiations with the Bohemians and with the Greeks on the question of reunion, was created Cardinal of St Sixtus in 1439, and till the end of his life had a decisive share in ecclesiastical Papal policy. His most important works are the 'Commentarii in Decretum Gratiani' (pub. 1519) on canon law, and the 'Summa de Ecclesia' (pub. 1489), a systematic treatise on the Church, defending the infallibility and plenitude of the spiritual power of the Pope, but taking only a moderate view of his temporal power. An edition of his treatise *De Veritate Conceptionis B. Virginis* (pub. 1547; rejecting the *Immaculate Conception) was issued by E. B. *Pusey in 1869.

Modern edns. of his *Apparatus super decretum Florentinum Unionis Graecorum*, ed. E. Candal, SJ (Concilium Florentinum, Documenta et Scriptores, 2, fasc. 1; 1942); *Oratio Synodalis de Primatu*, ed. id. (ibid. 4, fasc 2; 1954), and of his *Tractatus contra Madianitas et Ismaelitas* by N. L. Martínez and V. P. Gil (Burgos, 1957). Eng. tr. of his 'Oratio Synodalis' as *A Disputation on the Authority of Pope and Council*, with introd., by T. M. Izbicki (Dominican Sources, 4; Oxford, 1988). V. Beltrám de Heredia, OP, 'Noticias y Documentos para la Biografía del Cardenal Juan de Torquemada', *Archivum Fratrum Praedicatorum*, 30 (1960), pp. 53–148. K. Binder, *Wesen und Eigenschaften der Kirche bei Kardinal Juan de Torquemada O.P.* (Innsbruck, 1955); id., *Konzilsgedanken bei Kardinal Juan de Torquemada, O.P.* (Wiener Beiträge zur Theologie, 49; 1976). P. Massi, *Magistero infallibile del Papa nella teologia di Giovanni da Torquemada* (Scrinium Theologicum, 8; 1957). U. Horst [OP], 'Grenzen der päpstlichen Autorität. Konziliare Elemente in der Ekklesiologie des Johannes Torquemada', *Freiburger Zeitschrift für Philosophie und Theologie*, 19 (1972), pp. 361–88. T. M. Izbicki, *Protector of the Faith: Cardinal Johannes de Turrecremata and the Defense of the Institutional*

Church (Washington, DC [1981]). Kaeppeli, 3 (1980), pp. 24–42 and 4 (1993), pp. 173–6, s.v. 'Iohannes de Turrecremata', with extensive bibl. H. J. Sieben, SJ, in *Dict. Sp.* 15 (1991), cols. 1048–54, s.v.

Torquemada, Tomás (1420–98), Spanish Inquisitor General. A nephew of Juan de *Torquemada, he entered the *Dominican Order at Valladolid at an early age and was prior there by 1474. He was an enthusiast for the reform of the Order and *c*.1474 became prior of Segovia, where the reform was being introduced. He retained this office until his death. In 1482 he founded a new, reformed priory in Ávila, where he introduced the first statute of 'limpieza' ('purity of blood') into a Dominican house. For many years he was (at least titular) confessor to *Ferdinand V and *Isabella. In 1482 he was appointed an inquisitor in the newly established Spanish *Inquisition; he became its first Inquisitor General in 1483, with a concentration of power never equalled by his successors. Between 1484 and 1498 he issued a series of instructions for the practice of the Inquisition, which were gathered together and published in 1537; these left an indelible mark on the character and operation of the institution. Under Torquemada's leadership, the Spanish Inquisition rapidly became an extremely powerful force used particularly in the repression of the only nominally Christianized Jews (the 'conversos'). (Torquemada's ancestors were apparently of Jewish origin, converts to Christianity.) He was also influential in the decision made in 1492 to expel the Jews from Spain. See also INQUISITION.

E. de Molènes (ed.), *Documents inédits: Torquemada et l'Inquisition, la Jurisprudence du Saint-Office, l'Enfant de la Guardia, le Cœur et l'Hostie, Sortilèges et vénéfices, Sentences et autodafés, l'Expulsion des Juifs, les Procès à la mort* (1897). His 'Instructions' on the operation of the Inquisition are pr. in M. Jiménez Monteserín (ed.), *Introducción a la Inquisición española* [1980], pp. 82–121. There is no satisfactory biog. of Torquemada. J. Meseguer Fernández, 'Tomás de Torquemada, inquisidor general (1483–1498)', in J. Pérez Villanueva and B. Escandell Bonet (eds.), *Historia de la Inquisición en España y América*, 1 (Biblioteca de autores cristianos, 2nd edn., 1984), pp. 310–42. Quétif and Échard, 1, pp. 892 f.

Torres, Francisco, also 'Turrianus' (*c*.1509–1584), patristic scholar and RC controversialist. After studying at Alcalá, he went to Rome, where he became a well-known controversial author. From 1562 to 1563 he was at the Council of *Trent as Papal theologian. In 1563 he brought out the first edition of the '*Apostolic Constitutions', attributing them to St *Clement of Rome. In 1567 he entered the Society of Jesus (*Jesuits), and later was appointed professor at the Roman College, where he was one of the scholars entrusted with the revision of the official *Vulgate. He sought to defend the authenticity of the '*Apostolic Canons', the *False Decretals, and the 80 *Nicene Canons, all of them spurious, as well as that of the (genuine) Acts of the Sixth and Seventh General Councils. He was a very voluminous writer, but he had little critical sense. In his controversial writings he upheld the *Immaculate Conception, the superiority of the Pope over Councils, and the Divine origin of episcopal authority.

C. Gutiérrez, SJ, *Españoles en Trento* (Corpus Tridentinum Hispanicum, 1; Valladolid, 1951), pp. 446–72 [in Lat. and Sp.].

Sommervogel, 8 (1898), cols. 113–26. J. P. Grausem, SJ, in *DTC* 15 (pt. 1; 1946), cols. 1239 f., s.v., with bibl.

Tosefta (Heb., 'supplement'). A collection of early Jewish traditions of the same character as and contemporary with, but not incorporated in, the *Mishnah (q.v.). It contains so-called *baraita* material (i.e. material which pre-dates the formation of the Mishnah, but was not included in the Mishnah). Like the Mishnah it has six main divisions, each of which is subdivided into tractates. It contains a much larger proportion of *Haggadic elements than the Mishnah.

Eng. tr. by J. Neusner and others (6 vols., New York, etc., 1977–86). A. Goldberg in S. Safrai (ed.), *The Literature of the Sages*, 1 (Compendia Rerum Iudaicarum ad Novum Testamentum, Section 2, vol. 3, pt. 1; Assen and Philadelphia, 1987), pp. 283–302.

total depravity. A term in common use esp. in *Calvinism to express the extreme wretchedness of man's condition as the result of the *Fall. It emphasizes the belief that this result was not a mere loss or *deprivation* of a supernatural endowment possessed by unfallen man, but a radical corruption or *depravation* of his whole nature, so that apart from Christ he can do nothing whatever pleasing to God. Even his reason has been radically vitiated, so that, acc. to Calvinism, all natural knowledge of God (such as obtains in the system of St *Thomas Aquinas) is held to be impossible.

total immersion. See SUBMERSION.

totemism. A phenomenon partly social, partly magical (or, acc. to some, religious), allegedly found among 'primitive' peoples, by which the members of a tribe believe themselves to be associated with and named after a species of animal or plant. Proponents of totemism held that the totem had a holy and sacrosanct nature and was therefore an object of worship, and that its flesh was untouchable save at a tribal feast where the eponymous animal was ritually slain and eaten by the members of the tribe who thus identified themselves with their god. Some 19th-cent. anthropologists held that totemism was an early phase of all religion, and it was suggested that the prevalence of animal and plant names among Canaanite place-names and the fact that the tribes of Israel were descended from Leah ('wild cow') and Rachel ('ewe') indicate a totemic ancestry for the religion of the Hebrews and therefore for Christianity; but the evidence for this thesis is altogether too slender to give it any show of probability and it has now been generally abandoned.

J. G. Frazer, *Totemism and Exogamy: A Treatise on Certain Early Forms of Superstition and Society* (4 vols., 1910; suppl. vol., *Totemica*, 1937). A. R. Radcliffe-Brown, 'The Sociological Theory of Totemism', repr. in his *Structure and Function in Primitive Society* (1952), pp. 117–32. C. Lévi-Strauss, *Le Totémisme aujourd'hui* (1962; Eng. tr., 1964). W. R. Smith, *Kinship and Marriage in Early Arabia* (Cambridge, 1885; 2nd edn. by S. A. *Cook, London, 1903), esp. ch. 7; id., *Lectures on the Religion of the Semites* (Edinburgh, 1889; 3rd edn. by S. A. Cook, London, 1927). J. W. Rogerson, *Anthropology and the Old Testament* (Oxford, 1978), pp. 22–45.

touching for the King's evil. See KING'S EVIL, TOUCHING FOR THE.

Tower of Babel. See BABEL, TOWER OF.

tract (liturgical). The chant formerly sung or recited at Mass on certain penitential days instead of the *Alleluia. It is already mentioned in the oldest Roman *Ordines. It was originally the Psalm chanted after the second Lesson, but this was later supplanted by the Alleluia, though preserved on days of penance and mourning. It differed from the *Gradual in that it was chanted without a responsory (Lat. *tractim*, 'straight through'), but acc. to recent scholars its name is probably not derived from this, as formerly assumed, but is connected with the Greek εἱρμός ('train', 'series'), a technical term of Greek musical theory denoting a typical tune by which the several parts of a hymn are joined together. Some tracts such as that of the First Sunday in *Lent and of *Palm Sunday preserved almost the whole Psalm, whereas most others were reduced to a few verses. The tract was said on the Sundays from Septuagesima till Easter and on the Mondays, Wednesdays, and Fridays of Lent; also on the Saturdays in Ember Weeks (when it replaced the Gradual), and in Masses for the Dead. It was suppressed by the *Ordo Missae* of 1969.

Jungmann (1958 edn.), 1, pp. 550–2 (Eng. tr., 1 (1951), pp. 430 f.). M. Huglo in *NCE* 14 (1967), pp. 221 f., s.v. On the musical settings, also H. Hucke in S. Sadie (ed.), *New Grove Dictionary of Music and Musicians*, 19 (1980), pp. 108–10, s.v.

tract (propagandist) (Lat. *tractare*, 'to treat of the matter'). A pamphlet, usually issued with a religious or moral purpose. Its early history is obscure, but many medieval works, e.g. the lesser English works of J. *Wycliffe, come under this heading. The religious controversies of the 16th and 17th cents. stimulated the production of tracts which often (e.g. under the Commonwealth) reached vast proportions. The abusive *Marprelate Tracts (1588) are an instance from the age of *Elizabeth I. The *Bangorian Controversy also inspired a number of tracts. On the *Tracts for the Times* (1833–41) see following entry. Various tract societies have been formed, among them the *SPCK (1698) and the *Religious Tract Society (1799).

Tractarianism. A name for the earlier stages of the *Oxford Movement, derived from the *Tracts for the Times* issued under its aegis. The purpose of the tracts was to disseminate Church principles 'against Popery and Dissent'. The first, written by J. H. *Newman and published with two others on 9 Sept. 1833, was a 4-page leaflet entitled 'Thoughts on the Ministerial Commission respectfully addressed to the Clergy' and containing a defence of the Apostolic Succession. Others followed rapidly and on 21 Dec. appeared E. B. *Pusey's first tract ('Thoughts on the Benefits of the System of Fasting enjoined by our Church'; no. 18 of the series). The other tract writers included J. *Keble, J. W. Bowden (1798–1844), A. P. *Perceval, R. H. *Froude, C. *Marriott, and I. *Williams. They secured a wide circulation, and their influence, as the first public utterances of the Oxford Movement, was enormous. Their form gradually changed from brief leaflets to learned treatises and catenae

assembled from the 17th-cent. Anglican divines in support of Catholic theology and practice in the C of E. On 25 Jan. 1841 Newman's famous Tract 90 ('Remarks on Certain Passages in the Thirty-Nine Articles') appeared; the storm which it provoked brought the series to an end.

The tracts were issued in bound vols. as follows: vol. 1, nos. 1–46 (1834); 2, nos. 47–70 (1836); 3, nos. 71–7 (1836); 4, nos. 78–82 (1838); 5, nos. 83–8 (1840); 6, nos. 89–90 (1841). D. Croly, *An Index to the Tracts for the Times* (1842). Full discussion and attribution of authorship by R. Imberg, *In Quest of Authority: The 'Tracts for the Times' and the Development of the Tractarian Leaders, 1833–1841* (Bibliotheca Historico-Ecclesiastica Lundensis, 16 [1987]); id., *Tracts for the Times: A Complete Survey of all the Editions* (ibid. 17; 1987). R. D. Middleton, 'Tract Ninety', *JEH* 2 (1951), pp. 81–101. See also bibl. on OXFORD MOVEMENT.

Tractatus Origenis (Lat., 'Tractates of Origen'). A collection of 20 Homilies on the Scriptures, 19 of them on OT texts, first published in 1900 by P. *Batiffol and A. *Wilmart, OSB. In the 10th-cent. Orléans MS and the 12th-cent. St-Omer MS where they are preserved, they are ascribed to *Origen. Batiffol held that their Gk. originals were really the work of Origen; but it is now generally agreed, following G. *Morin's earlier view, that they were the work of *Gregory, Bp. of Elvira (q.v.).

P. Batiffol and A. Wilmart, OSB, *Tractatus Origenis de Libris SS. Scripturarum* (Paris, 1900); also ed. by V. Bulhart (CCLS, 69, 1967, pp. 1–146). G. Morin, OSB, 'Les Nouveaux *Tractatus Origenis* et l'héritage littéraire de l'évêque espagnol Grégoire d'Illiberis', *Revue d'Histoire et de Littérature religieuses*, 5 (1900), pp. 145–61. H. Koch, 'Zu Gregors von Elvira Schrifttum und Quellen', *ZKG* 51 (1932), pp. 238–72. Altaner and Stuiber (1978), pp. 370 and 627.

tractoria. Originally a 'letter of summons' (from Lat. *trahere*, 'to convey', i.e. by the *cursus publicus* or postal service), the word was applied also to letters containing the decisions of Councils. It is used esp. of the (lost) 'Epistola Tractoria' of *Zosimus (417–18), in which that Pope reversed his previous support of *Pelagianism.

The chief frags. of Zosimus' *Ep. Tractoria* are preserved in *Augustine, *Ep.* 190. 23, and in *Prosper of Aquitaine, *Auctoritates*, cap. 9; repr. with others in J. P. Migne, *PL* 20. 693–5.

Tracts for the Times. See TRACTARIANISM.

Traditio-Historical Criticism (Ger. *Überlieferungsgeschichte*), also called 'History of Traditions Method'. The study of the development of texts and motifs (often with particular reference to oral transmission), the circumstances in the life of the community in which they were created and its cultural background. It largely overlaps with *Form Criticism, which draws inferences about the transmission and community use of tradition by studying the oral and literary processes behind most biblical texts. The roots of this approach lie in the 18th cent., but the modern pioneer was H. *Gunkel, whose work was continued by M. *Noth and G. von *Rad in the OT and by R. *Bultmann and M. *Dibelius in the NT, esp. the Synoptic Gospels. In Scandinavia I. Engnell led a group who elevated this approach to the exclusion of more literary methods. See also FORM CRITICISM.

E. Nielsen, *Oral Tradition: A Modern Problem in Old Testament. Introduction* (Studies in Biblical Theology, 11; 1954 [Eng. tr. of arts. published in *Dansk Theologisk Tidsskrift*, 1950 and 1952]).

D. A. Knight (ed.), *Tradition and Authority in the Old Testament* (Philadelphia, 1977). G. Thiessen, *Lokalkolorit und Zeitgeschichte in den Evangelien* (Novum Testamentum et Orbis Antiquus, 8; 1989; Eng. tr., *The Gospels in Context*, Minneapolis, 1991). R. [C.] Morgan and J. Barton, *Biblical Interpretation* (Oxford, 1988), pp. 96–132. I. Engnell in *Svenskt Bibliskt Uppslagsverk* (2nd edn.), 2 (1962), cols. 1254–61, s.v. 'Traditionshistorisk metod'; Eng. tr. as 'The Traditio-Historical Method in Old Testament Research', in his *Critical Essays on the Old Testament* (1970), pp. 3–11. D. A. Knight in *Anchor Bible Dictionary*, 6 (1992), pp. 633–8, s.v. 'Tradition History'.

Traditio Symboli (Lat., the 'delivery' or 'handing over of the Creed'). During early times candidates for Baptism, who were mainly adults, were subjected to a long course of instruction before admission to the sacrament. Their training was both practical and doctrinal, as in modern 'Confirmation classes', and the latter part of it consisted of explanations of the Creed. This was the 'delivery' or *traditio*, made by the teacher to the candidates, who thus 'received the creed' into their own keeping. At their Baptism they were required to recite and profess the Creed, thus 'returning it' (*redditio symboli*) to the presiding bishop. The ceremony has been restored in the 1972 RC Order for Adult Baptism.

For main lit. see histories of Baptism, cited s.v. J. Barbet and C. Lambot, OSB, 'Nouvelle Tradition du symbole de rit gallican', *R. Bén.* 75 (1965), pp. 335–45.

tradition. In the early Christian Fathers, tradition (παράδοσις, *traditio*) means the revelation made by God and delivered by Him to His faithful people through the mouth of His prophets and apostles. It does not mean something 'handed down' but something 'handed over'. Similarly in the NT the word, or its corresponding verb, is applied equally to the betrayal of Christ by *Judas to the Jews, and to the delivery of Christian teaching by St *Paul to his converts. The tradition was at first called 'apostolic', because delivered by the apostles to the Churches which they founded, and later also 'ecclesiastic', because delivered again in each generation by the Church's teachers to their people. Its substance was held to consist of the central facts and beliefs crystallized in the creeds of the great orthodox bishoprics. From the beginning of the 3rd cent. the tradition was sometimes expressly identified with the Gospel record contained in Scripture. The occasional references in early Christian literature to an 'unwritten tradition' left by the apostles appear to relate not to any body of information independent of Scripture, but to the evidence of primitive Christian institutions and customs which confirms scriptural teaching.

In a more modern sense, tradition means the continuous stream of explanation and elucidation of the primitive faith, illustrating the way in which Christianity has been presented and understood in past ages. That is to say, it is the accumulated wisdom of the past. Sometimes, again, it means simply customs and ideas which have grown up imperceptibly and been accepted more or less uncritically. All tradition in these modern senses needs to have its true value proved by the double test—(1) whether it is in accordance with the principles embodied in divine revelation, and (2) whether it can be justified by right reason.

In the Reformation era the relation of unwritten tradition to the scriptural revelation was the subject of acute controversy between Protestants and Catholics. As against the Protestant belief in the sole sufficiency of the Bible, the Council of *Trent (Sess. 4. 1; 8 Apr. 1546) laid down that Scripture and unwritten traditions were to be received as of equal authority (*pari pietatis affectu ac reverentia*). In recent years it has been argued that, contrary to popular belief, the Tridentine decision did not imply that Scripture and tradition were the two sources (*fontes*) of revelation, and some RC writers have held that all revelation is materially contained in the Scriptures. The Dogmatic Constitution on Revelation of the Second *Vatican Council minimizes the distinction, stating that Scripture and tradition 'flow from the same divine wellspring, merge into a unity and tend to the same end' (Section 9).

J.-B. *Bossuet, *Défense de la tradition et des saints pères* (2 vols., 1763); J. B. *Franzelin, *Tractatus de Divina Traditione et Scriptura* (Rome, 1870). Extracts from the Fathers ed., with Fr. tr., by W. Rordorf and A. Schneider, *L'évolution du concept de tradition dans l'Église ancienne* (Traditio Christiana, 5 [1982]; with Ger. tr. [1983]). G. L. Prestige, *Fathers and Heretics* (1948), pp. 1–22 ('Tradition'); W. *Sanday and N. P. *Williams, *Form and Content in the Christian Tradition: A Friendly Discussion* (1916); C. H. *Turner, *Catholic and Apostolic* (1931); A. Deneffe, SJ, *Der Traditionsbegriff* (Münsterische Beiträge zur Theologie, Heft 18; 1931); O. *Cullmann, *La Tradition: Problème exégétique, historique et théologique* (1953); Y. M. J. *Congar, OP, *La Tradition et les traditions* (2 vols., 1960–3; Eng. tr., 1966); R. P. C. Hanson, *Tradition in the Early Church* (1962); J. R. Geiselmann, *Die Heilige Schrift und die Tradition* (Quaestiones Disputatae, 18; 1962; Eng. tr., 1966); J. P. Mackey, *The Modern Theology of Tradition* (1962); id., *Tradition and Change in the Church* (Dublin, 1968); *De Scriptura et Traditione*, ed. C. Balić, OFM (Rome, 1963); V. *Lossky, *À l'Image et à la ressemblance de Dieu* [1967], pp. 139–66 ('La Tradition et les traditions'); Eng. tr. (New York, 1974; London, 1975), pp. 141–68; F. F. Bruce, *Tradition Old and New* (Exeter, 1970); N. Lash, *Change in Focus: A Study of Doctrinal Change and Continuity* (1973). P. Longfield, M. Feiner, and others in *Mysterium Salutis*, ed. J. Feiner and M. Löhrer, 1 (Einsiedeln [1965]), pp. 239–88 and 463–605.

Tradition of the Instruments. See INSTRUMENTS, TRADITION OF THE.

Traditionalism. In its strict sense a theory proposed by a group of 19th-cent. RC thinkers, acc. to which all metaphysical, moral, and religious knowledge is based on a primitive revelation of God to man handed down in an unbroken tradition. Denying to human reason the power of attaining by itself to any truths, esp. those of natural theology, it makes an act of faith in a revealed tradition the origin of all knowledge. It was historically a reaction from 18th-cent. rationalism in the direction of the other extreme and flourished chiefly in France and Belgium. Among its advocates were L. G. A. de Bonald (1754–1840) and F. R. de *Lamennais and of esp. influence was the latter's *Essai sur l'indifférence en matière de religion* (4 vols., 1817–23) with its doctrine of the 'sens commun'. To restore belief to the modern world the Traditionalists aimed at removing it from discussion by individual reason and at imposing it by the authority of the common consent of mankind, which, acc. to Lamennais, is invested with infallibility. Modified forms of the doctrine were held by L. E. M. Bautain (1796–1867), A. Bonnetty (1798–1879), and G. C. *Ubaghs (q.v.) and the philosophers of the Louvain school. Though the insistence on the social nature of man and on the importance of tradition in religion were orthodox elements in the teaching of Traditionalism, its fundamental distrust of human reason could not but eventually lead to scepticism. It was officially condemned by a number of decrees, and finally ruled out as a possible Catholic system by the constitution 'De fide catholica' at the First *Vatican Council in 1870.

The word is also used less strictly by liberal theologians, usually with a more or less opprobrious *nuance*, of what they consider unduly conservative beliefs.

The condemnations of E. Bautin and A. Bonnetty are conveniently repr. in Denzinger and Hünermann (37th edn., 1991), pp. 762–4 (nos. 2751–6) and 776 f. (nos. 2811–14). J. Lupus, *Le Traditionalisme et le rationalisme examinés au point de vue de la philosophie et de la doctrine catholique* (3 vols., Liège, 1858). J. Henry, 'Le Traditionalisme et l'ontologisme à l'université de Louvain (1835–1865)', *Annales de l'Institut Supérieur de Philosophie* [at Louvain], 5 (1924), pp. 41–149, with bibl. refs. B. [M. G.] Reardon, *Liberalism and Tradition: Aspects of Catholic Thought in Nineteenth-Century France* (Cambridge, 1975), esp. pp. 43–61, 71–82, 113–16, and 175–81; G. A. McCool, *Catholic Theology in the Nineteenth Century* (New York, 1977), esp. pp. 37–58 ('French Traditionalism'). S. A. Matczak in *NCE* 14 (1967), pp. 228–30, s.v.

traditors. The name given in Africa in early times to Christians who surrendered the Scriptures when their possession was forbidden in the persecution of *Diocletian. The controversy between Catholics and *Donatists which followed the persecution was centred chiefly in the refusal of the Donatists to recognize *Caecilian, Bp. of Carthage, on the ground that he had been consecrated by traditors.

Traducianism (Lat. *tradux*, 'shoot', 'sprout'). The theory acc. to which the human soul is transmitted by the parents to the children. The term is sometimes restricted to the crudely materialistic view which asserts that this happens in the physical act of generation; it is then distinguished from opinions which refrain from dogmatizing on this point, collectively styled 'Generationism'. Traducianism was advocated by some of the Fathers, esp. *Tertullian in his 'De Anima' (chs. 23–41). For St *Augustine it suggested a simple explanation for *Original Sin, though he was unable to decide between it and *Creationism (q.v.). Pope Anastasius II condemned the theory in his Ep. to the Gallican bishops (498). In the Middle Ages Creationism was the almost universally accepted doctrine, but in the 19th cent. Traducianism was revived in a modified form by several RC theologians, e.g. A. *Rosmini, who argued that the parents generate a sensitive soul which God changes by illumination into a spiritual one. The theory in its crude form is incompatible with the spiritual nature of the soul, and even in the attenuated form of Generationism is widely held to be heretical.

A. Michel in *DTC* 15 (pt. 1; 1946), cols. 1350–65.

Traherne, Thomas (*c.*1636–74), English *Metaphysical poet and divine. Probably a native of Hereford, he entered Brasenose College, Oxford, in 1652, which he left after taking his degree in 1656. In 1657 he became rector of Credenhill, nr. Hereford, and in 1667 private chaplain to Sir Orlando Bridgman, Lord Keeper of the Great Seal, and 'minister' in the parish of Teddington. Only one work,

Roman Forgeries (1673), a controversial treatise on forged documents of the RC Church, appeared before his death. His *Christian Ethics*, issued in 1675 and until recently almost unknown, is an eloquent description of Christian virtue, though sometimes over-subtle in discussing theological niceties. In 1699 a friend published a little devotional book of Traherne, *A Serious and Pathetical Contemplation of the Mercies of God*, but his poems, for which he is now famous, remained in MS until they were published by B. Dobell in 1903. They were followed in 1908 by four *Centuries of Meditations*, a collection of reflections on ethics and religion which have proved more attractive than the verse.

Traherne, who was an ardent admirer and constant reader of the '*Hermetic Books', is the least orthodox of the metaphysical poets. From his essentially optimistic and 'vitalistic' conception of experience, the elements of sin and suffering are almost entirely excluded. His poetry, remarkable for a penetrating sense of the glory of nature and childhood, is clearly pantheistic in feeling. Among his more famous poems are 'The Rapture' and 'An Hymn upon St Bartholomew's Day'.

Centuries, Poems, and Thanksgivings, ed. H. M. Margoliouth (2 vols., Oxford, 1958). *Poems, Centuries and Three Thanksgivings*, ed. A. Ridler ('Oxford Standard Authors', 1966). Modern edn. of *Christian Ethics* by G. R. Guffey, with introd. by C. L. Marks (New York, 1968). Studies by G. E. Willett (Cambridge, 1919), [H.] Q. Iredale (Oxford, 1935), G. I. Wade (Princeton, NJ, 1944), and K. W. Salter (London, 1964). A. L. Clements, *The Mystical Poetry of Thomas Traherne* (Cambridge, Mass., 1969). A. M. Allchin and others, *Profitable Wonders: Aspects of Thomas Traherne* (3 lectures, Oxford [1989]); G. Dowell, *Enjoying the World: The Rediscovery of Thomas Traherne* [1990].

transcendentals (*transcendentalia*, *transcendentia* in *Scholastic philosophy), those properties which belong to all beings, as opposed to the categories (belonging only to finite beings) which they 'transcend'. They are usually held to include 'unity' (*unum*), goodness (*bonum*), truth (*verum*), and beauty (*pulchrum*), but the list varies.

transenna (Lat., properly a 'net'). In ecclesiastical architecture, a wall, usually of marble, which is pierced with holes in a regular pattern. Apart from purely ornamental purposes, transennae were also used to surround the tomb of a martyr (e.g. in the confessio), and thus to enable the worshipper to see it, and sometimes also touch it, through the grating.

Transfiguration, the. The appearing of the Lord in glory during His earthly life, related in the first three Gospels (Mt. 17: 1–13, Mk. 9: 2–13, Lk. 9: 28–36), and alluded to in 2 Pet. 1: 16–18. This vision of the Lord, transfigured, with *Moses and *Elijah, was witnessed by Sts *Peter, *James, and *John, and is described by the Evangelists as an historic event; some critics have suggested that it is a misplaced *Resurrection appearance. Tradition locates it on Mount Tabor, but many scholars prefer Mount Hermon, and some have even suggested the Mount of *Olives. The event was significant as showing the testimony of the Jewish Law and Prophets to the Messiahship of Christ, as furnishing a further Divine proclamation of His Sonship, and as foreshadowing His future glory. The Feast of the Transfiguration is observed on 6 Aug. It originated in the E. Church, where it appears to have been at first a local and unofficial feast, but it had become widely adopted before AD 1000. In the W., where the feast was not introduced till a much later date, its general observance goes back to 1457, when *Callistus III ordered its universal celebration in commemoration of the victory gained over the Turks at Belgrade on 22 July 1456, news of which reached Rome on 6 Aug. In a number of Protestant Churches the Transfiguration is commemorated on the last Sunday after Epiphany.

G. H. Boobyer, *St Mark and the Transfiguration Story* (1942); H. Riesenfeld, *Jésus transfiguré: L'Arrière-plan du récit évangélique de la transfiguration de Notre-Seigneur* (Acta Seminarii Neotestamentici Upsaliensis, 16; 1947); A. M. *Ramsey, *The Glory of God and the Transfiguration of Christ* (1949); H. Baltensweiler, *Die Verklärung Jesu* (Abhandlungen zur Theologie des Alten und Neuen Testaments, 33; 1959); J. A. McGuckin, *The Transfiguration of Christ in Scripture and Tradition* (Studies in the Bible and Early Christianity, 9; Lewiston, NY [1986]), incl. Eng. tr. of relevant texts from the Fathers; B. E. Reid, OP, *The Transfiguration: A Source- and Redaction-Critical Study of Luke 9: 28–36* (Cahiers de la *Revue Biblique*, 32; 1993). R. W. Pfaff, *New Liturgical Feasts in Later Medieval England* (Oxford Theological Monographs, 1970), pp. 13–39.

Transitorium. A prayer in the *Ambrosian rite corresponding to the *Communion anthem in the Roman Mass. It is apparently so named because the celebrant passes over (*transit*) to the S. side of the altar to recite it.

translation. In ecclesiastical contexts the word is used in various senses:

(1) The transference of the relics of a saint either from their original place of burial into an altar tomb or shrine, or from one shrine to another. The solemnities connected with it frequently gave rise to a new liturgical feast. Thus the translation of St Thomas *Becket, observed on 7 July, commemorates the reburial of the saint's relics at *Canterbury on 7 July 1220.

(2) The transference to a different day of a feast when a particular season (e.g. *Holy Week) prohibits its observance, or a feast of higher rank occurs on the same day. Acc. to the *Calendarium Romanum* of 1969 the Sundays of Lent and Eastertide, all days in Holy Week and the last eight days of Advent take absolute precedence, and the impeded feast is transferred to the nearest free day.

(3) In canon law the transference of a cleric from one ecclesiastical office to another. The translation of a bishop from one see to another was forbidden by can. 15 of the Council of *Nicaea (325), but the decree was never rigorously adhered to, and in the Middle Ages the translation of bishops became one of the prerogatives of the Popes and the practice has continued down to modern times.

transmigration of souls. See METEMPSYCHOSIS.

transubstantiation. In the theology of the *Eucharist, the conversion of the whole substance of the bread and wine into the whole substance of the Body and Blood of Christ, only the *accidents (i.e. the appearances of the bread and wine) remaining. The word was in widespread use in the later part of the 12th cent., and at the *Lateran Council of 1215 the Eucharistic elements were said to be 'transubstantiated' into the Body and Blood of Christ; but the elaboration of the doctrine was not achieved till after the acceptance of the *Aristotelian metaphysics later in the 13th cent., when it found classic formulation in the teach-ing of St *Thomas Aquinas. At the Council of *Trent (sess. 13, cap. 4) the medieval doctrine was reaffirmed, but with a minimum of technical philosophical language; 'transubstantiation' was confirmed as the 'most apt' term to describe the conversion. Since the 15th cent. the E. Church has used the word μετουσίωσις to denote an essentially identical doctrine and has on occasion given it formal approval, e.g. at the Synod of *Jerusalem (1672); but many modern Orthodox theologians avoid the term, because of its close associations with Latin Scholasticism. The *Anglican–Roman Catholic International Commission in 1971 reached agreement on Eucharistic doctrine, relegating the term 'transubstantiation' to a footnote, in which it is said to affirm the fact of the 'mysterious and radical change' rather than to explain how the change takes place. See also DECLARATION AGAINST TRANSUBSTANTIATION.

For main bibl. see works cited s.v. EUCHARIST. H. Jorissen, *Die Entfaltung der Transsubstantiationslehre bis zum Beginn der Hochscholastik* (Münsterische Beiträge zur Theologie, 28, Heft 1; 1965), with bibl. J. F. McCue, 'The Doctrine of Transubstantiation from Berengar through Trent: The Point at Issue', *HTR* 61 (1968), pp. 385–430. B. F. Byron, *Sacrifice and Symbol: A New Theology of the Eucharist for Catholic and Ecumenical Consideration* (Faith and Culture, 19; Sydney, 1991), pp. 89–149 passim. J. de Ghellinck, 'A propos du premier emploi du mot transsubstantiation', *Rech. S.R.* 2 (1911), pp. 466–9, 570–2; 3 (1912), pp. 255–9. A. Michel in *DTC* 15 (pt. 1; 1946), cols. 1396–406, s.v.

Trappists. Since the French Revolution the popular name for the reformed *Cistercians belonging to foundations originating from the exiled community of *la Trappe, the sole survivor of the Order in France. The union of three Trappist congregations in 1893, soon followed by the recovery of *Cîteaux, which became the mother house of the newly independent Order, led in 1902 to its current official designation as the Order of Reformed Cistercians, or Cistercians of the Strict Observance (OCSO), omitting any mention of la Trappe. The name Trappistines, popularly applied to nuns of the Order, also originates from Revolutionary times, when Cistercian nuns fleeing persecution rallied under the leadership of the Trappist Abbot Augustin Lestrange, and eventually formed new foundations under Trappist direction. They now form a single order with the monks.

See bibl. to CISTERCIAN ORDER and LA TRAPPE.

Travers, Walter (c.1548–1635), *Puritan divine. He was educated at Christ's College, Cambridge, and elected a Fellow of Trinity in 1567. Having formed a friendship with T. *Beza on a visit to *Geneva, Travers returned to England an acknowledged leader of the movement of Reform. Owing to his unwillingness to subscribe the *Thirty-Nine Articles, he was refused a licence to preach and returned to the Continent, where he was ordained to serve the English congregation at Antwerp. In 1581, through the influence of Lord Burghley, he became afternoon lecturer at the Temple, and three years later he would have been made Master had he not declined to receive orders in the C of E. Continuing as afternoon lecturer, he was soon engaged in controversy with R. *Hooker, the new Master, which lasted until he was inhibited by J. *Whitgift. Throughout the 1580s, he was one of the leaders of *Presbyterian activity in London. In 1594 he was made Provost of *Trinity College, Dublin. His principal works were the *Ecclesiasticae Disciplinae, et Anglicanae Ecclesiae . . . Explicatio* (pub. anon. at La Rochelle in 1574 and later in the same year in an Eng. tr. by T. *Cartwright), and the *Disciplina Ecclesiae Sacra ex Dei Verbo descripta* (written by 1587 and circulating in MS until an Eng. tr., *A *Directory of Church Government* was printed early in 1645). These both defended the Presbyterian form of Church government as of Dominical institution and proposed a scheme for practical implementation; they provided the most important English exposition of the Presbyterian case, and as such exercised great influence in that wing of the Puritan movement.

Disciplina Ecclesiae Sacra is pr. by F. *Paget, *An Introduction to the Fifth Book of Hooker's Treatise of the Laws of Ecclesiastical Polity* (Oxford, 1899), pp. 238–51. S. J. Knox, *Walter Travers: Paragon of Elizabethan Puritanism* (1962), with refs. P. [G.] Lake, *Anglicans and Puritans? Presbyterianism and English Conformist Thought from Whitgift to Hooker* (1988), pp. 71–87. R. Bauckham, 'Hooker, Travers and the Church of Rome in the 1580s', *JEH* 29 (1978), pp. 37–50.

Traversari, Ambrogio (*c*.1386–1439), also Fra Ambrogio, scholar and theologian. In 1400 he entered the *Camaldolese Order at the monastery of Sta Maria degli Angioli at Florence and in 1431 became its General. From about 1414 he devoted himself to the study of the Fathers, whom he regarded as a model for the contemporary Church. As well as bringing to light numerous patristic MSS, he translated into Latin the works of several Greek Fathers, notably John *Chrysostom and *Dionysius the Pseudo-Areopagite. Between *c*.1431 and 1435 he was active in promulgating monastic reforms instituted by Pope *Eugenius IV. In 1435 he defended Papal supremacy at the Council of *Basle. As a Greek expert, Traversari provided textual and linguistic material in the discussions on the *Filioque at the Council of *Florence and was responsible for the Greek version of the Decree of Union (*Laetentur Coeli) signed on 5 July 1439.

His correspondence and other material was pub. from different 15th-cent. collections by E. *Martène, OSB, and U. Durand, OSB (eds.), *Veterum Scriptorum et Monumentorum ... Amplissima Collectio*, 3 (Paris, 1724), cols. 1–728, and ed. P. Canneti, with Life by L. Mehus (2 vols., Florence, 1759). F. P. Luiso, *Riordinamento dell'Epistolario di Ambrogio Traversari con lettere inedite e note storico-cronologiche* (3 fascs., Florence, 1898–1903). Twelve further letters ed. L. Bertalot in *RQ* 29 (1915), pp. *91–*106. Further letters in G. *Mercati, *Ultimi contributi alla storia degli umanisti*, fasc. 1: *Traversariana* (ST 90; 1939). A. Dini Traversari, *Ambrogio Traversari e i suoi tempi* (Florence, 1912), incl. text of the *Hodoeporicon*. C. Somigli, Camaldolese, *Un amico dei Greci: Ambrogio Traversari* (Arezzo, 1964). C. L. Stinger, *Humanism and the Church Fathers: Ambrogio Traversari (1386–1439) and Christian Antiquity in the Italian Renaissance* (Albany, NY, 1977). G. C. Garfagnini (ed.), *Ambrogio Traversari nel VI Centenario della Nascita: Convegno Internazionale di Studi (Camaldoli–Firenze, 15–18 settembre 1986)* (Florence, 1988).

Treacle Bible. A popular title for M. *Coverdale's '*Great Bible' (q.v.; 1539) from its rendering of Jer. 8: 22, 'There is no more *triacle* [AV, 'balm'] in Gilead'.

Trecanum (from Gk. τρικάνων, 'triple canon'). In the *Gallican liturgy the title of the Communion chant. It

consisted in an act of faith in the Trinity. The name is found already in pseudo-*Germanus of Paris.

Tre Fontane. This monastery, now *Trappist, is some 3 miles south of Rome and the traditional site of St *Paul's martyrdom. Acc. to legend, St Paul's head, on severance from his body, rebounded from the ground at three points, from which issued the three springs that give the site its name.

Dom Marie Gabriel [Montbet], Abbé d'Aiguebelle, *L'Abbaye des Trois Fontaines située aux Eaux-Salviennes, près de Rome, et dédiée aux saints martyrs Vincent et Anastase* (1869). A. Sartorio, 'L'abbazia cistercense delle Tre Fontane', *Nuova Antologia*, 167 (5) (1913), pp. 50–65. C. Bertelli, 'L'Enciclopedia delle Tre Fontane', *Paragone*, 235 (1969), pp. 24–49.

Tregelles, Samuel Prideaux (1813–75), biblical scholar. A boy of exceptional talent, he devoted his spare time while at the Neath Abbey Iron Works in S. Wales to learning Greek, Hebrew, Aramaic, and Welsh. Returning to his native Falmouth, he joined the *Plymouth Brethren, although he subsequently became a *Presbyterian. In 1838 Tregelles formed the design for a new critical text of the NT which should replace the '*textus receptus', and thenceforward he was engaged in the collation of Greek texts, making very extensive travels for the purpose. *An Account of the Printed Text of the Greek New Testament* appeared in 1854, to be followed by the publication of all the NT, with the exception of Rev., by 1870. From 1862 Tregelles was in receipt of a Civil List pension.

F. G. Kenyon, *Handbook to the Textual Criticism of the New Testament* (1901), pp. 82–100 *passim*, 248 f. E. C. Marchant in *DNB* 57 (1899), pp. 170 f.; C. Bertheau in *PRE* (3rd edn.), 20 (1908), pp. 90–5, s.v., with further refs.

Tremellius, John Immanuel (1510–80), Hebrew scholar. The son of a Ferrarese Jew, he was educated at the University of Pavia and converted to Christianity in 1540 through the influence of R. *Pole. In 1541 he was persuaded by *Peter Martyr to become a Protestant and, leaving Italy, he taught at Strasbourg under Johannes *Sturm. After the peace of *Schmalkalden he came to England at the invitation of Abp. T. *Cranmer (1547), and in 1549 succeeded Paul Fagius as the King's Reader of Hebrew at Cambridge University. Having returned to the Continent on the death of *Edward VI (1553), he became professor of OT studies at the University of Heidelberg in 1561. In 1577 he was expelled by Louis VI, the Lutheran Count Palatine, on account of his *Calvinistic opinions, and finally appointed by the Duc de Bouillon as a teacher of Hebrew at his newly founded college at Sedan. Tremellius's greatest work is his translation of the Old and New Testaments into Latin from Hebrew and Syriac respectively. This was long the standard Protestant Latin translation of the Bible. The NT (Syriac text with Lat. tr.) appeared in 1569; the OT (Lat. tr. only) in 5 parts between 1575 and 1579. Among his other works are a Hebrew and Greek Catechism (1551) and a Chaldean and Syriac Grammar (1569).

W. Becker, *Immanuel Tremellius, ein Proselytenleben im Zeitalter der Reformation* (1887; 2nd edn., 1890). G. Lloyd Jones, *The Discovery of Hebrew in Tudor England: A Third Language* (Manchester

[1983]), pp. 50–52. E. I. Carlyle in *DNB* 57 (1899), pp. 186 f. T. J. Ney in *PRE* (3rd edn.), 20 (1908), pp. 95–8, s.v.

Trench, Richard Chenevix (1807–86), Abp. of *Dublin. Educated at Harrow and Trinity College, Cambridge, he was ordained deacon in 1832. For a brief time he was curate at Hadleigh to H. J. *Rose and later (1841–4) to S. *Wilberforce at Alverstoke. He became rector of Itchenstoke (1844–5), professor of divinity at *King's College, London (1846–58), Dean of *Westminster (1856–1863), and finally Abp. of Dublin (1863–84). His two books on the Gospels, *Notes on the Parables of our Lord* (1841) and *Notes on the Miracles of our Lord* (1846), at once scholarly and stimulating, created a fresh interest in the Gospels in many quarters. Trench also took a keen interest in philology, the fruits of which included his *Study of Words* (1851) and *Synonyms of the NT* (1854). He also exercised a decisive influence in the early stages of the *Oxford English Dictionary*. In addition, he wrote much religious poetry. As Abp. of Dublin he vigorously opposed W. E. *Gladstone's proposals for disestablishing the Irish Church. His other publications included *Sacred Latin Poetry* (1849) and many volumes of sermons and poetry.

Letters and Memorials [ed. M. Trench] (2 vols., 1888). J. Bromley, *The Man of Ten Talents: A Portrait of Richard Chenevix Trench 1807–86* (1959). R. Bayne in *DNB* 57 (1899), pp. 191–4.

Trent, Council of (1545–63). This Council, reckoned by RC theologians the Nineteenth *Oecumenical Council, was the most impressive embodiment of the ideals of the *Counter-Reformation.

The spread of Protestantism and the drastic need of moral and administrative reforms within the RC Church led to widespread demand among Catholics for a Universal Council, but disputes between *Charles V and others who favoured such action, and the Popes, who were generally averse to it, long prevented a move. At last *Paul III summoned a council to Mantua for 23 May 1537, but the plan fell through owing to French resistance. In 1538 further proposals for a council at Vicenza were frustrated by the unexpected indifference of the Emperor. In 1542 the Pope again convoked the Council, this time to Trent. After yet another postponement it eventually met on 13 Dec. 1545. At the outset it was a very small assembly, composed of 3 legates, 1 cardinal, 4 archbishops, 21 bishops, and 5 generals of orders.

PERIOD I (1545–7; Sessions 1–8). As it was decided that voting should be by individual heads rather than (as at *Constance, 1415) by nations, the bishops from the Italian states had a preponderant influence on account of their numbers. The principal preliminary, whether the Council should first discuss dogma or disciplinary reform, was settled by the compromise that the subjects should be treated concurrently. The control of the presiding legates was then asserted and subsequently maintained through all the Sessions.

At Session 3 (4 Feb. 1546), the *Niceno-Constantinopolitan Creed was formally reaffirmed as the basis of faith. At Session 4 (8 Apr. 1546) the validity of both Scripture and unwritten *traditions as sources of truth, the sole right of the Church to interpret the Bible, and the authority of the text of the *Vulgate were asserted. The decrees of Session 5 (17 June 1546) on *Original Sin and of

Session 6 (13 Jan. 1547) on *justification and merit struck at the root of the Protestant system. No decision was reached, however, on many of the points in dispute on these matters in the Catholic schools. At Session 7 (3 Mar. 1547) the theology of the Sacraments in general was defined. The institution of all seven by Christ and their necessity to salvation were affirmed. Baptism and Confirmation were also treated in detail and a number of decrees on administrative reforms were also passed.

Meanwhile, renewed political tension between Charles V and the Pope hindered progress. An epidemic at Trent offered a pretext for transferring the Council to *Bologna (Session 8, 11 Mar. 1547). The Council was now virtually suspended for four years, until *Julius III (1550–5) reconvoked the assembly to Trent, which some prelates had refused to abandon.

PERIOD II (1551–2; Sessions 9–14). Important decisions were reached at Session 13 (11 Oct. 1551) on the *Eucharist and at Session 14 (25 Nov. 1551) on *Penance and Extreme *Unction. *Transubstantiation was affirmed and the *Lutheran, *Calvinist, and *Zwinglian Eucharistic doctrines repudiated. The Protestants present demanded renewed discussion of the subjects previously defined, the release of the bishops from their oaths of allegiance to the Papacy, and the supremacy of General Councils over the Pope.

The revolt of the princes against Charles V led to the suspension of the Council on 28 Apr. 1552. Under the austere and violently anti-Protestant *Paul IV (1555–9, Carafa) there was no hope of its reassembly, and it first met again ten years later under his more tolerant successor, *Pius IV.

PERIOD III (1562–3; Sessions 15–25). When the Council reassembled on 18 Jan. 1562, all hope of conciliating the Protestants had gone and the *Jesuits were now a strong force. The proceedings were henceforward hampered by struggles between the Papal and the opposition bishops, Imperial, Spanish, and French. A far-reaching plan of reform, devised by the Emp. Ferdinand II and advocated by the Cardinal of Lorraine (a Guise), failed. The Papal party owed its success largely to the diplomatic skill of the legate, Cardinal G. *Morone. At Session 21 (16 July 1562) the subject of Eucharistic Communion was treated and the presence of the undivided Christ under either species (*concomitance) and the adequacy of Communion in one kind was affirmed. Session 22 (17 Sept. 1562) issued a series of important definitions on the sacrificial doctrine of the Mass. Session 23 (15 July 1563) dealt with Orders and Session 24 (24 Nov. 1563) with the Sacrament of *Matrimony. Other work was done on the reform of the *Index and the residence of bishops. Of great practical significance was the legislation establishing clerical seminaries and regulating the appointment of bishops, provincial and diocesan synods, preaching of sermons, etc. Finally, Session 25 (3–4 Dec. 1563) dealt cursorily with *purgatory, the invocation of *saints, the veneration of *relics and *images, and *indulgences.

The Council ended on 4 Dec. 1563. The decrees were confirmed in a body on 26 Jan. 1564 by Pius IV, who in the same year published the 'Profession of the Tridentine Faith', a brief summary of doctrine, generally known as the *Creed of Pius IV.

Several important works, which the Council recommended or initiated but could not effectually carry through, were handed over to the Pope for completion. The revision of the Vulgate, ordered at Trent in 1546, was concluded under *Clement VIII in 1592; and *Pius V founded the Congregation of the Index in 1571 to carry out other unfinished work, having himself issued the '*Roman Catechism' (1566) and revised *Breviary (1568) and *Missal (1570).

Though the Council failed to satisfy the Protestants and its reforms were less comprehensive than many Catholics had hoped for, it had established a solid basis for the renewal of discipline and the spiritual life in the RC Church, which emerged from Trent with a clearly formulated doctrinal system and an enhanced religious strength for the subsequent struggle with Protestantism.

The *Acta* of the Council ed. A. Theiner (2 vols., Leipzig, 1874); the decrees have frequently been repr. and are conveniently available, with Eng. tr., in Tanner, *Decrees*, 2 (1990), pp. 657–799. The principal collections of docs. are J. Le Plat (ed.), *Monumentorum ad Historiam Concilii Tridentini Illustrandam Spectantium Collectio* (7 vols., Louvain, 1781–7) and the *Concilium Tridentinum: Diariorum, Actorum, Epistolarum, Tractatuum nova Collectio. Edidit Societas Goerresiana* (Freiburg i.B., 1901 ff.). J. Šusta (ed.), *Die römische Curie und das Concil von Trient unter Pius IV.: Actenstücke zur Geschichte des Concils von Trient* (4 vols., Vienna, 1904–14). S. Kuttner (ed.), *Decreta septem priorum sessionum Concilii Tridentini sub Paulo III Pont. Max.* (Washington, DC, 1945), reproducing in facsimile the autograph of A. Massarelli, Secretary of the Council, with important introd. H. Jedin, *Das Konzil von Trient: Ein Ueberblick ueber die Erforschung seiner Geschichte* (1948). J. Olazarán, SJ (ed.), *Documentos inéditos tridentinos sobre la Justificación* (Madrid, 1957). Early histories by P. *Sarpi, *Servite (under the pseudonym of P. S. Polano), *Historia del Concilio Tridentino* (London, 1619; Eng. tr. by N. Brent, Warden of Merton College, Oxford, Oxford, 1620; very hostile), and S. Pallavicino, SJ, *Istoria del Concilio di Trento* (2 vols., Rome, 1656–7; reply to preceding work). H. Jedin, *Geschichte des Konzils von Trient* (4 vols. in 5, 1949–75; Eng. tr., 1957 ff.); G. Schreiber (ed.), *Das Weltkonzil von Trient: Sein Werden und Wirken* (2 vols., 1951). H. Jedin, *Krisis und Abschluss des Trienter Konzils 1562/3* (Freiburg, 1964; Eng. tr., 1967). J. Lecler, SJ, and others in *Latran V et Trente* (Histoire des Conciles Œcuméniques publiée sous la direction de G. Dumeige, SJ, 10; 1975), pp. 115–470; idd., *Trente* (ibid. 11; 1981). J. M. R. Belloso, *Trento: Una Interpretación Teológica* (Colectánea San Paciano, 25; Barcelona, 1979); A. Duval, *Des Sacrements au Concile de Trente* (1985). R. V. Laurence in *CMH* 2 (1903), pp. 639–89, with bibl. pp. 818–24. P. Richard and A. Michel in Hefele and Leclercq, 9 and 10 (pt. 1) (1930–38). L. Cristiani in Fliche and Martin, 17 (1948), pp. 13–242. A. Michel in *DTC* 15 (pt. 1; 1946), cols. 1414–508, s.v. 'Trente (Concile de)'; H. Jedin in *NCE* 14 (1967), pp. 271–8, s.v., with further bibl. See also bibl. to COUNTER-REFORMATION.

Trental. A set of thirty *Requiem Masses for the repose of a soul, whether said on a single or on successive days. The word was also formerly in occasional use for a Mass or other service (also 'Month's Mind') on the 30th day after death or burial.

Treuga Dei. See TRUCE OF GOD.

Triad (Gk. τριάς). A word first used of the *Trinity in the Godhead by *Theophilus of Antioch, who names as the Triad 'God and His Word and His Wisdom' (*ad Autol*. 2. 15).

Tridentine. Having reference to the Council of *Trent (*Concilium Tridentinum*), 1545–63.

Triduum Sacrum (Lat., 'the sacred three days'). The three concluding days of *Holy Week commemorating the Last Supper, Passion, and Death of Christ, i.e. *Maundy Thursday (evening only, acc. to modern RC reckoning), *Good Friday, and *Holy Saturday.

Triers and Ejectors. Persons appointed to ensure the theological and political reliability of the English clergy. In 1640 a committee of Parliament was formed to eject 'scandalous' ministers [i.e. those with *Laudian or '*Arminian' sympathies] and in 1642 Parliament replaced it with a Committee for Plundered Ministers, which had the additional task of providing substitutes. Local committees were then formed to eject further 'scandalous ministers', particularly those who would not accept the *Solemn League and Covenant. A national commission of Triers was appointed by O. *Cromwell, under an Ordinance of 20 Mar. 1654, for the 'approbation' of all public preachers and lecturers before their admission to benefices. It consisted of 29 clerics and 9 laymen drawn from various regional bodies. On 28 Aug. 1654 new county commissions of Ejectors were appointed. Both Triers and Ejectors ceased work at the *Restoration of Charles II.

The 1654 Ordinance for appointing Triers is pr. in C. H. Firth and R. S. Rait (eds.), *Acts and Ordinances of the Interregnum, 1642–1660*, 2 (1911), pp. 855–8; that for appointing Ejectors, ibid., pp. 968–90. Much information on ejected clergy is collected in A. G. Matthews (ed.), *Walker Revised, being a Revision of John Walker's Sufferings of the Clergy during the Grand Rebellion 1642–60* (Oxford, 1948). Primary docs. concerning the committees in one county are ed. by C. Holmes, *The Suffolk Committees for Scandalous Ministers 1644–1646* (Suffolk Records Society, 13; 1970), with introd.

Trimmer, Sarah (1741–1810), authoress, known as 'Good Mrs. Trimmer'. Sarah Kirby was born at Ipswich, where her father, J. J. Kirby (1716–74), was an artist of some standing. She married in 1762 and had six sons and six daughters, whom she educated herself except for the boys' classics. She later interested herself esp. in the establishment of *Sunday Schools, a project which she ventilated in her book *The Oeconomy of Charity* (1786). In 1793 began her connection with the *SPCK, which published two of her books in the same year, *The Abridgment of the Old Testament* and *The Abridgment of the New Testament*, which were designed as textbooks for charity schools. The best known of her writings, *The History of the Robins* (1786; originally in *Fabulous Histories*), long remained a favourite children's book for the upper classes, whereas her numerous school books were intended for the instruction of the poor.

Some Account of the Life and Writings of Mrs. Trimmer (2 vols., 1814) contains mainly extracts from her private journals. E. Lee in *DNB* 57 (1899), pp. 231 f.

Trinitarian. A person who believes in the doctrine of the Holy *Trinity, esp. as contrasted with a *Unitarian. In the 15th and 16th cents., however, the word was occasionally applied to those who held heretical, as opposed to orthodox, views on the Trinity.

Trinitarians (Order of the Most Holy Trinity). This order was founded in 1198 at Cerfroid in the diocese of Meaux by St *John of Matha (d. 1213) and St Felix of Valois (d. 1212) with the approval of *Innocent III. Its members, also known as 'Mathurins', followed an austere form of the *Augustinian Rule, wearing a white habit with a cross 'flory' (upright *red*, crossbar *blue*) on the *scapular and cloak. They devoted themselves esp. to the ransoming of countless captives to which one third of their revenue was devoted; at the height of their influence in the 15th cent. they possessed about 800 houses. In 1596 a reform called the Barefooted Trinitarians was started in Spain by Fr. Juan Bautista of the Immaculate Conception. It became a distinct order and is the only body of Trinitarians that now survives (with some 400 priests and 40 lay brothers in 1993). Its members are engaged in education, nursing, and pastoral work. There were nuns affiliated to the order at an early date and other communities were founded in the 16th cent. The various contemplative communities (Calced and *Discalced) were united in 1972. There are a number of other Trinitarian communities of women engaged in educational and other social work.

Acta Ordinis S. Trinitatis, vol. 1 (Rome, 1919–23) includes important primary docs. P. Deslandres, *L'Ordre des Trinitaires pour le rachat des captifs* (2 vols., Toulouse, 1903). C. Mazzarisi di Gesù, OSST, *L'Ordine Trinitario nella Chiesa e nella Storia* (Turin [1964]). Antoninus ab Assumptione, Ord. Trinit., *Les Origines de l'ordre de la Très Sainte Trinité d'après les documents* (Rome, 1925). Id., *Ministrorum Generalium Ordinis SS. Trinitatis Series* (Isola del Liri, 1936), and other works of this author. G. Cipollone, OSST, *Studi intorno a Cerfroid, prima casa dell'ordine trinitario (1198–1429)* (Ordinis Trinitatis Institutum Historicum, 1st ser. 1; Rome, 1978); id., *La casa della Santa Trinità di Marsiglia (1202–1547): Prima fondazione sul mare dell'ordine trinitario* (ibid. 2; Vatican City, 1981). Further vols. planned. J. Pujana, OST, in *Dict. Sp.* 15 (1991), cols. 1259–87, s.v. 'Trinitaires', with extensive bibl.

Trinity, doctrine of the. The central dogma of Christian theology, that the one God exists in three Persons and one substance, Father, Son, and Holy Spirit. God is one, yet self-differentiated; the God who reveals Himself to mankind is one God equally in three distinct modes of existence, yet remains one through all eternity.

Though the word 'Trinity', first used in its Greek form τριάς by *Theophilus of Antioch (c. AD 180), is not found in Scripture, Christian theologians have seen adumbrations of the doctrine in the biblical narratives; in the OT, for example, the appearance of the three men to *Abraham (Gen. 18) was held by the Fathers to foreshadow the revelation of the threefold nature of God. In the NT the most influential text was the reference to the three Persons in the baptismal formula at the end of Mt. (28: 19), but there are other passages held to have Trinitarian overtones, such as the Pauline benediction of 2 Cor. 13: 14. From the biblical language concerning Father, Son (or *Logos), and Spirit, Trinitarian doctrine developed, as the Church's expansion led to the need for reflection, confession, and dialogue.

Finding the appropriate concepts was not easy, and many 2nd- and 3rd-cent. Christians adopted views that were later considered unorthodox. These included the so-called 'economic Trinity', in which the distinctions between the Persons depended solely on their distinct functions (or 'economies') towards the created universe.

*Tertullian taught that the divine Word existed originally within the Father's mind, and first became a distinct Person when the world was created; the Spirit's Personality was subsequent to that of the Word; they were thus not strictly co-eternal with the Father. *Origen conceived the Word (or Son) as the offspring of the Father and the Spirit as coming into being through the Word; their special roles were respectively to control the universe and inspire the saints. Such *subordinationism is not counterbalanced by Origen's affirmation of the eternal generation of the Word from the Father, since Origen held that the whole universe of created spirits had always existed in some form, so that the Word's co-eternity with the Father does not entail equality. These subordinationist views echoed those of contemporary *Platonists, who envisaged three eternal divine powers arranged in descending order of dignity. The opposite deviation, extreme *Modalism, pictured only one divine Person who acted successively as creator, redeemer, and sanctifier.

At the Councils of *Nicaea (325) and *Constantinople (381) the doctrine was defined in its simplest outlines, by negative rather than positive pronouncements, affirming against *Sabellianism the real distinction of the divine Persons, and against *Arianism and *Macedonianism their equality and co-eternity. The Persons differ only in origin, in that the Father is ungenerated, the Son is generated by the Father, and the Holy Spirit proceeds from the Father. Some E. Fathers (notably St *Gregory of Nyssa and St *Cyril of Alexandria) understood the Spirit to proceed from the Father through the Son; others are less explicit (e.g. St *Gregory of Nazianzus) or deny any '*double procession' altogether (e.g. *Theodoret). Later, from the time of *Photius, the doctrine of the procession of the Holy Spirit from the Father alone became characteristic of E. theology. In a 7th-cent. work on the Trinity, attributed to Cyril of Alexandria and largely incorporated in the *De Orthodoxa Fide* of St *John of Damascus, the doctrine of the mutual indwelling of the Persons of the Trinity (περιχώρησις or *circumincession), already implicit in the Trinitarian theology of the Cappadocian Fathers and in *Dionysius the Pseudo-Areopagite, was developed.

In the W., the doctrine was developed in a somewhat different manner. Starting not from the difference of the Persons, as did many of the more philosophically minded Greek Fathers, but from the unity of the Substance, it readily safeguarded the co-equality of the Persons. The procession of the Holy Spirit was attributed both to the Father and the Son. The chief exponent of the teaching of the Latin Church during the patristic period was St *Augustine, esp. in his 'De Trinitate'; his great contribution was the comparison of the two processes of the Divine life (the later 'filiation' and 'spiration') to the analogical processes of human self-knowledge and self-love. Whereas his conception of the generation of the Son as the act of thinking on the part of the Father was based on Tertullian, the explanation of the Holy Spirit as the mutual love of the Father and the Son was the fruit of his own reflections. This so-called 'psychological theory of the Trinity' was taken over from him and developed by medieval Scholasticism. In its more formal aspects, medieval teaching on the Trinity reasserted the doctrines of the *Athanasian Creed. It received classical exposition in the writings of St *Thomas Aquinas.

The Trinitarian teaching thus elaborated by the School-men, though challenged in the 17th cent. by *Socinianism and *Unitarianism, has remained the central strand of subsequent W. theology. In the 20th cent. both K. *Barth and K. *Rahner have made considerable contributions to the subject, both emphasizing the essential unity of the immanent and the economic Trinity. Other scholars, e.g. G. W. H. Lampe, have sought to maintain the Divinity of Christ while regarding Trinitarian doctrine as basically outdated. J. *Moltmann has developed a distinctive doctrine of the social Trinity, reviving a version of the patristic theory of circumincession to express the self-differentiation of God as the crucified God. A number of scholars, notably Walter Kasper, have re-examined the *Filioque controversy in an ecumenical context.

Discussions of the doctrine of the Trinity figure in all works on Christian dogmatics and in writings concerned with the nature of God. Modern studies devoted to the subject as a whole incl. F. C. *Baur, *Die christliche Lehre von der Dreieinigkeit und Menschwerdung Gottes in ihrer geschichtlichen Entwicklung* (3 vols., 1841–3); T. de Régnon, SJ, *Études de théologie positive sur la Sainte Trinité* (4 vols., 1892–8); J. Lebreton, SJ, *Histoire du dogme de la Trinité* (Bibliothèque de Théologie Historique, 2 vols., 1910–28; Eng. tr. of vol. 1; 1939); A. E. J. Rawlinson (ed.), *Essays on the Trinity and the Incarnation* (1928); K. Barth, *Kirchliche Dogmatik*, 1. 1 (Munich, 1932), pp. 311–514; Eng. tr. (Edinburgh, 1975), pp. 295–489; P. Galtier, SJ, *De SS. Trinitate in se et in nobis* (Paris, 1933); G. L. Prestige, *God in Patristic Thought* (1936), *passim*; L. Hodgson, *The Doctrine of the Trinity* (Croall Lectures, 1942–3; 1943); V. *Lossky, *Essai sur la théologie mystique de l'Eglise d'Orient* (1944), pp. 43–86 and 131–69; Eng. tr. (1957), pp. 44–90 and 135–73; R. S. Franks, *The Doctrine of the Trinity* (1953); C. C. Richardson, *The Doctrine of the Trinity* (New York, 1958); A. W. Wainwright, *The Trinity in the New Testament* (1962); E. Jüngel, *Gottes Sein ist im Werden* (Tübingen, 1965; Eng. tr., 1976); K. Rahner, 'Der dreifaltige Gott als transzendenter Urgrund der Heilsgeschichte', in J. Feiner and M. Löhrer (eds.), *Mysterium Salutis*, 2 (1967), pp. 317–401; separate Eng. tr., *The Trinity* (1970); also other arts. in *Mysterium Salutis*, 2, esp. pp. 47–220; B. de Margérie, SJ, *La Trinité Chrétienne dans l'Histoire* (Théologie Historique, 31 [1975]); G. W. H. Lampe, *God as Spirit* (Bampton Lectures, 1976; Oxford, 1977); J. Moltmann, *Trinität und Reich Gottes* (Munich, 1980; Eng. tr., 1981); W. [J.] Kasper, *Der Gott Jesu Christi* (Glaubensbekenntnis der Kirche, 1; 1982; Eng. tr., New York, 1983; London, 1984); D. Brown, *The Divine Trinity* (1985); T. F. Torrance, *The Trinitarian Faith: The Evangelical Theology of the Ancient Catholic Church* (Edinburgh, 1988); id., *The Christian Doctrine of God, One Being Three Persons* (ibid., 1996); F. Courth, *Trinität in der Schrift und Patristik* (Handbuch der Dogmengeschichte, ed. M. Schmaus and others, 2, fasc. 1a; 1988). G. Bardy and A. Michel in *DTC* 15 (pt. 2; 1950), cols. 1545–855, s.v. 'Trinité', with detailed bibl.

Trinity College, Dublin.

The (one) College in the University of *Dublin, founded in 1591. Membership was long confined to Anglicans but religious tests were eventually abolished in 1873. Since 1904 women have been admitted to degrees. The College is governed by a Provost and Fellows and is represented in Seanad Eireann. The library has a very valuable collection of Irish and other MSS, among them the 'Book of *Kells', and the 'Book of *Armagh' (qq.v.).

J. P. Mahaffy and others, *The Book of Trinity College, Dublin* (1892); J. P. Mahaffy, *An Epoch in Irish History: Trinity College, Dublin, its Foundation and Early Fortunes, 1591–1660* (1903). C. Maxwell, *A History of Trinity College, Dublin, 1591–1892* (Dublin,

1946); K. C. Bailey, *A History of Trinity College, Dublin, 1892–1945* (ibid., 1947); R. B. Dowell and D. A. Webb, *Trinity College, Dublin 1592–1952* (Cambridge, 1982). J. V. Luce, *Trinity College, Dublin, the first 400 years* (Dublin, 1992). G. D. Burtchaell and T. U. Sadleir (eds.), *Alumni Dublinenses: A Register of the Students, Graduates, Professors and Provosts of Trinity College, in the University of Dublin* (1924; rev. and cont., 1935).

Trinity Sunday.

The first Sunday after *Pentecost or *Whitsun. It was not till the Middle Ages that the Sunday was at all widely observed as a separate feast in honour of the Holy Trinity. Its observance, introduced to mark the conclusion of the liturgical commemorations of the life of Christ and the descent of the Holy Spirit by a celebration embracing God in all three Persons, was universally enjoined by Pope *John XXII in 1334. The feast became specially popular in England, perhaps by its association with St Thomas *Becket, who was consecrated bishop on that day (1162). The restriction of the feast to a single day by the absence of an octave is appropriate to the Unity of the Godhead which the feast commemorates. Sundays are reckoned after Trinity in the *Sarum Missal and in the BCP. They were formerly also reckoned after Trinity (or after the first Sunday after Trinity) in the *Carmelite, *Dominican, and *Carthusian Orders and not after *Pentecost as was usual in the Roman Rite until 1969.

A. Klaus, OFM, *Ursprung und Verbreitung der Dreifaltigkeitsmesse* (1938). F. *Cabrol, OSB, 'Le Culte de la Trinité dans la liturgie de la fête de la Trinité', *EL* 45 (1931), pp. 270–8. P. Browe, SJ, 'Zur Geschichte des Dreifaltigkeitsfestes', *Archiv für Liturgiewissenschaft*, 1 (1950), pp. 65–81.

Triodion

(Gk. τριῴδιον). In the Byzantine rite, the liturgical book containing the variable portions of the services from the 4th Sunday before *Lent till the Saturday before *Easter. It is so named because during this season the *canons ordinarily contain only three odes (ᾠδαί) instead of the usual nine. In the Slavonic Churches the Triodion is called the 'Fasting Triodion' to distinguish it from the 'Flowery Triodion', the Slavonic term for the *Pentecostarion.

Partial Eng. tr. by Mother Mary and K. [T. R.] Ware, *The Lenten Triodion* (1978). H. J. Schulz in *L.Th.K.* (2nd edn.), 10 (1965), cols. 363 f.

triple candlestick.

The candlestick used until 1955 in the Latin Rite at the 'Lumen Christi', in the liturgy of *Holy Saturday, to hold the three candles which were successively lighted in the course of the procession up to the altar. It was commonly mounted on a long pole. A triple candlestick (together with a double candlestick) is also used in the E. Church for episcopal blessings at the Liturgy. The bishop holds one candlestick in each hand, the one symbolizing the Trinity, the other the two natures of Christ.

Trisagion

(Gk. τρισάγιον, 'thrice holy'). The refrain 'Holy God, Holy and strong, Holy and immortal, have mercy upon us' is a characteristic feature of *Orthodox worship. It is solemnly chanted in all E. liturgies before the lections, except at certain great feasts, and is recited at all other services. It occurred also in the *Gallican liturgy, and in the Roman rite it is sung as part of the *Reproaches on Good Friday. The earliest datable occurrence of the word is in the Acts of the Council of *Chalcedon (451). At Jerusalem, Constantinople, and in the W. the Trisagion was taken to be addressed to the Trinity; in Syria, parts of Asia Minor and in Egypt in the 5th cent. it was understood as referring to Christ. These differing interpretations were reflected in the controversy over *Theopaschism.

J. M. Hanssens, SJ, *Institutiones Liturgicae de Ritibus Orientalibus*, 3 (pt. 2; Rome, 1932), pp. 96–156. L. Brou, OSB, 'Études sur la liturgie mozarabe. Le Trisagion de la Messe d'après les sources manuscrites', *EL* 61 (1947), pp. 309–34. V.-S. Janeras, 'Les Byzantins et le Trisagion Christologique', in *Miscellanea Liturgica in onore di sua Eminenza il Cardinale Giacomo Lercaro*, 2 (1967), pp. 469–99. E. Klum-Böhmer, *Das Trishagion als Versöhnungsformel der Christenheit: Kontroverstheologie im V. und VI. Jahrhundert* (Munich, 1979). S. [P.] Brock, 'The thrice-holy hymn in the Liturgy', *Sobornost/Eastern Churches Review*, vol. 7, no. 2 (1985), pp. 24–34.

Tritheism. The heretical teaching about the Trinity which denies the unity of substance in the Three Divine Persons. The name is esp. applied to the teaching of a group of 6th-cent. *Monophysites, the best known of whom was *John Philoponus; he taught that the common nature shared by the Three Persons is an intellectual abstraction, and that though the Father, Son, and Holy Spirit have a common nature and substance (are 'consubstantial'), they are as individuals distinct substances or natures and also distinct in their properties. This teaching was condemned as tritheism at the Third Council of *Constantinople (680–1). In the Middle Ages the extreme *Nominalism of *Roscelin and the exaggerated *Realism of *Gilbert de la Porrée caused both these Schoolmen to be accused of teaching tritheistic doctrines; and they were condemned by the Councils of *Soissons (c.1092) and of *Reims (1148) respectively. Gilbert's doctrines later influenced *Joachim of Fiore and issued in a firm declaration of the numerical unity of the Divine Nature by the Fourth *Lateran Council (1215). A more recent exponent of tritheistic teaching was A. *Günther, who, in his struggle against *Hegelian pantheism, affirmed the existence of three absolute realities in the Trinity, distinct from each other and bound together only by a unity of origin. Popular ideas about the Trinity, in intention orthodox, often tend to be tritheistic in expression.

Trithemius, Johannes (1462–1516), Abbot of Sponheim, so named from his birthplace, Trittenheim, on the Moselle. After harsh treatment at the hands of his stepfather, he fled to Würzburg, where his intellectual powers developed rapidly and he came into close contact with the humanist movement. A chance visit to the monastery of Sponheim in 1482 led him to join the community, and in 1483 he was elected its abbot. He rapidly brought about its reform, collecting a library of MSS which soon made it one of the most famous in Europe. In 1506, however, through dissensions caused by the stringency of his discipline, he was induced to resign his abbacy, and for his last ten years he presided over the Scottish abbey of St Jakob at Würzburg. His writings include many useful historical compilations, e.g. *De Viris Illustribus Germaniae* (1495); works on natural science and magic, e.g. *Steganographia* (pub. 1606); and some fine sermons.

Theological writings first pub., Mainz, 1604 and 1605; Historical writings, Frankfurt, 1601; Letters, Dresden, 1536. Modern edn. of his *De Laude Scriptorum* by K. Arnold (Mainfränkische Heft, 10; Würzburg, 1973; repr., with Eng. tr., Lawrence, Kan., 1974). Studies by id. (Quellen und Forschungen zur Geschichte des Bistums und Hochstifts Würzburg, 23; 1971; 2nd edn., 1991) and N. L. Brann [in Eng.] (Studies in the History of Christian Thought, 24; Leiden, 1981), both with bibl. of earlier works. P. Séjourné, OSB, in *DTC* 15 (pt. 2; 1950), cols. 1862–7.

Trito-Isaiah. The name coined by B. *Duhm in 1892 for the author of the last 11 chapters of Isaiah (56–66), in the belief that they were written by a later prophet than the 6th-cent. 'Deutero-Isaiah' who wrote chs. 40–55. The term is also in current use for chs. 56–66 themselves, even when they are not held to be the work of a single individual.

triumphant, the Church. The body of Christians in heaven, i.e. the perfected saints, distinguished from those still on earth (*militant) and those in *purgatory (*expectant). See COMMUNION OF SAINTS.

trivium. The medieval name for the group of three sciences consisting of grammar, rhetoric, and dialectic, which together constituted the inferior group of the *seven liberal arts.

Troas. A city of NW Asia Minor visited several times by St *Paul. It was on his first visit here that he saw the vision of 'a man of Macedonia' which led him to carry the Gospel into Europe (Acts 16: 8–11).

Troeltsch, Ernst (1865–1923), theologian and philosopher. A native of Augsburg, he taught theology successively at Göttingen (1891–2), Bonn (1892–4), and Heidelberg (1894–1915). From 1915 until his death he was professor of the history of philosophy and civilization at Berlin.

In theological outlook Troeltsch was much influenced by A. *Ritschl, in philosophy by the Neo-Kantian Wilhelm Windelband (1848–1915) and Heinrich Rickert (1863–1936), and in the religious understanding and assessment of culture by W. *Dilthey. His originality as a theologian lay in his application of sociological theory to theology, notably in *Die Soziallehren der christlichen Kirchen und Gruppen* (1912; Eng. tr., 2 vols., 1931). He was also among the first seriously to consider the claims to truth of other world religions alongside Christianity in *Die Absolutheit des Christentums und die Religionsgeschichte* (1902; Eng. tr., 1972) and *Der Historismus und seine Probleme* (1922). This position led him into increasing relativism, esp. in *Christian Thought: Its History and Application* (1923). Close students of Troeltsch in Britain included F. *von Hugel and C. C. J. *Webb.

Gesammelte Schriften (4 vols., Tübingen, 1912–25). Eng. tr. of his *Writings on Theology and Religion* by R. Morgan and M. Pye (1977), and *Religion in History* by J. L. Adams and W. F. Bense (Edinburgh, 1991). Studies by E. Vermeil (Études d'Histoire et de Philosophie religieuses, 2; 1922), W. [E.] Köhler (Tübingen, 1941), W. Bodenstein (Gütersloh, 1959), W. F. Kasch (Beiträge zur historischen Theologie, 34; 1963), J. P. Clayton (ed.), *Ernest Troeltsch and the Future of Theology* (1976), S. Coakley, *Christ without Absolutes: A Study of the Christology of Ernst Troeltsch* (Oxford, 1988), W. E. Wyman (American Academy of Religion,

Academy Series, 44; Chico, Calif., 1983), and H.-G. Drescher (Göttingen, 1991; Eng. tr., 1992). H. Renz and F. W. Graf (eds.), *Troeltsch-Studien* (Gütersloh, 1982 ff.). F. W. Graf and H. Ruddies, *Ernst Troeltsch Bibliographie* (Tübingen, 1982).

troparion (Gk. τροπάριον). In the E. Church, a generic term to designate a stanza of religious poetry. In particular it is applied to the *Apolytikion, which is often known as the 'troparion of the day'.

E. [J.] Wellesz, *A History of Byzantine Music and Hymnography* (1949), pp. 144–52. L. Clugnet, *Dictionnaire grec-français des noms liturgiques* (1895), pp. 153–5, s.v. τροπάριον. Bardenhewer, 4, pp. 130–2 ('Tropariendichter'). A. Raes, SJ, in *EC* 12 (1954), cols. 571 f.

trope. In the W. Church, a phrase or sentence, with its music, introducing, or interpolated into, any of the chants of the Mass and some of those of the Divine *Office. The words are often highly poetic. They were intended to embellish, increase the solemnity, and deepen understanding of the texts to which they were attached. Some 200 trope MSS have survived, a tenth of them dating from the 10th cent. Tropes for the *Proper flourished particularly in the 11th cent. and then went out of use; those for the *Ordinary continued and developed until tropes were forbidden by the Council of *Trent. The 'Troper' is a collection of such pieces, and can also contain *sequences.

C. Blume, SJ, and H. M. Bannister (eds.), *Tropen des Missals im Mittelalter* (AHMA 47 and 49; 1905–6); R. Jonsson and others (eds.), *Corpus Troporum* (Acta Universitatis Stockholmiensis, Studia Latina Stockholmiensia, 21, 22, 25, 26, 31, 32, 34, etc.; 1975 ff.), with extensive bibl. in vol. 3, pp. 363–77. W. H. *Frere (ed.), *The Winchester Troper* (HBS 8; 1894), with introd. L. Gautier, *Histoire de la poésie liturgique au moyen âge: Les Tropes*, 1 (1886; all pub.). *Liturgische Tropen: Referate zweier Colloquien des Corpus Troparum in München (1983) und Canterbury (1984)*, ed. G. Silagi (Münchener Beiträge zur Mediävistik und Renaissance-Forschung, 36; 1985); *Pax et Sapientia: Studies in Text and Music of Liturgical Tropes and Sequences in Memory of Gordon Anderson*, ed. R. Jacobsson (Studia Latina Stockholmiensia, 29; 1986). H. Husmann, *Tropen- und Sequenzenhandschriften* (Répertoire international des sources musicales, B.5.1 [1964]); A. E. Planchart, *The Repertory of Tropes at Winchester* (2 vols., Princeton, NJ, 1977). J. Szövérffy, *Die Annalen der Lateinischen Hymnendichtung*, 1 (1964), esp. pp. 275–81. B. Stäblein in *Die Musik in Geschichte und Gegenwart*, 13 (1966), cols. 797–826, s.v. 'Tropus'; R. Steiner in S. Sadie (ed.), *New Grove Dictionary of Music and Musicians*, 19 (1980), pp. 172–87, s.v.

Trophimus, St. (1) Acc. to Acts 20: 4 and 21: 29, he was an Ephesian Gentile, who accompanied St *Paul on part of his third missionary journey and to *Jerusalem, where Paul's introduction of him into the Temple was the chief ground for the riot. He is also mentioned at 2 Tim. 4: 20 ('Trophimus I left at Miletum sick'). In the Gk. *Menology he is reckoned one of the Seventy (cf. Lk. 10: 1) and commemorated with St Aristarchus (cf. Acts 19: 29, etc.) and St *Pudens on 14 Apr.

(2) St Trophimus, traditionally reckoned the first Bp. of Arles, is first mentioned in 417 in an Ep. of Pope *Zosimus to Patroclus, Bp. of Arles, as an early preacher of the Gospel sent from Rome to Gaul. Acc. to St *Gregory of Tours he was one of the bishops who came to Gaul with St *Dionysius of Paris. At Arles as early as the 5th cent. he was identified with the Trophimus of the NT in

furtherance of the city's claim to primatial status, and he became greatly venerated. Feast day, 29 Dec.

(1) See comm. to Acts, cited s.v., and to Titus, Epistle to, cited s.v. TIMOTHY AND TITUS, EPISTLES TO. J. Polien in *Anchor Bible Dictionary*, 6 (1992), pp. 667 f., s.v.

(2) L. *Duchesne, *Fastes épiscopaux de l'ancienne Gaule*, 1 (1894), pp. 246 f., with refs. E. Caspar, *Geschichte des Papsttums*, 1 (1930), esp. pp. 347 f. and 449 f. E. Griffe, *La Gaule chrétienne à l'époque romaine*, 1 (2nd edn., 1964), pp. 104–8. L. Levillain, 'Saint Trophime, confesseur et métropolitain d'Arles et la Mission des Sept en Gaule. Étude d'un texte de Grégoire de Tours et d'un passage de la Passion de Saint Saturnin', *Revue d'Histoire de l'Église de France*, 13 (1927), pp. 145–89. S. A. Bennett in *DCB* 4 (1887), p. 1055, s.v.; M.-O. Garrigues in *Bibliotheca Sanctorum*, 12 (1969), cols. 665–72, s.v. 'Trofimo di Arles'.

Truce of God (Lat. *pax*, *treuga Dei*). In medieval times, a suspension of hostilities ordered by the Church on certain days and during certain seasons. The institution goes back to attempts to remedy the feudal anarchy of the 11th cent. By a canon of the Council of Elne of 1027, the conduct of hostilities between Saturday night and Monday morning was forbidden. At a later date *Advent and *Lent were also brought within the Truce.

Trullan Synod. The synod held in 692 by the E. bishops to pass disciplinary canons to complete the work of the Fifth (553) and Sixth (680–1) General Councils (hence its other name of Πενθέκτη, 'Quinisext', or Fifth-Sixth, Council). It sat in the domed room ('trullus') of the Emp. Justinian II's palace at *Constantinople, where the Sixth General Council had also met. The disciplinary decrees of the synod were rejected by the Pope and, though by no means completely observed in the E., served to accentuate the growing division between W. and E. practice. They are sometimes quoted (wrongly) as having been passed by the Sixth General Council, and as such seem to have received some sort of recognition by Pope *Hadrian I (772–95). The subjects legislated on included clerical marriage, ecclesiastical dress, the age of ordination, and affinity and other impediments to matrimony.

There survive only the Council's allocution to the Emperor and the 102 Canons, with the signatures of the participants of the Council. Hardouin, 3, cols. 1645–712; Mansi, 11 (Florence, 1765), cols. 929–1006. Texts also pr., with Fr. tr., in Joannou, 1, pt. 1 (1962), pp. 98–241. Hefele and Leclercq, 3 (pt. 1; 1909), pp. 560–81. V. Laurent, 'L'Œuvre canonique du Concile in Trullo (691–692), source primaire du droit de l'Église orientale', *Revue des Études byzantines*, 23 (1965), pp. 7–41. H. Ohme, *Das Concilium Quinisextum und seine Bischofsliste: Studien zum Konstantinopeler Konzil von 692* (Arbeiten zur Kirchengeschichte, 56; 1990). J. M. Hussey, *The Orthodox Church in the Byzantine Empire* (Oxford History of the Christian Church, 1986), pp. 24–9. *CPG* 4 (1980), p. 184 (nos. 9443 f.). G. Fritz in *DTC* 13 (pt. 2; 1937), cols. 1581–97, s.v. 'Quinisexte (Concile)'. See also bibl. to SERGIUS I.

Trumpets, Feast of. A Jewish feast kept on the first day of the seventh month (i.e. Tishri, Oct.), the observance of which is ordained in Lev. 23: 24 and Num. 29: 1. It is now regarded by the Jews as New Year's Day ('Rosh ha-Shanah').

Truro. The Anglican diocese of Truro was created in 1877, out of the Archdeaconry of Cornwall, previously in the diocese of *Exeter. Until Anglo-Saxon times the Cornish Church had been independent, and it is probable that the British bishops who assisted in St *Chad's consecration (664) were Cornish. In 931 the Cornish Church was finally incorporated with the English Church and Cornwall became an English diocese. In 1027 it was annexed to the see of *Crediton, and in 1050 the see of the united diocese was fixed at Exeter. In 1877, when Truro became the see of the reconstituted diocese, E. W. *Benson became its first bishop. The fine cathedral church of St Mary, designed by J. L. *Pearson in the Early English style and incorporating the south aisle of the old parish church, was begun in 1880 and completed in 1910. The Community of the Epiphany, founded in London c.1880 by G. H. Wilkinson, the second Bp. of Truro, when Vicar of St Peter's, Eaton Square, London, has its mother house at Truro.

A. B. Donaldson, *The Bishopric of Truro: The First Twenty-Five Years, 1877–1902* (1902); H. M. Brown, *A Century for Cornwall: The Diocese of Truro, 1877–1977* (Truro, 1976). [L.] F. Barham, *The Creation of a Cathedral: The Story of St Mary's, Truro* (Falmouth [1976]).

Truth, Gospel of. See EVANGELIUM VERITATIS.

Tübingen. The university for Württemberg, founded in 1477, soon grew in importance and numbered many celebrities among its early teachers, e.g. G. *Biel and P. *Melanchthon (1514–18). When Württemberg was made Protestant by Duke Ulrich in 1534–5, Tübingen became a centre of *Lutheran orthodoxy and increased the number and standard of its students through the famous 'Stift', a kind of public school at which later G. W. F. *Hegel and F. W. J. *Schelling were educated. In the 18th cent. G. C. Storr founded the older 'Tübingen School' of theology. Its chief characteristic was a 'biblical supranaturalism', which put the guarantee of Christ and the Apostles in the place of the orthodox Protestant doctrine of the inspiration of Scripture and regarded the Bible as the exclusive source and law book of Christianity, from which the tenets of faith were to be derived by purely deductive methods. In the early part of the 19th cent. another school of theology was formed under the influence of Hegel, F. C. *Baur being its leader and chief representative (see TÜBINGEN SCHOOL). In 1817 a Catholic faculty of theology was opened which soon became one of the most important centres of Catholic scholarship in Germany, counting among its members J. A. *Möhler and K. J. *Hefele and, in recent times, K. *Adam and H. *Küng. The Catholic school has been characterized by a combination of the historical and speculative methods, and by its emphasis on the need for relating modern thought to the data of the faith.

J. Haller, *Die Anfänge der Universität Tübingen 1477–1537* (2 vols., Stuttgart, 1927–9). H. *Rashdall, *The Universities of Europe in the Middle Ages*, 2 (ed. F. M. Powicke and A. B. Emden, 1936), pp. 278–80, with full bibl. H. Hermelink, *Die theologische Fakultät in Tübingen vor der Reformation 1477–1534* (1906). M. Brecht (ed.), *Theologen und Theologie an der Universität Tübingen: Beiträge zur Geschichte der Evangelisch-Theologischen Fakultät* (Contubernium. Beiträge zur Geschichte der Eberhard-Karls-Universität Tübingen, 15; 1977). On the Catholic faculty, see E. Vermeil, *Jean-Adam Möhler et l'école catholique de Tubingue, 1815–1840* (1913), the special number of *Th.Q.* to mark the 450th anniversary of the foundation of the university (*Th.Q.* 128; 1927, pp.

1–220), J. R. Geiselmann, *Die katholische Tübinger Schule: Ihre theologische Eigenart* (Freiburg, etc., 1964), J. T. Burtchaell, CSC, 'Drey, Möhler and the Catholic School of Tübingen', in [R.] N. Smart and others (eds.), *Nineteenth Century Religious Thought in the West*, 2 (Cambridge, 1985), pp. 111–39, and D. McCready, *Jesus Christ for the Modern World: The Christology of the Catholic Tübingen School* (American University Studies, 7th ser. 77; 1991).

Tübingen School. A school of German NT theologians founded by F. C. *Baur. Among its most prominent members were Eduard Zeller, who edited its organ, the *Tübinger Theologische Jahrbücher* (1842–57), and A. *Hilgenfeld, who continued it as the *Zeitschrift für wissenschaftliche Theologie* (1858–1914). The principal endeavour of the School was to apply G. W. F. *Hegel's conception of development to primitive Christianity. The early Church was to be divided into 'Petrinists' (Jewish Christians) and 'Paulinists' (Gentile Christians), the cleavage between them being healed only in the later 2nd cent. ('Catholicism'). This state of things is reflected in the books of the NT, several of which represent the views of one or other of the parties, the bulk, however, being products of the 2nd cent. synthesis and therefore of practically no historical value for the period to which they profess to refer. These theories were expressed most vigorously in A. *Schwegler's *Nachapostolisches Zeitalter* (1846), which assigns to Mk. a date later than St *Justin Martyr, and sees in Baptism and the Episcopate substitutes introduced by the Judaizers for circumcision and the aristocracy of Israel respectively. The school was at the height of its influence in the 1840s, but it soon lost its prestige through the discrepancy between its axioms and historical fact. A. *Ritschl, who for a time belonged to the group, later founded a school of his own. Since A. *Harnack the Tübingen position has been generally abandoned. For the Catholic Tübingen School, see the previous entry.

The chief sources are, besides the writings of its leading members (qq.v.), the *Theologische Jahrbücher* mentioned above. R. W. Mackay, *The Tübingen School and its Antecedents* (1863). E. Zeller, *Vorträge und Abhandlungen* (1865), pp. 267–353 ('Die Tübinger historische Schule'). H. Harris, *The Tübingen School* (Oxford, 1975).

Tuckney, Anthony (1599–1670), *Puritan divine. He was educated at Emmanuel College, Cambridge, where he was elected a Fellow in 1619. In 1633 he became vicar of Boston, Lincs. In 1643 he was nominated to the *Westminster Assembly, where as chairman of committee he took a leading part in the drawing-up of its doctrinal formularies, the section on the Decalogue in the 'Larger Catechism' being his work. He then became master successively of Emmanuel (1645) and St John's (1653) colleges, Cambridge, and in 1656 also Regius professor of divinity. After the Restoration he was superseded in his mastership and his chair, and passed the rest of his life in retirement. He published little and his chief works are posthumous, but his four letters to B. *Whichcote, published with the replies as an appendix to the latter's *Moral and Religious Aphorisms* (1753), illustrate the strength of his Puritan convictions, his fear of the rationalistic tendencies of the *Cambridge Platonists, and his charity towards the opinions of his opponents.

Forty Sermons upon Several Occasions, ed. by his son, J. Tuckney (London, 1676); *Praelectiones Theologicae*, ed. id. (Amsterdam,

1679), with short biog. preface by W. D[illingham] (no pagination). 'Eight Letters of Dr. Anthony Tuckney and Dr. Benjamin Whichcote' are appended to Whichcote's *Moral and Religious Aphorisms*, ed. S. Salter (1753; separate pagination), with preface, pp. i–xl. J. *Tulloch, *Rational Theology and Christian Philosophy in England in the Seventeenth Century*, 2 (1872), pp. 47, 53–5, and 59–84; J. B. Mullinger, *The University of Cambridge*, 3 (1911), pp. 529–32, 576–8, 591–4, and *passim*. J. D. Roberts, *From Puritanism to Platonism in Seventeenth Century England* (The Hague, 1968), pp. 42–65. A. Gordon in *DNB* 57 (1899), pp. 286–8.

Tulchan Bishops. Term contemptuously applied to the titular bishops introduced into the Reformed Church of Scotland after a concordat in the Assembly of Leith (1572). They were to be responsible to the General Assembly, but they became tools of the lay nobles who drew the revenues of their sees. The term derives from the Gaelic *tulachan*, 'little hillock', used to describe the device of stuffing a calf's skin with straw to deceive a cow into giving milk: a reference to the bishops' diversion of revenues. On his return from Geneva (1574), A. *Melville condemned episcopacy in any form as incompatible with a pure Church, and the office of bishop was abolished in the *Second Book of *Discipline* (1581); however, the ban was never fully enforceable, and from the late 1580s the episcopal office was put on an increasingly strong footing until swept away by the violent reaction to the ecclesiastical policies of *Charles I expressed in the Scottish *National Covenant (1638).

Tulloch, John (1823–86), Scottish theologian. Ordained in the Church of Scotland, he became in 1854, after several years' parochial work, Principal and professor of theology at St Mary's College, St Andrews. From about 1875 he was the most prominent member of his Church, and in 1878 was elected *Moderator. He is chiefly remembered for the prominent part he took in trying to awaken a spirit of liberal orthodoxy in the Church of Scotland. He sought to defend its comprehensiveness in doctrine and did not wish its members to be bound to the letter of its credal formularies. His most important treatise was his *Rational Theology and Christian Philosophy in England in the Seventeenth Century* (2 vols., 1872).

Memoir by Mrs [M. O. W.] Oliphant (Edinburgh, 1888). T. Bayne in *DNB* 57 (1899), pp. 307–10.

tunicle. In the W. rite the outer liturgical garment of the *subdeacon. Until 1968 it was also worn by the bishop under his *dalmatic and *chasuble. It seems to have developed out of the ordinary overcoat (*tunica*) of the later Empire, though without the usual girdle. St *Gregory I (*Ep*. 9. 26) suppressed it at Rome, but it survived in other places and was reintroduced at Rome *c.*1000. Its further development was closely parallel with that of the dalmatic. The tunicle formerly differed from it in possessing no *clavi* or stripes of coloured material and in having narrower sleeves, but the two garments came to be identical. When the office of subdeacon was suppressed in the RC Church the garment was rendered obsolete.

Braun, *LG*, pp. 247–305. J. Braun, SJ, *Handbuch der Paramentik* (1912), pp. 108–19; id. in *CE* 15 (1912), pp. 87 f., s.v. 'Tunic', with bibl.

Tunkers, also known as Dunkers, Dunkards (from Old Ger. *tunken*, 'to dip') and as German Baptists, a Protestant sect so named from its distinctive baptismal rite. Originating in Germany in 1708 under Alexander Mack (1679–1735), they quickly gathered adherents in Germany, the Netherlands, and Switzerland; but persecution compelled them to emigrate to America (1719–29), where they have been settled ever since. In the 1880s the Tunkers became divided into three bodies: (1) the very conservative Old German Baptist Brethren; (2) the majority, who continued to be known as the German Baptist Brethren until 1908, when the title 'Church of the Brethren' was adopted; and (3) the more liberal 'Brethren Church', which in 1939 divided into the 'Brethren Church (Ashland, Ohio)' and the 'National Fellowship of Brethren Churches (Grace Brethren)'. They all profess no creed other than the NT, reject infant baptism, insist on total immersion, accompany the Lord's Supper by an *agape*, and generally refuse to bear arms or take oaths.

In Canada the term 'Tunkers' was applied to a group of *Mennonite origin that arose out of a religious awakening in Lancaster County, Pennsylvania, in the 18th cent., now known as the 'Brethren in Christ'.

D. F. Durnbaugh (ed. and tr.), *European Origins of the Brethren: A source book on the beginnings of the Church of the Brethren in the early eighteenth century* (Elgin, Ill. [1958]). M. G. Brumbaugh, *A History of the German Baptist Brethren in Europe and America* (Mount Morris, Ill., 1899). J. L. Gillin, *The Dunkers: A Sociological Interpretation* (Columbia University thesis; New York, 1906). J. H. Moore in S. M. Jackson (ed.), *The New Schaff-Herzog Encyclopedia of Religious Knowledge*, 4 (1909), pp. 24–7; E. Boardman in *EB* (1969 edn.), 4, pp. 156 f., s.v. 'Brethren, Church of the'.

Tunstall, Cuthbert (1474–1559), Bp. of *Durham. He was educated at Cambridge and Padua. His interest in learning won him the friendship of Abp. W. *Warham, who appointed him his chancellor *c.*1508. The width of his early academic achievement is reflected in his mathematical work, *De Arte Supputandi* (London, 1522). After holding a series of preferments and being employed on various political missions by *Henry VIII, he was made Bp. of London in 1522 and translated to Durham in 1530. In the divorce question he was one of the counsel of the Queen, but during the following years, though continuing sympathetic to Catholic doctrine, he lacked strength of purpose. He yielded in the matter of the Royal Supremacy after first opposing it, and introduced into his diocese the religious changes confirmed by Parliament. In 1537 he was made president of the Council of the North, but continued to take an active part in ecclesiastical affairs, writing in favour of auricular confession, using his influence to keep the '*Bishops' Book' (1537) as Catholic as possible, and assisting with the preparation of the '*Great Bible' of 1539. Under *Edward VI his position became more and more difficult. In 1547 he voted against the abolition of *chantries, and in 1549 against the Act of *Uniformity and the Act permitting priests to marry. In 1551 he was imprisoned in his house in London, where he wrote his treatise *De Veritate Corporis et Sanguinis Domini Nostri Jesu Christi in Eucharistia* (pub. Paris, 1554), a careful exposition of Catholic Eucharistic doctrine. In 1552 he was tried by a lay commission for high treason and deprived of his bishopric, but reinstated by *Mary in 1554, when he refrained from taking part in the persecution of Protestants. On the accession of *Elizabeth I he refused to take the Oath of Supremacy and declined to consecrate M. *Parker to the Archbishopric of Canterbury (1559). He was then deprived of his see and kept a prisoner under the care of Parker in *Lambeth Palace, where he died shortly afterwards.

The Register of his Durham episcopate was ed. and calendared by G. Hinde (Surtees Society, 161 for 1951; 1952, pp. 1–131, with introd., pp. xi–xxxv). A collection of *Certain Godly and Devout Prayers* written by Tunstall in Lat., tr. into Eng. by T. Paynell, Augustinian Friar (London, 1558; ed. R. Hudleston, OSB, 'Orchard Books', extra series, 1; 1925). Full Life by C. Sturge (London, 1938). M. Thomas, 'Tunstall—Trimmer or Martyr?', *JEH*, 24 (1973), pp. 337–55; D. M. Loades, 'The Last Years of Cuthbert Tunstall, 1547–1559', *Durham University Journal*, NS 35 (1973–4), pp. 10–21. A. F. Pollard in *DNB* 57 (1899), pp. 310–15; H. Gee in *DECH*, pp. 603–5, s.v. *BRUO* 3 (1959), pp. 1913–15; *BRUC*, pp. 597–8 and 684–5.

Tur 'Abdin (literally 'mountain for the servants [of God]'). An area in SE Turkey noted for the survival of a number of early *Syrian Orthodox monasteries and parish churches still in use. Among the most notable are the monasteries of Mar Gabriel at Kartmin (said to have been founded in 394 and from *c*.614 to 1089/90 the residence of the Bp. of Tur 'Abdin) and Deir Za'faran, near Mardin (which existed in the 6th cent., and from the Middle Ages until the 1920s was the seat of the Syrian Orthodox Patr. of Antioch), and the parish churches of Kefr Zeh and Arnas (both before the 8th cent.). The buildings are of great interest in tracing the history of early Christian architecture.

G. Bell, *The Churches and Monasteries of the Tur 'Abdin* (expanded edn. by M. M. Mango, 1982). H. Anschütz, *Die syrischen Christen vom Tur 'Abdin* (Das östliche Christentum, NF 34; 1984). O. H. Parry, *Six Months in a Syrian Monastery* [Deir Za'faran], *Being the Record of a Visit to the Head Quarters of the Syrian Church in Mesopotamia* (1895). A. [N.] Palmer, *Monk and Mason on the Tigris Frontier: The early history of Tur 'Abdin* (Cambridge, 1990).

Turner, Cuthbert Hamilton (1860–1930), *patristic and NT scholar. Educated at *Winchester and at New College, Oxford, he was a Fellow of Magdalen from 1889 until his death. In 1920 he was elected Dean Ireland's professor of exegesis at Oxford in succession to W. Lock; he was the first layman to hold the office. An early interest in chronology bore fruit in 'The Day and Year of St. *Polycarp's Martyrdom [Saturday, 22 Feb. 156]', in *Studia Biblica*, 2 (1890), pp. 105–55; this was followed by a comprehensive article 'Chronology of the NT' in J. *Hastings' *Dictionary of the Bible*, 1 (1898). His main life-work was *Ecclesiae Occidentalis Monumenta Iuris Antiquissima*, a very painstaking and accurate edition of the early Latin ecclesiastical canons. Six fascicules (1899–1930) appeared at intervals during his life; the 7th fascicule came out in 1939, leaving the work incomplete. His writings also include *Studies in Early Church History* (1912), and an important essay on 'The Apostolic Succession' in *Essays on the Early History of the Church and the Ministry* (1918; ed. H. B. *Swete).

Catholic and Apostolic: Collected Papers by . . . Cuthbert Hamilton Turner, ed. H. N. Bate (1933), with Memoir by id., pp. 1–65. Id. *DNB, 1922–1930*, pp. 861–4.

Turrecremata, Juan de; Tomás. See TORQUEMADA, JUAN DE; TOMÁS.

Tutiorism (also termed **Rigorism**). The system of moral theology acc. to which, in cases of doubt or perplexity, the 'safer opinion' (*opinio tutior*; i.e. that in favour of the moral principle) must be followed unless there is a degree of probability amounting to moral certitude in the 'less safe opinion' (*opinio minus tuta*; i.e. that against the principle). A kind of Tutiorism was the normal position held by Catholic moral theologians before the notion of 'probability' achieved its full development in the 17th and 18th cents. As against *Probabilism, many of the *Jansenists (e.g. P. *Nicole) maintained Tutiorist doctrines; but the system was obsolescent by 1690, when the *Holy Office included statements of Tutiorism in a list of condemned rigorist propositions. Its critics urge that the system, if strictly practised, would render life intolerable, its requirement of absolute certainty before taking action making moral decisions in many cases impossible.

Twelfth Night. The evening preceding Twelfth Day (the *Epiphany), 12 days after *Christmas, formerly kept as a time of merry-making and associated with many old customs such as taking down the Christmas decorations. In Herefordshire there was a tradition of lighting 12 bonfires, representing the Twelve Apostles, to secure a blessing on the fruits of the earth, and similar practices prevailed elsewhere. The 'Twelfth Cake' was an ornamented cake made for the occasion, containing a bean or coin, the drawer of which became the 'King' or 'Queen' of the festivities.

Twelve Apostles, Teaching of the. See DIDACHE.

Twelve Articles. The main charter of the *Peasants' War, in the form of 'Twelve Articles' adopted at Memmingen in Mar. 1525. Among the peasants' demands were the right to appoint their own pastors, control over tithes, abolition of serfdom, proper rights in the matters of fishing (in streams, but not in ponds), game, and woodcutting, just conditions of work and rent, justice in the courts and abolition of *Todfall* ('heriot', i.e. the usage whereby the landlord appropriated the most valuable chattel of a deceased tenant). M. *Luther formally professed his agreement with the Articles, though he opposed the attempt to achieve their demands by revolt.

Crit. edn. of the text by A. Götze in *Historische Vierteljahrsschrift*, 5 (1902), pp. 1–33; text also in H. Böhmer, *Urkunden zur Geschichte des Bauernkrieges und der Wiedertäufer* (H. *Lietzmann (ed.), *Kleine Texte*, no. 50/1; 1910; Eng. tr. in Kidd, no. 83, pp. 174–9. A variant form is ed. by P. Blickle in R. Postel and F. Kopitzsch (eds.), *Reformation und Revolution* (1989), pp. 90–100. G. Franz, 'Die Entstehung der "Zwölf Artikel" der deutschen Bauernschaft', *Archiv für Reformationsgeschichte*, 36 (1939), pp. 195–213; M. Brecht, 'Der theologische Hintergrund der Zwölf Artikel der Bauernschaft in Schwaben von 1525', *ZKG* 85 (1974), pp. 174–208.

Twelve Great Feasts, the. In the E. Church, the 12 principal feast days in the liturgical year: *Epiphany (6 Jan.), *Presentation of Christ in the Temple (2 Feb.), *Annunciation of the BVM (25 March), *Palm Sunday, *Ascension Day, *Pentecost, *Transfiguration (6 Aug.), *Dormition of BVM (15 Aug.), *Nativity of BVM (8 Sept.), *Holy Cross (14 Sept.), *Presentation of BVM in the Temple (21 Nov.), and *Christmas Day (25 Dec.). *Easter Day, the 'Feast of Feasts', stands in a class by itself, and is not reckoned as one of the 12.

Twelve Patriarchs, Testaments of the. See TESTAMENTS OF THE TWELVE PATRIARCHS.

Tychicus. Acc. to Acts 20: 4 he was a native of Asia who accompanied St *Paul on his third missionary journey. He is mentioned as the bearer of the letters to Colossae (Col. 4: 7 f.) and *Ephesus (Eph. 6: 21 f.) and also at 2 Tim. 4: 12 and Tit. 3: 12. Several cities claim him as bishop, while some martyrologies make him a deacon. Feast day in the E., 8 Dec.; in the W., 29 Apr.

Tychon, St. See TIKHON, ST.

Tyconius (d. *c*.400), *Donatist theologian. He seems to have been a layman of considerable importance in his community, but was attacked for his catholicizing views by the Donatist bishop, Parmenian (*c*.378), and condemned by a Donatist Council at *Carthage *c*.380; he refused, however, to join the Catholic Church. His condemnation was probably caused by two works, 'De Bello Intestino Libri Tres' and 'Expositiones Diversarum Causarum', now lost, in which he seems to have taught that the Church must be a society spread over the whole earth and contain both good and bad. Tyconius' chief work was his 'Liber Regularum' (*c*.380), which propounded seven rules for the interpretation of Scripture, which St *Augustine, who greatly esteemed him despite his being a Donatist, incorporated in his 'De Doctrina Christiana'; hence they played an important part in medieval exegesis. His commentary on Rev. no longer exists in its original form, but it is quoted and used by a number of subsequent commentators, notably *Primasius, *Bede, and the Spanish presbyter, Beatus of Liebana (*c*.776). Fragments of an anonymous commentary on Rev. in a Turin MS (Codex F. iv. 18; formerly at *Bobbio) appear to be directly derived from Tyconius' commentary.

Editio princeps of the 'Liber Regularum' by J. J. Grynaeus, *Monumenta Patrum Orthodoxographa* (Basle [1569]), pp. 1352–87; the 'Rules' are also repr. from a later edn. in J. P. Migne, *PL* 18. 13–66. Discussion and crit. text in F. C. *Burkitt, *The Book of Rules of Tyconius* (Texts and Studies, 3, pt. 1; Cambridge, 1894); text repr., with Eng. tr. by W. S. Babcock (Texts and Translations, 31; Atlanta [1989]). *The Turin Fragments of Tyconius' Commentary on Revelation*, ed. F. Lo Bue (Texts and Studies, NS 7; 1963). On his comm. on Rev., see also J. Haussleiter, 'Die lateinische Apokalypse der alten Afrikanischen Kirche', in T. *Zahn, *Forschungen zur Geschichte des neutestamentlichen Kanons und der altkirchlichen Literatur*, 4 (1891), pp. 1–244; and K. B. Steinhauser, *The Apocalypse Commentary of Tyconius: A History of its Reception and Influence* (European University Studies, 23rd ser. 301; Frankfurt etc. [1987]). P. [M.] Bright, *The Book of Rules of Tyconius: Its Purpose and Inner Logic* (Christianity and Judaism in Antiquity, 2; Notre Dame, Ind. [1988]; to be used with caution). T. Hahn, *Tyconius-Studien* (Studien zur Geschichte der

Theologie und der Kirche, 6, Heft 2; 1900). P. Monceaux, *Histoire littéraire de l'Afrique chrétienne*, 5 (1920), pp. 165–219. M. Simonetti in Quasten (cont.), *Patrology*, 4 (1986), pp. 119–22, with bibl. E. Dinkler in *PW*, Zweite Reihe, 6 (pt. 1; 1936), cols. 849–56, s.v. 'Ticonius'; E. Romero Pose in *DPAC* 2 (1984), cols. 3447–50, s.v. 'Ticonio'; Eng. tr. in *Encyclopedia of the Early Church*, 2 (1992), pp. 838 f., s.v. 'Tichonius'.

Tyndale or **Tindale, William** (1494?–1536), translator of the Bible and Reformer. He sometimes used the pseudonym 'William Huchyns'. A native of Gloucestershire, he studied from 1510 to 1515 at Magdalen Hall, Oxford, and later at Cambridge. About 1522 he conceived the project of translating the Bible; but when C. *Tunstall, Bp. of London, refused his support, Tyndale went to Germany and settled at Hamburg (1524), never to return to his own country. The printing of his first translation of the NT, which was begun at *Cologne in 1525, was interrupted by the local magistrates, but completed at Worms the same year. On its arrival in England in 1526, it was bitterly attacked by Abp. W. *Warham, C. Tunstall, and T. *More. Tyndale spent most of his remaining years at Antwerp, where he frequently revised the NT. His other writings include *A Prologue on . . . Romans* (1526; largely derived from M. *Luther), *Parable of the Wicked Mammon* (1528), and *Obedience of a Christian Man* (1528). Like Luther, he insisted on the authority of Scripture, but in the course of his work on the Bible, he moved away from Luther's teaching on *justification by faith alone towards the idea of double justification by faith and works. His Eucharistic teaching came to resemble that of H. *Zwingli, although the tract *The Souper of the Lorde* (1535), formerly thought to be by Tyndale, is now generally attributed to his associate G. Joye (1495?–1553). He wrote also against T. *Wolsey and the 'Divorce' (*Practice of Prelates*, 1530) and against T. More, his ablest opponent. Besides his NT, Tyndale printed translations of the Pentateuch (1530) and Jonah (1531), and left Jos.–2 Chron. in MS. His biblical translations, made direct from the Greek and Hebrew into straightforward, vigorous English, remain the basis of both the AV and the RV. In 1535 he was arrested, imprisoned at Vilvorde, nr. Brussels, and strangled and burnt at the stake prob. on 6 Oct. 1536. Feast day in some Anglican Churches, 6 Oct.

Collection of his works pub. London, 1573. Doctrinal Treatises ed. H. Walter (*Parker Society, 1848); selections from his works ed. S. L. Greenslade (London, 1938) and G. E. Duffield (Courtenay Library of Reformation Classics, 1; 1964). Complete text of the 1534 revision of the NT, with introd. by N. Hardy Wallis (Cambridge, 1938), and in modernized spelling, with introd. by D. Daniell (New Haven, Conn., and London, 1989). Modern Lives by R. Demaus (London [1871]), J. F. Mozley (ibid., 1937), and D. Daniell (New Haven, Conn., and London [1994]). W. A. Clebsch, 'More Evidence that George Joye wrote The Souper of the Lorde', *HTR* 55 (1962), pp. 63–6; W. D. J. Cargill Thompson, 'The Two Regiments: the Continental Setting of William Tyndale's Political Thought', in D. Baker (ed.), *Reform and Reformation: England and the Continent c.1500–c.1750* (Studies in Church History, Subsidia, 2; Oxford, 1979), pp. 17–33; M. McGiffert, 'William Tyndale's Conception of Covenant', *JEH*, 32 (1981), pp. 167–84; E. Ní Chuilleanáin, 'The Debate between Thomas More and William Tyndale, 1528–33: Ideas on Literature and Religion', ibid., 39 (1988), pp. 382–411; J. A. R. Dick and A. Richardson (eds.), *William Tyndale and the Law* (Sixteenth Century Essays & Studies, 25; Kirksville, Mo. [1994]);

C. R. Trueman, *Luther's Legacy: Salvation and English Reformers, 1525–1556* (Oxford, 1994), esp. pp. 9–14 and 83–120. See also bibl. to BIBLE (ENGLISH VERSIONS).

types (Gk. τύποι, 'examples', 'figures'). In theology, the foreshadowings of the Christian dispensation in the events and persons of the OT. Just as Christ Himself could refer to *Jonah as a symbol of His *Resurrection, so St *Paul found in the Israelites' crossing of the *Red Sea (1 Cor. 10: 1 6) the 'type' of Baptism, while to the author of the Ep. to the Hebrews *Melchizedek was the foreshadowing of Christ (Heb. 7). A Christian type differs from an *allegory in that the historical reference is not lost sight of. Types are looked upon, however, as having a greater significance now than was apparent in their pre-Christian OT context. Typology, with an increasingly allegorical emphasis, was much employed in the early Church, esp. by the *Alexandrian Fathers, for whom almost everything in the OT was capable of interpretation by this method.

W. J. Phythian-Adams, *The Fulness of Israel: A Study of the Meaning of Sacred History* (Warburton Lectures for 1935–1937; 1938); L. Goppelt, *Typos: Die typologische Deutung des Alten Testaments im Neuen* (Beiträge zur Förderung christlicher Theologie, 43; 1939; Eng. tr., Grand Rapids, Mich. [1982]). A. G. Hebert, SSM, *The Throne of David: A Study of the Fulfilment of the Old Testament in Jesus Christ and His Church* (1941); P. Lundberg. *La Typologie baptismale dans l'ancienne Église* (Acta Seminarii Neotestamentici Upsaliensis, 10; 1942); J. *Daniélou, SJ, *Sacramentum Futuri: Études sur les origines de la typologie biblique* (1950; Eng. tr., 1960); G. W. H. Lampe and K. J. Woollcombe, *Essays on Typology* (Studies in Biblical Theology, 22; 1957); P. Grelot, *Sens chrétien de l'ancien testament* (Bibliothèque de théologie, Série 1; théologie dogmatique, 3; 1962); A. C. Charity, *Events and their Afterlife: The Dialectics of Christian Typology in the Bible and in Dante* (Cambridge, 1966); R. T. France, *Jesus and the Old Testament: His Application of Old Testament Passages to Himself and His Mission* (1971); A. T. Hanson, *The Living Utterances of God: The New Testament Exegesis of the Old* (1983). J. E. Alsup in *Anchor Bible Dictionary*, 6 (1992), pp. 682–5, s.v. 'Typology'.

typicon (Gk. τυπικόν). In the E. Church, a liturgical manual which indicates how the services are to be recited during the ecclesiastical year, with directions as to the rules to be followed when two or more feasts fall on the same day. The term is also used of the Rule of a monastic house.

Typos, the. The Imperial edict issued by Constans II in Sept. 647 or 648 to supersede *Heraclius' *Ecthesis. It was prob. the work of Paul, Patr. of *Constantinople, 641–53. With a view to securing peace, it forbade anyone to assert either *Monothelite or *Dyothelite beliefs, and required that teaching should be limited to what had been defined in the first Five Oecumenical Councils. The refusal of Pope *Martin I (649–55; q.v.) to accept it led to his deposition.

The text is preserved in the Acts of the Lateran Council of 649; crit. edn., with Lat. tr., by R. Riediger (ACO, 2nd ser. 1; 1984), pp. 208–11. Hefele and Leclercq, 3 (pt. 1; 1909), pp. 432–4. J. M. Hussey, *The Orthodox Church in the Byzantine Empire* (Oxford History of the Christian Church, 1986), pp. 19–22. See also bibl. to MARTIN I.

tyrannicide. The murder of a tyrant whose rule has become insupportable. On the ethical question, three opinions have been current among Christians:

(1) Those who hold that the sixth commandment is to be interpreted as forbidding killing in any form, e.g. in police action or in war, naturally believe tyrannicide to be included in the prohibition.

(2) Those who (e.g. on the basis of Rom. 13: 1 f.) hold that force is by Divine authority wholly invested in the *de facto* civil government also believe tyrannicide to be morally unjustifiable.

(3) Those who hold that rebellion, including tyrannicide, is defensible and right in circumstances where, if the oppressor were an alien, war would be justified, and provided that the grievance is considerable, that the circumstances offer no milder means of redress, and that the killing is not simply an act of revenge. Such is the general view of Catholic moral theologians.

A. Bride in *DTC* 15 (pt. 2; 1950), cols. 1988–2016, s.v.

Tyre and Sidon. The two chief cities of the Phoenicians, on the coast of Lebanon. In OT times they carried on a lucrative maritime trade, and the Israelites knew them as rich heathen neighbours, whence in the time of King Ahab (c.875–853 BC) the worship of the Tyrian *Baal was introduced into Israel, and combated by *Elijah (1 Kgs. 16: 31 ff.; 18: 18 ff.). In the Gospels inhabitants of the region of Tyre and Sidon are mentioned among the multitudes attracted to Christ (Lk. 6: 17), and He Himself visited the district and healed the daughter of a Gentile woman there (Mk. 7: 24–30). In His comparison of the final judgement on these two cities with that being incurred by the towns of Palestine (Mt. 11: 22), it would appear that Tyre and Sidon represented the heathen world. Tyre was held by the *Crusaders, 1124–1291.

N. Jidejian, *Tyre through the Ages* (Beirut, 1969); id., *Sidon through the Ages* (ibid., 1971). H. J. Katzenstein, *The History of Tyre from the Beginning of the Second Millenium B.C.E. until ... 538 B.C.E.* (Jerusalem, 1973). J.-P. Rey-Coquais, *Inscriptions grecques et latines découvertes dans les Fouilles de Tyr (1963–1974)*, 1: *Inscriptions de la Nécropole* (Bulletin du Musée de Beyrouth, 29; 1977); M. H. Chébab, *Fouilles de Tyre: La Nécropole* (ibid. 33–6; 1983–6); id., *Tyre à l'Époque des Croisades* (ibid. 27–8 and 31–2; 1975–9). [E.] Honigmann in *PW*, 2. Reihe, 2 (pt. 2; 1923), cols. 2216–29, s.v. 'Sidon'; [O.] Eissfeldt, ibid. 6 (pt. 2; 1948), cols. 1876–907, s.v. 'Tyros (3)'; P. C. Schmitz in *Anchor Bible Dictionary*, 6 (1992), pp. 17 f., s.v. 'Sidon'; H. J. Katzenstein and D. R. Edwards ibid., pp. 686–92, s.v. 'Tyre'.

Tyrrell, George (1861–1909), English *Modernist theologian. He was a native of Dublin, of Evangelical upbringing, and educated at Trinity College. At an early age he had come under High Church influence, esp. that of R. W. R. *Dolling, and was later received into the RC Church (1879). In 1880 he entered the *Jesuit novitiate and in 1891 was priested and became lecturer in moral theology at *Stonyhurst. In 1896 he was transferred to Farm Street, the principal church of his order in London, where he was a sought-after confessor and made a name by writing, publishing two collections of Meditations, *Nova et Vetera* (1897) and *Hard Sayings* (1898), and a series of Lectures, *On External Religion* (1899). His friendship with F. *von Hügel led to his acquaintance with the writings

of H. *Bergson, M. *Blondel, L. *Laberthonnière, and
A. *Loisy, which contributed to his increasing hostility to
*Scholasticism and his stress on the anti-intellectual and
experiential aspects of religion. From 1899 he moved further and further from traditional RC orthodoxy, notably in
an article on hell, entitled 'A Perverted Devotion', which
appeared in the *Weekly Register* (1899). Though its publication led to his removal from Farm Street and his retirement to the Jesuit mission house at Richmond in N. Yorks,
Tyrrell did not cease to feel a strong attraction to the devotional aspects of Catholicism, for which he continued to
work as a keen apologist. In 1900 he wrote *Oil and Wine*
(printed 1902; new preface, 1907), another book of meditations, but its immediate publication was prohibited by his
episcopal superiors on account of its immanentist tendencies. In 1901 he published *The Faith of the Millions* and
in 1903 his *Lex Orandi*, his last work to appear with an
'*imprimatur'. After he had in vain asked for his secularization (1905), the final rupture with the Society of Jesus
came in 1906, following the publication of extracts from
an anon. 'Letter to a Professor' by the *Corriere della Sera*.
This writing, in which he contrasted living faith with dead
theology, he published with amplifications in 1906 as *A
Much Abused Letter*. Though expelled from his order and
suspended 'a divinis', Tyrrell continued his literary activities. *Lex Credendi* (1906) is for the most part a devotional
exposition of the 'Our Father' with a strong anti-
intellectual and anti-theological bias, and *Through Scylla*

and Charybdis (1907) a collection of essays which reflected
his increasing sympathy with a thoroughgoing symbolism.
After *Pius X's issue of the encyclical 'Pascendi', Tyrrell
wrote two letters of protest to *The Times* of 30 Sept. and
1 Oct. 1907; they drew upon him the minor excommunication. In 1908 Tyrrell published his *Medievalism*, a bitter
attack on Card. D. J. *Mercier and a violent denunciation
of the contemporary RC Church. His posthumous work,
Christianity at the Cross-Roads (1909), questioned whether
Christianity was the final religion and held out hopes of a
universal religion of which Christianity was but the germ.
Many of his articles were published under assumed names.
Tyrrell died with the last rites of the Church, but was
refused Catholic burial. His remains were deposited in the
Anglican churchyard at Storrington, where H. *Bremond
took part in the funeral.

M. D. Petre, *Autobiography and Life of George Tyrrell* (2 vols.,
1912); id., *Letters* (1920); id., *Von Hügel and Tyrrell: The Story of
a Friendship* (1937). A. Loisy, *Georges Tyrrell et Henri Bremond*
(1936); J. J. Stam, *George Tyrrell 1861–1909* (Utrecht, 1938); J.
Ratté, *Three Modernists* (1968), pp. 143–256; D. G. Schultenover,
SJ, *George Tyrrell in Search of Catholicism* (Shepherdstown,
W. Va., 1981); E. Leonard, CSJ, *George Tyrrell and the Catholic
Tradition* (1982); N. Sagovsky, *'On God's Side': A Life of George
Tyrrell* (Oxford, 1990). T. M. Loome, 'A Bibliography of the
Published Writings of George Tyrrell (1861–1909)', *Heythrop
Journal*, 10 (1969), pp. 280–314; 11 (1970), pp. 161–9; and in id.,
Liberal Catholicism, Reform Catholicism, Modernism (Tübinger
Theologische Studien, 14; 1979), pp. 218–27. Polgár, 3 (1990),
pp. 576–82. J. M. Rigg in *DNB, 1901–1911*, 2, pp. 542–5, s.v.

U

Ubaghs, Gerhard Casimir (1800–75), chief representative of the *Traditionalist *Ontologism of Louvain. He became professor of philosophy at Louvain in 1834 and from 1846 onwards was editor of the *Revue Catholique*, the principal organ of Ontologism. Among his most important works are his *Logicae seu Philosophiae Rationalis Elementa* (1834), *Ontologiae seu Metaphysicae Generalis Elementa* (1835), and *Theodiceae seu Theologiae Naturalis Elementa* (1841) in which he expounds a mitigated Traditionalism acc. to which the knowledge of metaphysical and moral truths is based on a primitive Divine teaching handed on by oral tradition. This teaching he combined with the Ontologist doctrine of the direct contemplation of God by the intellect in the 'objective ideas'. Though his books were not placed on the *Index, his teaching was censured by the *Holy Office on 21 Sept. 1864, and soon afterwards Ubaghs submitted and resigned his chair. See also TRADITIONALISM.

J. Jacops, 'Notice sur la vie et les travaux de M. le Chanoine G. C. Ubaghs, Professeur Émérite à la Faculté de Philosophie et Lettres de l'Université Catholique de Louvain', *Annuaire de l'Université Catholique de Louvain* (1876), pp. 417–66. A. Simon, 'Le Cardinal Sterckx et la condamnation de Ubaghs en 1843', *Collectanea Mechliniensia*, 31 (1946), pp. 639–44; id., *Le Cardinal Sterckx et son temps (1792–1867)*, 2 (Wetteren, 1950), pp. 162–97, passim. J. Henry in *Biographie nationale publiée par l'Académie Royale des Sciences, des Lettres et des Beaux-Arts de Belgique*, 25 (1930–2), cols. 889–92; L. Ceyssens, OFM, in *Nationaal Biografisch Woordenboek*, 9 (1981), cols. 767–70, both s.v., with bibl. See also works cited under TRADITIONALISM.

Ubertino of Casale (1259–*c*.1330), a leader of the '*Spiritual Franciscans' (q.v.). He became a *Franciscan in 1273, studied at *Paris, and returned to Italy as a preacher and lecturer. Here *John of Parma and Peter John *Olivi, then leading figures among the Spirituals, with whom he became acquainted, gained a strong influence on him. In 1305 he wrote his principal work, 'Arbor vitae crucifixae Jesu Christi', a mystical work with a strong apocalyptic vein, later used by a number of orthodox writers. From 1306 to 1308 he was chaplain to Cardinal N. Orsini, pontifical legate in N. and Central Italy, and in 1310 was called to *Avignon by *Clement V to defend the Spirituals in the controversy on poverty. Having failed to obtain the erection of convents and provinces for his party, he was allowed, in 1317, to be transferred to the *Benedictines of Gembloux. In 1322 *John XXII asked his opinion in the question of 'theoretical poverty', then a matter of dispute between the *Dominicans and the Franciscans. Two years later he was still at the *Curia, in the service of Cardinal Orsini. He fled, however, in 1325, probably because accused of heresy; in 1328 he was probably among the Franciscans who accompanied Louis the Bavarian on his journey to Rome; and in 1329 he seems to have preached against John XXII at Como. Nothing is known of his death. He is mentioned by *Dante in canto 12 of the 'Paradiso', and was venerated by the *Fraticelli of the 15th century.

His *Arbor Vitae Crucifixae Jesu* was pr. at Venice, 1485; repr. (Monumenta politica et philosophica rariora, 1st ser. 1; Turin, 1961), with introd. and bibl. by C. T. Davis. F. Callaey, *L'Idéalisme franciscain spirituel au XIVᵉ siècle: Étude sur Ubertin de Casale* (Université de Louvain. Recueil de travaux publiés par les membres des Conférences d'Histoire et de Philologie, fasc. 28; 1911). G. L. Potestà, *Storia ed escatologia in Ubertino da Casale* (Milan, 1980). M. Damiata, *Pietà e Storia nell'*Arbor Vitae *di Ubertino da Casale* (Biblioteca di Studi Francescani, 19; Florence, 1988). M. D. Lambert, *Franciscan Poverty* (1961), esp. pp. 174–6, 184–97. P. Godefroy in *DTC* 15 (pt. 2; 1950), cols. 2021–34, s.v.; G. L. Potestà in *Dict. Sp.* 16 (1994), cols. 3–16, s.v.

ubiquitarianism. The doctrine held by M. *Luther and many of his followers that Christ in His human nature is everywhere present. Luther employed it, e.g., in his two writings *Das diese Worte Christi, 'Das ist mein Leib', noch fest stehen wider die Schwarmgeister* (1527) and *Bekenntnis vom Abendmahl Christi* (1528), to uphold his belief in the real presence of Christ in the Eucharist; and it was formally defended by J. *Brenz at a Lutheran synod at Stuttgart in 1559.

Udall, John (*c*.1560–92), also 'Uvedale', *Puritan pamphleteer and Hebrew scholar. Matriculating at Christ's College, Cambridge, in 1578, he was chiefly educated at Trinity College, where he became strongly inclined to Puritanism. While curate of Kingston-on-Thames (1584–8) he was charged before the Court of *High Commission in 1586 for his criticism of Episcopacy. In 1588 he published anonymously a widely read pamphlet on *The State of the Church of England, laid open in a Conference between Diotrephes a Bishop, Tertullus a Papist, Demetrius a Usurer, Pandochus an Inn-keeper and Paul a Preacher of the Word of God*. Suspected of complicity in the *Marprelate Tracts, he was summoned before the Privy Council in 1589. In 1590, on his refusal to clear himself on oath, he was found guilty of the authorship of *A Demonstration of the Truth of that Discipline which Christ hath Prescribed for the Government of His Church* [1588]; but the sentence of death was not executed. He died in prison in Southwark, shortly after his pardon had been procured.

He published several volumes of his sermons, including *Amendment of Life* [1584], *The True Remedy against Famine and Wars* [1588], and *The Combat betwixt Christ and the Devil* (1588). In 1593 his *Commentary upon the Lamentations of Jeremy* (anon.) was published posthumously. In the same year there appeared at *Leiden his *Key of the Holy Tongue*, which comprised a Hebrew Grammar translated from Petrus Martinius and a Hebrew dictionary of his own compilation; the work was highly valued by *James I.

The State of the Church of England was repr. by E. Arber (The English Scholar's Library of Old and Modern Works, 5; 1880); *A Demonstration of the Truth of that Discipline which Christ hath*

Prescribed, also ed. id. (ibid. 9; 1880). S. Lee in *DNB* 58 (1899), pp. 4–6, s.v., with refs.

Udall, Nicholas (*c*.1505–56), also 'Uvedale', alias 'Randall', reformer and dramatist. Born at Southampton, he was admitted a scholar of *Winchester in 1517 and of Corpus Christi College, Oxford, in 1520, where he became a probationary Fellow in 1524. His *Lutheran sympathies prob. forced him to leave Oxford in 1529 and prevented his proceeding to MA until 1534. In 1533 he joined John Leland (d. 1552) in the composition of verses for the coronation of *Anne Boleyn. He was appointed Headmaster of Eton in 1534, but dismissed in 1541 on charges of complicity in the theft of silver images and college plate and of unsuitable behaviour, which led to a short imprisonment in the Marshalsea. In 1547, with the patronage of Catherine Parr, he was appointed to assist with Princess (later Queen) *Mary in translating the first volume of the *Paraphrases* of *Erasmus (pub. 1548). Through the favour of *Edward VI he became a Canon of *Windsor in 1551 and in 1553 he became rector of Calbourne (Isle of Wight). Possibly because of his association with Mary over the translation of Erasmus' *Paraphrases* he remained in favour in the next reign, continuing to write for the Court stage and in 1555 being appointed Headmaster of *Westminster (in succession to Alexander *Nowell).

Udall is a significant example of the influence of Protestantism on the new humanist movement. His other published works include translations of Erasmus' *Apophthegms* (1542), of *Peter Martyr's *Tractatio de Sacramento Eucharistiae* [1550], and of T. Gemini's *Compendiosa Totius Anatomiae Delineatio* (1553). His play *Ezekias*, performed before *Elizabeth I in 1564, has been lost. His *Ralph Roister Doister*, however, a Christmas comedy, originally written for a London school, prob. between 1545 and 1552 (*c*.1566), although lost since the 16th cent. and has been frequently reprinted.

Ralph Roister Doister ed. for the Shakespeare Society by W. D. Cooper (London, 1847), with memoir, pp. xi–xxxiv. Later edns. incl. those of W. C. Hazlitt (ibid., 1874), J. S. Farmer (ibid., 1906, with notes on his other dramatic works), C. G. Child (ibid., 1913; with introd.), and G. Scheurweghs (Materials for the study of Old English Drama, ed. H. de Vocht, 16; Louvain, 1939), with biog. introd. pp. xi–l. N. Pocock (ed.), *Troubles Connected with the Prayer Book of 1549* (Camden Society, NS 37; 1884), pp. xviii–xxv, 141–93. W. L. Edgerton, *Nicholas Udall* (Twayne's English Author Series, 30; New York [1965]). *BRUO, 1506–1546*, pp. 586–88, with bibl. S. Lee in *DNB* 58 (1899), pp. 7–9, s.v. D. S. Bland in *NCBEL* 1 (1974), cols. 1414–16.

Uganda, Christianity in. The first Christian missionaries were sent to the kingdom of Buganda by the *CMS in 1877 in response to an appeal by H. M. *Stanley. The RC mission was inaugurated by the arrival of the *White Fathers in 1879. Despite the rivalry between the C of E and RC missionaries, exacerbated by the royal refusal to allow either to settle away from the court and focused in the tension between two outstanding missionaries, Père S. Lourdel and A. M. *Mackay, the early preaching was welcomed by many younger men at the court of King Mutesa. Under his successor, Mwanga, both Churches suffered persecution. J. *Hannington, the Anglican Bishop of Eastern Equatorial Africa, was killed on Mwanga's orders in 1885 before even entering the country. Over 40 RCs and

Anglicans were martyred together between 1885 and 1887, the RCs being canonized in 1964. In the period before the establishment of the British Protectorate in 1894, the political instability erupted into armed conflict between parties nominally Muslim, RC, and Protestant. Missionaries had been expelled from the country and the young leadership established among both RCs and Protestants during the period of civil war would be decisive in establishing a major lay role in subsequent Church life, as well as encouraging the first movement of mass Christian conversion in modern African history. British rule reinforced and extended the political dominance of the Christian (and esp. Protestant) minority. It also enabled evangelism to move out from Buganda to cover all parts of the newly created Protectorate of Uganda. In this Ugandan lay catechists and quickly ordained clergy, such as the outstandingly holy Anglican missionary Apolo Kivebulaya (d. 1933), played a leading role. Upon the RC side the mostly French White Fathers were reinforced by British and Dutch *Mill Hill Fathers and, later, for the north of the country, Italian *Verona Fathers. Impressive networks of schools were established, and by the latter part of the 20th cent. 75 per cent of the population professed Christianity.

Uganda was notable for the speed with which a local clergy developed. The first Anglican ordinations of Ugandans took place in 1893; the first RC priests were ordained in 1913; and in 1910 the *Bannabikira* (Daughters of the Virgin) became the first RC religious sisterhood in sub-Saharan Africa. In 1939 an entire Vicariate Apostolic, Masaka, was already handed over to African priests and Joseph Kiwanuka consecrated as its bishop, the first black African RC bishop of modern times. The first Anglican Ugandan bishop was Aberi Balya, consecrated in 1947. In 1961 what was hitherto known as the 'Native Anglican Church' became the Church of Uganda, an autonomous Province of the Anglican Communion (until 1980 this also included the Churches in Rwanda and Burundi). From the 1930s the E. African Revival Movement (*Balokole*, 'saved ones') had a considerable effect on the Church of Uganda, stimulating its spiritual life but at times threatening to split the Church.

Before Uganda became independent in 1962, there were few other Christian denominations, apart from a small *Seventh-day Adventist Church dating from 1926, and an *Orthodox Church which originated in a breakaway movement from the Church of Uganda led by Reuben Spartas in 1929. Spartas secured ordination from a bishop in the J. R. *Vilatte succession line and his Church was recognized by the Greek Orthodox Church in 1946. During the tyrannical rule of Idi Amin (President 1971–9) Christians in Uganda suffered badly, Benedicto Kiwanuka, the Chief Justice and a leading RC lawyer, and Janani Luwum, the Anglican Abp. of Uganda, being among many murdered.

J. V. Taylor, *The Growth of the Church in Buganda* (1958); A. D. T. Tuma and P. Mutibwa (eds.), *A Century of Christianity in Uganda, 1877–1977* (Nairobi, 1978). E. Stock, *The History of the Church Missionary Society*, 3 (1899), pp. 94–112, 402–27, and 735–46; 4 (1916), pp. 83–104; G. Hewitt, *The Problems of Success: A History of the Church Missionary Society 1910–1942*, 1 (1971), pp. 205–60. Y. Tourigny, WF, *So Abundant a Harvest: The Catholic Church in Uganda 1879–1979* (1979). J. F. Faupel, *African Holocaust: The Story of the Uganda Martyrs* (1962). H. P. Gale,

Uganda and the Mill Hill Fathers (1959). M. L. Pirouet, *Black Evangelists: The spread of Christianity in Uganda 1891–1914* (1978); A. D. T. Tuma, *Building a Ugandan Church: African Participation in Church Growth and Expansion in Busoga 1891–1940* (Nairobi, 1980). R. Oliver, *The Missionary Factor in East Africa* (1952), *passim.* H. B. Hansen, *Mission, Church and State in a Colonial Setting: Uganda 1890–1925* (1984). F. B. Welbourn, *East African Rebels: A Study of Some Independent Churches* (1961), pp. 15–110. A. Hastings, *Mission and Ministry* (1971), pp. 144–76; id., *The Church in Africa 1450–1950* (Oxford History of the Christian Church, 1994), *passim.*

Ukrainian Churches. These comprise both the Orthodox Churches of the Ukraine and certain *Uniat Churches, mostly found in the west of the Ukraine, Slovakia, *Hungary, and *Poland, with colonies in N. America and elsewhere. The latter were formerly known as the Ruthenian Churches, but now more often as Ukrainian. Their ancestors, who were Slavonic converts of St *Vladimir, formed part of the *Russian Church under the jurisdiction of the Metropolitan of Kiev until the destruction of Kievan Russia by the Mongols in 1237–40 and the absorption of the Ukraine by Lithuania and Poland. After the Council of *Florence, Isidore, Metropolitan of Kiev, was delegated by the Pope to secure the acceptance of the Union in the countries of his jurisdiction, but in Moscow he was repudiated by Prince Vasili, who deposed him and appointed a successor (1448). In 1458 *Pius II appointed a Catholic Metropolitan of Kiev, who, by agreement with Casimir IV of Poland (1447–92), was permitted to exercise jurisdiction over the eight *eparchies of the province under the control of Poland and Lithuania. Although these Churches reverted to Orthodoxy at the beginning of the 16th cent., RC influence revived with the closer union of Poland and Lithuania in 1569, under which the Ukraine was attached to Poland, and in 1595 the Metropolitan of Kiev and the Bps. of Vladimir, Lutsk, Polotsk, Pinsk, and Kholm petitioned for communion with Rome; this was achieved on 23 Dec. 1595 by the Union of *Brest-Litovsk (q.v.). They were joined in 1694 by the Bp. of Przemysl and in 1700 by the Bp. of Lvov. Despite a decree of *Urban VIII (1624), during the 17th cent. the majority of the Ruthenian (Ukrainian) nobility and landowners in Poland adopted the Latin rite. Those who remained Orthodox in Polish Ukraine suffered severe repression. After the partitions of Poland (1772–95) most of the Ruthenians, except those of Galicia, passed under the sovereignty of Russia and their Churches were gradually suppressed in the early 19th cent. in favour of the Orthodox Church; in the Kholm district (ceded by Austria in 1815), they survived until *c.*1875. When toleration was granted to RCs in Russia in 1905, Catholic Byzantines still being illegal, the survivors passed to the Latin rite.

After the Ruthenians of Galicia had come under the sovereignty of Austria, Lvov was constituted an Archbishopric in 1807. During the 19th cent. the Galician Ruthenians enjoyed religious toleration; so, in theory at least, did the Uniat Ruthenians (now more generally known as Ukrainians) in the independent Poland reconstituted after 1918. At the time of the Russian Revolution, the Orthodox Church in the Ukraine was declared a self-governing exarchate of the Russian Orthodox Church, and this situation was confirmed in 1941 by the formation of an Autonomous Orthodox Church of the Ukraine. It was formed in response to the creation in the Ukraine in 1919 of a Ukrainian Autocephalous Orthodox Church, associated with the 'Living Church' movement in Russia; this was never recognized by other Orthodox Churches. At the end of the Second World War, the Ukrainian Uniat Church in the Soviet Union and in Poland was suppressed after a Council at Lvov (then under Soviet jurisdiction) in 1946 was forced to declare the 'reunion' of the Uniats with the Autonomous Orthodox Church of the Ukraine. They, however, maintained a clandestine existence in the Soviet Union until 1987, when a number of bishops, priests, and laity in the Ukraine declared their intention of seeking legal status; the campaign gathered strength during the millennial celebration of Christianity in E. Slav lands in 1988 and in Dec. 1989 the Uniat Church in the Ukraine was restored. The monastic element appears to be strong, and is esp. fostered by the austere Studites (see STUDIOS) founded *c.*1900. The liturgy is based on the Byzantine rite with certain modifications from Rome. In 1992 Metropolitan Filaret of Kiev, of the Autonomous Orthodox Church, was suspended and joined forces with the Autocephalous (now 'Unified') Church, which has the support of the political authorities of the Ukraine. There are now three Churches of the Byzantine Rite in the Ukraine claiming legitimacy: the Greek-Catholic Ukrainian Church (the 'Uniats'), the Ukrainian Orthodox Church (the 'Autonomous' Orthodox), and the 'Unified' Ukrainian Orthodox Church (the 'Autocephalous' Orthodox).

There is a further Ukrainian community (the Podcarpathian Ruthenians), which was created when a majority of the Ruthenian population south of the Carpathians was brought into communion with Rome in 1646 by the Union of Užhorod. It was granted a separate jurisdiction by the erection of the eparchy of Mukachevo, subject to the primacy of Hungary, by Pope *Clement XIV in 1771. Since 1945 this community has been split between the Transcarpathian Ukraine; Slovakia, where it was first suppressed and then reconstituted in 1968; and Hungary, which has a single largely Magyarized Uniat diocese.

There are considerable Ukrainian communities of all jurisdictions in the USA (since *c.*1876), *Canada (from the 1890s), *Brazil, and *Argentina. At Rome, a Ruthenian College, founded in 1897 by *Leo XIII and run since 1904 by Basilian monks, has done much to sustain the traditions of the Ukrainian Uniats in recent decades.

O. Zinkevych and A. Sorokowski (eds.), *A Thousand Years of Christianity in the Ukraine: An encyclopedic chronology* (New York, 1988); N. L. Chirovsky (ed.), *The Millennium of Ukrainian Christianity* (ibid. [1988]). I. Wlasowsky, *Outline History of the Ukrainian Orthodox Church*, vol. 1 [to 1596] (New York, 1956; 2nd edn., 1974), vol. 2 [17th cent.] (ibid., 1979) (Eng. tr. of earlier part of a larger work in Ukrainian). A. Theiner, *Die neuesten Zustände der katholischen Kirche beider Ritus in Polen und Russland seit Katherina II bis auf unsere Tage* (Augsburg, 1841). J. Pelesz, *Geschichte der Union der ruthenischen Kirche mit Rom* (2 vols., Würzburg, 1878–81). M. Lacko, SJ, *Unio Užhorodensis Ruthenorum Carpaticorum cum Ecclesia Catholica* (Orientalia Christiana Analecta, 143; 1955). A. B. Pekar, OSBM, *Narysy istoriji cerkvy Zakarpattja,* 1: *Jerarchične oformlennja* (Prague, 1967; rev. Eng. tr., *The History of the Church in Carpathian Rus'*, Classics of Carpathian-Rusyn Scholarship, 4; New York, 1992). D. Attwater, *The Catholic Eastern Churches* (Milwaukee, Wis. [1935]), pp. 76–95, rev. as *The Christian Churches of the East*, 1 (London, 1961), pp. 72–101. J. Krajcar, SJ, 'The Ruthenian Patriarchate. Some remarks on the project for its establishment in the 17th century', *OCP* 30 (1964), pp. 65–84. E. Likowski, *Geschichte des allmaeligen Verfalls der Unirten Ruthenischen Kirche im XVIII. und XIX. Jahrhundert unter polnischem und russischem Scepter* (Ger. tr., 2 vols., 1885–7). F. Heyer, *Die Orthodoxe Kirche in der Ukraine von 1917 bis 1945* (Osteuropa und der Deutsche Osten, 3; 1953). I. Kirillova, 'The Orthodox Church in the Ukraine: Divisions and Conflicts', *Sourozh*, 54 (Nov. 1993), pp. 12–22. P. R. Magocsi, *The Shaping of a National Identity: Subcarpathian Rus', 1848–1948* (Cambridge, Mass., and London, 1978), esp. pp. 178–87; id., *Galicia: A Historical Survey and Bibliographical Guide* (Toronto and London, 1983), esp. pp. 33 f., 61 f., 81–4, and 159 f. O. Subtelny, *Ukraine: A History* (Toronto, 1988). N. Andrusiak in *DTC* 14 (pt. 1; 1939), cols. 382–407, s.v. 'Ruthène (Église)'; M. M. Wojnar in *NCE* 14 (1967), pp. 372–5, s.v. 'Ukrainian (Ruthenian) Rite'.

UIODG (sometimes **IODG**), i.e. the initial letters of (*ut*) *in omnibus Deus glorificetur* ('that God may be glorified in all things'), one of the mottoes of the *Benedictine Order. It occurs in the 'Rule of St Benedict', ch. 57.

Ullathorne, William Bernard (1806–89), RC Bp. of Birmingham. He was a direct descendant of St Thomas *More. After over three years as a cabin-boy, Ullathorne entered the *Benedictine monastery at *Downside in 1824. He was ordained priest in 1831 and, in 1832, volunteered for the mission in *Australia, of which he was made *Vicar General. He organized the RC Church there, working esp. among the convicts, whose cause he defended vigorously during a stay in England. His tract *The Catholic Mission in Australasia* (1837), as the first popular attack on the convict system, earned him much hostility in Australia. In 1840 he returned to England and in the next year was put in charge of the Benedictine mission at Coventry. Having repeatedly refused a see in Australia, he was appointed *Vicar Apostolic for the Western District of England in 1846. Transferred to the Central District in 1848, he took an active part in the negotiations for establishing the hierarchy in England. During these years he worked together with Cardinal N. *Wiseman to bring about the fusion of the old Catholics with the recent Oxford converts and the Italian priests of the modern congregations, taking up an intermediate position and forming a firm friendship with J. H. *Newman. On the restoration of the hierarchy in 1850 he became Bp. of Birmingham, and later engaged in the controversies about the *Rambler and E. B. *Pusey's *Eirenicon* (1866). At the First *Vatican Council, though a firm *Ultramontane, he occupied an independent position and was a member of the deputation on ecclesiastical discipline. In 1888 he resigned his see and became titular Abp. of Cabasa. His most popular work, the *Autobiography*, ending with the year 1851, which was written in 1868–9 and revised in the last year of his life, was published together with his *Letters* in 1891–2.

[E.] C. Butler, OSB, *The Life and Times of Bishop Ullathorne* (2 vols., 1926); id., *The Vatican Council: The Story told from inside in Bishop Ullathorne's Letters* (2 vols., 1930). A. Austin, OSB, in D. H. Farmer (ed.), *Benedict's Disciples* (Leominster, 1980), pp. 308–26. T. Cooper in *DNB* 58 (1899), pp. 19–21.

Ulphilas (*c.*311–83), Apostle of the Goths. Of Cappadocian ancestry, he was completely at one with the Goths, among whom he was born, in both language and sympathy. He spent much of his life as a young man at *Constantinople, and *c.*341 was consecrated bishop in the city by *Eusebius (formerly Bp. of Nicomedia), then bishop of the capital. Shortly afterwards he returned to his native country to spend the rest of his life as a keen missionary, at first beyond the confines of the Empire, and later among the Goths settled in Moesia II. He translated the Bible into the *Gothic language for the first time, omitting (acc. to *Philostorgius) only the Books of Kings, as their warlike deeds might have a bad influence upon a nation so fond of war as the Goths. Through his connections with Eusebius of Nicomedia, he was led into *Arianism; and it was esp. through his influence that for several centuries the Goths continued attached to that heresy. An Arian confession of faith, of which Ulphilas was the author, has survived in an imperfect form.

Auxentius, Bp. of Dorostorum, *Epistola de Fide, Vita et Obitu Ulfilae*, pr. in J. P. Migne, *PL*, Supplementum, ed. A. Hamman, OFM, 1 (1958), cols. 703–7; with text of creed col. 707; Eng. tr. of this and the relevant portions of Philostorgius, with introd., in P. [J.] Heather and J. [F.] Matthews, *The Goths in the Fourth Century* (Translated Texts for Historians, 11; Liverpool, 1991), pp. 133–53. F. Kauffmann, *Aus der Schule des Wulfila* (Texte und Untersuchungen zur altgermanischen Religionsgeschichte, 1; 1899). J. Zeiller, *Les origines chrétiennes dans les provinces danubiennes de l'Empire romain* (Bibliothèque des Écoles françaises d'Athènes et de Rome, 112; 1918), esp. pp. 440–74. M. Simonetti, 'L'arianesimo di Ulfila', *Romanobarbarica*, 1 (1976), pp. 297–323, with summary in Eng. E. A. Thompson, *The Visigoths in the Time of Ulfila* (Oxford, 1966), *passim*. M. Simonetti in Quasten (cont.), *Patrology*, 4 (1986), pp. 95–7. G. Bardy in *DTC* 15 (pt. 2; 1950), cols. 2048–57, s.v. 'Ulfila'; A. Lippold in *PW*, 2te Reihe, 17 (1961), cols. 512–31, s.v. 'Ulfila'. For works on his version of the Bible see bibl. to GOTHIC VERSION.

Ulrich, St (*c.*890–973), Bp. of Augsburg from 923. He took a prominent part in the political and ecclesiastical history of his time. Staunchly loyal to the Emp. Otto I, he supported him in the Swabian uprising of 953, and he led the defence of Augsburg against the Magyars in 955. He was an effective administrator of his diocese and took his pastoral duties seriously, upholding a high standard of clerical morality. He had himself been educated at St Gall, and during his episcopacy the school at Augsburg flourished. He is the first person known to have been formally canonized by a Pope; at the instigation of a delegation from Augsburg John XV pronounced him a saint at the *Lateran synod of 29 Jan. 993. Feast day, 4 July.

A *Sermo Synodalis* of Ulrich is repr. from P. *Labbe in J. P. Migne, *PL* 135. 1071–4. The 'Epistola de Continentia Clericorum' (a forged letter opposing clerical celibacy ascribed to him in the 11th cent.), ed. L. von Heinemann in *MGH*, Libelli de Lite Imperatorum et Pontificum Saeculis XI et XII, 1 (1891), pp. 254–60. The principal source for his life is the biog. by Gerhard, Provost of Augsburg, which was taken to Rome in 993 in support of his canonization; it is pr. in *AASS*, Jul. 2 (1721), pp. 97–131; also ed. G. Waitz in *MGH*, Scriptores, 4 (1841), pp. 377–425; Ger. tr., with introd., by H. Kallfelz, *Lebensbeschreibungen einiger Bischöfe des 10.–12. Jahrhunderts* (Ausgewählte Quellen zur deutschen Geschichte des Mittelalters, 22; Darmstadt, 1973), pp. 35–167. The Life by Bernard of *Reichenau (d. 1248), tr. into Ger. *c.*1200, ed. in Ger. and Lat. by J. A. Schmeller (Munich, 1844). K. Haupt, 'Die Ulrichsvita in der mittelalterlichen Malerei', in *Bischof Ulrich und der Augsburger Religionsfriede: Neue Quellenforschungen zum Augsburger Gedenkjahr 955 + 1555 + 1955* (Zeitschrift des historischen Vereins für Schwaben, 61; 1955), pp. 1–159, incl. illustr. F. Zoepfl, *Das Bistum Augsburg und seine Bischöfe im Mittelalter* [1955], pp. 61–77. A. Finck von

Finkenstein, 'Ulrich von Augsburg und die ottonische Kirchen-politik in der Alemannia', in I. Eberl and others (eds.), *Früh- und hochmittelalterlicher Adel in Schwaben und Bayern* (Regio. Forschungen zur schwäbischen Regionalgeschichte, 1; Sigmaringendorf, 1988), pp. 261–9; G. Althoff, *Amicitiae und Pacta: Bündnis, Einung, Politik und Gebetsgedenken im beginnenden 10. Jahrhundert* (*MGH*, Schriften, 37; 1992), pp. 295–306.

Ultramontanism. The name widely given to a tendency in the RC Church which favours the centralization of authority and influence in the Papal *Curia, as opposed to national or diocesan independence. The word is found as early as the 11th cent., but opinions differ as to whether it was used in an ecclesiastical as distinguished from a geographical sense before the rise of *Gallicanism in France in the 17th cent. In this cent. and the next, Ultramontanism became a definite point of view which gained more and more power as national and centrifugal movements such as Gallicanism, *Jansenism, and *Josephinism became discredited either as involved in definite heresy or as lending countenance to the new liberal and anti-Christian movements of which the French Revolution of 1789 was the logical and most systematic expression. The 19th cent., therefore, saw the triumph of the Ultramontane cause, since there rallied to it all those elements in the RC Church which were most opposed to the rising theological liberalism of the age. In France the Gallican party was overpowered by the reproach of having conformed to the Revolution; in Germany the Ultramontanes seized the part of defenders of the Church against the interference of the State in spiritual affairs; in England the new missionary element among the RCs, little hampered by national traditions of the past, had every inducement, in spite of opposition from the hereditary RC families, to support to the utmost the policy of the Curia. The stages of the triumph of Ultramontanism were roughly as follows:

1814. The revival of the *Jesuit Order, which was always the mainstay of curial as opposed to local authority.

1864. The issuing by *Pius IX of the *Syllabus, in which Catholicism and any form of liberalism were held to be incompatible.

1870. The declaration by the First *Vatican Council that the Pope is infallible when he makes, by virtue of his office, a solemn pronouncement on faith or morals. This declaration, though not conceding the claim of administrative infallibility which many Ultramontanes would have wished, marked a substantial triumph for their point of view.

F. Nielsen, *Pavedømmet i den nittende Hundredaar* (2 vols., 1876; 2nd edn. rev., 1895–8; Eng. tr., *The History of the Papacy in the XIXth Century*, 2 vols., 1906); J. B. Bury, *History of the Papacy in the Nineteenth Century* (1930); J. D. Holmes, *The Triumph of the Holy See: A Short History of the Papacy in the Nineteenth Century* (1978). A. Gough, *Rome and Paris: The Gallican Church and the Ultramontane Campaign 1848–1853* (Oxford, 1986). H. Linn, *Ultramontanismus in Köln* (Studien zur Kölner Kirchengeschichte, 22; Siegburg, 1987); E. Garhammer, *Seminaridee und Klerusbildung bei Karl August Graf von Reisach: Eine pastoralgeschichtliche Studie zum Ultramontanismus des 19. Jahrhunderts* (Münchener Kirchenhistorische Studien, 5 [1990]). R. Aubert in Fliche and Martin, 21 (1952), pp. 262–310, with bibl.

UMCA. The (Anglican) Universities' Mission to Central Africa. It was founded in response to an appeal by D.

*Livingstone in the Senate House at Cambridge in 1857 and has received continuous support from members of the universities. The first expedition was led by C. F. Mackenzie, who was consecrated Bp. in South Africa on the way out, but died in Nyasaland within two years of sailing up the Zambezi river. In 1864 the second bishop, W. G. Tozer (Bp. 1863–73), moved the Mission to the island of Zanzibar. Reports from the Mission were instrumental in rousing opinion against the slave trade, which was centred at Zanzibar; in 1873 the Sultan was persuaded to abolish it, and the foundation-stone of the cathedral was laid on the site of the slave market. In the same year work was re-established on the mainland; it extended through what are now Tanzania, Malawi, and *Zambia. Owing to the climate there was a high rate of mortality among the missionaries, and from the first the training of a native ministry has been in the forefront of the Mission's work. The first African (a former slave given to Bp. Tozer by the Sultan) was ordained deacon in 1879. Nearly all the clergy and bishops in the countries served by the Mission are now nationals. The Community of the Sacred Passion, founded by Bp. F. *Weston of Zanzibar in 1910, has African and British nuns.

The formation in the 1950s of the Provinces of East and Central Africa cut across the area of the Mission's activities. In 1965 the UMCA joined with the *SPG to form the United Society for the Propagation of the Gospel (*USPG).

R. Keable, *Darkness or Light* (1912); G. H. Wilson, *History of the Universities' Mission to Central Africa* (1936); *The History of the Universities' Mission to Central Africa*: vol. 1 by A. E. M. Anderson-Morshead, covering 1859–96 (1897; 5th edn., covering 1859–1909, 1909); vol. 2 by A. G. Blood, covering 1907–32 (1957); vol. 3 by id., covering 1933–57 (1962). M. Dewey, *The Messengers: A Concise History of the United Society for the Propagation of the Gospel* (1975).

Una Sancta (Lat., 'One Holy'). Two of the *Notes of the Church in the *Nicene Creed, and often used, esp. in quite recent times, substantively for the Church, usually with emphasis upon its corporate aspect.

Unam Sanctam. The bull (so named from its opening words) which *Boniface VIII issued on 18 Nov. 1302 during his quarrel with Philip IV of France, declaring that there was 'One Holy Catholic and Apostolic Church' outside which there was 'neither salvation nor remission of sins'. It strongly emphasized the position of the Pope as the Supreme Head of the Church; and it maintained that to reject his authority was to cease to belong to the Church. It further declared that the 'temporal sword' and the 'spiritual sword' were alike committed to the Church. Of these the spiritual sword was in the hands of the clergy, while the temporal sword was delegated to the secular authority, to be wielded on behalf of the Church and under its direction. Since what was spiritual was greater than what was temporal, the temporal power was to be subject to the spiritual, which was itself subject only to the judgement of God. As the authority of the spiritual power had been divinely granted to St *Peter and his successors, to oppose it was to oppose the law of God Himself. The bull concluded by affirming that it was necessary to salvation for every human creature to be subject to the Roman

Pontiff. Although the text of the bull contained nothing new, it brought to a point the ever-growing claims of the Papacy and marks the zenith of medieval Papal ecclesiastical polity.

Crit. edn. of text in G. Digard, M. Faucon, A. Thomas, and R. Fawtier (eds.), *Les Registres de Boniface VIII* (Bibliothèque des Écoles Françaises d'Athènes et de Rome, 2nd ser. 4), 3 (1921) cols. 888–90 (no. 5382); text also in Mirbt and Aland, 1 (1967), pp. 458–60 (no. 746); Eng. tr. of operative portions in Bettenson, pp. 159–61. T. S. R. Boase, *Boniface VIII* (1933), esp. ch. 12, pp. 313–37; J. Rivière, *Le Problème de l'Église et de l'État au temps de Philippe le Bel* (SSL 8; 1926), esp. pp. 79–91, 150–5.

uncial script. A form of majuscule script used for books in Greek and Latin from about the 4th to the 8th cents. AD. Greek examples are the *Codices Sinaiticus, Vaticanus, and Alexandrinus; Latin examples are the Codex of *Eusebius of Vercelli and the *Codices Fuldensis and Amiatinus (qq.v.). Its name is derived from a passage in *Jerome's preface to Job, but its present meaning is that assigned to it by the *Maurist authors of the *Nouveau Traité de diplomatique* (1765). See also CURSIVE SCRIPT.

Uncreated Light. In the *Hesychast system, the mystical light of God's visible Presence (also known as the **Light of Tabor**) which the soul was held to be capable of apprehending by submitting to an elaborate process of ascetic purification and devotion. Its attainment was considered the highest end of man on earth. See also HESYCHASM.

unction. The process of anointing with oil with a religious significance, usually by a bishop or priest, e.g. at the *Coronation of a monarch. In the RC and E. Orthodox Churches unction is used both at *Baptism and *Confirmation. The word is most commonly applied, however, to the Sacrament of the Unction (or Anointing) of the Sick. This rite was long known in the W. Church as 'extreme unction' (*unctio extrema*), the word 'extreme' being explained either by the fact that it was the last of the three Sacramental Unctions or because it was normally administered only when the patient was *in extremis*. The 'Constitution on Liturgy' of the Second *Vatican Council recommended the title 'Anointing of the Sick' and this has been adopted in the Ordo issued in 1972 ('Ordo Unctionis Infirmorum eorumque Pastoralis Curae').

In the NT the anointing of the sick is referred to in Mk. 6: 13 and Jas. 5: 14 f. There is a prayer for the Blessing of Oil in St *Hippolytus, *Apostolic Tradition*, 5, and in the *Euchologion* of St *Serapion of Thmuis (d. *c.*365). From the 5th cent. references are more frequent. *Innocent I, in his Ep. to Decentius of Eugubium (416), describes the rite of unction with both spiritual and physical effects from which those undergoing canonical *penance are excluded. In St *Caesarius of Arles the rite is found in connection with the reception of Holy Communion; *Bede represents it as a well-established custom; and from the 10th cent. it is frequently discussed in connection with the theology of the Sacraments. Since *Peter Lombard, the first known author to use the term 'extreme unction', it has been numbered among the *Seven Sacraments. According to developed medieval doctrine, as expounded by St

*Thomas Aquinas, the remote matter of the Sacrament is the oil consecrated by the bishop, its proximate matter the anointing of the five senses, its form prayer and its minister the priest.

In the first seven cents. recovery from illness was commonly expected as a result of unction. In the early Middle Ages, however, the rite became so closely connected with repentance and the whole penitential system that it was commonly postponed until death was approaching, and in practice bodily recovery was not ordinarily looked for. The 1972 RC Ordo lays much greater emphasis on healing and underlines the position of sickness in the normal life of Christians and its part in the redemptive work of the Church. The Ordo provides for a blessing of the room (with *Holy Water if desired), a brief address, a penitential act (which may include sacramental *confession), the reading of one of a selection of scriptural passages, with commentary if circumstances permit, intercession for the sick person and his attendants, and the laying on of hands in silence; the patient is then anointed on the forehead and hands with a formula in two parts, to each of which he replies 'Amen'; the rite closes with a collect asking for healing, the *Lord's Prayer (after which the sick person may receive Communion if appropriate), and a special blessing. Normally oil blessed by the bishop on *Maundy Thursday is used, but in cases of necessity the priest administering the Sacrament may bless the oil. In the past olive oil was required, but oil from any plant may now be used. The Sacrament may be administered to all who are seriously ill, more than once during the same illness if a new crisis arises, to old people who are weak but not ill, and to children old enough to appreciate the nature of the Sacrament. RC Canon Law on the subject is contained in *CIC* (1983) cans. 998–1007.

In the Greek Church the rite is called *Euchelaion* (Gk. εὐχέλαιον, εὐχή, 'prayer', and ἔλαιον, 'oil') and administered in church by seven, five, or three priests, or by a single priest. Here its primary end is held to be the physical cure, though it is in fact frequently received as a preparation for Communion even by those who are not ill, esp. on the Wednesday in *Holy Week.

In the First English BCP (1549) a form of unction was included in the Order for the Visitation of the Sick for use 'if the sick person desire'. It contained an accompanying prayer for healing of body and mind, forgiveness, and spiritual strengthening. In 1552 and later versions of the BCP there has been no provision for unction. In modern times a desire for its restoration has been widely expressed in the Anglican Communion. The revised Scottish and American Prayer Books (1929) and most later Anglican liturgies make provision for unction of the sick. In Britain in 1935 a 'Form of Unction and the Laying on of Hands' was approved by the *Convocations of Canterbury and York 'for provisional use subject to due diocesan sanction'. The 1969 Canons (can. B 37) allows that if the sick 'person so desires, the priest may lay hands upon him and may anoint him with oil upon the forehead with the sign of the Cross using the form of service sanctioned by lawful authority'. The ASB includes provision for the Blessing of the Oils on Maundy Thursday, and the Alternative Services *Ministry to the Sick* (1983) allows other parts of the body to be anointed in addition to the forehead.

J. Kern, SJ, *De Sacramento Extremae Unctionis Tractatus Dogmaticus* (Ratisbon, 1907). A. Chavasse, *Étude sur l'onction des infirmes dans l'église latine du iii* au xi* siècle*, 1. *Du iii* siècle à la réforme carolingienne* (Lyons, 1942). P. Murray, 'The Liturgical History of Extreme Unction', *Studies in Pastoral Liturgy*, 2, ed. V. Ryan, OSB (Dublin, 1963), pp. 18–38 [based on unpub. 2nd pt. of Chavasse's work]. B. Poschmann, *Busse und Letzte Ölung* (Handbuch der Dogmengeschichte, ed. M. Schmaus and others, 4, Fasz. 3; Freiburg i.B., 1951), pp. 125–38; Eng. tr. rev. by F. Courtney, SJ, *Penance and Anointing of the Sick* (1964), pp. 234–57; H. Vorgrimler, *Busse und Krankensalbung* (Handbuch der Dogmengeschichte, 4, Fasz. 3; 1978), pp. 215–34. H. B. Porter, 'The Origin of the Medieval Rite for Anointing the Sick or Dying', *JTS* NS 7 (1956), pp. 211–25; id., 'The Rites for the Dying in the Early Middle Ages', ibid. 10 (1959), pp. 43–62 and 299–307. A special number of *Maison-Dieu* (no. 113; 1973), 'Le Nouveau Rituel des malades', incl. bibl. by J. C. Didier, pp. 81–5. E. J. Lengeling, ' "Per istam sanctam unctionem … adiuvet te Dominus gratia Spiritus Sancti". Die heilige Geist und die Krankensalbung', in *Lex Orandi, Lex Credendi: Miscellanea in onore di P. Cipriano Vagaggini*, ed. G. Békés and G. Farnedi (Studi Anselmiana, 79; 1980), pp. 235–94. B. Kranemann, *Die Krankensalbung in der Zeit der Aufklärung: Ritualien und pastoralliturgische Studien im deutschen Sprachgebiet* (Liturgiewissenschaftliche Quellen und Forschungen, 72 [1990]). K. M. Rallis, Περὶ τῶν μυστηρίων τῆς μετανοίας καὶ τοῦ εὐχελαίου κατὰ τὸ δίκαιον τῆς ὀρθοδόξου ἀνατολικῆς ἐκκλησίας (1905). T. Spáčil, SJ, *Doctrina Theologiae Orientis Separati de Sacra Infirmorum Unctione* (Orientalia Christiana, 24, Heft 2; no. 74; 1931), with bibl. B. J. Groen, *'Ter Genezing van Ziel en Lichaam': Die viering van het oliesel in de Grieks-Orthodoxe kerk* (Theology & Empire, 11 [1990]), with Eng. summary, pp. 255–7. C. W. Gusmer, *The Ministry of Healing in the Church of England: An Ecumenical-Liturgical Study* (Alcuin Club Collections, 56; 1973). G. Martimort in id. (ed.), *L'Église en Prière*, new edn., 3 [1984], pp. 132–53; Eng. tr. (1988), pp. 117–37, with further bibl. C. Ruch and L. Godefroy in *DTC* 5 (1913), cols. 1897–2022, s.v. 'Extrême-Onction'; H. *Leclercq, OSB, in *DACL* 5 (1922), cols. 1029–37, s.v. 'Extrême-Onction', and ibid. 12 (pt. 2; 1936), cols. 2116–30, s.v. 'Onction'; E. Cothenet in *Dict. Bibl.*, Suppl. 6 (1960), cols. 701–32, s.v. 'Onction'; T. A. Vismans, OP, in *LW* 2 (1968), cols. 2988–92, s.v. 'Ziekenzalving', with extensive bibl. See also bibl. to SPIRITUAL HEALING and VISITATION OF THE SICK.

Underhill, Evelyn (1875–1941), exponent of the mystical life. The daughter of a distinguished barrister, she was educated at *King's College, London, and later travelled much on the Continent. In 1907 she underwent an experience of religious conversion; she was drawn to the RC Church, but after the condemnation of *Modernism felt unable to join it and in her spiritual struggles turned to the study of the mystics. The first literary fruit of her newly awakened interest was her well-known book *Mysticism* (1911; 13th edn., 1940). Its range extended from St *Teresa to J. *Boehme and from Christian mystical experience to *Neoplatonist speculations, and its comprehensive approach to religious experience at once made it a standard work. In 1911 she came under the influence of F. *von Hügel, and about the same time began to undertake individual spiritual direction, but it was not until 1921 that she formally put herself under von Hügel's direction, and became a communicant member of the C of E. From 1924 onwards she was a much sought-after retreat-conductor. In 1927 she was made a Fellow of King's College, London. She was a prolific writer, the most important work of her later years being *Worship* (1936), which embodied her general outlook in a broad review of

the subject. She also published valuable modernized editions of the *Cloud of Unknowing* (1912) and W. *Hilton's *Scale of Perfection* (1923), and wrote a study of *Jacopone da Todi (1919). In her later years she was a keen pacifist. She is commemorated in the *Episcopal Church in the United States of America on 15 June.

The Letters of Evelyn Underhill, ed. with introd. by C. [W. S.] *Williams (1943). A collection of her arts., ed. with introd. and bibl. by D. Greene, *Evelyn Underhill: Modern Guide to the Ancient Quest for the Holy* (New York [1988]). Lives by M. [B.] Cropper (London, 1958) and C. J. R. Armstrong (ibid., 1975). Study by D. Greene (New York, 1990; London, 1991). M. Vernon in *DNB*, *1941–1950*, pp. 897 f.

Uniat Churches. The Churches of E. Christendom in communion with *Rome, which yet retain their respective languages, rites, and canon law in accordance with the terms of their union; these last in most cases provide for *Communion in both kinds, *Baptism by *immersion, and marriage of the clergy. In 1972 a commission was set up to prepare a code of canon law for all Uniat Churches; this was promulgated in 1990 and came into force in 1991. The term 'Uniat' (Lat. *Unio*, so Polish *Unia*) was first used by the opponents of the Union of *Brest-Litovsk (1595), and has been consistently disowned by the Churches concerned. The main groups covered by the designation are the *Maronites (united 1182), the *Syrians under the Patriarch of *Antioch, and the *Malankarese (1930), all of the Antiochene rite; the *Armenians under the Patriarch of Cilicia (united 1198–1291 and 1741); the *Chaldeans (1551 and 1830) and the *Malabarese (before 1599) of the Chaldean rite; the *Copts (1741) and *Ethiopians (1839), both of the Alexandrian rite; and of the Byzantine rite the Polish Ruthenians (now called *Ukrainians; 1595), the *Hungarians (1595), the Serbs in Croatia (1611), the Podcarpathian Ruthenians (1646), the *Romanians (1701), the Melkites (1724), and certain Bulgars (1860) and *Greeks (1860). Of these the largest body is the Ukrainians. The term is also applied to the Italo-Greek-Albanian community of S. Italy which, although never separated from Rome, is permitted to follow similar practices. In 1946 the Uniat Church in the Ukraine, and in 1948 that in Romania, were suppressed and their faithful forced to join the *Russian and Romanian Orthodox Churches respectively. They continued an underground existence and were legalized in 1989 and 1990. The total number of Uniats or Eastern Rite Catholics is prob. some 15 million. See also under separate groups.

D. Attwater, *The Catholic Eastern Churches* (Milwaukee, 1937), rev. as *The Christian Churches of the East*, 1 (London, 1961). C. de Clercq, *Les Églises unies d'Orient* (Bibliothèque Catholique des Sciences Religieuses; 1934). J. Hajjar, *Les Chrétiens uniates du Proche-Orient* (1962). Maximos IV Sayegh (ed.), *The Eastern Churches and Catholic Unity* (Freiburg and Edinburgh [1963]). J. Madey and S. T. Erackel (eds.), *The Future of the Oriental Catholic Churches* (Tiruvalla, India [1979]). C. A. Frazee, *Catholics and Sultans: The Church and the Ottoman Empire 1453–1923* (1983). S. Gaselee, *The Uniats and their Rites* (*Alcuin Club Tracts, 16; 1925). The 'Codex Canonum Ecclesiarum Orientalium' is pr. in *AAS* 82 (1990), pp. 1045–363. V. J. Pospishil, *Eastern Catholic Church Law according to the Code of Canons of the Eastern Churches* (Brooklyn, N.Y., 1993). On the Melkites and Uniats of S. Italy, A. *Fortescue, *The Uniate Eastern Churches*, ed. G. D. Smith (1923).

Uniformity, Acts of. There have been four:

(1) UNIFORMITY ACT 1548. This was passed on 21 Jan. 1549, and imposed the exclusive use of the First BCP of *Edward VI from the ensuing *Whitsunday (9 June) in the 'celebration of the Lord's Supper, commonly called the Mass' and in all public services. Holders of benefices who did not comply were punishable for a first offence with forfeiture of a year's income and six months' imprisonment, for a second offence with deprivation and a year's imprisonment, and for a third offence with imprisonment for life. Penalties of the same order were imposed for depraving or speaking against the Book. The public services were to be in English, with the exception that at the universities, 'for the encouragement of learning', all services other than the Mass might be said in Latin, Greek, or Hebrew; and in private use of the Book everyone was at liberty to use those languages as he wished. Only eight bishops and three lay peers voted against the Bill.

(2) UNIFORMITY ACT 1551. This was passed on 14 Apr. 1552. It stated that, owing to doubts occasioned by the interpretation of the 'very godly order' of the first Act, the BCP had been revised; and the use of the Second BCP of Edward VI was ordered from *All Saints' Day (1 Nov.) 1552. Absence from church on Sundays and Holy Days by all not reasonably hindered was now made punishable by ecclesiastical censures, and attendance at any other form of service by imprisonment.

(3) ACT OF UNIFORMITY 1558. This Act, *Primo Elizabethae*, which forms part of the 1662 BCP, received the Royal Assent on 8 May 1559. After repealing the legislation of *Mary's reign reimposing the forms of worship in use under *Henry VIII, it ordered the use of the Book of 1552, with three modifications and omission of the *Black Rubric, from 24 June 1559. The penalties for depraving the Book were increased, and absence from church made punishable by a fine of 12 pence as well as ecclesiastical censures. The *Ornaments Rubric was inserted in the Book, modified by a proviso in the Act itself.

(4) ACT OF UNIFORMITY 1662. As part of the Restoration settlement, a Bill for reintroducing the BCP passed the Commons in July 1661, but as the *Convocations did not complete the revision of the Book until December, the Bill was again considered in 1662. The Book itself (i.e. the 1662 BCP still in use), which was annexed to the Bill, was not discussed by either Commons or Lords. The Bill received the Royal Assent on 19 May. Before the ensuing St *Bartholomew's Day (24 Aug.), all ministers were required publicly to assent to the Book, from which day its exclusive use was ordered. Ministers not episcopally ordained by that date were to be deprived. All ministers and schoolmasters were also required to make a declaration of the illegality of taking up arms against the King and to repudiate the *National Covenant. Some 2,000 Presbyterian ministers who refused to conform were ejected from their livings.

This Act still remains on the Statute Book. It has been modified at a few points by the *Clerical Subscription Act 1865, the *Universities Tests Act 1871, the Prayer Book (Table of Lessons) Act 1871, the Act of *Uniformity Amendment Act 1872 and, more radically, by the Church of England (*Worship and Doctrine) Measure 1974.

The texts are pr. in Gee and Hardy as follows: (1) pp. 358–66 (no. 69); (2) pp. 369–72 (no. 71); (3) pp. 458–67 (no. 80); and (4), pp. 600–19 (no. 117).

Uniformity Amendment Act 1872, Act of. More generally known as the 'Shortened Services Act', this Act, passed by Parliament after its approval by the *Convocations of *Canterbury and *York, provided for the optional use of shortened forms of Morning and Evening Prayer, as additional services, in parish churches on Sundays and certain other days, and in cathedrals on any day, and as substitutes for the full services in parish churches on weekdays. The chief omissions sanctioned were the Exhortation 'Dearly beloved brethren', all but one of the appointed *Psalms, one of the *Canticles, and the State Prayers. It also provided that Morning Prayer, the Litany, and the Communion Service might be recited separately. The Act was repealed by the Church of England (*Worship and Doctrine) Measure 1974.

For exact details see the 'Schedule' to the Act, pr. in R. *Phillimore, *Ecclesiastical Law* (2nd edn., 1895), 1, pp. 757–61.

Unigenitus (1343). The bull of *Clement VI, issued on 27 Jan. 1343, which gave official approval to the teaching of the Schoolmen that *indulgences owed their efficacy to the Pope's dispensation of the accumulated *merit of the Church. In 1518 Cardinal T. de Vio *Cajetan accused M. *Luther of contravening its contents.

Text in *Corpus Iuris Canonici*, ed. A. Friedberg, 2 (Leipzig, 1881), cols. 1304–6, repr. in Mirbt and Aland, 1 (1967), pp. 472–4 (no. 760).

Unigenitus (1713). The Constitution of *Clement XI, pub. 8 Sept. 1713, condemning 101 propositions extracted from P. *Quesnel's *Réflexions morales sur le Nouveau Testament*. Some of these propositions contain doctrine previously condemned in the works of M. *Baius (1567) and C. O. *Jansen (1653). Most of the others are reactionary criticisms of modern developments in Catholic faith and practice. Many French Jansenists appealed from Clement's verdict to a 'future Council'.

Text in *Bullarum, Diplomatum et Privilegiorum Sanctorum Romanorum Pontificum Taurinensis Editio*, 21 (1871), pp. 567–75 (no. 187); abbrev. text in Denzinger and Hünermann (37th edn., 1991), pp. 670–82 (nos. 2400–502). J. Parguez, *La Bulle Unigenitus et le jansénisme politique* (1936); J. F. Thomas, *La Querelle de l'Unigenitus* (1950). L. Ceyssens and J. A. G. Tans, *Autour de l'Unigenitus: Recherches sur la Genèse de la Constitution* (Bibliotheca Ephemeridum Theologicarum Lovaniensium, 76; 1987 [repr. series of arts. orig. pub. 1981–4]). Further collection of arts. by L. Ceyssens and M. Lamberigts, *Le Sort de la Bulle Unigenitus* (ibid. 104; 1992). J. M. Gres-Gayer, 'The *Unigenitus* of Clement XI: A Fresh Look at the Issues', *Theological Studies*, 49 (1988), pp. 259–82. J. Carreyre, PSS, in *DTC* 15 (pt. 2; 1950), cols. 2061–162, s.v. 'Unigenitus (Bulle)'.

Union of Brest. See BREST-LITOVSK, UNION OF.

Union of Christendom. See REUNION.

Union Theological Seminary, New York City. An institution for the training of ministers founded in 1836, by the independent action of 'New School' Presbyterians, for 'men of moderate views' of any denomination. It has always encouraged critical studies and advocated toleration. Temporarily under Presbyterian control after 1870, it reclaimed its independence in 1892 and refused to dismiss C. A. *Briggs. Twelve years later it became a fully non-denominational institution. Its professors have regularly been scholars of international reputation, a number of them from abroad.

R. T. Handy, *A History of Union Theological Seminary in New York* (New York, 1987).

Unitarianism. A type of Christian thought and religious observance which rejects the doctrines of the Trinity and the Divinity of Christ in favour of the unipersonality of God. Unitarians have no formal creed. Originally their teaching was based on scriptural authority, but J. *Martineau (1805–1900) in England and T. *Parker (1810–60) in the USA led the way from biblical to rational Unitarianism. Hence reason and conscience have now become the criteria of belief and practice for Unitarians. Owing to their belief in the abiding goodness of human nature, they are critical of the orthodox doctrines of the *Fall, the *Atonement, and eternal punishment.

Though the unipersonality of God was voiced in the early Church in the various forms of *Monarchianism, modern Unitarianism dates historically from the Reformation era. It soon attracted adherents among those of extreme reforming views, esp. in the sects. Probably its earliest exponent was Martin Cellarius (1499–1564), a pupil of J. *Reuchlin, who defended Unitarian views in *De Operibus Dei* (Strasbourg, 1527). Other early Unitarians were J. de *Valdés (at least in sympathy), M. *Servetus, and B. *Ochino. As an organized community, it became established in the 16th–17th cents. in Poland, Hungary, and England.

In Poland George Blandrata, a Piedmontese physician, became leader of an active group of Unitarians in 1558. They continued to grow until 1565, when anti-Trinitarians were excluded from the synod of the Reformed Church and henceforward compelled to hold their own synods as the 'Minor Church'. From 1579 until his death (1604) Faustus *Socinus led the party. In 1605 the *Racovian Catechism (q.v.) was issued. Towards the middle of the 17th cent. they had to face strong opposition. In 1638 the *Jesuits secured the suppression of the Unitarian college at Raków; in 1658 Socinians were expelled from the realm and all traces of Unitarianism disappeared from Poland.

In Hungary also, Blandrata, who arrived in the country in 1563, was largely responsible for the spread of anti-Trinitarianism, and the King himself, John Sigismund, was converted. But after Sigismund's death (1570) the sect was persecuted. In 1638 the Unitarians put forward a common confession and were recognized as a legitimate religion.

In England John *Biddle (q.v.; 1615–62) is generally reckoned the father of Unitarianism. He published Unitarian tracts and in 1652–4 and 1658–62 held conventicles in London. Rather more than 100 years later J. *Priestley defended Unitarian principles in his *Appeal to the Serious and Candid Professors of Christianity* (1770). But until T. *Lindsey seceded from the C of E in 1773 and formed for the first time a Unitarian denomination, there was only one other Unitarian conventicle in England. In 1774 Lind-

sey opened Essex Chapel in London. Penal Acts continued in force against Unitarians until 1813. In the 18th cent. Unitarian views were also widely accepted by Dissenting congregations, esp. among the English *Presbyterians. The long disputes as to the endowments of chapels, once orthodox but now in the hands of the Unitarians, were ended in 1844 by the *Nonconformists' Chapels Act, which allowed the Unitarians to keep chapels founded on an Open Trust where over 25 years' usage could be proved for their opinions. In the later 19th cent. much influence was exercised by J. Martineau, who insisted that the term 'Unitarian' could be only the name of the belief of individuals and should never be adopted as the restrictive title of a denomination. In 1888 Manchester College was moved from London to Oxford with the aim of establishing it there as a college of liberal education without denominational ties. The *Hibbert Trust (founded 1853) devoted its income to promoting public lectures on comparative religion and similar subjects and to supporting a journal of liberal theology (the *Hibbert Journal*, 1902–68). The first quarter of the 20th cent., however, witnessed a swing towards more radical Unitarianism in some quarters. In 1925 the British and Foreign Unitarian Association (founded in 1825) and the National Conference (long the stronghold of the anti-dogmatic party) united into the 'General Assembly of Unitarian and Free Churches', the British and Foreign Unitarian Association remaining in existence only as a legal custodian of funds. From this time the Unitarians in England have been a distinctive and organized denomination, whose numbers have dwindled markedly in modern times.

In America the first definitely Unitarian congregation was King's Chapel, Boston. In 1785 it adopted a form of the American liturgy, revised to meet the needs of Unitarians. In the early 19th cent. Unitarianism was also adopted in *Congregationalist Churches. The American Unitarian Association was formed in 1825 and in 1865 the first National Conference of Unitarian Churches. The ethical and philosophical aspects of Unitarianism were emphasized in different ways by W. E. *Channing (1780–1842) and R. W. *Emerson (1803–82). Before the end of the 19th cent. Unitarianism in America had become a very liberal or rationalistic movement, accepting scientific methods and ideas and recognizing the truth of non-Christian religions. It came to exercise an influence disproportionate to the number of its adherents largely through the Divinity School at Harvard University as reconstituted by Charles W. Eliot (1869–1909). In 1961 the American Unitarian Association joined with the Universalist Church of America to form the Unitarian Universalist Association.

Collection of the works of F. Socinus, J. Crellius, J. Stichling, and L. Wolzogen in the *Bibliotheca Fratrum Polonorum quos Unitarios Vocant* (8 vols., Amsterdam, 1656). F. S. Bock, *Historia Antitrinitariorum, maxime Socinianismi et Socinianorum* (2 vols., Königsberg, 1774–8). F. Trechsel, *Die Protestantischen Antitrinitarier vor Faustus Socin* (2 vols., 1839–44); O. Fock, *Der Socinianismus nach seiner Stellung in der Gesammtentwickelung des christlichen Geistes* (2 vols., Kiel, 1847). *The Polish Brethren: Documentation of the History and Thought of Unitarianism in the Polish-Lithuanian Commonwealth and in the Diaspora, 1601–1685*, ed. and tr. G. H. Williams (Harvard Theological Studies, 30; 2 parts, Missoula, Mont. [1980]). J. H. Allen, *An Historical Sketch of the Unitarian Movement since the Reformation* (New York, 1894). J. E. *Carpenter (ed.), *Freedom and Truth: Modern Views of*

Unitarianism (1925). H. Gow, *The Unitarians* ('The Faiths', 1928). E. M. Wilbur, *A History of Unitarianism: Socinianism and its Antecedents* (Cambridge, Mass., 1946); id., *A History of Unitarianism in Transylvania, England, and America* (ibid., 1952). K. Twinn (ed.), *Essays in Unitarian Theology* (1959). R. Wallace, *Antitrinitarian Biography* (3 vols., 1850). H. J. McLachlan, *Socinianism in Seventeenth-Century England* (1951); H. McLachlan, *The Unitarian Movement in the Religious Life of England*, 1: *Its Contribution to Thought and Learning, 1700–1900* (1934); R. V. Holt, *The Unitarian Contribution to Social Progress in England* (1938). C. G. Bolam, J. Goring, H. L. Short, and R. Thomas, *The English Presbyterians from Elizabethan Puritanism to Modern Unitarianism* (1968). J. H. Allen in id. and R. Eddy, *A History of the Unitarians and the Universalists in the United States* (American Church History Series, 10; 1894), pp. 1–249; C. Wright, *The Liberal Christians: Essays on American Unitarian History* (Boston [1970]); C. E. Wright (ed.), *American Unitarianism, 1805–1865* (Massachusetts Historical Society Studies in American History and Culture, 1 [1989]). D. Robinson, *The Unitarians and the Universalists* (Denominations in America, 1; Westport, Conn., and London, 1985). W. J. Kühler, *Socinianisme in Nederland* (Leiden, 1912); J. C. van Slee, *De Geschiedenis van het Socinianisme in Nederlanden* (Haarlem, 1914). S. Kot, *Ideologia polityczna i społeczna Braci Polskich zwanych Arjanami* (Warsaw, 1932; Eng. tr., *Socinianism in Poland*, Boston [1957]). J. E. Carpenter in *HERE* 12 (1921), pp. 519–27, s.v. (also issued separately, London, 1922). J. C. Godbey in M. Eliade (ed.), *Encyclopedia of Religion*, 15 (1987), pp. 143–7, s.v. 'Unitarian Universalist Association'.

Unitas Fratrum. The Latinized form of the Czech *jednota bratrská* ('society of brethren'), the title assumed by the branch of the *Hussites known as the *Bohemian Brethren (q.v.) and their successors, the *Moravian Brethren.

United Church of Christ. A Church in the USA formed in 1957 by the union of the Evangelical and Reformed Church with the *Congregational Christian Churches. The Evangelical and Reformed Church was itself the result of a union in 1934 between the Evangelical Synod of North America and the Reformed Church of America. The former of these bodies was composed mainly of immigrants from Germany who were in sympathy with the Union of Lutheran and Reformed (Calvinist) traditions ordered by King Frederick of Prussia in 1817; the latter drew on refugees driven from the Palatinate region of Germany as a result of the devastations of the *Thirty Years War and on the Reformed Churches of Switzerland and the Netherlands. The Congregational Christian Churches were formed by a union in 1931 between the Congregational National Council and the Christian Churches, the latter being a small group of Churches holding similar principles of Churchmanship. Negotiations between the Evangelical and Reformed Church and the Congregational Christian Churches were authorized in 1942. After various legal difficulties the United Church of Christ was formed in a Uniting General Synod on 25 June 1957; its constitution came into force in 1961. About 85 per cent of the Congregational Christian Churches and nearly all the Evangelical and Reformed Churches joined to form the United Church of Christ, which originally had nearly 2 million members (by the early 1990s, some 1.6 million). The union has a particular significance owing to the wide differences in styles of Churchmanship, as well as in historical and social background, of the two bodies participating.

D. Horton, *The United Church of Christ: Its Origins, Organization and Role in the World Today* (New York [1962]); L. H. Gunnemann, *The Shaping of the United Church of Christ* (ibid. [1977]); R. S. Paul, *Freedom with Order: The Doctrine of the Church in the United Church of Christ* (ibid. [1987]). D. Dunn [and others], *A History of the Evangelical and Reformed Church* (Philadelphia [1961]). G. G. Atkins and F. L. Fagley, *History of American Congregationalism* (Boston [1942]). J. R. Willis in *NCE* 14 (1967), pp. 415–17; L. E. Wilshire in D. G. Reid and others (eds.), *Dictionary of Christianity in America* (Downers Grove, Ill. [1990]), pp. 1199–201, s.v.

United Free Church of Scotland. The Church formed in 1900 by the union of the *United Presbyterian Church and the *Free Church of Scotland. In 1929 the greater part of the United Free Church of Scotland joined with the Established Church of Scotland. A small minority, however, remained outside this union; it retained the name 'United Free Church of Scotland', for five years adding 'Continuing' to its title. For training of its ministry it shares the Scottish Congregational College in Edinburgh. It ordains women, and has about 6,500 communicant members.

United Methodist Church. (1) The branch of English Methodism formed in 1907 by the union of the *Methodist New Connexion, the *Bible Christians, and the *United Methodist Free Churches (qq.v.), and itself embodied in the *Methodist Church (q.v.) in 1932.

The possibility of reunion in Methodism was discussed throughout the 19th cent. and towards its end negotiations between various bodies took place. In 1901 the third Methodist Ecumenical Conference recommended that reunion in British Methodism was desirable and in 1902 active steps to that end were taken. Although other Methodist Churches were consulted and agreed in principle to the plan of reunion, only the above-named three Churches took part in the union of 1907.

The constitution accepted for the new Church closely followed that common to all branches of Methodism. Central government was in the hands of a conference meeting annually and presided over by a president elected each year. The missionary and social activities of the uniting Churches were maintained and increased.

The achievement of the union increased the desire for wider reunion in Methodism, and proposals in this direction were made by the Wesleyan Conference in 1913. In 1932 the United Methodist Church finally united with the *Wesleyan and *Primitive Methodist Churches to form a Methodist Church including almost the whole of English Methodism.

(2) In the *United States of America the United Methodist Church was formed in 1968 by a union between the Methodist Church and the Evangelical United Brethren Church. It is the principal Methodist Church in the USA and the largest Methodist community in the world, with nearly 10 million members.

On (1) see foll. entry; on both see bibl. to METHODIST CHURCHES; on (2) see also works cited under UNITED STATES OF AMERICA, CHRISTIANITY IN .

United Methodist Free Churches. One of the bodies which went to form the *United Methodist Church in 1907. It originated in the amalgamation of smaller communities which had broken away from *Wesleyan Methodism. In every case the reason for division was not doctrinal but constitutional, the Free Churches embodying the most democratic elements of Methodism.

The *Protestant Methodists*, formed in 1827, arose from discontent of long standing with the government of the Methodist Church. The great power vested in the annual Conference of ministers was oppressive to those who wished the laity to have a share in the government of their Church, and feeling ran high when Dr Jabez *Bunting (q.v.) asserted at the Conference: 'Methodism knows nothing of democracy; Methodism hates democracy as it hates sin.' The immediate occasion of their secession was trifling—the erection of an organ at Brunswick Chapel, Leeds. After much dissension the Protestant Methodists were founded at Leeds, with a few associated societies, mostly in Yorkshire.

The next group, the *Wesleyan Methodist Association*, was formed in 1835 through a dispute about the founding of a Theological Institution for the training of ministers. The principal ground of offence was that the Conference had acted contrary to its constitution and not consulted the people before taking a step of such importance; objection to the theological institution as such was of secondary importance. The expulsions which followed led to the formation of the new democratic association. In 1836 it was joined by the 'Protestant Methodists' and a year later by a small body of secessionists at Derby.

Further dissension was brought to a head at the Wesleyan Conference of 1849. For some years Methodism had been disturbed by the circulation of anonymous pamphlets, known as the Fly Sheets, containing accusations of favouritism, narrowness, and the mismanagement of Connexional funds against the predominant party in Methodism. Vigorous and, as some thought, unjust steps were taken to discover their authors, and finally, in the Conference of 1849, three ministers were expelled for refusing to answer questions. At the same time some 80,000 members left the Wesleyan Church. At first they were content to agitate for reform in Wesleyanism; but when it became apparent that they would not gain their end, a separate body, the *Wesleyan Reformers*, was formed.

After several years of discussion, largely on the subject of their constitution, the 'Wesleyan Methodist Association' and the bulk of the 'Wesleyan Reformers' united in 1857, taking the name of the 'United Methodist Free Churches'. Some Reformers stayed out of the union and formed the Wesleyan Reform Union which still continues. Peace and a settled constitution contributed to solid progress both in England and in foreign missions. As early as 1837 the Wesleyan Association had commenced work in Jamaica, and in 1851 the first missionary had been sent to Australia. In both West and East Africa missions were established and maintained in spite of much hardship. From 1864 stations were supported in China.

The constitution adopted by the United Methodist Free Churches reflects the opposition to autocratic rule by the ministry which led to their separation from the parent Church. The annual Assembly, unlike the Wesleyan Conference, was not composed wholly of ministers. It was composed, with the exception of a very small number of officials elected at the previous Assembly, of representatives elected by their own circuits. In organization an endeavour was made to combine the congregational with the connexional system, and great authority was given to the circuits in dealing with their own affairs, e.g. the Assembly did not determine the circuits to which ministers should be appointed.

In 1907 the United Methodist Free Churches united with the *Methodist New Connexion and the *Bible Christians to form the *United Methodist Church.

G. Eayrs in W. J. Townsend, H. B. Workman, and G. Eayrs (eds.), *A New History of Methodism*, 1 (1909), pp. 514–51. H. Smith, J. E. Swallow, and W. Treffy (eds.), *The Story of the United Methodist Church* [1932]. O. A. Beckerlegge, *The United Methodist Free Churches: A Study in Freedom* (1957). R. Currie, *Methodism Divided: A Study in the Sociology of Ecumenicalism* (1968), *passim*. D. A. Gowland, *Methodist Secessions: The origins of Free Methodism in three Lancashire towns: Manchester, Rochdale, Liverpool* (Chetham Society, 3rd ser. 26; 1979).

United Presbyterian Church. The Church formed in Scotland in 1847 by the union of two earlier groups, the *United Secession Church and the Relief Synod. The latter body had been formed in 1761 after difficulties over the system of patronage in the Church of Scotland. In 1900, apart from a very small minority (the *Wee Frees), the United Presbyterians united with the Free Church of Scotland to form the *United Free Church of Scotland.

United Reformed Church. The Church formed in 1972 by the union of a large majority of the *Congregational Church of England and Wales with the *Presbyterian Church of England. In 1981 the majority of the *Disciples of Christ in Britain joined it; as some of these congregations were in Scotland, the Church took the name 'United Reformed Church in the United Kingdom'. In government it combines elements from its constituent traditions (e.g. *Church Meeting and the office of *elder); in belief and practice it stands in the mainstream of *Reformed Churches. It belongs to the *Council for World Mission, the *World Alliance of Reformed Churches, the *World Council of Churches, and the *Council of Churches for Britain and Ireland (the successor of the *British Council of Churches, to which it had previously belonged).

The United Reformed Church issued *A Book of Services* (Edinburgh, 1980), rev. as the *Service Book* (Oxford, 1989); its use was recommended, though not prescribed. The 'Scheme of Union' is pr. in the Church's *Manual* (1973), pp. 3–29, with the Act of Parliament which effected the union, pp. 31–65; a summary of sections 1–10 and the complete text of the remaining part of the Scheme are pr. in *The Manual* (2nd edn. [1984]), pp. 2–24, with the 1972 Act (but not its schedules), pp. 25–47, and the 1981 Act (which made obsolete the schedules of the 1972 one), pp. 48–69. The Basis of the Union of the United Reformed Church, with amendments approved in 1981, is pr. in D. M. Thompson (ed.), *Stating the Gospel* (Edinburgh, 1990), pp. 248–65. K. Slack, *The United Reformed Church* (Exeter, 1978).

United Secession Church. The Church formed in Scotland in 1820 by the fusion of the 'New Lichts' of the *Burghers and *Antiburghers. These two groups had divided into 'Auld Lichts' and 'New Lichts' in 1799 and 1806 respectively, and the 'New Lichts' of both groups joined to form the United Secession Church. In 1847 this united with the Relief Synod to form the *United Presbyterian Church (q.v.).

United Society for Christian Literature. A Society founded in 1935 by the fusion of the *Religious Tract Society (q.v.), the Christian Literature Society for India and Africa (founded 1858), and the Christian Literature Society for China (founded 1884) for the spread of the Christian faith through literature in Britain and overseas. It works closely with 'Feed the Minds', a charity founded in 1964, which gives grants for Christian literature and communications projects in developing countries and Eastern Europe.

G. Hewitt, *Let the People Read: A Short History of the United Society for Christian Literature, Religious Tract Society, 1799, Christian Literature Society for India and Africa, 1858, Christian Literature Society for China (British Support), 1887* (1949). Annual Reports (London, 1937 ff.).

United Society for the Propagation of the Gospel. See USPG.

United States of America, Christianity in. Since its introduction into the geographical areas now comprising the United States, Christianity has left its mark in both public and private spheres, exercising influence upon society in general and upon the lives of individuals. At the same time American Christianity has been shaped in distinctive ways by its peculiar socio-political context.

The transplantation of W. Christianity to America began when European explorers sailed across the Atlantic in pursuit of fortune and national honour. Both profit and religion motivated these adventurers and their patrons. Christopher Columbus's choice of San Salvador as the name for the first island he encountered in 1492 reflected his personal zeal. Subsequent explorers carried the Christian traditions of their respective nations to the New World where they attempted to convert the native 'Indians'.

The colonial settlement of North America produced a patchwork pattern of religious diversity reflecting the fragmented and strife-torn state of European Christianity. In 1565 on the Florida peninsula the Spanish founded St Augustine, the oldest Christian settlement in what would become the United States. Later they established other RC missions in the SW part of the continent. At the time Spanish Catholicism was characterized by a close association between the Church and the Crown, as well as by a fervent, enthusiastic spirituality. The *Dominican, *Franciscan, and *Jesuit orders played a major role in the settlement of New Spain. Fur traders carried the flag of France into the upper regions of North America, accompanied by RC missionaries. Despite heroic efforts by Jesuit priests, conversions by the French among the natives were limited. The English joined the exploration and colonization effort relatively late. Land companies chartered by the Crown organized the first successful settlements at Jamestown (1603) in Virginia and at Plymouth (1620) and Massachusetts Bay (1630) in New England. In Virginia the C of E was legally established. In New England *Puritanism, in its separating and non-separating congregational forms, was initially the official religion. During the next 100 years the English settled much of the eastern seaboard of North America. Lord Baltimore (1606–47), a RC nobleman, founded Maryland (1634) under a grant from *Charles I. Roger *Williams, a separatist exiled from

Massachusetts Bay who became a *Baptist, organized Rhode Island (1636) for dissenters. The *Quaker William *Penn received a charter for Pennsylvania (1681), which became a haven for the oppressed. The Dutch and the Swedish, engaging in more limited colonial enterprises, brought the Dutch Reformed and *Lutheran Churches respectively to New Netherland (1626) and New Sweden (1638).

By the end of the 17th cent. regional patterns were evident among the Churches. The C of E was dominant in the southern English colonies where it faced the challenge of adapting the parish system to the new context. Anglicanism was also nominally established in other royal colonies, although that fact had little practical effect. In the Puritan colonies of New England, where Church and State cooperated closely, Reformed ideas, as modified by covenant theology, held sway. Among the Puritans biblical *covenants provided models for reflection on the process of redemption as well as on the nature of ecclesiastical and political order. The English colonies between New England and Virginia were religiously more disparate and more tolerant of that diversity. In these middle colonies *Presbyterians and Quakers, RCs and Lutherans, Jews and *Baptists, lived side by side. In the Spanish and French regions of North America, RCism remained the established Church.

The 18th cent. witnessed the consolidation and expansion of the Churches in the English colonies. The C of E, for example, tried to strengthen its position by supporting missionaries sent by the *SPG. RCs struggled to maintain the semblance of a sacramental life. Both Anglicans and RCs desperately needed resident bishops. The most significant religious event of the first half of the 18th cent. was the *Great Awakening, a series of religious revivals originating in isolated Dutch Reformed, *Congregational, and Presbyterian congregations in the 1720s and 1730s. At the beginning of the 1740s a general surge of religious activity swept through the English colonies, producing a spate of evangelical conversions and recommitments. George *Whitefield, then an Anglican priest from England, was the most celebrated itinerant preacher associated with the Awakening, Jonathan *Edwards of Massachusetts its foremost theologian. Gilbert Tennent (1703–64) led the revivals in the middle colonies, as did Samuel Davies (1723–61) and Shubal Stearns (1706–71) in the South. The 'New Light' movement, arising out of the Great Awakening, featured the necessity of a 'new birth', a describable spiritual experience of transforming grace. This evangelical principle provided grounds for an assault upon the traditional authority of the clergy and the integrity of the parish system by supporting lay exhorters and itinerant preachers. It also gave expanded religious opportunities to women and new impetus for Christianizing Blacks and Indians.

The Great Awakening was not without its critics. Drawing upon intellectual currents fed by the *Enlightenment, opponents charged that the excessive emotionalism and the divisive tendencies of the revivals were detrimental to religion and social order. These rationalists, adopting an *Arminian theological perspective, affirmed human capacity, the notion of progress, and the centrality of morality and virtue in the religious life. Later the same optimism about the moral order of the universe and an even sharper criticism of 'enthusiasm' informed the views of a small but articulate group of *Deists. Radical expressions of an anti-ecclesiastical and anticlerical variety surfaced in the writings of Thomas *Paine at the end of the 18th cent. The rationalists shared with the evangelicals a strong anti-Catholic and anti-episcopal bias.

The effects of the American Revolution (1776–83) upon the Churches were mixed. The Presbyterians, Congregationalists, and Baptists who enthusiastically supported the patriotic cause enjoyed some cultural advantage. The Anglicans, by contrast, were devastated by defections of clergy, the destruction of facilities, and general ill-will against them. The *Methodists experienced similar hostility because of their close association with Anglicanism and because of John *Wesley's counsel against rebellion. The peace Churches, incl. the Quakers and *Mennonites, suffered for their pacifism. The years of the War of Independence and the following decades were not prosperous times for the Churches, though they witnessed developments of importance for the future. The Anglicans secured the first American bishop with the consecration in 1784 of Samuel *Seabury, and the Protestant *Episcopal Church in the United States of America became an autonomous organization, no longer dependent on the C of E. The Methodists, who had held their first American Conference in 1773, decisively broke with Anglicanism when Wesley appointed a Superintendent for America in 1784. In the same year the RCs ceased to be dependent on the *Vicars Apostolic in England, acquiring a bishop of their own with the consecration in 1790 of John *Carroll (q.v.). The most significant direct result of the Revolution for the history of Christianity in the United States was the adoption of the new nation's Constitution with its Bill of Rights (1791) guaranteeing religious liberty. The First Amendment proscribed religious establishments (although they continued to exist on a state level as late as 1833) and articulated the principle of the free exercise of religion, thereby laying the foundation of the system of religious pluralism and for the further expansion of diversity within American Christianity.

The 19th cent. opened on a more positive note for the Churches, despite lingering fears that disestablishment would lead to irreligion and that Deism was making inroads into the population. The evangelical Churches experienced a new surge of revivalism at the same time that thousands of migrants were leaving the seaboard areas for the transappalachian regions. No portion of the new republic escaped the Second Great Awakening (1800–35). This evangelical movement flourished in the colleges of New England and the remote hamlets of the Northwest Territory, in the urban centres on the seaboard as well as in the backwoods of the SW frontier. The revivalists stimulated innovations or 'new measures' such as the use of the 'anxious bench' during protracted meetings and the gathering of rural *camp meetings. Ecstatic behaviour became commonplace. Theological change occurred, too, as evangelicalism, under the influence of Wesleyanism, adopted a more Arminian perspective with strains of perfectionism and optimistic *Millenarianism. Lyman *Beecher, Peter Cartwright (1785–1872), and Charles G. *Finney were prominent revivalists. The Methodists and Baptists benefited most from this activity. The Awakening produced an informal evangelical alliance which remained a powerful religious and cultural force throughout the 19th cent.

An increasing stream of immigrants from N. and W. Europe added to the diversity and complexity of America's religious scene after 1820. Germans by thousands—RC, Lutheran, Reformed, and Jewish—left their homeland for the United States. Nearly a million Irish, most fervently RC, also arrived before 1860. The situation of the RC Church in America was transformed: in 1800 there had been c.50,000 RCs, too few clergy, and only one bishop (John Carroll, Bp. of Baltimore). By 1860 the RC Church was the largest single denomination (3.5 million members) in the nation. This rapid growth fanned the fears of 'nativist' Protestants who mounted an anti-Catholic drive. Lutheran and Reformed immigrants likewise prospered, but as outsiders they too faced pressures.

A remarkable burst of reformist activity occurred in the first half of the 19th cent. The vast expanse of unsettled territory and the large influx of immigrants stimulated efforts to 'Christianize' and civilize the young nation. Evangelicals formed voluntary associations to convert RCs, *Unitarians, and the unchurched. An elaborate network of local and state societies aimed at eradicating particular sins, such as intemperance, profanity, and sabbath-breaking, through the dissemination of Bibles and religious tracts, the education of children in Sunday Schools, and the legislation of morals. Some of the same reforming zeal was evident in the RC Church which sought to improve educational opportunities for the immigrants and to assist the poor. In 1808 Elizabeth Bayley Seton (1774–1821) established the Sisters of Charity, a teaching order. Liberal Protestants, incl. the Quakers, Unitarians, and Universalists, joined campaigns for peace, prison reform, and women's rights.

The United States proved a fertile seedbed for new religious movements. The principle of the 'free exercise' of religion, the presence of open land, and the energy of revivalism all contributed to the proliferation of such groups. Some were imported from abroad, such as the *Harmonists led by the German *Pietist George Rapp (1757–1847). Many more were indigenous. They often centred on charismatic leaders who laid claim to special revelations and chose patterns of life at odds with conventional mores, seeking economic independence and isolation from the 'world'. The *Shakers, founded by the English Ann Lee (c.1736–84), established celibate communities which accepted a male–female principle in the Deity and sexual equality. By contrast, the Perfectionists (or *Oneida Community), led by John H. Noyes (1811–86), called for community both of goods and of persons, the latter structured in a system of complex marriage. The 'Christians' (later *Disciples of Christ), followers of Barton Stone (1772–1844), Alexander *Campbell, and others, sought to restore primitive Christianity. The Latter-day Saints (*Mormons) accepted the authority of Joseph Smith (1805–44) as a prophet of God, the scriptural status of the Book of Mormon (1830), and the goal of the establishment of Zion on earth. The historic denominations viewed these new groups as heretical and often persecuted them.

No issue proved more divisive to Americans in the 19th cent. than racial *slavery, a problem with roots in the earliest days of colonization. Christians split over slavery and their religious obligations towards slaves. Some argued for freeing them; others justified enslavement both as having biblical sanction and as a means to Christianization. In the North free Blacks organized independent Churches, the first of which was the African Methodist Episcopal Church founded in 1816 by Richard Allen (1760–1831). In the South after 1830 the Churches ministered to the slaves in various ways, filling religious and social needs. The crisis over slavery came to a head in the middle of the century. By that time the Presbyterians, Methodists, and Baptists had split over the conflict. The conclusion of the Civil War (1861–5) brought an end to racial slavery, but the failure of Reconstruction (1865–77) signalled the beginning of the system of racial segregation. After the war the *Black Churches continued to play a major socio-political role, at the same time nurturing a unique Afro-American heritage of spirituality in word, action, and song.

The period after the Civil War was marked by tremendous social change. The agrarian South, devastated by the war, struggled slowly to rebuild. In the North urbanization moved forward rapidly, fed by the growth of industrialization and by waves of new immigrants, mainly from S. and E. Europe, over 23 million arriving between 1865 and 1910. These included large numbers of RCs, Jews, and *Orthodox Christians. Poverty, crime, and other problems plagued urban residents, challenging society and the Churches to help. Some religious leaders proposed adapting evangelicalism to the new setting, establishing 'rescue missions' or organizing urban revivals. In this vein the revivalist Dwight L. *Moody utilized Sunday Schools and the *YMCA. Proponents of the Gospel of Wealth such as Russell Conwell (1843–1925) identified individual effort as the key to success. By contrast, advocates of a '*Social Gospel', including the theologian Walter *Rauschenbusch, criticized the individualistic ethic of capitalism, calling upon the Churches to 'Christianize' the social order. The solutions proposed by the Churches varied widely, from the radical application of the '*Golden Rule' to support for trade unions, socialism, and settlement houses, such as Hull House founded by Jane Addams (1860–1935). RC supporters of social Christianity drew upon the teachings of Pope *Leo XIII, channelling their efforts through Church-sponsored charities.

Modernization was accompanied by an intellectual revolution. Modern science, symbolized by the publication of Charles *Darwin's *Origin of Species* (1859), contested old ways of thinking about the universe. Protestant Modernists, such as the theologian Shailer Mathews (1863–1914), though few in number, sought to embrace science and use it as a measure of the religious traditions, including the Bible. Conservative Protestants, led by theologians at Princeton Theological Seminary, rejected the new science in the name of tradition, formulating their position on the basis of *Baconian science, the notion of biblical inerrancy, and assumptions drawn from common-sense realism. These Conservatives, later identified as *Fundamentalists, became embroiled in ecclesiastical controversies, incl. celebrated heresy trials in the Presbyterian Church. Protestant Liberalism, also known as the 'New Theology' or Progressive Orthodoxy, anticipated in the writings of Horace *Bushnell, attempted a reconciliation of science and tradition in support of an optimistic perspective on human nature and progress, emphasizing the immanence of God. There were few RC *Modernists in

the United States, for the American Church was firmly in the control of doctrinal conservatives. The condemnation of Modernism by *Pius X in 1907, following the Papal condemnation of '*Americanism' in 1899, stifled liberal activity even further.

Changing socio-economic patterns in modern America transformed the role of many middle-class women, reshaping popular ideas about the family and contributing to the 'feminization' of the Churches. As economic production moved outside the home, the patriarchal household gave way to the notion of the domestic world as woman's proper sphere. Religion was increasingly viewed as the particular province of women who were regarded as morally superior to men and who were responsible for the spiritual nurture of children and the moral rehabilitation of men. The Churches became the special forum for women, and the clergy, experiencing their own crisis of authority, directed greater attention to them. Religious societies, convents, and female schools provided unique opportunities for sisterhood, as did some sectarian groups. Large numbers of religiously motivated women organized campaigns within the Churches against slavery and alcoholism and for women's rights.

The expanding urban environment proved no less productive of new religious movements than had the frontier. The stress and uncertainties of the situation nurtured sects. Advocates of the New Thought movement, echoing Transcendentalist ideas, affirmed the power of constructive thinking. *Christian Science, founded by Mary Baker Eddy (1820–1910), provided its followers, predominantly women, with an idealistic metaphysical outlook and an antidote to the sense of ill-being in its practice of mental healing set out in *Science and Health* (1875). *Seventh-day Adventism, led by Ellen Harmon White (1827–1915), sought an answer in traditional eschatology and dietary regimens. The followers of Charles Taze *Russell, later called *Jehovah's Witnesses, found apocalyptic signs of an impending destruction of the world from which only members of their organization would be spared. *Holiness and *Pentecostal Churches arose in scattered locations, both urban and rural, in response to a perceived loss of spiritual vitality. They stressed the possibility of sinlessness and the restoration of the ecstatic patterns of the primitive Church. At the same time the Latter-day Saints were prospering in the western inter-mountain region as they accommodated to American society, renouncing the practice of polygamy and the creation of an earthly kingdom. These sectarian developments both fuelled ecclesiastical conflict and energized the Churches.

The religious and cultural hegemony exercised by Protestantism during the 19th cent.—an 'unofficial establishment'—was eroded in the early decades of the 20th cent. The rapid increase of the RC, Orthodox, Jewish, and sectarian communities; the theological divisions within Protestantism itself, esp. the Modernist–Fundamentalist struggle which gained notoriety during the Scopes Trial of 1925 when the teaching of evolution in state schools was tested; the failure of the Interchurch World Movement, a sweeping evangelical strategy for benevolence and mission; the repeal of the constitutional amendment prohibiting the manufacture and sale of alcohol after the failure of Prohibition as a social and moral experiment—these developments contributed to the loss of Protestant authority and influence. Additionally, the First World War and subsequent economic depression destroyed the cultural basis for optimism which had fuelled religious and social movements in the 19th cent.

In the early decades of the 20th cent. a growing effort to overcome divisions among denominations drew upon the legacy of earlier co-operative international missionary undertakings, incl. the Student Volunteer Movement (1888), and upon wide support for the expanding global involvement of America justified in terms of a 'Manifest Destiny'. Representatives from liberal Protestant denominations formed the Federal Council of Churches in 1908, a step encouraged by the growing worldwide interest in Christian unity. The American Council of Christian Churches (1941) and the National Association of Evangelicals (1942) were formed as alternative federations of conservative Protestant Churches. Ecclesiastical mergers among Presbyterians, Methodists, and Lutherans took place around the middle of the cent. After the formation of the *World Council of Churches in 1948, the Federal Council was reorganized into the National Council of Churches (1950). Although it expanded to include Orthodox Christian bodies, which by 1950 numbered c.2 million members in America, it remained predominantly liberal Protestant. The earliest representatives of Orthodoxy in the United States were primarily of Russian and Greek background. After the Second World War large numbers of immigrants from E. Europe and the Middle East brought other branches of Orthodoxy and also members of the *Oriental Orthodox Churches to America.

By 1950 the United States had recovered from the 'Great Depression' and had emerged from the Second World War (a military effort which the Churches had supported vigorously), only to find itself involved in a new conflict in Korea and in the larger East–West 'Cold War'. During the 1950s organized religion prospered in America. It became fashionable for middle-class Americans in the suburbs to attend church. The RC Church, for example, became a powerful institutional force in American life. Led by a hierarchy noted for its practicality, the Church prospered. Although it retained its theological conservatism and its traditional loyalty to Rome, these factors no longer antagonized Americans to the same degree as they did earlier. The election of the RC John Kennedy to the Presidency in 1960 was a measure of that change. Conservative evangelicalism experienced a resurgence during this period. Billy *Graham, its most prominent revivalist, rose to influence by his effective use of the media. Rivalling him was Oral Roberts (b. 1918), a Pentecostal faith healer. In Protestant seminaries another kind of reassessment was under way, influenced by European theological developments. Neo-orthodox theologians, including R. *Niebuhr and his brother H. R. *Niebuhr, re-examined the assumptions of Liberalism, calling for a more realistic assessment of human nature and reaffirming traditional Reformation emphases in the light of modern developments. During the 1950s popular religion prospered too, as the teachings of Norman Vincent Peale (1898–1993) on the power of 'positive thinking' testifies. In 1954 the phrase 'under God' was added to the national pledge of allegiance.

The prosperity of the Churches during the 1950s contrasted sharply with the situation in the 1960s, a time of radical change in American society and among the denominations. Social conflict developed over the involvement of the United States in the Vietnam War, the role of the government in the civil rights movement, the legitimacy of the youth culture, and the general shift towards a more secular life-style. The RC Church experienced revolutionary changes of its own, leaving behind patterns dominant since the Council of *Trent. The Second *Vatican Council (1962–5) seemed to point to a new way of being a Catholic, emphasizing the responsibility of individuals to follow the dictates of conscience, renewing and altering liturgical practice, encouraging ecumenical contacts, and generally promoting a climate for questioning in a less authoritative Church. Among American RC theologians none was more influential in anticipating these developments than John Courtney Murray (1904–67). A charismatic movement with similarities to Protestant Pentecostalism and a revival of mystical spirituality associated with Thomas *Merton also developed within the Church. Activist priests and nuns represented the Church in the social arena. Radical theologians among the Protestants celebrated the onset of the new secularism as a liberating force. The Baptist theologian Harvey Cox (b. 1929) extolled the virtues of the new urban environment and its revelatory possibilities. Others spoke of the '*death of God' in a world come of age, a world where traditional theological language was no longer meaningful. Still others called for a 'new morality' combined with responsible ethical decisions. These voices did not gain wide support among the Protestant Churches which were experiencing difficult times on an institutional level, suffering losses both in membership and finance. Ecumenical efforts among mainline Protestant Churches, which during this decade included the *Consultation on Church Union (COCU) supported by nine denominations, surged and then ultimately faltered. The more conservative Churches (notably the Southern Baptists), however, continued to grow, as did sectarian communities. The most important religious figure was Martin Luther *King, whose leadership of the civil rights drive symbolized the continuing commitment of Black Christians to the social aims of Christianity.

Increasing conflict characterized the Churches in the United States after the 1960s. Conservative and liberal factions organized themselves for both religious and political action. Through organizations such as the Moral Majority headed by the Baptist television evangelist Jerry Falwell (b. 1933), Fundamentalists carried their programme to the electorate. The agenda of the Religious Right included support for prayer and Bible reading in the state schools and for 'traditional' family values as well as opposition to *abortion, to equal rights for women and homosexuals, to the teaching of evolution in the schools, and to pornography. Television preachers, dubbed the 'electronic church', disseminated these ideas widely (see BROADCASTING, RELIGIOUS). Conservative leadership in the RC Church joined in support of some of these causes, most notably opposition to abortion and equal rights for women. *Feminist Theology became a potent influence. The idea of ordaining women, practised in some Protestant bodies for many years and in the Episcopal Church since 1977, remained a matter of controversy among RCs, as did a host of post-Vatican II developments. Liberal Protestant Churches addressed themselves to issues involving freedom of choice, gender, minority rights, and nuclear disarmament. *Liberation theologians, such as James Cone (b. 1938) and Mary Daly (b. 1928) spoke to these issues across denominational lines. During this period White denominations in America drew back from involvement in the flagging civil rights movement, leaving Black Churches relatively isolated in the quest for full citizenship. Sectarian groups, with some exceptions, drifted closer to the positions of the older traditional communities. Nevertheless, religious pluralism in America became more diverse than ever before, esp. with the growth of religious traditions of E. origin as well as with continuing interest in Native American religions and the occult. Christianity no longer exercises the hegemony in American life that it did before the middle of the 20th cent.

The literature has grown as a result of expanding and changing interests. Earlier concerns with denominational and intellectual history and with Protestantism, esp. Puritanism in New England and its offshoots, have been complemented by new approaches employing social history as well as regional, thematic, and comparative studies.

Instructive general surveys inc. S. E. Ahlstrom, *A Religious History of the American People* (New Haven, Conn., and London, 1972); R. T. Handy, *A History of the Churches in the United States and Canada* (Oxford History of the Christian Church, 1976), pp. 1–115, 136–227, 262–343, and 377–427; C. L. Albanese, *America: Religions and Religion* (Belmont, Calif. [1981]). M. A. Noll, *A History of Christianity in the United States and Canada* (1992) presents a sociological and cultural approach. On particular denominations, J. P. Dolan, *The American Catholic Experience: A History from Colonial Times to the Present* (Garden City, NY, 1985); P. Gleason, *Keeping the Faith: American Catholicism Past and Present* (Notre Dame, Ind. [1987]); E. S. Bucke (ed.), *The History of American Methodism* (3 vols., New York, 1964); F. A. Norwood, *The Story of American Methodism: A History of the United Methodists and their Relations* (Nashville and New York, 1974); A. R. Wentz, *A Basic History of Lutheranism in America* (Philadelphia, 1955); E. T. Thompson, *Presbyterians in the South* (3 vols., Richmond, Va. [1963–73]); R. E. Miller, *The Larger Hope* (2 vols., Boston, 1979–86 [on the Universalists]), and D. Robinson, *The Unitarians and the Universalists* (Denominations in America, 1; Westport, Conn., and London, 1985). See also under individual denominations mentioned in the article. E. S. Gaustad, *Historical Atlas of Religion in America* (New York [1962]; rev. edn. [1976]); M. E. Marty, *Pilgrims in their own Land: 500 Years of Religion in America* (Boston, 1984); J. W. Smith and A. L. Jamison (eds.), *Religion in American Life* (Princeton Studies in American Civilization, no. 5; vols. 1, 2, and 4 in 2 parts, 1961), esp. vol. 4 (N. R. Burr, *A Critical Bibliography of Religion in America*). Documentary histories incl. H. S. Smith, R. T. Handy, and L. A. Loetscher (eds.), *American Christianity: An Historical Interpretation with Representative Documents* (2 vols., New York [1960–3]); E. S. Gaustad (ed.), *A Documentary History of Religion in America* (2 vols., Grand Rapids, Mich. [1982–3]); J. T. Ellis (ed.), *Documents of American Catholic History* (Milwaukee [1956]; rev. edn., 2 vols., Chicago, 1967); M. C. Sernett (ed.), *Afro-American Religious History: A Documentary Witness* (Durham, NC, 1985); and R. R. Ruether and R. S. Keller (eds.), *Women and Religion in America* (3 vols., San Francisco, etc. [1981–6]).

Representative publications in the general chronological order of topics are C. H. Lippy and others, *Christianity Comes to the Americas, 1492–1776* (New York, 1992); P. [G. E.] Miller, *The New England Mind: The Seventeenth Century* (New York, 1939); C. E. Hambrick-Stowe, *The Practice of Piety: Puritan Devotional Disciplines in Seventeenth-Century New England* (Chapel Hill, NC [1982]); D. S. Lovejoy, *Religious Enthusiasm in the New World: Heresy to Revolution* (Cambridge, Mass., and London, 1985); S. Bercovitch, *The American Jeremiad* (Madison, Wis., 1978); J. Butler, *Power, Authority, and the Origins of American Denomina-*

tional Order: The English Churches in the Delaware Valley 1680–1730 (Transactions of the American Philosophical Society, 68, pt. 2; Philadelphia, 1978); A. [E.] Heimert, *Religion and the American Mind from the Great Awakening to the Revolution* (Cambridge, Mass., 1966); R. Isaac, *The Transformation of Virginia 1740–1790* (Chapel Hill, NC, 1982), *passim*; J. D. Marietta, *The Reformation of American Quakerism, 1748–1783* (Philadelphia [1984]); S. A. Marini, *Radical Sects of Revolutionary New England* (Cambridge, Mass., and London, 1982); H. F. May, *The Enlightenment in America* (New York, 1976); S. E. Mead, *The Lively Experiment: The Shaping of Christianity in America* (ibid. [1963]); J. B. Boles, *The Great Revival 1787–1805: The Origins of the Southern Evangelical Mind* (Lexington, Ky. [1972]); E. B. Holifield, *The Gentlemen Theologians: American Theology in Southern Culture 1795–1860* (Durham, NC, 1978); W. R. Cross, *The Burned-over District: The Social and Intellectual History of Enthusiastic Religion in Western New York, 1800–1850* (Ithaca, NY, 1950); P. E. Johnson, *A Shopkeeper's Millennium: Society and Revivals in Rochester, New York, 1815–1837* (New York, 1978); J. P. Dolan, *Catholic Revivalism: The American Experience 1830–1900* (Notre Dame, Ind., and London [1978]); R. J. Carwardine, *Evangelicals and Politics in Antebellum America* (New Haven, Conn., and London, 1993); D. G. Mathews, *Religion in the Old South* (Chicago and London, 1977); A. J. Raboteau, *Slave Religion: The 'Invisible Institution' in the Antebellum South* (New York, 1978); C. L. Albanese, *Corresponding Motion: Transcendental Religion and the New America* (Philadelphia, 1977), *passim*; B. Kuklich, *Churchmen and Philosophers from Jonathan Edwards to John Dewey* (New Haven, Conn. [1985]); C. R. Wilson, *Baptized in Blood: The Religion of the Lost Cause 1865–1920* (Athens, Ga. [1980]); R. M. Miller and T. D. Marzik (eds.), *Immigrants and Religion in Urban America* (Philadelphia, 1977); A. I. Abell, *American Catholicism and Social Action: A Search for Social Justice, 1865–1950* (Garden City, NY, 1960); E. R. Sandeen, *The Roots of Fundamentalism: British and American Millenarianism 1800–1930* (Chicago and London, 1970); S. Gottschalk, *The Emergence of Christian Science in American Religious Life* (Berkeley, Calif., and London [1973]); R. T. Handy, *Undermined Establishment: Church-State Relations in America 1880–1920* (Princeton, NJ [1991]); W. R. Hutchison, *The Modernist Impulse in American Protestantism* (Cambridge, Mass., 1976; Oxford, 1982); G. M. Marsden, *Fundamentalism and American Culture: The Shaping of Twentieth-Century Evangelicalism: 1870–1925* (New York and Oxford, 1980); P. A. Carter, *The Spiritual Crisis of the Age* (DeKalb, Ill., 1971); R. D. Cross, *The Emergence of Liberal Catholicism in America* (Cambridge, Mass., 1958); R. M. Anderson, *Vision of the Disinherited: The Making of American Pentecostalism* (New York and Oxford, 1979); S. S. Hill, *Southern Churches in Crisis* (New York [1967]); D. J. O'Brien, *American Catholics and Social Reform: The New Deal Years* (New York, 1968); I. I. Zaretsky and M. P. Leone (eds.), *Religious Movements in Contemporary America* (Princeton, NJ [1974]); M. E. Marty, *A Nation of Behavers* (Chicago and London [1976]); D. F. Wells and J. D. Woodbridge (eds.), *The Evangelicals: What They Believe, Who They Are, Where They are Changing* (Nashville [1975]); M. J. Weaver, *New Catholic Women: A Contemporary Challenge to Traditional Religious Authority* (San Francisco, 1985); D. W. Lotz and others (eds.), *Altered Landscapes: Christianity in America, 1935–1985. Essays in Honor of Robert T. Handy* (Grand Rapids, Mich. [1989]); S. Bruce, *The Rise and Fall of the New Christian Right: Conservative Protestant Politics in America 1978–1988* (Oxford, 1988).

Examples of thematic interpretations incl. R. L. Moore, *Religious Outsiders and the Making of Americans* (New York, 1986); W. G. McLoughlin, *Revivals, Awakenings, and Reform: An Essay on Religion and Social Change in America 1607–1977* (Chicago and London [1978]); P. W. Williams, *Popular Religion in America: Symbolic Change and the Modernization Process in Historical Perspective* (Englewood Cliffs, NJ [1980]); A. Porterfield, *Feminine Spirituality in America from Sarah Edwards to Martha Graham* (Philadelphia, 1980); J. W. James (ed.), *Women in American*

Religion (ibid., 1980); J. J. Kenneally, *The History of American Catholic Women* (New York, 1990). N. O. Hatch and M. A. Noll (eds.), *The Bible in America: Essays in Cultural History* (New York and Oxford, 1982); H. W. Bowden, *American Indians and Christian Missions: Studies in Cultural Conflict* (Chicago and London [1981]); E. L. Tuveson, *Redeemer Nation: The Idea of America's Millennial Role* (Chicago and London, 1968); E. A. Smith, *Religious Liberty in the United States: The Development of Church–State Thought since the Revolutionary Era* (Philadelphia [1972]); L. I. Sweet (ed.), *The Evangelical Tradition in America* (Macon, Ga. [1984]).

There is material on the contemporary situation in F. S. Mead, *Handbook of Denominations in the United States* (New York [1951]; 7th edn., Nashville [1980]); *Yearbook of the American Churches* (ibid., 1933–72); *Yearbook of the American and Canadian Churches* (1973 ff.); J. G. Melton, *The Encyclopedia of American Religions* (2 vols., Wilmington, NC [1978]). *Church History* (Scottdale, Pa., 1932 ff.), *Journal of the American Academy of Religion* (Philadelphia, 1957 ff. [previously called *Journal of the National Association of Biblical Instructors* (Wolcott, NY, 1933–6) and *Journal of Bible and Religion* (ibid., 1937–57)], and *American Quarterly* (Philadelphia, 1949 ff.) carry scholarly articles and reviews on Christianity in the USA. C. H. Lippy and P. W. Williams (eds.), *Encyclopedia of Religious Experience: Studies of Traditions and Movements* (3 vols., New York [1988]); D. G. Reid and others (eds.), *Dictionary of Christianity in America* (Downers Grove, Ill. [1990]).

unitive way. The third and final stage of the spiritual life. See PURGATIVE, ILLUMINATIVE, AND UNITIVE WAYS.

Univers, L'. The organ of the violently *Ultramontane opinions of Louis *Veuillot, who took over its editorship in 1843. Though many Catholics were offended by its virulent tone, it forced the anticlerical French Government to make some concessions to the Church, esp. in the much-debated issue of religious education. In later days its claims for the Church and the Papacy exceeded those commonly defended even at Rome. The paper was suppressed by the French Government in 1860 for publishing *Pius IX's encyclical *Nullis certe*, but it was revived in 1867, only to be again suppressed in 1874.

Universalism. (1) The teaching of certain of the later Hebrew prophets (e.g. *Deutero-Isaiah, *Jonah) that God's purposes covered not only the Jewish race but also at least some people of other nations.

(2) The doctrine, also known as ἀποκατάστασις, that hell is in essence purgative and therefore temporary and that all intelligent beings will therefore in the end be saved. See APOCATASTASIS.

universals. In metaphysics, general concepts, representing the common elements belonging to individuals of the same genus or species. The medieval doctrine of universals traces its origin to Greek philosophy, esp. to *Porphyry's 'Introduction to the Categories of Aristotle', which poses three questions: whether the universals exist substantially or only in the human mind; if the former, whether they have bodies or are disembodied beings; and lastly, whether they exist separated from the objects of sense or only in them. These problems were combined with the question treated by *Boethius whether the universals are things (*res*) or only names (*voces, nomina*), and acc. to the answer given philosophers subscribed to the systems of either *Realism or *Nominalism (qq.v.) which

were developed in manifold variations during the Middle Ages. Among the best-known representatives of early Realism are John Scottus *Erigena, St *Anselm, and *William of Champeaux; in the 13th cent. St *Thomas Aquinas and *Duns Scotus developed a doctrine which has come to be known as 'Moderate Realism'. Among the Nominalist opponents of the earlier forms of Realism were *Roscelin and *Abelard, whilst the Realist system of the 13th cent. was attacked by *William of Ockham, Gabriel *Biel, and others.

Universities' Mission to Central Africa. See UMCA.

Universities Tests Act 1871. By this Act it was laid down that no person taking any degree at *Oxford, *Cambridge or *Durham University other than a degree in divinity, holding lay academical or collegiate office, should henceforward be required to subscribe any article or formulary of faith.

Unknowing, The Cloud of. See CLOUD OF UNKNOWING, THE.

unleavened bread. See BREAD, LEAVENED AND UNLEAVENED.

Upper Room. See CENACULUM.

Uppsala. Long after the introduction of Christianity into *Sweden by St *Anskar, Old Uppsala (now a neighbouring town to the north) continued a centre of pagan religious rites. Old Uppsala Church was built on and contains remains of a pagan temple, probably that mentioned by Adam of Bremen (d. c.1085). In 1164 Pope *Alexander III made it the head of an ecclesiastical province, separate from *Lund. The see was transferred from Old Uppsala to its present site (Aros) under Abp. Folke (1274–7). The cathedral, still the largest church in Sweden, dates from 1287 to 1435. The archbishop, who from the middle of the 15th cent. until the Reformation bore the title of 'Primate of Sweden' ('Primas Sueciae'), is still accorded a certain primacy, though his position is now only that of a 'primus inter pares'. The university, modelled on that of *Bologna, was founded in 1477, and became in the 19th cent. the home of a liberal and 'Low Church' theology as contrasted with the orthodoxy of Lund. Among its most notable bishops of recent times was N. *Söderblom (d. 1931). The *World Council of Churches held its fourth Assembly in Uppsala in 1968.

The 'Historia Pontificum Metropolitanae Ecclesiae Upsalensis' of Johannes Magnus Gothus (Rome, 1560) is conveniently pr. in the *Scriptores Rerum Svecicarum Medii Aevi*, 3 (pt. 2; Uppsala, 1871), pp. 1–97, with other material pp. 97–102. G. Kallstenius, *Blad ur Uppsalasangens Historia* (Stockholm, 1913). N. J. and E. Söderberg, *Studier till Uppsala Domkyrkas Historia* (3 pts., Kyrkohistoriska Föreningen Skrifter, Ser. 1, Arg. 35 and 36; 1936–7). Ö. Sjöholm (ed.), *Uppsala Domkyrka* (Uppsala, 1982), with summaries in Eng. C. Annerstedt, *Uppsala Universitets Historia* [1477–1792] (3 vols. in 6 parts, 1877–1914, + register by E. Colliander, 1931; in Swedish); S. Lindroth, *A History of Uppsala University 1477–1977* (Stockholm, 1976). H. Lundh (ed.), *Uppsala Stads Historia* (3 vols., Uppsala, 1953–8), esp. 1, pp. 369–427; 2, pp. 220–41; and 3, pp. 409–17. G. Armfelt in *CE* 15 (1912), pp. 207 f., s.v. 'Upsala, Ancient See of'; K. Hoeber, ibid., p. 208, s.v.

'Upsala, University of'; S. Göransson in *NCE* 14 (1967), pp. 475 f., s.v. 'Uppsala, Royal University of'. See also works cited under SWEDEN, CHRISTIANITY IN.

Urban II (*c*.1035–99), Pope from 1088. Odo of Lagery studied at *Reims under St *Bruno, who afterwards became his most trusted adviser. Having early been canon and archdeacon, *c*.1070 he entered the monastery of *Cluny, where he became prior. He was later called to Rome by *Gregory VII, who made him Cardinal Bp. of Ostia in 1080. Sent as Papal legate to France and Germany, he held a synod at Quedlinburg in Saxony in 1085, at which the *antipope, Guibert of Ravenna (Clement III), was anathematized. Elected to the Papacy in 1088, he expressed his intention of adhering closely to the principles of Gregory VII, which he did, though in a more measured and diplomatic form than his predecessor. The three great difficulties of his pontificate were the antipope, the interference of secular princes in the question of *investiture, and the simony and incontinence of the clergy. Owing to the presence in the city of Guibert and his followers, Urban could not at first enter Rome. He held a Council at Melfi in 1089 which promulgated 16 canons against simony, lay investiture, and clerical marriage. In the same year his position was temporarily strengthened by the marriage of his ardent supporter, Matilda of Tuscany, with Guelph V of Bavaria, which enabled Urban to enter Rome and expel Guibert. The latter was brought back, however, by *Henry IV in 1090, and Urban was once more an exile in S. Italy. But from 1093 Henry's power began to weaken, esp. through the defection of his son Conrad, who went over to the Pope and was crowned King of Italy. In the same year Urban re-entered Rome and took possession of the *Lateran in 1094. In 1095 he held two Councils at Piacenza and *Clermont, whose chief object was the general reform of the Church, esp. on the subjects of simony and clerical marriage. At Clermont the '*Truce of God' was proclaimed a law of the Church, and Philip I of France, who had put away his queen Bertha and married Bertrada, wife of the Count of Anjou, was anathematized. Having received an appeal for help against the Seljuk Turks from the Greek Emperor, Alexius I Comnenus, Urban proclaimed the First *Crusade. His call, which was received with enthusiasm by the people, initiated the great medieval Crusading movement that was to become a source of strength and prestige to the Papacy. Having returned to Rome in 1096 he held a synod at the Lateran and, in 1098, one at Bari with the object of healing the E. schism. At the latter St *Anselm defended the *Filioque clause against the Greeks. Urban died in 1099 before the news of the capture of *Jerusalem by the Crusaders could reach him. His cult was sanctioned in 1881. Feast day, 29 or 30 July.

304 of his letters are pr. in J. P. Migne, *PL* 151. 283–552. Jaffé, 1, pp. 657–701, and 2, pp. 713 and 752 f. Life by Peter of Pisa in *LP* (Duchesne), 2 (1892), pp. 293 f. R. Somerville, *The Councils of Urban II*, 1: *Decreta Claromentensia* (Annuarium Historiae Conciliorum, Suppl. 1; Amsterdam, 1972). A. Becker, *Papst Urban II. (1088–1099)* (Schriften der Monumenta Germaniae Historica, 19; 2 vols., 1964–88). B. Leib, *Rome, Kiev et Byzance à la fin du XI*e *siècle: Rapports religieux des Latins et des Gréco-Russes sous le pontificat d'Urbain II* (1924). H. Fuhrmann, *Papst Urban II. und der Stand der Regularkanoniker* (Sb. (Bayr.), 1984, Heft 2). W. Holtz-

mann, 'Die Unionsverhandlungen zwischen Kaiser Alexios I und Papst Urban II im Jahre 1089', *BZ* 28 (1928), pp. 38–66. R. Crozet, 'Le Voyage d'Urbain II et ses négotiations avec le clergé de France (1095–1096)', *Revue historique*, 175 (1937), pp. 271–310. Mann, 7 (1910), pp. 245–346; A. Fliche in Fliche and Martin, 8 (1946), pp. 199–337, both with bibl. Hefele and Leclercq, 5 (pt. 1; 1912), pp. 337–465. É. Amann in *DTC* 15 (pt. 2; 1950), cols. 2269–85, s.v. 'Urbain II'; G. Mollat in *EC* 12 (1954), cols. 905 f., s.v. 'Urbano II'. See also works cited under CRUSADES.

Urban V (1309/10–70), Pope from 1362. Guillaume de Grimoard, born at Grisac in Languedoc of a noble family, became a *Benedictine monk at the priory of Chirac and studied at *Paris and *Avignon. After ordination, he taught canon law at Montpellier and Avignon and later became Vicar General at Clermont and Uzès. In 1352 Clement VI named him Abbot of St-Germain d'Auxerre and entrusted him with several legations in Italy; in 1361 he was appointed Abbot of St-Victor at Marseilles; and in 1362 was elected Pope. In many ways the best of the Avignon Popes, Urban seriously undertook the reform of the Church, esp. with regard to the distribution of benefices. He made peace with Barnabo Visconti in 1364, and endeavoured to suppress the *condottieri* in France and Italy, but without success. His plans for a Crusade against the Turks, despite the temporary occupation of Alexandria by Peter de Lusignan in 1365, came to nothing. In preparation for a return to Rome, Urban had already appointed a separate Bp. of Avignon on 12 Dec. 1363. After Cardinal Albornoz had reconquered the States of the Church, Urban, encouraged by the Roman Emperor, Charles IV, went to Italy in 1367, disregarding the remonstrances of the French court and cardinals, who feared the loss of their influence on the *Curia. He was enthusiastically received by the Roman people and began at once to restore the badly neglected city and to establish discipline among clergy and laity. In 1368 he crowned the consort of Charles IV Empress, and in 1369 received the Greek Emperor, John V Palaeologus, into communion. In the same year Perugia revolted and war broke out between England and France, two facts which added weight to the wish of Urban's advisers to go back to Avignon. Against the admonitions of St *Bridget, who foretold his early death if he were to leave Rome, he returned to France in 1370, where he died soon after. Urban was a great benefactor of the universities and generously assisted poor scholars. His cult was confirmed in 1870. Feast day, 19 Dec.

A. Fierens and C. Tihou (eds.), *Lettres d'Urbain V, 1362–1370* (Analecta Vaticano-Belgica, 9 and 15; 1928–32); P. Lecacheux and G. Mollat (eds.), *Lettres secrètes et curiales du pape Urbain V (1362–1370) se rapportant à la France* (Bibliothèque des Écoles Françaises d'Athènes et de Rome, sér. 3, 1955); M. Dubrulle (ed.), *Les Registres d'Urbain V* (ibid., 1926 ff.; fasc. 1 only pub. to date); M.-H. Laurent, M. Hayez, and others (eds.), *Urbain V (1362–1370): Lettres communes* (ibid., 12 vols., 1954–89); D. T. Leccisotti (ed.), *Documenti Vaticani per la storia di Montecassino: Pontificato di Urbano V* (Miscellanea Cassinese, 28; Montecassino, 1952); J. Prochno (ed.), *Acta Urbani V. (1362–1370)* (Monumenta Vaticana Res Gestas Bohemicas illustrantia, 3; 1944; index by V. Jensovská, 1954); A. L. Tăutu (ed.), *Acta Urbani PP. V (1362–1370)* (Pontificia Commissio ad Redigendum Codicem Iuris Canonici Orientalis, Fontes, 3rd ser. 11; 1964). A. Fierens (ed.), *Suppliques d'Urbain V, 1362–1370* (Analecta Vaticano-Belgica, 7; 1914). É. *Baluze, *Vitae Paparum Avenionensium*, ed. G. Mollat, 1 (1914), pp. 349–414. Modern Lives by J. B. Magnan (Paris,

1862), M. Chaillon ('Les Saints', 1911), E. de Lanouvelle (Paris, 1928), and P. Armagier (Marseilles, 1987). J. M. Prou, *Étude sur les relations politiques du pape Urbain V avec les rois de France Jean II et Charles V* (Bibliothèque des Hautes Études, 76; 1888). J. P. Kirsch, *Die Rückkehr der Päpste Urban V und Gregor XI von Avignon nach Rom* (Quellen und Forschungen aus dem Gebiete der Geschichte, 6; 1898), pp. 1–165. É. Delaruelle, 'La Translation des reliques de saint Thomas d'Aquin à Toulouse (1369) et la politique universitaire d'Urbain V', *Bulletin de Littérature ecclésiastique*, 56 (1955), pp. 129–46. J. Gill, SJ, 'Pope Urban V (1362–1370) and the Greeks of Crete', *OCP* 39 (1973), pp. 461–8. M. and A.-M. Hayez, 'Juifs d'Avignon au tribunal de la cour temporelle sous Urbain V', *Provence Historique*, 23, fasc. 93–4 (1973), pp. 165–73. G. Mollat, *Les Papes d'Avignon* (10th edn., 1965), pp. 116–29, with bibl.; Eng. tr. (from 9th edn. of 1949; 1963), pp. 52–8. N. Housely, *The Avignon Papacy and the Crusades, 1305–1378* (Oxford, 1986), esp. pp. 40–6, 77 f., 139 f., 185 f., and 248–50. G. Mollat in *DTC* 15 (pt. 2; 1950), cols. 2295–302, s.v. 'Urbain V', with extensive bibl. See also works cited under AVIGNON.

Urban VI (1318–89), Pope from 8 Apr. 1378. Bartolommeo Prignano became Abp. of Acerenza in 1363 and was translated to Bari in 1377. On the death of *Gregory XI (1378), under whom he had been head of the Papal chancery, he was elected Pope under pressure from the Roman populace, who demanded an Italian. Hitherto he had been an ecclesiastic noted for his austerity and his aptitude for affairs, but his pontificate became a series of grave imprudences and extravagances, frequently attributed to partial mental derangement. During the first months of his reign he estranged the cardinals by his violent and overbearing manner, his irritation culminating in the threat to establish an Italian. majority in the Sacred College. The French members, therefore, in Aug. 1378 announced the nullity of the election on account of its having been performed under duress, and in Sept., by electing Clement VII (Robert of Geneva) as antipope, began the *Great Schism in the W. Among Clement's adherents was Queen Joanna of Naples, whom Urban excommunicated (1380), putting in her place Charles of Durazzo. With him, too, he soon began to quarrel, and personally led an expedition against him during which he was almost captured (1383–4). After his escape, Urban had six of his cardinals tortured and five of them executed for conspiracy. From that time the conquest of Naples became his chief preoccupation, but various attempted expeditions came to nothing. He appointed the *Holy Year to be celebrated every 33 years and on 6 Apr. 1389 extended the Feast of the *Visitation of the BVM to the whole Catholic Church (decree pub. by Boniface IX, 9 Nov. 1389).

The principal authority is *Dietrich of Niem (d. 1418), *De Schismate*, bk. 1 (ed. G. Erler, Leipzig, 1890), pp. 7–123. 'Aktenstücke zur Geschichte des Papstes Urban VI' mitgeteilt von H. B. Sauerland, *Hist. J.* 14 (1893), pp. 820–32. L. Macfarlane, 'An English Account of the Election of Urban VI, 1378', *Bulletin of the Institute of Historical Research*, 26 (1953), pp. 75–83, incl. text. O. Přerovsky, *L'elezione di Urbano VI e l'insorgere dello scisma d'Occidente* (Miscellanea della Società Romana di Storia Patria, 20; 1960). M. Seidlmayer, *Die Anfänge des grossen abendländischen Schismas* (Spanische Forschungen der Görresgesellschaft, Reihe 2, Band 5; Munster, 1940). S. Fodale, *La Politica Napoletana di Urbano VI* [1973]. W. Brandmüller, 'Zur Frage nach der Gültigkeit der Wahl Urbans VI.', *Annuarium Historiae Conciliorum*, 6 (1974), pp. 78–120, repr. in id., *Papst und Konzil im Grossen Schisma (1378–1431)* (Paderborn, 1990), pp. 1–41. M. Dykmans,

SJ, 'La troisième élection du pape Urbain VI', *Archivum Historiae Pontificiae*, 15 (1977), pp. 217–64. M. Harvey, 'The Case for Urban VI in England to 1390', in J. Favier and others, *Genèse et débuts du Grand Schisme d'Occident* (Colloques Internationaux du Centre National de la Recherche Scientifique, no. 586; 1980), pp. 541–60, and other papers in this vol. Pastor, 1 (1891), pp. 117–37. G. Mollat in *DTC* 15 (pt. 2; 1950), cols. 2302–5, s.v. 'Urbain VI', with detailed bibl. See also works cited under GREAT SCHISM (2).

Urban VIII (1568–1644), Pope from 1623. Maffeo *Barberini, descendant of one of the oldest Florentine families, distinguished himself early by his literary activities. Having been twice Papal Nuncio in France he became titular Abp. of *Nazareth in 1604, Cardinal in 1606, and Bp. of Spoleto in 1608. In 1617 *Paul V appointed him legate of *Bologna and prefect of the Segnatura di Giustizia. He was elected in 1623, and, though essentially a 'political' Pope, was a zealous promoter of ecclesiastical reforms. By canonizing and beatifying a number of saints, e.g. Elizabeth of Portugal (1625) and Francis *Borgia (1624), and by approving new religious orders such as the *Visitation (1626) and St *Vincent de Paul's *Lazarists (1632), he encouraged the religious life. He fostered missionary efforts by founding the Urban College of *Propaganda in 1627 and in the same year gave its final form to the bull '*In coena Domini' which consisted of a number of excommunications against heretics and others, ordered to be read on every *Maundy Thursday. His decrees on *canonization (1625; confirmed by brief of 1634) still have a place in the present law, and the revisions he introduced into the *Breviary in 1632 remained in force till the Breviary Reform of *Pius X (1912). He also revised the *Missal and the *Pontifical and much reduced the number of *Feasts of Obligation (1642). Under him G. *Galilei was condemned for the second time (1633), and the '*Augustinus' of C. O. *Jansen declared heretical by the bull 'In eminenti' of 1642. Urban, who was much interested in military matters, had St Angelo and Civitavecchia fortified and built the new Fort Urban. From 1625 he favoured the policy of Cardinal *Richelieu against the House of Habsburg and deprived the Catholic League of sufficient subsidies against the Protestant powers, an attitude that earned him the unfounded reproach of sympathizing with *Gustavus Adolphus and estranged the Emperor; on the other hand he tried to prevent the alliance between France and Sweden (1631), thus straining his relations with Richelieu. Urban's greatest fault was his nepotism, which lost him the sympathies of the Romans and involved him in an unfortunate war against the Duke of Parma (1642–4). He established close contact with the English Court through *Henrietta Maria by means of his agents, G. Panzani (1634) and G. Conn (1638), in a vain endeavour to re-establish the RC Church in England. Both before and after he became Pope he was a notable patron of the artist Giovanni Lorenzo Bernini (1598–1680); in 1629 he made him architect of *St Peter's (in which he designed Urban's tomb). Urban himself was a highly gifted classical scholar. His Latin poems were published at Paris in 1623 and often reprinted.

The official acts of his pontificate are pr. in the *Bullarum, Diplomatum et Privilegiorum Sanctorum Romanorum Pontificum Taurinensis Editio*, 13 (Turin, 1858), 14 (ibid., 1858), and 15 (ibid., 1858), pp. 1–428. A. Leman, *Urbain VIII et la rivalité de la France et de la Maison d'Autriche de 1631 à 1635* (Mémoires et Travaux publiés par les professeurs des Facultés Catholiques de Lille, 16; 1920). O. Pollak, *Die Kunsttätigkeit unter Urban VIII* (2 vols., Quellenschriften zur Geschichte der Barockkunst in Rom, 1928–[31]). G. Hofmann, SJ, *Griechische Patriarchen und römische Päpste: Untersuchungen und Texte*, 3. 1: *Theophanes III Patriarch von Jerusalem und Papst Urban VIII* (Orientalia Christiana, 30, pt. 1 [no. 84]; 1933). J. Grisar, 'Päpstliche Finanzen, Nepotismus und Kirchenrecht unter Urban VIII', in *Xenia Piana SSmo Dno Nro Pio Papae XII* (Rome, 1943), pp. 207–366 (also separately pub. as Miscellanea Historiae Pontificiae, 14; 1943). L. Ceyssens, OFM, *La Première Bulle contre Jansénius: Sources relatives à son histoire (1644–1653)* (Bibliothèque de l'Institut historique Belge de Rome, 9–10; 1961–2). A. Kraus, *Das päpstliche Staatssekretariat unter Urban VIII. 1623–1644* (RQ, Supplementheft, 29; 1964). T. Magnuson, *Rome in the Age of Bernini*, 1 (Kungl. Vitterhets Historie och Antikvitets Akademiens Hanglingar, Antikvariska Serien, 34; 1982), pp. 215–360. L. Nussdorfer, *Civic Politics in the Rome of Urban VIII* (Princeton, NJ [1992]). Pastor, 28 and 29 (both 1938). M. Ott in *CE* 15 (1912), pp. 218–21, s.v.; R. Ciasca in *EC* 12 (1954), cols. 912–16, s.v. 'Urbano VIII'; V. Ponko, Jun., in *NCE* 14 (1967), pp. 482 f., s.v. See also bibl. to THIRTY YEARS WAR.

Urbi et Orbi (Lat., 'to the City [i.e. of Rome] and for the World'). A phrase used esp. of the solemn blessing which the Pope imparts from time to time from the balcony of one of the Roman basilicas (now from *St Peter's church). The custom, which fell into abeyance after 1870, was revived by *Pius XI after his election in 1922.

Urbs Beata Hierusalem. A 6th–7th cent. hymn celebrating the Heavenly Jerusalem in terms suggested by Rev. 21. In medieval Breviaries it was the *office hymn for the dedication of a church. In the revised Roman Breviary of 1632, its crude rhythm was changed into quantitative iambic metre beginning 'Coelestis Urbs Jerusalem', and much of its beauty was lost. The earlier text was restored in 1971. As printed in modern Breviaries and Hymnals it consists of two parts, the first four stanzas (with an added doxology) being used for *Vespers, the second part, beginning 'Angularis fundamentum' (in the revised version: 'Alto ex Olympi vertice') for *Lauds. Of the many Eng. translations of the original hymn, J. M. *Neale's 'Blessed City, heavenly Salem' is probably the best known.

Text, with introd., notes, and refs., in A. S. Walpole, *Early Latin Hymns* (1922), no. 119, pp. 377–80. H. Ashworth, OSB, ' "Urbs Beata Ierusalem". Scriptural and Patristic Sources', *EL* 70 (1956), pp. 238–41.

Urbs Sion Aurea. A set of extracts from the 'Hora novissima, tempora pessima' of *Bernard of Cluny (q.v.) in use as a well-known hymn ('Jerusalem the golden'). The familiar Eng. rendering is by J. M. *Neale. The hymn is not to be confused with that of the preceding entry.

Urgeschichte (Ger.), 'prehistory'. A term much used in the *Dialectical Theology for events which, from the standpoint of faith, are seen to be the means of God's direct supernatural revelation to man, though viewed from the human angle they appear merely as historical occurrences. This use of the word apparently derives from F. *Overbeck.

Uriel. Acc. to Jewish apocryphal writings, one of the four chief *archangels. In 1 *Enoch 20 he is said to have charge of Tartarus.

Urim and Thummim. Prob. originally 'lots', used in early Heb. divination to interpret the will of God to the people. There are several refs. in the OT, and from the *Septuagintal text of 1 Sam. 14: 41 it would seem that the lots were cast so as to yield a negative or affirmative answer to the question posed. Their nature is not stated; but the Arabic custom of divination by headless arrows (cf. Ezek. 21: 21 f.), with the alternatives written on them, may indicate the procedure followed.

Their divinatory use is nowhere mentioned after the time of *Solomon, perhaps because it was replaced by the living voice of the Prophets, who disapproved of all mechanical oracles (cf. Hos. 4: 12), and Ez. 2: 63 and Neh. 7: 65 expressly suggest that such divination had ceased in post-exilic times. The inclusion of Urim and Thummim in the breastplate worn by the *High Priest in later times (cf. Exod. 28: 30, Lev. 8: 8) was prob. a traditional survival (note the association of 'Thummim and Urim' with Levi in Deut. 33: 8). They were numbered by the Rabbis among the five things no longer possessed by the Second Temple. By the time of *Josephus they were so little understood as to be confused with the breastplate itself (*Ant.* 3. 214–18).

Etymologically the meaning of the words, which was unknown to the ancient translators of the Bible, is obscure; LXX has δήλωσις and ἀλήθεια, Vulg. *doctrina* and *veritas*. In RV marg. they are rendered 'the Lights and the Perfections'. It has been suggested (G. R. *Driver) that 'Urim' is to be connected with a word meaning 'to give oracular response'.

R. de Vaux, OP, *Les Institutions de l'Ancien Testament*, 2 (1960), pp. 204–6, with bibl. p. 447; Eng. tr. (2nd edn., 1965), pp. 352 f., with bibl. p. 544. G. F. Moore in *E.Bi.* 4 (1903), cols. 5235–7, s.v., with bibl.; E. F. Kautzsch in *PRE* (3rd edn.), 20 (1908), pp. 328–36, s.v., also with bibl.; M. Greenberg in *Encyclopaedia Judaica*, 16 (Jerusalem, 1972), cols. 8 f., s.v. See also works cited under EPHOD.

Urmarcus (Ger.), 'primitive Mark', a supposed early and lost draft of St *Mark's Gospel. The case for its existence is based partly on apparent signs of revision in the Gospel as we have it, partly on the study of the other *Synoptics (Mt. and Lk.), which (it is argued) presuppose knowledge of a variant, and earlier, form of Mk. The theory was popular in the 19th cent., but is now only weakly reflected in the view that the earliest versions of Mk. may have varied.

E. Wendling, *Urmarcus* (1905); id., *Die Entstehung des Marcus-Evangeliums* (1908). F. C. *Burkitt, *The Gospel History and its Transmission* (1906), pp. 40–61. N. P. *Williams, *Studies in the Synoptic Problem* (ed. W. *Sanday, 1911), pp. 387–421 (a critique of Wendling). V. Taylor, *The Gospel according to St Mark* (1952; 2nd edn., 1966), pp. 68–72. See also other comm. to MARK, GOSPEL OF ST, cited s.v.

Ursacius (*fl.* *c.*335–71), Bp. of Singidunum (now Belgrade). Leader with *Valens, Bp. of Mursa, of the *Arians in the W. See VALENS.

Ursinus, Zacharias (1534–83), *Calvinist theologian. A native of Breslau, he studied at *Wittenberg (1550–7) and came under the influence of P. *Melanchthon. During a tour of various universities, he met H. *Bullinger, J. *Calvin, S. *Castellio, and other Calvinists whose views he gradually adopted. He taught at Breslau before he went to Heidelberg in 1561. Here, at the behest of the Elector *Frederick III, with K. Olevian he drew up the *Heidelberg Catechism (q.v.). On the death of Frederick he left Heidelberg for Neustadt, where he wrote his *Admonitio Christiana* (see NEOSTADIENSIUM ADMONITIO), intended as a rebuttal of the Formula of *Concord.

Collected edns. of his Theological Works pub. in 2 vols., Neustadt, 1587–9, and ed. Q. Reuter, 3 vols., Heidelberg, 1612. K. Sudhoff, *C. Olevianus und Z. Ursinus: Leben und ausgewählte Schriften* (Elberfeld, 1857). E. K. Sturm, *Der junge Zacharias Ursin: Sein Weg vom Philippismus zum Calvinismus (1534–1562)* (Beiträge zur Geschichte und Lehre der Reformierten Kirche, 33; Neukirchen [1972]). D. Visser, *Zacharius Ursinus: The Reluctant Reformer. His Life and Times* (New York [1983]). C. J. Burchill, 'On the Consolation of a Christian Scholar: Zacharius Ursinus (1534–83) and the Reformation in Heidelberg', *JEH* 37 (1986), pp. 565–83.

Ursula, St. The legend of the martyr St Ursula and her 11,000 virgins developed from the veneration of some nameless virgin martyrs at *Cologne. Its earliest basis is a 4th–5th-cent. inscription formerly at Cologne, acc. to which a certain Clematius restored an old basilica on the site where holy virgins had shed their blood for Christ. The next mention of the martyrs occurs in a sermon of the 8th or 9th cent. in honour of several thousand virgins who had perished in the persecution of Maximian. Acc. to a later form of the story, Ursula, whose name now came to be affixed to their leader, was a British princess who, accompanied by 11,000 virgins, went on a pilgrimage to Rome, and on her return was massacred with her companions at Cologne by the Huns. This legend was a favourite of the Middle Ages, and the discovery, in 1106, of a burial ground near the church of St Ursula, believed to contain the relics of the martyrs, gave rise to many further embellishments. St Ursula became the patron of many educational institutions; in modern times her name is chiefly known through the teaching order of the *Ursulines (q.v.). Feast day, 21 Oct., suppressed in 1969.

Texts ed., with full discussion, by V. de Buck, SJ, in *AASS*, Oct. 9 (1885), pp. 73–303. W. Levison, 'Das Werden der Ursula-Legende', *Bonner Jahrbücher*, 132 (1927), pp. 1–164; also separately issued, Cologne, 1928. Extensive refs. to other lit. in the discussion of Levison's book by M. Coens in *Anal. Boll.* 47 (1929), pp. 89–110. Studies in Eng. incl. M. (Mrs T. F.) Tout, 'The Legend of St. Ursula and the Eleven Thousand Virgins', *Historical Essays by Members of Owens College, Manchester*, ed. T. F. Tout and J. Tait (1902), pp. 17–56. Good modern popular study by J. Solzbacher and V. Hopmann, *Die Legende der hl. Ursula: Die Geschichte der Ursula-Verehrung* (Cologne, 1964). On the representation of the legend in art, G. de Tervarent, *La Légende de sainte Ursule dans la littérature et l'art du moyen âge* (2 vols., 1931). A. Poncelet, SJ, in *CE* 15 (1912), pp. 225–8, s.v.

Ursulines. The oldest and most considerable teaching order of women in the the RC Church. It was founded at Brescia in 1535 by St *Angela Merici. The original members lived in their own houses, continuing their normal occupations in addition to pastoral work which included catechetics. Approved by *Paul III in 1544, community life and simple vows were introduced in 1572 by *Gregory XIII at the instigation of St *Charles Borromeo. In 1612

*Paul V allowed the Ursulines of Paris solemn vows and strict enclosure, and convents were erected on these lines, following a modified form of the Rule of St *Augustine. From this time the pastoral work of the order developed into the institutional form of schools for girls, esp. in 17th-cent. France, where Ursulines became noted for their educational work. The order spread not only in Europe, but to the New World and the Far East. Most houses were autonomous, but in 1900 at a Congress in Rome of Ursulines from all over the world, the union was effected of a great number of convents belonging to different congregations in the 'Roman Union'. There have since been a number of other unions, of which the largest is that of Eastern Quebec, formed in 1953 of all convents founded from Quebec. A union of Ursulines in German-speaking countries, constituted in 1907, became a federation in 1964. There are also autonomous houses in many parts of the world. Since the Second *Vatican Council removed the obligation of strict enclosure from nuns leading an active (as opposed to a contemplative) life, Ursulines have been able to live more closely among the people and to undertake a wider range of pastoral work, in addition to their educational undertakings. One of the most famous members of the order was the mystic, Marie *Guyard ('Mary of the Incarnation'), who founded the house at Quebec in 1639.

Annales de l'ordre de Ste Ursule …: avec une préface par M. C. Ste-Foi (2 vols., Clermont-Ferrand, 1857). M. Aron, *Les Ursulines* (Les Grands Ordres monastiques et instituts religieux, 1937; Eng. tr., New York, 1947). T. Ledóchowska, OSU, *Angèle Merici et la Compagnie de Sainte-Ursule* (2 vols., Rome [1968]; Eng. tr., ibid. [1970]), with bibl. M. de Chantal Gueudré, OSU, *Histoire de l'ordre des Ursulines en France* [to 1802] (3 vols., 1958–64). H. Albisser, *Die Ursulinen zu Luzern: Geschichte, Leben und Werk, 1659–1847* (Stans, 1938). *Les Ursulines des Trois Rivières* (3 vols., Three Rivers, Canada, 1888–98; vol. 4, Quebec, 1911); *Les Ursulines de Québec* (4 vols., Quebec, 1864–6). P. G. Roy, *À travers l'histoire des Ursulines de Québec* (Lévis, 1939). C. J. Beaumier, *L'Union romaine des Ursulines d'après les documents pontificaux* (Three Rivers, 1951); D. Dunkerley and others in *NCE* 14 (1967), pp. 491–5, s.v.; T. Ledóchowska and others in *DIP* 6 (1980), cols. 836–57, s.v. 'Orsoline, II'; L. Mariani, OSU, and others in *Dict. Sp.* 16 (1994), cols. 78–99, s.v. 'Ursulines, II–III'.

Usagers. The section of the *Nonjurors who in 1719 accepted the Communion Service which had been newly drawn up by J. *Collier, T. *Brett, and T. Deacon on the basis partly of the primitive Christian liturgies and partly of the 1549 BCP. They were so named from four 'usages' which the new rite contained, namely: (1) the *mixed chalice; (2) prayers for the dead; (3) a prayer for the descent of the Holy Spirit on the elements (see EPICLESIS); and (4) an Oblatory prayer. The schism between the 'Usagers' and 'Non-Usagers' was healed in 1732.

J. H. Overton, *The Nonjurors: Their Lives, Principles, and Writings* (1902), pp. 290–308, 321 f., 443–5; H. Broxap, *The Later Non-Jurors* (1924), pp. 35–65 and *passim*; and W. J. Grisbrooke, *Anglican Liturgies of the Seventeenth and Eighteenth Centuries* (*Alcuin Club Collections, 40; 1958), esp. pp. 71–112.

use. In liturgiology, a local modification of the standard (esp. the Roman) rite. In Latin Christendom such uses arose partly through the absorption of *Gallican features by the Roman rite as it spread through Europe and partly through later local developments in the Roman rite itself. These uses, which differed from the Roman rite only in details, were gradually consolidated and codified in metropolitan and diocesan cathedrals and in some of the religious orders and, after ritual books came to be printed, were often used over wide areas. In the Preface to the BCP of 1549, where the five uses of *Hereford, *York, *Lincoln, *Bangor, and *Salisbury are referred to, it was ordered that 'from henceforth all the whole realm shall have but one use'. In the RC Church all uses, except those which could prove an existence of two centuries (notably the *Ambrosian use at Milan, the *Mozarabic use at Toledo, and those of some religious orders), were abolished by the Council of *Trent.

USPG. The United Society for the Propagation of the Gospel was formed in 1965 by the amalgamation of the SPG and the UMCA (qq.v.). It continues to work in the areas previously covered by these societies.

M. Dewey, *The Messengers: A Concise History of the United Society for the Propagation of the Gospel* (1975), esp. pp. 121–42.

Ussher, James (1581–1656), Abp. of *Armagh. Educated at the newly founded *Trinity College, Dublin, he was ordained in 1601 and appointed chancellor of St Patrick's Cathedral in 1606 and first professor of divinity at Dublin in 1607. Subsequently he became Bp. of Meath (1621) and Abp. of Armagh (1625). A scholar and historian of vast learning, he was intimate with most of the English writers and divines of the day and was an authority on such diverse topics as the letters of St *Ignatius of Antioch (of which he distinguished the 7 genuine from the later spurious ones, whose existence had previously discredited them all) and the early history of Ireland. Although a *Calvinist in theology, he was not unfriendly with W. *Laud, and advised *Charles I against the execution of Strafford. After the Irish rebellion of 1641 he remained in England, endeavouring to bring about a reconciliation between Churchmen and Dissenters. So great was his repute for scholarship, tolerance, and sincerity that on his death he was given a state funeral in *Westminster Abbey by O. *Cromwell. See also IRISH ARTICLES (1615).

Ussher's published writings include: *A Discourse of the Religion anciently professed by the Irish* (1623); *Gotteschalci et Prædestinatianæ Controversiæ . . . Historia* (1631); *Britannicarum Ecclesiarum Antiquitates* (1639); *The Original of Bishops* (1641); *Polycarpi et Ignatii Epistolæ* (1644); *De Græca Septuaginta Interpretum Versione Syntagma* (1655); *Chronologia Sacra* (1660; ed. T. *Barlow); *The Power communicated by God to the Prince* (1661); *Historia Dogmatica Controversiæ inter Orthodoxos et Pontificios de Scripturis* (1690; ed. H. *Wharton). His *Annales Veteris et Novi Testamenti* (1650–4) are said to be the source of the dates later inserted in the margins of the AV of the Bible (edns. 1701 onwards).

Works ed. C. R. Elrington and J. H. Todd (17 vols., Dublin and London, 1847–64), with Life by C. R. Elrington in vol. 1, pp. 1–324. Early Lives by N. Bernard (Ussher's chaplain; London, 1656) and R. Parr (also chaplain; ibid., 1686, mainly important for letters). Modern studies by J. A. Carr, *The Life and Times of James Ussher, Archbishop of Armagh* (1895), and R. B. Knox, *James Ussher, Archbishop of Armagh* (Cardiff, 1967). J. Barr, 'Why the World was created in 4004 B.C.: Archbishop Ussher and

Biblical Chronology', *Bulletin of the John Rylands Library*, 67 (1984–5), pp. 575–608. H. Trevor-Roper, *Catholics, Anglicans and Puritans* (1987), pp. 120–65. A. Gordon in *DNB* 58 (1899), pp. 64–72.

Usuard, Martyrology of. The most widely circulated of the *martyrologies in the Middle Ages and the basis of the current '*Roman Martyrology'. Its compiler, Usuard (d. *c.*875), who was commissioned for the work by Charles the Bald, was a Benedictine monk of the abbey of *St-Germain-des-Prés at Paris. He seems to have based his work on the somewhat earlier Martyrology of *Ado of Vienne (d. 875). It was edited at Paris in 1718 by Dom Jacques Bouillart from a MS contemporary with its compiler and possibly the autograph.

The most important earlier edns. are those of J. Molanus (Louvain, 1563 and 1573, and Antwerp, 1583) and J. B. du Sollier, SJ (*AASS*, Jun. 7, 1714, and Venice, 1745, repr. in J. P. Migne, *PL* 123. 453–992, and 124. 9–860). Crit. edn., with comm., by J. Dubois, OSB (Subsidia Hagiographica, 40; 1965). P. Grosjean, SJ, 'Sur les éditions de l'Usuard de Jean Molanus', *Anal. Boll.* 70 (1952), pp. 327–33; J. Dubois, OSB, 'À la recherche de l'état primitif du martyrologe d'Usuard. Le manuscrit de Fécamp', ibid. 95 (1977), pp. 43–71, repr. in id., *Martyrologes d'Usuard au Martyrologe Romain* (Abbeville, 1990), pp. 121–49. É Amann in *DTC* 15 (pt. 2; 1950), cols. 2313–16, s.v. 'Usuard'. See also works cited under MARTYROLOGY.

usury. The exacting of interest was forbidden in the OT in the case of Jewish debtors (Exod. 22: 25, Deut. 23: 19 f.). The NT is not explicit on the subject, but during the patristic age all lending on interest was forbidden to clerics by the Councils of *Arles (314) and *Nicaea (325). The first Council of *Carthage (348) and the Council of Aix (789) objected to this method of making profit even in the case of laymen; and in the Decree of *Gratian, and subsequently at the Third *Lateran Council (1179) and the Second of *Lyons (1274), the practice was formally condemned, though it was allowed to the Jews by the Fourth Lateran Council of 1215. The condemnation was justified by the medieval view of money as solely a medium of exchange for articles of consumption, the use of which is adequately repaid by the return of a sum equal to that which was lent. This doctrine, founded on *Aristotle's theory of the 'barren' nature of money, was elaborated by the Schoolmen, esp. St *Thomas Aquinas (*Summa Theol.*, II/IIae, q. 78, art. 1) and held sway in the RC Church till the 19th cent. It was restated, e.g., by *Benedict XIV in 1745.

With the rise of capitalism the principle had to be gradually abandoned. M. *Luther and U. *Zwingli, as well as the 16th-cent. Anglican divines, still condemned the lending of money for interest, but J. *Calvin permitted it in the case of wealthy debtors, and the civil legislation, which had hitherto followed canon law, began to provide for moderate charges of interest in England in 1571, in Germany in the same century, but in many Continental countries much later, in France e.g. not until 1789. Today money is no longer thought of, as in the Middle Ages, as a barren means of exchange but as capital productive of wealth like other property. Since the exaction of a reasonable interest for its loan has been tolerated by the Christian Church, the term 'usury' has tended to be restricted to excessive rates.

R. H. Tawney, *Religion and the Rise of Capitalism* (Holland Memorial Lectures for 1922; 1926). B. N. Nelson, *The Idea of Usury* (Princeton, NJ, 1949; rev. edn., Chicago and London, 1969), with bibl. J. T. Noonan, Jun., *The Scholastic Analysis of Usury* (Cambridge, Mass., 1957). T. F. Divine, SJ, *Interest: An Historical and Analytical Study in Economics and Modern Ethics* (Milwaukee, 1959), pp. 3–116. J. W. Baldwin, *Masters, Princes, and Merchants* (2 vols., Princeton, NJ, 1970), 1, pp. 270–311, with notes, 2, pp. 185–211 [on the 12th cent.]. L. Poliakov, *Les Banchieri juifs et le Saint-Siège du XIIIe au XVIIe siècle* (1965; Eng. tr., 1977). O. Langholm, *The Aristotelian Analysis of Usury* (Bergen [1984]). N. Jones, *God and the Moneylenders: Usury and Law in Early Modern England* (Oxford, 1989). H. Siems, *Handel und Wucher im Spiegel frühmittelalterlicher Rechtsquellen* (*MGH*, Schriften, 35; 1992). A. Bernard, G. Le Bras, and H. du Passage, SJ, in *DTC* 15 (pt. 2; 1950), cols. 2316–90; s.v. 'Usure', with refs.

Utica, the Martyrs of. A group of early African martyrs of uncertain date who suffered at the Massa Candida (lit. 'White Farm'). The place, misunderstood as 'White Lump', gave rise to the legend that in the time of Valerian (*c.*258) they were thrown alive into slaking quicklime and their bodies reduced to a white mass of powder. Acc. to St *Augustine (*Serm.* 306, preached on their anniversary) there were 153 (cf. Jn. 21: 11), and the massacre took place at Utica, 35 miles from Carthage, though the *Roman Martyrology increases the number to 300 and assigns it to Carthage. *Prudentius, who extols the purity (*candor*) of their souls reflected in the whiteness (*candor*) of their bodies, prob. had a decisive influence on the legend. Feast day, 24 Aug.

Prudentius, *Peristephanon*, 13, lines 76–87; Augustine, *Sermones*, 306 and 311. 10; also *Sermones post Maurinos reperti*, ed. G. *Morin, OSB (Miscellanea Agostiniana, 1; Rome, 1930), pp. 645 f. (no. 14); also *Enarrationes in Pss.*, 49. 9, and 144. 17; and among the Ps.-Augustinian sermons no. 317. P. Monceaux, 'Les Martyrs d'Utique et la légende de la "Massa Candida" ', *Revue archéologique*, 3rd ser. 37 (1900), pp. 404–11; F. P. de' Cavalieri, 'I martiri della Massa Candida', in *Nuove Note agiografiche* (ST 9; 1902), pp. 39–51. H. *Leclercq, OSB, in *DACL* 10 (pt. 2; 1932), cols. 2649–53, s.v. 'Massa Candida', and 15 (pt. 2; 1953), cols. 2878 f., s.v. 'Utique'; G. D. Gordini in *Bibliotheca Sanctorum*, 9 (Rome, 1967), cols. 4–6, s.v. 'Massa Candida'.

Utilitarianism. The doctrine in ethics which identifies the good with happiness and maintains those actions to be right which bring the greatest happiness to the greatest number. In principle it was maintained by T. *Hobbes, B. de Mandeville, D. *Hume, and C. A. Helvetius, but it came into prominence with J. Bentham, J. S. Mill, and the Philosophical Radicals. H. *Rashdall sought to interpret the Christian ethic as an 'Ideal Utilitarianism'.

J. S. Mill's classic defence of the doctrine was originally pub. in three arts. in *Fraser's Magazine*, 64 (1861; pt. 2), pp. 391–406 (Oct.), 525–34 (Nov.), 659–73 (Dec.); they were reissued in book form as *Utilitarianism* (1863). L. Stephen, *The English Utilitarians* (3 vols., 1900). E. Albee, *A History of English Utilitarianism* (1902). D. Baumgardt, *Bentham and the Ethics of Today, with Bentham Manuscripts hitherto unpublished* (Princeton, NJ, 1952). A. [M.] Quinton, *Utilitarian Ethics* (1973; 2nd edn., 1989), with bibl. Good account by A. W. Hastings in *HERE* 12 (1921), pp. 558–67.

Utraquism. The Hussite doctrine that the laity, like the clergy, should receive the Holy Communion under the forms of both bread and wine (*sub utraque specie*). It was first formally defended by Jacob of Mies, a professor of the University of Prague, in 1414. John *Huss did not personally press the thesis, but, despite condemnation at the Councils of *Constance (1415) and *Basle (1432), it was maintained by his followers, including the more moderate group of them (who were also called *Calixtines, from their demand for the cup, *calix*). Communion in both kinds was conceded to the laity of Bohemia by the Compactata of Prague (1433), which, though formally cancelled by *Pius II in 1462, were maintained by the Bohemian Diet until 1567. At that stage, with most of the country Protestant, the RC authorities continued to turn a blind eye to Utraquist practice; but they were able to abolish it after the defeat of the Bohemian revolt in 1620.

See bibl. to CALIXTINES and HUSS, J.

Utrecht, Declaration of. The Profession of Faith which is the doctrinal basis of the *Old Catholic Church. It was drawn up by an assembly of the Old Catholic bishops at Utrecht on 24 Sept. 1889. Professing adherence to the beliefs of the primitive Church, esp. as formulated in the decrees of the *Oecumenical Councils down to AD 1000, it is mainly concerned with controverting specific doctrines of the RC Church. Among the formulae repudiated are the decrees on the Papacy of the First *Vatican Council in 1870, the dogma of the *Immaculate Conception, the encyclicals '*Unigenitus' and '*Auctorem fidei', and the *Syllabus of 1864. Positively it maintains the sacrificial element in the *Eucharist and the *Real Presence, though without mention of the propitiatory nature of sacrifice or of *transubstantiation.

Eng. tr. in the *Report* of the *Lambeth Conference for 1930, pp. 142–4; repr. in C. B. Moss, *The Old Catholic Movement* (1948), pp. 281 f.

Uvedale, John and Nicholas. See UDALL, JOHN and NICHOLAS.

V

Vacancy-in-See Committee. Under an Act of the General *Synod promulgated in 1977, when a diocese in the C of E becomes vacant, the Vacancy-in-See Committee of the diocese draws up a statement setting out the needs of the diocese and providing factual information about it, discusses possible candidates for the vacancy, and elects four representatives to sit on the *Crown Appointments Commission. The Committee consists of the *suffragan bishop(s) of the diocese, the Dean or Provost of the Cathedral (or if he cannot serve, a residentiary canon), one of the archdeacons, the diocesan proctors in the Lower House of *Convocation, the diocesan representatives in the House of Laity of the General Synod, and the chairman and not less than two elected members each of the Houses of Clergy and Laity of the Diocesan Synod. Two additional persons, one in *Orders and one lay, may be nominated by the Bishop's Council to represent some special interest in the diocese.

Vaison, Councils of. Two important ecclesiastical synods were held at Vaison (*c.*25 miles NE of Avignon, in SE France):

(1) On 13 Nov. 442. It enacted ten canons which provided *inter alia* that clergy should receive the *chrism at Easter from their own bishops (can. 3), that any unwilling to accept the judgements of their bishop should resort to the Synod (can. 5), and that there should be no intimacy with those hostile to the bishop (can. 6). It also regulated the adoption of children (cans. 9 and 10). Acc. to St *Ado, Abp. of Vienne (9th cent.), his predecessor, Nectarius of Vienne, presided at the Council.

(2) On 5 Nov. 529. It enacted five canons of liturgical import, ordering the frequent repetition of *Kyrie Eleison in the Office and at Mass (can. 3), the regular use of prayer for the Pope (can. 4) and of *Sicut erat* after *Gloria Patri* (can. 5). Twelve bishops were present, among them St *Caesarius of Arles.

(1) Hardouin, 1, cols. 1787–90; Mansi, 6 (Florence, 1761), cols. 451 f.; C. Munier (ed.), *Concilia Galliae A. 314–A. 506* (CCSL 148; 1963), pp. 94–104. Hefele and Leclercq, 2 (pt. 1; 1908), pp. 454–60.
(2) Hardouin, 2, cols. 1105 f.; Mansi, 8 (Florence, 1762), cols. 725–8; C. de Clercq (ed.), *Concilia Galliae A. 511–A. 695* (CCSL 148 A; 1963), pp. 82 f., repr., with Fr. tr. and notes by J. Gaudemet and B. Basdevant, *Les Canons des Conciles Mérovingiens (VIᵉ–VIIᵉ siècles)*, 1 (SC 353; 1989), pp. 186–93. O. Pontal, *Die Synoden im Merowingerreich* (1986), pp. 56–8; rev. Fr. tr. [1989], pp. 82–4. Hefele and Leclercq, 2 (pt. 2; 1908), pp. 1110–15.

Valdés, Juan de (?1490–1541), Spanish religious writer. A native of Cuenca in New Castile, he studied at Alcalá, fled from the Spanish *Inquisition to Italy in 1531, and became *camerario* to *Clement VII in 1533. From 1534 he lived in Naples, where he became the spiritual centre of a group of prominent men and women anxious for reforms and spiritual revival in the Church, among them Giulia Gonzaga and Vittoria Colonna. Though at least outwardly

he remained a Catholic, his conception of personal religion and interiority was largely Protestant in character and later had wide appeal for the Reformed traditions. After his death various of his friends, incl. *Peter Martyr and B. *Ochino, left the RC Church. Besides an important work on the Spanish language, *Diálogo de la lengua* (pub. 1737), he wrote a number of religious works, expounding Christian doctrine and the Scriptures. Among these are the *Diálogo de doctrina cristiana* (1529) and the *Alfabeto cristiano* (1536). He also translated the Hebrew Psalter into Castilian. His *Las ciento diez divinas consideraciones*, published in Italian in 1550, was translated into English by N. *Ferrar (1638).

His brother, **Alfonso de Valdés** (?1490–1532), who became Latin Secretary to the Emp. *Charles V, was a noted humanist and admirer of *Erasmus. After the Sack of Rome in 1527, he wrote the *Diálogo de Lactancio y un arcediano* (otherwise, *Diálogo de las cosas acaecidas en Roma*) (prob. first pub. 1529; Eng. tr. 1590) to justify the event; it vigorously attacks the Papacy for its part in contemporary international politics and for the corrupt state of the Church over which it presided, esp. the Curia, setting in contrast the fundamentals of New Testament Christianity as Erasmus interpreted them. The same themes recur in his *Diálogo de Mercurio y Carón* (1529), where he attacks religion that has become a matter of empty outward forms, devotion to inanimate objects, and good works undertaken on a *quid pro quo* basis. It contains a powerful apologia for lay Christianity as embodied in an ideal ruler. The work was long, but erroneously, attributed to Juan de Valdés.

Modern crit. edns. of Juan de Valdés, *Diálogo de la lengua* by C. Barbolini de García (Messina and Florence, 1967; rev., Madrid, 1982), which J. M. Lope Blanch (Clásicos Castalia, 11; 1969) follows; also by J. F. Montesinos (Clásicos Castellanos, 86; 1928); of his *Alfabeto cristiano* by B. *Croce (Bari, 1938); photographic repr. of the 1529 edn. of his *Diálogo de doctrina cristiana* with introd. and notes by M. Bataillon (Coimbra, 1925; repr., Paris, 1981); further edn. of this work, with his tr. of the Psalter, by D. Ricart (Mexico, 1964). Edns. of *Las ciento diez divinas consideraciones* by L. Usoz y Río (Reformistas Antiguos Españoles, 17; 1863), E. Cione (Milan, 1944) and, following MS of Juan Sánchez (1558), by J. I. Tellechea Idígoras (Salamanca, 1975). Unpub. letters to Card. Gonzaga, ed. J. F. Montesinos (Anejos de la *Revista de Filología Española*, 14; 1931). Modern Life by E. Cione (Bari, 1938; 2nd edn., Naples, 1963), with good bibl. J. E. Longhurst, *Erasmus and the Spanish Inquisition: The Case of Juan de Valdés* (Albuquerque, NM, 1950). M. Bataillon, *Érasme et l'Espagne* (1937; rev. edn., 3 vols., Travaux d'Humanisme et Renaissance, 250; Geneva, 1991), ch. 7; id., *Erasmo y el Erasmismo* (Barcelona, 1977), pp. 245–85. Domingo de Sta. Teresa, OCD, *Juan de Valdés, 1498(?)–1541* (Analecta Gregoriana, 85; 1957). P. McNair, *Peter Martyr in Italy* (Oxford, 1967), esp. pp. 17–28. J. H. Bakhuizen van den Brink, *Juan de Valdés, réformateur en Espagne et en Italie 1529–1541* (Geneva, 1969). J. C. Nieto, *Juan de Valdés and the Origins of the Spanish and Italian Reformation* (ibid., 1970; rev. Sp. tr., 1979). M. Firpo, *Tra Alumbrados e 'Spirituali': Studi su Juan de Valdés e il Valdesianesimo nella Crisi religiosa del '500 Italiano* (Studi e Testi per la Storia Religiosa del

Cinquecento, 3; Florence, 1990). A. [A. H.] Hamilton, *Heresy and Mysticism in Sixteenth-Century Spain* (Cambridge, 1992), esp. pp. 40–2, 86–8, and 129 f. J. C. Nieto in P. G. Bietenholz and T. B. Deutscher (eds.), *Contemporaries of Erasmus*, 3 (Toronto, etc., 1987), pp. 368–70, s.v.

Modern edns. of Alfonso de Valdés, *Diálogo de Lactancio* by J. F. Montesinos (Clásicos Castellanos, 89; 1928), and of *Diálogo de Mercurio y Carón* by id. (ibid. 96; 1929) and by R. Navarro Durán (Barcelona [1987]). M. Bataillon, 'Alonso de Valdés, auteur du "Diálogo de Mercurio y Carón" ', in *Homenaje ofrecido a Menéndez Pidal*, 1 (1925), pp. 403–15; id., *Erasme et l'Espagne* (cited above), ch. 8; D. Donald and E. Lázaro, *Alfonso de Valdés y su época* (Cuenca [1983]). J. C. Nieto in *Contemporaries of Erasmus* (cited above), pp. 366–8.

Valdes, Peter. See WALDENSES.

Valence, Councils of.
Of the many Councils held at Valence in Dauphiné, the three most important were:

(1) 12 July 374. A Council of 30 bishops, summoned to deal with various disciplinary problems, among them the refusal of Acceptus to become Bp. of Forum Iulii (Fréjus). It issued four disciplinary canons. Can. 1 forbade the ordination of digamists, can. 2 easy penance to lapsed virgins, and can. 3 absolution until death to those who had lapsed into idolatry or received second baptism. Can. 4 dealt with clerics who falsely accused themselves of crime to escape office.

(2) *c.*530. Its Acts are lost, and it is uncertain whether it was held before or after the Council of *Orange (529). Like the latter, it was directed against *Pelagianism and *Semipelagianism. Its president was *Cyprian of Toulon, who represented St *Caesarius of Arles.

(3) 8 Jan. 855. The Council was convoked by the Emp. Lothair (817–55) to try the Bp. of Valence on various counts. It then proceeded to discuss *predestination, upholding against *Hincmar of Reims and the Council of *Quiercy (853) 'double predestination' and rejecting the view that the redemptive work of Christ extended to the whole human race.

(1) Hardouin, 1, cols. 795–8; Mansi, 3 (Florence, 1759), cols. 491–500; C. Munier (ed.), *Concilia Galliae A. 314–A. 506* (CCSL 148; 1963), pp. 35–45; repr., with Fr. tr. and introd. by J. Gaudemet, *Conciles Gaulois du IVᵉ Siècle* (SC 241; 1977), pp. 100–11. Hefele and Leclercq, 1 (pt. 2; 1907), p. 982.

(2) Hardouin, 2, cols. 1103 f.; Mansi, 8 (Florence, 1762), cols. 723–6. C. de Clercq (ed.), *Concilia Galliae A. 511–A. 695* (CCSL 148 A; 1963), pp. 82 f. Hefele and Leclercq, 2 (pt. 2; 1908), p. 1110. O. Pontal, *Die Synoden im Merowingerreich* (1986), pp. 61–7; revised Fr. tr. [1989], pp. 89–94. See also works cited s.v. ORANGE, COUNCILS OF.

(3) Hardouin, 5, cols. 87–96; Mansi, 15 (Venice, 1770), cols. 1–16; W. Hartmann (ed.), *Die Konzilien der Karolingischen Teilreiche 843–859* (MGH, Concilia, 3; 1984), pp. 347–65. Hefele and Leclercq, 4 (pt. 1; 1911), pp. 204–10, and 4 (pt. 2; 1911), pp. 1326 and 1390–8, with further refs. See also works cited s.v. HINCMAR.

Valens
(4th cent.), Bp. of Mursa, who with *Ursacius, Bp. of Singidunum, was an *Arian leader in the W. Pupils of *Arius, they became bitter enemies of St *Athanasius, whom they opposed, e.g. at the Council of Tyre in 335. After retracting their charges at the Council of Milan in 347, owing to a temporary change in the policy of the Emp. Constantius, they resumed their opposition to him at *Arles in 353 and at Milan in 355, and at Sirmium (357) maintained the extreme Arian ('Anomoean') position.

Again in acc. with Imperial policy they took up a compromising attitude in 359 at the Synod of *Ariminum, where they were responsible for the victory of the *Homoean party. Though frequently excommunicated in the W. Church, they seem to have retained considerable influence at the court of Constantius. The last mention of Valens dates from 367.

There are scattered refs. in *Hilary of Poitiers, Athanasius, *Socrates, and *Sozomen. Frags of a treatise of Hilary, 'Adv. Valentem et Ursacium', known to St *Jerome (*De Vir. Ill.* 100), survive; text in J. P. Migne, *PL* 10. 627–724; crit. edn. by A. L. Feder, SJ, in CSEL 65 (1916), pp. 39–193. M. Meslin, *Les Ariens d'Occident 335–430* (Patristica Sorbonensia, 8; 1967), pp. 71–84. See also bibl. to ARIMINUM AND SELEUCIA, SYNODS OF.

Valentine, St.
The commemoration formerly observed on 14 Feb. appears to refer to two Valentines: a Roman priest martyred on the Flaminian Way under the Emp. Claudius (*c.*269) and a Bp. of Terni (Interamna) who was taken to Rome and martyred, and whose remains were later conveyed back to Terni. Though the surviving accounts of both martyrdoms are clearly legendary, there are indications that each contains a nucleus of fact; and it is just possible that the kernel of truth in the two legends refers to a single person. The traditional association of St Valentine's day with courtship and the choosing of a 'Valentine' of the opposite sex is connected perhaps with certain customs of the pagan festival of *Lupercalia (mid-Feb.) at Rome, or with the natural season, not with any tradition concerning either saint of the name.

'Acta' of both SS. Valentine in *AASS*, Feb. 2 (1658), pp. 751–62. Note on the SS. Valentine in *Anal. Boll.* 11 (1892), pp. 471–3. E. M. Fusciardi, *Vita di S. Valentino, V. e M., patrono di Terni: Con messa, novena, triduo e preghiere* (Terni, 1936). O. *Marucchi, *Il cimitero e la basilica di S. Valentino* (1890); R. Krautheimer and S. Corbett in R. Krautheimer and others, *Corpus Basilicarum Christianarum Romae*, 4 (Rome, 1970), pp. 289–311 (in Eng.). On the origin of the association of St Valentine's day with courtship, H. A. Kelly, *Chaucer and the Cult of Saint Valentine* (Davis Medieval Texts and Studies, 5; Leiden, 1986).

Valentinus
(2nd cent.), *Gnostic theologian and founder of the Valentinian sect. Acc. to St *Irenaeus and others he was a native of Egypt whose disciples claimed that he had been taught by Theodas, a pupil of St *Paul. He came to Rome *c.*136 and is said to have had hopes of being elected Bishop 'on account of his intellectual force and eloquence' (*quia et ingenio poterat et eloquio*; *Tertullian, *Adv. Valentinianos*, 4), but was passed over in favour of a '*confessor', seceded from the Church, and went to the E., perhaps to *Cyprus. Later he returned to Rome, where he died *c.*165.

Valentinus produced a variety of writings, but we have only fragments, preserved chiefly by *Clement of Alexandria, which are insufficient to allow us to reconstruct his teaching, except in broad outline. The Coptic texts from *Nag Hammadi include several which clearly derive from the Valentinian school (*Evangelium Veritatis*, the 'Tripartite Tractate', Gospel of *Philip, 'On the Resurrection', etc.), but none of them can be assigned to Valentinus himself with any confidence. *Hippolytus (*Haer.* 6. 37. 7) preserves one of his hymns. His system is known to us only in the developed and modified form given to it by his disciples. It appears to have been based on earlier systems (perhaps including the *Ophite), and to incorporate

*Platonic and Pythagorean elements. The spiritual world or 'pleroma' comprises 30 'aeons' emanated by the Primal Ground of Being, who form a succession of pairs (*syzygies). The visible world owes its origin to the fall of Sophia, the last of these aeons; this fall is variously described, but results in the emergence of her offspring the *Demiurge or creator, identified with the God of the OT. The Valentinian myth is intended to explain the human predicament by showing how a divine element has come to be imprisoned in this alien and hostile world, at the mercy of the Demiurge and his 'archons', the rulers of the planetary spheres. Redemption is effected by another aeon, Christ, who unites with the man Jesus (either at his conception or at his baptism) to bring mankind the saving knowledge ('gnosis') of its true origin and destiny. This gnosis, however, is given only to the 'spiritual' or 'pneumatics', i.e. the Valentinians, who through it are destined to return to the pleroma; other Christians, described as 'psychics' (cf. 1 Cor. 2: 14 etc.), can attain by faith and good works to a form of salvation, but only in a lower realm below the pleroma; the rest of mankind, called 'hylics' as merely material and not 'spiritual', are doomed to eternal perdition.

Valentinus was probably the most influential of the Gnostics and had a very large following (*frequentissimum plane collegium inter haereticos*; Tertullian, op. cit. 1). Later the school divided into two branches (Hippolytus, *Haer.* 6. 35), an E. one including *Theodotus, and an Italian or W. one including *Ptolemaeus, *Heracleon, and Marcus (see MARCOSIANS). The patristic reports frequently mention the divergent views of 'others' in describing the system, and thus show how easily and quickly modifications could be introduced or differences of opinion arise within the school.

The chief Christian sources are Irenaeus, *Adv. Haer.* 1, *passim*, and 3. 4; Tertullian, *Adv. Valentinianos*; Clement of Alexandria, *Stromateis* (several refs.) and *Excerpta ex Theodoto*; Hippolytus, *Haer.* 6. 20–55; Pseudo-Tertullian, *Adversus Omnes Haereses*, 4 [*De Praescriptione*, 49]; *Eusebius, *HE* 4. 11; *Epiphanius, *Haer.* 31, 33 f., and 56. Most of these, together with other material on the Valentinians, are conveniently collected in W. Völker, *Quellen zur Geschichte der christlichen Gnosis* (1932), pp. 57–141. Eng. tr. of primary texts, with brief introd., in W. Foerster, *Gnosis*, 1 (Eng. tr. by R. McL. Wilson, 1972), pp. 121–243. There are comprehensive studies by F.-M.-M. Sagnard, OP, *La Gnose valentinienne et le témoignage de saint Irénée* (Études de Philosophie médiévale, 36; 1947); A. Orbe, SJ, *Estudios Valentinianos* (Analecta Gregoriana, 65, 99, 100, 113, and 158; 1955–66); and C. Markschies, *Valentinus Gnosticus? Untersuchungen zur valentinianischen Gnosis* (Wissenschaftliche Untersuchungen zum Neuen Testaments, 65; Tübingen [1992]). Other important studies incl. C. Barth, *Die Interpretation des Neuen Testaments in der valentinianischen Gnosis* (TU 37, Heft 3; 1911); W. Foerster, *Von Valentin zu Herakleon: Untersuchungen über die Quellen und die Entwicklung der valentinianischen Gnosis* (Beihefte zu *ZNTW*, 7; 1928); G. Quispel, 'The Original Doctrine of Valentine', *VC* 1 (1947), pp. 43–73; G. C. Stead, 'The Valentinian Myth of Sophia', *JTS* NS 20 (1969), pp. 75–104; and B. Layton (ed.), *The Recovery of Gnosticism: Proceedings of the International Conference on Gnosticism at Yale, New Haven, Connecticut, March 28–31, 1978*, 1: *The School of Valentinus* (Numen, 41; Leiden, 1980). Convenient summary in K. Rudolph, *Die Gnosis* (Leipzig, 1977), pp. 339–47; Eng. tr. (1983), pp. 317–25. R. A. Lipsius in *DCB* 4 (1887), pp. 1076–99, s.v. 'Valentinus (1)'; G. Bardy in *DTC* 15 (pt. 2; 1950), cols. 2497–519, s.v. 'Valentin'. See also works cited under GNOSTICISM.

Valerian, St (d. after 450), Bp. of Cemele (now Cimiez, nr. Nice) in S. Gaul. He may have been a monk of *Lérins before he became bishop, and he is perhaps to be identified with the Valerian to whom *Eucherius addressed his 'De contemptu mundi'. The only facts known of his life are that he was present at the Councils of Riez (439) and *Vaison (442), and upheld the ancient jurisdictional claims of the see of *Arles against Pope *Leo the Great. He was the author of 20 homilies which, apart from one already known ('De bono disciplinae'), were discovered by J. *Sirmond in a *Corbie MS early in the 17th cent. Their subjects are mainly moral and ascetic. Written in a highly rhetorical but effective style, they are valuable for the light they throw on the history of their age. Valerian was also the author of an 'Epistola ad Monachos de Virtutibus et Ordine Doctrinae Apostolicae'. Theologically he seems to have inclined to *Semipelagianism. Feast day, 23 July.

'Homiliae' and 'Epistola', first ed. J. Sirmond, SJ, Paris, 1612; repr. in J. P. Migne, *PL* 52. 691–758. J.-P. Weiss, 'La Personalité de Valérien de Cimiez', *Annales de la Faculté des Lettres et Sciences Humaines de Nice*, 11 (1970), pp. 141–62. R. W. Mathisen, 'Petronius, Hilarius and Valerianus: Prosopographical Notes on the Conversion of the Roman Aristocracy', *Historia*, 30 (Wiesbaden, 1981), pp. 106–12, esp. pp. 110–12. C. Tibiletti, 'Valeriano di Cimiez e la teologia dei Maestri Provenzali', *Augustinianum*, 22 (1982), pp. 513–32. A. Hamman in Quasten (cont.), *Patrology*, 4 (1986), pp. 543 f. G. Bardy in *DTC* 15 (pt. 2; 1950), cols. 2520–2, s.v.

Valesius, Henricus (1603–76), French historian. Henri de Valois was a native of Paris who, after being educated by the *Jesuits at Verdun and Paris, spent nearly all his life in the capital. In 1630 he abandoned a career in law to devote himself exclusively to learning. In his earlier years he issued editions of many classical authors, including Ammianus Marcellinus (1636). In 1650 he began an intensive study of the early ecclesiastical historians, which bore fruit in his celebrated editions of the Church histories of *Eusebius (1659), *Socrates and *Sozomen (1668), and *Theodoret and *Evagrius (1673).

His edns. of Eusebius, Socrates, Sozomen, Theodoret, and Evagrius were reissued at Amsterdam, 3 vols., 1695–1700, and are repr. in J. P. Migne, *PG* (see under separate authors); rev. by W. Reading (3 vols., Cambridge, 1720). His minor works ed. P. Burmann, *Henrici Valesii … Emendationum Libri Quinque et de Critica Libri Duo* (Amsterdam, 1740). Life by his brother, A. Valesius, was appended to a Lat. tr. of his edn. of Eusebius, Socrates, etc., pub. Paris, 1677, pp. i–viii; repr. in G. Bates, *Vitae Selectorum Aliquot Virorum* (London, 1681), pp. 719–33; by P. Burmann, op. cit. (no pagination); and by W. Reading, op. cit. 3, pp. 615–22. E. *Schwartz (ed.), *Eusebius Werke*, Band 2, Teil 3 (GCS; 1909), pp. xliii–xlv. H. Hurter, SJ, *Nomenclator Literarius Theologiae Catholicae*, 4 (Innsbruck, 1910), cols. 173–7. P. Lejay in *CE* 15 (1912), pp. 263 f., s.v. 'Valois, Henri'; É. Amann in *DTC* 15 (pt. 2; 1950), cols. 2526 f., s.v. 'Valois, Henri de'.

validation of marriage. A marriage null by reason of defective consent or some *diriment impediment can be validated in canon law (1) by simple renewal of consent or (2) by *dispensation. Simple renewal of consent is sufficient when the marriage is null because of defective consent or when the impediment has ceased to exist. If the impediment is a public one, i.e. if it can be proved in the external *forum, then, the renewal must be public; if secret, it may be private. But if the marriage is null because of a persisting removable diriment impediment, the marriage may be validated by a simple dispensation followed by renewal of consent. In certain cases, esp. where a renewal of consent is difficult to obtain, a marriage can be validated by a *sanatio in radice* (q.v.). The validation of marriage is treated in *CIC* (1983), cans. 1156–65.

validity. A term used in W. *Sacramental theology denoting the fact that a Sacrament is genuine if certain formal conditions have been fulfilled. It is distinguished from fruitfulness (or efficacy) and regularity. Thus a Sacrament, even if celebrated irregularly (e.g. outside the unity of the Church), and even if unfruitful in that the participants will not receive *grace through the Sacrament, may still be a real Sacrament, conferring membership of the Church (in the case of *Baptism), Holy *Orders (in the case of Ordination), or the Real Presence of Christ in the Eucharist. The formal conditions are that the minister of the Sacrament be himself validly ordained (if necessary), that the essential part of the Church's liturgy be used (see FORM), and that there be a proper *intention (q.v.) on the part of the minister (i.e. to do what the Church intends in celebrating the Sacrament). The concept of validity was developed in the W. in connection with the problem of the Church's attitude to Sacraments conferred in heresy or schism. It is first found in the Roman insistence in controversy with St *Cyprian, Bp. of Carthage, that Baptism is validly conferred by heretics and therefore may not be repeated; it achieved its classic formulation by St *Augustine in his controversy with *Donatism. Augustine developed the concept of validity as a way of opposing the Donatist notion that the Sacraments were the possession of the perfect Church, insisting against them that the true minister of the Sacrament is Christ and thus the unworthiness of the minister (or the Church) does not affect the validity of the Sacrament. By thus enabling him to recognize Donatist Baptism and Ordination, it made easier the reconciling of repentant Donatists. At the Reformation most Protestants abandoned the concept of validity, regarding Sacraments as established by a true preaching of pure doctrine; it is affirmed in the *Thirty-Nine Articles of the C of E (art. 26). More recently the notion has been criticized (e.g. by C. H. *Turner and A. M. *Ramsey) as driving a wedge between the doctrine of the Church and the doctrine of the ministry, or as being a merely legalistic concept inadequate to deal with the problems of a divided Church.

The concept is discussed in most works on Sacramental theology, e.g. B. Leeming, SJ, *Principles of Sacramental Theology* (1956; 2nd edn., 1960), pp. 215–73. *Doctrine in the Church of England* (1938), pp. 130–6. C. H. Turner, 'Apostolic Succession', in H. B. *Swete (ed.), *Essays on the Early History of the Church and the Ministry* (1918), pp. 93–214; A. M. Ramsey, *The Gospel and the Catholic Church* (1936; 2nd edn., 1956), pp. 152–4, 218 f., and 223; K. E. *Kirk, 'The Apostolic Ministry', pt. 5: 'The Meaning of Validity', in id. (ed.), *The Apostolic Ministry* (1946), pp. 33–46. G. G. Willis, *Saint Augustine and the Donatist Controversy* (1950), pp. 144–68 and 176–86. J. A. Gurrieri, 'Sacramental Validity: The Origins and Use of a Vocabulary', *The Jurist*, 41 (1981), pp. 21–58; id., 'Sacraments Shaping Faith: The Problem of Sacramental Validity Today', in G. Austin (ed.), *Fountain of Life: In Memory of Niels K. Rasmussen, O.P.* (Washington, DC [1991]), pp. 165–81. See also works cited under ANGLICAN ORDINATIONS.

Valla, Lorenzo (*c.*1406–57), Italian humanist. He became an excellent classical scholar, through studies in Rome. In 1431 he accepted a chair of eloquence at Pavia, but had to leave the city in 1433 owing to quarrels with the jurists of the university. In 1435 he obtained a position in Naples at the court of Alfonso of Aragon, who was his protector for the next ten years. The King's controversy with the Pope over the legitimacy of his kingdom perhaps lay behind Valla's famous attack on the authenticity of the '*Donation of Constantine'. In 1447 Valla went to Rome, where he became 'scriptor' and later Apostolic Secretary, and in 1450 professor of eloquence at the university.

Valla's earliest work of importance, *De Voluptate*, is a dialogue between representatives of the *Stoic, *Epicurean, and Christian views, in which he defends the pleasures of the senses as the greatest good, though not perfectly attainable in this life. The first version was written in 1431; like many of his works, it was revised later. His *Dialecticae Disputationes contra Aristoteles* (the first version dates from 1439) ridicules the dialectic method of *Scholasticism. The work by which he has long been best known is *De Falso Credita et Ementita Constantini Donatione Declamatio* (1440) in which, using methods of modern historical criticism, he demonstrated the spuriousness of the 'Donation of Constantine'; it contained a bitter attack on the temporal power of the Papacy and led to his being summoned for trial before a tribunal of the *Inquisition in 1444. He was saved from imprisonment by Alfonso. His *De Elegantiis Linguae Latinae* (the first version dates from 1441) long remained a standard work on humanist Latin. He also undertook a critical comparison between the *Vulgate and the Greek NT in *Collatio Novi Testamenti* (first version completed in 1442). In his *De Libero Arbitrio* (completed by 1444), he denies the possibility of understanding the harmony of God's omnipotence with human free will. His other works include *De Professione Religiosorum*, a sustained attack on the ideals of the religious life (not printed until 1869), an account of the reign of Ferdinand of Aragon (written in 1446), and a defence of his historical writings, *Antidotum in Facium* (1447). His audacious views had a deep influence on Renaissance scholars. His work on the text of the NT was valued by *Erasmus (who published his *Collatio* in 1505), and his writings were held in high esteem by the Reformers, esp. M. *Luther.

Works, pub. Basle, 1540; anastatic repr., 2 vols., Turin, 1962. Modern edns. of his *De Constantini Donatione*, with Eng. tr. by C. B. Coleman (New Haven, Conn., 1922), by W. Schwahn (Teub., 1928) and W. Setz (*MGH*, Quellen zur Geistesgeschichte des Mittelalters, 10; 1976); of *De Libero Arbitrio* by M. Anfossi (Opuscoli Filosofici: Testi e Documenti Inediti o Rari Pubblicati da Giovanni Gentile, 6; Florence, 1934); and of *De Voluptate*, with later corrections, as *De Vero Falsoque Bono*, by M. de Panizza Lorch (Bari, 1970 [with notes in Eng.]); previously unpub. recension of *Collatio Novi Testamenti* ed. A. Perosa (Istituto Nazionale di Studi sul Rinascimento, Studi e Testi, 1; Florence, 1970), and *Defensio Questionum in Philosophia* (hitherto unpub.) ed. G. Zippel, 'L'Autodifesa di Lorenzo Valla per il processo dell'inquisizione napoletana (1444)', *Italia Medioevale e Umanistica*, 13 (1970), pp. 59–94. More recent edns. of *Antidotum Primum: La Prima Apologia contro Poggio Bracciolini*, ed. A. Wesseling (Respublica Literaria Neederlandica, 4; Assen and Amsterdam, 1978); *Antidotum in Facium*, ed. M. Regoliosi (Thesaurus Mundi, 20; Padua, 1981); *Repastinatio Dialectice et Philosophie*, ed. G. Zippel (ibid. 21 and 22; 1982); *Gesta Ferdinandi Regis Aragonum*, ed. O. Besomi (ibid. [no vol. no.]; 1983); and *Epistole*, ed. O. Besomi and M. Regoliosi (ibid. 24; 1984).

G. Mancini, *Vita di Lorenzo Valla* (Florence, 1891). L. Barozzi and R. Sabbadini, *Studi sul Panormita e sul Valla* (Pubblicazioni del R. Istituto di Studi Superiori Practici di Perfezionamento in Firenze, Sezione di Filosofia e Filologia, 25; 1891). J. Vahlen, 'Laurentii Vallae Opuscula Tria', *Sb.* (Wien), 61 (1869), pp. 7–66, 357–444, and 62 (1869), pp. 93–149; also pub. separately, ibid., 1869. G. Antonazzi, 'Lorenzo Valla e la Donazione di Costantino nel secolo XV con un testo inedito di Antonio Cortesi', *Rivista di Storia della Chiesa in Italia*, 4 (1950), pp. 186–234. F. Gaeta, *Lorenzo Valla: Filologia e storia nell'umanesimo italiano* (Istituto Italiano per gli Studi Storici in Napoli, 8; 1955). Giovanni di Napoli, *Lorenzo Valla: Filosofia e religione nell'umanesimo Italiano* (Uomini e Dottrine, 17; 1971). S. I. Camporeale, *Lorenzo Valla: Umanesimo e Teologia* (Florence, 1972). W. Setz, *Lorenzo Vallas Schrift gegen Konstantinische Schenkung De falso credita et ementita Constantini donatione: Zur Interpretation und Wirkungsgeschichte* (Bibliothek des deutschen historischen Instituts in Rom, 44; 1975). *Lorenzo Valla e l'Umanesimo Italiano: Atti del Convegno Internazionale di Studi Umanistici (Parma, 18–19 ottobre 1984)*, ed. O. Besomi and M. Regoliosi (Medioevo e Umanesimo, 59; 1986). G. Radetti, 'La religione di Lorenzo Valla', in *Medioevo e Rinascimento: Studi in onore di Bruno Nardi*, 2 (Florence [1955]), pp. 595–620. G. Zippel, 'Lorenzo Valla e le origini della storiografia umanistica a Venezia', *Rinascimento*, 7 (1956), pp. 93–133. C. Trinkaus, *In Our Image and Likeness* (2 vols., 1970), pp. 103–78 and 765 f. M. Lorsch, 'Lorenzo Valla', in A. Rabil (ed.), *Renaissance Humanism*, 1 (Philadelphia, 1988), pp. 332–49. R. Montano in *NCE* 14 (1967), pp. 522 f., s.v.

Vallarsi, Domenico (1702–71), editor of St *Jerome's writings. He was a native of *Verona, where he spent most of his life. His edition of Jerome (11 vols., 1734–42), was considerably superior to that of the *Maurists (Paris, 1693–1706) and long remained the standard text.

His edn. of the works of Jerome was repr., in J. P. Migne, *PL* 22–30; the edn. of the works of St *Hilary, in which Vallarsi assisted F. S. *Maffei (Verona, 1730), was repr., ibid. 9, 10; the first vol. of his edn. of the works of *Rufinus (Verona, 1745; vol. 2 not pub.) was repr., ibid. 21. 45–632. L. Federici, *Elogi istorici de' più illustri ecclesiastici veronesi*, 3 (Verona, 1819), pp. 134–48. É. Amann in *DTC* 15 (pt. 2; 1950), col. 2525, s.v.

Valley of Jehoshaphat, the. See JEHOSHAPHAT, THE VALLEY OF.

Vallumbrosans. A monastic *Congregation, formerly a separate order, so named from the mother-house at Vallombrosa, some 20 miles E. of Florence. The order was founded *c.*1036 by St *John Gualbert and confirmed by Pope Victor II in 1056. After the death of the founder, the order spread rapidly. In the 15th cent. a reform of the order through *Cassinese Benedictines was instigated by *Eugenius IV, and another was effected in the 17th cent. by Bl John Leonardi. The mother-house at Vallombrosa was burnt by the soldiers of *Charles V in 1527, plundered by Napoleon's troops in 1808 and suppressed by the Italian government in 1866, but restored in 1949. The order has declined, but it still has a few houses in Italy. The Vallumbrosans joined the *Benedictine Confederation in 1966. The Vallumbrosan way of life is based on the Rule of St *Benedict, but with greater stress on austerity and penance. The order has been noted for its contribution to ascetical literature, art, and science, and for a time counted *Galileo among its novices.

There are also a few houses of Vallumbrosan nuns, at Florence and elsewhere in Italy. They trace their origin to St Bertha Bardi (d. 1163), but the real foundress was St Humilitas (d. 1310).

F. Tarani, *L'ordine vallombrosano* (Florence, 1921). E. Lucchesi, OSB, *I Monaci Benedettini Vallombrosani nella diocesi di Pistoia e Prato* (ibid., [1941]), and other works of this author. [R.] N. Vasaturo, OSBV, 'L'espansione della Congregazione Vallombrosana fino alla metà del secolo XII', *Rivista di Storia della Chiesa in Italia*, 16 (1962), pp. 456–85; J. R. Gaborit, 'Les Plus Anciens Monastères de l'Ordre de Vallombreuse (1037–1115). Étude archéologique', *Mélanges d'Archéologie et d'Histoire*, 86 (1964), pp. 451–90; 87 (1965), pp. 179–208. R. N. Vasaturo and others, *Vallombrosa nel IX Centenario della Morte del Fondatore Giovanni Gualberto 12 Iulio 1073* (Florence [1973]). T. Sala, *Dizionario storico biografico di scrittori, letterati ed artisti dell'ordine di Vallombrosa* (ibid., 1929). R. Webster, OSB, in *CE* 15 (1912), pp. 262 f.; E. Baccetti in *NCE* 14 (1967), p. 526, both s.v. See also works cited under JOHN GUALBERT, ST.

Valois, Henri de. See VALESIUS, HENRICUS.

Valor Ecclesiasticus. The official valuation of ecclesiastical and monastic revenues made in 1535. It became necessary through the legislation of *Henry VIII, and esp. the First Fruits and Tenths Act 1534, whereby the *annates of every benefice, which had formerly been paid to the Pope, together with a tenth of the annual income, were appropriated to the Crown. Its importance to the ecclesiastical historian, with its details of every benefice, may be compared with that of the Domesday Survey of 1086 to the student of secular history. It became popularly known as the 'King's Books'.

It was ed. by J. Caley for the Record Commission (6 vols., 1810–34), with general introd. by J. Hunter in vol. 1, pp. i–viii. A. Savine, 'English Monasteries on the Eve of the Dissolution', in P. Vinogradoff (ed.), *Oxford Studies in Social and Legal History*, 1 (1909), pp. 1–217, esp. bk. 1, pp. 1–75. [M.] D. *Knowles, *The Religious Orders in England*, 3 (Cambridge, 1959), pp. 241–54. S. L. Ollard in *DECH* (1912), p. 609, s.v. See also works cited under DISSOLUTION OF THE MONASTERIES.

van den Steen, Cornelis Cornelissen. See CORNELIUS A LAPIDE.

van der Kemp, Johannes Theodorus (1747–1811), missionary. A native of Rotterdam, he resigned from the Dutch army on making an unsuitable marriage; he then studied medicine in Edinburgh and there in 1781 published *Parmenides*, a work on philosophy. He underwent a spiritual conversion after his wife and daughter drowned in his presence in 1791. Soon after the formation of the *LMS (1795), van der Kemp took a leading part in the foundation of a similar body, the Netherlands Missionary Society, at Rotterdam in 1797. He was ordained as a minister in the Church of Scotland and went as leader of the three missionaries sent by the LMS to *South Africa in 1799. Though conditions prevented sustained work among the Xhoso people, his preaching was prob. heard by Ntsikana (*c.*1760–1820), the visionary Xhosa prophet and spiritual fount of all later Xhosa Christianity. Van der Kemp finally settled among the Khoi (Hottentots, later known as 'Cape Coloured') whose cause he championed. His mission settlement for them at Bethelsdorp, near Vitenhage, came under much White criticism and was the subject of a government inquiry in 1811. He lived in conditions of extreme poverty but his marriage late in life to a former slave was bitterly criticized. He was the first of the great African missionary linguists of the 19th cent.

I. H. Enklaar, *Life and Work of Dr. J. Th. van der Kemp 1747–1811, Missionary Pioneer and Protagonist of Racial Equality in South Africa* (Cape Town and Rotterdam, 1988). J. Sales, *Mission Stations and the Coloured Communities of the Eastern Cape 1800–1852* (ibid., 1975), *passim*. P. B. Hinchliff in W. J. Kock and D. W. Krüger (eds.), *Dictionary of South African Biography*, 2 (Cape Town, 1972), pp. 774–8, s.v.

Van Espen, Zeger Bernhard (1646–1728), Belgian canonist.

A native of Louvain, he was ordained priest in 1673 and became professor of canon law at Louvain university in 1675. His comprehensive knowledge soon made him a much-consulted adviser of princes and bishops, and his works, the most important of which is *Jus Ecclesiasticum Universum* (2 vols., 1700), are remarkable for their learning and lucidity. Van Espen vigorously defended *Gallican theories and was an ardent upholder of secular power against religious authority. In the question of the 'Chapter of Utrecht' he gave his opinion in favour of the validity of the ordination of a *Jansenist bishop, an act which led to his suspension *a divinis* and deprivation of his academic functions in 1728. Summoned by the Abp. of Utrecht to retract, he fled to the Jansenist colony at Amersfoort, where he died soon afterwards. All his works were placed on the *Index in 1704, and again in 1714 and 1732.

Best collected edn. of works [by J. Barre] (4 vols., 'Louvain' [Paris], 1753); [id.,] *Supplementum ad Varias Collectiones Operum clar. viri Z. B. van Espen* (Brussels, 1758). Anon. Life by G. du Parc de Bellegarde (Louvain, 1767; also appended to suppl. vol. of works [separate pagination]). M. Nuttinck, *La Vie et l'œuvre de Zeger-Bernard Van Espen* (Université de Louvain. Recueil de travaux d'histoire et de philosophie, 4th ser. 43; 1969), with bibl. E. [W.] Kemp, 'Zeger Bernhard Van Espen', *Theology*, 49 (1946), pp. 194–200 and 227–32, with further refs. A. Depreester in *DDC* 5 (1953), cols. 457–61, s.v. 'Espen'.

van Eyck, Hubert (d. 1426) and Jan (d. 1441),

Flemish painters, renowned esp. for the Ghent Altarpiece. They were prob. natives of Maasiek, a small town on the R. Meuse downstream from Maastricht. Hubert is thought to have been the elder brother and is prob. the painter in Ghent referred to in five documents between 1424 and 1426 and buried in the cathedral at Ghent; nevertheless his connection with the Altarpiece has sometimes been denied. Jan is well documented from 1422 until his death: he was in the service of John of Bavaria (1422–4), became court painter to Philip, Duke of Burgundy in 1425, and prob. in 1430 settled in Bruges. Several signed paintings are extant. The Ghent Altarpiece, still in the cathedral of St *Bavon in Ghent, has a quatrain on the frame which asserts that it was begun by Hubert and finished by Jan, *arte secundus*, in May 1432. It is a very large polyptych of 12 oak panels arranged in two layers, the outer panels painted on both sides, making 24 scenes in all. The panels on the lower tier of the inside depict the Adoration of the Lamb by all conditions of men, largely derived from Rev.; other panels show Christ enthroned between St *John the Baptist and the BVM, the *Annunciation, *Adam and *Eve, and other figures. The iconography is extremely complicated; the ideas expressed have been linked with

*Rupert of Deutz. Since at least the 16th cent. the van Eycks have been believed to be the inventors of oil painting; this is clearly untrue since pigments mixed with oil were in use before their time, but nevertheless they (or Jan, since no work is known as certainly Hubert's) made technical advances which permitted unprecedented realism of detail and richness of colour. All Jan's known works are in this style, and the religious ones are similar to the Ghent Altarpiece, but there are a few pictures, notably the *Three Maries at the Tomb* (Boymans-van Beuningen Museum, Rotterdam) and the *Annunciation* (Metropolitan Museum, New York), which appear more archaic in style and have been attributed to Hubert. Jan's unblinking realism is esp. notable in portraits, such as the *Arnolfini Wedding* (1434; National Gallery, London) and his influence as a religious artist was therefore less widespread than that of Roger van der Weyden (c.1400–64), whose emotional style was attuned to the spirit of pathos notable in Flemish and German devotional practices in the 15th cent.

The first scholarly investigation of the problems surrounding the work of the two brothers was W. H. J. Weale, *Hubert and John van Eyck* (1908; 2nd edn., abridged, with the co-operation of M. W. Brockwell, *The van Eycks and their Art*, 1912). L. Baldass, *Jan van Eyck* (London, 1952); E. Dhanens, *Hubert and Jan van Eyck* (New York [1980]), both with numerous illustrations. The case against the existence of Hubert was argued by E. Renders, *Hubert van Eyck: Personnage de légende* (1933), and in other works of this author, but is not widely accepted. The results of a laboratory examination of the Ghent Altarpiece were pub. by P. Coremans, *L'Agneau Mystique au Laboratoire* (Les Primitifs Flamands, Série 3, tome 2; Antwerp, 1953). E. Dhanens, *Van Eyck: The Ghent Altarpiece* (1973). C. J. Purtle, *The Marian Paintings of Jan van Eyck* (Princeton, NJ [1982]). C. Harbison, *Jan van Eyck: The Play of Realism* (1991). E. Panofsky, *Early Netherlandish Painting* (Charles Eliot Norton Lectures, 1947–8; Cambridge, Mass., 1953), 1, pp. 178–246, with notes, pp. 427–57, and illustrations, 2, plates 109–68.

van Manen, Willem Christiaan (1842–1905), Dutch biblical critic.

After studying at Utrecht and holding pastorates in the Dutch Reformed Church, he was professor of Old Christian literature and NT exegesis at *Leiden from 1885 till his death. He was also co-editor of the *Theologisch Tijdschrift*. The opinions of van Manen, who was among the most radical biblical critics of the 19th cent., attracted attention more as curiosities than for their intrinsic importance. He maintained, e.g., that all the NT writings belong to the Sub-Apostolic period. His methods are most fully exhibited in his *Paulus* (3 vols., 1890–6), in which he rejected the authenticity of St *Paul's Epistles, arguing that they were the creation of a group of theologians who sought to transform primitive Christianity, which was originally a movement in Judaism, into a universal religion, with a system closely akin to *Gnosticism. He admitted that there was a historic St Paul, totally unlike the author of the Epp., but why he was taken by this school as its patron must, van Manen held, remain an insoluble mystery. Van Manen's views became widely known in Great Britain through his contributions to the *Encyclopaedia Biblica* (ed. T. K. *Cheyne and J. S. Black, 1899–1903).

T. Whittaker, *The Origins of Christianity with an Outline of van Manen's Analysis of the Pauline Literature* (1904; 3rd edn., 1914, with additional prologue, pp. xi–xxxii; 4th edn., rev., 1933).

A. Meyer in *RGG* (2nd edn.), 3 (1929), cols. 1958 f., s.v. 'Manen, W. C. van'.

Van Mildert, William (1765–1836), Bp. of *Durham. Of Dutch descent, he was appointed Regius professor of divinity at Oxford in 1813, made Bp. of *Llandaff in 1819, Dean of *St Paul's (in plurality) in 1820, and Bp. of Durham in 1826. He was the last Bp. of Durham with palatine rank, and was one of the founders of the university of Durham (1832). His chief works were *An Historical View of the Rise and Progress of Infidelity* (*Boyle Lectures, 2 vols., 1806) and an elaborate edition of the *Works* of D. *Waterland (10 vols., 1823–8), prefaced by a Life.

A Collection of his *Sermons on Several Occasions and Charges* (Oxford, 1838), with Memoir by C. Ives, pp. 3–158. E. A. Varley, *The Last of the Prince Bishops* (Cambridge, 1992). W. P. Courtney in *DNB* 58 (1899), pp. 1333 f.

Vane, Henry (1613–62), English politician. To distinguish him from his father, Henry Vane (1589–1655), he is commonly known as 'the Younger'. He was educated at Westminster and at Magdalen College, Oxford, and for a time travelled abroad, esp. in France and Switzerland, where he found encouragement for his already latent antiepiscopal and anti-monarchical views. On returning to England he decided to emigrate to America, where he became Governor of Massachusetts (1636). Before long he came back again and was appointed co-treasurer of the Navy, elected MP for Hull and made a knight (1640). In the Long Parliament he was a vigorous and bitter opponent of W. *Laud and Strafford, and one of the commissioners chiefly responsible for the *Solemn League and Covenant. He strongly disliked, however, the Presbyterian system of state-enforced discipline. He became a member of the Council of State in 1649 and its president in 1652, but latterly lost influence, owing to his opposition to O. *Cromwell's dictatorial methods. At the Restoration he was arrested, imprisoned, tried, and executed on Tower Hill, 14 July 1662.

[G. Sikes], *The Life and Death of Sir Henry Vane* (1662). Modern Life by V. A. Rowe (London, 1970). R. Spalding, *Contemporaries of Bulstrode Whitelocke 1605–1675* (Records of Social and Economic History, NS 14; Oxford, 1990), pp. 390 f. C. H. Firth in *DNB* 58 (1899), pp. 116–29.

Vangeon, Henri Léon. See GHÉON, HENRI.

Vásquez, Gabriel. See VÁZQUEZ, GABRIEL.

Västerås, Ordinance of. The regulations passed by the Diet of Västerås, which Gustavus Vasa assembled on 24 June 1527 to carry through the Protestant Reformation in *Sweden. Their effect was to transfer to the Crown the enormous power hitherto possessed by the Swedish episcopate, to alienate its property, and to make the Church completely subservient to the King.

Text in *Svenska Riksdagsakter jämte andra handlingar som höra till statsförfattningens historia under tidehvarfvet 1521–1718*, 1, ed. E. Hildebrand and O. Alin (1887), pp. 89–95; Eng. tr. in Kidd, pp. 234–6 (no. 101). See also works on the Reformation in Sweden, cited under SWEDEN, CHRISTIANITY IN.

Vatican. The modern Papal residence in Rome on the ancient 'Mons Vaticanus', once adorned with the Circus

of Nero. A Papal domicile is said to have been erected near the court of the old basilica of St Peter's by Pope *Symmachus (498–514). An earlier residence on the site was rebuilt by *Innocent III (c.1200) and extended by Nicholas III (1277–80). During the *Avignonese captivity (1308–77) it fell into disrepair; but as the *Lateran palace had also been seriously damaged by fire in 1309, the Vatican became the principal Papal residence after the return in 1377. The first *conclave was held here in the following year. Little of the existing building is earlier than the 15th cent. In 1410 *John XXIII restored the covered passage to the Castle of S. Angelo and in 1447 *Nicholas V began an extensive plan of building which included administrative offices and residences for the cardinals. This programme was actively carried into effect by Nicholas's successors. *Sixtus IV erected the *Sistine Chapel (1473–81), Innocent VIII the Belvedere (c.1490), *Julius II and *Leo X Bramante's *cortile* and the *stanze* of *Raphael, and *Paul III the *Sala Regia*. (For the building of the basilica, see ST PETER'S.) The present palace was completed by *Clement VIII (d. 1605), the Braccio Nuovo (designed by Raffael Stern) by *Pius VII in 1821. By the Law of *Guarantees (13 May 1871) the Vatican, the Lateran, and the Papal villa at *Castel Gandolfo were granted extraterritoriality, and additional privileges were conceded by the *Lateran Treaty of 1929. The Vatican Museum houses valuable collections of early Christian art and other antiquities, including much that was formerly in the Lateran Museum; a collection of modern religious art was opened by *Paul VI in 1973. The celebrated Library ('Bibliotheca Apostolica Vaticana') is administered by a Cardinal Prefect. Among its more famous collections of MSS are the *Palatini* (presented by the Elector Maximilian on the capture of Heidelberg; 1623), the *Reginenses* (formerly the property of Queen *Christina of Sweden; 1690), and the *Ottoboniani* (purchased by *Alexander VIII, Ottoboni; incorporated, 1746). See also CODEX VATICANUS.

Much information is to be found in the many good guides to the Vatican palace, intended in the first place for tourists. There are also countless monographs on the various collections. Modern general works incl. F. Ehrle, SJ, and H. Egger, *Der vaticanische Palast in seiner Entwicklung bis zur Mitte des XV. Jahrhunderts* (Studi e Documenti per la Storia del Palazzo Apostolico Vaticano, 2; 1935); K. B. Steinke, *Die mittelalterlichen Vatikanpaläste und ihre Kapellen: Baugeschichtliche Untersuchung anhand der schriftlichen Quellen* (ibid. 5; 1984); G. Fallani and M. Escobar (eds.), *Vaticano* (Florence [1946]); D. Redig de Campos, *I palazzi vaticani* (Roma Cristiana, 18 [1967]); and J. Daley and others, *The Vatican: Spirit and Art of Christian Rome* (New York [1982]). C. Pietrangeli, *I musei vaticani: Cinque secoli di storia* (Rome [1985]). The catalogues of Gk. MS collections are listed in M. Richard, *Répertoire des bibliothèques et des catalogues des manuscrits grecs* (Publications de l'Institut de Recherche et d'Histoire des Textes, 1; 2nd edn., 1958), pp. 198–202; the Lat. ones by P. O. Kristeller, *Latin Manuscript Books before 1600: A List of the Printed Catalogues and Unpublished Inventories of Extant Collections* (3rd edn., New York [1965]), pp. 209–14 and 279 f. J. Bignami Odier, *La Bibliothèque Vaticane de Sixte IV à Pie XI* (ST 272; 1973). There are also numerous studies on Vatican MSS in other vols. of ST. L. E. Boyle, OP, 'The Future of Old Libraries. The Vatican Library', *Ligue des Bibliothèques Européennes de Recherche, Bulletin*, 29 (1987), pp. 42–5. *Biblioteca Apostolica Vaticana*, ed. under the patronage of A. M. Stickler and L. E. Boyle, OP (Florence, 1985; Eng. tr., *The Vatican Library*, Yorktown Heights, NY, 1989 [popular]). P. M. Baumgarten in *CE* 15 (1912), pp. 276–302, s.v.;

G. Caraci and others in *EC* 12 (1954), cols. 1040–140, s.v. 'Vaticano'. See also bibls. to ST PETER'S, ROME; SISTINE CHAPEL.

Vatican Council, First. The Council held at Rome in 1869–70 and reckoned in the RC Church as the Twentieth *Oecumenical Council. Convoked by *Pius IX by a bull of Indiction dated 29 June 1868, it was planned to deal with a vast variety of subjects including faith and dogma, ecclesiastical discipline and canon law, religious orders, oriental Churches and foreign missions, and the relations between the Church and the civil powers. Even before the Council began, two bodies of opinion stood out clearly. The majority party, usually designated the '*Ultramontanes', were in favour of the heightening of Papal authority and of the definition of Papal infallibility. They included such distinguished laymen as W. G. *Ward in England and L. *Veuillot in France, and, among members of the Council, Abps. H. E. *Manning of Westminster and V. A. Dechamps of Malines, and Bps. L. Pie of Poitiers and I. von Senestrey of Ratisbon. The liberal minority was represented by J. H. *Newman in England and J. J. I. von *Döllinger in Bavaria, and, among the members of the Council, by F. *Dupanloup, Bp. of Orléans, and most German and many Austrian and American bishops. Of the governments none except the Russian, which forbade the Catholic bishops to attend, interfered with the Council; the French attitude, one of benevolent neutrality, was largely influenced by E. Ollivier (1825–1913), the French premier, who later embodied his views in *L'Église et l'État au concile du Vatican* (2 vols., 1879).

After elaborate preparations the Council began with a pre-synodal congregation on 2 Dec. 1869 at which Pius IX nominated the presidents. It was followed by the issue of the brief 'Multiplices inter' which established the procedure, acc. to which the Pope had the right of proposing questions (*ius proponendi*), though bishops might suggest subjects for discussion to congregations set up for this purpose. Four Deputations—on dogma, on ecclesiastical discipline, on religious orders, and on the oriental Churches—were appointed.

The business of the Council was opened by Pius IX on 8 Dec. 1869 in the presence of nearly 700 bishops. It began with a discussion on the schema 'De Fide' which had been drawn up against rationalism, naturalism, materialism, pantheism, and kindred errors. While this schema, which was criticized as too cumbrous, was being revised by the Deputation on dogma, the Council discussed matters of ecclesiastical discipline with special reference to canon law and repeatedly listened to the desire for a reform of the *Breviary.

In Feb. 1870 the procedure, which had proved very slow, was hastened by new regulations. Long debates were prevented by the application of closure and the quicker method of voting by standing up was adopted. Both measures were later much criticized by the minority. The revised constitution on Faith, 'Dei Filius', was laid before the Council on 1 Mar., and after detailed discussion was promulgated in its final form on 24 Apr. It consists of a proemium deploring the pantheism, materialism, and atheism of the time, followed by four chapters on God the Creator of all things, on Revelation, on Faith, and on Faith and Reason. The respective spheres of reason and faith were defined, esp. with a view to excluding *Traditionalism and other doctrines anathematized in the appended canons.

The public announcement that the question of Papal infallibility was to be discussed at the Council had been made on 6 Mar. After some controversy it was decided that this subject and the Primacy of the Pope, both of which divided the members of the Council, should be dealt with before the other points of the schema 'De Ecclesia'. From 27 Apr. the Deputation on dogma worked on the schema 'De Romano Pontifice'; and the debate on the 'opportunity' of the definition, which lasted from 13 May to 3 June, was ended by closure. In the debate on the Primacy which followed, the point to which the minority esp. objected was the definition of the Pope's jurisdiction as ordinary, immediate, and truly episcopal. In the debate on infallibility, the minority party desired to see the Pope's infallibility linked more closely with the infallibility of the Church by the use of some such expression as St *Antoninus of Florence's formula that the Pope 'using the counsel and seeking for the help of the universal Church' cannot err. The infallibility debate was closed on 4 July. On 13 July the definition received 451 placets, 88 non-placets, and 62 placets *juxta modum*, and at the Fourth Public Session on 18 July the constitution '*Pastor Aeternus' was passed by 533 placets to 2 non-placets, the remainder of the minority having abstained from voting. The definition as finally accepted disappointed the extremists of both sides. It stated plainly the infallibility of the Roman Pontiff, affirming that his definitions are 'irreformable of themselves, and not from the consent of the Church', but it restricted this infallibility only to those occasions 'when he speaks *ex cathedra*, that is, when in discharge of the office of Pastor and Doctor of all Christians, by virtue of his supreme Apostolic authority he defines a doctrine regarding faith or morals to be held by the Universal Church'.

On 19 July, the day after the promulgation, war broke out between France and Prussia, and the removal of the French troops from Rome and the Italian occupation of the city brought the Council to an end. It was formally suspended on 20 Oct. 1870.

The definitions of the Council, which were accepted by all the minority bishops, roused serious opposition only in Germany and Austria. In these countries some small groups organized themselves as the '*Old Catholics', and in Germany the opposition of Bismarck to the increased consolidation of Papal power issued in the *Kulturkampf*. J. J. I. von Döllinger, who had vigorously opposed the Council throughout, esp. in his articles in the *Augsburger Allgemeine Zeitung* and his book *The Pope and the Council* (1869), also refused to submit and was excommunicated, though he did not join the Old Catholic body. The chief result in Austria was the renouncing of the Concordat by the State.

In the RC Church itself, the result of the definition of the Papal primacy and infallibility was the final settlement of the controversies that began at the Council of *Constance (1415) and had been sustained by *Gallican theologians in later times, while the constitution 'Dei Filius' provided the principles on which Catholicism was soon to make its stand against the infiltration of *Modernism into its own ranks.

Acta et Decreta Sacrosancti Concilii Oecumenici Vaticani cum permultis aliis Documentis ad Concilium eiusque Historiam Spectantibus auctoribus Presbyteris SJ e Domo BVM sine Labe Conceptae ad Lacum (Collectio Lacensis Conciliorum Recentiorum, 7; Freiburg i.B., 1892); Mansi (continuation), 49–53 (Arnhem and Leipzig, 1923–7). Decrees, with Eng. tr., in Tanner, *Decrees* (1990), 2, pp. 800–16. E. Cecconi, *Storia del concilio ecumenico vaticano* (2 vols. in 4 parts, to end of second session, 1872–9; all pub.). J. *Friedrich, *Geschichte des vatikanischen Konzils* (3 vols., 1877–87); T. Granderath, SJ, *Geschichte des vatikanischen Konzils*, ed. K. Kirch, SJ (3 vols., 1903–6). E. Campana, *Il concilio vaticano* (2 vols., Lugano, 1926). [E.] C. Butler, OSB, *The Vatican Council: The Story Told from Inside in Bishop Ullathorne's Letters* (2 vols., 1930). R. Aubert, *Vatican I* (Histoire des Conciles Œcuméniques, 12; 1964). K. Schatz, *Vaticanum I. 1869–1870* (Konziliengeschichte, Reihe A, Darstellung; 3 vols., 1992–4). F. J. Cwiekowski, SS, *The English Bishops and the First Vatican Council* (Bibliothèque de la *Revue d'histoire ecclésiastique*, 52; 1971); M. O'Gara, *Triumph in Defeat: Infallibility, Vatican I, and the French Minority Bishops* (Washington, DC [1988]). T. *Mozley, *Letters from Rome on the Occasion of the Oecumenical Council, 1869–1870* (1891; hostile). H. E. Manning, *The True Story of the Vatican Council* (1877). A. Vacant, *Études théologiques sur les constitutions du concile du Vatican, d'après les actes du concile* (2 vols., 1895). A. B. Hasler, *Pius IX. (1846–1878), Päpstliche Unfehlbarkeit und 1. Vatikanische Konzil* (Päpste und Papsttum, 12; 2 vols., Stuttgart, 1977). G. Thils, *Primauté et infaillibilité du pontife romain à Vatican I et autres études d'ecclésiologie* (Bibliotheca Ephemeridum Theologicarum Lovaniensium, 89; 1989). J. Brugerette and É. Amann in *DTC* 15 (pt. 2; 1950), cols. 2536–85, s.v. 'Vatican (Concile du)'.

Vatican Council, Second (1962–5).

The proposal to hold this Council was apparently entirely due to Pope *John XXIII, who attributed the idea of convening such an assembly to a sudden inspiration of the Holy Spirit. He defined its immediate task as renewing the life of the Church and bringing up to date its teaching, discipline, and organization, with the unity of all Christians as the ultimate goal.

On 25 Jan. 1959 at *St Paul's outside the Walls John first made public his intention to summon a Council. Preparatory commissions and secretariats were set up by the *motu proprio* of 5 June 1960 and the Council was formally summoned by the Apostolic Constitution 'Humanae Salutis' of 25 Dec. 1961. The norms and procedures of the Council were settled by the Apostolic Constitution 'Appropinquante Concilio' of 5 Sept. 1962. The members of the Council were assisted by several thousand experts in theology, canon law, and Church history. There were also present in an official capacity (though without the right to speak or vote) observers from the main Churches not in communion with the RC Church.

SESSION I. 11 Oct.–8 Dec. 1962. Already on the second day of the Council the assembled prelates adjourned to elect their own commission members in place of those on the prepared list, and thus indicated their independence of the Roman *Curia. On 20 Oct. the Council issued a 'Message to Humanity', but when it adjourned in Dec. it had reached no formal decision.

John XXIII died on 3 June 1963 and was succeeded on 21 June by *Paul VI, who announced on his election his intention to continue the Council.

SESSION II. 29 Sept.–4 Dec. 1963. On 30 Oct. votes were taken which showed support for the *collegiality of the bishops, the Divine right of the episcopal college, and the restitution of the diaconate as a separate and permanent order. After the close of the session the Council promulgated a Constitution on the Sacred Liturgy and a decree on the Instruments of Social Communication.

During the recess Paul VI made an ecumenical journey to the Holy Land and met the *Oecumenical Patriarch, *Athenagoras (4–6 Jan. 1964). On 17 May 1964 the Secretariat for Non-Christian Religions was set up.

SESSION III. 14 Sept.–21 Nov. 1964. At the close of this session the Council promulgated the Dogmatic Constitution on the Church, the Decree on Ecumenism, and the Decree on the Eastern Catholic Churches; and the Pope proclaimed the BVM to be the 'Mother of the Church'.

SESSION IV. 14 Sept.–8 Dec. 1965. In an Apostolic Constitution on 15 Sept. ('Apostolica Sollicitudo') the Pope formulated the norms for the new episcopal synod which was to be established to assist him to govern the Church. On 28 Oct. the following documents were promulgated: the Decree on the Bishops' Pastoral Office in the Church, the Decree on the Appropriate Renewal of the Religious Life, the Decree on Priestly Formation, the Declaration on Christian Education, the Declaration on the Relationship of the Church to Non-Christian Religions. To these were added on 18 Nov. the Dogmatic Constitution on Divine Revelation and the Decree on the Apostolate of the Laity. The Pope also announced the beginning of the reform of the Roman Curia and the introduction of the process for the beatification of *Pius XII and John XXIII. On 4 Dec. a 'Service of Prayer (*Sacra Celebratio*) for Promoting Christian Unity' took place at St Paul's outside the Walls. In this the delegated observers and guests took part. On 7 Dec. were promulgated: a Declaration on Religious Freedom, the Decree on the Ministry and Life of Priests, the Decree on the Church's Missionary Activity, and the Pastoral Constitution on the Church in the Modern World. The next day the Council was solemnly closed.

The consequences of the Council have been far-reaching. The most obvious effect has been the almost complete replacement of Latin by the vernacular in the liturgy throughout the 'Latin rite', together with very considerable revision of almost all liturgical texts. The process of translation went with an increased pluralism in liturgy and in many other ways. Added to this were other changes, such as the extension of *Communion in both kinds to the laity, which collectively have brought the public worship of the RC Church fairly closely into line with that of many other W. Churches. Almost equally striking is the change in relationship with most other Churches from frigidity to warmth, including regular consultations with *Orthodox, *Anglican, *Lutheran, *Methodist, and other Churches, and close co-operation in various areas of work. Thirdly, the 'Constitution on the Church in the Modern World', while not in itself very radical, inaugurated a major shift in Church concern, esp. in 'Third World' countries, towards social and political issues (manifest above all in the work of 'Justice and Peace' Commissions). The development of a permanent married diaconate has significantly altered the shape of the RC Church's ministry, esp. in N. America. The Council's central theological debate over collegiality led to the establishment of an advisory episcopal synod meeting in Rome every two or three years, but in practice both collegiality and several other major conciliar themes, such as that of 'the People of God', have made little permanent impact upon the Church as a whole. The division between a 'minimizing' and a 'maximizing' interpretation of the meaning of the Council had become, 25 years later, the central underlying issue within the RC Church, dividing Rome and 'Conservatives' on the one hand from 'progressive theologians' and vocal opinion in many local Churches on the other.

For details of legislation implementing the decision of the Council, see PAUL VI.

Acta Synodalia Sacrosancti Concilii Oecumenici Vaticani Secundi (4 sections in 25 vols. + index, Vatican City, 1970–1980). The *Constitutiones, Decreta, Declarationes* were issued, ibid., 1966. They are also pr. in *AAS* 56 (1964), pp. 97–157; 57 (1965), pp. 5–112; 58 (1966), pp. 673–744, 817–64 and 929–1120. The Acts of the various commissions appointed after the Council are contained in subsequent volumes of *AAS*. Convenient Eng. trs. of the official docs. by W. M. Abbott, SJ, and J. Gallagher, *The Documents of Vatican II* (London and Dublin, 1966), and ed. A. Flannery, OP, *Vatican Council II: The Conciliar and Post Conciliar Documents* (Grand Rapids, Mich., 1975; Dublin, 1981); id. (ed.), *Vatican Council II: More Postconciliar Documents* (Grand Rapids and Dublin [1982]). Decrees, with Eng. tr., in Tanner, *Decrees* (1990), 2, pp. 817–1135. H. Vorgrimler (ed.), *Das Zweite Vatikanische Konzil, Dokumente und Kommentare* (3 vols., Freiburg, etc., 1966–8; abridged Eng. tr., 5 vols., 1967–9). C. Butler [OSB], *The Theology of Vatican II* (Sarum Lectures, 1966; 1967; enlarged edn., 1981). G. Alberigo and J.-P. Jossua (eds.), *La réception de Vatican II* (1985; Eng. tr., with additional ch. by A. Dulles, Washington, DC [1987]). *Le deuxième Concile du Vatican (1959–65): Actes du colloque organisé par l'École française (Rome 28–30 mai 1986)* (Collection de l'École française de Rome, 113; 1989); *Paolo VI e i problemi ecclesiologici al Concilio: Colloquio internazionale di Studio, Brescia 19-20-21 settembre 1986* (Pubblicazioni dell'Istituto Paolo VI, 7; Brescia, 1989). G. Alberigo (ed.), *History of Vatican II* (Louvain, 1995 ff.). A. Stacpoole [OSB] (ed.), *Vatican II by those who were there* (1986). A. Hastings (ed.), *Modern Catholicism* (1991). Three suppl. vols. of *L.Th.K.* (2nd edn.) are devoted to the Council, incl. Lat. text and Ger. tr. of docs. (1966–8).

Vaudois. See WALDENSES.

Vaughan, Charles John (1816–97), Dean of *Llandaff. Educated at Rugby under T. *Arnold and at Trinity College, Cambridge, he was ordained in 1841. From 1844 to 1859 he was Headmaster of Harrow, where he made a considerable reputation as the person who restored the prestige of the school. After withdrawing his acceptance of the bishopric of *Rochester he became vicar of Doncaster in 1860, where he undertook to prepare graduates for ordination. He carried on this work all through his life, so that by his death over 450 young men, popularly known as 'Vaughan's Doves', had gone through his training. In 1869 he became Master of the Temple and in 1879 Dean of Llandaff. Here his sympathies with Nonconformity gained him considerable influence in S. Wales, and he took an active part in the foundation of the University College at Cardiff (1883/4). Vaughan was a notable preacher who combined force and lucidity of expression with warmth of feeling and conviction. He opposed contemporary critical views in biblical scholarship, but maintained close friendship with notable liberals such as A. P. *Stanley. Among his numerous publications are commentaries on Rom. (1859), Phil. (1885), and Heb. (1890) and collections of

sermons, including *Lessons of Life and Godliness* (1862) and *Words from the Gospels* (1863).

Vaughan left strict instructions that no biog. should be published. Brief sketch by F. D. How, *Six Great Schoolmasters* (1904), pp. 138–80 ('Charles J. Vaughan, D.D., Headmaster of Harrow, 1844–1859'). R. R. Williams, 'A Neglected Victorian Divine, Vaughan of Llandaff', *CQR* 154 (1943), pp. 72–85. C. E. Vaughan in *DNB* 58 (1899), pp. 159–61.

Vaughan, Henry (1622–95), 'Silurist', English poet. Born near Brecon of an ancient Welsh family, in 1638 he was entered at Jesus College, Oxford, where he was an ardent supporter of *Charles I. He left without taking a degree, studied medicine in London and *c*.1645 began to practise at Brecon, and from *c*.1650 at his native place Newton-by-Usk. About this time a spiritual transformation took place in his life, partly due perhaps to the death of a brother and a severe illness. The poetical outcome was the *Silex Scintillans* (2 parts, 1650 and 1655), a collection of spiritual poems, influenced by G. *Herbert, which are marked by an atmosphere of intense and sustained religious fervour. The first volume of *Silex* was followed in 1652 by *The Mount of Olives*, a small collection of prayers and meditations, and in 1654 by *Flores Solitudinis*, translations from J. E. Nieremberg (1595–1658) and St *Eucherius, with a Life of St *Paulinus of Nola by Vaughan himself. Apparently through the neglect of his works by the public, he published nothing after the second volume of the *Silex* except a heterogeneous collection of verse which was brought out by one of his friends, 'J. W.' (prob. John Williams), under the title *Thalia Rediviva*, in 1678. Vaughan is usually numbered among the '*Metaphysical Poets' of the 17th cent., but his style is simpler than that of J. *Donne and less abstract than T. *Traherne's. The likeness between Vaughan's poem 'The Retreat' and W. *Wordsworth's 'Ode on Intimations of Immortality' has often been remarked but is sometimes disputed.

Crit. edn. of his Works by L. C. Martin (2 vols., Oxford, 1914; 2nd edn., 1957). Poems also ed. F. Fogle (New York, 1964) and A. Rudrum (Harmondsworth, 1976). J. D. Simmonds, *Masques of God: Form and Theme in the Poetry of Henry Vaughan* (Pittsburgh [1972]); T. O. Calhoun, *Henry Vaughan: The Achievement of Silex Scintillans* (Newark, Del., etc. [1981]); J. F. S. Post, *Henry Vaughan: The Unfolding Vision* (Princeton, NJ [1982]). R. D. Dunn and J. Horden in *NCBEL* 1 (1974), cols. 1230–4. See also METAPHYSICAL POETS.

Vaughan, Herbert (1832–1903), Abp. of *Westminster. Descended from an old English RC family, Vaughan was ordained to the priesthood at Lucca in 1854. For a time he was vice-president of the seminary of St Edmund's College, Ware. Having conceived the idea of founding a college in England to train missionaries, he toured S. America in 1863–5 to raise money for the purpose. In 1866 he founded St Joseph's College, *Mill Hill, whose members were commissioned to work among the Black population of the United States. At the height of the controversies prior to the First *Vatican Council he bought the *Tablet (1868) and for three years acted as editor, championing the *Ultramontane cause. In 1872 he was appointed Bp. of Salford, and in 1892 Abp. of Westminster. He became a cardinal in 1893. The most notable events of Vaughan's archiepiscopacy were his obtaining the permission of the authorities at Rome for RCs to attend the ancient English universities, the building of *Westminster Cathedral (begun 1895), the discussions regarding *Anglican Ordinations, which ended in their condemnation by *Leo XIII (1896), and his activities in connection with the Education Bill of 1902, which recognized his main thesis, i.e. that all schools, whether denominational or public schools, are equally the concern of the state.

Of Vaughan's family, six of his eight brothers became priests, and all six sisters entered convents. His eldest brother, **Roger William Bede Vaughan** (1834–83), was educated at *Downside and entered the *Benedictine Order in 1853. Appointed Prior of St Michael's, Belmont, nr. Hereford, in 1862, in 1873 he was consecrated with the title of Abp. of Nazianzus as coadjutor to the Abp. of Sydney, whom he succeeded in 1877. **Bernard John Vaughan** (1847–1922), who was educated at *Stonyhurst and entered the Society of Jesus [*Jesuits] in 1866, was a notable preacher. Several volumes of his Sermons have been published.

S. Leslie (ed.), *Letters of Herbert Cardinal Vaughan to Lady Herbert of Lea, 1867 to 1903* (1942). Life of Herbert Vaughan by J. G. Snead-Cox (2 vols., London, 1910; abridged edn., 1934). Modern studies by A. McCormack (London, 1966) and R. O'Neil, MHM (Tunbridge Wells, 1995). E. [R.] Norman, *The English Catholic Church in the Nineteenth Century* (Oxford, 1984), esp. pp. 345–73. J. G. Snead-Cox in *DNB, 1901–11*, 3 (1912), pp. 550–4. Of Roger William Bede Vaughan there is a memoir [by J. C. Hedley] in *Downside Review*, 3 (1884), pp. 1–27; A. E. Cahill in *Australian Dictionary of Biography*, 6 (Melbourne, 1976), pp. 327–9, s.v. Life of Bernard John Vaughan by C. C. Martindale, SJ (London, 1923).

Vaughan Williams, Ralph (1872–1958), English composer. The son of an Anglican priest, he was born at Down Ampney, Glos. (from which he named a hymn tune), and received his musical training at the Royal College of Music and at Trinity College, Cambridge; later he studied abroad with Max Bruch and Ravel. Apart from four years of active service during the First World War (1914–18), his life was devoted to composition, teaching, conducting, and the promotion of public interest in music. His enthusiasm for folk song and his work in that field made a distinctive contribution to English music, and markedly influenced his own style and outlook. He composed works of every kind, including nine symphonies, six operas, and many songs and choral works.

Although Vaughan Williams held only one ecclesiastical appointment, being for about three years organist at St Barnabas's in Lambeth (1895–7), he was music editor of The *English Hymnal, and helped in the preparation of *Songs of Praise and The Oxford Book of Carols. He wrote a number of hymn tunes, among them the notable *Sine Nomine* ('For all the saints'); his occasional works include the *Te Deum in G for the enthronement at *Canterbury of C. G. *Lang and a *Festival Te Deum* for the coronation of George VI. He also composed a superb *Mass in G minor, organ pieces, *canticle settings, and *anthems. He himself was a man of mystical inclination rather than specifically Christian commitment who did not fit comfortably into the Anglican choral tradition, and some of his settings for religious texts may better be described as spiritual music than as Church music designed for performance in choir.

Vaughan Williams's *National Music* (Flexner Lectures, 1932; pub. 1934) was repr., with other essays, 1963. His correspondence with Gustav Holst was ed. by U. Vaughan Williams (widow) and I. Holst, *Heirs and Rebels* (1959). [G.] M. [S] Kennedy, *The Works of Ralph Vaughan Williams* (1964; rev. edn., 1980); U. Vaughan Williams, *R. V. W.: A Biography of Ralph Vaughan Williams* (1964); these two works were written in accordance with the express wish of Vaughan Williams. The *Catalogue* of Vaughan Williams's Works, orig. incl. in the former, rev. as a separate vol. in 1982. H. [J.] Foss, *Ralph Vaughan Williams: A Study* (1950), incl. Vaughan Williams's 'Musical Autobiography', pp. 18–30; F. Howes, *The Music of Ralph Vaughan Williams* (1954); J. Day, *Vaughan Williams* ('Master Musicians' Series), 1961). N. Butterworth, *Ralph Vaughan Williams: A Guide to Research* (New York and London, 1990). F. Howes in *DNB, 1951–1960*, pp. 1006–9; H. Ottaway in S. Sadie (ed.), *The New Grove Dictionary of Music and Musicians*, 19 (1980), pp. 569–80, both s.v.

Vázquez, Gabriel (1549–1604), less correctly 'Vásquez', Spanish theologian. From his birthplace near Belmonte, he is sometimes known as **Bellomontanus**. He became a *Jesuit in 1569, and taught moral theology in the universities of Madrid, Ocaña, and Alcalá. He spent six years (1585–91) in Rome, but returned thence to Alcalá, where he taught till his death. His most important work is his commentary (*Commentarii ac Disputationes*) on the *Summa Theologiae* of St *Thomas Aquinas (8 vols. in all; 1598–1615), largely directed in its details against the theses of his co-Jesuit, F. *Suárez. In the discussion then raging as to the doctrine of grace, he opposed to the *Congruism of F. Suárez and R. *Bellarmine a strictly *Molinist position. His learning was immense; but it was often squandered on the discussion of useless questions and the defence of eccentric theories.

A. Astrain, SJ, *Historia de la Compañía de Jesús en la assistencia de España*, 4 (1913), pp. 68–73. F. Stegmüller, 'Zur Prädestinationslehre des jungen Vásquez', *BGPM*, Supplementband 3 (Halbband 2; 1935), pp. 1287–311. J. A. de Aldama, SJ (ed.), 'Un parecer inédito del P. Gabriel Vázquez sobre la doctrina augustiniana de la gracia eficaz', *Estudios eclesiásticos*, 23 (1949), pp. 515–20. L. Pereña Vicente (ed.), 'Importantes documentos inéditos de Gabriel Vázquez', *Revista Española de Teología*, 16 (1956), pp. 193–213. R. Araud, SJ, 'Une étape dans l'histoire du traité de la conscience morale; le 'traité de la conscience' chez G. Vasquez', *Mélanges de Science Religieuse*, 24 (1967), pp. 3–48 and 113–52. Sommervogel, 8 (1898), cols. 513–19; 12 (1911–30; repr. 1960), cols. 857 f. and 1239; Polgár, 3 (1990), pp. 608–10. J. Hellin, SJ, in *DTC* 15 (pt. 2; 1950), cols. 2601–10, s.v., with further bibl.

Vecchioni. Members of an ancient guild at Milan officially known as the 'Scuola di S. Ambrogio', consisting of 10 old men and 10 old women. Until recent times four of them (two of each sex) made public offerings of bread and wine on behalf of the laity at the solemn celebration of the (*Ambrosian) Liturgy in Milan Cathedral. The ceremony was a survival of the primitive offerings in kind by the faithful at Mass now represented by the offertory procession.

Vedast, St (d. 539), also 'Vaast', Bp. of Arras. He was ordained to the priesthood at Toul, where he was deputed to prepare King *Clovis I, returning from his victory over the Alemanni, for Baptism. For a time he assisted St *Remigius in his mission work among the Franks at *Reims. About 499 he was consecrated Bp. of Arras, where he successfully established Christianity; and he was also charged with the diocese of Cambrai. He was venerated in England as 'St Foster' (cf. the church of St Vedast in Foster Lane, London). Feast day, 6 Feb.

Two medieval Lives, the one ascribed to St Jonas of Bobbio (7th cent.), the other by *Alcuin, in *AASS*, Feb. 1 (1658), pp. 792–80; crit. edn. by B. Krusch in *MGH*, Scriptores Rerum Merovingicarum, 3 (1896), pp. 399–427. I. Deug-Su, 'L'opera agiografica di Alcuino: la "Vita Vedastis" ', *Studi Medievali*, 3rd ser. 21 (1980), pp. 665–706; repr. in id., *L'opera agiografica di Alcuino* (Spoleto, 1983), pp. 73–114. G. and W. Sparrow Simpson, *The Life and Legend of S. Vedast* (1896); E. Guilbert, *S. Vaast, fondateur de l'église d'Arras* (Arras, 1928). É. Brouette in *Bibliotheca Sanctorum*, 12 (1969), cols. 965–8, s.v. 'Vedasto', with bibl.

veil (1), Christian headdress. The veil, which was the customary feminine headdress among many ancient peoples, was worn by the Roman matron as a mark of distinction from the unmarried woman. In the Christian Church it was given to consecrated virgins by the bishop from the 3rd cent., as the symbol of their spiritual marriage to Christ. Since then it has come to be considered the most important part of the religious habit of women (cf. the expression 'to take the veil'). In most orders and congregations the veil of the professed sister is black, that of the novice white, but other colours, e.g. blue, are possible. Some modern congregations, such as the Sisters of Charity of St *Vincent de Paul, dispense with it altogether. In the C of E until about the middle of the 20th cent. female candidates usually wore a white veil at *Confirmation.

veil (2), liturgical cloths for covering various objects, e.g. the *chalice veil (q.v.), the veil used for the *ciborium while containing the sacred species, and the *humeral veil (q.v.). Acc. to a custom of the W. Church, traceable as far back as the 11th cent., all crucifixes, statues, and pictures were veiled during *Passiontide. In the Middle Ages the veiling lasted throughout *Lent, when the veils were usually of unbleached linen. In modern RC practice veiling is no longer obligatory; when used, it is from *Vespers preceding *Palm Sunday to the *Gloria in excelsis* of the *Paschal Vigil Service, and violet veils are used except for the crucifix on the high altar on *Maundy Thursday, which is veiled in white.

Velichkovsky, St Paisy (1722–94), Ukrainian monk and spiritual writer. In 1746 he became a monk on Mt. *Athos; his austerity attracted other Slavs and Romanians and his community grew so large that he transferred it to Moldavia. At Dragomirna, and later at Neamţ, he organized a huge monastery modelled on the life on Mt. Athos. He encouraged his monks to produce revisions and translations of the works of the Greek and Latin Fathers; he himself translated into Slavonic the *Philocalia* of Sts Macarius Notaras and *Nicodemus of the Holy Mountain (1793). Through his writings and the training of disciples who became spiritual guides and monastic superiors, he started a spiritual revival which continued the *hesychast tradition and is still of influence in the E. Orthodox world. He was proclaimed a saint by the 1988 Synod of the Russian Church; feast day, 15 Nov.

A.-E. N. Tachiaos, *The Revival of Byzantine Mysticism among Slavs and Romanians in the XVIIIth Century: Texts Relating to the Life and Activity of Paisy Velichkovsky* (Thessalonica, 1986).

Venantius Fortunatus (*c*.530–*c*.610), Latin poet. A native of Treviso, near *Venice, he was educated at *Ravenna. About 565 he set out on a pilgrimage to the tomb of St *Martin of Tours, in gratitude for the curing of an eye-complaint. On the way he was well received at the court of Sigebert of Austrasia at Metz, where he stayed until 567. By the time he had completed his pilgrimage, North Italy had been overrun by the Lombards, and Venantius settled at Poitiers. He became acquainted with the former Queen *Radegunde, by then a nun, and Agnes, the Abbess of her community; he entered the service of the community, first as steward and, after his ordination, as chaplain. He later became a friend of St *Gregory of Tours, who encouraged him to publish collections of his poetry. Towards the end of the 6th cent. he was elected Bp. of Poitiers.

Venantius Fortunatus was the author of 11 books of occasional verse, including epigrams, elegies, panegyrics, and epitaphs, as well as some hymns; a long metrical Life of Martin of Tours, prose Lives of St *Hilary of Poitiers, St *Germanus of Paris, Radegunde, and various local celebrities; the 'De Excidio Thoringiae', a touching lament on the extinction of the royal house of Thuringia and a moving monument to his friendship with Radegunde, and the hymns which stand out as the true expression of his genius. Venantius may be regarded 'not as the last of the Roman but as the first of the medieval poets' (Raby). The technique of his poetry was that of classical antiquity handled with exceptional formal skill, but the emotional and cultural content were imbued with the Christianized spirit of the Middle Ages. He was the first Christian poet to express himself in terms of erotic mysticism, and his hymns are steeped in the Catholic spirit and Catholic symbolism. The two greatest of them, '*Vexilla Regis' and '*Pange lingua gloriosi', became an integral part of the Passiontide Office of the W. Church.

Editio princeps of his poems pub. Cagliari, 1573; fuller edns. of his works by C. Brouwer, SJ (Mainz, 1603), and M. A. Luchi, OSB (2 vols., Rome, 1786–7), repr. in J. P. Migne, *PL* 88. 59–592, with addition, cols. 592–6; crit. edn. by F. Leo and B. Krusch in *MGH*, Auctores Antiquissimi, 4 (2 pts., 1881–5). Studies by W. Meyer (*Abh.* (Gött.), NF 4, Nr. 5; 1901), R. Koebner (Beiträge zur Kulturgeschichte des Mittelalters und der Renaissance, 22; 1915), D. Tardi (Paris thesis, 1927) and J. W. George (Oxford, 1992). S. Blomgren, *Studia Fortunatiana* (Uppsala Universitets Årsskrift, 1933, Filosofi, Språkvetenskap och Historiska Vetenskaper, 1, 1933 (in Band 2 of 1933), and ibid., 1934, 3, 1934 (in Band 2 of 1934)). G. M. Dreves, *Hymnologische Studien zu Venantius und Rabanus Maurus* (Veröffentlichungen aus dem kirchenhistorischen Seminar München, 3. Reihe, Nr. 3; 1908), pp. 1–54. B. de Gaiffier, 'S. Venance Fortunat, évêque de Poitiers. Les témoignages de son culte', *Anal. Boll.* 70 (1952), pp. 262–84. P. [J.] Godman, *Poets and Emperors: Frankish Politics and Carolingian Poetry* (Oxford, 1987), pp. 1–37, with bibl. Raby, pp. 86–95, with bibl. p. 489. *CPL* (3rd edn., 1995), pp. 337–41 (nos. 1033–52). J. Szövérffy, *Die Annalen der lateinischen Hymnendichtung*, 1 (1964), pp. 128–40; F. Brunhölzl, *Geschichte der lateinischen Literatur des Mittelalters*, 1 (Munich, 1975), pp. 118–28, with bibl. pp. 525 f.

Venerable. (1) In the RC Church, a title bestowed on a departed person when a certain stage in the process of *canonization has been reached. This stage has been fixed at different points in recent times; at present the title is granted only when the Pope declares that a person has led an heroically virtuous life or has been martyred. Formerly the title was popularly given on the introduction of the case before the Congregation of Sacred *Rites, and was the occasion of great celebrations; the regulations now insist that there are to be no solemn celebrations or laudatory prayers in church, and outside church all actions are to be avoided that might lead people to assume that the diocesan inquiry will certainly result in future canonization. In a less limited sense the word is used of other persons of marked holiness of life, esp. the 'Venerable *Bede'.

(2) In the C of E, the title of an *archdeacon.

Veneration of the Cross. A ceremony of the Latin Rite for *Good Friday, sometimes also called **Creeping to the Cross**, in which clergy and people solemnly venerate a crucifix, usually at the entrance to the sanctuary. It originated in the veneration of the relics of the True Cross in *Jerusalem (mentioned in the 'Pilgrimage of *Egeria'). Subsequently the custom was transferred to Rome with relics of the Cross deposited in the church of Santa Croce in Gerusalemme, and then it spread to churches which had no relics. The prayers were originally of an extra-liturgical character and appear to date from the Carolingian era. An early description of the ceremony occurs in the *Regularis Concordia. An analogous ceremony, consisting in a solemn procession, veneration, and elevation of the cross, takes place in the E. Church on *Holy Cross Day (14 Sept.) and on the 3rd Sunday in Lent.

H. Thurston, SJ, *Lent and Holy Week* (1904), pp. 345–62. L. Gjerlow, *Adoratio Crucis: The Regularis Concordia and the Decreta Lanfranci* (Oslo, 1961).

Veni Creator (Lat. 'Come, Creator'). A hymn to the Holy Spirit, prob. composed in the Frankish Empire in the 9th cent. and frequently attributed to *Rabanus Maurus. It was used as the Vespers Hymn of *Whitsuntide from the 10th cent., and from the 12th cent. came to be substituted during the Octave of the feast for the usual hymn of Terce, 'Nunc Sancte nobis Spiritus'. It is also widely used outside Pentecost, e.g. at the ordination of priests and of bishops. The best-known English version is that of Bp. John *Cosin, 'Come, Holy Ghost, our souls inspire', included since 1662 in the Anglican *Ordinal (to replace the earlier version in the 1550 Rite). Other versions of the 'Veni Creator' are due to J. *Dryden, R. *Mant, F. W. *Faber, and E. *Caswall.

Crit. text by G. M. Dreves, *Lateinische Hymnendichter des Mittelalters*, 2 (AHMA 50; 1907), pp. 193 f. A. *Wilmart, OSB, 'L'Hymne et la Séquence du Saint-Esprit', *La Vie et les Arts liturgiques*, 10 (1924), pp. 395–401, repr. in his *Auteurs dévots du moyen-âge latin* (1932), pp. 37–45. H. Lausberg, *Der Hymnus 'Veni Creator Spiritus'* (Abhandlungen der Rheinisch-Westfälischen Akademie der Wissenschaften, 64; 1979). Raby, p. 183.

Veni Sancte Spiritus. The *Sequence, sometimes called the 'Golden Sequence', for *Whitsunday. Its authorship is now usually attributed to Stephen *Langton (not *Innocent III). The most popular Eng. trs. are those of J. M. *Neale ('Come, Thou Holy Paraclete') and E. *Caswall ('Holy Spirit, Lord of Light').

Crit. text with notes by C. Blume, SJ, and H. M. Bannister, *Liturgische Prosen des Übergangsstiles und der zweiten Epoche,*

insbesondere die dem Adam von Sanct Victor zugeschriebenen (AHMA 54; 1915), pp. 234–9. H. Thurston, SJ, 'Notes on Familiar Prayers. IV, The *Veni, Sancte Spiritus* of Cardinal Langton', *The Month*, 121 (1915), pp. 602–16, repr. in his *Familiar Prayers* (ed. J. H. Crehan, SJ, 1953), pp. 54–72. A. *Wilmart, OSB, *Auteurs spirituels et textes dévots du moyen-âge latin* (1932), pp. 37–45 ('L'Hymne et la Séquence du Saint-Esprit'). Raby, pp. 342–4.

Veni, veni, Emmanuel ('O come, O come, Emmanuel'). The origins of both the words and the music of this well-known hymn (*AM* 49, *EH* 8), a versification of the *O-Antiphons (q.v.), are very obscure. The words have been traced back to the *Psalteriolum Cantionum Catholicarum* (Cologne, 1710). (J. M. *Neale's ascription of it to the 12th cent. seems wholly unfounded.) The tune, which first appeared in the *Hymnal Noted* (1854), is possibly founded on a reminiscence of a plainsong phrase.

The text of the words is pr. in H. A. Daniel (ed.), *Thesaurus Hymnologicus*, 2 (Leipzig, 1844), p. 336, and in J. M. Neale (ed.), *Hymni Ecclesiae e Breviariis quibusdam et Missalibus Gallicanis, Germanis, Hispanis, Lusitanis desumpti* (Oxford, 1851), pp. 57 f. P. *Dearmer, *Songs of Praise Discussed* (1933), pp. 43 f. For other Eng. trs. see J. Julian in J. Julian (ed.), *A Dictionary of Hymnology* (2nd edn., 1907), p. 74, s.v. 'Antiphon', with additional note p. 1551; J. Mearns, ibid., p. 1721, s.v.

venial sin. In moral theology, a sin which, though it disposes the soul to death and is the greatest of all evils except *mortal sin (q.v.), unlike mortal sin, does not wholly deprive the soul of sanctifying grace. The Fathers made a distinction (often supported by reference to 1 Jn. 5: 16) between grave (*mortalia, capitalia*) sins which could be remitted only by public *Penance and light (*levia*) sins, remitted by fasting, almsgiving, and esp. prayer. The modern distinction, however, goes back to the Schoolmen, esp. St *Thomas Aquinas (*Summa Theol.*, II (1), qq. 88, 89). It was formally approved (against M. *Luther) at the Council of *Trent (Sess. VI, cans. 23, 25, 27). Acc. to the theology of Penance, there is no obligation to confess venial sins when resorting to the Sacrament.

Venice. The present see of Venice goes back to the bishopric, founded in 774, on the isle of Olivolo, later known as Castello. It belonged to the patriarchate of Grado, the relations of which to the see of Castello were finally settled under Marco II Michele (1225–35). In 1328 Jacopo Albertini, Bp. of Castello, who was an adherent of Louis of Bavaria, crowned Louis with the *Iron Crown and was deposed in consequence. Half a century later Giovanni Piacentini (1376–78) met with the same fate for supporting the antipope Clement VII. Angelo Corrario, Bp. of Olivolo from 1380 to 1390, became (Latin) Patr. of *Constantinople and in 1406 Pope under the name of Gregory XII. Owing to constant disputes between the patriarch of Grado and the see of Olivolo both were suppressed and replaced by the patriarchate of Venice in 1451, St Lawrence Giustiniani being the first Patr. of Venice (1433–56). The *Tridentine reforms were introduced into the diocese by Giovanni Trevisano (1560), and later by Laurentius Priuli (1591–1600), who restored the cathedral and founded a seminary. The patriarchate was reorganized in 1818. Among its most important prelates of recent times were the learned Thomist, D. Agostini (1877–91), Giuseppe M. Sarto (1893–1903), later Pope *Pius X,

Angelo Giuseppe Roncalli (1953–8), later Pope *John XXIII, and Albino Luciani (1973–8), later Pope *John Paul I.

The most famous church of Venice is San Marco, originally the chapel of the Doges. Destined to receive the relics of St *Mark, it was begun c.830 and completed in 883. Burned down in 976, it was rebuilt after the model of the Basilica of the Apostles at Constantinople from 1063 to 1071. Its plan forms a Greek cross of equal arms, the centre and each of the arms being surmounted by a dome. The interior is richly decorated with many-coloured marbles and mosaics, dating from the end of the 11th to the 17th cents. The retable of the high altar is the famous Pala d'oro, a magnificent 10th-cent. piece of goldsmiths' and jewellers' art, with additions dating from the 12th to the 15th cents., representing Christ surrounded by angels, prophets, and saints. The treasury contains a unique collection of plate and jewellery, mostly of Byzantine origin. Immediately in front of the church stands the celebrated campanile, built in 1329 and rebuilt in 1910 after its fall in 1902. Since 1807 San Marco has been the cathedral church of the patriarchate in place of S. Pietro di Castello.

Among other famous Venetian churches are the *Franciscan Santa Maria Gloriosa (1250–1338), for which *Titian painted an *Assumption*, and the *Dominican SS. Giovanni e Paolo (1333–90), with the tombs of the Doges. Of the many religious orders that have houses in Venice the *Armenian Benedictine Congregation of the *Mechitarists is esp. remarkable; their convent on the island of San Lazzaro is a centre of Armenian education.

S. Romanin, *Storia documentata di Venezia* (10 vols., 1853–61). W. C. Hazlitt, *The Venetian Republic: Its Rise, its Growth, and its Fall, 421–1797* (2 vols., 1900); H. Kretschmayr, *Geschichte von Venedig* (3 vols., 1905–34); A. Battistella, *La repubblica di Venezia ne' suoi undici secoli di storia* (1921); R. Cessi, *Storia della repubblica di Venezia* (Bibliotheca Storica Principato, 23 and 24; 1944–6); *La Civiltà Veneziana*, pub. under the auspices of the Centro di Cultura della Fondazione Giorgio Cini (11 vols., Florence [1955–65]; repr., ed. V. Branca, *Storia della Civiltà Veneziana*, 3 vols. [1979]); P. Longworth, *The Rise and Fall of Venice* (1974); J. J. Norwich, *Venice: The Rise to Empire* (1977); id., *Venice: The Greatness and the Fall* (1981). M. Muraro and A. Grabar (Eng. tr. by J. Emmons), *Treasures of Venice* [1963]. F. Ughelli, Ord. Cist., *Italia sacra*, 5 (Rome, 1652), cols. 1225–406; P. F. Kehr, *Regesta Pontificum Romanorum: Italia Pontificia sive Repertorium Privilegiorum et Litterarum a Romanis Pontificibus ante Annum MCLXXXXVIII Italiae Ecclesiis Monasteriis Civitatibus Singulisque Personis Concessorum*, 7 (pt. 2; Berlin, 1925), esp. pp. 1–26 and 124–99. F. Tonon (ed.), *Le Origini della Chiesa di Venezia* (Contributi alla Storia della Chiesa di Venezia, 1; Venice [1987]), and other vols. in this series. U. Franzoi and D. Di Stefano, *Le Chiese di Venezia* (Venice, 1976). F. Schillmann, *Venedig: Geschichte und Kultur Venetiens* (1933). There are copious illustrations in *La basilica di San Marco in Venezia*, ed. F. Ongania with various others (15 vols., 1881–6); O. Demus, *The Church of San Marco in Venice* (Dumbarton Oaks Studies, 6; 1960). *Archivio veneto* (Venice, 1871 ff.). V. Piva, P. Paschini, and M. Muraro in *EC* 12 (1954), cols. 1205–21, s.v. 'Venezia', with further bibl.

Venite. Ps. 95 [Vulg. 94], from its first words ('Venite exultemus'). In the Rule of St *Benedict (ch. 9), it is prescribed at the 'vigil' (i.e. the night service which became commonly known as *Mattins), whence it found its way into the Roman, Sarum, and other *Breviaries; and in 1549 it was set in its familiar place in the BCP at the beginning of Mattins. The version of the BCP is that of the '*Great Bible'. The stern language of the concluding four verses led the revisers of the BCP of 1927–8 to propose their excision, and in the ASB the last three verses are replaced by Ps. 96: 13.

Venn, Henry (1725–97), *Evangelical divine. In 1749 he was elected a Fellow of Queens' College, Cambridge, and after holding several curacies he became vicar of Huddersfield from 1759 to 1771. Here his piety and zeal made a great impression. His *The Complete Duty of Man* (1763), designed to combat *The *Whole Duty* of Man, became popular among Evangelicals. Forced by ill-health to retire from Huddersfield in 1771, for the rest of his life he held the living of Yelling, Cambs, where he influenced C. *Simeon. His son, **John Venn** (1759–1813), also a prominent Evangelical and rector of Clapham from 1792 till his death, was one of the founders of the *CMS.

H. *Venn (grandson, ed.), *The Life and a Selection from the Letters of the late Rev. Henry Venn* (1834), with Memoir of his life mainly by John Venn (son), pp. 1–57, and list of his works, pp. 58–60. M. L. Loane, *Cambridge and the Evangelical Succession* (1952), pp. 119–71. M. [M.] Hennell, *John Venn and the Clapham Sect* (1958). J. Venn in *DNB* 58 (1899), pp. 207 f. See also bibl. s.v. CLAPHAM SECT.

Venn, Henry (1796–1873), *Evangelical missionary statesman. The son of John Venn and grandson of Henry *Venn of Huddersfield, he was a leading Evangelical in his generation and secretary to the *CMS from 1841 to 1872. His aim was that overseas Churches should become 'self-supporting, self-governing and self-extending'. He was instrumental in securing the appointment of the first Black Anglican bishop, S. A. *Crowther, in 1864.

Selections from his writings ed. M. [A. C.] Warren, *To Apply the Gospel* (Grand Rapids, Mich. [1971]), with introd., pp. 15–34, and list of his works, pp. 35–47. W. Knight, *Memoir of the Rev. H. Venn* (1880). T. E. Yates, *Venn and Victorian Bishops Abroad* (Studia Missionalia Upsaliensia, 33; Uppsala and London, 1978). M. [M.] Hennell, *Sons of the Prophets* (1979), pp. 68–90. W. R. Shenk, *Henry Venn—Missionary Statesman* (American Society of Missiology Series, 6; Maryknoll, NY, and Ibadan [1983]). C. P. Williams, *The Ideal of the Self-Governing Church* (Studies in Christian Mission, 1; Leiden, 1990). J. Venn in *DNB* 58 (1899), pp. 208 f.

verger. Strictly the official who carries a mace or 'verge' (Lat. *virga*) before a dignitary. Today the term is commonly used for one who takes care of the interior fabric of the church. In the *Sarum Rite the verger headed the procession. The form 'virger', formerly also in general use, has been occasionally revived in a few places.

Vergil. See VIRGIL.

Vergilius of Salzburg, St. See VIRGILIUS OF SALZBURG, ST.

Veritatis Splendor. The *encyclical issued by *John Paul II on 6 Aug. 1993 expounding the fundamental principles of the ethical teaching of the RC Church. It affirms the importance of morality for humanity, and the mission of the Church to exhort, judge, and explain. It repeats earlier condemnations of *contraception, artificial insemination, and *homosexual acts. *Evangelium Vitae*, an encyclical issued by John Paul II on 25 Mar. 1995, applied these ethical principles to issues concerning the value and inviolability of human life.

Text pr. in *AAS* 85 (1993), pp. 1133–228; that of *Evangelium Vitae*, ibid., 87 (1995), pp. 401–522.

Vermigli, Pietro Martire. See PETER MARTYR.

Vermittlungstheologie. A school of 19th cent. German Protestant theologians. The name derives from a memorandum drawn up by F. Lücke in 1827 and published in 1828 in the first issue of the *Theologische Studien und Kritiken*, the leading organ of the movement. Among its chief representatives were J. A. W. *Neander, K. I. *Nitzsch, F. A. G. *Tholuck, I. A. *Dorner, R. *Rothe, H. L. *Martensen, and W. *Beyschlag. The term is also used of the speculative theology of the Hegelians K. Daub and P. *Marheineke. All endeavoured in various ways to combine the traditional Protestantism of the Reformation Confessions with modern science, philosophy and historical scholarship. Most of them owed much to F. D. E. *Schleiermacher. The mediating aspirations of the school were vigorously attacked by A. *Ritschl and his disciples, and, more recently, by the theologians of the school of K. *Barth.

E. Hirsch, *Geschichte der neuern evangelischen Theologie im Zusammenhang mit den allgemeinen Bewegungen des europäischen Denkens*, 5 (Gütersloh, 1954), esp. pp. 364–430. F. Traub in *RGG* (2nd edn.), 5 (1931), cols. 1548–51, s.v. For further bibl. see under separate representatives of the school.

Vernazza, Battista (1497–1587), *Augustinian canoness and mystic. She was the daughter of Ettore Vernazza, the friend and disciple of St *Catherine of Genoa (who was Battista's godmother). From 1510 till her death she lived in a convent at Genoa. She wrote letters, some verses, many 'Spiritual Discourses' or homilies, and some 'Colloquies' on her mystical experiences. It was at one time thought that she was the final redactor of Catherine's works, but recent scholarship has discredited this suggestion.

Opere spirituali, ed. D. Gaspare da Piacenza, 3 vols., Venice, 1588; additional vol. 4, Verona, 1602; 6th edn., 6 vols., Genoa, 1755. F. *von Hügel, *The Mystical Element of Religion as Studied in Saint Catherine of Genoa and her Friends*, 1 (1908), pp. 336–67. Umile Bonzi de Genova, OFM Cap., 'La Vénérable Battistina Vernazza', *Revue d'Ascétique et de Mystique*, 16 (1935), pp. 147–79. C. Carpaneto da Langasco, OFM Cap., in *Dict. Sp.* 16 (1994), cols. 461–6, s.v. See also recent works cited under CATHERINE, ST, OF GENOA.

Verona. The beginnings of Christianity in Verona are described in the legendary 9th-cent. 'Carmen Pipinianum', which gives a list of its churches and of its early bishops. As its first bishop the city venerates St Euprepius (probably 3rd cent.). Its first historically attested bishop is Lucilius, who took part in the Council of *Sardica in 343. Its patron is St *Zeno (Bp., *c*.362–*c*.375). Among its later bishops were Nottingus (*c*.840), who opposed *Gottschalk; Francesco Condulmer (1439), who founded the College of Acolytes; and L. Lippomano (1548–58), who was one of the presidents of the Council of *Trent. An important synod was held at Verona in 1184, which introduced the

episcopal inquisition. Till 1752 the see was suffragan of *Aquileia, then of Udine, and since 1818 of *Venice. Among the famous churches of the city are the cathedral (12th cent.), which houses *Titian's painting of the Assumption; S. Zeno Maggiore, also 12th cent.; and the 13th-cent. *Dominican church, S. Anastasia. The Chapter Library has a notable collection of MSS, including MSS of St *Augustine's *De Civitate Dei* (XXVIII [26]), St *Hilary of Poitiers' *Super Psalmos* (XIII [11]) and *De Trinitate* (XIV [12])—all dating from the 5th cent.; the famous 'Verona *palimpsest' in which part of St *Isidore of Seville's *Sententiae* has been written on leaves from a 5th-cent. MS which contained Latin versions of the *Didascalia Apostolorum*, the '*Apostolic Church Order', and the '*Apostolic Tradition' (LV [53]); the 6th-cent. so-called *Leonine Sacramentary (LXXXV [80]); the *Theodosian Collection [LX [58]]; and a MS dated 517 containing works of St *Sulpicius Severus, copied by the earliest known scribe of the Library, Ursicinus (XXXVIII [36]). The city suffered severely in the Second World War in the spring of 1945 but has since been splendidly restored.

'Annales Veronenses Antiqui', ed. C. Cipolla, in *Bullettino dell'Istituto Storico Italiano*, 29 (1908), pp. 7–81. F. S. *Maffei, *Verona illustrata* (4 vols., Verona, 1731–2). G. Venturi, *Compendio della storia sacra e profana di Verona* (ibid., 1820); A. M. Allen, *A History of Verona* (1910); L. Simeoni, *Verona* (Rome, 1929). *Verona e il suo Territorio* (4 vols. in 6, Verona, 1960–84). L. Franzoni, *Verona: Testimonianze Archeologiche* (Collana 'Monografie d'Arte', 7, ibid., 1965); also other vols. in this series. F. Ughelli, *Italia sacra*, 5 (Rome, 1653), cols. 523–1090. P. F. Kehr, *Regesta Pontificum Romanorum: Italia Pontificia sive Repertorium Privilegiorum et Litterarum a Romanis Pontificibus ante Annum MCLXXXXVIII Italiae Ecclesiis Monasteriis Civitatibus Singulisque Personis Concessorum*, 7 (pt. 1; Berlin, 1923), pp. 212–304. G. B. G. Biancolini, *Notizie storiche delle chiese di Verona* (8 vols., 1749–71). A. da Lisca, *La Basilica di San Zenone in Verona* (Verona, 1956); P. Brugnoli (ed.), *La Cattedrale di Verona nelle sue vicende edilizie dal secolo IV al secolo XVI* (ibid., 1987). On the Council of 1184, Hardouin, 6, pt. 2, cols. 1881 f.; Mansi, 22 (Venice, 1778), cols. 487–94; Hefele and Leclercq, 5 (pt. 2; 1913), pp. 1117–27. G. Turrini, *Indice dei Codice Capitolari di Verona* (Verona, 1965). P. L. Zovatti and G. Turrini in *EC* 12 (1954), cols. 1289–98, s.v., with further bibl.

Verona Fathers. The popular name for the Comboni Missionaries of the Heart of Jesus, a RC religious society of priests and lay brothers dedicated exclusively to missionary work. The Verona Fathers, founded by D. *Comboni (q.v.) in 1867, received Papal approbation in 1910. The Comboni Missionary Sisters (formerly called Verona Sisters), founded by him in 1871, were approved in 1906. In the mission work of both communities priority is given to work among the Black populations of Africa and other parts of the world. The Verona Fathers began work in Egypt and the *Sudan, and later expanded their activities to *Uganda, *Ethiopia and Mozambique, *Zaire and Togo. The Comboni Missionary Sisters have missions in *Mexico, *Brazil, and Ecuador, and they also work among Black Americans in the *United States of America.

A. Gilli [MCCJ], *L'Istituto Missionario Comboniano dalla fondazione alla morte di Daniele Comboni* (Bologna, 1979; Eng. tr., Rome, 1979). See also works cited under COMBONI, D.

Veronica, St. A woman of Jerusalem who, acc. to a legend (prob. of French origin) first found in its present

form in the 14th cent., offered her head-cloth to the Lord
to wipe the blood and sweat from His face on the way
to Calvary. He returned it with His features impressed
upon it.

The name is applied in a late version of the 'Acts of
*Pilate' to the woman 'diseased with an issue of blood'
(Mt. 9: 20–2). In this account she is said to have cured
the Emp. Tiberius with a miraculous portrait of Christ.
*Giraldus Cambrensis mentions that she had long wanted
to see Him, and that, accepting a cloth, He returned it
with His features impressed upon it. He applies the word
'veronica' to the cloth, suggesting *vera εἰκών* ('true image')
as its etymology. *Matthew Paris also applies the name to
the portrait, but says that it was so called after the woman
at whose request the Lord's features were impressed upon
it. A portrait professing to be the original imprint, which
seems to have been at Rome since the 8th cent., was translated by *Boniface VIII to St Peter's in 1297. The relic at
Rome was greatly venerated throughout the Middle Ages,
esp. in the 14th and 15th cents., and Milan and Jaen also
claimed possession of the original head-cloth. The incident
now occupies a recognized position in the *Stations of the
Cross. Although St Veronica is not mentioned in the
*Roman Martyrology, her feast is kept on 12 July.

The identification of Veronica with the woman 'with an issue
of blood' occurs in ch. 7 of the Acts of Pilate (ed. C. Tischendorf,
Evangelia Apocrypha, 2nd edn., Leipzig, 1876, p. 239, with note;
Eng. tr. in J. K. Elliott, *The Apocryphal New Testament*, 1993, p.
175); the account of the cure of the Emp. Tiberius is preserved
in the Lat. legend of the Death of Pilate (text in C. Tischendorf,
op. cit., pp. 456 f.; Eng. tr. in M. R. James, *The Apocryphal New
Testament*, 1924, pp. 157 f., with further information, p. 158; a
similar text is tr. by J. K. Elliott, op. cit., pp. 215 f.). Giraldus
Cambrensis, *Speculum Ecclesiae*, cap. 6 (*Opera*, ed. J. S. Brewer,
RS, 1873, pp. 278 f.); Matthew Paris, *Chronica Majora*, ed. H. R.
Luard, 3 (RS, 1876), pp. 7 f. *AASS*, Feb. 1 (1668), pp. 449–57,
and Jul. 3 (1723), pp. 273–9. E. von Dobschütz, *Christusbilder:
Untersuchungen zur christlichen Legende* (TU 18; 1899), ch. 4, 'Die
Veronica-Legende', pp. 197–263, with docs. and bibl. pp. 250*–
335* and 157**–203**. K. Pearson, *Die Fronica: Ein Beitrag zur
Geschichte des Christusbildes im Mittelalter* (Strasbourg, 1887); A.
Grabar, *La Sainte Face de Laon: Le Mandylion dans l'art orthodoxe*
(Prague, 1931; orig. pub. in Russian, Prague, 1930); E. Kuryluk,
Veronica and her Cloth (Oxford, 1991). H. *Leclercq, OSB, in
DACL 15 (pt. 2; 1953), cols. 2962–6, s.v. 'Véronique'; A. P.
Frutaz in *EC* 12 (1954), cols. 1299–303, s.v. See also works cited
under PILATE, ACTS OF.

versicle. A short sentence, often taken from the Pss.,
which is said or sung antiphonally in Christian worship. It
is answered by a 'response' on the part of the congregation
or other half of the choir. Thus, in the services of *Mattins
and *Evensong in the BCP, the words 'O Lord, open
Thou our lips' and 'And our mouth shall shew forth Thy
praise' are respectively versicle and response.

Vesperale. (1) A liturgical book containing the psalms,
hymns, etc., used at *Vespers with their appropriate
chants. For convenience the corresponding items at
*Compline are also commonly added.

(2) In the W. Church, the cloth spread over the altar
when not in use to keep the white linen altar-cloths free
from dirt and dust. The name is derived from the circumstance that the front part of it used to be turned back when

the altar was being censed at Vespers. It is now removed
before the service.

Vespers. The evening service of both the E. and the W.
Church and one of the oldest parts of the Divine *Office
(q.v. for references to morning and evening prayers in the
early Church). It was also known as 'lucernarium' (Gk.
λυχνικόν), because candles were lit at its celebration. From
the time of St *Benedict, however, the Office was recited
before dark, and since the later Middle Ages in the afternoon and until recently on weekdays in *Lent even before
midday. Until the recent rearrangement of the Offices, in
the W. Church the structure of Vespers resembled that of
Lauds, with five Psalms (in the Monastic Breviary, four),
with their antiphons, followed by a short lesson
(*capitulum*), hymn, the canticle *Magnificat, collect and
concluding versicles. On the ferias of Advent and Lent, on
certain Vigils and Ember Days the 'preces feriales' were
added after the Magnificat. In the 1971 Breviary a hymn
is followed by two Psalms, a NT canticle, a short lesson,
short responsory, Magnificat with antiphon, intercessions,
*Lord's Prayer, collect, and blessing. Acc. to the present
RC rite, all Sundays and solemn feasts have a first and
second Vespers; in the case of concurrence of the first and
second Vespers of two succeeding feasts, the celebration is
governed by the rules regulating the rank of the feasts.
Vespers is, together with Lauds, the most important Day
Office and is frequently celebrated with great solemnity,
culminating in the chanting of the Magnificat, during
which the celebrant censes the altar. The service of Evensong in the BCP was partly formed on the model of Vespers, with important additions from *Compline.

In the E. Church (following the Jewish custom) the day
is reckoned to begin at sunset, and Vespers ('Hesperinos')
is the first service of the liturgical day. The central point
is the singing of the *Phos Hilaron (after a procession with
incense [the 'Entrance'] on Sundays and feast days). It is
preceded by the singing of Psalms, litanies and *troparia,
and followed by Scriptural readings (on feast days and in
Lent), more litanies, prayers and troparia and the *Nunc
Dimittis. In Lent the latter part of the service is extended
and includes a prayer attributed to St *Ephraem Syrus,
said with prostrations. Incense is always used.

P. *Batiffol, *Histoire du bréviaire romain* (1893), esp. pp. 84–8
(3rd edn., 1911, pp. 108–14; Eng. tr., 1912, pp. 70–4). C.
Callewaert, *Sacris Erudiri* (1940), no. 5, 'Vesperae Antiquae in
Officio praesertim Romano', pp. 91–117. A. G. Martimort in id.
(ed.), *L'Église en Prière* (édition nouvelle), 4 [1983], esp. pp. 279–
83; Eng. tr. (1986), pp. 262–6. 'D. G. M.' [perh. Dom G. *Morin]
in *DACL* 15 (pt. 2; 1953), cols. 2939–49, s.v. 'Vêpres'; P. C.
Langeveld, OSB, and A. Hollaardt, OP, in *LW* 2 (1968), cols.
2798–808, s.v. See also works cited under OFFICE, DIVINE.

Vespers, the Sicilian. See SICILIAN VESPERS.

Vestiarian Controversy. The dispute concerning clerical dress begun under *Edward VI, which under
*Elizabeth I became one of the foundations of the *Puritan
party. Already discussed before the publication of the First
BCP of Edward VI (1549), the question of vestments
became acute when John *Hooper, on being nominated to
the bishopric of *Gloucester (1550), refused to be consecrated in the surplice and rochet prescribed in the *Ordinal.

Although he eventually agreed to wear the appropriate vestments on public occasions, considerable laxity seems to have existed for the rest of the reign.

The restoration of vestments in 1559, and esp. the vestments in the Chapel Royal, excited opposition. Acc. to the *Interpretations* of 1560/1, an order apparently issued by the bishops, a cope was to be worn in the celebration of Holy Communion and a surplice at other times. Strong opposition to any vestments was voiced in the Convocation of 1563. After the failure of M. *Parker's attempts in 1564 to reach a compromise with the most learned of the returned exiles, he issued his *Advertisements* (q.v.) in 1566 and required the use of a 'four-cornered cap, a scholar's gown priestly and in the church a linen surplice' and a cope in cathedral and collegiate churches. Thirty-seven of the London clergy who refused to promise compliance were deprived. Serious disturbances followed. Parker tried to enforce the *Advertisements* in other dioceses, but, with the bishops divided, laxity remained. Polemical literature and some bitterness continued throughout the reign.

The controversy was of purely ministerial origin, concerning a subject which one party regarded as indifferent and therefore fit for the legislation of the magistrate and the other a matter of real importance because of its connection with Popery. In the end most of the latter group, on the advice of the Continental reformers, acquiesced. Such opposition as remained was based less on the use of vestments as such than on the claim to freedom of conscience against the attempts of the bishops to enforce conformity, and before the end of the 16th cent. had become merged in the disputes about Church government.

J. H. Primus, *The Vestments Controversy* (Amsterdam diss., Kampen, 1960). W. P. Haugaard, *Elizabeth and the English Reformation: The Struggle for a Stable Settlement of Religion* (Cambridge, 1968), esp. pp. 182–232. See also Lives of PARKER, MATTHEW, cited s.v.

vestments. The distinctive dress worn by the clergy when performing the liturgical and other services of the Church. This dress did not, as formerly believed, derive from the vestments of the Aaronic priesthood, but originated in the ordinary secular costume of the world of antiquity in which the early Church grew up. During the first centuries a better kind of dress was probably set aside for the sacred functions, but the development of a specific priestly costume took place only between the 4th and 9th cents., one of the chief reasons being the abandonment of long tunics and cloaks by laymen and their continued use in the Church. By the 10th cent. the principal liturgical vestments and their use had been established in the W. From the 10th to the 13th cents. further minor additions and alterations were made. The *surplice was introduced as a substitute for the *alb on many occasions, the *chasuble came to be almost reserved to the celebration of Mass, and the *tunicle became the distinctive vestment of the *subdeacon. In the same period the bishops, owing to their enhanced importance in the medieval world, received additional vestments such as *sandals, *mitre, and *gloves. Since the 13th cent. the vestments have varied in form and material, the general tendency being towards reducing their size for the sake of convenience. The *Liturgical Movement, however, advocated a return to the 'Gothic' style, based on late medieval models. Sub-

sequently there has been a revival of the earlier more flowing and ample style, which is now generally used.

The precise shape and adornment of vestments are largely dependent on the artistic style and taste of the period. In the past the RC Church has regulated the material and colour in some detail, but much is now left to the judgement of local conferences of bishops. In the Middle Ages the several Eucharistic vestments were endowed with symbolic meaning, being variously interpreted as signifying the Passion of Christ or the priestly virtues. From the 9th cent. onwards they were regularly blessed. Until 1969 special prayers were provided for recitation while they were being put on.

The principal vestments of the E. Church are similar to those of the W., though tunicle, dalmatic, and some others are not represented, whereas there is no equivalent of *epigonation and *epimanikion in the W. For the use of vestments in the C of E, see COPE, EUCHARISTIC VESTMENTS, and ORNAMENTS RUBRIC.

J. Braun, SJ, *Die liturgische Gewandung im Occident und Orient nach Ursprung und Entwicklung, Verwendung und Symbolik* (1907). C. E. Pocknee, *Liturgical Vesture, Its Origins and Development* (1960). J. Mayo, *A History of Ecclesiastical Dress* (1984). F. E. *Brightman in *DECH*, pp. 611 f., s.v.; H. *Leclercq, OSB, in *DACL* 15 (pt. 2; 1953), cols. 2989–3007, s.v. 'Vêtement', with bibl.; G. Cope in J. G. Davies (ed.), *A New Dictionary of Liturgy and Worship* (1986), pp. 521–40, s.v.

vestry. A room in or attached to a church in which the vestments, vessels, and other requisites for Divine worship are kept and in which the clergy robe. From the fact that it was here that the parishioners formerly met to transact the business of the parish, the word came to be used both of the parochial body (which consisted of the incumbent or curate-in-charge, the persons rated for relief of the poor in the parish, whether resident or not, and the occupiers of the property so rated), and of the actual meeting. By the Local Government Act 1894 and subsequent legislation, vestries in the C of E lost all their powers except those concerned with the administration of the church and of ecclesiastical charities. In 1921 (as a result of the *Enabling Act) the administration of the church passed to the newly formed *Parochial Church Councils, though the 'meeting of the parishioners', which since 1964 has been charged with the responsibility for choosing *churchwardens jointly with the incumbent, is in substance a continuation of the former vestry meeting. In the *Episcopal Church of the USA every parish has a 'vestry', consisting of the incumbent, two wardens, and a number of 'vestrymen'. This vestry is responsible for the financial administration of the parish and exercises control over the appointment of the incumbent (subject to the bishop's approval).

Veuillot, Louis (1813–83), *Ultramontane French journalist. Born at Boynes in Loiret, of poor parents, he entered journalism in 1831. He was converted to a living Catholic faith at Rome in 1838, and in 1843 he became editor until his death of L'*Univers*, a newspaper at that time of little importance, which increased in authority and acquired an international significance through his defence of the Church. The violence of his views led to his imprisonment in 1844. From 1860 to 1867 *L'Univers* was suspended by the French Government, but Veuillot continued in books and pamphlets to advocate his views, esp. his dislike of attempts to reconcile religion with modern ideas and his belief in Papal infallibility. During the First *Vatican Council he was so closely in the confidence of the Pope that *L'Univers* became an almost official organ. During the siege of 1870 Veuillot elected to remain in Paris.

His brilliant and incisive style, together with his single-minded devotion to Catholicism, made him one of the foremost defenders of the Church in 19th-cent. France. In his original stand for the freedom of Catholic teaching he was supported by the majority of French Catholics, but from *c*.1844, when he defended the temporal sovereignty of the Papacy, and esp. when he advocated Papal infallibility, he was opposed not only by freethinkers but also by moderate Catholics such as F. *Dupanloup. His published works include *Le Parfum de Rome* (1861), *Les Satires* (1863), *Les Odeurs de Paris* (1866) and *Rome pendant le Concile* (2 vols., 1872), as well as 18 vols. of *Mélanges* (1842–75).

Collected edn. of his works by F. Veuillot, nephew (39 vols., Paris, 1924–38). The primary Life is that by E. Veuillot (brother), cont. by F. Veuillot (4 vols., Paris, 1899–1913). The numerous other studies incl. those of E. Tavernier, Veuillot's secretary and later ed. of *L'Univers* (Paris, 1913), E. Lecigne (ibid., 1913), G. Bontoux (ibid., 1914), M. M. McDevitt (ibid., 1935), F. Veuillot (ibid., 1937), M. L. Brown, Jun. (Durham, NC, 1977), and B. Le Roux (Paris, 1984). E. Gauthier, *Le Vrai Louis Veuillot* [1939]; id., *Le Génie satirique de Louis Veuillot* [1953]. P. Fernessole, *Les Origines littéraires de Louis Veuillot, 1813–43* (1923); id., *Bio-bibliographie de la jeunesse de Louis Veuillot, 1813–43* (2 parts of a thesis, 1923). W. Gurian, 'Louis Veuillot', *Catholic Historical Review*, 36 (1951), pp. 385–414. *Louis Veuillot et son temps: Colloque historique organisé à l'occasion du 100ᵉ anniversaire de sa mort* (Revue de l'Institut Catholique de Paris, 10; 1984). É. Tavernier in *CE* 15 (1912), pp. 394–6, s.v.; É. Amann in *DTC* 15 (pt. 2; 1950), cols. 2799–835, s.v.

Veuster, Joseph de. See DAMIEN, FATHER.

Vexilla Regis. The Latin hymn by *Venantius Fortunatus celebrating the mystery of Christ triumphant on the tree of the Cross. In the Roman Rite it is sung at *Vespers during *Holy Week and on the *Exaltation (14 Sept.) of the Holy Cross. The fine Eng. trans., 'The royal banners forward go', is due to J. M. *Neale.

Text, with notes and introd., in A. S. Walpole, *Early Latin Hymns* (1922), no. 34, pp. 173–7; text also in W. Bulst, *Hymni Latini Antiquissimi LXXV* (Heidelberg [1956]), p. 129. J. Szövérffy, *Die Annalen der lateinischen Hymnendichtung*, 1 (1964), pp. 135–7, with refs.; id., *Hymns of the Holy Cross* (Medieval Classics: Texts and Studies, 7; Brookline and Leiden, 1976), pp. 15–18.

Via Appia. See APPIAN WAY.

Via Dolorosa. The route in *Jerusalem which Christ is believed to have followed from the judgement-hall of *Pilate, where He received the sentence of death, to Mount *Calvary, the site of the Crucifixion. It is marked by 14 'Stations of the Cross', and it is the traditional custom for *Franciscans resident in Jerusalem to conduct devotions along it every Friday.

via media (Lat., 'the middle way'). A term in use esp. by J. H. *Newman and other *Tractarians for the *Anglican

system as a middle road between 'Popery' and 'Dissent'. This conception of Anglicanism is already found in English divines of the 17th cent., e.g. G. *Herbert and S. *Patrick.

Via Ostiensis. See OSTIAN WAY.

Vianney, St Jean-Baptiste Marie. See CURÉ D'ARS, THE.

Viaticum (Lat., 'provision for a journey'; Gk. ἐφόδιον). The Holy Communion given to those in likelihood of immediate death to strengthen them with grace for their journey into eternity. Acc. to W. usage it can be given at any time of the day and the ordinary regulation requiring fasting (until 1955, from the preceding midnight) is dispensed.

P. Browe, SJ, 'Die Sterbekommunion im Altertum und Mittelalter', *ZKT* 60 (1936), pp. 1–54 and 211–40. G. Grabka, OFM Conv., 'Christian Viaticum: A Study of its Cultural Background', *Traditio*, 9 (1953), pp. 1–43. R. Rutherford, *The Death of a Christian* (Studies in the Reformed Rites of the Catholic Church, 7; New York [1980]), esp. pp. 42 f. and 66. A. Bride in *DTC* 15 (pt. 2; 1950), cols. 2842–58, s.v.

vicar. In the C of E, every incumbent of a parish is now a rector or a vicar. Originally, all incumbents were *rectors, entitled to the tithes and other revenues of the parish without deduction. In medieval times, these profits were often *appropriated to other bodies, such as monasteries, who would then be compelled to appoint and endow a vicar (Lat. *vicarius*, 'a substitute') as their deputy for performance of the parochial duties. About one third of the *tithes were usually set apart for the vicar's maintenance (the 'vicarial' or 'small' tithes), the remainder ('rectorial' or 'great' tithes) being reserved for the monastery or other appropriator. In certain cases, the rector was permitted to put in a curate, who was not endowed and had no security, but at the *dissolution of the monasteries these curacies became *perpetual. They were given the title of vicar by the Incumbents Act 1868 and were converted into vicarages in law by the Pastoral Measure 1968 s. 87. As parish priest a vicar has exactly the same spiritual status as a rector, and the forms of *institution and *induction are identical, since in both cases he holds his full spiritual jurisdiction from the *bishop. Subject to the personal rights of the bishop and to the Extra-Parochial Ministry Measure 1967, he has the exclusive cure of souls and conduct of divine service in his parish, unless he is in a *team or group ministry.

Vicar Apostolic. The name given to a RC ecclesiastic who is entrusted with the pastoral care of certain people in an area, generally in missionary countries, which for special reasons has not yet been constituted into a *diocese. He governs in the name of the Pope, and is usually a titular bishop. The origins of the office go back to the 17th cent., but the 1983 *Codex Iuris Canonici* (can. 371) does not specify the legal position of the Vicar Apostolic in any detail. The RC community in England was ruled by Vicars Apostolic from 1623 until 1850. At present there are Vicars Apostolic in Kuwait, Tripoli, and Istanbul, for example.

B. Hemphill, OSB, *The Early Vicars Apostolic of England 1685–1750* (1954).

Vicar of Christ. A title of the Roman Pontiff dating from the 8th cent. From the 13th cent. it completely superseded the older title, 'Vicar of St *Peter'. It expresses his claim to universal jurisdiction in virtue of Christ's words to Peter, 'Feed my lambs. . . . Feed my sheep' (Jn. 21: 15 ff.). Down to the 9th cent. other bishops sometimes called themselves Vicars of Christ, though probably not as a formal title. For another four centuries kings and even judges were sometimes so described.

A. *Harnack, 'Christus Praesens—Vicarius Christi. Eine kirchengeschichtliche Skizze', *Sb.* (Berl.), 1927, pp. 415–46. M. Maccarrone, *Vicarius Christi: Storia del titolo papale* (Lateranum, NS 18; 1952), with refs.

Vicar General. An official whom a bishop deputes to represent him in the exercise of his jurisdiction. In early times his functions were mostly performed by the *archdeacons, but by the end of the 13th cent. the office had become well established and its duties were exactly defined in the *Sext of *Boniface VIII. No member of a *mendicant order was permitted to fill the office.

In the C of E the office is nowadays ordinarily committed to the *Chancellor of the Diocese, together with that of *Official Principal. In *Sodor and Man, however, it survives as a separate office. Each archbishop also has a Vicar General who holds a court for the confirmation of bishops which 'praeconizes' opposers to appear and produce evidence against the validity of the election or the qualifications of the elected candidate.

In the RC Church it is now obligatory for a bishop to appoint a Vicar General. For current legislation, see *CIC* (1983), cans. 475–81.

M. A. Campagna, *Il vicario generale del vescovo: Una sinossi storica e commento* (Catholic University of America, Canon Law Studies, 66; Washington, DC, 1931). E. Fournier, *Les Origines du vicaire général* (1922; also in id., *L'Origine du vicaire général et des autres membres de la Curie diocésaine*, 1940, pp. 283–400).

Vicelin, St (*c.*1090–1154), 'Apostle of Holstein'. A native of Hameln, he studied at the Paderborn cathedral school and from *c.*1123 to 1126 in Laon. He was ordained priest by St *Norbert in 1126 and in the same year was sent by Adalbero, Bp. of Bremen, as a missionary to the pagan Wagrians. From 1127 he worked in Holstein, and despite constant revolts of the Wend population founded the monasteries of *Augustinian Canons at Neumünster and Faldera and a great number of other churches. After the unfortunate Crusade of the Wends in 1147 had destroyed all his labours, he was consecrated Bp. of Oldenburg in 1149, but, declining to be *invested by Henry the Lion, Count of Saxony, was not recognized by him as bishop. The ensuing political dissensions darkened his last years; he became partly paralysed and lost the use of his tongue two years before his death. Feast day, 12 Dec.

The principal sources are Helmold of Bosau, *Chronica Slavorum*, capp. 42–79 (ed. B. Schmeidler, Scriptores Rerum Germanicarum, 1909, pp. 84–149; Eng. tr. by F. J. Tschan, Records of Civilization, 21, New York, 1935, pp. 140–208), and a metrical Life ascribed to Sidon of Neumünster and a letter of the same Sidon (pr. by B. Schmeidler, op. cit., pp. 219–45). R. Haupt, *Nachrichten über Wizelin den Apostel der Wagern und seine Kirchen-* bauten (3 vols., 1913–16). F. Hestermann, *Sankt Vizelin, Apostel der Holsten und Wagrier* (Dülmen i.W., 1926).

Vico, Giovanni Battista (1668–1744), Italian jurist and philosopher. The son of a Neapolitan bookseller, he was educated in a *Jesuit school and at Naples University, where he became Professor of Rhetoric in 1697. In 1734 he was appointed historiographer to Charles III. He died after a period of mental disturbance.

Vico's chief work was his *Principii di una scienza nuova d'intorno alla natura comune delle nazioni* (1725; 2nd edn., enlarged, 1730; 3rd edn., further enlarged, 1744). The treatise (commonly known as the *Scienza nuova*) was the first attempt in modern times to expound a philosophy of history. Vico responded to R. *Descartes's attack on the value of historical study by drawing a distinction between the aims and methods of natural science and those of history; the realm of nature, he argued, being a divine and not a human creation, is largely obscure to human beings, whereas history, which describes the behaviour of human beings, is a human creation and therefore open to human understanding: 'the world of civil society has certainly been made by men, and its principles are therefore to be found in the modifications of our human mind'. In his understanding of the past, Vico distinguished three ages: that of the gods, of heroes, and of men. In the age of gods men interpreted the world around them in terms of divine beings; the heroic age was a 'barbarous' age in which might was right; the age of men is the period of civil society. Each age has its good and bad points; their succession is not progress, and regression (*ricorso*) is observable (e.g. the Middle Ages was a return to the heroic age). Language and the nature of ritual and myth are keys to the understanding of society; esp. through the use of metaphor, they reveal its values. Vico also resisted the tendency among his contemporaries to explain similarities between geographically remote areas in terms of influence or diffusion.

Vico's immensely suggestive ideas have appealed to many later thinkers. The great French historian J. Michelet (1798–1874) claimed him as the inspiration for his romantic understanding of history with its emphasis on the character of peoples; B. *Croce found warrant in Vico for his cultural relativism; more recently Vico's support has been sought for the notion of social science, as well as for the impossibility of such a study.

Standard edn. of his works by G. *Gentile, F. Nicolini, and B. Croce (Scrittori d'Italia, 11, 67, 112, 113, 135, 160–2, 168, 174, and 183; Bari, 1914–41). *Opere Filosofiche*, also ed. P. Cristofolini (Florence [1971]). Eng. tr. of *Selected Writings*, ed. and tr. by L. Pompa (Cambridge, 1982); also of his autobiog. by M. H. Fisch and T. G. Bergin (Ithaca, NY, 1944), and of *Scienza nuova* by idd. (ibid., 1948; rev. edn., 1968). R. Flint, *Vico* (Blackwood's Philosophical Classics, 9; 1884). B. Croce, *La filosofia di Giambattista Vico* (Saggi Filosofici, 2; Bari, 1911; Eng. tr. by R. G. Collingwood, 1913). H. P. Adams, *The Life and Writings of Giambattista Vico* (1935). I. Berlin, *Vico and Herder* (1976), pp. 1–142. G. Tagliacozzo and D. P. Vereme (eds.), *Giambattista Vico's Science of Humanity* (Baltimore and London [1976]). B. A. Haddock, *Vico's Political Thought* (Swansea, 1986). J. Milbank, *The Religious Dimension in the Thought of Giambattista Vico 1668–1774* (Studies in the History of Philosophy, 23 and 32; Lewiston, NY, etc. [1991–2]). J. Mali, *The Rehabilitation of Myth: Vico's 'New Science'* (Cambridge, 1992). Introd. by [U.] P. Burke, *Vico* (Past Masters, Oxford, 1985). B. Croce, *Bibliografia vichiana*, ed. F. Nicolini (2 vols., Naples, 1947–8); M. Donzelli, *Contributo alla* *bibliografia vichiana (1948–70)* (Studi vichiani, 9; 1973); A. Battistini, *Nuovo contributo alla bibliografia vichiana (1971–80)* (ibid. 14; 1983). G. Tagliacozzo and others, *A Bibliography of Vico in English 1884–1984* (Bowling Green, Oh. [1986]). P. Gardiner in P. Edwards (ed.), *Encyclopedia of Philosophy*, 8 (1967), pp. 247–51, s.v.

Victimae Paschali (Lat., 'To the Paschal Victim'). The Easter *Sequence in the W. Church. It is a short, dramatic hymn celebrating Christ's triumphant conquest of death, and was composed by *Wipo (d. after 1046).

Crit. edn. of text in C. Blume, SJ (ed.), *Sequentiae Ineditae: Liturgische Prosen des Mittelalters*, 4 (AHMA 34; 1900), no. 23, pp. 27 f. J. Szövérffy, *Die Annalen der lateinischen Hymnendichtung*, 1 (1964), pp. 372–4, with refs.

Victor I, St (d. 198), Pope from 189. Acc. to the '*Liber Pontificalis' he was an African by birth. His name is chiefly connected with the *Quartodeciman controversy, for the settlement of which he ordered synods to be held throughout Christendom. He himself assembled a Council at *Rome and threatened *Polycrates of Ephesus and other bishops of Asia Minor with excommunication if they refused to give up their practice of keeping *Easter on 14 Nisan instead of the following Sunday. When he actually carried out his threat, St *Irenaeus and other bishops blamed his severity, but the fact that the Churches in Asia Minor remained in communion with Rome would suggest that the Pope took back his sentence. The whole incident is an important step in the history of the Papal supremacy. Among other incidents of Victor's pontificate were the deposition of the presbyter Florinus for defending *Valentinian doctrines and the excommunication of the leather merchant, *Theodotus, the founder of Dynamic *Monarchianism. Acc. to St *Jerome, Victor was the first Latin ecclesiastical writer, but it seems that he wrote nothing but his encyclicals, which would naturally have been issued in both Latin and Greek. Though venerated as a martyr in the Liturgy, there is no other evidence that he died by violence. Feast day, 28 July; suppressed in 1969.

Jaffé, 1, pp. 11 f. The principal authorities are *LP* (ed. Duchesne), 1 (1886), pp. 137 f., and *Eusebius, *HE* 5. 23 f. E. Caspar, *Geschichte des Papsttums von den Anfängen bis zur Höhe der Weltherrschaft*, 1 (1930), esp. 19–22. H. von Campenhausen, 'Ostertermin oder Osterfasten? Zum Verständnis des Irenäusbriefs an Viktor', *VC* 28 (1974) pp. 114–38, with bibl. Fliche and Martin, 2 (1935), pp. 90–3, with bibl. p. 87. É. Amann in *DTC* 15 (pt. 2; 1950), cols. 2862 f., s.v. See also bibl. to PASCHAL CONTROVERSIES and QUARTODECIMANISM.

Victor (5th cent.), presbyter of *Antioch. His name is attached to what has been described as a Gk. commentary on Mk., but is really a compilation from earlier exegetical writings (*Origen, *Titus of Bostra, *Theodore of Mopsuestia, *Chrysostom, *Cyril of Alexandria) on Mt., Lk., and Jn. *Catena fragments on other biblical Books, notably on Jer., are also ascribed to him.

No crit., or even complete, text exists. Older edns. of the commentary on Mk. by P. Possinus, SJ (Rome, 1673), C. F. Matthaei (Moscow, 1775), and J. A. *Cramer, *Catenae in Evangelia S. Matthaei et S. Marci* (Oxford, 1840), pp. 259–447. Modern discussion of problems in J. Reuss, *Matthäus-, Markus- und Johannes-Katenen nach den handschriftlichen Quellen untersucht* (Neutestamentliche Abhandlungen, 18, Hefte 4–5; 1941), pp. 118–41. H. Smith, 'The Sources of Victor of Antioch's Comment-

ary on Mark', *JTS* 19 (1918), pp. 350–70. *CPG* 3 (1979), pp. 255 f. (nos. 6529–34). G. Bardy in *DTC* 15 (pt. 2; 1950), cols. 2872–4, s.v.

Victor, St (d. 554), Bp. of Capua from 541. He was the author of many writings, including a treatise on Noah's ark ('Reticulus') and a Paschal cycle; but his most celebrated work is a Harmony of the Gospels, made on the basis of the *Vulgate text, preserved in the so-called *Codex Fuldensis (q.v.). Feast day, 17 Oct.

Apart from the 'Codex Fuldensis', Victor's writings survive only in frags. Texts collected by J. B. *Pitra from 'De Reticulo seu de Arca Noe' in *Spicilegium Solesmense*, 1 (1852), pp. 287–9; from 'De Cyclo Paschali', ibid., pp. 296–301; from 'De Resurrectione Domini', ibid., p. liv. *CPL* (3rd edn., 1995), p. 308 f. (nos. 953a–956). G. Bardy in *DTC* 15 (pt. 2; 1950), cols. 2874–6; V. Loi in *DPAC* 2 (1984), cols. 3606 f.; Eng. tr., *Encyclopedia of the Early Church*, 2 (1992), p. 868. See also bibl. to CODEX FULDENSIS.

Victor (late 5th cent.), 'Vitensis', Bp. of Vita in N. Africa. He wrote 'Historia Persecutionis Africanae Provinciae', a history of the persecution of the Catholic Church in Africa by the Arian Vandals under Gaiseric and Huneric (429–84). Its 2nd and 3rd books, based on contemporary material and the author's own experiences, are of special value as giving not only a trustworthy account of the historical events, but also a vivid picture of the political and religious civilization of the country. The work, which was written *c*.488 in exile, contains several official documents, and appended to it is a 'Notitia Africae' for 484, i.e. a list of the Catholic bishops of the African Vandal Empire. The 'Passio Septem Monachorum', added to the history in some older editions, is not by Victor but belongs to a later period.

Editio princeps of his 'Historia' by Jehan Petit, Paris, *c*.1510. Later edn. by T. *Ruinart, OSB, ibid., 1694, repr., with dissertations by J. *Sirmond, SJ, and others, in J. P. Migne, *PL* 58. 125–434. Crit. edns. by C. Halm in *MGH*, Auctores Antiquissimi, 3 (pt. 1; 1879), and M. Petschenig in CSEL 7, 1881. C. Courtois, *Victor de Vita et son œuvre* (Algiers, 1954). H.-J. Diesner, 'Sklaven und Verbannte, Märtyrer und Confessoren bei Victor Vitensis', *Philologus*, 106 (1962), pp. 101–120. S. Costanza, 'Vittore di Vita e la *Historia persecutionis Africanae provinciae*', *Vetera Christianorum*, 17 (1980), pp. 229–68. L. *Duchesne, *Histoire ancienne de l'Église*, 3 (1910), pp. 625–45; Eng. tr. (1924), pp. 430–41. Bardenhewer, 4, pp. 550–2. S. Costanza in *DPAC* 2 (1984), cols. 3609–12, s.v. 'Vittore di Vita'; Eng. tr., *Encyclopedia of the Early Church*, 2 (1992), pp. 868 f., with bibl.

Victoria, Tomás Luis de (1548–1611), Spanish composer. A native of Ávila, he studied in Rome at the Collegio Germanico, of which he became 'maestro di cappella' in 1573. Ordained priest in 1575, he joined St *Philip Neri's *Oratorians before returning to Spain by 1587 to become chaplain to the Dowager Empress Maria (sister of *Philip II), and 'maestro' of the choir of the Madrid convent where she lived. Here he remained until his death, serving in the less demanding role of organist from 1604. His compositions, which were mostly printed in his lifetime, consist entirely of sacred music. Imbued with a strong mystical Iberian feeling, they rank among the greatest music of the Renaissance. His best-known works include a six-part Requiem, and music for *Holy Week, including the motet 'O vos omnes'.

Complete works ed. F. Pedrell (8 vols., Leipzig, 1902–13); rev. edn. by H. Anglés (Monumentos de la música española, 25, 26, 30, 31, etc.; Rome, 1965 ff.). F. Pedrell, *Tomás Luis de Victoria Abulense* (Valencia, 1918). R. [M.] Stevenson, *Spanish Cathedral Music in the Golden Age* (Berkeley and Los Angeles, Calif., 1961), pp. 345–464. Id. in S. Sadie (ed.), *The New Grove Dictionary of Music and Musicians*, 19 (1980), pp. 703–9.

Victorines. The *canons regular of the former abbey dedicated to St *Victor at *Paris. The house was founded by *William of Champeaux (the most famous scholar of his day and teacher of *Abelard) and built in 1113 at the cost of King Louis VI. The 'customs' of the house, which were drawn up under the influence of St *Bernard, acquired considerable prestige. But though the Victorines enjoyed great respect, they never became large in numbers. Many famous scholars, mystics, and poets were found in their ranks, esp. during the 12th cent., among them *Adam of St-Victor, *Hugh of St-Victor, *Richard of St-Victor, and *Walter of St-Victor (qq.v.). The abbey was secularized at the outbreak of the French Revolution.

Liber Ordinis Sancti Victoris Parisiensis, ed. L. Jocqué and L. Milis (CCCM 61; 1984). F. Bonnard, *Histoire de l'abbaye royale et de l'ordre des chanoines réguliers de Saint-Victor de Paris* (2 vols. [1904–8]). J. Chatillon, 'De Guillaume de Champeaux à Thomas Gallus. Chronique d'histoire littéraire et doctrinale de l'école de Saint-Victor', *Revue du moyen âge latin*, 8 (1952), pp. 139–62 and 249–72. J. Longère (ed.), *L'Abbaye Parisienne de Saint-Victor au Moyen Âge: Communications présentées au XIIIᵉ Colloque d'Humanisme médiéval de Paris (1986–1988)* (Bibliotheca Victorina, 1; 1991).

Victorinus, St (d. *c*.304), Bp. of Pettau (Poetovio) in Pannonia. Acc. to St *Jerome he was martyred, probably under *Diocletian. Victorinus is the earliest known exegete of the Latin Church, but nearly all his works are lost, probably on account of his *millenarianist tendencies, which caused them to be condemned as apocryphal by the '*Decretum Gelasianum'. He followed *Origen and other Greek commentators, but Jerome finds fault with both his style and his erudition. Of his many commentaries only that on Rev. survives. It has come down in a 15th-cent. *Vatican MS (Ottob. lat. 3288 A) and in a working-over of it by Jerome. The treatise 'De Fabrica Mundi', though not, as formerly believed, part of his commentary on Gen., is almost certainly also to be assigned to him. The attribution of the Pseudo-Tertullianic 'Adversus omnes haereses' (*De Praescr.* 46–53), to Victorinus (A. *Harnack) is improbable. Acc. to E. *Schwartz, however, Victorinus translated it from a Greek original. Feast day, 2 Nov.

Crit. edns. by J. Haussleiter (CSEL 49; 1916) and M. Dulaey (SC 423; 1997), with Fr. tr. Older texts, with prolegomena, partly repr. in J. P. Migne, *PL* 5. 281–344. M. Dulaey, *Victorin de Poetovio, premier exégète latin* (2 vols., Études Augustiniennes, 1993). E. Schwartz, *Zwei Predigten Hippolyts* (*Sb.* (Bayr.), 1936, Heft 3), p. 43. Bardenhewer, 2, pp. 657–63; Altaner and Stuiber (1966), pp. 182 f. *CPL* (3rd edn., 1995), pp. 22 f. (nos. 79–83). J. Haussleiter in *PRE* (3rd edn.), 20 (1908), pp. 614–19; G. Bardy in *DTC* 15 (pt. 1; 1950), cols. 2882–7; C. Curti in *DPAC* 2 (1984), cols. 3612–5, s.v. 'Vittorino di Petovio'; Eng. tr. in *Encyclopedia of the Early Church*, 2 (1992), p. 867, s.v., with bibl.

Victorinus Afer, Caius (or **Fabius**) **Marius** (4th cent.), rhetor and theologian. A native of Africa, he taught in Rome, where he gained a great reputation. About the middle of the century he became a Christian, resigned his rhetorship under *Julian in 362 (an event which excited much comment, and contributed towards determining *Augustine to follow his example in 386), and wrote theological works against the *Arians. The notorious obscurity of his manner of writing is very largely due to the fact that he was translating difficult philosophical Greek into Latin in an attempt to make use of a form of 4th-cent. *Neoplatonic metaphysics to elucidate and defend the Nicene doctrine of the Trinity. Modern research has shown that it is probable that he was closely following *Porphyry's development of the thought of *Plotinus in a direction very different from that taken by later Neoplatonists. The result is a philosophical theology of great power, though restricted in its influence because of the difficulty of the language and thought. Both in method and in conclusions he occasionally anticipates Augustinian positions, e.g. in his treatment of the Pauline doctrine of *justification.

In his pagan period Victorinus commented extensively on Cicero; translated some writings of *Aristotle and the 'Isagoge' of Porphyry, and prob. also part of Plotinus' 'Enneads'; and wrote some original philosophical works. His surviving Christian writings consist of what are collectively known as his works on the Trinity, namely a letter to Candidus, an Arian (*De Generatione Verbi Divini*), four books *Adversus Arium* (also addressed to Candidus), to which are appended a short treatise *De Homoousio recipiendo* and three hymns on the Trinity; and comm. on Eph., Gal., and Phil.

Apart from the collected edn. in J. P. Migne, *PL* 8. 993–1310, which is a compilation from earlier edns. of particular works by J. *Sirmond, SJ, J. *Mabillon, OSB, A. *Mai, and others, the first complete edn. is that projected in CSEL, of which two vols. have so far appeared (*Opera Theologica*, i.e. the writings on the Trinity, ed. P. Henry, SJ, and P. Hadot, CSEL 83/1; 1971, and *Opera Exegetica*, i.e. the comm. on Eph., Gal., and Phil., ed. F. Gori, ibid. 83/2; 1986). An earlier edn. of the treatises on the Trinity, ed. P. Henry, SJ, with introd., notes, and Fr. tr. by P. Hadot (SC 68–9; 1960). Eng. tr. by M. T. Clark, RSCJ (Fathers of the Church, 69; Washington DC, 1981). *Ars grammatica*, ed., with Italian tr., by I. Mariotti (Florence, 1967). E. Benz, *Marius Victorinus und die Entwicklung der abendländischen Willensmetaphysik* (1934). P. Hadot, *Marius Victorinus: Recherches sur sa vie et ses œuvres* (1971). Id., *Porphyre et Victorinus* (2 vols. [1968]). A. Ziegenaus, *Die trinitarische Ausprägung der göttlichen Seinsfülle nach Marius Victorinus* (Münchener Theologische Studien, Abteilung II, Bd. 41; 1972). A. *Souter, *The Earliest Commentaries on the Epistles of St Paul* (1927), pp. 8–38. W. Erdt, *Marius Victorinus Afer, der erste lateinische Pauluskommentator* (Europäische Hochschulschriften, Reihe 23, Bd. 135; 1980). P. Monceaux, *Histoire littéraire de l'Afrique chrétienne*, 3 (1905), pp. 373–422. Altaner and Stuiber (1978 edn.), pp. 368 f. and 626. C. *Gore in *DCB* 4 (1887), pp. 1129–38, s.v. 'Victorinus (6)'; P. Séjourné, OSB, in *DTC* 15 (pt. 2; 1950), cols. 2887–954, s.v.

Victorius, Claudius Marius (d. 425/30), rhetor. A native of Marseilles, he wrote, in three books of hexameters, the poem *Alethia*, a paraphrastic commentary on Gen. from the Creation to the fall of *Sodom. It owes much to St *Ambrose's *Hexaemeron*.

Crit. edns. of *Alethia* by C. Schenkl (CSEL 16, 1888, pp. 335–498) and by P. F. Hovingh (CCSL 128, 1960, pp. 115–93). H. H. Homey, *Studien zur Alethia des Claudius Marius Victorius* (Diss., Bonn, 1972). Altaner and Stuiber (1978 edn.), pp. 411 f., and 636.

Victricius, St (*c*.330–*c*.407), Bp. of Rouen from *c*.386. As a young man he entered the army. Becoming a Christian not long afterwards, he renounced the military profession as incompatible with his new faith and, acc. to St *Paulinus of Nola, narrowly escaped execution on a charge of desertion. He is next heard of as Bp. of Rouen, where he became a zealous defender of the faith against pagans and heretics, and undertook mission work as far afield as Flanders, Hainault, and Brabant. About 396 he was called to Britain to settle some ecclesiastical dispute. He also visited Rome. He was the recipient of a celebrated decretal ('Liber Regularum') on disciplinary matters sent by Pope *Innocent I in 404. His 'De Laude Sanctorum' (based on a sermon) provides valuable evidence concerning the cult of relics and other aspects of contemporary religious life. He was a close friend of Paulinus of Nola and an admirer of St *Martin of Tours. Feast day, 7 Aug.

The *Liber de Laude Sanctorum* is pr. in J. P. Migne, *PL* 20. 443–58; crit. edn. by J. Mulders, SJ, and R. Demeulenaere in CCSL 64 (1985), pp. 53–93, with bibl. on p. 64 f. Text also pr., with Fr. tr., in R. Herval, *Origines Chrétiennes* [1966], pp. 108–53. The principal source for his life is the two letters by Paulinus of Nola, *Epistolae*, 18 (ed. W. Hartel, CSEL 29, 1894, pp. 128–37) and 37 (ibid., pp. 316–23). The letter from Innocent to Victricius is repr. in J. P. Migne, *PL* 20. 469–81. Study by J. Mulders, SJ (Rome diss., Nijmegen, 1956). P. Andrieu-Guitrancourt, 'Essai sur saint Victrice, l'Église et la province ecclésiastique de Rouen aux derniers temps gallo-romains', *Année Canonique*, 14 (1970), pp. 1–23; C. Pietri, *Roma Christiana: Recherches sur l'Église de Rome . . . (311–440)* (Bibliothèque des Écoles françaises d'Athènes et de Rome, 244; 2 vols., 1976), 2, pp. 982–91. J. Fontaine, 'Victrice de Rouen et les origines du monachisme dans l'Ouest de la Gaule (IVᵉ–VIᵉ siècles)', in L. Musset (ed.), *Aspects du Monachisme en Normandie (IVᵉ–XVIIIᵉ siècles): Actes du Colloque Scientifique de l''Année des Abbayes Normandes', Caen, 18–20 octobre 1979* (Bibliothèque de la Société d'Histoire ecclésiastique de la France, 1982), pp. 9–29. S. Prete in *Bibliotheca Sanctorum*, 12 (Rome, 1969), cols. 1310–15, s.v. 'Vittricio'.

Vidi Aquam (Lat., 'I beheld water'). In the W. Church, the anthem traditionally sung in Eastertide during the sprinkling of the congregation at Mass on Sundays, in place of the *Asperges sung during the rest of the year. Both anthems may now be replaced by other suitable chants. The words of the 'Vidi aquam' are based on a combination of verses from Ezek. 47.

L. Eisenhofer, *Handbuch der katholischen Liturgik*, 1 (1932), pp. 479 f.

Vieira, António (1608–97), Portuguese theologian. Of humble origins, Vieira was born in Lisbon, but when he was 6 his family moved to Bahia in Brazil. Here he was educated by the *Jesuits and entered the Society of Jesus in 1623. From an early age he was drawn towards missionary work, but in 1641 he was sent back to Lisbon. His preaching gained him considerable influence at court and King John IV appointed him preacher of the royal chapel in 1644 and sent him on a number of (not altogether successful) diplomatic missions. On Vieira's advice the King organized a chartered company (incorporated in 1649) for the Brazilian trade, financed by Jewish capital; the capital invested was to be exempted from confiscation by the *Inquisition.

In 1652 Vieira was sent by the Jesuits to refound the missions to the Maranhão and Grão Pará which had lapsed on the death of the last missionaries in 1649. His most notable achievement in this field was the conversion of the Nheengaíbas on the island of Marajó. His persistent efforts to uphold the freedom of the Amerindians against the attempts of the colonists to exploit them created difficulties, especially after the death of John IV in 1656, and in 1661 he was compelled to return to Portugal. After a palace revolution he was arraigned before the Inquisition on account of a work in which he prophesied the resurrection of John IV; he was imprisoned for two years and suffered much humiliation. In 1669 he went to Rome to plead his own cause and on behalf of the Jews converted to Christianity (the 'New Christians' as they were called). In Rome his preaching won him fame, and he was later invited by Queen *Christina of Sweden to be her confessor. The Pope imposed a seven-year ban on Inquisitorial trials and *autos de fe in Portugal (1674) and Vieira returned to Portugal with a brief (1675) exempting him from the jurisdiction of the Portuguese Inquisition. In 1681 he sailed for Bahia, where he spent the rest of his life. From 1688 to 1691 he was Visitor-General of the Brazil and Maranhão missions, and he continued to espouse the cause of the Amerindians.

Vieira's sermons are masterpieces of Baroque pulpit oratory, famous in their time and since for their brilliant flights of imagination and compelling style. Vieira was a man of considerable political acumen, but was also strongly influenced by Messianic and *chiliastic beliefs. In both his sacred and his secular writings there appears his conviction that the Catholic Church, through the agency of Portugal, would soon prevail throughout the world and prepare the way for the Second Coming.

Sermões pub. in 16 vols., Lisbon, 1679–1748; *Obras escolhidas*, ed. A. Sérgio and H. Cidade (12 vols., ibid., 1951–4); *Cartas* ed. J. L. de Azevedo (3 vols., Coimbra, 1925–8); *História do Futuro*, ed. M. L. Carvalhão Buescu (Lisbon, 1982); crit. edn. of his *Sermão pelo bom sucesso das armas de Portugal contra as de Holanda* (preached in 1640), by F. Smulders (Nijmegen diss., Middleburg, 1989), with introd. (in Eng.) and extensive bibl. R. Cantel, *Prophétisme et messianisme dans l'œuvre d'António Vieira* (Paris, 1960); J. [J.] van den Besselaar, *António Vieira: o homem, a obra, as ideias* (Biblioteca Breve, 58; Amadora, 1981); M. Vieira Mendes, *A oratória barroca de Vieira* (Lisbon, 1989); S. Leite, SJ, *História da Companhia de Jesus no Brasil*, 9 (Rio de Janeiro, 1949), pp. 192–363. In Eng. there is a lecture by C. R. Boxer (London, 1957). Further bibl. in Polgár, 3 (1990), pp. 620–36.

Vienne, Council of (1311–12). Accounted in the RC Church as the Fifteenth *Oecumenical Council, it was summoned by *Clement V in 1308 primarily to deal with the question of the *Templars, who were being accused of heresy and immorality by those who coveted their wealth. The Council, which eventually met at Vienne on 16 Oct. 1311, also aimed at providing assistance for the Holy Land and reforming the Church. The majority of the Council at first held that the evidence against the Templars was insufficient. But owing to the transference of the Papacy to *Avignon the Council was under French dominance; and, when Philip IV of France appeared with an army before Vienne in Feb. 1312, the Pope by an administrative ordinance suppressed the Order in the bull 'Vox Clamantis' (22 Mar. 1312), and this was promulgated at the next session of the Council. The King then undertook to go on a Crusade within six years. On the question of *Franciscan poverty the Council decided in favour of the more austere party. It also issued a large number of miscellaneous decrees, relating *inter alia* to the *Beguines and the *Inquisition, which were later partly incorporated in the '*Clementines' by *John XXII. Another decree sought to further the missionary objects fostered by R. *Llull by providing for *studia* in oriental languages (Arabic, Chaldee, and Hebrew, and prob. also Greek) to be set up in five universities (*Paris, *Oxford, Salamanca, *Bologna, and the Roman Court). In the event Philip IV never went on the Crusade, but appropriated to his own use the tithe levied for the purpose, and also managed to obtain much of the property of the Templars.

Hardouin, 7, cols. 1321–62; Mansi, 25 (Venice, 1782), cols. 367–426. Relevant bulls and constitutions, with Eng. tr. and introd., in Tanner, *Decrees* (1990), pp. 333–401. F. Ehrle, SJ, 'Zur Vorgeschichte des Concils von Vienne', *Archiv für Litteratur- und Kirchengeschichte des Mittelalters*, 2 (1886), pp. 353–416 and 672, and 3 (1887), pp. 1–195. Id., 'Ein Bruchstück der Acten des Concils von Vienne', ibid. 4 (1888), pp. 361–470. Hefele and Leclercq, 6 (pt. 2; 1915), pp. 643–719, with bibl. to date. E. Müller, *Das Konzil von Vienne, 1311–1312: Seine Quellen und seine Geschichte* (Vorreformationsgeschichtliche Forschungen, 12; 1934), with further refs. J. Lecler, SJ, *Vienne* (Histoire des conciles œcuméniques, 8; 1964). J. Leclercq, OSB, in *DTC* 15 (pt. 2; 1950), cols. 2973–9, s.v. See also works cited under TEMPLARS.

Vietnam, Christianity in.

Vietnam comprises those portions of the Indo-Chinese peninsula formerly known as Cochin China, Annam, and Tonkin; the predominant religion is Mahayana Buddhism. Christianity was first preached by Spanish *Franciscans from the *Philippines and Portuguese *Dominicans in the 1580s or perhaps as early as the 1530s. The mission of Cochin China was founded in 1615 by *Jesuits, who had been driven out of *Japan by persecution. An influential figure among the early missionaries was Alexander de Rhodes (1591–1660), a French Jesuit and outstanding linguist who achieved the feat of writing Vietnamese phonetically in the Latin alphabet supplemented by five signs (the quốc ngũ)—a legacy adopted by the whole nation ever since. He sought to create a Church adapted to Vietnamese culture and made extensive use of celibate lay *catechists who lived in community. After his expulsion from Cochin China in 1645, Rhodes returned to France and assisted in the foundation of the 'Société des Missions Étrangères de Paris' (c.1660). In 1658 the Congregation of *Propaganda Fidei created two apostolic *vicariates, one for the north and one for the south. The first Vietnamese priests were ordained in 1668, and an indigenous religious order of women was formed in 1690. By the end of the 18th cent. the Christian community numbered 300,000. Throughout this period Christians suffered waves of severe persecution, which continued until in the 1860s the King of Annam granted partial toleration; the number of martyrs has been estimated at 130,000. In the face of this persecution, in the 1780s, Pierre Pigneau de Béhaine (1741–99), a member of the Société des Missions Étrangères de Paris and Vicar Apostolic of West Tonkin, encouraged French political intervention in the region. During the 19th cent. French influence increased and in 1884 Cochin China became a French colony. By 1912 RCs (mainly in the north, in the Hanoi delta region) comprised over 5 per cent of the total population of Vietnam. The number of Vietnamese clergy grew rapidly and the first Vietnamese bishop was appointed in 1933. Protestant missionary work was begun by the Christian and Missionary Alliance in 1911. The Evangelical Church of Vietnam was formed in 1927.

During the colonial war against the French (1945–54) the great majority of RCs were opposed to the nationalist movement because of its association with Communists. After the defeat of the French in 1954 the country was divided along the 17th degree of latitude: the (Communist) Democratic Republic of Vietnam in the north and the Republic of Vietnam, supported by the USA, in the south. A large migration of RCs from north to south followed, led by their bishops. In South Vietnam, under the rule of Presidents Ngo Dinh Diem and Nguyen Van Thieu, the RC Church prospered and held an influential position as a bulwark of anti-Communism. After the collapse of the Thieu government in 1975 and the withdrawal of United States forces, foreign missionaries were expelled. Since 1975 in the Communist state of Vietnam the public activities of the RC Church have been severely restricted. Christians, who numbered 3.6 million in 1980, comprise 7 per cent of the population; more than 90 per cent of them are RCs.

A. Launay, *Histoire de la Mission de Cochinchine, 1658–1823: Documents historiques* (3 vols., Paris, 1923–5); id., *Histoire de la Mission du Tonkin: Documents historiques*, 1: *1658–1717* (ibid., 1927; no more pub.). N. H. Lai, 'Vietnam', in A. Hastings (ed.), *The Church and the Nations* (1959), pp. 171–92. B. E. Colless, 'The Traders of the Pearl. The Mercantile and Missionary Activities of Persian and Armenian Christians in South-East Asia', 4: 'The Indochina Peninsula', *Abr-Nahrain*, 13 (for 1972–3; Leiden, 1972), pp. 115–35; see also vol. 18 (for 1978–9; 1980), pp. 13 f. E. F. Irwin, *With Christ in Indo-China: The Story of Alliance Missions in French Indo-China and Eastern Siam* (Harrisburg, Pa. [1937]), pp. 25–108; H. E. Dowdy, *The Bamboo Cross: Christian Witness in the Jungles of Viet Nam* (New York [1964]; London, 1965). R. De Roeck in G. H. Anderson (ed.), *Christ and Crisis in Southeast Asia* (New York [1968]), pp. 55–71. A. Gélinas in *NCE* 14 (1967), pp. 661–3.

Vigil

Vigil (Lat. *vigilia*, 'wakefulness', 'watchfulness', 'watch'), a service held at night (i.e. later at night, overnight, or before dawn), and by extension used of the day before a festival. Acc. to *Philo, the *Essenes spent a third of the night in prayer and reading, but nocturnal prayer formed no part of regular Jewish worship. Among Christians there was a widespread belief that the *Parousia would take place at midnight, and this may be reflected in the accounts of prayer at night in Acts 12: 12 and 16: 25. The letter of *Pliny to Trajan (c.111–23) provides clear evidence of Christians gathering for worship before daybreak, though here the practice may have been dictated by the fact that Sunday was a working day. In his sermon 'On the Pasch' *Melito of Sardis (c.160–70) speaks of *Easter as a Christian *Passover, still clearly celebrated at night. From an early date, the *Paschal Vigil Service (q.v.) comprised a lengthy series of readings and culminated in a Eucharist at dawn. By the early 3rd cent. it was seen as the most appropriate occasion for Baptism, and when in the 4th cent. Baptism was administered at *Whitsun, a similar Vigil emerged. By this time there is also evidence of regular weekly Vigils, on Saturday night to Sunday morning or perhaps from early on Sunday morning; such Vigils, recorded by *Egeria, were popular services of prayer which reached their climax in the reading of the Gospel account of the Resurrection. The opening of this so-called 'Cathedral Vigil' is connected with the custom of greeting the evening light or lamp with a hymn and/or prayer, from which, in the W., the tradition of the *Paschal Candle appears to have developed. From the 4th cent. Vigils on other occasions became popular, esp. on the feasts of local martyrs or Apostles. St *Augustine is a witness to such practices in N. Africa. Some night services were marred by unseemly behaviour and from the Synod of *Elvira (c.306) conciliar legislation increasingly restricted the participation of women at the Vigils. Their popularity continued. In some places, e.g. at *Constantinople, the Vigil took the form of an extension to *Vespers; elsewhere it sometimes, by a long series of readings, extended the morning office backwards into the early hours.

From the 8th cent. it became common to anticipate the Vigil on the evening of the previous day, and then the Vigil was gradually put back to the morning of that day. Thus the Paschal Vigil came to be celebrated on the morning of *Holy Saturday until, in the W. Church, it was restored to its position as a night service in 1951. By a similar process, in the Middle Ages many feasts had a Vigil, which came to be little more than a special Mass on the previous day, a relic of the time when the day was marked by a fast broken only by Communion in the evening. The BCP allotted fasts for the eves or vigils of 16 feast days, but modern Anglican liturgies mention few vigils apart from those of *Christmas and Easter. The RC *Calendar of 1969 retained only the Easter Vigil, but special texts are provided for an evening Mass on the days before Christmas and Whitsun and the Feasts of the Nativity of St *John the Baptist, St *Peter and St *Paul, and the *Assumption of the BVM, and there are some texts for the Vigils of Sundays and Feasts in the Breviary.

The custom of watching through the night in prayer in expectation of the Parousia, attested from the early 3rd cent. by *Tertullian and others, may have influenced the Vigils of the early Egyptian monks. When they began to live in communities, it became customary for them to spend the greater part of the night in prayer and psalmody. The urban based ascetics, whose practices were described by St *Basil and St John *Chrysostom, appear to have assembled for prayer and the recitation of psalms before the public services at dawn. Esp. in the W., with the development of *Benedictine monasticism, these psalms came to be interspersed with readings. The monastic Vigils tended to be simple and scriptural in form, but they adopted some of the more ceremonial features of non-monastic churches when they were in contact with them. Similarly, the non-monastic churches progressively adopted practices that were monastic in origin. The Rule of St *Benedict refers to the night office as 'vigiliae', and this remains the common name for the service before the morning office among the *Cistercians.

In the E. the Vigil service, or ἀγρυπνία (consisting of Vespers, *Apodeipnon, Midnight Office, and *Orthros), has retained its importance. In monasteries major Vigils (e.g. of great feasts or the dedication feast of the monastery) are celebrated with great solemnity and can last up to 15 hours (from Vespers at 6 p.m.). In Slav usage a shortened 'All-Night Vigil' (Vsenoshchnye bdenie, lit. 'all-night service') is regularly celebrated in parishes on Saturday evening in preparation for the Sunday Liturgy.

A. Gastoué, Les Vigiles nocturnes (Science et Religion, 295; 1908). C. Callewaert, 'De Vigiliarum Origine', Collationes Brugenses, 23 (1923), pp. 425–66, repr. in his Sacris Erudiri (Steenbrugge, 1940), no. 31, pp. 329–33. C. Marcora, La vigilia nella liturgia: Ricerche sulle origini e sui primi sviluppi (Sec. I–VI) (Archivio Ambrosiano, 6; 1954). A. *Baumstark and O. Heiming [OSB], Nocturna Laus: Typen frühchristlicher Vigilienfeier und ihr Fortleben vor allem im römischen und monastischen Ritus (Liturgiegeschichtliche Quellen und Forschungen, 32; 1957). J. Mateos, SJ, 'La vigile cathédrale chez Egérie', OCP 27 (1961), pp. 281–312. R. Taft, SJ, The Liturgy of the Hours in East and West (Collegeville, Minn. [1986]), esp. pp. 165–90. P. C. Langeveld, OSB, in LW 2 (1968), cols. 2815–24, s.v. 'Vigilie', with extensive bibl. See also bibl. to MATTINS.

Vigilantius (fl. c.400), a presbyter of Aquitaine. Most of our knowledge of him comes from his bitter opponent, St *Jerome, who nicknamed him 'Dormitianus' (i.e. 'the dormant', instead of 'the vigilant'). He was a native of Calagurris in Aquitania. Having paid Jerome a visit at *Bethlehem which ended in a quarrel, Vigilantius on his return to the W. attacked Jerome as an *Origenist. Jerome replied with his 'Contra Vigilantium' (406), accusing his adversary of rejecting such practices as the cult of the saints and martyrs, the observance of vigils, and celibacy and monasticism. As Jerome's writings against him are full of invective and his opponent's replies have not survived, the justice of these allegations cannot be assessed. It is possible that Vigilantius did not go further than attack certain excesses which threatened the practice of asceticism at that period.

Jerome also attacked him in Epp. 61 (ad Vigilantium) and 109 (ad Riparium). A. Réville, Vigilance de Calagurris: Un chapitre de l'histoire de l'ascétisme monastique (Paris, 1902). H. Crouzel [SJ], 'Saint Jérôme et ses Amis Toulousains', Bulletin de Littérature Ecclésiastique, 73 (1972), pp. 125–46, esp. pp. 140–5. G. Bardy in DTC 15 (pt. 2; 1950), cols. 2992–4, s.v.

Vigilius (d. 555), Pope from 537. Of a noble Roman family, he was a deacon in 531, when Boniface II nominated him his successor. The nomination, however, was nullified in 532 as uncanonical and in 535–6 Vigilius became *apocrisarius at the court of *Constantinople. Here, induced, it is said, by the Empress *Theodora, he promised his help to restore the deposed *Monophysite patriarch, Anthimus, and to condemn the Council of *Chalcedon. In 537 the legitimate Pope Silverius was deposed with the help of the Byzantine commander Belisarius, and Vigilius consecrated in his place. The new Pope, however, neither reinstalled Anthimus nor did he favour Monophysitism. The letter addressed to the deposed patriarchs Anthimus, Severus, and Theodosius privately supporting the Monophysite position is perhaps a forgery, and in letters to *Justinian and *Menas of Constantinople Vigilius certainly upheld the doctrine of Chalcedon quite decisively. A letter which he addressed to Profuturus, Bp. of Braga, in 538 provides important evidence for the early history of the Roman *Canon of the Mass (q.v.). The Emperor's religious policy soon involved him in the *Three Chapters Controversy (q.v.) raised by Justinian's edict of 543–4, which condemned writings of *Theodore of Mopsuestia, *Theodoret, and *Ibas of Edessa. Vigilius, in accordance with the opinion of the W., refused at first to assent to the condemnation, in which he saw a repudiation of Chalcedon. But, brought to Constantinople by order of Justinian, he repudiated the Three Chapters after considerable resistance and waverings in his 'Iudicatum' of 548, though not without reservations in favour of the Council of Chalcedon. His capitulation met with violent opposition in the W. The Pope was even excommunicated at a synod at Carthage, presided over by its bishop, Reparatus, and in consequence he retracted the 'Iudicatum'. After his protest against another Imperial edict in 551 he fled to Chalcedon, and in 553 refused to preside at the Second Council of *Constantinople. He again declined to condemn the Three Chapters in the 'Constitutum', in the drawing-up of which his deacon, the future Pope Pelagius I, had a large share. The Council, however, finally condemned the Three Chapters, leaving intact the authority of Chalcedon. Pressed by the Emperor, who would not allow him to return to Rome unless he accepted the decrees of Constantinople, Vigilius consented to them after six months' consideration and departed for Italy in 555, dying before he reached Rome.

The case of Pope Vigilius was adduced at the First *Vatican Council by the opponents of Papal *infallibility. It is generally held by RC theologians that infallibility was not involved and that the condemnation of the Three Chapters was in itself justified on account of their *Nestorian tendencies, though inopportune under the circumstances.

Correspondence and decrees in J. P. Migne, *PL* 69. 12–328. E. *Schwartz, *I. Vigiliusbriefe. II. Zur Kirchenpolitik Justinians* (Sb. (Bayr.), 1940, Heft 2), pp. 1–32. Vigilius' correspondence connected with the Second Council of Constantinople also ed. J. Straub in *ACO* 4. 1 (1971). Jaffé, 1, pp. 117–24. *LP* (ed. Duchesne), 1 (1886), pp. 296–302. A. Chavasse, 'Messes du Pape Vigile (537–555) dans le sacramentaire léonien', *EL* 64 (1950), pp. 161–213; 66 (1952), pp. 145–215. L. Magi, *La Sede Romana nella corrispondenza degli imperatori e patriarchi bizantini (VI–VII sec.)* (Bibliothèque de la *RHE*, 57; 1972), pp. 132–58. E. Zettl, CSSR, *Die Bestätigung des V. Ökumenischen Konzils durch Papst Vigilius* (Antiquitas, Reihe 1, Bd. 20; 1974). L. *Duchesne, *L'Église au VI*ᵉ* siècle* (1925), pp. 151–218. E. Caspar, *Geschichte des Papsttums von den Anfängen bis zur Höhe der Weltherrschaft*, 2 (1933), pp. 229–286. É. Amann in *DTC* 15 (pt. 2; 1950), cols. 2994–3005, s.v., with further bibl.; F. X. Murphy in *NCE* 14 (1967), pp. 664–7, s.v.; A. Lippold in *PW*, Suppl. 14 (1974), cols. 864–85, s.v. See also bibl. to THREE CHAPTERS.

Vigilius (*fl. c.*500), Bp. of Thapsus. Banished from Africa in 484 by the Arian king, Huneric, he fled to Constantinople. His chief work, 'Against Eutyches', attacks *Monophysitism and defends the *Tome of St *Leo and the *Chalcedonian Definition. He also wrote several anti-Arian works, but all that survives is the 'Dialogue against Arians, Sabellians, and Photinians' and the pseudo-Augustinian *Contra Felicianum* which is prob. Vigilius' work. Other writings, notably a 'De Trinitate', have been wrongly attributed to him, while P. *Quesnel held that he was the author of the *Athanasian Creed.

Works ed. P. F. Chifflet, SJ (Dijon, 1664), repr. in J. P. Migne, *PL* 62. 93–544. G. Ficker, *Studien zu Vigilius von Thapsus* (1897). M. Simonetti, 'Letteratura antimonofisita d'Occidente', *Augustin-*

ianum, 18 (1978), pp. 487–532, esp. pp. 505–22. *CPL* (3rd edn., 1995), pp. 272–4 (nos. 806–12). Bardenhewer, 4, pp. 553–7. G. Ficker in *PRE* (3rd edn.), 20 (1908), pp. 640–4, s.v.; G. Bardy in *DTC* 15 (pt. 2; 1950), cols. 3005–8.

Vilatte, Joseph René (1854–1929), '*episcopus vagans'. A Frenchman by birth, he joined the RC Church on several separate occasions, to leave it each time for a different Protestant denomination. In 1892, on the authority of an apparently forged bull, he was consecrated at Colombo in Sri Lanka by Abp. Alvarez, a schismatic from the Church of Antioch, as *Old Catholic bishop in America, and took the name of 'Mar Timotheos'. He himself consecrated a large number of bishops who have been recognized by no other Christian body. In 1898 he ordained 'Father *Ignatius' to the priesthood at Llanthony.

J. Parisot, OSB, *Monseigneur Vilatte, fondateur de l'Église Vieille-Catholique aux États-Unis d'Amérique* (Tours, 1899). H. R. T. Brandreth, OGS, *Episcopi Vagantes and the Anglican Church* (2nd edn., 1961), pp. 47–69, with bibl. pp. 126–9.

Vilmar, August Friedrich Christian (1800–60), *Lutheran theologian. A native of Solz in Kurhessen, he held a number of pastoral and administrative appointments until in 1855 he was appointed professor of theology at Marburg. He was a vigorous opponent of all forms of rationalism, upholding dogmatic and confessional Lutheranism by opposing to the prevalent 'theology of rhetoric' (as he termed it) a 'theology of facts' (*Theologie der Tatsachen*). He defended the retention of the ancient creeds in worship. In addition to a widely read *Geschichte der deutschen Nationalliteratur* (1845; rev. by J. Rohr, 1936), he wrote many theological works, largely dealing with the contemporary situation in Church politics. He also compiled a hymn-book (*Kleines evangelisches Gesangbuch*, 1838) embodying improved ideals in hymnology.

Selected Essays ed. K. Ramge (Munich [1939]). Studies by J. H. Leimbach (Hanover, 1875) and W. Hopf (2 vols., Marburg, 1912–13). P. Dietz, *Dr. August Friedrich Christian Vilmar als Hymnolog* (ibid., 1899). U. Asendorf, *Die Europäische Krise und das Amt der Kirche: Voraussetzungen der Theologie von A. F. C. Vilmar* (Arbeiten zur Geschichte und Theologie des Luthertums, 18; 1967), with bibl. J. Haussleiter in *PRE* (3rd edn.), 20 (1908), pp. 649–61, s.v.; K. Scholder in *RGG* (3rd edn.), 6 (1962), cols. 1401–3, s.v.

Vincent, St (4th cent.), the protomartyr of Spain. Acc. to a tradition of the late 4th cent. onwards, referred to by St *Augustine and by *Prudentius, St Vincent was educated and ordained deacon by Valerius, Bp. of Saragossa, and suffered in the *Diocletianic persecution. The details surrounding his death were considerably developed in later times. Feast day, in the W., 22 Jan.; in the E., 11 Nov.

Prudentius, *Peristephanon*, 5; St Augustine, *Sermones*, 274–7; *Sermo in Natali S. Vincentii Martyris* attributed to *Leo I (Sermo 13 in J. P. Migne, *PL* 54. 501–6). A 'Passio Sancti Vincentii Levitae', which Ruinart suggested was used by St Augustine, is pr. in T. *Ruinart, OSB, *Acta Primorum Martyrum Sincera et Selecta* (Paris, 1689), pp. 387–404; various 'Acta S. Vincentii Martyris' in *Anal. Boll.* 1 (1882), pp. 259–78, incl. the 'Passio Brevior', more prob. used by St Augustine, pp. 260–2. *AASS*, Jan. 2 (1647), pp. 397–414. É. Hurault, *Saint Vincent, martyr, patron de vignerons et son culte dans le diocèse de Châlons* (Châlons-sur-Marne, 1910). P. F. de' Cavalieri, *Note agiografiche*, 8 (ST 65; 1935), pp. 117–25. Marquise de Maillé, *Vincent d'Agen* *et saint Vincent de Saragosse: Étude de la 'Passio S. Vincentii Martyris'* (Melun, 1949). A. de Waal, 'Zum Kult des hl. Vinzenz von Saragossa', *RQ* 21 (1907), pp. 135–8. T. Moral in *Bibliotheca Sanctorum*, 12 (Rome, 1969), cols. 1149–55, s.v. 'Vincenzo di Saragozza', with further bibl.

Vincent of Beauvais

Vincent of Beauvais (*c.*1194–1264), author of the vast popular encyclopaedia and *florilegium, the *Speculum Maius*, which draws on some 450 authors. He studied in Paris, and it was probably there that he entered the *Dominican Order. He may have been associated with the foundation of the Dominican house in Beauvais in 1225; his presence there is attested from *c.*1230, and in 1246 he was subprior. Later in 1246 he was appointed lector to the *Cistercian abbey of Royaumont, near Paris, where he came into close contact with King *Louis IX. He left this position some time before 1260.

His main work, the *Speculum Maius*, was conceived and partly written by *c.*1244. From *c.*1245 he was supported financially and in other ways by Louis IX and was enabled to visit the libraries of France. He also received help from the Cistercians in collecting material. He retained links with the Dominicans in Paris and was able to make prompt use of some of the work of St *Thomas Aquinas. Originally envisaged as a two-part compendium, the book grew far beyond its author's expectations and was completed *c.*1259 in three sections, the *Speculum Naturale*, *Speculum Doctrinale*, and *Speculum Historiale*. A supposed fourth part, the *Speculum Morale*, is not authentic; it was added towards the end of the 13th cent. Vincent's other works include a treatise *De eruditione filiorum nobilium* (written 1246–9), the *Liber consolatorius*, written for Louis IX on the death of the crown prince in 1260, and the *Tractatus de morali principis institutione* (written 1260–3).

Speculum Historiale was pub. Strasbourg, 4 vols., 1473; *Speculum Naturalis*, ibid., not later than 1477; *Speculum Doctrinale*, ibid., not later than 1478; *Speculum Morale*, ibid., 1476. *Speculum Maius* ed., 4 vols. bound in 3, Venice, 1591. The latest, and least satisfactory, edn. is that by the Benedictines of *Douai, 4 vols., Douai, 1624. Collected *Opuscula* pub. Basle, 1481. Crit. edns. of the *De Eruditione* by A. Steiner (Mediaeval Academy of America Publication 32; Cambridge, Mass., 1938); of his *Apologia totius operis* [i.e. of *Speculum Maius*] by A.-D. v. den Brincken in *Deutsches Archiv*, 34 (1978), pp. 410–99, with extensive refs., and by S. Lusignan, *Préface au* Speculum Maius *de Vincent de Beauvais, Réfraction et diffraction* (Cahiers d'Études médiévales, 5; Montreal and Paris, 1979); and of *De Morali Principis Institutione* by R. J. Schneider (CCCM, 137; 1995). Parts of his work are still unpub. B. L. Ullman, 'A Project for a New Edition of Vincent of Beauvais', *Speculum*, 8 (1933), pp. 312–26, with discussion of existing edns. J. Échard, OP, *Sancti Thomae Summa suo auctori vindicata sive de V. F. Vincentii Bellovacensis scriptis* (Paris, 1708). J. B. Bourgeat, *Études sur Vincent de Beauvais* (Paris thesis, 1856). L. Lieser, *Vincenz von Beauvais als Kompilator und Philosoph: Eine Untersuchung s. Seelenlehre im* Speculum Maius (1928). G. Göller, *Vinzenz von Beauvais O.P. (um 1194–1264) und sein Musiktraktat im* Speculum doctrinale (Kölner Beiträge zur Musikforschung, 15; 1959), incl. text of *Speculum Doctrinale*, 17. 10–35, pp. 86–118. P. von Moos, 'Die Trotschrift des Vinzenz von Beauvais für Ludwig IX.', *Mittellateinische Jahrbuch*, 6 (1967), pp. 173–218, incl. text of *Liber consolatorius*, 1–3. A. L. Gabriel, *The Educational Ideas of Vincent of Beauvais* (Texts and Studies in the History of Mediaeval Education, 4; Notre Dame, Ind., 1956; rev. Ger. tr., Frankfurt, 1967); J. M. McCarthy, *Humanistic Emphases in the Educational Thought of Vincent of Beauvais* (Studien und Texte zur Geistesgeschichte des Mittelalters, 10; Leiden, 1976). J.

Schneider, 'Un encyclopédie du XIIIe siècle: Le "Speculum Maius" de Vincent de Beauvais', in G. Hasenohr and J. Longère (eds.), *Culture et travail intellectuel dans l'Occident médiéval: Bilan des 'Colloques d'humanisme médiéval' (1960–1980)* (1981), pp. 187–96. W. J. Aerts and others (eds.), *Vincent of Beauvais and Alexander the Great: Studies on the* Speculum Maius *and its Translators into Medieval Vernaculars* (Mediaevalia Groningana, 7; 1987). M. Paulmier-Foucart, S. Lusignan, and A. Nadeau (eds.), *Vincent de Beauvais: Intentions et réception d'une œuvre encyclopédique au Moyen-Age. Actes du XIVe Colloque de l'Institut d'études médiévales . . . 27–30 avril 1988* (Cahiers d'études médiévales, 4; Cahier spécial, 4; 1990). *Spicae: Cahiers de l'atelier Vincent de Beauvais* (Paris, 1978 ff., with bibl. in vol. 1). Kaeppeli, 4 (1993), pp. 435–58.

Vincent Ferrer

Vincent Ferrer, St (1350–1413), *Dominican mission preacher. In 1367 he entered the Dominican Order in his native city, Valencia. His talents as a preacher quickly became apparent, but until 1390 much of his time was devoted to academic life. He lectured on logic at Lerida, where between 1370 and 1372 he wrote two philosophical works, the *Tractatus de Suppositionibus* and the *Quaestio de Unitate Universalis*. In 1380 he wrote a treatise on the schism. Later (1385–90) he taught theology at the cathedral school at Valencia. Probably while he was a student at Barcelona he won the confidence of Card. Pedro de Luna (later *Benedict XIII), who employed him in his curia for several years (1394–8). He worked hard to end the schism and later abandoned Benedict because of his intransigence. From 1399 until his death he toured much of Europe as a preacher, generally accompanied by a group of followers who helped by hearing confessions, giving instruction and leading processions of *flagellants. His preaching was notably scriptural and aroused great popular support; he also converted heretics, Jews, and Moors. He died at Vannes in Brittany. He was canonized in 1455. Feast day, 5 Apr.

Works ed. H. Fages, OP (2 vols., Paris, 1909). Separate edns. of sermons preached at Valencia during Lent 1413, *Quaresma*, ed. J. Sanchez Sivera (Barcelona, 1927; repr., with introd. by M. Sanchez Guarner, 2 vols., Valencia, 1973); other sermons ed. J. Sanchez Sivera and G. Schib (4 vols., Barcelona, 1932–77). *Tractatus de Suppositionibus*, ed. J. A. Trentman (Grammatica Speculativa, 2; Stuttgart and Bad Cannstatt, 1977); *Quaestio de Unitate Universalis*, ed. id., *Mediaeval Studies*, 44 (1982), pp. 110–37. Sp. tr. of these two works by V. Forcada [OP], *Tractados Filosóficos*, with notes and introd. by A. Robles [OP] (Valencia, 1987). Process of canonization, ed. H. Fages, OP (Paris, 1904); id., *Notes et documents de l'histoire de saint Vincent Ferrier* (1905). Id., *Histoire de saint Vincent Ferrier* (2 vols., 1894). M.-M. Gorce, OP, *Saint Vincent Ferrier, 1350–1419* (Paris thesis, 1923); id., *Les Bases de l'étude historique de saint Vincent Ferrier* (Thèse Complémentaire, Paris, 1923). S. Brettle, *San Vicente Ferrer und sein literarischer Nachlass* (Vorreformationsgeschichtliche Forschungen, 10; 1924). J. M. de Garganta, OP, and V. Forcada, OP, *Biografía y escritos de San Vicente Ferrer* (Madrid, 1956). Popular Life by V. Forcada, OP (Valencia, 1987). B. Montagnes, OP, 'Prophétisme et eschatologie dans la prédication méridionale de saint Vincent Ferrier', in *Fin du Monde et Signes des Temps* (Cahiers de Fanjeaux, 27; 1992), pp. 331–49. Eng. Life by S. M. Hogan, OP (London, 1911). Kaeppeli, 4 (1993), pp. 458–74. M.-M. Gorce, OP, in *DTC* 15 (pt. 2; 1950), cols. 3033–45, s.v. 'Vincent Ferrier (Saint)'.

Vincent of Lérins

Vincent of Lérins, St (d. before 450), the author of the 'Commonitorium'. Little is known for certain about his life beyond the fact that, after a period in secular employment, he became a monk on the island of *Lérins. Although the view has recently been challenged, it is generally thought that here, as a *Semipelagian, he opposed the teaching of St *Augustine on *predestination and was prob. the object of *Prosper of Aquitaine's 'Responsiones ad capitula objectionum Vincentianarum' (which preserve the substance of the 'objectiones'). J. Madoz discovered and in 1940 published a text of Vincent's 'Excerpta', the earliest known Augustinian *florilegium. Vincent's main work, the 'Commonitorium', written under the pseudonym 'Peregrinus', was designed to provide a guide to the determination of the Catholic faith; it embodies the famous *Vincentian Canon (q.v.). Despite his emphasis on *tradition, Vincent maintained that the final ground of Christian truth was Holy Scripture, and that the authority of the Church was to be invoked only to guarantee its right interpretation. He did not, however, preclude a development in matters of doctrine, maintaining that in the process of history the truth of Scripture often became more fully explicated. Feast day, 24 May.

Crit. edn. of his surviving works ('Commonitorium' and 'Excerpta') by R. Demeulenaere (CCSL 64, 1985, pp. 125–231), with introd. [in Fr.] and bibl. The numerous earlier edns. of the 'Commonitorium' incl. that of É. *Baluze (Paris, 1663; 3rd edn., 1684 [excellent for its period], repr. in J. P. Migne, *PL* 50. 637–86) and R. S. Moxon (Cambridge Patristic Texts, 1915). Eng. trs. by C. A. Heurtley (NPNCF, 2nd ser. 11, 1894, pp. 123–59), T. H. Bindley ('Early Church Classics', 1914) and others. *Excerpta Vincentii Lirinensis según el Códice de Ripoll, No. 151*, ed., with introd., by J. Madoz, SJ (Estudios Onienses, 1st ser. 1; Madrid, 1940). Id., *El concepto de la tradición en S. Vicente de Lerins* (Analecta Gregoriana, 5; Rome, 1933). W. O'Connor, C.S.Sp., 'Saint Vincent of Lerins and Saint Augustine', *Doctor Communis*, 16 (1963), pp. 123–257. H. J. Sieben, *Die Konzilsidee der Alten Kirche* (1979), pp. 148–70 ('Der Konzilsbegriff des Vinzenz von Lerin'). A. Hamman in Quasten (cont.), *Patrology*, 4 (1986), pp. 546–51. G. Bardy in *DTC* 15 (pt. 2; 1950), cols. 3045–55, s.v.

Vincent de Paul (or Depaul), St (1581–1660), founder of the *Lazarist Fathers and of the 'Sisters of Charity'. Born of a peasant family in Pouy in the Département of Landes in SW France, he was at first a shepherd; he later went to school in Dax and then studied theology in Toulouse. He was ordained priest in 1600. According to his own account, he was captured by pirates and spent two years as a slave in Tunisia before returning to *Avignon with his former master, whom he had converted. After visiting Rome, in 1608 he went to *Paris and, coming under the influence of P. de *Bérulle, he decided to devote his life to the service of the poor. From 1613 to 1626 he was attached to the household of the Count de Gondi, General of the galleys; at the same time he undertook pastoral work in the parishes of Clinchy (near Paris) and Châtillon-les-Dombes (near Lyons), conducted missions in NE France, founded Confraternities of Charity for men and women, and as chaplain of the galleys from 1619 did much to relieve the lot of the prisoners. In 1622 St *Francis de Sales gave him charge of the convents of the *Visitation Order in Paris. In 1625 Vincent founded the Congregation of the Mission, usually called Lazarists (q.v.) or Vincentians, for giving missions among country people and for the training of priests. The first of the seminaries grew out of the Collège des Bons-Enfants, founded as a school for young boys. In 1633, together with St Louise

de Marillac, he founded the Sisters of Charity, the first congregation of women who were not enclosed, and who took no final vows; they were entirely devoted to the care of the sick and poor in a way that was impossible for the Ladies of the Confraternity of Charity. In 1638 he created the first viable home for foundlings. In 1643 the Queen Regent, Anne of Austria, appointed him a member of Louis XIV's Council of Conscience during the King's minority; during the Wars of the Fronde he organized relief work among the suffering populations. He had for some time been a friend of *Saint-Cyran and, in spite of some misgivings, he refused to make any accusation against him when he appeared as a witness after his imprisonment. He was, however, entirely opposed to *Jansenism and in particular the views of A. *Arnauld. His manner of simple preaching was widely followed. He was canonized in 1737. Feast day, 27 Sept. (formerly 19 July). In 1833 the 'Society of St Vincent de Paul', a lay association for personal service of the poor, was founded by A. F. *Ozanam and others.

P. Coste, CM (ed.), *Saint Vincent de Paul, correspondance, entretiens, documents* (14 vols., 1920–5; supplementary vol. 15, ed. A. Dodin, in the periodical *Mission et Charité*, 19–20; 1970); Eng. tr. (Brooklyn, NY [1985 ff.]). Earlier Eng. trs. of selected letters and addresses as *St Vincent de Paul and Mental Prayer* (1925), of further letters (1937), and of the *Conferences of St Vincent de Paul to the Sisters of Charity* (4 vols., 1938–40), all by J. Leonard, CM. L. Abelly, *La Vie du vénérable serviteur de Dieu, Vincent de Paul* (1664); P. Collet, *La Vie de saint Vincent de Paul* (2 vols., 1748); U. Maynard, *Saint Vincent de Paul: Sa vie, son temps, ses œuvres, son influence* (4 vols., 1860); L. E. Bougaud, *Histoire de saint Vincent de Paul* (2 vols., 1889; Eng. tr., 2 vols., 1899). P. Coste, CM, *Le Grand Saint du grand siècle, Monsieur Vincent* (3 vols., 1932; Eng. tr., 3 vols., 1934–5). Other studies by J. Calvet (Paris, 1948; Eng. tr., 1952), with bibl., A. Dodin (Maîtres Spirituels, Paris, 1960), L. Cognet and L. von Matt (Bruges, 1959; Eng. tr., 1960), M. Purcell (London, 1963), and L. Mezzadri (tr. into Fr., Paris [1985]). L. Mezzadri, *Fra giansenisti e antigiansenisti: Vincent Depaul et la Congregazione della Missione (1624–1737)* (Florence, 1977), pp. 1–118. *Vincent de Paul: Actes du Colloque International d'Études Vincentiennes, Paris 25–26 septembre 1981* (Rome [1983]). Bremond, 3 (1921), pp. 222–57, with refs.; Eng. tr., 3 (1936), pp. 193–222; Pourrat, 3 (1925), pp. 575–86; Eng. tr., 3 (1927), pp. 387–94. A. Dodin in *Dict. Sp.* 16 (1994), cols. 841–63, s.v. 'Vincent (7) de Paul'.

Vincentian Canon. The threefold test of Catholicity laid down by St *Vincent of Lérins in his 'Commonitorium' (2. 3), namely *quod ubique, quod semper, quod ab omnibus creditum est* ('what has been believed everywhere, always, and by all'). By this triple test of ecumenicity, antiquity, and consent, the Church is to differentiate between true and false traditions. The order of the tests is to be noted, as the canon was very frequently misquoted with 'antiquity' (*quod semper*) first by English writers in the 19th century.

Vinci, Leonardo da. See LEONARDO DA VINCI.

vincible ignorance. In moral theology, the converse of *invincible ignorance (q.v.).

Vineam Domini Sabaoth. The Constitution issued by *Clement XI on 16 July 1705 against the French *Jansenists. Besides confirming the three earlier Papal bulls—

'*Cum Occasione' (1653), 'Ad Sanctam' (1656), and 'Regiminis Apostolici' (1664)—it maintained that the Pope could determine questions of historic fact (the case in point being whether or not certain propositions, condemned by the Pope, were in fact contained in *Jansen's *Augustinus) as well as matters of doctrine, and that when such a determination had been made by the Pope, it must be accepted 'by the heart' of the believer, and not merely received 'with a respectful silence'. As its issue was believed to infringe the liberties of the French clergy, its promulgation in France was accompanied by a Declaration of the *Assembly of the Clergy that maintained the prerogatives of the bishops to judge with the Pope on matters of faith.

The orig. text, which incorporates the earlier bulls mentioned above, is pr. in *Bullarum, Diplomatum et Privilegiorum Sanctorum Pontificum Taurinensis Editio*, 21 (Turin, 1871), pp. 233–6; part repr. in Denzinger and Hünermann (37th edn., 1991), pp. 669 f. (no. 2390). A. Le Roy, *Le Gallicanisme au XVIIIᵉ Siècle: La France et Rome de 1700 à 1715* (1892), pp. 161–234. L. Ceyssens, 'La bulle *Vineam Domini* (1705) et le Jansénisme français', *Antonianum*, 64 (1989), pp. 398–430. M. Ott in *CE* 15 (1912), pp. 445 f., s.v.; B. Matteucci in *EC* 12 (1954), cols. 1446 f., s.v. See also works cited under GALLICANISM and JANSENISM.

Vinegar Bible. A popular name for the fine folio edition of the Bible, printed at Oxford in 1716–17 by John Baskett (d. 1742), the King's Printer. The headline of Lk. 20 reads 'The Parable of the Vinegar' instead of 'The Parable of the Vineyard'.

Darlow and Moule, ed. A. S. Herbert, 1 (1968), p. 244.

Vines, Richard (1600?–56), *Puritan divine. Educated at Magdalene College, Cambridge, where he became a good Greek scholar, he was a schoolmaster and non-resident rector of two parishes. On 30 Nov. 1642 he preached before the House of Commons and in 1643 was nominated a member of the *Westminster Assembly, where he became a member of the committee which drafted the Confession. In 1644 he became Master of Pembroke College, Cambridge. In the same year he was put on the Parliamentary Committee of Accommodation, and, though episcopally ordained, defended *Presbyterian ordinations. He was opposed, however, to lay elders as Church governors. In 1645 he was present at the negotiations between *Charles I and Parliament, and in 1648 he took part in a written discussion with the King on episcopacy. In 1649 he opposed the abolition of the kingly office and the House of Peers, and being ejected from Pembroke College and Watton Rectory he became minister of St Lawrence Jewry.

XII Sermons Preached upon Several Public Occasions: By . . . Mr. Richard Vines (1658), 'To which is adjoined, the Sermon Preached at his Funeral, By Mr. Thomas Jacomb' (orig. pub. 1656; sep. pagination). S. Clarke, *The Lives of Sundry Eminent Persons in this Later Age* (1683), pp. 48–56. B. Brook, *The Lives of the Puritans*, 3 (1813), pp. 230–5. A. Gordon in *DNB* 58 (1899), pp. 369–71, s.v.

Vinet, Alexandre Rudolf (1797–1847), Swiss Reformed theologian. A native of Ouchy, nr. Lausanne, from 1817 he taught French language and literature at Basle, where he came under the influence of W. M. L. *de Wette, and was ordained minister in 1819. He became professor of pastoral theology in 1837 at Lausanne, where he remained

till 1847, when he attached himself to the newly constituted Free Church in Canton Vaud. He was a strenuous defender of liberty of worship and the separation of Church and State and advocated these principles in his *Mémoire sur les libertés des cultes* (1826), *Essai sur la manifestation des convictions religieuses* (1842; Eng. tr., 1843), and *Du socialisme considéré dans son principe* (1846). His conception of Christianity was thoroughly individualistic, the seat of religion being the conscience and dogma important only in so far as it issued in moral action. Vinet gave forceful expression to these views in his sermons, collected in *Discours sur quelques sujets religieux* (1831 and 1841; Eng. tr. of both, 1846), which have had a lasting influence on Swiss and French Protestants, owing to their combination of classic form with modern scholarship and warmth of feeling. Shortly after his death appeared his brilliant *Études sur Blaise *Pascal* (1848; Eng. tr., 1859), with whom Vinet had certain affinities in his emphasis on the heart as the chief organ of religion and in his use of psychology in apologetics. Other formative influences on his theology were I. *Kant and T. *Erskine. He has sometimes been designated the 'Swiss Schleiermacher'.

Œuvres pub. under the auspices of the Société d'Édition Vinet, founded 23 April 1908, with introd. by various authors (30 vols., Lausanne, 1910–64). Selections ed. P. Bridel, *La Pensée de Vinet* (Lausanne, 1944), with refs. E. Rambert, *Alexandre Vinet: Histoire de sa vie et ses ouvrages* (ibid., 1875). L. M. Lane, *The Life and Writings of Alexandre Vinet* (1890). L. Molines, *Études sur Alexandre Vinet: Critique littéraire* (1890). P. A. Robert, *La flamme sur l'autel: Essai sur la crise religieuse d'Alexandre Vinet* (Lausanne, 1948); F. Jost, *Alexandre Vinet: Interprète de Pascal* (ibid., 1950). P. T. Fuhrmann, *Extraordinary Christianity: The Life and Thought of Alexander Vinet* (Philadelphia, 1964). A. Ruegg in *PRE* (3rd edn.), 20 (1908), pp. 680–92, s.v.

Vio, Thomas de. See CAJETAN, THOMAS DE VIO.

Viret, Pierre (1511–71), Reformer of W. Switzerland. Born in Orbe, he studied in Paris, where he adopted Protestantism. On returning to Orbe in 1531 he was ordained by G. *Farel and assisted him in establishing the Reformation in Geneva and in the Canton of Vaud (1534–6). From 1537 to 1559 he was in charge of the Lausanne Church. Expelled in 1559 because of a quarrel over Church discipline, he worked as a preacher in Geneva, Montpellier, Lyons, and elsewhere, playing a leading part in the affairs of the French Reformed Church. His *Instruction chrestienne* (Geneva, 1564) and other vernacular treatises are mostly popularizations of J. *Calvin's doctrine.

Letters were pub. in A. L. Herminjard (ed.), *Correspondance des réformateurs* (9 vols., 1866–97), *passim*. J. Barnaud (ed.), *Quelques Lettres inédites de Pierre Viret* (1911). *Pierre Viret d'après lui-même: Pages extraites des œuvres du réformateur à l'occasion du 4ᵉ centenaire de sa naissance* (Lausanne, 1912). *Quatre Sermons français sur Esaïe 65 (mars 1559)*, ed. H. Meylan (Publications de la Faculté de Théologie, Université de Lausanne, 3; 1961); *L'Interim fait par dialogues*, ed. G. R. Mermier (Berne and New York, 1985). J. Barnaud, *Pierre Viret: Sa vie et son œuvre* (1911), with bibl. of his writings, pp. 677–96. Other studies by P. Godet (Lausanne, 1892), H. Vuilleumier (ibid., 1911), and G. Bavaud (Geneva, 1986; uncritical). R. D. Linder, *The Political Ideas of Pierre Viret* (Geneva, 1964). C. Schmidt and C. Schetzler in *PRE* (3rd edn.), 20 (1908), pp. 693–5, s.v.

virger. See VERGER.

Virgil (70–19 BC), Roman poet. Publius Vergilius Maro, the son of a rich citizen of Mantua, was educated at Cremona, Milan, and Rome, with a view to a political career. He soon abandoned rhetoric and politics to study philosophy under the Greek *Epicurean Siron, near Naples (?49–45 BC). He intended, after completing the *Aeneid*, to devote himself to philosophy. He was the author of ten pastorals, *Bucolica* (?45–37 BC), known as the *Eclogues* (i.e. occasional poems); the *Georgics* (36–31 BC), on Italy and its agricultural wealth, the fourth book of which deals with the ordered civil life of the beehive and how it may be restored to life by a magical process of sacrifice, and culminates in the story of Orpheus' descent into the Underworld to recover his wife Eurydice; and the *Aeneid* (26–19 BC), an epic in 12 books on the foundation of Rome by the exiled Trojan. This work is a fusion of Homer's two poems, *Iliad* and *Odyssey*, into a prophetic sequel, looking forward to the inauguration of a golden age by Aeneas' descendant, the Emp. Augustus, under the providential guidance of Jupiter. It was at first criticized as plagiaristic, but by the time of the Emp. Tiberius' death (AD 37) the *Aeneid* was recognized as the epic of Rome and had become the staple of literary education in the Roman West.

Virgil's language and style were widely influential in the next 1,500 years and frequently imitated, with Christians writing Virgilian centos to tell biblical stories. The Emp. *Constantine tried to appropriate the Fourth ('Messianic') Eclogue as a prophecy of Christ, born of a virgin (1. 6: *iam redit et virgo*), and *Lactantius went some way towards accepting such a view (*Inst.* 1. 19. 5; 7. 24. 1). This, and the fact that Virgil was nicknamed Parthenias (Gk. παρθένος, 'virgin') and lived at Parthenope (Naples), led to the alteration of the spelling of his name. St *Jerome protested against the facile Christianization of Virgil, and St *Augustine made him his chief target in his *De Civitate Dei*. During the last period of serious pagan opposition at Rome, and in the struggle over the 'Altar of Victory' in the Senate House (AD 384), the pagans came to regard Virgil as a philosophical authority and a source of oracles (*Sortes Vergilianae*). But in the subsequent period whatever in Virgil resisted Christianization was explained by *allegory (e.g. by *Fulgentius, *John of Salisbury, and *Dante).

Later Christian writers accorded Virgil a unique position among pagan authors, partly because of their naïve acceptance of the *Sibylline Oracles and the Sibylline Fourth Eclogue, but also because of the poet's genuine qualities. The *pietas* of Aeneas (his loyal devotion to his gods, to his father, wife, and son, and to his city and its 'remnant', his companions), his responsibility and warmth of emotion, his consideration for Dido, his goodness and wisdom in spite of lapses and errors, and his eventual faith in Providence, evince a moral standard with appeal to Christians. Aeneas' creator could be taken as *anima naturaliter Christiana*, separated only by a few years from the faith for which he was ready. In the *Divine Comedy* Dante makes Virgil his guide through Hell and Purgatory, but excludes him from salvation. Virgil sinks back to Limbo, but only after hearing that he has mediated the light of faith to Statius, and after seeing Beatrice's cortège in the Earthly Paradise.

The numerous edns. of Virgil's works incl. those by O. Ribbeck (4 vols., Leipzig, 1859–68; rev., Teub., 3 vols., 1894–5), and R. A. B. Mynors (Oxford, 1969). Comm. on individual books of the *Aeneid*: Book 1 by R. G. Austin (Oxford, 1971), Book 2 by id. (ibid., 1964), Book 3 by R. D. Williams (ibid., 1962), Book 4 by R. G. Austin (ibid., 1955), Book 5 by R. D. Williams (ibid., 1960), Book 6 by E. Norden (Leipzig, 1903; 4th edn., Stuttgart, 1957) and by R. G. Austin (Oxford, 1977), and Book 8 by K. W. Gransden (Cambridge, 1976); on the *Eclogues* by R. Coleman (Cambridge, 1977); and on the *Georgics* by R. A. B. Mynors (Oxford, 1990). General studies incl. W. F. J. Knight, *Roman Vergil* (London, 1944; rev. edn., Harmondsworth, 1966); V. Pöschl, *Die Dichtkunst Virgils* (Innsbruck and Vienna [1950]; 3rd edn., Berlin and New York, 1977; Eng. tr., Ann Arbor, Mich. [1962]); G. N. Knauer, *Die Aeneis und Homer: Studien zur poetischen Technik Vergils* (Hypomnemata, 7 [1964]); B. Otis, *Virgil: A Study in Civilized Poetry* (Oxford, 1964); D. R. Dudley (ed.), *Virgil* (Studies in Latin Literature and its influence, 1969); R. D. Williams and T. S. Pattie, *Virgil: His poetry through the ages* [1982]. Studies more specifically concerned with his religious significance incl. E. Norden, *Die Geburt des Kindes* (Studien der Bibliothek Warburg, 3; 1924); H. Jeanmaire, *Le Messianisme de Virgile* (1930); C. N. Smiley, 'Vergil—his Philosophic Background and his Relation to Christianity', *Classical Journal*, 26 (1930–31), pp. 660–75; C. Bailey, *Religion in Virgil* (Oxford, 1935); H. J. Rose, *The Eclogues of Vergil* (Berkeley and Los Angeles, Calif., 1942); I. S. Ryberg, 'Vergil's Golden Age', *Transactions and Proceedings of the American Philological Association*, 89 (1958), pp. 112–31; P. Boyancé, *La Religion de Virgile* (1963); E. A. Hahn, 'Body and Soul in Vergil', *Transactions and Proceedings of the American Philological Association*, 92 (1961), pp. 193–219; F. A. Sullivan, SJ, 'Virgil and the mystery of suffering', *American Journal of Philology*, 90 (1969), pp. 161–77; G. Luck, 'Virgil and the mystery religions', ibid. 94 (1973), pp. 147–66; G. Williams, *Virgil's Fourth Eclogue* (Center for Hermeneutical Studies in Hellenistic and Modern Culture; Berkeley, Calif., 1975). D. Comparetti, *Virgilio nel medio evo* (2 vols., Livorno, 1872; Eng. tr., 1895); V. Zabughin, *Vergilio nel Rinascimento italiano de Dante a Torquato Tasso* (2 vols., Bologna [1921–3]); J. W. Spargo, *Virgil the Necromancer* (Harvard Studies in Comparative Literature, 10; Cambridge, Mass., 1934).

Virgilius of Salzburg, St (c.700–84), 'Apostle of Carinthia'. An Irishman—the Gaelic form of his name was prob. 'Fergal'—he was one of the most learned men of his age, esp. in mathematical matters. The facts of his early life are uncertain; but acc. to one tradition he was at first a monk of Aghaboe, where he later became abbot. He may have had some early association with *Iona. Having made his way to the Continent in 743, for several years he governed the diocese of Salzburg without becoming bishop. St *Boniface, who disapproved of this ecclesiastical arrangement no less than of some of Virgilius' scientific doctrines, in 748 accused him to Pope *Zacharias for heretical views about the spherical shape of the earth and the existence of the antipodes. Virgilius was, however, eventually consecrated to the see of Salzburg in either 755 or 767 (the sources are not clear). In 772 he took advantage of the fact that the inhabitants of Carinthia were seeking protection from the Avars to secure conversion of the Alpine Slavs, and in 774 he dedicated the first cathedral at Salzburg. He established a famous scriptorium here, where an Irishman (perhaps Virgilius himself) wrote under the pseudonym Aethicus Ister a fictitious cosmography, which claimed the authority of St *Jerome. Virgilius has been held in continuous repute in his diocese and was canonized by *Gregory IX in 1233. Feast day, 27 Nov.

A 12th-cent. Life ed. G. H. Pertz in *MGH*, Scriptores, 11 (1854), pp. 86–95; of greater historical importance is the epitaph by *Alcuin, ibid., Poetae, 1 (1881), p. 340. F. S. Betton, SJ, *St Boniface and St Virgil: A Study from the Original Sources of Two Supposed Conflicts* (Benedictine Historical Monographs, 2; Washington, DC, 1927). P. Grosjean, SJ, 'Virgile de Salzburg en Irlande', *Anal. Boll.* 78 (1960), pp. 92–123. H. Dopsch and R. Juffinger (eds.), *Virgil von Salzburg, Missionär und Gelehrter: Beiträge der Internationalen Symposiums von 21.–24. Sept. 1984 in der Salzburger Residenz* (Salzburg, 1985). H. Löwe, 'Ein literarischer Widersacher des Bonifatius. Virgil von Salzburg und die Kosmographie des Aethicus Ister', *Akademie der Wissenschaften und der Literatur in Mainz, Abhandlungen der Geistes- und Sozialwissenschaftlichen Klasse*, 1951, pp. 899–988 (Nr. 11). É Amann in *DTC* 14 (pt. 2; 1950), cols. 3093–7, s.v.

Virgin Birth of Christ. The belief that Jesus Christ had no human father, but was conceived by the Blessed Virgin Mary by the power of the Holy Spirit, is clearly stated in the two narratives of Christ's Infancy recorded in the Gospels (Mt. 1 f. and Lk. 1 f.), and has been a consistent tenet of orthodox Christian theology. It is also implied in the *Apostles' and *Nicene Creeds. It has generally been regarded by Christian theologians as altogether congruous with the Catholic doctrine of the *Incarnation, with its stress on the uniqueness of Christ.

In early times the fact was questioned only by a few heretical sects (*Psilanthropists, *Adoptionists). Within the last hundred years, however, it has been challenged by a number of liberal theologians on such grounds as: (1) a general suspicion of everything miraculous and in particular the belief that the LXX of Is. 7: 14 (παρθένος, 'virgin'), as an inexact rendering of the Heb., gave rise to, or at least promoted, the legend; (2) the absence of reference to the Virgin Birth in other parts of the NT, notably the Christological teaching of the Epp. and the Fourth Gospel; and (3) the contention that it would have been more congruous with the full Humanity of Christ for His Birth to have been like that of other men. It is answered: (1) that belief in miracle is integral to the Christianity of the NT and, as regards the supposed influence of Is. 7: 14, the more circumstantial account of the Birth of Christ in Lk. (as contrasted with that in Mt.) is in no way associated with this OT passage; (2) it was the kind of fact which from its nature would at first have become known in the Church much less rapidly than the public facts of the Lord's life; and (3) it is rash to suppose that the Son of God needed two parents in order to assume human nature. Yet it should be observed that the acceptance of Christ's Divine Sonship is not theologically dependent on the fact that He was not the son of Joseph, and in any case the doctrine of the Virgin Birth is to be clearly distinguished from that of the Incarnation itself.

(In current RC usage, the term 'Virgin Birth' has a wider connotation, covering both virginal conception (as described above) and the belief, attested since the 2nd cent., that the BVM gave birth as a virgin, i.e. that she remained *virgo intacta*).

Modern works defending the traditional belief incl. C. *Gore, *Dissertations on Subjects connected with the Incarnation* (1895), pp. 3–68; W. M. *Ramsay, *Was Christ born at Bethlehem? A Study on the Credibility of St Luke* (1898); J. G. Machen, *The Virgin Birth of Christ* (1930); D. [A.] Edwards, CR, *The Virgin Birth in History and Faith* (1943); T. Boslooper, *The Virgin Birth* (1962); R. E. Brown, *The Virginal Conception & Bodily Resurrection of Jesus* (1973), pp. 1–68; and id., *The Birth of the Messiah: A Commentary on the Infancy Narratives in Matthew and Luke* ([1977]; rev. ed.,

1993). J. McHugh, *The Mother of Jesus in the New Testament* (1975), esp. pp. 157–347, with list of the main opponents and defenders of the historicity of the Virgin Birth, pp. 456–8. Useful crit. examination of the NT evidence in V. Taylor, *The Historical Evidence for the Virgin Birth* (1920; no conclusion drawn and belief must be determined by dogmatic considerations). Study of the development of the doctrine in the early Church by H. von Campenhausen, *Die Jungfrauengeburt in der Theologie der alten Kirche* (*Sb.* (Heid.), 1962, Abt. 3; Eng. tr., Studies in Historical Theology, 2; 1964), takes it for granted that the Virgin Birth is unhistorical, similarly, A. R. C. Leaney, 'The Virgin Birth in Lucan Theology and in the Classical Creeds', in R. [J.] Bauckham and B. Drewery (eds.), *Scripture, Tradition and Reason: . . . Essays in Honour of Richard P. C. Hanson* (Edinburgh, 1988), pp. 65–100. L. G. Owens in *NCE* 14 (1967), pp. 692–7, and F. M. Jelly, ibid. 17 (1979), pp. 691 f., both s.v., with bibl. See also comm. to Gospels, ad locc., and bibl. to INCARNATION and MARY, THE BLESSED VIRGIN.

Virgin Mary, the Blessed. See MARY, THE BLESSED VIRGIN.

virtualism. A form of *Eucharistic doctrine acc. to which, while the bread and wine continue to exist unchanged after consecration, the faithful communicant receives together with the elements the virtue or power of the Body and Blood of Christ. Its classical exponent was J. *Calvin.

virtues, cardinal. See CARDINAL VIRTUES.

virtues, theological. See THEOLOGICAL VIRTUES.

Visigothic rite. Another name, used e.g. by Dom M. Férotin (1855–1914), for the *Mozarabic rite, derived from its use in Spain when the country was dominated by the Visigoths (5th–7th cents.).

Visitandine Order. See VISITATION ORDER.

Visitatio Liminum Apostolorum. See AD LIMINA APOSTOLORUM.

visitation, episcopal. Episcopal visitations are designed for the periodic inspection of those temporal and spiritual affairs of a diocese under the bishop's control. From the 6th cent., such visitations were regulated by several ecclesiastical councils. Triennial visitation, which was the usual medieval practice, was exacted by the Anglican *Canons of 1604 (can. 60); can. G 5 of the 1969 canons is less specific, although can. C 22 requires an archdeacon to hold yearly visitations unless inhibited by a visitation of the bishop or archbishop. Biennial visitation is the minimum stipulated by the Council of *Trent. In the later Middle Ages, when the work of visitation was already conducted by commissaries of the bishop, including archdeacons, there developed elaborate legal forms centring in the presentation of offenders by both clergy and laity, to whom articles of inquiry had been previously administered. The cases were then tried by canon law in much the same form as that of the *consistory court. The Abps. of *Canterbury and *York have the right to visit all the dioceses within their respective provinces, e.g. W. *Laud in 1634 instituted a visitation of all his suffragan dioceses. See also CHARGE.

C. R. Cheney, *Episcopal Visitation of Monasteries in the Thirteenth Century* (Manchester, 1931; 2nd edn., ibid. and Philadelphia, 1983). N. Coulet, *Les visites pastorales* (Typologie des sources du moyen âge occidental, 23; 1977). P. M. Smith, 'Points of Law and Practice concerning Ecclesiastical Visitations', *Ecclesiastical Law Journal*, 2 (1992), pp. 189–212.

Visitation of Our Lady. The feast, formerly observed on 2 July, commemorates the Blessed Virgin's visit to her cousin *Elizabeth, recorded in Lk. 1: 39–56. It made its first appearance in the 13th cent., when it was introduced into the *Franciscan Order by the General Chapter of 1263 at the instigation of St *Bonaventure. Its extension to the universal Church in order to obtain the end of the *Great Schism was decided upon by *Urban VI and prescribed by Boniface IX in 1389, but accepted only by the part of the Church under his obedience. The Council of *Basle, in 1441, again ordered its celebration, and *Pius V finally established it for the whole RC Church. In 1969 it was moved to 31 May. In the C of E, 2 July was inserted as a *Black Letter Day into the calendar of the 1662 BCP, but the ASB and various other modern Anglican liturgies assign the feast to 31 May.

J. V. Polc, *De origine festi Visitationis B.M.V.* (Corona Lateranensis, 9 A; 1967). B. Fischer, 'Why is the Feast of the Visitation Celebrated on July 2?', in J. N. Alexander (ed.), *Time and Community: In Honor of Thomas Julian Talley* (Washington, DC [1990]), pp. 77–80. R. W. Pfaff, *New Liturgical Feasts in Later Medieval England* (Oxford Theological Monographs, 1970), pp. 40–61.

Visitation Order (also known as the **Visitandines**). The order of contemplatives founded in 1610 by St *Francis de Sales and St *Jane Frances de Chantal. It was designed to include women unable to bear the austerities of the older orders and devoted itself to the special cultivation of humility, gentleness, and sisterly love. Originally the Visitandines were a congregation with simple vows. Only the novices were strictly enclosed, while the professed sisters went out on works of mercy, esp. nursing the sick. But this innovation was received unfavourably by the Abp. of Lyons, D. S. de Marquemont, who refused to admit the sisters to his diocese unless they kept to the enclosure. St Francis gave way, and on 23 Apr. 1618 Pope *Paul V constituted the congregation an order with full privileges ('Ordo Visitationis BMV'). It was solemnly approved by *Urban VIII in 1626 and has remained primarily contemplative. The 'constitutions' drawn up by St Francis were an adaptation of the *Augustinian Rule, with the characteristic substitution of the *Little Office of Our Lady for the Canonical Hours. This feature disappeared in the new constitutions finally approved in 1987. The house at Annecy has a primacy of honour in the order, but each house is under the jurisdiction of the diocesan bishop. Since 1957 the houses have been grouped into federations to reinforce the bonds of charity which unite them to each other and to Annecy. The most notable saint of the order is St *Margaret Mary Alacoque, whose visions had a large share in the institution of the Feast of the *Sacred Heart.

C. F. Ménestrier, SJ, *Projet de l'histoire de l'ordre de la Visitation de Sainte-Marie* (Annecy, 1701). *La Visitation Sainte-Marie* (Les Grands Ordres religieux, Paris, 1923); E. Lecouturier, *La Visitation* (Les Grands Ordres monastiques et instituts religieux, 1935). F. A. *Gasquet, OSB, *The Order of the Visitation: Its Spirit and*

its Growth in England [1910]. F. M. de Chaugy, *Les Vies des quatre premières mères de l'ordre de la Visitation Sainte-Marie* (1659; repr. as vol. 1 of the Œuvres historiques de la Mère Françoise-Madeleine de Chaugy, 1892); also other works by this author. R. Devos, *L'origine sociale des Visitandines d'Annecy aux XVIIe et XVIIIe siècles* (Mémoires et documents publiés par l'Académie Salésienne, 84; 1973). For the early history of the order see also *The Life of Jeanne Charlotte de Bréchard* by the Sisters of the Visitation, Harrow (1924). M. L. Lynn, VHM, in *NCE* 14 (1967), pp. 719–21, s.v.; M.-P. Burns, VSM, *Dict. Sp.* 16 (1994), cols. 1002–10, s.v. 'Visitandines'.

Visitation of the Sick. The 'Order for the Visitation of the Sick' in the BCP follows in arrangement that in the *Sarum *Manuale, but with considerable omissions, e.g. of the *Seven Penitential Psalms formerly recited on the way to the sick person's house. In the 1662 Book the minister of the parish, after an opening versicle and response on entering the sick person's presence, says the *Lord's Prayer, followed by further versicles and responses, collects for the sick person's faith, repentance, and perseverance, an exhortation (added in 1549, and partly based on the *Homilies* of 1547), a profession of faith in the articles of the *Apostles' Creed in an interrogatory form, an exhortation to confession of sin, followed by a form prescribed for priestly absolution, a further collect for the sick person's forgiveness, Psalm 71, 'O Saviour of the world', a final collect, and the Blessing (in the form in Num. 6: 24–6). Four occasional collects are appended. In the 1549 Book provision was also made for the *unction of the sick person, but this has been omitted since 1552. The 'Communion of the Sick', included as a separate item since 1549, originally provided either for the elements consecrated at the Communion Service in church to be taken to the sick person and those who were to communicate with him, or for a celebration in the sick-room with a special collect, Epistle (Heb. 12: 5), and Gospel (Jn. 5: 24); from 1552 only the latter option was permitted. The form of priestly absolution provided in the Order for the Visitation of the Sick formed the basis of the 19th-cent. revival of the sacrament of *Penance in the C of E. Modern Anglican liturgies have abandoned much of the ethos of the BCP Order, with its expectation of imminent death and its suggestion that sickness itself might be a deserved punishment from God. They include prayers for healing and provide for the laying on of *hands, unction, and Communion either from the Reserved Sacrament or a celebration in the presence of the sick person. Whereas provision for the reservation of the consecrated elements (at least ostensibly for the Communion of the sick) in the proposed BCP of 1927–8 was one of the factors leading to its rejection, the Alternative Services *Ministry to the Sick* (1983) encouraged such 'extended communion', as it is frequently called, without arousing old controversies. In many parts of the Anglican Communion lay people bring and administer the consecrated elements to the sick person.

In the RC Church the 1972 'Order for Anointing the Sick and their Pastoral Care' (*Ordo Unctionis Infirmorum eorumque Pastoralis Curae*), now slightly revised, provides for a comparable rite consisting of prayers, readings from Scripture, Psalms, and a blessing, with laying on of hands. In cases of serious illness this is followed by unction and Communion, and, when death approaches, by *Viaticum and the *Commendatio animae* (called in the new Ordo

Commendatio morientium). The 1972 Ordo replaces similar provisions contained in the *Rituale (Tit. 5, cap. 4).

F. Procter and W. H. *Frere, *A New History of the Book of Common Prayer* (1919), esp. pp. 622–9. C. Harris, 'Visitation of the Sick', in W. K. L. Clarke and C. Harris (eds.), *Liturgy and Worship: A Companion to the Prayer Books of the Anglican Communion* (1932), pp. 472–541; id., 'The Communion of the Sick, Viaticum, and Reservation', ibid., pp. 541–615. Forms of Service for 'Unction and the Laying-on of Hands' and for 'the Laying-on of Hands without Unction' were approved by both Houses of the *Convocation of Canterbury on 6 June 1935; they are repr in A. F. Smethurst and H. R. Wilson (eds.), *Acts of the Convocations of Canterbury and York . . . passed since . . . 1921* (1948), pp. 72–83; for somewhat similar provision made by both Houses of the Convocations of York, see ibid., pp. 83–6. See also bibl. to UNCTION and SPIRITUAL HEALING.

Vitalian (d. 672), Pope from 657. Despite the strained relations between Rome and *Constantinople during the *Monothelite controversy, he kept on good terms with the E. during the earlier part of his pontificate, exchanging the customary compliments with the E. Emp. Constans II at his consecration, and receiving him at Rome in 663. Later, however, Vitalian's name was removed from the *Diptychs at Constantinople for his adhesion to 'Dyothelite', i.e. orthodox, views. It was he who consecrated *Theodore of Tarsus Abp of *Canterbury in 668. Feast day, 27 Jan.

Jaffé, 1 (1885), pp. 235–7. *LP* (Duchesne), 1 (1886), pp. 343–5. Mann, 1 (pt. 2; 1902), pp. 1–16, with notes on sources. E. Caspar, *Geschichte des Papsttums von den Anfängen bis zur Höhe der Weltherrschaft*, 2 (1933), pp. 580–6, 588 f., 600, and 681 f. J. N. D. Kelly, *Oxford Dictionary of Popes* (1986), pp. 75 f.

Vitalis, St. St *Ambrose relates that in 393 he attended the exhumation, at *Bologna, of the remains of Sts Agricola and Vitalis which lay buried in the Jewish cemetery there, and that both Vitalis and Agricola (whose slave Vitalis was) had suffered death together. The cult of Vitalis spread rapidly through W. Christendom and famous churches were dedicated to his honour at *Ravenna (5th cent.; rebuilt in 6th) and *Rome (5th cent., formerly the basilica of the *titulus Vestinae*). Two historically valueless later accounts of the death of St Vitalis exist, in one of which he is associated not with Agricola but with his wife Valeria. Feast days: Vitalis and Valeria, 28 Apr.; Vitalis and Agricola, 4 Nov.

Ambrose, *Exhortatio virginitatis*, 1–2; *Paulinus of Milan, *Vita S. Ambrosii*, 29, who attributes the discovery of the martyrs' remains to Ambrose himself. F. Savio, SJ, 'Due lettere falsamente attribuite a S. Ambrogio', *Nuovo Bullettino di Archeologia cristiana*, 3 (1897), pp. 153–77. On the legend associating St Vitalis with Agricola, see also *AASS*, Nov. 2 (pt. 1; 1894), pp. 233–53; H. *Delehaye, SJ, 'L'Hagiographie ancienne de Ravenne', *Anal. Boll.* 47 (1929), pp. 5–30, esp. pp. 7–10; id., *Les Origines du culte des martyrs* (2nd edn., Subsidia Hagiographica, 20; 1933), esp. pp. 324 f. and 328 f. On the legends associating St Vitalis with Valeria, id., 'Trois Dates du calendrier romain', *Anal. Boll.* 46 (1928), sect. 2, 'Saint Vital (28 avril)', pp. 55–9. On the *titulus Vestinae*, C. Pietri, *Roma Christiana: Recherches sur l'Église de Rome . . . 311–440* (Bibliothèque des Écoles françaises d'Athènes et de Rome, 224; 1976), pp. 476 f.

Vitalis, Ordericus. See ORDERICUS VITALIS.

vitandi (Lat., 'persons to be avoided'). The technical name formerly used in *canon law for those *excommunicated persons with whom members of the Church were debarred from having any kind of intercourse unless there was reasonable cause. They were distinguished from the *tolerati*, with whom relations of a personal kind were more readily allowed. Unless he had laid violent hands upon the Pope, in which case *ipso facto* he was *vitandus*, an offender acquired this status only when he was expressly so named by the Roman see. These rulings are embodied in the *Codex Iuris Canonici* (1917), cans. 2258, 2259, and 2343. The category is not used in the 1983 *Codex*.

Vitoria, Francisco de (1483–1546), Spanish theologian. He entered the *Dominican Order in 1505 and studied in Burgos and Paris. In Paris he came under the influence of Pieter Crockaert, OP (*c*.1470–1514). He prob. taught philosophy at the Dominican convent of S. Jacques in Paris from 1513 to 1516 and thereafter taught theology there, receiving his doctorate in theology in 1522. After his return to Spain he lectured on theology at Valladolid from 1523 to 1526, and from 1526 held the Prime Chair of Theology at the University of Salamanca.

Vitoria may be considered a forerunner of the '*Salmanticenses'. By substituting the '*Summa Theologiae' of St *Thomas Aquinas for *Peter Lombard's 'Sentences' as the theological textbook, he inaugurated a new school at Salamanca which, under his pupils Dominic *Soto, Andreas de Vega (1498–1560), Melchior *Cano, and others, became the chief university in Europe in the 16th cent. for the study of *Scholasticism. A humanist as well as a philosopher and theologian, he developed a method which, without disregarding philosophical speculation, made the Scriptures and the Fathers the foundation of theological teaching. He is often also regarded today as the 'Father of International Law', and at some points H. *Grotius was dependent on him. In his famous 'Relectiones', lectures given between 1527 and 1540, he dealt *inter alia* with the chief problem of his day in international morality, namely the conquest of the Indies. He was critical of the Spanish methods of colonization in America and also laid down the conditions of a just war. On this last matter, basing himself on St *Augustine and St Thomas, he confined legitimate warfare to the redressing of a wrong received; and, indeed, he went further than St Thomas in holding that no war would be permissible if it should bring serious evil to Christendom and the world at large.

The early edns. of Vitoria's writings are very rare, and part of his work is still unpub. Modern edns. of his comm. on the Secunda Secundae of St Thomas by V. Beltrán de Heredia, OP (Bibliotheca de Teólogos Españoles, 2–6 and 17; 1932–52); of the sections 'De Indis' and 'De Jure Belli' of his *Relectiones Theologicae XII* (orig. pub. Lyons, 1557) by L. Pereña and others (Corpus Hispanorum de Pace, 5 and 6 respectively; Madrid, 1967–81). The *Relectiones*, ed., with Sp. tr., by T. Urdánoz, OP (Biblioteca de Autores Cristianos, 1960). Eng. tr. of selections, *Political Writings*, ed. A. Pagden and J. Lawrance (Cambridge Texts in the History of Political Thought, 1991). L. G. A. Getino, *El Mro. Francisco de Vitoria* (1930); J. B. Scott, *Francisco de Vitoria and his Law of Nations* (The Spanish Origin of International Law; 1934); V. Beltrán de Heredia, OP, *Francisco de Vitoria* (Barcelona, 1939); R. Hernández, OP, *Francisco de Vitoria* (Burgos, 1983); id., 'Documento más antiguo, inédito, de

Francisco de Vitoria', *Archivo Dominicano*, 11 (1990) pp. 69–84. F. Stegmüller, *Francisco de Vitoria y la doctrina de la gracia en la escuela salmantina* (Biblioteca histórica de la Biblioteca Balmes, 2nd ser. 10; 1934). Bruno de S. José, OCD, *El Dominico Burgalés P. Maestro Fray Francisco de Vitoria y Compludo (1485–1546)* (Burgos, 1946). B. Hamilton, *Political Thought in Sixteenth-Century Spain: A Study of the Political Ideas of Vitoria, De Soto, Suárez, and Molina* (Oxford, 1963). M. Andrés [Martín], *La teología española en el Siglo XVI* (Biblioteca de Autores Cristianos, 13–14; 1976–7), esp. 2, pp. 356–61. R. C. Gonzales, OP, *Francisco de Vitoria: Estudio bibliográfico* (Buenos Aires, 1946). J. K. Farge, *Biographical Register of Paris Doctors of Theology 1500–1536* (Pontifical Institute of Mediaeval Studies, Subsidia Mediaevalia, 10; Toronto, 1980), pp. 424–31, with bibl. V. Beltrán de Heredia, OP, and J.-G. Menendez-Rigada, OP, in *DTC* 15 (pt. 2; 1950), cols. 3117–44, s.v.; R. García Villoslada in Q. Aldea Vaquero and others (eds.), *Diccionario de Historia de España*, 4 (1975), pp. 2776–8, s.v.

Vitringa, Campegius (1659–1722), biblical exegete. A native of Leeuwarden in Friesland, he was educated at Franeker and *Leiden universities and in 1680 was offered a teaching post at Franeker. Here he lectured with great success for the rest of his life, repeatedly refusing to leave the town for a more prominent position at Utrecht. His fame rests on his biblical exegesis, which, though inspired by the *Calvinistic orthodoxy of his age, succeeded in interpreting the sacred text with unusual freshness and penetration. His principal work was a commentary on Isaiah (2 vols. fol., Leeuwarden, 1714, 1720). Among his other writings were *De Synagoga Vetere* (1696; Eng. tr., *The Synagogue and the Church*, 1842), *Anakrisis Apocalypios Joannis Apostoli* (1705), and *Observationum Sacrarum libri septem* (1727).

H. Bauch, *Die Lehre vom Wirken des heiligen Geistes im Früh-pietismus* (Theologische Forschungen, 55; 1974), pp. 14–33. K. M. Witteveen in *Biografisch Lexikon voor de Geschiedenis van het Nederlandse Protestantsime*, 3 (1988), pp. 379–82.

Vitus, St (d. perhaps 303), martyr. The common legend about him is much later, and exists in several forms. He is generally supposed to have been born of pagan parents in Lucania, S. Italy, and secretly brought up as a Christian by Crescentia, his nurse, and Modestus, her husband, all three being martyred under *Diocletian. St Vitus is invoked against sudden death, hydrophobia, and the convulsive disorder known as St Vitus' dance. The association of his cultus with bodily health appears already in the *Gelasian Sacramentary, and an early S. Italian Gospel *pericope* appointed for his feast (Mt. 9: 35–10: 1) connects him with the cure of sickness and of demonic possession. He is one of the 14 *Auxiliary Saints. Feast day, 15 June.

AASS, Jun. 2 (1699), pp. 1013–42; *BHL* 2, pp. 1257–9 (nos. 8711–23), and *novum supplementum* (1986), pp. 870–2. Eng. tr. of Church Slavonic material by M. Kantor, *The Origins of Christianity in Bohemia* (Evanston, Ill., 1990), pp. 113–29, with notes pp. 282–7. Text of the *Translatio S. Viti* also ed. F. Stentrup in F. Philippi (ed.), *Abhandlungen über Corveyer Geschichtsschreibung* (Veröffentlichungen der historichen Kommission für Westfalen, 1906), pp. 51–100 (text, pp. 75–100), and, with Ger. tr., by I. Schmale-Ott (Veröffentlichen der Historischen Kommission für Westfälen, 41; 1979). J. Oswald in *L.Th.K.* (2nd edn.), 10 (1965), cols. 825–7, s.v.

Vladimir, St (d. 1015), the Apostle of the Russians and Ukrainians. Though he was a grandson of St Olga, he was brought up a pagan. In 980 he took Kiev from his elder brother, and subsequently conquered Polotsk, subjugated large districts of White Russia, and was involved in many other wars. Having assisted the Byzantine Emp. Basil II in quelling a revolt, he married *c.*989 the Emperor's sister Anne. Henceforth he was an ardent promoter of Christianity and erected many churches and monasteries; but his work of evangelism owed part of its success to physical compulsion, and those who refused Baptism were punished. Vladimir's later years were troubled by insurrections of his sons by his former pagan wives, and he died on an expedition against one of them. Feast day, 15 July.

The principal authority is the chronicle attributed to Nestor, monk of Kiev (11th–12th cent.); Eng. tr., with introd. and notes of edns. in Russ. and Ger. and Fr. trs., by S. H. Cross in *Harvard Studies and Notes in Philology and Literature*, 13 (1930), pp. 77–309 (text, pp. 178–214). N. de Baumgarten, *Saint Vladimir et la conversion de la Russie* (Orientalia Christiana, vol. 27, fasc. 1; num. 79; 1932), with full bibl. J. Fennell, 'The Canonization of Saint Vladimir', in K. C. Felmy and others (eds.), *Tausend Jahre Christentum in Russland* (Göttingen, 1988), pp. 299–304. I. Dujčev in *Bibliotheca Sanctorum*, 12 (Rome, 1969), cols. 1323–9, s.v., with further bibl.

Voetius, Gisbert (1589–1676), Dutch Reformed theologian. A native of Heusden in the Netherlands, he was educated at the University of *Leiden, where he was deeply influenced by F. *Gomar. A minister successively at Vlijmen (1611) and Heusden (1617), he was a delegate to the Synod of *Dort (1618–19). From the first he fought against *Arminianism and defended an uncompromising *Calvinistic predestinarianism. In 1634 he was appointed professor of theology and oriental languages at Utrecht, and in 1637 also pastor of the Reformed Church there. A man of strong convictions and violently hostile to everything Catholic, he was involved in frequent controversies. A proponent of Reformed scholasticism, he defended strict Calvinism against the freer school represented by J. *Cocceius, carried on bitter and often unfair attacks against R. *Descartes, and at the end of his life quarrelled with J. de *Labadie because of his separatist tendencies. Greatly influenced by the works of Willem Teellinck (1579–1629) and those of English *Puritans, esp. W. *Ames, Voetius did much to promote the rise of Dutch *Pietism. His writings include *Disputationes Theologicae Selectae* (5 vols., Utrecht, 1648–69), *Politica Ecclesiastica* (4 vols., Amsterdam, 1663–76) and *Diatribae de Theologia* (Utrecht, 1668).

Eng. tr. of extracts from his *Disputationes Theologicae Selectae* by J. W. Beardslee, *Reformed Dogmatics* (Library of Protestant Theology, New York, 1965), pp. 263–334. Life by A. C. Duker (3 vols. + index vol., Leiden, 1897–1915; repr., with introd. by A. de Groot, ibid., 1989). M. Bouwman, *Voetius over het Gezag der Synoden* (Amsterdam, 1937). C. Steenblok, *Gisbertus Voetius: zijn leven en werken* (Gouda, 1942; 2nd edn., 1976). J. van Oort (ed.), *De onbekende Voetius: voordrachten wetenschappelijk symposium, Utrecht 3 maart 1989* (Kampen, 1989). D. Nauta in *Biografisch Lexicon voor de Geschiedenis van het Nederlandse Protestantisme*, 2 (1983) pp. 443–9.

Voltaire, pseudonym of **François-Marie Arouet** (1694–1778), French writer. His burning desire for social reform and his biting pen made him the most celebrated of the French 'Philosophes'. Educated by the Paris *Jesuits, throughout his life he was violently opposed to the Catholic Church, in whose institutions he saw nothing but deceit, superstition, and fanaticism; on the other hand he undertook the defence of *Deism with, as Lanson wrote, 'determination, warmth and courage'. After a quarrel with the Chevalier de Rohan, Voltaire went into exile in London from 1726 to 1729. His *Lettres philosophiques* or *Lettres sur les Anglais* (1734; originally published in England as *Letters concerning the English Nation*, 1733) held up an idealized picture of England as a land of rationalist philosophy, just social institutions, and religious toleration, as an object-lesson to the French reader. He also praised J. *Locke and I. *Newton, the authors who, with Samuel *Clarke, had the greatest influence on his Deism, although whenever possible he reduced metaphysical problems to matters of ethics. An attack on B. *Pascal, whom Voltaire selected as representative of the strain in Christianity most opposed to his own ethical optimism, was added to the letters as an appendix. When the book was publicly burnt in Paris, he fled to Cirey in Champagne, the country house of Madame du Châtelet, where he wrote his (posthumously pub.) *Traité de métaphysique* (1734) and *Éléments de la philosophie de Newton* (1738), and completed several of his most successful plays, among them *Mahomet* (1742), as well as the blasphemous epic on St *Joan of Arc, *La Pucelle* (1739; pub. 1755). From 1750 to 1752 he lived at the court of Frederick II of Prussia, and in 1758 bought the estate of Ferney, on the Swiss frontier, where he led the life of a country gentleman. The problem of *Theodicy always preoccupied him. At first inclined towards the solution of G. *Leibniz, he then violently rejected it, delivering its *coup de grâce* in *Candide* (1759); after this he attempted to set aside metaphysical inquiry for positive social action, taking up in particular the cause of the victims of religious intolerance, such as the Huguenot Jean Calas. During the last 15 or so years of his life his views came increasingly into conflict with those of the younger generation of 'Philosophes', notably P. H. D. d'Holbach (1723–1789), who were materialists and atheists and considered Voltaire's Deism retrograde. Voltaire bitterly attacked atheism not, as is sometimes maintained, because he regarded belief in the existence of God and personal immortality as necessary simply for the government of the masses, but out of a pragmatic conviction that without these beliefs human existence would be one of meaningless anarchy. The Irish Catholic writer Alfred Noyes described Voltaire as a true son of the Church 'whose criticisms, like those of Erasmus, were only letters to the family'. While this view is clearly untenable, it should nevertheless not be overlooked that the belief in absolute moral values which Voltaire's Deism subserved, his championship of religious toleration, and even the faint stirrings of personal faith which occasionally diversified his scepticism, were qualities often sadly lacking in the official institutions and representatives of Christianity in his day.

Voltaire's *Complete Works* are being newly ed. by T. Besterman and others (Geneva and Toronto, 1968–9; Geneva, 1970–1; Thorpe Mandeville, Banbury, 1971–6; Oxford 1976 ff.); they are expected to run to some 150 vols. Individual works have frequently been ed. and tr., incl. Correspondence, ed. T. Besterman (107 vols., Geneva, 1953–65). The extensive lit. incl., besides the well-known Life by J. Morley (London, 1872), studies by G. Lanson ('Les Grands Écrivains français', 1906), H. N. Brailsford

(HUL, 1935), N. L. Torrey (New York, 1938), R. Naves (Paris, 1942), P. [J.] Gay (Princeton, NJ, 1959), I. O. Wade (ibid., 1969), and H. [T.] Mason (London, 1981). R. Pomeau, *La Religion de Voltaire* (1956; new edn., 1969), and other works of this author. G. Bengesco, *Voltaire: Bibliographie de ses œuvres* (4 vols., 1882–90); M. M. H. Barr, *A Century of Voltaire: A Bibliography of Writings on Voltaire, 1825–1925* (New York, 1929); id., *Quarante Années d'Études Voltairiennes: . . . 1926–1965* (1968); F. A. Spear, *Bibliographie analytique des écrits relatifs à Voltaire 1966–1990* (Oxford, 1992). C. Constantin in *DTC* 15 (pt. 2; 1950), cols. 3387–471, s.v.

voluntary. A piece of music played on the organ at the beginning or end of (and, occasionally, during) a religious service. Those played at the beginning and close are sometimes distinguished as the in- and out-voluntaries.

Voluntaryism. Esp. in *Scotland, the doctrine that the Church ought to be spiritually independent of the State. It rests on the theses that the establishment of a particular denomination is unjust and that State endowments are devitalizing.

von Harnack, Adolf. See HARNACK, ADOLF.

von Hofmann, J. C. K. See HOFMANN, J. C. K. VON

von Hügel, Baron Friedrich (1852–1925), RC theologian and philosopher. He was born at Florence, the elder son of Carl Alexander Anselm, Baron von Hügel (1795–1870), and of Elizabeth, *née* Farquharson, a Scottish Presbyterian lady who was a convert to the RC Church. After a cosmopolitan education he settled in England in 1867. In 1870 an attack of typhus left him deaf and permanently weakened in health. After a religious crisis he was brought to a firm faith at Vienna through the influence of Raymond Hocking, a Dutch *Dominican (1870). He married in 1873 and for the rest of his life lived at Hampstead (1876–1903) and Kensington (1903–25), though he constantly travelled abroad. In 1884 he met for the first time H. *Huvelin at *Paris, who made a profound spiritual impression on him.

Meanwhile von Hügel had become a keen student of science (esp. geology), philosophy, biblical criticism, and religious history. Having become convinced of the critical view of the OT, he defended it in 1897 in a Congress at Fribourg (Switzerland). He found himself in growing accord with the cultural and liberalizing tendencies in the RC Church and several of the leaders of the *Modernist Movement (A. *Loisy, G. *Tyrrell) became his lifelong friends. In 1904 he founded the London Society for the Study of Religion, which brought him into touch with thinkers and scholars of the most diverse views. In 1908 he published *The Mystical Element of Religion as studied in St Catherine of Genoa and her Friends*. This was followed in 1911 by an article on St John's Gospel in the *Encyclopaedia Britannica* (11th edn.) and in 1912 by his book *Eternal Life*. In 1921 appeared his *Essays and Addresses on the Philosophy of Religion*; a second series followed in 1926, after his death. He was appointed *Gifford Lecturer at Edinburgh for 1924–6, but owing to ill-health was unable to deliver the course; portions of it were published posthumously in *The Reality of God* (1931).

Among the problems with which von Hügel constantly wrestled were the relation of Christianity to history (in which field he found a kindred spirit in E. *Troeltsch), the place of human culture in the Christian life, the Christian conception of time, and the significance of eschatology for the modern world. He saw the Institutional, the Intellectual, and the Mystical as the three abiding elements in religion. In his earlier life he had much sympathy with the activist philosophy of M. *Blondel, but believing that the essence of religion was 'adoration', he came in his later years to emphasize the Divine transcendence and the 'givenness' of faith. 'The Baron' became one of the chief religious influences in cultured circles in England, more so outside the RC Church than within it, though his 'Modernism' escaped formal condemnation. The confidence which he inspired as a spiritual counsellor may be clearly discerned in his published correspondence.

Von Hügel's *Selected Letters, 1896–1924*, ed. B. Holland (1927), with Memoir by id., pp. 1–68; *Letters from Baron Friedrich von Hügel to a Niece*, ed. G. Greene (1928), with introd., pp. vii–xlv; *The Letters of Baron Friedrich von Hügel and Professor Norman Kemp Smith*, ed. L. F. Barmann (New York, 1981). Much of his correspondence with G. Tyrrell is pr. in M. D. Petre, *Von Hügel and Tyrrell: The Story of a Friendship* (1937). Life by M. de la Bedoyère (London, 1951). Studies by M. Nédoncelle (Paris thesis, 1935; Eng. tr., 1937), J. Steinmann (Paris, 1962), J. J. Heaney (Washington, DC, 1968; London, 1969), J. P. Whelan, SJ (London, 1971), and L. F. Barmann (Cambridge, 1972). P. Neuner, *Religiöse Erfahrung und geschichtliche Offenbarung: Friedrich von Hügels Grundlegung der Theologie* (Beiträge zur ökumenischen Theologie, 15; 1977); J. J. Kelly, *Baron Friedrich von Hügel's Philosophy of Religion* (Bibliotheca Ephemeridum Theologicarum Lovaniensium, 62; 1983). T. M. Loome, *Liberal Catholicism, Reform Catholicism, Modernism* (Tübingen Theologische Studien, 14; 1979), esp. pp. 123–92 and 209–17. C. C. J. *Webb in *DNB, 1922–1930*, pp. 874–6.

Vonier, Anscar (1875–1938), *Benedictine theologian. Born in Württemberg, he entered *Buckfast Abbey as a boy. After surviving a shipwreck in which his abbot died, Vonier was elected to succeed him in 1906 and immediately undertook to rebuild the abbey church. His theological writings were noted for their clear exposition of abstruse questions. They covered a wide range of subjects, including Christology and spirituality. The most influential was *A Key to the Doctrine of the Eucharist* (1925) which, at a time when it was not usual to do so, emphasized the corporate nature of the liturgy.

Collected Works (3 vols., 1952–3). E. Graf, OSB, *Anscar Vonier: Abbot of Buckfast* (1957).

Vorstius, Conradus (1569–1622), Konrad von der Vorst, *Arminian theologian. He was a native of *Cologne. After abandoning his early intention of entering business, he studied theology at Herborn and Heidelberg, and later proceeded to Basle and Geneva, where he greatly impressed T. *Beza by his abilities. In 1596 he accepted a teaching post at Count Arnold of Bertheim's academy at Steinfurt. Certain of his writings gave rise to a charge of Socinianism; but having successfully cleared himself before the Theological Faculty at Heidelberg, he continued to teach at Steinfurt, where his reputation rose from year to year. In 1610, after the death of J. Arminius, he accepted, after much hesitation, a call by J. Uitenbogaert to the vacant chair at *Leiden. In the same year he issued a treatise against R. *Bellarmine and also the

second, greatly expanded, edition of a work (orig. pub. in 1606), *Tractatus Theologicus de Deo, sive de Natura et Attributis Dei*, which at once provoked attention on account of its rationalist tendencies. Strict Calvinists led by F. *Gomar pronounced it heretical; the Heidelberg theologians, and even H. a *Saravia, professed themselves shocked; and when *James I's attention was drawn to it he drew up a list of its theological errors, had Vorstius' books publicly burned in England, and instructed Ralph Winwood, the British Ambassador at The Hague, to oppose their author's appointment. Vorstius in consequence found himself compelled to retire from Leiden to Gouda (1612). Meanwhile he increased suspicion by translating certain of the works of F. *Socinus; and at the Synod of *Dort (1618–19) he was condemned as a heretic and banished from the territory of the States-General. He was the author of a long series of writings, including a commentary on most of St Paul's Epp. (posthumous, 1631). He was more sympathetic to the Fathers than most Protestant theologians of his age.

A. Schweizer, 'Conradus Vorstius. Vermittlung der reformirten Centraldogmen mit den socinianischen Einwendungen', *Theologische Jahrbücher*, 15 (1856), pp. 435–86, and 16 (1857), pp. 153–84. F. Shriver, 'Orthodoxy and diplomacy: James I and the Vorstius affair', *EHR* 85 (1970), pp. 449–74. C. van der Woude in *Biografisch Lexicon voor de Geschiedenis van het Nederlandse Protestantisme*, 1 (1978), pp. 407–10, s.v.

Voss, Gerhard Jan (1577–1649), Gerardus Joannes Vossius, Dutch humanist theologian. Born in Germany of Dutch parents, he was educated at *Leiden. In 1600 he became rector of the Latin School at Dordrecht and *c*.1615 regent of the States' College at Leiden. In common with his lifelong friend, H. *Grotius, he believed that the religious disputes of the day could be solved only by a profound study of Christian antiquity. He became involved in the disputes between the *Remonstrants and their opponents; and as himself suspected of Remonstrant leanings, he was compelled to resign his post in 1619. In 1622 he accepted a professorship of rhetoric and chronology, and later also of Greek, at Leiden University. He twice refused a call to Cambridge, but accepted a non-residential prebend at *Canterbury Cathedral from Abp. W. *Laud, being installed in 1629, and made a DCL at Oxford. In 1632 he was appointed professor of general and Church history at the newly founded Athenaeum at Amsterdam.

Voss's *Historia Pelagiana* (1618), *De Theologia Gentili* (1641), and *Dissertationes Tres de Tribus Symbolis* (1642) were all solid contributions to learning. In the last he was among the first to argue that the *Apostles' Creed was the work, not of the Apostles themselves, but of the early Roman Church. He also decisively disproved the traditional authorship of the *Athanasian Creed. He was one of the first scholars to apply the historical method to Christian dogmatics.

His son, **Isaac Voss** (1618–89), who became a residentiary Canon of Windsor in 1673, was also a classical and ecclesiastical historian of much erudition. He edited Pomponius Mela (1658), Marcus Junianus Justinus (1664), and Catullus (1684) and also zealously defended the genuineness of St *Ignatius's Epistles.

Collected edn. of G. J. Voss's *Opera*, pub. in 6 vols., Amsterdam, 1695–1701. P. Colomesius (ed.), *Gerardi Joan. Vossii et*

Clarorum Virorum ad eum Epistolae (London, 1690). G. A. C. van der Lem and C. S. M. Rademaker, SSCC (eds.), *Inventory of the Correspondence of Gerardus Joannes Vossius (1577–1649)* (Respublica Literaria Neederlandica, 7; Assen, 1993). C. S. M. Rademaker, *Life and Work of Gerardus Joannes Vossius (1577–1649)* (ibid. 5; 1981). N. Wickenden, *G. J. Vossius and the Humanist Concept of History* (ibid. 8; 1993).

On Isaac Voss, see T. Seccombe in *DNB* 58 (1899), pp. 392–6.

Votive Masses. In the past Latin Missals have provided Votive Masses for a wide variety of occasions and objects, such as the election of a Pope or the restoration of peace, or in honour of particular mysteries, such as the Passion of our Lord. In the 1970 Roman Missal there are 15 Votive Masses, including those of the Trinity, the Holy Spirit, the Blessed Sacrament, the BVM, *angels, St *Joseph, the Apostles, St *Peter and St *Paul, and All Saints. Their purpose is defined as to encourage the piety of the people, and this consideration alone is to govern their use. They may be said at the discretion of the celebrant on any day on which there is no feast or obligatory *memoria, though the trend of contemporary practice is to discourage the celebration of Votive Masses in favour of observing the ecclesiastical calendar. The Solemn Votive Masses (for a 'grave cause'), which were usually prescribed by the bishop, have now been replaced by prayers or Masses for Various Needs and Occasions (46 of these, some with alternative texts) which may be said on any days except *Solemnities and the Sundays of Advent, Lent, and Eastertide, while the *Ritual Masses (q.v.) provide for particular needs, such as marriage (see NUPTIAL MASS).

vowel points. In common with some other Semitic languages, *Hebrew was originally written without vowel signs. In early inscriptions, certain consonant signs were used to represent vowels as well as consonants, especially at the end of words, and in course of time these 'vowel letters' were increasingly used to represent both final and medial vowels. Later, when the language was no longer spoken and there was a danger of the traditional pronunciation being forgotten, a system of 'vowel points' was introduced. These are dots or strokes, superimposed upon the consonantal text. Similar points are used to harden the pronunciation of certain consonants and to distinguish the letters 'Sin' (שׂ) and 'Shin' (שׁ), which are otherwise identical. In the Babylonian and Palestinian systems pointing signs are exclusively superlinear, but in the Tiberian system the signs came to be placed above, below and within the consonants. The Tiberian system, which largely replaced the earlier systems, is attributed to the *Massoretes. It was probably completed by *c.* AD 900. However, this system of vowel points has never been widely used in non-biblical texts, and certain biblical texts, such as synagogue scrolls, are also unvocalized. Modern (Israeli) Hebrew is normally written without vowel points. See also HEBREW (TONGUE).

E. Würthwein, *Der Text des Alten Testaments* (4th edn., 1973), pp. 23–30; Eng. tr. of this edn. (Grand Rapids, Mich., 1979; London, 1980), pp. 21–7. J. Barr, 'Vocalization and the Analysis of Hebrew among the Ancient Translators', in *Hebräische Wortforschung: Festschrift zum 80. Geburtstag von Walter Baumgartner* (Supplements to *Vetus Testamentum*, 16; 1967), pp. 1–11.

vows. Solemn and voluntary promises to perform something not otherwise required but believed to be acceptable to the person to whom the vows are made. Such promises to the Deity are common in many religions.

In the OT vows are sometimes explicitly dependent upon the performance of certain favours by Yahweh (e.g. the oath of Jacob at Bethel, Gen. 28: 20–2; Hannah's dedication of Samuel, 1 Sam. 1: 11); others appear to have been made unconditionally (cf. Ps. 132: 2–5). In the former case the vow was conceived less as a payment than as an offering of thankfulness (cf. the custom which still survives in some countries of vowing the model of a ship after deliverance from shipwreck). The special kind of vows made by the *Nazirites (q.v.) were prob. in origin an extension of such vows of self-dedication as are found in Ps. 132 and in Saul's prohibition against eating before sundown (1 Sam. 14: 24). The obligation to fulfil a vow once undertaken could be seen as absolute, as appears in the case of Jephthah's daughter (Jgs. 11: 30–9). This obligation was emphasized in the Law (Deut. 23: 21–3), though it was recognized that things unlawful should not be offered to Yahweh even in fulfilment of a vow (Deut. 23: 18). However, in Lev. 27: 1–8 (attributed by those scholars who favour a 'documentary hypothesis' to *P, *c.* 5th cent. BC), a system was elaborated whereby persons under vows might evade a direct offering of themselves by the payment of a fixed sum; things vowed might be redeemed by the payment of their value together with an extra sum in compensation. Later Jewish practice can be found in the tractate 'Nedarim' of the *Talmud.

In the NT Christ condemned the Jewish rule which enabled a man to escape his duty to his parents on the pretext of a vow (Mk. 7: 9–13), thus emphasizing that the matter of a vow pleasing to God must itself be acceptable. St *Paul is recorded to have been under a vow on his own account on one occasion (Acts 18: 18) and on another occasion to have joined others in fulfilling one (Acts 21: 23 f.). Vows of virginity, which were taken from a very early date, may be implied in 1 Cor. 7.

Acc. to Catholic moral theologians a vow to be valid must be freely made by a person who has a sufficient use of reason, be within the bounds of possibility of performance and tending to some future good. By definition it cannot relate to matters of precept. With the development of monasticism the threefold vow to follow the evangelical *counsels of perfection, taken on entering the religious life, came to occupy special prominence. Those most commonly taken outside religious profession include vows to go on a pilgrimage, vows of chastity, and vows dedicating property, but they may cover a variety of subjects. A vow may be private, in which case it is usually taken with the consent of a confessor, or public, when it is accepted in the name of the Church by a legitimate authority, such as an Abbot receiving a vow of profession. Since *c.* the 13th cent. *canon law has also distinguished between 'simple' and 'solemn' vows. The exact scope of the distinction is disputed, but acc. to a common view the solemnity of vows is determined by their irrevocable acceptance. In practice the distinction is determined in the RC Church by whether a vow is instituted and accepted as solemn by the Church. In the religious life, however, the main distinction is now between temporary and perpetual vows (rather than between simple and solemn ones). Current legislation on vows is contained in *CIC* (1983), cans. 1191–8.

L. I. Rabinowitz in *Encyclopaedia Judaica*, 16 (Jerusalem, 1972), cols. 227 f., s.v. 'Vows and Vowing'. P. Séjourné, OSB, in *DTC* 15 (pt. 2; 1950), cols. 3182–281, s.v. 'Vœu, Vœux de Religion'.

Voysey, Charles (1828–1912), Theistic preacher. He was educated at St Edmund Hall, Oxford. After ordination in the C of E he held a number of curacies in London and elsewhere, at one of which (St Mary's, Victoria Docks) he preached a sermon denying the doctrine of eternal punishment. From 1864 to 1871 he was vicar of Healaugh, nr. Tadcaster. Here his heterodox opinions led to his citation before the Chancellor of *York, and the sentence of deprivation which followed was upheld on his appeal to the Privy Council. Removing to London, Voysey began holding services in St George's Hall, Langham Place, and founded the 'Theistic Church', whose headquarters from 1885 were in Swallow Street, off Regent Street. On Voysey's death some of his followers formed a schism, the 'Free Religious Movement'.

D. Wright in *DNB, 1912–1921*, pp. 545 f., s.v.

Vulgate. The Latin version of the Bible (*editio vulgata*) most widely used in the W. It was for the most part the work of St *Jerome, and its original purpose was to end the great differences of text in the *Old Latin MSS circulating in the latter part of the 4th cent.

Jerome began his work, at the request of Pope *Damasus in 382, with a revision of the Gospels which was completed in 384. Here he seems to have used as the basis of his revision a Greek MS closely akin to the *Codex Sinaiticus. That he revised the remaining books of the NT is unlikely.

In revising the Latin text of the OT, Jerome began with the Psalms. He records that he had made a 'hasty' attempt to translate the *Psalter from the *Septuagint before *c*.392, when he completed the '*Gallican Psalter', using as his basis Origen's *Hexaplaric text of the Septuagint. Further work on other books of the OT on the same lines convinced him that a satisfactory version could only be made by working directly from the Hebrew original and making a completely fresh translation, which should be entirely independent of the Greek. This translation occupied him intermittently for some 15 years and included a third recension of the Psalter (the 'Hebrew Psalter'). The 'Hebrew Psalter', however, never won general acceptance; the 'Gallican Psalter' was adopted for liturgical use and came to be included in Vulgate MSS and so became standard in the printed texts.

Jerome's translations had at first to face considerable opposition through the long and sacred associations of the earlier texts; both the old and the new versions remained in use together for some time, but the excellence of Jerome's work was gradually recognized. When (prob. in the 6th cent.) the various books came to be collected into a single Bible (the Vulgate as we know it), it consisted of Jerome's translation from the Hebrew of the Jewish canonical books except the Psalter; the Gallican Psalter; Jerome's translation of Tobit and Judith; Old Latin translations of the rest of the Apocrypha; Jerome's revision of the Gospels; and a revised text of Acts, Epistles, and Rev. Various suggestions have been made about the identity of the

reviser or revisers of the latter part of the NT, but all that can be said with certainty is that the earliest evidence for its existence is found in quotations in the writings of *Pelagius and his circle. The first unambiguous reference to a collection of biblical books within one cover occurs in the work of *Cassiodorus (*Institutes*, 1. 12. 3); the oldest known MS containing the whole Vulgate is the *Codex Amiatinus.

From the first, the translations which came to form the Vulgate were liable to easy corruption by reminiscence of Old Latin readings, esp. in the NT. Confusion was also caused by the practice of inserting into Old Latin MSS the more important of Jerome's corrections; the NT contained in the Book of *Armagh provides an example of the type of 'mixed' text which resulted. Attempts to standardize the text were made from the time of Cassiodorus onwards: notable among these were that associated with the name of *Alcuin and the work of *Theodulf of Orléans. A fresh, but corrupt, standard text (the 'Exemplar Parisiense') was put forth by the University of Paris in the 13th cent. Further efforts to preserve a standard text were made by the various '*correctoria' (q.v.).

The first printed edition was the *Mazarin (or 'Gutenberg') Bible (1456). A great many printed editions followed. The first critical text was that of Robert *Stephanus (Paris, 1528). At its Fourth Session (8 Apr. 1546) the Council of *Trent pronounced the Vulgate the only authentic Latin text of the Scriptures, and an edition eventually issued under the authority of *Sixtus V in 1590 was intended to be definitive. As, however, it contained many errors, existing copies, as far as possible, were called in and a revised text issued in 1592 by *Clement VIII, with some 3,000 corrections. Since, however, Sixtus had declared in his Bull authorizing the 1590 edition that that alone was the approved edition and its text was unalterable, the revised edition of 1592 bore the title-page: *Biblia Sacra Vulgatae Editionis Sixti Quinti Pont. Max. jussu recognita atque edita*, though it is commonly known as the 'Clementine edition'.

Later research has shown that the Clementine edition departs at many points from Jerome's text, and several attempts have been made to revise it. An emended text was printed by D. *Vallarsi in 1734; but owing to Papal prohibitions against further emendation of the Bible he included it in his edition of Jerome as the 'Divina Biblioteca'. A fresh edition projected by R. *Bentley was never completed. A critical edition of the NT, by John *Wordsworth (d. 1911), H. J. White (d. 1934), H. F. D. Sparks, and A. W. Adams was pub. in the years 1889–1954. In 1908 *Pius X appointed a Commission with F. A. *Gasquet as president to produce a new edition. Publication began with Genesis at the Vatican Press in 1926, and is in progress. A handy, two-volume edition, prepared by R. Weber, OSB, and four collaborators, was pub. by the Württemberg Bibelanstalt at Stuttgart in 1969. There is a concordance ed. B. Fischer, OSB (5 vols., ibid., 1977).

Edns. of the Clementine Vulgate are innumerable. Besides the two crit. texts (Papal Commission; J. Wordsworth, H. J. White, etc.) and the two Stuttgart volumes, there is a convenient students' edn., *Novum Testamentum Latine: Editio Minor* (Oxford, 1911), by H. J. White. S. Berger, *Histoire de la Vulgate pendant les premiers siècles du moyen âge* (1893). F. Stummer, *Einführung in die lateinische Bibel* (1928). H. *Quentin, OSB, *Mémoire sur *l'établissement du texte de la Vulgate*, 1, Octateuque (Collectanea Biblica Latina, 6; Rome and Paris, 1922). J. *Chapman, OSB, *Notes on the Early History of the Vulgate Gospels* (1908); H. J. Vogels, *Vulgatastudien: Die Evangelien der Vulgata, untersucht auf ihre lateinische und griechische Vorlage* (Neutestamentliche Abhandlungen, 14, Hefte 2–3; 1928); H. Glunz, *Britannien und Bibeltext: Der Vulgatatext der Evangelien in seinem Verhältnis zu irisch-angelsächsischen Kultur des Frühmittelalters* (Kölner anglistische Arbeiten, 12; 1930); id., *History of the Vulgate in England from Alcuin to Roger Bacon: Being an Inquiry into the Text of some English Manuscripts of the Vulgate Gospels* (1933). B. Smalley, *The Study of the Bible in the Middle Ages* (1941; 3rd edn. [1983]), *passim*; J. Fontaine and C. Pietri (eds.), *Le Monde latin antique et la Bible* (Bible et tous les temps, 2 [1985]). T. Stramare (ed.), *La Bibbia 'Vulgata' dalle origini ai nostri giorni: Atti del Simposio Internazionale in onore di Sisto V, Grottammare, 29–31 agosto 1985* (Collectanea Biblica Latina, 16; 1985). B. Fischer [OSB], *Die lateinischen Evangelien bis zum 10. Jahrhundert* (Vetus Latina, Aus der Geschichte der Lateinischen Bibel, 13, 15, 17, and 18; 1988–91). R. Loewe, 'The Medieval History of the Latin Vulgate' in *The Cambridge History of the Bible*, 2 (ed. G. W. H. Lampe; Cambridge, 1969), pp. 102–54; H. F. D. Sparks, 'Jerome as a Biblical Scholar', ibid. 1 (ed. P. R. Ackroyd and C. F. Evans; 1970), 510–41, esp. pp. 517–26. B. Fischer, OSB, 'Das Neue Testament in lateinischer Sprache', in K. Aland (ed.), *Die alten Übersetzungen des Neuen Testaments, die Kirchenväterzitate und Lektionare* (Arbeiten zur Neutestamentlichen Textforschung, 5; 1972), pp. 1–92, repr. in id., *Beiträge zur Geschichte der lateinischen Bibeltexte* (Aus der Geschichte der lateinischen Bibel, 12; 1986), pp. 156–274; also other items in this vol. P.-M. Bogaert, OSB, 'La Bible latine des origines au moyen âge. Aperçu historique, état des questions', *Revue Théologique de Louvain*, 19 (1988), pp. 137–59 and 276–314. B. Kedar, 'The Latin Translations', in M. J. Mulder (ed.), *Mikra* (Compendia Rerum Iudaicarum ad Novum Testamentum, 2. 1; Assen/Maastricht and Philadelphia, 1988), pp. 299–338, esp. pp. 313–38. W. E. Plater and H. J. White, *A Grammar of the Vulgate* (1926). H. J. White in *HDB* 4 (1902), pp. 873–90, s.v.; E. Mangenot in *Dict. Bibl.* 5 (1912), cols. 2456–500, s.v.; V. Reichmann in *TRE* 6 (1980), pp. 178–81, s.v. 'Bibelübersetzungen', 3. 3. 'Zum Geschichte der Vulgata'. See also CODEX AMIATINUS and CODEX FULDENSIS.

W

Wace, Henry (1836–1924), Dean of *Canterbury. He was educated at Rugby and Brasenose College, Oxford, and ordained in 1862. In 1863 he became a regular contributor to *The Times*. He was chaplain (1872–80), and then (1880–96) preacher, of Lincoln's Inn; Principal of *King's College, London (1883–96); rector of St Michael's, Cornhill (1896–1903); and from 1903 until his death Dean of Canterbury. He was a staunch Evangelical and supporter of the Reformation settlement, an admirer of M. *Luther, and equally opposed to the modern methods of 'higher criticism' of the Bible and to the High Church attempts at revising the BCP. He was the editor, with W. Smith, of the *Dictionary of Christian Biography* (4 vols., 1880–6), with P. *Schaff of the second series of the *Nicene and Post-Nicene Fathers* (14 vols., 1890–1900), and with C. A. Buchheim of *Luther's Primary Works* (1896). His own writings include lectures on *The Gospel and its Witnesses* (1883), and *The Bible and Modern Investigations* (1903), as well as numerous articles in newspapers and periodicals.

A. Cochrane in *DNB, 1922–1930*, pp. 876 f., s.v.

Wadding, Luke (1588–1657), *Franciscan historian. A native of Waterford, he made his profession in the Franciscan Order at Matozinhos, nr. Oporto, in 1608, studied at Lisbon and Coimbra, and was ordained priest in 1613. In 1617 he became president of the Irish College at Salamanca, and in 1618 theologian to the Spanish Embassy sent to Rome to promote the definition of the *Immaculate Conception. His studies led to his *Legatio Philippi III et IV pro definienda controversia Immaculatae Conceptionis* (1624). In 1625 he took over the new friary of St Isidore in Rome, which he developed into a college for Irish Franciscans. The establishment of the Ludovician College for Irish secular clergy followed in 1627. He served as consultor to the *Holy Office, was appointed a member of the commission set up to reform the *Breviary (1629) and the *Missal (1631), and advised the Sacred Congregation of the *Propaganda over the reorganization of the RC Church in Ireland, to which he was largely instrumental in securing the dispatch of a Papal Nuncio. In 1652 he was a member of the commission set up by *Innocent X to investigate *Jansenism. His principal works were the *Annales Ordinis Minorum* (8 vols., 1625–1654; 3rd edn., 25 vols., 1931–5), a monumental collection of material on the history of the Franciscan Order to 1540, with its subsidiary *Scriptores Ordinis Minorum* (1650; new edn., 1906), which is still indispensable for students of Franciscan history; and his edition of the works of *Duns Scotus (16 vols., 1639; new edn., 26 vols., 1891–5, repr. Farnborough, 1969).

B. Jennings, OFM (ed.), *Wadding Papers 1614–38* (Irish Manuscripts Commission, Dublin, 1953); id., 'Some Correspondence of Father Luke Wadding, O.F.M.', *Collectanea Hibernica*, 2 (1959), pp. 66–94. Life by F. Harold (nephew) orig. pr. in Epitome to *Annales* (Rome, 1662), prefixed to *Annales*, 1 (2nd edn., Rome, 1731), pp. i–clxxx. J. A. O'Shea, OSF, *The Life of Father Luke*

Wadding (Dublin, 1885). F. Casolini, *Luca Wadding, O.F.M.: L'annalista dei Francescani* (Milan, 1936). G. Cleary, *Father Luke Wadding and St Isidore's College, Rome* (Rome, 1925). *Father Luke Wadding: Commemorative Volume*, edited by the Franciscan Fathers of Dún Mhuire, Killeney (1957). C. Mooney, OFM, 'The Writings of Father Luke Wadding, O.F.M.', *Franciscan Studies*, 18 (1958), pp. 225–39. E. Pásztor, 'Luca Wadding, editore della "Vita Anselmi episcopi Lucensis"', *AFH* 54 (1961), pp. 303–28. B. Millett, OFM, in *NCE* 14 (1967), pp. 761 f. s.v., with further bibl.

Wailing Wall, known in Jewish tradition as the 'Western Wall', in *Jerusalem. Originally part of the *Temple structure erected by *Herod the Great, since the 7th cent. it has formed the W. wall of the Haram-es-Sherif ('The Noble Sanctuary'), which is the third most holy place in the world to Muslims after Mecca and Medina. The wall has been venerated by Jews since the destruction of the Temple in AD 70. They have been accustomed, prob. since the Middle Ages, to lament at this wall the downfall of the Temple and the Holy City and to pray, esp. on the *Sabbath, for their restoration; it is this custom which has given rise to the popular name.

J. Auerbach in *Encyclopaedia Judaica*, 16 (Jerusalem, 1972), cols. 467–72, s.v. 'Western Wall'.

wake. A vigil, and hence a holiday. The name (from Lat. *vigilia*) was originally applied to the all-night *vigil kept, from Anglo-Saxon times onwards, before certain holy days, but it early came to refer to the feasting and merry-making on the holy day itself, and then (by the 16th cent.) to a fair held annually at the festival of the local patron saint. The word survives as the name of annual local holidays of two or three days observed by a whole town or village in the Northern and West Midland districts of England. In Ireland a wake is a vigil and feast at a funeral.

Wake, William (1657–1737), Abp. of *Canterbury. Educated at *Christ Church, Oxford, he went to Paris as chaplain of the English ambassador in 1682, an office to which he owed his acquaintance with *Gallicanism. After his return to England in 1685 he held various ecclesiastical appointments, being made Canon of Christ Church in 1689 and Dean of *Exeter in 1703. In 1705 he became Bp. of *Lincoln and in 1716 Abp. of Canterbury. From 1717 to 1720 he was engaged in negotiations with representatives of Gallicanism, notably L. E. *Dupin, on a plan of reunion between the C of E and the French Church, in which both parties showed themselves ready for concessions. The death of Dupin in 1719, however, checked the project, which would probably have proved unacceptable in any case to both the English and the French clergy. A man of liberal views, Wake was in sympathy with the Nonconformists, and even advocated changes in the BCP to meet their difficulties, though he opposed, in 1718, a bill for modification of the *Corporation and *Test Acts. Among his numerous writings the most important is *The*

State of the Church and Clergy of England (1703), a history of English ecclesiastical synods which was intended as a reply to F. *Atterbury's theories of Convocation. His *Principles of the Christian Religion* (1700), a commentary on the BCP Catechism, became very popular. Wake bequeathed his valuable collections and library to Christ Church, which also possesses a large number of his unpublished manuscripts.

William Wake's Gallican Correspondence and Related Documents, 1716–1731, ed. L. Adams (American University Studies, Series 7, vols. 26 [in 2 parts], 55–8, and 134; New York, etc., 1988–93). J. Gres-Gayer (ed.), *Paris-Cantorbéry (1717–1720): Le Dossier d'un oecuménisme* [1989]. Life by N. Sykes (2 vols., Cambridge, 1957). J. H. Lupton, *Archbishop Wake and the Project of Union (1717–20) between the Gallican and Anglican Churches* (1896); E. Préclin, *L'Union des Églises gallicane et anglicane: Une tentative au temps de Louis XV. P.-F. le Courayer (de 1681 à 1732) et Guillaume Wake* (1928). J. H. Lupton in *DNB* 58 (1899), pp. 445 f., s.v.

Walafrid Strabo (*c.*808–49), i.e. 'Walafrid the Squinter', poet and biblical exegete. Of a local family, he spent his childhood and adolescence in the monastery of *Reichenau, where he wrote his first major poem, the *Visio Wettini*. After completing his education with *Rabanus Maurus at *Fulda (827–9), he became tutor to the Emperor's son Charles (the future King and Emp. Charles the Bald) in 829. His reward was the abbacy of Reichenau itself in 839 (confirmed in 842). He was drowned crossing the Loire on 18 Aug. 849. Walafrid wrote occasional verse for members of the court and the higher clergy, and a more ambitious poem *De Cultura Hortorum* (on gardening) that draws heavily on *Virgil and Ovid. He developed Rabanus' exegetical writings and followed him too in his liturgical treatise *De Exordiis et Incrementis quarundam in Observationibus Ecclesiasticis Rerum*. He wrote saints' Lives in verse and prose, and several sermons. He abridged Rabanus' commentaries on the Pentateuch and perhaps himself commented on the Psalter and Catholic Epistles; but the long-standing scholarly belief that he wrote the *Glossa Ordinaria* to the Bible is unfounded. A Reichenau letter-collection refers to him both as a young monk ('Straboni strionico') and as abbot, and his own commonplace book of grammar, metrics, and computistica—the raw material of Charles the Bald's education—is still preserved at St *Gall.

Works collected in J. P. Migne, *PL* 113–14; crit. edn. of his verse by E. Duemmler in *MGH, Poetae*, 2 (1884), pp. 259–423; of the *De Exordiis et Incrementis* by A. Boretius and V. Krause in *MGH, Leges*, Section 2, vol. 2 (1897), pp. 473–516; of *Visio Wettini*, with Eng. tr., by D. A. Traill (Lateinische Sprache und Literatur des Mittelalters, 2; Berne and Frankfurt, 1974). Six of his poems are pr., with Eng. tr., by P. [J.] Godman, *Poetry of the Carolingian Renaissance* (1985), pp. 214–29. The Reichenau letter-collection is ed. K. Zeumer in *MGH, Leges*, Section 5 (1886), pp. 364–77, the passages on Walafrid, pp. 368 f. Analysis of the commonplace book by B. Bischoff, 'Eine Sammelhandschrift Walahfrid Strabos (Cod. Sangall. 878)', in *Aus der Welt des Buches: Festgabe zum 70. Geburtstag von Georg Leyh* (Beiheft zum Zentralblatt für Bibliothekswesen, 75; 1950), pp. 30–48; rev. in his *Mittelalterliche Studien*, 2 (1967), pp. 34–51. H. Sierp, 'Walafried Strabos Gedicht über den Gartenbau', in K. Beyerle (ed.), *Die Kultur der Abtei Reichenau*, 2 (Munich, 1925), pp. 756–72. On other aspects of his life and work, K. Beyerle, ibid. 1 (1925), pp. 92–108, K. Künstle, ibid. 2 (1925), pp. 706–10, and A. Bergmann,

ibid., pp. 712–38. E. S. Duckett, *Carolingian Portraits* (Ann Arbor, Mich. [1962]), pp. 121–60. A. Önnerfors, 'Philologisches zu Walahfrid Strabo', *Mittellateinisches Jahrbuch*, 7 (1972), pp. 41–92. P. [J.] Godman, *Poets and Emperors: Frankish Politics and Carolingian Poetry* (Oxford, 1987), pp. 129–48. Raby (1953), pp. 183–9; F. J. Raby, *A History of Secular Latin Poetry in the Middle Ages*, 1 (2nd edn., Oxford, 1957), pp. 229–34; J. Szövérffy, *Weltliche Dichtungen des lateinischen Mittelalters*, 1 (1970), pp. 571–89. F. Stegmüller, *Repertorum Biblicum Medii Aevi*, 5 (Madrid, 1955), pp. 426–31 (nos. 8316–31). Manitius, 1, pp. 302–15; F. Brunhölz, *Geschichte der lateinischen Literatur des Mittelalters*, 1 (Munich, 1975), pp. 345–58 and 557–9. H. Peltier in *DTC* 15 (pt. 2; 1950), cols. 3498–505; K. Langosch in Stammler, 4 (1953), cols. 734–69, both s.v.

Walburga, St (*c.*710–79), sister of St *Willibald and St Wynnebald (d. 761) and Abbess of Heidenheim. Born in England and educated at the abbey at Wimborne, she went at the wish of St *Boniface to assist in his mission work in Germany. On Wynnebald's death she assumed the direction of his double monastery at Heidenheim, and remained there till her death. Her feast day is observed on 25 Feb. and 1 May. The coincidence of the latter date with an old pagan feast commemorating the beginning of summer, with rites protecting from witchcraft, has given to 1 May the name 'Walpurgis [i.e. Walburga's] Night', e.g. in Goethe's *Faust*.

AASS, Feb. 3 (1658), pp. 511–72. The account of her miracles by Wolfhard of Herrieden, written at the end of the 9th cent., is ed., with Ger. tr., by A. Bauch, *Quellen zur Geschichte der Diözese Eichstätt*, 2 (Eichstätter Studien, NF 12; 1979), pp. 141–348. F. M. Steele, *The Life of Saint Walburga* [1921]. M. Coens, 'Le Séjour légendaire de sainte Walburge à Anvers d'après son office à la collégiale de Zutphen', *Anal. Boll.* 80 (1962), pp. 345–60. A. Bauch, 'Monheim, ein Wallfahrtszentrum der Karolingerzeit. Frühe Walpurgisverehrung', *Studien und Mitteilungen zur Geschichte des Benediktiner-Ordens*, 90 (1979), pp. 32–44; M. Mengs, 'Schrifttum zum Leben und zur Verehrung der heiligen Walburga', ibid., pp. 121–46. A. Bang-Kaup in *L.Th.K.* (2nd edn.), 10 (1965), col. 928, s.v., with further bibl. See also bibl. to St Willibald, for whom the sources are historically more reliable.

Walden, Roger (d. 1406), Abp. of *Canterbury. A native of Essex, he rose to a position of importance in the *Channel Islands and held livings at Fenny Drayton, Leicestershire, and Burton in Kendal. In 1387 he became Archdeacon of *Winchester and from then onwards, under court influence, advanced rapidly. From 1387 to 1392 he was treasurer of Calais. In 1395 he was created Treasurer of England and, continuing to hold numerous other preferments, Dean of *York. On *Arundel's banishment in 1397 Richard II secured his provision to the see of Canterbury from the Pope; but when Arundel returned with Henry of Lancaster (1399), Walden's property was plundered and his register destroyed. On 10 Jan. 1400 he was committed to the Tower on a charge of complicity in the Epiphany plot against Henry IV, but liberated about a month later. In 1405 he succeeded Robert Braybrooke as Bp. of London. He died at Much Hadham, Herts, on 6 Jan. 1406. A MS collection of chronological tables (Cotton MS Julius B. XIII), known as the 'Historia Mundi', has been wrongly attributed to him.

J. H. Wylie, *History of England under Henry the Fourth*, 3 (1896), pp. 123–8. J. Tait in *DNB* 59 (1899), pp. 24–6, s.v., with further refs.

Waldenses, also **Vaudois**. The name 'Waldenses' has since the late 12th cent. been applied to several groups of similar and possibly interrelated heretics. Since some Waldenses in the valleys of Piedmont adopted the creeds and structures of Genevan *Calvinism in the 16th cent., they and their descendants formed an organized 'Waldensian' Protestant Church, the 'Chiesa Evangelica Valdese', taking the name and inhabiting some of the same regions as their medieval predecessors.

The earliest medieval sources attribute the foundation of the 'Waldensian' heresy to one called *Valdensis, Valdesius*, or 'Valdes'; the form 'Waldo' and the addition of 'Peter' to his name are later. The suggestion that the heresy originated earlier, in the 4th or 9th cent., can be discounted. Acc. to the Chronicle of Laon (*c.* 1220) and the nearly contemporary Richard of Poitiers, Valdes was a rich citizen of Lyons, either a merchant or a farmer of feudal revenues (hence technically a usurer); around 1170–3 he was converted, perhaps by hearing a street performer retell the story of St Alexis (a 5th-cent. Roman patrician who left a wealthy bride for a life of mendicancy and almsgiving in Syria), and gave all his wealth to the poor. He settled an income on his wife, placed his daughters in Robert of Abrissel's abbey of *Fontevrault, and began to live on alms and to preach, as well as having a translation (now lost) of parts of the Bible and the Fathers made for himself. His way of life was approved by Pope *Alexander III at the Third *Lateran Council in 1179, so long as he and his followers refrained from preaching except at the invitation of the clergy. In 1180 Valdes subscribed a profession of orthodox belief in the presence of the Cardinal Henry of Clairvaux and Abp. Guichard of Lyons. However, shortly afterwards he and his followers broke the Church's ban on unofficial preaching and in 1182 or 1183 they were excommunicated and expelled from Lyons by Abp. Jean Bellesmains. Summoned to the Council of *Verona in 1184, they were declared 'pertinacious and schismatic', and included with the *Cathars, *Humiliati, and others in the general condemnation of heretics pronounced at that Council. This condemnation was progressively echoed throughout W. and S. Europe. At this stage Valdes's movement was characterized essentially by itinerant lay preaching (esp. against the Cathars), voluntary poverty, and works of charity; hence the earliest Waldenses' alternative title of 'Poor men of Lyons'. Valdes himself died sometime between 1205 and 1218.

Around the time of Valdes's death the movement was split by a series of schisms. Some heretics known as 'Poor Lombards', perhaps originally separate and later under Valdes's leadership, established themselves in and around Milan and Piacenza. In 1205 these Lombards, under the leadership of Giovanni di Ronco, broke with the 'Lyonnais' poor over several issues, esp. manual labour (practised by the Lombards) and the validity of Catholic sacraments. The two groups aired their differences at Bergamo in 1218. Meanwhile the 'Lyonnais' themselves split; after a dispute at Pamiers in Languedoc in 1207, Valdes's former follower Durand of Osca led a group of Lyonnais Waldenses back into the Catholic obedience; he had made a profession of Catholic orthodoxy in 1208, and in 1210 he was authorized by *Innocent III to establish a community of 'Catholic Poor'. In 1210 Bernard Prim

returned other Waldenses to Catholicism as the 'Reconciled Poor'.

By the 1220s Waldenses were also found in the (*Holy Roman) Empire, presumably due to missions from Lombardy. They suffered under the inquisitor *Conrad of Marburg, and were described in detail by such authors as the 'Passauer Anonymous' and works attributed to *David of Augsburg. Such authors portrayed a Waldensianism in which the preachers (often called 'Brethren') did not preach openly to Catholics, but reserved their services for known sympathizers called 'friends'. These writers also established a scheme of Waldensian beliefs: '*Donatist' distrust of the 'Roman' [i.e. Catholic] clergy, esp. those in mortal sin, and of sacraments offered by them; doubts regarding prayers for the *dead and *purgatory; rejection of *oaths and of homicide; and insistence on their right to preach. After the middle of the 13th cent. persecution abated, leaving a gap in the sources of the movement. From the 1290s groups of 'Waldenses' were found and investigated in the SW Alps; others were widely scattered in the Empire, from Brandenburg and Pomerania to the regions of Austria; from the 14th cent. onwards detailed *inquisitorial proceedings against these groups survive. The Germans and Lombards occasionally corresponded, as in 1368. These later medieval movements were characterized by a more attenuated form of heresy: they entertained doubts about the Church's rites, but in many cases continued to participate in and receive the sacraments. Their pastors (called 'Brethren' in Germany and 'Barbes' in the Alps) travelled and taught in secret as far as possible.

Shortly after the outbreak of the *Hussite schism in Bohemia, the Swabian heretic pastor Friedrich Reiser established contacts between some German Waldenses and the Bohemian heretics. By the mid-15th cent. the Bohemian 'Unity of Brethren' was also known as the 'Waldensian Brethren'; that title was used when their confession was printed by the *Lutherans in 1538, and when they subscribed the Consensus of Sandomierz in 1570. The Bohemians may also have influenced the Waldenses in Latin Europe through the missions of their theologian Lukasz of Prague.

The Waldenses of the SW Alps, who before 1500 had spread to parts of Provence, Calabria, and Apulia, quickly took an interest in the Protestant *Reformation; reformed pamphlets circulated among them and in 1530 two of their pastors went to Neuchâtel, Berne, Basle and Strasbourg to take advice from leading reformers. In the autumn of 1532 several reformers, incl. Antoine Saunier and Pierre Robert (*Olivetan), and prob. G. *Farel, went to Piedmont to dispute with them and teach them. It has traditionally been held that at a meeting on 12 Sept. 1532 a gathering of 'barbes' at Chanforan in the Val d'Angrogna adopted a statement of beliefs based on Farel's teaching. However, the sources for this tradition are contradictory, and the 'statement of beliefs' is ambiguous; no historian located this meeting at 'Chanforan' before 1847. Protestant preachers were certainly heard, not always with approval, by the Waldenses in the 1530s; but the latter did not change their way of life and cease to receive Catholic sacraments, either in Provence or in the Alps, until they formed distinct Protestant Churches, with special buildings, settled pastors sent by J. *Calvin from *Geneva, and a

Genevan confession and Church ordinance, between c.1555 and c.1564.

With the advent of Protestantism in France, Germany, and Bohemia, the Waldenses lost their separate identity, except in that part of their Alpine valleys which fell under the Dukes of Savoy rather than the Kings of France. There they were attacked by Duke Emanuele Filiberto in 1560–61; they defended themselves so successfully that by the Treaty of Cavour (5 June 1561) they were given limited freedom of worship. Thereafter they were tolerated, but occasionally savagely persecuted. In 1655 Duke Carlo Emanuale II permitted a massacre which led to O. *Cromwell's intervention and the collection of a large fund for their relief in England; in 1686 Duke Vittorio Amedeo II, copying Louis XIV's revocation of the Edict of *Nantes, expelled them from their valleys, but some of them fought their way back in 1689 under their pastor Henri Arnaud. Only in 1848 were they given full civil rights within Piedmont-Savoy, where they still practise a form of worship based closely on 16th-cent. Genevan Protestantism. Their Church structure comprehends urban Churches in such cities as Turin, Florence, and Rome, as well as emigré communities in S. America. Their theological college, the 'Facoltà Valdese di Teologia', founded in 1855 at Torre Pèllice near Turin, was moved in 1861 to Florence and in 1920 to Rome.

Useful collection of docs. ed. A. Patschovsky and K.-V. Selge, *Quellen zur Geschichte der Waldenser* (Texte zur Kirchen- und Theologiegeschichte, 18 [1973]). The earliest evidence is found in the Chronicle of Laon (*Chronicon universale anonymi Laudunensis*), ed. A. Cartellieri and W. Stechele (Leipzig and Paris, 1909), pp. 20–2; also ed. G. Waitz in MGH, Scriptores, 26 (1882), pp. 442–57, at pp. 447 f.; other early medieval sources are pr. by A. Lecoy de la Marche (ed.), *Anecdotes historiques, légendes et apologues tirés du recueil inédit d'Étienne de Bourbon, dominicain du XIIIe siècle* (Société de l'Histoire de France, 1887), pp. 290–3; A. Dondaine, OP, 'Aux origines du valdéisme. Une profession de foi de Valdès', *Archivum Fratrum Praedicatorum*, 16 (1946), pp. 191–235; G. Gonnet (ed.), *Enchiridion Fontium Valdensium*, 1 (Collana della Facoltà Valdese de Teologia, Roma; Turin, 1958 [all pub.]); id., *Le Confessioni de Fede Valdesi prima della Riforma* (ibid., 1967); K.-V. Selge, *Die ersten Waldenser* (Arbeiten zur Kirchengeschichte, 37; 2 vols., 1967), incl. edn. of the *Liber Antiheresis* of Durandus of Osca.

Modern works on the early Waldenses incl. H. Grundmann, *Religiöse Bewegungen im Mittelalters* (Historische Studien, 267; 1935; 2nd edn., Hildesheim, 1961), esp. pp. 91–127, 161–7; C. Thouzellier, *Catharisme et Valdéisme en Languedoc à la fin du XIIe siècle et au début du XIIIe siècle* (Publications de la Faculté des Lettres et Sciences humaines de Paris, Série 'Recherches', 27; 1966); *Vaudois languedociens et Pauvres Catholiques*, with introd. by M.-H. Vicaire (Cahiers de Fanjeaux, 2 [1967]); A. Patschovsky, *Der Passauer Anonymus* (Schriften der Monumenta Germaniae historica, 22; Stuttgart, 1968); W. Erk (ed.), *Waldenser: Geschichte und Gegenwart* (Frankfurt am Main, 1971); J. Gonnet and A. Molnar, *Les Vaudois au Moyen Âge* (Turin [1974]); A. Molnar, *Storia dei Valdesi, 1: Dalle origini all'adhesione alla Riforma* (ibid. [1974]); G. G. Merlo, *Valdesi e valdisimi medievali: Itinerari e proposte di ricerca* (ibid. [1984]); id., *Valdesi e valdismi medievali, 2: Identità valdesi nella storia e nella storiografia* (ibid., 1991); and G. Audisio, *Les 'Vaudois': Naissance, vie et mort d'une dissidence (XIIme–XVIme siècles)* (ibid. [1989]).

Texts and studies on the later medieval movements in Ger.-speaking lands incl. D. Kurze (ed.), *Quellen zur Ketzergeschichte Brandenburgs und Pommerns* (Veröffentlichungen des Historischen Kommission zu Berlin, 45; 1975), *passim*; A. Patschovsky, *Die Anfänge einer ständigen Inquisition in Böhmen: Ein*

Prager Inquisitoren-Handbuch aus der ersten Hälfte des 14. Jahrhunderts (Beiträge zur Geschichte und Quellenkunde des Mittelalters, 3; 1975); and R. Kieckhefer, *Repression of Heresy in Medieval Germany* (Liverpool [1979]), pp. 13 f., 53–73. On the later Middle Ages and Reformation, J. H. Todd, *The Books of the Vaudois: The Waldensian Manuscripts Preserved in the Library of Trinity College, Dublin* (1865); J. Marx, *L'Inquisition en Dauphiné: Étude sur le développement et la répression de l'hérésie et de la sorcellerie du XIVe siècle au début du règne de François I* (Bibliothèque de l'École des Hautes Études, Sciences historiques et philologiques, 206; 1914), esp. pp. 11–27 and 145 200, A. Armand Hugon, *Storia dei Valdesi, 2: Dal sinodo di Chanforan all'Emancipazione* (Turin [1974]); V. Vinay, *Le Confessioni di fede dei Valdesi Reformati* (Collana della Facoltà Valdese di Teologia, 12; Turin [1975]); G. G. Merlo, *Eretici e Inquisitori nella Società Piemontese del Trecento* (ibid. [1977]), with edn. of primary texts; G. Audisio, *Le Barbe et l'inquisiteur: Procès du barbe vaudois Pierre Griot par l'inquisiteur Jean de Roma (Apt, 1532)* (Aix-en-Provence [1979]); E. Cameron, *The Reformation of the Heretics: The Waldenses of the Alps, 1450–1580* (Oxford Historical Monographs, 1984); G. Audisio, *Les Vaudois du Luberon: Une minorité en Provence (1460–1560)* (1984); id., *Procès-Verbal d'un Massacre: Les Vaudois du Luberon (avril 1545)* (Aix-en-Provence [1992]); A. de Lange (ed.), *Dall'Europa alle Valli Valdesi. Atti del XXIX Convegno storico internazionale: 'Il Glorioso Rimpatrio (1689–1989) . . .', Torre Pellice (To), 3–7 settembre 1989* (Collana della Società di Studi Valdesi, 11; Turin [1990]). Late medieval and early modern MSS associated with the Waldenses are discussed in E. Balmas and M. Dal Corso, *I Manoscritti valdesi di Ginevra* (Turin [1977]); several texts ed. by the former. On the modern Waldensian Church see V. Vinay, *Storia dei Valdesi, 3: Dal movimento evangelico italiano al movimento ecumenico (1848–1978)* (Turin [1980]). *Bulletin de la Société d'histoire vaudoise*, later *Bollettino della Società di Studi Valdesi* (1884 ff.). A. Armand Hugon and G. Gonnet, *Bibliografia valdese* (Torre Pellice, 1953). H. Grundmann, *Bibliographie zur Ketzergeschichte des Mittelalters, 1900–1966* (Sussidi eruditi, 20; 1967), pp. 41–5. L. Cristiani in DTC 15 (pt. 2; 1950), cols. 2586–600, s.v. 'Vaudois'.

Waldenström, Paul Peter (1838–1917), Swedish preacher and Free Churchman. As a young man he held various teaching appointments. In 1864 he was ordained a pastor. Attaching himself to the revivalist movement of C. O. Rosenius (d. 1868), he succeeded him as editor of the *Pietisten*, a widely circulating revivalist newspaper. In various writings between 1872 and 1875 he put forward a theory of the *Atonement inconsistent with *Lutheran orthodoxy: man had to be reconciled to God, not God to man, and God sent His Son, not in wrath but in love. He also rejected the doctrine that when Christ died His atoning work was finished. A long controversy ensued, and Waldenström became the founder of the largest sectarian movement in *Sweden. In 1905 he took over the direction of the separatist Swedish Mission Society (Svenska Missionsförbundet), which, besides work in Sweden, established missions in the *Congo, *China, and Chinese Turkestan. From 1884 to 1905 he was a member of the Swedish Riksdag.

Collected Sermons, 2 vols., Stockholm, 1918–19; Memoirs, 1838–75, ed. B. Nyrén (ibid., 1928). There are Eng. trs. by J. G. Princell, with notes and introds., of Waldenström's meditations on *The Blood of Jesus* (Chicago, 1888) and on *The Reconciliation* (ibid., 1888). Studies by N. P. Ollén (Stockholm, 1917), ed. A. Ohldén (Uppsala, 1917), E. Leufvén (ibid., 1920), E. Newman (Stockholm, 1932), and W. Bredberg (Uppsala, 1948). C. Olsson, *Försoningen enlight C. O. Rosenius och P. Waldenström* (1928). E. Beyreuther in RGG (3rd edn.), 6 (1962), col. 1534, s.v.

Wales, Christianity in. The early history of Christianity in Wales is obscure. The archaeological and literary evidence for the period before 500 is slight, but the writings of *Gildas (though he names no single ecclesiastic of his own times) have been held to suggest continuity of belief and organization from late Roman times. The 6th cent. is known as 'The Age of the Saints', but their lives, compiled at least five centuries later, are unsafe foundations for detailed historical reconstruction. In SE Wales Cadoc (founder of the monastery of Llancarfan), *Dubricius, and *Illtyd were apparently followed elsewhere in the south by a more ascetic group, *Teilo, Padarn, and *David; Seiriol, Cadfan, Cybi, and *Deiniol were active in the north. According to the Lives of these saints their journeys along the western sea-routes linked *Scotland, *Ireland, Cornwall, and Brittany with Wales; inscribed stones provide independent evidence of this activity. The monasteries they founded (esp. *Bangor Iscoed) were at first very large and were the religious centres of large districts; in time they came into the hands of smaller communities (*clasau*) of often hereditary clergy, clerical marriage being widespread in Wales. Those on the coast were despoiled by the Norsemen. Some of the early monasteries were also the seat of a bishop, and three of them (*St Asaph, *St Davids, and *Bangor), together with the later foundation of *Llandaff, eventually emerged as territorial bishoprics, though others (esp. Llanbadarn Fawr) are said to have been ruled by abbot-bishops for some time. There are, however, many gaps in the Welsh episcopal lists until the 12th cent.

The meeting of British bishops with St *Augustine *c.*603 failed to produce any union between the *Celtic and Roman missions. The Welsh Church remained stubbornly conservative, but eventually adopted the Roman date for Easter from 768, though it resisted the claims of *Canterbury to supremacy over Wales and maintained closer contacts with the Church in Ireland and Brittany than with England.

The Norman conquest of England and the subsequent conquest of parts of Wales by Norman lords reopened the Church in Wales to English and Continental influences. Abp. *Anselm won the first successes in the long struggle to subject all four Welsh sees to Canterbury; this was eventually achieved despite the efforts of *Giraldus Cambrensis to gain metropolitan status for St Davids. Twelfth-cent. bishops began the definition of diocesan and parochial boundaries: parishes in the north were generally large and in episcopal patronage; those in the south were small and in lay or monastic patronage. The system of *tithes was instituted, and by the end of the 13th cent. an administrative and judicial organization was in being and *clasau* replaced by cathedral chapters. Leadership in learning passed from notable individual families (esp. that of Sulien) to the religious houses. Latin monasticism came to Wales when the early Norman invaders founded *Benedictine houses (e.g. Chepstow, *c.*1071) on the borders of the S. and SE; later Normans founded some *Cistercian houses (e.g. *Tintern), but the Cistercians' initial austerity and their lack of Norman connections appealed strongly to the Welsh princes, who gave them a ready welcome and liberal endowments at Strata Florida (1164) and elsewhere. Houses of other orders were also established.

Pressure from the last native Welsh prince, Llewelyn ap Gruffydd (d. 1282), led the Welsh bishops to support Edward I, whose conquest of Wales was followed by a relatively stable and prosperous half-century for the Welsh Church. But plague and economic depression, and resentment at the exploitation of ecclesiastical revenues and appointments in the interests of the English state, led many of the Welsh secular clergy and religious to support the revolt of Owain Glyn Dwr against Henry IV in 1400. Its failure strengthened the position of the secular administration and the bishops (many of them English). The pre-*Reformation Church in Wales suffered to a special degree from inertia; *Lollardy, humanism, and *Lutheranism made little impression, and the religious houses became seriously undermanned.

The Tudor monarchs enjoyed the advantage of Welsh descent; higher clergy and *parvenu* gentry accepted their policies, and the breach with Rome and the *Dissolution of the Monasteries (whose lands found ready buyers) aroused little opposition; the greatest upheaval was caused by *Mary Tudor's brief attempt to impose clerical *celibacy. *Elizabeth I appointed resident, active, Welsh-speaking bishops, who imposed the 1559 settlement. The *Counter-Reformation made little impact in Wales, though some families of gentry remained *recusant and a few RCs were executed. The educational standards of the Welsh clergy were improved; medieval Welsh students had frequented Oxford, where Jesus College, founded in 1571, developed spontaneously into a college for Wales attended by future Welsh clergy. Nine-tenths of the output of the Tudor and Stuart printing presses in Wales consisted of religious works, esp. the *Welsh Bible and Prayer Book, authorized by an Act of 1563; Welsh became the language of Protestantism in Wales and a rift gradually developed between the anglicized squires and clergy and their Welsh-speaking parishioners.

The foundation of the 'gathered' Church at Llanfaches (west of Chepstow) in 1639 represents the faint beginnings of Nonconformity, which spread from England. Wales was mainly Royalist in the Civil War, but a more rapid growth of sects followed the Commonwealth's Act for the Propagation of the Gospel in Wales (1650) and the consequent activities of such new 'saints' as the *Fifth Monarchist Vavasor Powell (1617–70) from Heyop (near Knighton). After the Anglican reaction of 1660–2, Nonconformists (mainly in the SE) formed only 5 per cent. of the population in 1676; these were mostly *Baptists and *Independents, with some *Presbyterians and *Quakers, but in and after 1682 many Welsh Quakers and Baptists emigrated to Pennsylvania. The Welsh sees were poor and for well over a century after the Restoration they were often held by absentees hopeful of translation: that of Llandaff was for some time held with the Deanery of *St Paul's. The undoubted distinction as scholars of such bishops as B. *Hoadly, T. *Tanner, S. *Horsley, and E. *Copleston did not benefit their dioceses, and no Welsh bishop between 1715 and 1870 could preach in Welsh when appointed. Lay impropriation of tithes ensured that most parish clergy remained poor and ill-educated, though Bp. T. Burgess of St Davids tried to raise the standards of the clergy by the foundation of St David's College, Lampeter, in 1822. Great work had also been done in promoting popular education by Griffith *Jones (q.v.).

In the early 19th cent. the influence of the Church was at its lowest ebb. *Methodism, preached by H. *Harris, organized by Thomas Charles (1755–1814) and assisted by the popular hymns of William Williams of Pantycelyn (1717–91), spread widely, but its adherents remained within the Church until the (predestinarian) *Calvinistic Methodists (the only Christian denomination to originate in Wales) broke away in 1811. The (abortive) proposal to amalgamate the sees of Bangor and St Asaph in the 1840s was unpopular, while the zeal and teaching of *Tractarian clergy (such as I. *Williams) met with little sympathy. While the Church failed to adapt to a great increase in population, Nonconformity grew: in 1800 there were 50 Nonconformist chapels in the diocese of Llandaff, but in 1850 there were some 550. A split developed in Wales: the landowners and many ironmasters were English-speaking, Anglican, and Tory; the tenant farmers and the new miners and industrial workers were Welsh-speaking, Nonconformist, and radical. Nonconformists appear to have formed about three-quarters of the Church- or chapel-going population in 1851, but there was an Anglican revival under Bps. C. *Thirlwall at St Davids (1840–74), T. Vowler Short at St Asaph (1846–70), A. Ollivant at Llandaff (1849–82), and J. C. Campbell at Bangor (1859–90). In Llandaff, the most industrialized diocese, Dissent and the Church under the Evangelical Ollivant at first co-operated, esp. in the religious revival of 1859, but the co-operation ended after 1862. The *Temperance Movement (mainly Nonconformist) won a victory with the Sunday Closing (Wales) Act 1881, some of the effects of which are still felt to this day.

The Disestablishment of the Irish Church (1869), the Englishness of the Church in Wales, and Nonconformist fears that the reviving Church might become the largest single religious body in Wales, led to demands for the disestablishment of the Welsh Church, whose privileged position led to a tithe war, e.g. in NE Wales, in 1886–8, and to disputes over education. The demand for disestablishment was ably resisted by A. G. Edwards, Bp. of St Asaph 1889–1934, and John Owen, Bp. of St Davids 1897–1926; but Nonconformist numbers increased again with the religious revival of 1904, and an Act of 1914 disestablished the Welsh Church. (In parliament three English bishops, including C. *Gore, supported the measure.) With financial safeguards added by the Welsh Church (Temporalities) Act 1919, disestablishment took effect in 1920, when a separate province was created. There are six dioceses (Monmouth, and Swansea and Brecon having been carved out of Llandaff and St Davids respectively); the bishops are nominated by electors representing various elements in the Church, and one of the diocesans is similarly elected to the rank of Archbishop of Wales, A. G. Edwards (1920) being the first. The Church in Wales is no longer *Eglwys Loegr* (the 'English Church') over-dependent on the landowners, and it provides regular services in Welsh as well as in English; after 1920 it increased in both influence and numbers. Welsh Nonconformity lost a unifying objective, and modern Welsh nationalism has turned to secular objectives. Of Free Church bodies the Calvinistic Methodists are the most numerous; their Church is Presbyterian in government and is a member of the *World Alliance of Reformed Churches. The Baptists and Independents also remain strong, but in the *United Reformed Church and among Wesleyans there has been a particularly marked decline in numbers. The RCs are a small but vigorous community, recruited chiefly from Irish immigrant stock in the SE; there is a RC Abp. of Cardiff and Bps. of Menevia (whose cathedral is in Swansea) and Wrexham. There is a Greek Orthodox community in Cardiff.

See also ROMAN CATHOLIC CHURCH IN ENGLAND AND WALES AFTER THE REFORMATION and WELSH BIBLE AND PRAYER BOOK.

There are a number of studies in Welsh. Works in Eng. incl. A. G. Edwards, *Landmarks in the History of the Welsh Church* (1912); J. E. de Hirsch-Davies, *A Popular History of the Church in Wales from the Beginning to the Present Day* (1912); D. A. Jones, *A History of the Church in Wales* (Carmarthen, 1926); J. W. James, *A Church History of Wales* (Ilfracombe, 1945); D. Walker (ed.), *A History of the Church in Wales* (Penarth, 1976). A. W. Wade-Evans, *Welsh Christian Origins* (Oxford, 1934). E. G. Bowen, *The Settlements of the Celtic Saints in Wales* (Cardiff, 1954; 2nd edn., 1956). N. K. Chadwick and others, *Studies in the Early British Church* (Cambridge, 1958). Lives of St Dubricius, St Illtyd, St Paulinus, St Teilo and St Oudoceus, by G. H. Doble, orig. pub. between 1942 and 1944, collected and ed. by D. S. Evans, *Lives of the Welsh Saints* (Cardiff, 1971), with introd. essay and extensive refs., pp. 1–55. G. Williams, *The Welsh Church from Conquest to Reformation* (1962). J. C. Davies (ed.), *Episcopal Acts and Cognate Documents relating to Welsh Dioceses 1066–1272* (1946 ff.). L. Thomas, *The Reformation in the Old Diocese of Llandaff* (Cardiff, 1930). E. T. Davies, *Religion in the Industrial Revolution in South Wales* (Pantyfedwen Lectures, 1962; Cardiff, 1965). D. T. W. Price, *A History of Saint David's University College, Lampeter* (2 vols., Cardiff, 1977–90). C. A. H. Green, *The Setting of the Constitution of the Church in Wales* (1937). N. Doe (ed.), *Essays in Canon Law: A Study of the Law of the Church in Wales* (Cardiff, 1992). P. M. H. Bell, *Disestablishment in Ireland and Wales* (CHS, 1969), pp. 226–329. D. T. W. Price, *A History of the Church in Wales in the Twentieth Century* ([Penarth] 1990). J. E. de Hirsch-Davies, *Catholicism in Mediaeval Wales* (1916). D. Attwater, *The Catholic Church in Modern Wales: A Record of the Past Century* (1935). T. Rees, *History of Protestant Nonconformity in Wales from its Rise to the Present Time* (1861; enlarged edn., 1883). H. E. Lewis, *Nonconformity in Wales* (1904). G. F. Nuttall, *The Welsh Saints 1640–1660* (Cardiff, 1957). There is also much information in the Report of the Royal Commission on the Church of England and Other Religious Bodies in Wales and Monmouthshire (Parliamentary Papers, England, 1910, vols. 14–19 [Cd. 5432–9]) and many relevant entries in *The Dictionary of Welsh Biography down to 1940* (1959). *Journal of the Historical Society of the Church in Wales* (1947 ff.). See also bibl. to CELTIC CHURCHES; also to METHODISM, etc.

Wall, William

Wall, William (1647–1728), Anglican theologian. Educated at Queen's College, Oxford, he became vicar of Shoreham, Kent, in 1674, and rector of Milton-next-Gravesend in 1708. His chief work is *The History of Infant Baptism* (2 vols., 1705). Designed to combat the arguments of the *Baptists against Infant Baptism, it consisted in a learned exposition of the teaching of the Fathers, supported by ample quotations and taking into account recent controversies. It has remained the English classic on the subject. His other works include *Brief Critical Notes, especially on the Various Readings of the New Testament Books* (1730) and *Critical Notes on the Old Testament* (1734).

The History of Infant Baptism ... Together with Mr. Gale's Reflections, and Dr. Wall's Defence, ed. H. Cotton (4 vols., Oxford, 1835–6), with introd., vol. 1, pp. v–xxvii; an abridged edn. of the History was pub. by W. H. Spencer (London, 1848). T. Cooper in *DNB* 59 (1899), p. 97, s.v., with refs.

Walloon Confession (1561). See BELGIC CONFESSION.

Walsingham (Norfolk), place of pilgrimage. A replica of the Holy House of *Nazareth, said to have been built there in the 11th cent., made the Walsingham pilgrimage one of the most important in England in the Middle Ages. The shrine was destroyed in 1538. In 1922 A. H. Patten, the vicar of Walsingham, placed in the church a statue of the BVM, which became the nucleus of a new shrine, and soon afterwards pilgrimages were organized. Until recently, they were the subject of much controversy. A separate building to house the shrine, known as the Holy House, was erected in 1931; in the considerable extensions to this building in 1938 a small Orthodox chapel was incorporated. The Medieval Slipper Chapel was opened as a RC shrine in 1934.

*Erasmus, *Pilgrimages to Saint Mary of Walsingham and Saint Thomas of Canterbury*, tr. into Eng. by J. G. Nichols (1849), pp. 11–43 and 82–110. *The Foundation of the Chapel of Walsingham*, orig. pr. by R. Pynson (c.1493), repr. in H. Huth (ed.), *Fugitive Tracts Series*, 1 (1875), no. 2 (sep. pagination). H. M. Gillet, *Walsingham and its Shrine* (1934); J. C. Dickinson, *The Shrine of Our Lady of Walsingham* (1956). [J.] C. Stephenson, *Walsingham Way* (1970). J. C. Cox in *VCH*, Norfolk, 2, ed. W. Page (1906), pp. 394–401, with refs.

Walter, Hubert. See HUBERT WALTER.

Walter de Stapeldon. See STAPELDON, WALTER DE.

Walter of St-Victor (d. after 1180), prior of the *Augustinian Canons of St-Victor (see VICTORINES). His 'Contra Quatuor Labyrinthos Franciae' (after 1179) was a violent attack on the dialectical method, directed chiefly against *Abelard, *Peter Lombard, Peter of Poitiers (d. 1205), and *Gilbert de la Porrée. He also wrote some 21 sermons, mostly for feast days, that show an ordinary piety reflecting little of the concern with contemplation found in *Hugh and *Richard of St-Victor.

The 'Contra Quatuor Labyrinthos Franciae', ed. P. Glorieux, *AHDLMA* 19 (for 1952; 1953), pp. 187–335. R. Studeny, SVD, 'Walter of St. Victor and the *Apologia de Verbo Incarnato*', *Gregorianum*, 18 (1937), pp. 579–85. J. Chatillon, 'Un sermon théologique de Gauthier de Saint-Victor égaré parmi les œuvres du Prieur Richard', *Revue du Moyen Âge latin*, 8 (1952), pp. 43–50. P. Glorieux, 'Mauvaise Action et mauvais travail. Le "Contra quatuor labyrinthos Franciae"', *RTAM* 21 (1954), pp. 179–93. J. de Ghellinck, SJ, *Le Mouvement théologique du XIIᵉ siècle* (Études d'Histoire des Dogmes et d'ancienne Littérature ecclésiastique, 1914), pp. 158–60 and 268 f. (2nd edn., Museum Lessianum, Section Historique, 10, 1948, pp. 260–3 and 404 f.). J. Châtillon, 'Sermons et prédicateurs victorins de la seconde moitié du xiiᵉ siècle', *AHDLMA* 32 (for 1965; 1966), pp. 7–60, esp. pp. 40–4; J. B. Schneyer, *Repertorium der lateinische Sermones des Mittelalters* (BGPM 43, Heft 2; 2nd edn., 1970), pp. 118 f.

Walton, Brian (c.1600–61), Bp. of *Chester and editor of the 'London *Polyglot Bible'. Educated at Magdalene College and Peterhouse, Cambridge, in 1628 he became rector of St Martin's Orgar in London. His zealous defence of the claims of the clergy in the controversy with the citizens over the city tithes, added to his Laudian sympathies, led to his being accused in Parliament and deprived of his livings (1641). After a short imprisonment, he lived for some years in Oxford. The *Biblia Sacra Poly-*

glotta, which is among the first books in England to have been printed by subscription, was begun in 1653, and its six vols. of OT, Apocrypha, NT, and appendices were completed in 1657. Altogether nine languages are represented, though no individual book of the Bible is printed in more than eight versions. The work, which has not yet been superseded, is esp. useful because of its lucid arrangement. It was criticized by J. *Owen in his *Considerations*, to which Walton replied in an able defence entitled *The Considerator Considered* (1659). At the Restoration, he was appointed Bp. of Chester in 1660.

H. J. Todd, *Memoirs of the Life and Writings of the Right Rev. Brian Walton, Lord Bishop of Chester* (2 vols., 1821). A. Fox, *John Mill and Richard Bentley: A Study of the Textual Criticism of the New Testament, 1675–1729* (1954), pp. 47–9 and *passim*. D. S. Margoliouth in *DNB* 59 (1899), pp. 268–71, s.v.

Walton, Izaak (1593–1683), English author. Born in Stafford, he set up shop as a linen-draper in London (although a freeman of the Ironmongers' Company), and in the late 1620s came to know the vicar of his parish, St Dunstan-in-the-West, J. *Donne, and his friend Henry King, poet and later Bp. of *Chichester. Walton married first into the Cranmer family (deriving thence much information about R. *Hooker), and then the elder half-sister of T. *Ken. A passionate Royalist (but no Laudian), he nevertheless espoused toleration, his friendship embracing the spectrum from *Calvinists to RCs, though principally firm C of E men such as W. *Chillingworth, H. *Hammond, R. *Sanderson, and G. *Sheldon. Retiring from business after the battle of Marston Moor (1644), he spent most of the rest of his life in the households of eminent ecclesiastics such as G. *Morley, Bp. of Worcester and Winchester, whose Steward he was. His *Compleat Angler* (1653; rewritten and greatly enlarged, 1655) combines practical handbook and idealized picture of country life. Though his Lives of J. Donne (1640; enlarged, 1658, 1670, 1675), H. Wotton (1651), R. Hooker (1665), G. *Herbert (1670), and R. *Sanderson (1678), were enduringly influential as Anglican hagiography, he was praised by S. *Johnson merely as a 'great panegyrist', and subsequent scholarship has revealed how he sometimes selected, conflated, transposed, distorted, and invented ideas, speeches, and events to produce ingenious propaganda for pious ends.

Waltoniana: Inedited Remains in Verse and Prose, ed. R. H. Shepherd (London, 1878). *The Compleat Angler, the Lives of Donne, Wotton, Hooker, Herbert, & Sanderson, with Love and Truth & Miscellaneous Writings*, ed. G. [L.] Keynes (ibid., 1929). *The Compleat Angler, 1653–1676*, ed. J. Bevan (Oxford and New York, 1983); also ed. J. Buxton (World's Classics, 1982). Lives also ed. G. Saintsbury (World's Classics, 1927) and S. B. Carter (London, 1951). D. Novarr, *The Making of Walton's Lives* (Ithaca, NY, 1958); J. Bevan, *Izaak Walton's The Compleat Angler: The Art of Recreation* (Brighton, 1988). H. Gardner, 'Dean Donne's Monument in St. Paul's', in R. Wellek and A. Ribeiro (eds.), *Evidence in Literary Scholarship: Essays in Memory of James Marshall Osborn* (Oxford, 1979), pp. 29–44; C. D. Lein, 'Art and Structure in Walton's *Life of Mr. George Herbert*', *University of Toronto Quarterly*, 46 (1976–7), pp. 162–76. N. J. Endicott in *NCBEL* 1 (1974), cols. 2222 f. A. Lang [and X] in *DNB* 59 (1899), pp. 273–7.

Wandering Jew, the. A Jew who, acc. to popular legend, taunted Christ on His way to crucifixion and was doomed to wander over the earth till the Last Day. The legend, which first appeared in a pamphlet published in 1602, professedly at *Leiden, immediately became popular throughout the Protestant world and was known in Britain by 1625. Recorded meetings with the Jew in various places and at various dates range from one at Hamburg in 1542 (mentioned in the original pamphlet) to one at Salt Lake City in 1868; but whether they were purely fictitious or some impostor played the part is uncertain. There existed in the 13th cent. a somewhat similar legend. Roger of Wendover, e.g., chronicles that some natives of Armenia who visited England in 1228 alleged that St *Joseph of Arimathaea had been recently seen in their own country under the name of 'Cartaphilis', and that he had confessed to having taunted Christ as He went to His death.

L. Neubaur, *Die Sage vom Ewigen Juden untersucht* (1884; rev. edn., 1893); W. Zirus, *Der ewige Jude in der Dichtung vornehmlich in der englischen und deutschen* (Palaestra, 162; 1928), and other works of this author; G. K. Anderson, *The Legend of the Wandering Jew* (Providence, RI, 1965); G. Hasan-Rokem and A. Dundes (eds.), *The Wandering Jew: Essays in the Interpretation of a Christian Legend* (Bloomington, Ind. [1986]).

war, Christian attitude to. It has always been recognized that in a world wholly governed by Christian principles war would be ruled out as at variance with the moral teaching of Christ, esp. as contained in the *Sermon on the Mount (Mt. 5–7), and the theology of the *Incarnation. But since Christians are also citizens of a secular order in which the exercise of force is necessary to maintain the authority of law it has been widely, but far from universally, held that the method of war and the active participation of Christians in it are on occasion morally defensible and even praiseworthy. In early times, when the form of civil government was essentially pagan, some ecclesiastical enactments were made which seemed to forbid Christians to take part in military service (St *Hippolytus' *Ap. Trad.* 17–19; *Nicaea, can. 12), while *Tertullian (*De Corona Militis*; from his *Montanist period) and *Lactantius (*Div. Inst.* 6. 20. 16) also expressly condemned it. On the other hand, there were numbers of Christians in the army from the 2nd cent. onwards (see THUNDERING LEGION, also THEBAN LEGION).

From the time of *Constantine, Christians were less troubled by scruples about participation in war. St *Augustine defended it when undertaken for the good of society (*Ep.* 138, to Volusianus) arguing that it was justified when the end of war is peace (*Ep.* 189, to Boniface). The *Crusades are the classic instance of warfare in defence of supposed religious ends. But the constant wars of all kinds in which Christians in the Middle Ages found themselves engaged led to a discrimination by moral theologians between wars in which a Christian legitimately could and could not take part. *Thomas Aquinas lays down three conditions for a 'just war': (1) it must be on the authority of the sovereign (*auctoritas principis*); (2) the cause must be just (*justa causa*); and (3) the belligerents should have a rightful intention (*recta intentio*), intending the advancement of good or the avoidance of evil (*Summa Theol.* 2. 2, q. 40, *de bello*). Similar lists of conditions were drawn up by other medieval moralists. F. de *Vitoria (d. 1546) insisted on the further condition, of which much has been made by recent Catholic moralists, that the war must be

waged by 'proper means' (*debito modo*). The Anglican Reformers dealt with the subject briefly in the *Thirty-Nine Articles (art. 37; note *justa bella* in the Latin text).

In modern times 'Absolute Pacifism', i.e. the doctrine that warfare is in all circumstances forbidden by the Gospel, has been upheld by the *Anabaptists, the *Quakers, and L. *Tolstoy. In comparatively recent times, esp. in Great Britain, it has been widely defended on humanitarian, and sometimes even on frankly hedonistic, grounds as well as on Christian principles. Leading exponents of it in the inter-War years (1918–39) were C. J. Cadoux, H. R. L. *Sheppard, and C. E. Raven. Another group of (mainly RC) moralists (F. Stratmann, G. Vann, E. I. Watkin, E. *Gill) argued against the permissibility of participation in modern warfare on the ground that a 'just war' is nowadays not possible, since, e.g., the means (bombing of civilians, etc.) are never 'proper' (*debito modo*). The development of total methods of warfare during the Second World War (1939–1945), culminating in the use of nuclear weapons, gave new perspectives to the debate. In Great Britain the most widely based expression by Christians of opposition to war has been in the Campaign for Nuclear Disarmament (a secular organization founded in 1958), in which such leading Churchmen as G. K. A. *Bell, Canon L. J. Collins of *St Paul's, and Donald (later Lord) Soper aligned themselves with a wide spectrum of political opinion. The Campaign for Nuclear Disarmament gained wide publicity through the Easter Marches from Aldermaston in the early 1960s and to a lesser extent from the Greenham Common camp in the later 1980s. There were similar 'peace movements' in Continental Europe, notably in West Germany against the stationing of nuclear weapons there in the 1950s and again in the 1980s. Prominent figures in the *Lutheran Church, including M. *Niemöller, took part in the earlier protests. Though 'peace movements' in the Soviet Union and E. Europe were seldom independent of the ruling Communist parties, in East Germany an unofficial movement under the protection of the Church became a serious challenge to the regime. With the end of the Cold War, anti-nuclear protest movements lost their traditional rationale, but the underlying question of the legitimacy of the use of force, and of the kind of force which may be used, remain. These are questions of debate among Christians, though the main stream of Christian thought has not supported the modern pacifist movements, on the ground that there are even worse evils than physical destruction.

Eng. tr. of selected passages from the Fathers, L. J. Swift, *The Early Fathers on War and Military Service* (Message of the Fathers of the Church, 19; Wilmington, Del., 1983). A. *Harnack, *Militia Christi: Die christliche Religion und der Soldatenstand in den ersten drei Jahrhunderten* (Tübingen, 1905; Eng. tr., Philadelphia [1981]). C. J. Cadoux, *The Early Christian Attitude to War* (1919); F. Stratmann, OP, *Weltkirche und Weltfriede* (1924; Eng. tr., *The Church and War*, 1928); R. Regout, SJ, *La Doctrine de la guerre juste de saint Augustin à nos jours* (1935); C. E. Raven, *War and the Christian* (1938); G. Vann, OP, *Morality and War* (1939); R. *Niebuhr, *Why the Christian Church is not Pacifist* (1940); A. Sampson (ed.), *This War and Christian Ethics: A Symposium* (1940); J. Lasserre, *La Guerre et l'évangile* (1953; Eng. tr., 1962); R. H. Bainton, *Christian Attitudes to War and Peace: A Historical Summary and Critical Re-evaluation* (New York [1960]; London, 1961); J.-M. Hornus, *L'Évangile et Labarum: Étude sur l'attitude du* *christianisme primitif devant les problèmes de l'État, de la guerre et de la violence* (Geneva, 1960; Eng. tr., *It is Not Lawful for Me to Fight*, Scottdale, Pa., 1980); J. D. Tooke, *The Just War in Aquinas and Grotius* (1965); P. Brock, *Pacificism in Europe to 1914* (Princeton, 1972); id., *Pacificism in the United States from the Colonial Era to the First World War* (ibid., 1968); id., *Twentieth-Century Pacificism* (New York, etc. [1970]); F. H. Russell, *The Just War in the Middle Ages* (Cambridge, 1975); W. J. Sheils (ed.), *The Church and War: Papers read to the . . . Ecclesiastical History Society* (Studies in Church History, 20; 1983); R. G. Musto, *The Catholic Peace Tradition* (Maryknoll, NY [1986]).

war, participation of the clergy in. Since the Middle Ages clerics in *major orders have been expressly forbidden to take a direct part in the shedding of blood. The prohibition was based on the grounds that it was unseemly for the ministers of the altar to shed blood and that the military life was detrimental to the discharge of pastoral duties. This teaching is embodied in the present RC canon law (*CIC* (1983), can. 289). In the modern state, however, clerics are permitted to conform to the *force majeure* of military law both in peace-time and in war. The C of E has commonly upheld the medieval discipline, though ecclesiastical penalties have not been imposed on the few clerics who have entered the services and such clerics have been allowed to resume their clerical life when the war has ended.

Warburton, William (1698–1779), Bp. of *Gloucester. After being apprenticed for five years to an attorney, he decided on an ecclesiastical career and was ordained priest in 1727. He held various livings, was made Dean of Bristol in 1757 and Bp. of Gloucester in 1759. He was a figure in the literary world of his time. His first theological work of importance was *The Alliance between Church and State* (1736), which defended the *Establishment of the C of E on essentially utilitarian grounds but justified the restrictions imposed upon dissenters by the operation of the *Test Act. In his most famous book, *The Divine Legation of Moses* (2 vols., 1737–41), he professed to uphold the Divine origin of the Mosaic Law against the *Deists by the singular argument that it contained no doctrine of eternal life. The doctrine of future rewards and punishments being essential to the well-being of humanity, its absence from the OT can only be explained by a special Divine inspiration. This eccentric argumentation involved him in a series of controversies. The 'enthusiasm' of *Methodism being esp. repugnant to him, he published in 1762 *The Doctrine of Grace* against J. *Wesley. Warburton's works are remarkable for paradox rather than for scholarship, and his arrogance in the conduct of his literary feuds made him many enemies. He is, however, more creditably remembered for having preached against the slave trade as early as 1766.

Works, ed. R. Hurd (7 vols., London, 1788); id., *A Discourse by Way of General Preface to the Quarto Edition of Bishop Warburton's Works, Containing some Account of the Life, Writings and Character of the Author* (1794). D. W. Nichol (ed.), *Pope's Literary Legacy: The Book-Trade Correspondence of William Warburton and John Knapton with other Letters and Documents 1774–1780* (Oxford Bibliographical Society Publications, 23; 1992). J. S. Watson, *Life of Warburton* (1863). J. N. *Figgis, 'William Warburton', in W. E. Collins (ed.), *Typical English Churchmen from Parker to Maurice* (1902), no. 9, pp. 215–53. A. W. Evans, *Warburton and the Warburtonians: A Study in some Eighteenth-Century Controver-*

sies (1932). S. Taylor, 'William Warburton and the Alliance of Church and State', *JEH* 43 (1992), pp. 271–86.

Ward, Mary (1585–1645), foundress of the Institute of the Blessed Virgin Mary. Born at Mulwith, N. Yorkshire, she entered the Convent of the *Poor Clares of *St-Omer in 1606, and founded from there a daughter-house in Gravelines. In 1609, feeling called to 'some other thing', she left the convent. Returning to St-Omer after a brief stay in England, she began with five other Englishwomen what would later become a religious congregation modelled on the *Jesuit order. In subsequent years, she opened houses in Liège, *Cologne, *Rome, and elsewhere. Her project involved freedom from enclosure and from *office in choir; the Institute was also to be free from episcopal jurisdiction, subject directly to the Pope. Since these innovations were perceived as unacceptable, the Institute was suppressed in 1631, and Mary Ward herself imprisoned in the Convent of the Poor Clares in Munich. On regaining her liberty she went back to Rome, and, after securing the approval of *Urban VIII, resumed her activity on an informal basis. She returned to England in 1639, dying at Heworth, near York. Her Institute has had a complex canonical history, and survives today in three branches, each with their own General Superior.

Selection of writings, *Till God Will*, ed., with biog. comm., by M. E. Orchard, IBVM (1985). M. C. E. Chambers, IBVM, and H. J. Coleridge, SJ, *The Life of Mary Ward, 1585–1645* ('Quarterly Series', 35 and 52; 1882–5). H. Peters, IBVM, *Mary Ward: Ihre Persönlichkeit und ihr Institut* (Innsbruck and Vienna [1991]; Eng. tr., Leominster, 1994). Brief study of her theological significance by L. Byrne, IBVM (Dublin, 1984). M. I. Wetter, IBMV, in *Dict. Sp.*, 16 (1994), cols. 1317–24, s.v. 'Ward (1), Mary'.

Ward, Reginald Somerset (1881–1962), priest and spiritual director. Born in Newcastle-under-Lyme, he studied at Pembroke College, Cambridge. Ordained priest in 1905, he worked in parishes, mainly in London, and for the Sunday School Institute, until 1915, when he felt called to devote his life to spiritual direction. He spent the rest of his life at 'Ravenscroft' in Farncombe, Surrey, supported financially by an anonymous group of friends. Besides conducting a wide correspondence, he regularly heard confessions in various parts of the country. He exerted considerable influence in the C of E, esp. on the clergy, among whom the use of a spiritual director and the sacrament of *Penance became widespread. His appeal was not confined to *Anglo-Catholics. He published a number of books on the spiritual life, notably *The Way* (1922), *Following the Way* (1925), *To Jerusalem* (1931), and his *Guide for Spiritual Directors* (1957), all issued anonymously.

Life and Letters, ed. E. R. Morgan (London, 1963).

Ward, Seth (1617–89), Bp. of *Salisbury. He was educated at Sidney Sussex College, Cambridge, where he became a Fellow in 1640, but was deprived of his fellowship in 1644 for his opposition to the '*Solemn League and Covenant'. In 1649, however, he took the oath to the English Commonwealth when he became Savilian professor of astronomy at Oxford, and was one of the group of natural scientists at Oxford which foreshadowed the Royal

Society, of which he later became one of the original members. The fruits of his scientific studies included two works *In Ismaelis Bulliaidi Astronomiae Philolaicae Fundamenta Inquisitio Brevis* (1653) and *Astronomia Geometrica* (1656), in which he expounded a theory of planetary motions, and a philosophical controversy with T. *Hobbes. Resigning his professorship in 1660, he subsequently held several ecclesiastical offices. He was consecrated Bp. of *Exeter in 1662 and translated to Salisbury in 1667. In 1671 he became Chancellor of the Order of the Garter, being the first Anglican bishop to hold this office. In both dioceses he did much for the improvement of the cathedral. He was also a determined opponent of the dissenters and as a vigorous supporter of the *Conventicles and *Five Mile Acts he was so severe that the Nonconformists brought an unsuccessful petition against him in 1669. Among his theological works are *A Philosophical Essay towards an Eviction of the Being and Attributes of God* (1652) and *Seven Sermons* (1673); he also edited several works of Samuel Ward, Master of Sidney Sussex College, Cambridge (d. 1643), a strong *Calvinist, to whom Seth was not related.

Life by W. Pope (London, 1697), repr. with brief addenda, but some omissions, in S. H. Cassan, *Lives and Memoirs of the Bishops of Sherborne and Salisbury* (1824), pt. 2, pp. 31–163; also ed. J. B. Bamborough (Luttrell Society Reprints, 21; 1961). W. M. J. Fletcher, 'Seth Ward, Bishop of Salisbury, 1667–1689', *Wiltshire Archaeological and Natural History Magazine*, 49 (1942), pp. 1–16. S. Probst, 'Infinity and Creation: The Origin of the Controversy between Thomas Hobbes and the Savilian Professors Seth Ward and John Wallis', *British Journal for the History of Science*, 26 (1993), pp. 271–9. H. R. McAdoo, *The Spirit of Anglicanism* (1965), pp. 200–203; W. G. Simon, *The Restoration Episcopate* (New York, 1965), pp. 54–8 and 143–6. E. I. Carlyle in *DNB* 59 (1899), pp. 336–40.

Ward, Wilfrid (1856–1916), biographer and RC critic. The son of W. G. *Ward, he was trained for the priesthood but, not finding his vocation there, took up literary work. After controversial writings against H. *Spencer and F. *Harrison, he first wrote his father's Life in two separate books, *W. G. Ward and the Oxford Movement* (1889) and *W. G. Ward and the Catholic Revival* (1893). A biography of Card. N. *Wiseman followed in 1897. Under his direction the *Dublin Review* (of which he became editor in 1906) rose to distinguished rank among the quarterlies. In his Life of J. H. *Newman (dealing almost wholly with the RC period of his life; 2 vols., 1912) he showed considerable sympathy with the *Modernist Movement, and in so far departed from the rigidly orthodox opinions of his father.

Last Lectures, ed. J. and M. Ward (widow and daughter) (1918), with introd. study by his widow, pp. vii–lxxi. M. Ward, *The Wilfrid Wards and the Transition* (2 vols., 1934–7). S. Leslie in *DNB, 1912–1921*, pp. 552 f.

Ward, William George (1812–82), theologian and philosopher. He held a fellowship of Balliol College, Oxford, from 1834 to 1845, during which period he became an ardent follower of J. H. *Newman. A keen logician, lacking Newman's concern with history, he pushed *Tractarian principles to their furthest extremes. In 1844 he published *The Ideal of a Christian Church*, strongly praising the RC Church. In 1845 he was deprived of his degrees for heresy and in the same year entered the RC

Church. From 1851 to 1858 he was lecturer in moral philosophy at St Edmund's College, Ware. In later life he was a supporter of the *Ultramontane party, upholding Papal infallibility and maintaining fiercely anti-liberal views. He successfully opposed Newman's scheme to open a RC college in Oxford. In the last 30 years of his life he was constantly engaged in controversial writing.

Wilfrid Ward [q.v.], *W. G. Ward and the Oxford Movement* (1889) and *W. G. Ward and the Catholic Revival* (1893). J. M. Rigg in *DNB* 59 (1899), pp. 344–8.

Warham, William (c.1456–1532), Abp. of *Canterbury. He was educated at *Winchester and New College, *Oxford, of which he became a Fellow in 1475. After taking his doctor's degree, in 1488 he went to London, where he practised in the Court of *Arches. A rapid career followed. He was in turn moderator in the civil law school at Oxford (c.1490), precentor of *Wells (1493), Master of the Rolls (1494), and Archdeacon of Huntingdon (1496), and employed on several notable commercial and diplomatic missions, esp. between 1496 and 1502, when he became Bp. of London. Nominated Abp. of Canterbury by *Julius II in 1503, he received the pallium in 1504, after having been made Lord Chancellor by Henry VII in the same year. From this time he took a leading part in all affairs of national importance. He was also a recognized patron of the New Learning. In 1506 he negotiated a marriage for the King to Margaret of Savoy (which, however, did not take place), and in the same year was elected chancellor of Oxford University. In 1509 he crowned *Henry VIII and Catherine of Aragon, and in 1515 conferred the cardinal's hat on T. *Wolsey, who in the same year replaced him as Lord Chancellor.

After Wolsey's appointment as Papal legate (1518) official friction between archbishop and legate was continuous, though their personal relations remained friendly. In 1527 he was Wolsey's assessor in the secret inquiry into the validity of the King's marriage, and later the chief of the counsel for the Queen, whom, however, he in no way assisted. In 1530 he signed the petition to the Pope asking him to grant the King the divorce, his attitude in the matter being probably decided by the King's threat to destroy all ecclesiastical authority in the country unless his wishes were complied with. When, in 1531, the English clergy were bidden to acknowledge Henry as the Supreme Head of the Church, Warham introduced the amendment 'so far as the law of Christ will allow'. In 1532 he formally though ineffectually protested against all Acts of Parliament prejudicial to the authority of the Pope. He was a generous benefactor, esp. to scholars (*Erasmus, etc.), but without sympathy for the Protestant movement.

The principal sources are the State Papers and Calendars of the State Papers of the reigns of Henry VII and Henry VIII. See also 'Archbishop Warham's Letters', *Archaeologia Cantiana*, 1 (1858), pp. 9–41; 2 (1859), pp. 149–74, esp. 149–52. Calendar of Warham's Canterbury demesne leases, 1503–32, by F. R. H. Du Boulay in id. (ed.), *Documents illustrative of Medieval Kentish Society* (Kent Archaeological Society, Kent Records, 18; 1964), pp. 266–97. K. L. Wood-Legh (ed.), *Kentish Visitations of Archbishop William Warham and his Deputies, 1511–1512* (ibid. 24; 1984). The only Life is that in W. F. *Hook, *Lives of the Archbishops of Canterbury*, 6 (1888), pp. 155–421. J. Gairdner in *DNB* 59 (1899), pp. 378–83; *BRUO* 3 (1959), pp. 1988–92, s.v.

Wartburg. The 12th-cent. castle near Eisenach in Thuringia where M. *Luther was hidden for safety after being seized (with his own connivance) by the Elector *Frederick III on his way home from the Diet of *Worms in 1521. In his letters he described the Wartburg as his '*Patmos'; and during his ten months' residence he prepared his translation of the NT and also issued a number of polemical works.

Washington Cathedral. The cathedral church of St *Peter and St *Paul, Washington, DC, is the seat of the Bp. of Washington in the *Episcopal Church in the United States of America. It is known as the 'National Cathedral', but it has no extra-diocesan status. The diocese was founded in 1893, and the foundation stone of the cathedral, designed by G. F. *Bodley and Henry Vaughan of Boston, was laid in 1907. Building work began at the east end with the construction of the Bethlehem chapel and apse and continued westward under the direction of Philip Hubert Frohman, who modified the original design in detail, but adhered to the broad outline of the original plan. The cathedral, which was completed in 1990, is a vast cruciform building, in 14th-cent. Gothic style; it has a central 'Gloria in excelsis' tower, 301 feet high, and two west towers, each 235 feet high. Its position on the crown of Mount St Albans, overlooking the city, makes it visible for miles around. The interior is notable for its soaring proportions, magnificent collection of 20th-cent. stained glass, and fine craftsmanship in wood, stone, and metal.

T. Harrington, *The Last Cathedral* (Engelwood Cliffs, NJ [1979]); R. T. Feller, *Completing Washington Cathedral for Thy Great Glory* (Washington, DC, 1989).

Watch Tower Bible and Tract Society. See JEHOVAH'S WITNESSES.

water. See HOLY WATER.

Waterland, Daniel (1683–1740), Anglican theologian. He was educated at Magdalene College, Cambridge, of which he became a Fellow in 1704 and Master in 1713. In 1717 he was appointed chaplain to the King and in 1722 chancellor of the diocese of *York. In the following years he received many preferments, becoming a Canon of *Windsor in 1727 and Archdeacon of Middlesex in 1730. He took an active part in the theological controversies of his time, esp. those on the Divinity of Christ and the Trinity, on *Deism, and on the *Eucharist. His principal works were *A Vindication of Christ's Divinity* (1719), directed against S. *Clarke; *Eight Sermons in Defence of the Divinity of Our Lord Jesus Christ* (1720), his most popular work, in which he argued that the Divinity of Christ in no way impaired the unity of the Godhead; *Scripture Vindicated* (finished 1732), against M. *Tindal's *Christianity as Old as the Creation*, in which he defended the OT accounts of the Fall, of the origin of circumcision, and of the sacrifice of Isaac against the attacks of the Deists; *The Nature, Obligation and Efficacy of the Christian Sacraments* (1732); and his *Review of the Doctrine of the Eucharist* (1737). In this last work he sought to steer a middle course between the high views of the *Real Presence represented by T. *Brett and other *Nonjurors, and the minimizing opinions of *Socinians and Deists. The Eucharist was a commem-

orative and representative service, which possessed a sacrificial aspect from the remembrance of Christ's death, and the sacramental Presence was to be understood as the virtue and grace of the Lord's Body and Blood communicated to the worthy receiver. Waterland was a theologian of considerable learning, widely read not only in the Fathers but also in RC and Continental Protestant theologians, though hostile alike to philosophy and mysticism. His influence did much to restore sound Trinitarian teaching against the Arianizers, and his intermediate position in the Eucharistic controversy was for long widely accepted in the C of E.

Collected edn. of his Works pub. in 10 vols., Oxford, 1823, with 'Review of the Author's Life and Writings' by W. *Van Mildert as vol. 1, pt. 1. R. T. Holtby, *Daniel Waterland 1683–1740: A Study in Eighteenth Century Orthodoxy* (Carlisle, 1966). B. C. Rosendall, OFM Conv., *The Eucharistic Doctrine of Daniel Waterland: A Roman Catholic Study* (Fribourg thesis; Collegeville, Minn., 1970). J. M. Rigg in *DNB* 59 (1899), pp. 446–8.

Watson, Richard (1737–1816), Bp. of *Llandaff. He was educated at Trinity College, Cambridge, where he became a Fellow in 1760. In 1764 he was elected professor of chemistry, a subject of which he then knew nothing but in which he soon became an adept, and in 1769 a Fellow of the Royal Society. In 1771 he became Regius Professor of Divinity. In 1776 he published a reply to E. *Gibbon's attack on Christianity which Gibbon himself commended for its candour. In 1779 he was made Archdeacon of *Ely, and in 1782 Lord Shelburne offered him, as a known opponent of the American War, the see of Llandaff. Proposals for radical ecclesiastical reforms, including a redistribution of church revenues, combined with sympathy for the American colonists and—initially—for the French Revolution, brought him into disfavour with the government and put an end to his hopes of a better see. He settled at Calgarth Park in his native Westmorland, where he devoted himself largely to forestry and agriculture. He continued to write, issuing in 1796 *An Apology for the Bible* against T. *Paine, and in 1798 a work encouraging resistance to the French claims. He was one of the most versatile men of his age.

Anecdotes of the Life of Richard Watson . . . written by himself at different Intervals and revised in 1814, ed. R. Watson, son (London, 1817). J. R. Guy, 'Richard Watson and the Role of a Bishop', in B. Vogler (ed.), *Miscellanea Historiae Ecclesiasticae*, 8 (Bibliothèque de la *Revue d'Histoire Ecclésiastique*, 72; 1987), pp. 390–97, with further bibl. A. Gordon in *DNB* 60 (1899), pp. 24–7, with further refs.

Watts, Isaac (1674–1748), Nonconformist hymn-writer. A native of Southampton, he was educated at the local grammar school, where his unusual abilities induced a local benefactor to offer him a university education. He preferred, however, to enter the Dissenting Academy at Stoke Newington (1690–4), the high educational standard of which left a permanent mark on his mind. After holding a post as a private tutor, he was appointed assistant (1699) and then full pastor (1702) to the *Independent congregation at Mark Lane, London. But Watts's health deteriorated from 1703 onwards, and his pastoral duties devolved increasingly on his assistant. In 1712 he resigned and spent the rest of his life at Abney Park, Stoke Newington. In his later years he seems to have inclined towards

*Unitarianism. In 1719 he opposed the imposition of the doctrine of the *Trinity on dissenting ministers.

Watts deservedly holds a very high place among English hymn-writers. His hymns reflect his strong and serene faith and did much to make hymn-singing a powerful devotional force, esp. in Nonconformity, where hitherto the use of music in worship, apart from the *metrical Psalms, had been regarded with suspicion. They include many still in common use, among them 'Jesus shall reign where'er the sun', 'When I survey the wondrous Cross', and 'Our God, our help in ages past'. The two principal collections were *Hymns and Spiritual Songs* (1707) and *The Psalms of David* (1719). His other writings include *Horae Lyricae* (1706; poems), *Divine Songs* (1715; the first children's hymn-book), *The Improvement of the Mind* (1741), and a number of educational manuals, among them a *Logic* (1725).

Works ed. D. Jennings and P. *Doddridge (6 vols., London, 1753), 'with some account of the Author's life and character' in vol. 1, pp. iii–x; repr. with corrections (6 vols., ibid., 1810–11), with memoirs of the Life of the Author by G. Burder, vol. 1, pp. ix–lxxx. New edn. of his *Horae Lyricae* (London, 1837), with memoir by R. Southey, pp. i–lii. Abridged edn. of his *A Guide to Prayer* (orig. pub. 1715) by H. Escott (London, 1948). *Hymns and Spiritual Songs, 1707–1748*, ed. S. L. Bishop (London, 1962). T. Gibbons, *Memoirs of the Rev. Isaac Watts* (1830); T. Milner, *The Life, Times and Correspondence of the Rev. Isaac Watts* (1834); A. P. Davis, *Isaac Watts: His Life and Works* (New York, 1943; London, 1948). B. L. Manning, *The Hymns of Wesley and Watts* (1942), pp. 78–105. H. Escott, *Isaac Watts Hymnographer* (1962). [F.] J. Hoyles, *The Waning of the Renaissance 1640–1740* (International Archives of the History of Ideas, 39; The Hague, 1971), pp. 143–250. I. Rivers, *Reason, Grace, and Sentiment: A Study of the Language of Religion and Ethics in England, 1660–1780*, 1 (Cambridge, 1991), esp. pp. 164–204. H. L. Bennett in *DNB* 60 (1899), pp. 67–70.

Waynflete, William. See WILLIAM OF WAYNFLETE.

Wazo (980/90–1048), Bp. of Liège. Educated at the abbey school of Lobbes, he was appointed head of the cathedral school of Liège in 1008 on the recommendation of *Notker, and dean in 1015. Later he became provost of Liège and in 1042 he was elected bishop. His brother Gonzo was abbot of Florennes. A man of great energy and austere habits, Wazo was a faithful adherent of the Emperor Henry III, whose rights he defended against Henry I of France. In the incipient conflict between Papacy and Empire, however, he upheld the superiority of the spiritual authority, denied the Emperor the right to interfere in the appointment of bishops, and generally defended the independence of the Church. Having warned Henry before the Synod of Sutri that no one could judge the Pope save God, he regarded the deposition of Gregory VI as unjustifiable.

The chief source is the account written shortly after his death by Anselm of Liège, which forms the last part of Anselm's continuation of the *Gesta Episcoporum Tungrensium et Leodiensium* begun by Heriger of Lobbes; it is ed. R. Koepke in *MGH*, Scriptores, 7 (1846), pp. 210–34; repr. from E. *Martène in J. P. Migne, *PL* 142. 725–64. R. Huysmans, *Wazo van Luik in de Ideeënstrijd zijner Dagen* (Nijmegen, 1932). C. Hoerschelmann, *Bischof Wazo von Lüttich und seine Bedeutung für den Beginn des Investiturstreites* (Frankfurt am Main diss.; Düsseldorf, 1955). J.-L. Kupper, *Liège et l'Église imperiale, XIᵉ–XIIᵉ siècles*

(Bibliothèque de la Faculté de Philosophie et Lettres de l'Université de Liège, 228; 1981), esp. pp. 130–4, with refs. A. Fliche, *La Réforme grégorienne*, 1 (SSL 6; 1924), pp. 113–28. É. Amann in *DTC* 15 (pt. 2; 1950), cols. 3520–4, s.v. 'Wazon de Liège'.

Wearmouth and Jarrow. The twin *Benedictine abbeys between the Tyne and the Wear, of St Peter at Wearmouth and St Paul at Jarrow, founded respectively in 674 and 682 by St *Benedict Biscop, soon became one of the chief centres of learning and culture in W. Christendom. Benedict himself and Ceolfrid, deputy Abbot of Jarrow, who made numerous journeys to Rome, were great collectors of books which formed the nucleus of the celebrated library at Jarrow. The '*Codex Amiatinus' (q.v.) was written at Jarrow at the end of the 7th cent. The abbeys were made widely known through the writings of the Venerable *Bede (d. 735), who was educated in them and carried on the traditions of scholarship. In 867–70 they were destroyed by the Danes, but restored c.1074 by Aldwin, former prior of Winchcombe. He and two of his friends settled there for a time, and soon the monasteries began to flourish once more, later becoming cells to the priory of *Durham. The houses were secularized at the Reformation, and today part of their site is occupied by the parish churches.

J. Raine (ed.), *The Inventories and Account Rolls of the Benedictine Houses or Cells of Jarrow and Monk-Wearmouth* (Surtees Society, 29; 1854). W. *Dugdale, *Monasticon Anglicanum*, 1 (1817 edn.), pp. 501–4. H. E. Savage, 'Jarrow Church and Monastery', *Archaeologia Aeliana*, 22 (1900), pp. 30–60. R. Cramp, 'Monkwearmouth and Jarrow. The Archaeological Evidence', in G. [I.] Bonner (ed.), *Famulus Christi: Essays in Commemoration of the Thirteenth Centenary of the Birth of the Venerable Bede* (1976), pp. 5–18. M. E. Cornford in *VCH*, Durham, 2, ed. W. Page (1907), pp. 81–5, with refs.

Webb, Benjamin (1819–85), ecclesiologist. In 1838 he entered Trinity College, Cambridge, and while still an undergraduate founded with J. M. *Neale the *Cambridge Camden Society for the revival of ecclesiology. In this and other ways he did much to promote the revival of ritual that followed the *Oxford Movement, though Webb himself was a strictly moderate ceremonialist and never wore the Eucharistic vestments. From 1862 till his death he held the living of St Andrew's, Wells Street, London, which became famed for its music and parochial organizations. See also following entry.

C. C. J. *Webb, 'Benjamin Webb', *CQR* 75 (1913), pp. 329–48. Id. in *DNB* 60 (1899), pp. 96 f., with further refs.

Webb, Clement Charles Julian (1865–1954), *Anglican religious philosopher. The son of Benjamin *Webb (q.v.), he was educated at *Christ Church, Oxford. From 1889 to 1922 he was a Fellow of Magdalen College, Oxford, and from 1920 to 1930 (the first) Oriel (now Nolloth) Professor of the Philosophy of the Christian Religion at Oxford. His philosophical writings include *Problems in the Relations of God and Man* (1911), two sets of *Gifford Lectures, *God and Personality* (1918) and *Divine Personality and Human Life* (1920), and his Wilde Lectures for 1911–13, *Studies in the History of Natural Theology* (1915). His standpoint was in essentials that of orthodox Theism, with stress on the ultimate significance of personality against the *pantheism of *Hegelian Idealism. Webb also made important contributions to the study of medieval philosophy, incl. critical editions of *John of Salisbury's *Policraticus* (2 vols., 1909) and *Metalogicon* (1929). Among his other writings were *Religious Thought in the Oxford Movement* (1928), *John of Salisbury* (1932), and *A Study of Religious Thought in England from 1850* (1933; Olaus Petri Lectures).

C. C. J. Webb, *Religious Experience: A Public Lecture delivered ... on Friday 19 May 1944, ... with a Foreword by L. W. Grensted ... together with a Bibliography of his published Writings* (1945). F. M. Powicke in *DNB, 1951 1960*, pp. 1026–8.

Wednesday (originally so named in English after the Norse god 'Woden' or 'Odin'). From early times, as is shown by the *Didache* (8. 1), Wednesday was, together with *Friday, a Christian fast day; it long remained so in *Embertide and still is in the E. In the time of *Tertullian (*De jejunio*, 14), both these days were observed as *station days in Africa, as was the custom later elsewhere. In *Alexandria (Soc., *HE* 5. 22), and also in Rome until the 5th cent., there was a service of prayers and lessons without any Eucharistic celebration; the Liturgy of the *Presanctified is still the principal service of the E. Orthodox Churches on Wednesdays and Fridays during Lent. It is not clear why Wednesday was originally chosen as a fast day, but a tradition, first mentioned by St *Peter of Alexandria (*Ep. can.* 15) says that it was because it was the day of the week on which Judas and the chief priests planned the betrayal of Christ (cf. Mk. 14: 1; 10 f.).

G. Schreiber, *Die Wochentage im Erlebnis der Ostkirche und des christlichen Abendlandes* (Wissenschaftliche Abhandlungen der Arbeitsgemeinschaft für Forschung des Landes Nordrhein-Westfalen, 11; 1959), pp. 136–48.

Wee Frees. A popular name for the tiny minority of the *Free Church of Scotland which refused to countenance the action of the rest of their number in uniting in 1900 with the *United Presbyterian Church to form the *United Free Church.

week. The week as a liturgical institution derived from the Jewish observance of the *Sabbath day. The conception of a day of worship specially dedicated to God was taken over by the first Christians, but soon transferred to the first day of the week (Acts 20: 7, 1 Cor. 16: 2) in honour of the *Resurrection. The Jewish fasts on Tuesday and Thursday were translated to *Wednesday, the day of the Betrayal, and *Friday, the day of the Crucifixion (*Didache*, 8). Thursday as a day of rejoicing on account of the *Ascension and of the Institution of the Eucharist came into prominence in the early Middle Ages. About the same time in the W. *Saturday began to be dedicated to the BVM, and later other days, too, had their particular devotion, e.g. Monday became the day of the Holy Souls.

Possibly in NT times (cf. Rev. 1: 10), and certainly very early, the first day of the week was known as ἡ ἡμέρα κυριακή or τοῦ Κυρίου ('the Lord's Day'), but the other days retained their Jewish designations, namely ἡμέρα δευτέρα ('second day', i.e. 'Monday'), etc. In Latin these became *dies dominica, feria secunda*, etc. with *sabbatum* for Saturday. As fast days, Wednesday and Friday came to be known in the W. as 'stationes' (see STATION DAYS). The planetary names, which had been introduced into Roman usage shortly before the Christian era, were occasionally used by early Christian authors, but almost entirely in writings intended for non-Christians. Never adopted in the E., they gained currency in W. Christian usage only from the late 3rd cent. The English names are the Teutonic equivalents of the Roman planetary names.

G. Schreiber, *Die Wochentage im Erlebnis der Ostkirche und des christlichen Abendlandes* (Wissenschaftliche Abhandlungen der Arbeitsgemeinschaft für Forschung des Landes Nordrhein-Westfalen, 11; 1959). J. A. Jungmann, SJ, in *NCE* 14 (1967), pp. 841–3, s.v.

Week, Holy. See HOLY WEEK.

Weeks, Feast of. The Jewish celebration (Exod. 23: 16) of the completion of the grain harvest. It was held on the 50th day (hence the Greek title 'Pentecost') after the offering of the barley-sheaf at the feast of unleavened bread (i.e. in the late spring or early summer). Two loaves of leavened bread were presented as a 'wave-offering', accompanied by a 'peace-offering', a 'burnt-offering', and a 'sin-offering'. The fullest account in the OT of the ceremonies surrounding it is in Lev. 23: 9–21. In later times the feast was regarded both by Jews (e.g. *Maimonides) and Christians (e.g. *Jerome, *Augustine) as commemorating the Giving of the Law on Sinai (Exod. 20).

R. de Vaux, OP, *Les Institutions de l'Ancien Testament*, 2 (1960), pp. 395–7; Eng. tr. (2nd edn., 1965), pp. 493–5. H.-J. Kraus, *Gottesdienst in Israel* (2nd edn., Munich, 1962), pp. 72–8; Eng. tr., *Worship in Israel* (Oxford, 1966), pp. 55–61.

Weigel, Valentin (1533–88), *Lutheran mystical writer. From 1567 he was pastor at Zschopau, nr. Chemnitz. Not till the 17th cent., however, when from 1609 onwards his writings (not all genuine) were printed at Halle, did his doctrines become generally known. These books consisted esp. of attacks on the 'Bibliolaters' (*Buchstabentheologen*) and of cosmological speculations incompatible with dogmatic Lutheranism. In the history of mysticism his ideas, largely the outcome of the prolonged study of such writers as *Dionysius the Pseudo-Areopagite and *Paracelsus, are important for the considerable influence which they exercised on J. *Boehme.

Sämtliche Schriften, ed. W.-E. Peuckert and W. Zeller (Stuttgart, 1962 ff.). A. Israel, *M. Valentin Weigels Leben und Schriften* (Zschopau, 1888). H. Maier, *Der mystische Spiritualismus Valentin Weigels* (Beiträge zur Forderung christlicher Theologie, 29, Heft 4; 1926). A. Koyré, 'Un Mystique protestant. Maître Valentin Weigel' in *Revue d'Histoire et de Philosophie religieuses* [8] (1928), pp. 227–48 and 329–48. W. Zeller, *Die Schriften Valentin Weigels* (Historische Studien, 370; 1940). F. Lieb, *Valentin Weigels Kommentar zur Schöpfungsgeschichte und das Schrifttum seines Schülers Benedikt Biedermann* (Zurich, 1962), pp. 17–46 and 143–53, with refs. G. Wehr, *Valentin Weigel: Der Pansoph und esoterische Christ* (Fermenta Cognitionis, 7; Freiburg i.B, 1979), with bibl. R. H. Grützmacher in *PRE* (3rd edn.), 21 (1908), pp. 37–44, s.v.

Weiss, Bernhard (1827–1918), German NT critic and theologian. Educated at the universities of Königsberg, Halle, and Berlin, he became professor of NT exegesis at Kiel (1863–77) and Berlin (1877–1908). His *Lehrbuch der biblischen Theologie des Neuen Testaments* (1868; Eng. tr., *Biblical Theology of the New Testament*, 1882–3), which accepted the methods and conclusions of the then new historical study of Christian origins to the extent of distinguishing between different doctrinal systems within the NT, nevertheless remained the standard conservative work for a generation. His *Das Leben Jesu* (1882; Eng. tr., *The Life of Christ*, 1883–4) and *Lehrbuch der Einleitung in das Neue Testament* (1886; Eng. tr., *A Manual of Introduction to the New Testament*, 1887–8) were also widely read. He undertook several of the later editions of the commentaries of H. A. W. *Meyer on Books of the NT; these were notable for their careful exegesis, their attention to the history of interpretation, and their interest in the *Synoptic Problem. He also issued a critical edition of the NT text (3 parts, 1894–1900; 2nd edn., 1902–5).

His autobiog., *Aus neunzig Lebensjahren, 1827 bis 1918*, ed. H. Weiss (Leipzig, 1927). *Theologische Studien* (Festschrift to Weiss on his 70th birthday, with contributions by C. R. Gregory, A. *Harnack and others, Göttingen, 1897).

Weiss, Johannes (1863–1914), German NT scholar. The son of Bernhard *Weiss, he was educated at the universities of Marburg, Berlin, Göttingen, and Breslau, and became Privatdozent at Göttingen in 1888 and associate professor in 1890, full professor at Marburg in 1895 and at Heidelberg in 1908. His *Die Predigt Jesu vom Reiche Gottes* (1892; 2nd edn., 1900) was the first attempt at a consistent eschatological interpretation of the Gospel, defending the thesis that the central purpose of Christ's mission was to proclaim the imminence of a transcendental Kingdom of God, in which He Himself was to be manifested as the Messiah. He further elaborated this view in his *Kommentar zum Lukasevangelium* (1893) and elsewhere. In *Paulus und Jesus* (1909), *Christus, die Anfänge des Dogmas* (1909), and in his last and most comprehensive work, *Das Urchristentum* (1917; completed by R. Knopf; Eng. tr. 1937), he traced the growth of early Christianity. His commentary on 1 Cor. (KEK, 1910; repr. 1970) remains a classic. In his article 'Literaturgeschichte des NT', in *Religion in Geschichte und Gegenwart* (1912), he expounded for the first time the principles of *Form Criticism which were elaborated later by M. *Dibelius, his successor at Heidelberg, R. *Bultmann, his pupil, and others. He also edited, and contributed to, *Die Schriften des Neuen Testaments* (1905 ff.).

Eng. tr. of *Die Predigt Jesu vom Reiche Gottes* as *Jesus' Proclamation of the Kingdom of God*, with introd., by R. H. Hiers and D. L. Holland (1971), with list of Weiss's major works, pp. 138–42. F. C. *Burkitt, 'Johannes Weiss. In Memoriam', *HTR* 8 (1915), pp. 291–5. B. Lannert, *Die Wiederentdeckung der neutestamentlichen Eschatologie durch Johannes Weiss* (Tübingen, 1989).

Wellhausen, Julius (1844–1918), biblical critic and orientalist. A native of Hameln, he studied under H. G. A. *Ewald at Göttingen, where he became Privatdozent in 1870. In 1872 he became Professor of OT at Greifswald, but in 1882 resigned his chair on conscientious grounds. In the same year he became Privatdozent in Semitics at Halle and later Professor in Semitics at Marburg (1885–92) and Göttingen (1892–1913). After original study of the texts of *Samuel (1871) and other parts of the OT, he devoted the greater part of his life to *Higher Criticism on lines foreshadowed by E. Reuss. He elaborated the problem of the structure of *Genesis by a close analysis of '*J' and '*E' (qq.v.), while his thesis on the relative dating of the component documents of the Pentateuch, acc. to

which '*P' (the 'Priestly Code') was the latest, completely transformed OT studies. It sought to establish the development of Hebrew religion from a nomadic stage through that of the Prophets to the religion of the Law. Wellhausen's analysis of the Pentateuch became the established orthodoxy in OT scholarship; though challenged by many from the 1930s onwards, it still has numerous supporters. In his later years he devoted himself largely to a critical study of the NT on similar lines. He upheld the priority of the Gospel of St *Mark over '*Q', its composite nature and its original Aramaic form. In spite of his insight into philological problems, his conclusions in the NT field met with less ready acceptance, though his pregnant commentaries on the Gospels laid down many of the lines for the later development of *Form Criticism.

His most important works on the OT are *Die Geschichte Israels* (1878; 2nd edn. issued as *Prolegomena zur Geschichte Israels*, 1883; Eng. tr., 1885) and *Die Komposition des Hexateuchs und der historischen Bücher des Alten Testaments* (1885). His chief works on the NT were *Das Evangelium Marci* (1903), *Einleitung in die drei ersten Evangelien* (1905), and *Kritische Analyse der Apostelgeschichte* (1914).

K. Marti (ed.), *Studien zur semitischen Philologie und Religionsgeschichte Julius Wellhausen zum siebzigsten Geburtstag am 17. Mai 1914 gewidmet* (Beihefte zur *ZATW*, 27; 1914). E. *Schwartz, 'Julius Wellhausen', *Nachr.* (Gött. Gesch. Mitt., 1918), pp. 43–70. W. Baumgartner, 'Wellhausen und der heutige Stand der alttestamentlichen Wissenschaft', *Theologische Rundschau*, 2 (1930), pp. 287–307. H.-J. Kraus, *Geschichte der historisch-kritischen Erforschung des Alten Testaments* (Neukirchen, 1956), pp. 235–49; 3rd edn. (1982), pp. 255–74. R. Smend, 'Wellhausen in Greifswald', *Zeitschrift für Theologie und Kirche*, 78 (1981), pp. 141–76; id., 'Wellhausen in Göttingen', in B. Moeller (ed.), *Theologie in Göttingen* (Göttingen, 1987), pp. 306–25; id., *Deutsche Alttestamentler im drei Jahrhunderten* (ibid., 1989), pp. 99–113. *Semeia*, 25 (1982 [1983]) is devoted to assessments of various aspects of Wellhausen's work. J. W. Rogerson, *Old Testament Criticism in Nineteenth Century England and Germany* (1984), pp. 257–89; E. [W.] Nicholson, *The Pentateuch in the Twentieth Century: The Legacy of Julius Wellhausen* (Oxford, 1998).

Wells. A minster dedicated to St *Andrew existed in Wells by the third quarter of the 8th cent., and perhaps as early as 705. About 909 this church became the cathedral of the newly created diocese of the Somerset people. Its endowments were greatly increased by Bp. Giso (1061–88), who reorganized the canons under a modified form of the rule of St *Chrodegang. After the removal of the see to *Bath between 1088 and 1091, the establishment at Wells fell into neglect, but Bp. Robert of Lewes (1136–66) refounded the chapter on the lines of the constitution at *Salisbury and endowed the deanery and 22 *prebends, later increased to 55, of which 49 survived the Reformation. To settle legal questions arising from the surrender of the deanery and the alienation of capitular properties at the time of the Reformation, *Elizabeth I granted a charter to Wells in 1591 which also had the effect of assimilating its constitution partly to that of a New Foundation church (see *CATHEDRAL).

The present cathedral was begun *c*.1180 and the main structure was consecrated on 23 Oct. 1239; it lies to the north of the earlier Saxon church. The octagonal chapter house, the east end of the quire, the Lady chapel, and the central tower were added in the first half of the 14th cent., and the cloisters were rebuilt in the 15th cent. The magnificent 13th-cent. west front has 293 medieval figures (angels, saints, kings, and queens) and reliefs. There are *misericords with fine 14th-cent. woodwork and a 14th-cent. astronomical clock. The most striking interior feature is the inverted arches (14th cent.) by which the piers of the tower are strengthened.

The Vicars' Close and Hall, the moated Palace, the old Deanery, and the four great gates erected by Bp. Beckington form, with the cathedral, a unique group of medieval ecclesiastical buildings.

The Theological College, founded in 1840, was moved to Salisbury and united with the theological college there in 1971; recognition by the House of Bishops for full-time training of ordinands was withdrawn in 1994.

W. H. B. Bird and W. P. Baildon, (eds.), *Calendar of the Manuscripts of the Dean and Chapter of Wells* (Historical Manuscripts Commission, 2 vols., 1907–14). D. S. Bailey (ed.), *Wells Cathedral Chapter Acts Book 1666–83* (Somerset Record Society, 72; 1973). For the Statutes of Wells, A. Watkin, OSB, *Dean Cosyn and Wells Cathedral Miscellanea* (ibid., 56; 1941). J. A. *Robinson, *Somerset Historical Essays* (1921), pp. 54–72 ('The First Deans of Wells'). H. E. Reynolds (ed.), *Wells Cathedral: Its Foundation, Constitutional History and Statutes* (1881); C. M. Church, *Chapters in the Early History of the Church of Wells, A.D. 1136–1333* (1894); L. S. Colchester (ed.), *Wells Cathedral: A History* (West Compton, Somerset, 1982). Id., *Wells Cathedral* (New Bell's Cathedral Guides, 1987). T. S. Holmes, 'The Cathedral of Wells', *VCH*, Somerset, 2, ed. W. Page (1911), pp. 162–9. For edns. of Episcopal Registers see bibl. to BATH AND WELLS.

Welsh Bible and Prayer Book.

In 1567 the New Testament first appeared in Welsh, translated from the Greek mainly by William Salesbury (c.1529–95). It served as the basis for the complete Bible published in 1588 by William *Morgan (q.v.). This was revised by Richard Parry (1560–1623; Morgan's successor in the see of St Asaph), probably with the help of John Davies (1570–1644), his chaplain, and published in 1620. This Bible, which used the language of the bards, was an important formative influence on the Welsh prose language. It was the Welsh Bible in general use until 1988, when a fresh translation from the original languages was published: *Y Beibl Cymraeg Newydd* (*The New Welsh Bible*).

The English Prayer Book of 1559 was translated into Welsh by Richard Davies (1501–81), Bp. of *St Davids, and appeared in 1567. The Psalms were translated direct from the Hebrew, and the first lesson continued to be read in English. A translation of the new Book of 1662 which was provided for in the Act of *Uniformity appeared in 1664. Minor revisions were made at intervals until 1841. In 1956 the Governing Body of the Church in Wales approved a Canon authorizing 'Experimental Use of Proposed Revisions of the Book of Common Prayer' for periods not exceeding ten years. Revisions of individual services were followed by a complete new 'Book of Common Prayer for use in the Church of Wales' (1984). This provides for services in Welsh and English.

J. Ballinger, *The Bible in Wales* (1906), with bibl. of Welsh Bibles [by J. I. Jones] appended (sep. paged pp. 1–90). Darlow and Moule, 4 (1911), pp. 1657–85. S. L. Greenslade in id. (ed.), *The Cambridge History of the Bible* [3] (Cambridge, 1963), pp. 170–2. J. G. Jones, *The Translation of the Scriptures into Welsh, 1588: Aim, Accomplishment and Achievement* (Lecture, Cardiff

[1988]). *The Bible in Wales*. Catalogue of the Exhibition held at the National Library of Wales, Aberystwyth (Aberystwyth, 1988). A. O. Evans, *A Chapter in the History of the Welsh Book of Common Prayer, or The Letters which were written preparatory to the Revised Edition of 1841* (3 vols., Bangor, 1922), with general introd., 1, pp. xiii–xxxix. W. Muss-Arnolt, *The Book of Common Prayer among the Nations of the World* (1914), pp. 69–76 (ch. 7, 'Richard Davies and the Welsh Translations'). R. G. Gruffydd, 'The Welsh Book of Common Prayer, 1567', *Journal of the Historical Society of the Church in Wales*, 17 (1967), pp. 43–55; G. H. Jones, 'The Welsh Psalter, 1567', ibid., pp. 56–61. A. O. Evans, *A Memorandum on the Legality of the Welsh Bible and the Welsh Version of the Book of Common Prayer* (Cardiff, 1925).

Wenceslas, St

(c.907–29 [or possibly 935]), Bohemian prince and martyr. The son of Duke Wratislaw and Drahomira, he received a good Christian education, supervised by his grandmother, St Ludmilla. After the death of his father (c.920) his mother became regent, but her violent actions so estranged the people that Wenceslas took over the government, probably c.922. Himself a man of much piety, he worked for the religious and cultural improvement of his people, which he sought to bring into closer connection with the W. world, and for this reason entertained friendly relations with Germany. It is likely that it was this policy, as well as the dissatisfaction of the pagan elements among his subjects, which led to his being murdered by his brother Boleslav, prob. in 929. He was soon venerated as a martyr, and Boleslav himself had his relics translated to the Church of St Vitus, at Prague. From 985 his feast is known to have been observed in Bohemia, whose patron he became. From the year 1000 his picture appeared on Bohemian coins, and the Crown of St Wenceslas came to be the symbol of Czech independence. The name of the saint has become familiar in England through J. M. *Neale's Christmas carol 'Good King Wenceslas', but its contents are wholly imaginary. Feast day, 28 Sept.

AASS, Sept. 7 (1760), pp. 770–844. J. Pekař, *Die Wenzels- und Ludmila-Legenden und die Echtheit Christians* (1906), with modern edn. of texts. Other primary texts listed in *BHL* 2 (1900–1), pp. 1273–5 (nos. 8821–44), and *Novum Supplementum* (1986), pp. 879–82. P. Devos, SJ, 'Le Dossier de S. Wenceslas dans un manuscrit du XIIIe siècle', *Anal. Boll.* 82 (1964), pp. 87–105, with text pp. 106–31. Eng. tr. of material on Wenceslas and Ludmilla from Church Slavonic and Latin by M. Kantor, *The Origins of Christianity in Bohemia* (Evanston, Ill., 1990), pp. 59–110 and 143–244. A. Naegle, *Der heilige Wenzel, der Landespatron Böhmens* (1928); F. Dvorník, *Zivot svatého Václava* (1929; also in Eng., *The Life of Saint Wenceslas*, Prague, 1929; the Ger. tr., ibid., 1929, contains additional information). H. Kølln, *Der Bericht über den Dänenkönig in den St.-Wenzels-Biographien des 13. und 14. Jahrhunderts* (Det Kongelige Danske Videnskabernes Selskab. Historisk-filosofiske Meddelelser, 52: 2; 1986), with refs. C. Parrott, 'St. Wenceslas of Bohemia', *History Today*, 16 (1966), pp. 225–33. R. Turek and V. Ryneš in *Bibliotheca Sanctorum*, 12 (Rome, 1969), cols. 991–1000, s.v. 'Venceslao', with extensive bibl.

Werburg, St

(d. c.699), less correctly 'Werburgh', English abbess. The daughter of the Mercian king, Wulfhere, and St Ermenilda, Werburg entered the *Benedictine abbey of *Ely, where she became abbess, and was later instigated by King Ethelred to reform the monasteries of nuns in his kingdom. She also established new monasteries at Trentham and Hanbury (in Staffordshire) and at Weedon (in Northants). She was renowned for her holy life and many miracles were reported to have occurred at her tomb. For fear of the Danes her body was removed to *Chester in 875. Her shrine, of which fragments are still to be seen in Chester Cathedral, was destroyed during the reign of *Henry VIII. The life by *Goscelin is almost entirely legendary. Feast day, 3 Feb.

Life by Goscelin pr. in *AASS*, Feb. 1 (1658), pp. 386–90; Florence of Worcester, *Chronicon ex Chronicis* (ed. B. Thorpe, London, 1, 1848, p. 32). Metrical Life by Henry Bradshaw (d. 1513), orig. pub. 1521, ed. E. Hawkins (Chetham Society, OS, 15; 1848) and C. Horstmann (EETS, orig. ser. 88; 1887). H. Chadwick, *St Werburgh of Chester* (Chester [1994] [pamphlet]). J. Tait (ed.), *The Chartulary or Register of the Abbey of St Werburgh, Chester*, 1 (Chetham Society, NS 79; 1920), pp. viii–xiv.

Wesel, John of. See JOHN OF WESEL.

Wesley, Charles (1707–88), 16th or 17th child and third surviving son of Samuel, and brother of John, *Wesley. Educated at Westminster School and *Christ Church, Oxford, he became a member of the Oxford *Methodists. In 1735 he was ordained and then accompanied his brother to Georgia, where he acted as secretary to J. E. Oglethorpe, the colony's leader; he returned to England in 1736. Like John he came under the influence of Peter Böhler and the *Moravians and experienced conversion on Whitsunday (21 May) 1738. Entering on the itinerant ministry in 1739, he occupied himself in preaching and travelled until 1756. He then settled in Bristol and from 1771 in London, where he ministered at the City Road Chapel. He was the most gifted and indefatigable of English hymnwriters (over 5,000 hymns in all); like his brother he understood the importance of hymns for missionary, devotional, and instructional purposes. The first collection, *Hymns and Sacred Poems* (with the original form of 'Hark! the herald angels sing' and 'Hail the day that sees Him rise') appeared in 1739, to be quickly followed by others, all professedly the joint work of the two brothers. They included *Hymns on the Lord's Supper* (1745), with a preface taken from D. Brevint's *Christian Sacrament and Sacrifice* (1673). Other well-known hymns include 'Jesu, Lover of my soul', 'Love divine, all loves excelling', and 'Lo! He comes, with clouds descending'. More emotional and less stable, but a warmer and more pastoral personality than his brother, Charles opposed all moves tending to separation from the C of E, esp. John's ordinations. Both are commemorated on 24 May in the ASB; on 3 May in the American BCP (1979). See also WESLEY, S. S.

His *Journal*, with selections from his Correspondence and Poetry, ed. T. Jackson (2 vols., London, 1849); first part (1736–9), with additional material, ed. J. Telford [1910]. *Representative Verse*, ed., with introd. by F. Baker (1962). J. Whitehead, *The Life of the Rev. John Wesley . . . To which is prefixed . . . The Life of the Rev. Charles Wesley*, 1 (1793), pp. 97–374. T. Jackson, *The Life of the Rev. Charles Wesley* (2 vols., 1841); J. Telford, *The Life of the Rev. Charles Wesley* ([1887]; rev. edn., 1900). Other studies by F. L. Wiseman (New York [1932]; London, 1933) and F. C. Gill (London, 1964). J. Telford, *Sayings and Portraits of Charles Wesley* (1927). F. Baker, *Charles Wesley as Revealed by his Letters* (1948). J. E. Rattenbury, *The Evangelical Doctrines of Charles Wesley's Hymns* (1941); id., *The Eucharistic Hymns of John and Charles Wesley* (1948); B. L. Manning, *The Hymns of Wesley and Watts* (1942), pp. 32–77; R. N. Flew, *The Hymns of Charles Wesley* (1953). R. Green, *The Works of John and Charles Wesley: A Bibliography* (1896); F. Baker, *A Union Catalogue of the Publications of*

John and Charles Wesley (Durham, NC, 1966); B. M. Jarboe, *John and Charles Welsey: A Bibliography* (Metuchen, NJ, and London, 1987). A. Gordon in *DNB* 60 (1899), pp. 298–302.

Wesley, John (1703–91), founder of the *Methodist Movement. The 13th or 14th child and second surviving son of the Revd Samuel Wesley (1662–1735), rector of Epworth, Humberside, and his wife Susanna, he was educated at Charterhouse and *Christ Church, Oxford. In 1726 he was elected to a fellowship at Lincoln College, Oxford, and also acted for a time (1727–9) as curate to his father. At Oxford he gathered round him a group which became known as the '*Holy Club' or Methodists; they included Charles *Wesley and G. *Whitefield. At this period he came much under the influence of W. *Law (whom he visited) and other *Nonjurors and RC writers who inspired him to follow an intensely ascetic pattern of life. In 1735 he set out with his brother Charles on a missionary journey to Georgia under the auspices of the *SPG, but his severe pastoral discipline, aggravated by an unsuccessful love affair, alienated the colonists and he fled home in 1737. After the *Moravian Peter Böhler had convinced him that he lacked saving faith, he underwent a conversion experience when his 'heart was strangely warmed' on 24 May 1738 during the reading of M. *Luther's Preface to Rom. at the meeting of a religious society in Aldersgate Street, London. This was followed by a visit to the Moravian colony at *Herrnhut. Henceforth Welsey's professed object was 'to promote as far as I am able vital practical religion and by the grace of God to beget, preserve, and increase the life of God in the souls of men', and the rest of his life was spent in evangelistic work.

Finding the churches closed to him, Wesley followed Whitefield in field-preaching to the Kingswood colliers in 1739. He broke with the Moravians in 1740 and in 1741 his opposition to the strict Calvinist view of election led to a breach with Whitefield also. Wesley then developed his own organization with the help of lay preachers and extended his activity to cover the whole of the British Isles by 1751. His chief centres were in London, Bristol, and Newcastle-upon-Tyne. He is alleged to have travelled over 200,000 miles and to have preached over 40,000 sermons, as well as writing thousands of letters. Though attracting large audiences, he also suffered mob violence and clerical hostility, but eventually became a tolerated national figure. From 1744 he held conferences of lay preachers which became annual events and for which a legal constitution was provided in 1784. From small beginnings in the 1760s the Methodist system gradually developed also in America. The needs of this new field induced Wesley in 1784 to ordain T. *Coke as *Superintendent or Bishop, and also to instruct him to ordain F. *Asbury in America as his colleague. Wesley himself still wished the Movement to remain within the C of E, but an increasingly independent system grew up. At the time of his death there were 294 preachers and 71,668 members in Great Britain, 19 missionaries and 5,300 members on mission stations, and 198 preachers and 43,265 members in America.

Theologically, Wesley combined the teaching of *justification by faith alone with an emphasis on the pursuit of holiness to the point of 'Christian *perfection'. Intellectually, he combined a strong belief in the supernatural with appeals to Scripture, reason, and the *Fathers of the Church, though increasingly also to experience. He placed great value on liturgical prayer and Eucharistic devotion as well as on extempore worship. Personal magnetism and an enormous capacity for self-discipline and organization enabled him to control his movement. Though he mixed easily in a variety of company, impressed Samuel *Johnson with his conversation, and was an effective spiritual counsellor to women, his marriage to Mary Vazeille was most unhappy. A High Church Tory in politics, Wesley engaged in extensive charitable work; for him the pursuit of money was only for the sake of giving, while he distrusted the rich and the effects of wealth on the spiritual life. His extensive writings and abridgements give him a role as a popular educator. He was the central figure in the rise of Methodism and one of the greatest Christians of his age. Feast day (with Charles) in the ASB, 24 May; in the American BCP (1979), 3 Mar.

Wesley himself ed. a collection of his works, 32 vols., Bristol, 1771–4; later edns. incl. those by T. Jackson (14 vols., London, 1829–31; 15 vols., ibid., 1856–62; and 14 vols., ibid., 1872, repr., Grand Rapids [1958–9]). New edn., known since 1984 as the 'Bicentennial Edition', by F. Baker and others (Oxford, 1975–82; Nashville, 1984 ff.). This incl., as vols. 1–4, Wesley's sermons, ed. A. C. Outler (1984–7). Until they are incl. in this edn., the standard text of his Journal (which extends from 1735 to 1790) is that of N. Curnock (8 vols., London, 1909–16); of his Letters that of J. Telford (8 vols., ibid., 1931). Collection of extracts, with introd., by A. C. Outler (New York, 1964) and of John and Charles Wesley by F. Whaling (Classics of Western Spirituality, 1981). Lives by J. Hampson (3 vols., London, 1791), T. Coke and H. Moore (ibid., 1792), J. Whitehead (2 vols., ibid., 1793–6), R. Southey (2 vols., ibid., 1820, and many later edns.), H. Moore (2 vols., ibid., 1824–5), L. Tyerman (3 vols., ibid., 1870–1; with much fresh material), R. D. Urlin (ibid., 1870), J. Telford (ibid., 1886; 3rd edn., 1910), J. H. Overton (ibid., 1891), J. S. Simon (5 vols., ibid., 1921–34; in the form of separate studies), M. Schmidt (2 vols., Zurich, 1953–66; Eng. tr., 3 vols., 1962–73), V. H. H. Green (London, 1964), S. Ayling (ibid., 1979), and H. D. Rack, *Reasonable Enthusiast* [1989]. R. P. Heitzenrater, *The Elusive Mr. Wesley* (2 vols., Nashville, 1984, with extensive docs.). J. Telford (ed.), *Sayings and Portraits of John Wesley* (1924). On his life, also: M. Piette, *La Réaction Wesléyenne dans l'évolution protestante* (Louvain thesis; Brussels, 1925; 2nd edn., with slightly different title, ibid., 1927; Eng. tr., 1937); V. H. H. Green, *The Young Mr. Wesley: A Study of John Wesley and Oxford* (1961); R. L. Moore, *John Wesley and Authority: A Psychological Perspective* (American Academy of Religion Dissertation Series, 29; Missoula, Mont. [1979]). On his teaching and significance, M. [L.] Edwards, *John Wesley and the Eighteenth Century: A Study of his Social and Political Influence* (1933; rev. edn., 1955); G. C. Cell, *The Rediscovery of John Wesley* (New York [1935]); W. R. Cannon, *The Theology of John Wesley, with Special Reference to the Doctrine of Justification* (ibid. [1946]); H. Lindström, *Wesley and Sanctification: A Study in the Doctrine of Salvation* (Stockholm, 1946); W. L. Doughty, *John Wesley, Preacher* (1955); C. W. Williams, *John Wesley's Theology Today* (1960); A. B. Lawson, *John Wesley and the Christian Ministry: The Sources and Development of his Opinions and Practice* (1963); R. C. Monk, *John Wesley: His Puritan Heritage* (1966); F. Baker, *John Wesley and the Church of England* (1970). M. Marquardt, *Praxis und Prinzipien der Sozialethik Wesleys* (Göttingen, 1977). H. A. Snyder, *The Radical Wesley and Patterns of Church Renewal* (Downers Green, Ill. [1980]). R. E. Brantley, *Locke, Wesley, and the Method of English Romanticism* (Gainesville, Fla. [1984]), pp. 1–128 and 215–25. A. Gordon in *DNB* 60 (1899), pp. 303–14, s.v. See also works cited under METHODISM and WESLEY, CHARLES.

Wesley, Samuel Sebastian (1810–76), English composer and organist. He was a son of the composer Samuel Wesley (1766–1837), who was himself a son of Charles *Wesley. A chorister of the *Chapel Royal from 1819, he afterwards became organist of *Hereford Cathedral (1832–5), *Exeter Cathedral (1835–42), Leeds Parish Church (1842–9), *Winchester Cathedral (1849–65), and *Gloucester Cathedral (1865–76). He was a strong advocate of reform in church music, although seemingly often unable to achieve with his own choirs the standards he demanded from others. He nevertheless wrote some of the finest English church music since H. *Purcell, including a Service in E, and such well-known anthems as 'The Wilderness', 'Blessed be the God and Father', and 'Thou wilt keep him in perfect peace'.

Life by P. Chappell (Great Wakering, Essex, 1977). Further study by D. Hunt (Bridgend, S. Wales [1990]). E. [R.] Routley, *The Musical Wesleys* (1968), pp. 102–249; W. J. Gatens, *Victorian Cathedral Music in Theory and Practice* (Cambridge, 1986), pp. 128–46. N. Temperley in S. Sadie (ed.), *The New Grove Dictionary of Music and Musicians*, 20 (1980), pp. 363–8, s.v.

Wesleyan Methodists. See METHODISM and other arts. there listed.

Wessel (*c.*1419–89), Dutch theologian. (He is also known as **Gansfort**, the name 'Wessel' having been given to him at his baptism; the designation 'John Wessel', by which he is sometimes described, appears to have arisen through confusion with *John of Wesel.) Educated by the *Brethren of the Common Life at Deventer, he was influenced by *Plato, St *Augustine, and St *Thomas Aquinas. For 16 years he studied and taught at Paris, where he defended the side of *Nominalism against *Realism, more, however, it appears, on ecclesiastical than on philosophical grounds. Later he visited Italy, where he came into contact with the Renaissance humanism, and finally returned home for his last years. He is commonly regarded by German Protestant writers as one of the 'Reformers before the Reformation', since in his attitude to the Papacy, to the authority of the Church, and to the superstitious tendencies of his age, he shared many of the sentiments of M. *Luther, who edited a collection of his writings (*c.*1521). His practical system of meditation was a remote influence on the *Spiritual Exercises* of St *Ignatius Loyola.

Works pub. Groningen, 1614; repr., Nieuwkoop, 1966 (Monumenta Humanistica Belgica, 1). E. W. Miller, *Wessel Gansfort: Life and Writings* (2 vols., Papers of the American Society of Church History, 1 and 2; New York and London, 1917), with Eng. tr. by J. W. Scudder of his Correspondence in vol. 1, pp. 231–333, of his treatise 'concerning the Blessed Sacrament of the Eucharist and the Hearing of the Mass' in vol. 2, pp. 3–70, and of the Farrago, pp. 75–315, and full bibl. C. Ullmann, *Reformatoren vor der Reformation*, book 4, vol. 2 (2nd edn., 1866), pp. 236–557; Eng. tr. (1885), pp. 263–615. J. *Friedrich, *Johann Wessel* (1862). M. van Rhijn, *Wessel Gansfort* (The Hague, 1917); id., *Studiën over Wessel Gansfort en zijn Tijd* (1933). R. R. Post, *The Modern Devotion* (Studies in Medieval and Reformation Thought, 3; Leiden, 1968), esp. pp. 476–86. S. D. Reeves in *TRE* 12 (1984), pp. 25–8, s.v. 'Gansfort, Wessel'; R. T. M. van Dijk, O.Cist., in *Dict. Sp.*, 16 (1994), cols. 1393–6, s.v. 'Wessel Gansfort'.

Wessenberg, Ignaz Heinrich von (1774–1860), *Febronianist reformer. He was educated at Augsburg by ex-Jesuits, and later at Dillingen and Würzburg. In 1802, though only a subdeacon, he was appointed his *vicar general by K. von Dalberg (1744–1817), then Coadjutor Prince-Bp. of Constance. He became an increasingly warm advocate of Febronianist principles and aimed at the creation of a National German Church, largely independent of Rome. As early as 1802 he began a monthly review, *Geistliche Monatsschrift* (1802–4), which was replaced after two years by the less aggressive *Konstanzer Pastoralarchiv* (1804–27). Among his reforms were the raising of standards in the clerical seminaries, frequent gatherings of the clergy for mutual encouragement, bi-weekly religious instruction in the state schools, systematic provision for the blind and deaf-mute, and the establishment of an inter-confessional house of refuge. His *Josephinistic principles and writings met with much opposition at Rome. In support of his cause he accompanied Dalberg to Paris in 1811 and in 1814–15 attended the Congress of Vienna as Dalberg's deputy, but without positive result. During his absence in Vienna, Rome separated the Swiss portion of the diocese from Constance and shortly afterwards brought pressure on Dalberg to depose Wessenberg. Though Dalberg obeyed, he sought Wessenberg's appointment as his Coadjutor with the right of succession. The acceptance of this proposal by the Government of Baden was invalidated by Rome. When, on Dalberg's death (1817), the chapter elected Wessenberg as vicar and administrator of the diocese, *Pius VII again resisted the appointment and refused Wessenberg an audience. From now onwards Wessenberg, in open disobedience to the Pope, acted as administrator until 1827, when the diocese of Constance, which had been suppressed in 1821 by the bull 'Provida sollersque', was incorporated into that of Freiburg. In 1833 he retired into private life. Wessenberg was a voluminous writer. His publications included a large treatise, *Die grossen Kirchenversammlungen des 15. und 16. Jahrhunderts in Bezug auf die Kirchenverbesserung* (4 vols., 1840), but they lacked solidity and are without enduring value.

Unveröffentlichte Manuskripte und Briefe, ed. K. Aland and W. Müller (Freiburg, 1968 ff.). Correspondence with Heinrich Zschokke, ed. R. Herzog and O. Pfyl (Quellen zur Schweizer Geschichte, NF, 3. Abt., 10; 1990). Life by J. Beck (Freiburg i.B., 1862; put on *Index on 11 June 1866). A. Rösch, *Das religiöse Leben in Hohenzollern unter dem Einfluss des Wessenbergianismus, 1800–1850* (1908). K. Aland, 'Wessenberg-Studien', *Zeitschrift für die Geschichte des Oberrheins*, 95 (1943), pp. 550–620; 96 (1948), pp. 450–567; id., 'Das Schrifttum I. H. v. Wessenbergs', ibid. 105 (1957), pp. 475–511. W. Müller, 'Ignaz Heinrich von Wessenberg', in H. Fries and G. Schwaiger (eds.), *Katholische Theologen Deutschlands im 19. Jahrhundert*, 1 (Munich, 1975), pp. 189–204, with bibl. M. Ott in *CE* 15 (1912), pp. 590 f.

West Africa, Christianity in. The first Europeans arrived on the coast of W. Africa at the end of the 15th cent., but for the most part they were involved in the slave trade rather than evangelization. The Portuguese, however, undertook missionary work in *Angola, but the success of this mission declined after the end of the 18th century.

The abolition of the slave trade in the early 19th cent. and the exploration of previously unknown parts of Africa was followed by sustained missionary activity by Churches of all denominations. Anglicans, *Methodists, and

*Baptists were active in *Sierra Leone and, with *Presbyterians, in *Nigeria, while Methodists set up missions also in *Ghana, Gambia, and Dahomey. Protestant missionaries from Continental Europe, such as the Basel Mission, were also active in the area. The RC Church enjoyed a favoured position in the *Congo, and RC missionaries established posts in practically every part of W. Africa during the latter part of the 19th cent. In French territory an active part was taken not only by RCs but also by French Evangelicals; their most famous missionary was A. *Schweitzer. An Anglican mission from the *West Indies (under *SPG direction) also operated in French West Africa. The missions in Liberia (RC, Episcopalian and Protestant) were exclusively American in origin.

During the 20th cent., in W. Africa as elsewhere, there has been growth in co-operation between the non-RC Churches engaged in missionary work, and the independence which most W. African states achieved after the Second World War has been matched by the establishment of independent national Churches by Protestant bodies and the replacement of the older *vicariates by hierarchies in the RC Church. In the Anglican Communion, in 1951 all the existing dioceses in the area, apart from Liberia, were organized into the Church of the Province of West Africa, with a constitution which, coming into force in 1963, made it entirely independent of the C of E. In 1979 a separate Nigerian Province was formed out of part of the Province of West Africa, but the Province of West Africa was joined by the diocese of Liberia in 1982. See also AFRICA, CHRISTIANITY IN.

For bibl. see AFRICA, CHRISTIANITY IN, and works cited under ANGOLA, CONGO, GHANA, NIGERIA, and SIERRA LEONE.

West Indies, Christianity in the. The earliest evangelization in the West Indies was carried out by the RC missionaries who accompanied the Spanish colonists from the end of the 15th cent. Large numbers of priests and religious went to work among the Indians. A bishopric was established at San Domingo in 1511 and further organization soon followed. The aboriginal population was, however, largely exterminated and replaced by Negro slaves from W. Africa. The wealth derived from the cultivation of sugar by these slaves in the 17th cent. led to colonization by other nations, notably the French, the British, and the Danes, in some cases as a result of war. In the French islands the *Code Noir* of 1685 prescribed that all slaves were to be instructed and baptized in the Catholic religion. The cruelty with which the slaves were treated, however, led to antagonism and revolts.

In the islands ruled by the British the Anglican Church was established. It ministered to a large part of the white population, but in the 17th and 18th cents. made only isolated attempts to evangelize the slaves, e.g. the building of the *Codrington Missionary College, Barbados, in 1714–42. Despite the antagonism of the planters, other bodies undertook missionary work among the slaves. The *Moravians, who arrived on the Danish island of St Thomas in 1732, met with a sympathetic reception there, and soon set up missions in the British West Indies, coming to Jamaica in 1754. *Methodist preaching began with the arrival of Nathaniel Gilbert in 1760. It was supported by the Wesleyan Missionary Society from England and met with considerable success. In 1883 two independent Methodist Conferences were set up, but owing to financial difficulties were taken over again by the Wesleyan Missionary Society in 1904. This situation continued until 1967 when an independent Methodist Conference was established with its headquarters in Antigua. The first *Baptist place of worship was opened in 1791 by George Liele, a manumitted slave from the USA; by 1813 responsibility for the work had been assumed by the British Baptists, but in 1842 the mission declared itself independent. In 1824 *Presbyterians arrived from the USA; they devoted themselves particularly to the East Indians of Trinidad and the inhabitants of the Cayman Islands. In 1846 Presbyterians from Jamaica began sending missionaries to *Nigeria, providing an early example of the substantial missionary endeavour which has come from the West Indies. In the Danish territories a royal ordinance of King Frederick V in 1755 provided that God's Word should be preached to the slaves and their children baptized like other people's children; Lutheran missions were subsequently established.

By the beginning of the 19th cent. the Anglican Church began to take its responsibilities to the slaves more seriously. In 1808 the Bp. of London issued a circular to all clergy recommending that Sunday Schools should be set up for the education of Negro children. In 1824 the first two bishoprics of Jamaica and Barbados were established. Between 1868 and 1870 the Anglican Church was disestablished everywhere except in Barbados but it continues to play an important role in the life of the former British colonies. The Province was created in 1883; it elects its own bishops, makes its own canons and regulations by synodical action and administers its own finances.

In those areas which were originally Spanish or French the RC Church retained its predominance. Though the RC Church was for a time proscribed in Jamaica, when Trinidad and Tobago were ceded to Britain in 1802 it was agreed that no change should be made in the status of the RC Church. The 19th cent. saw the creation of three *Vicariates Apostolic for the British West Indies in 1837, as well as the establishment in 1820 of a bishopric for the Port of Spain. This post, now an archbishopric, was filled by a West Indian for the first time in 1971. Other Churches also gradually developed indigenous ministries after the liberation of the slaves in 1833 and particularly as the colonies gained political independence in the 20th cent. The 20th cent. has also been marked by efforts of the non-RC denominations to form *ecumenical links, resulting, for instance, in the creation of the United Theological College of the West Indies at Kingston, Jamaica, in 1965; in this ten denominations (incl. Anglican, Presbyterians and Methodists) are involved.

In the 20th cent. *Pentecostalism flourished. Most types were introduced from the USA, but some derived from West Indian folk religion. While the mainstream Churches have suffered a decline since 1945, the Pentecostal movement has expanded phenomenally. The two largest groups are the Church of God and its daughter Church, the New Testament Church of God. The Pentecostal style of worship has exercised influence upon the RC and historical Protestant Churches in the West Indies. Most of the Negroes accepted some form of Christianity, but the Oriental immigrants, esp. Chinese and Indian, have largely retained their own religion.

A. Caldecott, The Church in the West Indies (Colonial Church Histories, 1898). J. B. Ellis, The Diocese of Jamaica (1913). H. L. Clarke, Constitutional Church Government in the Dominions beyond the Seas and other Parts of the Anglican Communion (1924), pp. 259–315. F. D. Walker, The Call of the West Indies: The Romance of Methodist Work and Opportunity in the West Indies and Adjacent Regions [1933]. F. X. Delany, SJ, A History of the Catholic Church in Jamaica, B.W.I., 1494 to 1929 (New York, 1930); F. J. Osborne, SJ, History of the Catholic Church in Jamaica (Aylesbury, Bucks [1977]; repr. Chicago [1988]). G. E. Simpson, 'Religions of the Caribbean', in M. L. Kilson and R. I. Rotberg (eds.), The Africa Diaspora: Interpretative Essays (Cambridge, Mass., and London, 1976), pp. 280–311, esp. pp. 280–91. B. Stanley, The History of the Baptist Missionary Society 1792–1992 (Edinburgh, 1992), pp. 68–105 and pp. 240–68.

Westcott, Brooke Foss (1825–1901), Bp. of *Durham. He was educated at King Edward VI's School at Birmingham under J. Prince Lee, where he became the lifelong friend of J. B. *Lightfoot and E. W. *Benson, and at Trinity College, Cambridge. Ordained in 1851, in 1852 he became assistant master under C. J. *Vaughan at Harrow, where he published a series of theological works, including the 1st edition of his History of the Canon of the New Testament (1855), the Introduction to the Study of the Gospels (1860), and a History of the English Bible (1868). In 1869 he left Harrow for a residentiary canonry at *Peterborough Cathedral, which he retained when, in 1870, he was elected Regius Professor of Divinity at Cambridge. Here he prepared together with F. J. A. *Hort the celebrated critical edition of the Greek NT, published in 1881. It was followed by his three great commentaries on St John's Gospel (1881), on the Epp. of St John (1883), and on the Ep. to the Hebrews (1889), the fruit of his Cambridge lectures. At the same time he devoted much of his energy to the training of his students and to the encouragement of missions, the Cambridge Clergy Training School (now 'Westcott House') and the Cambridge Mission to Delhi owing their existence to his inspiration and direction. From 1883, when he resigned his canonry at Peterborough, he combined his chair with a canonry at *Westminster. In 1890 he was consecrated Bp. of Durham. In the diocese he made social problems his special concern, and one of the most notable events of his episcopate was his mediation in the coal strike of 1892. He also continued the plan inaugurated by J. B. Lightfoot whereby six or eight ordinands read for a year at Auckland Castle, and himself lectured to them each week. In 1892 he published his doctrinal work, The Gospel of Life, based on his Cambridge lectures, which was followed by several volumes of collected sermons and addresses, among them The Incarnation and Common Life (1893) and Christian Aspects of Living (1897).

A. Westcott (son), Life and Letters of Brooke Foss Westcott (2 vols., 1903). Shorter Life by J. Clayton ('Leaders of the Church, 1800–1900', ed. G. W. E. Russell, 1906); brief sketch by A. G. B. West, Memories of Brooke Foss Westcott (1936). Bishop Westcott Memorial Lectures (all pub., Cambridge): C. K. Barrett, Westcott as Commentator (1958 Lecture; 1959); H. Chadwick, The Vindication of Christianity in Westcott's Thought (1960 Lecture; [1961]); [W.] O. Chadwick, Westcott and the University (1962 Lecture; 1963); G. [F. A.] Best, Bishop Westcott and the Miners (1965 Lecture; 1966); D. Newsome, Bishop Westcott and the Platonic Tradition (1968 Lecture; 1969). F. Olofsson, Christus Redemptor et Consummator: A Study of the Theology of B. F. Westcott (Studia

Doctrinae Christianae Upsaliensis, 19; 1979). D. L. Edwards, *Leaders of the Church of England, 1828–1944* (1971), pp. 207–22. V. H. Stanton in *DNB, 1901–1911*, pp. 635–41.

Western text of the NT.

A type of text of the Greek NT marked by a distinctive cluster of variant readings, so named because the chief witnesses to it were thought to be of W. provenance, i.e. some Graeco-Latin MSS (e.g. *Codex Bezae), the *Old Latin, and quotations in the Latin Fathers. It is now acknowledged that this type of text is not confined to the W.; some of its variants appear in E. versions such as the Sinaitic *Old Syrian and the *Coptic. Thus, where the designation 'Western' continues to be used by textual critics, it is more as a proper name than as a geographical term.

B. F. *Westcott and F. J. A. *Hort posited three early types of text which preceded the later standard text of the Greek Church: the *Neutral, the *Alexandrian, and the Western. The Western text, they claimed, represented a process of free handling by scribes, harmonizing, clarifying, and embellishing the text, which, unlike the other two types, was not subject to the restraint of conscious revision. It was therefore generally unreliable, except where, contrary to its tendency to make additions, it preserved original shorter readings (dubbed 'Western Non-interpolations', e.g. Mt. 9: 34; 21: 44; Lk. 22: 19b–20, 62; 24: 12, 40; Jn. 12: 8; Rom. 16. 25–7). This is probably too sweeping a judgement, for some of these omissions, represented by very few MSS, may also be explained by carelessness or tendentiousness.

The Western text of Acts has so many longer readings that it poses a separate problem. J. H. Ropes argued that it was the result of a deliberate revision and expansion produced in the E. *c.*150, but he found no particular theological motive behind it. More recently others (notably E. J. Epp) have claimed to detect a strong anti-Judaic bias. The language and style of the Western text have also been studied closely; some scholars argue that they are distinctive and imply a homogeneous revision, while others deny this. Certain Western readings reflect St *Luke's own style and perspective to such an extent that they have good claim to be treated as original. The problem then becomes how to explain how the abbreviated, non-Western text came to dominate the MS tradition. One solution to this, that Luke himself produced two versions of Acts, i.e. that he revised his own work at some later stage, has recently been revived.

Important discussions in B. F. Westcott and F. J. A. Hort, *The New Testament in the Original Greek*, 2 (1881); B. H. *Streeter, *The Four Gospels* (1924); F. J. Foakes Jackson and K. *Lake (eds.), *The Beginnings of Christianity*, pt. 1, vol. 3 (1926; The Text of Acts, by J. H. Ropes); C. H. *Turner, 'Western Readings in the Second Half of St Mark's Gospel', *JTS* 29 (1928), pp. 1–16; A. C. Clark, *The Acts of the Apostles* (1933); G. D. Kilpatrick, 'Western Text and Original Text in the Gospels and Acts', *JTS* 44 (1943), pp. 24–36; E. J. Epp, *The Theological Tendency of Codex Bezae Cantabrigiensis in Acts* (Cambridge, 1966); M.-É. Boismard and A. Lamouille, *Le Texte occidental des Actes des Apôtres: Reconstitution et Réhabilitation* (2 vols., 1984); W. A. Strange, *The Problem of the Text of Acts* (Cambridge, 1992). E. J. Epp in *Anchor Bible Dictionary*, 6 (1992), pp. 909–12, s.v.

Westminster Abbey.

Acc. to a legend, not mentioned by *Bede and prob. of 13th-cent. origin, a Benedictine abbey was founded in Thorney Island in 616 and miraculously consecrated by St *Peter, the patron of the Church. The abbey is mentioned in a charter of *Offa, dated 785, of which, however, the authenticity has been challenged. Acc. to *William of Malmesbury it was restored by St *Dunstan. The rebuilding and restoration of the abbey were undertaken by *Edward the Confessor in commutation of a vow to go on a pilgrimage to Rome, the new choir and transepts being dedicated in 1065. The nave was prob. completed by 1085 and the original cloister by 1100. After the canonization of Edward the Confessor (1161), his relics were translated to a shrine in the choir. A Lady chapel at the east end was built between 1220 and 1245. Henry III in 1245 began the erection of the present church in the French style. By 1269, when the relics of Edward the Confessor were translated to the shrine behind the High Altar, the eastern part of the church had been completed. Work on the nave, resumed in 1376, was finished *c.*1505. By 1519 the chapel planned by Henry VII as a shrine for *Henry VI had been added. The western towers, designed by C. *Wren and modified by N. Hawksmoor (1661–1736), were completed by 1745. The present choir-screen (reredos) was erected in 1867 after the designs of G. G. *Scott (d. 1878).

The Benedictine foundation of Edward the Confessor soon became one of the richest abbeys in the country, largely through the veneration accorded to the royal saint. As a royal foundation it occupied a special position in relation to the reigning sovereigns, and it was under the protection of the Holy See. From pre-Norman times until the reign of *James I it enjoyed wide rights of *sanctuary. Abbot Laurence (Abbot *c.*1158–73) obtained the right to wear a mitre. Complete exemption from the jurisdiction of the Bp. of London and the Abp. of *Canterbury was granted in 1222. Notable Abbots included Edwin (Abbot 1049–71), Gilbert Crispin (Abbot 1085–1117), Simon Langham (Abbot 1349–62), Nicholas Lytlington (Abbot 1362–86), and John Islip (Abbot 1500–32).

In 1540 the monastery was dissolved and a collegiate church under a Dean with 12 Prebendaries was founded, W. Boston (Abbot 1532–1540) becoming the first Dean (1540–49). The abbey became a Royal *Peculiar, retaining its independence of the see of London. At the same time most of the monastic quarters, rebuilt after a fire in 1298, were appropriated for the school founded by *Henry VIII in 1540. In the same year a see of Westminster was established under T. *Thirlby, covering most of the county of Middlesex; it was suppressed in 1550. A Benedictine community under J. Feckenham (d. 1584) was reinstated by *Mary in 1556; it was dissolved in 1559 when *Elizabeth I restored the collegiate church. From the time of J. Dolben (Dean 1662–83) to that of S. *Horsley (Dean 1793–1802) the Deanery was held in conjunction with the see of *Rochester. In 1840 the title of Prebendary was changed to that of Canon and the number reduced from 12 to 6. There are now normally four Canons. Notable Deans include L. *Andrewes (Dean 1601–5), J. *Williams (Dean 1620–44), J. *Ireland (Dean 1816–42), R. Chenevix *Trench (Dean 1856–63), and A. P. *Stanley (Dean 1864–81). Lord John Thynne, Sub-Dean from 1834 to 1881, did much to improve the standard of worship in the abbey.

Notable features in the abbey include the fan-vaulting in the chapel of Henry VII, the shrine of Edward the

Confessor, the mosaic pavement in the sanctuary, the Coronation Chair, the mural paintings of St Christopher and the Incredulity of St Thomas in the south transept, the 11th-cent. chapel of the Pyx in the cloisters, and the tombs of numerous sovereigns from Henry III to George II and celebrities of all kinds, esp. since the 18th cent. Since the time of *William I it has been the invariable place for the Coronation of the sovereign, the Abbot or Dean having a special part in the ceremony. Until 1395 the House of Commons frequently sat in the 13th-cent. octagonal Chapter House. Almost throughout its history the abbey has retained a unique position as a centre of the national life.

A. P. Stanley, *Historical Memorials of Westminster Abbey* (1868; 5th edn., 1882); W. R. Lethaby, *Westminster Abbey & the King's Craftsmen* (1906); id., *Westminster Abbey Re-examined* (1925); H. F. Westlake, *Westminster Abbey* (2 vols., 1923); J. [H. T.] Perkins, *Westminster Abbey: Its Worship and Ornaments* (Alcuin Club Collections, 33, 34, and 38; 1938–52); E. [F.] Carpenter (ed.), *A House of Kings: A History of Westminster Abbey* (1966), with bibl.; J. Betjeman and others, *Westminster Abbey*, commissioned by W. Annenberg [1972]; C. Wilson and others, *Westminster Abbey* (New Bell's Cathedral Guides, 1986); *Westminster Abbey Official Guide* (1987). W. R. Lethaby, 'Medieval Paintings at Westminster', *Proceedings of the British Academy*, 13 (1927), pp. 123–51; S. E. Rigold, *The Chapter House and the Pyx Chamber, Westminster Abbey* (Department of the Environment Official Handbook, 1976); H. M. Colvin (ed), *The History of the King's Works*, 1 (1963), pp. 14–17 and 130–57, and 3 (pt. 1; 1975), pp. 210–22. Cf. also W. *Dugdale, *Monasticon Anglicanum*, 1 (1817 edn.), pp. 265–330. E. Mason, ' "The Site of King-Making and Consecration": Westminster Abbey and the Crown in the Eleventh and Twelfth Centuries', in D. Wood (ed.), *The Church and Sovereignty c.590–1918: Essays in Honour of Michael Wilks* (Studies in Church History, Subsidia, 9; Oxford, 1991), pp. 57–76.

Westminster Assembly (1643). The synod appointed by the Long Parliament to reform the English Church. A bill passed on 15 Oct. 1642 convening a body of divines having failed to receive the Royal Assent, Parliament issued on 12 June 1643 an ordinance to the same effect. The conference consisted of 151 nominated members—30 lay assessors (named first) and 121 divines. Among the laymen were such notable persons as J. Pym, J. *Selden, Bulstrode Whitelock, and H. *Vane. The ecclesiastics were carefully selected from men of widely diverse views. They fell into four groups: (1) *Episcopalians*, a group of four bishops (R. Brownrigg of *Exeter, J. Prideaux of *Worcester, J. *Ussher of *Armagh, and T. Westfield of Bristol) and five DDs (D. Featley, H. *Hammond, R. Holdsworth, G. *Morley, and R. *Sanderson); (2) *Presbyterians*, much the largest group, which included E. *Calamy, E. *Reynolds (later Bp. of *Norwich), A. *Tuckney, W. Twisse, and R. *Vines; (3) a small group of *Independents* of disproportionate influence, through the favour of Oliver *Cromwell and the Army—among them were Thomas Goodwin and Philip Nye; and (4) *Erastians* such as J. *Lightfoot. Out of loyalty to the King the Episcopalians practically never attended the sessions. It should be noted that despite its importance in the history of the Presbyterian Churches, the Assembly was in no sense a creation of Presbyterianism, nor indeed a Church court at all.

It met originally on 1 July 1643 in the Henry VII Chapel of *Westminster Abbey. When the autumn weather set in, it moved to the Jerusalem Chamber, which was thereafter its regular meeting-place. After the adoption of the *Solemn League and Covenant (q.v.), it was increased by five clerical and three lay Commissioners from Scotland. Between 1 July 1643 and 22 Feb. 1649 it held 1163 sessions; but the last mention of the presence of the Scottish Commissioners is on 9 Nov. 1647. Under the Commonwealth meetings continued at very irregular intervals down to 1653, mainly for the trial of ministers. The Assembly was never formally dissolved.

The Assembly began by revising the *Thirty-Nine Articles. But the appearance of the Solemn League and Covenant led to the construction of a wholly new formula, the celebrated *Westminster Confession (q.v.). At the same time the Assembly prepared the Directory of Public *Worship (q.v.) and the two *Westminster Catechisms (q.v.). The proceedings were long delayed by violent controversies between Presbyterians and Independents over the Sacraments and the jurisdiction of Church courts, and between Presbyterians and Erastians over Church censures.

Although only partially and temporarily accepted in England, the documents issued were approved by the Church of Scotland and came into general use throughout the Presbyterian world. In the present constitution of the Church of Scotland they are expressly mentioned as subordinate standards.

A. F. Mitchell, *The Westminster Assembly* (1883); S. W. Carruthers, *The Everyday Work of the Westminster Assembly* (Philadelphia, 1943); J. H. Leith, *Assembly at Westminster: Reformed Theology in the Making* (Atlanta, 1973); R. S. Paul, *The Assembly of the Lord: Politics and Religion in the Westminster Assembly and the 'Grand Debate'* (Edinburgh, 1985).

Westminster Catechisms. The two Catechisms ('Larger' and 'Shorter') compiled by the *Westminster Assembly. They were completed in the autumn of 1647 and, with slight changes, approved by Parliament on 15 Sept. 1648. Meanwhile the Larger Catechism had been adopted by the General Assembly at Edinburgh on 20 July, the Shorter on 28 July.

The Larger Catechism, partly based on J. *Ussher's *Body of Divinity* (1645), was mainly the work of A. *Tuckney. It is in essence a popular restatement of the teaching of the *Westminster Confession. It suffers from being in places unnecessarily elaborate, e.g. in its specification of what is commanded and forbidden in the Ten Commandments.

The Shorter Catechism, which came to fill a much more important place in *Presbyterianism, was probably also largely the work of A. Tuckney, who was assisted by John Wallis. It opens with the well-known Question and Answer: 'What is the chief end of man?' 'Man's chief end is to glorify God and to enjoy Him for ever.' Its didactic usefulness is increased by its method, since the answer always embodies the question and forms a sentence complete in itself. It has been in regular use among *Congregationalists and *Baptists as well as Presbyterians.

The Catechisms have often been repr. Convenient text in T. F. Torrance, *The School of Faith: The Catechisms of the Reformed Church* (1959), pp. 183–234 and 261–78. The Shorter, with Latin translation, is in P. *Schaff, *The Creeds of Christendom*, 3 (1882), pp. 676–704.

Westminster Cathedral. The cathedral of the RC Abp. of Westminster, dedicated to the *Precious Blood of Our Lord Jesus Christ. The building was proposed in 1865, begun in 1895 under Card. H. *Vaughan and opened for his funeral in 1903. It was consecrated by Abp. (later Card.) Francis Bourne in 1910. Designed by J. F. Bentley (1839–1902) in early 'Christian-Byzantine style' and executed mainly in red brick, the principal features are the spaciousness of the nave, the massive *ciborium over the High Altar, the interior decoration of marble and mosaic (still incomplete), and the domed campanile, 284 ft. high.

W. de l'Hôpital, *Westminster Cathedral and its Architect* (2 vols., 1919). P. Doyle, *Westminster Cathedral 1895–1995* (1995). *Westminster Cathedral*, ed. by the Administrator (1930); *A Popular Guide to Westminster Cathedral* (*Catholic Truth Society [1930]). *Westminster Cathedral: Guide to the architecture and interior, the history and pastoral functions of the Metropolitan Cathedral of Westminster*, with preface by J. Betjeman [1968]. See also Life of H. Vaughan (cited s.v.) and E. Oldmeadow, *Francis Cardinal Bourne* (2 vols., 1940–4), *passim*.

Westminster Confession. The profession of *Presbyterian faith set forth by the *Westminster Assembly. Originally the Assembly had been directed to revise the *Thirty-Nine Articles of the C of E in a Puritan direction and changes were made with the help of the *Lambeth Articles of 1595 and the *Irish Articles of 1615. But when Art. 15 was reached, the *Solemn League and Covenant appeared, presupposing uniformity of doctrine between England and Scotland, and under Scottish influence Parliament ordered the suspension of the revision on 12 Oct. 1643 and the framing of 'a Confession of Faith for the three Kingdoms, according to the Solemn League and Covenant'. The task was entrusted to a large commission; it took 27 months in all and was completed on 4 Dec. 1646. After revision it was finally approved by Parliament on 20 June 1648. Meanwhile the General Assembly at Edinburgh had ratified it on 27 Aug. 1647.

The Confession expounded in 33 chapters all the leading articles of the Christian Faith from the creation of the world to the last judgement. It taught emphatically the Calvinistic doctrine of election, though it recognized freedom of the will and 'the liberty or contingency of second causes' in the Divine decrees. It distinguished the two covenants, that of works made with *Adam and his posterity and that of grace made in Christ with believers, with its offer of free salvation on condition of faith. The distinction between the invisible and the visible Church was upheld. Great stress was laid on the identification of the Jewish Sabbath with the Christian Sunday (*dies dominica*) and the due observance of the Sabbath rest.

The Confession at once established itself as the definitive statement of Presbyterian doctrine in the English-speaking world. It exercised a deep influence on other groups of Calvinists. Several of the 17th-cent. *Baptist Confessions are simply adaptations of it.

S. W. Carruthers, *The Westminster Confession of Faith: Being an Account of the Preparation and Printing of its Seven Leading Editions* (Presbyterian Historical Society of England. Extra Publications, no. 2 [1937]), with crit. edn. of text, pp. 89–157. G. S. Hendry, *The Westminster Confession Today: A Contemporary Interpretation* (1960). A. I. C. Heron (ed.), *The Westminster Confession in the Church Today* (Edinburgh, 1982). Text, with Lat. vers.,

also pr. in H. B. Smith and P. Schaff (eds.), *The Creeds of the Evangelical Protestant Churches* (1887), pp. 598–673.

Westminster Directory. See WORSHIP, DIRECTORY OF PUBLIC.

Weston, Frank (1871–1924), Anglican Bp. of Zanzibar. After several years' work in slum parishes in England, he joined the *UMCA in 1898, and was appointed principal of St Andrew's Training College, Kiungani, in 1901. Here he learned to live among Africans as one of themselves, and to understand their point of view as few Englishmen have done. In 1908 he was consecrated to the see of Zanzibar. He is chiefly remembered for the occasions on which he figured in controversy. Of these the most notable were (1) the *Kikuyu Dispute (1913), and (2) his severance of relations with the Bp. of Hereford (J. *Percival) in 1915, after the appointment of B. H. *Streeter to a canonry at Hereford. In 1920 he largely inspired the appeal for Christian unity put out by the *Lambeth Conference, and in the same year appeared his protest against forced labour in Africa, entitled *Serfs of Great Britain*. In 1923 he presided at the Second Anglo-Catholic Congress, where his personality made a great impression. Of his writings the most important is *The One Christ* (1907), an expression of the *kenotic view of the Incarnation.

H. Maynard Smith, *Frank, Bishop of Zanzibar* (1926). B. C. Cross, 'The Christology of Frank Weston', *JTS* NS 21 (1970), pp. 73–90. H. M. Smith in *DNB, 1922–1930*, pp. 902 f.

Westphalia, Peace of (1648). The treaty terminating the *Thirty Years War. Strictly it was a pair of treaties concluded by the Empire on 24 Oct. 1648: the one with France at Münster in Westphalia and the other with Sweden and the Protestant states at Osnabrück. Besides many territorial decisions, the formula of the *Augsburg Peace of 1555, 'cuius regio eius religio', was accepted as the basis of ecclesiastical settlement. But it was modified in two important respects. First, full protection was accorded to all religious minorities already established in a given territory by 1 Jan. 1624, with the exception of those formerly in the Habsburg lands of Austria, Bohemia, and Moravia, and in the Bavarian Palatinate. Secondly, *Calvinists were now regarded as being comprehended within the *Augsburg Confession, and therefore within the new settlement. These terms infuriated Pope *Innocent X, but his protest ('Zelo Domus Dei', 20 Nov. 1648) proved ineffectual. While the Peace proved unable to arrest the gradual dissolution of the *Holy Roman Empire, some of its provisions were strikingly advanced, particularly that for separate discussion of ecclesiastical issues by Catholic and Protestant member states, with an associated constitutional right of veto.

Text of Treaty of Münster pr. in J. Dumont, *Corps universel diplomatique du droit des gens*, 6 (pt. 1; Amsterdam, 1738), pp. 450–61; of that of Osnabrück, ibid., pp. 469–90. Treaty of Münster also pr., with introd., in H. Vast, *Les Grands Traités du règne de Louis XIV*, 1 (1893), pp. 1–64. 'Zelo Domus Dei' pr. in the *Bullarum, Diplomatum et Privilegiorum Sanctorum Romanorum Pontificum Taurinensis Editio*, 15 (Turin, 1868), pp. 603–6. Eng. tr. of the religious clauses of the Peace and of 'Zelo Domus Dei' in S. Z. Ehler and J. B. Morall (eds.), *Church and State Through the Centuries* (1954), pp. 189–98. J. G. von Meiern (ed.), *Acta Pacis Westphalicae Publica oder Westphälische Friedens-Handlungen und*

Geschichte (6 vols., Hanover, 1734–6, + Register, 1740). [J. Dumont (ed.)], *Négociations secrètes touchant la paix de Munster et d'Osnaburg: ou Recueil général des préliminaires, instructions, lettres, mémoires etc. concernant ces négociations depuis leur commencement en 1642 jusqu'à leur conclusion en 1648* (4 vols., The Hague, 1725–6). *Acta Pacis Westphalicae: Im Auftrage der Vereinigung zur Erforschung der Neueren Geschichte*, ed. M. Braumbach and K. Repgen (Munich, 1962 ff.). F. [O.] Dickmann, *Der Westfälische Frieden* (Münster i.W., 1959). See also works cited under THIRTY YEARS WAR.

westward position. The practice of the celebrant of the Eucharist standing on the far side of the altar and facing the people (i.e. normally facing westward) appears to have been customary in ancient Roman churches. From about the 8th or 9th cent. the *eastward position was increasingly adopted in the Roman rite. Since *c.*1947 the westward position has been gradually restored in the RC Church, and an Instruction of the Sacred Congregation of *Rites of 26 Sept. 1964 enjoined that altars should be free-standing in order that the celebrant might be able to face the people. The westward position is also used in many C of E churches.

Wetstein, J. J. See WETTSTEIN, J. J.

Wette, W. M. L. de. See DE WETTE, W. M. L.

Wettstein, Johann Jakob (1693–1754), NT critic. A native of Basle, where he became a Protestant pastor, he was twice removed from his office on the charge of *Socinianism. From 1733 onwards he was professor at Amsterdam. His edition of the Greek NT (2 vols., 1751–2), which marked a great advance on its predecessors, included in the critical apparatus innumerable important variants, hitherto unrecorded, and also the *sigla* for denoting the MSS since then in common use. On a visit to England in search of MSS in 1716, he made the acquaintance of R. *Bentley, who gave him considerable encouragement, though a rupture occurred between them a few years later.

C. L. Hulbert-Powell, *John James Wettstein* (CHS [1938]).

Weymouth New Testament. An English version of the NT, published in 1903 under the title *The New Testament in Modern Speech*. It was the work of R. F. Weymouth (1822–1902), a *Baptist who was for several years headmaster of Mill Hill School. Besides the translation, each book is provided with a short introduction, and there are footnotes to the text.

Wharton, Henry (1664–95), English medievalist. A native of Worstead in Norfolk, he was educated at Caius College, Cambridge. In 1686–7 he assisted W. *Cave in the compilation of his *Historia Literaria*, and in 1688 he published several controversial writings, including *A Treatise on the Celibacy of the Clergy*, as well as an edition of R. *Pecock's 'Book of Faith'. In the same year he became domestic chaplain to Abp. W. *Sancroft and began work on a catalogue of the MSS in *Lambeth Palace. His decision to take the oaths in 1689 antagonized some *Nonjurors, but did not disrupt his association with Sancroft, who entrusted him with the 'History', 'Diary' and other remains of W. *Laud when he died in 1694.

Meanwhile, Wharton's greatest work, the *Anglia Sacra*, had been published in two volumes in 1691. Still indispensable for medieval studies, it provided the first comprehensive collection of sources for the pre-Reformation history of the English sees whose cathedrals were served by *regular clergy. The first volume deals with the dioceses and gives editions of medieval chronicles; the second is chiefly a collection of texts bearing on the lives of English bishops. In it are printed for the first time various important texts, such as *William of Malmesbury's 'Life of St *Wulfstan' and *John of Salisbury's 'Life of St Aidan'. Editorial abridgements and errors of transcription restrict the value of the work in parts, but they do not detract from its pioneering importance. It was, however, severely criticized by G. *Burnet, who also did much to obstruct Wharton's later search for preferment. A third volume, intended to deal with cathedrals served by the *secular clergy, was only partly finished and published, incomplete, in 1695.

Fourteen Sermons preached . . . before William Sancroft . . . in the Years MDCLXXXVIII, MDCLXXXIX (1697), with Life of the author (no pagination); *One and Twenty Sermons Preached . . . in the years MDCLXXXIX, MDCXC* (1698). 'Excerpta ex Vita MS. Henrici Whartoni, A. M., a seipso scripta' pr. in G. D'Oyly, *The Life of William Sancroft*, 2 (1821), pp. 103–74. D. C. Douglas, *English Scholars* (1939), ch. 7, pp. 175–96; 2nd edn. (1951), pp. 139–55. W. H. *Hutton in *DNB* 60 (1899), pp. 404–7.

Whately, Richard (1787–1863), Anglican Abp. of *Dublin. Educated at Oriel College, Oxford, he became successively Fellow of Oriel (1811), vicar of Halesworth (1822), principal of St Alban Hall, Oxford (1825), Drummond professor of political economy at Oxford (1829), and Abp. of Dublin (1831). He was one of the best known of the '*Noetics', an anti-*Erastian, and an anti-*Evangelical; and almost certainly the author of *Letters on the Church by an Episcopalian* (1826). This had considerable influence on J. H. *Newman, for a time Whately's vice-principal at St Alban Hall, whom he asked to assist him in the preparatory work for his *Elements of Logic* (1826), over many generations a standard textbook for students. Later Whately became a vigorous opponent of the *Tractarians. Among his other writings were his *Historic Doubts relative to Napoleon Buonaparte* (1819), an attempted *reductio ad absurdum* of the principles of D. *Hume; his *Elements of Rhetoric* (1828); and his *Introductory Lectures on Political Economy* (1831–2). As Abp. of Dublin he took an active part in the religious and political life of *Ireland, and did valuable work as a Commissioner of National Education. It was on his advice that Lord John Russell nominated R. D. *Hampden (q.v.) to the Regius Professorship of Divinity at Oxford.

E. J. Whately (daughter; ed.), *Miscellaneous Remains from the Commonplace Book of Richard Whately* (1864). Id., *Life and Correspondence of Richard Whately* (2 vols., 1866). His *Historic Doubts Relative to Napoleon Buonaparte* ed., with crit. introd. and notes by R. S. Pomeroy (1985). W. J. Fitzpatrick, *Memoirs of Richard Whately . . . with a Glance at his Contemporaries and Times* (2 vols., 1864). J. M. Rigg in *DNB* 60 (1899), pp. 423–9.

Wheatly, Charles (1686–1724), English divine. Educated at St John's College, Oxford, of which he was a Fellow from 1707 to 1713, he was *lecturer at two London churches and from 1726 until his death vicar of Brent

Pelham with Furneaux Pelham in Herts. In 1733–4 he delivered the Moyer Lectures, pub. in 1738 as *The Nicene and Athanasian Creeds*, and in 1739 he preached one of the earliest sermons against the rise of *Methodism. He is best remembered for his commentary on the BCP, *The Church of England Man's Companion, or a Rational Illustration . . . of the Book of Common Prayer* (1710; from the 3rd edn., in 1720, entitled *A Rational Illustration of the Book of Common Prayer*), which remained a standard work until the mid-19th cent. It shows his *High Church sympathy with the liturgical preferences of *Nonjurors such as T. *Brett.

Fifty Sermons on Several Subjects and Occasions (3 vols., London, 1746), with preface by J. Berriman in vol. 1 (no pagination); his *A Rational Illustration of the Book of Common Prayer and Administration of the Sacraments*, ed., with notes, by G. E. Corrie (Cambridge, 1858). E. I. Carlyle in *DNB* 60 (1899), p. 435.

Whichcote, Benjamin (1609–83), Provost of King's College, Cambridge. A native of Stoke, Salop, he entered Emmanuel College, Cambridge, in 1628, becoming Fellow in 1633 and tutor in 1634. Ordained both deacon and priest on 5 March 1637, he was appointed Sunday afternoon preacher at Trinity Church, Cambridge, where his preaching met with immediate success. On his marriage (1643) he retired to a college living at North Cadbury, Somerset. The following year, as a result of the Parliamentary reform of the University, he returned as Provost of King's College, but alone among the newly appointed heads of houses avoided subscribing to the *National Covenant. Vice-Chancellor for 1650–1, in 1655 he advised O. *Cromwell on the question of toleration of the Jews. At the *Restoration he was ejected by royal command, but was restored to favour in 1662 on accepting the Act of *Uniformity. From 1662 he held the cure of St Anne's, Blackfriars, until the church was burnt in 1666. In 1668 he was appointed vicar of St Lawrence Jewry; while the church was being rebuilt he preached frequently before the Corporation of London in the Guildhall Chapel.

Whichcote was one of the leading *Cambridge Platonists (q.v.). A sermon preached at the Commencement of 1650 involved him in a controversy with his old tutor and friend, A. *Tuckney. Averse to the pessimistic view of human nature prevalent among the *Puritans, he exalted man as a child of reason. He saw in reason the test of Scripture, maintained that some matters on which good men disagreed were insoluble, and pleaded for freedom of thought; and he was charged at different times with *Latitudinarianism, *Arminianism, and *Socinianism. His works, nearly all posthumous, include Θεοφορούμενα Δόγματα, *or Some Select Notions of B. Whichcote* (1685), *Select Sermons* (with preface by the third Earl of Shaftesbury, 1689), *Several Discourses* (ed. J. Jeffery, 1701), and *Moral and Religious Aphorisms* (ed. J. Jeffery, 1703).

Works (4 vols., Aberdeen, 1751), with short Life in vol. 1, pp. i–viii; selections from his *Select Sermons and Aphorisms* in E. T. Campagnac (ed.), *The Cambridge Platonists* (1901), pp. 1–75, with introd., pp. ix–xxvii; his *Moral and Religious Aphorisms*, ed. S. Salter (London, 1753), with 'Eight Letters of Dr. Anthony Tuckney and Dr. Benjamin Whichcote' appended (separate pagination), with introd. preface, pp. i–xl; *Aphorisms* repr. (London, 1930), with introd. by W. R. *Inge, pp. iii–x. B. F. *Westcott, 'Benjamin Whichcote', in A. Barry (ed.), *Masters in*

English Theology (1877), pp. 147–73. J. D. Roberts, *From Puritanism to Platonism in Seventeenth Century England* (The Hague, 1968). J. B. Mullinger in *DNB* 61 (1900), pp. 1–3. See also other works cited under CAMBRIDGE PLATONISTS.

Whiston, William (1667–1752), mathematician and theologian. Educated at Clare Hall, Cambridge, he was appointed chaplain to J. Moore, Bp. of *Norwich (1696), and vicar of Lowestoft (1698). In 1703 he succeeded I. *Newton as Lucasian professor of mathematics at Cambridge. His Arianizing views, however, caused him to be expelled from the university in 1710, and in 1747 he finally deserted the C of E and joined the *General Baptists. He wrote a large number of treatises, many of them of a startlingly paradoxical kind, which include his *New Theory of the Earth* (1696), *Accomplishment of Scripture Prophecies* (1708; in which he affirms that all prophecies have but one meaning), *Primitive Christianity Revived* (4 vols., 1711), *Life of Samuel *Clarke* (1730), and *Primitive New Testament* (1745). He is best remembered now by his translation of *Josephus, with many useful notes and dissertations (1737; very often reprinted).

The principal sources for his life are the *Memoirs of the Life and Writings of Mr. William Whiston . . . written by himself* (1733) and his *An Account of the Convocation's Proceedings with Relation to Mr. Whiston* (1711). J. E. Force, *William Whiston, Honest Newtonian* (Cambridge, 1985). L. Stephen in *DNB* 61 (1900), pp. 10–14, s.v.; G. Crosse in *DECH* (1912), pp. 629 f.

Whitaker, William (1547/8–95), *Puritan divine. A nephew of A. *Nowell, he was educated at St Paul's School, London, and Trinity College, Cambridge, where in 1571 he was elected to a Major Fellowship. In 1580 he became Regius professor of divinity and in 1586 master of St John's College. A strict *Calvinist, he exercised a wide influence by his devotion to learning and his impartiality. A strong anti-Romanist, he held that the Pope was *Antichrist and attacked the writings of R. *Bellarmine and T. *Stapleton. In the last year of his life he was mainly responsible for drafting the *Lambeth Articles, though at one or two points J. *Whitgift softened the extreme Calvinism of Whitaker's original text. His writings include Greek versions of the BCP (1569) and of Nowell's *Larger Catechism* (1573).

Opera Theologica (2 vols., Geneva, 1610), with Life [by A. Assheton] in vol. 1, pp. 698–704. *A Disputation on Holy Scripture against the Papists*, also ed. W. Fitzgerald (*Parker Society, 1849). H. C. Porter, *Reformation and Reaction in Tudor Cambridge* (Cambridge, 1958), esp. pp. 183–203, 314–22, and 364–75; P. [G.] Lake, *Moderate Puritans and the Elizabethan Church* (ibid., 1982), esp. pp. 93–115 and 169–218. J. B. Mullinger in *DNB* 61 (1900), pp. 21–3.

Whitby, Synod of (664), a council held by King Oswiu of Northumbria in order to establish unity of practice in the date of observing *Easter (see PASCHAL CONTROVERSIES) and the style of *tonsure within his territory, where diversity had hitherto been accepted. Oswiu had grown up in N. Ireland and followed the *Celtic practice, as did his bishop, St *Colman; his queen Eanfleda, who had been brought up in Kent, and their son Alhfrith followed the Roman practice. Colman spoke in defence of the Celtic custom; the Roman view, represented by Bp. Agilbert, a Frank who had studied in S. Ireland and was in 664 bishop among the West Saxons, was put forward by his English disciple, the young St *Wilfrid. *Bede represents the debate as between the custom of St *John, founded on Mosaic law, and the authority of St *Peter. The king decided to follow Peter as being keeper of the keys of Heaven; Northumbria adopted the Roman practice, and those clergy who would not change withdrew to *Iona and later to Ireland. Colman's place was taken by Tuda, an Englishman trained in Roman practice in S. Ireland.

Bede made this council the turning-point of his history: until 664 Christianity came to the English through different traditions; from 664 the trend is towards unity and orthodoxy. Since the 17th cent. English historians have treated this synod as if it were a national decision against Ireland and for Rome, but this view misrepresents the state of affairs in both countries. Bede indicated only one sign of influence beyond Northumbria: St *Cedd, a Northumbrian who was bishop among the East Saxons, attended the council, was persuaded to adopt the Roman practice, and took this view back to Essex.

The principal sources are Bede, *HE* 3. 25 (cf. comm. by J. M. Wallace-Hadrill, Oxford, 1988, pp. 124–9 and 235 f.; also p. xxiii), and Stephanus' Life of St Wilfrid, 10, ed., with Eng. tr., B. Colgrave (Cambridge, 1927), pp. 20–3, and notes pp. 156–8. W. *Bright, *Chapters of Early English Church History* (1878), pp. 193–200. J. L. G. Meissner, *The Celtic Church in England after the Synod of Whitby* (1929), pp. 7–18 (ch. 2, 'The Synod of Whitby and its Immediate Results'). P. Grosjean, SJ, 'La Date du Colloque de Whitby', *Anal. Boll.* 78 (1960), pp. 233–74. H. Mayr-Harting, *The Coming of Christianity to Anglo-Saxon England* (1972), pp. 103–113. P. Hunter Blair, 'Whitby as a Centre of Learning in the Seventh Century', in M. Lapidge and H. Gneuss (eds.), *Learning and Literature in Anglo-Saxon England: Studies presented to Peter Clemoes* (Cambridge, 1985), pp. 3–32, esp. pp. 14–22. See also works cited under PASCHAL CONTROVERSIES.

Whitby, Daniel (1638–1726), English divine. Educated at Trinity College, Oxford, of which he was elected a Fellow in 1664, he was appointed in 1668 to a prebendal stall at *Salisbury, and in 1669 became rector of St Edmund's church in that city. He gained notoriety for his hostility to Popery, for his desire for reconciliation with the Nonconformists, and for his provocative writings, the best-known of which were *The Protestant Reconciler* (1682; subsequently publicly burnt at Oxford) and *Last Thoughts* (1727). This last showed that Whitby was a *Unitarian in his later years. His most considerable work was a *Paraphrase and Commentary on the NT* (2 vols., 1703). He also wrote in defence of B. *Hoadly in the *Bangorian Controversy.

Extracts from Whitby's writings in P. E. More and F. L. Cross (eds.), *Anglicanism* (1935), nos. 57, 95, 118, 294, pp. 116 f., 221 f., 270–2, and 634 f. A. A. Sykes, 'A Short Account of Dr. Whitby. To which is Added, A Catalogue of his Works', prefixed to 2nd edn. of Whitby's *Last Thoughts* (1728), pp. i–xvi. A. Gordon in *DNB* 61 (1900), pp. 28–30, s.v., with refs.

Whitchurch, Edward (d. 1561), *Protestant printer. A citizen of London, he became a warm adherent of the Reformed doctrines and in 1537 associated himself with R. *Grafton (q.v.) for circulating *Matthew's Bible (printed at Antwerp). In 1538 he and Grafton gave M. *Coverdale financial assistance in printing his NT at Paris and in 1539 published the *Great Bible at Greyfriars

House in London. Seven editions had appeared by 1541, some copies bearing Whitchurch's, others Grafton's, name. In 1543, with six other printers, they were imprisoned for Protestantism, but released four weeks later. In the last years of *Henry VIII's reign they continued to print religious books such as *Primers. Under *Edward VI Whitchurch printed both the First (1549) and Second (1552) Prayer Books. He was one of a consortium of printers who helped Abp. T. *Cranmer's family after his arrest in 1553, and he married his widow.

E. G. Duff, *A Century of the English Book Trade* (1905), p. 169, s.v. H. R. Plomer, *A Short History of English Printing, 1476–1900* (1915), pp. 57–9. L. E. Osborne, 'The Whitchurch compartment in London and Mexico', *The Library*, 4th ser. 8 (1928), pp. 301–11. S. Lee in *DNB* 61 (1900), pp. 30 f., s.v. See also bibl. under GRAFTON, R., and GREAT BIBLE.

White Fathers (Fr. *Pères Blancs*). The Society of Missionaries of Africa was founded by C.-M. A.-*Lavigerie at Algiers in 1868. It is composed of secular priests and coadjutor brothers living in community without vows, but bound by solemn oath to lifelong work in the African mission and obedience to their superiors. They wear a white tunic and a cloak or burnous with a rosary round the neck. Their constitutions were approved by the Holy See in 1885 and confirmed in 1908. The White Fathers devote themselves to a thorough four years' preparation of the Africans for Baptism and to the subsequent training of converts for trades, agriculture, missionary work, and for the priesthood. They began their missions in Algeria and Tunisia but soon extended them into the interior of W., Central, and E. Africa, often meeting with violent opposition. Apart from their missionary achievements the White Fathers have done much for the abolition of slavery, for the improvement of agriculture, and for the scientific exploration of Africa. They remain the most numerous group of RC missionaries at work in Africa. See also WHITE SISTERS.

T. Frey, *Die Gesellschaft der Missionare von Afrika in ihrem 50-jähr. Bestehen* (Trier, 1918). J. Bouniol, WF, *The White Fathers and their Missions* ([1929]; based on T. Frey, op. cit.). *La Société des Missionnaires d'Afrique (Pères Blancs)* (Les Ordres religieux; 1924); P. Lesourd, *Les Pères Blancs du Cardinal Lavigerie* (Les Grands Ordres monastiques et instituts religieux; 1935); D. Attwater, *The White Fathers in Africa* (1937); G. D. Kittler, *The White Fathers* (1957). R. Heremans, *L'Éducation dans les Missions des Pères Blancs en Afrique Centrale (1879–1914)* (Université Catholique de Louvain. Recueil travaux d'histoire et de philologie, sér. 6, fasc. 26; 1983). L. Volker in *NCE* 14 (1967), pp. 894 f., s.v.; J. Casier, WF, in *DIP* 5 (1978), cols. 1430–7, s.v. 'Missionari d'Africa'. See also bibl. to LAVIGERIE, C.-M. A.-, and WEST AFRICA, CHRISTIANITY IN.

White Friars. The *Carmelite friars, so called from their white cloaks and *scapulars. The term has been applied, less accurately, to the *Premonstratensians or White Canons.

White Ladies. A name popularly given to the following religious orders, from their white habits: (1) The Sisters of the Presentation of Mary, a teaching order founded at Theuyts, Ardèche, in France in 1796, by Marie Rivier, for the education of young girls. The mother-house is at Saint-Andéol, Ardèche. Since 1853 they have been established also in Canada. (2) The *Magdalens (q.v.). (3) In medieval England the *Cistercian nuns, the designation still surviving here and there in the place-name 'White-ladies'.

White Monks.

The *Cistercian monks, so named from the colour of their habit, which was of undyed wool.

White Sisters.

(1) The Congregation of the Missionary Sisters of Our Lady of Africa was founded by C.-M. A.-*Lavigerie in 1869 to work alongside the *White Fathers (q.v.) and was recognized by the Pope in 1909. They have simple perpetual vows, no lay sisters, and devote themselves to teaching, nursing, and pastoral work in urban areas. They have been instrumental in setting up 18 congregations of African sisters and in training them for pastoral work.

(2) The Congregation of the Daughters of the Holy Ghost, usually called the White Sisters from their white habit, was founded in 1706 at Plérin in Brittany, moving to St-Brieuc in 1834. Its chief objects are education and nursing. The Congregation spread rapidly, esp. during the 19th cent., but the Sisters were driven from many of their houses in France by the legislation of 1902. They established convents in Belgium, England, and the USA. From 1936–51 they worked in Manchuria and since then have set up missions in Cameroon, Nigeria, and Chile.

(1) Heimbucher, 2, pp. 630–2, with bibl. G. Rocca, SSP, in *DIP* 5 (1978), cols. 1580 f., s.v. 'Missionarie di Nostra Signora d'Africa'. See also works cited s.v. WHITE FATHERS.
(2) C. Lemercier, *Notice sur la congrégation des Filles du Saint-Esprit, 1706–1850* (Saint-Brieuc, 1888). A. du Bois de la Villerable, *Dom Jean Leuduger, fondateur de la Congrégation des Filles du Saint-Esprit* (2nd edn., ibid., 1924). R. Aubert in *DHGE* 17 (1971), cols. 106–8, s.v. 'Filles du Saint-Esprit'.

White, Francis

(c.1564–1638), Bp. of *Ely. Educated at Gonville and Caius College, Cambridge, he was ordained priest in 1588, and after filling several livings was appointed Dean of *Carlisle in 1622. He became bishop successively of Carlisle (1626), *Norwich (1629), and Ely (1631). As a noted *Arminian, he licensed R. *Montagu's *Appello Caesarem* for printing in 1625, and in the following year attacked *Calvinist teaching at the York House conference. He was also a prominent anti-Papist disputant. In 1617 he published *The Orthodox Faith and Way to the Church* (1617), in answer to a RC treatise entitled *White dyed Black*, and in 1622 he was engaged by *James I to support W. *Laud in presenting the Anglican case in a formal dispute with the Jesuit, 'John *Fisher'. His final works, *A Treatise of the Sabbath Day* (1635), dedicated to Laud, and *An Examination and Confutation of . . . a Briefe Answer to a late Treatise of the Sabbath Day* (1637; the unnamed author of the *Brief Answer* was Richard Byfield, c.1598–1664) were both written to refute the *Sabbatarian tendencies of his time.

Extracts from White's works repr. in P. E. More and F. L. Cross (eds.), *Anglicanism* (1935), pp. 8 f., 46, 58 f., 132–4, 415, 437, 441 f., 514 f., 559, 573 f., 634. N. [R. N.] Tyacke, *Anti-Calvinists: The Rise of English Arminianism c.1590–1640* (Oxford, 1987), pp. 108, 151, 159, 171 f., and 174–80. A. Gordon in *DNB* 61 (1900), pp. 34 f., s.v., with refs.

White, John

(1867–1951), Scottish Church leader. He was minister of Shettleston, Glasgow (1893–1904), South Leith (1904–11), and The Barony of Glasgow (1911–51). An original member from the Church of *Scotland of the committee appointed in 1909 to negotiate a possible union between the Church of Scotland, which was by law established, and the *United Free Church of Scotland, which was a recent union of those who had at various times dissented from *Establishment, he became acknowledged by both sides as the dominant leader of the movement which led to the union of 1929. To achieve the union he was instrumental in promoting legislation in Parliament which by two Acts (1921 and 1925) preserved the status of the Church of Scotland as the national Church but gave it freedom to govern its own affairs, both spiritual and temporal, independently of Parliament and the courts. He had been *Moderator of the General Assembly of the Church of Scotland in 1925 and was unanimously chosen to be Moderator of the first General Assembly of the united Church. A forceful evangelical preacher, who appreciated the value of a pastoral ministry, he gave a strong lead after the union to Church Extension with the aim of placing a church in each new housing area. He was made a Companion of Honour in 1936.

A. Muir, *John White* (1958).

White, Joseph Blanco

(1775–1841), theological writer. Born in Seville of an Irish RC family, he was ordained to the priesthood in 1800; but, becoming troubled by religious doubts, he came to England in 1810 and later became an Anglican. For a time he was attached to Oriel College, Oxford, where he became intimate with R. *Whately and was well known among the *Tractarians. Later he was again afflicted with doubts and, under the influence of J. *Martineau, became a *Unitarian. His writings include the *Letters from Spain* (1822), *Practical and Internal Evidence against Catholicism* (1825), and *Second Travels of an Irish Gentleman in Search of a Religion* (1833), and the sonnet 'Night and Death'.

Spanish translation of selections from his works, with introd. and extensive bibl., by V. Llorens (Barcelona, 1971). J. H. Thom, *The Life of the Rev. J. B. White* (3 vols., 1845). Modern study by M. Murphy (New Haven, Conn., and London, 1989).

White, William Hale.

The real name of 'Mark *Rutherford' (q.v.).

Whitefield, George

(1714–70), *Methodist evangelist. Born at *Gloucester of humble parentage, in 1732 he became a servitor at Pembroke, College, Oxford, where he came under the influence of John and Charles *Wesley. Ordained deacon in 1736, he followed the Wesleys to Georgia in 1738. He returned to England later the same year to obtain priest's orders and collect money to establish an orphanage in Georgia. His spectacular preaching (esp. at open-air meetings from early 1739) attracted a remarkable response in S. Wales and Scotland, as well as in England, despite opposition from ecclesiastical authority. His *Journal*, of which the first part was published in 1738, caused much scandal on account of its morbid asceticism and assertions of Divine guidance. In 1741 his *Calvinist theology led him to break with the Wesleys and build a 'Tabernacle' in Moorfields, London. His loose *Calvinistic

Methodist Connexion, mostly in southern England, with regular 'Association' meetings from 1743, was overseen mainly by others (notably Howel *Harris), since Whitefield himself was determined to act as an 'Awakener' to all the Churches. Consequently his followers were scattered after his death, most joining the *Congregationalists. From 1749, under Lady *Huntingdon's patronage, he gained a hearing from the aristocracy. He made many visits to the *United States of America, where he helped to stimulate the *Great Awakening. He died in Massachusetts on 30 Sept. 1770. He was the most striking orator of the Evangelical Revival and his influence in awakening the religious conscience of the 18th cent. went deep.

Works pr. in 6 vols. (London, 1771–2), with Life by J. Gillies; Life also issued separately (ibid., 1772). Vol. 1 of letters (from 1734–42) repr., with additions (Edinburgh, 1976). The fullest edn. of his *Journals* (covering 1737–41 and 1744–5, with *A Short Account* and *Further account of God's Dealings with George Whitefield*, which give his autobiog. 1714–37) is that of I. Murray (Edinburgh, 1960). His sermons have frequently been repr. Studies by R. Philip (London, 1837), J. P. Gledstone (ibid., 1871), L. Tyerman (2 vols., ibid., 1876–7), A. D. Belden (ibid. [1930]), S. C. Henry (New York [1957]), O. Riecker (Wuppertal, 1962), and A. A. Dallimore (2 vols., London, 1970–80). J. [C.] Pollock, *George Whitefield and the Great Awakening* (New York, 1972; London, 1973). H. S. Stout, *The Divine Dramatist: George Whitefield and the Rise of Modern Evangelicalism* (Grand Rapids, Mich. [1991]). R. Austin, 'Bibliography of the Works of George Whitefield', *Proceedings of the Wesley Historical Society*, 10 (1916), pp. 169–84 and 211–23. A. Gordon in *DNB* 61 (1900), pp. 85–92. See also works cited s.v. CALVINISTIC METHODISTS.

Whitgift, John (prob. 1532–1604), Abp. of *Canterbury. Educated at Queens' College and Pembroke Hall, Cambridge, he was elected a Fellow of Peterhouse in 1555 (like M. *Parker, he was not a Marian exile); he was ordained in 1560, and became later Lady Margaret (1563) and Regius (1567) professor of divinity, master of Trinity College (1567), Vice-Chancellor (1570), Dean of *Lincoln (1571), and Bp. of *Worcester (1577). His opposition as master of Trinity and Regius professor to the *Puritan, T. *Cartwright, had brought him to the notice of *Elizabeth I, who in 1583 nominated him Abp. of Canterbury in succession to the Puritan, E. *Grindal. His desire for a strong and unified C of E, impervious alike to Papal and extreme Puritan influence, was reflected in the 'Eleven Articles' which he issued in 1583, requiring subscription (Article 6) to three further articles of loyalty to the existing settlement. In repressing Puritanism (*Marprelate Tracts, etc.) he made great use of the Ecclesiastical Commission, summoning before it suspects for interrogation on oath *ex officio mero*. This form of oath left no right to refuse to answer incriminating questions. Whitgift also vigorously opposed the attempt of the extreme Puritans in 1584–89 to impose upon the Church a Presbyterian form of government. A determined advocate of episcopacy and ritual uniformity, he was theologically a *Calvinist (*Lambeth Articles of 1595). In his later years he concerned himself with various administrative reforms, e.g. fostering learning among the clergy, abolishing non-residence, and reforming the ecclesiastical courts. He is commemorated by the Whitgift schools and almshouses at Croydon, which he founded and endowed.

Works ed. J. Ayre (*Parker Society, 3 vols., 1851–3). Early Life by G. Paule, Controller of his Household (London, 1612). The fullest source, however, is the Life by J. *Strype (ibid., 1718; new edn., 3 vols., Oxford, 1822). P. M. Dawley, *John Whitgift and the Reformation* (Hale Lectures; New York, 1954; London, 1955); V. J. K. Brook, *Whitgift and the English Church* (1957). J. F. H. New, 'The Whitgift–Cartwright Controversy', *Archiv für Reformationsgeschichte*, 59 (1968), pp. 203–11. [J. E.] C. Hill, *Economic Problems of the Church from Archbishop Whitgift to the Long Parliament* (Oxford, 1956), *passim*. P. [G.] Lake, *Anglicans and Puritans? Presbyterianism and English Conformist Thought from Whitgift to Hooker* (1988), esp. pp. 1–87. S. Lee in *DNB* 61 (1900), pp. 129–37.

Whitsunday. The feast of the descent of the Holy Spirit upon the Apostles on the 50th day after Easter (see PENTECOST). It ranks, after *Easter, as the second greatest festival in the Church. Its celebration at *Jerusalem in the late 4th cent. is described in the 'Peregrinatio *Egeriae'. In the W. the vigil of Pentecost soon became a secondary date for Baptisms with a ceremony closely resembling that of the *Paschal Vigil Service, except for the omission of the blessing of the New Fire and the candle, and the association of the vigil of Pentecost with Baptism survived in the RC Church until 1955. The word 'Whitsunday' is said to derive from the white robes worn by the newly baptized on that day. That the feast was kept with an *octave from early times is shown by the *Gelasian and *Gregorian Sacramentaries, though the following Sunday was never reckoned as the octave day, and in the Roman rite the whole octave was dropped in 1969. In the BCP the Monday and Tuesday after Whitsunday are '*Red Letter Days' and the Wednesday, Friday, and Saturday are *Ember Days, but these provisions have largely disappeared from modern Anglican liturgies. The liturgical colour is red. In the RC Church the Sundays between Whitsunday and Advent were until 1969 reckoned as 'Sundays after Pentecost'; in the E. the Sundays outside the period of Lent–Eastertide are still so reckoned. In the E. Church, however, the feast itself is kept as that of the Holy Trinity, the Monday following being designated that of the Holy Spirit, and the Tuesday the 'third day of the Trinity'. Vespers on Whitsunday evening is a long service at which kneeling is introduced after being forbidden throughout the 50 days of Eastertide in accordance with the First Council of *Nicaea (can. 20). For current divisions of the ecclesiastical year, see YEAR, LITURGICAL.

R. Cabié, *La Pentecôte: L'Évolution de la cinquantaine pascale au cours des cinq premiers siècles* [1965]. J. [T. A.] Gunstone, *The Feast of Pentecost* (Studies in Christian Worship, 8; 1967), esp. pp. 48–56. E. Venables in *DCA* 2 (1880), pp. 1618 f., s.v. 'Pentecost'; H. *Leclercq, OSB, in *DACL* 14 (pt. 1; 1939), cols. 260–74, s.v. 'Pentecôte'; R. Cabié in *LW* 2 (1968), cols. 2196–204, s.v. 'Pinksteren', with extensive bibl.

Whittier, John Greenleaf (1807–92), American *Quaker poet. After working as a journalist until he was about 25, he became the poet-seer of the Anti-Slavery Movement, writing many poems and pamphlets in the cause of liberation, and suffering from mob-violence and political hate. His fervent Christianity, which shone through all his work, was esp. evident in many of his poems, verses from which have become well known as hymns, among them 'Dear Lord and Father of mankind', 'Immortal love, for ever full', and 'O Brother Man'.

Collected edn. of his Works, 7 vols., London, 1888–9; Poetical Works also pub. Cambridge, Mass., 1895, with biog. sketch by H. E. S[cudder], pp. xi–xix, and ed. W. G. Horder, London, 1892; 2nd edn., ibid., 1904. *Selected Poems* (World's Classics, 1913). *Letters*, ed. J. B. Pickard (3 vols., Cambridge, Mass., and London, 1975). S. T. Pickard, *Life and Letters of John Greenleaf Whittier* (2 vols., Cambridge, Mass., 1894; London, 1895). Other studies by F. H. Underwood (Boston, 1884), G. K. Lewis (London [1913]), A. Mordell (Boston, 1933), E. Wagenknecht (New York, 1967), and R. H. Woodwell (Haverhill, Mass., 1985). Bibl. by T. F. Currier (Cambridge, Mass., 1937).

Whittingham, William (*c.*1524–79), Dean of *Durham. Educated at Brasenose College, Oxford, he was elected a Fellow of All Souls in 1545 and two years later moved to Christ Church. His *Calvinistic views having forced him to flee from England in *Mary's reign, he took a leading part in the organization of the English congregation at Frankfurt, where he supported J. *Knox against R. *Cox, and, on Knox's defeat, followed him to Geneva. Here he succeeded him as minister in 1559, although he had apparently received no ordination of any kind. Returning to England in the following year, he was made Dean of Durham in 1563. His iconoclasm and repeated failures to conform to the BCP led eventually to an attempt by E. *Sandys, Abp. of *York, to deprive him on the ground that he had not been validly ordained, but he died before the proceedings were concluded. His chief literary work was in the field of biblical translation. In 1557 he published at Geneva an English version of the NT and he also took a leading part in the production of the *Geneva Bible, remaining behind to supervise its completion when most of the translators returned to England on Mary's death. He also rendered into metre a number of Psalms, the Lord's Prayer, and the Decalogue. He was long thought to be the author of *A Brief Discourse of the Troubles begun at Frankfort . . . Anno Domini 1554* (1574).

Modern edn. of *A Brief Discourse of the Troubles at Frankfort*, by E. Arber ('A Christian Library', 1; 1907). Contemporary Life ed. from MS by A. *Wood in *Bodleian Library, Oxford (MS Wood E 64, Art. 5) by M. A. Everett Green in *The Camden Miscellany*, 6 (1871), pp. 1–40, with other relevant material, pp. 41–6. J. H. Colligan, *The Honourable William Whittingham of Chester* (?1524–1579) (1934). Brief notes on the question of his ordination in E. Denny, *The English Church and the Ministry of the Reformed Churches* (*Church Historical Society, Tract 57; 1900). pp. 59–62, with refs. P. Collinson, 'The Authorship of *A Brieff Discours off the Troubles Begonne at Franckford*', *JEH* 9 (1958), pp. 188–208, repr. in id., *Godly People: Essays on English Protestantism and Puritanism* [1983], pp. 191–211. A. F. Pollard in *DNB* 61 (1900), pp. 150–3. *BRUO, 1501–1540*, pp. 625 f.

Whole Duty of Man, The. This devotional manual, first published *c.*1658 and formerly very widely used, contains 17 discourses, mainly on matters of Christian morals, 'one whereof being read every Lord's Day, the whole may be read over thrice in the year'. The identity of the author is not known with certainty, but among those to whom it has been ascribed are H. *Hammond (who certainly contributed the prefatory letter signed 'H. H.'), J. *Fell, and (with most probability) R. *Allestree. Its moral standards are exacting, though adapted to life in the world.

E. Elmen, 'Richard Allestree and *The Whole Duty of Man*', *The Library*, 5th ser. 6 (1951), pp. 19–27. C. J. Stranks, *Anglican Devotion* (1961), pp. 123–48.

Whyte, Alexander (1836–1921), Scottish *Evangelical. Minister of the *Free (later *United Free) Church of Scotland church of St George's, Edinburgh (1870–1916) and principal of New College, Edinburgh (1909–18), he was generally regarded as the finest preacher of late-Victorian Scotland. *Calvinist in his theology, and *Puritan in his piety, he was irenic and open-minded; he influenced many by the welcome he gave both to the biblical criticism of W. R. *Smith and the beginning of the *Ecumenical Movement in the *Edinburgh Conference of 1910. His writings include *Bible Characters* (6 vols., 1896–1902) and *Thirteen Appreciations* [1914], a collection of earlier studies on St *Teresa of Ávila (1897), W. *Law (1893), J. H. *Newman (1901), and others.

G. F. Barbour, *The Life of Alexander Whyte* (1923).

Wichern, Johann Hinrich (1808–81), founder of the German *Innere Mission. A native of Hamburg, he studied theology at Göttingen and Berlin, where he came under the influence of J. A. W. *Neander and F. D. E. *Schleiermacher. After his return to Hamburg he was deeply moved by the neglect from which the children suffered in the poor quarters of the city, and in 1833 founded an institute, the Rauhes Haus, based on the principle of family education, to provide for their spiritual and material needs. Under Wichern's powerful personality and educational gifts the house soon began to expand, and in 1842 he established a training-house of helpers. From 1844 he edited a periodical, *Die Fliegenden Blätter aus dem Rauhen Hause*, which became the central organ of all charitable undertakings in the German Protestant Churches. At his suggestion all these activities were co-ordinated in the central organization of the Innere Mission at the first congress of the Evangelical Churches (*Erster evangelischer Kirchentag*) at *Wittenberg in 1848. In 1857 he was entrusted with the Prussian prison reform, and in 1858 he founded the Johannisstift at Spandau, nr. Berlin, on the model of the Rauhes Haus. In the wars of 1864, 1866, and 1870–1 he and his 'Brothers' organized a service of assistance to the wounded, the Felddiakonie. In 1872 Wichern returned to the Rauhes Haus, where his last years were spent in illness.

Collected writings ed. J. Wichern (son) and F. Mahling (6 vols., Hamburg, 1901–8); also ed. P. Meinhold (5 vols. in 7, Berlin, 1958–71). Selections ed. K. Janssen (3 vols., Gütersloh, 1956–62). Diaries of his earlier years ed. M. Gerhardt with title *Der junge Wichern* (1925). Lives by F. Oldenberg (2 vols., Hamburg, 1882–7) and M. Gerhardt (3 vols., ibid., 1927–31). M. Hennig, *Das Lebenswerk Wicherns* (ibid., 1908). F. J. Leenhardt, *La Mission intérieure et sociale de l'Église d'après Wichern, 1808–1881* [1931]. R. Kramer, *Nation und Theologie bei Johann Hinrich Wichern* (Arbeiten zur Kirchengeschichte Hamburgs, 2; 1959); H. Lemke, *Wicherns Bedeutung für die Bekämpfung der Jugendverwahrlosung* (ibid. 7; 1964). H. Rahlenbeck in *PRE* (3rd edn.), 21 (1908), pp. 219–24; K. Janssen in *RGG* (3rd edn.), 6 (1962), cols. 1678–80, s.v.

Wiclif, John. See WYCLIFFE, JOHN.

widows. In NT times widows had an acknowledged claim to the charity of their fellow-Christians (Acts 6: 1). Before long they acquired, like virgins, a recognized status and privileges in the Church, though they do not seem to have been ordained or to have taken specific vows. 1 Tim. 5: 3–16, which contains a detailed account of what was expected of widows, restricted the privileges to those over 60, younger women being recommended to remarry. The early history of the office was closely connected with that of the *deaconess (q.v.).

J. Mayer (ed.), *Monumenta de Viduis Diaconissis Virginibusque Tractantia* (Florilegium Patristicum, 42; Bonn, 1938), with bibl. C. H. *Turner, 'Ministries of Women in the Primitive Church. Widow, Deaconess and Virgin in the First Four Christian Centuries', *Constructive Quarterly*, 7 (1919), pp. 434–59, esp. pp. 435–42 and 457–9; repr. in H. N. Bate (ed.), *Catholic and Apostolic* (1931), no. 11, pp. 316–51, esp. pp. 317–28 and 349–51. J. Viteau, 'L'Institution des diacres et des veuves', *RHE* 22 (1926), pp. 513–37. L. Bopp, *Das Witwentum als organische Gliedschaft im Gemeinschaftsleben der alten Kirche* (Mannheim, 1950). B. B. Thurston, *The Widows: A Women's Ministry in the Early Church* (Philadelphia, 1989).

Wied, Hermann von. See HERMANN OF WIED.

Wilberforce, Robert Isaac (1802–57), *Tractarian divine. The second son of W. *Wilberforce, he was educated at Oriel College, Oxford, where he was elected a Fellow in 1826 and was brought into close association with J. H. *Newman and R. H. *Froude. He gradually acquired an extensive theological knowledge which made him one of the most learned of the Tractarians. In 1841 he was appointed Archdeacon of the East Riding. By Oct. 1843 he was in close personal relations with H. E. *Manning, then rector of Lavington, and carried on with him an extended theological correspondence which was largely concerned with the Roman claims. On 1 Nov. 1854 he was received into the RC Church at Paris. At the time of his death he was preparing for the priesthood in Rome, where he is buried in Santa Maria sopre Minerva. Besides the Life of his father, which he published in conjunction with his brother Samuel in 1838, his writings include three major theological studies: *The Doctrine of the Incarnation* (1848), *The Doctrine of Holy Baptism* (1849), and *The Doctrine of the Holy Eucharist* (1853).

A. R. Ashwell and R. G. Wilberforce, *Life of the Right Reverend Samuel Wilberforce* (3 vols., 1880–2), *passim*. D. [H.] Newsome, *The Parting of Friends: A Study of the Wilberforces and Henry Manning* [1966]. On his Eucharistic theology, A. Härdelin, *The Tractarian Understanding of the Eucharist* (Acta Universitatis Upsaliensis, Studia Historico-Ecclesiastica Upsaliensia, 8; Uppsala, 1965), pp. 123–219 *passim*. F. Legge in *DNB* 61 (1900), pp. 201–4, s.v., with further refs.

Wilberforce, Samuel (1805–73), successively Bp. of *Oxford and *Winchester. The third son of W. *Wilberforce, he was educated at Oriel College, Oxford, and in 1828 ordained deacon. From 1830 to 1840 he was rector of Brighstone in the Isle of Wight. The repute of his eloquence and pastoral efficiency led to his appointment by the Prince Consort, in 1840, as one of his chaplains, which was the beginning of his influence at court. After holding the living of Alverstoke in Hants from 1840, he was appointed Dean of *Westminster in 1845 and later in the same year Bp. of Oxford. Though at first viewed with suspicion by both *Evangelicals and *Tractarians, esp. E. B. *Pusey, he soon gained general confidence by the many reforms he introduced in his diocese. He encouraged the building of churches and the formation of Anglican sisterhoods, and himself founded Cuddesdon Theological Col-

lege (1854). He also established the system of Lenten missions and interested himself in the education of the poor. The effective methods of pastoral administration adopted in his diocese were widely imitated elsewhere. He took a leading part in the revival of *Convocation and was active in promoting legislation to provide synodical structures for the colonial Church and to enable the appointment of missionary bishops. In 1869 Wilberforce was translated to Winchester. One of his main achievements in his last years was his initiation of the revision of the AV. Throughout his life, however, he attracted considerable criticism from those who regarded him as pre-eminently a compromiser. His reputation as an opponent of modern science, based on his famous debate with T. H. *Huxley on evolution, was both unfortunate and unfair.

E. P. Baker (ed.), *Bishop Wilberforce's Visitation Returns for the Archdeaconry of Oxford in the year 1854* (Oxfordshire Record Society, 35; 1954); R. K. Pugh and J. F. A. Mason (eds.), *The Letter-Books of Samuel Wilberforce 1843–68* (ibid. 47; 1970). Life by A. R. Ashwell and R. G. Wilberforce [son] (3 vols., London, 1880–2), incl. extensive extracts from his diaries and correspondence. Shorter Life, based on the above, by R. [G.] Wilberforce (London, 1888). Further Lives by G. W. Daniell (ibid., 1891), R. G. Wilberforce (ibid., 1905), J. C. Hardwick, *Lawn Sleeves* (Oxford, 1933), and S. Meacham (Cambridge, Mass., 1970). D. [H.] Newsome, *The Parting of Friends: A Study of the Wilberforces and Henry Manning* [1966]. J. W. *Burgon, *Lives of Twelve Good Men*, 2 (1888), pp. 1–70. F. Legge in *DNB* 61 (1900), pp. 204–8; G. W. E. Russell in *DECH*, pp. 633–6, s.v.

Wilberforce, William (1759–1833), philanthropist and advocate of the abolition of the slave trade. A native of Hull, he was educated at St John's College, Cambridge. In 1780 he became MP for Hull, later for Yorkshire, and formed an intimate friendship with W. Pitt, whose devoted supporter he became. In 1784–5 he travelled on the Continent. Under the influence of his NT reading he was converted to *Evangelicalism and determined to lead a more disciplined Christian life. In this purpose he was guided by John *Newton, who opposed his wish to take Holy Orders and persuaded him to serve the cause of Christianity in Parliament, a vocation for which he was particularly well fitted by his oratorical gifts. In 1787 he founded the Proclamation Society for the 'reformation of manners'. About the same time, under the influence of T. *Clarkson, he began to interest himself in the slave trade, which he determined to take up in Parliament. In 1797 he settled at Clapham, where he became a prominent member of the '*Clapham Sect'. His *Practical View of the Prevailing Religious System of Professed Christians* (1797)—a treatise promoting the view that religion depended on vital revealed truths and was not a matter of mere ethics and applied benevolence—enjoyed great popularity and established his reputation as the acknowledged leader of the Evangelical party. He contributed generously to the charities of Hannah *More and helped in the foundation of the *Church Missionary Society and the *British and Foreign Bible Society (1804). Throughout these years the abolition of the slave trade continued to be his chief concern, and after many vicissitudes the Bill, which had repeatedly been refused passage in the Lords, finally became law in 1807. Later he supported the movement for the complete abolition of slavery, which was effected by the Emancipation Act of 1833, shortly before his death. In 1813 he defended

*Catholic Emancipation; he also advocated the introduction of English missionaries into *India and long championed the cause of *Sunday observance. In 1825 he resigned his seat in Parliament owing to failing health. Feast day in the ASB, 29 July; in the American BCP (1979), 30 July.

William Wilberforce had four sons and three daughters. For Robert Isaac Wilberforce and Samuel Wilberforce see preceding entries. **Henry William Wilberforce** (1807–73), his youngest son, was received into the RC Church in 1850. From 1854 to 1863 he edited the *Catholic Standard*.

William Wilberforce's *Family Prayers*, ed. R. I. Wilberforce (son; London, 1834); *Correspondence*, ed. id. and S. Wilberforce (sons; ibid., 1840); *Private Papers*, ed. A. M. Wilberforce (ibid., 1897). The principal authority is the Life by R. I. and S. Wilberforce (5 vols. bound in 3, London, 1838; condensed edn., ibid., 1868). The best modern studies are those of R. Coupland (Oxford, 1923) and F. W. R. Smith, Viscount Furneaux, later Lord Birkenhead (ibid., 1974). Other Lives by J. S. Harford (London, 1864), J. C. Colquhoun (ibid., 1866), O. Warner (ibid., 1962) J. C. Pollock (ibid., 1977), and G. D. Lean (ibid., 1980). L. Stephen in *DNB* 61 (1900), pp. 208–17.

Wilfrid, St (634–709), Bp. of *York. He was the son of a Northumbrian thegn, and was educated at the monastery of *Lindisfarne. Dissatisfied, however, with the *Celtic way of religious life, he studied the Roman form at *Canterbury and in 653 he set out for Rome itself; on the first part of the journey he was accompanied by St *Benedict Biscop. After he had spent three years at Lyons, where he received the tonsure in the Roman manner, he returned to England and, being made Abbot of *Ripon, introduced the Benedictine Rule. At the Synod of *Whitby (664) he was largely responsible for the victory of the Roman party on the question of dating *Easter. Shortly afterwards he was consecrated Bp. of York at Compiègne by 12 Frankish bishops, to avoid consecration by the Celtic bishops whom he regarded as schismatical. On his return (666), which had been delayed, he found his see occupied by St *Chad and retired to Ripon, but was put in possession of it by St *Theodore of Tarsus, Abp. of Canterbury, in 669. When in 678 Theodore divided the diocese of York into three sees without Wilfrid's consent, he departed for Rome to appeal against the high-handed procedure, spending a year on the way preaching in Frisia. Though the synod, assembled by the Pope, declared in his favour, on his return to England he was imprisoned, and later retired to Sussex, where he carried out successful missionary work among the heathen population (681–6). Having become reconciled to Theodore, he was once more reinstated in his see, which he held from 686 to 691. When disputes with King Aldfrith compelled him to flee again, the King of Mercia asked him to administer the vacant see of *Lichfield. When, in 703, a synod called by Abp. Berhtwald of Canterbury decreed that he should resign his see of York and retire to Ripon, he went once more to Rome to appeal to the Holy See. Though his claims were completely vindicated, he agreed, on his return, to resign in favour of St *John of Beverley, contenting himself with the see of *Hexham, and spending the last years of his life in his monastery at Ripon. A cosmopolitan Churchman, a notable missionary, and a great defender of Papal authority, Wilfrid, despite many setbacks, succeeded in bringing England into closer touch with Rome, and in replacing the existing Celtic usages in the N. of England by the Roman liturgy, and Celtic by Benedictine monasticism. Feast day, 12 Oct.

Life by his disciple, Eddius Stephanus of Ripon, ed. J. Raine, *The Historians of the Church of York and its Archbishops*, 1 (RS, 1879), pp. 1–103, with introd., pp. xxxi–xxxviii; modern edn., with Eng. tr. and notes, by B. Colgrave (Cambridge, 1927; repr., 1985). Later authorities incl. *Bede, *HE* 5. 19 (comm. by J. M. Wallace-Hadrill, Oxford, 1988, pp. 51, 95, 106, 125–8, 133, 139, 142, 144, 150 3, 155 f., 159, 172, 180, 183 f., 191–5, 227 f., and 235–8); metrical Life by Frithegod of Canterbury (written between 948 and 958), called the 'Breviloquium Vitae Wilfridi', pr. in J. Raine, op. cit., pp. 105–59; also a Life by *Eadmer, pr., ibid., pp. 161–226, with introd. pp. xxxix–l, and notes on further sources, pp. l f.; modern edn. of Frithegod's Life by A. Campbell (Zurich, 1950). B. W. Wells, 'Eddi's Life of Wilfrid', *EHR* 6 (1891), pp. 535–50. G. F. Browne, *Theodore and Wilfrith* (1897). E. S. Duckett, *Anglo-Saxon Saints and Scholars* (New York, 1948), pp. 101–214. D. P. Kirby (ed.), *Saint Wilfrid at Hexham* (Newcastle, 1974); H. [M. R. E.] Mayr-Harting, 'St. Wilfrid in Sussex', in M. J. Kitch (ed.), *Studies in Sussex Church History* (1981), pp. 1–17; D. P. Kirby, 'Bede, Eddius Stephanus and the "Life of Wilfred" ', *EHR* 98 (1983), pp. 101–14. W. T. Foley, *Images of Sanctity in Eddius Stephanus' Life of Bishop Wilfrid* (Lewiston, Queenston, and Lampeter [1992]) W. *Bright, *Chapters of Early English Church History* (1878), pp. 187–200, 209–11, 280–308, 367–416, and 432 f. F. M. Stenton, *Anglo-Saxon England* (The Oxford History of England, 2; 1943; 3rd edn., 1971), pp. 123 f., 132–45. H. [M. R. E.] Mayr-Harting, *The Coming of Christianity to Anglo-Saxon England* (1972), esp. pp. 129–47. J. Raine in *DCB* 4 (1887), pp. 1179–85. See also HEXHAM.

Wilkes, Paget (1871–1934), Protestant missionary in Japan. The son of an Anglican clergyman, Wilkes was educated at Lincoln College, Oxford, where he associated with the Oxford Inter-Collegiate Christian Union, well known in his day for its evangelistic fervour and missionary zeal. In 1897 he sailed for Japan under the *CMS to work with B. F. Buxton, the CMS pioneer. Here he formed the idea of a Japanese Evangelistic Band (JEB) which, free of ecclesiastical organization, would be directed towards aggressive evangelism and the spread of scriptural holiness; and in 1903 the JEB was established under the name of the 'One by One Band' of Japan, with its centre at Kobe. Apart from a few visits to England, Wilkes spent all his active life in Japan, pursuing his missionary work with unabating fervour. His best-known works (translated into many languages) are *The Dynamic of Service* (1920), *The Dynamic of Faith* (1921), *The Dynamic of Redemption* (1923).

M. W. Dunn Pattison (Wilkes's sister), *Ablaze for God: The Life Story of Paget Wilkes* (1936). Shorter Life by I. R. G. Stewart (London, 1957).

Wilkins, David (1685–1745), editor of the 'Concilia'. His parentage was German and his name anglicized from Wilke. After studying at several Continental universities, he became professor of Arabic at Cambridge in 1724. His patron, Abp. W. *Wake, had meanwhile made him Librarian at *Lambeth Palace and in due course secured for him several promotions, including the rectory of Hadleigh, a prebend at *Canterbury, and the archdeaconry of Suffolk. A pioneer in oriental studies and in Anglo-Saxon, Wilkins was a versatile, though by modern standards somewhat inaccurate, scholar. His reputation rests principally upon his *Concilia Magnae Britanniae et Hiberniae* (4 vols., 1737), a monumental collection of documents which long remained a standard source for the British and Irish ecclesiastical councils.

D. C. Douglas, *English Scholars* (1939), pp. 276–84. E. F. Jacob, 'Wilkins's *Concilia* and the Fifteenth Century', *Transactions of the Royal Historical Society*, 4th ser. 15 (1932), pp. 91–131. J. M. Rigg in *DNB* 61 (1900), pp. 260 f., s.v., with refs.

Wilkins, John (1614–72), Bp. of *Chester. Born at Fawsley, Northants, he studied at New Inn Hall and at Magdalen Hall, Oxford. In 1637 he was appointed Vicar of Fawsley, but soon resigned and held a succession of private chaplaincies. He became increasingly interested in the new scientific movement. In 1638 he published *The Discovery of a World in the Moon*, which argued that the moon was a physical world that might be habitable. In 1640 followed *A Discourse concerning a New Planet*, maintaining that the earth was a planet. From *c.*1645 he was a member of R. *Boyle's 'Invisible College' of scientists in London. As his sympathies during the Civil War had been with the Parliamentarians, the Visitors made him Warden of Wadham College, Oxford, in 1648. Here his tolerant disposition won warm approval and attracted to Oxford a brilliant group of scientists, including many of his former London associates, which used to meet in Wilkins's rooms in Wadham. In 1659 he was appointed Master of Trinity College, Cambridge, but he was deprived at the Restoration (1660). He was given a succession of benefices, among them the Rectory of Cranford, Greater London (1660), the Vicarage of St Lawrence Jewry, London (1662), and the Deanery of the collegiate church of *Ripon (1663). But his chief interests remained the furtherance of science and philosophical linguistics. When the Royal Society received its charter from *Charles II (15 July 1662), Wilkins, who had been largely instrumental in its foundation, became its first Secretary. In 1668 he became Bp. of Chester, where he advocated the toleration of dissenters. Wilkins was a strong upholder of natural theology. He held that it was the conflicting contentions of fanatics which were the main cause of unbelief. His writings include *Mathematical Magick, or the Wonders that may be performed by Mechanical Geometry* (1648), *A Discourse concerning the Gift of Prayer* (1649), *An Essay towards a real Character and a Philosophical Language* (1668), and *On the Principles and Duties of Natural Religion* (1678; posthumous).

P. A. Wright Henderson, *The Life and Times of John Wilkins* (1910). B. J. Shapiro, *John Wilkins 1614–1672: An Intellectual Biography* (Berkeley, Calif., and Los Angeles, 1969). A. Chapman, ' "A World in the Moon". John Wilkins and his Lunar Voyage of 1640', *Quarterly Journal of the Royal Astronomical Society*, 32 (1991), pp. 121–32. F. Sanders in *DNB* 61 (1900), pp. 264–7.

Willehad, St (d. 789), Bp. of Bremen. A native of Northumbria, he was probably educated at *York. Apparently inspired by the examples of St *Boniface and St *Willibrord, he set out with the approval of King Alchred and a Northumbrian synod for missionary work in Frisia between 765 and 774 and for a time preached at Dockum. In 780 *Charlemagne sent him to preach to the Saxons at Wigmodia near the North Sea; but shortly afterwards his work was brought to an end by an insurrection under the Saxon chief, Widukind, in 782. After a journey to Rome, he returned to the abbey of *Echternach, then presided over by Beornred, a relative of Willibrord. Here he devoted himself to copying MSS; none of his work has been identified among those which have survived. Later, when Charlemagne restored peace, Willehad resumed his activities at Wigmodia. In 787 he was consecrated Bishop of the new see of Bremen, where he built a cathedral which was dedicated to St Peter on 1 Nov. 789. A few days later he succumbed to a fever. Feast day, 8 Nov.

The principal source is a Life written prob. soon after 838 at Echternach (commonly, but apparently erroneously, attributed to St *Anskar); best edn. in *AASS*, Nov. 3 (1910), pp. 842–6; Book of Miracles by St Anskar, ibid., pp. 847–51, with valuable introd. by A. Poncelet, SJ, ibid., pp. 835–42. O. H. May (ed.), *Regesten der Erzbischöfe von Bremen*, 1, Lieferung 1 (Veröffentlichungen der Historischen Kommission für Hannover, Oldenburg, Braunschweig, Schaumburg-Lippe und Bremen, 11; 1928), pp. 1–4. A letter addressed to him in friendly terms by *Alcuin is pr. among the latter's letters, ed. E. Duemmler (*MGH*, Epistulae, 4; 1895), p. 31. G. Niemeyer, 'Die Herkunft der Vita Willehadi', *Deutsches Archiv*, 12 (1956), pp. 17–35. W. Levison, *England and the Continent in the Eighth Century* (Ford Lectures, 1943; Oxford, 1946), p. 110. G. H. Klippel and A. Hauck in *PRE* (3rd edn.), 21 (1908), pp. 302–4, s.v.

William I (?1028–87), Duke of Normandy and King of England ('the Conqueror'). The illegitimate son of Duke Robert I (d. 1035), William after a stormy minority won and kept firm control of his duchy, whence in 1066 he was able to conquer England, which he ruled with equal firmness. In Normandy he presided over a continuing ecclesiastical revival in the archdiocese of Rouen: capitular organization developed under strong bishops (cf. *Odo of Bayeux) who were themselves almost all of aristocratic blood, and many new monastic houses (e.g. *Bec) were founded by William himself and by his greater subjects.

William had sought and obtained Pope *Alexander II's blessing in 1066; his relations with Rome were generally constructive and co-operative, and though he rejected *Gregory VII's demand for fealty (?1080), that Pope held the King in high regard for the support which he gave to reform. There was no conflict over lay *investiture, which William continued to practise; the episcopate in England was largely Normanized, several bishops (e.g. *Stigand) and abbots being deposed by canonical process, and the prelates nominated and invested by William were in most cases efficient and reputable. In co-operation with Abp. *Lanfranc the King saw to the implementation of Papal legislation on *simony, clerical immorality, and diocesan administration. As in Normandy (esp. at Lillebonne, 1080) William himself presided at important reforming councils. By a far-reaching writ of *c.*1072 William removed certain pleas (offences against the 'moral law') from the jurisdiction of the (lay) courts of the hundred to that of the Church courts.

William founded monastic houses at Caen (in penance for his marriage within the prohibited degrees) and Battle (in gratitude for his victory at Hastings). He knew how to use the sanctions of the Church to strengthen himself, and his domestic life was above reproach (no bastard can be attributed to him). Energetic, courageous, majestic, brutal, and avaricious, he exercised an enduring influence on three important provinces of the Church which he ruled at a critical time.

M. Fauroux (ed.), *Recueil des Actes des Ducs de Normandie de 911 à 1066* (Mémoires de la Société des Antiquaires de Normandie, 26; 1961), pp. 242–453 (nos. 92–234); H. W. C. Davis and R. J. Whitwell (eds.), *Regesta Regum Anglo-Normannorum 1066-1154*, I (Oxford, 1913), pp. 1–76 (nos. 1–288b). Early description of the Norman Conquest by William's Norman chaplain, William of Poitiers, *Gesta Guillelmi ducis Normannorum et Regis Anglorum*; mod. edn., with Fr. tr., by R. Foreville (Les Classiques de l'histoire de France, 23; 1952). D. Whitelock, M. Brett, and C. N. L. Brooke (eds.), *Councils & Synods with Other Documents Relating to the English Church*, vol. 1: *871–1204* (Oxford, 1981), pp. 563–634 Convenient Eng. tr. of the well-known assessments by the contemporary Anglo-Saxon Chronicler ('E') and by *Ordericus Vitalis in D. C. Douglas and G. W. Greenaway (eds.), *English Historical Documents 1042–1189* (English Historical Documents, 2; 1953), pp. 163–4 and 281–9. The description by the 'monk of Caen' (ibid., pp. 279–80), must be used with caution because much of it has been borrowed from the Lives of *Charlemagne and *Louis the Pious; L. J. Engels, 'De Obitu Willelmi ducis Normannorum regisque Anglorum: Texte, modèles, valeur et origine', in *Mélanges Christine Mohrmann*, Nouveau Recueil (Utrecht and Antwerp, 1973), pp. 209–55. Docs. on the Church in D. C. Douglas and G. W. Greenaway, op. cit., pp. 601–5 and 626–49. Modern studies by F. M. Stenton ('Heroes of the Nations', 1908; rev. edn., 1925), D. C. Douglas (London, 1964; with bibl.), F. Barlow ('Teach Yourself History', 1965), M. de Boüard (Paris, 1984), and D. Bates (London [1989]). E. A. Freeman, *History of the Norman Conquest of England* (6 vols., Oxford, 1867–79 [still valuable for its appendices]). F. M. Stenton, *Anglo-Saxon England* (3rd edn., ibid., 1971), pp. 584–667. D. J. A. Matthew, *The Norman Conquest* (1966), pp. 167–215 (on the Church); C. Morris, 'William I and the Church Courts', *EHR* 82 (1967), pp. 449–63. See also bibl. on LANFRANC.

William of Auvergne

William of Auvergne (*c.*1180–1249), also 'William of *Paris', French Scholastic philosopher and theologian. In 1223 he became a Canon of *Notre-Dame, and in 1228 Bp. of Paris. He was a protector of the *Mendicant Orders, an adversary of pluralism, and an influential personality at the court of St *Louis. His prolific writings mainly form a vast philosophico-theological encyclopedia, 'Magisterium Divinale ac Sapientale' (written between 1223 and 1240), consisting of 'De Trinitate', 'De Universo', 'De Anima', 'Cur Deus Homo', 'De Fide et Legibus', 'De Sacramentis', and 'De Virtutibus'. William used *Aristotelian language and principles of scientific procedure, but remained respectfully wary of many Aristotelian doctrines, esp. those he knew only through *Avicenna's commentaries. His advocacy of rational methods for discovering truth prepared the way for later *Scholasticism. But despite the boldness and originality of his approach, he was not entirely successful in synthesizing new terms with traditional ideas. He strongly opposed the superstitions, esp. on the subject of astronomy, rife among his contemporaries.

Collected edn. of his Works pub. Nuremberg, 2 vols., 1496; the most complete edn. is that of J. B. Le Féron (anon., 2 vols., Orléans and Paris, 1674; anastatic repr., 2 vols., Frankfurt, 1963). His two treatises *De Bono et Malo* were first ed. J. R. O'Donnell, CSB, in *Mediaeval Studies*, 8 (1946), pp. 245–99, and ibid. 16 (1954), pp. 219–71, and *Tractatus de Gratia* ed. G. Corti (Corona Lateranensis, 7; 1966). Modern edn. of *De Trinitate* by B. Switalski (Pontifical Institute of Mediaeval Studies, Texts and Studies, 34; Toronto, 1976); Eng. tr. by R. J. Teske, SJ, and F. C. Wade, SJ (Medieval Philosophical Texts in Translation, 28; Milwaukee, Wis. [1989]). The *De Immortalitate Animae*, an anonymous work prob. wrongly ascribed to him, ed. G. Bülow (BGPM 2, Heft 3;

1897). N. Valois, *Guillaume d'Auvergne . . .: Sa vie et ses ouvrages* (1880). M. Baumgartner, *Die Erkenntnislehre des Wilhelm von Auvergne* (BGPM 2, Heft 1; 1893). J. Kramp, SJ, 'Des Wilhelm von Auvergne "Magisterium Divinale"', *Gregorianum*, 1 (1920), pp. 538–616; 2 (1921), pp. 42–103 and 174–95, incl. text. P. Glorieux, 'Le Tractatus Novus De Poenitentia de Guillaume d'Auvergne', in *Miscellanea Moralia in Honorem Arthur Janssen*, 2 (Bibliotheca Ephemeridum Theologicarum Lovaniensium, 1st ser. 3 [1949]), pp. 551–65. E. A. Moody, *Studies in Medieval Philosophy, Science, and Logic* (Berkeley and Los Angeles, Calif., and London, 1975), pp. 1–109 ('William of Auvergne and his Treatise *De Anima*'). A. Quentin, *Naturkenntnisse und Naturanschauungen bei Wilhelm von Auvergne* (Arbor Scientiarum, Reihe A, 5; Hildesheim, 1976). H. Borok, *Der Tugendbegriff des Wilhelm von Auvergne (1180–1249): Eine moralhistorische Untersuchung zur ideengeschichtlichen Rezeption der aristotelischen Ethik* (Düsseldorf, 1979). J. Rohls, *Wilhelm von Auvergne und der mittelalterliche Aristotelismus* (Münchener Monographien zur historischen und systematischen Theologie, 5; 1980). S. P. Marrone, *William of Auvergne and Robert Grosseteste: New Ideas of Truth in the Early Thirteenth Century* (Princeton, NJ [1983]), pp. 25–134. P. Vernet in *DTC* 6 (1920), cols. 1967–76, s.v. 'Guillaume d'Auvergne', with bibl.

William of Auxerre

William of Auxerre (d. 1231), Scholastic theologian. At one time Archdeacon of Beauvais, he later taught at *Paris. He became a member of the Commission appointed by *Gregory IX in 1231 to examine and amend the physical treatises of *Aristotle, the reading of which had been unreservedly forbidden by the University of Paris in 1210. He is himself important as one of the first to make use of the doctrines of the newly discovered Aristotle, esp. in his chief work, the 'Summa Aurea'. This eclectic work, loosely based on the 'Sentences' of *Peter Lombard and influenced by *Anselm's *Ontological Argument, showed much originality, and, in its turn, influenced John of Treviso, one of the first Dominican theologians.

Summa Aurea pub. Paris, 1500 and 1518, and Venice, 1591; modern edn. of bks. 1 and 2 by J. Ribaillier (Spicilegium Bonaventurianum, 16–17; Paris and Grottaferrata, 1980–2). His other works remain unpub. P. Glorieux, *Répertoire des maîtres en théologie de Paris au XIII' siècle*, 1 (1933), pp. 293 f. C. Ottaviano, *Guglielmo d'Auxerre (d. 1231): La vita, le opere, il pensiero* (Rome [1930]). W. Breuning, *Die hypostatische Union in der Theologie Wilhelms von Auxerre, Hugos von St Cher und Rolands von Cremona* (Trier Theologische Studien, 11; 1962), pp. 1–161; W. H. Principe, CSB, *William of Auxerre's Theology of the Hypostatic Union* (Pontifical Institute of Mediaeval Studies, Studies and Texts, 7; Toronto, 1963), incl. relevant texts. P. Mandonnet, OP, 'Date de la mort de Guillaume d'Auxerre (3 Nov. 1231)', *AHDLMA* 7 (1935), pp. 39–46. J. A. St Pierre, 'The Theological Thought of William of Auxerre. An Introductory Bibliography', *RTAM* 33 (1966), pp. 147–55. G. Gál, OFM, in *NCE* 14 (1967), pp. 921 f., s.v.; J. Ribaillier in *Dict. Sp.* 6 (1967), cols. 1192–9, s.v. 'Guillaume d'Auxerre'.

William of Champeaux

William of Champeaux (*c.*1070–1121), Scholastic philosopher. After studying under *Anselm of Laon, and (probably) hearing *Roscelin of Compiègne, he began to teach in the cathedral schools of Paris, whence he was driven (1108) by *Abelard's ridicule of his exaggerated *Realism. In retirement at the (then) priory of Saint-Victor, he appears to have modified his extreme doctrines, and by his lectures there to have laid the foundations of the *Victorine school. In 1113 he became Bp. of Châlons.

In his last years he seems to have abandoned the distinctive tenets of Realism altogether, though without elaborating any significant philosophical alternative.

Some of William of Champeaux's writings in J. P. Migne, *PL* 163. 1039–72. E. Michaud, *Guillaume de Champeaux et les Écoles de Paris au XIIe siècle* (1867). G. Lefèvre, *Les Variations de Guillaume de Champeaux et la question des universaux: Étude suivie de documents originaux* (Travaux et Mémoires de l'Université de Lille, 6, no. 20; 1898; mainly texts). H. Weisweiler, SJ, *Das Schriftum der Schule Anselms von Laon und Wilhelms von Champeaux in deutschen Bibliotheken* (BGPM 33, Hefte 1–2; 1936), incl. a number of texts. K. M. Fredborg, 'The Commentaries on Cicero's de Inventione and Rhetorica ad Herennium by William of Champeaux', Université de Copenhague, *Cahiers de l'Institut du Moyen-Âge Grec et Latin*, 17 (1976), pp. 1–39, with extracts of texts. O. Lottin, OSB, *Psychologie et morale aux XIIe et XIIIe siècles*, 5 (1959), esp. pp. 189–227. J. Gross, *Geschichte des Erbsündendogmas*, 3 (1971), pp. 54–7. C. H. Lohr in *L.Th.K.* (2nd edn.), 10 (1965), cols. 1130 f., s.v. 'Wilhelm v. Champeaux', with further bibl.

William of Conches

William of Conches (*c*.1080–*c*.1154), medieval philosopher. He was a pupil of *Bernard of Chartres, whose efforts to encourage the study of the profane sciences and literature in the interests of a Christian humanism he sought to further. His writings, of which the 'Philosophia Mundi' and the 'Dragmaticon' became the most popular, deal mainly with natural philosophy. The former treatise was attacked by *William of St-Thierry for its supposed *Modalistic view of the Trinity. William of Conches's other writings include glosses on Priscian's *Institutiones Grammaticae*, *Plato's *Timaeus*, Macrobius' *In Somnium Scipionis*, and *Boethius' *De Consolatione Philosophiae*. A work on ethics, 'Moralium Dogma Philosophorum', has also been attributed to him.

The only edn. of the 'Dragmaticon' is that of G. Gratarolus pub. under the title *Dialogus de Substantiis Physicis . . . confectus a Willelmo Aneponymo . . .* [and other works] (Strasbourg, 1567; photographically repr., Frankfurt, 1967), pp. 1–312. The 'Philosophia Mundi' is pr. among the works of *Bede in *PL* 90. 1127–78, and among those of *Honorius 'of Autun', ibid. 171. 39–102; new edn., with Ger. tr., by G. Maurach (Studia, 16; Pretoria [1980]). Part of the text of his gloss on Boethius ed. C. Jourdain in *Notices et extraits des manuscrits de la Bibliothèque Impériale*, 20 (pt. 2; 1862), pp. 40–82; J. M. Parent, OP, *La Doctrine de la création dans l'École de Chartres* (Publications de l'Institut d'Études Médiévales d'Ottawa, 8; 1938), pp. 115–77, incl. further extracts of the text of the gloss on Boethius, pp. 124–36, and of that on the *Timaeus*, pp. 142–77. *Glosae super Platonem* ed. É. Jeauneau (Textes Philosophiques du Moyen Âge, 13; 1965). *Glosae super Iuvenalem*, ed. B. Wilson (ibid. 18; 1980). The 'Moralium Dogma Philosophorum' is pr. among the works of *Hildebert of Lavardin in J. P. Migne, *PL* 171. 1007–56; modern edn., attributing it to William of Conches, by J. Holmberg (Arbeten utgivna met Understöd av Vilhelm Ekmans Universitetsfond, Uppsala, 1929). T. Gregory, *Anima Mundi: La Filosofia di Guglielmo di Conches e la Scuola di Chartres* (Pubblicazioni dell'Istituto di Filosofia dell'Università di Roma, 3 [1955]). M.-D. Chenu, 'Nature ou histoire? Une controverse exégétique sur la création au XIIe siècle', *AHDLMA* 20 (for 1953; 1954), pp. 25–30. B. Lawn, *The Salernitan Questions* (Oxford, 1963), esp. pp. 50–6 and 205 f. (rev. Ital. tr., 1969, pp. 70–5 and 233 f.). É. Jeauneau, '*Lectio Philosophorum': Recherches sur l'École de Chartres* (Amsterdam, 1973), pp. 101–16, 125–92, 205–7, 267–78, and 335–70 (repr. articles previously pub. 1957 onwards). [E.] P. [M.] Dronke, *Fabula: Explorations into the Uses of Myth in Medieval Platonism* (Mittellateinische Studien und Texte, 9; 1974), esp. pp. 14–78

and 167–83. D. Elford, 'William of Conches', in [E.] P. [M.] Dronke (ed.), *A History of Twelfth-Century Western Philosophy* (Cambridge, 1988), pp. 308–27, with bio-bibliography, pp. 456 f. The attribution to William of Conches of a 'Tertia Philosophia' partly pr. by C. Ottaviano, *Un brano inedito della "Philosophia" di Guglielmo di Conches* (Collezione di Testi Filosofici inediti e rari, 1; Naples, 1935), pp. 19–52, has been disproved by T. Gregory, 'Sull'attribuzione a Guglielmo di Conches di un rimaneggiamento della *Philosophia Mundi*', *Giornale critico della Filosofia italiana*, 30 (1951), pp. 119–25.

William of Malmesbury

William of Malmesbury (*c*.1090–*c*.1143), the chief English historian of his generation. He appears to have spent most of his life at the monastery at *Malmesbury, where he was offered, but declined, the abbacy in 1140. His work, though credulous and often careless in its chronology, has literary merit. He was a man of immensely wide reading, which is reflected in his autograph manuscripts which have survived, and in his 'Polyhistor', a sort of commonplace book. His two most important books were his 'Gesta Regum Anglorum' (1120) and his 'Gesta Pontificum Anglorum' (1125), which, as their titles imply, dealt respectively with the secular and ecclesiastical history of England. They were considerably revised both by William himself and, after his death, by others. His 'Historia Novella', which continues the 'Gesta Regum', is a contemporary narrative also of first-rate historical importance. It goes up to the year 1142 and is unfinished. William also wrote several theological works, including a treatise on 'The Miracles of the Virgin' and an abridged edition of the 'De Ecclesiasticis Officiis' of *Amalarius of Metz.

Most of his Works, collected from various edns., in J. P. Migne, *PL* 179. 945–1774, with frags. also pr. ibid. 127. 375–84. Crit. edns. of his *De Gestis Pontificum Anglorum* by N. E. S. A. Hamilton (RS, 1870); of his *Vita Sancti Dunstani* in W. *Stubbs (ed.), *Memorials of Saint Dunstan* (ibid., 1874), pp. 250–324, with introd., pp. xxxv–xxxvii; of his *De Gestis Regum Anglorum* by id. (2 vols., ibid., 1887–9), with introd. prefaces in vol. 1, pp. ix–cxlvii, and vol. 2, pp. xv–cxlii, with refs.; of his *Vita Wulstani* by R. R. Darlington (first full edn., Camden Society, 3rd ser. 40; 1928); Eng. tr. by J. H. F. Peile (Oxford, 1934); modern edns., with Eng. tr., of his *Historia Novella* (also incl. in RS edn. of *De Gestis Regum Anglorum*) by K. R. Potter (London, 1955), of *De Antiquitate Glastonie Ecclesie* by J. Scott (Woodbridge, Suffolk, 1981), and of *Gesta Regum Anglorum* by R. A. B. Mynors, R. M. Thomson, and M. Winterbottom (Oxford Medieval Texts, 1998 ff.); modern edn. of his *Polyhistor* by H. Testroet Ouellette (Medieval & Renaissance texts and studies, 10; Binghamton, NY, 1982). H. Farmer, OSB, 'William of Malmesbury's Life and Works', *JEH* 13 (1962), pp. 39–54; id., 'William of Malmesbury's Commentary on Lamentations', *Studia Monastica*, 4 (1962), pp. 283–311; R. M. Thomson, *William of Malmesbury* (Woodbridge, Suffollk, 1987).

William of Moerbeke

William of Moerbeke (d. 1286), translator of Greek philosophical and scientific works. Nothing is known of his early life. He was in Greece, as a *Dominican, in 1260, when he completed his earliest dated translations (of *Aristotle, *De partibus animalium* and *Meteorologica*). By 1267 he was at Viterbo, and until 1279 was attached to the curia as Papal penitentiary. He took part in the Second Council of *Lyons in 1274. In 1278 he was consecrated Abp. of Corinth, and in Corinth he translated the *tria opuscula* of *Proclus, which survive only in his translations. By the end of 1283 he was back in Italy, once more attached to the Papal court, probably until his death. His friends included *Witelo. The extent of his relationship with St *Thomas Aquinas is a matter of controversy, but it seems certain that Thomas encouraged his work as a translator and that he in turn kept Thomas informed of what he was doing. His translation of Proclus' *Elementatio theologica* (completed in 1268) enabled Thomas to identify the true nature of the *Liber de Causis*. He translated or revised translations of many of the works of Aristotle, including some not previously translated into Latin (*Politics*, *Poetics*, and book K of the *Metaphysics*), several other works of Proclus (including the massive commentary on Plato's *Parmenides*), and works by other Greek philosophers and by some ancient commentators on Aristotle, such as Alexander of Aphrodisias, *John Philoponus, Simplicius, Archimedes and Galen. His translations of Proclus aroused an interest in him which is particularly evident in German Dominican writers such as *Eckhart and Berthold of Moosburg.

His trs. are listed, with notes of edns. and studies and biog. information, in J. Brams and W. Vanhamel (eds.), *Guillaume de Moerbeke: Recueil d'Études à l'occasion du 700ᵉ anniversaire de sa mort (1286)* (Ancient and Medieval Philosophy, de Wulf-Mansion Centre, 1st ser. 7; Louvain, 1989), pp. 301–83. M. *Grabmann, *Guglielmo di Moerbeke, O.P., il traduttore delle opere di Aristotele* (Miscellanea Historiae Pontificiae, vol. 11, Collectionis totius, n. 20; 1946). Kaeppeli, 2 (1975), pp. 122–9 (nos. 1586–616). G. Verbeke in *DHGE* 22 (1988), cols. 963–6, s.v. 'Guillaume (138) de Moerbeke'.

William of Norwich, St (1132–44), supposed victim of a Jewish ritual murder. A tanner's apprentice at *Norwich, he was enticed from home on Monday in Holy Week 1144 and on Holy Saturday, six days later, his body was found with marks of violence in a neighbouring wood. Acc. to Thomas of Monmouth, a monk of Norwich and the only authority for the legend, William had been crucified and murdered by the Jews during the Passover. This story was substantiated by a converted Jew, Theobald, who asserted that, acc. to Jewish religious tradition, a Christian must be sacrificed every year to obtain the deliverance of the people. This is the first known case of the blood accusation against the Jews; but as the authorities took no action, the account is open to much suspicion.

The cult of William of Norwich dates from the translation of his body from the chapter house of the monks, where it had been buried, to the cathedral (1151) amidst a wave of religious enthusiasm. Many visions and miracles were reported to have taken place at his tomb, and throughout the Middle Ages he enjoyed great popularity. Feast day at Norwich, 26 Mar.; commemoration elsewhere, 25 Mar.

The Life by Thomas of Monmouth ed., with Eng. tr., full introd., and notes, by A. Jessopp and M. R. James (Cambridge, 1896). John Capgrave's version of the Legend, which depends on Thomas of Monmouth, is repr. in *AASS*, Mar. 3 (1668), pp. 590 f. M. D. Anderson, *A Saint at Stake: The Strange Death of William of Norwich 1144* (1964). G. I. Longmuir, 'Thomas of Monmouth: Detector of Ritual Murder', *Speculum*, 59 (1984), pp. 820–46; id., 'Historiographic Crucifixion', in G. Dahan (ed.), *Les Juifs au regard de l'histoire: Mélanges en l'honneur de Bernhard Blumenkranz* (1985), pp. 109–27. R. Webster in *CE* 15 (1912), pp. 635 f., s.v.

William of Ockham (*c.*1285–1347), philosopher, theologian and polemicist, 'Venerabilis inceptor'. A native of Ockham in Surrey, William early entered the *Franciscan

Order and studied and taught at *Oxford. He never became a regent master, but remained an 'inceptor' (hence his title), prob. owing to the accusation of teaching dangerous doctrines made by John Lutterell, the chancellor of the University. Lutterell went to *Avignon in 1323 and denounced Ockham for maintaining heretical positions. Ockham was summoned there by Pope *John XXII, and a commission of six theologians was set up to examine the charges. It censured 51 propositions taken from his works, but no formal condemnation followed. Ockham's philosophical and theological writings were composed during his periods at Oxford and Avignon. They include commentaries on parts of the 'Organon' of *Aristotle, a 'Summa Logicae', a Commentary on the '*Sentences' and seven '*Quodlibets'. In 1327 the Minister General of the Franciscans, Michael of Cesena, was summoned to Avignon in connection with the dispute on Franciscan poverty. He charged Ockham to examine the Papal constitutions on this subject. Ockham concluded that the Pope, John XXII, had taken up heretical positions. In 1328 he fled from Avignon and joined Louis of Bavaria, under whose protection he remained until 1347. In 1331 he was sentenced to expulsion from his order and to perpetual imprisonment, having been excommunicated since 1328. To this period of his life belong his polemical writings against the Pope and in favour of Louis. In 1332/3 he wrote his 'Opus Nonaginta Dierum', a violent attack directed against the Pope on the question of poverty. During the next years other writings against the Pope and in favour of the Imperial policy followed, among them 'Dialogus super Dignitate Papali et Regia', of which the first part was completed before the death of John XXII in Dec. 1334, 'Octo quaestiones' (1340–1), 'Breviloquium de principatu tyrannico' (*c.*1340–2), and 'Tractatus de Imperatorum et Pontificum Potestate' (*c.*1347). The tradition that he lived until 1349, and that towards the end of his life he took steps to be reconciled to the Church, has been shown to rest on evidence that will not withstand critical examination.

William of Ockham was a vigorous, critical and independent thinker, and at the same time a theologian in the Augustinian–Franciscan tradition. He contributed to the development of formal logic, and a logician's approach runs through all his work. He made much use of the principle of economy ('Ockham's razor'). He eliminated the notion, then generally accepted, of the existence of *universals. Only individual things exist, and they are directly apprehended by the mind. This intuitive knowledge is naturally caused. On the theological side much of Ockham's thinking is determined by his resolute attempt to eliminate anything that limited God's omnipotence and freedom. He considered that the doctrine of eternal ideas in the Divine mind in accordance with which the world was created and ordered limited God's freedom. He made a distinction between the absolute power (*potentia absoluta*) of God and His ordained power (*potentia ordinata*). God could have created a different order, provided that it did not violate the law of contradiction. The moral order is dependent on the Divine *fiat*. But God's omnipotence cannot be philosophically proved. It has to be accepted on faith through revelation. The same is true of His omniscience. Ockham also criticized the traditional proofs of the existence of God as not philosophically demonstrable. In short, he destroyed the conception of the relationship between theology and philosophy elaborated in the 13th century.

Ockham saw his task as the purification of *Aristotle's teaching and Christian theology of unwarranted assumptions such as necessary categories and real universals. His radical criticism of the prevailing belief in the reality of universals, and his grounding of human knowledge in intuitive cognition, and his rethinking of the relation of theology to philosophy marked the beginning of what was later characterized as the *via moderna* as opposed to the *via antiqua* represented by the *Thomists and *Scotists. It is also now generally agreed that 'by his interest in singulars rather than universals, intuition rather than abstraction, and induction rather than deduction, he prepared the ground for a more scientific approach to reality' (Gál). His philosophical and theological influence pervaded the university world from about 1340, though resisted by Thomas *Bradwardine and numerous other theologians, and even opponents of the *via moderna* were unconsciously affected; he was acknowledged as a mentor by G. *Biel and M. *Luther and universally as the inspirer of *Nominalism. His political theories played an important part in the development of the *Conciliar Movement in the 14th and 15th cents. He refused to acknowledge that the Pope had any right to determine the validity of the election of the Emperor. The Emperor had the right and the duty to depose a heretical Pope.

Crit. edn. of his *Opera Philosophica et Theologica* by G. Gál, OFM, and others (St Bonaventure, NY, 1967 ff.) now incl. *Summa Logicae, Brevis Summa, Summulae in libros Physicorum,* comm. on Aristotle's logical works and *Physics, Quodlibeta Septem,* and the majority of his comm. on the *Sentences*; his *Opera Politica,* ed. J. G. Sikes, H. S. Offler, and others (3 vols., Manchester, 1940–63, vol. 4, Oxford, 1997; 2nd edn. of vol. 1, 1974) incl. *Opus Nonaginta Dierum, Octo Quaestiones, Contra Ioannem, Contra Benedictum, Compendium Errorum Ioannis Papae XXII, Breviloquium, De Imperatorum et Pontificum Potestate, Allegationes de Potestate Imperiali,* and *De Electione Caroli Quarti. Dialogus,* ed. M. Goldast, *Monarchia S. Romani Imperii,* 2 (Frankfurt, 1614), pp. 392–957; and *De Sacramento Altaris,* ed. (with Eng. tr.) by T. B. Birch (Burlington, Ia., 1930). The *Tractatus de Successevis* (ed. P. Boehner, OFM, Franciscan Institute Publications, 1; 1944), formerly attributed to Ockham, is an early compilation from the *Physics.* Eng. tr. of a selection of his *Philosophical Writings* by P. Boehner, OFM (Edinburgh, 1957); also of pt. 1 of his *Summa Logicae* by M. J. Loux (Notre Dame, Ind., and London [1974]); of *Quodlibetal Questions* by A. J. Freddoso and F. E. Kelley (2 vols., New Haven, Conn., and London [1991]) and of *Breviloquium* by J. Kilcullen, ed. A. S. McGrade (Cambridge, 1992).

L. Baudry, *Guillaume d'Occam,* 1 (Études de philosophie médiévale, 39 [no further vols. pub.]; 1949); E. A. Moody, *The Logic of William of Ockham* (1935); G. de Lagarde, *La Naissance de l'esprit laïque au déclin du moyen âge,* 4–6 (1942–6); rev. edn., 4–5 (1962–3); P. Boehner, OFM, *Collected Articles on Ockham,* ed. E. M. Buytaert, OFM (Franciscan Institute Publications, Philosophy Series, 12; 1958); H. Junghans, *Ockham im Lichte der neueren Forschung* (Arbeiten zur Geschichte und Theologie des Lutherthums, 21; 1968); J. Miethke, *Ockhams Weg zur Socialphilosophie* (1969); A. S. McGrade, *The Political Thought of William of Ockham* (Cambridge, 1974); G. [A.] Leff, *William of Ockham: The Metamorphosis of Scholastic Discourse* (Manchester, 1975); M. Damiata, *Guglielmo d'Ockham: Povertà e potere* (Studi Francescani, 75, nos. 1–4; 1978; 76, nos. 3–4; 1979); M. McC. Adams, *William of Ockham* (Publications in Medieval Studies, 26; 2 vols., Notre Dame, Ind., 1987). Commemorative vols. of *Franciscan Studies,* 44–6 (1984–6); *From Ockham to Wyclif,* ed. A. Hudson

and M. Wilks (Studies in Church History, Subsidia, 5; Oxford, 1987); *Die Gegenwart Ockhams,* ed. W. Vossenkuhl and R. Schönberger (Weinheim, 1990). L. Baudry, *Lexique Philosophique de Guillaume d'Ockham* (1958). Works on Ockham (1919–49) are listed by V. Heynck, OFM, in *Wilhelm Ockham (1349–1949): Aufsätze su seiner Philosophie und Theologie* (Franziskanische Studien, 32; 1950), pp. 164–83; J. P. Reilly, 'Ockham Bibliography: 1950–1967', *Franciscan Studies,* 28 (1968), pp. 197–214. G. Gál, OFM, in *NCE* 14 (1967), pp. 932–5, s.v.

William of St-Thierry (1075/80–1148), theologian and spiritual writer. Of noble family, he was born at Liège, probably educated there and at *Reims, *c.*1100 entered the *Benedictine Abbey of St-Nicasius at Reims, and *c.*1120 was elected Abbot of St-Thierry near Reims. In 1131 he took part in the first General Chapter of the Benedictines of the province of Reims, held in that city, and he appears to have held an influential position among the Benedictine Abbots of the area. Before his election as Abbot he made the acquaintance of St *Bernard, with whom he formed a close friendship. He was long anxious to join St Bernard at *Clairvaux, being dissuaded by the resistance of St Bernard himself; in 1135 he resigned his abbacy and joined a group of Cistercian monks from Igny who were establishing a house at Signy in the Ardennes.

Although he was drawn to the contemplative life, William devoted much of his energies to theological study. His first two treatises, *De Contemplando Deo* and *De Natura et Dignitate Amoris,* discuss the rapport between knowledge and love. After completing his first exposition on the Song of Songs, which he discussed with St Bernard when both were ill at Clairvaux, he turned to the Epistle to the Romans and the problem of grace: in what way does God give us His love and how do we receive it? In answer to his questions St Bernard drafted for him the *De Gratia et Libero Arbitrio* (1128), and in the same year William dedicated to Bernard his own *De Sacramento Altaris,* on man's encounter with God in the Eucharist. Before leaving St-Thierry he also compiled a treatise *De Natura Animae et Corporis* in which he tried to synthesize the teaching of the E. and W. Fathers on the relation of the body and soul. In 1138 he wrote to St Bernard pointing out the defects of Peter *Abelard's views on the Trinity and Redemption; he urged St Bernard to take up his pen against Abelard, and in defence of orthodoxy he himself wrote his *Disputatio adversus Abelardum* and attacked the teaching of *William of Conches in *De Erroribus Guillielmi de Conches.* These works were followed by two treatises on faith, *Speculum Fidei* and *Enigma Fidei,* written between 1140 and 1144. After he went to Signy he also wrote a second, much more individualistic, commentary on the Song of Songs and completed his *Meditativae Orationes.* The last years of his life were devoted to a synthesis of his doctrine and experience in the famous *Epistola ad Fratres de Monte Dei de Vita Solitaria,* known as the 'Golden Letter', which has often been attributed to St Bernard. His final work was devoted to a Life of Bernard, which he never completed. All his works, both ascetical and didactic, were remarkable for their wide knowledge of the Bible and the Fathers, Eastern as well as Western.

Opera ed. B. Tissier, Ord. Cist., *Bibliotheca Patrum Cisterciensium,* 4 (Bonnefontaine, 1662), pp. 1–237; repr. in J. P. Migne, *PL* 180. 201–726; other works among those of St Bernard, ibid. 182. 531–3, and 184. 307–436. Modern edns. by M.-M. Davy of the *Epistola ad Fratres de Monte Dei* (Études de Philosophie médiévale, 29; 2 vols., 1940–49), of his *De Contemplando Deo* and *De Natura et Diginitate Amoris* (Bibliothèque des Textes Philosophiques, 1953), of his Comm. on the Song of Songs (ibid., 1958), and of his *Speculum Fidei* and *Enigma Fidei* (ibid., 1959); by J.-M. Déchanet, OSB, of his Comm. on the Song of Songs, with Fr. tr. by M. Dumortier, OCSO (SC 82; 1962), and, with his own Fr. tr., of *Epistola ad Fratres de Monte Dei* (ibid. 223; 1975), and of *Speculum Fidei* (ibid. 301; 1982); modern edns., with Fr. tr., by J. Hourlier, OSB, of his *De Contemplando Deo* and *Oratio Domni Willelmi* (ibid. 61; 1959) and of his *Meditativae Orationes* (ibid. 324; 1985) and by M. Lemoine of his *De Natura du Corporis et Animae* (Auteurs latins du moyen âge, 1988). Comm. on Rom. ed. P. Verdeyen, SJ (CCCM 86; 1989). Eng. tr. of his works by Sr. Penelope, CSMV, and others (Cistercian Fathers Series, 3, 6, 9, 12, 15, 24 (pp. 104–80), 27, 30, etc.; 1970 ff.).

Life by an anonymous author (d. 1148), ed. A. Poncelet, SJ, 'Vie ancienne de Guillaume de Saint-Thierry', in *Mélanges Godefroid Kurth*, 1 (Liège, 1908), pp. 85–96. J.-M. Déchanet, OSB, *Guillaume de Saint-Thierry: L'homme et son œuvre* (Bibliothèque Médiévale; 1942; Eng. tr., Cistercian Studies Series, 10; Spencer, Mass., 1972); id., *Guillaume de Saint-Thierry: Aux sources d'une pensée* (Théologie Historique, 49 [1978]); M.-M. Davy, *Théologie et Mystique de Guillaume de Saint-Thierry*, 1: *La Connaissance de Dieu* (Études de Théologie et d'histoire de la Spiritualité, 14; 1954; all pub.). *Saint Thierry: Une Abbaye du VIᵉ au XXᵉ siècle* (Saint Thierry, 1979; Acts of a Colloquium at the Abbey in 1976); Eng. tr. by J. Carfantan, *William, Abbot of St Thierry* (Cistercian Studies Series, 94; Kalamazoo, Mich. [1987]). D. N. Bell, *The Image and Likeness: The Augustinian Spirituality of William of St Thierry* (Cistercian Studies, 78; 1984). P. Verdeyen, *La Théologie mystique de Guillaume de Saint-Thierry* (Paris [1990]). L. Bouyer, Cong. Orat., *La Spiritualité de Cîteaux* (1955; Eng. tr., 1958), chs. 4 and 5. M. B. Pennington, OCSO, *The Last of the Fathers* (Studies in Monasticism, 1; Still River, Mass., 1983), pp. 109–80. J.-M. Déchanet, OSB, in *Dict. Sp.* 6 (1967), cols. 1241–63, s.v. 'Guillaume de Saint-Thierry', with additional bibl. by R. Aubert in *DHGE* 22 (1988), cols. 1014–16.

William of Tyre (*c.*1130–prob. 1186) Abp. of Tyre, historian. He was born in Palestine, prob. of European (poss. Italian) parents of the merchant class. He studied at *Paris (1145–61) and *Bologna (1161–5) and was ordained priest before 1161. After returning to Tyre, he was appointed Archdeacon of Tyre in 1167 by Amaury, King of Jerusalem (1163–74), with an enhanced stipend on condition that he wrote the official 'History' of the reign ('Gesta Amalrici'). In 1168 he was sent on a diplomatic mission to *Constantinople and in 1169 summoned to Rome to answer charges of an obscure nature preferred by his Archbishop. He was appointed tutor to Amaury's son Baldwin (later Baldwin IV) in 1170 and Chancellor in 1174. In May 1175 he was consecrated Abp. of Tyre. In the next few years he took an important part in government. He led the ecclesiastical delegation from Jerusalem to the *Lateran Council of 1179, where he obtained some restriction of the independence of the military orders from the local hierarchy, and was entrusted by *Alexander III with a mission to Constantinople in connection with the union of the East and West. On his return to Palestine (1180) political intrigue prevented his being elected Patr. of Jerusalem. He continued, and prob. in 1182 revised, his 'History', adding the prologue in 1184.

William of Tyre's *Historia Rerum in Partibus Transmarinis Gestarum*, comprising the 'Gesta Regum' (begun *c.*1170) and the 'Gesta Amalrici', covers the period from 1095 (Preaching of the First *Crusade) to 1184. It is the primary authority from 1127 (where Fulcher of Chartres ends), and from *c.*1144 is a contemporary record. Although William's sympathies clearly lay with Raymond of Tripoli and the *pullani* (or native) crusaders, his work is marked by insight, tolerance, and the careful sifting of evidence from a wide range of sources, as well as by the clear delineation of the physical and mental features of the characters portrayed. It was translated into French in the 12th or 13th cent., and in this form had a wide circulation and many continuations. Another work by William of Tyre, the 'Gesta Orientalium Principum', partly based on the Arabic chronicle of Said-ibn-Batrik (d. 940), Patr. of Alexandria, has been lost.

Lat. text of History first pr. at Basle, 1549; repr. from edn. of J. Bongars (Hanover, 1611) in J. P. Migne, *PL* 201. 200–892; Lat. text, with Old Fr. tr. [ed. A. Beugnot and A. Prévost], in *Recueil des historiens des croisades: Historiens occidentaux*, 1 (Paris, 2 pts., 1844); Eng. tr., with notes and full bibl., by E. A. Babcock and A. C. Krey (2 vols., 'Records of Civilization', 35; 1943); crit. edn. of Lat. by R. B. C. Huygens (CCCM 63 and 63A; 1986). 13th-cent. Fr. version, ed. P. Paris (2 vols., Paris, 1879). P. W. Edbury and J. G. Rowe, *William of Tyre: Historian of the Latin East* (Cambridge Studies in Medieval Life and Thought, 4th ser. 8; 1988), with bibl.

The text of the Continuation of William of Tyre, covering the period 1184–97, ed. M. R. Morgan (Documents relatifs à l'histoire des croisades publiés par l'Academie des Inscription et Belles Lettres, 14; 1982). Id., *The Chronicle of Ernoul and the Continuations of William of Tyre* (Oxford Historical Monographs, 1973).

William of Waynflete (*c.*1395–1486), Bp. of *Winchester. Educated possibly at Winchester College and then at one of the colleges or halls in Oxford, in 1420 he was ordained priest and also appointed master of St Mary Magdalen Hospital, nr. Winchester. By 1430 he was headmaster of Winchester College and in 1442 he was made provost of the newly founded Eton College and shaped its educational development. On *Henry VI's recommendation he succeeded Cardinal H. *Beaufort as Bp. of Winchester in 1447, and in 1448 obtained licence for founding a hall at Oxford, dedicated to St Mary Magdalen, in order to foster the study of theology and philosophy; in 1457–8 it was refounded as Magdalen College. As a moderate Lancastrian and a favourite of the King, he took an increasingly prominent part in public affairs, being delegated to mediate with Jack Cade's rebels in 1450 and with the Duke of York in 1452. In 1456 Henry appointed him Chancellor, and in the next year he was assessor in the trial of Bp. R. *Pecock. He resigned the Chancellorship in 1460 and soon afterwards acquiesced in the accession of Edward IV, although he renewed his support for Henry VI in 1470–1. He completed the building of Eton College and Magdalen, which he left the largest and best endowed of any Oxford college, besides in 1480 founding (in conjunction with John Anwykill) Magdalen College School and a school at Wainfleet, Lincs.

There is a short panegyrical Life by J. Budden (Oxford, 1602; repr. by W. Bates (ed.), *Vitae Selectorum Aliquot Virorum qui Doctrina, Dignitate aut Pietate Inclaruere* (London, 1681), pp. 51–89); some further information added by P. *Heylyn in *Memorial of Bishop Waynflete*, ed. J. R. *Bloxam (Caxton Society, 1851). Fuller modern Life by R. Chandler (London, 1811). V. Davis, *William Waynflete: Bishop and Educationalist* (Studies in the

History of Medieval Religion, 6; Woodbridge, Suffolk, 1993). I. S. Leadham in *DNB* 60 (1899), pp. 85–9, s.v. 'Waynflete'; *BRUO* 3 (1959), pp. 2001–3, s.v. 'Waynflete, William'.

William of Wykeham (1324–1404), Bp. of *Winchester. He was born of a poor family at Wickham, Hants, and educated at Winchester. He passed *c*.1343 from the service of the Constable of Winchester Castle into that of Edward III, who appointed him chaplain and rector of Irstead, Norfolk, in 1349. In 1356 he became clerk of the royal works at Henley and Easthampstead and surveyor of the works at Windsor. He was also responsible for the erection of Queenborough Castle in the Isle of Sheppey. In 1364 he became Keeper of the Privy Seal. Elected Bp. of Winchester in 1366, he was consecrated in 1367 and became Chancellor in the same year. Being blamed for the disasters of the French war, he was driven from office during an attack of anticlericalism in 1371. He devoted himself to the organization of his diocese, the reform of abuses, esp. in religious houses, and the plans for his future academic foundations. In 1376, owing to the hostility of John of Gaunt, he was accused in Parliament of malversation. Although found guilty on only one minor count, he was deprived of the temporalities of his see and also expelled from court. Although restored to favour before the death of Edward III and declared guiltless by Richard II in 1377, he took little further interest in politics. As a member of the commission of regency appointed in 1386 and as Chancellor from 1389 to 1391, he endeavoured to exercise a moderating influence both on the lords appellant and the King.

At Oxford he founded a college of 100 members dedicated to St Mary, but soon known as New College, for which he obtained a royal and Papal charter of foundation in 1379 (formally opened, 1386). At Winchester he established a school for 70 poor scholars to feed his Oxford foundation (Papal bull, 1378; royal charter, 1382). This college, which was the first independent and self-governing school in the country, was opened in 1394.

His episcopal Register, ed. T. F. Kirby (2 vols., Hampshire Record Society, 1896–9). G. H. Moberly, *Life of William of Wykeham* (1887), with two brief Lives written shortly after his death, the one prob. by Dr Thomas Aylward, one of his executors, the other perh. by Robert Heete (d. 1422), pp. 286–92 and 293–308 respectively. [T. Martin], *Historica Descriptio Complectens Vitam ac Res Gestas Beatissimi Viri Guiliemi Wicami* (London, 1597). R. *Lowth, *The Life of William of Wykeham* (1758; short suppl., 1759). M. E. C. Walcott, *William of Wykeham and his Colleges* (1852), esp. 'The Life of William of Wykeham', pp. 3–100. G. C. Heseltine, *William of Wykeham: A Commentary* (1932), with bibl. W. [G.] Hayter, *William of Wykeham* (1970). J. Tait in *DNB* 63 (1900), pp. 225–31; A. F. Leach in *DECH*, pp. 659–61, both s.v. 'Wykeham'.

William of York, St (d. 1154), Abp. of *York. William FitzHerbert was the younger son of Herbert of Winchester, chamberlain and treasurer of Henry I; he was a chaplain to King Stephen and by 1138 (prob. by 1130), Canon and Treasurer of York Minster. Elected Abp. of York in 1141, he received the temporalities of the see from the King, but, being accused of simony by the *Cistercians, he was refused consecration by *Theobald, Abp. of *Canterbury. Both sides appealed to Innocent II, who, in 1143, decided that William might be consecrated if he was

cleared by the oath of himself and the Dean of York. Prob. consecrated by *Henry of Blois in 1143, he ruled his diocese conscientiously, but he failed to obtain from Card. Imar the *pallium which Lucius II had sent him in 1145. The whole history of his disputed election and subsequent deposition and restoration reflect the power struggle between Henry of Blois and St *Bernard within the Papal curia. In 1147 William was forced to go the Pope, *Eugenius III (a Cistercian), who suspended him from the exercise of his episcopal functions until the Dean of York (now Bp. of *Durham) cleared him in person, having previously done so by proxy. After William's relatives had attacked the Cistercian abbey of *Fountains, where Henry Murdac, the rival candidate for the archbishopric, was abbot, William was deposed at the Council of *Reims in 1147. Taking refuge with Henry of Blois, he lived in great austerity at *Winchester until the death of Eugenius in 1153, when he appealed for restoration. On the death of Henry Murdac in the same year, Anastasius IV restored him and gave him the pallium. As William entered York in 1154, the bridge collapsed, but the travellers escaped injury, supposedly through his sanctity and prayers. He was respected in his diocese, but died within a month of his return, possibly by poison. Buried in York Minister, he was regarded a martyr and miracles were reported at his tomb. He was canonized by *Honorius III in 1227; his relics were translated to a shrine behind the High Altar in 1284. Feast day, 8 June; that of his translation, 8 Jan., until 1478 when it was transferred to the first Sunday after *Epiphany. His cult remained local.

The earliest sources, besides the letters of St Bernard (q.v. for edns.), are the contemporary accounts by William of Newburgh, *Historia Rerum Anglicarum* (ed. R. Howlett, 1, RS, 1884, pp. 55–7 and 79–81) and (up to 1153) John of Hexham's continuation of *Simeon of Durham's *Historia Regum* (*Symeonis Monachi Opera Omnia*, ed. T. Arnold, 2, RS, 1885, pp. 306 f., 311, 313–21). An anonymous Life, preserved in a 13th-cent. MS in the Harleian collection (2, fols. 76–88), is pr. in J. Raine, *Historians of the Church of York and its Archbishops*, 2 (RS, 1886), pp. 270–91, with introd. pp. xviii f. and other material, pp. 220–7, 388–97, and 531–50.

The most important modern work is D. *Knowles, OSB, 'The Case of Saint William of York', *Cambridge Historical Journal*, 5 (1935–37), pp. 162–77 and 212–14, with bibl., repr. in *The Historian and Character and Other Essays* (Cambridge, 1963), pp. 76–97. Other arts. by C. T. Clay, 'The Early Treasurers of York', *Yorkshire Archaeological Journal*, 35 (1943), pp. 7–34, esp. pp. 8–10; C. H. Talbot, 'New Documents in the Case of Saint William of York', *Cambridge Historical Journal*, 10 (1950–2), pp. 1–15; A. Morey, 'Canonist Evidence in the Case of St William of York', ibid., pp. 352 f. T. F. Tout in *DNB* 19 (1889), pp. 173–6, s.v. 'Fitzherbert, William'.

Williams, Charles Walter Stansby (1886–1945), poet and theological writer. Educated at *St Albans and at University College, London, he worked from 1908 until his death in the London publishing business of the Oxford University Press. After some early poetry and plays, of which he later came to think poorly, he began to publish novels, largely devoted to supernatural themes, among them *War in Heaven* (1930), *Descent into Hell* (1937) and *All Hallows' Eve* (1944); and also a play, *Thomas Cranmer of Canterbury*, written for the Canterbury festival of 1936. Of his theological writings prob. the most significant was *The Descent of the Dove* (1939), an unconventional and penetrating study of the Church as governed by the activity of the Holy Spirit in history. His leading theological ideas were his concept of romantic love in which the image of God in the beloved is revealed to the lover (an idea most fully expounded in *The Figure of Beatrice*, 1943), and his quite literal understanding of substitution, of which the *Atonement was the culminating example. His poetic achievement culminated in his two volumes on the Arthurian theme, *Taliessin through Logres* (1938) and *The Region of the Summer Stars* (1944). Both in London and later in Oxford (in 1939–45) Williams by his life and writings did much, like his fellow-Anglicans T. S. *Eliot and C. S. *Lewis, to commend Christianity in a Catholic and sacramental form to many who would have been unmoved by conventional apologetic.

Williams's unfinished prose work 'The Figure of Arthur' ed., with comm. on his Arthurian poems, by C. S. Lewis and pub. as *Arthurian Torso* (1948). Further poems, ed. D. L. Dodds (Arthurian Studies, 24; Cambridge, 1991). *Collected Plays*, with introd. by J. Heath-Stubbs (1963). Selected essays ed., with biog. and crit. introd., by A. Ridler (London, 1958). *Essays Presented to Charles Williams*, by D. [L.] *Sayers and others, with preface by C. S. Lewis (1947). M. McD. Shideler, *The Theology of Romantic Love: A Study in the Writings of Charles Williams* (New York [1962]); G. [T.] Cavaliero, *Charles Williams: Poet of Theology* (1983); A. M. Hadfield, *Charles Williams: An Exploration of his Life and Work* (New York and Oxford, 1983). G. W. S. Hopkins in *DNB*, *1941–1950*, pp. 958 f., s.v.

Williams, Isaac (1802–65), *Tractarian poet and theologian. He was educated at Harrow and Trinity College, Oxford, where he was drawn into the Tractarian Movement through the influence of J. *Keble. He was ordained priest in 1831, became tutor of Trinity College in 1832 and dean in the next year, and about the same time curate to J. H. *Newman at St Mary's. Besides contributing poetry to the *Lyra Apostolica* (1836) he wrote the famous Tract 80 on 'Reserve in Communicating Religious Knowledge', which lost him the election to the chair of poetry (1842). The defeat caused him to withdraw from Oxford and spend the rest of his life in retirement, occupied chiefly with writing sermons and poetry. Among his best-known poetical writings are *The Cathedral* (1838), interpreting Gothic architecture as a symbol of Christian doctrine, and *The Baptistery* (1842), containing an attack on the RC Church.

The Autobiography of Isaac Williams, ed. Sir G. Prevost (1892). O. W. Jones, *Isaac Williams and his Circle* (1971). W. P. Courtney in *DNB* 61 (1900), pp. 408–11.

Williams, John (1582–1650), Abp. of *York. Descended from an ancient Welsh family, he was educated at St John's College, Cambridge, where he was elected Fellow in 1603. Through the patronage of *James I and Chancellor Ellesmere, he received a large accumulation of benefices, including the bishopric of *Lincoln (1621), and in addition the Lord Keepership. His accommodating and intriguing character occasioned the dislike of *Charles I and W. *Laud, leading to heavy fines in 1637 and 1639 in the Star Chamber. During the Long Parliament Williams headed a party of compromise in the Lords and, recovering royal favour, was translated to York in 1641. He proved an assiduous royalist throughout the Civil War,

but was allowed to spend his last years in retirement in Wales.

Works repr., mainly photographically, with introd. and notes by B. Williams (Courtenay Library of Reformation Classics, 14; Sutton Courtenay [1980]). J. Hacket, *Scrinia Reserata: A Memorial Offered to the Deservings of John Williams* (1693). Life by A. Philips (Cambridge, 1700). R. D. Roberts, *Mitre and Musket: John Williams, Lord Keeper, Archbishop of York, 1582–1650* (1938), with bibl. R. B. Knox, 'The Social Teaching of Archbishop John Williams', *Studies in Church History*, 8 (ed. G. J. Cuming and D. Baker; 1972), pp. 179–85; G. W. Thomas, 'James I, Equity and Lord Keeper John Williams', *EHR* 91 (1976), pp. 506–28; H. T. Blethen, 'Bishop John Williams's Recantation of his *Holy Table, Name and Thing*, 1638', *JTS*, NS 29 (1978), pp. 157–60. S. R. Gardiner in *DNB* 61 (1900), pp. 414–20.

Williams, John (1796–1839), missionary of the *LMS. Born in London, after a commercial education he was accepted in 1816 by the LMS, which had chosen the *South Pacific for its earliest work. In 1817 he sailed for the Society Islands, and in 1818 settled on Raiatea, where the missionaries opened a chapel and also published a code of laws. In 1822 he went further afield, visiting the Cook Islands, and claimed the discovery of Rarotonga. In 1830 he brought the first LMS teachers to Samoa. On 20 Nov. 1839 he landed at Dillon's Bay, Erromanga, in Vanuatu (New Hebrides), where he and John Harris were killed and became Protestant 'martyrs'. Williams is chiefly notable for his practical missionary skills, his advocacy of a missionary ship, and the burst of missionary enthusiasm that the news of his death aroused in England. A succession of ships of the name *John Williams* have been employed in furthering the evangelization of the South Pacific.

There is much autobiographical material in his *A Narrative of Missionary Enterprises in the South Sea Islands* (1837). E. Prout, *Memoirs of the Life of the Rev. John Williams* (1843). Other Lives by [W.] C. Northcott (London, 1939) and B. Mathews (ibid., 1947). J. Gutch, *Beyond the Reefs: The Life of John Williams, Missionary* (1974). E. I. Carlyle in *DNB* 61 (1900), pp. 423–5.

Williams, Norman Powell (1883–1943), Anglican theologian. Educated at *Durham School and at *Christ Church, Oxford, he was elected a Fellow of Magdalen College in 1906. From 1909 to 1927 he was Chaplain-Fellow of Exeter College, and from 1927 until his death Lady Margaret Professor of Divinity and Canon of Christ Church. He was a leading *Anglo-Catholic theologian. His principal works were *The Ideas of the Fall and of Original Sin* (1927; *Bampton Lectures for 1924) and *The Grace of God* (1930).

E. W. Kemp, *N. P. Williams* (1954; memoir, with sermons). Id. in *DNB*, *1941–1950*, pp. 959 f., s.v.

Williams, Ralph Vaughan. See VAUGHAN WILLIAMS, RALPH.

Williams, Roger (*c*.1603–83), champion of religious *toleration. Educated at Pembroke College, Cambridge, and apparently ordained in the C of E, he sailed for N. America in 1630 in search of religious liberty. When he discovered that restrictions on religious freedom existed also at Boston, he set up a schismatic Church. He soon found himself in conflict with the civil powers, and in 1635 was ordered to leave Massachusetts and took refuge with the Indians who dwelt beyond the confines of the state, where he founded a settlement to which he gave the name 'Providence' (1636). In 1639 he established there the first Baptist church in the colonies. In 1643 he came back to England to try to secure a title for the new colony, and in the following year his friend, Sir Henry *Vane, procured him the desired charter, and Williams returned. While in England he published anonymously his vigorous pamphlet in defence of religious liberty, *The Bloody Tenent of Persecution* (1644). The constitution of his colony (later 'Rhode Island') included wide religious latitude, and when the *Quakers came to America in 1656 Williams granted them political toleration, though he sharply attacked their doctrines. He was a friend of the American Indians and learnt the language of the Narragansett tribe.

Complete Writings ed. J. H. Trumbull and others for the Narragansett Club (6 vols., Providence, RI, 1866–74; facsimile repr., with additional matter in vol. 7; New York, 1963). Correspondence ed. G. W. LaFantasie (2 vols., Hanover, NH, and London, 1988). Studies by O. S. Straus (London and New York, 1894), E. J. Carpenter (New York, 1909), E. Easton (Boston, 1930), J. E. Ernst (New York, 1932), S. H. Brockunier (ibid., 1940), P. Miller (ibid., 1953), O. E. Winslow (ibid., 1957), H. Chupack (ibid. [1969]), and H. Spurgin (Studies in American Religion, 34; Lewiston, Queenston, and Lampeter [1989]). E. S. Morgan, *Roger Williams: The Church and the State* (New York [1967]). W. C. Gilpin, *The Millenarian Piety of Roger Williams* (Chicago and London, 1979). E. S. Gaustad, *Liberty of Conscience: Roger Williams in America* (Grand Rapids, Mich. [1991]). S. H. Brockunier in *Dict. Amer. Biog.* 20 (1936), pp. 286–9, s.v.

Williams, Rowland (1817–70), Anglican scholar. He was educated at Eton and King's College, Cambridge, of which he became a Fellow in 1839. Ordained priest in 1843, he was appointed tutor at King's College, and, in 1850, vice-principal and professor of Hebrew at St David's College, Lampeter. In 1856 he published his most important work, *Christianity and Hinduism*. In 1860 Williams contributed an article dealing with biblical criticism to *Essays and Reviews*, which caused him to be prosecuted for heterodoxy by the Bp. of Salisbury (W. K. *Hamilton). The Court of *Arches having sentenced him to one year's suspension, the sentence was annulled by the Privy Council in 1864. Having left Lampeter in 1862, he retired to the living of Broad Chalke, nr. Salisbury.

Life and Letters of Rowland Williams, D.D., ed. E. Williams (his widow; 2 vols., 1874). Short study by O. W. Jones (Llandysul, Cardiganshire, 1991). E. Williams in *DNB* 61 (1900), pp. 450–3.

Willibald, St (700–86), Bp. of Eichstätt. He was possibly a relative of St *Boniface. After education at an otherwise unknown monastery at Waltham in Hants, he made a pilgrimage to *Rome in 722 with his father, St Richard, who died on the way at Lucca, and his brother, St Wynnebald. In 724 he set out from Rome for the East (Sicily, Cyprus, the Holy Land, Tyre, *Constantinople, and Nicaea). He eventually arrived back at *Monte Cassino in 730, and spent the next ten years there. In 740 he was again in Rome, whence Gregory III sent him to Germany. Boniface ordained him priest in 741 or 742 and shortly afterwards bishop. Before 750, with the assistance of Wynnebald, he founded a double monastery at Heidenheim in Württemberg, of which his sister, St *Walburga (q.v.) became Abbess after Wynnebald's death. Willibald was one of the

27 bishops and 17 abbots who joined in the confraternity agreement at Attigny in 762. He continued until his death actively consolidating the Church in Franconia. His body still lies in the cathedral of Eichstätt. Feast day, 7 July.

St Willibald's *Vita* is contained in the 'Hodoeporicon', an early and valuable history of his travels, written by a nun of Heidenheim who was a relative of St Willibald; text, with introd., and other material, in *AASS*, Jul. 2 (1731), pp. 485–519; better ed. O. Holder-Egger in *MGH*, Scriptores, 15 (pt. 1; 1887), pp. 86–106; Eng. tr. by C. H. Talbot, *The Anglo-Saxon Missionaries in Germany* (1954), pp. 153–77. F. Heidingsfelder (ed.), *Die Regesten der Bischöfe von Eichstätt* (Veröffentlichungen der Gesellschaft für Fränkische Geschichte, 6. Reihe, 1; 1915–38), pp. 1–15 [1915]. The text of the Attigny agreement is pr. in *MGH*, Concilia, 2 (pt. 1; 1906), pp. 72 f. W. Grothe, *Der heilige Richard und seine Kinder* (Berlin diss., 1908). B. Bischoff, 'Wer ist die Nonne von Heidenheim?', *Studien und Mitteilungen zur Geschichte des Benediktiner-Ordens*, 49 (1931), pp. 387 f. [the nun's name was Hugeburc, concealed under a cryptogram in Clm. 1086]. M. Coens, 'Légende et miracles du roi S. Richard', *Anal. Boll.* 49 (1931), pp. 353–84 (text of *Vita Sancti Richardi*, pp. 385–97; but the introd. contains information and valuable texts on St Willibald). W. Levison, *England and the Continent in the Eighth Century* (Ford Lectures, 1943; Oxford, 1946), esp. pp. 43 f. and 81. H. Löwe, 'Bonifatius und die bayerisch-fränkische Spannung', *Jahrbuch für fränkische Landesforschung*, 15 (1955), pp. 85–127; K.-U. Jäschke, 'Die Gründungszeit der mitteldeutschen Bistümer und das Jahr des Concilium Germanicum', in H. Beumann (ed.), *Festschrift für Walter Schlesinger*, 2 (Cologne, 1974), pp. 71–136, esp. pp. 80–101 ('Die Bischofsweihe Willibalds'). See also works cited s.v. BONIFACE, ST.

Willibrord, St (658–739), 'Apostle of Frisia'. A native of Northumbria, he was educated at *Ripon under the direction of St *Wilfrid. In 678 he went to an Anglo-Saxon religious community in Ireland at 'Rath Melsigi' (now thought to be Clonmelsch, Co. Carlow), where he remained for 12 years and was ordained priest. In 690, with about a dozen companions, he made his way as a missionary to W. Frisia. In 693, on a visit to Rome, he secured Papal support for his mission, and on a second visit, in 695, was consecrated Abp. of the Frisians by Pope *Sergius. On his return *Pepin granted him a site for his cathedral just outside Utrecht, and in 698 he founded the monastery of *Echternach in Luxemburg. In 714 he was temporarily driven from Utrecht by Duke Radbod, but despite this and other difficulties Willibrord continued his mission with success, making his way as far as *Denmark, Heligoland, and Thuringia. He received staunch support from the Carolingian Mayors of the Palace in Austrasia, as well as assistance from St *Boniface. Feast day, 7 Nov.

The Society of St Willibrord, founded *c*.1910, exists to promote closer relations between the C of E and the *Old Catholic Churches.

Prose and metrical Lives by *Alcuin pr. in *AASS*, Nov. 3 (1910), pp. 435–57, with other primary material, pp. 458–500, and excellent introd. by A. Poncelet, SJ, pp. 414–35, incl. refs. to earlier works; prose Life of Alcuin also ed. W. Levison in *MGH*, Scriptores Rerum Merovingicarum, 7 (pt. 1; 1913), pp. 81–141. 'Miracula' also ed. id. in *MGH*, Scriptores, 30 (pt. 2; 1934), pp. 1368–71, with further refs. Eng. tr. of Alcuin's prose Life in C. H. Talbot, *The Anglo-Saxon Missionaries in Germany* (1954), pp. 3–22. G. H. Verbist, *Saint Willibrord, apôtre des Pays-Bas et fondateur d'Echternach* (Université de Louvain. Recueil des Travaux publiés par les membres des Conférences d'Histoire et de Philologie, 2nd ser. 59; 1939). Further Lives by M. A. Erens,

O.Praem. (Tongerloo, 1939) and C. Wampach (Luxembourg, 1953). W. Levison, 'St. Willibrord and his Place in History', *Durham University Journal*, 32 (1939–40), pp. 23–41, repr. in id., *Aus rheinischer und fränkischer Frühzeit* (Dusseldorf, 1948), pp. 314–29, with other papers on Willibrord, pp. 304–13 and 330–46; id., *England and the Continent in the Eighth Century* (Ford Lectures, 1943; Oxford, 1946), esp. pp. 53–69. G. Kiesel, *Der heilige Willibrord im Zeugnis der bildenden Kunst* (Luxembourg, 1969). N. Gauthier, *L'Évangélisation des Pays de la Moselle* (1980), esp. pp. 314–23. D. Ó Cróinín, 'Rath Melsigi, Willibrord, and the earliest Echternach Manuscripts', *Peritia*, 3 (1984), pp. 17–42. *Willibrord, Apostel der Niederlande, Gründer der Abtei Echternach: Gedenkgabe zum 1250. Todestag des angelsächsichen Missionars*, ed. G. Kiesel and J. Schroeder (Saint-Paul, Luxembourg, 1989). A. G. Weiler, *Willibrords Missie* (Hilversum [1989]). A. Bange and A. G. Weiler (eds.), *Willibrord . . .: Voordrachten gehouden tijdens het Willibrord-congres, Nijmegen, 28–30 september 1989* (Middeleeuwse Studies, 6; Nijmegen, 1990). Facsimile edn. of *The Calendar of St Willibrord*, ed. H. A. Wilson (HBS 55; 1918).

On the Society of St Willibrord see G. Huelin, *St Willibrord and his Society* (1960), pp. 49–77; J. Burley and J. Witten in G. Huelin (ed.), *Old Catholics and Anglicans 1931–1981* (Oxford, 1983), pp. 62–85.

Wilmart, André (1876–1941), *patristic scholar. A native of Orléans, he studied under P. *Batiffol, with whom he published the *Tractatus Origenis* (1900). In 1901 he entered the *Benedictine Order at *Solesmes and was ordained priest in 1906. His demonstration (1906) that the *Tractatus* were the work of *Gregory of Elvira helped to establish his reputation. From now on he contributed constantly to the *Revue Bénédictine*. His main interests were Latin patristics (esp. the Carolingian epoch) and also Latin (esp. *Gallican) liturgies, here stimulated by his friendship with E. *Bishop. His longer works include *L'Ancien Cantatorium de l'église de Strasbourg* (1928), an edition of twelve sermons of St *Augustine in the *Miscellanea Agostiniana* (vol. 1, 1930), and *Auteurs spirituels et textes dévots du moyen âge latin* (1932). In the field of liturgy special importance attaches to his contention that the letters attributed to St *Germanus of Paris, hitherto a primary authority for the Gallican rite, were spurious; to his edition of the *Bobbio Missal (1924); and to his work on medieval books of private prayers.

Lettres de Jeunesse et Lettres d'Amitié, ed. G. de Luca and M. L. Baud (Uomini e Dottrine, 6; 1963). J. Bignami Odier, L. Brou, OSB, and A. Vernet, *Bibliographie sommaire des travaux du père André Wilmart* (Sussidi Eruditi, 5; 1953), with biog. introd. pp. 7–10, docs. on his life pp. 13–27, and list of obituary notices p. 10.

Wilsnack. A former place of pilgrimage nr. *Wittenberg. After a fire in the church of Wilsnack in 1383 three consecrated hosts were said to have been found unharmed, but marked with drops of blood. The alleged miracle, followed by striking answers to prayer and other extraordinary events, soon drew to the spot crowds of pilgrims, which made of the small village a prosperous town. Though frequently suspected of fraud, e.g. by J. *Huss (1405) and *Nicholas of Cusa (1451), the pilgrimage was encouraged by *Eugenius IV (1447) and *Nicholas V (1453), and continued to flourish until, in 1552, Wilsnack became Protestant and the miraculous hosts were burnt by Joachim Ellefeld, an Evangelical preacher.

E. Breest, 'Das Wunderblut von Wilsnack, 1383–1552. Quellenmässige Darstellung seiner Geschichte', *Märkische Forschungen*, 16 (1881), pp. 193–248. B. Hennig, 'Kurfürst Friedrich II und das Wunderblut zu Wilsnack', *Forschungen zur Brandenburgischen und Preussischen Geschichte*, 19 (pt. 2; 1906), pp. 73–104. G. Wentz in *Germania Sacra*, herausg. vom Kaiser-Wilhelm-Institut für deutsche Geschichte, 1 (pt. 2; 1933), pp. 116–19, with full bibl. pp. 7 f. G. Kawerau in *PRE* 21 (1908), pp. 346–50, s.v.

Wilson, Daniel (1778–1858), Bp. of Calcutta. The son of a wealthy silk-merchant, whom he was expected to succeed in the business, he was ordained in 1801. In 1807 he became Vice-Principal of St Edmund Hall, Oxford. He resigned in 1812 to succeed Richard Cecil, by whom he had been much influenced, as minister of St John's, Bedford Row, in London. This chapel, now demolished, was a stronghold of *Evangelicalism. Its congregation included W. *Wilberforce and other members of the *Clapham Sect, and Wilson became the leading Evangelical clergyman in the capital. In 1824 he was appointed vicar of Islington, the living being in the gift of his family. Here he introduced an early celebration of the Holy Communion to supplement that at midday, founded the annual Islington Clerical Conference (1827), and the *Lord's Day Observance Society (1831). In 1832, at the age of 54, he accepted the bishopric of Calcutta, which extended over the entire presidency of Bengal and gave him some authority over the sees of Bombay and Madras; he had the title of Metropolitan but not Archbishop. He established his authority in *India, improved the provision of churches and chaplains for stations and regiments as well as improving the schools, excluded the caste system from the churches of southern India, and devoted much of his fortune and energies to the building of St Paul's cathedral in Calcutta (consecrated in 1847). Even in India he made known his criticism of the *Tractarians.

Bishop Wilson's Journal Letters, addressed to his family, during the first nine years of his Indian episcopate, ed. by his son, D. Wilson (1863). J. Bateman (son-in-law), *The Life of the Right Rev. Daniel Wilson, D.D., late Lord Bishop of Calcutta and Metropolitan of India* (2 vols., 1860). E. Stock, *The History of the Church Missionary Society*, esp. 1 (1899), pp. 290–332; 2 (1899), pp. 156–225. M. L. Loane, *Oxford and the Evangelical Succession* (1950), pp. 247–96. T. Seccombe in *DNB* 62 (1900), pp. 87–9.

Wilson, Thomas (1663–1755), Bp. of *Sodor and Man. Born at Burton, Cheshire, he was educated at Trinity College, *Dublin, for the medical profession. After ordination as deacon in 1686, he became curate to his uncle at Newchurch Kenyon, Cheshire (1687), and chaplain to the 9th Earl of Derby (1692). In 1697, after refusing a valuable plurality, he was persuaded by the Earl of Derby to accept the see of Sodor and Man. He was consecrated in 1698, installed in St German's cathedral, Peel, and, taking up his residence at Kirkmichael, held the bishopric for the rest of his long life. He promptly set himself to raise the standards of spiritual life and pastoral efficiency in the island, and was also active as church-builder, farmer, and founder of public libraries under the scheme of T. *Bray. Following his own high estimate of episcopal authority, and the freedom of the Manx Church from Acts of the English Parliament, he enforced Church discipline by his Ecclesiastical Constitutions of 1704, which inflicted public penance for slander, perjury, immorality, and other offences. This drew him into acrimonious legal disputes, notably during the governorship of Alexander Horne (1713–23), on whose wife Wilson had imposed penance for slander. In 1722 he suspended his archdeacon, R. Horrobin, for heresy, and on Horrobin's appeal to the governor Wilson was convicted and imprisoned for a time. When in 1724 the case was finally decided in his favour, Wilson was offered, but declined, the see of *Exeter in compensation. Theologically he had many affinities with the *Nonjurors. His devotional writings, esp. his *Sacra Privata* (posthumous, ed. C. Cruttwell, 1781), long enjoyed a wide circulation; and his *Principles and Duties of Christianity* (projected 1699, first printed 1707; 'the Manx Catechism') was the first book printed in Manx. Many of his sermons were also published.

He was commemorated in the Isle of Man by the 'Bishop Wilson Theological College' (closed, 1943) at Kirkmichael.

Works ed. C. Cruttwell (2 vols., London, 1781), with Life by id., vol. 1, pp. iii–xcvi; also in LACT (7 vols. bound in 8, 1847–63), with Life by J. *Keble, vol. 1 (pts. 1 and 2). H. Stowell, *The Life of . . . Thomas Wilson* (1819). A. B. Ziegler, *Thomas Wilson, Bischof von Sodor und Man, 1663–1755* (Seges. Philologische und literarische Studien und Texte herausgegeben von der Philosophischen Fakultät der Universität Freiburg Schweiz, 15; 1972). A. Gordon in *DNB* 62 (1900), pp. 248–51.

Winchelsea, Robert of (*c*.1245–1313), theologian and Abp. of *Canterbury. He studied arts at *Paris, becoming Master and, in 1267, Rector of the faculty, before returning to England in the mid-1270s to study theology at *Oxford. He was at the time rector of Wood Eaton and canon of *Lincoln. After a further period overseas from 1278, he incepted as Master and by 1288 was Regent-Master in theology and Chancellor of the University. He was then already Archdeacon of Essex, and from *c*.1290 he was resident at *St Paul's. His theological teaching, which was primarily concerned with the doctrine of the *Trinity, survives in a series of *quaestiones disputatae*, some of which were delivered at St Paul's, and two *quodlibeta*. Although a secular doctor, he was strongly influenced by the teaching of St *Thomas Aquinas and must have been involved in the disputes over the latter's doctrine which affected the University of Oxford in the 1280s. On 13 Feb. 1293 he was elected Abp. of Canterbury, but he returned from Rome only in Jan. 1295 after a lengthy papal vacancy. As Archbishop he was a determined upholder of ecclesiastical rights, reacting against the increasing control over the Church by royal government. He soon became involved in a struggle with Edward I, chiefly on the subject of taxation of the clergy in times of urgent *necessitas* or defence of the realm; he made vigorous use of *Boniface VIII's bull '*Clericis laicos' in order to defend the right of the English clergy to consent to clerical taxation for wars in Scotland, Gascony, and Flanders. His refusal to contribute towards the expenses of the French wars led to the temporary confiscation of his property in 1297, but his opposition bore fruit between 1297 and 1301, not least in helping the magnates to secure the King's Confirmation of Magna Carta and the Forest Charter. His strong hostility to the King's treasurer, Walter Langton, Bp. of *Lichfield, caused further deterioration in his relations with Edward, and the

King was able to take his revenge after the election of Bertrand Got, Abp. of Bordeaux and a former royal clerk, as *Clement V in 1305. Taking advantage of improved relations with the Papal court and of Clement's revocation of 'Clericis laicos' and his annulment of the Confirmation of Magna Carta, the King secured Winchelsea's suspension from Canterbury in 1306. It was only Edward I's death in 1307 that brought him back to his see at the request of Edward II, but he soon found himself again in opposition to both King and Pope and in association with baronial grievances in the Ordinances of 1311. In the tradition of Stephen *Langton and Robert *Grosseteste rather than of St Thomas *Becket, Winchelsea was assiduous in the pursuit of his pastoral duties, a generous almsgiver, and, despite serious ill-health in the last six years of his life, a zealous administrator of his diocese. Attempts were made to secure his canonization in 1319–21 and in 1327, but without success.

Registrum Roberti Winchelsey, Archiepiscopi Cantuariensis, ed. R. Graham (*Canterbury and York Society, 51–52; 1942–56). A. G. Little and F. Pelster, SJ, *Oxford Theology and Theologians* c. A.D. *1282–1302* (OHS 96; 1934), esp. pp. 122 f. and 137–45. C. Smith, OSB, 'Some Aspects of the Scholastic Career of Archbishop Winchelsey', *Dominican Studies*, 6 (1953), pp. 101–26. J. H. Denton, *Robert Winchelsey and the Crown 1294–1313* (Cambridge Studies in Medieval Life and Thought, 3rd ser. 14; 1980). P. Glorieux in *DTC* 15 (pt. 2; 1950), col. 3553, s.v., for refs. to MS sources. *BRUO* 3 (1959), pp. 2057–9, s.v., with further refs.

Winchester. Apart from legends of no authority, the history of Christianity in Winchester begins with the foundation by King Cenwealh of Wessex *c*.648 of a church dedicated to St *Peter and St *Paul and probably designed to serve a royal residence. A bishop, Wine, was first appointed in 660, possibly when the bishopric of Wessex was transferred thither from *Dorchester, Oxon. The association of the former Roman city with the kings of Wessex, and its refoundation by King *Alfred (871–99), coupled with the fame of St *Swithun (Bp. 852–62), assisted the growth in power of the see. St *Ethelwold (Bp. 963–84) replaced the secular canons, who had formerly ruled the cathedral, by *Benedictine monks, under a prior, with the bishop as titular abbot. He and his successor, St *Alphege (Bp. 984–1006), rebuilt the cathedral on a vast scale, with rededications in 980 and 993–4. Excavations in 1962–70 revealed the plan of successive stages of the Anglo-Saxon cathedral, including the place where St Swithun was prob. originally buried. New Minster, founded by Edward the Elder (King of Wessex, 899–924) in 901–3, and Nunnaminster, founded by Alfred's wife, Ealhswith, before 902, formed with the cathedral (Old Minster) the greatest ecclesiastical group in Anglo-Saxon England, an artistic, literary, and monastic centre without later parallel in the country. A century later the cathedral was wholly rebuilt in the Norman style by Walkelin (Bp. 1070–98) on an adjacent site. Of this building the transepts survive, but the remainder was gradually transformed from Norman to Gothic. *Henry of Blois (Bp. 1129–71), the brother of King Stephen, made valuable gifts of ornaments and furnishings to the cathedral and brought from the site of the Old Minster the remains of Saxon kings and bishops now in the mortuary-chests round the presbytery; he erected six episcopal residences, incl. Wolvesey Palace and Farnham Castle, which Henry II made indefensible, but which were subsequently rebuilt and later again restored by George *Morley (Bp. 1662–84); and he founded the Hospital of St Cross, the best extant example of a medieval almshouse. Godfrey de Lucy (Bp. 1189–1204) and his successor, Peter des Roches (Bp. 1205–38), built the retrochoir and Lady chapel of the cathedral in Early English style (much altered later). The W. front and perpendicular nave were the work of William Edington (Bp. 1346–66) and *William of Wykeham (Bp. 1367–1404), who also founded the college (charter, 1382; formal entry of warden and scholars, 1394). They and their successors were commemorated by a series of splendid *chantry chapels in the nave and near the shrine of St Swithun in the retrochoir. The magnificent stone screen was prob. completed by 1476. At the *Dissolution (1539) William Kingsmill, the last prior, became the first Dean of the new foundation.

The see of Winchester ranks fifth among the English bishoprics (after *Canterbury, *York, London, and *Durham) and the bishop always has a seat in the House of Lords (irrespective of his seniority). He is also Prelate of the Order of the Garter and Provincial Chancellor of Canterbury. Among later Bps. of Winchester of note are Henry *Beaufort (1404–47), *William of Waynflete (1447–86), Richard *Foxe (1501–28), T. *Wolsey (1529–30), S. *Gardiner (1531–51 and 1553–5), L. *Andrewes (1619–26), B. *Duppa (1660–2), G. Morley (1662–84), B. *Hoadly (1734–61), C. R. *Sumner (1827–69), S. *Wilberforce (1869–73), R. T. *Davidson (1895–1903), H. E. *Ryle (1903–11), E. S. *Talbot (1911–23), C. F. Garbett (1932–42), and A. T. P. Williams (1952–61). A Papal bull of 1500 transferring the *Channel Islands from the diocese of Coutances (in France) to Winchester was ineffective, and it was only on the orders of Queen *Elizabeth I in 1568–9 that they were united with the rest of the diocese. This was reduced in size in 1877, when the parliamentary divisions of East and Mid Surrey were separated from Winchester and joined to *Rochester, and much more drastically when the new sees of Guildford and Portsmouth were created in 1927. It now comprises most of Hants (except the SE and the Isle of Wight), a small part of Dorset, and the Channel Islands.

The Episcopal Registers of John de Pontois [Bp. 1282–1304], ed. C. Deedes (Canterbury and York Society, 19 and 30; 1915–24); Henry Woodlock [Bp. 1305–16], ed. A. W. Goodman (ibid. 43–4; 1940–41); John Sandale [Bp. 1316–19] and Rigaud of Assier [Bp. 1320–23], ed. F. J. Baigent (Hampshire Record Society [8]; 1897); William Edington [Bp. 1346–66], ed. S. F. Hockey, OSB (Hampshire Record Series, 7–8; 1986–7); William of Wykeham [Bp. 1367–1404], ed. T. F. Kirby (Hampshire Record Society, 11 and 13; 1896–9); Thomas Wolsey [Bp. 1529–30], ed. F. T. Madge and H. Chitty (Canterbury and York Society, 32; 1926); Stephen Gardiner [Bp. 1531–51 and 1553–5] and John Ponet [Bp. 1551–3], ed. H. Chitty and H. E. Malden (ibid. 37; 1930); and John White [Bp. 1556–9], with prefatory note by W. H. *Frere (ibid. 16; 1914). The Pipe Roll of the Bishopric of Winchester for the Fourth Year of the Pontificate of Peter des Roches, 1208–1209, ed. under the supervision of H. Hall (Studies in Economics and Political Science, ed. W. A. S. Hewins; 1903); N. R. Holt (ed.), The Pipe Roll of the Bishopric of Winchester 1210–1211 (Manchester [1964]). G. W. Kitchin and F. T. Madge (eds.), Documents Relating to the Foundation of the Chapter of Winchester A.D. 1541–1547 (Hampshire Record Society [1]; 1889); W. R. W. Stephens and F. T. Madge (eds.), Documents Relating to

the History of the Cathedral Church of Winchester in the Seventeenth Century (ibid. [10]; 1897). A. W. Goodman (ed. into Eng.), Chartulary of Winchester Cathedral (Winchester, 1927); id. and W. H. *Hutton (eds.), The Statutes Governing the Cathedral Church of Winchester given by King Charles I (Oxford, 1925). G. W. Kitchin (ed.), Compotus Rolls of the Obedientiaries of St Swithun's Priory, Winchester (Hampshire Record Society [5]; 1892). W. de Gray Birch (ed.), Liber Vitae: Register and Martyrology of New Minster and Hyde Abbey, Winchester (ibid. [6]; 1892). W. *Dugdale, *Monasticon Anglicanum, esp. 1 (1817 edn.), pp. 189–218. S. Gale, The History and Antiquities of the Cathedral Church of Winchester (1715); J. Milner, The History Civil and Ecclesiastical and Survey of the Antiquities of Winchester (2 vols. bound in one [1798]), esp. 2, pp. 11–157; J. Britton, The History and Antiquities of the See and Cathedral Church of Winchester (1817). F. Barlow and others, Winchester in the Early Middle Ages: An Edition and Discussion of the Winton Domesday (Winchester Studies, 1; Oxford, 1976); D. Keene, Survey of Medieval Winchester (ibid. 2; 2 vols., 1985); M. Biddle, Object and Economy in Medieval Winchester (ibid. 7. 2; 2 vols., 1990). Id., 'The Study of Winchester: Archaeology and History in a British Town, 1961–1983', Proceedings of the British Academy, 69 (1983), pp. 93–135, with bibl. Id., 'Winchester: The Rise of an Early Capital', in B. Ford (ed.), The Cambridge Guide to the Arts in Britain, 1 (Cambridge, 1988), pp. 195–205, with bibl. pp. 289 f. S. H. Cassan, The Lives of the Bishops of Winchester from Birinus, the first Bishop of the West Saxons, to the Present Time (2 vols., 1827). R. Willis, 'The Architectural History of Winchester Cathedral', Proceedings of the Annual Meeting of the Archaeological Institute of Great Britain and Ireland at Winchester, September, MDCCCXLV (1846), no. 2. J. Vaughan, Winchester Cathedral: Its Monuments and Muniments [c.1919]. J. Crook (ed.), Winchester Cathedral: Nine Hundred Years 1093–1993 (Winchester and Chichester, 1993). R. N. Quirk, 'Winchester Cathedral in the Tenth Century', Archaeological Journal, 114 (1957), pp. 28–68. Medieval Art and Architecture at Winchester Cathedral (British Archaeological Association Conference Transactions for the Year 1980; 1983). C. W. C. Oman in DECH (1912), pp. 643–7, s.v. There are also numerous arts. in the Papers and Proceedings of the Hampshire Field Club (Southampton, 1885–1955; Winchester, 1956 ff.) and the Winchester Cathedral Record (Winchester, 1932 ff.).

Windesheim, near Zwolle, in the Netherlands. Here a house of *Augustinian Canons was established in 1387 under the direction of *Florentius Radewijns by six of G. *Groote's disciples who had received their religious formation at Eemstein, a foundation of the community of Jan van *Ruysbroeck (q.v.). Their constitutions were approved by Boniface IX in 1395, and under their second great prior, Johannes Vos (1391–1424), they formed, with three other Dutch monasteries, the 'Congregation of Windesheim'. They were joined in 1413 by the seven houses of the Groenendael Congregation, and in 1430 by the Congregation of Neuss. Throughout the 15th cent. the congregation grew rapidly, esp. in the Netherlands, W. and N. Germany, and Switzerland. Their fervent aspirations to religious perfection, notably under the saintly priors J. *Busch (d. c.1480) and Johannes Mauburnus ('John of Brussels', d. 1501), became an example to many other communities.

The Canons of Windesheim were the chief monastic representatives of the '*Devotio Moderna' (q.v.). Their influence also reached out to the secular clergy and the laity, whom they exhorted to frequent Communion and veneration of the Blessed Sacrament. They included many fine scholars, copyists, and illuminators, and among their members were *Thomas à Kempis, the probable author of the *Imitation of Christ*, and the *scholastic philosopher G. *Biel. In the 16th cent. the Congregation suffered great losses and all the Dutch houses were destroyed, Windesheim itself in 1581. It was reorganized under a Prior General in 1573 and continued to exist in Belgium and the Catholic parts of Germany until the secularization of the monasteries in 1802.

Statuta Capituli Windesemensis ([Windesheim], 1508); *Ordinarius Divini Officii pro Ordine Canonicorum Regularium Capituli sive Congregationis Wyndesemensis* (Deventer, 1521); *Regula Beati Augustini Episcopi cum Constitutionibus Canonicorum Regularium Capituli Windesemensis* (Utrecht, 1553); *Acta Capituli Windeshemensis* [1387–1611], ed. S. van der Woude (Kerkhistorische Studien, 6; The Hague, 1953), with detailed bibl. refs. J. Busch, *Chronicon Windesemense*, ed. H. Rosweyde, SJ, Antwerp, 1621; also ed. K. Grube, *Geschichtsquellen der Provinz Sachsen und angrenzender Gebiete*, 19 (1886), pp. 1–375. J. G. R. Acquoy, *Het Klooster te Windesheim en zijn Invloed* (3 vols., Utrecht, 1875–80). J. Andriessen and others (eds.), *Geert Grote & Moderne Devotie: Voordrachten gehouden tijdens het Geert Grote congres, Nijmegen 22–27 september 1984* (Ons Geestelijk Erf, Middeleeuwse Studies, 1; Nijmegen, 1985), esp. section 4: 'Materiële cultuur en dagelijks leven in de frater- en zusterhuizen en de Windesheimse kloosters', pp. 299–343. W. Kohl and others (ed.), *Monasticon Windeshemense* (Archives et Bibliothèques de Belgique, Numéro spécial, 16; 4 vols., Brussels, 1976–84). R. T. M. van Dijk, O.Cist., in *Dict. Sp.* 16 (1994), cols. 1457–78, s.v. See also bibl. to BRETHREN OF THE COMMON LIFE and DEVOTIO MODERNA.

Windisch, Hans (1881–1935), NT scholar. He became a Privatdozent at Leipzig in 1908. Later he held professorships at *Leiden (1914–29), Kiel (1929–35), and Halle (1935). He was an adherent of the *Religionsgeschichtliche Schule. Among his writings were *Taufe und Sünde im ältesten Christentum bis auf Origenes* (1908); *Der Sinn der Bergpredigt* (1929; Eng. tr., 1951), and comm. on the Catholic Epistles (Hb. NT, 1911; 2nd edn., 1930) and Heb. (ibid., 1913; 2nd edn., 1931), and on 2 Cor. (KEK, 1924).

K. Prümm, SJ, 'Zur Früh- und Spätform der religionsgeschichtlichen Christusdeutung von H. Windisch', *Biblica*, 42 (1961), pp. 391–422, and 43 (1962), pp. 22–56.

Windsor, St George's Chapel. The 'Royal Free Chapel of Windsor', constituted by Edward III to take charge of the shrine of the Order of the Garter (founded *c*.1348), received its statutes from William Edington, Bp. of *Winchester (1346–66), on 30 Nov. 1352. Originally it was designed to consist of a warden (later 'Dean'), 12 canons, 13 vicars, 4 clerks, 6 choristers, 24 poor knights, and a virger; but the ideal was never fully realized. The present fine perpendicular chapel, with its elaborate stone vaulting, dates from 1475–1508. In 1840 the canons were reduced to four (later for a time to three), while the minor canons, as the vicars came to be called, have also been gradually reduced to three. The chapter is under the direct jurisdiction of the Sovereign, which is exercised through the Lord Chancellor. Until the Confirmation of Marriages Act 1822, the Dean possessed the right of granting faculties for marriage licences and for proving wills.

W. H. St J. Hope, *Windsor Castle: An Architectural Survey*, 2 (1913), pp. 375–477. S. L. Ollard, *Fasti Wyndesorienses: The Deans and Canons of Windsor* (Historical Monographs relating to St George's Chapel, ed. S. L. Ollard; 1950); E. H. Fellowes, *The Vicars or Minor Canons of His Majesty's Free Chapel of St George in Windsor Castle* (ibid. [1945]); id., *Organists and Masters of the Choristers of St George's Chapel in Windsor Castle* (ibid. [1939]). E. A. Jones, *The Plate of St George's Chapel, Windsor Castle* (ibid., 1939); M. F. Bond, *The Inventories of St George's Chapel, Windsor Castle, 1384–1667* (ibid., 1947); A. K. B. Roberts, *St George's Chapel, Windsor Castle, 1348–1416: A Study in early Collegiate Administration* (London thesis, ibid. [1947]); J. N. Dalton (ed.), *The Manuscripts of St George's Chapel, Windsor*, posthumously pub. by M. F. Bond (ibid., 1957); S. M. Bond (ed.), *The Monuments of St George's Chapel, Windsor Castle* (ibid., 1958); id. (ed.), *The Chapter Acts of the Dean and Canons of Windsor, 1430, 1523–1672* (ibid., 1966), and other volumes in this series. H. W. Blackburne and M. F. Bond, *The Romance of St George's Chapel, Windsor Castle* (1933). W. St J. Hope in *VCH*, Berks, 3, ed. W. Page, P. H. Ditchfield, and J. H. Cope (1923), pp. 36–41. S. L. Ollard in *DECH* (3rd edn., 1948), pp. 667–9, s.v.

Windthorst, Ludwig (1812–91), German Catholic politician. The descendant of a well-known Hanoverian family, he studied law at Göttingen and Heidelberg and settled as a lawyer at Osnabrück in 1836. In 1848 he became Councillor at the Hanoverian supreme Court of Appeal at Celle, and in 1849 entered on a political career, twice becoming Minister of Justice (1851–3 and 1862–5). Having acquiesced in the enforced union of Hanover with Prussia in 1866, he became a member of the N. German Diet in 1867 and later of the German Reichstag. In 1871 he helped to found the *Centre Party, whose leader he remained till his death. The growth of the party, which was constantly harassed by the bitter opposition of O. von Bismarck, was due chiefly to his devotion and initiative. He played a prominent part in the *Kulturkampf, and, after Bismarck's change of policy, was reconciled to the Chancellor in 1879. He had a considerable share in the negotiations for the repeal of the *May Laws, and, after Bismarck's retirement (1888), his relations with the new Emperor, William II, became very friendly. His last political success was the defeat of the School Bill in 1891.

Ausgewählte Reden (3 vols., Osnabrück, 1901–2). There is much primary material in K. Bachem, *Vorgeschichte, Geschichte und Politik der Deutschen Zentrumspartei*, 2–9 (1927–32). M. L. Anderson, *Windthorst: A Political Biography* (Oxford, 1981), with bibl. Later short study by H.-G. Aschoff (Hanover, 1991).

wine. Wine is frequently mentioned in the Bible and appears to have been in everyday use in Palestine in NT times. The vine figures in the Lord's teaching (e.g. Jn. 15: 1) and the miracle of the turning of water into wine at Cana (Jn. 2: 1–11) has been taken to foreshadow the use of wine in the *Eucharist. Apart from certain ascetic sects who used water (see AQUARIANS), wine has traditionally been held to be one of the essential materials for a valid Eucharist, though some have argued that unfermented grape-juice fulfils the Dominical command. The words of administration in the Eucharist imply that the consecrated wine conveys to the communicant the Blood of Christ, but RC theologians have held that both the Body and the Blood are present in each of the Eucharistic species (see CONCOMITANCE and COMMUNION IN BOTH KINDS).

From the earliest period it has been the custom to mix water with the wine in the Eucharist; it is taken for granted by *Justin, *Irenaeus, and *Hippolytus, while by the time of *Cyprian a mystical meaning was given to the practice. The only important exception is furnished by the *Armenians, whose practice was condemned by the

*Trullan Synod. In the C of E the admixture was not ordered after 1549, though its use was known in the 17th cent. and was generally revived in the 19th. It was sanctioned by the *Judicial Committee of the Privy Council in 1892, and referred to by the proposed Prayer Book of 1928 as 'an ancient tradition of the Church'. See also MIXED CHALICE.

Provided that the wine is wholesome, its colour has always been held a matter of indifference, though white has been favoured since the 16th cent., when *purificators became common.

A conscientious abstinence from wine has led to the use of grape-juice by *Nonconformists, a use earlier sanctioned by W. *Durandus in his *Rationale*. The matter has sometimes been an issue in ecumenical discussions, e.g. the *Anglican–Methodist Conversations.

V. Zapletal, OP, *Der Wein in der Bibel* (Biblische Studien, 20, Heft 1; 1920). P. Lebeau, SJ, *Le Vin Nouveau du Royaume: Étude exégétique et patristique sur la Parole eschatologique de Jésus à la Cène* (Museum Lessianum, Section Biblique, 5; 1966), with bibl. A. *Harnack, *Brod und Wasser: Die eucharistischen Elemente bei Justin* (TU 7, Heft 2, 1891, pp. 115–44). A. Scheiwiler, *Die Elemente der Eucharistie in den ersten drei Jahrhunderten* (Forschungen zur Christlichen Literatur- und Dogmengeschichte, 3, Heft 4; 1903). J. J. Farraher and T. D. Terry, 'Altar Wine', *American Ecclesiastical Review*, 146 (1962), pp. 73–88. See also works cited s.v. AQUARIANS and EUCHARIST.

Winer, Johann Georg Benedikt (1789–1858), German theologian. From 1832 he was professor of theology at Leipzig. His celebrity rests on his NT Greek grammar (*Grammatik des neutestamentlichen Sprachidioms*), first pub. in 1822. It went through a large number of editions, and was several times translated into English, e.g. by W. F. *Moulton (1870). Its elaborate collection of material is still valuable, though Winer's conclusions have been largely invalidated by increased knowledge of Hellenistic Greek.

G. Lechler in *PRE* (3rd edn.), 21 (1908), pp. 368–71, s.v.

Winfrid or **Winfrith, St.** See BONIFACE, ST.

Winifred, St (d. *c*.650), in Welsh 'Gwenfrewi', the patron saint of N. Wales. Acc. to legends (late and not worthy of credence) she was a maiden of great beauty and attainments, who was sought in marriage by the Prince Caradog of Hawarden. For refusing his advances, she was wounded (or killed) by him, but miraculously healed (or restored to life) by her uncle, St *Beuno. A spring marked the scene, at the present Holywell (Welsh, 'Tre Ffynnon') in Flintshire, and here Winifred established a nunnery of which she became abbess. In 1138 her relics were translated to Shrewsbury and in 1398 her feast was ordered to be observed throughout the province of *Canterbury. Holywell, for many centuries a famous place of pilgrimage, has continued to attract sufferers down to modern times; Dr S. *Johnson saw people bathing there on 3 Aug. 1774. Feast day, 3 Nov.

The principal sources incl. a Life preserved principally in the Brit. Lib., Cott. MS Claud. A. v, attributed to Elerius, a monk, in the year 660 (actually *c*. 12th cent.), pr. in W. J. Rees, *Lives of the Cambro-British Saints* (pub. for the Welsh MSS Society, 1853), pp. 198–209, and a Life by Robert, prior of Shrewsbury, principally preserved in the Bodleian MS Laud. Misc. 114, saec. XII (*c*.1139); they are both pr. in *AASS*, Nov. 1 (1887), pp. 702–8

and 708–31 respectively, with introd. and other material, pp. 691–701 and 732–59. Eng. tr. of Life attributed to Elerius, with abridgment of Life by Robert of Shrewsbury, by J. Dalton (London, 1857). Collection of later material, mainly in Eng., ed. C. de Smedt, SJ, in *Anal. Boll.* 6 (1887), pp. 305–52. Life by Philip Metcalfe, SJ (no place, 1712; modern edn. by H. Thurston, SJ, London, 1917).

Wipo (d. after 1046), poet and royal biographer. Apparently a native of the Swabian part of the kingdom of Burgundy, he became priest and chaplain to the Emps. Conrad II and Henry III. He wrote much verse, the greater part of which has been lost. There survive a 'Tetralogus' (completed 1041), a eulogy of Henry III; his 'Proverbs', a series of maxims written for Henry after his royal coronation in 1028; and, best known, the '*Victimae paschali laudes', the *Sequence for Easter Day. His 'Gesta Chuonradi Imperatoris', written between 1040 and 1046, is one of the principal sources for the reign of Conrad II (1024–39).

Crit. edn. of his works by H. Bresslau (Scriptores Rerum Germanicarum in usum Scholarum, Hanover and Leipzig, 1915), with introd. and refs. 'Gesta Chuonradi' rev., with Ger. tr. and introd., by W. Trillmich in id. and R. Buchner (eds.), *Quellen des 9. und 11. Jahrhunderts zur Geschichte der Hamburgischen Kirche und des Reiches* (1961), pp. 507–613. Eng. tr. in T. E. Mommsen and K. F. Morrison, *Imperial Lives and Letters of the Eleventh Century* (Records of Civilization, Sources and Studies, 67; 1962), pp. 52–100. R. Holtzmann, 'Wipo und die schwäbische Weltchronik', *NA* 35 (1910), pp. 55–104. Raby, pp. 217–19; J. Szövérffy, *Die Annalen der Lateinischen Hymnendichtung*, 1 (1964), pp. 372–4.

wisdom. In the OT wisdom, whether human or divine, occupies a prominent place. Fundamental to the OT teaching about human wisdom is the repeated affirmation that 'the fear of the Lord is the beginning of wisdom' (e.g. Ps. 111: 10 and Prov. 1: 7). Human wisdom is both essentially practical and speculative, and the terms 'wisdom' and 'wise' are used to cover a diversity of activities ranging from ability as a carpenter (Exod. 36: 4) to the fundamental principles of virtuous living (Ecclus. 1: 10–12). Similarly, divine wisdom is manifested in creation and in God's guidance of nations and individuals (Wisd. 10–19). It is more than a mere quality and tends increasingly to become a *hypostasis, so esp. in Prov. 8 and Wisd. 7: 22 ff. The so-called 'Wisdom Literature' is generally reckoned to include Job, Prov., Eccles., Ecclus., and Wisdom (qq.v.). Such literature is found in all ancient Near Eastern cultures, and the combination of practical advice on sensible living with speculation about divine wisdom is characteristic of the genre, as is the attribution of wisdom to an ancient ruler (in the OT usually *Solomon, but in later times often *Ezra or *Enoch).

In the NT Christ is portrayed as a teacher of wisdom and endowed with the Spirit (Mk. 1: 10, Lk. 4: 18); St *Paul calls Him 'the wisdom of God' (1 Cor. 1: 24), 'in whom are all the treasures of wisdom and knowledge hidden' (Col. 2: 3). Traditions of personified wisdom are echoed in the Christ hymn of Col. 1: 15–20, the Johannine prologue, and Heb. 1: 3, and the OT view of wisdom as a gift of the Spirit (Is. 11: 2) is found at 1 Cor. 12: 8. Among the Fathers most use 'Wisdom' as a synonym for the Incarnate Word or *Logos, but some (e.g. *Theophilus of

Antioch and *Irenaeus) equate 'Wisdom' with the Third Person of the Trinity. In *Gnostic thought, which saw in Wisdom a Divine emanation and a cause of the creation and redemption of the world, the conception played an important part, and was understood in various systems as the spouse of the Logos, the mother of the Demiurge, etc.

In modern times Wisdom has again become a subject of speculation in connection with the Deity in the thought of Russian authors such as V. *Solovyov and S. *Bulgakov. These authors distinguish a created from an uncreated wisdom, which together form the unity of God and the world, and which, in their teaching, is closely connected with the Platonic World-soul, the *Theotokos, and the Holy Spirit. It also plays a major role in *Feminist Theology.

H. H. Schmid, *Wesen und Geschichte der Weisheit: Eine Untersuchung zur altorientalischen und israelitischen Weisheitsliteratur* (Beihefte zur *ZNTW*, 101; 1966). G. von *Rad, *Weisheit in Israel* (Neukirchen, 1970; Eng. tr., 1972); J. L. Crenshaw, *Old Testament Wisdom* (Atlanta [1981]; London, 1982); J. Blenkinsopp, *Wisdom and Law in the Old Testament* (Oxford, 1983). E. Schüssler Fiorenza, *Jesus: Miriam's Child, Sophia's Prophet. Critical Issues in Feminist Christology* (1995). U. Wilckens and G. Fohrer in *TWNT* 7 (1964), pp. 465–529 (Eng. tr., 7, 1971, pp. 465–526), s.v. σοφία.

Wisdom of Solomon. One of the *Apocryphal Books of the OT. Though it has been variously divided, it may conveniently be considered in three parts. The opening chapters (1: 1–6: 8) describe the different destinies awaiting the righteous and the wicked. In opposition to the 'ungodly', who maintain that, since this life is all, the only sensible course is to live for pleasure, the writer maintains that the righteous will be rewarded by a blessed immortality, while the ungodly will certainly be punished. Some scholars regard this section as a reply to Eccles. (cf. Wisd. 2. 1–10 and Eccles. 1: 11, 3: 19–22, and 9: 7–9). The second part (6: 9–9: 18) contains the meditation on Wisdom which has given the Book its name. Wisdom is 'the breath of the power of God, and a pure influence flowing from the glory of the Almighty' (7: 25), and she comes forth from God to dwell among men that she may make those who receive her 'friends of God, and prophets' (7: 27); and the section ends with *Solomon's prayer for Wisdom (9). The last part of the Book (10–19) gives a review of Israel's history down to the *Exodus, interrupted in 13–15 by a description of the origin and evils of idolatry. The good fortune of Israel's forefathers and the disasters overtaking their enemies, attributed in 10 to the activity of Wisdom, are used to illustrate the theories that 'by what things their enemies were punished, by the same things they in need were benefited' (11: 5), and that 'that wherewithal a man sinneth, by the same also shall he be punished'.

The ascription of the Book to Solomon (already questioned in the early Church) is now generally regarded as a literary device. The Book shows the blending of Jewish religion and Greek philosophy characteristic of *Alexandrian theology and was almost certainly written by an Alexandrian Jew. It was written at a time when traditional Judaism was under attack (2: 12, 19 f.), and 14: 16–17 seems to show knowledge of Emperor worship. Most scholars date the Book in the Ptolemaic period, either in the 1st or 2nd cent. BC; recent attempts to date it in the

1st cent. AD have not been widely accepted. The unity of the Book has been challenged by some critics, but is defended by most commentators, though many think that the author used some already existing material (e.g., the prayer in ch. 9 and the polemic against idolatry in 13–15).

The Book has had a great influence on Christian thought. Many critics explain the undoubted resemblances to it in passages of the Pauline and deutero-Pauline Epistles (e.g. Rom. 9: 21–23, cf. Wisd. 12: 12–18; Eph. 6: 11–17, cf. Wisd. 5: 17–20) as due to direct use made of it, and there may be reminiscences of it in Heb. (e.g. 1: 3, cf. Wisd. 7: 26), Jas. (2: 6, cf. Wisd. 2: 10), 1 Pet. (1: 6 f., cf. Wisd. 3: 5 f.), and Jn. (17: 3, cf. Wisd. 15: 3). In later writers the terms used of the Divine Wisdom are freely applied to Christ and so passed into the vocabulary of Christian theology.

Modern comm. incl. those of S. Holmes in R. H. *Charles (ed.), *The Apocrypha and Pseudepigrapha of the Old Testament*, 1 (Oxford, 1913), pp. 518–68, J. von Fichtner (HAT, Reihe 2, 6; 1938), J. Reider (Jewish Apocryphal Literature, New York, 1959), E. G. Clarke (Camb. Bib., NEB, 1973), and D. Winston (Anchor Bible, 1979). P. Heinisch, *Die griechische Philosophie im Buch der Weisheit* (Alttestamentliche Abhandlungen, 1, Heft 4; 1908); C. Larcher, OP, *Études sur le Livre de la Sagesse* (Études Bibliques, 1969). J. M. Reese, OSFS, *Hellenistic Influence on the Book of Wisdom and its Consequences* (Analecta Biblica, 41; 1970). R. H. Pfeiffer, *History of New Testament Times with an Introduction to the Apocrypha* (New York [1949]; London [1954]), pp. 313–51, with bibl. p. 535. E. *Schürer, *The History of the Jewish People in the Age of Jesus Christ*, rev. Eng. tr. by G. Vermes and others, 3 (pt. 1; Edinburgh, 1986), pp. 568–79. M. Gilbert, SJ, in *Dict. Bibl.*, Suppl. 11 (1991), cols. 58–119, s.v. 'Sagesse de Salomon'; D. Winston in *Anchor Bible Dictionary*, 6 (1992), pp. 120–7, s.v. 'Solomon, Wisdom of'. See also works cited s.v. APOCRYPHA.

Wiseman, Nicholas Patrick Stephen (1802–65), English cardinal. Born in Seville, where his Irish grandfather had settled in the 18th cent., Wiseman was educated at Ushaw College, Durham, and at the English College, Rome, of which he became rector in 1828. He established a considerable reputation for learning, esp. in oriental languages, but his main interest was soon directed to the Catholic revival in England. On a visit there in 1834–5, he lectured widely on the RC faith and was one of the founders of the *Dublin Review*. In this journal he responded encouragingly to the *Tractarians and throughout his life he worked to attract converts to RCism. In 1840 he returned to England as President of Oscott College, Birmingham, and Coadjutor to Bp. Walsh, *Vicar Apostolic of the newly created Central District. In 1850 he became Pro-Vicar Apostolic of the London District, and soon presided there in his own right. When in 1850 *Pius IX restored the RC hierarchy in England and Wales, Wiseman became the first Abp. of *Westminster and was made a cardinal. His flamboyant announcement of the event contributed to the so-called '*Papal Aggression' crisis of 1850–1, but by tact he was subsequently able to allay much of the fear and suspicion that had been aroused. He was criticized by RCs as well as Protestants for his *Ultramontane views, his independent policies, and his attempts to impose Italian devotional life and practices in England. It is, however, generally acknowledged that he did much to organize and advance the cause of the RC Church in England. He presided over and framed the decrees of the first three provincial synods (1852, 1855, and 1859); he struggled to promote legislation to remove RC disabilities and encouraged RCs to support parliamentary candidates well disposed to their cause; he welcomed religious orders to the archdiocese and founded schools and orphanages; and he wrote articles, essays, sermons, and even a novel (*Fabiola; or the Church of the Catacombs*, 1854) to promote RCism and foster a genuine Catholic culture in England.

W. *Ward, *The Life and Times of Cardinal Wiseman* (2 vols., 1897). [A.] B. Fothergill, *Nicholas Wiseman* (1963); R. J. Schiefen, *Nicholas Wiseman and the Transformation of English Catholicism* (Sheperdstown, W.Va., 1984).

Wishart, George (*c*.1513–46), Scottish Reformer. The facts of his early life are obscure. Charged with heresy in 1538, he fled to England, where a similar accusation was preferred against him in 1539. After travelling on the Continent and studying for some time at Corpus Christi College, Cambridge, he returned to Scotland in 1543 and may have been the Wishart who approached the English government in 1544 with a view to the murder of Card. D. *Beaton. In 1544 he began active propaganda on behalf of Reformed doctrines, going from place to place in great danger of his life and denouncing current abuses. In this work he was assisted by J. *Knox. He was apprehended by Bothwell at Ormiston in Jan. 1546, soon afterwards transferred to Edinburgh Castle, and burnt by Beaton at St Andrews on 1 Mar. 1546. He made an English translation of the '*Helvetic Confession' which was published posthumously (prob. 1548).

The primary authorities incl. J. Knox, *History of the Reformation in Scotland* (ed. W. C. Dickinson, 2 vols., London, 1949, vol. 1, pp. 60–72), and for his trial and death, Robert Lindesay of Pitscottie (*c*.1532–*c*.1578), *Historie and Chronicles of Scotland* (ed. Æ. J. G. Mackay, Scottish Text Society, 42–43, with glossary and index, 60, 1899–1911, vol. 2, pp. 52–82, with notes, pp. 421 f.), and J. *Foxe, *Acts and Monuments* (ed. G. Townsend, 6, 1846, pp. 625–36). Notes by D. Laing appended to his edn. of *The Works of John Knox*, 1 (The Wodrow Society, 1864), pp. 534–7. C. Rogers, 'Memoir of George Wishart, the Scottish Martyr', *Transactions of the Royal Historical Society* [Original Series], 4 (1876), pp. 260–3, with his Eng. tr. of the Helvetic Confession, pp. 319–28. Æ. J. G. Mackay in *DNB* 62 (1900), pp. 248–51.

witchcraft. The alleged exercise of magical powers through the gift of supernatural beings other than God and His angels. The narrative of the witch of Endor (1 Sam. 28: 7–25) and the condemnation of witchcraft in the OT (Exod. 22: 18, Deut. 18: 10) and NT (Gal. 5: 20) have sometimes been adduced as scriptural proof of its existence. In the patristic age *Tertullian (*Apol.* 22) and St *Augustine (*De Civ. Dei*, 21. 6) believed in it. On the other hand, the belief was opposed by many of the Fathers, e.g. St *Hippolytus, St *Chrysostom, and St *Caesarius of Arles.

Before 1100 witchcraft in W. Europe consisted chiefly in the performance of certain pagan rituals divorced from their religious context, and the Church sought to minimize their importance, as when the (prob. 9th cent.) 'Canon Episcopi' denounced as illusory the claims of witches to be able to fly. In the 12th cent. learned, ritual magic, derived from Hellenistic and Arabic sources, reached the W., and the Church viewed this more seriously, con-

demning all rites which involved the invocation of spirits. Nevertheless, witches and sorcerers were arrested only if they were accused of conspiring to cause criminal damage. They were tried in bishops' courts and, if found guilty, were punished by civil magistrates in accordance with secular law. No attempt was made to seek such people out, and in 1258 Pope Alexander IV forbade the *Inquisition to deal with cases of witchcraft unless they were related to heresy. Theologians later argued that witchcraft was a form of heresy because it involved an overt or tacit pact with the *devil, and from 1398 the Inquisition was given jurisdiction over such cases. Few inquisitors sought to exercise these powers, but in 1484 two German inquisitors, Heinrich Kramer and Jacob Sprenger, meeting with obstruction from the S. German hierarchy, obtained from Pope Innocent VIII a bull giving them jurisdiction over witchcraft. There is no reason to suppose that the Pope had any central interest in this issue, or that his bull marked any new departure in Papal policy, but Kramer and Sprenger printed it at the front of their *Malleus Maleficarum* ('Hammer of Witches'), so that it appeared to give official approval to the contents of this naïve and obscurantist, but influential book, published at Speyer shortly before 5 Apr. 1487.

Although witchcraft trials steadily increased from the late 14th cent. onwards, they did not reach their height until the period between 1580 and 1630, and in countries such as *Hungary and *Poland not until the early 18th cent. Probably about 50,000 people were executed for the alleged crime but the pattern of prosecutions varied enormously, depending on the jurisdiction involved, the attitude of the local clergy and magistrates, and the willingness of the authorities in Church and State to co-ordinate witch-hunting. The so-called 'witch-craze' was not a simple or uniform historical development and it has often been exaggerated. All over Europe ordinary people were eager to denounce their female neighbours as witches in the sincere belief that they caused *maleficium* (harm). In combination with the fears of those in power, this could lead to panics, as occurred in parts of Germany. On the other hand, the territories covered by the Mediterranean Inquisition tribunals saw almost no witch-hunting and only a handful of executions. In France, in the area covered by the jurisdiction of the Parlement of Paris, appeals were made automatic in witchcraft cases in 1624 and acquittals thereafter were common. In the *Netherlands the death penalty ceased to be applied *c*.1600. In England the worst persecution occurred during the Civil War years, notably in 1645–6, when the activities of the witch-finder Matthew Hopkins led to *c*.200 executions. But for most people most of the time 'witchcraft' was a rather mundane affair—a cause of strange or unexpected illness, sudden misfortunes, and marital problems. Witch-hunting on any scale had ended everywhere by 1750 and the legislation dealing with witchcraft was repealed during this period. The last hanging for the crime in England was in 1685, the last burning in Scotland in 1727. The final legal execution took place in Switzerland in 1782.

The debates conducted in the *Malleus* continued to attract the attention of theologians, jurists, and philosophers for at least two centuries. Most accepted the reality of witchcraft, with important reservations, and gave what would then have been rational reasons for doing so. The belief was supported by a natural philosophy that allowed devils to cause physical events and by theocratic political ideologies. Above all, it was sustained by all the main Churches, who tried to extend the concept of alliance with the devil to include all the forms of religious error deemed to be 'magical' and 'superstitious'. During the 18th and 19th cents. a different set of intellectual and moral assumptions led to a dismissal of the belief in witchcraft as irrational. This did not prevent many people from continuing to fear the effects of *maleficium* and adopting measures to counteract it. The practice of benign forms of witchcraft ('Wicca') continues in the present day.

Materials Toward a History of Witchcraft collected by H. C. Lea, arranged and ed. A. C. Howland (3 vols., Philadelphia and London, 1939). The *Malleus Maleficarum* was repr., with brief introd. by A. Schnyder (Litterae. Göppinger Beiträge zur Textgeschichte, 113; Göppingen, 1991). [E.] G. [S.] Parrinder, *Witchcraft* (Harmondsworth, 1958); L. [P.] Mair, *Witchcraft* [1969]. J. Français, *L'Église et la sorcellerie* (Bibliothèque de Critique religieuse, 1910). J. B. Russell, *Witchcraft in the Middle Ages* (Ithaca, NY, and London, 1972). E. [M.] Peters, *The Magician, the Witch and the Law* (Hassocks, W. Sussex, 1978). B. Ankarloo and G. Henningsen (eds.), *Häxornas Europa 1400–1700* (Rattshistoriska Studier, 13; 1987; Eng. tr., *Early Modern Witchcraft*, New York, 1990; Oxford, 1993); B. P. Levack, *The Witch-Hunt in Early Modern Europe* (1987); G. Scarre, *Witchcraft and Magic in Sixteenth- and Seventeenth-Century Europe* (Basingstoke, 1987). G. L. Kittredge, *Witchcraft in Old and New England* (Cambridge, Mass., and London, 1928). W. Notestein, *A History of Witchcraft in England from 1558 to 1718* (Washington, DC, and London, 1911). C. L'E. Ewen (ed.), *Witch Hunting and Witch Trials: The Indictments for Witchcraft from the Records of 1373 Assizes held for the Home Circuit A.D. 1559–1736* (1929); id., *Witchcraft and Demonianism: A Concise Account derived from Sworn Depositions in the Courts of England and Wales* (1933); id., *Witchcraft in the Star Chamber* (privately pr., 1938). A collection of material on witchcraft in Elizabethan and Jacobean England ed., in modernized form, by B. Rosen, *Witchcraft* (Stratford-upon-Avon Library, 6; 1969). A. Macfarlane, *Witchcraft in Tudor and Stuart England: A Regional and Comparative Study* (1970). K. [V.] Thomas, *Religion and the Decline of Magic: Studies in popular beliefs in seventeenth century England* (1971), pp. 435–583. S. Anglo, *The Damned Art: Essays in the Literature of Witchcraft* (1977).

Witelo (b. *c*.1230), Polish mathematician and natural philosopher. A native of Silesia, he followed the arts course at the University of *Paris and later studied canon law at Padua. From there he went to the Papal court at Viterbo, where he joined a remarkable scientific circle that included *William of Moerbeke, famed for his translations of *Aristotle. Witelo's major work, the *Perspectiva*, was written (probably between 1270 and 1274) at Moerbeke's prompting and was dedicated to him. Treating of both mathematical optics and the physiological and psychological aspects of vision, it was largely based on the work of the Arabic scholar Alhazen (Ihn al-Haytham), and remained a standard text until the work of J. *Kepler. After his stay at Viterbo, Witelo probably spent the rest of his life in Poland. Only one other work by him is known to be extant, the *Epistula de primaria causa poenitentiae in hominibus et de substantia et natura daemonum*, written during his time at Padua. On some questions (e.g. prophecy and the future life) Witelo reveals the influence of *Avicenna and Algazel (al-Ghazzālī), who help to give his writings a *Neoplatonic slant. His teachings on the propagation of physical influence on the analogy of light are akin to those of R. *Grosseteste and R. *Bacon, who also may have influenced him.

The *Perspectiva* pub. Nuremberg, 1535 and 1551, and at Basle, 1572; the last was repr., with introd. by D. C. Lindberg (Sources of Science, 94; New York and London, 1972). Crit. edn., with Eng. tr. and useful introd., by S. Unguru and others (Studia Copernicana, 15, 23, 28, etc.; Wroclaw, 1977 ff.). Crit. edn. of *Epistula de primaria causa poenitentiae* by E. Paschetto, *Demoni e Prodigi: Note su alcuni scritti di Witelo e di Oresme* (Turin, 1978), pp. 81–132. C. Baeumker, *Witelo, ein Philosoph und Naturforscher des XIII. Jahrhunderts* (BGPM 3, Hett 2; 1908), incl. texts of the *Liber de intelligentiis* (pp. 1–71), which Baeumker then (erroneously) believed to be by Witelo, and of the philosophical preface and a few other passages of the *Perspectiva* (pp. 127–79). A. Birkenmajer, *Études d'Histoire des Sciences en Pologne* (Studia Copernicana, 4; Wroclaw, 1972), pp. 95–434 ('Études sur Witelo'), is fundamental. C. Baeumker, 'Zur Frage nach Abfassungszeit und Verfasser des irrtümlich Witelo zugeschriebenen Liber de Intelligentiis', *Miscellanea Francesco Ehrle*, 1 (ST 37; 1924), pp. 87–102. A. C. Crombie, *Robert Grosseteste and the Origins of Experimental Science 1100–1700* (Oxford, 1953), pp. 213–32; D. C. Lindberg, *Theories of Vision from al-Kindi to Kepler* (Chicago and London, 1976), pp. 116–21. Id. in *Dictionary of Scientific Biography*, 14 (1976), pp. 457–62.

Witnesses, the Three. See JOHANNINE COMMA.

Wittenberg, since 1922 officially known as **Lutherstadt Wittenberg,** the cradle of the *Reformation. At its university (founded, 1502; united with that of Halle, 1815) M. *Luther became professor in 1508. On 31 Oct. 1517 he affixed his Ninety-Five Theses to the door of the Schlosskirche, declaiming against the medieval doctrine of *indulgences; and at the beginning of 1522 Protestant public worship was celebrated here for the first time, in the parish church. The *Augustinian monastery in the town, where Luther lived first as a monk and later with his family, is now fitted up as a museum (Lutherhaus). Both Luther and P. *Melanchthon are buried in the Schlosskirche.

H. Junghans, *Wittenberg als Lutherstadt* (Göttingen, 1979). W. Friedensburg, *Geschichte der Universität Wittenberg* (Halle, 1917); *450 Jahre Martin-Luther-Universität, Halle-Wittenberg* (3 vols., Halle [1952–3]).

Wittenberg, Concord of (1536). An agreement reached by *Lutheran and *Zwinglian theologians in the disputed doctrine of the *Eucharist. After a preliminary conference between M. *Bucer and P. *Melanchthon at Cassel in Dec. 1534, a large and representative body of divines, including M. *Luther himself, met in May 1536 at Wittenberg, where a doctrinal statement drawn up by Melanchthon, which set forth an essentially Lutheran doctrine of the Eucharist, though without insistence on *ubiquity, was accepted. The reunion thus achieved soon collapsed, however, largely through the refusal of the Swiss Zwinglians to accept the 'Concord'.

Text pr. among P. Melanchthon's collected works ed. C. G. Bretschneider, 3 (Corpus Reformatorum, 3; Brunswick, 1836), cols. 75–7; mostly repr. in Kidd, pp. 318 f. (no. 127); Eng. tr. of most of text in D. *Stone, *A History of the Doctrine of the Holy Eucharist*, 2 (1909), pp. 46 f. M. Bucer, *Opera Omnia*, 1st ser.: *Deutsche Schriften*, 6. 1: *Wittenberger Konkordie (1536). Schriften* zur Wittenberger Konkordie (1534–1537), ed. R. Stupperich and others (Gütersloh, 1988) [23 docs., not all by Bucer, and introd. with full bibl. refs.]. E. Bizer, 'Die Wittenberger Konkordie in Oberdeutschland und der Schweiz', Archiv für Reformationsgeschichte, 36 (1939), pp. 214–52. T. Kolde in PRE (3rd edn.), 21 (1908), pp. 383–99, s.v. 'Wittenberger Konkordie'. See also works cited s.v. BUCER, M.

Wittgenstein, Ludwig (1889–1951), philosopher. Born in Vienna, with an immensely rich and cultivated family background, he took up mechanical engineering, studying in Berlin and Manchester. He then became interested in the principles of mathematics and in 1912 went to Cambridge to work with Bertrand Russell. In 1914 he returned home to join the Austrian army; he served on the Russian and then on the Italian fronts, becoming a prisoner of war. His Logisch-Philosophische Abhandlung, completed in August 1918, was published in 1921 and again, with C. K. Ogden's English translation, in 1922 under the more familiar title of Tractatus Logico-Philosophicus. Universally regarded as a philosophical classic, it concludes with the famous dictum: 'Whereof one cannot speak, thereof one must be silent'.

Thinking all philosophical problems solved, Wittgenstein trained as a teacher and worked in remote village schools in Lower Austria from 1920 to 1926. He then spent two years in Vienna, mostly engaged in supervising the building of a house for his sister. He was also being drawn back to philosophy by discussions with members of the Vienna Circle, who had founded logical positivism partly on what he considered to be a misunderstanding of his Tractatus. Early in 1929 he returned to Trinity College, Cambridge, as a research student, but he was able to submit the Tractatus and received his doctorate in June. From 1930 he lectured in the philosophy faculty in Cambridge, succeeding G. E. Moore as professor of philosophy in 1939. Having become a British subject in 1938, he worked throughout the Second World War (1939–45) as a hospital porter and laboratory assistant. In 1947 he gave up teaching to concentrate on writing. In 1949 he was found to have cancer. He continued writing copiously (in German) until a few days before his death.

Though notes that he had dictated had circulated semi-clandestinely for some years, it was only in 1953, with the posthumous publication of Philosophical Investigations (incl. Eng. tr. by G. E. M. Anscombe), that philosophers in general were able to study his later work properly. Much more of his writing has since appeared (in German, with Eng. tr.), notably such major texts as Remarks on the Foundation of Mathematics (1956; 3rd edn. rev., 1978); The Blue and Brown Books (1958; Preliminary Studies for the Philosophical Investigations), On Certainty (1969); and Culture and Value (1980; the original German had appeared in 1977 as Vermischte Bemerkungen), which contains a number of reflections on Christianity.

It has slowly become accepted that in these later writings Wittgenstein has important things to say about many of the traditional *metaphysical problems: the relationship between thought or language and the world, the nature of meaning and understanding, states of consciousness, and the will. How radically he criticized the Tractatus is much disputed. His later style of writing, though very different and equally inimitable, is just as cryptic: he never wanted his writings 'to spare other people the trouble of thinking'. His later work is perhaps best approached as a kind of 'therapy' for people who are inevitably dominated by scientific models of understanding. That he is anti-*Cartesian in his philosophy of mind is plain; but his intervention in the ancient dispute between realists and idealists, with all its ramifications, is not easy to assess.

Some philosophers of religion, seizing on his appeal to 'language-games' and 'forms of life', have developed theories that others have labelled 'Wittgensteinian fideism': namely the doctrine that only participants in religious forms of life can play the appropriate language-games, so that religion remains immune to criticism from outside. How far such views are grounded on Wittgenstein's work is disputed. His remarks on religious matters in Culture and Value are not easy to interpret. It may plausibly be argued that a certain 'fideism' is adumbrated in Lectures and Conversations on Aesthetics, Psychology and Religious Belief (1966) and Remarks on Frazer's Golden Bough (1979). It seems likely, however, that the consequences for theology of Wittgenstein's later work will become manifest only when its significance for metaphysics and epistemology has become clearer.

N. Malcolm, Wittgenstein: A Memoir, with a Biographical Sketch by G. H. von Wright (1958; 2nd edn., Oxford, 1984). Full Life by B. McGuinness (London, 1988 ff.). The very numerous works on his thought incl.: A. Kenny, Wittgenstein (1973); id., The Legacy of Wittgenstein (Oxford, 1984); W. D. Hudson, Wittgenstein and Religious Belief (1975); A. Keightly, Wittgenstein, Grammar and God (1976); P. Sherry, Religion, Truth and Language Games (1977); D. Bolton, An Approach to Wittgenstein's Philosophy (1979); B. McGuinness (ed.), Wittgenstein and his Times (Oxford, 1982); F. Kerr [OP], Theology after Wittgenstein (ibid., 1986); D. [F.] Pears, The False Prison: A Study of the Development of Wittgenstein's Philosophy (2 vols., ibid., 1987–8); R. Monk, Ludwig Wittgenstein: The Duty of Genius (1990); D. Z. Phillips, Wittgenstein and Religion (1993). G. H. von Wright in DNB, 1951–1960 (1971), pp. 1068–71, s.v.

Wolfenbüttel Fragments. The title under which G. E. *Lessing issued between 1774 and 1778 seven extracts from the long (unpub.) work in which H. S. *Reimarus (q.v.) had attacked historic Christianity. The most famous of them was the last, entitled Von dem Zwecke Jesu und seiner Jünger (1778), in which Reimarus interpreted the purpose of Christ's work, as set down in the Gospels, in terms of *eschatology. Widespread attention was again drawn to it by A. *Schweitzer's Von Reimarus zu Wrede (1906; Eng. tr., The Quest of the Historical Jesus, 1910).

For bibl. see REIMARUS, H. S.

Wolff, Christian (1679–1754), less correctly 'Wolf', German philosopher. In 1706 he became professor of mathematics and natural science at Halle, then a stronghold of *Pietism. In an attempt to systematize the principles of G. W. *Leibniz, he developed a comprehensive system of philosophy. His supreme confidence in reason offended the Pietists, who eventually persuaded Frederick William I to expel him from Halle in 1723, urging on the monarch that the spread of Wolff's teaching would be subversive of military discipline, since its determinism would justify desertion from the army. Wolff spent his exile at *Marburg. On the accession of Frederick the Great (1740), one of the new king's first acts was to recall Wolff, who re-entered Halle on 6 Dec. 1740 in triumph. Wolff's system won great popularity and was in substance that taught in most of the German universities in the latter half of the 18th cent. It also provided the background of the Critical Philosophy of I. *Kant. Wolff wrote a very long series of treatises (in form textbooks), the earlier ones in German and the later in Latin. Among the latter were a Logic (1728), an Ontology (1730), a Cosmology (1731), Psychologies (1731–4), a Natural Theology (1736–7), an Ethics (1750–3), and an Economics (1750). Together they covered nearly the whole field of speculative philosophy.

Gesammelte Werke photographically reprod. with introd. by J. École and H. W. Arndt (Hildesheim, 1962 ff.; Abteilung 3, *Materialen und Dokumente*, 1973 ff., incl. important refs.). Wolff himself assembled his *Kleine Schriften*, 6 vols., Halle, 1736–40. Autobiog. first ed. H. Wuttke, Leipzig, 1841. The 1764 edn. of Wolff's *Jus Gentium methodo scientifica pertractatum* (orig. pub. in 1749) was photographically repr., together with useful introd. by O. Nippold and Eng. tr. by J. H. Drake (2 vols., Classics of International Law, 13; Oxford, 1934). Wolff finds a place in all histories of modern German philosophy. W. Arnsperger, *Christian Wolff's Verhältnis zu Leibniz* (1897); M. Campo, *Cristiano Wolff e il Razionalismo Precritico* (Pubblicazioni dell'Università Cattolica del S. Cuore, Serie Prima: Scienze Filosofiche, 30; 2 vols., 1939); A. Bissinger, *Die Struktur der Gotteserkenntnis: Studien zur Philosophie Christian Wolffs* (Bonn, 1970); W. Schneiders (ed.), *Christian Wolff 1679–1754* (Studien zum Achtzehnten Jahrhundert, 4; Hamburg, 1983), with bibl. 1800–1982, pp. 321–45; C. Schröer, *Naturbegriff und Moralbegründung: Die Grundlegung der Ethik bei Christian Wolff und deren Kritik durch Immanuel Kant* (Münchener philosophische Studien, NF 3 [1988]); J. École, *Introduction à l'opus philosophicum de Christian Wolff* (1985 [collection of arts. orig. pub. in *Giornale di Metafisica*, 1961–83]). H. Stephan in *PRE* (3rd edn.), 21 (1908), pp. 452–64; G. Tonelli in P. Edwards (ed.), *Encyclopedia of Philosophy*, 8 (1967), pp. 340–44.

Wolfgang, St (*c*.924–94), Bp. of Ratisbon. Of Swabian descent, he was educated at the monastery of *Reichenau, taught in the cathedral school of Trier, and *c*.965 became a monk at *Einsiedeln. In 971 he set out to evangelize the Magyars. The following year he was elected Bp. of Ratisbon; he soon became an ardent reformer. His feast (31 Oct.) is widely observed in Central Europe.

The principal sources are the works of two monks of St Emmeran, Ratisbon: Arnold of Vohburg on St Emmeran, bk. 2 (written *c*.1037), and a Life of St Wolfgang by Othlo (written *c*.1052), which is more lively but less reliable; the best edn. of both these sources, with other material, and introd. and comm. by H. *Delehaye, SJ, in *AASS*, Nov. 2 (pt. 1; 1894), pp. 527–97. Festschrift to mark the 9th centenary of his death, ed. J. B. Mehler (Ratisbon, 1894). Other modern studies by I. Zibermayr (Linz, 1924; 2nd edn., Horn, 1961) and R. Zinnhobler and others (Linz, 1975). K. Bugmann, OSB, 'Der Mönch Wolfgang', *Studien und Mitteilungen zur Geschichte des Benediktiner-Ordens*, 78 (1968), pp. 9–27, with full refs. U. Schmid in *CE* 15 (1912), pp. 682 f., s.v.; K. Kunze in *Bibliotheca Sanctorum*, 12 (1969), cols. 1334–42, s.v. 'Volfango'.

Wolsey, Thomas (1472/4–1530), cardinal. The son of a prosperous Ipswich butcher, he was educated at *Oxford, elected Fellow of Magdalen College *c*.1497, and ordained priest in 1498. He soon held a number of benefices, becoming one of the domestic chaplains of Henry Dean, Abp. of *Canterbury, in 1501, and chaplain to Henry VII *c*.1507. He retained the royal favour under his successor, *Henry VIII, became a royal councillor in 1511, and Bp.

of *Lincoln in 1514. In the same year he was translated to *York, and in 1515 he was created cardinal. Three months later he was made Lord Chancellor of England, now wielding an almost royal power. His main interest was foreign politics, in which he frequently changed sides, skilfully holding the balance of power between the Empire and France, in a boldly conceived attempt to make England the arbiter of Europe. Though he himself was in favour of friendship with France, he had to sign a secret treaty of alliance with the Emperor (1521). The latter, however, on the death of *Leo X (1521), as well as on that of *Hadrian VI (1523), failed to exercise his influence to get Wolsey elected Pope. In the meantime the cardinal, though retaining the royal favour, had made himself enemies in the Church and among the nobility and gentry by his ruthless methods of obtaining money for the war with France, as well as by his arrogance and pomp. When, in 1527, Henry began to take steps to obtain his divorce, Wolsey endeavoured by all means to further the King's wishes. His plan to induce the Pope to cede to himself authority to decide the case proved a failure, however, and the cardinal, unable to obtain the Papal dispensation necessary for the divorce, was blamed by *Anne Boleyn and, through her, incurred the King's displeasure. In 1529 he pleaded guilty to a *praemunire. In the same year he had to resign the Great Seal and to give up all his property to the King, though later his archbishopric was restored to him. His last months, devoted to his diocese and to deeds of charity, were embittered by the knowledge that the King intended to suppress the two colleges he had founded at Ipswich and Oxford. Of these the latter, the present *Christ Church (q.v.), survived in somewhat different form. Owing to a denunciation by his Italian doctor he was arrested on a charge of high treason in Nov. 1530, but died soon afterwards on his way to London. A statesman rather than a Churchman, Wolsey had devoted his life to the aggrandizement of his king and country, fostering royal control of the Church by the use of his legatine powers and taking a vigorous interest in reform of the secular legal system; but his dream of making England the chief factor in European politics remained unrealized in his age.

Registrum Thome Wolsey Cardinalis Ecclesie Wintoniensis Administratoris transcribed by F. T. Madge and H. Chitty, ed., with introd., by H. Chitty (*Canterbury and York Society, 32; 1926). The primary sources for his official policies are the calendars of the State Papers for the reign of Henry VIII (cited s.v.). Important docs. connected with the divorce in S. Ehses (ed.), *Römische Dokumente zur Geschichte der Ehescheidung Heinrichs VIII. von England* (Quellen und Forschungen aus dem Gebiete der Geschichte . . . herausgegeben von der Görres-Gesellschaft, 2; Paderborn, 1893). The primary authority for his personal life is the record of George Cavendish (1500–*c*.1561), pr. as *The Negotiations of Thomas Wolsey, the Great Cardinall of England* (1641); this Life has very frequently been repub.; crit. edn. by R. S. Sylvester (EETS 243; 1959; also, with modernized spelling, New Haven, Conn., and London, 1962). The best modern Life is that of A. F. Pollard (London, 1929). Other Lives by M. *Creighton (ibid., 1888), E. L. Taunton (ibid., 1902), N. Williams (ibid., 1975), and P. Gwyn (ibid., 1990). J. Ridley, *The Statesman and the Fanatic: Thomas More and Thomas Wolsey* (1982). J. A. Guy, *The Cardinal's Court: The Impact of Thomas Wolsey in Star Chamber* (Hassocks, W. Sussex [1977]). S. J. Gunn and P. G. Lindley (eds.), *Cardinal Wolsey: Church, State and Art* (Cambridge, 1991). J. *Gairdner in

DNB 62 (1900), pp. 325–43, s.v.; *BRUO* 3 (1959), pp. 2077–80, s.v. See also bibl. to HENRY VIII.

women, ordination of. Although there is no doubt that there were women of standing among Christ's followers, and that in the apostolic and sub-apostolic period women exercised roles of leadership within the emerging local communities, it is not clear how these roles relate to the threefold ministry of *bishops, *priests, and *deacons that was in place by the 2nd cent. *Epiphanius asserts that some *Montanists had women priests and bishops (*Pan.* 49. 2), perhaps echoing *Firmilian's report of a prophetess who celebrated the Eucharist, preached, and baptized, but it is plain from these and a few other possible references to women fulfilling priestly functions in heretical bodies that such behaviour was regarded as an outrage in orthodox circles. There is evidence for a distinct order of *deaconesses (q.v.) in the Church during the patristic period. They had charge of female candidates for Baptism, washing them, anointing them, and helping them to change their clothes. They also sometimes instructed women *catechumens, visited the sick of their own sex and, where women entered the church by a different door from men, were sometimes employed as doorkeepers. It is, however, by no means clear that they should be seen as women in deacon's orders, while their precise relationship to formal groups of *widows and virgins is obscure and in some places overlapped. The order disappeared, in the W. by the 11th cent., in the E. slightly later. In the medieval period the ministry of women found its greatest expression in the authority of some *abbesses who came to wield far-reaching power and influence within and beyond their own communities, in some cases even over the local secular clergy.

The first Churches to admit women to official ministry were those who had abandoned the threefold order of bishop, priest, and deacon at the *Reformation and which had little or no centralized hierarchical structure. In 1611, for example, the *Declaration of Faith* of English Baptists (written in Amsterdam) provided for 'Deacons, men and women'. It was not, however, until the 19th cent. that the ordination of women became a serious concern in the life of some Churches. It was given considerable emphasis by the women's suffrage movement in the early 20th cent. and by subsequent liberal and radical movements in theology and biblical studies and by the *Ecumenical Movement. Nevertheless, such ordinations did not become common for some decades because many of the Churches which began to accommodate women into their leadership tended to embrace a tradition of biblical interpretation which in the view of many of its holders made the ecclesiastical 'headship' of women a theological impossibility. The chronology of women in ministry is complicated by the phenomena of unordained and unofficial women's ministries (e.g. as preachers, catechists, founders of local congregations) which in almost every denomination preceded their admission into the ranks of ordained clergy.

The office of deaconess was first revived at *Kaiserswerth in Germany in 1836, and soon spread from there to other countries. A. C. *Tait, Bp. of London, 'set apart' Elizabeth Ferard as the first deaconess in the C of E in 1862; she had founded the Deaconess Community of St Andrew the previous year. Although there had been

several groups of women in the *Episcopal Church in the United States of America who had been calling themselves deaconesses since the 1850s, it was only in 1889 that the office was established by canon in the General Convention, which incidentally stipulated that deaconesses must be unmarried; in the following year three graduates of the recently established New York School for Deaconesses were set apart for the office by H. C. Potter, Bp. of New York. An American *Methodist deaconess institute was established in 1888, to be followed by the Wesley Deaconess Institute in England in 1890.

The first woman to be ordained as a minister of a recognized denomination was Antoinette Louisa Brown (later Mrs Blackwell), ordained as minister of the First Congregational Church in Butler and Savannah, Wayne County, NY, in 1853, but she was dismissed a year later. The next woman to be ordained was Olympia Brown in the Universalist Association (later joined with the *Unitarians) and from the later 19th cent. women were ordained in the USA by the *Disciples of Christ (Christian Church; 1888), some Baptist Churches, the *Methodist Protestant Church, the Cumberland *Presbyterian Church (an isolated instance in 1889), and the *Congregationalists who had nine women ordained by 1893. In England Congregationalists did not ordain a woman until 1917 and in Scotland not until 1929. In England the first woman minister was ordained to pastoral charge of a local Baptist church in 1918, and in 1925 the Baptist Union of Great Britain and Ireland formally accredited women as ministers for the first time. Presbyterians in England accepted the ordination of women in principle in 1921, but the first woman ordained after the regular training was made a minister in 1965. The first woman minister in the Presbyterian Church of the USA was ordained in 1956. The Church of Scotland admitted women as *elders in 1966 and ministers in 1968. English Methodists had known women as preachers since the earliest days of the Wesleyan movement, and in 1924 women were allowed to be made local preachers in the Methodist Episcopal Church in the USA, but they entered the fully ordained ministry in the Methodist Church in the USA only in 1956 and in England in 1974. The *Mennonites in the USA ordained a woman in 1973. Other Protestant bodies have followed the same trend.

The first of the *Lutheran Churches to ordain a woman to full ministry was the Evangelisch-Lutherse Kerk in the *Netherlands in 1929. Since then member Churches of the Lutheran World Federation have gradually admitted woman to their ordained ministry, though some still do not do so. The most significant decision was taken in 1958 when the *Swedish Church, which claims to maintain the apostolic succession, became the first such Lutheran body to permit the ordination of women to the priesthood; the first ordinations took place in 1960. In the USA the Lutheran Church in America and the American Lutheran Church ordained their first women pastors in 1970, and the Association of Evangelical Lutheran Churches did so in 1977.

Florence Tim Oi Li became the first woman priest in the Anglican Communion when in 1944 she was ordained by R. O. Hall, Bp. of Hong Kong, to serve Christians who were cut off by war or revolution in *China. His action was condemned by the *Lambeth Conference in 1948, and

Li ceased to function as a priest until her orders were recognized by the diocese of Hong Kong in 1970. In the meantime the Lambeth Conference of 1968 had affirmed that those who had 'been made deaconess by the laying on of hands with the appropriate prayer should be regarded as within the order of deacons' and opened the way for canonical regulations on the subject within each province. In the Episcopal Church in the USA, for instance, legislation to this effect was passed by the General Convention in 1970. In 1971 G. Baker, Bp. of Hong Kong, ordained two women deacons to the priesthood. In the USA in 1974 eleven women deacons were irregularly ordained to the priesthood by bishops who had either retired or resigned their jurisdiction, followed by four more in 1975. In 1976 the General Convention passed legislation to permit the ordination of women to the priesthood and the episcopate, and the 15 earlier ordinations were regularized. The first ordinations to the priesthood under the new legislation occurred in 1977. In the C of E legislation was passed in 1986 allowing women to be ordained deacon; in 1993 it was followed by legislation allowing them to become priests, with the first such ordinations taking place in 1994. Women have regularly been ordained as priests in the following Provinces of the Anglican Communion: Hong Kong and Macao (1971), Canada (1976), USA (1977; then incl. *Mexico, 1983), *New Zealand (1977), *Brazil (after 1984), Burundi (1989), *Kenya (1990), *Uganda (1990), *Ireland (1990), the *Philippines (1991), *West Africa (by 1992), *Southern Africa (1992), *Australia (1992), England (1994), *Scotland (1994) and *Wales (1997). Various other Provinces have agreed in principle to the ordination of women to the priesthood, though no such ordinations have taken place to date (1995), and in some Provinces women ordained elsewhere are permitted to officiate.

The first woman to be ordained to the episcopate in the historic succession was Barbara Harris, who was consecrated Suffragan Bishop of Massachusetts in the Episcopal Church in the USA in 1989. The first diocesan bishop was Penelope Jamieson, consecrated Bp. of Dunedin, New Zealand, in 1990. These consecrations followed the establishment of the Abp. of *Canterbury's Commission on Communion and Women in the Episcopate in 1988 to examine the consequences for the Anglican Communion of the admission of women to the episcopate. The United Methodist Church (USA) ordained Marjorie Matthews as their first woman bishop in 1980, the first woman bishop in any major denomination. The Lutherans ordained two women as bishops in 1992, and a third in 1993.

Of the Churches which possess the historic succession, only some Anglicans and some Lutherans admit women to the priesthood and to the episcopate. The German, Swiss, and Austrian *Old Catholic Churches admit women to the diaconate, but this move has not been universally accepted by other Old Catholic Churches. The subject has been a matter of discussion in ecumenical, RC and some Orthodox circles, but the RC Church, the E. *Orthodox and the *Oriental Orthodox Churches maintain an ordained ministry which is exclusively male, holding such to be of the essence of orders. In the RC Church discussion was restricted when *John Paul II issued an apostolic letter *Ordinatio Sacerdotalis* (22 May 1994) declaring that the Church had no authority to confer priestly ordination on women; on 28 Oct. 1995 the Congregation for the

*Doctrine of the Faith stated that the teaching excluding women from priestly ordination had been set forth by the ordinary and *infallible magisterium. Belief in the inherent impossibility of ordaining women to the priesthood held by some members of the Anglican Communion account for some of the controversy and schisms which have followed such ordinations in some Provinces.

Primary sources for statistics and events are contained in official reports and histories of the various Churches. Introductions to the questions surrounding the ordination of women incl.: P. Moore and others, *Man, Woman, and Priesthood* (1978); V. L. Brereton and C. R. Klein, 'American Women in Ministry: A History of Protestant Beginning Points', in R. Ruether and E. McLaughlin (eds.), *Women of Spirit* (New York [1979]), pp. 301–32; N. Carter and R. Ruether, 'Entering the Sanctuary: The Struggle for Priesthood in Contemporary Episcopalian and Roman Catholic Experience', ibid., pp. 356–83; E. M. Howe, *Women and Church Leadership* (Grand Rapids [1982]); J. W. Carroll and others, *Women of the Cloth: A New Opportunity for the Churches* (San Francisco [1983]); E. Schüssler Fiorenza, *In Memory of Her: A Feminist Theological Reconstruction of Christian Origins* (New York and London, 1983), pp. 243–342; T. Hopko (ed.), *Women and the Priesthood* (Crestwood, NY, 1983); M. Hauke, *Die Problematik am das Frauenpriestertum vor dem Hintergrund der Schöpfungs- und Erlösungsordnung* (1986; Eng. tr., *Women in the Priesthood? A Systematic Analysis in the Light of the Order of Creation and Redemption*, San Francisco, 1988); J. G. Melton (ed.), *The Churches Speak on Women's Ordination: Official Statements from Religious Bodies and Ecumenical Organizations* (Detroit [1991]); J. Field-Bibb, *Women towards Priesthood: Ministerial Politics and Feminine Praxis* (Cambridge, 1991); id., 'Women and Ministry: The Presbyterian Church of England', *Heythrop Journal*, 31 (1990), pp. 150–64. B. K. Stendahl, *The Force of Tradition: A Case Study of Women Priests in Sweden* (Philadelphia [1985]). E. C. Lehman, *Women Clergy in England: Sexism, Modern Consciousness, and Church Viability* (Studies in Religion and Society, 16; Lewiston, NY [1987]). C. M. Prelinger (ed.), *Episcopal Women: Gender, Spirituality, and Commitment in an American Mature Denomination* [the Episcopal Church] (New York and Oxford, 1992). *Ordinatio Sacerdotalis* is pr. in *AAS* 86 (1994), pp. 545–8 and the subsequent ruling of the Congregation for the Doctrine of the Faith, ibid., 87 (1995), p.1114. See also bibls. to DEACON, DEACONESS, ORDERS AND ORDINATION; also FEMINIST THEOLOGY.

Wood, Anthony (1632–95), antiquary and historian of *Oxford. In his later years he called himself 'Anthony à Wood'. He lived for most of his life in a house opposite the gate of Merton College, of which he became a member in 1647. He was an assiduous collector of facts, and, though his judgements were often prejudiced, his writings contain a mine of information about the university of Oxford and very many of its otherwise little-known members. In 1674 he issued *Historia et Antiquitates Universitatis Oxoniensis*, printed in two folios at the expense of John *Fell, and in 1691–2 his *Athenae Oxonienses; An Exact History of all the Writers and Bishops who have had their Education in the University of Oxford from 1500 to 1690, to which are added the Fasti or Annals of the said University for the same time* (also in two folios).

His *Athenae Oxonienses ... to which are added the Fasti, or Annals of the said University*, ed. P. Bliss (5 vols., London, 1813–20), with his autobiog. in vol. 1, pp. i–cxxv, and T. *Hearne's account of him, pp. cxxvii–cxxx. His *Survey of the Antiquities of the City of Oxford* (composed in 1661–6), ed. A. Clark (OHS 15, 17, 27; 1889–99); *The Life and Times of Anthony Wood, Antiquary of Oxford, 1632–1695, described by himself*, ed. id. (ibid. 19, 21, 26,

30, 40; 1891–1900); abridged edn. by L. Powys (London, 1932). A. Clark in *DNB* 62 (1900), pp. 349–53.

Woodard, Nathaniel (1811–91), founder of the 'Woodard Schools'. He was born at Basildon Hall, Essex, educated at Magdalen Hall, Oxford, and ordained in 1841. While a curate in E. London he became convinced of the necessity of establishing public schools which would provide a sound middle-class education on a definite Anglican basis. When, in 1847, he was appointed curate at New Shoreham, he founded his first day school, and in 1848 outlined his ideas in his *Plea for the Middle Classes*, which aroused much controversy, but also received warm approval. In the same year he established the St Nicolas Society for the realization of his plans, and many schools were founded, among them St Nicolas's, Lancing (1848), and St John's, Hurstpierpoint (1850). There was at the time much discussion about provision of schools for the middle and working classes and strong views were expressed, esp. about how to combine a national educational system with various ecclesiastical interests. Woodard's organizing abilities, combined with his devoted service, won him wide moral and financial support, esp. among High Churchmen, and in recognition of his work he was made Canon of Manchester and Rector of St Philip's, Salford, in 1870. In 1873 he founded Denstone, the first of the Midland schools, in 1880 King Alfred's School, Taunton, and in 1887 a girls' school at Bangor (N. Wales).

Life by J. Otter (London, 1925). K. E. *Kirk, *The Story of the Woodard Schools* (1937); B. Heeney, *Mission to the Middle Classes: The Woodard Schools 1848–1891* (1969); L. and E. Cowie, *That One Idea: Nathaniel Woodard and his Schools* (Ellesmere, Shropshire, 1991). J. A. Atkinson in *DNB* 62 (1900), pp. 383–5; A. L. Woodard in *DECH*, p. 649, s.v.

Woolman, John (1720–72), American *Quaker preacher. A native of Northampton, nr. Burlington, NJ, he led a long campaign against slavery from 1743 till his death, constantly travelling among the Quaker communities in America in support of Negro rights. In 1772 he crossed to England to further the interests of his cause and died at *York a few weeks after his arrival. His writings, remarkable for their unadorned sincerity and restrained but strong religious feeling, are among the best literary expressions of the Quaker ideal. The best-known, his *Journal* which he began writing in 1756, records his 'Life, Gospel-Labours and Christian Experiences'; it was pub. at Philadelphia in 1774.

The *Journal*, as well as Woolman's other writings, has been often repr. J. G. *Whittier issued an edn. with introduction (1871). *Journal and Essays* also ed., with biog. introd., by A. M. Gummere (1922); *Journal and Major Essays*, ed. P. P. Moulton (Library of Protestant Theology, New York, 1971). W. Teignmouth Shore, *John Woolman: His Life and our Times* (1913); J. Whitney, *John Woolman, Quaker* (Boston, 1942; London, 1943). H. J. *Cadbury, *John Woolman in England: A Documentary Supplement* (Journal of the Friends Historical Society, Supplement '31' [32]; 1971).

Woolston, Thomas (1670–1733), *Deistical writer. Educated at Sidney Sussex College, Cambridge, he was elected a Fellow of his college in 1691 and after ordination held a succession of college appointments. In various writings he defended the *Origenistic modes of exegesis of the

OT, and in some polemical writings upheld the *Quakers as their modern exponents. His provocative methods led to the loss of his fellowship in 1721, whereupon Woolston announced his intention of founding a new sect. He entered the lists on the Deistical side in the controversy between A. *Collins and Edward Chandler (c.1668–1750, Bp. of *Durham from 1730) with his *A Moderator between an Infidel and an Apostate* (1725). This was soon followed by two supplements in which he maintained that the Virgin Birth and the Resurrection were allegories.

Collection of his Works in 5 vols., London, each work being separately paginated and dated, incl. [T. Stackhouse?,] *The Life of Mr. Woolston, with an Impartial Account of his Writings* (London, 1733); C. C. Woog, *De Vita et Scriptis Thomae Woolstoni* (Leipzig, 1743). *Memoirs of the Life and Writings of Mr. William *Whiston, containing Memoirs of Several of his Friends also Written by himself* (2nd edn., 1749), pp. 231–5. J. Leland, *A View of the Principal Deistical Writers that have Appeared in England in the Last and Present Century*, 1 (1754), pp. 126–43. L. Stephen, *History of English Thought in the Eighteenth Century* (2 vols., 1876), esp. vol. 1, pp. 230–8; E. Sayous, *Les Déistes anglais et le christianisme principalement depuis Toland jusqu'à Chubb, 1696–1738* (1882), pp. 122–45. R. M. Burns, *The Great Debate on Miracles* (Lewisburg, London, and Toronto [1981]), esp. pp. 77–82. A. Gordon in *DNB* 62 (1900), pp. 437–9.

Worcester. The diocese was founded c.680 on the initiative of St *Theodore, Abp. of Canterbury, for the tribe of the Hwicce, when the diocese of Mercia was divided into five. The first cathedral, which was dedicated to St *Peter, was richly endowed by the Mercian kings. The secular canons, who originally served it, were gradually replaced by *Benedictine monks under St *Oswald, who also built a new cathedral. This church, which was dedicated to the BVM, was completed in 983. Destroyed by the Danes in 1041, it was rebuilt (1084–9) by St *Wulfstan, but the only remaining parts of his work are the crypt and a few walls, much of it having perished by fire and by the fall of the central tower in 1175. In 1218 the cathedral, which contained the tomb of King *John between the shrines of Oswald and Wulfstan, was restored and reconsecrated. In the course of time several alterations were made in its structure, the choir being a particularly fine example of the Early English style, whereas the nave, redone in the 14th cent., shows chiefly Perpendicular work. From 1497 to 1534 the see was held by absentee Italian bishops who were the King's representatives at Rome. The monastery was suppressed in 1540 and a secular chapter was in place by 1542, the last of the priors, Henry Holbeach, becoming the dean. The size of the diocese was much reduced in 1541 and 1542 by the foundation of the sees of *Gloucester and Bristol. Among the better-known Bps. of Worcester are, besides those already named, St *Dunstan, *Wulfstan (d. 1023), T. *Bourchier, H. *Latimer, J. *Hooper, E. *Sandys, J. *Whitgift, G. *Morley, J. *Gauden, J. *Earle, E. *Stillingfleet, and C. *Gore. Every third year the Three Choirs Festival is held at Worcester.

Episcopal Register for the periods of vacancy of the See ('Registrum Sede Vacante'), 1301–1435, ed. J. W. Willis Bund (Worcestershire Historical Society, 3 vols., 1893–7); Registers of Godfrey Giffard [Bp. 1268–1301], ed. id. (ibid., 2 vols., 1902); of William Ginsborough (more usually Gainsborough) [Bp. 1303–7], ed. id. (ibid., 1907); of Walter Reynolds [Bp. 1308–13], ed. R. A. Wilson (ibid., 1927); of Thomas de Cobham [Bp. 1317–27], ed.

E. H. Pearce (ibid., 1930); calendars of the Registers of Adam de Orleton [Bp. 1327–33] by R. M. Haines (ibid., 1979), of Wolstan de Bransford [Bp. 1339–49] by id. (ibid., 1966); of Henry Wakefield [Bp. 1375–95] by W. P. Marett (ibid., 1972); and of Richard Clifford [Bp. 1401–7] by W. E. L. Smith (Pontifical Institute of Mediaeval Studies, Subsidia Mediaevalia, 6; Toronto, 1976). E. S. Fegan (ed.), *Journal of Prior William More* [1518–36] (Worcestershire Historical Society, 1914). J. M. Wilson, *The Liber Albus of the Priory of Worcester*. Parts 1 and 2, Priors John de Wyke, 1301–17, and Wulfstan de Bransford, 1317–39 (ibid., 1919). M. Hollings (ed.), *The Red Book of Worcester containing Surveys of the Bishop's Manors and other Records chiefly of the Twelfth and Thirteenth Centuries* (ibid., 4 pts., 1934–50). J. M. Wilson (ed.), *Accounts of the Priory of Worcester for the Year . . . 1521–2*, and J. H. Bloom and S. G. Hamilton, *A Catalogue of the Rolls of Obedientiaries* (ibid., 1907); J. M. Wilson and C. Gordon (eds.), *Early Compotus Rolls of the Priory of Worcester* (ibid., 1908); S. G. Hamilton (ed.), *Compotus Rolls of the Priory of Worcester of the XIVth and XVth Centuries* (ibid., 1910). C. Price (ed.), *Liber Pensionum Prioratus Wigorn: Being a Collection of Documents Relating to Pensions from Appropriated Churches and other Payments Receivable by the Prior and Convent of Worcester and to the Privileges of the Monastery* (ibid., 1925). J. Atkins, *The Early Occupants of the Office of Organist and Master of the Choristers of the Cathedral Church of Christ and the Blessed Virgin Mary, Worcester* (ibid., 1918). R. R. Darlington (ed.), *The Cartulary of Worcester Cathedral Priory (Register I)* (Publications of the Pipe Roll Society, 76 for 1962–3; 1968). W. *Dugdale, *Monasticon Anglicanum*, 1 (1817 edn.), pp. 567–622. P. H. Sawyer, 'Charters of the Reform Movement: the Worcester Archive', in D. Parsons (ed.), *Tenth-Century Studies* (1975), pp. 84–93. W. Thomas, *A Survey of the Cathedral Church of Worcester: With an Account of the Bishops thereof from the Foundation of the See to the Year 1660* (1736). J. Noake, *The Monastery and Cathedral of Worcester* (1866). W. M. Ede, *The Cathedral Church of Christ and the Blessed Virgin Mary of Worcester: Its Monuments and their Stories* (Worcester, 1925). P. Barker, *Worcester Cathedral: A Short Architectural History* (ibid., 1994). M. M. C. Calthorp in *VCH*, Worcs, ed. J. W. Willis-Bund and W. Page, 2 (1906), pp. 94–112, and F. M. Stenton and H. Brakspear, ibid. 4 (1924), pp. 394–408. H. W. Yeatman-Biggs in *DECH* (1912), pp. 649–53, s.v.

Worcester House Declaration (1660). See DECLARATIONS OF INDULGENCE.

Word of God. See LOGOS.

Wordsworth, Christopher (1807–85), Bp. of *Lincoln. He was the youngest son of Christopher Wordsworth (1774–1846), Master of Trinity College, Cambridge, and thus a nephew of W. *Wordsworth, the poet. Elected a Fellow of his father's college in 1830, he was Headmaster of Harrow from 1836 to 1844, and after holding various ecclesiastical appointments was consecrated Bp. of Lincoln in 1869. Throughout his life he remained a conservative *High Churchman, with great veneration for the early Church Fathers. In this field perhaps his most important study was *St Hippolytus and the Church of Rome* (1853), a reply to C. C. J. *Bunsen's book (1852). He also wrote a commentary on the Bible (NT, 1856–60; OT, 1864–71) and a series of hymns, published in *The Holy Year* (1862); several of these are still in use, among them 'Hark! the sound of holy voices' and 'Songs of thankfulness and praise'.

He pub. a collection of his works as *Miscellanies Literary and Religious* (3 vols., 1879). J. H. Overton and E. Wordsworth (daughter), *Christopher Wordsworth, Bishop of Lincoln, 1807–1885*

(1888). A. C. Benson, *The Leaves of the Tree: Studies in Biography* (1911), ch. 11, 'Bishop Wordsworth of Lincoln', pp. 260–83. V. Strudwick, *Christopher Wordsworth: Bishop of Lincoln, 1869–85* (Lincoln, 1987 [slight]). J. H. Overton in *DNB* 63 (1900), pp. 9–11.

Wordsworth, John (1843–1911), Bp. of *Salisbury. The elder son of Christopher *Wordsworth, Bp. of *Lincoln (q.v.), he was educated at *Winchester and New College, *Oxford, became a Fellow of Brasenose College in 1867, and a prebendary of Lincoln in 1870. One of the best Latin scholars of his day, he worked assiduously from 1878 onwards at producing a critical edition of the *Vulgate NT (Mt. to Rom. pub. 1889–1911; minor edition of whole NT, 1911). In 1881 he was *Bampton Lecturer, and from 1883 to 1885 the first Oriel Professor of the Interpretation of Holy Scripture at Oxford. From 1885 until his death he was Bp. of Salisbury. As a bishop he proved an invaluable adviser to Abp. E. W. *Benson (with whom he was intimate) and an enthusiastic worker in the cause of Reunion, esp. with the *Swedish and *Old Catholic Churches. To the latter end he published two treatises on the validity of *Anglican Ordinations, *De successione episcoporum in ecclesia anglicana* (1890) and *De validitate ordinum anglicanorum* (1894). In 1897 he composed the Latin *Responsio* sent by the Abps. of *Canterbury and *York in reply to '*Apostolicae Curae'.

Life by E. W. Watson (London, 1915). Id. in *DNB, 1901–1911*, 3, pp. 705–7.

Wordsworth, William (1770–1850), English poet. He was educated at St John's College, Cambridge, and went in 1791–2 to France, where he became a radical in politics and sympathized with the revolutionaries. In these years he went through a period of moral laxity and religious unbelief. After his return to England he devoted himself entirely to poetry. In 1797 began his friendship with S. T. *Coleridge, and in 1798 the two published jointly *Lyrical Ballads*, which contain the famous 'Lines written . . . above Tintern Abbey'. Wordsworth's chief aim in this collection, which was a landmark in English poetry, was to bring out the deeper spiritual meaning in everyday persons and events, a task for which he was particularly fitted by his capacities for minute observation and for the detection of the emotional qualities in commonplace things. In 1799 he settled at Grasmere. Among his later works are *The Prelude*, his spiritual autobiography (of which there are three texts—an early draft of 1799, a revised text of 1805, not published in his lifetime, and the final text published in 1850), and the *Poems in Two Volumes* (1807), containing the famous 'Ode to Duty' and 'Ode on the Intimations of Immortality'. In the poetry written after 1810 there is a marked decline of poetic power, e.g. in much of *The Excursion* (1814), on which he had been working for many years. The great inspiration of Wordsworth's art was nature, which he invested with spiritual qualities; this process at times brought his thought near to *pantheism. In his later years, however, he returned to a more orthodox form of creed. His *Ecclesiastical Sonnets* (1822), which give an account of the Church in England from the introduction of Christianity to the reign of *Charles I, are an eloquent expression of his devotion to the C of E, containing, at the same time, a fair appreciation of medieval English

Catholicism. He was in sympathy with the *Oxford Movement and esp. with J. *Keble, whose *Christian Year* he admired. Having been little valued in his youth, Wordsworth's genius came to be recognized in his later years, and he was made Poet Laureate in 1843.

Edns. of Poems pub. by Wordsworth himself incl. those of 1807 (2 vols., London; repr. by T. Hutchinson, 1897, and ed. H. Darbishire, Oxford, 1914), 1827 (5 vols., London), 1832 (4 vols., ibid.), and 1849–50 (7 vols., ibid.). Modern edns. by T. Hutchinson (London, 1895, ed. E. de Selincourt, 1936), E. de Selincourt and H. Darbishire (6 vols., ibid., 1940–9), and S. Parrish and others ('The Cornell Wordsworth', Ithaca, NY, and Hassocks, Sussex, 1975 ff.). The 1805 text of *The Prelude* also ed. E. de Selincourt (Oxford, 1933); the texts of 1799, 1805, and 1850, together with recent critical essays, ed. Jonathan Wordsworth and others (New York and London [1979]). Modern edn. of his Prose Works by W. J. B. Owen and J. W. Smyser (3 vols., Oxford, 1974). [D.] W. Knight (ed.), *Letters of the Wordsworth Family from 1787 to 1855* (3 vols., 1907). E. de Selincourt (ed.), *The Early Letters of William and Dorothy Wordsworth (1787–1805)* (Oxford, 1935; 2nd edn. by C. L. Shaver, 1967); E. de Selincourt (ed.), *The Letters of William and Dorothy Wordsworth: The Middle Years* (2 vols., ibid., 1937; 2nd edn. by M. [C.] Moorman and A. G. Hill, 1969–70) and *The Later Years* (3 vols., ibid., 1939; 2nd edn. by A. G. Hill, 4 vols., 1978–88). C. *Wordsworth, *Memoirs of William Wordsworth* (2 vols., 1851). Modern biog. studies by M. [C.] Moorman (2 vols., Oxford, 1957–65), M. L. Reed (2 vols., Cambridge, Mass., 1967–75), and S. Gill (Oxford, 1989). Crit. studies by E. C. Batho (Cambridge, 1933), H. Darbishire (Clark Lectures, 1949; Oxford, 1950), F. [N.] W. Bateson (London, 1954), [H.] J. [F.] Jones (ibid., 1954), M. Rader (Oxford, 1967), M. Jacobus (ibid., 1976), J. Wordsworth (ibid., 1982), J. K. Chandler (Chicago and London, 1984), and K. R. Johnston (New Haven, Conn., and London, 1984). S. Prickett, *Coleridge and Wordsworth: The Poetry of Growth* (Cambridge, 1970); N. Roe, *Coleridge and Wordsworth: The Radical Years* (Oxford English Monographs, 1988). *Bicentenary Wordsworth Studies*, ed. J. Wordsworth (Ithaca, NY, and London, 1970). *Critical Essays on William Wordsworth*, ed. G. H. Gilpin (Boston [1990]). A. D. Martin, *The Religion of Wordsworth* (1936). T. J. Wise, *A Bibliography of the Writings in Prose and Verse of William Wordsworth* (1916); M. Jones and K. Kroeber, *Wordsworth Scholarship and Criticism, 1973–1984: An Annotated Bibliography, with Selected Criticism 1809–1972* (New York and London, 1985). W. J. B. Owen in *NCBEL* 3 (1969), cols. 182–211.

World Alliance of Reformed Churches. This body, officially called 'The World Alliance of Reformed Churches (Presbyterian and Congregational)', was formed in 1970 by the amalgamation of the (*Presbyterian) World Alliance of Reformed Churches, founded in 1875 (from 1877 to 1954 officially called 'The Alliance of the Reformed Churches throughout the World holding the Presbyterian System'; its title was slightly changed in 1954), with the International Congregational Council, founded in 1891. In 1990 it had 157 member Churches, representing some 60 million members. Its headquarters are in *Geneva.

M. Pradervand, *A Century of Service: A History of the World Alliance of Reformed Churches 1875–1975* (Edinburgh, 1975). A. P. F. Sell, *A Reformed, Evangelical, Catholic Theology: The Contribution of the World Alliance of Reformed Churches, 1875–1982* (Grand Rapids, Mich., 1991). Id. in D. K. McKim (ed.), *Encyclopedia of the Reformed Faith* (Louisville, Ky., and Edinburgh, 1992), pp. 403–7, s.v.

World Council of Churches. The 'fellowship of Churches which accept our Lord Jesus Christ as God and Saviour', formally constituted at *Amsterdam on 23 Aug. 1948. The organization arose from the fusion of the two earlier movements, *Life and Work and *Faith and Order, the first practical steps being taken at their respective conferences at *Oxford and *Edinburgh in 1937. A further stage was reached at a conference at Utrecht in 1938, when a constitution was drawn up and a provisional organization ('The World Council of Churches in Process of Formation') established. Because of the Second World War the formal constitution was delayed until 1948. At that time it was decided that the International Missionary Council (see EDINBURGH CONFERENCE, 1910) should be considered as being in association with the World Council of Churches; it was finally integrated in 1961. Also in 1961 the constitution of the World Council of Churches was amended, so that the Council was defined as 'A fellowship of churches which confess the Lord Jesus as God and Saviour according to the Scriptures and therefore seek to fulfil together their common calling to the glory of the one God, Father, Son and Holy Spirit'. The work of the Council is reviewed at six- to eight-yearly intervals by a representative Assembly and from this is elected the Council's highest governing body, its 150-member Central Committee, which meets annually. Advisory committees give oversight to the various programmes and activities of the Council. Assemblies have been held at Amsterdam (1948), *Evanston, Ill. (1954), New Delhi (1961), *Uppsala (1968), Nairobi (1975), Vancouver (1983), and Canberra (1991). The headquarters of the World Council of Churches is in *Geneva.

At its formation in 1948 the Council had 147 member Churches; by 1993 the number had risen to 322. With the exception of the RC Church and the *Unitarians, the Council includes Churches from all the main Christian confessions and denominations, including nearly all the E. *Orthodox Churches (incl. since 1961 the Patriarchate of Moscow). Many of the member Churches are from the non-Western world. Although the RC Church is not a member, since 1961 the Vatican has appointed accredited observers to Assemblies; in 1965 a Joint Working Group was established between the Vatican and the World Council of Churches to discuss questions of common concern, and in 1968 the RC Church accepted full membership of the Faith and Order Commission and was thus involved in the production of the 1982 report on '*Baptism, Eucharist and Ministry'. Many national and regional Councils of Churches are Associate Members of the World Council, and there are many contacts with the Christian world communions.

A reorganization in 1992 gathered most of the work of the World Council into four programme units: (1) Unity and Renewal, including Faith and Order and work on worship, theological education, the laity and the nature of community; (2) Mission, Education and Witness, continuing the Commission on World Mission and Evangelism and work on education, health, and the theological significance of religions; (3) Justice, Peace, and Creation, covering a broad range of ecumenical social witness and action (one component enjoying consultative status at the United Nations); and (4) Sharing and Service, continuing the work of the Commission on Inter-Church Aid, Refugee and World Service. A General Secretariat co-ordinates the relationships of the Council with its member Churches and other bodies, including other faiths. The Ecumenical Institute at *Bossey is an integral part of the World Council.

G. K. A. *Bell, *The Kingship of Christ: The Story of the World Council of Churches* (Harmondsworth, 1954). D. P. Gaines, *The World Council of Churches: A Study of its background and history* (Peterborough, NH [1966]). M. van Elderen, *Introducing the World Council of Churches* (Geneva [1990]). W. A. Visser 't Hooft, *The Genesis and Formation of the World Council of Churches* (ibid., 1982). H. Krüger, 'The Life and Activities of the World Council of Churches', in H. E. Fey (ed.), *The Ecumenical Advance* (1970), pp. 27–62; 2nd edn. (Geneva, 1986) is unchanged apart from additional bibl., pp. 514–36. M. E. Brinkman, *Progress in Unity? Fifty Years of Theology within the World Council of Churches: 1945–1995* (Louvain Theological and Pastoral Monographs, 18; 1995). See also other works cited under ECUMENICAL MOVEMENT.

World Evangelical Fellowship. See EVANGELICAL ALLIANCE.

Worms, Concordat of (1122), also the 'Pactum Calixtinum'. The agreement which was reached between Pope *Callistus II and the Emp. Henry V through the mediation of the German princes on 23 Sept. 1122; it ended the *Investiture Controversy. The Emperor's 'Precept' to the Church explicitly renounced all investiture by ring and staff in his dominions, and granted canonical election and free consecration. The Pope's 'Privilege' to Henry conceded that elections of bishops and abbots in the German kingdom were to take place (without simony or violence) in the Emperor's presence, and that before his consecration the elect was to receive the *regalia* from the Emperor by investiture with the sceptre. In cases of dispute the Emperor, with the counsel or judgement of the metropolitan and comprovincials, was to lend his assent and aid to the *sanior pars*. However, in the other parts of the Empire (i.e. Italy and Burgundy) no form of election in the Emperor's presence was granted; and consecration of the elect was to precede his investiture by the Emperor with the *regalia*, which should follow within six months.

Text ed. L. Weiland in *MGH*, Leges, Sectio 4, Constitutiones et Acta Publica Imperatorum et Regum, 1 (1893), pp. 159–61; conveniently repr. in Mirbt and Aland (1967), pp. 296 f. (no. 571); Eng. tr. in Bettenson, pp. 154 f. W. Fritz (ed.), *Quellen zum Wormser Konkordat* (Kleine Texte, 177; 1955). E. Bernheim, *Das Wormser Konkordat und seine Vorurkunden hinsichtlich Entstehung, Formulierung, Rechtsgültigkeit* (Untersuchungen zur Deutschen Staats- und Rechtsgeschichte, 81; 1906); H. Rudorff, *Zur Erklärung des Wormser Konkordats* (Quellen und Studien zur Verfassungsgeschichte des Deutschen Reiches, 1, Heft 4; 1906). A. Hofmeister, 'Das Wormser Konkordat. Zum Streit um seine Bedeutung', in *Forschungen und Versuche zur Geschichte des Mittelalters und der Neuzeit: Festschrift Dietrich Schäfer zum siebzigsten Geburtstag* (Jena, 1915), pp. 64–148; repr. separately, Darmstadt, 1962; P. Classen, 'Das Wormser Konkordat in der deutschen Verfassungsgeschichte', in J. Fleckenstein (ed.), *Investiturstreit und Reichsverfassung* (1973), pp. 411–60; M. Minninger, *Von Clermont zum Wormser Konkordat* (Forschungen zur Kaiser- und Papstgeschichte des Mittelalters, Beihefte zu J. F. Böhmer, Regesta Imperii, 2; 1978), esp. pp. 189–209. See also works cited under INVESTITURE CONTROVERSY.

Worms, Conference of (1540–1). The colloquy arranged, after the failure of the Conference of *Hagenau (q.v.), with a view to reuniting the Catholics and Protestants in Germany. The conference met on 25 Nov. 1540,

with 11 representatives on each side. After a long debate on procedure, it was finally agreed that one theologian should speak for each party, J. *Eck being selected by the Catholics and P. *Melanchthon by the Protestants. In Jan. 1541 an agreed formula was reached on the disputed matter of *original sin; but on 18 Jan. it was decided to end the discussions at Worms in view of the forthcoming Reichstag at *Ratisbon.

W. H. Neuser (ed.), *Die Vorbereitung der Religionsgespräche von Worms und Regensburg 1540/41* (Texte zur Geschichte der evangelischen Theologie, 4; Neukirchen [1974]). C. Augustijn, *De Godsdienstgespprekken tussen Rooms-Katholieken en Protestanten van 1538 tot 1541* (Haarlem, 1967), pp. 46–72, with bibl., pp. 142–6. P. Fraenkel, *Einigungsbestrebungen in der Reformationszeit* (Institut für Europäische Geschichte, Mainz, Vorträge 41; Wiesbaden, 1965), pp. 37–70. V. Pfnür, 'Die Einigung bei den Religionsgesprächen von Worms und Regensburg 1540/41 eine Täuschung?', in G. Müller (ed.), *Die Religionsgespräche der Reformationszeit* (Schriften des Vereins für Reformationsgeschichte, 191; Gütersloh, 1980), pp. 55–88. G. Kawerau in *PRE* (3rd edn.), 21 (1908), pp. 489–92, s.v. 'Wormser Religionsgespräche I'.

Worms, Diet of (1521). The most celebrated of the long series of Imperial diets held at Worms, at which M. *Luther defended his doctrines before the Emp. *Charles V. It took place in the Bischofshof from 27 Jan. to 25 May. The Papal legate, *Aleander, who had arrived at Worms on 30 Nov. 1520, having put the case against Luther on 13 Feb. 1521, Luther was then summoned and arrived on 16 Apr. On 18 Apr. he made his final refusal to recant his doctrines, acc. to an early but unreliable tradition concluding his answer with the famous words 'Hie stehe ich. Ich kan nicht anders. Gott helff mir. Amen.' Charles V having announced on the following day his resolve to take firmer measures against his doctrines, Luther departed from Worms on 26 Apr. On 26 May his teachings were formally condemned in the Edict of Worms.

Many of the primary docs. are pr. in P. Balan (ed.), *Monumenta Reformationis Lutherana ex Tabulariis S. Sedis Secretis, 1521–1525* (Ratisbon, 1883); extracts from these and other collections, with further refs., in Kidd, pp. 79–89 (nos. 39–46). P. Kalkoff, *Der Wormser Reichstag von 1521* (1922), with full refs. F. Reuter (ed.), *Der Reichstag zu Worms von 1521: Reichspolitik und Luthersache* (Worms, 1971). R. Bäumer (ed.), *Lutherprozess und Lutherbann* (Katholisches Leben und Kirchenreform im Zeitalter der Glaubensspaltung, 32; 1972). [E.] G. Rupp, *Luther's Progress to the Diet of Worms, 1521* (1951). Detailed bibl. in Schottenloher, 3 (1938), pp. 12–14 (nos. 27923–50), with refs. to other lists of specialized items, and on the Edict of Worms, ibid. 4 (1938), pp. 753 f. (nos. 44534–42). See also works cited under ALEANDER; LUTHER, M.; and REFORMATION.

Worms, Disputation of (1540–1). See WORMS, CONFERENCE OF.

Worms, Synod of (1076). The synod convened by King *Henry IV of Germany to secure the deposition of Pope *Gregory VII at the beginning of the *Investiture Controversy. Henry invited to the assembly, which met on 24 Jan. 1076, the Abps. of Mainz and Trier and a large number of other (mainly German) bishops. It issued a strong anti-Papal statement, charging Gregory with many serious crimes and calling upon the people of Rome to depose him; and an offensively worded letter was despatched by Henry to the Pope personally. As a result, the Pope excommunicated Henry at his Lenten synod.

Relevant texts ed. L. Weiland in *MGH, Leges*, Sect. 4, Constitutiones et Acta Publica Imperatorum et Regum, 1 (1893), pp. 106–13. G. Meyer von Knonau (ed.), *Jahrbücher des deutschen Reiches unter Heinrich IV. und Heinrich V.*, 2 (1894), pp. 613–28. A. Fliche, *La Réforme grégorienne*, 3 (SSL 16; 1937), pp. 50–9, with important notes. H. Zimmermann, 'Wurde Gregor VII. 1076 in Worms abgesetzt?', *Mitteilungen des Instituts für Österreichische Geschichtsforschung*, 78 (1970), pp. 121–31. See also works cited under INVESTITURE CONTROVERSY.

Worship, Directory of Public (1645). The 'Directory for the Public Worship of God', compiled by the *Westminster Assembly (q.v.), was designed on *Presbyterian principles to replace the BCP. An Ordinance requiring its use was passed by both houses of Parliament on 4 Jan. 1645. For the most part it contained general instructions rather than set forms of service. The principal service consisted of prayers, two lessons, Psalms and a sermon. The Holy Communion was to follow the morning sermon, with the people seated round the Holy Table. Instructions were provided for Baptism, visitation of the sick, and a form of marriage, but the burial of the dead was to be performed without ceremony, and feast days, apart from Sunday, were abolished. Penalties for using the BCP or failure to follow the Directory were imposed on 26 Aug. 1645.

The 'Ordinance for taking away the Book of Common Prayer, and for establishing and putting into execution of the Directory for the Public Worship of God' [incl. text of Directory] is pr. in C. H. Firth and R. S. Rait (eds.), *Acts and Ordinances of the Interregnum, 1642–1660* (1911), pp. 582–607. It is also repr., with introd., by I. Breward (Grove Liturgical Study, 21; Bramcote, 1980).

Worship and Doctrine Measure. The Church of England (Worship and Doctrine) Measure 1974 came into force on 1 Sept. 1975 and gives the General *Synod power to regulate by *Canon all matters of worship, including *Alternative Services, provided that the forms of service in the BCP 'continue to be available for use'. It also lays down that decisions as to the forms used in churches be taken by the incumbent and guild or *Parochial Church Council jointly, with provisions slanted in favour of the BCP in default of agreement. In the case of occasional services, the choice lies with the conducting minister, subject to a right of appeal to the diocesan bishop where there is a dispute. The Measure also allows the General Synod to oblige clergy and lay officers to assent to the doctrine of the C of E in a prescribed form (see ASSENT, DECLARATION OF).

The text is pr. in *Halsbury's Statutes of England and Wales*, 14 (4th edn., 1986), pp. 776–83; also in R. D. H. Bursell, *Liturgy, Order and the Law* (Oxford, 1996), pp. 261–5.

Wounds, the Five Sacred. Though the Passion narratives of the Gospels expressly record only the opening of the Lord's side, the piercing of His hands and feet, a normal practice in contemporary crucifixions, is attested in the Resurrection appearances (Lk. 24: 39 and Jn. 20: 20 and 27). Devotion to the Five Wounds developed in the Middle Ages, esp. under the influence of St *Bernard's love for the humanity of Christ and His Passion, and was fostered by the *stigmatization of St *Francis of Assisi.

Preference was soon given to the wound in the side from which the Church and the Sacraments, esp. Baptism ('water') and Eucharist ('blood'), were said to have sprung, and which led gradually to the cult of the *Sacred Heart. In the 14th and 15th cents. prayers to the Five Wounds became numerous in popular religious literature. *Portugal adopted the emblem on her coat of arms, the members of the *Pilgrimage of Grace wore it on their clothes, and the 'wells of pity' were engraved on many English rings in the 15th cent. The devotion figured prominently in the thought of N. L. Graf von *Zinzendorf and his followers. Today it is fostered esp. by the *Passionists, who observe a feast on the second Friday after Easter.

L. Gougaud, OSB, *Dévotions et pratiques ascétiques du moyen âge* (Pax, 21; 1925), pp. 78–128 (Eng. tr., 1927, pp. 80–130). A. Franz, *Die Messe im deutschen Mittelalter* (1902), pp. 155–61 and 703 f. R. W. Pfaff, *New Liturgical Feasts in Later Medieval England* (Oxford Theological Monographs, 1970), pp. 84–91. G. F. Holweck in *CE* 15 (1912), pp. 714 f., s.v.; O. Schmucki and E. Sauser in *L.Th.K.* (2nd edn.), 10 (1965), cols. 1249–51, s.v. 'Wunden Christi', with further bibl. See also works cited under SACRED HEART and STIGMATIZATION.

wrath of God, the. An anthropomorphic phrase for the Divine attitude towards sin. The expression is frequent in the Bible, esp. in the OT (e.g. Exod. 15: 7, Ps. 2: 12), where wrath is attributed to God not only when He punishes sinners but also when He sends trials to the just (e.g. Job 14: 13). In the NT the wrath of God is particularly connected with the Judgement on the Last Day, which St *Paul calls the 'day of wrath' (Rom. 2: 5, cf. 1: 18 and Mt. 3: 7), a conception elaborated in the Book of Rev., esp. under the metaphors of the 'wrath of the Lamb' (6: 16) and the 'wine-press of the fierceness of the wrath of Almighty God' (19: 15).

Patristic discussion in *Lactantius' *De Ira Dei*. M. Pohlenz, *Vom Zorne Gottes: Eine Studie über den Einfluss der griechischen Philosophie auf das alte Christentum* (Forschungen zur Religion und Literatur des Alten und Neuen Testaments, 12; 1909). R. V. G. Tasker, *The Biblical Doctrine of the Wrath of God* (1951 lecture [1952]). A. T. Hanson, *The Wrath of the Lamb* (1957). See also comm. to Romans, cited s.v., ad loc. H. Kleinert and others in *TWNT* 5 (1954), pp. 382–448 (Eng. tr., 1967, pp. 382–447), s.v. ὀργή, with bibl. G. A. Herion and S. H. Travis in *Anchor Bible Dictionary*, 6 (1992), pp. 989–98, s.v.

Wrede, William (1859–1906), German NT scholar. He was professor of NT at Breslau from 1895 until his death. A member of the '*Religionsgeschichtliche Schule', he pioneered the 'history of traditions' approach to the Gospels in *Das Messiasgeheimnis in den Evangelien* (1901; Eng. tr., 1971). In this work, which gave its name to the whole discussion of the so-called *Messianic Secret (q.v.), Wrede challenged the current critical view that St *Mark's Gospel was an unadorned record of historical fact, and maintained that Jesus in His earthly life did not claim to be the Messiah, the Gospel story being a reading back of later beliefs about His Person into the narrative. His other influential writings are *Über Aufgabe und Methode der sogenannten Neutestamentlichen Theologie* (1897; Eng. tr., 1973), which reduced this theological discipline to a purely historical account of early Christian religion, and *Paulus* (1905; Eng. tr., 1907), which argued that the Christian religion received its essential form through St *Paul's radical transformation of the teaching of Christ. Penetrating, but less influential, were his *Charakter und Tendenz des Johannesevangeliums* (1903) and *Die Echtheit des zweiten Thessalonicherbriefs* (1903).

Wrede's *Vorträge und Studien*, ed. A. Wrede (brother; Tübingen, 1907), with introd., pp. iii–xiv. Eng. tr. of *Über Aufgabe und Methode der sogenannten Neutestamentlichen Theologie* by R. [C.] Morgan, *The Nature of New Testament Theology* (Studies in Biblical Theology, 2nd ser. 25; 1973), pp. 68–116. A. *Schweitzer, *Geschichte der Leben-Jesu-Forschung* (2nd edn., 1913), pp. 368–89 (Eng. tr. of 1st edn., 1910, pp. 328–49). G. Strecker, 'William Wrede zur hundertsten Wiederkehr seines Geburtstages', *Zeitschrift für Theologie und Kirche*, 57 (1960), pp. 67–91, incl. list of his works. H. Räisänen, *Beyond New Testament Theology* (1990), pp. 13–18. A. *Jülicher in *PRE* (3rd edn.), 21 (1908), pp. 506–10.

Wren, Christopher (1632–1723), architect of *St Paul's Cathedral. The son of a future bishop, Wren was brought up and remained a *High Churchman. He was educated at Westminster School and Wadham College, Oxford. In 1653 he was elected to a fellowship at All Souls and in 1657 appointed professor of astronomy at Gresham College, London. Three years later he became Savilian professor of astronomy at Oxford, and in 1661 assistant, and later full, surveyor general. He was one of the founders, and from 1680 to 1682 president, of the Royal Society. His designs for the chapel of Pembroke College, Cambridge (1663) and the Sheldonian Theatre, Oxford (1664) having disclosed his outstanding ability, after the Great Fire of 1666 he was chosen as one of the rebuilders of the city. Besides his great work, St Paul's Cathedral, begun in 1675 and completed in 1716, Wren was responsible for building 52 London city churches, the Monument (1671–6), Trinity College Library, Cambridge (1676–84), Chelsea Hospital (1682–92), Hampton Court Palace (1689–94), and Greenwich Naval Hospital (begun in 1696). His great achievement as a church designer was to produce models specifically suited to the Anglican rite. In a Memorandum on Church Building (1708), he explains that for RCs 'it is enough if they hear the Murmur of the Mass, and see the Elevation of the Host, but ours are to be fitted for Auditories', allowing 'all to hear the Service, and both to hear distinctly, and see the Preacher' (*Parentalia*, p. 320). The need to maintain the centrality of the altar rendered Calvinist patterns of church-building equally unsuitable. His 52 churches, almost all built on the pre-Reformation foundations of the destroyed City churches, are examples of adaptation to difficult sites, while providing accommodation and audibility. In the case of St Paul's, and esp. his preferred Great Model (1673; in St Paul's), which was rejected but later adapted, he felt that grandeur in the classical style was essential, and he deliberately introduced echoes of *St Peter's, Rome.

Parentalia: or Memoirs of the Family of the Wrens: . . . but chiefly of Sir Christopher Wren. . . . Compiled by his son Christopher (London, 1750; repr., Farnborough, 1965), pp. 181–368; *Life and Works of Sir Christopher Wren, from the Parentalia or Memoirs of his son Christopher* [ed. E. J. Enthoven] (London and New York [1903]). J. Elmes, *Memoirs of the life and works of Sir Christopher Wren* (1823). Other studies by G. [F.] Webb (London, 1937), J. Summerson (ibid., 1953), E. F. Sekler (ibid., 1956), M. [D.] Whinney (ibid., 1971), K. Downes (ibid., 1971), and B. [D. G.] Little (ibid., 1975). *Sir Christopher Wren A.D. 1632–1723: Bicen-*

tenary Memorial Volume published under the Auspices of the Royal Institute of British Architects (1923). P. Waterhouse and others, *Sir Christopher Wren, 1632–1723* (1923). K. Downes, *Sir Christopher Wren: The Design of St Paul's Cathedral* (1988). Publications of the Wren Society (20 vols., Oxford, 1924–43). H. [M.] Colvin, *A Biographical Dictionary of British Architects 1600–1840* (1978), pp. 917–31, s.v.

Wroth, William (1570 or 1576–1641), the first Welsh Nonconformist pastor. Educated at Oxford, he became rector of Llanfaches, to the west of Chepstow, in 1611 or perhaps 1617, and after a sudden conversion in 1620 became famous as a Puritan preacher. In 1635 he was summoned before the Court of *High Commission, but his case was delayed. In 1639, however, after he had ceased to hold his living, he established at Llanfaches with some associates the first separatist church in Wales.

T. Watts, 'William Wroth (1570–1641)', *Congregational History Magazine*, 2, no. 5 (1989), pp. 1–69. T. Richards in *Dictionary of Welsh Biography down to 1940* (1959), p. 1093, s.v.

Wulfila. See ULPHILAS.

Wulfric, St (d. 1154), also 'St Ulrich', anchorite. He was born at Compton Martin, nr. Bristol, and ordained priest to the charge of Deverill, nr. Warminster. (It is not clear which village of this name is intended by his biographer.) After a conversion attributed to an interview with a beggar, who told him the contents of his purse and prophesied a life of sanctity for him, he returned to Compton Martin. He was enclosed *c.*1125 in a cell at Haselbury Plucknett, Somerset, where he practised very severe austerities and became renowned for his prophecies and miracles, e.g. that at his prayers the suit of mail which he wore was once cut with scissors as cloth. The statement that he was a *Cistercian seems to rest on a confusion. His cult was mainly confined to SW England, and he was never formally canonized. Feast day, 20 Feb.

Earliest account, written during his lifetime, by Henry of Huntingdon, *Historia Anglorum*, 9. 23 (ed. T. Arnold, RS, 1879, pp. xxix f.). Life by John, Abbot of Ford, prob. written between 1180 and 1190, ed. M. Bell, OSB (Somerset Record Society, 47; 1933), with full introd.

Wulfstan (d. 1023), Bp. of London from 996 to 1002 and Abp. of *York from 1002; homilist and law-writer. (He is not to be confused with the Wulfstan of the following entry.) He probably came from the eastern Danelaw, and was a monk, though it is not known where. He held the see of *Worcester as well as that of York from 1002 to 1016, and was a prominent royal counsellor. Wulfstan was a distinguished writer in Old English, probably surpassed only by his correspondent, *Aelfric. He was the author of numerous homilies (the exact canon is disputed), which are simple practical hortatory expositions of essential doctrines; the best-known, though not the most typical, bears the Latin rubric 'Lupi Sermo ad Anglos quando Dani maxime prosecuti sunt eos, quod fuit anno 1014'; this vividly depicts the miseries of the time and ascribes them, in traditional style, to God's anger at the sustained wickedness of all classes. His longest work is his 'Institutes of Polity, Civil and Ecclesiastical', an interesting attempt at a general work of political theory which is mainly concerned with the duties of the different ranks and classes of society. Wulfstan composed much of the legislation issued after 1008 by Kings Ethelred II and Canute, and drafted or influenced various private law-codes. There is much similarity of ideas and even of wording between these codes and Wulfstan's other writings. A number of MSS have survived which were either written or annotated by Wulfstan. He was a learned man of orderly mind, a conscientious prelate who stamped an ecclesiastical reformer's mark on Old English law. He was regarded as a saint at Ely (where he was buried); but his cult did not spread or become official.

Homilies ed. A. [S.] Napier (Sammlung Englischer Denkmäler in kritischen Ausgaben, 4, Abt. 1; 1883) [no more pub.] and D. Bethurum (Oxford, 1957), with introd. and notes; crit. edn. of 'Sermo Lupi ad Anglos' by D. Whitelock (Methuen's Old English Library, 1939; 3rd edn., 1963), with introd. 'Institutes of Polity' ed. K. Jost (Schweizer Anglistische Arbeiten, 47; 1959). The Laws of Ethelred II and Canute are ed., with modern Eng. tr., by A. J. Robertson, *The Laws of the Kings of England from Edmund to Henry I* (Cambridge, 1925), pp. 45–219. *Wulfstan's Canons of Edgar* separately ed. by R. Fowler (EETS 266; 1972). K. Jost, *Wulfstanstudien* (Schweizer Anglistische Arbeiten, 23; 1950), with detailed bibl. D. Whitelock, 'Archbishop Wulfstan, Homilist and Statesman', *Transactions of the Royal Historical Society*, 4th ser. 24 (1942), pp. 25–45; repr. in id., *History, Law and Literature in 10th–11th Century England* (1981), no. 11; more specialized arts. repr. as nos. 5, 8–10, 12–15. *A Wulfstan Manuscript* containing Institutes, Laws and Homilies. British Library Cotton Nero A I, ed. H. R. Loyn (Early English Manuscripts in Facsimile, 17; Copenhagen, 1971); N. [R.] Ker, 'The Handwriting of Archbishop Wulfstan' in P. Clemoes and K. Hughes (eds.), *England Before the Conquest: Studies in Primary Sources presented to Dorothy Whitelock* (Cambridge, 1971), pp. 315–31. P. Wormald in *Dict. Sp.*, 16 (1994), cols. 1497–1500, s.v. 'Wulfstan (2) d'York'.

Wulfstan, St (c.1009–95), also 'Wulstan', Bp. of *Worcester. After ordination he spent some 25 years in a monastery at Worcester, where he became greatly respected for his humility and asceticism. Elected Bp. of Worcester in 1062, he accepted the office with extreme reluctance, but having resigned himself to it, administered the diocese with great effectiveness till his death. Largely through uncertainty as to the status of the see of Worcester in relation to *Canterbury and *York, Wulfstan found himself opposed at the beginning of his episcopate to both archbishops; but later *Lanfranc was won by the simple goodness of Wulfstan, and together they suppressed the slave trade between England and Ireland. In the secular struggles of the time he assisted *William I against the barons and William II against both the barons and the Welsh. His Life was written by Coleman, a monk of Worcester. Feast day, 19 Jan.

The Old English Life by Coleman, written between 1095 and 1113, has not survived; a Lat. rendering by *William of Malmesbury ed. R. R. Darlington (Camden Society, 3rd ser. 40; 1928; Eng. tr. by J. H. F. Peile, Oxford, 1934). J. W. Lamb, *Saint Wulstan, Prelate and Patriot: A Study of his Life and Times* (CHS, 1933); E. Mason, *St Wulfstan of Worcester c.1008–1095* (Oxford, 1990).

Württemberg Confession. A Protestant confession of faith in 35 articles, compiled by J. *Brenz on the model of the *Augsburg Confession for presentation to the Council of *Trent in 1552. It contained some *Calvinist elements, but it was predominantly *Lutheran, with certain approximations (in view of its purpose) to the specifically Catholic position. Use was made of it by Abp. M. *Parker in preparing the Thirty-Eight Articles of 1563 (see THIRTY-NINE ARTICLES).

Text in H. Heppe (ed.), *Die Bekenntnisschriften der altprotestantischen Kirche Deutschlands* (Cassel, 1855), pp. 491–554. E. Bizer, *Confessio Virtembergica: Das Württembergische Bekenntniss von 1551* (Stuttgart, 1952). P. *Schaff, *A History of the Creeds of Christendom*, 1 (1877), pp. 343 f. and 627–9, with table illustrating the connexion with the Thirty-Nine Articles. See also works cited s.v. THIRTY-NINE ARTICLES.

Wycliffe, John (c.1330–84), English philosopher, theologian, and reformer. John Wycliffe was probably a member of the Wycliffe family who owned property near Richmond in N. Yorks. He was a Fellow of Merton in 1356, Master of Balliol (c.1360–1), and Warden of Canterbury Hall (later incorporated into *Christ Church), Oxford (1365–7); his expulsion from Canterbury Hall by Abp. Simon Langham in favour of a monastic establishment led to a bitter lawsuit and lasting disenchantment with monasticism. Wycliffe was rector of Fillingham (1361–8), of Ludgershall (1368–84) and of Lutterworth (1374–84), but until 1381 he lived mainly in Oxford, from 1363 in Queen's College. He was in the service of the Black Prince and of John of Gaunt after 1371, acting as envoy in negotiations with the Curia in 1374 and as propagandist for the government in 1376 and 1378; Gaunt and the Black Prince's widow protected him against ecclesiastical censures in 1377, 1378, and probably in 1382.

Wycliffe's early reputation was as a philosopher. Reacting against the prevailing scepticism of Oxford thought, which divorced the spheres of natural and supernatural knowledge, he returned to the philosophical realism of St *Augustine and R. *Grosseteste; in his *Summa de Ente* (c.1365–72) he argued that individual beings derived from God through a hierarchy of universals and were therefore in essence changeless and indestructible. From the beginning his philosophy was religious in character, and it was fed by a sense of the spiritual sterility of scepticism. As a theologian he sought inspiration in the Bible and the Fathers rather than in the speculation of the schools, and he fulfilled his doctoral obligations by an unprecedented, if unoriginal, series of lectures commenting on the whole Bible. His growing repugnance at the religious institutions of his time led to his gradual elaboration, on the basis of his philosophy, of a concept of the Church which distinguished its eternal, ideal reality from the visible, 'material' Church, and denied to the latter any authority which did not derive from the former. In his *De Civili Dominio* (1375–6) he maintained that secular and ecclesiastical authority depended on grace and that therefore the clergy, if not in a state of grace, could lawfully be deprived of their endowments by the civil power. This doctrine was condemned in 1377 by Pope *Gregory XI on the initiative of the English Benedictines, though Wycliffe escaped any punishment. In his *De Ecclesia, De Veritate Sacrae Scripturae* and *De Potestate Papae* (1377–8) he maintained that the Bible, as the eternal 'exemplar' of the Christian religion, was the sole criterion of doctrine, to which no ecclesiastical authority might lawfully add, and that the authority of the Pope was ill-founded in Scripture; and in *De Apostasia* (*c*.1382) he denied, in violent terms, that the religious life had any foundation in Scripture, and appealed to the government to reform the whole order of the Church in England. The friars in particular were the object of his denunciation. At the same time in *De Eucharistia* he attacked the doctrine of *transubstantiation as philosophically unsound and as encouraging a superstitious attitude to the Eucharist; he sought to free the Eucharist of the popular cult which conceived of it as miraculous and to inculcate a consciousness of its moral and spiritual effects.

These publicly proclaimed doctrines gradually lost him substantial support in Oxford and reduced his following to a small but loyal group of scholars, prob. with some friends at court. His Eucharistic doctrine was the breaking-point. It was condemned by the University in 1381; and after Wycliffe's public refusal to comply in his *Confessio* had created scandal, and the Peasants' Revolt, popularly though erroneously attributed to his teaching, had magnified the affair, a wide range of his doctrines and the persons of his followers (though not Wycliffe himself) were condemned by Abp. W. *Courtenay at the Blackfriars Council (the '*Earthquake Synod') in 1382. Wycliffe had to retire to Lutterworth, where he revised his works and produced a prolific series of pamphlets attacking his enemies. After his death the continued activity of his disciples, who, as they gained less educated support, became known as *Lollards (q.v.), led to further condemnations of Wycliffe's doctrine in 1388, 1397, and finally at the Council of *Constance in 1415.

Wycliffe aimed at propagating his views widely and was an energetic preacher in Latin and in English, as his surviving sermons show. Though he wrote in English, probably none of the English works attributed to him is really his. He apparently played no direct part in the translation of the Bible undertaken by his disciples (*c*.1380–92), though he undoubtedly inspired the project.

Wycliffe's philosophical influence in Oxford was considerable for at least a generation; his later influence in England, whether on the Lollards or in general, is less clear. However, his philosophical and theological writings from *c*.1380 exercised a major influence on Czech scholars, esp. John *Huss, and many of them survive only in Czech MSS. Though the 16th-cent. Reformers appealed to Wycliffe, his preoccupations were rather different from theirs. Outside the field of philosophy his ideas were not original and can be compared with the similar views of contemporary European reformers. His importance lies in his role in propagating them. Feast day in the ASB, 31 December.

Most of Wycliffe's works are published by the Wyclif Society (35 vols., London, 1883–1914); his *Tractatus de Officio Pastorali*, ed. G. V. Lechler (Leipzig, 1863); *Trialogus*, ed. id. (Oxford, 1869); *De Iuramento Arnaldi*, ed. id., *Johann von Wiclif*, 2 (Leipzig, 1873), pp. 575–9; *De Christo et suo Antichristo*, ed. R. Buddensieg (Gotha, 1880); *Summa de Ente*, ed. S. H. Thomson (Oxford, 1930); *Tractatus de Trinitate*, ed. A. du P. Breck (Boulder, Colo., 1962); *Tractatus de Universalibus*, ed. I. J. Mueller, with Eng. tr. by A. Kenny (2 vols., Oxford, 1985); other controversial pieces preserved in the *Fasciculi Zizaniorum* attributed to T. *Netter, ed. W. W. Shirley (RS, 1858); minor works ed. I. H. Stein in *Speculum*, 7 (1932), pp. 87–94; 8 (1933), pp. 503–10; and in *EHR* 47 (1932), pp. 95–103. The Eng. tracts ed. T. Arnold, *Select English Works* (Oxford, 1867–71), and F. D. Matthew, *English Works . . . hitherto Unprinted* (EETS 74; 1880), are probably not by Wycliffe. W. R. Thomson, *The Latin Writings of John Wyclyf: An Annotated Catalog* (Pontifical Institute of Mediaeval Studies, Subsidia Mediaevalia, 14; Toronto, 1983). Valuable modern studies incl. H. B. Workman, *John Wyclif* (2 vols., Oxford, 1926); K. B. McFarlane, *John Wycliffe and the Beginnings of English Nonconformity* ('Teach Yourself History', 1952); and the standard biog., J. A. Robson, *Wyclif and the Oxford Schools* (Cambridge, 1961). A. Kenny, *Wyclif* (Past Masters, Oxford, 1985). Id., *Wyclif in his Times* (Oxford, 1986). B. Smalley, 'John Wyclif's *Postilla super totam bibliam*', *Bodleian Library Record*, 4 (1953), pp. 186–205; id., 'John Wyclif's *Postilla* on the Old Testament and his *Principium*', in *Oxford Studies presented to Daniel Callus* (Oxford Historical Society, NS 16; 1964), pp. 253–96; id., 'The Bible and Eternity: John Wyclif's Dilemma', *Journal of the Warburg and Courtauld Institutes*, 27 (1964), 73–89; G. A. Benrath, *Wyclifs Bibelkommentar* (Arbeiten zur Kirchengeschichte, 36; 1966). J. H. Dahmus, *The Prosecution of John Wyclif* (New Haven, Conn., and London, 1952). G. [A.] Leff, *Heresy in the Later Middle Ages*, 2 (1967), pp. 494–573. *BRUO* 3 (1959), pp. 2103–6, with bibl. See also bibl. to LOLLARDY.

Wycliffites. See LOLLARDY.

Wynfrith, St. See BONIFACE, ST.

Wyttenbach, Thomas (1472–1526), Swiss Reformer. A native of Biel (Bienne), Switzerland, after studying at *Tübingen he lectured at Basle, teaching the new, philological method of Biblical study. U. *Zwingli was among his pupils. From 1507 to 1515 he was priest in Biel and then canon at Berne until 1519. In 1520 he returned to Biel and publicly supported the Reformation from 1523. Marriage in 1524 led to his deposition and the Reformation was carried through by his successor Jakob Würben in 1528. Wyttenbach left no writings, apart from some letters.

[S. Scheurer], 'Lebens Beschreibung Doctor Thomas Wittenbachs von Biel in der Schweiz', *Bernerisches Mausoleum*, 1 (Berne, 1740), pp. 1–110. F. A. Haller and H. Hermelink in *PRE* (3rd edn.), 21 (1908), pp. 574–7, s.v.

X

Xavier, St Francis. See FRANCIS XAVIER, ST.

Xian. See SIGAN-FU STONE.

Ximénez de Cisneros, Francisco (1436–1517), Cardinal Abp. of Toledo. A native of Torrelaguna in Castile, after studying at Alcalá de Henares and Salamanca, he spent some years in Rome, returning to Spain in 1465 with a letter from *Sixtus IV which provided him with the archpriestship of Uzeda in 1473. His diocesan, Carillo, Abp. of Toledo, who was offended by the appointment, incarcerated him, but in 1480 eventually gave way. Ximénez, restored to his benefice, promptly exchanged it for a chaplaincy in the diocese of Siguenza, where Cardinal Mendoza (later Abp. of Toledo) made him his vicar general. After fulfilling this office with distinction, he unexpectedly gave it up to become an *Observantine friar and entered the convent of San Juan de los Reyes at Toledo, recently founded by *Ferdinand and *Isabella. His life of extreme austerity soon attracted large crowds of penitents and he took refuge in a remote monastery, living for considerable periods as an anchorite.

In 1492 a new epoch in his life began when he reluctantly accepted the office of confessor to Queen Isabella, to whom he had been recommended by Mendoza. His advice was soon sought on affairs of state as well as on strictly spiritual matters. In 1494 he was appointed under the Queen's influence Provincial of the *Franciscans in Castile and in the face of formidable opposition carried through drastic reforms esp. among the *Conventuals. With royal support, he also encouraged reform in other Orders. On the death of Mendoza (1495), he succeeded, again with great reluctance, to the archbishopric of Toledo, the primatial and most influential see in Spain, and an office which carried with it the High Chancellorship of Castile. Behind the outward splendour of his position, Ximénez continued to live a severely ascetic life. In 1499 he followed the court to Granada, where he was active in promoting measures to convert the Moors.

On the death of Isabella (24 Nov. 1504), Ferdinand resigned his title of King of Castile, and Ximénez was faced with the delicate political task of establishing concord between Ferdinand and his son-in-law, the Archduke Philip of Burgundy, who succeeded to the throne. Ferdinand eventually agreed to retire from Castile. On the sudden death of Philip in 1506, Ximénez found himself the virtual ruler of Castile, until Ferdinand returned from Naples in Aug. 1507, bringing for the Archbishop a cardinal's hat. In that year he also became *Inquisitor General. In 1509 he led a Spanish force to Oran in Morocco for purposes partly religious and partly territorial. On the death of Ferdinand (23 Jan. 1516), Ximénez became regent of Castile during the minority of the later *Charles V (q.v.). Intrigues at home and in Flanders, where Charles was then living, made his position extremely difficult, but his vigorous measures enabled him to maintain his authority. On his way to meet Charles, who had landed in Asturias and virtually dismissed him from his office, he died at Roa on 8 Nov. 1517, not without a suspicion of poison.

In addition to his services to the Church, Ximénez was a zealous patron of learning. In 1500 he founded on a lavish scale out of his private income the University of Alcalá (opened 1508), to which he brought distinguished scholars from Paris, Bologna, and Salamanca. With his active encouragement, many devotional classics were published, some translated into Spanish; these were to influence the development of Spanish spirituality. At Toledo he revived the *Mozarabic rite and endowed a chapel in the cathedral for its survival. His chief contribution to scholarship was the famous *Complutensian Polyglot (q.v.; Lat. 'Complutum', i.e. Alcalá).

P. Gayangos and V. de la Fuente (eds.), *Cartas del Cardenal Don Fray Francisco Jimenez de Cisneros, dirigidas á Don Diego Lopez de Ayala* (1867); V. de la Fuente (ed.), *Cartas de los Secretarios del Cardenal D. Fr. Francisco Jimenez de Cisneros durante su Regencia en los años de 1516 y 1517* (1875). The other principal materials are to be found in A. Gómez de Castro, *De Rebus Gestis a F. Ximenio Cisnerio* (fol. 'Compluti' [Alcalá], 1569). There is also an account written by a member of the Cardinal's household, J. de Vallejo, *Memorial de la vida de Fray Francisco Jimenes de Cisneros*, first ed. A. de la Torre y del Cerro (Madrid, 1913). Other early Lives by E. de Robles (Toledo, 1604), M. Baudier (Paris, 1635; Eng. tr., 1671), P. de Quintanilla y Mendoza (Palermo, 1653), J. Marsollier (Toulouse, 1694), and [V.] E. Fléchier (Paris, 1693; also 2 vols., Amsterdam, 1693). Important modern studies by C. J. *Hefele (Tübingen, 1844; Eng. tr., 1860), [Jerónimo López de Alvarez de Toledo y del Hierro], Conde de Cedillo (3 vols., Madrid, 1921–8), and J. García Oro (Biblioteca de Autores Cristianos, 520 and 528; 1992–3). Other studies by J. P. R. Lyell (London, 1917, with good bibl.), R. Merton (ibid., 1934), and J. García Mercadal (2nd edn., Madrid, 1941). W. Starkie, *Grand Inquisitor: Being an Account of Cardinal Ximenez de Cisneros and his Times* (1940; popular). L. F. de Retana, CSSR, *Cisneros y su siglo* (2 vols., 1929–30). J. García Oro, OFM, *Cisneros y la reforma del clero español en tiempo de los reyes católicos* (1971); P. Sáinz Rodríguez, *La siembra mística del cardenal Cisneros y las reformas en la Iglesia* (1979).

Xystus. See SIXTUS.

Y

Yah, abbreviation of *Yahweh (q.v.). This form of the word is confined to poetical passages in the OT.

Yahweh. The Hebrew proper name of the Deity, formerly rendered in English as '*Jehovah'. It probably represents the correct original pronunciation of the *Tetragrammaton (q.v.).

year, liturgical. In the W. the Christian year is based on the week and the two festivals of *Easter and *Christmas. Easter, by its Passover connection, forms a link with the Jewish liturgical calendar, which is lunar; Christmas was fixed on 25 Dec. by the 4th cent., coinciding with the winter solstice according to the Roman calendar, and is thus a link with the Roman civil year which began on 1 Jan., and is solar.

The liturgical year in the W. Church begins with the period leading up to Christmas. The ASB reckons nine Sundays before Christmas, but in most calendars the year starts on *Advent Sunday. There are four Sundays in Advent and either one or two Sundays after Christmas bridge the gap to the *Epiphany (6 Jan.). Acc. to the calendar introduced in the RC Church in 1969, the 'Sundays of the Year' begin after Epiphany and are numbered consecutively, excluding the period from the beginning of *Lent to *Whitsunday. There are thus 33 or 34 'Sundays of the Year' (acc. to the date of Advent), six Sundays of Lent, and eight Sundays of Eastertide (the last being Whitsunday). The C of E retains the general pattern of the numeration of Sundays previously current in the whole W. Church: Sundays 'after Epiphany' are reckoned until *Septuagesima, *Sexagesima, and *Quinquagesima (called in the ASB the 9th, 8th, and 7th Sundays 'before Easter'); *Ash Wednesday introduces the 40 days of Lent, with its six Sundays; and five Sundays 'after Easter' lead up to *Ascension Day with its following Sunday and Whitsunday. The RC Church used to number the Sundays 'after Pentecost' to Advent, and this usage is adopted in the ASB and some other modern liturgies; in the BCP, as in the *Sarum Use, they are reckoned 'after *Trinity', i.e. the Sunday after Pentecost.

The liturgical year in the E. Orthodox Church has much the same shape as in W., with the following modifications: it begins on 1 Sept. (the beginning of the tax year in the Byzantine Empire), and the Sundays outside the period of Lent–Eastertide are numbered 'after Pentecost'. The period of Lent–Eastertide embraces the ten weeks before Easter to the Sunday after Pentecost (called the Sunday of All Saints); during this time the *Triodion and *Pentecostarion are used.

N. Nilles, SJ, *Kalendarium Manuale Utriusque Ecclesiae Orientalis et Occidentalis* (2 vols., Innsbruck, 1896–7). K. A. H. Kellner, *Heortologie oder das Kirchenjahr und die Heiligenfeste in ihrer geschichtlichen Entwicklung* (1901). J. Dowden, *The Church Year and Kalendar* (1910). F. *Cabrol, OSB, *Les Origines liturgiques* (1906). A. A. McArthur, *The Evolution of the Christian Year* (1953). J. van Goudoever, *Biblical Calendars* (Leiden, 1959), esp. pts. 2 and 3. J. Pascher, *Das liturgische Jahr* (Munich, 1962). T. J. Talley, *The Origins of the Liturgical Year* (New York [1986]). A. Adam, *Das Kirchenjahr mitfeiern* [1979]; Eng. tr., *The Liturgical Year* (New York [1981]) (on the changes following the Second Vatican Council). G. *Dix, OSB, *The Shape of the Liturgy* [1945], ch. 11, pp. 303–96; P. Jounel in A. G. Martimort, *L'Église en Prière* (édition nouvelle), 4: *La Liturgie et le temps* [1983], pp. 45–166; Eng. tr. (1986), pp. 31–150. P. G. Cobb, 'The History of the Christian Year', in C. [P. M.] Jones and others, *The Study of Liturgy* (2nd edn., 1992), pp. 455–72; K. Donovan, SJ, 'The Sanctoral', ibid., pp. 472–84. H. Thurston, SJ, in *CE* 3 (1908), pp. 158–66, s.v. 'Calendar'; T. A. Vismans, OP, and A. Hollaardt, OP, in *LW* 2 (1962), cols. 1303–10, s.v. 'Kerkelijk jaar', with further bibl.

Yew Sunday. A medieval name for *Palm Sunday, so called because branches of yew were carried in the liturgical procession.

Yiddish. A language used by Ashkenazi Jews which originated in the 10th cent. from a combination of German city dialects. Approximately 10 per cent. of its vocabulary is drawn from *Hebrew (and *Aramaic), 5 per cent. from Romance, Slavic, and international elements. Four periods of the language may be roughly designated: Earliest Yiddish, to 1250; Old Yiddish, 1250–1500, when the first contact with Slavs and Slavic-speaking Jews was made; Middle Yiddish, 1500–1700, a period of expansion; and Modern Yiddish, from 1700 onwards. It has a considerable literature, extending back to the Old period, and is still spoken and written. The Hebrew alphabet is used for writing Yiddish.

U. Weinreich in *Encyclopaedia Judaica*, 16 (Jerusalem, 1972), cols. 789–98, s.v., with bibl.

YMCA ('Young Men's Christian Association'). An association founded in London in 1844 by George Williams (1821–1905) out of his meetings for prayer and Bible-reading. It has always had an essentially lay and interdenominational character, and has become increasingly interconfessional. At its centre are Christians who wish to share their faith with others, but those of different or no religious faith are welcomed. Most local YMCA associations in Great Britain and Ireland follow one of two patterns of membership: either a single membership, admitting all who accept the aims and purposes of the movement; or a mixture of 'full' members—Christians, who have a part in defining policy—and 'associate' members, who are not necessarily Christian and have no voice in management. Women and girls have been accepted as YMCA members since 1964. The movement aims to foster a world-wide fellowship based on mutual respect and tolerance and seeks to develop stimulating activities in a welcoming environment. Since its early years it has worked to develop young people in body, mind, and spirit. It provides hostels (some of which take in people who have been sleeping rough), sports and leisure facilities, vocational training for the unemployed, drugs counselling, and summer day camps for children and Christian youth groups and camps. It used to work extensively with the Armed Forces at home and abroad, and still does so in Cyprus and Germany. YCare, the overseas development agency of the YMCAs of Great Britain and Ireland, was founded in 1984; it raises funds to help YMCAs in developing countries. The association is active in over 100 countries, of which 85 are affiliated to the World's Alliance of YMCAs, which dates from 1855.

L. L. Doggett, *History of the Young Men's Christian Association* (New York, 1922). [J.] C. [G.] Binfield, *George Williams and the Y.M.C.A.* (1973). C. P. Shedd and others, *History of the World's Alliance of Young Men's Christian Associations* (1955); [J.] C. [G.] Binfield, *This has been Tomorrow: The World Alliance of YMCAs since 1955* (Geneva, 1991). R. C. Morse, *History of the North American Young Men's Christian Association* (New York, 1913); C. H. Hopkins, *History of the Y.M.C.A. in North America* (ibid., 1951).

yoga. A Sanskrit word from the root *yuj*, meaning 'bind together' or 'yoke' and used of any ascetic technique or discipline of meditation. The name is applied in a technical sense to an Indian system of religious philosophy aiming at the union of the soul with the Divine Spirit by means of concentration to the exclusion of all sense-perception. The earliest known description of the system occurs in the *Upanishads* (6th cent. BC); the technique was fully developed by Patanjali in the *Yogasutras* (either 2nd cent. BC or 5th cent. AD). It had considerable influence within Christian devotion (esp., perhaps, within RC monasticism). The term is used more loosely to describe a system of health culture involving ascetic aspects and postures, usually in connection with meditation, which has developed in modern times, esp. in the W. world.

M. Eliade, *Le Yoga: Immortalité et liberté* (1954; Eng. tr., 1958; 2nd edn., with additional material, 1969). J.-M. Déchanet, OSB, *La voie du silence* (1956; Eng. tr., 1960), and other works of this author. M. Eliade in id. (ed.), *Encyclopedia of Religion*, 15 (1987), pp. 519–23, s.v.

Yom Kippur (יוֹם כִּפּוּר). The Hebrew name of the Day of *Atonement (q.v.).

Yonge, Charlotte Mary (1823–1901), novelist. She was born at Otterbourne, near *Winchester, where she lived throughout her life. Imbued by her father with great devotion to the Church, she taught for 71 years in the village Sunday school. When in 1836 J. *Keble became vicar of Hursley (with which parish Otterbourne was then united) she soon fell under his influence, became an enthusiastic supporter of the *Oxford Movement, and determined to apply her remarkable talents as a storyteller to spreading the faith in fiction. Her first success was *The Heir of Redclyffe* (1853). Among those which followed were *Heartsease* (1854), *The Daisy Chain* (1856), *The Trial* (1864), *The Pillars of the House* (1873), and *Magnum Bonum* (1879). She also wrote Lives of Bp. J. C. *Patteson (2 vols., 1873) and of Hannah *More (1888), and from 1851 onwards she edited *The Monthly Packet*, a periodical which aimed esp. at commending Anglican ideals to young women. She issued in all some 160 books.

Collected edn. of her *Novels and Tales* (16 vols., London, 1879–80). C. Coleridge, *Charlotte Mary Yonge: Her Life and Letters* (1903), with text of her autobiog. of her childhood and early youth, pp. 1–119, and list of her works, pp. 355–68. E. Romanes, *Charlotte Mary Yonge: An Appreciation* (1908). G. Battiscombe, *Charlotte Mary Yonge: The Story of an Uneventful Life* (1943). M. Mare and A. C. Percival, *Victorian Best Seller: The World of Charlotte M. Yonge* (1947). G. Battiscombe and others, *A Chaplet for Charlotte Yonge* (1965), incl. genealogical tables and bibl. B. Dennis, *Charlotte Yonge (1823–1901), Novelist of the Oxford Movement* (Lewiston, Queenston, and Lampeter [1992]).

York. The Romans made York ('Eboracum') their military headquarters in N. Britain; *Constantine the Great was first acclaimed there in 306. The first mention of a Bp. of York occurs in the acts of the Council of *Arles (314). The original Christian community was destroyed in the Saxon invasions, though Roman defences and buildings were still in use and determined the pattern of royal and ecclesiastical occupation when Christianity was restored in the 7th cent. In 625 St *Paulinus was consecrated Bp. of York; he baptized the Northumbrian King, *Edwin, in 627 and received the *pallium in 631, but in 633 after another pagan invasion Paulinus fled to *Rochester, and York came under the care of the bishops of *Lindisfarne. The see was finally restored in 664 with the consecration of *Wilfrid, who reintroduced Roman usages and favoured *Benedictine monasticism. Among the early bishops was St *John of Beverley. In 735, under *Egbert, the brother of the King, the see was raised to archiepiscopal dignity and its archbishops became the primates of the Northern Province, as *Gregory the Great had originally intended. Egbert also founded the famous School of York; its pupils included his successor Ethelbert and the famous scholar *Alcuin. From 867 to 954 York was ruled by kings of Scandinavian origin; the archiepiscopal succession was unbroken. Later English kings regarded the Abps. of York (e.g. St *Oswald, *Wulfstan) as useful agents in a dubiously loyal region, and appointed them from outside the North; from 972 to 1016 the impoverished Abps. also held the rich see of *Worcester. They fostered the four great secular minsters (York itself, *Ripon, *Beverley, and *Southwell) which served as local centres of Church life, but it was only after the Norman Conquest that monasticism north of the Humber revived with new foundations, of which St Mary's (Benedictine, 1089), just outside the wall of York, was the richest.

Under the first Norman Archbishop, Thomas of Bayeux (1070–1100), began the long drawn out struggle for precedence between *Canterbury and York. In 1071, in a discussion at Rome between *Lanfranc of Canterbury and Thomas of York, Pope *Alexander II decided in favour of the former, who was to consecrate the Archbishops of York and receive their oath of obedience. But in 1118 Thurstan, Abp. elect of York, refused to submit and appealed to *Callistus II, who in 1119 consecrated him and released him and his successors from the supremacy of Canterbury. The controversy continued for two centuries, its influence being shown in the opposition of Abp. Roger (1154–81) to Abp. T. *Becket, and was finally settled by Innocent VI (1352–62), who decided that the Abp. of Canterbury was to have precedence and the title of 'Primate of All England', and that the Abp. of York should be styled 'Primate of England'. Either archbishop was allowed to carry his cross in the other's province. Only after this decision did some Abps. of York accept translation to Canterbury, T. *Arundel (1396) being the first, and F. D. Coggan (1974) the tenth.

At the height of its prosperity medieval York (much larger than Roman York) contained well over 40 parish churches (12 were pre-Norman; a few were demolished before 1410), nine religious houses, the great hospital of St Leonard, several lesser hospitals and 16 chapels. The city was one of the two largest provincial towns in England and long remained important as a regional capital. The Archbishop's role in regional affairs was most strikingly shown when Abp. Thurstan (1119–40) commanded the army which defeated the Scots at the Battle of the Standard (1138). Other medieval Archbishops included connections of the royal family (*William of York, 1143–7 and 1153–4; Geoffrey Plantagenet, 1191–1212), members of great northern families (Alexander Neville, 1374–88; Richard le *Scrope, who was executed for rebellion; George Neville, 1465–76), and civil servants who were cardinals (J. *Kempe, C. *Bainbridge, and T. *Wolsey).

There is evidence of *Lollard views in early 16th-cent. York, but the city was deeply conservative during the Reformation; it admitted R. *Aske, leader of the *Pilgrimage of Grace, without difficulty in 1536 and the cathedral clergy conducted him to the high altar, where Aske made his oblation. The Reformation brought not only the end of the York *Use, the dissolution of religious houses and of the city's hundred or more chantries, with consequent losses of buildings, furnishings, and books, but also the demolition of 14 parish churches and (after 1580) the end of the famous medieval drama of York. The house of the abbot of St Mary's (the 'King's Manor') became (1539) the seat of the royal Council of the North, of which the Archbishops were members and sometimes Presidents. Elizabethan York contained a few active *recusants, esp. women (see CLITHEROW, M). Puritanism became strong in York in the 17th cent., but the city supported *Charles I until its surrender to Parliament after a short siege in 1644; Methodism took firm root in the 18th cent. During the 20th cent. a number of the city churches were declared redundant and put to other uses. In the 1970s the Evangelical preaching of David Watson (1933–84) at St Cuthbert's and St Michael-le-Belfrey attracted attention. Among post-Reformation Abps. were E. *Grindal, E. *Sandys, L. Blackburne, 1724–43 (whose enemies accused him of buccaneering), T. *Herring, C. G. *Lang, W. *Temple, and A. M. *Ramsey.

No churches in York can be traced back to Roman times, though Roman materials were reused in several. The alignment of St Michael-le-Belfrey, unlike that of the adjoining Minster, follows the Roman street-plan. Since it lies near the centre of the Roman fortress, it may conceivably cover the wooden church and later stone basilica of King Edwin, of which no traces have been found under the present Minster. The Saxon cathedral, wherever it lay, was destroyed by the Normans during the rebellion of 1069. Abp. Thomas then began and Abp. Roger completed the great Norman church which preceded the present York Minster, rebuilt on the same site between c.1227 and 1472. Like its predecessors it was dedicated to St Peter. There were four restorations in the 19th cent. The foundations of the Central Tower and West Front, which rest on

Roman rubbish, were strengthened between 1967 and 1972; serious damage was done by a fire in 1984. York contains much distinguished medieval glass, esp. in All Saints', North Street, and in the Minster, the windows of which were restored after 1945 under the guidance of Dean E. Milner-White (d. 1963).

Little remains of the medieval Archbishops' palace, which stood north of the Minster, near the site of the Roman legionary commandant's house. Abp. Young (1561–8) began its destruction; it was replaced by the present palace at Bishopthorpe.

In the 11th cent. York put forward claims to supremacy over English dioceses to its south and over dioceses in *Scotland. For four cents. it had only two English suffragans (*Durham and *Carlisle) until the addition of *Sodor and Man and the transfer of *Chester from Canterbury in 1542; the creation of new sees (beginning with Ripon, 1836) has at last brought the number of suffragans up to and beyond the twelve envisaged over 13 centuries earlier by Gregory the Great.

A university was founded at York in 1963. There is no faculty of theology, but the Borthwick Institute of Historical Research specializes in work on ecclesiastical archives.

Registers of Walter Gray [Abp. 1215–55], ed. J. Raine (Surtees Society, 56; 1872); of Walter Giffard [Abp. 1266–79], ed. W. Brown (ibid. 109; 1904); of William Wickwane [Abp. 1279–85], ed. id. (ibid. 114; 1907); of John le Romeyn [Abp. 1286–96] and Henry Newark [Abp. 1296–99], ed. id. (ibid. 123 and 128; 1913–17); of Thomas Corbridge [Abp. 1300–4], ed. id. (ibid. 138 and 141; 1925–8); of William Greenfield [Abp. 1306–15], ed. id. and A. H. Thompson (ibid. 145, 149, 151–3; 1931–40); and of William Melton [Abp. 1317–40], ed. R. M. T. Hill and others (Canterbury and York Society, 70, 71, 76, etc.; 1977 ff.). J. Raine (ed.), The Fabric Roll of York Minster (Surtees Society 35; 1859). 'York Statutes' in H. Bradshaw and C. *Wordsworth (eds.), Statutes of Lincoln Cathedral, 2 (1897), pp. 90–135. W. *Dugdale, *Monasticon Anglicanum, 6, pt. 3 (1830 edn.), pp. 1172–1209. C. T. Clay (ed.), York Minster Fasti, Being Notes on the Dignitaries, Archdeacons and Prebendaries in the Church of York prior to the Year 1307 (Yorkshire Archaeological Society, Record Series, 133–4, for 1957–8; 1958–9). J. Raine (ed.), The Historians of the Church of York and its Archbishops (3 vols., RS, 1879–94). W. H. Dixon and J. Raine, Fasti Eboracenses: Lives of the Archbishops of York, 1 (1863). J. W. Lamb, The Archbishopric of York: The Early Years (1967). J. M. Cooper, The Last Four Anglo-Saxon Archbishops of York (Borthwick Papers, 38; 1970); D. L. Douie, Archbishop Geoffrey Plantagenet and the Chapter of York [Abp. 1191–1212] (St Anthony's Hall Publications, ibid. 18; 1960). J. Hughes, Pastors and Visionaries: Religion and Secular Life in Late Medieval Yorkshire (Woodbridge, Suffolk, 1988). D. M. Palliser, The Reformation in York 1534–1553 (Borthwick Papers, 40; 1971); id., Tudor York (Oxford Historical Monographs, 1979); A. G. Dickens, The Marian Reaction in the Diocese of York (St Anthony's Hall Publications, 11 and 12; 1957). F. Drake, Eboracum, or the History and Antiquities of the City of York (1736), esp. bk. 2, 'The History and Antiquities of the Church of York', pp. 399–627. A. Raine, Mediaeval York: A Topographical Survey Based on Original Sources (1955). VCH, Yorks. The City of York, ed. P. M. Tillott (1961), esp. pp. 337–419; A. Stacpoole, OSB, and others (eds.), The Noble City of York (York, 1972). City of York (Royal Commission on Historical Monuments, 5 vols., 1962–81). P. Addyman, 'Archaeology in York 1831–1981', in C. H. Feinstein (ed.), York 1831–1981 (1981), pp. 53–87; E. Royle, 'Religion in York 1831–1981', ibid., pp. 205–33. J. Browne, The History of the Metropolitan Church of St Peter, York (2 vols., 1847). G. E. Aylmer and R. [C.] Cant (eds.), A History of York Minster (Oxford, 1977). H. Gee in DECH (1912), pp. 662–6, s.v.

Young Men's Christian Association. See YMCA.

Young Women's Christian Association. See YWCA.

Young, Patrick (1584–1652), biblical and patristic scholar. He was educated at St Andrews. After incorporation at Oxford in July 1605, he was ordained and became a chaplain at All Souls College. A year or two later he settled in London, where he was appointed Royal Librarian and prob. assisted *James I in preparing the Latin edition of his Works which appeared in 1619. From 1623 to 1647 he was rector of Hayes, Greater London. In 1633 he published from the *Codex Alexandrinus, which had reached the Royal Library from Cyril *Lucar in 1628, the *editio princeps* of St *Clement of Rome's *Ep. I ad Cor.* and in 1637 a folio *Catena Graecorum Patrum in Jobum* on the basis of two Bodley MSS; but these works, though important, embody only a fraction of his great erudition. On his title-pages he Latinized his name as 'Patricius Junius'.

Letters calendared and ed. J. Kemke (Sammlung Bibliothekswissenschaftlicher Arbeiten, ed. K. Dziatzko, 12; 1898), with Life, pp. v–xxix. *'Catalogus Librorum Manuscriptorum Bibliothecae Wigorniensis' made in 1622–1623 by Patrick Young,* ed. I. Atkins and N. R. Ker (Cambridge, 1944). Life in T. Smith, *Vitae Quorundam Eruditissimorum et Illustrium Virorum* (London, 1707; sep. pagination). A. H. Millar in *DNB* 63 (1900), pp. 385 f.

yule. The word, of Teutonic ancestry, which etymologically seems to imply 'noise' or 'clamour', was prob. originally applied to a Scandinavian feast of obscure origin, possibly connected with the turn of the year, and hence in Old English to the season of Dec. and Jan. In later usage it came to denote *Christmas and its attendant festivities. Except in the north of England the term is now archaic, but it is still found in compounds such as 'yule-log' connected with old-fashioned Christmas celebrations. Until the middle of the 19th cent. it was also used as an exclamation of joy and revelry at Christmastide.

Yvo, St, of Chartres. See IVO, ST.

YWCA ('Young Women's Christian Association'). A charitable body devoted to the needs of young women, esp. those who are at risk or suffering discrimination; it sees its work as the practical expression of its Christian values. It is entirely separate from the *YMCA. It was founded in 1855 by Miss Emma Robarts, who started a Prayer Union, and Lady Mary Jane Kinnaird, who opened the first hostel for Florence *Nightingale's nurses in London. The two organizations united in 1877, and the YWCA is now a world-wide body. In Great Britain it is known primarily for its national network of safe, affordable accommodation, but it also provides education, training, counselling, and support through its women's and community centres.

A. V. Rice, *A History of the World's Young Women's Christian Association* (New York, 1948). C. Seymour-Jones, *Journey of Faith: The history of the World YWCA 1945–94* (1994). F. Kinnaird in *HERE* 12 (1921), pp. 838–41, s.v. 'Young Women's Christian Association'.

Z

Zabarella, Francesco (1360–1417), Italian canonist. Having studied jurisprudence at *Bologna, he taught canon law at Florence from 1385 to 1390 and at Padua from 1390 to 1410, being at the same time employed in both the Paduan and the Venetian diplomatic services. Called to Rome by Boniface IX to tender advice in the matter of the *Great Schism, he took part in the Council of *Pisa in 1409. Though not in major orders, in 1410 he received the bishopric of Florence, which he resigned on being created cardinal by *John XXIII in 1411. After supporting John at the Council of Rome in 1412–13, he conducted the negotiations with the Emp. Sigismund for the Council of *Constance. His courageous conduct at the Council, which he continued to attend after John XXIII had fled (1415), contributed largely to the final healing of the schism. Though a supporter of John, he advised the Pope to abdicate, and until his death made continuous efforts to bring about the election of a new Pope. His collection of proposals for ending the schism entitled 'De schismate' (1402–8) was first printed in 1545. It was placed on the *Index, however, because it asserted the supremacy of the General Council over the Pope. His writings on canon law, the 'Lectura super *Clementinis' and the 'Commentaria in libros *Decretalium', long remained standard works.

G. Vedova, *Memorie intorno alla vita ed alle opere del cardinale F. Zabarella* (Padua, 1829). G. Zonta, *Francesco Zabarella* (ibid., 1915). W. Ullmann, *The Origins of the Great Schism: A Study in Fourteenth-century Ecclesiastical History* (1948), pp. 191–231; B. Tierney, *Foundations of the Conciliar Theory: The Contribution of the Medieval Canonists from Gratian to the Great Schism* (Cambridge, 1955), esp. pp. 220–37; T. E. Morrissey, 'Franciscus Zabarella (1360–1417): Papacy, Community, and Limitations upon Authority', in G. F. Lytle (ed.), *Reform and Authority in the Medieval and Reformation Church* (Washington, DC [1981]), pp. 37–54. See also works cited under CONSTANCE, COUNCIL OF.

Zacchaeus. The chief 'publican' (tax-collector), who was the subject of an incident related in Lk. 19: 1–10. Having climbed a sycamore tree to see Christ, he was called by name to come down and give Him lodging in his house.

Zachariah. The father of St *John the Baptist (Lk. 1 and 3: 2). A Jewish priest, he is said to have received a vision in the *Temple promising him and his aged wife, *Elizabeth, a son, who would be 'filled with the Holy Ghost, even from his mother's womb' (Lk. 1: 15). He celebrated the birth of the child and the coming redemption of Israel in the '*Benedictus'. Acc. to later tradition he was murdered in the Temple at the command of Herod. Feast day, 5 Nov.

Zacharias, St (d. 752), Pope from 741. Born in Calabria, he was the last Greek Pope and the last Pope to send letters to the E. capital to announce his election. Revising the policy of his predecessor, Gregory III, he gave up the alliance with Duke Trasamund of Spoleto, and, through his personal influence, induced Liutprand, King of the Lom-

bards, to return four cities and all her patrimonies to the Church. He also obtained a 20-year truce, caused the King to abandon his attack on *Ravenna and persuaded him to restore what he had already taken of his possessions. King Ratchis confirmed this truce, but his successor, Aistulf, captured Ravenna in 751. His relations with the Frankish kingdom were very cordial, esp. through the influence of St *Boniface, to whose missionary activities he gave full support. In 747 he addressed a long letter to *Pepin III in answer to questions about Church reform, and in 751 he sanctioned the deposition of the last Merovingian, Childeric III, in Pepin's favour. Zacharias vigorously denounced the *Iconoclastic policy of the Emps. *Leo III and Constantine V, to whom he addressed two letters on the subject. He held synods at Rome in 743 and 745, the latter confirming the condemnation of the two heretics, Adalbert and Clement, by St Boniface. He made an influential Greek translation of the 'Dialogues' of St *Gregory the Great. Feast day in the E., 5 Sept.; in the W., formerly 15 Mar.

Two letters to Constantine V, ed. W. Gundlach in *MGH*, Epistolae, 3 (1892), pp. 479–87, 709–11. Jaffé, 1, pp. 262–70. R. Rau (ed.), *Briefe des Bonifatius, Willibalds Leben des Bonifatius* (Ausgewählte Quellen zur Deutschen Geschichte des Mittelalters, 4b; Darmstadt, 1968), pp. 140–84, 210–12, 234–8, 256–70, 272–84, 288–306, 391–436 (incl. acts of the two Roman Synods). *LP* (Duchesne), 1 (1886), pp. 426–39. Eng. tr., with valuable introd., by R. Davis, *The Lives of the Eighth-Century Popes* (Translated Texts for Historians, 13; Liverpool, 1992), pp. 29–50. O. Bertolini, *Roma di fronte a Bisanzio e ai Longobardi* (1941), pp. 493–513; id., 'I Rapporti di Zaccaria con Costantino V e con Artavasdo nel racconto del biografo del papa e nella probabile realtà storica', *Archivio della Società romana di Storia patria*, 78 (1955), pp. 1–21. T. F. X. Noble, *The Republic of St Peter: The Birth of the Papal State, 680–825* (Philadelphia [1984]), esp. pp. 49–57 and 65–71.

Zacharias Scholasticus (d. after 536), also 'Zacharias of Mitylene' and 'Zacharias Rhetor', *Monophysite writer. He was a native of Maiuma, nr. Gaza, and hence known, with *Procopius and *Aeneas of Gaza, as one of the 'Gaza Triad'. About 492 he became a lawyer at *Constantinople and is known to have been in later life Bp. of Mitylene. His most important work was a Church History, valuable for the years 450–91. It survives in *Syriac embedded in a later compilation. Zacharias was also the author of biographies of *Severus of Antioch, Peter the Iberian and others; of a dialogue, 'De Opificio Mundi', directed against the *Neoplatonists; and of a Refutation of the *Manichees. In recent years a collection of *anathemas against the Manichees, known as the 'Seven Chapters', has been ascribed to Zacharias.

His 'De Opificio Mundi', ed., with Lat. tr. and notes, by C. Barth (Leipzig, 1655; with Aeneas of Gaza's 'De Immortalitate Animae', pp. 164–326); it was repr. from the edn. of A. *Gallandi in J. P. Migne, *PG* 85. 1011–44; crit. edn. by M. M. Colonna (Naples, 1973). His Refutation of the Manichees was ed. A. Demetracopulos, *Bibliotheca Ecclesiastica*, 1 (Leipzig, 1866), pp. 1–18. His 'Church History', incorporated in a later Syriac Chronicle in which alone it survives, ed., with Lat. tr., by E. W. Brooks (CSCO, Syriaci Scriptores, 3rd ser. 5–6; 1919–24); Eng. tr. by F. J. Hamilton and E. W. Brooks (London, 1899). Syriac tr. of Lives of Severus of Antioch ed., with Fr. tr., by M.-A. Kugener in *PO* 2 (1907), pp. 5–115; of an Egyptian monk named Isaias ed. E. W. Brooks, *Vitae Virorum apud Monophysitas Celeberrimorum* (CSCO, Syriaci Scriptores, 3rd ser. 25; 1907), pp. 3–16, with Lat. tr., pp. 3–10; of a fragment of Life of Peter the Iberian, ibid., p. 18, with Lat. tr., p. 12. The 'Seven Chapters' are ed. M. Richard, *Iohannis Caesariensis . . . Opera* (CCSG 1; 1977), pp. xxx–xli; repr., with Eng. tr., introd., and comm., by S. N. C. Lieu in *Jahrbuch für Antike und Christentum*, 26 (1983), pp. 152–218. M.-A. Kugener, 'La Compilation historique de Pseudo-Zacharie le Rhéteur', *Revue de l'Orient chrétien*, 5 (1900), pp. 201–14 and 461–80; id., 'Observations sur la vie de l'ascète Isaïe et sur les vies de Pierre l'Ibérien et de Théodore d'Antinoë par Zacharie le Scolastique', *BZ* 9 (1900), pp. 464–70. T. Nissen, 'Eine christliche Polemik gegen Julians Rede auf den König Helios', ibid. 40 (1940), pp. 15–22. E. Honigmann, *Patristic Studies* (ST 173; 1953), pp. 194–204 (no. 21: 'Zacharias of Mitylene'). P. Allen, 'Zachariah Scholasticus and the *Historia Ecclesiastica* of Evagrius Scholasticus', *JTS* NS 31 (1980), pp. 471–88. *CPG* 3 (1979), pp. 323 f. (nos. 6995–7001). G. Bardy in *DTC* 15 (pt. 2; 1950), cols. 3676–80, s.v. 'Zacharie le Rhéteur'; K. Wegenast in *PW*, Zweite Reihe, 18 (1967), cols. 2212–16, s.v.

Zadokite Fragments. See DEAD SEA SCROLLS.

Zahn, Theodor (1838–1933), NT and patristic scholar. Born at Mörs, he was Privatdozent (1868) and extraordinary Professor (1871) at Göttingen and Professor successively at Kiel (1877), Erlangen (1878), Leipzig (1888), and Erlangen (again, 1892). He retired in 1909. His standpoint was that of sober conservatism and all his work was characterized by vast erudition and great thoroughness. His long series of studies on the NT *canon, embodied in his *Geschichte des neutestamentlichen Kanons* (2 vols., 1888–92) and the successive fascicles of *Forschungen zur Geschichte des neutestamentlichen Kanons* (10 parts, 1881–1929), contained much pioneer work. He edited a Commentary on the NT, to which he himself contributed the volumes on Mt. (1903), Lk. (1913), Jn. (1908), Acts (2 vols., 1919–21), Rom. (1910), Gal. (1905) and Rev. (2 vols., 1924–6); he also wrote an Introduction to the NT (2 vols., 1897–9; Eng. tr., 3 vols., 1909). His studies in the field of patristics included *Marcellus von Ancyra* (1867), *Der Hirt des Hermas untersucht* (1868), *Ignatius von Antiochien* (1873) and the *Acta Joannis* (1880). With A. *Harnack and O. von Gebhardt he edited *Patrum Apostolicorum Opera* (major edn., 1875–8; minor edn., 1877). Among his many works addressed to a less specialized public were *Geschichte des Sonntags vornehmlich in der alten Kirche* (1878) and *Skizzen aus dem Leben der alten Kirche* (1894).

Festschriften for Theodor Zahn, Leipzig, 1908, with contributions by N. Bonwetsch and others; and ibid., 1928, with contributions by P. Bachmann and others. *Zahnbibliographie* (ibid., 1918). E. Stange (ed.), *Die Religionswissenschaft der Gegenwart in Selbstdarstellungen*, 1 (1925), last item (28 pp.). A. Meyer in *RGG* (2nd edn.), 5 (1931), cols. 2070 f., s.v.

Zaire, Christianity in. This huge area of central Africa was formed into a single country through the combined efforts of King Leopold II king of the Belgians, who wanted to establish a major colony in Africa, and H. M. *Stanley, the explorer, who returned to the Congo in 1879 in the employment of Leopold. The Congo Independent State, with Leopold as its king, was recognized by the European powers in 1885; it was annexed by Belgium in 1908, becoming the Belgian Congo.

The former RC missionary efforts dating from the 15th cent. in the extreme W. of modern Zaire and parts of Angola had effectively ceased at the end of the 18th cent. (see CONGO), but the late 19th-cent. exploration was quickly followed by missionary endeavour, both Protestant and RC. In 1878 a mission of the British *Baptist Missionary Society, led by George Grenfell, began work in the lower Congo region. In 1880 the *White Fathers, arriving in this part of Africa from the E. Coast, founded a mission at Mulweva (on Lake Tanganyika) in the E. of modern Zaire. The Baptists were soon followed by numerous other Protestant missions, mostly British and American, but including the Svenska Mission Forbundet from *Sweden. American *Methodists were active in Katanga, the American Presbyterian Congo Mission and the Congo Inland Mission in Kasai, and the Africa Inland Mission and the Heart of Africa Mission in the NE. Among RCs the Scheut Fathers, the national Belgian missionary society, were entrusted with a Vicariate Apostolic of the Congo in 1888; they were joined by Belgian Jesuits who took over the lower Congo in 1893, leaving Scheut the Kasai. *Trappists followed in 1895 and *Premonstratensians in 1898, while in 1910 *Benedictines from the abbey of Saint-André began work in Katanga. At Leopold's insistence, RC missionaries were almost exclusively of Belgian nationality.

From the mid-1890s Leopold's policy of financing the Independent State through a trading monopoly enforced with much brutality made missionary work difficult and provoked protest from Protestant missionaries, Swedish, American, and British. The ensuing international agitation led to Belgium's annexation of the Congo in 1908. Both before and after 1908, however, there was a relationship of close co-operation between the government and the RC Belgian missionaries, who were granted extensive privileges, esp. in the areas of education, health, and land grants. It was formalized by the Concordat of 1906, which was maintained by the Act of Annexation. Only in 1946 did the Protestants obtain equal treatment in regard to health and education. In general the alliance between the RC Church and the State was weakened in the 1950s when there was a socialist government in Brussels. At the same time independent African Churches and prophetic movements, which had all been banned since the trial of Simon *Kimbangu in 1921, but which had spread clandestinely throughout the country under various influences, including 'Watch Tower' ('Kitawala') and the 'Khaki movement' of Simon Mpadi in the 1940s, were allowed to come into the open.

After Independence in 1960 there was much popular resentment against missionaries, esp. RCs, and in subsequent disorders many were murdered. The attack at Kisangani in 1964 was led by a Kitawalan pastor. After 1965, when President Mobutu re-established an ordered and highly authoritarian state (named Zaire in 1971), the Churches recovered some security. The Churches were largely Africanized, Joseph Malula becoming the RC Abp. of Leopoldville (named Kinshasa) in 1964. In the following year, by presidential decree only three Churches were recognized: the RC Church, the 'Church of Christ in Zaire' (a loose federation of mission-founded Protestant

Churches), and the Kimbanguists, to which the Greek Orthodox Church was added later. All other independent Churches were again proscribed. By far the most powerful Church remained the RC, which controlled the majority of the country's schools. In 1972 the campaign for Zairean 'Authenticity' led to a new Church–State conflict. Crucifixes were removed from schools and hospitals and all religious instruction was forbidden. By 1976 much of this was reversed. An uneasy balance in which the Churches remain effectively the only free organizations within the country but say little about human rights violations has remained the pattern.

W. H. Bentley, *Pioneering on the Congo* (2 vols., 1900), F. de Meus, OSB, and R. Steenberghen, OSB, *Les Missions religieuses au Congo Belge* (Antwerp, 1947). R. M. Slade, *English-Speaking Missions in the Congo Independent State (1878–1908)* (Académie royale des Sciences coloniales, Classe des sciences morales et politiques, Mémoires in-8°, NS 16, fasc. 2; Brussels, 1959). A. Andersson, *Messianic Popular Movements in the Lower Congo* (Studia Ethnographica Upsaliensia, 14; Uppsala, 1958). E. M. Braekman, *Histoire du Protestantisme au Congo* (Brussels, 1961). D. Lagergren, *Mission and State in the Congo: A Study of the Relations between Protestant Missions and the Congo Independent State Authorities with Special Reference to the Equator District, 1885–1903* (Uppsala, 1970). M. Sinda, *Le Messianisme congolais et ses incidences politiques* (Bibliothèque historique, 1972). M. D. Markowitz, *Cross and Sword: The Political Role of Christian Missions in the Congo, 1908–1960* (Stanford, Calif. [1973]). C. Irvine, *The Church of Christ in Zaire: A Handbook of Protestant Churches, Missions, and Communities, 1878–1978* (Indianapolis [1978]). A. Hastings, *The Church in Africa 1450–1950* (Oxford History of the Christian Church, 1994), *passim*; id., *A History of African Christianity 1950–1975* (Cambridge, 1979), *passim*.

Zambia, Christianity in. Missionary work began relatively late in the area of central Africa which came to be known as Northern Rhodesia until it was renamed Zambia when it became independent in 1964. The first effective mission was that of François Coillard of the Paris Evangelical Missionary Society who, after 20 years in Lesotho, began work among the Lozi at the court of King Lewanika in 1886. At much the same time the *LMS established a mission in the north of the country and Scottish *Presbyterians, advancing from Livingstonia, came in the east. The main RC missions were the *White Fathers in the north, esp. strong in Bembaland, and in the south the *Jesuits, who moved up from the earlier mission in Southern Rhodesia. There were few local clergy before the Second World War, but one of the earliest was David Kaunda, ordained as a Church of Scotland minister in 1929, the father of Kenneth Kaunda, Zambia's first President.

Missionaries of different denominations multiplied, particularly in the towns developing on the Copperbelt, and an early attempt to unite them ecumenically in the 1930s resulted in the formation of the African United Church (the United Missions in the Copperbelt) and in the establishment in Kitwe of the Mindolo Ecumenical Foundation. In 1965, soon after political independence, the United Church of Zambia (UCZ), comprising *Congregationalists, *Methodists, and the Paris Mission, was inaugurated at Mindolo. Other major denominations are the Anglicans, African Reformed (founded by a Dutch Reformed Mission from *South Africa), and *Jehovah's Witnesses. In 1953 Alice 'Lenshina', after a visionary

experience, left the Presbyterian Church at Lubwa to found the Lumpa Church, whose membership grew very large over the next decade. In 1963 its followers came into armed conflict with the government and with Kaunda's party, UNIP; hundreds were killed, and the Lumpa Church was banned.

Most Zambians are members of one of the Christian Churches, the RC being the largest. Its first Zambian Abp. of Lusaka, Emmanuel Milingo, appointed in 1969, acquired a special following and international reputation on account of his ministry of healing and *exorcism, but he was in consequence made to resign in 1983 and has subsequently lived in Rome.

J. V. Taylor and D. Lehmann, *Christians of the Copperbelt: The Growth of the Church in Northern Rhodesia* (1961); R. I. Rotberg, *Christian Missionaries and the Creation of Northern Rhodesia 1880–1924* (Princeton, NJ, 1965); R. Henkel, *Christian Missions in Africa: A Social Geographical Study of the Impact of their Activities in Zambia* (Geographia Religionum, 3; Berlin, 1989). F. J. Verstraelen, *An African Church in Transition. From Missionary Dependence to Mutuality in Mission: A Case Study on the Roman Catholic Church in Zambia* (2 vols., Leiden, 1979). G. Verstraelen-Gilhuis, *From Dutch Mission Church to Reformed Church in Zambia: The Scope for African Leadership and Initiative in the History of a Zambian Mission Church* (Franeker, Netherlands [1982]). P. Bolink, *Towards Church Union in Zambia: A Study of Missionary Co-operation and Church-Union Efforts in Central Africa* (ibid. [1967]). E. Milingo, *The World in Between: Christian Healing and the Struggle for Spiritual Survival*, ed. M. Macmillan (1984).

Zanchi, Girolamo (1516–90), *Calvinist theologian. Born near Bergamo in N. Italy, he became an *Augustinian Canon in 1531 and was sent to Lucca. Here from 1541 he came under the influence of *Peter Martyr and the writings of P. *Melanchthon and H. *Bullinger. He left Italy and, after visiting J. *Calvin in Geneva in 1551, he became Professor of OT at Strasbourg in 1553. His Calvinist leanings led to disputes over the Lord's Supper and *predestination, and in 1563 he gave up his position and became preacher at the Reformed Church in Chiavenna in N. Italy. He was appointed Professor of Dogmatics at Heidelberg in 1567, but when *Lutheranism was imposed in the Palatinate in 1576, he went to Neustadt. He collaborated with Z. *Ursinus on work on a Reformed Confession which was incorporated in the *Harmonia Confessionum* issued at Geneva in 1581. His other writings include *De Religione Christiana* (Neustadt, 1585; Eng. tr., 1599) on predestination and treatises on the nature of God and on Creation.

Opera Theologica (8 vols. in 3, [Geneva] 1605). [C.] Schmidt, 'Girolamo Zanchi', *Theologische Studien und Kritiken*, 32 (1859), pp. 625–708. O. Gründler, *Die Gotteslehre Girolami Zanchis und ihre Bedeutung für seine Lehre von der Prädestination* (Beiträge zur Geschichte und Lehre der Reformierten Kirche, 20; 1965). C. J. Burchill, 'Girolamo Zanchi: Portrait of a Reformed Theologian and his Work', *Sixteenth Century Journal*, 15 (1984), pp. 185–207.

Zealots. A Jewish party of revolt. Acc. to *Josephus (*Bell. Jud.* 7. 8. 1), they were one of the revolutionary factions who, after the collapse of resistance to the Romans in Galilee, inspired the fanatical stand in *Jerusalem which led to its destruction in AD 70. They have been commonly identified with (1) the followers of Judas of Gamala who led a revolt at the time of the census of Quirinius (AD 6) and who, acc. to Josephus, was the 'author of the fourth sect of Jewish philosophy' whose members 'agree in all things with the Pharisaic notions' but 'have an inviolable attachment to liberty, and say that God is their only ruler and lord' (*Antiq.* 18. 1. 6) and (2) the Sicarii who, in the unsettled period before the outbreak of the Jewish war, tried to achieve their ends by assassinating their political opponents and whose refusal to surrender to the Romans at Masada is vividly described by Josephus (*Bell. Jud.* 7. 8. 2–7. 9. 1). His accounts of these groups, however, are not entirely consistent and leave room for doubt. The epithet ζηλωτής ('zealot'), applied in Lk. 6: 15 to Simon, one of the Twelve, is an accurate translation of an Aramaic word, derived from a root meaning 'to be zealous', which in Mk. 3: 18 is transliterated καναναῖος ('Cananaean'); it may mean that Simon belonged to the Zealot party, which in that case must have been already in existence in the lifetime of Jesus. But it may equally well be a description of his character, 'the zealous'.

W. R. Farmer, *Maccabees, Zealots and Josephus: An Inquiry into Jewish Nationalism in the Greco-Roman Period* (New York, 1956). M. Hengel, *Die Zeloten: Untersuchungen zur jüdischen Freiheitsbewegung in der Zeit von Herodes I. bis 70 n. Chr.* (Arbeiten zur Geschichte des Spätjudentums und Urchristentums, 1; Leiden and Cologne, 1961; 2nd edn., 1976; Eng. tr., Edinburgh, 1989). M. Smith, 'Zealots and Sicarii, their Origins and Relation', *HTR* 64 (1971), pp. 1–19; M. Borg, 'The Currency of the Term "Zealot"', *JTS*, NS 22 (1971), pp. 504–12; S. Applebaum, 'The Zealots: The Case for Revaluation', *Journal of Roman Studies*, 61 (1971), pp. 155–70. R. A. Horsley and J. S. Hanson, *Bandits, Prophets, and Messiahs: Popular Movements in the Time of Jesus* (Minneapolis, etc. [1985]), pp. 190–243. E. *Schürer, *The History of the Jewish People in the Age of Jesus Christ*, rev. Eng. tr. by G. Vermes and others, 1 (Edinburgh, 1973), p. 382, and 2 (1979), pp. 598–606. See also comm. on Mt. 10: 4. A. Stumpff in *TWNT* 2 (1935), pp. 886–9; Eng. tr., 2 (1964), pp. 884–6, s.v. ζηλόω. 'C. Der Zelotismus'; D. Rhoads in *Anchor Bible Dictionary*, 6 (1992), pp. 1043–54, s.v., with bibl.

Zechariah. The Hebrew form of the name rendered *Zachariah in Greek. It is widely used in modern English translations of the Bible for the father of St *John the Baptist.

Zechariah, Book of. One of the *Minor Prophets. The Book falls into two distinct sections, chs. 1–8 and 9–14.

The former, deriving for the most part from Zechariah himself, dates from the spring of 519 BC (1: 7) and the winter of 518/17 BC (7: 1). The Jews had returned from exile *c.*537, but the *Temple was not yet restored. After a short introductory prophecy (1: 1–6) there follow accounts of eight visions: (1) 1: 7–17, four horsemen who report that the whole earth is quiet; nevertheless the prophet declares that God will soon end the desolation of *Jerusalem; (2) 1: 18–21, four horns broken by four smiths, signifying the destruction of heathen powers; (3) 2: 1–13, a man with a measuring line who shows that the future glory of Jerusalem will not be confined by a city wall; (4) 3: 1–10, the cleansing of Joshua the High Priest from his 'filthy garments' (i.e. the removal of the nation's guilt) and his investiture with new dignity; (5) 4: 1–14, a seven-branched candlestick, supplied with oil from two olive trees. These are explained as two 'sons of oil', i.e. anointed persons who are prob. the High Priest and the Davidic prince (see MESSIAH). The latter seems to be identified with the person of Zerubbabel, the contemporary head of the royal line of Judah, who is exhorted to com-

plete the restoration of the Temple; (6) 5: 1–4, a flying roll symbolizing the curse which will light on evildoers; (7) 5: 5–11, a woman, named 'Wickedness', carried away in an *ephah* (a large dry measure) from the holy land to a far country; and (8) 6: 1–8, four chariots representing four winds (or spirits) carrying God's judgement to the corners of the earth. Joshua the High Priest (perhaps the original text referred also, or only, to Zerubbabel here) is to be crowned as Messiah (6: 9–15). In chs. 7–8 Zechariah declares that the observance of fasts should give place to true righteousness and prophesies the future glory of Judah when the *Diaspora should be gathered in and the Gentiles seeking God should voluntarily join themselves to the Jews.

Chs. 9–11 and 12–14 both begin (like the following Book of *Malachi) with the descriptive title *massah*, i.e. prophetic utterance (AV and RV, 'burden'). They are prob. both anonymous prophecies, not only different in style from chs. 1–8, but also reflecting the circumstances of an age later than Zechariah. Even chs. 1–8, however, have undergone extensive editing in the post-exilic age, perhaps to make them reflect the version of events recorded in Ezra 3–6.

Comm. by H. G. Mitchell (ICC on Hag., Zech., Mal., and Jon., 1912, pp. 81–362), M. Bič (Berlin, 1962), W. Rudolph (KAT, 13/4, on Hag., Zech., and Mal., 1976, pp. 59–243), and R. [A.] Mason (Camb. Bib., NEB, on Hag., Zech, and Mal., 1977, pp. 27–134), and on chs. 1–8 by A. Petitjean (Paris and Louvain, 1969), D. L. Peterson (London, on Hag. and Zech. 1–8, 1985, pp. 109–320), and C. L. and E. M. Meyers (Anchor Bible, 25B, on Haggai and Zech. 1–8, 1987, pp. 85–445) and on chs. 9–14 by idd. (Anchor Bible, 25C; 1993). L. G. Rignell, *Die Nachtgeschichte des Sacharja: Eine exegetische Studie* (Lund, 1950). B. Stade, 'Deuterozacharja. Eine kritische Studie', *ZATW* 1 (1881), pp. 1–96; 2 (1882), pp. 151–72 and 275–309; P. Lamarche, SJ, *Zacharie ix–xiv: Structure littéraire et messianisme* (Études Bibliques, 1961); B. Otzen, *Studien über Deuterosacharja*, tr. into Ger. by H. Leisterer (Acta Theologica Danica, 6; Copenhagen, 1964). W. A. M. Beuken, SJ, *Haggai-Sacharja 1–8: Studien zur Überlieferungsgeschichte der frühnachexilischen Prophetie* (Studia Semitica Neerlandica, 10; Assen, 1967), esp. pp. 15–20, 84–183, and 230–336. Eissfeldt, pp. 429–40.

Zeno (*c.*450?–91), Emp. of the E. from 474. His life was a tissue of treachery and violence, and his reign a succession of disastrous wars against his relations and ministers, and against the Ostrogoths (see THEODORIC). He took an active, but ill-advised, part in attempting to reconcile the *Monophysites; but his *Henoticon (482) did nothing to bring about the reunion for which it was devised, and occasioned a new schism between Constantinople and Rome.

Accounts of his reign in E. Stein and J. R. Palanque, *Histoire du Bas Empire*, 1 (1959), pp. 360–64, 2 (1949), pp. 7–76, and in A. H. M. Jones, *The Later Roman Empire*, 1 (Oxford, 1964), pp. 224–30. E. W. Brooks, 'The Emperor Zenon and the Isaurians', *EHR* 8 (1893), pp. 209–38. A. Lippold in *PW*, 2. Reihe, 19 (1972), cols. 149–213, s.v. 'Zenon (179)'.

Zeno, St (d. *c.*375), Bp. of *Verona from *c.*362. Beyond the fact that Zeno was an African by birth, very little is known of him. His sermons ('Tractatus') have affinities with the writings of such Africans as *Tertullian and *Cyprian, but, as they did not come into circulation until the earlier Middle Ages, they were unknown to St *Jerome and *Gennadius. The 8th-cent. Life by the Veronese presbyter Coronatus is devoid of historical value. He is commonly represented in art with a fish. Feast day, 12 Apr.

Editio princeps of his sermons by A. Castellanus, OP, and J. de Lenco (Venice, 1508); more accurate edn. by P. and H. *Ballerini (Verona, 1739), repr. in J. P. Migne, *PL* 11. 253–528; crit. edn. by B. Löfstedt (CCSL 22; 1971). A. Bigelmair, *Zeno von Verona: Habilitationsschrift* (1904). *Studi Zenoniani in occasione nel XVI centenario della morte di S. Zeno* (Verona, 1974). M. F. Stepanich, OFM, *The Christology of Zeno of Verona* (Catholic University of America, Studies in Sacred Theology, 2nd ser. 9; 1948). F. Segala, *Il Culto di San Zeno nella liturgia medioevale fino al secolo XII* (Studi e documenti di storia e liturgia, 1; Verona, 1982). M. Simonetti in Quasten (cont.), *Patrology*, 4 (1986), pp. 127–30. G. Bardy in *DTC* 15 (pt. 2; 1950), cols. 3685–90, s.v. 'Zénon'; A. Solignac, SJ, in *Dict. Sp.* 16 (1994), cols. 1628–39, s.v. 'Zénon (2) de Vérone'.

Zephaniah, Book of. One of the *Minor Prophets. This prophecy claims to have been delivered by Zephaniah, a descendant of (King?) Hezekiah, in the reign of Josiah, King of Judah (d. *c.*608 BC). The prophet announces the approaching judgement of all nations including Judah in the coming Day of the Lord, but he holds out the hope of future conversion among foreign nations and of a faithful remnant among the Jews (1: 2–3: 8). He concludes by encouraging Jerusalem to rejoice in the loving providence of God (3: 9–20). The prophecy, as originally delivered, probably belongs to the years immediately before the reformation of Josiah *c.*621 BC, and gives some valuable information on religion and society in Jerusalem and Judah at that time. From the religious point of view, the Book is evidence of Zephaniah's deep moral sense, of his awareness of the sin of his people, and of his implicit faith in the justice of God in the expected day of judgement. The opening words of the well-known Christian hymn '*Dies irae, dies illa' are taken from the *Vulgate version of 1: 15–16.

Comm. by J. M. P. Smith (ICC on Mic., Zeph., Nah., Hab., Obad., and Joel, 1912, pp. 159–263), J. H. Eaton (on Obad., Nah., Hab., and Zeph., London, 1961, pp. 119–59), and L. Sabottka (Biblica et Orientalia, 25; Rome, 1972). [J.] G. [H.] Gerleman, *Zephanja textkritisch und literarisch untersucht* (Lund thesis, 1942). P. R. House, *Zephaniah: A Prophetic Drama* (Journal for the Study of the Old Testament, Supplement Series, 69; Sheffield, 1988). E. B. Zvi, *A Historical-Critical Study of the Book of Zephaniah* (Beihefte zur ZATW, 198; 1991). Eissfeldt, pp. 423–5. C. L. Taylor in G. A. Buttrick and others (eds.), *The Interpreter's Bible*, 6 (New York [1956]), pp. 1007–34. J. S. Kselman in *Anchor Bible Dictionary*, 6 (1992), pp. 1077–80, s.v.

Zephyrinus, St (d. 217), Pope. He succeeded St *Victor as Bp. of Rome in 198, but despite his long pontificate relatively little is known of him. His critic, St *Hippolytus, described him as a simple man without education (ἀνὴρ ἰδιώτης καὶ ἀγράμματος; *Refut.* 9. 11). In his office he was closely associated with his deacon, *Callistus, who succeeded him as Pope. Hippolytus charged him with laxity in enforcing discipline and failure to assert his authority sufficiently in repressing the heresies (esp. *Sabellianism) then prevalent in the Roman Church. He is traditionally commemorated (on insufficient grounds) as a martyr. Feast day, 26 Aug.; dropped in 1969.

Jaffé, 1, p. 12. *LP* (Duchesne), 1 (1886), p. 139 f. B. *Capelle, OSB, 'Le Cas du pape Zéphyrin', *R. Bén.* 38 (1926), pp. 321–30. J. Wilpert, 'Beiträge zur christlichen Archäologie', 12, 'Das

Mausoleum des hl. Zephyrin', *RQ* 22 (1908), pp. 183–95; O. *Marucchi, 'La questione del sepolcro del papa Zefirino e del martire Tarsicio in seguito a una ultima scoperta', *Nuovo Bullettino di Archeologia cristiana*, 16 (1910), pp. 205–25; P. F. de' Cavalieri, *Note agiografiche*, 4 (ST 24; 1912), sect. 4, 'Del sepolcro di S. Zefirino', pp. 69–76. E. Caspar, *Geschichte des Papsttums von den Anfängen bis zur Höhe der Weltherrschaft*, 1 (1930), pp. 22–4 and 38–40. Fliche and Martin, 2 (1935), esp. p. 103. J. Quasten, *Patrology*, 1 (Utrecht, 1950), pp. 279 f. É. Amann in *DTC* 15 (pt. 2; 1950), cols. 3690 f., s.v.; J. N. D. Kelly, *The Oxford Dictionary of Popes* (1986), pp. 12 f.

Zerbolt, Gerhard. See GERHARD ZERBOLT OF ZUTPHEN.

Zernov, Nicolas (1898–1980), Russian scholar and ecumenist. Born in Moscow, he left Russia after the Revolution in 1921. From 1923 he was involved in the Russian Student Christian Movement, first in Belgrade (where he read theology) and later in Paris. He studied in Oxford (1930–2) and in 1934 settled in England. From 1934 to 1947 he was Secretary of the Fellowship of St *Alban and St Sergius (q.v.). In 1947 he was appointed first Spalding Lecturer in Eastern Orthodox Culture in the University of Oxford, a post he held until his retirement in 1966. In Oxford in 1959 he founded, and became the first warden of, the House of St Gregory and St Macrina. This was designed to provide a point of meeting between Christians of E. and W. traditions, with a library, residential accommodation for students (esp. those of Orthodox background), and a place of worship for the Russian Orthodox community in Oxford. Later a church was built (consecrated in 1973) which is shared by the Russian and Greek Orthodox parishes. In his many books and articles—most notably *Eastern Christendom* (1961) and *The Russian Religious Renaissance of the Twentieth Century* (1963)—Zernov made the world of Eastern Orthodoxy, and esp. Russian Orthodoxy, familiar in the W. Throughout his life he worked tirelessly for the unity of all Christians.

Zernov's final autobiographical work, completed by his widow, pub. Paris, 1981; Eng. tr., *Sunset Years* (1983). K. [T.] Ware, 'In Memoriam Nicolas Zernov', *Sobornost/Eastern Churches Review*, 3 (1981), pp. 11–38.

Zigabenus, Euthymius. See EUTHYMIUS ZIGABENUS.

Zillertal Evangelicals. A body of Protestants, resident in the Zillertal, one of the principal valleys of the Tyrol, who seceded from the RC Church in 1829 and the following years. Religious and social boycott from the RC clergy and laity culminated in a decree from the provincial estates of the Tyrol, ordering all nonconformists to leave the country. On appeal to Frederick William III of Prussia in 1837, they were allowed to sell their possessions and settle at Erdmannsdorf in Prussian territory, where they were assisted by a grant from the Prussian government. In 1945 their descendants were exiled and dispersed.

F. C. Arnold in *PRE* (3rd edn.), 21 (1908), pp. 675–8; E. Beyreuther in *RGG* (3rd edn.), 6 (1962), col. 1910, s.v. 'Zillertaler Emigranten'.

Zimbabwe, Christianity in. The earliest Christian mission to Zimbabwe (formerly Southern Rhodesia) was that of Fr. Gonçalo da Silviera, SJ, who was martyred at the court of Mutapa in 1561. In the early 17th cent.

*Dominican missionaries baptized several of the kings, but the ceremony seems to have been little more than a recognition of Portuguese protection. After the establishment of the Changamire state in the late 17th cent., the Christian missionary presence was eliminated, to be resumed only in the later 19th cent., when R. *Moffat of the *LMS received permission of the Ndebele king Mzilikazi to establish a mission at Inyati. In 1877 the Jesuit mission to the Zambezi was reconstituted under a Belgian, Henri Depelchin, and in 1879 established a station at the Ndebele capital of Bulawayo. However, little progress was made until the conquest of the country by Cecil Rhodes and the creation of Rhodesia. In the Shona Rising of 1896 Bernard Mizeki, an Anglican catechist of Mozambican origin, who refused to leave his post at Mangwende, was martyred. In the following years the Churches grew rapidly. British *Methodists worked in the central part of Mashonaland, where John White established the important Waddilove Training Institution (1898); American Methodists worked in the east; *Lutherans joined the LMS in Matabeleland; while Anglicans worked in all areas. The Jesuits, mostly British, were joined by German Mariannhill Fathers and, later, Swiss Bethlehem Fathers. John White, who was President of the Missionary Conference (1924–8), did much to defend African rights, as did Arthur Shearly Cripps, an Anglican priest, poet, and novelist who worked in the country from 1901 until his death in 1952. In 1979 Abel Muzorewa, Bp. of the American Methodist Church, became the country's first prime minister in alliance with Ian Smith and in opposition to the main nationalist forces. Nevertheless, relations between the government of Robert Mugabe and the Churches since independence in 1980 have been mostly good. Most Zimbabweans were linked to some Church, of which the largest is the RC. There are many 'Independent', Black-founded Churches, some of them extensions of the Zionist Churches of *South Africa, but others, such as the two Churches of Vapostori ('Apostles'), founded by Johane Maranke and Johane Masowe in the 1930s, are native to Zimbabwe.

The source material for the early period is pr., with Eng. tr., in *Documentos sobre os Portugueses em Moçambique e na Africa Central 1497–1840* (Documents on the Portuguese in Mozambique and Central Africa 1497–1840), 7 and 8 (Lisbon, 1971 and 1975), *passim*, and, in Eng. tr., in G. McC. Theal (ed.), *Records of South-eastern Africa* (9 vols., Cape Town, 1898–1903), *passim*. M. Gelfand, *Gubulawayo and Beyond: Letters and Journals of the Early Jesuit Missionaries to Zambesia (1879–1887)* (1968). General history of the early period by W. G. K. Randles, *L'Empire de Monomotapa du XV᷄ au XIX᷄ siècle* ([1975]; Eng. tr., Zambeziana, 7; Salisbury [1979]). M. W. Murphree, *Christianity and the Shona* (London School of Economics Monographs on Social Anthropology, 36; 1969). *Christianity South of the Zambesi*, 1, ed. A. J. Dachs (Salisbury, 1973); 2, ed. M. F. C. Bourdillon, SJ (ibid., 1977); 3, ed. C. F. Hallencreuty and A. M. Mayo, *Church and State in Zimbabwe* (ibid., 1988; deals with the period after 1921). A. J. Dachs and W. F. Rea, SJ, *The Catholic Church and Zimbabwe 1879–1979* (Zambeziana, 8; Salisbury, 1979). N. Bhebe, *Christianity and Traditional Religion in Western Zimbabwe 1859–1923* (1979). M. L. Daneel, *Old and New in Southern Shona Independent Churches* (1–2, The Hague, 1971–4; 3, Harare, 1988).

Zinzendorf, Nikolaus Ludwig Graf von (1700–60), founder of the Herrnhuter 'Brüdergemeine' or *Moravian Brethren. Born in Dresden, of an aristocratic family with *Pietist leanings, he was educated at A. H. *Francke's

Adelspädagogium and at *Wittenberg University (1716–19). He then travelled in the Netherlands and France and in 1721 entered the service of the Saxon Government. His chief interest, however, was evangelization. He organized religious assemblies in his home, and from 1722 received on one of his estates Protestant emigrants from Austria, many of them descendants of the *Bohemian Brethren. Giving up his Government post in 1727, he devoted himself entirely to the spiritual care of this colony, called *Herrnhut. Before long he was attacked as an innovator by *Lutheran orthodoxy, but his beliefs were examined and approved in 1734. Exiled from Saxony in 1736, he was permitted to return in 1747, and spent his last years in pastoral work at Herrnhut. During and after his exile he founded communities in the Baltic Provinces, the Netherlands, England, the West Indies, and N. America. His ideals of evangelism inspired many of his followers to work as missionaries, esp. among 'despised' races and peoples.

Opposed alike to the spirit of the *Enlightenment and of traditional Protestant orthodoxy, and also criticized by Pietists and *Methodists, Zinzendorf maintained a position of his own. In accordance with the 'Tropenlehre' which he elaborated ('God fulfils Himself in many ways') he was open to elements from Lutheran and Reformed sources as well as Moravian, and hoped to work pervasively from within the Protestant Churches, but circumstances forced his movement to adopt a separate organization. In 1737 he received episcopal orders from a Moravian bishop, D. E. Jablonski, and in England, where he was active from 1749 to 1755, the *Unitas Fratrum (the Moravian or United Brethren) was recognized by an Act of Parliament as an ancient Protestant Episcopal Church. For some time he had a considerable influence on *Evangelicals, esp. John *Wesley. Objection was taken, however, to his teaching on the relation between *justification and sanctification and to the emotionalism of his 'religion of the heart': the 'felt' fellowship with a Saviour conceived as at once creator, sustainer, and redeemer of the world found frequent expression in his hymns and in an almost playful cult of the Five *Wounds. Through F. D. E. *Schleiermacher his emphasis on the place of feeling in religion had an indirect influence on 19th-cent. theology.

Hauptschriften photographically reproduced from contemporary edns., ed. E. Beyreuther and G. Meyer (6 vols., Hildesheim, 1962–3, with Ergänzungsbande zu den Hauptschriften, 14 vols., ibid., 1964–85). Zinzendorf published his autobiog. under the title Περὶ ἑαυτοῦ. *Das ist naturelle Reflexiones über allerhand Materien* [c.1748]. Life by A. G. Spangenberg (8 Thle., [Barby] 1772–5; abridged Eng. tr., 1838; Ger. photographically repr. in the series of *Materialien und Documente* on Zinzendorf, ed. E. Beyreuther and G. Meyer, Reihe 2, vols. 1–8; Hildesheim and New York, 1971). L. K. von Schrautenbach, *Der Graf von Zinzendorf und die Brüdergemeine seiner Zeit* (written in 1782; ed. F. W. Kölbing, Gnadau, 1851). Modern Life by J. R. Weinlick (Nashville, 1956). H. Plitt, *Zinzendorfs Theologie* (3 vols., 1869–71). O. Uttendörfer, *Zinzendorfs Weltbetrachtung* (1929); id., *Zinzendorfs religiöse Grundgedanken* (Herrnhut, 1935); and other writings by id. W. Bettermann, *Theologie und Sprache bei Zinzendorf* (1935). L. Aalen, *Den Unge Zinzendorfs Teologi* (Oslo, 1952; Ger. tr., Arbeiten zur Geschichte und Theologie des Luthertums, 16; 1966). C. W. Towlson, *Moravian and Methodist: Relationships and Influences in the Eighteenth Century* (1957), *passim*. E. Beyreuther, *Zinzendorf und die sich allhier beisammen finden* (Marburg an der

Lahn, 1959); id., *Zinzendorf und die Christenheit 1732–1760* (ibid., 1961); id., *Studien zur Theologie Zinzendorfs* (Neukirchen and Vluyn Kries Moers, 1962). A. J. Lewis, *Zinzendorf the Ecumenical Pioneer: A Study in the Moravian Contribution to Christian Mission and Unity* (1962). H. Ruh, *Die christologische Begründung des ersten Artikels bei Zinzendorf* (Basler Studien zur historischen und systematischen Theologie, 7 [1967]). P. Deghaye, *La Doctrine ésotérique de Zinzendorf* [1969]. D. Meyer, *Der Christozentrismus des späten Zinzendorf* (Europäische Hochschulschriften, Reihe 23, Bd. 25; 1973). M. Gerland, *Wesentliche Vereinigung: Untersuchungen zum Abendmahlsverständnis Zinzendorfs* (Theologische Texte und Studien, 2; Hildesheim, etc., 1992). H. Schneider in M. Greschat (ed.), *Orthodoxie und Pietismus* (Gestalten der Kirchengeschichte, 7; Stuttgart, 1982), pp. 347–72, with bibl. D. Meyer (ed.), *Bibliographisches Handbuch zur Zinzendorf-Forschung* (Düsseldorf, 1987). B. Becker and J. T. Müller in *PRE* (3rd edn.), 21 (1908), pp. 679–703, s.v.; L. Cristiani in *DTC* 15 (pt. 2; 1950), cols. 3695–704, s.v.; E. Beyreuther in *RGG* (3rd edn) 6 (1962), cols. 1913–16, s.v., with extensive bibl. See also bibl. to MORAVIAN BRETHREN; also histories of PIETISM, cited s.v.

Zion. The citadel of *Jerusalem, taken by *David from the Jebusites (2 Sam. 5: 6–7). It was probably situated on the eastern ridge of the city, south of the site of the *Temple. The name came to signify the mount on which the Temple stood, 'God's holy hill' at Jerusalem (Ps. 2: 6); thence also, Jerusalem itself (Is. 1: 27), and allegorically the heavenly city (Heb. 12: 22, Rev. 14: 1). It has been inferred from certain references in Isaiah (e.g. 10: 24–6, 29: 5–8—where the name '*Ariel' is used for Zion—and 37: 22–9) and the Psalms (e.g. 46–8) that there was an ancient tradition of the 'inviolability' of Zion, perhaps celebrated in the pre-exilic cult of the Jerusalem Temple.

H. G. May (ed.), *Oxford Bible Atlas* (1962; 3rd edn. by J. Day, 1984), pp. 80 f. W. H. Mare in *Anchor Bible Dictionary*, 6 (1992), pp. 1096 f., s.v. On the inferences from Is. and Pss., W. H. Schmidt, *Alttestamentlicher Glaube in seiner Geschichte* (6th edn., Neukirchen, 1987), pp. 249–62; Eng. tr. (from 4th edn.), *The Faith of the Old Testament* (Oxford, 1983), pp. 207–20; R. E. Clements, *Isaiah and the Deliverance of Jerusalem* (Journal for the Study of the Old Testament, Supplement Series, 13; Sheffield, 1980), pp. 72–89.

Zita, St (*c.*1215–72), the patroness of domestic servants. At the age of 12 she entered the service of the Fatinelli family at Lucca, where she remained till her death. Misunderstood and maltreated at first, she later won, by her religious fervour, the respect, and even veneration, of the family. She was canonized in 1696. Feast day, 27 Apr.

The principal authority is the Life by Fatinellus de Fatinellis (anon.) pr. in *AASS*, Apr. 3 (1675), pp. 499–509; see also Propylaeum ad Dec. (1940), pp. 158 f., with further refs. Modern Lives by A. Guerra (Lucca, 1875) and P. Puccinelli (ibid., 1949). On the ref. to St Zita in *Dante's *Inferno*, see F. P. Luiso, *L'Anziano di Santa Zita* (Lucca, 1927); cf. B. de Gaiffier in *Anal. Boll.* 48 (1930), pp. 229 f.

Zonaras, Johannes (12th cent.), Byzantine canonist and historian. After holding high positions at *Constantinople in the Imperial administration, he retired from the court during the reign of John II Comnenus (1118–43) and spent the rest of his life in monastic retirement on the small island of Niandro. The chief of his writings, a universal History (᾽Επιτομὴ τῶν ῾Ιστοριῶν) in 18 books, preserves much material that would otherwise be lost. It extends to 1118, and includes events of which Zonaras was himself

an eyewitness. He also wrote a Commentary on Greek *canon law, starting with the *Apostolic Canons, notable for the aptness and directness of his comments. His other works include a commentary on the poems of St *Gregory of Nazianzus and a hymn to the Blessed Virgin (Κανὼν εἰς τὴν ὑπεραγίαν Θεοτόκον).

His Epitome of History, ed. M. Pinder and R. Büttner-Wobst (3 vols., C.S.H.Byz., 1841–97); also by L. Dindorf (6 vols., Teub., 1868–76). Collected edn. in J. P. Migne, *PG* 134 and 135. 9–438. M. DiMaio, Jun., 'Smoke in the Wind: Zonaras' Use of Philostorgius, Zosimos, John of Antioch, and John of Rhodes in his Narrative of the Neo-Flavian Emperors', *Byzantion*, 58 (1988), pp. 230–55, with refs. to recent lit. Krumbacher, pp. 370–6; G. Moravcsik, *Byzantinoturcica*, 1 (Berliner Byzantinische Arbeiten, 10; 2nd edn., 1958), pp. 344–6; Beck, pp. 656 f., both with bibl. P. Meyer in *PRE* (3rd edn.), 21 (1908), pp. 715–19; É. Amann in *DTC* 15 (pt. 2; 1950), cols. 3705–8, both s.v.

Zoroastrianism (also known as **Mazdaism**). The system of religious doctrine ascribed to Zoroaster (Zarathustra) which in later times became the dominant religion of Iran and under the Sassanian dynasty (AD 226–651) the official state religion. Its priests were called *magi* [Old Persian, *magu*]. After the conversion of Iran to *Islam, Zoroastrians sought religious freedom in *India, where they were called Parsis.

Of Zoroaster himself next to nothing is known with certainty. The *Gathas*, the oldest part of the *Avesta, the sacred writings of the Zoroastrians, are hymns ascribed to Zoroaster, an attribution accepted by many scholars. It would seem that his sphere of activity was what is now NE Iran, W. Afghanistan, and the Turkmen Republic of the former USSR. His dates have long been widely disputed, ranging from the traditional date of 258 years 'before Alexander' (which would place his *floruit* in the early 6th cent. BC) to some time in the middle, or at the end, of the second millennium BC.

Scholars are also divided about Zoroaster's original teaching, some regarding him as a monotheist and seeing later dualistic Zoroastrianism as a corruption of his teaching, others convinced of the essential continuity of Zoroastrian doctrine. According to Zoroastrianism, the world was made by one 'Wise Lord' (*Ahura Mazda* or *Ohrmuzd*) with the help of his holy spirit (*Spenta Mainyu*) and six other spirits, the *Amesha Spenta* or 'Holy Immortals'. *Ahura Mazda* is not, however, all-powerful, but opposed by an uncreated Evil Spirit (*Angra Mainyu* or *Ahriman*), who is supported by other evil spirits including the *daevas*, the ancient amoral gods of war. The created world is the arena for a combat between good and evil: human beings, having free will, have the duty to choose the good. At death each individual is judged according to his words and deeds on the 'bridge of decision': those who fail fall into hell. All human striving is to be directed towards the salvation of the world. In the last days of the world, the World Saviour, *Saoshyant*, will come in glory and there will be a final battle in which good will triumph over evil. A later teaching (first attested in the 9th cent. AD) holds that in this ordeal the wicked will be purified and saved.

Much of this teaching can be seen as a reform of earlier Iranian beliefs, and fire, regarded as present throughout the whole creation as a life-force, continues to play an important role in Zoroastrian ritual. Zoroastrian ideas, which underwent considerable development over the course of the centuries, are sometimes held to have influenced *Judaism and, less probably, Christianity and Islam. Beside the Parsis in India there is still a small Zoroastrian community in Iran.

Eng. tr. of primary texts by [N. E.] M. Boyce, *Textual Sources for the Study of Zoroastrianism* (Manchester [1984]). General studies incl. E. Herzfeld, *Zoroaster and his World* (2 vols., Princeton, NJ, 1947); R. C. Zaehner, *The Teaching of the Magi* (1956); id., *The Dawn and Twilight of Zoroastrianism* (1961); J. Duchesne-Guillemin, *The Western Response to Zoroaster* (Oxford, 1958); id., *La Religion de l'Iran ancien* (1962); id., *Symbols and Values in Zoroastrianism: Their Survival and Renewal* (New York [1966]), and other works; W. Hinz, *Zarathustra* (Stuttgart, 1961); G. Widengren, *Die Religionen Irans* (Die Religionen der Menschheit, 14; Stuttgart [1965]); [N. E.] M. Boyce (from vol. 3, with F. Grenet), *A History of Zoroastrianism* (Handbuch der Orientalistik, Abt. 1, Bd. 8, Abschnitt 1, Lieferung 2, Heft 2 (A); Leiden, 1975 ff.); id., *Zoroastrians: Their Religious Beliefs and Practices* (1979), and other works; G. Gnoli, *Zoroaster's Time and Homeland* (Istituto Universitario Orientale, Seminario di Studi Asiatici, Ser. Minor, 7; Naples, 1980). J. Duchesne-Guillemin in *The Cambridge History of Iran*, 3 (2), ed. E. Yarshater (1983), pp. 866–908. G. Gnoli in M. Eliade (ed.), *Encyclopedia of Religion*, 15 (1987), pp. 579–91; J. Baldick in F. Hardy (ed.), *The World's Religions: The Religions of Asia* (1988), pp. 20–36, s.v. 'Mazdaism'; [N. E.] M. Boyce in *Anchor Bible Dictionary*, 6 (1992), pp. 1168–74.

Zosimus (d. 418), Bp. of Rome from 417. He was a Greek by birth. His brief pontificate was marked by blunders. Thus his attempt to establish a vicariate of Arles, in disregard of already existing metropolitan rights in Gaul, had to be abandoned by his successor, and his policy twice suffered defeat in N. Africa. Having reopened the case of *Pelagius and his supporters (condemned by *Innocent I), he was forced by an Imperial edict to come into line with the views of St *Augustine and the African Church and issue his '*Tractoria' condemning Pelagianism. He was again outmanœuvred when, citing as *Nicene and therefore of oecumenical authority a canon which properly belonged to the Council of *Sardica (343), he tried to quash the sentence passed on the African priest *Apiarius by the Bp. of Sicca. Several of his letters survive. Feast day, 26 Dec.

Epp. ed. P. *Coustant, OSB, *Epistolae Romanorum Pontificum*, 1 (1721), cols. 933–1006; repr. J. P. Migne, *PL* 20. 639–704; see also Suppl. (ed. A. Hamman, OFM), 1 (1958), cols. 797 f. *LP* (Duchesne), 1, pp. 225 f. E. Caspar, *Geschichte des Papsttums von den Anfängen bis zur Höhe der Weltherrschaft*, 1 (1930), pp. 344–60. F. Floëri, 'Le Pape Zosime et la doctrine augustinienne du péché originel', in *Augustinus Magister: Congrès International Augustinien, Paris, 21–24 Septembre 1954. Communications*, 2 [1954], pp. 755–61. C. Pietri, *Roma Christiana: Recherches sur l'Église de Rome . . . (311–440)* (Bibliothèque des Écoles françaises d'Athènes et de Rome, 224; 1976), pp. 1212–44. *CPL* (3rd edn., 1995), pp. 530 f. (nos. 1644–7). É. Amann in *DTC* 15 (pt. 2; 1950), cols. 3708–16, s.v.; C. Munier in *Dict. Sp.* 16 (1994), cols. 1651–8, s.v. 'Zosime (1)'.

Zosimus (later 5th cent.), Greek historian. He held an administrative post at *Constantinople. His history of the Roman Empire, in six books, going down to 410 and written after 425, prob. c.500, is one of the primary sources for the secular history of the 4th cent. Though based throughout on earlier histories, esp. those of the *Neoplatonists Eunapius and Olympiodorus, whose philo-

sophical interests Zosimus shared, the history has a special interest because, without intentional distortion of facts, its author consistently developed a pagan and anti-Christian view of his subject-matter, attributing, e.g., the decline of the Empire as much to the neglect of the old religion as to any political cause. His account of ecclesiastical affairs also serves as an occasional corrective to the better-known accounts in Christian writers.

Ed. princeps of Gk. text by F. Sylburg (Frankfurt, 1590). Crit. edns. by L. Mendelssohn (Leipzig, 1887), with prolegomena; and, with Fr. tr. and introd., by F. Paschoud (Collection des Universités de France, 3 vols. in 5 parts, 1971–89). Eng. trs. by J. J. Buchanan and H. T. Davis (San Antonio, Tex., 1967) and R. T. Ridley (Byzantina Australiensia, 2; Sydney [1982]). F. Paschoud, *Cinq Études sur Zosime* (1975). W. Goffart, 'Zosimus, the First Historian of Rome's Fall', *American Historical Review*, 76 (1971), pp. 412–41. F. Paschoud in *PW* 19 (1972), cols. 795–841, s.v. 'Zosimos (8)'.

zucchetto. The small round skull-cap used by certain RC ecclesiastics. It has been customarily worn since the 13th cent., and varies in colour with the different grades of the hierarchy, the *Pope wearing white, *cardinals red, *bishops violet, and others black. It is worn at *Mass, except during the *Canon.

Zurich Consensus. See CONSENSUS TIGURINUS.

Zwickau Prophets. A group of early *Anabaptists which sought to establish a community of the elect at Zwickau, an industrial town in S. Saxony. The chief were N. *Storch, T. Drechsel, and M. Thoma (or Stübner). They claimed to be guided by the Holy Spirit, rejected *Infant Baptism, and embraced chiliastic beliefs. The source of their doctrines is uncertain; only Thoma is known to have had contacts with Bohemia and *Hussitism. The three leaders visited *Wittenberg in the winter of 1521; there they met and impressed both P. *Melanchthon and N. von *Amsdorf. Their influence in Zwickau, esp. among women, survived into the 1530s.

Brief reports on the Zwickau Prophets drawn up for the Kurfürst Friedrich by P. Melanchthon and N. von Amsdorf, ed. C. G. *Bretschneider, *Corpus Reformatorum*, 1 (Halle, 1834), cols. 533–55. P. Wappler, *Thomas Müntzer in Zwickau und die 'Zwickauer Propheten'* (Wissenschaftliche Beilage zu dem Jahresberichte des Realgymnasiums mit Realschule zu Zwickau; Zwickau, 1908) (repr. in Schriften des Vereins für Reformationsgeschichte, no. 182; Gütersloh [1966]). R. Schwarz, *Die apokalyptische Theologie Thomas Müntzers und der Taboriten* (Beiträge zur historischen Theologie, 55; Tübingen, 1977). S. Hoyer, 'Die Zwickauer Storchianer—Vorläufer der Täufer?', *Jahrbuch für Regionalgeschichte*, 13 (1986), pp. 60–78 (repr. in J.-G. Rott and S. L. Verheus (eds.), *Anabaptistes et dissidents au XVIᵉ siècle* (Bibliotheca Dissidentium, scripta et studia, 3; Baden-Baden and Bouxwiller, 1987), pp. 65–83). S. C. Karant-Nunn, *Zwickau in Transition, 1500–1547: The Reformation as an Agent of Change* (Columbus, Oh., 1987).

Zwingli, Ulrich (or Huldreich) (1484–1531), Swiss Reformer. A native of Wildhaus in the Toggenburg valley, canton St *Gall, Switzerland, he was educated at Berne (1496–8), Vienna (1498–1502), and Basle (under T. *Wyttenbach, 1502–6). He was ordained priest in 1506, and from 1506 to 1516 was pastor at Glarus. Already a devoted admirer of *Erasmus, he gave himself up at

Glarus largely to humanistic studies, taught himself Greek and prob. the rudiments of Hebrew, learned St Paul's Epp. by heart, and read the Fathers. In 1513 and 1515 he served as military chaplain to Swiss mercenaries in the Papal service and was present at the Battle of Marignano (13–14 Sept. 1515). In 1516 he left Glarus for *Einsiedeln, where the pilgrimage abuses at the famous shrine quickened his desire for reform; he also deepened his knowledge of the Greek NT with the aid of Erasmus' newly published *editio princeps* (1516) and improved his technique as a preacher. On 11 Dec. 1518 he was elected People's Preacher at the Old Minster in Zurich, where he remained for the rest of his life. Here, in an important office, he sought to carry through his political and religious ideals and met with strong local support. The rupture with ecclesiastical authority came gradually. The real beginning of the Reformation in Switzerland was Zwingli's sermons commenting on the NT in 1519. Attacks in his sermons on purgatory, invocation of saints, and monasticism soon followed. In April 1522 appeared his first Reformation tract, *Von Erkiesen und Fryheit der Spysen*, and later in the same year (22 Aug.) *Architeles*, advocating the liberation of believers from the control of the Papacy and bishops. The Bp. of Constance's Vicar General (Johann *Faber), sent to Zurich to deal with the situation, was silenced in a public disputation on 29 Jan. 1523, when Zwingli successfully upheld 67 theses before an audience of some 600. The sole basis of truth was the Gospel, and the authority of the Pope, the sacrifice of the Mass, the invocation of saints, times and seasons of fasting, and clerical celibacy were rejected. The city council gave Zwingli its full support and the Minster Chapter was reconstituted in independence of episcopal control. Matters were carried further at a second disputation on 26 Oct. 1523, which led to Zwingli's *Eine kurze christliche Einleitung*, expounding for the clergy the relations between the Gospel and the Law. Shortly afterwards steps were taken to abolish the Mass (eventually suppressed at Zurich in Apr. 1525), remove images and pictures from churches, and to institute the 'Prophezey', daily sessions of Bible-reading and exegesis for preachers and laymen. On 2 Apr. 1524 Zwingli publicly celebrated his marriage with Anna Meyer (*née* Reinhard) in the cathedral.

It was at this stage that Zwingli began to develop his characteristic theology ('Zwinglianism'). In 1522 he still accepted the traditional view of the Eucharist, but in a letter to Matthäus Alber of Reutlingen (16 Nov. 1524) he upheld a purely symbolic interpretation. He developed his teaching on the subject in a series of writings against M. *Luther from 1525 onwards. Against Luther's doctrine of *consubstantiation, he maintained that it is only the communicant's faith that makes Christ present in the Eucharist; there is no question of any physical presence. The Colloquy of *Marburg in 1529 failed to reconcile the opposing parties. Particularly in his *Responsio brevis* (1526), Zwingli distinguished more clearly than Luther between the human and the Divine nature in Christ. He also refused to admit the Lutheran distinction between the Law and the Gospel. This point of view led him to affirm, in the course of his disputes with the *Anabaptists in the 1520s that Infant Baptism was a natural development from the *circumcision prescribed in the OT. He was also unlike Luther in believing that the magistrate had the right to legislate in religious matters, and consequently he

acquiesced when the Council of Zurich put one of the Anabaptist leaders to death by drowning in 1527.

Meanwhile the movement had spread to other parts of Switzerland. In a public theological disputation at Berne in Jan. 1528 Zwingli successfully upheld ten theses (see BERNE, THESES OF), and the canton joined the movement. Basle, St Gall, and Schaffhausen followed shortly afterwards. The movement met, however, with fierce resistance elsewhere, notably in the Five Forest Cantons (Lucerne, Zug, Schwyz, Uri, Unterwalden). War was only just avoided in 1529 and finally broke out in 1531, when the Forest Cantons made a sudden and unexpected descent on Zurich. They were met by a small force at Cappel, where Zwingli, who as chaplain carried the banner, was killed (11 Oct. 1531).

Collected edns. of his works by R. Walther, 4 vols., Zurich, 1539; 4 vols., ibid., 1545, and 3 vols., ibid., 1581; ed. M. Schuler and J. Schulthess (8 vols., ibid., 1829–42); ed. E. Egli, G. Finsler, and others (Corpus Reformatorum, 88 ff.; 1904 ff.). *Zwingli Hauptschriften* also ed. F. Blanke and others (Zurich, 1940 ff.). Selections of his writings tr. into Eng. by S. M. Jackson (Philadelphia, 1901); also by G. W. Bromiley, *Zwingli and Bullinger* (Library of Christian Classics, 24; 1953), pp. 47–279, with introd., pp. 13–40, and by E. J. Furcha and H. W. Pipkin (2 vols., Allison Park, Pa., 1984). Life by O. *Myconius, written in 1532, pub. Basle, 1536. E. Egli, *Analecta Reformatoria*, 1: *Dokumente und Abhandlungen zur Geschichte Zwingli und seiner Zeit* (Zurich, 1899). Modern Lives by R. Christoffel (*Leben und ausgewählte Schriften der Väter und Begründer der reformirten Kirche*, 1; 1857; Eng. tr., 1858), O. Farner (4 vols., Zurich, 1943–60), and G. R. Potter (Cambridge, 1976). Shorter studies by O. Farner (Emmishofen, 1917; Eng. tr., 1952), J. Rilliet (Paris, 1959; rev. Eng. tr., 1964), F. Büsser (*Persönlichkeit und Geschichte*, 74–5; Göttingen, etc., 1973), U. Gäbler (Munich, 1983; Eng. tr., Edinburgh, 1987), and M. Haas (Zurich, 1983). A. Baur, *Zwinglis Theologie: Ihr Werden und ihr System* (2 vols., 1885–9). W. Köhler, *Zwingli und Luther: Ihr Streit über das Abendmahl nach seinen politischen und religiösen Beziehungen* (Quellen und Forschungen zur Reformationsgeschichte, 6 and 7; 1924–1953), and other works of this author. J. V. Pollet, OP, *Huldrych Zwingli et la Réforme en Suisse d'après les recherches récentes* (1963). R. C. Walton, *Zwingli's Theocracy* (Toronto [1967]). G. W. Locher, *Huldrych Zwingli in neuer Sicht: Zehn Beiträge zur Theologie der Zürcher Reformation* (Zurich and Stuttgart, 1969; Eng. tr., Studies in the History of Christian Thought, 25; Leiden, 1981); id., *Die Zwinglische Reformation im Rahmen der europäischen Kirchengeschichte* (Göttingen, 1979). A. Schindler, *Zwingli und die Kirchenväter* (Zurich, 1984). E. J. Furcha and H. W. Pipkin (eds.), *Prophet, Pastor, Protestant: The Work of Huldrych Zwingli after Five Hundred Years* (Pittsburgh theological monographs, NS 11; Allison Park, Pa., 1984). F. Büsser, *Wurzeln der Reformation in Zurich* (Studies in Medieval and Reformation Thought, 31; Leiden, 1985), pp. 20–105. W. P. Stephens, *The Theology of Huldrych Zwingli* (Oxford, 1986). J. V. Pollet, *Huldrych Zwingli et le Zwinglianisme: Essai de synthèse historique et théologique mis à jour d'après les recherches récentes* (1988), incl. repr. of his art. in *DTC*, cited below. I. Backus, *The Disputations of Baden, 1526, and Berne, 1528* (Studies in Reformed Theology and History, 1, no. 1; Princeton, NJ, 1993), *passim. Zwingliana: Mitteilungen zur Geschichte Zwinglis und der Reformation*, herausgegeben von der Vereinigung für das Zwinglimuseum in Zurich (Zurich, 1897 [1904] ff.; esp. 19: *Reformiertes Erbe: Festschrift für Gottfried W. Locher zu seinem 80. Geburtstag*, ed. H. A. Oberman and others, 2 Teile, 1992–3). G. Finsler, *Zwingli-Bibliographie* (ibid., 1897); U. Gäbler, *Hulrych Zwingli im 20. Jahrhundert: Forschungsbericht und annotierte Bibliographie 1897–1972* (ibid., 1975). E. Güder, R. Stähelin, and E. Egli in *PRE* (3rd edn.), 21 (1908), pp. 774–815, s.v.; L. Cristiani in *DTC* 15 (pt. 2; 1950), cols. 3716–44, s.v.; J.-V.-M. Pollet, OP, ibid., cols. 3745–928, s.v. 'Zwinglianisme'.

CHRONOLOGICAL LIST OF POPES
AND ANTIPOPES

Antipopes are indicated by indenting the names to the right in [   ]

until *c.*64	St *Peter	440–61	*Leo I	715–31	*Gregory II
	*Linus	461–8	Hilarus	731–41	Gregory III
	*Anacletus	468–83	*Simplicius	741–52	*Zacharias
*fl. c.*96	*Clement I	483–92	Felix III (II)	752	Stephen II
	Evaristus	492–6	*Gelasius I	752–67	*Stephen II (III)
	Alexander I	496–8	Anastasius II	757–67	Paul I
*c.*117–*c.*127	Sixtus I	498–514	*Symmachus	[767–9	Constantine]
*c.*127–*c.*137	*Telesphorus	[498–9, 501–6 Laurentius]		[768	Philip]
*c.*137–*c.*140	Hyginus	514–23	*Hormisdas	768–72	*Stephen III (IV)
*c.*140–*c.*154	*Pius I	523–6	John I	772–95	*Hadrian I
*c.*154–*c.*166	Anicetus	526–30	Felix IV (III)	795–816	*Leo III
*c.*166–*c.*175	Soter	530–2	Boniface II	816–17	Stephen V
*c.*175–89	Eleutherius	[530	Dioscorus]	817–24	Paschal I
189–98	*Victor I	533–5	John II	824–7	Eugenius II
198–217	*Zephyrinus	535–6	*Agapetus I	827	Valentine
217–22	*Callistus I	536–7	Silverius	827–44	Gregory IV
[217–*c.*235	*Hippolytus]	537–55	*Vigilius	844–7	Sergius II
222–30	Urban I	556–61	Pelagius I	[844	John]
230–5	Pontian	561–74	John III	847–55	*Leo IV
235–6	Anterus	575–9	Benedict I	855–8	Benedict III
236–50	*Fabian	579–90	Pelagius II	[855	*Anastasius
251–3	*Cornelius	590–604	*Gregory I		Bibliothecarius]
[251–257/8	*Novatian]	604–6	Sabinianus	858–67	*Nicholas I
253–4	Lucius I	607	Boniface III	867–72	Hadrian II
254–7	*Stephen I	608–15	Boniface IV	872–82	John VIII
257–8	*Sixtus II	615–18	Deusdedit or	882–4	Marinus I
259–68	*Dionysius		Adeodatus I	884–5	Hadrian III
269–74	Felix I	619–25	Boniface V	885–91	Stephen VI
275–83	Eutychianus	625–38	*Honorius I	891–6	*Formosus
283–96	Caius	640	Severinus	896	Boniface VI
296–304	Marcellinus	640–2	John IV	896–7	Stephen VII
*c.*307–308/9	Marcellus I	642–9	Theodore I	897	Romanus
310	Eusebius	649–55	*Martin I[1]	897	Theodore II
310/11–314	*Miltiades	654–7	Eugenius I	898–900	John IX
314–35	*Sylvester I	657–72	*Vitalian	900–3	Benedict IV
336	Mark	672–6	Adeodatus II	903	Leo V
337–52	*Julius I	676–8	Donus	[903–4	Christopher]
352–66	*Liberius	678–81	*Agatho	904–11	Sergius III
[355–65	Felix II]	682–3	Leo II	911–13	Anastasius III
366–84	*Damasus I	684–5	Benedict II	913–14	Lando
[366–7	Ursinus]	685–6	John V	914–28	John X
384–99	*Siricius	686–7	Cono	928	Leo VI
399–401	Anastasius I	[687	Theodore]	928–31	Stephen VIII
402–17	*Innocent I	[687	Paschal]	931–5	John XI
417–18	*Zosimus	687–701	*Sergius I	936–9	Leo VII
418–22	*Boniface I	701–5	John VI	939–42	Stephen IX
[418–19	Eulalius]	705–7	John VII	942–6	Marinus II
422–32	*Celestine I	708	Sisinnius	946–55	Agapetus II
432–40	Sixtus III	708–15	Constantine	955–64	*John XII

[1] After Martin's banishment his successor was elected and consecrated.

List of Popes and Antipopes

963–5	Leo VIII[1]	1159–81	*Alexander III	1471–84	*Sixtus IV
964	Benedict V	[1159–64	Victor IV[2]]	1484–92	Innocent VIII
965–72	John XIII	[1164–8	Paschal III]	1492–1503	*Alexander VI
973–4	Benedict VI	[1168–78	Callistus III]	1503	Pius III
[974, 984–5	Boniface VII]	[1179–80	Innocent III]	1503–13	*Julius II
974–83	Benedict VII	1181–5	Lucius III	1513–21	*Leo X
983–4	John XIV	1185–7	Urban III	1522–3	*Hadrian VI
985–96	John XV	1187	Gregory VIII	1523–34	*Clement VII
996–9	Gregory V	1187–91	Clement III	1534–49	*Paul III
[997–8	John XVI]	1191–8	*Celestine III	1550–5	*Julius III
999–1003	*Sylvester II	1198–1216	*Innocent III	1555	Marcellus II
1003	John XVII	1216–27	*Honorius III	1555–9	*Paul IV
1003/4–9	John XVIII	1227–41	*Gregory IX	1559–65	*Pius IV
1009–12	Sergius IV	1241	Celestine IV	1566–72	*Pius V
1012–24	Benedict VIII	1243–54	*Innocent IV	1572–85	*Gregory XIII
[1012	Gregory]	1254–61	Alexander IV	1585–90	*Sixtus V
1024–32	John XIX	1261–4	Urban IV	1590	Urban VII
1032–44	Benedict IX	1265–8	Clement IV	1590–1	Gregory XIV
1045	Sylvester III	1271–6	*Gregory X	1591	Innocent IX
1045	Benedict IX [for	1276	Innocent V	1592–1605	*Clement VIII
	the second time]	1276	Hadrian V	1605	Leo XI
1045–6	Gregory VI	1276–7	*John XXI[3]	1605–21	*Paul V
1046–7	Clement II	1277–80	Nicholas III	1621–3	Gregory XV
1047–8	Benedict IX [for	1281–5	*Martin IV	1623–44	*Urban VIII
	the third time]	1285–7	Honorius IV	1644–55	*Innocent X
1048	Damasus II	1288–92	Nicholas IV	1655–67	*Alexander VII
1048–54	*Leo IX	1294	*Celestine V	1667–9	Clement IX
1055–7	Victor II	1294–1303	*Boniface VIII	1670–6	Clement X
1057–8	Stephen X	1303–4	Benedict XI	1676–89	*Innocent XI
[1058–9	Benedict X]	1305–14	*Clement V	1689–91	*Alexander VIII
1059–61	Nicholas II	1316–34	*John XXII	1691–1700	Innocent XII
1061–73	*Alexander II	[1328–30	Nicholas V]	1700–21	*Clement XI
[1061–72	Honorius II]	1334–42	*Benedict XII	1721–4	Innocent XIII
1073–85	*Gregory VII	1342–52	*Clement VI	1724–30	*Benedict XIII
[1080, 1084–1100	Clement III]	1352–62	Innocent VI	1730–40	Clement XII
1086–7	Victor III	1362–70	*Urban V	1740–58	*Benedict XIV
1088–99	*Urban II	1370–8	*Gregory XI	1758–69	*Clement XIII
1099–1118	*Paschal II	1378–89	*Urban VI	1769–74	*Clement XIV
[1100–1	Theodoric]	[1378–94	Clement VII]	1775–99	*Pius VI
[1101	Albert]	1389–1404	Boniface IX	1800–23	*Pius VII
[1105–11	Sylvester IV]	[1394–1417	*Benedict XIII]	1823–9	Leo XII
1118–19	Gelasius II	1404–6	Innocent VII	1829–30	Pius VIII
[1118–21	Gregory VIII]	1406–15	Gregory XII	1831–46	*Gregory XVI
1119–24	*Callistus II	[1409–10	Alexander V]	1846–78	*Pius IX
1124–30	Honorius II	[1410–15	John XXIII]	1878–1903	*Leo XIII
[1124	Celestine II]	1417–31	*Martin V	1903–14	*Pius X
1130–43	Innocent II	[1423–9	Clement VIII]	1914–22	*Benedict XV
[1130–8	Anacletus II]	[1425–30	Benedict XIV]	1922–39	*Pius XI
[1138	Victor IV]	1431–47	*Eugenius IV	1939–58	*Pius XII
1143–4	Celestine II	[1439–49	Felix V]	1958–63	*John XXIII
1144–5	Lucius II	1447–55	*Nicholas V	1963–78	*Paul VI
1145–53	*Eugenius III	1455–8	*Callistus III	1978	*John Paul I
1153–4	Anastasius IV	1458–64	*Pius II	1978–	*John Paul II
1154–9	*Hadrian IV	1464–71	Paul II		

[1] His pontificate is dated from the deposition of his predecessor, but its legitimacy is contested.
[2] No account was taken of the previous antipope, who had resisted for a very short time.
[3] No Pope bearing the name of John XX ever existed.